WATERLOO
PUBLIC LIBRARY

TOTAL FOOTBALL

THE OFFICIAL ENCYCLOPEDIA OF THE NATIONAL FOOTBALL LEAGUE

BOB CARROLL, MICHAEL GERSHMAN,

DAVID NEFT, JOHN THORN

ELIAS SPORTS BUREAU

MATTHEW SILVERMAN, *MANAGING EDITOR*

HarperCollins*Publishers*

HarperCollins books may be purchased for educational, business, or sales promotional use. For information, please write to: Special Markets Department, HarperCollins Publishers, Inc., 10 East 53rd Street, New York, New York 10022.

ISBN 0-06-270174-6

99 00 01 02 03 10 9 8 7 6 5 4 3 2 1

Dedicated to Pete Rozelle and Ray Nitschke, who combined the will to win, on and off the field, with the stuff of greatness.

Contents

PART TWO

VII. The Register, Rosters, and Leaders

VIII. Appendixes

Acknowledgments

Like football, *Total Football* is a team game, and it is the product of a ongoing research effort that began more than 20 years ago and ultimately has involved thousands of people.

During that time, Bob Carroll and David Neft diligently researched every aspect of pro football. When either or both needed help, they were able to call on a long and varied list of organizations and individuals.

First and foremost among them is the Professional Football Researchers Association (PFRA), whose members have provided much of the historical data. Carroll founded the organization in the 1970s and discovered that other researchers and historians shared his enthusiasm for the early days of the NFL. PFRA members and many of the friends listed below helped fill in the blanks for the period from 1920, when the league was founded, through the 1932 season. Their efforts were given official recognition by the NFL in the first edition of *Total Football.* As a result, players active from 1920-1932 have become part of the league's statistical heritage.

The NFL was generous in lending its aid to this book in a variety of ways. John Wiebusch, who has logged more than 25 years overseeing NFL publishing efforts, proved to be invaluable in suggesting writers, story ideas, and editorial approaches. Jim Gigliotti of NFL Properties's Publishing Group in Los Angeles eyeballed every word of the first edition of *Total Football* and performed the same unglamorous function on this edition, turning in an all-pro performance. We also thank Chuck Garrity, Jr., who fulfilled a similar role on *Total Cowboys, Total Super Bowl,* and the four other books "spun off" from our debut edition.

Joel Bussert, the league's director of player personnel and an eminent football historian, spent countless hours refining our now-comprehensive list of NFL draft choices, and John Fawaz helped fact-check the manuscript, a role he also performed on the first edition of *Total Football* and its various offspring.

This project actually began in NFL Properties's New York office. Lori Quenneville has helped on a number of issues from the very beginning, and Bob O'Keefe has given us valuable marketing suggestions since he came over to lead the NFL's New York publishing department. Sara Levinson and Howard Handler "green-lighted" this project originally and personally have brought the book to the attention of NFL team owners, sponsors, and licensees.

Robert Wilson of HarperCollins has been a key player in our starting lineup since the beginning. He had the original inspiration for *Total Football* and worked with publisher Linda Cunningham to see it through to completion. Marketing director Carl Raymond, publicist Peter Shea, and special-market whizzes Frank Fochetta and Bill Huelster have added their support at different times to make sure the book reaches the widest possible audience.

We also thank the Elias Sports Bureau, particularly its president, Seymour Siwoff. As head of the company that has been the NFL's official statistician since 1961, he brought precision and dedication to an endeavor that was approached far more casually in the league's early years. Publication of *Total Football* is, therefore, for him the fulfillment of a lifelong dream.

Steve Hirdt, executive vice president of Elias, has spent a good portion of his life investigating and verifying the numbers that appear in this book and on *Monday Night Football.* Elias executives Peter Hirdt and Christopher Thorn helped organize the mountain of data that appears in the player register.

John Carson spent 16-hour days inputting that data, and Anthony Abilo transferred to computer code the research done by Santo Labombarda, Alex Stern, Tom Hirdt, Bob Waterman, and John Labombarda.

Special thanks go also to Carl Friedberg, a leading authority on programming design and presentation, and to Chris Slowik for keeping Elias's computers operational at all times. Also to Kevin Hines, Matt Martingale, Bob Rosen, Ken Hirdt, Brian Fodera, Sal D'Agostino, Frank Labombarda, Bill Foley, Mike Boyle, Matt Bazylewskyj, Matt Malm, Mike Donovan, Jonathan Steinberg, J. J. Gartland, and Pat O'Keefe. A very special thanks to two men, Jay Chesler and Rocky Avakian, who did much of the early work on this project but, unfortunately, did not live to see its publication.

The editors owe an equal debt of gratitude to the Pro Football Hall of Fame in Canton, Ohio. The Hall has become the official repository of pro football's storied past and the sport's keeper of the flame. Joe Horrigan, curator-director of research information; Don Smith, public relations director; Pete Fierle, research associate; and Tricia Trilli, archives clerk, have more than answered the call of duty and generously have shared their knowledge of the game.

Since the first edition of *Total Football,* we merged with Koz Sports of Raleigh, North Carolina, to become Total Sports and published the first edition of *Total Hockey* and the sixth edition of *Total Baseball,* the official encyclopedias of the National Hockey League and Major League Baseball. Our warmest thanks to Frank Daniels, George Schlukbier, and the many men and women in Raleigh, North Carolina, and Kingston, New York, who have helped us grow in the area of sports publishing.

We also are fortunate to extend our relationship with Starkey & Henricks, which has been the typographer by this time for 21 Total Sports volumes. Our admiration and gratitude go to Peter and Doug Bird, who have been generous with their advice and technical assistance, and Peter Compton, George Galgoczi, and Ellen Curcio.

We also thank pro football beat writers Jerry DiPaola

and Bob McGinn, who contributed work to the *Total Football* spinoffs.

Consultants Richard H. Bozzone, Jim J. Campbell, Bill Friedman, Shawn Gray, Stan Grosshandler, John G. Hogrogian, Rick Korch, and Michael Neft were standouts on "special teams" as were Bill Himmelman of Sports Nostalgia Research, and Gary Wright and Richard O. Brand on the high schools the pros attended. Our "safety," typist Melissa Hredocik, prepared this and many other features for publication.

We also thank a wide range of independent contributors. They are, in alphabetical order: Bob Allen, Hub Arkush, Bob Barnett, Mel Bashore, Scott Brofman, Richard Brown, Bill Carle, Stan Carlson, Jim W. Coleman, Tom Cooper, John Crelli, David Daugherty, Bob Davids, Bill Dolbier, Jamey Foster, Mike Gage, Jim Gallagher, William Garcia, Gordon Garlock, Morton Gerofsky, Lawrence M. Hoff, W. Lloyd Johnson, Harold Jones, Steve Jubyna, Joe Junod, Bob Kirlin, Gerald Kisiel, Jay Langhammer, Joe Lawler, Charles LeChorchick, Kevin Leonard, Ron McKenzie, Nancy McKinnon, Mark Maltby, Richard Musterer, Michael Neft, Naomi Neft, Bill Nusbaum, Bob Pence, Frank Phelps, Richard Piedmonte, Ray Queen, Libby Rehm, George R. Rekela, Marvin Scade, John Seaburn, Jack Selzer, Irwin Shapiro, Dan Sobczak, Tod Spieker, Jim Sumner, Frank Swain, George Treece, Lance Trusty, Chuck Wasserstrom, Jim Whalen, Dick Whittingham, Karl Wolf, and Randy Wooden.

Special mentions go to the Notre Dame International Sports and Games Research Collections and curator Jethrow Kyles, past curator Herb Juliano, and Rita Erskine. At the National Archives and Records Service of the General Services Administration, we thank Carmelita S. Ryan of the Scientific, Economic and Natural Resources Branch, Civil Archives Division.

We also thank the many colleges and universities who answered our questions and generously provided demographic information. Since so many schools have numerous names for departments which perform the same functions, we have abbreviated them to conserve space as follows:

Alum. - Alumni Services
Arch. - Archives, Libraries, and Special Collections
Ath. - Athletic Department
PR - Public Relations and Public Information
Reg. - Registrar's Office
SID - Sports Information Department

We are grateful for the cooperation of:

Abilene Christian University: Erma Jean Loveland, Arch.
Adrian College: Kristen Mickey, Arch.
Akron, University of: John V. Miller, Jr., Arch; former SID Ken McDonald
Alabama, University of: Cliff Davis, Alum.; Taylor Watson and Mrs. Gunetta R. Rich, Arch.; Rebecca Roberts, PR
Alabama State University: Arch.
Albright College: Edwin L. Bell, Arch.
Alfred University: Lawrence J. Casey, Reg.; Norma Higgins, Arch.
Allegheny College: Richard A. Stewart, Alum.; Arch.
American International College: Dale Labonte.
Amherst College: Daria D'Arienzo and Anne Ostendarp, Arch.
Arizona State University: Jeannette Frantz, Arch.
Arizona, University of: David P. Robrock, Peter Steere, Roger Myers, Arch.
Arkansas-Pine Bluff, University of: Arch.
Arkansas State University: Reg.
Arkansas Tech University: John Winkle, Arch.
Arkansas, University of: Tony Wappel, Arch.
Ashland University: David Roepke, Arch.
Auburn University: Reg.; David Rosenblatt; Pamela R. Pedersen, Alum.; Beverly S. Powers, Arch.
Augsburg College: Grace Sulerud; Irene Steenson.
Augustana College (Illinois): Judy Belan, Arch.; Reg.
Augustana College (South Dakota): Ann Smith, Arch.
Austin College: Laura McLemore and Martha Cox, Arch. Sue Sappenfield.
Baldwin-Wallace College: Beverly J. Lane, Arch.; Eloise Tressel.
Baylor University: Ellen Brown, Texas Collection; Reg.
Beloit College: Joseph Kobylka, Alum.; Laurel Nelson and Fred Burwell, Arch.; Pat Ortiz, Reg.
Benedictine College: Arch.
Bethany (West Virginia): Marilyn Shaver, Arch.
Bethune-Cookman College: Charles D. Jackson, SID
Bluffton College: Howard E. Krehbiel, Arch.
Boise State: Reg.; Arch.
Boston College: Reid Oslin, SID; Prof. Richard J. Schrader; Mary M. Hawes, Reg.; Amy Felker, Arch.
Boston University: Amy Shepardson, Arch.; Edward M. Carpenter, SID
Bowling Green State University: Reg.
Bradley University: Karen Deller and Sherri Schneider, Arch; Ruth Jass, Reg.; Casey Connors, SID
Brandeis University: Reg.
Brigham Young University: Mark Smith, Arch.; Gene F. Priday, Reg.
Brown University: Martha L. Mitchell, Arch and Gayle Lynch, Arch.
Bucknell, University: Bradley Tufts, PR; Arch.; Doris Dysinger; Kathy Gathman, Reg.
Buffalo, University of New York at: Stacy Askew, Arch.
Butler University: Reg.; Gisela Terrell, Arch and George Dellinger, Arch.
California-Berkeley, University of: William M. Roberts, Arch.; Reg.
California-Davis, University of: Gil Apaka; Reg.
California-Los Angeles, University of: Reg.; Dennis Bitterlich, Arch.
California-San Diego, University of: Bradley D. Westbrook, Arch.; Lisa M. Zullo, Reg.
California-Santa Barbara, University of: Reg.; Tanya Koepp, Alum.
California Polytech. State University: Ken Kenyon, University Arch.
California Polytechnic State University-Pomona: Arch.
California Polytechnic State University-San Luis Obispo: Thomas L. Zuur, Reg.
Cal State University-Bakersfield: D. Berona, Reg.
Cal State University-Chico:Pam Herman, Arch. Assistant; Bruce D. Reiver, Reg.
Cal State University-Fresno: Tina Beddall, Reg.
Cal State University-Long Beach: John A. Krecek, Reg.
Cal State University-Northridge: Ryan Finney, SID
Cal State University-Sacramento: Pamela Macas, Arch.
Canisius College: Gregory Coogan, Robert J.Nelson, S.J., and John D. Garvey, S.J., Arch.
Carleton College: Eric Hillemann and Mark A. Greene, Arch.
Carnegie Mellon University: Sharon E. Maclean, Arch.; Alum.; Mary C. Schall, Arch.
Carroll College: Jean Olsen, Reg.; James E. Van Ess, Arch.; Shawn Ama, SID
Carson-Newman College: Geoff Woolard, SID
Carthage College: Steve Marovich, SID; Ruth A. Johnson, Reg.
Case-Western Reserve University: Dennis Harrison, Arch.; Bob Psuik, Reg.

Catawba College: Brian Morrison, SID ; Reg.
Catholic University of America, The: Monica Cain, Reg.; Tim Meagher, Anthony Zitto, Brother David, and Lynn Conway, Arch.
Centenary College of Louisiana: Matthew Stephens, Arch.
Centenary College: Arch.
Central Arkansas, University of: Tony Sitz, Reg.; Tom W. Dillard, Arch.
Central College (Kansas): Linda Green, Alum.
Central Michigan University: Reg.; Evelyn Leasher, Reg.
Central Missouri State University: Vivian Richardson, Arch.; Nancy E. Littlejohn, Arch.
Central Oklahoma, University of: Jennifer McCullough, Arch. Technician; Reg.
Central State University: George T. Johnson, Arch.; Karen L. Davis, Alum.
Central Washington University:Carolyn Wells, Reg.
Centre College: Diane Fisher Johnson, Robert Glass, and Grace Doherty, Arch.
Chadron State College: Reg.
Chicago, University of: Caroline Coven, Arch.
Citadel, The: Jane Yates, Arch.
City College of the City University of New York: Thomas Jennings, Reg.; Barbara Dunlap, Arch.
Clark Atlanta University: Frederick A. Fresh, Reg.
Clarkson University: Sylina Hag, Arch.
Clemson; Office of Reg.; Arch.
Colgate University: Bob Cornell, SID; Carl Peterson, Arch.
Colorado at Boulder, University of: Sandra J. Trenka; Reg.
Colorado School of Mines: Arch.; Reg.
Colorado State University: Steve Dahl and S. Kay Jacks, Reg.
Columbia University: Curtis Pires, SID
Concordia College: Arch.
Connecticut College: Arch.
Connecticut, University of: Kathleen Shipton, Reg.; Randall Jimerson and Joanna Oudin, Arch.
Cornell College: Reg.; Anne Secor and Berta Ringold, Arch.
Cornell University: Elaine Engst, Kathleen Jacklin, Roberta M. Moudry, and Nancy Dean, Arch.
Creighton University: John A. Krecek, Reg.
Dartmouth College: Anne Ostendarp and Kenneth C. Cramer, Arch.; Joyce Pike.
Davidson College: Jan Blodgett, Arch.
Davis and Elkins College: M. Stellato and Beth Guye Kittle, Alum.
Dayton, University of: Kerrie A. Moore, Arch.
Delaware, University of: Jean K. Brown, Arch.; Joseph DiMartile, Reg.
Delaware State University: Reg.
Delta State University: Arch.; Reg.
Denison University: Florence W. Hoffman, Arch.; Larry R. Murdock, Reg.
DePaul University: Elisa Addlesperger, Eileen Ward, and Mary Zimmerman, Arch.
DePauw University: John R. Riggs, Arch.; Eleanor Ypma, Reg.; Virginia Brann and Roy O. West, Arch.
Detroit Mercy, University of: Andy Glatzman, SID; Rev. Edward J. Dowling S.J. and Christine Yancy, Arch.
Dickinson College: Shirley Soprano, Reg.; Marie Ferre and George Hing, Arch.
Drake University: Paul F. Morrison, Arch.; J. Elias Jones, Arch.
Duke University: Harry DeMik, Reg.; Pamela B. Vainadoe, Reg.
Duquesne University: Fr. Richard Wersing, Arch.
Earlham College: Sara Beth Terrell, Arch.; Thomas D. Hamm, Arch.
East Carolina University: Reg.
East Central University (Oklahoma): Arch.; Pamla Armstrong, Reg.; Dava Albertson, James A. Thomas, Sr.
East Texas State University: Richard C. Elliott, Reg.; Arch.
Eastern Illinois University: Robert V. Hillman, Arch.
Eastern Kentucky University: Arch.
Eastern Michigan University: Maria Davis, University Arch.
Eastern New Mexico University: Gene Bundy, Arch.
Elizabeth City State University: Leonard R. Ballou, Arch.
Elon College: Arch.; Connie L. Keller, Arch.
Emporia State University: James Meyer.
Evansville, University of: Arch.
Findlay, University of: Ann J. Cooper, Arch.; Reg.
Findley College: John C. Hutson.
Fisk University: Ann Allen Shockley, Arch.
Florida, University of
Florida State: Maxwell Carraway, Jr., Reg.
Fordham University: John J. Macisco Jr.; Rev. C. Gerard Commolly, S.J., Arch.; Rev. Edward Dunn, S.J., Arch.; Stephen Bordas, Reg.; Julio C. Diaz Jr.
Fort Hays State University: Bob Lowen, Alum.; Reg.; Ron Pflughoft, Alum.
Fort Valley State College: Reg.
Franklin and Marshall College: Anne Kenne, Arch.
Franklin College: Mary Alice Medlicott, Arch.; Reg.
Furman University: Arch.
Geneva College: Reg.; W. Lee Troup, PR
George Washington University, The: G. David Anderson, C.A., Arch.
Georgetown College: Jennifer Duvall, Arch.
Georgetown University: Reg.; John Reynolds, Arch.; Lynn Conway, Lisette Matano, Tricia Pyne.
Georgia, University of: Gilbert Head, Arch.; Robert M. Willingham, Jr., Arch.; Karlene Lawrence and Roy
Gatchell, Ath.; Reg.; Nicole Jebbia.
Georgia Institute of Technology: Michael Branch and Ruth Hale, Arch.; Reg.
Gettysburg College: Arch.; Reg.; Eileen Thomas.
Gonzaga University: Arch.
Grinnell College: Jim George, SID; Reg.; Anne Kintner, Arch.
Grove City College: Cindy Walheim, Alum.; John W. Cole, Reg.
Gustavus-Adolphus College: Denise A. Hudson, Arch.; Edi Thorstensson, Arch.; Reg.
Hamline University: Muriel McEachern, Arch.; Thelma Boeder, Consulting Arch.
Hampden-Sydney College: Arch.; Alan Zoelner, Arch.
Harvard University: Lee Fallontowne, Reg.; Patrice Donoghue, Harley P. Holden and John Trepasso, Arch.
Haskell Indian J.C.: Milton S. Overby.
Hawaii, University of: Reg.; Janice M. Joyce, Arch.
Heidelberg College: Carl G. Klopfenstein Arch.; Cindy Murphy, Reg.
Hillsdale College: Dr. Jerome A. Fallon, Arch.
Hobart and William Smith College: Charles P. Boswell, Reg.
Hofstra University: Kay Trudy, Reg.; Geri Solomon, Arch.
Holy Cross, College of the: Reg.; Rev. Eugene J. Harrington S.J., Arlene Long, and Cynthia Medina, Arch.
Houston, University of: Andrea Bean Hough, Arch.
Howard Payne University: Deborah Dill, Arch.
Humboldt State University: Arch.
Idaho, University of: Christine Gray, Arch.; M.E. Telin, Reg.
Illinois Institute of Technology: F. R. Eckford, Reg.
Illinois, University of: William Maher, Arch.; Robert T. Chapel, Arch.
Illinois Wesleyan University: Jack Horenberger, Ath.
Indiana University: J. William Baus, Arch.; Elisabeth R. Olesskar and Bryan Young, Arch.; Reg.
Indianapolis, University of: Jay L. Starks, Arch.
Iowa State University: Laura S. Kline, Arch.; Judy Casey, Arch.; Janis Meiers, Reg.
Iowa, University of: Earl M. Rogers, Arch.
Iowa Wesleyan College: Lynn Ellsworth, Arch.
John Carroll University: Arch.
Kalamazoo College: Thomas M. Myers, PR; Elizabeth Sloan Smith, Arch.
Kansas State University: Denise Wells, Reg.
Kansas, University of: John M. Nugent, Arch.; Barry Bunch, Arch.
Kent State University: Kenton Daniels, Arch.
Kentucky, University of: Frank B. Stranger, Jr., Arch.; Ty Halpin, SID

Kentucky Wesleyan College: Arch.
Kenyon College: Reg.; Thomas B. Greenslade, Arch.; Janie Peele, Arch.
Knox College: Reg.; Lynn Harlan, Arch.; Carley R. Robison, Arch.
Lafayette College: Albert W. Gendebein and Diane Windham Shaw, Arch.; David K. Thomas, Reg.
Lake Forest College: Martha Briggs, Arch.
Langston University: Reg.
La Salle University: Dominic J. Galante, Reg.; Bro. Joseph Grabenstein, Arch.
Lawrence University: Kathy Isaacson, Arch.
Lebanon Valley College: Bruce S. Correll, Reg.
Lehigh University: Fr. William Holberton, Arch.; Georgia E. Raynor, Arch.
Lenoir-Rhyne College: Dom Donnelly, SID
Lewis University: Br. Bernard Rapp, Arch.
Lincoln University (Missouri): Ronald G. Nelson, Reg.; SID; Carolyn F. Amos, Arch.
Lincoln University (Pennsylvania): Khalil Mahmud, Arch.
Linfield College: Sports Information Office; Arch.
Loras College: Michael D. Gibson, Arch.
Louisiana Tech University: Reg.; Arch.
Louisville, University of: Margaret Merrick, Arch.; Reg.; Thomas L. Owen, Arch.
Loyola College (Maryland): Nicholas Varga, Arch.
Loyola University (Chicago): Brother Michael Grace S.J., Arch.
Luther College: Kirk Johnson, Alum.; Duane W. Fenstermann, Reg.
Macalester College: Daniel J. Balik, Reg, Anna M. Theisen, and Marek Ciolko, Reg.; Harry Drake, Arch.
Maine, University of: Peter R. Reid, Reg.
Manchester College: Amy L. Taylor, SID , Ferne Baldwin, Arch.
Manhattan College: Reg.
Marietta College: Reg.; Judy Pannier, Arch.
Marquette University: John L. LeDoux, Arch., Charles Elston, Arch., and Terry Margherita.
Marshall University: Mrs. Teal, Arch.
Maryland, University of: Karla Koles, Reg.; Anne S.K. Turkos, Arch.
Massachusetts Institute of Technology: Elizabeth Kaplan, Arch.
McMurry College: Arch.
McNeese State University: Kathie Bordelon, Arch., Rodney Edwards, Arch.
McPherson College: Rowena Olsen, Arch.
Memphis, University of: Ed Frank, Arch.; Richard O'Bryan, Reg.; Barbara Rye, Reg.
Mercer University: Lee Twombly, Arch.
Miami (Florida), University of: William E. Brown, Jr., Arch.; SID; Kathy G. Uitvlugt, Alum.
Miami (Ohio) University: Arch.; Scott Parkinson and Bob Schmidt, Arch.
Michigan, University of: Matt Louis, SID
Michigan State University: Larry Ziewacz; Virginia M. Angell, Reg.
Michigan Technological University: Arch.
Middlebury College: College Arch.; Robert Buckeye and Danielle M. Rougeau, Arch.
Middle Tennessee State University: Arch.
Midwestern State University: Steve Holland, Ath.
Millikin University: Reggie Syrcle, PR
Minnesota, University of: Penny Krosch, Arch.
Minnesota-Duluth, University of: Reg.
Mississippi College: Ellen Poole, Alum.
Mississippi Valley State University: Reg.
Mississippi, University of: Kenneth L. Wooten, Reg.; Clay Cavett, Alum.; Langston Rosen and Jeff Romero, SID; Lisa Speer and Jennifer Ford, Arch.; Amanda Strickland.
Missouri, University of: D.J. Wade, Arch.
Missouri-Rolla, University of: Lynn Newman, Reg.; Wayne F. Bledsoe and Roberta E. Brown Morgan, Arch.
Monmouth College: Jill M. Munson, Reg.
Montana State University: Jean Smith, Kim Allen Scott, and Deborah S. Nash, Arch.; Joan L. Sweet, Ath.
Montana, University of: Dale L. Johnson, Arch.; Alita Phelps, Reg.; Dave Guffey,SID
Moorhead State University: Korella Selzler, Arch.
Morgan State University: Herbert S. Klinghoffer, Reg.
Morningside College: Candace Davies.
Morris Brown College: Reg.
Mount St. Mary's College: Reg.; Barbara D. Miles, Arch.
Mount Union College: Judy Kirchmeyer, Arch.; Reg.; Alan Aldinger, SID
Muhlenberg College: Joan Steiner, Reg.; Dr. Ralph S. Graber.
Murray State University: Reg.
Muskingum College: Reg.
Nebraska, University of: Lynn R. Beidrick, Arch.; Jane Jameson, Alum.; Ted Pfeifer, Reg.
Nebraska-Kearney, University of: Reg.
Nebraska-Omaha, University of: Cynthia A. Taylor, Arch.
Nebraska Wesleyan University: Arch.
Nevada, University of: Karen Gash, Arch.
New Hampshire, University of: Betty Aldrich, Reg.
New Mexico, University of: Jim Acosta, Reg.; Greg Remington, SID
New York University: Nancy Cricco, Rohinie Munzel, and Peter Braunstein, Arch.
Niagara University: Reg.: Alum.
Norfolk State University: Annette Montgomery, Arch.
North Alabama, University of: Dr. Sue J. Wilson, Reg.
North Carolina A & T: Mrs. Earla Thornhill, Reg.; Donald Bradsher, Arch.
North Carolina, University of: Michael G. Martin, Jr., Arch.
North Carolina Central University: B. T. McMillon, Arch.
North Carolina, Chapel Hill, University of: David C. Lanier, Reg.
North Carolina State University: Arch.; Maurice S. Toler.
North Central College: Michael Moser, Alum.
North Dakota, University of: Sandra J. Slater, Arch.; Reg.
North Dakota State University: John E. Bye, Arch.; Reg.; George Ellis, SID; Robert F. Entzion, Ath.
North Park College: Reg.
North Texas, University of: Richard L. Himmel, Arch.
Northeast Louisiana University: Arch.
Northeast Missouri State University: Judith May, Arch.; Elaine M. Doak, Arch.
Northeastern State University: Victoria Sheffler, Arch.
Northeastern University: Edmund J. Mullen, Reg.
Northern Illinois University: Reg.; Mike Korcek, SID
Northern Michigan University: Jim Pinar, SID; Reg.
Northwest Missouri State University: Thomas W. Carneal, Arch.; Reg.
Northwestern State University of Louisiana; Reg.
Northwestern University: Patrick M. Quinn, Arch.; Kevin Leonard and Matt McGarvey, Arch.
Notre Dame, University of: Daniel H. Winicur, Reg.; Charles Lamb, Arch.
Occidental College: Michael C. Sutherlond, Arch.
Oglethorpe University: Polly Perry, Alum.; Earle J. Moore, Sr.
Ohio Northern University: Robert L. Allen, Jr.
Ohio State University: Raimund E. Goerler, Arch.; Reg.
Ohio University: Sheppard Black, Arch.; Frank Morgan, SID ; Karen Jones, Reg.; Susie Rohrbough, Arch.
Ohio Wesleyan University: Catherine N. Schlichting, Arch; Pam Howard, Arch.; Sabrina Pollock, Reg.
Oklahoma, University of: Johnnie Williams, Reg.; Stephen H. Norwood; Laura Carter Teske, Arch.
Oklahoma City University: Larry McAlister, SID
Oklahoma State University: Heather Lloyd, Arch.; Kayla Barrett, Arch.; Robin A. Lacy, Reg.
Oregon State University: Elizabeth Nielsen and Georgia Scott, Arch.; Hal Cowan, SID; Russell G. Dix, Reg.
Oregon, University of: Keith Richard and Charla Davis, Arch.; Herbert R. Chereck, Reg.; Alisha Hunt, Reg.
Ottawa University: Annabelle Pence, Reg.
Otterbein College: John Berker.
Ouachita Baptist University: Wendy Richter, Arch.; Reg.

Pacific Lutheran University: Charles T. Nelson, Reg.; Kerstin Ringdahl, Arch.
Pacific University: Arch.
Pennsylvania, University of: Gail M. Pietrzyk, Arch.; Mandy Erickson, SID ; James Curtiss Ayers, Arch.
Pennsylvania State University: Arch.
Pepperdine University: Veronique Juhasz; Carmen Rodriguez, Arch.
Phillips University: Arch.; Nancy Smith, Reg.; Betty Ragsdell, Arch.; Kathryn S. Penland, Reg.
Pittsburg State University: Lee Christensen, Reg.; Randy Roberts, Arch.
Pittsburgh, University of: Arch.; Rebecca Abromitis, Arch.
Portland, University of: Martha V. Wachsmuth, Arch.
Presbyterian College: Arch.
Princeton University: Carl Esche, Arch; Dave Morgan, Alum.; Nicholas Donatiello, SID; Earl Coleman, Arch.; Ben Primer, Arch.; Terun Sabre Weed.
Providence College: Jane M. Jackson, Arch.; Teena Sullivan, Arch.
Purdue University: Linda Tye, Arch.; Brian Remsberg, SID
Redlands, University of: Reg.; Arch.
Rhode Island, University of: Arch.; David C. Masyln, Arch.; Richard Gelles.
Rhodes College: Elizabeth G. Kesler, Arch.
Richmond, University of: Robert A. Whitt, Darlene Slater, and Fred Anderson, Arch.; Reg.
Ripon College: Phil Rath, Arch.; William R. Brandt and Louise Schang, Arch.; Amy Lawless.
Rochester, University of: Karl Kabelac, Arch.
Rose-Hulman Institute of Technology: Bob Goldring and Dale Long, SID; John Robson, Arch.
Rutgers University: Ruth Simmons, Edward Skipworth and Susan Avallone, Arch.; Kenneth J. Iuso, Reg.
St. Ambrose College: Corinne Potter
St. Bonaventure University: Reg.; Malcolm V.T. Wallace, Arch.; Lorraine Welsh, Arch.; Alum.
St. Cloud State University: Jerry Westby, University Arch.; Keith J. Rauch, Reg.; Judy Nielson.
St. Edwards University (Texas): Ingrid Karklins and Inez Nira, Arch.; Reg.
St. Francis College: Barbara C. Doll, Arch.
St. John's University (Minnesota): Vincent Tegeder, Arch.
St. John's University (New York): Frank Ralaniello, SID ; Peggy L. McMullen, Arch.
St. Joseph's College (Indiana): Arch.; Reg.
St. Lawrence University: Lynn Case Ekfelt, Arch.
St. Louis University: Bruce W. Cunningham, Reg.; Stephen Smith, Arch.
St. Mary's College (California): Brother L. Dennis, F.S.C. Arch.; Linda Wobbe.
St. Mary's University (Minnesota): Bro. Paul J. Ostendorf, Arch.; Brother Richard Gerlach, Arch.
St. Mary's University of San Antonio: Bro. Robert Wood, S.M.
St. Norbert College: Jon Curtis, Reg.
St. Olaf College: Joan R. Olson, Arch.; Reg.
St. Thomas, College of: John Davenport, Arch.
St. Vincent College: Rev. Omer U. Kline, O.S.B., Arch.; Reg.
Samford University: Elizabeth C. Wells, Arch.; Shirley L. Hutchens, Arch.; Reg.
Sam Houston State University: Arch.; Reg.
San Diego, University of: Lisa M. Zullo, Reg.
San Diego State University: Samuel N. Goldman
San Francisco State University: Samuel N. Goldman
Santa Clara, University of: Julie O'Keefe, Arch.; Carol J. Lamoreaux, Reg.
Scranton, University of: Rich Ryczak, Arch.
Simpson College: Margaret Aten, Reg.
South Carolina, University of: Reg.
South Dakota State University: Barb Koenders, Alum.
South Dakota, University of: Arch.
Southeastern Louisiana: Lois Wagner, Arch.
Southeast Missouri State University: Arch.
Southern California, University of: Paul Christopher, University Arch.; Susan Hikida, Arch.; Tim Tessalone, SID
Southern Connecticut State University: Reg.
Southern Illinois University: Barbara J. Summers, Arch.
Southern Methodist University: Lee Milazzo, Arch.; P.J. Hunter; John Underwood, Ath.; SID
Southern Mississippi: Judy Kahler, Reg.
Southwest Missouri State University: Arch.
Southwest Texas State University: Margaret A. Vaverek, Iris T. Schumann, Jennifer B. Patterson, and Amanda Oates, Arch.
Southwestern College: Reg.
Southwestern Louisiana, University of: I. Bruce Turner, Head, Arch.
Southwestern Oklahoma State University: Bob Klaassen, Reg.
Southwestern University: Mrs. Jan Puskarich, Reg.
Springfield College: Gerald F. Davis, Arch.; Ms. Marjorie Fish; Tina Wuerthele, Reg.
Spring Hill College: Charles J. Boyle, Arch.
State University of New York at Buffalo; Stacey Askew, Arch.
Stephen F. Austin State University: Dennis Jones, Reg.
Sterling College: Frances Calderwood, Reg.
Sul Ross State University: Melleta R. Bell, Arch.
Swarthmore College: Arch.
Syracuse University: Amy Doherty, Mary O'Brien, Carolyn Davis, and Ann Atwater, Arch.; Cindy L. Curtis, Reg.
Tampa, University of: Art Bagley, Arch.
Temple University: Carol Ann Harris, Arch.
Tennessee-Chattanooga, University of: Harold Wilkes; Bill Prince.
Tennessee-Martin, University of: Dieter C. Ullrich and Paul Meek Arch.; Robert L. Carroll, Alum.
Tennessee, University of: H.D. (Bud) Ford, SID ; Office of Reg.
Texas A&M University: Charles R. Schultz, Arch.; Luke B. Spring, SID; Bradley Stevenson.
Texas Christian University: Arch.; Reg.
Texas Sports Hall of Fame: Jay Black, Arch.
Texas Tech University: Arch.; Reg.
Texas, University of, Arlington: William H. Richter, Arch.; Pete Carlon, Ath.
Thiel College: Mark R. McGrath, Reg.; John R. Hauser, Alum.; Dr. Paul Mueller, Arch.
Toledo, University of: Barbara Floyd, Arch.; Janice Hackbush; Arch.; Ral Brandt, SID
Trinity College (Connecticut): Peter J. Knapp, Arch.; Claire R. Brown, Reg.
Trinity University (Texas): Janice Sabec, Arch.; Richard C. Elliott, Reg.
Tufts University: Robert Johnson-Lally, Arch.; Mildred S. Eastwood, Reg.; Barbara Tringali, Arch.
Tulsa, University of: Toby Murray, Arch.; Elizabeth Flake, Alum.; SID
Tuskegee University (Texas): Daniel T. Williams, Arch.
U.S. Coast Guard Academy: Reg.; Lucinda Herrick, Arch.
U.S. Military Academy: Kenneth W. Rapp and Robert Schnare, Arch; Diane Baker; Jerry D. Cunningham, PR
U.S. Naval Academy: Brian D. Fors, Arch.; Jane H. Price, Arch.
Ursinus College: James R. Rue, Arch.; Reg.
Utah State University: Charles L. Olson, Reg.
Utah, University of: Clint Bailey, Arch.
Valparaiso University: Melvin H. Doering and Daniel R. Gahl, Arch.
Vanderbilt University: Suellen Stringer-Hye, Arch.; Sara J. Harwell, Arch.; Jami Awalt.
Vermont, University of: David J. Blow, Arch.
Villanova University: Kathryn L. Abraham, Arch.; Rev. Dennis J. Gallagher, Arch.
Virginia, University of: Jeanne C. Pardee, Justin P. Lowery, and Michael Plunkett, Arch.; Jane Desjardins, SID
Virginia Military Institute: Julie M. Gerke, Reg.; Diane B. Jacob, Arch.
Virginia Polytechnic Institute: Reg.
Virginia State University: Reg.
Virginia Union University: Reg.

Wabash College: Johanna Herring, Arch.; Reg.; Max Servies, Ath.
Wake Forest University: John R. Woodward, Arch.; Reg.; Jody Jones, SID.
Washburn University of Topeka: Charlene S. Hurt, Arch.; Martha Imparato, Arch.; Carla Rasch, Reg.
Washington College (Maryland): F.W. Dumschott.
Washington & Jefferson College: David W. Kraueter, Arch.
Washington & Lee University: Lisa M. Hamric, Arch.
Washington, University of: Gary Lundell, Arch.
Washington State University: Terry Abraham, Arch.; Michael Brooks, Reg.; Lawrence R. Stark, Arch.; Reg.
Washington University: Iris Wright, Reg.
Waynesburg College: Janice Brunazi; Teresa Verango; Mrs. Evalyn Black, Reg.; Ferdinand Dolfi, Alum.
Wayne State University: Patricia Bartkowski, Arch.
Weber State University: Julie A. Middlemas, Arch.; Reg.
West Texas State University: Arch.; Cesa Espinoza, Arch.
West Virginia Inst. of Tech.: Bob Scholl, Reg.; Arch.
West Virginia State College: Janice Young, Arch.
West Virginia University: John Antonik, SID; Bille Leach, Reg.
West Virginia Wesleyan College: Benjamin F. Crutchfield, Jr., Arch.
Western Kentucky University: Helen L. Knight, Arch.
Western Maryland College: Marylee Schmall, Arch.; Winifred S. Dulaney, Arch.
Western Michigan University: Jason Aikens, Arch.
Westminster College: Reg.; H. Dewey DeWitt, Arch.
Whittier College: Ann Topjon, Arch.; Betty Kenworthy, Reg.
Whitworth College: Ramona Kinnaman, Reg.; Gary Whisenand, Reg.
Wichita State University: Mary Nelson, Arch.; David Reagan, Reg.; Judi McBroom, Alum.; Kayla Barrett; Reg.
Widener University: Arch.; Reg.
Wiley College: M. Christian Jones, Alum.
Willamette University: Paul Olsen, Reg.; James Booth, Alum.
William and Mary, College of; Laura F. Parrish, Arch.; Dan Wakely, SID; Jeff Nygaard, SID
William Jewell College: Norris A. Patterson, Arch.; Iva Lea Durocher, Alum.
Williams College: Lynne K. Fonteneau, Arch.; Karen D. Drickamer; Catherine Curvin.
Wilmington College: Ina E. Kelley, Arch.; Karen M. Garman, Reg.
Wisconsin, University of: Debra Gansen, Reg.; SID ; Daniel C. Markeland and David M. Sieden, Arch.
Wisconsin-Eau Claire, University of: Richard L. Pifer, Arch.
Wisconsin-La Crosse, University of: Christina Cota, Arch.; Edwin L. Hill, Arch.; Alum.
Wisconsin-Milwaukee, University of: Allan Kovan, Arch.
Wisconsin-Oshkosh, University of: Reg.
Wisconsin-Platteville, University of: Mary Freymiller, Arch.
Wisconsin-Stevens Point, University of: Ray Stroik, Arch.
Wisconsin-Stout, University of: Arch.
Wittenberg University: Ms. Regina Entorf, Arch.; Kathy Schulz, Arch.; Mrs. Peggy Dalton, Alum.
Wofford College: Herbert Hucks, Jr., Arch.
Wooster, College of: Lowell W. Coolidge, Arch.; Reg.; Denise D. Monbarren, Arch.
Worcester Polytechnic Institute: Lora Bruick, Arch.
Wyoming, University of: Rebecca L. Macon, Reg.
Xavier University (Ohio): Ben Benedict, SID; Doris R. Wolf, Reg.
Yale University: Judith Ann Schiff, Arch.; Patricia Bodak Stark, Arch.; Tom Hyry, Arch.
Youngstown State University: Greg Gulas, SID

The Editors

Introduction

Pro football just keeps getting bigger, and so do books about pro football. Back in 1934, when the play-for-pay version of the game ranked far behind college football in fan interest (and even further behind baseball), former New York Giants president Dr. Harry March used fewer than 160 pages to relate the game's history in *Pro Football: Its "Ups" and "Downs."*

Things are different now. Relegated to newspapers' back sports pages in its early days, pro football now dominates the front pages of that section throughout much of the year. By any measurement—headlines, television ratings, water-cooler conversations—the National Obsession has surpassed the National Pastime in fan hysteria.

The game is big. It demands and deserves an encyclopedia of commensurate size.

Total Football, a publication parallel to its predecessor, *Total Baseball,* attempts to put a whole library of pro football knowledge into a single book. The first part of *Total Football* includes essays on the history of the game, its teams, its most significant games, and its greatest players. You'll find explanations of strategy through the years and detailed descriptions of key plays, as well as lists such as fathers and sons who both played pro football, players who enjoyed great second careers, and players who starred in other sports.

You'll also find the most complete compilation of yearly all-pro teams and individual awards ever printed, season rosters of every NFL, AAFC, and AFL team, and a complete listing of every drafted player. These features and others have been written or compiled by the foremost pro football historians and writers, people who care passionately about the game and about getting the facts right. The National Football League not only gave its endorsement to the project but also was an active participant in its creation, and the Pro Football Hall of Fame checked thousands of facts along the way. Some of the Hall's most knowledgeable employees contributed articles.

The heart of *Total Football,* of course, is the Player Register, with statistics provided by the redoubtable Elias Sports Bureau, the official NFL statistician, and a valuable "assist" from David Neft. For more than 30 years, Neft has been collecting demographic information on players' birthdates and places, colleges attended, heights, and weights. For *Total Football* he supplemented his research by contacting more than 400 colleges and universities and a like number of former players. There still are gaps in the demographic record, which we hope to close in the future, but, for now, we feel confident that we are presenting the most complete record ever assembled of the more than 17,000 men who have played in an NFL game.

Early on, we realized that football players' statistics could not be presented as easily as those for baseball players. Whereas a shortstop's complete batting record can be given in a single line of type across the page for each of his seasons, an offensive lineman may play a dozen years without earning a single statistical entry except his games played. On the other hand, a versatile halfback may play only a single year yet have entries in five or six categories. After many experiments, we settled on the format used here, which presents every player, regardless of position, in alphabetical order.

So here is *Total Football,* the very best way we know how to cram 79 years of intense competition between the covers of a book. We're not so foolish as to believe we could get through a project of this size without some errors of commission or omission. You, dear reader, are hereby designated an official volunteer proofreader. If you spot a mistake or a questionable statement, please write to us at *Total Football,* 12870 Route 30 North Huntingdon, PA 15642. All readers who correct errors or contribute in other ways will be acknowledged in future editions.

And, now, are you ready for some *Total Football?*

Bob Carroll
June 1999

THE HISTORY

CHAPTER 1

Pro Football Before the NFL

Beau Riffenburgh

The game known outside the United States as "American football" had its origins far from the homeland of the NFL and long before most Europeans even knew the Americas existed. More directly, it developed from two games popular throughout the rest of the world—association football (or soccer as it is known in the United States) and rugby. Varieties of games involving kicking a ball into a goal or beyond a line are known to have existed for more than 2,000 years, and the Spartans and Romans both played games that can be considered ancestors to modern soccer. Indeed, the Romans exported their game throughout much of Europe.

The first two major steps in the evolution of football occurred in the nineteenth century in England. According to legend, the first occurred at the Rugby School in 1823; in the midst of a soccer game, a student, William Webb Ellis, picked up the ball and ran with it. Since the rules forbade advancing the ball in any way other than kicking it, Ellis's move was considered outrageous. It did, however, help lead to the development of a totally new game—rugby—that dramatically would influence American football because players could both carry and kick the ball.

A second step came in 1863 with the formation in London of the Football Association (FA), established for the expressed purpose of establishing a uniform set of rules. This was followed eight years later by the formation of the Rugby Football Union, the governing body of that sport. These organizations set the precedent for having an overall body guiding the development of a sport.

Both sports spread across the ocean to North America. On November 6, 1869, Princeton and Rutgers competed in what has since been recognized as the first college football game. In reality, the rules of that contest bore little resemblance to the modern game and were modified FA rules. Each team had 25 players, the goal posts were 25 yards apart, and the ball was moved by kicking or butting it with one's head. The agreement was that the first team to score 6 goals would win, and Rutgers reached that mark first, outscoring Princeton 6-4.

Although the new game began to become popular at universities throughout the eastern parts of the United States and Canada, there were many variations in the rules, which caused regular confusion at the games, as had been the case with soccer before the formation of the FA. In 1876, following the lead of the FA and the Rugby Football Union, the first rules for American football were written and adopted at a convention in Springfield, Massachusetts. Concurrently, a new intercollegiate association was formed to assess the rules of the game on an annual basis.

That same year, Walter Camp, the man known today as "the father of American football," entered Yale University, where he became not only a sensational player but also a key figure in the rules meetings. Under Camp's guidance, in the next decade a number of significant rules changes were made that began to distinguish the game from rugby.

In 1880, for instance, the number of players allowed on the field at any one time was reduced from 15 per team to 11, and the center snap replaced the scrum to put the ball in play. Two years later, Camp championed the passage of a rule requiring a team to make five yards in three downs in order to maintain possession of the ball. In quick order, Camp developed the first prearranged plays and the first called signals, led the fight to establish set point values for different kinds of scoring, and hired referees to monitor the games and assess penalties.

In 1888, Camp proposed another rule change that would have a remarkable effect on the game: that tackling would be legal not only above the waist, but also down to the knees. Tackling became much more violent, and the change in the rules led to the era of mass formations, in which offensive players bunched themselves around the ball carrier. The wedge formation appeared, followed by Camp's shoving wedge and the famous flying wedge of Lorin Deland of Harvard. Play became brutal, fights were commonplace, and serious injuries and even deaths began to occur on the field. But by the 1890s, the game had risen to national prominence.

The Birth of Pro Football

During the same decades in which football was becoming popular, athletic clubs grew into an important part of American society; the first of these—the New York Athletic Club—was founded in 1868. Membership in athletic clubs not only allowed American men to participate in sporting events but also gave them the chance to engage in betting—with small sums or large—on those games. Membership in a successful athletic club also was seen as a potential route for a young man to gain acceptance into a more exclusive metropolitan men's club. However, this upward social mobility from athletic club to men's club was at least partially dependent upon the success of the athletic club on the field. Thus winning, rather than participation, became the key element of sports in the athletic clubs.

How to win while maintaining a socially desirable clientele, which meant keeping out those of "lower than desirable social station," became a key issue for the athletic clubs. This especially was true since many of the best athletes did not have the financial or social background desired by the clubs. By around 1890, a common solution for this problem had been found in the admission to clubs of athletes who did not become full members, but who competed in exchange for the use of facilities and the payment of "expenses." Although these special memberships and their attendant expense payments clearly were a step towards professionalism, the clubs were forced to maintain fronts of amateurism because of the public's negative attitude towards athletic professionalism.

The road to professionalism in football began in western Pennsylvania. In 1889, the Allegheny Athletic Association (AAA) was formed in Allegheny, Pennsylvania, in what is, today, part of Pittsburgh. The next year, the AAA found an athletic arena—football—in which it could compete for membership with the older, previously dominant East End Gymnasium Club (EEGC). Because the EEGC made only a one-game, half-hearted try at football, the AAA, which went 3-2-1 its initial season against strong competition, gained both new members and a considerable number of fans. The EEGC immediately followed suit and started its own team.

The next year, the AAA was not nearly as strong, while the EEGC, which was led by William Kirschner, a physical education instructor at the club, produced a powerful team that went 7-0. Calling for the two teams to meet—an event that did not occur—the Pittsburgh newspapers labeled the EEGC "semi-professional," while disapprovingly noting that Kirschner's salary nearly doubled during the football season, and that his classes were cut in half.

In 1892, the "Three A's," as the AAA locally was known, and the EEGC, which had been renamed the Pittsburgh Athletic Club (PAC), scheduled a game for October 21. The two teams were undefeated when they met, and more than 3,000 fans overflowed PAC Park. The game ended in a 6-6 tie, the two teams divided a healthy gate, and each added some 100 new members in the following months. The situation soon turned venomous. The PAC accused the AAA of deliberately trying to injure Kirschner, who had left the contest with an ankle injury. The AAA, in turn, argued that Kirschner should not have been playing anyway because he was a professional.

E.V. Paul of the AAA said that the PAC also had used a pro other than Kirschner. The PAC had played the game with a center whom PAC captain Charley Aull had introduced merely as "Stayer." Aull said Stayer had agreed to replace the regular center, who was out with an injury. A week later, it came to light that Stayer actually was A.C. Read, the captain of the Penn State team. No one could prove that Read actually had been paid, and Aull said that Read was not a regular member of the team, but bringing in a ringer of his ability clearly was another step toward the hiring of professionals.

When a rematch was scheduled for November 12, charges almost immediately began to surface that each side was trying to hire top-quality ringers. Indeed, on November 7, PAC manager George Barbour went to Chicago to convince William (Pudge) Heffelfinger and Knowlton (Snake) Ames, two former All-Americas playing with the traveling Chicago Athletic Association team, to join the PAC.

However, Barbour missed them both because they had quit the Chicago AA team over the benching of a teammate. Unfortunately for Barbour, they had gone to Pittsburgh, where they met AAA manager Billy Kountz. Five days later, when game time came at Recreation Park in Allegheny, not only Heffelfinger but his former Chicago teammates Ed Malley and Ben (Sport) Donnelly were representing the home side.

The PAC immediately protested their use, and its regulars walked off the field. While the sellout crowd waited anxiously and the regulars from both sides bickered, the substitutes began to play a game, which appeased no one. Finally, after more than half an hour, the real teams came back for a game that, because of the late start, was shortened to 30 minutes per half rather than the normal 45. The ringers played the major role expected. Midway through the first half Heffelfinger caused a fumble with a powerful hit, picked up the loose ball, and raced 35 yards to a touchdown for the game's only points. The AAA won 4-0.

Following the game, Heffelfinger was paid $500, plus $25 for expenses, while Malley and Donnelly each received expense money. Although it is almost certain that Heffelfinger and others had been paid by the Chicago AA, the AAA's expense account for this game is proof of the first acknowledged appearance of a professional football player.

Controversy over professionalism raged in the Pittsburgh newspapers for weeks, especially after the AAA paid Donnelly $250 to play against Washington and Jefferson College a week later. But, because each side had damaging evidence against the other regarding professionalism, neither filed grievances with the Amateur Athletic Union, the organization overseeing amateur sports. Instead, they decided to wait until the next season.

In 1893, the AAA and the PAC split two games, with the visitors winning each contest. More importantly, however, each almost certainly played a number of professionals. The PAC even signed one player to a formal contract, which read, "I agree to participate in all regularly scheduled football games of the Pittsburgh Athletic Club for the full season of 1893. As an active player I agree to accept a salary of $50 per contest and also acknowledge that I will play for no other club during PAC games." Although the existing contract was torn across the signature, the player was believed to be halfback Grant Dibert. Similarly, the Allegheny club also had at least three pros on its season roster—Ollie Rafferty, Jim Van Cleve, and Peter Wright—and also hired the first full-time professional football coach, Sport Donnelly.

The following season, professionalism began to spread outside of Pittsburgh. The Greensburg Athletic Association became the third team to turn professional when it paid former Princeton and AAA star Lawson Fiscus $20 per game.

Then, in 1895, 18-year-old John Brallier, who had quarterbacked Indiana Normal the previous year, agreed to play a game for the Latrobe YMCA team for $10 and expenses. None of Brallier's predecessors had admitted their professionalism, but Brallier was proud of the fact that he was (he thought) a trendsetter in being paid. He never told anything but the truth about his professionalism, for which he was later recognized for many years as the first pro football player.

It was not until the 1960s that a mysterious pro football researcher, believed to be Nelson Ross, gave Dan Rooney of the Pittsburgh Steelers a paper indicating that Heffelfinger actually had been paid in 1892. Ross's claims later were substantiated by Dick McCann of the Pro Football Hall of Fame, who found the 1892 account ledger of the AAA in which the payment to Heffelfinger was recorded.

The 1896 season saw at least five professional teams, the best of which was the AAA. The previous winter, the Amateur Athletic Union finally had come down on the club for paying its players, and had banned it from playing other AAU members. This signaled the death of the club, which, by the time of the football season, had lost virtually its entire membership.

The First Pro Team

In a desire to go out in a blaze of glory, the AAA decided not only to field a team in defiance of the AAU, but to make it entirely professional. Donnelly was hired as the coach, and he contacted some of the best pros in the country, including Heffelfinger, George Brooke, Langdon (Biffy) Lea, and Tom (Doggie) Trenchard. Each was offered $100 and expenses for the two games the Alleghenys scheduled. Donnelly's 12-man team had only one day of practice before playing back-to-back games in November. Nonetheless, they defeated the Duquesne Country and Athletic Club (DC&AC, or Duquesnes), a powerful team that had started paying players the year before, 12-0, and the PAC 18-0. The AAA then folded, but it had left a legacy as the first completely professional team.

In 1897, Latrobe, which had become the Latrobe Athletic Association, followed the AAA's example and went entirely professional, hiring players from as far away as Iowa. Following the Spanish-American War in 1898, one of the AAA's last rivals, the Duquesnes also hired many outstanding professionals. When it became apparent that the club could not survive financially with these costs, its chairman, sportsman William C. Temple, took over the payments, thus becoming, in effect, the first owner of a pro football team. (Temple also contributed a trophy, the Temple Cup, to winners of an early baseball world series from 1894-97.)

Under Temple, the Duquesnes became the finest pro team in Pennsylvania, which, in those days, generally meant in the country. In 1898, the DC&AC beat Washington and Jefferson, one of the college powerhouses, 11-0, as they did the next year, when they also beat Penn State and Bucknell. In so doing, they established themselves as perhaps the first pro team that could claim to be as strong as the top college teams.

Many of the top players from the DC&AC joined the Homestead Library and Athletic Club (HLAC) in the Pittsburgh suburb of Homestead in 1900 to go undefeated. The next year the HLAC went 11-0 and outscored its opponents 313-12; however, weak finances forced the team to break up. Similar money problems afflicted Latrobe, Greensburg, and a number of other western Pennsylvania teams. Then, oddly, it appeared that the sport might take off across the state, in Philadelphia, with the help of professional baseball.

The First Pro League

Strange goings-on occurred in Philadelphia in 1902. The Phillies of baseball's established National League had several of their players signed by manager Connie Mack of the young American League's champions, the Philadelphia Athletics. The Phillies had gone to court to get their players back, but emotions still ran high.

So when Phillies owner John I. Rogers organized a football team, Ben Shibe, the owner of the Athletics, asked Mack and former University of Pennsylvania tackle Charles (Blondy) Wallace to form another, better team. Since many of the best players were in the west of the state, the two new teams contacted Dave Berry, the former manager of Latrobe, who put together a team mainly consisting of the previous year's HLAC team, and the three united to form what they called the National Football League, the first professional football league.

The new NFL did not last long, but it did record the first night game in pro football history, when the Athletics defeated the Kanaweola Athletic Club 39-0 at Elmira, New York. The three teams split their league games, each going 2-2, and all three claimed the title. The Athletics then beat the Phillies once more, but Berry, who had served as league president, proclaimed his own team—the Pittsburgh Stars—as champions on the strength of their late-season victory over the Athletics.

The final standing was much less interesting to history buffs than Berry's signing of a fullback of some renown—Baseball Hall of Fame pitcher Christy Mathewson of the New York Giants. Mathewson, a great punter, played the first half of the season with Berry's team until, apparently, the Giants stepped in and ordered their star to stop risking his arm. Another future Baseball Hall of Fame pitcher, George Edward (Rube) Waddell was on the Athletics' roster, but only so that Connie Mack could keep an eye on his erratic star. According to contemporary accounts, Waddell stayed on the sideline and led cheers for the football team.

In December, 1902, Tom O'Rourke, the manager of Madison Square Garden, set up what he called the "World Series." The event was supposed to match the five best teams in the country. However, none of the NFL teams nor the Watertown (New York) Red and Blacks, who had claimed the national title two years in a row, were interested. Instead, the Syracuse Athletic Club won three straight games to claim the series over the Orange (New Jersey) AC, the Warlow (New York) AC, the Knickerbockers, and a team made up of players from both the Phillies and Athletics, but simply called "New York."

The first modern baseball World Series was played in 1903. O'Rourke also had a series in 1903, which was won by a team from Franklin, Pennsylvania, that was virtually an all-star team from the 1902 NFL. However, despite Franklin's success, pro football in Pennsylvania was on the wane. Late in 1903, four PAC players were hired by the Massillon Tigers, the first Ohio team openly to turn pro. By 1905, most of the western Pennsylvania and New York teams had declined or folded altogether. The best players in the country began to move to Ohio, the cradle of the sport.

The Beginning of the Ohio League

Athletic club football existed in Ohio as far back as 1889, when the Dayton AC developed a team. Athletic clubs or associations in Cleveland, Akron, Canton, and Youngstown all followed with teams, and state amateur champions were named by popular acclaim beginning in 1895. There were no playoffs as of 1902, and all games played by teams were considered in determining the unofficial champions. Victories over well-known or big-city teams were considered more significant than those against small-town teams, although a loss to a smaller team could be devastating to one's title hopes.

In 1903, a decision was made that would change football forever. For years, Massillon, the second-largest city in Stark County, Ohio, fielded amateur teams that unsuccessfully tried to compete on even terms with teams from Stark County's first city, Canton. The inevitable string of losses was demoralizing, embarrassing, and, for those who were betting men, costly. The football supporters of Massillon decided something had to change.

On September 3, 1903, the major football figures of Massillon held a meeting at the Hotel Sailor and established a new team, a team whose sole purpose was to defeat Canton. Lawyer Jack Goodrich was named manager and newspaperman Ed Stewart coach; the orange-and-black-striped sleeves of the jerseys supplied by the city's sporting goods store led to the team's nickname, the Tigers.

But this was not just any town team. First, the Tigers had considerable talent: Stewart not only was the editor of the *Massillon Evening Independent* and the coach of the Tigers, but also the team's quarterback; Goodrich was an effective halfback; Frank Botoner, a 32-year-old policeman, was one of the best guards anywhere; and, Mully Miller, the 170-pound fullback, was the team's big star. In addition, the Tigers were serious about winning, as evidenced by regular practices, something most other teams didn't do.

The Tigers lost their opener 6-0 to Wooster College, but then defeated four teams in a row before whipping Canton 16-0 and beating a team from Cleveland. They then challenged the East Ends of Akron to a game for the state title. The East Ends had been recognized as the state champions for several years running; in many people's minds they were as good as any other team in the country. They ultimately agreed to play the Tigers on December 5, with the winner taking 75 percent of the gate and the losers 25 percent.

Before the game was held, it was apparent that Massillon was determined to win, regardless of cost. They hired four professionals from the old PAC, including Bob Shiring, probably the best center in the country, and the McChesney brothers, Harry and Doc. The newest imports had a major impact on the game, as Doc McChesney recovered a fumble for the only touchdown of the first half. In the second half, the Tigers scored on a tackle-around play, and they cruised home with the state title 12-0.

Massillon's use of pros opened the floodgates, as at least five teams other than the Tigers openly began to pay players. One of them, Shelby, had professionals since 1902, but in 1904 made history by signing halfback Charles Follis, who thereby became professional football's first black player.

The influx of pros separated those teams playing for the traditional amateur championship from those now vying for the Ohio independent championship, as the professional title was known at the time. Those teams using professionals amalgamated into a loose group informally known as the Ohio League, and rules of determining a pro champion remained the same as they had been previously. The top teams in this league became so powerful that the champions called themselves the "U.S. Professional Champion."

Massillon repeated as champions in 1904, adding some more of the nation's top players to its roster (including guard Herman Kerchoffe, perhaps the top lineman in the country), and crushing six opponents by a combined score of 396-6 before defeating Akron 6-5 for the title.

The Tigers' second consecutive championship was too much for the folks in Canton, who hadn't even fielded a major team in 1904. They decided to sign all the talent they could and beat their neighbors to the west at their own game. Canton signed seven players from the Akron team, two members of Fielding Yost's "point-a-minute" teams at the University of Michigan, and the best pros they could find. Massillon, meanwhile, added four players from the Franklin team that won the 1903 World Series.

It became obvious from the beginning of the season that the two squads would battle for the title. For most of the season, building up to the Canton-Massillon game in late November, everything went as predicted. The Tigers thrashed four opponents before taking on the Carlisle Indians, a school that would become noted several years later for the coaching of Glenn (Pop) Warner and the play of Jim Thorpe. The Indians, reputed to be the fastest team in the nation, not only were outmuscled by the bigger, stronger Tigers, but also were beaten both in the speed department and on the scoreboard 8-4.

Canton, meanwhile, crushed six teams by a combined score of 409-0 before traveling to Latrobe to play the best team in Pennsylvania. A fumble on the second-half kickoff was returned 5 yards for a touchdown by Latrobe, John Brallier kicked the extra point, and the home team held on to win 6-0. Even more costly than the loss on the scoreboard, however, was a broken leg suffered by tackle, captain, and coach Bill Laub. To replace him, Canton immediately hired Blondy Wallace. Wallace had captained both the 1902 Philadelphia Athletics NFL team and the 1903 Franklin All-Stars. At 6 feet 2 inches, 240 pounds, he was a mammoth and exceptionally talented tackle.

Unfortunately, Wallace insisted on revamping the Canton team, and he brought in three new linemen and three new backs the week prior to the Massillon game. One was two-time All-America halfback Willie Heston, a star at Michigan; the $600 Heston was paid for the game was the most ever for a football player for one contest until Red Grange entered the NFL in 1926. The Tigers, meanwhile, decided to stick with the players who had practiced together throughout the season.

The teams played a tough first half, which ended with the score tied 4-4. In the second half, however, Doc Rayl, one of Canton's guards who had been with Akron the previous year, was ejected for slugging a Massillon player. Massillon thereupon took control offensively by running directly at Rayl's replacement. The strategy led to 2 touchdown runs by former Notre Dame fullback Red Salmon, and Massillon won the game and its third consecutive title 14-4.

Before the Ohio teams could get back together on the field in 1906, the game received a massive facelift. Late in 1905, President Theodore Roosevelt, horrified and revolted by the fact that 18 deaths and 149 major injuries had been recorded in the 1905 football season, threatened to ban the game if those running it did not make it safer. The result was the development of the Intercollegiate Athletic Association of the United States (IAAUS), organized to assist in the formation of sound requirements for intercollegiate athletics, particularly football. In 1910, the IAAUS changed its name to the National Collegiate Athletic Association (NCAA).

Colleges Change the Game

On January 12, 1906, rules were passed that forever changed the nature of football: the forward pass was legalized, the length of the game was reduced from 70 to 60 minutes; the neutral zone separating the offense from the defense by the length of the ball was established, the distance required for a first down was increased to 10 yards; and six men were required to be on the line of scrimmage.

Because the pros still followed collegiate rules, these changes were just as important to them as to college football. The new rules ultimately changed the game from one of brute power to one in which finesse and quickness also mattered. Requiring six men on the line eliminated the use of dangerous mass plays, such as the various wedges. Increasing the yardage for a first down encouraged outside running, and legalizing the forward pass ultimately refocused the entire concept of play.

The game might have changed, but one thing hadn't: Massillon and Canton still figured to be the best two teams in the country. Before the season started, Wallace signed four starters from the Tigers: Kerchoffe, quarterback Jack Hayden, tackle Jack Lang, and end Clark Schrontz. Massillon's new coach, Sherburn Wightman, tried to make up for the losses by signing 250-pound lineman Bob (Tiny) Maxwell and the great quarterback George (Peggy) Parratt.

As in the previous year, the two teams stormed through the early opposition. After eight games, Canton, now called the Bulldogs for the first time, held an imposing 285-0 scoring margin, which was nevertheless still far short of Massillon's 438-0. Although it didn't seem important at the time, a historical highlight occurred in a game between the Tigers and a combined Benwood-Moundsville team, when Parratt completed a forward pass to end (Bullet) Dan Riley, the first authenticated pass completion in a pro football game.

When, in late October, the teams finally worked out the schedule for their two November games, it turned out that they would play one game in Canton on November 16, and the other in Massillon on November 24. The conditions of the agreement showed the complete lack of trust between Wallace and Stewart: The two teams would divide the gate receipts from the two games, and each would put up a $3,000 guarantee to insure an appearance on both dates. There were additional guarantees built around Canton playing Latrobe on Thanksgiving Day, and Massillon not doing anything that would affect the Canton-Latrobe game.

The first game turned out to be the biggest in the history of Canton football. The Bulldogs built a 10-0 lead late in the game before Tiny Maxwell scored on a fumble return, and then the hosts held on to win 10-5 before a crowd of nearly 8,000 at Canton's Mahaffey Park.

The rematch was held at Massillon's Hospital Grounds Field, and an argument started before the game even began. Wallace protested the use of a Victor football, one that was lighter than the Spalding balls usually used. However, he had to accept the Massillon team's decision or lose his $3,000 guarantee. So the game was played, and the football turned out to be part of a brilliant strategy. With Peggy Parratt shifted to end, Homer Davidson moved in at quarterback for the Tigers, and his punting was the story of the game. Six times his punts, aided by the lightness of the Victor ball, sailed over the head of Bulldogs safety Jack Hayden, and the resulting field position helped Massillon gain a 5-0 halftime lead. Although the Bulldogs scored in the second half to take a 6-5 advantage, a blocked punt for a safety gave the Tigers the lead at 7-6, and another touchdown ultimately gave them a 13-6 victory and their fourth consecutive state championship.

A Charge of Bribery

On the Monday after the game, Ed Stewart announced in the *Massillon Evening Independent* that Blondy Wallace had been a key figure in attempting to fix the game, and that Wallace's plot revolved around splitting the two games, thereby forcing a third. Stewart wrote that he had found out about the plot earlier in the season, when Walter East, a Massillon end, had tried to bribe Tiny Maxwell and Bob Shiring to throw the first Canton-Massillon game. When the two other players reported the incident, Stewart and Wightman dropped East from the team.

Stewart's "revelations" were a sensation in the newspapers and caused an uproar throughout Ohio. During the days following the Canton-Massillon game, Wallace denied all charges to the satisfaction of a committee from Canton, and George Williams, the Bulldogs' manager, publicly supported Wallace's defense. Then East, recently returned to Akron from traveling, exonerated Wallace, accused Wightman of being behind the whole thing, and produced a contract in which Wightman had agreed to throw the game for $4,000. Wightman and Stewart immediately came up with a different story, saying they had entered into the contract to get the goods on East and his chief backer, John Windsor, one of the owners of the Akron baseball team. Canton officials then leveled charges that Stewart had deliberately set out to injure Canton football by destroying confidence in the team and thereby ruining the attendance at the Latrobe game the following week.

Nothing could be proven one way or another, but, through all of this, the one thing that was apparent was that there was absolutely no evidence that Blondy Wallace had been involved at all, while there was substantial indication that he not only was desperate to win the final game but also had no desire to play a third. Unfortunately for Wallace, Harry March, who later wrote the first published history of pro football, got only parts of the story, and wrote that Wallace fixed the game and that the discovery of this helped destroy pro football in Ohio for at least five years. Other historians later accepted March's comments as the truth, and his misinformation was perpetuated for decades before research showed it to be inaccurate. Wallace, basically an innocent bystander, was maligned for years before it was shown that he had nothing to do with any shady dealings.

While Wallace's name was dragged through the mud, Canton defeated Latrobe 16-0 before a crowd of only 939, less than one-sixth what had been predicted. With their huge payroll, the Bulldogs went broke because of the Latrobe game. Indeed, the players had to play a public pickup game several days later to earn enough to pay for railroad tickets home.

The Pro Game Suffers

While March wrote that the scandal over the second Canton-Massillon game had killed pro football, the reality is that the problem was financial. It simply had become too expensive regularly to play true all-star teams, as the Bulldogs and Tigers had done. Attendance could not support the high salaries because, after a couple of runaways, many fans grew bored and stopped coming to any but the games between the gridiron giants. The Bulldogs and Tigers thus ceased to exist, and Canton and Massillon, like the other Ohio teams, went back to playing mostly local athletes who were paid reduced salaries. Football wasn't dead, but it was regrouping.

In 1907, football in Ohio went back to being a game with a great deal of parity, with a number of teams having a shot at the title. However, the team that won it all came, yet again, from Massillon.

At the start of the season, Wightman gathered a number of the talented locals who were key figures in the 1903 and 1904 Tigers. Frank Botoner, Mully Miller, and Fred Haag came back, as did Peggy Parratt for part of the season. The result was four consecutive victories for the All-Massillons before a scoreless tie with the unbeaten Shelby Blues. A tough 6-4 victory over the rugged Columbus Panhandles followed by an easy victory set up a Thanksgiving rematch with the Panhandles, who had been reorganized before the year by Joe Carr. As it turned out, the game was a chance for the All-Massillons to win the state championship because the Blues also had tied the Panhandles. Falling back on old patterns, Wightman brought in some well-known talent for the one game, including Bob Shiring and Dan Riley. Massillon proceeded to win its fifth consecutive state title 13-4.

Although Columbus lost the game, it marked a key moment for the team, which had become the first pro team from southern Ohio to challenge for the state title. The team was to continue long enough to become charter members of the NFL in 1920. They had a great drawing card in the burly Nesser brothers—John, Phil, Ted, Fred, Frank, Raymond, and Al—all boilermakers for the Panhandle Division of the Pennsylvania Railroad.

The Parratt Era

Although the Nessers were most impressive, perhaps the key figure of the game then was Parratt, who had been considered the best all-around athlete in Ohio while a three-sport star at Case University, a major sports power at the time. In 1905 he was accused of playing professionally for Shelby under the name of Jimmy Murphy. Although this was common practice at the time, and players generally just denied the charges in order to maintain their college eligibility, Parratt openly admitted that he was doing so. He lost his eligibility at Case, but the esteem in which he was held was demonstrated by the fact that he still was awarded a varsity letter and named the All-Ohio college quarterback.

Parratt played for the Tigers in 1906 and started and finished the 1907 season with the All-Massillons, with a stint in the middle of 1907 with the Franklin AC in Cleveland. In 1908, he was hired back as coach and player by his first pro team, the Shelby Blues, to help them against Massillon. Parratt was not always well-liked, both because he drove exceedingly hard business bargains with his own players and with opposing teams and also because of his own natural ability, which was so enviable. But he had the connections and personality to put together a winning team, and he did. The Blues went undefeated, although they were outvoted for the state title by another undefeated side, the Akron Indians.

The Blues and Indians dominated their opposition the following season, too. This time, however, Parratt managed to set up a game between them so that the championship could be decided on the field. Parratt returned a fumble 45 yards for a touchdown to tie the game after Akron had jumped to a 6-0 lead, then Homer Davidson drop-kicked a field goal—changed from 4 points to 3 that year—late in the game to give Shelby a lead. But a series of desperation passes for the Indians led to the winning touchdown and another state title for Akron.

Shelby not only attained its long-sought championship in 1910, it had two teams in the running for it. The Shelby

Tigers went 7-0 in their first year, but the Blues were the better team. Parratt first combined them with a team from Mansfield, forming the Shelby-Mansfield Blues, and then he talked a number of the state's best former players, all of whom had gone into coaching, to come back and play for him. This remarkable combination of mental and physical skill helped the Blues twice defeat the Akron Indians—16-6 and 8-6—en route to the title.

Not only was Parratt's crew the best team in Ohio, but also, for the first time since 1906, the state probably had the best team in the country. For three years previous, that likely had been the Lyceums of Pittsburgh, where a number of old Canton and Massillon stars, including Bob Shiring and Doc McChesney, joined together with the Dillon brothers, former stars at Princeton, in a last fling of Pittsburgh glory. For nearly three years the Lyceum team went undefeated; the run ended with an upset by the Dayton Oakwoods in the final game of 1909, after which pro football in western Pennsylvania disappeared as a major force for more than two decades.

Parratt, meanwhile, went from success to success. In 1911, he combined his team with the Shelby Tigers and again won the state championship, shutting out the Akron Indians twice along the way. He learned when he was at Massillon that close, exciting games were more important to winning over fans than one-sided victories. So, in 1912, while leaving many of his best players at Shelby, he moved to Akron to rebuild the Indians. Some of the best talent moved on to the Elyria AC, which became a powerful contender. At the same time, 21-year-old Jack Cusack effectively took over the new Canton Professionals, which he built into a fourth team capable of challenging for the title.

The Game Stabilizes

Suddenly the teams started making profits, and the game began to stabilize. In a season in which new rules increased the value of a touchdown to 6 points, added a fourth down to each possession, and established end zones, while decreasing the actual playing field from 110 yards to 100, it was the Elyria Athletics who won the championship with an 8-0 record.

In 1913, Parratt brought back the title to Akron. In an Ohio League that was a picture of parity, Parratt's team won while going 8-1-2. The season included a tie with Canton and victories against Elyria and Shelby. The key game against Shelby showed that Parratt still was smiled on by the football gods. In early November, Shelby traveled to Akron, and the Blues, desperate for a win, hired a number of top college players for one week for $700. A snowstorm forced a postponement of the game, and, when Shelby returned the next week, they could no longer afford their expensive imports. Parratt's club won 20-0 to clinch the title.

The 1914 season started as if Parratt's rule had ended. In their third game, the Indians were beaten by the Columbus Panhandles 16-0, and a week later they were tied 7-7 by the Youngstown Pros. Meanwhile, Cusack's Canton team won its first six, including 31-0 against Youngstown and 40-10 over Columbus, the Panhandles' first loss of the season. After Akron got back in the championship picture with a 14-0 victory against Columbus, the Indians and Canton met for the first of two games. Parratt signed the left side of the Notre Dame line, including end Knute Rockne, but the Professionals overcame the Indians 6-0.

The game was marked by tragedy, however, when Canton captain Harry Turner fractured his back and almost completely severed his spinal cord while making a tackle. Turner died shortly after the game, the intensity of his desire to beat the inimitable Parratt made clear by his final words: "I know I must go, but I am satisfied, for we beat Peggy Parratt."

The death of Turner changed the season for Canton. Several players quit after the game, and Cusack considered closing down the operation. But the players decided to finish the season and bring the title to Canton. However, after a victory the next week over Shelby, they had one last game—a rematch with the Indians. Parratt's side won 21-0, and the ease of the victory convinced most of the experts that Akron, at 8-2-1, deserved the state championship over Canton, which finished 9-1.

Parratt thus won his fourth title in five years. And in many ways it was only just that he took home one last trophy, because—as a player, a coach, a manager, and a promoter—he managed to carry pro football through some of its bleakest periods, when many others had forsaken it.

Canton, Massillon, and Thorpe

A new team was launched in Massillon and was named the Tigers in honor of former glories. In response, Jack Cusack's Canton team changed its name from the Professionals to the Bulldogs. Canton and Massillon, after stockpiling some of the best talent in the country, went through their early schedules in 1915 looking like world-beaters, losing just one game apiece. As the teams approached the first of their two games against each other, one of the key moves in pro football history was made; Cusack signed Jim Thorpe, the former All-America at Carlisle Indian School and the man who won gold medals in the decathlon and the pentathlon at the 1912 Stockholm Olympics, to play for the Bulldogs.

The $250 Thorpe was paid for each game was an astronomical amount, especially considering the former All-America wasn't even currently playing football but was coaching the backs at the University of Indiana. Yet it was a wise business decision. Everyone wanted to see the greatest athlete in the world perform, and Canton's attendance rose from an average of 1,200 prior to signing Thorpe to 6,600 and 8,000 for the two Massillon games.

Despite Thorpe's presence, Massillon had its way in the first game, winning 16-0. But two weeks later, Thorpe kicked 2 field goals, one an 18-yard dropkick and the other 45 yards from placement, to lead the Bulldogs to a 6-0 victory. The Tigers almost pulled the game out at the very last, when their right end, Briggs, caught a pass and raced across the goal line into the midst of a crowd of standing-room-only fans. But the ground rules for the game stated that any player crossing the goal line into the crowd had to emerge with possession of the ball, and Briggs didn't have it. He insisted that a uniformed policeman had kicked the ball out of his hands! On the surface, that was ridiculous, because Canton had no uniformed policemen. The referee therefore ruled the play a touchback.

As the teams argued about the play, the fans pushed onto the field, and the officials could not clear the ground so they ended the game. The call as to whether the play was a touchdown or a touchback was all important, because a touchdown for Massillon would undoubtedly mean the state championship, while a victory for Canton would leave it open for dispute. With hostile fans on both sides, the officials agreed to make their determination, but said that they would only do so if it were read at 30 minutes after midnight by the manager of the Courtland Hotel, thereby allowing them all to leave town.

When the message was read at the jam-packed hotel that night, the fans learned that the officials had backed the decision that because Briggs did not have possession of the ball when he came out of the crowd, the play officially was a touchback and Canton had won 6-0. The conclusion of the story did not come until a decade later, however. It was at that time that Cusack, in a conversation with a streetcar conductor, learned that it was the uniformed conductor, not a policeman, who kicked the ball away from Briggs and into the arms of Canton's Charlie Smith. "I had thirty dollars bet on that game," the conductor admitted, "and, at my salary, I couldn't afford to lose that much money."

Ohio Rules Again

Although neither Canton nor Massillon ended as consensus champion, Thorpe's presence had brought the focus of professional football back to Ohio and particularly to Stark County. That emphasis continued in 1916, as the Bulldogs and Tigers again dominated the action. Despite the return of Parratt for a final season with his new Cleveland Indians, and despite the Columbus Panhandles and Youngstown Patricians both fielding strong teams, Canton and Massillon approached their final games unbeaten. In their first meeting, poor weather slowed both teams, and the result was a 0-0 tie. But, prior to the rematch, Cusack signed Pete Calac, Thorpe's former teammate at Carlisle. Calac immediately became the fullback, which allowed Thorpe to move to halfback, and the combination was lethal. The Bulldogs pounded the Tigers 24-0 for their first undisputed state championship.

The 1917 season brought more of the same, as Canton dominated a field that had been severely weakened by the United States's entry into World War I. The Patricians, for example, were relatively strong, but disbanded after several of their players enlisted following a second loss to the Bulldogs. Many of the remaining Youngstown players joined the Tigers, which raised that crew above the mediocrity of many of the teams. Nevertheless, Canton dominated Massillon in their first meeting, winning 14-3. A week later, however, former Notre Dame star Stanley Cofall kicked field goals of 34 and 31 yards as Massillon ended Canton's unbeaten season with a 6-0 victory. Despite Massillon's claims to the title, the Bulldogs, who ended with a 9-1 record while the Tigers had lost three times, retained their league championship.

Most teams lost considerable sums during the 1917 season, but 1918 was even leaner. With the combination of the "work or fight" orders during the First World War and the major influenza epidemic of 1918, the football season barely happened. Neither Canton nor Massillon fielded a team, and the champions, the Dayton Triangles, led by coach and fullback Earle (Greasy) Neale, won almost by default. The Triangles were the only major Ohio team to play a full season, and seven of their games were against inferior teams from Indiana. Of all the teams in Ohio, only Columbus managed a game against Dayton, and it was the Panhandles' only game of the year.

The 1919 Season

Prior to the 1919 season, the three major concerns that faced team managers in the past seemed to grow into greater problems. The first issue was rising salaries. With teams paying up to $2,000 a week in wages, and fans paying one dollar each to attend the games, most teams found that they were losing money from the start, as they could fill their small parks only for the most important games. A related problem was the players' ability to drive up salaries by jumping from one team to another. One year, the Nesser brothers claimed they faced Knute Rockne on five different occasions, playing for five different teams.

Although the managers were at fault for enticing the players from team to team, those running the clubs were willing to risk the financial problems because the teams would not draw fans and would collapse if they lost regularly. The third problem was the use of college players, who often played in professional games under assumed names. In an age when amateurism still had an aura of nobility to the general public, using collegians damaged the public perception of the sport.

Before the season started, the managers of Massillon and Akron met with Ralph Hay, who had taken over the Canton franchise from his friend Jack Cusack. They agreed not to steal each other's players, but they could not compromise on a salary limit, and no formal organization that would govern pro football was established.

The 1919 Ohio League season, though, turned out to be a thriller on the field. Canton, Massillon, Akron, and Cleveland all made a run for the title, while a new team in Hammond, Indiana, made a claim for national honors despite an early 6-0 loss to Cleveland. A regular with Hammond, which actually played its games in Chicago's Cub Park (now Wrigley Field), was former University of Illinois end George Halas. By the week that Canton and Massillon were scheduled to play their first game, Akron had suffered losses to Canton and Massillon, Cleveland had split two games with Massillon, and Hammond had tied Canton.

On November 16, with Thorpe and Calac having been joined in the backfield by another Native American, Joe Guyon, the Bulldogs put an exclamation point on their claim for the title with a 23-0 victory over the Tigers. In the next several weeks, Massillon ended Cleveland's hopes, Canton disposed of Akron, and, on Thanksgiving Day, the

Bulldogs dropped Hammond 7-0. It all came down to the second Canton-Massillon game, and Thorpe took over. In the third quarter, he kicked a 40-yard field goal for the only points of the game, and in the final period he launched a 95-yard punt to keep the Tigers away from Canton territory. The resulting 3-0 victory gave Canton a 9-0-1 record and an undisputed state and national championship.

Despite the excitement on the field, however, pro football and the Ohio League were in deep trouble. Attempts to control the league's problems prior to the season were not successful, and the problems were compounded by strong teams from other states signing Ohio's top players. The Youngstown Patricians had folded early in the season, and Massillon, Akron, and Cleveland appeared to be unstable. Even champion Canton had lost money during the 1919 season.

The Ohio League greatly added to the development of professional football, but something more was needed. It was time for all concerned to start thinking seriously about a national professional league.

CHAPTER 2

The History of the National Football League

Jack Clary

American football was just over a half century old on August 20, 1920, when seven men walked into Ralph Hay's Hupmobile automobile agency in the ground floor of the Odd Fellows Building in Canton, Ohio, and had a meeting. These seven men—Hay and Jim Thorpe from Canton, Frank Neid and Art Ranney from nearby Akron, Carl Storck from Dayton, and Jimmy O'Donnell and Stan Cofall from Cleveland—ran professional teams in their four gritty Ohio industrial cities. Their meeting was held primarily to consider survival of their teams, which formed the heart of the mythical "Ohio League," the real center of professional football at the time.

But bankruptcy was in the air. The biggest problem was salaries—$50 or $75 per game for most players, $100 for stars, and more for All-Americas of Thorpe's stature. The four Ohio clubs were confronted with escalating salaries to put stronger teams on the field; the problem was exacerbated when, in the wake of World War I, other strong Midwestern pro teams bid for top players' services. Clubs such as the Decatur Staleys, Racine Cardinals, and Rock Island Independents from Illinois, the Hammond Pros and Muncie Flyers from Indiana, and teams from Buffalo and Rochester, New York, hoped to replace the Ohioans as pro football's elite.

Each of those teams operated independently and without a league constitution, which forced every team to abide by the same rules. Player movement was rampant, with the highest bidder usually getting a player's service from a couple of games up to a season. That included good college players because it was not unusual for a collegian to play for his school on Saturday afternoon, then hop a train that night and assume a new identity to play again for a few bucks on Sunday. It was all done with a wink and a nod, yet the tenor of the times was such that pro football was being seen as a bad influence in enticing those "innocent" young lads to wrongdoing.

Thus, the meeting at Ralph Hay's showroom was convened. Along with the four teams represented in person, those from Buffalo, Rochester, and Hammond submitted letters of application to what, for a month, was called the American Professional Football Conference. The most important outcome of the August 20 meeting was that Hay was instructed to contact all the major professional teams in the country to meet and organize a league with a constitution of specific rules of operation.

Less than a month later, on September 17, 10 teams answered Hay's invitation to attend a second meeting. Added to the original group were the Decatur Staleys, with George Halas representing the interest of A.E. Staley; a second Chicago team, the Racine Cardinals (Racine was the street where they played); Hammond and Muncie, Indiana; Rochester, New York; and, Rock Island, Illinois. These men gathered in a crowded auto showroom without sufficient chairs so several, including Halas, sat on the fenders and running boards of the 1920 Hupmobiles. "It was a hot day," Halas recalled, "and we sat there drinking beer from buckets while we tried to plan the future of professional football."

A Cardinal by Any Other Name

Chris O'Brien's team was called the Racine Cardinals instead of the Chicago Cardinals because, at that time, there were numerous semipro teams in the Windy City. Until 1920, the Cardinals were only one of the many. However, the name caused some confusion at the September 17 meeting in Canton. Apparently, Art Ranney, who took the minutes, did not understand the nuances of Chicago football; he identified the team as "Racine, Wisconsin."

Ranney's misunderstanding has sometimes led some later historical writings to list Racine, Wisconsin, as a charter member of the National Football League. And, in at least one text, the team was listed as "Wisconsin."

The group, which adopted the name American Professional Football Association, had the stated purpose of "raising the standard of professional football . . . to eliminate bidding for players . . . and to secure cooperation in the formation of schedules, at least for the bigger teams." The teams also agreed to refrain from signing college players still in school or offering inducements to lure players from member clubs.

A $100 entry fee was set—and never paid by any team, according to Halas—and Thorpe was elected president after Hay demurred, rightly citing the need for the league to get visibility, which Thorpe would provide. (That's about all he did in the year he held the job, preferring to play rather than be an administrator.)

The 1920s: Less than Roaring

There were 14 teams in the first APFA season in 1920: Akron Pros, Decatur Staleys, Buffalo All-Americans, Racine (Chicago) Cardinals, Rock Island Independents, Dayton Triangles, Rochester Jeffersons, Canton Bulldogs, Detroit Heralds, Cleveland Tigers, Chicago Tigers, Hammond Pros, Columbus Panhandles, and Muncie Flyers. On October 3 at Dayton, in the first league game ever played, the Triangles defeated the Panhandles 14-0. Lou Partlow of Dayton ran 7 yards for the first touchdown ever scored in the league. At Rock Island later that same day, the Independents produced the league's first rout, shutting out Muncie 45-0.

But the first official professional football champion was not declared until April 30, 1921, five months after the conclusion of the season. At a special meeting, a consensus of the owners decided that the Akron Pros, with their 8-0-3 record, were the league's strongest team. Halas tried to claim the title for the Staleys after beating the Cardinals, avenging Decatur's only loss that season. But Halas's team spoiled its bid the following week, playing to a scoreless tie against the Pros. The Staleys ignored the ban on player movement by hiring Paddy Driscoll, the Cardinals' player-coach, to play against Akron.

Team owners were discouraged after the 1920 season because their new league accomplished little and many of them questioned the efficacy of the venture. But Joe Carr, the bright, innovative owner of the Columbus Panhandles, rode to the rescue, urging them to hold on, finally convincing them that an organized football league could succeed. They also became convinced that his leadership was needed to make all of this happen, and he was elected to succeed Thorpe. After the 1921 season the APFA name was dropped in favor of National Football League.

Mr. President

Joe Carr was one of the most interesting and well-rounded administrators in league history. He worked as a sportswriter and later assistant sports editor of the *Ohio State Journal* in Columbus, Ohio, while keeping his day job as a machinist for the Panhandle Division of the Pennsylvania Railroad in Columbus.

His career as a sports entrepreneur began when he was 20 years old, when he organized the famed Panhandle White Sox, one of the country's best semipro baseball teams. Four years later, he organized the Columbus Panhandles semipro football team, consisting of members of the railroad, and he directed their fortunes for two decades, right into the NFL as an original team.

While still president of the NFL, Carr served for three years as the first president of the American Basketball Association from 1925 to 1928 before becoming director of baseball's National Association's promotional department, where he was instrumental in building major league baseball's minor league system from 12 leagues in 1933 to 41 at the time of his death in 1939.

After Joe Carr became president of the league in 1921, he issued official standings. Supposedly, that was to eliminate disputes such as the one following the 1920 season when both Akron and the Decatur Staleys claimed the championship. Instead, titles had to be settled by vote at the league meetings following the 1921, 1924, and 1925 seasons. In 1921, Halas's Staleys were named champions over the Buffalo All-Americans, even though both teams had the same won-lost record and had split a pair of face-to-face meetings.

In 1924, Halas lost the championship when the owners ruled that a December victory over title-winning Cleveland had been played after the official season had ended and thus was only a postseason exhibition game. And late in 1925, the Pottsville Maroons were in first place when they were suspended from the league a week before the season ended for violating league rules by playing an exhibition game within another league team's franchised territory. The suspension ended the Maroons' eligibility for the championship. Only in 1922 and 1923, when the Canton Bulldogs finished undefeated, did the league championship go unchallenged.

Pottsville's Folly

The game that brought the Pottsville Maroons' 1925 suspension was played on December 12 against a team of Notre Dame graduates, including the famed "Four Horsemen," at Philadelphia's Shibe Park, well within the franchise territory of the Frankford Yellow Jackets. It promised to be a lucrative affair.

Earlier, Frankford and Pottsville had agreed that whichever team had the better record would play the Notre Dame stars. But when the Maroons reached December with a superior record and announced they would play the game at Shibe Park, Frankford filed a protest with the league. To shore up its case, Frankford scheduled a league game at its home field for the same day. League president Joe Carr had no choice but to uphold the protest. He warned Pottsville three times by telegram. When the Maroons went ahead and played, Carr suspended them, and they were not allowed to play a game with Providence the next day.

The Maroons defeated the Notre Dame players 9-7, but the game drew a disappointing crowd. During the summer of 1926, with Red Grange's American Football League posing a new threat to the NFL, Pottsville was reinstated after paying a fine.

During the first decade of the league, scheduling—particularly late-season games—was left to individual teams. The teams usually worked out their basic schedules at a late-summer meeting, although these were not cast in stone. In most seasons—1924 was an exception—teams still in the race that believed they could draw well in December could add a game or two with another league opponent, and those games would be counted in the league standings. A minimum number of games with league opponents was required to qualify for the league championship, though not for league membership. So from the beginning, there was a disparity in the number of games played by each team. It wasn't until 1936 that every team played the same number of games. It wasn't until 1932, when the Chicago Bears and Portsmouth (Ohio) Spartans finished in a tie for first place, that the league had a playoff game to decide its champion. The NFL didn't organize itself into a two-division setup until 1933, with a championship game between the division winners.

Carr Provides Leadership

Carr's gentle countenance belied a forceful leader. He wasted no time establishing his authority as APFA president, declaring a player under contract from the previous season could not be approached by another team unless first declared a free agent. He introduced a standard player's contract similar to that being used in baseball, and he appointed a committee to draft a new constitution and by-laws to govern the association.

His greatest achievement, which was supported by Halas, was passing a rule prohibiting any team from signing collegians whose original class had not yet graduated. He vigorously enforced the rule, fining teams $1,000 for violations. That included Halas's Bears on several occasions. He also established a league constitution and by-laws, gave teams territorial rights within the league, restricted player movements, and enforced more stringent membership criteria.

Carr's overriding principle was that the sport always should strive for the highest possible standards and that the public's interest and concern would always come first. When the Green Bay Packers, who joined the APFA in 1921, used college players under assumed names, Carr forced them to resign from the league.

A few months later, a group headed by Curly Lambeau applied for and was granted a new franchise that now is the third oldest in the NFL. Lambeau borrowed $50 for the entry fee and his group attempted, to no avail, to rename the team the Blues. The team went broke in 1922, but the city's businessmen realized the team's value, secured a $2,500 loan in 1923, and set up a public, nonprofit corporation to operate it. A share and an accompanying season ticket cost five dollars apiece. More than 75 years later, the Packers still are a community-owned team, now worth more than $150 million; the original shares are passed down from generation to generation.

Until the NFL was organized into two divisions in 1933 to begin the modern era, lack of stability was the biggest problem during most of the first dozen years as franchises came and went—more than 40 of them from 1920 through the 1932 season. Only two teams, the Decatur Staleys/Chicago Bears and Chicago Cardinals, started and stayed with the league. On the other hand, 19 teams lasted one season and 11 stayed for two.

Carr and several other league leaders believed that the NFL's future lay in the nation's larger cities rather than in pleasant, but limited, markets such as Canton, Evansville, or Rock Island. During its first half-dozen years, the league saw a slow but discernible movement toward replacing small towns with larger cities. After the 1926 season, most of the small cities were eliminated from the league. Ironically, that included three of the four Ohio teams—Canton, Akron, and Dayton—that had produced the league, as well as Carr's own Columbus club.

New York, New York

In 1925, Carr convinced Tim Mara to back a team in New York City. Mara knew nothing about football but a friend of Carr's, Dr. Harry March, was present at the sale, and he so impressed Mara with his knowledge that he was hired as the team's secretary. He immediately signed former Naval Academy coach Bob Folwell and some well-known players, including over-the-hill Jim Thorpe; Mara lost $40,000 even before the 1925 season had ended.

He tried to sign Red Grange, the great Illinois All-America running back, after his last college game for Illinois that fall, but Halas had the inside track because he had played for Bob Zuppke, Grange's coach. So after the Bears got him, Mara did the next best thing: he arranged for Grange to play in the Polo Grounds in New York against the Giants. After drawing record crowds in Chicago and Philadelphia, Grange and the Bears arrived in New York on December 6, and a crowd reported by some as more than 70,000 showed up. Gate receipts totaled $143,000, and the Giants' solvency was assured. Two years later, the team won the first of its six NFL titles.

Grange's appearance with the Bears coincided with the height of the Roaring Twenties, still referred to as the Golden Age of Sports, even though its world was a relatively small universe that was dominated by major league baseball, college football, and boxing. The NFL still was riding a bumpy road during that time, but it got a sizable boost in recognition when college football's two greatest players in those years—Grange, in 1925, and Ernie Nevers, in 1926—joined the league.

They didn't so much join it as unite with it. Both became the main attractions of traveling road shows that brought professional football to every part of the nation on the wildest barnstorming trips in pro football history. The publicity that they generated helped to lift the league from its mostly small-city existence.

Grange was decades ahead of his time when he hired a shrewd, tough-dealing agent named C.C. (Cash & Carry) Pyle to negotiate a contract with Halas that paid Grange a share of the gate receipts for the last few games of the 1925 season. That included that aforementioned game in New York City against the Giants, as well as those from a second tour that began in December and included 73,000 watching the Bears defeat the Los Angeles Tigers in the L.A. Coliseum in January. Grange played nine games at Illinois that season, then eight more with the Bears after signing his contract. He got a week off before he played another nine games before the end of January—a total of 26 in all.

Pyle and Grange demanded a five-figure salary and part of the team from Halas in 1926, but were rebuffed. When Pyle demanded the league give him a franchise in New York to showcase Grange's talents, Mara objected to the plan because he controlled the New York territory.

The First AFL

In another preview of the problems that would buffet the NFL later in the century, Pyle decided to compete with the NFL and formed the nine-team American Football League with Grange's New York Yankees franchise as the centerpiece. A war for talent ensued, and the AFL captured former college stars such as Harry Stuhldreher, one of the Four Horsemen, George Wilson of Washington, Doug Wycoff of Georgia Tech, and Joey Sternaman, who had played for the Bears. Overall, the AFL had marginal talent and poor coaching. Their football was dull (only 41 touchdowns were scored in 42 games), and only Grange was a top attraction. Further, the teams were undercapitalized, and some salaries never were paid. The Yankees lost the AFL title to the Quakers. Only four teams, three of them apparently underwritten by Pyle, still were operating by the end of the AFL's first, last, and only season.

There was one last postscript to the ill-fated American Football League in 1926. On December 12, 1926, the AFL-champion Quakers arranged a game against the seventh-place NFL Giants at the Polo Grounds. The Giants thrashed the AFL champions 31-0 before a meager crowd of about 5,000 on a cold, snowy day.

The 1926 season was a great one for Philadelphia. Not only did the Quakers win the AFL championship, but the Frankford Yellow Jackets won the NFL title (Frankford is a suburb of Philadelphia). The Yellow Jackets were coached by Guy Chamberlin, who had won championships in 1922 and 1923 with Canton and in 1924 with Cleveland.

The NFL's answer to Grange and the AFL in 1926 was the signing of Nevers, the star running back of Glenn (Pop) Warner's great Stanford teams. Nevers had great credentials and Warner, a master of hyperbole, already had called him a better player than his former pupil, Thorpe. "Nevers could run, pass, kick, and play defense on a par with Thorpe," Warner said, "but he had the edge in competitive spirit."

Ollie Haugsrud, the treasurer of the Duluth Kelleys, bought the franchise, then stunned an NFL owners meeting by announcing he had signed Nevers, a Minnesota native. His fellow owners stood up and cheered, and one told him, "You've saved the league." Although the team is remembered as the Duluth Eskimos, the official name was Ernie Nevers's Eskimos so no one would miss the connection.

Nevers got a Grange-like deal—a $15,000 contract and a share of the bigger gates, making him the NFL's highest-paid player. That so stretched Haugsrud's resources that he could afford to sign only 13 other players. But every team wanted the Eskimos and Nevers to play at their parks so the team played its first game at home on September 19, then played 13 league games and 15 exhibition games on the road. NFL teams then had that option and it was often more profitable, certainly for Haugsrud, than paying a share of gate receipts from a limited-capacity stadium. Haugsrud later claimed a $3,000 profit after the Eskimos barnstormed until February 5, 1927. In one stretch the team played four games in eight days and earned the nickname, "Iron Men of the North."

Remarkably, Ernie Nevers played all but 29 minutes of the 29 games during his first pro season. Those idle minutes came mostly in a game at Milwaukee when he had abdominal pains. On the field, he did nearly all of his team's running, passing, and kicking, and played linebacker on defense. While he thrilled tens of thousands with his great skills, the Eskimos never contended with their 6-5-3 record in games against NFL opponents.

In 1927, Pyle and Mara reached an uneasy compromise, and the New York Yankees, featuring Grange, moved over to the NFL. But Grange badly injured his knee against the Bears early in the season and the "Galloping Ghost" galloped a bit slower for the rest of his career. He later played several seasons with the Bears, where he still was good enough to make all-pro and earn induction into Pro Football's Hall of Fame.

The League Gets New Stars

Also entering the league in 1927 was Benny Friedman, the former University of Michigan All-America and the foremost passer of his day. The Cleveland-born Friedman was installed as the centerpiece of a new Cleveland team in hopes that his hometown popularity would spark a successful franchise where several others had failed. His passes brought victories, but attendance still lagged.

When Cleveland folded, Friedman joined the Detroit Wolverines in 1928. Again, his team was strong on the field and weak at the gate. However, he so impressed Tim Mara that the Giants' owner bought the floundering Wolverines to get him, leasing the Detroit franchise to Staten Island, one of New York City's five boroughs, where it played for four years as the Staten Island Stapletons. Mara then worked an in-house trade for Friedman and the other stars on Detroit's team. Friedman was paid a reported $10,000, a good investment because a strong Giants team helped Mara recoup the $40,000 he had lost the previous year. Friedman became the NFL's best passer.

Two years before Friedman joined the Giants, Mara's team won its first NFL championship with a team that boasted a powerful defense led by future Hall of Fame members Steve Owen and Cal Hubbard. New York shut out 10 of its 13 opponents. In 1928, while both Grange and Nevers sat out the season nursing injuries, the Providence Steam Roller, coached by Jimmy Conzelman, became the last franchise not currently a member of the NFL to win a championship.

Grange, Nevers and Friedman were joined by another great star during this time: Johnny (Blood) McNally. On Saturdays in 1924 at St. John's College in Minnesota, he was Johnny McNally; on Sundays he was Johnny Blood, a pseudonym that he chose while he played semipro football to protect his college eligibility. He and a college teammate were en route to sign up for a football payday when they passed a movie theater on which the marquee announced that *Blood and Sand* was the feature attraction. Needing a name to protect his eligibility, McNally chose "Blood," his pal took "Sand." For the rest of his career he was known as Johnny Blood, the name that he carried into the Hall of Fame in 1963 as one of its charter members.

He signed with the Milwaukee Badgers in 1925. For the

next 15 seasons, five teams—including Pittsburgh and Green Bay twice—had one of the game's truly unpredictable personalities. It is said that he never met a curfew that he liked or a party that bored him. When McNally was coach of the Pittsburgh Pirates in the late thirties, team owner Art Rooney once noted, "Usually, the coach checks up on the players. With John, the players had to check on the coach."

The 1930s: Surviving the Depression

McNally arrived in Green Bay in 1929 after playing for Milwaukee, Duluth, and Pottsville, and helped to form the National Football League's first real dynasty. The Packers won three consecutive NFL titles from 1929-1931 with a 34-5-2 record. Green Bay was coached by Curly Lambeau, a pioneer in featuring the forward pass. McNally became the NFL's top receiver, as well as a slashing inside runner, during his seasons with Green Bay. The team had a star-studded roster that also included future Hall of Fame linemen Mike Michalske, a former member of Grange's AFL team in New York, and Cal Hubbard, who had played for the Giants. Hubbard later became a member of the college and pro football Halls of Fame, as well as the National Baseball Hall of Fame after his distinguished career as an American League umpire and umpire-in-chief.

Green Bay's success also coincided with a shrinking process, later abetted by the Great Depression, that whittled the NFL from a high of 26 teams in 1926 to 12 teams in 1929 to 8 in 1932. By 1934, every NFL team except Green Bay was located in a city that also had a major league baseball team—and a major league stadium in which to play.

Carr gave the NFL a much-needed bit of fan appeal—a championship playoff. This came almost by accident because the Bears and Portsmouth tied for the NFL title in 1932 with 6-1 records (the Bears also tied six games and Portsmouth tied four, but the ties were not counted in won-lost percentage). Carr ordered the teams into a one-game playoff for the crown.

Because of heavy snow and bitter cold weather, the 1932 title game was played on an 80-yard field before 11,198 fans inside Chicago Stadium, a hockey arena that had last housed a circus; the dirt still on the floor was used for the game. A team was penalized 20 yards once it passed midfield to compensate for the short field. Goal posts were moved to the goal lines and inbound lines to put the ball in play were created 10 yards from the sideline. That temporary setup later was the basis by which the league revamped its playing field with the placement of hashmarks and placing the goal posts on the goal line. (Two years earlier, the Bears had nipped the Cardinals 9-7 on the same field in a charity exhibition, but the Bears-Spartans playoff was the first indoor NFL game that counted—and the last until 1968, when the Houston Oilers moved their games into the Astrodome.) The Bears won the 1932 championship over the Spartans 9-0.

Portsmouth was without star back Dutch Clark, who had already left to take a job as basketball coach at Colorado College. The game was scoreless until the fourth quarter when the Bears' Bronko Nagurski started to run with the ball, stopped and retreated, then threw a touchdown pass to Grange. Portsmouth vehemently protested that Nagurski had not retreated the requisite five yards behind the line of scrimmage before throwing the ball, to no avail. The following year, Halas pushed through a rule that allowed a pass to be thrown from any spot behind the line of scrimmage. Three years later, after Portsmouth had moved its franchise to Detroit in 1934, the team defeated the Giants 26-7 for the NFL championship.

The College All-Star Game

In 1934, imaginative Arch Ward, sports editor of the *Chicago Tribune* and father of baseball's All-Star game in 1933, arranged a game between the defending NFL champion Chicago Bears and a group of all-star collegians who had finished their careers the previous year. Thus the College All-Star game was born. It became an integral part of each season's schedule for more than 40 years.

The game drew huge crowds at Chicago's Soldier Field and for its first three decades, it was a boon to pro football's growth because it spun off the great popularity of the college game. The collegians won five of the first 15 games. But gradually, the game became one-sided in favor of the pros, and the reluctance of NFL coaches to risk injury to their high draft picks chosen to play for the All-Stars eventually led to its cancellation.

Halas's work as a rules maker underscored the dominance of the owners at this time—men of vision who, by a combination of artful design and absolute self-interest, crafted the NFL into a unique entity that enabled it to grow. The quartet of Carr, Halas, Lambeau, and Mara soon was joined by George Preston Marshall, Art Rooney, Bert Bell, and Charles Bidwill. Runyonesque characters all, they had much of the American pioneer spirit as sportsmen who loved to compete, and were fearless, unbridled by the norm, and notorious risk-takers. Those qualities helped the NFL to survive because, in the end, they did what was best for the league.

Marshall was the first to join the original quartet. In 1932, though he was operating a laundry in Washington, D.C., at the time, he led a group of investors that established the Boston Braves. The team lost $46,000 that season, and Marshall suddenly found himself sole owner of the team. He renamed it the Redskins, moved from Braves Field to Fenway Park, home of the Red Sox, and showcased one of the NFL's great stars of the thirties, running back Cliff Battles, who won the NFL's first official rushing title in 1932 and a second in 1937.

Marshall set new NFL standards for flamboyance and irascibility. He was a master promoter, of himself and his team. In Boston, he hired a full-blooded Indian coach, Will (Lone Star) Dietz, to lead his Redskins. Dietz lasted two seasons, and Marshall then hired a Boston athletic hero, Eddie Casey from Harvard. Casey won just two games so Marshall enlisted Ray Flaherty, an end with the Giants, who accepted the job on condition that Marshall stay in his seat and cease his penchant for barging onto the sidelines during a game and giving orders. "He never violated that agreement," said Flaherty, who coached the team for seven years and is its third-winningest coach behind Joe Gibbs and George Allen.

Marshall was a giant in the NFL's meetings, though his fellow owners often paid a fearful price when his arrogant independence disrupted meetings and caused great bouts of consternation. He proposed the split of the league into two divisions in 1933, with the winners playing each other in an NFL Championship Game. Halas, who battled Marshall more fiercely than any other owner during the nearly four decades they competed, immediately backed him. That year, Halas's Bears won the Western Division and then defeated the Giants, the Eastern Division winners, for the title.

Marshall also helped convince the owners to put the goal posts on the goal line, where they stayed until 1974, as a means to differentiate the NFL from college football. The goal posts became an integral part of NFL game strategy because they often became like two added defensive players on goal line stands, and pass receivers used them to screen off defenders when running patterns into the end zone.

Marshall also had a genius for promoting his team. He sold season tickets, and soon everyone followed suit. He established his own marching band when he moved the team to Washington in 1937 and outfitted it with colorful uniforms, topped by feathered Indian headdresses. His wife, Corrine Griffith, a silent screen star, and Barnee Breeskin, a Washington orchestra leader, co-opted the melody from an old revival song, *Yes, Jesus Loves Me,* and composed the words to *Hail to the Redskins.*

In 1936, Marshall's Boston Redskins team played six consecutive home games after midseason and defeated the Pittsburgh Pirates in the final game to break a first-place tie in the Eastern Division. Marshall raised ticket prices for that game without notice, and he was inundated by such a firestorm of press criticism that only 5,000 people showed up on a cold, snowy day. His team then finished the season by beating the Giants in New York, and Marshall, claiming lack of fan support, refused to play the title game against Green Bay in Boston. Instead, the game was played in New York, and the Packers won 21-6. The following year, Marshall moved his team to Washington. With a new star in quarterback Sammy Baugh and with a final season from Battles, the Redskins won their first NFL title in 1937.

Rooney and Bell

It was ironic that Pittsburgh made a run at the 1936 title because the Pirates (they didn't become the Steelers until 1940) then disappeared into the abyss of also-rans for most of the next three decades under the benevolent reign of Art Rooney, a Pittsburgh native who had played professional baseball, qualified for the 1920 U.S. Olympic boxing team, and had backed many different sports ventures as player and promoter around the Pittsburgh area. He loved to take risks, be it the stock market, the race track, or as a team owner. In 1932, knowing that the state of Pennsylvania would lift its blue laws and allow sports events to be held on Sunday, he heeded Joe Carr's plea to found a team in Pittsburgh for the next season, renamed his semipro team the Pirates, and moved it to the NFL in 1933.

It cost him $2,500, allegedly from a substantial pile of winnings he had accumulated during a month at Saratoga Race Track in New York. However, his Saratoga days also had helped to forge a close friendship with many fellow owners, including Halas, Charley Bidwill, Bert Bell, and Tim Mara, all of whom eagerly welcomed the 32-year-old Rooney to their madcap pro football world. Rooney often said that he and his NFL friends were involved "for kicks" and shrugged off losing thousands of dollars each season.

Their good times together stemmed from the respect and fellowship that bound all of them into a common purpose of surviving the adversity that often dogged the NFL. Rooney was the most cavalier about it because for 10 years he considered the league just another crapshoot among many. "Those were the times when the game on Sunday was incidental to making the payroll on Monday," Rooney said. "When we started making the payroll, the suspense went out of the game."

Such was the tenuous financial stability in the NFL in 1936, that the Boston Redskins unwittingly received a huge boost from Rooney when they played his Pittsburgh Pirates in their last home game of the season, with the Eastern Division title on the line. In May, with a guaranteed payday at hand, Rooney had agreed to play an exhibition game against an independent pro team in Los Angeles on a weekend between a game in Chicago against the Cardinals and his game in Boston. Pittsburgh lost a bruising battle 14-6 against Chicago, then traveled by train to the West Coast and lost again. After the game, they again traveled across the country by rail—day coach, no Pullman sleepers—to Boston for their title-deciding game against the Redskins. The travel-weary Pirates never had a chance and lost 30-0.

Matters didn't improve by 1940 when Rooney sold the Pirates to Alexis Thompson, a 27-year-old millionaire, and then bought a piece of the Philadelphia Eagles, owned by his pal, Bert Bell. Thompson, Rooney, and Bell swapped franchises and Rooney and Bell kept the Steelers for five years until Bell was elected NFL commissioner in January, 1946.

Donelli's Choice

After Rooney and Bell became co-owners of the Steelers in a complex deal in 1941, Bell became the head coach, even after posting a very mediocre record as the Eagles' head coach.

Pittsburgh was stomped in its first game. Bell telephoned coach Rooney and said, "We've got to do something drastic."

"I know," Rooney replied. "You've got to quit."

Bell coached one more game, lost it, and resigned. Rooney handed the job to Aldo (Buff) Donelli. Trouble was that Donelli also was the head coach at Duquesne University in Pittsburgh. After five winless games coaching the Steelers, he was faced with a problem: His Duquesne team was leaving by train for a Saturday game on the West Coast, and the Steelers were playing the next day in Pittsburgh.

"Make a choice," NFL commissioner Elmer Layden told him. "Duquesne or the Steelers."

Donelli chose Duquesne.

The Steelers enjoyed their first winning season in 1942, but World War II took an awful toll, and for most of the next 30 years, until the early seventies, the Steelers' survival was often a year-to-year matter. Yet, during that time, there was no more staunch and unselfish advocate for the game and the league than Rooney, often to the disadvantage of his own team.

Rooney's early teams had stars such as Blood, (Bullet Bill) Dudley, and Byron (Whizzer) White, whom he signed out of the University of Colorado in 1938 for the then-unheard of figure of $15,800, but who won the NFL rushing title in his only season with Pittsburgh. Rooney was just as much a hands-on owner as Marshall, hiring, firing, and rehiring coaches almost at will. Joe Bach coached for him in the 1930s and again in the 1950s; Walt Kiesling had two tours, and even McNally, still as zany as ever, lasted until early in the 1939 season as head coach.

Bell's background was in direct contrast to Rooney, but they shared a kindred spirit. Bell, whose first name actually was deBenneville, was raised on Philadelphia's ritzy Main Line. His grandfather was a congressman, his father was Pennsylvania's attorney general, and his brother served as its governor. The family had large hotel holdings on some of Philadelphia's prime real estate, and he could have enjoyed a life of power and prestige.

Instead, Bell was bitten by the football bug when he played at the University of Pennsylvania before and after World War I. Thereafter, he cared only for his part-time coaching jobs at Penn and Temple. He married beautiful Ziegfeld Follies stage star Frances Upton, then borrowed $2,500 in 1933 and became a partner with Lud Wray in the purchase of a Philadelphia franchise to replace the old Frankford Yellow Jackets team that had folded in 1931.

Bell became the general manager of the Eagles and Wray the head coach. The team lost its first three games in 1933 by a combined score of 116-9 and, until Bell left the Eagles and joined Rooney as a partner in 1941, never won more than five games in a season. Bell sometimes ran the team out of a downtown restaurant and gave the bartender tickets to sell while he tirelessly promoted the team in sports departments of the city's newspapers. He even sold tickets on the street to anyone willing to buy. After the team lost $80,000 in the first three seasons, Wray sold his share to Bell, and Bell also became head coach.

The First Draft

Bell's most notable achievement as an owner was convincing his fellow owners to adopt a draft of college players beginning in 1936. Without doubt, it was one of the most important ideas ever adopted by the NFL because, when used intelligently, it has maintained the NFL's competitiveness throughout the last six decades. It was a plan born of Bell's necessity because he simply wasn't getting any top-flight talent in the free-for-all system that existed then. It also was a tribute to the owners of that time, particularly Mara, Lambeau, and Halas, whose teams were attracting the best players, to agree to it for the good of the sport. His plan then, as now, called for the teams to draft in reverse order of their previous season's finish.

The first NFL player draft consisted of nine rounds, and was held February 8, 1936, at Philadelphia's Ritz-Carlton Hotel, which was owned by Bell's family. The Eagles, who had the NFL's worst record in 1935, had the first pick and chose University of Chicago running back Jay Berwanger, who had won the first Heisman Trophy (then called the Downtown Athletic Club Trophy). Berwanger showed no interest in playing pro football, so Bell traded his rights to the Bears, but George Halas's pleas had no impact on Berwanger, either. By the late forties, the draft had increased to 30 rounds, and by the mid-nineties it was reduced to just seven rounds.

Before the draft was instituted and for nearly 10 years after, the Bears, Giants, Packers, and Redskins dominated the league with an array of stars that brought added visibility to pro football. After the Bears beat Portsmouth for the 1932 NFL title, they played for the league championship seven times in the next 11 seasons, and, with Halas as the team's guiding hand (either as president or head coach), they won four of them during two distinct eras of dominance.

Bears and Giants

Halas often was cantankerous in his dealings. He drove his players to their limit of physical and emotional endurance. He bullied officials and tried to intimidate opponents, sometimes even shutting off the hot water to their dressing room showers. He coached for 40 years, in four different 10-year segments. When he finally stepped down after the 1967 season, he had won 324 games, a record unsurpassed until Don Shula broke it during the 1990s.

Yet, for all his stubbornness and rigidity, Halas never strayed from making pro football as exciting and entertaining as possible. A pantheon of Hall of Fame players made the Bears exciting in the early thirties: Grange, Bronko Nagurski, the legendary fullback; and Beattie Feathers, who in 1934 became the first man to rush for 1,000 yards in a season.

The Bears repeated their dominance in the forties when they earned the nickname "Monsters of the Midway" by winning four more NFL titles and five Western Division crowns. They were led by quarterback Sid Luckman, whose supporting cast included future Hall of Fame linemen Clyde (Bulldog) Turner, George Musso, Dan Fortmann, and Joe Stydahar plus end Ken Kavanaugh and backs George McAfee, and Bill Osmanski.

Luckman became the NFL's first great T-formation quarterback after joining the team in 1939. When Ralph Jones replaced Halas as coach from 1930-32, he livened up the T-formation with split ends and backs and men in motion. Halas continued to tinker with the T through the 1930s. Clark Shaughnessy, an advisor to the Bears while coaching the final days of football at the University of Chicago, helped Luckman make the transition from Single-Wing tailback to T-formation quarterback with such alacrity that he mastered the position by the end of his rookie season.

In 1940 Luckman led Chicago to its momentous 73-0 victory over Washington in the NFL title game. He followed a path that led him to the Hall of Fame by helping Chicago win titles the following year against the New York Giants, in 1943 against Washington, and his last, in 1946, again over New York. He was the first quarterback ever to throw for more than 400 yards and for 7 touchdown passes in a game.

The Giants challenged the Bears by winning eight division titles and two NFL championships in a 14-season period from 1933-1946 with some great players, including Alphonse (Tuffy) Leemans, Mel Hein, Ken Strong, and Ed Danowski. One of their most memorable wins was the famed "Sneakers Game" at the Polo Grounds, the1934 title game against a Bears team that had gone undefeated through the regular season. The field was frozen so badly that conventional cleats did not even dent the surface and players of both teams slipped and slid every time they tried to run.

Giants coach Steve Owen and his captain, end Ray Flaherty, talked about using sneakers instead of football shoes for better traction. Trainer Gus Mauch suggested that Manhattan College could provide some sneakers, and Owen dispatched assistant equipment man Abe Cohen to the college. By the time Cohen returned and New York players changed shoes early in the third quarter, the Giants trailed 13-3. But with better footing, New York roared back to win 30-13.

Owen, the team's winningest coach ever with a record of 155-108-17, was a master of defensive football that was underscored by a very basic coaching philosophy: "Football theory must be based on the inevitable fact that body contact is the basis of the game." He had the players to prove it, particularly Hein, considered the Giants' greatest two-way player after a 15-season career as a center and linebacker from 1931-1945. He frequently played 60 minutes per game and in 1938 he was chosen the NFL's first most valuable player, an astonishing feat for a lineman. Owen stressed "careful" offense, often punting on third down because he had great punters and he believed his defense could bottle up an opponent, making it possible to score field goals with such kickers as Strong and Ward Cuff.

Leemans, who current Giants' co-owner Wellington Mara scouted and still calls the franchise's greatest offensive player, wasn't fast, but he could explode into a hole. His strength, at 6 feet and 200 pounds, was such that few defenders ever tackled him below the waist. When the Giants selected Ed Danowski, who was a better passer than Leemans, Owen arranged them into two separate backfields; Leemans's group played the first and third quarters, and Danowski's group worked the second and fourth quarters. The scheme worked to beat the Packers for the 1938 title 23-17, as Danowski's passing and the running of Hank Soar, later a great American League baseball umpire, keyed the winning touchdown drive for the Giants at the Polo Grounds.

Hutson and Baugh

Beating the Packers was no mean feat in those years. Earl (Curly) Lambeau had founded a semipro team in Green Bay and convinced a local meat packing company to become its sponsor. He was the team's star runner and passer; two years later he brought the Packers into the NFL. Green Bay became the first team to win three consecutive NFL championships from 1929 to 1931. Over the next decade, the Packers added two Hall of Fame running backs, Tony Canadeo and Clarke Hinkle, and the great pass-catch combinations of Arnie Herber and Cecil Isbell throwing to Don Hutson.

Herber led the Packers to four NFL titles after joining them in 1930. He won the NFL's first official passing title in 1932 and added two more in the next four years. Hinkle, a triple-threat fullback, gained more yards rushing from 1932-1941 than any other player.

Then there was Hutson. He came to the Packers the year before the player draft went into effect so Green Bay had to outbid the Brooklyn Dodgers to sign him. He is arguably the best receiver in NFL history because he played in an era where the forward pass still was an evolving weapon. The 6-foot 1-inch, 185-pound Hutson also was a great two-way player. The team's kicker for most of his career, he was too light to play end on defense and was moved to the secondary, where he tied for the league lead in interceptions in 1940.

Hutson was the NFL's top receiver eight times, including five years in a row from 1941-45. He led the league in receiving yardage seven times, including four consecutive seasons, 1941-44, won or shared the lead in touchdowns in eight seasons, and was the top scorer six consecutive seasons, 1940-45. He also was the first receiver to gain more than 1,000 yards in a season with 1,211 in 1942, when he caught a then-record 74 passes. He finished his career in 1945 with 99 touchdown receptions, a record that lasted until Steve Largent of Seattle broke it in 1989.

Isbell and Luckman vied for prominence as passers with Washington's Sammy Baugh. He was the Redskins' number one draft pick in 1937 after leading Texas Christian University's "Aerial Circus" for three seasons. Baugh was a 6-2, 180-pound rawboned Texan who looked like he had been summoned from central casting for a Hollywood western. In his first game with the Redskins he completed 11 of 16 passes against the defense-minded Giants. With his amazing passing accuracy from any distance, he was the best passer of his era, and he led the league's passers six times. Baugh also was a great punter; more than four decades after retiring, he still holds several NFL records, including best career average (45.1) and highest season average (51.4, set in 1940). He also was an able defender in the era of two-way football, and for most of his early career, he was a Single-Wing tailback with some running responsibilities.

In 1937, helped by Cliff Battles, who won his second rushing title, Baugh helped the Redskins to their first NFL title in their first season in Washington. They defeated the Bears 28-21 in the championship game as Baugh threw 3 touchdown passes and completed 18 of 32 passes for 354 yards. The victory helped Marshall recoup the $80,000 he lost in Boston and turn a $40,000 profit.

Chicago got even two years later with a 73-0 victory. Bears quarterback Sid Luckman engineered the biggest blowout in NFL title-game history, and he did it while completing just 4 of 6 passes for 102 yards and 1 touchdown.

Washington had defeated the Bears 7-3 just three weeks earlier, but Redskins owner George Preston Marshall deprecated the losers and fired up Chicago for one of the most awesome performances ever seen in any NFL game. On the game's second play, Bill Osmanski ran 68 yards for a touchdown. The Bears led 28-0 at the half and as Washington tried to pass its way back into the game, Chicago intercepted 8 attempts, and 6 were turned into touchdowns.

In the fourth quarter, the referee, Red Friesell, asked Bears coach George Halas not to kick any more extra points because he had only two footballs left for the game.

Washington missed a scoring opportunity on its first possession when Charlie Malone dropped Sammy Baugh's pass at the goal line. Asked later if that might have made a difference, Baugh quipped, "Sure—the game would have wound up 73-7."

The Troubled 1940s

In 1939, while the Washington Redskins, Chicago Bears, and Green Bay Packers battled for domination, National Football League president Joe Carr died. Longtime league treasurer Carl Storck temporarily took over, and he was succeeded by Elmer Layden, then head coach and athletic director at Notre Dame. The owners wanted someone with a football background and instant visibility—Layden had been a member of Notre Dame's famed "Four Horsemen" backfield in 1925. To elevate their sport to the status enjoyed by major league baseball, the owners instituted the title "commissioner."

Also in 1939, the NFL attracted a million spectators for the first time, but, a few years later, at the height of its popularity, the NFL was affected severely by World War II. Fortunately for the pro football's continuity, President Franklin D. Roosevelt declared that all sports, pro and college, should continue wherever possible because of their morale benefits.

It wasn't easy in the NFL, which was stripped of many talented players. Most players worked in war plants, took weekend leave from military service to play, were draftees awaiting call-up, or were classified 4-F (physically unable to serve in the military). Cleveland Rams owner Dan Reeves was in the Navy, and the league allowed his team to suspend operations in 1943. To offset an awkward nine-team scheduling problem, Layden forced a reluctant merger of the Steelers and Eagles to give the league eight teams.

The team was popularly called the Steagles and played four games in each city. Surprisingly, it just missed tying Washington and New York for the Eastern Division title. The Steagles were dissolved after the season, and the NFL added a new franchise in Boston. The Cleveland Rams franchise returned, so Layden persuaded Rooney and Cardinals owner Charley Bidwill to merge their teams into one called Card-Pitt. The team lost every game, and Rooney called it the worst team in NFL history.

The Cleveland Rams, founded in 1937 by Homer Marshman, were purchased by Reeves and Fred Levy, Jr. In 1944 they drafted Bob Waterfield, an All-America tailback from UCLA who was even more famous for marrying voluptuous Hollywood star Jane Russell. Waterfield led the Rams to the 1945 Western Division title and then to a 15-14 victory over Washington in the title game. The deciding points came on a safety, when Baugh's pass struck the crossbar and hit the ground. Baugh left the game in the second quarter with injured ribs, and Waterfield threw a pair of touchdown passes and kicked the winning extra point.

The Cleveland Rams had drawn only about 70,000 during the entire 1945 season and early in 1946, they became the first major league team to relocate to the West Coast. That same year, NFL owners tapped Bert Bell to succeed Elmer Layden as commissioner for reasons that formed the strength of his 13-year reign. They liked Bell personally, he was never cowed or pushed to any rash decisions, he brought people together to work for the good of the sport, and they knew he was ardently dedicated to the game's prosperity.

A New League

The move was very timely because the NFL then was faced with its biggest challenge ever—the All-America Football Conference, with teams in New York City, Brooklyn, Los Angeles, San Francisco, Chicago, Cleveland, Miami, and Buffalo. The new league was the brain child of *Chicago Tribune* sports editor Arch Ward, who had conceived both the All-Star baseball game and the College All-Star football games. He had been the NFL owners' choice to succeed Joe Carr in 1939 but declined and backed his friend, Layden. Ward reasoned that since major league baseball had a two-league structure, then so should the NFL, including a season-ending "world series." When such a meeting was suggested to Layden after the AAFC had been formed, his reply became a rallying cry for the new league: "Tell them to get a football first."

There was no dearth of willing owners, many of whom had been rebuffed by the NFL, and they responded positively to Ward's call. Some, such as lumber tycoon Anthony Morabito in San Francisco and a group of movie stars in Los Angeles that included Don Ameche, Bing Crosby, Bob Hope, and movie studio tycoon Louis B. Mayer, were victims of the "train barrier," when three and four-day West Coast train trips weren't conducive to scheduling. But that problem disappeared after World War II because aviation made huge strides. Morabito joined the AAFC and called his team the 49ers. Ameche's group was joined by Ben Lindheimer, a wealthy Chicago racetrack owner, who had tried without success to become part of owner of the Bears and Cardinals, to found the Los Angeles Dons. They became more popular than the newly settled Rams for three of the AAFC's four years.

Jim Brueil withdrew his $25,000 deposit with the NFL for a new franchise in Buffalo, named his team the Bisons, and a year later changed it to the Bills. Arthur (Mickey) McBride, owner of the Yellow Cab Company in Cleveland, had been turned down by Dan Reeves with his offer to purchase the Rams. In New York City, Dan Topping, owner of the baseball Yankees, also owned the Brooklyn Dodgers, an NFL team since 1930. He merged it with the NFL's Boston Yanks in 1945 and then moved the franchise into the AAFC where it became the New York Yankees and played its games in Yankee Stadium. The AAFC then placed another franchise in Brooklyn. In Chicago, John Keeshin, a trucking company and race track owner, started the Chicago Rockets. Miami became the eighth team early in 1946, lasted just one season and was replaced by the Baltimore Colts in 1947.

There was also no scarcity of players. "There were enough players available to stock a dozen leagues," said Jim Crowley, the AAFC's first commissioner, who was appointed to the post to match the visibility of his fellow "Horseman" Layden. The AAFC didn't hold a draft for its 1946 season because its teams had been urged to go out and sign as many players as possible to compete on an equal footing with the NFL, and they particularly tapped the rich reserve of great collegiate talent playing football at the major military bases around the country while offering more money than had ever been paid before. Until that time, it was not uncommon for NFL linemen to receive $150 or $175 per game, and backs to get $250 or $300. Forty of the 67 players on the 1946 College All-Star team that defeated the NFL-champion Rams signed with the All-America Conference. However, allowing teams to pursue any players they wished instead of parceling them out in a draft proved a fatal move, Crowley later admitted, "because [a draft] would have equalized talent among all the teams, instead of permitting the ultimate domination by the Cleveland Browns."

The Browns' dominance was no accident. Coach Paul Brown hand-picked his team well—even paying many of them monthly retainers while they were in the service. One of those was Otto Graham, the Browns' quarterback, who became the preeminent star of the AAFC. Coach Brown always called him the greatest quarterback ever "because he got us to the championship game every year he played, and he won more of them than any other quarterback in history."

Graham, who won seven titles in both leagues, was the first player signed by Cleveland because Brown recalled his great ability to run and throw as a tailback for Northwestern, when he had played against the coach's Ohio State teams. He easily made the transition to quarterback, then teamed with great receivers such as Dante Lavelli, Mac Speedie, and Dub Jones in a passing attack that even Halas had his staff watch and copy. Brown complemented it with a great running attack led by fullback Marion Motley and other stars, including two other Hall of Fame players, linebacker Bill Willis and tackle/kicker Lou Groza, who played on all eight of Cleveland's AAFC/NFL championship teams.

The All-America Conference also had other great players, several of them future Hall of Fame members: Y.A. Tittle, Elroy (Crazylegs) Hirsch, Frank (Bruiser) Kinard, Arnie Weinmeister, and Joe Perry. A notch down were the likes of left-handed quarterback Frankie Albert, rusher/receiver Edgar (Special Delivery) Jones, triple threats Glenn Dobbs and Orban (Spec) Sanders, and Alyn Beals of the 49ers, who led the AAFC in touchdown catches all four seasons.

With such great talent, wealthier owners than the NFL, and the enthusiasm in new cities, the new league was a real threat. It might have had a greater impact had it not been for Cleveland's dominance. The Browns won all four league titles, and lost just four games during those four seasons. Its 1948 team was unbeaten and untied in 15 games, including the championship game.

One other significant factor saved the NFL; Bert Bell held all of his owners together during a multi-million dollar player war. The AAFC lacked Bell's leadership and the stability of the NFL owners, most of whom had raised their league from infancy and knew precisely what was needed to survive. After four years and millions of dollars of losses on both sides, the two leagues agreed to merge.

But there were some great benefits from their competition. Not only was the West Coast opened for pro football, but for the first time African-American players came into the sport in ever-increasing numbers. Black players had competed in the NFL prior to 1933. Fritz Pollard, Rube Marshall, Fred (Duke) Slater, Paul Robeson, Jay (Inky) Williams, and several others starred in the NFL during the 1920s. Moving the Rams to the West Coast helped African-Americans re-enter the NFL. The team signed former UCLA star Kenny Washington as a pre-condition to obtaining a lease to play in the Los Angeles Coliseum and later added lineman Woody Strode.

The AAFC had publicly stated there would be equal opportunity for everyone, but only Cleveland coach Paul Brown signed African-American players in the league's first season, getting Willis and Motley. Both had played for him previously, Willis as an All-America lineman at Ohio State and Motley at Great Lakes Naval Training Center. When other teams saw the talent they brought to the game, African Americans began to enter the sport in greater numbers.

Paul Brown, Innovator

Paul Brown's signing of Motley and Willis is but one instance of just how far ahead of everyone else he was in guiding a football team. Aside from George Halas, there has been no more influential coach in pro football history. While Halas was a mighty figure for the first part of the sport's history, Brown was the most influential during the postwar era and right up to his death in 1991.

Brown's greatest contributions to the game were his many innovations, most taken for granted now, that elevated pro football to a more sophisticated level. The list includes minutely detailed playbooks and classroom teaching techniques, year-round coaching staffs who set up complete statistical analyses of their team's performances and graded every player, and use of intelligence tests to measure a player's learning potential.

On the field, he established an intricate passing attack that was built on receivers running precision routes and reading opposing defenses to find the open spots; then he built a defense that could counteract that system. He was the first to develop a "two-minute drill" offense and the first to script opening sequences of plays. The basis of his offensive system still exists in the nineties as the West Coast offense, developed by Bill Walsh, one of Brown's assistant coaches in Cincinnati.

Walsh is one of some two dozen NFL and college coaches who either played for or coached with Brown who later went on to success in the NFL. (The head coaches of 13 NFL champions, including Super Bowl winners, either coached for or played for Brown, and 10 players in pro football's Hall of Fame also played for him in Cleveland.)

His genius was further reflected in the Browns' success after the team joined the NFL in 1950, along with the AAFC's San Francisco 49ers and Baltimore Colts. Players from the AAFC's other teams were distributed in a special draft and the result was a new NFL that propelled professional football to unimagined heights within a quarter century. The Browns were right in the middle of this surge, playing in the NFL title game during each of their first six seasons, and winning three of those games. Brown also had tremendous influence on the way the game developed as an original member of the NFL's prestigious Competition Committee, on which he served until his death.

The 1950s: Growth After the Merger

Upon joining the NFL, the Browns immediately were tested by defending-champion Philadelphia. The Eagles had won back-to-back NFL titles to close out the forties, when they had battled the Chicago Cardinals for league dominance. Chicago, with its Dream Backfield of Elmer Angsman, Charley Trippi, Pat Harder, and Paul Christman, won the 1947 title, beating Philadelphia 28-21. But the Eagles, led by Hall of Fame running back Steve Van Buren, won the next two championship games, 7-0 over the Cards in a blizzard at Philadelphia's Shibe Park in 1948 and 14-0 over the Rams in monsoon-like conditions in Los Angeles in 1949.

On the Saturday night before the other teams opened their seasons, more than 70,000 fans crammed Philadelphia's Municipal Stadium, most of them believing the prevailing NFL propaganda that the Browns were an inferior team from an inferior league. They expected to see the Eagles easily defeat Cleveland, even without Van Buren, who was injured. The Browns, seeking vengeance for the putdowns they had heard from the NFL for four years, stunned everyone as Graham coolly took apart the famed Eagle Defense. He completed 21 passes for 346 yards, and in the fourth quarter, he unleashed his running game. "We wanted to show them we could run better than they could," Graham said later. The final score was Browns 35, Eagles 10. Bell told everyone within earshot: "Cleveland is the best team I have ever seen."

The Browns continued to win, even beating the Eagles again without throwing a pass—a lone Cleveland completion was disallowed on a penalty—after Neale complained that all the Browns did was throw the ball. But Cleveland could not defeat the defense-minded New York Giants, thanks in part to the Umbrella Defense, designed by coach Steve Owen, that contained Cleveland's passing game. The two teams tied for the 1950 American Conference title, but the Browns won a playoff game in Cleveland 8-3, helped by Bill Willis's game-saving tackle of Eugene (Choo Choo) Roberts after he had run 47 yards to the Browns' 4-yard line.

Cleveland made one final exclamation mark on the NFL in its first season by defeating the Los Angeles Rams 30-28 (the Rams had beaten the Bears 24-14 in a National Conference playoff) in one of the most thrilling championship games ever played. The Rams had offensive stars such as Bob Waterfield and Norm Van Brocklin at quarterback. Waterfield was a do-everything player from his days as an all-America tailback at UCLA. He ran, passed, kicked extra points, punted, played defense, and even kicked off.

Van Brocklin, nicknamed the Dutchman, was the opposite in temperament, outgoing and gregarious in calm situations, defiant and challenging on the field. He wasn't as gifted as Waterfield athletically, but he was a better passer. Throughout their careers with the Rams, they were the centerpieces of a controversy over which one should start, but it didn't keep the Rams from going to three consecutive NFL title games.

The Browns and Rams met again for the title in 1951, and this time Los Angeles won 24-17 when Van Brocklin relieved Waterfield in the fourth quarter and threw a 73-yard TD pass to Tom Fears. In the next three seasons, the Rams, who lost a playoff to Detroit for the 1952 National Conference title, were chewed apart by coaching changes, but Sid Gillman restored order in 1955 and once more they played the Browns for the title. Cleveland won this one 38-14 in Graham's farewell game.

Layne's Lions

The Browns forged a gaudy 58-13-1 record during their first six seasons. Between Cleveland's bouts with the Rams, the Detroit Lions, a blue-collar team led by talented, hard-nosed Bobby Layne and coached by Buddy Parker, became a power. One key to Detroit's success—NFL titles in 1952 and 1953, and another in 1957—was the NFL's best secondary, with Hall of Fame members Jack Christiansen and Yale Lary, plus Jim David and Bob Smith, along with linebacker Joe Schmidt, another Hall of Fame honoree. After Detroit beat the Rams in the playoff for the conference title in 1952, they upset the Browns 17-7 for the championship, thanks largely to several great defensive stands and Doak Walker's 67-yard touchdown run. It was Detroit's first title since 1935, but they did it again in 1953 when Layne hit end Jim Doran with a late game-winning score for a 17-16 victory.

Their biggest victory thereafter was in a 1957 Western Conference playoff game against the San Francisco 49ers. They trailed 24-7 at halftime on 3 Y.A. Tittle touchdown passes, and as they tried to regroup during the halftime break, they heard the 49ers in the locker room next door doing some premature celebrating. Detroit roared out for the second half and after San Francisco kicked a field goal for a 27-7 lead, Detroit scored 24 points in 21 minutes for an astounding 31-27 victory. The Lions used that as a springboard for a 59-14 title game victory over the Browns, a great end to a tumultuous season. Parker had quit at a "Meet the Lions" banquet two days before the first preseason game and was replaced by George Wilson, and Layne was sidelined late in the year with a broken leg and was replaced by Tobin Rote.

The New York Giants put together a strong defense in 1956 and won the NFL championship. Jim Lee Howell was the Giants' head coach, but he left the defense to player-coach Tom Landry. For perhaps the first time ever, a defensive unit became the darlings of the fans and the cry "DEE-FENSE!" thundered throughout Yankee Stadium every Sunday when the Giants played at home. The term "front four" also became part of pro football's lexicon, and the Giants produced the first great one in 1956 with former Rams' all-pro Andy Robustelli and rookie Jim Katcavage at end and tackles Roosevelt Grier and Dick Modzelewski.

The middle linebacker position also became prominent at this time. New York's Sam Huff became the beneficiary of Landry's coordinated schemes and made tackle after tackle as running plays were funneled to him. Other great middle linebackers—Schmidt at Detroit, Bill George in Chicago, Les Richter in Los Angeles, Chuck Bednarik in Philadelphia, and Ray Nitschke in Green Bay—became stars.

1958: The Greatest Game?

A wide-open offense, epitomized by the Rams, and defense, popularized by the Giants, set the stage for a watershed 1958 season in which pro football leaped to the fore of America's sporting consciousness. The climax was played out on a frozen, grassless field at Yankee Stadium over a three-weekend span in December.

It began in the last game of the regular season at Yankee Stadium, with Cleveland holding a one-game lead over New York. Jim Brown, Cleveland's great fullback, ran 65 yards for a touchdown on the game's first play, but the Giants came from behind to win 13-10 when Pat Summerall kicked a 49-yard field goal through the wind, snow, and darkness of a mid-December Sunday afternoon.

That set up a playoff between the two teams the following week on the same field, and the media in New York City churned out tens of thousands of words that alerted an entire nation to the game and the teams. The game was televised nationally, and the Giants' defense shut down Brown again. Brown had set an NFL rushing record of 1,527 yards that season, but he ran for just 8 yards as New York won 10-0.

The following weekend, the NFL Championship Game between the Giants and Baltimore Colts became one of the most significant games ever played in terms of impact on the public and the future of football's popularity. Until then, pro football was a distinct second fiddle to major league baseball in fan popularity, and the impact of televised football was almost minimal, even in title games. The NFL didn't televise its first championship game nationally until 1951 when the Dumont Network paid the NFL $75,000 for the rights.

That all changed on December 28, 1958.

The Baltimore Colts were the successors of the original franchise that had come to the NFL from the AAFC and failed after just one season. Two years later, Baltimoreans proved they would support a new team by purchasing more than 15,000 season tickets within a month. Bell, ever wary of another failure, awarded the franchise to a group headed by his good friend, Carroll Rosenbloom, and then hand-picked another friend, Don Kellett, to be general manager.

Rosenbloom was unwilling to wait for his new team to grow its way to the top and sought the shortest cut to success. After his team finished with a 3-9 record in 1953, he tried to replicate the success of the Cleveland Browns and signed their long-time assistant coach, Wilbur (Weeb) Ewbank, who brashly promised the impatient Rosenbloom that he would have a championship team in five seasons. On the Sunday after Christmas in 1958, Ewbank had the Colts in the NFL title game with a group of players that included several future Hall of Fame inductees: quarterback Johnny Unitas, end Raymond Berry, halfback Lenny Moore, tackle Jim Parker, and defensive linemen Gino Marchetti and Art Donovan.

Unitas was the key. His daring leadership and last-minute heroics made him the NFL's first television poster boy. His trademarks were a crew cut, black high-top shoes in an era when low-cut football shoes had come into vogue, and an ice-water-in-his-veins approach to adversity. He didn't have the strongest arm and he couldn't run very fast, but he always seemed to make precise throws when he needed them, and he never shied from tacklers whenever he ran.

Unitas and his teammates jumped to a 14-3 lead and threatened to score again before the Giants' defense staged a great goal-line stand early in the second half. New York then scored 14 consecutive points and led 17-14 with just two minutes to play. In a classic display of two-minute offense, Unitas drove the Colts 73 yards against one of the NFL's best defenses, then watched as Steve Myhra kicked a 20-yard field goal with just seven seconds to play. The drive was a classic that astounded millions of television viewers, few of whom had ever seen such a precise display of offensive football.

Aside from a preseason game played under special rules in 1955, this was the first overtime game in NFL history and certainly the first with a championship on the line. The Giants won the coin toss in overtime but punted after their first series. The Colts got the ball at their 20-yard line, and never relinquished it. Once again, Unitas and his offense were perfect as they marched 80 yards for the winning touchdown, with Alan Ameche rushing 1 yard for the winning score 8:15 into the extra session.

As an ebullient Bert Bell burst out of his box, he shouted to all who could hear him, "This is the greatest day in the history of professional football." It was not only the game to which he was referring, but he knew the drama that had unfolded would have a profound impact on how the sport would be embraced by the nation. From that day onward, pro football began an ascendancy curve that carried it to the top of the nation's charts by the mid-seventies.

Bell always had been very judicious in his approach to television and built a strong foundation that later produced a solid relationship between the medium and the NFL. In 1956, Bell allowed the CBS network to televise selected games into specific market areas across the nation, and he instituted an automatic time out with two minutes to play in each half (the two-minute warning) to insure that television would get at least one commercial break per half.

Bell was careful not to overexpose the league. He convinced the owners to bar televising any home games by stations within 75 miles of the stadium site. The ban, which was upheld by a federal court in the mid-1950s, was in effect in New York, the nation's largest television market, when the Giants played their three memorable season-ending games in 1958. Millions in the Giants' hometown never saw their team's breathtaking exploits—and they couldn't read about them either because a major newspaper strike had closed all seven New York City daily newspapers during this time.

The total blackout rule stayed in effect until 1973, when the Washington Redskins became so popular that members of Congress resented not being able to see them play at home and threatened legislative action against the NFL. The league finally adopted a rule allowing the blackout to be lifted if a game is sold out 72 hours before kickoff.

The ripple effects of that 1958 title game and what it meant to the sport was felt throughout the early 1960s, as television rights fees rose from less than a million dollars for the entire NFL to $18.8 million for all regular season and playoff games in 1965.

Pete Rozelle Takes Over

Pete Rozelle, NFL commissioner from 1960 to 1989, was most responsible for the riches that accrued to the league from television. Bert Bell died in the fall of 1959 while watching the two teams he once owned—Philadelphia and Pittsburgh—play a game in Philadelphia, and finding his successor was not easy. It took 23 ballots before NFL owners finally chose Rozelle, then the 33-year-old general manager of the Los Angeles Rams, as a compromise candidate.

For the next three decades, Rozelle led the NFL through the most dramatic, and, at times, the most difficult period of its existence and became, without question, the most successful commissioner in pro sports history. The key to that success was his experience within pro football, and his ability to bend enough owners to his will, by persuasion if possible, by action when necessary.

As the sport prospered, his triumphs were many. League attendance zoomed from an average of 47,000 per game when he became commissioner to more than 65,000 when he retired during the 1989 season. His sport became number one among the nation's sporting preferences, and the Super Bowl became the single biggest one-day sports event in the nation and one that rivals World Cup soccer for international attention. Moreover, he established league-controlled entities to take advantage of fan interest, including NFL Properties as a league-wide marketing arm that became a multi-billion dollar worldwide enterprise.

War with the AFL

But Rozelle jumped into turbulent waters the day he became commissioner because the NFL faced competition from the American Football League. This eight-team league, like the All-America Football Conference 15 years earlier, was born of frustration, created this time by a rich, young Texan named Lamar Hunt. In 1958, Hunt had tried unsuccessfully to purchase the Chicago Cardinals, then in the throes of an ownership dispute, so he could move them to Dallas. Undaunted, Hunt decided to form his own league.

Like Arch Ward in 1944, he foresaw the growth of pro football to a second league and an eventual "world series." He received positive responses from such entrepreneurs as oilman Bud Adams in Houston; Bob Howsam, a veteran baseball executive from Denver who represented the Phipps Family; Barron Hilton, whose family owned the nation's largest hotel chain; famed sportscaster Harry Wismer, then a minority owner of the Redskins; and Max Winter and Bill Boyer in Minneapolis. Bill Sullivan, a former publicity man for Notre Dame and the Boston Braves, put together a group in Boston, and Ralph Wilson, an automobile executive and minority owner in the Detroit Lions, claimed a Buffalo franchise.

They placed teams in New York, Boston, Buffalo, Houston, Dallas, Denver, Los Angeles, and Minneapolis. The NFL, sensing that this was a serious threat, offered to expand to new franchises in Dallas and Houston, hoping to lure Hunt and Adams and cut down the venture. But the two Texans stayed with their group, though Winter's group defected and established the NFL's Minnesota Vikings franchise in 1961. It was replaced in the AFL by a group in Oakland headed by Y.C. (Chet) Soda, who affectionately called his group "The Foolish Club." Later, he applied the name to the AFL owners, and it stuck.

Joe Foss was the American Football League's first commissioner. Foss was governor of South Dakota and a much-decorated World War II fighter pilot. The owners hoped his squeaky-clean image would inspire public confidence.

The AFL went through some growing pains. Houston and Oakland played in high school stadiums for several years. There was sparse attendance in New York and Los Angeles, where the NFL had teams. The Boston Patriots scheduled many of their games on Friday night, because they couldn't compete with New York Giants games on television on Sunday afternoons. The Patriots played in four different stadiums during the first 11 years of their existence. The Los Angeles Chargers won the Western Division title in the league's first year and then moved down the coast to San Diego because they could not compete with a woeful Rams team. The Chargers appeared in five of the AFL's first six championship games. Even Hunt's flagship Dallas Texans moved to Kansas City in 1963, the year after they won the AFL championship in a double overtime victory against Houston.

Of course, the new league triggered a fierce war for star players, just as the AAFC had done in the forties. In the first couple of seasons, most of the AFL's leading players were retread NFL players. However, there also was an instant battle by both leagues to attract the top college stars. LSU's Billy Cannon won the 1959 Heisman Trophy and was signed to a contract by then-Rams general manager Rozelle, even though he still had a bowl game to play. After that game, Houston signed him to an AFL contract, and a judge finally ruled the latter was the valid pact.

War Stories

The war—and that's what it became—reached frantic proportions at times. The NFL started a group it called "Operation Hand Holding," which "babysat" prospective high draft picks to keep them away from AFL representatives. Sometimes the players and their escorts moved to three or four hotels in the same city the day before a contract was signed.

Dallas owner Lamar Hunt pursued quarterback Roman Gabriel, his number-one draft pick and also a first-round choice of the Los Angeles Rams, in 1962. He finally got an answer on Gabriel's phone and laid out the features of the contract. Years later, Hunt discovered that the voice on the other end of the phone belonged to Rams' general manager Elroy Hirsch, who was about to sign Gabriel to a contract.

Contracts included bonuses that ranged from hundreds of thousands of dollars to blue-chip stock portfolios to a honeymoon. Player drafts took days because a team would not select a player until after he signed a contract; that sometimes took an entire day while the player was hunted down, wooed, hidden, and finally given a pact that he accepted.

Despite the shenanigans, the AFL developed stars, some of them former NFL players whose second chance was a bonanza. George Blanda, the game's all-time leading scorer with 2,002 points, had played quarterback for the Chicago Bears until he "retired" after the 1958 season. Rejuvenated, he helped Houston win the AFL's first two titles and finished his career in 1975 after 340 games, the most ever.

Jack Kemp had failed in tryouts with several NFL teams, but he became a top AFL passer and led Buffalo to a pair of titles. Cookie Gilchrist was a star running back in the Canadian Football League, and he became the AFL's first 1,000-yard rusher for Buffalo. Two wide receivers—Don Maynard, who had been on the Giants' 1958 team, and Lance Alworth, an AFL "original" who played for San Diego—made it to the Hall of Fame.

The AFL's single most important player acquisition occurred in 1965 when New York Jets owner David (Sonny) Werblin signed Alabama quarterback Joe Namath to a $437,000 contract. That gave the AFL its most visible star in the nation's key media center. He became "Broadway Joe" in the fast lane of New York City's frenetic life, and a hero to an emerging generation. In 1967, he became the first quarterback to pass for 4,000 yards. Namath's greatest achievement came in Super Bowl III, when he brashly predicted that his 18-point underdog team would defeat the Baltimore Colts. It did, by a score of 16-7.

However, the survival and eventual success of the American Football League settled on four, and possibly, five events:

(1) Hunt moved his team in 1963 from Dallas to Kansas City, where the new Chiefs prospered.

(2) Oakland hired Al Davis as head coach and general manger in 1963. That stabilized the franchise, brought it great success, and placed it on a par with the 49ers in San Francisco.

(3) The New York Titans franchise, then bankrupt and a ward of the AFL, was sold in 1963 to a syndicate headed by Werblin for $1 million. Within a year, the renamed Jets moved into a new stadium built in connection with the 1964 World's Fair, drew record crowds, and, a year later, signed Namath, the AFL's biggest star.

(4) A five-year, $36 million contact signed with NBC in 1965 insured the AFL's financial survival.

Whether a fifth event helped or hindered bringing about the eventual merger still is argued hotly. In 1966, Pete Gogolak, pro football's first soccer-style kicker, was signed by the New York Giants. Gogolak had played out his option with the AFL's Buffalo Bills and his signing by the rival league triggered a war for established stars. The AFL named Al Davis commissioner, and he used Gogolak's defection as a reason to sign several of the NFL's best players to rich, future contracts. While some believe this escalation was the final shove needed to bring the two sides together, others insist it almost derailed an agreement that already had been reached.

Secret meetings were held in 1965 between Baltimore Colts owner Carroll Rosenbloom and Buffalo Bills owner Ralph Wilson to lay down the key points that would effect a merger. Hunt and Dallas Cowboys general manager Tex Schramm, ironed out the details. Rozelle, who became commissioner of the new entity, announced the merger on June 8, 1966, with interleague play set for the 1970 season—after the two leagues were combined into two conferences. A common draft began in 1967 and a long-awaited championship game between the two leagues, eventually dubbed the Super Bowl, began after the 1966 season.

Lombardi and the Packers

While the AFL-NFL war raged, the long-dormant the Packers surged back to championship status. Green Bay, which hadn't had a winning season since 1947, hired Giants assistant coach Vince Lombardi as head coach in 1959. Lombardi was a member of Fordham's famed Seven Blocks of Granite line in the late thirties and later coached under Earl (Red) Blaik at West Point and for the Giants for five years. At Green Bay, the fiery, demanding, and intimidating coach bullied and coaxed players with equal effectiveness. He was forceful and emotional, with a deep, rough voice that struck terror into even his toughest players. He had more bite than bark, too, and turned things upside down in his Green Bay first season by quickly dispatching players who did not respond to his ways.

Lombardi drove his players to the limits of their abilities while at the same time building up their confidence and self-esteem to the point they always believed they could win. His football was reminiscent of what he had learned at Fordham, and almost a self-portrait because it was a power-oriented running game that featured the Packers' sweep, not unlike the end runs and off-tackle plays during the heyday of Single-Wing football, in which linemen pulled out and led running backs through the tackles and around the corners with a crunching display of smash-mouth blocking.

The running roles were given to Jim Taylor, a tough fullback from LSU who resented being tackled, and a converted quarterback, Paul Hornung, the 1956 Heisman Trophy winner from Notre Dame. Lombardi taught them his run-to-daylight theories and both went on to the Hall of Fame. So did a once-reluctant, jittery quarterback named Bart Starr. He became a confident field general, willing to accept his coach's bullying without it affecting his steady performances. During their nine years together, the Packers had an 89-24-4 record, won five NFL championships and the first two Super Bowls, and six conference titles. Eleven members of those teams, including Lombardi, are enshrined in the Hall of Fame.

Lombardi got his team to the 1960 NFL title game but lost to the Philadelphia Eagles, led by Norm Van Brocklin, in the climactic farewell to his career, and linebacker Chuck Bednarik. But that was the Packers' last playoff stumble. They beat the Giants for the championship in 1961 and 1962, and just missed a fourth consecutive conference title in 1963 by losing twice to the eventual-champion Chicago Bears. After a year to regroup, Lombardi's team won three consecutive NFL titles from 1965 to 1967.

For the early part of the decade, their foremost rivals were the New York Giants, whose defense still was the National Football League's most formidable and whose offense had been revitalized by the acquisition in 1961 of quarterback Y.A. Tittle from San Francisco. New York added wide receiver Del Shofner from the Rams and tight end Joe Walton from Washington that same year, and in 1962, Frank Gifford, the Giants' running star of the 1950s, re-emerged as a wide receiver after sitting out a year with an injury.

Tittle was the key. He replaced the gallant Charlie Conerly during the 1961 season and injected a spark into the team with his spirit and his ability to utilize all the weapons at his command. Prematurely bald at age 35, he became the darling of New York's pro football fans. He passed for more than 10,000 yards, threw 96 touchdown passes, and twice led the NFL in touchdown passes in his four seasons in New York (1961-64).

Though Tittle and the defense helped the Giants to three consecutive conference titles from 1961-63, the team could not win the NFL championship. The Packers, playing an almost perfect game, demolished New York 37-0 in 1961 in Green Bay as Hornung set a playoff scoring record with 19 points. The following year, the teams met again in Yankee Stadium, but the slick New York attack was beaten as much by the howling wind and minus-39 degrees wind chill as it was by Green Bay's defense. The Packers won 16-7. "We were afraid to lose and have to face Lombardi afterward," one of the Packers said later. And in 1963, after another record-setting performance in the regular season, the Giants ran afoul of a brilliant Bears defense on a sub-freezing day in Chicago and lost 14-10 as Tittle sprained his knee in the second quarter and was ineffective thereafter. That victory was the last title-game win for Bears coach George Halas.

Peace Breaks Out

The AFL-NFL war ended before the 1966 season began and focused the entire year on the year's finale—the first clash between the champions of the two leagues. The Packers, of course, lived up to their role as favorites to represent the NFL as they won 12 of 14 games, but they had to beat the Dallas Cowboys to get there.

The Cowboys were born in 1960 as a result of the NFL's desire to blunt the formation of the AFL, and the franchise was awarded to Texas oilman Clint Murchison. During its first decade, the team was far from being America's Team. It tied just one of its 12 games in its first season and didn't have a winning season until 1966, when it won the Eastern Conference and played Green Bay for the right to go to the first Super Bowl. Green Bay didn't secure its trip to Super Bowl I until the final seconds when, with the Cowboys at the Packers' 2-yard line, Tom Brown intercepted a fourth-down pass in the end zone to preserve a 34-27 victory.

Two weeks later at the Los Angeles Coliseum, in the much-anticipated first game between the two rival leagues—the AFL-NFL World Championship Game, as Super Bowl I was known at the time—the Packers blew out the Kansas City Chiefs 35-10. The Chiefs stayed close to the heavily-favored Packers in the first half, trailing just 14-10 at halftime after Starr threw a 37-yard touchdown pass to Max McGee, and Taylor ran for a score. But Starr and McGee struck again in the second half, and running back Elijah Pitts scored twice while the Packers' blitzing defense crushed the Chiefs' offense.

The following year, Dallas and Green Bay set up the Packers' second consecutive Super Bowl appearance with a historic game dubbed the Ice Bowl. It is known almost as much for the ability of the teams and fans to survive the brutal weather conditions in Green Bay as for its tingling finish. The game was played in minus-31-degree wind chill conditions that not only froze the field but also the electric heating system that was installed beneath the turf. Green Bay took a 14-0 lead on a pair of touchdown passes from Starr to Boyd Dowler, but the Cowboys scored 17 consecutive points, the last on a halfback option pass from Dan Reeves to Lance Rentzel on the first play of the fourth quarter. With 16 seconds to play, Starr dove into the end zone between blocks by guard Jerry Kramer and center Ken Bowman to score the winning touchdown in a 21-17 victory. In Super Bowl II, the Packers scored the first three times they had the ball against the AFL-champion Oakland Raiders and went on to an easy 33-14 victory in Lombardi's final game as their coach.

Nearing Settlement

After the Packers resounding win against Oakland, there was general consternation within the NFL about whether the AFL was good enough to play on an even footing when the two leagues merged in 1970. But the New York Jets helped to answer that question when they upset the NFL champion Baltimore Colts 16-7 in Super Bowl III, and the Kansas City Chiefs put an exclamation point to the matter when they defeated the Minnesota Vikings 23-7 in Super Bowl IV.

The AFL now believed that it was at least the equal of its new partners and demanded that it retain its autonomy as a 10-team league and play the NFL only in the Super Bowl. The AFL had added Miami in 1966 and the Cincinnati Bengals in 1968. The latter was formed by Paul Brown, who returned from a five-year exile. The NFL wasn't in a hurry to realign either, because it had 16 of the 26 draft picks in each round of the common draft that had been instituted in 1967, and its teams were located in the nation's richest television markets. Thus, they could, over time, become stronger and richer than the smaller AFL. That stance also flew in the face of the original merger agreement that guaranteed that both leagues would be realigned into two conferences, with interconference play.

Paul Brown was outraged. He had endured two seasons in the AFL rather than holding out for an expansion slot among his former NFL brethren because he had been assured the merger agreement would take place in 1970 and every team would become part of the NFL. That was the basis of his selling pro football in Cincinnati to his partners, he said, and if it wasn't exercised, then he threatened to test the agreement in court.

Brown finally convinced a majority of AFL owners to back him. That, plus the threat of court action and Rozelle's decision to lock his 26 owners in a meeting room in NFL headquarters in New York City until they worked out a merger plan, finally solved the impasse. A suggestion from Raiders boss Al Davis that the NFL move three of its teams to the AFL, form two 13-team conferences, and pay each of the teams $3 million to make the move finally broke the impasse. Later, Paul Brown noted: "When that money went on the table, it was like barracudas going after raw meat." Three of the NFL's proudest teams—the Colts, Steelers, and Browns—joined the 10 AFL teams to form the American Conference. The other 13 NFL teams were grouped in the National Conference, and each of the conferences had three divisions and a schedule that permitted interconference play.

Davis then turned around and vetoed the proposal he had helped to craft—it required unanimous consent of all AFL teams—until he was given veto power over the NFL's realignment. But Oakland's majority owner, Wayne Valley, soured on his managing general partner's action and ended another uproarious session by voting with the others to ratify the proposal. The owners' other contentious problem—which teams went into which divisions—was settled in a rather bizarre fashion: Various combinations were drawn up on slips of paper, put into a hat, and the six divisions which became official were selected by Rozelle's secretary.

The result was an unparalleled era of prosperity for the NFL despite the fact that there have been two distinct eras of dominance by each entity. From 1970-1980, the three former NFL teams helped the American Conference to become dominant—Pittsburgh, with four titles, and Baltimore, with one in 1970, won five championships while Oakland and Miami won two each. From 1981 through 1996, the NFC was dominant and the Raiders, in the 1983 season, were the only AFC team to win an NFL championship.

The NFL hit it big that first season of its new look. It opened new stadiums in Pittsburgh and Cincinnati, where the Bengals became the earliest franchise team ever to qualify for a playoff when Brown led his three-year-old franchise to the AFC Central title. They lost to eventual-champion Baltimore, whose Johnny Unitas had one final hurrah. Unitas started Super Bowl V against the Cowboys, passed to tight end John Mackey for a touchdown, then left the game with a rib injury. He watched Earl Morrall, the goat of the Colts' Super Bowl III loss to the Jets, attain redemption as he guided the Colts to a 16-13 victory over the Dallas Cowboys. The winning points came with five seconds to play on Jim O'Brien's field goal.

Are You Ready for Some Football?

A new scheduling and television phenomenon swept the nation in 1970: *Monday Night Football.*

Before long, bowling leagues, social and civic meetings were rescheduled; movie houses showed a marked decline in box office business; streets became more deserted; and the national crime rate declined because much of America had stayed home to watch NFL football.

The first game matched the New York Jets and quarterback Joe Namath against the Cleveland Browns; the second one, the Baltimore Colts and Johnny Unitas against the Super Bowl-champion Kansas City Chiefs. The audience ratings were astounding. The show also developed a new hero in Don Meredith, the former Cowboys quarterback who showcased a pure "country-boy" personality with an incisive wit that delighted millions whenever he punctured the pretensions and pomposity of broadcasting partner Howard Cosell. Although Cosell's knowledgeable comments and "tell-it-like-it-is" style won him millions of fans, his overbearing manner had also made him a villain to many TV viewers. Suddenly, there was a game within a game, and it all worked with superb show business results.

The Cowboys' appearance in the 1966 NFL Championship Game launched a 20-season span during which Dallas had a record of 208-81-2, made the playoffs 18 times, played in five Super Bowls and won two, played in the NFL or NFC Championship Game 12 times, and won 13 division championships.

They often won in dramatic style, and, utilizing a multiple offense, they were one of the most entertaining teams in the NFL. Added to that was a new dimension of entertainment featuring cheerleaders clad as chorus girls, and television's insatiable desire to feature them as often as possible.

Landry, the mastermind of the Giants' great defenses in the late fifties, used his intricate knowledge of defense to build a complex, multi-pronged offensive system designed to destroy opposing defenses; and he perfected his "coordinated" defensive system, so effective with the Giants, into what later became popularly known as the Flex Defense, so named because one of its tackles was flexed a yard off the line of scrimmage.

He also had two great players to make it effective: tackle Bob Lilly and his successor, Randy White. Lilly and White represented the two eras of a 20-year Cowboys' dynasty. In the first, Landry also had a solid linebacking corps of Lee Roy Jordan, Chuck Howley, and Dave Edwards that played together for more than a decade, and great defensive backs Mel Renfro and Cornell Green. On offense, they were led by Meredith, Olympic sprint champion Bob Hayes, and running back Don Perkins, an explosive trio that helped produced 445 points in 1966, third most in NFL history to that time.

Part two of the Cowboys' dynasty came during the 1970s and early 1980s, when Landry introduced his Doomsday II defense, led by White, ends Harvey Martin and Ed (Too Tall) Jones, and defensive backs Charley Waters and Cliff Harris. On offense, the Cowboys drafted 1976 Heisman Trophy winner Tony Dorsett, college football's all-time leading rusher from the University of Pittsburgh, who was a well-muscled, but smallish back. At first, he bridled under Landry's restricted use, but Landry believed his career would be extended and more productive with fewer carries. Ultimately, he was correct because Dorsett played a dozen seasons and finished his career with 12,739 yards (at the time of his retirement, second only to Walter Payton in NFL history).

Much of the Cowboys' great success during the seventies is attributable to quarterback Roger Staubach, a 1964 tenth-round choice from Navy, where he also won the Heisman Trophy in 1963. Staubach attended the Cowboys' training camp whenever possible during his career as a naval officer. He had acquired the nickname "Roger the Dodger" while a collegian because of his incredible talent for escaping trouble and making big plays. That same excitement followed him into the NFL. He brought the Cowboys from behind 23 times in the fourth quarter to win, and 14 of those came in the final two minutes. It was the kind of grand entertainment that television craved, and the Cowboys were an almost weekly showcase for a national audience. Staubach later led Dallas to its Super Bowl victories over Miami and Denver, and he just missed in two more Super Bowls losses to Pittsburgh.

A Perfect Season

Though the Cowboys defeated Miami in Super Bowl VI, the game had unveiled the Dolphins as one of the NFL's premier teams. Don Shula had the five-year-old Dolphins in the playoffs in his first season as head coach in 1970, and in the next three years, they played in three Super Bowls, won two, and, in 1972, produced the only perfect season in NFL history. All the great parts were on hand when Shula arrived: running backs Larry Csonka, Jim Kiick, and Mercury Morris; quarterback Bob Griese; and a defense that soon was tagged No Name because it had no great stars but 11 very talented players who coalesced behind their leader, linebacker Nick Buoniconti. Two years later, they made famous a defensive system—the 3-4—that Shula and his defensive coordinator, Bill Arnsparger, had learned when they were assistant coaches during the late 1950s at the University of Kentucky.

The perfect season in 1972, capped by a 14-7 victory over Washington in Super Bowl VII, wasn't easy because Griese broke his ankle midway through the season. But Shula turned to Earl Morrall, the quarterback who had bailed out his Baltimore Colts in 1968 when Unitas was injured, and he carried Miami to the Super Bowl, where Griese finished off the Redskins. That year, Csonka and Kiick became the first teammates each to gain 1,000 rushing yards in the same season.

The Dolphins repeated their NFL championship in 1973, this time with a 12-2 record, and then they played an almost perfect game in beating the Minnesota Vikings 24-7 in the Super Bowl behind Csonka's record-setting 145 rushing yards. The Dolphins running game was so dominant that day that Griese threw only 7 passes, completing 6 for 73 yards. Miami lost a chance for a fourth consecutive Super Bowl appearance in 1974 with a playoff loss in the final minutes to the Oakland Raiders, and their dreams of more glory were shattered after that season when Csonka, Kiick, and wide receiver Paul Warfield fled to the newly formed World Football League.

The most notable personal achievement in 1973 belonged to Buffalo Bills running back O.J. Simpson, who became the first runner to exceed 2,000 yards in a single season. Playing against the New York Jets at Shea Stadium, Simpson ran through wind, snow, and rain in the season's final game and established the record (2,003 yards), while breaking Jim Brown's existing mark of 1,863 yards on the same day. Simpson broke the 2,000-yard barrier on his thirty-fourth and final carry of the game, a 7-yard run behind blocker Reggie McKenzie. Simpson's record was broken in 1984 by Eric Dickerson of the Rams, who amassed 2,105 yards.

A Pittsburgh Dynasty

After the Dolphins had their fling, the once-woeful Steelers gathered steam to dominate the last half of the seventies with four Super Bowl victories in as many appearances. Their triumphs were popular nationwide because owner Art Rooney, whose presence transcended team loyalties, had suffered so long with his team. Chuck Noll, an assistant to Shula at Baltimore, where he helped design the Colts' great defenses, became head coach in 1969. He was a tough, single-minded coach who could speak in esoteric terms but was downright basic in demanding perfection and never tolerating any excuses for failure. Noll coached the Steelers for 23 seasons and is the only coach to win four Super Bowls.

Noll keyed his team with a mighty defense, nicknamed the Steel Curtain, that included tackle Mean Joe Greene, linebackers Jack Lambert and Jack Ham, and defensive back Mel Blount, and an offense built around quarterback Terry Bradshaw and running back Franco Harris, who operated efficiently behind a small, but quick, offensive line. Bradshaw's strong arm particularly was effective when he threw long passes to his two tremendous wide receivers, John Stallworth and Lynn Swann. He isn't listed among the top 20 passers in the NFL's lifetime passing ratings, but he and Joe Montana of the 49ers are the only quarterbacks ever to start and win four Super Bowls.

The Steelers started slowly, finishing 1-13 in 1969, but three years later they won their first division title and then upset the Oakland Raiders in the divisional playoffs when Harris caught a deflected pass in the final seconds and ran for the winning touchdown. Pittsburgh won its first NFL title by defeating the Minnesota Vikings 16-6 in Super Bowl IX as Harris gained a record 158 rushing yards, and the Steel Curtain shut down the Vikings' offense with just 119 yards. In later Super Bowls, the Steelers defeated the Cowboys (twice) and the Los Angeles Rams.

The Steelers' defeat of the Vikings in Super Bowl IX was one of four Minnesota suffered in NFL title games, unfairly tarnishing the achievements of a great team. The Vikings mirrored their coach, Bud Grant, who didn't believe in frills such as sideline heaters when near-zero temperatures and snow piled around the sidelines at Metropolitan Stadium made games in December and January a survival test for his rivals. Its defense—ends Carl Eller and Jim Marshall, and tackles Alan Page and Gary Larsen—was nicknamed "the Purple People Eaters," and it ranks as one of the best in NFL history.

For many years, Fran Tarkenton was the Vikings' quarterback and he helped the team to three of their Super Bowl appearances. He epitomized the term "scrambler" with his evasive efforts to avoid pass rushers. Tarkenton finished his brilliant 18-season career as the NFL's all-time leader in career passing statistics.

Despite his individual accomplishments, Tarkenton never earned a championship ring, and weather may well have made the difference. The Vikings lost a big edge when they left frigid Minnesota and played in the temperate climates at Super Bowl sites. In those locales, their true grit was overmatched by physical teams such as the Dolphins, Steelers, and Raiders. Perhaps for the same reason, the Vikings' futility later was matched by two other Northern teams: the Denver Broncos in the 1980s (who went on to win back-to-back Super Bowls in the 1990s), and the Buffalo Bills.

Troubled Times

In poll after poll at this time, professional football was at the top of the nation's preference charts, but there was turmoil within the sport as the NFL dealt with new leagues, the National Football League Players Association, and legal actions that forced changes in the way sports leagues traditionally had done their business. Al Davis dealt the NFL a severe legal blow when a federal court ruled that he had the right to move the Oakland Raiders to Los Angeles without the consent of his fellow owners.

The NFL's constitution stipulated that three-quarters of the league's owners must approve the movement of any franchise. In 1980, Davis had asked permission of the league to move the Raiders to Los Angeles, and he was promised a hearing at the league's annual meeting. But when he arrived to plead his case, he was told that the owners already had voted to disallow the move. Davis, along with the Los Angeles Coliseum Commission, then sued the NFL for antitrust violations. Two years later, they won, and the team became the Los Angeles Raiders. In 1983, the Raiders won their third NFL championship with a 38-9 victory over the Washington Redskins in Super Bowl XVIII. But Davis never was content playing in the 92,000-seat Coliseum, which his team rarely filled. Moreover, promised renovations never materialized. He constantly sought a new stadium site until, in 1995, he moved his team back to Oakland.

That same year, the Rams ended a half century of tradition and vacated the Los Angeles area—they had played their games in nearby Anaheim since 1980—and moved to St. Louis. That city had been without a team since 1988, when owner Bill Bidwill moved the Cardinals to Phoenix.

The franchise shifting actually began in 1972 when Robert Irsay purchased the Los Angeles Rams, then swapped his new franchise with Carroll Rosenbloom and became owner of the Baltimore Colts. Twelve years later, in the middle of a March night, the Colts moved to Indianapolis to become the Indianapolis Colts. A dozen years passed before Baltimore could attract another NFL team, this one the Cleveland Browns, one of the NFL's most successful franchises. The new team was nicknamed the Ravens, while Cleveland was guaranteed another team by the NFL before the end of the century.

The NFL also added four teams after the merger in 1970. In 1976, the Tampa Bay Buccaneers and Seattle Seahawks came into existence. Seattle spent its first year in the NFC and Tampa Bay, which didn't win a game until near the end of its second season, was in the AFC. The teams shifted conferences in their second season. In 1995, the league added more teams in the Sun Belt with the Jacksonville Jaguars and Carolina Panthers, based in Charlotte, North Carolina. The Panthers exceeded all previous expansion teams by winning seven of their 16 games in the first season.

Labor unrest also rocked the NFL. Players began demanding free agency in 1974, and the players union and management signed a four-year agreement in 1977. When it expired, the unrest flared into a strike as the players walked out after the second game of the 1982 season and stayed on strike until a new collective bargaining agreement, running through 1986, was signed in mid-November. The stoppage reduced the league's 1982 schedule to nine games. A special playoff schedule was designed, and Washington and Miami emerged as the conference champs. The Redskins won Super Bowl XVII 27-17.

When that agreement ended and free agency demands again went unmet, the players staged a 24-day strike early in the 1987 season. Teams canceled one game and then replaced their strikers with free agents who played three games, all counting in the regular standings, until the strike was abandoned. This time, the owners came up with a plan of limited free agency, declaring all but 24 players on their rosters as free agents who could negotiate with any team, and a total of 229 free agents changed teams. In the meantime, a U.S. District Court in Minneapolis heard the NFL players' case that the NFL was in violation of antitrust laws for not allowing unrestricted movement of players. That led to a new collective bargaining agreement, with teams allowed to restrict just a few players in return for a hard cap on salaries and retention of the player draft.

Still THE Game

Despite off-the-field turmoil, the NFL has continued to grow in popularity. Some even have argued that the various legal and monetary wrangles have actually helped increase pro football's hold on the public by keeping the sport on the front pages year round. While that may be arguable, the game's strongest appeal still centers on record-setting players, exciting games, and great teams.

During the seventies and early eighties, the NFL also had several great running backs, all of whom surpassed Jim Brown's seemingly untouchable record of 12,312 yards. None was better than Chicago's Walter Payton, now the all-time leading rusher with 16,726 yards. Also surpassing Brown during this span was Eric Dickerson, whose 13,259 career yards includes a record-setting 2,105 yards in 1984, and Tony Dorsett (12,739 career yards).

The San Francisco 49ers, Washington Redskins, and the Raiders were the dominant teams of the eighties, winning eight NFL titles between them. The Chicago Bears jumped into the spotlight in 1985, coming within one game of a perfect season—a loss to the Miami Dolphins, the only NFL team ever to achieve such a feat. The Bears of that season were a very talented team on offense and defense but the spotlight centered on an overweight, yet nimble-footed 325-pound defensive tackle, William (Refrigerator) Perry. Perry played well in his primary job, but he became a national hero of sorts when coach Mike Ditka allowed him to carry the ball on goal-line situations. He scored several touchdowns, including one in the Bears' 46-10 victory over New England in Super Bowl XX.

The Giants, who had muddled along for nearly 20 years with little success, returned to their great defensive heritage to win two more championships in 1986 and 1990. Lawrence Taylor set a new standard for linebacking play, particularly as a pass rusher, and is credited with 132½ sacks. (Sacks didn't become an official statistic until 1982.)

In Washington, Redskins Fever had a renewal during the eighties under coach Joe Gibbs, who stressed a multi-dimensional offensive system, bulwarked by a stout defense. In his first season coaching the Redskins in 1981, he lost the first five games, but the following year his team won Washington's first NFL championship since 1942. The Redskins also won titles in 1987 against Denver, and in 1991 over Buffalo.

Joe Theismann quarterbacked Washington's first title run. He had plenty of help from Hall of Fame fullback John Riggins, who gained more than 11,300 yards during his career, and a big, mobile offensive line nicknamed "the Hogs," which stayed pretty much intact during the three title runs. Another constant of the last two titles was a swift wide receiver corps that included Art Monk, the NFL's number-two all-time receiver with 940 catches, Gary Clark, and Ricky Sanders.

Quarterback Doug Williams engineered the 1987 win in Super Bowl XXII, abetted by a 35-point second quarter and one of the greatest single-game performances in NFL championship play—204 rushing yards by Tim Smith, who had played sporadically that season and was out of pro football two years later. Four years later, in 1991, Washington won its third NFL title of the Gibbs era, this one behind quarterback Mark Rypien and running back Earnest Byner.

The 49ers were even more successful during this time. For 10 seasons, they were coached by Bill Walsh, a great teacher and innovator, during which time they won three NFL titles. Walsh was an unknown who had bounced around as an assistant coach in high school and college, had a year with the Oakland Raiders, and one as head coach of a minor league team before he was hired in 1968 by Paul Brown as receivers coach for the newly formed Cincinnati Bengals. For the next eight years, he absorbed Brown's very successful system of football, added some wrinkles from Don Coryell during a year with the San Diego Chargers, and designed what has been called the West Coast offense.

Walsh had the right quarterback in Joe Montana. Never known for a strong arm, Montana had terrific coaching from Walsh, and the instincts and mental skills to run his offense flawlessly. Ironically, two of the 49ers' titles came against the Bengals. The first was a 26-21 victory in Super Bowl XVI at the Pontiac Silverdome. The second came in Super Bowl XXIII in Miami, when Montana drove his team 92 yards in the final three minutes to pull out a 20-16 victory. The winning touchdown pass to John Taylor came with just 34 seconds to play. Sandwiched between them was a 38-16 victory in Super Bowl XIX over Miami and Dan Marino.

Walsh Departs

Walsh retired after his third NFL title and was succeeded by his top defensive aide, George Seifert. The beat didn't stop as Seifert guided the 49ers to their fourth and fifth titles. In his first year as head coach, San Francisco walloped Denver 55-10 as Montana threw a record 5 touchdown passes. Three of them went to wide receiver Jerry Rice, who rivals Don Hutson as the best receiver in NFL history. Rice holds all of the NFL's major pass receiving records and has been one of the great keys to the success of both the 49ers and the quarterbacks who guided them during their dynasty years, Montana and Steve Young. Young placed his own stamp on that dynasty when he led the team to its fifth NFL championship in 1994, climaxing a record-setting season with a momentous 49-26 victory over the San Diego Chargers in which he broke Montana's record with 6 touchdown passes.

During the 1990s, the 49ers vied with the Dallas Cowboys for supremacy. Oilman Jerry Jones purchased the Cowboys in 1989 and fired Tom Landry, the only coach the Cowboys ever had. Jimmy Johnson, who had produced a national collegiate championship at the University of Miami, replaced Landry and won just one game in his first season. But, with some good young players, including quarterback Troy Aikman, running back Emmitt Smith, and several big, talented linemen on both offense and defense, the Cowboys rebounded. Johnson won back-to-back NFL titles in 1992 and 1993. Then, in what was generally perceived as a battle of egos, Jones fired Johnson after the 1993 season.

Johnson was succeeded by Barry Switzer, who had been a successful coach at the University of Oklahoma. Switzer's first Cowboys team lost to eventual NFL-champion San Francisco in the 1994 NFC title game, but the following season won its third title in four seasons, again behind the steady play of Aikman, Smith, and great offensive and defensive lines.

When the Cowboys stumbled in 1996, the rejuvenated Packers became champions under the leadership of quarterback Brett Favre. Green Bay defensive end Reggie White earned his first Super Bowl ring as he neared the end of a long and distinguished career.

A similar scenario took place in 1997, when Denver's John Elway earned his first championship ring after 15 seasons and amid speculation that he was near retirement. But Elway returned to lead the Broncos to a second consecutive Super Bowl victory following the 1998 season. Denver's back-to-back championships broke the stranglehold the NFC held on the Super Bowl for more than a decade.

As stars such as White, Elway, Barry Sanders, Dan Marino, and Jerry Rice wound down their careers, new stars emerged. Drew Bledsoe, Terrell Davis, Jamal Anderson, Randy Moss, Peyton Manning, and dozens of others became fan favorites.

Without question, the NFL has become the most popular and most successful professional sports league. As a new century approaches, NFL football is at the heart of America's sporting passions, an outcome the men who met at Ralph Hay's Hupmobile showroom in 1920 could only have dreamed.

CHAPTER 3

Tools of the Trade

Beau Riffenburgh

The extensive protective equipment worn by football players is not only a necessary and accepted (indeed, required) part of the game, it also sets football apart from other sports. Hockey players wear shoulder pads, and, in baseball and cricket, the batter wears protective gear, but no other sport—even rugby—utilizes as much unique equipment.

That was not always so. In the 1869 game between Princeton and Rutgers, which the NCAA recognizes as the first college football game, there was no equipment other than the ball. The players merely took off their coats, vests, and hats and started playing. The only characteristic identifying either side was that some of the Rutgers players wore scarlet stocking caps. Five years later, when Harvard played McGill in a series of three games, McGill's players made the first serious attempts at uniforms, with white trousers, striped jerseys, and turbans, while the Harvard players wore sweaters and handkerchiefs around their heads.

In 1876, Princeton and Yale both began to use complete uniforms in their games; however, at that point, uniforms meant matching outfits, not extensive protective equipment. Perhaps the most important event in the development of protective gear for football players took place in 1888, when the annual rules convention for college football passed a rule permitting tackling below the waist.

Almost overnight, football changed dramatically. Teams no longer began to array themselves across the entire breadth of the field, but rather to bunch around the runner to block for him. The wedge and other mass plays made football a violent, dangerous sport that became marked by brawling, serious injuries, and even deaths. Grudgingly, football players began to accept the wearing of protective equipment.

A.G. Spalding & Company Sporting Goods was the first manufacturer of athletic equipment, although other suppliers quickly followed. Remarkably, not that much later it seemed that football equipment manufacturers might become unnecessary. Three years after the major rules changes of 1906 paved the way to opening up and modernizing the game, the *Spalding Guide* noted that, "the roughness of the game has been practically eliminated by the new rules. Still, shin guards and shoulder pads are sometimes needed."

But the need for equipment actually increased because of continuing concerns for safety as the game developed. Ultimately, the first major rules change the NFL made concerning equipment was the requirement (not made until 1943!) that players wear helmets. Two years later, Commissioner Elmer Layden pushed through a less safety-conscious, and almost comical, ruling requiring all players to wear long stockings, because he believed that many of the players in the league had unattractive legs.

Pants and Jerseys

Players had been flashing their legs at the spectators since the beginning of the game, and in the 1870s their knee-length breeches and jackets that laced up the front were made of canvas. Although canvas was incredibly sturdy and able to withstand the rigors of the game, it must not have been the most comfortable material for a uniform. It soon was replaced in pants by moleskin, then described as "a heavy-napped cotton twill fabric." Up top, players in the 1880s and 1890s began to wear turtleneck sweaters.

Near the turn of the century, a brief excursion was made into making pants and jerseys one unit, with canvas, moleskin, and leather combined in outfits that required the player to insert himself into them and lace them up all around. These short-lived commodities included the Smock football suit, the varsity union suit, and Whitley's Football Armor.

A wide variety of materials have been used in the manufacturing of football pants since those days. Khaki cloth or drill, fustian cloth (a coarse, sturdy cloth made of cotton and flax), and duckcloth all were used beginning in the second decade of the century, the last being the primary pants material for more than 30 years.

In the 1930s, new materials began to appear, including Spalding's Skookum Cloth, which quickly was followed by a number of new synthetic fibers. Knits first appeared in 1934. According to Rawlings Sporting Goods, "the first all-knit shell was introduced in 1936, and the first half-fabric, half-knit model made its bow in 1937. Many different combinations of knit materials have been developed through the years, with the latest knit incorporating the highly popular Spandex, a stretch polyurethane material." Spandex is the general term for fibers that resemble rubber since they have what scientists call "high extensibility and highly retractive forces that derive from their chemical nature." In lay terms, that means they are extremely flexible. Perhaps the most common kind of pant today is a nylon/LYCRA Spandex.

One development relating to pants was their relation to pads. As football became more and more violent, manufacturers began to take steps to make equipment safer, and there was a proliferation of new types of pads to protect knees, thighs, hips, ribs, and kidneys. Initially, the lower-body pads were laced into or hung from the player's pants. The process of properly holding the pads in place was one that took more than a quarter of a century to perfect. In 1906, for example, strips of cane were sewn into the lining of pants to serve as thigh pads. They might have protected the runner, but they were hard on tacklers. The next step was holding the thigh pads in place with laces tied around each leg.

In the second decade of the twentieth century, some manufacturers seemed to view pants as a shell onto which a wide variety of pads could be hung. In 1915, Spalding advertised a "complete padded harness with heavy felt hip pad connected with wide elastic belt at back, fiber thigh guards laced in special canvas and webbing-reinforced pockets all securely mounted on simple but strong skeleton pants." Ultimately, of course, a simpler pair of pants was developed, with pockets on the inside for thigh and knee pads. Hip and tail pads were strapped on with a belt or, more recently, inserted into a girdle worn under the pants. Like pants, jerseys originally were made of canvas. Players sometimes were called "canvasbacks" because of the sleeveless canvas vests they wore over their turtleneck sweaters.

The first modern jerseys came along after the turn of the century. They were made of wool or cotton, materials that dominated the market until the 1950s, when synthetic fabrics were developed. These synthetics included, according to Rawlings Sporting Goods, rayon-durene, nylon-durene, rayon-cotton, and nylon-cotton. Nylon-mesh jerseys were lighter and more comfortable than the rest; even the NFL teams in cool climates favored them, wearing them on cold days over long thermal underwear. Today, most jerseys are made of polyester of varying kinds of mesh, but with a yoke heavier than the rest of the body.

One jersey innovation that did not last long was Rawlings's 1928-29 model, which featured "grip-sure cloth, sewn to the jersey front to aid in holding onto the ball." Another was tear-away jerseys, allowing a runner to rip free from the grasp of tacklers holding onto his shirt. The costs were exorbitant, and Pro Football Hall of Fame running back Earl Campbell is said to have gone through six jerseys in a single game. In 1979, the year after Campbell entered the NFL, such jerseys were prohibited.

Insignia on game shirts go back almost as far as the game itself. By 1876, Princeton players were wearing a "P" on their sweaters in a game against the University of Pennsylvania. And by around 1905 either Amos Alonzo Stagg or Glenn (Pop) Warner had introduced numbers on jerseys. After this, numbers and stripes appeared in all sizes and locations before rules began to give uniforms a uniform appearance.

In 1937, the NFL determined that all players had to wear a minimum of six-inch numerals on the front of their jerseys and a minimum of eight-inch numerals on the back of their jerseys. Finally, the Cleveland Browns of the All-America Football Conference pioneered the notion of numbering players according to their positions, a rule that was not adopted universally by pro football until 1973. And in 1960, the American Football League added player names to the backs of all jerseys.

Pads

Underneath those colorful jerseys lie shoulder pads—equipment that not only gives football players their distinct appearance, but allows the game to be such an intense hitting sport. The goal of shoulder pads is to protect the clavicle, scapula, shoulder joint, anterior deltoid, and sternum. In doing so, they transform the look of small players into large players and large players into behemoths.

The original shoulder pads were little more than flimsy strips of leather over the crown of the shoulders. It wasn't until the mid-1930s that they took a quantum leap forward. Straps held the epaulets of the pads away from and high above the shoulders, absorbing the shock. It was these cantilever shoulder pads that began to turn slender young boys into fearsome-looking players.

Further developments in shoulder pads were elastic underarm straps, large and deep chest plates, "snubbers" to hold the flap in place under the epaulet, and nylon covering and stitching, as well as better production materials. Today's shoulder pads include a dual-density foam system that is heat-sealed for added impact displacement; extra thick, hinged pectoral pads for better shock attenuation; snubbers and cap connectors; and storm-proof, nylon taffeta outer and inner coverings to prevent moisture absorption.

The one-size-fits-all theory also disappeared through the years, as pads were developed for every size player and every position. As it became obvious that both the movement and the protection required by a quarterback or receiver were different from that by a lineman, manufacturers made appropriate design changes in the kinds and styles of shoulder pads. In recent years, shoulder-pad cushions, closed-cell foam accessories worn under shoulder pads for added protection, also have become more popular.

A major development came in the 1970s, when pads became lighter and less bulky than traditional pads. These pads, originally designed by Byron Donzis, use air-filled channels to absorb impact. Donzis's protective equipment was first used in the NFL in the 1978 playoffs, when Houston quarterback Dan Pastorini wore a flak jacket to protect his injured ribs. Donzis since has designed pads for a variety of players.

Other upper-body pads worn by some players include rib pads, a kickplate (which provides extended protection to lower-back areas), a neck roll, and bicep pads. Other pads required are thigh and knee pads, which are molded foam rubber or cross-linked polyethylene foam parts that are inserted into pockets inside playing pants. For decades, linemen wore elbow pads, forearm pads, and/or hand pads, but these have decreased in recent years. Meantime, in the 1980s, receivers began to wear gloves.

Helmets

The last major article of equipment players accepted was the helmet. There were even those who believed that helmets did not provide protection, but rather caused safety problems.

"Playing without helmets gives players more confidence, saves their heads from many hard jolts, and keeps their ears from becoming torn or sore," Glenn (Pop) Warner told his Carlisle players in 1912. "I do not encourage their use. I have never seen an accident to the head which was serious, but I have many times seen cases when hard bumps on the head so dazed the player receiving them that he lost his memory for a time and had to be removed from the game."

The helmet was not a required article of equipment in college football until 1939 and in the NFL until 1943, although by then players voluntarily wore them. The last NFL player to play in a game without a helmet probably was end Dick Plasman of the Chicago Bears in 1940 or 1941, before he went into the service in World War II. Certainly he was still not wearing a helmet when he played in the 1940 NFL Championship Game against the Washington Redskins.

One of the first protective devices for a part of the head was the nose protector, popularized (for a short period of time) by All-America back Edgar Allan Poe of Princeton (the grand-nephew of the author of the same name) in 1890. The nose protector was not an easy piece of equipment to use, however. A hard-leather proboscis hung from a strap around the forehead, fit over the nose, and had an extension at the bottom that the wearer clenched in his teeth to hold the device in place. This equipment interfered with vision and, significantly in a strenuous sport, the ability to breathe easily. "No player should wear a nose protector unless he has a sore nose," Warner said. The playing population tended to agree, and nose protectors ultimately disappeared.

In 1896, the head harness was developed, most likely by George Barclay of Lafayette College. His new headgear had three thick leather straps forming a tight fit around his head, and had been produced by a local harness maker. This strange contraption and its successors with an assortment of straps and pads ultimately turned into leather caps. These soon acquired ear flaps, which acquired ear holes. Nevertheless, there is no way that these devices could have provided anything more than rudimentary protection.

As the head harness gradually developed into a helmet, one basic problem remained. As long as it sat right down on the skull, it did not truly protect the wearer from serious blows. Then, in 1917, a helmet with suspension to cradle the skull away from the leather shell was produced. Straps of fabric formed a pattern inside the helmet. They better absorbed and distributed the impact, and they allowed for ventilation. It was a tremendous breakthrough for helmet-making. Rawlings introduced the Zuppke helmet, designed by famous Illinois coach Bob Zuppke, and in 1925 Spalding introduced the first of what would become a well-known line, its "ZH" helmets.

However, the most important step forward in safety occurred in 1939, the same year that the NCAA required helmets in college football. Gerry E. Morgan and other employees of the John T. Riddell Company in Chicago invented and patented a plastic football helmet. This was made of ABS (acrylonitrile-butadiene-styrene) and polycarbonate, materials that had been found to have excellent toughness and high-impact strength. The new helmet was made of a single molded shell with a revolutionary web suspension inside it. It was stronger, more durable, and lighter than leather helmets, and it would not rot or mildew the way leather did when damp.

Riddell's plastic helmets were worn for the first time by some of the players in the 1939 Chicago College All-Star Game. The next year, Riddell devised the first strap worn on the chin rather than the Adam's apple, and the first plastic facemask. The plastic helmet was a little flat on top initially, but it gradually changed to its characteristic teardrop shape, which allowed the impact of a blow to slide to one side or the other rather than be met head on. Its webbed suspension could be raised or lowered to fit the head of the wearer.

Riddell's production of plastic helmets was slowed by the war, but part of the military effort emphasized the advances of the new equipment. The United States Military Academy team of 1944 became the first team ever to wear the plastic helmets. Army, coached by Earl (Red) Blaik and featuring All-America backs Felix (Doc) Blanchard and Glenn Davis, won the national championship in 1944 and 1945.

There still were problems with the new helmets, however. The plastic in both Riddell's helmets and those of their competitors was brittle. A drill boring a hole to attach a facemask might pop right through. The material's resistance was questioned after linebacker Fred Naumetz of the Los Angeles Rams split nine plastic helmets in one season. Due to this—and the argument that they were more a weapon than a protective device—they were banned from use in the NFL in 1948. The plastic helmet was saved, however, by the intercession of George Halas of the Bears, who apparently argued forcefully for its return, which it made the next year.

The same year that plastic helmets were banned, halfback Fred Gehrke of the Rams, who had studied art at the University of Utah, painted a horn design on Los Angeles's helmets. It was the first helmet design in the NFL. Unfortunately, the paint on the Rams' helmets kept chipping off every game, and Gehrke and his teammates constantly were forced to repaint the headgear. The legalization of plastic helmets in 1949 made it possible to bake color into helmets and greatly expand its use on them. As a result, other teams followed the Rams' lead, and helmets became coordinated with jerseys and pants.

Also in 1949, all eligible pass receivers were given the option to wear different colored helmets than their teammates. Although this was not a widely adopted practice, it remained legal in the NFL until 1973.

As use of plastic helmets spread, so did the development of facemasks. Rubber-covered wire facemasks had been used in the 1930s, but the superior rigidity of the plastic made the universality of the facemask possible. The holes drilled for the bolts holding the mask would not expand the way they would if they had been drilled through leather.

And the sides of the plastic helmet would not collapse, driving the bolts into the wearer's face, as happened with leather helmets.

When Joe Perry of the San Francisco 49ers suffered a broken jaw in 1954, he was provided a facemask made of clear Lucite plastic. However, Lucite was prone to shattering, so it was banned shortly thereafter.

The major breakthrough in facemasks came the next year, when G.E. Morgan, the key figure at Riddell in developing the plastic helmet, joined with Paul Brown of the Cleveland Browns to develop the BT-5 facemask for Otto Graham. The name referred to "bar tubular," a single tubular bar that was a combination of rubber and plastic. The concept of the BT-5 was expanded to incorporate a vast number of facemasks with single bars, double bars, triple bars, and cages of various descriptions. Plastic and rubber tubing or welded steel or aluminum with a vinyl plasticol coating were used in their construction.

As with the adoption of helmets, many players did not want to change to the use of a facemask. Hall of Fame quarterback Bobby Layne still was not using a facemask when he retired following the 1962 season. More than a decade later, another gutsy leader, Billy Kilmer of the Washington Redskins, was one of the few men still playing with only a single bar facemask.

Morgan and Brown came up with a less-successful invention the year after the appearance of the BT-5. They put a citizen's band radio in the helmet of Browns quarterback George Ratterman, Graham's successor, in 1956. The plan was that Brown, who had a transmitter on the sideline, could talk to Ratterman, who had a receiver but no transmitter. These innovative plans went awry, however, when, expecting to hear Brown call the next play, all Ratterman could pick up was two women talking incoherently. The experiment ended, and the next year the NFL banned radio-equipped football helmets, although they returned in a different form in the 1990s.

The current form first was used in the World League in 1991. The NFL tried it in the 1994 and 1995 preseasons, and began using it in league games in 1996. The quarterback can hear but cannot talk with the bench. Fifteen seconds before the snap transmission shuts off and the coach cannot communicate with the quarterback. Only the quarterback can wear the helmet. (When backup quarterback Kordell Stewart went in at wide receiver for the Pittsburgh Steelers in 1995-96, he had to change helmets.)

In the intervening years, the NCAA led the way in equipment-related safety additions. Mouthpieces became a requisite in college football, and more and more players continued to wear them when they entered pro football. And chinstraps were improved by the addition of ribbed vinyl-coated chincups and then four-point attachment snaps.

In 1971, Morgan, by then the chairman of the board of Riddell, again moved helmet safety forward, when he was granted a patent for "energy absorbing and sizing means for helmets." The result was Riddell's microfit helmets, which had valves on the crown to allow air to be pumped into vinyl cushions that were crammed into every available space inside the helmet. This would allow the helmet to be pumped up while on the player's head so that it gave a more secure and firm fit. Similarly, fluid could also be pumped in, although these "water helmets" actually used an anti-freeze solvent to help prevent the helmet from freezing while being worn in the winter in northern NFL cities.

Despite the improved safety of the microhelmets, Riddell's older TK-2 web suspension helmets remained popular due to their lighter weight and better ventilation. How important is lighter? Norm Evans, a former tackle for the Seahawks and Dolphins, once gave the surprising answer: "Until I learned to do exercises to strengthen my neck, the hardest part of every training camp for me was starting to wear a helmet again. The first time I'd put the helmet on, my head would go *clunk!* over to one side. After a few days, I'd get to where I could draw my head down into my neck. Then there's a way I could tilt the facemask at a certain angle. Between the two positions, I could keep my helmet upright."

Riddell's PAC-3, the name standing for "padded aero cell," was popularized in 1974. In the PAC-3, the vinyl cushions did not have to be pumped up. It had 32 individual vinyl air cushions with layers of energy-absorbing foam. Small holes in the crown allowed the cushions inside to dissipate the force of the impact and carry it away through the holes in the surface.

Shoes

Few fans noticed football shoes until Jets quarterback Joe Namath gained attention not only for himself but also for his white footwear in New York's stunning victory over the Baltimore Colts in Super Bowl III. And yet, such styles were not new. Peck & Snyder, a sporting goods company, had advertised white shoes as its number-one model years before Namath came on the scene. How many years? Try 1886.

The first football shoes actually were baseball shoes. Early cowhide shoes were widely replaced by kangaroo leather as early as 1906. Even earlier (the 1890s), inverted truncated pyramid football cleats had appeared. They were made of a piece of leather glued together and nailed to the shoe. One-piece fiber cleats, also nailed to the shoe, were developed in 1915. And finally, in 1921, interchangeable cleats were developed, which screwed on and off a metal post jutting from the sole of the shoe. Such shoes were dangerous, should the cleats come off during a game. So, in 1939, the NCAA rules committee outlawed "female" football cleats; they determined that the cleat had to become the "male" part, with the metal post, while the shoe had the "female" part into which the post was inserted. Fiber cleats eventually gave way to rubber, and rubber gave way to aluminum and nylon, steel-tipped cleats. Aluminum shoe cleats, however, were banned in the NFL in 1951.

Meanwhile, the look of shoes also changed. Early shoes were heavy and high-topped. But John T. Riddell, a key figure in the development of helmets, joined with Bears owner/coach George Halas to devise low-cut football shoes, worn by the 1940 Bears for the first time.

Shoes changed even more dramatically when games

were played indoors on artificial turf, which first was used in the Houston Astrodome in 1965. Shoes began to have more and shorter cleats, which often were hard-rubber designed as part of the shoe.

The Ball

The most important piece of equipment that is not worn is, obviously, the football. Today, a football is officially defined as a prolate spheroid, which is a far cry from the round soccer-type ball that was used in the first 1869 game between Princeton and Rutgers.

Not long after that first game, perhaps in a contest between McGill and Harvard in 1874, a ball similar to a rugby ball began to be used rather than a round ball. Then, with the popularization of the forward pass beginning in the second decade of the twentieth century, the ball began to resemble what is used today. Five rules set by college football (at the time when the pros automatically followed the college rules) changed the game ball from a rugby ball to a football. In 1912, its weight was set at 14 to 15 ounces. The same year, its long axis was set at between 28 and 28½ inches, and its short axis (around the middle) at between 22½ and 23 inches. In 1929, the short axis was reduced to between 22 and 22½ inches, and five years later it dropped again, to between 21¼ and 21½ inches. Meanwhile its length became 11 to 11¼ inches. And the amount of air that could be pumped into it was set at 12½ to 13½ pounds.

The way air was pumped into a rubber bladder was a problem for more than half a century. In the second game between Rutgers and Princeton (also played in 1869), the ball kept losing its shape, and several times play had to be stopped, a key brought in from the sideline to unlock the small nozzle tucked into the ball, and players shared the chore of blowing it back up.

The actual blowing up of the ball slowly became easier. In 1886, the Peck & Snyder Sporting Goods catalog advertised a device resembling a syringe, which was called the "New Patent Foot Ball Inflator." It was, according to the advertising, "far superior, in every respect, to the old-style, large, brass pumps. With it, the largest ball can be inflated to its fullest capacity in five minutes time while the old way took half an hour."

Eventually, stem valves that protruded from the ball and had to be tucked in during play gave way to metal valves such as those on automobile tires. They were considered unsafe, however, so rubber valves were developed for footballs. The final step in making an efficient ball was prelacing; it developed about 1920, and after that the ball no longer had to be unlaced to be inflated.

Although footballs have almost always been referred to as "pigskins," the preferred material always has been steerhide. Cowhide has been considered second best. Rubber gained a foothold in the football world in 1951, but its stay was brief. In 1956, the NFL approved the use of white footballs in night games to make it easier to see them, and for the next 20 years there were "night footballs" with white stripes around each end. These were prohibited in 1976 because the paint made the balls slick. The rules continued to call for a ball that is "a pebble-grained, leather case of natural tan color."

From 1920 until 1940, the Spalding J5-V was the official football of the NFL, and it was also used by the American Football League from 1960 to 1969. Known as "The Duke" beginning in the 1930s—from a boyhood nickname of Wellington Mara, owner of the New York Giants—this name was sold to Wilson Sporting Goods when it became the manufacturer of official NFL footballs in 1941. "The Duke" stopped being used by the pros after 1969, when Wilson's official football became, simply, "NFL."

For decades, the leather Wilson used for its NFL footballs primarily came from the Horween Leather Company, originally owned and operated by Arnold Horween Sr., the coach at Harvard from 1926-1930. Wilson traditionally has used only full-grain steerhide, that is, the full thickness of the hide. The four panels of the ball are cut in such a way that any blemishes on the hide are avoided. The panels are cut to a specified thickness, weighed to make sure they meet specifications, and checked to make sure their appearance is uniform.

Linings for each panel and reinforcements for the bladder opening and the valve ring are added. The panels are sewn together inside out. The ball is then turned through the lace opening using an iron post, in an operation that requires strength and dexterity. The bladder is inserted and the ball is laced. It is inflated to 80 pounds—65 above its required pressure—so it can be examined for appearance, stitching, and shape. If it meets every requirement, it is stamped "NFL," deflated, delivered, and ready to make an appearance as the one totally essential piece of equipment in the game of football.

CHAPTER 4

Team Histories: NFC Teams

Jim J. Campbell

The National Football League's two parts—the American Football Conference and the National Football Conference—grew out of the historic 1966 merger between the NFL and the American Football League when the two leagues agreed to become one for the 1970 season. At the time there were 26 teams—16 in the NFL and 10 in the AFL. Despite some sentiment for keeping the two wings as they were, a more logical approach was to create two conferences, each with the same number of teams. After much discussion, three NFL teams—Baltimore, Cleveland, and Pittsburgh agreed to join the 10 American Football League teams to form the AFC.

Brief histories of all current NFC franchises follow. Histories of defunct NFL franchises may be found in Chapter 6.

(Statistical note: Prior to 1972, the NFL discounted ties when determining won-loss percentage. Since 1972, ties have been counted as half a win and half a loss. Overall team records reflect the latter method.)

Arizona Cardinals

The Arizona Cardinals began in Chicago as the Morgan Athletic Club in 1899. Twice relocated, they are the NFL's oldest franchise.

In 1901, owner-manager Chris O'Brien, a Chicago contractor, acquired a supply of used jerseys from the University of Chicago. The once-maroon jerseys had faded to a dull pink, but O'Brien declared them "cardinal red" and his team had a new name. As the Racine Cardinals—named for a Chicago street, not the Wisconsin city—they were 1920 charter members of the NFL, then called the American Professional Football Association (APFA). They became the Chicago Cardinals during the 1920 season.

In that first year, the Cardinals shared Chicago with the northside Tigers, another APFA member, but a 6-3 victory in early November, keyed by Paddy Driscoll's touchdown on a punt return, helped doom the Tigers to extinction.

Driscoll kept the club competitive in those early seasons. In 1925 the Cardinals won a controversial championship. Late in the season, they had a 9-1-1 record and engaged the upstart Pottsville Maroons in what was described by newspapers as a championship game. Pottsville held Driscoll in check and won, seemingly clinching the title. O'Brien, however, scheduled two extra games against also-rans in hopes of regaining first place and thus a rematch against the Bears and Red Grange. The Cardinals won those games, but an injury to Grange foiled O'Brien's plan.

Nonetheless, the Cardinals won the league title because, in defiance of league warnings, Pottsville played an exhibition against a team of Notre Dame alumni in Philadelphia, the franchise territory of the Frankford Yellowjackets. League president Joe Carr suspended the Maroons franchise, making it ineligible to win the NFL championship. The Cardinals had the best record of the remaining teams, and are considered champions for 1925, although they never were officially awarded the title because O'Brien made it clear he would not accept it.

Any celebration was short-lived. In 1926, the Bulls, Chicago's entry in the rival, Red Grange-led American Football League, leased Comiskey Park, where the Cardinals had played, and won over many of the Cardinals' fans. Strapped for cash, Chris O'Brien was forced to sell Paddy Driscoll's contract to the Bears. The Cardinals immediately took a nose dive in the standings.

O'Brien sold the Cardinals to dentist David Jones in 1929. Jones brought in some new players, most notably future Pro Football Hall of Fame fullback Ernie Nevers, and the Cardinals returned to respectability. By 1933, Nevers had retired, and Chicago businessman Charles Bidwill, Sr., bought the team and its heartaches from Jones. In 1935, player-coach Milan Creighton directed the Cardinals to a record of 6-4-2, their only winning season between 1932 and 1945.

Jimmy Conzelman became the coach in 1940, but had little success (8-22-3) before leaving after the 1942 season. However, some key players for future years began dotting the roster, among them center Vince Banonis, tackle Chet Bulger, and back Marshall (Biggie) Goldberg. Under Phil Handler in 1943 and Handler and Walt Kiesling (the team merged with Pittsburgh because of wartime player shortages) in 1944, the Cardinals endured back-to-back seasons of 0-10.

Conzelman returned to coach the Cardinals to a winning season in 1946. The next year, Bidwill signed Charley Trippi and added him to his self-proclaimed "Million-Dollar Backfield" of quarterback Paul Christman, fullback Pat Harder, and halfbacks Goldberg (who later moved to defense) and Elmer Angsman. That group led the Cardinals to the 1947 NFL championship, but Bidwill was not there to see it. He died April 19, leaving the club to his wife Violet. Receivers Mal Kutner and Bill Dewell and interior linemen Walt Szot, Stan Mauldin, and Buster Ramsey were other stars of what remains the franchise's most successful team.

In 1948, a pall hung over the season when Mauldin, an all-pro tackle, died of a heart attack after the opening game. The Cardinals repeated as champions of the West, but lost the title game 7-0 to the Eagles in a blizzard at Philadelphia. Conzelman retired after the championship game of 1948. Violet Bidwill married St. Louis businessman Walter Wolfner in 1949, and together they oversaw club operations. Buddy Parker and Handler eked out one more winning season, but more than a decade of frustration followed. With attendance dwindling, the Cardinals ceded Chicago to the Bears and moved the franchise to St. Louis in 1960.

Coach Frank (Pop) Ivy brought several good, young players with him to St. Louis—receivers Bobby Joe Conrad and Sonny Randle, runners John David Crow and Joe Childress, guard Ken Gray, and linebacker Dale Meinert, among others—but the team lacked a standout quarterback.

Violet Wolfner died in 1962, leaving the Cardinals to her sons, William and Charles Bidwill, Jr. Wally Lemm replaced Ivy as coach in 1962. He installed young Charley Johnson at quarterback, and the offense jelled. Crow and Childress piled up rushing yards, and Jackie Smith emerged as an outstanding tight end. Jim Bakken began a kicking career that eventually would make him the Cardinals' all-time scoring leader. Larry Wilson, Jimmy Hill, and Pat Fischer starred in the defensive backfield.

After a rebuilding year, Lemm posted nine-victory seasons in 1963 and 1964, but when the team slid back to mediocrity in 1965, he resigned. Charley Winner (35-30-5) narrowly missed winning a division title in 1968 with a 9-4-1 season that was one-half game behind Cleveland's 10-4, but it was under Winner that Jim Hart began a long and productive career at quarterback. After Winner was dismissed in 1970, Bob Hollway suffered through duplicate 4-9-1 seasons in 1971-72. By this time, William Bidwill had bought out his brother and taken control of the club. He hired a college coach, Don Coryell of San Diego State, to take over the Cardinals.

Coryell, an offensive-minded strategist, went 4-9-1 his first year, but the Cardinals took flight in 1974, winning the NFC Eastern Division title, and played in the postseason for the first time since 1948. They lost to the Vikings in a divisional playoff game.

Terry Metcalf, a multipurpose running back, earned his "Franchise" nickname that year—he led the team in rushing with 718 yards, caught 50 passes, returned 26 punts, and posted the league's highest kick-off-return average—31.2 yards. Fullback Jim Otis, a $100-waiver bargain, helped with the running, and Mel Gray caught 39 passes. The offensive line of tackles Dan Dierdorf and Ernie McMillan, guards Conrad Dobler and Bob Young, and center Tom Banks was one of the best. The Cardinals repeated as division champions in 1975, but lost to the Rams in their only playoff game. A 10-4 record in 1976 was not quite enough for a playoff berth, and when the team slipped to 7-7 in 1977, Coryell and the Cardinals parted company.

Fabled former University of Oklahoma college coach Bud Wilkinson came out of retirement to coach the team in 1978-79, but with little success. Under Jim Hanifan, the Cardinals made the 1982 playoffs (the year of the players' strike) but lost in the opening round. By then, Neil Lomax had succeeded Hart at quarterback, and versatile Roy Green—he played wide receiver and defensive back throughout 1981—was the star receiver. Hoping to build on a near-miss in 1984—the Cardinals missed the playoffs thanks to a 29-27 season-ending loss—the Cardinals expected big things in 1985. The team started well, but when Anderson and Green were injured the bottom fell out, and Hanifan was dismissed for his 5-11 mark. Gene Stallings was named to replace him.

Attendance had sagged as St. Louis fans became frustrated with unfulfilled promises. In March of 1988, the franchise received permission to move to Phoenix. The Cardinals' last season in St. Louis saw Lomax have a terrific year and J.T. Smith lead the league with 91 receptions. Things began well in the Valley of the Sun. Paced by runners Earl Ferrell and Stump Mitchell, the Cardinals streaked to a first-place tie and a 7-4 record, but then lost their last five games. An arthritic hip ended Lomax's career before the 1989 season. Joe Bugel, architect of the Washington Redskins' offensive line, was hired as head coach for 1990. Second-year quarterback Timm Rosenbach showed promise, and rookie Ricky Proehl's 56 catches were more than any other first-year player. Another rookie, Johnny Johnson, rushed for 926 yards. But four years passed without a winning record, and Bugel was dismissed after the 1993 season.

When former Philadelphia Eagles coach Buddy Ryan was hired to coach the Arizona Cardinals— the name change occurred in early 1994—he boasted, "Y'all got a winner in town." That wasn't exactly accurate. Buddy's first Cardinals team finished 8-8. Jay Schroeder, a Ryan import, split time at quarterback with Steve Beuerlein. Ryan, known as a defensive genius, beefed up his defense by adding two of his former Eagles—Seth Joyner and Clyde Simmons.

In 1995, veteran Dave Krieg became the seventh new quarterback in seven years. Running back Garrison Hearst gained 1,070 yards, backfield mate Larry Centers hauled in 101 passes, and rookie wide receiver Frank Sanders caught 52 passes for a 17-yard average. Former Jets receiver Rob Moore added 63 receptions. Nevertheless, the Cardinals scored only 275 points while yielding 422. That translated into a 4-12 record and a firing of Ryan.

New coach Vince Tobin brought the team back to respectability in 1996, compiling a record of 7-9. The high point of the season was a 522-yard passing performance by veteran quarterback Boomer Esiason in a 37-34 overtime victory over Washington in week 11. The Cardinals slipped to 4-12 in 1997, though rookie Jake Plummer established himself as one of the NFL's most exciting young quarterbacks. The former Arizona State star took over as the starter in midseason and passed for 2,203 yards and 15 touchdowns. Rob Moore was his favorite receiver and caught 97 passes.

In 1998, the Cardinals made the playoffs for the first time in 16 years. Plummer rallied his team from behind in eight of Arizona's nine regular-season victories. Kicker Chris Jacke, a midseason replacement for injured Joe Nedney, secured a wild-card playoff spot with a 52-yard field goal on the final game's final play, the third consecutive game he won with a last-play kick.

One week later, the Cardinals shocked the Cowboys 20-7 in an NFC Wild Card Game in Dallas. It was only the franchise's second postseason victory, and its first since the 1947 NFL Championship Game. The season ended with a 41-21 loss to the Vikings in the divisional-playoff round.

CARDINALS RECORD 1920-1998

YEAR	WON	LOST	TIED	PCT.	FIN	PF	PA
Chicago Cardinals							
1920	6	2	2	.750	4t	115	43
1921	3	3	2	.500	8t	54	53
1922	8	3	0	.727	3	96	50
1923	8	4	0	.667	6	161	56
1924	5	4	1	.556	9	90	67
1925a	11	2	1	.846	1	230	65
1926	5	6	1	.455	10	74	98
1927	3	7	1	.300	9	69	134
1928	1	5	0	.167	9	7	107
1929	6	6	1	.500	4t	154	83
1930	5	6	2	.455	7t	128	132
1931	5	4	0	.566	4	120	128
1932	2	6	2	.250	6t	72	114
1933	1	9	1	.100	5	52	101
1934	5	6	0	.455	4	80	84
1935	6	4	2	.600	3t	99	97
1936	3	8	1	.273	4	74	143
1937	5	5	1	.500	4	135	165
1938	2	9	0	.182	5	111	168
1939	1	10	0	.091	5	84	254
1940	2	7	2	.222	5	139	222
1941	3	7	1	.300	4	127	197
1942	3	8	0	.273	4	98	209
1943	0	10	0	.000	4	95	238
Card-Pitt (does not count in totals)							
1944	0	10	0	.000	5	108	328
Chicago Cardinals							
1945	1	9	0	.100	5	98	228
1946	6	5	0	.545	3t	260	198
1947b	9	3	0	.750	1	306	231
1948c	11	1	0	.917	1	395	226
1949	6	5	1	.545	3	360	301
1950	5	7	0	.417	5	233	287
1951	3	9	0	.250	6	210	287
1952	4	8	0	.333	5t	172	221
1953	1	10	1	.091	6	190	337
1954	2	10	0	.167	6	183	347
1955	4	7	1	.364	4t	224	252
1956	7	5	0	.583	2	240	182
1957	3	9	0	.250	6	200	299
1958	2	9	1	.182	5t	261	356
1959	2	10	0	.167	6	234	324
St. Louis Cardinals							
1960	6	5	1	.545	4	288	230
1961	7	7	0	.500	4	279	267
1962	4	9	1	.308	6	287	361
1963	9	5	0	.643	3	341	283
1964	9	3	2	.750	2	357	331
1965	5	9	0	.357	5t	296	309
1966	8	5	1	.615	4	264	265
1967	6	7	1	.462	3	333	356
1968	9	4	1	.692	2	325	289
1969	4	9	1	.308	3	314	389
1970	8	5	1	.615	3	325	228
1971	4	9	1	.308	4	231	279
1972	4	9	1	.321	4	193	303
1973	4	9	1	.321	4	286	365
1974d	10	4	0	.714	1	285	218
1975d	11	3	0	.786	1	356	276
1976	10	4	0	.714	3	309	267
1977	7	7	0	.500	3	272	287
1978	6	10	0	.375	4	248	296
1979	5	11	0	.313	5	307	358
1980	5	11	0	.313	4	299	350
1981	7	9	0	.438	5	315	408
1982e	5	4	0	.556	6	135	170
1983	8	7	1	.531	3	374	428
1984	9	7	0	.563	3	423	345
1985	5	11	0	.313	5	278	414
1986	4	11	1	.281	5	218	351
1987	7	8	0	.467	3	362	368
Phoenix Cardinals							
1988	7	9	0	.438	4	344	398
1989	5	11	0	.313	4	258	377
1990	5	11	0	.313	5	268	396
1991	4	12	0	.250	5	196	344
1992	4	12	0	.250	5	243	332
1993	7	9	0	.438	4	326	269
Arizona Cardinals							
1994	8	8	0	.500	3	235	267
1995	4	12	0	.250	5	275	422
1996	7	9	0	.438	4	300	397
1997	4	12	0	.250	5	283	379
1998f	9	7	0	.563	2	325	378
78 Years	415	562	39	.428	—	17,383	19,834

a NFL Champion; No Playoffs
b NFL Champion; 1-0 in Playoffs
c NFL Western Division Champion; 0-1 in Playoffs
d NFC Eastern Division Champion; 0-1 in Playoffs
e NFC Qualifier for Playoffs; 0-1 in Playoffs
f NFC Wild Card Qualifier for Playoffs; 1-1 in Playoffs

COACHING HISTORY
CHICAGO 1920-1943, 1945-1959; CARD-PITT 1944; ST. LOUIS 1960-1987; PHOENIX 1988-1993; ARIZONA 1994-98
(417-577-39)

1920-22	John (Paddy) Driscoll	17-8-4
1923-24	Arnold Horween	13-8-1
1925-26	Norman Barry	16-8-2
1927	Guy Chamberlin	3-7-1
1928	Fred Gillies	1-5-0
1929	Dewey Scanlon	6-6-1
1930	Ernie Nevers	5-6-2
1931	LeRoy Andrews*	0-1-0
1931	Ernie Nevers	5-3-0
1932	Jack Chevigny	2-6-2
1933-34	Paul Schissler	6-15-1
1935-38	Milan Creighton	16-26-4
1939	Ernie Nevers	1-10-0
1940-42	Jimmy Conzelman	8-22-3
1943-45	Phil Handler**	1-29-0
1946-48	Jimmy Conzelman	27-10-0
1949	Phil Handler-Buddy Parker***	2-4-0
1949	Raymond (Buddy) Parker	4-1-1
1950-51	Earl (Curly) Lambeau#	7-15-0
1951	Phil Handler-Cecil Isbell##	1-1-0
1952	Joe Kuharich	4-8-0
1953-54	Joe Stydahar	3-20-1
1955-57	Ray Richards	14-21-1
1958-61	Frank (Pop) Ivy###	15-31-2
1961	Chuck Drulis-Ray Prochaska-Ray Willsey†	2-0-0
1962-65	Wally Lemm	27-26-3
1966-70	Charley Winner	35-30-5
1971-72	Bob Hollway	8-18-2
1973-77	Don Coryell	42-29-1
1978-79	Bud Wilkinson††	9-20-0
1979	Larry Wilson	2-1-0
1980-85	Jim Hanifan	39-50-1
1986-89	Gene Stallings†††	23-34-1
1989	Hank Kuhlmann	0-5-0
1990-93	Joe Bugel	20-44-0
1994-95	Buddy Ryan	12-20-0
1996-98	Vince Tobin	21-29-0

* Resigned after one game in 1931
** Co-coach with Walt Kiesling in Chicago Cardinals-Pittsburgh merger in 1944
*** Co-coaches for first six games in 1949
# Resigned after 10 games in 1951
Co-coaches
Resigned after 12 games in 1961
† Co-coaches
†† Released after 13 games in 1979
††† Released after 11 games in 1989

Atlanta Falcons

Atlanta joined the NFL when a group headed by Rankin M. Smith was awarded a franchise in 1965, to begin play in 1966. The Falcons chose first overall in the 1966 draft, selecting Texas All-America linebacker Tommy Nobis. But Nobis also was drafted by Houston of the rival AFL, and he was implored to sign with the Oilers by NASA astronauts orbiting in outer space. Ultimately he chose the Falcons and went on to an outstanding 11-year career.

Atlanta also participated in an expansion draft, choosing non-protected players from existing NFL clubs. The draft didn't yield any long-term stars, but it did provide the team's first-year rushing leader in Junior Coffey from Green Bay, leading receiver in Baltimore's Alex Hawkins, and defensive captain in Bill Jobko from Minnesota.

In January, 1966, Norb Hecker was named head coach. Hecker, a defensive back during his NFL playing career, had been an assistant to Vince Lombardi in Green Bay for seven seasons. Predictably, the first season produced few victories—a 3-11 record. The Falcons lost their first nine games before defeating the Giants on November 20.

When Atlanta went 1-12-1 in 1967, then lost its first three games in 1968, Hecker was fired. Former Vikings coach Norm Van Brocklin was brought in and completed a 2-12 season. On defense, Nobis got some welcome help in rangy defensive end Claude Humphrey, the club's number-one draft pick in 1968. Young Greg Brezina, who would give a dozen years of quality service, joined Nobis at linebacker.

In 1971, Van Brocklin, a standout quarterback years earlier, was named to the Pro Football Hall of Fame and celebrated by taking the Falcons to their first winning season—7-6-1, good for third place in the NFC West. Art Malone gave the team excellent running, and rookie receiver Ken Burrow set the club's single-game record with 190 receiving yards against Detroit (he later matched that figure against New Orleans).

Atlanta had a 7-7 record in 1972. John Zook gave the team bookends on the defensive line, teaming with Humphrey. Dave Hampton surpassed 1,000 yards rushing late in the final game, was presented with the game ball, carried again, and was thrown for a loss. He finished the season with 995 yards. (Hampton kept the ball.)

Lacking only a talented quarterback, Atlanta rose to 9-5 in 1973. Dick Shiner began the season as the starter, but gave way to Bob Lee, who led the team to a 41-0 thrashing of San Diego. The Falcons won five straight games, including a victory over undefeated Minnesota, and were perched for a wild-card berth. Then they dropped two of three in December. When the Falcons won only two of their first eight games in 1974, Van Brocklin was replaced by Marion Campbell. He held the job through five games of 1976 when Pat Peppler came out of the front office to replace him. The Falcons got a star quarterback in 1975, drafting California's Steve Bartkowski first overall. By the time Leeman Bennett arrived to coach in 1977, Bartkowski was an established starter, but he was forced to miss six games with a knee injury. Still, Atlanta, by virtue of a defense that would set a team record by allowing only 129 points in 14 games, won four of the games Bartkowski missed. The next year Bennett gave Atlanta fans a winning season (9-7) and a postseason game. The Falcons' "Gritz Blitz" defense won a wild-card playoff game over the Eagles 14-13 but couldn't hold a 20-13 halftime lead in the next round and lost to Super Bowl-bound Dallas.

After regressing to 6-10 in 1979, Atlanta won the NFC West title in 1980. William Andrews, who had been mostly a blocker at Auburn, rushed for the second 1,000-yard season of his career. Partner Lynn Cain gained 914. Bartkowski filled the air with footballs, and Alfred Jenkins, Wallace Francis, Andrews, and Junior Miller caught many of them. Linebackers Al Richardson, Fulton Kuykendall, Buddy Curry, and Joel Williams keyed a blitzing defense. The Falcons led Dallas 24-10 after three quarters in a divisional playoff game, only to succumb to a 20-point Cowboy comeback in the fourth quarter en route to a 30-27 loss. The Falcons' 5-4 mark in the strike-shortened 1982 season got them into the extended playoffs. However, after they lost their opening playoff game, Bennett was fired. Dan Henning came on board for 1983, and although the team was only 7-9, Billy (White Shoes) Johnson was electrifying as a kick returner and receiver. Big Gerald Riggs joined Andrews to form a powerful running tandem. The offensive line was led by tackle Mike Kenn and center Jeff Van Note.

When the Falcons endured losing seasons from 1984-86, Henning was released. Defensive coordinator and former head coach Marion Campbell took over in 1987. Campbell lasted fewer than three seasons and was replaced by interim head coach Jim Hanifan with four games to go in 1989. Jerry Glanville, a Falcons' assistant from 1977-1982, returned to Atlanta as head coach in 1990. He immediately put some swagger into the team. Flamboyant cornerback Deion Sanders improved the defense, and wide receiver Andre Rison set club records with 82 catches for 1,208 yards and 10 touchdowns. Elbert Shelley, a non-starter who later would make the Pro Bowl as a special-teams player, blossomed under Glanville's aggressive approach to the game.

Atlanta gained a wild-card spot in the 1991 playoffs. Michael Haynes and Mike Pritchard joined Rison as receivers in the Red Gun (similar to the Run-and-Shoot) offense. Chris Miller settled in at quarterback, and rushing was by committee—Steve Broussard, Mike Rozier, and Erric Pegram. After beating New Orleans 27-20 on the road in the first round, Atlanta lost a divisional playoff game to Washington. A pair of disappointing 6-10 seasons in 1992 and 1993 cost Glanville his job.

Former Falcons backup quarterback June Jones was hired as coach in 1994, and quarterback Jeff George was acquired from the Colts by trade. Terance Mathis had a career season with 111 catches, Rison had 81, and veteran Ricky Sanders and youngster Bert Emanuel gathered in 67 and 46, respectively. Eric Metcalf, acquired by trade before the 1995 season, caught 104 passes and was an exciting punt returner. Morten Andersen, a free-agent acquisition, came over from New Orleans and scored 122 points. Chris Doleman recorded 7 sacks, and Craig (Ironhead) Heyward became a 1,000-yard rusher. The Falcons posted a 9-7 record and earned a spot in the playoffs with a victory over San Francisco in the final game, an outcome that cost the 49ers home-field advantage in the playoffs. In a wild-card playoff game, a George-to-Metcalf play produced a 65-yard touchdown and a 7-0 lead, but Green Bay scored 27 of the next 30 points to win 37-20.

After the surprise showing of 1995, the 1996 season was a disappointment. George and Jones erupted in a shouting match after the quarterback was replaced by Bobby Hebert in week 4. George was suspended and eventually released. And, after a 3-13 season, Jones followed him to the unemployment line, to be replaced by Dan Reeves.

Under Reeves, a native of Rome, Georgia, the Falcons started slow (1-7) but closed with a flurry (6-2) in 1997 in what was a portent of things to come. The offense was becoming a force. Running back Jamal Anderson recorded his second 1,000-yard season (1,002), a healthy Chris Chandler proved to be a reliable quarterback, and Emanuel (65 receptions) and Mathis (62) formed a quality receiving tandem.

Midway through the 1997 season, original owner Rankin Smith died at age 71. His son, Taylor Smith, took over the club.

The Falcons were the NFL's surprise team of 1998. They compiled a franchise-record 14 regular-season victories, unseated the 49ers as NFC Western Division champions, and reached the Super Bowl for the first time. Anderson ran for an NFC-best 1,846 yards and set a league record with 410 rushing attempts. Chandler passed for 3,154 yards and 25 touchdowns. Reeves, the consensus choice as NFL coach of the year, had heart surgery late in the season but was back on the sidelines as his team beat the 49ers 20-18 in the divisional playoff round. One week later, Chandler passed for 3 touchdowns and Atlanta rallied from a 20-7 first-half deficit to upset Minnesota 30-27 in overtime in the NFC title game.

The magic ran out against Denver in Super Bowl XXXIII in Miami. The Falcons were able to move the ball much of the game, but could not reach the end zone until the Broncos' 34-19 victory was secure.

FALCONS RECORD 1966-1998

YEAR	WON	LOST	TIED	PCT.	FIN	PF	PA
1966	3	11	0	.214	7	204	437
1967	1	12	1	.077	4	175	422
1968	2	12	0	.143	4	170	389
1969	6	8	0	.429	3	276	268
1970	4	8	2	.333	3	206	261
1971	7	6	1	.538	3	274	277
1972	7	7	0	.500	2	269	274
1973	9	5	0	.643	2	318	224
1974	3	11	0	.214	4	111	271
1975	4	10	0	.286	3	240	289
1976	4	10	0	.286	3	172	312
1977	7	7	0	.500	2	179	129
1978a	9	7	0	.563	2	240	290
1979	6	10	0	.375	3	300	388
1980b	12	4	0	.750	1	405	272
1981	7	9	0	.438	2	426	355
1982c	5	4	0	.556	5	183	199
1983	7	9	0	.438	4	370	389
1984	4	12	0	.250	4	281	382
1985	4	12	0	.250	4	282	452
1986	7	8	1	.469	3	280	280
1987	3	12	0	.200	4	205	436
1988	5	11	0	.313	4	244	315
1989	3	13	0	.188	4	279	437
1990	5	11	0	.313	4	348	365
1991a	10	6	0	.625	2	361	338
1992	6	10	0	.375	3	327	414
1993	6	10	0	.375	3	316	385
1994	7	9	0	.438	3	317	385
1995d	9	7	0	.563	2	362	349
1996	3	13	0	.188	4	229	339
1997	7	9	0	.438	3	320	361
1998e	14	2	0	.875	1	442	289
33 Years	196	295	5	.400	—	9,111	10,973

a NFC Wild Card Qualifier for Playoffs; 1-1 in Playoffs
b NFC Western Division Champion; 0-1 in Playoffs
c NFC Qualifier for Playoffs; 0-1 in Playoffs
d NFC Wild Card Qualifier for Playoffs; 0-1 in Playoffs
e NFC Champions; 2-1 in Playoffs

COACHING HISTORY
(200-300-5)

1966-68	Norb Hecker*	4-26-1
1968-74	Norm Van Brocklin**	37-49-3
1974-76	Marion Campbell***	6-19-0
1976	Pat Peppler	3-6-0
1977-82	Leeman Bennett	47-44-0
1983-86	Dan Henning	22-41-1
1987-89	Marion Campbell#	11-32-0
1989	Jim Hanifan	0-4-0
1990-93	Jerry Glanville	28-38-0
1994-96	June Jones	19-29-0
1997-98	Dan Reeves	23-12-0

* Released after three games in 1968
** Released after eight games in 1974
*** Released after five games in 1976
# Retired after 12 games in 1989

Carolina Panthers

The Carolina Panthers broke the mold for expansion teams; they won. In their first season they were 7-9. In doing so, they won four more games than any previous first-year expansion franchise.

Owner Jerry Richardson, a former Baltimore Colts receiver turned entrepreneur, and his partners began seeking a franchise in July, 1987. From then on, the organization (Richardson Sports) did the spadework to assure it was in contention for consideration for an NFL franchise. The diligent work was rewarded when the NFL owners, meeting in Chicago on October 23, 1993, unanimously selected the Panthers to be the league's twenty-ninth team.

The Panthers' owners had their work cut out for them. The team played its first season in Clemson University's famed "Death Valley" stadium, a tedious drive for fans from the Charlotte area, but the faithful came. Construction already had begun on the home of the Panthers—the first shovel of dirt was turned on April 22, 1994. Ericsson Stadium, the state-of-the-art, 72,500-seat facility opened on August 3, 1996, with the Panthers' preseason game against the Bears.

Richardson stocked the front office with tested football men such as president Mike McCormack, a Pro Football Hall of Fame tackle with coaching and administrative experience, and general manager Bill Polian, the man largely credited with building the Buffalo Bills' Super Bowl teams of the 1990s. Their decisions, from hiring former Steelers defensive coordinator Dom Capers as head coach to selecting Penn State's Kerry Collins as quarterback in the college draft, were thoughtful and effective. Previous expansion franchises frequently were populated with other teams' problems. Not so the Panthers of 1995. They took full advantage of the league's new free-agency system, signing veterans such as linebackers Carlton Bailey, Lamar Lathon, and Sam Mills, and receiver Willie Green.

Former Lions running back Derrick Moore was a surprising find. His 740 rushing yards represented the highest total ever for an expansion-team runner.

And all three Panthers first-round picks in the college draft came through. Texas tackle Blake Brockermeyer started immediately on offense, and Tyrone Poole, a cornerback from Fort Valley State, also started and played well. Collins quickly supplanted Frank Reich at quarterback and led the team to all seven first-year victories—including four consecutively. One of those was at the expense of the defending Super Bowl champion 49ers.

The promise of their first season was more than fulfilled in the Panthers' second year. Kerry Collins's increased maturity and a blitz-happy defense manned mainly by veterans such as Kevin Greene, Lathon, and Mills, pushed Carolina all the way to the NFC Championship Game before they were stopped by Green Bay. Capers was hailed as coach of the year by several news organizations, and seven players were named to the NFC Pro Bowl team.

But the Panthers took a step back in 1997, falling to 7-9, then won just four games in a tumultuous season the following year. Polian left before the 1998 season to head the day-to-day operations of the Indianapolis Colts. Collins was waived midway through the season. Capers was fired the day after the year ended with a 27-19 victory over the Colts.

Shortly thereafter, George Seifert, who led the 49ers to victories in Super Bowls XXIV and XXIX, was named the new head coach.

PANTHERS RECORD 1995-1998

YEAR	WON	LOST	TIED	PCT.	FIN	PF	PA
1995	7	9	0	.438	4	289	325
1996a	12	4	0	.750	1	367	218
1997	7	9	0	.438	2	265	314
1998	4	12	0	.250	4	336	413
4 Years	30	34	0	.469	—	1,257	1,270

a NFC Western Division champions; 1-1 in playoffs

COACHING HISTORY
(31-35-0)

1995-98	Dom Capers	31-35-0

Chicago Bears

For more than six decades, the Chicago Bears and George Halas were the embodiment of the NFL. In a sense, Halas's life was the history of the team and the league, beginning in 1920 when A. E. Staley of the starch works in Decatur, Illinois, that bore his name, hired Halas to work at his factory and coach a company football team. The team was known as the Staleys, and was represented by Halas at the organizational meeting of the American Professional Football Association in Canton, Ohio, in September of 1920. The APFA was the forerunner of the NFL.

In that inaugural season, the Staleys lost just once—7-6 to the Chicago Cardinals. By virtue of 10 victories and a scoreless tie with Akron, Halas and the team claimed the league championship. However, at a meeting the following spring, club owners voted the league title to undefeated (8-0-3) Akron. In 1921, Staley gave the club to Halas, who took the team approximately 100 miles north to Chicago to play at Wrigley Field (then called Cubs Park). To defray costs, Halas took his former Illinois teammate Dutch Sternaman as a partner, and Staley also gave Halas $5,000 to keep the starchmaker's name for a year. The Windy City's newest team, still referred to in some Chicago newspapers as "Decatur," won the league championship that year, but not without an argument from Buffalo, which insisted a late-season loss to the Staleys was really only an exhibition game.

In 1922, Staley let his league membership lapse. Halas and Sternaman secured their own franchise and renamed the team the "Bears," in keeping with their landlords—the baseball Cubs. Halas also was instrumental in the league's decision to change its name to the National Football League. From 1922-24, the Bears were one of the NFL's best franchises. Falling to seventh place in 1925, the Bears created a stir by signing Red Grange, who played for the Bears just days after his last game at Illinois. Grange made his debut in a Thanksgiving Day game against the Cardinals, and a record crowd of 36,000 turned out to see him. He was a non-factor in a 0-0 tie as the Cardinals' Paddy Driscoll kept the ball away from him with well-placed punts.

The Bears went coast-to-coast on a 17-game barnstorming tour. Grange, the best-known running back of his day, solidified the NFL's position as a major league by drawing an overflow crowd of an estimated 70,000 to New York's Polo Grounds for a December 6 game with the Giants. It was pro football's largest crowd to that point. Large crowds continued to show up as the barnstormers headed south and west, eventually finishing the widely publicized tour in California in early 1926. Grange and his agent, C.C. Pyle, struck off on their own, forming the short-lived American Football League for the 1926 season. Grange was the star of a new team, the Yankees, that played in New York's Yankee Stadium. The Bears acquired Paddy Driscoll from the Cardinals and built a 12-1-3 record, but finished just behind the champion Frankford Yellow Jackets. When Halas had his first losing season (4-9-2) in 1929, he retired as a player and stepped down as coach.

Ralph Jones was brought in to coach the team while Halas handled nearly every other aspect of the operation. Jones's refinement of the T-formation with a man-in-motion changed the team's fortunes. Jones took the 1932 team to a tie for first, which was broken in a game against the Portsmouth Spartans, played indoors on the truncated field of Chicago Stadium because of inclement weather. The Bears won 9-0.

Halas returned as coach and sole owner in 1933, having bought out Dutch Sternaman's interest in the franchise before the start of the season. The team won the Western Division and defeated the Eastern Division-champion Giants 23-21 in the first official NFL Championship Game.

In 1934, the Bears finished the regular season undefeated and untied (13-0). Behind the awesome blocking of fullback Bronko Nagurski in the regular season, rookie halfback Beattie Feathers became the league's first 1,000-yard rusher (1,004), but the Bears were defeated in the championship game—the "Sneakers Game"—30-13 by the Giants.

By drafting future Hall-of-Fame inductees tackle Joe Stydahar (first) and guard Dan Fortmann (last) in the NFL's first college draft in 1936, the Bears laid a foundation for future greatness. Those players joined end Bill Hewitt and guard-tackle George Musso to form a strong nucleus. The Bears advanced to the title game in 1937, but were beaten 28-21 by a Redskins' team led by Sammy Baugh.

The Bears missed the division title in 1938 and 1939, but 1940 was a watershed season. Under the tutelage of assistant coach Clark Shaughnessy, Sid Luckman ran the refined man-in-motion T to perfection. The football world took notice as the Bears overwhelmed the Redskins 73-0 in the 1940 title game, the most lopsided game in NFL history. Helping the team achieve the success were rookie draft picks: running back George McAfee, center Clyde (Bulldog) Turner, and ends Ken Kavanaugh and Hampton

Pool. The Bears and Halas repeated as champions in 1941 with a 37-9 pounding of the Giants and roared through the 1942 regular season undefeated despite losing Halas to the U.S. Navy after five games. But the Redskins exacted a measure of revenge for the 73-0 thrashing by upsetting Chicago 14-6 in the championship game.

Nagurski, who retired after the 1937 season to pursue a professional wrestling career, was coaxed out of retirement to play tackle in 1943. However, in a key, late-season game against the crosstown rival Cardinals, with his team behind, Bronk returned to his old fullback position and powered two decisive scoring drives to put the Bears into the championship game. Chicago defeated Washington 41-21 for the 1943 crown. Luke Johnsos and Heartley (Hunk) Anderson, who had taken over for Halas in 1942, remained as co-coaches for two more seasons before Halas was discharged and returned as coach.

Returning with Halas in 1946 was the old Bears magic. Arguably the most successful NFL franchise to this point, the Monsters of the Midway—as the team became known—won another title. The Bears defeated the Giants 24-14 in the championship game on the passing and running of Sid Luckman. However, it would be the Bears' last championship appearance for a decade. Halas, absent as coach in 1956-57, returned in 1958, and Bill Wade's passing, Johnny Morris's and Mike Ditka's catching, and the running of Ronnie Bull and Willie Galimore, gave him a final championship in 1963. In the title game, the defense stopped quarterback Y.A. Tittle and the Giants 14-10.

Tragedy struck the Bears in training camp the next summer when Galimore and end John (Bo) Farrington were killed in a car crash in rural Indiana, but fortune smiled on the club in 1965 when the Bears outbid the AFL and signed first-round draft picks Gale Sayers and Dick Butkus, both destined for the Hall of Fame. Sayers, a nifty running back, scored 22 touchdowns as a rookie, including a record-tying 6 in one game; middle linebacker Butkus hammered away at opponents ferociously. Halas retired for the last time after the 1967 season, having coached longer and won more games than any other man in NFL history—40 years and 324 victories.

Offensive assistant Jim Dooley succeeded Halas, and the team made Soldier Field its home field beginning with the 1971 season. Sayers's meteoric career was ended prematurely in 1972 by knee injuries, as was Butkus's two years later. Without marquee players, Dooley found it difficult to win. He was replaced, in turn, by Abe Gibron, Jack Pardee, and Neill Armstrong. The Bears earned wild-card playoff berths in 1977 and 1979, but were ousted in the first game each time.

Halas, who died October 31, 1983, hired former Bears tight end Mike Ditka as coach in 1982. Ditka steadily built a winner. In 1985, with Walter Payton, the NFL's all-time rushing leader, and quarterback Jim McMahon, Ditka had a solid attack. Even more responsible for the club's 15-1 record was the disruptive 46 Defense. The Bears shut out the Giants 21-0 in a divisional playoff game and whitewashed the Rams 24-0 for the NFC championship. They won Super Bowl XX, crushing New England 46-10. William (Refrigerator) Perry, a 300-pound defensive tackle, became an overnight folk hero when Ditka used the rotund rookie as a running back near the goal line.

Payton retired after the 1987 season, but the team, paced by a defense still led by intense middle linebacker Mike Singletary, was a playoff fixture. The club rebounded from a losing season in 1989 to make the postseason in 1990 and 1991, but slipped in 1992. Ditka was replaced by Dave Wannstedt, and with Erik Kramer at quarterback, the Bears again contended in 1994-95, but injuries slowed their progress in 1996.

By 1997, the Bears had fallen to 4-12. Still, there was reason for optimism the following year when Chicago selected running back Curtis Enis, an All-America from Penn State, with the fifth pick of the draft. A prolonged holdout kept Enis out of training camp and limited his playing time once he did show up, but he exhibited flashes of brilliance. However, soon after he was given the starting role, a knee injury ended his season, and the Bears limped to another 4-12 finish.

Wannstedt was one of five NFL coaches fired on Black Monday—the day after their seasons ended. He was replaced by Dick Jauron, the defensive coordinator of the Jacksonville Jaguars.

BEARS RECORD 1920-1998

YEAR	WON	LOST	TIED	PCT.	FIN	PF	PA
Decatur Staleys							
1920	10	1	2	.909	2	164	21
Chicago Staleys							
1921a	9	1	1	.900	1	128	53
Chicago Bears							
1922	9	3	0	.750	2	123	44
1923	9	2	1	.818	2	123	35
1924	6	1	4	.857	2	122	44
1925	9	5	3	.643	7	158	96
1926	12	1	3	.923	2	216	63
1927	9	3	2	.750	3	149	98
1928	7	5	1	.583	5	175	85
1929	4	9	2	.308	9	119	227
1930	9	4	1	.692	3	169	71
1931	8	5	0	.615	3	145	92
1932a	7	1	6	.875	1	151	44
1933b	10	2	1	.833	1	133	82
1934c	13	0	0	1.000	1	286	86
1935	6	4	2	.600	3t	192	106
1936	9	3	0	.750	2	222	94
1937c	9	1	1	.900	1	201	100
1938	6	5	0	.545	3	194	148
1939	8	3	0	.727	2	298	157
1940b	8	3	0	.727	1	238	152
1941d	10	1	0	.909	1	396	147
1942c	11	0	0	1.000	1	376	84
1943b	8	1	1	.889	1	303	157
1944	6	3	1	.667	2t	258	172
1945	3	7	0	.300	4	192	235
1946b	8	2	1	.800	1	289	193
1947	8	4	0	.667	2	363	241
1948	10	2	0	.833	2	375	151
1949	9	3	0	.750	2	332	218
1950e	9	3	0	.750	2	279	207
1951	7	5	0	.583	4	286	282
1952	5	7	0	.417	5	245	326
1953	3	8	1	.273	4	218	262
1954	8	4	0	.667	2	301	279
1955	8	4	0	.667	2	294	251
1956f	9	2	1	.818	1	363	246
1957	5	7	0	.417	5	203	211
1958	8	4	0	.667	2t	298	230
1959	8	4	0	.667	2	252	196
1960	5	6	1	.455	5	194	299
1961	8	6	0	.571	3t	326	302
1962	9	5	0	.643	3	321	287
1963b	11	1	2	.917	1	301	144
1964	5	9	0	.357	6	260	379
1965	9	5	0	.643	3	409	275
1966	5	7	2	.417	5	234	272
1967	7	6	1	.538	2	239	218
1968	7	7	0	.500	2	250	333
1969	1	13	0	.071	4	210	339
1970	6	8	0	.429	3	256	261
1971	6	8	0	.429	3	185	276
1972	4	9	1	.321	4	225	275

YEAR	WON	LOST	TIED	PCT.	FIN	PF	PA
1973	3	11	0	.214	4	195	334
1974	4	10	0	.286	4	152	279
1975	4	10	0	.286	3	191	379
1976	7	7	0	.500	2	253	216
1977g	9	5	0	.643	2	255	253
1978	7	9	0	.438	4	253	274
1979g	10	6	0	.625	2	306	249
1980	7	9	0	.438	3	304	264
1981	6	10	0	.375	5	253	324
1982	3	6	0	.333	12	141	174
1983	8	8	0	.500	3	311	301
1984h	10	6	0	.625	1	325	248
1985i	15	1	0	.938	1	456	198
1986j	14	2	0	.875	1	352	187
1987j	11	4	0	.733	1	356	282
1988h	12	4	0	.750	1	312	215
1989	6	10	0	.375	4	358	377
1990h	11	5	0	.688	1	348	280
1991g	11	5	0	.688	2	299	269
1992	5	11	0	.313	4	295	361
1993	7	9	0	.438	4	234	230
1994k	9	7	0	.563	4	271	351
1995	9	7	0	.563	3	392	360
1996	7	9	0	.438	3	283	305
1997	4	12	0	.250	5	263	421
1998	4	12	0	.250	5	276	368
79 Years	606	418	42	.588	—	20,173	17,145

a NFL Champion
b NFL Champion; 1-0 in Playoffs
c NFL Western Division Champion; 0-1 in Playoffs
d NFL Champion; 2-0 in Playoffs
e NFL National Conference Runner-up; 0-1 in Playoffs
f NFL Western Conference Champion; 0-1 in Playoffs
g NFC Wild Card Qualifier for Playoffs; 0-1 in Playoffs
h NFC Central Division Champion; 1-1 in Playoffs
i Super Bowl Champion; 3-0 in Playoffs
j NFC Central Division Champion; 0-1 in Playoffs
k NFC Wild Card Qualifier for Playoffs; 1-1 in Playoffs

COACHING HISTORY
DECATUR STALEYS 1920, CHICAGO STALEYS 1921, CHICAGO BEARS 1922-1998
(620-432-42)

1920-29	George Halas	84-31-19
1930-32	Ralph Jones	24-10-7
1933-42	George Halas*	88-24-4
1942-45	Hunk Anderson-Luke Johnsos**	24-12-2
1946-55	George Halas	76-43-2
1956-57	John (Paddy) Driscoll	14-10-1
1958-67	George Halas	76-53-6
1968-71	Jim Dooley	20-36-0
1972-74	Abe Gibron	11-30-1
1975-77	Jack Pardee	20-23-0
1978-81	Neill Armstrong	30-35-0
1982-92	Mike Ditka	112-68-0
1993-98	Dave Wannstedt	41-57-0

* Retired after five games in 1942 to enter U.S. Navy
** Co-coaches

Dallas Cowboys

For a franchise that became known as "America's Team," the Dallas Cowboys had rather humble beginnings.

The NFL granted a franchise to Clint Murchison, Jr., and Bedford Wynne on January 28, 1960. The Cowboys—at first they were going to be called the Rangers—were the league's thirteenth franchise. Texas native Tom Landry, who had been a player and assistant coach with the New York Giants, was named head coach.

The Cowboys, admitted too late to take part in the 1960 college draft, initially were built through an expansion draft of players from other teams. Few quality players showed up in Dallas by this route. Dallas did, however, sign SMU All-America quarterback Don Meredith and obtained New Mexico fullback Don Perkins in a trade with the Colts.

Tex Schramm, a former Rams and television executive, was the team's first general manager. Gil Brandt, a successful photographer from Wisconsin, ran the scouting department in the early years. He logged thousands of miles evaluating and signing undrafted free agents.

When the Cowboys opened the 1960 NFL season, Landry used a unique system at quarterback. He alternated Meredith, a rookie, and veteran Eddie LeBaron on successive plays. Each took the field with the play that Landry wanted to run. The Cowboys lost their first 10 games. The highlight of the year was Landry's return to New York, where the Cowboys tied his old team 31-31. Dallas finished its inaugural year with an 0-11-1 record.

The Cowboys improved slightly in 1961. Perkins, who missed his rookie season with a foot injury, rushed for 815 yards. Defensive tackle Bob Lilly, who eventually would be inducted into the Pro Football Hall of Fame, was the team's first draft pick. The Cowboys finished 4-9-1, winning their first two games over Pittsburgh and the expansion Minnesota Vikings. Frank Clarke led the team in scoring with 9 touchdown catches, and linebacker Chuck Howley was obtained in a trade with the Bears. To show that Landry was the coach for the long haul, in 1964 Dallas extended his original contract, which had a year remaining, by 10 years. The next year, and succeeding years, proved the wisdom of stability at the top of the organization. The Cowboys went 7-7 and finished second in the Eastern Conference in 1965.

From 1966-1985, the Cowboys posted 20 consecutive winning records. During that span, Dallas won 13 division championships and appeared in Super Bowls V, VI, X, XII, and XIII, winning VI and XII.

By serving as hosts of a televised Thanksgiving Day game each year, beginning in 1966, the Cowboys increased the nation's awareness of their team. Landry's exciting, multiple-formation offense was the NFL's best show. The Doomsday Defense took shape as Lilly, George Andrie, Jethro Pugh, Lee Roy Jordan, Howley, Mel Renfro, and Cornell Green matured. Safeties Charlie Waters and Cliff Harris, both fearless hitters, came along in 1970.

Craig Morton led the Cowboys to their first Super Bowl, but after that it was Roger Staubach's team. Calvin Hill, Duane Thomas, and Walt Garrison were the team's top runners, and Drew Pearson and Tony Hill were young receivers who came to prominence.

The Cowboys reached Super Bowl V after the 1970 season, only to lose a mistake-laden game 16-13 to the Colts as time expired. Howley was chosen the game's most valuable player despite playing for the losing side. The team returned to win Super Bowl VI over the Miami Dolphins 24-3. Staubach, who had led the NFL in passing, threw 2 touchdown passes and was named the game's MVP.

After making the playoffs for eight consecutive years, the Cowboys missed in 1974. In 1975, a dozen draft choices made the team and had a dramatic impact on the Cowboys' fortunes. Randy White, Thomas (Hollywood) Henderson, Bob Breunig, Burton Lawless, and Herb Scott were the most notable of the rookies who helped propel Dallas to Super Bowl X, where the Cowboys were beaten 21-17 by Pittsburgh.

After the 1977 season, the team earned its second Super Bowl victory by stopping the Denver Broncos 27-10 in XII. Defensive linemen Harvey Martin and White were named co-MVPs as they battered former teammate Morton.

The Cowboys posted their thirteenth consecutive winning season in 1978. They shut out the Rams 28-0 for the NFC title but could not repeat as champions, losing to Pittsburgh 35-31 in Super Bowl XIII.

Staubach retired after the 1979 season. From 1980-88, Dallas enjoyed moderate success, but was not the dominant team that it was in the 1970s.

H.R. (Bum) Bright bought the team from Murchison in 1984 and in turn sold it to Jerry Jones on February 25, 1989. Jones replaced the legendary Landry with Jimmy Johnson, who had guided the University of Miami to the national title in 1987.

With the first overall draft pick in 1989, the Cowboys took quarterback Troy Aikman. Once the season got underway, they traded Herschel Walker, who gained 1,514 yards for Dallas in 1988, to Minnesota. The Cowboys acquired five veteran players and eight draft choices. The Cowboys finished the season 1-15, but those acquisitions proved to be the foundation for Dallas's brilliant 1992 season, which ended with a 52-17 victory over Buffalo in Super Bowl XXVII. In Super Bowl XXVIII, the Cowboys again defeated Buffalo 30-13 behind MVP Emmitt Smith.

Jones and Johnson parted ways before the 1994 season and former Oklahoma head coach Barry Switzer was hired to replace Johnson.

In 1994, Switzer led Dallas to a 12-4 mark. But in the NFC title game against San Francisco, the Cowboys quickly found themselves in a deep hole as a result of turnovers. They couldn't overcome a 21-0 first-period deficit and lost 38-28.

In 1995, the Cowboys seemed in disarray, but, at the very end of the season and through the playoffs, they were running like a well-oiled machine. Smith won his fourth rushing crown and set a league record with 25 touchdowns. For half of Super Bowl XXX, they continued to run smoothly. The Steelers made a game of it late, but Larry Brown's 2 second-half interceptions clinched a 27-17 victory and gave Dallas its third Super Bowl title in four years.

Problems off the field plagued the Cowboys in 1996. Smith and Aikman had subpar seasons, and Irvin was suspended for five games. However, the Cowboys remained among the NFL's elite organizations and won their division behind a strong defense. Carolina ended Dallas's hopes for another Super Bowl trip with a 26-17 victory in the divisional playoffs.

Injuries, age, and off-field distractions finally caught up with the Cowboys in 1997, when they missed the playoffs for the first time in seven years. Smith rushed for 1,074 yards, but was slowed by the pounding of carrying the ball more than 350 times a season. Aikman missed his favorite third-down receiver, tight end Jay Novacek, who retired when a back injury failed to respond to rest and treatment. A 45-17 manhandling in Green Bay started a five-game losing streak that dropped the Cowboys to 6-10. Switzer resigned at season's end and was replaced by former Steelers offensive coordinator Chan Gailey.

Under Gailey, the Cowboys rebounded to win the NFC East in 1998. In fact, they became the first NFC East team to sweep each of the other four division teams even though Aikman went down for a five-week stretch with a broken collarbone. In a wild-card game at Dallas, however, a strong performance by the upstart Cardinals led to an early postseason exit for the Cowboys.

COWBOYS RECORD 1960-1998

YEAR	WON	LOST	TIED	PCT.	FIN	PF	PA
1960	0	11	1	.000	7	177	369
1961	4	9	1	.308	6	236	380
1962	5	8	1	.385	5	398	402
1963	4	10	0	.286	5	305	378
1964	5	8	1	.385	5	250	289
1965	7	7	0	.500	2t	325	280
1966a	10	3	1	.769	1	445	239
1967b	9	5	0	.643	1	342	268
1968c	12	2	0	.857	1	431	186
1969c	11	2	1	.846	1	369	223
1970d	10	4	0	.714	1	299	221
1971e	11	3	0	.786	1	406	222
1972f	10	4	0	.714	2	319	240
1973g	10	4	0	.714	1	382	203
1974	8	6	0	.571	3	297	235
1975d	10	4	0	.714	2	350	268
1976h	11	3	0	.786	1	296	194
1977e	12	2	0	.857	1	345	212
1978d	12	4	0	.750	1	384	208
1979h	11	5	0	.688	1	371	313
1980i	12	4	0	.750	2	454	311
1981g	12	4	0	.750	1	367	271
1982j	6	3	0	.667	2	226	145
1983k	12	4	0	.750	2	479	360
1984	9	7	0	.563	4	308	308
1985h	10	6	0	.625	1	357	333
1986	7	9	0	.438	3	346	337
1987	7	8	0	.467	2	340	348
1988	3	13	0	.188	5	265	381
1989	1	15	0	.063	5	204	393
1990	7	9	0	.438	4	244	308
1991f	11	5	0	.688	2	342	310
1992e	13	3	0	.813	1	409	243
1993e	12	4	0	.750	1	376	229
1994g	12	4	0	.750	1	414	248
1995e	12	4	0	.750	1	435	291
1996g	10	6	0	.625	1	286	250
1997	6	10	0	.375	4	304	314
1998h	10	6	0	.625	1	381	275
39 Years	344	228	6	.600	—	13,264	10,991

a NFL Eastern Conference Champion; 0-1 in Playoffs
b NFL Eastern Conference Champion; 1-1 in Playoffs
c NFL Capitol Division Champion; 0-1 in Playoffs
d NFC Champion; 2-1 in Playoffs
e Super Bowl Champion; 3-0 in Playoffs
f NFC Wild Card Qualifier for Playoffs; 1-1 in Playoffs
g NFC Eastern Division Champion; 1-1 in Playoffs
h NFC Eastern Division Champion; 0-1 in Playoffs
i NFC Wild Card Qualifier for Playoffs; 2-1 in Playoffs
j NFC Qualifier for Playoffs; 2-1 in Playoffs
k NFC Wild Card Qualifier for Playoffs; 0-1 in Playoffs

COACHING HISTORY
(376-248-6)

1960-88	Tom Landry	270-178-6
1989-93	Jimmy Johnson	51-37-0
1994-97	Barry Switzer	45-26-0
1998	Chan Gailey	10-7-0

Detroit Lions

The Portsmouth (Ohio) Spartans, later to become the Detroit Lions, entered the NFL in 1930 as a fairly good "town team" that was looking to take a step up to the major leagues.

In 1931, they added the considerable talents of two Clarks. George (Potsy) Clark's eye for talent and no-nonsense approach helped make him one of the most successful pro coaches of the 1930s. The former Butler University coach quickly won his team's respect when he kicked star Roy (Father) Lumpkin off the field for "horseplay." Earl (Dutch) Clark was the premier triple-threat tailback of the decade and an All-NFL quarterback throughout most of his career. With the help of linemen such as George Christiansen, Gover (Ox) Emerson, and Clare Randolph, the team's record improved to 11-3 in 1931.

The next year the Spartans won six and lost only one during the regular season but were tied four times. That put them in a tie for first place with the Bears, who were 6-1-6. An extra game was scheduled, but it was forced indoors at Chicago Stadium by a snowstorm. It turned out to be one of the most significant games in NFL history because of the rules changes it created. However, for the Spartans it was just a frustrating 9-0 loss. Dutch Clark didn't play. He had to leave for his offseason job coaching basketball at Colorado College.

Clark stayed out of football altogether in 1933 directing athletics at Colorado College, but a strong year by tailback Glenn Presnell helped Portsmouth finish second in the NFL's new Western Division. The Spartans were winners on the field, but the Depression made them losers at the gate. The team was deep in debt when it was sold to radio executive George Richards, who moved the team to Detroit and rechristened them the Lions in 1934.

The coach and the core of the team remained the same, and Dutch Clark was lured out of retirement. The Lions roared out of the blocks with 10 consecutive victories, 7 by shutout. A highlight was Presnell's NFL-record 54-yard field goal to defeat Green Bay 3-0. The bubble burst with three losses at the end of the season, including two to the Bears. The first Bears game began a Detroit tradition when it was played on Thanksgiving Day. With his radio connections, Richards was able to get the game broadcast nationally over a 94-station network.

Everything came together for Detroit in 1935. The Lions won the West and defeated the Giants 26-7 in the NFL Championship Game. Detroit's ground attack was awesome. Three Lions were among the NFL's top five rushers: Ernie Caddell, Clark, and Bill Shepherd. The running game kicked into an even higher gear in 1936. The Lions amassed 2,885 yards—an NFL record that stood until 1972. Detroit remained competitive through the thirties, posting winning records from 1937-39. In 1940, the Lions paid a princely sum to acquire the rights to Byron (Whizzer) White from Pittsburgh. White, just back from his studies at Oxford, led the NFL in rushing in 1940—something he also did for Pittsburgh in 1938.

Heisman Trophy winner Frank Sinkwich debuted in 1943. In 1944, he was the NFL's Most Valuable Player as he led the team in rushing and to a winning record. Without much of a passing game in 1946, the team struggled. Bullet Bill Dudley, who led the league in rushing, interceptions, and punt returns with the Steelers in 1946, joined the Lions in a trade. Detroit's defense couldn't match its offense, and 1947 was a losing season.

Indiana's Bo McMillin was hired to coach the team in 1948. However, McMillin lasted only until 1950. Nevertheless, he had begun to build a defense that would assist the coming championship teams of the fifties. Les Bingaman, 349 pounds of middle guard, was the cornerstone of the Lions' defensive unit, and defensive backs Don Doll and Jim Smith were adept at intercepting passes.

Quarterback Bobby Layne and running back Doak Walker, a pair of Texans who joined the team in 1950, became the stars of the Lions' offense. In 1951, Buddy Parker quickly established himself as a players' coach. He continued the pipeline from Texas by bringing in defensive back-punter Yale Lary and guard Harley Sewell. Parker had an immediate impact, as did Layne's fiery leadership. Only a season-ending loss prevented Detroit from winning its division.

After losing two of their first three games to open the year in 1952, the Lions hit their stride. Bob Hoernschmeyer and Layne provided most of the ground game, Layne hit Cloyce Box for big gainers through the air, and Lary and Jim David joined Jack Christiansen in the secondary. Walker ran 67 yards for a touchdown in the title game, and the Lions and Parker got the best of Paul Brown and the Cleveland Browns 17-7 for Detroit's first championship since 1935.

It was business as usual in 1953—a Western Conference title and the NFL championship, which again came over the Browns. The championship-game victory was tougher this time, though. Trailing late, Layne accomplished what would become his signature—directing a winning drive in the final minutes. He hit 195-pound Jim Doran, used most of the year as a defensive end, for a 33-yard touchdown pass with 2:08 left to give the Lions a 17-16 victory.

The Lions breezed to a third title-game appearance, and a third confrontation with the Browns, in 1954. This time the Browns took out two years of frustration 56-10. Layne was hurt the next season and the team went from first to worst. Walker led the league in scoring but retired after the 1955 season.

In 1956, the Lions had a shot at another division title. But in the season's final game, Bears defensive end Ed Meadows knocked Layne out, and Chicago went on to win the game and the division. Gene Gedman and Howard (Hopalong) Cassady developed as runners, and Dave Middleton had another great season receiving.

Parker stunned the Lions by resigning on the eve of the 1957 season. Assistant George Wilson took over and acquired Tobin Rote, a good running quarterback, from Green Bay. That deal paid off when Layne broke his leg late in the season. Rote, with lots of help from a Joe Schmidt-led defense and halfback Tom (the Bomb) Tracy, guided the team past the 49ers in a stirring playoff comeback. The Lions blasted the Browns 59-14 in a rematch of earlier NFL Championship Games.

Layne followed Parker to Pittsburgh in 1958. A rash of injuries and the loss of their leader sent the Lions to the bottom of the West. Bill Glass, Alex Karras, and Wayne Walker were new faces on defense. While 1959 was another down year, the Lions were maturing on defense and by 1960 had a ferocious unit—big Roger Brown was up front and Dick (Night Train) Lane was in the secondary to steady youngsters Dick LeBeau and Gary Lowe. Tough as they were, the Packers forced the Lions to settle for second best in the West for three consecutive seasons, 1960-62.

William Clay Ford, who became Detroit's owner in 1964, hired Harry Gilmer in 1965. Gilmer was gone after 1966. Joe Schmidt took over in 1967, and, after a couple of rocky seasons, led the team to four consecutive second-place finishes before resigning after the 1972 season. Don

McCafferty and Rick Forzano continued the unbroken string of runner-up finishes through 1975. When the team dropped three of its first four games in 1976, Forzano resigned. Coaches Tommy Hudspeth (1977) and Monte Clark (1978) each finished third.

Clark and the Lions finally won their division in 1983, but lost their first playoff game. Darryl Rogers replaced Clark in 1984, but failed to reach .500 in any of his four seasons. Wayne Fontes replaced Rogers for the final five games of 1988. In Fontes's first full season, the Lions drafted Barry Sanders, the 1988 Heisman Trophy winner. Sanders led the NFC in rushing as a rookie. With its version of the Run-and-Shoot, called the Silver Stretch, Detroit won six of its final seven games to finish 7-9. Detroit's strong finish quieted Fontes's critics, who had been calling for his removal. That scenario would play out almost every year during Fontes's tenure.

Although Sanders led the league in rushing in 1990, Detroit had trouble winning. Lomas Brown was a fixture at left tackle, and Mel Gray became a fearsome kick returner.

After losing to the Redskins 45-0 to open 1991, the Lions caught fire, winning the NFC Central and a playoff game over Dallas before losing to Washington again, this time in the NFC title game. Erik Kramer, an undrafted free-agent quarterback, filled in for Rodney Peete and directed the team to a 38-6 playoff victory over the Cowboys. Sanders rushed for 1,548 yards, and wide receivers Brett Perriman, Robert Clark, and Mike Farr (son of Mel Farr, Sr.) had good seasons catching the ball.

The Lions went 5-11 in 1992, then had another up and down year in 1993. But Fontes's team won the division and made the playoffs by winning three of its final four games. The 1994 season was a replay of several previous. The Lions started poorly (2-4), Fontes was under fire again, then he resuscitated the team, which finished with a flurry (7-3) to make the playoffs.

The franchise paid a high price in 1994 to bring in free-agent quarterback Scott Mitchell, and in 1995 he showed why by passing for 4,338 yards. His improved play improved that of wide receiver Herman Moore and Perriman, too. Moore caught a record 123 passes and Perriman 108; no teammates ever caught more. The team started 2-5 and the wolves were howling for Fontes's job. But the Lions wound up 10-6 to make the playoffs, where they lost 58-37 to the Eagles.

The Lions began the 1996 season without Lomas Brown and linebacker Chris Spielman, who left via free agency. Sanders again led the league in rushing, but the team finished 5-11. Fontes was fired and replaced by Bobby Ross, who had led San Diego to Super Bowl XXIX.

Under Ross, the Lions reached the postseason with a 9-7 record, but the real story of the season was Sanders. The soft-spoken dynamo became the third runner in NFL history to rush for more than 2,000 yards in a season, averaging 6.1 yards per carry en route to 2,053 yards. The Lions boasted other weapons on offense, too. Herman Moore (104 catches) and Johnnie Morton (80) both were 1,000-yard receivers. Scott Mitchell passed for 3,484 yards.

But the following season was a disappointment. Mitchell, whose career had been a series of ups and downs, was replaced early in the schedule by Eastern Michigan rookie Charlie Batch. Batch showed mobility and maturity, but could generate just five victories. Sanders had his string of 1,500-yard rushing seasons ended at four when he gained 1,491. He reached 1,499 yards in the last game of the season against the Ravens before losing yardage on his final three carries.

LIONS RECORD 1930-1998

YEAR	WON	LOST	TIED	PCT.	FIN	PF	PA
Portsmouth Spartans							
1930	5	6	3	.455	7t	176	161
1931	11	3	0	.786	2	175	77
1932	6	2	4	.750	2	116	62
1933	6	5	0	.545	2	128	87
Detroit Lions							
1934	10	3	0	.769	2	238	59
1935a	7	3	2	.700	1	191	111
1936	8	4	0	.667	3	235	102
1937	7	4	0	.636	2t	180	105
1938	7	4	0	.636	2	119	108
1939	6	5	0	.545	3	145	150
1940	5	5	1	.500	3	138	153
1941	4	6	1	.400	3	121	195
1942	0	11	0	.000	5	38	263
1943	3	6	1	.333	3	178	218
1944	6	3	1	.667	2t	216	151
1945	7	3	0	.700	2	195	194
1946	1	10	0	.091	5	142	310
1947	3	9	0	.250	5	231	305
1948	2	10	0	.167	5	200	407
1949	4	8	0	.333	4	237	259
1950	6	6	0	.500	4	321	285
1951	7	4	1	.636	2t	336	259
1952b	9	3	0	.750	1	344	192
1953a	10	2	0	.833	1	271	205
1954c	9	2	1	.818	1	337	189
1955	3	9	0	.250	6	230	275
1956	9	3	0	.750	2	300	188
1957b	8	4	0	.667	1	251	231
1958	4	7	1	.364	5	261	276
1959	3	8	1	.273	5	203	275
1960	7	5	0	.583	2t	239	212
1961	8	5	1	.615	2	270	258
1962	11	3	0	.786	2	315	177
1963	5	8	1	.385	4t	326	265
1964	7	5	2	.583	4	280	260
1965	6	7	1	.462	6	257	295
1966	4	9	1	.308	6t	206	317
1967	5	7	2	.417	3	260	259
1968	4	8	2	.333	4	207	241
1969	9	4	1	.692	2	259	188
1970d	10	4	0	.714	2	347	302
1971	7	6	1	.538	2	341	286
1972	8	5	1	.607	2	339	290
1973	6	7	1	.464	2	271	247
1974	7	7	0	.500	2	256	270
1975	7	7	0	.500	2	245	262
1976	6	8	0	.429	3	262	220
1977	6	8	0	.429	3	183	252
1978	7	9	0	.438	3	290	300
1979	2	14	0	.125	5	219	365
1980	9	7	0	.563	2	334	272
1981	8	8	0	.500	2	397	322
1982e	4	5	0	.444	8	181	176
1983f	9	7	0	.563	1	347	286
1984	4	11	1	.281	4	283	408
1985	7	9	0	.438	4	307	366
1986	5	11	0	.313	3	277	326
1987	4	11	0	.267	5	269	384
1988	4	12	0	.250	4	220	313
1989	7	9	0	.438	3	312	364
1990	6	10	0	.375	3	373	413
1991g	12	4	0	.750	1	339	295
1992	5	11	0	.313	5	273	332
1993f	10	6	0	.625	1	298	292
1994d	9	7	0	.563	3	357	342
1995d	10	6	0	.625	2	436	336
1996	5	11	0	.313	5	302	366
1997d	9	7	0	.563	3	379	306
1998	5	11	0	.313	4	306	378
69 Years	440	457	32	.491	—	17,615	17,295

a NFL Champion; 1-0 in Playoffs
b NFL Champion; 2-0 in Playoffs
c NFL Western Conference Champion; 0-1 in Playoffs
d NFC Wild Card Qualifier for Playoffs, 0-1 in Playoffs
e NFC Qualifier for Playoffs; 0-1 in Playoffs
f NFC Central Division Champion; 0-1 in Playoffs
g NFC Central Division Champion; 1-1 in Playoffs

COACHING HISTORY
PORTSMOUTH SPARTANS 1930-33, DETROIT LIONS 1934-1998
(447-466-32)

1930	Hal (Tubby) Griffen	5-6-3
1931-36	George (Potsy) Clark	49-20-6
1937-38	Earl (Dutch) Clark	14-8-0
1939	Elmer (Gus) Henderson	6-5-0
1940	George (Potsy) Clark	5-5-1
1941-42	Bill Edwards*	4-9-1
1942	John Karcis	0-8-0
1943-47	Charles (Gus) Dorais	20-31-2
1948-50	Alvin (Bo) McMillin	12-24-0
1951-56	Raymond (Buddy) Parker	50-24-2
1957-64	George Wilson	55-45-6
1965-66	Harry Gilmer	10-16-2
1967-72	Joe Schmidt	43-35-7
1973	Don McCafferty	6-7-1
1974-76	Rick Forzano**	15-17-0
1976-77	Tommy Hudspeth	11-13-0
1978-84	Monte Clark	43-63-1
1985-88	Darryl Rogers***	18-40-0
1988-96	Wayne Fontes	67-71-0
1997-98	Bobby Ross	14-19-0

* Released after three games in 1942
** Resigned after four games in 1976
*** Released after 11 games in 1988

Green Bay Packers

The Green Bay Packers, though not a charter member of the NFL, enjoy a unique place in league history. They were among the first teams to enjoy corporate sponsorship. In 1919, the Indian Packing Company gave the team $500 for uniforms and equipment, so the nickname Packers was a natural. The Packers joined the league in 1921, owned by John Clair of the Acme Packing Company, which had bought out the Indian Packing Company.

The Packers are the only remaining "town team" (Green Bay, population: 102,179) in a league that was once composed almost entirely of midwestern town teams, such as the Canton (Ohio) Bulldogs and the Evansville (Indiana) Crimson Giants. Earl (Curly) Lambeau was the driving force behind the Packers. A Green Bay high school star who played a season at Notre Dame, he was similar to George Halas in that he wore many hats with the team—player, coach, general manager, and publicity director. The Packers lost their league membership in January, 1922, for using college players whose class had not yet graduated. But before the 1922 season began, Lambeau borrowed the money to buy a new NFL franchise. Initially, Lambeau renamed the team the Blues, but because people still referred to the Green Bay franchise as the Packers, he changed the team's name back to Packers.

Mounting debt, caused in part by rain on game days in 1922, led to the team becoming a nonprofit corporation in 1923. Citizens of the area subscribed to support the club. It remains the only publicly held franchise in the NFL.

Led by Lambeau, the team kept winning in the 1920s. Suffering only a tie in 13 games in 1929, the Packers were crowned league champions. Center Jug Earpe and future Pro Football Hall of Fame enshrinees Cal Hubbard and Mike Michalske fortified the line. Johnny (Blood) McNally, one of the game's true characters, quarterback Red Dunn, end Lavie Dilweg, halfback Verne Lewellen, and fullback Bo Molenda handled the offense. The defense was practically impenetrable, shutting out eight opponents, allowing only a safety to two more, and giving up six points to three others.

The Packers again were NFL champions in 1930. Tailback Arnie Herber debuted, but Lewellen and Dunn still were the main passers. In 1931, Green Bay became the first team to win three consecutive NFL championships.

Green Bay received new blood in 1932. Clarke Hinkle, an All-East fullback at Bucknell, immediately stepped into the starting lineup and led the team in rushing. Herber asserted himself and, in the first year the NFL kept official statistics, led the league in passing. Green Bay's 10 victories topped the league, but its .769 winning percentage ranked third to keep the Packers from winning their fourth consecutive title.

Another financial crisis in 1933 prompted another community bailout of the Packers. Local residents contributed $15,000, and the club was reorganized into its present structure. Six hundred shares were divided up, paying no dividends and with the proviso that if the club ever is sold, all profits go to local nonprofit organizations.

After a losing season in 1933 and a mediocre 1934, the Packers got a big boost in 1935 when Alabama's Rose Bowl hero, Don Hutson, joined the team. He was the league's most dangerous pass catcher from his first game. In fact, his first reception went for a long touchdown against the Bears. With Herber passing for 1,200 yards and Hutson on the receiving end for about half of them, Green Bay won the division and the NFL Championship Game from the Boston Redskins in 1936.

Hutson led the league in receiving in 8 of his first 11 seasons. Lambeau brought in Cecil Isbell to learn under Herber in 1938. Isbell and Herber sometimes played in the same backfield, both passing and running. After a stellar regular season, the team lost the NFL title game to the Giants 23-17. However, in 1939, Green Bay shut out New York 27-0 for the championship in Milwaukee, where the Packers had begun playing some home games in 1933.

The 1940 Packers were no match for the Bears, but the 1941 edition split with Chicago. The tie was broken when Chicago won a playoff game 33-14. It was the last season for Hinkle, who left for military service as the National Football League's all-time rushing leader. Hutson set or equaled season records for receptions, touchdown receptions, and points scored.

Green Bay finished second to Chicago in 1943 before winning another title in 1944. Hutson, as usual, led in receptions. Running back Ted Fritsch was the star of the championship game victory over the Giants. Hutson, considered by many to be the greatest receiver ever, retired after the 1945 season, prominently displayed in the NFL record book. The franchise played just better than .500 football through 1947, but then won only five games in the next two seasons. Lambeau, who had founded the club, resigned as coach in 1950 after a long-running dispute with the Packers' executive committee.

Gene Ronzani was hired as coach to make a fresh start in 1950, but really ushered in a decade of instability. Not until Vince Lombardi arrived in 1959 did the Packers have a winning season. When Lombardi came to town there was nowhere to go but up. Ray (Scooter) McLean had only a win and a tie to show for the 12-game 1958 season.

Lombardi found talent in Green Bay when he arrived, but it took him time to develop and mold it. Paul Hornung, Jim Taylor, Bart Starr, Ron Kramer, Jerry Kramer, and

Forrest Gregg all were there, as were Jim Ringo and Dave (Hawg) Hanner. Lombardi made Hornung his Frank Gifford-like left halfback and made the option sweep a Packer staple. Green Bay won its first three games in 1959, lost five in a row, and then won the final four to record its first winning season since 1947.

In 1959, Fred (Fuzzy) Thurston joined Jerry Kramer to form a tandem of star guards. In 1960, Hornung set an NFL scoring record with 176 points. Henry Jordan, Willie Davis, and Willie Wood were new to the defense. The team won the West, but for the only time in Lombardi's career, he lost a championship game, bowing to the Eagles.

By 1961, Starr was firmly in control at quarterback. Ron Kramer, a pioneer tight end, made 35 receptions. Taylor rushed for 1,307 yards. This time Lombardi annihilated his old team, the Giants, 37-0 in the title game. Hornung commuted from military duty at Fort Riley, Kansas, to Green Bay but still scored 146 points.

Former first-round draft pick Tom Moore filled in effectively for the injured Hornung in 1962, and only a Thanksgiving loss to Detroit marred a perfect season. The Packers defeated the Giants 16-7 in a title repeat.

In 1963, Hornung received a year's suspension for gambling. The Packers still had a great season, but the Bears won the division. Hornung was back in 1964 but was a little rusty. In 1965, kicker Don Chandler helped produce a championship by scoring the winning points in a 13-10 victory over Baltimore in the playoff for the Western Conference title. A week later, Green Bay beat Cleveland 23-12 in the NFL Championship Game.

Essentially, the same cast of heroes won the 1966 and 1967 NFL titles after titanic struggles with the Cowboys. Those victories in the NFL Championship Game earned Green Bay the right to face the AFL champions in Super Bowls I and II. In I, the Packers defeated Kansas City 35-10. In II, Oakland fell 33-14. After that game, Lombardi stepped down as coach.

Phil Bengtson took over in 1968, resigned after 1970, and was replaced by college coach Dan Devine, who was succeeded by Packers legends Starr and Gregg, neither of whom could match Lombardi's magic. Lindy Infante, a creative offensive coordinator from the Cleveland Browns, took over in 1988 and guided the Packers to a 10-6 record in 1989. Infante earned coach-of-the-year honors, and quarterback Don Majkowski led the NFL with 4,318 yards passing. Two years later, Infante was fired. In 1992, Mike Holmgren was hired from the 49ers' staff, and quarterback Brett Favre was obtained in a trade with the Atlanta Falcons. Sterling Sharpe caught 108 passes, an NFL record. Free agent Reggie White signed in 1993 to anchor the defense. The offense again featured Favre (3,303 yards passing) and Sharpe (112 catches). The Packers won wild-card playoff games in 1993 and 1994.

Favre was fabulous in 1995, winning league MVP honors. Sharpe was forced to retire because of a neck injury, but Robert Brooks made 102 catches and many new friends by jumping into the stands at Lambeau Field following touchdown catches. Edgar Bennett cracked 1,000 yards, the first Packer to rush for that total since 1978. Mark Chmura became a complete tight end. Green Bay showed how serious a contender it was by shocking defending Super Bowl champion San Francisco in the postseason before losing to Dallas in the NFC title game.

Despite a series of injuries to the receiving corps in 1996, the Packers marched to their first Super Bowl victory in 29 years. They scored the most points and gave up the fewest of any team in the NFL. Favre was league MVP for the second year in a row. Kick returner Desmond Howard was named the MVP of Super Bowl XXXI after his third-quarter, 99-yard kickoff return for a touchdown sealed Green Bay's 35-21 victory over New England.

A year later, the Packers won 13 regular-season games and successfully defended their NFC title, but fell 31-24 to Denver in Super Bowl XXXII. Favre was named the NFL's most valuable player by the Associated Press for the third consecutive year, sharing the award with Detroit running back Barry Sanders. Levens added nearly 1,000 yards to his run production—up to 1,435 yards from 566 in 1996. Antonio Freeman emerged as an explosive wide receiver.

Free-agency losses hurt in 1998, but perhaps not as much as a broken leg that kept Levens out of nine games. Without the benefit of a rushing attack, Favre was forced to do too much himself. He passed for a league-leading 4,212 yards, but the team was overtaken by Minnesota for the NFC Central title. The Packers finished 11-5 and earned a playoff berth, but lost in the final seconds to the 49ers in a titanic wild-card struggle.

A distraction all season was the persistent rumor that Holmgren would leave to become coach and general manager of another team. Shortly after Green Bay's elimination from the playoffs, Holmgren left for Seattle. He was replaced by former Eagles coach Ray Rhodes, who was Holmgren's defensive coordinator in Green Bay from 1992-93.

PACKERS RECORD 1921-1998

YEAR	WON	LOST	TIED	PCT.	FIN	PF	PA
1921	3	2	1	.600	6t	70	55
1922	4	3	3	.571	7	70	44
1923	7	2	1	.778	3t	85	34
1924	7	4	0	.636	6	102	38
1925	8	5	0	.615	9	151	110
1926	7	3	3	.700	5	151	60
1927	7	2	1	.778	2	113	43
1928	6	4	3	.600	4	120	92
1929a	12	0	1	1.000	1	198	24
1930a	10	3	1	.769	1	234	111
1931a	12	2	0	.857	1	291	94
1932	10	3	1	.769	3	152	63
1933	5	7	1	.417	3	170	107
1934	7	6	0	.538	3	156	112
1935	8	4	0	.667	2	181	96
1936b	10	1	1	.909	1	248	118
1937	7	4	0	.636	2t	220	122
1938c	8	3	0	.727	1	223	118
1939b	9	2	0	.818	1	233	153
1940	6	4	1	.600	2	238	155
1941d	10	1	0	.909	2	258	120
1942	8	2	1	.800	2	300	215
1943	7	2	1	.778	2	264	172
1944b	8	2	0	.800	1	238	141
1945	6	4	0	.600	3	258	173
1946	6	5	0	.545	3t	148	158
1947	6	5	1	.545	3	274	210
1948	3	9	0	.250	4	154	290
1949	2	10	0	.167	5	114	329
1950	3	9	0	.250	5t	244	406
1951	3	9	0	.250	5	254	375
1952	6	6	0	.500	4	295	312
1953	2	9	1	.182	6	200	338
1954	4	8	0	.333	5	234	251
1955	6	6	0	.500	3	258	276
1956	4	8	0	.333	5t	264	342
1957	3	9	0	.250	6	218	311
1958	1	10	1	.091	6	193	382
1959	7	5	0	.583	3t	248	246

YEAR	WON	LOST	TIED	PCT.	FIN	PF	PA
1960e	8	4	0	.667	1	332	209
1961b	11	3	0	.786	1	391	223
1962b	13	1	0	.929	1	415	148
1963	11	2	1	.846	2	369	206
1964	8	5	1	.615	2t	342	245
1965f	10	3	1	.769	1	316	224
1966g	12	2	0	.857	1	335	163
1967h	9	4	1	.692	1	332	209
1968	6	7	1	.462	3	281	227
1969	8	6	0	.571	3	269	221
1970	6	8	0	.429	4	196	293
1971	4	8	2	.333	4	274	298
1972i	10	4	0	.714	1	304	226
1973	5	7	2	.429	3	202	259
1974	6	8	0	.429	3	210	206
1975	4	10	0	.286	4	226	285
1976	5	9	0	.357	4	218	299
1977	4	10	0	.286	3	134	219
1978	8	7	1	.531	2	249	269
1979	5	11	0	.313	4	246	316
1980	5	10	1	.344	5	231	371
1981	8	8	0	.500	3	324	361
1982j	5	3	1	.611	3	226	169
1983	8	8	0	.500	2	429	439
1984	8	8	0	.500	2	390	309
1985	8	8	0	.500	2	337	355
1986	4	12	0	.250	4	254	418
1987	5	9	1	.367	3	255	300
1988	4	12	0	.250	5	240	315
1989	10	6	0	.625	2	362	356
1990	6	10	0	.375	4	271	347
1991	4	12	0	.250	4	273	313
1992	9	7	0	.563	2	276	296
1993k	9	7	0	.563	3	340	282
1994k	9	7	0	.563	2	382	287
1995l	11	5	0	.688	1	404	314
1996h	13	3	0	.813	1	456	210
1997m	13	3	0	.813	1	422	282
1998n	11	5	0	.688	2	408	319
78 Years	551	445	36	.551	—	19,743	17,584

a NFL Champion; No Playoffs
b NFL Champion; 1-0 in Playoffs
c NFL Western Division Champion; 0-1 in Playoffs
d NFL Western Division Runner-up; 0-1 in Playoffs
e NFL Western Conference Champion; 0-1 in Playoffs
f NFL Champion; 2-0 in Playoffs
g Super Bown Champion; 2-0 in Playoffs
h Super Bowl Champion; 3-0 in Playoffs
i NFC Central Division Champion; 1-1 in Playoffs
j NFC Qualifier for Playoffs; 1-1 in Playoffs
k NFC Wild Card Qualifier for Playoffs; 1-1 in Playoffs
l NFC Central Division Champion; 2-1 in Playoffs
m NFC Champion; 2-1 in Playoffs
n NFC Wild Card Qualifier for Playoffs; 0-1 in Playoffs

COACHING HISTORY
(573-455-36)

1921-49	Earl (Curly) Lambeau	212-106-21
1950-53	Gene Ronzani*	14-31-1
1953	Hugh Devore-Ray (Scooter) McLean**	0-2-0
1954-57	Lisle Blackbourn	17-31-0
1958	Ray (Scooter) McLean	1-10-1
1959-67	Vince Lombardi	98-30-4
1968-70	Phil Bengtson	20-21-1
1971-74	Dan Devine	25-28-4
1975-83	Bart Starr	53-77-3
1984-87	Forrest Gregg	25-37-1
1988-91	Lindy Infante	24-40-0
1992-98	Mike Holmgren	84-42-0

* Resigned after 10 games in 1953
** Co-coaches

Minnesota Vikings

The Minnesota Vikings were to be charter members of the American Football League, but on January 27, 1960, they withdrew from the AFL. One day later they were awarded an NFL franchise, to begin play in 1961. (Minnesota became the first NFL franchise to be named for a state.)

In addition to former Minneapolis Lakers owner Max Winter, E. William Boyer, Bernard Ridder, Jr., and H.P. Skoglund, one of the original owners was Ole Haugsrud, who owned the Duluth Eskimos in the early NFL. When he turned the franchise back to the league in 1928, he did so with the proviso that if pro football ever came back to Minnesota, he would have the option to purchase 10 percent of the team, which he did for $60,000 with the Vikings.

Norm Van Brocklin, fresh from leading the Eagles to an NFL title, was selected as the team's first head coach. The expansion draft produced some recognizable names, but not much talent. The college draft was a different story. Tommy Mason, a halfback from Tulane, was the team's first-round draft choice in 1961 and quickly became a Pro Bowl choice. Fran Tarkenton was drafted in the third round and beat out veteran George Shaw at quarterback. Tarkenton earned his place in club history when he replaced Shaw in the team's first regular-season game and passed for 4 touchdowns and ran for another to lead the Vikings to a 37-13 upset of the Bears. Jim Marshall, a fixture at defensive end for two decades, also came to the team that first year in a trade.

The Vikings strengthened their roster over the next several seasons, adding center Mick Tingelhoff, fullback Bill Brown, wide receiver Paul Flatley (the 1963 rookie of the year), and defensive end Carl Eller. In 1964, the Vikings finished 8-5-1.

Jim Finks, a successful general manager in the Canadian Football League, was hired as Minnesota's general manager in 1964. The 1965 Vikings were expected to contend, instead they finished .500, and the Vikings slid to 4-9-1 in 1966. Moreover, Van Brocklin and Tarkenton hardly were speaking to each other. Tarkenton suggested either he or the Dutchman should ply his trade elsewhere. Finks accommodated both. He accepted Van Brocklin's resignation and traded Tarkenton to the Giants. This trade and other moves helped Minnesota get a great group of rookies—defensive tackle Alan Page, wide receiver Gene Washington, running back Clint Jones, and defensive backs Bobby Bryant and Bob Grim. They joined a corps of veterans that now featured Gary Larsen, the fourth member of the Purple People Eaters defensive line, linebacker Lonnie Warwick, and running back Dave Osborn.

Finks's hiring of Bud Grant, a Minnesota multi-sport legend, was the catalyst the team needed. Grant had been a winning coach at Winnipeg in the Canadian League. Charismatic Joe Kapp, Grant's Blue Bombers' quarterback, came south of the border in 1967. The team was 3-8-3, but upset the eventual champion Packers. Ron Yary, a giant offensive tackle from USC, was the Vikings' first draft choice in 1968—and first overall selection. Paul Krause, ideally suited for "center field" in the team's deep-zone defense, came in a trade. Kapp pushed the team to the NFL Central Division championship. With Osborn injured, Brown shouldered the running game and produced 805 yards and 14 touchdowns. Baltimore defeated Minnesota in the Vikings' first postseason game.

The 1969 Vikings breezed through the regular season (12-2) with Kapp providing inspirational quarterbacking. Minnesota won two home playoff games and took on the Chiefs in Super Bowl IV. The Vikings were two-touchdown favorites, but they fell victim to Kansas City 23-7. It was Kapp's swan song—in 1970 he sat out the early part of the season in a contract dispute and was sold to the Patriots.

Tarkenton returned from New York in a 1972 trade. John Gilliam led the team in receiving, but the Vikings still managed to finish only .500. Helped by the addition of versatile number-one draft pick Chuck Foreman (a running back also adept at catching passes) in 1973, Minnesota regained stride with a 12-2 record in the regular season and playoff victories at home and in Dallas. Again the Vikings came up short in Super Bowl VIII, losing to Miami 24-7. Finks resigned the next spring, and Mike Lynn became general manager.

Fred McNeill, Matt Blair, Steve Riley, and Sam McCullum joined the team as 1974 draftees and the Vikings won the NFC, but for the third time they lost in the Super Bowl, bowing this time to Pittsburgh 16-6 in IX. Minnesota went 12-2 in 1975, but lost their first playoff game on the Cowboys' desperation pass in the final minute. Grant had the Vikings back in Super Bowl XI after the 1976 season, but they were beaten for the fourth time, this time 32-14 by the Oakland Raiders.

They came back in 1977 and, even with Tarkenton sidelined by an injury, defeated the Rams in the Los Angeles Coliseum in the first round of the playoffs. But Minnesota lost to Dallas for the NFC championship. The next two seasons resulted in first-game postseason losses. During this time, Page was waived, Eller lost his starting job, and Tarkenton, Tingelhoff, and Marshall retired.

Grant had a losing season in 1979, got back to the postseason in 1980, experienced another losing season in 1981, and retired after the 1983 season in favor of Les Steckel. The team also vacated "the Met" (Metropolitan Stadium) for the controlled climate of the Hubert H. Humphrey Metrodome in 1982. Steckel split his first four games in 1984, but then the losses mounted. Grant was back for a year in 1985 and then turned over the reins to Jerry Burns—a Minnesota assistant since 1968. Burns produced winning teams through 1989, getting to the NFC Championship Game in 1987. Burns retired after 6-10 and 8-8 seasons in 1990-91, and Dennis Green was hired to replace him in 1992.

It was during the 1989 season that Minnesota sent a covey of players and draft choices to Dallas in exchange for running back Herschel Walker. Walker, not really suited for the Vikings' offense, was in Philadelphia by 1992.

Under Green, Terry Allen emerged as a runner, tight end Steve Jordan became the club's career receptions leader, and Cris Carter emerged as a record-setting wide receiver. After up-and-down results with quarterbacks Rich Gannon, Wade Wilson, and Jim McMahon, the Vikings acquired Warren Moon in 1994 to lead the team. Waiting with open arms were wide receivers Jake Reed, Qadry Ismail, and Carter.

Green led the team to the playoffs in his first three seasons, but was unable to win a postseason game. In 1995, Minnesota was 8-8. The team entered the 1996 season without highly respected defensive coordinator Tony Dungy, who was hired as head coach of the Tampa Bay Buccaneers. Moon was injured much of the season, but Brad Johnson took over and showed he was ready to become the Vikings' regular quarterback. Once more, Green took Minnesota to the playoffs, and, once more, they lost their opening game. Moon signed with Seattle as a free agent following the 1996 season.

After Johnson was injured late the following season, backup Randall Cunningham led the Vikings to a stunning come-from-behind, wild-card victory over the Giants. Minnesota scored 10 points in the last 90 seconds to turn a 22-13 deficit into a 23-22 victory. The season ended with a loss at San Francisco in the divisional playoffs the following week. During the team's 9-7 regular season, defensive tackle John Randle solidified his reputation as one of the best in the game, and Robert Smith fulfilled his promise by staying healthy and running for 1,266 yards while averaging 5.5 yards per carry.

In the offseason, ownership was stabilized when Texan Red McCombs purchased the team after best-selling author Tom Clancy's attempt failed. With Johnson hurt again much of 1998, Cunningham stepped in to pass for 3,704 yards and 34 touchdowns while leading the team to an NFL-best 15-1 record.

Rookie receiver Randy Moss made an already potent offense even more explosive, and the Vikings set a new NFL record with 556 points. Moss was a near-unanimous choice as NFL rookie of the year. Kicker Gary Anderson was perfect during the regular season, connecting on each of his field-goal and extra-point attempts.

The Vikings easily dispatched the Cardinals 41-21 in the divisional playoffs. But after jumping to a 20-7 first-half lead over the Falcons in the NFC Championship Game, Minnesota faltered. Anderson missed a field-goal attempt late in the fourth quarter, opening the door for Atlanta's tying touchdown drive. The Falcons won 30-27 in overtime.

VIKINGS RECORD 1961-1998

YEAR	WON	LOST	TIED	PCT.	FIN	PF	PA
1961	3	11	0	.214	7	285	407
1962	2	11	1	.154	6	254	410
1963	5	8	1	.385	4t	309	390
1964	8	5	1	.615	2t	355	296
1965	7	7	0	.500	5	383	403
1966	4	9	1	.308	6t	292	304
1967	3	8	3	.273	4	233	294
1968a	8	6	0	.571	1	282	242
1969b	12	2	0	.857	1	379	133
1970c	12	2	0	.857	1	335	143
1971c	11	3	0	.786	1	245	139
1972	7	7	0	.500	3	301	252
1973d	12	2	0	.857	1	296	168
1974d	10	4	0	.714	1	310	195
1975c	12	2	0	.857	1	377	180
1976d	11	2	1	.821	1	305	176
1977e	9	5	0	.643	1	231	227
1978c	8	7	1	.531	1	294	306
1979	7	9	0	.438	3	259	337
1980c	9	7	0	.563	1	317	308
1981	7	9	0	.438	4	325	369
1982f	5	4	0	.556	4	187	198
1983	8	8	0	.500	4	316	348
1984	3	13	0	.188	5	276	484
1985	7	9	0	.438	3	346	359
1986	9	7	0	.563	2	398	273
1987g	8	7	0	.533	2	336	335
1988h	11	5	0	.688	2	406	233
1989c	10	6	0	.625	1	351	275
1990	6	10	0	.375	5	351	326
1991	8	8	0	.500	3	301	306
1992c	11	5	0	.688	1	374	249
1993i	9	7	0	.563	2	277	290
1994c	10	6	0	.625	1	356	314
1995	8	8	0	.500	4	412	385
1996i	9	7	0	.562	2	298	315

YEAR	WON	LOST	TIED	PCT.	FIN	PF	PA
1997h	9	7	0	.563	4	354	359
1998e	15	1	0	.938	1	556	296
38 Years	313	244	9	.561	—	12,262	11,024

a NFL Central Division Champion; 0-1 in Playoffs
b NFL Champion; 2-1 in Playoffs
c NFC Central Division Champion; 0-1 in Playoffs
d NFC Champion; 2-1 in Playoffs
e NFC Central Division Champion; 1-1 in Playoffs
f NFC Qualifier for Playoffs; 1-1 in Playoffs
g NFC Wild Card Qualifier for Playoffs; 2-1 in Playoffs
h NFC Wild Card Qualifier for Playoffs; 1-1 in Playoffs
i NFC Wild Card Qualifier for Playoffs; 0-1 in Playoffs

COACHING HISTORY
(328-265-9)

1961-66	Norm Van Brocklin	29-51-4
1967-83	Bud Grant	161-99-5
1984	Les Steckel	3-13-0
1985	Bud Grant	7-9-0
1986-91	Jerry Burns	55-46-0
1992-98	Dennis Green	73-47-0

New Orleans Saints

With 29-year-old John Mecom, Jr., as president, the New Orleans Saints came marching into the NFL in 1967 as the second expansion franchise in two years.

The Saints selected Paul Hornung, left unprotected by the Packers in the expansion draft, and signed former Louisiana State great Jim Taylor, who had played out his Packers option. If coach Tom Fears thought he could reconstruct Green Bay's big-back attack, he was thwarted when Hornung retired before training camp. Taylor led the Saints in rushing (390 yards) that first year and then also retired.

As with other expansion teams of the sixties, the Saints got little value from the expansion draft. Only Billy Kilmer, Steve Stonebreaker, and Dave Whitsell had any lasting effect on the team. Bears defensive end Doug Atkins was signed before the season started and gave the Saints three quality seasons before retiring. In the last round of the collegiate draft, the Saints got Dan Abramowicz, who led the team in receiving in each of its first five years.

Things began well when John Gilliam took the opening kickoff of the Saints' first game 94 yards for a touchdown against the Rams. Los Angeles eventually won that game, and the Saints won just three times that season. After only a win and a tie in the first seven games of 1970, Fears was out of a job. J.D. Roberts took control, and his first game was memorable. Tom Dempsey provided the victory with an NFL-record 63-yard field goal on the final play against Detroit.

In 1971, Kilmer was traded to the Redskins, and New Orleans drafted Mississippi All-America Archie Manning, who had an outstanding pro career. In 1975, the team moved into the Louisiana Superdome, and Hank Stram, out of coaching for two seasons, was hired to lead the Saints in 1976.

In that year's college draft, New Orleans took a pair of running backs with their first two choices—Chuck Muncie, who had seriously contended for the Heisman Trophy at California, and Tony Galbreath, a durable fullback from Missouri. Muncie was fast and elusive, Galbreath was powerful and a good receiver. One or the other led the team in rushing from 1976-79 with Muncie peaking at 1,198 in 1979. The pair, however, left New Orleans by 1981; Muncie was traded to San Diego in mid-1980, and Galbreath was traded to the Vikings in 1981.

Wes Chandler, a quick and sure-handed receiver, was the Saints' first draft choice in 1978. He contributed 35 catches as a rookie and gained 993 yards on punt and kickoff returns. In 1979, he led the team in receptions (65 for 1,069 yards) and was selected to play in the Pro Bowl. More important, it was the Saints' first non-losing season. Coach Dick Nolan took them to 8-8 and second place in the NFC West. Much was expected in 1980, but the Saints plummeted to 1-15, and assistant Dick Stanfel coached the team for the last four games.

O.A. (Bum) Phillips was hired as head coach in 1981. Perhaps envisioning another Earl Campbell, he drafted South Carolina Heisman Trophy winner George Rogers as the first overall choice. Rogers became NFL rushing champion as a rookie and broke Ottis Anderson's first-year record with 1,674 yards. Manning played his last full season with the franchise, after never experiencing a winning season (he was traded in 1982). The Saints were 4-12 under Phillips in 1981, 4-5 in the strike year, and only kicker Morten Andersen was a draftee of any consequence. Phillips coached the team to 8-8 in 1983, only the second non-losing season in history. The next year, the team slid back to 7-9 and Phillips resigned after a 4-8 start in 1985. He was replaced by his son Wade.

Tom Benson assumed ownership of the franchise in 1985 and Jim Finks, with a proven track record in the Canadian League and with the Vikings and Bears, became president and general manager. He hired Jim Mora, who had been a winner in the USFL as head coach. Mora elevated the Saints' record to 7-9. Runner Rueben Mayes was the rookie of the year after gaining 1,353 yards.

In 1987, 20 years after the franchise was founded, Mora produced a winner. He got help from Pro Bowl linebackers Rickey Jackson and Vaughan Johnson and by bringing in linebacker Sam Mills from the USFL. He aided the offense with another USFL player—quarterback Bobby Hebert, a Louisiana native from Baton Rouge. Dalton Hilliard took some of the running burden from Mayes, and the Saints were 12-3. The only sour note was a 44-10 loss to Minnesota in the 1987 NFC Wild Card Game, their first playoff game.

New Orleans qualified for the postseason three more times (including its first division title in 1991), but the Saints made early exits each time. After posting 7-9 marks in 1994 and 1995, Mora retired in frustration midway through the 1996 season. Interim coach Rick Venturi failed to turn things around, as the team finished with its worst record since 1980. Following the season, former Bears coach Mike Ditka was named to coach the Saints.

Ditka's first team won four of six games in a late-season stretch to finish 6-10 despite coping with an unsettled quarterback situation. Heath Shuler, Billy Joe Hobert, Danny Wuerffel, and Doug Nussmeier all played the position.

Although the Saints finished 6-10 again in 1998, there were encouraging signs, such as a 3-0 start to the season and a 22-3 rout of the Cowboys in December. William Roaf provided a stable anchor at the key left tackle spot, and 272-pound rookie tight end Cam Cleeland got rave reviews for his steady play. Tackle La'Roi Glover and end Joe Johnson helped give the Saints a defensive front line that caused problems for opposing offensive coordinators.

SAINTS RECORD 1967-1998

YEAR	WON	LOST	TIED	PCT.	FIN	PF	PA
1967	3	11	0	.214	4	233	379
1968	4	9	1	.308	3	246	327
1969	5	9	0	.357	3	311	393
1970	2	11	1	.154	4	172	347
1971	4	8	2	.333	4	266	347
1972	2	11	1	.179	4	215	361
1973	5	9	0	.357	3	163	312
1974	5	9	0	.357	3	166	263
1975	2	12	0	.143	4	165	360
1976	4	10	0	.286	4	253	346
1977	3	11	0	.214	4	232	336
1978	7	9	0	.438	3	281	298
1979	8	8	0	.500	2	370	360
1980	1	15	0	.063	4	291	487
1981	4	12	0	.250	4	207	378
1982	4	5	0	.444	10	129	160
1983	8	8	0	.500	3	319	337
1984	7	9	0	.438	3	298	361
1985	5	11	0	.313	3	294	401
1986	7	9	0	.438	4	288	287
1987a	12	3	0	.800	2	422	283
1988	10	6	0	.625	3	312	283
1989	9	7	0	.563	3	386	301
1990a	8	8	0	.500	2	274	275
1991b	11	5	0	.688	1	341	211
1992a	12	4	0	.750	2	330	202
1993	8	8	0	.500	2	317	343
1994	7	9	0	.438	2	348	407
1995	7	9	0	.438	5	319	348
1996	3	13	0	.188	5	229	339
1997	6	10	0	.375	4	237	327
1998	6	10	0	.375	3	305	359
32 Years	189	288	5	.397	—	8,719	10,518

a NFC Wild Card Qualifier for Playoffs; 0-1 in Playoffs
b NFC Western Division Champion; 0-1 in Playoffs

COACHING HISTORY
(189-288-5)

1967-70	Tom Fears*	13-34-2
1970-72	J.D. Roberts	7-25-3
1973-75	John North**	11-23-0
1975	Ernie Hefferle	1-7-0
1976-77	Hank Stram	7-21-0
1978-80	Dick Nolan***	15-29-0
1980	Dick Stanfel	1-3-0
1981-85	O.A. (Bum) Phillips#	27-42-0
1985	Wade Phillips	1-3-0
1986-96	Jim Mora##	93-78-0
1996	Rick Venturi	1-7-0
1997-98	Mike Ditka	12-20-0

* Released after seven games in 1970
** Released after six games in 1975
*** Released after 12 games in 1980
# Resigned after 12 games in 1985
Resigned after 8 games in 1996

New York Giants

The NFL started primarily as a collection of midwestern town teams. Nothing would help give it credibility as much as a franchise in New York City. In 1925, Tim Mara paid $500 for the New York franchise, stating that exclusive rights to anything in New York was worth the price.

The New York Football Giants, like their more-established baseball namesakes, began play in the Polo Grounds. The team struggled at the turnstiles at first, but the season was saved when the Chicago Bears, featuring the legendary Red Grange, came to town on December 6. A crowd estimated at more than 70,000 saw a game generally credited with giving the NFL a big boost.

When Mara objected to Grange and his manager forming a team to play in Yankee Stadium, the Galloping Ghost and C.C. Pyle started a rival league—the first American Football League—in 1926, and Giants coach Bob Folwell also jumped to the new circuit. Joe Alexander, a physician and center, coached the 1926 Giants, then gave up coaching in 1927 in favor of Earl Potteiger, who led the team to a championship. The Giants yielded only 20 points while compiling an 11-1-1 record. Cal Hubbard, the only man enshrined in both the Pro Football Hall of Fame and the Baseball Hall of Fame, teamed with Steve Owen to form a nearly impregnable line, and no opponent scored more than seven points.

Potteiger was gone after posting a 4-7-2 record in 1928. Benny Friedman, the league's best passer, played for Detroit. Mara wanted him, but couldn't swing a deal. So, he bought the entire franchise and brought Friedman, a group of other players, and coach LeRoy Andrews to New York for 1929. Unofficially, Friedman passed for more than 1,000 yards—a milestone for the time, and the Giants went 13-1-1. They lost a midseason game to the Packers that cost them the NFL title. The season was notable in that attendance, spurred by the exciting play of Friedman, averaged 25,000.

Owen became the Giants' coach in 1931 on a handshake. (He never had a contract in the 23 years he was their head coach.) Rookie Mel Hein began his 15-year career at center for the team, but the Giants were nothing special until 1933 when they lost the championship game to the Bears, a 23-21 thriller that saw six lead changes.

After winning the East again, the Giants were in a rematch in the 1934 championship game against the undefeated Bears. The Polo Grounds field was a sheet of ice at kickoff. Team captain Ray Flaherty suggested to Owen that basketball shoes might offer better traction. Equipment man Abe Cohen was dispatched to Manhattan College. He returned at halftime with several bags of basketball shoes. The shoes helped the Giants rally from a 13-3 deficit and defeat the Bears 30-13 in the "Sneakers Game." The Giants were in the title game again in 1935, but they were out-slogged by the Lions in rain, mud, and snow.

Only a season-ending loss prevented the Giants from winning their division again in 1936. On Wellington Mara's suggestion, the Giants drafted Tuffy Leemans, who led the league in rushing. In 1937, the Giants made wholesale changes. There were 17 rookies on the 25-man roster, including storied names such as backs Ward Cuff and Hank Soar and ends Jim Lee Howell and Jim Poole. The rookies of 1937 were veterans in 1938 as the Giants won the championship with a 23-17 victory over Green Bay. Hein was chosen the first official NFL Most Valuable Player.

The duel with the Redskins continued in 1939. For the fourth consecutive year, the Giants met the Redskins in the final game with the division title on the line. The Giants won 9-7 when the referee ruled a late Redskins' field-goal attempt was wide. Many people at the Polo Grounds—including players from both teams—thought it was good. A week later, the Giants were shut out by the Packers in Milwaukee.

The Giants went to the title game in 1994, but weakened the following year. In 1946, the squad rebounded to get into the championship game. Frankie Filchock, traded by the Redskins, put life in the passing game. Drama surrounded the title game. Gamblers approached Merle Hapes to fix the outcome of the game. He refused the bribe and he related the incident to Filchock, though neither reported the attempt. Hapes was suspended. Filchock, with all eyes on him, gave his all in a losing effort. After the game, Filchock was suspended, too.

To replace Filchock, the Giants traded for Paul Governali in 1947. But an 0-7-2 start doomed the season, and the next two seasons were noteworthy only in that the draft rights to Charlie Conerly were obtained from Washington, and Emlen Tunnell was given a successful tryout.

With the NFL-AAFC merger in 1950, Owen got three ball-hawking defensive backs from the AAFC Yankees—Tom Landry, Otto Schnellbacher, and Harmon Rowe—as well as a great defensive tackle in Arnie Weinmeister. This enabled Owen to devise his Umbrella Defense; the four defensive backs—the three AAFC newcomers and Tunnell—were the umbrella's spokes. That, and the running of Eddie Price and Gene (Choo-Choo) Roberts, allowed the team to defeat the Cleveland Browns twice and force a divisional playoff game. The Browns won the teams' third meeting and went on to take the championship.

After the 1953 season, Jim Lee Howell assumed control. A fine coach and administrator, he brought in Vince Lombardi to handle the offense and made Landry a defensive player-coach. Howell was fond of saying that with those two, all he did was "blow up the footballs."

Frank Gifford, who played everywhere under Owen, found a home at left halfback in 1954. Kyle Rote ran a little and caught a lot. A slow start hampered the team in 1955, but a strong finish set the stage for a title run in 1956. Gifford had a truly golden year and earned MVP honors. Mel Triplett and Alex Webster helped run the ball, and Jimmy Patton and Rosey Grier aided the defense.

The big defensive addition, though, was rookie linebacker Sam Huff. With the others keeping the blockers away from him, Huff made numerous tackles. The tailor-made defense earned him much acclaim and a niche in Canton, Ohio. Andy Robustelli and Dick Modzelewski, half of the front four, came in trades. Using sneakers once again, the Giants romped over the Bears 47-7 in the championship game. Essentially, this same squad challenged for the championship for the next three years. In 1958, they defeated the Browns in a playoff, but then lost to Baltimore in the famous overtime game. The 1959 season saw a rematch with the Colts and another defeat for the Giants.

Allie Sherman took over following Howell's retirement after the 1960 season. During his first three seasons Sherman had the team in the title game, but couldn't win. He replaced Conerly with Y.A. Tittle, who found new life after coming from the 49ers. After 1963, five non-winning seasons followed, and when New York lost all of its preseason games in 1969, Sherman was fired. Alex Webster became head coach. The change worked somewhat, especially when Fran Tarkenton was effective at quarterback and running back Ron Johnson produced, but Webster couldn't win consistently and resigned in frustration after the 1973 season.

In 1974, for the first time, the franchise went outside the Giants' family to find a head coach. Bill Arnsparger, from Don Shula's staff in Miami, lasted 2½ seasons, John McVay the same, and Ray Perkins four years.

General manager George Young joined the Giants in 1979 and began drafting and acquiring quality young players. When Bill Parcells took over as coach in 1983, a nucleus was there. By 1984, quarterback Phil Simms, linebackers Lawrence Taylor and Harry Carson, runner Joe Morris, and defensive end Leonard Marshall were helping the Giants win. Tight end Mark Bavaro arrived in 1985. In 1986, linebacker Carl Banks and nose tackle Jim Burt made the defense even tougher, and Simms and Morris took care of the offense that produced a lopsided 39-20 victory over Denver in Super Bowl XXI.

In 1990, with Jeff Hostetler at quarterback for the injured Simms and O.J. Anderson a solid runner, they returned to the Super Bowl and defeated Buffalo 20-19. Parcells then retired. Ray Handley succeeded Parcells, but soon he was gone in favor of Dan Reeves, who came in 1993, the last season for Simms and Taylor.

Reeves had the team in contention in his first two years, albeit with a different cast—Dave Brown for Simms, Howard Cross for Bavaro, Rodney Hampton as the chief runner. Reeves, who wanted more control, feuded with Young. After the 1996 season, Reeves was let go, and former Arizona Cardinals offensive coordinator Jim Fassel was named the Giants' coach.

Fassel quickly became the darling of New York by taking the Giants to the top of the NFC East in 1997 for the first time since 1990. Quarterback Danny Kanell guided the offense. Fullback Charles Way was a path-clearing blocker and the leading rusher with 698 yards. But the key to the Giants' success was a superior defense led by Pro Bowl selections Michael Strahan and Jessie Armstead.

New York went undefeated within the division (only a 7-7 tie with Washington marred their divisional record), and finished 10-5-1. But with a wild-card game against Minnesota seemingly safe in hand, the Giants lost 23-22. Hopes were high for 1998, but talented cornerback Jason Sehorn suffered a knee injury during the preseason and was lost for the year. After a season-opening victory over Washington, the Giants lost seven of nine games. Kent Graham replaced Kanell at quarterback, and the Giants closed with a four-game winning streak to finish 8-8. The team's wild-card hopes were alive until the season's final day.

GIANTS RECORD 1925-1998

YEAR	WON	LOST	TIED	PCT.	FIN	PF	PA
1925	8	4	0	.667	4t	122	67
1926	8	4	1	.667	6t	147	51
1927a	11	1	1	.917	1	197	20
1928	4	7	2	.364	6	79	136
1929	13	1	1	.929	2	312	86
1930	13	4	0	.765	2	308	98
1931	7	6	1	.538	5	164	100
1932	4	6	2	.400	5	93	113
1933b	11	3	0	.786	1	244	101
1934c	8	5	0	.615	1	147	107
1935b	9	3	0	.750	1	180	96
1936	5	6	1	.455	3	115	163
1937	6	3	2	.667	2	128	109
1938c	8	2	1	.800	1	194	79
1939b	9	1	1	.900	1	168	85
1940	6	4	1	.600	3	131	133
1941b	8	3	0	.727	1	238	114
1942	5	5	1	.500	3	155	139
1943d	6	3	1	.667	2	197	170

YEAR	WON	LOST	TIED	PCT.	FIN	PF	PA
1944b	8	1	1	.889	1	206	75
1945	3	6	1	.333	3t	179	198
1946b	7	3	1	.700	1	236	162
1947	2	8	2	.200	5	190	309
1948	4	8	0	.333	3t	297	388
1949	6	6	0	.500	3	287	298
1950e	10	2	0	.833	2	268	150
1951	9	2	1	.818	2	254	161
1952	7	5	0	.583	2t	234	231
1953	3	9	0	.250	5	179	277
1954	7	5	0	.583	3	293	184
1955	6	5	1	.545	3	267	223
1956c	8	3	1	.727	1	264	197
1957	7	5	0	.583	2	254	211
1958f	9	3	0	.750	1	246	183
1959f	10	2	0	.833	1	284	170
1960	6	4	2	.600	3	271	261
1961f	10	3	1	.769	1	368	220
1962f	12	2	0	.857	1	398	283
1963f	11	3	0	.786	1	448	280
1964	2	10	2	.167	7	241	399
1965	7	7	0	.500	2t	270	338
1966	1	12	1	.077	8	263	501
1967	7	7	0	.500	2	369	379
1968	7	7	0	.500	2	294	325
1969	6	8	0	.429	2	264	298
1970	9	5	0	.643	2	301	270
1971	4	10	0	.286	5	228	362
1972	8	6	0	.571	3	331	247
1973	2	11	1	.179	5	226	362
1974	2	12	0	.143	5	195	299
1975	5	9	0	.357	4	216	306
1976	3	11	0	.214	5	170	250
1977	5	9	0	.357	5	181	265
1978	6	10	0	.375	5	264	298
1979	6	10	0	.375	4	237	323
1980	4	12	0	.250	5	249	425
1981g	9	7	0	.563	3	295	257
1982	4	5	0	.444	10	164	160
1983	3	12	1	.219	5	267	347
1984g	9	7	0	.563	2	299	301
1985g	10	6	0	.625	2	399	283
1986h	14	2	0	.875	1	371	236
1987	6	9	0	.400	5	280	312
1988	10	6	0	.625	2	359	304
1989i	12	4	0	.750	1	348	252
1990h	13	3	0	.813	1	335	211
1991	8	8	0	.500	4	281	297
1992	6	10	0	.375	4	306	367
1993g	11	5	0	.688	2	288	205
1994	9	7	0	.563	2	279	305
1995	5	11	0	.313	4	290	340
1996	6	10	0	.375	5	242	297
1997i	10	5	1	.656	1	307	265
1998	8	8	0	.500	3	287	309
74 Years	531	437	33	.547	—	18,728	17,463

a NFL Champion; No Playoffs
b NFL Eastern Division Champion; 0-1 in Playoffs
c NFL Champion; 1-0 in Playoffs
d NFL Eastern Division Runner-up; 0-1 in Playoffs
e NFL American Conference Runner-up; 0-1 in Playoffs
f NFL Eastern Conference Champion; 0-1 in Playoffs
g NFC Wild Card Qualifier for Playoffs; 1-1 in Playoffs
h Super Bowl Champion; 3-0 in Playoffs
i NFC Eastern Division Champion; 0-1 in Playoffs

COACHING HISTORY
(545-456-33)

1925	Bob Folwell	8-4-0
1926	Joe Alexander	8-4-1
1927-28	Earl Potteiger	15-8-3
1929-30	LeRoy Andrews*	24-5-1
1930	Benny Friedman	2-0-0
1931-53	Steve Owen	155-108-17
1954-60	Jim Lee Howell	55-29-4
1961-68	Allie Sherman	57-54-4
1969-73	Alex Webster	29-40-1
1974-76	Bill Arnsparger**	7-28-0
1976-78	John McVay	14-23-0
1979-82	Ray Perkins	24-35-0
1983-90	Bill Parcells	85-52-1
1991-92	Ray Handley	14-18-0
1993-96	Dan Reeves	32-34-0
1997-98	Jim Fassel	18-14-1

* Released after 15 games in 1930
** Released after seven games in 1976

Philadelphia Eagles

The Philadelphia Eagles, who joined the NFL in 1933, took their name from the symbol for the National Recovery Administration, an integral part of the New Deal.

Although not a continuation of the Frankford Yellow Jackets (an NFL team from a section of Philadelphia), the Eagles filled a void created in 1931 when Frankford disbanded. The franchise was purchased for $2,500 plus payment of 25 percent of Frankford's debts by Bert Bell and Lud Wray, former Penn teammates.

Wray coached the team, with little success, for three seasons. Bell, who became sole owner, tried his hand for the next five (1936-1940), with even less. It was during that time that Bell proposed the college player draft that gave teams the opportunity to choose star players in reverse order of team standings. Bell made Heisman Trophy winner Jay Berwanger of the University of Chicago the first selection of the draft, then traded him to the Chicago Bears.

The early Eagles had very few quality players. Much of the early teams consisted of Penn, Temple, and Villanova players putting in a year or two before getting on with their life's work. The 1940 team, despite winning only one game, was an exception to the rule. Heisman Trophy winner Davey O'Brien and his former Texas Christian teammate Don Looney formed a great pass-catch combination. Looney led the league in receiving as a rookie, while O'Brien set an NFL single-game record with 60 pass attempts in the 1940 season finale.

Before the start of the 1941 season, ownership passed to Alexis Thompson in a complicated series of deals that saw Thompson first purchase the Pittsburgh Pirates, Bell take on former Pittsburgh owner Art Rooney as a partner, and then Bell and Rooney swap franchises with Thompson. A Yale man through and through, Thompson tapped Earle (Greasy) Neale from Yale's staff to lead the team. Neale installed the T-formation upon his arrival in Philadelphia. To direct the offense, he had quarterback Tommy Thompson.

By 1943, the shortage of players brought on by World War II forced the merger of the Eagles and Steelers rosters. The press was fond of calling the combined teams the "Steagles." The merger lasted only a year and the combine went 5-4-1—the first time the Eagles could claim a winning record. End Larry Cabrelli, tackles Vic Sears and Al Wistert, and running backs Bosh Pritchard and Ernie Steele gave the team credibility.

The Eagles had a breakthrough year in 1944—7-1-2, good for second in the East. The big difference was Steve Van Buren. A blocker at LSU who seldom carried the ball until his senior year, Van Buren had not earned a star reputation in college, but he soon became the outstanding pro runner of his time. In 1945, Van Buren led the NFL in scoring and rushing as the Eagles again placed second in the East. Linemen Frank (Bucko) Kilroy and Vic Lindskog played important roles as Philadelphia was finally building a winner.

After another second-place finish in 1946, the Eagles won the East in 1947, beating the Steelers in a playoff game. Key to the team's success was the Eagles Defense. It looked like a seven-man line, but the ends dropped off to cover passes. Alex Wojciechowicz, acquired from Detroit, was a master at the technique. The franchise played in the next three championship games. It lost 28-21 to the Cardinals on an ice rink-like surface in Chicago in 1947, but won 7-0 at home in the snow in 1948 and won 14-0 in Los Angeles in the rain and mud in 1949. The Eagles are the only team in league history to post back-to-back championship-game shutouts. Van Buren became the second man in NFL history to surpass 1,000 yards rushing in 1947 and repeated the feat in 1949.

In 1949, Thompson sold the team to a group headed by Jim Clark. Van Buren was hurt part of the 1950 season, and much of the Eagles' core was aging. The low point came in a 7-3 loss to the Giants. After the game, in front of players and media, Clark told Neale, "Greasy, you need more than a field goal to win in the NFL." Neale and a few of his fiercely loyal players had to be restrained. Essentially, it was the end of the championship reign. Neale was gone at the end of the season. Van Buren's career was all but over, and Thompson had thrown his last pass.

In 1951, Bo McMillin was hired to coach the team, to be followed by Wayne Millner and Jim Trimble. By this time only a few players from the glory days remained. Pete Pihos was an effective receiver, and Chuck Bednarik was an all-pro linebacker. Young defensive end Norm (Wildman) Willey perfected the sack before the term was in use.

After three second-place finishes, Trimble went 4-7-1 in 1955 and was replaced. Likable, always-available Hugh Devore coached for two losing seasons, but his last, 1957, produced a remarkable draft— the first four choices, Clarence Peaks, Billy Ray Barnes, Sonny Jurgensen, and Tommy McDonald composed the starting backfield in the early 1960s. Barnes, described as "a tumbleweed in a wind storm," finished among the league's leading rushers and made the Pro Bowl in each of his first three seasons.

Lawrence T. (Buck) Shaw, the 49ers' original coach, was lured away from the Air Force Academy to coach the Eagles in 1958. Veteran quarterback Norm Van Brocklin came from the Rams. The Dutchman had great receivers in Bobby Walston, Pete Retzlaff, and McDonald. In 1959, the Eagles tied the Browns for second place.

Alex Karras is fond of saying, "No one played quarterback like the Dutchman in 1960." Van Brocklin was first or second in most passing categories and won MVP honors. But the catalyst was the 35-year-old Bednarik, who played center and linebacker and averaged 58 minutes a game over a stretch of key games that decided the division. Rookie Ted Dean sparked the running game, Tom Brookshier and Don Burroughs steadied a young secondary, and rookie Maxie Baughan played linebacker like a veteran. The Eagles handed Vince Lombardi his only championship game loss as they won 17-13. Coach Shaw and quarterback Van Brocklin left winners, both retiring after the game.

Van Brocklin had been all but promised the head coaching job, but assistant Nick Skorich was given the position. Sonny Jurgensen stepped in at quarterback and had a record-setting year to carry the team to a second-place finish, but after two dismal years in 1962-63 Skorich was fired. The team was sold to builder Jerry Wolman late in 1963. He brought in Joe Kuharich as coach and general manager. Fans, never patient, were irked in 1967 when Wolman gave Kuharich a 15-year contract after two losing years out of three. Kuharich lasted through 1968, when new owner Leonard Tose fired him, although he agreed to pay him for the duration of his contract.

Jerry Williams took over in 1969, but was replaced by assistant Eddie Khayat after three lopsided losses in 1971. Like Williams, Khayat had few quality players, although receivers Harold Carmichael, Harold Jackson, and Ben Hawkins were exceptions. Khayat was replaced by Mike McCormack for 1973, but another losing season in 1975 cost McCormack his job, and UCLA coach Dick Vermeil took charge. After two rebuilding years, the energetic Vermeil got the Eagles to the 1978 playoffs.

The Eagles won the NFC East in 1980 and advanced to the Super Bowl for the first time. Halfback Wilbert Montgomery was on fire in the postseason, churning for 268 yards and 3 touchdowns in 2 playoff games at Veterans Stadium. Ron Jaworski established himself at quarterback, and the 6-foot 7-inch Carmichael was an inviting target. However, the team went flat in Super Bowl XV and lost 27-10 to the Raiders.

Again in 1981, the Eagles made the playoffs, but were shocked by the Giants 27-21 in the first game. The 1982 strike had a disastrous effect on the team—they went 3-6. Vermeil, citing "coaching burnout," resigned after the season.

Long-time defensive coordinator Marion Campbell succeeded him. A seven-game losing streak ruined Campbell's first year, although Mike Quick led the NFL in receiving yards. Campbell never found the key to winning and after Norman Braman bought the team from Tose in 1985, Campbell was released. Buddy Ryan, defensive coordinator of the Super Bowl-champion Bears, was hired as coach.

Ryan immediately cleaned house and brought in younger players, but one Eagles veteran that he kept was sack specialist Reggie White. Ryan built a defense modeled after his famed "46" defensive unit in Chicago. Jaworski and Randall Cunningham shared playing time, but the team still lost in Ryan's first year. Cunningham was the starter in 1987. Ryan openly sided with his veteran players during the strike. Whatever he gained in team loyalty after the strike was settled, he lost all three strike games. The Eagles finished 7-8.

The next year the Eagles went 10-6. Cunningham was hailed in some corners as the ultimate weapon. His pure athleticism resulted in 3,808 passing yards and a team-leading 624 yards rushing. Tight end Keith Jackson and running back Keith Byars caught 81 and 72 passes, respectively. But in fog-shrouded Soldier Field, the Bears slipped by the Eagles in the postseason.

Ryan got the team into the playoffs again in 1989, but again lost the first game. In 1990, Cunningham rushed for 942 yards, the second-highest total ever for a quarterback. But Ryan had become controversial and confrontational with management. After Ryan's third consecutive one-game playoff exit, Braman had enough.

Rich Kotite, whom Ryan had hired in 1990 to help with

the offense, was given the job. Cunningham suffered a season-ending knee injury in the first quarter of the first game in 1991. Using four quarterbacks and a remarkable performance by their defense, the Eagles still went 10-6, but missed the playoffs.

Displaying splendid form, Cunningham was back in 1992. The defense, which tragically lost tackle Jerome Brown in an auto accident before the season, remained solid with defensive linemen White and Clyde Simmons, linebacker Seth Joyner, and defensive back Eric Allen. Free agent Herschel Walker rushed for 1,070 yards, and young receiver Fred Barnett had his first 1,000-yard season. In the playoffs, the Eagles scored 26 points in the fourth quarter to defeat the New Orleans Saints, but they couldn't get past the Dallas Cowboys in the divisional playoffs.

Free agency took away key players in 1993, and Cunningham was lost early to injury. The team finished 8-8. Braman sold the team to Jeffery Lurie in 1994, who initially kept Kotite but fired him after the season and hired 49ers defensive coordinator Ray Rhodes.

A student of the game and a motivator, Rhodes took the team to a 10-6 mark—much better than expected. He played Rodney Peete instead of Randall Cunningham at quarterback. In the playoffs, his team shocked the Detroit Lions 58-37. Unfortunately, the magic ran out against the Cowboys in Dallas the next week.

The workaholic Rhodes returned the club to the playoffs in 1996, for one game only. Peete was knocked out for the season early, but Ty Detmer came off the bench to produce a strong passing attack. The Eagles fell to 6-9-1 in 1997. Neither Peete nor Detmer solidified the quarterback position. However, young Bobby Hoying played well toward the end of the year. Workhorse running back Ricky Watters got his usual 1,000 yards (1,110) but left after the season via the free-agent route. Charlie Garner gained 547 yards while averaging a solid 4.7 yards per carry. Irving Fryar, a 14-year veteran, caught 83 passes and earned a trip to the Pro Bowl, as did linebacker William Thomas.

The 1998 season began with a 38-0 home loss to Seattle, and things did not get any better from there. Philadelphia averaged only 10 points per game and finished 3-13. Rhodes, the 1995 coach of the year, was fired the day after the season ended (he eventually took over as Green Bay's head coach). Rhodes's replacement, Andy Reid, became the twentieth head coach in franchise history. Reid joined the Eagles after spending the last seven seasons as an assistant coach with the Packers.

EAGLES RECORD 1933-1998

YEAR	WON	LOST	TIED	PCT.	FIN	PF	PA
1933	3	5	1	.375	4	77	158
1934	4	7	0	.364	3t	127	85
1935	2	9	0	.182	5	60	179
1936	1	11	0	.083	5	51	206
1937	2	8	1	.200	5	86	177
1938	5	6	0	.455	4	154	164
1939	1	9	1	.100	4t	105	200
1940	1	10	0	.091	5	111	211
1941	2	8	1	.200	4	119	218
1942	2	9	0	.182	5	134	239
Phil-Pitt (does not count in totals)							
1943	5	4	1	.556	3	225	230
Philadelphia Eagles							
1944	7	1	2	.875	2	267	131
1945	7	3	0	.700	2	272	133
1946	6	5	0	.545	2	231	220
1947a	8	4	0	.667	1	308	242
1948b	9	2	1	.818	1	376	156
1949b	11	1	0	.917	1	364	134
1950	6	6	0	.500	3t	254	141
1951	4	8	0	.333	5	234	264
1952	7	5	0	.583	2t	252	271
1953	7	4	1	.636	2	352	215
1954	7	4	1	.636	2	284	230
1955	4	7	1	.364	4t	248	231
1956	3	8	1	.273	6	143	215
1957	4	8	0	.333	5	173	230
1958	2	9	1	.182	5t	235	306
1959	7	5	0	.583	2t	268	278
1960b	10	2	0	.833	1	321	246
1961	10	4	0	.714	2	361	297
1962	3	10	1	.231	7	282	356
1963	2	10	2	.167	7	242	381
1964	6	8	0	.429	3	312	313
1965	5	9	0	.357	5t	363	359
1966	9	5	0	.643	2t	326	340
1967	6	7	1	.462	2	351	409
1968	2	12	0	.143	4	202	351
1969	4	9	1	.308	4	279	377
1970	3	10	1	.231	4	241	332
1971	6	7	1	.462	3	221	302
1972	2	11	1	.179	5	145	352
1973	5	8	1	.393	3	310	393
1974	7	7	0	.500	4	242	217
1975	4	10	0	.286	5	225	302
1976	4	10	0	.286	4	165	286
1977	5	9	0	.357	4	220	207
1978c	9	7	0	.563	2	270	250
1979d	11	5	0	.688	2	339	282
1980e	12	4	0	.750	1	384	222
1981c	10	6	0	.625	2	368	221
1982	3	6	0	.333	13	191	195
1983	5	11	0	.313	4	233	322
1984	6	9	1	.406	5	278	320
1985	7	9	0	.438	4	286	310
1986	5	10	1	.344	4	256	312
1987	7	8	0	.467	4	337	380
1988f	10	6	0	.625	1	379	319
1989c	11	5	0	.688	2	342	274
1990c	10	6	0	.625	2	396	299
1991	10	6	0	.625	3	285	244
1992d	11	5	0	.688	2	354	245
1993	8	8	0	.500	3	293	315
1994	7	9	0	.438	4	308	308
1995d	10	6	0	.625	2	318	338
1996c	10	6	0	.625	2	363	341
1997	6	9	1	.406	3	317	372
1998	3	13	0	.188	5	161	344
65 Years	385	464	24	.455	—	16,551	17,267

a NFL Eastern Division Champion; 1-1 in Playoffs
b NFL Champion; 1-0 in Playoffs
c NFC Wild Card Qualifier for Playoffs; 0-1 in Playoffs
d NFC Wild Card Qualifier for Playoffs; 1-1 in Playoffs
e NFC Champion; 2-1 in Playoffs
f NFC Eastern Division Champion; 0-1 in Playoffs

COACHING HISTORY
PHILADELPHIA 1933-1942, 1944-1998; PHIL-PITT 1943
(400-479-25)

1933-35	Lud Wray	9-21-1
1936-40	Bert Bell	10-44-2
1941-50	Earle (Greasy) Neale*	66-44-2
1951	Alvin (Bo) McMillin**	2-0-0
1951	Wayne Millner	2-8-0
1952-55	Jim Trimble	25-20-3
1956-57	Hugh Devore	7-16-1
1958-60	Lawrence (Buck) Shaw	20-16-1
1961-63	Nick Skorich	15-24-3
1964-68	Joe Kuharich	28-41-1
1969-71	Jerry Williams***	7-22-2
1971-72	Ed Khayat	8-15-2
1973-75	Mike McCormack	16-25-1
1976-82	Dick Vermeil	57-51-0
1983-85	Marion Campbell#	17-29-1
1985	Fred Bruney	1-0-0
1986-90	Buddy Ryan	43-38-1
1991-94	Rich Kotite	37-29-0
1995-98	Ray Rhodes	30-36-1

* Co-coach with Walt Kiesling in Philadelphia-Pittsburgh merger in 1943
** Retired after two games in 1951
*** Released after three games in 1971
# Released after 15 games in 1985

St. Louis Rams

In Cleveland, Los Angeles, or St. Louis, the Rams have been one of the glamour franchises of the NFL. Numerous players in the Pro Football Hall of Fame have Rams connections, including Bob Waterfield, Elroy (Crazylegs) Hirsch, Norm Van Brocklin, Tom Fears, David (Deacon) Jones, and Merlin Olsen.

The franchise was born in 1937 as the Cleveland Rams, who were coached that year and part of the next by Hugo Bezdek—the only man ever to be an NFL head coach and a major league baseball manager (Pittsburgh Pirates, 1917-19). Dan Reeves and Fred Levy bought the franchise in 1941 from original owner Homer Marshman. Reeves bought the team with the intent to move it to the West Coast, but World War II delayed his plan. With the war causing a manpower shortage, the Rams suspended operations in 1943. The team came back in 1944 and went 4-6.

Adam Walsh was named head coach in 1945. He switched to the T-formation with rookie Bob Waterfield at quarterback. In one game, Waterfield connected with Jim Benton 10 times for 303 yards, setting an NFL record that stood for 40 years. Waterfield, husband of Hollywood film star Jane Russell, was league MVP as he led his team to an NFL championship. Despite the winning season, Reeves lost money and felt the time was right to take the Rams west and make the National Football League truly national.

In 1946 Reeves signed former UCLA stars Kenny Washington and Woody Strode, the NFL's first black players since 1933. Waterfield and Benton led the league in their departments, and the Rams, who competed with the AAFC's Dons for Los Angeles's allegiance, posted another winning record in their first year on the coast.

Linebacker Don Paul joined tackle Dick Huffman to anchor the defense in 1949. Norm Van Brocklin added depth at quarterback. Waterfield and Van Brocklin each had their supporters among the fans and the players. Waterfield started, but Van Brocklin played long enough and well enough to feed a controversy that would remain unsettled until Waterfield retired in 1952. Hirsch was in his first year with the team, and Fears led the NFL in receiving for the second consecutive season. Los Angeles went 8-2-2 and won the West, but they were shut out in the championship game by the Eagles. Bickering led to coach Clark Shaughnessy's firing before the 1950 season.

Joe Stydahar became head coach with Hampton Pool as his assistant. Heisman Trophy winner Glenn (Mr. Outside) Davis of Army, Deacon Dan Towler, Bob Boyd, and Woodley Lewis all came in as rookies. Van Brocklin, playing more than Waterfield, led the league in passing, and Fears won his third consecutive receiving title with 84 catches for 1,116 yards. Fears set an NFL record with 18 receptions in a game (the record still stands). The 9-3 Rams set 22 league scoring records, but couldn't win the championship. Back in their former hometown, the Browns won the NFL title on Lou Groza's late field goal.

In 1951, Van Brocklin passed for 554 yards in one game, Fears and Hirsch were hauling in bombs from both quarterbacks, and the Bull Elephant Backfield (Towler, Tank Younger, and Dick Hoerner, all in the 225-pound range) ran roughshod over opponents. The Rams amassed 5,506 total yards in a 12-game schedule. This time, the Rams defeated the Browns for the title 24-17.

Los Angeles tied Detroit for the West title in 1952 but lost a playoff game. The big news was the Rams' trade of 11 players for California linebacker Les Richter. Dick (Night Train) Lane, with only junior college and service football experience, walked into the Rams' office and asked for a tryout. He made the team and set a still-standing NFL single-season record with 14 interceptions.

Pool replaced Stydahar after one game in 1952, but resigned after 1954. Reeves hired little-known Sid Gillman, a college coach at Cincinnati, who got the team to the championship game in his first year, though the Rams again lost to the Browns. A new quarterback controversy arose. Gillman and Van Brocklin were incompatible, and young Bill Wade showed that he warranted playing time. Gillman struggled for three years before taking the team to an 8-4 record in 1958, the year he sent Van Brocklin to the Eagles.

Rams general manager Pete Rozelle made a trade in 1959 almost as big as the Richter deal—nine players for Cardinals all-pro Ollie Matson. The coaches were undecided where to play him—flanker, fullback, halfback, split end, or defensive back, and the future Hall of Fame inductee never really found a niche with the Rams. After going 2-10 in 1959, Gillman was gone. He would resurface with the Los Angeles Chargers of the new AFL in 1960.

Cat-quick Jon Arnett, deep receiver Del Shofner, quarterback Frank Ryan, linebacker Larry Morris, tight end Jim (Red) Phillips, and star runner Dick Bass all developed in the Gillman era. Nearly all would be traded. Defensive end Andy Robustelli was traded to the Giants so he could be closer to his Connecticut home. While the team kept losing, there were sideshows to grab the fans' attention, including the never-ending quarterback controversies. After a Wade-Zeke Bratkowski controversy, there was Bratkowski-Roman Gabriel, which gave way to Gabriel-Bill Munson.

The Rams weren't without good players. Gene Brito was a quality defensive end. Jack Pardee was a far-ranging linebacker. Eddie Meador and Will Sherman were excellent defensive backs. The Fearsome Foursome defensive line was in place by 1963—David (Deacon) Jones, Merlin Olsen, Rosey Grier, and Lamar Lundy. George Allen came from the Bears to coach the team in 1966. He traded for Eagles linebacker Maxie Baughan and defensive back Irv Cross. Roger Brown, from the Lions, took Grier's spot in the front four, and Jack Snow, Tom Mack, Charlie Cowan, and Les Josephson came aboard.

Allen went 11-1-2 in 1967, his second season, and advanced to a Western Conference playoff game with the Packers, but lost. Allen successfully melded a strong defense with a conservative offense, a far cry from the point-a-minute bombers of the early 1950s. After the 1968 season, another winner, Allen was fired by Reeves, who said that it wasn't "fun" winning with Allen. The players backed Allen and loudly clamored for his return until Reeves relented. Allen had two more winning seasons, then Reeves refused to renew his contract and Allen was gone.

Successful UCLA coach Tommy Prothro replaced Allen. Reeves died shortly afterwards. Jack Youngblood, a number-one draft choice, was a rookie in 1971 and split playing time with Deacon Jones. Prothro won in his first season, was a game under .500 in 1972, then was dismissed by new owner Carroll Rosenbloom. Rosenbloom, the Colts' owner, swapped franchises with Robert Irsay, who purchased the Rams in 1972 from the Reeves's estate.

Rosenbloom brought Chuck Knox in as coach. He traded Gabriel to Philadelphia and dealt for John Hadl, who had fine receivers in Snow and Harold Jackson, but the Rams relied heavily on steady runners Lawrence McCutcheon and Jim Bertelsen. Los Angeles went 12-2, best in club history, but lost a playoff game to Dallas. Knox coached four more years, winning division titles every season. But the Rams could not make it to the Super Bowl, as Hadl gave way to James Harris, who gave way to Pat Haden. Rosenbloom was impatient, and Knox resigned to take over the Buffalo Bills. With much fanfare, George Allen was brought back for the 1978 season, but Rosenbloom fired him after two preseason losses.

Respected defensive coordinator Ray Malavasi led the team to the playoffs, but then tragedy struck. In April of 1979, Rosenbloom drowned in Florida. His widow Georgia became majority owner.

In 1979, Haden was hurt and the team struggled to a 9-7 record, but still won its seventh consecutive division title. Moreover, the Rams made it to Super Bowl XIV, and gave heavily favored Pittsburgh a scare before falling 31-19. A new quarterback controversy marred the 1980 season: young Vince Ferragamo or Haden? Ferragamo fired 30 touchdown passes to lead the team to a wild-card game, another loss to Dallas. The Rams had losing seasons in 1981 and 1982, and Malavasi was fired. Ferragamo, seeking more money, fled to Canada. Jeff Rutledge, who took over for an injured Haden, was hurt. Dan Pastorini took a turn. Bert Jones was signed, but no one seemed to work out.

Former USC coach John Robinson was hired and drafted Eric Dickerson in 1983 after trading running back Wendell Tyler. Dickerson was the main runner in Robinson's one-back attack. He blazed to an NFL rookie-record 1,808 yards rushing, and Ferragamo, back from Canada, passed for 3,276 yards. The Rams beat Dallas in a wild-card game before losing big to Washington. Jeff Kemp, who with his father Jack became pro football's first father-son quarterbacks, replaced Ferragamo, who got hurt in 1984. Dickerson set the NFL rushing record with 2,105 yards, and the team again suffered a wild-card loss.

Another fine season, another new quarterback—Dieter Brock of the CFL—and another disappointing postseason followed in 1985, though Dickerson set a playoff record with 248 yards rushing in a victory over Dallas. With stars Jim Everett, Henry Ellard, Jackie Slater, and Nolan Cromwell, Robinson would continue to coach through 1991. Knox came back in 1992, and, by 1993, he had Jerome Bettis spearheading his rushing attack. However, Knox couldn't find a winning combination, and, after his contract expired at the end of 1994, he was released.

Owner Frontiere announced that the team planned to move to St. Louis for the 1995 season. After 50 years, the first NFL team to go west came back east—at least part way. Rich Brooks, after a Rose Bowl appearance with Oregon, was named to head the team in its first year in St. Louis. Under Brooks, the team embraced a more wide-open attack, and Bettis, the line-smashing runner, virtually disappeared from the offense. Chris Miller, a first-rate passer, suffered a series of concussions that ended his season prematurely.

Tony Banks, a rookie, became the starting quarterback in 1996. An obvious talent, he was prone to rookie mistakes. Several other rookies became regulars, and they, too, had typical growing pains. The team went 6-10, and Brooks was fired. Former Eagles coach Dick Vermeil was hired as the twentieth head coach in the history of the franchise.

Vermeil, back on the sidelines for the first time in 15 years, struggled to a 5-11 finish in his first year, a season that included an eight-game losing streak. Banks was streaky at quarterback, but Orlando Pace, the top pick of the draft, became a force at tackle. Running back Amp Lee led the Rams with 61 receptions, and was the team's MVP. Cornerback Ryan McNeil led the NFL with 9 interceptions.

The Rams were disappointing again in 1998, winning only four games. Banks remained inconsistent. At times he was spelled by backup Steve Bono. Banks's quarterback rating of 68.6 was near the NFC's bottom, and the team signed Redskins free agent Trent Green to take over at quarterback in 1999.

RAMS RECORD 1937-1998

YEAR	WON	LOST	TIED	PCT.	FIN	PF	PA
Cleveland Rams							
1937	1	10	0	.091	5	75	207
1938	4	7	0	.364	4	131	215
1939	5	5	1	.500	4	195	164
1940	4	6	1	.400	4	171	191
1941	2	9	0	.182	5	116	244
1942	5	6	0	.455	3	150	207
1943 The Rams suspended operations							
1944	4	6	0	.400	4	188	224
1945a	9	1	0	.900	1	244	136
Los Angeles Rams							
1946	6	4	1	.600	2	277	257
1947	6	6	0	.500	4	259	214
1948	6	5	1	.545	3	327	269
1949b	8	2	2	.800	1	360	239
1950c	9	3	0	.750	1	466	309
1951a	8	4	0	.667	1	392	261
1952d	9	3	0	.750	2	349	234
1953	8	3	1	.727	3	366	236
1954	6	5	1	.545	4	314	285
1955e	8	3	1	.727	1	260	231
1956	4	8	0	.333	5t	291	307
1957	6	6	0	.500	4	307	278
1958	8	4	0	.667	2t	344	278
1959	2	10	0	.167	6	242	315
1960	4	7	1	.364	6	265	297
1961	4	10	0	.286	6	263	333
1962	1	12	1	.077	7	220	334
1963	5	9	0	.357	6	210	350
1964	5	7	2	.417	5	283	339
1965	4	10	0	.286	7	269	328
1966	8	6	0	.571	3	289	212
1967f	11	1	2	.917	1	398	196
1968	10	3	1	.769	2	312	200
1969f	11	3	0	.786	1	320	243
1970	9	4	1	.692	2	325	202
1971	8	5	1	.615	2	313	260
1972	6	7	1	.464	3	291	286
1973g	12	2	0	.857	1	388	178
1974h	10	4	0	.714	1	263	181
1975h	12	2	0	.857	1	312	135
1976h	10	3	1	.750	1	351	190
1977g	10	4	0	.714	1	302	146
1978h	12	4	0	.750	1	316	245
1979i	9	7	0	.563	1	323	309
1980j	11	5	0	.688	2	424	289
1981	6	10	0	.375	3	303	351

YEAR	WON	LOST	TIED	PCT.	FIN	PF	PA
1982	2	7	0	.222	14	200	250
1983k	9	7	0	.563	2	361	344
1984j	10	6	0	.625	2	346	316
1985h	11	5	0	.688	1	340	277
1986j	10	6	0	.625	2	309	267
1987	6	9	0	.400	3	317	361
1988j	10	6	0	.625	2	407	293
1989l	11	5	0	.688	2	426	344
1990	5	11	0	.313	3	345	412
1991	3	13	0	.188	4	234	390
1992	6	10	0	.375	4	313	383
1993	5	11	0	.313	4	221	367
1994	4	12	0	.250	4	286	365
St. Louis Rams							
1995	7	9	0	.438	3	309	418
1996	6	10	0	.375	3	303	409
1997	5	11	0	.313	5	299	359
1998	4	12	0	.250	5	285	378
61 Years	420	391	20	.517	—	17,865	16,838

a NFL Champion; 1-0 in Playoffs
b NFL Western Division Champion; 0-1 in Playoffs
c NFL National Conference Champion; 1-1 in Playoffs
d NFL National Conference Runner-up; 0-1 in Playoffs
e NFL Western Conference Champion; 0-1 in Playoffs
f NFL Coastal Division Champion; 0-1 in Playoffs
g NFC Western Division Champion; 0-1 in Playoffs
h NFC Western Division Champion; 1-1 in Playoffs
i NFC Champion; 2-1 in Playoffs
j NFC Wild Card Qualifier for Playoffs; 0-1 in Playoffs
k NFC Wild Card Qualifier for Playoffs; 1-1 in Playoffs
l NFC Wild Card Qualifier for Playoffs; 2-1 in Playoffs

COACHING HISTORY
CLEVELAND 1937-45, LOS ANGELES 1946-1994, ST. LOUIS 1995-98 (433-411-20)

1937-38	Hugo Bezdek*	1-13-0
1938	Art Lewis	4-4-0
1939-42	Earl (Dutch) Clark	16-26-2
1944	Aldo (Buff) Donelli	4-6-0
1945-46	Adam Walsh	16-5-1
1947	Bob Snyder	6-6-0
1948-49	Clark Shaughnessy	14-8-3
1950-52	Joe Stydahar**	19-9-0
1952-54	Hampton Pool	23-11-2
1955-59	Sid Gillman	28-32-1
1960-62	Bob Waterfield***	9-24-1
1962-65	Harland Svare	14-31-3
1966-70	George Allen	49-19-4
1971-72	Tommy Prothro	14-12-2
1973-77	Chuck Knox	57-20-1
1978-82	Ray Malavasi	43-36-0
1983-91	John Robinson	79-74-0
1992-94	Chuck Knox	15-33-0
1995-96	Rich Brooks	13-19-0
1997-98	Dick Vermeil	9-23-0

* Released after three games in 1938
** Resigned after one game in 1952
*** Resigned after eight games in 1962

San Francisco 49ers

Frustrated in attempts to obtain an NFL franchise, brothers Vic and Tony Morabito became charter members of the newly formed All-America Football Conference in 1946. The 49ers had a decidedly Bay Area flavor from the start; former Stanford stars quarterback Frankie Albert, fullback Norm Standlee, and guard Bruno Banducci were members of the charter team, which was coached by ex-Santa Clara coach Buck Shaw.

This group, augmented by jet-propelled runner Joe Perry, was the second-best team in the league, but couldn't wrest a championship away from Cleveland in the four years the league existed. San Francisco was merged into the expanded NFL for the 1950 season. Two standout rookies from Minnesota, future Pro Football Hall of Fame tackle Leo (the Lion) Nomellini and kicker-receiver Gordy Soltau, joined the team. The next year two more San Francisco legends signed on—unflappable quarterback Y.A. Tittle, drafted from defunct Baltimore, and blistering broken-field runner Hugh (the King) McElhenny.

Solid performers such as league-leading receiver Billy Wilson, thumping fullback John Henry Johnson, and giant tackle Bob St. Clair were added to the roster about this time, but still the team couldn't get past the Rams or Lions to take a Western Division title.

In 1954, Perry became the first NFL player to rush for more than 1,000 yards in two consecutive seasons, but the 49ers could not reach the playoffs under Buck Shaw or Red Strader. Frankie Albert, the 49ers' former quarterback, took over in 1956. In 1957, the 49ers finished in a tie with the Lions for first in the West, but in the division playoff, after leading Detroit 24-7 at the half, the 49ers collapsed and lost 31-27.

Added to the disappointment of 1957 was the death of co-owner Tony Morabito at a home game with the Bears. Behind 17-7 when they got the sad news, the 49ers rallied to win 21-17. The game was the key in tying for the division championship. Runner J.D. Smith, basketball-player-turned-receiver R.C. Owens, and linebacker Matt Hazeltine were new and vital parts of this team. Owens's leaping ability served him well on the "Alley Oop," a high, floating pass from Tittle that Owens caught by outjumping the defensive backs.

Albert stepped down after a .500 season in 1958, and Red Hickey replaced him. Stanford quarterback John Brodie, receiver Bernie Casey, defensive tackle Charlie Krueger, and kick returner Abe Woodson improved the team, and Hickey experimented with the Shotgun formation. The 49ers took the NFL by storm. They won four of their first five games—including 49-0 over the Lions and 35-0 over the Rams. The firepower was taken out of the Shotgun in the sixth game when crafty Bears defensive coordinator George Allen put middle linebacker Bill George up in the line, on the center's nose, instead of a yard or two behind scrimmage as normal. George's immediate pressure on the center disrupted the offensive scheme, and the Bears won 31-0. The 49ers won only three more games.

By 1970, Jimmy Johnson, a Hall of Fame defensive back, and Gene Washington, a reliable receiver and still another Stanford product, emerged as stars. Sensational kick returner and defensive back Bruce Taylor was rookie of the year, and the 49ers' 10-3-1 record was their best in years. San Francisco's trip to the Super Bowl was thwarted when they were beaten in the NFC Championship Game by the Cowboys. They again won the division in 1971, only to lose again to Dallas. The 1972 season was even more frustrating. San Francisco won the division, but lost in the first round, again to the Cowboys on a miracle finish engineered by Dallas quarterback Roger Staubach.

In March, 1977, the team was sold to Edward DeBartolo, Jr. After a succession of short-term coaches, Bill Walsh was brought in for 1979 and took over as coach and general manager. The won-lost record didn't improve immediately, but the passing game ranked first in the NFC. Rookie Joe Montana was on the team, but Steve DeBerg was the man under center. By the end of 1980, Montana had the controls. Fullback Earl Cooper and sure-handed wide receiver Dwight Clark were Montana's primary targets, along with wide receiver Freddie Solomon and running back Paul Hofer.

Things fell into place in 1981. San Francisco got off to a 1-2 start, but won 12 of the next 13. Behind a line anchored by Randy Cross and Keith Fahnhorst, Montana executed Walsh's complex offense to near perfection. Pass-rushing defensive end Fred Dean from the Chargers and savvy linebacker Jack (Hacksaw) Reynolds from the Rams, coupled with a young secondary featuring three rookies—Ronnie Lott, Eric Wright, and Carlton Williamson—formed a stubborn defense. In the NFC Championship Game, Montana found a leaping Clark for a deciding last-minute touchdown to defeat Dallas 28-27. It will be known forever simply as "The Catch." Playing in their first Super Bowl, the 49ers scored early and held off a Bengals' rally to win 26-21.

In strike-shortened 1982, the wheels fell off, but in 1983 the addition of Wendell Tyler and Roger Craig gave Montana a running game that had been missing. The 49ers were back in the playoffs but lost the NFC Championship Game to the Redskins. They were near-perfect in 1984, winning a record-setting 15 regular-season games, and capped the season by winning Super Bowl XIX over Miami 38-16 in Stanford Stadium.

San Francisco reached the playoffs in 1985, but as a wild card. The defense faltered. Craig became the first NFL player to gain 1,000 yards rushing and 1,000 yards receiving in the same season. Jerry Rice, a first-round draft choice from Mississippi Valley State, caught 49 passes as a rookie.

Montana missed significant playing time in 1986 with a back injury, and veteran backup Jeff Kemp filled in admirably. Rice, Craig, and Clark kept the passing game airborne. Lott and Tim McKyer keyed the defense. The 49ers again reached the playoffs, but were defeated by the Giants in the first round. Rice set a record with 23 touchdown catches to garner MVP honors in 1987, and the team, which went 13-2, was a Super Bowl favorite. But the Vikings shocked the 49ers in the playoffs, and Montana was benched during the game in favor of Steve Young, creating doubts about Montana's future.

A 6-5 start in 1988 intensified those doubts, but Montana registered four late-season victories to reach the playoffs, then led the 49ers to one-sided playoff victories over Minnesota and Chicago. In Super Bowl XXIII, sparked by Jerry Rice, San Francisco scored two fourth-quarter touchdowns to defeat the Bengals. Montana's 10-yard touchdown pass to John Taylor with 34 seconds left won it 20-16. After the game, Walsh retired with his third Vince Lombardi Trophy.

Defensive coordinator George Seifert was chosen to fill Walsh's shoes for 1989. The defense improved, Montana was at his best statistically, and Rice and Taylor were more than any defense could handle. Craig again rushed for 1,000 yards. Tom Rathman proved valuable as a blocker and receiver. Montana was brilliant in Super Bowl XXIV as the 49ers buried Denver 55-10.

The 49ers sought an unprecedented third consecutive Super Bowl title in 1990, but it didn't happen. They went 14-2 during the regular season, but an injury to Craig stymied the running game. In the NFC Championship Game, the Giants edged San Francisco 15-13, scoring all their points on field goals, the last as time ran out.

Montana missed the entire 1991 season due to an elbow injury, and Young also was knocked out with a sprained knee. Steve Bono was inserted as the starting quarterback and led the 49ers to five victories in six games, but the 49ers were third in their four-team division and failed to qualify for the playoffs for the first time since 1982. Montana played only in the 1992 season finale—he completed 15 of 21 passes in a victory over Detroit. Young won his second consecutive passing title and Ricky Watters ran for 1,013 yards. But the 49ers lost the NFC title game to Dallas. In a gut-wrenching move for 49ers' fans, Montana was traded to Kansas City. In 1993, San Francisco lost the NFC Championship Game for the third time in four years. Rice was the NFL's offensive player of the year.

Things changed dramatically in 1994. The franchise signed key free agents Ken Norton, Jr., Deion Sanders, and Gary Plummer. Safety Merton Hanks made huge plays in the secondary. Fullback William Floyd and defensive tackle Dana Stubblefield, both rookies, contributed greatly. After eliminating the Cowboys 38-28 in the NFC title game, San Francisco beat San Diego 49-26 in Super Bowl XXIX.

Sanders and Watters left the team via free agency in 1995. With Floyd injured, the 49ers' running game was more Young scrambling than anything else. In the stretch drive, the team could not pull off enough big plays to get back to the Super Bowl. The 49ers were eliminated by Green Bay in the divisional playoffs.

Bill Walsh was rehired to be an offensive consultant in 1996. The team still lacked a reliable running game, and Young was injured much of the season. The 49ers still finished 12-4, but placed second to Carolina in the West. After beating Philadelphia in the wild-card round, the 49ers lost to Green Bay on muddy Lambeau field. Young missed most of the game with injured ribs. Ten days later, Seifert resigned as the 49ers' coach. Steve Mariucci, the University of California head coach, was named to replace him.

Mariucci's career got off to an inauspicious start when Young and Rice both were injured in a season-opening loss at Tampa Bay. Young would return two weeks later, but Rice missed most of the season. However, the defense—led by defensive tackle Dana Stubblefield, who had 15 sacks and was named the NFL's defensive player of the year—rose to the occasion. The loss of Rice was tempered by the emergence of young wide receivers Terrell Owens and J.J. Stokes, who had 60 and 58 receptions, respectively. Garrison Hearst gained 1,019 yards and gave the 49ers their most potent rushing threat since Watters's departure. San Francisco won 11 consecutive games after its opening loss, finished 13-3, and advanced to the NFC title game for the seventh time in 10 seasons, losing 23-10 to Green Bay.

In 1998, Young had still another banner year: 4,170 yards, 36 touchdown passes, and a rating of 101.1. Rice returned to catch 82 passes, but continuity was interrupted in midseason when executives Carmen Policy and Dwight Clark left to become involved with the new Cleveland Browns.

The 49ers finished second to the Falcons in the NFC West, but earned a playoff berth with a 12-4 record. In a classic heavyweight battle, the 49ers beat the Packers in an NFC Wild Card Game 30-27 on a 25-yard touchdown pass from Young to Owens with three seconds left. One week later, the 49ers lost Hearst to a broken leg on the first play of a divisional-playoff game against Atlanta and eventually lost the game to the Falcons 20-18.

49ERS RECORD 1946-1998

YEAR	WON	LOST	TIED	PCT.	FIN	PF	PA
1946	9	5	0	.643	2	307	189
1947	8	4	2	.667	2	327	264
1948	12	2	0	.857	2	495	248
1949a	9	3	0	.750	2	416	227
1950	3	9	0	.250	5t	213	300
1951	7	4	1	.636	2t	255	205
1952	7	5	0	.583	3	285	221
1953	9	3	0	.750	2	372	237
1954	7	4	1	.636	3	313	251
1955	4	8	0	.333	5	216	298
1956	5	6	1	.455	3	233	284
1957b	8	4	0	.667	2	260	264
1958	6	6	0	.500	4	257	324
1959	7	5	0	.583	3t	255	237
1960	7	5	0	.583	2t	208	205
1961	7	6	1	.538	5	346	272
1962	6	8	0	.429	5	282	331
1963	2	12	0	.143	7	198	391
1964	4	10	0	.286	7	236	330
1965	7	6	1	.538	4	421	402
1966	6	6	2	.500	4	320	325
1967	7	7	0	.500	3	273	337
1968	7	6	1	.538	3	303	310
1969	4	8	2	.333	4	277	319
1970c	10	3	1	.769	1	352	267
1971c	9	5	0	.643	1	300	216
1972d	8	5	1	.607	1	353	249
1973	5	9	0	.357	4	262	319
1974	6	8	0	.429	2	226	236
1975	5	9	0	.357	2	255	286
1976	8	6	0	.571	2	270	190
1977	5	9	0	.357	3	220	260
1978	2	14	0	.125	4	219	350
1979	2	14	0	.125	4	308	416
1980	6	10	0	.375	3	320	415
1981e	13	3	0	.813	1	357	250
1982	3	6	0	.333	11	209	206
1983c	10	6	0	.625	1	432	293
1984e	15	1	0	.938	1	475	227
1985f	10	6	0	.625	2	411	263
1986d	10	5	1	.656	1	374	247
1987d	13	2	0	.867	1	459	253
1988e	10	6	0	.625	1	369	294
1989e	14	2	0	.875	1	442	253
1990c	14	2	0	.875	1	353	239
1991	10	6	0	.625	3	393	239
1992c	14	2	0	.875	1	431	236
1993c	10	6	0	.625	1	473	295
1994e	13	3	0	.813	1	505	296
1995d	11	5	0	.688	1	457	258
1996g	12	4	0	.750	2	398	257
1997c	13	3	0	.813	1	375	265
1998g	12	4	0	.750	2	479	328
4 AAFC	38	14	2	.722		1,545	928
49 NFL	393	292	13	.572	—	16,000	13,746
53 Pro	431	306	15	.583	—	17,943	14,674

a AAFC Runner-up; 1-1 in Playoffs
b NFL Western Conference Runner-up; 0-1 in Playoffs
c NFC Western Division Champion; 1-1 in Playoffs
d NFC Western Division Champion; 0-1 in Playoffs
e Super Bowl Champion; 3-0 in Playoffs
f Wild Card Qualifier for Playoffs; 0-1 in Playoffs
g Wild Card Qualifier for Playoffs; 1-1 in Playoffs

COACHING HISTORY
(417-307-13)

1950-54	Lawrence (Buck) Shaw	33-25-2
1955	Norman (Red) Strader	4-8-0
1956-58	Frankie Albert	19-17-1
1959-63	Howard (Red) Hickey*	27-27-1
1963-67	Jack Christiansen	26-38-3
1968-75	Dick Nolan	56-56-5
1976	Monte Clark	8-6-0
1977	Ken Meyer	5-9-0
1978	Pete McCulley**	1-8-0
1978	Fred O'Connor	1-6-0
1979-88	Bill Walsh	102-63-1
1989-96	George Seifert	108-35-0
1997-98	Steve Mariucci	27-9-0

* Resigned after three games in 1963
** Released after nine games in 1978

Tampa Bay Buccaneers

The Tampa Bay Buccaneers lost every game in their first year, 1976, and went on to lose another 12 before finally winning, but they became a playoff team in their fourth season. In 1979, they advanced to the NFC Championship Game (a 9-0 loss to the Rams kept them from Super Bowl XIV), and they returned to the playoffs in 1981 and 1982.

Tampa Bay was awarded the NFL's twenty-seventh franchise on April 24, 1974. Part of the deal was to enlarge Tampa Stadium to a capacity of 72,000, and the stadium later hosted Super Bowls XVIII and XXV.

John McKay, winner of four national collegiate titles at USC, signed on to coach the Buccaneers. The team played its first game in Tampa Stadium on August 21, 1976. A crowd of 67,466 saw the Buccaneers drop a 28-21 preseason decision to Miami. The Buccaneers opened the regular season on the road at Houston and lost 20-0.

Playing the 1976 season as an AFC West team (Tampa Bay shifted to the NFC Central the following season), the Buccaneers went 0-14. They had few stars in that dismal season. An exception was Tampa Bay's first draft choice, Lee Roy Selmon of Oklahoma. The tenacious defensive end played at a level that earned him induction into the Pro Football Hall of Fame in 1995.

On offense the first year, Steve Spurrier took most of the snaps from center, but couldn't do much. The Buccaneers scored as many as 20 points only once, while giving up 28 or more in half their games. When asked about his team's execution, the glib McKay replied, "I'm in favor of it."

After 26 consecutive league defeats, the Buccaneers surprised the Saints by winning 33-14 on December 12, 1977. Defenders Mike Washington, Richard Wood, and Greg Johnson all scored touchdowns on interception returns to provide the points necessary for victory. Tampa Bay closed out the season by defeating the Cardinals 17-7 at home. Gary Huff teamed with Morris Owens on touchdown passes of 61 and 62 yards.

Tampa Bay began the 1979 season on fire, winning its first five games. The Buccaneers cooled somewhat, but after dropping three consecutive games and in danger of missing the playoffs, the defense shut out the Chiefs on the last day of the season. Neil O'Donoghue's 19-yard, fourth-quarter field goal was the only score of the day.

Quarterback Doug Williams, who took his lumps as a rookie in 1978, matured nicely in 1979. He relied on former USC tailback Ricky Bell, a 1,000-yard runner, and tight end Jimmie Giles. In the 24-17 playoff victory over the Eagles, Bell carried the load. The ill-fated back (he would die from a rare muscle disease before reaching 30) carried a playoff-record 38 times for 142 yards.

Offense deserted the Buccaneers in the NFC Championship Game. Williams and backup Mike Rae each were 2 of 13 passing, and Bell ran for only 59 yards on 20 carries. Although the defense gave up only 3 field goals, that was enough to spell defeat.

Tampa Bay was down in 1980, but back in 1981, winning the Central Division. In the playoffs, the Buccaneers were shut out by the Cowboys 38-0. They would make the playoffs in 1982, but then the lean years returned. McKay resigned after the 1984 season and was succeeded by Leeman Bennett, who won four games in two seasons. Ray Perkins took a turn in 1987 and lasted 13 games into the 1990 season. Richard Williamson, an assistant, finished the season and coached in 1991 without success. Sam Wyche was given the task of righting the Bucs' ship in 1992, but after the 1995 season, he, too, was out.

The Buccaneers have had quality players—just not enough at any one time. All-purpose running back James Wilder, linebacker Hugh Green, wide receiver Mark Carrier, and heavy-hitting linebacker Hardy Nickerson all made the Pro Bowl, some more than once. In 1995 the NFL approved the transfer of ownership from the estate of original owner Hugh Culverhouse to businessman Malcolm Glazer.

Tony Dungy, a low-key but no-nonsense defensive coordinator, was selected to lead Tampa Bay in 1996. The Buccaneers were strong defensively, but punchless on offense. Quarterback Trent Dilfer began showing signs of developing into a major talent. Errict Rhett gave the Buccaneers a strong running game. The team started 1-9, but provided hope for the future by winning five of seven games down the stretch.

The Buccaneers picked up from there in 1997, and began the season with five consecutive victories. Rookie running back Warrick Dunn gave a new dimension to an offense badly in need of pizzazz—he darted and dashed for 978 yards and caught a team-high 39 passes for 462 yards. If Dunn was lightning, fullback Mike Alstott was thunder, both blocking and running (665 yards). Dilfer was efficient, passing for 21 touchdowns while throwing only 11 interceptions.

The defense was stingy. Warren Sapp and Chidi Ahanotu constituted a force up front, and people began to notice just how good middle linebacker Hardy Nickerson really was. The Buccaneers finished 10-6, then defeated the Lions 20-10 in a wild-card game at home. The season ended with a 21-7 loss to Green Bay in the divisional playoffs.

Tampa Bay entered 1998 with Super Bowl aspirations in new Raymond James Stadium, but the Buccaneers started 4-7 before finishing with four victories in five games to close at 8-8. They were in playoff contention through their final game.

BUCCANEERS RECORD 1976-1998

YEAR	WON	LOST	TIED	PCT.	FIN	PF	PA
1976	0	14	0	.000	5	125	412
1977	2	12	0	.143	5	103	223
1978	5	11	0	.313	5	241	259
1979a	10	6	0	.625	1	273	237
1980	5	10	1	.344	4	271	341
1981b	9	7	0	.563	1	315	268
1982c	5	4	0	.556	7	158	178
1983	2	14	0	.125	5	241	380
1984	6	10	0	.375	3	335	380
1985	2	14	0	.125	5	294	448
1986	2	14	0	.125	5	239	473
1987	4	11	0	.267	4	286	360
1988	5	11	0	.313	3	261	350
1989	5	11	0	.313	5	320	419
1990	6	10	0	.375	2	264	367
1991	3	13	0	.188	5	199	365
1992	5	11	0	.313	3	267	365
1993	5	11	0	.313	5	237	376
1994	6	10	0	.375	5	251	351
1995	7	9	0	.438	5	238	335
1996	6	10	0	.375	4	221	293
1997d	10	6	0	.625	2	299	263
1998	8	8	0	.500	3	314	295
23 Years	118	237	1	.333	—	5,752	7,738

a NFC Central Division Champion; 1-1 in Playoffs
b NFC Central Division Champion; 0-1 in Playoffs
c NFC Qualifier for Playoffs; 0-1 in Playoffs
d NFC Wild Card Qualifier for Playoffs; 1-1 in Playoffs

COACHING HISTORY
(120-241-1)

1976-84	John McKay	45-91-1
1985-86	Leeman Bennett	4-28-0
1987-90	Ray Perkins*	19-41-0
1990-91	Richard Williamson	4-15-0
1992-95	Sam Wyche	23-41-0
1996-98	Tony Dungy	25-25-0

* Released after 13 games in 1990

Washington Redskins

Before moving to the nation's capital in 1937 and winning the NFL championship, the Redskins hailed from Boston.

George Preston Marshall and a group purchased a franchise in 1932. Because they played in the home park of the baseball Braves, they also were known as the Braves. Lud Wray was their first coach and guided the team to a 4-4-2 record. Cliff Battles, a rookie halfback, led the NFL in rushing with 576 yards. Tackle Turk Edwards, also a rookie, was a force in the line.

The team lost money. Marshall's partners wanted out, and he accommodated them. He moved the team into the baseball Red Sox's Fenway Park and renamed it the Redskins. He also hired Native American coach William (Lone Star) Dietz to replace Wray. Jim Musick and Battles were one-two in the league in rushing, but the Redskins still were a .500 team in 1933. Edwards was an iron man—he missed three minutes in the first game, seven minutes in the last, and played all the rest (a total of 710 minutes of a possible 720).

Another .500 season followed in 1934, and Marshall dismissed Dietz in favor of local Harvard hero Eddie Casey, who was 2-8-1 in his only season. In 1936, Ray Flaherty, a great end with the Giants, was hired as coach. Battles and Pug Rentner, a fullback, powered the team to an Eastern Division championship, but attendance still lagged.

The division-champion Redskins were to host the Packers in the 1936 NFL Championship Game. Marshall, fed up with poor attendance, moved the game to a neutral site—New York's Polo Grounds. The final straw, he said, was the Boston papers' ignoring his pro football game in favor of a high school field hockey contest. Shortly after the title game, which his team lost, Marshall moved the team to Washington, D.C.

It was more than just a change of scenery. The Redskins took on a whole new attack when Marshall brought in rookie Texan (Slingin') Sammy Baugh. Baugh, throwing to Wayne Millner, gave the Redskins a potent offense. The threat of passing spread the defense so much that it allowed Battles to win the NFL rushing title with an astounding (for then) 874 yards. Baugh passed the Bears dizzy 28-21 in the title game of 1937. But Battles couldn't get Marshall to raise his salary to $5,000 for 1938, so he retired to take a job as an assistant at Columbia.

Baugh was hurt in the first game of 1938 and was not effective when he did come back. The next year, Flaherty alternated Baugh and Frank Filchock at tailback, and Filchock led the league in touchdown passes. With the Eastern Division title at stake, the Redskins and Giants played in the final regular-season game. In the waning minutes of the game, Bo Russell attempted a field goal, which most players—Washington and New York—thought was good. The referee ruled otherwise, and the Redskins lost 9-7.

There was nothing controversial about the 73-0 pasting Washington took from the Bears in the 1940 Championship Game. Ironically, the Redskins had beaten the Bears 7-3 in a regular-season game a few weeks before. When the Bears complained about officiating, Marshall called Halas's team "quitters" and "crybabies." To make matters worse, the title game was the first NFL championship broadcast on a coast-to-coast radio network.

After a late-season collapse in 1941, the Redskins exacted revenge for the Bears' 1940 humiliation by winning the 1942 championship game over Chicago. It was Flaherty's last game before entering military service. Never much for locker-room oration, he simply chalked "73-0" on the blackboard before the game.

Arthur (Dutch) Bergman filled Flaherty's shoes in 1943. Baugh led the Redskins past the Giants in a divisional playoff, but got hurt in the championship-game loss to the Bears. For the season, though, he led the league in passing, punting, and interceptions—a rare triple crown. New coach Dudley DeGroot brought in Clark Shaughnessy to install the modern T-formation. Baugh, long a tailback, took a while to adjust, but Filchock adapted immediately and split time with Slingin' Sam. The team faltered late and missed the championship game, but Baugh had no trouble with the T in 1945. He completed a record 70.3 percent of his passes. In the championship game, Baugh's team lost to the Cleveland Rams 15-14. The difference was a safety against the Redskins when Baugh's pass from his end zone hit the goal post. (The rule was changed the next year.)

The 1946 season began a dismal stretch. From then until Vince Lombardi took over as coach in 1969, the Redskins had only three winning seasons. Lombardi, out of coaching and antsy as Packers general manager, came to the rescue. He duplicated, to a point, his Packers running game. Rookie Larry Brown and former Browns fullback Charlie Harraway gained more than 1,300 yards between them. Sonny Jurgensen again led the NFL in passing, and Lombardi gave the team its first winner since 1955.

Lombardi was hospitalized with cancer in the summer of 1970. Bill Austin, his Packers assistant who came with him, was to take over until Lombardi recovered. But Lombardi died September 3.

George Allen came from California with his future-is-now philosophy for the 1971 season. It looked like the answer—he went 9-4-1 in his first year. He brought in quarterback Billy Kilmer, who played a great deal with Jurgensen hurt. His Over-the-Hill-Gang, as his new veterans were affectionately called, included future Redskins head coaches Jack Pardee and Richie Petitbon.

With Jurgensen again hurt, Kilmer directed the team in 1972. Larry Brown rushed for 1,216 yards. Brown had more carries than the team had pass attempts. Pardee, Pat Fischer, and Chris Hanberger keyed a strong defense. The Redskins dethroned the Cowboys in the division, but, when they got to Super Bowl VII, they couldn't keep the Dolphins from completing a perfect 17-0 season.

Jurgensen was healthy and split time with Kilmer most of the next season. Ken Houston and Dave Robinson were the latest seasoned veterans to join Allen. Washington made the playoffs, but lost the first game. Another first-game playoff loss ended 1974, and the Redskins missed the postseason in 1975, although they had a winning record. Jack Kent Cooke took over controlling interest in the team in 1974. Allen, dealing off future draft choices, brought in even more veterans in 1976. John Riggins and Calvin Hill were the latest. The team made the playoffs, but lost in the first round.

After splitting time with Kilmer in 1977, Joe Theismann was at the controls in 1978, when Riggins cracked the 1,000-yard mark. Allen left for the West Coast to take a brief fling with the Rams, and Jack Pardee became coach. In 1979, the Redskins were on the verge of winning the division. But Roger Staubach led the last comeback of his career to beat Washington 35-34 in the season finale, a crushing defeat for Pardee's crew. Pardee would end his tenure at 24-24 after the 1980 season. Before his final season, he did something no other Redskins coach had done since 1968: He had a number-one draft choice and used it by taking Syracuse wide receiver Art Monk.

Joe Gibbs was hired from Don Coryell's staff for 1981. After losing the first five games, he righted the team to break even. He acquired Joe Washington, who led the team in rushing (916 yards) and receiving (70 catches).

The 1982 strike didn't hurt the Redskins. They lost only one game, rolled through the playoffs, and broke open Super Bowl XVII when Riggins rumbled 43 yards on a fourth-and-1 to score. The Hogs (as the large and mobile offensive line was known) became celebrities. It was back to Super Bowl XVIII the next year, but the Raiders prevailed. Gibbs led the team to the playoffs twice between 1984-86, but couldn't return to the Super Bowl.

Jay Schroeder started the 1987 season at quarterback, but was rescued by Doug Williams a few times. Gary Clark and Ricky Sanders joined Monk as reliable, active receivers. Dexter Manley and Charles Mann were forces on defense. In Super Bowl XXII, Williams directed a record 35-point second quarter in a 42-10 romp over Denver.

The Redskins stumbled in 1988. Williams had an appendectomy, and young Mark Rypien stepped in. The next season he started most of the games. Though erratic at times, Rypien got the ball to Monk, Clark, and Sanders enough for each to gain 1,000 yards. In 1991, Gibbs's team won a third Super Bowl trophy with a victory over Buffalo in XXVI. Each of his Super Bowl victories came with a different starting quarterback—Theismann, Williams, and Rypien.

After losing the second playoff game in 1992, Gibbs stepped away from coaching to become a television analyst. Most of the nucleus of the championship team was gone or going. Respected defensive coordinator Richie Petitbon took over, but a 4-12 record limited his tenure to one season. Dallas assistant Norv Turner was brought in in 1994 and set about rebuilding. Although Tennessee's Heath Shuler was drafted as the future quarterback, unheralded Gus Frerotte took over in 1996 and led the team to a string of early season victories. Reality caught up with the Redskins in the season's second half, and the team missed the playoffs.

Jack Kent Cooke, only the second owner in Redskins' history, died of congestive heart failure in April, 1997. He was 84. The Redskins announced that their new stadium would be named after him, and on September 14, 1997, Washington christened Jack Kent Cooke Stadium with a 19-13 overtime victory over the Cardinals. The Redskins could not win with any consistency, however. Frerotte struggled and veteran Jeff Hostetler saw considerable action. The optimism of the previous season gave way to disappointment as Washington finished 8-7-1 and narrowly missed the playoffs again.

In an effort to shore up their rushing defense, the Redskins made a major investment the following offseason in defensive tackles Dana Stubblefield and Dan Wilkinson. But the team still finished twenty-eighth in the league against the run. Trent Green became the new starting quarterback. After seven games, the Redskins were winless. A late-season, four-game winning streak helped them finish 6-10.

REDSKINS RECORD 1932-1998

YEAR	WON	LOST	TIED	PCT.	FIN	PF	PA
Boston Braves							
1932	4	4	2	.500	4	55	79
Boston Redskins							
1933	5	5	2	.500	3	103	97
1934	6	6	0	.500	2	107	94
1935	2	8	1	.200	4	65	123
1936a	7	5	0	.583	1	149	110
Washington Redskins							
1937b	8	3	0	.727	1	195	120
1938	6	3	2	.667	2	148	154
1939	8	2	1	.800	2	242	94
1940a	9	2	0	.818	1	245	142
1941	6	5	0	.545	3	176	174
1942b	10	1	0	.909	1	227	102
1943c	6	3	1	.667	1	229	137
1944	6	3	1	.667	3	169	180
1945a	8	2	0	.800	1	209	121
1946	5	5	1	.500	3t	171	191
1947	4	8	0	.333	4	295	367
1948	7	5	0	.583	2	291	287
1949	4	7	1	.364	4	268	339
1950	3	9	0	.250	6	232	326
1951	5	7	0	.417	3	183	296
1952	4	8	0	.333	5t	240	287
1953	6	5	1	.545	3	208	215
1954	3	9	0	.250	5	207	432
1955	8	4	0	.667	2	246	222
1956	6	6	0	.500	3	183	225
1957	5	6	1	.455	4	251	230
1958	4	7	1	.364	4	214	268
1959	3	9	0	.250	5	185	350
1960	1	9	2	.100	6	178	309
1961	1	12	1	.077	7	174	392
1962	5	7	2	.417	4	305	376
1963	3	11	0	.214	6	279	398
1964	6	8	0	.429	3t	307	305
1965	6	8	0	.429	4	257	301
1966	7	7	0	.500	5	351	355
1967	5	6	3	.455	3	347	353
1968	5	9	0	.357	3	249	358
1969	7	5	2	.583	2	307	319
1970	6	8	0	.429	4	297	314
1971d	9	4	1	.692	2	276	190
1972e	11	3	0	.786	1	336	218
1973d	10	4	0	.714	2	325	198
1974d	10	4	0	.714	2	320	196
1975	8	6	0	.571	3	325	276
1976d	10	4	0	.714	2	291	217
1977	9	5	0	.643	2	196	189
1978	8	8	0	.500	3	273	283
1979	10	6	0	.625	3	348	295
1980	6	10	0	.375	3	261	293
1981	8	8	0	.500	4	347	349
1982f	8	1	0	.889	1	190	128
1983e	14	2	0	.875	1	541	332
1984g	11	5	0	.688	1	426	310
1985	10	6	0	.625	3	297	312
1986h	12	4	0	.750	2	368	296
1987i	11	4	0	.733	1	379	285
1988	7	9	0	.438	3	345	387
1989	10	6	0	.625	3	386	308
1990j	10	6	0	.625	3	381	301
1991i	14	2	0	.875	1	485	224
1992j	9	7	0	.563	3	300	255
1993	4	12	0	.250	5	230	345
1994	3	13	0	.188	5	320	412
1995	6	10	0	.375	3	326	359
1996	9	7	0	.562	3	364	312
1997	8	7	1	.531	2	327	289
1998	6	10	0	.375	4	319	421
67 Years	462	409	27	.530	—	17,826	17,522

a NFL Eastern Division Champion; 0-1 in Playoffs
b NFL Champion; 1-0 in Playoffs
c NFL Eastern Division Champion; 1-1 in Playoffs
d NFC Wild Card Qualifier for Playoffs; 0-1 in Playoffs
e NFC Champion; 2-1 in Playoffs
f Super Bowl Champion; 4-0 in Playoffs
g NFC Eastern Division Champion; 0-1 in Playoffs
h NFC Wild Card Qualifier for Playoffs; 2-1 in Playoffs
i Super Bowl Champion; 3-0 in Playoffs
j NFC Wild Card Qualifier for Playoffs; 1-1 in Playoffs

COACHING HISTORY
BOSTON BRAVES 1932,
BOSTON REDSKINS 1933-36,
WASHINGTON REDSKINS 1937-1998
(482-424-27)

1932	Lud Wray	4-4-2
1933-34	William (Lone Star) Dietz	11-11-2
1935	Eddie Casey	2-8-1
1936-42	Ray Flaherty	56-23-3
1943	Arthur (Dutch) Bergman	7-4-1
1944-45	Dudley DeGroot	14-6-1
1946-48	Glen (Turk) Edwards	16-18-1
1949	John Whelchel*	3-3-1
1949-51	Herman Ball**	4-16-0
1951	Dick Todd	5-4-0
1952-53	Earl (Curly) Lambeau	10-13-1
1954-58	Joe Kuharich	26-32-2
1959-60	Mike Nixon	4-18-2
1961-65	Bill McPeak	21-46-3
1966-68	Otto Graham	17-22-3
1969	Vince Lombardi	7-5-2
1970	Bill Austin	6-8-0
1971-77	George Allen	69-35-1
1978-80	Jack Pardee	24-24-0
1981-92	Joe Gibbs	140-65-0
1993	Richie Petitbon	4-12-0
1994-98	Norv Turner	32-47-0

* Released after seven games in 1949
** Released after three games in 1951

CHAPTER 5

Team Histories: AFC Teams

Ed Gruver

The American Football Conference (AFC) grew out of the old American Football League (AFL). When the AFL and NFL agreed to merge in 1966, the two circuits became one unified league beginning with the 1970 season. At the time of the merger there had been 26 pro teams—16 in the NFL and 10 in the AFL. Although some urged that the two leagues be retained, a more balanced approach was chosen—the creation of two conferences, each with the same number of teams. To effect this balance, three NFL franchises—the Baltimore Colts, Cleveland Browns, and Pittsburgh Steelers—agreed to join the ten American Football League teams to form the AFC. Histories of each AFC franchise follow.

(Statistical note: Prior to 1972, the NFL discounted ties when determining won-loss percentage. Since 1972, ties have been counted as half a win and half a loss. Overall team records reflect the latter method.)

Baltimore Ravens

From the moment the Colts relocated to Indianapolis in 1984, Baltimore fans worked and prayed for another NFL franchise. On November 6, 1995, they learned one was headed their way after Cleveland Browns owner Art Modell announced he was moving his team to Baltimore. This produced a blizzard of criticism and several lawsuits by the city of Cleveland. Eventually, NFL Commissioner Paul Tagliabue worked out a compromise whereby Cleveland would receive a replacement franchise by no later than 1999 and would retain the Browns' records and heritage.

Baltimore went in search of a name for its new team. In March, 1996, the team was named the Ravens after a *Baltimore Sun* telephone poll received an overwhelming number of calls supporting that name. The reference was to the famous poem by Baltimore native son Edgar Allan Poe. Team colors were black, purple, and gold.

Browns coach Bill Belichick was not retained, and Ted Marchibroda, who had taken the Baltimore Colts (in the 1970s) and the Indianapolis Colts (in 1995) to the playoffs, was named the Ravens' first head coach.

The Ravens' initial season was less than a triumph on the field, as they settled for a 4-12 mark. However, there were several bright spots. Quarterback Vinny Testaverde had his best season and was chosen to the Pro Bowl. Running back Bam Morris, acquired as a free agent, gave the team a strong running attack. And wide receivers Michael Jackson and Derrick Alexander were a formidable duo.

Baltimore struggled to a 6-9-1 finish in its second season, losing six games by a combined total of 15 points. But the Ravens fielded some stars, notably Pro Bowl tackle Jonathan Ogden and linebacker Ray Lewis. The promise of rookie linebacker Peter Boulware, the addition of veteran quarterback Jim Harbaugh, and the opening of a new state-of-the-art stadium in the Inner Harbor gave fans reason for optimism.

The Ravens' struggles continued in 1998, however, and Baltimore finished a disappointing 6-10. The team escaped the AFC Central Division cellar for the first time, but head coach Ted Marchibroda was fired the day after the season finale, a 19-10 victory over Detroit. On January 19, the Ravens named Vikings offensive coordinator Brian Billick their new head coach.

RAVENS RECORD 1996-98

YEAR	WON	LOST	TIED	PCT.	FIN	PF	PA
1996	4	12	0	.250	5	371	444
1997	6	9	1	.406	5	326	345
1998	6	10	0	.375	4	269	335
3 Years	16	31	1	.344	—	966	1,124

COACHING HISTORY (16-31-1)

1996-98	Ted Marchibroda	16-31-1

Buffalo Bills

When Ralph C. Wilson, a minority stockholder in the Detroit Lions, sought to put an American Football League franchise in Miami in 1959, he was turned down by civic leaders who felt pro football never would successfully challenge the college game in south Florida.

Miami's loss was Buffalo's gain. Bolstered by a pledge of personal and civic support from influential *Buffalo Evening News* editor Paul Neville, Wilson phoned AFL founder Lamar Hunt in October of 1959 and issued a five-word statement that put upstate New York on the pro football map: "Count me in with Buffalo."

The Bills became the seventh of the eight charter AFL franchises, and, from the start of their inaugural training camp in 1960 in Aurora, New York, they were something of an oddity in the fledgling league—a team built to win with defense. On September 11, the Bills opened their first regular season with a 27-3 loss to the New York Titans. Two weeks later, they earned their first victory, a 13-0 shutout of the Patriots.

The team finished 5-8-1 its first season and 6-8 the following year. Lou Saban, who had been a member of the Cleveland teams that won four consecutive championships in the All-America Football Conference from 1946-49, became coach in 1962. Saban signed 6-foot 2-inch, 243-pound Carlton (Cookie) Gilchrist, a bruising fullback who had starred for several years in Canada. Gilchrist paid immediate dividends, running over AFL defenses for 1,099 yards to become the league's first 1,000-yard back.

Inconsistent quarterbacking hurt the Bills in their first years. Then, an error in the San Diego front office left star quarterback Jack Kemp on the waiver list, and the Bills were able to claim him for a mere $100. With Gilchrist and Kemp aboard, Saban directed Buffalo to a 7-6-1 record in 1962 for its first winning season.

The team repeated its 7-6-1 record the following season, but reached the playoffs for the first time in franchise history by tying the Patriots for first place. The Bills lost 26-8 to the Patriots in a divisional playoff in snow-covered War Memorial Stadium. The highlight of the season was Cookie Gilchrist's pro record 243 yards rushing against the Jets late in the year.

In 1964, Saban's team established itself as one of the AFL's best. The Bills were the AFL's first great ball-control team, featuring Gilchrist, who ran for a league-high 981 yards, and an offensive line that included all-pro guard Billy Shaw. Buffalo's ground attack topped the league in both rushing yards (2,040) and touchdowns (25). Kemp passed judiciously, and speedy Elbert (Golden Wheels) Dubenion owned an AFL-high 27-yards per catch average.

The backbone of the team, however, was its bruising defense, the best in the league. Key contributors included tackle Tom Sestak, linebacker Mike Stratton, and safety George Saimes. The team won its first nine games of the 1964 season and won its first division title with a 12-2 mark. The Bills met defending league champion San Diego in the AFL title game at frozen War Memorial, and defeated the Chargers 20-7.

Gilchrist was traded in the offseason, but the defense keyed the team to a second consecutive division title in 1965 with a 10-3-1 record. At San Diego in a championship game rematch, Saban confused the Chargers with innovative wrinkles that included a double-tight end offense and 3-4 defense, and the Bills repeated as AFL champions with a 23-0 shutout.

Saban surprised the Bills by resigning in the offseason to become head coach at the University of Maryland, and assistant coach and defensive coordinator Joe Collier replaced him. Under Collier, the Bills won a third consecutive division title and made their fourth straight appearance in the playoffs. Buffalo's rock-ribbed defense continued to excel, and the team earned its third consecutive appearance in the AFL title game. The Bills' reign as league champions ended with a 31-7 loss to Kansas City in a game to determine the AFL's first Super Bowl representative.

Age and injuries caught up with the Bills. The team spent the rest of the AFL years in decline, winning a combined 9 games over the next three seasons. Collier was fired in the midst of a disastrous 1-12-1 season in 1968, and former Raiders coach John Rauch was hired for 1969. Rauch arrived in time to preside over one of the most significant drafts in franchise history, when the Bills selected Heisman Trophy running back O.J. Simpson of USC as their number-one choice.

But the Bills endured losing seasons from 1970-72, and it wasn't until the team rehired Saban in 1972 that a turnaround began.

Saban molded the 1970s Bills in the same fashion as the title teams he'd built in the 1960s—a mobile offensive line, a feature back, and a sturdy defense. Simpson ran for a league-high 1,251 yards in 1972, the club's last season in War Memorial Stadium. The Bills moved to Rich Stadium in Orchard Park in 1973. Simpson set an NFL record that year by rushing for 2,003 yards. The Bills went 9-5 for their first winning season in eight years, and followed with a playoff appearance in 1974—the team's first since the 1966 AFL title game—where they lost 32-14 to eventual Super Bowl champion Pittsburgh.

Though the Bills followed with another winning season in 1975, the team was lapsing into another slump. Saban resigned five games into the 1976 season, and was replaced by Jim Ringo, the Hall of Fame center from Vince Lombardi's Packers. Ringo was unable to kindle any Lombardi-like flames. He was fired following a 3-11 season in 1977.

Former Los Angeles Rams head coach Chuck Knox was hired. The aging Simpson was dealt to San Francisco in March of 1978, and the Bills spent the next two seasons rebuilding. Buffalo broke through in 1980 with an 11-5 record to win their first division title in 14 years, but was knocked from the playoffs in its first game, falling to San Diego 20-14.

Led by quarterback Joe Ferguson and 1,000-yard back Joe Cribbs, the Bills went 10-6 the following season to earn a wild-card playoff spot, then beat the Jets 31-27 for their first postseason victory since 1965. Their season ended the next week with a 28-21 loss to Cincinnati in the divisional playoff game. That game marked Buffalo's last playoff appearance until 1988, when head coach Marv Levy directed the team to the Eastern Division title with a 12-4 mark.

Under Levy, the club featured several superstars: quarterback Jim Kelly, all-purpose halfback Thurman Thomas, defensive end Bruce Smith, and linebacker Cornelius Bennett. They took measured steps, dropping the 1988 AFC title game to Cincinnati 21-10, then falling to Cleveland 34-30 in a 1989 playoff game.

The Bills popularized the No-Huddle offense in 1990, a maneuver that enabled them to limit their opponents' defensive substitutions. Buffalo won its division that year with a franchise-best 13-3 record. In the playoffs, the Bills beat Miami 44-34, then bombed the Raiders 51-3 in the AFC title game. In Super Bowl XXV in Tampa, the Bills battled the favored New York Giants down to the wire before succumbing 20-19.

The club repeated its 13-3 division-winning mark in 1991, then beat Kansas City and Denver en route to Super Bowl XXVI. Once again, the Bills came up short, losing 37-24 to the Washington Redskins in Minneapolis's Metrodome. Their route to Super Bowl XXVII in Pasadena was more difficult. An 11-5 record placed them second to

Miami in the AFC East and ended their division title string at four. Backup quarterback Frank Reich rallied the Bills from a 32-point deficit in the third quarter to a 41-38 victory over Houston, and they followed with a 24-3 victory over Pittsburgh. The Bills earned their third consecutive AFC title with a 29-10 win at Miami, but were blitzed by Dallas 52-17 in the Super Bowl.

In 1993 the Bills earned a record fourth straight Super Bowl appearance, after first regaining their division title with a 12-4 record. They edged the Raiders in a playoff game, then topped Kansas City 30-13 for their fourth consecutive AFC championship. They also lost their fourth consecutive Super Bowl, bowing to the Cowboys 30-13 in XXVIII, played in the Georgia Dome.

A string of injuries led to a losing season in 1994, when the Bills fell to 7-9 and missed the playoffs for the first time in six years. Levy and his resilient squad, which now included free-agent linebacker Bryce Paup, bounced back in 1995, regaining the division championship with a 10-6 record. They beat Miami 37-22 in a wild-card playoff game that turned out to be Don Shula's last as head coach before losing to eventual AFC champion Pittsburgh 40-21.

The Bills bolstered their defense in the offseason, signing free agent linebacker Chris Spielman of Detroit and using four of their first five picks in the college draft on defensive players. Despite a rash of injuries that sometimes crippled the offense, the Bills qualified for the playoffs again in 1996. However, the team was upset by Jacksonville in a wild-card game, losing for the first time in 10 playoff games at Rich Stadium.

The following season was a year of transition. Kelly retired, and Thomas finished second on the team in rushing to rookie Antowain Smith. Buffalo scrapped its trademark 3-4 defense for a 4-3 design, and the Bills ended the season 6-10 and in fourth place in the AFC East.

Levy retired at the end of the season, and defensive coordinator Wade Phillips took over. Buffalo enjoyed a renaissance in 1998, thanks to the continuing emergence of Smith at running back and the inspired play veteran CFL quarterback Doug Flutie. "Flutie Flakes," a breakfast cereal, became the rage as the diminutive quarterback guided the Bills to a 10-6 record and a wild-card playoff berth.

The season ended with a 24-17 loss at Miami in the wild-card round. Flutie, who had been exiled to the CFL earlier by teams that believed he was too small for the NFL, was named the league's comeback player of the year.

BILLS RECORD 1960-1998

YEAR	WON	LOST	TIED	PCT.	FIN	PF	PA
1960	5	8	1	.385	3	296	303
1961	6	8	0	.429	4	294	342
1962	7	6	1	.538	3	309	272
1963a	7	6	1	.538	2	304	291
1964b	12	2	0	.857	1	400	242
1965b	10	3	1	.769	1	313	226
1966c	9	4	1	.692	1	358	255
1967	4	10	0	.286	3	237	285
1968	1	12	1	.077	5	199	367
1969	4	10	0	.286	4	230	359
1970	3	10	1	.231	4	204	337
1971	1	13	0	.071	5	184	394
1972	4	9	1	.321	4	257	377
1973	9	5	0	.643	2	259	230
1974d	9	5	0	.643	2	264	244
1975	8	6	0	.571	3	420	355
1976	2	12	0	.143	5	245	363
1977	3	11	0	.214	5	160	313
1978	5	11	0	.313	4	302	354
1979	7	9	0	.438	4	268	279
1980e	11	5	0	.688	1	320	260
1981f	10	6	0	.625	3	311	276
1982	4	5	0	.444	9	150	154
1983	8	8	0	.500	3	283	351
1984	2	14	0	.125	5	250	454
1985	2	14	0	.125	5	200	381
1986	4	12	0	.250	4	287	348
1987	7	8	0	.467	4	270	305
1988g	12	4	0	.750	1	329	237
1989e	9	7	0	.563	1	409	317
1990h	13	3	0	.813	1	428	263
1991h	13	3	0	.813	1	458	318
1992i	11	5	0	.688	2	381	283
1993h	12	4	0	.750	1	329	242
1994	7	9	0	.438	4	340	356
1995g	10	6	0	.625	1	350	335
1996d	10	6	0	.625	2	319	266
1997	6	10	0	.375	4	255	367
1998d	10	6	0	.625	3	400	333
39 Years	277	295	8	.484	—	11,572	12,034

a AFL Eastern Division Runner-up; 0-1 in Playoffs
b AFL Champion; 1-0 in Playoffs
c AFL Eastern Division Champion; 0-1 in Playoffs
d AFC Wild Card Qualifier for Playoffs; 0-1 in Playoffs
e AFC Eastern Division Champion; 0-1 in Playoffs
f AFC Wild Card Qualifier for Playoffs; 1-1 in Playoffs
g AFC Eastern Division Champion; 1-1 in Playoffs
h AFC Eastern Division Champion; AFC Champion; 2-1 in Playoffs
i AFC Wild Card Qualifier for Playoffs; AFC Champion; 3-1 in Playoffs

COACHING HISTORY
(291-309-8)

1960-61	Buster Ramsey	11-16-1
1962-65	Lou Saban	38-18-3
1966-68	Joe Collier*	13-17-1
1968	Harvey Johnson	1-10-1
1969-70	John Rauch	7-20-1
1971	Harvey Johnson	1-13-0
1972-76	Lou Saban**	32-29-1
1976-77	Jim Ringo	3-20-0
1978-82	Chuck Knox	38-38-0
1983-85	Kay Stephenson***	10-26-0
1985-86	Hank Bullough#	4-17-0
1986-97	Marv Levy	123-78-0
1998	Wade Phillips	10-7-0

* Released after two games in 1968
** Resigned after five games in 1976
*** Released after four games in 1985
\# Released after nine games in 1986

Cincinnati Bengals

The groundwork for the Cincinnati Bengals' franchise was established on December 14, 1965, when Paul Brown, the legendary founder and former head coach of the Cleveland Browns, met with Ohio governor James Rhodes to bring the idea of a professional football franchise before a gathering of Cincinnati's civic leaders.

One year and one day after that meeting, the Cincinnati City Council officially set aside a 48-acre downtown tract of land bordered by Second Street and the Ohio River for the construction of Riverfront Stadium, the future home of the baseball Reds and a pro football team. With the promise of a spacious new stadium, Brown was awarded an AFL expansion franchise on September 27, 1967. Brown named the franchise the Bengals, honoring the memory of the 1937 Bengals that were part of one of the earlier American Football Leagues.

Brown was allowed to choose 40 players out of an allocation draft arranged by AFL owners in 1968. Brown landed some solid veterans, shoring up his defense with linebacker Sherrill Headrick and safety Bobby Hunt. The college draft proved that Brown's eye for talent was as sharp as ever. The club's first choice was Bob Johnson, an All-America center out of Tennessee who became one of the NFL's top centers over the next few years. The 1968 draft also yielded running backs Paul Robinson and Essex Johnson, tight end Bob Trumpy, linebacker Al Beauchamp, and defensive back Jess Phillips.

The Bengals opened the 1968 regular season with a 29-13 loss at San Diego, then thrilled their fans with home victories over Denver and Buffalo. Cincinnati dropped seven consecutive games to finish 3-11 and in last place in the AFL's Western Division. Despite its record, the team showed promise. Robinson earned AFL rookie-of-the-year honors by rushing for a league-high 1,023 yards.

Brown made talented hometown quarterback Greg Cook of the University of Cincinnati the Bengals' top choice in the draft. The defense was aided by the addition of middle linebacker Bill Bergey and cornerback Ken Riley. The Baby Bengals, as they were known around the AFL, started fast with a victory over Miami in their regular-season opener.

Cook passed for 3 touchdowns the next week as the Bengals beat the Chargers, and Cincinnati improved to 3-0 when it handed the eventual Super Bowl-champion Chiefs one of their three losses on the season. The win was a costly one, however. A hard tackle by Chiefs middle linebacker Willie Lanier forced Cook out of the lineup for the next four games with a sore throwing arm, and the Bengals dropped all four. Cook came back to lead Cincinnati past the powerful Oakland Raiders, and then passed for 4 touchdowns to salvage a tie with Houston. Cincinnati went 4-9-1 and again finished in last place in its division, but postseason honors went to Brown, who was named AFL coach of the year, and Bergey, who was tabbed AFL defensive rookie of the year. However, the major find was Cook, who led the AFC in passing. Veteran observers predicted he would become one of pro football's greatest quarterbacks.

With the merger of the AFL and NFL, the Bengals were moved into the AFC Central Division. Although the 1970 season was to end with the Bengals celebrating their first playoff berth, the campaign opened on a down note when Cook's troubled right arm went dead in training camp. Although he hung on for a few years, his promising career essentially was over.

Stepping in for Cook was Virgil Carter, a former member of both the Bears and Bills. In their first game at Riverfront Stadium, the Bengals downed Washington 27-12 in a preseason contest on August 8. A six-game losing streak early in the regular season left the Bengals in last place in the Central Division, but a 14-10 victory over Cleveland before a Cincinnati record crowd of 60,007 signaled a remarkable turnaround that saw the Bengals close the regular season with seven victories to win the division with an 8-6 record. No expansion team ever had come so far so fast. Rookies Mike Reid and Lemar Parrish led a defense that held three of its last five opponents to 7 points or less. The Bengals clinched their first title with a 45-7 victory at home against Boston, but fell to eventual Super Bowl-champion Baltimore 17-0 a week later in the first round of the playoffs.

Cincinnati missed the postseason the next two years, but Brown continued to build through the draft. Added to the fold was quarterback Ken Anderson, wide receiver Isaac Curtis, running back Boobie Clark, and safety Tommy Casanova. The team returned to the playoffs in 1973, as Cincinnati featured a balanced attack that saw Anderson set club passing records and Clark and Essex Johnson combining for nearly 2,000 yards rushing. By season's end the Bengals had their best record ever (10-4) but they again they fell to an eventual Super Bowl champion when they dropped a 34-16 decision to the powerful Miami Dolphins.

Following a .500 season in 1974, the Bengals returned to the playoffs in 1975, winning a club-record 11 games and earning a wild-card berth. Cincinnati's season ended with a 31-28 loss to the Raiders in a first-round game in Oakland on December 28. Four days later, Paul Brown announced his retirement from coaching and named line coach Bill Johnson to succeed him.

The team began the Johnson era by winning 9 of its first 11 games in 1976, but late-season losses to Pittsburgh and Oakland helped knock the Bengals out of the playoffs. They finished with a 10-4 record, then endured mixed results the next four seasons.

The 1981 season saw the emergence of the new-look Bengals. The team unveiled flashy new uniforms that included tiger stripes on its helmets, jerseys, and pants. The offense was rebuilt with young draft choices such as tackle Anthony Munoz of USC and receiver Cris Collinsworth of Florida. Forrest Gregg, the Packers' Hall of Fame tackle during the Green Bay glory years, instilled a Lombardi-like discipline and approach to the game. Anderson, whose 98.5 passer rating was highest in the league, led Cincinnati to its first playoff victory with a 28-21 win over Buffalo.

Making their first appearance in the AFC title game, the Bengals faced the San Diego Chargers in polar conditions—minus-11 degrees temperature with a wind-chill of minus-59. Cincinnati won 27-7 to wrap up its first Super Bowl berth. Their dream season ended in the Pontiac Silverdome, when they fell to San Francisco 26-21 in Super Bowl XVI.

A 57-day players' strike forced the NFL to shorten its 1982 season to nine games and restructure its playoff format. The Bengals reached the playoffs with a 7-2 record, thanks to Anderson, who led the NFL in passing for the fourth time, and set NFL records by completing 20 consecutive passes and hitting on 70.55 percent of his passes, to erase the mark previously held by the Redskins' Sammy Baugh. Cincinnati's hopes of a second straight Super Bowl appearance ended when the Bengals lost 44-17 to the New York Jets.

The club struggled the next three seasons, but came back in 1986 as head coach Sam Wyche blended the talents of Munoz, quarterback Boomer Esiason, and running back James Brooks into a 10-6 squad. The Bengals posted a franchise-best 12-4 record in 1988. Esiason won the NFL MVP honors, and fullback Ickey Woods won the hearts of Bengals' fans with his patented touchdown dance, the "Ickey Shuffle." In the postseason, the Bengals dispatched Seattle 21-13, then beat Buffalo 21-10 for the AFC title as Woods bulled for a pair of 1-yard touchdowns.

Super Bowl XXIII in Miami matched Wyche against his mentor, 49ers boss Bill Walsh, who was coaching his final NFL game. The underdog Bengals led 16-13 with 3:20

left, then fell victim to a late touchdown drive orchestrated by San Francisco quarterback Joe Montana, who capped a 20-16 victory with a touchdown pass to John Taylor with 34 seconds left.

Following an off-year in 1989, the Bengals won the division title in 1990 with a 9-7 record. Cincinnati crushed rival Houston 41-14 in the opening round of the playoffs, then saw its season end with a 20-10 loss to the Los Angeles Raiders. A 3-13 finish cost Wyche his job in 1991, and the Bengals replaced him with 32-year-old Dave Shula, son of legendary coach Don Shula and the youngest head coach in modern NFL history. Shula won five games in 1992, then endured consecutive 3-13 campaigns in 1993-94.

The team returned to respectability in 1995, as the exciting tandem of quarterback Jeff Blake and wide receiver Carl Pickens keyed Cincinnati to a 7-9 finish. Shula continued to concentrate on offense in the 1996 draft, using his top three choices on offensive players, including number-one pick Willie Anderson, a tackle out of Auburn. Free-agent running backs Garrison Hearst and Eric Bieniemy joined 1995 number-one pick, Ki-Jana Carter, in the backfield.

Nevertheless, Cincinnati stumbled out of the gate. After losing six of its first seven games, the Bengals replaced Shula with Bruce Coslet. The former Jets' head coach went 7-2 the rest of the way. Important in the reformation were a return to form of Blake and Pickens, strong running by Hearst, and a large improvement by the defense.

But high expectations gave way to disappointment the following year. Hearst left via free agency, and Blake struggled as Cincinnati stumbled out of the gate again, winning only one of its first eight games. The 36-year-old Esiason, who spent the previous four years with the Jets and Cardinals, replaced Blake at quarterback midway through the season, and rallied the Bengals to six wins in their final eight games. Esiason passed for 13 touchdowns in a five-game span, and rookie running back Corey Dillon gained 1,129 yards on the ground. The strong finish helped Coslet post a 7-9 record in his first full season as coach.

Esiason retired following the season to become an analyst on the *Monday Night Football* announcing crew. Neil O'Donnell took over at quarterback and ranked third among AFC passers in 1998 after throwing 15 touchdowns and just 4 interceptions. But back and hip injuries slowed Dillon, the Bengals' point production fell from 355 in 1997 to 268 in 1998, and Cincinnati went 3-13 for the fourth time in the nineties.

BENGALS RECORD 1968-1998

YEAR	WON	LOST	TIED	PCT.	FIN	PF	PA
1968	3	11	0	.214	5	215	329
1969	4	9	1	.308	5	280	367
1970a	8	6	0	.571	1	312	255
1971	4	10	0	.286	4	284	265
1972	8	6	0	.571	3	299	229
1973a	10	4	0	.714	1	286	231
1974	7	7	0	.500	2	283	259
1975b	11	3	0	.786	2	340	246
1976	10	4	0	.714	2	335	210
1977	8	6	0	.571	3	238	235
1978	4	12	0	.250	4	252	284
1979	4	12	0	.250	4	337	421
1980	6	10	0	.375	4	244	312
1981c	12	4	0	.750	1	421	304
1982d	7	2	0	.778	3	232	177
1983	7	9	0	.438	3	346	302
1984	8	8	0	.500	2	339	339
1985	7	9	0	.438	2	441	437
1986	10	6	0	.625	2	409	394
1987	4	11	0	.267	4	285	370
1988c	12	4	0	.750	1	448	329
1989	8	8	0	.500	4	404	285
1990e	9	7	0	.563	1	360	352
1991	3	13	0	.188	4	263	435
1992	5	11	0	.313	4	274	364
1993	3	13	0	.188	4	187	319
1994	3	13	0	.188	3	267	406
1995	7	9	0	.438	2	349	374
1996	8	8	0	.500	3	372	369
1997	7	9	0	.438	4	355	405
1998	3	13	0	.188	5	268	452
31 Years	210	257	1	.450	—	9,715	10,056

a AFC Central Division Champion; 0-1 in Playoffs
b Wild Card Qualifier for Playoffs; 0-1 in Playoffs
c Central Division Champion; AFC Champion; 2-1 in Playoffs
d Qualifier for Playoffs; 0-1 in Playoffs
e AFC Central Division Champion; 1-1 in Playoffs

COACHING HISTORY
(215-264-1)

1968-75	Paul Brown	55-59-1
1976-78	Bill Johnson*	18-15-0
1978-79	Homer Rice	8-19-0
1980-83	Forrest Gregg	34-27-0
1984-91	Sam Wyche	64-68-0
1992-96	Dave Shula**	19-52-0
1996-98	Bruce Coslet	17-24-0

* Resigned after five games in 1978
** Replaced after seven games in 1996

Cleveland Browns

The Browns began operations in 1946, when Arthur (Mickey) McBride, a Cleveland entrepreneur, founded the franchise in the newly formed All-America Football Conference. McBride named Paul Brown, a man who had produced winning programs at Massillon High School, Ohio State, and the Great Lakes Naval Training Station during World War II, head coach and general manager. McBride's team originally was going to be called the Panthers, but Brown vetoed the nickname because a Cleveland football team named the Panthers had failed during the 1920s.

A contest was held through a local newspaper and "Browns" emerged as the leading choice, but whether that referred to the team's coach, to Joe Louis—the heavyweight boxing champion nicknamed "The Brown Bomber"—or simply to a color preference never was made clear.

Brown's innovative coaching earned him recognition as the father of the modern pro game. He was the first head coach to give his players written tests. He and his assistants scientifically studied films to learn why a play worked or not, then graded the players on their performances. His pass patterns were revolutionary, and he invented the "cup" blocking system that soon became standard for protecting the passer. He called all plays from the sideline by sending in "messenger" guards. He even designed the team's uniform and color scheme—brown, burnt orange, and white.

Brown signed a number of players whom he was familiar with from his coaching days at Ohio State and the Naval Station. Otto Graham, a Single-Wing tailback out of Northwestern, was signed to play quarterback. Guard Bill Willis had been a star lineman for Brown at Ohio State. Tackle Lou Groza and end Dante Lavelli had played there briefly before entering the service. Brown had been impressed by end Mac Speedie's play for a service team. Fullback Marion Motley had been seen both in high school and in the service. Motley and Willis were the first black players to be signed by an AAFC team.

The Browns opened the first AAFC regular season with a 44-0 victory over the Miami Seahawks in Cleveland's Municipal Stadium. They won their first seven games, and claimed the Western Division title with a 12-2 record, then won the inaugural AAFC title game by defeating the New York Yankees 14-9.

With Graham earning AAFC MVP honors, the Browns roared through the 1947 regular season with a 12-1-1 record, and faced the Yankees again for the AAFC championship. Motley ran for 109 yards as Cleveland beat New York again 14-3.

The Browns hit their AAFC peak in 1948, going 14-0 and defeating the Buffalo Bills 48-7 in the championship game.

Cleveland went 9-1-2 in 1949, the last year of the AAFC, and claimed its fourth consecutive league title with a 21-7 victory over the San Francisco 49ers in the title game. But so much success had its down side. The Browns' dominance hurt attendance all over the league. Even Browns' fans saw little reason to pay to watch their team run roughshod over the victim of the week.

Just before the AAFC's final championship game, a merger with the NFL was announced. The Browns, 49ers, and Baltimore Colts were admitted to the NFL for the 1950 season. NFL schedule makers matched the four-time AAFC-champion Browns against the two-time defending NFL-champion Philadelphia Eagles in a special Saturday night contest the evening before the regular season opened. The Browns stunned a record crowd of 71,237 in Philadelphia's Municipal Stadium with an easy 35-10 victory.

Cleveland finished 10-2 and beat the New York Giants 8-3 in a playoff to decide the Eastern Division crown. One week later, Groza made a field goal with 28 seconds left to give the Browns a 30-28 victory over the Los Angeles Rams in the NFL Championship Game.

Cleveland repeated as division champions in 1951 with an 11-1 record, but lost to the Rams 24-17 in the title game. The Browns won their division again in 1952, but fell to the Detroit Lions 17-7 in the championship game.

The 1953 season began with McBride selling the franchise to Cleveland industrialist David Jones for a record sum of $600,000. The Browns started the season with 11 consecutive wins, but fell short of their second perfect season when the Eagles beat them in the season finale. Then, for the third straight year, the Browns lost in the NFL Championship Game, dropping a 17-16 decision to the Lions.

Cleveland went 9-3 in 1954 and returned to the title game to face the Lions for the third consecutive time. Graham, who announced his retirement before the game, passed for 3 touchdowns and ran for 3 as the Browns routed the Lions 56-10.

Brown coaxed Graham into coming back for the 1955 season, and the Browns went 9-2-1 for their sixth consecutive division title. Facing the Rams in the NFL title game—his second "farewell appearance"—Graham accounted for 4 touchdowns in a 38-14 victory. This time Graham retired for good, leaving behind a legacy of having played in his league's championship game 10 consecutive years—and winning seven.

Graham's retirement left a vacuum at quarterback that was intensified when heir apparent George Ratterman suffered a career-ending knee injury early in the 1956 season. Many of the stars who had brought the Browns to prominence were either retired or nearing the end of their careers. To shore up the offense, Brown drafted Syracuse star Jim Brown in 1957, and the 6-foot 2-inch, 230-pound fullback used his size and speed to lead the NFL in rushing and earn rookie-of-the-year honors. Cleveland claimed the Eastern Division with a 9-2-1 record but then was bombed 59-14 by its old nemesis, Detroit, in the NFL title game. The following year, a 10-0 loss to the Giants in a playoff prevented the team from returning to the championship game, and the Browns endured mixed results the next four years. Art Modell, a New York advertising executive, purchased the franchise in 1961 for $3.925 million.

Brown traded talented running Bobby Mitchell to Washington in 1962 for the rights to Heisman Trophy runner Ernie Davis of Syracuse in order to create a dream backfield of Brown and Davis. But Davis died from leukemia having never played a down of pro football.

When the Browns finished just above .500 with a 7-6-1 record in 1962, Modell shocked the football world by firing his coach and replacing him with former Browns assistant Blanton Collier.

Jim Brown rushed for an NFL-record 1,863 yards as Cleveland went 10-4 in 1963, the team's best record since 1953. In 1964, the Browns drafted Ohio State's Paul Warfield, and the addition of Warfield, combined with flanker Gary Collins, gave Cleveland one of the best receiving tandems in the NFL. At the same time, quarterback Frank Ryan emerged as a strong passer and leader. Cleveland won its division with a 10-3-1 record, and upset the Baltimore Colts 27-0 in the NFL Championship Game as Collins hauled in 3 touchdown passes from Ryan.

Postseason shoulder injuries to Ryan and Warfield hurt the Browns offensively in 1965, but Collier's team still won the Eastern Conference with an 11-3 mark. Seeking their second straight NFL title, the Browns met the Green Bay Packers on a snowy field in Green Bay but lost 23-12.

Still at the top of his game, Jim Brown retired before the start of the 1966 season to pursue an acting career. Though he played just nine years, Brown left behind records that marked him as arguably the greatest runner ever—12,312 yards rushing, 126 touchdowns, and 8 rushing titles. With Brown gone, halfback Leroy Kelly stepped forward as the team's top running threat, and he led the NFL in touchdowns with 16 in 1966, and the Browns went 9-5.

The Browns returned to the postseason in 1967 by winning the realigned Century Division with a 9-5 mark. Kelly spearheaded the NFL's best rushing attack with a league-high 1,205 yards, but the Browns lost to Dallas 52-14 in the playoffs. Lou (The Toe) Groza retired before the start of the 1968 season after a 21-year career in which he scored 1,608 points and established himself as one of the greatest kickers of all time.

A shoulder injury sidelined Collins for most of the

season, but the club rallied behind Kelly, who repeated as NFL rushing champion with a career-high 1,239 yards, and quarterback Bill Nelsen, who was obtained from Pittsburgh. Despite playing with bad knees, Nelsen led his team to a 10-4 mark and its second straight Century Division title. The Browns faced the Cowboys in the first round of the playoffs again and pulled off a 31-20 upset. In the NFL Championship Game, the Browns lost to the Baltimore Colts 34-0. Cleveland won a third consecutive division title in 1969, and, after defeating Dallas 38-14 in a playoff game, lost to the Minnesota Vikings 27-7 in the championship game.

The Browns struggled to a 7-7 finish in 1970, their first season in the AFC season. Warfield was traded to Miami for the rights to draft Purdue quarterback Mike Phipps. Collier resigned as head coach at season's end and was replaced by assistant coach Nick Skorich.

Skorich led the team to the playoffs in 1971, winning the Central Division with a 9-5 record, but the Browns' season ended with a 20-3 loss to the defending world-champion Colts in a first-round playoff game. The following year saw Phipps become the team's number-one quarterback, and he led the Browns into the playoffs with a 10-4 mark. The Browns blew a fourth-quarter lead and lost to the eventual Super Bowl-champion Miami Dolphins 20-14.

Phipps never was able to deliver consistently at quarterback, and age caught up with some of the team's longtime stars. The club endured a six-year absence from the playoffs. But in 1980, quarterback Brian Sipe led a "Kardiac Kids" offense that saw 13 of the Browns' 16 regular-season games decided by a touchdown or less, most in the final moments. Sipe led the NFL in passing and was named NFL player of the year after becoming just the third quarterback to throw for more than 4,000 yards in a season. Under head coach Sam Rutigliano, the Browns clinched their first division title since 1971. However, their dream season came to an end in their opening playoff game, when Sipe was intercepted in the Oakland end zone with 41 seconds left as the Browns lost 14-12 to the Raiders.

In 1985, head coach Marty Schottenheimer led the Browns to the Central Division title with an 8-8 record. The Cleveland attack was powered by running backs Earnest Byner and Kevin Mack, who became just the third backfield duo to rush for more than 1,000 yards in the same season, and rookie quarterback Bernie Kosar, who two seasons earlier led the University of Miami to the national championship. In the playoffs, the Browns led the Dolphins 21-3 in the second half, but lost 24-21.

Kosar became one of the AFC's top young passers in 1986, and despite being rocked by the death of safety Don Rogers, Cleveland won the division with a 12-4 record. The Browns edged the Jets 20-17 in a double overtime playoff game, then lost to Denver 23-20 in overtime in the AFC title game.

Kosar led the AFC in passing in 1987, and the team earned its third consecutive Central Division title by going 10-5. Linebacker Clay Matthews and cornerbacks Hanford Dixon and Frank Minnifield emerged as defensive standouts. Kosar threw for 3 touchdowns in a 38-21 victory over the Indianapolis Colts in a playoff game, but the Browns again lost to the Broncos in the AFC Championship Game, this time by a 38-33 margin.

Injuries decimated the team's quarterbacks in 1988, but 38-year-old backup Don Strock guided the team into the postseason with a 10-6 record. Once again, the Browns came up short in the playoffs, losing to division rival Houston 24-23. Schottenheimer resigned at the end of the season.

Bud Carson, who helped design Pittsburgh's Steel Curtain defense of the 1970s, was named head coach for the 1989 season. He did a solid job holding together a unit that was plagued by Kosar's recurring arm injuries. The defensive front was shored up by young Michael Dean Perry, and the club won its fifth division title of the decade with a 9-6-1 mark. The Browns topped the Bills 34-30 in a divisional playoff game, but for the third time in four years lost to the Broncos 37-21 in the AFC title game.

The Browns began the nineties by winning a club-low three games in 1990. Carson was fired and replaced by Bill Belichick, a defensive coach on the Giants' Super Bowl XXV champions. Under Belichick, the club suffered three losing seasons from 1991-93.

Modell stuck with Belichick in 1994, and, behind a defense that allowed an AFC-low 204 points, the Browns went 11-5 and beat New England 20-13 in a first-round playoff game. But the Browns' season ended short of the Super Bowl when they lost 29-9 to the Steelers the next week.

Early in the 1995 season, Modell stunned Cleveland fans when he announced he was moving the franchise to Baltimore. Some NFL owners frowned on Modell's move, but they voted to approve it after NFL Commissioner Paul Tagliabue arranged a compromise with the city that promised Cleveland a new team within three years. The new or relocated franchise would assume the Browns' name, colors, history, and records. The lame-duck Browns endured a disastrous season, finishing 5-11. Worst of all, Cleveland fans endured three years without their beloved team.

Billionaire banker Al Lerner was awarded the restored Browns franchise that was to begin play in 1999. Lerner looked west to build his new team, and signed two men who had been key to the long-time success of the San Francisco 49ers, Carmen Policy and Dwight Clark. Policy joined the Browns as team president, Clark as director of football operations. On January 21, 1999, the Browns introduced former Jaguars offensive coordinator Chris Palmer as the team's new head coach. Lions center Jim Pyne was Cleveland's first pick in the expansion draft.

BROWNS RECORD 1946-1995

YEAR	WON	LOST	TIED	PCT.	FIN	PF	PA
1946a	12	2	0	.857	1	423	137
1947a	12	1	1	.923	1	410	185
1948a	14	0	0	1.000	1	389	190
1949b	9	1	2	.900	1	339	171
1950c	10	2	0	.833	1	310	144
1951d	11	1	0	.917	1	331	152
1952d	8	4	0	.667	1	310	213
1953e	11	1	0	.917	1	348	162
1954f	9	3	0	.750	1	336	162
1955f	9	2	1	.818	1	349	218
1956	5	7	0	.417	4t	167	177
1957e	9	2	1	.818	1	269	172
1958g	9	3	0	.750	2	302	217
1959	7	5	0	.583	2t	270	214
1960	8	3	1	.727	2	362	217
1961	8	5	1	.615	3	319	270

YEAR	WON	LOST	TIED	PCT.	FIN	PF	PA
1962	7	6	1	.538	3	291	257
1963	10	4	0	.714	2	343	262
1964f	10	3	1	.769	1	415	293
1965e	11	3	0	.786	1	363	325
1966	9	5	0	.643	2t	403	259
1967h	9	5	0	.643	1	334	297
1968i	10	4	0	.714	1	394	273
1969i	10	3	1	.769	1	351	300
1970	7	7	0	.500	2	286	265
1971j	9	5	0	.643	1	285	273
1972k	10	4	0	.714	2	268	249
1973	7	5	2	.571	3	234	255
1974	4	10	0	.286	4	251	344
1975	3	11	0	.214	4	218	372
1976	9	5	0	.643	3	267	287
1977	6	8	0	.429	4	269	267
1978	8	8	0	.500	3	334	356
1979	9	7	0	.563	3	359	352
1980j	11	5	0	.688	1	357	310
1981	5	11	0	.313	4	276	375
1982l	4	5	0	.444	8	140	182
1983	9	7	0	.563	2	356	342
1984	5	11	0	.313	3	250	297
1985j	8	8	0	.500	1	287	294
1986m	12	4	0	.750	1	391	310
1987m	10	5	0	.667	1	390	239
1988k	10	6	0	.625	2	304	288
1989m	9	6	1	.594	1	334	254
1990	3	13	0	.188	4	228	262
1991	6	10	0	.375	3	293	298
1992	7	9	0	.438	3	272	275
1993	7	9	0	.438	3	304	307
1994n	11	5	0	.688	2	340	204
1995	5	11	0	.313	4	289	356
4 AAFC	47	4	3	.922	—	1,561	683
46 NFL	374	266	10	.583	—	11,004	9,404
50 Pro	421	270	13	.607	—	12,565	10,087

a AAFC Champion; 1-0 in Playoffs
b AAFC Champion; 2-0 in Playoffs
c NFL American Conference Champion; NFL Champion; 2-0 in Playoffs
d NFL American Conference Champion; 0-1 in Playoffs
e NFL Eastern Conference Champion; 0-1 in Playoffs
f NFL Eastern Conference Champion; NFL Champion; 1-0 in Playoffs
g NFL Eastern Conference Runner-up; 0-1 in Playoffs
h NFL Century Division Champion; 0-1 in Playoffs
i NFL Eastern Conference Champion; 1-1 in Playoffs
j AFC Central Division Champion; 0-1 in Playoffs
k AFC Wild Card Qualifier for Playoffs; 0-1 in Playoffs
l AFC Qualifier for Playoffs; 0-1 in Playoffs
m AFC Central Division Champion; 1-1 in Playoffs
n AFC Wild Card Qualifier for Playoffs; 1-1 in Playoffs

COACHING HISTORY
(385-285-10)

1950-62	Paul Brown	115-49-5
1963-70	Blanton Collier	79-38-2
1971-74	Nick Skorich	30-26-2
1975-77	Forrest Gregg*	18-23-0
1977	Dick Modzelewski	0-1-0
1978-84	Sam Rutigliano**	47-52-0
1984-88	Marty Schottenheimer	46-31-0
1989-90	Bud Carson***	12-14-1
1990	Jim Shofner	1-6-0
1991-95	Bill Belichick	37-45-0

* Resigned after 13 games in 1977
** Released after eight games in 1984
*** Released after nine games in 1990

Denver Broncos

The Denver Broncos have become one of the most successful franchises in the AFC, winning back-to-back Super Bowls following the 1997 and 1998 seasons.

The Broncos were founded on August 14, 1959, when principal owner Bob Howsam gained charter membership in the fledgling AFL. Denver joined the Dallas Texans, Los Angeles Chargers, and Oakland Raiders in the AFL's Western Division, and played their home games at Bears Stadium, a minor-league baseball park.

Under successful Canadian Football League coach Frank Filchock, Denver beat the Boston Patriots in their AFL opener 13-10 when Gene Mingo returned a punt 73 yards for a crucial touchdown. Quarterback Frank Tripucka and wide receiver Lionel Taylor were the cornerstones of the early Broncos. The pair formed a prolific passing attack, and Taylor made history in 1961 when he became the first player to catch 100 passes in a season.

With their pass-oriented offense, porous defense, and bargain-basement brown-and-gold uniforms that featured vertical-striped socks, the Broncos symbolized the growing pains of the AFL's early years. Their best record in their first 13 seasons came in 1962, when new head coach Jack Faulkner led them to a 7-7 finish.

In 1961, Howsam sold his stock in the club to a group headed by Cal Kunz and Gerry Phipps. Faulkner set the tone for his new regime by burning the Broncos' striped socks at a public bonfire in the 1962 preseason and introduced the team's new colors, a bright orange-and-blue scheme. Despite the addition of all-pro stars such as halfback Floyd Little and defensive end Rich Jackson, the team won just 25 games over the next seven seasons. Their few highlights included a 13-7 victory over Detroit in a 1967 preseason game, the first victory for an AFL team over an NFL opponent; the renovation and renaming of Bears Stadium to Mile High Stadium in 1968; and Marlin Briscoe, who in 1968 became pro football's first black quarterback to play regularly.

In 1965, the team came close to moving to Atlanta before Denver fans responded with a huge season ticket sale, and, with the hiring of Robert (Red) Miller as head coach in 1977, the Broncos became a consistent contender. Miller's defense, known as the Orange Crush, was one of the best in the AFC, and Miller beefed up the offense by acquiring quarterback Craig Morton.

In 1977, with an offense that featured Morton, tight end Riley Odoms, and wide receiver Haven Moses, and a defense headed by end Lyle Alzado and linebacker Randy Gradishar, the Broncos clinched their first division title with an NFL-best 12-2 record. A Christmas Eve crowd of 75,011, the largest audience to that point for a sporting event in Colorado, filled Mile High Stadium as the Orange Crush outplayed Pittsburgh's Steel Curtain 34-21 in the Broncos' first playoff game.

One week later, Denver fans enjoyed a festive New Year's Day as Morton passed for 2 touchdowns and the Broncos edged the defending Super Bowl-champion Raiders 20-17 in the AFC title game. The Broncos showed little of their swashbuckling style in Super Bowl XII, however, turning over the ball 8 times in a 27-10 loss to the Dallas Cowboys in the Louisiana Superdome. Denver repeated as Western Division champs in 1978 with a 10-6 record, but lost to the Steelers 33-10 in the playoffs.

Alzado was traded to Cleveland in 1979, and the club was upended by the Houston Oilers 13-7 in their playoff opener. After an 8-8 season in 1980, the 1981 Denver season saw a change in both ownership and coaching, as Edgar F. Kaiser bought the club in March and Dan Reeves, the offensive coordinator of the Dallas Cowboys, was named head coach. Under Reeves, the club finished 10-6 but missed the playoffs.

Injuries and turnovers dropped Denver to a disappointing 2-7 in the strike-marred 1982 season, but the Broncos buoyed their fans in the offseason by acquiring

Stanford All-America quarterback John Elway from the Colts in the biggest trade in Broncos' history. Combining a winning attitude with one of the strongest throwing arms in league history, Elway helped the Broncos to a 9-7 record and a wild-card berth in the playoffs, where they lost to Seattle 31-7.

Denver real estate magnate Patrick Bowlen became majority owner of the franchise in 1984, and the team produced a club-record 13 victories and a division title. But Denver's hopes were dashed when the Broncos lost to the Steelers 24-17 in the divisional playoffs. The Broncos regained the division title in 1986 with an 11-5 record. Elway paced the offense and standout linebacker Karl Mecklenburg headed the defense. Denver defeated the Patriots 22-17 in the playoffs. In the AFC Championship Game in Cleveland, Elway engineered "The Drive," a 98-yard, fourth-quarter march that resulted in a game-tying touchdown pass to Mark Jackson. The Broncos won 23-20 in overtime, but lost to the Giants 39-20 at Pasadena in Super Bowl XXI.

Denver repeated as division champs in 1987, as the Three Amigos receiving corps of Mark Jackson, Vance Johnson, and Ricky Nattiel helped produce a 10-4-1 record. The Broncos defeated the Oilers 34-10 in a divisional playoff game, and won their second consecutive AFC title when Jeremiah Castille made the play of the season by stripping Browns' halfback Earnest Byner of the ball 2 yards short of a game-tying touchdown late in the fourth quarter of a 38-33 win. Against Washington in Super Bowl XXIII in San Diego, the Redskins scored a Super Bowl-record 35 points in the second quarter en route to a 42-10 victory.

Denver won its third division title in four years with an AFC-best 11-5 record in 1989 as rookie back Bobby Humphrey rushed for more than 1,000 yards. In the playoffs, the Broncos beat the Steelers 24-23, then downed the Browns 37-21 in the AFC title game as Elway passed for 395 yards and 3 touchdowns. Playing in their third Super Bowl in four years, the Broncos lost 55-10 to the 49ers in the Louisiana Superdome.

In 1991, Denver went 12-4 and regained the Western Division crown as the defense allowed an AFC-low 235 points. The Broncos beat the Oilers in a divisional playoff game but lost to the Bills 10-7 in the AFC title game. Reeves was fired following an 8-8 season in 1992 and was replaced by defensive coordinator Wade Phillips. The team improved only slightly to 9-7 but lost 42-24 to the Raiders in a wild-card game.

Mike Shanahan replaced Phillips as coach in 1995, and the Broncos went 8-8. But in 1996, the team roared to a 13-3 mark, tying Green Bay for the best regular-season record in the NFL. Terrell Davis led the AFC in rushing, Elway had one of his best seasons, and the defense topped the AFC. With home-field advantage lined up through the playoffs, the Broncos seemed poised for another Super Bowl trip. It all came crashing down when Denver was upset 30-27 by Jacksonville in the Broncos' opening playoff game.

One year later, however, the Broncos were Super Bowl champions for the first time in franchise history. Denver went 12-4 during the regular season to earn a wild- card playoff berth, then avenged the previous season's loss to the Jaguars in the first round. Back-to-back road victories against Kansas City and Pittsburgh gave the Broncos the conference title. In Super Bowl XXXII, Denver ended 13 years of AFC frustration with a 31-24 victory over the favored Green Bay Packers. With the victory, Denver joined the 1980 Oakland Raiders and 1969 Kansas City Chiefs as the only teams to win the Super Bowl without the benefit of a division title.

Elway had a career year by passing for 3,635 yards and 27 touchdowns. Davis led the AFC in rushing with 1,750 yards and 15 touchdowns, and tight end Shannon Sharpe had 72 receptions.

Having finally captured the elusive Super Bowl title, Elway mulled retirement, but he returned to help the Broncos defend their world championship in 1998. Denver breezed through the regular season, winning its first 13 games. A loss to the New York Giants in the Meadowlands ended the Broncos' bid for a perfect season, but they finished 14-2. Elway surpassed 50,000 yards and 300 touchdowns for his career. Davis rushed for 2,008 yards, the third-highest mark in league history. Denver's franchise-record 501 points topped the AFC.

On the same day he was named *Associated Press's* NFL MVP, Davis rushed for 199 yards to lift the Broncos into the AFC title game for the second consecutive year with a 38-3 victory over Miami in a divisional playoff game at Mile High Stadium. Denver overcame a 10-0 third-quarter deficit to defeat the visiting Jets 23-10 to repeat as AFC champions. Two weeks later, Elway earned most-valuable-player honors as Denver won its second consecutive Super Bowl, 34-19 over Atlanta.

BRONCOS RECORD 1960-1998

YEAR	WON	LOST	TIED	PCT.	FIN	PF	PA
1960	4	9	1	.308	4	309	393
1961	3	11	0	.214	3	251	432
1962	7	7	0	.500	2	353	334
1963	2	11	1	.154	4	301	473
1964	2	11	1	.154	4	240	438
1965	4	10	0	.286	4	303	392
1966	4	10	0	.286	4	196	381
1967	3	11	0	.214	4	256	409
1968	5	9	0	.357	4	255	404
1969	5	8	1	.385	4	297	344
1970	5	8	1	.385	4	253	264
1971	4	9	1	.308	4	203	275
1972	5	9	0	.357	3	325	350
1973	7	5	2	.571	2	354	296
1974	7	6	1	.536	2	302	294
1975	6	8	0	.429	2	254	307
1976	9	5	0	.643	2	315	206
1977a	12	2	0	.857	1	274	148
1978b	10	6	0	.625	1	282	198
1979c	10	6	0	.625	2	289	262
1980	8	8	0	.500	4	310	323
1981	10	6	0	.625	2	321	289
1982	2	7	0	.222	12	148	226
1983c	9	7	0	.563	3	302	327
1984b	13	3	0	.813	1	353	241
1985	11	5	0	.688	2	380	329
1986a	11	5	0	.688	1	378	327
1987a	10	4	1	.700	1	379	288
1988	8	8	0	.500	2	327	352
1989a	11	5	0	.688	1	362	226
1990	5	11	0	.313	5	331	374
1991d	12	4	0	.750	1	304	235
1992	8	8	0	.500	3	262	329
1993c	9	7	0	.563	3	373	284
1994	7	9	0	.438	4	347	396
1995	8	8	0	.500	4	388	345
1996b	13	3	0	.813	1	391	275
1997e	12	4	0	.750	2	472	287
1998f	14	2	0	.875	1	501	309
39 Years	295	275	10	.518	—	12,241	12,362

a AFC Western Division Champion; AFC Champion; 2-1 in Playoffs
b AFC Western Division Champion; 0-1 in Playoffs
c AFC Wild Card Qualifier for Playoffs; 0-1 in Playoffs
d AFC Western Division Champion; 1-1 in Playoffs
e Super Bowl Champion; 4-0 in Playoffs
f Super Bowl Champion; 3-0 in Playoffs

COACHING HISTORY
(311-286-10)

1960-61	Frank Filchock	7-20-1
1962-64	Jack Faulkner*	9-22-1
1964-66	Mac Speedie**	6-19-1
1966	Ray Malavasi	4- 8-0
1967-71	Lou Saban***	20-42-3
1971	Jerry Smith	2- 3-0
1972-76	John Ralston	34-33-3
1977-80	Robert (Red) Miller	42-25-0
1981-92	Dan Reeves	117-79-1
1993-94	Wade Phillips	16-17-0
1995-98	Mike Shanahan	54-18-0

* Released after four games in 1964
** Resigned after two games in 1966
*** Resigned after nine games in 1971

Indianapolis Colts

Like the Cleveland Browns and San Francisco 49ers, the Indianapolis Colts can trace their heritage to the All-America Football Conference.

The original Colts were founded in 1947, when the owners of the Miami Seahawks gave up their AAFC franchise after a disastrous 3-11 season that saw the team lose badly on the field and at the gate. With the city of Miami unwilling to support a marginal pro team, Robert Rodenberg transferred the franchise to Baltimore, where they were renamed the Colts. When the young team faced bankruptcy, Baltimore Mayor Thomas D'Alesandro, Jr., formed a citizen's syndicate that kept it from going out of business. In 1948, the club tied for the AAFC Eastern title with a 7-7 record before losing a playoff to the Bills.

When the AAFC and NFL merged following the 1949 season, the Colts joined the Browns and 49ers as the three AAFC teams were admitted to the NFL. After losing 11 games in 1950 and considerable money at the box office, Colts owner Abraham Watner gave his franchise back to the NFL on January 18, 1951. Baltimore fans protested the loss of their team, and, on January 23, 1952, a second incarnation of the Colts became a National Football League franchise.

Headed by businessman Carroll Rosenbloom, the club selected blue, silver, and white as its colors, then pulled off one of the biggest trades in league history by agreeing to a 15-player deal with the Browns. Keith Molesworth was named head coach, and the club went 3-9. The Colts repeated that record in 1954, this time under former Browns assistant Wilbur (Weeb) Ewbank. Molesworth was switched to chief scout, and his keen eye for talent paid off in 1955 when 12 rookies made the squad, among them end Raymond Berry and fullback Alan Ameche.

Bolstered by young talent, the Colts improved to 5-6-1, then drafted halfback Lenny Moore, plucked defensive tackle Eugene (Big Daddy) Lipscomb off the waiver wire, and took a chance on stoop-shouldered semipro quarterback John Unitas. Unitas had been cut from the Steelers and was plying his trade for $6 a game on the dirt fields of Pittsburgh for the Bloomfield Rams. He was signed as a backup to George Shaw but became a starter four games into the 1956 season when Shaw went down with an injury. The Colts continued to struggle on the field, and, with Ewbank's job reportedly on the line, Unitas launched a 53-yard touchdown pass to beat the Rams in the season finale.

They added another offensive star in 1957, drafting Ohio State's Jim Parker, a massive but agile 275-pound tackle who was regarded as the best college lineman in 1956. In 1957, their 7-5 mark was the first winning record for any Baltimore Colts team. Ewbank had promised a championship within five years when he took over. In 1958, the Colts claimed their first division title with a 9-3 record, then met the New York Giants for the NFL championship in Yankee Stadium on December 28. In what has been called "the greatest game ever played," Unitas put together two textbook drives, one to tie the game with 7 seconds left, the second to win it 23-17 on Ameche's 1-yard run in the NFL's first official overtime.

With a defense that included future Hall-of-Fame inductees in end Gino Marchetti and tackle Art Donovan, the Colts duplicated their record from the previous year and retained the division championship in 1959. They rematched with the Giants in the NFL title game, this time played in Baltimore. Again, the Colts trailed in the fourth quarter, this time 9-7, but Unitas keyed a comeback that produced 24 unanswered points and a 31-16 victory.

Injuries and old age ended the Colts' championship run in 1960, and Ewbank was fired following the 1962 campaign and replaced by Don Shula, a defensive back with the Colts in the early 1950s and then a defensive coach for the Detroit Lions. The franchise rebuilt with young stars such as Tom Matte and John Mackey. The Colts returned to the top of the Western Division pack in 1964 as the aging Moore led the league in rushing touchdowns. The Colts scored a club-record 428 points and led the NFL in both scoring offense and defense, but were upset by Cleveland 27-0 in the NFL Championship Game.

Unitas and his backup, Gary Cuozzo, both were sidelined by injuries in 1965, but Baltimore made another run at the division title as Shula built his late-season offense around the multitalented Matte, a running back who had been a quarterback at Ohio State. Wearing a plastic wrist brace that carried the Colts' list of plays, Matte led Baltimore to a 20-17 victory in Los Angeles in the regular-season finale, giving the Colts a 10-3-1 record and a tie with Green Bay for the Western Division title. In a playoff in frigid Green Bay, the Colts lost to the Packers 13-10 in overtime.

Shula and his club recorded one of the greatest regular seasons in NFL history in 1968. Ironically, the Colts' success came without Unitas, who was sidelined with a chronic sore elbow. Journeyman Earl Morrall threw a league-high 26 touchdowns and ranked number one among NFL quarterbacks as he led the Colts to a 13-1 season and was named league MVP. The defense featured all-pros in linebacker Mike Curtis, cornerback Bobby Boyd, and safety Rick Volk. Shula and assistants Bill Arnsparger and Chuck Noll installed a scheme of shifting fronts and rotating zones buttressed by an eight-man maximum blitz that shut out three opponents and tied an NFL record by allowing just 144 points.

Baltimore's only blemish in the 1968 regular season was a 30-20 loss to the Browns on October 20, but, after mauling the Minnesota Vikings in the mud of Memorial Stadium 24-14 in a first-round playoff game, the Colts got revenge on the Browns, routing them 34-0 in Cleveland to win the NFL Championship Game. Considered by experts one of the greatest teams ever, the Colts entered Super Bowl III in Miami as 18-point favorites over the AFL's New York Jets. The Jets stunned the experts by pulling off a 16-7 upset.

The Colts finished with an 8-5-1 record in 1969. Shula fell out of favor with Rosenbloom, and on February 18, left to become head coach of the Miami Dolphins. Don McCafferty, a career assistant with the Colts, was named head coach as the club moved into the realigned AFC Eastern Division. The addition of wide receivers Eddie Hinton and Roy Jefferson lent speed to the offense, and the defense got younger with the emergence of end Roy Hilton and linebacker Ted Hendricks. Jim O'Brien, a 23-year-old, took over the kicking chores.

The Colts led the AFC in scoring with 321 points, and displayed a flair for the dramatic by earning 6 of their 11 victories by 7 points or less. Highlights of the season included a victory over their Super Bowl III nemesis, Namath and the Jets, in Shea Stadium, and a 35-0 shelling of Shula and the Miami Dolphins. Baltimore defeated the Cincinnati Bengals 17-0 in an AFC playoff game, then won the conference title with a 27-17 victory over Oakland as Norm Bulaich ran for 2 touchdowns.

The Colts arrived at Super Bowl V in the Miami Orange Bowl eager to atone for their poor showing in the same setting two years prior. O'Brien booted a 32-yard field goal with five seconds left to give the Colts a 16-13 victory over the Cowboys.

Baltimore returned to the playoffs in 1971 as the defense allowed a club-record low 140 points. The Colts shut down Cleveland 20-3 in a first-round playoff game the day after Christmas, but Baltimore's hopes of returning to the Super Bowl ended a week later in the Orange Bowl, when they lost to Miami 21-0 in the AFC title game.

On July 26, 1972, Robert Irsay, a 49-year-old Illinois businessman, acquired the Colts from Rosenbloom in exchange for his Los Angeles Rams' franchise. Joe Thomas was named vice president and general manager. Baltimore endured three consecutive losing seasons from 1972-74 as many of the old stars left the team via retirements or trades. The painful process of rebuilding saw Unitas dealt away to San Diego on January 22, 1973.

Ted Marchibroda, a low-key and long-time assistant to George Allen, was named head coach of the Colts on January 15, 1975. They won the division with a 10-4 record behind an explosive offense headed by 23-year-old quarterback Bert Jones, and Lydell Mitchell, who became the first 1,000-yard running back in franchise history. Their surprising season ended in the first round of the playoffs, when they lost to the defending Super Bowl-champion Steelers 28-10.

The 1976 season began on an ominous note when Marchibroda and Irsay clashed following a preseason loss. Marchibroda resigned, the team threatened mutiny, and Marchibroda was reinstated September 7. The turmoil had little effect on the Colts as Mitchell ran for a club-record 1,200 yards and the offense, bolstered by George Kunz, an all-pro tackle from Atlanta, generated a conference-high 417 points. Baltimore repeated as Eastern Division champions with an 11-3 record, but once again ran into the Steelers in the first round of the playoffs. The Colts lost 40-14 in Baltimore.

The 1977 offseason was brightened by the return of Unitas as a special consultant to the team. The Colts claimed their third consecutive division crown with a 30-24 victory over the Patriots in the final game of the regular season. Before a festive Christmas Eve crowd in Baltimore, the Colts had the defending Super Bowl-champion Raiders on the ropes late in the game but lost 37-31 in double overtime in one of the greatest games ever played.

After a three-year playoff run, Irsay's team suffered six consecutive losing seasons, including an 0-8-1 mark in the 1982 strike season. The Colts rebounded the following year to go 7-9, the best turnaround ever in the NFL for a winless team, and capped their season with a 20-10 victory at home over Houston on December 18 in the season finale. Few realized it at the time, but that game marked the final time the Colts would play as the home team in Memorial Stadium. In 1984, the Colts moved to Indianapolis.

While their surroundings changed, the club continued its losing ways, going 4-12 in 1984, the Colts' first year in the Hoosier Dome. They finally gave their new Midwest fans something to cheer about in 1987, when Ron Meyer coached them to the Eastern Division title with a 9-6 record. Key to the season was the acquisition of running back Eric Dickerson on Halloween. The Colts went 6-3 after Dickerson arrived via a trade with the Rams. The Colts lost in the playoffs 38-21 in Cleveland.

Meyer was fired five games into a 1-15 season in 1991 as the Colts scored just 143 points, the lowest total ever in a 16-game NFL season. Marchibroda was brought back to coach the team in 1992, and the team improved to 9-7. The Colts struggled the next season, going 4-12 in 1993, then improved to 8-8 in 1994 when rookie halfback Marshall Faulk, who was the second pick in the draft, ran for 1,282 yards.

The 1995 season saw the Colts achieve Cinderella status when former Bears quarterback Jim Harbaugh played with guts and guile in leading the team to the playoffs with a 9-7 record. Indianapolis upset the Chargers in San Diego and the Chiefs in Kansas City, then narrowly missed beating the Steelers in Pittsburgh in the AFC title game when Harbaugh's last-second desperation pass barely fell incomplete in the end zone. Marchibroda left the team at season's end and was replaced by offensive coordinator Lindy Infante.

In some ways, the Colts' 1996 season was even a greater effort than their Cinderella run the year before. No team in the league suffered more injuries. Marshall Faulk missed large blocks of playing time and was seldom healthy when he could play. Harbaugh, playing behind an often makeshift offensive line, spent much of the season on his back or running for his life. Through it all, the club still qualified for the playoffs. But in a rematch of their 1995 AFC title tilt, the Colts were outmuscled by the bigger, stronger, and healthier Steelers 42-14 in a wild-card playoff game.

One year later, the Colts slumped to 3-13, dropping seven games by six points or less. General manager Bill Tobin subsequently was replaced by Bill Polian, and Infante gave way to former Saints coach Jim Mora.

Indianapolis went 3-13 again in 1998 but offered promise. Former Tennessee All-America quarterback Peyton Manning was the club's top pick in the draft and showed flashes of brilliance in his rookie season. He teamed with Faulk to give the offense spark. Faulk finished second among AFC rushers with 1,319 yards and led the NFL with 2,227 yards rushing and receiving.

COLTS RECORD 1953-1998

YEAR	WON	LOST	TIED	PCT.	FIN	PF	PA
Baltimore Colts							
1953	3	9	0	.250	5	182	350
1954	3	9	0	.250	6	131	279
1955	5	6	1	.455	4	214	239
1956	5	7	0	.417	4	270	322
1957	7	5	0	.583	3	303	235
1958a	9	3	0	.750	1	381	203
1959a	9	3	0	.750	1	374	251
1960	6	6	0	.500	4	288	234
1961	8	6	0	.571	3t	302	307
1962	7	7	0	.500	4	293	288
1963	8	6	0	.571	3	316	285
1964b	12	2	0	.857	1	428	225
1965c	10	3	1	.769	2	389	284
1966	9	5	0	.643	2	314	226
1967	11	1	2	.917	2	394	198
1968d	13	1	0	.929	1	402	144
1969	8	5	1	.615	2	279	268
1970e	11	2	1	.846	1	321	234
1971f	10	4	0	.714	2	313	140
1972	5	9	0	.357	3	235	252
1973	4	10	0	.286	4	226	341
1974	2	12	0	.143	5	190	329
1975g	10	4	0	.714	1	395	269
1976g	11	3	0	.786	1	417	246
1977g	10	4	0	.714	1	295	221
1978	5	11	0	.313	5	239	421
1979	5	11	0	.313	5	271	351
1980	7	9	0	.438	4	355	387
1981	2	14	0	.125	4	259	533
1982	0	8	1	.056	14	113	236
1983	7	9	0	.438	4	264	354
Indianapolis Colts							
1984	4	12	0	.250	4	239	414
1985	5	11	0	.313	4	320	386
1986	3	13	0	.188	5	229	400
1987g	9	6	0	.600	1	300	238
1988	9	7	0	.563	2	354	315
1989	8	8	0	.500	2	298	301
1990	7	9	0	.438	3	281	353
1991	1	15	0	.063	5	143	381
1992	9	7	0	.563	3	216	302
1993	4	12	0	.250	5	189	378
1994	8	8	0	.500	3	307	320
1995h	9	7	0	.563	2	331	316
1996i	9	7	0	.562	3	317	334
1997	3	13	0	.188	5	313	401
1998	3	13	0	.188	5	310	444
46 Years	313	342	7	.478	—	13,300	13,935

a NFL Western Conference Champion; NFL Champion; 1-0 in Playoffs
b NFL Western Conference Champion; 0-1 in Playoffs
c NFL Western Conference Runner-up; 1-1 in Playoffs
d NFL Western Conference Champion; NFL Champion; 2-1 in Playoffs
e AFC Eastern Division Champion; Super Bowl Champion; 3-0 in Playoffs
f AFC Wild Card Qualifier for Playoffs; 1-1 in Playoffs
g AFC Eastern Division Champion; 0-1 in Playoffs
h AFC Wild Card Qualifier for Playoffs; 2-1 in Playoffs
i AFC Wild Card Qualifier for Playoffs; 0-1 in Playoffs

COACHING HISTORY
BALTIMORE 1953-1983, INDIANAPOLIS 1984-1998
(323-352-7)

1953	Keith Molesworth	3-9-0
1954-62	Weeb Ewbank	61-52-1
1963-69	Don Shula	73-26-4
1970-72	Don McCafferty*	26-11-1
1972	John Sandusky	4-5-0
1973-74	Howard Schnellenberger**	4-13-0
1974	Joe Thomas	2-9-0
1975-79	Ted Marchibroda	41-36-0
1980-81	Mike McCormack	9-23-0
1982-84	Frank Kush***	11-28-1
1984	Hal Hunter	0-1-0
1985-86	Rod Dowhower#	5-24-0
1986-91	Ron Meyer##	36-36-0
1991	Rick Venturi	1-10-0
1992-95	Ted Marchibroda	32-35-0
1996-1997	Lindy Infante	12-21-0
1998	Jim Mora	3-13-0

* Released after five games in 1972
** Released after three games in 1974
*** Resigned after 15 games in 1984
# Released after 13 games in 1986
Released after five games in 1991

Jacksonville Jaguars

Jacksonville became the NFL's thirtieth franchise on November 30, 1993, headed by shoe magnate Wayne Weaver.

Tom Coughlin, a former New York Giants' assistant under Bill Parcells and the former head coach at Boston College, took over at the helm of the expansion Jaguars, who began play in 1995. Jacksonville was aligned in the AFC Central Division, and earned its first victory with a 17-16 win over the Oilers in week 5. The Jaguars finished the season 4-12. Several players enjoyed solid seasons, including quarterback Mark Brunell, wide receiver Willie Jackson, and defensive end Jeff Lageman.

Coughlin went for defense in the 1996 draft, taking Illinois All-America linebacker Kevin Hardy with his first pick. Jacksonville signed free agents Leon Searcy, a tackle from the Steelers, and claimed Chargers running back Natrone Means off waivers. Far from behaving like a second-year expansion team, the Jaguars opened their season with a home victory over Pittsburgh, then closed with a rush to qualify for the playoffs. Brunell was dangerous running or passing all season, but his play down the stretch particularly was effective. Means, after a slow start, also came on strong at the end.

The club also had some luck going for it. Jacksonville was able to win its final regular-season game and qualify for the playoffs when Atlanta's Morten Andersen missed a short field-goal attempt on the last play of the game. In the Jaguars' wild-card victory over Buffalo, a field goal by Mike Hollis bounced off the upright and through to provide the margin in a 30-27 victory. But an even bigger upset followed in the divisional playoffs. Again by a 30-27 score, the 14-point underdog Jaguars upset the Broncos, the team with the AFC's best record, at Denver. Jacksonville's Cinderella season ended the following week when they were beaten 20-6 by the Patriots.

The Jaguars were back in the playoffs the following year. Brunell passed for 18 touchdowns and directed the team to an 11-5 record and a second-place finish in the AFC Central. The offense revolved around Brunell, tackle Tony Boselli, wide receivers Keenan McCardell and Jimmy Smith (who combined for 167 receptions and 2,488 yards), and Means (who rushed for 9 touchdowns). But the Jaguars were routed 42-17 by eventual Super Bowl-champion Denver in a wild-card playoff game.

In 1998, rookie running back Fred Taylor emerged as

the team's top offensive threat. Taylor took over for injured James Stewart three games into the season and rushed for 1,223 yards and 14 touchdowns. The Jaguars won their first AFC Central Division title with an 11-5 record. Brunell, who missed the final three games of the regular season with an ankle injury, returned for the playoffs. He passed for a touchdown and Taylor ran for 162 yards in a 25-10 victory over visiting New England in the wild-card round. One week later, Jacksonville dropped a hard-fought, 34-24 decision to the host New York Jets in a divisional playoff game.

JAGUARS RECORD 1995-1998

YEAR	WON	LOST	TIED	PCT.	FIN	PF	PA
1995	4	12	0	.250	5	275	404
1996a	9	7	0	.562	2	325	335
1997b	11	5	0	.688	2	394	318
1998c	11	5	0	.688	1	392	338
4 Years	35	29	0	.547	—	1,386	1,395

a AFC Wild Card Qualifier for Playoffs; 2-1 in Playoffs
b AFC Wild Card Qualifier for Playoffs; 0-1 in Playoffs
c AFC Central Division Champion; 1-1 in Playoffs

COACHING HISTORY
(38-32-0)

1995-98	Tom Coughlin	38-32-0

Kansas City Chiefs

The Kansas City Chiefs, and to a larger extent, the American Football League, were born out of the frustration of Texas millionaire Lamar Hunt, who tried to get an NFL franchise in the 1950s. Hunt, the son of oilman H.L. Hunt, tried unsuccessfully for several years to obtain ownership of the downtrodden Chicago Cardinals franchise, and to excite NFL owners with the idea of adding expansion teams, particularly in the Southwest.

When Hunt learned other wealthy entrepreneurs had not been able to join the NFL, he decided in 1959 to contact each one with the proposition of forming a new league. Hunt succeeded, and the six-team AFL was officially founded on August 22, 1959. The AFL added Buffalo in October, and Boston in November.

Hunt named his franchise the Dallas Texans and selected Hank Stram, who had been an assistant coach at Purdue and the University of Miami, as head coach. The Texans and expansion Dallas Cowboys of the NFL shared the Cotton Bowl for their home games in 1960. To identify with Dallas fans, the Texans stocked their roster with local players, including quarterback Cotton Davidson of Baylor University and halfback Abner Haynes from North Texas State.

They lost their regular season opener 21-20 to the Chargers in Los Angeles, then earned their first victory with a 34-16 win at Oakland. Haynes won the AFL rushing title in an 8-6 season. The Texans added more homegrown talent in 1961 when they signed All-America center E.J. Holub of Texas Tech, then added defensive tackle Jerry Mays of Southern Methodist. Inconsistent play at quarterback slowed the offense in 1961, however, and Dallas fell to 6-8.

Stram signed quarterback Len Dawson, who had been released by the NFL's Browns. Dawson had spent five NFL seasons riding the bench and was considered by many to be a pro washout. Once Stram gave him a chance to play, Dawson showed how wrong his critics had been. He led the league in completion percentage and touchdowns, and Haynes rushed for 1,049 yards and a league-high 13 touchdowns. End Chris Burford caught an AFL-best 12 touchdowns.

The Texans won their first division title with an 11-3 record. In the AFL title game, the Texans and Oilers staged a 77-minute, 54-second classic. Dallas survived Haynes's disastrous coin-flip decision to give the Oilers both the ball and the wind at the start of the first overtime, and Dallas eventually dethroned the two-time defending league champions 20-17 on rookie Tommy Brooker's 25-yard field goal.

In 1963, Hunt and Stram selected Grambling tackle Buck Buchanan, a future Hall-of-Fame member, as their number-one pick in the college draft. In later rounds, they chose future Hall-of-Fame linebacker Bobby Bell, star guard Ed Budde, and Jerrel Wilson, an outstanding punter. Though they outshone the NFL's Cowboys on the field, the Cowboys won the battle at the gate. When Kansas City mayor H. Roe Bartle invited Hunt to move his franchise out of Dallas with a guarantee of increased ticket sales, Hunt agreed. On May 14, Hunt announced his team would move to Kansas City and the team would be called Chiefs, in honor of Bartle, whose nickname was "Chief."

The move to Kansas City was resisted by many of the players, who had ties to the Dallas area. The players' resentment and the preseason death of rookie Stone Johnson put the team under a cloud. The team finished under .500, but the outlook was brightened by the play of rookies Buchanan, Bell, Budde, and Wilson.

Off-field misfortune continued when a mugging cost tight end Fred Arbanas sight in his left eye. Although he continued to star as a blocker, his pass-catching ability was reduced. Free agent running back Mack Lee Hill averaged a league-best 5.5 yards per carry, but tragedy continued to stalk the club in 1965, when Hill died on the operating table during what was supposed to be routine knee surgery.

The Chiefs continued to draft well. In 1965, they lost Kansas star halfback Gale Sayers to the Chicago Bears but drafted wide receiver Otis Taylor of Prairie View. The next year, Hunt signed Heisman Trophy halfback Mike Garrett of USC away from the NFL's Los Angeles Rams. Dawson led the league in touchdown passes with 26, Garrett topped the team in rushing, and Taylor led AFL receivers with a 22.4-yard average per catch.

The Chiefs hosted the defending AFL champion Bills at Municipal Stadium before a record crowd of 43,885, the largest ever to see a sporting event in Kansas City. The Chiefs lost 29-14, but the day was not a total loss. Stram negotiated a trade with Bills coach Joe Collier on the field after the game, obtaining kicker Mike Mercer.

In 1966, Mercer went on to lead the league in field goals, and Kansas City stormed to the Western Division title with a 12-2 record. On New Year's Day, the Chiefs faced the Bills in the AFL Championship Game. With the right to represent the AFL against the NFL in the first Super Bowl on the line, Kansas City routed the Bills 31-7.

Kansas City advanced to meet Vince Lombardi's Green

Bay Packers in the first AFL-NFL World Championship Game, played in the Los Angeles Memorial Coliseum on January 15, 1967. The Chiefs surprised observers by playing the heavily favored NFL champions close early on, but lost the historic contest 35-10.

They added blue-chip rookie linebackers Willie Lanier and Jim Lynch in 1967 and signed Norwegian soccer-style kicker Jan Stenerud. Injuries to Taylor and Garrett crippled the Kansas City offense in 1968, but the team still went 12-2 to tie the Raiders for first place in the West. The defense set an AFL record by allowing only 170 points. But the Chiefs lost to Oakland 41-6 in a divisional playoff.

The Chiefs opened the 1969 regular season with easy victories over San Diego and Boston, but the latter proved to be costly. Dawson injured his knee against the Patriots, and the next week, backup quarterback Jacky Lee broke a bone in his ankle in a 24-19 upset loss at Cincinnati. Third-string quarterback Mike Livingston took over the reins of Stram's multiple offense and helped lead Kansas City to a 26-13 victory at Denver. With his quarterback situation unsettled, Stram relied on his ground game more than ever. The team had a deep stable of runners, including the "mini-back" trio of Garrett, Robert (The Tank) Holmes, and Warren McVea. Wendell Hayes, a 220-pound power back, balanced the rushing attack, which led the AFL in rushing yards and touchdowns. Led by All-AFL performers Mays, Buchanan, and safety Johnny Robinson, the defense allowed a league-low 177 points.

The Chiefs closed the season with an 11-3 record. Kansas City advanced to the playoffs to meet the defending Super Bowl-champion New York Jets. On a wind-swept, icy afternoon in Shea Stadium, Lanier and the Chiefs staged the most famous goal-line stand in league history, stopping the Jets on three tries from the 1-yard line to highlight a 13-6 victory. Kansas City then defeated the Raiders 17-7 in the final AFL Championship Game, stopping several Oakland drives deep in Chiefs' territory.

The Chiefs took the field in Tulane Stadium for the final AFL-NFL Super Bowl wearing patches on their uniform sleeves to commemorate the 10-year existence of their league. Dawson's play-calling kept Minnesota's vaunted defense off-balance, and the Chiefs' defense manhandled Vikings quarterback Joe Kapp in a 23-7 victory.

Stram proclaimed his offense the "Offense of the Seventies," but his strategies were hurt by the loss of Garrett, who fell out of favor and was traded to San Diego. Kansas City fell to 7-5-2, but the emergence of young offensive stars such as running back Ed Podolak and end Elmo Wright sparked the club to a 10-3-1 record and the division title in 1971. The Chiefs hosted Miami in the first round of the playoffs on Christmas Day, and for the second time in their franchise history, engaged in a double-overtime classic. Unlike the 1962 AFL title game, however, the Chiefs lost 27-24 after 82 minutes and 40 seconds, the longest game in NFL history.

Stram was fired following a 5-9 season in 1974, and the organization endured mixed results through 1985. Kansas City rode its special-teams play to a playoff berth in 1986. Albert Lewis had 4 of the team's 11 blocked kicks, and the Chiefs had 6 touchdown returns. Special teams accounted for 3 Kansas City scores in a 24-19 victory over the Steelers in the season finale, giving the Chiefs a 10-6 record and a wild-card berth in the playoffs. Their season ended with a 35-15 loss to the Jets. Head coach John Mackovic was fired at season's end and replaced by special teams coach Frank Gansz.

In 1989, Hunt named Marty Schottenheimer head coach, and the team finished above .500 behind talented players such as 1,000-yard fullback Christian Okoye and rookie linebacker Derrick Thomas. In his second season, Shottenheimer's Chiefs began a run of six consecutive playoff appearances.

In 1990, Thomas fueled a big-play defense and quarterback Steve DeBerg and 1,000-yard back Barry Word headed a conservative offense as the club earned a playoff berth with an 11-5 record. The Chiefs lost to Miami 17-16 in a first-round game. They followed with a 10-6 record and second consecutive wild-card berth, then beat the Raiders 10-6 for their first postseason victory since Super Bowl IV, but lost 37-14 to the Bills the following week. Veteran Dave Krieg quarterbacked the Chiefs to another 10-6 record and playoff spot in 1992, but San Diego eliminated them with a 17-0 defeat.

The Chiefs traded for legendary quarterback Joe Montana in 1993, and paced by old pros Montana and former Raiders running back Marcus Allen, they went 11-5 and won their first division title in 22 years. Nick Lowery's 32-yard field goal in overtime gave Kansas City a 27-24 victory over Pittsburgh in the Chiefs' playoff opener, then they topped Houston 28-20 as Montana beat Buddy Ryan's blitzing defenses with 3 touchdown passes. Playing in their first AFC title game, the Chiefs lost 30-13 at Buffalo after Montana left the game with a concussion.

The club slipped to 9-7 in 1994, and lost 27-17 at Miami in a first-round playoff game. Montana retired at season's end and was replaced by Steve Bono, his long-time backup. Displaying poise and leadership in his first starting role, Bono led the Chiefs to an NFL-best 13-3 record, but they were upset in the playoffs, losing at home to the underdog Colts 10-7.

Bono failed to play up to his standard of the year before and was replaced by Rich Gannon late in the 1996 season. The Chiefs failed to qualify for the playoffs for the first time since 1989.

The Chiefs surged past division-leading Denver in December to capture the 1997 AFC West title with a stellar 13-3 record. But a stunning divisional playoff to those same Broncos brought an early end to the season.

The Chiefs started fast in 1998, but a mid-season slump doomed them to a 7-9 finish, their first losing season under Schottenheimer in 10 years. Schottenheimer resigned at season's end, and on January 22, the Chiefs named Gunther Cunningham head coach.

CHIEFS RECORD 1960-1998

YEAR	WON	LOST	TIED	PCT.	FIN	PF	PA
Dallas Texans							
1960	8	6	0	.571	2	362	253
1961	6	8	0	.429	2	334	343
1962a	11	3	0	.786	1	389	233
Kansas City Chiefs							
1963	5	7	2	.417	3	347	263
1964	7	7	0	.500	2	366	306
1965	7	5	2	.583	3	322	285
1966b	11	2	1	.846	1	448	276
1967	9	5	0	.643	2	408	254

YEAR	WON	LOST	TIED	PCT.	FIN	PF	PA
1968c	12	2	0	.857	2	371	170
1969d	11	3	0	.786	2	359	177
1970	7	5	2	.583	2	272	244
1971e	10	3	1	.769	1	302	208
1972	8	6	0	.571	2	287	254
1973	7	5	2	.571	3	231	192
1974	5	9	0	.357	3	233	293
1975	5	9	0	.357	3	282	341
1976	5	9	0	.357	4	290	376
1977	2	12	0	.143	5	225	349
1978	4	12	0	.250	5	243	327
1979	7	9	0	.438	5	238	262
1980	8	8	0	.500	3	319	336
1981	9	7	0	.563	3	343	290
1982	3	6	0	.333	11	176	184
1983	6	10	0	.375	5	386	367
1984	8	8	0	.500	4	314	324
1985	6	10	0	.375	5	317	360
1986f	10	6	0	.625	2	358	326
1987	4	11	0	.267	5	273	388
1988	4	11	1	.281	5	254	320
1989	8	7	1	.531	2	318	286
1990f	11	5	0	.688	2	369	257
1991g	10	6	0	.625	2	322	252
1992f	10	6	0	.625	2	348	282
1993h	11	5	0	.688	1	328	291
1994f	9	7	0	.563	2	319	298
1995e	13	3	0	.813	1	358	241
1996	9	7	0	.562	2	297	300
1997e	13	3	0	.813	1	375	232
1998	7	9	0	.438	4	327	363
39 Years	306	262	12	.538	—	12,410	11,103

a AFL Champion; 1-0 in Playoffs
b AFL Champion; 1-1 in Playoffs
c AFL Western Division Runnerup; 0-1 in Playoffs
d Super Bowl Champion; 3-0 in Playoffs
e AFC Western Division Champion; 0-1 in Playoffs
f AFC Wild Card Qualifier for Playoffs; 0-1 in Playoffs
g AFC Wild Card Qualifier for Playoffs; 1-1 in Playoffs
h AFC Western Division Champion; 2-1 in Playoffs

COACHING HISTORY
DALLAS TEXANS 1960-62, KANSAS CITY 1963-1998
(314-273-12)

1960-74	Hank Stram	129-79-10
1975-77	Paul Wiggin*	11-24-0
1977	Tom Bettis	1-6-0
1978-82	Marv Levy	31-42-0
1983-86	John Mackovic	30-35-0
1987-88	Frank Gansz	8-22-1
1989-98	Marty Schottenheimer	104-65-1

* Released after seven games in 1977

Miami Dolphins

If Joe Robbie had his way in 1965, his AFL expansion franchise would have been situated in historic Philadelphia, rather than his part-time home of Miami.

A Minneapolis lawyer who owned a summer home in Miami, Robbie was a classmate of AFL Commissioner Joe Foss when the two were at the University of South Dakota. In 1965, Robbie approached Foss with the idea of putting an AFL expansion franchise in Philadelphia. Foss rejected the proposal because the NFL Eagles were firmly entrenched there and owned exclusive rights to Franklin Field. Foss suggested Robbie locate in Miami instead, noting the city's favorable climate and growing population. Robbie enlisted the backing of entertainer Danny Thomas and Vice President Hubert Humphrey, and eventually gained the support of Miami mayor Robert King. With a promise that the new franchise could play its home games at the Orange Bowl, the AFL Executive Committee voted on August 16, 1965 to award its first expansion franchise to Robbie and Thomas for $7.5 million.

The new franchise was named the Dolphins in a contest that included 20,000 entries, and former Detroit Lions coach George Wilson was named head coach. Miami opened its first regular season in the Orange Bowl on September 2 against the Oakland Raiders. Although the Dolphins' Joe Auer returned the opening kickoff 95 yards for a touchdown, Miami lost 23-14. The Dolphins earned their first victory in week 6, a 24-7 decision at home against Denver. They finished their inaugural season with a 3-11 record.

Having employed four different quarterbacks during their first season, including Wilson's son, George, Jr., the club made quarterback a priority in the 1967 draft, selecting Purdue star Bob Griese. When starting quarterback John Stofa was injured in the season opener against Denver, Griese ran the offense in a 35-21 victory. The Dolphins improved slightly, finishing 4-10.

Miami strengthened its backfield in 1968 by drafting fullback Larry Csonka and halfback Jim Kiick. Griese set club records for passing and Miami continued to improve, winning five games. General manager Joe Thomas traded for all-pro middle linebacker Nick Buoniconti and guard Larry Little, and drafted speedy halfback Eugene (Mercury) Morris. When the team fell to 3-10-1 in 1969, Wilson was fired as head coach.

Don Shula was named head coach and vice-president of the team on February 18, 1970. Thomas added wide receiver Paul Warfield via trade and drafted safety Jake Scott. The Dolphins won six straight games down the stretch to finish 10-4 and earn their first playoff berth. Miami lost 21-14 to the Raiders on a muddy field in the Oakland Coliseum.

The Dolphins went 10-3-1 and won the Eastern Division in 1971. Griese ranked first in passing among AFC quarterbacks, Csonka became the club's first 1,000-yard back, and Warfield led AFC receivers with 11 touchdowns. The Dolphins won their first playoff contest when Garo Yepremian, who scored a league-high 117 points, kicked a 37-yard field goal to beat the Chiefs 27-24 after 82 minutes, 40 seconds—the longest game ever played. They hosted the Colts in the AFC title game, and used big plays to stun the defending Super Bowl champions 21-0. However, Miami played one of its worst games of the season against the Dallas Cowboys in Super Bowl VI, losing 24-3 in New Orleans.

The Dolphins rebounded from their Super Bowl defeat to Dallas with the greatest season in NFL history. Miami lost Griese to a broken leg in week 5, but, with backup Earl Morrall becoming the top-ranked quarterback in the AFC, they went 14-0 during the regular season and led the AFC in both offense and defense. Csonka and Morris became the first backfield tandem to each rush for 1,000 yards in the same season, and Morris led the AFC in rushing touchdowns with 12. Miami rallied to beat Cleveland 20-14 in a playoff game on Christmas Eve, and followed with a 21-17 victory over Pittsburgh in the AFC title game. The Dolphins completed a 17-0 season with a 14-7 win over the Redskins in Super Bowl VII in Los Angeles. Kiick scored his fourth touchdown of the postseason and Scott earned game MVP honors with 2 interceptions.

Miami's 16-game regular-season win streak ended in week 2 of the 1973 season with a 12-7 loss to the Raiders. They followed by reeling off 10 consecutive victories to clinch their third consecutive Eastern Division title. Behind a stellar offensive line that included center Jim Langer and guard Larry Little, Csonka bulled his way to his third consecutive 1,000-yard season, and Morris averaged an AFC-high 6.4 yards per carry. Bill Arnsparger's celebrated "53" defense, which featured an intricate zone pass defense, allowed just 150 points, a club record for a 14-game season.

Playing with hard-hitting precision, the Dolphins advanced to the playoffs for the fourth consecutive time. Fielding a team that many observers considered better than their 1972 undefeated squad, Miami crushed Cincinnati 34-16 in a playoff game, then dominated the Raiders 27-10 in the AFC Championship Game as Csonka ran for 117 yards and 3 touchdowns. The Dolphins crushed Minnesota in Super Bowl VIII in Houston's Rice Stadium, as Csonka ran for a record 145 yards and 2 touchdowns in a 24-7 victory. Miami joined Lombardi's Packers as the only teams to win back-to-back Super Bowls, and the Dolphins' 32-2 record in 1972-73 is the best two-year mark in NFL history.

The rival World Football League signed stars Csonka, Kiick, and Warfield to 1975 contracts, and that distraction, plus injuries, helped slow the Miami machine in 1974. Even with their three stars for one last season, the Dolphins no longer dominated opponents with regularity. They pulled out three wins in the final 20 seconds, and had to rally from a 24-point deficit to beat the visiting Patriots 34-27 in the final regular-season game. The victory was the Dolphins' thirty-first consecutive win at the Orange Bowl. Miami won its fourth consecutive division title with an 11-3 record, but the Dolphins' season ended with a last-minute 28-26 playoff loss at Oakland.

With Csonka, Kiick, and Warfield gone to the WFL, Shula's club no longer was dominant. The Dolphins didn't return to the playoffs until 1978, when Delvin Williams ran for 1,258 yards and helped the team finish 11-5. Miami lost to Houston 17-9 in a wild-card game. Csonka returned to the Dolphins for the 1979 season and led the team in rushing, and Shula combined old stars such as Griese and Little with youngsters A.J. Duhe and linebacker Kim Bokamper. Shula guided the team to a 10-6 record and its first division title since 1974, but the Dolphins were ousted from the playoffs by a 34-14 divisional-playoff loss to the eventual Super Bowl-champion Steelers.

Griese and Little retired after the Dolphins went 8-8 in 1980, but the club rallied in 1981 to claim the Eastern Division title with an 11-4-1 record. Miami lost a classic playoff battle to San Diego 41-38 after 13:52 of overtime. In 1982, 10 years after he earned distinction as the architect of the No-Name Defense, defensive coordinator Bill Arnsparger built another standout unit that relied on teamwork and precision rather than individual brilliance. The "Killer Bees" defense was so named because of the surnames of its starters—Betters, Bokamper, Baumhower, linebacker Brudzinski, and the Blackwood brothers, Glenn and Lyle, at the safety spots. The Dolphins allowed a conference-low 131 points in the strike-shortened nine-game season, finishing with a 7-2 mark.

David Woodley quarterbacked the team to a 28-13 win over New England in a first-round game, and the defense forced 7 turnovers in a 34-13 victory over the Chargers the following week. Miami shut out the Jets 14-0 in the AFC title game. Seeking their first NFL title since the 1973 season, the Dolphins lost to Washington 27-17 in Super Bowl XVII.

The Dolphins made one of the great decisions in franchise history when they drafted University of Pittsburgh quarterback Dan Marino with the twenty-seventh overall pick in 1983. Marino led the AFC in passing, and the team won 9 of 10 games to end the season with a 12-4 record, good enough for the Eastern Division title. Miami lost to Seattle 27-20 in the playoffs.

The Dolphins served notice of things to come when they opened the 1984 season with a 35-17 victory over the two-time defending NFC-champion Washington Redskins. Marino and his "Marks Brothers" receivers—Mark Duper and Mark Clayton—set NFL records by the handful, including completions (362), yards passing (5,084), and touchdown passes (48). Clayton set another league record with 18 touchdown catches. With their offense seemingly unstoppable, the Dolphins dominated the AFC, winning their second consecutive division title and finishing 14-2. They dominated Seattle 31-10 in a playoff game, then beat the Steelers 45-28 in the AFC title game. They were stopped by San Francisco in Super Bowl XIX, however, losing 38-16.

The Dolphins weren't as awesome the following season, but they won the division with a 12-4 mark that included a 38-24 Monday night victory over Chicago, the Bears' lone loss of the year. Marino again led the NFL in passing yards and touchdowns, and he rallied the Dolphins to a 24-21 victory over Cleveland in their playoff opener. With an eye on a rematch against the Bears in Super Bowl XX, the Dolphins turned over the ball 6 times and lost to New England 31-14 in the AFC title game.

Marino enjoyed another spectacular season in 1986, filling the air with footballs an NFL-record 623 times, but he finally found a defense even he couldn't overcome—his own. The Dolphins yielded 405 points, most in the AFC, and Miami slumped to 8-8. The story was similar the following three seasons when, despite Marino's excellence and the new surroundings of Joe Robbie Stadium, Miami missed the playoffs all three years. The organization was saddened when owner Joe Robbie, who founded the team in 1965, passed away on January 7, 1990.

Shula tightened his defense in 1990 and halfback Sammie Smith gave life to the ground game. The result was a 12-4 record and a return to the playoffs after a four-season absence. Marino passed for 2 fourth-quarter touchdowns to beat Kansas City 17-16 in a first-round playoff game, but the Dolphins were outgunned the next week by the division-rival Bills 44-34.

An 11-5 record in 1992 gave Shula his first division title since 1985. The defense came up big in a 31-0 shutout of San Diego in the playoffs, but the Dolphins lost to the Bills 29-10 in the AFC title game. Miami started the 1993 season with an NFL-best 9-2 record, but with Marino out with a torn Achilles tendon suffered in week 5 at Cleveland, the Dolphins lost their last five games to finish 9-7. Marino returned in 1994 to pass for a conference-high 30 touchdowns and Miami won the Eastern Division with a

10-6 record. Marino won a shootout with Joe Montana in a wild-card playoff game as the Dolphins beat the Chiefs 27-17. But they blew a 21-6 halftime lead and fell to San Diego 22-21 in the divisional playoffs.

Shula guided Miami to the playoffs with a 9-7 record in 1995, but the team was considered a disappointment after spending heavily for free agents. After the Dolphins' 37-22 playoff loss to the Bills, Shula retired, ending a 33-year NFL coaching career. Team owner Wayne Huizenga, who purchased the franchise from the Robbie family in 1994, signed former Cowboys coach Jimmy Johnson to a four-year contract.

The new coach used his first season to weed out playing personnel he considered unproductive and to replace them with less experienced, but hungrier, athletes. But an injury that sidelined Marino for part of the season contributed to a lackluster 8-8 finish.

Johnson's second season came to a crashing end when the Dolphins dropped their final three games of 1997, including a 17-3 wild-card decision at New England. Marino led the AFC with 319 completions and running back Karim Abdul-Jabbar rushed for a conference-best 15 touchdowns, but the Dolphins' offense was held to an average of 5 points per game in the season-ending losing streak. Miami's young defense featured emerging stars such as 24-year old linebacker Zach Thomas.

The defense blossomed in 1998, allowing just 265 points as Miami went 10-6 and earned another wild-card playoff berth. On offense, wide receiver O.J. McDuffie caught 90 passes to lead the AFC. The highlight of Miami's regular season was a 31-21 Monday night victory over Denver, a game in which Marino threw 4 touchdown passes to outduel John Elway. Miami edged visiting Buffalo 24-17 in a wild-card matchup, but the Dolphins were defeated by Denver 38-3 in the divisional playoffs.

DOLPHINS RECORD 1966-1998

YEAR	WON	LOST	TIED	PCT.	FIN	PF	PA
1966	3	11	0	.214	5	213	362
1967	4	10	0	.286	3t	219	407
1968	5	8	1	.385	3	276	355
1969	3	10	1	.231	5	233	332
1970a	10	4	0	.714	2	297	228
1971b	10	3	1	.769	1	315	174
1972c	14	0	0	1.000	1	385	171
1973c	12	2	0	.857	1	343	150
1974d	11	3	0	.786	1	327	216
1975	10	4	0	.714	2	357	222
1976	6	8	0	.429	3	263	264
1977	10	4	0	.714	2	313	197
1978a	11	5	0	.688	2	372	254
1979d	10	6	0	.625	1	341	257
1980	8	8	0	.500	3	266	305
1981d	11	4	1	.719	1	345	275
1982e	7	2	0	.778	2	198	131
1983d	12	4	0	.750	1	389	250
1984b	14	2	0	.875	1	513	198
1985f	12	4	0	.750	1	428	320
1986	8	8	0	.500	3	430	405
1987	8	7	0	.533	3	362	335
1988	6	10	0	.375	5	319	380
1989	8	8	0	.500	3	331	379
1990g	12	4	0	.750	2	336	242
1991	8	8	0	.500	3	343	349
1992f	11	5	0	.688	1	340	281
1993	9	7	0	.563	2	349	351
1994f	10	6	0	.625	1	389	327
1995a	9	7	0	.563	3	398	332
1996	8	8	0	.500	4	339	325
1997a	9	7	0	.563	2	339	327
1998g	10	6	0	.625	2	321	265
33 Years	299	193	4	.607	—	10,989	9,466

a AFC Wild Card Qualifier for Playoffs; 0-1 in Playoffs
b AFC Eastern Division Champion; AFC Champion; 2-1 in Playoffs
c AFC Eastern Division Champion; Super Bowl Champion; 3-0 in Playoffs
d AFC Eastern Division Champion; 0-1 in Playoffs
e AFC Champion; 3-1 in Playoffs
f AFC Eastern Division Champion; 1-1 in Playoffs
g AFC Wild Card Qualifier for Playoffs; 1-1 in Playoffs

COACHING HISTORY
(317-209-4)

1966-69	George Wilson	15- 39-2
1970-95	Don Shula	274-147-2
1996-98	Jimmy Johnson	28-23-0

New England Patriots

The New England Patriots were founded on November 22, 1959, when William H. Sullivan, Jr., and his associates were awarded a charter membership in the American Football League. The franchise was originally called the Boston Patriots, the team nickname originating from a local newspaper contest. In accordance with the nickname, Sullivan chose red, white, and blue for the team colors. Boston College head coach Mike Holovak was named director of player personnel and Lou Saban, a member of Paul Brown's championship Cleveland teams in the 1950s and the coach at Western Illinois, became the team's first head coach.

The Patriots and Denver Broncos made history when they met on Friday night, September 9, 1960, at Boston University Field in the first AFL regular-season game. A crowd of 21,597 was on hand for the game, which saw Boston drop a 13-10 decision. The Patriots earned their first victory one week later, edging the New York Titans 28-24 when defensive back Chuck Shonta scooped up a New York fumble on the last play of the game and scored a touchdown. Boston lost its last four games to finish 5-9.

The Patriots swung a five-player deal with Oakland, obtaining quarterback Vito (Babe) Parilli, and the 31-year-old signal-caller gave the young franchise leadership and experience. The addition of Parilli and the move of cornerback Gino Cappelletti to wide receiver opened up the Boston offense in 1961, and the defense improved with the signing of end Larry Eisenhauer and tackle Houston Antwine.

When his team won just two of its first five games and fan interest fell off, Sullivan fired Saban on October 19 and installed Holovak as his head coach. The Patriots tied powerful Houston 31-31 in Holovak's first game, then routed Buffalo 51-21. The blowout spurred Boston to seven wins in its final eight games en route to a 9-4-1 record. Cappelletti led the team in receptions and, because he also kicked extra points and field goals, he set an AFL record by totaling 147 points.

Middle linebacker Nick Buoniconti strengthened the defense, and the club repeated its 9-4-1 mark in 1962. After playing bridesmaid to the Oilers for two consecutive seasons, the Patriots endured a season-long struggle with the Bills in 1963. The team had an up-and-down season, relying on Cappelletti to kick field goals when the offense bogged down, and on an all-out blitzing defense designed by coordinator Marion Campbell. Boston and Buffalo ended the regular season tied for the division lead with 7-6-1 records.

The teams met to decide the title in Buffalo on December 28, and the Patriots triumphed 26-8 in snow-filled War Memorial Stadium to claim its first division title. One week later, they headed to San Diego to meet the Chargers for the AFL championship. Boston's blitzing defense was ravaged in a 51-10 loss as Chargers fullback Keith Lincoln ran for a title-game record 206 yards. Cappelletti led the league in scoring the following season, registering 155 points, and the team posted its best record of the decade with a 10-3-1 record. But they fell short of repeating as division champs, placing second in the East to 12-2 Buffalo.

Holovak drafted Jim Nance, a 235-pound fullback from Syracuse University, in 1965. Cappelletti continued to carry the team with his kicking and receiving, and Jim Colclough was a solid wide receiver. But injuries and advancing age rendered the team inconsistent, and the Patriots finished 4-8-2.

Nance rushed for an AFL-record 1,458 yards in 1966 as Boston went 8-4-2. The Patriots were knocked out of the championship picture by the New York Jets in the regular-season finale. Nance continued to be the workhorse of the team's ground game in 1967, running for 1,216 yards. The rest of the club slipped below par, and Boston fell to 3-10-1 and last place in the division.

Parilli was traded to the Jets in 1968, Nance was slowed by an ankle injury, and bad knees limited the playing time of former all-pros Buoniconti and Eisenhauer. When the club finished 4-10, Holovak was fired and replaced by Clive Rush, the offensive coordinator for the Jets' Super Bowl champions. Nance rebounded from his poor 1968 season to lead the team in rushing, but Boston lost its first seven games and finished 4-10.

Boston took up residence in the new American Football Conference in 1970, and sought a quick fix for its quarterback problems by signing Joe Kapp, who had led Minnesota to Super Bowl IV following the 1969 season but left the Vikings after a bitter contract dispute. Kapp bombed in Boston, throwing 17 interceptions and just 3 touchdowns. The Patriots finished 2-12, and Rush was fired and replaced by John Mazur.

In its twelfth year of existence, the franchise finally had a suitable place to call home, Schaefer Stadium. The team changed its name from Boston to New England. The Patriots not only had a new stadium, they also had a new look when they drafted Heisman Trophy quarterback Jim Plunkett of Stanford. Plunkett opened his first regular season in style, upsetting the Oakland Raiders, but the club lost five of the next six games and finished 6-8.

In 1973, Sullivan lured University of Oklahoma head coach Chuck Fairbanks to New England, and Fairbanks responded by engineering a youth movement. Fullback Sam (Bam) Cunningham, wide receiver Darryl Stingley, and guard John Hannah were rookies who made an immediate impact. New England improved to 5-9 in Fairbanks's first season, then went 7-7 in 1974.

A quarterback controversy the following season erupted between the injury-plagued Plunkett and rookie Steve Grogan. The controversy split the team and its fans, and the club fell to a disappointing 3-11 in 1975. The quarterback controversy was resolved when Plunkett was dealt to San Francisco. New England went 11-3, the first 11-victory season in franchise history, and handed the eventual Super Bowl-champion Raiders their lone loss of the season, a 48-17 drubbing in Oakland. Cunningham led the ground game, and nose tackle Ray (Sugar Bear) Hamilton anchored the club's 3-4 defense. The Patriots entered the playoffs on a six-game win streak, but lost to the Raiders 24-21 in the final seconds.

A paralyzing hit by Raiders safety Jack Tatum on Stingley in week 3 of the 1978 preseason shook the organization. The Patriots recovered to win seven consecutive games in midseason, and clinched their first AFC divisional title with an 11-5 record. Fairbanks rocked the team before the season finale by announcing he had accepted an offer to coach the University of Colorado in 1979. Sullivan became enraged over the ill-timed announcement, and ordered Fairbanks out of the locker room prior to the season finale, a 23-3 loss to the Dolphins in which the team was coached by assistants Hank Bullough and Ron Erhardt. Fairbanks returned to the sidelines for the playoffs, but the distracted Patriots lost to Houston 31-14.

Following a 2-14 season in 1981, Sullivan named Southern Methodist University's Ron Meyer to replace Erhardt as head coach. Quarterback Steve Grogan set club records for career completions and passing yardage in a 26-13 loss at Chicago on December 5. The Patriots finished 5-4, good enough to earn a playoff berth in the strike-shortened season, but lost to Miami 28-13.

Schaefer Stadium was renamed Sullivan Stadium on May 23, 1983, in honor of the club's founder, William H. Sullivan, Sr. The Patriots went 8-8 in 1983, and Meyer, who angered Sullivan by firing defensive coordinator Rod Rust following a loss to Miami, was replaced by Raymond Berry, the Colts' Hall-of-Fame wide receiver. Young quarterback Tony Eason matured quickly, and linebacker Andre Tippett spearheaded the defense in a 9-7 season.

In 1985, New England rode a six-game winning streak to an 11-5 record and a wild-card berth in the playoffs. Grogan often spelled Eason, and together they directed an offense that included all-pro guard John Hannah, running back Craig James, and wide receiver Irving Fryar. The Patriots clinched a wild-card berth with a 34-23 victory at home against Cincinnati. New England earned its first playoff win since 1963 when Tony Franklin kicked 4 field goals in a 26-14 victory over the Jets at Giants Stadium. The following week in Los Angeles, James rushed for 104 yards and 1 touchdown as New England beat the Raiders 27-20. The Patriots earned their first trip to the Super Bowl with a 31-14 victory over Miami in the AFC title game. Their memorable season ended with a 46-10 loss to the Chicago Bears in Super Bowl XX at the Louisiana Superdome.

The next year, Berry led the club to an 11-5 record and the Eastern Division title, but the Patriots lost 22-17 at Denver in a divisional playoff game. New England followed with an 8-7 record in the strike-shortened 1987 season, and the franchise changed hands in 1988 when Victor Kiam bought the club from the Sullivan family. Grogan and Eason split time at quarterback in a 9-7 season.

Preseason injuries hampered the defense and receiving corps the next season, and New England fell to 5-11. Berry was fired and replaced by Rod Rust, and the 1990 Patriots endured the worst season in franchise history, going 1-15. In 1991, Syracuse University head coach Dick MacPherson took over as the team's third coach in as many years, and his enthusiastic style helped improve the team to 6-10. Running back Leonard Russell garnered NFL offensive rookie-of-the-year honors. MacPherson was hospitalized with diverticulitis during the 1992 season, missing seven games as the team fell to 2-14.

The franchise changed owners in 1992 when James B. Orthwein purchased controlling interest. In 1993, New England switched coaches again, hiring Bill Parcells, who had led the New York Giants to two Super Bowl victories. Parcells made quarterback Drew Bledsoe his number-one pick in the draft. Leonard Russell ran for 1,088 yards and tight end Ben Coates led the team with 53 catches in a 5-11 season.

Robert Kraft, a Patriots' season-ticket holder since 1972, purchased the franchise from Orthwein in January, 1994. Parcells continued to rebuild, and the club responded by going 10-6 and earning a wild-card playoff berth. Bledsoe set a league record with 691 pass attempts, and his team took a seven-game winning streak into the playoffs, where they lost 20-13 to the Browns.

In 1995, rookie of the year Curtis Martin ran for 1,487 yards, but the team struggled and fell to 6-10. Another draft pick, Terry Glenn, set an NFL rookie record with 90 receptions in 1996, helping New England claim its first division title since 1986. The Patriots then blew out the Pittsburgh Steelers 28-3 in a divisional playoff game. New England advanced to Super Bowl XXXI with a 20-6 victory over Jacksonville, but the Patriots did not enjoy their second trip to New Orleans any more than their first, losing 35-21 to Green Bay. Parcells left to coach the New York Jets and was replaced by former Jets coach Pete Carroll.

Carroll led the Patriots to a 10-6 record and a first-place finish in the AFC East in 1997. New England defeated division-rival Miami 17-3 in a wild-card playoff game in Foxboro, but the injury-plagued Patriots were held to just 2 field goals in a 7-6 divisional-playoff loss at Pittsburgh the following weekend.

Bledsoe continued to develop into one of the league's top quarterbacks, passing for a career-high 28 touchdowns. Martin gained 1,160 yards, and Coates had a team-high 66 receptions. The defense was led by end Willie McGinest, linebacker Chris Slade, and free safety Willie Clay, who led the club with 6 interceptions.

Martin left via free agency, but rookie Robert Edwards stepped in to rush for 1,115 yards in 1998. The Patriots went 9-7 and made the playoffs as a wild-card entrant. But Bledsoe broke a finger on his passing hand late in the season. Scott Zolak directed a victory over the 49ers to clinch the playoff berth, but New England's season came to an end with a 25-10 wild-card loss at Jacksonville.

PATRIOTS RECORD 1960-1998

YEAR	WON	LOST	TIED	PCT.	FIN	PF	PA
Boston Patriots							
1960	5	9	0	.357	4	286	349
1961	9	4	1	.692	2	413	313
1962	9	4	1	.692	2	346	295
1963a	7	6	1	.538	1	327	257
1964	10	3	1	.769	2	365	297
1965	4	8	2	.333	3	244	302
1966	8	4	2	.677	2	315	283
1967	3	10	1	.231	5	280	389
1968	4	10	0	.286	4	229	406
1969	4	10	0	.286	3	266	316
1970	2	12	0	.143	5	149	361
New England Patriots							
1971	6	8	0	.429	3	238	325
1972	3	11	0	.214	5	192	446
1973	5	9	0	.357	3	258	300
1974	7	7	0	.500	3	348	289
1975	3	11	0	.214	4	258	358
1976b	11	3	0	.786	2	376	236
1977	9	5	0	.643	3	278	217
1978c	11	5	0	.688	1	358	286
1979	9	7	0	.563	2	411	326
1980	10	6	0	.625	2	441	325
1981	2	14	0	.125	5	322	370
1982d	5	4	0	.556	7	143	157
1983	8	8	0	.500	2	274	289
1984	9	7	0	.563	2	362	352
1985e	11	5	0	.688	3	362	290
1986c	11	5	0	.688	1	412	307
1987	8	7	0	.533	2	320	293
1988	9	7	0	.563	3	250	284
1989	5	11	0	.313	4	297	391
1990	1	15	0	.063	5	181	446
1991	6	10	0	.375	4	211	305
1992	2	14	0	.125	5	205	363
1993	5	11	0	.313	4	238	286
1994b	10	6	0	.625	2	351	312
1995	6	10	0	.375	4	294	377
1996f	11	5	0	.688	1	418	313
1997g	10	6	0	.625	1	369	289
1998b	9	7	0	.563	4	337	329
39 Years	267	304	9	.468	—	11,724	12,429

a AFL Eastern Division Champion; 1-1 in Playoffs
b AFC Wild Card Qualifier for Playoffs; 0-1 in Playoffs
c AFC Eastern Division Champion; 0-1 in Playoffs
d Qualifier for Playoffs; 0-1 in Playoffs
e AFC Champion; 3-1 in Playoffs
f AFC Eastern Division Champion; AFC Champion; 2-1 in Playoffs
g AFC Eastern Division Champion; 1-1 in Playoffs

COACHING HISTORY
BOSTON 1960-1970, NEW ENGLAND 1971-1998
(274-314-9)

1960-61	Lou Saban*	7-12-0
1961-68	Mike Holovak	53-47-9
1969-70	Clive Rush**	5-16-0
1970-72	John Mazur***	9-21-0
1972	Phil Bengtson	1-4-0
1973-78	Chuck Fairbanks#	46-41-0
1978	Hank Bullough-Ron Erhardt##	0-1-0
1979-81	Ron Erhardt	21-27-0
1982-84	Ron Meyer###	18-16-0
1984-89	Raymond Berry	51-41-0
1990	Rod Rust	1-15-0
1991-92	Dick MacPherson	8-24-0
1993-96	Bill Parcells	34-34-0
1997-98	Pete Carroll	20-15-0

* Released after five games in 1961
** Released after seven games in 1970
*** Resigned after nine games in 1972
# Suspended for final regular-season game in 1978
Co-coaches
Released after eight games in 1984

New York Jets

Harry Wismer, who had a long history of involvement in sports as a broadcaster, headed the New York franchise that was founded in the American Football League's first organizational meeting in Chicago on August 14, 1959. Wismer named his team the Titans, declaring that titans are bigger than giants, a veiled reference at his NFL neighbors across town.

Seeking a big-name head coach, Wismer chose Sammy Baugh, who had a Hall-of-Fame career as a quarterback for the Washington Redskins in the 1930s and 1940s. Don Maynard, a former New York Giant and a free agent from

Canada, became the first player to sign a contract with the Titans. Wismer announced the team would play its home games at the Polo Grounds, a structure that housed the baseball Giants until they left for San Francisco in 1958.

New York's first victory came against the Bills in the regular-season opener, a 27-3 win before 10,200 in New York. The Titans relied heavily on quarterback Al Dorow launching bombs to ends Maynard and Art Powell. Dorow threw a league-high 26 touchdown passes and Powell led AFL receivers with 14 touchdown catches. New York went 7-7 and led the AFL with 382 points.

Offense remained the Titans' strong suit in 1961, as Dorow led the league in completions, and fullback Bill Mathis led the league with 846 yards rushing. New York endured an up-and-down season, going 7-7 and making more news off the field than on as Wismer openly feuded with Baugh, AFL Commissioner Joe Foss, and the New York media. In 1962, Wismer replaced Baugh with Clyde (Bulldog) Turner, but the Titans dropped to 5-9 and last place in the East. They again made more off-field news than on. Players' checks bounced, Wismer continued to feud with Foss and the media, and the organization became a shambles. By November, Wismer was bankrupt, and AFL owners stepped in and assumed operating costs to prevent the franchise from folding.

The franchise took its first step toward respectability in 1963, when show-business magnate David (Sonny) Werblin headed a five-man syndicate that purchased the team for $1 million. Eager to erase the memories of Wismer's Titans, Werblin changed the team's name to the Jets and the team colors from blue-and-gold to kelly green-and-white. Werblin named Wilbur (Weeb) Ewbank as head coach. Ewbank had led the Baltimore Colts to consecutive NFL titles in 1958-59, and he gave the Jets instant credibility.

Werblin continued to improve the franchise when he signed Ohio State fullback Matt Snell, the team's number-one pick in the 1964 draft, and the Jets moved from the rusting Polo Grounds to state-of-the-art Shea Stadium that same year. An AFL-record crowd of 44,497 filled Shea for the season opener against Denver, and the Jets responded with a rousing 30-6 victory. The addition of Snell, who earned AFL rookie-of-the-year honors with 948 yards rushing, and colorful players such as linebacker Edward (Wahoo) McDaniel renewed fan interest in the club, and 61,929 were on hand in November when the Jets lost 20-7 to the Buffalo Bills. Unfortunately, that defeat began a string of six losses in seven games that left New York with a 5-8-1 record.

The Jets then made the most important trade in franchise history when it dealt quarterback Jerry Rhome (who never played for the Jets) to Houston for the Oilers' number-one pick in the 1965 draft. With that choice, the Jets selected University of Alabama quarterback Joe Namath.

The Jets signed Namath away from the NFL's St. Louis Cardinals for a then-record sum of $427,000. The Namath signing had a major impact on pro football, helping to speed up the eventual merger between the two warring leagues. Werblin added to his quarterback talent by signing Notre Dame star John Huarte for $200,000. Namath underwent knee surgery and was in the lineup for the first time on September 18 against Kansas City in Shea Stadium. The Jets lost 14-10, then fell to Buffalo, 33-21, as Namath made his first official pro start. New York went 5-8-1 again, but Namath earned rookie-of-the-year honors, and other rookies making an impact included wide receiver George Sauer and linebacker Al Atkinson.

The Jets continued to upgrade their talent in 1966, adding rookie halfback Emerson Boozer. New York hammered Houston 52-13 in the regular-season home opener, setting a club record for points scored. The club started fast, going 4-0-1 before finishing with a 6-6-2 record.

The Jets put together another strong start in 1967, going 5-1-1 through the first half of the season. They clinched their first winning season in week 10 with a 29-24 victory over Boston, and were 7-2-1 and battling the Oilers for the division lead. But the running game suffered without Boozer, who had been lost for the season following a knee injury suffered in week 8. The Jets lost three of their last four games to finish second with an 8-5-1 record. The club set AFL attendance records while selling out all home games at Shea, and Namath passed for 4,007 yards, the first quarterback ever to accumulate more than 4,000 yards in a season.

Werblin sold his interest in the Jets in 1968. New York won their first Eastern Division title that year with an 11-3 record. The Jets led the AFL in defense, and the team set a franchise record by scoring 419 points. Maynard led the league by averaging 23 yards per catch, and the ground game produced an AFL-best 22 touchdowns. The Jets lost 43-32 at Oakland in the "Heidi Game," and later faced the Raiders in Shea Stadium on December 29 in the AFL Championship Game. Namath passed for 3 touchdowns, and linebacker Ralph Baker scooped up an Oakland lateral late in the game to give New York a 27-23 victory. The Jets entered Super Bowl III in Miami as 18-point underdogs to the powerful Baltimore Colts, and Namath made national headlines by predicting a Jets' victory. New York stunned the experts with a 16-7 win.

Namath shocked the football world for the second time in six months when he tearfully announced in June that he was retiring because of a controversy concerning his ownership of a New York nightclub, Bachelors III. Namath eventually sold his shares in the nightclub and returned to lead the Jets to a 10-4 record and their second consecutive Eastern Division title in 1969. The Jets fell to Kansas City 13-6 in a first-round playoff game at Shea Stadium.

The Jets opened the 1970 season in historic fashion, playing the Cleveland Browns in the first Monday night television game. New York lost 31-21, a harbinger of their season. Injuries prevented the team from competing in the realigned American Football Conference. Namath and Snell both were sidelined for the second half of the season, and the team finished with a 4-10 record.

From 1971-1980, the Jets never finished above .500, despite a succession of changes. Ewbank resigned after the 1973 season, and Charley Winner, Ken Shipp, Lou Holtz, Mike Holovak, and Walt Michaels took their turns as head coach. Michaels led the club to the playoffs in 1981, when the Jets went 10-5-1 for their first winning season since 1969. Defense keyed the club's resurgence, as linemen Mark Gastineau and Joe Klecko headed New York's heralded Sack Exchange. The Jets fell to Buffalo 31-27 in a first-round playoff game.

The Jets returned to the playoffs in 1982 after posting a 6-3 record in the strike-shortened season. They stunned the Bengals and the Raiders on the road in the playoffs before falling to the Dolphins 14-0 at Miami in the AFC Championship Game.

New York didn't return to the postseason until 1985, when head coach Joe Walton presided over a turnaround that saw his team go from 7-9 in 1984 to 11-5. The defense set a club record by allowing an average of just 16.5 points per game. The Jets failed to make it out of the first round of the playoffs, losing 26-14 to New England.

Walton guided his team to a 10-6 finish in 1986. Quarterback Jim O'Brien passed for 25 touchdowns, 20 of them to wide receivers Al Toon and Wesley Walker. The franchise earned its first playoff victory since Super Bowl III when the Jets beat Kansas City 35-15 in a first-round game. New York's season ended the following week with a 20-17 loss at Cleveland in double overtime.

Walton was replaced in 1990 by Bruce Coslet, who guided the club to a 6-10 record his first season. The Jets went 8-8 in 1991 and made the playoffs as a wild-card team, losing 17-10 at Houston. Boomer Esiason, who quarterbacked the Bengals to Super Bowl XXIII, joined the Jets before the 1993 season. Another 8-8 finish cost Coslet his job, and longtime owner Leon Hess installed Pete Carroll as his head coach for the 1994 season. Carroll had the Jets on the verge of first place at 6-5, but a crushing defeat to Miami started a season-ending five-game losing streak that cost Carroll his job.

Enter former Eagles coach Rich Kotite, who worked no miracles in 1995, when the Jets won just 3 of 16 games. The team showed promise for the 1996 season when it signed free-agent quarterback Neil O'Donnell and offensive coordinator Ron Erhardt from AFC-champion Pittsburgh, and made USC star wide receiver Keyshawn Johnson the number-one pick in the college draft. Johnson had an effective rookie year, but O'Donnell was injured most of the year. Little went right. New York finished 1-15, Kotite stepped aside, and Hess brought in former Giants and Patriots coach Bill Parcells to turn around a franchise that entered 1997 having lost 33 of its previous 37 games.

Parcells's influence was immediate and dramatic. New York carried an 8-4 record beyond Thanksgiving before finishing the 1997 season at 9-7. Adrian Murrell led the team in rushing with 1,086 yards and Johnson had 70 catches for 963 yards. Glenn Foley replaced O'Donnell as the team's top quarterback, and a defense that gave up an AFC-high 454 points the year before yielded just 287 under the guidance of Parcells's long-time friend and coordinator Bill Belichick.

One year later, the Jets reached the AFC Championship Game. New York went 12-4 during the regular season and won its first AFC Eastern Division title. The Jets' balance was evident: They finished second in the AFC in both points scored (416) and points allowed (266). Vinny Testaverde took over at quarterback and turned in a Pro Bowl performance, leading AFC signal callers with a 101.6 passer rating. Curtis Martin, a free-agent acquisition, ranked fourth in the AFC with 1,287 rushing yards; Johnson was fourth in receiving with 83 catches for 1,131 yards and tied for the conference lead with 10 receiving touchdowns.

Martin and Johnson each scored 2 touchdowns in a 34-24 victory over Jacksonville in the divisional playoffs. One week later, in their first conference championship game in 16 years, the Jets led Denver 10-0 in the third quarter before falling 23-10.

JETS RECORD 1960-1998

YEAR	WON	LOST	TIED	PCT.	FIN	PF	PA
N.Y. Titans							
1960	7	7	0	.500	2	382	399
1961	7	7	0	.500	3	301	390
1962	5	9	0	.357	4	278	423
N.Y. Jets							
1963	5	8	1	.385	4	249	399
1964	5	8	1	.385	3	278	315
1965	5	8	1	.385	2	285	303
1966	6	6	2	.500	3	322	312
1967	8	5	1	.615	2	371	329
1968a	11	3	0	.786	1	419	280
1969b	10	4	0	.714	1	353	269
1970	4	10	0	.286	3	255	286
1971	6	8	0	.429	4	212	299
1972	7	7	0	.500	2	367	324
1973	4	10	0	.286	5	240	306
1974	7	7	0	.500	4	279	300
1975	3	11	0	.214	5	258	433
1976	3	11	0	.214	4	169	383
1977	3	11	0	.214	4	191	300
1978	8	8	0	.500	3	359	364
1979	8	8	0	.500	3	337	383
1980	4	12	0	.250	5	302	395
1981c	10	5	1	.656	2	355	287
1982d	6	3	0	.667	6	245	166
1983	7	9	0	.438	5	313	331
1984	7	9	0	.438	3	332	364
1985c	11	5	0	.688	2	393	264
1986e	10	6	0	.625	2	364	386
1987	6	9	0	.400	5	334	360
1988	8	7	1	.531	4	372	354
1989	4	12	0	.250	5	253	411
1990	6	10	0	.375	4	295	345
1991c	8	8	0	.500	2	314	293
1992	4	12	0	.250	4	220	315
1993	8	8	0	.500	3	270	247
1994	6	10	0	.375	5	264	320
1995	3	13	0	.188	5	233	384
1996	1	15	0	.063	5	279	454
1997	9	7	0	.563	3	348	287
1998f	12	4	0	.750	1	416	266
39 Years	252	320	8	.441	—	11,807	13,026

a AFL Eastern Division Champion; AFL Champion; Super Bowl Champion; 2-0 in Playoffs
b AFL Eastern Division Champion; 0-1 in Playoffs
c AFC Wild Card Qualifier for Playoffs; 0-1 in Playoffs
d AFC Qualifier for Playoffs; 2-1 in Playoffs
e AFC Wild Card Qualifier for Playoffs; 1-1 in Playoffs
f AFC Eastern Division Champion; 1-1 in Playoffs

COACHING HISTORY
NEW YORK TITANS 1960-62, NEW YORK JETS 1963-1998
(258-327-8)

1960-61	Sammy Baugh	14-14-0
1962	Clyde (Bulldog) Turner	5-9-0
1963-73	Weeb Ewbank	73-78-6
1974-75	Charley Winner*	9-14-0
1975	Ken Shipp	1-4-0
1976	Lou Holtz**	3-10-0
1976	Mike Holovak	0-1-0
1977-82	Walt Michaels	41-49-1
1983-89	Joe Walton	54-59-1
1990-93	Bruce Coslet	26-39-0
1994	Pete Carroll	6-10-0
1995-96	Rich Kotite	4-28-0
1997-98	Bill Parcells	22-12-0

* Released after nine games in 1975
** Resigned after 13 games in 1976

Oakland Raiders

When the American Football League was formed on

August 14, 1959, it included a Minneapolis franchise. In January, 1960, however, Minneapolis suddenly pulled out of the AFL, joined the rival NFL, and became the Minnesota Vikings. The move infuriated AFL owners, in particular Los Angeles Chargers owner Barron Hilton, who informed his fellow owners that unless they replaced Minneapolis with a West Coast franchise, he would withdraw from the league. AFL owners satisfied Hilton's demand when they gave the eighth and final charter franchise to an Oakland group led by businessman Y.C. (Chet) Soda.

Soda and his seven partners considered various nicknames for their new team, including Senors and Dons, before settling on Raiders. Former Navy coach Eddie Erdelatz was named the team's first head coach, and the club shared Kezar Stadium with the NFL's San Francisco 49ers as its home site. The Raiders began the season with a few solid players, including quarterbacks Tom Flores and Babe Parilli, and linemen Jim Otto and Wayne Hawkins.

The Raiders' first regular-season game ended in a 37-22 loss at home to Houston, and it wasn't until week 3 that the franchise claimed its first victory, a 14-13 rematch over the Oilers. The club ended its inaugural campaign with a 6-8 record as Flores completed a league-high 54 percent of his passes. The Raiders moved their home games in 1961 to Candlestick Park in San Francisco, but their 2-12 record gave their dwindling fan base little to cheer about. Erdelatz was fired when the club lost to Houston and San Diego on consecutive weekends by a combined 99-0. The team took up residence in Frank Youell Field, a high school complex in Oakland named after an undertaker, and hired Marty Feldman as head coach in 1962, but the Raiders continued to be the worst in the West, dropping their first 13 games of the season to extend their losing streak to 19 games. Feldman was replaced by Red Conkright, and the losing streak finally ended in the last regular-season game, when the Raiders beat Boston 20-0.

In 1963, the Raiders named San Diego assistant coach Al Davis as head coach and general manager. Davis engineered one of the most startling turnarounds in pro football history when he led the Raiders to a 10-4 record and a second-place finish in the Western Division. New stars emerged on the Oakland scene as running back Clem Daniels and end Art Powell fueled Davis's explosive offense. The team slumped the following season, falling to 5-7-2, then added future stars in wide receiver Fred Biletnikoff and defensive tackle Tom Keating while compiling consecutive 8-5-1 records in 1965 (under Davis) and 1966 (under John Rauch).

Davis left in 1966 for a short stint as AFL commissioner, then returned to Oakland as managing general partner. He traded for Buffalo quarterback Daryle Lamonica prior to the 1967 season, acquired backup quarterback-kicker George Blanda and cornerback Willie Brown, and drafted guard Gene Upshaw. Each played a key role as the team, coached by Rauch, won an AFL-record 13 games and crushed the Houston Oilers 40-7 in the league title game. Oakland advanced to Super Bowl II in Miami, losing to the NFL-champion Green Bay Packers 33-14.

Behind the deep passing of Lamonica and a fearsome defense, the Raiders won the Western Division the following two seasons, but dropped AFL title-game decisions to the Jets (27-23) and Chiefs (17-7). John Madden replaced Rauch in 1969, and in 1970, Oakland reached the title game of the newly-realigned American Football Conference, but lost to Baltimore 27-17.

The Raiders' postseason woes continued in 1972, when they suffered a heartbreaking 13-7 loss at Pittsburgh in a first-round playoff game remembered for Steelers back Franco Harris's Immaculate Reception. Keyed by southpaw quarterback Ken Stabler, and a hard-hitting defense headed by Jack Tatum, the Raiders made five consecutive appearances in the AFC title game following the 1973-77 seasons. Madden's team was frustrated by great teams in Miami and Pittsburgh, but gained a measure of revenge in 1976, when they defeated the two-time defending world-champion Steelers 24-7 to win the conference title. The Raiders made their first trip to the Super Bowl since the 1967 season, and, behind MVP Fred Biletnikoff, manhandled the Minnesota Vikings 32-14 in Super Bowl XI in Pasadena.

Madden guided his club back to the AFC title game in 1977, where they lost 20-17 to division-rival Denver. With many of its stars in decline, the team missed the playoffs in 1978 with a 9-7 record. Madden retired, and Flores, who quarterbacked the Raiders in the 1960s, was named head coach. Flores finished 9-7 his first season, then led the team to an 11-5 record in 1980. Led by quarterback Jim Plunkett, running back Mark van Eeghen, and all-pro cornerback Lester Hayes, the Raiders earned a wild-card playoff berth and beat Houston, Cleveland, and San Diego en route to Super Bowl XV in Louisiana. Plunkett was named MVP as Oakland claimed its second Super Bowl title in five seasons with a 27-10 victory over the Philadelphia Eagles, becoming the first wild-card team to win a Super Bowl.

Flores saw his team struggle to a 7-9 record the following season, but owner Al Davis emerged a big winner off the field when he was allowed to move his franchise to Los Angeles. The team reached the play offs in 1982 with an 8-1 record and beat Cleveland 27-10 in a first-round game. The Jets ended the Raiders' playoff run the following weekend with a 17-14 defeat before 90,688 at the Los Angeles Memorial Coliseum.

The 1983 Raiders fielded one of the great teams of the modern era. Plunkett, former Heisman Trophy running back Marcus Allen of USC, and tight end Todd Christiansen keyed the offense, and Hayes and end Lyle Alzado led the defense. Flores coached the club to a 12-4 record, and the Raiders advanced through the playoffs with victories over Pittsburgh (38-10) and Seattle (30-14) to win the AFC title. Allen rushed for a Super Bowl-record 191 yards in a 38-9 victory over the Washington Redskins in Super Bowl XVIII at Tampa Stadium.

The Raiders followed their Super Bowl season with an 11-5 record, but were upset by Seattle 13-7 in a wild-card playoff game. The team went 12-4 in 1985, but again was upset in the playoffs, this time 27-20 by New England.

An 8-8 season followed in 1986, and, despite the addition of game-breaking running back Bo Jackson the following season, the Raiders fell to 5-10 in 1987. Mike Shanahan took over as head coach in 1988, but the club missed the playoffs again, going 7-9. The team went 8-8 the following season, then won the Western Division in 1990 with a 12-4 mark under new head coach Art Shell. Shell, a former all-pro tackle for the Raiders, was the first African-American in the modern era to coach an NFL team. Los Angeles defeated Cincinnati 20-10 in a playoff game, then was annihilated by the Buffalo Bills 51-3 in the AFC title game.

Shell led the team back to the playoffs in 1991 with a 9-7 record, but a 10-6 loss to division-rival Kansas City in the first round of the playoffs ended the Raiders' season. The team fell below .500 the next season with a 7-9 record, but Shell brought Los Angeles back to the playoffs in 1993 with a 10-6 record. The Raiders bombed division-foe Denver 42-24 in a wild-card game, then were eliminated by Buffalo 29-23. Shell was fired in 1994 after the club went 9-7 and missed the playoffs.

Davis returned the Raiders to Oakland in 1995, but the team struggled in its old home, going 8-8. The team dropped to 7-9 in 1996, and never was a factor in the division race. After two disappointing seasons in a row, coach Mike White was fired and replaced by former Cardinals coach Joe Bugel.

Wearing Lamonica's number 3, quarterback Jeff George gave a passable impression of the "Mad Bomber" in 1997, when he passed for an AFC-leading 29 touchdowns and 3,917 yards. Tim Brown was his prime target, and led the NFL with 104 catches and 1,408 receiving yards. Napoleon Kaufman rushed for 1,294 yards, but the Raiders surrendered 419 points and finished 4-12, their worst record in 35 years.

Bugel was released at season's end and was replaced by Eagles offensive coordinator Jon Gruden. The Raiders began the 1998 season with a 7-3 record, but lost five of their last six games to finish 8-8.

RAIDERS RECORD 1960-1998

YEAR	WON	LOST	TIED	PCT.	FIN	PF	PA
Oakland Raiders							
1960	6	8	0	.429	3	319	388
1961	2	12	0	.143	4	237	458
1962	1	13	0	.071	4	213	370
1963	10	4	0	.714	2	363	282
1964	5	7	2	.417	3	303	350
1965	8	5	1	.615	2	298	239
1966	8	5	1	.615	2	315	288
1967a	13	1	0	.929	1	468	233
1968b	12	2	0	.857	1	453	233
1969b	12	1	1	.923	1	377	242
1970c	8	4	2	.667	1	300	293
1971	8	4	2	.667	2	344	278
1972d	10	3	1	.750	1	365	248
1973c	9	4	1	.679	1	292	175
1974c	12	2	0	.857	1	355	228
1975c	11	3	0	.786	1	375	255
1976e	13	1	0	.929	1	350	237
1977f	11	3	0	.786	2	351	230
1978	9	7	0	.563	2	311	283
1979	9	7	0	.563	4	365	337
1980g	11	5	0	.688	2	364	306
1981	7	9	0	.438	4	273	343
Los Angeles Raiders							
1982h	8	1	0	.889	1	260	200
1983e	12	4	0	.750	1	442	338
1984i	11	5	0	.688	3	368	278
1985d	12	4	0	.750	1	354	308
1986	8	8	0	.500	4	323	346
1987	5	10	0	.333	4	301	289
1988	7	9	0	.438	3	325	369
1989	8	8	0	.500	3	315	297
1990c	12	4	0	.750	1	337	268
1991i	9	7	0	.563	3	298	297
1992	7	9	0	.438	4	249	281
1993f	10	6	0	.625	2	306	326
1994	9	7	0	.563	2	319	298
Oakland Raiders							
1995	8	8	0	.500	4t	348	332
1996	7	9	0	.438	4t	340	293
1997	4	12	0	.250	4	324	419
1998	8	8	0	.500	2	288	356
39 Years	340	229	11	.596	—	12,888	11,589

a AFL Western Division Champion; AFL Champion; 1-1 in Playoffs
b AFL Western Division Champion; 1-1 in Playoffs
c AFC Western Division Champion; 1-1 in Playoffs
d AFC Western Division Champion; 0-1 in Playoffs
e AFC Western Division Champion; Super Bowl Champion; 3-0 in Playoffs
f AFC Wild Card Qualifier for Playoffs; 1-1 in Playoffs
g Super Bowl Champion; 4-0 in Playoffs
h AFC Qualifier for Playoffs; 1-1 in Playoffs
i AFC Wild Card Qualifier for Playoffs; 0-1 in Playoffs

COACHING HISTORY
OAKLAND 1960-1981, 1995-98
LOS ANGELES 1982-1994
(361-244-11)

1960-61	Eddie Erdelatz*	6-10-0
1961-62	Marty Feldman**	2-15-0
1962	Red Conkright	1-8-0
1963-65	Al Davis	23-16-3
1966-68	John Rauch	35-10-1
1969-78	John Madden	112-39-7
1979-87	Tom Flores	91-56-0
1988-89	Mike Shanahan***	8-12-0
1989-94	Art Shell	56-41-0
1995-96	Mike White	15-17-0
1997	Joe Bugel	4-12-0
1998	Jon Gruden	8-8-0

* Released after two games in 1961
** Released after five games in 1962
*** Released after four games in 1989

Pittsburgh Steelers

Pennsylvania's legalization of professional sports on Sunday and Art Rooney's winning day at the racetrack were two factors in the birth of the Pittsburgh franchise in 1933.

Rooney was a 32-year-old former semipro football player when Pennsylvania lawmakers announced the legalization of Sunday pro sports in 1933. Rooney purchased an NFL franchise for $2,500, money he had gained from a good day at the track. Rooney named the team the Pirates, after the city's National League baseball club. The Pirates went 3-6-2 in their inaugural season, and, despite colorful players such as Johnny (Blood) McNally, Byron (Whizzer) White, and Frankie Filchock, never finished above .500 during the 1930s.

A name change to "Steelers" before the 1940 season didn't change the team's luck. To Rooney, they looked like "the same old Pirates." At the end of the season, a discouraged Rooney sold the franchise to Alexis Thompson and bought a half-interest in the Philadelphia Eagles from his close friend Bert Bell. By April of 1941, however, Thompson had been blocked by the league in his efforts to move his team to Boston, and was unhappy in Pittsburgh. Meanwhile, Rooney was anxious to return to his hometown, and Bell, who had enjoyed little success in Philadelphia, was willing. A deal was worked out whereby Rooney and Bell swapped franchises with Thompson. Rooney was back home. All but a few of the players also switched uniforms.

One year later, the Steelers enjoyed their first winning season when tailback (Bullet Bill) Dudley led the squad to a 7-4 record. World War II siphoned the ranks of the NFL, and Rooney merged his roster with that of the Eagles in 1943. The team, officially the Phil-Pitt Combine but popularly known as the "Steagles," went 5-4-1, splitting its home games between Philadelphia and Pittsburgh. Rooney followed by merging his club with the Chicago Cardinals in 1944. The Card-Pitt Combine went 0-10, and it was so bad that it was derided as the "Carpets."

The Steelers resumed being an entirely Pittsburgh team in 1945, and the club endured mixed results over the next 10 years. The team's highlight of this period was the 1947 season, when head coach John (Jock) Sutherland installed tailback Johnny Clement in his Single-Wing offense, and the Steelers went 8-4. They played in their first postseason game, a 21-0 loss to the Eagles.

Quarterback Jim Finks and defensive tackle Ernie Stautner were two of the team's better players of the 1950s, a decade that saw the club manage just two winning seasons. It also was a decade in which the Steelers cut rookie quarterback John Unitas, passed on drafting rookie running back Jim Brown, and traded quarterback Len Dawson.

The team's tough luck and losing ways continued in the 1960s. The team did have some quality players, including quarterback Bill Nelsen, halfback Dick Hoak, and receiver Roy Jefferson, but managed just two winning seasons, the highlight being a 9-5 record in 1962, the best record in club history to that point. In 1969, Rooney named Chuck Noll, a 37-year-old former assistant with the Colts and Chargers whose specialty was defense, as head coach. Pittsburgh's losing ways continued through Noll's first three seasons, but Noll patiently built through the draft.

In 1969, Noll drafted defensive tackle Joe Greene, quarterback Terry Hanratty, offensive lineman Jon Kolb, and defensive end L.C. Greenwood. In 1970, he selected quarterback Terry Bradshaw and defensive back Mel Blount. In 1971, the Steelers drafted wide receiver Frank Lewis, linebacker Jack Ham, offensive lineman Gerry Mullins, defensive end Dwight White, tight end Larry Brown, and defensive tackle Ernie Holmes. The 1972 draft yielded Franco Harris, offensive lineman Gordon Gravelle, defensive lineman Steve Furness, and quarterback Joe Gilliam.

Pittsburgh's patient rebuilding process yielded franchise "firsts" in 1972—its first division championship and first playoff victory. The latter was a 13-7 victory over Oakland in a game made famous by Harris's Immaculate Reception with 5 seconds left in the game. Pittsburgh's season ended with a 21-17 loss to Miami in the AFC Championship Game.

The Steelers returned to the playoffs in 1973 with a 10-4 record, but quickly were dispatched 33-14 by the revenge-minded Raiders. Noll's 1974 draft is considered by some football observers as the best draft in NFL history. Pittsburgh's first five selections yielded two future-Hall-of-Fame players in middle linebacker Jack Lambert and center Mike Webster, and two great receivers, Lynn Swann and John Stallworth.

Lambert was the final piece of the Steel Curtain puzzle, and Pittsburgh rode its defense to a 10-3-1 mark and its second AFC Central Division title in 1974. The Steelers defeated Buffalo 32-14 and Oakland 24-13 to win the AFC title and earn their first berth in the Super Bowl. Pittsburgh ended 40 years of frustration for venerable owner Art Rooney with a 16-6 victory over Minnesota in Super Bowl IX. Harris earned MVP honors by rushing for a Super Bowl-record 158 yards.

With a team considered one of the greatest in league history, the 1975 Steelers rolled to a 12-2 record and another Central Division championship. Pittsburgh battered Baltimore 28-10 in a playoff game, then repeated as AFC champs with a 16-10 victory over Oakland in sub-zero temperatures in Pittsburgh. In Super Bowl X, the Steelers beat Dallas 21-17 for their second consecutive title. Bradshaw threw 2 touchdown passes, including the game winner to the acrobatic Swann, who was named MVP for his 4 catches for 161 yards.

An injury to Bradshaw in 1976 slowed the offense, which relied more than ever on its famed trapping game. Harris and Rocky Bleier joined the 1972 Dolphins as just the second backfield tandem in NFL history to both rush for more 1,000 or more yards in the same season. But the big story was the Steel Curtain, which kept the team in the playoff hunt with one of the greatest defensive campaigns ever. The Steelers tallied three consecutive shutouts, did not allow a touchdown for 22 consecutive quarters, did not yield a touchdown in eight of their last nine games, and shut out three of their final five opponents. With the defense peaking, Pittsburgh claimed its third consecutive division title, then beat Baltimore 40-14 in the playoffs. But the victory over the Colts was costly, as both Harris and Bleier suffered injuries that kept them out of the AFC title game against the Raiders. Oakland ended Pittsburgh's reign as world champions with a 24-7 victory.

The Steelers repeated as division champs the following season, but lost to Denver 34-21 in the playoffs. The club had its greatest season in 1978, going 14-2. The defense was aging but still effective, leading the league in fewest points allowed. On offense, Noll took advantage of the NFL's new liberalized pass-blocking rules and opened up Pittsburgh's passing attack. Bradshaw led the AFC in passing and led the Steelers to a 33-10 victory over Denver in the playoffs and a 34-5 victory over division-rival Houston in the AFC Championship Game. In Super Bowl XIII in Miami, he threw 4 touchdown passes to beat Dallas 35-31 and garner MVP honors.

Noll's team claimed its sixth consecutive division title in 1979 and led the NFL in scoring with 416 points. Harris produced his seventh 1,000-yard season to tie Cleveland great Jim Brown's NFL record. The Steelers eliminated Miami 34-14 in the playoffs, then defeated the Oilers 27-13 in a rematch of the 1978 title game. Pittsburgh then earned its record fourth Super Bowl victory behind game MVP Bradshaw, who rallied the team past the upset-minded Los Angeles Rams 31-19 in Super Bowl XIV in Pasadena.

Advancing age and injuries ended the Steelers' dynasty in 1980, as the team slumped to a 9-7 record and missed the playoffs. In 1983, the team won its first Central Division title since 1979, going 10-6 as Bradshaw ignored an aching elbow and led the Steelers past the Jets 34-7 to clinch the division. Pittsburgh lost its first playoff game for the second year in a row, falling 38-10 to the Raiders.

Bradshaw retired in 1984, but Mark Malone stepped in at quarterback and led the team to its second consecutive division title, despite a mediocre 9-7 record. Malone combined with Stallworth and rookie of the year Louis Lipps to lead the offense, and the team earned its first playoff victory since Super Bowl XIV with a 24-17 win at Denver. Playing in their first AFC title game in five years, the Steelers lost 45-28 at Miami.

The 1991 season marked Noll's last as head coach, as the longtime Steelers boss and future Hall of Fame inductee retired following a 7-9 season. Pittsburgh native Bill Cowher, a 35-year-old former assistant with the Browns and Chiefs, was named head coach. Cowher's enthusiasm and Barry Foster's AFC-best 1,690 yards rushing and 11 touchdowns led the Steelers to an 11-5 record and their first Central Division title since 1984. In their first playoff game at Three Rivers Stadium since the 1982 season, the Steelers lost to Buffalo 24-3.

The Steelers went 9-7 in 1993 as quarterback Neil O'Donnell broke Bradshaw's club records for attempts and completions. Tight end Eric Green was a favorite target, leading the club in receptions. For the second year in a row, the Steelers lost their first playoff game, this time a 27-24 overtime defeat at Kansas City.

Cowher's conservative offense and blitzing defense helped Pittsburgh build a 12-4 record in 1994, the club's best since their 1979 Super Bowl season. Pittsburgh led the NFL in rushing, and its defense, keyed by linebackers Greg Lloyd and Kevin Greene and cornerback Rod Woodson, ranked second in the league. A 29-9 victory over division-rival Cleveland put the Steelers in the AFC title game for the first time in 11 years, but Pittsburgh's hopes of returning to the Super Bowl ended with a 17-13 loss to the underdog Chargers.

The Steelers made up for their title-game loss the following season, repeating as Central Division champions with an 11-5 record despite losing all-pro cornerback Woodson in their opening game. With rookie Kordell (Slash) Stewart jump-starting the attack, the offense scored an AFC-high 407 points. A 40-21 victory over Buffalo in the playoffs put the Steelers back in the AFC title game against the Indianapolis Colts. O'Donnell led a late touchdown drive, and the Colts just missed completing a long pass on the final play of the Steelers' 20-16 victory. Making their first Super Bowl appearance in 16 years, the Steelers lost 27-17 to the Dallas Cowboys in Super Bowl XXX at Sun Devil Stadium at Tempe, Arizona.

The 1996 season began badly. Quarterback Neil O'Donnell and offensive tackle Leon Searcy left through free agency. Defensive end Ray Seals and Pro Bowl linebacker Greg Lloyd were lost for the season to injury before the first quarter of the opening game ended. Still, after losing the opener, the team won five consecutive games and went on to win the Central Division crown. Jerome Bettis gave the Steelers a strong rushing attack, but the strength of the team still was the defense, where linebackers Chad Brown and Levon Kirkland and defensive backs Carnell Lake and Woodson all made the Pro Bowl. The Steelers opened the playoffs by crushing Indianapolis, but lost 28-3 at New England in the divisional round.

The next year, the Steelers won their fifth division title and advanced to the AFC title game for the fourth time in six seasons under Cowher. Stewart ran and passed for 29 touchdowns in his first full season as a starting quarterback, and wide receiver Yancey Thigpen had 79 receptions. Bettis rushed for 1,665 yards behind an offensive line anchored by Pro Bowl center Dermontti Dawson. The Steelers fashioned an 11-5 regular-season record, then edged New England 7-6 in the divisional playoffs. But the season ended with a 24-21 loss to Denver in the AFC title game at Three Rivers Stadium.

In 1998, Pittsburgh fell to 7-9 and failed to make the playoffs for the first time in Cowher's tenure as coach. Stewart wasn't as productive and suffered through an emotional season that featured a sideline flareup with Cowher. The Steelers' offense struggled, netting just 263 points. To shore up the offense, Cowher named former Chargers head coach Kevin Gilbride as his new offensive coordinator for the 1999 season.

STEELERS RECORD 1933-1998

YEAR	WON	LOST	TIED	PCT.	FIN	PF	PA
Pittsburgh Pirates							
1933	3	6	2	.333	5	67	208
1934	2	10	0	.167	5	51	206
1935	4	8	0	.333	3	100	209
1936	6	6	0	.500	2	98	187
1937	4	7	0	.364	3	122	145
1938	2	9	0	.182	5	79	169
1939	1	9	1	.100	5	114	216
Pittsburgh Steelers							
1940	2	7	2	.222	4	60	178
1941	1	9	1	.100	5	103	276
1942	7	4	0	.636	2	167	119
Phil-Pitt (does not count in totals)							
1943	5	4	1	.556	3	225	230
Card-Pitt (does not count in totals)							
1944	0	10	0	.000	5	108	328
Pittsburgh Steelers							
1945	2	8	0	.200	5	79	220
1946	5	5	1	.500	4	136	117
1947a	8	4	0	.667	2	240	259
1948	4	8	0	.333	4	200	243
1949	6	5	1	.545	2	224	214
1950	6	6	0	.500	4	180	195
1951	4	7	1	.364	4	183	235
1952	5	7	0	.417	4	300	273
1953	6	6	0	.500	4	211	263
1954	5	7	0	.417	4	219	263
1955	4	8	0	.333	6	195	285
1956	5	7	0	.417	5	217	250
1957	6	6	0	.500	3	161	178
1958	7	4	1	.636	3	261	230
1959	6	5	1	.545	4	257	216
1960	5	6	1	.455	5	240	275
1961	6	8	0	.429	5	295	287
1962	9	5	0	.643	2	312	363
1963	7	4	3	.636	4	321	295
1964	5	9	0	.357	6	253	315
1965	2	12	0	.143	7	202	397
1966	5	8	1	.385	6	316	347
1967	4	9	1	.308	4	281	320
1968	2	11	1	.154	4	244	397
1969	1	13	0	.071	4	218	404
1970	5	9	0	.357	3	210	272
1971	6	8	0	.429	2	246	292
1972b	11	3	0	.786	1	343	175
1973c	10	4	0	.714	2	347	210
1974d	10	3	1	.750	1	305	189
1975d	12	2	0	.857	1	373	162
1976b	10	4	0	.714	1	342	138
1977e	9	5	0	.643	1	283	243
1978d	14	2	0	.875	1	356	195
1979d	12	4	0	.750	1	416	262
1980	9	7	0	.563	3	352	313
1981	8	8	0	.500	2	356	297
1982f	6	3	0	.667	4	204	146
1983e	10	6	0	.625	1	355	303
1984b	9	7	0	.563	1	387	310
1985	7	9	0	.438	3	379	355
1986	6	10	0	.375	3	307	336
1987	8	7	0	.533	3	285	299
1988	5	11	0	.313	4	336	421
1989g	9	7	0	.563	3	265	326
1990	9	7	0	.563	3	292	240
1991	7	9	0	.438	2	292	344
1992e	11	5	0	.688	1	299	225
1993c	9	7	0	.563	2	308	281

YEAR	WON	LOST	TIED	PCT.	FIN	PF	PA
1994b	12	4	0	.750	1	316	234
1995h	11	5	0	.688	1	407	327
1996b	10	6	0	.625	1	344	257
1997b	11	5	0	.688	1	372	307
1998	7	9	0	.438	3	263	303
64 Years	420	429	19	.495	—	16,046	16,516

a NFL Eastern Division Runnerup; 0-1 in Playoffs
b AFC Central Division Champion; 1-1 in Playoffs
c AFC Wild Card Qualifier for Playoffs; 0-1 in Playoffs
d AFC Central Division Champion; Super Bowl Champion; 3-0 in Playoffs
e AFC Central Division Champion; 0-1 in Playoffs
f AFC Qualifier for Playoffs; 0-1 in Playoffs
g AFC Wild Card Qualifier for Playoffs; 1-1 in Playoffs
h AFC Central Division Champion; AFC Champion; 2-1 in Playoffs

COACHING HISTORY
PITTSBURGH PIRATES 1933-1940; PITTSBURGH STEELERS 1940-42, 1945-1998; PHIL-PITT 1943; CARD-PITT 1944
(446-458-20)

1933	Forrest (Jap) Douds	3-6-2
1934	Luby DiMelio	2-10-0
1935-36	Joe Bach	10-14-0
1937-39	Johnny (Blood) McNally*	6-19-0
1939-40	Walt Kiesling	3-13-3
1941	Bert Bell**	0-2-0
	Aldo (Buff) Donelli***	0-5-0
1941-44	Walt Kiesling****	13-20-2
1945	Jim Leonard	2-8-0
1946-47	Jock Sutherland	13-10-1
1948-51	Johnny Michelosen	20-26-2
1952-53	Joe Bach	11-13-0
1954-56	Walt Kiesling	14-22-0
1957-64	Raymond (Buddy) Parker	51-47-6
1965	Mike Nixon	2-12-0
1966-68	Bill Austin	11-28-3
1969-91	Chuck Noll	209-156-1
1992-98	Bill Cowher	76-47-0

* Released after three games in 1939
** Resigned after two games in 1941
*** Released after five games in 1941
**** Co-coach with Earle (Greasy) Neale in Philadelphia-Pittsburgh merger in 1943 and with Phil Handler in Chicago Cardinals-Pittsburgh merger in 1944

San Diego Chargers

More than any other team, the San Diego Chargers symbolized the wide-open style of play that characterized the American Football League.

The Chargers' quick-strike scoring capability was symbolized not only by the jagged lightning bolts that adorned their uniforms, but also by the explosive talent of stars such as Lance Alworth, Paul Lowe, and Keith Lincoln.

The Chargers were founded in 1959 by hotel magnate Barron Hilton. One of the eight original AFL franchises, the team originally was located in Los Angeles. The club's nickname was submitted by Gerald Courtney of Hollywood in a local contest, and Hilton agreed to it in part because it coincided with the arrival of the new Hilton Carte Blanche charge card.

Hilton hired legendary Notre Dame coach Frank Leahy as general manager and former NFL coach Sid Gillman as his first head coach. Leahy resigned soon after for health reasons, and Gillman assumed general-manager duties as well. He surrounded himself with talented, young coaches such as Al Davis, Chuck Noll, and Jack Faulkner, and they pieced together a championship team out of largely unknown players. On the first play of the team's first preseason game August 6, free-agent halfback Paul Lowe returned the opening kickoff 105 yards for a touchdown against the New York Titans. Lowe and former NFL quarterback Jack Kemp became the focal points of Gillman's offense, and the Chargers clinched the Western Division title with a 41-33 win over Denver before just 9,928 people in the cavernous Los Angeles Coliseum. They finished 10-4 in the regular season but fell short in the first AFL Championship Game, losing to the Houston Oilers 24-16 on New Year's Day.

Hilton, who lost more than $900,000 his first year, was lured out of Los Angeles by the Greater San Diego Sports Association. The renamed San Diego Chargers scheduled their home games at Balboa Stadium, then improved their defense by drafting two standout rookies in 320-pound tackle Ernie (Big Cat) Ladd and end Earl Faison. Faison and Ladd made an immediate impact, heading a pass rush that helped the club record 49 interceptions. The Chargers won their second consecutive Western Division title with a 12-2 record, then played the Oilers again for the AFL title. The Chargers lost 10-3 in San Diego.

The Chargers won an important battle for the AFL in 1962 when they signed two blue-chip college stars—Arkansas flanker Lance Alworth and Kansas quarterback John Hadl—away from the NFL. Both became AFL stars, and Alworth lent credit to the young league by becoming arguably the best receiver of the 1960s. Injuries slowed the team that season, but a much bigger loss was the death of linebacker Bob Laraba, killed in an offseason car accident. After two championship seasons, Kemp was lost to Buffalo when Gillman tried to maneuver the quarterback, who had suffered a broken hand in preseason, through waivers to the reserve list. The Bills quickly claimed him for a mere $100.

Determined to toughen his team mentally and physically for the 1963 campaign, Gillman quartered them at a deserted dude ranch 40 miles from San Diego called "Rough Acres." The Chargers emerged from the camp ready to reclaim their division title, and, with former NFL quarterback Tobin Rote on board, San Diego had all the pieces in place to make a run at the league title. They finished the season with an AFL-best 11-3 mark. Rote led the AFL in passing, Lowe ran for more than 1,000 yards, and Lincoln had a league-high 6.5 yards-per-carry average. The offensive line was headed by all-pro tackle Ron Mix. In the AFL title game against Boston on January 5, game-MVP Lincoln ran for a league championship-record 206 yards and scored 2 touchdowns in a 51-10 rout.

San Diego repeated as division champions in 1964 with an 8-5-1 record, but with Lincoln sidelined early in the championship game by Buffalo linebacker Mike Stratton's crushing tackle, the Chargers lost 20-7. Gillman's team won its fifth division title in 1965, going 9-2-3. Lowe ran for an AFL-record 1,121 yards, Alworth led AFL receivers with 1,602 yards and 14 touchdowns, and Hadl led the league in passing. The Chargers hosted the Bills in Balboa Stadium for the AFL title, but again were stymied 23-0.

The club remained a contender from 1966-69, but endured four consecutive third-place finishes as the Chiefs and Raiders rose to prominence. Wide receiver Gary Garrison and halfback Dickie Post joined Gillman's celebrated offense the next two seasons, but the lack of a solid defense doomed hopes of returning to the top. Hilton sold the team in 1966 to a business group headed by Eugene Klein. Other changes saw the Chargers leave Balboa Stadium for San Diego Stadium in 1967 while Gillman retired as head coach in 1969 due to a stomach ulcer. Gillman returned briefly in 1971, but resigned late in the season. A series of patchwork moves that brought in aging stars such as John Unitas, Duane Thomas, and Deacon Jones, but the team remained out of contention throughout much of the 1970s.

The turnaround didn't begin until 1979, with head coach Don Coryell building a winner around quarterback Dan Fouts, tight end Kellen Winslow, and wide receiver John Jefferson. Coryell rebuilt the team in the image of the Gillman Chargers of the 1960s, a quick-strike aerial attack and a defense whose strength was its pass rush. Defensive end Fred Dean and tackle Louie Kelcher were Coryell's version of Faison and Ladd.

Fouts passed for 4,082 yards in 1979 to become the first quarterback since Joe Namath to surpass 4,000 yards in a season. San Diego went 12-4 to win its first division title since 1965, but the Chargers lost to Houston 17-14 in a divisional playoff game.

The offense continued to set records in 1980 and San Diego went 11-5 to repeat as division champs. Fouts set a record with 4,715 yards passing, and Winslow, Jefferson, and Charlie Joiner each surpassed the 1,000-yard mark in receptions. Fullback Chuck Muncie, acquired in a trade with New Orleans, led the team in rushing. The Chargers earned their first playoff victory since the 1963 AFL title game when they beat Buffalo 20-14 in a first-round game. San Diego lost to eventual Super Bowl champion Oakland 34-27 in the AFC title game.

Jefferson was traded and replaced by Wes Chandler, and Air Coryell hardly missed a beat. Winslow led the AFC in receptions for the second consecutive year, and Chandler joined Winslow and Joiner as a 1,000-yard receiver. Muncie ran for more than 1,000 yards. Fouts broke his record by passing for 4,802 yards, and the team went 10-6 to claim its third consecutive division title. The Chargers defeated Miami 41-38 in one of the greatest games ever, then fell to Cincinnati 27-7 in minus-59 degree wind chill in the AFC title game.

The Chargers qualified for the 1982 strike-expanded playoffs with a 6-3 mark as the offense remained the NFL's best. Fouts tied for the league lead in touchdown passes, and Winslow led the AFC in receiving for the third consecutive season. Chandler averaged an NFL-record 129 yards receiving per game. San Diego rallied to beat Pittsburgh 31-28 in a first-round game, but Coryell's post-season frustration continued with a 34-13 loss to Miami.

The team came under new ownership in 1984 when Alex Spanos bought the club from Klein. San Diego struggled the rest of the decade, and in 1990 hired Bobby Beathard as its new general manager.

The 1992 season marked the end of the team's 10-year playoff drought. Head coach Bobby Ross produced an 11-5 record and the first division title since 1981. Former Redskins quarterback Stan Humphries ran the offense, and fullback Marion Butts powered a ground game that tied for the conference lead with 18 touchdowns. Linebacker Junior Seau and end Leslie O'Neal keyed the defense. San Diego defeated Kansas City 17-0 in its playoff opener, then was shut out by Miami 31-0.

Ross guided the club to an 11-5 record and a division title in 1994. Fullback Natrone Means ran for a franchise-record 1,350 yards. The Chargers beat the Miami Dolphins 22-21 in the playoffs, then upset the Pittsburgh Steelers 17-13 on a pair of 43-yard touchdown passes by Humphries to claim the AFC title. Playing in their first Super Bowl, the Chargers were overwhelmed by the San Francisco 49ers 49-26 in Super Bowl XXIX in Miami.

San Diego returned to the playoffs in 1995, earning a wild-card berth with a 9-7 record. Tony Martin set a club record with 90 catches. A 35-20 playoff loss to Indianapolis spurred Ross and Beathard to make changes. O'Neal, Means, and third-down running back Ronnie Harmon were not retained. The Chargers signed defensive end Marco Coleman and traded their 1997 number-one pick to Tampa Bay for the rights to draft Virginia Tech wide receiver Bryan Still. But San Diego slipped another notch in 1996, dropping to .500. Humphries was hurt much of the season, after which Ross resigned. Kevin Gilbride was hired as the new head coach.

No fewer than 14 Chargers spent time on the injured reserve list in 1997, but the biggest blow was the loss of quarterback Stan Humphries. After suffering numerous concussions, Humphries retired eight games into the season. San Diego nosedived from 4-4 to 4-12 and finished in last place in the AFC West.

The Chargers traded two players and three draft choices to Arizona to move up one spot and take Washington State quarterback Ryan Leaf with the second selection of the 1998 draft. But Leaf struggled much of his rookie season before giving way to Craig Whelihan. San Diego was 2-4 when Gilbride was fired and replaced by quarterbacks coach June Jones. The Chargers stumbled home at 5-11. Jones departed at season's end to become head coach at the University of Hawaii. Oregon State's Mike Riley was named head coach of the Chargers on January 7, 1999.

CHARGERS RECORD 1960-1998

YEAR	WON	LOST	TIED	PCT.	FIN	PF	PA
Los Angeles Chargers							
1960a	10	4	0	.714	1	373	336
San Diego Chargers							
1961a	12	2	0	.857	1	396	219
1962	4	10	0	.286	3	314	392
1963b	11	3	0	.786	1	399	256
1964a	8	5	1	.615	1	341	300
1965a	9	2	3	.818	1	340	227
1966	7	6	1	.538	3	335	284
1967	8	5	1	.615	3	360	352
1968	9	5	0	.643	3	382	310
1969	8	6	0	.571	3	288	276
1970	5	6	3	.455	3	282	278
1971	6	8	0	.429	3	311	341
1972	4	9	1	.321	4	264	344
1973	2	11	1	.179	4	188	386
1974	5	9	0	.357	4	212	285
1975	2	12	0	.143	4	189	345
1976	6	8	0	.429	3	248	285
1977	7	7	0	.500	3	222	205
1978	9	7	0	.563	4	355	309
1979c	12	4	0	.750	1	411	246
1980d	11	5	0	.688	1	418	327
1981d	10	6	0	.625	1	478	390
1982e	6	3	0	.667	5	288	221
1983	6	10	0	.375	4	358	462
1984	7	9	0	.438	5	394	413
1985	8	8	0	.500	4	467	435
1986	4	12	0	.250	5	335	396
1987	8	7	0	.533	3	253	317
1988	6	10	0	.375	4	231	332
1989	6	10	0	.375	5	266	290
1990	6	10	0	.375	4	315	281
1991	4	12	0	.250	5	274	342
1992d	11	5	0	.688	1	335	241
1993	8	8	0	.500	4	322	290
1994f	11	5	0	.688	1	381	306

YEAR	WON	LOST	TIED	PCT.	FIN	PF	PA
1995g	9	7	0	.563	2	321	323
1996	8	8	0	.500	3	310	376
1997	4	12	0	.250	5	266	425
1998	5	11	0	.313	5	241	342
39 Years	282	287	11	.496	—	12,463	12,485

a AFL Western Division Champion; 0-1 in Playoffs
b AFL Western Division Champion; AFL Champion; 1-0 in Playoffs
c AFC Western Division Champion; 0-1 in Playoffs
d AFC Western Division Champion; 1-1 in Playoffs
e AFC Qualifier for Playoffs; 1-1 in Playoffs
f AFC Western Division Champion; AFC Champion; 2-1 in Playoffs
g AFC Wild Card Qualifier for Playoffs; 0-1 in Playoffs

COACHING HISTORY
LOS ANGELES 1960, SAN DIEGO 1961-1998
(289-298-11)

1960-69	Sid Gillman*	83-51-6
1969-70	Charlie Waller	9-7-3
1971	Sid Gillman**	4-6-0
1971-73	Harland Svare***	7-17-2
1973	Ron Waller	1-5-0
1974-78	Tommy Prothro#	21-39-0
1978-86	Don Coryell##	72-60-0
1986-88	Al Saunders	17-22-0
1989-91	Dan Henning	16-32-0
1992-96	Bobby Ross	50-36-0
1997-98	Kevin Gilbride###	6-16-0
1998	June Jones	3-7-0

* Retired after nine games in 1969
** Resigned after 10 games in 1971
*** Resigned after eight games in 1973
# Resigned after four games in 1978
Resigned after eight games in 1986
Resigned after six games in 1998

Seattle Seahawks

A group of business leaders formed Seattle Professional Football, Inc., an organization designed to lure pro football to their city. The group was headed by Portland Trail Blazers owner Herman Sarkowsky and, in November, 1972, it began construction on the $67 million Kingdome. On December 5, 1974, Seattle was awarded an NFL franchise for $16 million. The nickname "Seahawks" was selected in a local contest, with blue, silver, and green being chosen as the team's colors. Minnesota Vikings assistant Jack Patera was named the Seahawks' first head coach. The club played its first preseason game on August 1, 1976, losing to San Francisco 27-20 before 60,825 in the Kingdome.

Seattle's inaugural season was spent in the NFC West. The Seahawks opened the regular season at home with a 30-24 loss to St. Louis, the first of five consecutive defeats. The Seahawks' first victory came in week 6, when they beat Tampa Bay 13-10. Patera's team added another win on November 7, defeating Atlanta 30-13, but went winless the rest of the season and finished 2-12.

Seattle was switched to the AFC Western Division for the 1977 season, and improved to 5-9. The improvement continued in 1978, when Patera was named NFC coach of the year after guiding his team to a 9-7 record. Zorn led the AFC in completions and passing yardage, wide receiver Steve Largent led the AFC with 71 catches, and halfback David Sims ran for a conference-best 14 touchdowns. Seattle repeated its 9-7 record the following season, then slumped the next two seasons as injuries hurt the offense, and the defense failed to improve.

To strengthen the defense, Seattle drafted All-America defensive back Kenny Easley of UCLA in 1981. Patera was fired during the 1982 season and replaced by Mike McCormack. The Seahawks continued to struggle, going 4-5 in strike-shortened 1982. Chuck Knox, who had coached both the Rams and Bills to the playoffs, was named head coach of the Seahawks on January 26, 1983. Knox drafted All-America running back Curt Warner of Penn State, who led the AFC in rushing with 1,449 yards in 1983.

Dave Krieg replaced Zorn at quarterback, and led Seattle to a 9-7 record that year to put the team in the postseason for the first time in franchise history. Krieg threw 3 touchdown passes in a 31-7 victory over Denver in a wild-card game. The Seahawks then rallied to beat the Dolphins 27-20 in a divisional playoff game at Miami. Seattle's surprising run ended the next week, when they lost to the eventual Super Bowl-champion Los Angeles Raiders 30-14 in the AFC title game.

The Seahawks opened the 1984 season with a 33-0 victory over the Cleveland Browns—their first season-opening win—en route to a franchise-best 12-4 record. The team lost Curt Warner to a season-ending knee injury in the opener, but the defense, led by Easley, picked up the slack by notching three shutouts and allowing a club-low 282 points. The Seahawks returned to the postseason, and gained a measure of revenge over the Raiders by eliminating the defending Super Bowl champions 13-7 in the wild-card round. But Seattle fell short in the next round, losing to the Miami Dolphins 31-10.

Warner returned to the ranks of 1,000-yard backs the following season, and Largent broke his club records for receptions and yards in a season. The team was erratic on both offense and defense however, and missed the playoffs with an 8-8 record. Krieg, Warner, and Largent continued to excel in 1986, and Largent set an NFL record by catching at least 1 pass in 139 consecutive games. Despite going 10-6, Seattle again missed the playoffs. The club looked to bolster its defense in 1987 by signing Oklahoma linebacker Brian Bosworth, but the controversial "Boz" took second billing to Largent, who became the NFL's all-time receptions leader with 752. Knox coached the team to a 9-6 record and a berth in the playoffs, but the team lost 23-20 in overtime to Houston in a first-round game.

The 1988 season saw Seattle's Ground Chuck offense reach its zenith. Warner and fullback John L. Williams formed a one-two running punch that accounted for almost 2,000 yards rushing. The defense was led by end Jacob Green, and the Seahawks went 9-7 and won their first Western Division title. The team suffered another disappointing postseason, however, losing to Cincinnati 21-13 in the divisional playoffs.

Turnovers caused a decline in 1989. Seattle was minus-15 in turnovers, and fell to 7-9. Largent retired as the game's leading receiver, owning NFL records for receptions, yards, and touchdowns. The much-publicized "Boz" also stepped down, forced to retire by a nagging shoulder injury.

Knox led the team to a 9-7 record in 1990, but the up-and-down ride continued the following season when the team fell to 7-9. Knox left the team to return to the Rams, and was replaced by Tom Flores. Bolstered by young stars such as defensive tackle Cortez Kennedy, the NFL's defensive player of the year in 1992, quarterback Rick Mirer, 1,000-yard running back Chris Warren, and wide receiver Brian Blades, the team improved to 6-10 in 1993, but was 6-10 again in 1994.

University of Miami head coach Dennis Erickson replaced Flores at the helm of the Seahawks in 1995, and the club improved to 8-8. Warren was named team MVP after rushing for 1,346 yards, and rookie wide receiver-punt returner Joey Galloway of Ohio State flashed game-breaking abilities. Team owner Ken Behring looked to move the Seahawks to Los Angeles for the 1996 season, but backed off in the face of stiff opposition from the league and a lease that bound the club to Seattle through the year 2005. The controversy was defused at least temporarily when Microsoft co-founder Paul Allen signed an agreement with Behring giving Allen the option to purchase the club.

In the 1996 draft, Erickson sought to strengthen his offensive line by drafting tackle Pete Kendall of Boston College with the Seahawks' first pick and Rutgers tackle Robert Barr with their third. But with Chris Warren suffering an off-year, the Seahawks' 7-9 season in 1996 largely was forgettable.

Forty-year-old quarterback Warren Moon led the Seahawks to a 6-4 start in 1997, but four consecutive losses led to an 8-8 finish, third in the AFC West. Moon's 25 touchdown passes headed the NFL's most prolific passing attack, and Seattle finished third in the league in total offense.

The Seahawks were 8-8 again in 1998. Free-agent acquisition Ricky Watters ran for 1,239 yards, Galloway tied for the conference lead in receiving touchdowns (10), and developing quarterback Jon Kitna replaced Moon during the season and showed promise. Seattle opened the season with a 38-0 rout of the Eagles in Philadelphia, and followed with victories over Arizona and Washington. But the Seahawks lost six of their next eight games and could not recover.

Erickson was fired the day after a 28-21 season-ending loss at Denver. On January 8, the Seahawks signed former Green Bay coach Mike Holmgren to a four-year contract as their new head coach and general manager.

SEAHAWKS RECORD 1976-1998

YEAR	WON	LOST	TIED	PCT.	FIN	PF	PA
1976	2	12	0	.143	5	229	429
1977	5	9	0	.357	4	282	373
1978	9	7	0	.563	3	345	358
1979	9	7	0	.563	3	378	372
1980	4	12	0	.250	5	291	408
1981	6	10	0	.375	5	322	388
1982	4	5	0	.444	10	127	147
1983a	9	7	0	.563	2	403	397
1984b	12	4	0	.750	2	418	282
1985	8	8	0	.500	3	349	303
1986	10	6	0	.625	3	366	293
1987c	9	6	0	.600	2	371	314
1988d	9	7	0	.563	1	339	329
1989	7	9	0	.438	4	241	327
1990	9	7	0	.563	3	306	286
1991	7	9	0	.438	4	276	261
1992	2	14	0	.125	5	140	312
1993	6	10	0	.375	5	280	314
1994	6	10	0	.375	5	287	323
1995	8	8	0	.500	3	363	366
1996	7	9	0	.438	4t	317	376
1997	8	8	0	.500	3	365	362
1998	8	8	0	.500	3	372	310
23 Years	164	192	0	.461	—	7,167	7,630

a AFC Wild Card Qualifier for Playoffs; 2-1 in Playoffs
b AFC Wild Card Qualifier for Playoffs; 1-1 in Playoffs
c AFC Wild Card Qualifier for Playoffs; 0-1 in Playoffs
d AFC Western Division Champion; 0-1 in Playoffs

COACHING HISTORY
(167-196-0)

1976	Jack Patera*	35-59-0
1982	Mike McCormack	4- 3-0
1983-91	Chuck Knox	83-67-0
1992-94	Tom Flores	14-34-0
1995-98	Dennis Erickson	31-33-0

* Released after two games in 1982

Tennessee Titans

Had Houston oilman K.S. (Bud) Adams, Jr., not decided to join Lamar Hunt in his venture to start the American Football League in 1959, there may not have been an AFL at all.

When Hunt began looking for partners in his new league in 1959, Adams was the first man he sought. Hunt, who was planning on situating his team in Dallas, believed the cornerstone of the new league would be a rivalry, preferably in the Southwest, Hunt's home territory and an area that was a hotbed for football.

Adams had been turned down by NFL owners when he approached them with expansion ideas, and he agreed to field a team in the new league. The home field was Jeppesen Stadium, an old high school structure, and, since Adams had made his fortune in oil, he named his team appropriately.

Adams outmaneuvered the Los Angeles Rams for the contract rights to Heisman Trophy back Billy Cannon of LSU. While the Cannon signing was important to AFL prestige, the Oilers signing of former Chicago Bear George Blanda gave the Oilers the AFL's best quarterback. With Blanda launching rockets to ends Charley Hennigan and Bill Groman, the Oilers won five of their first six games and the first Eastern Division title with a 10-4 record in 1960. In the AFL Championship Game, played on New Year's Day in Houston, Blanda hit Cannon with an 88-yard touchdown that clinched a 24-16 victory over the Los Angeles Chargers.

Lou Rymkus was fired after a 1-3-1 start in 1961 and was replaced by former assistant Wally Lemm. The club reeled off nine wins in a row and became the first team in pro history to score more than 500 points in a season (513). Blanda led the league with 3,330 yards passing and 36 touchdowns and also booted a record 55-yard field goal to earn AFL MVP honors. Hennigan led the league with 1,746 receiving yards, and Cannon ran for a league-high 948 yards. On a sunny Christmas Eve in San Diego, the Oilers and Chargers rematched in the AFL title game. Blanda and Cannon again combined for the winning touchdown, and Houston earned a 10-3 victory in a defense-dominated game.

The club's revolving door at head coach continued as Lemm jumped leagues to become head coach of the St. Louis Cardinals, and Adams hired Frank (Pop) Ivy. Blanda threw 42 interceptions, but Charley Tolar, nicknamed the "Human Bowling Ball," boosted the ground game as he became the team's first 1,000-yard back. Houston went 7-0 down the stretch, finished 11-3, and wrapped up its third straight Eastern Division title. The two-time defending-champion Oilers hosted the Texans with the AFL title on the line, and they hooked up in a classic—a six-quarter thriller that saw Dallas finally prevail 20-17 on Tommy Brooker's 25-yard field goal at 2:54 of the second overtime.

Houston suffered losing seasons the next four years, but surprised observers in 1967, winning the Eastern Division with a 9-4-1 record to become the first AFL team to go from last to first in one season. The key to the Houston turnaround was the defense, which featured rookie outside linebacker George Webster and defensive back Ken Houston, while fullback Hoyle Granger led the team in both rushing and receiving. Houston's hopes of representing the AFL in Super Bowl II came to a crashing end on New Year's Eve in Oakland, when they lost to the Raiders 40-7.

The big story in Houston in 1968 was the Oilers' long-awaited move into the Astrodome. They finished 7-7 in 1968, and closed out their AFL years with a 6-6-2 record in 1969. Thanks to a revamped playoff system that allowed second-place teams to advance to the postseason, the Oilers were matched with the Western Division-champion Raiders in the first round. Houston hadn't defeated an opponent with a winning record all season, and they lost to Oakland 56-7.

From 1970-77, the Oilers managed just two winning seasons, but regained lost glory in 1978, drafting Heisman Trophy back Earl Campbell, a 225-pound Texas bull who dominated college defenses with power and speed. Campbell's impact on both the Oilers and the AFC were immediate. He led the AFC in rushing with 1,450 yards, and head coach O.A. (Bum) Phillips installed a 3-4 defense tailor-made for the unique talents of nose tackle Curley Culp. The Oilers finished the season at 10-6, and their resurgence thrilled Houston fans, who packed the Astrodome with "Luv Ya Blue" banners.

Returning to the playoffs for the first time since their AFL days, the Oilers rode the arm of quarterback Dan Pastorini and the legs of Campbell to a 17-9 victory over the Dolphins. One week later, Houston beat New England 31-14 to advance to the AFC title game opposite division-rival Pittsburgh. The game was played in a cold, driving rain that drenched Three Rivers Stadium, and the Oilers played as miserably as the weather, turning over the ball to the Steel Curtain defense 9 times in a 34-5 loss.

With Campbell hammering defenses by rushing for 100 or more yards in 11 games, the Oilers went 11-5 in 1979, their best season since 1962. Campbell rushed for an AFC-high 1,697 yards, and Houston advanced through the first round of the playoffs with a 13-7 victory over Denver. One week later, the Oilers upset the San Diego Chargers 17-14 as defensive back Vernon Perry intercepted 4 of Dan Fouts's passes. Facing the Steelers again in the AFC title game, Pastorini's apparent touchdown pass to Mike Renfro in the back of the end zone was waived off by an official, and the Steelers went on to win 27-13.

Pastorini was traded to the Raiders for veteran Ken Stabler, and the Oilers traded for another Raider, tight end Dave Casper. Houston produced another 11-5 season, as Campbell led the AFC in rushing for the third consecutive year, posting a career-high 1,934 yards that was second in NFL history to O.J. Simpson's 2,003 yards in 1973. The Oilers advanced to the playoffs for the third straight season, but again were eliminated by the eventual Super Bowl champions, losing this time to the Raiders 27-7.

The 1980s was a decade of decline. Phillips was fired; Campbell, the club's workhorse back, was traded in 1984 to New Orleans; and the "Luv Ya Blue" hysteria faded away. The franchise endured six consecutive losing seasons and four straight last-place finishes from 1983-86. A turnaround began in 1987, when head coach Jerry Glanville and ex-Canadian League quarterback Warren Moon directed the team to a 9-7 record. Houston earned its first playoff victory since 1979 by defeating Seattle 23-20 in a first-round game, but was eliminated by Denver 34-10.

The Oilers started 7-1 in 1988 and finished with a 10-6 record. With Mike Rozier rushing for 1,002 yards, they reached the playoffs for the second straight season and proved they could win away from the Astrodome with a 24-23 victory over the division-rival Browns. Their season ended with a 17-10 loss at Buffalo. They closed the decade with a 9-7 record in 1989 and lost to the Steelers 26-23 in overtime in the playoffs.

Glanville was replaced for the 1990 season by University of Houston coach Jack Pardee, and the Oilers, despite three losses in their first five games, still managed a 9-7 season while featuring their "Run-and-Shoot" offense. Wide receivers Haywood Jeffires and Drew Hill each hauled in 74 passes to lead the AFC. Backup quarterback Cody Carlson produced a 34-14 victory over the Steelers in the season finale to give the Oilers a postseason berth, but their season ended with a 41-14 playoff loss at Cincinnati.

Pardee directed the team to an 11-5 record in 1991 and its first Central Division title. Moon's 655 pass attempts and 404 completions were NFL records, and he passed for more than 4,600 yards. Jeffires snared 100 receptions to become the fifth player in league history to hit the century mark in a season. Fronted by pass-rushing ends William Fuller and Sean Jones, the defense allowed just 251 points, second lowest in the AFC. Moon passed for 2 touchdowns in a 17-10 victory over the Jets in the opening round, but the Oilers, who were the only NFL team to make the playoffs every year from 1987-1991, again fell in the second round, blowing a fourth-quarter lead in Denver and losing to the Broncos 26-24.

Thanks to a beefed-up ground game that saw Lorenzo White rush for 1,226 yards, the team finished second in the division with a 10-6 record and reached the playoffs for the sixth consecutive season in 1992. Despite Moon's injury-plagued season, the passing attack continued to prosper. Carlson stepped in and completed an AFC best 65.6 percent of his passes. Jeffires again led the conference in receptions, pulling in 90. With a defense ranked first in the conference and an offense ranked second, the Oilers were in position to make a run at their first Super Bowl. They looked to be on their way when they took a 35-3 lead over the two-time defending AFC-champion Bills in Buffalo in a first-round playoff game, but they blew that 32-point lead and lost 41-38 in overtime.

The Oilers began the 1993 season with just one win in their first five games. But they rallied to win their last 11 regular-season games and the Central Division championship. The team lost 1,000-yard back Lorenzo White to injuries, but found another in Gary Brown, who ran for 1,002 and averaged a conference-best 5.1 yards per carry. Under Ryan, the defense gave up an AFC-low 238 points, but their postseason futility continued as the Chiefs eliminated the Oilers 28-20 in the Astrodome.

Moon and defensive stars Sean Jones and William Fuller left the team in 1994, and the club's run of seven consecutive playoff appearances came to a crashing halt as the Oilers fell to 2-14 in the worst one-season turnaround in league history. Pardee was fired after a 1-9 start and was replaced by defensive coordinator Jeff Fisher.

Fisher improved the team to 7-9 in 1995, and provided hope for the future by using his number-one draft pick on Heisman Trophy running back Eddie George of Ohio State. However, when Adams announced his plans to move the team to Nashville for the 1998 season, fan interest in the Oilers almost disappeared. The Astrodome was filled to less than half of capacity for some 1996 home games.

Still, George rushed for 1,368 yards and earned NFL rookie-of-the-year honors. After a 5-2 start, the Oilers finished 8-8.

After the season, the franchise moved up its timetable and relocated to Tennessee in time for the 1997 season. The Oilers won six of eight games in their new home in Memphis in 1997, but lost six of eight on the road and finished 8-8. George rushed for 1,399 yards to head the league's third-best ground attack, but the passing game struggled behind an inconsistent Steve McNair, who passed for 14 touchdowns but was intercepted 13 times.

Tennessee moved its home games to Vanderbilt Stadium in Nashville for 1998, but the club finished 8-8 for the third consecutive year.

Late in the season, Tennessee unveiled a new club nickname, which was to be implemented for the 1999 season. Ironically, the new moniker chosen by owner Bud Adams, an original AFL owner, was "Titans," the original nickname of the New York Jets.

OILERS RECORD 1960-1998

YEAR	WON	LOST	TIED	PCT.	FIN	PF	PA
1960a	10	4	0	.714	1	379	285
1961a	10	3	1	.769	1	513	242
1962b	11	3	0	.786	1	387	270
1963	6	8	0	.429	3	302	372
1964	4	10	0	.286	4	310	355
1965	4	10	0	.286	4	298	429
1966	3	11	0	.214	4t	335	396
1967b	9	4	1	.692	1	258	199
1968	7	7	0	.500	2	303	248
1969c	6	6	2	.500	2	278	279
1970	3	10	1	.231	4	217	352
1971	4	9	1	.308	3	251	330
1972	1	13	0	.071	4	164	380
1973	1	13	0	.071	4	199	447
1974	7	7	0	.500	3	236	282
1975	10	4	0	.714	3	293	226
1976	5	9	0	.357	4	222	273
1977	8	6	0	.571	2	299	230
1978d	10	6	0	.625	2	283	298
1979d	11	5	0	.688	2	362	331
1980e	11	5	0	.688	2	295	251
1981	7	9	0	.438	3	281	355
1982	1	8	0	.111	13	136	245
1983	2	14	0	.125	4	188	460
1984	3	13	0	.188	4	240	437
1985	5	11	0	.313	4	284	412
1986	5	11	0	.313	4	274	329
1987f	9	6	0	.600	2	345	349
1988f	10	6	0	.625	3	424	365
1989e	9	7	0	.563	2	365	412
1990e	9	7	0	.563	2	405	307
1991g	11	5	0	.688	1	386	251
1992e	10	6	0	.625	2	352	258
1993h	12	4	0	.750	1	368	238
1994	2	14	0	.125	4	226	352
1995	7	9	0	.438	3	348	324
1996	8	8	0	.500	4	345	319
1997	8	8	0	.500	3	333	310
1998	8	8	0	.500	2	330	320
39 Years	267	307	6	.466	—	11,914	12,518

a AFL Champion; 1-0 in Playoffs
b AFL Eastern Division Champion; 0-1 in Playoffs
c AFL Eastern Division Runner-up; 0-1 in Playoffs
d AFC Wild Card Qualifier for Playoffs; 2-1 in Playoffs
e AFC Wild Card Qualifier for Playoffs; 0-1 in Playoffs
f AFC Wild Card Qualifier for Playoffs; 1-1 in Playoffs
g AFC Central Division Champion; 1-1 in Playoffs
h AFC Central Division Champion; 0-1 in Playoffs

COACHING HISTORY
HOUSTON OILERS 1960-1996, TENNESSEE OILERS 1997-98, TENNESSEE TITANS 1999-
(276-320-6)

1960-61	Lou Rymkus*	12-7-1
1961	Wally Lemm	10-0-0
1962-63	Frank (Pop) Ivy	17-12-0
1964	Sammy Baugh	4-10-0
1965	Hugh Taylor	4-10-0
1966-70	Wally Lemm	28-40-4
1971	Ed Hughes	4-9-1
1972-73	Bill Peterson**	1-18-0
1973-74	Sid Gillman	8-15-0
1975-80	O.A. (Bum) Phillips	59-38-0
1981-83	Ed Biles***	8-23-0
1983	Chuck Studley	2-8-0
1984-85	Hugh Campbell****	8-22-0
1985-89	Jerry Glanville	35-35-0
1990-94	Jack Pardee#	44-35-0
1994-98	Jeff Fisher	32-38-0

* Released after five games in 1961
** Released after five games in 1973
*** Resigned after six games in 1983
**** Released after 14 games in 1985
\# Released after 10 games in 1994

CHAPTER 6

Team Histories: Defunct Franchises

Joe Horrigan

While the National Football League today is, by almost any measure, America's most popular sport, its success was neither immediate nor without tremendous growing pains. Now a successful 30-team league, the NFL has had 48 failed franchises that have operated in such unlikely locations as Muncie, Indiana; Akron, Ohio; and Tonawanda, New York. Even successful NFL cities such as New York, Detroit, Chicago, and Dallas were, at one time or other, homes to now-defunct NFL franchises.

Obviously, the vast majority of washouts occurred during the league's first decade. During that period, 35 franchises folded. The major reason was that the young NFL primarily operated in small cities with populations and/or playing facilities that couldn't support major league teams.

Even winning a championship during the league's early years wasn't enough to insure a team's future. The NFL's first champions, the Akron Pros, were gone by 1926. The Canton Bulldogs, after winning consecutive championships in 1922 and 1923, failed to field a team in 1924 and two years later were out of business. The Frankford Yellow Jackets won the league championship in 1926, but folded part way through the 1931 season. The last team not currently in the NFL to win a championship was the 1928 Providence Steam Roller. After 1931, they were gone.

A migration to larger cities, however, was essential if pro football was to survive. Joe Carr, NFL president from 1921 until his death in 1939, understood that fact. It was Carr who guided the league through much of the futility of its early years.

Aaron Hertzman, reflecting on his years as the owner of the defunct Louisville Brecks, once wrote, "The majority of present-day owners know nothing of the hardships Joe Carr went through in finding new clubs each year, most of which only lasted one season, but," Hertzman continued, "they did contribute dues and assessments, which were essential to the continuance of the league until it finally got on its feet. The three or four or five games they filled in the schedules of the ruling clubs enabled the league to keep going."

It was Carr who, in 1927, directed the NFL through a much-needed reorganization that saw the league reduce its numbers from 22 teams to a more solid 12-team operation. This was the most significant move toward stability the NFL had taken to that point.

Through the 1930s, the number of franchise failures was reduced to eight, and most of those were victims of the Great Depression. From 1935 until 1952, just five franchises ceased operations. The last to go belly-up in the NFL was the 1952 Dallas Texans. Since then, no NFL franchise has failed.

The following is a brief description of the NFL's failed franchises.

Akron Pros/Indians (1920-25/26) The Akron Pros, charter members of the NFL, were managed by Frank Neid, a local cigar store owner, and Art Ranney, a former Buchtel College (University of Akron) athlete. The 1920 Pros, the NFL's first champions, featured the play of former Brown University All-America running back Fritz Pollard. Pollard was one of only two African-Americans playing pro football during the league's inaugural season. In 1921, Pollard and 1920 Pros' coach Elgie Tobin were named co-coaches of the Akron squad, earning Pollard the distinction of becoming the first African-American head coach in the NFL.

While Pollard, who left the team after the 1921 season, clearly was the Pros' star performer, the team was not without other quality players. Rip King, a fullback from West Virginia, was a fine backfield compliment to Pollard in 1920 and 1921. Durable Al Nesser, the next-to-youngest of the seven Nesser Brothers—six of whom played in the league—anchored the Pros' line from 1920 through 1925 and served as the team's player-coach in 1926. Other big-name players included Bob (Nasty) Nash and Paul Robeson. Both former Rutgers All-America ends, Nash played for Akron in 1920 and Robeson in 1921.

AKRON PROS/INDIANS RECORD

YEAR	WON	LOST	TIED	PCT.	FIN	PF	PA
1920a	8	0	3	1.000	1	151	7
1921	8	3	1	.727	3	148	31
1922	3	5	2	.375	10	146	95
1923	1	6	0	.143	15t	25	74
1924	2	6	0	.250	13t	59	132
1925	4	2	2	.667	5	65	51
1926	1	4	3	.200	16t	23	89
7 yrs	27	26	11	.509	-	617	479

a - record versus league teams only = 6-0-3

Baltimore Colts (1950) The Baltimore Colts were born

in 1947 as a replacement franchise for the defunct Miami Seahawks of the All-America Football Conference. During their three AAFC seasons, the Colts posted unimpressive 2-11-1, 7-7-0 and 1-11-0 records, making them a surprise choice to join the NFL in 1950 as a part of the NFL/AAFC merger settlement.

In their first and only NFL season, the 1-11-0 Colts finished in the NFL's basement. Owner Abe Watner, no longer able to absorb the team's financial losses, turned the Baltimore franchise back to the NFL following the 1950 season. Still, the Colts weren't without a couple bright spots, namely quarterback Y. A. Tittle and defensive tackle Art Donovan. Both went on to have Hall of Fame careers with other teams.

BALTIMORE COLTS RECORD

YEAR	WON	LOST	TIED	PCT.	FIN	PF	PA
1950	1	11	0	.083	7-N	213	462

Boston Yanks (1944-48) On June 19, 1943, the NFL granted a new Boston franchise to Ted Collins. Originally wanting to secure a team to play in New York's Yankee Stadium, Collins named his Boston team the Yanks. In 1944, their inaugural season, the Yanks managed just two victories, both against an equally bad Brooklyn Tigers team owned by Dan Topping, who also owned Yankee Stadium.

In 1945, due to a manpower shortage caused by World War II, Collins and Topping merged their teams for one season. The team, known as the Yanks, played four home games in Boston and one in New York. While the Yanks did play better football, fans from neither city seemed to notice or care.

In 1946, Topping deserted the NFL and joined the upstart All-America Football Conference as owner of the New York franchise which he named the Yankees. The NFL's response was to cancel his Brooklyn franchise and award all players previously assigned to the franchise to Collins's Boston Yanks. After three more seasons of financial losses, Collins asked the league to cancel his Boston franchise and grant him a new one to operate in New York City. (See New York Bulldogs)

BOSTON YANKS RECORD

YEAR	WON	LOST	TIED	PCT.	FIN	PF	PA
1944	2	8	0	.200	4-E	82	233
1945a	3	6	1	.333	3t-E	123	211
1946	2	8	1	.200	5-E	189	273
1947	4	7	1	.364	3-E	168	256
1948	3	9	0	.250	5-E	174	372
5 yrs	14	38	3	.269	-	736	1345

a - Merged with Brooklyn Tigers for 1945 only.

Brooklyn Dodgers/Tigers (1930-1943/44; merged with Boston 1945) In 1930, John Dwyer, a Brooklyn businessman, purchased the Dayton Triangles franchise, moved it, and renamed the team the Brooklyn Dodgers. Three years later, Dwyer and partner-coach John Depler sold the franchise to Chris Cagle and John (Shipwreck) Kelly. The Kelly-Cagle operation lasted just one season before selling to New Yorker Dan Topping.

The Dodgers' best years came in 1940 and 1941, when they finished second in the NFL's Eastern Division. Tackle Bruiser Kinard anchored a solid line, while quarterback Ace Parker and end Perry Schwartz made a pass-catch combination worthy of league-wide recognition.

Beginning in 1942, however, the Dodgers went into a steep decline. The demands of military service caused by World War II hit the Dodgers' roster so hard that when training camp opened in 1943, only seven players from the 1942 squad were available. Although Kinard remained and continued to shine, gone were stars Parker and Schwartz. The Dodgers finished last in their division.

The 1944 Brooklyn team—renamed the Tigers—went winless in 10 games. In a desperate attempt for survival, the Tigers merged for one season with the equally troubled Boston Yanks. The merger team, known as the Yanks, played four home games in Boston and one in New York. Though the team was improved, fan support continued to wane.

Topping dropped a bombshell of his own in 1945, when he announced that he was joining the upstart All-America Football Conference as the owner of that league's New York franchise. The NFL's response was to cancel his NFL franchise and award all those players previously assigned to the franchise to the Boston Yanks.

BROOKLYN DODGERS/TIGERS RECORD

YEAR	WON	LOST	TIED	PCT.	FIN	PF	PA
1930	7	4	1	.636	4	154	59
1931	2	12	0	.143	9t	64	199
1932	3	9	0	.250	6	63	131
1933	5	4	1	.556	2-E	93	54
1934	4	7	0	.364	3t-E	61	153
1935	5	6	1	.455	2-E	90	141
1936	3	8	1	.273	4-E	92	161
1937	3	7	1	.300	4-E	82	174
1938	4	4	3	.500	3-E	131	161
1939	4	6	1	.400	3-E	108	219
1940	8	3	0	.727	2-E	186	120
1941	7	4	0	.636	2-E	158	127
1942	3	8	0	.273	4-E	100	168
1943	2	8	0	.200	4-E	65	234
1944	0	10	0	.000	5-E	69	166
1945a	3	6	1	.333	4-E	123	211
16 yr	63	106	10	.373	-	1639	2478

a - Merged with Boston Yanks.

Brooklyn Lions (1926) The biggest name in pro football in 1925 was Red Grange. In 1926, Grange and his manager, C. C. Pyle, formed the American Football League to compete with the then-young NFL. The AFL fielded teams in such NFL cities as Chicago, New York, Los Angeles (both league's Los Angeles entries were road teams only), Philadelphia, and Rock Island. Rock Island actually had defected from the NFL. Rounding out the AFL were teams in Cleveland, Newark, Boston, and Brooklyn.

A countermove by the NFL was to challenge the AFL in Brooklyn. While the AFL-NFL war would eventually be for fan support, the first battle in Brooklyn was for Ebbets Field. On July 20, the NFL emerged victorious with a signed lease for their Brooklyn Lions.

Neither the NFL Lions nor Grange's AFL squad, however, met with much success. In fact, after just four games, the AFL's Brooklyn Horsemen merged with the NFL's Lions. The team finished the 1926 NFL season as the Brooklyn Lions. Both the AFL and the NFL's Brooklyn franchise ceased to operate following the 1926 season.

BROOKLYN LIONS/HORSEMEN RECORD

YEAR	WON	LOST	TIED	PCT.	FIN	PF	PA
1926	3	8	0	.273	14	60	150

Buffalo All-Americans/Bisons/Rangers/Bisons (1920-23/24-25 / 26 / 27, 1929) The Buffalo All-Americans, led by former college stars Tommy Hughitt, Lud Wray, Lou Little, and Swede Youngstrom, were a formidable team in 1920 and 1921, barely missing league titles in both years.

During the 1921 season, however, several key Buffalo players deserted their NFL team to play for the independent Philadelphia Quakers. Because Pennsylvania had blue laws prohibiting professional sports on Sundays, Buffalo players had been earning extra income by playing for the nonleague Quakers on Saturdays before suiting up as the All-Americans on Sunday. Learning of the practice, league President Joe Carr enforced an NFL rule that prohibited players from playing for more than one team during the same week. The defections forced Buffalo management to scramble for enough players to finish the season. Eventually, players from the Detroit Panthers, who had ended their season early, were added to the All-Americans' roster.

After two mediocre seasons in 1922 and 1923, team owner Frank McNeil sold his franchise to Warren Patterson and player-coach Hughitt, who renamed the team the Bisons. Hughitt remained for one more season before retiring from his owner-coach-player role. Other ownership and name changes followed, but nothing seemed to help the struggling franchise. Finally, after failing to field a team in 1928 and unable to meet its financial obligations in 1929, the franchise was disbanded.

BUFFALO ALL-AMERICANS/BISONS/RANGERS/BISONS RECORD

YEAR	WON	LOST	TIED	PCT.	FIN	PF	PA
1920a	9	1	1	.900	3	258	32
1921	9	1	2	.900	2	211	29
1922	5	4	1	.556	9	87	41
1923	5	4	3	.556	9	94	43
1924	6	5	0	.545	9	120	140
1925	1	6	2	.143	15	33	113
1926	4	4	2	.500	9	53	62
1927	0	5	0	.000	12	6	123
1928b	-	-	-	-	-	-	-
1929	1	7	1	.125	10	48	142
9 yr	40	37	12	.519	-	910	725

a - record versus league teams only = 4-1-1
b - no team

Canton Bulldogs (1920-23, 1925-26) In 1920, when the NFL was founded, the Canton Bulldogs already owned the proudest heritage of any team of the league's founding group. However, their inaugural NFL season was not up to Canton standards despite the presence of the legendary Jim Thorpe as its star and coach. The Bulldogs' 7-4-2 record was good only for a mid-level finish in a 14-team league.

But by 1922, the Bulldogs were ready to write the first bright chapter in the young league's book. That year, led by coach and end Guy Chamberlin and with two other future Hall of Fame players in Wilbur Henry and Roy (Link) Lyman at tackles, the undefeated team finished first, posting a 10-0-2 record. With virtually the same lineup, the 1923 Bulldogs marched to their second consecutive undefeated season with an 11-0-1 record.

Though successful on the field, the team suffered financially. Ralph Hay, the Hupmobile Agency owner who brought the Bulldogs into the league, sold out to a group of Canton business men after the 1922 season. Before the 1924 season, unable to find sufficient financial support, the Bulldogs were forced to sell off their assets, including player contracts to Sam Deutsch, the owner of the league's Cleveland franchise. Deutsch combined the best of his Cleveland Indians team with the best Canton players and renamed his Cleveland team the Bulldogs. While Deutsch's Bulldogs went on to win a league title, the once-proud Canton franchise sat dormant.

In 1925, the Canton franchise was reactivated with Henry and several other players in charge. After a mediocre 1925 season and a disastrous 1926 that produced just one victory, the proud Canton Bulldogs disbanded for good.

CANTON BULLDOGS RECORD

YEAR	WON	LOST	TIED	PCT.	FIN	PF	PA
1920a	7	4	2	.636	8	208	57
1921	5	2	3	.714	4	106	55
1922	10	0	2	1.000	1	184	15
1923	11	0	1	1.000	1	246	21
1924b	-	-	-	-	-	-	-
1925	4	4	0	.500	11	50	73
1926	1	9	3	.100	20	46	161
6 yr	38	19	11	.667	-	840	382

a - record versus league teams only = 4-3-1
b - no team

Chicago Tigers (1920) The Chicago Tigers were one of two NFL teams calling Chicago home in 1920. The other Windy City entry was the Chicago (Racine) Cardinals. Popular legend contends that the two teams played a late-season game in which it was agreed that the losing team would fold, leaving the winner the exclusive rights to the Chicago market. The Cardinals won the game and presumably the sole rights to the city. Lost in the legend, however, is the fact that the Tigers didn't fold, but in fact went on to finish the season. A more likely cause for the Tigers' eventual demise was the general lack of attendance caused by their increasingly poor play, coupled with an increased interest in the better-performing Cardinals.

CHICAGO TIGERS RECORD

YEAR	WON	LOST	TIED	PCT.	FIN	PF	PA
1920a	2	5	1	.286	11t	49	63

a - Record versus league teams only = 1-5-1

Cincinnati Celts (1921) The Cincinnati Celts, a moderately successful club team dating from before World War I, played just four games during their brief stay in the NFL. Their only victory, and their only points, came at the expense of the Muncie Flyers, whom they defeated 14-0. The game was Muncie's last in the NFL, while the Celts suffered through two more shutouts before folding.

CINCINNATI CELTS RECORD

YEAR	WON	LOST	TIED	PCT.	FIN	PF	PA
1921	1	3	0	.250	13t	14	117

Cincinnati Reds (1933-34) The Cincinnati Reds were one of three NFL expansion teams in 1933. Unlike the other two, the Philadelphia Eagles and the Pittsburgh Steelers, the Reds' NFL tenure was short. Poor attendance, caused by bad weather and a bad team, plagued the Reds during their inaugural season. Although a second season was attempted, the Reds were unable to meet financial obligations and folded after eight games of the 1934 season. The St. Louis Gunners, an independent pro team, were granted an NFL franchise during the season and finished the remaining games on the Reds' 1934 schedule.

CINCINNATI REDS RECORD

YEAR	WON	LOST	TIED	PCT.	FIN	PF	PA
1933	3	6	1	.333	4-W	38	110
1934	0	8	0	.000	6-W	10	243
2 yr	3	14	1	.176	-	48	353

Cleveland Indians (1931) The Cleveland Indians were a league-sponsored road team. The team was managed by a league appointee, Jerry Corcoran, the former manager of the Columbus Tigers. The NFL's intention was to locate the franchise permanently in Cleveland after a suitable backer was found. No backer surfaced, however, and the franchise was canceled at the end of the season.

CLEVELAND INDIANS RECORD

YEAR	WON	LOST	TIED	PCT.	FIN	PF	PA
1931	2	8	0	.200	8	45	137

Cleveland Indians/Bulldogs (1923/24-25, 1927) On August 28, 1923, Cleveland was granted its second franchise in the NFL. This version, owned by Cleveland's Sam Deutsch, was christened the Indians. While the 1923 roster included a few big-name players such as Ohio State's Pete Stinchcomb, the Indians were not a very good team. That changed in 1924, however, when Deutsch purchased the financially struggling Canton Bulldogs.

Deutsch combined the best of the Bulldogs—NFL champions in 1922 and 1923—with his Indians team to form the Cleveland Bulldogs. The Bulldogs went on to win the 1924 NFL title. The following season, Deutsch sold the dormant Canton franchise back to Canton and the Cleveland franchise to a new local owner, Herbert Brandt.

Without most of the Canton players, the 1925 Cleveland Bulldogs struggled to a 5-8-1 record. Prior to the start of the 1926 season, Brandt requested and received permission from the league to suspend operations for a year.

The Bulldogs' franchise returned in 1927 stocked with many players from the defunct Kansas City Cowboys. With the addition of All-America quarterback Benny Friedman, the Bulldogs were vastly improved and led the league in scoring. It wasn't enough, however, as financial woes continued and the team folded following an impressive 8-4-1 season.

CLEVELAND INDIANS/BULLDOGS RECORD

YEAR	WON	LOST	TIED	PCT.	FIN	PF	PA
1923	3	1	3	.750	5	52	49
1924	7	1	1	.875	1	229	50
1925	5	8	1	.385	12	75	135
1926a	-	-	-	-	-	-	-
1927	8	4	1	.667	4	209	107
4 yr	23	14	6	.622	-	565	341

a - no team

Cleveland Tigers/Indians (1920-21) The Cleveland Tigers were charter members of the NFL. Although the team was stocked with several name players, it got off to a disappointing 0-3 start. As a result, manager Jimmy O'Donnell cleaned house. The following week, minus several key players, including player-coach Stan Cofall, the Tigers recorded the first of two victories. The 2-4-2 Tigers finished tenth in the 14-team league.

In 1921, three former Canton Bulldogs—Jim Thorpe, Joe Guyon and Pete Calac—were signed by Cleveland. Capitalizing on the fact that all three were Native Americans, the team changed its name to Indians. Although improved, the Indians struggled both on and off the field. Following a season-ending loss to the Washington Senators, the 3-5-0 Cleveland Indians folded.

CLEVELAND TIGERS/INDIANS RECORD

YEAR	WON	LOST	TIED	PCT.	FIN	PF	PA
1920a	2	4	2	.333	10	28	46
1921	3	5	0	.375	11	95	58
2 yr	5	9	2	.357	-	123	104

a - Record versus league teams only = 1-4-2

Columbus Panhandles/Tigers (1920-22/1923-26) The Columbus Panhandles were a pro team long before the founding of the NFL in 1920. Organized in the early 1900s by Joe Carr, who served as NFL president from 1921 until his death in 1939, the Panhandles already were a well-known team when they joined the new league in its inaugural season. However, it wasn't their play that earned the Panhandles their notoriety, but rather the colorful nature of their player personnel.

In their pre-NFL years, the team featured seven brothers—Al, Ted, Phil, John, Raymond, Fred, and Frank—of the Nesser family. During those years it wasn't uncommon for five and occasionally six of the brothers to play in the same game. But by 1920, the Nessers had already begun to go their separate ways. However, on December 4, 1921, in a game against the Louisville Brecks in which five of the brothers—Fred, Ted, Phil, John, and Frank—suited up for the Panhandles, the Nessers made NFL history in yet another way. In that game, Ted's son Charles played tailback. Thus the two became the first and only father-son combination to play in an NFL game together.

The Panhandles had one financial advantage over other NFL teams. Because most of the players were railroad employees, they rode the rails free of charge. Additionally, by playing most of their games on the road, they had no stadium expenses. However, having no practice field to call their own affected their play. Reorganized as the Tigers in 1923 with Joe Carr's right-hand man Jerry Corcoran as manager and younger players replacing the Nessers, the team tried playing some home games before disappointing crowds. During their seven NFL seasons the Panhandles/Tigers had only one winning season.

COLUMBUS PANHANDLES/TIGERS RECORD

YEAR	WON	LOST	TIED	PCT.	FIN	PF	PA
1920a	2	6	2	.250	13	41	121
1921	1	8	0	.111	17	47	222
1922	0	8	0	.000	18	24	174
1923	5	4	1	.556	8	119	35
1924	4	4	0	.500	10	91	68
1925	0	9	0	.000	20	28	124
1926	1	6	0	.143	19	26	93
7 yr	13	45	3	.224	-	376	837

a - Record versus league teams only = 0-5-0

Dallas Texans (1952) The Texans seemingly were born of failure. They were actually a transplanted version of the failed New York Yanks franchise which earlier had been sold back to the NFL by owner Ted Collins. While some questioned the league's decision to attempt to place a team in an area so devoted to college football, others questioned team owner Giles Miller's sanity for purchasing the assets of the failed franchise.

The critics were right. Miller didn't last the season. After just seven games he was forced to return the financially strapped franchise to the league. For the final five games the Texans were operated by the league out of Hershey, Pennsylvania, and played as a road team. Their only win came against the Chicago Bears on Thanksgiving Day in Akron, Ohio. The team, however, was not bereft of talent. It had Buddy Young, a speedy running back, and future Hall of Fame members Gino Marchetti and Art Donovan.

DALLAS TEXANS RECORD

YEAR	WON	LOST	TIED	PCT.	FIN	PF	PA
1952	1	11	0	.083	6-N	182	427

Dayton Triangles (1920-29) Managed by Carl Storck, who would serve as NFL secretary for nearly two decades and succeed Joe Carr as league president upon Carr's death, the Dayton Triangles were charter members of the NFL. The 1920 Triangles were an inconsistent team that featured a fairly effective offense led by running backs Francis Bacon and Lou Partlow and the passing of Al Mahrt. When they were good, the Triangles could score at least 20 points a game, as they did five times, or shut out the opposition, as they did five times. However, on three occasions, the erratic team failed to cross their opponent's goal line. This inconsistency left them with a good, but not great, 5-2-2 record and a fourth-place tie in the new league.

The Triangles' inaugural season was followed by respectable back-to-back, four-win seasons in 1921 and 1922. However, 1922 was the last time the team would experience a winning season. With a small playing field and a team that featured mostly home-grown talent, the Triangles were unable to attract the top teams to Dayton. As a result, they were forced to play the majority of their games on the road. Finally, after winless seasons in 1928 and 1929, the franchise was sold to interests in Brooklyn, where the team was relocated and renamed the Brooklyn Dodgers.

DAYTON TRIANGLES RECORD

YEAR	WON	LOST	TIED	PCT.	FIN	PF	PA
1920a	5	2	2	.714	6	150	50
1921	4	4	1	.500	8t	96	67
1922	4	3	1	.571	7t	80	62
1923	1	6	1	.143	16t	16	95
1924	2	6	0	.250	13t	45	148
1925	0	7	1	.000	16t	3	84
1926	1	4	1	.200	16t	15	82
1927	1	6	1	.143	10	15	57
1928	0	7	0	.000	10	9	131
1929	0	6	0	.000	12	7	136
10 yr	18	51	8	.261	-	436	912

a - Record versus league teams only = 4-2-2

Detroit Heralds (1920) The Detroit Heralds were members of the NFL during its inaugural season of 1920. Although they had been the Michigan independent champions before World War I, those days long were past when they joined the league under veteran manager Billy Marshall. A weak team, the Heralds' only wins came against an equally bad Columbus Panhandles team and the semi-pro Cleveland Panthers.

DETROIT HERALDS RECORD

YEAR	WON	LOST	TIED	PCT.	FIN	PF	PA
1920a	2	3	3	.400	9	53	82

a - Record versus league teams only = 1-3-0

Detroit Panthers (1925-26) In 1925, desirous of having the NFL represented in Detroit, NFL president Joe Carr offered then-Milwaukee Badgers player-coach Jimmy Conzelman a franchise for the Motor City. The price tag was $100. Conzelman accepted the offer and christened the team the Panthers.

Conzelman, as owner, coach, and tailback, built a strong team in 1925. In fact it was the league's best defensive club, posting eight shutouts in 12 contests and finishing third in the 20-team league. After a successful debut, the 1926 Panthers didn't reach the high expectations of Conzelman or the Detroit fans. A disappointing 4-6-2 finish in 1926, coupled with the inability to compete with the popularity of the University of Michigan Wolverines, resulted in the Panthers folding after their second NFL season.

DETROIT PANTHERS RECORD

YEAR	WON	LOST	TIED	PCT.	FIN	PF	PA
1925	8	2	2	.800	3	129	39
1926	4	6	2	.400	12	107	60
2 yr	12	8	4	.600	-	236	99

Detroit Tigers (1921) The Detroit Tigers were the NFL's second effort in the Motor City in as many years. Managed by former Heralds leader Billy Marshall, the new Detroit team fared even worse than the first, winning just one game, a surprise 10-7 victory over the Dayton Triangles.

DETROIT TIGERS RECORD

YEAR	WON	LOST	TIED	PCT.	FIN	PF	PA
1921	1	5	1	.167	16	19	109

Detroit Wolverines (1928) After lying dormant for one season, the Detroit franchise was reactivated under new ownership, a consortium of Detroit businessmen. Stocked by several players from the defunct Cleveland Bulldogs, including quarterback Benny Friedman, the Detroit Wolverines were the surprise of the season. Friedman, the league leader in scoring with 55 points, led Detroit to an impressive 7-2-1 third-place finish in 1928. Still, the franchise suffered tremendous financial losses.

New York Giants owner Tim Mara was so impressed by Friedman that prior to the start of the 1929 season, he purchased the financially struggling Detroit franchise just to obtain Friedman's contract rights.

DETROIT WOLVERINES RECORD

YEAR	WON	LOST	TIED	PCT.	FIN	PF	PA
1928	7	2	1	.778	3	189	76

Duluth Kelleys/Eskimos (1923-25/1926-27) The Duluth franchise originally operated as an independent pro team prior to joining the NFL in 1923. Officially, the team was named the Kelley Duluths, after the Kelley-Duluth Hardware Store, where team co-owner M.C. Gebert worked as manager.

Gebert and partner Dewey Scanlon operated the franchise through the end of the 1923 season when Gebert dropped out and the players took over, running the team on a cooperative basis. Scanlon was the coach. Following the 1925 season, the players sold the franchise to Scanlon and team treasurer Ole Haugsrud for $1 and assumption of the team's debt.

Haugsrud and Scanlon scored a major victory when they signed Stanford All-America Ernie Nevers to a contract. In an attempt to capitalize on Nevers's fame, the duo renamed the team Ernie Nevers' Eskimos. The Eskimos became a traveling team. They hit the road on September 20, 1926 and didn't return until February 5, 1927. The Nevers-led squad, which often numbered as few as 15, played 29 league and exhibition games. Nevers, who played in all but 29 minutes of the tour, almost single-handedly led the team to a respectable 6-5-3 league record.

Although Nevers continued to shine in 1927, his supporting cast was unable to provide any consistency, and the team plummeted to a 1-8-0 record. Duluth suspended operations prior to the 1928 season and in 1929 the franchise was sold to a group from Orange, New Jersey.

DULUTH KELLEYS/ESKIMOS RECORD

YEAR	WON	LOST	TIED	PCT.	FIN	PF	PA
1923	4	3	0	.571	7	35	33
1924	5	1	0	.833	4	56	16
1925	0	3	0	.000	16t	6	25
1926	6	5	3	.545	8	113	61
1927	1	8	0	.111	11	68	134
5 yr	16	20	3	.444	-	278	269

Evansville Crimson Giants (1921-22) The Evansville Crimson Giants, organized in 1921 by Franklin Fausch, "surprised local fans in developing a winning team," according to a local tabloid. Although the Giants' 3-2-0 league record was good, the Giants' one-sided victories over several inferior nonleague clubs may have created some false hopes for the local fans.

The Giants' second season was much more telling. It was a disaster. First they lost their home field to a local semipro team. Then they lost all their games, including a 60-0 shellacking by the Rock Island Independents in the second week of the season. In that game, the Independents tallied 9 rushing touchdowns. The Crimson Giants folded after a final loss to the Louisville Brecks two weeks later.

EVANSVILLE CRIMSON GIANTS RECORD

YEAR	WON	LOST	TIED	PCT.	FIN	PF	PA
1921	3	2	0	.600	6	57	46
1922	0	3	0	.000	15t	6	88
2 yr	3	5	0	.375	-	63	134

Frankford Yellow Jackets (1924-1931) The Frankford Yellow Jackets, a successful independent pro team sponsored by the nonprofit Frankford Athletic Association, joined the NFL in 1924. Because of Pennsylvania blue laws, the Yellow Jackets could not play on Sundays. Still the team drew large crowds on Saturdays even though they faced the competition of area college and high school football. Often they would play at home on Saturday, then jump on a train for a game in another city on Sunday. As a result, Frankford played more games than any other NFL team nearly every season.

The Yellow Jackets finished their first NFL season with an impressive 11-2-1 record, good for a third-place finish in the 18-team league. With high hopes for the 1925 season, the F.A.A. hired Guy Chamberlin as a player-coach. Chamberlin had been player-coach of three consecutive NFL champions: the Canton Bulldogs in 1922 and 1923 and the Cleveland Bulldogs of 1924. Chamberlin's Yellow Jackets posted a 13-7 record in 1925 and in 1926 he led the team to the NFL title. Frankford's 14 victories (against one defeat and one tie) were not surpassed by an NFL team until 1984, when the mark was eclipsed by the San Francisco 49ers (15-1).

The Yellow Jackets eventually became another casualty of the Great Depression. By 1929, most of the team's top players had retired or moved on to greener pastures. Due to lack of funds and a stadium left in disrepair, the Yellow Jackets disbanded after only eight games of the 1931 season.

FRANKFORD YELLOW JACKETS RECORD

YEAR	WON	LOST	TIED	PCT.	FIN	PF	PA
1924	11	2	1	.846	3	326	109
1925	13	7	0	.650	6	190	169
1926	14	1	1	.933	1	236	49
1927	6	9	3	.400	7	152	166
1928	11	3	2	.786	2	175	84
1929	9	4	5	.692	3	139	128
1930	4	13	1	.222	9	113	321
1931	1	6	1	.143	10	13	99
8 yr	69	45	14	.605	-	1344	1125

Hammond Pros (1920-26) Charter members of the NFL, the Hammond Pros were organized by Dr. Alva Andrew Young. Not a very good team, the Pros won only two of their seven games in 1920. Both of those victories came against inferior nonleague teams. Against recognized league teams, Hammond lost by sizable margins. During their seven NFL seasons, only once did the Pros win more than one game, that coming in 1924 when the team went 2-2-1.

While the team made no lasting marks on the field, Young made a significant contribution of another sort—a willingness to hire African-American players. Of the six African-Americans in the league in 1922, two played for the Pros, a fact not missed by the *Milwaukee Journal's* pregame coverage of a 1922 match between the Pros and the Milwaukee Badgers. "Other collegians on the squad," reported the newspaper, "are Williams, once an end on the Brown University eleven, and Shelburne, colored, formerly with Dartmouth. Inky Williams, the left end for Hammond, also is a colored player." During the Pros' NFL years, only nine African-Americans played in the league. At one time or another, all but three played for Young's Hammond Pros.

HAMMOND PROS RECORD

YEAR	WON	LOST	TIED	PCT.	FIN	PF	PA
1920a	2	5	0	.286	12	41	154
1921	1	3	1	.250	13t	17	45
1922	0	5	1	.000	15t	0	69
1923	1	5	1	.167	15	14	59
1924	2	2	1	.500	10t	18	45
1925	1	4	0	.200	14	23	87
1926	0	4	0	.000	21t	3	56
7 yr	7	28	4	.200	-	116	515

a - Record versus league teams only = 0-3-0

Hartford Blues (1926) The Hartford Blues, an independent pro team in 1925, joined the NFL in 1926. Managed by promoter George Mulligan, the Blues played home games in the Velodrome, a bicycle-racing arena.

The 3-7 Hartford team was composed mostly of local talent and was not very competitive. Because of bad weather and a bad team, attendance dipped to as low as

500 for a game against the Kansas City Cowboys. Two games actually were canceled due to weather conditions.

Although Mulligan was willing to continue in 1927, the NFL had voted to cut back from 22 franchises to 12 strong entries. Hartford was not counted among them.

HARTFORD BLUES RECORD

YEAR	WON	LOST	TIED	PCT.	FIN	PF	PA
1926	3	7	0	.300	13	57	99

Kansas City Blues/Cowboys (1924/1925-26) The Kansas City Blues of 1924 featured the line play of future Hall of Famer Steve Owen, but not much else. In 1925 the team, renamed the Cowboys, left town and played all of its games on the road. After an opening-day victory over the Kelleys in Duluth, Minnesota, the Cowboys went winless until the final game of the season, when they defeated the Cleveland Bulldogs 17-0 to finish 2-5-1.

The Cowboys continued their odyssey in 1926, playing all but their final two games on the road. In a two-season span, the team played 17 road games before returning home to Kansas City. Traveling must have agreed with the 1926 team, however, as it performed much better. After winning just one of their first four games, they went on to win seven in a row and finish fourth in the 22-team league. After the season, the Cowboys failed to survive the NFL's cut to 12 teams.

KANSAS CITY BLUES/COWBOYS RECORD

YEAR	WON	LOST	TIED	PCT.	FIN	PF	PA
1924	2	7	0	.222	15	46	124
1925	2	5	1	.286	13	65	97
1926	8	3	0	.727	4	76	53
3 yr	12	15	1	.444	-	187	274

Kenosha Maroons (1924) Prior to the start of the 1924 NFL season, the Toledo Maroons' franchise was ordered by the league to transfer or suspend operations. It appears, though no conclusive evidence exists, that the Toledo franchise was transferred to Kenosha. In addition to the same nickname and common players, both franchises were managed by George Johnson.

In any event, the Kenosha Maroons folded after posting no victories in five games (with one tie) in their only season in the NFL.

KENOSHA MAROONS RECORD

YEAR	WON	LOST	TIED	PCT.	FIN	PF	PA
1924	0	4	1	.000	16t	12	117

Los Angeles Buccaneers (1926) The Los Angeles Buccaneers actually were a road team that played out of Chicago, Illinois. The squad was led by Harold (Brick) Muller, former University of California star and Rose Bowl hero. Tut Imlay, another University of California star, shared the coaching duties with Muller. Backed by Lew Cody, an actor, and Fritz Burns, a Los Angeles real-estate dealer, the team was stocked with players from California schools.

Although fairly successful on the field in 1926, the financially troubled and road-weary Buccaneers folded following their 6-3-1 season.

LOS ANGELES BUCCANEERS RECORD

YEAR	WON	LOST	TIED	PCT.	FIN	PF	PA
1926	6	3	1	.667	6t	67	57

Louisville Brecks/Colonels (1921-23/1926) The Brecks kept going by playing semipro teams at home for most of their schedule. Occasionally they would visit NFL teams to pick up guarantees and beatings. When their home park burned down in 1923, they went out of business.

Not only did the Brecks help fill the schedules of the ruling clubs from 1921 through 1923, but in 1926, when the rival American Football League threatened the NFL, the dormant Louisville franchise was reactivated to fill the schedules of the expanded NFL. The team was known as the Colonels and played out of Chicago as a road team.

LOUISVILLE BRECKS/COLONELS RECORD

YEAR	WON	LOST	TIED	PCT.	FIN	PF	PA
1921	0	2	0	.000	18t	0	27
1922	1	3	0	.250	12t	13	140
1923	0	3	0	.000	19t	0	83
1924-25a	-	-	-	-	-	-	-
1926	0	4	0	.000	21t	0	108
4 yr	1	12	0	.077	-	13	358

a - no team

Milwaukee Badgers (1922-26) Perhaps the most surprising thing about the 1922 Milwaukee Badgers was their modest 2-4-3 record. With a roster that, at least early on, featured the likes of Fritz Pollard and Paul Robeson, and later included veteran stars Duke Slater, Bo McMillin, and future Hall of Fame enshrinee Jimmy Conzelman, a stronger showing was expected.

In 1923, with player-coach Conzelman leading the way, the Badgers, even without Pollard, Robeson, and Slater, were much improved. A strong defense provided the Badgers with a fourth-place, seven-victory season. Unfortunately, the team never again experienced much success. In 1925, the league ordered team manager Ambrose McGurk to sell his franchise.

The order came after McGurk, desirous of an opportunity for another payday, agreed to play the Chicago Cardinals even though his Badgers had disbanded for the season. Unable to provide enough players, McGurk allowed four high school boys to play for the Badgers. The Cardinals easily won the farcical game in which the quarters were shortened and no admission was charged.

The Milwaukee franchise later was transferred to former Chicago Bears back Johnny (Red) Bryan, but the Badgers folded after just two wins in nine games in 1926.

MILWAUKEE BADGERS RECORD

YEAR	WON	LOST	TIED	PCT.	FIN	PF	PA
1922	2	4	3	.333	11	51	71
1923	7	2	3	.778	3t	100	49
1924	5	8	0	.385	12	142	188
1925	0	6	0	.000	16t	7	191
1926	2	7	0	.222	15	41	66
5 yr	15	27	6	.357	-	341	565

Minneapolis Marines/Red Jackets (1921-24/1929-30) The Minneapolis Marines operated as a semipro or pro team for many years before joining the NFL in 1921. Not quite ready for the jump to the NFL, the Marines of 1921 and 1922 played as many nonleague as league-sanctioned games. Although they managed to win the majority of their nonleague contests, they won just two league games in two years.

Definitely a second-division team, the Marines relied on the sandlot players who had won games for them in their pre-NFL years. They suspended operations in 1924, following two seasons of on-the-field and box-office losses. Minneapolis franchise holders Johnny Dunn and Val Ness, however, continued to maintain membership in the league by paying their annual fees and assessments. Dunn, in fact, was NFL vice president.

Then in 1929, Dunn and Ness reactivated their dormant franchise as the Minneapolis Red Jackets. Although they employed more college-trained players, the Red Jackets fared no better than their predecessor and folded after two seasons with a combined 2-16-1 record.

MINNEAPOLIS MARINES/REDJACKETS RECORD

YEAR	WON	LOST	TIED	PCT.	FIN	PF	PA
1921	1	3	1	.250	13t	37	41
1922	1	3	0	.250	12t	19	40
1923	2	5	2	.286	13	48	51
1924	0	6	0	.000	16t	14	108
1925-28a	-	-	-	-	-	-	-
1929	1	9	0	.100	11	48	185
1930	1	7	1	.125	10	27	165
6 yr	6	33	4	.154	-	193	590

a - no team

Muncie Flyers (1920-21) The Muncie Flyers were charter members of the NFL. However, their 45-0 loss to the Rock Island Independents on October 3 was their only game of the season. Of historical note, that game and one played between the Dayton Triangles and the Columbus Panhandles on the same day were the first played between recognized NFL teams.

The Flyers tried again in 1921 but folded after losing their first two games of the season to the Cincinnati Celts and the Evansville Crimson Giants.

MUNCIE FLYERS RECORD

YEAR	WON	LOST	TIED	PCT.	FIN	PF	PA
1920	0	1	0	.000	14	0	45
1921	0	2	0	.000	18t	0	28
2 yr	0	3	0	.000	-	0	73

New York Bulldogs/Yanks (1949/1950-51) After five financially unsuccessful seasons, Boston Yanks owner Ted Collins requested that the NFL cancel his Boston franchise and issue him a new one to operate in New York City. The league granted the new franchise only after Collins agreed to stipulations made by the New York Giants, in whose protected territory Collins would operate. It was agreed that the Giants would have first choice of all home-game dates and Collins would pay $25,000 annually for the right to operate in New York.

Collins's new team, the New York Bulldogs, continued to play to empty seats, however. Then in 1950, as part of the merger between the All-America Football Conference and the National Football League, Collins purchased the assets of Dan Topping's AAFC Yankees, including player contracts and the lease for Yankee Stadium. The merger provided that the Giants had first choice of six players from the Yankees' roster, but even without the best Yankee players, Collins's team, renamed the Yanks, was much improved. Quarterback George Ratterman and a number of fine runners gave the Yanks an exciting offense. Still, the team went virtually unnoticed in New York.

In 1951, Ratterman jumped to the Canadian League and the always weak Yanks' defense became even more porous. Finally, following the 1951 season, Collins sold his franchise back to the league for $100,000.

NEW YORK BULLDOGS/YANKS RECORD

YEAR	WON	LOST	TIED	PCT.	FIN	PF	PA
1949	1	10	1	.091	5-E	153	365
1950	7	5	0	.583	3-N	366	367
1951	1	9	2	.100	6-N	241	382
3 yr	9	24	3	.297	-	760	1114

New York Giants (1921) The 1921 New York Giants were organized by former Harvard great Charley Brickley and sports promoter Billy Gibson. Brickley also served as the team's coach.

While the Gibson-Brickley team played a full schedule in 1921, only two games, both losses, were against NFL opponents. After failing to post the necessary league fees for the 1922 season, the New York franchise was canceled by the league.

NEW YORK BRICKLEY GIANTS RECORD

YEAR	WON	LOST	TIED	PCT.	FIN	PF	PA
1921	0	2	0	.000	18t	0	72

New York Yankees (1927-28) In 1927, the NFL reorganized and reduced itself from a 22- team league in 1926 to a more efficient 12-team circuit. Gone were many of the small-town teams that lacked suitable playing facilities and fans. Also gone was the rival American Football League, which operated during the 1926 season.

One AFL team, the Red Grange-C.C. Pyle New York Yankees, however, was granted permission to join the NFL. New York Giants owner Tim Mara, who held the territorial rights to New York, permitted the Yankees to operate under the Brooklyn Lions franchise, which he also held in lieu of payments owed him. However, as part of the agreement, the Yankees were to operate primarily as a road team.

The Yankee road team, with Grange as the box-office attraction, was expected to draw large crowds. Grange, however, suffered a leg injury early in the season. While the injury caused him to miss just three games, the "Galloping Ghost" was never the same. Neither were the crowds.

In 1928, with Grange out of football for the year, the Yankees continued to slide and, prior to the start of the 1929 season, the club folded.

NEW YORK YANKEES RECORD

YEAR	WON	LOST	TIED	PCT.	FIN	PF	PA
1927	7	8	1	.467	6	142	174
1928	4	8	1	.333	7	103	179
2 yr	11	16	2	.407	-	145	353

Oorang Indians (1922-23) Perhaps the most unusual NFL team ever was the Oorang Indians. The team, which was composed entirely of American Indians, was led by the incomparable Jim Thorpe. The idea of an all-Indian team was conceived by Walter Lingo, who owned the Oorang Dog Kennels located in tiny LaRue, Ohio. Lingo, who was more interested in selling dogs than in winning football games, staged wild halftime shows that featured the Indians and his dogs.

The Oorang squad operated for two seasons as a traveling franchise. Their roster was filled with the likes of such players as Long Time Sleep, Ted Lone Wolf, Laughing

Gas, and Baptiste Thunder, who hailed from Native American tribes ranging from the Cherokee to the Iroquois.

During their two-season stay in the NFL, the Indians played only one of 20 games at home and even that one wasn't played in LaRue, which lacked a suitable playing field. It was played in neighboring Marion, Ohio.

The Indians were not a very good team. After posting a 3-6-0 record in 1922 and going 1-10-0 in 1923, the novelty of Lingo's squad had pretty much worn off and the team disbanded.

OORANG INDIANS RECORD

YEAR	WON	LOST	TIED	PCT.	FIN	PF	PA
1922	2	6	0	.250	12t	69	190
1923	1	10	0	.091	18	43	257
2 yr	3	16	0	.188	-	112	447

Orange/Newark Tornadoes (1929/1930) On July 27, 1929, the NFL approved the sale of the defunct Duluth franchise to the Orange Athletic Club of New Jersey. The OAC had operated a strong independent pro team known as the Tornadoes. Managed by Eddie Simandl, the Tornadoes were perhaps a better team than their inaugural NFL record indicates. Although they won only three games, they tied four times and stayed close in two of their four losses.

The Tornadoes relocated to Newark in 1930, but the move didn't help as the team finished in last place. Unable to field a team, the franchise was forfeited to the league prior to the 1931 season.

ORANGE/NEWARK TORNADOES RECORD

YEAR	WON	LOST	TIED	PCT.	FIN	PF	PA
1929	3	4	4	.429	6t	35	80
1930	1	10	1	.091	11	51	190
2 yr	4	14	5	.222	-	86	270

Pottsville Maroons/Boston Bulldogs (1925-28/1929) The Pottsville Maroons, a strong independent pro team, joined the NFL in 1925 and immediately emerged as one of the strongest teams on the pro circuit. A late-season favorite to win the 1925 NFL title, the Maroons scheduled a much-ballyhooed game with the Chicago Cardinals, another strong contender. Pottsville defeated the Cardinals 21-7, earning them, at least temporarily, bragging rights as the best team in the pro league.

With two weeks remaining in the season, the Maroons were scheduled to play an exhibition game in Philadelphia's Shibe Park with a nonleague team billed as the Notre Dame All-Stars. The Frankford Yellow Jackets, with a game scheduled that same day at Frankford Stadium, lodged a formal protest, claiming its territorial rights were being violated. League president Joe Carr agreed, and in advance of the game, ordered Pottsville not to play. To do so, Carr warned, would result in Pottsville's expulsion from the league. The Maroons' management, however, ignored Carr's warning and went ahead with the heavily promoted game. Immediately, Carr notified Pottsville manager J.G. Striegel that his membership in the NFL was revoked. The Cardinals, with their 11-2-1 record, were declared NFL champions for 1925.

Pottsville fans lobbied for years, claiming their team had been robbed. As late as 1963, they petitioned the league to have the Maroons declared 1925 champions. Unfortunately, the Pottsville sportswriter who championed the cause neglected to inform his readers that the team had been warned three times before the game of the consequences of violating league rules, or that a suspended team cannot win a league crown. He did, however, manage to erect an elaborate conspiracy theory with Carr serving as the evil genius behind a dark plot to cheat Pottsville. Sadly, several nationally known writers later took up Pottsville's quest, apparently after ending their research with the Pottsville sportswriter's columns.

Pottsville's expulsion from the NFL, however, did not last long. Carr, fearing that the newly formed American Football League would add Pottsville to its ranks, reinstated the Maroons prior to the start of the 1926 season.

Pottsville played well in 1926, finishing third with a 10-2-2 record. However, after two unsuccessful seasons, Striegel relocated his franchise to Boston, where the team played as the Bulldogs for a final season before folding.

POTTSVILLE MAROONS/BOSTON BULLDOGS RECORD

YEAR	WON	LOST	TIED	PCT.	FIN	PF	PA
1925	10	2	0	.833	2	270	45
1926	10	2	1	.833	3	155	29
1927	5	8	0	.385	8	80	163
1928	2	8	0	.200	8	74	134
1929	4	4	0	.500	4	98	73
5 yr	31	24	1	.564	-	677	444

Providence Steam Roller (1925-1931) The Providence Steam Roller, a successful independent pro team, joined the NFL in 1925. The team played in a stadium built not for football but for bicycle racing. The Cyclodrome featured a steeply banked wooden track with an enclosed area just large enough for a football field. The seats were so close to the field that players often found themselves among the fans, and one end zone was only five yards deep. Despite these minor drawbacks, the Steam Roller was a successful team from the start.

Providence's roster got a significant boost in 1927, when several players from the defunct Detroit Panthers joined the team. Included among them was player-coach Jimmy Conzelman. From the collapsed AFL came another important addition: star tailback George (Wildcat) Wilson.

With Conzelman in charge, and Wilson having a career year, the Steam Roller went 8-1-2 in 1928 and won the NFL title. However, the team would never match that success again, and within only a few years, the Steam Roller was flattened by the Depression.

Following the 1931 season, Providence received permission from the league to suspend operations for a year. But the Steam Roller never played in the NFL again, and in 1933, the franchise was forfeited to the league.

Of historical note, on November 3, 1929, the Steam Roller played the Chicago Cardinals at Providence's Kinsley Park in the NFL's first night game played under lights.

PROVIDENCE STEAM ROLLER RECORD

YEAR	WON	LOST	TIED	PCT.	FIN	PF	PA
1925	6	5	1	.545	10	111	101
1926	5	7	1	.417	11	99	103
1927	8	5	1	.615	5	105	88
1928	8	1	2	.889	1	128	42
1929	4	6	2	.400	8	107	117
1930	6	4	1	.600	5	90	125
1931	4	4	3	.500	6	78	127
7 yr	41	32	11	.562	-	718	703

Racine Legion/Tornadoes (1922-24/1926) The Racine Legion, a team sponsored by American Legion Post 76 of Racine, Wisconsin, entered the NFL in 1922 to promote "both the club's activities and the city of Racine." After a 1-3 start, Legion manager Babe Ruetz bolstered his roster by adding some new faces, including quarterback Chuck Dressen, better known for his later efforts as a baseball player and manager. Dressen, along with Colgate All-America Hank Gillo, sparked the team to a respectable 6-4-1 record.

Though the team had improved as the season wore on, attendance did not. In 1923, the Legion sponsors found it necessary to have a fund-raising dinner to bail out the financially strapped team. It was merely a temporary solution, however, as the team's financial burden eventually proved too heavy.

Unable to field a team in 1925, the Legion sold the franchise in 1926 to the Racine Exchange Club, which operated the team as the Racine Tornadoes. After a disastrous 1-4 start, the Tornadoes folded.

RACINE LEGION/TORNADOES RECORD

YEAR	WON	LOST	TIED	PCT.	FIN	PF	PA
1922	6	4	1	.600	6	122	56
1923	4	4	2	.500	9t	86	76
1924	4	3	3	.571	7	69	47
1925a	-	-	-	-	-	-	-
1926	1	4	0	.200	16t	8	92
4 yr	15	15	6	.500	-	285	271

a - no team

Rochester Jeffersons (1920-25) The Rochester Jeffersons began as a neighborhood team around 1912 and eventually grew into city champions. Charter members of the NFL, the Jeffersons' only game against a recognized NFL opponent in 1920 was a 17-6 loss to the Buffalo All-Americans. In 1921, the Jeffersons beat the Columbus Panhandles and Tonawanda Kardex during a 2-3 season. But, the 1922 team went 0-4-1 and was shut out four times. The following season, Rochester played just two games and lost by a cumulative score of 116-0. In 1924 it was more of the same, as the Jeffersons were outscored 156-7 in seven league contests. After an 0-6-1 campaign in 1925, team owner Leo Lyons could hold on no longer and the franchise ceased operations.

ROCHESTER JEFFERSONS RECORD

YEAR	WON	LOST	TIED	PCT.	FIN	PF	PA
1920a	6	3	2	.667	7	156	57
1921	2	3	0	.400	10	85	76
1922	0	4	1	.000	15t	13	76
1923	0	4	0	.000	19t	6	141
1924	0	7	0	.000	16t	7	156
1925	0	6	1	.000	16t	26	111
6 yr	8	27	4	.229	-	293	617

a - Record versus league teams only = 0-1-0

Rock Island Independents (1920-25) The Rock Island Independents were a good pro football team even before the formation of the NFL in 1920. Charter members of the new league, the Independents finished their inaugural NFL season with a disappointing 21-0 loss to the Dayton Triangles. Clearly a better team than Dayton, the Independents' loss was attributable directly to the physical battering they had received from the Decatur Staleys a week earlier.

Although the Independents played the Staleys to a 0-0 tie, four Rock Island players were knocked out of the game by an aggressive Decatur squad. The Independents got some revenge in 1921, however, when they lured Staleys star Jimmy Conzelman away from Decatur to Rock Island. Conzelman, who was handed the team's coaching responsibilities during a time out in the third game of the season, directed the 1921 team to a 4-2-1 record. Both losses were to the Staleys, who by then played out of Chicago.

In 1922, the Independents again were outflanked by Chicago, who by then had become the Bears. Not only did the Bears maul Rock Island twice that season, but Chicago's shrewd owner-coach-player, George Halas, purchased the contract of Rock Island tackle Ed Healey. Dissatisfied with Healey's play, Independents manager Walt Flanigan sold his contract for just $200. While Flanigan left pro football following the 1922 season, Healey went on to have a Hall-of-Fame career with the Bears.

The Independents finally beat Chicago in 1923, which, ironically, was the Independents' only losing season in the NFL. In 1924, a revamped Independents team that included aging Jim Thorpe posted a 6-2-2 record. In 1925, it was 5-3-3.

Then in 1926, the Independents management surprised the NFL by jumping leagues and joining Red Grange's rival American Football League. It was a bad move. Amid much red ink, the AFL and the Independents folded following the 1926 season.

ROCK ISLAND INDEPENDENTS RECORD

YEAR	WON	LOST	TIED	PCT.	FIN	PF	PA
1920a	4	2	1	.667	3	-	-
1921	4	2	1	.667	5	65	30
1922	4	2	1	.667	5	154	27
1923	2	3	3	.400	12t	84	62
1924	6	2	2	.750	5	88	38
1925	5	3	3	.625	8	99	58
6 yr	27	14	12	.659	-	691	264

a - Record versus league teams only = 4-2-1

St. Louis All-Stars (1923) The St. Louis All-Stars, organized by Ollie Kraehe, a former Washington University of St. Louis player, began their brief stay in the NFL by playing the Green Bay Packers to a 0-0 tie. The following week, the All-Stars returned home to face the Hammond Pros. Only 719 fans witnessed the All-Stars' home debut, which they lost 6-0.

Though the All-Stars' defense performed well in most games, the offense virtually was nonexistent and failed to score a point until the sixth game of the season, when they defeated the Oorang Indians 14-3. Not only would this be the All-Stars' only victory of the season, but the only points scored by the team during its seven-game NFL existence.

ST. LOUIS ALL-STARS RECORD

YEAR	WON	LOST	TIED	PCT.	FIN	PF	PA
1923	1	4	2	.200	14	14	39

St. Louis Gunners (1934) Although not a member of the NFL in 1933, the independent St. Louis Gunners did play exhibition games against some NFL teams. The Gunners defeated the Chicago Cardinals and Brooklyn Dodgers, and played the defending champion Chicago Bears to a scoreless tie.

In 1934, while the Gunners were enjoying a winning season among the independents, over in the NFL the second-year Cincinnati Reds were experiencing quite the opposite, losing their first eight games. After their eighth loss, the Reds, unable to pay their players, were ordered by the league to suspend operations. The independent Gunners then purchased the Cincinnati franchise. As a new NFL team, the Gunners were scheduled to play the Reds' three remaining games. The Gunners won their first game 6-0 over Pittsburgh. Then they added five former Reds players to their roster and lost the two remaining contests.

Unable to meet their new, higher payroll and forced to file bankruptcy, the Gunners disbanded in May, 1935.

ST. LOUIS GUNNERS RECORD

YEAR	WON	LOST	TIED	PCT.	FIN	PF	PA
1934	1	2	0	.333	5-W	27	61

Staten Island Stapletons (1929-1932) The Staten Island Stapletons, so named because they represented the Stapleton area of the Island, featured the play of future Hall of Fame member Ken Strong and player-coach Doug Wycoff. Although the Stapletons managed only one .500 season in their four NFL years, they were usually respectable losers. The Stapletons developed a strong rivalry with the other New York team, the Giants. In fact, a visit to Staten Island became somewhat of a nightmare for the Giants, who were winless on the Island from 1930 to 1932.

On Thanksgiving Day, 1930, 12,000 fans packed Staten Island's tiny Thompson Stadium, where the Stapletons surprised the visiting Giants 7-6. Almost a year-to-the-day later, they again bested the visiting New Yorkers, this time 9-6. In 1932, however, the Stapletons had to settle for a 13-13 tie. Their home-field dominance of the Giants was not enough to offset the financial losses suffered throughout much of the rest of the season, and the Stapletons left the NFL following the 1932 season.

STATEN ISLAND STAPLETONS RECORD

YEAR	WON	LOST	TIED	PCT.	FIN	PF	PA
1929	3	4	3	.429	6t	89	65
1930	5	5	2	.500	6	95	112
1931	4	6	1	.400	7	79	118
1932	2	7	3	.222	8	77	143
4 yr	14	22	9	.389	-	340	438

Toledo Maroons (1922-23) The Toledo Maroons, like several other NFL teams of its day, were more successful on the field than in the box office. Although they finished the 1922 season with a respectable 5-2-2 record, the level of competition was, to say the least, suspect. The combined record of their five victims was 7-23-2, with six of the seven wins belonging to one opponent, the Racine Cardinals of Chicago.

The Maroons' 1923 schedule for the most part featured equally inept teams. However, their final two games did match them up against the talented Buffalo All-Americans and powerful Canton Bulldogs. Toledo managed a 3-3 tie with the All-Americans, but reality hit as the Bulldogs defeated the Maroons 28-0. The loss was Toledo's final game.

TOLEDO MAROONS RECORD

YEAR	WON	LOST	TIED	PCT.	FIN	PF	PA
1922	5	2	2	.714	4	94	59
1923	3	3	2	.500	11t	41	56
2 yr	8	5	4	.615	-	135	115

Tonawanda Kardex (1921) Tonawanda, New York, was granted an NFL franchise on July 27, 1921. The team known as the Kardex featured mostly local talent and was destined to be a traveling team. They didn't travel far. The Kardex folded after playing just one NFL game, a 45-0 loss to the Rochester Jeffersons.

TONAWANDA KARDEX RECORD

YEAR	WON	LOST	TIED	PCT.	FIN	PF	PA
1921	0	1	0	.000	18t	0	45

Washington Senators (1921) Although the Washington Senators played a full football schedule in 1921, only four of their 11 games were against recognized NFL opponents. In fact, their NFL debut did not occur until November 27, when they played the Canton Bulldogs. Washington coach Jack Hegerty so wanted to defeat Canton that he signed three former Bulldogs—Joe Guyon, Johnny Gilroy, and Pete Calac—for the game. Still, the Canton team had little trouble beating the upstart Senators 15-0. In a late-season rematch the Canton Bulldogs once again defeated the District of Columbia representative, this time by an equally decisive 28-14 margin.

The Senators beat the Cleveland Indians 7-0 for one of their two victories, but the second came in the form of a forfeit by the Rochester Jeffersons that never made it into the official league standings. In fact, no game actually was played. The Jeffersons refused to take the field because of a Washington snowstorm, and the referee gave the decision to the home team.

WASHINGTON SENATORS RECORD

YEAR	WON	LOST	TIED	PCT.	FIN	PF	PA
1921	2	2	0	.500	12	21	43

CHAPTER 7

The Road to the Super Bowl and Super Sunday

Ted Brock, Bob Carroll, Michael Gershman, and Matthew Silverman

By 1966, the battle for talent between the upstart American Football League (formed in 1960) and the more established National Football League threatened the existence of both as salaries skyrocketed. Secret talks were underway to achieve a merger between the two leagues, which had agreed to a "no-tampering" rule on players who had not played out their option year. However, peace was threatened when the New York Giants signed kicker Pete Gogolak away from the AFL Buffalo Bills.

On April 8, 1966, Al Davis took over as commissioner of the AFL and created a "war chest" specifically to sign NFL quarterbacks. The Oakland Raiders quickly signed the Los Angeles Rams' Roman Gabriel, and the Houston Oilers began negotiating with the San Francisco 49ers' John Brodie.

But, on June 8, just when hope seemed lost, the leagues announced plans to merge in 1970, with a common draft beginning in 1967 and—most important from the fans' standpoint—a game matching the AFL and NFL champions, to be played in a neutral, warm-weather site.

The first AFL-NFL World Championship Game—its official name, though some in the media already called it the Super Bowl—was close for a half before the Green Bay Packers eventually wore down the Kansas City Chiefs at the Los Angeles Coliseum. The second game wasn't even close for a half as the Packers did the same thing to the Oakland Raiders. All that changed in Super Bowl III—the first official Super Bowl—when the AFL's New York Jets shocked the Baltimore Colts and forever transformed the game and pro football. But the game is only part of what the biggest day in sports is all about. No other major league sport has a two-week waiting period to decide a champion, yet it is hardly two weeks of inactivity. Every day is spent publicizing not only the players and the teams, but the game of football itself. Even countries that think of the final of the World Cup as the ultimate football game watch the Super Bowl with heightened interest.

Every Super Bowl story line is different. There are no "reruns" even when the game features a rematch of a previous Super Bowl (Pittsburgh-Dallas, Washington-Miami, San Francisco-Cincinnati, Dallas-Buffalo). One constant has been dominance by one conference. The NFC won 13 straight Super Bowls from 1985-1997, but the AFL/AFC won 11 times in 13 years from 1969-1981. Denver has started a new winning streak for the AFC with triumphs in Super Bowls XXXII and XXXIII.

The story lines may be different, but some clearly are better than others. Debates rage about which Super Bowl stands above the rest (New York Jets-Baltimore Colts in Super Bowl III, Pittsburgh-Dallas in Super Bowl X, San Francisco-Cincinnati in Super Bowl XXIII, New York Giants-Buffalo in Super Bowl XXV, Green Bay-Denver in Super Bowl XXXII). None have gone to overtime yet, so until that happens we may not have a definitive winner.

Reaching the Super Bowl is the culmination of a season's worth of work, not to mention the years of groundwork required to assemble the right personnel and coaching staff. This section of *Total Super Bowl* not only explains what happened in the Super Bowl, but also details how each team got there, who was on the team roster, who played in the game, and even the quarter-by-quarter score of each playoff game the team played.

Each left-hand page in this section chronicles how both the NFL/NFC and AFL/AFC entry from each season reached the Super Bowl. A linescore of each playoff game for both teams is included. Also detailed are the regular-season results of each game that season with the day, date, location, opponent, and score. In the schedule listing, N stands for a night game, H is home, and A is away. Special sites—such as Green Bay Packers' games played in Milwaukee—are noted at the bottom of that season's schedule.

On each right-hand page is a detailed summary of every Super Bowl, including the date, place, and attendance for the game. At the end of each summary is the linescore, how each team scored, and team statistics. Also on that page will be complete rosters for both teams that year. Players who appeared in the Super Bowl—and whose names appear in the Super Bowl Register—are noted with an asterisk.

The Super Bowl: At a Glance

No.	Score	Site	Attendance	Winning Coach	MVP
I	Packers 35, Chiefs 10	Los Angeles Coliseum	61,946	Lombardi	Starr
II	Packers 33, Raiders 14	Orange Bowl	75,546	Lombardi	Starr
III	Jets 16, Colts 7	Orange Bowl	75,389	Ewbank	Namath
IV	Chiefs 23, Vikings 7	Tulane Stadium	80,562	Stram	Dawson
V	Colts 16, Cowboys 13	Orange Bowl	79,204	McCafferty	Howley
VI	Cowboys 24, Dolphins 3	Tulane Stadium	81,023	Landry	Staubach
VII	Dolphins 14, Redskins 7	Los Angeles Coliseum	90,182	Shula	Scott
VIII	Dolphins 24, Vikings 7	Rice Stadium	71,882	Shula	Csonka
IX	Steelers 16, Vikings 6	Tulane Stadium	80,997	Noll	Harris
X	Steelers 21, Cowboys 17	Orange Bowl	80,187	Noll	Swann
XI	Raiders 32, Vikings 14	Rose Bowl	103,438	Madden	Biletnikoff
XII	Cowboys 27, Broncos 10	Louisiana Superdome	75,583	Landry	White, Martin
XIII	Steelers 35, Cowboys 31	Orange Bowl	79,484	Noll	Bradshaw
XIV	Steelers 31, Rams 19	Rose Bowl	103,985	Noll	Bradshaw
XV	Raiders 27, Eagles 10	Louisiana Superdome	76,135	Flores	Plunkett
XVI	49ers 26, Bengals 21	Pontiac Silverdome	81,270	Walsh	Montana
XVII	Redskins 27, Dolphins 17	Rose Bowl	103,667	Gibbs	Riggins
XVIII	Raiders 38, Redskins 9	Tampa Stadium	72,920	Flores	Allen
XIX	49ers 38, Dolphins 16	Stanford Stadium	84,059	Walsh	Montana
XX	Bears 46, Patriots 10	Louisiana Superdome	73,818	Ditka	Dent
XXI	Giants 39, Broncos 20	Rose Bowl	101,063	Parcells	Simms
XXII	Redskins 42, Broncos 10	S.D. Jack Murphy Stadium	73,302	Gibbs	Williams
XXIII	49ers 20, Bengals 16	Joe Robbie Stadium	75,179	Walsh	Rice
XXIV	49ers 55, Broncos 10	Louisiana Superdome	72,919	Seifert	Montana
XXV	Giants 20, Bills 19	Tampa Stadium	73,813	Parcells	Anderson
XXVI	Redskins 37, Bills 24	Metrodome	63,130	Gibbs	Rypien
XXVII	Cowboys 52, Bills 17	Rose Bowl	98,374	Johnson	Aikman
XXVIII	Cowboys 30, Bills 13	Georgia Dome	72,817	Johnson	E. Smith
XXIX	49ers 49, Chargers 26	Joe Robbie Stadium	74,107	Seifert	S. Young
XXX	Cowboys 27, Steelers 17	Sun Devil Stadium	76,347	Switzer	Brown
XXXI	Packers 35, Patriots 21	Louisiana Superdome	72,301	Holmgren	Howard
XXXII	Broncos 31, Packers 24	Qualcomm Stadium	68,912	Shanahan	Davis
XXXIII	Broncos 34, Falcons 19	Pro Player Stadium	74,803	Shanahan	Elway

Future Super Bowl Sites

XXXIV — January 30, 2000 — Georgia Dome, Atlanta, Georgia
XXXV — January 28, 2001 — Raymond James Stadium, Tampa, Florida

1966 AFL Champions
Kansas City Chiefs

The 1966 Chiefs won the first championship in Kansas City history, but not the first championship in franchise history. The team, originally known as the Dallas Texans, had beaten the Houston Oilers for the American Football League title in their final game in Texas in 1962. After three so-so seasons, the Chiefs went 11-2-1 in 1966 to win the AFL West under Hank Stram, who had coached the team since day one in Dallas.

The Chiefs featured a strong running game, led by rookie sensation Mike Garrett of USC and the solid play of fellow AFL All-Star Curtis McClinton. They helped soften up defenses for the lethal aerial attack of Len Dawson to Otis Taylor.

On the other side of the ball, the Chiefs snared 33 interceptions, with Johnny Robinson and Bobby Hunt collecting 10 apiece. The All-AFL linebacking corps of Sherrill Headrick, E.J. Holub, and Bobby Bell, plus linemen Buck Buchanan and Jerry Mays, helped the Chiefs to a 7-0 mark on the road.

On New Year's Day, the Chiefs traveled to Buffalo to face a Bills' team that was playing in its third straight AFL Championship Game. Buffalo had 4 turnovers and Garrett put the game away with 2 late touchdowns as the Chiefs won 31-7 to represent the AFL against the NFL in the first Super Bowl.

Regular Season

Sun	S-11	A	Buffalo Bills	42-20	W
Sun	S-18	A	Oakland Raiders	32-10	W
Sun	S-25	A	Boston Patriots	43-24	W
Sun	O-2	H	Buffalo Bills	14-29	L
Sat	O-8	H N	Denver Broncos	37-10	W
Sun	O-16	H	Oakland Raiders	13-34	L
Sun	O-23	A	Denver Broncos	56-10	W
Sun	O-30	H	Houston Oilers	48-23	W
Sun	N-6	H	San Diego Chargers	28-14	W
Sun	N-13	H	Miami Dolphins	34-16	W
Sun	N-20	H	Boston Patriots	27-27	T
Sun	N-27	A	New York Jets	32-24	W
Sun	D-11	A	Miami Dolphins	19-18	W
Sun	D-18	A	San Diego Chargers	27-17	W

Postseason

1966 AFL Championship Game
January 1, 1967
Kansas City 31, Buffalo 7 at Buffalo

Kansas City	7	10	0	14	—	31
Buffalo	7	0	0	0	—	7

1966 NFL Champions
Green Bay Packers

A Packers team that had won three NFL championships in the previous five years was no less dominating in 1966, winning 12 games and losing 2 by a total of 4 points.

The NFL Championship Game matched Green Bay's power sweep and the Cowboys' multiple-formation offense. The game was decided when Green Bay's Tom Brown intercepted a pass in the end zone with 28 seconds left, to preserve the Packers' 34-27 victory.

The Packers appeared ready to make a runaway of it early on. Bart Starr threw a 17-yard touchdown pass to Elijah Pitts. Mel Renfro fumbled the ensuing kickoff and Green Bay's Jim Grabowski returned it 18 yards for a touchdown. The Cowboys, however, tied the score on touchdown runs by Dan Reeves and Don Perkins.

Starr passed for 3 touchdowns in the second half, the final one covering 28 yards to Max McGee, to give Green Bay a 34-20 lead with 5:20 remaining. But the Cowboys came right back, scoring on a 68-yard pass from Don Meredith to Frank Clarke. A short punt gave Dallas the ball at the Packers' 47, and Dallas advanced to the 22 before Brown was called for pass interference in the end zone. Dallas received a first down at the Green Bay 2, but on fourth down Meredith's pass was intercepted by Brown, ending the Cowboys' chances of upsetting Vince Lombardi's Packers.

Regular Season

Sat	S-10	H N (m)	Baltimore Colts	24-3	W
Sun	S-18	A	Cleveland Browns	21-20	W
Sun	S-25	H	Los Angeles Rams	24-13	W
Sun	O-2	H	Detroit Lions	23-14	W
Sun	O-9	A	San Francisco 49ers	20-21	L
Sun	O-16	A	Chicago Bears	17-0	W
Sun	O-23	H (m)	Atlanta Falcons	56-3	W
Sun	O-30	A	Detroit Lions	31-7	W
Sun	N-6	H	Minnesota Vikings	17-20	L
Sun	N-20	H	Chicago Bears	13-6	W
Sun	N-27	A	Minnesota Vikings	28-16	W
Sun	D-4	H (m)	San Francisco 49ers	20-7	W
Sat	D-10	A	Baltimore Colts	14-10	W
Sun	D-18	A	Los Angeles Rams	27-23	W

(m) - Milwaukee, Wisconsin

Postseason

1966 NFL Championship Game
January 1, 1967
Green Bay 34, Dallas 27 at Dallas

Green Bay	14	7	7	6	—	34
Dallas	14	3	3	7	—	27

Super Bowl I

Green Bay 35, Kansas City 10
January 15, 1967, Memorial Coliseum, Los Angeles, California
Attendance: 61,946

The first AFL-NFL World Championship Game on January 15, 1967, between Green Bay and Kansas City—"Super Bowl" did not become official until III in 1969—was the most anticipated pro football game ever.

The reputation of the mighty NFL against the upstart "Mickey Mouse League," as the AFL had been dubbed by NFL adherents, was at stake, and NFL owners exhorted Packers coach Vince Lombardi to win—and win big—because raw feelings still existed after the intense war the two leagues had fought since 1960.

The game was played in the 94,000-seat Los Angeles Memorial Coliseum, Though the game was blacked out locally, only 61,946 attended after L.A. newspapers ranted against the "exorbitant" $12 ticket price and instructed fans how to rig home TV antennas to pirate the signal from stations outside Los Angeles.

There was competition from every angle. Two networks—NBC and CBS—televised the game across the country and used their own announcers (Ray Scott, Frank Gifford, Jack Whitaker and Pat Summerall for CBS; Curt Gowdy and Paul Christman for NBC).

During the game, each league's official football was used whenever its champion was on offense, and there was a mixed crew of officials from both leagues. Norm Schachter of the NFL was the referee.

The game attracted scores of media, who were entertained by Kansas City defensive back Fred Williamson. The "Hammer" boasted he would manhandle the Packers. "Two hammers to [end Boyd] Dowler, one to [end Carroll] Dale should be enough," he bragged.

He should have gone after end Max McGee, instead.

McGee made a spectacular one-handed catch of a pass that Bart Starr (the game's most valuable player) threw slightly behind him and ran 23 yards to complete a 37-yard play for the game's first touchdown. But the Chiefs, undaunted and clever with their multiple offense, soon tied it on a pass from Len Dawson to running back Curtis McClinton. Green Bay came right back for a 14-7 lead in the second quarter on Jim Taylor's 14-yard run, but the Chiefs' Mike Mercer kicked a field goal, and Green Bay led only 14-10 at the half.

The upstart Chiefs clearly had "won" the first half because they'd kept Green Bay's offense off balance by stacking their linebackers behind the tackles, making them hard to block on running plays. On offense, Kansas City's play-action passes made the Packers' pass rush and coverage seem tentative. Lombardi ordered an all-out attack by his offense and his defense in the second half.

On the Chiefs' first possession of the second half, linebackers Lee Roy Caffey and Dave Robinson blitzed and hit Dawson as he threw. The ball floated into the hands of free safety Willie Wood, who returned it 50 yards. On the next play, Elijah Pitts scored on a 5-yard run, and a second-half blowout ensued. Starr passed 13 yards to McGee for his second touchdown; McGee caught 7 passes for 138 yards that day after grabbing only 4 all season. Pitts's second touchdown in the last quarter polished off the scoring in the Packers' 35-10 victory.

The media hounded Lombardi for a postgame verdict on who was best—the NFL or AFL? "I don't think Kansas City compares with the best teams in the NFL," he said. "Dallas is a better team." Then with eyes flashing, he added: "There. That's what you wanted me to say, isn't it?"

Kansas City (AFL)	**0**	**10**	**0**	**0**	**—**	**10**
Green Bay (NFL)	**7**	**7**	**14**	**7**	**—**	**35**

GB—McGee 37 pass from Starr (Chandler kick)
KC—McClinton 7 pass from Dawson (Mercer kick)
GB—Taylor 14 run (Chandler kick)
KC—FG Mercer 31
GB—Pitts 5 run (Chandler kick)
GB—McGee 13 pass from Starr (Chandler kick)
GB—Pitts 1 run (Chandler kick)

TEAM STATISTICS	**KC**	**GB**
First Downs	17	21
Rushing	4	10
Passing	12	11
Penalty	1	0
Total Yardage	239	361
Net rushing yardage	72	133
Net passing yardage	167	228
Passes att.-comp.-had int.	32-17-1	24-16-1

RUSHING
Kansas City—Dawson 3 for 24; Garrett 6 for 17; McClinton 6 for 16; Beathard 1 for 14; Coan 3 for 1.
Green Bay—J. Taylor 17 for 56, 1 TD; Pitts 11 for 45, 2 TDs; D. Anderson 4 for 30; Grabowski 2 for 2.
PASSING
Kansas City—Dawson 16 of 27 for 211, 1 TD, 1 int.; Beathard 1 of 5 for 17.
Green Bay—Starr 16 of 23 for 250, 2 TDs, 1 int.; Bratkowski 0 of 1.
RECEIVING
Kansas City—Burford 4 for 67; O. Taylor 4 for 57; Garrett 3 for 28; McClinton 2 for 34, 1 TD; Arbanas 2 for 30; Carolan 1 for 7; Coan 1 for 5.
Green Bay—McGee 7 for 138, 2 TDs; Dale 4 for 59; Pitts 2 for 32; Fleming 2 for 22; J. Taylor 1 for -1.

1966 Team Rosters

Green Bay	Kansas City
Herb Adderley*	Bud Abell*
Lionel Aldridge*	Fred Arbanas*
Donny Anderson*	Pete Beathard*
Bill Anderson*	Bobby Bell*
Ken Bowman*	Denny Biodrowski*
Zeke Bratkowski*	Solomon Brannan
Allen Brown	Tommy Brooker
Robert Brown*	Aaron Brown*
Tom Brown*	Buck Buchanan*
Lee Roy Caffey*	Ed Budde*
Don Chandler*	Chris Burford*
Tommy Crutcher*	Reggie Carolan*
Bill Curry*	Bert Coan*
Carroll Dale*	Walt Corey*
Willie Davis*	Len Dawson*
Boyd Dowler*	Tony DiMidio*
Marv Fleming*	Wayne Frazier*
Gale Gillingham*	Mike Garrett*
Jim Grabowski*	Jon Gilliam*
Forrest Gregg*	Sherrill Headrick*
Doug Hart*	Dave Hill*
Dave Hathcock*	Jimmy Hill
Paul Hornung	E.J. Holub*
Bob Jeter*	Bobby Hunt*
Henry Jordan*	Chuck Hurston*
Ron Kostelnik*	Ed Lothamer
Jerry Kramer*	Jerry Mays*
Bob Long*	Curtis McClinton*
Red Mack*	Mike Mercer*
Max McGee*	Curt Merz*
Ray Nitschke*	Willie Mitchell*
Elijah Pitts*	Frank Pitts*
Dave Robinson*	Bobby Ply*
Bob Skoronski*	Al Reynolds*
Bart Starr*	Andy Rice*
Jim Taylor*	Johnny Robinson*
Fuzzy Thurston*	Hatch Rosdahl
Phil Vandersea*	Fletcher Smith*
Jim Weatherwax*	Smokey Stover*
Willie Wood*	Otis Taylor*
Steve Wright*	Emmitt Thomas*
	Gene Thomas*
	Jim Tyrer*
	Fred Williamson*
	Jerrel Wilson*

1967 AFL Champions Oakland Raiders

The Oakland Raiders had three winning seasons in their first seven years of existence in the American Football League, but they had no postseason appearances. That changed in 1967.

The Raiders traded for Buffalo quarterback Daryle Lamonica, acquired backup quarterback-kicker George Blanda and cornerback Willie Brown, and drafted guard Gene Upshaw.

Under second-year coach John Rauch, the Raiders opened the 1967 season with a 51-0 demolition of the Denver Broncos and never looked back. Oakland suffered its lone setback in New York in week four, then reeled off 10 straight wins, including a 38-29 victory in a rematch with the Jets.

With an American Football League-record 13 wins under their belt, the Raiders hosted Houston in the AFL Championship Game. The Raiders led 10-0 in the second quarter when Blanda lined up for a field-goal attempt from the Houston 17.

Lamonica instead took the snap and threw to a wide open Dave Kocourek for a touchdown with 18 seconds remaining in the first half. The demoralized Oilers didn't score until the fourth quarter in the Raiders' 40-7 rout. Oakland was now on its way to Miami to face Vince Lombardi's formidable Green Bay Packers in Super Bowl II in the Orange Bowl.

Regular Season

Sun	S-10	H	Denver Broncos	51-0	W
Sun	S-17	H	Boston Patriots	35-7	W
Sun	O-1	H	Kansas City Chiefs	23-21	W
Sat	O-7	A N	New York Jets	14-27	L
Sun	O-15	A	Buffalo Bills	24-20	W
Sun	O-22	A	Boston Patriots	48-14	W
Sun	O-29	H	San Diego Chargers	51-10	W
Sun	N-5	A	Denver Broncos	21-17	W
Sun	N-19	H	Miami Dolphins	31-17	W
Thu	N-23	A	Kansas City Chiefs	44-22	W
Sun	D-3	A	San Diego Chargers	41-21	W
Sun	D-10	A	Houston Oilers	19-7	W
Sun	D-17	H	New York Jets	38-29	W
Sun	D-24	H	Buffalo Bills	28-21	W

Postseason

1967 AFL Championship Game
December 31, 1967
Oakland 40, Houston 7 at Oakland

Houston	0	0	0	7	—	7
Oakland	3	14	10	13	—	40

1967 NFL Champions Green Bay Packers

When Green Bay turned the ball over 3 times in the Western Conference Playoff Game against the Los Angeles Rams, anxiety was palpable at Milwaukee County Stadium.

But, with the Packers trailing 7-0, momentum shifted when Dave Robinson blocked a 24-yard field-goal attempt. In the second quarter, Travis Williams ran 46 yards for the tying score. Bart Starr then found Carroll Dale for 17 yards and the go-ahead touchdown, and the Packers ran for 2 more scores in the second half to put the game away.

The NFL Championship Game went down in history as "The Ice Bowl." The temperature at kickoff was minus-13 degrees with a 15-mile-per-hour wind. Bart Starr scored on a 1-yard quarterback sneak with 13 seconds left to give the Packers a 21-17 victory over the Dallas Cowboys.

Starr found Boyd Dowler with 8- and 46-yard scoring tosses in the first half to give Green Bay a 14-0 lead. Dallas rallied when defensive end George Andrie scooped up a fumble by Starr and returned it 7 yards for a touchdown. On the first play of the fourth quarter, the Cowboys took a 17-14 lead when halfback Dan Reeves threw a 50-yard touchdown pass to Lance Rentzel.

The Packers started at their 32 with 4:50 left. The big gain in the 12-play drive came when Chuck Mercein took a short pass from Starr and ran 19 yards to the Cowboys' 11. Four plays later, behind blocks by guard Jerry Kramer and center Ken Bowman, Starr sneaked across the goal line for the victory.

Regular Season

Sun	S-17	H	Detroit Lions	17-17	T
Sun	S-24	H	Chicago Bears	13-10	W
Sun	O-1	H (m)	Atlanta Falcons	23-0	W
Sun	O-8	A	Detroit Lions	27-17	W
Sun	O-15	H (m)	Minnesota Vikings	7-10	L
Sun	O-22	A	New York Giants	48-21	W
Mon	O-30	A N	St. Louis Cardinals	31-23	W
Sun	N-5	A	Baltimore Colts	10-13	L
Sun	N-12	H (m)	Cleveland Browns	55-7	W
Sun	N-19	H	San Francisco 49ers	13-0	W
Sun	N-26	A	Chicago Bears	17-13	W
Sun	D-3	A	Minnesota Vikings	30-27	W
Sat	D-9	A	Los Angeles Rams	24-27	L
Sun	D-17	H	Pittsburgh Steelers	17-24	L

(m)—Milwaukee, Wisconsin

Postseason

1967 NFL Western Conference Playoff Game
December 23, 1967
Green Bay 28, Los Angeles Rams 7 at Milwaukee

L.A. Rams	7	0	0	0	—	7
Green Bay	0	14	7	7	—	28

1967 NFL Championship Game
December 31, 1967
Green Bay 21, Dallas 17 at Green Bay

Dallas	0	10	0	7	—	17
Green Bay	7	7	0	7	—	21

Super Bowl II

Green Bay 33, Oakland 14
January 14, 1968, Orange Bowl, Miami, Florida
Attendance: 75,546

The Green Bay Packers won their second consecutive AFL-NFL World Championship Game. In besting the Oakland Raiders 33-14, Vince Lombardi's team followed a script similar to the one it used the year before in its victory over Kansas City: Take a lead in the first half and wrap up the game in the third quarter.

Green Bay took their first possession 34 yards in 9 plays to the Oakland 32. Don Chandler kicked a 39-yard field goal to put the Packers in front 3-0. The next time they got the ball, the Packers started at their 3 and went 84 yards in a drive that consumed 8:40. From the 20, Chandler kicked his second field goal, raising the score to 6-0.

The Raiders were held without a first down, and Green Bay took the ball at its 38. On the first play from scrimmage, Starr passed to Boyd Dowler. Dowler cut inside Kent McCloughan, who was playing a tight man-for-man, took the football on the fly, and raced the rest of the way for a touchdown.

In danger of being blown out, Oakland fought back, driving 78 yards in 8 plays. Daryle Lamonica's 23-yard pass to Bill Miller tightened the score to 13-7. However, shortly before the end of the first half, Oakland's Rodger Bird fumbled a fair catch at midfield, and the Packers recovered. With one second on the clock, Chandler kicked his third field goal, this one from 43 yards to make it 16-7.

Any hopes the Raiders might have harbored for a second-half comeback were dashed on the Packers' second possession of the third quarter. Green Bay rumbled 82 yards in 11 plays. Starr kept the drive alive twice by completing third-down passes. Donny Anderson wrapped up the drive by slashing 2 yards into the end zone. Before the third quarter ended, Chandler added his fourth field goal of the day (from 31 yards) to make it 26-7.

Oakland desperately tried to catch up with Lamonica passes, but early in the final quarter, Green Bay's Herb Adderley stepped in front of Fred Biletnikoff for an interception and ran 60 yards for the Packers' final touchdown. Lamonica's 23-yard touchdown pass to Miller with 9:13 remaining was too little and far too late.

With the Packers' second convincing victory, several critics argued that the AFL was not ready to compete with the stronger NFL teams. That idea was underscored when Lombardi allowed that his club's victory "wasn't our best." Bart Starr completed 13 of 24 passes for 202 yards and a touchdown to earn the game's most valuable player award for the second time.

A few days after the game, celebrations in Titletown, U.S.A., were tempered by Lombardi's announcement that he would retire as Green Bay coach and devote his time exclusively to being the team's general manager.

Team	1	2	3	4		Total
Green Bay (NFL)	3	13	10	7	—	33
Oakland (AFL)	0	7	0	7	—	14

GB—FG Chandler 39
GB—FG Chandler 20
GB—Dowler 62 pass from Starr (Chandler kick)
Oak—Miller 23 pass from Lamonica (Blanda kick)
GB—FG Chandler 43
GB—Anderson 2 run (Chandler kick)
GB—FG Chandler 31
GB—Adderley 60 interception return (Chandler kick)
Oak—Miller 23 pass from Lamonica (Blanda kick)

TEAM STATISTICS	**GB**	**OAK**
First Downs	19	16
Rushing	11	5
Passing	7	10
Penalty	1	1
Total Yardage	322	293
Net rushing yardage	160	107
Net passing yardage	162	186
Passes att.-comp.-had int.	24-13-0	34-15-1

RUSHING
Green Bay—Wilson 17 for 62; Anderson 14 for 48, 1 TD; Williams 8 for 36; Starr 1 for 14; Mercein 1 for 0.
Oakland—Dixon 12 for 54; Todd 2 for 37; Banaszak 6 for 16.

PASSING
Green Bay—Starr 13 of 24 for 202, 1 TD.
Oakland—Lamonica 15 of 34 for 208, 2 TDs, 1 int.

RECEIVING
Green Bay—Dale 4 for 43; Fleming 4 for 35; Dowler 2 for 71, 1 TD; Anderson 2 for 18; McGee 1 for 35.
Oakland—Miller 5 for 84, 2 TDs; Banaszak 4 for 69; Cannon 2 for 25; Biletnikoff 2 for 10; Wells 1 for 17; Dixon 1 for 3.

1967 Team Rosters

Green Bay
Herb Adderley*
Lionel Aldridge*
Donny Anderson*
Ken Bowman*
Zeke Bratkowski*
Allen Brown
Robert Brown*
Tom Brown*
Lee Roy Caffey*
Dick Capp*
Don Chandler*
Tommy Crutcher*
Carroll Dale*
Willie Davis*
Boyd Dowler*
Jim Flanigan*
Marv Fleming*
Gale Gillingham*
Jim Grabowski
Forrest Gregg*
Doug Hart*
Don Horn
Bob Hyland*
Claudis James
Bob Jeter*
Henry Jordan*
Ron Kostelnik*
Jerry Kramer*
Bob Long*
Max McGee*
Chuck Mercein*
Ray Nitschke*
Elijah Pitts
Dave Robinson*
John Rowser*
Bob Skoronski*
Bart Starr*
Fuzzy Thurston*
Jim Weatherwax*
Travis Williams*
Ben Wilson*
Willie Wood*
Steve Wright

Oakland
Dan Archer*
Pete Banaszak*
Estes Banks
Duane Benson*
Fred Biletnikoff*
Rodger Bird*
Dan Birdwell*
George Blanda*
Willie Brown*
Bill Budness*
Billy Cannon*
Dan Conners*
Clem Daniels
Ben Davidson*
Hewritt Dixon*
Mike Eischeid*
Bill Fairband*
Dave Grayson*
Roger Hagberg*
Jim Harvey*
Wayne Hawkins*
Ken Herock*
Tom Keating*
Dave Kocourek*
Bob Kruse*
Daryle Lamonica*
Bill Laskey*
Ike Lassiter*
Kent McCloughan*
Bill Miller*
Carleton Oats*
Gus Otto*
Jim Otto*
Warren Powers*
Harry Schuh*
Rod Sherman
Richard Sligh*
Bob Svihus*
Larry Todd*
Gene Upshaw*
Warren Wells*
Howie Williams*
J.R. Williamson*

1968 AFL Champions
New York Jets

The New York Jets, coming off their first winning season the year before, were the class of the American Football League in 1968. The Jets led the AFL in defense, and the team set a franchise record by scoring 419 points. Don Maynard led the league by averaging 23 yards per catch, and the ground game produced an AFL-best 22 touchdowns. Plus the team had the most charismatic—if not the most talented—quarterback in the American Football League in Joe Namath.

Even when the Jets lost it was exciting. With just 1:05 left and the Jets leading the Raiders 32-29 on November 17, NBC switched to the film *Heidi* in the Eastern and Central time zones as incredulous football fans rubbed their eyes in disbelief. Even more amazing was Oakland's unseen comeback victory in what became known as the "Heidi Game." The Jets shook off that defeat to win their final four games to complete the season with an 11-3 record.

The Raiders and Jets met again on December 29 in Shea Stadium for the AFL Championship Game. Namath passed for 3 touchdowns, including a 6-yard pass to Maynard in the fourth quarter to erase a 3-point deficit. Linebacker Ralph Baker scooped up an errant lateral late in the game to help preserve New York's 27-23 victory and a trip to Super Bowl III against the heavily favored Baltimore Colts.

Regular Season

Sun	S-15	A	Kansas City Chiefs	20-19	W
Sun	S-22	A (b)	Boston Patriots	47-31	W
Sun	S-29	A	Buffalo Bills	35-37	L
Sat	O-5	H N	San Diego Chargers	23-20	W
Sun	O-13	H	Denver Broncos	13-21	L
Sun	O-20	A	Houston Oilers	20-14	W
Sun	O-27	H	Boston Patriots	48-14	W
Sun	N-3	H	Buffalo Bills	25-21	W
Sun	N-10	H	Houston Oilers	26-7	W
Sun	N-17	A	Oakland Raiders	32-43	L
Sun	N-24	A	San Diego Chargers	37-15	W
Sun	D-1	H	Miami Dolphins	35-17	W
Sun	D-8	H	Cincinnati Bengals	27-14	W
Sun	D-15	A	Miami Dolphins	31-7	W

(b) - Birmingham, Alabama

Postseason

1968 AFL Championship Game
December 29, 1968
New York Jets 27, Oakland 23 at New York

Oakland	0	10	3	10	—	23
N.Y. Jets	10	3	7	7	—	27

1968 NFL Champions
Baltimore Colts

Baltimore recorded one of the greatest regular seasons in NFL history in 1968. Johnny Unitas was sidelined with a chronic sore elbow, but Earl Morrall stepped in to pass for a league-high 26 touchdowns. Morrall ranked number one among NFL quarterbacks while leading the Colts to a 13-1 season. Morrall, who had spent much of his career as a backup, earned league MVP honors.

During the regular season, the Colts beat Minnesota 21-9, and in the mud of Memorial Stadium, the team's rematch in the Western Conference Playoff Game was not much different.

Morrall passed for 2 touchdowns, and linebacker Mike Curtis picked up a fumble and raced 60 yards for the clinching score in Baltimore's 24-14 victory.

The only blemish on coach Don Shula's regular season had been a 30-20 loss to the Browns on October 20. In the NFL Championship Game, the Colts got revenge with a 34-0 rout in Cleveland.

The Browns had their best chance to score in the first quarter, but defensive end Bubba Smith blocked Don Cockcroft's 41-yard field-goal attempt.

After a 28-yard field goal by Lou Michaels put Baltimore ahead 3-0 in the second quarter, Tom Matte scored the first of his 3 touchdowns on the day. Meanwhile, Baltimore's defense held NFL rushing leader Leroy Kelly to just 28 yards on 13 carries.

Regular Season

Sun	S-15	H	San Francisco 49ers	27-10	W
Sun	S-22	A	Atlanta Falcons	28-20	W
Sun	S-29	A	Pittsburgh Steelers	41-7	W
Sun	O-6	H	Chicago Bears	28-7	W
Sun	O-13	A	San Francisco 49ers	42-14	W
Sun	O-20	H	Cleveland Browns	20-30	L
Sun	O-27	H	Los Angeles Rams	27-10	W
Sun	N-3	A	New York Giants	26-0	W
Sun	N-10	A	Detroit Lions	27-10	W
Sun	N-17	H	St. Louis Cardinals	27-0	W
Sun	N-24	H	Minnesota Vikings	21-9	W
Sun	D-1	H	Atlanta Falcons	44-0	W
Sat	D-7	A	Green Bay Packers	16-3	W
Sun	D-15	A	Los Angeles Rams	28-24	W

Postseason

1968 NFL Western Conference Playoff Game
December 22, 1968
Baltimore 24, Minnesota 14 at Baltimore

Minnesota	0	0	0	14	—	14
Baltimore	0	7	14	3	—	24

1968 NFL Championship Game
December 29, 1968
Baltimore 34, Cleveland 0 at Cleveland

Baltimore	0	17	7	10	—	34
Cleveland	0	0	0	0	—	0

Super Bowl III

N.Y. Jets 16, Baltimore 7
January 12, 1969, Orange Bowl, Miami, Florida
Attendance: 75,377

At a Miami Touchdown Club dinner three days before the Super Bowl III, Jets quarterback Joe Namath told the audience, "We're going to win Sunday. I guarantee it." His chutzpah made national headlines, though most experts passed it off as bluster or self-delusion.

Not only had the NFL handily won the first two Super Bowls, but the 13-1 Baltimore Colts also were considered one of the greatest teams in football history. Namath's Jets generally were regarded as only third-best in the American Football League. One columnist predicted a 55-0 Colts' win, and oddsmakers made the Jets 18- to 20-point underdogs.

From the opening kickoff, the Jets established a strong ground game, led by 220-pound fullback Matt Snell. Meanwhile, the Colts couldn't get untracked.

Quarterback Earl Morrall, the NFL's regular-season MVP, had one of the worst games of his career. For the day, he completed 6 of 17 passes for 71 yards, with 3 interceptions. By the third quarter, he was replaced by Johnny Unitas, who had missed most of the regular season with an elbow injury.

In the second quarter, Snell's 35 yards on 6 carries and Namath's 4 completions for 43 yards accounted for most of an 80-yard drive that culminated in Snell's 4-yard plunge for a touchdown. The 7-0 lead stood up to halftime. The New Yorkers' supposedly porous pass defense held the high-flying Colts in check, and the AFL team actually outmuscled the NFL team.

The Jets built on their lead in 3-point increments. Jim Turner kicked field goals of 32, 30, and 9 yards to make it 16-0 in the fourth quarter.

The Colts finally scored with 3:19 left. Jerry Hill ran 1 yard to complete an 80-yard drive. A successful onside kick gave the ball back to Baltimore, but the Colts could not capitalize.

Namath, who completed 17 of 28 passes for 206 yards, was voted the most valuable player, but equally deserving was Snell, who rushed for 121 yards on 30 carries and caught 4 passes for 40 yards.

New York Jets (AFL)	0	7	6	3	—	16
Baltimore (NFL)	0	0	0	7	—	7

NYJ—Snell 4 run (Turner kick)
NYJ—FG Turner 32
NYJ—FG Turner 30
NYJ—FG Turner 9
Bal—Hill 1 run (Michaels kick)

TEAM STATISTICS	NYJ	BALT
First Downs	21	18
Rushing	10	7
Passing	10	9
Penalty	1	2
Total Yardage	337	324
Net rushing yardage	142	143
Net passing	195	181
Passes att.-comp.-had int.	29-17-0	41-17-4

RUSHING
N.Y. Jets—Snell 30 for 121, 1 TD; Boozer 10 for 19; Mathis 3 for 2.
Baltimore—Matte 11 for 116; Hill 9 for 29, 1 TD; Unitas 1 for 0; Morrall 2 for -2.

PASSING
N.Y. Jets—Namath 17 of 28 for 206; Parilli 0 of 1.
Baltimore—Unitas 11 of 24 for 110, 1 int.; Morrall 6 of 17 for 71, 3 int.

RECEIVING
N.Y. Jets—Sauer 8 for 133; Snell 4 for 40; Mathis 3 for 20; Lammons 2 for 13.
Baltimore—Richardson 6 for 58; Orr 3 for 42; Mackey 3 for 35; Matte 2 for 30; Hill 2 for 1; Mitchell 1 for 15.

1968 Team Rosters

N.Y. Jets
Al Atkinson*
Bill Baird*
Ralph Baker*
Randy Beverly*
Verlon Biggs*
Emerson Boozer*
Earl Christy*
Paul Crane*
Mike D'Amato*
John Dockery*
John Elliott*
Cornell Gordon*
Larry Grantham*
Ray Hayes
Karl Henke
Dave Herman*
Winston Hill*
Jim Hudson*
Billy Joe
Curley Johnson*
Pete Lammons*
Bill Mathis*
Don Maynard*
Carl McAdams*
Joe Namath*
John Neidert*
Babe Parilli*
Gerry Philbin*
Bill Rademacher*
Randy Rasmussen*
Jim Richards*
Jeff Richardson*
Paul Rochester*
Johnny Sample*
George Sauer*
John Schmitt*
Mark Smolinski*
Matt Snell*
Mike Stromberg
Bob Talamini*
Steve Thompson*
Jim Turner*
Bake Turner*
Sam Walton*
Lee White

Baltimore
Ocie Austin*
Sam Ball*
Bobby Boyd*
Ordell Braase*
Timmy Brown*
Gail Cogdill
Terry Cole*
Bill Curry*
Mike Curtis*
Dennis Gaubatz*
Bob Grant
Alex Hawkins*
Jerry Hill*
Roy Hilton*
Cornelius Johnson*
David Lee*
Jerry Logan*
Lenny Lyles*
John Mackey*
Tom Matte*
Lou Michaels*
Fred Miller*
Tom Mitchell*
Earl Morrall*
Jimmy Orr*
Preston Pearson*
Ray Perkins*
Ron Porter*
Glenn Ressler*
Willie Richardson*
Don Shinnick*
Billy Ray Smith Sr.*
Bubba Smith*
Charles Stukes*
Dan Sullivan*
Dick Szymanski*
Johnny Unitas*
Bob Vogel*
Rick Volk*
Jim Ward
John Williams*
Sid Williams*

1969 AFL Champions Kansas City Chiefs

The Chiefs opened the 1969 regular season with two victories in three games, but they lost two quarterbacks in the process. Len Dawson injured his knee against the Patriots, and the next week, backup quarterback Jacky Lee broke a bone in his ankle in Cincinnati. Third-string quarterback Mike Livingston took over the reins.

With his quarterback situation unsettled, coach Hank Stram relied heavily on his ground game. The "mini-back" trio of Mike Garrett, Robert (The Tank) Holmes, and Warren McVea led the AFL in rushing yards and touchdowns. The defense, powered by Curley Culp, Buck Buchanan, and Willie Lanier, allowed a league-low 177 points as the Chiefs finished the season with an 11-3 record.

In the playoffs, the Chiefs staged the most famous goal-line stand in league history. On a wind-swept, icy afternoon in Shea Stadium, the Chiefs stopped the defending Super Bowl champion Jets on three tries from the 1-yard line to highlight a 13-6 victory.

Kansas City then faced Oakland, which had beaten the Chiefs twice during the regular season. Dawson came up with huge passes when he needed them and the defense stopped several Oakland drives deep in Chiefs' territory. Kansas City held on for a 17-7 victory in the final AFL Championship Game, earning the Chiefs their second trip to the Super Bowl.

Regular Season

Sun	S-14	A	San Diego Chargers	27-9	W
Sun	S-21	A	Boston Patriots	31-0	W
Sun	S-28	A	Cincinnati Bengals	19-24	L
Sun	O-5	A	Denver Broncos	26-13	W
Sun	O-12	H	Houston Oilers	24-0	W
Sun	O-19	H	Miami Dolphins	17-10	W
Sun	O-26	H	Cincinnati Bengals	42-22	W
Sun	N-2	A	Buffalo Bills	20-7	W
Sun	N-9	H	San Diego Chargers	27-3	W
Sun	N-16	A	New York Jets	34-16	W
Sun	N-23	H	Oakland Raiders	24-27	L
Thu	N-27	H	Denver Broncos	31-17	W
Sun	D-7	H	Buffalo Bills	22-19	W
Sat	D-13	A	Oakland Raiders	6-10	L

Postseason

1969 AFL Divisional Playoff Game
December 20, 1968
Kansas City 13, New York Jets 6
at New York

Kansas City	0	3	3	7	—	13
N.Y. Jets	3	0	0	3	—	6

1969 AFL Championship Game
January 4, 1970
Kansas City 17, Oakland 7 at Oakland

Kansas City	0	7	7	3	—	17
Oakland	7	0	0	0	—	7

1969 NFL Champions Minnesota Vikings

In 1968, the Vikings drafted USC offensive tackle Ron Yary and added Pro Bowl defensive back Paul Krause in a trade to complement the Purple People Eaters—defensive linemen Carl Eller, Alan Page, Gary Larsen, and Jim Marshall.

The Vikings won 12 in a row behind quarterback Joe Kapp in the regular season, and he shined in the playoffs as well. In the Western Conference Playoff Game, Kapp passed for 40 yards and ran for 14 on the winning drive in the fourth quarter as the Vikings came from behind to defeat the Rams 23-20.

The field was slick for the NFC Championship Game; the sidelines of Metropolitan Stadium were stacked with snow, and it was only 8 degrees when the Minnesota Vikings defeated the Cleveland Browns 27-7.

On the Vikings' first possession, cornerback Walt Sumner slipped on the icy field, and Gene Washington caught a 33-yard pass from Kapp to set up a Vikings' first touchdown. Kapp again found Washington, who went 75 yards with the catch for a touchdown and a 14-0 first-quarter lead.

The Vikings then turned to their ground game, and Dave Osborn's 108 yards led a rushing attack that netted 222 yards. Osborn's 20-yard touchdown run late in the second quarter increased the Vikings' margin to 24-0 and ended any hopes of a Cleveland comeback.

Regular Season

Sun	S-21	A	New York Giants	23-24	L
Sun	S-28	H	Baltimore Colts	52-14	W
Sun	O-5	H	Green Bay Packers	19 -7	W
Sun	O-12	A	Chicago Bears	31 -0	W
Sun	O-19	A	St. Louis Cardinals	27-10	W
Sun	O-26	H	Detroit Lions	24-10	W
Sun	N-2	H	Chicago Bears	31-14	W
Sun	N-9	H	Cleveland Browns	51 -3	W
Sun	N-16	A (m)	Green Bay Packers	9 -7	W
Sun	N-23	H	Pittsburgh Steelers	52-14	W
Thu	N-27	A	Detroit Lions	27 -0	W
Sun	D-7	A	Los Angeles Rams	20-13	W
Sun	D-14	H	San Francisco 49ers	10 -7	W
Sun	D-21	A	Atlanta Falcons	3-10	L

(m)—Milwaukee, Wisconsin

Postseason

1969 NFL Western Conference Playoff Game
December 27, 1969
Minnesota 23, Los Angeles Rams 20
at Bloomington, Minnesota

L.A. Rams	7	10	0	3	—	20
Minnesota	7	0	7	9	—	23

1969 NFL Championship Game
January 4, 1970
Minnesota 27, Cleveland 7 at Bloomington, Minnesota

Cleveland	0	0	0	7	—	7
Minnesota	14	10	3	0	—	27

Super Bowl IV

Kansas City 23, Minnesota 7
January 11, 1970, Tulane Stadium, New Orleans, Louisiana
Attendance: 80,562

Despite the Jets' shocking victory over the Colts in Super Bowl III, many people remained unconvinced that the AFL really had pulled even with the NFL. Partisans of the NFL considered the Jets' win a fluke. They fully expected the balance of power to be restored when the NFL title-winning Minnesota Vikings played the Kansas City Chiefs, losers of the first Super Bowl, in Game IV. The oddsmakers agreed; at kickoff, the Chiefs were 2-touchdown underdogs.

The Vikings relied on a marvelous defensive front four of Carl Eller, Alan Page, Gary Larsen, and Jim Marshall, nicknamed the Purple People Eaters. Not only had Minnesota led the league in fewest opponents' points scored, but, largely because the defense kept giving the offense the ball, the ground-based attack topped the NFL in scoring.

Kansas City finished behind Oakland during the regular season before coming on strong in the playoffs. But five days before the Super Bowl, word leaked out that quarterback Len Dawson's name had been linked to a federal gambling investigation in Detroit. Although he eventually was cleared of any wrongdoing, the pressure of the investigation added to the pressure he already was under as a Super Bowl quarterback, causing him to lose sleep, weight, and concentration.

The Chiefs took the field wearing a patch on their jerseys reading "AFL-10," signifying the American Football League's 10-year existence. Super Bowl IV was the last game to be played by an AFL team.

Despite Minnesota's defensive reputation, it was Kansas City's huge defensive linemen who outmuscled the smaller Vikings on the line of scrimmage and kept Minnesota from establishing a running game. Buck Buchanan and Curley Culp overpowered Vikings' all-pro center Mick Tingelhoff to clog the middle, and the Chiefs' linebacking crew of Willie Lanier, Bobby Bell, and Jim Lynch stopped anyone who filtered through.

Just past midway of the opening quarter, Kansas City's Jan Stenerud connected on a 48-yard field goal. He added 2 more field goals in the second quarter to increase the lead to 9-0. On the kickoff following Stenerud's third field goal, Minnesota's Charlie West fumbled, and Remi Prudhomme recovered for Kansas City at the Vikings' 19, third down from the 5, Mike Garrett scored for Kansas City.

Trailing 16-0, the Vikings forced the Chiefs to punt to start the second half, then drove 69 yards in 10 plays for a touchdown. Minnesota quarterback Joe Kapp went 4-for-4 for 47 yards on the drive. With slightly more than 10 minutes of the third quarter gone, Dave Osborn scored to make it 16-7.

The Chiefs took the kickoff to their 18, moving to the Minnesota 46. Then Dawson tossed a short pass to Otis Taylor, who took the ball at the 41 and ran through Vikings cornerback Earsell Mackbee. Safety Karl Kassulke had a shot at him at the 10, but Taylor's fake left Kassulke lying on the ground and allowed Taylor to reach the end zone.

In the fourth quarter, the Vikings had three possessions, with little choice but to pass, and each possession ended in an interception. For the Chiefs, the 23-7 victory avenged their Super Bowl I loss. For the AFL, it proved it really was ready to compete evenly with the NFL. And for Len Dawson, who had survived the pregame pressure to be named MVP, the game stamped him as a great quarterback.

Minnesota (NFL)	0	0	7	0	—	7
Kansas City (AFL)	3	13	7	0	—	23

KC—FG Stenerud 48
KC—FG Stenerud 32
KC—FG Stenerud 25
KC—Garrett 5 run (Stenerud kick)
Minn—Osborn 4 run (Cox kick)
KC—Taylor 46 pass from Dawson (Stenerud kick)

TEAM STATISTICS	**MINN**	**KC**
First Downs	13	18
Rushing	2	8
Passing	10	7
Penalty	1	3
Total Yardage	239	273
Net rushing yardage	67	151
Net passing yardage	172	122
Passes att.-comp.-had int.	28-17-3	17-12-1

RUSHING
Minnesota—Brown 6 for 26; Reed 4 for 17; Osborn 7 for 15, 1 TD; Kapp 2 for 9.
Kansas City—Garrett 11 for 39, 1 TD; Pitts 3 for 37; Hayes 8 for 31; McVea 12 for 26; Dawson 3 for 11; Holmes 5 for 7.
PASSING
Minnesota—Kapp 16 of 25 for 183, 2 int.; Cuozzo 1 of 3 for 16, 1 int.
Kansas City—Dawson 12 of 17 for 142, 1 TD, 1 int.
RECEIVING
Minnesota—Henderson 7 for 111; Brown 3 for 11; Beasley 2 for 41; Reed 2 for 16; Osborn 2 for 11; Washington 1 for 9.
Kansas City—Taylor 6 for 81, 1 TD; Pitts 3 for 33; Garrett 2 for 25; Hayes 1 for 3.

1969 Team Rosters

Kansas City	**Minnesota**
Fred Arbanas*	Grady Alderman*
Bobby Bell*	John Beasley*
Ceasar Belser*	Bookie Bolin
Aaron Brown*	Bill Brown*
Buck Buchanan*	Bobby Bryant
Ed Budde*	Fred Cox*
Curley Culp*	Gary Cuozzo*
George Daney*	Doug Davis
Len Dawson*	Paul Dickson*
Tom Flores	Carl Eller*
Mike Garrett*	Bob Grim*
Wendell Hayes*	Dale Hackbart*
Dave Hill*	Tom Hall
Robert Holmes*	Jim Hargrove*
E.J. Holub*	Billy Harris*
Chuck Hurston*	John Henderson*
Jim Kearney*	Wally Hilgenberg*
Willie Lanier*	Clint Jones*
Jacky Lee	Joe Kapp*
Mike Livingston*	Karl Kassulke*
Ed Lothamer*	John Kirby
Paul Lowe	Kent Kramer*
Jim Lynch*	Paul Krause*
Jim Marsalis*	Gary Larsen*
Jerry Mays*	Bob Lee*
Mickey McCarty	Jim Lindsey*
Curtis McClinton*	Earsell Mackbee*
Warren McVea*	Jim Marshall*
Willie Mitchell*	Mike McGill*
Mo Moorman*	Dave Osborn*
Frank Pitts*	Alan Page*
Ed Podolak*	Oscar Reed*
Remi Prudhomme*	Mike Reilly
Gloster Richardson*	Ed Sharockman*
Johnny Robinson*	Steve Smith*
Goldie Sellers*	Milt Sunde*
Noland Smith	Mick Tingelhoff*
Bob Stein*	Jim Vellone*
Jan Stenerud*	Lonnie Warwick*
Otis Taylor*	Gene Washington*
Emmitt Thomas*	Charlie West*
Gene Trosch*	Ed White*
Jim Tyrer*	Roy Winston*
Jerrel Wilson*	Ron Yary*

1970 AFC Champions Baltimore Colts

Baltimore, which left the NFL and joined the AFC (along with Pittsburgh and Cleveland) when the NFL and AFL merged, wound up as the conference's first champion.

Besides playing in a new division in a new conference, the AFC East, Baltimore also had a new coach. Don McCafferty, a career assistant with the Colts, replaced Don Shula, who left to become coach of the Dolphins.

The offense revolved around venerable Johnny Unitas at quarterback with receivers Eddie Hinton and Roy Jefferson. The defense got younger with the emergence of end Roy Hilton and linebacker Ted Hendricks. Jim O'Brien, a 23-year-old rookie, took over the kicking chores for Baltimore.

The Colts led the AFC in scoring with 321 points, and displayed a flair for the dramatic by earning 6 of their 11 victories by 7 points or less. Highlights of the 11-2-1 campaign included two victories over the New York Jets, their Super Bowl III nemesis and new division rival, and a 35-0 shelling of Shula's Dolphins.

Baltimore defeated the Cincinnati Bengals 17-0 in an AFC Divisional Playoff Game on long touchdown passes to Hinton and Jefferson. The Colts won the conference title with a 27-17 victory over Oakland as Norm Bulaich ran for 2 touchdowns. Baltimore, which just two years earlier had suffered one of the great upsets in profootball history at the hands of the Jets at the Orange Bowl, was headed back to Miami for Super Bowl V.

Regular Season

Sun	S-20	A	San Diego Chargers	16-14	W
Mon	S-28	H N	Kansas City Chiefs	24-44	L
Sun	O-4	H	Boston Patriots	14-6	W
Sun	O-11	A	Houston Oilers	24-20	W
Sun	O-18	A	New York Jets	29-22	W
Sun	O-25	A	Boston Patriots	27-3	W
Sun	N-1	H	Miami Dolphins	35-0	W
Mon	N-9	A N (m)	Green Bay Packers	13-10	W
Sun	N-15	H	Buffalo Bills	17-17	T
Sun	N-22	A	Miami Dolphins	17-34	L
Sun	N-29	H	Chicago Bears	21-20	W
Sun	D-6	H	Philadelphia Eagles	29-0	W
Sun	D-13	A	Buffalo Bills	20-14	W
Sat	D-19	H N	New York Jets	35-20	W

(m)—Milwaukee, Wisconsin

Postseason

1970 AFC Divisional Playoff Game
December 26, 1970
Baltimore 17, Cincinnati 0 at Baltimore

Cincinnati	0	0	0	0	—	0
Baltimore	7	3	0	7	—	17

1970 AFC Championship Game
January 3, 1971
Baltimore 27, Oakland 17 at Baltimore

Oakland	0	3	7	7	—	17
Baltimore	3	7	10	7	—	27

1970 NFC Champions Dallas Cowboys

The Cowboys struggled through early disappointments, but coach Tom Landry guided Dallas to its first of eight NFC titles in 1970.

Landry's multiple-formation offense was the NFL's best show, with Craig Morton at quarterback, Bob Hayes at wide receiver, and Calvin Hill carrying the ball. The Doomsday Defense took shape around Bob Lilly, Lee Roy Jordan, and Chuck Howley. Safeties Charlie Waters and Cliff Harris came along in 1970, as did running back Duane Thomas.

The Cowboys went 10-4 and faced the Lions in an NFC Divisional Playoff Game. Dallas pounded out 209 yards on the ground against the NFL's best rushing defense, but it took a field goal, a safety, and some stellar defensive play for the Cowboys to defeat the Lions 5-0.

Eight days later, Thomas rushed for 143 yards on 27 carries as the Cowboys defeated San Francisco 17-10 to end four years of postseason frustration by winning their first championship game.

In the third quarter, San Francisco quarterback John Brodie threw a short pass over the middle that was intercepted by linebacker Lee Roy Jordan at the 49ers' 13. Thomas ran for a touchdown on the next play. San Francisco responded with an impressive drive, but Mel Renfro intercepted Brodie at the Cowboys' 18. Dallas then drove 82 yards, scoring on a 5-yard pass from Morton to Garrison.

Regular Season

Sun	S-20	A	Philadelphia Eagles	17-7	W
Sun	S-27	H	New York Giants	28-10	W
Sun	O-4	A	St. Louis Cardinals	7-20	L
Sun	O-11	H	Atlanta Falcons	13-0	W
Sun	O-18	A	Minnesota Vikings	13-54	L
Sun	O-25	A	Kansas City Chiefs	27-16	W
Sun	N-1	H	Philadelphia Eagles	21-17	W
Sun	N-8	A	New York Giants	20-23	L
Mon	N-16	H N	St. Louis Cardinals	0-38	L
Sun	N-22	A	Washington Redskins	45-21	W
Thu	N-26	H	Green Bay Packers	16-3	W
Sun	D-6	H	Washington Redskins	34-0	W
Sat	D-12	A	Cleveland Browns	6-2	W
Sun	D-20	H	Houston Oilers	52-10	W

Postseason

1970 NFC Divisional Playoff Game
December 26, 1970
Dallas 5, Detroit 0 at Dallas

Detroit	0	0	0	0	—	0
Dallas	3	0	0	2	—	5

1970 NFC Championship Game
January 3, 1971
Dallas 17, San Francisco 10 at San Francisco

Dallas	0	3	14	0	—	17
San Francisco	3	0	7	0	—	10

Super Bowl V

Baltimore 16, Dallas 13
January 17, 1971, Orange Bowl, Miami, Florida
Attendance: 79,204

This was the Super Bowl no one wanted to win. At least, that's how it seemed. Between them, the Baltimore Colts and Dallas Cowboys had 14 penalties and 10 turnovers.

The offenses were so ineffective that the MVP award went to a defensive player on the losing side! Cowboys linebacker Chuck Howley intercepted 2 passes and caused a fumble to win the honor.

If the game was less than artistic, it made up for it by remaining suspenseful to the end.

Defense and mistakes dominated the first quarter, but Dallas managed to score on a 14-yard field goal by Mike Clark. Early in the second quarter, Clark added a 30-yard field goal to make the score 6-0.

The play that most typified the afternoon came a few moments later. Colts quarterback Johnny Unitas launched a pass down the center intended for receiver Eddie Hinton, who reached for it and tipped it. Dallas cornerback Mel Renfro took a turn at the deflected football but only succeeded in changing its direction slightly. The ball fell into the hands of Colts tight end John Mackey, who completed a 75-yard touchdown play. Jim O'Brien's extra-point attempt was blocked, leaving the score knotted at 6-6.

The next time Baltimore got the ball, Unitas received a sound thwacking to the ribs from Cowboy George Andrie. The blow was sufficient to separate Unitas from the football at the 25-yard line and to send him to the sideline for the remainder of the day.

Dallas recovered at Baltimore's 28, and Craig Morton moved his team to the 7. Morton, despite a sore arm and suffering through a 12-for-26, 3-interception day, threw a touchdown pass to Duane Thomas. The Cowboys led 13-6 at the half.

Baltimore's Jim Duncan fumbled away the second-half kickoff, but Thomas fumbled the ball back at the 1. After that, things settled into a pattern of futility, with neither Morton nor Earl Morrall, subbing for Unitas, able to move his team.

Midway through the fourth quarter, Morton was rushed and his overthrown pass to Walt Garrison was tipped to Baltimore's Rich Volk at Dallas's 33. Volk ran the interception back to the 3, and Tom Nowatzke scored from the 2 two plays later to tie the game.

With only 1:09 left, Mike Curtis intercepted Morton's pass at the Dallas 41, and returned it to the 28. With five seconds remaining, rookie O'Brien kicked a 32-yard field goal to settle the game in favor of the Colts 16-13.

Baltimore (AFC)	0	6	0	10	—	16
Dallas (NFC)	3	10	0	0	—	13

Dall—FG Clark 14
Dall—FG Clark 30
Balt—Mackey 75 pass from Unitas (kick blocked)
Dall—Thomas 7 pass from Morton (Clark kick)
Balt—Nowatzke 2 run (O'Brien kick)
Balt—FG O'Brien 32

TEAM STATISTICS	BALT	DALL
First Downs	14	10
Rushing	4	4
Passing	6	5
Penalty	4	1
Total Yardage	329	215
Net rushing yardage	69	102
Net passing yardage	260	113
Passes att.-comp.-had int.	25-11-3	26-12-3

RUSHING
Baltimore—Nowatzke 10 for 33, 1 TD; Bulaich 18 for 28; Unitas 1 for 4; Havrilak 1 for 3; Morrall 1 for 1.
Dallas—Garrison 12 for 65; Thomas 18 for 35; Morton 1 for 2.

PASSING
Baltimore—Morrall 7 of 15 for 147, 1 int.; Unitas 3 of 9 for 88, 1 TD, 2 int.; Havrilak 1 of 1 for 25.
Dallas—Morton 12 of 26 for 127, 1 TD, 3 int.

RECEIVING
Baltimore—Jefferson 3 for 52; Mackey 2 for 80, 1 TD; Hinton 2 for 51; Havrilak 2 for 27; Nowatzke 1 for 45; Bulaich 1 for 5.
Dallas—Reeves 5 for 46; Thomas 4 for 21, 1 TD; Garrison 2 for 19; Hayes 1 for 41.

1970 Team Rosters

Baltimore
Jim Bailey
Sam Ball*
Norm Bulaich*
Larry Conjar
Bill Curry*
Mike Curtis*
Tom Curtis
Jim Duncan*
Ron Gardin*
Tom Goode*
Bob Grant*
Sam Havrilak*
Ted Hendricks*
Jerry Hill*
Roy Hilton*
Eddie Hinton*
Roy Jefferson*
Cornelius Johnson*
David Lee*
Jerry Logan*
John Mackey*
Jack Maitland*
Tom Matte
Tommy Maxwell*
Ray May*
Fred Miller*
Tom Mitchell*
Earl Morrall*
Dennis Nelson
Billy Newsome*
Robbie Nichols*
Tom Nowatzke*
Jim O'Brien*
Jimmy Orr
Ray Perkins*
Glenn Ressler*
Billy Ray Smith Sr.*
Bubba Smith*
Charles Stukes*
Dan Sullivan*
Johnny Unitas*
Bob Vogel*
Rick Volk*
John Williams*
George Wright

Dallas
Herb Adderley*
Margene Adkins
George Andrie*
Bob Asher*
Mike Clark*
Larry Cole*
Mike Ditka*
Ron East*
Dave Edwards*
Richmond Flowers*
Walt Garrison*
Cornell Green*
Halvor Hagen
Cliff Harris*
Bob Hayes*
Calvin Hill*
Dennis Homan*
Chuck Howley*
Lee Roy Jordan*
Steve Kiner*
D.D. Lewis*
Bob Lilly*
Tony Liscio
Dave Manders*
Craig Morton*
Ralph Neely*
John Niland*
Pettis Norman*
Blaine Nye*
Jethro Pugh*
Dan Reeves*
Mel Renfro*
Lance Rentzel
Reggie Rucker*
Roger Staubach
Thomas Stincic*
Duane Thomas*
Pat Toomay*
Mark Washington*
Charlie Waters*
Claxton Welch*
Ron Widby*
Rayfield Wright*

1971 AFC Champions Miami Dolphins

The Miami Dolphins lost 10 or more games in three of their first four years of existence, but when Don Shula arrived from Baltimore in 1970, the team won 10 games and reached the playoffs. The next year Miami went 10-3-1 and won the AFC Eastern Division.

Bob Griese ranked first in passing among AFC quarterbacks, Larry Csonka became the club's first 1,000-yard back, and Paul Warfield led AFC receivers with 11 touchdowns. After starting the 1971 season with a win, a loss, and a tie, the Dolphins reeled off eight straight wins to secure the division title.

The Dolphins won their first playoff contest when Garo Yepremian, who scored a league-high 117 points, kicked a 37-yard field goal to beat the Chiefs 27-24 on Christmas Day after 82 minutes, 40 seconds—the longest NFL game ever played.

Miami hosted the Baltimore Colts in the AFC title game as Shula faced his former team in the biggest game in Miami history. The Dolphins, known for their grind-it-out-style of attack, used big plays to stun the defending Super Bowl champions 21-0 and earn a trip to Super Bowl VI.

Regular Season

Sun	S-19	A	Denver Broncos	10-10	T
Sun	S-26	A	Buffalo Bills	29-14	W
Sun	O-3	H	New York Jets	10-14	L
Sun	O-10	A	Cincinnati Bengals	23-13	W
Sun	O-17	H	New England Patriots	41-3	W
Sun	O-24	A	New York Jets	30-14	W
Sun	O-31	A	Los Angeles Rams	20-14	W
Sun	N-7	H	Buffalo Bills	34-0	W
Sun	N-14	H	Pittsburgh Steelers	24-21	W
Sun	N-21	H	Baltimore Colts	17-14	W
Mon	N-29	H N	Chicago Bears	34-3	W
Sun	D-5	A	New England Patriots	13-34	L
Sat	D-11	A N	Baltimore Colts	3-14	L
Sun	D-19	H	Green Bay Packers	27-6	W

Postseason

1971 AFC Divisional Playoff Game
December 25, 1971
Miami 27, Kansas City 24 (OT)
at Kansas City

Miami	0	10	7	7	0	3	—	27
Kansas City	10	0	7	7	0	0	—	24

1971 AFC Championship Game
January 2, 1972
Miami 21, Baltimore 0 at Miami

Baltimore	0	0	0	0	—	0
Miami	7	0	7	7	—	21

1971 NFC Champions Dallas Cowboys

In 1971, the Cowboys moved into their new home in Irving, Texas, with a quarterback controversy brewing. Craig Morton and Roger Staubach alternated until Staubach took control in midseason. After a 4-3 start, the suddenly revved-up Cowboys roared into the playoffs, winning their last seven regular-season games.

In their first 1971 playoff game, Dallas scored 13 points following turnovers plus another touchdown set up by a punt return. Despite being outgained 311-183, the Cowboys defeated the Vikings 20-12.

The Doomsday Defense earned the spotlight in the NFC Championship Game against the 49ers. Dallas held San Francisco to 9 first downs and intercepted 3 passes by John Brodie, including 1 that led to the game's first touchdown, as the Cowboys won their second consecutive NFC title game over the 49ers 14-3.

George Andrie's interception in the second quarter put Dallas at San Francisco's 2. Shortly thereafter, Calvin Hill scored on a 1-yard run. The 49ers cut the margin to 4 points on Bruce Gossett's 28-yard field goal in the third quarter, but Dallas drove 80 yards in 14 plays to the clinching score, a 2-yard run by Duane Thomas.

Regular Season

Sun	S-19	A	Buffalo Bills	49-37	W
Sun	S-26	A	Philadelphia Eagles	42-7	W
Sun	O-3	H	Washington Redskins	16-20	L
Mon	O-11	H N	New York Giants	20-13	W
Sun	O-17	A	New Orleans Saints	14-24	L
Sun	O-24	H	New England Patriots	44-21	W
Sun	O-31	A	Chicago Bears	19-23	L
Sun	N-7	A	St. Louis Cardinals	16-13	W
Sun	N-14	H	Philadelphia Eagles	20-7	W
Sun	N-21	A	Washington Redskins	13-0	W
Thu	N-25	H	Los Angeles Rams	28-21	W
Sat	D-4	H	New York Jets	52-10	W
Sun	D-12	A	New York Giants	42-14	W
Sat	D-18	H	St. Louis Cardinals	31-12	W

Postseason

1971 NFC Divisional Playoff Game
December 25, 1971
Dallas 20, Minnesota 12
at Bloomington, Minnesota

Dallas	3	3	14	0	—	20
Minnesota	0	3	0	9	—	12

1971 NFC Championship Game
January 2, 1972
Dallas 14, San Francisco 3 at Irving, Texas

San Francisco	0	0	3	0	—	3
Dallas	0	7	0	7	—	14

Super Bowl VI

Dallas 24, Miami 3
January 16, 1972, Tulane Stadium, New Orleans, Louisiana
Attendance: 81,023

In retrospect, Super Bowl VI can be seen as a contest between Miami coach Don Shula's overachievers, still a year away from greatness, and Dallas coach Tom Landry's team, which was ready to blossom. The Cowboys had talent, experience, and a new quarterback. Roger Staubach had warmed the bench behind Craig Morton in 1970; in 1971 he took his first steps toward the Pro Football Hall of Fame by earning the most-valuable-player award in Super Bowl VI.

In the opening quarter, Chuck Howley, the Super Bowl MVP of the previous year, recovered Dolphin Larry Csonka's fumble at midfield. Csonka did not fumble once during the regular season. Dallas turned it into a 9-yard field goal.

The Cowboys executed a dominating, 76-yard drive in the second quarter to increase their lead to 10-0. Only 1 of the 10 plays in the drive gained fewer than 5 yards. The touchdown came on a 7-yard pass from Staubach to Lance Alworth with 1: 15 to go.

There still was enough time for Miami to tighten the score by driving 44 yards to Garo Yepremian's 31-yard field goal as the half ended. That also ended Miami's scoring for the day.

The Cowboys wrapped up the game by taking the second-half kickoff and driving 71 yards to another touchdown in 8 plays, 7 of them runs. Duane Thomas, Dallas's leading rusher for the day (95 of the Cowboys' 252 yards on the ground), scored the touchdown on a 3-yard dash.

The Cowboys shut down the Dolphins throughout the rest of the third quarter, allowing a mere 13 yards on 8 plays. Early in the final period, Howley intercepted Bob Griese's pass and returned it 41 yards to the Miami 9-yard line. Two plays gained 2 yards, and then Staubach passed 7 yards to Mike Ditka for Dallas's final touchdown.

After the game, Shula said, "My biggest disappointment was that we never challenged. They completely dominated."

Dallas (NFC)	3	7	7	7	—	24
Miami (AFC)	0	3	0	0	—	3

Dall—FG Clark 9
Dall—Alworth 7 pass from Staubach (Clark kick)
Mia—FG Yepremian 31
Dall—D. Thomas 3 run (Clark kick)
Dall—Ditka 7 pass from Staubach (Clark kick)

TEAM STATISTICS	**DALL**	**MIA**
First Downs	17	21
First Downs	23	10
Rushing	15	3
Passing	8	7
Penalty	0	0
Total Yardage	352	185
Net rushing yardage	252	80
Net passing yardage	100	105
Passes att.-comp.-had int.	19-12-0	23-12-1

RUSHING
Dallas—D. Thomas 19 for 95, 1 TD; Garrison 14 for 74; Hill 7 for 25; Staubach 5 for 18; Ditka 1 for 17; Hayes 1 for 16; Reeves 1 for 7.
Miami—Csonka 9 for 40; Kiick 10 for 40; Griese 1 for 0.

PASSING
Dallas—Staubach 12 of 19 for 119, 2 TDs.
Miami—Griese 12 of 23 for 134, 1 int.

RECEIVING
Dallas—D. Thomas 3 for 17; Alworth 2 for 28, 1 TD; Ditka 2 for 28, 1 TD; Hayes 2 for 23; Garrison 2 for 11; Hill 1 for 12.
Miami—Warfield 4 for 39; Kiick 3 for 21; Csonka 2 for 18; Fleming 1 for 27; Twilley 1 for 20; Mandich 1 for 9.

1971 Team Rosters

Dallas
Herb Adderley*
Margene Adkins
Lance Alworth*
George Andrie*
Lee Roy Caffey
Mike Clark*
Larry Cole*
Mike Ditka*
Dave Edwards*
John Fitzgerald*
Richmond Flowers
Toni Fritsch
Walt Garrison*
Cornell Green*
Forrest Gregg
Bill Gregory*
Cliff Harris*
Bob Hayes*
Calvin Hill*
Chuck Howley*
Lee Roy Jordan*
D.D. Lewis*
Bob Lilly*
Tony Liscio*
Dave Manders*
Craig Morton
Ralph Neely
John Niland*
Blaine Nye*
Jethro Pugh*
Dan Reeves*
Mel Renfro*
Gloster Richardson
Reggie Rucker
Tody Smith*
Roger Staubach*
Thomas Stincic*
Don Talbert
Duane Thomas*
Ike Thomas*
Pat Toomay*
Billy Truax*
Rodney Wallace
Mark Washington
Charlie Waters*
Claxton Welch*
Ron Widby*
Joe Williams*
Rayfield Wright*

Miami
Dick Anderson*
Nick Buoniconti*
Terry Cole*
Frank Cornish*
Doug Crusan*
Larry Csonka*
Bob DeMarco*
Vern Den Herder*
Norm Evans*
Dale Farley
Manny Fernandez*
Marv Fleming*
Tim Foley*
Hubert Ginn*
Bob Griese*
Bob Heinz*
Curtis Johnson*
Ray Jones
Jim Kiick*
Mike Kolen*
Bob Kuechenberg*
Jim Langer*
Charlie Leigh
Larry Little*
Jim Mandich*
Wayne Mass
Bob Matheson*
George Mira
Wayne Moore*
Mercury Morris*
Lloyd Mumphord*
Karl Noonan*
Bob Petrella*
Jesse Powell*
John Richardson
Jim Riley*
Jake Scott*
Larry Seiple*
Bill Stanfill*
Otto Stowe*
Doug Swift*
Howard Twilley*
Paul Warfield*
Garo Yepremian*

1972 AFC Champions Miami Dolphins

Simply put, the 1972 Dolphins had the greatest season in NFL history. Rebounding from a loss to Dallas in Super Bowl VI, the Dolphins became the first team to finish the season with a 14-0 record.

Miami lost quarterback Bob Griese to a broken leg in week five, but 38-year-old Earl Morrall, who was picked up on waivers from Baltimore, became the top-ranked quarterback in the AFC. Coach Don Shula's Dolphins led the AFC in both offense and defense.

Larry Csonka and Mercury Morris became the first backfield tandem to each rush for 1,000 yards in the same season. The No-Name Defense racked up three shutouts, including two against Shula's former team, the Colts, plus a 52-0 shellacking of New England.

The third member of the vaunted Miami backfield, Jim Kiick, ran for an 8-yard touchdown in the fourth quarter to rally the Dolphins past Cleveland 20-14 in a playoff game on Christmas Eve.

Miami trailed Pittsburgh 7-0 in the first half of the AFC Championship Game until punter Larry Seiple, seeing the Steelers fall back, took off on a 37-yard run out of punt formation. The fake punt set up the tying touchdown, a 9-yard run by Csonka.

The game remained tied until Griese came off the bench and threw a 52-yard pass to Paul Warfield in the third quarter. Kiick scored on 2 short touchdown runs for a 21-17 victory for Miami's second straight AFC title.

Regular Season

Sun	S-17	A	Kansas City Chiefs	20-10	W
Sun	S-24	H	Houston Oilers	34-13	W
Sun	O-1	A	Minnesota Vikings	16-14	W
Sun	O-8	A	New York Jets	27-17	W
Sun	O-15	H	San Diego Chargers	24-10	W
Sun	O-22	H	Buffalo Bills	24-23	W
Sun	O-29	A	Baltimore Colts	23-0	W
Sun	N-5	A	Buffalo Bills	30-16	W
Sun	N-12	H	New England Patriots	52-0	W
Sun	N-19	H	New York Jets	28-24	W
Mon	N-27	H N	St. Louis Cardinals	31-10	W
Sun	D-3	A	New England Patriots	37-21	W
Sun	D-10	A	New York Jets	23-13	W
Sat	D-16	H N	Baltimore Colts	16-0	W

Postseason

1972 AFC Divisional Playoff Game
December 24, 1972
Miami 20, Cleveland 14 at Miami

Cleveland	0	0	7	7	—	14
Miami	10	0	0	10	—	20

1972 AFC Championship Game
December 31, 1972
Miami 21, Pittsburgh 17 at Pittsburgh

Miami	0	7	7	7	—	21
Pittsburgh	7	0	3	7	—	17

1972 NFC Champions Washington Redskins

The Redskins went 11-3 in the regular season by outscoring their opponents 42 touchdowns to 23. Larry Brown rushed for 1,216 yards. Brown had more carries (285) than the team had pass attempts (284). Future Redskins head coaches Jack Pardee and Richie Petitbon led The Over-the-Hill Gang defensively with help from Pat Fischer and Chris Hanburger.

In an NFC Divisional Playoff Game, the Redskins' five-man defensive line shut down the Green Bay Packers' powerful running game, and Curt Knight kicked 3 field goals as Washington won 16-3. John Brockington, the Packers' star running back, was held to just 9 yards on 13 carries.

The Redskins qualified for their first Super Bowl with a 26-3 victory over the Cowboys. Charley Taylor caught 2 touchdown passes and Washington's defense did not allow Dallas beyond midfield in the second half. The Redskins wanted to pressure Cowboys quarterback Roger Staubach, who had missed nearly the entire season with an injury before coming off the bench the week before against San Francisco, started against Washington. Staubach managed 59 yards on scrambles, but he also was sacked for 25 yards in losses and passed for only 98 yards.

Offensively, Taylor beat Charlie Waters for 51 yards, then scored a touchdown on a 15-yard catch. When Waters suffered a broken arm, Taylor scored on a 45-yard against Mark Washington in the fourth quarter.

Regular Season

Mon	S-18	A N	Minnesota Vikings	24-21	W
Sun	S-24	H	St. Louis Cardinals	24-10	W
Sun	O-1	A	New England Patriots	23-24	L
Sun	O-8	H	Philadelphia Eagles	14-0	W
Sun	O-15	A	St. Louis Cardinals	33-3	W
Sun	O-22	H	Dallas Cowboys	24-20	W
Sun	O-29	A	New York Giants	23-16	W
Sun	N-5	A	New York Jets	35-17	W
Sun	N-12	H	New York Giants	27-13	W
Mon	N-20	H N	Atlanta Falcons	24-13	W
Sun	N-26	H	Green Bay Packers	21-16	W
Sun	D-3	A	Philadelphia Eagles	23-7	W
Sat	D-9	A	Dallas Cowboys	24-34	L
Sun	D-17	H	Buffalo Bills	17-24	L

Postseason

1972 NFC Divisional Playoff Game
December 24, 1972
Washington 16, Green Bay 3 at Washington

Green Bay	0	3	0	0	—	3
Washington	0	10	0	6	—	16

1972 NFC Championship Game
December 31, 1972
Washington 26, Dallas 3 at Washington

Dallas	0	3	0	0	—	3
Washington	0	10	0	16	—	26

Super Bowl VII

Miami 14, Washington 7
January 14, 1973, Memorial Coliseum, Los Angeles, California
Attendance: 90,182

Miami entered Super Bowl VII seeking to make history. Don Shula's Dolphins had won all 16 regular-season and postseason games to that point—and no NFL team ever had completed a perfect season.

Still, Miami was a slight underdog against George Allen's Redskins, a savvy, veteran team known as the Over-the-Hill Gang.

The Dolphins built a 14-0 lead at the half. Griese hit Howard Twilley for a 28-yard touchdown just before the first quarter ended. Then in the second period, Jim Kiick ran 1 yard for a touchdown, capping a short Miami drive set up by an interception.

Meanwhile, the Miami defense, led by tackle Manny Fernandez, held the Redskins' runners in check and treated quarterback Billy Kilmer shabbily. Kilmer threw 3 interceptions, was sacked twice, and harried continuously. Miami defensive back Jake Scott, who had 2 of the interceptions, was named the game's MVP.

Although the Dolphins had dominated the first half, Washington was only a break or two away. In the second half, the Redskins' Larry Brown began running for consistent gains, and Kilmer connected on several passes. But Washington missed a short field-goal attempt in the third quarter, and Miami kept the Redskins scoreless.

Then, with barely more than two minutes left, Miami's Cypriot kicker, Garo Yepremian, trotted onto the field to attempt a 42-yard field goal that would secure the Dolphins' victory.

Yepremian's kick was blocked. He picked up the rolling ball and comically tried to throw a pass. But the ball squirted out of Yepremian's hands and into the arms of Redskins defensive back Mike Bass, who raced 49 yards for a touchdown.

Trailing by a touchdown, Washington had one chance to tie after forcing a punt and taking over at its 30-yard line with no time outs left and 1:14 on the clock. But on fourth down from the 26, Kilmer was sacked, and the Dolphins had their perfect season.

Miami (AFC)	**7**	**7**	**0**	**0**	**—**	**14**
Washington (NFC)	**0**	**0**	**0**	**7**	**—**	**7**

Mia—Twilley 28 pass from Griese (Yepremian kick)
Mia—Kiick 1 run (Yepremian kick)
Was—Bass 49 fumble return (Knight kick)

TEAM STATISTICS	**MIA**	**WASH**
First Downs	12	16
Rushing	7	9
Passing	5	7
Penalty	0	0
Total Yardage	253	228
Net rushing yardage	184	141
Net passing yardage	69	87
Passes att.-comp.-had int.	11-8-1	28-14-3

RUSHING
Miami—Csonka 15 for 112; Kiick 12 for 38, 1 TD; Morris 10 for 34.
Washington—Brown 22 for 72; Harraway 10 for 37; Kilmer 2 for 18; C. Taylor 1 for 8; Smith 1 for 6.

PASSING
Miami—Griese 8 of 11 for 88, 1 TD, 1 int.
Washington—Kilmer 14 of 28 for 104, 3 int.

RECEIVING
Miami—Warfield 3 for 36; Kiick 2 for 6; Twilley 1 for 28, 1 TD; Mandich 1 for 19; Csonka 1 for -1.
Washington—Jefferson 5 for 50; Brown 5 for 26; C. Taylor 2 for 20; Smith 1 for 11; Harraway 1 for -3.

1972 Team Rosters

Miami
Dick Anderson*
Charlie Babb*
Larry Ball*
Marlin Briscoe*
Nick Buoniconti*
Doug Crusan*
Larry Csonka*
Jim Del Gaizo
Vern Den Herder*
Jim Dunaway
Norm Evans*
Manny Fernandez*
Marv Fleming*
Tim Foley
Hubert Ginn*
Bob Griese*
Bob Heinz*
Mike Howell
Al Jenkins
Ed Jenkins*
Curtis Johnson*
Jim Kiick*
Howard Kindig*
Mike Kolen*
Bob Kuechenberg*
Jim Langer*
Charlie Leigh*
Larry Little*
Billy Lothridge
Jim Mandich*
Bob Matheson*
Maulty Moore*
Wayne Moore*
Earl Morrall*
Mercury Morris*
Lloyd Mumphord*
Jesse Powell*
Jake Scott*
Larry Seiple*
Bill Stanfill*
Otto Stowe
Henry Stuckey*
Doug Swift*
Howard Twilley*
Paul Warfield*
Garo Yepremian*

Washington
Mack Alston*
Mike Bass*
Verlon Biggs*
Mike Bragg*
Larry Brown*
Bill Brundige*
Bob Brunet*
George Burman*
Speedy Duncan
Mike Fanucci*
Pat Fischer*
Chris Hanburger*
Charlie Harraway*
Len Hauss*
Alvin Haymond*
Terry Hermeling*
Mike Hull*
Jon Jaqua*
Roy Jefferson*
Jimmie Jones
Jeff Jordan
Sonny Jurgensen
Billy Kilmer*
Curt Knight*
Paul Laaveg*
Bill Malinchak
Ron McDole*
Harold McLinton*
Clifton McNeil*
Herb Mul-key*
George Nock
Brig Owens*
Jack Pardee*
Richie Petitbon
Myron Pottios*
Walt Rock*
Ray Schoenke
Jeff Severson*
Manny Sistrunk*
Jerry Smith*
Diron Talbert*
Charley Taylor*
Rosey Taylor*
Rusty Tillman*
Ted Vactor*
John Wilbur*
Sam Wyche*

1973 AFC Champions Miami Dolphins

The 1973 Dolphins weren't perfect, but they were close enough. The Dolphins, coming off a season in which they went 17-0, including playoffs, finally lost a game, but they won the AFC title for the third straight year.

Miami's 16-game regular-season win streak ended in week two with a 12-7 loss to the Raiders. The Dolphins then reeled off 10 consecutive victories and finished the season at 12-2 to clinch their third consecutive Eastern Division title. Behind a stellar offensive line that included center Jim Langer and guard Larry Little, Larry Csonka bulled his way to his third consecutive 1,000-yard season, and Mercury Morris averaged an AFC-high 6.4 yards per carry.

Bill Arnsparger's celebrated 53 Defense, which featured an intricate zone pass defense, allowed just 150 points, a club record for a 14-game season. Special teams also played a key role as Garo Yepremian scored 113 points and Tom Foley returned 2 blocked punts for touchdowns in a game against Baltimore, Miami's fourth straight shutout of the Colts.

Miami made it look easy by beating Cincinnati 34-16 in a playoff game. The Dolphins mounted touchdown drives of 80, 80, and 75 yards to build a 21-16 halftime lead over the Bengals.

In the AFC Championship Game, the Dolphins gained revenge on the Raiders as Csonka ran for 117 yards and 3 touchdowns for a 27-10 victory.

Regular Season

Sun	S-16	H	San Francisco 49ers	21-13	W
Sun	S-23	A (b)	Oakland Raiders	7-12	L
Sun	S-30	H	New England Patriots	44-23	W
Sun	O-7	A	New York Jets	31-3	W
Mon	O-15	A N	Cleveland Browns	17-9	W
Sun	O-21	H	Buffalo Bills	27-6	W
Sun	O-28	A	New England Patriots	30-14	W
Sun	N-4	H	New York Jets	24-14	W
Sun	N-11	H	Baltimore Colts	44-0	W
Sun	N-18	A	Buffalo Bills	17-0	W
Thu	N-22	A	Dallas Cowboys	14-7	W
Mon	D-3	H N	Pittsburgh Steelers	30-26	W
Sun	D-9	A	Baltimore Colts	3-16	L
Sat	D-15	H N	Detroit Lions	34-7	W

(b)—Berkeley, California

Postseason

1973 AFC Divisional Playoff Game
December 23, 1973
Miami 34, Cincinnati 16
at Miami

Cincinnati	3	13	0	0	—	16
Miami	14	7	10	3	—	34

1973 AFC Championship Game
December 30, 1973
Miami 27, Oakland 10 at Oakland

Oakland	0	0	10	0	—	10
Miami	7	7	3	10	—	27

1973 NFC Champions Minnesota Vikings

Minnesota was nearly invincible in 1973, losing only 2 road games to go 12-2 on the season. Number-one draft pick Chuck Foreman accounted for 1,163 yards rushing and receiving.

Minnesota looked listless in the first half of the NFC Divisional Playoff Game, but defensive end Carl Eller went into a frenzy at halftime, smashing the team's chalkboard. The Vikings drove 79 yards to start the third quarter, with a 46-yard run by Oscar Reed preceding Bill Brown's short touchdown run.

After the Redskins retook the lead on 2 field goals, Fran Tarkenton capped a 71-yard drive with a 28-yard touchdown pass to John Gilliam. Nate Wright intercepted Billy Kilmer on the first play after the kickoff, and Tarkenton teamed with Gilliam again. Minnesota added a field goal and won 27-20.

The NFC Championship Game was no contest. Running back Calvin Hill and defensive tackle Bob Lilly couldn't play, and the Cowboys could neither run effectively nor stop the Vikings from pounding up the middle. Minnesota won easily 27-10.

Minnesota led at the half 10-0, the only touchdown coming when Foreman ran 5 yards to cap an 86-yard drive. In the fourth quarter, after Dallas had narrowed the deficit to 17-10, Bobby Bryant returned an interception 63 yards for a touchdown. Another interception set up a 34-yard field goal by Fred Cox.

Regular Season

Sun	S-16	H	Oakland Raiders	24-16	W
Sun	S-23	A	Chicago Bears	22-13	W
Sun	S-30	H	Green Bay Packers	11-3	W
Sun	O-7	A	Detroit Lions	23-9	W
Sun	O-14	A	San Francisco 49ers	17-13	W
Sun	O-21	H	Philadelphia Eagles	28-21	W
Sun	O-28	H	Los Angeles Rams	10-9	W
Sun	N-4	H	Cleveland Browns	26-3	W
Sun	N-11	H	Detroit Lions	28-7	W
Mon	N-19	A N	Atlanta Falcons	14-20	L
Sun	N-25	H	Chicago Bears	31-13	W
Sun	D-2	A	Cincinnati Bengals	0-27	L
Sat	D-8	A N	Green Bay Packers	31-7	W
Sun	D-16	A (+)	New York Giants	31-7	W

(+)—New Haven, Connecticut

Postseason

1973 NFC Divisional Playoff Game
December 22, 1973
Minnesota 27, Washington 20
at Bloomington, Minnesota

Washington	0	7	3	10	—	20
Minnesota	0	3	7	17	—	27

1973 NFC Championship Game
December 30, 1973
Minnesota 27, Dallas 10 at Irving, Texas

Minnesota	3	7	7	10	—	27
Dallas	0	0	10	0	—	10

Super Bowl VIII

Miami 24, Minnesota 7
January 13, 1974, Rice Stadium, Houston, Texas
Attendance: 71,882

Miami became the first team to appear in three Super Bowls and equaled Green Bay's feat of back-to-back victories with a 24-7 triumph over Minnesota. The Dolphins jumped out to a 2-touchdown lead in the first quarter and scored all their points in the first three quarters before finally allowing Minnesota a meaningless touchdown in the fourth period.

For the Vikings, the game marked their second Super Bowl, their second loss, and the second time they were held to a single touchdown. Vikings quarterback Fran Tarkenton actually passed for more than twice the yardage than did the Dolphins' Bob Griese, but he didn't have Miami's rushing attack to control the game.

Griese threw only 7 passes in the game, but he completed 6. Most valuable player Larry Csonka smashed for 145 yards and 2 touchdowns on 33 carries to double the rushing yardage of the entire Minnesota backfield.

The Dolphins took the opening kickoff 62 yards to a 5-yard touchdown smash by Csonka. Minnesota went three plays and out. Miami came right back with a 56-yard drive for another touchdown. This time Jim Kiick did the honors with a 1-yard plunge.

In the second quarter, the Dolphins marched down the field again. The drive culminated in a 28-yard field goal by Garo Yepremian.

Trailing 17-0, Minnesota finally put its offense in gear. Paced by Tarkenton (4 completions for 66 yards), the Vikings drove 74 yards, only to lose the ball when Oscar Reed fumbled on a fourth-and-1 at the Miami 6.

Minnesota opened the second half with John Gilliam's 65-yard kickoff return, but the play was called back by a Vikings' penalty. When the Dolphins got the ball, they cemented their lead with a drive from midfield climaxed by Csonka's 2-yard smash to score.

The Vikings' only touchdown came early in the final quarter. Tarkenton's 4-yard run finished off a drive from the Minnesota 43. Although it was much too late, Minnesota put together another strong drive in the quarter. It was foiled by Curtis Johnson's interception at the Miami goal line. The Dolphins used their ground game to hold the ball for the final 6:24 of the game.

Minnesota (NFC)	**0**	**0**	**0**	**7**	**—**	**7**
Miami (AFC)	**14**	**3**	**7**	**0**	**—**	**24**

Mia—Csonka 5 run (Yepremian kick)
Mia—Kiick 1 run (Yepremian kick)
Mia—FG Yepremian 28
Mia—Csonka 2 run (Yepremian kick)
Minn—Tarkenton 4 run (Cox kick)

TEAM STATISTICS	MINN	MIA
First Downs	14	21
Rushing	5	13
Passing	8	4
Penalty	1	4
Total Yardage	238	259
Net rushing yardage	72	196
Net passing yardage	166	63
Passes att.-comp.-had int.	28-18-1	7-6-0

RUSHING
Minnesota—Reed 11 for 32; Foreman 7 for 18; Tarkenton 4 for 17, 1 TD; Marinaro 1 for 3; B. Brown 1 for 2. Miami—Csonka 33 for 145, 2 TDs; Morris 11 for 34; Kiick 7 for 10, 1 TD; Griese 2 for 7.

PASSING
Minnesota—Tarkenton 18 of 28 for 182, 1 int.
Miami—Griese 6 of 7 for 73.

RECEIVING
Minnesota—Foreman 5 for 27; Gilliam 4 for 44; Voigt 3 for 46; Marinaro 2 for 39; B. Brown 1 for 9; Kingsriter 1 for 9; Lash 1 for 9; Reed 1 for -1.
Miami—Warfield 2 for 33; Mandich 2 for 21; Briscoe 2 for 19.

1973 Team Rosters

Miami
Dick Anderson*
Charlie Babb*
Larry Ball*
Bruce Bannon*
Marlin Briscoe*
Nick Buoniconti*
Doug Crusan*
Larry Csonka*
Vern Den Herder*
Norm Evans*
Manny Fernandez*
Marv Fleming*
Tim Foley*
Hubert Ginn
Irv Goode*
Bob Griese*
Bob Heinz*
Curtis Johnson*
Jim Kiick*
Mike Kolen*
Bob Kuechenberg*
Jim Langer*
Charlie Leigh
Larry Little*
Jim Mandich*
Bob Matheson*
Maulty Moore*
Wayne Moore*
Earl Morrall*
Mercury Morris*
Lloyd Mumphord*
Ed Newman*
Don Nottingham*
Jesse Powell
Bo Rather
Jake Scott*
Larry Seiple*
Ron Sellers
Tom Smith
Bill Stanfill*
Henry Stuckey*
Doug Swift*
Howard Twilley*
Paul Warfield*
Larry Woods
Garo Yepremian*
Willie Young

Minnesota
Grady Alderman*
Gary Ballman
John Beasley
Bob Berry
Terry Brown*
Bill Brown*
Bobby Bryant*
Fred Cox*
Carroll Dale*
Rhett Dawson
Mike Eischeid*
Carl Eller*
Chuck Foreman*
Frank Gallagher*
John Gilliam*
Charlie Goodrum*
Wally Hilgenberg*
Doug Kingsriter*
Paul Krause*
Gary Larsen*
Jim Lash*
Steve Lawson
Bob Lurtsema*
Ed Marinaro*
Jim Marshall*
Amos Martin*
Brent McClanahan
Dave Osborn*
Alan Page*
Ron Porter*
Al Randolph
Oscar Reed*
Jeff Siemon*
Milt Sunde
Doug Sutherland*
Fran Tarkenton*
Mick Tingelhoff*
Stu Voigt*
John Ward
Charlie West*
Ed White*
Roy Winston*
Jeff Wright*
Nate Wright*
Ron Yary*
Godfrey Zaunbrecher

1974 AFC Champions
Pittsburgh Steelers

Coach Chuck Noll's 1974 draft is considered by some football observers as the best draft in NFL history. Pittsburgh's first five selections yielded two future Hall of Fame players in middle linebacker Jack Lambert and center Mike Webster, and two great receivers, Lynn Swann and John Stallworth. Lambert was the final piece of the Steel Curtain, and Pittsburgh rode its defense to a 10-3-1 mark and its second AFC Central Division title.

The Steelers rolled past Buffalo 32-14 in an AFC Divisional Playoff Game to set up a meeting against bitter rival Oakland in the AFC Championship Game. The Steelers scored 3 touchdowns in the fourth quarter to break open a game in which they trailed 10-3 after three periods, and won a title game for the first time in Pittsburgh franchise history 24-13.

Early in the final period, the Steelers tied the game 10-10 on Franco Harris's 8-yard run. Then the defense took over, intercepting a pass to set up a 6-yard touchdown pass from Bradshaw to Swann. Oakland had a chance to tie the score again, but Ken Stabler was forced to throw the ball away under heavy pressure and the Raiders settled for a 24-yard field by George Blanda. Harris's 21-yard touchdown run clinched the victory. The Raiders netted only 29 rushing yards.

Regular Season

Sun	S-15	H	Baltimore Colts	30-0	W
Sun	S-22	A	Denver Broncos (OT)	35-35	T
Sun	S-29	H	Oakland Raiders	0-17	L
Sun	O-6	A	Houston Oilers	13-7	W
Sun	O-13	A	Kansas City Chiefs	34-24	W
Sun	O-20	H	Cleveland Browns	20-16	W
Mon	O-28	H N	Atlanta Falcons	24-17	W
Sun	N-3	H	Philadelphia Eagles	27-0	W
Sun	N-10	A	Cincinnati Bengals	10-17	L
Sun	N-17	A	Cleveland Browns	26-16	W
Mon	N-25	A N	New Orleans Saints	28-17	W
Sun	D-1	H	Houston Oilers	10-13	L
Sun	D-8	A	New England Patriots	21-17	W
Sat	D-14	H	Cincinnati Bengals	27-3	W

Postseason

1974 AFC Divisional Playoff Game
December 22, 1974
Pittsburgh 32, Buffalo 14
at Pittsburgh

Buffalo	7	0	7	0	—	14
Pittsburgh	3	26	0	3	—	32

1974 AFC Championship Game
December 29, 1974
Pittsburgh 24, Oakland 13
at Oakland

Pittsburgh	0	3	0	21	—	24
Oakland	3	0	7	3	—	13

1974 NFC Champions
Minnesota Vikings

Fred McNeill, Matt Blair, Steve Riley, and Sam McCullum joined the Vikings as 1974 draftees, and Minnesota won three games in a row to end the season as NFC Central champions.

The St. Louis Cardinals dominated the first half of an NFC Divisional Playoff Game but the teams were tied 7-7 at the half. On the opening drive of the third quarter, Jeff Wright intercepted a pass, and Minnesota went ahead 10-7 on a Fred Cox field goal. Two plays later, Terry Metcalf fumbled and Nate Wright picked up the ball and ran 20 yards for a touchdown.

Later in the quarter, Fran Tarkenton hit John Gilliam with a 38-yard touchdown pass that finished off the Cardinals; Minnesota won 30-14.

In the NFC Championship Game, against the Los Angeles Rams, the Vikings scored when Tarkenton found Jim Lash for a 29-yard touchdown pass.

In the third quarter, the Rams' James Harris completed a pass to Harold Jackson, who went 73 yards before safety Jeff Wright knocked him out of bounds at the Vikings' 2. The Rams were denied when linebacker Wally Hilgenberg intercepted Harris's third-down pass in the end zone. Minnesota subsequently scored on Dave Osborn's 4-yard touchdown run.

Regular Season

Sun	S-15	A	Green Bay Packers	32-17	W
Sun	S-22	A	Detroit Lions	7-6	W
Sun	S-29	H	Chicago Bears	11-7	W
Sun	O-6	A	Dallas Cowboys	23-21	W
Sun	O-13	H	Houston Oilers	51-10	W
Sun	O-20	H	Detroit Lions	16-20	L
Sun	O-27	H	New England Patriots	14-17	L
Sun	N-3	A	Chicago Bears	17-0	W
Mon	N-11	A N	St. Louis Cardinals	28-24	W
Sun	N-17	H	Green Bay Packers	7-19	L
Sun	N-24	A	Los Angeles Rams	17-20	L
Sun	D-1	H	New Orleans Saints	19-9	W
Sat	D-7	H	Atlanta Falcons	23-10	W
Sat	D-14	A	Kansas City Chiefs	35-15	W

Postseason

1974 NFC Divisional Playoff Game
December 21, 1974
Minnesota 30, St. Louis 14
at Bloomington, Minnesota

St. Louis	0	7	0	7	—	14
Minnesota	0	7	16	7	—	30

1974 NFC Championship Game
December 29, 1974
Minnesota 14, Los Angeles Rams 10
at Bloomington, Minnesota

L.A. Rams	0	3	0	7	—	10
Minnesota	0	7	0	7	—	14

Super Bowl IX

Pittsburgh 16, Minnesota 6
January 12, 1975, Tulane Stadium, New Orleans, Louisiana
Attendance: 80,997

The Steelers were making their first appearance in the Super Bowl, and were playing for the NFL championship for the first time in franchise history.

The veteran Vikings, meanwhile, had been to the Super Bowl twice before. The Vikings had a savvy leader in quarterback Fran Tarkenton. The Steelers also had a strong defense, but their quarterback, Terry Bradshaw, was unproven.

The first half was dominated by the defenses. Pittsburgh concentrated on the middle of the Minnesota defensive line. One defensive tackle, Ernie Holmes, played over Vikings center Mick Tingelhoff, while the other tackle, Joe Greene, lined up at an angle pointed directly at Tingelhoff. Holmes sometimes took on the Vikings' center directly, allowing Greene to knife through and pursue Tarkenton. At other times, Greene would smash into Tingelhoff while Holmes looped behind him.

The only score in the half was a safety registered by the Steelers. Tarkenton fumbled a handoff to Dave Osborn, scrambled to recover the ball in the end zone, and was downed by Pittsburgh defensive end Dwight White.

Leading 2-0, Pittsburgh kicked to Minnesota to open the second half, and the Vikings' Bill Brown fumbled; Marv Kellum recovered for Pittsburgh at the Minnesota 30. The Steelers took four plays to go the distance, with Franco Harris taking the ball in from the 9.

Harris, the game's MVP, ran for 158 yards on 34 tries to set Super Bowl records in both categories. Rocky Bleier also added 65 yards on 17 carries for the Steelers. Minnesota, meanwhile, managed only 17 yards rushing.

Denied on the ground, the Vikings weren't much better in the air. Tarkenton, under constant pressure from Greene, Holmes, White, and L.C. Greenwood, completed only 11 of 26 attempts for 102 yards—an average of fewer than 4 yards per pass.

Despite their dominance, Pittsburgh's 9-0 lead was far from safe; it narrowed to 9-6 in the final quarter when Matt Blair blocked Bobby Walden's punt, and Terry Brown recovered in the end zone.

After Terry Brown's touchdown, Pittsburgh put the game on ice with a drive that began on its 34. The big play of the drive was a 30-yard toss from Bradshaw to Larry Brown. Harris and Bleier moved the ball to the 4, where, on third down, Bradshaw passed to Larry Brown for the touchdown.

Soon after the ensuing kickoff, Pittsburgh's Mike Wagner intercepted a Tarkenton pass, and the Steelers maintained possession until the game was nearly over.

Pittsburgh (AFC)	**0**	**2**	**7**	**7**	**—**	**16**
Minnesota (NFC)	**0**	**0**	**0**	**6**	**—**	**6**

Pitt—Safety, White downed Tarkenton in end zone
Pitt—Harris 9 run (Gerela kick)
Minn—T. Brown recovered blocked punt in end zone (kick failed)
Pitt—L. Brown 4 pass from Bradshaw (Gerela kick)

TEAM STATISTICS	**PITT**	**MINN**
First Downs	17	9
Rushing	11	2
Passing	5	5
Penalty	1	2
Total Yardage	333	119
Net rushing yardage	249	17
Net passing yardage	84	102
Passes att.-comp.-had int.	14-9-0	26-11-3

RUSHING
Pittsburgh—Harris 34 for 158, 1 TD; Bleier 17 for 65; Bradshaw 5 for 33; Swann 1 for -7.
Minnesota—Foreman 12 for 18; Tarkenton 1 for 0; Osborn 8 for -1.

PASSING
Pittsburgh—Bradshaw 9 of 14 for 96, 1 TD.
Minnesota—Tarkenton 11 of 26 for 102, 3 int.

RECEIVING
Pittsburgh—L. Brown 3 for 49, 1 TD; Stallworth 3 for 24; Bleier 2 for 11; Lewis 1 for 12.
Minnesota—Foreman 5 for 50; Voigt 2 for 31; Osborn 2 for 7; Gilliam 1 for 16; Reed 1 for -2.

1974 Team Rosters

Pittsburgh	Minnesota
Jimmy Allen*	Grady Alderman*
Rocky Bleier*	Scott Anderson*
Mel Blount*	Bob Berry
Ed Bradley*	Joe Blahak
Terry Bradshaw*	Matt Blair*
Larry Brown*	Dave Boone
Jim Clack*	Terry Brown*
Dick Conn*	Bill Brown*
Charles Davis*	Bobby Bryant
Sam Davis*	Fred Cox*
Steve Davis*	Steve Craig*
Rich Druschel*	Mike Eischeid*
Glen Edwards*	Carl Eller*
John Fuqua	Chuck Foreman*
Steve Furness*	John Gilliam*
Reggie Garrett*	Charlie Goodrum*
Roy Gerela*	Wally Hilgenberg*
Joe Gilliam	John Holland
Gordon Gravelle*	Doug Kingsriter*
Joe Greene*	Paul Krause*
L.C. Greenwood*	Gary Larsen*
Randy Grossman*	Jim Lash*
Jack Ham*	Steve Lawson*
Terry Hanratty	Bob Lurtsema*
Franco Harris*	Ed Marinaro*
Reggie Harrison*	Jim Marshall*
Ernie Holmes*	Larry Marshall
Marv Kellum*	Amos Martin*
Jon Kolb*	Andy Maurer*
Jack Lambert*	Brent McClanahan*
Frank Lewis*	Sam McCullum*
Ray Mansfield*	Fred McNeill*
John McMakin*	Dave Osborn*
Gerry Mullins*	Alan Page*
Preston Pearson*	Randy Poltl*
Dave Reavis*	Oscar Reed*
Andy Russell*	Steve Riley
Ron Shanklin*	Jeff Siemon*
Donnie Shell*	Milt Sunde*
John Stallworth*	Doug Sutherland*
Lynn Swann*	Fran Tarkenton*
J.T. Thomas*	Mick Tingelhoff*
Loren Toews*	Stu Voigt*
Mike Wagner*	Jackie Wallace*
Bobby Walden*	Ed White*
Mike Webster*	Roy Winston*
Dwight White*	Jeff Wright*
Jim Wolf	Nate Wright*
	Ron Yary*

1975 AFC Champions Pittsburgh Steelers

In 1974, the Steelers won the first championship in their 42-year history; the next year they went about establishing a dynasty. With a team considered one of the greatest in league history, the 1975 Steelers rolled to a 12-2 record and another Central Division championship.

In an AFC Divisional Playoff Game against Baltimore, the Steel Curtain defense totally dominated the Colts, scoring once, setting up 2 other scores, recording 5 sacks, forcing 4 turnovers, and holding the Colts to 154 total yards as the Steelers won 28-10.

The Steelers won their second consecutive AFC title with a 16-10 victory over the Raiders. The Steelers led 3-0 in the fourth quarter, when, in a span of 6 minutes, the teams combined for 23 points.

Franco Harris raced 25 yards for a touchdown, but the Raiders came right back, with Ken Stabler throwing a 14-yard touchdown pass to Mike Siani. Finally, Terry Bradshaw connected with John Stallworth for a 20-yard touchdown. The Raiders drove down the field again and, with 17 seconds left, 48-year-old George Blanda, playing in his final game, kicked a 41-yard field goal to cut the lead to 6 points. Marv Hubbard of the Raiders then recovered an onside kick with 7 seconds remaining. Oakland reached the Pittsburgh 15, but the clock ran out before wide receiver Cliff Branch could get out of bounds.

Regular Season

Sun	S-21	A	San Diego Chargers	37-0	W
Sun	S-28	H	Buffalo Bills	21-30	L
Sun	O-5	A	Cleveland Browns	42-6	W
Sun	O-12	H	Denver Broncos	20-9	W
Sun	O-19	H	Chicago Bears	34-3	W
Sun	O-26	A (m)	Green Bay Packers	16-13	W
Sun	N-2	A	Cincinnati Bengals	30-24	W
Sun	N-9	H	Houston Oilers	24-17	W
Sun	N-16	H	Kansas City Chiefs	28-3	W
Mon	N-24	A N	Houston Oilers	32-9	W
Sun	N-30	A	New York Jets	20-7	W
Mon	D-7	H N	Cleveland Browns	31-17	W
Sun	D-13	H	Cincinnati Bengals	35-14	W
Sun	D-20	A	Los Angeles Rams	3-10	L

(m)—Milwaukee, Wisconsin

Postseason

1975 AFC Divisional Playoff Game
December 27, 1975
Pittsburgh 28, Baltimore 10 at Pittsburgh

Baltimore	0	7	3	0	—	10
Pittsburgh	7	0	7	14	—	28

1975 AFC Championship Game
January 4, 1976
Pittsburgh 16, Oakland 10 at Pittsburgh

Oakland	0	0	0	10	—	10
Pittsburgh	0	3	0	13	—	16

1975 NFC Champions Dallas Cowboys

The Cowboys missed the playoffs in 1974, but, in 1975, a dozen draft choices made an immediate impact in Dallas. Behind rookie linebackers Randy White, Thomas (Hollywood) Henderson, and Bob Breunig, and guards Burton Lawless and Herb Scott, Dallas won its last two games to capture a wild-card playoff berth, and the Cowboys-Vikings game proved to be as wild as any postseason NFL contest has ever been.

With 24 seconds left, Roger Staubach completed a 50-yard touchdown pass to Drew Pearson as Dallas defeated Minnesota 17-14 on a play that has become known as the Hail Mary.

Trailing 14-10, Dallas took over on its 15 with only 1:51 remaining. On fourth-and-16, Staubach found Pearson at midfield for a first down and connected with him again at the 5 on a desperation heave; Pearson backed into the end zone to score the winning touchdown.

In the NFC Championship Game, Staubach threw 4 touchdown passes, and the Cowboys shocked the favored Los Angeles Rams 37-7.

Staubach teamed with running back Preston Pearson on 3 scores and found Golden Richards for another touchdown in the rout of the Rams at the Los Angeles Memorial Coliseum. In doing so, Dallas became the first wild-card team to reach the Super Bowl.

Regular Season

Sun	S-21	H	Los Angeles Rams	18-7	W
Sun	S-28	H	St. Louis Cardinals (OT)	37-31	W
Mon	O-6	A N	Detroit Lions	36-10	W
Sun	O-12	A	New York Giants	13-7	W
Sun	O-19	H	Green Bay Packers	17-19	L
Sun	O-26	A	Philadelphia Eagles	20-17	W
Sun	N-2	A	Washington Redskins (OT)	24-30	L
Mon	N-10	H N	Kansas City Chiefs	31-34	L
Sun	N-16	A	New England Patriots	34-31	W
Sun	N-23	H	Philadelphia Eagles	27-17	W
Sun	N-30	H	New York Giants	14-3	W
Sun	D-7	A	St. Louis Cardinals	17-31	L
Sat	D-13	H	Washington Redskins	31-10	W
Sun	D-21	A	New York Jets	31-21	W

Postseason

1975 NFC Divisional Playoff Game
December 28, 1975
Dallas 17, Minnesota 14 at Bloomington, Minnesota

Dallas	0	0	7	10	—	17
Minnesota	0	7	0	7	—	14

1975 NFC Championship Game
January 4, 1976
Dallas 37, Los Angeles Rams 7 at Los Angeles

Dallas	7	14	13	3	—	37
L.A. Rams	0	0	0	7	—	7

Super Bowl X

Pittsburgh 21, Dallas 17
January 18, 1976, Orange Bowl, Miami, Florida
Attendance: 80,187

What were, at the time, the two most popular teams in the NFL met in Super Bowl X, and the contrast between their styles was as great as the hue of their jerseys.

The glitzy, white-clad Dallas Cowboys—"America's Team"—combined a high-tech offense and a state-of-the-art Flex Defense to put on a dazzling show each Sunday. They were easy to like, and, for once, they even had something of an underdog aura, having reached the Super Bowl as a wild-card team. The black-clad Pittsburgh Steelers, out to defend their Super Bowl victory of the year before, lived by a steel-hard defense occasionally spelled by a grind-it-out running attack.

The Cowboys struck first. Roger Staubach zeroed in on Drew Pearson for a 29-yard touchdown pass. Before the first quarter ended, Pittsburgh evened the score on a 7-yard pass from Terry Bradshaw to tight end Randy Grossman. Setting up the score was a 32-yard pass to Lynn Swann, whose health was questionable because of a concussion he had suffered in the AFC Championship Game. Swann outleaped a Dallas defender, then magically kept both feet inside the sideline to make his catch.

Dallas reclaimed the lead at 10-7 only 15 seconds into the second quarter when Toni Fritsch booted a 36-yard field goal. Later, Pittsburgh's Roy Gerela, playing at less than 100 percent because of a cracked rib he suffered making a tackle on the opening kickoff, shanked a field-goal try. Dallas led 10-7 at halftime.

Defense continued to dominate in the scoreless third quarter. Pittsburgh sacked Staubach 7 times during the game and forced him to scramble on numerous occasions. Moreover, they pressured him into 3 interceptions.

One of the interceptions set up another field-goal try by Gerela, but he pulled it left from 33 yards. Dallas safety Cliff Harris mockingly patted him on the helmet, only to be unceremoniously dumped on his hip pads by irate Pittsburgh linebacker Jack Lambert. The inspired Steelers dominated after that.

In the fourth quarter, Steelers reserve fullback Reggie Harrison blocked Mitch Hoopes's punt. The ball rolled through the end zone for a safety to cut the Cowboys' lead to 10-9. Gerela, who'd donned a corset to protect his ribs, regained his kicking touch with field goals of 36 and 18 yards to put the Steelers in front 15-10.

With 3:02 left in the game, Bradshaw lofted a long pass to Swann, who caught the ball at the 5 and took it over the goal line to complete a 64-yard lightning strike. Swann, the game's MVP, finished the day with 161 yards on 4 catches, a 40.3 average-per-catch. Gerela missed the extra point.

Now it was Dallas's turn. It took Staubach only 1:14 to get the touchdown back, completing a drive with a 34-yard bullseye to Percy Howard—the only pass Howard caught during his entire career.

Terry Hanratty replaced Bradshaw, still woozy from a hit suffered after his touchdown pass to Swann, but the Steelers were stalled on fourth-and-9 at the Dallas 41 with almost a minute-and-a-half to go. Coach Chuck Noll feared a blocked kick and called for a Rocky Bleier run that gained only 2 yards.

Trailing only 21-17, Staubach had the ball back with more time than he usually needed to negotiate 61 yards. The Cowboys reached Pittsburgh's 38. With five seconds left, Staubach launched his final pass into the end zone. Steeler Mike Wagner batted the ball, which was caught by another Steeler, Glen Edwards.

Dallas (NFC)	**7**	**3**	**0**	**7**	**—**	**17**
Pittsburgh (AFC)	**7**	**0**	**0**	**14**	**—**	**21**

Dall—D. Pearson 29 pass from Staubach (Fritsch kick)
Pitt—Grossman 7 pass from Bradshaw (Gerela kick)
Dall—FG Fritsch 36
Pitt—Safety, Harrison blocked punt through the end zone
Pitt—FG Gerela 36
Pitt—FG Gerela 18
Pitt—Swann 64 pass from Bradshaw (kick failed)
Dall—P. Howard 34 pass from Staubach (Fritsch kick)

TEAM STATISTICS	**DALL**	**PITT**
First Downs	14	13
Rushing	6	7
Passing	8	6
Penalty	0	0
Total Yardage	270	339
Net rushing yardage	108	149
Net passing yardage	162	190
Passes att.-comp.-had int.	24-15-3	19-9-0

RUSHING
Dallas—Newhouse 16 for 56; Staubach 5 for 22; Dennison 5 for 16; P. Pearson 5 for 14.
Pittsburgh—Harris 27 for 82; Bleier 15 for 51; Bradshaw 4 for 16.

PASSING
Dallas—Staubach 15 of 24 for 204, 2 TDs, 3 int.
Pittsburgh—Bradshaw 9 of 19 for 209, 2 TDs.

RECEIVING
Dallas—P. Pearson 5 for 53; Young 3 for 31; D. Pearson 2 for 59, 1 TD; Newhouse 2 for 12; P. Howard 1 for 34, 1 TD; Fugett 1 for 9; Dennison 1 for 6.
Pittsburgh—Swann 4 for 161, 1 TD; Stallworth 2 for 8; Harris 1 for 26; Grossman 1 for 7, 1 TD; L . Brown 1 for 7.

1975 Team Rosters

Pittsburgh	Dallas
Jimmy Allen*	Benny Barnes*
John Banaszak*	Bob Breunig*
Rocky Bleier*	Warren Capone*
Mel Blount*	Larry Cole*
Ed Bradley*	Kyle Davis*
Terry Bradshaw*	Doug Dennison*
Dave Brown*	Pat Donovan*
Larry Brown*	Billy Joe DuPree*
Jim Clack*	Dave Edwards*
Mike Collier*	John Fitzgerald*
Sam Davis*	Toni Fritsch*
Glen Edwards*	Jean Fugett*
John Fuqua*	Bill Gregory*
Steve Furness*	Cliff Harris*
Reggie Garrett*	Tom Henderson*
Roy Gerela*	Mitch Hoopes*
Joe Gilliam	Percy Howard*
Gordon Gravelle*	Ron Howard*
Joe Greene*	Randy Hughes*
L.C. Greenwood*	Too Tall Jones*
Randy Grossman*	Lee Roy Jordan*
Jack Ham*	Scott Laidlaw
Terry Hanratty*	Burton Lawless*
Franco Harris*	D.D. Lewis*
Reggie Harrison*	Clint Longley
Ernie Holmes*	Harvey Martin*
Marv Kellum*	Ralph Neely*
Jon Kolb*	Robert Newhouse*
Jack Lambert*	Blaine Nye*
Frank Lewis*	Drew Pearson*
Ray Mansfield*	Preston Pearson*
Gerry Mullins*	Cal Peterson*
Dave Reavis*	Jethro Pugh*
Andy Russell*	Mel Renfro*
Donnie Shell*	Golden Richards*
John Stallworth*	Herbert Scott*
Lynn Swann*	Roger Staubach*
J.T. Thomas*	Bruce Walton
Loren Toews*	Mark Washington*
Mike Wagner*	Charlie Waters*
Bobby Walden*	Randy White*
Mike Webster*	Roland Woolsey*
Dwight White*	Rayfield Wright*
	Charley Young*

1976 AFC Champions Oakland Raiders

From 1972-75, the Raiders played the Steelers in the playoffs each year. They lost to Pittsburgh in 1972 on the disputed Immaculate Reception; they beat the Steelers in 1973, but lost to the Dolphins in the AFC Championship Game; Oakland hosted the 1974 AFC Championship Game and lost to Pittsburgh; and in 1975, they had the ball at the Steelers' 15 as time ran out in a 16-10 loss in another title game. Nothing made in Pittsburgh would stop the Raiders in 1976.

The Raiders, who equaled a club record with 13 victories in 1976, almost didn't get their rematch with the Steelers. Oakland had to score 2 fourth-quarter touchdowns, the final score coming on a bootleg into the end zone by Ken Stabler with 10 seconds left, to beat the Patriots 24-21 in an AFC Divisional Playoff Game.

In the AFC Championship Game, the Raiders shut down the Steelers' ground game—minus Franco Harris and Rocky Bleier—to dethrone the two-time Super Bowl champions 24-7. Led by the short passing of Stabler and the pounding running of Mark van Eeghen, Clarence Davis, and Pete Banaszak, the Raiders jumped to a 10-0 lead. After the Steelers pulled within 10-7, Oakland scored a touchdown 19 seconds before the first half ended. The Raiders finished off the Steelers with a 12-play, 63-yard drive in the third quarter, with Banaszak scoring on a 5-yard touchdown pass.

Regular Season

Sun	S-12	H	Pittsburgh Steelers	31-28	W
Mon	S-20	A	Kansas City Chiefs	24-21	W
Sun	S-26	A	Houston Oilers	14-13	W
Sun	O-3	A	New England Patriots	17-48	L
Sun	O-10	A	San Diego Chargers	27-17	W
Sun	O-17	A	Denver Broncos	17-10	W
Sun	O-24	H	Green Bay Packers	18-14	W
Sun	O-31	H	Denver Broncos	19-6	W
Sun	N-7	A	Chicago Bears	28-27	W
Sun	N-14	H	Kansas City Chiefs	21-10	W
Sun	N-21	A	Philadelphia Eagles	26-7	W
Sun	N-28	H	Tampa Bay Buccaneers	49-16	W
Mon	D-6	H	Cincinnati Bengals	35-20	W
Sun	D-12	H	San Diego Chargers	24-0	W

Postseason

1976 AFC Divisional Playoff Game
December 18, 1976
Oakland 24, New England 21
at Oakland

New England	7	0	14	0	—	21
Oakland	3	7	0	14	—	24

1976 AFC Championship Game
December 26, 1976
Oakland 24, Pittsburgh 7
at Oakland

Pittsburgh	0	7	0	0	—	7
Oakland	3	14	7	0	—	24

1976 NFC Champions Minnesota Vikings

The Vikings lost just twice by a total of 5 points on the way to winning the NFC Central, and their NFC Divisional Playoff Game was a romp.

Running backs Chuck Foreman and Brent McClanahan each rushed for better than 100 yards as Minnesota dominated George Allen's Washington Redskins, coasting to a 35-20 victory.

With a 7-3 lead late in the first quarter, Fran Tarkenton threw to Sammy White, who grabbed the ball, juggled it as he fell, maintained possession, and rolled into the end zone. Drives of 66, 51, and 76 yards finished off any Redskins' hopes.

Minnesota qualified for its fourth Super Bowl with a 24-13 victory over the Rams on an afternoon in which the wind-chill factor plummeted to 12 degrees below zero by game's end.

The tone of the game was set early when Nate Allen blocked a Los Angeles Rams' field-goal attempt and defensive back Bobby Bryant returned the ball 90 yards for a touchdown.

Later in the quarter, a fumble by John Cappelletti ended another drive and Matt Blair, who recovered the fumble, also blocked a punt in the second quarter. The Rams scored 2 late touchdowns, but lost any chance for redemption when a Pat Haden pass was intercepted at Minnesota's 8-yard line.

Regular Season

Sun	S-12	A	New Orleans Saints	40-9	W
Sun	S-19	H	Los Angeles Rams (OT)	10-10	T
Sun	S-26	A	Detroit Lions	10-9	W
Mon	O-4	N H	Pittsburgh Steelers	17-6	W
Sun	O-10	H	Chicago Bears	20-19	W
Sun	O-17	H	New York Giants	24-7	W
Sun	O-24	A	Philadelphia Eagles	31-12	W
Sun	O-31	A	Chicago Bears	13-14	L
Sun	N-7	H	Detroit Lions	31-23	W
Sun	N-14	H	Seattle Seahawks	27-21	W
Sun	N-21	A (m)	Green Bay Packers	17-10	W
Mon	N-29	N A	San Francisco 49ers	16-20	L
Sun	D-5	H	Green Bay Packers	20-9	W
Sat	D-11	A	Miami Dolphins	29-7	W

(m)—Milwaukee, Wisconsin

Postseason

1976 NFC Divisional Playoff Game
December 18, 1976
Minnesota 35, Washington 20
at Bloomington, Minnesota

Washington	3	0	3	14	—	20
Minnesota	14	7	14	0	—	35

1976 NFC Championship Game
December 26, 1976
Minnesota 24, Los Angeles Rams 13
at Bloomington, Minnesota

L.A. Rams	0	0	13	0	—	13
Minnesota	7	3	7	7	—	24

Super Bowl XI

Oakland 32, Minnesota 14
January 9, 1977, Rose Bowl, Pasadena, California
Attendance: 103,438

The attack-and-destroy Raiders of the mid-1970s came of age in 1976, and won their first Super Bowl.

It was the Vikings' fourth loss in four Super Bowl appearances.

The Raiders' swagger was at work from the beginning—even if their precision lacked something in the opening 15 minutes. When Errol Mann attempted a 29-yard field goal in the first quarter, the ball bounced off the left upright. Late in the first quarter, Minnesota's Fred McNeill blocked Ray Guy's punt at the Oakland 28; it was the first time Guy had a punt blocked in his four-year National Football League career.

McNeill recovered the loose ball at the Raiders' 3. Instead of capitalizing, however, Minnesota's Brent McClanahan fumbled two plays later, and the Raiders were off on a 90-yard drive that led to their first score, a 24-yard field goal by Mann.

After the Vikings punted, wide receiver Fred Biletnikoff's reception across the middle got the Raiders to the Vikings' 1, the first of Biletnikoff's 4 receptions for 79 yards (he was named the game's most valuable player). Stabler's 1-yard touchdown pass to tight end Dave Casper completed the Raiders' march of 64 yards in 10 plays. Another Raiders' touchdown three-and-a-half minutes later made it 16-0 at halftime.

Midway through the fourth quarter, the Raiders completed a 54-yard drive, 48 of them on a pass from Stabler to Biletnikoff. Banaszak ran for a touchdown from the 2, and it was 26-7 with 7:39 to play.

The Raiders set a Super Bowl record with 429 total yards. Running back Clarence Davis gained 137 yards on the ground. The "left-handed" style of the Raiders confused the Vikings all day, with left tackle Art Shell and left guard Gene Upshaw clearing paths for Davis, Banaszak, and fullback Mark van Eeghen (18 carries, 73 yards), and lefty quarterback Stabler completing passes to Biletnikoff, Casper, Cliff Branch, and running back Carl Garrett.

The Vikings failed to score until late in the third quarter, when they drove 68 yards and scored on Fran Tarkenton's 8-yard pass to Sammy White.

In the fourth quarter, Tarkenton twice drove the Vikings into Raiders' territory but was intercepted—first by Willie Hall, whose interception at the 30 began a drive that ended with Banaszak's 2-yard touchdown run. Later, from the Oakland 28, Tarkenton attempted to hit White near the left sideline. Cornerback Willie Brown intercepted and returned it 75 yards for a touchdown (a Super Bowl record) and a 32-7 margin.

Tarkenton completed 17 of 35 passes for 205 yards, and his backup, Bob Lee, threw a 13-yard touchdown pass to Stu Voigt for the final points.

Oakland (AFC)	**0**	**16**	**3**	**13**	**—**	**32**
Minnesota (NFC)	**0**	**0**	**7**	**7**	**—**	**14**

Oak—FG Mann 24
Oak—Casper 1 pass from Stabler (Mann kick)
Oak—Banaszak 1 run (kick failed)
Oak—FG Mann 40
Minn—S. White 8 pass from Tarkenton (Cox kick)
Oak—Banaszak 2 run (Mann kick)
Oak—Brown 75 interception return (kick failed)
Minn—Voigt 13 pass from Lee (Cox kick)

TEAM STATISTICS	**OAK**	**MINN**
First Downs	21	20
Rushing	13	2
Passing	8	15
Penalty	0	3
Total Yardage	429	353
Net rushing yardage	266	71
Net passing yardage	163	282
Passes att.-comp.-had int.	19-12-0	44-24-2

RUSHING
Oakland—Davis 16 for 137; van Eeghen 18 for 73; Garrett 4 for 19; Banaszak 10 for 19, 2 TDs; Ginn 2 for 9; Rae 2 for 9.
Minnesota—Foreman 17 for 44; Johnson 2 for 9; S. White 1 for 7; Lee 1 for 4; Miller 2 for 4; McClanahan 3 for 3.
PASSING
Oakland—Stabler 12 of 19 for 180, 1 TD.
Minnesota—Tarkenton 17 of 35 for 205, 1 TD, 2 int.; Lee 7 of 9 for 81, 1 TD.
RECEIVING
Oakland—Biletnikoff 4 for 79; Casper 4 for 70, 1 TD; Branch 3 for 20; Garrett 1 for 11.
Minnesota—S. White 5 for 77, 1 TD; Foreman 5 for 62; Voigt 4 for 49, 1 TD; Miller 4 for 19; Rashad 3 for 53; Johnson 3 for 26.

1976 Team Rosters

Oakland
Butch Atkinson*
Pete Banaszak*
Warren Bankston*
Rodrigo Barnes*
Fred Biletnikoff*
Greg Blankenship
Rik Bonness*
Morris Bradshaw*
Cliff Branch*
Willie Brown*
George Buehler*
Dave Casper*
Neal Colzie*
Dave Dalby*
Clarence Davis*
Carl Garrett*
Hubert Ginn*
Ray Guy*
Willie Hall*
Ted Hendricks*
David Humm*
Rick Jennings
Monte Johnson*
Terry Kunz
Ted Kwalick
Henry Lawrence*
Errol Mann*
John Matuszak*
Herb McMath*
Dan Medlin*
Manfred Moore*
Charlie Phillips*
Charles Philyaw*
Mike Rae*
Mike Reinfeldt
Floyd Rice*
Dave Rowe*
Art Shell*
Mike Siani*
Otis Sistrunk*
Ken Stabler*
Fred Steinfort
Steve Sylvester*
Jack Tatum*
Skip Thomas*
Gene Upshaw*
Mark van Eeghen*
John Vella*
Phil Villapiano*

Minnesota
Nate Allen*
Scott Anderson
Autry Beamon*
Bob Berry
Matt Blair*
Bobby Bryant*
Bart Buetow
Neil Clabo*
Fred Cox*
Steve Craig*
Doug Dumler*
Carl Eller*
Chuck Foreman*
Charlie Goodrum*
Bob Grim*
Ron Groce*
Windlan Hall*
Wes Hamilton*
Wally Hilgenberg*
Sammy Johnson*
Mark Kellar
Paul Krause*
Jim Lash
Bob Lee*
Bob Lurtsema
Jim Marshall*
Amos Martin*
Brent McClanahan*
Fred McNeill*
Robert Miller*
Mark Mullaney*
Alan Page*
Ahmad Rashad*
Steve Riley*
Jeff Siemon*
Willie Spencer
Doug Sutherland*
Fran Tarkenton*
Mick Tingelhoff*
Stu Voigt*
Ed White*
James White*
Sammy White*
Leonard Willis*
Roy Winston*
Jeff Wright*
Nate Wright*
Ron Yary*

1977 AFC Champions
Denver Broncos

The Denver defense, known as the Orange Crush, was one of the best in the AFC, and new coach Red Miller beefed up the offense by acquiring quarterback Craig Morton. With Morton throwing bombs to tight end Riley Odoms and wide receiver Haven Moses, plus a defense headed by end Lyle Alzado and linebacker Randy Gradishar, the Broncos clinched their first division title with an AFC-best 12-2 record.

A Christmas Eve crowd of 75,011, the largest audience to that point for a sporting event in Colorado, filled Mile High Stadium as the Orange Crush outplayed Pittsburgh's Steel Curtain 34-21 in the Broncos' first playoff game.

On New Year's Day, Denver hosted the Raiders, the defending Super Bowl champions and the only team to beat the Broncos at Mile High Stadium in 1977. The Broncos held off Oakland to win the AFC title 20-17.

After the Raiders had gone ahead 3-0 on their opening drive, Denver scored on a 74-yard touchdown pass from Morton to Moses. In the third period, Rob Lytle was hit by Jack Tatum at the goal line and lost the ball. Raiders nose tackle Mike McCoy picked it up and began running the other way, but the play had been blown dead. John Keyworth scored for Denver on the next play. The Raiders scored twice in the fourth quarter on touchdown passes from Ken Stabler to Dave Casper, but Bob Swenson's interception led to a Morton-Moses touchdown pass.

Regular Season

Sun	S-18	H	St. Louis Cardinals	7-0	W
Sun	S-25	H	Buffalo Bills	26-6	W
Sun	O-2	A	Seattle Seahawks	24-13	W
Sun	O-9	H	Kansas City Chiefs	23-7	W
Sun	O-16	A	Oakland Raiders	30-7	W
Sun	O-23	A	Cincinnati Bengals	24-13	W
Sun	O-30	H	Oakland Raiders	14-24	L
Sun	N-6	H	Pittsburgh Steelers	21-7	W
Sun	N-13	A	San Diego Chargers	17-14	W
Sun	N-20	A	Kansas City Chiefs	14-7	W
Sun	N-27	H	Baltimore Colts	27-13	W
Sun	D-4	A	Houston Oilers	24-14	W
Sun	D-11	H	San Diego Chargers	17-9	W
Sun	D-18	H	Dallas Cowboys	6-14	L

Postseason

1977 AFC Divisional Playoff Game
December 24, 1977
Denver 34, Pittsburgh 21 at Denver

Pittsburgh	0	14	0	7	—	21
Denver	7	7	7	13	—	34

1977 AFC Championship Game
January 1, 1978
Denver 20, Oakland 17 at Denver

Oakland	3	0	0	14	—	17
Denver	7	0	7	6	—	20

1977 NFC Champions
Dallas Cowboys

The Cowboys won their first eight games, and, after two losses, took their last four to go into the playoffs under a full head of steam.

Dallas's NFC Divisional Playoff Game, against the Chicago Bears, was a 37-7 rout. Dallas dominated from the opening gun as safety Charlie Waters set a divisional playoff record by intercepting 3 passes.

The Cowboys' defensive line held Chicago to 13 yards and no first downs on the Bears' first three possessions while the Dallas offense drove 79 and 74 yards to touchdowns.

In the National Football Conference Championship Game, Dallas held the Minnesota ground game to 66 yards as the Cowboys won 23-6 to earn their fourth Super Bowl appearance.

Defensive end Harvey Martin recovered Robert Miller's fumble at the Minnesota 39 on the third play of the game, and two downs later, Roger Staubach teamed with Golden Richards on a 32-yard touchdown pass.

Thc margin increased to 13 points in the second quarter when the Cowboys scored on running back Robert Newhouse's 5-yard run.

Dallas put the game away midway through the fourth quarter. Manfred Moore fumbled a punt and Dallas tight end Jay Saldi recovered. Five plays later, Tony Dorsett ran 11 yards for a touchdown.

Regular Season

Sun	S-18	A	Minnesota Vikings (OT)	16-10	W
Sun	S-25	H	New York Giants	41-21	W
Sun	O-2	H	Tampa Bay Buccaneers	23-7	W
Sun	O-9	A	St. Louis Cardinals	30-24	W
Sun	O-16	H	Washington Redskins	34-16	W
Sun	O-23	A	Philadelphia Eagles	16-10	W
Sun	O-30	H	Detroit Lions	37-0	W
Sun	N-6	A	New York Giants	24-10	W
Mon	N-14	H N	St. Louis Cardinals	17-24	L
Sun	N-20	A	Pittsburgh Steelers	13-28	L
Sun	N-27	A	Washington Redskins	14-7	W
Sun	D-4	H	Philadelphia Eagles	24-14	W
Mon	D-12	A N	San Francisco 49ers	42-35	W
Sun	D-18	H	Denver Broncos	14-6	W

Postseason

1977 NFC Divisional Playoff Game
December 26, 1977
Dallas 37, Chicago Bears 7 at Irving, Texas

Chicago	0	0	0	7	—	7
Dallas	7	10	17	3	—	37

1977 NFC Championship Game
January 1, 1978
Dallas 23, Minnesota 6 at Irving, Texas

Minnesota	0	6	0	0	—	6
Dallas	6	10	0	7	—	23

Super Bowl XII

Dallas 27, Denver 10
January 15, 1978, Louisiana Superdome, New Orleans, Louisiana
Attendance: 75,583

How dominant was the Cowboys' defense in Super Bowl XII?

- No defensive player had been voted the Super Bowl's most valuable player since Miami Dolphins safety Jake Scott in Super Bowl VII. This time, the Cowboys supplied the voters with a tie: defensive end Harvey Martin and defensive tackle Randy White.
- The Cowboys' defense intercepted 4 passes and recovered 3 fumbles in the first half alone.
- Denver finished with only 156 total yards, and its 35 yards passing were the fewest in Super Bowl history.
- Under the constant, gap-closing pressure of head coach Tom Landry's Flex Defense, Broncos starting quarterback Craig Morton (who formerly quarterbacked Dallas) and Norris Weese, who relieved Morton early in the second half, completed only 8 of 25 pass attempts.

Things went Dallas's way from the start, when the Cowboys' defense set up a first-quarter touchdown with Randy Hughes's interception. Tony Dorsett scored five plays later on a 3-yard run. Two field goals by Efren Herrera made it 13-0 at the half.

Jim Turner kicked a 47-yard field goal for the Broncos, but Dallas took a 20-3 lead when Butch Johnson flew parallel to the ground, stretching out to catch a 45-yard touchdown pass from Roger Staubach. But Denver's Rick Upchurch returned the kickoff 67 yards to set up a touchdown, and the Broncos were within 10 when the third quarter ended.

With less than eight minutes to play, Martin forced Weese's fumble at the Denver 29, and the Cowboys' Aaron Kyle recovered. Dallas running back Robert Newhouse took a handoff and threw a touchdown pass to wide receiver Golden Richards to secure the victory.

Dallas (NFC)	10	3	7	7	—	27
Denver (AFC)	0	0	10	0	—	10

Dall—Dorsett 3 run (Herrera kick)
Dall—FG Herrera 35
Dall—FG Herrera 43
Den—FG Turner 47
Dall—Johnson 45 pass from Staubach (Herrera kick)
Den—Lytle 1 run (Turner kick)
Dall—Richards 29 pass from Newhouse (Herrera kick)

TEAM STATISTICS	DALL	DEN
First Downs	17	11
Rushing	8	8
Passing	8	1
Penalty	1	2
Total Yardage	325	156
Net rushing yardage	143	121
Net passing yardage	182	35
Passes att.-comp.-had int.	28-19-0	25-8-4

RUSHING
Dallas—Dorsett 15 for 66, 1 TD; Newhouse 14 for 55; White 1 for 13; P. Pearson 3 for 11; Staubach 3 for 6; Laidlaw 1 for 1; Johnson 1 for -9.
Denver—Lytle 10 for 35, 1 TD; Armstrong 7 for 27; Weese 3 for 26; Jensen 1 for 16; Keyworth 5 for 9; Perrin 3 for 8.
PASSING
Dallas—Staubach 17 of 25 for 183, 1 TD; Newhouse 1 of 1 for 29, 1 TD; D. White 1 of 2 for 5.
Denver—Morton 4 of 15 for 39, 4 int.; Weese 4 of 10 for 22.
RECEIVING
Dallas—P. Pearson 5 for 37; DuPree 4 for 66; Newhouse 3 for -1; Johnson 2 for 53, 1 TD; Richards 2 for 38, 1 TD; Dorsett 2 for 11; D. Pearson 1 for 13.
Denver—Dolbin 2 for 24; Odoms 2 for 9; Moses 1 for 21; Upchurch 1 for 9; Jensen 1 for 5; Perrin 1 for -7.

1977 Team Rosters

Dallas
Benny Barnes*
Bob Breunig*
Larry Brinson*
Guy Brown*
Larry Cole*
Jim Cooper*
Doug Dennison*
Pat Donovan*
Tony Dorsett*
Billy Joe DuPree*
John Fitzgerald*
Andy Frederick*
Bill Gregory*
Cliff Harris*
Mike Hegman*
Tom Henderson*
Efren Herrera*
Tony Hill*
Randy Hughes*
Bruce Huther*
Butch Johnson*
Too Tall Jones*
Aaron Kyle*
Scott Laidlaw*
Burton Lawless*
D.D. Lewis*
Harvey Martin*
Ralph Neely*
Robert Newhouse*
Drew Pearson*
Preston Pearson*
Jethro Pugh*
Tom Rafferty*
Mel Renfro*
Golden Richards*
Jay Saldi
Herbert Scott*
Dave Stalls*
Roger Staubach*
Mark Washington*
Charlie Waters*
Randy White*
Danny White*
Rayfield Wright*

Denver
Hank Allison*
Lyle Alzado*
Otis Armstrong*
Rich Baska
Billy Bryan
Rubin Carter*
Barney Chavous*
Bucky Dilts*
Jack Dolbin*
Ron Egloff*
Larry Evans*
Steve Foley*
Tom Glassic*
Randy Gradishar*
John Grant*
Paul Howard*
Glenn Hyde*
Bernard Jackson*
Tom Jackson*
Jim Jensen*
Jon Keyworth*
Jim Kiick
Rob Lytle*
Brison Manor*
Bobby Maples*
Andy Maurer*
Claudie Minor*
Mike Montler*
Craig Morton*
Haven Moses*
Rob Nairne*
Riley Odoms*
Chris Pane
Craig Penrose
Lonnie Perrin*
Randy Poltl*
Randy Rich*
Larry Riley
Joe Rizzo*
Steve Schindler
John Schultz*
Paul Smith*
Bob Swenson*
Billy Thompson*
Godwin Turk*
Jim Turner*
Rick Upchurch*
Norris Weese*
Louis Wright*

1978 AFC Champions
Pittsburgh Steelers

The 14-2 Steelers were led by a defense that was aging but still effective. Eight opponents scored 10 or fewer points as the Steelers led the league in fewest points allowed.

On offense, coach Chuck Noll took advantage of the National Football League's new liberalized pass-blocking rules and opened up Pittsburgh's passing attack. Quarterback Terry Bradshaw led the AFC in passing while running back Franco Harris, who, like Bradshaw, would end up in the Pro Football Hall of Fame, rushed for more than 1,000 yards.

The Steelers dominated Denver 33-10 in an AFC Divisional Playoff Game.

Pittsburgh racked up 425 yards of offense, but it was a 34-second span in the fourth quarter that did in the defending AFC champion Broncos. In the final period, Bradshaw completed a 45-yard touchdown pass to John Stallworth, who caught an AFC divisional playoff-record 10 passes.

The first play after the kickoff was fumbled back to the Steelers and Bradshaw found Lynn Swann with a 38-yard touchdown pass.

The AFC Championship Game wasn't even close. Division-rival Houston turned the ball over 9 times in the freezing rain in a 34-5 rout.

Regular Season

Sun	S-3	A	Buffalo Bills	28-17	W
Sun	S-10	H	Seattle Seahawks	21-10	W
Sun	S-17	A	Cincinnati Bengals	28-3	W
Sun	S-24	H	Cleveland Browns (OT)	15-9	W
Sun	O-1	A	New York Jets	28-17	W
Sun	O-8	H	Atlanta Falcons	31-7	W
Sun	O-15	A	Cleveland Browns	34-14	W
Mon	O-23	H N	Houston Oilers	17-24	L
Sun	O-29	H	Kansas City Chiefs	27-24	W
Sun	N-5	H	New Orleans Saints	20-14	W
Sun	N-12	A	Los Angeles Rams	7-10	L
Sun	N-19	H	Cincinnati Bengals	7-6	W
Mon	N-27	A N	San Francisco 49ers	24-7	W
Sun	D-3	A	Houston Oilers	13-3	W
Sat	D-9	H	Baltimore Colts	35-13	W
Sat	D-16	A	Denver Broncos	21-17	W

Postseason

1978 AFC Divisional Playoff Game
December 30, 1978
Pittsburgh 33, Denver 10 at Pittsburgh

Denver	3	7	0	0	—	10
Pittsburgh	6	13	0	14	—	33

1978 AFC Championship Game
January 7, 1979
Pittsburgh 34, Houston 5 at Pittsburgh

Houston	0	3	2	0	—	5
Pittsburgh	14	17	3	0	—	34

1978 NFC Champions
Dallas Cowboys

Inspired by a vicious hit that knocked Roger Staubach out of the game, the Cowboys shut down Atlanta in the second half of the NFC Divisional Playoff Game and came from behind for a 27-20 victory.

Robert Pennywell's hit on Staubach after he had already thrown the ball ended the quarterback's day; it was the beginning of the end of Atlanta's day as well. The Falcons, who had scored on their first four possessions, were stopped cold thereafter. In the third quarter, Danny White took Dallas 54 yards, throwing to tight end Jackie Smith for a touchdown. In the fourth period, Scott Laidlaw's 1-yard touchdown run put Dallas ahead for good.

The Dallas defense came up with 5 second-half turnovers as the Cowboys defeated the Los Angeles Rams 28-0 in the NFC Championship Game. Late in the third quarter of a scoreless defensive struggle, Dallas safety Charlie Waters intercepted Pat Haden twice to set up a pair of touchdowns.

After Harvey Martin recovered a fumble, the Cowboys drove 89 yards in 7 plays, the touchdown coming on Staubach's 11-yard strike to Billy Joe DuPree. The final score came when linebacker Thomas Henderson raced 68 yards with an interception.

Regular Season

Mon	S-4	H N	Baltimore Colts	38-0	W
Sun	S-10	A	New York Giants	34-24	W
Sun	S-17	A	Los Angeles Rams	14-27	L
Sun	S-24	H	St. Louis Cardinals	21-12	W
Mon	O-2	A N	Washington Redskins	5-9	L
Sun	O-8	H	New York Giants	24-3	W
Sun	O-15	A	St. Louis Cardinals (OT)	24-21	W
Sun	O-22	H	Philadelphia Eagles	14-7	W
Thu	O-26	H	Minnesota Vikings	10-21	L
Sun	N-5	A	Miami Dolphins	16-23	L
Sun	N-12	A	Green Bay Packers	42-14	W
Sun	N-19	H	New Orleans Saints	27-7	W
Thu	N-23	H	Washington Redskins	37-10	W
Sun	D-3	H	New England Patriots	17-10	W
Sun	D-10	A	Philadelphia Eagles	31-13	W
Sun	D-17	A	New York Jets	30-7	W

Postseason

1978 NFC Divisional Playoff Game
December 30, 1978
Dallas 27, Atlanta 20 at Irving, Texas

Atlanta	7	13	0	0	—	20
Dallas	10	3	7	7	—	27

1978 NFC Championship Game
January 7, 1979
Dallas 28, Los Angeles Rams 0 at Los Angeles

Dallas	0	0	7	21	—	28
L.A. Rams	0	0	0	0	—	0

Super Bowl XIII

Pittsburgh 35, Dallas 31
January 21, 1979, Orange Bowl, Miami, Florida
Attendance: 79,484

This was more than just the first rematch in Super Bowl history: It restaged what many still consider the most enjoyable and dramatic Super Bowl battle to that point (game X).

Opportunity—recognizing it and capitalizing on it—was the theme. Failure to embrace it would play a hand, as well.

Dallas had its chances. The Cowboys took a 14-7 lead in the second quarter when linebacker Mike Hegman simply took the ball away from Steelers quarterback Terry Bradshaw and ran 37 yards to score. But Bradshaw countered immediately with a 75-yard touchdown strike to John Stallworth.

In the third quarter, trailing 21-14, Dallas marched from its 42 to the Steelers' 10. On third-and-3, Cowboys quarterback Roger Staubach saw tight end Jackie Smith alone in the end zone. Smith slipped and fell reaching for Staubach's pass and couldn't hold it. Rafael Septien kicked a 27-yard field goal.

Pittsburgh scored 2 touchdowns early in the fourth quarter—a 22-yard run by Franco Harris and an 18-yard pass from Bradshaw to Swann. Harris's score followed a pass-interference call against Dallas cornerback Benny Barnes, who was covering Swann. The mistake cost the Cowboys 33 yards.

Frantically, albeit courageously, Dallas scored touchdowns with 2:27 and 22 seconds to play, on passes from Staubach to tight end Billy Joe DuPree and Butch Johnson, but Pittsburgh held on to win 35-31.

With the victory, the Steelers became the first team to win three Super Bowls. The two teams set a Super Bowl record for points scored.

Pittsburgh (AFC)	7	14	0	14	—	35
Dallas (NFC)	7	7	3	14	—	31

Pitt—Stallworth 28 pass from Bradshaw (Gerela kick)
Dall—Hill 39 pass from Staubach (Septien kick)
Dall—Hegman 37 fumble recovery return (Septien kick)
Pitt—Stallworth 75 pass from Bradshaw (Gerela kick)
Pitt—Bleier 7 pass from Bradshaw (Gerela kick)
Dall—FG Septien 27
Pitt—Harris 22 run (Gerela kick)
Pitt—Swann 18 pass from Bradshaw (Gerela kick)
Dall—DuPree 7 pass from Staubach (Septien kick)
Dall—B. Johnson 4 pass from Staubach (Septien kick)

TEAM STATISTICS	PITT	DALL
First Downs	19	20
Rushing	2	6
Passing	15	13
Penalty	2	1
Total Yardage	357	330
Net rushing yardage	66	154
Net passing yardage	291	176
Passes att.-comp.-had int.	30-17-1	30-17-1

RUSHING
Pittsburgh—Harris 20 for 68, 1 TD; Bleier 2 for 3; Bradshaw 2 for -5.
Dallas—Dorsett 16 for 96; Staubach 4 for 37; Laidlaw 3 for 12; P. Pearson 1 for 6; Newhouse 8 for 3.
PASSING
Pittsburgh—Bradshaw 17 of 30 for 318, 4 TDs, 1 int.
Dallas—Staubach 17 of 30 for 228, 3 TDs, 1 int.
RECEIVING
Pittsburgh—Swann 7 for 124, 1 TD; Stallworth 3 for 115, 2 TDs; Grossman 3 for 29; Bell 2 for 21; Harris 1 for 22; Bleier 1 for 7, 1 TD.
Dallas—Dorsett 5 for 44; D. Pearson 4 for 73; Hill 2 for 49, 1 TD; Johnson 2 for 30, 1 TD; DuPree 2 for 17, 1 TD; P. Pearson 2 for 15.

1978 Team Rosters

Pittsburgh
Fred Anderson*
Larry Anderson*
John Banaszak*
Tom Beasley*
Theo Bell*
Rocky Bleier*
Mel Blount*
Terry Bradshaw*
Larry Brown*
Robin Cole*
Craig Colquitt*
Steve Courson*
Bennie Cunningham
Sam Davis*
Jack Deloplaine*
Tony Dungy*
Gary Dunn*
Steve Furness*
Wentford Gaines
Roy Gerela*
Joe Greene*
L.C. Greenwood*
Randy Grossman*
Jack Ham*
Franco Harris*
Ron Johnson*
Jon Kolb*
Mike Kruczek
Jack Lambert*
Jim Mandich*
Alvin Maxson
Rick Moser*
Gerry Mullins*
Ray Oldham*
Ted Petersen*
Ray Pinney*
Randy Reutershan
Donnie Shell*
Jim Smith*
John Stallworth*
Lynn Swann*
Nat Terry
Sidney Thornton*
Loren Toews*
Mike Wagner*
Mike Webster*
Dwight White*
Dennis Winston*

Dallas
Benny Barnes*
Larry Bethea*
Alois Blackwell*
Bob Breunig*
Larry Brinson*
Guy Brown*
Glenn Carano
Larry Cole*
Jim Cooper*
Doug Dennison
Pat Donovan*
Tony Dorsett*
Billy Joe DuPree*
John Fitzgerald*
Andy Frederick*
Cliff Harris*
Mike Hegman*
Tom Henderson*
Tony Hill*
Randy Hughes*
Bruce Huther*
Butch Johnson*
Too Tall Jones*
Aaron Kyle*
Scott Laidlaw*
Burton Lawless*
D.D. Lewis*
Harvey Martin*
Robert Newhouse*
Drew Pearson*
Preston Pearson*
Jethro Pugh
Tom Rafferty*
Tom Randall*
Golden Richards
Jay Saldi
Herbert Scott*
Rafael Septien*
Jackie Smith*
Dave Stalls*
Roger Staubach*
Robert Steele*
Dennis Thurman*
Mark Washington
Charlie Waters*
Randy White*
Danny White*
Rayfield Wright*

1979 AFC Champions Pittsburgh Steelers

Pittsburgh claimed its sixth consecutive division title in 1979 and led the NFL in scoring with 416 points. Franco Harris produced his seventh 1,000-yard season to tie Jim Brown's NFL record.

In the divisional playoffs, Pittsburgh held Miami to 25 rushing yards in a 34-14 victory. Touchdowns on Pittsburgh's first three possessions—on a 1-yard run by Sidney Thorton and passes from Terry Bradshaw to John Stallworth and Lynn Swann, respectively—gave the Steelers a commanding lead.

For the second straight year, Pittsburgh met Houston in the AFC Championship Game; and for the second straight year, the Steelers won, but the 27-13 victory over the Oilers didn't come easily.

Houston led 7-0 after rookie safety Vernon Perry scored on a 75-yard interception return, but Bradshaw responded with touchdown passes to Bennie Cunningham and Stallworth for a 17-10 halftime lead.

The key play of the game came at the end of the third quarter when Houston quarterback Dan Pastorini passed to Mike Renfro at the back of the end zone. The officials ruled the pass incomplete, saying Renfro didn't have possession. Houston had to settle for a field goal and Pittsburgh put the game away with 10 points in the final quarter for their fourth AFC title in six seasons.

Regular Season

Mon	S-3	A N	New England Patriots (OT)	16-13	W
Sun	S-9	H	Houston Oilers	38-7	W
Sun	S-16	A	St. Louis Cardinals	24-21	W
Sun	S-23	H	Baltimore Colts	17-13	W
Sun	S-30	A	Philadelphia Eagles	14-17	L
Sun	O-7	A	Cleveland Browns	51-35	W
Sun	O-14	A	Cincinnati Bengals	10-34	L
Mon	O-22	H N	Denver Broncos	42-7	W
Sun	O-28	H	Dallas Cowboys	14-3	W
Sun	N-4	H	Washington Redskins	38-7	W
Sun	N-11	A	Kansas City Chiefs	30-3	W
Sun	N-18	A	San Diego Chargers	7-35	L
Sun	N-25	H	Cleveland Browns (OT)	33-30	W
Sun	D-2	H	Cincinnati Bengals	37-17	W
Mon	D-10	A N	Houston Oilers	17-20	L
Sun	D-16	H	Buffalo Bills	28-0	W

Postseason

1979 AFC Divisional Playoff Game
December 30, 1979
Pittsburgh 34, Miami 14 at Pittsburgh

Miami	0	0	7	7	—	14
Pittsburgh	20	0	7	7	—	34

1979 AFC Championship Game
January 6, 1980
Pittsburgh 27, Houston 13 at Pittsburgh

Houston	7	3	0	3	—	17
Pittsburgh	3	14	0	10	—	27

1979 NFC Champions Los Angeles Rams

In 1979, the Los Angeles Rams lost quarterback Pat Haden for six games and struggled to a 9-7 record but still won their record seventh consecutive division title.

Vince Ferragamo, filling in for Haden, passed for 3 touchdowns, the last covering 50 yards with 2:06 to play to spark a 21-19 victory over Dallas in an NFC Divisional Playoff Game. It was Roger Staubach's last game.

The Cowboys scored first when Ferragamo slipped in the end zone for a safety, but he later found Wendell Tyler with a 32-yard touchdown pass. Shortly before halftime, Ferragamo moved the Rams 70 yards on 4 plays, throwing a 43-yard pass to Ron Smith, who made an acrobatic catch in the end zone with three seconds left. Trailing 19-14 in the fourth quarter, Ferragamo found Billy Waddy over the middle and he outlegged several Dallas defenders for the winning touchdown.

The Rams qualified for their first Super Bowl by defeating Tampa Bay 9-0 in the first championship game in which no touchdowns were scored. The Rams' defense dominated the Buccaneers, holding them without a first down until midway through the second period, and allowing Tampa Bay quarterbacks to complete only 4 of 26 passes for 54 yards. Behind the running of Cullen Bryant and Wendell Tyler, the Rams gained 369 total yards and scored all their points on 3 field goals by Frank Corral.

Regular Season

Sun	S-2	H	Oakland Raiders	17-24	L
Thu	S-6	N A	Denver Broncos	13-9	W
Sun	S-16	H	San Francisco 49ers	27-24	W
Sun	S-23	A	Tampa Bay Buccaneers	6-21	L
Sun	S-30	H	St. Louis Cardinals	21-0	W
Sun	O-7	A	New Orleans Saints	35-17	W
Sun	O-14	A	Dallas Cowboys	6-30	L
Sun	O-21	H	San Diego Chargers	16-40	L
Sun	O-28	H	New York Giants	14-20	L
Sun	N-4	A	Seattle Seahawks	24-0	W
Sun	N-11	A	Chicago Bears	23-27	L
Mon	N-19	H N	Atlanta Falcons	20-14	W
Sun	N-25	A	San Francisco 49ers	26-20	W
Sun	D-2	H	Minnesota Vikings (OT)	27-21	W
Sun	D-9	A	Atlanta Falcons	34-13	W
Sun	D-16	H	New Orleans Saints	14-29	L

Postseason

1979 NFC Divisional Playoff Game
December 30, 1979
Los Angeles Rams 21, Dallas 19 at Irving, Texas

L.A. Rams	0	14	0	7	—	21
Dallas	2	3	7	7	—	19

1979 NFC Championship Game
January 6, 1980
Los Angeles Rams 9, Tampa Bay 0 at Tampa Bay

L.A. Rams	0	6	0	3	—	9
Tampa Bay	0	0	0	0	—	0

Super Bowl XIV

Pittsburgh 31, Los Angeles 19
January 20, 1980, Rose Bowl, Pasadena, California
Attendance: 103,985

There was a moment of self-sacrifice when Rams defensive end Jack Youngblood, announced he would play in his team's first Super Bowl despite a fractured leg.

There was a rush of "What if?" euphoria as the underdog Rams took a 19-17 lead into the fourth quarter.

And there was cold reality: Pittsburgh, with as much patience as talent, struck quickly for 2 touchdowns in the fourth quarter, and it was over. The Steelers Super Bowl victory was their fourth in the last six seasons.

The game's signature image is of Steelers wide receiver John Stallworth at the Rams' 32, looking back over his head for a lofty Terry Bradshaw pass, catching it just over the outstretched arms of cornerback Rod Perry, and continuing into the end zone for a 73-yard touchdown.

The Steelers had taken the lead and then surrendered it in the third quarter. Bradshaw hit Lynn Swann over the middle for a 47-yard score. The Rams came back with a surprise—a 24-yard halfback pass from Lawrence McCutcheon to Ron Smith that made it 19-17 before Bradshaw-to-Stallworth put Pittsburgh ahead for good.

The Rams intercepted Bradshaw 3 times, but it was the Steelers' lone interception—by linebacker Jack Lambert—that punctuated the ending. With the score 24-19 and Los Angeles driving, Lambert intercepted a pass from Rams quarterback Vince Ferragamo at the Steelers' 14.

For the second year in a row, Bradshaw was named the game's most valuable player after passing for 309 yards and 2 touchdowns.

Los Angeles (NFC)	7	6	6	0	—	19
Pittsburgh (AFC)	3	7	7	14	—	31

Pitt—FG Bahr 41
LA —Bryant 1 run (Corral kick)
Pitt—Harris 1 run (Bahr kick)
LA —FG Corral 31
LA —FG Corral 45
Pitt—Swann 47 pass from Bradshaw (Bahr kick)
LA —Smith 24 pass from McCutcheon (kick failed)
Pitt—Stallworth 73 pass from Bradshaw (Bahr kick)
Pitt—Harris 1 run (Bahr kick)

TEAM STATISTICS	**RAMS**	**PITT**
First Downs	16	19
Rushing	6	8
Passing	9	10
Penalty	1	1
Total Yardage	301	393
Net rushing yardage	107	84
Net passing yardage	194	309
Passes att.-comp.-had int.	26-16-1	21-14-3

RUSHING
LA Rams—Tyler 17 for 60; Bryant 6 for 30, 1 TD; McCutcheon 5 for 10; Ferragamo 1 for 7.
Pittsburgh—Harris 20 for 46, 2 TDs; Bleier 10 for 25; Bradshaw 3 for 9; Thornton 4 for 4.

PASSING
LA Rams—Ferragamo 15 of 25 for 212, 1 int.; McCutcheon 1 of 1 for 24, 1 TD.
Pittsburgh—Bradshaw 14 of 21 for 309, 2 TDs, 3 int.

RECEIVING
LA Rams—Waddy 3 for 75; Bryant 3 for 21; Tyler 3 for 20; Dennard 2 for 32; Nelson 2 for 20; D. Hill 1 for 28; Smith 1 for 24, 1 TD; McCutcheon 1 for 16.
Pittsburgh—Swann 5 for 79, 1 TD; Stallworth 3 for 121, 1 TD; Harris 3 for 66; Cunningham 2 for 21; Thornton 1 for 22.

1979 Team Rosters

Pittsburgh
Anthony Anderson*
Larry Anderson*
Matt Bahr*
John Banaszak*
Tom Beasley*
Theo Bell*
Rocky Bleier*
Mel Blount*
Terry Bradshaw*
Larry Brown*
Robin Cole*
Craig Colquitt*
Steve Courson*
Bennie Cunningham*
Sam Davis*
Jack Deloplaine
Thom Dornbrook*
Gary Dunn*
Steve Furness*
Tom Graves*
Joe Greene*
L.C. Greenwood*
Randy Grossman*
Jack Ham
Franco Harris*
Greg Hawthorne*
Ron Johnson*
Jon Kolb*
Mike Kruczek
Jack Lambert*
Rick Moser*
Gerry Mullins*
Ted Petersen*
Donnie Shell*
Jim Smith*
John Stallworth*
Lynn Swann*
J.T. Thomas*
Sidney Thornton*
Loren Toews*
Zack Valentine*
Mike Wagner
Mike Webster*
Dwight White*
Dennis Winston*
Dwayne Woodruff*

LA Rams
George Andrews*
Bill Bain*
Larry Brooks*
Eddie Brown*
Bob Brudzinski*
Cullen Bryant*
Ken Clark*
Frank Corral*
Nolan Cromwell*
Preston Dennard*
Reggie Doss*
Fred Dryer*
Bill Dunstan
Ken Ellis*
Dave Elmendorf*
Mike Fanning*
Vince Ferragamo*
Doug France*
Gordon Gravelle*
Pat Haden
Dennis Harrah*
Joe Harris*
Drew Hill*
Eddie Hill*
Kent Hill*
Ron Jessie
Jim Jodat*
Sidney Justin
Bob Lee
Lawrence McCutcheon*
Kevin McLain
Willie Miller
Terry Nelson*
Ricky Odom
Dwayne O'Steen*
Elvis Peacock
Rod Perry*
Jack Reynolds*
Jeff Rutledge
Dan Ryczek*
Rich Saul*
Jeff Severson
Jackie Slater*
Doug Smith
Ron Smith*
Ivory Sully*
Pat Thomas*
Wendell Tyler*
Billy Waddy*
Jackie Wallace*
Greg Westbrooks*
Jerry Wilkinson*
John Williams
Charle Young*
Jack Youngblood*
Jim Youngblood*

1980 AFC Champions Oakland Raiders

Tom Flores joined John Rauch and John Madden as coaches who won championships with the Raiders. Flores, however, was the first coach to navigate a team through three rounds of playoffs to win the AFC title.

In the AFC Wild Card Game, the Oilers had more yards, more first downs, and more time of possession, but the Raiders came away with a 27-7 win in Oakland thanks to 7 sacks of former Raiders quarterback Ken Stabler. Lester Hayes intercepted 2 passes, including a 20-yard return for a touchdown, and Jim Plunkett passed for 2 touchdowns.

It was safety Mike Davis's turn to save the day in an AFC Divisional Playoff Game. Davis intercepted a Brian Sipe pass in the end zone with 41 seconds left to preserve Oakland's 14-12 win over the Browns. Mark van Eeghen battled through heavy winds and a temperature of 1 degree to score 2 touchdowns.

For the AFC Championship Game, Plunkett threw 3 touchdowns in the first quarter as Oakland upended the Chargers 34-27. The Raiders built a 28-7 lead and withstood San Diego's second-half charge to earn a trip to their third Super Bowl.

Regular Season

Sun	S-7	A	Kansas City Chiefs	27-14	W
Sun	S-14	A	San Diego Chargers (OT)	24-30	L
Sun	S-21	H	Washington Redskins	24-21	W
Sun	S-28	A	Buffalo Bills	7-24	L
Sun	O-5	H	Kansas City Chiefs	17-31	L
Sun	O-12	H	San Diego Chargers	38-24	W
Mon	O-20	A N	Pittsburgh Steelers	45-34	W
Sun	O-26	H	Seattle Seahawks	33-14	W
Sun	N-2	H	Miami Dolphins	16-10	W
Sun	N-9	H	Cincinnati Bengals	28-17	W
Mon	N-17	A N	Seattle Seahawks	19-17	W
Sun	N-23	A	Philadelphia Eagles	7-10	L
Mon	D-1	H N	Denver Broncos	9-3	W
Sun	D-7	H	Dallas Cowboys	13-19	L
Sun	D-14	A	Denver Broncos	24-21	W
Sun	D-21	A	New York Giants	33-17	W

Postseason

1980 AFC Wild Card Game

December 28, 1980

Oakland 27, Houston 7 at Oakland

Houston	7	0	0	0	—	7
Oakland	3	7	0	17	—	27

1980 AFC Divisional Playoff Game

January 4, 1981

Oakland 14, Cleveland 12 at Cleveland

Oakland	0	7	0	7	—	14
Cleveland	0	6	6	0	—	12

1980 AFC Championship Game

January 11, 1981

Oakland 34, San Diego 27 at San Diego

Oakland	21	7	3	3	—	34
San Diego	7	7	10	3	—	27

1980 NFC Champions Philadelphia Eagles

Quarterback Ron Jaworski led the Eagles to a 12-4 record in 1980 and was named NFL player of the year by the Maxwell Football Club.

In an NFC Divisional Playoff Game, the Vikings turned the ball over 8 times in a span of 22 minutes. Philadelphia, which once trailed 14-0, wound up with a 31-16 victory. The Eagles tied the game on the opening drive of the third quarter. After the Vikings regained the lead on a safety, Wilbert Montgomery scored his second touchdown for the Eagles. Two fumbles—Minnesota's first in eight weeks—set up 10 points, and each of the Vikings' final 4 possessions ended with an interception.

Gusting winds helped stall the passing game in the NFC Championship Game, but Montgomery pounded for 194 yards to lead the Eagles into their first Super Bowl with a 20-7 victory over Dallas. Montgomery finished the Eagles' opening drive with a 42-yard touchdown after only 2:11 of play. Dallas tied the game in the second period, but the Cowboys didn't move beyond the Eagles' 39 again. In the second half, a pair of Dallas fumbles led to the final 10 points of the day.

Regular Season

Sun	S-7	H	Denver Broncos	27-6	W
Sun	S-14	A	Minnesota Vikings	42-7	W
Mon	S-22	H N	New York Giants	35-3	W
Sun	S-28	A	St. Louis Cardinals	14-24	L
Sun	O-5	H	Washington Redskins	24-14	W
Sun	O-12	A	New York Giants	31-16	W
Sun	O-19	H	Dallas Cowboys	17-10	W
Sun	O-26	H	Chicago Bears	17-14	W
Sun	N-2	A	Seattle Seahawks	27-20	W
Sun	N-9	A	New Orleans Saints	34-21	W
Sun	N-16	A	Washington Redskins	24-0	W
Sun	N-23	H	Oakland Raiders	10-7	W
Sun	N-30	A	San Diego Chargers	21-22	L
Sun	D-7	H	Atlanta Falcons	17-20	L
Sun	D-14	H	St. Louis Cardinals	17-3	W
Sun	D-21	A	Dallas Cowboys	27-35	L

Postseason

1980 NFC Divisional Playoff Game

January 3, 1981

Philadelphia 31, Minnesota 16 at Philadelphia

Minnesota	7	7	2	0	—	16
Philadelphia	0	7	14	10	—	31

1980 NFC Championship Game

January 11, 1981

Philadelphia 20, Dallas 7 at Philadelphia

Dallas	0	7	0	0	—	7
Philadelphia	7	0	10	3	—	20

Super Bowl XV

Oakland 27, Philadelphia 10
January 25, 1981, Louisiana Superdome, New Orleans, Louisiana
Attendance: 76,135

The lasting image from this Super Bowl is that of Raiders running back Kenny King dashing down the left sideline with a pass from Jim Plunkett for the Super Bowl-record 80-yard touchdown that gave the Raiders a 14-0 lead in the first quarter.

It came on third-and-4, two plays after Max Runager's punt backed the Raiders to their 14-yard line.

The pass to King was the second of 3 touchdown passes for Plunkett, who was voted the game's most valuable player. The 10-year veteran had been picked up by owner Al Davis in 1978. Said Raiders head coach Tom Flores: "All Jim needed was for someone to believe in him."

Plunkett's first strike in Super Bowl XV, a 2-yard touchdown pass to Cliff Branch, came on the seventh play of a short drive. Linebacker Rod Martin set it up when he intercepted Ron Jaworski's pass at the Philadelphia 47 and returned it 17 yards.

The Eagles managed a field goal as the second quarter began, as Tony Franklin's 30-yard kick finished a drive inside the Raiders' 20. Philadelphia put together an even deeper drive later in the half, moving 62 yards to the 11 before Franklin's attempt from 28 yards was blocked by linebacker Ted Hendricks.

The Raiders' third touchdown drive, a 76-yard dash in 5 plays at the outset of the third quarter, took only 2 minutes 36 seconds. Plunkett completed passes to King (13 yards) and Bob Chandler (32 yards) before hitting Branch for 29 yards and the score.

Martin intercepted his second pass of the game on the Eagles' next drive. The Raiders turned it into a 46-yard field goal by Chris Bahr. The Eagles took 12 plays to go 88 yards for their only touchdown of the day. Jaworski threw 8 yards to tight end Keith Krepfle for the score. Then the Raiders went on a clock-killing drive, moving 72 yards before Bahr kicked a 35-yard field goal to finish the scoring.

Oakland (AFC)	**14**	**0**	**10**	**3**	**—**	**27**
Philadelphia (NFC)	**0**	**3**	**0**	**7**	**—**	**10**

Oak—Branch 2 pass from Plunkett (Bahr kick)
Oak—King 80 pass from Plunkett (Bahr kick)
Phil—FG Franklin 30
Oak—Branch 29 pass from Plunkett (Bahr kick)
Oak—FG Bahr 46
Phil—Krepfle 8 pass from Jaworski (Franklin kick)
Oak—FG Bahr 35

TEAM STATISTICS	OAK	PHIL
First Downs	17	19
Rushing	6	3
Passing	10	14
Penalty	1	2
Total Yardage	377	360
Net rushing yardage	117	69
Net passing yardage	260	291
Passes att.-comp.-had int.	21-13-0	38-18-3

RUSHING
Oakland—van Eeghen 18 for 75; King 6 for 18; Jensen 4 for 17; Plunkett 3 for 9; Whittington 3 for -2.
Philadelphia—Montgomery 16 for 44; Harris 7 for 14; Giammona 1 for 7; Harrington 1 for 4; Jaworski 1 for 0.
PASSING
Oakland—Plunkett 13 of 21 for 261, 3 TDs.
Philadelphia—Jaworski 18 of 38 for 291, 1 TD, 3 int.
RECEIVING
Oakland—Branch 5 for 67, 2 TDs; Chandler 4 for 77; King 2 for 93, 1 TD; Chester 2 for 24.
Philadelphia—Montgomery 6 for 91; Carmichael 5 for 83; Smith 2 for 59; Krepfle 2 for 16, 1 TD; Spagnola 1 for 22; Parker 1 for 19; Harris 1 for 1.

1980 Team Rosters

Oakland
Chris Bahr*
Jeff Barnes*
Morris Bradshaw*
Cliff Branch*
Dave Browning*
Joe Campbell*
Dave Casper
Mario Celotto*
Bob Chandler*
Raymond Chester*
Todd Christensen*
Dave Dalby*
Bruce Davis*
Mike Davis*
Ray Guy*
Cedrick Hardman*
Dwight Harrison
Lester Hayes*
Ted Hendricks*
I.M. Hipp
Monte Jackson*
Derrick Jensen*
Willie Jones*
Kenny King*
Reggie Kinlaw*
Henry Lawrence*
Alva Liles
Rod Martin*
Rich Martini*
Mickey Marvin*
Lindsey Mason*
Ira Matthews*
John Matuszak*
Randy McClanahan*
Odis McKinney*
Matt Millen*
Keith Moody*
Bob Nelson*
Dwayne O'Steen*
Burgess Owens*
Dan Pastorini
Dave Pear*
Jim Plunkett*
Derrick Ramsey*
Art Shell*
Mike Spivey
Steve Sylvester*
Gene Upshaw*
Mark van Eeghen*
Greg Westbrooks
Art Whittington*
Marc Wilson

Philadelphia
Ron Baker*
Bill Bergey*
Richard Blackmore*
Luther Blue
Thomas Brown*
John Bunting*
Billy Campfield*
Harold Carmichael*
Al Chesley*
Ken Clarke*
Jim Culbreath
Zachary Dixon
Ken Dunek
Herman Edwards*
Scott Fitzkee
Tony Franklin*
Louie Giammona*
Lewis Gilbert
Carl Hairston*
Perry Harrington*
Leroy Harris*
Dennis Harrison*
Zac Henderson*
Wally Henry*
Mike Hogan
Claude Humphrey*
Ron Jaworski*
Charlie Johnson*
Steve Kenney*
Keith Krepfle*
Frank LeMaster*
Randy Logan*
Wilbert Montgomery*
Guy Morriss*
Rod Parker*
Woody Peoples*
Petey Perot*
Ray Phillips*
Joe Pisarcik
Jerry Robinson*
Max Runager*
John Sciarra*
Jerry Sisemore*
Mark Slater*
Charlie Smith*
John Spagnola*
Bob Torrey
Steve Wagner
Stan Walters*
Reggie Wilkes*
Brenard Wilson*
Roynell Young*

1981 AFC Champions Cincinnati Bengals

The 1981 season saw the emergence of the new-look Bengals. The team unveiled flashy new uniforms that included tiger stripes on its helmets, jerseys, and pants. The offense was rebuilt with young draft choices such as tackle Anthony Munoz of USC and receiver Cris Collinsworth of Florida. Coach Forrest Gregg, the Packers' Hall of Fame tackle during the Green Bay glory years, instilled a Lombardi-like discipline and approach to the game. Ken Anderson posted a league-high 98.4 passer rating.

Anderson threw the game-winning touchdown pass to Collinsworth for a 28-21 win over Buffalo in an AFC Divisional Playoff Game. The Bills had the ball at the Cincinnati 21 in the final three minutes of the game when Joe Ferguson completed a fourth-down pass to Lou Piccone for a first down. But Buffalo was penalized for delay of game, and Ferguson's pass on the next snap was incomplete. The Bengals ran out the clock for their first-ever playoff victory.

A temperature of 9 degrees below zero and a 35-mile-per-hour wind created a wind-chill factor of minus 59 in the AFC Championship Game at Riverfront Stadium. Anderson passed for 2 touchdowns and the defense, not to mention the weather, grounded San Diego's potent passing attack in Cincinnati's 27-7 victory.

Regular Season

Sun	S-6	H	Seattle Seahawks	27-21	W
Sun	S-13	A	New York Jets	31-30	W
Sun	S-20	H	Cleveland Browns	17-20	L
Sun	S-27	H	Buffalo Bills (OT)	27-24	W
Sun	O-4	A	Houston Oilers	10-17	L
Sun	O-11	A	Baltimore Colts	41-19	W
Sun	O-18	H	Pittsburgh Steelers	34-7	W
Sun	O-25	A	New Orleans Saints	7-17	L
Sun	N-1	H	Houston Oilers	34-21	W
Sun	N-8	A	San Diego Chargers	40-17	W
Sun	N-15	H	Los Angeles Rams	24-10	W
Sun	N-22	H	Denver Broncos	38-21	W
Sun	N-29	A	Cleveland Browns	41-21	W
Sun	D-6	H	San Francisco 49ers	3-21	L
Sun	D-13	A	Pittsburgh Steelers	17-10	W
Sun	D-20	A	Atlanta Falcons	30-28	W

Postseason

1981 AFC Divisional Playoff Game
January 3, 1982
Cincinnati 28, Buffalo 21 at Cincinnati

Buffalo	0	7	7	7	—	21
Cincinnati	14	0	7	7	—	28

1981 AFC Championship Game
January 10, 1982
Cincinnati 27, San Diego 7 at Cincinnati

San Diego	0	7	0	0	—	7
Pittsburgh	10	7	3	7	—	27

1981 NFC Champions San Francisco 49ers

Bill Walsh led the 49ers to their first Western Division title since 1972. Despite Scott Brunner's 3 touchdown passes for the New York Giants in a divisional playoff game, the 49ers won 38-24.

Ronnie Lott had 2 interceptions, including a 20-yard interception return for a touchdown. Joe Montana teamed with Freddie Solomon on a 58-yard touchdown pass. Following Keena Turner's fumble recovery, Ricky Patton scored on a 25-yard sweep to increase the lead to 24-7.

The 49ers won a championship game for the first time as Dwight Clark made "The Catch," a leaping grab at the back of the end zone with 51 seconds remaining. Starting from San Francisco's 11 with only 4:54 remaining, Montana led the 49ers 89 yards in 13 plays to the Dallas 6; on third down, he threw a high pass that the 6-foot 4-inch Clark just managed to pull in. Ray Wersching's extra point provided the 28-27 win.

The Cowboys led 10-7 after one quarter. Montana's second touchdown pass of the day (20 yards to Clark) put San Francisco back in front, but Tony Dorsett scored to give the Cowboys the lead at the half.

A field goal and a touchdown pass from Danny White to tight end Doug Cosbie moved Dallas briefly in front of San Francisco 27-21.

Regular Season

Sun	S-6	A	Detroit Lions	17-24	L
Sun	S-13	H	Chicago Bears	28-17	W
Sun	S-20	A	Atlanta Falcons	17-34	L
Sun	S-27	H	New Orleans Saints	21-14	W
Sun	O-4	A	Washington Redskins	30-17	W
Sun	O-11	H	Dallas Cowboys	45-14	W
Sun	O-18	A (m)	Green Bay Packers	13-3	W
Sun	O-25	H	Los Angeles Rams	20-17	W
Sun	N-1	A	Pittsburgh Steelers	17-14	W
Sun	N-8	H	Atlanta Falcons	17-14	W
Sun	N-15	H	Cleveland Browns	12-15	L
Sun	N-22	A	Los Angeles Rams	33-31	W
Sun	N-29	H	New York Giants	17-10	W
Sun	D-6	A	Cincinnati Bengals	21-3	W
Sun	D-13	H	Houston Oilers	28-6	W
Sun	D-20	A	New Orleans Saints	21-17	W

(m)—Milwaukee, Wisconsin

Postseason

1981 NFC Divisional Playoff Game
January 3, 1982
San Francisco 38, New York Giants 24 at San Francisco

N.Y. Giants	7	3	7	7	—	24
San Francisco	7	17	0	14	—	38

1981 NFC Championship Game
January 10, 1982
San Francisco 28, Dallas 27 at San Francisco

Dallas	10	7	0	10	—	27
San Francisco	7	7	7	7	—	28

Super Bowl XVI

San Francisco 26, Cincinnati 21
January 24, 1982, Pontiac Silverdome, Pontiac, Michigan
Attendance: 81,270

The dramatic sequence that put the 49ers in this game featured a tense, precise, improbable 89-yard drive against Dallas in the NFC Championship Game, climaxed by "The Catch," Dwight Clark's leaping grab of Joe Montana's pass in the right rear corner of the Cowboys' end zone.

But with a Super Bowl championship to win, the 49ers' sometimes opportunistic, sometimes rock-stingy defense, staged a four-play goal-line stand. It came late in the third quarter, with San Francisco leading 20-7 and a first-and-goal for the Bengals at the 49ers' 3.

Fullback Pete Johnson got 2 yards on first down. The next three plays gained nothing. The 49ers' stand was the day's crowning moment, complementing and outshining even the field generalship of Montana, the game's most valuable player, and kicker Ray Wersching, whose leg produced 14 points.

The 49ers' defense had its resiliency tested in the early going. It passed magnificently, averting an early Cincinnati score after San Francisco's Amos Lawrence fumbled the opening kickoff and the Bengals recovered at the 49ers' 26. Free safety Dwight Hicks stepped in front of Cincinnati's Isaac Curtis at the 5, intercepted Ken Anderson's pass, and returned it to the 32.

San Francisco coach Bill Walsh gave his players something to cut the tension of their first Super Bowl: a gadget play with Montana handing off to running back Ricky Patton, who handed to wide receiver Freddie Solomon, who pitched to Montana, who threw to tight end Charle Young for 14 yards. The drive was scripted and steady and covered 68 yards in 11 plays, with Montana carrying 1 yard for the 49ers' first touchdown.

The Bengals were driving early in the second quarter when San Francisco cornerback Eric Wright stripped the ball from wide receiver Cris Collinsworth at the 49ers' 8. Cornerback Lynn Thomas recovered, and Montana took the 49ers 92 yards in 12 plays, throwing to running back Earl Cooper for a 14-0 lead.

San Francisco added 6 points in a 13-second span. Wersching made a 22-yard field goal with 15 seconds left in the half. Bengals running back Archie Griffin fumbled the ensuing squib kickoff, and Wersching kicked a 26-yard field goal with 2 seconds to go.

San Francisco (NFC)	7	13	0	6	—	26
Cincinnati (AFC)	0	0	7	14	—	21

SF—Montana 1 run (Wersching kick)
SF—Cooper 11 pass from Montana (Wersching kick)
SF—FG Wersching 22
SF—FG Wersching 26
Cin—Anderson 5 run (Breech kick)
Cin—Ross 4 pass from Anderson (Breech kick)
SF—FG Wersching 40
SF—FG Wersching 23
Cin—Ross 3 pass from Anderson (Breech kick)

TEAM STATISTICS	**SF**	**CIN**
First Downs	20	24
Rushing	9	7
Passing	9	13
Penalty	2	4
Total Yardage	275	356
Net rushing yardage	127	72
Net passing yardage	148	284
Passes att.-comp.-had int.	22-14-0	34-25-2

RUSHING
San Francisco—Patton 17 for 55; Cooper 9 for 34; Montana 6 for 18, 1 TD; Ring 5 for 17; Davis 2 for 5; Clark 1 for -2.
Cincinnati—Johnson 14 for 36; Alexander 5 for 17; Anderson 4 for 15, 1 TD; A. Griffin 1 for 4.

PASSING
San Francisco—Montana 14 of 22 for 157, 1 TD.
Cincinnati—Anderson 25 of 34 for 300, 2 TDs, 2 int.

RECEIVING
San Francisco—Solomon 4 for 52; Clark 4 for 45; Cooper 2 for 15, 1 TD; Wilson 1 for 22; Young 1 for 14; Patton 1 for 6; Ring 1 for 3.
Cincinnati—Ross 11 for 104, 2 TDs; Collinsworth 5 for 107; Curtis 3 for 42; Kreider 2 for 36; Johnson 2 for 8; Alexander 2 for 3.

1981 Team Rosters

San Francisco
Dan Audick*
John Ayers*
Matt Bahr
Guy Benjamin
Dwaine Board*
Matt Bouza
Dan Bunz*
John Choma*
Ricky Churchman
Dwight Clark*
Earl Cooper*
Randy Cross*
Johnny Davis*
Fred Dean*
Walt Downing*
Walt Easley
Lenvil Elliott
Keith Fahnhorst*
Rick Gervais*
Willie Harper*
John Harty*
Dwight Hicks*
Paul Hofer
Arrington Jones
Allan Kennedy*
Pete Kugler
Amos Lawrence*
Bobby Leopold*
Jim Looney
Ronnie Lott*
Saladin Martin
Milt McColl*
Jim Miller*
Joe Montana*
Ricky Patton*
Brian Peets
Lawrence Pillers*
Craig Puki*
Fred Quillan*
Eason Ramson*
Archie Reese*
Jack Reynolds*
Bill Ring*
Mike Shumann*
Freddie Solomon*
Jim Stuckey*
Terry Tautolo
Lynn Thomas*
Keena Turner*
Ray Wersching*
Carlton Williamson*
Mike Wilson*
Eric Wright*
Charle Young*

Cincinnati
Charles Alexander*
Ken Anderson*
Don Bass*
Jim Breech*
Louis Breeden*
Greg Bright
Ross Browner*
Glenn Bujnoch
Gary Burley*
Blair Bush*
Glenn Cameron*
Clarence Chapman
Cris Collinsworth*
Isaac Curtis*
Oliver Davis*
Tom Dinkel*
Eddie Edwards*
Guy Frazier*
Mike Fuller*
Archie Griffin*
Ray Griffin*
Jim Hargrove*
Bo Harris*
M.L. Harris*
Bryan Hicks*
Rod Horn*
Pete Johnson*
Bobby Kemp*
Steve Kreider*
Dave Lapham*
Jim LeClair*
Pat McInally*
Max Montoya*
Blake Moore*
Anthony Munoz*
Brad Oates
Mike Obrovac*
Elvis Peacock
Rick Razzano*
Ken Riley*
Dan Ross*
Turk Schonert
Jeff Schuh
John Simmons*
Mike St. Clair*
Jack Thompson
David Verser*
Wilson Whitley*
Bobby Whitten
Reggie Williams*
Mike Wilson*

1982 AFC Champions Miami Dolphins

In 1982, a decade after he earned distinction as the architect of Miami's No-Name Defense, defensive coordinator Bill Arnsparger built another standout unit that relied on teamwork and precision rather than on individual brilliance.

The Killer Bees defense was so named because of the surnames of its starters—Doug Betters, Kim Bokamper, Bob Baumhower, Bob Brudzinski, and the Blackwood brothers, Glenn and Lyle.

The Dolphins allowed an AFC-low 131 points in the strike-shortened season, finishing with a 7-2 mark. One of those losses was a controversial 3-0 loss in a snowstorm at New England in which a vagabond snowplow driver made an unexpected visit to the field just before the winning field-goal attempt.

David Woodley quarterbacked the team to a 28-13 win over New England in a first-round game. Miami forced 7 turnovers in a 34-13 victory over the Chargers the following week as the Killer Bees sacked Dan Fouts twice and intercepted him 4 times in the second half.

It was not a Killer Bee, but linebacker A.J. Duhe who killed the New York Jets in the American Football Conference Championship Game. Duhe had 3 interceptions, including a 35-yard interception return for a touchdown at the muddy Orange Bowl.

In all, the Dolphins intercepted quarterback Richard Todd 5 times in the 14-0 victory to reach the Super Bowl for the first time since their 12-2 1973 season.

Regular Season

Sun	S-12	A	New York Jets	45-28	W
Sun	S-19	H	Baltimore Colts	24-20	W
Sun	N-21	A	Buffalo Bills	9-7	W
Mon	N-29	A	Tampa Bay Buccaneers	17-23	L
Sun	D-5	H	Minnesota Vikings	22-14	W
Sun	D-12	A	New England Patriots	0-3	L
Sat	D-18	H	New York Jets	20-19	W
Mon	D-27	H N	Buffalo Bills	27-10	W
Sun	Ja-2	A	Baltimore Colts	34-7	W

Postseason

1982 AFC First-Round Playoff Game
January 8, 1983
Miami 28, New England 13 at Miami

New England	0	3	3	7	—	13
Miami	0	14	7	7	—	28

1982 AFC Divisional Playoff Game
January 16, 1983
Miami 34, San Diego 13 at Miami

San Diego	0	13	0	0	—	13
Miami	7	20	0	7	—	34

1982 AFC Championship Game
January 23, 1983
Miami 14, New York Jets 0 at Miami

N.Y. Jets	0	0	0	0	—	0
Miami	0	0	7	7	—	14

1982 NFC Champions Washington Redskins

The Redskins, in their second season under head coach Joe Gibbs, lost just once in the strike-shortened regular season and breezed into the playoffs.

John Riggins ran for 119 yards and Joe Theismann completed 14 of 19 passes for 210 yards and 3 touchdowns as the Redskins proved too much for Detroit 31-7 in a first-round playoff game. Theismann threw 3 touchdown passes to Alvin Garrett.

In an NFC Divisional Playoff Game, Riggins, who had asked to be given the ball more in the playoffs, carried 37 times for 185 yards to lead Washington to a 21-7 victory against Minnesota.

On the game's opening possession, the Redskins drove 66 yards in 10 plays, with Theismann hitting tight end Don Warren with a 3-yard touchdown pass. Riggins followed with a 2-yard scoring run for a 14-0 first-quarter lead. After the Vikings responded with a second period touchdown, Theismann found Garrett with a scoring pass that proved to be the final score of the afternoon.

The Washington defense and special teams made the big plays as the Redskins defeated the Cowboys 31-17 in the NFC Championship Game. Monte Coleman recovered a fumbled punt at the Dallas 11, leading to a 1-yard touchdown by Riggins for a 14-3 Washington lead.

After Dallas cut the lead to 21-17, Mel Kaufman's interception led to a Washington field goal. Then, Dexter Manley tipped Gary Hogeboom's pass to Darryl Grant, who lumbered 10 yards for the clinching touchdown.

Regular Season

Sun	S-12	A	Philadelphia Eagles (OT)	37-34	W
Sun	S-19	A	Tampa Bay Buccaneers	21-13	W
Sun	N-21	A	New York Giants	27-17	W
Sun	N-28	H	Philadelphia Eagles	13-9	W
Sun	D-5	H	Dallas Cowboys	10-24	L
Sun	D-12	A	St. Louis Cardinals	12-7	W
Sun	D-19	H	New York Giants	15-14	W
Sun	D-26	A	New Orleans Saints	27-10	W
Sun	Ja-1	H	St. Louis Cardinals	28-0	W

Postseason

1982 NFC First-Round Playoff Game
January 8, 1983
Washington 31, Detroit 7 at Washington

Detroit	0	0	7	0	—	7
Washington	10	14	7	0	—	31

1982 NFC Divisional Playoff Game
January 15, 1983
Washington 21, Minnesota 7 at Washington

Minnesota	0	7	0	0	—	7
Washington	14	7	0	0	—	21

1982 NFC Championship Game
January 22, 1983
Washington 31, Dallas 17 at Washington

Dallas	3	0	14	0	—	17
Washington	7	7	7	10	—	31

Super Bowl XVII

Washington 27, Miami 17
January 30, 1983, Rose Bowl, Pasadena, California
Attendance: 103,667

Climaxing a season shortened by a 57-day players' strike, teams with regular-season records of 8-1 (Redskins) and 7-2 (Dolphins) completed a special postseason format. Division standings were abandoned in 1982 in favor of overall conference standings. The top eight teams in both the AFC and NFC entered a four-round tournament.

The route to Super Bowl XVII may have been unique, but the Redskins' deliberate, methodical disposal of the Dolphins stuck to a formula that has seldom failed: Control the football and win. Most valuable player John Riggins rushed for 166 yards behind an offensive line dubbed The Hogs by Redskins offensive coordinator Joe Bugel. The Hogs were left tackle Joe Jacoby, left guard Russ Grimm, center Jeff Bostic, right guard Fred Dean, and right tackle George Starke.

The play of the game came in the final quarter. Trailing 17-13, Washington faced fourth-and-1 at the Miami 43. Riggins carried at left end, shook off a Dolphins defender, and rumbled the rest of the way to put the Redskins ahead.

That 43-yard touchdown burst may have made a lasting impression, but it was during the Redskins' final drive that the running back from Kansas put his mark on the game. Riggins carried on 8 of the 12 plays of the Redskins' next possession, a drive that ended with a 6-yard touchdown pass from Joe Theismann to Charlie Brown.

Miami flashed speed in the first quarter. The second time the Dolphins had the ball, quarterback David Woodley hit wide receiver Jimmy Cefalo in a seam in the Redskins' zone, and Cefalo dashed the final 55 yards of a 76-yard touchdown play.

Fulton Walker's 42-yard kickoff return followed Washington's first score on Mark Moseley's 31-yard field goal. Walker's return led to a 20-yard field goal by Uwe von Schamann. Washington came back with a drive that went mostly through the air, with Theismann completing 4 of 4 passes, including a 4-yard toss to wide receiver Alvin Garrett for the Redskins' first touchdown.

Walker's 98-yard return for a touchdown on the ensuing kickoff was the last fun the Dolphins would have. The second half proved to be a nightmare for Miami, which gained only 34 yards and passed 11 times without a completion. In the end, the Redskins outgained the Dolphins, 400 yards to 176.

The Redskins got a 20-yard field goal from Moseley midway through the third quarter, after a 44-yard reverse by Garrett got them to the Dolphins' 9. Later in the quarter, Theismann, on first-and-10 at his 18, alertly made the defensive play of the game. Dolphins linebacker Kim Bokamper deflected Theismann's pass in the air and tried to control it. But the Redskins' quarterback got a hand on the ball and knocked it loose, saving a touchdown.

Miami (AFC)	7	10	0	0	—	17
Washington (NFC)	0	10	3	14	—	27

Mia—Cefalo 76 pass from Woodley (von Schamann kick)
Wash—FG Moseley 31
Mia—FG von Schamann 20
Wash—Garrett 4 pass from Theismann (Moseley kick)
Mia—Walker 98 kickoff return (von Schamann kick)
Wash—FG Moseley 20
Wash—Riggins 43 run (Moseley kick)
Wash—Brown 6 pass from Theismann (Moseley kick)

TEAM STATISTICS	**MIA**	**WASH**
First Downs	9	24
Rushing	7	14
Passing	2	9
Penalty	0	1
Total Yardage	176	400
Net rushing yardage	96	276
Net passing yardage	80	124
Passes att.-comp.-had int.	17-4-1	23-15-2

RUSHING
Miami—Franklin 16 for 49; Nathan 7 for 26; Woodley 4 for 16; Vigorito 1 for 4; Harris 1 for 1.
Washington—Riggins 38 for 166, 1 TD; Garrett 1 for 44; Harmon 9 for 40; Theismann 3 for 20; Walker 1 for 6.

PASSING
Miami—Woodley 4 of 14 for 97, 1 TD, 1 int.; Strock 0 of 3.
Washington—Theismann 15 of 23 for 143, 2 TDs, 2 int.

RECEIVING
Miami—Cefalo 2 for 82, 1 TD; Harris 2 for 15.
Washington—Brown 6 for 60, 1 TD; Warren 5 for 28; Garrett 2 for 13, 1 TD; Walker 1 for 27; Riggins 1 for 15.

1982 Team Rosters

Washington
Stuart Anderson
Jeff Bostic*
Perry Brooks*
Charlie Brown*
Dave Butz*
Rich Caster
Monte Coleman*
Pete Cronan*
Fred Dean*
Vernon Dean*
Clint Didier*
Alvin Garrett*
Nick Giaquinto*
Darryl Grant*
Russ Grimm*
Clarence Harmon*
Jeff Hayes*
Bob Holly
Wilbur Jackson*
Joe Jacoby*
Curtis Jordan*
Mel Kaufman*
Larry Kubin*
Don Laster*
Joe Lavender*
Todd Liebenstein*
Quentin Lowry*
Dexter Manley*
Mark May*
LeCharls McDaniel*
Tony McGee*
Mat Mendenhall*
Rich Milot*
Art Monk
Mark Moseley*
Mark Murphy*
Mike Nelms*
Pat Ogrin
Neal Olkewicz*
Tony Peters*
Garry Puetz
John Riggins*
Virgil Seay*
George Starke*
Joe Theismann*
Rick Walker*
Don Warren*
Joe Washington
Jeris White*
Greg Williams*
Mike Williams
Otis Wonsley*

Miami
Bill Barnett
Bob Baumhower*
Woody Bennett*
Doug Betters*
Richard Bishop
Glenn Blackwood*
Lyle Blackwood*
Kim Bokamper*
Charles Bowser*
Bob Brudzinski*
Jimmy Cefalo*
Steve Clark
Larry Cowan
Vern Den Herder*
Mark Dennard*
Rich Diana*
A.J. Duhe*
Mark Duper
Roy Foster*
Andra Franklin*
Jon Giesler*
Larry Gordon*
Cleveland Green*
Bruce Hardy*
Duriel Harris*
Vince Heflin*
Ron Hester*
Eddie Hill*
Jim Jensen*
William Judson*
Mike Kozlowski*
Bob Kuechenberg*
Eric Laakso*
Paul Lankford*
Ronnie Lee*
Don McNeal*
Nat Moore*
Tony Nathan*
Ed Newman
Tom Orosz*
Steve Potter*
Earnest Rhone*
Joe Rose*
Steve Shull*
Gerald Small*
Dwight Stephenson*
Don Strock*
Jeff Toews*
Tommy Vigorito*
Uwe von Schamann*
Fulton Walker*
David Woodley*

1983 AFC Champions
Los Angeles Raiders

The 1983 Raiders fielded one of the great teams of the modern era. Quarterback Jim Plunkett and running back Marcus Allen, both former Heisman Trophy winners, and tight end Todd Christensen keyed the offense, while Lester Hayes and end Lyle Alzado led the defense.

Since the formation of the AFC in 1970, one of the great playoff rivalries existed between the Raiders and the Steelers. An NFL playoff-record 90,380 packed the Los Angeles Coliseum for the 1983 AFC Divisional Playoff Game between the teams and the fans were on their feet when the Raiders forced the Steelers to kick a field goal on fourth-and-inches in the first quarter.

The Los Angeles defensive line accounted for the first touchdown when Hayes ran an interception 18 yards for a touchdown. Rushing touchdowns followed by Kenny King, Frank Hawkins, and Marcus Allen, who scored twice, as the Raiders cruised to an easy 38-10 victory.

The AFC Championship Game was against a relatively new yet familiar foe. The Raiders, who had lost to division-rival Seattle Seahawks twice during the regular season, held American Football Conference rookie of the year Curt Warner to 26 yards on 11 carries, while Marcus Allen responded with 154 yards rushing as Los Angeles defeated Seattle 30-14.

Regular Season

Sun	S-4	A	Cincinnati Bengals	20-10	W
Sun	S-11	H	Houston Oilers	20-6	W
Mon	S-19	H N	Miami Dolphins	27-14	W
Sun	S-25	A	Denver Broncos	22-7	W
Sun	O-2	A	Washington Redskins	35-37	L
Sun	O-9	H	Kansas City Chiefs	21-20	W
Sun	O-16	A	Seattle Seahawks	36-38	L
Sun	O-23	A N	Dallas Cowboys	40-38	W
Sun	O-30	H	Seattle Seahawks	21-34	L
Sun	N-6	A	Kansas City Chiefs	28-20	W
Sun	N-13	H	Denver Broncos	22-20	W
Sun	N-20	A	Buffalo Bills	27-24	W
Sun	N-27	H N	New York Giants	27-12	W
Thu	D-1	A	San Diego Chargers	42-10	W
Sun	D-11	H	St. Louis Cardinals	24-34	L
Sun	D-18	H	San Diego Chargers	30-14	W

Postseason

1983 AFC Divisional Playoff Game
January 1, 1984
Los Angeles Raiders 38, Pittsburgh 10, at Los Angeles

Pittsburgh	3	0	7	0	—	10
L.A. Raiders	7	10	21	0	—	38

1984 AFC Championship Game
January 8, 1984
Los Angeles Raiders 30, Seattle 14 at Los Angeles

Seattle	0	0	7	7	—	14
L.A. Raiders	3	17	7	3	—	30

1983 NFC Champions
Washington Redskins

The Redskins, 14-2 in the regular season, scored on their first five possessions in the NFC Divisional Playoff Game to build a 38-7 halftime lead, then turned the game over to a defense that held NFL-rushing champion Eric Dickerson to 16 yards on 10 carries. Washington's defense also intercepted Vince Ferragamo 3 times and scored once in a 51-7 victory, the worst defeat ever for the Rams.

The 49ers Joe Montana attempted to turn the NFC Championship Game into the greatest fourth-quarter rebound in playoff history, but Mark Moseley kicked a 25-yard field goal with 40 seconds left to give Washington a 24-21 victory.

Two touchdown runs by John Riggins and a 70-yard bomb from Joe Theismann to Charlie Brown gave the Redskins a 21-0 lead. But Moseley missed 4 field-goal attempts, and a penalty nullified Darrell Green's punt return for a touchdown.

In the fourth period, the 49ers came to life. Behind Montana's NFC Championship Game-record 27 completions in 48 attempts, the 49ers scored 3 times.

But the Redskins engaged in some heroics of their own. Starting at the Washington 14, Theismann led a 13-play, 78-yard drive that took 6:12 off the clock and set up the winning kick.

Regular Season

Mon	S-5	H N	Dallas Cowboys	30-31	L
Sun	S-11	A	Philadelphia Eagles	23-13	W
Sun	S-18	H	Kansas City Chiefs	27-12	W
Sun	S-25	A	Seattle Seahawks	27-17	W
Sun	O-2	H	Los Angeles Raiders	37-35	W
Sun	O-9	A	St. Louis Cardinals	38-14	W
Mon	O-17	A N	Green Bay Packers	47-48	L
Sun	O-23	H	Detroit Lions	38-17	W
Mon	O-31	A N	San Diego Chargers	27-24	W
Sun	N-6	H	St. Louis Cardinals	45-7	W
Sun	N-13	A	New York Giants	33-17	W
Sun	N-20	A	Los Angeles Rams	42-20	W
Sun	N-27	H	Philadelphia Eagles	28-24	W
Sun	D-4	H	Atlanta Falcons	37-21	W
Sun	D-11	A	Dallas Cowboys	31-10	W
Sat	D-17	H	New York Giants	31-22	W

Postseason

1983 NFC Divisional Playoff Game
January 1, 1984
Washington 51, Los Angeles Rams 7 at Washington

L.A. Rams	0	7	0	0	—	7
Washington	17	21	6	7	—	51

1983 NFC Championship Game
January 8, 1984
Washington 24, San Francisco 21 at Washington

San Francisco	0	0	0	21	—	21
Washington	0	7	14	3	—	24

Super Bowl XVIII

Los Angeles Raiders 38, Washington 9
January 22, 1984, Tampa Stadium, Tampa, Florida
Attendance: 72,920

Not since Super Bowl III had the event been marked with its own signature pregame quote. Then it was Joe Namath saying, "I guarantee it." Now it was Raiders owner Al Davis sticking his head inside his team's locker room not much longer than the time it took to tell them, "Just win, baby."

The Raiders took him up on it, to the point of scoring on offense, defense, and special teams in a 21-3 first half. The climactic moment, Marcus Allen's record-breaking 74-yard touchdown run on the last play of the third quarter, reminded some observers of Willie Brown's door-slamming 75-yard interception return in the Raiders' rout of Minnesota seven Super Bowls earlier.

In the early going of this one, a sure sign of excitement was punt formation. The Redskins were forced to punt from their 30. Derrick Jensen of the Raiders burst through, blocked the punt by Jeff Hayes, and recovered it in the end zone for the day's first score.

The Raiders were on their way to the widest margin of victory in a Super Bowl to that time. But they nearly paused to let the Redskins get their bearings. Raiders punter Ray Guy saved a high snap with a basketball-like jump, barely snaring the ball with his right hand, then punting in one motion to avert disaster.

When they got the ball back, the Raiders scored on a 12-yard pass from Jim Plunkett to Cliff Branch. Two plays before the touchdown, Plunkett passed over the middle to Branch for 50 yards.

The Redskins cut their deficit to 14-3 with Mark Moseley's 24-yard field goal, then regained possession at their 12 with 12 seconds left in the first half. On the Redskins' first play, Raiders linebacker Jack Squirek picked off Theismann's swing pass to running back Joe Washington at the 5-yard line and strode into the end zone to give the Raiders a 21-3 halftime lead.

The Redskins' second-half effort began and ended with a long drive to a 1-yard touchdown run by fullback John Riggins. The magic of a year earlier was nowhere in sight, however. Raiders reserve tight end Don Hasselbeck blocked Moseley's extra-point attempt, and the Redskins were scoreless for the duration. Quarterback Jim Plunkett took the Raiders 70 yards in 8 plays, with Allen running in from the 5 for a 28-9 lead.

Later, after Allen's long touchdown run, a 21-yard field goal by Chris Bahr broke the scoring record previously held by Green Bay (Super Bowl I) and Pittsburgh (Super Bowl XIII). Allen finished the game with 191 yards rushing, another record, and was named the game's most valuable player.

Raiders cornerbacks Mike Haynes and Lester Hayes also deserved special mention for holding the Redskins' vaunted receivers, Art Monk and Charlie Brown, to a mere 4 catches combined—none in the first half when the game was decided.

Washington (NFC)	0	3	6	0	—	9
L.A. Raiders (AFC)	7	14	14	3	—	38

Raid—Jensen recovered blocked punt in end zone (Bahr kick)
Raid—Branch 12 pass from Plunkett (Bahr kick)
Wash—FG Moseley 24
Raid—Squirek 5 interception return (Bahr kick)
Wash—Riggins 1 run (kick blocked)
Raid—Allen 5 run (Bahr kick)
Raid—Allen 74 run (Bahr kick)
Raid—FG Bahr 21

TEAM STATISTICS	WASH	RAIDERS
First Downs	19	18
Rushing	7	8
Passing	10	9
Penalty	2	1
Total Yardage	283	385
Net rushing yardage	90	231
Net passing yardage	193	154
Passes att.-comp.-had int.	35-16-2	25-16-0

RUSHING
Washington—Riggins 26 for 64, 1 TD; Theismann 3 for 18; J. Washington 3 for 8.
L.A. Raiders—Allen 20 for 191, 2 TDs; Pruitt 5 for 17; King 3 for 12; Willis 1 for 7; Hawkins 3 for 6; Plunkett 1 for -2.

PASSING
Washington—Theismann 16 of 35 for 243, 2 int.
L.A. Raiders—Plunkett 16 of 25 for 172, 1 TD.

RECEIVING
Washington—Didier 5 for 65; Brown 3 for 93; J. Washington 3 for 20; Giaquinto 2 for 21; Monk 1 for 26; Garrett 1 for 17; Riggins 1 for 1.
L.A. Raiders—Branch 6 for 94, 1 TD; Christensen 4 for 32; Hawkins 2 for 20; Allen 2 for 18; King 2 for 8.

1983 Team Rosters

L.A. Raiders
Marcus Allen*
Lyle Alzado*
Chris Bahr*
Jeff Barnes*
Malcolm Barnwell*
Rick Berns
Don Bessillieu
Cliff Branch*
Darryl Byrd*
Tony Caldwell*
Todd Christensen*
Dave Dalby*
Bruce Davis*
James Davis*
Mike Davis*
Ray Guy*
Charley Hannah*
Don Hasselbeck*
Frank Hawkins*
Lester Hayes*
Mike Haynes*
Ted Hendricks*
Kenny Hill*
David Humm*
Derrick Jensen*
Shelby Jordan*
Kenny King*
Reggie Kinlaw*
Henry Lawrence*
Howie Long*
Rod Martin*
Mickey Marvin*
Vann McElroy*
Odis McKinney*
Matt Millen*
Cleo Montgomery*
Don Mosebar*
Calvin Muhammad*
Ed Muransky
Bob Nelson*
Irvin Phillips
Bill Pickel*
Jim Plunkett*
Greg Pruitt*
Derrick Ramsey
Archie Reese
Johnny Robinson*
Jim Romano
Jack Squirek*
Dave Stalls*
Steve Sylvester*
Greg Townsend*
Ted Watts*
Dokie Williams*
Chester Willis*
Marc Wilson*

Washington
Stuart Anderson*
Jeff Bostic*
Perry Brooks*
Charlie Brown*
Dave Butz*
Brian Carpenter*
Ken Coffey*
Monte Coleman*
Pete Cronan*
Vernon Dean*
Clint Didier*
Reggie Evans*
Alvin Garrett*
Nick Giaquinto*
Darryl Grant*
Darrell Green*
Russ Grimm*
Jeff Hayes*
Bob Holly
Ken Huff*
Joe Jacoby*
Curtis Jordan*
Mel Kaufman*
Bruce Kimball*
Larry Kubin*
Todd Liebenstein*
Quentin Lowry
Dexter Manley*
Charles Mann*
Mark May*
Tony McGee*
Mark McGrath
Rich Milot*
Art Monk*
Mark Moseley*
Mark Murphy*
Mike Nelms
Neal Olkewicz*
John Riggins*
John Sawyer
Virgil Seay
Roy Simmons*
George Starke*
Dave Stief
Joe Theismann*
Rick Walker*
Don Warren*
Anthony Washington*
Joe Washington*
Greg Williams*
Mike Williams*
Otis Wonsley*

1984 AFC Champions Miami Dolphins

Dan Marino and the Marks Brothers—receivers Mark Duper and Mark Clayton—set NFL records by the handful in 1984, including completions (362), passing yards (5,084), and touchdown passes (48). Clayton set another league record with 18 touchdown catches. With their seemingly unstoppable offense, the Dolphins dominated the AFC, winning their second consecutive division title and finishing 14-2.

In an AFC Divisional Playoff Game, Seattle wanted to play ball control, but it was the Dolphins who ran off 70 plays, netted 405 yards, and produced a 31-10 victory. Miami clung to a 14-10 halftime lead, and seemed to be in trouble when the Seahawks embarked on an 11-play drive in the third quarter. But Norm Johnson missed a field-goal attempt, and Marino found Bruce Hardy and then Clayton for touchdown passes to seal the game.

Marino completed 21 of 32 passes for 421 yards and 4 touchdowns to lead the Dolphins to a 45-28 victory over the Steelers. He found Duper twice and Clayton and Nat Moore once apiece to outduel Pittsburgh's Mark Malone, who passed for 312 yards and 3 touchdowns. Tony Nathan and Woody Bennett also ran for touchdowns for Miami.

Regular Season

Sun	S-2	A	Washington Redskins	35-17	W
Sun	S-9	H	New England Patriots	28-7	W
Mon	S-17	A N	Buffalo Bills	21-17	W
Sun	S-23	H	Indianapolis Colts	44-7	W
Sun	S-30	A	St. Louis Cardinals	36-28	W
Sun	O-7	A	Pittsburgh Steelers	31-7	W
Sun	O-14	H	Houston Oilers	28-10	W
Sun	O-21	A	New England Patriots	44-24	W
Sun	O-28	H	Buffalo Bills	38-7	W
Sun	N-4	A	New York Jets	31-17	W
Sun	N-11	H	Philadelphia Eagles	24-23	W
Sun	N-18	A	San Diego Chargers (OT)	28-34	L
Mon	N-26	H N	New York Jets	28-17	W
Sun	D-2	H	Los Angeles Raiders	34-45	L
Sun	D-9	A	Indianapolis Colts	35-17	W
Mon	D-17	H N	Dallas Cowboys	28-21	W

Postseason

1984 AFC Divisional Playoff Game
December 29, 1984
Miami 31, Seattle 10 at Miami

Seattle	0	10	0	0	—	10
Miami	7	7	14	3	—	31

1984 AFC Championship Game
January 6, 1985
Miami 45, Pittsburgh 28, at Miami

Pittsburgh	7	7	7	7	—	28
Miami	7	17	14	7	—	45

1984 NFC Champions San Francisco 49ers

San Francisco set a league record by winning 15 regular-season games and losing only once, to the Steelers.

In their NFC Divisional Playoff Game, Joe Montana passed for 3 touchdowns and San Francisco defeated the New York Giants 21-10. The 49ers scored twice in the first seven minutes of the game. Soon after Montana passed 21 yards to Dwight Clark for a touchdown on San Francisco's first possession, linebacker Dan Bunz tipped New York quarterback Phil Simms's pass. It was intercepted by Ronnie Lott, who returned it 38 yards to the 12. Montana then threw a 9-yard touchdown pass to Russ Francis.

Defense dominated the NFC Championship Game, as San Francisco sacked Bears' quarterback Steve Fuller 9 times, to earn a 23-0 victory. The 49ers scored twice on field goals by Ray Wersching in the first half, but San Francisco couldn't break the game open in the second half. Wendell Tyler scored a 9-yard touchdown run in the third quarter.

In the fourth quarter, the 49ers drove 88 yards as Roger Craig burst off left tackle for a 39-yard run and Montana completed 4 of 4 passes, including a 10-yard completion to Freddie Solomon for the clinching score.

Regular Season

Sun	S-2	A	Detroit Lions	30-27	W
Mon	S-10	H N	Washington Redskins	37-31	W
Sun	S-16	H	New Orleans Saints	30-20	W
Sun	S-23	A	Philadelphia Eagles	21-9	W
Sun	S-30	H	Atlanta Falcons	14-5	W
Mon	O-8	A N	New York Giants	31-10	W
Sun	O-14	H	Pittsburgh Steelers	17-20	L
Sun	O-21	A	Houston Oilers	34-21	W
Sun	O-28	A	Los Angeles Rams	33-0	W
Sun	N-4	H	Cincinnati Bengals	23-17	W
Sun	N-11	A	Cleveland Browns	41-7	W
Sun	N-18	H	Tampa Bay Buccaneers	24-17	W
Sun	N-25	A	New Orleans Saints	35-3	W
Sun	D-2	A	Atlanta Falcons	35-17	W
Sat	D-8	H N	Minnesota Vikings	51-7	W
Fri	D-14	H N	Los Angeles Rams	19-16	W

Postseason

1984 NFC Divisional Playoff Game
December 29, 1984
San Francisco 21, New York Giants 10 at San Francisco

N.Y. Giants	0	10	0	0	—	10
San Francisco	14	7	0	0	—	21

1984 NFC Championship Game
January 6, 1985
San Francisco 23, Chicago 0 at San Francisco

Chicago	0	0	0	0	—	0
San Francisco	3	3	7	10	—	23

Super Bowl XIX

San Francisco 38, Miami 16
January 20, 1985, Stanford Stadium, Stanford, California
Attendance: 84,059

The NFL's premier offensive forces of the mid-1980s—Bill Walsh's imaginative script-and-improvise, wide-field artistry and Don Shula's turn-'em-loose yardage machine—met head-on.

And a defensive decision turned the game into a rout.

San Francisco's response to the lightning strikes of Miami quarterback Dan Marino was a configuration of six defensive backs, one of whom lined up as a virtual outside linebacker. Marino passed 50 times, completing 29 for 318 yards, with 1 touchdown and 2 interceptions. But the Dolphins' running game netted only 25 yards.

Meanwhile, San Francisco quarterback Joe Montana threw 3 touchdown passes, 2 of them to running back Roger Craig, as part of a 24-for-35 performance that netted Montana a Super Bowl-record 331 passing yards and the game's most-valuable-player award. It was the second time Montana received the honor, tying him with Green Bay's Bart Starr and Pittsburgh's Terry Bradshaw as the only double recipients.

Craig scored on an 8-yard pass from Montana early in the second quarter and added a 2-yard scoring run early in the third quarter. A 16-yard reception from Montana midway through the fourth quarter was Craig's third touchdown of the game, a Super Bowl record.

The Dolphins held a 10-7 lead at the end of the first quarter as the teams combined for a Super Bowl record for total points in the opening 15 minutes. Miami led 3-0 on Uwe von Schamann's 37-yard field goal 7:36 into the game. San Francisco running back Carl Monroe took a 33-yard scoring pass from Montana four minutes later.

The Dolphins went ahead for the last time on Marino's 2-yard pass to tight end Dan Johnson in the quarter's final minute. By then, Walsh and his coaching staff had demystified Marino, and the 49ers' defense saw to it that Montana and the offensive unit had plenty of playing time. San Francisco's time-of-possession advantage over Miami was 37:11 to 22:49.

Miami (AFC)	10	6	0	0	—	16
San Francisco (NFC)	7	21	10	0	—	38

Mia—FG von Schamann 37
SF—Monroe 33 pass from Montana (Wersching kick)
Mia—D. Johnson 2 pass from Marino (von Schamann kick)
SF—Craig 8 pass from Montana (Wersching kick)
SF—Montana 6 run (Wersching kick)
SF—Craig 2 run (Wersching kick)
Mia—FG von Schamann 31
Mia—FG von Schamann 30
SF—FG Wersching 27
SF—Craig 16 pass from Montana (Wersching kick)

TEAM STATISTICS	**MIA**	**SF**
First Downs	19	31
Rushing	2	16
Passing	17	15
Penalty	0	0
Total Yardage	314	537
Net rushing yardage	25	211
Net passing yardage	289	326
Passes att.-comp.-had int.	50-29-2	35-24-0

RUSHING
Miami—Nathan 5 for 18; Bennett 3 for 7; Marino 1 for 0.
San Francisco—Tyler 13 for 65; Montana 5 for 59, 1 TD; Craig 15 for 58, 1 TD; Harmon 5 for 20; Solomon 1 for 5; Cooper 1 for 4.

PASSING
Miami—Marino 29 of 50 for 318, 1 TD, 2 int.
San Francisco—Montana 24 of 35 for 331, 3 TDs.

RECEIVING
Miami—Nathan 10 for 83; Clayton 6 for 92; Rose 6 for 73; D. Johnson 3 for 28, 1 TD; Moore 2 for 17; Cefalo 1 for 14; Duper 1 for 11.
San Francisco—Craig 7 for 77, 2 TDs; D. Clark 6 for 77; Francis 5 for 60; Tyler 4 for 70; Monroe 1 for 33, 1 TD; Solomon 1 for 14.

1984 Team Rosters

San Francisco
John Ayers*
Dwaine Board*
Greg Boyd
Dan Bunz*
Michael Carter*
Matt Cavanaugh
Dwight Clark*
Mario Clark
Earl Cooper*
Roger Craig*
Randy Cross*
Fred Dean*
Al Dixon
Riki Ellison*
Jim Fahnhorst
Keith Fahnhorst*
Ron Ferrari
Russ Francis*
John Frank
Jeff Fuller*
Derrick Harmon*
Dwight Hicks*
Tom Holmoe*
Gary Johnson*
Louie Kelcher*
Allan Kennedy*
Ronnie Lott*
John Macaulay
Milt McColl*
Guy McIntyre*
Dana McLemore*
Carl Monroe*
Joe Montana*
Blanchard Montgomery*
Renaldo Nehemiah*
Tom Orosz
Bubba Paris*
Lawrence Pillers*
Fred Quillan*
Jack Reynolds*
Bill Ring*
Max Runager*
Jesse Sapolu
Todd Shell*
Billy Shields*
Freddie Solomon*
Jeff Stover*
Jim Stuckey*
Manu Tuiasosopo*
Keena Turner*
Wendell Tyler*
Michael Walter*
Ray Wersching*
Carlton Williamson*
Mike Wilson*
Eric Wright*

Miami
Bill Barnett*
Bob Baumhower*
Woody Bennett*
Charles Benson*
Doug Betters*
Glenn Blackwood*
Lyle Blackwood*
Kim Bokamper*
Charles Bowser*
Jay Brophy*
Bud Brown*
Mark Brown*
Bob Brudzinski*
Fernanza Burgess
Joe Carter*
Jimmy Cefalo*
Mike Charles*
John Chesley
Steve Clark*
Mark Clayton*
A.J. Duhe*
Mark Duper*
Roy Foster*
Andra Franklin
Jon Giesler*
Cleveland Green*
Bruce Hardy*
Vince Heflin*
Eddie Hill*
Jim Jensen*
Dan Johnson*
Pete Johnson
Ed Judie
William Judson*
Mike Kozlowski*
Eric Laakso
Paul Lankford*
Ronnie Lee*
Dan Marino*
Don McNeal*
Nat Moore*
Tony Nathan*
Ed Newman*
Earnest Rhone*
Reggie Roby*
Joe Rose*
Jackie Shipp*
Sanders Shiver*
Robert Sowell*
Dwight Stephenson*
Don Strock*
Rodell Thomas
Jeff Toews*
Uwe von Schamann*
Fulton Walker*

1985 AFC Champions
New England Patriots

In 1985, New England rode a six-game winning streak to an 11-5 record and a wild-card playoff berth. In the postseason, coach Raymond Berry's club became the first team to win three road playoff games and they did it by beating three teams they lost to during the regular season.

The Patriots earned their first playoff win since 1963 when Tony Franklin kicked 4 field goals in a 26-14 victory over the Jets at Giants Stadium. The turning point came in the third quarter when the Patriots' lead grew by 10 points in a matter of seconds. Franklin kicked his third field goal and Johnny Rembert recovered a fumble on the ensuing kickoff and waltzed 15 yards for a touchdown.

The following week in Los Angeles, Craig James rushed for 104 yards and 1 touchdown as the Patriots beat the Raiders 27-20. Again turnovers were the difference as New England converted 6 miscues into 17 points.

The Patriots earned their first trip to the Super Bowl with a 31-14 victory over Miami in the AFC title game.

Regular Season

Sun	S-8	H	Green Bay Packers	26-20	W
Sun	S-15	A	Chicago Bears	7-20	L
Sun	S-22	A	Buffalo Bills	17-14	W
Sun	S-29	H	Los Angeles Raiders	20-35	L
Sun	O-6	A	Cleveland Browns	20-24	L
Sun	O-13	H	Buffalo Bills	14-3	W
Sun	O-20	H	New York Jets	20-13	W
Sun	O-27	A	Tampa Bay Buccaneers	32-14	W
Sun	N-3	H	Miami Dolphins	17-13	W
Sun	N-10	H	Indianapolis Colts	34-15	W
Sun	N-17	A	Seattle Seahawks	20-13	W
Sun	N-24	A	New York Jets (OT)	13-16	L
Sun	D-1	A	Indianapolis Colts	38-31	W
Sun	D-8	H	Detroit Lions	23-6	W
Mon	D-16	A N	Miami Dolphins	27-30	L
Sun	D-22	H	Cincinnati Bengals	34-23	W

Postseason

1985 AFC Wild Card Game
December 28, 1985
New England 26, New York Jets 14
at East Rutherford, New Jersey

New England	3	10	10	3	—	26
N.Y. Jets	0	7	7	0	—	14

1985 AFC Divisional Playoff Game
January 5, 1986
New England 27, Los Angeles Raiders 20
at Los Angeles

New England	7	10	10	0	—	27
L.A. Raiders	3	17	0	0	—	20

1985 AFC Championship Game
January 12, 1986
New England 31, Miami 14
at Miami

New England	3	14	7	7	—	31
Miami	0	7	0	7	—	14

1985 NFC Champions
Chicago Bears

In 1985, with Walter Payton, the NFL's all-time rushing leader, and quarterback Jim McMahon, coach Mike Ditka had a solid offense to complement the Bears' 46 Defense, led by Hall of Fame linebacker Mike Singletary.

Following a 15-1 regular season, the Bears shut out the Giants 21-0 in the NFC Divisional Playoff Game, holding the Giants without a first down for the first 28 minutes. The first touchdown came on a 5-yard punt return by Shaun Gayle after Sean Landeta whiffed a punt in the cold and wind. McMahon hit wide receiver Dennis McKinnon with 2 third-quarter touchdown passes to ice the victory.

The Bears were just as dominant in the NFC Championship Game, whitewashing the Rams 24-0. The Bears held Rams running back Eric Dickerson to 46 yards—202 fewer than the previous week—and limited quarterback Dieter Brock to 10 completions in 31 attempts. It was the first time a team had recorded successive postseason shutouts in the same year.

Regular Season

Sun	S-8	H	Tampa Bay Buccaneers	38-28	W
Sun	S-15	H	New England Patriots	20-7	W
Thu	S-19	A	Minnesota Vikings	33-24	W
Sun	S-29	H	Washington Redskins	45-10	W
Sun	O-6	A	Tampa Bay Buccaneers	27-19	W
Sun	O-13	A	San Francisco 49ers	26-10	W
Mon	O-21	H N	Green Bay Packers	23-7	W
Sun	O-27	H	Minnesota Vikings	27-9	W
Sun	N-3	A	Green Bay Packers	16-10	W
Sun	N-10	H	Detroit Lions	24-3	W
Sun	N-17	A	Dallas Cowboys	44-0	W
Sun	N-24	H	Atlanta Falcons	36-0	W
Mon	D-2	A N	Miami Dolphins	24-38	L
Sun	D-8	H	Indianapolis Colts	17-10	W
Sat	D-14	A	New York Jets	19-6	W
Sun	D-22	A	Detroit Lions	37-17	W

Postseason

1985 NFC Divisional Playoff Game
January 5, 1986
Chicago Bears 21, New York Giants 0
at Chicago

N.Y. Giants	0	0	0	0	—	0
Chicago	7	0	14	0	—	21

1985 NFC Championship Game
January 12, 1986
Chicago Bears 24, Los Angeles Rams 0
at Chicago

L.A. Rams	0	0	0	0	—	0
Chicago	10	0	7	7	—	24

Super Bowl XX

Chicago 46, New England 10
January 26, 1986, Louisiana Superdome,
New Orleans, Louisiana
Attendance: 73,818

On the second play of the game, the Bears were in trouble on a fumble by running back Walter Payton. Larry McGrew picked it up, and four plays later the New England Patriots led 3-0.

That was the Patriots' lone bright spot. By halftime, the game was out of New England's reach. The Patriots had minus-19 yards total offense and trailed 23-3 on 3 field goals by Kevin Butler and touchdown runs of 11 yards by Bears fullback Matt Suhey and 2 yards by quarterback Jim McMahon.

Early in the third quarter, a 60-yard pass to wide receiver Willie Gault led to McMahon's second score on a 1-yard sneak for a 30-3 lead.

The Patriots, who arrived in New Orleans as only the third wild-card playoff team ever to reach the Super Bowl (following the Dallas Cowboys in X and Oakland Raiders in XV) were given little hope to match the Raiders by winning.

Buddy Ryan, the Bears' defensive coordinator, and his attacking 46 Defense opened the door to the rout. It was the Super Bowl's largest margin of victory. Led by Super Bowl XX's most valuable player, defensive end Richard Dent, the Bears' defense allowed the Patriots just 116 yards through the air and 7 yards rushing, the latter a Super Bowl low.

The Bears' defense created 6 turnovers, including Reggie Phillips's 28-yard interception return in the third quarter for a touchdown that made it 37-3. Two plays after the ensuing kickoff, New England wide receiver Cedric Jones fumbled.

Linebacker Wilber Marshall returned it to the Patriots' 31, and the Bears drove to the 1. In came 318-pound defensive tackle William (Refrigerator) Perry, who lined up at fullback, took a handoff from McMahon, and ran for the touchdown.

Perry's massive windmill spike in the end zone was the game's final punctuation, though more than a quarter remained. After New England's Steve Grogan threw an 8-yard touchdown pass to Irving Fryar, the final scoring play came, appropriately, when Bears defensive tackle Henry Waechter chased down Grogan in the end zone for a safety.

Chicago (NFC)	13	10	21	2	—	46
New England (AFC)	3	0	0	7	—	10

NE—FG Franklin 36
Chi—FG Butler 28
Chi—FG Butler 24
Chi—Suhey 11 run (Butler kick)
Chi—McMahon 2 run (Butler kick)
Chi—FG Butler 24
Chi—McMahon 1 run (Butler kick)
Chi—Phillips 28 interception return (Butler kick)
Chi—Perry 1 run (Butler kick)
NE—Fryar 8 pass from Grogan (Franklin kick)
Chi—Safety, Waechter tackled Grogan in end zone

TEAM STATISTICS	CHI	NE
First Downs	23	12
Rushing	13	1
Passing	9	10
Penalty	1	1
Total Yardage	408	123
Net rushing yardage	167	7
Net passing yardage	241	116
Passes att.-comp.-had int.	24-12-0	36-17-2

RUSHING
Chi. Bears—Payton 22 for 61; Suhey 11 for 52, 1 TD; Gentry 3 for 15; Sanders 4 for 15; McMahon 5 for 14, 2 TDs; Thomas 2 for 8; Perry 1 for 1, 1 TD; Fuller 1 for 1.
New England—Collins 3 for 4; Weathers 1 for 3; Grogan 1 for 3; C. James 5 for 1; Hawthorne 1 for -4.

PASSING
Chi. Bears—McMahon 12 of 20 for 256; Fuller 0 of 4.
New England—Grogan 17 of 30 for 177, 1 TD, 2 int.; Eason 0 of 6 for 0.

RECEIVING
Chi. Bears—Gault 4 for 129; Gentry 2 for 41; Margerum 2 for 36; Moorehead 2 for 22; Suhey 1 for 24; Thomas 1 for 4.
New England—Morgan 6 for 51; Starring 2 for 39; Fryar 2 for 24, 1 TD; Collins 2 for 19; Ramsey 2 for 16; Jones 1 for 19; C. James 1 for 6; Weathers 1 for 3.

1985 Team Rosters

Chi. Bears
Brad Anderson
Tom Andrews*
Kurt Becker
Mark Bortz*
Maury Buford*
Kevin Butler*
Brian Cabral*
Jim Covert*
Richard Dent*
Dave Duerson*
Gary Fencik*
Leslie Frazier*
Andy Frederick*
Steve Fuller*
Willie Gault*
Shaun Gayle*
Dennis Gentry*
Dan Hampton*
Mike Hartenstine*
Jay Hilgenberg*
Stefan Humphries*
Tyrone Keys*
James Maness
Ken Margerum*
Wilber Marshall*
Dennis McKinnon*
Jim McMahon*
Steve McMichael*
Emery Moorehead*
Jim Morrissey*
Keith Ortego*
Walter Payton*
William Perry*
Reggie Phillips*
Mike Richardson*
Ron Rivera*
Thomas Sanders*
Mike Singletary*
Matt Suhey*
Ken Taylor*
Tom Thayer*
Calvin Thomas*
Cliff Thrift*
Mike Tomczak*
Keith Van Horne*
Henry Waechter*
Otis Wilson*
Tim Wrightman*

New England
Julius Adams*
Don Blackmon*
Jim Bowman*
Pete Brock*
Rich Camarillo*
Raymond Clayborn*
Tony Collins*
Tom Condon
Smiley Creswell*
Lin Dawson*
Tony Eason*
Paul Fairchild*
Tony Franklin*
Irving Fryar*
Ernest Gibson*
Steve Grogan*
John Hannah*
Greg Hawthorne*
Brian Holloway*
Brian Ingram*
Craig James*
Roland James*
Cedric Jones*
Ronnie Lippett*
Fred Marion*
Trevor Matich
Larry McGrew*
Rod McSwain*
Steve Moore*
Stanley Morgan*
Guy Morriss*
Steve Nelson*
Dennis Owens*
Art Plunkett*
Derrick Ramsey*
Johnny Rembert*
Ed Reynolds*
Kenneth Sims
Stephen Starring*
Mosi Tatupu*
Ben Thomas*
Andre Tippett*
Garin Veris*
Robert Weathers*
Derwin Williams
Ed Williams*
Lester Williams*
Toby Williams
Ron Wooten*

1986 AFC Champions
Denver Broncos

The Broncos won their second division title in three years in 1986. Although Denver finished with an 11-5 record, the team went just 3-4 to close out the season. To make things more difficult, the Broncos drew the defending AFC champion Patriots in a divisional playoff game.

John Elway staked the Broncos a 10-0 lead over New England when he scrambled 22 yards for a touchdown in the second quarter. He gave Denver the lead for good with a 48-yard touchdown pass to Vance Johnson. The Broncos tacked on a safety by Rulon Jones to complete the 22-17 win at Mile High Stadium.

In the AFC Championship Game, it looked like it might be Cleveland's day when Bernie Kosar completed a 48-yard touchdown pass to Brian Brennan that gave the Browns a 20-13 lead with only 5:43 remaining in the fourth quarter.

Denver took over at its 2 and embarked on what became known as "The Drive." The 15-play odyssey included 9 passes and 2 runs by Elway, who, on third-and-1, found Mark Jackson with a 5-yard touchdown pass to tie the game.

On Denver's first possession in overtime, Elway took the Broncos 60 yards in 9 plays to set up the winning 33-yard field goal by Rich Karlis.

Regular Season

Sun	S-7	H	Los Angeles Raiders	38-36	W
Mon	S-15	A	Pittsburgh Steelers	21-10	W
Sun	S-21	A	Philadelphia Eagles	33-7	W
Sun	S-28	H	New England Patriots	27-20	W
Sun	O-5	H	Dallas Cowboys	29-14	W
Sun	O-12	A	San Diego Chargers	31-14	W
Mon	O-20	A N	New York Jets	10-22	L
Sun	O-26	H	Seattle Seahawks	20-13	W
Sun	N-2	A	Los Angeles Raiders	21-10	W
Sun	N-9	H	San Diego Chargers	3-9	L
Sun	N-16	H	Kansas City Chiefs	38-17	W
Sun	N-23	A	New York Giants	16-19	L
Sun	N-30	H	Cincinnati Bengals	34-28	W
Sun	D-7	A	Kansas City Chiefs	10-37	L
Sat	D-13	H	Washington Redskins	31-30	W
Sat	D-20	A	Seattle Seahawks	16-41	L

Postseason

1986 AFC Divisional Playoff Game
January 4, 1987
Denver 22, New England 17
at Denver

New England	0	10	7	0		—	17
Denver	3	7	10	2		—	22

1986 AFC Championship Game
January 11, 1987
Denver 23, Cleveland 20 (OT)
at Cleveland

Denver	0	10	3	7	3	—	23
Cleveland	7	3	0	10	0	—	20

1986 NFC Champions
New York Giants

The Giants rambled to a 14-2 season and won their first playoff game just as easily, routing the 49ers 49-3. Phil Simms passed for 4 touchdowns and New York's defense held San Francisco to 29 yards rushing

On the 49ers' first drive, Jerry Rice caught a pass and was on his way to a 50-yard touchdown but dropped the ball and New York recovered. The Giants went 80 yards, scoring on a 24-yard touchdown pass from Simms to Mark Bavaro. In the second period, an interception by Herb Welch led to Joe Morris's 45-yard touchdown run. At the end of the half, Lawrence Taylor intercepted Joe Montana and rambled 34 yards for a touchdown.

In the NFC Championship Game at Giants Stadium, New York took advantage of a wind gusting up to 35 miles per hour to blow past the Redskins 17-0.

After winning the coin toss, the Giants elected to kick off with the wind. The Redskins punted into the wind, and New York took over at the Washington 47. Six plays later, Raul Allegre kicked a 47-yard field goal.

A second punt into the wind gave the Giants the ball at the Redskins' 38, and Simms hit Lionel Manuel with an 11-yard touchdown pass. In the second period, the Giants scored again on Joe Morris's 1-yard touchdown run. The New York defense made it stand up.

Regular Season

Mon	S-8	A N	Dallas Cowboys	28-31	L
Sun	S-14	H	San Diego Chargers	20-7	W
Sun	S-21	A	Los Angeles Raiders	14-9	W
Sun	S-28	H	New Orleans Saints	20-17	W
Sun	O-5	A	St. Louis Cardinals	13-6	W
Sun	O-12	H	Philadelphia Eagles	35-3	W
Sun	O-19	A	Seattle Seahawks	12-17	L
Mon	O-27	H N	Washington Redskins	27-20	W
Sun	N-2	H	Dallas Cowboys	17-14	W
Sun	N-9	A	Philadelphia Eagles	17-14	W
Sun	N-16	A	Minnesota Vikings	22-20	W
Sun	N-23	H	Denver Broncos	19-16	W
Mon	D-1	A N	San Francisco 49ers	21-17	W
Sun	D-7	A	Washington Redskins	24-14	W
Sun	D-14	H	St. Louis Cardinals	27-7	W
Sat	D-20	H	Green Bay Packers	55-24	W

Postseason

1986 NFC Divisional Playoff Game
January 4, 1987
New York Giants 49, San Francisco 3
at East Rutherford, New Jersey

San Francisco	3	0	0	0	—	3
N.Y. Giants	7	21	21	0	—	49

1986 NFC Championship Game
January 11, 1987
New York Giants 17, Washington 0
at East Rutherford, New Jersey

Washington	0	0	0	0	—	0
N.Y. Giants	10	7	0	0	—	17

Super Bowl XXI

New York Giants 39, Denver 20
January 25, 1987, Rose Bowl, Pasadena, California
Attendance: 101,063

This was Denver quarterback John Elway's first trip to the Super Bowl, and he was on fire. Exhibiting the same brilliance that led the Broncos to a 23-20 overtime victory over Cleveland in the AFC Championship Game, Elway managed to get in 30 minutes' worth of Super Bowl heroics. He completed 13 of 20 passes for 187 yards as the Broncos took a 10-9 halftime advantage.

But the day belonged to New York's Phil Simms, whose Super Bowl-record 10 consecutive completions highlighted a 30-point second half for the Giants, another Super Bowl record.

"I felt good when we were warming up before the game," Simms said. "I was telling the guys, 'I've got it today.' "

Statistically, that translated to 22 completions in 25 pass attempts (a Super Bowl-record completion percentage of 88 percent) for 268 yards and 3 touchdowns.

The first of Simms's scoring throws came 9:33 into the game, a 6-yard pass to tight end Zeke Mowatt that finished a 9-play, 78-yard drive.

The Giants' quarterback hit tight end Mark Bavaro with a 13-yard scoring pass early in the third quarter to give New York a 16-10 lead. Meanwhile, the Giants' defense was holding the Broncos to 2 net yards in 7 offensive plays in the third period, and New York built a 26-10 lead.

Simms's third scoring pass went 6 yards to wide receiver Phil McConkey early in the fourth quarter to make it 33-10 with 10:56 left. The Broncos could answer only with a 28-yard field goal by Karlis, and the teams traded touchdowns to finish it.

Simms was voted the game's most valuable player, then unloaded an albatross: years of criticism in the New York media since his arrival with the Giants in 1979. "After all I've taken over the years," Simms said, "this makes everything worth it."

Denver (AFC)	10	0	0	10	—	20
N.Y. Giants (NFC)	7	2	17	13	—	39

Den—FG Karlis 48
NYG—Mowatt 6 pass from Simms (Allegre kick)
Den—Elway 4 run (Karlis kick)
NYG—Safety, Martin tackled Elway in end zone
NYG—Bavaro 13 pass from Simms (Allegre kick)
NYG—FG Allegre 21
NYG—Morris 1 run (Allegre kick)
NYG—McConkey 6 pass from Simms (Allegre kick)
Den—FG Karlis 28
NYG—Anderson 2 run (kick failed)
Den—V. Johnson 47 pass from Elway (Karlis kick)

TEAM STATISTICS	DEN	NYG
First Downs	23	24
Rushing	5	10
Passing	16	13
Penalty	2	1
Total Yardage	372	399
Net rushing yardage	52	136
Net passing yardage	320	263
Passes att.-comp.-had int.	41-26-1	25-22-0

RUSHING
Denver—Elway 6 for 27, 1 TD; Willhite 4 for 19; Sewell 3 for 4; Lang 2 for 2; Winder 4 for 0.
N.Y. Giants—Morris 20 for 67, 1 TD; Simms 3 for 25; Rouson 3 for 22; Galbreath 4 for 17; Carthon 3 for 4; Anderson 2 for 1, 1 TD; Rutledge 3 for 0.

PASSING
Denver—Elway 22 of 37 for 304, 1 TD, 1 int.; Kubiak 4 of 4 for 48.
N.Y. Giants—Simms 22 of 25 for 268, 3 TDs.

RECEIVING
Denver—V. Johnson 5 for 121, 1 TD, Willhite 5 for 39; Winder 4 for 34; M. Jackson 3 for 51; Watson 2 for 54; Sampson 2 for 20; Mobley 2 for 17; Sewell 2 for 12; Lang 1 for 4.
N.Y. Giants—Bavaro 4 for 51, 1 TD; Morris 4 for 20; Carthon 4 for 13; Robinson 3 for 62; Manuel 3 for 43; McConkey 2 for 50, 1 TD; Rouson 1 for 23; Mowatt 1 for 6, 1 TD.

1986 Team Rosters

N.Y. Giants	Denver
Raul Allegre*	Ken Bell*
Ottis Anderson*	Keith Bishop*
Billy Ard*	Tony Boddie
Carl Banks*	Billy Bryan*
Mark Bavaro*	Rubin Carter
Brad Benson*	Tony Colorito*
Jim Burt*	Darren Comeaux*
Harry Carson*	Mark Cooper*
Maurice Carthon*	Rick Dennison*
Mark Collins*	John Elway*
Joe Cooper	Simon Fletcher*
Eric Dorsey*	Steve Foley*
Tom Flynn*	Mike Freeman*
Tony Galbreath*	Freddie Gilbert*
Chris Godfrey*	Joey Hackett*
Andy Headen*	Mike Harden*
Kenny Hill	Mark Haynes*
Jeff Hostetler	Winford Hood
Erik Howard*	Mike Horan*
Byron Hunt*	Paul Howard
Bobby Johnson*	Ricky Hunley*
Damian Johnson*	Daniel Hunter
Pepper Johnson*	Mark Jackson*
Brian Johnston*	Tom Jackson*
Robbie Jones*	Vance Johnson*
Terry Kinard	Rulon Jones*
Sean Landeta*	Rich Karlis*
Greg Lasker*	Clarence Kay*
Lionel Manuel*	Greg Kragen*
Leonard Marshall*	Gary Kubiak*
George Martin*	Gene Lang*
Phil McConkey*	Ken Lanier*
Solomon Miller*	Tony Lilly*
Joe Morris*	Karl Mecklenburg*
Zeke Mowatt*	Bobby Micho*
Karl Nelson*	Orson Mobley*
Bart Oates*	Chris Norman
Elvis Patterson*	Dan Remsberg*
Gary Reasons*	Randy Robbins*
William Roberts*	Jim Ryan*
Stacy Robinson*	Clint Sampson*
Lee Rouson*	Steven Sewell*
Jeff Rutledge*	Dennis Smith*
Jerome Sally*	Dave Studdard*
Phil Simms*	Andre Townsend*
Lawrence Taylor*	Steve Watson*
Bob Thomas	Jack Weil
Vince Warren	Gerald Willhite*
John Washington	Steve Wilson*
Herb Welch*	Sammy Winder*
Perry Williams*	Ken Woodard*
	Louis Wright*

1987 AFC Champions
Denver Broncos

Denver repeated as division champs for the second straight year in 1987, as the Three Amigos receiving corps of Mark Jackson, Vance Johnson, and Ricky Nattiel helped produce a 10-4-1 record.

The Broncos defeated the Oilers 34-10 in a divisional playoff game as Denver's defense set up 2 first-quarter touchdowns with a fumble recovery and an interception. The Broncos jumped out to a 24-3 lead as John Elway teamed up with tight end Clarence Kay twice for touchdowns before halftime.

Reserve cornerback Jeremiah Castille forced a fumble by Earnest Byner and then recovered it at the Denver 3 with 65 seconds left to preserve the Broncos' second consecutive AFC title game victory over the Cleveland Browns 38-33. It was the second straight year the Browns seemed poised to go to the Super Bowl only to have Denver snatch it away each time; this time Denver almost let it get away, blowing a 21-3 halftime lead.

The Browns scored 4 touchdowns in a little over a quarter, but Elway responded by driving the Broncos 75 yards and hitting Sammy Winder with a 20-yard touchdown pass with only 4:01 remaining. After Castille's big play averted disaster, punter Mike Horan took a safety with 8 seconds left to finish the scoring.

Regular Season

Sun	S-13	H	Seattle Seahawks	40-17	W
Sun	S-20	A	Green Bay Packers (OT)	17-17	T
Sun	O-4	H	Houston Oilers	10-40	L
Mon	O-12	H N	Los Angeles Raiders	30-14	W
Sun	O-18	A	Kansas City Chiefs	26-17	W
Mon	O-26	A N	Minnesota Vikings	27-34	L
Sun	N-1	H	Detroit Lions	34-0	W
Sun	N-8	A	Buffalo Bills	14-21	L
Mon	N-16	H N	Chicago Bears	31-29	W
Sun	N-22	A	Los Angeles Raiders	23-17	W
Sun	N-29	A	San Diego Chargers	31-17	W
Sun	D-6	H	New England Patriots	31-20	W
Sun	D-13	A	Seattle Seahawks	21-28	L
Sat	D-19	H	Kansas City Chiefs	20-17	W
Sun	D-27	H	San Diego Chargers	24-0	W

Postseason

1987 AFC Divisional Playoff Game
January 10, 1988
Denver 34, Houston 10 at Denver

Houston	0	3	0	7	—	10
Denver	14	10	3	7	—	34

1987 AFC Championship Game
January 17, 1988
Denver 38, Cleveland 33 at Denver

Cleveland	0	3	21	9	—	33
Denver	14	7	10	7	—	38

1987 NFC Champions
Washington Redskins

With Jay Schroeder and Doug Williams sharing the quarterbacking duties, the Redskins went 11-4 in the regular season and overcame an early deficit to come back and beat the Bears for the second year a row in a divisional playoff game 21-17.

Chicago held a 14-0 lead, but George Rogers got Washington on the scoreboard with a 3-yard touchdown run. Williams connected with tight end Clint Didier to tie the game shortly before halftime, and early in the third quarter, Darrell Green returned a Bears' punt 52 yards for the deciding touchdown.

The Redskins defeated Minnesota 17-10 in the NFC Championship Game, holding the Vikings to 76 rushing yards and sacking quarterback Wade Wilson 8 times.

The Redskins scored in the first quarter on a 42-yard touchdown pass from Williams to Kelvin Bryant. The Vikings tied it before halftime when Wilson hit Leo Lewis with a 23-yard touchdown strike.

With the score tied 10-10, Washington put together an 18-play, 70-yard drive that ended with a 7-yard touchdown pass from Williams to Gary Clark with 5:06 left. Minnesota drove to the Washington 6, but Wilson's fourth-down pass into the end zone fell incomplete and the Redskins were headed to their third Super Bowl in six years.

Regular Season

Sun	S-13	H	Philadelphia Eagles	34-24	W
Sun	S-20	A	Atlanta Falcons	20-21	L
Sun	O-4	H	St. Louis Cardinals	28-21	W
Sun	O-11	A	New York Giants	38-12	W
Mon	O-19	A	Dallas Cowboys	13-7	W
Sun	O-25	H	New York Jets	17-16	W
Sun	N-1	A	Buffalo Bills	27-7	W
Sun	N-8	A	Philadelphia Eagles	27-31	L
Sun	N-15	H	Detroit Lions	20-13	W
Mon	N-23	H N	Los Angeles Rams	26-30	L
Sun	N-29	H	New York Giants	23-19	W
Sun	D-6	A	St. Louis Cardinals	34-17	W
Sun	D-13	H	Dallas Cowboys	24-20	W
Sun	D-20	A	Miami Dolphins	21-23	L
Sat	D-26	A	Minnesota Vikings (OT)	27-24	W

Postseason

1987 NFC Divisional Playoff Game
January 10, 1988
Washington 21, Chicago Bears 17 at Chicago

Washington	0	14	7	0	—	21
Chicago	7	7	3	0	—	17

1987 NFC Championship Game
January 17, 1988
Washington 17, Minnesota 10 at Washington

Minnesota	0	7	0	3	—	10
Washington	7	0	3	7	—	17

Super Bowl XXII

Washington 42, Denver 10
January 31, 1988, San Diego Jack Murphy Stadium, San Diego, California
Attendance: 73,302

It looked from the beginning like another Super Bowl blowout—with Denver finally getting its licks.

Ricky Nattiel, one of the Broncos' Three Amigos at wide receiver, scored on his team's first play from scrimmage, a 56-yard pass from quarterback John Elway. Rich Karlis added a 24-yard field goal to give Denver a 10-0 lead after one quarter.

Then came a scoring outburst unseen in Super Bowl history. Washington quarterback Doug Williams, the game's most valuable player, led his team on a 35-0 binge in the game's second 15 minutes. The shock was decisive. The Redskins intercepted Elway 3 times (twice by cornerback Barry Wilburn) and sacked him 5 times (twice by strong safety Alvin Walton) en route to winning 42-10.

Williams, who left the game late in the first quarter with a hyperextended left knee, came back with 14:17 left in the second quarter and began striking with accuracy and abandon. Before halftime, he directed scoring drives of 80, 64, 74, 60, and 79 yards. All but the middle one, the 74-yard march highlighted by Timmy Smith's 58-yard touchdown run, ended in touchdown passes from Williams. The first went 80 yards to Ricky Sanders. The second went 27 yards to Gary Clark. The third was a 50-yard bomb to Sanders, and the fourth went to Clint Didier for 8 yards.

Smith, who ran for a Super Bowl-record 204 yards on 22 carries—78 yards more than he gained the entire regular season—closed out the scoring with a 4-yard touchdown run in the final quarter.

Washington (NFC)	0	35	0	7	—	42
Denver (AFC)	10	0	0	0	—	10

Den—Nattiel 56 pass from Elway (Karlis kick)
Den—FG Karlis 24
Wash—Sanders 80 pass from Williams (Haji-Sheikh kick)
Wash—Clark 27 pass from Williams (Haji-Sheikh kick)
Wash—Smith 58 run (Haji-Sheikh kick)
Wash—Sanders 50 pass from Williams (Haji-Sheikh kick)
Wash—Didier 8 pass from Williams (Haji-Sheikh kick)
Wash—Smith 4 run (Haji-Sheikh kick)

TEAM STATISTICS	WASH	DEN
First Downs	25	18
Rushing	13	6
Passing	11	10
Penalty	1	2
Total Yardage	602	327
Net rushing yardage	280	97
Net passing yardage	322	230
Passes att.-comp.-had int.	30-18-1	39-15-3

RUSHING
Washington—Smith 22 for 204, 2 TDs; Bryant 8 for 38; Clark 1 for 25; Rogers 5 for 17; Griffin 1 for 2; Williams 2 for -2; Sanders 1 for -4.
Denver—Lang 5 for 38; Elway 3 for 32; Winder 8 for 30; Sewell 1 for -3.
PASSING
Washington—Williams 18 of 29 for 340, 4 TDs, 1 int.; Schroeder 0 of 1.
Denver—Elway 14 of 38 for 257, 1 TD, 3 int.; Sewell 1 of 1 for 23.
RECEIVING
Washington—Sanders 9 for 193, 2 TDs; Clark 3 for 55, 1 TD; Warren 2 for 15; Monk 1 for 40; Bryant 1 for 20; Smith 1 for 9; Didier 1 for 8, 1 TD.
Denver—Jackson 4 for 76; Sewell 4 for 41; Nattiel 2 for 69, 1 TD; Kay 2 for 38; Winder 1 for 26; Elway 1 for 23; Lang 1 for 7.

1987 Team Rosters

Washington
Anthony Allen
Obed Ariri
Jess Atkinson
Dan Benish
Cliff Benson
Keiron Bigby
Jeff Bostic*
Todd Bowles*
Reggie Branch*
Darrick Brilz
Kelvin Bryant*
Derek Bunch
Danny Burmeister
Dave Butz*
Ravin Caldwell*
Joe Caravello
Mark Carlson
Gary Clark*
Joe Cofer
Monte Coleman*
Anthony Copeland
John Cowne
Steve Cox*
Eric Coyle
Bobby Curtis
Brian Davis*
Vernon Dean*
Glenn Dennison
Clint Didier*
K.D. Dunn
Dave Etherly
Frank Frazier
Steve Gage
Alec Gibson
Kurt Gouveia*
Darryl Grant*
Darrell Green*
Keith Griffin*
Russ Grimm*
Ali Haji-Sheikh*
Dean Hamel*
Steve Hamilton*
Allen Harvin
Ray Hitchcock
Walter Holman
Charles Jackson
Joe Jacoby*
Tim Jessie
Richard Johnson
Anthony Jones*
David Jones
Ted Karras
Mel Kaufman*
Rick Kehr*
Garry Kimble
Jon Kimmel
Markus Koch*
Skip Lane
Kit Lathrop
Dexter Manley*
Charles Mann*
Steve Martin
Mark May*
Craig McEwen
Curtis McGriff
Raleigh McKenzie*
Dan McQuaid
Rich Milot*
Michael Mitchell
Art Monk*
Tim Morrison
Neal Olkewicz*
Terry Orr*
Phil Pettey
Joe Phillips
Tony Robinson
George Rogers*
Carlton Rose
Ed Rubbert
Anthony Sagnella
Ricky Sanders*
Jay Schroeder*
Willard Scissum
Tony Settles
Derrick Shepard
Ed Simmons
Timmy Smith*
R.C. Thielemann*
Steve Thompson
Brendan Toibin
Dave Truitt
Clarence Vaughn*
Clarence Verdin
Lionel Vital
Henry Waechter
Alvin Walton*
Don Warren*
Jack Weil
Barry Wilburn*
Doug Williams*
Marvin Williams
Eric Wilson
Ted Wilson
Wayne Wilson
David Windham
Dennis Woodberry*
Mike Wooten
Eric Yarber*

Denver
Mitch Andrews
John Ayers
Kevin Belcher
Ken Bell*
Keith Bishop*
Tony Boddie*
Walt Bowyer*
Tyrone Braxton*
Michael Brooks*
Laron Brown
Steve Bryan
Billy Bryan
Scott Caldwell
Jeremiah Castille*
Kevin Clark*
Mike Clendenen
Mark Cooper
Rick Dennison*
Kirk Dodge
Joe Dudek
John Elway*
Steve Fitzhugh
Simon Fletcher*
Mike Freeman*
Ralph Giacomarro
Freddie Gilbert*
Sam Graddy
Mike Harden
Archie Harris
Mark Haynes*
Winford Hood
Mike Horan*
Stefan Humphries*
Ricky Hunley*
Mark Jackson*
Roger Jackson
Earl Johnson
Vance Johnson*
Tim Joiner
Daryll Jones
David Jones
Leonard Jones
Rulon Jones*
Ken Karcher
Rich Karlis*
Keith Kartz*
Clarence Kay*
Bruce Klosterman*
Mike Knox
Greg Kragen*
Gary Kubiak*
Gene Lang*
Ken Lanier*
Larry Lee
Zeph Lee
Tony Lilly*
Bill Lobenstein
Kerry Locklin
Tim Lucas*
Dan MacDonald
Warren Marshall
Rick Massie
Dean May
Monte McGuire
Ron McLean
Karl Mecklenburg*
Bobby Micho*
Orson Mobley*
Marc Munford
Ricky Nattiel*
Russell Payne
Jack Peavey
Lyle Pickens
Bruce Plummer*
Nathan Poole
Dan Remsberg
Randy Robbins*
Martin Rudolph
Darryl Russell
Jim Ryan*
Steven Sewell*
Dennis Smith*
Matt Smith
Dave Studdard*
Shane Swanson
Bob Thompson
Andre Townsend*
Jeff Tupper
Steve Watson*
Gerald Willhite
Steve Wilson*
Sammy Winder*
Bryant Winn
Ray Woodard

1988 AFC Champions
Cincinnati Bengals

The Bengals posted a franchise-best 12-4 record in 1988. Quarterback Boomer Esiason won NFL MVP honors, and fullback Ickey Woods won the hearts of Bengals' fans with his patented touchdown dance, the "Ickey Shuffle."

In the postseason, Cincinnati dominated the line of scrimmage, pounding out 254 yards on the ground while holding Seattle to only 18. The Bengals, who took a 21-0 lead in the second period, withstood a fourth-quarter rally to defeat the Seahawks 21-13. Woods bulled for 126 yards and James Brooks ran for 72, but it was Stanley Wilson who scored Cincinnati's first 2 touchdowns on a pair of 3-yard runs. Woods finished the Bengals' scoring with a 1-yard touchdown in the second quarter.

In the AFC Championship Game, the Bengals limited the Bills to only 45 yards rushing and 136 passing. Woods, meanwhile, did the heavy-duty work for the Bengals, rushing for 102 yards on 29 carries.

The Bengals established their defensive dominance from the start against the Bills, with Lewis Billups and Eric Thomas intercepting 2 of Jim Kelly's first 3 passes. David Fulcher added another interception in the end zone in the fourth quarter to put the game on ice.

The end result was a 21-10 victory that sent Cincinnati to its second Super Bowl of the decade.

Regular Season

Sun	S-4	H	Phoenix Cardinals	21-14	W
Sun	S-11	A	Philadelphia Eagles	28-24	W
Sun	S-18	A	Pittsburgh Steelers	17-12	W
Sun	S-25	H	Cleveland Browns	24-17	W
Sun	O-2	A	Los Angeles Raiders	45-21	W
Sun	O-9	H	New York Jets	36-19	W
Sun	O-16	A	New England Patriots	21-27	L
Sun	O-23	H	Houston Oilers	44-21	W
Sun	O-30	A	Cleveland Browns	16-23	L
Sun	N-6	H	Pittsburgh Steelers	42-7	W
Sun	N-13	A	Kansas City Chiefs	28-31	L
Sun	N-20	A	Dallas Cowboys	38-24	W
Sun	N-27	H	Buffalo Bills	35-21	W
Sun	D-4	H	San Diego Chargers	27-10	W
Sun	D-11	A	Houston Oilers	6-41	L
Sat	D-17	H	Washington Redskins (OT)	20-17	W

Postseason

1988 AFC Divisional Playoff Game
December 31, 1988
Cincinnati 21, Seattle 13 at Cincinnati

Seattle	0	0	0	13	—	13
Cincinnati	7	14	0	0	—	21

1988 AFC Championship Game
January 8, 1989
Cincinnati 21, Buffalo 10 at Cincinnati

Buffalo	0	10	0	0	—	10
Cincinnati	7	7	0	7	—	21

1988 NFC Champions
San Francisco 49ers

Stumbling with a 6-5 record and two games out of first place, the 49ers then won four straight to take the Western Division title.

In the playoffs, the 49ers avenged their postseason defeat of the year before by routing Minnesota 34-9 in a divisional playoff game. Joe Montana and Jerry Rice connected for 3 first-half touchdowns, from 2, 4, and 11 yards, and after the Vikings finally scored a touchdown in the third quarter, the 49ers turned the game over to Roger Craig. For the day, Craig gained 135 yards on 21 carries. He scored on a 4-yard run in the final period, and later had an 80-yard touchdown run.

It was 17 degrees with a wind-chill factor of minus-26, but San Francisco paid the weather no mind. The 49ers scored in every period, gaining 406 total yards, losing only 1 turnover, and having no penalties to defeat the Bears 28-3 in the NFC Championship Game. Montana and Rice teamed up for 2 touchdowns, 61 yards in the first quarter, and 27 yards in the second. Chicago was able to respond only with a 25-yard field goal by Kevin Butler. Montana drove the 49ers 78 yards on 13 plays in the third quarter, passing to tight end John Frank for 5 yards and a touchdown. San Francisco's final score came on fullback Tom Rathman's 4-yard run in the fourth quarter.

Regular Season

Sun	S-4	A	New Orleans Saints	34-33	W
Sun	S-11	A	New York Giants	20-17	W
Sun	S-18	H	Atlanta Falcons	17-34	L
Sun	S-25	A	Seattle Seahawks	38-7	W
Sun	O-2	H	Detroit Lions	20-13	W
Sun	O-9	H	Denver Broncos (OT)	13-16	L
Sun	O-16	A	Los Angeles Rams	24-21	W
Mon	O-24	A N	Chicago Bears	9-10	L
Sun	O-30	H	Minnesota Vikings	24-21	W
Sun	N-6	A	Phoenix Cardinals	23-24	L
Sun	N-13	H	Los Angeles Raiders	3-9	L
Mon	N-21	H N	Washington Redskins	37-21	W
Sun	N-27	A	San Diego Chargers	48-10	W
Sun	D-4	A	Atlanta Falcons	13-3	W
Sun	D-11	H	New Orleans Saints	30-17	W
Sun	D-18	H N	Los Angeles Rams	16-38	L

Postseason

1988 NFC Divisional Playoff Game
January 1, 1989
San Francisco 34, Minnesota 9 at San Francisco

Minnesota	3	0	6	0	—	9
San Francisco	7	14	0	13	—	34

1988 NFC Championship Game
January 8, 1989
San Francisco 28, Chicago 3 at Chicago

San Francisco	7	7	7	7	—	28
Chicago	0	3	0	0	—	3

Super Bowl XXIII

San Francisco 20, Cincinnati 16
January 22, 1989, Joe Robbie Stadium, Miami, Florida
Attendance: 75,129

Trailing 16-13 with 3:10 to play, Joe Montana led the 49ers on an 11-play, 92-yard drive that ended when Montana hit wide receiver John Taylor in the back of the Cincinnati end zone with a 10-yard touchdown pass with 34 seconds left. In this Super Bowl, however, Montana's mastery of clock management and his record 357 passing yards rode shotgun next to most-valuable-player Jerry Rice and his 11 receptions for a Super Bowl-record 215 yards—on a sprained ankle.

Cincinnati's reward for keeping the 49ers contained most of the game was a short-lived 16-13 lead following Jim Breech's 40-yard field goal.

After a 3-3 halftime tie, the teams traded field goals in the latter half of the third quarter—a 43-yard kick by Breech and a 32-yard kick by San Francisco's Mike Cofer.

The Bengals took a 13-6 lead when Stanford Jennings returned Cofer's kickoff 93 yards for a touchdown. A minute and 31 seconds later, Montana connected with Rice on a 14-yard touchdown pass to tie the game, the fourth play of an 85-yard drive. Appropriately, Rice got the march started with a 31-yard reception from Montana.

On his scoring play, Rice caught the ball at the Bengals' 5, and his momentum appeared to be carrying him out of bounds near the goal line. But at the last second, Rice reached out and broke the goal line's invisible plane with the ball. Next to Taylor's game-decider, it was Rice's 27-yard reception on second-and-20 from the Cincinnati 45 that highlighted the 49ers' final drive.

In the end, 49ers guard Randy Cross put into perspective the feeling of the 10 men who accompanied Montana for the game's most memorable 92 yards. "Even if we had to pick up Joe en masse and carry him over the goal line," Cross said, "we were going to get a touchdown."

Cincinnati (AFC)	0	3	10	3	—	16
San Francisco (NFC)	3	0	3	14	—	20

SF—FG Cofer 41
Cin—FG Breech 34
Cin—FG Breech 43
SF—FG Cofer 32
Cin—Jennings 93 kickoff return (Breech kick)
SF—Rice 14 pass from Montana (Cofer kick)
Cin—FG Breech 40
SF—Taylor 10 pass from Montana (Cofer kick)

TEAM STATISTICS	CIN	SF
First Downs	13	23
Rushing	7	6
Passing	6	16
Penalty	0	1
Total Yardage	229	453
Net rushing yardage	106	112
Net passing yardage	123	341
Passes att.-comp.-had int.	25-11-1	36-23-0

RUSHING
Cincinnati—Woods 20 for 79; Brooks 6 for 24; Jennings 1 for 3; Esiason 1 for 0.
San Francisco—Craig 17 for 71; Rathman 5 for 23; Montana 4 for 13; Rice 1 for 5.
PASSING
Cincinnati—Esiason 11 of 25 for 144, 1 int.
San Francisco—Montana 23 of 36 for 357, 2 TDs.
RECEIVING
Cincinnati—Brown 4 for 44; Collinsworth 3 for 40; McGee 2 for 23; Brooks 1 for 20; Hillary 1 for 17.
San Francisco—Rice 11 for 215, 1 TD; Craig 8 for 101; Frank 2 for 15; Rathman 1 for 16; Taylor 1 for 10, 1 TD.

1988 Team Rosters

San Francisco
Harris Barton*
Dwaine Board
Jeff Bregel
Chet Brooks
Michael Carter*
Wes Chandler
Mike Cofer*
Bruce Collie*
Greg Cox*
Roger Craig*
Randy Cross*
Doug DuBose
Riki Ellison*
Kevin Fagan*
Jim Fahnhorst*
Terrence Flagler
John Frank*
Jeff Fuller*
Terry Greer*
Don Griffin*
Ron Hadley
Charles Haley*
Ron Heller*
Barry Helton*
Tom Holmoe*
Pierce Holt*
Brent Jones*
Sam Kennedy*
Pete Kugler*
Kevin Lilly
Ronnie Lott*
Guy McIntyre*
Tim McKyer*
Doug Mikolas
Joe Montana*
Calvin Nicholas
Tory Nixon
Bubba Paris*
Darryl Pollard*
Tom Rathman*
Jerry Rice*
Larry Roberts*
Del Rodgers*
Bill Romanowski*
Max Runager
Jesse Sapolu*
Jeff Stover*
Danny Stubbs*
Harry Sydney*
John Taylor*
Chuck Thomas*
Keena Turner*
Steve Wallace*
Michael Walter*
Mike Wilson*
Eric Wright*
Steve Young

Cincinnati
Leo Barker*
Lewis Billups*
Brian Blados*
Ed Brady*
Jim Breech*
James Brooks*
Eddie Brown*
Jason Buck*
Barney Bussey*
Cris Collinsworth*
Ellis Dillahunt
Rickey Dixon*
David Douglas*
Eddie Edwards*
Boomer Esiason*
David Fulcher*
Scott Fulhage
David Grant*
Ira Hillary*
Rodney Holman*
Ray Horton*
Tim Inglis
Stanford Jennings*
Lee Johnson*
Eric Kattus
Joe Kelly*
Emanuel King*
Bruce Kozerski*
Tim Krumrie*
Marc Logan*
Mike Martin
Curtis Maxey
Skip McClendon*
Tim McGee*
Max Montoya*
Anthony Munoz*
Mike Norseth
Carl Parker*
Bruce Reimers*
Jim Riggs*
Rich Romer
Jim Rourke*
Turk Schonert*
Jim Skow*
Daryl Smith*
Dave Smith*
Eric Thomas*
Kevin Walker
Joe Walter
Leon White*
Solomon Wilcots*
Reggie Williams*
Stanley Wilson
Ickey Woods*
Carl Zander*

1989 AFC Champions Denver Broncos

Denver won its third division title in four years with an AFC-best 11-5 record in 1989. Rookie running back Bobby Humphrey rushed for more than 1,000 yards and John Elway had his fifth consecutive 3,000-yard passing season.

In a tooth-and-nail divisional playoff game, Elway took the Broncos 71 yards in 9 plays to set up Melvin Bratton's 1-yard touchdown run with 2:27 to play. Rookie David Treadwell then added the winning extra point as the Broncos edged the Steelers 24-23.

Pittsburgh led most of the way, but Denver tied the game in the third quarter when Elway connected with Vance Johnson for a 37-yard touchdown pass on the first play following a turnover. Pittsburgh's Gary Anderson kicked 2 field goals to give the Steelers a 23-17 lead, but Elway quickly marched Denver to the winning score.

The Broncos and Browns met for the third time in four years in the AFC Championship Game. Like the first three meetings, Denver won, but this time it didn't come down to the closing minutes of the game. The Broncos led 24-7 before the Browns cut the lead to 3 points in the third quarter. Elway, who passed for 395 yards and 3 touchdowns, led the team on 3 scoring drives in the fourth quarter for a 37-21 win.

Regular Season

Sun	S-10	H	Kansas City Chiefs	34-20	W
Mon	S-18	A N	Buffalo Bills	28-14	W
Sun	S-24	H	Los Angeles Raiders	31-21	W
Sun	O-1	A	Cleveland Browns	13-16	L
Sun	O-8	H	San Diego Chargers	16-10	W
Sun	O-15	H	Indianapolis Colts	14-3	W
Sun	O-22	A	Seattle Seahawks (OT)	24-21	W
Sun	O-29	H	Philadelphia Eagles	24-28	L
Sun	N-5	H	Pittsburgh Steelers	34-7	W
Sun	N-12	A	Kansas City Chiefs	16-13	W
Mon	N-20	A N	Washington Redskins	14-10	W
Sun	N-26	H	Seattle Seahawks	41-14	W
Sun	D-3	A	Los Angeles Raiders (OT)	13-16	L
Sun	D-10	H	New York Giants	7-14	L
Sat	D-16	A	Phoenix Cardinals	37-0	W
Sun	D-24	A	San Diego Chargers	16-19	L

Postseason

1989 AFC Divisional Playoff Game
January 7, 1990
Denver 24, Pittsburgh 23 at Denver

Pittsburgh	3	14	3	3	—	23
Denver	0	10	7	7	—	24

1989 AFC Championship Game
January 14, 1990
Denver 37, Cleveland 21 at Denver

Cleveland	0	0	21	0	—	21
Denver	3	7	14	13	—	37

1989 NFC Champions San Francisco 49ers

George Seifert, the 49ers' new head coach, led the team to a 14-2 record in the regular season.

The postseason was just as dominating as Joe Montana completed 17 of 24 passes for 241 yards and 4 first-half touchdown passes to lead San Francisco to a 41-13 victory over Minnesota in an NFC Divisional Playoff Game. First, he found Jerry Rice with a 72-yard touchdown pass. Then, he fired 3 more scoring passes in the second period: 8 yards to Brent Jones, 8 yards to John Taylor, and 13 yards to Rice. Roger Craig ran for 118 yards and a touchdown. Ronnie Lott intercepted a pass in the final period and returned it 58 yards for a touchdown.

San Francisco dominated the Los Angeles Rams 30-3 to reach the Super Bowl for the fourth time. The Rams took a 3-0 lead on Mike Lansford's 23-yard field goal, but the 49ers exploded for 3 second-quarter touchdowns. Montana, who completed 26 of 30 attempts for 262 yards, fired a 20-yard touchdown pass to Jones and an 18-yard touchdown strike to Taylor sandwiched around Craig's 1-yard touchdown run.

In the second half, the 49ers slowly built their advantage as Mike Cofer kicked 3 field goals, 8 receivers caught passes, 6 players carried the ball, and 3 defenders intercepted passes.

Regular Season

Sun	S-10	A	Indianapolis Colts	30-24	W
Sun	S-17	A	Tampa Bay Buccaneers	20-17	W
Sun	S-24	A	Philadelphia Eagles	38-28	W
Sun	O-1	H	Los Angeles Rams	12-13	L
Sun	O-8	A	New Orleans Saints	23-20	W
Sun	O-15	A	Dallas Cowboys	31-14	W
Sun	O-22	H	New England Patriots	37-20	W
Sun	O-29	A	New York Jets	23-10	W
Mon	N-6	H N	New Orleans Saints	31-13	W
Sun	N-12	H	Atlanta Falcons	45-3	W
Sun	N-19	H	Green Bay Packers	17-21	L
Mon	N-27	H N	New York Giants	34-24	W
Sun	D-3	A	Atlanta Falcons	23-10	W
Mon	D-11	A N	Los Angeles Rams	30-27	W
Sun	D-17	H	Buffalo Bills	21-10	W
Sun	D-24	H	Chicago Bears	26-0	W

Postseason

1989 NFC Divisional Playoff Game
January 6, 1990
San Francisco 41, Minnesota 13 at San Francisco

Minnesota	3	0	3	7	—	13
San Francisco	7	20	0	14	—	41

1989 NFC Championship Game
January 14, 1990
San Francisco 30, Los Angeles Rams 3 at San Francisco

L.A. Rams	3	0	0	0	—	3
San Francisco	0	21	3	6	—	30

Super Bowl XXIV

San Francisco 55, Denver 10
January 28, 1990, Louisiana Superdome, New Orleans, Louisiana
Attendance: 72,919

George Seifert joined Baltimore's Don McCafferty (Super Bowl V) as the only coaches to win the Super Bowl in their first year as an NFL head coach, and Joe Montana was named Super Bowl MVP for the record third time in the 49ers' rout. The 49ers matched Pittsburgh's four Super Bowl victories.

Montana completed 22 of 29 passes for 297 yards and a Super Bowl-record 5 touchdowns. Three of those went to Jerry Rice, who had 7 receptions for 148 yards.

Montana threw a 20-yard touchdown pass to Jerry Rice 4:54 into the game, and the 49ers went on to score on six of their first eight possessions, including a 1-yard run by fullback Tom Rathman and touchdown passes of 38 yards (to Rice) and 7 yards (to Brent Jones). San Francisco led 27-3 at halftime.

Rice added a 28-yard scoring catch in the third quarter, and John Taylor caught a 35-yard pass from Montana for the 49ers' sixth touchdown. By the time the Broncos reached the end zone—on a 3-yard run by Elway midway through the third quarter—it was 41-10.

The 49ers added touchdowns early in the fourth quarter on a 3-yard run by Rathman and a 1-yard run by Roger Craig. San Francisco finished with a 28-12 advantage in first downs and an impressive margin of 39:31 to 20:29 in time of possession.

So marked was the imbalance between the teams that San Francisco tackle Bubba Paris said afterward, "It got to the point where, being a Christian and being a person who loves people, I actually felt sorry for the Broncos."

San Francisco (NFC)	13	14	14	14	—	55
Denver (AFC)	3	0	7	0	—	10

SF—Rice 20 pass from Montana (Cofer kick)
Den—FG Treadwell 42
SF—Jones 7 pass from Montana (kick failed)
SF—Rathman 1 run (Cofer kick)
SF—Rice 38 pass from Montana (Cofer kick)
SF—Rice 28 pass from Montana (Cofer kick)
SF—Taylor 35 pass from Montana (Cofer kick)
Den—Elway 3 run (Treadwell kick)
SF—Rathman 3 run (Cofer kick)
SF—Craig 1 run (Cofer kick)

TEAM STATISTICS	SF	DEN
First Downs	28	12
Rushing	14	5
Passing	14	6
Penalty	0	1
Total Yardage	461	167
Net rushing yardage	144	64
Net passing yardage	317	103
Passes att.-comp.-had int.	32-24-0	29-11-2

RUSHING
San Francisco—Craig 20 for 69, 1 TD; Rathman 11 for 38, 2 TDs; Montana 2 for 15; Flagler 6 for 14; Sydney 1 for 2; Young 4 for 6.
Denver—Humphrey 12 for 61; Elway 4 for 8, 1 TD; Winder 1 for -5.

PASSING
San Francisco—Montana 22 of 29 for 297, 5 TDs; Young 2 of 3 for 20.
Denver—Elway 10 of 26 for 108, 2 int.; Kubiak 1 of 3 for 28.

RECEIVING
San Francisco—Rice 7 for 148, 3 TDs; Craig 5 for 34; Rathman 4 for 43; Taylor 3 for 49, 1 TD; Sherrard 1 for 13; Walls 1 for 9; Jones 1 for 7, 1 TD; Williams 1 for 7; Sydney 1 for 7.
Denver—Humphrey 3 for 38; Sewell 2 for 22; Johnson 2 for 21; Nattiel 1 for 28; Bratton 1 for 14; Winder 1 for 7; Kay 1 for 6.

1989 Team Rosters

San Francisco
Michael Barber
Harris Barton*
Steve Bono
Jeff Bregel
Chet Brooks*
Jim Burt*
Michael Carter*
Mike Cofer*
Bruce Collie*
Roger Craig*
Dave Cullity
Keith DeLong*
Kevin Fagan*
Jim Fahnhorst
Terrence Flagler*
Jeff Fuller
Antonio Goss
Terry Greer
Don Griffin*
Charles Haley*
Barry Helton*
Keith Henderson
Steve Hendrickson*
Tom Holmoe
Pierce Holt*
Johnnie Jackson*
Brent Jones*
Pete Kugler*
Kevin Lilly
Ronnie Lott*
Guy McIntyre*
Tim McKyer*
Matt Millen*
Joe Montana*
Bubba Paris*
Darryl Pollard*
Rollin Putzier
Tom Rathman*
Jerry Rice*
Mike Richardson
Larry Roberts*
Bill Romanowski*
Jesse Sapolu*
Mike Sherrard*
Danny Stubbs*
Harry Sydney*
Terry Tausch*
John Taylor*
Chuck Thomas*
Spencer Tillman*
Keena Turner*
Steve Wallace*
Wesley Walls*
Michael Walter*
Jamie Williams*
Mike Wilson*
Eric Wright*
Steve Young*

Denver
Jeff Alexander
Steve Atwater*
Ken Bell*
Keith Bishop*
Mel Bratton*
Tyrone Braxton*
Michael Brooks*
Alphonso Carreker*
Darren Carrington*
Kip Corrington*
Scott Curtis*
Rick Dennison*
John Elway*
Simon Fletcher*
Paul Green*
Mark Haynes*
Wymon Henderson*
Brad Henke*
Ron Holmes*
Mike Horan*
Bobby Humphrey*
Mark Jackson*
Vance Johnson*
Jim Juriga*
Keith Kartz*
Clarence Kay*
Patrick Kelly
Bruce Klosterman*
Greg Kragen*
Gary Kubiak*
Ken Lanier*
Tim Lucas*
Jake McCullough
Karl Mecklenburg*
Orson Mobley*
Marc Munford*
Ricky Nattiel*
Gerald Perry*
Warren Powers*
Randy Robbins*
Mike Ruether
Steven Sewell*
Richard Shelton
Dennis Smith*
Monte Smith*
Andre Townsend*
David Treadwell*
Doug Widell*
Sammy Winder*
Chris Woods*
Mike Young*

1990 AFC Champions
Buffalo Bills

The Bills popularized the No-Huddle Offense in 1990, a maneuver that enabled them to limit their opponents' defensive substitutions. Buffalo won its division that year with a franchise-best 13-3 record.

In the divisional playoff against Miami, Buffalo jumped to a 13-3 first-quarter lead, then the two teams matched each other almost score for score as the Bills outlasted the Dolphins 44-34. Jim Kelly completed 19 of 29 passes for 339 yards and 3 touchdowns to offset Dan Marino's 3 touchdown passes and a touchdown run.

The closest the Dolphins came was 30-27 in the opening minute of the fourth quarter. The Bills responded quickly as Thurman Thomas scored from the 5, and Kelly found Andre Reed for a 26-yard touchdown pass to put the Dolphins away for good.

The Bills romped past the Los Angeles Raiders 51-3 in the AFC Championship Game at Rich Stadium for Buffalo's first title since the team won the AFL championship a quarter of a century earlier.

Thomas had a sensational day, rushing for 138 yards on 25 carries and catching 5 passes for 61 yards. Kenneth Davis, meanwhile, tied an AFC playoff record by scoring 3 touchdowns. The Bills ran up 41 first-half points, establishing an NFL postseason-game record.

Regular Season

Sun	S-9	H	Indianapolis Colts	26-10	W
Sun	S-16	A	Miami Dolphins	7-30	L
Mon	S-24	A N	New York Jets	30-7	W
Sun	S-30	H	Denver Broncos	29-28	W
Sun	O-7	H N	Los Angeles Raiders	38-24	W
Sun	O-21	H	New York Jets	30-27	W
Sun	O-28	A	New England Patriots	27-10	W
Sun	N-4	A	Cleveland Browns	42-0	W
Sun	N-11	H	Phoenix Cardinals	45-14	W
Sun	N-18	H	New England Patriots	14-0	W
Mon	N-26	A N	Houston Oilers	24-27	L
Sun	D-2	H	Philadelphia Eagles	30-23	W
Sun	D-9	A	Indianapolis Colts	31-7	W
Sat	D-15	A	New York Giants	17-13	W
Sun	D-23	H	Miami Dolphins	24-14	W
Sun	D-30	A	Washington Redskins	14-29	L

Postseason

1990 AFC Divisional Playoff Game
January 12, 1991
Buffalo 44, Miami 34
at Orchard Park, New York

Miami	3	14	3	14	—	34
Buffalo	13	14	3	14	—	44

1990 AFC Championship Game
January 20, 1991
Buffalo 51, Los Angeles Raiders 3
at Orchard Park, New York

L.A. Raiders	3	0	0	0	—	3
Buffalo	21	20	0	10	—	51

1990 NFC Champions
New York Giants

With starting quarterback Phil Simms lost to injuries late in the season, the Giants still finished at 13-3 with the less experienced, but more mobile, Jeff Hostetler. The defense and running game took up the slack.

New York held Chicago to only 27 rushing yards, while the Giants' offense methodically cut up the Bears for a 31-3 victory in a divisional playoff game. Hostetler, playing in his first postseason game, completed 10 passes for 112 yards and 2 touchdowns and ran for 43 yards and another touchdown.

The NFC Championship Game was a classic. San Francisco held New York without a touchdown, but Matt Bahr kicked 5 field goals in 6 attempts, including the game-winner from 42 yards as time ran out, to lead the Giants to a 15-13 upset of the two-time defending Super Bowl-champion 49ers.

San Francisco went ahead 13-6 in the third period when Joe Montana connected with John Taylor on a 61-yard scoring pass. Behind Hostetler and running back Ottis Anderson, the Giants set up 2 more field goals to cut the margin to 1 point. Late in the game, nose tackle Erik Howard forced Roger Craig to fumble and Lawrence Taylor recovered. Hostetler took the Giants 33 yards in 6 plays to set up the winning kick.

Regular Season

Sun	S-9	H	Philadelphia Eagles	27-20	W
Sun	S-16	A	Dallas Cowboys	28-7	W
Sun	S-23	H	Miami Dolphins	20-3	W
Sun	S-30	H	Dallas Cowboys	31-17	W
Sun	O-14	A	Washington Redskins	24-20	W
Sun	O-21	H	Phoenix Cardinals	20-19	W
Sun	O-28	H	Washington Redskins	21-10	W
Mon	N-5	A N	Indianapolis Colts	24-7	W
Sun	N-11	A	Los Angeles Rams	31-7	W
Sun	N-18	H	Detroit Lions	20-0	W
Sun	N-25	A	Philadelphia Eagles	13-31	L
Mon	D-3	A N	San Francisco 49ers	3-7	L
Sun	D-9	H	Minnesota Vikings	23-15	W
Sat	D-15	H	Buffalo Bills	13-17	L
Sun	D-23	A	Phoenix Cardinals	24-21	W
Sun	D-30	A	New England Patriots	13-10	W

Postseason

1990 NFC Divisional Playoff Game
January 13, 1991
New York Giants 31, Chicago Bears 3
at East Rutherford, New Jersey

Chicago	0	3	0	0	—	3
N.Y. Giants	10	7	7	7	—	31

1990 NFC Championship Game
January 20, 1991
New York Giants 15, San Francisco 13
at San Francisco

N.Y. Giants	3	3	3	6	—	15
San Francisco	3	3	7	0	—	13

Super Bowl XXV

New York Giants 20, Buffalo 19
January 27, 1991, Tampa Stadium, Tampa, Florida
Attendance: 73,813

Scott Norwood's 47-yard field-goal attempt in the final seconds sailed wide to the right, and the New York Giants held on to beat the Buffalo Bills in the Super Bowl's Silver Anniversary game.

What made this game most interesting was the contrast of styles. The Giants, pounding away with their ball-control offense, kept the ball for 40 minutes and 33 seconds. The Bills, on the other hand, used a frenetic No-Huddle attack whose main weapon was running back Thurman Thomas, who ran for 135 yards on 15 carries and caught 5 passes for 55 yards.

Giants coach Bill Parcells kept the Bills' defense on the field by utilizing a running game that featured the game's most valuable player, fullback Ottis Anderson, who gained 102 yards on 21 carries. Much of that yardage came in the second half, as the Giants maintained possession for all but eight minutes.

A recycling success story like no other in Super Bowl history, Anderson had come over from the St. Louis Cardinals in 1986. When starter Joe Morris was injured in 1989, Anderson stepped in. By the time his Super Bowl opportunity arrived, Anderson had turned 34.

The Giants were able to move the ball as exhibited by a 14-yard touchdown pass to Stephen Baker shortly before halftime that narrowed the Bills' lead to 12-10.

New York's first drive of the third quarter consumed 9 minutes and 29 seconds, a Super Bowl record. Giants quarterback Jeff Hostetler kept the drive alive with three third-down completions, and Anderson gave New York a 17-12 lead with a 1-yard touchdown run. Hostetler finished with 222 yards passing, completing 20 of 32 attempts.

Thomas's 31-yard touchdown run to open the fourth quarter put the Bills in front 19-17, but midway through the quarter Matt Bahr's 21-yard field goal gave the Giants a 20-19 lead. In the final minutes, Buffalo drove from its 10 to New York's 29, but Norwood's field-goal try went awry with four seconds left.

Buffalo (AFC)	**3**	**9**	**0**	**7**	**—**	**19**
N.Y. Giants (NFC)	**3**	**7**	**7**	**3**	**—**	**20**

NYG—FG Bahr 28
Buff—FG Norwood 23
Buff—D. Smith 1 run (Norwood kick)
Buff—Safety, B. Smith tackled Hostetler in end zone
NYG—Baker 14 pass from Hostetler (Bahr kick)
NYG—Anderson 1 run (Bahr kick)
Buff—Thomas 31 run (Norwood kick)
NYG—FG Bahr 21

TEAM STATISTICS	**BUFF**	**NYG**
First Downs	18	24
Rushing	8	10
Passing	9	13
Penalty	1	1
Total Yardage	371	386
Net rushing yardage	166	172
Net passing yardage	205	214
Passes att.-comp.-had int.	30-18-0	32-20-0

RUSHING
Buffalo—Thomas 15 for 135, 1 TD; Kelly 6 for 23; K. Davis 2 for 4; Mueller 1 for 3; D. Smith 1 for 1, 1 TD.
N.Y. Giants—Anderson 21 for 102, 1 TD; Meggett 9 for 48; Carthon 3 for 12; Hostetler 6 for 10.

PASSING
Buffalo—Kelly 18 of 30 for 212.
N.Y. Giants—Hostetler 20 of 32 for 222, 1 TD.

RECEIVING
Buffalo—Reed 8 for 62; Thomas 5 for 55; K. Davis 2 for 23; McKeller 2 for 11; Lofton 1 for 61.
N.Y. Giants—Ingram 5 for 74; Bavaro 5 for 50; Cross 4 for 39; Baker 2 for 31, 1 TD; Meggett 2 for 18; Anderson 1 for 7; Carthon 1 for 3.

1990 Team Rosters

N.Y. Giants
Bobby Abrams*
Raul Allegre
Ottis Anderson*
Matt Bahr*
Stephen Baker*
Carl Banks*
Mark Bavaro*
Roger Brown*
Maurice Carthon*
Matt Cavanaugh
Mark Collins*
Johnie Cooks*
Howard Cross*
Steve DeOssie*
Eric Dorsey*
Dave Duerson*
Jumbo Elliott*
Mike Fox*
Myron Guyton*
Rodney Hampton
Jeff Hostetler*
Erik Howard*
Mark Ingram*
Greg Jackson*
Pepper Johnson*
Bob Kratch*
Troy Kyles*
Sean Landeta*
Lionel Manuel
Leonard Marshall*
Larry McGrew*
Dave Meggett*
Eric Moore*
Bob Mrosko*
Bart Oates*
Gary Reasons*
Tom Rehder
Doug Riesenberg*
William Roberts*
Stacy Robinson*
Lee Rouson*
Phil Simms
Lawrence Taylor*
Reyna Thompson*
Lewis Tillman*
Odessa Turner
Everson Walls*
John Washington*
Kent Wells*
David Whitmore*
Brian Williams*
Perry Williams*

Buffalo
Carlton Bailey*
Gary Baldinger*
Howard Ballard*
Don Beebe
Cornelius Bennett*
Ray Bentley*
Richard Carey
Shane Conlan*
John Davis*
Kenneth Davis*
Dwight Drane*
Al Edwards*
Mitch Frerotte*
Carwell Gardner*
Hal Garner*
Gale Gilbert
John Hagy*
Chris Hale
Cliff Hicks*
Kent Hull*
Jeff Hunter
Kirby Jackson*
Jim Kelly*
Mark Kelso*
Larry Kinnebrew
Adam Lingner*
Mike Lodish*
James Lofton*
Keith McKeller*
Pete Metzelaars*
Matt Monger
Jamie Mueller*
John Nies
Scott Norwood*
Nate Odomes*
Glenn Parker*
Marvcus Patton
Kim Phillips
Mark Pike*
David Pool
Andre Reed*
Frank Reich*
Jim Ritcher*
Butch Rolle*
Leon Seals*
Bruce Smith*
Don Smith*
Leonard Smith*
Darryl Talley*
Steve Tasker*
Thurman Thomas*
Vernon Turner
Rick Tuten*
James Williams*
Will Wolford*
Jeff Wright

1991 AFC Champions
Buffalo Bills

Buffalo had its second consecutive 13-3 season in 1991, on the way to the Bills' second consecutive AFC title.

Buffalo's defense knocked out Kansas City's starting quarterback, Steve DeBerg, and the offense rolled past the Chiefs both on the ground and through the air in a 37-14 playoff victory. Jim Kelly completed 23 of 35 passes for 273 yards and 3 touchdowns, 2 of them to Andre Reed. Thurman Thomas carried the ball 22 times for 100 yards, the fourth consecutive postseason game in which he reached the century mark. Meanwhile, the defense intercepted Mark Vlasic, DeBerg's replacement, 4 times.

In the AFC Championship Game, linebacker Carlton Bailey scored on an 11-yard interception return to lead the Bills to a 10-7 victory over the Broncos. The Bills were also helped by the kicking of Denver's unfortunate David Treadwell, who missed 3 field goals during the game, 2 of which bounced off the uprights. Scott Norwood kicked a 44-yard field goal to give the Bills the lead with only 4:18 left in the game.

With John Elway injured, Gary Kubiak came on to complete 11 of 12 passes and ran for a touchdown in what he had already announced would be his last game. Denver recovered the subsequent onside kick at its 49, but the Broncos fumbled and Kirby Jackson recovered.

Regular Season

Sun	S-1	H	Miami Dolphins	35-31	W
Sun	S-8	H	Pittsburgh Steelers	52-34	W
Sun	S-15	A	New York Jets	23-20	W
Sun	S-22	A	Tampa Bay Buccaneers	17-10	W
Sun	S-29	H	Chicago Bears	35-20	W
Mon	O-7	A N	Kansas City Chiefs	6-33	L
Sun	O-13	H	Indianapolis Colts	42-6	W
Mon	O-21	H N	Cincinnati Bengals	35-16	W
Sun	N-3	H	New England Patriots	22-17	W
Sun	N-10	A	Green Bay Packers	34-24	W
Mon	N-18	A N	Miami Dolphins	41-27	W
Sun	N-24	A	New England Patriots	13-16	L
Sun	D-1	H	New York Jets	24-13	W
Sun	D-8	A	Los Angeles Raiders (OT)	30-27	W
Sun	D-15	A	Indianapolis Colts	35-7	W
Sun	D-22	H	Detroit Lions (OT)	14-17	L

Postseason

1991 AFC Divisional Playoff Game
January 4, 1992
Buffalo 37, Kansas City 14 at Orchard Park, New York

Kansas City	0	0	7	7	—	14
Buffalo	7	10	7	13	—	37

1991 AFC Championship Game
January 12, 1992
Buffalo 10, Denver 7 at Orchard Park, New York

Denver	0	0	0	7	—	7
Buffalo	0	0	7	3	—	10

1991 NFC Champions
Washington Redskins

Head coach Joe Gibbs led his Redskins to a 14-2 record and set about winning his third Super Bowl with a different starting quarterback—Joe Theismann, Doug Williams, and Mark Rypien.

Washington scored 2 touchdowns in a span of 3:11 of the second quarter to dispatch Atlanta 24-7 in a divisional playoff game. Washington drove 81 yards and finished its drive with a 17-yard run by rookie Ricky Ervins. A short time later, James Geathers recovered a fumble at the Atlanta 39. Gerald Riggs then scored on a 2-yard run. The Falcons came back with a touchdown before halftime, but the Redskins scored in both the third and fourth quarters to put the game away.

Washington scored twice in the first five minutes of the NFC Championship Game and rolled to a 41-10 victory over the Lions. On Detroit's first play from scrimmage, defensive end Charles Mann forced a fumble by Erik Kramer. Two plays later, Riggs scored. Kurt Gouveia then intercepted a pass by Kramer and returned it 38 yards to set up a 20-yard field goal by Chip Lohmiller.

In the third quarter, Rypien broke the game open with a 45-yard scoring strike to Gary Clark and a 21-yard touchdown pass to Art Monk as Washington qualified for its fifth Super Bowl berth.

Regular Season

Sun	S-1	H	Detroit Lions	45-0	W
Mon	S-9	A N	Dallas Cowboys	33-31	W
Sun	S-15	H	Phoenix Cardinals	34-0	W
Sun	S-22	A	Cincinnati Bengals	34-27	W
Mon	S-30	H	Philadelphia Eagles	23-0	W
Sun	O-6	A	Chicago Bears	20-7	W
Sun	O-13	H	Cleveland Browns	42-17	W
Sun	O-27	A	New York Giants	17-13	W
Sun	N-3	H	Houston Oilers (OT)	16-13	W
Sun	N-10	H	Atlanta Falcons	56-17	W
Sun	N-17	A	Pittsburgh Steelers	41-14	W
Sun	N-24	H	Dallas Cowboys	21-24	L
Sun	D-1	A	Los Angeles Rams	27-6	W
Sun	D-8	A	Phoenix Cardinals	20-14	W
Sun	D-15	H	New York Giants	34-17	W
Sun	D-22	A	Philadelphia Eagles	22-24	L

Postseason

1991 NFC Divisional Playoff Game
January 4, 1992
Washington 24, Atlanta 7 at Washington

Atlanta	0	7	0	0	—	7
Washington........	0	14	3	7	—	24

1991 NFC Championship Game
January 12, 1992
Washington 41, Detroit 10 at Washington

Detroit............	0	10	0	0	—	10
Washington........	10	7	10	14	—	41

Super Bowl XXVI

Washington 37, Buffalo 24
January 26, 1992, Hubert H. Humphrey Metrodome, Minneapolis, Minnesota
Attendance: 63,130

If his team's convincing victories in Super Bowls XVII and XXII hadn't ensured Joe Gibbs of enshrinement in the Pro Football Hall of Fame (he was inducted in 1996), this game was a message to begin casting his bust for shipment to Canton, Ohio.

Gibbs became the third coach to win three Super Bowls, joining Pittsburgh's Chuck Noll, who won four, and San Francisco's Bill Walsh.

The Redskins' third Super Bowl championship in 10 years was sparked by their offense. Quarterback Mark Rypien's MVP performance—18 completions in 33 attempts for 292 yards and 2 touchdowns—highlighted his team's 417 yards of total offense. Gary Clark caught 7 passes for 114 yards and Art Monk had 7 receptions for 113 yards.

The Bills' afternoon got off to a horrible start as running back Thurman Thomas—the AFC's rushing leader in 1991 with 1,407 yards and the NFL's leader in yards from scrimmage with 2,038 yards—lost his helmet. Thomas missed Buffalo's first possession and finished the game with just 13 yards rushing on 10 carries and 27 yards on 4 receptions.

After a scoreless first quarter, the Redskins took a 17-0 halftime lead on a 34-yard field goal by Chip Lohmiller (the first of 3 for Lohmiller, who hit 25-and 39-yard field goals in the second half), a 10-yard pass from Rypien to running back Earnest Byner, and a 1-yard run by to fellow running back Gerald Riggs.

Riggs scored another touchdown, from 2 yards, 16 seconds into the third quarter, after Redskins linebacker Kurt Gouveia intercepted Jim Kelly's pass at the 25 and returned it 23 yards.

Kelly and the Bills made the score respectable from then on, and the Buffalo quarterback finished with 28 completions in a Super Bowl-record 58 attempts for 275 yards.

Washington (NFC)	0	17	14	6	—	37
Buffalo (AFC)	0	0	10	14	—	24

Wash—FG Lohmiller 34
Wash—Byner 10 pass from Rypien (Lohmiller kick)
Wash—Riggs 1 run (Lohmiller kick)
Wash—Riggs 2 run (Lohmiller kick)
Buff—FG Norwood 21
Buff—Thomas 1 run (Norwood kick)
Wash—Clark 30 pass from Rypien (Lohmiller kick)
Wash—FG Lohmiller 25
Wash—FG Lohmiller 39
Buff—Metzelaars 2 pass from Kelly (Norwood kick)
Buff—Beebe 4 pass from Kelly (Norwood kick)

TEAM STATISTICS	WASH	BUFF
First Downs	24	25
Rushing	10	4
Passing	12	18
Penalty	2	3
Total Yardage	417	283
Net rushing yardage	125	43
Net passing yardage	292	240
Passes att.-comp.-had int.	33-18-1	59-29-4

RUSHING
Washington—Ervins 13 for 72; Byner 14 for 49; Riggs 5 for 7, 2 TDs; Sanders 1 for 1; Rutledge 1 for 0; Rypien 6 for -4.
Buffalo—K. Davis 4 for 17; Kelly 3 for 16; Thomas 10 for 13, 1 TD; Lofton 1 for -3.

PASSING
Washington—Rypien 18 of 33 for 292, 2 TDs, 1 int.
Buffalo—Kelly 28 of 58 for 275, 2 TDs, 4 int.; Reich 1 of 1 for 11.

RECEIVING
Washington—Clark 7 for 114, 1 TD; Monk 7 for 113; Byner 3 for 24, 1 TD; Sanders 1 for 41.
Buffalo—Lofton 7 for 92; Reed 5 for 34; Beebe 4 for 61, 1 TD; K. Davis 4 for 38; Thomas 4 for 27; McKeller 2 for 29; Edwards 1 for 11; Metzelaars 1 for 2, 1 TD; Kelly 1 for -8.

1991 Team Rosters

Washington
Mark Adickes*
Jeff Bostic*
John Brandes*
Jason Buck*
Earnest Byner*
Ravin Caldwell*
Gary Clark*
Monte Coleman*
Andre Collins*
Danny Copeland*
Travis Curtis
Brad Edwards*
Ricky Ervins*
Jumpy Geathers*
Kelly Goodburn*
Kurt Gouveia*
Darrell Green*
Russ Grimm*
Terry Hoage*
Stephen Hobbs*
Joe Jacoby*
James Jenkins*
A.J. Johnson*
Jimmie Johnson
Joe Johnson
Sidney Johnson*
Tim Johnson*
Markus Koch
Jim Lachey*
Chip Lohmiller*
Charles Mann*
Wilber Marshall*
Martin Mayhew*
Alvoid Mays*
Raleigh McKenzie*
Ron Middleton*
Matt Millen
Brian Mitchell*
Art Monk*
Terry Orr*
Gerald Riggs*
Jeff Rutledge*
Mark Rypien*
Ricky Sanders*
Mark Schlereth*
Ed Simmons*
Fred Stokes*
Ralph Tamm
Clarence Vaughn
Alvin Walton
Don Warren*
Eric Williams*
Bobby Wilson*

Buffalo
Mike Alexander
Carlton Bailey*
Gary Baldinger
Howard Ballard*
David Bavaro
Don Beebe*
Cornelius Bennett*
Ray Bentley*
Shane Conlan*
Brad Daluiso*
John Davis
Kenneth Davis*
Dwight Drane*
Al Edwards*
Mitch Frerotte*
Eddie Fuller
Carwell Gardner*
Hal Garner*
Odell Haggins
Chris Hale*
Phil Hansen*
Cliff Hicks*
Kent Hull*
Kirby Jackson*
Henry Jones*
Jim Kelly*
Mark Kelso*
Adam Lingner*
Mike Lodish*
James Lofton*
Keith McKeller*
Pete Metzelaars*
Chris Mohr*
Scott Norwood*
Nate Odomes*
Chris Oldham
Glenn Parker*
Marvcus Patton*
Mark Pike*
Andre Reed*
Frank Reich*
Jim Ritcher*
Reggie Rogers
Butch Rolle*
Leon Seals*
Bruce Smith*
Leonard Smith
Joe Staysniak*
Darryl Talley*
Steve Tasker*
Brian Taylor
Thurman Thomas*
James Williams*
Will Wolford*
Jeff Wright*

1992 AFC Champions
Buffalo Bills

The Bills captured their third straight AFC title, but this one proved to be the most difficult.

Warren Moon staked the Oilers to a 35-3 lead in an AFC Wild Card Game with 4 touchdown passes, but Frank Reich, subbing for injured Jim Kelly, threw 4 touchdown passes in the second half as the Bills mounted the greatest comeback in NFL history to stun Houston 41-38. Within 6:54 of their first touchdown in the third quarter, the Bills scored 3 more times. Later, Reich threw a 17-yard touchdown pass to Andre Reed for Buffalo's first lead, but Moon led the Oilers to a tying field goal. Nate Odomes intercepted Moon in overtime to set up Steve Christie's 32-yard winning kick.

Given new life in the postseason, the Bills cruised past the Steelers 24-3. Reich threw 2 more touchdowns and Pittsburgh turned the ball over 4 times.

Turnovers also were Miami's undoing in the AFC Championship Game. The Bills recovered 3 fumbles, intercepted 2 passes, and sacked Dan Marino 4 times in Buffalo's 29-10 victory. Christie kicked a record-tying 5 field goals, and Kelly, back from injury, completed 17 of 24 passes.

Regular Season

Sun	S-6	H	Los Angeles Rams	40-7	W
Sun	S-13	A	San Francisco 49ers	34-31	W
Sun	S-20	H	Indianapolis Colts	38-0	W
Sun	S-27	A	New England Patriots	41-7	W
Sun	O-4	H	Miami Dolphins	10-37	L
Sun	O-11	A	Los Angeles Raiders	3-20	L
Mon	O-26	A N	New York Jets	24-20	W
Sun	N-1	H	New England Patriots	16-7	W
Sun	N-8	H	Pittsburgh Steelers	38-20	W
Mon	N-16	A N	Miami Dolphins	26-20	W
Sun	N-22	H	Atlanta Falcons	41-14	W
Sun	N-29	A	Indianapolis Colts (OT)	13-16	L
Sun	D-6	H	New York Jets	17-24	L
Sat	D-12	H	Denver Broncos	27-17	W
Sun	D-20	A	New Orleans Saints	20-16	W
Sun	D-27	A	Houston Oilers	3-27	L

Postseason

1992 AFC Wild Card Game
January 3, 1993
Buffalo 41, Houston 38 (OT) at Orchard Park, New York

Houston	7	21	7	3	0	—	38
Buffalo	3	0	28	7	3	—	41

1992 AFC Divisional Playoff Game
January 9, 1993
Buffalo 24, Pittsburgh 3 at Pittsburgh

Buffalo	0	7	7	10	—	24
Pittsburgh	3	0	0	0	—	3

1992 AFC Championship Game
January 17, 1993
Buffalo 29, Miami 10 at Miami

Buffalo	3	10	10	6	—	29
Miami	3	0	0	7	—	10

1992 NFC Champions
Dallas Cowboys

The Cowboys won their first NFC Eastern Division title since 1985 by posting a 13-3 mark.

In the divisional playoffs, Dallas sacked Eagles quarterback Randall Cunningham 5 times and rolled to a 34-10 victory. Philadelphia took a 3-0 lead, but the Cowboys took over later in the first period when Troy Aikman threw a 1-yard touchdown pass to Derek Tennell. Aikman's 6-yard scoring pass to Jay Novacek 47 seconds before the end of the half made it 14-3. When Vai Sikahema fumbled away the ensuing kickoff, Dallas increased its lead to 17-3.

Dallas won the NFC Championship Game 30-20 by forcing 4 San Francisco turnovers. The game was tied 10-10 at halftime. After taking the second-half kickoff, the Cowboys scored on a 3-yard run by Daryl Johnston. San Francisco responded with a field goal, but the Cowboys took nine minutes off the clock with a drive that ended with Aikman's 16-yard touchdown pass to Emmitt Smith.

With less than five minutes left, Steve Young hit Jerry Rice with a 5-yard scoring pass to make it 24-20. But on the next play from scrimmage, Alvin Harper caught a short pass from Aikman and burst loose for 70 yards. That set up a 6-yard touchdown pass to Kelvin Martin.

Regular Season

Mon	S-7	H N	Washington Redskins	23-10	W
Sun	S-13	A	New York Giants	34-28	W
Sun	S-20	H	Phoenix Cardinals	31-20	W
Mon	O-5	A N	Philadelphia Eagles	7-31	L
Sun	O-11	H	Seattle Seahawks	27-0	W
Sun	O-18	H	Kansas City Chiefs	17-10	W
Sun	O-25	A	Los Angeles Raiders	28-13	W
Sun	N-1	H	Philadelphia Eagles	20-10	W
Sun	N-8	A	Detroit Lions	37-3	W
Sun	N-15	H	Los Angeles Rams	23-27	L
Sun	N-22	A	Phoenix Cardinals	16-10	W
Thu	N-26	H	New York Giants	30-3	W
Sun	D-6	A	Denver Broncos	31-27	W
Sun	D-13	A	Washington Redskins	7-20	L
Mon	D-21	A N	Atlanta Falcons	41-17	W
Sun	D-27	H	Chicago Bears	27-14	W

Postseason

1992 NFC Divisional Playoff Game
January 10, 1993
Dallas 34, Philadelphia 10 at Irving, Texas

Philadelphia	3	0	0	7	—	10
Dallas	7	10	10	7	—	34

1992 NFC Championship Game
January 17, 1993
Dallas 30, San Francisco 20 at San Francisco

Dallas	3	7	7	13	—	30
San Francisco	7	3	3	7	—	20

Super Bowl XXVII

Dallas 52, Buffalo 17
January 31, 1993, Rose Bowl, Pasadena, California
Attendance: 98,374

The very thought of committing 9 turnovers in a game—5 fumbles and 4 interceptions—fits better with a high school junior varsity than a Super Bowl team. But the Buffalo Bills did the unthinkable, set a Super Bowl record in doing so, and paid for it.

Ironically, it was Buffalo that struck first when Steve Tasker blocked a punt to give the Bills possession at the Dallas 16. Thurman Thomas's 2-yard run five minutes into the game gave Buffalo a 7-0 lead.

Then Dallas began forcing turnovers. Safety James Washington intercepted Jim Kelly's pass, returned it 13 yards to the Bills' 47, and with 1:36 left in the first quarter, the Cowboys tied the game on a 23-yard pass from Troy Aikman, the game's most valuable player, to tight end Jay Novacek.

On the Bills' next play, defensive end Charles Haley sacked Kelly, who fumbled. Cowboys defensive tackle Jimmie Jones picked it out of the air at the 2-yard line, and Dallas led for the first time at 14-7.

The Bills lost Kelly on the next series when Dallas linebacker Ken Norton fell on the quarterback's knee, which had been sprained twice in the first two rounds of the playoffs. Frank Reich came on, and the Bills settled for Steve Christie's 21-yard field goal.

The Cowboys went on a long drive that ended with a 19-yard touchdown pass from Aikman to Michael Irvin. Soon, Buffalo's Thomas fumbled, and an Aikman-to-Irvin pass produced an 18-yard touchdown and a solid 28-10 halftime lead.

The Bills actually outscored the Cowboys 7-3 in the third quarter, getting a 40-yard touchdown pass from Reich to Don Beebe on the quarter's final play to make it 31-17. But Dallas struck for 3 touchdowns in the fourth period: a 45-yard pass from Aikman to Alvin Harper, a 10-yard run by Emmitt Smith, and a 9-yard fumble recovery and return by Norton.

Buffalo (AFC)	7	3	7	0	—	17
Dallas (NFC)	14	14	3	21	—	52

Buff—Thomas 2 run (Christie kick)
Dall—Novacek 23 pass from Aikman (Elliott kick)
Dall—J. Jones 2 fumble recovery return (Elliott kick)
Buff—FG Christie 21
Dall—Irvin 19 pass from Aikman (Elliott kick)
Dall—Irvin 18 pass from Aikman (Elliott kick)
Dall—FG Elliott 20
Buff—Beebe 40 pass from Reich (Christie kick)
Dall—Harper 45 pass from Aikman (Elliott kick)
Dall—E. Smith 10 run (Elliott kick)
Dall—Norton 9 fumble recovery return (Elliott kick)

TEAM STATISTICS	BUFF	DALL
First Downs	22	20
Rushing	7	9
Passing	11	11
Penalty	4	0
Total Yardage	362	408
Net rushing yardage	108	137
Net passing yardage	254	271
Passes att.-comp.-had int.	38-22-4	30-22-0

RUSHING
Buffalo—K. Davis 15 for 86; Thomas 11 for 19, 1 TD; Gardner 1 for 3; Reich 2 for 0.
Dallas—E. Smith 22 for 108, 1 TD; Aikman 3 for 28; Gainer 2 for 1; Beuerlein 1 for 0; Johnston 1 for 0.

PASSING
Buffalo—Reich 18 of 31 for 194, 1 TD, 2 int.; Kelly 4 of 7 for 82, 2 int.
Dallas—Aikman 22 of 30 for 273, 4 TDs.

RECEIVING
Buffalo—Reed 8 for 152; Thomas 4 for 10; K. Davis 3 for 16; Beebe 2 for 50, 1 TD; Tasker 2 for 30; Metzelaars 2 for 12; McKeller 1 for 6.
Dallas—Novacek 7 for 72, 1 TD; Irvin 6 for 114, 2 TDs; E. Smith 6 for 27; Johnston 2 for 15; Harper 1 for 45, 1 TD.

1992 Team Rosters

Dallas
Bobby Abrams
Tommie Agee*
Troy Aikman*
Bill Bates
Steve Beuerlein*
Larry Brown*
Tony Casillas*
Frank Cornish*
Dixon Edwards*
Lin Elliott*
Thomas Everett*
Derrick Gainer*
Kenneth Gant*
John Gesek*
Kevin Gogan*
Charles Haley*
Alvin Harper*
Dale Hellestrae*
Chad Hennings*
Tony Hill
Clayton Holmes*
Issiac Holt*
Ray Horton*
Michael Irvin*
Jim Jeffcoat*
Daryl Johnston*
Jimmie Jones*
Robert Jones*
Leon Lett*
Kelvin Martin*
Russell Maryland*
Godfrey Myles*
Nate Newton*
Danny Noonan
Ken Norton*
Jay Novacek*
Mickey Pruitt*
Curvin Richards
Alfredo Roberts
Mike Saxon*
Emmitt Smith*
Jimmy Smith*
Kevin Smith*
Vinson Smith*
Mark Stepnoski*
Derek Tennell*
Tony Tolbert*
Mark Tuinei*
Alan Veingrad
James Washington*
Erik Williams*
Robert Williams
Darren Woodson*
Alexander Wright

Buffalo
Rob Awalt*
Carlton Bailey*
Gary Baldinger
Howard Ballard*
Don Beebe*
Cornelius Bennett*
Steve Christie*
Shane Conlan*
Jerry Crafts
Matt Darby*
John Davis*
Kenneth Davis*
Al Edwards
John Fina*
Mitch Frerotte*
Eddie Fuller
Carwell Gardner*
Keith Goganious*
Chris Hale*
Phil Hansen*
Richard Harvey
Cliff Hicks*
Kent Hull*
Kirby Jackson*
Henry Jones*
Jim Kelly*
Mark Kelso*
Brad Lamb*
Adam Lingner*
Mike Lodish*
James Lofton*
Mark Maddox*
Keith McKeller*
Pete Metzelaars*
Chris Mohr*
Nate Odomes*
Glenn Parker*
Marvcus Patton*
Mark Pike*
Andre Reed*
Frank Reich*
Jim Ritcher*
Kurt Schulz
Bruce Smith*
Darryl Talley*
Steve Tasker*
Thurman Thomas*
Chris Walsh
James Williams*
Keith Willis
Will Wolford*
Jeff Wright*

1993 AFC Champions Buffalo Bills

On their way to a 12-4 season, the Bills went 7-1 in their division, but lost to a pair of teams in the AFC West, the Chiefs and the Raiders. Buffalo got a shot at redemption in the postseason.

With the temperature zero degrees and a wind-chill factor of minus-32, Buffalo fell behind 17-6 before taking charge for a 29-23 victory over the Raiders. After being dominated for most of the first half, Buffalo quickly moved 76 yards to a touchdown shortly before halftime.

In the second half, Jim Kelly teamed with Bill Brooks on a 25-yard touchdown pass that gave Buffalo a 19-17 lead. A fumble recovery and Steve Christie's field goal stretched the lead to 5 points. Two plays later, the Raiders took an 23-22 lead when Tim Brown took a short pass 86 yards for a touchdown. But the Bills came right back, driving 71 yards, with Kelly hitting Brooks from 22 yards for the game-winning touchdown pass.

In the American Football Conference Championship Game, Thurman Thomas carried the ball 33 times for 186 yards and 3 touchdowns to lead Buffalo to a 30-13 victory over Kansas City.

Joe Montana, who later left the game with an injury, had a chance to get the Chiefs within a touchdown just before halftime, but his pass bounced off Kimble Anders's hands at the goal line and was intercepted by Buffalo's Henry Jones.

Regular Season

Sun	S-5	H	New England Patriots	38-14	W
Sun	S-12	A	Dallas Cowboys	13-10	W
Sun	S-26	H	Miami Dolphins	13-22	L
Sun	O-3	H	New York Giants	17-14	W
Mon	O-11	H N	Houston Oilers	35-7	W
Sun	O-24	A	New York Jets	19-10	W
Mon	N-1	H N	Washington Redskins	24-10	W
Sun	N-7	A	New England Patriots (OT)	13-10	W
Mon	N-15	A N	Pittsburgh Steelers	0-23	L
Sun	N-21	H	Indianapolis Colts	23-9	W
Sun	N-28	A	Kansas City Chiefs	7-23	L
Sun	D-5	H	Los Angeles Raiders	24-25	L
Sun	D-12	A	Philadelphia Eagles	10-7	W
Sun	D-19	A	Miami Dolphins	47-34	W
Sun	D-26	H	New York Jets	16-14	W
Sun	Ja-2	A	Indianapolis Colts	30-10	W

Postseason

1993 AFC Divisional Playoff Game
January 15, 1994
Buffalo 29, Los Angeles Raiders 23
at Orchard Park, New York

L.A. Raiders	0	17	6	0	—	23
Buffalo	0	13	9	7	—	29

1993 AFC Championship Game
January 23, 1994
Buffalo 30, Kansas City 13
at Orchard Park, New York

Kansas City	6	0	7	0	—	13
Buffalo	7	13	0	10	—	30

1993 NFC Champions Dallas Cowboys

Dallas lost its first two regular-season games as Emmitt Smith held out for a new contract, but the Cowboys rebounded to a 12-4 record.

In the postseason, Dallas scored 10 points in the final 23 seconds of the first half to defeat Green Bay 27-17 in a divisional playoff game. The Cowboys trailed 3-0 before Troy Aikman connected with Alvin Harper on a 25-yard touchdown pass. With 23 seconds left in the half, Eddie Murray kicked a 41-yard field goal. The Packers fumbled the ensuing kickoff, and the Cowboys recovered at the 14. Aikman teamed with tight end Jay Novacek on a 6-yard scoring pass with only five seconds remaining in the second quarter.

Midway through the third quarter, Aikman came back with his third scoring strike, a 19-yard pass to Michael Irvin that shut the door on the Packers.

In the NFC Championship Game, the Cowboys scored touchdowns on 4 of their first 5 possessions to take a 28-7 lead at halftime, then coasted to a 38-21 victory over San Francisco to qualify for their record seventh Super Bowl.

In the second period, an 11-play, 80-yard drive ended with Daryl Johnston's 4-yard touchdown run. Three plays later, safety Thomas Everett intercepted Steve Young, and the Cowboys turned that into an 11-yard touchdown pass to Smith. In the final minute of the half, Aikman hit Novacek for a 19-yard touchdown.

Regular Season

Mon	S-6	A N	Washington Redskins	16-35	L
Sun	S-12	H	Buffalo Bills	10-13	L
Sun	S-19	A	Phoenix Cardinals	17-10	W
Sun	O-3	H	Green Bay Packers	36-14	W
Sun	O-10	A	Indianapolis Colts	27-3	W
Sun	O-17	H	San Francisco 49ers	26-17	W
Sun	O-31	A	Philadelphia Eagles	23-10	W
Sun	N-7	H	New York Giants	31-9	W
Sun	N-14	H	Phoenix Cardinals	20-15	W
Sun	N-21	A	Atlanta Falcons	14-27	L
Thu	N-25	H	Miami Dolphins	14-16	L
Mon	D-6	H N	Philadelphia Eagles	23-17	W
Sun	D-12	A	Minnesota Vikings	37-20	W
Sat	D-18	A	New York Jets	28-7	W
Sun	D-26	H	Washington Redskins	38-3	W
Sun	Ja-2	A	New York Giants (OT)	16-13	W

Postseason

1993 NFC Divisional Playoff Game
January 16, 1994
Dallas 27, Green Bay 17
at Irving, Texas

Green Bay	3	0	7	7	—	17
Dallas	0	17	7	3	—	27

1993 NFC Championship Game
January 23, 1994
Dallas 38, San Francisco 21
at Irving, Texas

San Francisco	0	7	7	7	—	21
Dallas	7	21	7	3	—	38

Super Bowl XXVIII

Dallas 30, Buffalo 13
January 30, 1994, Georgia Dome, Atlanta, Georgia
Attendance: 72,817

There were a number of milestones in Super Bowl XXVIII. It was the first Super Bowl in the state of Georgia. The Cowboys won their fourth Super Bowl, tying Pittsburgh and San Francisco. Dallas also became the first team to begin the regular season 0-2 and wind up Super Bowl champions.

It also was the Bills' fourth Super Bowl loss, tying them with Minnesota and Denver. Worse, it was the Bills' fourth consecutive loss in the Super Bowl, something no team ever had suffered.

The first half went to Buffalo. Not long after Eddie Murray put Dallas on the board with a 41-yard field goal 2:19 into the game, the Bills tied it on Steve Christie's 54-yard kick, the longest in Super Bowl history.

Murray came back with a 24-yard field goal, but early in the second quarter Bills running back Thurman Thomas ran in from 4 yards out to give Buffalo a 10-6 lead. Christie added a 28-yard field goal as the half ended for a 13-6 advantage.

The second half belonged to Dallas. Fifty-five seconds into the third quarter, Cowboys defensive tackle Leon Lett stripped Thomas of the ball, and safety James Washington took it 46 yards to tie the game at 13-13.

The Cowboys soon forced the Bills to punt and went on a 64-yard scoring drive. Dallas running back Emmitt Smith, the game's most valuable player, accounted for all but 3 yards of the drive and scored on a 15-yard burst to put his team ahead 20-13.

Washington victimized the Cowboys again, intercepting Jim Kelly's pass at the Buffalo 46 and returning it to the 34. A penalty moved the ball back to the 39, but Dallas, with Smith carrying twice for 10 yards and catching a screen pass for 9 yards, set up a 16-yard pass from Troy Aikman to Alvin Harper that moved the ball to the Buffalo 6. Smith's 1-yard run on fourth-and-goal with 9:50 to play and Murray's 20-yard field goal seven minutes later sealed the victory.

Dallas (NFC)	6	0	14	10	—	30
Buffalo (AFC)	3	10	0	0	—	13

Dall—FG Murray 41
Buff—FG Christie 54
Dall—FG Murray 24
Buff—Thomas 4 run (Christie kick)
Buff—FG Christie 28
Dall—Washington 46 fumble return (Murray kick)
Dall—E. Smith 15 run (Murray kick)
Dall—E. Smith 1 run (Murray kick)
Dall—FG Murray 20

TEAM STATISTICS	DALL	BUFF
First Downs	20	22
Rushing	6	6
Passing	14	15
Penalty	0	1
Total Yardage	341	314
Net rushing yardage	137	87
Net passing yardage	204	227
Passes att.-comp.-had int.	27-19-1	50-31-1

RUSHING
Dallas—E. Smith 30 for 132, 2 TDs; K. Williams 1 for 6; Aikman 1 for 3; Johnston 1 for 0; Kosar 1 for -1; Coleman 1 for -3.
Buffalo—K. Davis 9 for 38; Thomas 16 for 37, 1 TD; Kelly 2 for 12.
PASSING
Dallas—Aikman 19 of 27 for 207, 1 int.
Buffalo—Kelly 31 of 50 for 260, 1 int.
RECEIVING
Dallas—Irvin 5 for 66; Novacek 5 for 26; E. Smith 4 for 26; Harper 3 for 75; Johnston 2 for 14.
Buffalo—Brooks 7 for 63; Thomas 7 for 52; Reed 6 for 75; Beebe 6 for 60; K. Davis 3 for -5; Metzelaars 1 for 8; McKeller 1 for 7.

1993 Team Rosters

Dallas
Bobby Abrams
Tommie Agee
Troy Aikman*
Bill Bates*
Kelly Blackwell
Larry Brown*
Tony Casillas*
Lincoln Coleman*
Frank Cornish*
Dixon Edwards*
Lin Elliott
Thomas Everett*
Joe Fishback*
Derrick Gainer*
Scott Galbraith*
Kenneth Gant*
Jason Garrett
John Gesek*
Kevin Gogan*
Charles Haley*
Chris Hall
Alvin Harper*
Dale Hellestrae*
Chad Hennings*
Michael Irvin*
Jim Jeffcoat*
John Jett*
Daryl Johnston*
Jimmie Jones*
Robert Jones*
Bernie Kosar*
Derrick Lassic
Leon Lett*
Brock Marion
Russell Maryland*
Joey Mickey
Eddie Murray*
Godfrey Myles*
Nate Newton*
Ken Norton*
Jay Novacek*
Elvis Patterson*
Jim Price
John Roper
Darrin Smith*
Emmitt Smith*
Kevin Smith*
Mark Stepnoski
Dave Thomas*
Tony Tolbert*
Mark Tuinei*
Matt Vanderbeek*
James Washington*
Erik Williams*
Kevin Williams*
Robert Williams
Tyrone Williams
Darren Woodson*

Buffalo
Rob Awalt
Howard Ballard*
Oliver Barnett*
Don Beebe*
Cornelius Bennett*
Bill Brooks*
Monty Brown*
Steve Christie*
Russell Copeland*
Jerry Crafts*
Matt Darby*
John Davis*
Kenneth Davis*
Mike Devlin*
John Fina*
Eddie Fuller
Carwell Gardner*
Gale Gilbert
Keith Goganious*
Phil Hansen*
Richard Harvey*
Jerome Henderson*
Kent Hull*
Henry Jones*
Jim Kelly*
Mark Kelso*
Brad Lamb
Adam Lingner*
Mike Lodish*
Mark Maddox*
Keith McKeller*
Pete Metzelaars*
Chris Mohr*
Tom Myslinski
Nate Odomes*
Glenn Parker*
John Parrella
James Patton
Marvcus Patton*
Mark Pike*
David Pool
Andre Reed*
Frank Reich*
Jim Ritcher*
Kurt Schulz*
Bruce Smith*
Thomas Smith*
Darryl Talley*
Steve Tasker*
Thurman Thomas*
Nate Turner
Chris Walsh
Mickey Washington*
James Williams
Jeff Wright*

1994 AFC Champions
San Diego Chargers

Since the Chargers were founded in 1960, the team had played in five AFL Championship Games, going 1-4, but the team had never won an AFC championship. Coach Bobby Ross changed that in 1994.

In a divisional playoff game, Miami's Dan Marino passed for 206 yards in the first two periods, but was held to just 56 yards in the second half. With the Chargers trailing 21-6 in the third quarter, defensive tackle Reuben Davis dropped Bernie Parmalee for a safety. Natrone Means scored a touchdown after the ensuing free kick. The Chargers scored the go-ahead touchdown with 35 seconds left as Stan Humphries connected with Mark Seay, then watched anxiously as Pete Stoyanovich's 48-yard field-goal attempt fell short on the final play as the Chargers won 22-21.

Pittsburgh quarterback Neil O'Donnell set AFC Championship Game records by completing 32 of 54 passes, but the Chargers came up with the important plays and shocked the favored Steelers 17-13. Pittsburgh led 13-3 in the third quarter, but Humphries completed a pair of 43-yard touchdown passes, the first to Alfred Pupunu and the second to Tony Martin. On fourth-and-goal at the 3, linebacker Dennis Gibson deflected O'Donnell's pass with 1:04 remaining to send San Diego to the Super Bowl for the first time.

Regular Season

Sun	S-4	A N	Denver Broncos	37-34	W
Sun	S-11	H	Cincinnati Bengals	27-10	W
Sun	S-18	A	Seattle Seahawks	24-10	W
Sun	S-25	A	Los Angeles Raiders	26-24	W
Sun	O-9	H	Kansas City Chiefs	20-6	W
Sun	O-16	A	New Orleans Saints	36-22	W
Sun	O-23	H	Denver Broncos	15-20	L
Sun	O-30	H	Seattle Seahawks	35-15	W
Sun	N-6	A	Atlanta Falcons	9-10	L
Sun	N-13	A	Kansas City Chiefs	14-13	W
Sun	N-20	A	New England Patriots	17-23	L
Sun	N-27	H	Los Angeles Rams	31-17	W
Mon	D-5	H N	Los Angeles Raiders	17-24	L
Sun	D-11	H	San Francisco 49ers	15-38	L
Sun	D-18	A	New York Jets	21-6	W
Sat	D-24	H	Pittsburgh Steelers	37-34	W

Postseason

1994 AFC Divisional Playoff Game
January 8, 1995
San Diego 22, Miami 21 at San Diego

Miami	7	14	0	0	—	21
San Diego	0	6	9	7	—	22

1994 AFC Championship Game
January 15, 1995
San Diego 17, Pittsburgh 13 at Pittsburgh

San Diego	0	3	7	7	—	17
Pittsburgh	7	3	3	0	—	13

1994 NFC Champions
San Francisco 49ers

The 49ers scored a club-record 505 points to roll to a 13-3 record, then dominated in the postseason as well.

After a turnover on their first possession in an NFC Divisional Playoff Game led to a Bears' field goal, the 49ers' offense scored on six consecutive possessions to blow out the Bears 44-15.

Rookie fullback William Floyd scored 3 touchdowns. Steve Young completed an 8-yard touchdown pass to tight end Brent Jones for the 49ers' second score, then ran for a 6-yard touchdown to make it 30-3 at halftime.

San Francisco exploded for 3 touchdowns in the opening minutes of the NFC Championship Game, then held on to defeat Dallas 38-28. It was sweet revenge for the 49ers, who had lost to Dallas in the title game the past two years.

On the third play of the game, cornerback Eric Davis intercepted a pass by Troy Aikman and returned it 44 yards for a touchdown. Three plays later, Davis forced a fumble, leading to Steve Young's 29-yard touchdown pass to Ricky Watters. When Kevin Williams fumbled the following kickoff, 49ers kicker Doug Brien recovered at the Dallas 35. A 7-play drive was climaxed by William Floyd's 1-yard touchdown run.

After 2 touchdowns shaved San Francisco's lead to 24-14, Young fired a 28-yard touchdown pass to Jerry Rice eight seconds before halftime.

Regular Season

Mon	S-5	H N	Los Angeles Raiders	44-14	W
Sun	S-11	A	Kansas City Chiefs	14-24	L
Sun	S-18	A	Los Angeles Rams	34-19	W
Sun	S-25	H	New Orleans Saints	24-13	W
Sun	O-2	H	Philadelphia Eagles	8-40	L
Sun	O-9	A	Detroit Lions	27-21	W
Sun	O-16	A	Atlanta Falcons	42-3	W
Sun	O-23	H	Tampa Bay Buccaneers	41-16	W
Sun	N-6	A	Washington Redskins	37-22	W
Sun	N-13	H	Dallas Cowboys	21-14	W
Sun	N-20	H	Los Angeles Rams	31-27	W
Sun	N-27	A	New Orleans Saints	35-14	W
Sun	D-4	H	Atlanta Falcons	50-14	W
Sun	D-11	A	San Diego Chargers	38-15	W
Sun	D-18	H	Denver Broncos	42-19	W
Mon	D-26	A N	Minnesota Vikings	14-21	L

Postseason

1994 NFC Divisional Playoff Game
January 7, 1995
San Francisco 44, Chicago 15 at San Francisco

Chicago	3	0	0	12	—	15
San Francisco	7	23	7	7	—	44

1994 NFC Championship Game
January 15, 1995
San Francisco 38, Dallas 28 at San Francisco

Dallas	7	7	7	7	—	28
San Francisco	21	10	7	0	—	38

Super Bowl XXIX

San Francisco 49, San Diego 26
January 29, 1995, Joe Robbie Stadium, Miami, Florida
Attendance: 74,107

Smoke from a pregame fireworks show still hung inside Joe Robbie Stadium on the third play of the game when Jerry Rice cut to the wide-open middle of the San Diego secondary and took a pass from Steve Young for a 44-yard touchdown.

When sportswriters write about "setting the tone," this is what they mean.

Young would throw a record 6 touchdown passes, part of a 24-for-36 performance that generated 325 yards and earned him the game's most-valuable-player award. After the initial touchdown to Rice, he threw:

- a 51-yard touchdown pass to running back Ricky Watters with 10:05 left in the first quarter, giving the 49ers a 14-0 lead;
- a 5-yard touchdown pass to fullback William Floyd with 13:02 left in the second quarter, finishing off a 70-yard drive and giving the 49ers a 21-7 lead. That came after the Chargers had gobbled up more than seven minutes with a 13-play, 78-yard drive that ended with Natrone Means's 1-yard touchdown run;
- an 8-yard touchdown pass to Watters with 4:44 left in the second quarter to make it 28-7. The Chargers got a 31-yard field goal from John Carney shortly before halftime, and the 18-point gap at intermission was the closest they would get.

Young added 15- and 7-yard scoring passes to Rice in the second half. In all, the 49ers' excess came to 449 total yards, more than enough against a San Diego defense that centered around all-pro linebacker Junior Seau. The 49ers built their game plan on the understanding that the Chargers' defense allowed Seau to freelance liberally. The 49ers kept one eye on him, and Seau, playing with a neck injury aggravated by a season of painful collisions, made just 2 tackles.

San Diego's final touchdown, a 30-yard pass from Stan Humphries to wide receiver Tony Martin, meant the two teams' total of 75 points surpassed the Super Bowl record of 69 set by Dallas and Buffalo in Super Bowl XXVII.

San Diego (AFC)	7	3	8	8	—	26
San Francisco (NFC)	14	14	14	7	—	49

SF—Rice 44 pass from S. Young (Brien kick)
SF—Watters 51 pass from S. Young (Brien kick)
SD—Means 1 run (Carney kick)
SF—Floyd 5 pass from S. Young (Brien kick)
SF—Watters 8 pass from S. Young (Brien kick)
SD—FG Carney 31
SF—Watters 9 run (Brien kick)
SF—Rice 15 pass from S. Young (Brien kick)
SD—Coleman 98 kickoff return (Seay pass from Humphries)
SF—Rice 7 pass from S. Young (Brien kick)
SD—Martin 30 pass from Humphries (Pupunu pass from Humphries)

TEAM STATISTICS	**SD**	**SF**
First Downs	20	28
Rushing	5	10
Passing	14	17
Penalty	1	1
Total Yardage	354	449
Net rushing yardage	67	133
Net passing yardage	287	316
Passes att.-comp.-had int.	55-27-3	38-25-0

RUSHING
San Diego—Means 13 for 33, 1 TD; Jefferson 1 for 10; Harmon 2 for 10; Gilbert 1 for 8; Bieniemy 1 for 3; Humphries 1 for 3.
San Francisco—S. Young 5 for 49; Watters 15 for 47, 1 TD; Floyd 9 for 32; Rice 1 for 10; Carter 2 for -5.

PASSING
San Diego—Humphries 24 of 49 for 275, 1 TD, 2 int.; Gilbert 3 of 6 for 30, 1 int.
San Francisco—S. Young 24 of 36 for 325, 6 TDs; Musgrave 1 of 1 for 6; Grbac 0 of 1.

RECEIVING
San Diego—Harmon 8 for 68; Seay 7 for 75; Pupunu 4 for 48; Martin 3 for 59, 1 TD; Jefferson 2 for 15; Bieniemy 1 for 33; Means 1 for 4; D. Young 1 for 3.
San Francisco—Rice 10 for 149, 3 TDs; Taylor 4 for 43; Floyd 4 for 26, 1 TD; Watters 3 for 61, 2 TDs; Jones 2 for 41; Popson 1 for 6; McCaffrey 1 for 5.

1994 Team Rosters

San Francisco
Harris Barton*
Harry Boatswain
Brian Bollinger
Doug Brien*
Dennis Brown*
Brett Carolan
Dexter Carter*
Toi Cook*
Chris Dalman*
Eric Davis*
Derrick Deese*
Richard Dent
Dedrick Dodge
Tyronne Drakeford*
William Floyd*
Antonio Goss*
Elvis Grbac*
Dana Hall*
Rhett Hall*
Merton Hanks*
Adrian Hardy
Tim Harris*
Rickey Jackson*
Brent Jones*
Darin Jordan*
Todd Kelly
Marc Logan*
Derek Loville*
Charles Mann*
Ed McCaffrey*
Tim McDonald*
Rod Milstead
Kevin Mitchell*
Bill Musgrave*
Ken Norton*
Bart Oates*
Tony Peterson
Gary Plummer*
Frank Pollack*
Ted Popson*
Jerry Rice*
Deion Sanders*
Jesse Sapolu*
Nate Singleton*
Artie Smith
Dana Stubblefield*
Ralph Tamm*
John Taylor*
Mark Thomas
Adam Walker*
Steve Wallace*
Ricky Watters*
Klaus Wilmsmeyer*
Troy Wilson*
Lee Woodall*
Bryant Young*
Steve Young*

San Diego
Johnnie Barnes
Eric Bieniemy*
David Binn*
Stan Brock*
Lewis Bush*
John Carney*
Darren Carrington*
Eric Castle*
Willie Clark*
Joe Cocozzo*
Andre Coleman*
Rodney Culver*
Isaac Davis*
Reuben Davis*
Dennis Gibson*
Gale Gilbert*
Darrien Gordon*
David Griggs*
Courtney Hall*
Ronnie Harmon*
Dwayne Harper*
Rodney Harrison*
Steve Hendrickson*
Stan Humphries*
Shawn Jefferson*
Raylee Johnson*
Eric Jonassen*
John Kidd
Aaron Laing
Shawn Lee*
Tony Martin*
Deems May
Natrone Means*
Joe Milinichik
Doug Miller*
Les Miller*
Chris Mims*
Shannon Mitchell*
Leslie O'Neal*
Vaughn Parker*
John Parrella*
Alfred Pupunu*
Stanley Richard*
Junior Seau*
Mark Seay*
Harry Swayne*
Cornell Thomas
Sean Vanhorse*
Bryan Wagner*
Reggie White
Curtis Whitley
Blaise Winter
Duane Young*
Lonnie Young

1995 AFC Champions Pittsburgh Steelers

Since the 1970s, fans in Pittsburgh had grown accustomed to winning. When the favored Steelers lost to the Chargers in the 1994 AFC Championship Game, the pressure on the club to reach the Super Bowl only increased. Pittsburgh got its wish in 1995.

Byron (Bam) Morris ran for 2 touchdowns in the closing minutes to thwart Buffalo's comeback attempt and help Pittsburgh to a 40-21 playoff victory. Holding a slim 26-21 lead, the Steelers mounted a 76-yard scoring drive followed by Levon Kirkland's interception to set up another touchdown.

The Steelers withstood a last-minute drive to beat stubborn Indianapolis 20-16 to win their fifth AFC title. Except for a 5-yard touchdown pass from O'Donnell to multi-talented Kordell Stewart, the scoring was all field goals until the fourth quarter.

Jim Harbaugh staked the Colts to a 16-13 lead with a 47-yard touchdown pass. Taking over at his 33 with 3:03 left, O'Donnell made a 9-yard completion on fourth-and-3. He then hit Ernie Mills with a 37-yard strike to the 1 to set up the touchdown by Morris. The Colts still nearly won as Harbaugh passed for 38 yards and scrambled for 17 more to guide his team to the Pittsburgh 29. Harbaugh's pass to Aaron Bailey in the end zone was juggled before falling incomplete as the game ended.

Regular Season

Sun	S 3	H	Detroit Lions	23-20	W
Sun	S-10	A	Houston Oilers	34-17	W
Mon	S-18	A N	Miami Dolphins	10-23	L
Sun	S-24	H	Minnesota Vikings	24-44	L
Sun	O-1	H	San Diego Chargers	31-16	W
Sun	O-8	A	Jacksonville Jaguars	16-20	L
Thu	O-19	H N	Cincinnati Bengals	9-27	L
Sun	O-29	H	Jacksonville Jaguars	24-7	W
Sun	N-5	A	Chicago Bears (OT)	37-34	W
Mon	N-13	H N	Cleveland Browns	20-3	W
Sun	N-19	A	Cincinnati Bengals	49-31	W
Sun	N-26	A	Cleveland Browns	20-17	W
Sun	D-3	H	Houston Oilers	21-7	W
Sun	D-10	A	Oakland Raiders	29-10	W
Sat	D-16	H	New England Patriots	41-27	W
Sun	D-23	A	Green Bay Packers	19-24	L

Postseason

1995 AFC Divisional Playoff Game
January 6, 1996
Pittsburgh 40, Buffalo 21 at Pittsburgh

Buffalo	0	7	7	7	—	21
Pittsburgh	7	16	3	14	—	40

1995 AFC Championship Game
January 14, 1996
Pittsburgh 20, Indianapolis 16 at Pittsburgh

Indianapolis	3	3	3	7	—	16
Pittsburgh	3	7	3	7	—	20

1995 NFC Champions Dallas Cowboys

Emmitt Smith set an NFL record for touchdowns in a season (25), and the Cowboys rolled right through the playoffs to their third NFC title in four years.

The Eagles, playing without injured quarterback Rodney Peete, couldn't keep pace as Dallas defeated Philadelphia 30-11 in the divisional playoffs. In the second quarter, Deion Sanders ran 21 yards on an end-around to cap a 70-yard drive, then Smith smashed in from the 1 to finish off a 79-yard march.

Smith rushed for 150 yards and 3 touchdowns, 2 of them in the fourth quarter, to overcome a 27-24 deficit and power Dallas to a 38-27 victory over Green Bay in the NFC Championship Game.

Troy Aikman teamed with Michael Irvin on 2 first-quarter touchdown passes. But Brett Favre led the Packers back with a 73-yard scoring pass to Robert Brooks and a 24-yard touchdown toss to Keith Jackson. With 4:05 left in the half. Smith capped an 11-play, 99-yard drive with a 1-yard scoring run.

Favre's third touchdown pass gave the Packers a 27-24 lead after three quarters, but Dallas drove 90 yards on 14 plays, with Smith scoring from the 5 for a 31-27 lead. Then, after cornerback Larry Brown intercepted Favre and returned the ball 28 yards, Smith scored from the 16 to clinch the victory and send the Cowboys into their record eighth Super Bowl.

Regular Season

Mon	S-4	A N	New York Giants	35-0	W
Sun	S-10	H	Denver Broncos	31-21	W
Sun	S-17	A	Minnesota Vikings (OT)	23-17	W
Sun	S-24	H	Arizona Cardinals	34-20	W
Sun	O-1	A	Washington Redskins	23-27	L
Sun	O-8	H	Green Bay Packers	34-24	W
Sun	O-15	A	San Diego Chargers	23-9	W
Sun	O-29	A	Atlanta Falcons	28-13	W
Mon	N-6	H N	Philadelphia Eagles	34-12	W
Sun	N-12	H	San Francisco 49ers	20-38	L
Sun	N-19	A	Oakland Raiders	34-21	W
Thu	N-23	H	Kansas City Chiefs	24-12	W
Sun	D-3	H	Washington Redskins	17-24	L
Sun	D-10	A	Philadelphia Eagles	17-20	L
Sun	D-17	H	New York Giants	21-20	W
Mon	D-25	A N	Arizona Cardinals	37-13	W

Postseason

1995 NFC Divisional Playoff Game
January 7, 1996
Dallas 30, Philadelphia 11 at Irving, Texas

Philadelphia	0	3	0	8	—	11
Dallas	3	14	6	7	—	30

1995 NFC Championship Game
January 14, 1996
Dallas 38, Green Bay 27 at Irving, Texas

Green Bay	10	7	10	0	—	27
Dallas	14	10	0	14	—	38

Super Bowl XXX

Dallas 27, Pittsburgh 17
January 28, 1996, Sun Devil Stadium, Tempe, Arizona
Attendance: 76,347

After producing 10 lopsided outcomes in its last 12 editions, the Super Bowl was due for some drama. Pittsburgh was up to the task and made a game of it, but the game turned on 2 interceptions by the game's most valuable player, Dallas cornerback Larry Brown.

The first of Brown's interceptions came midway through the third quarter. No Steelers receiver was within 10 yards when Brown accepted Neil O'Donnell's misfired pass at the Cowboys' 38 and returned it 44 yards to the Steelers' 18. Troy Aikman's pass to Michael Irvin took Dallas to the 1, and Emmitt Smith scored to give the Cowboys a 20-7 lead.

The Steelers made it 20-10 with Norm Johnson's 46-yard field goal, then recovered an onside kick. They reduced the gap to 20-17 when Bam Morris scored from the 1 with 6:36 to play. With 4:15 left, Pittsburgh had the ball again at its 32 after forcing Dallas to punt.

Two plays later, Brown intercepted O'Donnell at the Steelers' 39 and returned it to the 6. Smith scored from the 4 two plays later, and the Cowboys had locked up their record-tying fifth Super Bowl.

The Steelers never led, as Dallas scored on its first three possessions—on a 3-yard pass from Aikman to tight end Jay Novacek and 2 field goals by Chris Boniol—for a 13-0 lead. Shortly before halftime, the Steelers made it 13-7 when O'Donnell threw a 6-yard touchdown pass to Yancey Thigpen.

The statistical irony of the day was that O'Donnell entered the game as the NFL's career leader in fewest interceptions per pass attempt. On the game's final play, he was intercepted for the third time.

Dallas (NFC)	10	3	7	7	—	27
Pittsburgh (AFC)	0	7	0	10	—	17

Dall—FG Boniol 42
Dall—Novacek 3 pass from Aikman (Boniol kick)
Dall—FG Boniol 35
Pitt—Thigpen 6 pass from O'Donnell (N. Johnson kick)
Dall—E. Smith 1 run (Boniol kick)
Pitt—FG N. Johnson 46
Pitt—Morris 1 run (N. Johnson kick)
Dall—E. Smith 4 run (Boniol kick)

TEAM STATISTICS	DALL	PITT
First Downs	15	25
Rushing	5	9
Passing	10	15
Penalty	0	1
Total Yardage	254	310
Net rushing yardage	56	103
Net passing yardage	198	207
Passes att.-comp.-had int.	23-15-0	49-28-3

RUSHING
Dallas—E. Smith 18 for 49, 2 TDs; Johnston 2 for 8; K. Williams 1 for 2; Aikman 4 for -3.
Pittsburgh—Morris 19 for 73, 1 TD; Pegram 6 for 15; Stewart 4 for 15; O'Donnell 1 for 0; J. Williams 1 for 0.
PASSING
Dallas—Aikman 15 of 23 for 209, 1 TD.
Pittsburgh—O'Donnell 28 of 49 for 239, 1 TD, 3 int.
RECEIVING
Dallas—Irvin 5 for 76; Novacek 5 for 50, 1 TD; K. Williams 2 for 29; Sanders 1 for 47; Johnston 1 for 4; E. Smith 1 for 3.
Pittsburgh—Hastings 10 for 98; Mills 8 for 78; Thigpen 3 for 19, 1 TD; Morris 3 for 18; Holliday 2 for 19; J. Williams 2 for 7.

1995 Team Rosters

Dallas
Troy Aikman*
Larry Allen*
Robert Bailey*
Jon Baker
Reggie Barnes
Bill Bates*
Michael Batiste
Darren Benson
Eric Bjornson*
Chris Boniol*
Alundis Brice*
Greg Briggs*
Larry Brown*
Shante Carver*
Scott Case*
Billy Davis*
Ray Donaldson
Dixon Edwards*
Anthony Fieldings
Cory Fleming*
Oronde Gadsden
Jason Garrett*
Charles Haley*
Darryl Hardy
George Hegamin
Dale Hellestrae*
Chad Hennings*
Clayton Holmes
Michael Irvin*
John Jett*
Daryl Johnston*
Robert Jones*
Derek Kennard*
David Lang*
Leon Lett*
Brock Marion*
Russell Maryland*
Hurvin McCormack*
Godfrey Myles*
Nate Newton*
Jay Novacek*
Dominique Ross
Deion Sanders*
Jim Schwantz*
Darrin Smith*
Emmitt Smith*
Kevin Smith
Ron Stone*
Oscar Sturgis
Tony Tolbert*
Greg Tremble
Mark Tuinei*
Kendell Watkins*
Charlie Williams*
Erik Williams*
Kevin Williams*
Sherman Williams
Wade Wilson
Darren Woodson*

Pittsburgh
Steve Avery
Johnnie Barnes
Myron Bell*
Chad Brown*
Mark Bruener*
Brentson Buckner*
Dermontti Dawson*
Ta'ase Faumui
Deon Figures*
Lethon Flowers*
Randy Fuller*
Kendall Gammon*
Oliver Gibson
Jason Gildon*
Kevin Greene*
Tracy Greene
Andre Hastings*
Jonathan Hayes*
Kevin Henry*
Corey Holliday*
John Jackson*
Charles Johnson
Norm Johnson*
Bill Johnson*
Donta Jones*
Levon Kirkland*
Carnell Lake*
Tim Lester*
Greg Lloyd*
Alvoid Mays
Fred McAfee*
Jim Miller
Ernie Mills*
Bam Morris*
Tom Newberry*
Neil O'Donnell*
Chris Oldham*
Jerry Olsavsky*
Lonnie Palelei
James Parrish*
Erric Pegram*
Darren Perry*
Eric Ravotti
Ray Seals*
Leon Searcy*
Ariel Solomon*
Brenden Stai*
Rohn Stark*
Joel Steed*
Kordell Stewart*
Justin Strzelczyk*
Yancey Thigpen*
Mike Tomczak
John L. Williams*
Willie Williams*
Rod Woodson*

1996 AFC Champions New England Patriots

Fog shrouded Foxboro Stadium, but it couldn't dim the Patriots' first half offensive fireworks in their 28-3 victory over the defending AFC champion Steelers in a divisional playoff game.

The Patriots exploded for 226 yards and 3 touchdowns on their first 14 plays, including a 53-yard bomb from Drew Bledsoe to Terry Glenn to open the game. Curtis Martin followed with the first of his 3 touchdowns on the day. Keith Byars added a 34-yard touchdown on a screen pass to polish off Pittsburgh.

A week later, a mid-game power failure replaced the fog in Foxboro, but the Patriots still couldn't be stopped. In the AFC Championship Game, a bad snap on a first-quarter punt gave the Patriots the ball inside the Jacksonville 5. Martin scored on a 1-yard run to give New England a lead it never relenquished.

The teams traded field goals to make it 13-6 entering the fourth quarter. Jacksonville appeared on its way to the tying touchdown, but the Patriots' Willie Clay intercepted Mark Brunell in the end zone with 3:43 remaining. When Jacksonville got the ball again, Otis Smith returned a fumble 47 yards to put the finishing touches on a 20-6 victory.

Regular Season

Sun	S-1	A	Miami Dolphins	10-24	L
Sun	S-8	A	Buffalo Bills	10-17	L
Sun	S-15	H	Arizona Cardinals	31-0	W
Sun	S-22	H	Jacksonville Jaguars (OT)	28-25	W
Sun	O-6	A	Baltimore Ravens	46-38	W
Sun	O-13	H	Washington Redskins	22-27	L
Sun	O-20	A	Indianapolis Colts	27-9	W
Sun	O-27	H	Buffalo Bills	28-25	W
Sun	N-3	H	Miami Dolphins	42-23	W
Sun	N-10	A	New York Jets	31-27	W
Sun	N-17	H	Denver Broncos	8-34	L
Sun	N-24	H	Indianapolis Colts	27-13	W
Sun	D-1	A	San Diego Chargers	45-7	W
Sun	D-8	H	New York Jets	34-10	W
Sun	D-15	A	Dallas Cowboys	6-12	L
Sat	D-21	A	New York Giants	23-22	W

Postseason

1996 AFC Divisional Playoff Game
January 5, 1997
New England 28, Pittsburgh 3
at Foxboro, Massachusetts

Pittsburgh	0	0	3	0	—	3
New England	14	7	0	7	—	28

1996 AFC Championship Game
January 12, 1997
New England 20, Jacksonville 6
at Foxboro, Massachusetts

Pittsburgh	0	3	3	0	—	6
New England	7	6	0	7	—	20

1996 NFC Champions Green Bay Packers

The Packers went 13-3, scoring the most points (456) and giving up the fewest (210) of any team in the NFL.

Desmond Howard led Green Bay to a 35-14 win over San Francisco on a muddy Lambeau Field in a divisional playoff game. The first time Howard touched the ball, he returned a punt 71 yards for a touchdown. Then he sped 46 yards with another punt to set up Brett Favre's 4-yard touchdown pass to Andre Rison. Green Bay led 14-0 although it had only gained 9 yards from scrimmage.

San Francisco had 5 turnovers, but the 49ers closed the margin to 21-14. The Packers reacted by marching 72 yards for another touchdown, then added an 11-yard touchdown run by Edgar Bennett in the fourth quarter.

The Packers ended Carolina's hopes for a Super Bowl with a workmanlike 30-13 victory in the NFC Championship Game. The Panthers had an early 7-0 lead, but Favre countered with touchdown passes to Dorsey Levens and Antonio Freeman. An interception in the closing seconds of the half allowed Chris Jacke to add a 31-yard field goal before intermission.

The second half was a matter of staying warm for the presentation of Green Bay's first conference championship trophy since the NFL-AFL merger.

Regular Season

Sun	S-1	A	Tampa Bay Buccaneers	34-3	W
Mon	S-9	H N	Philadelphia Eagles	39-13	W
Sun	S-15	H	San Diego Chargers	42-10	W
Sun	S-22	A	Minnesota Vikings	21-30	L
Sun	S-29	A	Seattle Seahawks	31-10	W
Sun	O-6	A	Chicago Bears	37-6	W
Mon	O-14	H N	San Francisco 49ers (OT)	23-20	W
Sun	O-27	H	Tampa Bay Buccaneers	13-7	W
Sun	N-3	H	Detroit Lions	28-18	W
Sun	N-10	A	Kansas City Chiefs	20-27	L
Mon	N-18	A N	Dallas Cowboys	6-21	L
Sun	N-24	A N	St. Louis Rams	24-9	W
Sun	D-1	H	Chicago Bears	28-17	W
Sun	D-8	H	Denver Broncos	41-6	W
Sun	D-15	A	Detroit Lions	31-3	W
Sun	D-22	H	Minnesota Vikings	38-10	W

Postseason

1996 NFC Divisional Playoff Game
January 4, 1997
Green Bay 35, San Francisco 14
at Green Bay

San Francisco	0	7	7	0	—	14
Green Bay	14	7	7	7	—	35

1996 NFC Championship Game
January 12, 1997
Green Bay 30, Carolina 13
at Green Bay

Carolina	7	3	3	0	—	13
Green Bay	0	17	10	3	—	30

Super Bowl XXXI

Green Bay 35, New England 21
January 26, 1997, Louisiana Superdome, New Orleans, Louisiana
Attendance: 72,301

For the first time in Super Bowl history, a special teams player was chosen MVP. Former Heisman Trophy winner Desmond Howard, rescued off the NFL scrap heap before the season, re-wrote the record book in leading the Green Bay Packers to a 35-21 victory over the New England Patriots, the thirteenth consecutive Super Bowl win for the NFC. After New England had pulled to within a touchdown in the third quarter and seemed to have momentum, Howard's record 99-yard kickoff return re-established Green Bay's 14-point lead. His 244 return yards total equalled another Super Bowl record.

Green Bay began the game as though they would blow the Patriots out of Louisiana. On the second play of their first possession, Packers quarterback Brett Favre found Andre Rison for a 54-yard touchdown pass. As soon as Green Bay got the ball back, Chris Jacke booted a 37-yard field goal to widen the lead.

That woke up the Patriots. In six plays, they drove 79 yards to a touchdown. Quarterback Drew Bledsoe completed key passes to Keith Byars for 32 yards and Curtis Martin for 20, but the play that set up a touchdown pass to Byars was an interference penalty that put the ball on the 1. Moments later, New England scored again to go in front 14-10 on a 4-yard toss to Ben Coates after a 44-yard pass to Terry Glenn had moved the ball into position.

Less than a minute into the second quarter, Favre hit Antonio Freeman for a Super Bowl-record 81-yard touchdown pass down the right sideline. Before the period ended, Jacke added a 31-yard field goal and Favre ran 2 yards for a touchdown to cap a 74-yard drive. The score at intermission was 27-14.

New England began to gain control in the third quarter. Midway through the period, the Patriots drove 53 yards, with Martin scoring on an 18-yard run up the middle. But, on the ensuing kickoff, Howard crushed New England with his 99-yard sprint. A two-point conversion pass to Mark Chmura put the margin at 14 points. From there on, the Green Bay defense took over and the rest of the game was scoreless. Reggie White collected 3 of the Packers' 5 sacks on the day and helped hurry Bledsoe into 4 costly interceptions.

New England (AFC)	14	0	7	0	—	21
Green Bay (NFC)	10	17	8	0	—	35

GB—Rison 54 pass from Favre (Jacke kick)
GB—FG Jacke 37
NE—Byars 1 pass from Bledsoe (Vinatieri kick)
NE—Coates 4 pass from Bledsoe (Vinatieri kick)
GB—Freeman 81 pass from Favre (Jacke kick)
GB—FG Jacke 31
GB—Favre 2 run (Jacke kick)
NE—Martin 18 run (Vinatieri kick)
GB—Howard 99 kickoff return (Chmura pass from Favre)

TEAM STATISTICS	**NE**	**GB**
First Downs	16	16
Rushing	3	8
Passing	12	6
Penalty	1	2
Total Yardage	257	323
Net rushing yardage	43	115
Net passing yardage	214	208
Passes att.-comp.-had int.	48-25-4	27-14-0

RUSHING
New England—Martin 11 for 42, 1 TD; Bledsoe 1 for 1; Meggett 1 for 0.
Green Bay—Levens 14 for 61; Bennett 17 for 40; Favre 4 for 12; Henderson 1 for 2.

PASSING
New England—Bledsoe 25 of 48 for 253, 2 TD, 4 int.
Green Bay—Favre 14 of 27 for 245, 2 TD.

RECEIVING
New England—Coates 6 for 67, 1 TD; Glenn 4 for 62; Byars 4 for 42, 1 TD; Jefferson 3 for 34; Martin 3 for 28; Meggett 3 for 8; Brisby 2 for 12.
Green Bay—Freeman 3 for 105, 1 TD; Levens 3 for 23; Rison 2 for 77, 1 TD; Henderson 2 for 14; Chmura 2 for 13; Jackson 1 for 10; Bennett 1 for 4.

1996 Team Rosters

Green Bay
Mike Arthur
Don Beebe*
Edgar Bennett*
Robert Brooks
Bucky Brooks
Gary Brown
Gilbert Brown*
LeRoy Butler*
Mark Chmura*
Shannon Clavelle
Ron Cox*
Jeff Dellenbach*
Earl Dotson*
Santana Dotson*
Corey Dowden
Doug Evans*
Brett Favre*
Antonio Freeman*
Bernardo Harris*
Chris Hayes*
William Henderson*
Craig Hentrich*
Darius Holland*
Lamont Hollinquest*
Desmond Howard*
Chris Jacke*
Keith Jackson*
Travis Jervey*
Calvin Jones*
Sean Jones*
Lindsay Knapp*
George Koonce
Bob Kuberski
Dorsey Levens*
Derrick Mayes
Gene McGuire
Keith McKenzie*
Jim McMahon
John Michels*
Terry Mickens*
Anthony Morgan
Roderick Mullen*
Craig Newsome*
Doug Pederson
Mike Prior*
Andre Rison*
Eugene Robinson*
Mike Robinson
Ken Ruettgers
Brian Satterfield
Wayne Simmons*
Kevin Smith*
Aaron Taylor*
Jeff Thomason*
Adam Timmerman*
Reggie White*
Bruce Wilkerson*
Gabe Wilkins*
Brian Williams*
Tyrone Williams*
Frank Winters*

New England
Bruce Armstrong*
Troy Barnett
Mike Bartrum*
Drew Bledsoe*
Vincent Brisby*
Corwin Brown*
Monty Brown
Troy Brown
Tedy Bruschi*
John Burke*
Keith Byars*
Willie Clay*
Ben Coates*
Todd Collins*
Ferric Collons*
Jeff Dellenbach
Chad Eaton*
Sam Gash
Mike Gisler*
Terry Glenn*
Hason Graham*
Marrio Grier*
Jerome Henderson*
Jimmy Hitchcock
Shawn Jefferson*
Dietrich Jells
Ted Johnson*
Mike Jones*
Bob Kratch*
Max Lane*
Ty Law*
Vernon Lewis
Ray Lucas*
Curtis Martin*
Willie McGinest*
Mike McGruder*
Dave Meggett*
Lawyer Milloy*
Marty Moore*
Will Moore
Lovett Purnell
Terry Ray*
Ricky Reynolds
David Richards
William Roberts*
Todd Rucci*
Dwayne Sabb*
Pio Sagapolutele*
Walter Scott
Chris Slade*
Otis Smith*
Chris Sullivan*
Tom Tupa*
Adam Vinatieri*
Mark Wheeler*
Larry Whigham*
Dave Wohlabaugh*
Devin Wyman
Scott Zolak

1997 AFC Champions
Denver Broncos

The 1996 Broncos went 13-3 and appeared headed to the Super Bowl until suffering a stunning first-round playoff defeat. They returned in 1997 determined to do better, and despite entering the playoffs as a wild-card team, they did exactly that.

After building up a 21-0 first-half lead, Denver allowed Jacksonville, which had surprised the Broncos in the 1996 playoffs, to make it 21-17 by the end of the third quarter in the wild-card game. The backfield tandem of Terrell Davis (184 yards and 2 touchdowns) and Derek Loville (103 yards and a pair of touchdowns), helped Denver run away with a 42-17 victory.

The Broncos trailed the Chiefs 10-7 in an AFC Divisional Playoff Game, but a personal foul on a kickoff gave Denver the ball at midfield. Elway connected with Ed McCaffrey for 43 yards to the 1. Davis scored and Denver held on for the 14-10 victory.

In the AFC Championship Game, Elway led 2 scoring drives that put the Broncos ahead 24-14 at the end of the first half. But the play that crushed Pittsburgh was Elway's strike to Shannon Sharpe on third down that allowed the Broncos to run out the clock for the 24-21 win as Davis had his third straight 100-yard playoff day.

Regular Season

Sun	A-31	H	Kansas City Chiefs	19-3	W
Sun	S-7	A	Seattle Seahawks	35-14	W
Sun	S-14	H	St. Louis Rams	35-14	W
Sun	S-21	H	Cincinnati Bengals	38-20	W
Sun	S-28	A	Atlanta Falcons	29-21	W
Mon	O-6	H N	New England Patriots	34-13	W
Sun	O-19	A	Oakland Raiders	25-28	L
Sun	O-26	A	Buffalo Bills	23-20	W
Sun	N-2	H	Seattle Seahawks	30-27	W
Sun	N-9	H	Carolina Panthers	34-0	W
Sun	N-16	A	Kansas City Chiefs	22-24	L
Mon	N-24	H N	Oakland Raiders	31-3	W
Sun	N-30	A	San Diego Chargers	38-28	W
Sun	D-7	A	Pittsburgh Steelers	24-35	L
Mon	D-15	A N	San Francisco 49ers	17-34	L
Sun	D-21	H	San Diego Chargers	38-3	W

Postseason

1997 AFC Wild Card Game
December 27, 1997
Denver 42, Jacksonville 17 at Denver

Jacksonville	0	7	10	0	—	17
Denver	14	7	0	21	—	42

1997 AFC Divisional Playoff Game
January 4, 1998
Denver 14, Kansas City 10 at Kansas City

Denver	0	7	0	7	—	14
Kansas City	0	0	10	0	—	10

1997 AFC Championship Game
January 11, 1998
Denver 24, Pittsburgh 21 at Pittsburgh

Denver	7	17	0	0	—	24
Pittsburgh	7	7	0	7	—	21

1997 NFC Champions
Green Bay Packers

The defending NFC champion Packers won 10 of their last 11 games to breeze into the playoffs.

The Packers limited Tampa Bay to 90 rushing yards and only 12 completions in 37 attempts to win a divisional playoff game 21-7. The Buccaneers tallied 3 turnovers and 4 sacks, but they also botched 3 field-goal attempts. After Mike Alstott's 6-yard touchdown run cut the Green Bay lead to 13-6, Brett Favre and the Packers answered. On third-and-18 from the Buccaneers' 45, Favre found Derrick Mayes for 23 yards and a first down. Levens ended the drive with a 2-yard touchdown run.

For the third season in a row, the Packers knocked the San Francisco 49ers out of the playoffs 23-10. Green Bay limited the 49ers to a miniscule 33 yards on the ground and sacked Steve Young 4 times in the NFC Championship Game.

With less than a minute to play in the first half, the Packers had the ball on their 27. An 8-yard burst by Dorsey Levens and a 40-yard bomb to Antonio Freeman set up Ryan Longwell's 40-yard field goal to give the Packers a 13-3 halftime lead. Levens, who ran for a club-playoff-record 114 yards, iced the victory with a 5-yard touchdown run in the fourth quarter.

Regular Season

Mon	S-1	H N	Chicago Bears	38-24	W
Sun	S-7	A	Philadelphia Eagles	9-10	L
Sun	S-14	H	Miami Dolphins	23-18	W
Sun	S-21	H	Minnesota Vikings	38-32	W
Sun	S-28	A	Detroit Lions	15-26	L
Sun	O-5	H	Tampa Bay Buccaneers	21-16	W
Sun	O-12	A	Chicago Bears	24-23	W
Mon	O-27	A N	New England Patriots	28-10	W
Sun	N-2	H	Detroit Lions	20-10	W
Sun	N-9	H	St. Louis Rams	17-7	W
Sun	N-16	A	Indianapolis Colts	38-41	L
Sun	N-23	H	Dallas Cowboys	45-17	W
Mon	D-1	A N	Minnesota Vikings	27-11	W
Sun	D-7	A	Tampa Bay Buccaneers	17-6	W
Sun	D-14	A	Carolina Panthers	31-10	W
Sat	D-20	H	Buffalo Bills	31-21	W

Postseason

1997 NFC Divisional Playoff Game
January 4, 1998
Green Bay 21, Tampa Bay 7 at Green Bay

Tampa Bay	0	0	7	0	—	7
Green Bay	7	6	0	8	—	21

1997 NFC Championship Game
January 11, 1998
Green Bay 23, San Francisco 10 at San Francisco

Green Bay	3	10	0	10	—	23
San Francisco	0	3	0	7	—	10

Super Bowl XXXII

Denver 31, Green Bay 24
January 25, 1998, Qualcomm Stadium,
San Diego, California
Attendance: 68,912

In a Super Bowl that lived up to its adjective, the underdog Denver Broncos defeated the Green Bay Packers to (1) give the Coloradans their first Super Bowl win in five tries, (2) hand the Wisconsin club its first loss in four attempts, and (3) cap John Elway's long and legendary career. It also broke an AFC losing streak that dated back to Super Bowl XVIII.

The Broncos entered the game as at least 12-point underdogs for several reasons. The Super Bowl had become an annual NFC tour-de-force. Previous Denver trips to the big game had bordered on the embarrassing. The Packers, as defending champions, had experience in coping with Super Bowl Hype, a dreaded malady that often fatally infects first-time participants, such as most of the Denver roster. But, most of all, Green Bay was simply seen going in as the better team. Particularly, the Packers' huge defensive line was expected to easily manhandle the Broncos' relatively smaller offensive counterparts.

Instead, the Denver Diminutives proved the race is not always to the brawny. Featuring quickness and durability over brawn and oxygen on the sideline, the Broncos' blockers asserted themselves early and by the fourth quarter, they were clearly in charge. Their efforts allowed Terrell Davis to win MVP honors with 157 rushing yards and a Super Bowl-record 3 rushing touchdowns. His superlative effort was all the more remarkable in that Davis missed nearly the whole second quarter because of a blinding migraine.

In the duel of quarterbacks, Brett Favre, the current king, had the better of the statistics, but Elway, nearing the end of his storied career, avoided making critical mistakes and let his team do its thing. His most inspirational moment, and one of the game's greatest moments, came near the end of the third quarter, after Green Bay had tied the game 17-17 on Ryan Longwell's field goal. Elway drove the Broncos down the field. On third-and-6 from the 12, he scrambled to his right, drove into a pair of Green Bay tacklers, spun through the air, and landed on the 4. His willingness to risk a body nearing 40 years old was rewarded a few moments later when Davis scored Denver's go-ahead touchdown.

Yet the game was far from over. Favre brought the Packers back for a tying touchdown early in the final quarter as he capped an 85-yard drive by throwing his third touchdown pass of the day. Neither team could get anything going on their next two possessions. With 3:27 to go, Denver took over at the Green Bay 49. A facemask penalty, a 17-yard run by Davis, and a 23-yard pass from Elway to Howard Griffith moved the ball to the 8. Three plays later, Davis scored the winning touchdown.

Denver (AFC)	7	10	7	7	—	31
Green Bay (NFC)	7	7	3	7	—	24

GB—Freeman 22 pass from Favre (Longwell kick)
Den—Davis 1 run (Elam kick)
Den—Elway 1 run (Elam kick)
Den—FG Elam 51
GB—Chmura 6 pass from Favre (Longwell kick)
GB—FG Longwell 27
Den—Davis 1 run (Elam kick)
GB—Freeman 13 pass from Favre (Longwell kick)
Den—Davis 1 run (Elam kick)

TEAM STATISTICS	**DEN**	**GB**
First Downs	21	21
Rushing	14	4
Passing	5	14
Penalty	2	3
Total Yardage	302	350
Net rushing yardage	179	95
Net passing yardage	123	255
Passes att.-comp.-had int.	22-12-1	42-25-1

RUSHING
Denver—Davis 30 for 157, 3 TD; Elway 5 for 17, 1 TD; Hebron 3 for 3; Griffith 1 for 2.
Green Bay—Levens 19 for 90; Brooks 1 for 5.

PASSING
Denver—Elway 12 of 22 for 123, 1 int.
Green Bay—Favre 25 of 42 for 256, 1 int, 3 TD.

RECEIVING
Denver—Sharpe 5 for 38; McCaffrey 2 for 45; Davis 2 for 8; Griffith 1 for 23; Hebron 1 for 5; Carswell 1 for 4.
Green Bay—Freeman 9 for 126, 2 TD; Levens 6 for 56; Chmura 4 for 43, 1 TD; Brooks 3 for 16; Henderson 2 for 9; Mickens 1 for 6.

1997 Team Rosters

Denver
Allen Aldridge*
Flipper Anderson
Steve Atwater*
Scott Bentley
Tyrone Braxton*
Bubby Brister
Jamie Brown
Keith Burns*
Glenn Cadrez*
Dwayne Carswell*
Byron Chamberlain
Ray Crockett*
Terrell Davis*
David Diaz-Infante*
Dedrick Dodge*
Jason Elam*
John Elway*
David Gamble
Darrien Gordon*
Willie Green*
Howard Griffith*
Brian Habib*
Harald Hasselbach*
Vaughn Hebron*
Randy Hilliard*
Patrick Jeffers*
Darrius Johnson*
Ernest Jones
Tony Jones*
Jeff Lewis
Mike Lodish*
Derek Loville*
Anthony Lynn*
Ed McCaffrey*
Tim McKyer*
John Mobley*
Tom Nalen*
Dan Neil
Michael Dean Perry
Trevor Pryce*
David Richie
Bill Romanowski*
Tom Rouen*
Mark Schlereth*
Shannon Sharpe*
Detron Smith*
Neil Smith*
Rod Smith*
Harry Swayne*
Maa Tanuvasa*
Keith Traylor*
Tony Veland*
Alfred Williams*
Gary Zimmerman*

Green Bay
Joe Andruzzi
Don Beebe
Edgar Bennett
Steve Bono
Robert Brooks*
Gilbert Brown*
LeRoy Butler*
Mark Chmura*
Mark Collins*
Brett Conway
Chris Darkins*
Rob Davis*
Tyrone Davis*
Jeff Dellenbach
Earl Dotson*
Santana Dotson*
Doug Evans*
Brett Favre*
Paul Frase
Antonio Freeman*
Bernardo Harris*
Aaron Hayden*
William Henderson*
Craig Hentrich*
Anthony Hicks
Darius Holland*
Lamont Hollinquest*
Travis Jervey*
Seth Joyner*
George Koonce*
Bob Kuberski*
Dorsey Levens*
Ryan Longwell*
Derrick Mayes*
Blaine McElmurry
Keith McKenzie*
John Michels
Terry Mickens*
Roderick Mullen*
Craig Newsome
Doug Pederson
Mike Prior*
Marco Rivera*
Eugene Robinson*
Bill Schroeder
Darren Sharper*
Jermaine Smith
Aaron Taylor*
Jeff Thomason*
Adam Timmerman*
Ross Verba*
Reggie White*
Bruce Wilkerson*
Gabe Wilkins*
Brian Williams*
Tyrone Williams*
Frank Winters*

1998 NFC Champions Atlanta Falcons

Atlanta entered the 1998 season as a team on the rise, having won six of its last eight games to finish with a 7-9 record in 1997. Powered by veteran quarterback Chris Chandler and running back Jamal Anderson, who set an NFL record for rushing attempts (410), the 1998 Falcons soared to a franchise-best 14-2 record, losing only on the road to the 49ers and Jets.

Coach Dan Reeves, who had quadruple-bypass heart surgery in December, returned to lead his upstart team past the 49ers 20-18 in an NFC Divisional Playoff Game. Anderson rushed for 113 yards and 2 touchdowns, and the Falcons intercepted 49ers quarterback Steve Young 3 times in the second half, the last on a desperation bomb as time expired.

There were more heroics in store for Atlanta the following week. Morten Andersen's 38-yard field goal 11:52 into overtime lifted the Falcons to a 30-27 upset of the Minnesota Vikings in the NFC Championship Game. Atlanta qualified for its first trip to the Super Bowl in the 33-year history of the franchise by rallying from a 10-point fourth-quarter deficit.

The Falcons scored the tying touchdown with 49 seconds left in regulation when Chandler drilled a 16-yard touchdown pass to Terance Mathis. Atlanta held Minnesota's record-setting offense twice on downs in overtime before Andersen's game-winning kick.

Regular Season

Sun	S-6	A	Carolina Panthers	19-14	W
Sun	S-13	H	Philadelphia Eagles	17-12	W
Sun	S-27	A	San Francisco 49ers	20-31	L
Sun	O-4	H	Carolina Panthers	51-23	W
Sun	O-11	A	New York Giants	34-20	W
Sun	O-18	H	New Orleans Saints	31-23	W
Sun	O-25	A	New York Jets	3-28	L
Sun	N-1	H	St. Louis Rams	37-15	W
Sun	N-8	A	New England Patriots	41-10	W
Sun	N-15	H	San Francisco 49ers	31-19	W
Sun	N-22	H	Chicago Bears	20-13	W
Sun	N-29	A	St. Louis Rams	21-10	W
Sun	D-6	H	Indianapolis Colts	28-21	W
Sun	D-13	A	New Orleans Saints	27-17	W
Sun	D-20	A	Detroit Lions	24-17	W
Sun	D-27	H	Miami Dolphins	38-16	W

Postseason

1998 NFC Divisional Playoff Game
January 9, 1999
Atlanta 20, San Francisco 18 at Atlanta

San Francisco	0	10	0	8	-	18
Atlanta	7	7	3	3	-	20

1998 NFC Championship Game
January 17, 1999
Atlanta 30, Minnesota 27 (OT) at Minnesota

Atlanta	7	7	3	10	3	-	30
Minnesota........	7	13	0	7	0	-	27

1998 AFC Champions Denver Broncos

Defending Super Bowl-champion Denver started the 1998 season by becoming only the third NFL team (along with the 1934 Chicago Bears and the 1972 Miami Dolphins) to win its first 13 games. The Broncos lost a last-minute thriller to the Giants in game 14 and a second road game to the Dolphins a week later, but recovered to beat the Seahawks and finish 14-2.

Any doubts that Denver had lost its edge quickly were dispelled in an AFC Divisional Playoff Game against Miami. Davis rushed for a career playoff-high 199 yards and 2 touchdowns on just 21 carries to lead the Broncos to a 38-3 rout of the Dolphins, who absorbed their worst postseason loss.

In the AFC Championship Game against the resurgent New York Jets, the Broncos awoke from a first-half slumber and showed the Jets the heart of a champion. The Broncos took advantage of a fierce wind at Mile High Stadium and exploded for 20 third-quarter points to defeat the Jets 23-10.

Davis had another big game with 167 yards on 32 carries and capped the third-quarter uprising with a 31-yard touchdown run. It was his sixth consecutive 100-yard playoff game, tying an NFL record. The Broncos also forced 6 turnovers, including 2 on interceptions by cornerback Darrien Gordon, and held New York running back Curtis Martin to 14 yards on 13 carries.

Regular Season

Mon	S-7	H N	New England Patriots	27-21	W
Sun	S-13	H	Dallas Cowboys	42-23	W
Sun	S-20	A	Oakland Raiders	34-17	W
Sun	S-27	A	Washington Redskins	38-16	W
Sun	O-4	H	Philadelphia Eagles	41-16	W
Sun	O-11	A	Seattle Seahawks	21-16	W
Sun	O-25	H	Jacksonville Jaguars	37-24	W
Sun	N-1	A	Cincinnati Bengals	33-26	W
Sun	N-8	H	San Diego Chargers	27-10	W
Mon	N-16	A N	Kansas City Chiefs	30-7	W
Sun	N-22	H	Oakland Raiders	40-14	W
Sun	N-29	A	San Diego Chargers	31-16	W
Sun	D-6	H	Kansas City Chiefs	35-31	W
Sun	D-13	A	New York Giants	16-20	L
Mon	D-21	A N	Miami Dolphins	21-31	L
Sun	D-27	H	Seattle Seahawks	28-21	W

Postseason

1998 AFC Divisional Playoff Game
January 9, 1999
Denver 38, Miami 3 at Denver

Miami	0	3	0	0	-	3
Denver	14	7	3	14	-	38

1998 AFC Championship Game
January 17, 1999
Denver 23, New York Jets 10 at Denver

N.Y. Jets	0	3	7	0	-	10
Denver	0	0	20	3	-	23

Super Bowl XXXIII

Denver 34, Atlanta 19
January 31, 1999, Pro Player Stadium, Miami, Florida
Attendance: 74,803

John Elway passed for 336 yards and 1 touchdown to earn most-valuable-player honors in the Broncos' 34-19 victory over the Falcons. Denver, which defeated Green Bay in Super Bowl XXXII, became the seventh team (including Pittsburgh twice) to win back-to-back Super Bowls.

Elway completed 18 of 29 passes and had plenty of help from his teammates. Terrell Davis ran for more than 100 yards (102) for a record seventh consecutive postseason game, Darrien Gordon intercepted 2 passes, Rod Smith snagged a back-breaking, 80-yard touchdown pass, and the Broncos' defense came through with big plays. The flip side of Denver's defensive performance was the Falcons' failure to come up with the plays on offense that could have kept them in the game.

Atlanta took the opening kickoff and marched 48 yards before settling for Morten Andersen's 32-yard field goal. Denver countered with a 10-play, 80-yard touchdown drive highlighted by Elway's 41-yard pass to Rod Smith. Blocking back Howard Griffith crossed up the Falcons, who were keying on Davis, by driving over from the 1 for the touchdown.

Denver's Jason Elam widened the lead to 10-3 with a 26-yard field goal in the second quarter, but late in the period Atlanta drove 65 yards to the Broncos' 8. Once again, the key play eluded the Falcons, and Andersen came in for a 26-yard field-goal try. Shockingly, the ball sailed wide right. On Denver's next play, Elway and Smith teamed on their 80-yard touchdown to give Denver a 14-point lead. Andersen's successful 28-yard field goal before the half ended was small consolation for the Falcons.

In the third quarter, Atlanta drove to Denver's 21, only to have Chris Chandler's pass batted into the hands of Gordon, who returned the interception 58 yards. Five plays later, Griffith scored again from the 1. Shortly after that, Gordon made his second interception. Elway led a 48-yard drive that culminated in his 3-yard touchdown run for a 31-6 lead. Tim Dwight ran back the ensuing kickoff 94 yards for a touchdown to give Atlanta its last hurrah. Denver took the challenge in stride, adding another Elam field goal that made a final Atlanta touchdown no more than a footnote.

Denver (AFC)	7	10	0	17	—	34
Atlanta (NFC)	3	3	0	13	—	19

Atl—FG Andersen 32
Den—Griffith 1 run (Elam kick)
Den—FG Elam 26
Den—R. Smith 80 pass from Elway (Elam kick)
Atl—FG Andersen 28
Den—Griffith 1 run (Elam kick)
Den—Elway 3 run (Elam kick)
Atl—Dwight 94 kickoff return (Andersen kick)
Den—FG Elam 37
Atl—Mathis 3 pass from Chandler (Chandler pass failed)

TEAM STATISTICS	DEN	ATL
First Downs	22	21
Rushing	8	8
Passing	14	12
Penalty	0	1
Total Yardage	457	337
Net rushing yardage	121	131
Net passing yardage	336	206
Passes att.-comp.-had int.	29-18-1	35-19-3

RUSHING
Denver—Davis 25 for 102; Griffith 4 for 9, 2 TD; Loville 2 for 8; Elway 3 for 2, 1 TD; R.Smith 1 for 1; Brister 1 for -1.
Atlanta—Anderson 18 for 96; Chandler 4 for 30; Dwight 1 for 5.

PASSING
Denver—Elway 18 of 29 for 336, 1 TD, 1 int.
Atlanta—Chandler 19 of 35 for 219, 1 TD, 3 int.

RECEIVING
Denver—R. Smith 5 for 152, 1 TD; McCaffrey 5 for 72; Chamberlain 3 for 29; Davis 2 for 50; Sharpe 2 for 26; Griffith 1 for 7.
Atlanta—Mathis 7 for 85, 1 TD; Martin 5 for 79; Anderson 3 for 16; Harris 2 for 21; Santiago 1 for 13; Kozlowski 1 for 5.

1998 Team Rosters

Atlanta
Morten Andersen*
Darren Anderson
Jamal Anderson*
Lester Archambeau*
Chris Bayne
Cornelius Bennett*
Juran Bolden
Michael Booker*
Ronnie Bradford*
Keith Brooking*
Omar Brown
Ray Buchanan*
John Burrough*
Devin Bush*
Chris Chandler*
Bob Christian
Calvin Collins*
Henri Crockett*
Steve DeBerg
Gary Downs*
Shane Dronett*
Tim Dwight*
Antonio Edwards*
Randy Fuller*
Jammi German
Tony Graziani
Harold Green*
Travis Hall*
Bob Hallen*
Ruffin Hamilton*
Ronnie Harris*
Todd Kinchen
Brian Kozlowski
Tony Martin*
Terance Mathis*
Ken Oxendine
Jose Portilla*
Eugene Robinson*
Ephraim Salaam*
O.J. Santiago*
Craig Sauer*
Adam Schreiber*
Chuck Smith*
Ed Smith*
Dan Stryzinski*
Shawn Swayda
Ben Talley*
Robbie Tobeck*
Esera Tuaolo*
Jessie Tuggle*
William White*
Bob Whitfield*
Dave Widell
Elijah Williams*
Gene Williams*

Denver
Justin Armour
Steve Atwater*
Chris Banks
Tyrone Braxton*
Bubby Brister*
Cyron Brown
Eric Brown
Keith Burns*
Glenn Cadrez*
Dwayne Carswell*
Byron Chamberlain*
George Coghill*
Ray Crockett*
Terrell Davis*
David Diaz-Infante*
Jason Elam*
John Elway*
Darrien Gordon*
Willie Green*
Brian Griese
Howard Griffith*
Harald Hasselbach*
Vaughn Hebron*
Tory James*
Darrius Johnson*
Ernest Jones
Tony Jones*
Seth Joyner*
Matt Lepsis*
Mike Lodish*
Derek Loville*
Anthony Lynn*
Ed McCaffrey*
John Mobley*
Tom Nalen*
Marcus Nash*
Dan Neil*
Tito Paul*
Trevor Pryce*
Bill Romanowski*
Tom Rouen*
Mark Schlereth*
Shannon Sharpe*
Detron Smith*
Neil Smith*
Rod Smith*
Harry Swayne*
Maa Tanuvasa*
Keith Traylor*
Marvin Washington*
Nate Wayne
Alfred Williams*

CHAPTER 8

Championships & Playoffs

Beau Riffenburgh

The Chicago Bears and Portsmouth Spartans ended the regularly scheduled portion of the 1932 season with identical 6-1 records. (The Bears tied 6 games and the Spartans tied 4, but, at the time, ties were discounted when computing winning percentage). So league officials arranged for the two teams to play one week later in Chicago to determine the NFL champion.

Chicago beat Portsmouth 9-0 to claim the title. Though the game is not considered a postseason game (it counts in the regular-season standings), its success did prompt NFL owners to split the league into two divisions and create an official championship game beginning in 1933.

Another item of note: The Bears-Spartans game in 1932 was played indoors at Chicago Stadium because of a snowstorm. But weather never has forced the movement or cancellation of an official championship game. The weather has, however, played a crucial role in numerous championships over the years; how the players adapted to the conditions helped the legend of the NFL grow. With expansion of the number of teams and number of games required to reach the championship game, a season that once ended in December stretched into January; the weather in the northern cities that dominated the league for many years did not improve.

The uncontrollable elements led to the term "home field advantage," which is perhaps more important in football than in any other professional sport. Teams like the Green Bay Packers, Chicago Bears, New York Giants, can attribute part of their success over the years to their location and the intimidation it had on visiting teams. Likewise, the Miami Dolphins, San Francisco 49ers, and Dallas Cowboys have had their finest seasons when they forced opponents to come to their stadiums for crucial games in January. There is, however, more to the NFL playoffs than just a weather report.

Injuries, unsung heroes, and players thriving under the scrutiny of the championship season have created some of the most memorable games in sport. The following list details those games, with expanded reports since 1996.

1933 NFL CHAMPIONSHIP GAME
Chicago Bears 23, New York Giants 21

December 17, 1933, at Chicago
Attendance: 26,000

Fog hung low over Wrigley Field as the Chicago Bears came from behind to defeat the New York Giants 23-21 in the first official NFL Championship Game. The Giants led 7-6 at the half, with Harry Newman's 29-yard touchdown pass to Morris (Red) Badgro and Ken Strong's extra point overcoming two earlier field goals by Jack Manders.

In the third quarter the lead started bouncing back and forth. The Bears went ahead on Manders's third field goal, but the Giants came back with a 61-yard drive for a score. The Bears retaliated, scoring on an 8-yard touchdown pass from Bronko Nagurski to end Bill Karr.

On the first play of the fourth quarter, with the ball at the Chicago 8, Strong took a handoff, became trapped near the sideline, and lateraled to the surprised Newman. Newman scrambled for a while himself, then threw a desperation pass to Strong, who had slipped free for the touchdown catch.

Down 21-16, the Bears came back again. From the New York 33, Nagurski threw a jump pass to end Bill Hewitt, who gained 14 yards before lateraling to Karr, who covered the remaining 19 yards for the winning score.

N.Y. Giants	0	7	7	7	-	21
Chi. Bears	3	3	10	7	-	23

ChiB - FG Manders 16
ChiB - FG Manders 40
NYG - Badgro 29 pass from Newman (Strong kick)
ChiB - FG Manders 28
NYG - Krause 1 run (Strong kick)
ChiB - Karr 8 pass from Nagurski (Manders kick)
NYG - Strong 8 pass from Newman (Strong kick)
ChiB - Karr 19 lateral from Hewitt, who caught 14 pass from Nagurski (Brumbaugh kick)

1934 NFL CHAMPIONSHIP GAME
New York Giants 30, Chicago Bears 13

December 9, 1934, at New York
Attendance: 35,059

In a rematch of the first NFL Championship Game, the Giants scored 27 points in the fourth quarter to register a 30-13 victory in what has come to be known as the "Sneakers Game."

A freezing rain the night before and a temperature of 9 degrees turned the field into a virtual sheet of ice, so an equipment man was sent to Manhattan College to borrow sneakers for better footing.

The home team did not don the rubber-soled shoes until the third quarter, by which time they trailed, 10-3. It was 13-3 before the Giants exploded. First, rookie tailback Ed Danowski threw a 28-yard touchdown pass to Ike Frankian. On their next possession, after taking over at Chicago's 42, the Giants took only one play to score, as Ken Strong burst straight up the middle for a touchdown. A short while later, Strong scored again, this time from 11 yards, and Danowski finished the romp over the stunned Bears with a 9-yard dash around right end.

Chi. Bears	0	10	3	0	-	13
N.Y. Giants	3	0	0	27	-	30

NYG - FG Strong 38
ChiB - Nagurski 1 run (Manders kick)
ChiB - FG Manders 17
ChiB - FG Manders 24
NYG - Frankian 28 pass from Danowski (Strong kick)
NYG - Strong 42 run (Strong kick)
NYG - Strong 11 run (kick failed)
NYG - Danowski 9 run (Molenda kick)

1935 NFL CHAMPIONSHIP GAME
Detroit 26, New York Giants 7

December 15, 1935, at Detroit
Attendance: 15,000

On a day on which wind, rain, sleet, and snow turned the University of Detroit field into a quagmire, the Lions dominated the Giants in the very early and very late going, and that was enough to bring Detroit an NFL title only two months after the Tigers had won their first World Series.

The Lions scored on the opening series of the game, helped by their only 2 pass completions of the day. Ace Gutowsky scored from 2 yards out, and, later in the first period, Earl (Dutch) Clark made a twisting, swirling 40-yard touchdown run to increase the lead to 13-0. The Giants scored in the second period when Ed Danowski passed to Ken Strong, who broke away on a 42-yard scoring romp.

The Giants threatened several times in the second half, but could not get the ball into the end zone. With three minutes left, Danowski's quick kick hit the back of one of his teammates, and the Lions took over at the New York 26. Six plays later, Ernie Caddel put the game away when he swept in from 4 yards out, a feat that was equaled in the final seconds of the game by Raymond (Buddy) Parker.

N.Y. Giants	0	7	0	0	-	7
Detroit	13	0	0	13	-	26

Det - Gutowsky 2 run (Presnell kick)
Det - Clark 40 run (kick failed)
NYG - Strong 42 pass from Danowski (Strong kick)
Det - Caddel 4 run (Clark kick)
Det - Parker 4 run (kick failed)

1936 NFL CHAMPIONSHIP GAME
Green Bay 21, Boston 6

December 13, 1936, at New York
Attendance: 29,545

George Preston Marshall, the owner of the Redskins, moved the title game from Boston to the Polo Grounds in New York to show his contempt for the lack of fan support, but the Redskins' performance was as poor as that of the fans, and the Packers won easily 21-6.

On the tenth play of the game, Boston's all-league halfback Cliff Battles was injured, Riley Smith fumbled, and Lou Gordon recovered for the Packers. Three plays later, Arnie Herber combined with Don Hutson for a 48-yard touchdown pass. Battles's replacement, Ernest (Pug) Rentner, scored on a 2-yard run in the second quarter, but Smith missed the extra-point attempt, and the Packers led 7-6 at halftime.

In the third quarter, Herber went to work again. First, he found halfback Johnny (Blood) McNally on a 52-yard pass play, then passed 8 yards to Milt Gantenbein for a touchdown that increased Green Bay's lead to 14-6.

The Packers' defense put the game away in the fourth quarter. Lon Evans blocked a punt at Boston's 22-yard line, which was recovered by Clarke Hinkle at the 3. Two plays later, Bob Monnett scored from the 2.

Green Bay	7	0	7	7	-	21
Boston	0	6	0	0	-	6

GB - Hutson 48 pass from Herber (E.Smith kick)
Bos - Rentner 2 run (kick failed)
GB - Gantenbein 8 pass from Herber (E.Smith kick)
GB - Monnett 2 run (Engebretsen kick)

1937 NFL CHAMPIONSHIP GAME
Washington 28, Chicago Bears 21

December 12, 1937, at Chicago
Attendance: 15,870

Rookie Sammy Baugh completed 18 of 33 passes for a championship-game record 354 yards and 3 third-quarter touchdowns as the Redskins won their first title.

It was 15 degrees and the field was icy when Baugh marched the Redskins 53 yards for their first score. However, the Bears responded with 2 quick touchdowns for a 14-7 lead after one period. In the third quarter, Baugh hit Wayne Millner on a crossing pattern, and the all-pro end broke loose to complete a 55-yard scoring play that tied the game. But Chicago took back the lead on a 13-play, 73-yard drive that ended with a 4-yard touchdown pass from Bernie Masterson to Edgar (Eggs) Manske.

Baugh struck back quickly, throwing a 78-yard touchdown pass to Millner on the first play after the ensuing kickoff. Then, on their next possession, the Redskins drove 80 yards in 11 plays, with the payoff coming on a 35-yard pass from Baugh to Ed Justice. The game was not locked away, however, and the Bears drove deep into Washington territory twice in the fourth quarter, only to be held on downs both times.

Washington	7	0	21	0	-	28
Chi. Bears	14	0	7	0	-	21

Was - Battles 7 run (R.Smith kick)
ChiB - Manders 10 run (Manders kick)
ChiB - Manders 37 pass from Masterson (Manders kick)
Was - Millner 55 pass from Baugh (R.Smith kick)
ChiB - Manske 4 pass from Masterson (Manders kick)
Was - Millner 78 pass from Baugh (R.Smith kick)
Was - Justice 35 pass from Baugh (R.Smith kick)

1938 NFL CHAMPIONSHIP GAME
New York Giants 23, Green Bay 17

December 11, 1938, at New York
Attendance: 48,120

A record championship-game crowd of 48,120 in the Polo Grounds saw the Giants manhandled in almost every way (they were outgained 378 yards to 212) by the Green Bay Packers. However, that was not the case on the scoreboard, where the Giants came out ahead 23-17.

On the Packers' second possession of the day, end Jim Lee Howell blocked Clarke Hinkle's punt to set up the game's first score, Ward Cuff's 14-yard field goal. The Giants extended their lead following another blocked punt, with Alphonse (Tuffy) Leemans scoring on a 6-yard run. The Packers cut the Giants' lead to 2 points before the end of the first quarter, however, scoring on a 40-yard pass.

In the second quarter, the teams exchanged scores, with Ed Danowski throwing a 21-yard touchdown pass to rookie Hap Barnard, and Green Bay responding with Hinkle's 1-yard scoring run.

A 15-yard field goal by Paul (Tiny) Engebretsen put Green Bay ahead for the first time in the third quarter, but halfback Hank Soar led the Giants right back downfield. He carried the ball 5 times and caught 1 pass before making a leaping grab at the goal line, and dragging Hinkle over for the winning score.

Green Bay	0	14	3	0	-	17
N.Y. Giants	9	7	7	0	-	23

NYG - FG Cuff 14
NYG - Leemans 6 run (kick failed)
GB - C. Mulleneaux 40 pass from Herber (Engebretsen kick)
NYG - Barnard 21 pass from Danowski (Cuff kick)
GB - Hinkle 1 run (Engebretsen kick)
GB - FG Engebretsen 15
NYG - Soar 23 pass from Danowski (Cuff kick)

1939 NFL CHAMPIONSHIP GAME
Green Bay 27, New York Giants 0

December 10, 1939, at Milwaukee
Attendance: 32,278

Winds blowing 35 miles per hour through the open ends of Milwaukee's State Fair Park seemed to bother the Giants considerably more than the Packers, as the visiting team threw 6 interceptions and missed 3 field goals en route to being shut out 27-0. Green Bay, meanwhile, completed 7 of 10 passes and kicked 2 field goals.

The Packers jumped ahead early when Arnie Herber threw a 7-yard touchdown pass to Milt Gantenbein, alone between the goal posts due to double coverage on Don Hutson. The Giants looked for their first score after Jim Poole blocked Clarke Hinkle's punt and Jim Lee Howell recovered. However, Ward Cuff's field-goal attempt missed from 42 yards, and the score remained 7-0 at halftime.

A 29-yard field goal by Paul (Tiny) Engebretsen increased Green Bay's lead to 10-0 in the third quarter, then, after Gantenbein intercepted Ed Danowski at the New York 33, Cecil Isbell found halfback Joe Laws with a 31-yard touchdown pass. Green Bay scored twice more in the fourth quarter, with Ernie Smith booting a 42-yard field goal, and Ed Jankowski plowing in from 1 yard.

N.Y. Giants	0	0	0	0	-	0
Green Bay	7	0	10	10	-	27

GB - Gantenbein 7 pass from Herber (Engebretsen kick)
GB - FG Engebretsen 29
GB - Laws 31 pass from Isbell (Engebretsen kick)
GB - FG E.Smith 42
GB - Jankowski 1 run (E.Smith kick)

1940 NFL CHAMPIONSHIP GAME
Chicago Bears 73, Washington 0

December 8, 1940, at Washington
Attendance: 36,034

After Washington's ninth game of the 1940 season, a 7-3 victory over the Chicago Bears, the Redskins had been quoted as calling the Bears "crybabies." George Halas intended to have his team ready for the rematch, and brought in T-formation mastermind Clark Shaughnessy to help his offense. In a showcase for the T, Halas's crew played virtually a flawless game, destroying the Redskins 73-0.

The Bears did not wait to show their dominance. On the second play of the game, fullback Bill Osmanski swept around left end for 68 yards and a touchdown. The next time the Bears had the ball, they moved steadily downfield, going 80 yards in 17 plays, with Sid Luckman scoring on a quarterback sneak. Then, on the first play of their third possession, fullback Joe Maniaci raced 42 yards for a score that made it 21-0 in the first quarter.

Chicago rushed for 381 yards, completed 7 of 10 passes for 138 yards, and intercepted 8 passes—3 of which were returned for touchdowns in the third quarter—en route to a record romp.

Chi. Bears	21	7	26	19	-	73
Washington	0	0	0	0	-	0

ChiB - Osmanski 68 run (Manders kick)
ChiB - Luckman 1 run (Snyder kick)
ChiB - Maniaci 42 run (Martinovich kick)
ChiB - Kavanaugh 30 pass from Luckman (Snyder kick)
ChiB - Pool 15 interception return (Plasman kick)
ChiB - Nolting 23 run (kick failed)
ChiB - McAfee 34 interception return (Stydahar kick)
ChiB - Turner 24 interception return (kick failed)
ChiB - Clark 44 run (kick failed)
ChiB - Famiglietti 2 run (Maniaci pass from Sherman)
ChiB - Clark 1 run (pass failed)

1941 NFL WESTERN DIVISION PLAYOFF GAME
Chicago Bears 33, Green Bay 14

December 14, 1941, at Chicago
Attendance: 43,425

In the first divisional playoff game in NFL history, the Chicago Bears won the rubber match between two teams that had gone 10-1 in the regular season. The Green Bay Packers jumped ahead quickly, recovering a fumble on the opening kickoff and driving 18 yards to score on a 1-yard run by fullback Clarke Hinkle.

But then the Bears exploded. Late in the first quarter, rookie halfback Hugh Gallarneau returned a punt 81 yards for a touchdown. In the second period, the Bears took the lead on Bob Snyder's 24-yard field goal, then scored on three dominating drives, with fullback Norm Standlee rushing for 2 touchdowns and backup halfback Bob Swisher dashing 9 yards up the middle for the score that made it 30-7 at halftime.

Flooding the field with reserves in the second half, the Bears still held their own, cruising to a 33-14 victory.

Green Bay	7	0	7	0	-	14
Chi. Bears	6	24	0	3	-	33

GB - Hinkle 1 run (Hutson kick)
ChiB - Gallarneau 81 punt return (kick blocked)
ChiB - FG Snyder 24
ChiB - Standlee 3 run (Stydahar kick)

ChiB	-	Standlee 2 run (Stydahar kick)
ChiB	-	Swisher 9 run (Stydahar kick)
GB	-	Van Every 10 pass from Isbell (Hutson kick)
ChiB	-	FG Snyder 26

1941 NFL CHAMPIONSHIP GAME
Chicago Bears 37, New York Giants 9

December 21, 1941, at Chicago
Attendance: 13,341

In another masterful performance, the Bears' line dominated the game on both sides of the ball on the way to defeating the Giants 37-9.

Chicago led only 9-6 at halftime despite having controlled the ball for the first 10:34 of the game and for 53 of the half's 63 plays. Three field goals by Bob Snyder had been, to a great extent, offset by Alphonse (Tuffy) Leemans's 31-yard touchdown pass to George Franck.

But after Ward Cuff tied the game 9-9 with a 16-yard field goal, the Bears started finishing their drives, going 71, 66, and 54 yards for touchdowns, with Norm Standlee scoring twice and Ken McAfee once. Then, in the final seconds of the game, the Bears' defense upped the margin. New York's Hank Soar lateraled to Andy Marefos, who attempted a halfback pass. But Marefos fumbled when hit by several Chicago defenders, and Ken Kavanaugh picked up the ball and ran 42 yards for a touchdown.

N.Y. Giants	6	0	3	0	-	9
Chi. Bears	3	6	14	14	-	37

ChiB	-	FG Snyder 14
NYG	-	Franck 31 pass from Leemans (kick failed)
ChiB	-	FG Snyder 39
ChiB	-	FG Snyder 37
NYG	-	FG Cuff 16
ChiB	-	Standlee 2 run (Snyder kick)
ChiB	-	Standlee 7 run (Maniaci kick)
ChiB	-	McAfee 5 run (Artoe kick)
ChiB	-	Kavanaugh 42 fumble return (McLean drop kick)

1942 NFL CHAMPIONSHIP GAME
Washington 14, Chicago Bears 6

December 13, 1942, at Washington
Attendance: 36,006

The Bears rolled into Washington looking for their third title in a row and to become the first team in NFL history to record a perfect season. They went home with a 14-6 loss.

After a scoreless first quarter, Chicago jumped ahead when tackle Lee Artoe picked up a fumble by Dick Todd and rumbled 50 yards for a touchdown. Artoe's extra-point attempt was wide, however. The Redskins struck back immediately. A long kickoff return set them up at the Chicago 42, and, after two plays, Sammy Baugh found Wilbur Moore with a 38-yard touchdown pass. Bob Masterson's kick put Washington ahead 7-6 at halftime.

Andy Farkas ran 1 yard for a touchdown in the third quarter to make it 14-6, and the Redskins held on. One Chicago drive that reached the Washington 12 ended when Baugh intercepted a pass in the end zone. As the game wound down, another Chicago drive went 79 yards from the Bears' 20 to the Washington 1. But when halfback Hugh Gallarneau scored on the next play, the Bears were penalized for backfield in motion. They surrendered the ball on downs, and the Redskins ran out the clock.

Chi. Bears	0	6	0	0	-	6
Washington	0	7	7	0	-	14

ChiB	-	Artoe 50 fumble return (kick failed)
Was	-	Moore 38 pass from Baugh (Masterson kick)
Was	-	Farkas 1 run (Masterson kick)

1943 NFL EASTERN DIVISION PLAYOFF GAME
Washington 28, New York Giants 0

December 19, 1943, at New York
Attendance: 42,800

Sammy Baugh put on a one-man show and displayed why he had been able to lead the NFL in passing, interceptions, and punting, as he used each of those talents to lead the Redskins to a 28-0 victory over the Giants on a frozen field at the Polo Grounds. Baugh completed 16 of 21 passes for 199 yards, intercepted 2 passes, and averaged more than 40 yards per punt.

After neither team could score in the first quarter, Baugh's passing to Bob Masterson and Wilbur Moore set up 2 short touchdown runs by Andy Farkas in the second period.

The Giants threatened to get back into it in the third quarter, but Baugh intercepted a pass by Alphonse (Tuffy) Leemans and returned it 28 yards, setting up Farkas's third touchdown early in the final period. Then Baugh took to the air, finishing an impressive drive with an 11-yard strike to backup end Ted Lapka.

Washington	0	14	0	14	-	28
N.Y. Giants	0	0	0	0	-	0

Was	-	Farkas 2 run (Masterson kick)
Was	-	Farkas 2 run (Masterson kick)
Was	-	Farkas 1 run (Masterson kick)
Was	-	Lapka 11 pass from Baugh (Masterson kick)

1943 NFL CHAMPIONSHIP GAME
Chicago 41, Washington 21

December 16, 1943, at Chicago
Attendance: 34,320

Sammy Baugh came into the game having had one of the great seasons of all time, but it was Bears quarterback Sid Luckman who had the great day, completing 15 of 26 passes for 286 yards and 5 touchdowns and rushing for 64 yards while leading the Bears to their third title in four years 41-21.

Baugh was knocked out of the game with a concussion early in the first quarter, but, behind the play-calling of George Cafego, the Redskins drove 60 yards for the first score of the day, a 1-yard touchdown run by Andy Farkas. Then Bears' quarterback Luckman took over, finding Harry Clark with a 31-yard touchdown pass and setting up Bronko Nagurski's 3-yard scoring run that made the score 14-7 at halftime.

The second half was pass crazy. Luckman found Dante Magnani with touchdown passes of 36 and 66 yards before Baugh, back in action after halftime, connected with Farkas from 17 yards. But Luckman tossed 2 more touchdown passes (to Jim Benton and Clark) in the fourth quarter to secure the victory.

Washington	0	7	7	7	-	21
Chi. Bears	0	14	13	14	-	41

Was	-	Farkas 1 run (Masterson kick)

ChiB	-	Clark 31 pass from Luckman (Snyder kick)
ChiB	-	Nagurski 3 run (Snyder kick)
ChiB	-	Magnani 36 pass from Luckman (Snyder kick)
ChiB	-	Magnani 66 pass from Luckman (kick failed)
Was	-	Farkas 17 pass from Baugh (Masterson kick)
ChiB	-	Benton 26 pass from Luckman (Snyder kick)
ChiB	-	Clark 10 pass from Luckman (Snyder kick)
Was	-	Aguirre 25 pass from Baugh (Aguirre kick)

1944 NFL CHAMPIONSHIP GAME
Green Bay 14, New York Giants 7

December 17, 1944, at New York
Attendance: 46,016

The Packers rebounded from a 24-0 drubbing by the Giants four weeks earlier to defeat the team that had finished the regular season with the NFL's best record. The Giants' offense, hampered by the loss of Bill Paschal, the league's leading rusher, could score only once in the 14-7 loss.

The Packers took control of the game in the second quarter. After driving to first-and-goal at the 1, they were stopped for three plays before fullback Ted Fritsch banged in for the touchdown on fourth down. Later in the quarter, Irv Comp found Don Hutson for a 24-yard gain to the New York 30. Three plays later, at the 28, Hutson ran a crossing pattern that drew the Giants' secondary with him, and Fritsch looped out of the backfield to catch a long touchdown pass from Comp to make it 14-0.

The Giants, with former Green Bay great Arnie Herber doing the passing, drove to a touchdown in the fourth quarter. Following a 41-yard pass to Frank Liebel, Ward Cuff ran 1 yard for a touchdown. However, the Packers held off the other Giants' drives, in large part due to 4 intercepted passes.

Green Bay	0	14	0	0	-	14
N.Y. Giants	0	0	0	7	-	7

GB	-	Fritsch 1 run (Hutson kick)
GB	-	Fritsch 28 pass from Comp (Hutson kick)
NYG	-	Cuff 1 run (Strong kick)

1945 NFL CHAMPIONSHIP GAME
Cleveland 15, Washington 14

December 16, 1945, at Cleveland
Attendance: 32,178

Two footballs that hit the goal-post crossbar were the difference as the Cleveland Rams defeated the Washington Redskins 15-14 in the last game played in Cleveland before the Rams moved to Los Angeles.

In the first quarter, with the ball at the Washington 5, Sammy Baugh dropped into the end zone to pass, but his throw hit the crossbar and bounced back into the end zone for a safety. Baugh left the game in the first quarter and was replaced by Frank Filchock, who, in the second period, threw a 38-yard touchdown pass to halfback Steve Bagarus. The Rams came back just before the half, however, as rookie quarterback Bob Waterfield found Jim Benton with a 37-yard touchdown pass. Waterfield's extra point was partially blocked and struck the crossbar, teetering before it dropped over for a 9-7 halftime lead.

The Rams increased their lead in the third quarter when Waterfield teamed with Jim Gillette on a 44-yard TD.

But the Redskins came back to cut the lead to one, as Filchock fired an 8-yard scoring strike to Bob Seymour. In the fourth quarter, Joe Aguirre attempted 2 field goals that could have won the game, but both kicks failed.

Washington	0	7	7	0	-	14
Cleveland	2	7	6	0	-	15

Cle	-	Safety, Baugh's pass hit goal post
Was	-	Bagarus 38 pass from Filchock (Aguirre kick)
Cle	-	Benton 37 pass from Waterfield (Waterfield kick)
Cle	-	Gillette 44 pass from Waterfield (kick failed)
Was	-	Seymour 8 pass from Filchock (Aguirre kick)

1946 AAFC CHAMPIONSHIP GAME
Cleveland 14, New York Yankees 9

December 22, 1946, at Cleveland
Attendance: 41,181

Otto Graham led Cleveland to a come-from-behind, 14-9 victory over the New York Yankees to win the first All-America Football Conference Championship Game. The Browns' passing ace completed 16 of 27 passes for 213 yards and stemmed a late Yankees' rally with a pass interception.

The Yankees led off the scoring with a first-quarter field goal by Harvey Johnson, but the lead lasted only into the second period. The Browns launched a long drive with Marion Motley scoring the touchdown on a 2-yard smash.

In the third quarter, New York drove 80 yards to score. Spec Sanders bolted over from 2 yards to register the touchdown. Cleveland tackle Lou Rymkus broke through to block Johnson's try for the conversion.

With the fourth quarter draining away, Graham led the Browns downfield. There were only about five minutes left when Graham shot a 16-yard scoring pass to Dante Lavelli to put Cleveland back in front. The Yankees rallied on the passing arm of Ace Parker, but Graham snuffed the threat with an interception.

Cleveland	0	7	0	7	-	14
N.Y. Yankees	3	0	6	0	-	9

NYY	-	FG H.Johnson 21
Cle	-	Motley 2 run (Groza kick)
NYY	-	Sanders 2 run (kick blocked)
Cle	-	Lavelli 16 pass from Graham (Groza kick)

1946 NFL CHAMPIONSHIP GAME
Chicago Bears 24, New York Giants 14

December 15, 1946, at New York
Attendance: 58,346

The day of the championship game began with the suspension of New York fullback Merle Hapes, who, despite having declined a bribe to throw the game, had not reported the attempt. With a playoff record crowd of 58,346 watching at the Polo Grounds, the Giants gave it their best shot before falling short 24-14.

The Bears raced to a 14-0 lead when Sid Luckman threw a touchdown pass to Ken Kavanaugh and Dante Magnani returned an interception 19 yards for a score. It was 1 of 6 passes by Frank Filchock that the Bears intercepted. Nevertheless, Filchock brought back his team, throwing a 38-yard touchdown pass to Frank Liebel late in the first quarter.

In the third period, the Giants tied the score following Jim Lee Howell's recovery of Joe Osmanski's fumble at the Bears' 20. Three plays later, Filchock threw a 5-yard touchdown pass to Steve Filipowicz.

With the score tied in the fourth quarter, Luckman faked a handoff to George McAfee, hid the ball on his hip, and bootlegged around right end for 19 yards and a touchdown. A short while later, Frank Maznicki clinched the victory with a 26-yard field goal.

Chi. Bears	**14**	**0**	**0**	**10**	**-**	**24**
N.Y. Giants	**7**	**0**	**7**	**0**	**-**	**14**

ChiB - Kavanaugh 21 pass from Luckman (Maznicki kick)
ChiB - Magnani 19 pass interception (Maznicki kick)
NYG - Liebel 38 pass from Filchock (Strong kick)
NYG - Filipowicz 5 pass from Filchock (Strong kick)
ChiB - Luckman 19 run (Maznicki kick)
ChiB - FG Maznicki 26

1947 NFL EASTERN DIVISION PLAYOFF GAME
Philadelphia 21, Pittsburgh 0

December 21, 1947, at Pittsburgh
Attendance: 35,729

The Eagles of coach Earle (Greasy) Neale were on the rise, destined to play in the next three NFL title games, whereas Jock Sutherland's Steelers—the last of the Single-Wing offenses to make the playoffs—would have only one winning season in the next decade.

The Eagles capitalized early on a Pittsburgh error. Pete Pihos blocked a punt by Bob Cifers, and the Eagles gained possession at the Steelers' 14. Two plays later, Tommy Thompson threw a 15-yard touchdown pass to Steve Van Buren. The next period, Thompson went to the air again and found Jack Ferrante for 28 yards and a touchdown that made it 14-0.

In the third quarter, the punting game again got the Steelers into trouble. Cifers outkicked his coverage, and Bosh Pritchard wound his way through Pittsburgh's defense, going 79 yards for the final score.

Going into the game, the Steelers were torn by controversy. The players demanded an extra paycheck for the playoff. Although they got their money, they outraged Sutherland, who held his pregame practices outdoors in the snow and ice.

Philadelphia	**7**	**7**	**7**	**0**	**-**	**21**
Pittsburgh	**0**	**0**	**0**	**0**	**-**	**0**

Phi - Van Buren 15 pass from Thompson (Patton kick)
Phi - Ferrante 28 pass from Thompson (Patton kick)
Phi - Pritchard 79 punt return (Patton kick)

1947 AAFC CHAMPIONSHIP GAME
Cleveland 14, New York Yankees 3

December 14, 1947, at New York
Attendance: 60,103

Otto Graham and the Cleveland Browns ignored the near-freezing temperature at Yankee Stadium to defeat New York and win their second consecutive AAFC title 14-3.

In the opening period, the teams jockeyed back and forth until Marion Motley broke loose on a 51-yard run to give Cleveland a first down at the Yankees' 13. After a couple of running plays gained 4 yards, Graham zipped a pass to Mac Speedie at the 1. From there, Graham took the ball over with two minutes left in the quarter.

Buddy Young brought the ensuing kickoff back to New York's 32, where the Yankees started a drive paced by the running of Young and Spec Sanders. New York reached the Cleveland 6 before settling for a 12-yard field goal by Harvey Johnson to make the score 7-3.

Late in the third quarter, Edgar Jones ran 4 yards for Cleveland's second touchdown.

N.Y. Yankees	**0**	**3**	**0**	**0**	**-**	**3**
Cleveland	**7**	**0**	**7**	**0**	**-**	**14**

Cle - Graham 1 run (Groza kick)
NYY - FG H.Johnson 12
Cle - Jones 4 run (Saban kick)

1947 NFL CHAMPIONSHIP GAME
Chicago Cardinals 28, Philadelphia 21

December 28, 1947, at Chicago
Attendance: 30,759

The Cardinals went into the game at Comiskey Park convinced they could run up the middle on the Eagles, who played a 5-2-4 defense, with no middle linebacker. They proved their point and won the NFL title 28-21.

A frozen field did not seem to hamper either team, and, midway through the first quarter, the Cardinals double-teamed the Eagles' middle guard as Charley Trippi roared up the middle for 44 yards and a touchdown. Early in the second period, the Cardinals ran a similar play, and Elmer Angsman blew through the line for a 70-yard scoring run. Meanwhile, the Cardinals were stopping the Eagles' ground game cold, and the visitors did not score until the final minute of the first half, when Tommy Thompson found Pat McHugh on a 53-yard scoring pass.

Big plays by the Cardinals did not let the determined Eagles catch up in the second half. Trippi went 75 yards for a score on a punt return on which he slipped down twice but managed to get to his feet both times. Then, after Steve Van Buren ran 1 yard for a touchdown, Angsman again ran 70 yards straight up the middle for a touchdown.

Philadelphia	**0**	**7**	**7**	**7**	**-**	**21**
Chi. Cardinals	**7**	**7**	**7**	**7**	**-**	**28**

ChiC - Trippi 44 run (Harder kick)
ChiC - Angsman 70 run (Harder kick)
Phi - McHugh 53 pass from Thompson (Patton kick)
ChiC - Trippi 75 punt return (Harder kick)
Phi - Van Buren 1 run (Patton kick)
ChiC - Angsman 70 run (Harder kick)
Phi - Craft 1 run (Patton kick)

1948 AAFC EASTERN DIVISION PLAYOFF
Buffalo 28, Baltimore 17

December 12, 1948, at Baltimore
Attendance: 27,327

Quarterback George Ratterman rallied his Buffalo Bills to three fourth-quarter touchdowns to win the AAFC's Eastern Division title and break the hearts of Baltimore fans.

The Colts took a three-point lead in the opening quarter on Rex Grossman's 16-yard field goal. But Buffalo came back in the second period to go in front on a 5-yard pass from Ratterman to Zeke O'Connor.

Baltimore built a 17-7 lead in the third quarter behind the passing of rookie quarterback Y.A. Tittle and the running of Bus Mertes, who scored both touchdowns.

The Bills narrowed the gap early in the fourth quarter on

a 66-yard touchdown pass from Ratterman to Bill Gompers.

With a little over five minutes left, the Bills began a drive from their own 25. Ratterman's passes brought them to the Baltimore 25, where the Bills' ace passed to Alton Baldwin for the score. Buckets Hirsch intercepted Tittle's pass and returned it 20 yards for the clinching touchdown as time ran down.

Buffalo	0	7	0	21	-	28
Baltimore	3	0	14	0	-	17

Bal - FG Grossman 16
Buf - O'Connor 5 pass from Ratterman (Armstrong kick)
Bal - Mertes 9 run (Grossman kick)
Bal - Mertes 1 run (Grossman kick)
Buf - Gompers 66 pass from Ratterman (Armstrong kick)
Buf - Baldwin 25 pass from Ratterman (Armstrong kick)
Buf - Hirsch 20 pass interception (Armstrong kick)

1948 AAFC CHAMPIONSHIP GAME
Cleveland 49, Buffalo 7

December 19, 1948, at Cleveland
Attendance: 22,981

The Cleveland Browns completed un unbeaten and untied season with a 49-7 thrashing of the Buffalo Bills before a disappointing, but hardly disappointed, crowd of 22,981 at Municipal Stadium. The Browns thus became the first professional football team in a major league to win every game of the regular season and then continue victorious through the championship game.

The rout of the Bills was fully expected. That anticipation no doubt held down the crowd.

The first half was played on comparatively even terms, but Cleveland scored once in each quarter. First, Edgar (Special Delivery) Jones ran 3 yards for a touchdown with 10 seconds left in the opening quarter. Early in the second quarter, Browns end George Young returned Rex Bumgardner's fumble 18 yards for Cleveland's second touchdown.

The second half was all Browns. Barely two minutes into the third quarter, Otto Graham passed 9 yards to Jones to make the score 21-0. Marion Motley, Cleveland's 238-pound fullback, took over from there and scored 3 touchdowns on runs of 29, 31, and 5 yards.

Cleveland	7	7	14	21	-	49
Buffalo	0	0	7	0	-	7

Cle - E.Jones 3 run (Groza kick)
Cle - Young 18 fumble return (Groza kick)
Cle - E.Jones 9 pass from Graham (Groza kick)
Cle - Motley 29 run (Groza kick)
Buf - Baldwin 10 pass from Still (Armstrong kick)
Cle - Motley 31 run (Groza kick)
Cle - Motley 5 run (Groza kick)
Cle - Saban 39 pass interception (Groza kick)

1948 NFL CHAMPIONSHIP GAME
Philadelphia 7, Chicago Cardinals 0

December 19, 1948, at Philadelphia
Attendance: 28,864

A heavy snow that blanketed the field at Shibe Park made for near-impossible playing conditions in which chains could not be used for measurements, the sidelines were marked by ropes tied to stakes, and piles of snow lay on the sidelines. Neither team could pass effectively—the Cardinals, playing without injured quarterback Paul Christman, threw for only 35 yards, and the Eagles' Tommy Thompson was held to 7.

Turnovers gave both teams chances to score throughout the game, but tough defenses and missed field goals kept the game scoreless until the fourth quarter. In the final minute of the third period, Elmer Angsman fumbled at his 17-yard line, and Frank (Bucko) Kilroy recovered for the Eagles. Bosh Pritchard ran to the 11 on the final play of the quarter, and the fourth period opened with runs by Joe Muha and Thompson, giving Philadelphia a first down at the 5. Steve Van Buren, who powered to 98 yards for the day, then brought the Eagles their first victory in an NFL Championship Game by bulling 5 yards for the game's only touchdown.

Chi. Cardinals	0	0	0	0	-	0
Philadelphia	0	0	0	7	-	7

Phi - Van Buren 5 run (Patton kick)

1949 AAFC FIRST-ROUND ROUND GAME
Cleveland 31, Buffalo 21

December 4, 1949, at Cleveland
Attendance: 17,240

With the AAFC down to seven teams for 1949, the East and West Divisions were dispensed with in favor of a single, league-wide race. That also called for a new championship-game format. In the first round, the first-place team played the fourth-place team, while the teams finishing second and third played each other.

The first-place Browns had more trouble than expected from the fourth-place Bills. Buffalo quarterback George Ratterman had a hot hand and threw 3 touchdown passes, but ultimately Cleveland's Otto Graham made the difference.

Graham put the Browns in front in the opening quarter by firing a 51-yard touchdown pass to Dante Lavelli. Lou Groza widened the lead to 10-0 with a 31-yard field goal.

The Bills came roaring back. Ratterman passed 4 yards to Lou Tomasetti for a touchdown in the second period, then added an 8-yard scoring toss to Chet Mutryn to put the Bills in front at the half.

Ratterman's third touchdown pass in the third quarter wasn't enough to keep up with the Joneses. First Edgar (Special Delivery) Jones plunged 2 yards for one Browns' touchdown, Then Dub Jones put Cleveland in front to stay by catching a 49-yard touchdown pass from Graham. In the final quarter, Warren Lahr intercepted a Ratterman pass and ran it 52 yards for the clinching touchdown.

Buffalo	0	14	7	0	-	21
Cleveland	10	0	14	7	-	31

Cle - Lavelli 51 pass from Graham (Groza kick)
Cle - FG Groza 31
Buf - Tomasetti 4 pass from Ratterman (Adams kick)
Buf - Mutryn 8 pass from Ratterman (Adams kick)
Cle - E.Jones 2 run (Groza kick)
Buf - Mutryn 30 pass from Ratterman (Adams kick)
Cle - D.Jones 49 pass from Graham (Groza kick)
Cle - Lahr 52 pass interception (Groza kick)

1949 AAFC FIRST-ROUND PLAYOFF GAME
San Francisco 17, New York Yankees 7

December 4, 1949, at San Francisco
Attendance: 41,393

The second-place 49ers and third-place Yankees struggled through a defensive battle at San Francisco, with the 49ers—better known for their ability to score—coming out ahead 17-7.

The 49ers scored a touchdown in the opening quarter when halfback Verl Lillywhite broke through right tackle and ran 40 yards. New York bounced back in the second quarter with a 64-yard drive to Sherman Howard's 1-yard touchdown run. A few minutes later, San Francisco broke the deadlock on Joe Vetrano's 38-yard field goal.

The only score of the second half was Frankie Albert's 10-yard touchdown pass to Don Garlin. Albert kept the Yankees on their heels all day, deftly mixing passes and runs. He and New York's Tom Landry put on a spectacular punting duel. Landry averaged 55 yards per kick, including 1 of 75 yards; Albert had 2 of 60 yards.

N.Y. Yankees	0	7	0	0	-	7
San Francisco	7	3	7	0	-	17

SF - Lillywhite 40 run (Vetrano kick)
NYY - Howard 1 run (H.Johnson kick)
SF - FG Vetrano 38
SF - Garlin 10 pass from Albert (Vetrano kick)

1949 AAFC CHAMPIONSHIP GAME
Cleveland 21, San Francisco 7

December 11, 1949, at Cleveland
Attendance: 22,550

The fourth and final All-America Football Conference Championship Game took place only a few days after word leaked out that a merger agreement had been reached between the AAFC and the NFL, one that would close the AAFC forever. The fact that this was a lame-duck championship game dampened attendance.

The field was a mixture of mud and slush, but, surprisingly, neither team lost the ball on a turnover. Only 1 penalty was walked off all afternoon, a mere 5 yards against the Browns. Cleveland's Edgar (Special Delivery) Jones scored the only touchdown of the first half on a 2-yard plunge midway through the first quarter.

Marion Motley, Cleveland's big fullback, scored the Browns' second touchdown on the game's most spectacular play in the third quarter. He burst up the middle on a trap play for 63 yards.

The 49ers responded with a 74-yard drive culminating in Frankie Albert's 23-yard touchdown pass to Paul Salata. That allowed Joe Vetrano to kick his 107th consecutive extra point and preserve his record of having scored in every San Francisco game since they began.

With the score narrowed to 14-7, the Browns began a march of their own to clinch the victory. It ended successfully 69 yards later on Dub Jones's 4-yard smash for a touchdown. Groza kicked the final AAFC point.

Cleveland	7	0	7	7	-	21
San Francisco	0	0	0	7	-	7

Cle - E.Jones 2 run (Groza kick)
Cle - Motley 63 run (Groza kick)
SF - Salata 23 pass from Albert (Vetrano kick)
Cle - D.Jones 4 run (Groza kick)

1949 NFL CHAMPIONSHIP GAME
Philadelphia 14, LA Rams 0

December 18, 1949, at Los Angeles
Attendance: 22,245

Despite a muddy field caused by three inches of rain in Los Angeles the day before the game, Steve Van Buren set playoff records with 31 carries and 196 yards rushing, as he and a defense that recorded its second consecutive title-game shutout led the Eagles to another championship.

Although it was Van Buren who effectively kept the ball away from the high-powered Rams' offense throughout the game, the Eagles' first touchdown, in the second quarter, came as a result of their only effective passing of the day. Tommy Thompson, who threw for 68 yards in the game, completed 3 passes on the drive for 58 yards: first to end Jack Ferrante for 11 yards and a first down, then to Ferrante again for 16 yards and another first down, and finally a 31-yard scoring strike to end Pete Pihos.

In the third quarter, the Eagles trapped the Rams deep in their own end, and, when Bob Waterfield tried to punt, Don Paul's snap was high. Waterfield's kick was blocked by defensive end Leo Skladany, who picked the ball up at the 2 and scored.

Philadelphia	0	7	7	0	-	14
LA Rams	0	0	0	0	-	0

Phi - Pihos 31 pass from Thompson (Patton kick)
Phi - Skladany 2 blocked-punt return (Patton kick)

1950 NFL AMERICAN CONFERENCE PLAYOFF GAME
Cleveland 8, New York Giants 3

December 17, 1950, at Cleveland
Attendance: 33,754

In a game played in a strong wind off Lake Erie, a temperature of only 10 degrees, and a rock-hard, icy field, the Browns edged the Giants 8-3.

Cleveland scored in the first quarter on an 11-yard field goal by Lou Groza, and, for more than three quarters, it appeared that would hold up for the victory. But in the final period, fleet halfback Gene (Choo-Choo) Roberts broke loose on a reverse for what could have been the winning touchdown. Amazingly, Cleveland middle guard Bill Willis chased Roberts down at the 4-yard line, and New York had to settle for a tie on a 20-yard field goal by Randy Clay.

Late in the game, Browns quarterback Otto Graham finally found a play that the Giants could not stop: the quarterback draw. Graham's running set up Groza's winning field goal of 28 yards. Moments later, Charlie Conerly, trying to pass, was tackled in his end zone for a safety.

N.Y. Giants	0	0	0	3	-	3
Cleveland	3	0	0	5	-	8

Cle - FG Groza 11
NYG - FG Clay 20
Cle - FG Groza 28
Cle - Safety, Willis tackled Conerly in end zone

1950 NFL NATIONAL CONFERENCE PLAYOFF GAME

Los Angeles Rams 24, Chicago Bears 14

December 17, 1950, at Los Angeles
Attendance: 83,501

Bob Waterfield, unable to practice all week because of the flu, came off the bench to complete 14 of 21 passes for 280 yards and 3 touchdowns and lead the Rams to a 24-14 victory over the Bears.

Waterfield replaced Norm Van Brocklin in the second quarter with the Rams trailing 7-3. Almost instantly, the complexion of the game changed as Waterfield found Tom Fears alone for a 43-yard touchdown pass. The next time the Rams had possession, Waterfield led the team 76 yards, most of it coming on a 68-yard strike to Fears that gave the Rams a 17-7 halftime lead.

In the third quarter, Waterfield built the margin to 17 points when he found Fears for a 27-yard touchdown pass. The Bears, who outgained the Rams 422-371, hurt their own cause by losing 3 interceptions and 2 fumbles.

Chi. Bears	0	7	0	7	-	14
L.A. Rams	3	14	7	0	-	24

Rams - FG Waterfield 43
ChiB - Campana 23 run (Lujack kick)
Rams - Fears 43 pass from Waterfield (Waterfield kick)
Rams - Fears 68 pass from Waterfield (Waterfield kick)
Rams - Fears 27 pass from Waterfield (Waterfield kick)
ChiB - Morrison 4 run (Lujack kick)

1950 NFL CHAMPIONSHIP GAME

Cleveland 30, Los Angeles Rams 28

December 24, 1950, at Cleveland
Attendance: 29,751

In perhaps the most exciting NFL Championship Game that had yet been played, Lou Groza kicked a 16-yard field goal with 28 seconds left to give the Browns a 30-28 victory and their first NFL title.

On the first play from scrimmage, Bob Waterfield threw an 82-yard touchdown pass to Glenn Davis, but Cleveland came right back to score on a 27-yard touchdown pass from Otto Graham to Dub Jones. Eight plays after the kickoff, the Rams scored again, with Dick Hoerner pounding in from 3 yards out.

Trailing 14-13 at halftime, the Browns took their first lead in the third quarter when Graham threw his third touchdown pass, and second to Dante Lavelli. But then the Rams scored twice in 21 seconds. First, Hoerner scored from the 1 on his seventh consecutive carry, then, on the first play after the kickoff, Larry Brink scooped up Marion Motley's fumble and returned it 6 yards for a touchdown.

With 4:35 remaining in the game, the Browns closed to within a point when Graham completed 5 consecutive passes to Lavelli, then threw a 14-yard scoring strike to Rex Bumgardner. Two minutes remained when the Browns got the ball back, just enough time to drive to Groza's winning kick.

L.A. Rams	14	0	14	0	-	28
Cleveland	7	6	7	10	-	30

Rams - Davis 82 pass from Waterfield (Waterfield kick)
Cle - Jones 27 pass from Graham (Groza kick)
Rams - Hoerner 3 run (Waterfield kick)
Cle - Lavelli 37 pass from Graham (kick failed)
Cle - Lavelli 39 pass from Graham (Groza kick)
Rams - Hoerner 1 run (Waterfield kick)
Rams - Brink 6 fumble return (Waterfield kick)
Cle - Bumgardner 14 pass from Graham (Groza kick)
Cle - FG Groza 16

1951 NFL CHAMPIONSHIP GAME

Los Angeles Rams 24, Cleveland 17

December 23, 1951, at Los Angeles
Attendance: 57,522

The Rams avenged their title-game defeat to Cleveland a year earlier with a 24-17 victory. Norm Van Brocklin connected with Tom Fears for a 73-yard touchdown pass midway through the fourth quarter for the winning score. Fears split defenders Cliff Lewis and Tom James, caught the ball at midfield, and raced to the end zone.

The game was close from the start. The Rams scored first in the second period on a 1-yard run by Dick Hoerner, but the Browns came back to lead 10-7 at halftime on a playoff-record 52-yard field goal by Lou Groza and a 17-yard touchdown pass from Otto Graham to Dub Jones.

The Rams regained the lead in the third quarter when Larry Brink blindsided Graham, causing a fumble that Andy Robustelli returned from the Cleveland 24 to the 2. On third down, Deacon Dan Towler scored from the 1 for a 14-10 lead.

Early in the fourth quarter, the Rams' Bob Waterfield kicked a 17-yard field goal, but the Browns came back to tie the score when an 8-play, 70-yard drive ended with Ken Carpenter's 5-yard touchdown run. Twenty-five seconds later, Van Brocklin and Fears teamed for the title-winning touchdown.

Cleveland	0	10	0	7	-	17
L.A. Rams	0	7	7	10	-	24

Rams - Hoerner 1 run (Waterfield kick)
Cle - FG Groza 52
Cle - Jones 17 pass from Graham (Groza kick)
Rams - Towler 1 run (Waterfield kick)
Rams - FG Waterfield 17
Cle - Carpenter 5 run (Groza kick)
Rams - Fears 73 pass from Van Brocklin (Waterfield kick)

1952 NFL NATIONAL CONFERENCE PLAYOFF GAME

Detroit 31, Los Angeles Rams 21

December 21, 1952, at Detroit
Attendance: 47,645

Detroit fullback Pat Harder scored 2 touchdowns and kicked 4 extra points and a field goal for a postseason-record 19 points to lead the Lions to a 31-21 victory in a cold, wet fog.

The first time the Lions had the ball, Bobby Layne completed passes of 22 and 13 yards to Leon Hart before Harder scored on a 12-yard sweep around left end. The next quarter, Harder scored again to make it 14-0.

The Rams cut into Detroit's lead before the half, but the third quarter belonged to Detroit, as Doak Walker's halfback pass to Hart was good for 24 yards and a touchdown, then Harder kicked a 43-yard field goal.

Two touchdowns by the Rams in the fourth quarter put them back in the game at 24-21, but an interception in the final minute set up Bob Hoernschemeyer's clinching 9-yard touchdown run.

L.A. Rams	0	7	0	14	-	21
Detroit	7	7	10	7	-	31

Det - Harder 12 run (Harder kick)
Det - Harder 4 run (Harder kick)
Rams - Fears 14 pass from Van Brocklin (Waterfield kick)
Det - Hart 24 pass from Walker (Harder kick)
Det - FG Harder 43
Rams - Towler 5 run (Waterfield kick)
Rams - Smith 56 punt return (Waterfield kick)
Det - Hoernschemeyer 9 run (Harder kick)

1952 NFL CHAMPIONSHIP GAME
Detroit 17, Cleveland 7

December 28, 1952, at Cleveland
Attendance: 50,934

A series of impressive defensive stands gave Detroit its first NFL title since 1935. The Lions held at their 21-, 21-, 24-, 5-, and 8-yard lines, and allowed the Browns to reach the end zone only once.

Detroit scored first following a short punt to midfield in the second period. Bobby Layne's 2-yard quarterback sneak gave the Lions a 7-0 advantage. Detroit increased its margin to 14 in the third quarter when Doak Walker ran out of the grasp of Bert Rechichar and raced 67 yards for a touchdown. The Browns followed with their only successful drive of the day, the 11-play, 67-yard march ending in fullback Harry (Chick) Jagade's 7-yard run.

Pat Harder kicked a 36-yard field goal in the fourth quarter for the final margin, and the Lions then held the Browns on downs at the 5 and the 8. The final threat ended when Otto Graham passed to Ray Renfro, who deflected the ball to Darrel (Pete) Brewster in the end zone, only to have it ruled an illegal catch because the ball had been touched by two offensive players.

Detroit	0	7	7	3	-	17
Cleveland	0	0	7	0	-	7

Det - Layne 2 run (Harder kick)
Det - Walker 67 run (Harder kick)
Cle - Jagade 7 run (Groza kick)
Det - FG Harder 36

1953 NFL CHAMPIONSHIP GAME
Detroit 17, Cleveland 16

December 27, 1953, at Detroit
Attendance: 54,577

Bobby Layne did what he did best—improvising a play in the huddle—to lead the Lions to their second consecutive NFL title.

The Lions opened the scoring on Doak Walker's 1-yard touchdown run, and the teams exchanged field goals in the second period. In the third quarter, Harry (Chick) Jagade's 9-yard touchdown run tied the score. Lou Groza's second field goal put the Browns ahead for the first time in the fourth quarter, and he extended the lead to 6 points with a 43-yard field goal with a little more than four minutes left.

Then Layne took over. From the Detroit 20, he passed 20 yards to Jim Doran, who was substituting for injured Leon Hart. After two incompletions, Layne teamed with Doran again for 18 yards to the Cleveland 45. Layne passed 9 yards to Cloyce Box and picked up the first down with a 3-yard run to the 33. After a time out and a conference with coach Raymond (Buddy) Parker, Layne returned to the huddle, ignored Parker's decision of a screen, and called a fly to Doran, who made the catch all alone at the 10 and raced in for the score. Walker's extra point provided the final margin.

Cleveland	0	3	7	6	-	16
Detroit	7	3	0	7	-	17

Det - Walker 1 run (Walker kick)
Cle - FG Groza 13
Det - FG Walker 23
Cle - Jagade 9 run (Groza kick)
Cle - FG Groza 15
Cle - FG Groza 43
Det - Doran 33 pass from Layne (Walker kick)

1954 NFL CHAMPIONSHIP GAME
Cleveland 56, Detroit 10

December 26, 1954, at Cleveland
Attendance: 43,827

The Browns took out three years of frustration in title games by smashing the Lions 56-10 in what Otto Graham claimed would be his last game. Graham completed 9 of 12 passes for 163 yards and 3 touchdowns and scored 3 times to lead the onslaught.

The Browns were not only an offensive juggernaut. The defense intercepted Bobby Layne 6 times and recovered 3 Detroit fumbles, setting up 6 touchdowns. A penalty on Gil Mains for roughing kicker Horace Gillom set up another touchdown, a 35-yard pass from Graham to Ray Renfro that gave Cleveland a 7-3 lead in the first quarter. Graham passed for another touchdown in the first quarter and ran for 2 and passed for 1 in the second period. His third touchdown pass, of 31 yards to Renfro, increased the Browns' lead to 35-10 at halftime.

Prior to the game, the Browns had lost four games in a row to the Lions, including a 14-10 defeat in the final minute of the regular season game the week before.

Detroit	3	7	0	0	-	10
Cleveland	14	21	14	7	-	56

Det - FG Walker 36
Cle - Renfro 35 pass from Graham (Groza kick)
Cle - Brewster 8 pass from Graham (Groza kick)
Cle - Graham 1 run (Groza kick)
Det - Bowman 5 run (Walker kick)
Cle - Graham 5 run (Groza kick)
Cle - Renfro 31 pass from Graham (Groza kick)
Cle - Graham 1 run (Groza kick)
Cle - Morrison 12 run (Groza kick)
Cle - Hanulak 10 run (Groza kick)

1955 NFL CHAMPIONSHIP GAME
Cleveland 38, Los Angeles Rams 14

December 26, 1955, at Los Angeles
Attendance: 85,693

Otto Graham again announced that this was his last game, and this time it really was. He went out in style, passing for 209 yards and 2 touchdowns and running for a pair of scores to lead the Browns to a 38-14 victory over the Rams before a championship game record crowd of 85,693.

As they had the year before with Bobby Layne, the Browns intercepted Norm Van Brocklin 6 times, and they converted the errors into 24 points, the margin of difference. The first score of the game, Lou Groza's 26-yard field goal, followed an interception by Ken Konz. In the second quarter, Don Paul set a playoff record with a 65-yard interception return for a touchdown. Then, after Van

Brocklin connected with Volney (Skeet) Quinlan on a 67-yard touchdown pass to pull the Rams within 10-7, Tom James' interception set up Graham's 50-yard touchdown pass to Dante Lavelli, giving the Browns a 17-7 halftime lead.

Graham scored twice in the third quarter, the second time after Sam Palumbo intercepted Van Brocklin, and he teamed with Ray Renfro on a 35-yard touchdown pass 11 seconds into the final period.

Cleveland	3	14	14	7	-	38
L.A. Rams	0	7	0	7	-	14

Cle - FG Groza 26
Cle - Paul 65 interception return (Groza kick)
Rams - Quinlan 67 pass from Van Brocklin (Richter kick)
Cle - Lavelli 50 pass from Graham (Groza kick)
Cle - Graham 15 run (Groza kick)
Cle - Graham 1 run (Groza kick)
Cle - Renfro 35 pass from Graham (Groza kick)
Rams - Waller 4 run (Richter kick)

1956 NFL CHAMPIONSHIP GAME
New York Giants 47, Chicago Bears 7

December 30, 1956, at New York
Attendance: 56,836

The Giants, as usual, started quarterback Don Heinrich, who would probe the defenses so that star quarterback Charlie Conerly could watch from the sideline and know where to attack. The Bears must have figured that they were in trouble when Conerly came in at the end of one quarter and New York already led 13-0. The Giants went on to win 47-7.

The game marked the fifth time that the Bears and the Giants had played in the NFL Championship Game, and the second time that New York won.

The Giants' first quarter points came on a 17-yard touchdown run by fullback Mel Triplett and 2 field goals by Ben Agajanian. But when Conerly entered the game, the tempo really picked up. He directed 2 second-quarter touchdown drives and then threw 2 touchdown passes in the second half. In between, at the end of the second quarter, the Giants' special team scored itself when Henry Moore recovered a blocked punt in the end zone for a touchdown. By the end of the game, third-string quarterback Bobby Clatterbuck had seen his first postseason action for the Giants.

Chi. Bears	0	7	0	0	-	7
N.Y. Giants	13	21	6	7	-	47

NYG - Triplett 17 run (Agajanian kick)
NYG - FG Agajanian 17
NYG - FG Agajanian 43
NYG - Webster 3 run (Agajanian kick)
ChiB - Casares 9 run (Blanda kick)
NYG - Webster 1 run (Agajanian kick)
NYG - Moore blocked punt recovery in end zone (Agajanian kick)
NYG - Rote 9 pass from Conerly (kick failed)
NYG - Gifford 14 pass from Conerly (Agajanian kick)

1957 NFL WESTERN CONFERENCE PLAYOFF GAME
Detroit 31, San Francisco 27

December 22, 1957, at San Francisco
Attendance: 60,118

The Lions trailed 24-7 at halftime when they overheard a premature celebration in San Francisco's locker room. Fired up, Detroit scored 3 touchdowns in a span of 4:29 of the third and fourth quarters to shock the 49ers 31-27.

San Francisco jumped on top early, as Y.A. Tittle threw touchdown passes to three different receivers in the first half. At the start of the third period, it looked as if it might be more of the same, when McElhenny broke loose for a 71-yard run to the Detroit 7. The Lions' defense held, however, and forced Gordy Soltau to kick a field goal.

Now it was Detroit's turn. First, Tom Tracy ended a 73-yard drive with a 1-yard scoring run. Then he burst loose up the middle for a 58-yard touchdown run. Gene Gedman finished off another drive with a 2-yard touchdown run. The 49ers had four possessions in the final 14 minutes, but they turned over the ball each time.

Detroit	0	7	14	10	-	31
San Francisco	14	10	3	0	-	27

SF - Owens 34 pass from Tittle (Soltau kick)
SF - McElhenny 47 pass from Tittle (Soltau kick)
Det - Junker 4 pass from Rote (Martin kick)
SF - Wilson 12 pass from Tittle (Soltau kick)
SF - FG Soltau 25
SF - FG Soltau 10
Det - Tracy 1 run (Martin kick)
Det - Tracy 58 run (Martin kick)
Det - Gedman 2 run (Martin kick)
Det - FG Martin 13

1957 NFL CHAMPIONSHIP GAME
Detroit 59, Cleveland 14

December 29, 1957, at Detroit
Attendance: 55,263

The Detroit Lions thrashed the Cleveland Browns 59-14 to complete a crusade started when head coach Raymond (Buddy) Parker resigned at a preseason banquet with the words, "I don't want to get involved in another losing season, so I'm leaving Detroit."

The key figure for the Lions was quarterback Tobin Rote, a backup until Bobby Layne was hurt late in the season. Rote completed 12 of 19 passes for 280 yards and 4 touchdowns.

Detroit wasted no time mounting a big lead, as a field goal by Jim Martin and touchdown runs by Rote and halfback Gene Gedman put the Lions ahead 17-0 at the end of one quarter. Then, after the Browns pulled within 10 points, Rote snatched back control of the game with a 26-yard touchdown pass to Steve Junker on a fake field goal. When the Browns scored in the third quarter to cut the Lions lead to 31-14, Rote countered again, firing a 78-yard touchdown pass to wide receiver Jim Doran to end any thought of a comeback, and then passing for 2 more scores as a salve for those players who had suffered through the Lions' 56-10 title-game loss to the Browns three years before.

Cleveland	0	7	7	0	-	14
Detroit	17	14	14	14	-	59

Det - FG Martin 31
Det - Rote 1 run (Martin kick)
Det - Gedman 1 run (Martin kick)
Cle - Brown 29 run (Groza kick)
Det - Junker 26 pass from Rote (Martin kick)
Det - Barr 19 interception return (Martin kick)
Cle - L. Carpenter 5 run (Groza kick)
Det - Doran 78 pass from Rote (Martin kick)
Det - Junker 23 pass from Rote (Martin kick)
Det - Middleton 32 pass from Rote (Martin kick)
Det - Cassady 16 pass from Reichow (Martin kick)

1958 NFL EASTERN CONFERENCE PLAYOFF GAME
New York Giants 10, Cleveland 0

December 21, 1958, at New York
Attendance: 61,274

The Giants' defense dominated the Browns, holding Jim Brown to 8 yards on 7 carries and limiting Cleveland to 86 total yards. The previous weekend, Pat Summerall had kicked a 49-yard field goal in the final minute to give the Giants a 13-10 victory over the Browns, forcing the playoff.

The one long, successful drive of the game came late in the first quarter. The Giants drove 84 yards for a touchdown that came on an unusual play. From the Browns' 18-yard line, quarterback Charlie Conerly handed off to fullback Alex Webster, who gave the ball to Frank Gifford on a reverse. Gifford reached the 10 before lateraling to Conerly, who was trailing the play. Conerly covered the remaining distance to score.

Summerall kicked a 26-yard field goal in the second quarter, and the Giants' defense made the 10-point advantage stand for the rest of the game.

Cleveland	0	0	0	0	-	0
N.Y. Giants	7	3	0	0	-	10

NYG - Conerly 10 lateral from Gifford, who had run 8 (Summerall kick)
NYG - FG Summerall 26

1958 NFL CHAMPIONSHIP GAME
Baltimore 23, New York Giants 17 (OT)

December 28, 1958, at New York
Attendance: 64,185

In one of the greatest games of all time, Steve Myhra of Baltimore kicked a 20-yard field goal with seven seconds left in regulation time to produce the first overtime in NFL Championship Game history. The Colts went on to defeat the Giants 23-17.

Baltimore led 14-3 at halftime after converting 2 fumbles by Frank Gifford into touchdowns—a 2-yard run by Alan Ameche and a 15-yard pass from Johnny Unitas to Raymond Berry.

In the third quarter, the Colts drove to the Giants' 1, but on fourth down Ameche was stopped at the 5 by linebacker Cliff Livingston, and the fired-up Giants responded with a 95-yard drive to a touchdown. The big play was a 62-yard pass from Charlie Conerly to Kyle Rote; when Rote fumbled at the Colts' 25, teammate Alex Webster picked up the ball and ran to the 1. Mel Triplett scored on the next play. Four minutes later the Giants went ahead when Conerly threw a 15-yard touchdown pass to Gifford.

With two minutes left, the Colts took over at their 14. In one of the most masterful drives in football history, Unitas drove them to Myhra's field goal. After Baltimore forced the Giants to punt in overtime, Unitas went to work again, moving his team 80 yards in 13 plays, with Ameche scoring the game-winner 8:15 into the overtime.

Baltimore	0	14	0	3	6	-	23
N.Y. Giants	3	0	7	7	0	-	17

NYG - FG Summerall 36
Bal - Ameche 2 run (Myhra kick)
Bal - Berry 15 pass from Unitas (Myhra kick)
NYG - Triplett 1 run (Summerall kick)
NYG - Gifford 15 pass from Conerly (Summerall kick)
Bal - FG Myhra 20
Bal - Ameche 1 run

1959 NFL CHAMPIONSHIP GAME
Baltimore 31, New York Giants 16

December 27, 1959, at Baltimore
Attendance: 57,545

The Colts exploded for 24 points in the fourth quarter to open up a tight contest and win their second consecutive NFL title game over the Giants 31-16.

The Colts scored first, on a 60-yard touchdown pass from Johnny Unitas to Lenny Moore. But the Giants patiently moved ahead as Pat Summerall kicked a field goal in each of the first three quarters.

Early in the fourth quarter, the Colts suddenly came to life. After the defense stopped Alex Webster on fourth-and-inches, Unitas took his team downfield, scoring himself on a 4-yard sweep around right end. Shortly thereafter, Andy Nelson intercepted a pass by Charlie Conerly and returned it to the Giants' 14, setting up a 12-yard scoring strike from Unitas to Jerry Richardson.

Defensive back Johnny Sample then took charge. First, he returned an interception 42 yards for a touchdown. A short while later, he intercepted another pass to set up Steve Myhra's 25-yard field goal and a 31-9 lead. The Giants' lone touchdown came with 32 seconds left.

N.Y. Giants	3	3	3	7	-	16
Baltimore	7	0	0	24	-	31

Bal - Moore 60 pass from Unitas (Myhra kick)
NYG - FG Summerall 23
NYG - FG Summerall 37
NYG - FG Summerall 23
Bal - Unitas 4 run (Myhra kick)
Bal - Richardson 12 pass from Unitas (Myhra kick)
Bal - Sample 42 interception return (Myhra kick)
Bal - FG Myhra 25
NYG - Schnelker 32 pass from Conerly (Summerall kick)

1960 AFL CHAMPIONSHIP GAME
Houston 24, Los Angeles Chargers 16

January 1, 1961, at Houston
Attendance: 32,183

One sensational play by rookie halfback Billy Cannon, the previous season's Heisman Trophy winner, was the difference, as the Houston Oilers defeated the Los Angeles Chargers 24-16 in the first AFL Championship Game.

The Chargers took the early lead on 2 field goals by Ben Agajanian, but George Blanda brought the Oilers back, throwing a 17-yard touchdown pass to Dave Smith and kicking an 18-yard field goal to put Houston ahead 10-9 at halftime.

The teams exchanged touchdowns in the third quarter, with Blanda throwing a 7-yard scoring pass to Bill Groman and Chargers halfback Paul Lowe pounding over from the 2. Early in the final period, Blanda threw a short pass from the Oilers' 12 to Cannon, who broke a tackle and outran the Chargers' secondary to complete an 88-yard scoring play. In the final minute of the game, the Chargers—knowing they could tie and send the game into overtime with a touchdown and two-point conversion—drove to Houston's 22. But the Oilers held on fourth down to win.

L.A. Chargers	6	3	7	0	-	16
Houston	0	10	7	7	-	24

LAC - FG Agajanian 38
LAC - FG Agajanian 22
Hou - Smith 17 pass from Blanda (Blanda kick)
Hou - FG Blanda 18
LAC - FG Agajanian 27
Hou - Groman 7 pass from Blanda (Blanda kick)
LAC - Lowe 2 run (Agajanian kick)
Hou - Cannon 88 pass from Blanda (Blanda kick)

1960 NFL CHAMPIONSHIP GAME
Philadelphia 17, Green Bay 13

December 26, 1960, at Philadelphia
Attendance: 67,325

It was the last playoff game for Norm Van Brocklin and the first for Vince Lombardi as a head coach. Experience won out as the Eagles administered the only loss Lombardi would suffer in a championship game 17-13.

The Eagles turned over the ball twice deep in their own territory in the opening moments. The defense held, however, and the Packers managed only a 20-yard field goal from Paul Hornung. After Hornung kicked another short field goal in the second period, Van Brocklin showed his passing wizardry. From Philadelphia's 43, he found Tommy McDonald for 22 yards and then for 35 yards and a touchdown. Bobby Walston's 15-yard field goal put the Eagles ahead 10-6 at halftime.

Green Bay regained the lead in the fourth quarter when Bart Starr found Max McGee with a 7-yard touchdown pass, but the Eagles, boosted by Ted Dean's 58-yard kickoff return, came right back. Their 39-yard drive culminated in Dean's 5-yard touchdown run and a 17-13 advantage with 5:21 left.

The Packers drove to the Eagles' 22 with eight seconds left. Starr then passed to Jim Taylor, who reached the 8 before being dropped by Chuck Bednarik on the game's last play.

Green Bay	3	3	0	7	-	13
Philadelphia	0	10	0	7	-	17

GB - FG Hornung 20
GB - FG Hornung 23
Phil - McDonald 35 pass from Van Brocklin (Walston kick)
Phil - FG Walston 15
GB - McGee 7 pass from Starr (Hornung kick)
Phil - Dean 5 run (Walston kick)

1961 AFL CHAMPIONSHIP GAME
Houston 10, San Diego 3

December 24, 1961, at San Diego
Attendance: 29,556

The Houston Oilers defeated the San Diego Chargers 10-3 to win the AFL title in a sloppily played game. Houston had 7 turnovers and San Diego 6.

The only score of the first half came on a 46-yard field goal by George Blanda, which followed San Diego's 9-yard punt.

In the third quarter, the Oilers put together the only sustained drive of the game, moving 80 yards. On third-and-5 at San Diego's 35, Blanda rolled to his right and found Billy Cannon open at the 17. Cannon jumped to make the catch, shrugged off a would-be tackler, and ran into the end zone for a touchdown that put Houston ahead 10-0.

The Chargers scored early in the fourth quarter on a 12-yard field goal by George Blair, but they could not score again.

Houston	0	3	7	0	-	10
San Diego	0	0	0	3	-	3

Hou - FG Blanda 46
Hou - Cannon 35 pass from Blanda (Blanda kick)
SD - FG Blair 12

1961 NFL CHAMPIONSHIP GAME
Green Bay 37, New York Giants 0

December 31, 1961, at Green Bay
Attendance: 39,029

The Packers, and Paul Hornung in particular, dominated the Giants to win their first NFL title in 17 years, 37-0. The Packers outgained New York in 345 total yards to 130, and intercepted Y.A. Tittle 4 times, while Hornung rushed for 89 yards, caught 3 passes, and tied an NFL postseason record with 19 points.

The Giants had some early chances, but they slipped away. Kyle Rote dropped a sure touchdown pass deep in Green Bay territory, and halfback Bob Gaiters overthrew a wide-open Rote in the end zone later in the contest.

The Packers erupted for 24 points in the second quarter, starting with Hornung's 6-yard touchdown run six seconds into the period. Bart Starr then threw touchdown passes to Boyd Dowler and Ron Kramer before Hornung kicked a 17-yard field goal just before end of the half.

Two short field goals by Hornung and another touchdown pass from Starr to Kramer completed the scoring in the second half.

N.Y. Giants	0	0	0	0	-	0
Green Bay	0	24	10	3	-	37

GB - Hornung 6 run (Hornung kick)
GB - Dowler 13 pass from Starr (Hornung kick)
GB - R. Kramer 14 pass from Starr (Hornung kick)
GB - FG Hornung 17
GB - FG Hornung 22
GB - R. Kramer 13 pass from Starr (Hornung kick)
GB - FG Hornung 19

1962 AFL CHAMPIONSHIP GAME
Dallas Texans 20, Houston 17 (2 OT)

December 23, 1962, at Houston
Attendance: 37,981

In what was, at the time, the longest game in the history of professional football, the Dallas Texans dethroned the two-time defending AFL-champion Houston Oilers when Tommy Brooker kicked a 25-yard field goal after 2:54 of the sixth quarter, or 17:54 of sudden-death overtime.

Regulation time was dominated for one half by the Texans, who led 17-0 after two quarters, and one half by the Oilers, who tied it with 17 second-half points.

The overtime started with a potentially damaging gaffe by Dallas. Texans captain Abner Haynes, who had scored 2 touchdowns, won the coin toss but elected to "kick to the clock." What Haynes wanted was the strong wind behind his team, but by saying "kick" first, he gave the Oilers the chance to decide which end to take, and they chose to have the wind behind them. As it turned out, it didn't matter.

After an interception near the end of the first overtime period, the Texans took over at midfield. Two big plays by fullback Jack Spikes moved the ball to Houston's 19, and, on fourth-and-9, Brooker's field goal won it.

Dal. Texans	3	14	0	0	0	3	-	20
Houston	0	0	7	10	0	0	-	17

Dal - FG Brooker 16
Dal - Haynes 28 pass from Dawson (Brooker kick)
Dal - Haynes 2 run (Brooker kick)
Hou - Dewveall 15 pass from Blanda (Blanda kick)
Hou - FG Blanda 31
Hou - Tolar 1 run (Blanda kick)
Dal - FG Brooker 25

1962 NFL CHAMPIONSHIP GAME
Green Bay 16, New York Giants 7

December 30, 1962, at New York
Attendance: 64,892

The Giants outgained the Packers 291 yards to 244 but lost in the NFL Championship Game for the fourth time in five years, bowing to Green Bay 16-7.

The key figure for the Packers was fullback Jim Taylor, who tied an NFL playoff record with 31 carries while gaining 85 yards and scoring the Packers' only touchdown. That came in the second quarter and increased the Packers' lead to 10-0. With Green Bay leading 3-0, linebacker Dan Currie forced a fumble by Giants halfback Phil King, and the Packers recovered at New York's 28. On first down, Paul Hornung threw a halfback pass to Boyd Dowler for 21 yards. On the next play, Taylor blasted through the middle for a touchdown.

The Giants tried to rally in the third quarter. The Packers had to punt from deep in their own territory, and Erich Barnes blocked Max McGee's punt, which Jim Collier recovered in the end zone for a touchdown. However, New York could not score again, while Jerry Kramer added 2 field goals to insure the Packers' second consecutive championship.

Green Bay	3	7	3	3	-	16
N.Y. Giants	0	0	7	0	-	7

GB - FG J. Kramer 26
GB - Taylor 7 run (J. Kramer kick)
NYG - Collier blocked punt recovery in end zone (Chandler kick)
GB - FG J. Kramer 29
GB - FG J. Kramer 30

1963 AFL EASTERN DIVISION PLAYOFF GAME
Boston 26, Buffalo 8

December 28, 1963, at Buffalo
Attendance: 33,044

Boston fullback Larry Garron turned 2 short passes from Babe Parilli into touchdowns, and Gino Cappelletti kicked 4 field goals, as Boston won 26-8.

Cappelletti kicked a 28-yard field goal on the Patriots' second drive. On Boston's next possession, Parilli dumped a pass in the flat to Garron, who broke two tackles and sprinted to a 59-yard touchdown. Two more field goals by Cappelletti put the Patriots ahead 16-0 at the half.

The Bills changed quarterbacks in the third quarter, and Daryle Lamonica teamed with Elbert Dubenion on a 93-yard touchdown pass. A two-point conversion trimmed the deficit to 16-8.

In the fourth quarter, the Patriots eliminated any Buffalo hopes for a comeback. After driving to the Bills' 17, Parilli again went to the flat to Garron, who raced in for the touchdown.

Boston	10	6	0	10	-	26
Buffalo	0	0	8	0	-	8

Bos - FG Cappelletti 28
Bos - Garron 59 pass from Parilli (Cappelletti kick)
Bos - FG Cappelletti 12
Bos - FG Cappelletti 33
Buf - Dubenion 93 pass from Lamonica (Tracey pass from Lamonica)
Bos - Garron 17 pass from Parilli (Cappelletti kick)
Bos - FG Cappelletti 36

1963 AFL CHAMPIONSHIP GAME
San Diego 51, Boston 10

January 5, 1964, at San Diego
Attendance: 30,127

Fullback Keith Lincoln had one of the greatest days in the history of the playoffs to lead San Diego to a smashing 51-10 victory over Boston. Lincoln rushed for 206 yards on 13 carries, caught 7 passes for 123 yards, and completed his lone pass attempt for 20 yards.

Lincoln got the Chargers off to a quick start. On the second play from scrimmage, he raced up the middle for a 56-yard gain. Seven plays later, Tobin Rote scored on a quarterback sneak. The next time Lincoln touched the ball, he rambled 67 yards for a score. After the Patriots cut the margin to 14-7, halfback Paul Lowe reeled off another long run, going 58 yards for the Chargers' third touchdown of the first quarter.

The Chargers' continued to flex their offensive muscle, and a short field goal and a 14-yard touchdown pass from Rote to Don Norton built the lead to 31-10 at halftime. In the second half, Rote teamed with Lance Alworth on a 48-yard touchdown pass, backup quarterback John Hadl connected with Lincoln on a 25-yard touchdown pass, and Hadl scored on a 1-yard keeper, all contributing to an AFL-playoff-record 610 yards total offense.

Boston	7	3	0	0	-	10
San Diego	21	10	7	13	-	51

SD - Rote 2 run (Blair kick)
SD - Lincoln 67 run (Blair kick)
Bos - Garron 7 run (Cappelletti kick)
SD - Lowe 58 run (Blair kick)
SD - FG Blair 11
Bos - FG Cappelletti 15
SD - Norton 14 pass from Rote (Blair kick)
SD - Alworth 48 pass from Rote (Blair kick)
SD - Lincoln 25 pass from Hadl (pass failed)
SD - Hadl 1 run (Blair kick)

1963 NFL CHAMPIONSHIP GAME
Chicago Bears 14, New York Giants 10

December 29, 1963, at Chicago
Attendance: 45,801

Chicago's defense intercepted Y.A. Tittle 5 times, twice setting up short drives that provided all of the Bears' points, and George Halas won the last NFL title of his coaching career 14-10.

The Giants scored first, an impressive 83-yard drive culminating in a 14-yard touchdown pass from Tittle to

Frank Gifford. A short while later, the Giants had a chance to build their lead after they recovered halfback Willie Galimore's fumble at Chicago's 31. But Del Shofner dropped a pass in the end zone, and New York came away with nothing.

The Bears evened the game after linebacker Larry Morris intercepted a screen pass late in the first quarter and ran 61 yards to New York's 5. Quarterback Billy Wade scored on a sneak from the 2. The Giants regained the lead before the half on a 13-yard field goal by converted punter Don Chandler.

Another errant screen pass proved the Giants' undoing, as defensive end Ed O'Bradovich intercepted and returned the ball to New York's 14. Five plays later, Wade scored his second touchdown for the decisive points.

N.Y. Giants	**7**	**3**	**0**	**0**	**-**	**10**
Chi. Bears	**7**	**0**	**7**	**0**	**-**	**14**

NYG - Gifford 14 pass from Tittle (Chandler kick)
ChiB - Wade 2 run (Jencks kick)
NYG - FG Chandler 13
ChiB - Wade 1 run (Jencks kick)

1964 AFL CHAMPIONSHIP GAME
Buffalo 20, San Diego 7

December 26, 1964, at Buffalo
Attendance: 40,242

Keith Lincoln started the game as if he were going to match his record-setting performance of the year before, but a crushing tackle by Buffalo linebacker Mike Stratton left Lincoln with a broken rib and the Chargers struggling offensively. The result was a 20-7 victory for the Bills and their first AFL title.

The Chargers scored on a 26-yard pass from Tobin Rote to tight end Dave Kocourek on their first possession, a play set up by Lincoln's dazzling 38-yard run. San Diego was driving again, when Lincoln, who already had rushed for 47 yards on only 3 carries, caught a pass and gained 11 yards before being leveled by Stratton. And that, to a great extent, was the day offensively for San Diego.

The Bills slowly established their dominance, and took a 13-7 halftime lead on two short field goals by Pete Gogolak and a 4-yard touchdown run by halfback Wray Carlton. Then, after a scoreless third period, Jack Kemp hit end Glenn Bass with a 48-yard pass to set up Kemp's 1-yard quarterback sneak for the final score of the day.

San Diego	**7**	**0**	**0**	**0**	**-**	**7**
Buffalo	**3**	**10**	**0**	**7**	**-**	**20**

SD - Kocourek 26 pass from Rote (Lincoln kick)
Buf - FG Gogolak 12
Buf - Carlton 4 run (Gogolak kick)
Buf - FG Gogolak 17
Buf - Kemp 1 run (Gogolak kick)

1964 NFL CHAMPIONSHIP GAME
Cleveland 27, Baltimore 0

December 27, 1964, at Cleveland
Attendance: 79,544

The Colts had the NFL's top offense and the top defense in 1964 and were heavy favorites to beat the Browns in the title game. But Cleveland won handily, 27-0.

A conservatively played first half saw neither team able to score, but the Browns turned up the tempo in the third quarter. The game's first score, a 43-yard field goal by Cleveland's Lou Groza, followed Tom Gilburg's poor punt. When the Browns got the ball back, Jim Brown powered 46 yards to set up Frank Ryan's 18-yard touchdown pass to Gary Collins. Before the quarter ended, the two teamed on another touchdown pass, this one for 42 yards.

The game turned into a rout in the fourth quarter. First, Groza kicked a 10-yard field goal, then Ryan threw his third touchdown pass of the day, 51 yards to Collins. For the day, Collins had 130 yards on 5 receptions, and Cleveland outgained the Colts 339-181.

Baltimore	**0**	**0**	**0**	**0**	**-**	**0**
Cleveland	**0**	**0**	**17**	**10**	**-**	**27**

Cle - FG Groza 43
Cle - Collins 18 pass from Ryan (Groza kick)
Cle - Collins 42 pass from Ryan (Groza kick)
Cle - FG Groza 10
Cle - Collins 51 pass from Ryan (Groza kick)

1965 NFL WESTERN CONFERENCE PLAYOFF GAME
Green Bay 13, Baltimore 10 (OT)

December 26, 1965, at Green Bay
Attendance: 50,484

Green Bay's Don Chandler kicked 2 field goals, the first to tie the game with 1:58 remaining in regulation, and the other to win it after 13:39 of overtime, as the Packers defeated Baltimore 13-10.

Baltimore quarterbacks Johnny Unitas and Gary Cuozzo both were injured, so halfback Tom Matte took over the position, helped by a list of plays taped to his wrist. On the Packers' first play from scrimmage, quarterback Bart Starr threw a pass to Bill Anderson, who fumbled. The ball was picked up by Don Shinnick, who returned it 25 yards for a touchdown. Starr was injured on the play and missed the rest of the game.

Trailing 10-0 at halftime, the Packers cut the lead to 3 points after a high snap on a punt allowed them to take over at Baltimore's 35. Then, with nine minutes left, Green Bay started a 15-play drive that ended with Chandler's 22-yard field goal.

Baltimore	**7**	**3**	**0**	**0**	**0**	**-**	**10**
Green Bay	**0**	**0**	**7**	**3**	**3**	**-**	**13**

Bal - Shinnick 25 fumble return (Michaels kick)
Bal - FG Michaels 15
GB - Hornung 1 run (Chandler kick)
GB - FG Chandler 22
GB - FG Chandler 25

1965 AFL CHAMPIONSHIP GAME
Buffalo 23, San Diego 0

December 26, 1965, at San Diego
Attendance: 30,361

A blitzing, stunting defense that included an unusual three-man line, a defensive end dropping into a zone, and constant double coverage on Lance Alworth, confused the Chargers' offense and helped the Bills to a 23-0 victory. San Diego had scored 54 points and gained 816 yards in their two regular-season games against Buffalo.

The Chargers never penetrated beyond Buffalo's 24,

and, although Alworth had 4 receptions for 82 yards, Paul Lowe, whose 1,121 yards rushing in the regular season had set an AFL record, was held to 57 yards, including a 47-yard run.

After the defenses dominated most of first half, the Bills broke open the game five minutes before halftime. The first touchdown came when Jack Kemp teamed with Ernie Warlick on an 18-yard touchdown pass. Shortly thereafter, George (Butch) Byrd returned a punt 74 yards for a touchdown to give the Bills a 14-0 lead.

Buffalo slowly extended its advantage in the second half on 3 field goals by Pete Gogolak.

Buffalo	0	14	6	3	-	23
San Diego	0	0	0	0	-	0

Buf - Warlick 18 pass from Kemp (Gogolak kick)
Buf - Byrd 74 interception return (Gogolak kick)
Buf - FG Gogolak 11
Buf - FG Gogolak 39
Buf - FG Gogolak 32

1965 NFL CHAMPIONSHIP GAME
Green Bay 23, Cleveland 12

January 2, 1966, at Green Bay
Attendance: 50,777

After four inches of snow had been removed from Lambeau Field, a freezing rain turned the playing surface into thick mud. Conditions helped slow Cleveland's Jim Brown, but did not have the same effect on Green Bay's Paul Hornung and Jim Taylor, as the Packers slowly pulled away to defeat the defending champion Cleveland Browns 23-12.

The Packers jumped ahead on their first possession on a 47-yard touchdown pass from Bart Starr to Carroll Dale. The Browns came right back on an 18-yard touchdown pass from Frank Ryan to Gary Collins, the heroes of the previous year's title game. Lou Groza missed the extra point, however, and the Packers led 7-6. Each team added 2 field goals before halftime, and Green Bay led 13-12 at intermission.

The Packers used Taylor to control the ball in the second half. He carried 12 times out of 24 plays on drives that led to a touchdown and a field goal. Hornung's 13-yard touchdown run in the third quarter was the decisive play in a drive that increased Green Bay's advantage to 20-12.

Cleveland	9	3	0	0	-	12
Green Bay	7	6	7	3	-	23

GB - Dale 47 pass from Starr (Chandler kick)
Cle - Collins 17 pass from Ryan (kick failed)
Cle - FG Groza 24
GB - FG Chandler 15
GB - FG Chandler 23
Cle - FG Groza 28
GB - Hornung 13 run (Chandler kick)
GB - FG Chandler 29

1966 AFL CHAMPIONSHIP GAME
Kansas City 31, Buffalo 7

January 1, 1967, at Buffalo
Attendance: 42,080

The Kansas City Chiefs dominated the two-time defending AFL-champion Buffalo Bills 31-7 to earn the right to represent the AFL in the first Super Bowl.

Kansas City led 14-7 late in the first half when Bills quarterback Jack Kemp was intercepted by Chiefs safety Johnny Robinson in the end zone. Robinson returned the ball 72 yards to set up Mike Mercer's 32-yard field goal for a 17-7 advantage at halftime.

While the Chiefs' defense shut down the Bills in the second half, Kansas City's offense turned to its running game. Rookie halfback Mike Garrett scored on 2 fourth-quarter touchdown runs to put the game away.

Kansas City	7	10	0	14	-	31
Buffalo	7	0	0	0	-	7

KC - Arbanas 29 pass from Dawson (Mercer kick)
Buf - Dubenion 69 pass from Kemp (Lusteg kick)
KC - Taylor 29 pass from Dawson (Mercer kick)
KC - FG Mercer 32
KC - Garrett 1 run (Mercer kick)
KC - Garrett 18 run (Mercer kick)

1966 NFL CHAMPIONSHIP GAME
Green Bay 34, Dallas 27

January 1, 1967, at Dallas
Attendance: 74,152

In a match between the old power and the new, Green Bay's Tom Brown intercepted a pass in the end zone with 28 seconds left, and the Packers held on to defeat the Dallas Cowboys 34-27.

The Packers appeared ready to make a runaway of it early on. Bart Starr threw a 17-yard touchdown pass to Elijah Pitts. On the ensuing kickoff, Mel Renfro fumbled and Green Bay's Jim Grabowski picked up the ball and returned it 18 yards for a touchdown and a 14-0 lead. The Cowboys were undaunted, however, and tied the score at the end of one quarter on touchdown runs by Dan Reeves and Don Perkins.

Starr threw 3 touchdown passes in the second half, the final one of 28 yards to Max McGee to give Green Bay a 34-20 lead with 5:20 remaining in the game. But the Cowboys came right back, scoring on a 68-yard pass from Don Meredith to Frank Clarke. A short punt gave Dallas the ball at the Packers' 47, and Dallas advanced to the 22 before Brown was called for pass interference in the end zone. Dallas received a first down at the Green Bay 2, but on fourth down Meredith's pass was intercepted by Brown.

Green Bay	14	7	7	6	-	34
Dallas	14	3	3	7	-	27

GB - Pitts 17 pass from Starr (Chandler kick)
GB - Grabowski 18 fumble return (Chandler kick)
Dal - Reeves 3 run (Villanueva kick)
Dal - Perkins 23 run (Villanueva kick)
GB - Dale 51 pass from Starr (Chandler kick)
Dal - FG Villanueva 11
Dal - FG Villanueva 32
GB - Dowler 16 pass from Starr (Chandler kick)
GB - McGee 28 pass from Starr (kick blocked)
Dal - Clarke 68 pass from Meredith (Villanueva kick)

1967 NFL EASTERN CONFERENCE PLAYOFF GAME
Dallas 52, Cleveland 14

December 24, 1967, at Dallas
Attendance: 70,786

Dallas thoroughly dominated Cleveland on offense, defense, and special teams to easily win the most one-sided conference playoff game yet played 52-14.

Despite the early loss of halfback Dan Reeves with an injury, the Cowboys didn't miss a beat as his replacement, rookie Craig Baynham, caught a 3-yard touchdown pass from Don Meredith and Don Perkins scored from the 4 to make it 14-0 after one quarter. In the second period, Bob Hayes scored on an 86-yard touchdown pass from Meredith. Hayes also set up two other scores with punt returns of 68 and 64 yards. The Cowboys jumped to a 24-0 lead before Cleveland finally scored.

Dallas erupted again in the second half, with Baynham and Perkins scoring on 1-yard runs before Cornell Green returned an interception 60 yards for a touchdown that built the lead to 45-7.

Cleveland	0	7	0	7	-	14
Dallas	14	10	21	7	-	52

Dal - Baynham 3 pass from Meredith (Villanueva kick)
Dal - Perkins 4 run (Villanueva kick)
Dal - Hayes 86 pass from Meredith (Villanueva kick)
Dal - FG Villanueva 10
Cle - Morin 13 pass from Ryan (Groza kick)
Dal - Baynham 1 run (Villanueva kick)
Dal - Perkins 1 run (Villanueva kick)
Dal - Green 60 interception return (Villanueva kick)
Dal - Baynham 1 run (Villanueva kick)
Cle - Warfield 75 pass from Ryan (Groza kick)

1967 NFL WESTERN CONFERENCE PLAYOFF GAME
Green Bay 28, Los Angeles Rams 7

December 23, 1967, at Milwaukee
Attendance: 49,861

The Packers shut down the NFL's leading offense while moving effectively themselves, and Green Bay avenged a last-minute defeat by the Rams two weeks earlier, winning 28-7.

The Rams were the dominant team in the early going, as Roman Gabriel staked them to a lead with a 29-yard touchdown pass to Bernie Casey. Shortly thereafter, a 24-yard field goal attempt was blocked by Dave Robinson, and the momentum shifted to the Packers.

In the second quarter, big plays gave Green Bay the lead. A 39-yard punt return by Tom Brown set up Travis Williams's 46-yard run for the tying score. Then, after Willie Wood returned a short field-goal attempt 44 yards, Bart Starr found Carroll Dale for 17 yards and the go-ahead touchdown.

The Packers' defense smothered the Rams in the second half, while their punishing ground game produced 2 touchdowns.

L.A. Rams	7	0	0	0	-	7
Green Bay	0	14	7	7	-	28

Rams - Casey 29 pass from Gabriel (Gossett kick)
GB - Williams 46 run (Chandler kick)
GB - Dale 17 pass from Starr (Chandler kick)
GB - Mercein 6 run (Chandler kick)
GB - Williams 2 run (Chandler kick)

1967 AFL CHAMPIONSHIP GAME
Oakland 40, Houston 7

December 31, 1967, at Oakland
Attendance: 53,330

Big plays turned a close game into a rout, and the Raiders won their first AFL title with a 40-7 victory over Houston.

A 69-yard touchdown run by Hewritt Dixon, who had been converted to fullback after three years at tight end with Denver, helped Oakland to a 10-0 advantage in the second quarter. Late in the first half, the Raiders lined up for a field-goal attempt from Houston's 17, but quarterback Daryle Lamonica took the snap and instead threw to wide-open Dave Kocourek for a touchdown with 18 seconds remaining to build the lead to 17-0.

The Oilers' Zeke Moore fumbled the second-half kickoff and Oakland recovered deep in Houston territory, leading to Lamonica's 1-yard quarterback sneak. George Blanda kicked 3 field goals in the second half to give him 16 points for the day, and Lamonica threw a touchdown pass to Bill Miller as Oakland cruised into its first Super Bowl.

Houston	0	0	0	7	-	7
Oakland	3	14	10	13	-	40

Oak - FG Blanda 37
Oak - Dixon 69 run (Blanda kick)
Oak - Kocourek 17 pass from Lamonica (Blanda kick)
Oak - Lamonica 1 run (Blanda kick)
Oak - FG Blanda 40
Oak - FG Blanda 42
Hous - Frazier 5 pass from Beathard (Wittenborn kick)
Oak - FG Blanda 36
Oak - Miller 12 pass from Lamonica (Blanda kick)

1967 NFL CHAMPIONSHIP GAME
Green Bay 21, Dallas 17

December 31, 1967, at Green Bay
Attendance: 50,861

In some of the most difficult conditions in the history of the playoffs—a temperature at kickoff of minus-13 degrees and a 15-mile-per-hour wind—Bart Starr scored on a 1-yard quarterback sneak with 13 seconds left to give the Packers a 21-17 victory against the Dallas Cowboys in a game that came to be known as the Ice Bowl.

The Packers jumped to a 14-0 lead in the first half when Starr found Boyd Dowler with an 8-yard touchdown pass in the first period and a 46-yard scoring toss in the second. But the Cowboys rallied when defensive tackle Willie Townes drilled Starr, who fumbled. Defensive end George Andrie scooped up the ball and returned it 7 yards for a touchdown. A field goal by Danny Villanueva narrowed the margin to 14-10 at halftime.

On the first play of the fourth quarter, the Cowboys took the lead. Halfback Dan Reeves, who had been a quarterback at South Carolina, threw a 50-yard touchdown pass to Lance Rentzel.

The Packers started their final drive at their 32 with 4:50 left. The big gain in the 12-play drive came when fullback Chuck Mercein took a short pass from Starr and ran 19 yards to Dallas's 11. Mercein then powered to the 3. Three plays later, behind blocks by guard Jerry Kramer and center Ken Bowman, Starr sneaked across the goal line for the victory.

Dallas	0	10	0	7	-	17
Green Bay	7	7	0	7	-	21

GB - Dowler 8 pass from Starr (Chandler kick)
GB - Dowler 46 pass from Starr (Chandler kick)
Dal - Andrie 7 fumble return (Villanueva kick)
Dal - FG Villanueva 21
Dal - Rentzel 50 pass from Reeves (Villanueva kick)
GB - Starr 1 run (Chandler kick)

1968 AFL WESTERN DIVISION PLAYOFF GAME
Oakland 41, Kansas City 6

December 22, 1968, at Oakland
Attendance: 53,605

Daryle Lamonica threw 5 touchdown passes as the Raiders destroyed the AFL's stingiest defense 41-6.

Lamonica, who passed for 347 yards, threw touchdown passes on three of Oakland's first four possessions to help stake his team to a 21-0 lead in the first quarter. He took the Raiders on scoring drives of 80 and 70 yards, and one in between that had to go only 25 yards after a shanked punt. The Chiefs threatened to get back into the game in the second quarter, driving to the Raiders' 3- and 2-yard lines on separate possessions. But each time they had to settle for short field goals, then Lamonica landed the knockout punch, throwing a 54-yard touchdown pass to Fred Biletnikoff with 28 seconds left in the first half.

Kansas City	0	6	0	0	-	6
Oakland	21	7	0	13	-	41

Oak - Biletnikoff 24 pass from Lamonica (Blanda kick)
Oak - Wells 23 pass from Lamonica (Blanda kick)
Oak - Biletnikoff 44 pass from Lamonica (Blanda kick)
KC - FG Stenerud 10
KC - FG Stenerud 8
Oak - Biletnikoff 54 pass from Lamonica (Blanda kick)
Oak - Wells 35 pass from Lamonica (Blanda kick)
Oak - FG Blanda 41
Oak - FG Blanda 40

1968 NFL EASTERN CONFERENCE PLAYOFF GAME
Cleveland 31, Dallas 20

December 21, 1968, at Cleveland
Attendance: 81,497

The Cleveland Browns turned 5 turnovers by the favored Cowboys into 24 points—including 2 touchdowns in the first three minutes of the second half—for a 31-20 victory.

On Dallas's first possession, Mike Howell intercepted a pass by Don Meredith to set up a 38-yard field goal by rookie Don Cockroft. But the Cowboys responded when Chuck Howley returned Bill Nelsen's fumble 44 yards for a touchdown, and Mike Clark kicked a 16-yard field goal following an interception by Dave Edwards. The Browns tied the game at halftime, going 85 yards on 6 plays, and scoring on a 45-yard pass from Nelsen to Leroy Kelly.

Cleveland exploded early in the third quarter. On the first play from scrimmage, Dale Lindsey returned an interception 27 yards for a touchdown. Three scrimmage plays later, Ben Davis intercepted Meredith to set up Kelly's 35-yard touchdown run. The Browns scored in the fourth quarter after Erich Barnes intercepted a pass from Craig Morton.

Dallas	7	3	3	7	-	20
Cleveland	3	7	14	7	-	31

Cle - FG Cockroft 38
Dal - Howley 44 fumble return (Clark kick)
Dal - FG Clark 16
Cle - Kelly 45 pass from Nelson (Cockroft kick)
Cle - Lindsey 27 interception return (Cockroft kick)
Cle - Kelly 35 run (Cockroft kick)
Dal - FG Clark 47
Cle - Green 2 run (Cockroft kick)
Dal - Garrison 2 pass from Morton (Clark kick)

1968 NFL WESTERN CONFERENCE PLAYOFF GAME
Baltimore 24, Minnesota 14

December 22, 1968, at Baltimore
Attendance: 60,238

Baltimore scored twice in 2:01 of the third period to break open a close game, and the Vikings came up short in their first-ever playoff game 24-14.

The Colts led 7-0 at halftime after Earl Morrall put together an impressive passing drive. First, he threw 39 yards and 33 yards to flanker Willie Richardson. He ended the drive with a 3-yard completion to tight end Tom Mitchell for the touchdown.

Midway through the third quarter, the Colts broke open the game. First, Morrall hit John Mackey with a short pass, and the Hall-of-Fame tight end slipped a tackle and ran 49 yards for a touchdown. On the ensuing drive, defensive end Bubba Smith pounded Minnesota quarterback Joe Kapp, who fumbled. Line-backer Mike Curtis grabbed the ball and raced 60 yards for a touchdown and a 21-0 lead.

Minnesota	0	0	0	14	-	14
Baltimore	0	7	14	3	-	24

Bal - Mitchell 3 pass from Morrall (Michaels kick)
Bal - Mackey 49 pass from Morrall (Michaels kick)
Bal - Curtis 60 fumble return (Michaels kick)
Min - Martin 1 pass from Kapp (Cox kick)
Bal - FG Michaels 33
Min - Brown 7 pass from Kapp (Cox kick)

1968 AFL CHAMPIONSHIP GAME
New York Jets 27, Oakland 23

December 29, 1968, at New York
Attendance: 62,627

With two minutes left, the Raiders were driving to the potential winning touchdown when, with the ball at New York's 24, Daryle Lamonica threw a swing pass to rookie halfback Charlie Smith. Smith did not catch the ball, nor did he cover it, and the play was ruled a lateral rather than a forward pass. Jets linebacker Ralph Baker recovered for the Jets, who were able to run out the clock for a 27-23 victory.

Despite icy winds, the Jets scored on their first drive, with Joe Namath hitting Don Maynard with a 14-yard touchdown pass. New York increased its lead to 10-0 before Lamonica responded with a 29-yard touchdown pass to Fred Biletnikoff.

New York led 13-10 at halftime, but George Blanda tied the game at 13-13 with a 9-yard field goal early in the third quarter. Namath got the lead right back when he hit tight end Pete Lammons with a 20-yard touchdown pass.

Midway through the fourth quarter, the only interception of the game was returned by Oakland's George Atkinson to New York's 5. Pete Banaszak then scored to give the Raiders a 23-20 lead. But Namath took less than a minute to lead his team to another touchdown, finishing with a 6-yard toss to Maynard.

Oakland	0	10	3	10	-	23
N.Y. Jets	10	3	7	7	-	27

NYJ - Maynard 14 pass from Namath (J. Turner kick)
NYJ - FG J. Turner 33
Oak - Biletnikoff 29 pass from Lamonica (Blanda kick)
NYJ - FG J. Turner 36
Oak - FG Blanda 26

Oak - FG Blanda 9
NYJ - Lammons 20 pass from Namath (J. Turner kick)
Oak - FG Blanda 20
Oak - Banaszak 5 run (Blanda kick)
NYJ - Maynard 6 pass from Namath (J. Turner kick)

1968 NFL CHAMPIONSHIP GAME
Baltimore 34, Cleveland 0

December 29, 1968, at Cleveland
Attendance: 78,410

Remembering that four years previously they had been highly favored but had lost 27-0 to the Browns in the NFL Championship Game, the Baltimore Colts came into the 1968 title game with something to prove. They played like it, dominating every aspect of the game while administering only the second shutout the Cleveland Browns ever had received 34-0.

The Browns had their best chance to score in the first quarter, but defensive end Bubba Smith blocked Don Cockcroft's 41-yard field-goal attempt. The Colts then broke open the game in the second period. After a 28-yard field goal by Lou Michaels put Baltimore ahead 3-0, Tom Matte culminated a 10-play, 60-yard drive with a 1-yard touchdown run. Following an interception by Mike Curtis that he returned to the Cleveland 33, Matte scored again on a 12-yard run.

The Colts continued to dominate in the second half. Matte scored his third touchdown while Baltimore's defense was holding NFL rushing leader Leroy Kelly to a total of 28 yards on 13 carries.

Baltimore	0	17	7	10	-	34
Cleveland	0	0	0	0	-	0

Bal - FG Michaels 28
Bal - Matte 1 run (Michaels kick)
Bal - Matte 12 run (Michaels kick)
Bal - Matte 2 run (Michaels kick)
Bal - FG Michaels 10
Bal - Brown 4 run (Michaels kick)

1969 AFL DIVISIONAL PLAYOFF GAME
Kansas City 13, New York Jets 6

December 20, 1969, at New York
Attendance: 62,977

Frigid conditions and a gusting wind helped slow two of the best passing attacks in the game, but 2 passes by Len Dawson that did click were the difference as the Chiefs became the first AFL team to return to the Super Bowl.

The game was tied 3-3 at halftime, but Jan Stenerud's second field goal gave Kansas City a 6-3 lead after three periods. In the fourth quarter, the Jets drove to a first-and-goal at the Chiefs' 1 after Emmitt Thomas was called for pass interference in the end zone. However, two runs and a pass didn't produce a score, and Jim Turner tied the game with a short field goal.

Following the kickoff, Kansas City took possession at its 20. On first down, Dawson threw long to Otis Taylor, who raced to the Jets' 19 before being tackled by Al Atkinson. On the next play, Dawson found Gloster Richardson alone in the end zone for the winning touchdown.

Kansas City	0	3	3	7	-	13
N.Y. Jets	3	0	0	3	-	6

NYJ - FG J. Turner 27
KC - FG Stenerud 23
KC - FG Stenerud 25
NYJ - FG J. Turner 7
KC - Richardson 19 pass from Dawson (Stenerud kick)

1969 AFL DIVISIONAL PLAYOFF GAME
Oakland 56, Houston 7

December 21, 1969, at Oakland
Attendance: 53,539

Oakland scored 4 touchdowns in a span of 4:22 of the first quarter, jumping to a 28-0 lead before coasting to a 56-7 victory.

The key figure was quarterback Daryle Lamonica, who threw 6 touchdown passes. On their second possession, the Raiders moved 50 yards in 5 plays, with Lamonica throwing a 13-yard scoring pass to Fred Biletnikoff. On the first play after the kickoff, George Atkinson intercepted Pete Beathard's pass and returned it 57 yards for a touchdown. The Oilers again lost the ball the first play after the kickoff, when Hoyle Granger fumbled and Carleton Oats recovered at Houston's 24. On first down, Lamonica threw a 24-yard touchdown pass to Rod Sherman. Following the next kickoff, Houston again fumbled— this time by Beathard on the fourth play—and Tom Keating recovered. Again it took the Raiders just one play to score, Lamonica finding Biletnikoff for a 31-yard touchdown pass.

Houston	0	0	0	7	-	7
Oakland	28	7	14	7	-	56

Oak - Biletnikoff 13 pass from Lamonica (Blanda kick)
Oak - Atkinson 57 interception return (Blanda kick)
Oak - Sherman 24 pass from Lamonica (Blanda kick)
Oak - Biletnikoff 31 pass from Lamonica (Blanda kick)
Oak - Smith 60 pass from Lamonica (Blanda kick)
Oak - Sherman 23 pass from Lamonica (Blanda kick)
Oak - Cannon 3 pass from Lamonica (Blanda kick)
Hou - Reed 8 pass from Beathard (Gerela kick)
Oak - Hubbard 4 run (Blanda kick)

1969 NFL EASTERN CONFERENCE PLAYOFF GAME
Cleveland 38, Dallas 14

December 28, 1969, at Dallas
Attendance: 69,321

The Cleveland Browns played a nearly flawless game to romp over the favored Dallas Cowboys for the second year in a row 38-14.

The Browns dominated the first half, building a 17-0 lead behind quarterback Bill Nelsen, who completed 15 of 22 passes for 184 yards in the first two periods. One of those completions was a 6-yard touchdown pass to tight end Milt Morin to give Cleveland a 14-0 lead in the second quarter. The Browns had started the scoring with the first of two 2-yard touchdown runs by Bo Scott.

The Cowboys never put together a successful drive until the third quarter, when Craig Morton scored on a 2-yard run. But linebacker Jim Houston stopped Dallas's next threat with an interception, and cornerback Walt Sumner later returned another interception of a Morton pass 88 yards for a touchdown.

Cleveland	7	10	7	14	-	38
Dallas	0	0	7	7	-	14

Cle - Scott 2 run (Cockroft kick)
Cle - Morin 6 pass from Nelsen (Cockroft kick)
Cle - FG Cockroft 29
Cle - Scott 2 run (Cockroft kick)
Dal - Morton 2 run (Clark kick)

Cle	-	Kelly 1 run (Cockroft kick)
Cle	-	Sumner 88 interception return (Cockroft kick)
Dal	-	Rentzel 5 pass from Staubach (Clark kick)

1969 NFL WESTERN CONFERENCE PLAYOFF GAME
Minnesota 23, Los Angeles Rams 20

December 27, 1969, at Bloomington
Attendance: 47,900

Quarterback Joe Kapp passed for 40 yards and ran for 14 to lead Minnesota on a 65-yard touchdown drive in the fourth quarter as the Vikings came from behind to defeat the Rams 23-20.

Thirty-five seconds after Kapp's 2-yard run gave the Vikings a 21-20 lead, defensive end Carl Eller tackled NFL most valuable player Roman Gabriel for a safety to secure the upset victory.

The Rams scored early on a 45-yard touchdown drive following Richie Petitbon's recovery of Bill Brown's fumble. The Vikings then drove 75 yards to tie the score on Dave Osborn's 1-yard run. But the Rams got a 20-yard field goal from Bruce Gossett and took a 17-7 lead on a 2-yard touchdown pass from Gabriel to tight end Billy Truax only 48 seconds before the half.

The Vikings drove 71 yards to a touchdown on their first possession of the second half, the big play a 41-yard pass from Kapp to Gene Washington. Then, late in the game, Kapp took over.

L.A. Rams	7	10	0	3	-	20
Minnesota	7	0	7	9	-	23

Rams	-	Klein 3 pass from Gabriel (Gossett kick)
Min	-	Osborn 1 run (Cox kick)
Rams	-	FG Gossett 20
Rams	-	Truax 2 pass from Gabriel (Gossett kick)
Min	-	Osborn 1 run (Cox kick)
Rams	-	FG Gossett 27
Min	-	Kapp 2 run (Cox kick)
Min	-	Safety, Eller tackled Gabriel in end zone

1969 AFL CHAMPIONSHIP GAME
Kansas City 17, Oakland 7

January 4, 1970, at Oakland
Attendance: 53,564

The Kansas City Chiefs won the last championship of the AFL 17-7 by slowing down Oakland's passing attack and capitalizing on big plays.

The Raiders seemed on their way to their third win of the season against Kansas City when Charlie Smith scored on a 3-yard run in the first quarter. But then Len Dawson, who had thrown 7 incompletions in a row, hit Frank Pitts for a 41-yard gain to the Raiders' 1. Three plays later, Wendell Hayes scored the tying touchdown.

Dawson made another big play with the game tied 7-7 in the third quarter. Facing third-and-14 at Kansas City's 2, the Chiefs' quarterback scrambled out of trouble and fired a 35-yard pass to Otis Taylor. That was the key to a 94-yard drive that culminated in a 5-yard scoring run by Robert Holmes.

The Chiefs turned over the ball inside their own 30 three times in the fourth quarter, but each time they intercepted Raiders quarterback Daryle Lamonica, who was playing despite having severely jammed his throwing hand on the helmet of Aaron Brown early in the final period.

Kansas City	0	7	7	3	-	17
Oakland	7	0	0	0	-	7

Oak	-	Smith 3 run (Blanda kick)
KC	-	Hayes 1 run (Stenerud kick)
KC	-	Holmes 5 run (Stenerud kick)
KC	-	FG Stenerud 22

1969 NFL CHAMPIONSHIP GAME
Minnesota 27, Cleveland 7

January 4, 1970, at Bloomington
Attendance: 46,503

The field was slick, the sidelines of Metropolitan Stadium were stacked with snow, and it was only 8 degrees when the Minnesota Vikings defeated the Cleveland Browns 27-7 for the NFL title.

On the Vikings' first possession, Gene Washington broke open when cornerback Walt Sumner slipped on the icy field. Washington caught a 33-yard pass from Joe Kapp to set up the Vikings' first touchdown. The score came on a 7-yard run by Kapp, who collided with Bill Brown while trying to hand off, then blasted through the middle of Cleveland's defense, shedding tacklers into the end zone. On the Vikings' next possession, Kapp again found Washington, who came open when Erich Barnes fell trying to cover him, and the wide receiver went 75 yards with the catch for a touchdown and a 14-0 first quarter lead.

The Vikings then turned to their tough ground game, and Dave Osborn's 108 yards led a rushing attack that netted 222 yards. Osborn's 20-yard touchdown run late in the second quarter increased the Vikings' margin to 24-0 and ended any hopes of a Cleveland comeback.

Cleveland	0	0	0	7	-	7
Minnesota	14	10	3	0	-	27

Min	-	Kapp 7 run (Cox kick)
Min	-	Washington 75 pass from Kapp (Cox kick)
Min	-	FG Cox 30
Min	-	Osborn 20 run (Cox kick)
Min	-	FG Cox 32
Cle	-	Collins 3 pass from Nelsen (Cockroft kick)

1970 AFC DIVISIONAL PLAYOFF GAME
Baltimore 17, Cincinnati 0

December 26, 1970, at Baltimore
Attendance: 51,127

Baltimore's veteran defense dominated the young Bengals, who were making their first playoff appearance. Cincinnati never crossed Baltimore's 42 and gained only 139 yards in the 17-0 shutout.

The Colts scored the second time they had the ball. The power running of Norm Bulaich took them into Cincinnati territory, but, with a third-and-9, Johnny Unitas went long to Roy Jefferson, who caught the pass on Cincinnati's 12 and sped into the end zone to complete a 45-yard touchdown. The next time the Colts had possession, they drove 35 yards to set up rookie Jim O'Brien's 44-yard field goal into a stiff wind.

Baltimore's third score score came in the final period. With a third-and-long, Unitas passed to Eddie Hinton, who made the catch, eluded a tackler, and, behind a block by Bulaich, raced 35 yards to complete a 53-yard scoring play.

Cincinnati	0	0	0	0	-	0
Baltimore	7	3	0	7	-	17

Bal - Jefferson 45 pass from Unitas (O'Brien kick)
Bal - FG O'Brien 44
Bal - Hinton 53 pass from Unitas (O'Brien kick)

1970 AFC DIVISIONAL PLAYOFF GAME
Oakland 21, Miami 14

December 27, 1970, at Oakland
Attendance: 54,401

The Raiders overcame numerous mistakes to beat the Dolphins 21-14 in Miami's first playoff game.

Both teams missed short field goals in the first quarter, but the Raiders continued to make mistakes. Charlie Smith fumbled at the Oakland 20 and Bill Stanfill recovered for Miami. Two plays later, Bob Griese threw a 16-yard touchdown pass to Paul Warfield. Late in the quarter, Oakland finally put a drive together. Daryle Lamonica found Raymond Chester for 21 yards, Fred Biletnikoff for 11, then Biletnikoff again for 22 and the tying touchdown.

The Raiders opened the third quarter by driving to the Miami 2, but Smith fumbled again. A short while later, Willie Brown intercepted a pass by Griese and returned it 50 yards for the go-ahead touchdown. In the fourth quarter, Lamonica saw flanker Rod Sherman with man-for-man coverage; the result was an 82-yard touchdown pass and a 21-14 lead.

Miami	0	7	0	7	-	14
Oakland	0	7	7	7	-	21

Mia - Warfield 16 pass from Griese (Yepremian kick)
Oak - Biletnikoff 22 pass from Lamonica (Blanda kick)
Oak - Brown 50 interception return (Blanda kick)
Oak - Sherman 82 pass from Lamonica (Blanda kick)
Mia - W. Richardson 7 pass from Griese (Yepremian kick)

1970 NFC DIVISIONAL PLAYOFF GAME
Dallas 5, Detroit 0

December 26, 1970, at Dallas
Attendance: 73,167

Dallas pounded out 209 yards on the ground against the NFL's best rushing defense, but it took a field goal, a safety, and some stellar defensive play for the Cowboys to defeat the Lions 5-0.

The Cowboys led 3-0 at halftime after Mike Clark kicked a 26-yard field goal to end a drive that began when Detroit quarterback Greg Landry fumbled near midfield, with safety Charlie Waters recovering.

Early in the final period the Cowboys put together a 15-play, 76-yard drive that took almost eight minutes off the clock. With a fourth-and-goal one foot from the end zone, rookie halfback Duane Thomas, who gained 135 yards in the game, stumbled over his blocker, forcing Dallas to give up the ball. But three plays later, defensive end George Andrie tackled Landry for a safety. In the final moments, with Detroit at the Dallas 29, Mel Renfro made an interception to preserve the victory.

Detroit	0	0	0	0	-	0
Dallas	3	0	0	2	-	5

Dal - FG Clark 26
Dal - Safety, Andrie tackled Landry in end zone

1970 NFC DIVISIONAL PLAYOFF GAME
San Francisco 17, Minnesota 14

December 27, 1970, at Bloomington
Attendance: 45,103

John Brodie passed for 1 touchdown and ran for another to lead the 49ers to their first NFL playoff victory.

Minnesota took an early lead when San Francisco fullback Ken Willard fumbled, and Paul Krause caught the ball in midair and raced 22 yards for a touchdown. The 49ers came back to score before the end of the first period, following a 30-yard punt return by Bruce Taylor. Brodie teamed with Dick Witcher on a 24-yard touchdown pass.

With less than four minutes remaining in the half, Dave Osborn fumbled, and the 49ers converted it into Bruce Gossett's 40-yard field goal.

Midway through the fourth quarter, Steve Spurrier punted Minnesota back to the 1. When the Vikings couldn't move and punted, Taylor returned it 23 yards to the 14. Five plays later, on third-and-goal, Brodie scored on a sneak with 1:20 remaining, and Minnesota's touchdown in the final seconds wasn't enough.

San Francisco	7	3	0	7	-	17
Minnesota	7	0	0	7	-	14

Min - Krause 22 fumble return (Cox kick)
SF - Witcher 24 pass from Brodie (Gossett kick)
SF - FG Gossett 40
SF - Brodie 1 run (Gossett kick)
Min - Washington 24 pass from Cuozzo (Cox kick)

1970 AFC CHAMPIONSHIP GAME
Baltimore 27, Oakland 17

January 3, 1971, at Baltimore
Attendance: 54,799

Baltimore, which joined the AFC with Pittsburgh and Cleveland when the AFL and NFL merged, won the first AFC title, defeating Oakland 27-17.

The Colts took a 10-0 lead when Jim O'Brien kicked a short field goal and Norm Bulaich ran 2 yards for a touchdown. The Raiders came back under the guidance of George Blanda, who entered the game at quarterback after Daryle Lamonica pulled a thigh muscle on a tackle by Bubba Smith early in the second period.

Blanda's 48-yard field goal cut the margin to 10-3 at halftime. Then, in the third quarter, he tied it with a 38-yard touchdown pass to Fred Biletnikoff. But another field goal by O'Brien and another touchdown run by Bulaich extended the Colts' lead to 10 points again.

Early in the fourth quarter, Blanda passed to Warren Wells for a touchdown, but the Raiders could not score again. Twice they went into Baltimore territory, only to have Blanda intercepted in the end zone. Then, late in the game, Johnny Unitas shut the door on the Raiders when he teamed with Ray Perkins on a 68-yard touchdown pass.

Oakland	0	3	7	7	-	17
Baltimore	3	7	10	7	-	27

Bal - FG O'Brien 16
Bal - Bulaich 2 run (O'Brien kick)
Oak - FG Blanda 48
Oak - Biletnikoff 38 pass from Blanda (Blanda kick)
Bal - FG O'Brien 23
Bal - Bulaich 11 run (O'Brien kick)
Oak - Wells 15 pass from Blanda (Blanda kick)
Bal - Perkins 68 pass from Unitas (O'Brien kick)

1970 NFC CHAMPIONSHIP GAME
Dallas 17, San Francisco 10

January 3, 1971, at San Francisco
Attendance: 59,364

Rookie halfback Duane Thomas rushed for 143 yards on 27 carries as the Cowboys beat San Francisco 17-10 and ended four years of frustration in the playoffs with their first victory in a championship game.

The Cowboys made 70 percent of their yards on the ground, and the 49ers made 80 percent of theirs through the air, but neither team could move effectively in a first half that ended in a 3-3 tie.

In the third quarter, San Francisco quarterback John Brodie, under heavy pressure from defensive end Larry Cole, threw a short pass over the middle that was intercepted by linebacker Lee Roy Jordan at the 49ers' 13. Thomas ran for a touchdown on the next play. San Francisco responded with an impressive drive, but Mel Renfro intercepted Brodie at the Dallas 18. The Cowboys then drove 82 yards, scoring on a 5-yard pass from Craig Morton to fullback Walt Garrison.

The 49ers came back before the end of the quarter, when Brodie threw a 26-yard touchdown pass to Dick Witcher. But Dallas's defense dominated the final period, which marked the end of the 49ers' history at Kezar Stadium, where they had been playing since the team was formed in 1946. San Francisco would begin playing its home games in Candlestick Park in 1971.

Dallas	0	3	14	0	-	17
San Francisco	3	0	7	0	-	10

SF - FG Gossett 16
Dal - FG Clark 21
Dal - Thomas 13 run (Clark kick)
Dal - Garrison 5 pass from Morton (Clark kick)
SF - Witcher 26 pass from Brodie (Gossett kick)

1971 AFC DIVISIONAL PLAYOFF GAME
Miami 27, Kansas City 24 (OT)

December 25, 1971, at Kansas City
Attendance: 50,374

Garo Yepremian kicked a 37-yard field goal after 7:40 of the second period of overtime to give Miami a 27-24 victory against Kansas City in the longest game ever played.

The Chiefs jumped ahead 10-0 after one quarter, but the Dolphins tied the score at 10-10 at halftime. After the teams exchanged touchdowns in the third quarter, Kansas City drove 91 yards, capped by Ed Podolak's 3-yard touchdown run in the fourth period. The Dolphins countered by marching 71 yards, with Bob Griese's 5-yard touchdown pass to tight end Marv Fleming tying the game at 24-24.

Podolak, who finished the day with 350 all-purpose yards—85 rushing, 110 receiving, and 155 on kick returns—returned the ensuing kickoff to Miami's 22 with 1:25 left, but Jan Stenerud missed a field goal. In the fifth period, Stenerud had a field goal attempt blocked, while Yepremian missed a long attempt.

Miami	0	10	7	7	0	3	-	27
Kansas City	10	0	7	7	0	0	-	24

KC - FG Stenerud 24
KC - Podolak 7 pass from Dawson (Stenerud kick)
Mia - Csonka 1 run (Yepremian kick)
Mia - FG Yepremian 14
KC - Otis 1 run (Stenerud kick)
Mia - Kiick 1 run (Yepremian kick)
KC - Podolak 3 run (Stenerud kick)
Mia - Fleming 5 pass from Griese (Yepremian kick)
Mia - FG Yepremian 37

1971 AFC DIVISIONAL PLAYOFF GAME
Baltimore 20, Cleveland 3

December 26, 1971, at Cleveland
Attendance: 74,082

Baltimore's defense came up with big plays on both ends of the field to shut down the Browns and lead the Colts to a 20-3 victory over Cleveland.

The Browns had their chances early. On the fourth play of the game, Bill Nelsen hit Fair Hooker with a 39-yard pass to the Baltimore 12, but cornerback Rex Kern stole the ball from Hooker. On the Browns' next drive, they moved to the Baltimore 4, but Bubba Smith blocked Don Cockroft's field-goal attempt.

The Colts then put together a 17-play, 92-yard drive that ended with a 1-yard scoring blast by Don Nottingham. Midway through the second quarter, the Colts' defense struck again. Safety Rick Volk intercepted a pass intended for Hooker and returned it 37 yards to the Cleveland 15. After a pass-interfer-ence penalty, Nottingham ran 7 yards for a touchdown.

Baltimore	0	14	3	3	-	20
Cleveland	0	0	3	0	-	3

Bal - Nottingham 1 run (O'Brien kick)
Bal - Nottingham 7 run (O'Brien kick)
Cle - FG Cockroft 14
Bal - FG O'Brien 42
Bal - FG O'Brien 15

1971 NFC DIVISIONAL PLAYOFF GAME
Dallas 20, Minnesota 12

December 25, 1971, at Bloomington
Attendance: 49,100

Dallas scored 13 points following turnovers, and another touchdown was set up by a punt return as the Cowboys defeated the Vikings 20-12 despite being outgained in yardage 311-183.

The Cowboys led 6-3 after a fumble recovery and an interception led to 2 field goals by Mike Clark.

Dallas opened up the game up with 2 touchdowns in the third quarter. On the second play of the second half, Cliff Harris intercepted a pass and returned it 30 yards to the Minnesota 13. On first down, Duane Thomas sprinted up the middle for 13 yards and a touchdown. Then, after a 24-yard punt return by Charlie Waters, Dallas started at its 48. On third-and-15, Roger Staubach found Lance Alworth for 30 yards. Five plays later, Staubach threw a 9-yard touchdown pass to Bob Hayes.

Dallas	3	3	14	0	-	20
Minnesota	0	3	0	9	-	12

Dal - FG Clark 26
Min - FG Cox 27
Dal - FG Clark 44
Dal - D. Thomas 13 run (Clark kick)
Dal - Hayes 9 pass from Staubach (Clark kick)
Min - Safety, Page tackled Staubach in end zone
Min - Voigt 6 pass from Cuozzo (Cox kick)

1971 NFC DIVISIONAL PLAYOFF GAME
San Francisco 24, Washington 20
December 26, 1971, at San Francisco
Attendance: 45,364

San Francisco's defense came up with the big plays, leading to a 24-20 victory against Washington.

The Redskins scored first after Jon Jaqua blocked Steve Spurrier's punt at the San Francisco 28. Washington led 10-3 in the final minute of the first half when Ted Vactor returned a punt 47 yards to the 49ers' 12. But Johnny Fuller blocked Curt Knight's field-goal attempt, and the Redskins led by 7 points at halftime.

Early in the third quarter, the Redskins drove to the 49ers' 11. But on fourth-and-inches, Frank Nunley dropped Larry Brown for a 2-yard loss. Three plays later, John Brodie found Gene Washington for a 78-yard touchdown pass. On the fourth play after the kickoff, Roosevelt Taylor intercepted Billy Kilmer, setting up Brodie's go-ahead touchdown pass to Bob Windsor.

San Francisco put the game away in the fourth quarter when Washington punter Mike Bragg had a poor snap roll through his legs, and 49ers defensive tackle Bob Hoskins recovered in the end zone for a touchdown.

Washington	7	3	3	7	-	20
San Francisco	0	3	14	7	-	24

Was - Smith 5 pass from Kilmer (Knight kick)
SF - FG Gossett 23
SF - FG Knight 40
SF - G. Washington 78 pass from Brodie (Gossett kick)
SF - Windsor 2 pass from Brodie (Gossett kick)
Was - FG Knight 36
SF - Hoskins, fumble recovery in end zone (Gossett kick)
Was - Brown 16 pass from Kilmer (Knight kick)

1971 AFC CHAMPIONSHIP GAME
Miami 21, Baltimore 0
January 2, 1972, at Miami
Attendance: 76,622

The Miami Dolphins, known for their grind-it-out style of attack, used big pass plays to shut down the defending Super Bowl-champion Baltimore Colts 21-0.

Although Dolphins' quarterback Bob Griese threw only 8 passes, he was very effective. The first big play came midway through the first quarter, Griese hit Paul Warfield in full stride, and the Hall-of-Fame receiver turned it into a 75-yard touchdown.

With the score still 7-0 in the third period, the Colts went to the deep game themselves, but Johnny Unitas's pass to an open Eddie Hinton was short. Hinton managed to knock the ball away from cornerback Curtis Johnson, but the tip was intercepted by Dick Anderson, who weaved his way 62 yards for a touchdown.

Any hopes the Colts had for a comeback ended in the fourth quarter when Griese found Warfield again for a 50-yard gain. That pass set up the game's final score, a 5-yard touchdown run by Larry Csonka.

Baltimore	0	0	0	0	-	0
Miami	7	0	7	7	-	21

Mia - Warfield 75 pass from Griese (Yepremian kick)
Mia - Anderson 62 interception return (Yepremian kick)
Mia - Csonka 5 run (Yepremian kick)

1971 NFC CHAMPIONSHIP GAME
Dallas 14, San Francisco 3
January 2, 1972, at Irving, Texas
Attendance: 63,409

Dallas held San Francisco to 9 first downs and intercepted 3 passes by John Brodie, including 1 that led to the game's first touchdown, as the Cowboys won their second consecutive NFL title game over the 49ers 14-3.

In the second quarter, the Cowboys had San Francisco pinned deep in its own territory. Brodie threw a screen pass to fullback Ken Willard, but defensive end George Andrie, who had been hidden from Brodie's view by tackle Len Rohde, stepped in the way, intercepted, and returned it 8 yards to the San Francisco 2. Shortly thereafter, Calvin Hill scored on a 1-yard run to give Dallas a 7-0 lead.

The 49ers cut the margin to 4 points on Bruce Gossett's 28-yard field goal in the fourth quarter, but then Dallas flexed its offensive muscle, driving 80 yards in 14 plays to the clinching score, a 2-yard run by Duane Thomas. On that drive, the Cowboys converted 4 third-down plays, giving them 8 of 14 for the day, compared to the 49ers' 1 of 11 third-down conversions.

San Francisco	0	0	3	0	-	3
Dallas	0	7	0	7	-	14

Dal - Hill 1 run (Clark kick)
SF - FG Gossett 288
Dal - Thomas 2 run (Clark kick)

1972 AFC DIVISIONAL PLAYOFF GAME
Pittsburgh 13, Oakland 7
December 23, 1972, at Pittsburgh
Attendance: 50,327

In perhaps the most fantastic finish ever, Pittsburgh defeated Oakland 13-7 on Franco Harris's touchdown catch that came to be known as the Immaculate Reception.

In a fierce defensive struggle, the first score did not come until Roy Gerela capped a 55-yard drive with an 18-yard field goal in the third quarter. Gerela kicked another field goal, from 29 yards, in the fourth quarter. But then the Raiders started their best drive of the day. From the Pittsburgh 30, Ken Stabler, who had replaced Daryle Lamonica at quarterback, read a Pittsburgh blitz, circled left end, and raced 30 yards untouched for a touchdown and a 7-6 lead with 1:13 left.

In the final seconds, the Steelers faced fourth-and-10 on their own 40. Terry Bradshaw was forced out of the pocket and threw to John (Frenchy) Fuqua, but the pass ricocheted off Oakland's Jack Tatum and was caught by Harris at his shoelaces. Harris raced 42 yards to complete the amazing 60-yard scoring play.

Oakland	0	0	0	7	-	7
Pittsburgh	0	0	3	10	-	13

Pit - FG Gerela 18
Pit - FG Gerela 29
Oak - Stabler 30 run (Blanda kick)
Pit - Harris 60 pass from Bradshaw (Gerela kick)

1972 AFC DIVISIONAL PLAYOFF GAME
Miami 20, Cleveland 14

December 24, 1972, at Miami
Attendance: 80,010

The Dolphins sputtered, but kept alive their hopes for the first unbeaten and untied season in NFL history.

Miami jumped to an early lead when Charlie Babb blocked a punt by Don Cockroft at the 17, picked it up at the 5, and ran it in for a touchdown. The Dolphins still led 13-7 in the fourth quarter when Cleveland started a 90-yard drive. The big play came when Miami's Dick Anderson intercepted Mike Phipps, but fumbled, and the ball was recovered by Fair Hooker. Two plays later, Phipps teamed with Hooker on a 27-yard touchdown pass for a 14-13 lead.

Miami then put together its most impressive drive. Earl Morrall hit Paul Warfield for 15 and 35 yards before a pass-interference penalty gave the Dolphins a first down at the 8. Jim Kiick then powered into the end zone from there for the winning touchdown.

Cleveland	0	0	7	7	-	14
Miami	10	0	0	10	-	20

Mia - Babb 5 blocked punt return (Yepremian kick)
Mia - FG Yepremian 40
Cle - Phipps 5 run (Cockroft kick)
Mia - FG Yepremian 46
Cle - Hooker 27 pass from Phipps (Cockroft kick)
Mia - Kiick 8 run (Yepremian kick)

1972 NFC DIVISIONAL PLAYOFF GAME
Dallas 30, San Francisco 28

December 23, 1972, at San Francisco
Attendance: 61,214

Roger Staubach came off the bench to lead Dallas to 17 points in the fourth quarter as the Cowboys eliminated San Francisco from the playoffs for the third year in a row 30-28.

The 49ers jumped to a quick lead when Vic Washington returned the game's opening kickoff 97 yards for a touchdown. A fumble by Dallas quarterback Craig Morton and an interception by Skip Vanderbundt led to 1-yard touchdown runs by Larry Schreiber that gave San Francisco a 21-3 lead. The Cowboys pulled within 8 points by halftime, but Schreiber's third 1-yard touchdown run of the day came in the third quarter and increased the 49ers' advantage to 28-13.

Enter Staubach. First, he led the Cowboys 60 yards to a field goal. Then, with less than two minutes left in the game, he drove Dallas 55 yards, passing 20 yards to Billy Parks for a touchdown that cut the deficit to 28-23. And, after Mel Renfro recovered an onside kick, Staubach ran for 21 yards, passed 19 yards to Parks, and found Ron Sellers for 10 yards and the winning touchdown with 52 seconds remaining.

Dallas	3	10	0	17	-	30
San Francisco	7	14	7	0	-	28

SF - V. Washington 97 kickoff return (Gossett kick)
Dal - FG Fritsch 37
SF - Schreiber 1 run (Gossett kick)
SF - Schreiber 1 run (Gossett kick)
Dal - FG Fritsch 45
Dal - Alworth 28 pass from Morton (Fritsch kick)
SF - Schreiber 1 run (Gossett kick)
Dal - FG Fritsch 27
Dal - Parks 20 pass from Staubach (Fritsch kick)
Dal - Sellers 10 pass from Staubach (Fritsch kick)

1972 NFC DIVISIONAL PLAYOFF GAME
Washington 16, Green Bay 3

December 24, 1972, at Washington
Attendance: 53,140

A five-man defensive line shut down the Packers' powerful running game, and Curt Knight kicked 3 field goals as Washington defeated Green Bay 16-3. John Brockington, the Packers' star running back, was held to 9 yards on 13 carries.

The Green Bay Packers scored first when Chester Marcol capped a 60-yard drive with a 17-yard field goal late in the second quarter. But the Redskins came right back. Billy Kilmer threw a 32-yard touchdown pass over the middle to Roy Jefferson. A short punt put Knight in range for a 42-yard field goal 33 seconds before halftime.

Tough defense and the outstanding punting of Mike Bragg kept the Packers contained throughout the second half, and Knight kicked 2 more field goals to shut the door on any hopes for a Green Bay comeback.

Green Bay	0	3	0	0	-	3
Washington	0	10	0	6	-	16

GB - FG Marcol 17
Was - Jefferson 32 pass from Kilmer (Knight kick)
Was - FG Knight 42
Was - FG Knight 35
Was - FG Knight 46

1972 AFC CHAMPIONSHIP GAME
Miami 21, Pittsburgh 17

December 31, 1972, at Pittsburgh
Attendance: 50,845

Miami quarterback Bob Griese, sidelined since the fifth game of the season with a broken ankle, came off the bench in the second half and directed 2 touchdown drives to lead the Dolphins to a 21-17 victory over the Steelers.

Pittsburgh took the lead in the first quarter. Steelers quarterback Terry Bradshaw fumbled into the end zone, and the ball was recovered by tackle Gerry Mullins for a touchdown. The hit on Bradshaw knocked him out of the game.

In the second quarter, the Dolphins evened the score after a big special-teams play. With the ball at the Pittsburgh 49, punter Larry Seiple took off on a fake punt, gaining 37 yards to the Pittsburgh 12. Shortly thereafter, Earl Morrall found Larry Csonka with a 9-yard touchdown pass.

A short field goal by Roy Gerela put Pittsburgh ahead in the third quarter, but Griese teamed with Paul Warfield on a 52-yard pass that set up Jim Kiick's 2-yard touchdown run. Then Griese led a 49-yard drive that culminated in a 3-yard scoring run by Kiick. Bradshaw came back late in the game to throw a touchdown pass, but he also was intercepted twice.

Miami	0	7	7	7	-	21
Pittsburgh	7	0	3	7	-	17

Pit - Mullins fumble recovery in end zone (Gerela kick)
Mia - Csonka 9 pass from Morrall (Yepremian kick)
Pit - FG Gerela 14

Mia - Kiick 2 run (Yepremian kick)
Mia - Kiick 3 run (Yepremian kick)
Pit - Young 12 pass from Bradshaw (Gerela kick)

1972 NFC CHAMPIONSHIP GAME
Washington 26, Dallas 3

December 31, 1972, at Washington
Attendance: 53,129

Charley Taylor caught 2 touchdown passes and Washington's defense did not allow Dallas beyond midfield in the second half as the Redskins qualified for their first Super Bowl with a 26-3 victory.

Washington coach George Allen had one goal for his offense and one for his defense, and both worked to perfection. Defensively, the Redskins wanted to pressure Cowboys quarterback Roger Staubach, who had missed nearly the entire season with an injury before coming off the bench the week before against San Francisco. Staubach managed 59 yards on scrambles against the pressure defense, but he also was sacked for 25 yards in losses and passed for only 73 yards.

Offensively, the Redskins thought they could take advantage of the Cowboys' left cornerback position with Taylor. In the first quarter, Taylor beat Charlie Waters for 51 yards, then scored a touchdown on a 15-yard catch. When Waters suffered a broken arm, Taylor continued his performance against Mark Washington, scoring on a 45-yard reception in the fourth quarter. Sixteen points in the final period—on Taylor's touchdown catch and 3 field goals by Curt Knight—broke open a close game.

Dallas	0	3	0	0	-	3
Washington	0	10	0	16	-	26

Was - FG Knight 18
Was - Taylor 15 pass from Kilmer (Knight kick)
Dal - FG Fritsch 35
Was - Taylor 45 from Kilmer (Knight kick)
Was - FG Knight 39
Was - FG Knight 46
Was - FG Knight 45

1973 AFC DIVISIONAL PLAYOFF GAME
Oakland 33, Pittsburgh 14

December 22, 1973, at Oakland
Attendance: 51,110

Oakland used a powerful running attack and a controlled passing game to dominate the Pittsburgh Steelers 33-14. The Raiders drove 82, 60, 68, 57, 62, and 58 yards for scores.

Oakland took 16 plays in the first quarter to move to Marv Hubbard's 1-yard touchdown run off left tackle. Early in the second period, the Raiders increased the lead to 10 points, but Terry Bradshaw finished off a Pittsburgh drive with a touchdown pass to Barry Pearson that made the score 10-7 at halftime.

The Raiders put together three long, time-consuming drives that ended in field goals in the second half, but the big play came when cornerback Willie Brown intercepted Bradshaw's pass and raced 54 yards down the sideline for a touchdown. Bradshaw's fourth-quarter touchdown pass was offset by another 1-yard scoring plunge by Hubbard.

Pittsburgh	0	7	0	7	-	14
Oakland	7	3	13	10	-	33

Oak - Hubbard 1 run (Blanda kick)
Oak - FG Blanda 25
Pit - B. Pearson 4 pass from Bradshaw (Gerela kick)
Oak - FG Blanda 31
Oak - FG Blanda 22
Oak - W. Brown 54 interception return (Blanda kick)
Oak - FG Blanda 10
Pit - Lewis 26 pass from Bradshaw (Gerela kick)
Oak - Hubbard 1 run (Blanda kick)

1973 AFC DIVISIONAL PLAYOFF GAME
Miami 34, Cincinnati 16

December 23, 1973, at Miami
Attendance: 74,770

The Miami Dolphins made it look easy, slicing through the Cincinnati Bengals on touchdown drives of 80, 80, and 75 yards on three of their first four possessions en route to a 34-16 victory.

On their first possession, the Dolphins put together a 10-play drive capped by Bob Griese's 13-yard touchdown pass to Paul Warfield. After the Bengals retaliated with a field goal, the Dolphins came right back with a 12-play drive capped by Larry Csonka's 1-yard scoring burst. Another drive was finished off by Eugene (Mercury) Morris's 4-yard touchdown run.

Neal Craig's 45-yard interception return and 2 field goals pulled the Bengals within 21-16 at halftime. But the Dolphins drove to a touchdown and a field goal the first two times they had the ball in the second half to secure the victory.

Cincinnati	3	13	0	0	-	16
Miami	14	7	10	3	-	34

Mia - Warfield 13 pass from Griese (Yepremian kick)
Cin - FG Muhlmann 24
Mia - Csonka 1 run (Yepremian kick)
Mia - Morris 4 run (Yepremian kick)
Cin - Craig 45 interception return (Muhlmann kick)
Cin - FG Muhlmann 46
Cin - FG Muhlmann 10
Mia - Mandich 7 pass from Griese (Yepremian kick)
Mia - FG Yepremian 50
Mia - FG Yepremian 46

1973 NFC DIVISIONAL PLAYOFF GAME
Minnesota 27, Washington 20

December 22, 1973, at Bloomington
Attendance: 45,475

The Vikings awoke from their slumber when defensive end Carl Eller went into a frenzy at halftime, smashing the team's chalkboard. The result was a 27-20 victory.

Washington led 7-3 after a sloppy Minnesota first half. The Redskins' touchdown came on a 3-yard run by Larry Brown after Bob Brunet recovered Bobby Bryant's fumbled punt at the Minnesota 21. With a chance to take the lead in the closing moments of the first half, the Vikings were stymied when Fran Tarkenton threw an interception.

But the Vikings drove 79 yards to start the third quarter, with a 46-yard run by Oscar Reed preceding Bill Brown's short touchdown run. Then, after the Redskins retook the lead on 2 field goals, Tarkenton capped a 71-yard drive with a 28-yard touchdown pass to John Gilliam. Nate Wright intercepted Billy Kilmer on the first play after the kickoff, following which Tarkenton again teamed with Gilliam for a touchdown.

Washington	0	7	3	10	-	20
Minnesota	0	3	7	17	-	27

Min - FG Cox 19
Was - L. Brown 3 run (Knight kick)
Min - B. Brown 2 run (Cox kick)
Was - FG Knight 52
Was - FG Knight 42
Min - Gilliam 28 pass from Tarkenton (Cox kick)
Min - Gilliam 8 pass from Tarkenton (Cox kick)
Was - Jefferson 28 pass from Kilmer (Knight kick)
Min - FG Cox 30

1973 NFC DIVISIONAL PLAYOFF GAME
Dallas 27, Los Angeles Rams 16

December 23, 1973, at Irving, Texas
Attendance: 64,291

Turnovers by the Rams on their first two plays of the game gave Dallas a 14-0 lead, and the Cowboys went on to win 27-16.

On the game's first play from scrimmage, Lee Roy Jordan intercepted John Hadl; Calvin Hill gave Dallas a 7-0 lead with a 3-yard touchdown run. When Lawrence McCutcheon fumbled on the first play after the ensuing kickoff, Mel Renfro recovered, and the Cowboys built their lead to 14 points when Roger Staubach found Drew Pearson with a 4-yard touchdown pass.

David Ray kept the Rams in the game with 3 field goals. Then, in the fourth quarter, Hill fumbled and Fred Dryer recovered at the Dallas 17. Two plays later, Tony Baker blasted into the end zone to make the score 17-16.

But on third-and-14 on Dallas's next possession, Staubach went deep to Pearson, who caught the ball between Steve Preece and Eddie McMillan and raced away to complete an 83-yard touchdown play.

L.A. Rams	0	6	0	10	-	16
Dallas	14	3	0	10	-	27

Dal - Hill 3 run (Fritsch kick)
Dal - Pearson 4 pass from Staubach (Fritsch kick)
Dal - FG Fritsch 39
Rams - FG Ray 33
Rams - FG Ray 37
Rams - FG Ray 40
Rams - Baker 5 run (Ray kick)
Dal - Pearson 83 pass from Staubach (Fritsch kick)
Dal - FG Fritsch 12

1973 AFC CHAMPIONSHIP GAME
Miami 27, Oakland 10

December 30, 1973, at Miami
Attendance: 74,384

Miami controlled the game on the ground and Larry Csonka ran for 117 yards and scored 3 touchdowns as the Dolphins won their third consecutive AFC title with a 27-10 victory over Oakland.

The Dolphins scored the first time they had the ball when Csonka ran 11 yards for a touchdown one play after Bob Griese scrambled 27 yards. Griese finished the day with 39 yards rushing but only 34 passing on 6 attempts. Csonka scored again late in the first half, when his 2-yard run capped a 63-yard drive.

The Raiders, who had had their only threat of the first half stymied by a holding penalty, finally scored in the third quarter on a 21-yard field goal by George Blanda. Then they cut the lead to 17-10 when Ken Stabler found Mike Siani with a 25-yard touchdown pass.

Late in the game, after Miami had driven to a second field goal by Garo Yepremian, the Raiders were stopped on fourth-and-inches, and the Dolphins marched to Csonka's third touchdown, which clinched the game.

Oakland	0	0	10	0	-	10
Miami	7	7	3	10	-	27

Mia - Csonka 11 run (Yepremian kick)
Mia - Csonka 2 run (Yepremian kick)
Oak - FG Blanda 21
Mia - FG Yepremian 42
Oak - Siani 25 pass from Stabler (Blanda kick)
Mia - FG Yepremian 26
Mia - Csonka 2 run (Yepremian kick)

1973 NFC CHAMPIONSHIP GAME
Minnesota 27, Dallas 10

December 30, 1973, at Irving, Texas
Attendance: 59,688

Two key Dallas players—running back Calvin Hill and defensive tackle Bob Lilly—couldn't play, and the result was that the Cowboys could neither run effectively nor stop the Vikings from pounding up the middle. Minnesota won easily 27-10.

Minnesota led at the half 10-0, the only touchdown coming when Chuck Foreman ran 5 yards to cap an 86-yard drive, most of which came on runs up the middle. The Cowboys, meanwhile, could get nothing going offensively as Roger Staubach threw 4 interceptions.

In the third quarter, the Cowboys finally scored when Golden Richards returned a punt 63 yards for a touchdown. But the Vikings came right back, with Fran Tarkenton finding John Gilliam open behind Mel Renfro for a 54-yard touchdown pass.

In the fourth quarter, 2 interceptions knocked the Cowboys out. After Dallas had narrowed the deficit to 17-10, Bobby Bryant returned one interception 63 yards for a touchdown. Another interception set up a 34-yard field goal by Fred Cox. Walt Garrison concluded a forgettable day for the Cowboys by fumbling the ball away at the Minnesota 2 late in the game.

Minnesota	3	7	7	10	-	27
Dallas	0	0	10	0	-	10

Min - FG Cox 44
Min - Foreman 5 run (Cox kick)
Dal - Richards 63 punt return (Fritsch kick)
Min - Gilliam 54 pass from Tarkenton (Cox kick)
Dal - FG Fritsch 17
Min - Bryant 63 interception return (Cox kick)
Min - FG Cox 34

1974 AFC DIVISIONAL PLAYOFF GAME
Oakland 28, Miami 26

December 21, 1974, at Oakland
Attendance: 53,023

The Raiders dethroned the two-time defending Super Bowl-champion Dolphins 28-26 as Ken Stabler threw 4 touchdown passes, the last to triple-teamed Clarence Davis with 26 seconds remaining as Stabler was about to be sacked.

The game was marked by almost non-stop excitement, beginning on the opening kickoff, which Nat Moore returned 89 yards for a touchdown.

A field goal early in the fourth quarter gave Miami a 19-

14 lead, but Stabler took the Raiders 83 yards in only 2 plays to take the lead. From the 28, Stabler threw long for Cliff Branch, who made a diving catch at the Miami 27, got to his feet before any defenders could reach him, and sped off for a touchdown.

Miami came right back, going 68 yards in 4 plays, with Benny Malone sweeping right end for the 23 yards and a touchdown with 2:08 to play. But in a minute-and-a-half, Stabler converted two third-down plays while driving the Raiders to the winning touchdown.

Miami	7	3	6	10	-	26
Oakland	0	7	7	14	-	28

Mia - N. Moore 89 kickoff return (Yepremian kick)
Oak - C. Smith 31 pass from Stabler (Blanda kick)
Mia - FG Yepremian 33
Oak - Biletnikoff 13 pass from Stabler (Blanda kick)
Mia - Warfield 16 pass from Griese (kick failed)
Mia - FG Yepremian 46
Oak - Branch 72 pass from Stabler (Blanda kick)
Mia - Malone 23 run (Yepremian kick)
Oak - Davis 8 pass from Stabler (Blanda kick)

1974 AFC DIVISIONAL PLAYOFF GAME
Pittsburgh 32, Buffalo 14

December 22, 1974, at Pittsburgh
Attendance: 48,321

Franco Harris scored 3 touchdowns in 4:52 of the second quarter as Pittsburgh easily defeated the wild-card Bills 32-14.

The two sides alternated scoring before Harris took over. Pittsburgh went ahead on its first possession with a field goal by Roy Gerela. Buffalo responded with a 56-yard drive that ended with Joe Ferguson's 22-yard touchdown pass to tight end Paul Seymour. The Steelers quickly came back with a 63-yard march resulting in a 27-yard touchdown pass from Terry Bradshaw to running back Rocky Bleier.

The next time the Steelers had the ball, they drove 66 yards to Harris's first touchdown, a 1-yard run. On the first play after the kickoff, Jack Ham recovered Jim Braxton's fumble, setting up Harris's 4-yard touchdown run. And after holding the Bills following the kickoff, the Steelers took over at their 46 and raced downfield, with Harris scoring from the 1 only 16 seconds before the half.

Buffalo	7	0	7	0	-	14
Pittsburgh	3	26	0	3	-	32

Pit - FG Gerela 21
Buf - Seymour 22 pass from Ferguson (Leypoldt kick)
Pit - Bleier 27 pass from Bradshaw (kick blocked)
Pit - Harris 1 run (Gerela kick)
Pit - Harris 4 run (kick blocked)
Pit - Harris 1 run (Gerela kick)
Buf - Simpson 3 pass from Ferguson (Leypoldt kick)
Pit - FG Gerela 22

1974 NFC DIVISIONAL PLAYOFF GAME
Minnesota 30, St. Louis 14

December 21, 1974, at Bloomington
Attendance: 44,626

The Vikings scored 16 points in less than 7 minutes of the third quarter as they put away St. Louis 30-14 after the Cardinals had dominated play in the first half.

The Cardinals missed several opportunities in a first half that ended 7-7. In the second quarter, they had a third-and-1 deep in Minnesota territory, only to come up short on 2 running plays. Then, with 3 seconds left in the half, Jim Bakken missed a 23-yard field goal.

On the opening drive of the second half, Jeff Wright intercepted a pass, and 5 plays later Fred Cox put Minnesota ahead 10-7. Two plays later, Terry Metcalf fumbled and Nate Wright picked up the ball and ran 20 yards for a touchdown. After Minnesota held St. Louis on the next series, Fran Tarkenton hit John Gilliam with a 38-yard touchdown pass that finished off the Cardinals.

St. Louis	0	7	0	7	-	14
Minnesota	0	7	16	7	-	30

StL - Thomas 13 pass from Hart (Bakken kick)
Min - Gilliam 16 pass from Tarkenton (Cox kick)
Min - FG Cox 37
Min - N. Wright 20 fumble return (Cox kick)
Min - Gilliam 38 pass from Tarkenton (kick failed)
Min - Foreman 4 run (Cox kick)
StL - Metcalf 11 run (Bakken kick)

1974 NFC DIVISIONAL PLAYOFF GAME
Los Angeles Rams 19, Washington 10

December 22, 1974, at Los Angeles
Attendance: 80,118

With the game on the line, Los Angeles defensive tackle Merlin Olsen put heavy pressure on Sonny Jurgensen, who underthrew his receiver. Linebacker Isiah Robertson intercepted and returned it 59 yards for the clinching touchdown as the Rams defeated the Redskins 19-10.

The Rams went ahead on their opening possession, with James Harris completing 4 of 4 passes for 60 yards, including a 10-yard touchdown pass to tight end Bob Klein. But the Redskins came back to lead at halftime. First, Billy Kilmer passed to Charley Taylor for 41 yards to set up Mike Bragg's 35-yard field goal. Then, Pat Fischer intercepted Harris and returned the ball 40 yards to help set up a 1-yard touchdown run by Moses Denson.

Two field goals by David Ray put the Rams ahead 13-10, and Robertson's fourth-quarter interception sealed the victory.

Washington	3	7	0	0	-	10
L.A. Rams	7	0	3	9	-	19

Rams - Klein 10 pass from Harris (Ray kick)
Was - FG Bragg 35
Was - Denson 1 run (Bragg kick)
Rams - FG Ray 37
Rams - FG Ray 26
Rams - Robertson 59 interception return (pass failed)

1974 AFC CHAMPIONSHIP GAME
Pittsburgh 24, Oakland 13

December 29, 1974, at Oakland
Attendance: 53,023

The Steelers scored 3 touchdowns in the fourth quarter to break open a game in which they trailed 10-3 after three periods, and won its first-ever title game 24-13.

The game was tied 3-3 at halftime. In the third quarter, the Raiders went ahead on a 38-yard touchdown pass from Ken Stabler to Cliff Branch. Early in the final period, the Steelers tied the game 10-10 on Franco Harris's 8-yard run. Then the defense took over, as linebacker Jack Ham intercepted a pass by Stabler, and Pittsburgh converted it into a 6-yard touchdown pass from Terry Bradshaw to

Lynn Swann. Oakland had a chance to tie the score again, but, on third-and-6 at the Pittsburgh 12, Stabler had to throw the ball away under heavy pressure. The Raiders settled for a 24-yard field by George Blanda.

As the game wound down, the Steelers drove to the clinching touchdown, a 21-yard run by Harris. By contrast, the Raiders netted only 29 yards rushing.

Pittsburgh	0	3	0	21	-	24
Oakland	3	0	7	3	-	13

Oak - FG Blanda 40
Pit - FG Gerela 23
Oak - Branch 38 pass from Stabler (Blanda kick)
Pit - Harris 8 run (Gerela kick)
Pit - Swann 6 pass from Bradshaw (Gerela kick)
Oak - FG Blanda 24
Pit - Harris 21 run (Gerela kick)

1974 NFC CHAMPIONSHIP GAME
Minnesota 14, Los Angeles Rams 10

December 29, 1974, at Bloomington
Attendance: 48,444

The Vikings returned to their third Super Bowl in six years after holding off the Rams. The Vikings scored in the second quarter when Fran Tarkenton found Jim Lash for a 29-yard touchdown pass. The Rams responded with a 27-yard field goal by David Ray.

In the third quarter, the Rams took over at their 1 after Mike Eischeid got off a superb punt. They moved to their 25, and then James Harris completed a pass to Harold Jackson, who went 73 yards before safety Jeff Wright knocked him out of bounds at the Vikings' 2. On second down at the 1, left guard Tom Mack was called for illegal motion, and the ball was moved back to the 6. Harris ran for 4 yards to the 2, but on third down, his pass for tight end Pat Curran was intercepted in the end zone by linebacker Wally Hilgenberg. The Vikings took over at their 20, and in 15 plays, they marched to Dave Osborn's 4-yard touchdown run.

The Rams came back with a 44-yard touchdown pass from Harris to Jackson, but the Vikings ran out the final 5:37 of the game.

LA Rams	0	3	0	7	-	10
Minnesota	0	7	0	7	-	14

Min - Lash 29 pass from Tarkenton (Cox kick)
Rams - FG Ray 27
Min - Osborn 4 run (Cox kick)
Rams - Jackson 44 pass from Harris (Ray kick)

1975 AFC DIVISIONAL PLAYOFF GAME
Pittsburgh 28, Baltimore 10

December 27, 1975, at Pittsburgh
Attendance: 49,053

The Steel Curtain totally dominated the Baltimore offense, scoring once, setting up 2 other scores, recording 5 sacks, forcing 4 turnovers, and holding the Colts to 154 yards as the Steelers won 28-10.

The Steelers' defense made its presence felt early, when Jack Ham intercepted a Marty Domres pass to set up Franco Harris's 8-yard touchdown run. The Colts' defense returned the favor when Lloyd Mumphord's 58-yard interception return set up a touchdown pass from Domres to Glenn Doughty. After Baltimore went ahead in the third quarter, the Steelers' defense took over. Mel Blount intercepted Domres and returned the ball to the 7, from where Rocky Bleier scored.

In the fourth quarter, a short Baltimore punt set up a touchdown run by Terry Bradshaw, and, when Baltimore responded by driving deep into Pittsburgh territory, Ham knocked the ball loose from Bert Jones. Andy Russell picked it up and rambled 93 yards for a touchdown.

Baltimore	0	7	3	0	-	10
Pittsburgh	7	0	7	14	-	28

Pit - Harris 8 run (Gerela kick)
Bal - Doughty 5 pass from Domres (Linhart kick)
Bal - FG Linhart 21
Pit - Bleier 7 run (Gerela kick)
Pit - Bradshaw 2 run (Gerela kick)
Pit - Russell 93 fumble return (Gerela kick)

1975 AFC DIVISIONAL PLAYOFF GAME
Oakland 31, Cincinnati 28

December 28, 1975, at Oakland
Attendance: 53,039

The Oakland Raiders jumped to a 31-14 lead, then barely held off a Cincinnati Bengals' comeback 31-28. Ken Stabler led a virtually unstoppable offense in the first half, throwing 2 touchdown passes and setting up a 27-yard field goal by George Blanda. On the Raiders' other possessions, Blanda missed 1 field-goal attempt and had another blocked.

The Raiders continued their domination in the third quarter, scoring the first time they had the ball for a 24-7 lead. Then, after a 91-yard touchdown drive cut the Oakland lead to 10 points, Stabler threw his third touchdown pass of the day, 2 yards to Dave Casper.

With 10 minutes left, Ken Riley intercepted Stabler, leading to a touchdown pass from Ken Anderson to Charlie Joiner. After Oakland punted, Anderson cut the lead to 3 points with another touchdown strike. A fumble by Pete Banaszak gave Cincinnati its final chance, but the Raiders' defense held.

Cincinnati	0	7	7	14	-	28
Oakland	3	14	7	7	-	31

Oak - FG Blanda 27
Oak - Siani 9 pass from Stabler (Blanda kick)
Cin - Fritts 1 run (Green kick)
Oak - Moore 8 pass from Stabler (Blanda kick)
Oak - Banaszak 6 run (Blanda kick)
Cin - Elliott 6 run (Green kick)
Oak - Casper 2 pass from Stabler (Blanda kick)
Cin - Joiner 25 pass from Anderson (Green kick)
Cin - Curtis 14 pass from Anderson (Green kick)

1975 NFC DIVISIONAL PLAYOFF GAME
Los Angeles Rams 35, St. Louis 23

December 27, 1975, at Los Angeles
Attendance: 72,650

Lawrence McCutcheon set NFC playoff records with 37 carries for 202 yards rushing, and the Los Angeles defense scored 2 touchdowns in the first 16 minutes as the Rams defeated the Cardinals 35-23.

The Rams led from the beginning, taking the opening kickoff and driving 79 yards in 13 plays to quarterback Ron Jaworski's 5-yard scoring run. On the second play after the kickoff, defensive end Jack Youngblood intercepted a pass from Jim Hart and returned it 47 yards for a touchdown.

The Rams increased their lead on the first play of the second quarter, when safety Bill Simpson returned an interception 65 yards for a touchdown. St. Louis came back with a touchdown of its own, but the Rams immediately asserted themselves, blocking the extra point and then, on the first play after the kickoff, scoring on a 66-yard pass from Jaworski to Harold Jackson.

St. Louis	0	9	7	7	-	23
L.A. Rams	14	14	0	7	-	35

Rams - Jaworski 5 run (Dempsey kick)
Rams - Jack Youngblood 47 interception return (Dempsey kick)
Rams - Simpson 65 interception return (Dempsey kick)
StL - Otis 3 run (kick blocked)
Rams - H. Jackson 66 pass from Jaworski (Dempsey kick)
StL - FG Bakken 39
StL - Gray 11 pass from Hart (Bakken kick)
Rams - Jessie 2 fumble return (Dempsey kick)
StL - Jones 3 run (Bakken kick)

1975 NFC DIVISIONAL PLAYOFF GAME
Dallas 17, Minnesota 14

December 28, 1975, at Bloomington
Attendance: 46,425

Roger Staubach completed a 50-yard touchdown pass to Drew Pearson with 24 seconds left as Dallas defeated Minnesota 17-14 on a miracle play that has become known as the Hail Mary.

Despite outgaining the Vikings 158-78, the Cowboys trailed 7-0 at the intermission. Minnesota had scored on a 1-yard run by Chuck Foreman after a punt hit Cliff Harris, and Fred McNeill recovered for Minnesota at the Dallas 4.

The Cowboys went ahead by scoring on their first two possessions of the second half. But with five minutes left, Minnesota regained the lead with a 70-yard touchdown drive.

Dallas took over on its 15 with 1:51 remaining. On third-and-1, Staubach completed a pass to Pearson for 7 yards. Then, on fourth-and-16, he found Pearson at midfield for another first down. Finally, with a desperation heave, Staubach connected with Pearson again at the 5, and the receiver scored.

Dallas	0	0	7	10	-	17
Minnesota	0	7	0	7	-	14

Min - Foreman 1 run (Cox kick)
Dal - Dennison 4 run (Fritsch kick)
Dal - FG Fritsch 24
Min - McClanahan 1 run (Cox kick)
Dal - D. Pearson 50 pass from Staubach (Fritsch kick)

1975 AFC CHAMPIONSHIP GAME
Pittsburgh 16, Oakland 10

January 4, 1976, at Pittsburgh
Attendance: 50,609

A three-quarter defensive struggle turned into an offensive slugfest in the final period as the Steelers won their second consecutive AFC title with a 16-10 victory over the Raiders.

For 45 minutes neither team could move consistently on the icy field, with the only score being a 36-yard field goal by Roy Gerela. Then, in a span of 6 minutes, the two teams scored 3 times. First, Franco Harris broke through the Oakland defense, racing 25 yards for a touchdown. The Raiders came right back, with Ken Stabler concluding a drive with a 14-yard touchdown pass to Mike Siani. Finally, Terry Bradshaw connected with John Stallworth for a 20-yard touchdown.

The Raiders drove down the field again and, with 17 seconds left, had a third-and-2 at the Pittsburgh 24. Forty-eight-year-old George Blanda kicked a 41-yard field goal to cut the lead to 6 points. Marv Hubbard of the Raiders then recovered an onside kick with 7 seconds remaining. Stabler completed a pass to Cliff Branch for a 37-yard gain to the Pittsburgh 15, but the clock ran out before the wide receiver could get out of bounds.

Oakland	0	0	0	10	-	10
Pittsburgh	0	3	0	13	-	16

Pit - FG Gerela 36
Pit - Harris 25 run (Gerela kick)
Oak - Siani 14 pass from Stabler (Blanda kick)
Pit - Stallworth 20 pass from Bradshaw (kick failed)
Oak - FG Blanda 41

1975 NFC CHAMPIONSHIP GAME
Dallas 37, Los Angeles Rams 7

January 4, 1976, at Los Angeles
Attendance: 88,919

Roger Staubach threw 4 touchdown passes, including 3 to running back Preston Pearson, and the wild-card Cowboys shocked the favored Rams 37-7.

The Cowboys led from the start. Linebacker D.D. Lewis intercepted the first pass of the day by James Harris, and, on first down, Staubach threw a short pass to Pearson, who dashed 18 yards through the Rams' defenders to score. After Staubach teamed with Golden Richards for a touchdown in the second period, Staubach found Pearson again, this time from 15 yards for a touchdown with 54 seconds remaining in the half to put Dallas ahead 21-0. The Rams' only threats of the first half ended in a missed field-goal attempt and a blocked field-goal try.

The Cowboys continued their relentless pressure in the third quarter, driving 69 yards to a touchdown on their first possession. Staubach hit Pearson 2 yards deep in the backfield, and the running back weaved his way through the Rams for a 19-yard touchdown. A short touchdown run by John Cappelletti in the fourth quarter allowed the Rams to avoid their first home-field shutout in 30 years.

Dallas	7	14	13	3	-	37
L.A. Rams	0	0	0	7	-	7

Dal - P. Pearson 18 pass from Staubach (Fritsch kick)
Dal - Richards 4 pass from Staubach (Fritsch kick)
Dal - P. Pearson 15 pass from Staubach (Fritsch kick)
Dal - P. Pearson 19 pass from Staubach (Fritsch kick)
Dal - FG Fritsch 40
Dal - FG Fritsch 26
Rams - Cappelletti 1 run (Dempsey kick)
Dal - FG Fritsch 26

1976 AFC DIVISIONAL PLAYOFF GAME
Oakland 24, New England 21

December 18, 1976, at Oakland
Attendance: 53,045

In a game marked by numerous significant penalties, Ken Stabler rolled left from the 1 and dived into the end zone with 10 seconds left to give Oakland a 24-21 victory against New England.

The Patriots took an early lead after an 86-yard touchdown drive, but the Raiders went ahead 10-7 with 39 seconds left in the first half on a 31-yard touchdown pass from Stabler to Fred Biletnikoff, who made a leaping, one-handed catch.

The Patriots regained the lead with 2 touchdown drives in the third quarter, each of which was aided by an Oakland penalty on fourth down. With the score 21-17 late in the game, the Patriots were moving toward the clinching touchdown, but an illegal motion penalty stopped their drive.

The Raiders then drove 68 yards to Stabler's winning touchdown, assisted by 2 penalties, including 1 for roughing the passer following an incomplete pass on third-and-long.

New England	7	0	14	0	-	21
Oakland	3	7	0	14	-	24

NE - A. Johnson 1 run (Smith kick)
Oak - FG Mann 40
Oak - Biletnikoff 31 pass from Stabler (Mann kick)
NE - Francis 26 pass from Grogan (Smith kick)
NE - Phillips 3 run (Smith kick)
Oak - van Eeghen 1 run (Mann kick)
Oak - Stabler 1 run (Mann kick)

1976 AFC DIVISIONAL PLAYOFF GAME
Pittsburgh 40, Baltimore 14

December 19, 1976, at Baltimore
Attendance: 60,020

The Pittsburgh Steelers flexed their muscles to gain a divisional playoff record 526 yards while rolling to an easy 40-14 victory against the Colts, whom the Steel Curtain held to 170 yards.

Pittsburgh dominated from the start. On the game's first possession, faced with a third-and-8 at the Pittsburgh 24, Terry Bradshaw saw the Colts rotate their double coverage to Lynn Swann. Bradshaw immediately went deep to Frank Lewis, who caught a 76-yard touchdown pass.

Late in the first quarter, Bert Jones drove the Colts 69 yards to a touchdown to cut the Steelers' lead to 9-7, but Pittsburgh responded with a sparkling second quarter. The Steelers drove 68 and 54 yards for touchdowns and, following Glen Edwards's interception, Ray Gerela kicked a 25-yard field goal with 7 seconds left in the first half to make the score 26-7.

Pittsburgh	9	17	0	14	-	40
Baltimore	7	0	0	7	-	14

Pit - Lewis 76 pass from Bradshaw (kick failed)
Pit - FG Gerela 45
Bal - Carr 17 pass from Jones (Linhart kick)
Pit - Harrison 1 run (Gerela kick)
Pit - Swann 29 pass from Bradshaw (Gerela kick)
Pit - FG Gerela 25
Pit - Swann 11 pass from Bradshaw (Gerela kick)
Bal - Leaks 1 run (Linhart kick)
Pit - Harrison 9 run (Mansfield kick)

1976 NFC DIVISIONAL PLAYOFF GAME
Minnesota 35, Washington 20

December 18, 1976, at Bloomington
Attendance: 47,221

Chuck Foreman and Brent McClanahan each rushed for more than 100 yards as Minnesota dominated the Redskins while building a 35-6 lead, then coasting to a 35-20 victory.

On the first scrimmage play, McClanahan rumbled 41 yards. Three plays later, Fran Tarkenton threw short to tight end Stu Voigt, who ran over two tacklers on his way to an 18-yard touchdown.

With a 7-3 lead late in the first quarter, the Vikings had a third-and-9 at the Washington 27. Tarkenton threw to Sammy White, who, despite Ken Houston's deflection of the pass, somehow grabbed it, juggled it as he fell, maintained possession, and rolled into the end zone.

Minnesota's dominating drives of 66, 51, and 76 yards in the second and third periods ended Redskins' hopes.

Washington	3	0	3	14	-	20
Minnesota	14	7	14	0	-	35

Min - Voigt 18 pass from Tarkenton (Cox kick)
Was - FG Moseley 47
Min - White 27 pass from Tarkenton (Cox kick)
Min - Foreman 2 run (Cox kick)
Min - Foreman 30 run (Cox kick)
Was - FG Moseley 35
Min - White 9 pass from Tarkenton (Cox kick)
Was - Grant 12 pass from Kilmer (Moseley kick)
Was - Jefferson 3 pass from Kilmer (Moseley kick)

1976 NFC DIVISIONAL PLAYOFF GAME
Los Angeles Rams 14, Dallas 12

December 19, 1976, at Irving, Texas
Attendance: 62,436

The Los Angeles Rams overcame a series of breakdowns in their punting game to edge the Cowboys, 14-12. Late in the first half, with Dallas trailing 7-3, Charlie Waters blocked a punt by Rusty Jackson, and the Cowboys turned it into a 10-7 lead.

Early in the fourth quarter, on fourth-and-5 at the 18, Tom Dempsey kicked a field goal to tie the score 10-10. However, Cliff Harris was penalized for running into the kicker, and the Rams took the first down. With a third-and-goal at the 1, Lawrence McCutcheon ran through Thomas Henderson's tackle for a 14-10 lead.

With less than two minutes to go, Waters again blocked a punt by Jackson. On first down at the 17, Roger Staubach hit Butch Johnson, who could get only one foot in bounds as he came down in the end zone. Los Angeles eventually took over on downs, and then, on fourth down with four seconds left, Jackson took a snap in the end zone and ran to the right sideline, giving the Cowboys a safety, but ending the game.

L.A. Rams	0	7	0	7	-	14
Dallas	3	7	0	2	-	12

Dal - FG Herrera 44
Rams - Haden 4 run (Dempsey kick)
Dal - Laidlaw 1 run (Herrera kick)
Rams - McCutcheon 1 run (Dempsey kick)
Dal - Safety, R. Jackson ran out of end zone

1976 AFC CHAMPIONSHIP GAME
Oakland 24, Pittsburgh 7

December 26, 1976, at Oakland
Attendance: 53,739

The Raiders shut down the Steelers' ground game— which

was missing Franco Harris and Rocky Bleier—to dethrone the two-time Super Bowl champions and win their first title since 1967 with a 24-7 victory.

Led by the short passing of Ken Stabler and the pounding running of Mark van Eeghen, Clarence Davis, and Pete Banaszak, the Raiders jumped to a 10-0 lead, then, after the Steelers pulled within 10-7, scored an important touchdown 19 seconds before the first half ended. With a first down at the Pittsburgh 4, the Raiders lined up with three tight ends as if to power the ball in. Stabler faked a handoff to the right and then hit tight end Warren Bankston, who had slipped free to the left side, for a touchdown that increased the margin to 17-7.

The Raiders finished off the Steelers with a 12-play, 63-yard drive in the third quarter, the touchdown coming on a 5-yard pass to Banaszak. Although Stabler was shaken up on the play and didn't return, his replacement, Mike Rae, helped the Raiders' run out the clock in the fourth quarter.

Pittsburgh	0	7	0	0	-	7
Oakland	3	14	7	0	-	24

Oak	-	FG Mann 39
Oak	-	Davis 1 run (Mann kick)
Pit	-	Harrison 3 run (Mansfield kick)
Oak	-	Bankston 4 pass from Stabler (Mann kick)
Oak	-	Banaszak 5 pass from Stabler (Mann kick)

1976 NFC CHAMPIONSHIP GAME
Minnesota 24, Los Angeles Rams 13

December 26, 1976, at Bloomington
Attendance: 47,191

Minnesota qualified for its fourth Super Bowl with a 24-13 victory against the Rams on a day on which the wind-chill factor was 12 degrees below zero.

The tone for the day was set early, when, behind the running of Lawrence McCutcheon, the Rams drove to a first down at the Minnesota 6. On fourth down, inches short of the goal line, the Rams attempted a field goal, which was blocked by Nate Allen. The ball was picked up at the 10 by Bobby Bryant, who raced 90 yards for a touchdown.

Late in the first quarter, the Rams drove to the Minnesota 21, but John Cappelletti fumbled, and Matt Blair recovered for the Vikings. In the second period, Blair blocked a punt by Rusty Jackson, and Fred Cox's subsequent field goal gave Minnesota a 10-0 lead at halftime.

The Vikings upped their lead in the third period after Chuck Foreman broke off right tackle and raced 62 yards to the Rams' 2. Two plays later he scored to increase the lead to 17-0. The Rams quickly responded with 2 touchdowns, but their last gasp ended with two minutes to play when Pat Haden's pass was intercepted at the Minnesota 8.

LA Rams	0	0	13	0	-	13
Minnesota	7	3	7	7	-	24

Min	-	Bryant 90 blocked field goal return (Cox kick)
Min	-	FG Cox 25
Min	-	Foreman 2 run (Cox kick)
Rams	-	McCutcheon 10 run (kick failed)
Rams	-	H. Jackson 5 pass from Haden (Dempsey kick)
Min	-	Johnson 12 run (Cox kick)

1977 AFC DIVISIONAL PLAYOFF GAME
Oakland 37, Baltimore 31 (2 OT)

December 24, 1977, at Baltimore
Attendance: 59,925

In the third-longest game played at the time, Ken Stabler threw 3 touchdown passes to tight end Dave Casper, the last 43 seconds into the sixth period, as the Raiders defeated the Colts 37-31.

The Colts led 10-7 at halftime, the big play a 61-yard interception return for a touchdown by Bruce Laird.

On the Raiders' first possession of the third quarter, Stabler hit Casper with an 8-yard touchdown pass, but Baltimore's Marshall Johnson returned the ensuing kickoff 87 yards for a touchdown. Another touchdown pass to Casper, after Ted Hendricks blocked a Baltimore punt, made it 21-17 after three periods.

Two touchdown runs by Ron Lee, sandwiched around Pete Banaszak's scoring run for Oakland, put the Colts ahead 31-28. With time running out in regulation, Stabler found Casper on a 42-yard pass to the 14. Errol Mann kicked the tying field goal with 29 seconds left in the fourth period.

Oakland	7	0	14	10	0	6	-	37
Baltimore	0	10	7	14	0	0	-	31

Oak	-	Davis 30 run (Mann kick)
Bal	-	Laird 61 interception return (Linhart kick)
Bal	-	FG Linhart 36
Oak	-	Casper 8 pass from Stabler (Mann kick)
Bal	-	Johnson 87 kickoff return (Linhart kick)
Oak	-	Casper 10 pass from Stabler (Mann kick)
Bal	-	R. Lee 1 run (Linhart kick)
Oak	-	Banaszak 1 run (Mann kick)
Bal	-	R. Lee 13 run (Linhart kick)
Oak	-	FG Mann 22
Oak	-	Casper 10 pass from Stabler

1977 AFC DIVISIONAL PLAYOFF GAME
Denver 34, Pittsburgh 21

December 24, 1977, at Denver
Attendance: 75,059

Denver linebacker Tom Jackson set up 17 points as the Broncos, in their first playoff game ever, defeated Pittsburgh 34-21.

The Steelers were the dominant team in the first half, outgaining the Broncos, 183-44. But two big plays allowed the Broncos to come out tied 14-14 at halftime. Denver scored first after John Schultz blocked a punt at the Pittsburgh 17. Rob Lytle carried the ball 4 consecutive times, the last for 4 yards and a touchdown. In the second quarter, Jackson picked up Franco Harris's fumble at the Pittsburgh 45 and returned it to the 10, from which point Otis Armstrong blasted it in.

In the fourth quarter, two plays after Jim Turner had put Denver ahead 24-21 with a 44-yard field goal, Jackson intercepted a pass from Terry Bradshaw and returned it 32 yards, setting up another field goal. Then Jackson intercepted Bradshaw again, leading to Craig Morton's 34-yard touchdown pass to Jack Dolbin.

Pittsburgh	0	14	0	7	-	21
Denver	7	7	7	13	-	34

Den	-	Lytle 7 run (Turner kick)
Pit	-	Bradshaw 1 run (Gerela kick)
Den	-	Armstrong 10 run (Turner kick)
Pit	-	Harris 1 run (Gerela kick)

Den	-	Odoms 30 pass from Morton (Turner kick)
Pit	-	Brown 1 pass from Bradshaw (Gerela kick)
Den	-	FG Turner 44
Den	-	FG Turner 25
Den	-	Dolbin 34 pass from Morton (Turner kick)

1977 NFC DIVISIONAL PLAYOFF GAME
Dallas 37, Chicago Bears 7

December 26, 1977, at Irving, Texas
Attendance: 63,260

Dallas thoroughly dominated the Chicago Bears, and safety Charlie Waters set a divisional playoff record by intercepting 3 passes as the Cowboys rolled to a 37-7 victory.

The Cowboys' defense held Chicago to 13 yards and no first downs on the Bears' first three possessions. The Cowboys, meanwhile, drove 79 and 74 yards to touchdowns. On the first drive, Roger Staubach completed 2 passes for 44 yards, and on the second it was 2 completions for 59 yards.

The Cowboys continued their performance in the second half. On the first play, linebacker D.D. Lewis intercepted a pass from Bob Avellini, and, two plays later, rookie Tony Dorsett ran 23 yards for a touchdown. Two fumbles by Avellini, 1 recovered by Lewis and the other by Bill Gregory, led to 10 more Dallas points. The Bears didn't score until well into the final period.

Chi. Bears	0	0	0	7	-	7
Dallas	7	10	17	3	-	37

Dal	-	Dennison 2 run (Herrera kick)
Dal	-	DuPree 28 pass from Staubach (Herrera kick)
Dal	-	FG Herrera 21
Dal	-	Dorsett 23 run (Herrera kick)
Dal	-	FG Herrera 31
Dal	-	Dorsett 7 run (Herrera kick)
Dal	-	FG Herrera 27
ChiB	-	Schubert 34 pass from Avellini (Thomas kick)

1977 NFC DIVISIONAL PLAYOFF GAME
Minnesota 14, Los Angeles Rams 7

December 26, 1977, at Los Angeles
Attendance: 70,203

In a game that has become know as the Mud Bowl, Chuck Foreman ran for 101 yards in a torrential rainstorm to lead the Vikings to a 14-7 victory over the Rams.

Early in the game, Minnesota quarterback Bob Lee— playing for the injured Fran Tarkenton— completed 5 of 6 passes to drive the Vikings 70 yards to Foreman's 5-yard touchdown run. The Rams moved the ball well, but Pat Haden was intercepted in the end zone, and Rafael Septien later missed a short field goal.

Early in the fourth quarter, Manfred Moore's 21-yard punt return set up a 1-yard touchdown run by Sammy Johnson. The Rams came right back, but Haden was intercepted.

Late in the game, the Rams scored on a 1-yard pass to Harold Jackson, and they had a chance to pull even when Jim Jodat recovered an onside kick with 53 seconds left. But Haden again was intercepted.

Minnesota	7	0	0	7	-	14
L.A. Rams	0	0	0	7	-	7

Min	-	Foreman 5 run (Cox kick)
Min	-	S. Johnson 1 run (Cox kick)
Rams	-	H. Jackson 1 pass from Haden (Septien kick)

1977 AFC CHAMPIONSHIP GAME
Denver 20, Oakland 17

January 1, 1978, at Denver
Attendance: 74,982

The Broncos won the first title in club history with a 20-17 victory over the Raiders.

After the Raiders had gone ahead 3-0 on their opening drive, Denver scored in only two plays, the second a 74-yard touchdown pass from Craig Morton to Haven Moses. The score remained 7-3 until the Broncos scored on a 1-yard run by Jon Keyworth in the third period. On the play before the touchdown, with a first-and-goal at the 2, Rob Lytle was hit by Jack Tatum as he dived over the line. Lytle lost the ball; Raiders nose tackle Mike McCoy picked it up and began running the other way. The play was blown dead, however, and the officials ruled it was Denver's ball.

The Raiders scored early in the final period on the fourth touchdown pass from Ken Stabler to Dave Casper in two playoff games. Then Bob Swenson intercepted a pass on Oakland's next drive and returned it to the 17. Three plays later, Morton connected with Moses for 12 yards and the clinching touchdown. Stabler completed the scoring with another touchdown strike to Casper.

Oakland	3	0	0	14	-	17
Denver	7	0	7	6	-	20

Oak	-	FG Mann 20
Den	-	Moses 74 pass from Morton (Turner kick)
Den	-	Keyworth 1 run (Turner kick)
Oak	-	Casper 7 pass from Stabler (Mann kick)
Den	-	Moses 12 pass from Morton (pass failed)
Oak	-	Casper 17 pass from Stabler (Mann kick)

1977 NFC CHAMPIONSHIP GAME
Dallas 23, Minnesota 6

January 1, 1978, at Irving, Texas
Attendance: 61,968

Defensive ends Harvey Martin and Ed (Too Tall) Jones led a defensive effort that held the Minnesota ground game to 66 yards, including only 22 in the second half, as the Cowboys defeated the Vikings 23-6 to earn their fourth Super Bowl appearance.

The Cowboys jumped ahead right at the start. Martin recovered Robert Miller's fumble at the Minnesota 39 on the third play of the game, and two downs later, Roger Staubach teamed with Golden Richards on a 32-yard touchdown pass.

The margin increased to 13 points in the second quarter when the Cowboys drove 46 yards and scored on Robert Newhouse's 5-yard run. The drive was kept alive by Danny White's 14-yard run out of punt formation.

Dallas put the game away midway through the fourth quarter. On fourth-and-11 at the Dallas 12, White punted, but the ball was fumbled by Manfred Moore and recovered by Dallas tight end Jay Saldi. Five plays later, Tony Dorsett ran 11 yards for a touchdown.

For the game, Martin recovered 2 of the 3 fumbles the Vikings lost, while Jones made a team-high 12 tackles and also had a sack.

Minnesota	0	6	0	0	-	6
Dallas	6	10	0	7	-	23

Dal	-	Richards 32 pass from Staubach (kick blocked)

Dal	-	Newhouse 5 run (Herrera kick)
Min	-	FG Cox 33
Min	-	FG Cox 37
Dal	-	FG Herrera 21
Dal	-	Dorsett 11 run (Herrera kick)

1978 AFC WILD CARD GAME
Houston 17, Miami 9

December 24, 1978, at Miami
Attendance: 72,445

Dan Pastorini completed 20 of 30 passes for 306 yards to lead Houston to an upset of Miami in the first AFC Wild Card Game. The Dolphins did a good job of slowing rookie of the year Earl Campbell but seemed unprepared for Pastorini's precision passing.

Miami opened the scoring two plays after Earnie Rhone recovered a fumbled punt at the Houston 21. Pastorini responded with a 10-play, 71-yard drive on which he completed 6 of 7 passes for 66 yards, including the touchdown to fullback Tim Wilson from 13 yards.

Neither team scored again until the fourth quarter, when Pastorini completed 4 passes for 45 yards to set up Toni Fritsch's 35-yard field goal. Then, after Gregg Bingham intercepted Bob Griese on the first play after the kickoff, Campbell and Wilson carried the ball on 9 consecutive plays, with Campbell scoring from the 1.

Houston	7	0	0	10	-	17
Miami	7	0	0	2	-	9

Mia	-	Tillman 13 pass from Griese (Yepremian kick)
Hou	-	T. Wilson 13 pass from Pastorini (Fritsch kick)
Hou	-	FG Fritsch 35
Hou	-	Campbell 1 run (Fritsch kick)
Mia	-	Safety, Pastorini ran out of end zone

1978 NFC WILD CARD GAME
Atlanta 14, Philadelphia 13

December 24, 1978, at Atlanta
Attendance: 59,403

The Falcons won the first playoff game in club history when Steve Bartkowski threw 2 touchdown passes in the final 5 minutes to overcome a 13-0 Philadelphia lead.

The only score of the first half came after Atlanta's Billy Ryckman fumbled Mike Michel's punt at the Falcons' 13. Cleveland Franklin recovered for Philadelphia, setting up Ron Jaworski's touchdown pass to Harold Carmichael. Michel missed the extra point. In the third quarter, the Eagles drove 60 yards to Wilbert Montgomery's 1-yard touchdown run.

Late in the game, Bartkowski got Atlanta moving. He completed 4 of 6 passes for 88 yards, including a touchdown pass to tight end Jim Mitchell. On Atlanta's next possession, Bartkowski completed 3 of 4 passes, including a 37-yard touchdown strike to Wallace Francis with 1:39 to play.

Passing on eight consecutive plays, Jaworski drove the Eagles to the Atlanta 16, but with 13 seconds left, Michel missed a 34-yard field-goal attempt.

Philadelphia	6	0	7	0	-	13
Atlanta	0	0	0	14	-	14

Phi	-	Carmichael 13 pass from Jaworski (kick failed)
Phi	-	Montgomery 1 run (Michel kick)
Atl	-	Mitchell 20 pass from Bartkowski (Mazzetti kick)
Atl	-	Francis 37 pass from Bartkowski (Mazzetti kick)

1978 AFC DIVISIONAL PLAYOFF GAME
Pittsburgh 33, Denver 10

December 30, 1978, at Pittsburgh
Attendance: 50,230

The Steelers dominated the Broncos, gaining 425 yards to 218, and used two big pass plays in a span of 34 seconds to knock off the defending AFC champions 33-10.

The Broncos scored first, but then the Steelers drove 66 yards in 8 plays and scored on a 1-yard run by Franco Harris. The next time the Steelers had the ball, Harris scored again when he broke around right end for 18 yards. Pittsburgh built its lead to 19-10 at halftime, and that's how the score stood until the fourth quarter.

In the final period, Terry Bradshaw completed a 45-yard touchdown pass to John Stallworth, who caught an AFC divisional playoff-record 10 passes for the day. On the first play after the kickoff was fumbled back to the Steelers, Bradshaw found Lynn Swann with a 38-yard touchdown pass.

Denver	3	7	0	0	-	10
Pittsburgh	6	13	0	14	-	33

Den	-	FG Turner 37
Pit	-	Harris 1 run (kick failed)
Pit	-	Harris 18 run (Gerela kick)
Pit	-	FG Gerela 24
Den	-	Preston 3 run (Turner kick)
Pit	-	FG Gerela 27
Pit	-	Stallworth 45 pass from Bradshaw (Gerela kick)
Pit	-	Swann 38 pass from Bradshaw (Gerela kick)

1978 AFC DIVISIONAL PLAYOFF GAME
Houston 31, New England 14

December 31, 1978, at Foxboro
Attendance: 60,735

Dan Pastorini had his second successive sizzling performance, completing 12 of 15 passes for 200 yards and 3 touchdowns, as the Oilers jumped to a 21-0 halftime lead and coasted to a 31-14 victory over the Patriots.

Houston exploded in the second period. First, Pastorini found Ken Burrough one-on-one with Mike Haynes; Burrough made a catch, sidestepped Haynes, and raced 71 yards for a touchdown. After the kickoff, the Patriots drove deep into Houston territory, only to have Mike Reinfeldt intercept Steve Grogan's pass on the 1. The Oilers pounded out a 99-yard drive, scoring on Pastorini's 19-yard pass to tight end Mike Barber. Following another interception by Reinfeldt, Pastorini again threw a touchdown pass to Barber, from 13 yards with 36 seconds in the half.

The Oilers used the running of Earl Campbell, who gained 118 yards and scored once, to control the tempo of the game in the second half.

Houston	0	21	3	7	-	31
New England	0	0	7	7	-	14

Hou	-	Burrough 71 pass from Pastorini (Fritsch kick)
Hou	-	Barber 19 pass from Pastorini (Fritsch kick)
Hou	-	Barber 13 pass from Pastorini (Fritsch kick)
Hou	-	FG Fritsch 30
NE	-	Jackson 24 pass from Johnson (Posey kick)
NE	-	Francis 24 pass from Owens (Posey kick)
Hou	-	Campbell 2 run (Fritsch kick)

1978 NFC DIVISIONAL PLAYOFF GAME
Dallas 27, Atlanta 20

December 30, 1978, at Irving, Texas
Attendance: 63,406

Inspired by a vicious hit that knocked Roger Staubach out of the game and by the play of backup quarterback Danny White, the Cowboys shut down explosive Atlanta in the second half and came from behind for a 27-20 victory.

The Falcons seemed unstoppable in the first half, when they scored on their first four possessions. The Cowboys, meanwhile, had scored their only touchdown on a drive that was kept alive when White ran for a first down from punt formation.

When, late in the half, linebacker Robert Pennywell knocked out Staubach after he had already thrown the ball, the Cowboys became fired up, and the defense stopped the Falcons cold. In the third quarter, White took Dallas 54 yards, throwing to tight end Jackie Smith for 2 yards and a touchdown. In the fourth period, following a hurried punt, Dallas took over at the Atlanta 30. Four consecutive carries by Scott Laidlaw, the last a 1-yard touchdown run, put Dallas ahead for good.

Atlanta	7	13	0	0	-	20
Dallas	10	3	7	7	-	27

Dal - FG Septien 34
Atl - Bean 14 run (Mazzetti kick)
Dal - Laidlaw 13 run (Septien kick)
Atl - FG Mazzetti 42
Dal - FG Septien 48
Atl - Francis 17 pass from Bartkowski (Mazzetti kick)
Atl - FG Mazzetti 22
Dal - Smith 2 pass from D. White (Septien kick)
Dal - Laidlaw 1 run (Septien kick)

1978 NFC DIVISIONAL PLAYOFF GAME
Los Angeles Rams 34, Minnesota 10

December 31, 1978, at Los Angeles
Attendance: 70,436

The Los Angeles Rams avenged four consecutive playoff losses to Minnesota with a dominating second half that broke a 10-10 tie and led to a 34-10 laugher.

Despite the score, the Rams controlled Minnesota for most of the first half. In the second period, Pat Haden led the Rams 59 yards for a touchdown that came on a 9-yard pass to Willie Miller. Minnesota's touchdown came following Bobby Bryant's interception; Fran Tarkenton threw a 1-yard touchdown pass to Ahmad Rashad with 6 seconds left in the half.

The Rams overpowered the Vikings in the second half. Early in the third quarter, a 21-yard punt return by Jackie Wallace set up Cullen Bryant's 3-yard, go-ahead touchdown. The next time they had the ball, the Rams went 60 yards in 5 plays, with Haden throwing a 27-yard touchdown pass to Ron Jessie, who dodged through the Vikings' defense for the last 20 yards.

Minnesota	3	7	0	0	-	10
L.A. Rams	0	10	14	10	-	34

Min - FG Danmeier 42
Rams - Miller 9 pass from Haden (Corral kick)
Rams - FG Corral 43
Min - Rashad 1 pass from Tarkenton (Danmeier kick)
Rams - Bryant 3 run (Corral kick)
Rams - Jessie 27 pass from Haden (Corral kick)
Rams - FG Corral 28
Rams - Jodat 3 run (Corral kick)

1978 AFC CHAMPIONSHIP GAME
Pittsburgh 34, Houston 5

January 7, 1979, at Pittsburgh
Attendance: 49,417

The Pittsburgh Steelers scored 17 points in a 48-second span of the second quarter, and their defense accounted for 9 turnovers en route to a 34-5 victory against their AFC Central rivals.

The Steelers led from the beginning, driving 57 yards to a 7-yard touchdown run by Franco Harris. Later in the first quarter, Earl Campbell fumbled and Jack Ham recovered at the Houston 17. Rocky Bleier ran in from the 15.

With 1:23 to go in the first half and Pittsburgh holding a 14-3 lead, Houston's Ronnie Coleman fumbled. Moments later, Terry Bradshaw found Lynn Swann with a 29-yard touchdown pass. Johnny Dirden fumbled the ensuing kickoff, and the Steelers recovered at the Houston 17. Two plays later, Bradshaw hit John Stallworth with a 17-yard touchdown pass. After the Oilers took the kickoff, Coleman fumbled again on the first play from scrimmage, and the Steelers recovered, setting up Roy Gerela's field goal with 4 seconds left in the half.

The Steel Curtain dominated the second half, intercepting Dan Pastorini 4 times in the Oilers' 6 possessions and holding the formidable Earl Campbell to less than 3 yards per carry.

Houston	0	3	2	0	-	5
Pittsburgh	14	17	3	0	-	34

Pit - Harris 7 run (Gerela kick)
Pit - Bleier 15 run (Gerela kick)
Hou - FG Fritsch 19
Pit - Swann 29 pass from Bradshaw (Gerela kick)
Pit - Stallworth 17 pass from Bradshaw (Gerela kick)
Pit - FG Gerela 37
Pit - FG Gerela 22
Hou - Safety, Washington tackled Bleier in end zone

1978 NFC CHAMPIONSHIP GAME
Dallas 28, Los Angeles Rams 0

January 7, 1979, at Los Angeles
Attendance: 67,470

Dallas's defense came up with 5 second-half turnovers, setting up 3 touchdowns and scoring a fourth, as the Cowboys defeated the Los Angeles Rams 28-0.

With only 1:52 remaining in the third quarter of a tight defensive struggle, Dallas safety Charlie Waters intercepted a pass by Pat Haden and returned it to the Los Angeles 10. Five plays later, Tony Dorsett ran in from 5 yards. Shortly before the end of the period, Waters intercepted again and returned the ball 29 yards to the Los Angeles 20. That led to Roger Staubach's 4-yard touchdown pass to Scott Laidlaw in the opening moments of the final period.

With Vince Ferragamo replacing the injured Haden, the Rams got their offense going in the fourth quarter. But on first down at the Dallas 10, the Rams fumbled, and it was recovered by Harvey Martin at the 11. The Cowboys drove 89 yards in 7 plays, the touchdown coming on Staubach's 11-yard strike to Billy Joe DuPree. The final score came with 1:19 remaining when linebacker Thomas Henderson intercepted a pass from Ferragamo and raced 68 yards down the left sideline for a touchdown that sealed the victory.

Dallas	0	0	7	21	-	28
L.A. Rams	0	0	0	0	-	0

Dal - Dorsett 5 run (Septien kick)
Dal - Laidlaw 4 pass from Staubach (Septien kick)
Dal - DuPree 11 pass from Staubach (Septien kick)
Dal - Henderson 68 interception return (Septien kick)

1979 AFC WILD CARD GAME
Houston 13, Denver 7

December 23, 1979, at Houston
Attendance: 48,776

The Oilers' defense owned the day as Houston managed to win 13-7 despite the loss of Earl Campbell and Dan Pastorini with injuries.

Denver's only successful drive followed a field goal by Toni Fritsch of Houston on the game's opening series. Denver marched 80 yards in 13 plays, with Craig Morton passing 7 yards to running back Dave Preston for the touchdown.

With 2:33 remaining before halftime, the Oilers took over at the 26, and Pastorini quickly moved them 74 yards. On the drive, Pastorini passed for 39 yards and Campbell ran for 20, including the final 3. Campbell was injured on his touchdown run, however, and didn't return. Pastorini was injured on the Oilers' first drive of the second half.

Late in the game, Gregg Bingham intercepted Morton and returned the ball to the Denver 20. Rob Carpenter carried 5 consecutive times, setting up Fritsch's 20-yard field goal.

Denver	7	0	0	0	-	7
Houston	3	7	0	3	-	13

Hou - FG Fritsch 31
Den - Preston 7 pass from Morton (Turner kick)
Hou - Campbell 3 run (Fritsch kick)
Hou - FG Fritsch 20

1979 NFC WILD CARD GAME
Philadelphia 27, Chicago Bears 17

December 23, 1979, at Philadelphia
Attendance: 69,397

Ron Jaworski threw 3 touchdown passes to bring the Eagles from behind as they defeated the Bears 27-17 for their first postseason victory in 19 years.

The game was relatively even in the first half. Philadelphia scored early after Wally Henry returned a punt 34 yards to Chicago's 26. Jaworski found Harold Carmichael for a 17-yard touchdown. The Bears came back with an 82-yard drive on which Mike Phipps completed 5 of 6 passes for 60 yards, and Walter Payton scored from the 2.

A second touchdown run by Payton and a field goal in the final minute of the half put the Bears ahead 17-10.

Jaworski took to the air in the second half. In the third quarter, he completed 3 consecutive passes for 53 yards, including 29 on a touchdown to Carmichael. On the Eagles' next possession, Jaworski teamed with running back Billy Campfield for the go-ahead touchdown.

Chi. Bears	7	10	0	0	-	17
Philadelphia	7	3	7	10	-	27

Phi - Carmichael 17 pass from Jaworski (Franklin kick)
ChiB - Payton 2 run (Thomas kick)
Phi - FG Franklin 29
ChiB - Payton 1 run (Thomas kick)
ChiB - FG Thomas 30
Phi - Carmichael 29 pass from Jaworski (Franklin kick)
Phi - Campfield 63 pass from Jaworski (Franklin kick)
Phi - FG Franklin 34

1979 AFC DIVISIONAL PLAYOFF GAME
Houston 17, San Diego 14

December 29, 1979, at San Diego
Attendance: 51,192

Rookie safety Vernon Perry set a postseason record with 4 interceptions as the Houston Oilers upset the San Diego Chargers 17-14 despite the absence of Earl Campbell and Dan Pastorini.

The Chargers' high-powered offense moved easily early on, with Dan Fouts passing the first 7 plays to set up a Chargers' touchdown. On San Diego's next possession, however, Perry intercepted at the Houston 18.

In the second quarter, Perry blocked a field-goal attempt and returned it 57 yards to the San Diego 28. Six plays later, Toni Fritsch cut the margin to 7-3 with a 26-yard field goal. On the third play after the kickoff, Perry intercepted again, setting up Boobie Clark's 1-yard touchdown run for the lead.

Lydell Mitchell scored for the Chargers in the third quarter, but J.C. Wilson later intercepted Fouts. Gifford Nielsen then passed to Mike Renfro for a 47-yard touchdown and a 17-14 lead. Perry intercepted on each of the Chargers' last two possessions.

Houston	0	10	7	0	-	17
San Diego	7	0	7	0	-	14

SD - C. Williams 1 run (Wood kick)
Hou - FG Fritsch 26
Hou - Clark 1 run (Fritsch kick)
SD - Mitchell 8 run (Wood kick)
Hou - Renfro 47 pass from Nielsen (Fritsch kick)

1979 AFC DIVISIONAL PLAYOFF GAME
Pittsburgh 34, Miami 14

December 30, 1979, at Pittsburgh
Attendance: 50,214

Pittsburgh's offense scored on its first three possessions, while the defense held Miami to 25 yards rushing as the Steelers whipped the Dolphins 34-14.

The first quarter was all Steelers. Taking the opening kickoff, they moved 62 yards in 13 plays, with Sidney Thornton scoring from the 1. After holding Miami without a first down, they went 62 yards again, this time in 9 plays, with Terry Bradshaw passing to John Stallworth for the touchdown. Again, the Dolphins couldn't get a first down, and on the sixth play, Bradshaw passed 20 yards to Lynn Swann for a touchdown.

The Dolphins tried to get back in the game in the third period, when they recovered a punt touched by Dwayne Woodruff. Two plays later, Bob Griese found Duriel Harris for a 7-yard touchdown pass. But the Steelers asserted themselves, driving 69 yards on 12 plays to a touchdown to put the game out of reach.

Miami	0	0	7	7	-	14
Pittsburgh	20	0	7	7	-	34

Pit - Thornton 1 run (Bahr kick)
Pit - Stallworth 17 pass from Bradshaw (kick blocked)
Pit - Swann 20 pass from Bradshaw (Bahr kick)
Mia - D. Harris 7 pass from Griese (von Schamann kick)
Pit - Bleier 1 run (Bahr kick)
Pit - F. Harris 5 run (Bahr kick)
Mia - Csonka 1 run (von Schamann kick)

1979 NFC DIVISIONAL PLAYOFF GAME
Tampa Bay 24, Philadelphia 17

December 29, 1979, at Tampa
Attendance: 71,402

Ricky Bell carried a playoff record 38 times for 142 yards, while the Tampa Bay defense held Philadelphia to 48 yards on the ground as the Buccaneers won 24-17.

The Buccaneers set the tone on their opening possession, moving 80 yards on 18 plays, and using up 9:34 before Bell scored from the 4. Tampa Bay extended its lead to 10-0 in the second quarter, and on the second play after the ensuing kickoff, Wilbert Montgomery fumbled with Randy Crowder recovering. A short drive culminated in Bell's 1-yard touchdown run and a 17-0 lead.

An interception that Jerry Robinson returned 37 yards to the 11 set up Ron Jaworski's touchdown pass to Charles Smith just before the end of the first half, and the Eagles cut the margin to 7 points in the third period. But then Doug Williams passed to Jimmie Giles for a touchdown and a 24-10 lead that the Eagles couldn't overcome.

Philadelphia	0	7	3	7	-	17
Tampa Bay	7	10	0	7	-	24

TB - Bell 4 run (O'Donoghue kick)
TB - FG O'Donoghue 40
TB - Bell 1 run (O'Donoghue kick)
Phi - Smith 11 pass from Jaworski (Franklin kick)
Phi - FG Franklin 42
TB - Giles 9 pass from Williams (O'Donoghue kick)
Phi - Carmichael 37 pass from Jaworski (Franklin kick)

1979 NFC DIVISIONAL PLAYOFF GAME
Los Angeles Rams 21, Dallas 19

December 30, 1979, at Irving, Texas
Attendance: 64,792

Vince Ferragamo, starting due to an injury to Pat Haden, threw 3 touchdown passes, and the Rams came from behind in what proved to be Roger Staubach's final game for a 21-19 victory.

The Cowboys scored first when Ferragamo slipped in the end zone for a safety. But Ferragamo then found Wendell Tyler with a 32-yard touchdown pass down the sideline. A 33-yard field goal cut Dallas's deficit to 2 points with 52 seconds left before halftime, but Ferragamo moved the Rams 70 yards on 4 plays, throwing a 43-yard pass to Ron Smith, who made an acrobatic catch in the end zone with 3 seconds left.

Two touchdowns put the Cowboys ahead 19-14, but with time running out, the Rams forced a punt. On first down from midfield, Ferragamo's pass was tipped by linebacker Mike Hegman. But Billy Waddy made the catch and outlegged the Dallas defenders to the end zone for the winning touchdown with 2:06 left.

L.A. Rams	0	14	0	7	-	21
Dallas	2	3	7	7	-	19

Dal - Safety, R. White tackled Ferragamo in end zone
Rams - Tyler 32 pass from Ferragamo (Corral kick)
Dal - FG Septien 33
Rams - R. Smith 43 pass from Ferragamo (Corral kick)
Dal - Springs 1 run (Septien kick)
Dal - Saldi 2 pass from Staubach (Septien kick)
Rams - Waddy 50 pass from Ferragamo (Corral kick)

1979 AFC CHAMPIONSHIP GAME
Pittsburgh 27, Houston 13

January 6, 1980, at Pittsburgh
Attendance: 50,475

The Steelers held the Oilers to only 24 yards rushing, but had to withstand Dan Pastorini's outstanding passing to clinch their fourth Super Bowl appearance with a 27-13 victory.

The Oilers jumped ahead quickly when rookie safety Vernon Perry, the hero of the playoff victory against San Diego, intercepted a pass by Terry Bradshaw and returned it 75 yards to score. However, Bradshaw threw touchdown passes to Bennie Cunningham and John Stallworth as the Steelers built a 17-10 lead at halftime.

The key play of the game came at the end of the third quarter. With a first-and-goal at the Pittsburgh 6, Pastorini passed to Mike Renfro at the back of the end zone. The officials ruled the pass incomplete, saying Renfro didn't have possession until he crossed the end line. The Oilers protested, and the television replays were not conclusive. Houston had to settle for a field goal on the first play of the fourth quarter, and Pittsburgh maintained its lead.

The Steelers then reasserted themselves, driving 78 yards to a field goal by Matt Bahr. They clinched the game in the final minute after Donnie Shell recovered a fumble by Guido Merkens at the Houston 45.

Houston	7	3	0	3	-	13
Pittsburgh	3	14	0	10	-	27

Hou - Perry 75 interception return (Fritsch kick)
Pit - FG Bahr 21
Hou - FG Fritsch 27
Pit - Cunningham 16 pass from Bradshaw (Bahr kick)
Pit - Stallworth 20 pass from Bradshaw (Bahr kick)
Hou - FG Fritsch 23
Pit - FG Bahr 39
Pit - Bleier 4 run (Bahr kick)

1979 NFC CHAMPIONSHIP GAME
Los Angeles Rams 9, Tampa Bay 0

January 6, 1980, at Tampa
Attendance: 72,033

The Los Angeles Rams, who had lost four of the previous five NFC title games, qualified for their first Super Bowl by defeating Tampa Bay 9-0 in the first championship game in which no touchdowns were scored.

The Rams' defense dominated the Buccaneers, holding them without a first down until midway through the second period, limiting Ricky Bell to 59 yards rushing, and allowing the Tampa Bay quarterbacks to complete only 4 of 26 passes for 54 yards.

The Rams, meanwhile, moved the ball effectively, although they were not able to get into the end zone. Emphasizing the power running of Cullen Bryant and Wendell Tyler, they picked up 369 total yards. The Rams' initial score came on the first play of the second quarter, when Frank Corrall ended a 68-yard drive to the Tampa Bay 1 with a field goal. The Rams also put together a 58-yard drive at the end of the half, resulting in a 21-yard field goal with 47 seconds remaining.

Los Angeles clinched the game midway through the final period, using Eddie Brown's 16-yard punt return to set up a 45-yard drive that culminated in Corral's 23-yard field goal.

L.A. Rams	0	6	0	3	-	9
Tampa Bay	0	0	0	0	-	0

Rams - FG Corral 19
Rams - FG Corral 21
Rams - FG Corral 23

1980 AFC WILD CARD GAME
Oakland 27, Houston 7

December 28, 1980, at Oakland
Attendance: 53,333

The Raiders used big plays on both sides of the ball to defeat Houston 27-7 despite the Oilers having more yards, more first downs, and more time of possession.

On the first play from scrimmage, Earl Campbell fumbled and Mike Davis recovered, setting up Chris Bahr's 47-yard field goal. The Oilers then went 55 yards in 9 plays, 7 of them runs by Campbell, including his 1-yard touchdown run. In the second quarter, Jim Plunkett found running back Kenny King with a 37-yard pass to set up the Raiders' first touchdown, Plunkett's 1-yard toss to Todd Christensen for a 10-7 lead at halftime.

In the third quarter, Lester Hayes intercepted Oilers quarterback Ken Stabler's pass in the end zone. On the last play of the period, Plunkett found Cliff Branch with a 33-yard completion. Then he threw a 44-yard touchdown strike to running back Arthur Whittington. And with six minutes left, Hayes shut the door by intercepting another pass and returning it 20 yards for a touchdown.

Houston	7	0	0	0	-	7
Oakland	3	7	0	17	-	27

Oak - FG Bahr 47
Hou - Campbell 1 run (Fritsch kick)
Oak - Christensen 1 pass from Plunkett (Bahr kick)
Oak - Whittington 44 pass from Plunkett (Bahr kick)
Oak - FG Bahr 37
Oak - Hayes 20 interception return (Bahr kick)

1980 NFC WILD CARD GAME
Dallas 34, Los Angeles Rams 13

December 28, 1980, at Irving, Texas
Attendance: 63,052

Danny White broke open a game tied at halftime by throwing a touchdown pass on each of the Cowboys' first three drives of the second half, and Dallas pulled away to defeat Los Angeles 34-13.

The Rams, who had defeated the Cowboys 38-14 late in the regular season, moved ahead 6-3 in the first quarter when Jewerl Thomas ran 1 yard for a touchdown to cap a 73-yard drive propelled by 3 completions from Vince Ferragamo to Preston Dennard.

Rafael Septien's 29-yard field goal tied the game at 6-6, but Los Angeles went ahead 13-6 in the second period when Ferragamo threw a 21-yard touchdown pass to Dennard. The Cowboys came back to tie the game 13-13 at halftime on Tony Dorsett's 12-yard touchdown run.

In the second half, White threw touchdown passes to end two quick drives and a sustained 95-yard march that ended any doubts about the final result.

L.A. Rams	6	7	0	0	-	13
Dallas	3	10	14	7	-	34

Dal - FG Septien 28
Rams - Thomas 1 run (kick blocked)
Dal - FG Septien 29
Rams - Dennard 21 pass from Ferragamo (Corral kick)
Dal - Dorsett 12 run (Septien kick)
Dal - Dorsett 10 pass from White (Septien kick)
Dal - Johnson 35 pass from White (Septien kick)
Dal - D. Pearson 11 pass from White (Septien kick)

1980 AFC DIVISIONAL PLAYOFF GAME
San Diego 20, Buffalo 14

January 3, 1981, at San Diego
Attendance: 52,253

Dan Fouts teamed with Ron Smith on a 50-yard touchdown pass with 2:08 remaining in the game to lift San Diego to a 20-14 victory over Buffalo. On the play, Fouts sent his three 1,000-yard receivers—John Jefferson, Charlie Joiner, and Kellen Winslow—to the left, while Smith lined up on the right. Smith cut over the middle and beat safety Bill Simpson.

The Bills led 14-3 at halftime, but Fouts moved the Chargers 70 yards in 4 plays on the opening drive of the third quarter, capping the march with a 9-yard scoring pass to Joiner following a 45-yard pass to the same receiver. A field goal early in the final period cut the margin to 1 point, and, with less than four minutes remaining, San Diego took over at its 31. On the play before the touchdown, Buffalo cornerback Charles Romes had a chance to make an interception, but the ball bounced off his chest.

Buffalo	0	14	0	0	-	14
San Diego	3	0	7	10	-	20

SD - FG Benirschke 22
Buf - Leaks 1 run (Mike-Mayer kick)
Buf - Lewis 9 pass from Ferguson (Mike-Mayer kick)
SD - Joiner 9 pass from Fouts (Benirschke kick)
SD - FG Benirschke 22
SD - Smith 50 pass from Fouts (Benirschke kick)

1980 AFC DIVISIONAL PLAYOFF GAME
Oakland 14, Cleveland 12

January 4, 1981, at Cleveland
Attendance: 78,245

Strong safety Mike Davis intercepted Brian Sipe's pass for Ozzie Newsome in the end zone with 41 seconds remaining to preserve the Raiders' 14-12 victory. The second-down play ended a drive that had taken the Browns from their 14 to the Oakland 13 in the final two minutes.

Heavy winds and a temperature of 1 degree helped shut down both big-play offenses. The Browns scored first when Ron Bolton intercepted a pass by Jim Plunkett and returned it 42 yards for a touchdown in the second quarter. Ted Hendricks blocked Don Cockroft's extra-point attempt. The Raiders drove 64 yards after the ensuing kickoff to score with 22 seconds left in the first half.

Two field goals in the third period regained the lead for

the Browns, but the Raiders established the final margin when they moved 80 yards in 12 plays, ending in Mark van Eeghen's second 1-yard touchdown run of the day.

Oakland	**0**	**7**	**0**	**7**	**-**	**14**
Cleveland	**0**	**6**	**6**	**0**	**-**	**12**

Cle - Bolton 42 interception return (kick blocked)
Oak - van Eeghen 1 run (Bahr kick)
Cle - FG Cockroft 30
Cle - FG Cockroft 30
Oak - van Eeghen 1 run (Bahr kick)

1980 NFC DIVISIONAL PLAYOFF GAME
Philadelphia 31, Minnesota 16

January 3, 1981, at Philadelphia
Attendance: 70,178

The Vikings turned the ball over 8 times in a span of 22 minutes of the second half to help Philadelphia, once trailing 14-0, to an improbable 31-16 victory.

The Vikings scored the first time they had the ball, when Tommy Kramer threw a 30-yard touchdown pass to Sammy White. In the second quarter, Minnesota added a 1-yard touchdown run by Ted Brown, but an 85-yard touchdown drive—which included 10 passes by Ron Jaworski—cut the halftime margin to 7 points.

The Eagles tied the game on the opening drive of the third quarter. After the Vikings regained the lead on a safety, Wilbert Montgomery scored his second touchdown for a lead that Philadelphia wouldn't relinquish. And then everything went to pieces for the Vikings. Two fumbles—their first in eight weeks— set up 10 points, and each of the Vikings' final 4 possessions ended with an interception.

Minnesota	**7**	**7**	**2**	**0**	**-**	**16**
Philadelphia	**0**	**7**	**14**	**10**	**-**	**31**

Min - S. White 30 pass from Kramer (Danmeier kick)
Min - Brown 1 run (Danmeier kick)
Phi - Carmichael 9 pass from Jaworski (Franklin kick)
Phi - Montgomery 8 run (Franklin kick)
Min - Safety, Jaworski tackled in end zone by Martin and Blair
Phi - Montgomery 5 run (Franklin kick)
Phi - FG Franklin 33
Phi - Harrington 2 run (Franklin kick)

1980 NFC DIVISIONAL PLAYOFF GAME
Dallas 30, Atlanta 27

January 4, 1981, at Atlanta
Attendance: 59,793

Dallas exploded for 3 touchdowns in the fourth quarter, the final one with only 42 seconds remaining, to come from behind and defeat Atlanta 30-27.

The Falcons controlled the early stages of the game, jumping to a 10-0 lead in the first quarter, and, after the Cowboys had come back to tie the contest, going up 24-10 after three periods.

Then the Cowboys caught fire. First, they drove 85 yards to score on Robert Newhouse's 1-yard touchdown run. Then, after Atlanta increased its lead to 27-17, Danny White completed 4 of 5 passes to take the Cowboys 62 yards, finishing the drive with a 14-yard touchdown strike to Drew Pearson. With less than two minutes left, White took over again, completing 4 of 6 passes for 70 yards, with the winning touchdown again going to Pearson, this time from 23 yards.

Dallas	**3**	**7**	**0**	**20**	**-**	**30**
Atlanta	**10**	**7**	**7**	**3**	**-**	**27**

Atl - FG Mazzetti 38
Atl - Jenkins 60 pass from Bartkowski (Mazzetti kick)
Dal - FG Septien 38
Dal - DuPree 5 pass from White (Septien kick)
Atl - Cain 1 run (Mazzetti kick)
Atl - Andrews 12 pass from Bartkowski (Mazzetti kick)
Dal - Newhouse 1 run (Septien kick)
Atl - FG Mazzetti 34
Dal - D. Pearson 14 pass from White (Septien kick)
Dal - D. Pearson 23 pass from White (Septien kick)

1980 AFC CHAMPIONSHIP GAME
Oakland 34, San Diego 27

January 11, 1981, at San Diego
Attendance: 52,428

Jim Plunkett accounted for 3 touchdowns in the first quarter as the Raiders jumped ahead of San Diego 28-7 and held on to defeat their AFC West rivals 34-27.

Plunkett, who completed 14 of 18 passes for 260 yards, opened the scoring with a 65-yard touchdown pass to tight end Raymond Chester. After the Chargers had evened the score on a 48-yard touchdown pass from Dan Fouts to Charlie Joiner, Plunkett scored on a 5-yard run. He then teamed with Kenny King on a 21-yard touchdown pass that made the score 21-7.

Trailing 28-7 late in the second period, the Chargers started their comeback on a drive that culminated in an 8-yard touchdown pass from Fouts to Joiner. They also scored on each of their first two possessions of the second half to cut the margin to 28-24.

However, the Raiders came alive, driving to 2 field goals by Chris Bahr. San Diego put together a 72-yard drive in the fourth quarter, but had to settle for a field goal. Then the Raiders made sure the Chargers couldn't get any closer by holding onto the ball for the last 6:43 of the game.

Oakland	**21**	**7**	**3**	**3**	**-**	**34**
San Diego	**7**	**7**	**10**	**3**	**-**	**27**

Oak - Chester 65 pass from Plunkett (Bahr kick)
SD - Joiner 48 pass from Fouts (Benirschke kick)
Oak - Plunkett 5 run (Bahr kick)
Oak - King 21 pass from Plunkett (Bahr kick)
Oak - van Eeghen 3 run (Bahr kick)
SD - Joiner 8 pass from Fouts (Benirschke kick)
SD - FG Benirschke 26
SD - Muncie 6 run (Benirschke kick)
Oak - FG Bahr 27
Oak - FG Bahr 33
SD - FG Benirschke 27

1980 NFC CHAMPIONSHIP GAME
Philadelphia 20, Dallas 7

January 11, 1981, at Philadelphia
Attendance: 70,696

Heavy, gusting winds and 16-degree temperature helped stall both teams' passing attacks, but Wilbert Montgomery took up the slack for Philadelphia, pounding for 194 yards to lead the Eagles to a 20-7 victory over Dallas and into their first Super Bowl.

Montgomery sent a message to the Cowboys from the start. He finished the Eagles' opening drive by running through the Dallas defense for 42 yards and a touchdown after only 2:11 of play. Dallas tied the game in the second period when Tony Dorsett ran in from the 3, but the Cowboys didn't move beyond the Eagles' 39 again.

In the second half, the Philadelphia defense set up 2 scores. Tony Franklin put the Eagles up by 3 points with a 26-yard field goal 4 plays after Dennis Harrison sacked Danny White and then recovered his fumble at the Dallas 11. The next Dallas drive ended when Dorsett fumbled and linebacker Jerry Robinson returned the ball 22 yards to the Dallas 38. Six plays later, Leroy Harris (who ran for 60 yards) pounded off tackle at the 9, cut to the middle of the field, and blasted into the end zone for a 17-7 lead.

Dallas	0	7	0	0	-	7
Philadelphia	7	0	10	3	-	20

Phi - Montgomery 42 run (Franklin kick)
Dal - Dorsett 3 run (Septien kick)
Phi - FG Franklin 26
Phi - Harris 9 run (Franklin kick)
Phi - FG Franklin 20

1981 AFC WILD CARD GAME
Buffalo 31, New York Jets 27

December 27, 1981, at New York
Attendance: 57,050

The Bills cruised to a 24-0 lead in the second quarter, then had to hold on desperately as a comeback by the Jets fell just short.

The Bills scored immediately when Bruce Harper fumbled the opening kickoff, and Charles Romes picked the ball up at the 26 and returned it for a touchdown. On Buffalo's second possession, Joe Ferguson found Frank Lewis with a 50-yard touchdown pass. Two interceptions led to 10 more points, and Buffalo was ahead 24-0.

Quarterback Richard Todd helped the Jets pull within 24-13, but a Buffalo touchdown with 10 minutes left put the Bills ahead 31-13. Then Todd found Bobby Jones with a 30-yard touchdown pass, and a 1-yard touchdown run by Kevin Long made it 31-27. New York regained possession with 2:36 left, and, passing on every play, Todd drove the Jets 69 yards to the 11. But Bill Simpson intercepted on the 1 with 2 seconds left to preserve the victory.

Buffalo	17	7	0	7	-	31
N.Y. Jets	0	10	3	14	-	27

Buf - Romes 26 fumble recovery return (Mike-Mayer kick)
Buf - Lewis 50 pass from Ferguson (Mike-Mayer kick)
Buf - FG Mike-Mayer 29
Buf - Lewis 26 pass from Ferguson (Mike-Mayer kick)
NYJ - Shuler 30 pass from Todd (Leahy kick)
NYJ - FG Leahy 26
NYJ - FG Leahy 19
Buf - Cribbs 45 run (Mike-Mayer kick)
NYJ - B. Jones 30 pass from Todd (Leahy kick)
NYJ - Long 1 run (Leahy kick)

1981 NFC WILD CARD GAME
New York Giants 27, Philadelphia 21

December 27, 1981, at Philadelphia
Attendance: 71,611

In a game similar to its AFC counterpart, the New York Giants jumped to a 20-0 lead in the first quarter and then withstood a furious comeback by the Philadelphia Eagles to win 27-21.

Early in the game, Philadelphia kick returner Wally Henry fumbled a punt at the Eagles' 26. Beasley Reece recovered for the Giants, who scored on a pass from Scott Brunner to Leon Bright. After the Giants drove 62 yards for another touchdown, Henry fumbled the kickoff. Mark Haynes recovered in the end zone for a 20-0 lead.

Brunner's third touchdown pass of the game gave New York at 27-7 halftime lead, but the Eagles opened the third quarter with an impressive 15-play, 82-yard drive, culminating in Wilbert Montgomery's 6-yard touchdown run. Montgomery scored again to cap a fourth-quarter drive on which Ron Jaworski passed on 11 consecutive plays, but the Giants then ran out the clock.

N.Y. Giants	20	7	0	0	-	27
Philadelphia	0	7	7	7	-	21

NYG - Bright 9 pass from Brunner (kick failed)
NYG - Mistler 10 pass from Brunner (Danelo kick)
NYG - Haynes recovered fumble in end zone (Danelo kick)
Phi - Carmichael 15 pass from Jaworski (Franklin kick)
NYG - Mullady 22 pass from Brunner (Danelo kick)
Phi - Montgomery 6 run (Franklin kick)
Phi - Montgomery 1 run (Franklin kick)

1981 AFC DIVISIONAL PLAYOFF GAME
San Diego 41, Miami 38 (OT)

January 2, 1982, at Miami
Attendance: 73,735

In one of the most thrilling games in pro football history, Rolf Benirschke kicked a 29-yard field goal after 13:52 of overtime to give San Diego a 41-38 victory over Miami.

The Chargers exploded out of the blocks, scoring on a run, a pass, a punt return, and a field goal to lead 24-0 after one period. But Don Strock replaced David Woodley at quarterback for Miami in the second period, and the Dolphins rallied. On the final play of the first half, Strock passed 15 yards to Duriel Harris, who lateraled to Tony Nathan, who ran 25 yards for a touchdown to pull Miami within 24-17. Strock's third touchdown pass of the day tied the score at 24-24 in the third quarter.

Each team then scored twice more, with Dan Fouts capping an 82-yard drive to tie the game with a touchdown pass to James Brooks in the final minute. Miami came right back, but Kellen Winslow blocked Uwe von Schamann's field-goal attempt on the last play of regulation. In overtime, Benirschke missed a field-goal attempt and von Schamann had another blocked before Fouts led the Chargers 74 yards to the game winner.

San Diego	24	0	7	7	3	-	41
Miami	0	17	14	7	0	-	38

SD - FG Benirschke 32
SD - Chandler 56 punt return (Benirschke kick)
SD - Muncie 1 run (Benirschke kick)
SD - Brooks 8 pass from Fouts (Benirschke kick)
Mia - FG von Schamann 34
Mia - Rose 1 pass from Strock (von Schamann kick)
Mia - Nathan 25 lateral from Harris after 15 pass from Strock (von Schamann kick)
Mia - Rose 15 pass from Strock (von Schamann kick)
SD - Winslow 25 pass from Fouts (Benirschke kick)
Mia - Hardy 50 pass from Strock (von Schamann kick)
Mia - Nathan 12 run (von Schamann kick)
SD - Brooks 9 pass from Fouts (Benirschke kick)
SD - FG Benirschke 29

1981 AFC DIVISIONAL PLAYOFF GAME
Cincinnati 28, Buffalo 21

January 3, 1982, at Cincinnati
Attendance: 55,420

Trailing by a touchdown and with the ball at the Cincinnati 21 in the final 3 minutes of the game, Joe Ferguson of the Bills completed a fourth-down pass to Lou Piccone for a first down. But Buffalo was penalized for delay of game, and Ferguson's pass on the next snap was incomplete. The Bengals took over and ran out the clock for their first playoff victory ever.

Cincinnati took an early lead, driving 58 and 52 yards to touchdowns in the first quarter. But with less than 2 minutes left in the first half, Ferguson passed 54 yards to Jerry Butler to set up a touchdown run by Joe Cribbs.

Buffalo tied the game on its first possession of the second half, but the Bengals drove 65 yards to a touchdown to go back ahead. The Bills tied the game at 21-21 in the fourth quarter, but Cincinnati again responded, going 78 yards for the winning score.

Buffalo	0	7	7	7	-	21
Cincinnati	14	0	7	7	-	28

Cin - Alexander 4 run (Breech kick)
Cin - Johnson 1 run (Breech kick)
Buf - Cribbs 1 run (Mike-Mayer kick)
Buf - Cribbs 44 run (Mike-Mayer kick)
Cin - Alexander 20 run (Breech kick)
Buf - Butler 21 pass from Ferguson (Mike-Mayer kick)
Cin - Collinsworth 16 pass from Anderson (Breech kick)

1981 NFC DIVISIONAL PLAYOFF GAME
Dallas 38, Tampa Bay 0

January 2, 1982, at Irving, Texas
Attendance: 64,848

The Dallas defensive line of ends Ed (Too Tall) Jones and Harvey Martin and tackles John Dutton and Randy White thoroughly dominated the Buccaneers, limiting them to 74 yards rushing, just 2 in the second half. The Cowboys held Doug Williams to 10 of 29 passing, intercepted him 4 times, sacked him 4 times, and forced him into 2 intentional grounding penalties. The result was a 38-0 victory for the Cowboys.

After a scoreless first quarter, the Cowboys' offense got going in the second period when Danny White threw a 9-yard touchdown pass to Tony Hill and Rafael Septien booted a 32-yard field goal. Then Dallas exploded for 3 touchdowns in the third period, driving 80 yards with the second-half kickoff for 1 touchdown and scoring 2 touchdowns in the final moments of the quarter following a pair of interceptions.

Tampa Bay	0	0	0	0	-	0
Dallas	0	10	21	7	-	38

Dal - Hill 9 pass from White (Septien kick)
Dal - FG Septien 32
Dal - Springs 1 run (Septien kick)
Dal - Dorsett 5 run (Septien kick)
Dal - Jones 5 run (Septien kick)
Dal - Newsome 1 run (Septien kick)

1981 NFC DIVISIONAL PLAYOFF GAME
San Francisco 38, New York Giants 24

January 3, 1982, at San Francisco
Attendance: 58,360

Scott Brunner threw 3 touchdown passes for New York, but the 49ers put together an outstanding all-around game, scoring on the ground, through the air, and on defense to win easily 38-24.

The San Francisco offense showed its prowess early, marching 85 yards in 13 plays after taking the opening kickoff. The Giants tied the score later in the period on Brunner's 72-yard touchdown pass to Earnest Gray.

The 49ers took charge in the second period. With San Francisco leading 10-7, Ronnie Lott intercepted Brunner, and three plays later Joe Montana teamed with Freddie Solomon on a 58-yard touchdown pass. Keena Turner pounced on a fumble on the ensuing kickoff, and Ricky Patton immediately scored on a 25-yard sweep to increase the lead to 24-7.

When the Giants cut the margin to 7 points in the third period, the 49ers responded with a long touchdown drive, followed by Lott's 20-yard interception return for a touchdown.

N.Y. Giants	7	3	7	7	-	24
San Francisco	7	17	0	14	-	38

SF - Young 8 pass from Montana (Wersching kick)
NYG - Gray 72 pass from Brunner (Danelo kick)
SF - FG Wersching 22
SF - Solomon 58 pass from Montana (Wersching kick)
SF - Patton 25 run (Wersching kick)
NYG - FG Danelo 48
NYG - Perkins 59 pass from Brunner (Danelo kick)
SF - Ring 3 run (Wersching kick)
SF - Lott 20 interception return (Wersching kick)
NYG - Perkins 17 pass from Brunner (Danelo kick)

1981 AFC CHAMPIONSHIP GAME
Cincinnati 27, San Diego 7

January 10, 1982, at Cincinnati
Attendance: 46,302

It certainly was not football weather, as a temperature of 9 degrees below zero and a 35-mile-per-hour wind created a wind-chill factor of minus 59. The conditions, and a fired-up Cincinnati defense, combined to stop San Diego's record-setting passing attack, while Cincinnati quarterback Ken Anderson threw 2 touchdown passes for a 27-7 victory.

The Bengals led virtually the entire way, driving 51 yards to Jim Breech's 31-yard field goal on their second possession. James Brooks then fumbled the ensuing kickoff and Don Bass recovered for the Bengals at the 12. On second down, Anderson found M.L. Harris for an 8-yard touchdown.

The Chargers came back in the second quarter on a 33-yard touchdown pass from Dan Fouts to Kellen Winslow, but the Bengals responded immediately. David Verser returned the kickoff to the 45, Anderson completed 4 of 5 passes for 52 yards, and Pete Johnson finished the drive by scoring from the 1.

The San Diego Chargers couldn't get anything going in the game's second half, while the Cincinnati Bengals used a fumble recovery to set up another field goal and then drove downfield 68 yards in 14 plays for the clinching touchdown.

San Diego	0	7	0	0	-	7
Cincinnati	10	7	3	7	-	27

Cin - FG Breech 31
Cin - M. L. Harris 8 pass from Anderson (Breech kick)
SD - Winslow 33 pass from Fouts (Benirschke kick)
Cin - Johnson 1 run (Breech kick)
Cin - FG Breech 38
Cin - Bass 3 pass from Anderson (Breech kick)

1981 NFC CHAMPIONSHIP GAME
San Francisco 28, Dallas 27

January 10, 1982, at San Francisco
Attendance: 60,525

Dwight Clark made "The Catch," a leaping grab at the back of the end zone with 51 seconds remaining, as the 49ers won their first championship game 28-27 over the Dallas Cowboys. Starting from the San Francisco 11 with only 4:54 remaining, Joe Montana led the 49ers 89 yards in 13 plays to the Dallas 6; on third down, he threw a high pass that the 6-foot 4-inch Clark just managed to pull in.

The game had seesawed back and forth, with the 49ers scoring first but the Cowboys leading 10-7 after one quarter. Montana's second touchdown pass of the day (20 yards to Clark) put San Francisco back in front, but Tony Dorsett scored to give the Cowboys the lead at the half.

The 49ers went ahead 21-17 in the third quarter, but a field goal and a touchdown pass from Danny White to tight end Doug Cosbie moved Dallas ahead 27-21 in the final period. Even when the 49ers scored in the final minute, they were not safe. White completed a pass that almost went for a touchdown before the 49ers' defense forced a fumble to secure the victory.

Dallas	10	7	0	10	-	27
San Francisco	7	7	7	7	-	28

SF - Solomon 8 pass from Montana (Wersching kick)
Dal - FG Septien 44
Dal - Hill 26 pass from D. White (Septien kick)
SF - Clark 20 pass from Montana (Wersching kick)
Dal - Dorsett 5 run (Septien kick)
SF - Davis 2 run (Wersching kick)
Dal - FG Septien 22
Dal - Cosbie 21 pass from D. White (Septien kick)
SF - Clark 6 pass from Montana (Wersching kick)

1982 AFC FIRST-ROUND PLAYOFF GAME
Miami 28, New England 13

January 8, 1983, at Miami
Attendance: 68,842

A balanced offense helped Miami put together four long touchdown drives, as the Dolphins eliminated the Patriots in the first round of the extended playoffs 28-13.

The Patriots jumped ahead early in the second quarter, but Miami built a pair of 9-play, 79-yard drives to lead at halftime 14-3. The passing attack was led by David Woodley, who completed 16 of 19 attempts and threw a 2-yard touchdown pass to Bruce Hardy, who juggled the ball before controlling it at the back of the end zone; the ground game was led by Andra Franklin, who pounded out 112 yards and scored the Dolphins' second touchdown.

After the Patriots cut the lead to 14-6 in the third period, the Dolphins drove 74 yards in 11 plays for 1 touchdown and then put the game away in the final period with Woodley's second touchdown pass to Hardy.

New England	0	3	3	7	-	13
Miami	0	14	7	7	-	28

NE - FG Smith 23
Mia - Hardy 2 pass from Woodley (von Schamann kick)
Mia - Franklin 1 run (von Schamann kick)
NE - FG Smith 42
Mia - Bennett 2 run (von Schamann kick)
Mia - Hardy 2 pass from Woodley (von Schamann kick)
NE - Hasselbeck 22 pass from Grogan (Smith kick)

1982 AFC FIRST-ROUND PLAYOFF GAME
Los Angeles Raiders 27, Cleveland 10

January 8, 1983, at Los Angeles
Attendance: 56,555

The Raiders netted 510 yards but found it difficult to get in the end zone for much of the day. However, two lengthy second-half drives finally subdued the Browns 27-10.

On the game's first play, Jim Plunkett found Cliff Branch for 64 yards. But the Raiders stalled and Chris Bahr kicked a 27-yard field goal. The Raiders threatened twice more in the first period, but each time Plunkett was intercepted.

After the Browns tied the score, the Raiders drove 88 yards to take a 10-3 lead on Marcus Allen's 2-yard touchdown run. With less than two minutes left in the first half, Paul McDonald teamed with Ricky Feacher on a 43-yard touchdown pass that tied the game. But the Raiders quickly marched to Bahr's 37-yard field goal with six seconds left.

In the second half, the Raiders asserted themselves, driving 89 yards in 12 plays to Allen's second touchdown, then moving 80 yards in 11 plays for their final score.

Cleveland	0	10	0	0	-	10
L.A. Raiders	3	10	7	7	-	27

Raid - FG C. Bahr 27
Cle - FG M. Bahr 52
Raid - Allen 2 run (C. Bahr kick)
Cle - Feacher 43 pass from McDonald (M. Bahr kick)
Raid - FG C. Bahr 37
Raid - Allen 3 run (C. Bahr kick)
Raid - Hawkins 1 run (C. Bahr kick)

1982 AFC FIRST-ROUND PLAYOFF GAME
New York Jets 44, Cincinnati 17

January 9, 1983, at Cincinnati
Attendance: 57,560

Freeman McNeil ran for 202 yards on 21 carries, and New York scored 3 touchdowns in the fourth quarter to turn a close game into a runaway, defeating the Bengals 44-17.

The Bengals dominated the early action, when Ken Anderson threw 2 first-quarter touchdown passes for a 14-3 lead. But the Jets asserted themselves in the second quarter. After McNeil threw a 14-yard touchdown pass to Derrick Gaffney, Johnny Lynn intercepted a pass by Anderson to set up a drive that ended in a 4-yard touchdown pass from Richard Todd to Wesley Walker for the Jets' first lead.

The game was still close (23-17) when the fourth quarter began. But McNeil scored on a 20-yard run, and, when it looked like Cincinnati was about to get back into the game, Darrol Ray returned an interception 98 yards for the clinching touchdown.

N.Y. Jets	3	17	3	21	-	44
Cincinnati	14	0	3	0	-	17

Cin - Curtis 32 pass from Anderson (Breech kick)
NYJ - FG Leahy 32
Cin - Ross 2 pass from Anderson (Breech kick)
NYJ - Gaffney 14 pass from McNeil (Leahy kick)
NYJ - Walker 4 pass from Todd (Leahy kick)
NYJ - FG Leahy 24
NYJ - FG Leahy 47
Cin - FG Breech 20
NYJ - McNeil 20 run (Leahy kick)
NYJ - Ray 98 interception return (Leahy kick)
NYJ - Crutchfield 1 run (Leahy kick)

1982 AFC FIRST-ROUND PLAYOFF GAME
San Diego 31, Pittsburgh 28

January 9, 1983, at Pittsburgh
Attendance: 53,546

Dan Fouts threw 2 touchdown passes to Kellen Winslow in the fourth quarter, the second with only a minute left, as the Chargers came from behind on the road to defeat the Steelers 31-28.

Pittsburgh jumped ahead immediately when James Brooks of San Diego fumbled the opening kickoff in his end zone and Guy Ruff recovered it for a touchdown. Brooks fumbled the next kickoff, but recovered at his 1-yard line. The Chargers managed to overcome this start to lead 17-14 at halftime, as Brooks ran 18 yards for a touchdown and Fouts took San Diego 64 yards in 7 plays, and fired a 10-yard touchdown pass to backup tight end Eric Sievers with 32 seconds left in the half.

Terry Bradshaw threw touchdown passes in the third and fourth quarters to give Pittsburgh a 28-17 lead, but then Fouts and Winslow took over.

San Diego	3	14	0	14	-	31
Pittsburgh	14	0	7	7	-	28

Pit	-	Ruff fumble recovery in end zone (Anderson kick)
SD	-	FG Benirschke 25
Pit	-	Bradshaw 1 run (Anderson kick)
SD	-	Brooks 18 run (Benirschke kick)
SD	-	Sievers 10 pass from Fouts (Benirschke kick)
Pit	-	Cunningham 2 pass from Bradshaw (Anderson kick)
Pit	-	Stallworth 9 pass from Bradshaw (Anderson kick)
SD	-	Winslow 8 pass from Fouts (Benirschke kick)
SD	-	Winslow 2 pass from Fouts (Benirschke kick)

1982 NFC FIRST-ROUND PLAYOFF GAME
Washington 31, Detroit 7

January 8, 1983, at Washington
Attendance: 55,045

John Riggins ran for 119 yards and Joe Theismann completed 14 of 19 passes for 210 yards and 3 touchdowns as the Redskins proved too much for outmanned Detroit 31-7.

Washington dominated the first half, starting on Detroit's second possession, when safety Jeris White intercepted a pass intended for Billy Sims and raced 77 yards for a touchdown. On Detroit's next series, Eric Hipple fumbled when sacked by blitzing cornerback Vernon Dean, and Darryl Grant recovered to set up a field goal by Mark Moseley.

Theismann then threw 3 touchdown passes to Alvin Garrett, who was only starting due to an injury to Art Monk. Garrett caught a pair for 21-yard touchdowns in the second quarter, then pulled one in from 27 yards in the third period. For the day, he had 6 receptions for 110 yards.

Detroit	0	0	7	0	-	7
Washington	10	14	7	0	-	31

Was	-	White 77 interception return (Moseley kick)
Was	-	FG Moseley 26
Was	-	Garrett 21 pass from Theismann (Moseley kick)
Was	-	Garrett 21 pass from Theismann (Moseley kick)
Was	-	Garrett 27 pass from Theismann (Moseley kick)
Det	-	Hill 15 pass from Hipple (Murray kick)

1982 NFC FIRST-ROUND PLAYOFF GAME
Green Bay 41, St. Louis 16

January 8, 1983, at Green Bay
Attendance: 54,282

Green Bay scored touchdowns on 4 consecutive possessions to post an easy 41-16 victory over a St. Louis team that gained more yards (453 to 394) but kept failing on chances to score.

The Cardinals moved to the Green Bay 1 on the first possession of the game, but had to settle for a field goal. The Packers then took over, moving 73 yards on successive drives that were concluded with touchdown passes by Lynn Dickey. St. Louis turnovers at the Cardinals' 39- and 12-yard lines set up the next 2 Packers' touchdowns, short runs by Eddie Lee Ivery. When the Cardinals scored 9 seconds before the end of the first half, they missed the extra point.

In the second half, Dickey threw his fourth touchdown pass, while the Cardinals' woes continued with a missed field goal, a first down at the Green Bay 13 that led to no points, and an interception at the 1-yard line.

St. Louis	3	6	0	7	-	16
Green Bay	7	21	10	3	-	41

StL	-	FG O'Donoghue 18
GB	-	Jefferson 60 pass from Dickey (Stenerud kick)
GB	-	Lofton 20 pass from Dickey (Stenerud kick)
GB	-	Ivery 2 run (Stenerud kick)
GB	-	Ivery 4 pass from Dickey (Stenerud kick)
StL	-	Tilley 5 pass from Lomax (kick blocked)
GB	-	FG Stenerud 46
GB	-	Jefferson 7 pass from Dickey (Stenerud kick)
GB	-	FG Stenerud 34
StL	-	Shumann 18 pass from Lomax (O'Donoghue kick)

1982 NFC FIRST-ROUND PLAYOFF GAME
Dallas 30, Tampa Bay 17

January 9, 1983, at Irving, Texas
Attendance: 65,042

Dallas more than doubled Tampa Bay's yardage (445 to 218), but it took a touchdown by the Cowboys' defense to make up for numerous offensive mistakes and to propel them past the Buccaneers 30-17.

The Cowboys scored on a pair of field goals, but Tampa Bay moved ahead in the second quarter when linebacker Hugh Green grabbed Danny White's fumble in midair and returned it 60 yards for a touchdown. The Cowboys regained the lead when White hit running back Ron Springs with a 6-yard touchdown pass 35 seconds before halftime.

The Dallas offense continued to have problems in the third period, moving 84 yards to the Tampa Bay 1, but having to settle for a field goal. Then White was intercepted, setting up the Buccaneers' go-ahead touchdown.

In the fourth quarter, rookie backup safety Monty Hunter intercepted a pass by Doug Williams and returned it 19 yards for the touchdown that put the Cowboys ahead for good.

Tampa Bay	0	10	7	0	-	17
Dallas	6	7	3	14	-	30

Dal	-	FG Septien 33
Dal	-	FG Septien 33
TB	-	Green 60 fumble return (Capece kick)
TB	-	FG Capece 32
Dal	-	Springs 6 pass from D. White (Septien kick)

Dal	-	FG Septien 19
TB	-	Jones 49 pass from Williams (Capece kick)
Dal	-	Hunter 19 interception return (Septien kick)
Dal	-	Newsome 10 pass from D. White (Septien kick)

1982 NFC FIRST-ROUND PLAYOFF GAME
Minnesota 30, Atlanta 24

January 9, 1983, at Minneapolis
Attendance: 60,560

The Vikings drove 72 yards in 10 plays, capped by a 5-yard touchdown run by Ted Brown with 1:44 left, to overcome Atlanta 30-24.

The Falcons went ahead in the first 2 minutes of the game when Paul Davis blocked a punt that Doug Rogers recovered for a touchdown in the Minnesota end zone. However, Minnesota bounced back to lead 13-7 at halftime.

In the third period, Atlanta kicker Mick Luckhurst took a lateral on a fake field goal and scrambled 17 yards for the go-ahead touchdown. Less than 2 minutes later, safety Bob Glazebrook intercepted a pass by Tommy Kramer and returned it 35 yards for a touchdown. Although Minnesota retook the lead in the final period, a field goal by Luckhurst put Atlanta ahead again and set up the need for the Vikings' impressive winning drive.

Atlanta	7	0	14	3	-	24
Minnesota	3	10	3	14	-	30

Atl	-	Rogers recovered blocked punt in end zone (Luckhurst kick)
Min	-	FG Danmeier 33
Min	-	White 36 pass from Kramer (Danmeier kick)
Min	-	FG Danmeier 30
Atl	-	Luckhurst 17 run (Luckhurst kick)
Atl	-	Glazebrook 35 interception return (Luckhurst kick)
Min	-	FG Danmeier 39
Min	-	McCullum 11 pass from Kramer (Danmeier kick)
Atl	-	FG Luckhurst 41
Min	-	Brown 5 run (Luckhurst kick)

1982 AFC DIVISIONAL PLAYOFF GAME
New York Jets 17, Los Angeles Raiders 14

January 15, 1983, at Los Angeles
Attendance: 90,038

Wide receiver Wesley Walker scored 1 touchdown and set up 2 other scores, while Lance Mehl intercepted 2 passes late in the game to preserve New York's 17-14 victory.

The Jets led 10-0 at halftime after Walker caught a 20-yard touchdown pass from Richard Todd, then set up Pat Leahy's 30-yard field goal with a 37-yard catch.

In the third quarter, the Raiders took control. They drove 77 yards on 12 plays, with Marcus Allen scoring on a 3-yard touchdown run. Then Jim Plunkett hit Malcolm Barnwell with a 57-yard touchdown pass. Los Angeles had another chance after Lester Hayes intercepted Todd, but Allen fumbled deep in New York territory.

The Jets regained the lead with 3:45 left, after Walker caught a 45-yard pass to the 1, setting up Scott Dierking's touchdown run. Mehl then twice picked off passes by Plunkett.

N.Y. Jets	7	3	0	7	-	17
L.A. Raiders	0	0	14	0	-	14

NYJ	-	Walker 20 pass from Todd (Leahy kick)
NYJ	-	FG Leahy 30
Raid	-	Allen 3 run (Bahr kick)
Raid	-	Barnwell 57 pass from Plunkett (Bahr kick)
NYJ	-	Dierking 1 run (Leahy kick)

1982 AFC DIVISIONAL PLAYOFF GAME
Miami 34, San Diego 13

January 16, 1983, at Miami
Attendance: 71,383

Miami turned 3 first-half turnovers into points and went on to defeat the Chargers 34-13. Only 1 of the Dolphins' first 4 scores came following a drive of more than 30 yards.

The turnovers, which included 2 fumbled kickoffs, combined with 2 touchdown passes by David Woodley and a short scoring run by Andra Franklin to give the Dolphins a 24-0 lead in the second period. San Diego cut its deficit to 27-13 at halftime, with Dan Fouts throwing 1 touchdown pass and Chuck Muncie running for another, but then Miami's Killer Bees defense, the NFL's top-ranked unit, took charge.

In the second half, the Dolphins sacked Fouts twice and intercepted him 4 times, including 2 by strong safety Glenn Blackwood. The Dolphins knocked out the Chargers when Woodley scored on a 7-yard quarterback draw on the second play of the fourth quarter.

San Diego	0	13	0	0	-	13
Miami	7	20	0	7	-	34

Mia	-	Moore 3 pass from Woodley (von Schamann kick)
Mia	-	Franklin 3 run (von Schamann kick)
Mia	-	Lee 6 pass from Woodley (von Schamann kick)
Mia	-	FG von Schamann 24
SD	-	Joiner 28 pass from Fouts (kick failed)
Mia	-	FG von Schamann 23
SD	-	Muncie 1 run (Benirschke kick)
Mia	-	Woodley 7 run (von Schamann kick)

1982 NFC DIVISIONAL PLAYOFF GAME
Washington 21, Minnesota 7

January 15, 1983, at Washington
Attendance: 54,593

John Riggins, who earlier had asked to be given the ball in the playoffs, carried 37 times for 185 yards to lead the Washington Redskins to a 21-7 victory against the Minnesota Vikings.

Behind Riggins's power running, the Redskins controlled the ball for nearly 12 minutes of the first quarter. On the game's opening possession, they drove 66 yards in 10 plays, with Joe Theismann hitting tight end Don Warren with a 3-yard touchdown pass. They then moved 71 yards on only 7 plays, the key a 46-yard pass from Theismann to Alvin Garrett. Riggins blasted in from the 2 on fourth down.

After the Vikings responded with a touchdown in the second period, Theismann found Garrett with an 18-yard scoring pass that proved to be the final points of the game.

Minnesota	0	7	0	0	-	7
Washington	14	7	0	0	-	21

Was	-	Warren 3 pass from Theismann (Moseley kick)
Was	-	Riggins 2 run (Moseley kick)
Min	-	T. Brown 18 run (Danmeier kick)
Was	-	Garrett 18 pass from Theismann (Moseley kick)

1982 NFC DIVISIONAL PLAYOFF GAME
Dallas 37, Green Bay 26

January 16, 1983, at Irving, Texas
Attendance: 63,972

Dallas cornerback Dennis Thurman intercepted 3 of Lynn

Dickey's passes to help lead the Cowboys to a 37-26 victory over Green Bay.

Dallas led 6-0 on 2 field goals in the first quarter, but the Packers drove 79 yards to take the lead on a 6-yard pass from Dickey to James Lofton in the second quarter. Dallas responded with an 80-yard touchdown drive. Then, on the first play after the ensuing kickoff, Thurman intercepted at the Green Bay 39 and returned it for a touchdown that made it 20-7 at halftime.

The Packers trailed 23-13 at the end of three periods, but, on the first play of the final quarter, Lofton ran 71 yards for a touchdown on a reverse. Dallas responded with an 80-yard scoring drive, but Green Bay's Mark Lee scored on a 22-yard interception return. Thurman's third interception of the day preserved Dallas's lead.

Green Bay	**0**	**7**	**6**	**13**	**-**	**26**
Dallas	**6**	**14**	**3**	**14**	**-**	**37**

Dal	-	FG Septien 50
Dal	-	FG Septien 34
GB	-	Lofton 6 pass from Dickey (Stenerud kick)
Dal	-	Newsome 2 run (Septien kick)
Dal	-	Thurman 39 interception return (Septien kick)
GB	-	FG Stenerud 30
GB	-	FG Stenerud 33
Dal	-	FG Septien 24
GB	-	Lofton 71 run (kick failed)
Dal	-	Cosbie 7 pass from D. White (Septien kick)
GB	-	Lee 22 interception return (Stenerud kick)
Dal	-	Newhouse 1 run (Septien kick)

1982 AFC CHAMPIONSHIP GAME
Miami 14, New York Jets 0

January 23, 1983, at Miami
Attendance: 67,396

Miami linebacker A.J. Duhe intercepted 3 passes, scoring 1 touchdown and setting up another, to lead the Dolphins to a 14-0 victory over the New York Jets. The Killer Bees defense intercepted 5 Richard Todd passes and held the Jets to 139 total yards, including only 46 from NFL rushing leader Freeman McNeil.

A rainy day, a muddy field, and a slick ball limited both teams' effectiveness on offense. In the first half, neither team even drove deep enough to attempt a field goal.

On the opening drive of the third quarter, Duhe intercepted a pass intended for running back Mike Augustyniak. With a third-and-3 at the New York 28, David Woodley hit Duriel Harris for 14 yards, and an unsportsmanlike conduct penalty moved the ball to the 7. On first down, Woody Bennett powered through the middle for a touchdown.

The next time the Jets attained decent field position, at their 41, Duhe intercepted again to kill their hopes. Then, early in the fourth quarter, he intercepted a screen pass for Bruce Harper in the left flat and raced down the sideline 35 yards for the clinching touchdown.

N.Y. Jets	**0**	**0**	**0**	**0**	**-**	**0**
Miami	**0**	**0**	**7**	**7**	**-**	**14**

Mia	-	Bennett 7 run (von Schamann kick)
Mia	-	Duhe 35 interception return (von Schamann kick)

1982 NFC CHAMPIONSHIP GAME
Washington 31, Dallas 17

January 22, 1983, at Washington
Attendance: 55,045

The Washington defense and special teams made the big plays, and the offense took advantage of them, as the Redskins defeated the Cowboys 31-17.

The Cowboys scored early, marching 75 yards to a field goal. However, the Redskins mounted an 84-yard drive to Joe Theismann's 19-yard touchdown pass to Charlie Brown. In the second quarter, the Redskins' special teams went to work. Rod Hill bobbled a punt and Monte Coleman recovered at the Dallas 11, leading to a 1-yard touchdown by John Riggins, which made it 14-3.

The Cowboys' offense picked up in the second half behind the play of Gary Hogeboom, who came in late in the second period when Danny White suffered a concussion. Hogeboom led a drive that culminated in his 6-yard touchdown pass to Drew Pearson. Mike Nelms responded with a 76-yard kickoff return to the Dallas 20, leading to Riggins's 4-yard touchdown run. But Hogeboom brought Dallas back, moving 84 yards, culminating in a 23-yard touchdown pass to Butch Johnson.

In the final period, Mel Kaufman's interception led to a Washington field goal. Then, Dexter Manley tipped Hogeboom's pass to Darryl Grant, who lumbered 10 yards for the touchdown that clinched the game.

Dallas	**3**	**0**	**14**	**0**	**-**	**17**
Washington	**7**	**7**	**7**	**10**	**-**	**31**

Dal	-	FG Septien 27
Was	-	Brown 19 pass from Theismann (Moseley kick)
Was	-	Riggins 1 run (Moseley kick)
Dal	-	Pearson 6 pass from Hogeboom (Septien kick)
Was	-	Riggins 4 run (Moseley kick)
Dal	-	Johnson 23 pass from Hogeboom (Septien kick)
Was	-	FG Moseley 29
Was	-	Grant 10 interception return (Moseley kick)

1983 AFC WILD CARD GAME
Seattle 31, Denver 7

December 24, 1983, at Seattle
Attendance: 64,275

Dave Krieg completed 12 of 13 passes for 200 yards and 3 touchdowns, and the normally conservative Seahawks opened up their game in the second half as Seattle defeated Denver 31-7 for the franchise's first playoff victory.

The first half was relatively even. The Seahawks scored on their first possession, with Krieg passing 17 yards to Steve Largent for the touchdown. But the Broncos came back before the end of the first quarter, driving 76 yards in 9 plays, with Steve DeBerg passing 13 yards to Wilbur Myles for the equalizer.

Leading 10-7 at halftime, the Seahawks dropped their two-tight-end offense, and proceeded to score on their first three possessions of the second half, going 73 yards in 5 plays to Krieg's 5-yard touchdown pass to tight end Pete Metzelaars on their initial drive. Kreig threw an 18-yard touchdown pass to Paul Johns and then set up Seattle's final touchdown with a 41-yard pass to Johns.

Denver	**7**	**0**	**0**	**0**	**-**	**7**
Seattle	**7**	**3**	**7**	**14**	**-**	**31**

Sea	-	Largent 17 pass from Krieg (N. Johnson kick)

Den	-	Myles 13 pass from DeBerg (Karlis kick)
Sea	-	FG N. Johnson 37
Sea	-	Metzelaars 5 pass from Krieg (N. Johnson kick)
Sea	-	Johns 18 pass from Krieg (N. Johnson kick)
Sea	-	Hughes 2 run (N. Johnson kick)

1983 NFC WILD CARD GAME
Los Angeles Rams 24, Dallas 17

December 26, 1983, at Irving, Texas
Attendance: 62,118

The opportunistic Rams turned 3 second-half turnovers by the Cowboys into 17 points and came away surprise winners 24-17.

The Rams jumped ahead immediately, driving 85 yards to a touchdown behind the passing of Vince Ferragamo. But, taking over at the Dallas 30 with only 1:07 left in the first half, Danny White completed 5 of 6 passes, concluding with a 14-yard touchdown strike to Tony Hill to tie the game at 7-7.

Dallas moved ahead 10-7 in the third period, but then the Rams started taking advantage of the Cowboys' errors. After Greg Allen muffed a punt that Mike Witcher recovered at the Dallas 16, Ferragamo hit Preston Dennard for a touchdown. An interception by Jim Collins set up another touchdown drive. Finally, LeRoy Irvin intercepted a pass by White to set up a 20-yard field goal by Mike Lansford, and a last-minute touchdown couldn't save Dallas.

L.A. Rams	7	0	7	10	-	24
Dallas	0	7	3	7	-	17

Rams	-	D. Hill 18 pass from Ferragamo (Lansford kick)
Dal	-	T. Hill 14 pass from D. White (Septien kick)
Dal	-	FG Septien 41
Rams	-	Dennard 16 pass from Ferragamo (Lansford kick)
Rams	-	Farmer 8 pass from Ferragamo (Lansford kick)
Rams	-	FG Lansford 20
Dal	-	Cosbie 2 pass from White (Septien kick)

1983 AFC DIVISIONAL PLAYOFF GAME
Seattle 27, Miami 20

December 31, 1983, at Miami
Attendance: 74,136

Seattle took advantage of Miami mistakes in the second half to defeat the Dolphins 27-20. Miami looked strong early on, as Dan Marino took the Dolphins 80 yards for 1 touchdown and threw a spectacular 32-yard pass to Mark Duper for another. Seattle's first-half score came in between, set up by a 59-yard kickoff return.

In the second half, Miami started making mistakes. Curt Warner scored after the Seahawks recovered David Overstreet's fumble at the Miami 45. An interception of a Marino pass set up a field goal that gave Seattle a 17-13 advantage.

When the Dolphins scored to regain the lead, Seattle responded by driving to Curt Warner's second touchdown run. A fumble on the ensuing kickoff by Fulton Walker set up a field goal by Norm Johnson, and another fumble by Walker on the next kickoff made certain Miami wouldn't get a chance to tie the game.

Seattle	0	7	7	13	-	27
Miami	0	13	0	7	-	20

Mia	-	Johnson 19 pass from Marino (kick failed)
Sea	-	C. Bryant 6 pass from Krieg (N. Johnson kick)
Mia	-	Duper 32 pass from Marino (von Schamann kick)
Sea	-	Warner 1 run (N. Johnson kick)
Sea	-	FG N. Johnson 27
Mia	-	Bennett 3 run (von Schamann kick)
Sea	-	Warner 2 run (N. Johnson kick)
Sea	-	FG N. Johnson 37

1983 AFC DIVISIONAL PLAYOFF GAME
Los Angeles Raiders 38, Pittsburgh 10

January 1, 1984, at Los Angeles
Attendance: 90,380

The Los Angeles Raiders crushed the Pittsburgh Steelers 38-10 before an NFL playoff-record crowd of 90,380 at Los Angeles Memorial Coliseum.

The first score of the game, although it was by Pittsburgh, gave a huge emotional advantage to the Raiders. The Steelers drove 78 yards, but, on fourth-and-inches near the goal line, Gary Anderson kicked a 17-yard field goal.

"When they decided to take the three," Raiders head coach Tom Flores said, "it gave us a huge lift." Three minutes later, Lester Hayes returned an interception 18 yards for a touchdown, and the Raiders were off and running.

Los Angeles drove 80 yards for a 4-yard second-period touchdown run by Marcus Allen, then added a field goal for a 17-3 halftime lead. In the third period, the Raiders turned the game into a rout, driving 72, 58, and 65 yards for touchdowns.

Pittsburgh	3	0	7	0	-	10
L.A. Raiders	7	10	21	0	-	38

Pit	-	FG Anderson 17
Raid	-	Hayes 18 interception return (Bahr kick)
Raid	-	Allen 4 run (Bahr kick)
Raid	-	FG Bahr 45
Raid	-	King 9 run (Bahr kick)
Raid	-	Allen 49 run (Bahr kick)
Pit	-	Stallworth 58 pass from Stoudt (Anderson kick)
Raid	-	Hawkins 2 run (Bahr kick)

1983 NFC DIVISIONAL PLAYOFF GAME
San Francisco 24, Detroit 23

December 31, 1983, at San Francisco
Attendance: 59,979

Detroit's Eddie Murray kicked 3 field goals, including one for a playoff-record 54 yards, but with 5 seconds remaining he missed a 43-yard attempt, allowing San Francisco to escape with a 24-23 victory.

The Lions jumped up 3-0 on their first drive. They threatened again in the first quarter, but Gary Danielson was intercepted, setting up the 49ers' first touchdown. On the first play after the kickoff, Danielson was intercepted again, and the 49ers turned it into a 14-3 lead. The Lions managed 2 field goals in the second period despite 2 more interceptions of Danielson.

In the final period, Billy Sims scored on 2 touchdown runs for a 23-17 lead with five minutes left. But Joe Montana completed 6 of 6 passes, including a 14-yard touchdown strike to Freddie Solomon for the lead. Danielson completed 4 passes in a last-gasp drive to set up Murray's field-goal attempt.

Detroit	3	6	0	14	-	23
San Francisco	7	7	3	7	-	24

Det	-	FG Murray 37
SF	-	Craig 1 run (Wersching kick)
SF	-	Tyler 2 run (Wersching kick)
Det	-	FG Murray 21
Det	-	FG Murray 54
SF	-	FG Wersching 19
Det	-	Sims 11 run (Murray kick)
Det	-	Sims 3 run (Murray kick)
SF	-	Solomon 14 pass from Montana (Wersching kick)

1983 NFC DIVISIONAL PLAYOFF GAME
Washington 51, Los Angeles Rams 7

January 1, 1984, at Washington
Attendance: 54,440

The Redskins scored on their first five possessions to build a 38-7 halftime lead, then turned the game over to a defense that held NFL-rushing champion Eric Dickerson to 16 yards on 10 carries (and only 9 yards on 6 receptions). Washington's defense also intercepted Vince Ferragamo 3 times and scored once in a 51-7 victory, the worst defeat ever for the Rams.

John Riggins pounded for 119 yards—his fifth consecutive playoff game over the 100-yard mark— and Joe Theismann completed 18 of 23 passes as the Redskins did virtually anything they wanted in jumping ahead 24-0 before the Rams could score. Mark Moseley's extra point after Riggins' third touchdown run gave the Redskins an NFL playoff-game record for most first-half points (38).

The highlight of the second half was a scintillating 72-yard interception return for a touchdown by Darrell Green.

L.A. Rams	0	7	0	0	-	7
Washington	17	21	6	7	-	51

Was	-	Riggins 3 run (Moseley kick)
Was	-	Monk 40 pass from Theismann (Moseley kick)
Was	-	FG Moseley 42
Was	-	Riggins 1 run (Moseley kick)
Rams	-	Dennard 32 pass from Ferragamo (Lansford kick)
Was	-	Monk 21 pass from Theismann (Moseley kick)
Was	-	Riggins 1 run (Moseley kick)
Was	-	FG Moseley 36
Was	-	FG Moseley 41
Was	-	Green 72 interception return (Moseley kick)

1983 AFC CHAMPIONSHIP GAME
Los Angeles Raiders 30, Seattle 14

January 8, 1984, at Los Angeles
Attendance: 91,445

The Raiders, who had lost to the Seahawks twice during the regular season, held AFC rookie of the year Curt Warner to 26 yards on 11 carries, while Marcus Allen responded with 154 yards rushing as Los Angeles defeated Seattle 30-14.

The Raiders jumped ahead 20-0 at halftime. Each of their 4 scores was set up by a big play, 2 by the offense and 2 by the defense. On Seattle's first possession of the game, Lester Hayes intercepted Dave Krieg to set up Chris Bahr's 20-yard field goal. In the second period, long passes by Jim Plunkett set up short scoring runs by Frank Hawkins, and another turnover set up Bahr's 45-yard field goal.

Jim Zorn replaced Krieg in the second half and threw 2 touchdown passes, but it was too little, too late. By the time of Zorn's first scoring toss, 11 yards to Dan Doornink, the Raiders already led 27-0. Los Angeles's third-period touchdown came on a 2-play, 49-yard drive.

Seattle	0	0	7	7	-	14
L.A. Raiders	3	17	7	3	-	30

Raid	-	FG Bahr 20
Raid	-	Hawkins 1 run (Bahr kick)
Raid	-	Hawkins 5 run (Bahr kick)
Raid	-	FG Bahr 45
Raid	-	Allen 3 pass from Plunkett (Bahr kick)
Sea	-	Doornink 11 pass from Zorn (N. Johnson kick)
Raid	-	FG Bahr 35
Sea	-	Young 9 pass from Zorn (N. Johnson kick)

1983 NFC CHAMPIONSHIP GAME
Washington 24, San Francisco 21

January 8, 1984, at Washington
Attendance: 55,363

Joe Montana attempted to turn this game into the greatest fourth-quarter comeback in playoff history, but Mark Moseley kicked a 25-yard field goal with 40 seconds left to give Washington a 24-21 victory over San Francisco.

For three quarters, Washington, the NFL's dominant team in the regular season, continued to play that way. Two touchdown runs by John Riggins and a 70-yard bomb from Joe Theismann to Charlie Brown gave the Redskins a 21-0 lead. But the normally consistent Moseley missed 4 field-goal attempts, and Darrell Green's punt return for a touchdown was called back due to a penalty.

In the fourth period, the 49ers came to life. Behind Montana's NFC Championship Game-record 27 completions in 48 attempts, the 49ers scored 3 times. Montana threw touchdown passes to Mike Wilson, Freddie Solomon, and Wilson again to tie the score at 21-21.

But then the Redskins engaged in some heroics of their own. Starting at the Washington 14, Joe Theismann led a 13-play, 78-yard drive that took 6:12 off the clock. The drive was helped by 2 controversial penalties: pass interference against Eric Wright and holding against Ronnie Lott.

San Francisco	0	0	0	21	-	21
Washington	0	7	14	3	-	24

Was	-	Riggins 4 run (Moseley kick)
Was	-	Riggins 1 run (Moseley kick)
Was	-	Brown 70 pass from Theismann (Moseley kick)
SF	-	Wilson 5 pass from Montana (Wersching kick)
SF	-	Solomon 76 pass from Montana (Wersching kick)
SF	-	Wilson 12 pass from Montana (Wersching kick)
Was	-	FG Moseley 25

1984 AFC WILD CARD GAME
Seattle 13, Los Angeles Raiders 7

December 22, 1984, at Seattle
Attendance: 62,049

Seattle, which had been one of the most productive passing teams in the NFL, controlled the ball with a slow-but-sure ground game that netted 205 yards en route to a 13-7 victory against AFC West rival Los Angeles.

Dave Krieg, who passed for 3,671 yards and 32 touchdowns in the regular season, completed only 4 passes in 10 attempts. The only time he connected with a wide receiver all day came in the second quarter, when his 26-yard touchdown strike to Daryl Turner provided the only score of the first half.

The Seahawks' plan was to let Dan Doornink and David Hughes run off tackle and cut back against the Raiders' attacking front. Doornink compiled 126 yards on 29 carries, and the Seahawks added a pair of field goals in the second half. Meanwhile, Seattle's defense intercepted Jim Plunkett twice and sacked him 6 times.

L.A. Raiders	0	0	0	7	-	7
Seattle	0	7	3	3	-	13

Sea - Turner 26 pass from Krieg (N. Johnson kick)
Sea - FG N. Johnson 35
Sea - FG N. Johnson 44
Raid - Allen 46 pass from Plunkett (Bahr kick)

1984 NFC WILD CARD GAME
New York Giants 16, Los Angeles Rams 13

December 23, 1984, at Anaheim, California
Attendance: 67,037

In a tough defensive struggle, the Rams gave up fewer yards (192 to 214), but the Giants gave up fewer points to win 16-13.

The Giants led the entire way, taking the lead early on Ali Haji-Sheikh's 37-yard field goal. Later in the first period, Eric Dickerson fumbled, and Bill Currier recovered at the Los Angeles 23. A 9-play drive was capped by Rob Carpenter's 1-yard touchdown run to give New York a 10-0 lead.

After swapping field goals, the Rams drove 78 yards in the third quarter, scoring on Dickerson's 14-yard run. Trailing, 16-10 in the final period, they drove deep into New York territory. But with a second-and-goal at the 4, the Rams tried to surprise the Giants by giving the ball to Dwayne Crutchfield instead of Dickerson. A 3-yard loss meant the Rams had to settle for a Mike Lansford field goal, and the Giants' defense made certain Los Angeles didn't score again.

N.Y. Giants	10	0	6	0	-	16
L.A. Rams	0	3	7	3	-	13

NYG - FG Haji-Sheikh 37
NYG - Carpenter 1 run (Haji-Sheikh kick)
Rams - FG Lansford 38
NYG - FG Haji-Sheikh 39
Rams - Dickerson 14 run (Lansford kick)
NYG - FG Haji-Sheikh 36
Rams - FG Lansford 22

1984 AFC DIVISIONAL PLAYOFF GAME
Miami 31, Seattle 10

December 29, 1984, at Miami
Attendance: 73,469

Seattle wanted to play ball control, but it was the Dolphins who ran off 70 plays, netted 405 yards, and produced a 31-10 victory.

The Dolphins couldn't shake the Seahawks in the first half. Miami went ahead on Tony Nathan's 14-yard run, but Seattle responded with a field goal. Then Dan Marino's 34-yard scoring pass to Jimmy Cefalo was matched by a 56-yard touchdown pass from Dave Krieg to Steve Largent.

In the third period, Seattle had an 11-play drive to the Miami 24, but Norm Johnson missed a field goal. The Dolphins responded by driving to Seattle's 3. On third down, Marino's pass was batted down, but a pass-interference penalty gave Miami a first down, and two plays later Marino threw a touchdown pass to Bruce Hardy. The next time Miami had the ball, Marino found Mark Clayton with a 33-yard touchdown pass for the clinching score.

Seattle	0	10	0	0	-	10
Miami	7	7	14	3	-	31

Mia - Nathan 14 run (von Schamann kick)
Sea - FG N. Johnson 27
Mia - Cefalo 34 pass from Marino (von Schamann kick)
Sea - Largent 56 pass from Krieg (N. Johnson kick)
Mia - Hardy 3 pass from Marino (von Schamann kick)
Mia - Clayton 33 pass from Marino (von Schamann kick)
Mia - FG von Schamann 37

1984 AFC DIVISIONAL PLAYOFF GAME
Pittsburgh 24, Denver 17

December 30, 1984, at Denver
Attendance: 74,981

With a little more than 3 minutes left in a tied game, Pittsburgh safety Eric Williams intercepted a pass by John Elway and returned it to the Denver 2-yard line. Three plays later Frank Pollard scored his second touchdown of the day to provide the Steelers with a 24-17 victory.

The Broncos took the early lead on a touchdown pass from Elway to Jim Wright 5 plays after Tom Jackson had recovered a fumble by Mark Malone. Then the Steelers began to dominate the line of scrimmage (they rushed for 169 yards to Denver's 51). Pittsburgh led at halftime after Pollard ran 1 yard for a touchdown with 1:14 left in the second quarter.

Denver tied the game in the third period, then Elway threw a 20-yard touchdown pass to Steve Watson. But Pittsburgh came right back, tying the score by marching 66 yards, the last 10 on a touchdown pass from Malone to Louis Lipps.

Pittsburgh	0	10	7	7	-	24
Denver	7	0	10	0	-	17

Den - J. Wright 9 pass from Elway (Karlis kick)
Pit - FG Anderson 28
Pit - Pollard 1 run (Anderson kick)
Den - FG Karlis 21
Den - Watson 20 pass from Elway (Karlis kick)
Pit - Lipps 10 pass from Malone (Anderson kick)
Pit - Pollard 2 run (Anderson kick)

1984 NFC DIVISIONAL PLAYOFF GAME
San Francisco 21, New York Giants 10

December 29, 1984, at San Francisco
Attendance: 60,303

Joe Montana threw 3 touchdown passes, and San Francisco beat New York 21-10.

The 49ers scored twice in the first 7 minutes of the game. Soon after Montana passed 21 yards to Dwight Clark for a touchdown on San Francisco's first possession, linebacker Dan Bunz tipped Phil Simms's pass. The ball bounced off linebacker Riki Ellison and was intercepted by Ronnie Lott, who returned it 38 yards to the 12. Montana then threw a 9-yard touchdown pass to Russ Francis for a 14-0 lead.

After the Giants kicked a field goal, linebacker Harry Carson intercepted a pass by Montana and returned it 14 yards for a touchdown. But Montana responded with a 5-play, 72-yard drive that culminated in his 29-yard touchdown pass to Freddie Solomon. The defenses then toughened and allowed no points in the second half.

N.Y. Giants	0	10	0	0	-	10
San Francisco	14	7	0	0	-	21

SF - D. Clark 21 pass from Montana (Wersching kick)

SF	-	Francis 9 pass from Montana (Wersching kick)
NYG	-	FG Haji-Sheikh 46
NYG	-	Carson 14 interception return (Haji-Sheikh kick)
SF	-	Solomon 29 pass from Montana (Wersching kick)

1984 NFC DIVISIONAL PLAYOFF GAME
Chicago Bears 23, Washington 19

December 30, 1984, at Washington
Attendance: 55,431

The Chicago defense held John Riggins to 50 yards rushing, sacked Joe Theismann 7 times, and created 3 turnovers as the Bears pulled a 23-19 upset.

Surprisingly, it was the Bears' passing game that made much of the difference. With the score tied 3-3 late in the first half, Walter Payton took a pitchout, faked a reverse to Dennis McKinnon, and threw a 19-yard touchdown pass to tight end Pat Dunsmore, who was alone in the end zone.

Chicago quarterback Steve Fuller led the way in the second half. On the second play of the third quarter, he threw a short pass to Willie Gault, who raced past Darrell Green for a 75-yard touchdown. Fuller subsequently threw a 16-yard pass to McKinnon for the clinching touchdown.

Chi. Bears	0	10	13	0	-	23
Washington	3	0	14	2	-	19

Was	-	FG Moseley 25
ChiB	-	FG B. Thomas 34
ChiB	-	Dunsmore 19 pass from Payton (B. Thomas kick)
ChiB	-	Gault 75 pass from Fuller (kick failed)
Was	-	Riggins 1 run (Moseley kick)
ChiB	-	McKinnon 16 pass from Fuller (B. Thomas kick)
Was	-	Riggins 1 run (Moseley kick)
Was	-	Safety, Finzer stepped out of end zone

1984 AFC CHAMPIONSHIP GAME
Miami 45, Pittsburgh 28

January 6, 1985, at Miami
Attendance: 76,029

Pittsburgh's Mark Malone passed for 312 yards and 3 touchdowns, but Miami's Dan Marino completed 21 of 32 passes for 421 yards and 4 touchdowns to lead the Dolphins to a 45-28 victory.

Miami scored on its first possession, going 67 yards in only 4 plays, with Marino teaming with Mark Clayton on a 40-yard touchdown pass. Behind a powerful ground game and a 65-yard touchdown pass from Malone to John Stallworth, the Steelers came back to lead 14-10 late in the second period. Then Marino went to work again, as the Dolphins marched 77 yards in 5 plays, scoring on a 41-yard touchdown pass to Mark Duper. A 2-yard touchdown run by Tony Nathan after an interception put Miami ahead 24-14 at halftime.

On the first series of the third quarter, Marino worked his magic again, driving his team 78 yards in 4 plays, culminating with a 36-yard pass to Duper. After Malone came back with another touchdown pass to Stallworth, Marino led the Dolphins to 2 more touchdowns, the last a 6-yard strike to Nat Moore.

Pittsburgh	7	7	7	7	-	28
Miami	7	17	14	7	-	45

Mia	-	Clayton 40 pass from Marino (von Schamann kick)
Pit	-	Erenberg 7 run (Anderson kick)
Mia	-	FG von Schamann 26
Pit	-	Stallworth 65 pass from Malone (Anderson kick)
Mia	-	Duper 41 pass from Marino (von Schamann kick)
Mia	-	Nathan 2 run (von Schamann kick)
Mia	-	Duper 36 pass from Marino (von Schamann kick)
Pit	-	Stallworth 19 pass from Malone (Anderson kick)
Mia	-	Bennett 1 run (von Schamann kick)
Mia	-	Moore 6 pass from Marino (von Schamann kick)
Pit	-	Capers 29 pass from Malone (Anderson kick)

1984 NFC CHAMPIONSHIP GAME
San Francisco 23, Chicago Bears 0

January 6, 1985, at San Francisco
Attendance: 61,336

The San Francisco defense sacked Steve Fuller 9 times and shut down the Bears' attack, while the 49ers' offense slowly overcame the outstanding Chicago defense to record a 23-0 victory.

The first half was a tough defensive struggle. The 49ers scored twice on field goals by Ray Wersching, but they came up empty on two other excellent scoring opportunities when safety Gary Fencik intercepted passes by Joe Montana, 1 in the end zone and the other on the Chicago 5.

The 49ers started to break the game open in the third period. A 15-yard punt return by Dana McLemore set them up at the Chicago 35, and, 5 plays later, Wendell Tyler ran in from the 9. Chicago then drove to the 49ers' 21, but sacks by Dwaine Board and Gary Johnson ended the drive.

With Montana completing 4 of 4 passes and Roger Craig bursting off left tackle for 39 yards on 1 play, the 49ers drove 88 yards to the clinching touchdown. Montana passed 10 yards to Freddie Solomon for the score.

Chi. Bears	0	0	0	0	-	0
San Francisco	3	3	7	10	-	23

SF	-	FG Wersching 21
SF	-	FG Wersching 22
SF	-	Tyler 9 run (Wersching kick)
SF	-	Solomon 10 pass from Montana (Wersching kick)
SF	-	FG Wersching 34

1985 AFC WILD CARD GAME
New England 26, New York Jets 14

December 28, 1985,
at East Rutherford, New Jersey
Attendance: 70,958

The Patriots won their first playoff game since 1963 as their defense accounted for 4 turnovers, 5 sacks, and the clinching touchdown in a 26-14 victory over the Jets.

The Jets led 7-6 late in the first half and apparently were driving to another score when safety Fred Marion intercepted a pass by Ken O'Brien and returned it to the 33. Six plays later, Tony Eason hit Stanley Morgan with a 36-yard touchdown pass, and the Patriots led 13-7. Then, when the Jets tried to race down the field in the final 2 minutes, linebacker Andre Tippett dropped O'Brien with such a jarring tackle that the NFL's leading passer missed the rest of the game.

In the third quarter, Tony Franklin kicked his third field goal. On the ensuing kickoff, Johnny Rembert stripped the ball from Johnny Hector, picked it up, and went 15 yards for a touchdown.

New England	3	10	10	3	-	26
N.Y. Jets	0	7	7	0	-	14

NE	-	FG Franklin 33
NYJ	-	Hector 11 pass from O'Brien (Leahy kick)
NE	-	FG Franklin 41
NE	-	Morgan 36 pass from Eason (Franklin kick)

NE	-	FG Franklin 20
NE	-	Rembert 15 fumble return (Franklin kick)
NYJ	-	Shuler 12 pass from Ryan (Leahy kick)
NE	-	FG Franklin 26

1985 NFC WILD CARD GAME
New York Giants 17, San Francisco 3

December 29, 1985,
at East Rutherford, New Jersey
Attendance: 75,842

The Giants' defense was punctured for 362 yards, but it came up with big plays when needed, holding San Francisco to a single field goal, while the offense moved the ball well enough to defeat the 49ers 17-3.

The Giants took the lead the first time they had the ball, when Eric Schubert kicked a 47-yard field goal. In the second quarter, Terry Kinnard intercepted a pass from Joe Montana, setting up Phil Simms's 18-yard touchdown pass to Mark Bavaro, who made a sensational one-handed grab. Late in the period, the 49ers put together their best drive, moving 85 yards in 16 plays, but still had to settle for a field goal.

With Joe Morris doing the heavy-duty work on the opening series of the second half—he gained 141 yards for the day—the Giants drove 77 yards to the game's final touchdown.

San Francisco	0	3	0	0	-	3
N.Y. Giants	3	7	7	0	-	17

NYG	-	FG Schubert 47
NYG	-	Bavaro 18 pass from Simms (Schubert kick)
SF	-	FG Wersching 21
NYG	-	Hasselbeck 3 pass from Simms (Schubert kick)

1985 AFC DIVISIONAL PLAYOFF GAME
Miami 24, Cleveland 21

January 4, 1986, at Miami
Attendance: 75,128

Miami trailed Cleveland 21-3 midway through the third quarter, but the Dolphins exploded for 3 touchdowns, the last score with only 1:57 left in the game, to win 24-21.

The Dolphins kicked a field goal on their first possession, but their offense disappeared for the rest of the half. Meanwhile, the Browns were on their way to piling up 251 yards on the ground. In the first period, they drove 82 yards in 10 plays. In the second period, it was 55 yards in 8 plays after Don Rogers intercepted Dan Marino.

Earnest Byner ran 66 yards to make it 21-3 midway through the third period, but the Dolphins exploded with Marino passing to Nat Moore from 6 yards to climax a 74-yard drive. The next time Miami had the ball, Ron Davenport scored on a 31-yard run, and then an 8-play, 73-yard game-winning drive ended when Davenport plowed in from the 1.

Cleveland	7	7	7	0	-	21
Miami	3	0	14	7	-	24

Mia	-	FG Reveiz 51
Cle	-	Newsome 16 pass from Kosar (Bahr kick)
Cle	-	Byner 21 run (Bahr kick)
Cle	-	Byner 66 run (Bahr kick)
Mia	-	N. Moore 6 pass from Marino (Reveiz kick)
Mia	-	Davenport 31 run (Reveiz kick)
Mia	-	Davenport 1 run (Reveiz kick)

1985 AFC DIVISIONAL PLAYOFF GAME
New England 27, Los Angeles Raiders 20

January 5, 1986, at Los Angeles
Attendance: 88,936

New England collected 6 turnovers, converted them into 17 points, and upset the Raiders 27-20.

The Patriots wasted little time taking advantage of a Raiders' miscue. When Fulton Walker fumbled a punt at the Los Angeles 21, backup safety Jim Bowman recovered, setting up Tony Eason's 13-yard touchdown pass to tight end Lin Dawson. The Raiders charged back for 17 points, the second touchdown set up by Mosi Tatupu's lost fumble at the New England 17. New England drove 80 yards for a touchdown, then tied the game after Ronnie Lippett intercepted a pass from Marc Wilson. But the Raiders regained the lead on a field goal 6 seconds before halftime.

Late in the third quarter, the Patriots drove 54 yards to Tony Franklin's tying 32-yard field goal. On the ensuing kickoff, Sam Seale fumbled and Bowman recovered in the end zone for the winning points.

New England	7	10	10	0	-	27
L.A. Raiders	3	17	0	0	-	20

NE	-	Dawson 13 pass from Eason (Franklin kick)
Raid	-	FG Bahr 29
Raid	-	Hester 16 pass from Wilson (Bahr kick)
Raid	-	Allen 11 run (Bahr kick)
NE	-	C. James 2 run (Franklin kick)
NE	-	FG Franklin 45
Raid	-	FG Bahr 32
NE	-	FG Franklin 32
NE	-	Bowman recovered fumble in end zone (Franklin kick)

1985 NFC DIVISIONAL PLAYOFF GAME
Los Angeles Rams 20, Dallas 0

January 4, 1986, at Anaheim, California
Attendance: 66,581

Eric Dickerson set a postseason record by rushing for 248 yards to lead the Rams to a 20-0 victory over the Cowboys.

A defensive struggle in the first half ended with the Rams ahead 3-0. In the first quarter, Henry Ellard returned a punt 23 yards to the Dallas 38, then caught a 21-yard pass from Dieter Brock to set up Mike Lansford's 33-yard field goal.

The Rams scored twice to start the second half. On first down, after Charles White returned the kickoff to the 45, Dickerson blasted straight through the middle and raced 55 yards for a touchdown. Kenny Duckett fumbled the following kickoff, and the ball was recovered by Vince Newsome, setting up Lansford's second field goal and giving the Rams a 13-0 lead.

Late in the period, Gordon Banks fumbled a punt and Tony Hunter recovered for the Rams. Dickerson then raced down the right sideline 40 yards for his second touchdown.

Dallas	0	0	0	0	-	0
L.A. Rams	3	0	10	7	-	20

Rams	-	FG Lansford 33
Rams	-	Dickerson 55 run (Lansford kick)
Rams	-	FG Lansford 34
Rams	-	Dickerson 40 run (Lansford kick)

1985 NFC DIVISIONAL PLAYOFF GAME
Chicago Bears 21, New York Giants 0

January 5, 1986, at Chicago
Attendance: 62,076

The Chicago defense was phenomenal, holding the Giants without a first down for the first 28 minutes, recording almost twice as much sack yardage (60) as it gave up rushing yards (32), and limiting the Giants to minus-11 yards in the third quarter. With some help from the offense, the result was a 21-0 victory.

The only score of the first half came when the Giants were forced to punt from their 12. The wind caught the ball, which barely grazed off the side of punter Sean Landeta's foot, and Shaun Gayle picked it up and ran 5 yards for a touchdown.

Chicago quarterback Jim McMahon applied the knock-out punch in the third quarter. First, he found Dennis McKinnon for a 23-yard touchdown pass. Six minutes later, 1 play after he hit Tim Wrightman for a 46-yard gain, McMahon went back to McKinnon for 20 yards and another touchdown.

N.Y. Giants	0	0	0	0	-	0
Chi. Bears	7	0	14	0	-	21

ChiB	-	Gayle 5 punt return (Butler kick)
ChiB	-	McKinnon 23 pass from McMahon (Butler kick)
ChiB	-	McKinnon 20 pass from McMahon (Butler kick)

1985 AFC CHAMPIONSHIP GAME
New England 31, Miami 14

January 12, 1986, at Miami
Attendance: 74,978

New England converted 6 Miami turnovers into 24 points, and Tony Eason threw 3 touchdown passes as the Patriots defeated the Dolphins 31-14 to snap an 18-game losing streak in Miami.

The Dolphins' first turnover came on their first offensive play. Tony Nathan fumbled and Garin Veris recovered, setting up Tony Franklin's 23-yard field goal. After Dan Marino fired a touchdown pass to give Miami a lead, the Patriots came storming back. Robert Weathers carried the ball 4 times for 57 yards in a 66-yard drive that culminated in Eason's 4-yard pass to Tony Collins. Marino fumbled 2 plays after the kickoff, and the Patriots recovered. Eason ultimately threw a 1-yard touchdown pass to tight end Derrick Ramsey for a 17-7 lead.

A fumble of the second-half kickoff knocked out the Dolphins. Lorenzo Hampton's fumble was recovered for New England by Greg Hawthorne at the Miami 25. Eason threw a 2-yard touchdown pass to Weathers for a 24-7 lead.

Marino passed on 23 of Miami's 24 plays in the fourth quarter, but the Dolphins could score only once. Meanwhile, the Patriots concentrated on their ground game, finishing the day with 255 yards rushing.

New England	3	14	7	7	-	31
Miami	0	7	0	7	-	14

NE	-	FG Franklin 23
Mia	-	Johnson 10 pass from Marino (Reveiz kick)
NE	-	Collins 4 pass from Eason (Franklin kick)
NE	-	D. Ramsey 1 pass from Eason (Franklin kick)
NE	-	Weathers 2 pass from Eason (Franklin kick)
Mia	-	Nathan 10 pass from Marino (Reveiz kick)
NE	-	Tatupu 1 run (Franklin kick)

1985 NFC CHAMPIONSHIP GAME
Chicago Bears 24, Los Angeles Rams 0

January 12, 1986, at Chicago
Attendance: 63,522

In a game that ended in snow flurries, the Bears' defense held Rams running back Eric Dickerson to 46 yards—202 fewer than the previous week—and limited quarterback Dieter Brock to 10 completions in 31 attempts in a 24-0 rout. It was the first time a team had recorded successive shutouts in the same playoff year.

The Bears took the lead at the start, driving 66 yards on their first possession. Jim McMahon finished the drive by scrambling 16 yards around left end for a touchdown. On their next possession, the Bears moved 33 yards to set up Kevin Butler's 34-yard field goal.

Los Angeles's best chance to score came late in the second quarter, but the half ended with the Rams inside the Chicago 3-yard line.

The Bears built their lead to 17 points in the third quarter, when McMahon ended a 52-yard drive by passing 22 yards to Willie Gault. Then, in the final period, Richard Dent forced a fumble by Brock, which Wilber Marshall scooped up and returned 52 yards for a touchdown.

L.A. Rams	0	0	0	0	-	0
Chi. Bears	10	0	7	7	-	24

ChiB	-	McMahon 16 run (Butler kick)
ChiB	-	FG Butler 34
ChiB	-	Gault 22 pass from McMahon (Butler kick)
ChiB	-	Marshall 52 fumble return (Butler kick)

1986 AFC WILD CARD GAME
New York Jets 35, Kansas City 15

December 28, 1986,
at East Rutherford, New Jersey
Attendance: 69,307

Pat Ryan, who only started twice during the regular season, threw 3 touchdown passes and set up New York's first score with a fourth-down run to lead the Jets to a 35-15 victory against Kansas City. The Jets made the playoffs despite losing their last five games of the regular season.

The Chiefs drove 67 yards for a touchdown on their first possession. On the following series, the Jets faced a fourth-and-6 at the Kansas City 33. Eschewing the long field-goal attempt, Ryan faked a pitchout to the left and ran through a huge hole, gaining 24 yards before being dragged down at the 9. Two plays later Freeman McNeil barged in from 4 yards, and the Jets took a 7-6 lead.

The momentum, which in the early stages seemed to belong to the Chiefs, clearly shifted to the Jets. Ryan threw a pair of touchdown passes in the second quarter, then another in the fourth.

Kansas City	6	0	0	9	-	15
N.Y. Jets	7	14	7	7	-	35

KC	-	J. Smith 1 run (kick failed)
NYJ	-	McNeil 4 run (Leahy kick)
NYJ	-	McNeil 1 pass from Ryan (Leahy kick)
NYJ	-	Toon 11 pass from Ryan (Leahy kick)
NYJ	-	McArthur 21 interception return (Leahy kick)
KC	-	Lewis recovered blocked punt in end zone
NYJ	-	Griggs 6 pass from Ryan (Leahy kick)
KC	-	Safety, Jennings ran out of end zone

1986 NFC WILD CARD GAME
Washington 19, Los Angeles Rams 7

December 28, 1986, at Washington
Attendance: 54,180

The Rams had more yards rushing than the Redskins (198-138) and more yards passing (126-90), but they also turned over the ball 6 times. Washington did not commit a turnover and won 19-7.

Los Angeles wasted no time in helping the Redskins take the lead. After the Rams drove to the Washington 40 early in the game, Eric Dickerson fumbled, and safety Alvin Walton recovered, setting up a 25-yard field goal by Jess Atkinson. After the Redskins scored their only touchdown of the game, the Rams helped them build their lead even further. First Dickerson lost the ball at the Washington 17, then tight end David Hill fumbled at the Washington 26, leading to Atkinson's second field goal and a 13-0 halftime score.

The pattern continued in the second half as, after finally scoring in the fourth quarter, the Rams suffered turnovers on their next three possessions, one of them setting up Atkinson's fourth field goal.

L.A. Rams	0	0	0	7	-	7
Washington	10	3	3	3	-	19

Was	-	FG Atkinson 25
Was	-	Bryant 14 pass from Schroeder (Atkinson kick)
Was	-	FG Atkinson 20
Was	-	FG Atkinson 38
Rams	-	House 12 pass from Everett (Lansford kick)
Was	-	FG Atkinson 19

1986 AFC DIVISIONAL PLAYOFF GAME
Cleveland 23, New York Jets 20 (2 OT)

January 4, 1987, at Cleveland
Attendance: 78,106

Bernie Kosar set NFL playoff records by throwing 64 passes for 489 yards to lead Cleveland to a 23-20 victory in the third-longest game in NFL history. Mark Moseley ended the stalemate with a 27-yard field goal after 17:02 of overtime.

The Jets scored first when Pat Ryan teamed with Wesley Walker on a 42-yard touchdown pass to cap an 82-yard drive. Although the ensuing kickoff was returned only to the Cleveland 2, it took Kosar just 6 plays to move his team 98 yards to tie the score.

The Jets took a 20-10 lead with 4:14 remaining in regulation, but Kosar brought his team back, driving the Browns 68 yards to a touchdown on Kevin Mack's 1-yard run. Kosar threw a 37-yard pass to Webster Slaughter to set up Moseley's 22-yard field goal with 7 seconds left, sending the game into overtime.

N.Y. Jets	7	3	3	7	0	0	-	20
Browns	7	3	0	10	0	3	-	23

NYJ	-	Walker 42 pass from Ryan (Leahy kick)
Cle	-	Fontenot 37 pass from Kosar (Moseley kick)
Cle	-	FG Moseley 38
NYJ	-	FG Leahy 46
NYJ	-	FG Leahy 37
NYJ	-	McNeil 25 run (Leahy kick)
Cle	-	Mack 1 run (Moseley kick)
Cle	-	FG Moseley 22
Cle	-	FG Moseley 27

1986 AFC DIVISIONAL PLAYOFF GAME
Denver 22, New England 17

January 4, 1987, at Denver
Attendance: 76,105

John Elway ran for 1 touchdown and passed for another to lead Denver to a 22-17 victory over New England.

Elway got going early, hitting successive passes to Steve Sewell and Steve Watson to set up the only score of the first period, Rich Karlis's 27-yard field goal. After New England drove 87 yards to a touchdown to take the lead, Elway moved the Broncos 82 yards in 13 plays. When Elway was trapped, he scrambled out of pressure and ran 22 yards for a touchdown.

After an exchange of field goals, New England retook the lead in third period on Tony Eason's second touchdown pass to Stanley Morgan. But Elway again retaliated, hitting Vance Johnson for 48 yards and the go-ahead touchdown. The only score of the final period came when Rulon Jones sacked Eason for a safety.

New England	0	10	7	0	-	17
Denver	3	7	10	2	-	22

Den	-	FG Karlis 27
Den	-	Elway 22 run (Karlis kick)
NE	-	FG Franklin 38
NE	-	Morgan 19 pass from Eason (Franklin kick)
Den	-	FG Karlis 22
NE	-	Morgan 45 pass from Eason (Franklin kick)
Den	-	Johnson 48 pass from Elway (Karlis kick)
Den	-	Safety, Eason sacked in end zone by R.Jones

1986 NFC DIVISIONAL PLAYOFF GAME
Washington 27, Chicago Bears 13

January 3, 1987, at Chicago
Attendance: 65,141

A methodical attack by the Redskins and a string of miscues by the Bears combined to lead Washington to a 27-13 victory.

Kevin Butler missed a field-goal attempt on the Bears' opening drive, and Washington responded with Jay Schroeder's 28-yard touchdown pass to Art Monk. In the second period, Doug Flutie teamed with Willie Gault on a 50-yard touchdown pass. But when Chicago went ahead on Butler's 23-yard field goal, it represented a moral victory for the Redskins, who held the Bears without a touchdown after a first-and-goal at the 4.

Leading 13-7, Chicago continued its self-destructive pattern in the third period. An interception of Flutie set up Schroeder's 23-yard touchdown pass to Monk. The Bears then drove to the Washington 17, but Walter Payton fumbled. Washington responded with an 11-play, 83-yard drive to a 1-yard touchdown run by George Rogers.

Washington	7	0	7	13	-	27
Chi. Bears	0	13	0	0	-	13

Was	-	Monk 28 pass from Schroeder (Atkinson kick)
ChiB	-	Gault 50 pass from Flutie
ChiB	-	FG Butler 23
ChiB	-	FG Butler 41
Was	-	Monk 23 pass from Schroeder (Atkinson kick)
Was	-	Rogers 1 run (Atkinson kick)
Was	-	FG Atkinson 35
Was	-	FG Atkinson 25

1986 NFC DIVISIONAL PLAYOFF GAME
New York Giants 49, San Francisco 3

January 4, 1987, at East Rutherford, New Jersey
Attendance: 76,034

Phil Simms threw 4 touchdown passes and the New York defense held San Francisco to 29 yards rushing as the Giants routed the 49ers 49-3.

From the beginning, San Francisco helped the Giants with turnovers. On the 49ers' first drive, Jerry Rice caught a pass and was on his way to a 50-yard touchdown but inexplicably dropped the ball and New York recovered. The Giants then went 80 yards, scoring on a 24-yard touchdown pass from Simms to Mark Bavaro. In the second period, an interception by Herb Welch led to Joe Morris's 45-yard touchdown run.

Only 50 seconds before the end of the first half, Simms hit Bobby Johnson with a 15-yard touchdown pass. Two plays later Lawrence Taylor intercepted Joe Montana and rambled 34 yards for a touchdown. On the same play, Montana was knocked out of the game with a concussion.

San Francisco	3	0	0	0	-	3
N.Y. Giants	7	21	21	0	-	49

NYG - Bavaro 24 pass from Simms (Allegre kick)
SF - FG Wersching 26
NYG - Morris 45 run (Allegre kick)
NYG - B. Johnson 15 pass from Simms (Allegre kick)
NYG - Taylor 34 interception return (Allegre kick)
NYG - McConkey 28 pass from Simms (Allegre kick)
NYG - Mowatt 29 pass from Simms (Allegre kick)
NYG - Morris 2 run (Allegre kick)

1986 AFC CHAMPIONSHIP GAME
Denver 23, Cleveland 20 (OT)

January 11, 1987, at Cleveland
Attendance: 79,915

John Elway guided the Broncos 98 yards to tie the game with 37 seconds left in regulation, and Rich Karlis kicked a 33-yard field goal 5:38 into overtime as Denver beat Cleveland 23-20.

In a game that neither team led by more than 7 points, Cleveland scored first when Bernie Kosar fired a 6-yard touchdown pass to Herman Fontenot to cap an 86-yard drive. Two second-quarter turnovers by the Browns led to 10 Denver points, and the score was tied 10-10 at halftime.

After an exchange of field goals, Kosar threw a 48-yard touchdown pass to Brian Brennan to give Cleveland a 20-13 lead with only 5:43 remaining in the fourth quarter.

The Broncos began their next drive at the 2, and Elway took over. The 15-play drive included 9 passes and 2 runs by Elway, who, on third-and-1, found Mark Jackson with a 5-yard touchdown pass to tie the game. On Denver's first possession in overtime, Elway took the Broncos 60 yards in 9 plays to set up Karlis's winning field goal.

Denver	0	10	3	7	3	-	23
Cleveland	7	3	0	10	0	-	20

Cle - Fontenot 6 pass from Kosar (Moseley kick)
Den - FG Karlis 19
Den - Willhite 1 run (Moseley kick)
Cle - FG Moseley 29
Den - FG Karlis 26
Cle - FG Moseley 24
Cle - Brennan 48 pass from Kosar (Moseley kick)
Den - M. Jackson 5 pass from Elway (Karlis kick)
Den - FG Karlis 33

1986 NFC CHAMPIONSHIP GAME
New York Giants 17, Washington 0

January 11, 1987, at East Rutherford, New Jersey
Attendance: 76,633

The Giants took advantage of a wind gusting up to 35 miles per hour to grab an early lead, then blunted Jay Schroeder's passing barrage to defeat the Redskins 17-0.

After winning the coin toss, the Giants elected to kick off with the wind. When the Redskins couldn't move, they punted into the wind, and New York took over at the Washington 47. Six plays later, Raul Allegre kicked a 47-yard field goal.

After the ensuing kickoff, the Giants again stopped the Redskins, and another punt into the teeth of the wind gave New York possession at the Redskins' 38. A 25-yard pass from Phil Simms to Lionel Manuel bailed the Giants out of a third-and-long, and Simms then hit Manuel with an 11-yard touchdown pass.

In the second period, the Giants put the Redskins in a big hole by driving 51 yards to Joe Morris's 1-yard touchdown run. Then New York's defense took over. Schroeder passed 34 times in the second half while the Redskins ran the ball only once, but the Giants' defense limited them to 150 yards through the air for the game, while the offense successfully ran time off the clock.

Washington	0	0	0	0	-	0
N.Y. Giants	10	7	0	0	-	17

NYG - FG Allegre 47
NYG - Manuel 11 pass from Simms (Allegre kick)
NYG - Morris 1 run (Allegre kick)

1987 AFC WILD CARD GAME
Houston 23, Seattle 20 (OT)

January 31, 1988, at Houston
Attendance: 49,622

The Oilers outgained the Seahawks 427 yards to 250 and held onto the ball more than twice as long, but still needed a 42-yard field goal by Tony Zendejas 8:05 into overtime to defeat Seattle 23-20.

The Seahawks jumped ahead in the first quarter on a 20-yard touchdown pass from Dave Krieg to Steve Largent, but a pair of long field goals by Zendejas sandwiched around a touchdown run by Mike Rozier gave the Oilers a 13-10 halftime lead.

Seattle tied it up in the third quarter, only to see Warren Moon hit Willie Drewrey with the receiver's first-ever NFL touchdown reception from 29 yards. The Seahawks sent the game into overtime with Krieg's second touchdown pass to Largent with only 1:47 to play. Zendejas then atoned for a missed 29-yard field-goal attempt in the final period with his winning kick.

Seattle	7	3	3	7	0	-	20
Houston	3	10	7	0	3	-	23

Sea - Largent 20 pass from Krieg (N. Johnson kick)
Hou - FG Zendejas 47
Hou - Rozier 1 run (Zendejas kick)
Hou - FG Zendejas 49
Sea - FG Johnson 33
Sea - FG Johnson 41
Hou - Drewrey 29 pass from Moon (Zendejas kick)
Sea - Largent 12 pass from Krieg (N. Johnson kick)
Hou - FG Zendejas 42

1987 NFC WILD CARD GAME
Minnesota 44, New Orleans 10

January 3, 1988, at New Orleans
Attendance: 68,127

New Orleans's first playoff appearance was a forgettable one as Minnesota dominated the game in every category to defeat the Saints 44-10.

The Saints scored first, with Bobby Hebert firing a 10-yard touchdown pass to Eric Martin. But from that point on the Vikings' defense stopped the Saints, making 4 interceptions, recovering 2 fumbles, and recording 2 sacks, while giving up only 149 yards the entire game.

With the score 7-3, Anthony Carter put Minnesota ahead for good in the first period when he returned a punt 84 yards for a touchdown, the longest return in postseason history. In the second quarter, Carter continued his work, catching a 10-yard halfback pass from Allen Rice for a touchdown. Wade Wilson also threw 2 touchdown passes to build the Vikings' margin to 31-10 at halftime.

Minnesota	10	21	3	10	-	44
New Orleans	7	3	0	0	-	10

NO - Martin 10 pass from Hebert (Andersen kick)
Min - FG C. Nelson 42
Min - Carter 84 punt return (C. Nelson kick)
Min - Jordan 5 pass from Wilson (C. Nelson kick)
Min - Carter 10 pass from Rice (C. Nelson kick)
NO - FG Andersen 40
Min - Jones 44 pass from Wilson (C. Nelson kick)
Min - FG C. Nelson 42
Min - FG C. Nelson 19
Min - Dozier 18 run (C. Nelson kick)

1987 AFC DIVISIONAL PLAYOFF GAME
Cleveland 38, Indianapolis 21

January 9, 1988, at Cleveland
Attendance: 78,586

Felix Wright intercepted a pass deep in Cleveland territory midway through the third quarter to swing the momentum from Indianapolis to Cleveland, and the Browns went on to defeat the Colts 38-21.

The score was tied 14-14 at halftime after Bernie Kosar and Jack Trudeau matched touchdown passes. The Browns scored first to end an 86-yard drive on their opening possession. After the Colts tied it, Cleveland grabbed the lead with only 1:51 to go before the end of the first half. But Trudeau fired a touchdown pass to Eric Dickerson 1:07 later to tie it again.

The Colts were driving again in the third period, but Wright's interception was the prelude to an 86-yard scoring drive. The Browns built their lead to 31-14, and after Indianapolis scored to close the margin, Frank Minnifield returned an interception 48 yards for a touchdown to eliminate any chances of a comeback.

Indianapolis	7	7	0	7	-	21
Cleveland	7	7	7	17	-	38

Cle - Byner 10 pass from Kosar (Bahr kick)
Ind - Beach 2 pass from Trudeau (Biasucci kick)
Cle - Langhorne 39 pass from Kosar (Bahr kick)
Ind - Dickerson 19 pass from Trudeau (Biasucci kick)
Cle - Byner 2 rush (Bahr kick)
Cle - FG Bahr 22
Cle - Brennan 2 pass from Kosar (Bahr kick)
Ind - Bentley1 run (Biasucci kick)
Cle - Minnifield 48 interception return (Bahr kick)

1987 AFC DIVISIONAL PLAYOFF GAME
Denver 34, Houston 10

January 10, 1988, at Denver
Attendance: 75,968

The Denver defense set up 2 first-quarter touchdowns with a fumble recovery and an interception as the Broncos jumped ahead quickly and never looked back.

Safety Steve Wilson recovered Warren Moon's lateral to Mike Rozier at the Oilers' 1-yard line to set up Gene Lang's 1-yard touchdown run. On Houston's next possession, Karl Mecklenburg intercepted a pass, and John Elway quickly turned it into points with a 27-yard touchdown pass to tight end Clarence Kay. Elway came back to Kay in the second period, finding him with a touchdown pass from the 1 after a 55-yard completion to Vance Johnson moved Denver deep into Houston territory.

The normally explosive Oilers finally scored a touchdown in the fourth quarter, but the Broncos came back with a drive that culminated in Elway's 3-yard touchdown run with 4:23 left.

Houston	0	3	0	7	-	10
Denver	14	10	3	7	-	34

Den - Lang 1 run (Karlis kick)
Den - Kay 27 pass from Elway (Karlis kick)
Den - FG Karlis 43
Hou - FG Zendejas 46
Den - Kay 1 pass from Elway (Karlis kick)
Den - FG Karlis 23
Hou - Givins 19 pass from Moon (Zendejas kick)
Den - Elway 3 run (Karlis kick)

1987 NFC DIVISIONAL PLAYOFF GAME
Minnesota 36, San Francisco 24

January 9, 1988, at San Francisco
Attendance: 62,457

Anthony Carter caught 10 passes for a playoff-record 227 yards, and Chuck Nelson made all 5 of his field-goal attempts to lead Minnesota to a convincing 36-24 victory over the 49ers, who lost in their first playoff game for the third year in a row.

The Vikings broke open the game in the second quarter as Wade Wilson found tight end Carl Hilton with a 7-yard touchdown pass, Nelson kicked his second field goal, and rookie cornerback Reggie Rutland intercepted a pass and returned it 45 yards for a touchdown.

The 49ers responded with some defensive heroics in the third period, with safety Jeff Fuller returning an interception 48 yards for a touchdown. But Wilson responded with a touchdown pass to Hassan Jones. Then, each time backup quarterback Steve Young drove San Francisco to a score, Nelson kicked a field goal to keep the 49ers at bay.

Minnesota	3	17	10	6	-	36
San Francisco	3	0	14	7	-	24

Min - FG C. Nelson 21
SF - FG Wersching 43
Min - Hilton 7 pass from Wilson (C. Nelson kick)
Min - FG C. Nelson 23
Min - Rutland 45 interception return (C. Nelson kick)
SF - Fuller 48 interception return (Wersching kick)
Min - H. Jones 5 pass from Wilson (C. Nelson kick)
SF - Young 5 run (Wersching kick)
Min - FG C. Nelson 40
Min - FG C. Nelson 40
SF - Franklin 16 pass from Young (Wersching kick)
Min - FG C. Nelson 23

1987 NFC DIVISIONAL PLAYOFF GAME
Washington 21, Chicago Bears 17

January 10, 1988, at Chicago
Attendance: 58,153

The Redskins overcame an early deficit and went on to defeat the Bears in a divisional playoff game for the second year a row 21-17.

Chicago dominated the early action, jumping to a 14-0 lead. Calvin Thomas ran in from 2 yards out for the first touchdown, and then Jim McMahon hit rookie Ron Morris for 14 yards and a touchdown in the second period. The Redskins got going behind the power running of George Rogers, who ran 3 yards for a touchdown, and the erratic, but timely, passing of Doug Williams, who connected with tight end Clint Didier for an 18-yard touchdown to tie the game at halftime.

The crucial play came early in the third quarter. With Chicago pinned in its own territory, Darrell Green took a punt at his 48 and raced 52 yards for a touchdown. The Bears responded with Kevin Butler's 25-yard field goal, but neither team could score in the tense final period.

Washington	0	14	7	0	-	21
Chicago	7	7	3	0	-	17

ChiB - Thomas 2 run (Butler kick)
ChiB - Morris 14 pass from McMahon (Butler kick)
Was - Rogers 3 run (Haji-Sheikh kick)
Was - Didier 18 pass from Williams (Haji-Sheikh kick)
Was - Green 52 punt return (Haji-Sheikh kick)
ChiB - FG Butler 25

1987 AFC CHAMPIONSHIP GAME
Denver 38, Cleveland 33

January 17, 1988, at Denver
Attendance: 75,993

Reserve cornerback Jeremiah Castille forced a fumble by Earnest Byner and then recovered it at the Denver 3 with 1:05 left to preserve the Broncos' second consecutive AFC title game victory over the Cleveland Browns 38-33. The play was a cruel end for Byner, who had a sensational day, with 67 yards rushing, 7 receptions for 120 yards, and 2 touchdowns.

The Broncos dominated the early going and led 21-3 at halftime. But behind Bernie Kosar's passing (26 completions in 41 attempts for 356 yards), the Browns stormed back. Early in the third period, Kosar found Reggie Langhorne for 18 yards and a touchdown. Then, after John Elway struck back with an 80-yard bomb to Mark Jackson, Kosar threw a 32-yard touchdown pass to Byner. A short while later Byner scored again on a 4-yard run.

Early in the final period, Kosar passed to Webster Slaughter for 4 yards and a touchdown that made it 31-31. Elway again responded, driving the Broncos 75 yards and hitting Sammy Winder with a 20-yard touchdown pass with only 4:01 remaining. The Browns were driving to even the score until Castille's big play sent Denver to its third Super Bowl. Punter Mike Horan took a safety with 8 seconds left to finish the scoring.

Cleveland	0	3	21	9	-	33
Denver	14	7	10	7	-	38

Den - Nattiel 8 pass from Elway (Karlis kick)
Den - Sewell 1 run (Karlis kick)
Cle - FG Bahr 24
Den - Lang 1 run (Karlis kick)
Cle - Langhorne 18 pass from Kosar (Bahr kick)
Den - Jackson 80 pass from Elway (Karlis kick)
Cle - Byner 32 pass from Kosar (Bahr kick)
Cle - Byner 4 run (Bahr kick)
Cle - Slaughter 4 pass from Kosar (Bahr kick)
Den - Winder 20 pass from Elway (Karlis kick)
Cle - Safety, Horan ran out of end zone

1987 NFC CHAMPIONSHIP GAME
Washington 17, Minnesota 10

January 17, 1988, at Washington, D.C.
Attendance: 55,212

Minnesota quarterback Wade Wilson's fourth-down pass into the end zone was incomplete in the final minute, and the Redskins held on to defeat Minnesota 17-10. On a day in which the defenses were dominant, the Redskins' unit was slightly better, holding the Vikings to 76 yards rushing while sacking Wilson 8 times.

The Redskins moved ahead in the first quarter, driving 98 yards in 8 plays and scoring on Doug Williams's 42-yard pass to running back Kelvin Bryant. The Vikings tied it before halftime when Wilson hit Leo Lewis with a 23-yard touchdown strike.

In the third quarter, linebacker Mel Kaufman made the game's only interception, returning it 10 yards to the Minnesota 17 to set up a field goal by Ali Haji-Sheikh. Early in the final period, Anthony Carter returned a punt 26 yards to midfield, and Minnesota drove to the 1 before settling for Chuck Nelson's equalizing field goal.

Washington then put together an 18-play, 70-yard drive that ended with a 7-yard touchdown pass from Williams to Gary Clark with 5:06 left. Minnesota drove to the Washington 6, but the Vikings could not get into the end zone.

Minnesota	0	7	0	3	-	10
Washington	7	0	3	7	-	17

Was - Bryant 42 pass from Williams (Haji-Sheikh kick)
Min - Lewis 23 pass from Wilson (C. Nelson kick)
Was - FG Haji-Sheikh 28
Min - FG C. Nelson 18
Was - Clark 7 pass from Williams (Haji-Sheikh kick)

1988 AFC WILD CARD GAME
Houston 24, Cleveland 23

December 24, 1988, at Cleveland
Attendance: 74,977

Houston halfback Allen Pinkett scored 2 touchdowns in a 15-second span of the second quarter to help lead the Oilers to a 24-23 victory over Cleveland.

The Browns went ahead 3-0 early, but the Oilers pieced together a 17-yard, 91-play drive culminated 7 seconds into the second period with Warren Moon's 14-yard touchdown pass to Pinkett. On the first play after the kickoff, nose tackle Richard Byrd recovered Don Strock's fumble, and Pinkett immediately turned it into a 16-yard touchdown run.

After trailing 14-9 at halftime, the Browns went ahead when Mike Pagel, in for the injured Strock, threw a 14-yard touchdown pass to Webster Slaughter. The Oilers responded with a 76-yard drive that ended with Lorenzo White's 1-yard touchdown run. Cornerback Richard Johnson intercepted on the Browns' next possession to set up the clinching 49-yard field goal by Tony Zendejas with 1:54 remaining.

Houston	0	14	0	10	-	24
Cleveland	3	6	7	7	-	23

Cle - FG Bahr 33
Hou - Pinkett 14 pass from Moon (Zendejas kick)
Hou - Pinkett 16 run (Zendejas kick)
Cle - FG Bahr 26
Cle - FG Bahr 28
Cle - Slaughter 14 pass from Pagel (Bahr kick)
Hou - White 1 run (Zendejas kick)
Hou - FG Zendejas 49
Cle - Slaughter 2 pass from Pagel (Bahr kick)

1988 NFC WILD CARD GAME
Minnesota 28, Los Angeles Rams 17

December 26, 1988, at Minneapolis
Attendance: 57,666

Minnesota safety Joey Browner made 2 first-quarter interceptions that set up touchdowns only 21 seconds apart to give the Vikings a lead they would never relinquish en route to defeating the Rams 28-17.

Browner's first interception set the Vikings up at their 27, and they marched 73 yards to Alfred Anderson's 7-yard touchdown run. On the first play after the subsequent kickoff, Browner again intercepted Rams quarterback Jim Everett and brought the ball back to the Los Angeles 17. On first down, Allen Rice ran for a touchdown.

A touchdown pass from Everett to tight end Damone Johnson cut the margin in half at the intermission, but the Vikings responded in the third period with a drive culminating in a 1-yard touchdown run by Anderson. A 5-yard touchdown pass from Wade Wilson to tight end Carl Hilton guaranteed the Vikings the victory.

L.A. Rams	0	7	3	7	-	17
Minnesota	14	0	7	7	-	28

Min - Anderson 7 run (C. Nelson kick)
Min - Rice 17 run (C. Nelson kick)
Rams - D. Johnson 3 pass from Everett (Lansford kick)
Min - Anderson 1 run (C. Nelson kick)
Rams - FG Lansford 33
Min - Hilton 5 pass from Wilson (C. Nelson kick)
Rams - Holohan 11 pass from Everett (Lansford kick)

1988 AFC DIVISIONAL PLAYOFF GAME
Cincinnati 21, Seattle 13

December 31, 1988, at Cincinnati
Attendance: 58,560

Cincinnati dominated the line of scrimmage, pounding out 254 yards on the ground while holding Seattle to only 18, and the Bengals, who took a 21-0 lead in the second period, withstood a fourth-quarter rally to defeat the Seahawks 21-13.

Ickey Woods bulled for 126 yards and James Brooks ran for 72 to power the Bengals' ground game. However, it was Stanley Wilson who scored Cincinnati's first 2 touchdowns on a pair of 3-yard runs. Woods then ran in from the 1. Meanwhile, the Bengals held the Seahawks to a paltry 47 total yards in the first half.

With Dave Krieg taking to the air, Seattle made a comeback in the final period. First, Krieg teamed with John L. Williams on a 7-yard touchdown pass; it was one of 11 receptions for Williams. Then, Krieg scored on a 1-yard quarterback sneak, but it still wasn't enough to catch the Bengals.

Seattle	0	0	0	13	-	13
Cincinnati	7	14	0	0	-	21

Cin - Wilson 3 run (Breech kick)
Cin - Wilson 3 run (Breech kick)
Cin - Woods 1 run (Breech kick)
Sea - Williams 7 pass from Krieg (N. Johnson kick)
Sea - Krieg 1 run (kick failed)

1988 AFC DIVISIONAL PLAYOFF GAME
Buffalo 17, Houston 10

January 1, 1989, at Orchard Park, New York
Attendance: 79,532

Splendid efforts on offense, defense, and special teams led Buffalo to a 17-10 victory over Houston as the Bills advanced to their first AFC Championship Game.

After a scoreless first period, the Bills took the lead after safety Leonard Smith blocked a punt by Greg Montgomery. Robb Riddick ran in from the 1 for the touchdown. The Bills increased the lead to 14-3 in the third period, when rookie Thurman Thomas, who had 75 yards on only 7 carries, ran 11 yards for a touchdown.

With the Oilers playing catch-up in the final period, the Bills' defense made several big plays. First, Mark Kelso intercepted a pass from Warren Moon to end one drive. Then, on Houston's next possession, Derrick Burroughs recovered a fumble. Scott Norwood's short field goal gave Buffalo enough cushion that even a late score by Mike Rozier left the Oilers trailing by 7 points.

Houston	0	3	0	7	-	10
Buffalo	0	7	7	3	-	17

Buf - Riddick 1 run (Norwood kick)
Hou - FG Zendejas 35
Buf - Thomas 11 run (Norwood kick)
Buf - FG Norwood 27
Hou - Rozier 1 run (Zendejas kick)

1988 NFC DIVISIONAL PLAYOFF GAME
Chicago 20, Philadelphia 12

December 31, 1988, at Chicago
Attendance: 65,534

In a fog so heavy that at times fans couldn't see across the field, the Bears' defense bent, but kept the Eagles out of the end zone for a 20-12 victory. Philadelphia moved effectively all day, getting inside the Bears' 25 nine times and reaching their 11 five times. Yet, the Eagles had only 4 field goals to show for their efforts.

Chicago's Mike Tomczak connected with Dennis McKinnon for a 64-yard touchdown pass only 3:02 into the game. The Eagles, led by Randall Cunningham's passing (27 completions in 54 attempts for 407 yards) responded with a pair of field goals by Luis Zendejas. However, the Bears scored again on a 4-yard run by Neal Anderson. The teams exchanged field goals to make it 17-9 at halftime. Each team came away with but 1 short field goal in the second half.

Philadelphia	3	6	3	0	-	12
Chicago	7	10	0	3	-	20

ChiB - McKinnon 64 pass from Tomczak (Butler kick)
Phi - FG Zendejas 42
Phi - FG Zendejas 29
ChiB - Anderson 4 run (Butler kick)
ChiB - FG Butler 46
Phi - FG Zendejas 30
Phi - FG Zendejas 35
ChiB - FG Butler 27

1988 NFC DIVISIONAL PLAYOFF GAME
San Francisco 34, Minnesota 9

January 1, 1989, at San Francisco
Attendance: 61,848

San Francisco's offense dominated Minnesota through the air in the first half and on the ground in the second half as the 49ers routed the Vikings 34-9.

After an early field goal by the Vikings, the story of the first half was Joe Montana throwing to Jerry Rice; they connected for touchdowns 3 times, from 2, 4, and 11 yards. Montana completed 11 of 14 passes for 111 yards in the first half, which ended with San Francisco leading 21-3. Meanwhile, the 49ers' defense stopped Minnesota with 5 sacks in the first half.

After the Vikings finally scored a touchdown in the third quarter, the 49ers turned the game over to Roger Craig. For the day, Craig gained 135 yards on 21 carries. He scored on a 4-yard run in the final period, and later had a post-season-record 80-yard touchdown run.

Minnesota	3	0	6	0	-	9
San Francisco	7	14	0	13	-	34

Min - FG Nelson 47
SF - Rice 2 pass from Montana (Cofer kick)
SF - Rice 4 pass from Montana (Cofer kick)
SF - Rice 11 pass from Montana (Cofer kick)
Min - H. Jones 5 pass from Wilson (kick failed)
SF - Craig 4 run (Cofer kick)
SF - Craig 80 run (kick failed)

1988 AFC CHAMPIONSHIP GAME
Cincinnati 21, Buffalo 10

January 8, 1989, at Cincinnati
Attendance: 59,747

Cincinnati shut down Buffalo's explosive attack, limiting the Bills to only 45 yards rushing and 136 yards passing, while Ickey Woods did the heavy-duty work for the Bengals, rushing for 102 yards on 29 carries. The end result was a 21-10 win that sent Cincinnati to its second Super Bowl.

The Bengals established their defensive dominance from the start, with Lewis Billups and Eric Thomas intercepting 2 of Jim Kelly's first 3 passes. The first score of the game, a 1-yard plunge by Woods, followed Thomas's 26-yard return. The Bills came back to tie the game on Kelly's touchdown pass to Andre Reed, but the Bengals immediately responded with a 10-yard touchdown pass from Boomer Esiason to halfback James Brooks.

Late in the third quarter, the Bengals had a fourth-and-4 at the Buffalo 33. After lining up in punt formation, backup quarterback Turk Schonert moved behind center, took the snap, and handed off to Stanley Wilson, who gained 6 yards. The Bengals then drove to Woods's second touchdown. With Buffalo desperately trying to get back in the game midway through the final period, Dave Fulcher intercepted Kelly in the end zone to seal the victory.

Buffalo	0	10	0	0	-	10
Cincinnati	7	7	0	7	-	21

Cin - Woods 1 run (Breech kick)
Buf - Reed 9 pass from Kelly (Norwood kick)
Cin - Brooks 10 pass from Esiason (Breech kick)
Buf - FG Norwood 39
Cin - Woods 1 run (Breech kick)

1988 NFC CHAMPIONSHIP GAME
San Francisco 28, Chicago 3

January 8, 1989, at Chicago
Attendance: 64,830

In a game played in 17-degree temperatures with a wind-chill factor of minus-26, the San Francisco offense put together a near-flawless game, scoring in every period, gaining 406 total yards, losing only 1 turnover, and having no penalties to slowly grind up the Bears 28-3.

The 49ers' initial scores came the same way they had in the first half the week before: Joe Montana throwing to Jerry Rice. After catching 3 touchdowns against Minnesota, Rice had 5 catches for 133 yards and 2 touchdowns against the Bears. The first touchdown, for 61 yards, came in the first quarter, and the second, in the next period, was from 27 yards. Chicago was able to respond only with a 25-yard field goal by Kevin Butler, which marked one of two times that the Bears were able to cross the San Francisco 40-yard line.

At the beginning of the third period, Montana drove the 49ers 78 yards on 13 plays, passing to tight end John Frank for 5 yards and the touchdown. Their final score came on fullback Tom Rathman's 4-yard run in the fourth quarter.

San Francisco	7	7	7	7	-	28
Chicago	0	3	0	0	-	3

SF - Rice 61 pass from Montana (Cofer kick)
SF - Rice 27 pass from Montana (Cofer kick)
ChiB - FG Butler 25
SF - Frank 5 pass from Montana (Cofer kick)
SF - Rathman 4 run (Cofer kick)

1989 AFC WILD CARD GAME
Pittsburgh 26, Houston 23 (OT)

December 31, 1989, at Houston
Attendance: 58,306

Gary Anderson kicked his fourth field goal of the game, from 50 yards after 3:26 of overtime, to give Pittsburgh a 26-23 victory over a Houston team that had won both regular-season meetings.

The Steelers opened the scoring on Tim Worley's 9-yard run before the two teams spent more than half the game exchanging 6 field goals. In the fourth period, the Oilers took their first lead when Warren Moon threw 2 touchdown passes to Ernest Givins, who had 11 receptions for the day. But the Steelers responded in the final 6 minutes, moving 82 yards on 11 plays to a 2-yard touchdown run by Merrill Hoge with 46 seconds left.

The Steelers took the kickoff in overtime, but were forced to punt. Then Rod Woodson recovered Lorenzo White's fumble on the Oilers' first play, setting up Anderson's winning field goal.

Pittsburgh	7	3	3	10	3	-	26
Houston	0	6	3	14	0	-	23

Pit - Worley 9 run (Anderson kick)
Hou - FG Zendejas 26
Hou - FG Zendejas 35
Pit - FG Anderson 25
Hou - FG Zendejas 26
Pit - FG Anderson 30
Pit - FG Anderson 40
Hou - Givins 18 pass from Moon (Zendejas kick)
Hou - Givins 9 pass from Moon (Zendejas kick)
Pit - Hoge 2 run (Anderson kick)
Pit - FG Anderson 50

1989 NFC WILD CARD GAME
Los Angeles Rams 21, Philadelphia 7

December 31, 1989, at Philadelphia
Attendance: 57,869

Jim Everett threw 2 first-quarter touchdown passes to stake Los Angeles to a 14-0 lead, then both defenses took over as the Rams defeated the Eagles 21-7.

The Rams wasted no time grabbing their lead. Early in the first period, Everett found Henry Ellard with a 39-yard touchdown pass. He came back to throw a 4-yard scoring pass to tight end Damone Johnson midway through the period.

Led by linebacker Kevin Greene, the Rams' defense controlled the Eagles most of the way. Greene had 2 sacks of quarterback Randall Cunningham and also recovered a fumble. When Anthony Toney of the Eagles finally did reach the end zone in the fourth quarter, Los Angeles drove back to the clinching score, a 7-yard touchdown run by Greg Bell, who had 27 carries for 124 yards.

L.A. Rams	14	0	0	7	-	21
Philadelphia	0	0	0	7	-	7

Rams	-	Ellard 39 pass from Everett (Lansford kick)
Rams	-	Johnson 4 pass from Everett (Lansford kick)
Phi	-	Toney 1 run (Ruzek kick)
Rams	-	Bell 7 run (Lansford kick)

1989 AFC DIVISIONAL PLAYOFF GAME
Cleveland 34, Buffalo 30

January 6, 1990, at Cleveland
Attendance: 77,706

Jim Kelly passed for 405 yards and 4 touchdowns, but his pass to the Cleveland 1-yard line was intercepted by Clay Matthews with 3 seconds remaining in the game, and the Browns held on to defeat the Bills 34-30.

Buffalo scored on its sixth play when Kelly teamed with Andre Reed on a 72-yard touchdown pass. In the second and third periods, Kelly threw 2 more touchdown passes, but Bernie Kosar threw for 3. Combined with Eric Metcalf's 90-yard kickoff return for a touchdown, Kosar's passing led Cleveland to a 31-21 lead after three quarters.

An exchange of field goals preceded Kelly's second touchdown pass to Thurman Thomas, who tied an NFL postseason record with 13 receptions for 150 yards. But the kick failed, which meant that the Bills couldn't tie with a field goal on their final drive.

Buffalo	7	7	7	9	-	30
Cleveland	3	14	14	3	-	34

Buf	-	Reed 72 pass from Kelly (Norwood kick)
Cle	-	FG Bahr 45
Cle	-	Slaughter 52 pass from Kosar (Bahr kick)
Buf	-	Lofton 33 pass from Kelly (Norwood kick)
Cle	-	Middleton 3 pass from Kosar (Bahr kick)
Cle	-	Slaughter 44 pass from Kosar (Bahr kick)
Buf	-	Thomas 6 pass from Kelly (Norwood kick)
Cle	-	Metcalf 90 kickoff return (Bahr kick)
Buf	-	FG Norwood 30
Cle	-	FG Bahr 47
Buf	-	Thomas 3 pass from Kelly (Norwood kick)

1989 AFC DIVISIONAL PLAYOFF GAME
Denver 24, Pittsburgh 23

January 7, 1990, at Denver
Attendance: 75,868

John Elway led the Broncos 71 yards in 9 plays, with the drive ending on Melvin Bratton's 1-yard touchdown run with 2:27 to play. Rookie David Treadwell then added the game-winning extra point as the Broncos edged the Steelers 24-23.

Pittsburgh led most of the way, being up 10-0 at one stage and 17-10 at halftime. Denver tied it at 17-17 after Tyrone Braxton recovered a fumble at the Pittsburgh 37 midway through the third period. On the next play, Elway connected with Vance Johnson for a 37-yard touchdown pass.

Pittsburgh's Gary Anderson came back with 2 field goals to give the Steelers a 23-17 lead, but Elway quickly marched Denver to the winning score. After the ensuing kickoff, Randy Robbins recovered a fumble at the Pittsburgh 18 with 2:02 left to clinch the game for the Broncos.

Pittsburgh	3	14	3	3	-	23
Denver	0	10	7	7	-	24

Pit	-	FG Anderson 32
Pit	-	Worley 7 run (Anderson kick)
Den	-	Bratton 1 run (Treadwell kick)
Pit	-	Lipps 9 pass from Brister (Anderson kick)
Den	-	FG Treadwell 43
Den	-	V. Johnson 37 pass from Elway (Treadwell kick)
Pit	-	FG Anderson 35
Pit	-	FG Anderson 32
Den	-	Bratton 1 run (Treadwell kick)

1989 NFC DIVISIONAL PLAYOFF GAME
San Francisco 41, Minnesota 13

January 6, 1990, at San Francisco
Attendance: 64,585

Minnesota's 71 sacks in the regular season were the second-most in NFL history, but the Vikings' defense came nowhere near Joe Montana in this game as he completed 17 of 24 passes for 241 yards and 4 first-half touchdown passes to lead San Francisco to a 41-13 victory.

After Minnesota jumped ahead on Rich Karlis's 38-yard field goal in the first quarter, the rest of the half belonged to Montana. First, he found Jerry Rice with a 72-yard touchdown pass. Then, he threw 3 more touchdown passes in the second period: 8 yards to Brent Jones, 8 yards to John Taylor, and 13 yards to Rice.

The game wasn't all Montana, but, rather, all San Francisco. Ronnie Lott intercepted a pass in the final period and returned it 58 yards for a touchdown. And Roger Craig gained 118 yards rushing and scored a touchdown late in the fourth quarter.

Minnesota	3	0	3	7	-	13
San Francisco	7	20	0	14	-	41

Min	-	FG Karlis 38
SF	-	Rice 72 pass from Montana (Cofer kick)
SF	-	Jones 8 pass from Montana (Cofer kick)
SF	-	Taylor 8 pass from Montana (Cofer kick)
SF	-	Rice 13 pass from Montana (kick failed)
Min	-	FG Karlis 44
SF	-	Lott 58 interception return (Cofer kick)
SF	-	Craig 4 run (Cofer kick)
Min	-	Fenney 3 run (Karlis kick)

1989 NFC DIVISIONAL PLAYOFF GAME
Los Angeles Rams 19, New York Giants 13 (OT)

January 7, 1990, at East Rutherford, New Jersey
Attendance: 76,325

Jim Everett threw a 30-yard touchdown pass to Willie (Flipper) Anderson after only 1:06 of overtime as the

Rams upset the New York Giants 19-13.

The Giants were the dominant team for most of the first half and led 6-0 on 2 field goals by Raul Allegre; then, with only 17 seconds remaining in the second period, the Rams finally scored on a 20-yard touchdown pass from Everett to Anderson.

New York regained the lead in the third quarter on a 2-yard touchdown run by Ottis Anderson. But behind the passing of Everett, who completed 25 of 44 attempts for 315 yards, the Rams drove to 2 field goals in the fourth quarter. The second, from 22 yards away by Mike Lansford with only 3:01 remaining in the game, evened the score at 13-13.

L.A. Rams	0	7	0	6	6	- 19
N.Y. Giants	6	0	7	0	0	- 13

NYG - FG Allegre 35
NYG - FG Allegre 41
Rams - F. Anderson 20 pass from Everett (Lansford kick)
NYG - O. Anderson 2 run (Allegre kick)
Rams - FG Lansford 31
Rams - FG Lansford 22
Rams - F. Anderson 30 pass from Everett

1989 AFC CHAMPIONSHIP GAME
Denver 37, Cleveland 21

January 14, 1990, at Denver
Attendance: 76,005

John Elway passed for 385 yards and 3 touchdowns and led all rushers in the game with 39 yards to lead Denver to its third AFC Championship Game victory against Cleveland in four years 37-21. Unlike the previous two encounters, the Broncos led from start to finish.

The game was played close to the vest for much of the first half, and the Broncos led only 3-0 until Elway found backup wide receiver Michael Young with a 70-yard scoring bomb.

The offenses erupted in the third period. Bernie Kosar threw a touchdown pass to Brian Brennan, but Elway responded with a touchdown strike to tight end Orson Mobley, which was set up by a 53-yard pass to Young. A 7-yard touchdown run by Sammy Winder built the score to 24-7. Then Cleveland closed the gap by scoring twice in a span of 2:11, a short touchdown run by Tim Manoa following the second touchdown pass from Kosar to Brennan.

Elway kept the Broncos composed, driving them to a touchdown and 2 field goals on 4 possessions in the final period; the key play was a 39-yard touchdown pass to Winder that increased the lead to 31-21.

Cleveland	0	0	21	0	- 21
Denver	3	7	14	13	- 37

Den - FG Treadwell 29
Den - Young 70 pass from Elway (Treadwell kick)
Cle - Brennan 27 pass from Kosar (Bahr kick)
Den - Mobley 5 pass from Elway (Treadwell kick)
Den - Winder 7 run (Treadwell kick)
Cle - Brennan 10 pass from Kosar (Bahr kick)
Cle - Manoa 2 run (Bahr kick)
Den - Winder 39 pass from Elway (Treadwell kick)
Den - FG Treadwell 34
Den - FG Treadwell 31

1989 NFC CHAMPIONSHIP GAME
San Francisco 30, Los Angeles Rams 3

January 14, 1990, at San Francisco
Attendance: 64,769

San Francisco dominated Los Angeles in every way for a 30-3 victory that led the 49ers to their fourth Super Bowl berth. The 49ers outgained the Rams in yards 442 to 156, in first downs 29 to 9, and in possession 39:48 to 20:12.

The Rams took a 3-0 lead when Mike Lansford kicked a 23-yard field goal to cap their first drive. But after that the 49ers allowed them virtually nothing and exploded for 3 second-quarter touchdowns. Joe Montana, who completed 26 of 30 attempts for 262 yards, fired a 20-yard touchdown pass to tight end Brent Jones and an 18-yard touchdown strike to John Taylor. Between those scores, Roger Craig scored on a 1-yard run.

In the second half, the 49ers slowly built their advantage as Mike Cofer kicked 3 field goals. In a true team effort, 8 receivers caught passes, 6 players carried the ball, and 3 defenders intercepted passes to lead San Francisco to the one-sided victory.

L.A. Rams	3	0	0	0	- 3
San Francisco	0	21	3	6	- 30

Rams - FG Lansford 23
SF - Jones 20 pass from Montana (Cofer kick)
SF - Craig 1 run (Cofer kick)
SF - Taylor 18 pass from Montana (Cofer kick)
SF - FG Cofer 28
SF - FG Cofer 36
SF - FG Cofer 25

1990 AFC WILD CARD GAME
Miami 17, Kansas City 16

January 5, 1991, at Miami
Attendance: 67,276

Nick Lowery's 52-yard field-goal attempt with 49 seconds remaining in the game was short, allowing Miami to escape with a 17-16 victory against Kansas City.

Kansas City led almost the entire way, taking the lead in the first period on Lowery's 27-yard field goal. Pete Stoyanovich kicked an NFL-playoff record 58-yard field goal for Miami's only points of the first half, but the Chiefs responded with a 26-yard touchdown pass from Steve DeBerg to Stephone Paige.

Two field goals by Lowery in the third quarter built Kansas City's advantage to 13 points before Dan Marino launched a magnificent comeback. First, he threw a 1-yard scoring pass to Tony Paige, then drove the Dolphins 85 yards to a 12-yard touchdown throw to Mark Clayton with only 2:28 left in the game.

Kansas City	3	7	6	0	- 16
Miami	0	3	0	14	- 17

KC - FG Lowery 27
Mia - FG Stoyanovich 58
KC - Paige 26 pass from DeBerg (Lowery kick)
KC - FG Lowery 25
KC - FG Lowery 38
Mia - Paige 1 pass from Marino (Stoyanovich kick)
Mia - Clayton 12 pass from Marino (Stoyanovich kick)

1990 AFC WILD CARD GAME
Cincinnati 41, Houston 14

January 6, 1991, at Cincinnati
Attendance: 60,012

Cincinnati had defeated Houston 40-20 in the next-to-last week of the regular season, and the Bengals gave the Oilers more of the same in the playoffs, building a 34-0 lead in the third quarter on the way to a 41-14 victory.

The Bengals slowly ground up the Oilers, scoring twice in each of the first three quarters while building their lead. Ultimately, they had big advantages in time of possession (39:45 to 20:15) and first downs (24 to 13).

Cincinnati quarterback Boomer Esiason completed a 2-yard touchdown pass to Harold Green in the second period, scored on a 10-yard keeper after James Francis recovered a Houston fumble in the third quarter, and threw a touchdown to Eric Kattus in the final period.

Houston	0	0	7	7	-	14
Cincinnati	10	10	14	7	-	41

Cin - Woods 1 run (Breech kick)
Cin - FG Breech 27
Cin - Green 2 pass from Esiason (Breech kick)
Cin - FG Breech 30
Cin - Ball 3 run (Breech kick)
Cin - Esiason 10 run (Breech kick)
Hou - Givins 16 pass from Carlson (Garcia kick)
Cin - Kattus 9 pass from Esiason (Breech kick)
Hou - Givins 5 pass from Carlson (Garcia kick)

1990 NFC WILD CARD GAME
Washington 20, Philadelphia 6

January 5, 1991, at Philadelphia
Attendance: 65,287

The Eagles had their chances early and couldn't convert 2 turnovers into touchdowns, leaving Washington within easy striking distance. Once the Redskins got moving, they took advantage of the breaks for a 20-6 victory.

Philadelphia threatened in the early stages of the game but could show only 2 field goals by Roger Ruzek for their efforts. When Mark Rypien came back to throw a 16-yard touchdown pass to Art Monk, it proved to be all the Redskins would need to win the game. However, the Redskins increased their margin 8 seconds before halftime when Chip Lohmiller booted a 20-yard field goal.

The third quarter saw two more effective Washington drives. On the first, Lohmiller again hit a short field goal, and on the second Rypien threw a 3-yard touchdown pass.

Washington	0	10	10	0	-	20
Philadelphia	3	3	0	0	-	6

Phi - FG Ruzek 37
Phi - FG Ruzek 28
Was - Monk 16 pass from Rypien (Lohmiller kick)
Was - FG Lohmiller 20
Was - FG Lohmiller 19
Was - Clark 3 pass from Rypien (Lohmiller kick)

1990 NFC WILD CARD GAME
Chicago 16, New Orleans 6

January 6, 1991, at Chicago
Attendance: 60,767

Chicago's defense held New Orleans to 65 yards rushing and 6 first downs and allowed only 2 field goals to defeat the wild card Saints 16-6. Offensively, the story for the Bears was Neal Anderson, who pounded out 166 yards on 27 carries, caught 4 passes for 42 yards, and also completed a halfback pass for 22 yards.

The Bears netted 365 yards. However, other than an 18-yard touchdown pass from Mike Tomczak to tight end James Thornton in the second quarter, they demonstrated a lack of ability to finish off drives. Chicago reached the New Orleans 2-, 5-, and 4-yard lines before stalling and having Kevin Butler kick short field goals.

In the final minutes of the game, the Bears finally came up with a big play. Tomczak hit wide receiver Dennis Gentry for a 38-yard gain that clinched the victory.

New Orleans	0	3	0	3	-	6
Chicago	3	7	3	3	-	16

ChiB - FG Butler 19
ChiB - Thornton 18 pass from Tomczak (Butler kick)
NO - FG Andersen 47
ChiB - FG Butler 22
NO - FG Andersen 38
ChiB - FG Butler 21

1990 AFC DIVISIONAL PLAYOFF GAME
Buffalo 44, Miami 34

January 12, 1991, at Orchard Park, New York
Attendance: 77,087

Buffalo jumped to a 13-3 first-quarter lead, then the two teams matched each other score for score as the Bills outlasted the Dolphins 44-34. Jim Kelly completed 19 of 29 passes for 339 yards and 3 touchdowns to offset Dan Marino's 3 touchdown passes and a touchdown run.

Kelly teamed with Andre Reed from 40 yards for the first touchdown. After the Bills had built their second-quarter lead to 20-3, Marino got his team moving. First he threw a 64-yard touchdown pass to Mark Duper, then, after Kelly hit James Lofton for a score, Marino ran it in himself from the 2.

In the opening minute of the fourth quarter, Marino fired a 2-yard touchdown pass to Roy Foster to cut Miami's deficit to 30-27. But Thurman Thomas scored from the 5, and Kelly found Reed for a 26-yard touchdown pass to put the Dolphins away.

Miami	3	14	3	14	-	34
Buffalo	13	14	3	14	-	44

Buf - Reed 40 pass from Kelly (Norwood kick)
Mia - FG Stoyanovich 49
Buf - FG Norwood 40
Buf - FG Norwood 22
Buf - Thomas 5 run (Norwood kick)
Mia - Duper 64 pass from Marino (Stoyanovich kick)
Buf - Lofton 13 pass from Kelly (Norwood kick)
Mia - Marino 2 run (Stoyanovich kick)
Mia - FG Stoyanovich 22
Buf - FG Norwood 28
Mia - Foster 2 pass from Marino (Stoyanovich kick)
Buf - Thomas 5 run (Norwood kick)
Buf - Reed 26 pass from Kelly (Norwood kick)
Mia - Martin 8 pass from Marino (Stoyanovich kick)

1990 AFC DIVISIONAL PLAYOFF GAME
Los Angeles Raiders 20, Cincinnati 10

January 13, 1991, at Los Angeles
Attendance: 92,045

The Raiders moved most effectively on the ground, but they scored through the air while defeating the Central Division-champion Bengals 20-10.

The Raiders totaled 235 yards rushing, including 140 by Marcus Allen on 21 carries and 77 by Bo Jackson on only

6. But it took a 13-yard touchdown pass from Jay Schroeder to Mervyn Fernandez to give Los Angeles a 7-3 halftime lead after the Bengals had gone ahead in the second period on Jim Breech's 27-yard field goal.

Los Angeles increased its lead in the third period on a 49-yard field goal by Jeff Jaeger. The Bengals came back to tie it at 10-10 early in the final period when Boomer Esiason hit Stanford Jennings with an 8-yard touchdown pass. However, the Raiders scored 10 unanswered points, the big play being Schroeder's 41-yard scoring pass to Ethan Horton.

Cincinnati	0	3	0	7	-	10
L.A. Raiders	0	7	3	10	-	20

Cin - FG Breech 27
Raid - Fernandez 13 pass from Schroeder (Jaeger kick)
Raid - FG Jaeger 49
Cin - Jennings 8 pass from Esiason (Breech kick)
Raid - Horton 41 pass from Schroeder (Jaeger kick)
Raid - FG Jaeger 25

1990 NFC DIVISIONAL PLAYOFF GAME
San Francisco 28, Washington 10

January 12, 1991, at San Francisco
Attendance: 65,292

Joe Montana passed for 200 yards and 2 touchdowns in the first half to lead San Francisco to a 21-10 advantage, and neither offense scored again as the 49ers went on to defeat Washington 28-10.

Washington, which outgained San Francisco 441-338, scored quickly when Mark Rypien found Art Monk for 31 yards and a touchdown in the first quarter. The 49ers matched that score on Tom Rathman's 1-yard run, but Chip Lohmiller gave the Redskins the lead with a 44-yard field goal 36 seconds before the end of the period.

Then Montana took charge. He threw a 10-yard touchdown pass to Jerry Rice, then came back with an 8-yard strike to backup wide receiver Mike Sherrard. The only score of the second half came when nose tackle Michael Carter returned a deflected pass 61 yards for a touchdown.

Washington	10	0	0	0	-	10
San Francisco	7	14	0	7	-	28

Was - Monk 31 pass from Rypien (Lohmiller kick)
SF - Rathman 1 run (Cofer kick)
Was - FG Lohmiller 44
SF - Rice 10 pass from Montana (Cofer kick)
SF - Sherrard 8 pass from Montana (Cofer kick)
SF - M. Carter 61 interception return (Cofer kick)

1990 NFC DIVISIONAL PLAYOFF GAME
New York Giants 31, Chicago Bears 3

January 13, 1991, at East Rutherford, New Jersey
Attendance: 77,025

The New York defense held Chicago to only 27 yards rushing (Neal Anderson had only 19 yards on 12 carries), while the offense methodically cut up the Bears in a 31-3 victory.

Giants quarterback Jeff Hostetler, playing because of injuries to starter Phil Simms, completed 10 of 17 passes for 112 yards and 2 touchdowns and ran for 43 yards and another touchdown to pace the Giants' attack. Hostetler hit Stephen Baker with a 21-yard touchdown pass in the first quarter to build a 10-0 lead. He came back in the next period to find tight end Howard Cross for 5 yards and a touchdown. And he eliminated any hopes the Bears might have by running in from 3 yards out in the third quarter, building the New York lead to 24-3.

Chicago	0	3	0	0	-	3
N.Y. Giants	10	7	7	7	-	31

NYG - FG Bahr 46
NYG - Baker 21 pass from Hostetler (Bahr kick)
ChiB - FG Butler 33
NYG - Cross 5 pass from Hostetler (Bahr kick)
NYG - Hostetler 3 run (Bahr kick)
NYG - Carthon 1 run (Bahr kick)

1990 AFC CHAMPIONSHIP GAME
Buffalo 51, Los Angeles Raiders 3

January 20, 1991, at Orchard Park, New York
Attendance: 80,324

Running backs Thurman Thomas and Kenneth Davis combined to lead the Bills to a 51-3 romp over the Raiders for Buffalo's first title in a quarter of a century. Thomas had a sensational day, rushing for 138 yards on 25 carries and catching 5 passes for 61 yards. Davis, meanwhile, tied an AFC playoff record by scoring 3 touchdowns.

The game essentially was over in the first quarter. The Bills drove to a quick touchdown, with Jim Kelly passing to James Lofton from 13 yards. The Raiders came back with Jeff Jaeger's 41-yard field goal, but that was their high point for the day. When Thomas scored from the 12, the rout was on. Linebacker Darryl Talley made it 21-3 in the first period by returning an interception of Jay Schroeder 27 yards for a touchdown.

Davis, Buffalo's short-yardage specialist, scored on a pair of touchdown runs in the second period, and Kelly again went to Lofton as the Bills ran up 41 first-half points, establishing an NFL postseason-game record.

L.A. Raiders	3	0	0	0	-	3
Buffalo	21	20	0	10	-	51

Buf - Lofton 13 pass from Kelly (Norwood kick)
Raid - FG Jaeger 41
Buf - Thomas 12 run (Norwood kick)
Buf - Talley 27 interception return (Norwood kick)
Buf - K. Davis 1 run (kick blocked)
Buf - K. Davis 3 run (Norwood kick)
Buf - Lofton 8 pass from Kelly (Norwood kick)
Buf - K. Davis 1 run (Norwood kick)
Buf - FG Norwood 39

1990 NFC CHAMPIONSHIP GAME
New York Giants 15, San Francisco 13

January 20, 1991, at San Francisco
Attendance: 65,750

San Francisco held New York without a touchdown, but Matt Bahr kicked 5 field goals in 6 attempts, including the game-winner from 42 yards as time ran out, to lead the Giants to a 15-13 upset of the two-time defending Super Bowl-champion 49ers.

The game began as an exchange of field goals, as Bahr and Mike Cofer kicked 1 in each of the first two periods. The Giants, however, had showed a stronger offense, based on a running attack that pounded for 152 yards in the game, while the 49ers were held to only 39 yards rushing.

Nevertheless, San Francisco went ahead 13-6 in the third period when Joe Montana connected with John Taylor on a 61-yard scoring pass. Behind the running of Ottis Anderson and the passing and leadership of Jeff Hostetler, the Giants set up 2 more field goals to cut the margin to 1 point.

As the game wound down, nose tackle Erik Howard forced a fumble by Roger Craig that was recovered by Lawrence Taylor. Hostetler took the Giants 33 yards in 6 plays to set up Bahr's winning field goal.

N.Y. Giants	3	3	3	6	-	15
San Francisco	3	3	7	0	-	13

SF - FG Cofer 47
NYG - FG Bahr 28
NYG - FG Bahr 42
SF - FG Cofer 35
SF - Taylor 61 pass from Montana (Cofer kick)
NYG - FG Bahr 46
NYG - FG Bahr 38
NYG - FG Bahr 42

1991 AFC WILD CARD GAME
Kansas City 10, Los Angeles Raiders 6

December 28, 1991, at Kansas City
Attendance: 75,827

The Chiefs and Raiders had engaged in a 27-21 slugfest the previous week, but the defenses controlled this game, and Kansas City scored the game's lone touchdown to win 10-6.

Rookie Todd Marinovich had been outstanding the week before, but the Chiefs' defense intercepted him 4 times. The first 2 were by Deron Cherry, who, late in the second quarter, returned the second to the Raiders' 11. On the next play, Steve DeBerg hit Fred Jones for a touchdown.

The Raiders cut the margin to 1 point at the end of the third quarter with 2 field goals by Jeff Jaeger. In the final period, the Chiefs reached the 1 before Nick Lowery kicked an 18-yard field goal. The Raiders drove to the Kansas City 24-yard line in the closing minutes, but 4 penalties in a 5-play span preceded linebacker Lonnie Marts's interception that sealed the victory.

L.A. Raiders	0	3	3	0	-	6
Kansas City	0	7	0	3	-	10

KC - Jones 11 pass from DeBerg (Lowery kick)
Raid - FG Jaeger 32
Raid - FG Jaeger 26
KC - FG Lowery 18

1991 AFC WILD CARD GAME
Houston 17, New York Jets 10

December 29, 1991, at Houston
Attendance: 61,485

The Houston defense stopped New York twice inside the 5-yard line in the second half to preserve a 17-10 victory over the Jets. The Oilers led 14-10 at halftime after Warren Moon threw 2 touchdown passes to Ernest Givens.

New York took the second-half kickoff and consumed more than eight minutes while driving to the Houston 8. But on third down, O'Brien's pass was intercepted at the 2 by Bubba McDowell. After a 53-yard field goal by Al Del Greco increased the Oilers' lead to 7 points, the Jets again drove deep into Houston territory. With a third-and-inches at the 3, Al Smith stopped Brad Baxter for no gain, and, on fourth down, Freeman McNeil was gang-tackled for no gain. New York had one more chance after recovering Moon's fumble at the Houston 26, but the Jets could not pick up a first down.

N.Y. Jets	0	10	0	0	-	10
Houston	7	7	0	3	-	17

Hou - Givins 5 pass from Moon (Del Greco kick)
NYJ - Toon 10 pass from O'Brien (Allegre kick)
Hou - Givins 20 pass from Moon (Del Greco kick)
NYJ - FG Allegre 33
Hou - FG Del Greco 53

1991 NFC WILD CARD GAME
Atlanta 27, New Orleans 20

December 28, 1991, at New Orleans
Attendance: 68,794

Chris Miller threw 3 touchdown passes, the last a 61-yard strike to Michael Haynes with 2:41 remaining in the game, as Atlanta knocked New Orleans, which had won its first-ever division title, out of the playoffs 27-20.

The Saints jumped to a 10-0 lead, but Miller, who completed 18 of 30 passes for 291 yards, hit Andre Rison with a 24-yard touchdown to open Atlanta's scoring, then came back in the third quarter to give the Falcons their first lead with a 20-yard strike to Haynes.

With the score tied 20-20 late in the game, Miller hit Haynes with a short pass, and the wide receiver spun away from the Saints' defenders and raced to the end zone for the winning points. Bobby Hebert drove the Saints back to the Falcons' 35-yard line, but was intercepted by cornerback Tim McKyer.

Atlanta	0	10	7	10	-	27
New Orleans	7	6	0	7	-	20

NO - Turner 26 pass from Hebert (Andersen kick)
NO - FG Andersen 45
Atl - Rison 24 pass from Miller (Johnson kick)
Atl - FG Johnson 44
NO - FG Andersen 35
Atl - Haynes 20 pass from Miller (Johnson kick)
NO - Hilliard 1 run (Andersen kick)
Atl - FG Johnson 36
Atl - Haynes 61 pass from Miller (Johnson kick)

1991 NFC WILD CARD GAME
Dallas 17, Chicago 13

December 29, 1991, at Chicago
Attendance: 62,594

The Dallas Cowboys used a big defensive play to jump to a 10-0 first-quarter lead and went on to win their first playoff game since 1982, narrowly defeating the Chicago Bears 17-13.

With Dallas leading 3-0, linebacker Darrick Brownlow blocked Maury Buford's punt, and it was recovered by linebacker Ken Norton at the Chicago 10, setting up a 1-yard touchdown run by Emmitt Smith, who gained 105 yards on 26 carries for the day.

The Bears cut the margin to 4 points on 2 field goals by Kevin Butler, but in the third period, the Cowboys drove 75 yards, scoring on Steve Beuerlein's 3-yard pass to tight end Jay Novacek. Chicago responded with its own scoring pass with only 2:42 remaining in the game—Jim Harbaugh finding Tom Waddle from the 6—but the Bears couldn't catch up.

Dallas	10	0	7	0	-	17
Chicago	0	3	3	7	-	13

Dal - FG Willis 27
Dal - E. Smith 1 run (Willis kick)
ChiB - FG Butler 19

ChiB	-	FG Butler 43
Dal	-	Novacek 3 pass from Beuerlein (Willis kick)
ChiB	-	Waddle 6 pass from Harbaugh (Butler kick)

1991 AFC DIVISIONAL PLAYOFF GAME
Denver 26, Houston 24

January 4, 1992, at Denver
Attendance: 75,301

John Elway worked his fourth-quarter magic, leading 2 long scoring drives as Denver beat Houston 26-24.

Warren Moon threw 3 touchdown passes in the first half while Houston built a 21-6 lead. But in the second half, the Broncos' defense limited the Oilers to a field goal, which moved Houston ahead 24-16 in the fourth quarter.

Elway then directed an 80-yard drive culminating in Greg Lewis's second 1-yard touchdown run. When Greg Montgomery punted the Broncos back to their 2 with 2:07 left, Elway took over. First he hit Michael Young for 22 yards. Then, on fourth-and-6 at the 28, he scrambled 7 yards. And on fourth-and-10, Elway passed to Vance Johnson for 44 yards. With 16 seconds remaining, David Treadwell kicked a 28-yard field goal for the victory.

Houston	14	7	0	3	-	24
Denver	6	7	3	10	-	26

Hou	-	Jeffires 15 pass from Moon (Del Greco kick)
Hou	-	Hill 9 pass from Moon (Del Greco kick)
Den	-	V. Johnson 10 pass from Elway (Treadwell kick failed)
Hou	-	Duncan 6 pass from Moon (Del Greco kick)
Den	-	Lewis 1 run (Treadwell kick)
Den	-	FG Treadwell 49
Hou	-	FG Del Greco 25
Den	-	Lewis 1 run (Treadwell kick)
Den	-	FG Treadwell 28

1991 AFC DIVISIONAL PLAYOFF GAME
Buffalo 37, Kansas City 14

January 6, 1992, at Orchard Park, New York
Attendance: 80,182

Buffalo avenged a 33-6 defeat to Kansas City in the regular season by dominating virtually every phase of the game and beating the Chiefs 37-14.

The Chiefs' hopes were dealt a severe blow in the second quarter, when quarterback Steve DeBerg was knocked out of the game with a sprained thumb; his backup, Mark Vlasic, was intercepted 4 times. Meanwhile, Jim Kelly completed 23 of 35 passes and threw a touchdown pass in each of the first three quarters while staking the Bills to a 24-0 lead.

Thurman Thomas also starred for the Bills, carrying the ball 22 times for 100 yards, the fourth consecutive postseason game in which he reached the century mark. Andre Reed, who caught the first 2 touchdown passes of the game, finished with 100 yards on 4 receptions.

Kansas City	0	0	7	7	-	14
Buffalo	7	10	7	13	-	37

Buf	-	Reed 25 pass from Kelly (Norwood kick)
Buf	-	Reed 53 pass from Kelly (Norwood kick)
Buf	-	FG Norwood 33
Buf	-	Lofton 10 pass from Kelly (Norwood kick)
KC	-	Word 3 run (Lowery kick)
Buf	-	FG Norwood 20
Buf	-	FG Norwood 47
Buf	-	Davis 5 run (Norwood kick)
KC	-	F. Jones 20 pass from Vlasic (Lowery kick)

1991 NFC DIVISIONAL PLAYOFF GAME
Washington 24, Atlanta 7

January 4, 1992, at Washington
Attendance: 55,181

Washington scored 2 touchdowns in a span of 3:11 of the second quarter to take a lead it never relinquished in dispatching Atlanta 24-7. The conditions—rainy, windy, and muddy—were conducive for turning over the ball, but whereas the Falcons were plagued by 6 turnovers, the Redskins seemed not to notice the weather as they ran virtually at will.

After a scoreless first quarter, Washington scored first, driving 81 yards and finishing its drive with a 17-yard run by rookie Ricky Ervins. A short while later, James Geathers recovered a fumble at the Atlanta 39-yard line, and it took the Redskins only 4 plays to score on Gerald Riggs's 2-yard run.

The Falcons came back with a touchdown before halftime, but the Redskins scored in both the third and fourth quarters to put the game away. Washington maintained possession for more than 36 minutes.

Atlanta	0	7	0	0	-	7
Washington	0	14	3	7	-	24

Was	-	Ervins 17 run (Lohmiller kick)
Was	-	Riggs 2 run (Lohmiller kick)
Atl	-	T. Johnson 1 run (Johnson kick)
Was	-	FG Lohmiller 24
Was	-	Riggs 1 run (Lohmiller kick)

1991 NFC DIVISIONAL PLAYOFF GAME
Detroit 38, Dallas 6

January 5, 1992, at Detroit
Attendance: 78,290

With all eyes watching Barry Sanders, Detroit quarterback Eric Kramer completed 29 of 38 passes for 341 yards and 3 touchdowns to shock the Cowboys 38-6. Sanders carried the ball only 12 times for 69 yards (with 47 coming on a fourth-quarter touchdown run).

Detroit jumped in front early when Kramer teamed with Willie Green on a 31-yard touchdown pass. The Cowboys responded with a field goal, but the next time they had the ball, Melvin Jenkins inter-cepted a pass from Troy Aikman and returned it 41 yards for a touchdown.

With the score 17-6 at the start of the third period, Detroit put the game away with 2 touchdowns in a span of 1:05. First, Kramer hit Green with a 9-yard touchdown pass. Then Aikman fumbled at the Dallas 27, and linebacker Victor Jones recovered. That led to Kramer's 7-yard touchdown pass to Herman Moore.

Dallas	3	3	0	0	-	6
Detroit	7	10	14	7	-	38

Det	-	Green 31 pass from Kramer (Murray kick)
Dal	-	FG Willis 28
Det	-	Jenkins 41 interception return (Murray kick)
Dal	-	FG Willis 28
Det	-	FG Murray 36
Det	-	Green 9 pass from Kramer (Murray kick)
Det	-	Moore 7 pass from Kramer (Murray kick)
Det	-	Sanders 47 run (Murray kick)

1991 AFC CHAMPIONSHIP GAME
Buffalo 10, Denver 7

January 12, 1992, at Orchard Park, New York
Attendance: 80,272

Denver shut down Buffalo's explosive offense, but linebacker Carlton Bailey scored on an interception return to lead the Bills to a 10-7 victory over the Broncos.

In a tough defensive match, neither team was able to score in the first half, although the Bills were helped by the kicking of Denver's unfortunate David Treadwell, who missed 3 field goals during the game, 2 of which bounced off the uprights.

Late in the third quarter, nose tackle Jeff Wright tipped a screen pass by John Elway, and Bailey intercepted and returned it 11 yards for a touchdown. It was the only score of the game until Scott Norwood increased Buffalo's margin with a 44-yard field goal with only 4:18 left in the game.

With Elway out due to a deep thigh bruise, Gary Kubiak came on to complete 11 of 12 passes in what he had already announced would be his last game. Kubiak led the Broncos 85 yards and scored himself on a 3-yard run with 1:43 left. Denver recovered the subsequent onside kick at its 49, but on first down Steve Sewell fumbled and the ball was recovered by Kirby Jackson. It was only Denver's second turnover.

Denver	0	0	0	7	-	7
Buffalo	0	0	7	3	-	10

Buf - Bailey 11 interception return (Norwood kick)
Buf - FG Norwood 44
Den - Kubiak 3 run (Treadwell kick)

1991 NFC CHAMPIONSHIP GAME
Washington 41, Detroit 10

January 12, 1992, at Washington
Attendance: 55,585

The Redskins had defeated the Lions 45-0 on the same field on the opening day of the regular season, and Detroit was determined things were going to be different this time. They weren't, as Washington scored twice in the first 5 minutes of the game and went on to a 41-10 victory.

On the Lions' first play from scrimmage, defensive end Charles Mann forced a fumble by Erik Kramer, and 2 plays later the Redskins turned it into a touchdown on a 2-yard run by Gerald Riggs. Several minutes later Kurt Gouveia intercepted a pass by Kramer and returned it 38 yards to set up a 20-yard field goal by Chip Lohmiller.

Although Detroit responded with a touchdown pass from Kramer to Willie Green in the second quarter, the Redskins came right back with a 3-yard scoring run by Riggs for a 17-10 lead at halftime.

In the third quarter, Mark Rypien, who completed 12 of 17 passes for 228 yards, broke the game open with a 45-yard scoring strike to Gary Clark and a 21-yard touchdown pass to Art Monk as Washington qualified for its fifth Super Bowl berth.

Detroit	0	10	0	0	-	10
Washington	10	7	10	14	-	41

Was - Riggs 2 run (Lohmiller kick)
Was - FG Lohmiller 20
Det - Green 18 pass from Kramer (Murray kick)
Was - Riggs 3 run (Lohmiller kick)
Det - FG Murray 30
Was - FG Lohmiller 28
Was - Clark 45 pass from Rypien (Lohmiller kick)
Was - Monk 21 pass from Rypien (Lohmiller kick)
Was - Green 32 interception return (Lohmiller kick)

1992 AFC WILD CARD GAME
San Diego 17, Kansas City 0

January 2, 1993, at San Diego
Attendance: 58,278

The Chargers were ready for the only team that had defeated them in the final 12 weeks of the regular season. With the San Diego defense shutting down the Chiefs, it was only a matter of time before the Chargers scored to put the game away, which they ultimately did 17-0.

There was no scoring until midway through the third quarter, when Marion Butts broke loose for a 54-yard touchdown run. On Kansas City's subsequent possession, defensive tackle Blaise Winter tipped a pass by Dave Krieg, and end Leslie O'Neal intercepted to set up John Carney's 34-yard field goal.

The Chargers applied the knockout punch in the final period, driving 90 yards on 10 plays and scoring on Steve Hendrickson's 5-yard run. A linebacker who also doubled as a blocking back in goal-line situations, Hendrickson had not carried the ball all year.

Kansas City	0	0	0	0	-	0
San Diego	0	0	10	7	-	17

SD - Butts 54 run (Carney kick)
SD - FG Carney 34
SD - Hendrickson 5 run

1992 AFC WILD CARD GAME
Buffalo 41, Houston 38 (OT)

January 3, 1993, at Orchard Park, New York
Attendance: 75,141

Warren Moon staked the Oilers to a 35-3 lead in the third period with 4 touchdown passes, but Frank Reich, subbing for injured Jim Kelly, threw 4 touchdown passes in the second half as the Bills mounted the greatest comeback in NFL history to stun Houston 41-38.

Houston built its lead to 32 points after Bubba McDowell returned an interception 58 yards for a touchdown only 1:41 into the third quarter. Then Reich started the comeback, guiding the Bills 50 yards to Kenneth Davis's 1-yard touchdown run. Steve Christie then recovered his own onside kick, and, within 6:54 of their first touchdown, the Bills had scored 3 more times.

Late in the game, Reich drove the Bills 74 yards to their first lead, achieved on a 17-yard touchdown pass to Andre Reed. But Moon led the Oilers to a field goal with 12 seconds left that sent the game into overtime. When Moon was intercepted by Nate Odomes on the first possession of overtime, it set up Christie for the 32-yard field goal that won the game.

Houston	7	21	7	3	0	-	38
Buffalo	3	0	28	7	3	-	41

Hou - Jeffires 3 pass from Moon (Del Greco kick)
Buf - FG Christie 36
Hou - Slaughter 7 pass from Moon (Del Greco kick)
Hou - Duncan 26 pass from Moon (Del Greco kick)
Hou - Jeffires 27 pass from Moon (Del Greco kick)
Hou - McDowell 58 interception return (Del Greco kick)
Buf - K. Davis 1 run (Christie kick)
Buf - Beebe 38 pass from Reich (Christie kick)
Buf - Reed 26 pass from Reich (Christie kick)
Buf - Reed 18 pass from Reich (Christie kick)

Buf	-	Reed 17 pass from Reich (Christie kick)
Hou	-	FG Del Greco 26
Buf	-	FG Christie 32

1992 NFC WILD CARD GAME
Washington 24, Minnesota 7

January 2, 1993, at Minneapolis
Attendance: 57,353

Brian Mitchell, playing only because of injuries to teammates, rushed for 109 yards and had 100 yards on receptions and punt returns to lead the Redskins to a 24-7 victory over the Vikings. Mitchell's 16 carries were only 2 short of the total he had managed in his first three years in the NFL.

Minnesota grabbed a quick lead, going 79 yards after taking the opening kickoff and scoring on Terry Allen's 1-yard run. But the Washington defense asserted itself after that, holding Minnesota to just 69 total yards the rest of the game.

Washington moved ahead 10-7, then Mitchell broke open the game late in the second quarter. On fourth down at the Minnesota 44, he took the snap on a fake punt and raced 36 yards. He scored on an 8-yard run.

Washington	3	14	7	0	-	24
Minnesota	7	0	0	0	-	7

Min	-	Allen 1 run (Reveiz kick)
Was	-	FG Lohmiller 44
Was	-	Byner 3 run (Lohmiller kick)
Was	-	Mitchell 8 run (Lohmiller kick)
Was	-	Clark 24 pass from Rypien (Lohmiller kick)

1992 NFC WILD CARD GAME
Philadelphia 36, New Orleans 20

January 3, 1993, at New Orleans
Attendance: 68,893

After trailing 20-7 late in the third quarter, the Eagles erupted for 29 points—26 in the final period against a team that had not allowed more than 21 in a game all year—to defeat the Saints 36-20.

The Saints led 20-10 with less than 11 minutes left, then Randall Cunningham found Fred Barnett for 35 yards and a touchdown. On the first play after the kickoff, linebacker Seth Joyner intercepted a pass by Bobby Hebert and returned it to the New Orleans 26. That set up Heath Sherman's 6-yard touchdown run, which put Philadelphia ahead 24-20 with 6:48 left. On New Orleans's next possession, Reggie White sacked Hebert for a safety. Cornerback Eric Allen closed the door on New Orleans 19 seconds after Roger Ruzek kicked a 39-yard field goal by making his second interception of the game and returning it 18 yards for a touchdown.

Philadelphia	7	0	3	26	-	36
New Orleans	7	10	3	0	-	20

NO	-	Heyward 1 run (Andersen kick)
Phil	-	Barnett 57 pass from Cunningham (Ruzek kick)
NO	-	FG Andersen 35
NO	-	Early 7 pass from Hebert (Andersen kick)
NO	-	FG Andersen 42
Phil	-	FG Ruzek 40
Phil	-	Barnett 35 pass from Cunningham (Ruzek kick)
Phil	-	Sherman 6 run (Ruzek kick)
Phil	-	Safety, Hebert sacked by White in end zone
Phil	-	FG Ruzek 39
Phil	-	Allen 18 interception return (Ruzek kick)

1992 AFC DIVISIONAL PLAYOFF GAME
Buffalo 24, Pittsburgh 3

January 9, 1993, at Pittsburgh
Attendance: 60,407

Pittsburgh, which led the NFL with 43 takeaways during the regular season, lost the ball 4 times while never getting a turnover, and Buffalo methodically won, 24-3.

The Steelers took the lead in the first period on Gary Anderson's 38-yard field goal. But when defensive tackle Phil Hansen recovered a fumble by Pittsburgh quarterback Neil O'Donnell, it helped kick the Bills into gear. Buffalo drove 59 yards, scoring on Frank Reich's 1-yard touchdown pass to eligible lineman Mitch Frerotte.

Late in the third quarter, Reich—who completed 16 of 23 passes for 160 yards in his substitute role—found James Lofton with a 17-yard touchdown pass that gave the Bills what turned out to be a safe cushion. Two fourth-quarter scores made the final outcome seem more one-sided than it really was.

Buffalo	0	7	7	10	-	24
Pittsburgh	3	0	0	0	-	3

Pit	-	FG Anderson 38
Buf	-	Frerotte 1 pass from Reich (Christie kick)
Buf	-	Lofton 17 pass from Reich (Christie kick)
Buf	-	FG Christie 43
Buf	-	Gardner 1 run (Christie kick)

1992 AFC DIVISIONAL PLAYOFF GAME
Miami 31, San Diego 0

January 10, 1993, at Miami
Attendance: 71,224

Dan Marino threw 3 touchdown passes in just over six minutes of the second period to break open a defensive struggle and lead Miami to a 31-0 victory against San Diego.

The game was scoreless in the second quarter when Miami cornerback Troy Vincent intercepted a pass from San Diego's Stan Humphries that he returned to the Chargers' 48. Marino finished the subsequent drive with a 1-yard touchdown pass to running back Tony Paige. After Vincent intercepted again, Marino took only two plays to score, the second a 9-yard pass to tight end Keith Jackson with 1:46 remaining in the half. Linebacker Bryan Cox then intercepted another Humphries pass. With 27 seconds remaining, Marino again connected with Jackson, this time for a 30-yard touchdown.

Miami controlled the ball on the ground in the second half, while the Chargers never really got going.

San Diego	0	0	0	0	-	0
Miami	0	21	0	10	-	31

Mia	-	Paige 1 pass from Marino (Stoyanovich kick)
Mia	-	Jackson 9 pass from Marino (Stoyanovich kick)
Mia	-	Jackson 30 pass from Marino (Stoyanovich kick)
Mia	-	FG Stoyanovich 22
Mia	-	Craver 25 run (Stoyanovich kick)

1992 NFC DIVISIONAL PLAYOFF GAME
San Francisco 20, Washington 13

January 9, 1993, at San Francisco
Attendance: 64,991

Steve Young turned over the ball 4 times, but passed for 227 yards and 2 touchdowns and ran for 73 yards, and the

49ers held off Washington for a 20-13 victory.

The 49ers led at halftime 17-3 as Young threw a 5-yard touchdown pass to John Taylor in the first quarter and hit tight end Brent Jones for a 16-yard touchdown in the second period.

Late in the third quarter, Young lost a fumble at his 15, and the Redskins converted it into Mark Rypien's 1-yard quarterback sneak to make it 17-13. The Redskins then put together a drive that reached the San Francisco 23 before Rypien fumbled trying to hand off. San Francisco's ensuing 14-play, 59-yard drive took more than seven minutes, so that Mike Cofer's 33-yard field goal came with only 2:22 left.

Washington	3	0	3	7	-	13
San Francisco	7	10	0	3	-	20

SF - Taylor 5 pass from Young (Cofer kick)
Was - FG Lohmiller 19
SF - FG Cofer 23
SF - Jones 16 pass from Young (Cofer kick)
Was - FG Lohmiller 32
Was - Rypien 1 run (Lohmiller kick)
SF - FG Cofer 33

1992 NFC DIVISIONAL PLAYOFF GAME
Dallas 34, Philadelphia 10

January 10, 1993, at Irving, Texas
Attendance: 63,721

A stingy Dallas defense held Philadelphia to only 178 yards and sacked Eagles quarterback Randall Cunningham 5 times, as the Cowboys rolled over the Eagles 34-10.

Philadelphia took a lead 7:15 into the game when Roger Ruzek kicked a 32-yard field goal. However, the Cowboys took the lead for good later in the period when Troy Aikman threw a 1-yard touchdown pass to backup tight end Derek Tennell. Aikman's second touchdown pass, of 6 yards to Jay Novacek, came 47 seconds before the end of the half, and when Vai Sikahema fumbled away the ensuing kickoff, Dallas was able to increase its lead to 17-3 on Lin Elliott's 20-yard field goal as the clock ran out.

In the second half, the Cowboys kept the ball mainly on the ground and built a 34-3 lead.

Philadelphia	3	0	0	7	-	10
Dallas	7	10	10	7	-	34

Phi - FG Ruzek 32
Dal - Tennell 1 pass from Aikman (Elliott kick)
Dal - Novacek 6 pass from Aikman (Elliott kick)
Dal - FG Elliott 20
Dal - Smith 23 run (Elliott kick)
Dal - FG Elliott 43
Dal - Gainer 1 run (Elliott kick)
Phi - Williams 18 pass from Cunningham (Ruzek kick)

1992 AFC CHAMPIONSHIP GAME
Buffalo 29, Miami 10

January 17, 1993, at Miami
Attendance: 72,703

The Buffalo defense held Miami to 33 yards rushing while recovering 3 fumbles, intercepting 2 passes, sacking Dan Marino 4 times, and setting up 13 points. Combined with a versatile offense and a record-tying 5 field goals by Steve Christie, this spelled a 29-10 victory for the Bills.

The score was 3-3 at the end of one period, but, 40 seconds into the second quarter, Jim Kelly hit Thurman Thomas with a 17-yard touchdown pass that put the Bills ahead for good. Kelly, just back from a sprained knee that had forced him to miss the Bills' first two playoff games, completed 17 of 24 passes.

The back-breaking play for Miami came when the Dolphins fumbled the second-half kickoff, and the Bills recovered at the 24. Five plays later, Kenneth Davis scored from the 2 to make it 20-3. Two more field goals by Christie built the lead to 23 points before Marino finally hit Mark Duper with a 15-yard touchdown pass.

The victory made the Bills only the second team to earn three consecutive Super Bowl appearances.

Buffalo	3	10	10	6	-	29
Miami	3	0	0	7	-	10

Buf - FG Christie 21
Mia - FG Stoyanovich 51
Buf - Thomas 17 pass from Kelly (Christie kick)
Buf - FG Christie 33
Buf - Davis 2 run (Christie kick)
Buf - FG Christie 21
Buf - FG Christie 31
Mia - Duper 15 pass from Marino (Stoyanovich kick)
Buf - FG Christie 38

1992 NFC CHAMPIONSHIP GAME
Dallas 30, San Francisco 20

January 17, 1993, at San Francisco
Attendance: 64,920

San Francisco and Dallas were even in first downs (24), and the Cowboys had only 1 more yard (416-415), but the 49ers had 4 critical turnovers and the Cowboys none. That was the difference as Dallas won 30-20.

The game was tied 10-10 at halftime, but all of the Cowboys' points had come after a pair of fumbles by the 49ers. In the second half, Troy Aikman took charge. Starting from their 22 after taking the second-half kickoff, the Cowboys scored in 8 plays, the big gainer a 38-yard pass from Aikman to Alvin Harper.

San Francisco responded with a field goal, but the Cowboys had a dominating drive that took nine minutes off the clock and ended with Aikman's 16-yard touchdown pass to Emmitt Smith.

With less than five minutes left, Steve Young hit Jerry Rice with a 5-yard scoring pass to cut the score to 24-20. But on the first play from scrimmage after that, Harper caught a short pass from Aikman and burst loose for a 70-yard gain that set up the clinching 6-yard touchdown pass to Kelvin Martin.

Dallas	3	7	7	13	-	30
San Francisco	7	3	3	7	-	20

Dal - FG Elliott 20
SF - Young 1 run (Cofer kick)
Dal - E. Smith 4 run (Elliott kick)
SF - FG Cofer 28
Dal - Johnston 3 run (Elliott kick)
SF - FG Cofer 42
Dal - E. Smith 16 pass from Aikman (Elliott kick)
SF - Rice 5 pass from Young (Cofer kick)
Dal - Martin 6 pass from Aikman (kick blocked)

1993 AFC WILD CARD GAME
Kansas City 27, Pittsburgh 24 (OT)

January 8, 1994, at Kansas City
Attendance: 74,515

Nick Lowery atoned for missing a 43-yard field-goal attempt at the end of regulation time with a 32-yard kick after 11:03 of overtime to give Kansas City a 27-24 victory.

The Steelers scored first, but the Chiefs tied it when, on his only pass of the game, Dave Krieg—who had temporarily replaced injured Joe Montana—connected with J.J. Birden for a 23-yard touchdown. The Steelers moved ahead 17-7 when Neil O'Donnell fired a 26-yard touchdown pass to Ernie Mills 18 seconds before halftime. That came after the Steelers stopped the Chiefs on a fourth-down situation near midfield.

The Chiefs tied it in the fourth quarter, but the Steelers retook the lead when O'Donnell capped a 74-yard drive with his third touchdown pass. As regulation wound down, Keith Cash blocked a Pittsburgh punt, and Fred Jones returned it to the 9. On fourth down, Montana hit Fred Barnett for a 7-yard touchdown.

Pittsburgh	7	10	0	7	0	-	24
Kansas City	7	0	3	14	3	-	27

Pit - Cooper 10 pass from O'Donnell (Anderson kick)
KC - Birden 23 pass from Krieg (Lowery kick)
Pit - FG Anderson 30
Pit - Mills 26 pass from O'Donnell (Anderson kick)
KC - FG Lowery 23
KC - Allen 2 run (Lowery kick)
Pit - Green 22 pass from O'Donnell (Anderson kick)
KC - Barnett 7 pass from Montana (Lowery kick)
KC - FG Lowery 32

1993 AFC WILD CARD GAME
Los Angeles Raiders 42, Denver 24

January 9, 1994, at Los Angeles
Attendance: 65,314

John Elway and Jeff Hostetler each threw 3 touchdown passes in the first half, but the Broncos had no answer for 3 touchdown runs by Napoleon McCallum in the second half, and the Raiders won 42-24.

The first half ended tied at 21-21; each time Hostetler threw a scoring pass, Elway matched it. But field position was the key after intermission. Early in the third quarter Denver took over inside its 5 after an excellent punt by Jeff Gossett. A short punt by Tom Rouen set up the Raiders at the Denver 35. On third-and-1, McCallum broke loose for a 26-yard touchdown run. Another short punt gave L.A. the ball at its 48, and a 33-yard pass from Hostetler to Ethan Horton led to McCallum's 2-yard touchdown run.

Denver	7	14	0	3	-	24
L.A. Raiders	14	7	14	7	-	42

Raid - Horton 9 pass from Hostetler (Jaeger kick)
Den - Sharpe 23 pass from Elway (Elam kick)
Raid - T. Brown 65 pass from Hostetler (Jaeger kick)
Den - R. Johnson 16 pass from Elway (Elam kick)
Raid - Jett 54 pass from Hostetler (Jaeger kick)
Den - Russell 6 pass from Elway (Elam kick)
Raid - McCallum 26 run (Jaeger kick)
Raid - McCallum 2 run (Jaeger kick)
Den - FG Elam 33
Raid - McCallum 1 run (Jaeger kick)

1993 NFC WILD CARD GAME
Green Bay 28, Detroit 24

January 8, 1994, at Pontiac, Michigan
Attendance: 68,479

Brett Favre threw 3 touchdown passes to Sterling Sharpe, the last a 40-yard strike with 55 seconds left, and Green Bay rallied from a 17-7 third-quarter deficit to a 28-24 victory over Detroit.

The Lions led 10-7 at halftime, and Melvin Jenkins increased the advantage when he intercepted Favre midway through the third period and returned it 15 yards to score. Favre countered with his second touchdown pass to Sharpe. Then, when the Lions were on the verge of scoring again, rookie safety George Teague intercepted Erik Kramer's short pass in the end zone and raced 101 yards for a touchdown and a 21-17 advantage.

Detroit retook the lead in the final period. But Favre drove Green Bay to the 40. Unable to find Mark Clayton, he scrambled to his left and threw across field to Sharpe, who scored.

Green Bay	0	7	14	7	-	28
Detroit	3	7	7	7	-	24

Det - FG Lohmiller 47
GB - Sharpe 12 pass from Favre (Jacke kick)
Det - Perriman 1 pass from Kramer (Hanson kick)
Det - Jenkins 15 interception return (Hanson kick)
GB - Sharpe 28 pass from Favre (Jacke kick)
GB - Teague 101 interception return (Jacke kick)
Det - D. Moore 5 run (Hanson kick)
GB - Sharpe 40 pass from Favre (Jacke kick)

1993 NFC WILD CARD GAME
New York Giants 17, Minnesota 10

January 9, 1994, at East Rutherford, New Jersey
Attendance: 77,328

Freezing temperatures and a howling, gusting wind dominated the action and thwarted the team moving into the face of the flurries. All the points were scored with the wind, and the Giants scored 2 touchdowns in the third period to defeat the Vikings 17-10.

The Giants led 3-0 after one period, but the Vikings came back with 10 points in the second quarter, when Jim McMahon teamed with Cris Carter on a 40-yard scoring pass and Fuad Reveiz kicked a 52-yard field goal.

The Giants tied the score on their opening possession of the third period, when Rodney Hampton blasted over right end and rambled 51 yards for a touchdown. A short while later, a 21-yard punt gave New York the ball at the Minnesota 26. Six plays later, Hampton barreled in from the 2 for the final points of the day.

Minnesota	0	10	0	0	-	10
N.Y. Giants	3	0	14	0	-	17

NYG - FG Treadwell 26
Min - C. Carter 40 pass from McMahon (Reveiz kick)
Min - FG Reveiz 52
NYG - Hampton 51 run (Treadwell kick)
NYG - Hampton 2 run (Treadwell kick)

1993 AFC DIVISIONAL PLAYOFF GAME
Buffalo 29, Los Angeles Raiders 23

January 15, 1994, at Orchard Park, New York
Attendance: 61,923

With the temperature zero degrees and a wind-chill factor of minus-32, Buffalo fell behind 17-6 before taking charge for a 29-23 victory over the Los Angeles Raiders.

The Raiders dominated the second quarter, and Napoleon McCallum's second 1-yard touchdown run gave them a 17-6 lead 1:57 before halftime. But Buffalo quickly moved 76 yards to a touchdown, the big play a 37-yard pass-interference penalty. Thurman Thomas scored on an 8-yard run with 50 seconds left.

Four scores in a span of 6:18 of the third and fourth

quarters changed the complexion of the game. First, Jim Kelly teamed with Bill Brooks on a 25-yard touchdown pass that gave Buffalo a 19-17 lead. Moments later, Henry Jones recovered McCallum's fumble, setting up Steve Christie's field goal. Two plays later, the Raiders' Tim Brown took a short pass and dashed 86 yards for a touchdown to give his team a 23-22 lead. But the Bills came right back, driving 71 yards, with Kelly hitting Brooks from 22 yards for the game-winning touchdown pass.

L.A. Raiders	0	17	6	0	-	23
Buffalo	0	13	9	7	-	29

Raid - FG Jaeger 30
Buf - Davis 1 run (kick failed)
Raid - McCallum 1 run (Jaeger kick)
Raid - McCallum 1 run (Jaeger kick)
Buf - Thomas 8 run (Christie kick)
Buf - Brooks 25 pass from Kelly (kick blocked)
Buf - FG Christie 29
Raid - T. Brown 86 pass from Hostetler (kick failed)
Buf - Brooks 22 pass from Kelly (Christie kick)

1993 AFC DIVISIONAL PLAYOFF GAME
Kansas City 28, Houston 20

January 16, 1994, at Houston
Attendance: 64,011

Joe Montana threw 3 second-half touchdown passes to help the Chiefs snap the Oilers' winning streak at 11.

Houston jumped to a 10-0 lead in the first period, and the Oilers still led 13-7 with less than 10 minutes left in the game. But, helped by a 38-yard pass interference penalty, the Chiefs moved 71 yards to take the lead on Montana's 11-yard touchdown pass to J.J. Birden. On Houston's first play, linebacker Derrick Thomas recorded 1 of Kansas City's 9 sacks of Warren Moon, who fumbled, and defensive tackle Dan Saleaumua recovered at the Houston 12. Three plays later, Montana fired an 18-yard scoring strike to Willie Davis.

Houston drove 80 yards to pull within a point with 3:45 remaining, but the Chiefs put together a 79-yard drive, capped by Marcus Allen's game-clinching touchdown.

Kansas City	0	0	7	21	-	28
Houston	10	0	0	10	-	20

Hou - FG Del Greco 49
Hou - G. Brown 2 run (Del Greco kick)
KC - K. Cash 7 pass from Montana (Lowery kick)
Hou - FG Del Greco 43
KC - Birden 11 pass from Montana (Lowery kick)
KC - W. Davis 18 pass from Montana (Lowery kick)
Hou - Givins 7 pass from Moon (Del Greco kick)
KC - Allen 21 run (Lowery kick)

1993 NFC DIVISIONAL PLAYOFF GAME
San Francisco 44, New York Giants 3

January 15, 1994, at San Francisco
Attendance: 67,143

Ricky Watters scored an NFL postseason-record 5 touchdowns—all on short runs—to lead the 49ers to a 44-3 rout of the Giants. No player had previously scored more than 3 touchdowns in a postseason game.

The 49ers led from the start, as they took the opening kickoff and drove 80 yards in 8 plays, 4 of them completions by Steve Young for 63 yards. Watters's 1-yard run capped the drive. After the Giants punted, a 31-yard return by Dexter Carter set up Mike Cofer's field goal. Then safety Tim McDonald intercepted Phil Simms on the Giants' first play to set up another touchdown run by Watters that made the score 16-0 two seconds into the second period.

San Francisco's defense was just as effective as the offense, holding the Giants' NFL-leading rushing attack to 41 yards.

N.Y. Giants	0	3	0	0	-	3
San Francisco	9	14	14	7	-	44

SF - Watters 1 run (kick failed)
SF - FG Cofer 29
SF - Watters 1 run (Cofer kick)
SF - Watters 2 run (Cofer kick)
NYG - FG Treadwell 25
SF - Watters 6 run (Cofer kick)
SF - Watters 2 run (Cofer kick)
SF - Logan 2 run (Cofer kick)

1993 NFC DIVISIONAL PLAYOFF GAME
Dallas 27, Green Bay 17

January 16, 1994, at Irving, Texas
Attendance: 64,790

Dallas scored 10 points in the final 23 seconds of the first half to open up a close game, then went on to defeat Green Bay 27-17.

The Cowboys trailed 3-0 before Aikman connected with Alvin Harper midway through the second period on a 25-yard touchdown pass. With only 23 seconds left in the half, the Cowboys scored again, as veteran placekicker Eddie Murray booted a 41-yard field goal. Corey Harris of the Packers fumbled the ensuing kickoff when hit by Kenneth Gant, and Joe Fishback recovered for the Cowboys at the 14. Aikman hit tight end Jay Novacek with a 6-yard scoring pass with only five seconds remaining in the second quarter.

Aikman came back midway through the third quarter with his third scoring strike, a 19-yard pass to Michael Irvin that shut the door on the Packers. Brett Favre threw 2 second-half touchdown passes, but it was too little, too late.

Green Bay	3	0	7	7	-	17
Dallas	0	17	7	3	-	27

GB - FG Jacke 30
Dal - Harper 25 pass from Aikman (Murray kick)
Dal - FG Murray 41
Dal - Novacek 6 pass from Aikman (Murray kick)
Dal - Irvin 19 pass from Aikman (Murray kick)
GB - Brooks 13 pass from Favre (Jacke kick)
Dal - FG Murray 38
GB - Sharpe 29 pass from Favre (Jacke kick)

1993 AFC CHAMPIONSHIP GAME
Buffalo 30, Kansas City 13

January 23, 1994, at Orchard Park, New York
Attendance: 76,642

Thurman Thomas carried the ball 33 times for 186 yards and 3 touchdowns, and Steve Christie added 3 field goals to lead Buffalo to a 30-13 victory over Kansas City and into its record fourth consecutive Super Bowl.

The Bills dominated from the start, with Thomas scoring on runs of 12 and 3 yards and Christie kicking a pair of field goals as Buffalo took a 20-6 halftime advantage. The Chiefs lost a huge opportunity at the close of the half, after they moved 75 yards to the Buffalo 5. Joe Montana hit wide-open running back Kimble Anders in the hands at the goal line, but the ball popped up in the air and was intercepted in the end zone by safety Henry Jones.

With Dave Krieg replacing an injured Montana in the third period, the Chiefs drove 90 yards to Marcus Allen's 1-yard touchdown run, which cut the margin to 7 points. But Buffalo answered with a 14-play, 79-yard drive to the Kansas City 1 that resulted in Christie's third field goal. Thomas's third touchdown of the day came with only 5:30 remaining and shut the door on the Chiefs.

Kansas City	6	0	7	0	-	13
Buffalo	7	13	0	10	-	30

Buf - Thomas 12 run (Christie kick)
KC - FG Lowery 31
KC - FG Lowery 31
Buf - Thomas 3 run (Christie kick)
Buf - FG Christie 23
Buf - FG Christie 25
KC - Allen 1 run (Lowery kick)
Buf - FG Christie 18
Buf - Thomas 3 run (Christie kick)

1993 NFC CHAMPIONSHIP GAME
Dallas 38, San Francisco 21

January 23, 1994, at Irving, Texas
Attendance: 64,902

The Cowboys scored touchdowns on 4 of their first 5 possessions to take a 28-7 lead at halftime, then coasted to a 38-21 victory over San Francisco to qualify for their record seventh Super Bowl.

On the opening kickoff, Dallas drove 75 yards in 11 plays, scoring on Emmitt Smith's 5-yard touchdown run. The 49ers tied the score on the first play of the second period, but Dallas blew open the game. First, an 11-play, 80-yard drive ended with Daryl Johnston's 4-yard touchdown run. Three plays later, safety Thomas Everett intercepted Young and returned to the 49ers' 14; the Cowboys turned that into Troy Aikman's 11-yard touchdown pass to Smith. In the final minute of the half, Aikman hit tight end Jay Novacek to build the lead to 28-7.

The 49ers responded with a touchdown in the third quarter, but Dallas shut the door with a 7-play, 82-yard drive led by Bernie Kosar, who had replaced Aikman after the starter received a concussion. Kosar passed for 74 yards on the drive, including the touchdown, a 42-yard strike to Alvin Harper.

San Francisco	0	7	7	7	-	21
Dallas	7	21	7	3	-	38

Dal - Smith 5 run (Murray kick)
SF - Rathman 7 pass from Young (Cofer kick)
Dal - Johnston 4 run (Murray kick)
Dal - Smith 11 pass from Aikman (Murray kick)
Dal - Novacek 19 pass from Aikman (Murray kick)
SF - Watters 4 run (Cofer kick)
Dal - Harper 42 pass from Kosar (Murray kick)
Dal - FG Murray 50
SF - Young 1 run (Cofer kick)

1994 AFC WILD CARD GAME
Miami 27, Kansas City 17

December 31, 1994, at Miami
Attendance: 67,487

Dan Marino and Joe Montana were virtually unstoppable in the first half, but the Miami defense asserted itself after the intermission and the Dolphins went on to defeat the Chiefs 27-17.

The Chiefs and Dolphins each had 3 possessions in the first half (other than Kansas City's kneel-down on the final play), and Montana and Marino each took his team to 2 touchdowns and a field goal for a 17-17 score at halftime.

In the third quarter, Marino kept moving his team, taking the Dolphins 64 yards in 6 plays to a 7-yard touchdown pass to Irving Fryar, and setting up a 40-yard field goal by Pete Stoyanovich. Meanwhile, cornerback J.B. Brown intercepted Montana at the goal line, and safety Michael Stewart wrestled the ball away from Marcus Allen to stop Kansas City's major threats in the final period.

Kansas City	14	3	0	0	-	17
Miami	7	10	10	0	-	27

KC - D. Walker 1 pass from Montana (Elliott kick)
Mia - Parmalee 1 run (Stoyanovich kick)
KC - Anders 57 pass from Montana (Elliott kick)
Mia - FG Stoyanovich 40
KC - FG Elliott 21
Mia - R. Williams 1 pass from Marino (Stoyanovich kick)
Mia - Fryar 7 pass from Marino (Stoyanovich kick)
Mia - FG Stoyanovich 40

1994 AFC WILD CARD GAME
Cleveland 20, New England 13

January 1, 1995, at Cleveland
Attendance: 77,452

Just when it appeared that the Patriots might be on the verge of a sensational comeback, the Browns shut down New England's passing game to clinch a 20-13 victory.

The game was tied 10-10 at halftime, as both Drew Bledsoe and Vinny Testaverde threw a touchdown pass in the second quarter. Leroy Hoard's 10-yard scoring run in the third period put the Browns ahead for good, and Matt Stover kicked a 21-yard field goal with 3:36 left to give Cleveland what seemed a safe 10-point margin.

But the Patriots weren't finished. Bledsoe moved his team 63 yards to Matt Bahr's 33-yard field goal with 1:30 remaining, then New England recovered the ensuing on-side kick. The Patriots picked up 1 first down before 4 consecutive incompletions turned the ball back to the relieved Browns.

New England	0	10	0	3	-	13
Cleveland	3	7	7	3	-	20

Cle - FG Stover 30
NE - Thompson 13 pass from Bledsoe (Bahr kick)
Cle - Carrier 5 pass from Testaverde (Stover kick)
NE - FG Bahr 23
Cle - Hoard 10 run (Stover kick)
Cle - FG Stover 21
NE - FG Bahr 33

1994 NFC WILD CARD GAME
Green Bay 16, Detroit 12

December 31, 1994, at Green Bay
Attendance: 58,125

An inspired Green Bay defense held NFL rushing leader Barry Sanders to minus-1 yard on 13 carries and allowed him just 4 yards on 3 receptions en route to a 16-12 victory against the Lions, who had scored 30 or more points in both regular-season meetings between the teams.

Green Bay took the lead early, with Dorsey Levens scoring on a 3-yard run in the first quarter. Three field goals by Chris Jacke, including an attempt from 51 yards, kept the Packers in front. Jacke's final kick gave Green Bay a 16-10 lead with 5:35 remaining in the game.

However, Eric Lynch returned the ensuing kickoff to the Green Bay 49, and the Lions drove to Packers' 11 by the two-minute warning. Linebacker Bryce Paup sacked Dave Krieg, and, on fourth-and-14 from the 17, Herman Moore caught Krieg's pass at the back of the end zone but came down out of bounds, just past the end line.

Detroit	0	0	3	9	-	12
Green Bay	7	3	3	3	-	16

GB	-	Levens 3 run (Jacke kick)
GB	-	FG Jacke 51
Det	-	FG Hanson 38
GB	-	FG Jacke 32
Det	-	Perriman 3 pass from Krieg (Hanson kick)
GB	-	FG Jacke 28
Det	-	Safety, Hentrich ran out of end zone

1994 NFC WILD CARD GAME
Chicago 35, Minnesota 18

January 1, 1995, at Minneapolis
Attendance: 60,347

The Bears, after finishing fourth in the NFC Central, upset the division-winning Vikings 35-18 behind the passing of Steve Walsh, who completed 15 of 23 passes for 221 yards and 2 touchdowns.

The Bears had turnovers on their first 2 possessions, but they came back with 2 touchdowns in the second period, a 1-yard run by Lewis Tillman and a 9-yard pass from Walsh to tight end Keith Jennings. Warren Moon's touchdown pass to Cris Carter just 19 seconds before the half cut Chicago's margin to 14-9.

Walsh continued his sizzling play in the second half, completing 2 passes for 41 yards to set up Raymont Harris's 29-yard touchdown run, then finding Jeff Graham with a 21-yard touchdown pass to build the Bears' lead to 28-12. Kevin Minniefield capped the Bears' day with a 48-yard fumble return for a touchdown.

Chicago	0	14	7	14	-	35
Minnesota	3	6	3	6	-	18

Min	-	FG Reveiz 29
ChiB	-	Tillman 1 run (Butler kick)
ChiB	-	K. Jennings 9 pass from Walsh (Butler kick)
Min	-	C. Carter 4 pass from Moon (2-point attempt failed)
ChiB	-	R. Harris 29 run (Butler kick)
Min	-	FG Reveiz 48
ChiB	-	Graham 21 pass from Walsh (Butler kick)
Min	-	A. Lee 11 pass from Moon (2-point attempt failed)
ChiB	-	Minniefield 48 fumble return (Butler kick)

1994 AFC DIVISIONAL PLAYOFF GAME
Pittsburgh 29, Cleveland 9

January 7, 1995, at Pittsburgh
Attendance: 58,185

The game was the ninety-first meeting between the Steelers and the Browns, but the first in the postseason. Pittsburgh scored on its first 3 possessions to take a 17-0 advantage and went on to a convincing 29-9 win in which the Steelers controlled the ball for 42:27 of the game.

Barry Foster's power running that eventually garnered 133 yards, and a hot start by Neil O'Donnell, who completed 8 of his first 9 passes, led the Steelers to their quick lead. After the Browns scored on a 22-yard field goal by Matt Stover, the Steelers knocked them out right before halftime. Tim McKyer intercepted a pass by Vinny Testaverde and returned it 21 yards to the Cleveland 6. Sixteen seconds before the intermission, O'Donnell turned that into his second touchdown pass of the day, a 9-yard toss to Yancey Thigpen.

Cleveland	0	3	0	6	-	9
Pittsburgh	3	21	3	2	-	29

Pit	-	FG Anderson 39
Pit	-	E. Green 2 pass from O'Donnell (Anderson kick)
Pit	-	J.L. Williams 26 run (Anderson kick)
Cle	-	FG Stover 22
Pit	-	Thigpen 9 pass from O'Donnell (Anderson kick)
Pit	-	FG Anderson 40
Cle	-	McCardell 20 pass from Testaverde (2-point attempt failed)
Pit	-	Testaverde sacked by C. Lake for safety

1994 AFC DIVISIONAL PLAYOFF GAME
San Diego 22, Miami 21

January 8, 1995, at San Diego
Attendance: 63,381

The San Diego offense and defense both solved the mysteries of Miami in the second half as the Chargers edged the Dolphins 22-21.

Miami had built a 21-6 halftime lead on 3 touchdown passes by Dan Marino. But in the second half, Marino, who had thrown for 206 yards in the first two periods, was held to 56 yards, while the Chargers allowed the Dolphins only 16 plays.

San Diego's offense, meanwhile, learned how to finish a drive. The Chargers stalled twice inside the Miami 5 in the first half, then again at the 1 after driving 71 yards to open the third quarter. However, defensive tackle Reuben Davis dropped Bernie Parmalee for a safety after that last failure, and San Diego scored its first touchdown after the ensuing free kick. The Chargers scored the go-ahead touchdown with 35 seconds left, then watched as Pete Stoyanovich's 48-yard field-goal attempt fell short on the final play.

Miami	7	14	0	0	-	21
San Diego	0	6	9	7	-	22

Mia	-	K. Jackson 8 pass from Marino (Stoyanovich kick)
SD	-	FG Carney 20
Mia	-	K. Jackson 9 pass from Marino (Stoyanovich kick)
SD	-	FG Carney 21
Mia	-	M. Williams 16 pass from Marino (Stoyanovich kick)
SD	-	Parmalee tackled by R. Davis for safety
SD	-	Means 24 run (Carney kick)
SD	-	Seay 8 pass from Humphries (Carney kick)

1994 NFC DIVISIONAL PLAYOFF GAME
San Francisco 44, Chicago 15

January 7, 1995, at San Francisco
Attendance: 64,644

After a turnover on their first possession led to a Chicago field goal, the 49ers' offense buckled down, scored on 6 consecutive possessions to blow out the Bears 44-15.

Rookie fullback William Floyd scored 3 touchdowns, the first putting San Francisco ahead with 3:41 left in the first quarter. The other major player was Steve Young, who threw an 8-yard touchdown pass to tight end Brent Jones for the 49ers' second score, then kept for 6 yards and a touchdown with 1:17 left in the second quarter to increase San Francisco's halftime lead to 30-3.

The 49ers' first possession of the third period resulted in a 70-yard drive capped by Floyd's third touchdown of the day. At that point, San Francisco reserves replaced most of the starters, and the 49ers coasted home.

Chicago	3	0	0	12	-	15
San Francisco	7	23	7	7	-	44

ChiB - FG Butler 39
SF - Floyd 2 run (Brien kick)
SF - Jones 8 pass from Young (kick failed)
SF - Floyd 4 run (Brien kick)
SF - FG Brien 36
SF - Young 6 run (Brien kick)
SF - Floyd 1 run (Brien kick)
ChiB - Flanigan 2 pass from Walsh (2-point attempt failed)
SF - Walker 1 run (Brien kick)
ChiB - Tillman 1 run (2-point attempt failed)

1994 NFC DIVISIONAL PLAYOFF GAME
Dallas 35, Green Bay 9

January 8, 1995, at Irving, Texas
Attendance: 64,745

Troy Aikman completed 23 of 30 passes for 337 yards, and 3 Dallas players—Michael Irvin, Alvin Harper, and Jay Novacek—each had more than 100 yards receiving as the Cowboys built a 28-9 halftime lead and coasted to a 35-9 victory over the Packers.

Dallas actually started pounding out the yardage with Emmitt Smith, but, after gaining 44 yards in the first period and scoring the game's opening touchdown, the star running back went out with a hamstring injury.

Aikman then turned to the air and found Harper with a 94-yard touchdown pass, the longest play from scrimmage in NFL postseason history. Two 1-yard touchdown plays, 1 on a run by Smith's replacement Blair Thomas and the other on a pass from Aikman to reserve tight end Scott Galbraith, finished off the Packers before halftime.

Thomas scored again in the final period and finished the game with 70 yards rushing.

Green Bay	3	6	0	0	-	9
Dallas	14	14	0	7	-	35

Dal - Smith 5 run (Boniol kick)
GB - FG Jacke 50
Dal - Harper 94 pass from Aikman (Boniol kick)
Dal - Thomas 1 run (Boniol kick)
GB - Bennett 1 run (2-point attempt failed)
Dal - Galbraith 1 pass from Aikman (Boniol kick)
Dal - Thomas 2 run (Boniol kick)

1994 AFC CHAMPIONSHIP GAME
San Diego 17, Pittsburgh 13

January 15, 1995, at Pittsburgh
Attendance: 61,545

Neil O'Donnell set AFC title-game records by completing 32 of 54 passes while leading Pittsburgh to huge advantages in plays (80-47), yards (415-226), and time of possession (37:13-22:47). But the Chargers came up with the important plays and shocked the favored Steelers 17-13 to advance to their first Super Bowl.

The Steelers went ahead in the first period on O'Donnell's 16-yard touchdown pass to John L. Williams, and increased their margin to 13-3 early in the third quarter. But midway through the period, Stan Humphries hit Alfred Pupunu over the middle, and the tight end broke loose to complete a 43-yard touchdown play. With 5:13 left in the game, Humphries found Tony Martin for a 43-yard touchdown pass that put San Diego ahead for the first time.

O'Donnell completed 7 consecutive passes while marching the Steelers from their 17 to a first-and-goal at the 9. Three plays later, with a fourth-and-goal at the 3, O'Donnell's pass intended for Barry Foster was knocked down at the goal line by linebacker Dennis Gibson with 1:04 remaining.

San Diego	0	3	7	7	-	17
Pittsburgh	7	3	3	0	-	13

Pit - J.L. Williams 16 pass from O'Donnell (Anderson kick)
SD - FG Carney 20
Pit - FG Anderson 39
Pit - FG Anderson 23
SD - Pupunu 43 pass from Humphries (Carney kick)
SD - T. Martin 43 pass from Humphries (Carney kick)

1994 NFC CHAMPIONSHIP GAME
San Francisco 38, Dallas 28

January 15, 1995, at San Francisco
Attendance: 69,125

San Francisco exploded for 3 touchdowns and a 21-0 lead in the opening minutes of the game, then withstood the Cowboys' rallies to defeat Dallas 38-28.

On the third play of the game, cornerback Eric Davis intercepted a pass by Troy Aikman and returned it 44 yards for a touchdown, with just 1:02 gone. Three plays later, Davis forced a fumble that safety Tim McDonald recovered, leading to Steve Young's 29-yard touchdown pass to Ricky Watters. When Kevin Williams fumbled the following kickoff, 49ers kicker Doug Brien recovered at the Dallas 35. The ensuing 7-play drive was climaxed by William Floyd's 1-yard touchdown run.

Two touchdowns shaved the San Francisco lead to 24-14 late in the second period. But Dallas threw incomplete on 3 successive passes, and a short punt left the 49ers with the ball and time to score. Young threw a 28-yard touchdown pass to Jerry Rice 8 seconds before halftime.

In the second half, Young scored on a 3-yard run and the 49ers' defense held the Cowboys twice on downs in the final period to stop Dallas from getting closer than 10 points.

Dallas	7	7	7	7	-	28
San Francisco	21	10	7	0	-	38

SF - Davis 44 interception return (Brien kick)
SF - Watters 29 pass from Young (Brien kick)
SF - Floyd 1 run (Brien kick)
Dal - Irvin 44 pass from Aikman (Boniol kick)
SF - FG Brien 34
Dal - Smith 4 run (Boniol kick)
SF - Rice 28 pass from Young (Brien kick)
Dal - Smith 1 run (Boniol kick)
SF - Young 3 run (Brien kick)
Dal - Irvin 10 pass from Aikman (Boniol kick)

1995 AFC WILD CARD GAME
Buffalo 37, Miami 22

December 30, 1995, at Buffalo
Attendance: 73,103

In a wild offensive game, Buffalo's playoff-record 341 yards rushing proved more valuable than Dan Marino's 422 yards passing, and the Bills easily defeated the Dolphins 37-22.

The Bills scored on their first possession, driving 58 yards in only 7 plays, with Thurman Thomas blasting in from the 1. Less than 3 minutes later they added a 48-yard field goal by Steve Christie, and second-quarter touchdown drives of 68 and 62 yards boosted Buffalo's lead to 24-0 at halftime.

Marino completed 33 of 64 passes to lead the Dolphins

67, 68, and 73 yards for touchdowns in the fourth period, but it was too late. Third-string running back Tim Tindale roared 44 yards for a touchdown to keep Miami at bay after the Dolphins' first score, and Christie added his third field goal after Miami's second touchdown.

Miami	0	0	0	22	-	22
Buffalo	10	14	3	10	-	37

Buf - Thomas 1 run (Christie kick)
Buf - FG Christie 48
Buf - Holmes 21 run (Christie kick)
Buf - Tasker 37 pass from Kelly (Christie kick)
Buf - FG Christie 23
Mia - McDuffie 5 pass from Marino (Stoyanovich kick)
Buf - Tindale 44 run (Christie kick)
Mia - Hill 45 pass from Marino (Stoyanovich kick)
Buf - FG Christie 42
Mia - Kirby 1 run (McDuffie pass from Marino)

1995 AFC WILD CARD GAME
Indianapolis 35, San Diego 20

December 31, 1995, at San Diego
Attendance: 61,182

Rookie Zack Crockett, who had carried the ball only once in the regular season, rushed for 147 yards and 2 touchdowns to lead the Colts to their first playoff victory in 24 years. Crockett entered the game because Marshall Faulk was injured on the Colts' first play from scrimmage.

San Diego jumped ahead early on John Carney's 54-yard field goal, and the lead exchanged hands regularly until Jim Harbaugh threw his second touchdown pass of the day, 42 yards to Sean Dawkins, in the third quarter.

Carney kicked a 30-yard field goal in the final period to draw the Chargers to within 1 point, but on the next play from scrimmage Crockett burst away for a 66-yard touchdown and a 28-20 lead. Jason Belser's 33-yard interception return set up Harbaugh's clinching 3-yard touchdown run.

Indianapolis	0	14	7	14	-	35
San Diego	3	7	7	3	-	20

SD - FG Carney 54
Ind - Dilger 2 pass from Harbaugh (Blanchard kick)
SD - Pupunu 6 pass from Humphries (Carney kick)
Ind - Crockett 33 run (Blanchard kick)
SD - Jefferson 11 pass from Humphries (Carney kick)
Ind - Dawkins 42 pass from Harbaugh (Blanchard kick)
SD - FG Carney 30
Ind - Crockett 66 run (Blanchard kick)
Ind - Harbaugh 3 run (Blanchard kick)

1995 NFC WILD CARD GAME
Philadelphia 58, Detroit 37

December 30, 1995, at Philadelphia
Attendance: 66,492

Philadelphia erupted for 31 points in the second quarter en route to shocking Detroit 58-37. The keys for the Eagles were 3 touchdown passes by Rodney Peete and 6 interceptions by the defense.

The game was tied 7-7 after one period, but Gary Anderson's 21-yard field goal began the second-quarter onslaught. First, Peete capped a 3-play drive with a 22-yard pass to Fred Barnett. Two plays later, Barry Wilburn intercepted Scott Mitchell and returned the ball 24 yards for a touchdown. Kurt Gouveia's interception set up a 1-yard touchdown run by Ricky Watters. With no time left on the clock, Peete hit Rob Carpenter with a 43-yard touchdown pass.

A 45-yard touchdown pass from Peete to Watters and 2 more field goals by Anderson built the lead to 51-7 before the Lions produced Don Majkowski's 3 touchdown passes.

Detroit	7	0	14	16	-	37
Philadelphia	7	31	13	7	-	58

Phi - Garner 15 run (Anderson kick)
Det - Sloan 32 pass from Mitchell (Hanson kick)
Phi - FG Anderson 21
Phi - Barnett 22 pass from Peete (Anderson kick)
Phi - Wilburn 24 interception return (Anderson kick)
Phi - Watters 1 run (Anderson kick)
Phi - Carpenter 43 pass from Peete (Anderson kick)
Phi - Watters 45 pass from Peete (Anderson kick)
Phi - FG Anderson 31
Phi - FG Anderson 39
Det - Moore 68 pass from Majkowski (Hanson kick)
Det - Morton 7 pass from Majkowski (Hanson kick)
Phi - Thomas 30 interception return (Anderson kick)
Det - Sloan 2 pass from Majkowski (Rivers run)
Det - Rivers 1 run (Moore pass from Majkowski)

1995 NFC WILD CARD GAME
Green Bay 37, Atlanta 20

December 31, 1995, at Green Bay
Attendance: 60,453

Antonio Freeman returned a punt 76 yards for a touchdown, and Brett Favre threw a touchdown pass with 49 seconds left in the first half to break open a close game and lead Green Bay to a 37-20 victory against the Atlanta Falcons.

The Packers led 14-10 midway through the second quarter, having taken a lead on Edgar Bennett's 8-yard touchdown run and Favre's 14-yard touchdown pass to Robert Brooks. Then Freeman shook loose for his long punt return, and soon thereafter the Packers started a 14-play, 85-yard drive that culminated in Favre's 2-yard touchdown pass to tight end Mark Chmura for a 27-10 lead.

After a scoreless third quarter, Favre led a matching drive each time the Falcons cut into Green Bay's lead.

Atlanta	7	3	0	10	-	20
Green Bay	14	13	0	10	-	37

Atl - Metcalf 65 pass from J. George (Andersen kick)
GB - Bennett 8 run (Jacke kick)
GB - Brooks 14 pass from Favre (Jacke kick)
Atl - FG Andersen 31
GB - Freeman 76 punt return (2-point attempt failed)
GB - Chmura 2 pass from Favre (Jacke kick)
Atl - Birden 27 pass from J. George (Andersen kick)
Atl - FG Andersen 22
GB - FG Jacke 25

1995 AFC DIVISIONAL PLAYOFF GAME
Pittsburgh 40, Buffalo 21

January 6, 1996, at Pittsburgh
Attendance: 59,072

Byron (Bam) Morris ran for 2 touchdowns in the closing minutes to thwart a Buffalo comeback and help Pittsburgh to a 40-21 victory.

The Steelers' offense dominated the game early, driving 76 and 58 yards to touchdowns. A pair of field goals by Norm Johnson built the lead to 20-0 before the Bills finally scored on a 1-yard run by Thurman Thomas 45 seconds before halftime. But a 53-yard drive in only 38 seconds allowed Anderson to increase the lead to 23-7 just before the intermission.

Two touchdown passes by the Bills cut the Steelers' lead

to 26-21 in the fourth quarter. Pittsburgh put the game away by driving 76 yards in 9 plays, the last a 13-yard run by Morris. Moments later, linebacker Levon Kirkland's interception set up Morris's second touchdown with less than 2 minutes left.

Buffalo	0	7	7	7	-	21
Pittsburgh	7	16	3	14	-	40

Pit - J.L. Williams 1 run (Johnson kick)
Pit - Mills 10 pass from O'Donnell (Johnson kick)
Pit - FG Johnson 45
Pit - FG Johnson 38
Buf - Thomas 1 run (Christie kick)
Pit - FG Johnson 39
Buf - Cline 2 pass from Van Pelt (Christie kick)
Buf - Thomas 9 pass from Kelly (Christie kick)
Pit - Morris 13 run (Johnson kick)
Pit - Morris 2 run (Johnson kick)

1995 AFC DIVISIONAL PLAYOFF GAME
Indianapolis 10, Kansas City 7

January 7, 1996, at Kansas City
Attendance: 77,594

Kansas City had 4 turnovers and Lin Elliott missed 3 field goals as the Chiefs, after posting the NFL's best record during the regular season, were upset at home by Indianapolis 10-7.

Neither team managed much offense, and the game was tied at halftime 7-7 after Steve Bono's 20-yard touchdown pass to Lake Dawson was matched by Jim Harbaugh's 5-yard pass to Floyd Turner. Harbaugh's scoring pass climaxed an 18-play, 77-yard drive that he kept alive by completing passes in two third-and-long situations.

Late in the third quarter, Bono was intercepted by Ashley Ambrose, setting up the Colts at the Kansas City 48. On third-and-3, Harbaugh ran for a first down. Harbaugh hit Sean Dawkins twice for 25 yards before Cary Blanchard broke the tie with a 30-yard field goal.

In the fourth period, Elliott missed 2 field goals, the second from 42 yards with 37 seconds left.

Indianapolis	0	7	3	0	-	10
Kansas City	7	0	0	0	-	7

KC - Dawson 20 pass from Bono (Elliott kick)
Ind - Turner 5 pass from Harbaugh (Blanchard kick)
Ind - FG Blanchard 30

1995 NFC DIVISIONAL PLAYOFF GAME
Green Bay 27, San Francisco 17

January 6, 1996, at San Francisco
Attendance: 69,311

Brett Favre completed 15 of 17 passes for 222 yards in the first half, when the Packers opened a 21-0 lead, to lead Green Bay to a 27-17 victory over the 49ers.

Green Bay took the opening kickoff and held onto the ball for more than seven minutes before Chris Jacke's field-goal attempt was blocked by Tim McDonald. But on San Francisco's first play, Adam Walker fumbled a pass from Steve Young, and cornerback Craig Newsome returned it 31 yards for a touchdown.

On the Packers' next possession, Favre ended a 4-play, 62-yard drive with a 3-yard touchdown pass to Keith Jackson. On their third possession, they drove 72 yards, Favre hitting Mark Chmura for a 13-yard touchdown.

In the second half, San Francisco drove 80 and 47 yards to touchdowns, but Jacke kicked 2 field goals to keep the 49ers at arm's length, and the Packers withstood Young's playoff-record 65 pass attempts.

Green Bay	14	7	3	3	-	27
San Francisco	0	3	7	7	-	17

GB - Newsome 31 fumble return (Jacke kick)
GB - Jackson 3 pass from Favre (Jacke kick)
GB - Chmura 13 pass from Favre (Jacke kick)
SF - FG Wilkins 21
SF - Young 1 run (Wilkins kick)
GB - FG Jacke 27
GB - FG Jacke 26
SF - Loville 2 run (Wilkins kick)

1995 NFC DIVISIONAL PLAYOFF GAME
Dallas 30, Philadelphia 11

January 7, 1996, at Irving, Texas
Attendance: 64,371

The Cowboys' offense slowly asserted itself, and the Eagles, without injured quarterback Rodney Peete, couldn't keep pace as Dallas defeated NFC East rival Philadelphia 30-11.

The score was tied 3-3 after the first quarter, as each team hit a short field goal. But the Cowboys put together two long scoring drives to open up the game in the second period. First, Deion Sanders ran 21 yards on an end-around to cap a 70-yard drive, then Emmitt Smith, who pounded for 99 yards in the game, smashed in from the 1 to finish off a 79-yard march. The big plays on the second drive were a 37-yard pass from Troy Aikman to wide receiver Kevin Williams and a 26-yard completion to fullback Daryl Johnston.

In the second half, Chris Boniol kicked 2 field goals before Aikman passed 9 yards to Michael Irvin for a 30-3 lead.

Philadelphia	0	3	0	8	-	11
Dallas	3	14	6	7	-	30

Dal - FG Boniol 24
Phi - FG Anderson 26
Dal - Sanders 21 run (Boniol kick)
Dal - Smith 1 run (Boniol kick)
Dal - FG Boniol 18
Dal - FG Boniol 51
Dal - Irvin 9 pass from Aikman (Boniol kick)
Phi - Cunningham 4 run (R. Johnson pass from Cunningham)

1995 AFC CHAMPIONSHIP GAME
Pittsburgh 20, Indianapolis 16

January 14, 1996, at Pittsburgh
Attendance: 61,062

Byron (Bam) Morris bulled into the end zone from 1 yard out with 1:34 left in the game, and the Steelers withstood a last-minute drive to beat stubborn Indianapolis 20-16.

The game was mainly one of field goals until the fourth quarter—Cary Blanchard of Indianapolis kicked 3 and Norm Johnson of Pittsburgh had 2. The Steelers' 13-9 lead had been built on a 5-yard touchdown pass from Neil O'Donnell to Kordell Stewart.

In the final period, Jim Harbaugh staked the Colts to a lead with a 47-yard touchdown pass to Floyd Turner. The Steelers took the ball at their 33 with 3:03 left. Five plays later, O'Donnell kept the drive alive with a 9-yard completion on fourth-and-3. He then hit Ernie Mills with a 37-yard strike to the 1. Two plays later, Morris scored.

The Colts were not done, however. Harbaugh passed for 38 yards and scrambled for 17 more as he guided his team to the Pittsburgh 29 with 5 seconds left. On the final play, his pass to Aaron Bailey in the end zone was juggled before falling incomplete.

Indianapolis	3	3	3	7	-	16
Pittsburgh	3	7	3	7	-	20

Ind - FG Blanchard 34
Pit - FG Johnson 31
Ind - FG Blanchard 36
Pit - Stewart 5 pass from O'Donnell (Johnson kick)
Ind - FG Blanchard 37
Pit - FG Johnson 36
Ind - Turner 47 pass from Harbaugh (Blanchard kick)
Pit - Morris 1 run (Johnson kick)

1995 NFC CHAMPIONSHIP GAME
Dallas 38, Green Bay 27

January 14, 1996, at Irving, Texas
Attendance: 65,135

Emmitt Smith rushed for 150 yards and 3 touchdowns, 2 of them in the fourth quarter to overcome a 27-24 deficit and power Dallas to a 38-27 victory and into their record eighth Super Bowl.

The Cowboys dominated the early going, with Troy Aikman throwing 2 touchdown passes to Michael Irvin. But Brett Favre led the Packers back with a 73-yard scoring pass to Robert Brooks and a 24-yard touchdown toss to Keith Jackson. The game was tied 17-17 when the Cowboys took over at their 1 with 4:05 left in the half. Smith blasted 25 yards to get them going, and the 11-play, 99-yard drive was capped 24 seconds before halftime by Smith's 1-yard scoring run.

Favre threw his third touchdown pass to rally the Packers to a 27-24 lead after three quarters. But Smith, who had 35 carries, asserted himself again. First, Dallas drove 90 yards on 14 plays, with Smith scoring from the 5 for a 31-27 lead. Then, after cornerback Larry Brown intercepted Favre and returned the ball 28 yards, Smith scored from the 16 to clinch the victory.

Green Bay	10	7	10	0	-	27
Dallas	14	10	0	14	-	38

GB - FG Jacke 46
Dal - Irvin 6 pass from Aikman (Boniol kick)
Dal - Irvin 4 pass from Aikman (Boniol kick)
GB - Brooks 73 pass from Favre (Jacke kick)
GB - Jackson 24 pass from Favre (Jacke kick)
Dal - FG Boniol 34
Dal - Smith 1 run (Boniol kick)
GB - FG Jacke 37
GB - Brooks 1 pass from Favre (Jacke kick)
Dal - Smith 5 run (Boniol kick)
Dal - Smith 16 run (Boniol kick)

1996 AFC WILD CARD GAME
Jacksonville 30, Buffalo 27

December 28, 1996, at Buffalo
Attendance: 70,213

Second-year Jacksonville shocked Buffalo with a 30-27 victory in the Bills' ballpark. The Bills had been 9-0 in previous playoff games at Rich Stadium. The Jaguars, who advanced to the playoffs when Atlanta's Morten Andersen missed a chip-shot field goal in their final regular season game, scored their winning points ahainst Buffalo with another strange kick—Mike Hollis' 45-yard field goal that hit the upright and caromed through with just over 3 minutes to play.

The Bills came out firing, as Jim Kelly marched them smartly down the field to a 7-0 lead, scoring on his 7-yard toss to Thurman Thomas. A little later, the Bills were moving again when the Jaguars' Clyde Simmons intercepted Kelly's weak shovel pass and ran it in for a touchdown. That play changed the momentum.

The score see-sawed the rest of the way until Hollis' winning kick. Jacksonville's attack featured the running of Natrone Means who had a 30-yard touchdown run and another dash good for 62 yards. Another key was the play of offensive tackle Tony Boselli who neutralized Bruce Smith's pass rush.

Jacksonville	10	7	3	10	-	30
Buffalo	14	3	3	7	-	27

Buf - Thomas 7 pass from Kelly (Christie kick)
Jack - Simmons 20 interception return (Hollis kick)
Buf - Thomas 2 run (Christie kick)
Jack - FG Hollis 27
Jack - Means 30 run (Hollis kick)
Buf - FG Christie 33
Buf - FG Christie 47
Jack - FG Hollis 24
Buf - Burris 38 interception return (Christie kick)
Jack - Smith 2 pass from Brunell (Hollis kick)
Jack - FG Hollis 45

TEAM STATISTICS	JACK	BUF
First Downs	18	19
Rushing	5	5
Passing	13	14
Penalty	0	0
Total Yardage	409	308
Net rushing yardage	184	92
Net passing yardage	225	216
Passes att.-comp.-had int.	33-18-2	36-22-1

RUSHING
Jacksonville - Means 31 for 175, 1 TD; Brunell 3 for 9; Stewart 1 for 0.
Buffalo - Thomas 14 for 50, 1 TD; Kelly 4 for 18; Holmes 9 for 10; Tasker 1 for 9; Tinsdale 1 for 5.

PASSING
Jacksonville - Brunell 18 of 33 for 239, 1 TD, 2 int.
Buffalo - Kelly 21 of 32 for 239, 1 TD 1 int; Collins 1 of 4 for 7.

RECEIVING
Jacksonville - Smith 5 for 58, 1 TD; McCardell 4 for 76; Mitchell 3 for 64; Maston 2 for 21; Jackson 1 for 11; Brown 1 for 8; Stewart 1 for 5; Means 1 for -4.
Buffalo - Early 9 for 122; Reed 3 for 32; Tasker 3 for 30; Johnson 3 for 27; Thomas 3 for 24, 1 TD; Holmes 1 for 11.

1996 AFC WILD CARD GAME
Pittsburgh 42, Indianapolis 14

December 29, 1996, at Pittsburgh
Attendance: 58,078

Pittsburgh blew a 13-point first-half lead but returned to crush Indianapolis in the second half with 29 unanswered points. The Colts were missing a couple of defensive linemen because of injuries and the Steelers' offensive line took full advantage, opening holes for Jerome Bettis and protecting quarterback Mike Tomczak. Change-up quarterback Kordell Stewart dazzled the crowd with his ad-lib running in the final quarter.

In the meantime, the Pittsburgh defense, led by Chad Brown who had 3 sacks and 5 tackles, held the Colts to a paltry 146 yards.

Pittsburgh dominated the first 25 minutes but Eugene Daniel picked off a Tomczak pass in the flat and returned it 59 yards for the Colts' first touchdown. On Pittsburgh's next possession, Tomczak's pass was tipped into the hands of a Colt defender. Indianapolis quarterback Harbaugh followed with a 48-yard pass completion and a 9-yard scoring strike to give the Colts an improbable 14-13 lead at the half. However, Pittsburgh opened the second half with a 16-play, 91-yard drive of nearly 10 minutes to regain the lead for good.

Indianapolis	0	14	0	0	-	14
Pittsburgh	10	3	8	21	-	42

Pitt - FG N. Johnson 29
Pitt - Stewart 1 run (N. Johnson kick)
Pitt - FG N. Johnson 50
Ind - Daniel 59 interception return (Blanchard kick)
Ind - Bailey 9 pass from Harbaugh (Blanchard kick)
Pitt - Bettis 1 run (Farquhar pass from Stewart)
Pitt - Bettis 1 run (N. Johnson kick)
Pitt - Witman 31 run (N. Johnson kick)
Pitt - Stewart 3 run (N. Johnson kick)

TEAM STATISTICS	IND	PITT
First Downs	8	24
Rushing	0	16
Passing	7	7
Penalty	1	1
Total Yardage	146	407
Net rushing yardage	41	231
Net passing yardage	105	176
Passes att.-comp.-had int.	33-13-1	22-14-0

RUSHING
Indianapolis - Faulk 9 for 25; Groce 2 for 11; Harbaugh 3 for 6; Warren 1 for -1.
Pittsburgh - Bettis 25 for 102, 2 TDs; Stewart 9 for 48, 2 TDs; Witman 7 for 48, 1 TD; McAfee 5 for 21; Hastings 2 for 7; Mills 1 for 4; Lester 1 for 2; Tomczak 1 for -1.

PASSING
Indianapolis - Harbaugh 12 of 32 for 134, 1 TD, 1 int.; Justin 1 of 1 for 6.
Pittsburgh - Tomczak 13 of 21 for 176, 2 int.; Stewart 1 of 1 for 0.

RECEIVING
Indianapolis - Harrison 3 for 71; Stablein 3 for 28; Faulk 3 for 10; Dawkins 2 for 18; Bailey 1 for 9, 1 TD; Dilger 1 for 4.
Pittsburgh - C. Johnson 5 for 109; Hastings 3 for 30; Botkin 2 for 26; Lester 2 for 7; Bettis 1 for 4; McAfee 1 for 0.

1996 NFC WILD CARD GAME
Dallas 40, Minnesota 15

December 28, 1996, at Irving, Texas
Attendance: 64,682

The Dallas Cowboys forced 5 Minnesota turnovers and converted them into 23 points on their way to a 40-15 blitzing of the Vikings.

On offense, Troy Aikman ran for 1 touchdown, passed for another, and completed 19 of 29 passes for 178 yards. Michael Irvin caught 8 passes for 103 yards. Emmitt Smith scored twice and rushed for 116 yards on 17 carries.

But the star of the day for Dallas was safety George Teague. In the first quarter, after Dallas had scored, Minnesota's Amp Lee took a short pass over the middle and appeared on his way to a 43-yard touchdown. But Teague caught him at the 1-yard line and poked the ball out of his hands and out of the end zone for a touchback. In the second quarter, Teague forced a fumble, and on the next play Smith ran 37 yards for a touchdown. A few moments later, Teague intercepted a pass and returned it 29 yards for a touchdown to put Dallas in front 24-0.

Chris Boniol kicked 4 field goals for the Cowboys.

Minnesota	0	0	7	8	-	15
Dallas	7	23	7	3	-	40

Dall - Aikman 2 run (Boniol kick)
Dall - FG Boniol 28
Dall - E. Smith 37 run (Boniol kick)
Dall - Teague 29 interception return (Boniol kick)
Dall - FG Boniol 31
Dall - FG Boniol 22
Minn - Carter 30 pass from B. Johnson (Sisson kick)
Dall - E. Smith 1 run (Boniol kick)
Dall - FG Boniol 25
Minn - B. Johnson 5 run (Carter pass from B. Johnson)

TEAM STATISTICS	MINN	DALL
First Downs	12	27
Rushing	3	16
Passing	7	10
Penalty	2	1
Total Yardage	268	438
Net rushing yardage	63	255
Net passing yardage	205	183
Passes att.-comp.-had int.	27-15-2	31-21-1

RUSHING
Minnesota - Lee 7 for 26; Hoard 3 for 21; B. Johnson 3 for 14; Graham 2 for 2.
Dallas - E. Smith 17 for 116, 2 TDs; Williams 17 for 67; Walker 8 for 62; Johnston 1 for 5, 1 TD; K. Williams 1 for 1.

PASSING
Minnesota - B. Johnson 15 of 27 for 208, 1 TD, 2 int.
Dallas - Aikman 19 of 29 for 178, 1 int; Garrett 2 of 2 for 14.

RECEIVING
Minnesota - Ismail 3 for 78; Carter 3 for 36, 1 TD; Evans 3 for 9; Lee 2 for 59; Jordan 1 for 10; Reed 1 for 10; Hoard 1 for 7; Graham 1 for -1.
Dallas - Irvin 8 for 103; E. Smith 4 for 26; Bjornson 3 for 16; Martin 2 for 30; Johnston 2 for 7; Walker 1 for 8; Williams 1 for 2.

1996 NFC WILD CARD GAME
San Francisco 14, Philadelphia 0

December 29, 1996, at San Francisco
Attendance: 56,460

Playing in a steady rain with winds gusting up to 51 miles per hour, San Francisco shut out Philadelphia 14-0. For the 49ers, it was their first playoff whitewash since the 1984 season. The Eagles never had been shut out in the playoffs.

Quarterback Steve Young provided most of the offense for the 49ers, completing 14 of 21 passes for 161 yards. Young's 3-yard pass to Jerry Rice in the third quarter gave San Francisco its second touchdown. Young created the first score in the second quarter, dashing 9 yards into the end zone to complete a 75-yard drive. The 49ers' quarterback finished as the game's leading rusher with 65 yards.

Philadelphia outgained San Francisco, but 2 costly interceptions of Eagles quarterback Ty Detmer cost them their best scoring chances. Detmer was knocked out of the game with an injured hamstring after a third-quarter sack by San Francisco tackle Bryant Young.

Philadelphia	0	0	0	0	-	0
San Francisco	0	7	7	0	-	14

SF - S. Young 9 run (Wilkins kick)
SF - Rice 3 pass from S. Young (Wilkins kick)

TEAM STATISTICS	PHIL	SF
First Downs	16	17
Rushing	3	9
Passing	13	8
Penalty	0	0
Total Yardage	283	279
Net rushing yardage	71	118
Net passing yardage	212	161
Passes att.-comp.-had int.	33-19-3	21-14-0

RUSHING
Philadelphia - Watters 20 for 57; Garner 3 for 10; Turner 3 for 4.
San Francisco - S. Young 11 for 65; Kirby 16 for 43; Floyd 5 for 13; Loville 2 for -3.

PASSING
Philadelphia - Detmer 14 of 21 for 148, 2 int.; Rypien 5 of 12 for 77, 1 int.
San Francisco - S. Young 14 of 21 for 161, 1 TD.

RECEIVING
Philadelphia - Fryar 5 for 62; Watters 5 for 45; J. Johnson 3 for 37; C. Williams 2 for 40; Jones 2 for 23; Turner 2 for 18.
San Francisco - Rice 4 for 50, 1 TD; Floyd 4 for 41; Kirby 2 for 24; Jones 2 for 22; Cooper 1 for 17; Owens 1 for 7.

1996 AFC DIVISIONAL PLAYOFF GAME
Jacksonville 30, Denver 27

January 4, 1997, at Denver
Attendance: 75,678

Jacksonville, a 14-point underdog at kickoff, overcame a

12-0 Denver lead and pulled off the biggest upset of the season. The Jaguars scored on 6 consecutive possessions before running out the clock at the end.

Form appeared to hold when the Broncos scored a pair of first-quarter touchdowns, but a missed extra point and a failed 2-point conversion attempt left the door open for Jacksonville. The Jaguars, led by quarterback Mark Brunell and running back Natrone Means, rallied to take a 13-12 lead at the half on an 8-yard touchdown run by Means and 2 field goals by Mike Hollis. In the third quarter, Brunell's 31-yard touchdown pass to Keenan McCardell widened the lead. Hollis kicked another field goal 4 minutes into the fourth quarter.

Denver mounted a comeback in the final period and closed the gap to 23-20, but Brunell took his team back down the field and opened a 10-point margin with a perfectly thrown fade pass to Jimmy Smith for a 16-yard touchdown. The Broncos' John Elway rallied his team to another touchdown, but a failed onside kick left Jacksonville in charge.

Jacksonville	**0**	**13**	**7**	**10**	**-**	**30**
Denver	**12**	**0**	**0**	**15**	**-**	**27**

Den - Hebron 1 run (kick blocked)
Den - Sharpe 18 pass from Elway (pass failed)
Jack - FG Hollis 46
Jack - Means 8 run (Hollis kick)
Jack - FG Hollis 42
Jack - McCardell 31 pass from Brunell (Hollis kick)
Jack - FG Hollis 22
Den - Davis 2 run (Davis run)
Jack - Smith 16 pass from Brunell (Hollis kick)
Den - McCaffrey 15 pass from Elway (Elam kick)

TEAM STATISTICS JACK DEN		
First Downs	22	21
Rushing	9	7
Passing	11	13
Penalty	2	1
Total Yardage	443	351
Net rushing yardage	203	126
Net passing yardage	240	225
Passes att.-comp.-had int.	29-18-0	38-25-0

RUSHING
Jacksonville - Means 21 for 140, 1 TD; Brunell 7 for 44; Stewart 8 for 19.
Denver - Davis 14 for 91, 1 TD; Elway 5 for 30; Hebron 2 for 5, 1 TD.

PASSING
Jacksonville - Brunell 18 of 29 for 245, 2 TD.
Denver - Elway 25 of 38 for 226, 2 TD.

RECEIVING
Jacksonville - McCardell 5 for 59, 1 TD; Means 4 for 46; Smith 3 for 71, 1 TD; Jackson 3 for 35; Mitchell 2 for 9; Stewart 1 for 25.
Denver - Davis 7 for 24; Miller 5 for 67; McCaffrey 5 for 54, 1 TD; Craver 3 for 17; Sharpe 2 for 31, 1 TD; Carswell 2 for 18; Smith 1 for 15.

1996 NFC DIVISIONAL PLAYOFF GAME
Green Bay 35, San Francisco 14

January 4, 1997, at Green Bay
Attendance: 60,787

Desmond Howard led Green Bay to a 35-14 win over San Francisco on a rain-swept, muddy Lambeau Field. Howard put the Packers up early with his punt returns. The first time he touched the ball, he went 71 yards for a touchdown. Then, after a fair catch on the next punt, he sped 46 yards to set up Brett Favre's 4-yard touchdown pass to Andre Rison. Green Bay led 14-0 although it only had 9 yards from scrimmage.

The rest of the game was mistake-filled, largely because of the rain and mud. San Francisco had 5 turnovers. The 49ers' Steve Young started at quarterback but had to leave the game with a rib injury suffered in the previous week's NFC Wild Card Game. The Packers scored their third touchdown on Edgar Bennett's 2-yard run following an interception of Elvis Grbac's pass.

The 49ers closed the margin to 21-14 on 2 touchdowns within 40 seconds covering the end of the second quarter and the beginning of the third. Both resulted from miscues by Green Bay's special teams.

The Packers reacted by marching 72 yards for another touchdown, then added an 11-yard touchdown run by Bennett in the fourth quarter.

San Francisco	**0**	**7**	**7**	**0**	**-**	**14**
Green Bay	**14**	**7**	**7**	**7**	**-**	**35**

GB - Howard 71 punt return (Jacke kick)
GB - Rison 4 pass from Favre (Jacke kick)
GB - Bennett 2 run (Jacke kick)
SF - Kirby 8 pass from Grbac (Wilkins kick)
SF - Grbac 2 run (Wilkins kick)
GB - Freeman recovered fumble in end zone (Jacke kick)
GB - Bennett 11 run (Jacke kick)

TEAM STATISTICS	**SF**	**GB**
First Downs	12	15
Rushing	4	10
Passing	8	5
Penalty	0	0
Total Yardage	196	210
Net rushing yardage	68	139
Net passing yardage	128	71
Passes att.-comp.-had int.	41-21-3	15-11-0

RUSHING
San Francisco - Grbac 4 for 32, 1 TD; Kirby 6 for 14; Floyd 5 for 13; Vardell 2 for 6; S. Young 1 for 3.
Green Bay - Bennett 17 for 80, 2 TD; Levens 15 for 46; Favre 5 for 9; Henderson 2 for 4.

PASSING
San Francisco - Grbac 19 of 36 for 125, 1 TD, 3 int.; S. Young 2 of 5 for 8.
Green Bay - Favre 11 of 15 for 79, 1 TD.

RECEIVING
San Francisco - Kirby 6 for 35, 1 TD; Floyd 6 for 30; Rice 5 for 36; Jones 4 for 32.
Green Bay - Freeman 2 for 26; Levens 2 for 16; Bennett 2 for 14; Rison 2 for 13, 1 TD; Henderson 1 for 4; Jackson 1 for 4; Beebe 1 for 2.

1996 AFC DIVISIONAL PLAYOFF GAME
New England 28, Pittsburgh 3

January 5, 1997, at Foxboro, Massachusetts
Attendance: 60,188

Fog shrouded Foxboro Stadium, but it couldn't dim the New England Patriots' first half offensive fireworks in their 28-3 victory over the Pittsburgh Steelers. The Patriots exploded for 226 yards and 3 touchdowns on their first 14 plays.

On New England's first play from scrimmage, Drew Bledsoe hit Terry Glenn with a 53-yard bomb down the right sideline. Curtis Martin ran in from the 2. When the Patriots next got the ball, Bledsoe completed 2 quick passes for 18 yards, Martin ran 7 yards, then Keith Byars took a screen pass from Bledsoe 34 yards for another touchdown.

The knockout blow came early in the second quarter when Martin sprinted 78 yards through the middle of the Steelers' defense. Martin added his third touchdown of the day on a 23-yard run in the final quarter.

While the famed Pittsburgh defense was being singed for 346 yards by New England's offense, the underrated Patriots' defense bottled up the Pittsburgh offense.

Pittsburgh	0	0	3	0	-	3
New England	14	7	0	7	-	28

NE - Martin 2 run (Vinatieri kick)
NE - Byars 34 pass from Bledsoe (Vinatieri kick)
NE - Martin 78 run (Vinatieri kick)
Pitt - FG N. Johnson 29
NE - Martin 23 run (Vinatieri kick)

TEAM STATISTICS	PITT	NE
First Downs	12	17
Rushing	7	9
Passing	5	6
Penalty	0	2
Total Yardage	213	346
Net rushing yardage	123	194
Net passing yardage	90	152
Passes att.-comp.-had int.	39-16-2	26-15-2

RUSHING
Pittsburgh - Bettis 13 for 43; McAfee 5 for 30; Tomczak 2 for 20; Stewart 4 for 19; Witman 3 for 11.
New England - Martin 19 for 166, 3 TDs; Meggett 2 for 18; Byars 2 for 8; Grier 5 for 7; Zolak 3 for -4; Bledsoe 1 for -1.

PASSING
Pittsburgh - Tomczak 16 of 29 for 110, 2 int.; Stewart 0 of 10.
New England - Bledsoe 14 of 24 for 164, 1 TD, 2 int.; Zolak 1 of 2 for 3.

RECEIVING
Pittsburgh - Hastings 5 for 55; Botkin 2 for 20; Arnold 2 for 16; Mills 2 for 15; McAfee 2 for 7; Bettis 2 for -1; Witman 1 for -2.
New England - Byars 4 for 53, 1 TD; Glenn 3 for 69; Coates 3 for 18; Jefferson 3 for 18; Martin 2 for 9.

1996 NFC DIVISIONAL PLAYOFF GAME
Carolina 26, Dallas 17

January 5, 1997, at Charlotte, North Carolina
Attendance: 72,808

The second-year Carolina Panthers upended the defending Super Bowl-champion Dallas Cowboys with a methodical 26-17 victory at Charlotte. The Cowboys received an early blow when wide receiver Michael Irvin was knocked out of the game by an injured shoulder. With his prime receiver missing, quarterback Troy Aikman passed for only 165 yards and was intercepted 3 times.

Dallas got off to a quick start on Chris Boniol's 22-yard field goal, but Carolina took the lead before the first quarter ended on a 68-yard drive that culminated in a 1-yard pass to Wesley Walls. In the second quarter, Kerry Collins threw his second touchdown pass to a diving Willie Green. The Cowboys answered with a 15-play, 73-yard drive that ended with a 2-yard touchdown pass from Aikman to Daryl Johnston.

Before the half ended, Dallas gained a safety when a bad snap on a Carolina punt attempt went out of the end zone, but John Kasay added a field goal for the Panthers, set up by safety Chad Cota's interception.

The second half was a battle of field goals, with Carolina's Kasay kicking 3 to Boniol's 2.

Dallas	3	8	3	3	-	17
Carolina	7	10	3	6	-	26

Dall - FG Boniol 22
Car - Walls 1 pass from Collins (Kasay kick)
Car - Green 10 pass from Collins (Kasay kick)
Dall - Johnston 2 pass from Aikman (pass failed)
Dall - Safety, bad snap by Carolina on a punt went out of end zone
Car - FG Kasay 24
Dall - FG Boniol 21
Car - FG Kasay 40
Car - FG Kasay 40
Dall - FG Boniol 21
Car - FG Kasay 32

TEAM STATISTICS	DALL	CAR
First Downs	21	18
Rushing	5	8
Passing	12	7
Penalty	4	3
Total Yardage	244	227
Net rushing yardage	96	127
Net passing yardage	148	100
Passes att.-comp.-had int.	36-18-3	22-12-1

RUSHING
Dallas - E. Smith 22 for 80; Sanders 1 for 16; Aikman 1 for 0.
Carolina - Johnson 26 for 104; Oliver 3 for 11; Ismail 1 for 7; Collins 6 for 5; Stark 1 for 0.

PASSING
Dallas - Aikman 18 of 36 for 165, 1 TD, 3 int.
Carolina - Collins 12 of 22 for 100, 2 TD, 1 int.

RECEIVING
Dallas - K. Williams 6 for 89; Johnston 4 for 18, 1 TD; Martin 3 for 31; E. Smith 3 for -2; Irvin 1 for 22; Bjornson 1 for 7.
Carolina - Green 5 for 53, 1 TD; Walls 3 for 25, 1 TD; Johnson 1 for 9; Carrier 1 for 7; Oliver 1 for 5; Griffith 1 for 1.

1996 AFC CHAMPIONSHIP GAME
New England 20, Jacksonville 6

January 12, 1997, at Foxboro, Massachusetts
Attendance: 60,190

Jacksonville's Cinderella season ended amid a cascade of late mistakes against the New England Patriots. The New England defense quashed the Jaguars just when they seemed geared for yet another postseason comeback.

The Patriots scored a touchdown off a Jaguars' mistake in the first quarter when the snap to punter Bryan Barker was high and he was tackled inside his 5-yard-line. Moments later, Curtis Martin scored on a 1-yard run.

Mike Hollis countered with a 32-yard field goal in the second quarter, but when Jacksonville punt returner Chris Hudson fumbled a punt, the Patriots' Adam Vinatieri kicked a 29-yard field goal. He added another field goal before the first half ended.

The Jaguars' defense shut down the Patriots' offense, and Hollis added another field goal in the third quarter to pull Jacksonville to within a touchdown.

Jacksonville appeared on its way to the tying touchdown late in the final quarter. But with 3:43 left, the Patriots' Willie Clay intercepted Mark Brunell's pass in the end zone. When Jacksonville got the ball again, James Stewart fumbled and Otis Smith raced 47 yards with the recovery for the clinching touchdown.

Jacksonville	0	3	3	0	-	6
New England	7	6	0	7	-	20

NE - Martin 1 run (Vinatieri kick)
Jack - FG Hollis 32
NE - FG Vinatieri 29
NE - FG Vinatieri 20
Jack - FG Hollis 28
NE - Smith 47 fumble return (Vinatieri kick)

TEAM STATISTICS	JACK	NE
First Downs	18	13
Rushing	6	6
Passing	12	7
Penalty	0	0
Total Yardage	289	234
Net rushing yardage	101	73
Net passing yardage	188	161
Passes att.-comp.-had int.	38-20-2	33-20-1

RUSHING
Jacksonville - Means 19 for 43; Stewart 7 for 40; Brunell 6 for 34; Barker 1 for -16.
New England - Martin 19 for 59, 1 TD; Meggett 3 for 9; Bledsoe 1 for 4; Byars 1 for 1.

PASSING
Jacksonville - Brunell 20 of 38 for 190, 2 int.
New England - Bledsoe 20 of 33 for 178, 1 int.

RECEIVING
Jacksonville - Mitchell 7 for 63; McCardell 6 for 62; Smith 3 for 45; Stewart 2 for 8; Brown 1 for 10; Barlow 1 for 2.
New England - Glenn 5 for 33; Jefferson 4 for 91; Byars 4 for 16; Martin 3 for 18; Meggett 3 for 15; Coates 1 for 5.

1996 NFC CHAMPIONSHIP GAME
Green Bay 30, Carolina 13

January 12, 1997, at Green Bay
Attendance: 60,216

After a slow start, the Green Bay Packers ended Carolina's hopes for a Super Bowl with a workmanlike 30-13 victory. The Packers' last appearance in the big game was in Super Bowl II, 29 years earlier.

Despite the energy generated by the Green Bay fans, the game lacked suspense after the first quarter as the Packers took charge. The main surprise was the effectiveness of the Green Bay running game, which accumulated 201 yards. The blitz-happy Panthers were able to get to Packers quarterback Brett Favre only once all day.

Kerry Collins's 3-yard touchdown pass to Howard Griffith put Carolina ahead in the opening quarter. Dorsey Levens's 29-yard touchdown catch from Favre tied the score early in the second period. John Kasay's field goal after a Favre fumble regained the lead temporarily for the Panthers, but Green Bay moved back in front on Favre's 6-yard touchdown pass to Antonio Freeman with less than a minute left in the half. An interception immediately after the kickoff allowed the Packers' Chris Jacke to add a 31-yard field goal before intermission.

The second half, keyed by the running of Levens and Edgar Bennett, was all Green Bay.

Carolina	7	3	3	0	-	13
Green Bay	0	17	10	3	-	30

Car - Griffith 3 pass from Collins (Kasay kick)
GB - Levens 29 pass from Favre (Jacke kick)
Car - FG Kasay 22
GB - Freeman 6 pass from Favre (Jacke kick)
GB - FG Jacke 31
GB - FG Jacke 32
Car - FG Kasay 23
GB - Bennett 4 run (Jacke kick)
GB - FG Jacke 28

TEAM STATISTICS	CAR	GB
First Downs	12	22
Rushing	1	10
Passing	11	12
Penalty	0	0
Total Yardage	251	479
Net rushing yardage	45	201
Net passing yardage	206	278
Passes att.-comp.-had int.	37-19-2	29-19-1

RUSHING
Carolina - Johnson 11 for 31; Oliver 2 for 15; Collins 1 for -1.
Green Bay - Bennett 25 for 99, 1 TD; Levens 10 for 88; Favre 5 for 14; McMahon 4 for 0; Henderson 1 for 0.

PASSING
Carolina - Collins 19 of 37 for 215, 1 TD, 2 int.
Green Bay - Favre 19 of 29 for 292, 2 TDs, 1 int.

RECEIVING
Carolina - Green 5 for 51; Carrier 4 for 65; Griffith 4 for 23, 1 TD; Walls 3 for 33; Ismail 1 for 24; Johnson 1 for 14; Oliver 1 for 5.
Green Bay - Levens 5 for 117, 1 TD; Freeman 4 for 43, 1 TD; Rison 3 for 53; Jackson 3 for 30; Bennett 2 for 5; Beebe 1 for 29; Chmura 1 for 15.

1997 AFC WILD CARD GAME
Denver 42, Jacksonville 17

December 27, 1997, at Denver
Attendance: 74,481

One year after being knocked out of the playoffs by a surprise home loss to the Jaguars, the Broncos appeared on their way to repeating history. After building a 21-0 first-half lead on Terrell Davis's running and John Elway's passing, Denver let Jacksonville climb back to make it 21-17 by the end of the third quarter, then turned over the ball twice. However, the Broncos' defense kept the Jaguars from taking advantage.

Denver went back to its overpowering running game despite losing Davis to bruised ribs. Derek Loville took over and added 103 yards and 2 touchdowns, and Denver won going away.

Jacksonville	0	7	10	0	-	17
Denver	14	7	0	21	-	42

Den - Te. Davis 2 run (Elam kick)
Den - R.Smith 43 pass from Elway (Elam kick)
Den - Te. Davis 5 run (Elam kick)
Jac - Means 2 run (Hollis kick)
Jac - FG Hollis 38
Jac - Tr. Davis 29 blocked punt return (Hollis kick)
Den - Loville 25 run (Elam kick)
Den - Loville 8 run (Elam kick)
Den - Hebron 6 run (Elam kick)

TEAM STATISTICS	JAC	DEN
First Downs	14	28
Rushing	3	18
Passing	9	8
Penalty	2	2
Total Yardage	237	511
Net rushing yardage	50	310
Net passing yardage	187	201
Passes att.-comp.-had int.	32-18-1	24-16-0

RUSHING
Jacksonville - Means 10 for 40, 1 TD; Stewart 1 for 6; Brunell 3 for 4
Denver - Te. Davis 31 for 184, 2 TDs; Loville 11 for 103, 2 TDs; Hebron 6 for 23, 1 TD; Elway 1 for 0.

PASSING
Jacksonville - Brunell 18 of 32 for 203, 1 int.
Denver - Elway 16 of 24 for 223, 1 TD.

RECEIVING
Jacksonville - McCardell 6 for 55; Smith 6 for 55; Stewart 3 for 46; Jones 1 for 37; Mitchell 1 for 7; Means 1 for 3.
Denver - Te. Davis 4 for 11; R. Smith 3 for 99, 1 TD; McCaffrey 2 for 33; Green 2 for 32; Sharpe 2 for 29; Griffith 2 for 9; Loville 1 for 10.

1997 AFC WILD CARD GAME
New England 17, Miami 3

December 28, 1997, at Foxboro, Massachusetts
Attendance: 60,041

Two plays into the second half, Miami quarterback Dan Marino called an audible. New England linebacker Todd Collins recognized the call: It was the same one used in each of the 2 previous meetings between the Dolphins and Patriots. Collins moved appropriately, Marino threw as expected, and Collins intercepted the pass, returning it 40 yards for the touchdown that stretched New England's lead to 14 points.

On a day when Miami's offense was held to a franchise-playoff-low 162 yards, that was more than enough for New England to win. The Patriots added a field goal before the third quarter ended. The Dolphins only score came on a fourth-quarter field goal.

New England's second-quarter touchdown came on a 24-yard pass from Drew Bledsoe to Troy Brown after an interception of a Marino pass by Chris Slade.

Miami	0	0	0	3	-	3
New England	0	7	10	0	-	17

NE - Brown 24 pass from Bledsoe (Vinatieri kick)
NE - Collins 40 interception return (Vinatieri kick)
NE - FG Vinatieri 22
Mia - FG Mare 38

TEAM STATISTICS	MIA	NE
First Downs	10	15

Rushing	2	7
Passing	6	7
Penalty	2	1
Total Yardage	162	228
Net rushing yardage	42	108
Net passing yardage	120	120
Passes att.-comp.-had int.	43-17-2	32-16-0

RUSHING
Miami - Parmalee 9 for 22; Abdul-Jabbar 5 for 16; McPhail 1 for 4; Marino 1 for 2; Pritchett 1 for-2.
New England - Cullors 22 for 86; Grier 6 for 16; Bledsoe 2 for 4; Meggett 1 for 2.

PASSING
Miami - Marino 17 of 43 for 141, 2 int.
New England - Bledsoe 16 of 32 for 139, 1 TD.

RECEIVING
Miami - McPhail 5 for 28; L. Thomas 3 for 62; Parmalee 3 for 13; McDuffie 3 for 6; Perriman 1 for 13; Jordan 1 for 11; Drayton 1 for 8.
New England - Glenn 4 for 57; Coates 4 for 25; T. Brown 2 for 32, 1 TD; Meggett 2 for 11; Jefferson 1 for 7; Purnell 1 for 4; Gash 1 for 3; Cullors 1 for 0.

1997 NFC WILD CARD GAME
Minnesota 23, New York Giants 22

December 27, 1997, at East Rutherford, New Jersey
Attendance: 77,710

The New York Giants led by 16 points at the half and still had a 9-point advantage with a minute-and-a-half left, but the Minnesota Vikings moved on in the playoffs with a spectacular comeback. New York built its 19-3 halftime lead in part on 3 turnovers by Vikings quarterback Randall Cunningham. But in the second half, the Giants' offense stagnated while Cunningham grew more effective.

Minnesota narrowed its deficit with Leroy Hoard's 4-yard touchdown run in the third quarter. The teams exchanged field goals in the final period. Then Cunningham teamed with Jake Reed on a 30-yard touchdown pass with only 90 seconds left. The Vikings recovered the onside kick when Chris Walsh grabbed Chris Calloway's muff. With only 10 seconds remaining, Eddie Murray booted the game-winning field goal from 24 yards.

Minnesota	**0**	**3**	**7**	**13**	**-**	**23**
N.Y. Giants	**6**	**13**	**0**	**3**	**-**	**22**

NYG - FG Daluiso 43
NYG - FG Daluiso 22
NYG - Pierce 2 pass from Kanell (Daluiso kick)
NYG - FG Daluiso 41
Min - FG Murray 26
NYG - FG Daluiso 51
Min - Hoard 4 run (Murray kick)
Min - FG Murray 26
NYG - FG Daluiso 22
Min - Reed 30 pass from Cunningham (Murray kick)
Min - FG Murray 24

TEAM STATISTICS	MIN	NYG
First Downs	16	13
Rushing	8	2
Passing	7	11
Penalty	1	0
Total Yardage	293	266
Net rushing yardage	106	76
Net passing yardage	187	190
Passes att.-comp.-had int.	36-15-1	32-16-0

RUSHING
Minnesota - R. Smith 16 for 40; Cunningham 7 for 38; Hoard 3 for 14, 1 TD; Evans 2 for 14.
NY Giants - Barber 17 for 29; Way 10 for 28; R. Hampton 8 for 18; Lane 1 for 1.

PASSING
Minnesota - Cunningham 15 of 36 for 203, 1 TD, 1 int.
NY Giants - Kanell 16 of 32 for 199, 1 TD.

RECEIVING
Minnesota-Carter 6 for 83; Reed 5 for 89, 1 TD; Glover 2 for 18; Hoard 1 for 9; Delong 1 for 4.
NY Giants-Calloway 6 for 53; Patten 5 for 86; Barber 3 for 31; Way 1 for 27; Pierce 1 for 2, 1 TD.

1997 NFC WILD CARD GAME
Tampa Bay 20, Detroit 10

December 28, 1997, at Tampa
Attendance: 73,361

The Tampa Bay Buccaneers made their first playoff appearance in 15 years and won in the postseason for the first time since 1979. Tampa Bay dominated Detroit all the way, building a 20-0 lead before the Lions could score.

Michael Husted kicked 2 first-half field goals and Trent Dilfer tossed a 9-yard touchdown pass to Horace Copeland to give Tampa Bay a 13-0 lead at the half. In the third quarter, Mike Alstott scored the Buccaneers' second touchdown on a 31-yard run.

Meanwhile, Detroit's Barry Sanders, who rushed for more than 2,000 yards during the regular season, was limited to 65 yards on 18 carries. Lions quarterback Scott Mitchell left the game in the third quarter with a mild concussion. Backup Frank Reich led Detroit to its only points.

Detroit	**0**	**0**	**3**	**7**	**-**	**10**
Tampa Bay	**3**	**10**	**7**	**0**	**-**	**20**

TB - FG Husted 22
TB - Copeland 9 pass from Dilfer (Husted kick)
TB - FG Husted 42
TB - Alstott 31 run (Husted kick)
Det - FG Hanson 33
Det - Vardell 1 run (J. Hanson kick)

TEAM STATISTICS	DET	TB
First Downs	18	15
Rushing	6	5
Passing	12	9
Penalty	0	1
Total Yardage	307	316
Net rushing yardage	109	141
Net passing yardage	198	175
Passes att.-comp.-had int.	40-21-1	26-13-1

RUSHING
Detroit - Sanders 18 for 65; Mitchell 4 for 20; Rivers 1 for 17; Reich 1 for 5; Vardell 2 for 1, 1 TD; Jett 1 for 1.
Tampa Bay - Dunn 18 for 72; Alstott 11 for 68, 1 TD; Anthony 1 for 1; Dilfer 2 for 0.

PASSING
Detroit - Mitchell 10 of 25 for 78, 1 int.; Reich 11 of 15 for 129.
Tampa Bay - Dilfer 13 of 26 for 181, 1 TD, 1 int.

RECEIVING
Detroit - Morton 7 for 69; Sanders 5 for 43; Moore 4 for 44; T. Boyd 2 for 11; Scroggins 1 for 19; Vardell 1 for 12; Sloan 1 for 9.
Tampa Bay - Anthony 3 for 62; Dunn 3 for 0; Thomas 2 for 66; Copeland 2 for 14, 1 TD; Williams 1 for 23; Alstott 1 for 12; Harris 1 for 4.

1997 AFC DIVISIONAL PLAYOFF GAME
Denver 14, Kansas City 10

January 4, 1998, at Kansas City
Attendance: 76,965

The game was played in Kansas City only because Denver's last-second loss to the Chiefs in the regular season cost the Broncos home-field advantage throughout the AFC playoffs. But Denver came through in Kansas City.

This was payback time for Denver, but it wasn't easy. Despite another 100-plus-yard rushing game by Terrell Davis, the Broncos trailed 10-7 after three quarters. Tight end Tony Gonzalez's 12-yard touchdown catch with only 10 seconds left in the third quarter put the Chiefs in front.

But Denver started its next possession on the Chiefs' 49-yard-line. Three plays later, John Elway teamed with Ed McCaffrey on a 43-yard completion to put the ball at the 1. It took three tries, but Davis scored on the third one.

Kansas City's last chance to win ended when Broncos cornerback Darrien Gordon batted down Elvis Grbac's final pass in the end zone on fourth-and-2 with 19 seconds left.

Denver	0	7	0	7	-	14
Kansas City	0	0	10	0	-	10

Den - Davis 1 run (Elam kick)
KC - FG Stoyanovich 20
KC - Gonzalez 12 pass from Grbac (Stoyanovich kick)
Den - Davis 1 run (Elam kick)

TEAM STATISTICS	DEN	KC
First Downs	16	18
Rushing	6	4
Passing	7	10
Penalty	3	4
Total Yardage	272	303
Net rushing yardage	109	77
Net passing yardage	163	226
Passes att.-comp.-had int.	19-10-0	37-24-0

RUSHING
Denver - Davis 25 for 101, 2 TDs; Griffith 4 for 9; Loville 2 for 0; Elway 1 for -1.
Kansas City - Allen 12 for 37; Grbac 4 for 22; Anders 3 for 9; Bennett 3 for 4; Aguiar 1 for 3; Hill 1 for 2.

PASSING
Denver - Elway 10 of 19 for 170.
Kansas City - Grbac 24 of 37 for 260, 1 TD.

RECEIVING
Denver - McCaffrey 3 for 56; Sharpe 2 for 33; R. Smith 2 for 19; Carswell 1 for 26; Green 1 for 19; Davis 1 for 17.
Kansas City - Rison 8 for 110; Popson 5 for 26; Gonzalez 3 for 26, 1 TD; Dawson 2 for 20; Anders 2 for 4; Horn 1 for 50; Hughes 1 for 13; Allen 1 for 8; Vanover 1 for 3.

1997 AFC DIVISIONAL PLAYOFF GAME
Pittsburgh 7, New England 6

January 3, 1998, at Pittsburgh
Attendance: 61,228

The Steelers advanced in the playoffs with a victory over the Patriots, the team that knocked them out of postseason in 1996. Pittsburgh scored its lone touchdown early and made it stand up by keeping New England out of the end zone. The Patriots settled for 2 field goals while registering a mere 36 yards on the ground.

The Steelers' touchdown came at 5:11 of the first quarter when quarterback Kordell Stewart rolled to his left and scampered 40 yards down the sideline to score.

Perhaps the play of the game came in the last few minutes. New England quarterback Drew Bledsoe, who passed for 264 yards but turned over the ball 4 times, was marching his team toward a possible go-ahead score. But with the ball on Pittsburgh's 42, Steelers defensive end Mike Vrabel sacked Bledsoe, forcing a fumble. Linebacker Jason Gildon recovered with 1:44 remaining, and Pittsburgh held on to win.

New England	0	3	0	3	-	6
Pittsburgh	7	0	0	0	-	7

Pit - Stewart 40 run (N. Johnson kick)
NE - FG Vinatieri 31
NE - FG Vinatieri 46

TEAM STATISTICS	NE	PIT
First Downs	15	16
Rushing	1	6
Passing	14	8
Penalty	0	2
Total Yardage	280	279
Net rushing yardage	36	145
Net passing yardage	244	134
Passes att.-comp.-had int.	44-23-2	31-14-1

RUSHING
New England - Shaw 10 for 22; Cullors 7 for 18; Bledsoe 2 for -4.
Pittsburgh - Stewart 11 for 68, 1 TD; Bettis 25 for 67; McAfee 1 for 10.

PASSING
New England - Bledsoe 23 of 44 for 264, 2 ints.
Pittsburgh - Stewart 14 of 31 for 134, 1 int.

RECEIVING
New England - Jefferson 9 for 104; Glenn 5 for 96; Brisby 3 for 37; Byars 2 for 1; Shaw 1 for 13; Brown 1 for 6; Gash 1 for 6; Cullors 1 for 1.
Pittsburgh - Hawkins 4 for 28; Thigpen 3 for 54; C. Johnson 3 for 28; Lester 2 for 3; Blackwell 1 for 14; Bettis 1 for 7.

1997 NFC DIVISIONAL PLAYOFF GAME
San Francisco 38, Minnesota 22

January 3, 1998, at San Francisco
Attendance: 65,018

With less than six minutes left to play in the first half, the 49ers led the Vikings just 14-7. Then Ken Norton, Jr., intercepted Randall Cunningham's pass and ran it 23 yards into the end zone. That put San Francisco ahead by 2 touchdowns and proved to be the key play of the game.

Playing without injured wide receiver Jerry Rice and running back Garrison Hearst, the 49ers found effective weapons in J.J. Stokes and Terry Kirby. Stokes caught a career-high 9 passes, and Kirby ran for a career-best 120 yards. Steve Young passed for 224 yards and led San Francisco to 394 total yards.

Minnesota, which had reached the divisional playoffs with an unlikely comeback victory over the Giants, looked for another miracle, but their prayers were hindered by an ineffective running game that managed only 57 yards. Randall Cunningham played an uneven game, teetering between his 66-yard touchdown pass to Cris Carter in the first quarter and his misdirected toss to Norton in the second.

Minnesota	7	0	7	8	-	22
San Francisco	7	14	10	7	-	38

SF - Floyd 1 run (Anderson kick)
Min - Carter 66 pass from Cunningham (Murray kick)
SF - Kirby 1 run (Anderson kick)
SF - Norton 23 interception return (Anderson kick)
SF - FG Anderson 34
Min - Carter 3 pass from Cunningham (Murray kick)
SF - Owens 15 pass from S. Young (Anderson kick)
SF - Kirby 1 run (Anderson kick)
Min - Hatchette 13 pass from Cunningham (Walsh pass from Cunningham)

TEAM STATISTICS	MIN	SF
First Downs	16	31
Rushing	2	15
Passing	13	11
Penalty	1	5
Total Yardage	378	394
Net rushing yardage	57	175
Net passing yardage	321	219
Passes att.-comp.-had int.	40-18-1	30-21-0

RUSHING
Minnesota - R. Smith 8 for 33; Cunningham 2 for 14; Hoard 5 for 11; Evans 1 for -1.
San Francisco - Kirby 25 for 120, 2 TDs; S. Young 4 for 37; Floyd 3 for 13, 1 TD; Levy 9 for 5.

PASSING
Minnesota - Cunningham 18 of 40 for 331, 3 TDs, 1 int.
San Francisco - S. Young 21 of 30 for 224, 1 TD.

RECEIVING
Minnesota - Carter 6 for 93, 2 TDs; Reed 5 for 114; Glover 3 for 84; R. Smith 3 for 27; Hatchette 1 for 13, 1 TD.
San Francisco - Stokes 9 for 101; Owens 4 for 49, 1 TD; Jones 3 for 39; Kirby 3 for 24; Levy 1 for 6; Floyd 1 for 5.

1997 NFC DIVISIONAL PLAYOFF GAME
Green Bay 21, Tampa Bay 7

January 4, 1998, at Green Bay
Attendance: 60,327

The Green Bay Packers won a mistake-filled game on the strength of Dorsey Levens's running. Levens set a Packers' playoff record by running for 112 yards and scored the final, clinching touchdown. The game was played in a temperature of 29 degrees; Tampa Bay never had won a game when the mercury dipped below 42.

Although Green Bay failed to take advantage of several opportunities, Tampa Bay made the most miscues. Three Buccaneers' field-goal tries went awry because of mistakes, and quarterback Trent Dilfer, who never did get untracked, contributed 2 pass interceptions. Packers quarterback Brett Favre did not have one of his best days (he passed for 190 yards), but did toss a touchdown pass to Mark Chmura in the opening quarter and ran for a 2-point conversion in the final period to put the game out of the Buccaneers' reach.

Tampa Bay defensive tackle Warren Sapp played brilliantly in a losing effort, sacking Favre 3 times, forcing 2 fumbles, and making 7 solo tackles.

Tampa Bay	0	0	7	0	-	7
Green Bay	7	6	0	8	-	21

GB - Chmura 3 pass from Favre (Longwell kick)
GB - FG Longwell 21
GB - FG Longwell 32
TB - Alstott 6 run (Husted kick)
GB - Levens 2 run (Favre run)

TEAM STATISTICS	TB	GB
First Downs	15	16
Rushing	4	6
Passing	9	10
Penalty	2	0
Total Yardage	263	289
Net rushing yardage	90	118
Net passing yardage	173	171
Passes att.-comp.-had int.	37-12-2	28-15-2

RUSHING
Tampa Bay - Dunn 18 for 64; Alstott 7 for 21, 1 TD; Anthony 1 for 5; Walsh 1 for 0.
Green Bay - Levens 25 for 112, 1 TD; Henderson 2 for 4; Favre 5 for 2.

PASSING
Tampa Bay - Dilfer 11 of 36 for 200, 2 ints.; Walsh 1 of 1 for 0.
Green Bay - Favre 15 of 28 for 190, 1 TD, 2 ints.

RECEIVING
Tampa Bay - Copeland 4 for 44; Moore 3 for 54; Dunn 2 for 34; Anthony 1 for 52; Thomas 1 for 16; Davis 1 for 0.
Green Bay - Freeman 4 for 75; Levens 4 for 29; Mayes 2 for 37; Chmura 2 for 20, 1 TD; Henderson 2 for 8; R. Brooks 1 for 21.

1997 AFC CHAMPIONSHIP GAME
Denver 24, Pittsburgh 21

January 11, 1998, at Pittsburgh
Attendance: 61,382

In a game that pitted a talented, but inexperienced, young quarterback against a talented and crafty veteran, Denver's John Elway made a solid case for experience.

By Elway's standards, he was not outstanding, but in leading 2 touchdown drives that put the Broncos ahead 24-14 at the end of the first half, he was magnificent. Still, the play that killed the Steelers' hopes came in the game's final two minutes. On third down in his own territory, Elway fired a strike to Shannon Sharpe for the first down that allowed the Broncos to run out the clock.

In contrast to Elway's performance, Pittsburgh quarterback Kordell Stewart showed his inexperience by throwing 3 interceptions—2 in the end zone—and losing a fumble.

In a battle of the AFC's two foremost runners, Denver's Terrell Davis had the edge on Pittsburgh's Jerome Bettis, 139 yards to 105. Each scored a touchdown.

Denver	7	17	0	0	-	24
Pittsburgh	7	7	0	7	-	21

Den - Davis 8 run (Elam kick)
Pit - Stewart 33 run (N. Johnson kick)
Pit - Bettis 1 run (N. Johnson kick)
Den - FG Elam 43
Den - Griffith 16 pass from Elway (Elam kick)
Den - McCaffrey 1 pass from Elway (Elam kick)
Pit - C. Johnson 15 pass from Stewart (N. Johnson kick)

TEAM STATISTICS	DEN	PIT
First Downs	23	23
Rushing	6	8
Passing	15	13
Penalty	2	2
Total Yardage	345	351
Net rushing yardage	150	161
Net passing yardage	195	190
Passes att.-comp.-had int.	31-18-1	36-18-3

RUSHING
Denver - Davis 26 for 139, 1 TD; Elway 2 for 9; Hebron 2 for 2.
Pittsburgh - Bettis 23 for 105, 1 TD; Stewart 3 for 44, 1 TD; McAfee 1 for 12.

PASSING
Denver - Elway 18 of 31 for 210, 2 TDs, 1 int.
Pittsburgh - Stewart 18 of 36 for 201, 1 TD, 3 ints.

RECEIVING
Denver - R. Smith 6 for 87; McCaffrey 5 for 37, 1 TD; Sharpe 3 for 49; Griffith 2 for 26, 1 TD; Hebron 1 for 9; Davis 1 for 2.
Pittsburgh - Thigpen 6 for 92; Hawkins 4 for 30; C. Johnson 3 for 34, 1 TD; Blackwell 2 for 19; Bruener 1 for 16; Lester 1 for 7; Bettis 1 for 3.

1997 NFC CHAMPIONSHIP GAME
Green Bay 23, San Francisco 10

January 11, 1998, at San Francisco
Attendance: 68,987

For the third consecutive season, the Green Bay Packers knocked the San Francisco 49ers out of the playoffs. Home-field advantage proved as ineffective as the 49ers' running attack.

Only the week before, San Francisco's runners had given Steve Young an alternative to his pinpoint passing. But Green Bay limited the 49ers to a miniscule 33 yards on the ground. Without a running threat, most of Young's 23 completions went for only short gains. In the second quarter, Young was intercepted by Packers safety Eugene Robinson, setting up Green Bay's first touchdown.

Leading 10-3 late in the first half, the Packers had the ball on their 27 with less than a minute to play. An 8-yard run by Dorsey Levens and a 40-yard bomb from Brett Favre to Antonio Freeman set up Ryan Longwell's 43-yard field goal to give the Packers all the points they would need to win. Levens, who ran for 114 yards and a touchdown, took over in the second half as Green Bay controlled the clock.

With less than 3 minutes to go, San Francisco got its only touchdown on a 95-yard kickoff return by Chuck Levy.

Green Bay	3	10	0	10	-	23
San Francisco	0	3	0	7	-	10

GB - FG Longwell 19
GB - Freeman 27 pass from Favre (Longwell kick)
SF - FG Anderson 28
GB - FG Longwell 43

GB	-	FG Longwell 25
GB	-	Levens 5 run (Longwell kick)
SF	-	Levy 95 kickoff return (Anderson kick)

TEAM STATISTICS	GB	SF
First Downs	19	15
Rushing	8	1
Passing	10	11
Penalty	1	3
Total Yardage	325	257
Net rushing yardage	106	33
Net passing yardage	219	224
Passes att.-comp.-had int.	27-16-0	38-23-1

RUSHING
Green Bay - Levens 27 for 114, 1 TD; Henderson 3 for 2; Favre 2 for -10.
San Francisco - Kirby 6 for 21; Hearst 8 for 12; S. Young 2 for 1; Floyd 2 for -1.

PASSING
Green Bay - Favre 16 of 27 for 222, 1 TD.
San Francisco - S. Young 23 of 38 for 250, 1 int.

RECEIVING
Green Bay - Freeman 4 for 107, 1 TD; Levens 4 for 27; R. Brooks 3 for 36; Chmura 2 for 18; Davis 1 for 17; Mayes 1 for 10; Henderson 1 for 7.
San Francisco - Owens 6 for 100; Stokes 6 for 87; Kirby 4 for 7; Hearst 3 for 14; Uwaezuoke 2 for 14; Clark 1 for 16; Jones 1 for 12.

1998 AFC WILD CARD GAME
Miami 24, Buffalo 17

January 2, 1999, at Miami
Attendance: 72,698

Miami held off Buffalo when defensive end Trace Armstrong sacked Bills quarterback Doug Flutie, forcing a fumble that Shane Burton recovered at the Dolphins' 3-yard line in the closing seconds.

When Miami quarterback Dan Marino threw an 11-yard touchdown pass to Lamar Thomas with 3:42 left, the Dolphins had a seemingly comfortable 24-14 lead. But Buffalo quickly drove to Steve Christie's 33-yard field goal with 1:33 left, then recovered the ensuing onside kick. The Bills reached Miami's 5-yard line with 17 seconds left before Armstrong's sack ended their last chance.

Flutie passed for 360 yards and wide receiver Eric Moulds set an NFL postseason record with 240 yards on 9 catches, but Miami earned its first playoff victory under Jimmy Johnson.

Buffalo	**0**	**7**	**7**	**3**	**-**	**17**
Miami	**3**	**3**	**8**	**10**	**-**	**24**

Mia	-	FG Mare 31
Mia	-	FG Mare 40
Buf	-	T. Thomas 1 run (Christie kick)
Mia	-	Abdul-Jabbar 3 run (Pritchett run)
Buf	-	Moulds 32 pass from Flutie (Christie kick)
Mia	-	FG Mare 23
Mia	-	L. Thomas 11 pass from Marino (Mare kick)
Buf	-	FG Christie 33

TEAM STATISTICS	BUF	MIA
First Downs	23	25
Rushing	7	10
Passing	13	10
Penalty	3	5
Total Yardage	416	352
Net rushing yardage	77	124
Net passing yardage	339	228
Passes att.-comp.-had int.	36-21-1	34-23-1

RUSHING
Buffalo - T. Thomas 7 for 33, 1 TD; Flutie 4 for 29; A. Smith 7 for 15.
Miami-Abdul - Jabbar 27 for 95, 1 TD; Parmalee 2 for 10; Pritchett 2 for 7; Z. Thomas 0 for 7; Avery 1 for 3; McDuffie 1 for 3; Marino 1 for-1.

PASSING
Buffalo - Flutie 21 of 36 for 360, 1 TD, 1 int.
Miami - Marino 23 of 34 for 235, 1 TD, 1 int.

RECEIVING
Buffalo - Moulds 9 for 240, 1 TD; Reed 5 for 60; Williams 2 for 20; Loud 1 for 12; A. Smith 1 for 12; Gash 1 for 9; Riemersma 1 for 4; T. Thomas 1 for 3.
Miami - McDuffie 6 for 53; Gadsden 5 for 85; L. Thomas 4 for 36, 1 TD; Drayton 3 for 20; Perry 2 for 29; Abdul-Jabbar 2 for 4; Ruddy 1 for 8.

1998 AFC WILD CARD GAME
Jacksonville 25, New England 10

January 3, 1999, at Jacksonville
Attendance: 71,139

Mark Brunell's 37-yard touchdown pass to Jimmy Smith early in the fourth quarter dashed New England's comeback attempt and assured Jacksonville's 25-10 victory. Brunell, who missed the Jaguars' final 3 regular-season games with a high ankle sprain, struggled most of the day until his clutch throw to Smith. It was rookie running back Fred Taylor, who gained 162 yards, who helped Jacksonville take a 12-0 lead at the half.

The Patriots moved the ball little in the first half but came alive in the second half and closed the deficit to 12-10. New England quarterback Scott Zolak, subbing for injured Drew Bledsoe, led the Patriots on two long drives in the third quarter that resulted in a touchdown and a field goal. But Smith's diving catch in the end zone with 12:24 remaining extended the Jaguars' lead to 9 points. Mike Hollis added 2 late field goals, giving him 4 on the day, to secure the victory.

New England	**0**	**0**	**7**	**3**	**-**	**10**
Jacksonville	**6**	**6**	**0**	**13**	**-**	**25**

Jac	-	FG Hollis 35
Jac	-	FG Hollis 24
Jac	-	Taylor 13 run (run failed)
NE	-	Edwards 1 run (Vinatieri kick)
NE	-	FG Vinatieri 27
Jac	-	Smith 37 pass from Brunell (Hollis kick)
Jac	-	FG Hollis 34
Jac	-	FG Hollis 21

TEAM STATISTICS	NE	JAC
First Downs	14	17
Rushing	3	6
Passing	11	9
Penalty	0	2
Total Yardage	206	308
Net rushing yardage	35	160
Net passing yardage	171	148
Passes att.-comp.-had int.	44-21-1	34-14-0

RUSHING
New England - Edwards 17 for 28, 1 TD; Shaw 1 for 4; Carter 1 for 3.
Jacksonville - Taylor 33 for 162, 1 TD; Brunell 4 for-2.

PASSING
New England - Zolak 21 of 44 for 190, 1 int.
Jacksonville - Brunell 14 of 34 for 161, 1 TD.

RECEIVING
New England - Brown 4 for 46; Jefferson 4 for 30; Simmons 3 for 42; Edwards 3 for 33; Cullors 2 for 17; Coates 2 for 10; Carter 2 for 3; Purnell 1 for 9.
Jacksonville - McCardell 6 for 72; Smith 5 for 56, 1 TD; Mitchell 1 for 22; Jones 1 for 8; Shelton 1 for 3.

1998 NFC WILD CARD GAME
Arizona 20, Dallas 7

January 2, 1999, at Irving, Texas
Attendance: 62,969

Jake Plummer passed for 2 touchdowns to lead the Cardinals to their first postseason victory since 1947, when the franchise was located in Chicago.

The Cowboys had beaten the Cardinals twice during the regular season, but Arizona grabbed the lead in the first quarter on Plummer's 12-yard shovel pass to Adrian Murrell. Chris Jacke's 37-yard field goal in the final seconds of the first half gave the Cardinals a 10-0 lead.

Two plays into the second half, Murrell raced 74 yards to set up Plummer's 3-yard touchdown pass to Larry Centers. Jacke kicked his second field goal in the final quarter before Dallas scored a late touchdown that failed to dim Arizona's superior defensive performance.

Arizona	7	3	7	3	-	20
Dallas	0	0	0	7	-	7

Ariz - Murrell 12 pass from Plummer (Jacke kick)
Ariz - FG Jacke 37
Ariz - Centers 3 pass from Plummer (Jacke kick)
Ariz - FG Jacke 46
Dal - B. Davis 6 pass from Aikman (Cunningham kick)

TEAM STATISTICS	ARIZ	DAL
First Downs	14	20
Rushing	2	5
Passing	11	12
Penalty	1	3
Total Yardage	346	260
Net rushing yardage	133	96
Net passing yardage	213	164
Passes att.-comp.-had int.	36-19-2	49-22-3

RUSHING
Arizona - Murrell 12 for 95; Bates 11 for 32; Centers 3 for 5; Plummer 3 for 1.
Dallas - E. Smith 16 for 74; S. Williams 3 for 22; Aikman 1 for 0.

PASSING
Arizona - Plummer 19 of 36 for 213; 2 TDs, 2 ints.
Dallas - Aikman 22 of 49 for 191, 1 TD, 3 ints.

RECEIVING
Arizona - Moore 5 for 41; F. Sanders 3 for 72; Metcalf 3 for 48; Centers 3 for 16, 1 TD; Murrell 2 for 16, 1 TD; Gedney 2 for 15; McWilliams 1 for 5.
Dallas - Jeffers 7 for 92; Irvin 4 for 32; B. Davis 4 for 25, 1 TD; Bjornson 2 for 12; S. Williams 2 for 6; E. Smith 1 for 10; Clay 1 for 9; Johnston 1 for 5.

1998 NFC WILD CARD GAME
San Francisco 30, Green Bay 27

January 3, 1999, at San Francisco
Attendance: 66,506

The 49ers ended a string of 5 consecutive losses to the Packers with one of the most spectacular finishes in postseason history. With 3 seconds left, San Francisco's Terrell Owens snagged Steve Young's 25-yard touchdown pass in the midst of 3 defenders to give his team a come-from-behind victory. It was a magnificent ending to what had been a terrible day for Owens, who had dropped 4 passes and fumbled once.

Until the 49ers' late touchdown, the game looked like a come-from-behind victory for Green Bay. Brett Favre's 15-yard touchdown pass to Antonio Freeman capped a 9-play, 76-yard drive and gave the Packers a 27-23 lead with only 1:56 left to play. But Young completed 7 of 9 passes on the ensuing 76-yard drive, and San Francisco put an end to Green Bay's hopes of a third consecutive trip to the Super Bowl.

Green Bay	3	14	0	10	-	27
San Francisco	7	3	10	10	-	30

GB - FG Longwell 23
SF - Clark 1 pass from Young (Richey kick)
GB - Freeman 2 pass from Favre (Longwell kick)
SF - FG Richey 34
GB - Levens 2 run (Longwell kick)
SF - Clark 8 pass from Young (Richey kick)
SF - FG Richey 48
GB - FG Longwell 37
SF - FG Richey 40
GB - Freeman 15 pass from Favre (Longwell kick)
SF - Owens 25 pass from Young (Richey kick)

TEAM STATISTICS	GB	SF
First Downs	24	20
Rushing	10	10
Passing	12	9
Penalty	2	1
Total Yardage	403	347
Net rushing yardage	121	178
Net passing yardage	282	169
Passes att.-comp.-had int.	35-20-2	32-18-2

RUSHING
Green Bay - Levens 27 for 116, 1 TD; Freeman 1 for 5.
San Francisco - Hearst 22 for 128; Kirby 5 for 32; Young 3 for 16; Edwards 1 for 2.

PASSING
Green Bay - Favre 20 of 35 for 292, 2 TDs, 2 ints.
San Francisco - Young 18 of 32 for 182, 3 TDs, 2 ints.

RECEIVING
Green Bay - Levens 6 for 37; Freeman 4 for 75, 2 TDs; Henderson 3 for 55; Bradford 2 for 53; Brooks 2 for 31; Mayes 1 for 20; Chmura 1 for 12; Davis 1 for 9.
San Francisco - Stokes 5 for 58; Owens 3 for 73, 1 TD; Hearst 3 for 15; Clark 3 for 13, 2 TDs; Kirby 2 for 14; Rice 1 for 6; Edwards 1 for 3.

1998 AFC DIVISIONAL PLAYOFF GAME
Denver 38, Miami 3

January 9, 1999, at Denver
Attendance: 75,729

In perhaps the last meeting between future Pro Football Hall of Fame quarterbacks John Elway and Dan Marino, it was Broncos running back Terrell Davis who sparked his team to the victory.

Davis ran for 199 yards and 2 touchdowns just three weeks after Miami held him to a season-low 29 yards. In week 16 of the regular season, the Dolphins handed the Broncos a 31-21 defeat, but in the playoffs, Miami's hopes for a repeat evaporated quickly.

The Dolphins' heralded defense was unable to stop Davis, who ran for both his touchdowns in the first quarter and gained 129 yards by halftime, at which point Denver led 21-3.

The Broncos' final touchdown came in spectacular fashion. Cornerback Darrius Johnson forced a Miami fumble; big defensive end Neil Smith picked up the ball and rumbled 79 yards down the sideline to score.

Miami	0	3	0	0	-	3
Denver	14	7	3	14	-	38

Den - Davis 1 run (Elam kick)
Den - Davis 20 run (Elam kick)
Mia - FG Mare 22
Den - Loville 11 run (Elam kick)
Den - FG Elam 32
Den - R. Smith 28 pass from Elway (Elam kick)
Den - N. Smith 79 fumble return (Elam kick)

TEAM STATISTICS	MIA	DEN
First Downs	14	24
Rushing	1	13
Passing	11	10
Penalty	2	1
Total Yardage	252	424
Net rushing yardage	14	250
Net passing yardage	238	174
Passes att.-comp.-had int.	37-26-2	23-14-0

RUSHING
Miami - Parmalee 7 for 14; Abdul-Jabbar 3 for 5; Huard 2 for -2; Pritchett 1 for -3.
Denver - Davis 21 for 199; 2 TDs; Loville 8 for 34, 1 TD; Elway 3 for 19; Brister 6 for -2.

PASSING
Miami - Marino 26 of 37 for 243, 2 ints.
Denver - Elway 14 of 23 for 182, 1 TD.

RECEIVING
Miami - McDuffie 9 for 118; Parmalee 5 for 24; Gadsden 4 for 36; L. Thomas 3 for 31; Pritchett 3 for 23; Jacquet 1 for 6; Abdul-Jabbar 1 for 5.
Denver - Sharpe 5 for 38; R. Smith 4 for 71, 1 TD; McCaffrey 3 for 52; Griffith 1 for 14; Davis 1 for 7.

1998 AFC DIVISIONAL PLAYOFF GAME
New York Jets 34, Jacksonville 24

January 10, 1999, at East Rutherford, New Jersey
Attendance: 78,817

Running back Curtis Martin and wide receiver Keyshawn Johnson each scored 2 touchdowns as the Jets reached the AFC Championship Game for the first time since 1982.

Martin rushed for 124 yards, and Johnson caught 9 passes, including a 21-yard touchdown to open the scoring in the first quarter. Johnson's second touchdown came on a 10-yard end-around play and gave the Jets a 17-0 lead in the second quarter.

Jacksonville's Mark Brunell, still recovering from a month-old ankle sprain, was not at his best. He threw 3 interceptions and had several passes blocked at the line of scrimmage. Nevertheless, an apparent rout turned into a close game in the fourth quarter. The Jaguars narrowed New York's lead to 7 points on Mike Hollis' 37-yard field goal with 6:38 left, but the Jets added a field goal of their own. New York closed out the day with an interception by Johnson, who was inserted on defense in the final minute to break up the long pass.

Jacksonville	0	7	7	10	-	24
N.Y. Jets	7	10	14	3	-	34

NYJ - K. Johnson 21 pass from Testaverde (Hall kick)
NYJ - FG Hall 52
NYJ - K. Johnson 10 run (Hall kick)
Jac - J. Smith 52 pass from Brunell (Hollis kick)
NYJ - C. Martin 1 run (Hall kick)
Jac - McCardell 3 pass from Brunell (Hollis kick)
NYJ - C. Martin 1 run (Hall kick)
Jac - J. Smith 19 pass from Brunell (Hollis kick)
Jac - FG Hollis 37
NYJ - FG Hall 30

TEAM STATISTICS	JAC	NYJ
First Downs	14	29
Rushing	5	11
Passing	8	17
Penalty	1	1
Total Yardage	251	429
Net rushing yardage	95	151
Net passing yardage	156	278
Passes att.-comp.-had int.	31-12-3	36-24-1

RUSHING
Jacksonville - Taylor 20 for 86; Brunell 2 for 9.
NY Jets - C. Martin 36 for 124, 2 TDs; K. Johnson 2 for 28, 1 TD; Testaverde 1 for -1.

PASSING
Jacksonville - Brunell 12 of 31 for 156, 3 TDs, 3 ints.
NY Jets - Testaverde 24 of 36 for 284, 1 TD, 1 int.

RECEIVING
Jacksonville - J. Smith 5 for 104, 2 TDs; McCardell 4 for 32, 1 TD; Mitchell 2 for 13; Banks 1 for 7.
NY Jets - K. Johnson 9 for 121, 1 TD; C. Martin 6 for 58; Chrebet 4 for 45; Byars 2 for 11; Ward 1 for 18; Brady 1 for 17; Meggett 1 for 14.

1998 NFC DIVISIONAL PLAYOFF GAME
Atlanta 20, San Francisco 18

January 9, 1999, at Atlanta
Attendance: 70,262

The Falcons advanced to the NFC Championship Game for the first time in franchise history with a grind-it-out victory over the 49ers. Atlanta took a 14-0 lead in the first half on a pair of touchdowns by Jamal Anderson, who rushed for 113 yards. But the 49ers closed within 14-10 by halftime on Steve Young's 17-yard touchdown pass to Jerry Rice and Wade Richey's 36-yard field goal.

Atlanta regained momentum in the third quarter when Eugene Robinson returned an interception 77 yards to set up Morten Andersen's 29-yard field goal. Andersen added another field goal in the final period to offset a 49ers' touchdown and 2-point conversion.

San Francisco received a severe blow on the game's first play, when running back Garrison Hearst suffered a broken leg.

San Francisco	0	10	0	8	-	18
Atlanta	7	7	3	3	-	20

Atl - Anderson 2 run (Andersen kick)
Atl - Anderson 34 run (Andersen kick)
SF - Rice 17 pass from Young (Richey kick)
SF - FG Richey 36
Atl - FG Andersen 29
Atl - FG Andersen 32
SF - Young 8 run (Clark pass from Detmer)

TEAM STATISTICS	SF	ATL
First Downs	15	16
Rushing	2	7
Passing	12	8
Penalty	1	1
Total Yardage	334	289
Net rushing yardage	46	136
Net passing yardage	288	153
Passes att.-comp.-had int.	37-23-3	19-13-1

RUSHING
San Francisco - Kirby 9 for 22; Young 6 for 19, 1 TD; Hearst 1 for 7; Edwards 3 for 4; Levy 1 for -6.
Atlanta - Anderson 29 for 113, 2 TDs; Downs 1 for 16; Chandler 3 for 7.

PASSING
San Francisco - Young 23 of 37 for 289, 1 TD, 3 ints.
Atlanta - Chandler 13 of 19 for 169, 1 int.

RECEIVING
San Francisco - Owens 8 for 73; Stokes 5 for 76; Rice 3 for 63, 1 TD; Levy 2 for 58; Kirby 2 for 7; Edwards 2 for 3; Clark 1 for 9.
Atlanta - Mathis 5 for 71; Martin 4 for 63; Kozlowski 2 for 3; Harris 1 for 22; Anderson 1 for 10.

1998 NFC DIVISIONAL PLAYOFF GAME
Minnesota 41, Arizona 21

January 10, 1999, at Minneapolis
Attendance: 63,760

Minnesota's high-octane offense fueled an easy victory over the outmatched Cardinals. After building a 24-7 lead at the half, the Vikings coasted to the victory.

Most of Minnesota's heralded weapons were in evidence: quarterback Randall Cunningham threw 3 touchdown passes, rookie wide receiver Randy Moss caught 4 passes for 73 yards and a touchdown, running back Robert Smith gained 124 yards, and kicker Gary Anderson continued his perfect season with 2 field goals and 5 extra points.

Jake Plummer provided most of the offense for the Cardinals but was guilty of 2 first-half interceptions. They came on back-to-back possessions and led to 10 points by the Vikings.

Arizona	0	7	7	7	-	21
Minnesota	7	17	10	7	-	41

Min - Hoard 1 run (Anderson kick)
Min - Glover 15 pass from Cunningham (Anderson kick)
Min - FG Anderson 34
Ariz - Bates 1 run (Jacke kick)
Min - Hoard 16 pass from Cunningham (Anderson kick)
Ariz - Bates 1 run (Jacke kick)
Min - FG Anderson 20
Min - Moss 2 pass from Cunningham (Anderson kick)
Ariz - Bates 1 run (Jacke kick)
Min - Hoard 6 run (Anderson kick)

TEAM STATISTICS	ARIZ	MIN
First Downs	23	26
Rushing	7	12
Passing	11	13
Penalty	5	1
Total Yardage	316	416
Net rushing yardage	74	188
Net passing yardage	242	228
Passes att.-comp.-had int.	41-23-2	28-17-1

RUSHING
Arizona - Murrell 15 for 62; Plummer 4 for 9; Bates 4 for 3, 3 TDs.
Minnesota - R. Smith 19 for 124; Hoard 11 for 44, 2 TDs; Palmer 2 for 13; Cunningham 3 for 6; Evans 1 for 1.

PASSING
Arizona - Plummer 23 of 41 for 242, 2 ints.
Minnesota - Cunningham 17 of 27 for 236, 3 TDs, 1 int.; Palmer 0 of 1 for 0.

RECEIVING
Arizona - Moore 6 for 91; Centers 6 for 45; Sanders 4 for 30; Murrell 3 for 52; Metcalf 2 for 9; Gedney 1 for 8; McWilliams 1 for 7.
Minnesota - Carter 5 for 82; Moss 4 for 73, 1 TD; Glover 3 for 22, 1 TD; Palmer 2 for 29; R. Smith 2 for 14; Hoard 1 for 16, 1 TD.

1998 AFC CHAMPIONSHIP GAME
Denver 23, New York Jets 10

January 17, 1999, at Denver
Attendance: 75,482

Broncos running back Terrell Davis and 6 Jets turnovers were too much for New York to overcome at Denver's Mile High Stadium.

Despite some sloppy play, New York led 10-0 in the third quarter on a field goal on the last play of the first half and Curtis Martin's 1-yard touchdown run early in the second half. Then the Broncos exploded for 20 points before the end of the third quarter to take the game.

In the first half, Davis rushed for more than 100 yards and the Jets' Vinny Testaverde connected on his first 13 passes. But Denver's John Elway completed only 3 of his passes, while the Jets lacked a rushing attack. So the game was scoreless until John Hall kicked a 32-yard field goal on the final play of the second quarter. New York increased its lead to 10-0 on Martin's touchdown run one play after a blocked punt.

Denver finally scored on Elway's 11-yard touchdown pass to Howard Griffith nearly 5 minutes into the third period. A 47-yard bomb to Ed McCaffrey was the key play on the drive. Jason Elam tied the game with a 44-yard field goal, then moved the Broncos in front for the first time with a 48-yard kick. Davis effectively wrapped up the victory with a 31-yard dash for a touchdown in the final minute of the third quarter. Three of the Jets' turnovers came in the fourth quarter, stifling their chances to rally.

N.Y. Jets	0	3	7	0	-	10
Denver	0	0	20	3	-	23

NYJ - FG Hall 32
NYJ - Martin 1 run (Hall kick)
Den - Griffith 11 pass from Elway (Elam kick)
Den - FG Elam 44
Den - FG Elam 48
Den - Davis 31 run (Elam kick)
Den - FG Elam 35

TEAM STATISTICS	NYJ	DEN
First Downs	18	14
Rushing	1	8
Passing	17	6
Penalty	0	0
Total Yardage	370	331
Net rushing yardage	14	178
Net passing yardage	356	153
Passes att.-comp.-had int.	52-31-2	34-13-0

RUSHING
NY Jets - Martin 13 for 14, 1 TD.
Denver - Davis 32 for 167, 1 TD; Elway 3 for 13; Loville 2 for 7; Rouen 1 for -9.

PASSING
NY Jets - Testaverde 31 of 52 for 356, 2 ints.
Denver - Elway 13 of 34 for 173, 1 TD.

RECEIVING
NY Jets - Chrebet 8 for 121; K. Johnson 7 for 73; Ward 5 for 61; Martin 4 for 39; Byars 3 for 33; Brady 2 for 11; Van Dyke 1 for 16; Meggett 1 for 2.
Denver - McCaffrey 3 for 66; R. Smith 3 for 37; Chamberlain 2 for 26; Sharpe 2 for 14; Davis 1 for 12; Griffith 1 for 11, 1 TD; Carswell 1 for 7.

1998 NFC CHAMPIONSHIP GAME
Atlanta 30, Minnesota 27 (OT)

January 17, 1999, at Minneapolis
Attendance: 64,060

The upstart Falcons won their first NFC championship with a shocking, come-from-behind, overtime victory.

The Vikings led 20-7 in the second quarter and still held a 27-17 advantage early in the fourth quarter. Morten Andersen narrowed Atlanta's deficit to 27-20 with a 24-yard field goal. Then, with 2:07 remaining, Minnesota kicker Gary Anderson, who had not missed an extra-point or field-goal try in the regular season or playoffs, pulled a 38-yard try to the left. Atlanta quarterback Chris Chandler took over and marched his team 71 yards. His 16-yard touchdown pass to Terance Mathis tied the score with 49 seconds left.

Minnesota could not move the ball in overtime, and 11:52 into the extra period, Andersen kicked a 38-yard, game-winning field goal.

Chandler passed for 340 yards and 3 touchdowns despite a leg injury that had him limping badly late in the game.

Atlanta	7	7	3	10	3	-	30
Minnesota	7	13	0	7	0	-	27

Atl - J. Anderson 5 pass from Chandler (Andersen kick)
Min - Moss 31 pass from Cunningham (G. Anderson kick)
Min - FG G. Anderson 29
Min - Cunningham 1 run (G. Anderson kick)
Min - FG G. Anderson 35
Atl - Mathis 14 pass from Chandler (Andersen kick)
Atl - FG Andersen 27
Min - Hatchette 5 pass from Cunningham (G. Anderson kick)
Atl - FG Andersen 24
Atl - Mathis 16 pass from Chandler (Andersen kick)
Atl - FG Andersen 38

TEAM STATISTICS	ATL	MIN
First Downs	25	26
Rushing	6	4
Passing	17	19
Penalty	2	3
Total Yardage	427	356
Net rushing yardage	110	102
Net passing yardage	317	254
Passes att.-comp.-had int.	43-27-0	48-29-0

RUSHING
Atlanta - J. Anderson 23 for 67; Dwight 3 for 28; Chandler 2 for 15; Oxendine 1 for 0.
Minnesota - R. Smith 21 for 71; Cunningham 6 for 13, 1 TD; Hoard 6 for 10; Evans 1 for 8.

PASSING
Atlanta - Chandler 27 of 43 for 340, 3 TDs.
Minnesota - Cunningham 29 of 48 for 266, 2 TDs.

RECEIVING
Atlanta - Mathis 6 for 73, 2 TDs; J. Anderson 6 for 33, 1 TD; Martin 5 for 129; Santiago 3 for 54; Kozlowski 3 for 11; Green 2 for 9; Harris 1 for 29; E. Smith 1 for 2.
Minnesota - Moss 6 for 75, 1 TD; Carter 6 for 67; Glover 4 for 34; Hatchette 4 for 34, 1 TD; Hoard 3 for 23; DeLong 2 for 17; Palmer 2 for 9; Evans 1 for 8; R. Smith 1 for -1.

CHAPTER 9

The 25 Most Memorable Regular Season Games

Jack Clary

A panel of 13 historians—Phil Barber, Tom Barnidge, Joel Bussert, Bob Carroll, Ray Didinger, Chuck Garrity, Sr., Michael Gershman, Joe Horrigan, David Neft, Beau Riffenburgh, Don Smith, Don Weiss, and John Wiebusch—was polled to pick the most memorable regular-season NFL games. Among the criteria used were historical significance, great individual efforts, and outstanding matchups. The results are presented here in chronological order.

December 7, 1925
Chicago Bears 19, New York Giants 7

"Out of a little Middle Western town came a fiery-haired youth who took the big city by storm."

That's how Richards Vidmer of *The New York Times* began his story after watching Red Grange and the Chicago Bears dazzle 73,000 spectators at the Polo Grounds and defeat the New York Giants 19-7.

It was Grange's fifth appearance as a pro football player after completing his college career at Illinois. Against the Giants, he played before the largest crowd ever to see a pro football game to that point, and he did a little bit of everything, including collecting about $30,000 as his share of the estimated $120,000 gate.

Grange rushed for 53 yards on 13 carries, returned 2 punts for 13 yards, completed 2 of 3 passes for 32 yards, and caught 1 pass for 23 yards. The coup de grace was his 35-yard interception return for Chicago's final touchdown in the fourth quarter.

Grange had played four games in the previous 10 days, including two in Chicago, one in St. Louis, and another in Philadelphia, and he had five more games scheduled the following week. That meant 10 games within a span of less than three weeks. Player-coach George Halas decided to give Grange some time off in New York. Grange played the first 20 minutes and didn't appear again until the fourth quarter. During his absence, there were constant chants of "We want Grange!" from the huge throng.

The crowd filled every bit of available space, sometimes standing three-deep in walkways behind the seats, and clogging every aisle. Hundreds of people spilled onto the sidelines. Blue-and-gold bunting, in tribute to the Bears, and red-and-blue bunting for the Giants was hung throughout the stadium. The weather was unusually balmy for early December, and the sky was cloudless. The playing field was sloppy from rains earlier in the week, so Grange couldn't display any of the hip-swiveling moves that had earned him the nickname, "The Galloping Ghost."

The Bears drove 62 yards on their first possession for a touchdown. Grange carried twice and gained 9 yards, with the bulk of the work going to Joe Sternaman and Laurie Walquist. On its next possession, Chicago drove 60 yards to another touchdown. Grange had runs of 6, 3, and 2 yards; caught a 23-yard pass; threw a 14-yard pass to Walquist; and then was the lead blocker as Sternaman scored his second touchdown.

When Grange reappeared in the final quarter, he played a key role in a Bears' drive that covered nearly 70 yards before being stopped. Then, a minute later, he intercepted a pass and raced untouched for a touchdown as the stadium erupted in cheers.

In the end it wasn't so much what he accomplished on the playing field as the effect he had on the emerging game of pro football. His drawing power supplied enough gate receipts to enable the Giants to survive in New York City, a locale the NFL desperately needed for its survival. News of Grange's feats and his effect on sports-mad New York City were like bolts of electricity when dispatched throughout the land.

November 28, 1929
Chicago Cardinals 40, Chicago Bears 6

There have been many great performances in NFL history, but none has topped Ernie Nevers's 40 points for the Chicago Cardinals against the Chicago Bears on Thanksgiving Day, 1929. It is the NFL's longest-standing individual record.

Nevers's mark of 6 touchdowns in that game later was tied by Dub Jones of the Cleveland Browns and Gale Sayers of the Chicago Bears, but the 4 extra points that Nevers kicked in the Cardinals' 40-6 victory at Comiskey Park give him the edge.

Nevers rarely is mentioned in the same breath as his

foremost rival of that time, Red Grange, though pound for pound there is little to distinguish between them as great football talent. Ironically, Nevers's record-setting day came against a Red Grange-led Bears' team whose only points were scored by Red's brother, Garland Grange.

Nevers, a great player at Stanford under Pop Warner, was a one-man gang when he came into the NFL in 1926, a year after Grange made his grand entrance with the Bears. Nevers signed with the Duluth Eskimos, whose owner, Ole Haugsrud, was hailed for "saving the league," because Grange left the Bears after a salary dispute with owner George Halas and started the rival American Football League.

Nevers labored for two seasons with the Eskimos, playing nearly all of his games on the road and playing nearly every minute of every game. When Duluth folded after the 1927 season, Nevers resumed playing major league baseball for two seasons. When the 1929 baseball season ended, he joined the Cardinals at the same time that Grange returned to the Bears, intensifying the already red-hot crosstown rivalry between the North Side Bears and the South Side Cardinals.

The estimated 8,000 who watched the game—mostly South Siders—couldn't get enough scoring. Wilfrid Smith of the *Chicago Tribune* noted: "From the time Nevers plunged for the first touchdown until he slid over for the sixth in the final period and then place-kicked the fortieth point, that crowd yelled for more touchdowns."

Nevers scored 20 points in each half. His first touchdown came on a 20-yard run in the first quarter, and he got his second just before the period ended on a 4-yard run. He kicked the extra point after his first touchdown but missed after the second. His third touchdown, in the second quarter, came on a 6-yard run, and then he added his twentieth point.

In the second half, Nevers had a pair of 1-yard touchdown plunges and broke off a 10-yard run in the fourth quarter for his final score. He kicked extra points after his first and third touchdowns in the second half. He left the game after his sixth touchdown.

While Nevers got the glory, that Cardinals also featured tackle Duke Slater, one of the few black players in pro football at that time, guard Walt Kiesling, and halfback Mickey McDonnell. To Cardinals fans, Nevers's big day especially was important because, after years of being trampled by their bitter rivals, they could claim at last to be champions of Chicago.

October 22, 1939
Brooklyn 23, Philadelphia 14

Few dates in NFL history are as important as October 22, 1939, the day that a game between the Philadelphia Eagles and Brooklyn Dodgers at Ebbets Field in Brooklyn was the first NFL game to be televised.

In 1939, no more than 1,000 television sets existed in New York City. Today, NFL football is seen in more than 150 countries around the world and the Super Bowl, presented in several languages, has become one of the most popular worldwide sporting events.

For the record, the Dodgers defeated the Eagles, then coached by future NFL commissioner Bert Bell, 23-14. The Dodgers' Ralph Kerchival kicked 3 field goals of more than 40 yards, and Ace Gutowsky set a National Football League record when his 7-yard run pushed his career rushing total to 3,399 yards. Notable for the Eagles was that future Hall of Fame inductee Bill Hewitt, playing without a helmet that day, caught a touchdown pass from Davey O'Brien.

Of course, there is no comparison as to how the game was televised on that fall Sunday and how today's high-tech package is sent worldwide by satellite. In 1939, there were just two cameras in use. Today, most games have at least a half dozen, and Monday night games and playoff games use twice that number.

In 1939, television-set owners had a small, grainy black-and-white picture. The voice they heard belonged to Allen Walz, a former New York City Golden Gloves champion and New York University football star who did sports for fledgling station W2XBS, the granddaddy of the CBS television network.

"It was late in October on a cloudy day, and when the sun crept behind the stadium, there wasn't enough light for the two cameras we used," Walz said. "The picture would get darker and darker, and eventually it would be completely blank and we'd revert to a radio broadcast."

Walz recalled using two iconoscope cameras. He sat with his chin on the railing in the mezzanine of Ebbets Field, boxes 143 and 145 in the balcony, and one camera was aimed over his shoulder at the field. There was another camera at field level on the 50-yard line, but it proved to be ineffective and was barely used.

"I did my own spotting, and when the play moved up and down the field on punts and kickoffs, I'd point to tell the cameraman what I'd be talking about. We also used hand signals for communication. Producer Burke Crotty was in the mobile unit truck, and he'd tell me over the headphones which camera he was using."

Walz, who never pursued a career as a sports play-by-play announcer when television began to boom after World War II, was savvy enough to know that he need not describe what was happening on the screen but was content to offer commentary instead. "Some of the fun of television was to tell the audience what was going to happen, to give them a clue of what to watch," Walz said. "For instance, the Dodgers used a buttonhook pass to Perry Schwartz all season and other variations of that pass. Well, sure enough you could feel they were going to use it, and we'd tell the audience to look for it. The game wasn't so complicated then, with only a few plays, and we got to know them pretty well.

"After a while, Potsy Clark, the Dodgers' coach, didn't like us calling the play before it was run, and we stopped doing it. Of course, Potsy also liked the medium because we had a monitor on the sidelines and he saw it as a means of scouting his opponent when the game was going on. He insisted that we keep the monitor near his bench where he could watch it."

Today, huge in-stadium television screens do the same thing for players and coaches on the sidelines, while millions more watch at home.

September 15, 1950
Cleveland 35, Philadelphia 10

This game on a balmy September Saturday night in Philadelphia at Municipal Stadium was the birth of the NFL's modern age. The league had just completed a merger with the rival All-America Football Conference after four years of a very costly war. The result was a new-look NFL that included the Browns, who had won all four of the AAFC's titles and were so dominant they probably hastened the demise of the league.

When the merger was official early in 1950, NFL commissioner Bert Bell immediately scheduled Cleveland to face the defending two-time NFL champion Philadelphia Eagles in the season's first game. It was the most anticipated matchup in pro football history, but one in which the Browns were given little chance of winning.

The Browns, coached by Paul Brown, stunned the Eagles and the rest of the NFL with an easy 35-10 victory. From that Saturday night in Philadelphia, pro football never was the same. Brown changed the way the game was played and made pro football a unique sport, separate and distinct from college football.

The Browns did it two ways: They dazzled and shredded Philadelphia's proud defense with their passing game for three quarters, and then turned loose their great running game. The Eagles also were handicapped as a result of injuries to their great running backs, Steve Van Buren and Bosh Pritchard. During the game, all semblance of their famed running game disappeared when another back, Clyde (Smackover) Scott, broke his shoulder.

The Eagles scored first when Cliff Patton kicked a 15-yard field goal for a 3-0 lead. It was their only lead of the game.

Cleveland's offense was geared to Brown's precision passing attack, the basic form of which still exists today as the West Coast offense. Early in the game, wide receiver Dub Jones worked on Philadelphia's best defensive back, Russ Craft, with a series of square-out moves. Each time he ran the patterns, Craft edged up to cover him until, finally, Jones ran the same pattern but broke it toward the end zone, and quarterback Otto Graham hit him with a 59-yard touchdown pass.

On Cleveland's next possession, Graham teamed with tight end Dante Lavelli, who easily shed the coverage of future Hall of Fame linebacker Alex Wojciechowicz and defensive back Frank Reagan and caught a 26-yard touchdown pass to give the Cleveland Browns a 14-3 lead at halftime.

Early in the third quarter, Graham bewildered the Eagles' defense by using swift halfback Rex Bumgardner as a fullback. The Eagles did not cover the fullback when he went in motion before the ball was snapped, and the Browns gained 30 yards in three plays. When the Eagles adjusted, they went back to their ill-fated scheme of trying to cover the Browns' outside receivers man-for-man, and Graham teamed with end Mac Speedie for a 12-yard touchdown.

Philadelphia got its only touchdown on Bill Mackrides's pass to end Pete Pihos to close to gap to 21-10. Then Brown took control of the game with his running attack. He ordered his linemen to set themselves wider on each play, knowing the Eagles would try to match the setup. It worked, because Philadelphia's linemen found themselves not only facing wider gaps but also trying to cope with better blocking angles by the Browns' linemen. Fullback Marion Motley, along with Bumgardner and Jones, then rolled through those openings for big gains. Cleveland ran the ball seven consecutive times at one point and Graham scored on a quarterback sneak. On the Browns' next possession, Jones ran 57 yards for the final touchdown.

"We just wanted to show them that we could run the ball better than they could," Graham said. It was a put down of the Eagles' proud boast that they were the best running team in football, as well as of an earlier put down that Philadelphia considered the Browns just a passing team. When the teams played each other a second time that season, the Browns didn't throw a pass in beating Philadelphia 13-7.

September 15, 1960
Denver 13, Boston 10

Early in 1959 Texas millionaires Lamar Hunt and Bud Adams wanted to join the NFL. Hunt sought to purchase the Chicago Cardinals and move them to Dallas, and Adams wanted to place a team in Houston.

When the NFL turned them down, they started their own league—the American Football League—and not only got their teams in Dallas and Houston but also got other men to secure franchises in Los Angeles, Buffalo, Oakland, New York, Boston, and Denver. The new league signed a television contract with ABC that guaranteed each team $95,000 a season, which ultimately helped assure its survival.

The AFL went toe-to-toe with the NFL to sign All-Americas, lured former NFL players out of retirement, and gathered enough talent to field eight teams.

The league's first game was in Boston between the Patriots and Denver Broncos on September 15, 1960. The teams had played each other five weeks earlier in an exhibition game in Providence, Rhode Island, and Boston won 43-6. The Patriots, after being refused use of Fenway Park, Harvard Stadium, and Alumni Field at Boston College, finally found a home at old Braves Field, where Boston University played its games.

Boston was coached by Lou Saban, who had been recommended by former Cleveland Browns teammate Otto Graham after Graham turned down a bid from owner Bill Sullivan to coach the team. The Broncos were led by Frank Filchock, who had coached for seven years at Saskatchewan of the Canadian Football League before being fired and replaced by his quarterback, Frank Tripucka. In one of many ironies that marked the AFL's early existence, Tripucka was Denver's quarterback its first three seasons.

Most memorable about the Broncos that first season was their uniforms—gold helmets, chocolate brown jerseys, and vertically-striped stockings. Those stockings created a stir that first season and finally were burned in a ceremonial funeral pyre in Denver two seasons later.

With commissioner Joe Foss looking on among 21,597

spectators—and with Hurricane Donna bearing down on the region—Boston won referee Harold Bourne's coin toss and elected to kick off. Thus, at 8:02 on that Friday night in September, the AFL officially began its first game.

Boston scored the league's first points when Gino Cappelletti kicked a 35-yard field goal midway through the first quarter.

Denver bounced right back after Cappelletti's field goal when Al Carmichael took a swing pass from Tripucka on the right sideline, then reversed his field to the left side and completed a 38-yard touchdown play. Gene Mingo, whose football experience was as a high school and service-team player, kicked the extra point, the first of his league-leading 123 points in 1960.

Denver upped its lead to 13-3 in the third quarter when Mingo returned a punt 76 yards for a touchdown. He missed the extra point.

Boston closed to within 3 points when Chuck Shonta returned an interception 52 yards to set up Butch Songin's 10-yard touchdown pass to Jim Colclough.

The Patriots had one last chance to win late in the fourth quarter, driving to the Broncos' 13-yard line on Jim Crawford's 40-yard run. But on third down, Songin's pass was intercepted by defensive back Goose Gonsoulin.

Hunt and Adams eventually got their wish. In 1970, they became part of the NFL in a merger of the two leagues that sent pro football soaring to the top of the nation's popularity charts.

December 12, 1965
Chicago 61, San Francisco 20

A San Francisco 49ers player said it best after his team was demolished by the Chicago Bears 61-20 at Wrigley Field.

"Watching the game films on Tuesday is going to be like watching the Chicago Bears' 1965 season highlight film. That guy did everything to us."

"That guy" was rookie Gale Sayers, the Bears' number-one draft choice that year. Sayers scored 6 touchdowns in a variety of ways. It was the signature of an all-too-short career that nonetheless landed him in the Pro Football Hall of Fame.

Sayers equaled the NFL record of 6 touchdowns in a single game, first set in 1929 by Ernie Nevers of the Cardinals, and equaled in 1951 by Dub Jones of the Browns. Sayers scored on an 80-yard pass, on 4 touchdown runs, and on an 85-yard punt return. He rushed for 113 yards on only 9 carries on that dark, soggy day, and, in all, he had 326 of the Bears' 586 total yards.

Sayers's incredible day began on the Bears' second possession. On second-and-10, he caught a screen pass from quarterback Rudy Bukich and, helped by blocks from Mike Rabold, Mike Pyle, and Ron Bull, threaded his way through the 49ers' defense for an 80-yard touchdown.

After the 49ers scored with five minutes to play in the second quarter, Sayers struck a second time. He got blocks from Rabold and guard Jim Cadile and ran 21 yards for his second touchdown. With a minute to play in the first half, he ended another drive with a 7-yard sweep for his third.

Early in the third quarter Sayers tied the club record for touchdowns in a game with a 50-yard run. He took a pitchout from Bukich and broke into the clear on his first step.

Sayers set the club record on the Bears' next possession, diving into the end zone from inside the 49ers' 1-yard line for his fifth touchdown. Chicago led 47-20.

In the fourth quarter, Sayers caught a wobbly punt by the 49ers' Tommy Davis on Chicago's 15-yard line. Seeing no coverage directly in front of him, he took off up the middle, cut to his left, broke back against the flow of players, and burst into the clear, completing an 85-yard return for his sixth touchdown. It also was his twenty-first touchdown of the season, breaking Lenny Moore's NFL mark of 20. Sayers added another the following week against Minnesota and finished the season with a record 22 touchdowns.

After his sixth score, Halas took him out of the game. "I'd never have forgiven myself if I allowed him to stay in and he was seriously injured," Halas said. Sayers's replacement, Jon Arnett, scored the Bears' final touchdown.

December 9, 1967
Los Angeles 27, Green Bay 24

Travis Williams was a like flaming meteor streaking over the NFL's sky in 1967—brilliant, astounding, and before long, gone.

For the last part of the 1967 season, Williams, a kickoff returner, arguably was the most exciting player in the NFL. Williams, a rookie from Arizona State who was timed in 9.3 seconds for the 100-yard dash, returned a record 4 of 18 kickoffs for touchdowns that year. He averaged a record 41.1 yards per return.

Williams returned 2 kickoffs for touchdowns against the Cleveland Browns during a November game in 1967, but perhaps his most electrifying play was a 104-yard return against the Los Angeles Rams on December 9. It didn't help the Packers win—the Rams came from behind for an exciting 27-24 victory—but it was the centerpiece of a great game.

The Packers had all but secured their second consecutive Central Division title en route to their third NFL title in a row, while the Rams were battling the Baltimore Colts for first place in the NFL's Coastal Division. The Rams, coached by George Allen, knew that a loss would all but doom their title chances.

Bart Starr tossed a 30-yard touchdown pass to Carroll Dale that gave Green Bay a 7-0 lead. The Rams' Roman Gabriel ended a 73-yard drive by throwing a 16-yard touchdown pass to Jack Snow. Don Chandler's 32-yard field goal, set up by Willie Wood's interception, put Green Bay ahead again. But Gabriel and Snow teamed on an 11-yard touchdown pass and Bruce Gossett kicked a 23-yard field goal that gave the Rams a 17-10 advantage.

The defending-NFL-champion Packers were undaunted. Williams, nicknamed "The Roadrunner," waited under the goal posts for Gossett's ensuing kickoff. Gossett and the Rams feared Williams's return ability and had been squib-kicking the ball to keep him at bay. This time, though, Gossett got off a strong boot that soared 4 yards into the end zone. Instead of downing the ball, as most returners would have done, Williams caught it and sped upfield. In the next 10 seconds, just one Rams player touched him as he zoomed 104 yards for a touchdown and a 17-17 tie.

Because the game was televised nationally, that one play immortalized Williams. But it was not a decisive factor in this game.

Early in the fourth quarter, Gossett's 16-yard field goal, set up by Clarence Williams's interception, put the Rams ahead 20-17. Back came the Packers. Following the recovery of a fumble by Rams running back Dick Bass, they drove 43 yards, finishing the drive with Chuck Mercein's 4-yard run for a 24-20 lead.

The Packers defense again came to the fore and took the ball away on four downs, seemingly dooming Los Angeles' chances to win with 2:19 to play. But the Rams' great defensive line, led by Deacon Jones and Merlin Olsen, stuffed the Packers' vaunted offense, and Donnie Anderson had to punt from his 27-yard line with 54 seconds to play.

One of the hallmarks of a George Allen-coached team was its ability to make big plays on special teams, and this time linebacker Tony Guillory broke through Green Bay's punt protection and blocked Anderson's punt. The ball was scooped up by Claude Crabbe, who raced 20 yards to the Packers' 5-yard line. On second down, with 34 seconds to play, Gabriel tossed his third touchdown pass of the afternoon to end Bernie Casey, and Gossett added the extra point to cap a 27-24 victory.

November 17, 1968
Oakland 43, New York Jets 32

The Oakland Raiders and New York Jets were just 50 seconds from finishing their game on November 17, 1968. The Jets were ahead 32-29 following Jim Turner's 26-yard field goal 15 seconds earlier. The Raiders launched a drive from their 22-yard line with a 20-yard pass to Charlie Smith and a 10-yard facemask penalty that moved the ball to the Jets' 43.

The next thing millions of viewers saw were 60 seconds of commercials and a musical billboard leading into the movie *Heidi,* televised nationally on NBC. Someone pulled the plug on the football game and caused the biggest uproar in sports television history.

The huge telephone switchboard lit up at NBC's New York City headquarters, as well as at other stations in its network where viewers were equally irate.

A decision actually had been made seven minutes before the scheduled termination of the game on television to allow it to continue until completion. But NBC officials said it was confusion in their network communications system that caused the cutoff.

The game was not a long one by current standards. It started at 1:07 P.M. Pacific time, and ended at 4:10 P.M. At that time, though, many games were completed within two-and-a-half hours. But this game had 19 penalties and 31 incomplete passes, and each team used all of its time outs.

Oakland scored 2 touchdowns in those unseen 50 seconds to win the game 43-32. The ensuing outrage that all but consumed the network for more than 24 hours. Within 90 minutes of the snafu, NBC president Julius Goodman had issued a statement from his home telling the world that he, too, lamented the fact that he hadn't seen the game to its conclusion, but that "it was a forgivable error committed by humans who were concerned about children expecting to see Heidi."

What he and millions of others missed seeing was a 43-yard touchdown pass from Daryle Lamonica to Smith that put Oakland ahead 35-32 with 42 seconds to play, and the fumbled kickoff by the Jets' Earl Christy that the Raiders recovered in the end zone with 33 seconds to play for the final score.

While that was happening, incoming calls from irate viewers to the NBC switchboard in New York were so crushing that the board ceased to function. It wasn't until 22 minutes after *Heidi* began that the network ran a crawl on the bottom of the screen giving the final score. That only touched off another bombardment from still-irate fans.

Seven years later, the Raiders and Washington Redskins were tied 23-23 at the end of regulation time, with *Willy Wonka and the Chocolate Factory* being eagerly awaited by millions of children when the game ended. Not a hand went near the cutoff switch at NBC, and the game continued for almost 45 minutes before George Blanda's field goal finally gave the Raiders a 26-23 victory. The network televised the movie in its entirety in all but the Eastern time zone, where viewers missed the movie's first 45 minutes while the game was in progress.

September 21, 1970
Cleveland 31, New York Jets 21

ABC's *Monday Night Football* debuted on September 21, 1970, when the Cleveland Browns hosted the New York Jets at Cleveland Stadium.

The Browns defeated the Joe Namath-led Jets 31-21, and fall Monday nights in America have not been the same since.

This wasn't the first time that NFL football was televised on Monday night. Commissioner Pete Rozelle had convinced CBS to televise a Dallas Cowboys-New York Giants game in 1968, and the Los Angeles Rams and St. Louis Cardinals also played on a Monday night in 1969. But neither CBS nor NBC, which was going to be the prime carrier for AFC games in the NFL's realigned structure, were interested in changing their profitable entertainment format on one of the biggest viewing nights of the week.

ABC, perennially the number-three network and scrambling to improve its position, was receptive. Roone Arledge, head of the network's sports division, was an imaginative and progressive thinker. He knew the value of promotion and was willing to showcase NFL football unlike anything the other networks had ever done.

He also was willing to devote twice as many technical resources as the other networks used for their Sunday coverage—not that difficult because he could concentrate on one game while they had to broadcast five or six—so he could present a product previously seen only in playoffs and Super Bowls.

For the first year, Arledge linked play-by-play announcer Keith Jackson with Howard Cosell and former Cowboys quarterback Don Meredith. Frank Gifford replaced Jackson after the first year, but the Cosell-Meredith tandem was a winning formula. Cosell maintained his reputation for being overbearing. He soon became the man that most viewers loved to hate. Some saloons even ran promotions in which the winner could throw a brick through a set while Cosell was on camera.

Meredith, on the other hand, was pure country from his Texas roots to his Texas boots. He was an unknown in broadcasting when he got the job, but he possessed a sense of humor that played off the pompous Cosell. He was beloved for his uncanny ability to puncture Cosell's pretensions. Their by-play became as popular as the game on the field.

The first game got the series off to a rousing start. Cleveland Stadium was jammed with more than 85,000 fans. Namath put on a good show, completing 18 of 29 passes for 284 yards.

The Browns took a 14-0 lead in the first quarter on Bill Nelsen's touchdown pass to Gary Collins and Bo Scott's 2-yard plunge, and led 14-7 at the half. Cleveland's Homer Jones returned the second-half kickoff 94 yards for a touchdown before Emerson Boozer's second touchdown run of the game pulled the Jets within 21-14 in the third quarter. It was 24-14 until Namath's 33-yard touchdown pass to George Sauer trimmed New York's deficit to 3 points late in the game. With two minutes to play, the Jets forced Cleveland to punt, but safety Mike Battle misjudged the ball. Instead of catching it at the Jets' 30-yard line, he allowed it to roll dead at the 4 with 90 seconds to play. Namath tried to pass the Jets downfield, but linebacker Bill Andrews intercepted a pass and returned it 25 yards for the clinching score.

November 8, 1970
New Orleans 19, Detroit 17

Until November 8, 1970, Bert Rechichar of the Baltimore Colts held the record for kicking the NFL's longest field goal—56 yards on September 27, 1953, against the Chicago Bears.

But along came stub-toed kicker Tom Dempsey, who had bounced around pro football's fringes for a couple of years, and he boomed a field goal 63 yards for the New Orleans Saints to defeat the Detroit Lions 19-17 on the final play of the game.

Dempsey was a straight-on kicker rather than the side-wheeling soccer-style kickers who were just beginning to infiltrate pro football. In 1966, when Garo Yepremian, a soccer-style kicker who had come from Cyprus, played with Detroit, he side-wheeled a winning kick against Norm Van Brocklin's Minnesota Vikings. The fiery Dutchman was asked what should be done against this very unorthodox style of kicking.

"Tighten the immigration laws," Van Brocklin snapped.

In a sense, Dempsey's kick really was the last hurrah for the conventional-style kickers, though even he was controversial at the time because of the special shoe that he wore. Dempsey was born without toes on his right foot, and, to accommodate his stump-like foot while kicking, he wore a heavy, square-toed shoe.

Detroit had taken a 17-16 lead with 18 seconds left after a 17-play, 86-yard drive capped by Errol Mann's 18-yard field goal. Al Dodd returned the ensuing kickoff 14 yards to the Saints' 28-yard line. There were just 8 seconds to play, and quarterback Bill Kilmer passed 17 yards to Dodd, who got out of bounds with just 2 seconds remaining.

"I looked at Tom," said J.D. Roberts, who was making his debut as head coach that day after relieving Tom Fears. " 'Give it your best shot,' I told him, and all he did was nod and say, 'I'm ready, Coach.' "

Joe Scarpati was the holder and he trotted onto the field with Dempsey, who had already kicked 3 field goals in the game. "Just hold them a little longer than usual," Scarpati pleaded with the kicking team's line.

"Then when we were setting up, I told Tom that I was back a yard deeper than usual so that he would have an instant longer to get into the kick and not worry about the rush," Scarpati said.

Dempsey said later that he was sure he could kick the ball 63 yards, but he wasn't certain whether he could kick it straight. "Naturally, I felt the pressure," Dempsey said. "But all I was thinking about was kicking it as hard as I could. I wanted to get it up because I'd had a line drive blocked earlier."

Dempsey never saw the ball go between the uprights because he lost track of the kick. He saw the officials raise their arms, signaling it was good. No one matched the distance of Dempsey's kick for almost three decades until Denver's Jason Elam tied the mark in 1998.

November 8, 1970
Oakland 23, Cleveland 20

The same day that Tom Dempsey kicked his record-setting 63-yard field goal, Oakland's 43-year-old George Blanda was in the midst of a magical five-game streak in which he produced a victory or a tie either from his kicking or his play at quarterback. On November 8, his 52-yard field goal gave the Raiders a 23-20 victory over the Cleveland Browns.

Two weeks before, Blanda relieved Daryle Lamonica at quarterback with the score tied 7-7 against the Pittsburgh Steelers, and went on to engineer a 31-14 victory. A week later against the Raiders' archrivals, the Kansas City Chiefs, Lamonica was back at quarterback, but, in the final seconds of the game, Blanda kicked a 48-yard field goal with 3 seconds to play for a 17-14 victory.

Against the Browns, he again relieved an injured Lamonica early in the fourth quarter with Oakland trailing 17-13. Cleveland's Don Cockroft kicked a field goal to increase the Browns' lead to 7 points with 4:10 left in the game.

Oakland began its next drive from its 30-yard line, and Blanda completed a 22-yard pass to Warren Wells. Three plays later, on fourth-and-16 with 1:55 to play, he scrambled and tossed a 17-yard pass to Fred Biletnikoff for a first down. From Cleveland's 17-yard line, he threw a low strike to Wells in the end zone, then kicked the extra point to tie the score at 17-17. There still was 1:34 to play.

After the kickoff, the Raiders' Kent McCloughan intercepted Bill Nelsen's pass for tight end Milt Morin and returned it to Cleveland's 49-yard line with 34 seconds left. On third-and-20, Blanda threw an incomplete pass. But the Raiders were whistled for an illegal procedure penalty, and, astonishingly, the Browns accepted it. So instead of facing a fourth-and-20 at Cleveland's 49-yard line, the Oakland Raiders had a third-and-25 at its 46-yard line.

"They weren't going to let us throw to get out of bounds," Blanda explained later, "but Hewritt [Dixon] kept saying, 'Give it to me, give it to me, I can get out.'" So Blanda did, hitting him with a 9-yard pass. Dixon got out of bounds with 7 seconds to play.

All Blanda could do at that point was try a 52-yard field goal. "We weren't on the temporary sod they had laid over the infield, so I had a good spot," Blanda said. His kick was good, giving Oakland a 20-17 victory.

Blanda's odyssey wasn't finished. The following week, he came off the bench with Oakland trailing the Denver Broncos 19-17. In a minute-and-a-half, he led a drive that ended with him throwing the winning touchdown pass to Biletnikoff. A week after that, he finished his astounding run when, with 7 seconds to play, he kicked a 19-yard field goal that gave Oakland a 20-17 victory over the San Diego Chargers.

"Anybody could have kicked that field goal," Blanda said later. "It kind of embarrassed me that everyone made such a fuss about it. Pressure? Nah. By then the pressure was on the other team."

September 24, 1972
New York Jets 44, Baltimore 34

The tremors that shook the NFL following the New York Jets' astounding victory over the Baltimore Colts in Super Bowl III still were reverberating four years later, at least in Baltimore.

The loss was humiliating to the proud franchise that had sparked the upward surge of NFL football with its overtime victory over the New York Giants in the 1958 NFL Championship Game. Nothing could be done to reverse the result of Super Bowl III, but every game that the Colts played against the Jets became a crusade of sorts.

Baltimore beat the Jets the first four times the teams played after Super Bowl III. But the Jets broke their skid with a 44-34 victory at Baltimore's Memorial Stadium on September 24, 1972.

Namath never was better as he passed for a whopping 496 yards and 6 touchdown passes on just 15 completions in 28 attempts. Unitas completed 26 passes for 376 yards and 2 touchdowns.

Big numbers abounded:

- Jets end Rich Caster caught 6 passes for 204 yards and 3 touchdowns;
- New York's other end, Ed Bell, caught 7 passes for 197 yards and a 65-yard touchdown pass in the first quarter;
- Baltimore's Don McCauley returned a kickoff 93 yards for a touchdown and also scored on a 1-yard run;
- Baltimore running back Tom Matte rushed for 42 yards on 9 carries and had 69 yards on 9 receptions, including an 8-yard touchdown catch;
- Colts flanker Sam Havrilak caught 4 passes for 115 yards, including a 40-yard touchdown;
- Unitas and Namath combined for 872 yards passing, an NFL record.

After Bell's touchdown gave the Jets a 6-0 lead, the Colts rolled off 13 points, including Unitas's touchdown pass to Havrilak. Starting with McCauley's kickoff return, the teams scored 21 points within a span of 89 seconds. McCauley's return quickly was matched by 2 touchdown passes from Namath, 28 yards to Don Maynard and 10 yards to Caster. The Jets added a field goal by Bobby Howfield for a 10-point lead late in the third quarter, and swapped scores with Baltimore the rest of the game to preserve their victory.

"It was a fun day," Namath said. "Baltimore played a zone defense, and all I did was to send one or two receivers into one area and another one deep underneath the zone. That underneath man always seemed to be open."

December 16, 1973
Buffalo 34, New York Jets 14

During the spring of 1973, O.J. Simpson called his best friend and roommate on the Buffalo Bills, guard Reggie McKenzie, and said, "I'm going after 1,700 yards this year." "Make it 2,000," McKenzie told him.

Simpson gained 2,003 yards, the first time any NFL running back had broken what once was seen as an impenetrable barrier.

It happened in the final game of the 1973 season on the frozen turf at Shea Stadium, then the home of the Jets. Simpson broke two barriers during the Bills' 34-14 victory—Jim Brown's 10-year-old NFL rushing mark of 1,863 yards, which he surpassed on his eighth carry of the game, and the 2,000 mark, which he reached on a 7-yard run on his thirty-fourth and final carry.

Leading him on those two record-setting plays was McKenzie, the bellwether of the Bills' offensive line, which had been dubbed "The Electric Company" by Bills public relations director L. Budd Thalman because "it turned on the Juice."

"We came out on the field for our first series thinking about the record," Bills quarterback Joe Ferguson said. "I think all of us wanted to get it over with, then settle down to the business of winning the game."

On the Bills' first series, Simpson carried the ball 7 times for 57 yards, helped by a 30-yard run, and he was just 4 yards short of Brown's record. That series ended with Jim Braxton barging through the Jets' defense for a touchdown. On the first play of the Bills' next possession,

Simpson set the single-season record. In the press box everyone, including the Bills' coaches, began keeping a play-by-play log of Simpson's yards. At the half, he had 108 yards, and after three quarters he had 147.

"They kept phoning downstairs from the press box so we knew just how much he needed," McKenzie said.

Simpson rattled off 8 yards, then a big gain of 22 yards. He added 9 yards, then 5, and suddenly he was at 1,996. With six-and-a-half minutes left, Simpson burst through another hole opened by McKenzie and gained 7 yards to raise his season total to 2,003.

November 28, 1974
Dallas 24, Washington 23

In the mid-seventies, the Dallas Cowboys were beginning to enthrall America with their last-minute victories. The chief perpetrator of these hair-breadth victories was quarterback Roger Staubach. But the character and makeup of the Cowboys was such that the entire team seemed capable of making the impossible at least probable—even a one-game rookie quarterback named Clint Longley.

That was the case on Thanksgiving Day, 1974, when Staubach was knocked from a game against the Washington Redskins in the third quarter. Dallas coach Tom Landry was forced to use Longley, a rookie from Abilene Christian who had been obtained in a trade with the Cincinnati Bengals. Dallas was desperate for quarterback help because they had traded away veteran Craig Morton to the Giants.

Staubach hadn't fared well against the Redskins' usually tenacious defense, and, when he was tackled hard by linebacker Dave Robinson midway through the third quarter, Longley entered the game. No one expected a 22-year-old rookie to turn in one of the great relief appearances in NFL history. But Longley drove Dallas to 3 touchdown passes, the final one coming with 28 seconds to play, to give Dallas a 24-23 victory.

Dallas trailed 16-3 when Longley entered the game. His first touchdown pass was for 35 yards to tight end Billy Joe DuPree, closing the Redskins' lead to 16-10. On Dallas's next possession, Longley drove the Cowboys to another touchdown, a 1-yard run by Walt Garrison. Dallas led 17-16.

Early in the fourth quarter, Washington's Duane Thomas swept left end for 19 yards and a touchdown that gave the Redskins a 23-17 lead. Neither team did much until, with 1:45 to play, Dallas got the ball for the last time. On fourth down, and needing 5 yards for a first down, Longley passed for 6 yards to flanker Bob Hayes at midfield. His next pass was incomplete but on second down, he found Pearson clear along the left sideline and hit him in stride. Pearson caught the ball and raced into the end zone to complete a 50-yard touchdown pass. Effren Herrera kicked the extra point, and Dallas won the game 24-23.

Landry was as astonished as everyone else. "Football is an incredible game," he said. "This is what makes it so unbelievable. Anything can happen in football."

November 20, 1977
Chicago 10, Minnesota 7

In 1977, Walter Payton was about 13,400 yards from becoming the NFL's all-time leading rusher when he faced the Minnesota Vikings in a late-season game.

Always a precise-thinking man, Payton hadn't even begun thinking about breaking Jim Brown's long-standing rushing mark of 12,312 yards. But he smashed O.J. Simpson's single-game record of 273 yards that was set the previous season with a still-standing record of 275 yards in Chicago's 10-7 victory over the Vikings.

It wasn't easy against the team that had reached Super Bowl XI the previous January, and the task was made that much harder because Payton had been burdened by a terrible case of the flu throughout the week of the game. He said afterward, "I wondered whether I could put on a Walter Payton-type performance when I left the dressing room."

Payton already had gained 1,404 yards on 239 carries that season, his third in the NFL. He didn't seem built for heavy duty work, but that afternoon he carried the ball 40 times. He accepted a lot of punishment, but he doled out as much as he took because he rarely evaded a tackler. He took them on with a massive pair of legs that were made stronger by a brutal routine of running up and down a railroad embankment near his Mississippi home every day during the offseason.

He scored the Bears' only touchdown on a 1-yard run in the second quarter en route to rolling up 144 yards on 26 first-half carries. Late in the game, he tore off a 58-yard run down the right side to reach a total of 268 yards, just 5 short of Simpson's record. He got 3 on his next carry, and then followed with a 4-yard run that broke the record.

"Don't get me wrong," he said after the game in which he gained 275 of the Bears' 343 yards, "but the record really doesn't mean that much right now. Maybe later, maybe in three or four years, or after I'm out of the game. All I can say is that this was a day when everything went right and we got a big win. The holes were there and I just ran."

September 10, 1978
Oakland 21, San Diego 20

In 1978, the following NFL rules were in effect: 1) Rule 8, Section 4, Article 2—It covered forward and backward passes and said: "If a runner intentionally fumbles forward, it is a forward pass." 2) Rule 12, Section 2, Article 17, Subsection a—"A player may not bat or punch a loose ball [in the field of play] toward opponent's goal line."

Both were applicable on September 10, 1978, when the Oakland Raiders rallied to beat the San Diego Chargers 21-20 in the final seconds at San Diego.

With just 10 seconds to play and the Chargers leading 20-14, Oakland had the ball at San Diego's 14-yard line. On fourth down, quarterback Ken Stabler dropped back to pass and a blitzing Chargers linebacker, Woody Lowe, was all over him. Stabler lost the ball, and it rolled toward San Diego's end zone, where Pete Banaszak tried to scoop it up. Banaszak botched his attempt and propelled the ball closer to the goal line, where it found the foot of tight end Dave Casper and caromed into the end zone. Casper fell on it, and the officials ruled the play a touchdown.

But that was far from the end of the story.

Any reasonable viewing of the play then—and the officials on the scene did not have replay—made it almost impossible to discern whether Stabler had intentionally, as stipulated by the rule, or unintentionally, which is not mentioned, fumbled the ball toward the end zone. Neither could it be discerned if Banaszak's attempt to pick it up was botched by his being off-balance and clumsily trying to scoop it up on the run, further pushing it along, nor whether the ball bounced off Casper's foot of its own momentum and into the end zone.

Finally, by the players' own admission, here is what really happened:

Stabler said as he was going down, he shoveled the ball forward in a motion that resembled a fumble. Banaszak, seeing he would have no chance to advance the ball because he was surrounded by Chargers' defenders, deliberately batted it toward the goal line, and Casper deliberately nudged the ball into the end zone with his foot where he fell on it for the touchdown.

When the NFL Competition Committee met the following year, it upheld the rules against illegally batting a ball and said that an intentional fumble is to be treated as a forward pass; hence, it is incomplete if it hits the ground without first being caught. Each of those circumstances should have negated the disputed touchdown a year earlier if the intentions of the participants had then been known.

Then the committee added a supplemental note under Rule 8, Section 4, Article 2: "After the two-minute warning, on any fumble that occurs during a down (including a PAT), the fumbled ball may only be advanced by the offensive player who fumbled the ball, or by any member of the defensive team." It was destined to be known forever after as the Raiders' fumble rule.

November 20, 1978
Houston 35, Miami 30

In 1977, Earl Campbell won the Heisman Trophy and All-America honors at the University of Texas. Five months later, the Houston Oilers made him the first player selected in the 1978 draft.

Campbell immediately was dubbed "The Franchise." Skeptics abounded, but, as his rookie season unfolded, only the most stubborn refused to become believers. Then came a Monday night in November when he unleashed his great talent to its fullest and steam rollered over the Miami Dolphins. After he had scored 4 touchdowns and gained 199 yards on 28 carries in Houston's 35-30 victory, those skeptics became believers because Campbell proved that he was even better than advertised.

Those were exciting times in Houston. The Oilers were flying high, and the Astrodome was packed for every game, with more than 56,000 fans happily waving their blue-and-white pompoms and singing their fight song, *Luv Ya Blue.* For added spice, their coach, O.A. (Bum) Phillips was pure country, from the top of his 10-gallon cowboy hat to the tips of his snakeskin boots. His Texas drawl and an almost endless litany of homey sayings and common-sense philosophy earned him celebrity status.

But Phillips was also a down-to-earth coach, and he knew a lethal weapon when he saw one. He used Campbell to the maximum, and the rookie was the second-leading NFL rusher when he faced the Dolphins, behind only Delvin Williams of Miami. Moreover, this shootout between the leading runners was on ABC's *Monday Night Football.*

Before the game, Oilers center Carl Mauck told Campbell, "We need you to score four touchdowns to win tonight. You do that, and the defense promises to hold Williams under a hundred yards." In the end, Campbell did his part, and the Oilers' defense reciprocated, holding Williams to 73 yards.

Miami grabbed a 7-0 lead when quarterback Bob Griese, who completed 23 of 33 passes for 349 yards, threw the first of 2 touchdown passes to Nat Moore. Campbell's 1-yard touchdown tied the score, and the teams were tied at the half 14-14.

To that point, Miami's defense had done a good job on Campbell, holding him to only 44 yards, but Campbell scored his second touchdown early in the third quarter on a 6-yard run. Miami again tied the score, then went ahead when defensive end A.J. Duhe tackled Oilers quarterback Dan Pastorini in the end zone for a safety. Miami got no points after getting the ball on a free kick, and that was a signal for Campbell to rev up his game.

Houston launched an 80-yard scoring drive on which Campbell tore off 6- and 8-yard runs to convert third downs and keep it going. He ended the march with a 12-yard touchdown run, first cutting inside, then dipping outside like a 170-pound scatback, not a 235-pound fullback.

That gave Houston the lead for good, but Campbell wasn't finished. With Miami trailing by only 5 points, Campbell carried 3 times for a first down at Houston's 19-yard line, giving him 27 rushing attempts for the game. The next play was a sweep to the right, with the option for him to cut up field whenever he saw an opening. For an instant, Miami safety Tim Foley had him lined up for a loss, but Campbell made a sudden turn downfield and got a key block from tackle Greg Sampson. Showing no sign of fatigue after so much work, he flashed into afterburner speed and ran away from the defense to complete an 81-yard touchdown run and a memorable night's work.

December 16, 1979
Dallas 35, Washington 34

With Roger Staubach at quarterback, Dallas never was out of a game: Staubach engineered 23 fourth-quarter comeback victories, 14 of them in the final two minutes or in overtime.

He saved one of his most electrifying performances for his final regular-season game. A division title and playoff berth were at stake when Dallas played its most hated rival, the Washington Redskins. Washington jumped to a 17-0 lead in the second quarter, but Dallas recovered and scored 3 touchdowns for a 21-17 lead as the fourth quarter began.

In the next 11 minutes, the Redskins ran off 17 straight points, including a 66-yard touchdown run by John Riggins, and seemingly had the game locked away 34-21.

But Dallas recovered Clarence Harmon's fumble, and, three plays later, Staubach passed 26 yards to Ron Springs for a touchdown to cut the deficit to 34-28. The Cowboys' defense then shut down Washington, helped by Larry Cole's tackle of Riggins on third-and-1, to force a punt with 1:46 to play.

Dallas got the ball at its 25-yard line, and Staubach worked another of his miracles. Five plays later, with less than a minute to play, he had the Cowboys at Washington's 8-yard line. With 50 seconds to play, he threw the ball in the end zone to wide receiver Tony Hill, but Redskins defensive back Ray Waddy broke up the play.

It was close enough for coach Tom Landry to order Staubach to try the same play again, but this time Hill was picked up by the Redskins' best defender, Lemar Parrish. Staubach rifled the ball to Hill just inside the corner of the end zone for the winning touchdown. There were 39 seconds left.

"Roger just knew he could win in that type of situation," Landry said. "There was something in him that brought out his best when everything seems hopeless."

December 7, 1980
San Francisco 38, New Orleans 35 (Overtime)

One of the worst blights on the proud heritage of the San Francisco 49ers was blowing a 27-7 third-quarter lead against the Detroit Lions in a 1957 playoff game and eventually losing the game and a chance to play for their first NFL championship. It is said the 49ers spent the halftime celebrating a victory not yet won, and their premature hootings were overheard by the furious Lions who were camped next door.

Some 15 years later, another San Francisco team held a 28-13 lead against the Dallas Cowboys with just 15 minutes to play in another playoff game. The 49ers blew that lead, too, and lost 30-28.

On the fourteenth weekend of the 1980 season, it was the 49ers who trailed the winless New Orleans Saints 35-7 at halftime. The 49ers scored 4 consecutive touchdowns in the second half and forced the game into overtime. Then they won it 38-35 on Ray Wersching's 36-yard field goal. It was the greatest regular-season comeback in NFL history.

Such a recovery seemed impossible in the first half because the Saints quarterback, Archie Manning, was on fire. He completed 14 of 22 passes for 248 yards and 3 touchdowns, and New Orleans outgained the 49ers 324-21. The Saints held a 21-0 lead even before the 49ers made a first down as Manning tossed a pair of touchdown passes and Jack Holmes scored on a 1-yard run. San Francisco scored on Freddie Solomon's 57-yard punt return for a touchdown, but the Saints then scored twice more in the first half, on Holmes' second touchdown run and Ike Harris's second touchdown catch from Manning.

In the 49ers' locker room, coach Bill Walsh didn't exhort his team to go out and stage a rally. Rather, he urged them to make a respectable showing. Only defensive tackle Archie Reese stood up and told his teammates there still was a chance to win.

The 49ers roared back. Four minutes into the second half, second-year quarterback Joe Montana, who had made comebacks part of his life with Notre Dame's football team, dove into the end zone to end an 88-yard drive. Then he threw a 71-yard touchdown pass to Dwight Clark, and the 49ers trailed 35-21.

The Saints wasted three chances to increase their lead in the third quarter, but San Francisco cooled off until Montana drove his team 83 yards in 14 plays, finishing with a 14-yard touchdown pass to Solomon in the fourth quarter. That cut the deficit to just 7 points. On their next possession, which began with 5:12 to play, the 49ers used just three minutes and 22 seconds to roll 78 yards and tie the score on Lenvil Elliott's 7-yard run. Elliott was the star of this comeback because he accounted for 91 of the 49ers' 161 yards in their two fourth-quarter drives.

In overtime, New Orleans took possession and, after one first down, punted to the 49ers. San Francisco never relinquished the ball, though a roughing penalty against Saints defensive lineman Steve Parker nullified a third-down stop that would have forced a punt. The drive ended eight plays later on Wersching's field goal with eight minutes gone in the overtime. It was the fourth time in four years that Wersching had beaten the Saints with a field goal, and three of them had come on the final play of the game.

October 2, 1983
Washington 37, Los Angeles Raiders 35

It is rare during any season that two teams preview a Super Bowl battle, but, in the fifth game of the 1983 season, the Washington Redskins and Los Angeles Raiders provided a look ahead to Super Bowl XVIII.

The Super Bowl was a blowout as the Raiders dominated the game from start to finish and won easily 38-9, but the regular-season game was difficult to top because big plays were the order of the day. There was a record-tying 99-yard touchdown pass from Raiders quarterback Jim Plunkett to Cliff Branch—only the fifth 99-yard score in NFL history—a 97-yard punt return by Los Angeles's Greg Pruitt, and a winning touchdown pass from Redskins quarterback Joe Theismann to Joe Washington with just 33 seconds to play.

The early October clash featured big leads by both teams, and then big comebacks by each of them. For example, Washington led 17-7 at halftime and 20-7 early in the third quarter. Theismann, who completed 23 of 39 passes for a career-high 417 yards and 3 touchdowns, had thrown a 5-yard touchdown pass to Washington after John Riggins ran 2 yards for a touchdown and Mark Moseley kicked a pair of field goals. Theismann paid a price, however, because the Raiders' defense sacked him 6 times and recovered 1 fumble.

Early in the third quarter, Plunkett caught fire. He threw

3 touchdown passes—35 and 22 yards to Calvin Muhammad, and a 2-yard toss to tight end Todd Christensen that gave the Raiders a 28-17 lead early in the fourth quarter. (Plunkett finished the day with 16 completions in 29 attempts for 372 yards, but the Redskins' defense sacked him 5 times, intercepted him 4 times, and forced 2 fumbles.)

Los Angeles upped its advantage to 35-17 on Pruitt's 97-yard punt return midway through the fourth quarter, but Washington, which finished that season as the NFL's winningest team, scored the game's final 17 points.

Theismann passed to Charlie Brown for an 11-yard touchdown and Moseley's third field goal cut the Raiders' lead to 5 points with less than four minutes to play. On the Redskins' final possession, Joe Washington made a leaping catch of Theismann's 6-yard pass for the winning touchdown.

December 2, 1985
Miami 38, Chicago 24

Don Shula won more games than any other coach in NFL history—328 in the regular season and 19 in the postseason—but there are 17 that please him the most. They are the victories which his Miami Dolphins tallied in 1972, the year they became the first team in NFL history to finish with a perfect record.

That was on Shula's mind on December 2, 1985, when his Dolphins played the unbeaten Chicago Bears. The Bears were 12-0 at the time. Keeping the record for themselves became a crusade for the Dolphins on that Monday night.

An entire nation tuned in to watch the battle. Chicago lived by a rough-and-tumble defense reminiscent of its glory days as Monsters of the Midway. The Bears featured the 46 Defense. It had eight men crowding the line of scrimmage, and it was run by brash assistant coach Buddy Ryan. Its heart and soul was middle linebacker Mike Singletary, but its media star was 350-pound defensive tackle William (Refrigerator) Perry.

Perry had wowed the nation when he also was turned loose as a lead blocker in goal-line situations. He was even allowed to crash into the end zone on one play and to catch a touchdown pass on another. Even teammate Walter Payton, en route to becoming the NFL's all-time leading rusher, was overshadowed by Perry's fame, to say nothing of his girth.

The pregame hype nearly equaled that of a Super Bowl, but lost in all the talk was the fact that Miami was considered the best team in the AFC and had feasted on Monday night competition—16 victories in the previous 19 games. Conversely, the Bears were winless in nine previous Monday night games away from Soldier Field.

The game was played before a roaring crowd of more than 75,000 at the Orange Bowl, which became all the more frenzied when the Dolphins scored on their first five possessions en route to a 38-24 victory that wasn't as close as the final score indicates.

The Bears featured the NFL's number-one scoring offense and the stingiest defense. Chicago had shut out its previous two opponents and hadn't allowed a touchdown in 13 quarters, but four minutes into the game, Dolphins quarterback Dan Marino threw a 33-yard touchdown pass to Nat Moore for a 7-0 lead. The Bears matched that a few minutes later on Steve Fuller's quarterback sneak for a touchdown. The Dolphins took the lead for good before the end of the first quarter on Fuad Reveiz's 47-yard field goal.

Ron Davenport ran for a touchdown early in the the second quarter for a 17-7 lead, and Miami scored 2 more touchdowns within 40 seconds late in the quarter to break open the game. Davenport's second rushing touchdown and Marino's second touchdown pass to Moore gave the Dolphins a 31-10 advantage at halftime.

The statistical battle overwhelmingly favored the losing Bears—they led in first downs 23-17 and in total yards 343-335. Payton put in a gallant effort with 121 yards on 23 carries. It was a record-setting eighth consecutive game in which he gained more than 100 yards. But the Dolphins' defense, vastly underrated in relation to that of its rival, intercepted 3 passes, sacked Bears quarterbacks 6 times, and recovered a fumble.

The loss was the only blemish on Chicago's record that year. The Bears went on to win the NFL championship with a rousing 46-10 victory over the New England Patriots in Super Bowl XX. Ironically, the Patriots spoiled a rematch between Chicago and Miami by upsetting the Dolphins in the AFC title game. But the Dolphins still had one consolation—they remain the only franchise in NFL history to have completed a perfect season.

September 21, 1986
New York Jets 51, Miami 45 (Overtime)

The most important person at Giants Stadium on September 21, 1986, may have been the scorekeeper. Final score: New York Jets 51, Miami Dolphins 45. The total of 96 points came on 13 touchdowns and 2 field goals during four full quarters and two minutes and 35 seconds of overtime.

After a quiet first quarter in which the Dolphins led 7-3, the teams erupted for 42 points in the second quarter. The Jets took a 17-7 lead on 2 touchdown runs by Johnny Hector; Miami regained the lead at 21-17 when Dan Marino threw 2 of his 6 touchdown passes that day. New York came back and scored 14 points on bombs of 65 and 50 yards from Ken O'Brien to Wesley Walker and held a 31-21 halftime lead.

The Dolphins opened the second half with a 17-point burst on a pair of touchdown passes by Marino—one of 46 yards to Mark Duper—and Fuad Reveiz's 44-yard field goal to regain the lead at 38-31.

After the Jets tied the score 38-38, Walker, who caught 6 balls that day for 194 yards and a club-record 4 touchdowns, fumbled and lost the ball after making a catch. That set up Marino's 4-yard touchdown pass to Mark Clayton, who caught 8 of Marino's 29 completions for 174 yards.

Clayton's touchdown gave Miami a 45-38 lead with three minutes to play, but the Jets were undaunted. O'Brien, who completed 29 of 43 passes for 479 yards, the second best single-game total in Jets' history, drove his team 80 yards in 7 plays and teamed with Walker on a 21-yard touchdown pass on the final play of regulation to force the game into overtime.

"I was down on myself for fumbling the ball that had set up Miami's last touchdown," Walker said. "I thought I lost the game for the team. I was just grateful I was given the opportunity to make it up."

Walker's heroics didn't end there. The Jets won the coin toss in overtime, and it took O'Brien just 5 plays to drive his team 78 yards for the winning touchdown—a 43-yard pass to Walker down the right sideline, over Dolphins safety Bud Brown.

When all the numbers finally were sorted out, the Dolphins and Jets had set an NFL record by accumulating a total of 884 net passing yards.

September 20, 1987
San Francisco 27, Cincinnati 26

There is a bewitching quality about the Cincinnati-San Francisco rivalry.

It always has seemed to manifest itself with hair-breadth finishes, usually in favor of the 49ers. Certainly, that was the case in Super Bowl XXIII, when the 49ers defeated the Bengals in the game's final minute. But the most outlandish example probably occurred in the second game of the 1987 season.

The Bengals seemed to have locked up a 26-20 victory with less than a minute to play, only to see the game slip away in a 27-26 loss in an almost surrealistic series of events in the final seconds at Riverfront Stadium.

The Bengals held a 20-7 halftime lead, but the 49ers, led by quarterback Joe Montana, tied the score in the third quarter. Two field goals by Jim Breech gave Cincinnati a 6-point lead, and the Bengals then turned aside the 49ers. Cincinnati had the ball and a 26-20 lead at its 45-yard line with 54 seconds to play.

Cincinnati quarterback Boomer Esiason took a 2-yard loss on first down, and the 49ers stopped the clock with 49 seconds to play. Esiason again knelt down on second play for a 3-yard loss, and the 49ers used their last time out with 45 seconds to play. Esiason lost 5 yards on third down, giving the Bengals a fourth-and-20 at their 35-yard line.

The 49ers couldn't stop the clock, and the Bengals let the play clock run down, content to take a 5-yard penalty. Now faced with fourth-and 25 with just 6 seconds to play, Bengals coach Sam Wyche disdained a punt and chose instead to let running back James Brooks try a sweep to eat up the final seconds.

But before Brooks had gotten started, San Francisco defensive lineman Kevin Fagen burst through the line and tackled him at the 25-yard line with two seconds still to play.

Montana had one last shot, and he played his ace, wide receiver Jerry Rice. Montana lined up three wide receivers on the left side and put Rice by himself on the right side. Rice ran into the end zone shadowed by rookie cornerback Eric Thomas, who earlier had been beaten for touchdowns by Rice and Mike Wilson. Rice took Thomas deep into the end zone, then freed himself of coverage by hooking back toward Montana. He easily caught the ball for the tying touchdown. Ray Wersching's extra point gave the 49ers an improbable 27-26 victory.

Rice was confused by the coverage he received. "He [Thomas] was covering me all by himself," Rice said. "At least, you'd expect them to give him some help."

"I expected help," Thomas said. "Rice ran, stopped, the ball was in the air. It didn't matter at that point."

"I knew the pass was there," Montana said. "It's tough to make a catch in that situation. The receiver has to outjump anyone around him but what's really amazing is that we got a chance to get a play like that off."

"I miscalculated two seconds," said Bengals coach Sam Wyche, who had coached under 49ers coach Bill Walsh at San Francisco. "I made a miscalculation that cost us the game. I don't blame anyone but me. This is a game of inches and seconds and that's what it was today. We decided to pitch to Brooks on our last play, figuring it would eat up the last few seconds. We had thought about a punt and thought about taking a safety but we were afraid of something going wrong with either one."

November 25, 1993
Miami 16, Dallas 14

Though Yogi Berra was a baseball player, his sage advice that "it's never over 'till it's over" is applicable for any sport.

Take Miami versus Dallas on Thanksgiving Day, 1993, at rainy, sleety, snowy, blustery Texas Stadium, where the Dallas Cowboys held a 14-13 lead, thanks to a pair of second-quarter touchdowns by Kevin Williams, the second a 64-yard punt return with 42 seconds to play in the first half.

The Cowboys missed a chance to increase their lead late in the fourth quarter when Eddie Murray missed a field goal. Miami quarterback Steve DeBerg came back with a wonderfully executed drive to set up Pete Stoyanovich's 41-yard field-goal attempt to win the game with just a few seconds to play.

But the kick was tipped, and the ball spun to the ground, rolling crazily over a slick, snow-covered field toward the Dallas end zone. Players from both teams stayed away from the ball.

Except for Cowboys defensive lineman Leon Lett.

This was the same Leon Lett who had picked up a Buffalo Bills fumble in Super Bowl XXVII, and romped toward the Bills' end zone. At the 10-yard line, he slowed to begin his touchdown celebration, and this enabled determined Bills wide receiver Don Beebe to catch up to him at the 1-yard line and knock the ball loose so that it rolled harmlessly through the end zone for a touchback.

This time, Lett had a well-intentioned, but ill-advised, notion of jumping on the careening football to secure it for the Cowboys. Instead, he slid on the slick turf, grazed the ball and sent it skittering toward the goal line. Jeff Dellenbach of Miami fell on it at the 2-yard line.

By rule, a blocked field goal by the defensive team (Dallas) at the line of scrimmage is ignored, but if the ball is touched down field by a member of the defense, then it is a live ball and the kicking team can keep possession upon recovery. The ball is dead at the spot of possession and cannot be advanced.

Stoyanovich then kicked a 20-yard field goal as time expired, and Miami won 16-14.

"The play by Lett was a mistake and we all make 'em," stunned Dallas coach Jimmy Johnson said. "It's part of the game . . . and it so happened that it came at the end of a game, and it will be remembered as the one that cost us the game."

October 17, 1994
Kansas City 31, Denver 28

At first the picture was a bit off-center when this Monday night shootout began. Quarterback Joe Montana's Kansas City Chiefs were stuck in a point drought early in the 1994 season—they hadn't scored a touchdown in more than 11 quarters. And John Elway's Denver Broncos were struggling, having won just one of their first five games.

During a scoreless first quarter, it appeared as if their struggles would continue because the game's first five possessions yielded nothing but punts. But on the Chiefs' third possession, Denver defensive tackle Ted Washington tipped Montana's pass into the hands of teammate Dan Williams at Kansas City's 21-yard line. Three plays later, Leonard Russell swept left end for a 12-yard touchdown, and the Broncos led 7-0.

For most of the next 20 minutes, the teams marched up and down the field as Montana and Elway played at a level that only quarterbacks of their ilk can attain. After Denver's first touchdown, the Chiefs responded with an 8-play, 45-yard drive, with Marcus Allen's 12-yard touchdown run tying the score. It stayed tied only as long as it took Elway to move the Broncos 60 yards in 7 plays, ending with his 27-yard touchdown pass to Anthony Miller for a 14-7 lead. The Chiefs tied the score just before the half as Montana directed a 9-play, 62-yard march that produced his 6-yard touchdown pass to J.J. Birden.

Kansas City took the lead for the first time in the third quarter when Montana directed a 10-play, 76-yard drive. He climaxed it with a bit of trickery by passing 4 yards to tackle-eligible Joe Valerio.

On Denver's second possession of the second half, he moved the Broncos 73 yards in 8 plays, capping the march with a 20-yard touchdown pass to reserve tight end Jerry Evans to tie the score 21-21.

The game settled back to a punting duel until midway in the fourth quarter, when Lin Elliott's 19-yard field goal gave the Chiefs a 24-21 lead after the Broncos had stopped the Chiefs on the 1-yard line on third down.

Denver's offense was momentarily thwarted when tight end Shannon Sharpe lost a fumble with 2:45 to play at the Chiefs' 41-yard line. But the Broncos took back the ball on the next play when Washington forced Allen to fumble, and the ball was recovered at the 39-yard line by linebacker Karl Mecklenberg. So Elway picked up where he had left off before Sharpe's fumble, and, six plays later, he scored on a masterful quarterback draw from the 4-yard line that put Denver ahead 28-24 with just 89 seconds to play.

Eighty-nine seconds was a lifetime to Montana. Starting at his 25-yard line, he masterfully carved apart Denver's defense. He completed 7 of 8 passes, using 6 of them to reach Denver's 5-yard line with 10 seconds to play. The last completion, with just 8 seconds to play, went to Willie Davis for the winning touchdown in Kansas City's 31-28 victory.

That pass also was the fifty-fourth of the game for Montana, who completed 34 for 393 of the Chiefs' 483 total yards. It was a masterful performance. Elway was a "modest" 18 of 29 for 263 yards.

The difference? The clock, of course.

MEN WHO MADE THE GAME

CHAPTER 10

The 300 Greatest Players Plus

Bob Carroll, Jim J. Campbell, Jack Clary, Pete Fierle, Matthew Silverman, and Don Smith

Choosing the greatest players of all time is a sure way to elicit screams of protest from fans. No matter how long the list, some worthy players will be omitted. No matter how liberal the criteria, a few players on the list won't belong, according to some critics.

In the first edition of *Total Football,* we kept the list to 300, because we wanted to include deserving players from all eras, all the players in the Pro Football Hall of Fame, players who were outstanding at all positions, and at least some players whose names might not spring readily to mind but who were nonetheless excellent in their time.

For this second edition, we've added 20 current players who have distinguished themselves in more recent years — hence the plus. The new selections are noted with an asterisk.

Who made these recent choices? Most of the same editors and writers who created the original list.

What were the criteria? We asked that the expert members of our panel use their best judgment based on whatever statistics, anecdotes, or personal observations they felt were significant. The results follow.

The bracketed initials following each entry corresponds to the author(s).

1 Herb Adderley
2 Troy Aikman
3 *Larry Allen
4 Marcus Allen
5 Lance Alworth
6 Alan Ameche
7 Morten Andersen
8 Dick Anderson
9 *Gary Anderson
10 Ken Anderson
11 Doug Atkins
12 Morris (Red) Badgro
13 Erich Barnes
14 Lem Barney
15 Dick Barwegan
16 Cliff Battles
17 Sammy Baugh
18 Maxie Baughan
19 Chuck Bednarik
20 Bobby Bell
21 Bill Bergey
22 Raymond Berry
23 *Jerome Bettis
24 Fred Biletnikoff
25 George Blanda
26 *Drew Bledsoe
27 Mel Blount
28 Al Blozis
29 Terry Bradshaw
30 Gene Brito
31 Charley Brock
32 John Brodie
33 Bob Brown
34 Hardy Brown
35 Jim Brown
36 Roger Brown
37 Roosevelt Brown
38 Willie Brown
39 Junious (Buck) Buchanan
40 Nick Buoniconti
41 Dick Butkus
42 Jack Butler
43 *LeRoy Butler
44 Earl Campbell
45 Tony Canadeo
46 Harry Carson
47 *Cris Carter
48 Dave Casper
49 Guy Chamberlin
50 Jack Christiansen
51 Earl (Dutch) Clark
52 Charlie Conerly
53 George Connor
54 Roger Craig
55 Lou Creekmur
56 Larry Csonka
57 Curley Culp
58 *Randall Cunningham
59 Mike Curtis
60 *Terrell Davis
61 Tommy Davis
62 Willie Davis
63 *Dermontti Dawson
64 Len Dawson
65 Joe DeLamielleure
66 Tom Dempsey
67 Eric Dickerson
68 Dan Dierdorf
69 Bobby Dillon
70 Lavern Dilweg
71 Mike Ditka
72 Art Donovan
73 Tony Dorsett
74 John (Paddy) Driscoll
75 Bill Dudley
76 Kenny Easley
77 Albert Glen (Turk) Edwards
78 Carl Eller
79 John Elway
80 Gover (Ox) Emerson
81 *Boomer Esiason
82 *Brett Favre
83 Tom Fears
84 Beattie Feathers
85 Pat Fischer
86 Len Ford
87 Chuck Foreman
88 Dan Fortmann
89 Joe Fortunato
90 Dan Fouts
91 Benny Friedman
92 Frank Gatski
93 Bill George
94 Abe Gibron
95 Frank Gifford
96 Carlton (Cookie) Gilchrist
97 Horace Gillom
98 Pete Gogolak
99 Randy Gradishar
100 Otto Graham
101 Harold (Red) Grange
102 Mel Gray
103 Cornell Green
104 *Darrell Green
105 Joe Greene
106 L.C. Greenwood
107 Forrest Gregg
108 Roosevelt Grier
109 Bob Griese
110 Lou Groza
111 Ray Guy
112 Joe Guyon
113 Charles Haley
114 Jack Ham
115 Dan Hampton
116 John Hannah
117 Franco Harris
118 Bob Hayes
119 Lester Hayes
120 Mike Haynes
121 Ed Healey
122 William (Pudge) Heffelfinger
123 Mel Hein
124 Ted Hendricks
125 Charley Hennigan
126 Wilbur (Pete) Henry
127 Arnie Herber
128 Bill Hewitt
129 Gene Hickerson
130 Clarke Hinkle
131 Elroy (Crazylegs) Hirsch
132 Paul Hornung
133 Ken Houston
134 Chuck Howley
135 Cal Hubbard
136 Sam Huff
137 Don Hutson
138 *Michael Irvin
139 Cecil Isbell
140 Joe Jacoby
141 Billy (White Shoes) Johnson
142 Jimmy Johnson
143 John Henry Johnson
144 Charlie Joiner
145 David (Deacon) Jones
146 Ed (Too Tall) Jones
147 Stan Jones
148 Henry Jordan
149 Lee Roy Jordan
150 Sonny Jurgensen
151 Alex Karras
152 Ken Kavanaugh
153 Jim Kelly
154 Leroy Kelly
155 Walt Kiesling
156 Frank (Bucko) Kilroy
157 Frank (Bruiser) Kinard
158 Jerry Kramer
159 Ron Kramer
160 Paul Krause
161 *Dave Krieg
162 *Carnell Lake
163 Jack Lambert
164 Dick (Night Train) Lane
165 Jim Langer
166 Willie Lanier
167 Steve Largent
168 Yale Lary
169 Dante Lavelli
170 Bobby Layne
171 Alphonse (Tuffy) Leemans
172 Bob Lilly
173 Gene (Big Daddy) Lipscomb
174 Larry Little
175 James Lofton
176 Howie Long
177 Ronnie Lott
178 Sid Luckman
179 Lamar Lundy
180 William Roy (Link) Lyman
181 Tom Mack
182 John Mackey
183 Gino Marchetti
184 Dan Marino
185 Jim Marshall
186 Harvey Martin
187 Ollie Matson
188 Bruce Matthews
189 Don Maynard
190 George McAfee
191 Mike McCormack
192 Tommy McDonald
193 Hugh McElhenny
194 Johnny (Blood) McNally
195 Mike Michalske
196 Wayne Millner

197 Bobby Mitchell
198 Ron Mix
199 Art Monk
200 Joe Montana
201 Warren Moon
202 Lenny Moore
203 Marion Motley
204 Anthony Muñoz
205 George Musso
206 Bronislaw (Bronko) Nagurski
207 Joe Namath
208 Ernie Nevers
209 Ozzie Newsome
210 Ray Nitschke
211 Tommy Nobis
212 Leo Nomellini
213 *Ken Norton, Jr.
214 Merlin Olsen
215 Jim Otto
216 Alan Page
217 Jack Pardee
218 Clarence (Ace) Parker
219 Jim Parker
220 Lemar Parrish
221 Walter Payton
222 Drew Pearson
223 Joe Perry
224 Pete Pihos
225 Jim Plunkett
226 Frederick (Fritz) Pollard
227 Garrard (Buster) Ramsey
228 *John Randle
229 *Andre Reed
230 Mel Renfro
231 Jerry Rice
232 Les Richter
233 John Riggins
234 Jim Ringo
235 Dave Robinson
236 Johnny Robinson
237 Andy Robustelli
238 Andy Russell
239 Bob St. Clair
240 Barry Sanders
241 Charlie Sanders
242 Deion Sanders
243 Orban (Spec) Sanders
244 Gale Sayers
245 Joe Schmidt
246 Jake Scott
247 Junior Seau
248 Lee Roy Selmon
249 Tom Sestak
250 *Shannon Sharpe
251 Sterling Sharpe
252 Billy Shaw
253 Art Shell
254 Donnie Shell
255 Phil Simms
256 O.J. Simpson
257 Mike Singletary
258 Fred (Duke) Slater
259 Bruce Smith
260 Emmitt Smith
261 Jackie Smith
262 Mac Speedie
263 Ed Sprinkle
264 Ken Stabler
265 John Stallworth
266 Dick Stanfel
267 Bart Starr
268 Roger Staubach
269 Ernie Stautner
270 Jan Stenerud
271 Dwight Stephenson
272 Ken Strong
273 Jack Stroud
274 Joe Stydahar
275 Lynn Swann
276 Fran Tarkenton
277 *Steve Tasker
278 Charley Taylor
279 Jim Taylor
280 Lawrence Taylor
281 Lionel Taylor
282 Otis Taylor
283 Thurman Thomas
284 Jim Thorpe
285 Mick Tingelhoff
286 Y.A. Tittle
287 George Trafton
288 Charley Trippi
289 Emlen Tunnell
290 Clyde (Bulldog) Turner
291 Jim Tyrer
292 Johnny Unitas
293 Rick Upchurch
294 Gene Upshaw
295 Norm Van Brocklin
296 Steve Van Buren
297 Doak Walker
298 Herschel Walker
299 Everson Walls
300 Paul Warfield
301 Bob Waterfield
302 Charlie Waters
303 Mike Webster
304 Roger Wehrli
305 Arnie Weinmeister
306 Byron (Whizzer) White
307 Randy White
308 Reggie White
309 Dave Wilcox
310 Bill Willis
311 Larry Wilson
312 Kellen Winslow
313 Al Wistert
314 Alex Wojciechowicz
315 Willie Wood
316 Abe Woodson
317 Rod Woodson
318 Ron Yary
319 Claude (Buddy) Young
320 Steve Young

HERB ADDERLEY

Defensive Back. 6-1, 200. Michigan State
Born June 8, 1939, Philadelphia, Pennsylvania.
1961-69 Green Bay, 1970-72 Dallas
Inducted into Pro Football Hall of Fame in 1980.

Adderley's 60-yard interception return for the Packers' clinching touchdown in Super Bowl II was the only interception return for a touchdown in the first 10 Super Bowls. The play was an appropriate highlight for the man who was a fixture at left cornerback during Green Bay's championship years of the 1960s. Adderley then concluded his career with another group of champions—the Dallas Cowboys of the early 1970s.

He was a fixture in postseason games. He played in seven NFL or NFC Championship Games in an 11-season span from 1961 through 1971, and his teams won every one—five with the Packers and two with the Cowboys. He also played in four of the first six Super Bowls, winning championship rings in three of them.

An All-Big Ten star at Michigan State before entering pro football as Green Bay's number-one draft pick in 1961, he immediately took command in the Packers' defensive backfield. He earned all-pro honors in 1963, 1965, 1966, and 1969. Adderley also played in five Pro Bowl games during the 1960s.

An exceptionally fast ball hawk, Adderley amassed 48 interceptions, returning them for 1,046 yards for a 21.8-yard average with 7 touchdowns during his 12-year career. Adderley doubled as a kickoff-return specialist during most of his Green Bay career and wound up with a 25.7-yard average on 120 returns. Included was a 103-yard return in 1962 and 98-yard return in 1963. [DS/PF]

TROY AIKMAN

Quarterback. 6-4, 218. Oklahoma, UCLA
Born November 21, 1966, West Covina, California.
1989-1998 Dallas

Troy Aikman could not have walked into a worse situation.

The Dallas Cowboys had just fired Tom Landry, the only coach the team ever had, and replaced him with Jimmy Johnson, a coach Aikman had once committed to play for at Oklahoma State before changing his mind and heading across the state.

When Aikman, the Oklahoma Sooner, next met Johnson on the football field, in 1985, Johnson was coach of the University of Miami and, as things turned out, the Hurricane defense broke Aikman's leg. Aikman was on the sidelines when Oklahoma won the national championship that season. When the two finally did get together in Dallas in 1989, Aikman went 0-11 as a starter, and Johnson was 1-15 as the coach.

Aikman was the star quarterback in high school for the Henryetta (Oklahoma) Hens, before he went to college in Norman, then transferred to UCLA. Unable to play in 1986 as a transfer student, he made up for lost time over the next two years with 5,298 yards passing, 41 touchdowns, and just 17 interceptions.

He was rewarded by being the first overall draft selection. Dallas then had its worst season since the city first received a National Football League expansion franchise in 1960. But, just three years after the nightmare beginning to his pro career, Aikman and the Cowboys went 13-3, swept through the playoffs, and trounced Buffalo 52-17 in Super Bowl XXVII. The next year Dallas beat the Bills 30-13. Super Bowl XXX made it three NFL championships for Aikman in four seasons. [MS]

***LARRY ALLEN**

Guard-Tackle. 6-3, 325. Sonoma State
Born November 27, 1971, Los Angeles, California.
1994-98 Dallas

The Cowboys selected big, versatile lineman Howard Richards out of Missouri in the first round of the 1981 draft. Following Richards's unspectacular six years in Dallas, the Cowboys did not select another offensive lineman that high until the 1994 draft, when they took big, versatile Larry Allen in the second round. No player ever had been drafted out of Division II Sonoma State, but there was little risk involved with the two-time All-America.

Injuries to Erik Williams forced Allen to start sooner than the Cowboys planned, but Allen proved he was ready. He started 10 games at right tackle as a rookie and helped the Cowboys set a club record with only 20 sacks allowed. The next season, with Allen switching to right guard, the Cowboys allowed just 18 sacks while Emmitt Smith set a franchise rushing record. Dallas went on to win Super Bowl XXX that season, beating Pittsburgh 27-17. The next week's Pro Bowl featured four members of the Dallas front line, led by Allen.

Allen was named to the Pro Bowl as a guard the next two seasons. The Cowboys rewarded him with a six-year contract in 1998, then switched him to tackle. He responded with his fourth consecutive Pro Bowl season. [MS]

MARCUS ALLEN

Running Back. 6-2, 205. Southern California
Born March 26, 1960, San Diego, California.
1982-1992 Los Angeles Raiders, 1993-97 Kansas City

Marcus Allen's career was a series of ups and downs. A highly recruited *Parade* All-America high school star, he chose to attend the University of Southern California, famous for its award-winning tailbacks. But, in his first two seasons, he served mostly as a blocking fullback for 1979 Heisman Trophy winner Charles White. Returned to tailback as a junior, he set 15 NCAA records and won the Heisman himself as a senior in 1981.

The tenth player chosen in the 1982 NFL draft, Allen broke in with the Raiders by leading the league in touchdowns and earning rookie-of-the-year honors. In 1983, he helped take the Raiders to a Super Bowl where he was named MVP, rushing for 191 yards, including a brilliant 74-yard run that cemented the Raiders' win in XVIII. Two years later, he led the NFL in rushing with 1,759 yards and was named player of the year.

Then things began to go sour for Allen. He found himself sharing running time with other backs. When Bo Jackson arrived in midseason of 1987, Allen went into further eclipse. For the next couple of seasons, he was shoved aside when Jackson finished his baseball commitment and joined the team. Even when Jackson's career was ended by an injury, Allen was used sparingly.

At age 33, Allen signed with Kansas City, where he made a remarkable turnaround to become his team's featured back. He retired in 1997 with 123 rushing touchdowns. [BC]

LANCE ALWORTH

Wide Receiver. 6-0, 184. Arkansas
Born August 3, 1940, Houston, Texas.
1962-1970 San Diego, 1971-72 Dallas
Inducted into Pro Football Hall of Fame in 1978.

He was known as "Bambi," the smooth and graceful fawn bounding free and easy among the behemoths of pro football. He was the sure-handed ace of the San Diego Chargers flashing that 9.6 speed in the 100-yard dash, that high jumper's spring, and those eager, grasping hands that spelled sudden disaster for even the best-prepared opponent.

He was the premier pass catcher of an entire decade and the first true superstar the American Football League produced. In 1978, he was the first "pure" AFL player to be elected to the Pro Football Hall of Fame.

Alworth's accomplishments are legendary. In 11 pro seasons, he caught 542 passes for 10,266 yards (an 18.9-yard average) and 85 touchdowns. He was named All-AFL seven consecutive years from 1963 to 1969 and played in the league's last seven all-star games. He caught at least one pass in every AFL game in which he played, including a record string of 96 consecutive regular-season games.

These rare deeds came as no surprise to Al Davis, the Chargers' assistant coach who signed Alworth to a $30,000 contract just prior to the 1962 Sugar Bowl game in New Orleans. The Chargers traded three draft picks to the Oakland Raiders for the rights to Alworth and felt they got a bargain.

"Lance was one of maybe three players in my lifetime who had what I would call 'it'," Davis declared. As the Houston Oilers' prize wide receiver, Charley Hennigan, once said, "A player comes along once in a lifetime who alone is worth the price of admission. Lance Alworth was that player." [DS/PF]

ALAN AMECHE

Fullback. 6-1, 217. Wisconsin
Born June 1, 1933, Kenosha, Wisconsin.
Died August 8, 1988, Houston, Texas.
1955-1960 Baltimore

Alan Ameche scored what may be the most famous touchdown in NFL history. At 8:15 of overtime in the 1958 NFL Championship Game, he bulled the final yard to give the Baltimore Colts a 23-17 victory.

Ameche was the Colts' bread-and-butter, up-the-middle fullback for six seasons until an Achilles tendon injury ended his career prematurely. He was the 1954 Heisman Trophy winner at the University of Wisconsin, where he broke all rushing records.

The quietly modest fullback came to Baltimore as a number-one draft choice in 1955, when the team was just beginning to struggle out of the NFL cellar. He took his first NFL carry 79 yards for a touchdown to help spark an upset of the Bears. Ameche went on to earn rookie-of-the-year honors by leading the league in rushing with 961 yards on 213 carries.

Ameche ran with a powerful straight-up, head-bobbing style that earned him the nickname "The Horse." In succeeding seasons, as the Colts' attack became more diversified, Ameche's role in the offense changed. No longer was he the main weapon and his number of carries and rushing yardage dropped accordingly. His strong blocking became as important as his running ability, particularly when Johnny Unitas emerged as the league's foremost quarterback and protecting him became the key to the Colts' success. [BC]

MORTEN ANDERSEN

Kicker. 6-2, 214. Michigan State
Born August 19, 1960, Struer, Denmark.
1982-1994 New Orleans, 1995-98 Atlanta

With Morten Andersen on your team, you may not always

win, but you will always score. Andersen holds the National Football League record for scoring in 238 consecutive games.

The New Orleans Saints never had finished above .500 when they drafted Andersen out of Michigan State in the fourth round of the 1982 draft. In Andersen's 13 years with the team, the Saints finished .500 or better eight times.

Andersen, a native of Denmark who immigrated to the United States as a youth, benefited from the vacuum-like conditions in the Louisiana Superdome, but his cannon of a left leg was the real reason for his success. No chip-shot artist, Andersen has kicked more field goals from beyond 50 yards than anyone else in NFL history (35). In 1995, he connected on a record 3 field goals of 50-plus yards (51, 55, and 55) in Atlanta's 19-14 victory against his former team, the Saints. Andersen, who has been named to the Pro Bowl seven times, also is one of a handful of kickers to have a 60-yard field goal on his resume.

He has surpassed 100 points 12 times, and ranks as the third-leading scorer in NFL history. The Saints paid Andersen the ultimate compliment for a kicker when they designated him a transitional player in 1993, but New Orleans released the veteran before the 1995 season. The Falcons picked him up and Andersen responded with a career-high 122 points.

He recorded 120 points during the 1998 regular season, then made the biggest kick of his career, a 38-yard field goal in overtime of the NFC Championship Game to send the Falcons to the Super Bowl for the first time. [MS]

DICK ANDERSON

Safety. 6-2, 198. Colorado
Born February 10, 1946, Midland, Michigan.
1968-1974, 1976-77 Miami

Dick Anderson came down from the mountains to help lead the Miami Dolphins to the promised land.

Anderson, who grew up in Boulder, Colorado, helped anchor the Dolphins' No-Name Defense in the 1970s. Anderson shadowed receivers from his safety position and often was in a better position to catch the ball than they were.

He was a big part of the Dolphins' undefeated season in 1972 when Miami held regular-season opponents to an NFL-low 171 points. Anderson played in three Super Bowls and tied National Football League records with 4 interceptions and 2 touchdowns against the Pittsburgh Steelers on December 3, 1973.

Anderson was switched to strong safety at the University of Colorado and excelled at the position, but he first caught national attention as a punt returner. He ran back 2 punts for touchdowns in the Blue-Gray Game to earn most-valuable-player honors.

He began his career as the American Football League defensive rookie of the year and was named an all-pro three times. He was chosen to the 1960-1984 AFL-NFL All-Star Second Team by the Pro Football Hall of Fame.

He missed the 1975 season with a knee injury and retired in 1977 with 34 interceptions, second only to Jake Scott in Miami history. After his career, Anderson was president of the NFL Players Association for three years, then served three years as a Florida state senator. [MS]

GARY ANDERSON

Kicker. 5-11, 178. Syracuse
Born, July 16, 1959, Parys, South Africa.
1982-1994 Pittsburgh, 1995-1996 Philadelphia, 1997 San Francisco, 1998 Minnesota

The Pittsburgh Steelers had their eye on Gary Anderson while he was at the University of Syracuse, and they had every intention of drafting him in the seventh round in 1982. After all, he had connected on a school-record 97.4 percent of his field goals (18 of 19) during his senior year. The Buffalo Bills drafted ahead of the Steelers that year and took Anderson earlier in the round. The Bills, though, decided to cut the rookie and keep veterans Efren Herrera and Nick Mick-Mayer. The Steelers pounced, claiming Anderson on waivers six days before the start of the season.

Anderson was named to the NFL all-rookie team, hitting 10 of 12 field-goal attempts in a strike-shortened season. In 1983, he led the AFC with 119 points and was named the Steelers' MVP in a playoff season.

Anderson's 1,343 points in Pittsburgh nearly doubled Roy Gerela's club scoring mark. Anderson connected on 309 of 395 field-goal attempts with the Steelers, missing only 4 of 420 extra-point kicks. Salary-cap constraints prompted Anderson and the Steelers to part company after the 1994 season.

He already was the NFL's all-time leader in field goals when he joined the Minnesota Vikings, his third team in four years, in 1998. Anderson responded with the finest season of his career—and the best season ever by an NFL kicker. He was perfect in the regular season, successfully converting all 94 attempts (35 field goals and 59 extra points) for an NFL-record 164 points. He added 8 extra points and 4 field goals in the playoffs before he finally missed in the closing minutes of the NFC Championship Game. [JD]

KEN ANDERSON

Quarterback. 6-3, 212. Augustana College (Illinois)
Born February 15, 1949, Batavia, Illinois.
1971-1986 Cincinnati

Ken Anderson was one of the most accurate passers in pro football history, completing more than 59 percent of his passes during his 16-season career with the Cincinnati Bengals.

Assistant coach Bill Walsh had scouted him at tiny Augustana College in Illinois, and Walsh raved so much about Anderson's ability that Cincinnati head coach Paul Brown made the quarterback the team's third-round draft pick in 1971.

"I knew little about the fine technical points of playing quarterback, like setting up in the pocket," Anderson said. "I spent the first two weeks of my first training camp without ever throwing a ball. Bill Walsh spent that time teaching me such mundane points as taking the snap, pivoting, stepping to make a correct handoff, learning how to make three-, five- and seven-yard pass drops, and the proper method of throwing the ball."

Once Anderson learned, he was deadly efficient. He still is the Bengals' all-time leader in touchdown passes (197) and passing yards (32,838). He led the Bengals to the playoffs in 4 of his 16 seasons, including Super Bowl XVI after the 1981 season, when he won NFL most-valuable-player honors. That year, Anderson set a club record with 29 touchdown passes and passed for 3,754 yards. He also led the league's passers four times, and appeared in four Pro Bowls. [JC]

DOUG ATKINS

Defensive End. 6-8, 275. Tennessee
Born May 8, 1930, Humboldt, Tennessee.
1953-54 Cleveland, 1955-1966 Chicago, 1967-69 New Orleans
Inducted into Pro Football Hall of Fame in 1982.

Opposing players faced Atkins with just one thought in mind: "Don't make him mad." Everyone knew that holding or tripping Atkins was an absolute no-no. When angered, Atkins inflicted the kind of devastation upon enemy linemen and quarterbacks that seldom has been equaled on any football field. For 17 years and 205 games the huge defensive end wreaked havoc on NFL quarterbacks.

Atkins attended the University of Tennessee on a basketball scholarship. He also filled in on the track team and won the Southeastern Conference high jump title. Later, he would use this ability to leap frog over blockers in his mad rush to get at NFL passers. One day the Tennessee football coach saw Atkins on the basketball court and quickly commandeered him for the football team. Atkins wound up as an All-America tackle as a senior.

The Cleveland Browns made Atkins their number-one draft choice in 1953 but two seasons later he was traded to Chicago, where he was all-pro three times and an eight-time Pro Bowl pick. His easy-going approach to practice often nettled Coach George Halas. Once he was ordered to "Take a lap. And wear your helmet!" Atkins took the lap wearing only his helmet. In 1967, Atkins demanded a trade and got it. He was sent to New Orleans, where he played the final three years of his career. [DS/PF]

MORRIS (RED) BADGRO

End. 6-0, 190. Southern California
Born December 1, 1902, Orilla, Washington.
Died July 13, 1998, Seattle, Washington.
1927 New York Yankees, 1930-35 New York Giants, 1936 Brooklyn
Inducted into Pro Football Hall of Fame in 1981.

In 1981, at age 78, Badgro, a two-way end who started his NFL career almost six decades earlier, became the oldest person ever elected to the Pro Football Hall of Fame. The 45-year span between his final NFL appearance with the 1936 Brooklyn Dodgers and his 1981 election also is a record.

Badgro began his NFL career with the 1927 New York Yankees before taking a two-year sabbatical to try his hand at professional baseball. He returned to the NFL with the 1930 New York Giants and played there through 1935 before ending his career with Brooklyn in 1936.

During his six seasons with the Giants, his team was a solid championship contender every year, and Badgro was one of the team's most-honored stars. He won unofficial all-pro designation in 1930, then official all-league acclaim in 1931, 1933, and 1934.

Although Badgro was regarded as a sure-tackling defender and an effective blocker on offense, he also was a talented receiver. In 1934, he tied for the NFL's individual pass-catching title with 16 receptions, a significant number in those defense-dominated days when most NFL teams concentrated on grind-it-out football.

Both Badgro's teammates and opponents lauded his performances. Typical was a statement by the fabled Red Grange: "I played with Red one year with the New York Yankees and against him the five seasons he was with the Giants. Playing both offense and defense, he was one of the half-dozen best ends I ever saw." [DS/PF]

ERICH BARNES

Defensive Back. 6-2, 198. Purdue
Born July 4, 1935, Elkhart, Indiana.
1958-1960 Chicago Bears, 1961-64 New York Giants, 1965-1971 Cleveland

Erich Barnes was a winner. A cornerback, he helped the New York Giants to the National Football League Championship Game in three of his four seasons with them; and he was a big factor in Cleveland reaching the NFL title game three more times during his seven seasons with the Browns.

Barnes was as fast as the men he covered, but he also was bigger than most of them. He brashly challenged his opponents to try to beat him, then backed up his talk with his aggressive style.

A fourth-round pick out of Purdue in 1958, he had 9 interceptions in three seasons with the Bears, but owner-coach George Halas packaged him in a three-way deal that sent him to the Rams and then on to the Giants. He was the perfect fit to a great defense that had already been to three NFL title games in five seasons.

While Barnes was a fan favorite with his rugged defense during his first season with the Giants, he still is best remembered as the recipient of a touchdown pass from Y.A. Tittle on a specially devised play called the "Pete Previte Special" because it was suggested by Giants clubhouse attendant Pete Previte.

Barnes, who appeared in six Pro Bowls, accumulated 18 interceptions during his seasons with the New York Giants. When he was sent to the Cleveland Browns as part of another three-way deal, he immediately assisted the Browns to a conference title. During his seven seasons with Cleveland, he intercepted 18 more passes. [JC]

LEM BARNEY

Cornerback. 6-0, 190. Jackson State
Born September 9, 1945, Gulfport, Mississippi.
1967-1977 Detroit
Inducted into Pro Football Hall of Fame in 1992.

Although he was a three-time All-Southwestern Conference star who had intercepted 26 passes in three seasons at Jackson State, Barney was a comparatively unknown player when he joined the NFL as the Lions' second-round draft pick in 1967.

It took only a few games, however, for him to become widely respected as one of the premier cornerbacks in pro football. After a sensational rookie season, he was named the NFL defensive rookie of the year and was selected to play in the Pro Bowl. He tied for the NFL interception lead with 10 and returned 3 for touchdowns, 1 short of the single-season record.

Barney also won acclaim as a kick-return specialist. The Mississippi native was highly feared as a big-play threat for good reason. In his 11-year tenure that ended after the 1977 season, Barney had a 98-yard kickoff return, a 94-yard field-goal return, a 74-yard punt return, and a 71-yard interception runback.

His career record includes 56 interceptions for 1,077 yards, 143 punt returns for 1,312 yards, and 50 kickoff returns for 1,274 yards. He scored 11 touchdowns on 7 interceptions, 2 punt returns, 1 kickoff return, and 1 field-goal return. He also recovered 11 opponents' fumbles and doubled as the Lions' punter in both 1967 and 1969. Barney played in seven Pro Bowls and was named all-pro in 1968 and 1969 and All-NFC in 1972. [DS/PF]

DICK BARWEGAN

Guard. 6-1, 230. Purdue
Born December 25, 1921, Chicago, Illinois.
Died September 3, 1966, Baltimore, Maryland.
1947 New York AAFC, 1948-49, 1953-54 Baltimore, 1950-52 Chicago Bears

"He was a helluva ballplayer, not real tall, but quick and tenacious," said former teammate Paul Stenn (Stenko), who played tackle alongside the much-honored Barwegan both with the Chicago Bears in the early 1950s and earlier on the crack March Field service team during World War II.

Stenn added, "All I worried about was my man. I knew Dick would get his with no help. His quickness made him an ideal pulling guard. Don't forget, he could play defense as good as the best, too."

In 1943, Barwegan was voted MVP as a freshman with an undefeated Purdue team. Because of wartime considerations, he was one of two men chosen to play in four consecutive Chicago College All-Star Games. The other was Pro Football Hall of Fame halfback Charley Trippi.

When Barwegan joined the New York Yankees of the All-America Football Conference AAFC in 1947, he immediately earned second-team all-league honors. But before the next season, the league tried to improve some of its weaker teams by adding players from the stronger clubs. Barwegan was sent to the Baltimore Colts. For the final two years of the AAFC, he was first-team all-league.

He joined Stenn and the Bears in 1950 and was consensus all-pro that year and again in 1951. All-pro offensive guards usually were taken from championship teams, but Barwegan made the Pro Bowl four consecutive years, 1951-54. His final two seasons were spent with the reconstituted Colts.

When the Pro Football Hall of Fame picked its all-1950s team in conjunction with the league's fiftieth anniversary, Barwegan was one of three guards named. [JJC]

CLIFF BATTLES

Halfback. 6-1, 200. West Virginia Wesleyan
Born May 1, 1910, Akron, Ohio.
Died April 28, 1981, Clearwater, Florida.
1932-36 Boston, 1937 Washington
Inducted into Pro Football Hall of Fame in 1968.

Battles, a sensational Phi Beta Kappa running back from West Virginia Wesleyan College, won the NFL rushing championship in his rookie season with the Boston Braves in 1932. A year later, the Braves became the Redskins, and Battles became the first NFL player to rush for 200 yards in a game.

In 1937, the Redskins were moved to Washington where fans eagerly anticipated the arrival of Sammy Baugh, a touted rookie quarterback from Texas Christian. Fans dreamed of a Battles-Baugh combo that would form a devastating ground-air offense and make the Redskins championship contenders for years to come.

For one season in 1937, Baugh and Battles combined their talents as everyone envisioned. On the season's final day, Battles scored 3 touchdowns to power the Redskins to a 49-14 win over the New York Giants for the Eastern Division championship. Against the Chicago Bears a week later, Battles scored the first touchdown in a 28-21 victory that gave the Redskins their first NFL championship. Battles was the NFL's leading rusher with 874 yards and he won All-NFL honors for the third time in six years.

In just six seasons, Battles totaled 3,542 yards rushing—really big numbers in those days—and happy Redskins fans looked forward to many more exciting days watching their superstar running back. But when team owner George Preston Marshall refused to raise Battles's salary above $3,000, the Akron, Ohio, native retired to accept a $4,000-a-year job as an assistant coach at Columbia University. Washington won only one more championship during Baugh's remarkable career while loyal Redskins fans only could ponder "what might have been" if Marshall had paid Battles that extra $1,000. [DS/PF]

SAMMY BAUGH

Quarterback. 6-2, 180. Texas Christian
Born March 17, 1914, Temple, Texas.
1937-1952 Washington
Inducted into Pro Football Hall of Fame in 1963.

Baugh arrived on the pro football scene in 1937, the same time the Redskins moved from Boston to Washington. He was the team's first-round pick that year. Over the next 16 seasons, "Slingin' Sammy" not only helped establish the pro game in the nation's capital, he was also a major influence in the offensive revolution that occurred in the National Football League in the late 1930s and early 1940s.

The "Texas Tornado" took the league by storm with his wide-open passing attack. As a rookie, Baugh led Washington to the league championship. He concluded his first year by firing 3 long touchdowns to lead Washington to a 28-21 victory over the Chicago Bears in the title game.

The All-America from Texas Christian University started his NFL career as a tailback. In 1944, he made the switch to the T-formation. Baugh won six NFL passing titles. While he was a man "ahead of his time" as far as passing accomplishments are concerned, he also was a remarkable all-around player, starring also as both a safety and a punter.

Baugh scored a rare "triple crown" in 1943. He led the league in passing, punting, and interceptions. In fact, the six-time all-league selection led the NFL in punting four consecutive years, 1940-43. He still ranks as history's leading punter.

Appropriately, Baugh saved perhaps his finest individual performance for the day the fans paid tribute to him. On "Sammy Baugh Day" in 1947, the Redskins faced the Chicago Cardinals. He passed for 355 yards and 6 touchdowns as Washington stunned that season's eventual champions 45-21. [DS/PF]

MAXIE BAUGHAN

Linebacker. 6-1, 227. Georgia Tech
Born August 3, 1947, Forkland, Alabama.
1960-65 Philadelphia, 1966-1970 Los Angeles Rams

Maxie Baughan helped turn George Allen into a "genius."

As captain of the Los Angeles Rams' defense in the late 1960s, Baughan was responsible for coordinating Allen's very complex defensive schemes. While it was complicated on paper—250 different defenses and 180 audibles—Baughan helped it click on the field. He was brilliant at recognizing offensive sets and reacting fast to counter them. The 1967 Rams allowed a league-low 196 points en route to the National Football League Coastal Division title.

Maxie—his real handle, not a nickname—started his pro career on the other coast. He was drafted by the Philadelphia Eagles in the second round in 1960 after an All-America senior year at Georgia Tech where he set a school single-season record for tackles. Combining quickness, aggressiveness, and intelligence, he quickly became one of the NFL's most respected linebackers. He was named to nine Pro Bowls. An all-pro linebacker with the Eagles in 1964, he was named to the team again in 1967, a year after he was traded to the Rams for three players.

Injuries in 1968 and 1969 slowed Baughan, but still he helped the Rams' defense remain among the league leaders. When Allen was hired to coach the Washington Redskins in 1971, he again traded for Baughan, but injuries forced the veteran defender to retire before the start of the season. An attempted comeback in 1974 died in training camp.

He finished with 18 career interceptions and 1 touchdown. Baughan is a member of the College Football Hall of Fame. [MS]

CHUCK BEDNARIK

Center-Linebacker. 6-3, 230. Pennsylvania
Born May 1, 1925, Bethlehem, Pennsylvania.
1949-1962 Philadelphia
Inducted into Pro Football Hall of Fame in 1967.

Long after the two-way player in the NFL had largely faded from the scene, Bednarik showed he could still excel both on offense and defense. In 1960, his twelfth pro season, the Philadelphia Eagles star responded to an injury-induced emergency by playing 694 minutes in a 12-game season. He finished the season with a 58-minute performance, capped by a game-saving tackle of the Packers' Jim Taylor in the Eagles' NFL Championship Game victory over Green Bay.

As an offensive center, Bednarik was a bulldozing blocker, both on rushing and passing plays. On defense, he was a true scientist in his field and the kind of a tackler who could literally stop even the best opposing runners "on a dime."

One such tackle not only gave the Eagles a crucial victory in 1960, but also put the New York Giants' Frank Gifford out of action for more than a year. Films of the play proved that Bednarik's tackle, while indicative of his "play for keeps" philosophy, was clean.

After a 30-month mission as a waist gunner on a B-24 bomber in World War II, Bednarik became a two-time All-America center at the University of Pennsylvania. He was the Eagles' bonus draft choice in 1949 and soon proved he could be an outstanding pro as well as a durable one. He missed his first two games as a rookie, then only one more in 14 seasons. He was an all-pro choice seven times and played in eight Pro Bowls. [DS/PF]

BOBBY BELL

Linebacker. 6-4, 225. Minnesota
Born June 17, 1940, Shelby, North Carolina.
1963-1974 Kansas City Chiefs
Inducted into Pro Football Hall of Fame in 1983.

Bell could do almost anything on a football field. He was an All-North Carolina high school quarterback, an All-America tackle at the University of Minnesota, and an excellent defensive end for the Kansas City Chiefs before he settled on the left outside linebacker position. It proved to be his perfect position, one that earned him a spot in the Pro Football Hall of Fame.

As versatile as he was—he even snapped the football on punts and kickoffs for the Chiefs—Bell also had the physique to survive against any opponent in the rugged world of pro football. Bell was built in the shape of an inverted pyramid with massive shoulders tapering down to a 32-inch waist on his 225-pound frame. He also had the strength that helped him withstand punishment and to deal out his own punishment in return. Bell had exceptional agility and speed: He regularly was timed at 4.5 seconds in the 40-yard dash.

Bell began his American Football League career as a defensive end because that is where the Chiefs needed him most. But in his third season, coach Hank Stram moved Bell to outside linebacker, where he quickly gained stardom. He won All-AFL/AFC designation the next eight seasons—he already had been All-AFL once as a defensive end. Bell also played in Super Bowls I and IV, the last six AFL All-Star games and the first three AFC-NFC Pro Bowls. He was named to the AFL's all-time team in 1969. [DS/PF]

BILL BERGEY

Linebacker. 6-2, 240. Arkansas State
Born February 14, 1945, South Dayton, Ohio.
1969-1973 Cincinnati, 1974-1980 Philadelphia

When God made middle linebackers, He had Bill Bergey in mind. He gave him all of the physical and emotional tools that the great players at the position ever have possessed.

Bergey was a one-man thundering herd who ruled the middle of his defense with a ferocity that was breathtaking and intimidating. He ranged sideline to sideline as he shed would-be blockers and slammed into running backs.

His first Eagles coach, Mike McCormack, once noted: "His whole attitude is contagious. It's like dropping a stone in a pond. It's that rippling effect where a good hit flows through the rest of the defense and everybody wants to get in on it."

Bergey had his own style. He developed a tackling technique he called his "shoulder punch," in which he exploded the final six inches before tackling a runner, delivering such a jolt that the back's head would snap back as if struck with a pole ax. He also was the Eagles' spiritual defensive leader and helped the team win the 1980 NFC title to earn a berth in Super Bowl XV.

Bergey was Cincinnati's second-round draft pick in 1969 after playing at Arkansas State University, near where the son of Bengals head coach and general manager, Paul Brown, had a ranch. Robin Brown, Paul's son, scouted him and delivered a ringing recommendation. Bergey played five seasons with the Bengals, helping them to a pair of AFC playoffs. But after he signed a future contract with Virginia of the World Football League, the Bengals traded him to Philadelphia. [JC]

RAYMOND BERRY

End. 6-2, 187. Southern Methodist
Born February 27, 1933, Corpus Christi, Texas.
1955-1967 Baltimore
Inducted into Pro Football Hall of Fame in 1973.

There was nothing in Berry's pre-NFL days to indicate he would become one of the game's true superstars.

At Paris (Texas) High School, where his dad was head coach, Berry didn't play as a regular until he was a senior. At Southern Methodist, he caught just 33 passes and scored only 1 touchdown in three years. For some reason, the Baltimore Colts drafted Berry, but, when he reported to camp in 1955, he was given little chance of making the team. Somehow, he managed to stay and, in his second season, he began to team with rookie quarterback Johnny Unitas. Soon, the Unitas-Berry duo was the most lethal in pro football. Berry caught 631 passes in his career, most of them from Unitas.

In his relentless drive for perfection, Berry, by actual count, developed 88 maneuvers for getting around defenders and to the ball. Insistent on practicing every move each week, he enlisted a variety of helpers: teammates, coaches, groundskeepers, writers, and even his wife.

Berry's hard work reaped huge rewards. He retired with a record 631 receptions. He was a game-saving hero many times, but he was never better than in the Colts' overtime NFL title victory over the New York Giants in 1958. Berry caught 12 passes for 178 yards, scored 1 touchdown, and made several critical catches in the Colts' game-tying drive in regulation time. In 1958, 1959, and 1960, Berry led the NFL in receiving and earned all-pro honors. He was a five-time Pro Bowl selection. [DS/PF]

***JEROME BETTIS**

Running Back. 5-11, 243. Notre Dame
Born February 16, 1972, Detroit, Michigan.
1993-94 Los Angeles Rams, 1995 St. Louis, 1996-98 Pittsburgh

Bettis likes to knock things down, whether it's bowling pins or defensive backs. His mother, Gladys, introduced him to bowling as a child as a way to keep him off the streets in inner-city Detroit. He thrived at the sport and even has a perfect 300 game to his credit, but Bettis became known as "The Bus" for bowling over tacklers on the way to the end zone.

Coming out of Detroit's Mackenzie High School, Bettis was rated the top player in the state by the *Detroit Free Press.* But the University of Michigan thought he was better suited to play linebacker, and since Bettis thought he was better suited to carrying the ball, he opted for Notre Dame.

Bettis was the tenth pick in the 1993 NFL draft, and he made an immediate friend in Rams head coach Chuck Knox, whose propensity for running the ball had long ago earned him the name "Ground Chuck." After Bettis had two 1,000-yard seasons in Los Angeles, Rich Brooks replaced Knox, and the Rams moved to St. Louis. Brooks thought Bettis was too slow and gave him just 183 carries in 1995. Brooks then traded him to the Steelers for two draft picks.

Right from the start Bettis fit in perfectly in Pittsburgh. He had five consecutive 100-yard games with the Steelers in 1996, plus a 129-yard performance in a 42-6 drubbing of Brooks and the Rams. Bettis rode his way to team MVP honors and even surpassed all the single-season yardage numbers put up by Franco Harris in his legendary 12-year career in Pittsburgh. "The Bus" remained right on schedule in 1997 as Bettis led the NFL in carries, finished third in rushing, and ended the season just 25 yards shy of Barry Foster's club record 1,690-yard season in 1992. He surpassed 1,000 yards for the fifth time in his six-year career in 1998, when he gained 1,185. [MS]

FRED BILETNIKOFF

Wide Receiver. 6-1, 190. Florida State
Born February 23, 1943, Erie, Pennsylvania.
1965-1978 Oakland
Inducted into Pro Football Hall of Fame in 1988.

Biletnikoff used deceptive speed and perhaps the best hands in football to catch 589 passes during his 14-year career in Oakland. He dominates the Raiders' record book for pass receiving. His 70 receptions, 1,167 yards receiving, and 10 touchdowns in 19 postseason games all were NFL postseason career records at the time of his retirement.

Biletnikoff reached the zenith of a career filled with outstanding achievements when he caught 4 passes for 79 yards to set up 3 touchdowns in the Raiders' 32-14 victory over Minnesota in Super Bowl XI. He was named the game's most valuable player. The Pennsylvania native was an All-AFL pick in that league's final 1969 season, then won All-AFC honors in 1970, 1972, and 1973. He played in two AFL All-Star games and four AFC-NFC Pro Bowl games as well as three AFL and five AFC Championship Games, plus Super Bowls II and XI.

The talented pass-catcher came to the Raiders as their second-round draft pick in 1965. A 1964 All-America at Florida State, Biletnikoff caught 4 touchdown passes in his team's Gator Bowl victory over Oklahoma. Biletnikoff started his pro career as a special teams player and did not see action as a flanker until the seventh game of his rookie campaign. When he did get a chance to start, he responded with a 7-catch, 118-yard performance and, in the process, became a regular for good. [DS/PF]

GEORGE BLANDA

Quarterback-Kicker. 6-2, 215. Kentucky
Born September 17, 1927, Youngwood, Pennsylvania.
1949-1958 Chicago Bears, 1950 Baltimore, 1960-66 Houston, 1967-1975 Oakland
Inducted into Pro Football Hall of Fame in 1981.

Although Blanda played pro football for 26 seasons—far longer than any other individual—he will be remembered best for his 1970 season with the Raiders.

In a five-game period, he provided Oakland with 4 victories and 1 tie with last-second touchdown passes or field goals—at age 43. The string started with a 3-touchdown passing outburst against Pittsburgh and continued with a 48-yard field goal with 3 seconds left to tie Kansas City. He threw a touchdown pass and added a 52-yard field goal in the last 96 seconds to defeat Cleveland. Next came a winning touchdown pass against Denver and a last-instant field goal to upend San Diego.

Through most of his long career, Blanda had two primary assignments: to pass the football and to kick it. On both jobs, he accumulated impressive credentials. He threw 236 touchdown passes and scored an incredible 2,002 points, most of them by kicking. In 1970, he became the oldest quarterback to play in a championship game. Although the Baltimore Colts won the AFC title 27-17, Blanda accounted for all of the Raiders' points.

Blanda's remarkable 340-game career was divided into three distinct parts, the first 10 years with the Chicago Bears from 1949 to 1958, the next seven with the Houston Oilers from 1960 to 1966 and the final nine years with the Oakland Raiders from 1967 to 1975. He was just a month shy of his forty-ninth birthday when he retired in August, 1976. In his storybook career, he had captured the fancy of fans of all ages but, for the over-40 set of an entire nation, Blanda had provided a new lease on life. [DS/PF]

***DREW BLEDSOE**

Quarterback. 6-5, 233. Washington State
Born February 14, 1972, Ellensburg, Washington.
1993-98 New England

Bill Parcells took over a 2-14 Patriots team and immediately began to rebuild. The centerpiece of that reconstruction was Drew Bledsoe, the top pick in the 1993 draft. Parcells's plan was to bring Bledsoe along slowly. But after he arrived in New England, the Patriots lost 11 of their first 12 games, and the rookie quarterback aired it out. He threw more than 40 passes seven times and amassed 2,494 yards in 12 starts. The Patriots won their last four games of the season.

Bledsoe passed even more in 1994 as he guided the Patriots to victories in their last seven games and a berth in the playoffs for the first time in eight years. Bledsoe led the NFL with 4,555 yards and had more attempts (691) that season than any quarterback in NFL history. Bledsoe became the youngest quarterback to reach 10,000 yards in 1995, and the following year he led the Patriots to Super Bowl XXXI against the Green Bay Packers, a 35-21 loss in Parcells's last game with the team. Under new coach Pete Carroll, Bledsoe passed for a career-high 28 touchdowns in 1997. He surpassed 3,000 yards for the fifth consecutive season in 1998, and at just 26 years of age, he reached the postseason for the fourth time in five years.

The son of two English teachers in Walla Walla, Washington, Bledsoe mastered reading books and reading defenses from an early age. Washington State coach Mike Price made him the first freshman quarterback to start for the Cougars in 30 years. Bledsoe finished his college career ranked second on the school's all-time passing charts (7,373 yards, 46 touchdowns) after just 28 games. [MS]

MEL BLOUNT

Cornerback. 6-3, 205. Southern University
Born April 10, 1948, Vidalia, Georgia.
1970-1983 Pittsburgh
Inducted into Pro Football Hall of Fame in 1989.

When the rule limiting defensive backs' bump-and-run tactics was initiated, many referred to it as the "Blount Rule." The Pittsburgh cornerback was the acknowledged master of the fine art of physically punishing a receiver running a route. But even shorn of his trademark technique, Blount continued as a top defender using more traditional man-for-man and zone coverages.

A pro scouts' All-America as both a safety and cornerback at Southern University, Blount was a third-round draft choice of the Steelers in 1970. Although he did not become a regular at right cornerback until his third season, Blount wound up his 14-season, 200-game pro career with 57 interceptions. The Georgia native also recovered 13 opponents' fumbles, 2 of which he returned for touchdowns. Blessed with excellent speed and strength, Blount also was durable, missing only one game because of injury in his pro career.

He led the league with 11 interceptions in 1975, when he was named the NFL's most valuable defensive player. Blount was an all-pro choice in 1975, 1977 and 1981 and also a four-time All-AFC selection. He played in five AFC-NFC Pro Bowls. In Super Bowl XIII, Blount's interception ignited a Pittsburgh drive that resulted in a go-ahead touchdown in the Steelers' 35-31 victory over the Dallas Cowboys. [DS/PF]

AL BLOZIS

Tackle. 6-6, 250. Georgetown.
Born August 15, 1919, Garfield, New Jersey.
Died January 31, 1945.
1942-44 New York Giants

Had Al Blozis lived, his bust might well be found today in the Enshrinees Hall at the Pro Football Hall of Fame. Certainly in his brief three-season career, he gave every evidence of becoming one of the great tackles in NFL history.

Ironically, football probably was not his best sport. Blozis was the best shot putter of his time. He won the national championship in that event from 1940 through 1942, setting both the world indoor and outdoor records along the way. He also won championships in the discus. His skill earned him such nicknames as "Big Bertha" (after a famous cannon) and "The Human Howitzer."

On the football field, Blozis won All-America honors at Georgetown University in both 1940 and 1941. The Hoyas went to the Orange Bowl in his senior year. In 1986, he was elected to the National Football Foundation College Hall of Fame.

Blozis joined the New York Giants in 1942 and became an immediate starter. The next year, he was named all-pro.

Blozis was initially rejected for military service because of his height, but in 1944 those restrictions were relaxed. Weekend leaves while he attended Officers' Candidate School allowed him to continue playing with the Giants as they won the 1944 NFL Eastern Division championship. Six weeks after playing in the championship game, he was in combat in France. When one of his men failed to return from a patrol, Lieutenant Blozis went out in a blinding snowstorm to find him. His body was never found. [BC]

TERRY BRADSHAW

Quarterback. 6-3, 210. Louisiana Tech
Born September 2, 1948, Shreveport, Louisiana.
1970-1983 Pittsburgh
Inducted into Pro Football Hall of Fame in 1989.

Bradshaw was at his best in big games. In the 1974 AFC Championship Game against Oakland, his fourth-quarter touchdown pass to Lynn Swann proved to be the winning score in a 24-13 victory. In the Super Bowl IX victory over Minnesota that followed, his fourth-quarter touchdown pass put the Steelers out of reach.

In Super Bowl X, Bradshaw again threw the winning touchdown pass on a 64-yard bomb to Swann. He was named the most valuable player in both Super Bowl XIII (35-31 over Dallas) and Super Bowl XIV (31-19 over the Los Angeles Rams). In four Super Bowls, he passed for 932 yards and 9 touchdowns. In 19 postseason games, he completed 261 passes for 3,833 yards.

But his career was not always the stuff of highlight films. Considered to be the most outstanding senior in 1969 by most pro scouts, Bradshaw was the first player selected in the 1970 NFL draft. Pittsburgh fans confidently expected him to lead the Steelers to a championship— immediately. He had the talent, but not the maturity. That took several seasons. He went through many rough learning experiences before emerging as a dominant quarterback. But once he blossomed, he led the Steelers to an unprecedented four Super Bowl titles in a six-year period from 1974-79.

In his 14-season career, Bradshaw completed 2,025 of 3,901 passes for 27,989 yards and 212 touchdowns. He also rushed 444 times for 2,257 yards and 32 touchdowns. Bradshaw, who was all-pro in 1978 and All-AFC in 1979, also was named to three Pro Bowls. [DS/PF]

GENE BRITO

End-Defensive End. 6-1, 230. Loyola (California)
Born October 23, 1925, Los Angeles, California.
Died June 6, 1965, Los Angeles, California.
1951-53, 1955-58 Washington, 1959-1960 Los Angeles

Gene Brito received the Presidential Seal of Approval from both Richard M. Nixon and John F. Kennedy when he played a consistently high level of defensive end for the Redskins. Both Nixon (especially as vice president) and Kennedy (going back to his Senate days) saw Brito play often and proclaimed him their favorite player.

Brito, a World War II veteran, was older than most rookies (25) when he reported to the Redskins in 1951. A two-way end in college, he was used more on offense than defense early on, but though more than adequate on offense, he shone on defense. By 1953, he was a defensive specialist. A contract dispute in 1954 sent him to the Canadian Football League for a year. Brito returned to play at an all-pro pace for the Redskins until 1959, when he was traded to his home-state Rams.

Brito, light even in his day, used quickness to the extreme. NFL folklore includes this story: Brito was beating a Steelers tackle and tattooing the quarterback so badly, the quarterback said to the hapless lineman that, even if the official was looking, he was to hold Brito. The lineman replied: "But I have been holding him!"

In the 1961 preseason, Brito was stricken by a disease similar to the ALS that felled baseball's Lou Gehrig. He died in 1965. Teammate Les Richter said at Brito's funeral, "He was never a cheerleader and he never was emotional—his cheerleading and emotional qualities appeared to us in the way he played the game." [JJC]

CHARLIE BROCK

Center. 6-2, 203. Nebraska
Born March 15, 1916, Columbus, Nebraska.
Died May 25, 1987, Green Bay, Wisconsin.
1939-1947 Green Bay

Football was a two-way game in the 1940s, and Charlie Brock was as good at it as anybody. As a center, he was considered one of the best in the game; as a linebacker, he was called a "ball thief." He played nine years with the Packers and was a key member of two world championship teams led by Hall of Fame coach Earl (Curly) Lambeau.

The National Football League was still relatively young when Brock was lettering in football and track at the University of Nebraska, but the Packers were already entrenched in tradition. Green Bay, which had been in the National Football League since 1921, already had four titles—and had missed a fifth by a touchdown to the New York Giants in 1938—the season before Brock joined the Packers. The team added another title in Brock's first year in 1939 with a 27-0 revenge win over the Giants. For the next four years, the Packers chased the great Chicago Bears teams down to the wire.

Brock, who was All-America at Nebraska, was named captain of the Packers in 1944 and the team responded with another title—again over the Giants. He stood out in era that featured legendary centers such as Mel Hein, Clyde (Bulldog) Turner, and Alex Wojciechowicz.

The two-way era took its toll on players, and Brock retired in 1947 at the age of 31. He was selected to the Nebraska Hall of Fame, the Packers' Hall of Fame, and was named to the Packers' Iron-Man Team in 1976. [MS]

JOHN BRODIE

Quarterback. 6-1, 210. Stanford
Born August 14, 1935, San Francisco, California.

1957-1973 San Francisco
Brodie may be the best pro golfer ever to play quarterback. Or the best quarterback ever to play professional golf. He melded both careers during most of his 17 years in the NFL, and, when his football days ended, he continued to compete on the PGA tour.

Brodie was always considered one of the NFL's most talented passers during his years with the 49ers, most of them frustrating seasons when the club would huff and puff and blow no one away. He made three passes at glory in the early seventies when the 49ers made three consecutive playoff appearances, twice losing to the Cowboys in the NFC title game and a third time incredibly blowing an 15-point lead with 16 minutes to play in a first-round 1972 playoff game against Dallas.

He was a homegrown 49er. He had been a ball boy for the team during the early fifties, worked his way up from the number-six quarterback slot at Stanford to achieve All-America status in 1957, and became the 49ers' number-one draft choice that season.

There were few nicer people in the NFL than Brodie, yet that nice mien masked toughness that enabled him to compete successfully for the starting job against future Hall of Fame quarterback Y.A. Tittle (traded to the Giants), Bill Kilmer (traded to the Saints), Steve Spurrier (a Heisman Trophy winner and the 49ers' number-one pick in 1967), and a few other interlopers.

During all of this, he still managed to throw 215 touchdown passes and for 31,548 yards. [JC]

BOB BROWN
Tackle. 6-4, 278. Nebraska
Born December 8, 1941, Cleveland, Ohio.
1964-68 Philadelphia, 1969-1970 Los Angeles, 1971-73 Oakland
"I'm about as subtle as a sixteen-pound sledgehammer," Bob Brown said of his style of offensive tackle play.

While the conventional wisdom on pass blocking calls for the tackle to absorb the rusher and neutralize him, the mammoth Brown pass blocked aggressively. He drove his shoulder into a defensive end; he didn't grapple with him. Brown exploded off the ball and into whatever got in his way. Richard Harris, a veteran of NFL trench warfare, said, "He fires out. He slams you with both forearms. After a while, that can take the wind out of you."

That's exactly what Brown wanted. He said, "I beat on people from the opening kickoff. I want to see results in the fourth quarter. I don't want them to have as much left. I want them to not be sure they want to keep coming. I try to take a toll on them."

Although a knee injury suffered in 1967 bothered him the rest of his career, he was All-NFL in seven of his ten seasons and named NFL/NFC offensive lineman of the year three times. He was chosen for six Pro Bowls—three with the Eagles, two with Rams, and one final time with the Raiders.

In his first Raiders camp, Brown got the attention of his new teammates. While warming up, he shattered a 4-by-4 wooden goal post with his brawny forearm. [JJC]

HARDY BROWN
Linebacker. 6-0, 193. SMU, Tulsa.
Born May 8, 1924, Childress, Texas.
Died November 8, 1991, Stockton, California.
1948 Brooklyn AAFC, 1949 Chicago AAFC, 1950 Baltimore, 1950 Washington, 1951-56 San Francisco, 1957 Chicago Cardinals, 1960 Denver AFL
Hardy Brown was a one-trick pony. But it was a heckuva trick. As a linebacker, Brown wasn't all that good at covering pass receivers and was a bit slow in pursuit. But he was one of the hardest hitters in the NFL's long history.

Brown's method was simplicity in itself. He would crouch in front of an oncoming ball carrier like a compressed spring. At the optimum moment, he would launch himself forward and upward, making no attempt to wrap up the ball carrier. Instead, he would smash his shoulder into the unfortunate player and knock him to the ground.

In one game, Brown's rugged technique knocked out the entire Washington backfield.

For his unusual skill, Brown gained the nickname "Thumper" and the distinction of being the most hated man in the league. Except for a six-season stay with the San Francisco 49ers, Thumper never lasted more than a season with any of the seven teams in three leagues in which he played. [BC]

JIM BROWN
Fullback. 6-2, 232. Syracuse
Born February 17, 1936, St. Simons, Georgia.
1957-1965 Cleveland
Inducted into Pro Football Hall of Fame in 1971.
When a reporter asked Cleveland Coach Paul Brown if he might be overusing his star fullback, the coach answered, "When you've got the biggest cannon, you shoot it." Jim Brown was several notches above any other runner of his time.

In nine years (before he quit for a movie career) he led the NFL in rushing eight times, totaled 12,312 yards, 106 rushing touchdowns, and 756 points. He set records for rushing attempts and was a marked man on every play, yet never missed a down because of injury.

Special defenses were designed to stop him, but none succeeded for long. On 58 occasions he rushed for more than 100 yards in a game. Four times he topped 200. He rushed for a career-high 1,863 yards in 1963. He was named to nine Pro Bowls, won the Maxwell Trophy in 1963, was chosen rookie of the year in 1957, and MVP in both 1958 and 1965.

Brown was one of the most versatile athletes ever. At Syracuse, he lettered in basketball and was an All-America in football and lacrosse. As a college sophomore, he finished fifth in the national decathlon championship and his marks actually surpassed those of Jim Thorpe in 6 of the 10 events.

He was the perfect combination of speed and size, a runaway boxcar at 6-2 and 232 pounds—with a 32-inch waist. Ironically, Cleveland had wanted to draft quarterback Len Dawson in the 1957 draft. When the Pittsburgh Steelers took Dawson first, Cleveland was forced to "settle" for Brown. [DS/PF/BC]

ROGER BROWN
Defensive Tackle. 6-5, 298. Maryland Eastern Shore
Born May 1, 1937, Surry County, Virginia
1960-66 Detroit, 1967-69 Los Angeles Rams
Roger Brown knew how to make an impact. Brown was drafted in the fourth round in 1960 out of Maryland Eastern Shore and quickly found himself a starter on the Detroit Lions' defensive line with Alex Karras and Darris McCord. That trio remained intact for the next six years. Although the Lions were not able to overtake the powerhouse Green Bay Packers in the standings, Detroit had its day—Thanksgiving Day.

The Lions beat the Packers twice, lost once and tied once on Thanksgiving Day from 1960 to 1963, but the game that everyone remembers occurred on November 22, 1962. The Packers came into Detroit on Thanksgiving with a 10-0 record and were looking to carve up the Lions on their way to their second straight title. Instead, the Lions beat Green Bay 26-14 to hand the Packers their only loss of the season.

After five consecutive Pro Bowl seasons with the Lions, Brown was sent to the Los Angeles Rams, where he had another Pro Bowl season in 1967. He went from a power trio in Detroit to the Fearsome Foursome in Los Angeles—and didn't miss a beat. Brown replaced Rosey Grier in the Rams' famous defensive front, and he played in the postseason in 1969 for the first and only time of his career. He retired after the season. [MS]

ROOSEVELT BROWN
Tackle. 6-3, 255. Morgan State
Born October 20, 1932, Charlottesville, Virginia.
1953-1965 New York Giants
Inducted into Pro Football Hall of Fame in 1975.
As the 1953 National Football League college draft entered its final stages, the New York Giants were wondering whom to pick next. Someone in the Giants' front office noticed a weekly newspaper, the *Pittsburgh Courier,* had picked a 6-3, 225-pound tackle named Brown to the Black All-America team of 1952. Deciding they had nothing to lose, the Giants chose him in the twenty-seventh round. It turned out to be one of the truly great "sleeper" picks of all time.

Brown quickly developed into one of the premier offensive lineman in history. He was the Giants' starting offensive right tackle for 13 years. He was an all-pro choice eight consecutive years from 1956 through 1963 and was named to the Pro Bowl nine times. In 1975, Brown became only the second player to be elected to the Pro Football Hall of Fame on the merits of his offensive line play alone.

The odds were astronomical that the 20-year-old recruit who first reported to the Giants' 1953 training camp would attain even a regular job, let alone the top honor of his profession. Brown had signed a $2,700 contract—there were no bonus provisions—but he wasn't afraid of being cut because he simply didn't know he could be.

Giants coach Steve Owen decided Rosey was big enough to deserve a "good look," which meant a scrimmage against all-pro defensive tackle Arnie Weinmeister. Brown took a frightful pounding, but Owen saw enough potential to keep Brown on the squad. A few weeks later, he became a starter, a job he held for the rest of his career. [DS/PF]

WILLIE BROWN
Defensive Back. 6-1, 210. Grambling
Born December 2, 1940, Yazoo City, Mississippi.
1963-66 Denver, 1967-1978 Oakland
Inducted into Pro Football Hall of Fame in 1984.
Sometimes the scouts miss them. Brown was an excellent end for four years at Grambling but was not drafted by either the NFL or AFL when his college career ended in 1963.

He was signed by the Houston Oilers as a free agent but cut before the end of summer camp. He then went to Denver where he became a starter midway into his rookie season. A year later, he intercepted 4 passes against the New York Jets to tie an all-time record, won All-AFL honors, and played in his first AFL All-Star game.

Brown's career with the Denver Broncos and the Oakland Raiders spanned 16 seasons and 205 games from 1963 through 1978. Even though the Broncos were not successful on the playing field during Brown's four years in Denver, the 6-foot 1-inch, 210-pound cornerback was an established star by the time he was traded to the Raiders in 1967. With a perpetually contending team in Oakland, Brown's outstanding abilities emerged into clear focus. Armed with speed, mobility, aggressiveness, determination, and a keen football sense, Brown became a key figure in every Raider success.

Altogether, Brown was named to an all-league team seven times. He was elected to the AFL's all-time team in 1969. He also played in five AFL All-Star games and four AFC-NFC Pro Bowls. During his career, he intercepted 54 passes, which he returned for 472 yards and 2 touchdowns. His biggest steal came in Super Bowl XI, when he returned an interception 75 yards for the clinching touchdown. [DS/PF]

JUNIOUS (BUCK) BUCHANAN
Defensive Tackle. 6-7, 274. Grambling
Born September 10, 1940, Gainesville, Alabama.
Died July 16, 1992, Kansas City, Missouri.
1963-1975 Kansas City
Inducted into Pro Football Hall of Fame in 1990.
Eddie Robinson, the legendary coach at Grambling where Buchanan was an NAIA All-America in 1962, called Buck "the finest lineman I have seen."

During an era when Kansas City possessed some of pro football's biggest stars, Buchanan was a team leader and defensive fixture for 13 years from 1963 through 1975. He was the first player selected in the 1963 AFL draft, and he quickly proved the rave notices that preceded him to Kansas City were not unfounded.

Buchanan had the physical size—6 feet 7 inches and 274 pounds—plus the athletic instincts to be exceptionally successful at his job of foiling opposition offenses. He was particularly effective at intimidating the passer and in 1967 alone, Buchanan batted down 16 passes at or behind the line of scrimmage. The Alabaman was clocked at 4.9 in the 40 and 10.2 in the 100 at Grambling. He could range from sideline to sideline to make tackles.

After dabbling briefly at defensive end as a rookie, Buchanan settled in as the Chiefs' defensive right tackle. For eight seasons beginning in 1964, he played in either the AFL All-Star game or the AFC-NFC Pro Bowl. He was a virtually unanimous All-AFL choice from 1966 through 1969 and then won All-AFC honors in 1970. He was particularly outstanding in Kansas City's 23-7 upset of Minnesota in Super Bowl IV that saw the Buchanan-led defense completely stifle the Vikings' attack. [DS/PF]

NICK BUONICONTI

Linebacker. 5-11, 220. Notre Dame
Born December 15, 1940, Springfield, Massachusetts.
1962-68 Boston, 1969-1976 Miami

"I've got nothing against hydrants," an American Football League fullback noted after a 1968 game against the Boston Patriots. "It's just that I don't enjoy being hit by one all afternoon."

That "hydrant" was Nick Buoniconti, the middle linebacker who for 15 seasons with both Boston and Miami defied all the numbers by which pro football scouts judge potential. At Notre Dame, he had been a 5-11, 210-pound guard who played linebacker on defense. He certainly didn't fit any of the ideal measurements for pro football linebackers even back in 1962 when he was the Patriots' thirteenth-round draft pick. The 14 NFL teams, then battling the fledgling AFL for all available collegiate talent, ignored him in their draft. But as many coaches later noted, Buoniconti "played bigger than his size."

"Every play is like life and death," he once said, when asked why he was so relentless even during practice sessions. "I can't think of anything except the play that is taking place at the moment."

Buoniconti made an immediate impact at middle linebacker while helping the Patriots to the 1963 AFL Eastern Division title. He had played in five postseason AFL All-Star games when Boston traded him to Miami after the 1968 season. He then had his greatest seasons under coach Don Shula as the linchpin of Miami's famed No Name Defense. The Dolphins made three straight Super Bowl appearances, and won the final two, one coming after an incredible unbeaten season in 1972. [JC]

DICK BUTKUS

Linebacker. 6-3, 245. Illinois
Born December 9, 1942, Chicago, Illinois.
1965-1973 Chicago
Inducted into Pro Football Hall of Fame in 1979.

From 1965 through 1973, the Bears' Butkus wreaked unprecedented havoc on other NFL teams. Possessed with a desire to excel that few others have ever known, the 6-foot 3-inch, 245-pound middle linebacker played with one goal in mind—to be the best. "When they say all-pro middle linebacker, I want them to mean Butkus!" he said.

A first-round draft choice of the Chicago Bears, he came to rookie camp needlessly fretting about his chances of beating out Bill George, the incumbent middle linebacker. As things turned out, Butkus had no challengers at his position and only one for rookie of the year: Bears teammate, running back Gale Sayers.

Butkus was named all-pro for the first of seven times, and the Chicago native also played in eight Pro Bowls. He even figured in the statistical columns with 47 takeaways, 22 on pass interceptions and 25 on recoveries of opponents' fumbles, including a recovery for a touchdown.

Butkus had drive, meanness, a consuming desire to pursue, tackle, and manhandle— anything he could do to thwart his opponent on every play. Still he was a clean player, totally devoted to his career, a man who by his own admission played every game as though it were his last one.

He had the speed and agility to make tackles from sideline to sideline and to cover the best tight ends and running backs on pass plays. There's no telling what heights Butkus might have realized had he not suffered a knee injury in 1970. The knee didn't totally respond to surgery, and, three years later, he limped off an NFL field for the last time. "I gave the game all I could for as long as I could, "Butkus said. "I guess my only regret is that my career was too short." [DS/PF]

JACK BUTLER

Defensive Back. 6-0, 195. St. Bonaventure
Born November 12, 1927, Pittsburgh, Pennsylvania.
1951-59 Pittsburgh

Pittsburgh football writer Pat Livingston described Jack Butler as "having the face of a choirboy and the heart of an arsonist."

Butler, a four-time Pro Bowl defensive back, described his style: "The best pass defense is the respect of the receivers. If they know they're gonna get hit as soon as they touch the ball, they're not so relaxed about catching it." No one relaxed much in Butler's territory, which was a considerable portion of the football field.

Some said only Hall of Fame defensive back Dick (Night Train) Lane was Butler's equal in the 1950s, and he finished his career in 1959 with 52 interceptions. Only Emlen Tunnell and Lane had more at the time. Tunnell called Butler "a defensive genius."

That Butler played in the NFL at all is surprising. He never played high school football, studying for the priesthood at a small Canadian Catholic seminary instead. When he enrolled at St. Bonaventure, he thought he would give football a try. At the first practice, he lined up with the ends because he was about their size. He turned out to be a pretty good end, but he wasn't flooded with pro offers. Father Dan Rooney, brother of Pittsburgh Steelers owner Art, recommended the baby-faced Butler. Art, who had played sandlot ball with Jack's father, took a chance. Many NFL receivers and runners wished he hadn't.

Butler was a fine clutch receiver himself when used in special situations. After a freak injury ended his career, he pioneered the use of computers in college player scouting. [JJC]

***LeROY BUTLER**

Safety. 6-0, 200. Florida State
Born July 19, 1968, Jacksonville, Florida.
1990-98 Green Bay

LeRoy Butler was born so pigeon-toed that doctors had to break bones in both of his feet before he was a year old. He spent much of his youth in Jacksonville watching other children play while confined to a wheelchair. When the braces came off, Butler made up for lost time in miraculous fashion to become one of the great playmaking safeties of the 1990s. "My biggest thing is not only making a big play but turning the whole game around," Butler said. "I expect to make the big play."

Drafted as a cornerback in the second round of the 1990 draft, Butler served as a Nickel back as a rookie and then started at cornerback in 1991. Mike Holmgren moved Butler to strong safety shortly after he was named coach in 1992. Butler responded by earning all-pro honors four times in seven seasons.

Butler is as gifted and complete a safety as any scout could draw up. His speed and man-for-man cover ability enable him to take even the best pass-catching tight ends out of the game. He anticipates well and has a nose for the interception. Despite ordinary size for stopping the run he is both a jarring and reliable tackler.

And, when defensive coordinator Fritz Shurmur really began to turn him loose, Butler registered 6 sacks in 1996 (the most ever by an NFL defensive back is 7). "The best description of LeRoy is that if the ball is there, he's near it," Shurmur said. "He has amazing instincts and feel for where the ball is going." [BM]

EARL CAMPBELL

Running Back. 5-11, 233. Texas
Born March 29, 1955, Tyler, Texas.
1978-1984 Houston, 1984-85 New Orleans
Inducted into Pro Football Hall of Fame in 1991.

"The Tyler Rose"—because he was a native of Tyler, Texas—took the NFL by storm right from the start. Earl Campbell, a ball-carrying dynamo with thighs like tree trunks, joined the Houston Oilers as the first player taken in the 1978 NFL draft.

At the University of Texas, he'd been an All-America and the Heisman Trophy winner in 1977. Few rookies make such an immediate impact. In 1978, he was named the NFL's most valuable player, all-pro and rookie of the year. He won the league rushing title and was named to the AFC Pro Bowl squad.

He repeated as MVP in 1979, but his best season came in 1980 when he rushed for 1,934 yards. In 1981, he won his fourth straight AFC rushing title. In his eight-season career, Campbell rushed for 9,407 yards and 74 touchdowns. He was picked for the Pro Bowl five of his first six NFL seasons.

In spite of the constant pounding he took from opposing defenders, Campbell missed only six games out of 115 because of injuries.

Although he had four games in which he gained more than 200 yards rushing, Campbell's most famous performance came in a Monday night game against Miami in his rookie season when he just missed 200. That night, he rushed for 199 yards and 4 touchdowns to lead the Oilers to a spectacular 35-30 victory. [DS/PF]

TONY CANADEO

Halfback. 5-11, 195. Gonzaga
Born May 5, 1919, Chicago, Illinois.
1941-44, 1946-1952 Green Bay
Inducted into Pro Football Hall of Fame in 1974.

During the 11 years Canadeo played for the Green Bay Packers, he played offense and defense, ran with the football, threw passes, caught passes, intercepted passes, punted, and returned punts and kickoffs.

Altogether, the hard-working star amassed 8,626 yards on 1,488 multi-categoried attempts with a football, almost 75 yards in each of his 116 NFL games.

A product of little-known Gonzaga University in Spokane, Washington, Canadeo was an unsung seventh-round draft choice of the Packers in 1941. From 1941 to 1944, the Packers were one of the NFL's premier teams with a cumulative 33-7-2 mark. During those years, Canadeo served as an understudy to the great Green Bay passer Cecil Isbell.

Canadeo's pro career was interrupted in his fourth season by a call to serve in World War II. When he returned, he found the post-war segment of his Packers career to be vastly different. In Canadeo's final seven years, after his return in 1946, the Packers record was 29-53-1. During those years, he became a heavy-duty running back and, in 1949, he became only the third player in NFL history to rush for 1,000 yards.

Nicknamed "The Gray Ghost of Gonzaga" because he was prematurely gray, Tony never looked the part of a football player, let alone a truly great one. He was small by pro gridiron standards and not exceptionally fast. Nevertheless, he employed determination, courage and tenacity to become a star. [DS/PF]

HARRY CARSON

Linebacker. 6-2, 240. South Carolina State
Born November 26, 1953, Florence, South Carolina.
1976-1988 New York Giants

Bill Arnsparger pointed at Harry Carson, who was going through a tortuous set of agility drills all by himself. "There is a future star," the Giants' head coach said. Arnsparger was absolutely correct.

In the tradition of great defensive players—long a hallmark of New York Giants football—Carson, a fourth-round draft pick in 1976, was an outstanding player for the team during 13 seasons. Often he was the only great player on a team that struggled through the first half of his National Football League career.

Carson was an inside linebacker and a ferocious run stopper. Later in his career when he was joined by outside linebackers Lawrence Taylor and Carl Banks, there was no better linebacking trio in the NFL and they proved it by helping the Giants win Super Bowl XXI after the 1986 season.

Carson, a defensive lineman in college, always retained the unique approach that position brings to the game. He freely slammed his body into onrushing blockers and often tossed them right back into the runner. Like Lawrence Taylor, he was difficult to stop man-for-man on blitzing pass rushes, and he had the speed and quickness to track down plays away from his position. He looked like a big jungle cat as he blithely sped through the melee of a play to make a tackle.

He was well-recognized by his peers, appearing in nine Pro Bowls during his career, including seven straight from

1981 through 1987 as a member of the Giants. [JC]

***CRIS CARTER**

Wide Receiver. 6-3, 216. Ohio State
Born November 25, 1965, Middletown, Ohio.
1987-89 Philadelphia, 1990-98 Minnesota

The Vikings claimed Cris Carter on waivers five days before the start of the 1990 season. He has gone on to set club records for most receiving yards, receptions, and touchdown receptions. Carter set an NFL record with 122 catches in 1994 and equaled that number the following year (Detroit's Herman Moore topped Carter's mark by 1 catch in 1995). The 207 combined receptions by Carter and teammate Jake Reed in 1994 were more than any other tandem in NFL history.

The Eagles drafted Carter, the younger brother of former NBA player Butch Carter, out of Ohio State in the fourth round of the 1987 supplemental draft. He caught 11 touchdown passes for Philadelphia in 1989, but was waived the following year.

In Minnesota, Carter has caught at least 50 passes each season since 1991, and he has been named to the Pro Bowl each of the past six seasons. The Vikings have reached the playoffs six times since Carter joined the team. In 1998, the Vikings drafted deep threat Randy Moss and reunited Carter with Randall Cunningham, who was Carter's quarterback in Philadelphia. The result was the NFL's most lethal passing attack and a franchise record 15-1 mark. [MS]

DAVE CASPER

Tight End. 6-4, 232. Notre Dame.
Born September 26, 1951, Bemidji, Minnesota.
1974-79, 1984 Raiders, 1980-83 Houston, 1983 Minnesota

Dave Casper was big enough to be a defensive lineman and quick enough to play tight end. In fact, he did both.

Casper spent his first two years at Notre Dame as a defensive tackle before he was switched to tight end as a junior. His size did not go unnoticed. Legendary coach Paul (Bear) Bryant called Casper "half a line by himself." Defenders found the best way to stop Casper was to hold him, a defensive tactic that followed Casper from college to the pros.

He helped push the Oakland Raiders from contender to Super Bowl champion. He was chosen in the second round of the 1974 draft but spent his first two years on special teams before he secured the starting tight end spot. At that point, he gave quarterback Kenny Stabler another reliable target to go along with wide receivers Cliff Branch and Fred Biletnikoff.

"The Ghost" (a play on Casper, the cartoon character) caught 4 passes, including a touchdown, in Super Bowl XI. On Christmas Eve, 1977, Casper made an over-the-shoulder touchdown catch in the final minutes of regulation to set up a tying field goal against the Baltimore Colts. Casper's third touchdown catch of the day, in the second overtime, lifted the Oakland Raiders over the Colts and into their fifth consecutive AFC Championship Game.

After six years with the Raiders, Casper played for the Houston Oilers (1980-83). He returned to his native Minnesota to complete 1983 with the Vikings, but he finished his career the way it started, in a Raiders uniform in 1984. Casper played in five Pro Bowls and was named to the Pro Football Hall of Fame's All-Pro Squad of the 1970s. [MS]

GUY CHAMBERLIN

End, Coach. 6-1, 210. Nebraska
Born January 16, 1894, Blue Springs, Nebraska.
Died April 4, 1967, Lincoln, Nebraska.
1920-21 Decatur/Chicago Staleys, 1922-23 Canton, 1924 Cleveland, 1925-26 Frankford, 1927 Chicago Cardinals
Inducted into Pro Football Hall of Fame in 1965.

As a player, Chamberlin was one of the best ends of his time. As a coach in the early days of the NFL when the only statistic kept was the team's won-lost record, Chamberlin compiled a 56-14-5 won-lost mark and an .824 winning percentage—a mark some of history's most famous coaches have not approached. In his six coaching seasons, five of which were spent as a player-coach, Chamberlin also won four NFL championships: for the Canton Bulldogs in 1922 and 1923, the Cleveland Bulldogs in 1924 and the Frankford Yellow Jackets in 1926.

A two-time All-America at the University of Nebraska, Chamberlin was lured into pro football by his idol, Jim Thorpe, to play with the pre-NFL Canton Bulldogs in 1919. When George Halas began lining up players for his first Decatur Staleys team in 1920, Chamberlin was his prime recruit.

He was big, tall, and fast, excellent on both offense and defense and a 60-minute player every game. Chamberlain played with the Chicago Staleys in 1921, when Halas won his first championship. A year later, Chamberlin began his career as a player-coach with the Canton Bulldogs.

Canton, with undefeated seasons in both 1922 and 1923, became the NFL's first two-time champion. The Bulldogs were sold to a Cleveland promoter in 1924 but Chamberlin, with a slightly different cast of players, led his team to a third straight title. He joined the Frankford Yellow Jackets in 1925 and a year later won another title, this time with a 14-1-1 mark. The 3-7-1 mark of the 1927 Chicago Cardinals was the lone blemish on an otherwise almost-perfect coaching record. [DS/PF]

JACK CHRISTIANSEN

Defensive Back. 6-1, 185. Colorado State
Born December 20, 1928, Sublette, Texas.
Died June 29, 1986, Stanford, California.
1951-58 Detroit
Inducted into Pro Football Hall of Fame in 1970.

During the 1950s, when Detroit dominated the NFL with four divisional and three world championships, the Lions boasted a fine offensive unit paced by Bobby Layne and Doak Walker. Yet it was the formidable defensive unit that set the Lions apart from the rest of the NFL pack.

The key was the defensive backfield foursome known as Chris's Crew because safety Jack Christiansen was the leader of the pack. He played with the Lions eight seasons from 1951-58 and was named all-pro six consecutive years. He played in five consecutive Pro Bowls. Christiansen contributed 46 interceptions to the Lions' cause.

Christiansen was considered a longshot when the Lions

drafted him in the sixth round in 1951. At Colorado State, he starred on offense, defense, and return teams, but he was not big enough to be a heavy-duty ball carrier in the NFL.

So defense is what Christiansen played. Two years later, Lions coach Buddy Parker was espousing a new theory: "If I had to lose four good backs, I'd rather give up the men on offense. You can always get someone to run the ball, but good defensive backs are hard to find."

Christiansen also excelled on the return units. As a rookie, he brought back 4 punts for touchdowns, and, before he retired, he added 4 more to that total. The standard rule around the NFL when playing the Lions was don't throw in Christiansen's area and don't kick to him, either. [DS/PF]

EARL (DUTCH) CLARK

Quarterback. 6-0, 185. Colorado College
Born October 11, 1906, Fowler, Colorado.
Died August 5, 1978, Canon City, Colorado.
1931-32 Portsmouth, 1934-38 Detroit
Inducted into Pro Football Hall of Fame in 1963.

Clark's story didn't fit the ordinary picture of an all-time pro football great. In 1929 he became the first Colorado College football star ever named All-America, yet he didn't play his first pro game until 1931, when he joined the Portsmouth Spartans. After two all-pro seasons, he retired to become head coach at another small college, the Colorado School of Mines.

By the time he returned to the NFL in 1934, the Spartans had become the Detroit Lions. From 1934 to 1938 calling signals from his tailback position, Clark was the mastermind behind the Lions' famed infantry attack that set a team rushing record in 1936 that stood for 36 years. He was an all-pro quarterback four more times.

Even before the year layoff in 1933, Clark was considered slow, and his eyesight was so poor he had trouble seeing receivers. Furthermore, the Spartans' star was so humble and unassuming that he hesitated to call his own signal, lest his teammates think he was hogging the limelight.

Nevertheless, in his seven NFL seasons, he was the Lions' true triple-threat, consistently finishing among the leaders in rushing and once completed 53.5 percent of his passes in a season when the league average was just 36.5 percent. He also led the league in scoring three times and, as the NFL's last great dropkicker, was Detroit's conversion and field-goal specialist.

Yet, if any one trait of Clark's stood out above the rest, it was his genius for quick thinking on the gridiron. "If Clark stepped on the field with Red Grange, Jim Thorpe, and George Gipp," a rival coach once said, "Dutch would be the general." [DS/PF]

CHARLIE CONERLY

Quarterback. 6-1, 185. Mississippi
Born September 19, 1923, Clarksdale, Mississippi.
Died February 13, 1996, Memphis, Tennessee.
1948-1961 New York Giants

Mississippi All-America "Chuckin' Charlie" Conerly was billed as "the new Sammy Baugh" when he came to New York in 1948. He lost no time in breaking the NFL record for most passes completed in a single game (36) against Pittsburgh. The bad news was that the Giants lost the game.

Though he had several fine seasons throwing the ball, the Giants' losing record soon brought him long and loud choruses of boos from impatient New York fans. After the Giants hit bottom in 1953, he was ready to retire.

But new coach Jim Lee Howell contacted him after the season, assured him he was still the Giants' number-one quarterback, and that an influx of talented supporting players was on the way. Conerly came back to New York for what turned out to be his greatest seasons.

Instead of throwing on down after down, Conerly was able to concentrate on directing the Giants' new-found running game featuring Frank Gifford and Alex Webster. Once the run was established, Conerly was able to use his occasional passes—he averaged fewer than 20 a game after 1953—with far more telling effect.

In 1956, he guided New York to an NFL championship, and in 1958 and 1959 he took them to division titles. In 1959—when he led the NFL in passing—he was named the league's most valuable player. [BC]

GEORGE CONNOR

Tackle-Defensive Tackle-Linebacker. 6-3, 240. Holy Cross, Notre Dame
Born January 21, 1925, Chicago, Illinois.
1948-1955 Chicago Bears
Inducted into Pro Football Hall of Fame in 1975.

When Connor was in college, he earned All-America honors three times, once at Holy Cross in 1943 and then at Notre Dame in 1946 and 1947. In his eight-year career with the Bears, he was named all-pro at three different positions—offensive tackle, defensive tackle, and linebacker. In 1952 and 1953, he was named all-league on both the offensive and defensive teams by different wire services.

Although Connor is remembered as one of the best of the post-World War II tackles, it was as a linebacker that he made his biggest mark in pro football. The Philadelphia Eagles were running roughshod over the NFL in 1949 and one end sweep with two guards and the fullback leading Steve Van Buren around the flank had been particularly successful. The Bears' coaching staff hit upon the idea of moving a big, fast, agile man like Connor into a linebacking slot to try to stop the play. The move was made, the experiment was successful, the Eagles were beaten and, Connor became a linebacker for keeps.

The Notre Dame graduate was always one of the smartest men on the field wherever he played. He seemed instinctively to know about keys—the tips that the movements of certain offensive players will provide to the alert defender as to which way the play is going—long before keys became the vogue.

Connor always played the game hard and clean and with exceptional effectiveness and he might have continued in a starring role for many years had not a knee injury cut short his career after eight seasons. [DS/PF]

ROGER CRAIG

Running Back. 6-0, 225. Nebraska.
Born July 10, 1960, Preston, Mississippi.
1983-1990 San Francisco, 1991 Raiders, 1992-93 Minnesota

Roger Craig was the perfect back for San Francisco's West Coast offense. He had the size to run inside, the speed to run wide, and the hands of a reliable pass receiver.

The versatile offense devised by 49ers coach Bill Walsh used short flare passes as a way to break a running back outside. Although the plays were counted statistically as passes, they were really an extension of a running play. The passes were better than traditional pitchouts that had been around forever in that the runner-receiver could be farther out and closer to the line of scrimmage when he received the ball.

Craig's running ability turned innumerable short flare passes into long gains. Not surprisingly, he led the 49ers in rushing yards and pass receptions three times each. In 1985, he became the first player in NFL history to gain more than 1,000 yards both rushing and receiving in a single season, running for 1,050 yards and accumulating 1,016 receiving. His 92 receptions that season led the NFL.

Coming out of the University of Nebraska, where he rushed for 1,060 yards, Craig had few chances to catch passes; the Cornhuskers relied on an overpowering running game. Nevertheless, San Francisco selected him in the second round of the 1983 NFL draft.

He immediately became a regular, rushing for 725 yards. The next year the 49ers won Super Bowl XIX, and Craig gained 135 yards rushing and receiving and scored a record 3 touchdowns. He went on to help the 49ers win Super Bowls XXIII and XXIV as well. [BC]

LOU CREEKMUR

Tackle-Guard-Defensive Guard. 6-4, 246. William & Mary
Born January 22, 1927, Hopetown, New Jersey.
1950-59 Detroit
Inducted into Pro Football Hall of Fame in 1996.

After starring at William & Mary, Creekmur joined the Detroit Lions in 1950 and quickly established himself as one of the most versatile and talented performers on a team loaded with outstanding stars. During the 1950s, when the Lions won three NFL championships, Creekmur was a perennial all-pro selection.

An outstanding blocker on both passing an rushing plays, Creekmur began his pro career as an offensive guard, winning all-league acclaim at that spot in 1951 and 1952. He then was shifted to offensive left tackle where he remained, except for one season, the rest of his 10-year career. At that position, Creekmur was named all-pro in 1953, 1954, 1956, and 1957. In 1955, he spent most of the season filling in capably, in an emergency situation, at defensive middle guard. Throughout his Detroit tenure, the versatile Creekmur was used in critical short-yardage defensive situations.

Extremely durable, Creekmur played every preseason, regular-season, and postseason game during his first nine campaigns. Besides two divisional playoff games and four NFL championship contests he played in as a Lion, Creekmur was selected to eight consecutive Pro Bowls from 1950-57.

He joins Bobby Layne and Doak Walker as only the third offensive player from the Lions vintage years to earn Pro Football Hall of Fame membership. Defensive teammates already in the Hall of Fame include Joe Schmidt, Jack Christiansen, and Yale Lary. [DS/PF]

LARRY CSONKA

Running Back. 6-3, 235. Syracuse
Born December 25, 1946, Stow, Ohio.
1968-1974, 1979 Miami, 1976-78 New York Giants
Inducted into Pro Football Hall of Fame in 1987.

A classic line-smashing fullback, Csonka provided the major rushing thrust in Miami's vaunted ball-control offense when the Dolphins were dominating the National Football League in the early 1970s. A consensus All-America at Syracuse and the Dolphins' number-one draft pick in 1968, Csonka contributed almost picture-perfect performances during Miami's three Super Bowl seasons in 1971, 1972, and 1973.

Csonka surpassed 1,000 yards in rushing all three seasons with his best production—1,117 yards—coming during Miami's perfect season in 1972. All-AFC three straight seasons (1971-73) and all-pro in 1971, Csonka was selected to play in five consecutive Pro Bowls from 1970-74, although injuries forced him to miss two of those games.

Perhaps his best single-game effort came in Super Bowl VIII, when he was selected as the most valuable player. Miami's powerful attack was at its best with Csonka carrying 33 times for a then-Super Bowl-record 145 yards and 2 touchdowns. He wound up his 11-year AFL-NFL career with 8,081 yards rushing. Extremely sure-handed, he fumbled only 21 of his 1,997 career ball-handling opportunities.

Csonka startled the pro football world by playing out his option with Miami in 1974 to join the Memphis Southmen of the World Football League. When the WFL folded, he joined the New York Giants as a free agent in 1976. He enjoyed moderate success for three seasons with the Giants before returning to the Dolphins for a final 1979 season. [DS/PF]

CURLEY CULP

Nose Tackle-Defensive Tackle. 6-1, 265. Arizona State
Born October 16, 1946, Yuma, Arizona.
1968-1974 Kansas City, 1974-1980 Houston

Curley Culp was the ideal nose tackle in an NFL 3-4 defense. As a youngster he hoisted 55-gallon drums on the family farm in Arizona. As a college wrestler he was NCAA heavyweight champion in 1968 with Arizona State and a member of the Olympic team. His training in Greco-Roman wrestling, where only the upper body and arms—no legs—can be used, helped him when he became a nose tackle.

Culp, a relatively short and compact man, did not fit the mold of a pro defensive tackle when drafted in the second round by the Broncos. Perhaps that is why he was traded to Kansas City before the first regular-season game. He fit in well in Hank Stram's over-shifted, stacked defense. Culp was on the center's nose in a four-man line. He received a lot of credit his second year when the Chiefs disrupted the Vikings' offense in Super Bowl IV.

The Chiefs traded Culp to the Oilers in mid-1974, where he continued to play head-up on the center—but in a 3-4. Culp "wrote the book" on playing nose tackle in Houston. He regarded the position as one that took a different mindset. Culp said, "A defensive lineman's first instinct is to rush the passer, but nose tackles don't have a chance to get a sack. You get off one blocker and there's another. Get off him and there's still another." [JJC]

***RANDALL CUNNINGHAM**

Quarterback. 6-4, 205. Nevada-Las Vegas
Born March 27, 1963, Santa Barbara, California.
1985-1995 Philadelphia, 1997-98 Minnesota

Randall Cunningham has had two NFL careers, and both of them have been successful.

His first career was as the NFL's most mobile quarterback. The brother of Patriots running back Sam (Bam) Cunningham (1973-1982), he arrived in Philadelphia as a running quarterback with a strong arm. A versatile athlete—he was a two-time All-America punter in college—Cunningham stands second in Eagles' history in passing yards and third in rushing yards. He led Philadelphia to the playoffs five times before he retired in 1996.

Cunningham's second NFL career technically began when he signed with the Vikings to be Brad Johnson's backup in 1997, but it did not truly begin until the fourth quarter of an NFC Wild Card Game that year at Giants Stadium. Starting in place of the injured Johnson, Cunningham led the Vikings to 10 points in the final 1:30 to pull out a 23-22 victory, Minnesota's first postseason victory in a decade.

Johnson began the 1998 season as the Vikings' starter, but when he broke his leg in the second game of the season, Cunningham stepped in and had the best season of his career. Cunningham, the NFL's all-time leader in rushing yards by a quarterback, always had been at his best when he took off running, but the Vikings convinced him to stay in the pocket, make the right reads, and make big plays with his arm.

With a receiving tandem of rookie Randy Moss and veteran Cris Carter, Cunningham led the Vikings to an NFL single-season record 556 points and a 15-1 record. Cunningham, who never lost his ability to throw the ball deep with ease and accuracy, passed for 3,704 yards and 34 touchdowns. He made the Pro Bowl for the first time since the 1990 season. [MS]

MIKE CURTIS

Linebacker. 6-2, 232. Duke
Born March 27, 1944, Rockville, Maryland.
1965-1975 Baltimore, 1976 Seattle

Mike Curtis was one of a kind. A linebacker for the Baltimore Colts for 11 seasons, he played on the outside for his first two-and-a-half seasons before coach Don Shula moved him to the middle to prevent opponents from constantly running away from his side of the field. It really didn't matter where he played because Curtis was an equal-opportunity destroyer.

"I play football because it's the only place you can hit people and get away with it," he once said. When a drunken fan ran onto the field during a Saturday afternoon game against the Miami Dolphins in 1971, a Curtis forearm sent him spinning head over heels. "He was on my territory," Curtis said afterward without the slightest show of contrition. He was never one to apologize for what happened in the field.

Curtis was an independent thinker who sometimes seemed to occupy a world apart from everyone else. Colts players often wondered during practice whether Curtis understood that they also were all on his team because he treated them like he treated the opposition on Sunday.

He was fast, smooth, and always under control until he met his target. Then he unleashed a ferocious explosion of punishment. For that, he got a reputation as a vicious player.

"I never went out to hurt another player," he said. "I just played hard. I preferred being called aggressive rather than vicious. I was a competitor, not a bully, and I concentrated all of my energies into first doing my job in a mistake-free manner, and then stopping the guy who was my target." [JC]

***TERRELL DAVIS**

Running Back. 5-11. 210. Long Beach State, Georgia
Born October 28, 1972, San Diego, California.
1995-98 Denver

Terrell Davis fulfilled a lifelong dream by playing in Super Bowl XXXII—and then he took it one step further. Davis not only set a Super Bowl record with 3 rushing touchdowns and earned most valuable player honors in Denver's 31-24 victory in Super Bowl XXXII, he did all this in his hometown of San Diego. He rushed for 157 yards while missing almost an entire quarter with an extremely painful migraine headache, a problem that has plagued him since he played Pop Warner football.

Davis, in mourning from the death of his father to lupus, didn't even play football his first two years of high school. When he transferred from Morse High to Abraham Lincoln Prep, he played nose tackle. Davis switched to running back as a senior. He didn't threaten any records held by Marcus Allen, Lincoln Prep's best known alum, but Davis was good enough to go to Long Beach State. His coach at Long Beach, the legendary George Allen, died in 1990, and the school soon after dropped football. Davis transferred to Georgia and he played well enough to be drafted, but not until the sixth round, after 20 backs had already been taken.

Davis entered the NFL like a seasoned pro instead of an overlooked rookie. He rushed for 1,117 yards in just 14 games in 1995, good for an AFC-leading 4.7 yards per carry. He topped the AFC in rushing the next two seasons, including 10 games of more than 100 yards and an NFL-high 15 touchdowns in 1997. He rushed for 100 yards in all three playoff games to lead the Broncos to the Super Bowl; then he helped them win it, headache and all.

Davis had an even better season in 1998, becoming the fourth running back to surpass 2,000 yards in a season. He rushed for more than 100 yards in three postseason games, including Super Bowl XXXIII, when the Broncos won their second consecutive NFL title with a victory over the

Falcons. He scored 3 postseason touchdowns in 1998. [MS]

TOMMY DAVIS

Kicker-Punter. 6-0, 215. Louisiana State.
Born October 13, 1934, Shreveport, Louisiana.
Died April 2, 1987, Milbrae, California.
1959-1969 San Francisco

Tommy Davis was a very good kicker on some very bad 49ers teams.

Davis, a native of Shreveport, Louisiana, was a standout at Louisiana State University and the 49ers hoped he would help kick them to a championship when they drafted him as a future pick in 1957. He was that rare kicker who was equally adept at punting and kicking, making him particularly valuable in the days of 33-man rosters. He turned out to be one of the NFL's steadiest performers. Unfortunately, San Francisco did not win more than seven games for a decade, even when the schedule expanded to 14 games in 1961.

Davis was the model of consistency, however. He led the NFL in field goals in 1960, kicked the most extra points in 1965, and was the league's top punter in 1962, including a career-long punt of 82 yards. The two-time Pro Bowl performer had only 2 of his 511 punts blocked during his 11-season career. Davis had a 44.7-yard punting average—second place in the all-time lists to the multi-talented Sammy Baugh.

As a kicker, Davis scored in 87 consecutive games and set the NFL record for most consecutive extra points (234) from 1959 to 1965, breaking George Blanda's mark. His 99.43 percent average on extra points is also an NFL record. A traditional, straight-ahead kicker, he connected on 130 field goals. In all, he racked up 738 points. [MS]

WILLIE DAVIS

Defensive End. 6-3, 245. Grambling
Born July 24, 1934, Lisbon, Louisiana.
1958-59 Cleveland, 1960-69 Green Bay
Inducted in Pro Football Hall of Fame in 1981.

Davis was blessed with the three attributes—speed, agility, and size—that Vince Lombardi considered most important for a successful pro football lineman. "Give a man any two of those dimensions and he'll do okay. But give him all three and he'll be a great football player," Lombardi summarized. Davis, a dynamic 6-3, 245-pound player, also had the intangibles—dedication, intelligence, leadership—that enabled him to climb almost everyone else.

By the nature of their assignments, linemen aren't expected to capture many headlines but Davis, with his big-play performance year after year, was an exception to this rule. In 10 seasons with the Packers, he was an all-pro selection five times. He played in six NFL Championship Games and the first two Super Bowls. He was a Pro Bowl choice five years in a row. He played 12 seasons—the first two with the 1958 and 1959 Cleveland Browns—and didn't miss one of the 162 games in that period. Davis recovered 21 opponents' fumbles, one shy of the all-time record at the time of his retirement in 1969.

In spite of his numerous individual honors, Davis also was considered a perfect team player who looked on Packers achievements with great zest. "Nothing will surpass the high points of the first championship, the first Super Bowl and things like that," Davis said. "And the leadership role I was fortunate to be able to play surely gave me great pleasure." Reminiscing about Super Bowl I, he declared: "We weren't playing just for the Packers but for the entire NFL. That was a game we simply had to win." [DS/PF]

***DERMONTTI DAWSON**

Center. 6-2, 288. Kentucky
Born June 17, 1965, Lexington, Kentucky.
1988-1998 Pittsburgh

Pittsburgh's seamless transition at center from Ray Mansfield to Mike Webster to Dawson is one of the reasons the Steelers have gone from perennial doormat to consistent contender over the past 30 years. But growing up in Lexington, Kentucky, Dawson didn't have Super Bowl aspirations; instead, he dreamed of competing in the Olympics.

Dawson was a state champion and high school All-America in the discus and shot put when the football coach at Bryan Station High spotted him walking in the corridor one day. The coach thought this large young man was looking for his child; he didn't realize Dawson was a student. He never made the same mistake again because from that day on, Dawson was an immovable object on the Defenders' offensive and defensive lines. He earned all-state honors and received numerous scholarship offers, but he stayed near home at the University of Kentucky.

The Steelers took Dawson, who played guard for the Wildcats, in the second round of the 1988 draft. He started his NFL career at guard next to the ageless Webster in 1988 and doubled as the Steelers' long snapper. Dawson moved to center in 1989 (after Webster moved to Kansas City) and has been there since. He hasn't missed a game in 11 seasons, but that's part of the job description for centers in Pittsburgh. Mansfield played in 182 consecutive games, while Webster, a member of the Pro Football Hall of Fame, played in 177 straight contests. Dawson, a Pro Bowl selection for seven consecutive seasons, is closing fast with 168 consecutive games. [MS]

LEN DAWSON

Quarterback. 6-0, 190. Purdue
Born June 20, 1935, Alliance, Ohio.
1957-59 Pittsburgh. 1960-61 Cleveland, 1962 Dallas AFL, 1963-1975 Kansas City
Inducted into Pro Football Hall of Fame in 1987.

Dawson ranks among the elite passers of all time with an 82.6 rating compiled over 19 seasons of pro play. However, he is perhaps best remembered for his courageous most-valuable-player performance in leading the Kansas City Chiefs to a 23-7 upset of the Minnesota Vikings in Super Bowl IV.

Although burdened by the pressures of a week-long gambling investigation that completely cleared him of any involvement, Dawson completed 12 of 17 passes for 142 yards, and his 46-yard touchdown to Otis Taylor was the clincher.

The number-one draft pick of the Pittsburgh Steelers in

1957—Dawson was selected ahead of running superstar Jim Brown—the former Purdue sharpshooter struggled through five seasons as a seldom-used backup with the Steelers and Cleveland Browns before finding his niche with the Dallas Texans of the American Football League in 1962. He paced the Texans, who became the Kansas City Chiefs the next year, to their first AFL championship in a double-overtime victory over the Houston Oilers.

Noted for his calm, poised approach to every situation, the Ohio native was often lauded by his coach, Hank Stram, as "the most accurate passer in pro football." Dawson won four AFL individual passing crowns—1962, 1964, 1966 and 1968. He was named to six AFL All-Star games and the 1972 AFC-NFC Pro Bowl. An All-AFL selection in both 1962 and 1966, he was named the AFL player of the year in 1962. [DS/PF]

JOE DeLAMIELLEURE

Guard. 6-3, 250. Michigan State.
Born March 16, 1951, Detroit, Michigan.
1973-79, 1985 Buffalo, 1980-84 Cleveland

Joe DeLamielleure was the foreman of Buffalo's Electric Company. DeLamielleure and the Bills' offensive line of the 1970s earned that nickname because "they turned the Juice loose." The "Juice," of course, was teammate O.J. Simpson, who always gave credit to the men who blocked for him. (After he became the first man to run for 2,000 yards in a season, Simpson graciously began the press conference by introducing his offensive line.)

An All-America and three-time All-Big Ten performer at Michigan State, DeLamielleure was picked by the Buffalo Bills in the first round of the 1973 draft. At first, when he failed his physical, it seemed he would never play pro football. Fortunately, further tests showed his irregular heartbeat was not serious, and DeLamielleure went on to win all-rookie honors. Running behind the Electric Company, Simpson continued to gain large totals of yardage over the next several years.

DeLamielleure was the most honored of a deserving line. In 1975, he began a string of six consecutive all-pro years and an equal number of Pro Bowl selections. He was traded to Cleveland in 1980 where he played four seasons and helped the Browns win a division title. Extremely durable, DeLamielleure had a streak of 185 consecutive games at one point. Tough-minded and dependable, he was best known for run blocking for Simpson, but DeLamielleure was also outstanding when it came to protecting passers. The Pro Football Hall of Fame named him to its All-Pro Squad of the 1970s. [MS]

TOM DEMPSEY

Kicker. 6-1, 285. Palomar Junior College
Born January 12, 1947, Milwaukee, Wisconsin.
1969-1970 New Orleans, 1971-74 Philadelphia, 1975-76 Los Angeles Rams

Dempsey was born with only half of his right foot and no right hand, but he kicked himself into football lore on November 8, 1970, when his game-winning 63-yard field goal for the New Orleans Saints against the Detroit Lions became the longest field goal in NFL history.

Dempsey's record-making kick was his fourth field goal of the game and came as time expired to give the Saints a 19-17 victory in J.D. Roberts's first game as New Orleans head coach. The Saints had the ball at their 45-yard line with just 2 seconds to play. Roberts looked at Dempsey, standing next to him on the sidelines and said, "Give it your best shot."

Holder Joe Scarpatti set up for the kick 8 yards behind the center, instead of the usual 7 yards to give him just an instant more time from the defensive rush.

"I knew I could kick it 63 yards," Dempsey said. "I wasn't sure that I could kick it straight." The ball exploded off his foot and soared over the crossbar.

"I'll always be thankful for my parents' attitude," Dempsey said later. "They wouldn't let me feel sorry for myself. They taught me to get out and compete and earn my place in life. I had to admit that the handicap is there; then I say I'm not handicapped . . . that I can do anything anyone else can do." [JC]

ERIC DICKERSON

Running Back. 6-3, 220. Southern Methodist
Born September 2, 1960, Sealy, Texas.
1983-87 Los Angeles Rams, 1987-91 Indianapolis, 1992 Raiders, 1993 Atlanta
Inducted into Pro Football Hall of Fame in 1999.

Eric Dickerson was a force to be reckoned with on the football field. He was a six-time Pro Bowl pick and had seven consecutive 1,000-yard seasons. He shattered the rookie rushing record with the Los Angeles Rams in 1983, then broke the mark for most yards in a season the following year.

"Whenever he doesn't do something unbelievable, you're disappointed," former Ram coach John Robinson said.

As a *Parade* high school All-America, Dickerson led his team to the state championship in Sealy, Texas, and he went on to greater heights at Southern Methodist University. He received All-America honors as both a junior and a senior at SMU and broke Earl Campbell's career rushing record in the Southwest Conference. And Dickerson alternated with Craig James at tailback all four years, considerably reducing his ball-carrying opportunities.

There was no doubt that Dickerson would get the ball enough in the NFL. He was a workhorse in Los Angeles before he was traded to the Indianapolis Colts in a blockbuster deal during the 1987 season. Indianapolis gave up the rights to Cornelius Bennett and a number of draft choices, but, spurred by Dickerson's arrival on Halloween night, went on to gain a spot in the playoffs.

He finished his career in 1993 after one-year stints with the Los Angeles Raiders and Atlanta Falcons. He averaged 4.4 yards per carry in his career and retired in 1993 with 13,259 yards, second only to Walter Payton. [MS]

DAN DIERDORF

Tackle. 6-3, 290. Michigan
Born June 29, 1949, Canton, Ohio.
1971-1983 St. Louis
Inducted into Pro Football Hall of Fame in 1996.

Dierdorf excelled as an offensive lineman for 13 seasons from 1971 through 1983. He seemed destined for stardom from the moment he joined the St. Louis Cardinals as a second-round choice and the forty-third player selected in the 1971 draft. Dierdorf, who had been a consensus All-America at Michigan in 1970, possessed size, speed, quickness, discipline, intelligence, and consistency, all necessary attributes for an outstanding lineman.

The 290-pound Dierdorf, from Canton, Ohio, played both guard and tackle his first two seasons before settling down as the permanent right tackle in his third season. Dierdorf, who was equally effective as a blocker on both running and passing plays, was the ring leader of the line that permitted the fewest sacks in the NFC for five straight years in the mid-1970s.

In 1975, the Cardinals set a record by allowing only 8 sacks in 14 games. Dierdorf proved his durability by playing in every game until a broken jaw forced him out of two games in his seventh season, 1977. In 1979, he missed 14 of 16 games because of a dislocated left knee. However, he bounced back strongly in 1980 with another all-pro caliber season.

Dierdorf was all-pro five seasons—from 1975 to 1978 and again in 1980. He played in six Pro Bowl games, missing only once from 1974 through 1980. For three consecutive years from 1976-78, he was picked as the best overall blocker in the NFL by the NFL Players Association. [DS/PF]

BOBBY DILLON

Defensive Halfback. 6-1, 180. Texas
Born February 23, 1930, Temple, Texas.
1952-59 Green Bay

No one ever questioned Bobby Dillon's timing on the football field—he retired after an eight-year career with 52 interceptions.

At the time, only Emlen Tunnell and Dick (Night Train) Lane had more. However, the timing of his retirement is subject to question. After playing one season for Vince Lombardi, Dillon retired quite young, just as the Packers were about to emerge as a dynasty. As it was, Dillon had been one of the few Packers stars—four consecutive Pro Bowls (1956-59)—on a below-average team.

Dillon's NFL story is remarkable in that there probably shouldn't have been an NFL story in the first place. He lost vision in one eye at age 10, and he was primarily a track and field athlete in high school. But Dillon made a smooth transition to football and became an All-America defensive back for the University of Texas.

Dillon never let the fact that he had sight in only one eye bother him. He compensated for his lack of depth perception by never being too far away from the intended receiver. "Cover guy" is what they call players today who play like Dillon. "He could stay with anybody," said Dick Szymanski, an old adversary.

Apparently, it took a while for coaches and quarterbacks to realize that a one-eyed Dillon was the equal of any full-sighted defensive back—they kept throwing, and Dillon kept picking them off and running them back. He led or tied for the lead in team interceptions in seven of his eight seasons. [JJC]

LAVERN DILWEG

End. 6-3, 199. Marquette.
Born January 11, 1903, Milwaukee.
Died January 2, 1968, St. Petersburg, Florida.
1926 Milwaukee, 1927-1934 Green Bay

Lavern Dilweg, by nearly all contemporary accounts, was the best end in pro football almost from his first game in 1926 until his last in 1934. He had an unusually long career for his era, played on the best team of his time, the three-time NFL champion Packers, and followed his playing days with a life of public service that took him all the way to Washington.

Today, he is nearly forgotten.

There are several reasons. First, the job of "end" has evolved into "wide receiver," with a premium on pass catching. Although Dilweg once caught 25 passes in a season—a terrific number at the time—his offensive contribution to Green Bay's success was mainly his blocking. On defense, he stopped the run, but spectacular sacks of passers weren't a major part of his game; teams didn't pass often enough to make that a big deal.

Second, by his own admission, he never had a "big" game. Apparently, he never had a bad one either. But steadiness and reliability are more prized by coaches than commentators.

And third, the year after Dilweg retired, Don Hutson arrived in Green Bay. His brilliance was such that the world virtually forgot that anyone else had ever played end for the Packers.

Dilweg's post-football career as a U.S. Congressman and later an official in the Kennedy administration earned points in citizenship but not on a football scoreboard. Dilweg may have been the best end of his time—contemporary all-pro teams say so—but it was the wrong time to be remembered. [BC]

MIKE DITKA

Tight End. 6-3, 225. Pittsburgh
Born October 18, 1939, Carnegie, Pennsylvania.
1961-66 Chicago Bears, 1967-68 Philadelphia,
1969-1972 Dallas
Inducted into Pro Football Hall of Fame in 1988.

Ditka introduced a new dimension to the tight-end position that once was viewed primarily as an assignment for a tough, talented blocker. He proved to be a superb blocker, but he also became one of the first tight ends to catch a large number of passes. He startled opposing defenses in 1961 with 56 catches for 1,076 yards and 12 touchdowns in his rookie-of-the-year season. Three years later, in 1964, he had 75 receptions, a season record for tight ends that lasted until 1980 and the era of the 16-game season.

A consensus All-America in 1960 for the University of Pittsburgh, he played middle linebacker and end on defense and as an offensive receiver. He also was one of the nation's premier punters. The number-one draft pick of the Chicago Bears in 1961, Ditka moved into the Bears' starting lineup at the beginning of his rookie season and didn't miss a start in 84 games with the Bears. He earned all-pro honors four consecutive seasons from 1961 through 1964 and was a Pro Bowl choice after each of his first five seasons. He wound up with 427 receptions.

In 1967, Ditka was traded to the Philadelphia Eagles for quarterback Jack Concannon. Two years later, he was traded to the Dallas Cowboys. The fiercely determined and competitive Ditka regained much of his old form in four years in Dallas. His best season there was in 1971, when he had 30 receptions during the season and scored the final touchdown in Dallas's 24-3 win over the Miami Dolphins in Super Bowl VI.

He later coached the Bears to victory in Super Bowl XX, becoming the second man to both play for and coach a Super Bowl winner. After four years as a studio analyst for NBC Sports, Ditka returned to the sidelines in 1997 in New Orleans to try to change the fortunes of the Saints. [DS/PF]

ART DONOVAN

Defensive Tackle. 6-3, 270. Boston College
Born June 5, 1925, Bronx, New York.
1950, 1953-1961 Baltimore, 1951 New York Yanks, 1952 Dallas
Inducted into Pro Football Hall of Fame in 1976.

Son of the famous boxing referee of the same name, Donovan did not have a particularly outstanding career at either St. Michael's High School in the Bronx or at Boston College. Then it got worse.

The 25-year-old rookie defensive tackle joined the original Baltimore Colts in 1950. The hapless Colts folded after one season, and Art moved to the New York Yanks in 1951, then played for the Dallas Texans in 1952. In 36 games over three years, Donovan's teams yielded a staggering 1,271 points and went 3-31-2.

In 1953, Art returned to Baltimore to play for a new Colts teams and, as the Colts developed toward championship status, Donovan developed even more rapidly into one of history's best defensive tackles. He was smart, strong, and quick. He rushed the passer, read the keys, closed off the middle, split the double-team blocks, and followed the flow of the play. He was all-pro four consecutive years from 1954 to 1957. He also played in five consecutive Pro Bowls.

As great as Art Donovan was on the field, he was at least as valuable as a morale-builder. Lovable, laughable, certainly one of the most universally popular athletes in the National Football League, Donovan's self-deprecating humor was the pressure safety valve whenever team tensions built up. [DS/PF]

TONY DORSETT

Running Back. 5-11, 184. Pittsburgh
Born April 7, 1954, Rochester, Pennsylvania.
1977-1987 Dallas, 1978 Denver
Inducted into Pro Football Hall of Fame in 1994.

On a Monday night against Minnesota at the end of the 1982 season, Dorsett set a record that may some day be tied, but will never be broken—a 99-yard touchdown run.

Dorsett already was a celebrity by the time he joined the Dallas Cowboys as their first-round draft pick in 1977. A four-time All-America at Pittsburgh, he also won the 1976 Heisman Trophy. Just as he had been at Pitt, he was an immediate NFL sensation in his rookie season. Dorsett rushed for 1,007 yards and 12 touchdowns and was a virtually unanimous choice for NFL offensive-rookie-of-the-year honors. He rushed for more than 1,000 yards eight of his first nine seasons—the only miss was the strike-shortened 1982 campaign which, ironically, saw him win his only NFC rushing championship. His top production came in 1981, when he rushed for 1,646 yards. Dorsett spent the first 11 seasons of his 12-year, 173-game NFL career with the Dallas Cowboys before being traded to the Denver Broncos for a fifth-round draft pick in 1988. He led the Broncos in rushing in 1988, but injuries prevented him from playing after that.

For his career, Dorsett rushed for 12,739 yards. He also totaled 16,326 yards from scrimmage. Dorsett, who was all-pro in 1981 and a veteran of four Pro Bowls, played in five NFC Championship Games and Super Bowls XII and XIII. He had impressive postseason statistical totals: 1,383 rushing yards and 1,786 yards from scrimmage in 17 games. [DS/PF]

JOHN (PADDY) DRISCOLL

Quarterback-Halfback. 5-11, 160. Northwestern
Born January 11, 1896, Evanston, Illinois.
Died June 29, 1968, Chicago, Illinois.
1920-25 Chicago Cardinals, 1926-29 Chicago Bears
Inducted into Pro Football Hall of Fame in 1965.

In 1920, the Chicago Cardinals had just become charter members of the American Professional Football Association (direct forerunner of the NFL), but they faced box-office competition from the Chicago Tigers.

Legend has it that Cardinals owner Chris O'Brien and the Tigers management decided to square off on the football field with the winner retaining exclusive territorial rights to Chicago. The Cardinals won 6-3 and the Tigers soon disappeared. The only touchdown was scored by triple-threat Driscoll whom O'Brien had hired for the then-princely sum of $300 a game. Thus, Driscoll became a true "franchise player."

Even by 1920 standards, Driscoll was not a big football player—just 5-11 and 160 pounds. But he was a brilliant field general who could run, pass, play defense, and was particularly effective as a punter and dropkicker. Driscoll seemed to be at his best when he faced the Bears, with whom he played in the late 1920s.

In 1922, Paddy twice flattened the Bears, 6-0 and 9-0, with all the points coming on dropkicks. He kicked 50-yard field goals in 1924 and 1925 that were NFL records at the time. When Red Grange made his NFL debut for the Bears on Thanksgiving Day, 1925, Driscoll, still with the Cardinals, angered fans by punting continually away from Grange. "I decided if one of us had to look bad, it wouldn't be me," Driscoll explained. "Punting to Grange is like grooving a pitch to Babe Ruth." [DS/PF]

BILL DUDLEY

Halfback. 5-10, 176. Virginia
Born December 24, 1921, Bluefield, Virginia.
1942, 1945-46 Pittsburgh, 1947-49 Detroit, 1950-51, 1953 Washington
Inducted into Pro Football Hall of Fame in 1966.

Although he weighed only 176 pounds and stood just 5-10, Dudley was the University of Virginia's first All-America and the number-one draft pick of the Pittsburgh Steelers in 1942.

From the start, he dispelled any thoughts he was too small to play with the "big boys" of the NFL. He ran for a 55-yard touchdown in his first game and scored on a kickoff return in his second. He won the NFL rushing title with 696 yards and was named to the All-NFL team.

Dudley was nicknamed "Bullet Bill," but that was misleading. Not only was he small and slow—he once finished fifteenth in a 15-man pregame exhibition sprint—but he passed with a sidearm motion that frustrated his coaches. His kicking style was unorthodox. He once was denied a tryout because his high school had no uniform small enough for him.

His nine-year NFL career was unique in that he played three seasons each with the Steelers, the Detroit Lions, and the Washington Redskins. He served in the Army Air Corps in 1943 and 1944, but returned to the Steelers late in the 1945 campaign. He reached his zenith in 1946 when he won a triple crown with individual statistical championships in rushing, punt returns, and interceptions. Naturally, he was named the NFL's most valuable player.

His versatility was never more evident than in 1947, when he scored 13 touchdowns for the Lions on 1 punt return, 1 kickoff return, 7 receptions and 4 rushes. Dudley also threw 2 touchdown passes as he helped the Steelers to an 8-4 mark, the franchise's best record to that point. [DS/PF]

KENNY EASLEY

Safety. 6-3, 206. UCLA

Born January 15, 1959, Chesapeake, Virginia.

1981-87 Seattle

Easley made it look easy from his safety position with the Seattle Seahawks. At 6-3 and 206 pounds, he seemed to glide across the field—and in front of unsuspecting receivers—but he was nearly always in a position to make the tackle with the kind of hit that receivers remembered the next time they ventured into his territory. He won AFC defensive-rookie-of-the-year honors in 1981 and was AFC defensive player of the year two seasons later.

Easley was voted NFL defensive player of the year in 1984. He led the NFL with 10 interceptions and ran 2 of them back for touchdowns as the Seahawks enjoyed their best season in franchise history (12-4). He also intercepted 3 passes in a Monday night game against the Chargers.

Easley was a three-sport athlete at Oscar Smith High School in Chesapeake, Virginia. He was offered basketball scholarships by schools in the Atlantic Coast Conference and Big Ten, but decided to head west and play football at UCLA. It was a good decision. Easley was a three-time consensus All-America pick with the Bruins. He was the first player selected All-Pac-10 for four years as a defensive back and kick returner. In 1981, he was selected by the Seahawks in the first round of the NFL draft.

A five-time Pro Bowl selectee, Easley was in his prime when a serious injury ended his career abruptly. In just seven seasons, he accumulated 32 interceptions. [MS]

ALBERT GLEN (TURK) EDWARDS

Tackle. 6-2, 260. Washington State

Born September 28, 1907, Mold, Washington.

Died January 12, 1973, Seattle, Washington.

1932-36 Boston, 1937-1940 Washington

Inducted into Pro Football Hall of Fame in 1969.

As an All-America tackle at Washington State, Edwards played a major role in leading the Cougars to the 1931 Rose Bowl. Upon graduation a year later, he received offers from three NFL teams—the Boston Braves, the New York Giants, and the Portsmouth Spartans. It was before the days of the draft so Turk could take his choice, and he chose the high offer—$1,500 for 10 games with the Braves.

Today, a 6-2, 260-pound professional football tackle would attract only passing attention, but in the decade of the 1930s, a player of that dimension stood out like the Rock of Gibraltar. For the rest of the decade, he was an outstanding leader of both the offensive and defensive lines of the Boston and Washington Redskins. He was named to the official All-NFL team in four of his first six seasons.

Edwards typified overwhelming strength and power, rather than speed. Yet he was agile enough to get the job done as well or better than all but a mere handful who played his position in the pre-World War II days of the NFL.

Almost unbelievably, the seemingly indestructible Edwards was injured at a coin-tossing ceremony prior to a game against the New York Giants early in the 1940 season. Edwards met his best friend, Mel Hein, the Giants' captain at midfield, called the flip of the coin, shook hands and pivoted toward the Redskins bench. Edwards caught his spikes in the turf and his oft-injured knee simply gave way. He never played again. [DS/PF]

CARL ELLER

Defensive End. 6-6, 247. Minnesota

Born February 25, 1942, Winston-Salem, North Carolina.

1964-1978 Minnesota, 1979 Seattle

After winning consensus All-America honors at Minnesota, Eller was drafted by both the Vikings and the Buffalo Bills. He chose to stay close to home and became a regular defensive end with the Vikings in 1964, his rookie year. He went on to hold that job for 15 seasons, becoming one of the most honored defenders in the game. He retired in 1979 after a final season with the Seattle Seahawks, having played in 225 regular-season games.

The winner of the George Halas Trophy as the NFL's top defensive player in 1971 was a 6-6, 247-pound terror to enemy passers because of his great speed and agility. During the 1975-77 seasons alone he totaled 44 sacks, according to unofficial statistics. He had 23 fumble recoveries, but his most famous fumble is one he caused as a rookie; teammate Jim Marshall picked it up and ran the wrong way with it.

With Marshall, Alan Page, and Gary Larsen, Eller formed the famous Purple People Eater defensive line that took Minnesota to four Super Bowls. During 10 of his Minnesota seasons the Vikings won their division crown.

Named all-pro in 1968, 1969, 1970, 1971, and 1973, he was All-NFL/NFC seven times and selected to six Pro Bowls.

Although justly famous for his ability to overcome pass

blockers, Eller faced a more dangerous foe when he developed a substance-abuse problem. With typical courage and determination, he turned his life around and came out, as he usually did, triumphant. [BC]

JOHN ELWAY

Quarterback. 6-3, 210. Stanford.
Born July 28, 1960, Port Angeles, Washington.
1983-1998 Denver

John Elway is the golden-armed quarterback whose fourth-quarter drives have led the Denver Broncos to so many victories, but for much of his career he was just as well remembered for the games he hadn't won: Super Bowls XXI, XXII, and XXIV. He finally put that to rest with an inspiring performance to help lead the Broncos to a 31-24 victory over the Packers in Super Bowl XXXII following the 1997 season. One year later, he led Denver to a 34-19 victory over the Falcons in Super Bowl XXXIII.

Against Atlanta, Elway passed for 336 yards, including an 80-yard touchdown to Rod Smith in the second quarter, and was named the game's most valuable player. Elway, one of the most mobile quarterbacks in NFL history, also scored on a 3-yard run for Denver's final touchdown of the game.

His father, Jack Elway, was a lifelong football coach, but John chose Stanford University because it was "the only school that actively encouraged me to play baseball." His baseball talents earned him $140,000 to play just 42 games for a New York Yankees' minor league affiliate at Oneonta, New York, in 1982. Elway's baseball ability gave him bargaining power when the Baltimore Colts picked him as the first player in the 1983 draft. He threatened to become a Yankee full time if he was not traded to a team located in the West. Baltimore traded its rights to Elway to Denver.

Elway has certainly made the trade pay off in Denver. He has won more regular-season games (148) than any other quarterback in NFL history, and Elway and Dan Marino are the only quarterbacks to pass for 50,000 yards.

The Broncos won the AFC title five times under Elway, but he still is perhaps best remembered for what he did on the road to Super Bowl XXI, when he engineered "The Drive." He led the Broncos 98 yards in the final 5:32 of regulation and his touchdown pass to Mark Jackson sent the 1986 AFC title game into overtime. Denver beat the Cleveland Browns 23-20 in overtime in one of the most memorable playoff games in NFL history. [MS]

GOVER (OX) EMERSON

Guard-Linebacker-Center. 5-11, 203. Texas
Born December 18, 1907, Douglas, Texas.
Died November 26, 1998, Austin, Texas.
1931-33 Portsmouth, 1934-37 Detroit, 1938 Brooklyn

Let it be known that the star guard for the Detroit Lions in the 1930s was Gover—not Grover—Emerson. He was named for the family pet, a mule named Governor. Of course, many writers of the time opted simply to use his nickname of "Ox," a moniker more suggestive of a hulking brute than of the lanky, agile Emerson.

Once the name is settled, all that remains is that Emerson was considered one of the foremost linemen of the Depression Decade. In those two-way days, Emerson was known for both strong blocking and fine defensive work, but stopping the foe was his greatest attribute.

He was a consensus all-pro pick in 1932, 1934, 1935, and 1936. In 1969, the Pro Football Hall of Fame chose him to its All-Pro Squad of the 1930s.

Ox was slated to captain the University of Texas team of 1931 when it was discovered that he had played two downs as a freshman, costing him his final year of eligibility. He took off for Portsmouth, Ohio, where he joined the NFL's Spartans. He played in the famous indoor playoff game in 1932 when the Spartans came close to winning the championship.

In 1935, the team—by then the Detroit Lions—won the title. Emerson retired after the 1937 season to become an assistant to coach Potsy Clark at Brooklyn, but when injuries depleted the Dodgers' line, he put on the pads for a final hurrah. [BC]

***BOOMER ESIASON**

Quarterback. 6-5, 228. Maryland
Born April 17, 1961, West Islip, New York.
1984-1992, 1997 Cincinnati, 1993-95 New York Jets, 1996 Arizona

Boomer Esiason needed only one year to take over for the great Ken Anderson as the quarterback of the Cincinnati Bengals. A second-round draft pick out of Maryland, Esiason played extensively as a rookie and then muscled his way into the starting lineup ahead of the man who led the NFL in passing four times.

Norman Julius Esiason earned his nickname before he was born because he kicked so much during his mother's pregnancy. Boomer also had a great left arm. In his first five years as a starter (1985-89), Esiason passed for more than 3,300 yards each season, with his best year coming in 1988, when he led the NFL in passing and took the Bengals to Super Bowl XXIII.

In 1993, with some saying he was washed up, Esiason moved to the New York Jets. He promptly set a personal mark by hitting 60.9 percent of his attempts, while passing for 3,421 yards and finishing fourth in the AFC in passing. After two more successful years in New York, he made another move in 1996, going to Arizona. He led the Cardinals to several improbable comeback victories, including the third-greatest passing day in NFL history with 522 yards in a 37-34 overtime win in Washington. His return to Cincinnati in 1997 also was successful. He ended the season as the starter and moved up to eighth all-time in career attempts (5,205) and completions (2,969), while his 37,920 passing yards ranked ninth all-time.

"He has always had one of the best throwing arms in the game," former Bengals coach Sam Wyche said. "Most importantly, though, Boomer is a smart quarterback. He never gets fazed in the slightest. If we were to ask him to call the plays for both teams one game he could do it." After the 1997 season, ABC asked Esiason to do just that as a broadcaster on *Monday Night Football.* [BR]

***BRETT FAVRE**

Quarterback. 6-2, 225. Southern Mississippi
Born October 10, 1969, Gulfport, Mississippi.

1991 Atlanta, 1992-98 Green Bay

Setting records in a football town like Green Bay is no easy feat, especially at the quarterback position. But after just seven seasons with the club, Brett Favre is near the top of the list on the hallowed scroll of Packer legend.

Favre already owns club records for most touchdown passes (213), most attempts (3,752), and most completions (2,318). Of course, he would trade all the records for back-to-back titles. Favre guided the Packers to victory in Super Bowl XXXI against New England, but Denver dashed Favre's hopes for a second consecutive title in Super Bowl XXXII in San Diego.

Favre was named NFL MVP by the Associated Press three straight years (1995-97), not bad for a man who started his career as a third-string quarterback in Atlanta. Packers general manager Ron Wolf surprised many by trading a first-round draft choice to the Falcons for Favre in 1992. Favre began his career in Green Bay by coming off the bench to lead the Packers to a 24-23 victory over Cincinnati, and he guided Green Bay to its second-best record in 20 years. The following year he led the Packers to their first playoff appearance since 1982.

With Green Bay trailing Detroit 24-21 in the final minute of the 1993 first-round contest, Favre scrambled out of the pocket to his left, threw across his body and found Sterling Sharpe for the game-winning score at the Pontiac Silverdome. Favre has led the Packers to the playoffs each of the past six seasons, and has helped return Green Bay to the NFL's elite. [MS]

TOM FEARS

End. 6-2, 215. Santa Clara, UCLA
Born December 3, 1923, Los Angeles, California.
1948-1956 Los Angeles Rams
Inducted into Pro Football Hall of Fame in 1970.

Fears was first ticketed for the defensive unit when he joined the Los Angeles Rams in 1948. In his first game, he intercepted 2 passes and returned 1 for a touchdown. Rams coach Clark Shaughnessy immediately decided Fears' talents could be utilized on the offensive unit.

It proved to be a wise decision. Fears caught 400 passes in his nine-season NFL career, but his biggest day came in 1950 when he caught 18 passes in a 51-14 rout of the Green Bay Packers. It was a single-game record that still stands almost five decades later.

The fact that the record was set against a cellar-dweller club was out of the Fears mold because Tom, as a rule, saved his best performances for the biggest games. In 1951, when the Rams defeated the Cleveland Browns for their first championship since moving from Ohio in 1946, it was Fears who scored the winning touchdown on a spectacular 73-yard pass-run play.

A year earlier in 1950, when the Rams had beaten the Chicago Bears 24-14 to win the NFL Western Division crown, Fears scored all 3 touchdowns on sensational pass plays of 43, 68, and 27 yards.

Fears, a native of Los Angeles who played college football at both Santa Clara and UCLA was the first player in college or pro ranks to catch large numbers of forward passes. In his first three seasons in the NFL, he led the league in receiving. He caught a then-record 84 passes during the 1950 season for the Rams. [DS/PF]

BEATTIE FEATHERS

Halfback. 5-10, 185. Tennessee
Born August 20, 1909, Bristol, Virginia.
Died March 11, 1979, Winston-Salem, North Carolina.
1934-37 Chicago Bears, 1938-39 Brooklyn, 1940 Green Bay

In 1934, Chicago Bears rookie Beattie Feathers did something no one had ever done before. As a rookie he led the NFL in rushing by gaining more than 1,000 yards.

It took 34 years to duplicate: Another rookie didn't reach the 1,000-yard mark until Paul Robinson in 1968. Amazingly, Feathers averaged nearly a first down—8.4 yards—every time he carried the ball. No full-time running back has ever come close to that for a season's average.

In addition to his maturity, elusiveness, and speed, Feathers undoubtedly benefited from a strong surrounding cast, most conspicuously Bronko Nagurski, the future Hall of Fame fullback. The Bronk threw the important lead block on many of Beattie's long jaunts. Feathers tended to minimize his own ability by saying, "Whichever way Bronko knocked them, I cut the other way into a nice opening.

"It takes two things to be a thousand-yarder," he said, "You've got to be lucky enough to avoid injuries, and you've got to be lucky enough to get good blocking—I had the best blocker who ever lived, Bronko Nagurski."

Feathers wasn't so lucky after that first year. A shoulder dislocation suffered late in his rookie season required him to play the rest of his career in an immobilizing brace. His numbers dropped drastically.

By 1938, he was a part-timer with the Brooklyn Dodgers and in 1940 carried just four times for the Packers. In the six seasons that followed his sensational debut, Feathers accumulated fewer than 1,000 yards. [JJC]

PAT FISCHER

Cornerback. 5-9, 170. Nebraska
Born January 2, 1940, St. Edward, Nebraska.
1961-67 St. Louis, 1968-1977 Washington

Pat Fischer proved that a player's ability, not his size, determines a career in the NFL.

Fischer was only 5 feet 9 inches tall and weighed about 170 pounds during 17 seasons of playing left cornerback for the St. Louis Cardinals and Washington Redskins. When he retired after the 1977 season, he had played 213 games as a defensive back, the most at that position in NFL history.

That wasn't bad for a seventeenth-round draft pick in 1961 from the University of Nebraska. Although he'd played both quarterback and defensive back in college, the Cardinals projected him as a wide receiver. As things turned out, he caught only 1 pass in his 17-year career. As a cornerback he proved he could cover receivers and that, despite his size, he could knock down the biggest running backs.

But it wasn't easy.

"In my first week at training camp, I ran around in shorts until the team found some pads to fit me," he said. "I remember in the first game, my pants fell down below the knee. I had to tape them up.

"Eventually, I showed the coaches I could tackle people and not get killed. Coaches have a predetermined idea of what a cornerback is supposed to look like. I never fit the description . . . but it never bothered me."

It certainly bothered a lot of receivers because Fischer accumulated 56 interceptions. After seven years in St. Louis, he became a free agent and signed with the Redskins. He became the prototype player in coach George Allen's Over-the-Hill-Gang philosophy and a starter on Washington's 1972 NFC championship team that played in Super Bowl VII. [JC]

LEN FORD

Defensive End. 6-5, 260. Michigan
Born February 18, 1926. Washington, D.C.
Died March 14, 1972, Detroit, Michigan.
1948-49 Los Angeles AAFC, 1950-57 Cleveland, 1958 Green Bay
Inducted into Pro Football Hall of Fame in 1976.

Len Ford, an All-America Michigan graduate, played pro football for 11 seasons, the first two with the Los Angeles Dons of the AAFC in 1948 and 1949, the next eight with the Cleveland Browns from 1950 to 1957, and a final campaign with the Green Bay Packers in 1958.

In the AAFC, he was used as a two-way end, excellent on defense and a favorite on offense with leaping, one-hand grabs that netted 67 receptions in two years. The Dons' coach, Jim Phelan, flatly predicted: "Len can become the greatest all-around end in history. He has everything—size, speed, strength, and great hands."

But the demise of the AAFC brought about a dramatic change in Ford's career. In 1950, he was picked up by the Cleveland Browns, who earmarked him for their defensive team. It wasn't long before Ford was recognized as the best of many stars on a unit that allowed the fewest points of any NFL team in six of the next eight seasons.

Ford developed into such a devastating pass rusher that the Browns changed their defensive alignment to take advantage of his rare talents. A serious face injury in 1950 almost ended Ford's career, but he returned to lead his team to a dramatic 30-28 victory in the 1950 NFL Championship Game.

He was an all-pro pick the next five seasons and played in four Pro Bowls. Always alert for the football, he recovered 20 opponents' fumbles. In the 1954 NFL Championship Game, he intercepted 2 passes in a 56-10 rout of Detroit. [DS/PF]

CHUCK FOREMAN

Running Back. 6-2, 207. Miami
Born October 26, 1950, Frederick, Maryland.
1973-79 Minnesota, 1980 New England

Chuck Foreman created a new offensive position when he played for the Minnesota Vikings during the 1970s. There never was a name for it but only a technical description that in essence said that he took "an extended handoff."

Foreman, the Vikings' fullback, would circle out of the backfield, catch a short pass, and gain whatever yardage he could. Vikings head coach Bud Grant said at the time: "We know that Chuck can get five yards on a running play so we throw him a five-yard pass and let him get even more. It is just an extension of our running game."

Foreman, who was the NFC's 1972 rookie of the year after being a first-round draft pick from the University of Miami, became a prolific yardage producer. He had three 1,000-yard rushing seasons and also held the Vikings' receiving record when he left the team after the 1979 season to finish his career with the New England Patriots.

Foreman was utilized well by quarterback Fran Tarkenton, who reveled in multiple-formation offenses, and together they helped the Vikings get to three Super Bowls. During his time as Vikings head coach when Foreman was his main running weapon, Grant deftly pinpointed his talents: "He's intense. He's strong enough to go inside and quick enough to go outside. There is no one thing in which he excels but there's not another player in the league who can do all of the things that he does so well." [JC]

DAN FORTMANN

Guard. 6-0, 207. Colgate
Born April 11, 1916, Pearl River, New York.
Died May 24, 1995, Los Angeles, California.
1936-1943 Chicago Bears
Inducted into Pro Football Hall of Fame in 1965.

When the first-ever NFL draft of college players took place in 1936, the league and its member clubs were unprepared. Team scouting departments were armed with a few newspaper clippings and perhaps a random tip from a friend familiar with college football. Accordingly, it was in that climate that George Halas of the Chicago Bears, on a hunch, selected Fortmann, a guard from Colgate, in the ninth and final round. "I like that name. I'll take him," Halas said as he made the selection.

On the surface, it appeared as if Halas had made a major mistake. At 6 feet and 210 pounds, Fortmann was too small for line play in the NFL. And he was just 19.

But one quality Fortmann had in abundance was determination. Combined with football instinct, his resolve led him to become the youngest starter in the NFL as a rookie. On offense, he called signals for the linemen and was battering-ram blocker. On defense, he was a genius at diagnosing plays and was a deadly tackler.

From 1936-1943, Fortmann was the top man at his position in pro football. He earned all-pro honors six consecutive years from 1938-1943. Fortmann and Halas developed a strong rapport over the years. Danny respected Halas for his coaching but also for another important reason. "George made it possible for me to pursue my medical studies while playing football," Dr. Fortmann said. [DS/PF]

JOE FORTUNATO

Linebacker. 6-0, 225. Mississippi State
Born March 28, 1931, Mingo Junction, Ohio.
1956-1966 Chicago Bears

Joe Fortunato suffered the fate of many great outside linebackers of the 1950s and 1960s. He, and they, were overshadowed by the more glamorous and highly publicized middle linebackers.

Observed Dick Szymanski, an offensive and defensive standout with the Baltimore Colts of the time: "Fortunato was as good as any linebacker—outside or inside, middle, whatever—but with the Bears he was in Bill George's shadow. And then Dick Butkus comes along at the end. I tell you, he couldn't win—but he was damn good."

Fortunato did eventually get enough recognition to make five Pro Bowls, four consecutively (1962-65 seasons). A tough two-way fullback, Fortunato found his way south from the Ohio River valley to Mississippi State in the late-1940s. Drafted in 1952, the ex-Bulldog delayed his pro debut to fulfill a military obligation.

If he didn't make an immediate impact on the media, he did on the Bears and their opponents. Fortunato seemed always to be where the action was, seldom out of position.

The Bears' 1963 championship team is testimony to Fortunato's ability. With only an adequate offense, the Bears got it done with defense, and Fortunato played a big role. Chicago led the NFL with the fewest yards allowed by rushing, fewest yards allowed by passing, and most interceptions. Fortunato called the signals. The unit gave no opponent more than 7 points in the second half of any game that year.

George Allen, the Bears' defensive coordinator, said of his linebacker, "He gave us generalship." [JJC]

DAN FOUTS

Quarterback. 6-3, 210. Oregon
Born June 10, 1951, San Francisco, California.
1973-1987 San Diego
Inducted into Pro Football Hall of Fame in 1993

An All-Pacific-8 quarterback at the University of Oregon, Fouts was the third-round draft pick of the San Diego Chargers in 1973. He started slowly, but his career took off when Don Coryell became the Chargers' coach in 1978. It was Fouts who put the air in the Chargers' Air Coryell offense. Although Fouts battled injuries for much of his career, he played a major role in transforming the Chargers from also-rans to AFC Western Division champions in 1979, 1980, and 1981.

In both 1980 and 1981, Fouts led the Chargers to the AFC Championship Game. The Oakland Raiders defeated the Chargers 34-27 in the 1980 game in spite of Fouts's 336-yard, 2-touchdown passing performance. In the 1981 AFC title game, played in a 59-below-zero wind chill, Fouts completed 15 passes for 185 yards and the Chargers' only touchdown, a 33-yard pass to Kellen Winslow, but the Cincinnati Bengals won 27-7.

In 15 seasons, Fouts completed 3,297 passes for 43,040 yards, 254 touchdowns, and an 80.2 passer rating. He was the third passer ever to throw for more than 40,000 yards. Fouts was the AFC player of the year in 1979 and then in 1982, he was named the NFL most valuable player by the Pro Football Writers of America, the AFC player of the year by United Press International, and the NFL offensive player of the year by Associated Press. He was an all-pro choice in 1979, 1982, and 1985 and all-AFC in 1979 and 1982 and played in six Pro Bowls from the 1979-1985 seasons. [DS/PF]

BENNY FRIEDMAN

Quarterback. 5-8, 172. Michigan
Born March 18, 1905, Cleveland, Ohio.
Died November 24, 1982, New York, New York.
1927 Cleveland, 1928 Detroit, 1929-1931 New York Giants, 1932-34 Brooklyn

Michigan's Fielding Yost said he was "one of greatest passers [and] smartest quarterbacks in history," and Red Grange said he was the best quarterback he ever played against. Benny Friedman was one of the greatest players of the 1920s according to his contemporaries, his coaches, historians, and, yes, Benny Friedman.

No doubt, Benny's insistence on his own greatness right up to the day he died actually hurt his case. Critics looked for pins to prick his boasts. He became tiresome—even though he probably was right.

At Michigan, Friedman was a clever, risk-taking quarterback, a dangerous runner, an adequate kicker, and—most important—the top passer of his time. Yost, his coach, also said he was the best defensive back around, but Benny was primarily a put-points-on-the-scoreboard player. Twice an All-America, only Grange and perhaps Ernie Nevers surpassed him in mystique by the time he graduated to the NFL.

In his first four seasons, he was phenomenal. Although official statistics were not kept, Benny appears to have completed more than half his passes (at a time when 35 percent was good) and each season launched many more touchdown passes than anyone else. He was the league scoring leader in 1928, and Tim Mara bought the entire Detroit team just to get Friedman for his Giants.

Friedman's teams were winners, but he could never quite bring them in first. A leg injury slowed him in 1931, and after that college coaching duties limited his appearances. The arrival of Sammy Baugh made a lot of people forget how good a passer Friedman had been, but he never forgot himself. [BC]

FRANK GATSKI

Center. 6-3, 240. Marshall, Auburn
Born March 18, 1922, Farmington, West Virginia.
1946-1956 Cleveland, 1957 Detroit
Inducted into Pro Football Hall of Fame in 1985.

When the Cleveland Browns were dominating first the AAFC from 1946 to 1949 and the NFL in the early 1950s, Gatski anchored an offensive line that powered pro football's most potent attack. He concluded his 11-year tenure with the Browns in 1956 and then was traded to the Detroit Lions for a final season in 1957.

The 6-foot 3-inch, 240-pound Gatski, who played three years at Marshall College before joining the U.S. Infantry in World War II, served a two-year apprenticeship behind veteran Mo Scarry before he took over the regular center job for good in 1948.

Early in his career, Gatski doubled as a linebacker, but it was as a center that he excelled. Strong, consistent, and blessed with a great attitude and exceptional pass-blocking abilities, he never missed a game or a practice in high school, college, or the pros. He was named to the all-pro honor roll from 1951-53 and in 1955, and played as the starting center in the Pro Bowl following the 1955 season.

Perhaps because the native West Virginian played at a comparatively obscure position, Gatski was relatively unsung through most of his career. However, he can claim one signal distinction—11 championship games in 12 seasons with his team, winning eight times. No other nonkicker can point to such a record. Gatski earned seven championship rings as a Brown and his eighth with Detroit in 1957, when the Lions overwhelmed his old team 59-14 in Gatski's final game in the NFL. [DS/PF]

BILL GEORGE

Linebacker. 6-2, 230. Wake Forest
Born October 27, 1930, Waynesburg, Pennsylvania.
Died September 30, 1982, Davis Junction, Illinois.
1952-1965 Chicago Bears, 1966 Los Angeles
Inducted into Pro Football Hall of Fame in 1974.

During the 1950s and early 1960s, the Chicago Bears were famed for ferocious defensive teams that made them perennial championship contenders in the NFL.

For most of those years, the Bears' defensive wheelhorse was middle linebacker Bill George, a 6-foot 2-inch, 230-pound Wake Forest product who stepped into a new position just evolving in pro football and did the job so well few have matched his proficiency. It can be debated whether George actually was the first to play middle linebacker, at least regularly. What cannot be disputed are his innovative contributions to the new position and the quality of his play.

George began his NFL career in 1952 as a middle guard in the standard five-man defensive front of the day. Two years later against he Eagles, George made a mid-game adjustment which permanently changed defensive strategy in the NFL. On passing plays, George's job was to bump the center, then drop back. This particular day, the Eagles were completing short passes right over George's head. George decided to omit the center bump and drop back immediately. Two plays later, George got his first of 18 pro interceptions.

Within three years, the wire services substituted a third linebacker for the middle guard on their all-league selections. George, who had been a two-time all-pro middle guard, became instead an all-league linebacker six times in the next seven years. He also played in eight consecutive Pro Bowls. In 1956, he became the Bears' defensive signal caller, a job he handled with near-perfection for almost a decade. [DS/PF]

ABE GIBRON

Guard. 5-11, 255. Valparaiso, Purdue
Born September 22, 1925, Michigan City, Indiana.
Died September 23, 1997, Bellaire, Florida.
1949 Buffalo AAFC, 1950-56 Cleveland, 1956-58 Philadelphia, 1958-59 Chicago Bears

Abe Gibron often is cited as one of the three or four best offensive guards of the 1950s. He was the first draft choice of the Buffalo Bills of the AAFC in a secret draft held in July, 1948—before his final season at Purdue. The AAFC hoped to get the jump on the rival NFL in signing college seniors. In the 1949 NFL draft, he was selected in the sixth round by the New York Giants, but he signed with Buffalo and became an immediate starter.

When the AAFC merged with the NFL after the 1949 season, the players from defunct AAFC clubs such as Buffalo were thrown into a general pool to be drafted by the remaining NFL teams. Cleveland coach Paul Brown remembered Gibron "had the fastest and quickest charge I ever saw" and "was very spirited." He grabbed Gibron.

The roly-poly Gibron became one of the Browns' "messenger guards," linemen who alternated in taking plays called by the coach to the quarterback. Eventually, he was deemed too valuable to play part time and stayed in the lineup while the other guards ran messages. He was selected for the Pro Bowl four times from 1952-55 and was named all-pro by the United Press in 1955. In the meantime, Cleveland played in six consecutive championship games, winning three. [BC]

FRANK GIFFORD

Halfback. 6-1, 195. Southern California
Born August 16, 1930, Santa Monica, California.
1952-1960, 1962-64 New York Giants
Inducted into Pro Football Hall of Fame in 1977

By the time Gifford joined the New York Giants as their first-round draft choice in 1952, he already had experienced unusual gridiron success at Bakersfield (California) High School, Bakersfield Junior College, and the University of Southern California. At USC, he was All-America as a senior.

It took only a few days for Giants coach Steve Owen to realize he had a prize. "Gifford is one of the most versatile athletes I have ever seen," the veteran coach said. "He has hard-running ability. He is an accurate passer, a strong blocker, a sensational receiver, a superior defensive back. He returns kicks and even placekicks."

At one time or another in the next nine seasons, Gifford did all of these things, and he did them extremely well. In 1956, he was the NFL's most valuable player as he led the Giants to a league championship. In four different seasons, he was named all-pro by one or more major wire services.

A severe head injury in 1960 caused by a Chuck Bednarik tackle led Gifford to retire before the 1961 season. A year later, he tried a comeback. Conquering the dual problem of regaining his touch after a long layoff and of learning a new position—he was switched from halfback to flanker to take advantage of his great pass-catching skills—Gifford attained star status once again.

The Giants won big during the Gifford years and, while the team was loaded with many great pro football names, no one played a more dynamic role year in and year out. [DS/PF]

CARLTON (COOKIE) GILCHRIST

Fullback. 6-3, 249. No college
Born May 25, 1935, Brackenridge, Pennsylvania.
1962-64 Buffalo, 1965, 1967 Denver, 1966 Miami

Gilchrist never went to college and never took the word of management as gospel. An independent thinker, he earned the nickname "Cookie" because of his love for sweets as a child and he learned to love football with equal fervor.

Gilchrist went straight from Har-Brack High School to the Cleveland Browns training camp, but management found him not quite ready for prime time. He headed north and played in the Ontario Rugby Football Union and the Canadian Football League. In Toronto, the last of his three stops in the CFL, Gilchrist had a dispute with management that led him back to the United States.

Gilchrist joined the Buffalo Bills in 1962 and became the first runner in AFL history to run for 1,000 yards. Huge, powerful, and fast, he earned AFL most-valuable-player honors in the process. Gilchrist never reached that plateau again, but he set a league record with 243 yards rushing against the New York Jets in 1963. The following season he led the league in rushing and helped the Bills to the AFL title. He also was a devastating blocker.

A dispute with Buffalo coach Lou Saban resulted in Gilchrist's relocation to Denver, where he set an AFL record for most carries, but a salary dispute with Broncos' management led Gilchrist to announce his retirement. An out-of-shape Gilchrist returned to the AFL in 1966 with the Miami Dolphins and had his worst season. He returned to the Broncos and played his last AFL game in a Broncos' uniform in 1967. [MS]

HORACE GILLOM

Punter-End. 6-1, 225. Nevada-Reno
Born March 3, 1921, Roanoke, Alabama.
1947-1956 Cleveland

Some NFL players of the late 1940s looked down their collective nose at Paul Brown's AAFC Cleveland Browns and dismissed them as "a high school team, with a high school coach, in a high school league." They would soon learn otherwise. One reason for that misguided assessment of "the other league" was Horace Gillom, who had played high school football for Brown at Washington High in Massillon, Ohio.

Gillom was the Browns' star punter after college and service in World War II. Remembered best as a punting specialist, Gillom was much more. Teammate Tommy James said, "Sure, he was the best punter that ever put a toe to the pigskin, but he was a lot more, too. He was a great two-way end. He made some great catches for us. Two things, make that three, kept him from being a fine offensive end—Dante Lavelli, Mac Speedie, and Paul Brown. Lavelli and Speedie were all-league, and P.B. didn't want to endanger his superstar punter. So, Horace just punted. Man, did he punt!"

Gillom was the first to take a 15-yard drop—other punters kicked from 10-12 yards. This deeper drop allowed the Browns' cover team to spread itself out and leave the line of scrimmage sooner as the rules allowed at the time. Although it wasn't called "hang time" in those days, Gillom was the first to get height and distance on his kicks consistently. Once he got to the NFL in 1950, he led the league twice in punting average before retiring. [JJC]

PETE GOGOLAK

Kicker. 6-2, 205. Cornell
Born April 18, 1942, Budapest, Hungary.
1964-65 Buffalo, 1966-1974 New York Giants

Pete Gogolak escaped one revolution and started another one. He and his family escaped Hungary with only the clothes on their backs in 1956 as Russian tanks crushed a revolt by the Hungarian people. Less than a decade later, Gogolak led a revolution that changed kicking in pro football.

When his family relocated in upstate New York, Gogolak, who had been kicking a soccer ball with earnest since age 3, went out for football. He had seen Lou Groza kick a field goal for the Browns on television, but thought "what a funny way to kick." Groza was a straight-on kicker like everyone else in that era. When Gogolak's prep school needed a kicker, he tried out. His unique style baffled his holder and coach, but he was so successful that he played at Cornell and caught the eye of pro scouts.

The "sidewinder," as writers began calling him, signed with the Bills in 1964, as pro football's first soccer-style kicker. Gogolak became the center of another confrontation in 1966. When he played out his option and jumped leagues to the Giants, the AFL-NFL war heated up.

Gogolak, who had been strafed by Soviet MIGs while escaping Hungary, was unruffled by kick rushers. On kicking in the blustery northeast, he said, "I'd see the flags really blowing and think if I missed one from forty yards out, no one could blame me, but then instantly I'd know I shouldn't think like that. I'd think of the other kicker and tell myself, 'Let him miss one from forty—I'll make it.' " [JJC]

RANDY GRADISHAR

Linebacker. 6-3, 232. Ohio State.
Born March 3, 1952, Warren, Ohio.
1974-1983 Denver

Randy Gradishar always was smart. He was an Academic All-America at Ohio State and after 10 seasons in the NFL, he quit while he was ahead.

Gradishar attended tiny Champion High School in Ohio and attracted few scholarship offers, but Ohio State coach Woody Hayes could smell talent—especially in-state talent—from a mile away. Gradishar averaged 103 tackles per season, played in two Rose Bowls, and was a consensus All-America in 1973. OSU defensive coordinator George Hill said he was able to "make plays that no other linebacker in the country can make."

The Denver Broncos thought so, too. They drafted him in the first round in 1974. Gradishar became the foundation on which the imposing Orange Crush defense was built. He made the country take notice when he returned an interception 44 yards for a touchdown in his first *Monday Night Football* appearance in 1975.

Two years later the country watched as the Broncos' defense allowed only 10 points per game—best in the AFC—and finished the regular season with a 12-2 mark. Denver mauled the Pittsburgh Steelers in the playoffs and defeated the defending Super Bowl-champion Oakland Raiders to win the AFC title. In Super Bowl XII, however, the Orange Crush was overshadowed by the Dallas defense in a 27-10 Cowboys' win.

Gradishar was the 1978 NFL defensive player of the year, and the Broncos made the playoffs in the next two seasons. After appearing in seven Pro Bowls, he retired after the 1983 season at age 31. [MS]

OTTO GRAHAM

Quarterback. 6-1, 195. Northwestern

Born December 6, 1921, Waukegan, Illinois.
1946-1955 Cleveland
Inducted into Pro Football Hall of Fame in 1965.
Graham had been an outstanding tailback for Northwestern University and the Chapel Hill, North Carolina, Pre-Flight team in the early 1940s. But when Paul Brown began planning for his new Cleveland Browns team that would play in the AAFC in 1946, he felt Graham would be the perfect quarterback for his new T-formation team.

This was a surprise choice because Graham wanted to concentrate on basketball in college. He was "discovered" playing intramural football as a freshman and, although he became an outstanding passer in three varsity seasons, he had no experience in the T.

Brown was firm in his decision: "Otto has the basic requirements of a T-quarterback—poise, ball-handling, and distinct qualities of leadership." Once Graham joined the Browns, he not only quickly mastered the mechanics of the formation, but he also became the heart of a dynamic football machine.

With Graham throwing touchdown passes at a sizzling pace with relatively few interceptions, the Browns won four consecutive AAFC titles and compiled an awesome 52-4-3 record (including postseason). The "experts," however, theorized the Browns would get their comeuppance when they faced the "real pros" in the NFL. The Browns were more than equal to the occasion. In their 30-28 victory over the Los Angeles Rams in the 1950 NFL title game, Graham threw 4 touchdown passes.

With Graham leading the Browns, the Cleveland team played in 10 consecutive title games and won four AAFC and three NFL championships. It is a record no other quarterback has matched. [DS/PF]

HAROLD (RED) GRANGE
Halfback. 6-0, 185. Illinois
Born June 13, 1903, Forksville, Pennsylvania.
Died January 28, 1991, Lake Wales, Florida.
1925, 1929-1934 Chicago Bears, 1926 New York Yankees AFL, 1927 New York Yankees
Inducted into Pro Football Hall of Fame in 1963.
The American Professional Football Association, the direct forerunner of the NFL, was organized in 1920. But by the mid-1920s, the young league was in desperate need of special gate attractions to help bring maximum attention to the NFL.

At about the same time, a whirling dervish halfback from the University of Illinois, Harold (Red) Grange, became the most famous football star of the decade. Many college stars ignored pro football, but George Halas of the Chicago Bears pondered just how much Grange would do for pro football and finally signed him to a contract.

Just days after his college career ended, on Thanksgiving Day 1925, Grange took the field for the Bears against the Chicago Cardinals before a crowd of 36,000 standing-room-only fans in Wrigley Field. Sensing a rare opportunity was at hand, Grange's agent, C.C. (Cash and Carry) Pyle, quickly lined up a coast-to-coast barnstorming tour. More than 400,000 fans saw the fabled "Galloping Ghost" in action.

With Grange as his star attraction, Pyle in 1926 organized a rival league, the AFL, and put a team featuring Grange in New York called the Yankees. The Yankees had moderate success but the rest of the league failed. In 1927, Grange, back in the NFL, suffered a crippling knee injury against the Bears. He didn't play at all in 1928, but Halas invited him back into the Bears camp in 1929.

Grange remained with the Bears through the 1934 season. By his own admission, Grange was just an ordinary ball carrier when he returned to the Bears, but "I did develop into a pretty good defensive back." [DS/PF]

MEL GRAY
Kick Returner. 5-9, 171. Purdue
Born March 16, 1961, Williamsburg, Virginia.
1986-88 New Orleans, 1989-1994 Detroit, 1995-97 Houston, 1997 Philadelphia
Mel Gray was the top kick returner of his era, and, perhaps, of all time. Throughout his career, he was a double threat. No one ever returned more kickoffs for so many yards or more touchdowns. Moreover, he ranks in the top 20 all-time in punt returns, punt-return yardage, and average gain per punt return. As great as his statistics were, the most amazing part of his career was its longevity. Returning kicks—either kickoffs or punts—ranks as one of the highest-risk occupations in sports. Yet did it for 12 NFL seasons.

After attending Coffeyville Junior College, Gray switched to Purdue for his final two college seasons. An all-around back, he led the Boilermakers in rushing both years, but it was his kick returning that really caught the eyes of pro scouts. He signed with Los Angeles of the USFL and in two seasons rolled up 2,075 combined yards (rushing, receiving, and kick returning).

Gray joined the Saints in 1986 as a kickoff-return specialist. He unleashed a 101-yard touchdown effort against San Francisco in his third game. In 1994, he topped that by going 102 yards for another touchdown. He didn't begin to return punts until his second season—and he led the NFL that year. In 1991 with Detroit, he became the only man ever to lead the NFL in kickoff returns and punt returns in the same season. [BC]

CORNELL GREEN
Defensive Back. 6-3, 205. Utah State
Born February 10, 1940, Oklahoma City, Oklahoma.
1962-1974 Dallas
The Dallas Cowboys pioneered evaluating and selecting personnel with non-football backgrounds. One of their most successful experiments was Cornell Green, a three-time All-Skyline Conference basketball player who became one of the team's greatest defensive backs. The Cowboys signed him as a free agent in 1962.

How successful was the experiment? Green played 168 games—including 145 consecutive starts—he played in four Pro Bowls, and, as part of its famed Doomsday Defense, he helped the team win Super Bowl VI.

"Basketball was no hindrance," Green said. "You come into the league and everybody has it all to learn anyway, whether they know it or not."

Green never believed he was beaten on any long touchdown passes. "Oh, maybe one of those receivers beat me once in a while, but while I'm walking off the field, I talk myself out of it," he once said.

Green played the corner during his first eight seasons and led the team in interceptions four times. A wondrous man-for-man defender, he stalked opposing pass receivers with the same tenacity that he did opposing forwards on the basketball court. "He had the athletic skills from basketball to become a fine defensive back,"Landry said. "His only transition was playing a sport where you could tackle someone with the ball, and Cornell never had a problem dealing with that."

He switched to strong safety in 1969 and the Cowboys went to two Super Bowls. Two years later, he made the Pro Bowl at that position. [JC]

***DARRELL GREEN**

Cornerback. 5-8, 184. Texas A&I
Born February 15, 1960, Houston, Texas.
1983-1998 Washington

At 37, an age when most cornerbacks long since have retired, Darrell Green signed a five-year contract with the Redskins in 1997. At the press conference announcing the new contract, his family wore T-shirts that read, "Darrell Green. Pro Bowl 2000." That same day Green ran the 40-yard dash in 4.28 seconds, nearly as fast as when he arrived in the NFL as Washington's first pick in the 1983 draft.

He started as a rookie for the defending Super Bowl champions and helped the team repeat as NFC champions with a 72-yard interception return for a touchdown in the playoffs against the Rams. That was one of a number of big plays he has made in the postseason. In the 1987 NFC Championship Game, Green's jarring hit at the goal line forced a fumble in the final minutes and kept the Vikings from tying the game. He had clinched the previous week's playoff game against the Bears with a 52-yard punt return for a touchdown in a 21-14 victory.

A veteran of seven Pro Bowl appearances, Green has started more games (232) than any other player in Redskins' history, and he also holds the club mark for most interceptions (47). In 1997, he became the oldest player in NFL history to return an interception for a touchdown, and the fact that it was an 83-yard return confirms that he still has speed to burn. He won the "NFL Fastest Man" competition four times. He also was named the NFL's Man of the Year in 1996 for his off-the-field contributions. [MS]

JOE GREENE

Defensive Tackle. 6-4, 260. North Texas State
Born September 24, 1946, Temple, Texas.
1969-1981 Pittsburgh
Inducted into Pro Football Hall of Fame in 1987.

Although he was a 1968 consensus All-America at North Texas State, Steelers' fans asked "Joe who?" when Greene was made Pittsburgh's first-round pick in the 1969 draft.

Almost from his first game, the big tackle showed the superstar talents that established him as the defensive foundation in coach Chuck Noll's program that produced four AFC titles and four Super Bowl victories in the 1970s. Greene was named the NFL defensive rookie of the year in 1969 when he received the first of his 10 Pro Bowl invitations. He won all-pro and/or All-AFC acclaim nine times in the 1970s as a part of Pittsburgh's Steel Curtain.

Greene was selected as the NFL defensive player of the year in both 1972 and 1974, playing a major role in his team's success. He had a career-high 11 sacks in 1972 when Pittsburgh won its first playoff game. In 1974, Pittsburgh won its first AFC championship and Super Bowl IX.

That year, Greene developed the new tactic of lining up at a sharp angle between the guard and center to disrupt the opposition's blocking assignment. Against Minnesota in Super Bowl IX, Greene virtually was unstoppable. His pass interception and a fumble recovery at Pittsburgh's 7-yard line were major factors in the Vikings' defeat.

Greene, who was born in Temple, Texas, was armed with speed, quickness, strength, and great determination and, at the peak of his career, could dominate a game almost single-handedly. He opened his career with a 91-game streak that was interrupted by injury in 1975. Greene fought off injuries through much of his 13 seasons, but still wound up playing in 181 of a possible 190 regular-season games. [DS/PF]

L.C. GREENWOOD

Defensive End. 6-6, 250. Arkansas-Pine Bluff
Born September 8, 1946, Canton, Mississippi.
1969-1981 Pittsburgh

The Pittsburgh Steelers were fined for a uniform violation every game Greenwood played. While his teammates wore the uniform's black shoes, Greenwood's shoes always were gold. The Steelers never complained about the fines; Greenwood was worth it.

A three-year regular at Arkansas Pine Bluff, he was named an Ebony magazine All-America. Nonetheless, Greenwood was not drafted until the tenth round in 1969. In 1971, he became a regular, combining with Joe Greene to form a nearly impregnable left side of the Steelers' defensive line. The right side—Ernie Holmes and Dwight White—was nearly as strong. The Steel Curtain formed the heart of a legendary defense that took Pittsburgh to four Super Bowl victories and seven division titles.

A nightmare for quarterbacks, Greenwood used his height and quick reflexes to bat down numerous passes. In Super Bowl IX, he swatted 3 of Fran Tarkenton's attempts. He had unusual speed and quickness for a man his size and, though his pass-rushing style was often described as "free-wheeling" and "reckless," he was remarkably consistent and undeniably effective. During his 13 seasons, he recorded 73½ sacks (unofficially) and 14 fumble recoveries. When the Steelers won Super Bowl X, he sacked Roger Staubach 3 times.

Greenwood was all-pro twice, All-AFC four times, and appeared in six Pro Bowls. Playing in some of the most hard-fought games of the 1970s, he was seldom injured until 1977 when he missed five games with a knee injury. He rebounded in 1978 with one of his best seasons as the Steelers won their third Super Bowl. [BC]

FORREST GREGG

Tackle-Guard. 6-4, 250. Southern Methodist
Born October 18, 1933, Birthright, Texas.
1956, 1958-1970 Green Bay, 1971 Dallas
Inducted into Pro Football Hall of Fame in 1977.

During his 15 seasons in the NFL, Gregg proved himself versatile, durable, extremely unselfish, and exceptionally talented. The native Texan starred at Southern Methodist and was the Green Bay Packers' second-round draft pick in 1956. Even though he was considered small for the job, he was ticketed from the start for offensive right tackle.

Realizing that he would never be able to overpower the NFL's monstrous defensive left ends, Gregg went right to work learning how to finesse them. He spent countless hours watching film of the NFL's most noted stars and it wasn't long before he knew the moves of every opponent and had perfected ways to combat them.

Gregg always was ready for combat. The only severe football injury he ever experienced was a broken arm as a high school sophomore. Forrest earned an "ironman" tag by playing in a then-record 188 consecutive NFL games from 1956 until 1971, his final season which he spent with the Super Bowl-bound Dallas Cowboys.

He won all-pro acclaim eight consecutive years from 1960-67 and also played in nine straight Pro Bowls.

In 1961 and again in 1965, when injuries created a crisis on the Packers' offensive line, Gregg willingly switched to guard to fill the void. He had to learn a completely new set of assignments, but he met the challenge successfully. In 1965, one major wire service named him an All-NFL guard, the other picked him as its all-league tackle.

Vince Lombardi, in his book *Run to Daylight,* wrote: "Forrest Gregg is the finest player I ever coached." [DS/PF]

ROOSEVELT GRIER

Defensive Tackle. 6-5, 285. Penn State
Born July 14, 1932, Cuthbert, Georgia.
1956-1962 New York Giants, 1963-66 Los Angeles Rams

Rosey Grier was a pioneer of sorts in the National Football League. As a 1955 third-round draft pick of the New York Giants, he was the first truly mammoth defensive tackle in the 4-3 defense that became popular in the NFL during the mid-1950s.

The Giants' philosophy deemed that each of the four linemen and three linebackers control seven of the eight "holes" along the line of scrimmage to shut down the run. (A designated defensive back, nicknamed "Tilly," got the eighth.) The pass rush came from big, mobile linemen who could overpower an offensive line. Grier fit perfectly with ends Andy Robustelli and Jim Katcavage, and tackle Dick Modzelewski.

Yankee Stadium rocked Sunday after Sunday with the cry of "DEE-fense!" and, for the first time in football history, defensive players became as popular as their offensive teammates. The defense helped the Giants win the 1956 NFL title and brought the team to five other NFL title games, four while Grier was one of its members. He was traded to the Los Angeles Rams in 1963. Again, he was a perfect fit with the Rams' great defensive line of ends Deacon Jones and Lamar Lundy and tackle Merlin Olsen, a group nicknamed the Fearsome Foursome.

Grier outweighed most of the offensive linemen of his time by 40 or 50 pounds. His toughest battles were with his weight, which sapped his stamina as the season progressed. In training camp, he was a permanent member of the "fat man" table, suffering through endless meals of lettuce and Jell-O salads as he tried to lose weight. [JC]

BOB GRIESE

Quarterback. 6-1, 190. Purdue
Born February 3, 1945, Evansville, Indiana.
1967-1980 Miami
Inducted into Pro Football Hall of Fame in 1990.

A two-time All-America at Purdue, Griese was the Dolphins' top draft choice in their second year in 1967. For the next 14 seasons, he was the poised leader of a classic ball-control offense that generated an awesomely efficient running attack, AFC championships in 1971, 1972, and 1973, and victories in Super Bowls VII and VIII.

In several of his best performances, Griese used the pass only sparingly. But when the defenses clogged up the Miami runners, he quickly and efficiently opened up things with his accurate passes. In Super Bowl VII, for instance, only 11 of Miami's 50 scrimmage plays were passes, but Griese's 8 completions accounted for 1 touchdown and set up the second.

In Super Bowl VIII, the rush-pass ratio for Miami was a startling 53-7 with Griese completing 6 of his 7 passes. The Dolphins won easily. In 14 seasons, Griese threw 3,429 passes, completing 1,926 for 25,092 yards and 192 touchdowns.

Honors came frequently for Griese—a six-time Dolphins MVP. He also was the NFL player of the year in 1971 and all-pro or all-AFC in 1971, 1973, and 1977. He played in two AFL All-Star games and six AFC-NFC Pro Bowls. His success came in spite of numerous injuries that constantly plagued him. During Miami's perfect 1972 season, Griese missed nine games but returned in time to lead his team to victories in both the AFC title game and Super Bowl VII. [DS/PF]

LOU GROZA

Tackle-Kicker. 6-3, 250. Ohio State
Born January 25, 1924, Martins Ferry, Ohio.
1946-1959, 1961-67 Cleveland
Inducted into Pro Football Hall of Fame in 1974.

With a host of outstanding stars, the Cleveland Browns enjoyed exceptional success during their four years in the AAFC and for 17 of their first 18 years in the NFL. More than any other player, tackle-kicker Lou Groza, who played for 21 seasons, epitomized that unforgettable era.

While many fans remember Groza primarily as the first great kicker who routinely won games with his field goals, he was also an outstanding tackle who earned all-league honors six of the first eight years the Browns were in the NFL. In 1954, he was named *The Sporting News* NFL player of the year. He played in the Pro Bowl nine years, six of them as a starting tackle.

In 1946, 33-man rosters prevented any team from carrying a specialist, but Groza was almost that, doing all of the kicking and playing on the scrimmage line only occasionally. Late in his second season, Lou made the starting lineup and he didn't give up that status until 1959. He sat out the entire 1960 season with a back injury, then returned in 1961 at the age of 37 for seven more campaigns as a kicker.

Regardless of their abilities, offensive linemen rarely made the headlines so, whether Groza liked it or not, a lion's share of fame was generated by his kicking achievements. In 21 years, "The Toe," as he became known, scored 1,608 points, including 259 in the AAFC. His most dramatic kick came in the 1950 NFL Championship Game, when his 16-yard field goal with time running out gave the Browns a 30-28 victory over the Los Angeles Rams. Groza admitted, "It was my biggest thrill." [DS/PF]

RAY GUY

Punter. 6-3, 190. Southern Mississippi
Born December 22, 1949, Swainsboro, Georgia.
1973-1986 Raiders

So far, there only has been one Ray Guy. When the Raiders drafted the Southern Mississippi all-around athlete in 1973, it marked the first time a pure punter was taken on the first round. To date, that hasn't been repeated.

The long, lean, right-footed kicker generated tremendous leg-whip with his near-perfect technique. He was the first of only a few punters to hit the hanging scoreboard in the Louisiana Superdome. Not only did Guy punt high and far—"hang time" came into the NFL lexicon during his tenure—he got the ball away quickly and surely. A blocked punt was a rarity; he had no kicks blocked in his first five NFL seasons and finished his career with a streak of 619 unblocked boots.

In three years—1974, 1975, and 1977—he led the AFC in punting average. But his raw yardage was secondary to his ability to kick the ball high and keep it there so long that there was little chance for a decent return. His 42.3 average yards per punt isn't in the top 20, but it was hang time and placement that made him so dangerous. He pinned down the opposition, and, if the defense upheld its part of the bargain, the Raiders invariably won the exchange of punts and the battle for field position.

From the 1973-1980 seasons, he played in seven of eight Pro Bowls. Pro Football Hall of Fame historian Joe Horrigan said, "He's the first punter you could look at and say, 'He won games.' " [JJC]

JOE GUYON

Halfback. 6-1, 180. Carlisle, Georgia Tech
Born November 26, 1892, Mahnomen, Minnesota.
Died November 27, 1971, Louisville, Kentucky.
1920 Canton, 1921 Cleveland, 1922-23 Oorang, 1924 Rock Island, 1924-25 Kansas City, 1927 New York Giants
Inducted into Pro Football Hall of Fame in 1966

While Jim Thorpe was the most famous Native-American athlete to play in the early NFL, a second, Joe Guyon, a full-blooded Chippewa, also was an outstanding football player. In fact, some contemporary players considered the multitalented Guyon superior to Thorpe because he played with more consistency.

Born O-Gee-Chidah on the White Earth Indian Reservation in Minnesota, Guyon used his athletic skills to gain an education. He played on two great collegiate teams, the Carlisle Indian School in 1912 and Georgia Tech in 1917. He joined the Canton Bulldogs in 1919, then played with six different teams in seven years.

Thorpe and Guyon played on the same team during Guyon's first six pro seasons, but they parted in 1925 when Guyon stayed with the Kansas City Cowboys and Thorpe moved to the New York Giants. Two years later, Guyon also became a Giant and played a major role in leading New York to the 1927 championship. Away from the shadow of Thorpe for the first time, Guyon enjoyed a banner season and gained the first significant publicity he had enjoyed since his college days.

The 1927 Giants compiled an 11-1-1 record largely on the strength of a superior defense that allowed only 20 points all season. But Guyon, flashing all of his many abilities— passing, running, punting, tackling, and blocking—played a leading role in putting the necessary points on the scoreboard. [DS/PF]

CHARLES HALEY

Defensive End. 6-5, 245. James Madison
Born January 6, 1964, Gladys, Virginia.
1986-1991, 1998 San Francisco, 1992-96 Dallas

Charles Haley went from a little school to the big time. Haley attended James Madison University in Virginia and did enough damage in the Yankee Conference to be drafted by the San Francisco 49ers in the fourth round of the 1986 draft. Haley holds the NFL record for the most Super Bowl appearances on the winning team. He is 5-0 in the Super Bowl; he was a member of the world champions with the San Francisco 49ers in 1988 and 1989 and with the Dallas Cowboys in 1992, 1993, and 1995. A shining example of the dominance of the Cowboys and 49ers from the late 1980s to the mid-1990s, Haley played in the NFC Championship Game seven times between 1988 and 1995.

While Haley has been more than adequate in stopping the run, his specialty is sacking the quarterback. Few do it better. The 6-foot 5-inch, 255-pound defensive end has 97½ career sacks. He has had 10 or more sacks six times and led the NFC with 16 in 1990. Haley also is the all-time Super Bowl sack leader.

As enjoyable as Haley's career has been on the field, it has not always gone so smoothly in his relationships with his coaches. He had several well-publicized clashes with the 49ers' coaching staff and was traded to the Cowboys for a second-round pick in 1992.

After almost two years away from the field, Haley returned to football and San Francisco to help the depleted 49ers during the 1998 postseason. He appeared in two playoff games. [MS]

JACK HAM

Linebacker. 6-1, 225. Penn State
Born December 23, 1948, Johnstown, Pennsylvania.
1971-1982 Pittsburgh
Inducted into Pro Football Hall of Fame in 1988.

A consensus All-America at Penn State and the thirty-fourth player taken in the 1971 draft, Ham used a sensational rookie training camp to become a starting left linebacker for the Pittsburgh Steelers in his first regular-season game. The clincher was a 3-interception performance against the New York Giants in the preseason finale. Ham started all 14 games as a rookie and he continued to hold a regular job with Pittsburgh until his retirement after the 1982 season.

Ham quickly earned the reputation as a big-play defender and one of the best outside linebackers in the game. He finished his career with 21 fumbles recovered and 32 interceptions. Blessed with speed, quickness, intelligence, and exceptional mobility, the Johnstown, Pennsylvania, native had the uncanny ability to diagnose plays and to be in the right defensive position at all times.

He played in Super Bowls IX, X, and XIII, but was forced to sit out Super Bowl XIV because of injuries. He also played in five AFC Championship Games and it was his 19-yard interception return to the Oakland 9-yard line that set up the Steelers' go-ahead touchdown in their first championship victory in 1974.

Ham was named to the All-AFC team for the first time in 1973, then was a universal all-pro choice the next six seasons through the 1979 campaign. In 1975, he was named the defensive player of the year by the Football News. He was the only linebacker of his decade to be named to eight consecutive AFC-NFC Pro Bowls. [DS/PF]

DAN HAMPTON

Defensive Tackle. 6-5, 264. Arkansas
Born September 19, 1957, Oklahoma City, Oklahoma
1979-1990 Chicago Bears

Dan Hampton played a dozen years in the NFL with the Chicago Bears, but he will always think of himself as a member of the 1985 defense.

In 1985 the Bears allowed only 198 points. The defense shut out both opponents in the NFC playoffs, and the Bears capped it off in the Super Bowl against the New England Patriots with 7 sacks and just 123 total yards allowed. The 46-10 final score only hinted at the Bears' dominance. "It was one year when a team transcended the game itself," Hampton said.

Hampton was one of the keys to the defense. He drew extra blockers from his defensive tackle position and allowed others to make the big plays.

Although 1985 surely was the high point of his career, Hampton was anything but a one-year wonder. The man who came to be known affectionately as "Danimal" among Bears' fans was a first-round draft choice out of the University of Arkansas in 1979. As a senior with the Razorbacks, he was chosen the Southwest Conference's defensive player of the year. With the Bears, he was several times all-NFL/NFC and played in four Pro Bowls.

He paid a price for his career—10 knee operations. Nevertheless, he ranks as one of the best tackles in the history of a franchise that can boast such greats as Ed Healey, Joe Stydahar, and George Connor. [MS]

JOHN HANNAH

Guard. 6-3, 285. Alabama
Born April 4, 1951, Canton, Georgia.
1973-1985 New England
Inducted into Pro Football Hall of Fame in 1991.

John Hannah went from Canton, Georgia, to Canton, Ohio, and the Pro Football Hall of Fame.

Starting his first 13 games before a freak leg injury forced him out of the final game of his rookie season, Hannah dispelled any concerns the New England Patriots might have had about his ability to adjust from the straight-ahead blocking of Alabama's Wishbone offense to the drop-back blocking and pulling required of guards in the pros. Hannah was the first-round pick of the Patriots and the fourth player selected in the 1973 NFL draft. The son of former New York Giants tackle Herb Hannah, John was an eight-letterman star in football, track, and wrestling and a two-time football All-America at Alabama.

In the next 12 years, Hannah became widely recognized as the premier guard of pro football. He was named all-pro 10 consecutive years from 1976-1985. He won the NFL Players Association's offensive-lineman-of-the-year award four straight years from 1978-1981. Hannah was named to nine Pro Bowls, but missed the game following the 1983 season because of an injury. In spite of the constant contact his body had to absorb, Hannah missed only five games out of a possible 191 because of injuries in 13 seasons. He also missed three games due to a contract dispute at the start of the 1977 season.

The Georgia native finished his career after the 1985 season on a high note. His final campaign had produced an AFC championship and Super Bowl XX appearance for the Patriots, all-pro honors, and a Pro Bowl invitation one last time. [DS/PF]

FRANCO HARRIS

Running Back. 6-2, 225. Penn State
Born March 7, 1950, Fort Dix, New Jersey.
1972-1983 Pittsburgh, 1984 Seattle
Inducted into Pro Football Hall of Fame in 1990.

Harris gained national attention in 1972 by making the famous Immaculate Reception on a deflected pass from Terry Bradshaw that gave the Steelers their first playoff victory, 13-7 over the Oakland Raiders. It capped a remarkable rookie year.

Considered somewhat of an underachiever at Penn State, he nevertheless was the Pittsburgh Steelers' number-one pick and the thirteenth player selected in the 1972 NFL draft. He established himself as a future superstar when he became only the fifth rookie in NFL history to rush for more than 1,000 yards. The 6-foot 2-inch, 225-pounder was sometimes criticized for running out of bounds instead of lowering his head for a few more yards. In truth, he'd blast when the yardage was vital, but his cerebral running style helped save his body for a long career.

In 13 seasons, Harris rushed 2,949 times for 12,120 yards and 91 touchdowns. He rushed for 1,000 yards or more eight times and for more than 100 yards in 47 games. He also caught 307 passes for 2,287 yards and 9 touchdowns.

The Fort Dix, New Jersey, native was an all-AFC choice in 1972, 1975, and 1977. He also earned all-pro honors in 1977. He played in eight Pro Bowls and missed a ninth because of an injury. Harris played in five AFC Championship Games—missing a sixth because of another injury—and four Super Bowls. In Super Bowl IX, when the Steelers won their first league title with a 16-6 victory over Minnesota, Harris rushed for 158 yards, compared to just 17 yards rushing for the entire Vikings team. He was named the game's most valuable player. [DS/PF]

BOB HAYES

Wide Receiver. 6-0, 185. Florida A&M
Born December 20, 1942, Jacksonville, Florida.
1965-1974 Dallas Cowboys

Bob Hayes was a rarity—a world-class track star who also was a great NFL wide receiver.

Hayes won a pair of gold medals in the 1964 Olympic Games in Tokyo, including the 100 meters to earn the title "World's Fastest Human."

Other sprinters followed him to the NFL as wide receivers but none ever did as well as Hayes. "Bullet Bob" terrorized defensive backs and demanded a kind of deep double coverage rarely seen in the NFL.

The biggest difference was that he also played running back at Florida A&M, so the game, with all of its nuances and its contact and pounding, were no mysteries whenever he battled NFL defensive backs. He sent a serious message in his rookie season, 1965, when he led the team with 46 receptions for 1,003 yards.

He led the Cowboys three times in receptions, including back-to-back titles in 1965-66 when he caught a total of 110 passes for more than 2,200 yards and 25 touchdowns. For his 10-season career, he accumulated 7,295 yards and 71 touchdowns.

Larry Wilson, the St. Louis Cardinals' Pro Football Hall of Fame free safety, who often was the last line of defense against the always-dangerous Hayes, said the difference between him and other Olympic sprinters who attempted playing in the NFL was his ability to use his speed in a football sense, rather than just trying to run as fast as he could. "He had several speeds, all of them fast, but defensive backs had to figure out which one he was using and which one he was going to use," Wilson said. [JC]

LESTER HAYES

Cornerback. 6-0, 200. Texas
Born December 22, 1955, Houston, Texas.
1977-1986 Raiders

Lester Hayes didn't let anyone off easy. A popular poster in the 1980s characterized the Raiders defensive back as a "judge" and NFL wide receivers as "law breakers." According to the poster, wide receivers were "sentenced to four quarters of relentless intimidation, bone-jarring hits, and masterful interceptions." The poster may have exaggerated the facts, but not by much.

Hayes, a linebacker at Texas A&M, was chosen in the fifth round in the 1977 draft. He switched to cornerback and intercepted 7 passes and had 2 touchdowns for the Raiders in 1979. In 1980, he had 13 interceptions, the second-highest single-season total in NFL history. And he had 4 other interceptions nullified by penalties. He added 5 interceptions in the postseason as the Raiders became the first wild-card team to win the Super Bowl. Hayes won NFL defensive-player-of-the-year honors.

Hayes continued to help the Raiders win after his stellar 1980 season. He intercepted a pass and returned it for a touchdown and also blocked a punt against the Pittsburgh Steelers in the 1983 playoffs. Two games later, he intercepted a pass and returned it 44 yards against the Seattle Seahawks as the Raiders won the AFC title. Hayes and fellow cornerback Mike Haynes helped stymie the Washington Redskins' passing attack in a 38-9 upset victory in Super Bowl XVIII.

His 8 interceptions in 13 postseason games ranks fourth on the all-time list. Hayes made five Pro Bowl appearances during his 12-year career with the Raiders. [MS]

MIKE HAYNES

Cornerback. 6-2, 195. Arizona State
Born July 1, 1953, Denison, Texas.
1976-1982 New England, 1983-89 Raiders
Inducted into Pro Football Hall of Fame in 1997.

To borrow a line Ralph Kiner once used to describe the ability of a great center fielder, three-fourths of the earth is covered by water, the other fourth is covered by Mike Haynes. At least it must have seemed that way to NFL receivers trying to evade Haynes's smothering pass coverage from 1976 through 1989.

No one played with less of a cushion than the in-your-jersey cornerback, who usually took on an opponents' top pass receiver man-for-man. Haynes was big for a cornerback at the time and not easily—if ever—outmuscled.

A first-round draft choice of the Patriots after an All-America career at Arizona State, Haynes was voted the AFC rookie of the year in 1976. He intercepted 8 passes and returned punts for a sparkling 13.5 average per return. Haynes's speed, quickness, vision, and field sense made him a dangerous man with the football, whether returning kicks or interceptions. After seven seasons in New England, he signed as a free agent with the Raiders. He and Lester Hayes provided one of the best cornerback tandems in NFL history. They were a big factor in the Raiders' Super Bowl XVIII victory.

Haynes did not fit the swaggering image of his hometown Raiders when he joined the team. He simply let his ability and talent speak for him. Very early in his career, teams learned not to test Mike Haynes. [JJC]

ED HEALEY

Tackle. 6-3, 220. Dartmouth
Born December 28, 1894, Indian Orchard, Massachusetts.
Died December 9, 1978, South Bend, Indiana.
1920-22 Rock Island, 1922-27 Chicago Bears
Inducted into Pro Football Hall of Fame in 1964.

Although he stood 6 feet 3 inches and weighed 220 pounds, Ed Healey enjoyed only moderate success as an end at Dartmouth College. After graduation, he moved to Omaha, Nebraska, where he worked loading meat into railroad cars. When he heard that a new professional football league was being formed, he decided to try out with the Rock Island Independents. After one game against the Chicago Tigers, he was given $100 and asked to join the team on a permanent basis.

In 1922, while playing tackle against George Halas, the Chicago Bears' player-coach, he dominated his opponent so thoroughly that Halas decided he had to have this player on his team. After the game, he bought Healey for $100. Healey liked his raise to $100 per game, but was impressed with the locker rooms at Wrigley Field, which he saw as a "warm place to dress and take a shower."

Throughout his NFL career, Healey was a true warrior, one who enjoyed the contact involved in the game. Halas often referred to him as "the most versatile tackle in history." He was an all-pro selection five times during his eight-year career.

Blessed with good speed for a tackle, Healey twice used this attribute to make game-saving tackles. Once he ran more than 30 yards to tackle a teammate who was running the wrong way. In 1925, on a barnstorming tour featuring Red Grange, Healey made a touchdown-saving tackle before 60,000 fans, a play he called his greatest pro football thrill. [BC]

WILLIAM (PUDGE) HEFFELFINGER

Guard. 6-3, 210. Yale

Born December 20, 1867, Minneapolis, Minnesota.

Died April 2, 1954, Blessing, Texas.

1892 Allegheny Athletic Association

Today, William (Pudge) Heffelfinger is regarded as the first professional football player. At the Pro Football Hall of Fame a large exhibit celebrates Heffelfinger's accomplishment with a life-size photo and a blow-up of a page from the Allegheny Athletic Association's 1892 ledger book showing his $500 salary for playing a single game

Heffelfinger was undoubtedly the best football player in the country. He began 1892 playing for the Chicago A.C. for "expenses"—liberal expenses, to say the least, but still within the guidelines for amateurs set by the Amateur Athletic Union, sports' ruling body at the time.

The Alleghenys asked him to come to Pittsburgh and earn $500 playing in their big game against archrival Pittsburgh Athletic Club on November 12, 1892. Heffelfinger turned out to be worth his wages, which were more than many steelworkers made in a year. He played brilliantly and won the game by stripping the opposing ball carrier and running for the only score.

Heffelfinger had been a three-time All-America at Yale (1889-1891), famous for stuffing opponents' flying wedges by leaping over blockers and landing on the ball carriers. Normally a guard, he sometimes dropped back and carried the ball himself. At 6 feet 3 inches, and more than 200 pounds, he was one of the biggest and fastest players of his time.

Although rumors of Heffelfinger's payday abounded, neither he nor the Allegheny Athletic Association ever admitted money had changed hands. Not until 70 years later was the A.A.A.'s ledger discovered. [BC]

MEL HEIN

Center. 6-2, 225. Washington State

Born August 22, 1909, Redding, California.

Died January 31, 1992, San Clemente, California.

1931-1945 New York Giants

Inducted into Pro Football Hall of Fame in 1963.

Mel Hein led Washington State to a Rose Bowl bid in 1930 and was named to Grantland Rice's All-America team as a utility lineman because he played tackle, guard, and center.

Yet Hein had to write to three NFL teams offering his services in 1931. Providence offered $135 per game so he signed and mailed the Steam Roller contract. Then he learned the Giants would give him $150 per game so he wired the Providence postmaster to ask him to return the Steam Roller contract. When Hein and his new wife Florence arrived broke in Gotham just before training camp opened, the Giants advanced him $200. He had to beat out two veterans to stay with the team.

Hein was included on the Giants' 25-man squad, and he became a fixture at center in New York for 15 seasons. He was one of the most durable players in NFL history during a time when there was no platoon football. Hein called time out just once during his career when he needed to fix his broken nose.

Hein combined great stamina, mental alertness, and superior athletic ability to become an exceptional star. He was named an all-NFL center eight times from 1933-1940. In 1938, he was named the NFL's most valuable player, a rare honor for a center. He was the Giants' captain for 10 years. The ultimate honor for Hein came in 1963 when he was elected as a charter member of the Pro Football Hall of Fame. [DS/PF]

TED HENDRICKS

Linebacker. 6-7, 235. Miami

Born November 1, 1947, Guatemala City, Guatemala

1969-1973 Baltimore, 1974 Green Bay, 1975-1983 Raiders

They called Ted Hendricks "The Mad Stork." Tall and comparatively skinny, Hendricks was strong, fast, and a devastating tackler who specialized in blocking punts, field goals, and extra-point attempts. In his career, Hendricks intercepted 26 passes. He also recovered 16 opponents' fumbles and totaled a record-tying 4 safeties. Hendricks scored 3 touchdowns, 1 on an interception, another on a fumble return, and 1 on a blocked punt.

A three-time All-America as a linebacker and defensive end at the University of Miami in Florida, Hendricks began his 15-year pro football career as the second-round selection of the Baltimore Colts in the 1969 AFL-NFL draft. After five seasons with the Colts, he was traded to the Green Bay Packers in 1974. Hendricks played out his option with the Packers and signed with the Oakland Raiders in 1975. He played nine seasons with the Raiders before retiring after the 1983 season.

Hendricks played 215 successive regular-season games and participated in eight Pro Bowl games, seven AFC championships, and four Super Bowls (V with the Colts, XI, XV, XVIII with the Raiders). He was named all-pro while with the Colts in 1971, as a Packer in 1974 and as a Raider in 1980 and 1982. He was selected All-AFC seven times and All-NFC once. In his final pro game, Hendricks was the starting left linebacker in the Los Angeles Raiders' 38-9 victory over the Washington Redskins in Super Bowl XVIII. [DS/PF]

CHARLEY HENNIGAN

Wide Receiver. 6-0, 187. LSU, Northwest Louisiana

Born March 19, 1935, Bienville, Lousiana.

1960-66 Houston

As a child, Charley Hennigan was told he couldn't play sports; as a rookie in the Houston Oilers' training camp, he was told he couldn't catch.

At age 11, Hennigan was told by doctors that a medical condition would keep him from ever participating in sports. He went on to become a three-sport athlete at Minden High School and a two-sport star in college. As a freshman at Louisiana State University, Hennigan ran on the Tigers' Southeastern Conference-champion mile relay team. He transferred to Northwest Louisiana and lettered in both football and track while earning his degree.

Hennigan was teaching high school biology when the American Football League formed. He signed with the Houston Oilers, but assistant coach Mac Speedie had to talk head coach Lou Rymkus into keeping him. In camp, he showed terrific speed, but had a problem catching the ball.

Hennigan justified Speedie's faith by becoming one of the outstanding receivers who helped the AFL earn the reputation as a "passer's paradise." He helped the Oilers win the first AFL championship in 1960, but he really blossomed the following year with 1,746 receiving yards. Houston again won the AFL title in 1961. Hennigan teamed with quarterback George Blanda for several more productive seasons and set another league record with 101 catches in 1964.

Injuries hindered Hennigan the next two years, and he was traded to the San Diego Chargers after the 1966 season. He retired instead. [MS]

WILBUR (PETE) HENRY

Tackle. 6-0, 250. Washington & Jefferson
Born October 31, 1897, Mansfield, Ohio.
Died February 7, 1952, Washington, Pennsylvania.
1920-23, 1925-26 Canton, 1927 New York Giants, 1927-28 Pottsville
Inducted into Pro Football Hall of Fame in 1963.

Wilbur (Pete) Henry was one of pro football's earliest superstars. He was such a big name that when he signed with the Bulldogs he was the lead story on page one of the Canton Repository on September 20, 1920, and relegated the birth of the NFL to page three.

Even if the newspaper's makeup man had known that the new league would turn into a giant in professional sports, the signing of the All-America tackle from Washington and Jefferson College undoubtedly would have received at least equal attention in a football hotbed such as Canton.

Henry was a 60-minute player in the NFL. Since he had been a fullback in high school, the Bulldogs used him occasionally on a powerful "tackle over tackle" play and on tackle-eligible passes. He was the outstanding performer on Canton's undefeated championship teams in 1922 and 1923. Henry, also known by his nickname "Fats," was a superior punter, kicker, and dropkicker. For many years, he held various NFL kicking record records. In 1922, he had a successful 45-yard dropkick for a field goal.

As good as he was offensively, it was on defense that Henry had the most impact. In a 1922 game, the Buffalo All-Americans decided to run straight at Henry on every play. On the first play, Henry flattened the entire side of the Buffalo line, then smothered the ball carrier for a big loss. The Buffalo coach quickly abandoned that game plan. [DS/PF]

ARNIE HERBER

Quarterback. 6-1, 200. Wisconsin, Regis College
Born April 2, 1910, Green Bay, Wisconsin.
Died October 14, 1969, Green Bay, Wisconsin.
1930-1940 Green Bay, 1944-45 New York Giants
Inducted into Pro Football Hall of Fame in 1966.

Many NFL historians think of Sammy Baugh as the first pro football star to use the forward pass with impressive results. A glance at the record book shows Arnie Herber was a pretty fair passer when "Slingin' Sam" still was in high school. The NFL kept detailed statistics for the first time in Herber's third season in 1932. He won the league passing title that year and two more times before Baugh joined the league in 1937.

The arrival of the sensational Don Hutson in 1935 gave pro football its first lethal quarterback-receiver tandem. In Hutson's second game in the NFL, against the Chicago Bears, he teamed with Herber for an 83-yard touchdown reception. In 1935, the Herber-to-Hutson duo connected 18 times for 420 yards and 7 touchdowns. Although Herber suffered a leg injury that sharply reduced his effectiveness in 1937, the Herber-Hutson mystique continued until Herber retired in 1940.

With many players serving in the military during World War II, the New York Giants brought Herber back for two more years in 1944 and 1945. He then retired for good with the reputation as pro football's first great long-distance passer.

As a teenager in Green Bay, Herber sold programs so he could watch the Packers play. He eventually migrated to tiny Regis College in Denver, but he soon was back in Green Bay, where he worked as a handyman in the Packers' clubhouse. One day, coach Curly Lambeau decided to give Herber a tryout. For $75 a game, the Packers gained a great player who'd been right in their own clubhouse. [DS/PF]

BILL HEWITT

End. 5-11, 191. Michigan
Born October 8, 1909, Bay City, Michigan.
Died January 14, 1947, Sellersville, Pennsylvania.
1932-36 Chicago Bears, 1937-39, 1943 Philadelphia
Inducted into Pro Football Hall of Fame in 1971.

Bill Hewitt made his mark in nine NFL seasons in a number of ways, but two stand out especially. First, he shunned the use of a helmet until the league finally forced him to wear this protective gear in 1939, his eighth season. Hewitt's reason was simple. He felt a helmet hampered his play.

Second, he was known as "The Offside Kid" because most people felt he was perpetually offside. In fact, he got such a terrific start when the center snapped the ball that many times he brought down ball carriers almost before they received the ball. Opponents felt he had to be offside to accomplish such a feat.

Hewitt was one of the most respected players of his day, an All-NFL player three of his five seasons with the Chicago Bears and again in his first season with the Philadelphia Eagles in 1937. Hewitt affectionately was known by his teammates as "Stinky." He always was conjuring up new gimmicks to foil the opposition. One of his special plays called for a jump pass from fullback Bronko Nagurski to Hewitt, who would then lateral to another end, Bill Karr, racing toward the goal line. It was this play that gave the Bears a victory in the NFL's first championship game in 1933, a 23-21 win over the Giants.

Hewitt, who died in an automobile accident in 1947, wasn't a very big player but he was tough as nails and possessed a strong upper body. [DS/PF]

GENE HICKERSON

Guard. 6-3, 250. Mississippi
Born February 15, 1936, Trenton, Tennessee.
1958-1960, 1962-1973 Cleveland

"He was the consummate guard." That's how fellow guard and NFL assistant coach Howard Mudd saw Gene Hickerson of the Browns. Hickerson, a somewhat mysterious man from Tennessee, who played at Ole Miss, is the man who paved the way for two Hall of Fame running backs—Jim Brown and Leroy Kelly—for 15 seasons.

Hickerson's strength was pulling out of the line and leading the sweep. He led the sweep so well that he was selected to play in the Pro Bowl six consecutive years (1965-1970). When the NFL, in conjunction with its fiftieth anniversary, named its All-Sixties team, Hickerson was one of the decade's all-star guards.

The Browns drafted Hickerson as a "future" pick in 1957. He joined the team the following year. Coach Paul Brown installed him as one of his "messenger guards," delivering plays to the quarterback. Although Hickerson was on the field only half the time, he still attracted attention, and was sorely missed when he suffered a broken leg before the 1961 season. After Brown was fired following the 1962 season, Hickerson played full time.

Hickerson had a great combination of speed, power, durability, and athletic ability. Few offensive linemen performed at the level and quality he did for so long a period of time. As the position's requirements changed, so did Hickerson—he came into the league at 230 pounds and left at 260. The added bulk never affected his overall speed.

"A high-quality football player for a long time," Mudd recalled. "When I came into the league, I said, 'Wow! That's the guy I want to be like.' " [JJC]

CLARKE HINKLE

Fullback. 5-11, 201. Bucknell
Born April 10, 1909, Toronto, Ohio.
Died November 9, 1988, Steubenville, Ohio.
1932-1941 Green Bay
Inducted into Pro Football Hall of Fame in 1964.

The intensity of pro football's oldest rivalry between the Chicago Bears and Green Bay Packers was best typified in the 1930s by the individual clashes of two fullbacks, Bronko Nagurski for the Bears and Clarke Hinkle for the Packers. Nagurski was the prototype power runner, but the rugged Hinkle, 30 pounds lighter, was determined to hold his own.

His creed was "get to the Bronk before he gets to me," a tactic he used to perfection one day in 1934. Trapped on the sidelines by Nagurski, Clarke escaped his tackle by driving directly into and over him. The Bears' superstar received a broken nose and fractured rib.

Hinkle, who retired in 1941 after 10 years in Green Bay, was one of the best all-around players of his era, a powerful runner with the speed to elude tacklers in the open field. He also was an outstanding blocker. He could catch the ball and throw it in option situations. His career statistics, though not impressive by modern standards, were significant for his time.

The four-time All-NFL star also was brilliant on defense. As a linebacker, he was a punishing tackler against the run and equally adept in pass coverage. As Green Bay's punter from 1939 to 1941, he had a 40.8-yard average. [DS/PF]

ELROY (CRAZYLEGS) HIRSCH

Halfback-End. 6-2, 190. Wisconsin, Michigan
Born June 17, 1923, Wausau, Wisconsin.
1946-48 Chicago AAFC, 1949-1957 Los Angeles Rams
Inducted into Pro Football Hall of Fame in 1968.

Pro football stardom was expected of Elroy (Crazylegs) Hirsch, an All-America halfback at both Wisconsin and Michigan, when he joined the Chicago Rockets of the new AAFC in 1946. But injuries delayed his ascension as one of the league's elite players. When his AAFC contract expired and he joined the Los Angeles Rams of the NFL in 1949, it wasn't earth-shaking news.

Hirsch, who was given the nickname "Crazylegs" in college because of his unique running style, saw only limited action in 1949. But in 1950, Rams coach Joe Stydahar shifted him from halfback to end, a position he had never played. Hirsch turned out to be a natural. He was a major contributor to the Rams' championship team in 1951.

Hirsch's brilliant first season as a receiver included a 91-yard touchdown reception against the Chicago Bears. With the Rams at their 9-yard line and trailing 14-0, quarterback Bob Waterfield faked a handoff, dropped back a few steps, and threw the ball downfield to connect with the speeding Hirsch. The Los Angeles Rams went on to a 42-17 victory. In addition to that 91-yard touchdown against Chicago, Hirsch also scored on catches of 34, 44, 47, 53, 70, 72, 76, 79, and 81 yards in 1951. His 66 catches for 1,495 yards and 17 touchdowns in 1951 represented the best single-season totals of his 12-year pro career. Overall, Hirsch caught 387 passes for 7,029 yards and 60 touchdowns. [DS/PF]

PAUL HORNUNG

Halfback. 6-2, 220. Notre Dame
Born December 23, 1935, Louisville, Kentucky.
1957-1962, 1964-66 Green Bay
Inducted into Pro Football Hall of Fame in 1986.

In his first two NFL seasons, Paul Hornung didn't live up to expectations.

A consensus All-America and the 1956 Heisman Trophy winner as a quarterback at Notre Dame, the Kentucky native was the Packers' bonus draft pick in 1957. Dividing his time between fullback and quarterback, Hornung was unimpressive until Vince Lombardi arrived as the Green Bay Packers' head coach in 1959. The fiery new coach moved Hornung to halfback permanently, and Hornung developed into a superstar.

Hornung was the epitome of the player who made the big plays when his team needed then most. He scored 760 points in nine seasons (62 touchdowns, 190 conversions, and 66 field goals). But Hornung did more than just score points. He gained 3,711 yards rushing and added 1,480 yards on pass receptions. Highly effective on the halfback-option play, the former quarterback accounted for 383 passing yards and 5 touchdowns with his arm.

The zenith of Hornung's NFL career came in 1959, 1960, and 1961, when he enjoyed exceptional seasons. He was the NFL's scoring leader in each season, including a league-record 176 points in 1960. He was the NFL's most valuable player in 1960 and 1961. In the 1961 NFL Championship Game, Hornung, on Christmas leave from the U.S. Army, startled the New York Giants by scoring a record 19 points in Green Bay's 37-0 victory.

He was suspended for 1963, along with Detroit defensive tackle Alex Karras, for gambling on NFL games, but was reinstated in 1964 and scored 5 touchdowns in one game against the Baltimore Colts in 1965. [DS/PF]

KEN HOUSTON

Safety. 6-3, 198. Prairie View A&M
Born November 12, 1944, Lufkin, Texas.
1967-1972 Houston, 1973-1980 Washington
Inducted into Pro Football Hall of Fame in 1986.

With 16 seconds left, Cowboys running back Walt Garrison took a short pass and turned for the end zone. A touchdown meant victory. Washington Redskins cornerback Ken Houston met Garrison at the 1, lifted him into the air, and dropped him short of the goal line. It was a victory for Washington in its storied rivalry with the Dallas Cowboys, and a perfect example of the impact Houston had during his 14-year NFL career.

Houston was the premier strong safety of his era, which began in 1967 with the Houston Oilers and concluded in 1980 with the Redskins. After six years with the Oilers, Houston was traded to the Redskins for five veteran players in 1973. He earned All-AFC honors with the Oilers in 1971 and was either all-pro or All-NFC with the Redskins every year from 1973-79. He was selected to either the AFL All-Star game or the AFC-NFC Pro Bowl for 12 consecutive years from 1968-1979.

Houston had the natural ability to be a sensational strong safety. With a long, fluid stride, he had excellent speed and quickness. His 6-foot 3-inch, 198-pound frame made him a big presence in the secondary. He was a punishing tackler and a good runner when he carried the ball.

With the Oilers, Houston set an NFL record by returning 9 interceptions for touchdowns. During his career, he intercepted 49 passes and returned them for 898 yards. He also recovered 19 opponents' fumbles. [DS/PF]

CHUCK HOWLEY

Linebacker. 6-2, 225. West Virginia.
Born June 28, 1936, Wheeling, West Virginia.
1958-59 Chicago Bears, 1961-1972 Dallas

Chuck Howley initially retired after the 1959 season, which may come as a surprise to fans who see his name in the Ring of Honor at Texas Stadium. After all, the Cowboys didn't play their first game until 1960.

Howley had been a star athlete at West Virginia University, lettering in diving, track, gymnastics, and wrestling. He also was a three-year All-Southern Conference selection in football. The Chicago Bears selected him in the first round of the 1958 NFL draft. But three games into the 1959 season, he injured his knee so badly that his career appeared over. In 1960, he managed a gas station in Wheeling, West Virginia.

However in the spring of 1961, he played in a West Virginia alumni game and his knee felt fine. Howley decided to give the NFL another shot.

One of Howley's former Bears teammates, who was playing for Dallas, recommended Howley to the Cowboys. Dallas signed Howley, and he made an immediate impact on the fledgling franchise.

Howley had a reputation as a risk-taking, big-play defender. Relying on exceptional speed, remarkable agility, and a sixth sense for where the ball was headed, he and Hall of Fame tackle Bob Lilly were sometimes allowed to freelance in the Cowboys' otherwise disciplined defense. Howley was an all-pro from 1966-1970 and went to six Pro Bowls.

In Super Bowl V, he became the first player to be named MVP while playing for the losing team. In 1971, he helped Dallas win Super Bowl VI. [BC]

CAL HUBBARD

Tackle, End, Linebacker. 6-5, 250. Centenary, Geneva
Born October 31, 1900, Keytesville, Missouri.
Died October 17, 1977, St. Petersburg, Florida.
1927-28, 1936 New York Giants, 1929-1933, 1935 Green Bay, 1936 Pittsburgh
Inducted into Pro Football Hall of Fame in 1963.

The New York Giants' 1927 NFL-championship team allowed only 20 points in 13 games. The Green Bay Packers won league titles in 1929, 1930, and 1931. Those teams had one thing in common—Cal Hubbard.

Hubbard played college football for three years at Centenary in Louisiana and a final season with Geneva in Pennsylvania. Three NFL teams offered him contracts, but his college coach, Bo McMillin, advised him to sign with the Giants.

In 1927, Hubbard joined the Giants and was paid $150 per game. He quickly made his mark in the NFL as an end on offense and linebacker on defense. At the time, it was unusual that a man of Hubbard's size could also be so fast. He continually filled holes other linemen could not have reached. In 1929, at his request, Hubbard was traded to Green Bay, where he liked the small-town atmosphere. He enjoyed his best pro years with the Packers from 1929-1933 and in 1935. Coach Curly Lambeau moved Hubbard to tackle and he was an All-NFL choice for five years.

By 1936, Hubbard realized his football days were numbered. He became a baseball umpire, one of the best ever. He was as an American League umpire for 15 seasons and spent another 15 years as the league's supervisor of umpires. Today, he is the only person to be enshrined in both the Pro Football Hall of Fame and the Major League Baseball Hall of Fame. [DS/PF]

SAM HUFF

Linebacker. 6-1, 230. West Virginia
Born October 4, 1934, Morgantown, West Virginia.
1956-1963 N.Y. Giants, 1964-67, 1969 Washington
Inducted into Pro Football Hall of Fame in 1982.

Because Sam Huff spent the early part of his NFL career with a highly successful team in a large media city, he became one of the league's most publicized players. He appeared on the cover of Time magazine at the age of 24. Later, he was the subject of a television special entitled *The Violent World of Sam Huff.*

He deserved the attention. Huff excelled as a middle linebacker for 13 pro seasons— eight with the New York Giants (1956-1963) and five with the Washington Redskins (1964-67, 1969).

Although Huff didn't appear to have great speed or great strength, he had enough of both to become the prototypical middle linebacker in the intricate Giants' defense. He was big enough to handle the power runners and fast enough to overtake swift halfbacks. The Giants reached the NFL title game six times in Huff's first eight years. He was named an all-pro middle linebacker four times and played in five Pro Bowls, the first four as a member of the Giants.

Huff lived by one code. "Get the man with the football," he said. "This is a man's game and any guy who doesn't want to hit hard doesn't belong in it." Huff also was good in pass coverage. He had 30 interceptions in his career. [DS/PF]

DON HUTSON

End-Safety. 6-1, 180. Alabama
Born January 31, 1913, Pine Bluff, Arkansas.
Died June 26, 1997, Rancho Mirage, California.
1935-1945 Green Bay
Inducted into Pro Football Hall of Fame in 1963.

Although Don Hutson had been an All-America at Alabama in 1934, doubts lingered over whether the 6-foot 1-inch, 180-pound speedster could survive the rigors of pro football. However, it wasn't long before Hutson's presence changed entire defensive strategies. In his second game as a member of the Packers, Hutson scored on an 83-yard pass from Arnie Herber against the Bears in 1935. He finished his career with an NFL-record 99 touchdown receptions. When he retired in 1945 after 11 brilliant seasons, he led all receivers with 488 career catches.

As the prime target for Herber and later Cecil Isbell, Hutson could outmaneuver and outrace virtually every defender in the league. Measures such as double coverage and triple-teaming were unheard of until Hutson entered the NFL. Jock Sutherland, the Brooklyn coach, once scoffed at the thought of putting more than one man on any receiver. In Hutson's first game against the Dodgers, he had 6 sensational catches and 2 touchdowns. Sutherland was stunned, but also convinced.

Like all players in the days before free substitution, Hutson played safety on defense. In his final four seasons, he intercepted 23 passes. He also was the Packers' kicking specialist. In 1941 and 1942, he was the NFL's most valuable player. [DS/PF]

*MICHAEL IRVIN

Wide Receiver. 6-2, 205. Miami
Born March 5, 1966, Fort Lauderdale, Florida.
1988-1998 Dallas

For many people, and in many ways, the great Cowboys teams of the 1990s boiled down to three simple facts: Troy Aikman passed, Emmitt Smith ran, and Michael Irvin caught.

That triumvirate of skill position players rivals any trio on any team in history. Among the three, Irvin has the toughest job; after all, Smith and Aikman have blockers. But Irvin seemed to like it out there all alone, especially when he made opponents pay for keying on Smith.

Defenses soon were keying on Irvin, with little discernible effect. Even though everyone knew the ball was going to Irvin, he still posted phenomenal numbers thanks to his speed, strength, and most of all, his size. Aikman had so much confidence in Irvin that he would throw to him even if the receiver was covered, figuring (correctly) that Irvin could outfight the cornerback for the ball.

Among the three, Irvin was the lone holdover from the Tom Landry era, joining the Cowboys in 1988 as a first-round draft choice. Success had followed Irvin at every stop, but he enjoyed anything but success during his first two years in Dallas. The team won just four times and Irvin missed 12 games with injuries.

That all began to change in 1990, Jimmy Johnson's second season as coach. Irvin, who had played for Johnson at the University of Miami, became the centerpiece of Johnson's pass offense, which involved precise timing, quick throws, and receivers who could pick up a lot of yards after the catch. Irvin fit the bill perfectly. By the end of the 1998 season his credits included club career records for catches (740) and receiving yards (11,737). Irvin shined even brighter in the postseason, entering the 1999 season with the second-most playoff catches (87) in NFL history, along with three Super Bowl rings. [MS]

CECIL ISBELL

Tailback. 6-1, 190. Purdue
Born July 11, 1915, Houston, Texas.
Died June 23, 1983, Hammond, Indiana.
1938-1942 Green Bay

While Don Hutson was setting all of the NFL's career pass-receiving records, Cecil Isbell was the quarterback throwing Hutson the ball from 1938-1942.

Isbell, a tailback in coach Curly Lambeau's Single-Wing formation, led all NFL passers in 1941-42. "[He] was a master at any range," Lambeau said. "He could throw soft passes, bullet passes, or long passes."

Isbell's favorite target was Hutson. When Isbell set an NFL record with 1,479 passing yards in 1941, Hutson tied an NFL mark with 58 catches for 738 yards; and the following season, Isbell became the first passer ever to surpass 2,000 yards when he completed 146 passes for 2,021 yards, and a league-record 24 touchdowns. Hutson set two NFL records by catching 74 of Isbell's passes for 1,211 yards and 17 touchdowns in 1942. Hutson was the first receiver in league history to gain more than 1,000 yards in a single season.

Isbell threw touchdown passes in 23 consecutive games

in 1941-42. He passed for 5 touchdowns in a 1942 game against the Cleveland Rams. In 1942, Isbell passed for 333 yards on just 10 completions against the Chicago Cardinals.

Amazingly, Isbell played his entire NFL career with a chain attached from his body to his left arm so he could not raise it too high. If Isbell lifted his left arm too high, his chronic dislocated shoulder would pop out of place. [JC]

JOE JACOBY
Tackle. 6-7, 305. Louisville
Born July 6, 1959, Louisville, Kentucky.
1981-1993 Washington
At his Pro Football Hall of Fame induction ceremony, Joe Gibbs had special words of praise for "the undrafted free agents." The Redskins' coach didn't mention Joe Jacoby by name, but the tall, quiet tackle certainly was the type of player to whom Gibbs referred.

Despite his mammoth size, Jacoby didn't arouse that much interest in pro scouts while playing at Louisville. Shortly after Gibbs became the Redskins' head coach in 1981, Jacoby signed with Washington.

At first, Jacoby played defensive tackle, an unfamiliar position. Because he was less than spectacular as a defensive tackle, the Redskins' coaches decided to move Jacoby to offense. The move proved to be a stroke of genius. Jacoby was Washington's starting left tackle for 13 seasons (1981-1993).

Jacoby was a vital part of the Hogs, the nickname of Washington's offensive line which was instrumental in helping the team earn four Super Bowl berths and win three NFC titles. From 1983-86, Jacoby went to four consecutive Pro Bowls. [JC]

BILLY (WHITE SHOES) JOHNSON
Wide Receiver-Kick Returner. 5-9, 170. Widener
Born January 27, 1952, Bouthwyn, Pennsylvania.
1974-1980 Houston, 1982-87 Atlanta, 1988 Washington
Billy (White Shoes) Johnson not only brought white shoes and end-zone dances to the NFL, he also turned the position of kick returner into an offensive weapon. Johnson retired as the NFL leader in punt-returns (282) and punt return yards (3,317). The flashy performer had 6 career punts returned for touchdowns, including 3 in 1975. He caught 300 passes for 25 touchdowns as a receiver.

In his 14-year career with the Houston Oilers, Atlanta Falcons, and Washington Redskins (he also spent one season in the Canadian Football League), Johnson had the potential to score a touchdown every time he touched the ball. There were faster players in the game, but Johnson combined great balance with speed, agility, and toughness. When the NFL selected an all-time team for its seventy-fifth anniversary, Johnson was chosen as the game's greatest return specialist.

As a halfback at Widener College, Johnson seemed an unlikely candidate for the NFL. But he averaged 9.1 yards per carry, totaled 5,404 all-purpose yards, and scored 62 touchdowns at Widener. The Oilers selected him in the fifteenth round of the 1974 NFL draft. [MS]

JIMMY JOHNSON
Cornerback-Wide Receiver. 6-2, 187. UCLA
Born March 31, 1938, Dallas, Texas.
1961-1976 San Francisco
Inducted into Pro Football Hall of Fame in 1994.
Jimmy Johnson initially had a tough time getting his family's attention, let alone the NFL's. His brother Rafer Johnson was the world decathlon champion and winner of a gold medal in the 1960 Olympics.

Jimmy played running back and defensive back at UCLA. He also was a track star who ran the 110-meter hurdles in 13.9 seconds and long jumped 25 feet. San Francisco made him a first-round draft choice in 1961. They tried him at defensive back as a rookie, moved him to offense in his second season, then back to the defensive unit to stay in his third year in 1963.

Johnson intercepted 5 passes in his rookie season, then he caught 34 passes for 627 yards and 4 touchdowns as a receiver in 1962. He played one season at safety in 1963, then moved to the left cornerback for the remainder of his 16-year career, which was concluded after the 1976 season. He played in 212 games, the most in 49ers history. Recognized as one of the best man-for-man defenders in league history, Johnson had so great a reputation that opposing quarterbacks rarely threw in his direction.

By the time he retired, Johnson had intercepted 47 passes and returned them 615 yards, both club records. He had his big moments as a receiver as well, including an 80-yard touchdown catch against the Chicago Bears and a 181-yard receiving day against Detroit in 1962. Johnson was named all-pro four years in a row from 1969-1972. He was selected to five Pro Bowls. [DS/PF]

JOHN HENRY JOHNSON
Fullback. 6-2, 225. St. Mary's, Arizona State
Born November 24, 1929, Waterproof, Louisiana.
1954-56 San Francisco, 1957-59 Detroit, 1960-65 Pittsburgh, 1966 Houston
Inducted into Pro Football Hall of Fame in 1987.
During his 13-year career, John Henry Johnson rushed for 6,803 yards, the fourth-highest total in NFL history at the time. However, Johnson may have been an even more impressive blocker.

A college star at St. Mary's and at Arizona State, Johnson was a second-round draft choice of the Pittsburgh Steelers in 1953, but he opted to play in Canada instead. After one season at Calgary, he returned to start his NFL career with the 49ers. For the next three years, he was an integral part of the "Million-Dollar Backfield" that included future Pro Football Hall of Fame members Hugh McElhenny, Y. A. Tittle, and Joe Perry.

Johnson was traded to Detroit in 1957, then to Pittsburgh in 1960. With the Lions, he participated in his only NFL title game. Detroit won the 1957 NFL championship by defeating the Cleveland Browns 59-14. Johnson enjoyed his best seasons with Pittsburgh. In 1962 and 1964, he rushed for more than 1,000 yards, the first Pittsburgh player to reach that lofty level. He also played in four Pro Bowls. [DS/PF]

CHARLIE JOINER
Wide Receiver. 5-11, 180. Grambling
Born October 14, 1947, Many, Louisiana.
1969-1971 Houston, 1972-75 Cincinnati, 1976-1986 San Diego
Inducted into Pro Football Hall of Fame in 1996.
Charlie Joiner played pro football for 18 years, longer than any other wide receiver in NFL history. When he retired at the age of 39 after the 1986 season with the San Diego Chargers, he was the league's all-time leading receiver with 750 catches. Blessed with excellent speed, Joiner accumulated 12,146 yards receiving and 65 touchdown catches during his career.

The Houston Oilers wanted Joiner to play defensive back when they selected him in the fourth round of the 1969 AFL-NFL draft. Joiner played briefly on defense and as a kick returner, but he soon became established as a premier pass receiver.

In 1972, Houston traded Joiner to the Cincinnati Bengals in a four-player swap. In 1976, he was traded to San Diego. With the Chargers, Joiner became a superstar. He and quarterback Dan Fouts formed a marvelous duo that accounted for plenty of offensive fireworks.

During his 11 years in San Diego, Joiner caught 50 or more passes seven times and had 70 or more receptions in three seasons. He was an all-pro selection in 1980 and a Pro Bowl choice three times. Joiner once was described by San Francisco 49ers coaching great Bill Walsh as "the most intelligent, the smartest, the most calculating receiver the game has ever known." [DS/PF]

DAVID (DEACON) JONES
Defensive End. 6-5, 250. South Carolina State Mississippi Vocational
Born December 9, 1938, Eatonville, Florida.
1961-1971 Los Angeles Rams, 1972-73 San Diego, 1974 Washington
Inducted into Pro Football Hall of Fame in 1980.
David (Deacon) Jones might never have played in the NFL had it not been for two Rams scouts who were watching films of Jones's opponents in college. When the scouts noted that the defensive tackle was outrunning the running backs they were scouting, they recommended that the Rams draft Jones.

Jones, who was selected by the Rams in the fourteenth round of the 1961 draft, had an obscure college career at South Carolina State and Mississippi Vocational. He quickly blossomed into a superb defensive end. Blessed with speed, agility, and quickness, Jones became one of the league's most feared pass rushers.

For most of a decade, Jones teamed with tackle Merlin Olsen to give Los Angeles a perennial all-pro left side of the defensive line that became known as the Fearsome Foursome. Jones won unanimous all-league honors six successive years from 1965-1970 and played in seven Pro Bowls in a row. In 1967 and 1968, he was chosen as the league's best defensive player. He is credited with coining the term "sack" for tackling opposing quarterbacks for losses.

In 1972, Jones was included in a multi-player trade with the San Diego Chargers. He was an instant success with his new team, leading all Chargers' defensive linemen in tackles and winning a berth on the AFC Pro Bowl squad. He also was named San Diego's defensive captain. He concluded his career with the Washington Redskins in 1974. [DS/PF]

ED (TOO TALL) JONES
Defensive End. 6-9, 271. Tennessee State
Born February 23, 1951, Jackson, Tennessee.
1974-78, 1980-89 Dallas
In the first five years of his NFL career, Ed (Too Tall) Jones helped the Cowboys make three Super Bowl appearances and win Super Bowl XII.

Jones abandoned football for a boxing career after the 1978 season. However, after six fights in two years, the 6-foot 9-inch athlete returned to Dallas and played another 10 years before retiring for good in 1989.

"At one time earlier in his career, Ed wasn't too excited about football," former Dallas Cowboys coach Tom Landry says. "That's why he went to boxing. And that wasn't very exciting either, so when he came back he appreciated football more."

Basketball seemed to be Jones's ticket to stardom as a teenager in Jackson, Tennessee. He did not play high school football, but he did receive 52 basketball scholarship offers. Jones decided to pursue football in college and discovered he was very good at it. He played in only one losing game in three years at Tennessee State.

He was first overall selection in the 1974 NFL draft and was a force at defensive end for 15 seasons in Dallas. [MS]

STAN JONES
Guard-Tackle-Defensive Tackle. 6-1, 250. Maryland
Born November 24, 1931, Altoona, Pennsylvania.
1954-1965 Chicago, 1966 Washington
Inducted into Pro Football Hall of Fame in 1991.
Stan Jones was one of the great guards in Chicago Bears' history. The rugged lineman from the University of Maryland played 13 seasons in the NFL, the first 12 with the Bears (1954-1965) and the 1966 season with the Washington Redskins. The Bears selected Jones as a future choice in the 1953 NFL draft. It proved to be an insightful move because later that year Jones earned consensus All-America honors with Maryland's 1953 national championship team.

Jones began his career as an offensive tackle with Chicago in 1954. He switched to guard in 1955 and, for the next eight seasons, was a fixture at that position. For most of those years, he was the Bears' offensive captain. Jones possessed impressive size, quickness, and strength. He was one of the first pro football players to use weight lifting as a means to improve his playing condition. Jones was disciplined and dependable. He missed only two games in his first 11 seasons. He was a four-time all-pro guard and played in seven successive Pro Bowls from 1955-61.

When the Bears needed defensive line help in 1962, assistant coach George Allen decided that Jones could play defensive tackle. Jones played both ways in 1962, then switched to defensive tackle permanently in 1963. After Jones's twelfth season in the league, Bears coach George Halas agreed, as a favor to Jones, to trade him to the

Washington Redskins so that he could play his final season near his home in Rockville, Maryland. [DS/PF]

HENRY JORDAN
Defensive Tackle. 6-3, 240. Virginia
Born January 26, 1935, Emporia, Virginia.
Died February 21, 1977, Milwaukee, Wisconsin.
1957-58 Cleveland, 1959-1969 Green Bay
Inducted into Pro Football Hall of Fame in 1995.
Henry Jordan was the fifth player from the Packers' vaunted defense of the 1960s to be elected to the Pro Football Hall of Fame. Defensive teammates Willie Davis, Ray Nitschke, Herb Adderley, and Willie Wood preceded the Packers' defensive tackle into the Hall of Fame.

A three-sport star at the University of Virginia where he was a captain of the football team as a senior and was a runner-up in the heavyweight class of the 1957 NCAA wrestling championships, Jordan began his pro football career as a fifth-round draft choice of the Cleveland Browns in 1957. He earned a spot on the Browns, who won the 1957 NFL Eastern Division title. But before the 1959 season, Cleveland sent him to the Packers for a fourth-round draft choice.

The acquisition of Jordan proved to be a key element in coach Vince Lombardi's ambitious building program. For the next decade, Jordan was a fixture at right defensive tackle as Green Bay won six divisional titles, five NFL championships, and the first two Super Bowls. Jordan earned all-pro honors six times and played in four Pro Bowls. Extremely durable, he missed only two games in his first 12 seasons. Jordan died on February 21, 1977, at age 42. [DS/PF]

LEE ROY JORDAN
Linebacker. 6-1, 215. Alabama
Born April 27, 1941, Excel, Alabama.
1963-1976 Dallas
For 14 seasons, Lee Roy Jordan always was the man in the middle in Dallas.

Jordan, an All-America center and linebacker at the University of Alabama, was the Cowboys' first-round draft choice in 1963. Landry made him his middle linebacker, the most critical position in his Flex Defense. Jordan became a five-time Pro Bowl selection and helped the Cowboys to five NFL/NFC Championship Games and three Super Bowls. He was a member of the Cowboys' championship team in 1971, and he holds the club record for starting 154 consecutive games from 1966-1976.

Extremely quick and agile, Jordan reflected the toughness of his college coach, Paul (Bear) Bryant. He was flanked by Dave Edwards and Chuck Howley, and they became arguably the NFL's best linebacking corps during the late sixties and early seventies.

Jordan covered the field from sideline to sideline to make plays in Landry's defense, a coordinated system that allowed the middle linebacker to make most of the tackles. No one did it better than Jordan. He also was an outstanding pass defender, and accumulated 32 interceptions during his 14 seasons. He returned 3 of his interceptions for touchdowns. [JJC]

SONNY JURGENSEN
Quarterback. 6-0, 203. Duke
Born August 23, 1934, Wilmington, North Carolina.
1957-1963 Philadelphia, 1964-1974 Washington
Inducted into Pro Football Hall of Fame in 1983
Sonny Jurgensen proved that a great player doesn't always have to compete on great teams to make it into the Pro Football Hall of Fame.

For 18 seasons—the first seven with the Philadelphia Eagles and the rest with the Washington Redskins—Jurgensen was widely recognized as the best passer of his time. But he participated in the postseason only four times in his career.

Jurgensen, a native of Wilmington, North Carolina, wanted more than anything else to play on a championship team. When the Eagles won the NFL championship in 1960, Jurgensen sat on the bench. With the Redskins 12 years later, he was sidelined with a torn Achilles tendon in both the NFC Championship Game and Super Bowl VII.

However, whether Jurgensen's teams won or lost, adoring fans knew that he would provide game-long excitement. A classic dropback passer, Jurgensen was known for his ability to deliver the ball at the last moment under the pressure of an intense pass rush. He completed 2,433 of 4,262 passes for 32,224 yards and 255 touchdowns in his career. [DS/PF]

ALEX KARRAS
Defensive Tackle. 6-2, 248. Iowa
Born July 15, 1935, Gary, Indiana.
1958-1962, 1964-1970 Detroit
Alex Karras probably is best known as a television and movie actor, but he first gained fame as a dominating defensive tackle for the Detroit Lions between 1958 and 1970.

Karras won the Outland Trophy in 1957 at the University of Iowa as the country's best lineman and easily made the transition to the NFL. Although he was relatively small for his position, he compensated for his lack of size by watching game films to learn the blocking techniques and tendencies of his opponents. His quickness off the ball earned him the nickname "Tippy Toes," but his intense attitude also earned him the name "Mad Duck."

Karras was an all-pro with the Lions from 1960-62, but he and Paul Hornung of the Green Bay Packers were suspended for the 1963 season for gambling on NFL games. Karras spent the year as a bartender and also wrestled professionally. He returned to the Lions in 1964.

Nowhere was Karras's personality more apparent than in the film *Paper Lion,* in which he played himself. Later he had a small, but memorable, role in the comedy *Blazing Saddles* and "knocked out" a horse with one punch in one of the film's most famous scenes. Karras spent three years as an announcer on *Monday Night Football* and later starred in the ABC situation comedy *Webster* with his second wife, Susan Clark, and Emanuel Lewis. [MS]

KEN KAVANAUGH
End. 6-3, 205. Louisiana State
Born November 23, 1916, Little Rock, Arkansas.
1940-41, 1945-1950 Chicago Bears

Kavanaugh caught too few passes to be considered seriously for the Pro Football Hall of Fame. His modest total of 162 receptions over an eight-year pro career would be eclipsed by some of today's wide receivers in less than two seasons.

But there's quantity, and then there's quality. Kavanaugh definitely was a quality receiver. It was never how many passes he caught but what he did with them that counted. On a Bears team that ran the ball against NFL defenses with thunderous effect, Kavanaugh was the big-play man. He averaged 1 touchdown nearly every 3 catches during his career with the Bears.

At Louisiana State, Kavanaugh was All-SEC each year, and starred in two Sugar Bowls. He joined the Bears in 1940, the same year Chicago won the championship with their historic 73-0 victory over the humiliated Washington Redskins. Sid Luckman's powerful arm and Kavanaugh's blazing speed made them a potent long-distance touchdown threat.

Kavanaugh helped the Bears win a second title in 1941, entered the U.S. Army Air Corps for three-and-a-half years, reaching the rank of captain, and flew 30 missions over Europe. By 1946, he was back to help the Bears to another championship.

Kavanaugh had perhaps his greatest season in 1947, catching 32 passes for 818 yards and a league-leading 13 touchdowns. He was an all-pro in 1946 and 1947. His best game came in 1950, his final season, when he caught 8 passes for 177 yards against the New York Yanks on October 29. [BC]

JIM KELLY

Quarterback. 6-2, 217. Miami
Born February 14, 1960, Pittsburgh, Pennsylvania.
1986-1996 Buffalo

Jim Kelly and the Buffalo Bills went to the Super Bowl four years in a row from 1990-93, but they always went home disappointed.

In his NFL career, Kelly put up numbers that place him among the game's greatest quarterbacks—35,467 career passing yards, 237 touchdown passes, and a winning percentage over .600—but he also is the only quarterback to start, and lose, four consecutive Super Bowls.

Kelly took his time getting to Buffalo, even though he starred at East Brady (Pennsylvania) High School, not that far away. Penn State's Joe Paterno tried to recruit him as a linebacker, so Kelly opted for Miami, where he became the first in a long line of outstanding Hurricanes quarterbacks. After passing for 5,233 yards and 32 touchdowns at Miami, Kelly spurned the Bills, who selected him with the fourteenth pick of the 1983 draft. Kelly's reason? "You can't be a great quarterback in snow and thirty-mile-per-hour wind." That is a statement Kelly proved wrong many times over.

He signed with the United States Football League and was a sensation, passing for 83 touchdowns in only two seasons. Only when the USFL disbanded did he join the Bills for a decade before retiring.

The irony is that Kelly and Buffalo were a perfect fit. Kelly, who grew up with six brothers in the blue-collar town of East Brady, about 70 miles northeast of Pittsburgh, was a rugged, hard worker, and was so courageous in the pocket that he was accused of being a quarterback with a linebacker's mentality. Maybe Paterno wasn't so wrong. [MS]

LEROY KELLY

Running Back. 6-0, 205. Morgan State
Born May 20, 1942, Philadelphia, Pennsylvania.
1964-1973 Cleveland
Inducted into Pro Football Hall of Fame in 1994

In his 10-year career with the Cleveland Browns from 1964-1973, Leroy Kelly established himself as one of the most feared ball carriers in the history of the NFL, rushing for 7,274 yards. He added 2,281 yards on 190 pass receptions and excelled as a punt-and kickoff-return specialist. His combined net yards total of 12,239 on rushes, receptions, and returns ranks him among pro football's elite.

Kelly was an eighth-round pick of the Browns in the 1964 draft after an excellent four-year career at Morgan State. For his first two years, he was an understudy to the fabled Jim Brown. When Brown retired just before the 1966 season, Kelly picked up where Brown left off. For the next three years, he rushed for 1,000 yards, winning all-pro honors each year. He also was selected as a starter in three consecutive Pro Bowls. In all, the Philadelphia native was selected to six Pro Bowls and named all-pro five times.

In 1965, Kelly won the NFL punt-return title, an honor he repeated in the AFC in 1971. He also won NFL rushing championships in 1967 and 1968. An exceptional runner on muddy fields, the 6-foot, 205-pound Kelly favored the famed Browns' trap play up the middle. His quick-starting ability, along with a sense of balance and a knack for evading direct hits by tacklers, kept him relatively injury free. He missed only four games in 10 years and never more than one game per season. [DS/PF]

WALT KIESLING

Guard. 6-2, 245. St. Thomas (Minnesota)
Born May 27, 1903, St. Paul, Minnesota.
Died March 2, 1962, Pittsburgh, Pennsylvania.
1926-27 Duluth, 1928 Pottsville, 1929-1933 Chicago Cardinals, 1934 Chicago Bears, 1935-36 Green Bay, 1937-38 Pittsburgh
Inducted into Pro Football Hall of Fame in 1966.

Walt Kiesling spent 34 years as an NFL player, assistant coach, and head coach. It's arguable which of the three pursuits gained his induction into the Hall of Fame because he had highlights in all three.

A two-way guard who was larger, stronger, and tougher than most of his opponents, he began his NFL career with the Duluth Eskimos (led by Ernie Nevers), the team that played 29 games in 1926, 28 of them on the road. Later he rejoined Nevers with the Chicago Cardinals and helped clear the way in the game in which Nevers scored 40 points. He was All-NFL in 1932. Although Kiesling played on some losing teams, he also was a member of the 1934 Bears, who went through the regular season undefeated, and the 1936 Packers, who were NFL champions.

In 1937, he joined Pittsburgh as a part-time player and assistant to head coach Johnny (Blood) McNally, whose escapades were more entertaining than the teams he produced. Kiesling, who proved himself an excellent line coach, succeeded McNally as head coach during the 1939 season.

In 1942, with the considerable help of star back "Bullet Bill" Dudley, he coached the Steelers to their first winning season. He was co-coach of the Pittsburgh-Philadelphia and Pittsburgh-Chicago Cardinal combined teams during World War II. In the 1950s, he served as Steelers' coach again. Although the team suffered through three losing seasons, it earned a reputation for rugged, hard-hitting football—much the same reputation its coach had earned during his fine playing career. [BC]

FRANK (BUCKO) KILROY

Guard-Middle Guard. 6-2, 240. Temple
Born May 30, 1921, Philadelphia, Pennsylvania.
1943 Phil-Pitt, 1944-1955 Philadelphia

Kilroy was a survivor in the National Football League for half a century—from the time he joined the wartime merger "Steagles," until he retired from the Patriots' front office.

At first, he was a two-way guard and sometime tackle. Then he took his place in the middle of the innovative Eagle Defense (a set that eventually led to the standard pro 4-3 alignment). As the middle man, he taught many opponents a new meaning to "Kilroy Was Here." A self-proclaimed "heavy hitter," he didn't make many friends on the other side of the ball. He was a relentless defender who never quit until the whistle had blown in an era when runners could crawl or get up and run again if their forward progress wasn't completely stopped.

Kilroy's aggressive style rankled some opponents. An article in Life magazine branded Kilroy as one of the league's "ornery critters." Kilroy, who was seldom penalized in his 14-year playing career, took exception to *Life's* statement and sued the weekly picture magazine. He won his lawsuit.

The Eagles of Kilroy's era were the class of the NFL—the only team to post back-to-back championship shutouts. Kilroy was an important part of the winning tradition. He became a player-coach in his final seasons, and later was a scout, personnel director, general manager, and club vice president in the NFL. [JJC]

FRANK (BRUISER) KINARD

Tackle. 6-1, 210. Mississippi
Born October 23, 1914, Pelahatchie, Mississippi.
Died September 7, 1985, Jackson, Mississippi.
1938-1944 Brooklyn Dodgers-Tigers, 1946-47 New York Yankees (AAFC)
Inducted into Pro Football Hall of Fame in 1971.

Today any pro football star nicknamed "Bruiser" would have to weigh at least 275 pounds. Five decades ago, however, a pro football great known as Bruiser Kinard punished his opposition for nine star-studded seasons. Kinard began his pro football career weighing a mere 195 pounds. Even in his final season, and still playing offensive and defensive tackle, he weighed only 218 pounds.

But he was a perennial all-star. Kinard earned a host of accolades during the nine years he played pro football, but one distinction stands out—he was the only player to win all-league honors in both the NFL and the AAFC.

Kinard was a two-time All-America at the University of Mississippi when he was drafted in the second round by the Brooklyn Dodgers in 1938. Kinard earned All-NFL honors four times with the Dodgers. In 1946, as a member of the New York Yankees, he won honors as All-AAFC.

On many offensive plays, and particularly on the Dodgers' shovel pass, Kinard was the key blocker. On defense, he was a crushing tackler. He rarely needed a rest and near-60-minute performances were the rule, rather than the exception. He missed only one game because of injury during his pro football career. [DS/PF]

JERRY KRAMER

Guard. 6-3, 245. Idaho
Born January 23, 1936, Jordan, Montana.
1958-1968 Green Bay

Even an offensive lineman, the epitome of anonymity in the National Football League, can gain a measure of fame if he takes part in one of the most celebrated plays of all time.

For Jerry Kramer, that play was Bart Starr's quarterback sneak for the winning score in the 1967 NFL Championship Game. The game, played under such frigid conditions in Green Bay that it was dubbed the Ice Bowl, sent the Packers rather than the Dallas Cowboys on to Super Bowl II. Starr's touchdown sneak came with only seconds left and was made possible by Kramer's block (with help from center Ken Bowman) on Dallas's Jethro Pugh. Through the then-new television technology of instant replay, American audiences witnessed the play again and again until Kramer became arguably the best known lineman in America.

The irony was that the block was only one in a long line of superior plays by Kramer, the kind of performance he had made routine in 10 years of National Football League play. That level of excellence had made Kramer a five-time All-NFL selection but it took the Ice Bowl block to make his name a household word among casual fans around the league.

Kramer was a legitimate star without television technology. Along with fellow pulling guard Fred (Fuzzy) Thurston, he put the power in the fabled Green Bay Sweep. Kramer endured 22 operations to play pro football. He had so many stitches that his team mates called him "Zipper." [JJC]

RON KRAMER

Tight End. 6-3, 250. Michigan
Born June 24, 1935, Girard, Kentucky.
1957, 1959-1964 Green Bay, 1965-67 Detroit

Norm Van Brocklin once referred to Ron Kramer as an "oaf." Kramer's teammates picked up on it, and it became his nickname, though not used much outside of the team. Others, kinder and gentler than the acid-tongued Van Brocklin, called him a third tackle—for it was Kramer who first played the tight end position as it is known today. After languishing as an oversized flanker in Green Bay before Lombardi arrived and missing the 1958 season due to military service, Kramer found a home on the right side of the offensive line in Lombardi's run-oriented, big-back offense.

Always a forceful blocker, Kramer probably reached his peak as a receiver in 1962 when he caught 37 passes for 555 yards and 7 touchdowns. He was a 250-pound receiver when some of the best offensive tackles and guards were 245 pounds or less.

The Packers' offense didn't feature Kramer as a receiver as the Bears' system did Mike Ditka, but Kramer was the first modern tight end and, for a time, the best. Injuries eventually took their toll on the two-time Michigan All-America, but when the ex-Detroit scholastic star was on top of his game, there were few in his class.

Defensive ends and linebackers met their match when Kramer blocked down on the storied Green Bay Power Sweep. Defensive backs felt his sting when they were unfortunate enough to meet up with him as a pass receiver in the secondary. [JJC]

PAUL KRAUSE

Defensive Back. 6-3, 195. Iowa
Born February 19, 1942, Flint, Michigan.
1964-67 Washington, 1968-1979 Minnesota
Inducted into Pro Football Hall of Fame in 1998.

Paul Krause didn't waste any time making a name for himself in the NFL. In his first game, he intercepted 2 of Frank Ryan's passes. When he finished playing 16 seasons later, he was the NFL's all-time interception leader with 81—2 more than former leader Emlen Tunnell.

Still, the NFL almost didn't have Krause's services. He played both football and baseball at Iowa. Major league baseball scouts awaited him with open checkbooks because of his great play as a center fielder (he once threw out four runners at home plate in one game for the Hawkeyes). But during a football game against Michigan in his junior year, Krause, who played wide receiver and defensive back, badly damaged his right shoulder. His prized arm no longer had the zip the big leagues required.

He played free safety for the Redskins, who drafted him in the second round in 1964, and led the NFL with 12 interceptions as a rookie. After four seasons with Washington, accumulating 28 interceptions, he was traded to Minnesota for linebacker Marlin McKeever and a draft pick. He had 53 interceptions during the rest of his career with the Vikings.

The key to his success? "You have to think interceptions," he said. "I analyzed quarterbacks. I knew some of the things they tried to do in certain situations. That wasn't gambling. It was being in the right place at the right time."

To be exact, 81 times. [JC]

***DAVE KRIEG**

Quarterback. 6-1, 193. Milton
Born October 20, 1958, Iola, Wisconsin.
1980-1991 Seattle, 1992-93 Kansas City, 1994 Detroit, 1995 Arizona, 1996 Chicago, 1997-98 Tennessee

After playing his first 12 pro seasons with the Seattle Seahawks, Dave Krieg saw the country in the twilight years of his career. He suited up for five teams in five seasons between 1993 and 1997. Krieg has posted numbers that have put him among the top 10 quarterbacks all-time in pass attempts, completions, yards, and touchdown passes albeit in relative anonymity. Krieg also holds a more dubious distinction: he is second on the all-time list for most fumbles in a career with 153.

After starring at both baseball and football at tiny Milton College in Wisconsin, Krieg joined the Seahawks as an undrafted free agent in 1980 and spent most of his first three seasons backing up Jim Zorn. But new coach Chuck Knox put Krieg in midway through the 1983 season, and the Seahawks caught fire. The club finished with a 9-7 record to reach the playoffs for the first time in their eight-year history. Once there, they pulled off two upset wins to reach the AFC Championship Game.

The following season, Krieg tossed a career-high 32 touchdown passes as the team finished with a franchise-best 12-4 record. Krieg led the Seahawks back to the playoffs in 1987 and 1988, often finding his favorite target, future Hall of Fame wide receiver Steve Largent.

Krieg left for Kansas City in 1992, and he stayed on the move. He went to the Detroit Lions in 1994, guiding Detroit into the playoffs with a great second half. He then went to the Arizona Cardinals in 1995 and the Chicago Bears in 1996 and saw plenty of action with rebuilding teams. Appropriately, Krieg caught on with the newly relocated Tennessee Oilers in 1997, serving as Steve McNair's backup and mentor. [DF]

***CARNELL LAKE**

Safety-Cornerback. 6-1, 210, UCLA
Born July 15, 1967, Salt Lake City, Utah.
1988-1998 Pittsburgh

Lake may be an all-pro safety, but he is willing to do what is best for the team, as he has proven time and again.

With all-pro cornerback Rod Woodson out for the season and the Steelers struggling in 1995, head coach Bill Cowher asked Lake to switch to cornerback. Lake said sure; he'd already changed positions twice. As a senior running back at California's Culver City High School, Lake rushed for 956 yards and 12 touchdowns in just 5 games before dislocating his elbow. He made the switch to outside linebacker at UCLA, where he racked up 24 career sacks and earned All-America and All-Pacific 10 honors as a senior. He played safety in a couple of college all-star games and did well enough to impress the Steelers, who surprised many by picking Lake in the second round of the 1988 draft.

He not only turned out to be a natural as an NFL safety, but he also proved to be a natural leader. That's why Cowher turned to Lake when the Steelers were in dire need at cornerback, a position where mistakes are quickly exploited. Lake came through splendidly and the Steelers reeled off 10 wins in their final 11 games to reach Super Bowl XXX.

Lake shifted between the two positions as needed again in 1997 to help the Steelers reach the AFC Championship Game for the third time in four years. His leadership and versatility are among the reasons why the Steelers dubbed him their franchise player. In Lake's case, that tag filters all the way to the locker room and, even more importantly, onto the field. [MS]

JACK LAMBERT

Linebacker. 6-4, 220. Kent State
Born July 8, 1952, Mantua, Ohio.
1974-1984 Pittsburgh
Inducted into Pro Football Hall of Fame in 1990

Even though he was the youngest starter on the Pittsburgh Steelers' defensive unit, many felt that Lambert's presence was the final ingredient needed to turn the team into a dynasty. Lambert helped shape and reinforce the Steel Curtain.

Lambert was a two-year All-Mid-America Conference linebacker at Kent State. A second-round draft selection of the Steelers in 1974, he immediately took charge by winning the starting middle linebacker assignment as a rookie and keeping it throughout his 11-year career in Pittsburgh that ended after the 1984 season. Lambert had all the necessary ingredients—intelligence, intensity, speed, quickness, range, durability—and used them all to his advantage.

Lambert was the NFL defensive rookie of the year in 1974. He was all-pro seven times and All-AFC six times in a nine-year span between 1975 and 1983. He missed all-star honors during that period only in 1977, when an injury kept him out of three games. He played in nine consecutive Pro Bowls from the 1975-1983 seasons and was the National Football League defensive player of the year in 1976 and 1979.

The Steelers' defensive captain for eight years, Lambert played in six AFC Championship Games and four Super Bowls. During his career, he had 28 interceptions. Lambert missed only six games because of injuries his first 10 years in the NFL but, in 1984, he suffered a severe toe injury which eventually forced him to retire at the end of the season. [DS/PF]

DICK (NIGHT TRAIN) LANE

Defensive Back. 6-2, 210. Scottsbluff Junior College
Born April 16, 1928, Austin, Texas.
1952-53 Los Angeles Rams, 1954-59 Chicago Cardinals, 1960-65 Detroit
Inducted into Pro Football Hall of Fame in 1974

Dick Lane was an Army veteran trying to find his niche in the post-World War II world when he entered the Los Angeles Rams office one day in 1952 to ask for a tryout. All he had for credentials was a battered scrapbook which chronicled his minimal football experience in high school, at Scottsbluff (Nebraska) Junior College, and in the Army. Coach Joe Stydahar saw just enough "good press" in the scrapbook to offer Lane a trial.

At first, Lane was tried at offensive end, but future Hall of Famer receivers Tom Fears and Elroy (Crazylegs) Hirsch were fixtures at those spots. His brief tryout on the offensive unit did produce his famous nickname. He spent a lot of time with Fears, who was continually playing the hit record "Night Train." One day a teammate came into Fears's room, saw Lane, and blurted out; "Hey, there's Night Train." Lane was known as Night Train from then on.

Once Stydahar moved Lane to defense, he quickly made an impression. Blessed with outstanding speed, exceptional agility, and great reflexes, Lane intercepted 14 passes in a 12-game schedule as a rookie, a league record that still stands. Almost all NFL secondary alignments were man-for-man during Lane's career, and he was one of the best. His career took him to the Chicago Cardinals in 1954 and then to the Detroit Lions, where he enjoyed his best years from 1960 to 1965. He was all-pro five times, four of them while with the Lions, and played in seven Pro Bowls, two as a starter. He intercepted 68 passes for 1,207 yards and 5 touchdowns in his career. [DS/PF]

JIM LANGER

Center. 6-2, 255. South Dakota State
Born May 16, 1948, Little Falls, Minnesota.
1970-79 Miami, 1980-81 Minnesota
Inducted into Pro Football Hall of Fame in 1987.

Hard-working and quick, center Jim Langer was a compact, low-driving blocker who had the strength to overpower bigger defensive linemen.

Langer joined the Miami Dolphins as a free agent in 1970, stayed with the club for 10 years through the 1979 season, and finished his career with the Minnesota Vikings in 1980 and 1981. In his decade with the Dolphins, Langer developed from an obscure substitute to one of the best centers ever to play in the NFL. As a Miami Dolphin, Langer was named all-pro or All-AFC six consecutive years from 1973 to 1978 and also was picked for the Pro Bowl each of those seasons. During that period, he started in three AFC Championship Games and Super Bowls VI, VII, and VIII.

Langer played middle linebacker at South Dakota State before signing with the Cleveland Browns as a free agent in 1970. When the Browns cut him, he joined the Dolphins. For two years, Langer saw only limited action, but in 1972 he switched to center, beat out veteran Bob DeMarco for the starting job, and played every offensive down in Miami's perfect season. In their postseason film review, Miami coaches discovered that while Langer had nearly 500 blocking assignments, he needed help on only three plays. [DS/PF]

WILLIE LANIER

Linebacker. 6-1, 245. Morgan State
Born August 21, 1945, Clover, Virginia.
1967-1977 Kansas City
Inducted into Pro Football Hall of Fame in 1986.

Willie Lanier played middle linebacker for the Kansas City Chiefs for 11 seasons from 1967-1977. As the first African-American to star at that demanding position, he not only was a true pioneer but also the key on one of the NFL's strongest defensive teams.

At 6 feet 1 inch and 245 pounds, he presented an awesome image to any quarterback who lined up against him. He become known and respected for his ability to track down enemy ball carriers and devastate them with the force of his tackles. His teammates affectionately called him "Bear" or "Honeybear" because he looked and acted like a bear—friendly, playful but also potentially dangerous. But he also was called "Contact" because of his powerful hits on the opposition.

Lanier was intelligent and disciplined and obviously much more than just a hitter in his role as quarterback of the defense. Except for the 1969 season, Lanier was all-pro, All-AFL, or All-AFC every year from 1968-1975. He played in the last two AFL All-Star games in 1968 and 1969 and was elected to the first six AFC-NFC Pro Bowl games. Lanier intercepted 27 passes in his career and returned them for 440 yards and 2 touchdowns. He also recovered 15 opponents' fumbles.

Lanier was a two-time Small College All-America at Morgan State. He was a second-round choice of the Chiefs in the 1967 AFL draft and won a starting job in the fourth game of his rookie season. [DS/PF]

YALE LARY

Defensive Back-Punter. 5-11, 189. Texas A&M
Born November 24, 1930, Fort Worth, Texas.
1952-53, 1956-1964 Detroit
Inducted into Pro Football Hall of Fame in 1979.

Detroit Lions' fans remember Yale Lary in many different ways. Some think of him as a superb right safety, a key in Detroit's fearsome defensive platoon in the 1950s and 1960s. Others consider him one of the NFL's great punters. Still others say it was his breakaway ability on punt returns that set him apart.

In reality, Lary, a multitalented Texas A&M product, did all of those things well during his 11-year tenure with the Lions. Lary's defensive play was exceptional. A fixture at right safety, he was named all-pro four times and he played in nine Pro Bowls. He intercepted 50 passes and he might well have had many more had not opposition quarterbacks avoided throwing in his area.

"If I had to pick one defensive back who had everything," quarterback Bobby Layne, the key offensive performer during the Lions' championship years, once said, "it would have to be Yale. He was the smartest, but the big thing was his quickness and his ability to recover and intercept after he had lulled the quarterback into thinking he had an open receiver."

Lary's career punting average of 44.3 yards places him third on the all-time list. He won three NFL punting titles and narrowly missed a fourth. [DS/PF]

DANTE LAVELLI

End. 6-0, 199. Ohio State
Born February 23, 1923, Hudson, Ohio.
1946-49 Cleveland (AAFC), 1950-56 Cleveland
Inducted into Pro Football Hall of Fame in 1975.

A quarterback in high school and a halfback as an Ohio State freshman, Dante Lavelli was switched to end by Buckeyes coach Paul Brown before his sophomore season. When Lavelli joined Brown's newly formed Cleveland Browns in 1946, injuries and a long stint in the U. S. Army had limited his college experience to just three games. To make the Browns, he had to beat our four more-experienced candidates. Lavelli not only prevailed but he led the league in receptions and won All-AAFC honors in his rookie season.

There were many more big moments in Lavelli's career. He was All-AAFC again in 1947 and, when the Browns moved to the NFL in 1950, he was all-league twice more and a starter in three Pro Bowl games. In the 1950 NFL Championship Game, he caught 11 passes, then an NFL postseason record, and scored 2 touchdowns as the Browns edged the Los Angeles Rams 30-28.

Through the years, Lavelli was a favorite target of legendary Browns quarterback Otto Graham. All but 20 of Lavelli's 386 career receptions (including 142 in the All-America Football Conference) came from Graham. [DS/PF]

BOBBY LAYNE

Quarterback. 6-2, 190. Texas
Born December 19, 1926, Santa Anna, Texas.
Died December 1, 1986, Lubbock, Texas.
1948 Chicago Bears, 1949 N.Y. Bulldogs, 1950-58 Detroit, 1958-1962 Pittsburgh
Inducted into Pro Football Hall of Fame in 1967.

Bobby Layne left pro football with a legend that may never be duplicated. Layne's story includes not only great moments on the field but also his penchant for enjoying every moment off the field, even if on occasion that meant a big night on the town just hours before a crucial game. There is no question he did not subscribe to the norm when it came to general football team deportment.

But during his 15-year career, Layne was an all-pro caliber quarterback who was exceptional in the intangibles—leadership, determination, guts, competitiveness, and esprit de corps. Layne was fortunate that he had a coach, Buddy Parker, who understood what made him tick. And the two combined their talents to produce the most successful years in Detroit Lions history.

The Lions, under Layne, won division titles in 1952, 1953, and 1954, defeating the Cleveland Browns for the NFL championship the first two years. Layne enjoyed his most dramatic—and famous—moment in the 1953 title game. With the ball on the Detroit 20, the Lions trailing 16-10, and 4:10 left to play, the native Texan directed the Lions on an 80-yard touchdown drive in two minutes. The climax was Layne's 33-yard pass to end Jim Doran. Doak Walker's extra point gave the Lions a 17-16 triumph.

In 1958, Layne was traded to Pittsburgh, where he provided the Steelers with some of their most successful years before his retirement in 1962. [DS/PF]

ALPHONSE (TUFFY) LEEMANS

Fullback. 6-0, 200. George Washington
Born November 12, 1912, Superior, Wisconsin.
Died January 19, 1979, Hillsboro Beach, Florida.
1936-1943 New York Giants
Inducted into Pro Football Hall of Fame in 1978.

As a triple-threat running back at George Washington in the mid-1930s, Tuffy Leemans was virtually a one-man show. Yet it is possible Leemans would have remained a comparative unknown had it not been for a vacationing high school boy, Wellington Mara, son of the New York Giants president, who "discovered" Leemans during a sensational performance against Alabama.

Wellington told his father about his find and, in the NFL's first draft in 1936, the Giants chose Leemans in the second round. Leemans quickly showed the Giants they had made a wise choice by winning most-valuable-player honors in the Chicago College All-Star game. In 1936, he led the NFL with 830 yards rushing and was the only rookie to win All-NFL honors.

Leemans played halfback and fullback and excelled on defense at a time the Giants were perennial contenders. During Leemans's career, New York won three division titles and the 1938 NFL championship. Leemans's career statistics are impressive—3,142 yards rushing, 422 yards on receptions, 167 pass completions for 2,324 yards and 16 touchdowns, and almost 14 yards per punt return.

His numbers are even more impressive when it is remembered that the Giants of that era employed a system that saw two separate units divide playing time both offensively and defensively. [DS/PF]

BOB LILLY

Defensive Tackle-Defensive End. 6-5, 260.
Texas Christian
Born July 26, 1939, Olney, Texas.
1961-1974 Dallas
Inducted into Pro Football Hall of Fame in 1980.

Bob Lilly, a consensus All-America at Texas Christian, was the Cowboys' first-ever draft choice in 1961. For the next 14 seasons, his play was so outstanding that he became popularly known as "Mr. Cowboy."

Lilly won rookie-of-the-year acclaim as a defensive end in 1961, but in 1963 moved to defensive tackle with even more sensational results. As a tackle, Lilly was an all-pro choice every year from 1964-69 and won All-NFC honors in 1971 and 1972. Equally effective as a pass rusher and a run defender, Lilly was continually double-teamed and even triple-teamed, but he rarely was delayed in his pursuit of the ball carrier.

Lilly even scored 4 touchdowns in his career. One came on a 17-yard interception return in 1964 while the other 3 came on fumble recoveries. Altogether, he returned 15 opponents' fumbles for 109 yards.

Extremely durable, he played in 196 consecutive regular-season games. Postseason play became a way of life for the 6-foot 5-inch, 260-pound Texan. The Cowboys played in seven NFL/NFC title games in an eight-year period from 1966 through 1973 and also played in Super Bowls V and VI. Lilly was selected to 11 Pro Bowls. He was the first player who spent his entire career with the Cowboys to be elected to the Pro Football Hall of Fame. [DS/PF]

GENE (BIG DADDY) LIPSCOMB

Defensive Tackle. 6-6, 282. No College
Born November 9, 1931, Detroit, Michigan. Died May 10, 1963, Baltimore, Maryland.
1953-55 Los Angeles Rams, 1956-1960 Baltimore, 1961-62 Pittsburgh

Few NFL players are feared by their opponents. Gene (Big Daddy) Lipscomb was an exception.

"Whatever you did, you never wanted to get him mad," observed Jack Stroud, a great offensive guard and tackle for the New York Giants who played against Lipscomb in some memorable games. "Big Daddy played in his own world and being bigger than everyone he played against, he sort of cruised through a game. But if he got upset, he went to another level that was truly awesome."

For all of his reputation as a tough player on the field, he usually was a remarkably gentle man off the field.

Lipscomb was unusual in that he had no college experience and was signed off the sandlots by the Los Angeles Rams. He played on the Rams' 1955 division-championship team, then was traded to the Baltimore Colts where he joined a great defensive line that included future Pro Football Hall of Fame inductees Gino Marchetti and Art Donovan. He played on two NFL championship teams for Baltimore in 1958-59.

In 1960, the Colts traded him to the Pittsburgh Steelers, where he joined another future Hall of Fame player, tackle Ernie Stautner. The always downtrodden Steelers suddenly were winners in 1962 and felt confident they could win a conference title the following year. But tragically, in May, 1963, Lipscomb was found dead in his apartment in Baltimore. [JC]

LARRY LITTLE

Guard. 6-1, 255. Bethune-Cookman
Born November 2, 1945, Groveland, Georgia.
1967-68 San Diego, 1969-1980 Miami
Inducted into Pro Football Hall of Fame in 1993.

Larry Little began his NFL career as an unheralded free agent with the San Diego Chargers in 1967. Little, who had been a two-way tackle, team captain, and an all-conference choice at Bethune-Cookman College, enjoyed only moderate success during his two years in San Diego. In 1969, he was traded to the Dolphins and it wasn't long before the 6-foot 1-inch, 255-pound guard was being lauded as one of the NFL's premier offensive linemen.

During the 1970s, when the Dolphins were a dominant team, Little became the epitome of the intimidating force of the vaunted Miami rushing attack. Also a superb pass blocker, Little was named all-pro and All-AFC seven consecutive years from 1971-77. Little was selected to five Pro Bowls in his career. He was named the NFL Players Association's AFC lineman of the year in 1970, 1971, and 1972.

A native of Georgia, Little displayed versatility, durability, and dedication throughout his career. Dolphins coach Don Shula called him "a real inspiration, not just for the way he performs but also for his influence on our younger players." [DS/PF]

JAMES LOFTON

Wide Receiver. 6-3, 192. Stanford
Born July 5, 1956, Fort Ord, California.
1978-1986 Green Bay, 1987-88 Raiders, 1989-1992 Buffalo, 1993 Los Angeles Rams, 1993 Philadelphia

James Lofton could run and catch as well as anyone from the moment he entered the National Football League, but the most amazing part of his career was how long he was able to remain a deep-receiving threat. At the stage where most receivers were retired or at best taking short gains as possession receivers, Lofton remained his team's best deep threat. In 16 seasons, Lofton caught 764 passes for 14,004 yards—an average of 18.3 yards per catch. Many of his 75 touchdown receptions came on long passes.

He began as a successful high school quarterback in Los Angeles and shifted to receiver at Stanford, where he became the best in the Pac-8 as a senior and earned All-America honors. He was also an accomplished track performer and won the NCAA long-jump title in 1978.

Green Bay selected Lofton in the first round of the 1978 draft, and he became a standout immediately. Lofton holds the Packers' record for most receiving yards (9,656) and his 83-yard run in 1983 is one of the longest plays in club history. During his time with the Packers, he was chosen to play in seven Pro Bowls.

He was traded to the Raiders in 1987, and after two years on the West Coast, he joined the Buffalo Bills, where he enjoyed some of his best seasons. He caught 7 passes for Buffalo in Super Bowl XXVI. [MS]

HOWIE LONG

Defensive End. 6-5, 268. Villanova
Born January 6, 1960, Somerville, Massachusetts.
1981-1993 Raiders

Howie Long joined the Raiders one year after the team won Super Bowl XV. Three years later, Long helped them win another NFL title with a 38-9 victory over Washington in Super Bowl XVIII. In between the two Super Bowls, the Raiders moved from Oakland to Los Angeles, and Long helped the Raiders establish a new identity.

At 6 feet 5 inches and 270 pounds, Long was big enough to blow past offensive linemen and fast enough to catch up to quarterbacks and ball carriers from his defensive end position. "As an inside rusher, he has outside speed and quickness," said former Bears coach Dave Wannstedt.

Long was voted the National Football League defensive lineman of the year in 1986 and was picked for the Pro Bowl eight times.

"Tough" is a good word to describe Howie Long. He grew up in a rough environment in Charlestown, Massachusetts, outside of Boston. He turned his energy to sports, however, and played football, basketball, and track at Milford High School. He earned a scholarship to Villanova University and capped off a solid college career by earning most-valuable-player honors in the 1980 Blue-Gray All-Star Game.

Long was one of the most popular Raiders in Los Angeles. He retired after the 1993 season with 84 career sacks and now is a studio analyst for NFL coverage on FOX. [MS]

RONNIE LOTT

Cornerback-Safety. 6-0, 200. Southern California
Born May 8, 1959, Albuquerque, New Mexico.
1981-1990 San Francisco, 1991-92 Raiders, 1993-94 New York Jets

Ronnie Lott titled his 1991 autobiography *Total Impact.* It was a suitable choice because that's exactly what Lott had when he took the field. The NFL may never have seen a harder-hitting defensive back. "He's like a middle linebacker playing safety," Cowboys coach Tom Landry once said. "He's devastating. He may dominate the secondary better than anyone I've seen."

After an All-America career at Southern California, Lott was San Francisco's first-round draft pick and the eighth player chosen overall in the 1981 draft. He made an immediate impression on the 49ers and was the starting left cornerback from the first day of training camp. Lott led the secondary that helped the 49ers to victory in Super Bowl XVI. The 1981 NFL rookie of the year, he also was a Pro Bowl choice that season and 9 times over the next 10 years. He was an all-pro pick four times.

During his career, Lott lined up at both corners and both safeties, but he was probably at his most intimidating as a free safety, where he had the freedom to cover the entire field.

Lott signed with the Raiders as a Plan B free agent in 1991 and led the NFL with 8 interceptions that season. His 63 career interceptions place him among the NFL's elite. He is now a studio analyst on FOX. [JJC]

SID LUCKMAN

Quarterback. 6-0, 195. Columbia
Born November 21, 1916, Brooklyn, New York.
Died July 5, 1998, North Miami Beach, Florida.
1939-1950 Chicago Bears
Inducted into Pro Football Hall of Fame in 1965.

Sid Luckman was selected by the Chicago Bears in the first round of the 1939 draft as a triple-threat tailback who had excelled in Columbia University's Single-Wing attack. Running was his strongest suit, but he was a fine passer and a better-than-average punter and kicker. Bears head coach George Halas had special ideas for Luckman. Even before Luckman reported to training camp, Halas presented him with a Bears' playbook that introduced Luckman to the T-formation.

Astonished by the complexities of the new system, Luckman failed his first "T" test. Halas temporarily abandoned the plan, but reintroduced it to Luckman later in the year. This time Halas's tutoring paid off. Because of Halas's patience, Luckman developed into the NFL's first great T-formation quarterback. In the 1940 NFL Championship Game, Luckman showed the world just how explosive the T-formation attack could be. Although he passed only 6 times, completing 4 of them for 102 yards and a touchdown, Luckman led the Bears to the most lopsided victory in pro football history, a 73-0 rout of the Washington Redskins. During Luckman's 12-year career, the Bears won four NFL championships.

Luckman had many more outstanding games but two, both in 1943, stood out above the rest. On November 14, "Sid Luckman Day" at the Polo Grounds, he passed for a record 7 touchdowns in a 56-7 massacre of the New York Giants. In the 1943 title game against Washington, Luckman passed for 286 yards and 5 touchdowns in a 41-21 triumph. [DS/PF]

LAMAR LUNDY

Defensive End. 6-7, 245. Purdue
Born April 17, 1935, Richmond, Indiana.
1957-1969 Los Angeles Rams

Lamar Lundy was the least known, but perhaps the most consistent member of the Los Angeles Rams' fabled Fearsome Foursome defensive line. His reliability allowed the others to gamble on defense.

An honor student who played both football and basketball at Purdue University, Lundy arrived in Los Angeles in 1957 as a fourth-round draft choice. At first the Rams used him as an offensive end—he caught 25 passes in his second season—but in 1959 he was switched to defensive end. Lundy endured several seasons with the mediocre Rams before he received help—one year at a time.

David (Deacon) Jones was a godsend in the fourteenth round of the 1961 draft. Merlin Olson arrived the next year after an All-America season at Utah State. Rosey Grier, who came from the New York Giants in 1963, was the final piece of the foursome.

The group made up its own signals, invented moves such as stunting and looping and even added the term "sack" to the football lexicon. The Rams also made progress in the standings—slowly but surely. Los Angeles had a 1-12-1 record in 1962, improved to 5-9 in 1963, were 5-7-2 in 1964, slipped to 4-10 in 1965, but the Rams resided near or at the top of their division for the rest of the decade. Lundy retired in 1969 after the Rams' second division title in three years. [MS]

WILLIAM ROY (LINK) LYMAN

Tackle. 6-2, 252. Nebraska
Born November 30, 1898, Table Rock, Nebraska.
Died December 16, 1972, Baker, California.
1922-23, 1925 Canton, 1924 Cleveland, 1925 Frankford, 1926-28, 1930-31, 1933-34 Chicago Bears
Inducted into Pro Football Hall of Fame in 1964.

Many football historians insist the constant shifting by defensive players before each play in modern professional football had its beginning more than seven decades ago in the early 1920s when a sensational 252-pound tackle, William Roy (Link) Lyman, regularly resorted to similar ploys. Steve Owen, himself an outstanding tackle who later became famous as the New York Giants coach, was among the first to be victimized by Lyman's tactics. "He was the first linemen I ever saw who moved from his assigned defensive position before the ball was snapped," Owen said. "It was difficult to play against him because he would vary his moves and no matter how you reacted, you could be wrong."

Lyman, who played with four NFL championship teams before joining the Chicago Bears for the final seven years of his career, said he began shifting as an instinctive move to fool a blocker. He had a unique ability to diagnose a play and many times he would make his move just as the ball was snapped.

A highly regarded college star at the University of Nebraska, Lyman was lured to the Canton Bulldogs in 1922 by another Nebraska graduate, player-coach Guy Chamberlin. In January, 1926, Lyman joined the Bears for their long barnstorming tour and remained with Chicago the rest of his career, which ended after the 1934 season. In his last two seasons, the Bears won the 1933 NFL championship and the 1934 divisional crown. Lyman played on just one losing team in 16 seasons of high school, college and professional football. [DS/PF]

TOM MACK

Guard. 6-3, 250. Michigan
Born November 1, 1943, Cleveland, Ohio.
1966-1978 Los Angeles Rams
Inducted into Pro Football Hall of Fame in 1999.

Guard Tom Mack was an essential part of the great Los Angeles Rams teams that rang up a record of 129-48-7 and won eight division titles from 1966-1978.

Mack reveled in being a powerful run blocker. "I've always thought that one of the best things I've had going for me is my speed," he said. "I'm not as big and strong as some guards, but one of the things I can do best is block on a sweep."

Mack always was amused by the anonymity afforded offensive linemen, even for some, like himself, who were perennial choices to play in the Pro Bowl. He played in 11 Pro Bowls during his 13 seasons, maintaining a path of excellence that reached back to his days as an All-America lineman at the University of Michigan where he played in the Rose Bowl, the East-West Shrine Game, the Hula Bowl, and the College All-Star game.

"It wasn't until instant replay became popular on television that people began to take notice of players other than quarterbacks, running backs, and receivers," Mack once observed. "The rest of us were spear-carriers—just part of the background, but in the public's eye, not necessary to the game.

"When I saw myself on some of those instant-replay shots, I always seemed to be blocking the wrong man. But that didn't matter. What mattered was that I was wiping out somebody—showing the world that a guard has a big job to do."

Few did it as well. [JC]

JOHN MACKEY

Tight End. 6-2, 224. Syracuse
Born September 24, 1941, New York, New York.
1963-1971 Baltimore, 1972 San Diego
Inducted into Pro Football Hall of Fame in 1992.

John Mackey was only the second player who performed strictly as a tight end to become a member of the Pro Football Hall of Fame. The 6-foot 2-inch, 224-pound Syracuse University graduate joined the Baltimore Colts as a second-round draft pick in 1963 and established himself as a premier performer at his position.

Mackey had all the attributes of the prototype tight end. A strong blocker, he also had breakaway speed and the tackle-breaking ability that made him a scoring threat on every play. In 1966, for instance, 6 of his 9 touchdown receptions came on plays of more than 50 yards. Mackey was durable, missing only one game in 10 years.

Mackey, who was born in New York City, started every game as a rookie and was selected to the first of his five Pro Bowls. For three consecutive years from 1966-68 Mackey was the all-league tight end. In 10 seasons, the one-time NFL Players Association president caught 331 passes for 5,236 yards and 38 touchdowns. As a rookie he returned kickoffs and averaged 30.1 yards on 9 returns. Perhaps Mackey's most famous play came in Super Bowl V, when he grabbed a deflected pass from Johnny Unitas and raced to a 75-yard touchdown, a Super Bowl record at the time. [DS/PF]

GINO MARCHETTI

Defensive End. 6-4, 245. San Francisco
Born January 2, 1927, Smithers, West Virginia.
1952 Dallas, 1953-1964, 1966 Baltimore
Inducted into Pro Football Hall of Fame in 1972.

Gino Marchetti's parents always feared that he would be hurt playing football and discouraged him from taking up the sport. Every quarterback who played in the NFL in the 1950s and early 1960s probably wishes Marchetti had heeded his parents' advice. Ironically, Gino suffered the most serious injury of his career in the famous 1958 overtime championship game at a time when his parents were watching him on television for the first time. Marchetti had made a key tackle that ended a New York Giants' drive and gave the Baltimore Colts a chance to tie the game in regulation when teammate Gene (Big Daddy) Lipscomb fell on him and broke his leg.

Marchetti began his career with the 1952 Dallas Texans as an offensive tackle before he starred for the Baltimore Colts at defensive end from 1953-1964. After a one-year retirement, he returned to the Colts for one final season in 1966 when the team was beset by injuries.

Marchetti was a brilliant all-around defender, adept at stopping the running play, but most famous for his pass-rushing techniques. He was known for clean but hard play and he was a particular terror in passing situations. When opponents double-teamed or even triple-teamed him, it only helped make the rest of the Colts' defensive line more effective.

The University of San Francisco product earned all-pro honors seven times and was selected to 10 Pro Bowls. In 1969, Marchetti was named the NFL's top defensive end in the league's first 50 years. [DS/PF]

DAN MARINO

Quarterback. 6-4, 216. Pittsburgh
Born September 15, 1961, Pittsburgh, Pennsylvania.
1983-1998 Miami

Dan Marino is the most prolific passer in NFL history. He holds the league's passing records for attempts, completions, yards, and touchdowns.

Marino also was a brilliant quarterback at the University of Pittsburgh, which was located only four blocks from where he grew up. Marino guided Pittsburgh to three consecutive 11-1 seasons and three consecutive bowl triumphs in his first three years with the Panthers. His senior year the team went 9-3. Marino passed for 8,597 yards and 79 touchdowns in college.

Early in his professional career, he was shattering records in the NFL. In 1984, he set single-season records for completions (362), yards (5,084), and touchdown passes (48). Miami went to Super Bowl XIX but lost to the San Francisco 49ers..

Marino has led the league in completions and passing yards four more times since then. He reached 40,000 career passing yards quicker than any other quarterback (153 games), and he was the first quarterback to surpass 50,000 yards and 400 touchdown passes. Marino has added 4,219 yards and 30 touchdown passes in 16 postseason games, but he has not made it back to the Super Bowl. He has seemingly has accomplished everything in football except one thing: win an NFL championship. [MS]

JIM MARSHALL

Defensive End. 6-4, 235. Ohio State
Born December 30, 1937, Danville, Kentucky.
1960 Cleveland, 1961-1979 Minnesota

Jim Marshall was the greatest ironman in NFL history. Marshall played a league-record 282 consecutive games for the Cleveland Browns and Minnesota Vikings—302 counting his playoff appearances—over 21 seasons, and that doesn't count one season in 1959 with Saskatchewan of the Canadian Football League while he was waiting to become eligible for the 1960 NFL draft (he left Ohio State a year before his class graduated).

Marshall's durability was amazing considering that, at 235 pounds, he usually faced players bigger than him. Bud Grant, his coach, called him a "physiological impossibility. He just doesn't rip, bust, or tear."

Twice he kept his streak intact by walking out of hospitals where he was recuperating from pneumonia and ulcers. On another occasion, he played after accidentally shooting himself in the side while cleaning his shotgun. Away from the game, Marshall was an avid sky diver, scuba diver, and snowmobiler.

There was little in pro football that he never did, including running 66 yards the wrong way for a safety in a 1964 game against the San Francisco 49ers. That never detracted from the respect his teammates showed him. Marshall was the Vikings' co-captain during his entire career. While he may have been outweighed by many opposing offensive linemen, he was more intense and quicker than most of them. [JC]

HARVEY MARTIN

Defensive End. 6-5, 260. East Texas State University
Born November 15, 1960, Dallas, Texas.
1973-1983 Dallas

Harvey Martin was one of the mainstays of the famed Doomsday II Defense that helped the Dallas Cowboys win Super Bowl XII, where he and teammate Randy White, a defensive tackle, were chosen as the game's most valuable players.

Martin was one of the quickest defensive ends in the NFL. His patented pass-rush move, one that allowed him to record 113 sacks (unofficially), was a quick step at the snap of the ball to freeze an offensive lineman, then another quick step to the outside followed by a crashing move toward the quarterback.

Cowboys coach Tom Landry called Martin the best pass-rushing defensive end in Cowboys' history. He also was the most athletic. Although he stood 6 feet 5 inches and weighed 252 pounds, Martin was timed in 4.8 seconds in the 40-yard dash.

In addition to White, a member of the Pro Football Hall of Fame, Martin also played on Doomsday II with Ed (Too Tall) Jones and Larry Cole, a holdover from the Cowboys' Doomsday I defense. Martin always played next to White, leaving opponents in a terrible dilemma because White demanded double-team blocking. Martin was almost unblockable man-for-man, so opponents either used a second tight end or a running back to help out, lessening the effectiveness of their passing game.

Martin always loved the spotlight and thrived in it. He became a well-known radio personality in Dallas, and once after a television interview with former Miss America Phyllis George on CBS, he turned around and interviewed her for his Dallas radio show. [JC]

OLLIE MATSON
Halfback. 6-2, 220. San Francisco
Born May 1, 1930, Trinity, Texas.
1952, 1954-58 Chicago Cardinals, 1959-1962 Los Angeles Rams, 1963 Detroit, 1964-66 Philadelphia
Inducted into Pro Football Hall of Fame in 1972.
Ollie Matson, a fleet-footed halfback from the University of San Francisco, excelled in the NFL for 14 seasons. When Matson began his pro career with the Chicago Cardinals in 1952, he was hailed as "The Messiah" who could lead the Cardinals out of the NFL wilderness. In 1959, he was traded to the Los Angeles Rams for a stunning total of nine players. He was expected to lead the Rams to a long-awaited championship.

Matson never led any of his teams to a title, but his career was exceptional. He gained 12,884 yards on rushing, receptions, and returns. He scored 40 touchdowns running, 23 on receptions, 9 on kick returns, and 1 on a fumble recovery. Matson was the Cardinals' top pick in 1952 but he opted to join the United States Olympic team. He returned from Helsinki with a bronze medal in the 400-meter race and a gold medal from the 1,600-meter relay.

Once in the NFL, he shared 1952 rookie-of-the-year honors with Hugh McElhenny. He was all-pro four consecutive years and played in the Pro Bowl five times. Matson finished his career in a blaze of glory by leading the 1966 Philadelphia Eagles to a 9-5 record, the best finish ever for a team on which Matson played. [DS/PF]

BRUCE MATTHEWS
Guard-Tackle-Center. 6-4, 290. Southern California
Born August 8, 1961, Arcadia, California.
1983-1996 Houston, 1997-98 Tennessee
At 6 feet 4 inches and 290 pounds, Bruce Matthews was perfectly suited for the family business.

The Matthews's preferred line of work is the National Football League. Among Clay Matthews, Sr., Clay Matthews, Jr., and Bruce Matthews, the family has spent more than 30 years in the NFL. Clay, Jr., a linebacker with the Cleveland Browns and Atlanta Falcons, has the most service time—19 seasons, but Bruce, who is five years younger, is runner-up in the family with 16. Clay, Sr., played end for three seasons with the San Francisco 49ers in the 1950s.

Bruce Matthews, equally adept playing guard or center, grew up in Arcadia, California, and followed in his brother's footsteps at the University of Southern California. And, just like his brother, he was selected in the first round of the NFL draft. Bruce signed with the Houston Oilers and has played every game of every season since 1983, except for eight games in 1987 when he did not sign with the team until November. He has 248 regular-season games under his belt, but still lags 30 games behind Clay, Jr.

With Matthews as the anchor of the Houston offensive line, the Oilers made the playoffs every year from 1987-1993. He has been named to the Pro Bowl 11 times. [MS]

DON MAYNARD
Wide Receiver. 6-1, 175. Texas Western
Born January 25, 1935, Crosbyton, Texas.
1958 New York Giants, 1960-62 New York Titans, 1963-1972 New York Jets, 1973 St. Louis
Inducted into Pro Football Hall of Fame in 1987.
Don Maynard had the biggest day of his career in the 1968 AFL Championship Game that preceded the Jets' stunning upset of the Baltimore Colts in Super Bowl III. In New York's 27-23 victory over Oakland, Maynard caught 6 passes for 118 yards and 2 touchdowns. His 14-yard catch in the first period gave the Jets the lead and his 6-yard catch in the fourth period proved to be the game winner.

The lanky receiver was not known for running precise patterns. In fact, many of his biggest gains came on improvised routes. Named to the American Football League's all-time team as a wide receiver in 1969, he recorded 633 receptions for 11,834 yards and 88 touchdowns in a 15-year career that began with the New York Giants in 1958 and concluded with a brief fling with the 1973 St. Louis Cardinals. The rest of his career was spent with the AFL's New York franchise, which was known as the Titans from 1960-62 and became the Jets in 1963.

A former Texas Western (now UTEP) track star who played halfback on offense and safety on defense during his college days, Maynard was a future draft pick of the Giants in 1957. He played only the 1958 season with the NFL club before moving to Hamilton in the Canadian Football League in 1959. A year later, he became the first signee of the Titans of the new AFL. [DS/PF]

GEORGE McAFEE
Halfback. 6-0, 177. Duke
Born March 13, 1918, Ironton, Ohio.
1940-41, 1945-1950 Chicago Bears
Inducted into Pro Football Hall of Fame in 1966.
When Gale Sayers joined the Chicago Bears in 1965, veteran writers immediately asked coach George Halas if the prized rookie was as good as former Bears star halfback George McAfee.

To Halas, the highest compliment that could be given any ball carrier was to compare him to McAfee, who was an all-purpose halfback during the Bears' best years in the 1940s. At 6 feet and 177 pounds, McAfee did not have the physique of an outstanding National Football League player but his achievements on the field make him one of the most memorable of all Chicago Bears.

From the start of his National Football League career, the former Duke star established himself as a game-breaker. In his first exhibition game, McAfee returned a punt 75 yards for a touchdown with 37 seconds left to beat the Brooklyn Dodgers. In the 1940 regular-season opener, he ran back a kickoff 93 yards and threw a touchdown pass in a 41-10 Bears victory. In the historic 73-0 rout of the Washington Redskins in the 1940 NFL Championship Game, McAfee contributed a 34-yard interception return for a touchdown.

McAfee's pro career was not particularly long—limited to just eight years before and after World War II. While his career statistics were not particularly impressive, they did show that McAfee did just about everything a player can do with a football. He was a speedy runner, a dangerous pass receiver, and one of history's best kick-return specialists.

His 12.78-yard average on 112 punt returns still stands as a record. He also recorded 21 interceptions. [DS/PF]

MIKE McCORMACK

Tackle. 6-4, 248. Kansas
Born June 21, 1930, Chicago, Illinois.
1951 New York Yanks, 1954-1962 Cleveland
Inducted into Pro Football Hall of Fame in 1984.

Mike McCormack, one of pro football's greatest offensive tackles, enjoyed perhaps his most memorable individual moment as a defensive player for Cleveland in the 1954 NFL Championship Game. He stole the ball from Detroit Lions quarterback Bobby Layne to set up one of the early touchdowns in the Browns' 56-10 rout.

In his first season in Cleveland, McCormack was asked to fill the middle guard position that had been vacated by the retirement of Bill Willis on the defensive unit. But as soon as he could, coach Paul Brown shifted McCormack back to offensive tackle. McCormack, who played 10 years in the NFL, was the Cleveland Browns' right tackle for eight years from 1955-1962. During that period, the Browns' forward wall played a major role in assuring a balanced offensive approach, and McCormack, equally adept as a blocker on rushing plays and as a pass protector, was a stabilizing factor.

The former University of Kansas star and Chicago native was drafted by the New York Yanks in 1951 and immediately became the club's regular right tackle. He made his first of six Pro Bowl appearances after his rookie season. McCormack was called into military service before another season and, in 1953, after the Baltimore Colts had acquired his contract, he was traded to the Cleveland Browns in a massive 10-player deal. Even though the Browns knew Mike would not be available for a full year, he was a key man in the trade. Coach Paul Brown always considered it one of his wisest personnel moves.

McCormack, formerly the president of the Seattle Seahawks, held the same position with the Carolina Panthers until retiring. [DS/PF]

TOMMY McDONALD

Wide Receiver. 5-9, 176. Oklahoma
Born July 26, 1934, Roy, New Mexico.
1957-1963 Philadelphia, 1964 Dallas, 1965-66 Los Angeles Rams, 1967 Atlanta, 1968 Cleveland
Inducted into Pro Football Hall of Fame in 1998.

McDonald was one of the most feared wide receivers in the National Football League. Single coverage on him invited disaster, and, when McDonald cut over the middle on post patterns and the passer hit him in stride, a touchdown was likely.

McDonald used his running skills brilliantly after making his catches, finishing his career with an average of nearly 17 yards per catch and 84 touchdowns. He was selected to play in six Pro Bowls.

College football's player of the year in 1956, McDonald spearheaded Oklahoma during its record-setting 47-game winning streak. McDonald never played in a losing contest at Oklahoma, and no one really knew how good he was because the Sooners were so powerful that he rarely played more than a half of a game.

The Eagles made him a third-round pick in 1957. They utilized him primarily as a kickoff- and punt-return specialist in his rookie season. When Buck Shaw became the Eagles' head coach in 1958, he put him at flanker, and then obtained quarterback Norm Van Brocklin in a trade with the Rams. In the next three seasons, the Van Brocklin-McDonald combination produced 115 receptions for 2,250 yards and 32 touchdowns. McDonald was the Eagles' primary weapon in their 1960 NFL championship.

Van Brocklin retired after winning the 1960 title, but Sonny Jurgensen took up the quarterbacking duties. Although opposing teams constructed their pass defenses to contain McDonald, Jurgensen utilized him even more. McDonald caught 119 passes for 2,290 yards and 23 touchdowns with the Eagles in 1961-62. [JC]

HUGH McELHENNY

Halfback. 6-1, 198. Washington
Born December 31, 1928, Los Angeles, California.
1952-1960 San Francisco, 1961-62 Minnesota, 1963 New York Giants, 1964 Detroit
Inducted into Pro Football Hall of Fame in 1970.

When Hugh McElhenny first decided to play pro football, he figured he would stay around "about three years, just enough to get a down payment on a house, a car, an investment. . . ." But as it turned out, he played 13 years in the National Football League and his accomplishments were so outstanding that he was elected to the Pro Football Hall of Fame in 1970, his first year of eligibility.

It was ample testimony to McElhenny's football abilities and it explains, too, why he was known as "The King" during his 13-year career. In his prime, McElhenny was the scourge of NFL defenses. He was the master at open-field running, he was an artist at running the draw, and he had sudden bursts of blinding speed.

McElhenny was the 49ers' first-round draft choice in 1952. From the start, he was a star—running 42 yards to a touchdown one of the first times he touched the ball in pro play. He unanimously was named the rookie of the year.

McElhenny was a great runner but he also was much more. When he retired after the 1964 season, he was one of only three players to have gained more than 11,000 combined yards. Altogether, on rushing, receiving, kickoff returns and punt returns, he totaled 11,369 yards. [DS/PF]

JOHNNY (BLOOD) McNALLY

Halfback. 6-0, 185. St. John's (MN)
Born November 27, 1903, New Richmond, Wisconsin.
Died November 28, 1985, Palm Springs, California.
1925-26 Milwaukee, 1926-27 Duluth, 1928 Pottsville, 1929-1933, 1935-36 Green Bay, 1934, 1937-39 Pittsburgh
Inducted into Pro Football Hall of Fame in 1963.

At 6 feet and 185 pounds, John McNally was unbelievably fast, a superb running back, and the finest receiver in the National Football League. He could throw passes and punt with the best. On defense he was a ball hawk and a deadly tackler. He played on five NFL teams in 15 seasons but his best years came with the Green Bay Packers, with whom he was a major contributor to championship juggernauts in 1929, 1930, 1931, and 1936.

His off-the-field antics, however, constantly drew attention away from his exceptional playing skills. When the Packers were ahead, he tended to coast and clown. He broke training rules and ignored curfews. Green Bay coach Curly Lambeau once offered McNally $10 more per game if he would give up drinking. McNally refused the extra money but did agree to drink only until Wednesday evening each week. Another time, he missed the team train but caught up with it by driving his car onto the tracks and then gleefully joining his teammates aboard the train.

McNally still had a year of college eligibility remaining when he decided to take a shot at pro football. To protect his eligibility, he needed an alias, a common practice in the 1920s. He and a friend passed a movie theater where the movie *Blood and Sand* was playing. McNally exclaimed to his friend: "That's it. You be Sand, I'll be Blood." So "Johnny Blood" it was for the next 15 seasons. His pro football days ended when he was a player-coach with the Pittsburgh Pirates in 1939. It was his wife Marguerite who described him most accurately: "Even when Johnny does the expected, he does it in an unexpected way."[DS/PF]

MIKE MICHALSKE

Guard. 6-0, 209. Penn State
Born April 24, 1903, Cleveland, Ohio.
Died October 26, 1983, Green Bay, Wisconsin.
1926 New York Yankees (AFL), 1927-28 New York Yankees, 1929-1935, 1937 Green Bay
Inducted into Pro Football Hall of Fame in 1964.

Some say that playing guard in the National Football League in the 1920s and 1930s was the toughest assignment of all. A guard in those days had to block head on the biggest of opposing linemen. He also had to pull from the line and lead interference for the ball carrier. On defense, the guard was the key man in stopping the opposition's running attack. But he also had to be capable of storming into the backfield to thwart a pass. During this time, Mike Michalske was the premier guard in the NFL, particularly adept at rushing the passer.

Christened August at birth, Michalske became known as "Iron Mike" because not only did he play nearly 60 minutes every game, he also never was injured. In high school and at Penn State, where he was an All-America pick in 1925, he played fullback, guard, end, and tackle. He first turned pro with the New York Yankees in the 1926 American Football League. After the Yankees folded in 1928, Michalske opted to become a free agent so that he could join the Packers. [DS/PF]

WAYNE MILLNER

End. 6-0, 191. Notre Dame
Born January 31, 1913, Roxbury, Massachusetts.
Died November 19, 1976, Arlington, Virginia
1936 Boston, 1937-1941, 1945 Washington
Inducted into Pro Football Hall of Fame in 1968.

Wayne Millner, who joined the Boston Redskins in 1936, was among the last of the outstanding two-way ends. When he wasn't playing strong defense, he was catching passes or blocking for the quarterback. The All-America from Notre Dame was competitive, determined, and known for cat-like reflexes and sure hands. He was at his best when the stakes were highest and pressure the greatest.

Those were the attributes that prompted Redskins coach Ray Flaherty to promise to resign "if we don't win the championship with that big Yankee playing end," his first comment after learning that Millner would be joining his 1936 team. The Redskins did win the NFL Eastern Division championship that season, and Millner was a big contributor. The Redskins lost the championship game to Green Bay.

In 1937, the Redskins moved to Washington and Sammy Baugh, the touted passer from Texas Christian, joined the team. For the next few seasons, the Redskins won two more divisional championships, as well as the 1937 NFL championship. Millner proved to be one of Baugh's favorite targets.

In the 1937 NFL championship showdown with the Chicago Bears (won by Washington 28-21), Baugh threw touchdown passes of 55 and 78 yards to Millner, then used Millner as a decoy when he threw the game's winning pass to Ed Justice.

Millner, a native of Roxbury, Massachusetts, caught 124 passes for 1,578 yards and 12 touchdowns in seven NFL seasons, meager fare today but impressive numbers in the 1930s. [DS/PF]

BOBBY MITCHELL

Running Back-Wide Receiver. 6-0, 195. Illinois
Born June 6, 1935, Hot Springs, Arkansas.
1958-1961 Cleveland, 1962-68 Washington
Inducted into Pro Football Hall of Fame in 1983.

Bobby Mitchell was blessed with exceptional speed, uncanny faking ability, and balance. These talents eventually would earn him a place in the Pro Football Hall of Fame.

Mitchell began his 11-year NFL career as a halfback with the Browns in 1958 and teamed with the incomparable Jim Brown to give Cleveland one of history's most potent running back combinations. Mitchell also was a breakaway threat as a punt- and kickoff-return specialist. Although Mitchell had several sensational games, coach Paul Brown wanted to pair another big back with Jim Brown. In 1962, he traded Mitchell to Washington for the rights to Syracuse All-America Ernie Davis.

Mitchell was a pioneer in Washington, the first African-American to star for the Redskins. He became a full-time flanker for Washington and one of the best catch-run yardage makers in pro football.

When he retired, his 14,078 combined net yards was the third-highest total in NFL history and his 91 touchdowns ranked fifth. Eighteen of his touchdowns came by rushing, 65 on receptions, 3 on punt returns, and 5 on kickoff returns. He amassed 7,954 yards on receptions and 2,735 yards on rushes. He won the NFL receiving title in 1962 with 72 catches. He didn't catch fewer than 58 passes his first six seasons in Washington. Mitchell was an all-pro pick in 1962 and 1964 and played in four Pro Bowls, one with the Browns and three with Washington. [DS/PF]

RON MIX

Tackle-Guard. 6-4, 250. Southern California
Born March 10, 1938, Los Angeles, California.
1960 Los Angeles Chargers, 1961-69 San Diego, 1971 Oakland
Inducted into Pro Football Hall of Fame in 1979.

Ron Mix excelled as an offensive tackle with the San Diego Chargers in the American Football League, but he always jokingly complained about the relatively little attention interior linemen received. While this lack of identity may be a reality for many offensive linemen, the finely tuned Mix combined determination and ability to rise above the line-of-scrimmage oblivion throughout his 10 years with the Chargers.

A powerful blocker who depended on superior technique—during his AFL career he was assessed only 2 holding penalties—Ron was nicknamed "The Intellectual Assassin." Out of uniform, he was articulate, intelligent, and modest. On the field, he eliminated defenders. He was an All-AFL selection eight times as a tackle and once as a guard, played in eight AFL All-Star games and five of the first six AFL championship games, and was unanimously chosen for the AFL's all-time team in 1969.

Perhaps the most surprising aspect of the Mix story is that he played football at all. In high school, he really wanted to play baseball and was fairly successful in track, but somehow ended up playing football, a sport he disliked. Ron did well enough to earn a scholarship to USC, where he gained almost 100 pounds and became an efficient tackle. When he signed with the Los Angeles Chargers in 1960, he intended to play only long enough "to get a start in life, just a year or two." But as he started to improve as a player, he began to enjoy football more. He decided to stick around. [DS/PF]

ART MONK

Wide Receiver. 6-3, 210. Syracuse
Born December 5, 1957, White Plains, New York.
1980-1993 Washington, 1994 New York Jets, 1995 Philadelphia

At various times during his career, Art Monk set NFL records for most catches in a career, most catches in a season, and most consecutive games with at least 1 catch. He was the prototype for today's bigger, stronger wide receivers. After starring at Syracuse, he came into the league at 6 feet 3 inches and 210 pounds. The average NFL wide receiver of the time was between 5-10 and 5-11 and weighed 175-185 pounds.

Monk, the Redskins' first first-round draft choice in 11 years in 1980, paid handsome and immediate dividends, peaking in the Redskins' Super Bowl years. He made "the dodge" pattern his signature. He got off the line quickly, took the ball 5 to 7 yards downfield before anyone could react, and went from there. He was fearless going into heavy traffic over the middle.

His coach for most of his career, Joe Gibbs, said this about Monk: "Art's the strongest outside receiver I have ever coached, and he's caught a lot of balls inside and taken the hit. He's big, he's strong, he's intelligent, he has everything. You don't get the whole package very often; he is it." Monk closed out his career with the Jets and Eagles after leaving the Redskins. [JJC]

JOE MONTANA

Quarterback. 6-2, 197. Notre Dame
Born June 11, 1956, Monongahela, Pennsylvania.
1979-1990, 1992 San Francisco, 1993-94 Kansas City

Joe Montana was compared to the legendary quarterbacks who came before him—including Bobby Layne, Sammy Baugh, Johnny Unitas, and Bart Starr—but all who follow Montana will be compared to him. Montana's time to shine was late-December and January when many other contemporary quarterbacks were at home polishing their trophies. The bigger the game, the better his performance.

His former mentor and coach with the San Francisco 49ers, Bill Walsh, said of his star pupil: "When the game is on the line, and you need someone to go in there and win it right now, I would rather have Joe Montana as my quarterback than anyone who ever played the game."

Montana engineered 31 winning fourth-quarter comebacks in his career, including a 92-yard drive in the closing seconds of Super Bowl XXIII.

Montana led his team to four Super Bowls triumphs in his 16-year career, and was named most valuable player of the game a record three times. Previously, he demonstrated his ability to direct comebacks at Notre Dame, where he led the Fighting Irish to the national championship in 1977, and capped his college career by bringing Notre Dame back from a 22-point deficit with five minutes left to win the 1979 Cotton Bowl. Despite his college heroics, he lasted until the third round of the 1979 NFL draft. [MS]

WARREN MOON

Quarterback. 6-3, 210. Washington
Born November 18, 1956, Los Angeles, California.
1984-1993 Houston, 1994-96 Minnesota, 1997-98 Seattle

Warren Moon is, in the words of former Houston Oilers wide receiver Butch Johnson, "a receiver's dream." To the rest of the NFL, he's a defensive coordinator's nightmare.

A former Rose Bowl most valuable player at the University of Washington, Moon led Edmonton to five Canadian Football League titles. He was the first player to pass for more than 20,000 yards in both the Canadian Football League and the NFL. Moon left the CFL after six seasons. "After winning and winning, it just wasn't the same challenge anymore," he said. "I needed something new."

Moon lost his first eight games with Houston, but he also set the club record for yards passing with 3,338 his first year with the team, a record he would break five more times.

Houston made the playoffs the first time with Moon during the strike-shortened 1987 season. The Oilers made the postseason six consecutive years with Moon, but they never advanced past the divisional playoffs.

Moon was traded to the Minnesota Vikings for two draft picks following the 1993 season. He responded with back-to-back 4,000-yard passing seasons in Minnesota. [MS]

LENNY MOORE

Halfback. 6-1, 198. Penn State
Born November 25, 1933, Reading, Pennsylvania.
1956-1967 Baltimore

Inducted into Pro Football Hall of Fame in 1975.
In pondering whom to pick first in the 1956 NFL draft, the Baltimore Colts asked the opinion of then-Penn State assistant coach Joe Paterno about Lenny Moore, the Nittany Lions' All-America halfback. Paterno's response was quick and decisive: "Go tell Weeb Ewbank not to miss this guy because if he does, it will be the greatest mistake he ever made." The Colts made Moore their choice and, just as Paterno had promised it would be, it was a wise one.

The speedy Moore won rookie-of-the-year honors in 1956 and amassed impressive credentials—including 12,393 combined net yards, 5,174 yards rushing, 363 pass receptions, and 113 touchdowns—in a 12-year career. He was first used as a combination flanker and running back but his primary responsibility was to catch passes. He soon became part of a lethal pass-catch team with Johnny Unitas.

In the Colts' drive to the 1958 NFL title, Moore was named all-pro for the first time. In the overtime championship game against the New York Giants, he grabbed 5 passes for 99 yards. In 1962, Moore returned to halfback. He seemed to be slowing down, but in 1964, he responded with his best season, scoring 20 touchdowns. For the fifth time, he was named all-pro and one wire service tabbed him the NFL player of the year. [DS/PF]

MARION MOTLEY
Fullback. 6-1, 238. South Carolina State, Nevada
Born June 5, 1920, Leesburg, Georgia.
1946-49 Cleveland (AAFC), 1950-53 Cleveland, 1955 Pittsburgh
Inducted into Pro Football Hall of Fame in 1968.
After studying miles of historic film, one football expert declared that Motley was not only the greatest fullback ever, but the greatest player.

Starting in 1946 and continuing into the 1950s, the Cleveland Browns, led by Motley, Otto Graham, Dante Lavelli, Mac Speedie, Bill Willis, and other stars, dominated pro football. Though justly honored for his running and blocking, Motley also was an exceptional linebacker. Even after free-substitution rules made him an offensive specialist, he would go in on goal-line defense.

Motley was a devastating pass-protection blocker, perhaps the best ever at his position. The Browns invented the "trap" play specifically for Motley. The play called for Graham to drop back to pass but then hand off to Motley when the opposing rush drew close. Motley would barrel straight ahead and, if necessary, over opponents who stood in his way. Once Motley's reputation was established, defenses never could concentrate solely on Graham again.

Blessed with speed as well as power, Motley, who played football at Canton McKinley High School, across the street from the present site of the Pro Football Hall of Fame, did much more than serve just as Graham's bodyguard. He was the leading rusher in the four-year history of the AAFC and was the NFL rushing champion in 1950. [DS/PF]

ANTHONY MUÑOZ
Tackle. 6-6, 285. Southern California
Born August 19, 1958, Ontario, California.
1980-1992 Cincinnati
Inducted into Pro Football Hall of Fame in 1998.
During his 13 seasons with the Cincinnati Bengals, Anthony Munoz defined his position. He played left tackle for the Bengals, giving him the responsibility of protecting right-handed quarterback Ken Anderson's blind side for the first six years of his career. When left-handed Boomer Esiason took over as quarterback, Munoz became his personal convoy on his rollout plays to the left. The southern Californian moved with seemingly effortless grace in the face of hard pass rushes from defensive ends, and he was awesome to watch as he simply crushed defenders on running plays. He helped the Bengals reach two Super Bowls.

Munoz was a bit of a gamble by the Bengals when they made him a first-round pick in 1980. He had missed most of his senior year at USC because of a knee injury, but Bengals general manager Paul Brown watched him put on a flawless performance against Ohio State in the Rose Bowl and decided to take a chance. Munoz missed just one game during his prolific career with the Bengals, and that game came in his final season.

Much of the reason for his good health came from his work ethic. He installed a complete set of weight equipment in the basement of his home and worked year round, every year, to improve his strength, even when he was at the peak of his career. He always was the top-graded blocker on his Bengals teams, twice helping Cincinnati to the Super Bowl, and he was named to the Pro Bowl 11 consecutive seasons.

"There has never been a lineman as great as Anthony Munoz, and I doubt whether we will see his equal again," said his line coach Jim McNally. [JC]

GEORGE MUSSO
Guard-Tackle. 6-2, 270. Millikin
Born April 8, 1910, Collinsville, Illinois.
1933-1944 Chicago Bears
Inducted into Pro Football Hall of Fame in 1982.
The Chicago Bears of the 1930s and 1940s were loaded with outstanding football players but it would be difficult to overlook the biggest star of them all—in size at least. George Musso stood 6 feet 2 inches and weighed 270 pounds. He specialized as a middle guard on defense and was far above average in all offensive assignments, particularly as a pass blocker and as a pulling guard on running plays.

Musso became the epitome of the powerful line play that made the Bears famous and fearsome. Opponents and teammates revered him as a quality two-way performer, someone who would force alterations to almost any team's game plan.

On offense, Musso began his NFL career as a tackle but, after four seasons, made the switch to guard when his team's personnel needs so dictated. He won All-NFL honors as a tackle in 1935 and as a guard in 1937.

Musso starred in football, basketball, baseball, and track at Millikin College, where he once lined up against Eureka College guard Ronald Reagan. Musso played well enough to earn a bid to the Chicago College All-Star Game, where his opponent was another future President, Gerald Ford.

When Musso joined the Bears in 1933, George Halas offered him a tryout and $90 per game if he made the squad. To seal the deal, Halas sent $5 for expenses—$3 for the train ride to Chicago and $2 for incidentals. Musso did make the team, and, eventually, Halas came through with the weekly $90 salary he first promised his big rookie. [DS/PF]

BRONISLAU (BRONKO) NAGURSKI

Fullback. 6-2, 225. Minnesota
Born November 3, 1908, Rainy River, Ontario, Canada.
Died January 7, 1990, International Falls, Minnesota
1930-37, 1943 Chicago Bears
Inducted into Pro Football Hall of Fame in 1963.

Bronko Nagurski, a bruising fullback for the Chicago Bears in the 1930s, was the symbol of football power. His exploits took on legendary proportions. In 1963, Nagurski unanimously was elected as a charter member of the Pro Football Hall of Fame.

Nagurski may be best remembered for his bull-like thrusts at the enemy line. Yet he had no peer as a blocker, and his tackling was as effective as any the game has seen. His offensive versatility is not well-known, but he also was quite a threat as a passer. He threw the winning touchdown pass in the 1932 playoff game against the Portsmouth Spartans. One year later, he led the Bears to another championship when he tossed a pair of touchdown passes in Chicago's 23-21 victory over the New York Giants.

Nagurski, who was born in Rainy River, Ontario, and grew up in International Falls, Minnesota, earned All-America honors at both tackle and fullback at the University of Minnesota. He starred for eight seasons in the NFL before he retired in 1937 to pursue a more profitable career in wrestling.

However, in 1943, player shortages caused by World War II forced the Bears to issue an SOS. Nagurski returned for one final season. He came back as a tackle but also carried the ball on key plays. Appropriately, he scored his final touchdown in the NFL title game and helped his teammates become champions. [DS/PF]

JOE NAMATH

Quarterback. 6-2, 200. Alabama
Born May 31, 1943, Beaver Falls, Pennsylvania.
1965-1976 New York Jets, 1977 Los Angeles Rams
Inducted into Pro Football Hall of Fame in 1985.

Although Joe Namath is best remembered for his sterling performance in the New York Jets' stunning 16-7 upset of the heavily favored Baltimore Colts in Super Bowl III, his 13-year tenure as one of the game's most exciting, proficient, and publicized quarterbacks clearly establishes his place in professional football history.

This was assured with his first pro football act, the signing of a $400,000 contract early in 1965 that gave the AFL its biggest victory in the costly interleague war of the 1960s. After that, his image as a swinging New York bachelor as much as his golden arm helped make him perhaps the most famous football player of his time.

In 1967, "Broadway Joe" became the first quarterback to pass for more than 4,000 yards in one season. In 1968, he was named AFL player of the year and a unanimous all-pro. He also was selected the most valuable player of Super Bowl III. Namath's pregame "guarantee" of victory, backed up by his 206 yards passing, was a major factor in assuring the competitive viability of the Super Bowl.

Namath excelled at Alabama, where he was hailed by veteran Crimson Tide coach Paul (Bear) Bryant as "the greatest athlete I have ever coached." But he was plagued with knee injuries through much of his pro career. Still, his career passing totals are impressive. In the 1968 AFL Championship Game, he threw 3 touchdown passes to lead New York to a 27-23 win over the Oakland Raiders that put the Jets in Super Bowl III. He was named to the All-Time AFL Team in 1969. [DS/PF]

ERNIE NEVERS

Fullback. 6-1, 205. Stanford
Born June 11, 1903, Willow River, Minnesota.
Died May 3, 1976, San Rafael, California.
1926-27 Duluth, 1929-1931 Chicago Cardinals
Inducted into Pro Football Hall of Fame in 1963.

Ernie Nevers, a star at Stanford and hero of the 1925 Rose Bowl, was in big demand when he finished his collegiate career. He signed pro basketball and baseball contracts. Pro football also beckoned, and Ole Haugsrud, owner of the Duluth Eskimos, signed the star to a then-incredible $15,000 contract in 1926.

Haugsrud promptly took his team on the road to showcase Nevers. Haugsrud named his team "Ernie Nevers's Eskimos." In 1926, the Eskimos played 29 games, 28 of them on the road, and traveled 17,000 miles. Nevers played all but 29 of a possible 1,740 minutes.

Injury forced Nevers to sit out the entire 1928 season but he returned as the do-everything man for the Chicago Cardinals in 1929. On Thanksgiving Day that season, Nevers set what today is the longest-standing National Football League individual record. The game—a rematch against the crosstown rivals, the Bears—was billed as a duel between Nevers and Red Grange, the Bears' legendary star. However, there was no duel as Nevers scored a remarkable 40 points to lead the Cardinals to a 40-6 victory. The following week, he scored all of his team's points again in a 19-0 win over Dayton to bring his total to 59 consecutive points scored.

Truly a 60-minute warrior, Nevers could do it all—run, pass, return kicks, punt, kick and call plays. In both 1930 and 1931, he also was the playing coach of the Cardinals. In each of the five years he played, he was named the all-league fullback. [DS/PF]

OZZIE NEWSOME

Tight End. 6-2, 232. Alabama
Born March 15, 1956, Muscle Shoals, Alabama.
1978-1990 Cleveland
Inducted into Pro Football Hall of Fame in 1999.

University of Alabama head coach Paul (Bear) Bryant called Ozzie Newsome "the best end I ever coached." The talented tight end did all he could to live up to the statement.

Newsome led Alabama in receptions all four years he was there and only got better in the National Football League. The Cleveland Browns drafted the 6-foot 2-inch,

232-pound Newsome in the first round of the 1978 draft and converted him from wide receiver to tight end. Newsome, who had been on two Southeastern Conference champions with the Crimson Tide, helped lead the Browns to the AFC Central Division title in his third season. Newsome only improved as he got more experience.

Against the New York Jets in 1984 Newsome set club single-game records with 14 receptions and 191 yards. The following year he passed Jackie Smith as the all-time NFL receiver among tight ends and also became just the tenth NFL player to catch at least 50 passes in six pro seasons. His 89 catches in both 1983 and 1984 were his career highs.

Although Newsome was chosen for three Pro Bowls and was All-AFC several times, he wasn't a typical tight end. He was more valuable as a receiver than as a blocker.

When he retired in 1991 after 13 seasons in the NFL, Newsome was fourth on the league's all-time list with 662 catches. He had 7,980 yards receiving and caught 47 touchdown passes. [MS]

RAY NITSCHKE

Linebacker. 6-3, 235. Illinois
Born December 29, 1936, Elmwood Park, Illinois.
Died March 8, 1998, Venice, Florida.
1958-1972 Green Bay
Inducted into Pro Football Hall of Fame in 1978.

The Green Bay Packers were the scourge of pro football during the 1960s, and Ray Nitschke was a large part of the reason.

The team's middle linebacker established himself as one of the Packers' most respected defensive performers. The former University of Illinois standout treasured the reputation he earned as one of the hardest hitters of all pro football players. "You want them to respect you when they run a play," Nitschke said. "You want them to remember you are there."

Nitschke certainly was remembered by his teammates and opponents. When the Packers, edged the New York Giants 16-7 in the 1962 NFL Championship Game, Nitschke was named the game's most valuable player. He was named to three all-pro teams in the 1960s, and in his lone Pro Bowl appearance following the 1964 season, he scored on a 42-yard interception return.

Although Nitschke was a rugged and fierce player, he also possessed fine-tuned athletic ability. He was quick enough to intercept 25 passes during his career. Off the field, Nitschke belied the fearsome image he portrayed during a game. In his dark horn-rimmed glasses and traditional business suit, he was thoughtful, intelligent, and soft-hearted, traits that his opponents never saw. [DS/PF]

TOMMY NOBIS

Linebacker. 6-2, 235. Texas
Born September 20, 1943, San Antonio, Texas.
1966-1976 Atlanta

"If he had been on a better team and had better legs—look out. He was everything you wanted in a linebacker. Nobody hit harder." That's how one pro football historian saw Tommy Nobis.

The Texas All-America was the first player chosen in the 1966 NFL draft by the expansion Falcons. But he was also the first choice of the Oilers of the AFL. When astronaut Frank Borman was orbiting the earth, he radioed back to NASA headquarters in Houston, "Tell Nobis to sign with the Oilers." Nobis ignored the advice from the heavens and signed with the Falcons. He became an immediate star, but about the only one the Falcons had. Although he earned the respect of his peers—the red-headed Texan made all-pro in his second season—he had little help.

"I would have liked to have been Jack Lambert behind the Steel Curtain, or even Sam Huff and lined up behind those guys [Andy Robustelli and Dick Modzelewski], or even Lee Roy Jordan behind Bob Lilly, but I wasn't and there's not a danged thing I could do about it," Nobis said.

What the five-time Pro Bowl selection did was play with a special relentlessness for 11 seasons—until his knees could take no more.

"After reading and hearing about Nobis [before his first game against him], I knew he could not be that good," Cowboys running back Don Perkins said. "Well, he was that good! He was the toughest middle linebacker I ever played against." [JJC]

LEO NOMELLINI

Defensive Tackle. 6-3, 264. Minnesota
Born June 19, 1924, Lucca, Italy.
1950-1963 San Francisco
Inducted into Pro Football Hall of Fame in 1969.

Leo Nomellini made life miserable for opponents for 14 seasons in the National Football League. From his first day in the NFL in 1950 until he retired after the 1963 season, Nomellini never missed a game as a member of the San Francisco 49ers. During his career, he was known as one of the best tackles in the game, both on offense and defense.

One of the 49ers' first decisions when they joined the NFL was to select Nomellini, a consensus All-America at the University of Minnesota, as their first pick in the 1950 draft.

Nomellini became one of the few players ever to be named all-pro both on offense and defense. "The Lion" won offensive honors in 1951 and 1952 and defensive laurels in 1953, 1954, 1957, and 1959. He also played in 10 Pro Bowl games during his first 12 seasons in pro football.

At 6 feet 3 inches and 264 pounds, Nomellini had everything needed to be an all-time great—size, speed, agility, aggressiveness and, perhaps most important, dedication to the game. He was one of the best pass rushers the NFL has seen and it wasn't often that opponents would run his way. On offense, he was an outstanding pass blocker and adept at opening holes. In 1955, he played nearly 60 minutes of every game when injuries created a severe personnel problem for the 49ers. [DS/PF]

***KEN NORTON, JR.**

Linebacker. 6-2, 241. UCLA
Born September 29, 1966, Lincoln, Illinois.
1988-1993 Dallas, 1994-98 San Francisco

Ken Norton, Sr., didn't take up boxing until he was 22. Similarly, Ken Norton, Jr., came late to football, but both have experienced undisputed championship careers.

Norton didn't even play football until he was a junior at

Westchester High in Los Angeles, California. He averaged 8.8 yards per carry as a senior tailback, but UCLA switched him to linebacker. He earned a letter as a freshman and was named first team All-America as a senior. He did not, however, find quick success in the NFL. Norton missed 13 games as a rookie because of a thumb injury, and an injured knee limited his playing time for the 1-15 Cowboys in 1989.

As the Cowboys got better and Norton became healthier (he hasn't missed a start since 1991), he found prosperity. In Super Bowl XXVII, Norton made 9 tackles, including a key stop of Kenneth Davis at the 1-yard line, and he capped off the day with a 9-yard fumble recovery for a touchdown. He helped the Cowboys win another Super Bowl the following year even though he played half the season with a torn right biceps muscle.

After he left Dallas for San Francisco in 1994, Norton's Midas touch made him the first player in history to win three straight Super Bowl rings. He got there by denying the Cowboys their third straight Super Bowl appearance with a game-high 10 tackles in the 1994 NFC Championship Game. In 1995, he scored a touchdown on an interception for the first time in his career, and then he did it again later in the same game. Norton, who holds the 49ers' record for most tackles in a season, made his third Pro Bowl appearance after the 1997 season. [MS]

MERLIN OLSEN

Defensive Tackle. 6-5, 270. Utah State
Born September 15, 1940, Logan, Utah.
1962-1976 Los Angeles Rams
Inducted into Pro Football Hall of Fame in 1982.

Merlin Olsen, an All-America and Outland Trophy winner from Utah State, was one of the NFL's dominant defensive stars during his 15-year career. He was big, fast, agile, and smart as the stabilizing leader of the famed Fearsome Foursome defensive line.

Olsen, the Rams' first-round draft pick in 1962, was an instant hit who won the starting left defensive tackle job in the third week of his rookie season. He never relinquished the starting role. Altogether, he played 208 regular-season games for the Rams, the last 198 in succession as a starter.

The 6-foot 5-inch, 270-pound Olsen was named to the Pro Bowl a league-record 14 consecutive times. He missed a bid only after 1976, his final season. Olsen was a unanimous all-pro selection five consecutive years during the heyday of the "Fearsome Foursome" from 1966-1970.

Olsen was honored as either the Rams' top defensive lineman or most valuable player six consecutive years and, in 1970, was named to the club's all-time team. In 1974, the Maxwell Club selected him as the NFL player of the year. In 1982, he was selected to the Pro Football Hall of Fame. His post-playing career as an actor and football broadcaster earned him additional fame. [DS/PF]

JIM OTTO

Center. 6-2, 255. Miami
Born January 5, 1938, Wausau, Wisconsin.
1960-1974 Oakland
Inducted into Pro Football Hall of Fame in 1980.

It is difficult to imagine one player dominating one position more thoroughly than Jim Otto did both in the American Football League and in the National Football League from 1960-1974. The Wausau, Wisconsin, native joined the newly founded Oakland Raiders in 1960 and for the next 15 seasons he was the Raiders' starting center.

Otto, who starred as a center and linebacker at the University of Miami in Florida, won All-AFL acclaim 10 consecutive seasons and was the All-AFC center for three more years from 1970-72. He was named to the All-Time All-AFL Team following the 1969 season. During his 15-year career, he participated in all nine AFL All-Star games and the first three AFC-NFC Pro Bowls.

When Otto retired following the 1974 season, he had started in 210 consecutive regular-season games. During Otto's career, the Raiders, who had once been AFL doormats, rose to prominence. Oakland won seven division championships in an eight-year period from 1967-1974. The 1967 Raiders were AFL champions and played against the Green Bay Packers in Super Bowl II. [DS/PF]

ALAN PAGE

Defensive Tackle. 6-4, 225. Notre Dame
Born August 7, 1945, Canton, Ohio.
1967-1978 Minnesota, 1978-1981 Chicago Bears
Inducted into Pro Football Hall of Fame in 1988.

Alan Page, a consensus All-America at Notre Dame in 1966, was the Minnesota Vikings' second pick in the first round of the first combined AFL-NFL draft in 1967. Although he had played defensive end, the Vikings moved him to defensive right tackle, where he played his entire 16-year NFL career.

Page, who was born in Canton, Ohio (the birthplace of the National Football League), had the rare honor in 1971 of being a defensive player who was named NFL most valuable player. He was named the National Football Conference's defensive player of the year four times. For nine consecutive seasons from 1969-1977, Page was all-pro. He also was named to nine consecutive Pro Bowls from 1968-1976.

Page excelled with the Vikings for 12 seasons. But after six games in 1978, Minnesota released him. The Chicago Bears quickly signed him, and he moved into the starting lineup without missing a game. Page finished his career in 1981 after playing 238 games, all but three of them as a starter. Included were 16 playoff games and Super Bowls IV, VIII, IX, and XI.

Unlike many stars who steadily build up their weight after turning pro, Page started his NFL career at 278 pounds and gradually pared down to a more mobile weight as his career progressed. Intelligent and hard-working, with amazing speed and quickness, Page accumulated some imposing career statistics. Unofficial figures show that he recovered 23 opponents' fumbles, blocked 28 kicks, and recorded 173 sacks.

After retiring from the National Football League, Page became a lawyer and was elected to the Minnesota Supreme Court. [DS/PF]

JACK PARDEE

Linebacker. 6-2, 230. Texas A&M
Born April 19, 1936, Exira, Iowa.

1957-1964, 1966-1971 Los Angeles, 1972 Washington
The NFL's best linebackers seem to enjoy long careers, and Jack Pardee was one of the really good ones. To reach the NFL, Pardee had to survive Paul (Bear) Bryant's legendary boot camp-style preseason practices at Texas A&M. Pardee excelled under Bryant and went on to play 15 seasons in pro football. He also successfully battled cancer along the way.

Pardee was chosen to play in only one Pro Bowl, but was consistently rated among the best at his position. "I never fully appreciated Pardee until I saw him with the Redskins," said National Football League linebacker Bob Walker, who played against Pardee. "He was at the end of his career, but he still did everything right. Talk about consistency; talk about Jack Pardee."

Pardee was part of George Allen's Over-the-Hill-Gang that played in Super Bowl VII.

Late in his career, the rawhide-tough linebacker still had so much savvy and played position defense so well that he intercepted 5 passes at age 35. After the end of his playing career, Pardee took his quiet strength into coaching. He had success at all levels and in nearly every league pro football had to offer. [JJC]

CLARENCE (ACE) PARKER

Quarterback. 5-11, 168. Duke
Born May 17, 1912, Portsmouth, Virginia.
1937-1941 Brooklyn, 1945 Boston, 1946 New York Yankees (AAFC)
Inducted into Pro Football Hall of Fame in 1972.
Clarence (Ace) Parker never intended to play pro football when he completed his career as an All-America tailback at Duke University in 1936. Instead, he signed a contract with the Philadelphia Athletics and hit a home run in his first major league at bat.

But, after the 1937 baseball season, he obtained permission from the Athletics to give pro football a try. He joined the Brooklyn Dodgers of the National Football League, still expecting to play just one pro football season.

However, baseball hits were scarce after his initial home run, while his football career blossomed with the Dodgers. The Dodgers of the early 1940s were a constant threat to the Giants and Redskins for Eastern Division supremacy in the NFL, and Parker was the driving force of the Dodgers' attack.

Military service in World War II interrupted his football career in 1942. He returned to the pros in 1945 with the Boston Yanks, then added a brilliant final campaign with the New York Yankees of the All-America Football Conference in 1946.

Parker wasn't exceptionally fast, but he performed many tasks, including running, passing, catching passes, punting, kicking, returning punts and kickoffs, and playing defense. In 1940, he was named the NFL's most valuable player. [DS/PF]

JIM PARKER

Guard-Tackle. 6-3, 273. Ohio State
Born March 3, 1934, Macon, Georgia.
1957-1967 Baltimore
Inducted into Pro Football Hall of Fame in 1973.
Jim Parker was an exceptional star with the Baltimore Colts from 1957-1967. The former All-America from Ohio State split his National Football League career between tackle and guard and became the first "pure" offensive lineman to be elected to the Pro Football Hall of Fame.

Parker, the Colts' first-round draft choice in 1957, specialized in protecting the quarterback. In Parker's case, he may have received more attention than most offensive line stars because he was helping to protect one of the NFL's greatest passers, Johnny Unitas. The fact that Parker and his teammates did the job well goes a long way toward explaining the unprecedented passing success of Unitas and the overall success of the Colts.

"It didn't take long to learn the one big rule," Parker said. "Just keep 'em away from John. I remember coach Weeb Ewbank telling me, 'You can be the most unpopular man on the team if the quarterback gets hurt.' How could I ever forget that?"

Parker, a native of Macon, Georgia, began his career at left tackle, where he earned all-league honors four times. In the middle of the 1962 season, he switched to left guard, where he was named all-pro four more times. During this period, Parker played in eight consecutive Pro Bowls. He ended his career late in the 1967 season because of a knee injury. [DS/PF]

LEMAR PARRISH

Cornerback. 5-11, 180. Lincoln (Missouri)
Born December 13, 1947, Riviera Beach, Florida.
1970-77 Cincinnati, 1978-1981 Washington, 1982 Buffalo
Lemar Parrish was a small defensive back from a small college who took his talent a long way in the NFL.

Parrish played his college football at Lincoln College in Missouri and impressed Paul Brown enough for the Cincinnati Bengals' head coach to draft him in the seventh round in 1970. He made an immediate impact with the Bengals, who lost six of their first seven games, but rallied to win the Central Division title in just their third season.

The Bengals also made the playoffs in 1973 and 1975 but couldn't advance past the divisional playoffs. Although Parrish anchored the Bengals' defense as a cornerback and Cincinnati's special teams as a kickoff returner, he moved to the Washington Redskins in 1978 and had his best season the following year. Parrish led the NFC with 9 interceptions in 1979, but the Redskins blew two leads to Dallas on the final day of the season to miss the playoffs.

Parrish had a six-game interception streak—the third-longest in NFL history—that overlapped the 1978 and 1979 seasons. He was named to the Pro Bowl eight times. After spending the 1982 season with Buffalo, Parrish retired with 47 career interceptions. [MS]

WALTER PAYTON

Running Back. 5-10, 202. Jackson State
Born July 25, 1954, Columbia, Mississippi.
1975-1987 Chicago Bears
Inducted into Pro Football Hall of Fame in 1993.
Walter Payton dominates the rushing section of the NFL record book. His records include 16,726 total yards, 10 seasons with 1,000 or more yards rushing, 275 yards rushing in one game against Minnesota in 1977, and 77

games with more than 100 yards rushing.

What the record book does not reflect was Payton's unselfish leadership. Nor does it mention his outstanding blocking. Nor does the book betray how dangerous he was on an option pass. And there should be a footnote about his personality—he was nicknamed "Sweetness"—which made him one of the most popular players ever to wear a Chicago Bears uniform, which he did for 13 seasons.

The record book tells us that Payton won the NFC rushing title five consecutive years from 1976 to 1980 and that his best season was in 1977 when he ran for 1,852 yards. He also led the NFC with 96 points in 1977.

He was named all-pro and All-NFC seven times and played in nine Pro Bowls. He was selected as the NFL's most valuable player and the NFL player of the year in 1977 and 1985, and the NFL offensive player of the year in 1977. Payton led Chicago to the playoffs six times, and helped the Bears win Super Bowl XX following the 1985 season. [DS/PF]

DREW PEARSON

Wide Receiver. 6-0, 183. Tulsa
Born January 12, 1951, South River, New Jersey.
1973-1983 Dallas

Drew Pearson caught 489 passes for the Dallas Cowboys during his 11-year career. He was the favorite target of quarterbacks Roger Staubach and Danny White.

Pearson also is a great success story. He played quarterback his first two years at the University of Tulsa, then labored in obscurity as a flanker his final two seasons when his team employed a running offense. Yet, midway through his rookie season with the Cowboys, he became the team's starting flanker and kept the job for the rest of his career. He was selected to three Pro Bowls.

"When Drew came to Dallas after he signed his contract and we watched him work out every day with Roger, we knew we had something different here," legendary former Dallas Cowboys' coach Tom Landry once observed. "Drew became the kind of receiver who could catch ten passes a game. He always could get open, he could get deep in a hurry, and he was a great, fluid receiver. He had a knack, a feel, for finding daylight. Add to that outstanding moves, and Roger's great confidence in him, and you had a great success story."

The Cowboys always pointed out that Pearson came to them with his only claim to fame being the son-in-law of Harlem Globetrotters basketball legend Marques Haynes. But before his career ended, opponents knew who Pearson was.

Roger Wehrli, an all-pro cornerback with the St. Louis Cardinals, summed up Pearson's talents: "Drew simply had great hands and really deceiving speed. He always had something extra, acceleration, or a little something. And anything he touched, he caught." [JC]

JOE PERRY

Fullback. 6-0, 200. Compton (California) Junior College
Born January 22, 1927, Stevens, Arizona.
1948-1960, 1963 San Francisco, 1961-62 Baltimore
Inducted into Pro Football Hall of Fame in 1969.

Joe Perry put Compton Junior College on the football map when he scored 22 touchdowns in one season. However, before he completed his college career, he was called into military service. He was playing for the Alameda, California, Naval Training Station team when he was spotted by a 49ers tackle who passed the word to the San Francisco hierarchy. In 1948, Perry joined the 49ers and immediately established himself as one of the premier running backs in the AAFC. Known for his blazing speed, he earned the nickname "The Jet" during his second pro season.

The flashy fullback became the first player in NFL history to rush for 1,000 yards in consecutive seasons when he accomplished the feat in 1953 and 1954. A veteran of three Pro Bowls, Perry was a small fullback unsuited for constantly pounding up the middle, but was able to slash through the line with his quickness.

In 1961, his fourteenth season, Perry was traded to Baltimore. He led the Colts in rushing during his first season with the team. He returned to the 49ers for one more season in 1962. [DS/PF]

PETE PIHOS

End. 6-1, 210. Indiana
Born October 22, 1923, Orlando, Florida.
1947-1955 Philadelphia
Inducted into Pro Football Hall of Fame in 1970.

Pihos began his NFL career as a two-way end. When the platoon system was instituted, he concentrated on offense until the Eagles needed a defensive end in 1952. He switched to defense for one year and earned all-pro honors. Then for the remaining three years of his career, he played offense and led the league in receiving all three seasons.

Pihos was Philadelphia's third-round draft pick in 1945, although military service prevented him from playing until 1947. Extremely durable, he missed just one game during his nine NFL seasons. Immediately after Pihos joined the Eagles, Philadelphia marched to its first divisional championship. In the playoff game against the Pittsburgh Steelers for the Eastern Division crown, he blocked a punt to set up the first touchdown in the Eagles' 21-0 victory.

Although the team failed to win the NFL title in 1947, the Eagles bounced back with league championships the next two years. In 1948, the Eagles defeated the Chicago Cardinals 7-0. One year later, Pihos caught a 31-yard touchdown pass in the Eagles' 14-0 victory over the Rams.

Pihos did not have great speed, but he was a consistent receiver with sure hands, clever moves, and courage. He led the NFL in receiving from 1953-55, catching 63, 60, and 62 passes. He earned all-pro honors six times in nine seasons and played in six Pro Bowls. [DS/PF]

JIM PLUNKETT

Quarterback. 6-2, 215. Stanford
Born December 5, 1947, Santa Clara, California.
1971-75 New England, 1976-77 San Francisco,
1978-1986 Raiders

Jim Plunkett was drafted to be the savior of the New England Patriots. Instead, he eventually led the Raiders to two Super Bowl victories.

Plunkett helped resurrect football at Stanford University and was expected to do the same with the Patriots in the National Football League. He led Stanford to its first Rose

Bowl victory in 30 years and finished his career as the NCAA all-time total-offense leader. The 1970 Heisman Trophy winner was selected by the Patriots with the first pick in the 1971 draft and responded by winning rookie-of-the-year honors.

Injuries, poor protection, and disagreements with former Patriots coach Chuck Fairbanks resulted in a trade that sent Plunkett back to California in 1976. After two years with the San Francisco 49ers, he was released. The Oakland Raiders, a team famous for finding stars among players no one else wanted, signed him. And when Dan Pastorini injured his leg in 1980, Plunkett got another chance. This time he fulfilled his promise.

The Raiders became the first wild-card team to win the Super Bowl. Plunkett, who was NFL comeback player of the year, threw a Super Bowl record 80-yard touchdown pass and earned most-valuable-player honors in a 27-10 victory over the Philadelphia Eagles in Super Bowl XV. Three years later Plunkett again helped guide the Raiders to the Super Bowl and engineered a 38-9 victory over the favored Redskins. Plunkett's Super Bowl quarterback rating of 122.8 is second only to Joe Montana. [MS]

FREDERICK (FRITZ) POLLARD

Halfback. 5-7, 149. Brown
Born January 27, 1894, Chicago, Illinois.
Died May 11, 1986, Silver Spring, Maryland.
1920-21, 1925-26 Akron, 1922 Milwaukee, 1923, 1925 Hammond, 1925 Providence

In 1921, Pollard became the first African-American to serve as an NFL head coach. But he not only was the Akron Pros' coach that year, he also was their star runner and a team leader.

A fast, elusive, and courageous runner, Pollard led Brown University to the Rose Bowl in 1915 and was a consensus All-America the next year—only the second African-American to be so honored. After army service in World War I, he joined Akron the year before the NFL was formed. In 1920, when the Pros went undefeated to win the league's first championship, defense was the team's strength, but contemporary accounts indicate Pollard was the most feared running back in the fledgling league.

After 1921, he played and sometimes coached for Milwaukee, Hammond, Providence, and Akron again through 1926. He played as many or more games for strong independent teams in the Pennsylvania coal district.

After his playing career ended, Pollard organized and coached the Chicago Brown Bombers, an independent team of African-Americans that played from 1927-1933. Then he went on to a successful business career. He was elected to the College Football Hall of Fame in 1954. [BC]

GARRARD (BUSTER) RAMSEY

Guard-Linebacker. 6-1, 215. William & Mary
Born March 16, 1920, Townsend, Tennessee.
1946-1950 Chicago Cardinals

Ramsey was a fiery guard-linebacker who helped the Chicago Cardinals to their greatest period of success in the half decade after World War II.

His reputation for line play was established early. His Knoxville (Tennessee) High School team played for the national prep championship in the Orange Bowl in 1937, and he was twice elected to the All-Southern High School Team. At William & Mary, he was All-Southern Conference guard for three years and named to several All-America teams in 1941 and 1942. After his final college season, he starred in the Blue-Gray Game and started in the 1943 Chicago College All-Star Game.

Before he could join the Cardinals, Ramsey spent two years in the U.S. Navy during World War II, twice being named to All-Service teams. He was chosen to play in a second College All-Star Game in 1946.

After years as also-rans, the Cardinals were on their way up when Ramsey arrived in 1946. They won the NFL championship in 1947 and the Western Division title in 1948. The 1948 squad narrowly lost the NFL Championship Game to the Eagles in a blizzard.

A reliable blocker on offense and a fearsome defender at linebacker, Ramsey won all-league honors from 1947 through 1949. In 1969, the Pro Football Hall of Fame Selection Committee named the durable Ramsey to its All-Pro Squad of the 1940s.

Retiring after the 1950 season, Ramsey served one year as an assistant coach for Chicago, then joined Buddy Parker at Detroit. He was widely credited with developing the staunch defense that helped the Lions win three NFL championships and four division titles. [BC]

*JOHN RANDLE

Defensive Tackle. 6-1, 272. Texas A&I
Born December 12, 1967, Hearne, Texas.
1990-98 Minnesota

The name of the game for John Randle is intimidation, and it works. With his face elaborately painted with eye-black—"It's my war paint," he says—Randle constantly is in motion, spinning past double teams and hurling himself at the ball carrier or the quarterback.

A seven-time Pro Bowl starter, Randle has 96 career sacks (95 since 1991). Only Reggie White and Bruce Smith have had as many consecutive 10-sack seasons (7). Randle also is durable: He did not miss a game in his first nine seasons, appearing in 144 consecutively.

Randle led the NFL with 15 sacks in 1997, but perhaps more impressive was his switch to defensive end for the last two regular-season games and the playoffs. Forced to change positions because of injuries, Randle had 6 sacks in 4 games, including 3 in his first start at end against Detroit. He was so effective there, the Vikings occasionally slipped him into that spot as a change of pace in 1998, as if Randle doesn't already keep opposing offenses guessing. [MS]

*ANDRE REED

Wide Receiver. 6-2, 190. Kutztown State
Born January 29, 1964. Allentown, Pennsylvania.
Buffalo 1985-1998

Andre Reed quietly has crept up the list of all-time receivers in the NFL. Only Jerry Rice and Art Monk have more career receptions, Rice is the only other player with a dozen seasons of 50 or more catches, and just six players have more career receiving yards. Reed, who has been named to the Pro Bowl seven times, has appeared in more games than any other player in Bills' history. His 14 years in Buffalo ties a club record with teammate Bruce Smith.

Reed was a cornerstone of Buffalo's No-Huddle offense that helped the Bills compile a record of 60-26 from 1988-1993. Reed has appeared in 20 career postseason games against a dozen different teams. He has caught a pass in all but 2 of those games and has averaged more than 14 yards per catch on 85 career postseason receptions.

Reed's 3 touchdown receptions in Buffalo's remarkable 41-38 comeback victory against the Oilers in the 1992 playoffs tied an NFL postseason record. In four Super Bowl starts, he caught 27 passes for 323 yards, including an 8-catch, 152-yard performance in a losing effort against Dallas in Super Bowl XXVII.

Reed was a high school quarterback in Allentown, Pennsylvania, but he shifted to receiver at Kutztown State, where he set nine school records. Reed was picked in the fourth round of the 1985 draft that also brought Bruce Smith to Buffalo. [MS]

MEL RENFRO

Cornerback-Safety. 6-0, 191. Oregon
Born December 30, 1941, Houston, Texas.
1964-1977 Dallas
Inducted into Pro Football Hall of Fame in 1996.

Renfro was an All-America halfback as well as an outstanding track star at the University of Oregon when the Dallas Cowboys selected him as their second-round pick in the 1964 draft. He went to camp expecting to score touchdowns, not prevent them. But, as coach Tom Landry explained, the Cowboys were well stocked on offense so Renfro would play safety until an offensive position on the team opened up. "I guess I made one fat mistake," Renfro said years later. "I played defense too well."

Renfro excelled as a defensive back for Dallas from 1964-1977. He began his career at safety but switched to cornerback in his fifth season. During his first three seasons, Renfro also starred as a punt- and kickoff-return specialist.

Renfro had a spectacular rookie season. He led the Cowboys with 7 interceptions, topped the NFL in both punt- and kickoff-return yardage, and culminated his great season with an invitation to the Pro Bowl. Blessed with 4.65 speed, he earned Pro Bowl invitations his first 10 seasons but missed the 1973 game because of injury. An all-pro choice in 1965 and 1969, he won all-pro honors in 1971 and 1973 and was a three-time All-NFC pick. Renfro played in eight NFL/NFC Championship Games—his interception set up the Cowboys winning touchdown in a 17-10 victory over the San Francisco 49ers in the 1970 NFC title game—and four Super Bowls.

He led the National Football League with 10 interceptions in 1969, and in his 14 seasons Renfro intercepted 52 passes. [DS/PF]

JERRY RICE

Wide Receiver. 6-2, 200. Mississippi Valley State.
Born October 13, 1962, Starkville, Mississippi.
1985-1998 San Francisco

Jerry Rice always has been good with his hands. He had to be. As a high school student, the future record-setting wide receiver helped his father painstakingly lay bricks in the sweltering summer months in Oktibbeha County, Mississippi.

"I would be standing on this tall scaffold and they would toss the bricks up to me," he said. "I was catching bricks all day. One of my brothers would stack four bricks on top of each other and toss them up. They might go this way and that, and I would catch all four. I did it so many times, it was just a reaction."

Rice has used that catching ability to become one of the greatest pass receivers in NFL history. He owns nearly every NFL career receiving record. Additionally, his 19 touchdowns, 124 receptions, and 1,811 receiving yards are all postseason records. But Rice's greatness goes far beyond his numbers. His work ethic is legendary, and he constantly strives to improve his game. Few receivers can match what he can do after catching the football. And, when it comes to clutch catches, he wrote the book.

Rice was the 49ers' first-round draft choice out of Mississippi Valley State in 1985. He has helped San Francisco to three Super Bowl victories, two with Joe Montana at quarterback and one with Steve Young. In Super Bowl XXIII, his 11 catches for 215 yards earned him most-valuable-player honors. [MS]

LES RICHTER

Linebacker. 6-3, 248. California
Born October 6, 1930, Fresno, California.
1954-1962 Los Angeles Rams

One of Les Richter's claims to fame is that he once was traded for an entire team. In 1952, the Rams sent 11 men (including players and draft choices) to the Dallas Texans, who had taken the California All-America linebacker second overall in the draft, for Richter. And Richter, because of a military obligation, couldn't even report to the Rams until 1954.

When he got to the team, he became an immediate starter at middle linebacker and remained so for his entire career. The NFL was filled with great middle linebackers during Richter's days in the league. The Giants' Sam Huff, the Lions' Joe Schmidt, and the Bears' Bill George were the most honored, and Ray Nitschke of the Packers was just establishing himself in Green Bay. But, despite formidable competition from middle linebackers with stronger teams, Richter played in eight consecutive Pro Bowls—every season but his ninth and final year.

At the beginning of his career, Richter doubled as the Rams' kicker and made 104 of 107 extra points and 29 field goals.

After their 1955 division title, the Rams slumped. Richter was a bulwark on some pretty poor teams throughout the late 1950s. Once, when things got really bad, he became a 60-minute man—he played middle linebacker and guard. The Rams wanted their best 11 players on the field at all times—and Richter was one of them. After football, he became an auto-racing executive. [JJC]

JOHN RIGGINS

Running Back. 6-2, 240. Kansas
Born August 4, 1949, Seneca, Kansas.
1971-75 New York Jets, 1976-79, 1981-85 Washington
Inducted into Pro Football Hall of Fame in 1992.

Riggins was not a spectacular running back, but he was a classic workhorse who specialized in the tough yardage in the big games—a runner for the long run, not for long runs. In 14 seasons and 175 games, he carried 2,916 times for 11,352 yards and 104 touchdowns. In spite of his long-term excellence, Riggins was named all-pro only in 1983 and played in just one Pro Bowl.

Riggins, a Big Eight Conference rushing champion who broke Gale Sayers's school rushing record at the University of Kansas, was the number-one pick of the New York Jets in the 1971 NFL draft. He played in New York for five years, but signed with the Redskins as a free agent in 1976. His nine-year tenure with the Redskins was interrupted in 1980, when he sat out the season in a contract dispute.

Riggins, who played in the 1982 and '83 NFC Championship Games and Super Bowls XVII and XVIII, made the most of his postseason appearances. He was named the most valuable player of Super Bowl XVII after carrying the ball 38 times for 166 yards, including a 43-yard touchdown run on fourth down that clinched Washington's 27-17 victory over Miami. He followed that success with a sensational season in 1983 when he rushed for a career-high 1,347 yards and an NFL-record 24 touchdowns. [DS/PF]

JIM RINGO

Center. 6-1, 235. Syracuse
Born November 21, 1931, Orange, New Jersey.
1953-1963 Green Bay, 1964-67 Philadelphia.
Inducted into Pro Football Hall of Fame in 1981.

Jim Ringo was an all-pro even before the Green Bay Packers began dominating the National Football League in the 1960s. The hard-working center played with the Packers from 1953-1963, then with the Philadelphia Eagles from 1964-67.

Ringo joined the Packers in 1953 as a seventh-round draft pick from Syracuse University. He steadily grew in stature and earned his first all-pro designation in 1957, his fifth season.

Ringo was one of the last of a vanishing breed in the National Football League, a lineman who didn't benefit from tremendous size. He reported to his rookie camp at 211 pounds and never weighed more than 235 pounds at any time during his long pro career. Yet, he responded to the constant challenge of facing much bigger opponents as he utilized his quickness and innate football intelligence to dominate his opponents. Ringo also established his durability and desire with an NFL-record 182 consecutive starts.

Ringo earned all-league honors 7 of his 11 years in Green Bay and was named the top NFL center of the 1960s. In 1964, he was traded to the Eagles. During his combined Packers-Eagles tenure, he played in 10 Pro Bowls and was one of the few players ever to start for both the East and West squads in the postseason classic. The 1968 Pro Bowl was the final game of his 15-season career. [DS/PF]

DAVE ROBINSON

Linebacker. 6-3, 245. Penn State
Born May 3, 1941, Mt. Holly, New Jersey.
1963-1972 Green Bay, 1973-74 Washington

During the Green Bay Packers' reign as three-time National Football League champions from 1965-67, Dave Robinson was perhaps the most unheralded member of their great linebacking trio that also included Ray Nitschke and Leroy Caffey.

Robinson was an extremely intelligent player. "All the keys we must read are the science and they are designed to get me close enough to play football. Then it's seek and destroy," he said.

Robinson was an all-America end at Penn State, where he played more like a third tackle on offense, rarely catching a pass but blocking aggressively, and was a demon on defense. Green Bay made him its first-round draft choice in 1963, and Packers coach Vince Lombardi made him a linebacker when Robinson reported to the team. Robinson was fast enough to cover running backs on pass patterns, big enough to blitz, and tough enough to battle the tight end.

Robinson had a knack for making big plays. In the 1966 NFL Championship Game against the Cowboys, the Packers had a 7-point lead in the final minute, but Dallas had the ball at Green Bay's 6-yard line. On fourth down, Robinson raced past a pair of Cowboys blockers as quarterback Don Meredith rolled out. Robinson forced Meredith to throw a poor pass that defensive back Tom Brown intercepted in the end zone to seal Green Bay's victory and a trip to Super Bowl I. [JC]

JOHNNY ROBINSON

Safety. 6-0, 195. Louisiana State
Born September 9, 1938, Dehli, Louisiana.
1960-62 Dallas Texans, 1963-1971 Kansas City

Johnny Robinson was the "other" halfback alongside Heisman Trophy winner Billy Cannon for Louisiana State University's 1958 national-championship team. Ultimately, his NFL career outshone Cannon's.

Robinson began his pro career as a running back with the Dallas Texans in the AFL, and he played well, totaling 658 yards on 150 carries and 1,212 yards on 77 catches in two seasons. However, when the Texans moved to Kansas City and became the Chiefs a year later, Robinson was switched to safety. He became an all-pro at his new position. "He was a chessmaster, and it's a chess match out there," said Chiefs Hall of Fame linebacker Willie Lanier. "You have to have the mindset of the quarterback. Johnny had that. He was intuitive. He just had a knack for the game."

Robinson, a Louisiana native, was All-AFL for five consecutive years, and when the league merged with the NFL in 1970, he was named as a safety on the All-Time All-AFL Team. His 53 interceptions were fifth on the NFL's all-time list when he retired.

Robinson was involved in a court battle before his rookie season. Like Cannon, he signed with both leagues—the AFL Texans and the NFL Detroit Lions. Robinson said he didn't prefer Dallas for the money, it was because he didn't want to live in the snow. "I had lived in Baton Rouge all my life and had never seen snow. That may not seem important now, but at the time it was a prime consideration." [JCC]

ANDY ROBUSTELLI

Defensive End. 6-0, 230. Arnold College
Born December 6, 1925, Stamford, Connecticut.
1951-55 Los Angeles Rams, 1956-1964 New York Giants
Inducted into Pro Football Hall of Fame in 1971.

The only "bonus" Robustelli received from the Los Angeles Rams when they drafted him in the nineteenth round in 1951 was his airfare to training camp—a fair investment in an obscure defensive end out of little Arnold College, a school that has long since dropped football. However, the first time the Rams held a scrimmage game, Robustelli was all over the field. He knocked down ball carriers, smothered passers, and left blockers sprawled on the turf.

He was a regular for Los Angeles's championship team in 1951, and the one game he missed that season was the only one he missed in his 14-year career. After five standout seasons in Los Angeles, Robustelli yearned to play closer to his home in Connecticut. The Rams, believing he might be slowing down, granted his wish and dealt him to the New York Giants for a number-one draft pick.

Robustelli performed even better in a Giants' uniform and is credited with molding the New York defense that helped win the 1956 NFL championship. He stayed with the Giants for nine seasons, the last three years as a player-coach. Robustelli, who excelled as a pass rusher, was named all-pro seven times and played in seven Pro Bowls. Perhaps his greatest individual honor during his playing days came when he was named the NFL's outstanding player by the Maxwell Club in 1962. [DS/PF]

ANDY RUSSELL

Linebacker. 6-3, 225. Missouri
Born October 29, 1941, Detroit, Michigan.
1963, 1966-1976 Pittsburgh

Andy Russell played 12 years in the NFL and earned two Super Bowl rings as "the thinking man's linebacker." Not particularly big or fast, he had to take a cerebral approach to the game.

He was patently equipped to do that—early in his career he earned an MBA from Missouri to go along with his bachelor's degree. When Russell, a star St. Louis high school fullback, chose to matriculate at Missouri instead of an Ivy League school, it was regarded as a recruiting coup for the Tigers.

Russell, who aspired to a business career, told pro scouts he wasn't interested in postgraduate football. The Steelers drafted him anyway, suggesting he deter his two-year military obligation a year and take a crack at the NFL. Russell did and played well enough to start for the 1963 Steelers—a team that made a serious run at the division title. Then came the army and a return to Pittsburgh.

The heady linebacker gained a solid reputation. He was selected for the Pro Bowl in the 1968 and 1970-75 seasons. In the mid-seventies, Russell, Jack Ham, and Jack Lambert formed one of the best linebacking trios in National Football League history as the Steelers won Super Bowls IX and X.

Steelers coach Chuck Noll summed up Russell this way, "You didn't fool Andy. He's about the best I've seen at reading a play and getting to the right place at the right time." [JJC]

BOB ST. CLAIR

Tackle. 6-9, 265. San Francisco, Tulsa
Born February 13, 1931, San Francisco, California.
1953-1963 San Francisco
Inducted into Pro Football Hall of Fame in 1990.

At 6 feet 9 inches and 265 pounds, Bob St. Clair's mere presence on the football field tended to intimidate many opponents. He was blessed with size, speed, intelligence, and a genuine love of hitting. Using these traits to the maximum, his on-the-field trademarks became violence, power, and strength. He was an outstanding blocker, both on passing plays and rushing attempts. Early in his career, he was used on defense in goal-line situations. He also excelled on the special teams. In 1956, he was credited with an amazing 10 blocked field goals.

Extremely popular with fans and his teammates, St. Clair served as the 49ers' captain for three seasons. He was named all-pro in 1955, 1956, and 1957, and was selected as a starter in five Pro Bowls. He was tough and durable and often played in spite of severe injuries that eventually cut short his career. An Achilles tendon injury in 1962 followed by a second Achilles tendon injury forced him to retire before the 1964 season.

St. Clair played college football at the University of San Francisco until that school dropped the game after the 1951 season. He transferred to Tulsa, where he was an All-Missouri Valley Conference star. He joined the San Francisco 49ers as a third-round draft selection in 1953, the ninth member of the 1951 USF team to enter the pros.

His teammates nicknamed him "The Geek" because of several of his unusual habits, such as eating raw meat. He also became active in politics and was both a councilman and the mayor of Daly City, California. [DS/PF]

BARRY SANDERS

Running Back. 5-8, 203. Oklahoma State
Born July 16, 1968, Wichita, Kansas.
1989-1998 Detroit

When Barry Sanders trots onto the field for the Detroit Lions, defenders shake their heads.

"He makes you miss [tackles] so bad, you kind of look up in the stands and wonder if anybody's looking at you," Atlanta Falcons cornerback D.J. Johnson said. "You've got 60,000 people in there, and you wonder if anyone saw you miss that tackle."

Sanders did the same thing in college. He set 13 NCAA rushing and scoring records at Oklahoma State en route to the 1988 Heisman Trophy. He entered the National Football League draft after his junior season and Detroit selected him with the third pick. Sanders responded with a string of eight consecutive 1,000-yard seasons. He led the NFL in rushing in 1990 with 1,304 yards and repeated in 1994 with 1,883 yards. He won his third NFL rushing title in 1996 with 1,553 yards, but the most impressive feat of his remarkable career came in 1997, when he became just the third running back to rush for 2,000 yards in a season (he had 2,053). In 10 NFL seasons, Sanders has been named to 10 Pro Bowls. He also has surpassed 1,000 yards each season.

What makes Sanders so dangerous is his ability to cut back and leave defenders in his wake. A weightlifter,

Sanders could squat 600 pounds at Oklahoma State, turning his legs into the tree trunks that many a defender has hit—only to find that those legs hit back.

"He's a 280-pound man who was cut off at the knees and had his shoes put back on," long-time NFL assistant Floyd Peters said. "People who hit him around those thunder thighs just bounce off . . . he's like a Walt Disney deer bouncing through the forest." [MS]

CHARLIE SANDERS

Tight End. 6-4, 235. Minnesota
Born August 13, 1946, Greensboro, North Carolina.
1968-1977 Detroit Lions

Charlie Sanders was nicknamed "Charlie Deep." The seven-time Pro Bowl selection went deep well enough to reach double figures in average yards per catch in each of his 10 seasons with the Detroit Lions. The durable tight end also led his team in receptions in four of those years, no small feat for someone at his position.

"There was no 'book' on Charlie," said former Detroit quarterback Greg Landry, who threw passes to him for most of his career. "Charlie was strong enough to work against anyone in the secondary, even linebackers who had him in coverage, and he was fast enough that strong safeties had problems coping with him in the open field. He was a wonderful target with his size, and an intelligent receiver who knew how to find open spots, or adjust routes to make it easier for me to reach him."

Sanders often was just as renowned for his run blocking as his pass receiving. He was almost as big as the offensive tackles of his time and rarely was outmanned by a defensive lineman. "He just crushed the corner when he came off the ball, regardless of whether he was lined up against a defensive lineman or a linebacker. It was like having a third tackle in the game," Landry said. [JC]

DEION SANDERS

Cornerback. 6-0, 187. Florida State
Born August 9, 1967, Ft. Myers, Florida.
1989-1993 Atlanta, 1994 San Francisco, 1995-98 Dallas

First Deion Sanders was a two-sport player; then he became a two-way player. Sanders lined up on both offense and defense in 1996 to help Dallas become the first team to win six Super Bowls. His ceaseless self-promotion has alienated some fans, but it has made him extremely popular with others. Moreover, he has backed his flash with superior play. He is widely regarded as one of the best coverage cornerbacks in the NFL.

"Prime Time," as Sanders refers to himself, was a can't-miss prospect at Florida State in three sports: track and field (he qualified for the 1988 Olympic Trials as a sprinter), baseball (he was a center fielder and played in the College World Series), and football (he played on four bowl-game winners with the Seminoles). He was a football All-America twice and won the Jim Thorpe Award as the nation's best defensive back.

Sanders has played with seven different professional teams—four major league baseball teams and three National Football League teams. He made the NFL playoffs as a member of the Atlanta Falcons and played on Super Bowl champions with the 49ers and Cowboys.

Sanders was the first person to play in both a Super Bowl and a World Series. He is also the only player to hit a home run and score a touchdown as a professional in the same week. In postseason play he has two Super Bowl rings and batted .533 in his lone World Series. [MS]

ORBAN (SPEC) SANDERS

Tailback. 6-1, 196. Texas
Born January 26, 1919, Temple, Oklahoma.
1946-48 New York Yankees AAFC, 1950 New York Yanks

Orban (Spec) Sanders did a little of everything, and he did it in a short period of time. Sanders actually spent more time in college than in the pros. He was a three-sport athlete at Temple High School in Oklahoma, but transferred to Cameron Junior College in Lawton, Oklahoma, where he finished his last two years of high school and spent his first two college years. He played four years of junior college football and then went on to the University of Texas for the 1940 and 1941 seasons.

Even though he did not start for the Longhorns, the Washington Redskins drafted Sanders in the first round. But he joined the U.S. Navy instead and continued to play football while serving in the military during World War II.

Sanders signed with the New York Yankees of the All-America Football Conference in 1946 and led the league in rushing and touchdowns. He set a professional mark the following season with 1,432 yards rushing and scored 19 touchdowns.

His 250 yards rushing against the Chicago Rockets stood as the single-game professional record for almost 30 years. He led the Yankees to the championship game twice in three years in the AAFC.

Knee surgery sidelined Sanders in 1949 and effectively ended his days as a running back. But he joined the National Football League the following year with the New York Yanks as a safety and punter. His 13 interceptions tied the NFL record at the time, and he was named an all-pro defensive back. Sanders retired after the season. [MS]

GALE SAYERS

Running Back. 6-0, 200. Kansas
Born May 30, 1943, Wichita, Kansas.
1965-1971 Chicago Bears
Inducted into Pro Football Hall of Fame in 1977.

In just seven National Football League seasons, Gale Sayers dazzled the pro football world. Whether running from scrimmage, returning kicks, or catching passes, he was a threat to go all the way every time he touched the football.

Incredibly, more than a few pro scouts questioned whether Sayers could make it in the pros. Everyone recognized the Kansas All-America's natural abilities, but some doubted the speedster could withstand the pounding he was sure to face in the NFL. The Chicago Bears' George Halas didn't share those concerns and selected Sayers in the first round of the 1965 draft.

Halas opted to bring his prize rookie along slowly as a confidence-building measure, but once Sayers got into heavy action, it was the opposition that suffered a confidence crisis. Whether he was rushing, receiving, or returning punts and kickoffs, Sayers immediately displayed the rocket-like form that soon was to shake up the entire pro football world. In his first preseason game against the Rams, Sayers raced 77 yards on a punt return, 93 yards on a kickoff return, then startled everyone with a 25-yard, left-handed touchdown pass. Later in his rookie season, he scored 4 touchdowns against Minnesota and a record-tying 6 touchdowns against San Francisco.

Sayers continued to dazzle Bears' foes until he suffered a severe knee injury in 1968. He bounced back for a second 1,000-yard season in 1969, but another knee injury in 1970 effectively ended the career of the man many insist was the most picture-perfect running back of all time. [DS/PF]

JOE SCHMIDT

Linebacker. 6-0, 222. Pittsburgh
Born January 19, 1932, Pittsburgh, Pennsylvania.
1953-1965 Detroit
Inducted into Pro Football Hall of Fame in 1973.

"If I were to start from scratch and pick out just one player," Vikings coach Norm Van Brocklin once said, "I'd pick Joe Schmidt to form the core of my team."

Schmidt won just about every honor a middle linebacker could earn during his 13 seasons with the Detroit Lions from 1953-1965. He was named all-pro eight times and was selected to play in nine consecutive Pro Bowls from the 1954-1962 seasons. His teammates named him their most valuable player in 1955, 1957, 1958, and 1961.

Because he had had a long history of injuries during his college days at the University of Pittsburgh, Schmidt was not selected by the Lions until the seventh round of the 1953 draft. Within two seasons, Schmidt was all-pro, and many eventually would consider him the ideal middle linebacker. As a nine-year defensive captain, Schmidt barked split-second assignments to his defensive cohorts. He was a ferocious tackler, and he was fast enough to defend against either the pass or the run.

Schmidt prided himself on having the uncanny knack of seemingly always knowing what the opposition was going to do. As John Henry Johnson, who had been both a teammate and an opponent of Schmidt, commented, "He is always in the way!" [DS/PF]

JAKE SCOTT

Defensive Back. 6-1, 188. Georgia
Born July 20, 1945, Greenwood, South Carolina.
1970-75 Miami, 1976-78 Washington

Around the NFL during the early 1970s they joked that free safety Jake Scott of the Miami Dolphins could only play in home games because airport metal detectors rejected him every time he tried to fly.

At one time, Scott had five stainless-steel screws holding together the bones of his right hand, and at least one other metal screw in an elbow. He went into Super Bowl VII nursing a separated shoulder. When he intercepted 2 passes in the Miami victory that gave the Dolphins a perfect 17-0 record, he was named the game's most valuable player. On another occasion, he played in the Pro Bowl with two broken hands in casts.

Scott left the University of Georgia a year before his class graduated and went to the Canadian Football League where, with the British Columbia Lions, he caught 35 passes for 596 yards and 3 touchdowns. He was offered a three-year, $100,000 contract by the Lions, but after he was picked in the seventh round of the 1970 draft by the Dolphins, he took a $5,000 salary cut to join Miami.

Scott not only was a savvy free safety, but also was a fine return man, averaging 10.5 yards on punt returns and 23 yards on kickoff returns. Though he may have been among the bravest men on the field, he also was no dummy: He set a single-game record (since broken) in 1970 with 6 fair catches against the Buffalo Bills. [JC]

JUNIOR SEAU

Linebacker. 6-3, 250. Southern California
Born January 19, 1969, San Diego, California.
1990-98 San Diego

Junior Seau, the San Diego Chargers' star linebacker, played most of the 1994 season with his left-side mobility restricted by a pinched nerve in his shoulder. He still played in all 16 games and was instrumental in getting the Chargers to the Super Bowl for the first time in franchise history. Seau had a career season with the Chargers, making 155 tackles (124 solo), including 5½ sacks, and recovering 3 fumbles.

"Football's a dangerous game, and everyone's going to get injured," he said. The [key] is what kind of shape you're in when it does happen."

Seau bench presses 500 pounds, and his workout routines are staggering. In the offseason, he rises at 6 A.M. and starts the day by lifting weights and running sprints for at least two hours. His workouts during the season also are grueling, but his mind is working hard, too.

Seau has been plugging holes with the best in the National Football League since he was San Diego's first-round draft pick out of USC in 1990. Not coincidentally, Seau has been named to the Pro Bowl every season since 1991.

"I can't settle for mediocrity," he said. "I have to put pressure on myself. I have to excel every practice, every game." [MS]

LEE ROY SELMON

Defensive End. 6-3, 250. Oklahoma
Born October 20, 1954, Eufaula, Oklahoma.
1976-1984 Tampa Bay
Inducted into Pro Football Hall of Fame in 1995.

Lee Roy Selmon, a consensus All-America in 1975 at the University of Oklahoma, was the first draft pick of the new Tampa Bay Buccaneers' franchise in 1976. The winner of both the Lombardi and Outland trophies as the outstanding college lineman in 1975, Selmon immediately established himself at right end as the leader of the Buccaneers' defensive unit that eventually would help produce NFC Central Division championships in 1979 and 1981.

Selmon joined his brother Dewey on Tampa Bay's first team. A defensive tackle-linebacker, Dewey played in Tampa Bay until 1980.

Lee Roy Selmon battled injuries during two of his first three seasons but, in his fourth year in 1979, he was named all-pro for the first of three times. He also was an all-NFC choice five years and was named to six consecutive Pro Bowls from the 1979-1984 seasons. Selmon was named the NFC defensive lineman of the year by the NFL Players Association four times, and he was the Associated Press NFL defensive player of the year in 1979.

Selmon had 3 sacks in a game four times. A back injury that forced him to miss the entire 1985 season brought a premature end to his outstanding career. [DS/PF]

TOM SESTAK

Defensive Tackle. 6-4, 270. Texas A&M, Baylor, McNeese State
Born March 9, 1936, Gonzales, Texas.
Died April 3, 1987, Buffalo, New York.
1962-68 Buffalo

Tom Sestak was more than the AFL's best defensive tackle, according to coach Lou Saban: "He's one of the very best I've ever seen, on any field in any league. For strength, interior pass rush, ability to read offensive keys, instinct to fight off traps, and raw courage, Tom is the absolute best." Sestak was named to the all-time All-AFL team in 1969.

It was a long and circuitous route for Sestak from Gonzales, Texas, to stardom in Buffalo. He was recruited to Texas A&M by Paul (Bear) Bryant. When the NCAA and the Southwest Conference judged Bryant's recruiting of Sestak and others as just a little too zealous, Sestak left. He was at Baylor for a short time, but then went into the army for a couple of years. After the service, Sestak enrolled at McNeese State. Drafted as a 245-pound defensive end by both the Bills and Detroit Lions, he bulked up to 270 and became a rock in the middle of the Bills' defensive line in their championship era.

Raw courage was a key ingredient in Sestak's game. Early in his career he had two operations to remove cartilage from his knees. Bills trainer Eddie Ambromoski said that without the cartilage, it was bone against bone, but the stoic Sestak said nothing. According to the trainer, "Most guys couldn't play under those circumstances. But Big Ses, he never says a word." [JJC]

***SHANNON SHARPE**

Tight End. 6-2, 230. Savannah State
Born June 26, 1968, Chicago, Illinois.
1990-98 Denver

It is hard to imagine Shannon Sharpe entering a room, much less a league, unnoticed, but the gregarious seven-time Pro Bowl tight end arrived in the NFL with little fanfare out of tiny Savannah State. Denver coach Dan Reeves drafted him in the seventh round in 1990 because Sharpe was a three-time All-America and his brother, Sterling, was a Pro Bowl wide receiver in Green Bay.

Shannon Sharpe earned a spot on the Broncos as a rookie and had more tackles (16 on special teams) than catches (7), but he started twice at the end of season. Two years later, he was the team's leading receiver. He and his brother teamed in the record books: In 1992, they became the first brothers to lead their respective teams in receiving in the same year, and later they became the all-time leading fraternal receiving tandem. They remain close; Shannon gave his Super Bowl XXXII ring to Sterling, who retired because of a spinal injury in 1994.

Shannon has as many 1,000-yard receiving seasons (3) as any other tight end in history, and a franchise-record seven consecutive seasons with 50 catches. He has 42 catches in 11 postseason games, including 13 against the Raiders in 1994 to tie an NFL postseason record. He brings Denver an added dimension, an extra receiver who also can block for Pro Bowl running back Terrell Davis. "I would like to think I'm one of the best," Sharpe says. Few would argue with him. [MS]

STERLING SHARPE

Wide Receiver. 5-11, 202. South Carolina
Born April 6, 1965, Chicago, Illinois.
1988-1994 Green Bay

Sterling Sharpe left the National Football League at the top of his game, but he didn't leave on his own terms.

Sharpe was sidelined after the 1994 season because of a serious neck injury. In his seven years with the Green Bay Packers, however, Sharpe made the most of the time he had on the field. He never missed a regular-season game and led the NFL in receptions three times, in touchdowns twice, and even managed to wrestle the receiving yards title from Jerry Rice in 1992. He surpassed the 1,000-yard mark five times in his career and had 28 games with 100 or more yards receiving.

He meant more than just numbers to Green Bay; Sharpe signaled the beginning of a rebirth of playoff football for one of the league's most storied franchises. The team had gone to the playoffs only twice since Vince Lombardi resigned as coach after the 1967 season, but the Packers qualified for the postseason in both 1993 and 1994 behind Sharpe and quarterback Brett Favre.

Sharpe, a native of Chicago, moved to Georgia with his family and became a standout at Glennville High. Sharpe set records at the University of South Carolina for career receptions, receiving yards, and touchdowns. His biggest play was a one-handed 80-yard touchdown grab that helped South Carolina upset Nebraska.

Sharpe now serves as a studio analyst for ESPN, but his family is still represented on the playing fields of the NFL. Younger brother Shannon is a tight end for the Denver Broncos. [MS]

BILLY SHAW

Guard. 6-3, 250. Georgia Tech
Born December 15, 1938, Natchez, Mississippi.
1961-69 Buffalo
Inducted into Pro Football Hall of Fame in 1999.

In 1961, Billy Shaw chose to sign with the Buffalo Bills of the year-old American Football League instead of the Dallas Cowboys of the established NFL, but not because the Bills chose him in a higher draft round or made him a better offer. He had heard Dallas planned to use him as a linebacker.

Although he had played both offense and defense at Georgia Tech, he believed his size and speed were better suited to guard, where the Bills wanted him to play. That Shaw went on to become one of the best and most-honored guards of the 1960s proves that he chose well.

All-AFL from 1963 through 1966, he played in eight AFL All-Star Games and was selected to the All-Time AFL Team. Shaw was a key member of the Bills teams that won league titles in both 1964 and 1965.

Shaw was perfectly suited to a Bills' offense that stressed the running game. His speed allowed him to pull and get out in front of runners on sweeps. In fact, because Buffalo's runners tended to be more durable than speedy, he sometimes was able to stay in front of them to make blocks far downfield.

Shaw credits Bills' all-star defensive tackle Tom Sestak with making him a better player. Good friends, the two always lined up against each other in one-on-one practice scrimmages. "Those were some battles," he says. "Sometimes I won, but mostly he did." But going against the best helped make Shaw one of the best himself. [BC]

ART SHELL

Tackle. 6-5, 285. Maryland State-Eastern Shore
Born November 25, 1946, Charleston, South Carolina.
1968-1982 Raiders
Inducted into Pro Football Hall of Fame in 1989.

Shell, the first African-American to serve as an NFL head coach in the modern era, coached the Raiders from 1989-1994. But he earned a place in the Pro Football Hall of Fame because of his play as one of the NFL's greatest offensive tackles.

A third-round draft pick of the Oakland Raiders in 1968, Shell excelled on special teams for two seasons before winning the starting offensive left-tackle job in his third year. Within a short time, he became widely recognized as one of the premier offensive linemen in the National Football League. Through much of his career, Shell teamed with left guard Gene Upshaw to power the Oakland offense of the 1970s.

Shell was an All-AFC selection six consecutive years from 1973 through 1978 and all-pro in 1973, 1974, and 1977. He also played in eight Pro Bowls and 24 postseason games, including eight AFL/AFC championships and the Raiders' victories in Super Bowls XI and XV. Shell was credited with a nearly perfect performance against Jim Marshall, the Minnesota Vikings' sterling defensive end, in Super Bowl XI.

A native of Charleston, South Carolina, Shell was all-state in both football and basketball at Bonds-Wilson High School in North Charleston. In college at Maryland State-Eastern Shore, Shell was named all-conference in football three years, All-America two years by the *Pittsburgh Courier* and *Ebony Magazine,* and little All-America as a senior in 1967. [DS/PF]

DONNIE SHELL

Safety. 5-11, 190. South Carolina State
Born August 26, 1952, Whitmire, South Carolina.
1974-1987 Pittsburgh

Donnie Shell intercepted at least 1 pass in each of his 14 Steelers' seasons, and had 51 total interceptions. He put up numbers like no other strong safety, and numbers like very few defensive backs, regardless of position. Shell, a fierce hitter, often gave away 50 pounds to the receivers he covered, but many of the NFL's best and biggest tight ends came out second-best in collisions with the compact South Carolinian.

Shell, who holds a master's degree in guidance and counseling, played an intelligent, if reckless, game. The team's leading tackler in 1984, he consistently was among the leaders in other years.

That Shell, and eight other undrafted free agents, made the Steelers in 1974 is attributable in all likelihood to a players' strike that summer. With the veterans not in camp, Shell and the others received a long look from the coaches. Before Shell settled into a starting position in Pittsburgh, he gained a reputation as a fast, tough special-teams player.

He tackled with such ferocity, a writer punned, "He just leaves 'em Shell-shocked." Shell was so good for so long only ironman center Mike Webster played more games in a Steelers uniform than Shell's 201.

Today, Shell uses his advanced degree as the Carolina Panthers' director of player development, coordinating four separate player programs. [JJC]

PHIL SIMMS

Quarterback. 6-3, 216. Moorhead State
Born November 3, 1955, Lebanon, Kentucky.
1979-1993 New York Giants

Phil Simms proved that quarterbacks need not come from major college football powers to succeed in the NFL. He was the New York Giants' first-round draft pick in 1979 after playing for Moorhead State College, a Division I-AA school in Kentucky.

It was a splendid choice. Simms owns nearly every major Giants' passing record, and he helped the team win two NFL championships. He led them to a victory in Super Bowl XXI by completing 22 of 25 passes while earning game MVP honors. He also brought them to the brink of their Super Bowl XXV victory, leading them to a division title before being sidelined with a foot injury. Jeff Hostetler took the Giants through the playoffs and to a 20-19 Super Bowl victory over Buffalo.

Yet for most of his career, Simms was vastly underappreciated by New York Giants fans, who awaited the second coming of Hall-of-Fame quarterback Y.A. Tittle.

Simms took the starting job midway through his rookie season and for the next several years—despite helping the team to the playoffs in 1981 for the first time in 18 years—he often was in and out of the lineup as a combination of injuries and spotty performances hampered his development.

The 1986 championship was a turning point. His leadership, his accuracy, and his mastery at spreading his passes among a number of receivers, and his fiery competitive spirit eventually won the affection of the fans. Now anyone else playing quarterback for the Giants is compared to Phil Simms. [JC]

O.J. SIMPSON

Running Back. 6-1, 212. Southern California
Born July 9, 1947, San Francisco, California.
1969-1977 Buffalo, 1978-79 San Francisco
Inducted into Pro Football Hall of Fame in 1985.

Simpson was a two-time All-America from Southern California and the 1968 Heisman Trophy winner. The Buffalo Bills selected him with the first pick in the 1969 draft. His career record for 11 seasons, the first nine in Buffalo and the 1978 and 1979 campaigns in San Francisco, showed his college greatness was just the beginning. Simpson rushed for 11,236 yards, added 2,142 yards on 203 pass receptions, returned 33 kickoffs for 990 yards (a 30.0-yard average), and amassed 14,368 combined net yards. He scored 456 points on 76 touchdowns.

Incredibly, Simpson was used sparingly as a running back for his first three years in the pros until Lou Saban took over the reins in 1972 and immediately decided to give the 6-foot 2-inch, 212-pound speedster the football as often as possible. Simpson responded with a sensational 1973 season when he became the first player to rush for more than 2,000 yards (2,003). Many say his 1975 season was even better—1,817 yards rushing, 428 yards on 28 receptions, and a then-record 23 touchdowns. He led the league in rushing in 1972, 1973, 1975, and 1976.

Honors came by the dozens for Simpson. He was named NFL player of the year in 1972, 1973, and 1975. He was all-pro five consecutive years from 1972 through 1976. Through it all, he never played for a championship team. His lone playoff appearance came in a wild-card game the Bills played in 1974. [DS/PF]

MIKE SINGLETARY

Linebacker. 6-0, 230. Baylor
Born October 9, 1958, Houston, Texas.
1981-1992 Chicago Bears
Inducted into the Pro Football Hall of Fame in 1998.

On a team built around great defense, Mike Singletary was the best—he had to be because this preacher's son was making good on a promise.

In a pre-draft interview with former Chicago Bears scout Jim Parmer in 1981, the Baylor University senior said, very matter-of-factly, "If you draft me, I'm going to be the best linebacker in the National Football League." The Bears drafted him in the second round and never regretted it.

Singletary was the cornerstone of the Bears' innovative 46 Defense. In an age of specialty substitution, Singletary was an every-down middle linebacker in the tradition of Dick Butkus. He was the NFL defensive player of the year in 1985 while playing for one of the best defensive teams ever. And more than anything else, Singletary was intense. "His eyes look like fifty-cent pieces," said former teammate Otis Wilson.

Singletary led a defense that allowed less than 11 points per game in 1985 and often brooded about the points it did allow in an 18-1 season that included two playoff shutouts and a 46-10 annihilation of the New England Patriots in Super Bowl XX.

Buddy Ryan, Singletary's defensive coach with the Bears, said, "To me, he's the MVP of the NFL. Hands down."

The Bears made the playoffs seven times in Singletary's 12-year career. Despite his relatively small size for his position—6 feet, 230 pounds—Singletary missed only two games in his career. He appeared in the Pro Bowl 10 times and was named 1990 NFL Man of the Year for his off-the-field community service. [MS]

FRED (DUKE) SLATER

Tackle. 6-1, 215. Iowa
Born December 9, 1898, Normal. Illinois.
Died August 14, 1966, Chicago, Illinois.
1922-25 Rock Island, 1922 Milwaukee, 1926 Rock Island (AFL), 1926-1931 Chicago Cardinals

In the pioneering days of the NFL, there were a handful of African-American players. They seldom played more than a few years, and there were seldom more than two per team. Given that, Fred (Duke) Slater's career was noteworthy on two counts. None of the early black players played as long as Slater (10 years) and none surpassed his level of performance.

Slater had been a consensus All-America tackle at Iowa before joining the Rock Island Independents in 1922. After the Independents disbanded for the season, he finished the year with the Milwaukee Badgers, then returned to Rock Island for three more years. In 1926, the Independents jumped to Red Grange's American Football League in what proved to be a bad move. The team went broke. Slater, however, was welcomed by the Chicago Cardinals, where he closed out the year.

The scholarly Slater—he would graduate from law school while still playing pro football—stayed with the Cardinals and was a force as a two-way tackle through the 1931 season. In 1930, the year before the first official All-NFL Team was named, he was a consensus choice among many such newspaper-selected teams.

Slater became a municipal court judge in Chicago and later a superior court judge.

A humble man, Slater's greatest thrill in pro football did not center around himself but was "when we defeated the Bears 40-6 in 1929, and Ernie Nevers scored all the points." [JJC]

BRUCE SMITH

Defensive End. 6-4, 281. Virginia Tech
Born July 18, 1963, Norfolk, Virginia.
1985-1998 Buffalo

Bruce Smith is intimidation squeezed into a 6-foot 4-inch, 281-pound frame. "Anybody who says they don't use two and three people [on me], I don't know what film they're watching," Smith said. "It's no secret."

Smith gets such attention because he has 164 career sacks with the Bills, and is tied with Reggie White as the NFL's all-time leader in postseason sacks.

Virginia Tech's football program was floundering when Smith arrived in 1981. By the time he left four years later, the Hokies had gone to the Independence Bowl, and Smith was the top prospect in the country (he had 46 career sacks and 25 tackles behind the line of scrimmage in college). Smith was named All-America as a Virginia Tech senior. As a senior at Booker T. Washington High School in Norfolk, Smith was also All-America and was on a state championship team—in basketball.

Smith exploded onto the NFL scene after the Bills made him the top pick in the 1985 draft. He was named the defensive rookie of the year that season with 6½ sacks; he since has had 10 seasons with sacks in double digits.

His greatest season came in 1990, when his 19 sacks led Buffalo to a 13-3 record and its first Super Bowl appearance. In Super Bowl XXV, a 20-19 Giants' victory, Smith sacked New York quarterback Jeff Hostetler for a safety in the second quarter to give Buffalo a 12-3 lead. [MS]

EMMITT SMITH

Running Back. 5-9, 205. Florida
Born May 15, 1969, Pensacola, Florida.
1990-98 Dallas

During Emmitt Smith's contract holdout with the Dallas Cowboys at the start of the 1993 season, the team's owner, Jerry Jones, said, "Emmitt Smith is a luxury, not a necessity for the Dallas Cowboys."

After the Cowboys lost their first two games that season, Jones made sure Smith's name was on the dotted line. It seems that winning was a luxury Dallas couldn't do without. Even after signing Smith, there was still the fact that no team had ever won the Super Bowl after starting out 0-2, another record Smith helped break.

He has broken records wherever he's been and done it fast. Smith shattered virtually every record at Escambia High School in Pensacola, Florida. Smith accomplished the same at the University of Florida, breaking the single-game rushing record in his first start as a freshman in an upset of Alabama in 1987. He broke the 1,000-yard barrier in seven games. By the end of his junior year, it was off to the National Football League. Dallas traded up in the draft for a shot at Smith, and selected him with the seventeenth overall pick.

After his rookie year, he began a remarkable streak of eight consecutive 1,000-yard seasons, punctuated with double-digit touchdown totals. Smith has led the league in rushing four times and was the top scorer in the NFL in 1992, 1994, and 1995. In the final game of the 1998 season, he scored 2 touchdowns to break Marcus Allen's NFL record of 123 career rushing touchdowns (Smith has 125).

Smith has played in four NFC Championship Games and three Super Bowls. He was named most valuable player following the Cowboys' 30-13 win over Buffalo in Super Bowl XXVIII. [MS]

JACKIE SMITH

Tight End. 6-4, 232. Northwestern Louisiana
Born February 23, 1940, Columbia, Mississippi.
1963-1977 St. Louis, 1978 Dallas
Inducted into Pro Football Hall of Fame in 1994.

Jackie Smith was a fixture at tight end for 15 years with the St. Louis Cardinals before finishing his career with the Dallas Cowboys in 1978. At the time of Smith's retirement, he ranked as the all-time top receiver among tight ends with 480 receptions for 7,918 yards and 40 touchdowns.

An outstanding football and track competitor at Northwestern Louisiana, Smith was the Cardinals' tenth-round draft pick in 1963.

He was a talented receiver, a punishing blocker, a fierce competitor, and an excellent runner after he caught the ball. He even handled the Cardinals' punting chores his first three seasons. Ironically, he may be better known to fans for the sure touchdown pass he muffed in Super Bowl XIII, the last pass ever directed his way.

Smith became the St. Louis Cardinals' starting tight end during his 1963 rookie season and held that spot the rest of his tenure in St. Louis. The teams' offensive co-captain from 1967-1970, Smith had a string of 45 consecutive games with at least 1 reception. He played in 121 consecutive games until a knee injury sidelined him in his ninth season in 1971. Injuries slowed him again in 1975 and 1976, but Smith still played in 198 games, third most in club history.

He played in five consecutive Pro Bowls from the 1966-1970 seasons, and was all-pro pick in 1967. [DS/PF]

MAC SPEEDIE

End. 6-3, 215. Utah
Born January 12, 1920, Odell, Illinois.
Died March 12, 1993, Laguna Hills, California.
1946-49 Cleveland AAFC, 1950-52 Cleveland

When Speedie was 8, doctors feared he'd never walk without a brace because of a bone deficiency in his left leg. But after four years of painful rehabilitation, he walked, then ran, without a support. Eventually, he ran himself into a brilliant pro football career.

At the University of Utah, Speedie twice was named an end on the All-Rocky Mountain Conference team, but he was best known for track, setting the conference record for the 220-yard low hurdles. He entered the U.S. Army in March, 1942, and served until June, 1946. While playing service football, he was "discovered" by Paul Brown. After the war, Brown built his great Cleveland Browns. The Browns won the AAFC Championship each year from 1946-49, and when the NFL and AAFC made peace for 1950, Cleveland was taken into the older league and continued to win titles.

Along with end Dante Lavelli, another unknown discovered by Brown, Speedie gave quarterback Otto Graham the best tandem of receivers in football. One or the other—and often both—made every important all-league team from 1946 through 1952. Speedie, who set the AAFC record for career receptions with 211, was most dangerous after catching the ball, when his speed and agility made him a breakaway threat. After leading the NFL in receiving with 62 catches in 1952, Speedie jumped to the Canadian Football League. [BC]

ED SPRINKLE

Defensive End. 6-1, 206. Hardin-Simmons, Navy
Born March 9, 1923, Tuscolo, Texas.
1944-1955 Chicago Bears

The Bears' Ed Sprinkle was named as "The Meanest Man in Football" by one national magazine, but he was also termed a "fine gentleman" by teammates. George Halas said he was "the greatest pass rusher I've ever seen" and "a rough, tough ballplayer, but not a dirty one."

Sprinkle was probably the first player to achieve fame for his pass-rushing ability. During his dozen seasons with the Bears, all NFL teams switched to the T-formation, and a strong pass rush was essential to defend against the improved passing attacks. Sprinkle was determined, extremely quick off the snap, and, as a left-handed right end, he could handle most blockers with his stronger arm.

Sprinkle was selected to play in four Pro Bowls, and named to several all-pro teams, although the practice of naming offensive and defensive teams was not established until late in his career, and such honors for ends usually went to pass catchers. [BC]

KEN STABLER

Quarterback. 6-3, 210. Alabama
Born December 25, 1945, Foley, Alabama.
1970-79 Raiders, 1980-81 Houston, 1982-84 New Orleans

Ken Stabler was born on Christmas Day, but "The Snake" had plenty of the devil in him. His swashbuckling, bad boy image was perfect for the Raiders, but his pinpoint passing was even a better match.

Stabler was a winner at every level. The agile left-handed passer guided his high school to two state championships, led the University of Alabama to an undefeated season and a victory in the Sugar Bowl, and crowned his career with a Super Bowl triumph.

Stabler began his professional career on the sidelines. Drafted by the Oakland Raiders in the second round in 1968, he did not get a starting assignment until 1973. He came in after the Raiders lost two of their first three games, then guided Oakland into the playoffs. Stabler and the Raiders went to five consecutive AFC Championship Games. In Super Bowl XI he completed 12 of 19 passes for 180 yards in the Raiders' 32-14 victory over the Minnesota Vikings.

Stabler's most famous play was a fumble. In a game against San Diego, the Chargers converged on Stabler for an apparent game-ending sack. Stabler purposely fumbled the ball forward. Running back Pete Banaszak "accidentally" muffed the ball farther forward, and tight end Dave Casper "inadvertently" knocked the rolling ball over the goal line and fell on it to win the game 21-20. (The rules later were changed to prevent this from happening.)

Stabler finished his career with the Houston Oilers and New Orleans Saints. He retired in 1984 having completed 60 percent of his career passes for 27,938 passing yards and 194 touchdowns. [MS]

JOHN STALLWORTH

Wide Receiver. 6-2, 202. Alabama A&M
Born July 15, 1952, Tuscaloosa, Alabama.
1974-1987 Pittsburgh

Stallworth battled a variety of fibula, foot, ankle, knee, and hamstring injuries throughout his career but still managed to play 14 seasons in the NFL and set almost every Pittsburgh Steelers' receiving record.

He seemed almost spindly compared with his beefier teammates, but the quiet, friendly receiver had wonderful hands, ran precise routes, and burned defensive backs with his deceptive speed.

But far more than his admirable career totals—537 receptions and 63 touchdown passes— he was a "big game" performer. He played in six AFC Championship Games and four Super Bowls and had 12 touchdown catches and 17 consecutive postseason games with at least 1 reception. In four Super Bowls, he caught 11 passes for an average of 24.4 yards per catch, including a 73-yard touchdown reception in the fourth quarter of Super Bowl XIV that gave the Steelers the lead for good.

Twice all-conference at Alabama A&M, Stallworth was a fourth-round pick in the same 1974 draft that brought the Steelers wide receiver Lynn Swann, linebacker Jack Lambert, and center Mike Webster. The Steelers emphasized the running game in Stallworth's first few years, limiting his chances to catch passes, but by the team's third and fourth trips to the Super Bowl, he was an integral part of a well-rounded, explosive offense.

He had a 67-game streak of catching at least 1 pass from 1977-1982, and led the AFC in receiving yards in 1984. Stallworth was an all-pro in 1979, played in four Pro Bowls, and his teammates twice chose him most valuable player. [BC]

DICK STANFEL

Guard. 6-3, 236. San Francisco
Born July 20, 1927, San Francisco, California.
1952-55 Detroit, 1956-58 Washington

Because he got a late start and retired early, Stanfel played only seven seasons in the NFL, but during that time he was on two championship teams, three division winners, was named all-pro five times, and was selected to five Pro Bowls.

After serving in the army, Stanfel played guard at the University of San Francisco under Coach Joe Kuharich from 1948-1950, captaining the team in his senior year. Selected by Detroit in the second round of the 1951 draft, he suffered a knee injury practicing for the College All-Star Game and missed the entire 1951 season. By the time Stanfel played his first NFL game in 1952, he was 25 years old.

Detroit won its first NFL championship in 20 seasons in Stanfel's rookie year. He solidified an offensive line that already included future Pro Football Hall of Fame member Lou Creekmur. Stanfel was taller than most guards of his day, and that, along with his speed, helped make him a devastating blocker on sweeps. In straight-ahead or pass blocking, he was considered among the league's best. When the Lions won a second consecutive championship in 1953, his teammates voted Stanfel the club's MVP.

Even though he missed half the 1955 season with an injury, he was still voted to the Pro Bowl. In 1956, Kuharich, then coaching the Redskins, worked a trade to bring Stanfel to Washington, where he enjoyed three more all-pro seasons. When Kuharich became head coach at Notre Dame in 1959, he took his star guard with him as line coach. [BC]

BART STARR

Quarterback. 6-1, 200. Alabama
Born January 9, 1934, Montgomery, Alabama.
1956-1971 Green Bay
Inducted into Pro Football Hall of Fame in 1977.

Starr started slowly. A seventeenth-round draft choice of the Green Bay Packers in 1956, his playing time still was limited three years later. But Vince Lombardi took over as the team's head coach in 1959 and, after tireless study of films, decided that he liked Starr's mechanics and would build his new team around him.

Under Lombardi's careful tutoring, Starr slowly gained confidence and in 1960 he led the Packers to the first of six division titles they would win in the 1960s. He led the league in passing three times and was the named the NFL's most valuable player in 1966.

From 1960-67, Starr's won-lost record as the starting quarterback was a sizzling 82-24-4, and the Packers won NFL championships in 1961, 1962, 1965, 1966, and 1967. They also won the first two Super Bowls. Strangely, Starr received only minimum fanfare while his more publicized teammates captured the headlines.

Maybe it was because Starr, the calm leader of a balanced, precision attack, made it all look so easy. He never threw as many as 300 passes in one season, a situation which may have helped create the illusion he was only an average passer. Perhaps it was because some felt, with the Green Bay's great array of talent in the 1960s, any quarterback could be successful.

But knowledgeable football observers knew better. One rival coach said: "I wish there were a way to ban Bart Starr from playing against us. For the Packers, he is the perfect quarterback." [DS/PF]

ROGER STAUBACH

Quarterback. 6-3, 202. Navy
Born February 5, 1942, Cincinnati, Ohio.
1969-1979 Dallas
Inducted into Pro Football Hall of Fame in 1985.

Roger Staubach joined the Dallas Cowboys as a 27-year-old rookie in 1969 but didn't become the regular quarterback until his third season in 1971.

For eight of the next nine seasons (he missed almost all of 1972 with an injury) he led the potent Cowboys' attack. Dallas played in six NFC Championship Games, winning four of them, and also won Super Bowls VI and XII during that span. The Cowboys racked up a sizzling .731 winning percentage with 95 wins against only 35 losses.

Staubach became a star quarterback at the U. S. Naval Academy, where he won the Heisman Trophy as a junior in 1963. Following his graduation, he spent a mandatory four years on active duty, including service in Vietnam, before he was able to turn his attention to pro football.

Making Staubach particularly dangerous was his ability to scramble out of trouble. His 410 career rushes netted him 2,264 yards and 20 touchdowns. He led the NFL in passing four times, was named to six Pro Bowls, and was named all-NFC four times.

During his best years with the Cowboys, Staubach had the reputation for making the big play. He was the MVP of Super Bowl VI and provided the offensive spark in a defense-dominated victory in Super Bowl XII. His ability to bring his team from behind was legendary and earned him the nickname "Captain Comeback."

He retired after the 1979 season with an 83.4 passer rating, the best mark up to that time. [DS/PF]

ERNIE STAUTNER

Defensive Tackle. 6-2, 235. Boston College
Born April 20, 1925, Prinzing-by-Cham, Bavaria, Germany.
1950-1963 Pittsburgh
Inducted into Pro Football Hall of Fame in 1969.

After his college career ended, Stautner was turned down by New York Giants coach Steve Owen because "you are too small for the pros, son." Fortunately, the Pittsburgh Steelers saw things differently.

The Steelers decided to take a chance on the smaller-than-average lineman from Boston College and picked Ernie Stautner in the 1950 NFL draft. It turned out to be a sensational pick. For the next 14 years, Stautner was a fixture at defensive tackle, a veritable folk hero with long-suffering Steelers fans and a major factor in the Pittsburgh defense, one of the most punishing in the NFL. During that period, Stautner played in nine Pro Bowls.

Stautner was extremely durable, missing only six games in 14 seasons—not that Ernie was never hurt, but he kept right on playing, even with assorted injuries such as broken ribs, shoulders, hands, and a nose broken too many times to count.

Perhaps Stautner's determination to play in the NFL regardless of injuries was a throwback to his days as a high school star in Albany, New York. He was introduced to football on grade-school sandlots, but when he came home one day badly battered, his father issued a quick order: "No more football." Ernie kept playing, a secret he kept from his parents until he was named to the All-Albany team as a junior. Fortunately, family pride came to the rescue and saved Ernie's gridiron career. [DS/PF]

JAN STENERUD

Kicker. 6-2, 190. Montana State
Born November 26, 1942, Fetsund, Norway.
1967-1979 Kansas City, 1980-83 Green Bay, 1984-85 Minnesota
Inducted into Pro Football Hall of Fame in 1991.

Jan Stenerud was an outstanding ski jumper who attended Montana State on a skiing scholarship. In his sophomore year, Stenerud was spotted kicking a football by the college's basketball coach, who relayed the news of the Norwegian native's abilities to the football coach. For the next two years, he starred as a kicker on the varsity football team. He had a then-record 59-yard field goal and scored 82 points as a senior. The Kansas City Chiefs drafted Stenerud in the third round of the AFL's 1966 future draft.

Stenerud excelled for 19 seasons and 263 games in pro football, never missing a game because of injury or illness. He kicked for the Chiefs for 13 years from 1967 until 1979, then moved to the Green Bay Packers, where he stayed for four seasons. In 1984, the Packers traded Stenerud to the Minnesota Vikings. He retired after the 1985 season.

He scored 1,699 points, and his 373 career field goals were an all-time high at the time of his retirement. He scored 100 or more points in seven seasons and kicked 17 field goals of 50 yards or longer, including one of 55 yards against Denver in 1970. In the Chiefs' upset victory over the Vikings in Super Bowl IV, Stenerud's 3 field goals, including a then-record-tying 48-yard kick, accounted for the first 9 points. He was named all-pro four times. Stenerud played in two AFL All-Star games and in four AFC-NFC Pro Bowls. He was named the outstanding offensive player of the 1972 Pro Bowl.

In 1991, Stenerud became the first full-time kicker to enter the Pro Football Hall of Fame. [DS/PF]

DWIGHT STEPHENSON

Center. 6-2, 255. Alabama
Born November 20, 1957, Murfreesboro, North Carolina.
1980-87 Miami
Inducted into Pro Football Hall of Fame in 1998.

Dwight Stephenson does not remember his childhood fondly, but his ability and desire on the football field ensured that he got more out of his adulthood.

"Even the girls pushed me around," he recalls of his youth in Hampton, Virginia. Stephenson's life took a turn for the better when he was hired at a supermarket at 14 to help his family pay the bills. The hard work, steady diet, and plenty of basketball helped sculpt Stephenson's frame. He went out for football his junior year and was all-state the next season. He arrived at the University of Alabama as a defensive end, but head coach Paul (Bear) Bryant switched him to center as a freshman.

Stephenson won the Jacobs Award as the best blocker in the Southeastern Conference as a senior and helped Alabama to a share of the 1978 national title and, after a 24-9 win over the University of Arkansas in the Cotton Bowl, sole possession of the number-one spot in the polls in 1979. It was Bryant's last national title, but Stephenson went on to win two AFC titles as a professional.

The Miami Dolphins selected Stephenson in the second round of the 1980 draft and he started every game. He was named all-pro five times and earned AFC lineman-of-the-year honors in 1983. He played in Super Bowls XVII and XIX (the Dolphins lost both times), but he was forced to retire at age 30 because of a serious knee injury. [MS]

KEN STRONG

Halfback. 5-11, 210. New York University
Born August 6, 1906, New Haven, Connecticut.
Died October 5, 1979, New York, New York.
1929-1932 Staten Island, 1933-35, 1939, 1944-47 New York Giants, 1936-37 New York Yankees (AFL)
Inducted into Pro Football Hall of Fame in 1967.

December 9, 1934, was a memorable day in NFL history. That was the day the New York Giants resorted to the use of basketball shoes on an ice-coated Polo Grounds field to upset the previously unbeaten Chicago Bears in the NFL Championship Game.

The sneakers did not arrive until halftime but, once the Giants' footing was assured they quickly turned the tide, erased a 10-3 halftime deficit, and rolled to a 30-13 victory. The architect of the stunning comeback was do-everything halfback Ken Strong, who kicked a 38-yard field goal, scored 2 touchdowns, and booted 2 extra points. His 17 points stood as an NFL Championship Game scoring record for almost 30 years.

The Sneakers Game was the most memorable performance in Strong's 14 NFL seasons, but not the only great one. Strong could do everything on the football field—run, pass, block, catch passes, punt, kick, and play defense with the best.

For all his brilliance, Strong had a tumultuous pro career. When he returned to the Giants during the World War II-induced manpower shortage, he set some unusual conditions. It was understood—and agreed—that he would wear no shoulder pads, and he even wore his wrist watch when he went onto the field as a member of the Giants.

After signing initially with the relatively unknown Staten Island Stapletons in 1929, he moved to the Giants in 1933, jumped to the rival AFL in 1936, played with the 1939 Giants, retired, and then came back as a kicking specialist for the Giants from 1944-47. [DS/PF]

JACK STROUD

Tackle-Guard. 6-1, 235. Tennessee
Born January 29, 1928, Fresno, California.
Died June 1, 1994, Flemington, New Jersey.
1953-1964 New York Giants

Jack Stroud had the respect of his Giants teammates, opponents, and anyone who closely observed the game. He was tough, strong, played through pain, and was a consummate team player. When the Giants needed a tackle, Stroud was a tackle. When they needed a guard, Stroud was a guard.

He learned to play basic football for General Bob Neyland at Tennessee. There was nothing fancy about the Volunteers' Single Wing. It was set 'em up and knock 'em down.

Stroud's approach to the game: "We played a different kind of football. It wasn't the dance steps you see now. We put the helmet or the shoulder pads right between the numbers and banged away. The rules were different then. Use your hands, get caught, stop a drive."

Delaying his rookie season two years to serve in the Korean War, Stroud joined the Giants in 1953 and soon became one of the league's best guards. He worked hard to reach that level. Stroud was a dedicated year-round weightlifter when he and Bears guards Ray Bray and Stan Jones were about the only players doing weight training. He was selected to just three Pro Bowls, but there's significance in the fact that each season the Giants were in the NFL title game.

Stroud said of his stellar career at an unglamorous position, "It was a job, and I did it because I had pride in my work. I thought I was lucky to play the game. I just loved football, and the people who mattered knew I did it well." [JJC]

JOE STYDAHAR

Tackle. 6-4, 230. West Virginia
Born March 3, 1912, Kaylor, Pennsylvania.
Died March 23, 1977, Beckley, West Virginia.
1936-1942, 1945-46 Chicago Bears
Inducted into Pro Football Hall of Fame in 1967.

By 1936, George Halas was steadily building the powerful Chicago Bears team that would dominate the NFL during the early 1940s. Halas sought only the finest talent so it was somewhat of a surprise when the NFL staged its first college draft before the 1936 season, and in the first round Halas proudly proclaimed, "The Chicago Bears select tackle Joe Stydahar from West Virginia."

It was not that the Stydahar did not have good credentials. He had earned various All-Eastern honors and played in the College All-Star game before joining the Bears. The surprise was that, in the days when most teams were relying on football magazines to select their players, the Bears ferreted out a potential blue-chip pro from a lesser-known college instead of choosing a more publicized star.

The choice, however, was as good as any the Bears ever made. By 1940, when the Bears earned their "Monsters of the Midway" reputation, Stydahar was firmly entrenched as the league's premier left tackle. He was the anchor of an exceptional line that included future Hall of Fame enshrinees Dan Fortmann, Clyde (Bulldog) Turner, and George Musso.

Fearless and huge by 1940 standards, "Jumbo Joe" possessed incredible power and remarkable speed. Flaunting his disdain for superstition by wearing jersey number 13, he was a near-60-minute performer who preferred not to wear a helmet until NFL rules forced him to comply. From 1937-1940, he was the left tackle on the NFL's official all-star team. [DS/PF]

LYNN SWANN

Wide Receiver. 6-0, 180. Southern California
Born March 7, 1952, Alcoa, Tennessee.
1974-1982 Pittsburgh

Swann was one of the most graceful receivers ever to play the game—a leaping, diving Nureyev of the gridiron. If NFL record keepers gave receivers style points, Swann probably would have led the league each year he played.

As a matter of fact, Swann studied ballet to improve his agility, but he was unlikely to lead the NFL in receptions while performing in the run-oriented Steelers' offense. His 336 receptions in nine seasons were the Pittsburgh career record until John Stallworth surpassed him, but other NFL receivers racked up many more catches each season.

Swann's specialty was the significant catch, the reception that wins the game. The best example of that was his performance in Super Bowl X when he was named most valuable player. He had only 4 receptions, but they were spectacular and good for 161 yards, including a game-winning 64-yard touchdown. In four Super Bowls his catches totaled 364 yards.

The former USC All-America joined the Steelers in 1974 and spent most of his first season returning kicks. By his second year, he took his place among the elite receivers of the NFL. His ability to turn a game around with a single catch earned him all-pro recognition in 1975 and 1978. He was All-AFC three times and was chosen to three Pro Bowls.

Swann has fashioned a successful second career as a television sports reporter. [BC]

FRAN TARKENTON

Quarterback. 6-0, 185. Georgia
Born February 3, 1940, Richmond, Virginia.
1961-66, 1972-78 Minnesota, 1967-1971 New York Giants
Inducted into Pro Football Hall of Fame in 1986.

In the expansion Minnesota Vikings' first game, Tarkenton threw 4 touchdown passes and ran for a touchdown in an upset of the Chicago Bears. In his early years, Tarkenton attracted widespread attention as an exciting scrambler who exasperated defenders almost as much as he exasperated his own coach with his evasive tactics. (His first coach at Minnesota, Norm Van Brocklin, had been a classic pocket passer who believed a quarterback should run only out of fear.) Tarkenton's running gave him an added dimension.

Tarkenton's career as an NFL quarterback started as a third-round draft pick with the fledgling Vikings in 1961, took him to the New York Giants in 1967, then back to Minnesota in 1972. In Tarkenton's final seven years with the Vikings, he led Minnesota to six NFC Central Division titles and three NFC championships.

As criticism of his scrambling died down, a new complaint emerged. Tarkenton's detractors derided the fact that he was on the losing side in three Super Bowls. His defenders pointed out that he was the quarterback who put his team into those games.

For 18 seasons, he never let up in his relentless quest of yardage and touchdowns. When he retired, Tarkenton held NFL career records with 3,686 pass completions, 47,003 passing yards, and 342 touchdown passes. Add his 3,674 yards rushing to his stunning passing totals and you have a combined total of 50,677 yards. [DS/PF]

***STEVE TASKER**

Special Teams-Wide Receiver. 5-9, 183. Northwestern
Born April 10, 1962, Leoti, Kansas.
Houston 1985-86, Buffalo 1986-1997

He was called the "patron saint of special teams players" by some, and the "greatest special teams player ever" by others, but all Steve Tasker originally wanted out of football was a conversation starter.

"I just wanted to make a team one time, so I could tell my kids and my grandkids that I actually did play on an NFL team," he said the day he announced his retirement in 1997. "I really just wanted to make a team so when you go out to dinner and people start talking about professional football, you can be one of the guys who can say, 'I did play,' and be one of the guys who can speak with authority."

Tasker made the Houston Oilers in 1985 but was released two games into the 1986 season. New Bills coach Marv Levy picked Tasker off waivers. Although Tasker spent most of the 1986 season thinking he'd be cut again, he actually was starting a Pro Bowl career in Buffalo. Over the next 11 seasons, Tasker and the Bills appeared in 19 postseason games, including 5 AFC Championship Games and 4 Super Bowls. Tasker became a perennial Pro Bowl participant, heading to Honolulu seven times, the most appearances by any special teams player. At the 1993 Pro Bowl he became the first true special teams player to be named the game's most valuable player. [MS]

CHARLEY TAYLOR

Running Back-Wide Receiver. 6-3, 210. Arizona State
Born September 28, 1941, Grand Prairie, Texas.
1964-1975, 1977 Washington
Inducted into Pro Football Hall of Fame in 1984.

Taylor might have made the Pro Football Hall of Fame as a running back, but as a pass receiver he was a lock.

In 1964, he was the Redskins' number-one draft choice out of Arizona State, and was rookie of the year with 755 yards rushing and 814 yards receiving. Although still rated as a premier ball carrier, Taylor was switched to split end in the seventh game of his third season in 1966. He wound up that year as the NFL leader with 72 receptions. Taylor was a fixture at that position for the next nine seasons through 1975. He sat out the entire 1976 campaign with injuries and then returned for a final year in 1977.

When he retired after 13 seasons, Taylor was the NFL's all-time leading pass receiver with 649 catches that accounted for 9,140 yards and 79 touchdowns. He led the NFL in receiving in both 1966 and 1967, his first two years as a wide receiver, and caught more than 50 passes in seven seasons. With 1,488 yards rushing and a smattering of kick-return yardage, he amassed 10,883 combined net yards. With 90 touchdowns, Taylor scored 540 points in his career.

Taylor was an All-Western Athletic Conference halfback at Arizona State. Following his senior season, he played in the East-West Shrine Game, the Hula Bowl, the All-American Bowl, and the Chicago College All-Star Game. As a Redskin, he earned all-pro honors in 1967, and was named All-NFC in both 1974 and 1975. He also played in eight Pro Bowls. [DS/PF]

JIM TAYLOR

Fullback. 6-0, 216. Louisiana State
Born September 20, 1935, Baton Rouge, Louisiana.
1958-1966 Green Bay, 1967 New Orleans
Inducted into Pro Football Hall of Fame in 1976.

Jim Taylor was a throwback to Bronko Nagurski. He ran with a fierce belligerence, he caught short swing passes, and he blocked with rugged dedication.

The Green Bay Packers of the 1960s, under coach Vince Lombardi, beat their opponents in a variety of ways—forward passes, big-yardage rushes, bone-jarring defense. But Jim Taylor, their rock-hard fullback, was the bread-and-butter guy, the man they looked to for 2 or 3 yards for a first down or for a single foot at the goal line. As the Packers dynasty grew, so, too, did the plaudits for Taylor, the symbol of power in the awesome Green Bay attack and the epitome of the ideal pro football fullback.

During his 10-year career—he spent nine seasons with the Packers and one year with the New Orleans Saints—Taylor amassed 8,597 yards rushing and scored 558 points. Taylor had the misfortune, however, of playing in the NFL at the same time a fellow fullback, Jim Brown of the Cleveland Browns, was piling up even bigger yardage totals, and it was Brown, instead of Taylor, who became the perennial all-pro fullback.

More than any other Packers runner, Taylor became adept at the favorite strategy of the Lombardi game-plan, "running to daylight," which meant that if a planned hole was clogged, the ball carrier simply ran to the nearest hole. That technique enabled Taylor to achieve five consecutive 1,000-yard seasons from 1960-64. [DS/PF]

LAWRENCE TAYLOR

Linebacker. 6-3, 241. North Carolina
Born February 4, 1959, Williamsburg, Virginia.
1981-1993 New York Giants
Inducted into Pro Football Hall of Fame in 1999.

Lawrence Taylor is the standard by which all future outside linebackers will be judged. In effect, he reinvented the position.

There had been versatile outside linebackers who could blitz, stuff the run, or cover passes before—Bobby Bell, Chuck Howley, Ted Hendricks, Jack Ham, and a few others—but they were primarily "read-and-react" defenders. With Taylor, linebacking went into an all-out "attack mode." He could disrupt the other team's offense so that they had to react to him.

In his 13 seasons with the New York Giants, Taylor relentlessly pursued anybody who had the ball. He used his blazing speed and powerful frame to hunt down quarterbacks, running backs and receivers, not to mention the headaches he caused blockers and coaches alike.

Taylor was an all-state linebacker and caught 10 touchdown passes on the state championship team in Williamsburg, Virginia, as a high school senior. He earned All-America honors at the University of North Carolina and was named Atlantic Coast Conference player of the year as a senior. The Giants made him the second pick of the 1981 draft, and he immediately paid dividends in New York. Taylor led the team to the playoffs his rookie season and helped the Giants triumph in the Super Bowl after the 1986 and 1990 seasons.

A 10-time Pro Bowl selection, "LT" became one of the most popular and most successful players in Giants' history. Taylor had his number 56 retired at Giants Stadium in 1994. He finished his career in second place on the NFL's all-time list with 132½ sacks. [MS]

LIONEL TAYLOR

Split End. 6-2, 205. New Mexico Highlands
Born August 15, 1936, Kansas City, Missouri.
1959 Chicago Bears, 1960-66 Denver, 1967-68 Houston

Taylor was an unlikely candidate to become the first pro receiver to catch 100 passes in a season, especially after the Chicago Bears used him infrequently as a defensive back in his rookie year, then released him.

Taylor cast his lot with the Denver Broncos in the new AFL. Not only did Taylor catch 100 balls in his second season with Denver, he led the AFL in receptions in five of his first six seasons. When the AFL closed its doors and joined the NFL in 1970, Taylor was the league's all-time leader in receptions.

If the AFL had had a record for one-handed catches, Taylor's name would have held that, too. He wasn't a speed burner, but his hands were among the best ever. He worked long and hard to perfect his ability to catch balls from all angles and speeds. Later, as a coach, he drilled his players on the same techniques.

Taylor had a knack for piling up yards after the catch. A perceived lack of strong secondaries in the early AFL caused some to minimize Taylor's numbers, but insiders know that he was among the best. [JJC]

OTIS TAYLOR

Wide Receiver. 6-3, 215. Prairie View A&M College
Born August 11, 1942, Houston, Texas.
1965-1975 Kansas City

There are many unusual stories of how players got to the NFL, but Otis Taylor's tale may top them all.

He was being hotly pursued by both the Philadelphia Eagles and Kansas City Chiefs during the AFL-NFL war in the mid-sixties, and was stashed in a Dallas hotel by Philadelphia, prior to his signing a contract with that NFL team. But scout Lloyd Wells of the Chiefs found the hideaway, pried open the window in Taylor's room where he sat alone watching television, and induced him to climb out and accompany him to sign a Kansas City contract.

Chiefs coach Hank Stram was so tired of being beaten by San Diego's great speedster, Lance Alworth, that he signed Taylor, who was a wide receiver with sprinter's speed at Prairie View. Taylor broke into Kansas City's starting lineup late in the 1966 season, his second year, after Chris Burford was injured. Taylor gained more than 1,000 yards in helping the Chiefs to Super Bowl I.

In that game, he caught a key pass in the first half to set up Kansas City's only touchdown. He had his biggest moment three Super Bowls later with an explosive 46-yard touchdown pass from Len Dawson that secured a 23-7 victory over the Minnesota Vikings in Super Bowl IV.

Despite his reputation as a sprinter, many defensive backs were fooled by his long running gait. He gobbled up more yards in fewer strides than any other receiver of his time. [JC]

THURMAN THOMAS

Running Back. 5-10, 198. Oklahoma State
Born May 16, 1966, Missouri City, Texas.
1988-1998 Buffalo

Thurman Thomas has been a consistent 1,000-yard rusher with the Buffalo Bills and holds the club record for most career touchdowns. In postseason play, he has had five 100-yard games, including 135 yards on 15 carries in Super Bowl XXV. That probably would have garnered him most-valuable-player honors, except his team lost to the New York Giants 20-19.

Still, those positive performances are not the things that critics remember. They focus on the 69 yards rushing on 37 carries he accumulated over the next three Super Bowls, his key fumble in Super Bowl XXVIII, and his infamous misplaced helmet at the start of Super Bowl XXVI.

Despite his Super Bowl errors, he has had a super career. "I love him dearly and I always will," said Bills general manager John Butler, putting things in perspective. "Thurman Thomas got us to four Super Bowls."

He was a 1,600-yard rusher as a senior at Oklahoma State, where Barry Sanders was Thomas's backup. But a knee operation at the end of his senior year forced many general managers to downgrade Thomas. He was picked by Buffalo in the second round of the 1988 draft. [MS]

JIM THORPE

Halfback. 6-1, 190. Carlisle
Born May 8, 1888, Prague, Oklahoma.
Died March 28, 1953, Lomita, California.
1915-17, 1919-1920, 1926 Canton, 1921 Cleveland, 1922-23 Oorang, 1923 Toledo, 1924 Rock Island, 1925 New York Giants, 1928 Chicago Cardinals
Inducted into Pro Football Hall of Fame in 1963.

Among the reasons the Pro Football Hall of Fame is located in Canton, Ohio, is the fact that the fabled Jim Thorpe, the first big-name American athlete to play pro football, began his pro football career in Canton in 1915.

Jack Cusack, the Canton Bulldogs' general manager, signed the most famous American athlete of the age for the princely sum of $250 a game. Thorpe was everything Cusack expected him to be—an exceptional talent and an unparalleled gate attraction. With Thorpe leading the way, the Bulldogs claimed unofficial world championships in 1916, 1917, and 1919.

While Thorpe's exploits tend to be exaggerated with the passing years, there is no question he was a superb football player. He could run with speed as well as bruising power. He could pass and catch passes with the best, punt long distances, and kick field goals either by dropkick or placekick. He blocked with authority and, on defense, was a bone-jarring tackler.

Thorpe, who was born in a one-room cabin in Prague, Oklahoma, had some French and Irish blood but he was mostly of Sac and Fox Indian heritage. His Native American Indian name was Wa-Tho-Huk, meaning "Bright Path," something he was destined to follow in sports.

He excelled in every sport he tried and won the decathlon in the 1912 Olympics, but was stripped of his gold medal because he had once been paid to play minor-league baseball (the medal was restored posthumously in 1982). But football was his favorite sport, and he firmly established his reputation when he scored 25 touchdowns in leading the Carlisle Indian School to the national collegiate championship in 1912. [DS/PF]

MICK TINGELHOFF

Center. 6-1, 237. Nebraska
Born May 22, 1940, Lexington, Nebraska.
1962-1978 Minnesota

Mick Tingelhoff had a date every Sunday. Tingelhoff lined up over the ball at Metropolitan Stadium as center for the Minnesota Vikings every Sunday for 16 years, regardless of the weather, the opponent, or the quarterback. Tingelhoff solidified the Vikings' line in the franchise's difficult early years and protected his quarterback through four Super Bowls (one with Joe Kapp as quarterback and three more with Fran Tarkenton). The Vikings lost all four games, but Minnesota qualified for the playoffs in 10 of Tingelhoff's last 11 years with the team.

Durability, toughness, and intelligence all were part of Tingelhoff's game, but his most distinguishing feature was his speed. He was one of the few centers in the National Football League who was fast enough to pull out of the line like a guard to lead a running play. Observers said it was almost as though he would snap the ball and be down the field cutting down a linebacker in one motion.

"He plays and plays well every week," his coach Bud Grant said. "He doesn't let the little injuries slow him down." Tingelhoff set a record for offensive linemen with 240 consecutive starts for the Vikings. The University of Nebraska graduate earned all-pro honors seven consecutive times from 1964-1970 and played in six Pro Bowls.

Despite playing a traditionally anonymous position on a team most noted for its Purple People Eaters defense, Tingelhoff was nevertheless able to carve out an enviable reputation as one of the best of his time. [MS]

Y.A. TITTLE
Quarterback. 6-0, 200. Louisiana State
Born October 24, 1926, Marshall, Texas.
1948-49 Baltimore (AAFC), 1950 Baltimore, 1951-1960 San Francisco, 1961-64 New York Giants
Inducted into Pro Football Hall of Fame in 1971.
Yelberton Abraham Tittle played as a pro quarterback for 17 seasons, but just four of them with the New York Giants. Yet, when he stepped down after the 1964 season, his Giants jersey (number 14) was retired, a tribute perhaps no other athlete ever earned in so short a time.

Tittle, who played three seasons with the Baltimore Colts—in the AAFC (1948, 1949) and NFL (1950)—and 10 seasons with the San Francisco 49ers (1951-1960), joined the Giants in 1961. Despite impressive individual statistics, Tittle never had played on a championship team.

But in New York that all changed. First, Tittle won over his new teammates. The Giants players were a close-knit outfit and, to them, Tittle seemed to be an outsider coming in to take over a job capably held by their friend, Charley Conerly, for most of a decade. As the 1961 season began, Tittle and Conerly shared the quarterback role, but as the Giants moved nearer to the Eastern Conference championship, it became more and more obvious that Tittle was the player who was making it all possible. He passed for 2,272 yards and 17 touchdowns and was named the NFL's most valuable player.

Tittle was even better the next two years. In 1962, he passed for a career-high 3,224 yards and 33 touchdowns. A year later, his touchdown figure went to 36. He completed 60.2 percent of his passes and again was named NFL player of the year. In his 17-season career, he passed for 33,070 yards and 242 touchdowns. [DS/PF]

GEORGE TRAFTON
Center. 6-2, 235. Notre Dame
Born December 6, 1896, Chicago, Illinois.
Died September 5, 1971, Los Angeles, California.
1920 Decatur, 1921 Chicago Staleys, 1923-1932 Chicago Bears
Inducted into Pro Football Hall of Fame in 1964.
In the NFL's early years, teams organized, joined the league, and disbanded with monotonous regularity. Players came quickly and left the same way. Those who did stick around for any length of time invariably played for several teams, often more than one every year.

But there was one notable exception to this general pattern. That was George Trafton, who was the durable, hard-hitting center of the Chicago Bears between 1920 and 1932. He started with the Decatur Staleys, forerunner of the Bears, in the first year of the American Professional Football Association, forerunner of the NFL. Trafton followed coach and new owner George Halas to Chicago when the team moved 100 miles north in 1921. Trafton missed only 1922 when he was an assistant coach at Northwestern. At that stage of history, he was the only player of note to have even played that long, let alone with one team.

Trafton was an excellent player and a superior competitor; he was named to various newspapers' all-pro teams in 6 of his 12 seasons. But there can be little doubt that he also held a deserved reputation as a player who was able to roughhouse with the best. [DS/PF]

CHARLEY TRIPPI
Halfback. 6-0, 185. Georgia
Born December 14, 1922, Pittston, Pennsylvania.
1947-1955 Chicago Cardinals
Inducted into Pro Football Hall of Fame in 1968.
When Chicago Cardinals owner Charles W. Bidwill, Sr., announced that he had signed Charley Trippi to a four-year contract worth a reported $100,000 early in 1947, it stunned the sports world.

Contracts of that size were unheard of in those days, and the signing proved to be a huge breakthrough for the NFL in its war with the All-America Football Conference. As a two-time All-America from the University of Georgia, Trippi was the most sought-after college athlete of his day.

Trippi's acquisition completed Bidwill's quest for a "Dream Backfield." Although Bidwill did not live to see it, Trippi became a gamebreaker in a talented corps that included quarterback Paul Christman, Pat Harder, Marshall Goldberg, and, later, Elmer Angsman. Never was Trippi more magnificent than in the 1947 NFL Championship Game, when the Cardinals defeated the Philadelphia Eagles 28-21. With the game played on an icy field in Chicago, Trippi wore basketball shoes for better traction and totaled 206 yards, including 102 yards on 2 punt returns. He scored touchdowns on a 44-yard run and a 75-yard punt return.

Trippi could do anything on a football field. He played as the Cardinals' left halfback for four years, switched to quarterback for two years, and went back to halfback for one season before changing almost exclusively to the defensive unit in 1954 and 1955. [DS/PF]

EMLEN TUNNELL
Safety. 6-1, 200. Toledo, Iowa
Born March 29, 1925, Bryn Mawr, Pennsylvania.
Died July 23, 1975, Pleasantville, New York.
1948-1958 New York Giants, 1959-1961 Green Bay
Inducted into Pro Football Hall of Fame in 1967.
During the decade of the 1950s, when the New York Giants were a perennial contender in the National Football League, Emlen Tunnell served as the key "strut" in the Giants' famed Umbrella Defense, and in so doing, put fear into the hearts of the opposition.

Tunnell entered the NFL as an obscure free agent in 1948 and soon emerged as an exceptional defensive back. He was known as the Giants' "offense on defense" through most of his 11-year tenure in New York. Never was this tag more appropriate, nor his contributions more spectacular, than in the early 1950s.

In 1952, for instance, Tunnell returned 30 punts for 411 yards, added 364 yards on 15 kickoff returns, and returned 7 interceptions for 149 yards.

When he entered the Pro Football Hall of Fame in 1967, he was both the first African-American and the first purely defensive player to be enshrined. [DS/PF]

CLYDE (BULLDOG) TURNER
Center. 6-2, 235. Hardin-Simmons

Born November 10, 1919, Sweetwater, Texas.
Died October 30, 1998, Gatesville, Texas.
1940-1952 Chicago Bears
Inducted into Pro Football Hall of Fame in 1966.
Coming from Hardin-Simmons, Turner was a surprise number-one draft choice for the Chicago Bears.

Back in 1940, the NFL draft was still in its infant stages, and scouts relied on football magazines for their information about potential pro football stars. Under this system, most attention was given to the big colleges. Rarely did a small-college star get much attention unless he was a big-yardage offensive star.

As it turned out, not one NFL team but two—the Detroit Lions and the Chicago Bears—had heard about Turner and eagerly sought his services. George Halas outmaneuvered the Lions to sign Turner, who quickly proved himself to be one of the best center-linebackers the NFL had yet seen. In his second season, Turner broke Mel Hein's string of eight consecutive years as the All-NFL center. In his career, Turner was named all-pro six times.

Turner was a versatile athlete who might well have played as an offensive back had he not excelled at center and linebacker. He was ready to play any position any time he was needed and learned everyone's assignment just in case. In 1942, Turner led the NFL in interceptions with 8 and, in 1947, in what he calls his favorite play in the pros, he intercepted a Sammy Baugh pass and returned it 96 yards for a touchdown. [DS/PF]

JIM TYRER

Tackle. 6-6, 283. Ohio State
Born February 25, 1939, Newark, Ohio.
Died September 15, 1980, Kansas City, Missouri.
1961-62 Dallas AFL, 1963-1973 Kansas City, 1974 Washington
Jim Tyrer was a man who would not let anything stand in his way. During 14 years as an offensive tackle, he made sure no one got in the way of his quarterback.

Tyrer was a three-sport athlete at Newark (Ohio) High School but decided on football over basketball and track for college. He was an All-America choice at Ohio State as a senior in 1960 and was drafted by both the Cleveland Browns in the NFL and the Dallas Texans in the AFL.

He chose the Texans and the AFL and became a starting tackle as a rookie. In 1963, the Texans moved to Kansas City to become the Chiefs. Tyrer appeared in two Super Bowls, two Pro Bowls, three AFL title games, and seven AFL All-Star games.

Tyrer played in Super Bowl I with the Kansas City Chiefs, a 35-10 loss to the Green Bay Packers, and played in the last game before the two leagues merged, a 23-7 victory over the Minnesota Vikings in Super Bowl IV. He left the Chiefs after the 1973 season and finished his career with the Washington Redskins.

He had great size, speed, and endurance; he played 12 consecutive years without missing a game. He was named to the Chiefs' Hall of Fame and by the Pro Football Hall of Fame to the All-Time AFL Team. [MS]

JOHNNY UNITAS

Quarterback. 6-1, 195. Louisville
Born May 7, 1933, Pittsburgh, Pennsylvania.
1956-1972 Baltimore, 1973 San Diego Chargers
Inducted into Pro Football Hall of Fame in 1979.
More than any other single event, the 1958 National Football League Championship Game, in which the Baltimore Colts defeated the New York Giants 23-17 in overtime, catapulted pro football toward the heights of fan popularity it knows today.

The game's most valuable player was young quarterback Johnny Unitas, who had his first chance to demonstrate to a nationwide television audience the attributes that would eventually make him one of the most fabled and followed NFL stars in history.

In addition to his undeniable abilities, Unitas grabbed the public's heart with his Cinderella story. He was the ninth-round pick of the Pittsburgh Steelers in 1955 but was cut. So he played semipro football for a year, then was signed as a free agent by the Colts in 1956. When regular quarterback George Shaw was injured in the fourth game, Unitas took over the job.

Unitas was a team player through and through. He never criticized his teammates publicly, but when someone let down on the field, it was a different story. There was never a question of who was running the show. As one Colt described being in the huddle with Unitas, "It's like being in the huddle with God."

His career statistics were awesome—2,830 pass completions, 40,239 yards, and 290 touchdown passes. His NFL record of at least 1 touchdown pass in 47 consecutive games may stand forever. He was an all-pro pick five times, the NFL player of the year three times, and a 10-time Pro Bowl selection. [DS/PF]

RICK UPCHURCH

Wide Receiver-Kick Returner. 5-10, 175. Minnesota
Born May 20, 1952, Toledo, Ohio.
1975-1983 Denver
Teams hate to punt the ball, and Rick Upchurch made them hate it even more. Upchurch gave his team a weapon on special teams—a weapon that could explode from any part of the field. Upchurch tied a 25-year-old NFL record with 4 punt returns for touchdowns in his second season with the Denver Broncos in 1976. He had returns of 73 and 47 yards for touchdowns against Cleveland, then scored on a club-record 92-yard return the following week against the San Diego Chargers. He added a 55-yard score against Kansas City Chiefs and set up another touchdown with a 64-yard return.

Upchurch had one of the most spectacular debuts in NFL history with 284 combined yards in the 1975 season opener against Kansas City. The 175-pound receiver caught 3 passes for 153 yards, including a 90-yard touchdown, had 4 returns for 118 yards, and added a flanker reverse for 13 yards.

Upchurch was a key member of Denver's 1977 AFC championship team and tied for the team lead with 4 receiving touchdowns. While mostly noted for his prowess as a return specialist—he scored 8 touchdowns on returns—Upchurch also was a talented receiver in his nine-year career. He is ranks among the Broncos' all-time leaders for most receiving yards (4,369), catches (267), and yards per catch (16.6). Not surprisingly, he is number one in nearly every kick-return category in franchise history. [MS]

GENE UPSHAW

Guard. 6-5, 255. Texas A&I
Born August 15, 1945, Robstown, Texas.
1967-1981 Oakland Raiders
Inducted into Pro Football Hall of Fame in 1987.

Gene Upshaw was the Oakland Raiders' first-round choice in the first combined AFL-NFL draft in 1967. The Raiders needed a big guard to take on such huge defensive tackles as Buck Buchanan and Ernie Ladd.

At 6 feet 5 inches and 255 pounds, he wasn't built along the lines of traditional guards; he had played center, tackle, and end while winning NAIA All-America honors at Texas A&I. Nevertheless, he won the starting left guard job in his rookie training camp. Soon other teams were drafting tall guards. He held onto the job for the next 15 seasons, starting 207 consecutive regular-season games until finally being forced out of action for one game in 1981, his final season.

Upshaw played 317 preseason, regular-season, and postseason games. Included in his 24 postseason games were three AFL and seven AFC Championship Games and Super Bowls II, XI, and XV. With an AFL championship in 1967 and victories in Super Bowls XI and XV, Upshaw was the only player to start on championship teams in both the AFL and NFL.

He was named all-pro or All-AFC eight times. He was selected for the 1968 AFL All-Star Game and six AFC-NFC Pro Bowls.

Upshaw, the NFL Players' Association executive director in his post-playing days, was an intense, intelligent, dedicated competitor who used his size and speed to best advantage. Extremely effective leading wide running plays, he was an integral part of the powerful offensive line that spawned the Raiders' lethal running attack of the 1970s. Upshaw captained the Raiders' offensive unit for eight seasons. [DS/PF]

NORM VAN BROCKLIN

Quarterback. 6-1, 190. Oregon
Born March 15, 1926, Eagle Butte, South Dakota.
Died May 2, 1983, Social Circle, Georgia.
1949-1957 Los Angeles Rams, 1958-1960 Philadelphia
Inducted into Pro Football Hall of Fame in 1971.

One of the most colorful and competitive individuals that pro football has seen, Van Brocklin blazed a sometimes stormy but always eventful path in his dozen NFL years as a player.

Van Brocklin spent his first nine seasons with the Rams, during which the team won four division titles and one league championship. He was traded to the Eagles in 1958 and, within three years, "The Dutchman" had guided the Eagles to the NFL championship.

Van Brocklin left the University of Oregon with a year's eligibility remaining to join the Rams in 1949. The only problem, from Van Brocklin's standpoint, was that the Rams already had one future Hall-of-Fame quarterback in Bob Waterfield. The net result was that two great quarterbacks had to share passing duties, a situation that any great competitor, which both men were, couldn't be expected to accept with any enthusiasm.

Still, Van Brocklin won the NFL passing title in both 1950 and 1952, even though he was playing only half the time on offense. He earned a third passing title in 1954. His greatest day as a passer came in 1951, when he threw for a record 554 yards against the New York Yanks.

If Van Brocklin always had to face the challenge of other quarterbacks with the Rams, he found just the opposite situation in Philadelphia, where he was given a free hand at running the offensive show. Behind Van Brocklin, the Eagles won the NFL title in 1960 in his last game before taking over as coach of the expansion Vikings. [DS/PF]

STEVE VAN BUREN

Halfback. 6-1, 200. Louisiana State
Born December 28, 1920, La Ceiba, Honduras.
1944-1951 Philadelphia
Inducted into Pro Football Hall of Fame in 1965.

A battering ram of a runner, Van Buren led the league in rushing four times. In 1947, he became only the second NFL ball carrier to rush for a 1,000 yards. He had a second 1,000-yard campaign in 1949.

Van Buren joined the Eagles in 1944. He wasn't particularly elusive, but his combination of bull-like strength and surprising speed made him the NFL's premier runner. Philadelphia dominated the NFL the next six years, culminating with three consecutive division titles and NFL championships in 1948 and 1949. Van Buren won all-league honors five of those six seasons.

Van Buren's early years were not particularly happy ones. Born in La Ceiba, Honduras, he was orphaned at an early age and sent to New Orleans to live with his grandparents. He failed to make the football team as a 125-pound high school sophomore, but as a senior he played well enough to win an LSU scholarship.

He had a splendid senior season at LSU when he rushed for 832 yards. The Eagles, tipped off by LSU coach Bernie Moore, drafted him in the first round in 1944. It was a break for Van Buren and, for the Eagles, possibly their most fortunate move ever. [DS/PF]

DOAK WALKER

Halfback. 5-10, 172. Southern Methodist
Born January 1, 1927, Dallas, Texas.
Died September 27, 1998, Steamboat Springs, Colorado.
1950-55 Detroit
Inducted into Pro Football Hall of Fame in 1986.

Doak Walker, a three-time All-America and the 1948 Heisman Trophy winner at Southern Methodist, brought glowing credentials to pro football when he joined the Detroit Lions in 1950. Yet many scouts honestly felt that, at 5 feet 11 inches and 175 pounds, Walker was too small and, while versatile, not a specialist at any phase of the game. They predicted the "big boys" of the NFL would simply overwhelm him.

Walker quickly erased any of the doubts that he belonged in pro football. In 1950, he was all-pro, the rookie of the year, the league scoring champion with a rookie-record 128 points, and a Pro Bowl participant. Walker retired after the 1955 season as a four-time all-pro and five-time Pro Bowl selection. It is no coincidence that the Lions enjoyed their best years with three divisional titles and two NFL championships with Walker on the team.

Just as he had done at SMU, Walker was a do-everything contributor for the Lions. His career chart shows entries in every possible statistical category—rushing, passing, receiving, punt and kickoff returns, punting, kicking, and even interceptions, for Walker also played defense whenever he was needed. Because he did so many things, his career figures are not overly impressive except in the scoring column. He scored 534 points.

Walker had the knack of making the big plays in the most important games. In the 1952 NFL title game, his 67-yard run proved to be the winning touchdown in a 17-7 victory. A year later, he scored the game's first touchdown, then kicked the winning extra point in a 17-16 triumph. [DS/PF]

HERSCHEL WALKER

Running Back. 6-1, 226. Georgia
Born March 3, 1962, Wrightsville, Georgia.
1986-89, 1996-97 Dallas, 1989-1991 Minnesota, 1992-94 Philadelphia, 1995 New York Giants

Despite having a career most players would envy, Herschel Walker always will be considered a disappointment by some fans.

As a freshman at the University of Georgia, Walker was All-America, Southeastern Conference player of the year and led his team to the national championship. By the time he was a junior he had three SEC player-of-the-year trophies, a coveted Heisman Trophy, held 80 NCAA, SEC, and Georgia records, and was ranked with the greatest runners ever.

In 1983, he skipped his senior year to turn professional and immediately became the greatest player in league history, recording 11 consecutive 100-yard games. That league, however, was the United States Football League, not the NFL.

When the USFL folded after three years, Walker joined the Dallas Cowboys. He responded with solid seasons in 1986 and 1987, but in 1988 he showed the form that had been predicted. He gained 1,514 yards rushing and earned 505 yards as a receiver.

The moribund Cowboys could have built the team around Walker, but they decided to use him to rebuild the team instead. In one of the most famous—or infamous—trades in NFL history, the Cowboys sent Walker to the Minnesota Vikings in the largest trade ever (18 players or draft picks were involved). The Cowboys won back-to-back Super Bowls in five years; in Minnesota, Walker was stuck in an offensive system unsuited to his talents. After three disappointing seasons with the Vikings, he signed with Philadelphia, where he surpassed 1,000 yards rushing in 1992. [MS]

EVERSON WALLS

Cornerback. 6-1, 194. Grambling
Born December 28, 1959, Dallas, Texas.
1981-89 Dallas, 1990-92 New York Giants, 1992-93 Cleveland

The Dallas Cowboys weren't smart enough to draft Everson Walls in 1981, but they were lucky enough that he lived nearby.

Walls was not selected by any team out of Grambling University after his senior season, so the Dallas native signed a free-agent contract with the hometown Cowboys. He not only made the team, he was a starter at defensive back. The undrafted rookie proceeded to lead the NFL with 11 interceptions.

Rookies often break in with high interception totals simply because they are the defensive backs who will be most tested by veteran quarterbacks. If they prove themselves up to the task, their subsequent interception marks drop as passers move on to other tempting targets.

Walls was an exception. He intercepted 57 passes in 13 years to tie for ninth place on the all-time list. He is the only person in NFL history to lead the league in interceptions three times (1981, 1982, and 1985).

Walls, after nine seasons and four Pro Bowls, left Dallas and went to the New York Giants as a free agent in 1990. Walls started at right cornerback in Super Bowl XXV and helped contain the Buffalo Bills' explosive No-Huddle offense in New York's 20-19 victory. He was released by the Giants in 1992 and finished his career with the Cleveland Browns the following season. [MS]

PAUL WARFIELD

Wide Receiver. 6-0, 188. Ohio State
Born November 28, 1942, Warren, Ohio.
1964-69, 1976-77 Cleveland Browns, 1970-74 Miami
Inducted into Pro Football Hall of Fame in 1983.

Picture a graceful athlete streaking downfield, leaping in the air, gently grasping the football, then heading toward the goal line. That was Paul Warfield at his prime.

Warfield had the good fortune to play with two extremely successful NFL teams, the Cleveland Browns at both the start and the end of his 13-year career and with the Miami Dolphins in the middle. He often was showcased in big games—four NFL championships and three AFC title games.

Although he was one of history's premier wide receivers, the former Ohio State star did not post big numbers. His career totals are impressive considering the time he played and the teams for which he played, but he does not crack the NFL's all-time top 20.

Warfield happened to play on ball-control teams that looked to the forward pass more as a threat to make the ground game effective than as a heavy-duty offensive weapon. A first-round draft pick of the Browns in 1964, Warfield played in Cleveland for six seasons before going to the Miami Dolphins in a blockbuster trade in 1970.

Two years later, the Dolphins became the first team ever to record a perfect season. Warfield's presence was considered a key factor for the 17-0 Dolphins, though he caught only 29 passes all season. The Dolphins rushed 613 times and went to the air just 280 times. But the constant threat of a Warfield reception (he averaged 20.9 yards per catch) kept opposing defenses on guard. [DS/PF]

BOB WATERFIELD

Quarterback. 6-2, 200. UCLA

Born July 26, 1920, Elmira, New York.
Died March 25, 1983, Burbank, California.
1945 Cleveland Rams, 1946-1952 Los Angeles Rams
Inducted into Pro Football Hall of Fame in 1965.
It is a long-standing adage that a rookie quarterback can't lead his team to a championship in the NFL but, somehow, Waterfield never got the word.

In 1944, Cleveland Rams owner Dan Reeves selected Waterfield, an All-America quarterback from UCLA, as a third-round future draft choice. The Rams had not finished above the .500 mark since joining the NFL in 1937 but Waterfield quickly changed that. He arrived in 1945 and led the Rams to a 27-14 lacing of the defending champion Green Bay Packers en route to a 9-1 regular-season record to earn a championship showdown against Sammy Baugh's Washington Redskins. Waterfield won the duel with a 15-14 victory in what turned out to be the last game for the Rams in Cleveland.

In the offseason, the Rams moved to Los Angeles and Waterfield, the hometown hero with movie star Jane Russell as his wife, stayed with them for seven more star-studded seasons. He won all-pro honors three times and won the league passing championship in 1946 and 1951.

He was, however, more than just an outstanding passer. He was a quadruple-threat performer. Besides his passing, he had a career punting average of 42.4 yards. He rushed for 13 touchdowns and added 495 points kicking for a career total of 573 points.

Unfortunately for Waterfield, the Rams had another future Hall-of-Fame quarterback, Norm Van Brocklin, and the two were forced to share playing time for much of Waterfield's career. Perhaps because of this situation, Waterfield retired after the 1952 season, while he was still in his prime. [DS/PF]

CHARLIE WATERS
Defensive Back. 6-1, 194. Clemson
Born July 10, 1948, Miami, Florida.
1970-78, 1980-81 Dallas
Charlie Waters played cornerback and free safety for the Dallas Cowboys before settling in at strong safety in his sixth season. He had played quarterback and strong safety at Clemson, and the Cowboys made him a third-round pick in the 1970 draft.

Waters and free safety Cliff Harris became a marvelous tandem in the deep secondary for Dallas because they complemented each other's skills so well. Waters was a cerebral player, the "brains" of the Cowboys' secondary. He was quick enough to avoid blockers and strong enough to force running plays to the inside or step into a hole and make a linebacker-like tackle. Harris was a daredevil free safety who flew around the field making plays, knowing Waters would back him up.

"The guys you have to beat when you play Dallas are Waters and Harris," Detroit running back Dexter Bussey once noted. "They come at you like linebackers, and you have to juke them, duck under them, or they'll knock your head off. They are so quick that even if you do beat them, they can recover and make the tackle."

Waters finished his career with 41 interceptions, third most in Cowboys history. He was picked for three Pro Bowls, including two when Harris was selected to play alongside him. A knee injury cost him the entire 1979 season. [JC]

MIKE WEBSTER
Center. 6-1, 250. Wisconsin
Born March 18, 1952, Tomahawk, Wisconsin.
1974-1988 Pittsburgh, 1989-1990 Kansas City
Inducted into Pro Football Hall of Fame in 1997.
Mike Webster was a partner in the firm of Swann, Lambert, Stallworth, and Webster. That was the Steelers' draft class of 1974. He outlasted the others in his 17-year career and earned a reputation as the best center of his day and one of the best of any day.

When Webster arrived in Pittsburgh, Ray Mansfield was the resident ironman at center; he had a consecutive-game streak of well over 150 games and would retire with a club-record 182. Webster was such an obvious talent that he and Mansfield soon were alternating quarters. Eventually, Webster would play in 177 consecutive games, second only to Mansfield. But Webster did something else noteworthy from a durability standpoint; he made every offensive snap for six consecutive seasons. Webster played more seasons (15) and more games (220) than any other Steeler.

As a center, it was Webster's job to make the line calls, commands that told all offensive linemen which of the Steelers' complex blocking schemes was in effect. Webster performed the task to near-perfection. Webster was a realist about the anonymity of offensive linemen. At an NFL Alumni player-of-the-year dinner, he said, "It isn't unusual for a center to be invited to something like this; they just don't tell us when or where it's being held." [JJC]

ROGER WEHRLI
Cornerback. 6-0, 194. Missouri
Born November 26, 1947, St. Louis, Missouri.
1969-1982 St. Louis
Whether the Cardinals were good or bad—and they were both during Wehrli's tenure in St. Louis—Wehrli was consistently among the NFL's upper echelon. His 40 career interceptions are second only to Hall of Fame free safety Larry Wilson on the team's all-time interception list.

A seven-time Pro Bowl selection and a former high school sprint champion, Wehrli maintained enough speed and savvy to play the demanding position for 14 seasons. He and Wilson formed half of the all-pro secondary for several seasons. When Wilson blitzed from safety, Wehrli shouldered even more coverage responsibility. The Missouri native was up to the task.

The nation's leading punt returner as a senior All-America at Missouri, Wehrli returned punts for the Cardinals for the first half of his career. Blessed with considerable talent, he also had a fine work ethic and sense of purpose. Don Coryell, who coached the Cardinals in the mid-1970s, once said of him, "I have never seen anyone with more determination to succeed." [JJC]

ARNIE WEINMEISTER
Defensive Tackle. 6-4, 235. Washington
Born March 23, 1923, Rhein, Saskatchewan, Canada.

1948-49 New York Yankees (AAFC), 1950-53 New York Giants
Inducted into Pro Football Hall of Fame in 1984.
Few players ever have been so dominant at their position in pro football than Arnie Weinmeister was in his six-year career as a defensive tackle. His career began with the New York Yankees of the AAFC in 1948 and ended with the New York Giants of the NFL in 1953. He won first team All-AAFC honors in 1949, then was a unanimous all-pro choice all four years with the Giants. He also was selected to play in the NFL's Pro Bowl four times.

Weinmeister was one of the first defensive players to captivate fans the way an offensive ball handler does. He had good size, exceptional strength, and was widely considered to be the fastest lineman in pro football. Blessed with an extremely keen football instinct, he was a master at diagnosing opposition plays, then thwarting whatever the opposition attempted, but it was as a pass rusher that he really caught the fans' notice.

His ability to pressure the opposing quarterback enabled New York Giants coach Steve Owen to institute the famed Umbrella Defense that called for the ends, the normal pass rushers, to often drop off the line into linebacking positions.

Weinmeister played end, fullback, and tackle in his four-year tenure at the University of Washington, a tenure interrupted by a four-year army stint during World War II. New York Yankees coach Ray Flaherty first spotted Weinmeister as a fullback but wisely made him into a two-way tackle when he turned pro in 1948. When he moved to the Giants after the AAFC-NFL war ended, Weinmeister was used almost exclusively on defense. [DS/PF]

BYRON (WHIZZER) WHITE
Halfback. 6-1, 187. Colorado
Born June 8, 1917, Ft. Collins, Colorado.
1938 Pittsburgh, 1940-41 Detroit
White raised the art of benchwarming to the ultimate—all the way to the U.S. Supreme Court.

White, a Heisman Trophy runner-up and consensus All-America tailback at Colorado in 1937, was not going to play pro football. He was a Phi Beta Kappa and had been awarded a Rhodes Scholarship to study at Oxford. But Johnny (Blood) McNally, coach of the Pittsburgh Pirates (now the Steelers) thought so much of White that he had team owner Art Rooney's permission to offer the future justice an unheard-of $15,800 to play a season in the NFL.

White learned that he could delay his graduate studies until after his rookie season and signed. He was the NFL's leading rusher by more than 100 yards, then departed for a year's study in England. Thinking White was through with football, Rooney sold his rights to the Lions. World War II heated up in Europe and White returned to the United States. He played the 1940 season with the Lions and again led the league in rushing. He also played in 1941, but he was a marked man on a mediocre team. After the season, he entered the military.

President John F. Kennedy appointed White to the highest court in the land in 1962. Ever the athlete, White, who also starred in baseball, basketball, and track in college, amazed law clerks 40 years his junior in pickup basketball games over lunch hour in the Supreme Court gym.

The NFL Players Association has named its award for humanitarianism for White. [JJC]

RANDY WHITE
Defensive Tackle. 6-4, 265. Maryland
Born January 15, 1953, Wilmington, Delaware.
1975-1988 Dallas
Inducted into Pro Football Hall of Fame in 1994.
Randy White was a disappointment—for a while. The former Maryland All-America was the Dallas Cowboys' first pick and the second player selected in the 1975 NFL draft.

The Cowboys envisioned him as a great middle linebacker. For his first two seasons he was tested at that position and found wanting. But in his third season, when he became the starting right defensive tackle, the position he'd starred at in college, he emerged as a superstar. For the remainder of his 14-season, 209-game NFL career, White was the anchor of the Dallas Cowboys' excellent defensive line.

White capped his first season as a regular by being named as the co-most valuable player in the Cowboys' 27-10 win over the Denver Broncos in Super Bowl XII. The next season in 1978, White was named the NFL defensive player of the year. That year he began a string of eight consecutive seasons as a virtually unanimous all-pro. White also was named to nine consecutive Pro Bowls from the 1977-1985 seasons.

Blessed with all the traits of a great defensive lineman—quickness, balance, toughness, ability, desire, intelligence, and durability—he missed only one game in 14 seasons. He played in three Super Bowls and six NFC championship games. White recorded 4 sacks in those three Super Bowls, including 2 in Super Bowl X against Pittsburgh. [DS/PF]

REGGIE WHITE
Defensive End-Defensive Tackle. 6-5, 289. Tennessee
Born December 19, 1961, Chattanooga, Tennessee.
1985-1992 Philadelphia, 1993-98 Green Bay
White has more sacks than any other player since the NFL began keeping that statistic officially in 1982. Although he is famous for his ability to pressure quarterbacks, White is an equal-opportunity destroyer of running backs.

"He's as good a player as ever to play the position in the history of the game," Packers general manager Ron Wolf said.

White was good enough to be named the NFL defensive player of the year in 1998, his final season. He had 16 sacks for the Packers that year, then announced his retirement after 14 NFL seasons.

White's NFL-topping regular-season career sack total of 192½ does not even count the 23½ sacks he amassed in the United States Football League in 1984 and 1985. He left the Memphis Showboats and the ill-fated USFL behind and headed to Philadelphia, where he helped change the Eagles' fortunes. In 1985, the year the USFL folded, White played a total of 31 games between the two leagues. That season was the only one of his NFL career that White was not named to the Pro Bowl, but he probably needed the rest anyhow.

From 1985-1992, the Eagles made four playoff appearances with White. He had 21 sacks in only 12 games in 1987, and just missed breaking Mark Gastineau's NFL mark of 22, which had been set during the 1984 season.

White was so revered at the University of Tennessee that he was named to the Volunteers' all-time team. He was a consensus All-America pick and the Southeastern Conference player of the year as a senior with the Vols.

The nickname White received at Tennessee, "The Minister of Defense," fits him perfectly. White is an ordained minister. His intensity and leadership on the field gave way to his spiritual side off the field. [MS]

DAVE WILCOX
Outside Linebacker. 6-3, 240. Oregon
Born September 29, 1942, Ontario, Oregon.
1964-1974 San Francisco

"Dave Wilcox is the best I've ever seen at his position," said long-time NFL player and coach Paul Wiggin, who saw a lot of outside linebackers. The former Oregon star was ideally suited for the position, mentally and physically. He simply wanted to be the greatest linebacker to play the game. His long arms and good speed helped greatly.

Wilcox played for the 49ers when they were not yet the team they would become in the eighties. Despite being all-pro four times and invited to seven Pro Bowls, Wilcox is somewhat of a forgotten man. As one pro football observer remarked in a group discussion, "No one played better and was forgotten faster than Dave Wilcox."

The NFL was full of tight ends who knew how difficult it was to run pass patterns against the strongside linebacker. He simply didn't let anybody off the line, whether to block or to get into a pass route.

Wilcox thrived on action and wanted it all directed his way, but he assessed his own game, "What I do best is not let people block me. I just hate to be blocked."

Rams quarterback Roman Gabriel paid the overlooked linebacker a supreme compliment, "He plays outside linebacker like Dick Butkus plays middle linebacker." [JJC]

BILL WILLIS
Guard. 6-2, 215. Ohio State
Born October 5, 1921, Columbus, Ohio.
1946-1953 Cleveland
Inducted into Pro Football Hall of Fame in 1977.

Willis came to the Cleveland Browns' tryout camp as a comparatively small man seeking a job in a big man's sport.

Any doubt that Willis could make the grade was permanently erased during his first scrimmage. Lined up as the middle man of a five-man defensive front, Willis eluded the center four consecutive times, each time crashing quickly into quarterback Otto Graham. Observers felt he had to be offside. But Paul Brown, who had coached Willis at Ohio State, checked and found out his new recruit hadn't been offside, just exceptionally fast and agile.

At 215 pounds, Willis was small by pro football standards, even in the 1940s. But for eight seasons with the Browns in both the All-America Football Conference and the National Football League, he was in a class by himself. He was all-league seven of the years he played from 1946-1953 and played in three NFL Pro Bowls beginning in 1950.

Willis and teammate Marion Motley, who joined the team a week later, were the first African-Americans in the All-America Football Conference.

Willis played both offense and defense for the Browns, but it was at middle guard on defense that he earned lasting acclaim. He was the hub of a Cleveland defense that annually allowed fewer points than any other team in the league. The Browns' press book once boasted that photographers had to shoot Willis at 1/600th of a second to stop the action. But at least they could stop him, something no opponent really ever did successfully. [DS/PF]

LARRY WILSON
Safety. 6-0, 190. Utah
Born March 24, 1938, Rigby, Idaho.
1960-1972 St. Louis
Inducted into Pro Football Hall of Fame in 1978.

During his 13-season career, Larry Wilson, the St. Louis Cardinals' dynamo safety earned the reputation of being "the toughest player in the NFL."

Fractures, stitches, broken teeth, bumps and bruises by the thousands—the never-say-die Wilson endured them all. In a game against Pittsburgh, he ignored doctor's orders and, while playing with casts on two broken hands, intercepted a pass for a go-ahead touchdown.

If Wilson suffered punishment himself, however, all the NFL's top passers also were battered at one time or another by the sterling free safety. If the league's passers weren't being smashed to the ground after a safety blitz, they were watching helplessly as Wilson was making one of his 52 career interceptions. A perennial all-pro, Wilson also played in eight Pro Bowls.

As a rookie, Wilson had serious doubts he could make the team. A two-way star in college, he quickly found offense in the NFL was not his cup of tea. But the late Chuck Drulis, the Cardinals' defensive coordinator, had been planning a daring defensive maneuver—soon to become famous as the safety blitz. Drulis was waiting for just the right man to come along to try it, and he decided Wilson was the guy who could do the job.

The play was code-named "Wildcat" and Wilson handled it so well that it soon became his nickname. Although historians disagree over what player first ran the safety blitz, there's no doubt who perfected it. [DS/PF]

KELLEN WINSLOW
Tight End. 6-5, 250. Missouri
Born November 5, 1957, St. Louis, Missouri.
1979-1987 San Diego Chargers
Inducted into Pro Football Hall of Fame in 1995.

Winslow brought a new dimension to the tight end position because he was big enough to block like a tight end, but had the speed and receiving ability to give the talent-laden San Diego Chargers an additional deep threat.

The Chargers engineered a draft-day trade with the Cleveland Browns to get the rights to the University of Missouri All-America. He was the thirteenth player selected in the 1979 NFL draft. He amassed 541 receptions for 6,741 yards and 45 touchdowns in just nine seasons from 1979-1987, and may have had more receptions if not for a serious knee injury in 1984.

Winslow was a consensus all-pro in 1980, 1981, and 1982, a four-time All-AFC choice and an AFC Pro Bowl selection five times. The Chargers' passing attack soared with the receiving corps of Charlie Joiner, Wes Chandler, and Winslow.

He had a career-high 89 receptions for 1,290 yards in 1980 and had 88 catches both in 1981 and 1982 to give him 319 receptions in his first four seasons. His most memorable performance came in a 41-38 overtime playoff victory over Miami in 1981. He caught 13 passes for 166 yards and blocked a field goal with four seconds to play to send the game into overtime.

A knee injury forced Winslow to miss 17 games in 1984 and 1985. He returned to his old form long enough to earn a Pro Bowl invitation after the 1987 season. It turned out to be his final game. [DS/PF]

AL WISTERT

Tackle. 6-1, 214. Michigan
Born December 10, 1920, Chicago, Illinois.
1943 Phil-Pitt, 1944-1951 Philadelphia

Great tackle play ran in the Wistert family. Al was an All-America tackle at Michigan in 1942, and his two older brothers were also Wolverine All-America tackles: Francis in 1933 and Alvin in the late 1940s after returning from military service. Only Al played professionally, but he was probably the most consistently honored lineman of his time. In his nine seasons with the Eagles (1943-1951), he received at least a second-team all-league selection in every year except his first. From 1944-48, he was consensus all-pro.

During the 1940s, the surest gain in the NFL was the Eagles' Steve Van Buren off right tackle. Van Buren was a phenomenal runner, but it was Wistert's key blocks at the line of scrimmage that sprang Van Buren into the opponent's secondary.

For much of his career, Wistert was a two-way star. At 214 pounds, he was one of the league's smallest tackles, but he more than made up for any lack of bulk with speed and fighting spirit. On defense, he used his speed to beat defenders. Sometimes Eagles coach Earle (Greasy) Neale had him drop back off the line because of his ability to cover pass receivers out of the backfield. On offense, where he really excelled, Neale called him "the greatest offensive tackle I have ever seen."

If the Eagles seemed flat before a game, Neale would sometimes turn the squad over to Wistert on Saturdays so that he could put them into a fighting mood for Sunday. [BC]

ALEX WOJCIECHOWICZ

Center-Defensive Back. 6-0, 235. Fordham
Born August 12, 1915, South River, New Jersey.
Died July 13, 1992, Forked River, New Jersey.
1938-1946 Detroit, 1946-1950 Philadelphia
Inducted into Pro Football Hall of Fame in 1968.

Alex Wojciechowicz first gained fame in college as a member of Fordham's famous Seven Blocks of Granite line, earning a two-time All-America status. Playing right next to "Wojie" was future coaching legend Vince Lombardi.

Wojciechowicz was the Detroit Lions' number-one draft choice in 1938 and won the starting center job in his first game as a Lion. During his years in Detroit, the Lions slipped from one of the NFL's strongest teams to one of its weakest. Wojciechowicz continued his strong blocking, and he was always the bulwark of the Detroit defense. Then, when "Wojie" was traded to the Eagles in the middle of the 1946 season, he became a defensive specialist and the ringleader of a formidable Philadelphia defensive platoon.

Wojciechowicz was the comic relief on the football team, the kind of guy every team likes to have around. On the field, however, he was all business, one of the last of the true ironmen of football, a center on offense and a sure tackler with good range in the secondary. In 1944, Wojciechowicz intercepted 7 passes, a Lions' record for several years.

Wojciechowicz's burning desire to play on a championship team never was realized in Detroit but when he moved to Philadelphia, he became revitalized in a defensive specialist role and was a major contributor to the Eagles' 1948 and 1949 NFL championship teams. He retired in 1950 after 13 seasons. [DS/PF]

WILLIE WOOD

Safety. 5-10, 190. Southern California
Born December 23, 1936, Washington, D.C.
1960-1971 Green Bay
Inducted into Pro Football Hall of Fame in 1989.

Willie Wood is another of the talented athletes who teamed to give Green Bay pro football dominance in the 1960s. Yet he had to seek a tryout and prove his worth before the Packers accepted him as a free agent in 1960.

At the University of Southern California, he had been a quarterback whose strong suit was running the football. There was no market for running quarterbacks in the NFL, and Wood went undrafted.

Recognizing his athleticism, the Packers moved him over to defense. Within a short time, Wood was recognized as a premier free safety. He became a starter in his second season (1961) and held that job for more than a decade until his retirement following the 1971 season.

Wood won all-pro honors five times in an eight-year stretch beginning in 1964 and continuing through his final 1971 season. A Pro Bowl participant eight times from 1962-1970, Wood also played in six NFL Championship Games. The Packers won all but the first one in 1960. He also was the starting free safety for Green Bay in Super Bowls I and II. His 50-yard interception return of a Len Dawson pass early in the third quarter of Super Bowl I broke open a close contest and paved the way for the Packers' 35-10 triumph over Kansas City.

Wood starred whenever he was given the chance to handle the football. He has 48 career interceptions and won the NFL interception title in 1962 with 9. Doubling on the punt-return team, he paced the league with a 16.1-yard punt-return average in 1961. [DS/PF]

ABE WOODSON

Kick Returner-Defensive Back. 5-11, 188. Illinois
Born February 15, 1934, Jackson, Mississippi.
1958-1964 San Francisco, 1965-66 St. Louis

For all of Abe Woodson's moves on the football field, he couldn't seem to shake losing. He missed the San Francisco 49ers' playoff appearance in 1957 during a hitch in the army and did not play for a team that won more than seven games until his final season with the St. Louis Cardinals in 1966.

Woodson was a track, football, and basketball star at Austin High School in Chicago and continued to impress with his speed in college. He twice tied the world record in the 50-meter hurdles and played both offense and defense at the University of Illinois. He was a speed demon out of the backfield (1,271 yards rushing) and had good hands (31 catches for 571 yards). His biggest game came against Michigan State in 1956. He scored 3 touchdowns, including a decisive 82-yard screen pass that led Illinois to a comeback victory.

Although he did not play offense in the NFL, Woodson still demonstrated the ability to make the big play as a return specialist and defensive back. Woodson went to five Pro Bowls and no one had led the league in kickoff returns more times than Woodson, who did it in 1959, 1962, and 1963. His 105-yard kickoff return in 1959 is the second-longest kickoff return in NFL history.

His 7 career returns for touchdowns (5 on kickoffs and 2 on punts) is tied for ninth on the all-time list. He returned 3 kickoffs for touchdowns in 1963, which is the third-best in NFL history, and his 28.7-yard career kickoff-return average trails only Gale Sayers (30. 6) and Lynn Chandnois (29.6). [MS]

ROD WOODSON

Cornerback. 6-0, 198. Purdue
Born March 10, 1965, Ft. Wayne, Indiana.
1987-1996 Pittsburgh, 1997 San Francisco, 1998 Baltimore

Born in 1965, Rod Woodson is too young to have been a member of Pittsburgh's famed Steel Curtain of the 1970s, but as a child in Fort Wayne, Indiana, he vividly remembers the image of the black-clad Steelers mauling quarterbacks, running backs, and receivers. In that respect, he could line up on the same side of the ball as Joe Greene or Mel Blount.

In 1995, Woodson tore his anterior cruciate ligament in the first game and was out the rest of the regular season, but he made a remarkable rehabilitation to play in Super Bowl XXX. Until that point, Woodson had missed only three games in seven seasons.

From 1991-94, he accumulated 12 sacks and 19 interceptions, including 3 he ran back for touchdowns. The first interception of his professional career in 1987 resulted in a 45-yard touchdown, Woodson has also scored twice as a punt returner and twice as a kickoff returner during his 12-year career.

The Steelers drafted Woodson in the first round out of Purdue in 1987, but he did not sign with the team until midway through the season. He spent a decade in Pittsburgh, where he was named to the Pro Bowl seven times. Woodson landed in San Francisco as a free agent in 1997 and stayed for a year before moving on to Baltimore. He had 6 interceptions for the Ravens in 1998, including 2 that he returned for touchdowns. [MS]

RON YARY

Tackle. 6-5, 260. Southern California
Born August 16, 1946, Chicago, Illinois.
1968-1982 Minnesota

When Ron Yary was made the NFL's first pick in the 1968 draft, he said, "I just can't see any other life than playing football." Had he been brash enough, he could have added ". . . and being the best offensive tackle in the NFL before my career ends."

In his senior year, Yary won the Outland Trophy as college football's best lineman while helping USC to the national championship. He had few peers during most of his 15 seasons with the Vikings. Ironically, Yary, who had been a defensive lineman during his first two seasons at USC, was such a great all-around player coming out of college that the Vikings had planned to try him on their defensive line as well as all three offensive line positions when he arrived at training camp.

Vikings coach Bud Grant ended any experiment as soon as he watched Yary play right tackle, where he handled the opposition's power rusher and crushed the corner of the defense for the Vikings' largely right-handed running offense.

Yary's hallmark was his always-steady play, which helped him earn seven consecutive Pro Bowl invitations during the seventies, and his tenaciousness as a pass blocker. His run blocking was superb, and his athletic skill enabled him to handle most pass rushers. [JC]

CLAUDE (BUDDY) YOUNG

Halfback. 5-4, 175. Illinois
Born January 5, 1926, Chicago, Illinois.
Died September 4, 1983, Terrell, Texas.
1947-49 New York Yankees-AAFC, 1950-51 New York Yanks, 1952 Dallas, 1953-55 Baltimore

Buddy Young was one of the quickest and most elusive runners ever to play pro football.

At 5 feet 4 inches and 170 pounds, he had to be tough to survive nine seasons. But Young had another disadvantage. As one of the first African-Americans to enter pro ball after World War II, he suffered more than casual prejudice. Through it all, Young not only survived, he excelled.

Curiously, he always maintained he found more prejudice against his height than his race. Perhaps that said more about Young's winning personality than about race relations. When he joined the AAFC's New York Yankees in 1947, Baltimore fans came to the game in blackface. Buddy ignored the insult. A few years later, when he was a member of the NFL's Colts, Baltimore fans voted him the team's most popular player.

As a freshman at the University of Illinois, Young tied Red Grange's one-season touchdown record with 13. Five of those touchdowns came on runs of 60 yards or more. In 1946, he led the Illini to a Rose Bowl victory over UCLA. He also tied the world indoor record for the 60-yard dash.

As a pro, Young was too small for heavy-duty running-back chores, but he proved most effective as a spot runner, pass receiver, and kick returner. In nine seasons, he rushed for 2,727 yards, caught 179 passes, averaged 27.7 yards per kickoff return, and had a 10.4 yard average on punt returns.

At the time of his death in an auto accident, he was director of player relations for the NFL. [BC]

STEVE YOUNG

Quarterback. 6-2, 205. Brigham Young
Born October 11, 1961, Salt Lake City, Utah.
1985-86 Tampa Bay, 1987-1998 San Francisco

A great-great-great-grandson of Brigham Young, the second president of the Church of Jesus Christ of Latter Day Saints and the first territorial governor of Utah, Young is a survivor. He was eighth string as a freshman at Brigham Young University, but as a senior finished as runner-up for the Heisman Trophy.

He set the NCAA single-season record for completion percentage (71.3) as a senior, then bypassed the NFL for the Los Angeles Express of the United States Football League. Two years and 4,102 yards later, Young bought out his Express contract and signed with the Tampa Bay Buccaneers, who owned his NFL rights.

"Tampa couldn't protect the passer, plus they were running a dated offense, so Steve looked bad there," said former 49ers coach Bill Walsh, who traded for Young in 1987. Young watched from the sidelines as Joe Montana won Super Bowls XXIII and XXIV.

Young eventually got his chance and was named the NFL's most valuable player in 1992 and 1994, but in San Francisco, anything less than a Super Bowl is not a successful season.

After two years as National Football Conference runner-up, the 49ers finally beat the Dallas Cowboys in the NFC Championship Game to earn a spot in Super Bowl XXIX. Young threw a record 6 touchdown passes, including 3 to Jerry Rice, to lead San Francisco to a 49-26 drubbing of San Diego. Young was MVP again—this time in the big game. [MS]

CHAPTER 11

The 30 Greatest Coaches

Jim J. Campbell and David Fischer

Ultimately, a coach's reputation—to say nothing of his job—depends on winning. No doubt in the history of pro football there have been coaches who might have ranked among the best had they only had the players. Perhaps they never received a second chance. Would we remember Tom Landry or Chuck Noll had their club owners pulled the plug after their first seasons?

Some of the 30 men profiled here were winners from the start; others built more slowly, but eventually found themselves at the height of their profession.

But winning is not enough for a coach to be included in this exclusive honor roll. Each of these coaches brought something more to pro football—such as method, innovation, or philosophy. They not only left a record, they also left a mark. [JJC]

GEORGE ALLEN
Marquette, Michigan
Born April 29, 1922, Detroit, Michigan.
Died December 31, 1990, Pasos Verde, California.
1966-1970 Los Angeles Rams, 1971-77 Washington
The title of George Allen's 1972 book is *The Future Is Now*. Not only did the book describe his thoughts on the game, but the title also was his credo.

Allen did not want youth on his teams, he wanted seasoned veterans. Wherever he was head coach, the future was mortgaged to win *now*. Usually it worked.

His first-head coaching job in the NFL was with the Rams in 1966. Before that, he was a highly successful defensive coordinator for the Bears.

Allen took along a few Bears—namely key defenders Bill George and Richie Petitbon. Allen, a master motivator, quickly built a winner. David (Deacon) Jones and Merlin Olsen keyed his defense; Roman Gabriel and Jack Snow paced his conservative offense. But owner Dan Reeves said that "winning with Allen wasn't fun." Reeves fired Allen in 1968, but player support at a tear-filled press conference forced Reeves to rehire Allen. Allen won big in 1969, but after 1970 Reeves fired him again.

Allen surfaced in Washington in 1971 with enough former Los Angeles players (Jack Pardee, Petitbon, Jones, and Myron Pottios) that the media dubbed the team the "Ramskins." Even better known was the tag "The Over-the-Hill-Gang" because the team had so many veterans. Nevertheless, Allen took the group to the NFC title and Super Bowl VII in 1972. [JJC]

PAUL BROWN
Miami (Ohio)
Born September 7, 1908, Norwalk, Ohio.
Died August 5, 1991.
1946-49 Cleveland (AAFC), 1950-1962 Cleveland, 1968-1975 Cincinnati
Inducted into Pro Football Hall of Fame in 1967.
"All football comes from [Amos Alonzo] Stagg," Knute Rockne said. That may be true for college football, but, had Rockne lived to see Paul Brown, he may have added: "But the pro game comes from Brown."

Much of what is taken for granted in pro football today—year-round coaching staffs, classroom practice sessions, tests, loose-leaf playbooks kept by players (requiring note-taking), advanced scouting methods, grading game performance from films, sending plays in from the bench, and even the passer's "pocket"—can be attributed to Brown.

Brown became a legend at Washington High in Massillon, Ohio, in the 1930s. His teams were so powerful that they once went an entire *season* without punting. When the head-coaching job opened at Ohio State, his opponents in the Ohio High School Coaches Association lobbied long and hard for Brown to get the post. Brown won a national title at Ohio State.

In 1945, Brown was hired by the Cleveland Browns of the newly organized All-America Football Conference. The success of the Browns often is cited as the reason for the demise of the AAFC. Cleveland had little competition. In the four seasons the Browns dominated the AAFC, they lost just four games, often playing before small crowds on the road. Brown said, "I'm primarily a football teacher, not a professional promoter. If we win before ten thousand, that's swell. If we lose before eighty thousand, that's awful."

When the NFL absorbed the Browns and two other AAFC teams in 1950, there was much anticipation surrounding the opening game: Cleveland at Philadelphia (winner of the last two NFL titles). The game, played the night before the rest of the league opened, wasn't even close. Cleveland won 35-10. NFL purists were not convinced. They called the squad "a basketball team in cleats" because of its precision passing game. Brown, who could be as stubborn as anyone, ordered his team not to throw a single pass in the return contest with the Eagles later that season. It was closer, but the Browns still won 13-7.

Brown left Cleveland following the 1962 season, and returned to football in 1968 as owner and coach of the expansion Bengals. He took Cincinnati to the postseason in just three years. [JJC]

JIMMY CONZELMAN
Washington (Missouri)
Born March 6, 1898, St. Louis, Missouri.
Died July 31, 1970, St. Louis, Missouri.
1921-22 Rock Island, 1922-23 Milwaukee, 1925-26 Detroit, 1927-1930 Providence, 1940-42, 1946-48 Chicago Cardinals
Inducted into Pro Football Hall of Fame in 1964.
Jimmy Conzelman was many things to many people—football player, football coach, team owner, pro baseball player, major league baseball executive, newspaper publisher, playwright, author, orator, and actor. He was a success at most endeavors but perhaps never more successful than as a football coach.

Conzelman was a versatile and effective halfback at Washington University in St. Louis and a teammate of George Halas and Paddy Driscoll on the World War I Great Lakes Naval Training Station team that played in the 1919 Rose Bowl. Conzelman joined Halas and the NFL in 1920 as a member of the Decatur Staleys, and moved on to the Rock Island Independents in 1921 and then to the Milwaukee Badgers. Offered an NFL franchise in Detroit for $100 in 1925, Conzelman became an NFL owner.

Though successful, Conzelman and his team received little support in the Motor City; eventually he turned the franchise back to the league and joined the Providence Steam Roller as a player-coach. Quarterback Conzelman suffered a knee injury in 1928, but coach Conzelman led his team to an 8-1-2 record and the NFL championship.

Conzelman left Providence after 1930 to pursue other interests. However, he returned to the pro game in 1940 to coach the Chicago Cardinals. He helped the team stay strong during the early years of World War II before leaving to work for the St. Louis Browns baseball team.

Conzelman's commencement address to the University of Dayton in 1942 was so uplifting that it was read into the *Congressional Record* and made required reading at West Point. When he returned to the Cardinals in 1946, several key parts of an outstanding team were in place. Conzelman had his passer, Paul Christman. He had his fullback, thumping runner and blocker Pat Harder. He had solid halfbacks Elmer Angsman and Marshall (Biggie) Goldberg. But he wanted more explosiveness. In 1947, he got Charley Trippi. Goldberg moved to defensive halfback, and Trippi ran from left halfback.

Conzelman's wisdom of teaming Trippi with Angsman in the Dream Backfield never was more evident than in the 1947 title game, won by the Cardinals 28-21. Trippi and Angsman scored 2 touchdowns each on long plays. Conzelman's second NFL title came nearly two decades after his first.

Conzelman did a fantastic job of keeping the team focused in 1948. Stan Mauldin, as good a tackle as the game had seen, collapsed and died of a heart attack after the first game. Still, the team only lost one regular-season game before losing the championship game to the Eagles 7-0 in a blinding blizzard in Philadelphia. After the game, Conzelman retired for good from pro coaching. [JJC]

BILL COWHER
North Carolina State
Born May 8, 1957, Pittsburgh, Pennsylvania.
1992-98 Pittsburgh
Since taking over for Chuck Noll before the 1992 season, Bill Cowher has won acclaim mostly for his intensity and leadership. A track record of six consecutive playoff appearances from 1992-97 testifies that his approach works.

Cowher's intensity helped make him a standout on special teams during his four seasons with the Cleveland Browns and Philadelphia Eagles. A knee injury ended Cowher's playing career in 1984, and a year later, Marty Schottenheimer hired Cowher, then 28, to coach Cleveland's special teams. After two seasons in that role, he became the Browns' secondary coach for two more years, then followed Schottenheimer to Kansas City in 1989 as the Chiefs' defensive coordinator.

Cowher, a Pittsburgh native who grew up cheering for Noll's great Steelers teams, became the fifteenth head coach in franchise history on January 21, 1992. During his tenure, the Steelers have lost numerous marquee players to free agency, yet they won five AFC Central titles in Cowher's first six seasons as coach (Pittsburgh also made the playoffs in 1993 as a wild-card team). Cowher also has seen many of his best assistant coaches, including Dom Capers, Ron Erhardt, and Chan Gailey, move on to other jobs.

But while the names have changed, the team's philosophy has stayed constant: an attacking 3-4 defense and a ball-control offense featuring dominant offensive line play and bruising running backs with nicknames like Bam (Byron Morris) and The Bus (Jerome Bettis). Cowher insists on players with as much commitment, intensity, and will to win as he exhibits pacing the sidelines each Sunday. [DF]

WEEB EWBANK
Miami (Ohio)
Born May 6, 1907, Richmond, Indiana.
1954-1962 Baltimore, 1963-1973 New York Jets
Inducted into Pro Football Hall of Fame in 1978.
Weeb Ewbank did what no other pro football coach did. He won championships in both the NFL and the AFL—with the Baltimore Colts in 1958 and 1959, and with the New York Jets in 1968, followed by the Jets' victory in Super Bowl III.

Ewbank was the winner in two of the most pivotal games in pro football history. The Colts' sudden-death victory over the Giants in the 1958 NFL Championship Game was viewed by millions on network television. It is called "the greatest game ever played," and it served as a wake-up call for millions of people to the excitement and spectacle of pro football. The huge upset by his upstart Jets in Super Bowl III largely was responsible for generating interest from younger fans. It also gave credence to the AFL-NFL merger.

Ewbank also developed two of the game's fabled quarterbacks—stoic Johnny Unitas and flamboyant (Broadway) Joe Namath. Each had great talent, but each blossomed under the careful cultivation of their thoughtful mentor.

Ewbank, one of many offspring from Miami (Ohio) University's Cradle of Coaches, was the first disciple of Paul Brown to coach in the National Football League. Brown's tackle coach, he took over a downtrodden Colts franchise in 1954. He had a five-year plan that worked to perfection; the Colts were world champions in 1958, his fifth season.

With the Colts, Ewbank showed a knack for bringing out the best in his players, many of them reclamation projects such as Gene (Big Daddy) Lipscomb. Lipscomb, who never played a down of college football, languished on the Rams' bench before being waived. The bargain-hunting Ewbank claimed him for $100 and turned him into an all-pro.

Ironically, when the Jets played in Super Bowl III, the game pitted Ewbank against his former team, the Colts. When asked if he attempted to get his players "to win one for the Weebster," he replied, "I never used that with my players. We had our own reasons to win, for ourselves and the AFL."

Ewbank had his own school of protegés. NFL Hall of Fame coaches Bud Grant, Chuck Noll, Don Shula, and Chuck Knox—all were from Weeb Ewbank's sphere of influence. [JJC]

RAY FLAHERTY

Gonzaga
Born September 1, 1903, Spokane, Washington.
Died July 19, 1994, Coeur d'Alene, Idaho.
1936 Boston, 1937-1942 Washington, 1946-48 New York (AAFC), 1949 Chicago (AAFC)
Inducted into Pro Football Hall of Fame in 1976.

Ray Flaherty was so quiet and low profile that his induction into the Pro Football Hall of Fame took place much later than it should have.

Flaherty, an all-pro end with the Giants, is remembered as the man whose suggestion won the storied "Sneakers Game" for the 1934 NFL championship. With the field covered by a sheet of ice, Flaherty recalled his days at Gonzaga (his alma mater) in the state of Washington, and how he had to wear basketball shoes to practice because of an injury. He discovered that the shoes provided great traction on a frozen turf. A Giants' equipment man was dispatched to secure the footgear. And once the Giants put them on in the third quarter, they literally ran away from the Bears, scoring 27 points in the final quarter to turn New York's 13-3 deficit into a 30-13 victory.

Flaherty entered the coaching ranks in 1936 as head coach of the Boston Redskins. One of the first things he did was point out to team owner George Preston Marshall that there was room for only one head coach on the sidelines. When asked how he got along with the meddlesome Marshall, Flaherty said, "Fine. He came down to the bench one game and I sent him back to the stands. He never came down again." Flaherty truly was a man of few words, but they usually carried considerable weight.

As a rookie coach, Flaherty got his team into the title game, but lost. The next season, after the team moved to Washington and with rookie Sammy Baugh passing, the Redskins won it all. After two second-place finishes, the Redskins were in the title game again in 1940, although it resulted in their infamous 73-0 loss to the Bears.

The Redskins lost only one game in 1942, and they again played the Bears in the NFL Championship Game. A believer in letting actions on the field speak louder than words in the locker room, Flaherty made no great oration before the game. In fact, he said next to nothing. He simply picked up a piece of chalk, went to the blackboard, and inscribed in large figures: 73-0. The strategy worked. The Redskins won 14-6.

Flaherty pioneered platoon football in the NFL with two two-way units. One of the units featured Baugh's passing, including a special screen pass devised by the coach; the other unit was spearheaded by a pounding ground game.

When Flaherty returned from military service in 1946, he became the head coach of the New York Yankees of the All-America Football Conference. His teams played the Browns for the championship twice, but like everyone else in the AAFC, he couldn't find the key to beating Paul Brown's team. During the AAFC years, Flaherty used a TV monitor on the sidelines to see what was happening at the moment, rather than waiting for Monday's or Tuesday's films. [JJC]

JOE GIBBS

Cerritos (California) Junior College, San Diego State
Born November 25, 1940, Mocksville, North Carolina.
1981-1992 Washington
Inducted into Pro Football Hall of Fame in 1996.

The success of some coaches can be attributed to their players. Joe Gibbs's success largely was the responsibility of one man—Joe Gibbs.

Nothing illustrates this better than Gibbs's three Super Bowl victories as head coach of the Redskins. Each was achieved with a different quarterback—Super Bowl XVIII, Joe Theismann; Super Bowl XXII, Doug Williams; and Super Bowl XXVI, Mark Rypien. Gibbs's teams were at their best in postseason, winning 16 of 21 games.

Gibbs assisted Don Coryell at San Diego State, St. Louis, and San Diego, but as a head coach did not limit his outlook of the game simply to Coryell's famed passing attack. Gibbs always seemed to have a big, powerful running back on his team—something he learned to value as an assistant to John McKay, both at USC and with Tampa Bay. Later, Gibbs, as much as anyone, was responsible for the one-back offense.

A native of North Carolina who grew up in California, Gibbs got his break as an NFL head coach in 1981 when he was hired by the Washington Redskins. Gibbs lost his first 5 games, but he was able to break even by winning 8 of the final 11 games.

Gibbs's work ethic was legendary. He said once, "To win at all, a team has to be obsessive about fundamentals and the little things." He routinely worked a 20-hour day during the season and often spent several nights a week sleeping in his Washington Redskins office. He retired in 1992. [JJC]

SID GILLMAN

Ohio State
Born October 26, 1911, Minneapolis, Minnesota.
1955-59 Los Angeles Rams, 1960 Los Angeles Chargers,

1961-69, 1971 San Diego, 1973-74 Houston
Inducted into Pro Football Hall of Fame in 1983.
"The big play comes from the pass," said Sid Gillman, the game's foremost authority on the passing game. "God bless those runners because they get you the first downs, give you ball control, and keep your defense off the field. But if you want to ring the cash register, you have to pass."

No one who saw Gillman's San Diego Chargers in the early AFL, with John Hadl throwing to Lance Alworth, doubted Gillman's belief in throwing the ball. Gillman took the AFL vertical. The league followed his lead.

It is unlikely Gillman learned much about the forward pass as a college end at run-oriented Ohio State. Nevertheless, Gillman was proficient enough to make All-Big Ten and play in the first Chicago College All-Star Game in 1934.

Gillman had success as a college coach at Miami (Ohio) and the University of Cincinnati. In 1955, he was named head coach of the Los Angeles Rams. As a rookie NFL coach, Gillman led the Rams to the NFL title game, but he was defeated by another coach with deep Ohio roots, Paul Brown.

When the AFL was formed in 1960, Gillman took over the Chargers. He guided them to the first two AFL title games, but lost both times to the Houston Oilers. The third time was the charm—his 1963 team was nearly perfect in defeating the Boston Patriots 51-10 for the AFL championship.

An ulcer forced Gillman to resign late in the 1969 season, although he returned to coach the Chargers for 10 games in 1971. Later he coached the Houston Oilers for two seasons, but after 1974—when he was named UPI's AFC coach of the year—he was never to be a head coach again. He assisted some teams, consulted for others, and kept his hand in the game. Many of today's leading proponents of the pass learned the rudiments of their systems from Gillman or his many disciples (both Chuck Noll and Al Davis were on his first Chargers' staff). Gillman's advice and counsel still are sought by coaches who want a better understanding of the passing game. [JJC]

BUD GRANT
Minnesota
Born May 20, 1927, Superior, Wisconsin.
1967-1983, 1985 Minnesota
Inducted into Pro Football Hall of Fame in 1994.
The public image of Bud Grant was stoic and unemotional. Those fortunate enough to get to know him knew another Bud Grant: a practical joker, an avid outdoorsman, a caring man who had a life away from football.

Grant was a legendary athlete at Superior (Wisconsin) Central High and at the University of Minnesota—a star in football, basketball, and baseball. Although a first-round draft choice of the Eagles in 1950, Grant postponed his NFL debut to play for the Minneapolis Lakers of the NBA. A 195-pound end, Grant joined the Eagles in 1951. In his second season, his 56 pass receptions were second best in the league.

The versatile Grant left Philadelphia for Winnipeg in the Canadian Football League in 1953. In four seasons, he led the CFL in receptions three times. By 1957, he was the Blue Bombers' coach, and when he came down from the north to coach the Vikings in 1967, he had four Grey Cups on his resume.

Grant quickly built a winner with Minnesota and then maintained a high level of excellence and consistency over 18 seasons. With a defense as solid as the frozen turf of Metropolitan Stadium in December, and an offense suited for the wintry weather of the Upper Midwest, Grant's Vikings were perennial Central Division winners.

Playing outdoors late in the season or in the playoffs, Grant's team seemed oblivious to the cold, while other teams—especially those from warmer climates—seemed to be more concerned with the elements than the Vikings. It was all part of Grant's coaching methods. He insisted cold was a state of mind. His Vikings wore regular jerseys. Vikings players who started the season with short sleeves finished the season in short sleeves. No Vikings wore gloves on the field or put on thermal mittens on the sidelines. There were no sideline heaters, either.

Some choose to remember Grant for being on the short end of the score in all four Super Bowls in which he coached, but in 1994 the Pro Football Hall of Fame selection committee chose to remember his 158 regular-season and 10 playoff victories. [JJC]

GEORGE HALAS
Illinois
Born February 2, 1895, Chicago, Illinois.
Died October 31, 1983, Chicago, Illinois.
1920 Decatur Staleys, 1921 Chicago Staleys, 1922-29, 1933-1942, 1946-1955, 1958-1967 Chicago Bears
Inducted into Pro Football Hall of Fame in 1963.
George Halas didn't invent pro football; it only seemed that way. He and a few comtemporaries were in Canton, Ohio, on a steamy Friday evening in 1920 when the NFL was formed in the Hupmobile showroom of car dealer Ralph Hay. Halas represented the Decatur Staleys, a squad sponsored by A.E. Staley's Staley Starch Works of Decatur, Illinois. Halas was coach, left end, and business manager for the company team.

After a year in Decatur, Halas—with Staley's blessings and $5,000 of his cash to keep the Staley name—took over the club and moved it to Chicago. In 1922, Halas and partner Ed Sternaman changed the name to the Bears.

Halas, who bought out Sternaman in the early 1930s, is given credit for many significant firsts, although at the time they might not have seemed that important. He held daily practices before other NFL teams followed suit. He used a tarpaulin to protect the playing surface of his field. He pioneered radio broadcasts of his games. He also was the first to take his team barnstorming—after signing Red Grange—in late 1925 and early 1926. Papa Bear, as he became known, is credited with the use of a public-address system to apprise fans at the stadium of who carried the ball, who made the tackle, and of the upcoming down and needed yardage.

As a coach, Halas believed in discipline. George Trafton, a Hall-of-Fame center for the Bears in the early days of the league, said, "He'd fine himself if he was late for a meeting or practice. You had better be there, and you had better be on time."

While Halas was associated with the Bears from their inception until his death in 1983, he was not always their head coach. He stepped away and gave the team a new perspective three separate times—1930-32, 1942-45 (to serve in the military), and 1956-57. Each time a rejuvenated Halas returned to the sidelines to coach and won an NFL championship. Twice, in 1934 and 1942, Halas's teams had undefeated regular-season records. Halas's 318 regular-season wins and 324 total victories were NFL records until broken by Don Shula in 1993.

Early on, Halas recognized the importance of employing good assistant coaches. Luke Johnsos was one of the first pro assistants to move up into the press box to observe game action and transmit his insights to the head coach on the sideline. Heartley (Hunk) Anderson was considered the best line coach in the business. And Clark Shaughnessy was influential. By adding a few new wrinkles to the T-formation, Shaughnessy awakened the world of football to the quick-strike possibilities of the offense. The Bears' stunning 73-0 victory over Washington in the 1940 NFL Championship Game received national attention, and Halas happily shared the credit with Shaughnessy. [JJC]

MIKE HOLMGREN

Southern California

Born June 15, 1948, San Francisco, California.

1992-98 Green Bay

The first Packers coach since Vince Lombardi to win a Super Bowl doesn't exactly fit the image of Green Bay's legendary tough guy. Lombardi ate, slept, and breathed football; Mike Holmgren often retains the air of the teacher he once was. Lombardi was the ultimate authoritarian, seemingly taking no guff from his players and projecting a strait-laced image; Holmgren appears more relaxed. Appearances, however, can be deceiving.

For all his stylistic differences with Lombardi, Holmgren has followed his predecessor to the pinnacle of success. In seven seasons on the sidelines at Lambeau Field, Holmgren transformed the Packers from the NFL's answer to Siberia into a dream destination for free agents, and restored the glory of a franchise steeped in legend.

Holmgren was drafted as a quarterback by the St. Louis Cardinals, but never played in the NFL. He returned to his high school alma mater to coach football and teach history. After coaching several high schools in San Francisco, Holmgren became an assistant coach at San Francisco State and then Brigham Young University. In 1986, he returned to San Francisco, this time with the 49ers. After six years as quarterbacks coach and offensive coordinator, the Bill Walsh protégé came to Green Bay.

Holmgren was quickly called upon to use his teaching skills after the Packers acquired quarterback Brett Favre in 1992. Strong-armed but undisciplined, Favre learned Holmgren's version of the West Coast offense and led the Packers to three consecutive 9-7 records from 1992-94. Holmgren even found the superstar defender to complement Favre: defensive end Reggie White. The team survived three straight playoff losses at the hands of rival Dallas, finally breaking through in 1996 as the Packers stormed to their NFL-record twelfth championship.

The Packers returned to the Super Bowl following the 1997 season, but Denver scored a late touchdown for a 31-24 victory. After guiding Green Bay to the postseason for the sixth consecutive year in 1998, Holmgren resigned to take over the dual role of coach and general manager in Seattle. [DF]

JIMMY JOHNSON

Arkansas

Born July 16, 1943, Port Arthur, Texas.

1989-1993 Dallas, 1996-98 Miami

Native Texan Jimmy Johnson has followed in the sizable footsteps of some of football's legendary winners—Howard Schnellenberger at the University of Miami, Tom Landry at Dallas, and Don Shula at Miami.

After winning a national championship at the University of Miami, Johnson came to the NFL in 1989 after the sale of the Cowboys to his former Arkansas linemate Jerry Jones. Johnson replaced Landry, who had been the only head coach in Cowboys' history. The new coach had a tough start in Dallas, posting a 1-15 record his first season. But a quick trip to the playoffs and back-to-back victories in Super Bowls XXVII and XXVIII established Johnson as one of the best in his business. A clash of egos caused Jones and Johnson to split after the second Super Bowl, but Johnson returned to the NFL in 1996 as Shula's successor in Miami.

The cherubic-looking Johnson is a hard disciplinarian. He also is a firm believer in team speed and mammoth linemen, and advocates relentless, attacking defense. With the speed of his defenders, no one got upfield penetration faster or deeper than his Super Bowl defensive units.

Johnson, one of only two coaches to win a national collegiate championship and a Super Bowl, earned the respect of his fellow pro coaches.

"Jimmy made a few adjustments along the way, but I didn't see a change in his philosophy," Jets head coach Bill Parcells said. "He knew what he wanted to do, and how he wanted to build things. He has a philosophy, he has put it in place, and he has acquired the people to implement that philosophy. I think that's the only way—the only way—to be successful. The people who constantly change plans, change people, change philosophies, are the ones who end up as also-rans. The ones who can stick to what they believe in are the ones who emerge on top." [JJC]

CHUCK KNOX

Juniata

Born April 27, 1932, Sewickley, Pennsylvania.

1973-77, 1992-94 Los Angeles Rams, 1978-1982 Buffalo, 1983-1991 Seattle

"It's eighth grade Sewickley." That was Chuck Knox's way of saying something is common sense. It's a reference to the mill town just outside of Pittsburgh in which Knox grew up. Knox made a great coaching career out of common sense and basic, fundamental football.

Knox is the only coach in NFL history to win division titles with three different teams (Rams, Bills, and Seahawks). Only Paul Brown matched his mark of going to the postseason in each of his first five seasons (1973-77) as a head coach.

Knox did all of this with very little razzle-dazzle. His

offense was predictable, but seldom stoppable. When the San Diego Chargers aerial circus was called "Air Coryell," media wags named Knox's rush-oriented attack "Ground Chuck."

Knox won in Los Angeles but resigned in 1978 to take over the Buffalo Bills, who had won five games in the previous two seasons.

In his third season in Buffalo, Knox got the team to the playoffs. Joe Cribbs was his workhorse running back. Cribbs was complemented by another Knox trademark—a stingy defense.

Knox moved to Seattle in 1983. With the Seahawks, Knox's star running back was Curt Warner. In his first year, Knox earned a wild-card berth in the playoffs and got all the way to the AFC Championship Game. He was a fixture in the Great Northwest for nearly a decade, getting back to the playoffs several more times.

Knox returned to the Rams in 1992. Despite 1,000-yard rusher Jerome Bettis, the Rams failed to become a playoff squad under Knox the second time around. [JJC]

EARL (CURLY) LAMBEAU

Notre Dame

Born March 9, 1898, Green Bay, Wisconsin.

Died June 1, 1965, Sturgeon Bay, Wisconsin.

1921-1949 Green Bay, 1950-51 Chicago Cardinals, 1952-53 Washington

Inducted into Pro Football Hall of Fame in 1963.

Earl (Curly) Lambeau, a star at Green Bay's East High, could throw the football. He did it against arch-rival West High to snap West's domination of East. He did it as a pioneer pro with the Packers. And when he could no longer play, he coached the passing game like no one before.

Despite rules that made it difficult to use the forward pass, Lambeau and the Packers were a team whose main offensive weapon was the pass—at any time, on any down, from anywhere on the field. At first, passing could only be done 5 yards behind the line of scrimmage. An incomplete pass out of bounds went over to the other team, much like a punt. A second incompletion in the same series resulted in the loss of possession. There were ample reasons why the early NFL game was a between-the-tackles affair.

Lambeau, never one to accept the conventional wisdom of the times, flew in the face of common practice. With his vaunted passing attack, Lambeau led the team to the 1929, 1930, and 1931 NFL championships. After signing the era's ultimate weapon, speedy receiver Don Hutson in 1935, Lambeau and the Packers won three other league titles.

When Lambeau retired as a player in 1929, he replaced himself with Arnie Herber and later Cecil Isbell. Before Hutson's arrival, the incomparable Johnny (Blood) McNally was streaking through baffled NFL secondaries for large chunks of yardage and numerous touchdowns. McNally still was playing well when Hutson first joined the team. NFL defenders didn't know whom to cover because both could break open a game. So advanced were Lambeau's offensive theories and Hutson's abilities that Hutson's records stood until Lance Alworth and Jerry Rice entered the NFL decades later.

Lambeau always got the most from his players. Tackle Cal Hubbard, guard Mike Michalske, and the free-spirited McNally were fine players who enjoyed Hall of Fame careers under Lambeau.

Lambeau resigned in 1950 and later coached the Chicago Cardinals and Redskins. For many years, his 229 career victories were second only to George Halas. [JJC]

TOM LANDRY

Texas

Born September 11, 1924, Mission, Texas.

1960-1988 Dallas

Inducted into Pro Football Hall of Fame in 1990.

"Emotion can cover up a lot of inadequacies, but in the end it also gets in the way of performance. An emotional team cannot stay that way consistently over a full season or even a few games," said Tom Landry at the height of his coaching career.

That explains why he appeared to be so stoic on the sidelines. A truer picture of Landry's demeanor on the coaching line was that he usually was thinking two plays ahead. While he seemed unemotional about a game-turning play, he was concerned more about the long-range effects than he was with instant reaction.

Who's to argue with him? No one coached with more sustained success for a longer period of time than the tall, lean Texan, who had 20 consecutive winning seasons (1966-1985). He won 13 divisional titles and five NFC championships in that time. His teams won two Super Bowls (VI and XII).

Things weren't always as easy as they later appeared for Landry and the Cowboys. In 1960, the expansion Cowboys had only a 31-31 tie against the Giants (Landry's old team) to show for the season; the other 11 games were losses. The Cowboys didn't have a .500 record until 1965.

Landry was an innovator. As a player and then a player-coach with the Giants, he helped develop what became the basic NFL defense—the 4-3. When everybody else adopted it, Landry further refined it into his Flex defense, which he used in Dallas.

Landry also introduced motion and movement to his offense. Seldom, if ever, did the Cowboys run a play from the formation they took upon first breaking the huddle. There always was at least one shift by one or more players. Later the Dallas mentor reloaded the old Shotgun formation and gave it more firepower than it ever had before. By inserting different players into the game for specific purposes, offensively and defensively, Landry popularized situation substitution. [JJC]

MARV LEVY

Coe

Born August 3, 1928, Chicago, Illinois.

1978-1982 Kansas City, 1986-1996 Buffalo

Marv Levy, who has a Master's degree from Harvard, is best known as an intelligent and analytical football coach.

Under Levy, the Bills made four consecutive trips to the Super Bowl from 1990-93. After a down year in 1994, perhaps Levy's greatest coaching accomplishment was bouncing back in 1995 to lead the Bills to the playoffs despite his battle with cancer in midseason. The Bills were back in the playoffs again in 1996.

The former Coe College halfback began his NFL career with Philadelphia in 1969 as one of the league's first special-teams coaches. In the mid-1970s, he won two Grey Cups (1974 and 1977) in five seasons with the Montreal Alouettes of the Canadian Football League. Levy then returned to the NFL in Kansas City (1978-1982),

Levy, a Phi Beta Kappa, developed a No-Huddle offense in Buffalo that had quarterback Jim Kelly calling most plays at the line of scrimmage. With the Chiefs, a young team without a potent passing game, Levy featured a full house-backfield T—a throwback to earlier decades.

Levy has won more games than any other Bills' head coach, and ranks in the top dozen of all-time winning NFL head coaches. [JJC]

VINCE LOMBARDI

Fordham

Born June 11, 1913, Brooklyn, New York.

Died September 3, 1970, Washington, D.C.

1959-1967 Green Bay, 1969 Washington

Inducted into Pro Football Hall of Fame in 1971.

Vince Lombardi—once a member of Fordham's legendary Seven Blocks of Granite line—made the Packers a mighty dynasty and himself a mythical figure. Not a true innovator, Lombardi simply borrowed and honed other coaches' methods. But no one ever ran the basics more to perfection than Lombardi. Just as the game was becoming complex, Lombardi simplified it. And with his success, others turned back to basics. While no one quite had his success, Lombardi had many disciples.

Lombardi learned the passing game from fellow Army assistant coach Sid Gillman. He remembered the power sweep from playing under Frank Leahy and Jim Crowley at Fordham. He learned execution and organization from Colonel Earl (Red) Blaik.

"Winning isn't everything, it's the only thing!" John Wayne said that first. It wasn't Lombardi, as is often suggested; it was Wayne as a coach in a 1953 football movie entitled *Trouble Along the Way.*

Lombardi then was hardly known outside of the West Point coaching staff, on which he was an assistant. Within the next decade, it would be a different matter. He moved into the NFL as Jim Lee Howell's offensive coach and helped the Giants win a title in 1956 and a division crown in 1958.

In 1959, in Green Bay, Lombardi revived a flagging Packers franchise—the NFL's only surviving town team. His offense was nothing fancy, just executed nearly flawlessly: Paul Hornung sweeping right with the added threat of a halfback-option pass behind pulling guards Fred (Fuzzy) Thurston and Jerry Kramer, Jim Taylor blasting over tackle Forrest Gregg or Bob Skoronski on a weakside slant, Bart Starr going deep to Max McGee after sucking in the defense on third-and-1 with play-action.

While many tried to sum up Lombardi's approach to the game, he stated it best, "They call it coaching, but it is teaching. You don't just tell them it is so. You show them the reasons why it is so, and then you repeat and repeat until they are convinced, until they know." Even minor changes in the running of a play were explained endlessly and then run exhaustively.

After winning the first two Super Bowls, Lombardi retired and became the Packers' general manager. A season away from the sidelines was tough for him. In 1969, he returned to coaching with the Redskins and led them to their first winning season in 14 years. Before he could complete his work, cancer claimed him in 1970. No coach who coached as long as Lombardi (10 seasons) ever had a better winning percentage—.728 regular season, .900 postseason, .740 overall. The only championship game Lombardi lost was his first, 17-13 to the Eagles in 1960. [JJC]

JOHN MADDEN

California Polytechnic College (San Luis Obispo)

Born March 10, 1936, Austin, Minnesota.

1969-1978 Oakland

Former Raiders coach John Madden learned the basics of pro football from Norm Van Brocklin. Madden was drafted by the Eagles in 1958, but a knee injury in training camp kept him from playing. Rather than return to the West Coast, he stayed in Philadelphia and spent much of his time with the Eagles' wily quarterback.

When the Dutchman talked football, Madden became a veritable sponge, soaking up as much as he could. He and the veteran quarterback often arrived early for practice and watched films. The next year, Madden began his coaching career at Allan Hancock Junior College in California.

In 1964, Madden joined Don Coryell's staff at San Diego State. Coryell remembered his dedication and intensity. "Sometimes our practices got a little heated, because John didn't even like to lose a scrimmage. He never let his players give up; he never allowed them to slough off one play just because it was practice."

In 1967, Raiders managing general partner Al Davis offered Madden a job as an assistant coach. Two years later, Madden became head coach in Oakland at 32, the youngest head coach in the history of the AFL.

As a coach, Madden realized good players help make good coaches. He said, "We look for players who can contribute to the organization over a long period of time." His offensive line was a prime example—Jim Otto, 1960-1974; Gene Upshaw, 1967-1981; and Art Shell, 1968-1982. All are in the Pro Football Hall of Fame.

Madden was the head coach of the Raiders for 10 years before retiring. He won 100 games faster than any other NFL coach at that time and led the Raiders to a victory over the Vikings in Super Bowl XI, but he walked away at the top of his game after the 1978 season. For several years, rumors of his return surfaced whenever a coaching vacancy occurred, but Madden had by then become a broadcasting icon. [JJC]

EARLE (GREASY) NEALE

West Virginia Wesleyan

Born November 5, 1891, Parkersburg, West Virginia.

Died November 2, 1973, Lake Worth, Florida.

1941-42, 1944-1950 Philadelphia Eagles, 1943 Phil-Pitt

Inducted into Pro Football Hall of Fame in 1969.

When Alexis Thompson, a graduate of Yale, hired Neale, an assistant at Yale, to coach Thompson's newly purchased Philadelphia Eagles in 1941, Neale requested, and received, from a friend the complete game film of the Bears' striking 73-0 championship-game victory over the Redskins in 1940. After studying the film endlessly, Neale became the first man in the NFL to imitate the Bears' modern T-formation.

It took Neale awhile to build a team, but once he built the Eagles to respectablility in 1944, they stayed among the league's elite teams the remainder of the decade. To execute his version of the T, Neale had Tommy Thompson throwing, Jack Ferrante and Pete Pihos catching, and Steve Van Buren slashing through the line and around the ends.

Defensively, Neale developed what was an NFL staple for years—the Eagle Defense. At first glance, it resembled an outdated seven-man line. But Neale deployed his troops differently. The ends really weren't ends. They often dropped into pass coverage or held up receivers attempting to get downfield. This defensive set eventually spawned another NFL staple, the 4-3, still used by many teams today.

From 1944-49, Neale and the Eagles placed second three times and first three times. The Eagles won the NFL championship in 1948 and 1949. They are the only franchise to win back-to-back championships by shutting out their opponents—the Cardinals 7-0 and the Rams 14-0.

The West Virginian starred as an end with Jim Thorpe's Canton Bulldogs before World War I and coached Washington and Jefferson College to the Rose Bowl in 1922. He was a major-league outfielder and batted .357 for the Cincinnati Reds in the 1919 World Series. [JJC]

CHUCK NOLL

Dayton

Born January 5, 1932, Cleveland, Ohio.

1969-1991 Pittsburgh

Inducted into Pro Football Hall of Fame in 1993.

Chuck Noll won his first game as an NFL head coach—then lost the remaining 13 games of the 1969 regular season. Fortunately, Noll's first year was not indicative of the rest of his career. He went on to develop some of the best teams in NFL annals.

Through shrewd drafts and strong guidance, Noll helped team owner Art Rooney and the Steelers shed their "lovable losers" image. Pittsburgh won four Super Bowls between 1974 and 1979 (IX, X, XIII, and XIV).

Noll, who for many years served as his own quarterback coach—and allowed his quarterbacks to call their plays long after it went out of style with the rest of the league—was a proponent of a strong, speedy, hard-hitting, but disciplined defense. All 11 black-helmeted Steelers flew to the ball. Few defenses ever have dominated a game like his Steel Curtain did in Super Bowl IX, when they allowed the Vikings a scant 17 yards rushing.

While other winning coaches seemed to relish the spotlight and attention, Noll avoided it intentionally. His typical reply when someone approached with an endorsement deal was, "Let one of the players do it."

During his career, Noll was secure in who he was and what he was. Actually, he was many things—winning football coach, connoisseur of fine wines, scuba diver, gourmet cook, lover of classical music, a reader of fine literature, gardener, and pilot. Rocky Bleier once said, "Chuck's so confident, he's the only person I know who bought a plane before he took flying lessons."

Noll was a good, if not spectacular, high school player in his native Cleveland. When Big Ten schools did not offer him a scholarship, he attended the University of Dayton. He was elected captain as a senior and was drafted in the twentieth round by the Browns in 1953. At first, he was one of Paul Brown's "messenger" guards, shuttling plays into Otto Graham. Later, he became a smart, tough linebacker.

After retiring as a player in 1959, Noll joined Sid Gillman's Chargers' staff. From there he moved to Baltimore under Don Shula, and took over the Steelers in January, 1969. [JJC]

STEVE OWEN

Phillips

Born April 21, 1898, Cleo Springs, Oklahoma.

Died May 17, 1964, New York, New York.

1930-1953 New York Giants

Inducted into Pro Football Hall of Fame in 1966.

To call Steve Owen a pioneer is not an overstatement. The sturdy tackle and head coach was born in Oklahoma before it was a state—it was still a territory in 1898.

After playing at Phillips, a small Oklahoma college, Owen became an outstanding tackle with the Kansas City Blues (later Cowboys), a touring NFL team, in 1924. He was sold to the Giants in 1926 for $500. He played at an all-pro level during his NFL career, and in 1931 became the Giants' head coach. Owen and the Mara family, who owned the Giants, never had a signed contract. He coached 23 years on just a handshake.

Owen believed in fundamental, basic football. He once said, "This game is essentially a game played by two men down in the dirt. The fella who hits first and harder usually wins." Owen's offensive approach was simple, too. He was successful with his basic style. The Giants played in 8 of the first 15 Championship Games of the National Football League. The victory in the 1934 "Sneakers Game" is well-documented. He coached the Giants to another championship in 1938. But Owen's forte was defense. He originated the Umbrella Defense—the secondary was likened to the rain-shielding device with the four deep backs representing the spokes of the umbrella. His four ball-hawking defenders were Tom Landry, future Hall of Fame safety Emlen Tunnell, Otto Schnellbacher, and Harmon Rowe. Owen successfully used this defense to thwart the pass-oriented Browns when they joined the NFL.

Owen left the Giants in 1953. He then coached in the CFL and became an Eagles' assistant in the mid-1950s. His 153 victories still rank in the all-time top 10 among NFL head coaches. [JJC]

BILL PARCELLS

Colgate, Wichita State

Born August 22, 1941, Englewood, New Jersey.

1983-1990 New York Giants, 1993-96 New England Patriots, 1997-98 New York Jets

In 1983, Duane Charles Parcells was named the head coach of the New York Giants, a once-proud franchise fallen on hard times. After one losing season in which he turned over the roster, installed his system, and designed the defense around superstar linebacker Lawrence Taylor, Parcells reversed the team's fortunes in dramatic fashion.

The Giants made the postseason as wild-card entrants the next two years, winning a game each time before bowing out against the eventual Super Bowl champion (San Francisco in 1984 and Chicago in 1985). Led by Taylor and quarterback Phil Simms in 1986, New York went 14-2 and crushed the Denver Broncos in Super Bowl XXI. After two down years, Parcells directed the team to NFC East titles in 1989 and 1990. With Simms hurt, Parcells called on backup Jeff Hostetler to take his team to the title. By using a ball-control offense that kept Buffalo's No-Huddle offense on the sidelines, the Giants earned a dramatic 20-19 victory over the favored Bills in Super Bowl XXV.

Citing health concerns, Parcells left the sidelines for the broadcast booth. He returned to coaching in 1993 with the Patriots, a team with a 14-50 record over the previous four years under three different coaches. With maturing quarterback Drew Bledsoe leading the way, New England was back in the postseason in 1994. Two years later, the Patriots reached the Super Bowl.

But Parcells, who had battled with owner Robert Kraft all season, was already rumored to be out the door, and a distracted Patriots team fell 35-21 to Green Bay in Super Bowl XXXI. Indeed, Parcells soon announced that he was moving on to the New York Jets, fresh off a nightmarish 1-15 season. Kraft protested, and the Jets ultimately had to pay a heavy price in draft picks as compensation. Parcells quickly proved worth it, working a stunning transformation as the Jets went 9-7 and barely missed the playoffs in 1997. He led the Jets to a franchise-record 12 victories and their first AFC East title in 1998. The Jets beat Jacksonville in the AFC divisional playoffs before falling to Denver in the AFC Championship Game. [DF]

BUDDY PARKER
Centenary
Born December 16, 1913, Kemp, Texas.
Died March 22, 1982, Kaufman, Texas.
1949 Chicago Cardinals, 1951-56 Detroit, 1957-1964 Pittsburgh

Buddy Parker had his greatest impact as an NFL head coach in the 1950s. He guided the Lions to NFL titles in 1952 and 1953.

Parker knew the NFL inside out. He was a slick and resourceful halfback for the Detroit Lions and Chicago Cardinals beginning in 1935, and was a fixture in the league until he retired after the 1964 season.

As a coach, he specialized in making his system fit his players, or at least acquiring players to fit his system. He made a career of trading for players deemed no longer useful and then getting several productive seasons from them. Parker was as good as the NFL ever has seen as a game-day coach. He could analyze what an opponent was doing on the field, and from his sideline vantage point quickly counter the move.

With quarterback Bobby Layne—a fellow Texan with whom he had a particularly close relationship—Parker developed what is known today as the "two-minute drill." No team controlled the clock better at the end of a half than the Lions in the Parker-Layne Era. Parker's offensive system of play calling was simplistic but effective. He modeled it after the Bears of the early 1940s.

Parker quit as Detroit's head coach at a Lions boosters' banquet on the eve of the 1957 season. He went to Pittsburgh and coached the Steelers for eight years. [JJC]

DAN REEVES
South Carolina
Born January 19, 1944, Rome, Georgia.
1981-1992 Denver, 1993-96 New York Giants, 1997-98 Atlanta

As a player for Tom Landry's Dallas Cowboys, Dan Reeves had neither great size nor exceptional speed. Too small to play quarterback, where he'd starred in college, he entered the NFL without a position. But his grit and intelligence helped him to a successful career as a running back. After earning a Super Bowl ring as a player, he joined Landry's staff as an offensive assistant, winning a second championship ring in that role.

As a rookie head coach in 1981, Reeves guided the Broncos to a 10-6 record and won the first of four coach of the year awards. In 1984, Reeves and John Elway led the Broncos to a franchise-best 13-3 record and the AFC West title. Denver won the division five times in eight years, and went on to the Super Bowl following the 1986, 1987, and 1989 seasons. But the team lost all three games by a combined score of 136-40. The humiliating Super Bowl defeats helped drive a wedge between the coach and his quarterback. After an 8-8 season in 1992, Reeves and the Broncos parted ways.

The New York Giants, fresh off a disappointing 6-10 season, retained his services in 1993, and Reeves directed the team to an 11-5 record and a playoff berth. The next season, with a much younger team, the Giants won their final six games to finish 9-7. But criticism of his conservative play-calling was already beginning to mount, and Reeves was out of a job after two sub-.500 seasons.

The Georgia native returned home in 1997 to coach the Atlanta Falcons, who shook off a 1-7 start to finish with a 7-9 record. The Falcons doubled their victory total in 1998, winning the second NFC West title in club history with a franchise-best 14-2 record. Although Reeves underwent quadruple bypass surgery on December 14, he was back on the sidelines for the playoffs. He guided the Falcons past the rival 49ers, followed by a stunning overtime victory over the Vikings in the Metrodome in the NFC Championship Game. Reeves participated in his ninth Super Bowl as a player, assistant coach, and head coach, but was undone by his former team when Denver beat Atlanta 34-19 in Super Bowl XXXIII. [DF]

MARTY SCHOTTENHEIMER
Pittsburgh
Born September 23, 1943, Canonsburg, Pennsylvania.
1984-88 Cleveland, 1989-1998 Kansas City

When Marty Schottenheimer was introduced as the Chiefs' head coach in January, 1989, after guiding the Browns for five years, he said, "The best way to establish a position of excellence in the NFL is to expect it."

Under Schottenheimer, the Chiefs were consistent winners. They made the playoffs six consecutive years (1990-95), and twice, in 1995 and 1997, the Chiefs had the NFL's best regular-season record at 13-3. Schottenheimer's teams did not finish below .500 or place lower than second in the division every year from 1985-1997. They reached the postseason 11 times in that span.

Not all of Schottenheimer's success came in Kansas City. He also had good results in Cleveland. He succeeded Sam Rutigliano in the middle of the 1984 season after serving as the Browns' defensive coordinator and guided Cleveland to the AFC Championship Game in 1985 and 1987.

Schottenheimer, an All-American linebacker while at the University of Pittsburgh and a linebacker for six seasons in the NFL with Buffalo and Boston, is known for his teams' rock-solid defenses. Under Schottenheimer, the Chiefs annually were among the league leaders in sacks and takeaways, and also among the NFL's best in fewest giveaways. Schottenheimer is a stickler for detail. "He is, without a doubt, the fiercest competitor I've ever known," Chiefs president Carl Peterson said.

The Chiefs averaged 10 wins per season under Schottenheimer, whose 145 regular-season victories rank eleventh in NFL history. He resigned as head coach in Kansas City after the 1998 season. [JJC]

GEORGE SEIFERT
Utah
Born January 22, 1940, San Francisco, California.
1989-1996 San Francisco
In eight seasons as coach of the 49ers, Seifert guided his teams to two Super Bowl titles (XXIV and XXIX) and 108 victories. He resigned as coach after taking San Francisco to the playoffs for the fifth consecutive season in 1996.

Before being named head coach in 1989, Seifert was the 49ers' defensive coordinator under Bill Walsh. Seifert, a native of San Francisco who once worked as an usher at 49ers' games at Kezar Stadium, led the team to a Super Bowl title in his first year. Don McCafferty, with the Baltimore Colts in 1970, is the only other head coach to win a Super Bowl in his first season.

Seifert's career winning percentage of .755 is the best in NFL history—only Vince Lombardi (.740) and John Madden (.731) come close. The low-profile Utah graduate (with a zoology degree) reached the 50-win, 75-win, and 100-win plateaus faster than any other coach in NFL history.

Seifert joined the 49ers in 1980 as secondary coach and had an immediate impact in his second season, when the team won Super Bowl XVI. Seifert's starting secondary that year consisted of three rookies and a three-year veteran. He was promoted to defensive coordinator in 1983. The 49ers consistently finished at or near the top in the NFL's defensive categories during Seifert's tenure as coordinator. Some critics dismissed Seifert's early success as a continuation of Walsh's system, but a closer look shows that he added his own stamp to the 49ers and eventually won with revamped offensive and defensive platoons.

After two years away from the sidelines, Seifert was hired as head coach of the Carolina Panthers in 1999. [JJC]

MIKE SHANAHAN
Eastern Illinois
Born August 24, 1952, Oak Park, Illinois.
1988-89 Los Angeles Raiders, 1995-98 Denver
Broncos coach Mike Shanahan got a precious gift for NFL coaches: a second chance. As an exceptionally successful quarterbacks coach and offensive coordinator with the Denver Broncos in the 1980s, Shanahan was instrumental in John Elway's development. As a result, Shanahan got his first head coaching opportunity with the Los Angeles Raiders in 1988. He went 7-9 that year, then was unceremoniously fired by Al Davis after a 1-3 start in 1989.

Shanahan returned to Denver as quarterbacks coach later that season, and was the team's offensive coordinator in 1991. He was hired by San Francisco's George Seifert as the 49ers' offensive coordinator in 1992 and presided over one of the most productive offenses in NFL history. Quarterback Steve Young was named the league's most valuable player twice in Shanahan's three years. In 1994, his offense pounded the Chargers 49-26 in Super Bowl XXIX.

Shanahan's name topped many teams' coaching wish lists that winter, but it was the Broncos and Elway who ultimately won his services. After an up-and-down first season highlighted by Elway's return to form and the emergence of rookie running back Terrell Davis, Denver joined the ranks of the NFL elite in 1996 with a league-best 13-3 record. But the Broncos were shocked in their playoff opener by the second-year Jacksonville Jaguars.

Shanahan went back to the drawing board and signed key players such as defensive end Neil Smith and cornerback/returner Darrien Gordon. The 1997 Broncos went 12-4, but finished in second place to Kansas City. Denver settled an old score against Jacksonville in the opening round of the playoffs. The Broncos then avenged regular-season losses by beating the Chiefs and Steelers to reach Super Bowl XXXII. Few gave them a chance against the defending-champion Packers, but an MVP performance from Davis lifted the Broncos to a 31-24 victory.

The 1998 Broncos won their first 13 games before losing, and Davis became the fourth 2,000-yard rusher in NFL history. The Broncos allowed just two offensive touchdowns in three postseason games, including a 34-19 win over Shanahan's former boss, Dan Reeves, and the Falcons in Super Bowl XXXIII. With the victory, Shanahan joined Vince Lombardi, Don Shula, Chuck Noll, and Jimmy Johnson as the only coaches to win back-to-back Super Bowls. [DF]

DON SHULA
John Carroll
Born January 4, 1930, Grand River, Ohio.
1963-69 Baltimore, 1970-1995 Miami
Don Shula retired as the Miami Dolphins' head coach after the 1995 season with more career victories (347) than any other coach in NFL history. He earned the respect of nearly everyone connected with professional football.

After an NFL playing career that was built more on dedication and hard work than athletic ability, Shula became a very young head coach in 1963 with the Baltimore Colts. From 1963-69, he compiled a 73-26-4 mark and guided the Colts to Super Bowl III. When Miami offered him its head-coaching job in 1970, he took it.

He immediately amplified his standing in the coaching community. In 1972, he coached the Dolphins to the only perfect season (17-0) in NFL history, including a victory in Super Bowl VII. He won Super Bowl VIII, too. Before he retired, Shula took six teams to the Super Bowl.

Throughout his career, Shula adapted to his personnel. With Larry Csonka, Jim Kiick, and Mercury Morris in the early 1970s, the Dolphins won mainly with a powerful rushing attack. With Dan Marino in 1980s, the Dolphins opened up the passing game.

"The secret of success is getting inside different personalities and getting the most out of them," Shula said. [JJC]

HANK STRAM
Purdue
Born January 3, 1924, Chicago, Illinois.
1960-62 Dallas (AFL), 1963-1974 Kansas City, 1976-77 New Orleans

Hank Stram was an obscure college assistant when Lamar Hunt tapped him to lead the Dallas Texans of the fledgling American Football League in 1960. The innovative Stram was an immediate winner in Dallas, and won the 1962 AFL championship.

The seeds for success in Kansas City (the Texans moved there in 1963 and were renamed the Chiefs) were sown in that final Texas season. Weary of having his quarterback harried and hassled by blitzing linebackers, Stram devised a two-tight end offense—it provided an extra blocker and slowed down the pass rush. It also was that year that the stocky, well-dressed mentor used a 3-4 defense, with linebackers stacked behind down linemen. When defensive end Buck Buchanan joined the team in 1963, Stram went back to a 4-3. Whatever the front, Stram's defense differed in that there was always a man head-up on the center. Linebackers Willie Lanier, Bobby Bell, and Jim Lynch were the game's best trio for a time.

On offense, Stram's Chiefs featured quarterback Len Dawson, a castoff from Pittsburgh and Cleveland who became a star in Kansas City. Mike Garrett developed into a 1,000-yard rusher, and Hall of Fame kicker Jan Stenerud gave Stram's Chiefs an added dimension.

The high point of Stram's career was Kansas City's 23-7 victory over Minnesota in Super Bowl IV. The previous year, the Jets' Super Bowl victory over the Colts was viewed as an upset. The Chiefs' defeat of the Vikings gave further credibility to the AFL. [JJC]

BILL WALSH
San Jose State
Born November 30, 1931, Los Angeles, California.
1979-1988 San Francisco
Inducted into Pro Football Hall of Fame in 1993.

Bill Walsh thought that his chance to be an NFL head coach may have slipped away when he was passed over as Paul Brown's successor in Cincinnati in 1976.

Discouraged, Walsh left the Bengals to join the Chargers' staff as an assistant coach. Then he spent two years as head coach at Stanford. Finally, at age 47, Walsh was tapped to be the head coach and general manager of the San Francisco 49ers in 1979. He went on to build the NFL's dominant team of the 1980s.

An offensive innovator, Walsh originated the pass-oriented West Coast offense, which has had a profound effect on modern football. The short-to-moderate passing game is predicated on coverage mismatches and passer-receiver options designed to turn short passes into long gainers. Walsh, a Los Angeles native, is known as a developer of quarterbacks. He had a hand in shaping the careers of Pro Football Hall of Fame member Dan Fouts and future Hall-of-Fame inductees Joe Montana and Steve Young.

Walsh took over a 2-14 team in 1979 and won Super Bowl XVI in his third season. The play that propelled them into their first Super Bowl was called "Brown Left, Slot-Sprint, Right Option." That's the technical name under Walsh's complex system. Forget the fancy nomenclature. San Francisco fans refer to the Montana-to-Dwight Clark play that stunned Dallas in the 1981 NFC Championship Game simply as "The Catch." The 49ers went on to win two more Super Bowls (XIX and XXIII) before Walsh retired following the 1988 season. After serving as a consultant to the 49ers, he was named the team's general manager in 1999. [JJC]

CHAPTER 12

Movers and Shakers

Jim Gigliotti

When National Football League Commissioner Pete Rozelle presented the Vince Lombardi Trophy to Steelers owner Art Rooney following Pittsburgh's 16-6 victory over Minnesota in Super Bowl IX, there wasn't a dry eye in the place.

"I'm not ashamed to admit that I had tears in my eyes," Rozelle said. "No man ever deserved it more."

The image of that presentation is a lasting one because it brought together two powerful and influential figures who had bridged the gap during professional football's emergence from its adolescent days into a sport that had made an indelible impression on the nation's consciousness during the sixties.

Rozelle was at the forefront as the NFL seized opportunities presented by television and revenue sharing; Rooney was one of a handful of patriarchs whose families helped mold the league since the early days.

The First Owners' Meeting

The NFL's first "owners' meeting" took place in 1920, in the showroom of a Hupmobile automobile dealership run by Ralph Hay, the business manager of the Canton Bulldogs. That meeting eventually led to the formation of the American Professional Football Conference, which was renamed the American Professional Football Association less than a month later. ("National Football League" was adopted in 1922.)

The legendary Jim Thorpe was named the league's first president, the precursor to today's commissioner. Joe Carr was elected to succeed Thorpe in 1921, and was the fledgling association's first strong leader. Carr actually was a sportswriter and promoter by trade, with a long resume that included stints as a pro basketball and minor-league baseball executive, as well as founder of professional football's Panhandles in his hometown of Columbus, Ohio, in 1904.

Carr created the league's first by-laws and gave a loose collection of teams structure lacking to that point. He set up a league office in Columbus, issued regular league standings, and, in 1927, reorganized the NFL into a stable, 12-team league. He also introduced the first standard player contract, and established membership criteria for franchises.

And, while Carr always wanted an NFL franchise in Columbus (the Panhandles lasted until 1926, the last four as the "Tigers"), he had the foresight to realize that if the NFL was to succeed the league had to expand outside the relatively small towns in the Midwest to large metropolitan areas. Thus, he scheduled more interstate games than ever before and brought pro football to the largest stadiums in the Midwest and East. He also established an NFL franchise in New York in 1925, bringing the Maras, one of the league's most influential and lasting families, into the fold.

Near the end of Carr's tenure as president, he hired Hugh (Shorty) Ray as technical advisor and supervisor of officials. Ray streamlined the game, making it faster and safer. He annually toured teams' training camps to clarify rules and he improved the techniques and quality of officiating. His efforts from 1938-1956 were recognized with his induction into the Pro Football Hall of Fame in 1966, 10 years after his death.

The Advent of the Commissioner

Joe Carr remained NFL president until his death in 1939. Carl Storck, the league's long-time secretary-treasurer, inherited the position, but in 1941 the title was shelved, and Elmer Layden (the head coach at Notre Dame and one of that university's legendary "Four Horsemen") took over as the league's first commissioner.

By 1946, the league was in direct competition with the upstart All-America Football Conference, and Bert Bell was selected to succeed Layden as commissioner and take up that fight. Bell, the man who proposed the college player draft in 1935, eventually established strong anti-gambling laws and imposed the NFL's television blackout rule. He also oversaw the agreement whereby the AAFC dissolved and three of its teams (the Baltimore Colts, Cleveland Browns, and San Francisco 49ers) were incorporated into the NFL.

But Bell died of a heart attack in 1959, just as the NFL was about to enter another battle with a new league, the American Football League. Dallas's Lamar Hunt was the driving force behind the AFL. A Texas native, Hunt repeatedly had tried to secure an NFL franchise for his home state, only to be turned down. So he did the next-best thing: He formed his own league—the American Football League.

Hunt, William H. Sullivan, Jr. (Boston), Ralph Wilson (Buffalo), Bob Howsam (Denver), Bud Adams (Houston), Barron Hilton (Los Angeles Chargers), Harry Wismer (New York Titans), and Wayne Valley (Oakland) formed an alliance Valley dubbed the "Foolish Club." Hunt (who moved his team to Kansas City in 1963), Wilson, and Adams remain in control of their franchises today.

While the Foolish Club was jumping into the professional football war head first—drafting players, naming former South Dakota governor and World War II flying ace Joe Foss the AFL's first commissioner, and throwing around large signing bonuses—the NFL owners were locked in a bitter, drawn-out struggle over who was to replace Bell.

The leading candidates in January, 1960, were Austin Gunsel, interim commissioner since Bell's death in October, 1959, and Marshall Leahy, an attorney for the San Francisco 49ers. But for seven days and 22 ballots, neither candidate could muster the three-fourths majority required for election.

Finally, New York Giants owner Wellington Mara and Cleveland Browns coach Paul Brown proposed a candidate upon whom everyone could agree: Pete Rozelle, 33, a former sports information director at the University of San Francisco and the general manager of the Los Angeles Rams.

Brown told an incredulous Rozelle, "You can grow into the job." That he did, ushering in the largest era of growth in the sport's history. Under Rozelle's direction, the NFL expanded from 12 teams in 1960 to 28 when he retired in 1989. He played the key role in the NFL-AFL merger and eventual restructuring of the league in 1970, and his ability to maintain cohesion and form unlikely alliances among the disparate owners is unparalleled.

He was the first to recognize that the marriage of football and television could elevate the game to a higher level than ever before. And perhaps his greatest legacy is the creation of the Super Bowl, which has progressed to the stature of an unofficial national holiday.

"The Super Bowl is his monument," Jim Murray wrote in the *Los Angeles Times.* "It exists because of Pete Rozelle. He built it from scratch. Michelangelo has his David, Da Vinci has his Mona Lisa, and Rozelle has the Super Bowl."

When Rozelle retired in 1989, the league turned to one of his closest confidants to replace him. Paul Tagliabue, a former basketball player at Georgetown University and the NFL's legal counsel, took over.

The seemingly disparate styles of Rozelle, who came from a public-relations background, and Tagliabue, from a legal background, have served the league well. "Pete was a man for his time," Saints owner Tom Benson said. "You've got to give him credit for what the National Football League is today. But it's a different era now, and the people are different. Paul couldn't have done Pete's job, and Pete couldn't have done Paul's. It's like any other business where the right person comes around at the right time. I think the right person came along for us in Paul Tagliabue."

To date, Tagliabue's lasting accomplishment has been securing labor peace through at least the end of the century while many other major sports have suffered player strikes and owner lockouts.

Tagliabue also expanded the NFL to 31 teams with the addition of the Carolina Panthers and Jacksonville Jaguars in 1995, and the Cleveland Browns in 1999 (returning professional football to that city after a five-year hiatus). In January, 1998, Tagliabue signed the heftiest television contract in entertainment history.

Powerful Bloodlines

Tim Mara never had any idea that he was about to purchase the New York Giants when he walked into the office of fight manager Billy Gibson in 1925. Mara was there to inquire about buying into one of Gibson's fighters, world lightweight champion Benny Leonard. "I won't sell you a piece of Leonard," Gibson said, "but here's a fellow who's selling franchises in pro football, and he tells me New York is open."

The fellow was Joe Carr, whose pitch to Gibson fell on deaf ears, but who piqued Mara's interest. "A New York franchise for anything is worth $500," Mara reasoned, and the Giants, as they would be known, were his.

A few months later, Mara may have had second thoughts when his franchise was floundering in a sea of red ink. But in December, 1925, the Bears brought recently signed legend Red Grange to the Polo Grounds, and a record crowd of 73,000 helped save the future of pro football in New York, the significance of which is not to be understated: The New York franchise helped put the league on the national map.

One year later, Mara opposed C.C. Pyle, Grange's manager, when Pyle attempted to bring another NFL franchise to New York to play in Yankee Stadium. Mara stood firm for his franchise's territorial rights—a cornerstone of the league—and blocked Pyle, who then formed the first incarnation of the American Football League. It lasted only one season.

In 1927, Mara agreed to let a chastened Pyle into the NFL on the stipulation that he play 13 of 16 games away from home, and the other three when the Giants were out of town. Pyle's Yankees could not break even financially or on the field, and at the end of the 1928 season, he abandoned the franchise.

In time, Mara turned over day-to-day control of the Giants to his sons Jack and Wellington. Wellington Mara remains co-owner of the club with business magnate Robert Tisch, who purchased 50 percent of the franchise from Jack's heirs in 1991.

In 1997, he was elected to the Pro Football Hall of Fame for his many contributions as a member of virtually every significant NFL committee. Wellington and Tim Mara are the first father-son combination to be enshrined.

Dan Reeves, a schoolmate of Jack Mara, had his interest in professional football sparked as a result of his friendship, capping it off with the purchase of the Cleveland Rams in 1941.

In 1945, the Rams went 9-1 and won the NFL title with a classic 15-14 victory over the Washington Redskins in the championship game. But when the franchise still lost $50,000 that year, Reeves petitioned the league to move to Los Angeles, a shift he long coveted. The league refused permission, but recanted when Reeves threatened to sell, and the next year the NFL (and AAFC) made pro football the first coast-to-coast major sport.

In 1933, Art Rooney parlayed his winnings from a good day at the racetrack ($2,500) into an NFL franchise. Rooney always denied it, but he admitted he had a couple of other days where he won at least that much. Pittsburgh (the club originally was known as the Pirates) managed only 24 victories in its first eight years and lost money every year, severely trying Rooney's patience—so much that he sold the team to Alexis Thompson following a 2-7-2 season in 1940.

But that was the only bump in the road for the relationship between the Rooney family and the Pittsburgh franchise. Shortly thereafter, Rooney bought into the Philadelphia Eagles with future NFL Commissioner Bert Bell and, by April, 1941, was so homesick for Pittsburgh that he swapped franchises with Thompson. The 1941 Steelers won only 1 of 11 games, and the franchise had only seven winning seasons until 1972.

Rooney was inducted into the Pro Football Hall of Fame in 1964, however, and his infinite patience was rewarded a decade later when the Steelers began an unprecedented run of four Super Bowl victories in six years. Rooney died in 1988 at age 87, and his son Dan is at the Steelers' helm today.

Mild-mannered Art Rooney often played an unsung but important role in the early days of the NFL by acting as a buffer between tempestuous owners such as Washington's George Preston Marshall and Chicago's George Halas. Halas was a player in the early days of the NFL, an end who returned a fumble 98 yards for a touchdown in 1923, a record that stood nearly half a century.

He spent 40 seasons on the sidelines as coach of the Chicago Bears, compiling 324 victories in four separate 10-year coaching stints, more victories than any other head coach until Don Shula broke the mark in 1993. And he was a powerful figure at league meetings. In fact, it was a letter from Halas to Hay that set in motion the wheels for the league's original organizational meeting.

Later, as president of the rules committee, Halas enacted legislation in February, 1933, that dramatically opened up the game and increased scoring: goal posts were moved from the end lines to the goal lines; on plays ending out of bounds or near the sideline, the ball was brought in 10 yards to start the next play; and passing was legal from anywhere behind the line of scrimmage (before that, the passer had to be five yards behind the line).

Halas owned the Bears from the time he and then-partner Ed (Dutch) Sternaman purchased the franchise in 1922 until his death in 1983 at age 88. His grandson, Michael McCaskey, now runs the club.

A decade after the purchase, Halas bought out Sternaman. Halas, however, may never have completed the purchase were it not for the financial assistance of Charles Bidwill, whose support helped him maintain control of the club in the early days of the Great Depression.

A short time later, Bidwill hosted a dinner party aboard his yacht. One of the guests suggested to another, Chicago Cardinals owner David Jones, that he sell his club to the party's host. Jones, a dentist who had purchased the franchise four years earlier for $25,000, was willing to sell because he had seen his team deteriorate (the Cardinals had a 1-9-1 record in 1933). Bidwill accepted his off-the-cuff sale price of $50,000.

Bidwill gutted the underachieving team, and it improved enough to win five games his first season in control. Rough times followed, but Bidwill kept trying. The new owner signed halfback Charley Trippi to a hefty, multi-year contract in 1947. That move and others indeed produced a winner. The Cardinals went 9-3 in 1947 and won the NFL title with a 28-21 victory over the Philadelphia Eagles in the championship game. Sadly, Bidwill was not around to see it; he had died in the spring. The Cardinals' franchise has remained in the Bidwill family ever since, passing from Bidwill's widow, Violet, in 1947 to sons Charles, Jr., and Bill in 1962, and solely to the latter in 1972.

Maverick Owners

George Preston Marshall was one of pro football's earliest showmen. Marshall was married to silent-movie star Corinne Griffith, and he reveled in the spotlight.

He purchased the Boston franchise in the NFL as head of a four-man syndicate in 1932. Marshall renamed the club from Braves to Redskins a year later, and, frustrated that the Boston fans failed to turn out in great numbers even when the team advanced to the league's title game in 1936, moved the club to Washington in 1937.

In the nation's capital, Marshall organized the Redskins' marching band and spectacular halftime shows, introduced cheerleaders, began a radio network that carried games throughout the South, and led thousands of supporters on pilgrimages to rival cities.

But Marshall was as innovative about the product on the field as he was about publicity. After a hastily arranged playoff game between the Chicago Bears and Portsmouth Spartans decided the league title in 1932, the Braves' owner recognized the value of an annual championship game and joined Bears owner George Halas in pushing through legislation that split the NFL into two divisions, with the winners meeting in a championship game. Marshall also backed Halas on other sweeping rules changes enacted in 1933 that opened up the game with more passing.

Marshall, however, endured his share of criticism for not integrating his team until 1962. That year, he drafted his club's first African-American player, Heisman Trophy-winning running back Ernie Davis from Syracuse. He promptly traded Davis to Cleveland for two more African-Americans, running backs Bobby Mitchell and Leroy Jackson.

Mitchell was switched to wide receiver by the Redskins and eventually earned induction into the Pro Football Hall of Fame after catching 521 passes in his 11-year career. He currently is the club's assistant general manager. Marshall maintained ownership of the Redskins until his death in 1969. Jack Kent Cooke owned the club from 1974 until his death in 1997.

Like Marshall, Oakland's Al Davis and Dallas's Jerry Jones are current owners who frequently have been at odds with league tradition (Davis over franchise relocation and Jones over marketing and revenue sharing). Davis holds the distinction of being the only man to serve as a personnel assistant, scout, assistant coach, head coach, general manager, commissioner, and team owner/chief executive officer.

He was only 33 when Oakland hired him away from head coach Sid Gillman's staff in San Diego to be the Raiders' head coach in 1963. Oakland had won just 9 of 42 games in its first three seasons, but Davis was 23-16-3 in three years before becoming American Football League commissioner in 1966. After the historic merger of the AFL and NFL was announced a short time later, Davis returned to guide Raiders' fortunes as managing general partner. Although some of his actions have angered his fellow NFL owners—for example, Davis moved the Raiders from Oakland to Los Angeles in 1982 and back to Oakland in 1995—he also helped the club to three Super Bowl victories.

Jones bought the Dallas Cowboys in 1989 and immediately replaced Pro Football Hall of Fame coach Tom Landry, the only coach in Dallas franchise history, with Jimmy Johnson. Though the move was immensely unpopular at the time, Johnson captured two Super Bowls before stepping down following the 1993 season. Johnson's successor Barry Switzer added another Super Bowl triumph in 1995.

Landry and Cowboys president and general manager Tex Schramm had helped build a dynasty in the seventies and eighties. Schramm, who represented the league in merger talks with the AFL's Lamar Hunt and chaired the NFL's competition committee for almost 25 years, was inducted into the Pro Football Hall of Fame in 1991.

Four years later, another former team president, the Saints' Jim Finks, was inducted into the Hall one year after his death. Finks spent more than 40 years in the NFL as a player, general manager, and team president. A consummate builder, he developed the Vikings, Bears, and Saints—all with losing records when he took over—into winners.

Stability in Ownership

Stability has been a cornerstone of the NFL in its years of immense growth. The Smith family has owned the Falcons since the inception of the franchise in 1965. (Rankin Smith founded the club; his son, Taylor Smith, took over after Rankin Smith's death in 1998.) The Brown family has owned the Bengals, beginning with Pro Football Hall of Fame coach Paul Brown in 1967 and continuing today with his son Mike. Art Modell owned the Cleveland Browns from 1961 until 1995 and now is the owner of the Baltimore Ravens. William Clay Ford has maintained control of the Lions since 1961. And the Irsay family, beginning with Robert Irsay and continuing with his son Jim, has owned the Colts since 1972.

And through it all, there has been nothing quite like the ownership of the Green Bay Packers. By virtue of a unique agreement that dates to 1923, when 400 townspeople bought shares in the franchise that cannot be sold for more than the original price ($5), the club is assured of remaining in the small Wisconsin town no matter how many big cities vie for franchises. And that makes the citizens of Green Bay rank right up there with the league's biggest movers and shakers.

ANNUAL AWARDS

CHAPTER 13

Pro Football Hall of Fame

David Pietrusza and John Hogrogian

Pro football was not born in Canton, Ohio, but Canton spearheaded its growth in the years before World War I, as the pro game grew from an autumn activity for Midwest town teams to a sport that drew superior players from all over the country.

It also was in Canton, in Ralph Hay's Hupmobile showroom on September 17, 1920, that the NFL (then called the American Professional Football Association) was founded. Four decades later, the newly established Pro Football Hall of Fame found a home in the northern Ohio city.

The Hall opened on September 7, 1963, with an inaugural class of 17 enshrinees. Canton Bulldog Jim Thorpe was among the original inductees, and a seven-foot high bronze statue of Thorpe now stands immediately inside the building's entrance.

Modern-era players nominated for the Hall must be retired from the game for five years. Coaches must also be retired, but contributors to the game (i.e., owners or officials) may still be active at the time of their selection. Writers and broadcasters are not eligible for enshrinement in the Pro Football Hall of Fame, but since 1969 writers have been honored by the Dick McCann Award (named after the Hall of Fame's first director). Since 1989, broadcasters have been honored through the Pete Rozelle Award. Voting is performed by a 36-member panel composed of a media representative from each NFL city, one Professional Football Writers of America (PFWA) representative, and five selectors-at-large. This panel first designates a list of finalists before choosing selectees. A Seniors Committee functions to review the qualifications of those players, coaches, and contributors whose careers occurred primarily more than 25 years ago. Each inductee is honored not only with a bronze bust in the Hall's Enshrinement Gallery, but also in the Enshrinee Mementos Room.

Induction ceremonies occur in late July or early August and are followed by a preseason NFL game at Canton's recently refurbished Fawcett Stadium. The address of the Pro Football Hall of Fame is 2121 George Halas Drive, Canton, Ohio 44708.

1963
Sammy Baugh - halfback, quarterback
Bert Bell - owner, NFL Commissioner
Joe Carr - NFL President
Earle (Dutch) Clark - quarterback
Harold (Red) Grange - halfback
George Halas - coach, owner
Mel Hein - center
Wilbur (Pete) Henry - tackle
Cal Hubbard - tackle, end
Don Hutson - end
Earle (Curly) Lambeau - coach
Tim Mara - owner
George Preston Marshall - owner
Johnny (Blood) McNally - halfback
Bronko Nagurski - fullback
Ernie Nevers - fullback
Jim Thorpe - halfback

1964
Jimmy Conzelman - coach
Ed Healey - tackle
Clarke Hinkle - fullback
William Roy (Link) Lyman - tackle
Mike Michalske - guard
Art Rooney - owner
George Trafton - center

1965
Guy Chamberlin - end, coach
John (Paddy) Driscoll - halfback
Danny Fortmann - guard
Otto Graham - quarterback
Sid Luckman - quarterback
Steve Van Buren - halfback
Bob Waterfield - quarterback

1966
Bill Dudley - halfback
Joe Guyon - halfback
Arnie Herber - halfback
Walt Kiesling - guard, coach
George McAfee - halfback
Steve Owen - coach
Hugh (Shorty) Ray - supervisor of officials
Clyde (Bulldog) Turner - center

1967
Chuck Bednarik - center, linebacker
Charles Bidwill, Sr. - owner
Paul Brown - coach
Bobby Layne - quarterback
Dan Reeves - owner
Ken Strong - halfback
Joe Stydahar - tackle
Emlen Tunnell - defensive back

1968
Cliff Battles - halfback
Art Donovan - defensive tackle
Elroy (Crazylegs) Hirsch - end
Wayne Millner - end
Marion Motley - fullback
Charley Trippi - halfback
Alex Wojciechowicz - center

1969
Albert Glen (Turk) Edwards - tackle
Earl (Greasy) Neale - coach
Leo Nomellini - defensive tackle
Joe Perry - fullback
Ernie Stautner - defensive tackle

1970
Jack Christiansen - safety
Tom Fears - end
Hugh McElhenny - halfback
Pete Pihos - end

1971
Jim Brown - fullback
Bill Hewitt - end
Frank (Bruiser) Kinard - tackle
Vince Lombardi - coach
Andy Robustelli - defensive end
Y.A. Tittle - quarterback
Norm Van Brocklin - quarterback

1972
Lamar Hunt - owner
Gino Marchetti - defensive end
Ollie Matson - halfback
Clarence (Ace) Parker - quarterback

1973
Raymond Berry - end
Jim Parker - tackle, guard
Joe Schmidt - linebacker

1974
Tony Canadeo - halfback
Bill George - linebacker
Lou Groza - tackle, kicker
Dick (Night Train) Lane - cornerback

1975
Roosevelt Brown - tackle
George Connor - linebacker, tackle
Dante Lavelli - end
Lenny Moore - halfback

1976
Ray Flaherty - end, coach
Len Ford - defensive end
Jim Taylor - fullback

1977
Frank Gifford - halfback
Forrest Gregg - tackle
Gale Sayers - halfback
Bart Starr - quarterback
Bill Willis - guard

1978
Lance Alworth - wide receiver
Weeb Ewbank - coach
Alphonse (Tuffy) Leemans - halfback
Ray Nitschke - linebacker
Larry Wilson - safety

1979
Dick Butkus - linebacker
Yale Lary - defensive back-punter
Ron Mix - tackle
Johnny Unitas - quarterback

1980
Herb Adderley - defensive back
David (Deacon) Jones - defensive end
Bob Lilly - defensive tackle
Jim Otto - center

1981
Morris (Red) Badgro - end
George Blanda - quarterback, kicker
Willie Davis - defensive end
Jim Ringo - center

1982
Doug Atkins - defensive end
Sam Huff - linebacker
George Musso - tackle
Merlin Olsen - defensive tackle

1983
Bobby Bell - linebacker
Sid Gillman - coach
Sonny Jurgensen - quarterback
Bobby Mitchell - wide receiver
Paul Warfield - wide receiver

1984
Willie Brown - cornerback
Mike McCormack - tackle
Charley Taylor - wide receiver
Arnie Weinmeister - defensive tackle

1985
Frank Gatski - center
Joe Namath - quarterback
Pete Rozelle - NFL Commissioner
O.J. Simpson - halfback
Roger Staubach - quarterback

1986
Paul Hornung - halfback
Ken Houston - safety
Willie Lanier - linebacker
Fran Tarkenton - quarterback
Doak Walker - halfback

1987
Larry Csonka - fullback
Len Dawson - quarterback
Joe Greene - defensive tackle
John Henry Johnson - fullback
Jim Langer - center
Don Maynard - wide receiver
Gene Upshaw - guard

1988
Fred Biletnikoff - wide receiver
Mike Ditka - tight end
Jack Ham - linebacker
Alan Page - defensive tackle

1989
Mel Blount - cornerback
Terry Bradshaw - quarterback
Art Shell - tackle
Willie Wood - safety

1990
Buck Buchanan - defensive tackle
Bob Griese - quarterback
Franco Harris - fullback
Ted Hendricks - linebacker
Jack Lambert - linebacker
Tom Landry - coach
Bob St. Clair - tackle

1991
Earl Campbell - halfback
John Hannah - guard
Stan Jones - guard
Tex Schramm - general manager
Jan Stenerud - kicker

1992
Lem Barney - cornerback
Al Davis - owner
John Mackey - tight end
John Riggins - fullback

1993
Dan Fouts - quarterback
Larry Little - guard
Chuck Noll - coach
Walter Payton - halfback
Bill Walsh - coach

1994
Tony Dorsett - halfback
Bud Grant - coach
Jimmy Johnson - cornerback
Leroy Kelly - halfback
Jackie Smith - tight end
Randy White - defensive tackle

1995
Jim Finks - general manager
Henry Jordan - defensive tackle
Steve Largent - wide receiver
Lee Roy Selmon - defensive end
Kellen Winslow - tight end

1996
Lou Creekmur - tackle-guard
Dan Dierdorf - tackle
Joe Gibbs - coach
Charlie Joiner - wide receiver
Mel Renfro - defensive back

1997
Mike Haynes - cornerback
Wellington Mara - owner
Don Shula - coach
Mike Webster - center

1998
Paul Krause - safety
Tommy McDonald - wide receiver
Anthony Muñoz - tackle
Mike Singletary - linebacker
Dwight Stephenson - center

1999
Eric Dickerson - running back
Tom Mack - guard
Ozzie Newsome - tight end
Billy Shaw - guard
Lawrence Taylor - linebacker

CHAPTER 14

Awards and Honors

John Hogrogian

For the first decades of major-league professional football, membership on an all-pro team was the only honor available to players. The NFL instituted an official most-valuable-player award in 1938 and awarded it through 1946. The rival AAFC named official MVPs in 1946, 1947, and 1948. Sportswriters had been selecting major-league baseball MVPs continuously since 1931 and naming a Heisman Trophy winner in college football since 1935. In the 1930s and 1940s, however, the pro football leagues had to fulfill this function themselves.

With the advent of television in the years after World War II, pro football attained new levels of public attention. Various publications and wire services began naming an annual MVP or Player of the Year during the 1950s. *United Press, The Sporting News,* Newspaper Enterprise Association, and the *Associated Press* conducted annual polls during that decade to select an outstanding player for the season. In 1959, the Maxwell Club of Philadelphia joined the field by awarding the first annual Bert Bell Trophy to its NFL most valuable player. In later decades, prestigious MVP awards were instituted by *Pro Football Weekly* and the Pro Football Writers of America. Since 1992, *PFW* and the PFWA awards have been presented jointly.

The various MVP awards coexist without any official status, unlike baseball's MVP award. The prestige of each award has fluctuated over the years. In the 1950s, the *United Press* award received the greatest media attention. In the 1990s, the *Associated Press* and Pro Football Writers of America awards appear to carry the most weight. At any rate, each award has its adherents as the most valid.

The various MVP awards have blossomed into a wide range of formats. There are NFL honorees, conference honorees, offensive honorees, and defensive honorees. Each is presented below.

Also springing into existence after World War II were rookie-of-the-year and coach-of-the-year awards. Like the MVP awards, there have been multiple selectors and multiple formats for these awards.

In the tables that follow, the winners of the major MVP, rookie-of-the-year, and coach-of-the-year awards are presented. Some awards, such as those honoring kickers, executives, and assistant coaches, also have been added for this edition. The legend for the selectors follows. When a "*t*" appears following the selector, it indicates that there was a tie for the award indicated.

Legend

In the following table, MVP refers to the most-valuable-player and player-of-the-year awards in all their different forms. Similarly, ROY refers to rookie-of-the-year awards and COY to coach-of-the-year awards.

AP *Associated Press:* MVP (1957-present), ROY (1964-present), COY (1957-present)
FW Pro Football Writers of America: MVP (1975-present), ROY (1982-present), COY (1982-present)
MX Maxwell Club of Philadelphia: MVP (1959-present), COY (1993-present)
NE Newspaper Enterprise Association: MVP (1955-1989), ROY (1964-1989)
OA official AAFC MVP (1946-48)
OF official NFL MVP (1938-1946)
PW *Pro Football Weekly:* MVP (1968-1984, 1986-present), ROY (1969-1984, 1986-present), COY (1968-1984, 1986-present)
SN *The Sporting News:* MVP (1954-present), ROY (1955-present), COY (1947-1953, 1955-56, 1961, 1963-present)
UP *United Press* and *United Press International:* MVP (1951, 1953-present), ROY (1955-present), COY (1953, 1955-present)

Most Valuable Player/Player of the Year

1938 Mel Hein, C, NYG (OF)
1939 Parker Hall, HB, Cle (OF)
1940 Ace Parker, QB, Bkn (OF)
1941 Don Hutson, E, GB (OF)
1942 Don Hutson, E, GB (OF)
1943 Sid Luckman, QB, ChiB (OF)
1944 Frank Sinkwich, HB, Det (OF)
1945 Bob Waterfield, QB, Cle (OF)
1946 NFL—Bill Dudley, HB, Pit (OF)
1946 AAFC—Glenn Dobbs, HB, Bk-A (OA)
1947 NFL—no selection
1947 AAFC—Otto Graham, QB, Cl-A (OA)
1948 NFL—no selection
1948 AAFC—Otto Graham, QB, Cl-A (OA*t*); Frankie Albert, QB, SF-A (OA*t*)
1949 NFL—no selection
1949 AAFC—no selection
1950 no selection
1951 Otto Graham, QB, Cle (UP)
1952 no selection
1953 Otto Graham, QB, Cle (UP)
1954 Joe Perry, FB, SF (UP); Lou Groza, OT, Cle (SN)
1955 Otto Graham, QB, Cle (UP, SN); Harlon Hill, OE, ChiB (NE)
1956 Frank Gifford, HB, NYG (UP, NE, SN)
1957 Y.A. Tittle, QB, SF (UP); Jim Brown, FB, Cle (AP, SN); John Unitas, QB, Bal (NE)
1958 Jim Brown, FB, Cle (UP, AP, NE, SN)
1959 Johnny Unitas, QB, Bal (UP, SN, MX); Charley Conerly, QB, NYG (AP, NE)

1960 NFL—Norm Van Brocklin, QB, Phi (UP*t*, AP, NE, SN, MX); Joe Schmidt, LB, Det (UP*t*)
1960 AFL—Abner Haynes, HB, DalT (UP, SN)
1961 NFL—Paul Hornung, HB, GB (UP, AP, SN, MX); Y.A. Tittle, QB, NYG (NE)
1961 AFL—George Blanda, QB, Hou (UP, SN)
1962 NFL—Y.A. Tittle, QB, NYG (UP, SN); Jim Taylor, FB, GB (AP, NE); Andy Robustelli, DE, NYG (MX)
1962 AFL—Cookie Gilchrist, FB, Buf (UP); Len Dawson, QB, DalT (SN)
1963 NFL—Jim Brown, FB Cle (UP, NE*t*, MX); Y.A. Tittle, QB, NYG (AP, NE*t*, SN)
1963 AFL—Lance Alworth, WR, SD (UP); Clem Daniels, HB, Oak (SN)
1964 NFL—Johnny Unitas, QB, Bal (UP, AP, SN, MX); Lenny Moore, HB, Bal (NE)
1964 AFL—Gino Cappelletti, WR, Bos (UP, SN)
1965 NFL—Jim Brown, FB, Cle (UP, AP, SN, NE); Pete Retzlaff, TE, Phi (MX)
1965 AFL—Jack Kemp, QB, Buf (UP); Paul Lowe, HB, SD (SN)
1966 NFL—Bart Starr, QB, GB (UP, AP, NE, SN); Don Meredith, QB, Dal (MX)
1966 AFL—Jim Nance, FB, Bos (UP, AP, SN)
1967 NFL—Johnny Unitas, QB, Bal (UP, AP, NE, SN, MX)
1967 AFL—Daryle Lamonica, QB, Oak (UP, AP, SN)
1968 NFL—Earl Morrall, QB, Bal (UP, AP, NE, SN, PW); Leroy Kelly, HB, Cle (MX)
1968 AFL—Joe Namath, QB, NYJ (UP, SN, PW)
1969 NFL—Roman Gabriel, QB, LARm (UP, AP, NE, SN, MX, PW)
1969 AFL—Daryle Lamonica, QB, Oak (UP, SN, PW); Joe Namath, QB, NYJ (AP)
1970 John Brodie, QB, SF (AP, NE); George Blanda, QB-K, Oak (MX)
1971 Alan Page, DT, Min (AP); Bob Griese, QB, Mia (NE); Roger Staubach, QB, Dal (MX)
1972 Larry Brown, RB, Was (AP, NE, MX)
1973 O.J. Simpson, RB, Buf (AP, NE, MX)
1974 Ken Stabler, QB, Oak (AP, NE); Merlin Olsen, DT, LARm (MX)
1975 Fran Tarkenton, QB, Min (FW, AP, NE, MX)
1976 Bert Jones, QB, Bal (FW, AP, NE); Ken Stabler, QB, Oak (MX)
1977 Walter Payton, RB, ChiB (FW, AP, NE); Bob Griese, QB, Mia (MX)
1978 Earl Campbell, RB, Hou (FW, NE); Terry Bradshaw, QB, Pit (AP, MX)
1979 Earl Campbell, RB, Hou (FW, AP, NE, MX)
1980 Brian Sipe, QB, Cle (FW, AP, SN); Earl Campbell, RB, Hou (NE); Ron Jaworski, QB, Phi (MX)
1981 Ken Anderson, QB, Cin (FW, AP, NE, SN, MX)
1982 Dan Fouts, QB, SD (FW, NE); Mark Moseley, K, Was (AP, SN); Joe Theismann, QB, Was (MX)
1983 Joe Theismann, QB, Was (FW, AP, NE); Eric Dickerson, RB, LARm (SN); John Riggins, RB, Was (MX)
1984 Dan Marino, QB, Mia (FW, AP, NE, SN, MX)
1985 Marcus Allen, RB, LARd (FW, AP, SN); Walter Payton, RB, ChiB (NE, MX)
1986 Lawrence Taylor, LB, NYG (FW, AP, SN, MX); Phil Simms, QB, NYG (NE)
1987 Jerry Rice, WR, SF (FW, NE, SN, MX); John Elway, QB, Den (AP)
1988 Boomer Esiason, QB, Cin (FW, AP, SN); Roger Craig, RB, SF (NE); Randall Cunningham, QB, Phi (MX)
1989 Joe Montana, QB, SF (FW, AP, NE, SN, MX)
1990 Randall Cunningham, QB, Phi (FW, MX); Joe Montana, QB, SF (AP); Jerry Rice, WR, SF (SN)
1991 Thurman Thomas, RB, Buf (FW, AP, SN); Barry Sanders, RB, Det (MX)
1992 Steve Young, QB, SF (FW, AP, SN, MX)
1993 Emmitt Smith, RB, Dal (FW, AP, SN, MX)
1994 Steve Young, QB, SF (FW, AP, SN, MX)
1995 Brett Favre, QB, GB (FW, AP, SN, MX)
1996 Brett Favre, QB, GB (FW, AP, SN)
1997 Brett Favre, QB, GB (AP*t*); Barry Sanders, RB, Det (AP*t*, FW, SN)
1998 Terrell Davis, RB, Den (AP, FW, SN)

AFC MVP/Player of the Year

1970 AFC—George Blanda, QB, Oak (UP, SN)
1971 AFC—Otis Taylor, WR, KC (UP); Bob Griese, QB, Mia (SN)
1972 AFC—O.J. Simpson, RB, Buf (UP); Earl Morrall, QB, Mia (SN)
1973 AFC—O.J. Simpson, RB, Buf (UP, SN)
1974 AFC—Ken Stabler, QB, Oak (UP, SN)
1975 AFC—O.J. Simpson, RB, Buf (SN)
1976 AFC—Ken Stabler, QB, Oak (SN)
1977 AFC—Craig Morton, QB, Den (SN)
1978 AFC—Earl Campbell, RB, Hou (SN)
1979 AFC—Dan Fouts, QB, SD (UP, SN)
1980 AFC—Brian Sipe, QB, Cle (UP)
1981 AFC—Ken Anderson, QB, Cin (UP)
1982 AFC—Dan Fouts, QB, SD (UP)
1983 AFC—Curt Warner, RB, Sea (UP)
1984 AFC—Mark Gastineau, DE, NYJ (UP)
No further conference selections

NFC MVP/Player of the Year

1970 NFC—John Brodie, QB, SF (UP, SN)
1971 NFC—Alan Page, DT, Min (UP); Roger Staubach, QB, Dal (SN)
1972 NFC—Larry Brown, RB, Was (UP, SN)
1973 NFC—John Hadl, QB, LARm (UP, SN)
1974 NFC—Jim Hart, QB, StL (UP); Chuck Foreman, RB, Min (SN)
1975 NFC—Fran Tarkenton, QB, Min (UP, SN)
1976 NFC—Chuck Foreman, RB, Min (UP); Walter Payton, RB, ChiB (SN)
1977 NFC—Walter Payton, RB, ChiB (UP, SN)
1978 NFC—Archie Manning, QB, NO (UP, SN)
1979 NFC—Ottis Anderson, RB, StL (UP, SN)
1980 NFC—Ron Jaworski, QB, Phi (UP)
1981 NFC—Tony Dorsett, RB, Dal (UP)
1982 NFC—Mark Moseley, K, Was (UP)
1983 NFC—Eric Dickerson, RB, LARm (UP)
1984 NFC—Eric Dickerson, RB, LARm (UP)
No further conference selections

Offensive MVP/Player of the Year

1970 John Brodie, QB, SF (NE, PW)
1971 Otis Taylor, WR, KC (PW)
1972 Larry Brown, RB, Was (AP, PW)
1973 O.J. Simpson, RB, Buf (AP, PW)
1974 Ken Stabler, QB, Oak (AP); Otis Armstrong, RB, Den (PW)
1975 Fran Tarkenton, QB, Min (AP, PW, UP-NFC); O.J. Simpson, RB, Buf (UP-AFC)
1976 Bert Jones, QB, Bal (AP, UP-AFC); Ken Stabler, QB, Oak (PW); Chuck Foreman, RB, Min (UP-NFC)
1977 Walter Payton, RB, ChiB (AP, PW, UP-NFC); Craig Morton, QB, Den (UP-AFC)
1978 Earl Campbell, RB, Hou (AP, PW, UP-AFC); Archie Manning, QB, NO (UP-NFC)
1979 Earl Campbell, RB, Hou (AP, PW)
1980 Earl Campbell, RB, Hou (AP); Brian Sipe, QB, Cle (PW)
1981 Ken Anderson, QB, Cin (AP, PW)
1982 Dan Fouts, QB, SD (AP, PW)
1983 Joe Theismann, QB, Was (AP, PW)
1984 Dan Marino, QB, Mia (AP, PW)
1985 Marcus Allen, RB, LARd (AP, UP-AFC); Walter Payton, RB, ChiB (UP-NFC)
1986 Eric Dickerson, RB, LARm (AP, UP-NFC); Jerry Rice, WR, SF (PW); Curt Warner, RB, Sea (UP-AFC)
1987 Jerry Rice, WR, SF (AP, PW, UP-NFC); John Elway, QB, Den (UP-AFC)
1988 Roger Craig, RB, SF (AP, UP-NFC); Boomer Esiason, QB, Cin (PW, UP-AFC)
1989 Joe Montana, QB, SF (AP, PW, UP-NFC); Christian Okoye, RB, KC (UP-AFC)
1990 Warren Moon, QB, Hou (AP, UP-AFC); Randall Cunningham, QB, Phi (PW, UP-NFC)
1991 Thurman Thomas, RB, Buf (AP, PW, UP-AFC); Mark Rypien, QB, Was (UP-NFC)
1992 Steve Young, QB, SF (AP, PW, UP-NFC); Barry Foster, RB, Pit (UP-AFC)
1993 Jerry Rice, WR, SF (AP); Emmitt Smith, RB, Dal (PW, UP-NFC); John Elway, QB, Den (UP-AFC)
1994 Barry Sanders, RB, Det (AP); Steve Young, QB, SF (PW, UP-NFC); Dan Marino, QB, Mia (UP-AFC)
1995 Brett Favre, QB, GB (AP, PW, UP-NFC); Jim Harbaugh, QB, Ind (UP-AFC)
1996 Terrell Davis, RB, Den (AP, UP-AFC); Brett Favre, QB, GB (UP-NFC)
1997 Barry Sanders, RB, Det (AP)
1998 Terrell Davis, RB, Den (AP)

Defensive MVP/Player of the Year

1966 NFL—Larry Wilson, S, StL (NE)
1966 AFL—no selection
1967 NFL—Deacon Jones, DE, LARm (NE)
1967 AFL—no selection
1968 NFL—Deacon Jones, DE, LARm (NE)
1968 AFL—no selection
1969 NFL—Dick Butkus, LB, ChiB (NE)
1969 AFL—no selection
1970 Dick Butkus, LB, ChiB (NE, PW)
1971 Alan Page, DT, Min (AP, NE, PW)
1972 Joe Greene, DT, Pit (AP, NE, PW)
1973 Dick Anderson, S, Mia (AP); Alan Page, DT, Min (PWt, NE); Paul Smith, DT, Den (PWt)
1974 Joe Greene, DT, Pit (AP, NE, PW)
1975 Mel Blount, CB, Pit (AP, UP-AFC); Curley Culp, DT, Hou (NE); Jack Ham, LB, Pit (PW); Jack Youngblood, DE, LARm (UP-NFC)
1976 Jack Lambert, LB, Pit (AP, PW, UP-AFC); Jerry Sherk, DT, Cle (NE); Wally Chambers, DT, ChiB (UP-NFC)
1977 Harvey Martin, DE, Dal (AP, NE, PW, UP-NFC); Lyle Alzado, DE, Den (UP-AFC)
1978 Randy Gradishar, LB, Den (AP, NE, PW, UP-AFC); Randy White, DT, Dal (UP-NFC)
1979 Lee Roy Selmon, DE, TB (AP, NE, PW, UP-NFC)
1980 Lester Hayes, CB, Oak (AP, NE, PW, UP-AFC); Nolan Cromwell, S, LARm (UP-NFC)
1981 Lawrence Taylor, LB, NYG (AP); Joe Klecko, DE, NYJ (NE, PW, UP-AFC); Fred Dean, DE, SF (UP-NFC)
1982 Lawrence Taylor, LB, NYG (AP); Mark Gastineau, DE, NYJ (NE); Dan Hampton, DT, ChiB (PW)
1983 Doug Betters, DE, Mia (AP); Jack Lambert, LB, Pit (NE); Bob Baumhower, DT, Mia (PW)
1984 Kenny Easley, S, Sea (AP, PW); Mike Haynes, CB, LARd (NE)
1985 Mike Singletary, LB, ChiB (AP, UP-NFC); Andre Tippett, LB, NE (NE*t*, UP-AFC); Howie Long, DE, LARd (NE*t*)
1986 Lawrence Taylor, LB, NYG (AP, NE, PW, UP-NFC); Rulon Jones, DE, Den (UP-AFC)
1987 Reggie White, DT, Phi (AP, NE, PW, UP-NFC); Bruce Smith, DE, Buf (UP-AFC)
1988 Mike Singletary, LB, ChiB (AP, NE, PW, UP-NFC); Bruce Smith, DE, Buf (UP-AFC*t*); Cornelius Bennett, LB, Buf (UP-AFC*t*)
1989 Keith Millard, DT, Min (AP, PW, UP-NFC); Tim Harris, LB, GB (NE); Michael Dean Perry, DT, Cle (UP-AFC)
1990 Bruce Smith, DE, Buf (AP, PW, UP-AFC); Charles Haley, LB, SF (UP-NFC)
1991 Pat Swilling, LB, NO (AP); Reggie White, DE, Phi (PW, UP-NFC); Cornelius Bennett, LB, Buf (UP-AFC)
1992 Cortez Kennedy, DT, Sea (AP, PW); Junior Seau, LB, SD (UP-AFC); Chris Doleman, DE, Min (UP-NFC)
1993 Rod Woodson, CB, Pit (AP, UP-AFC); Bruce Smith, DE, Buf (PW); Eric Allen, CB, Phi (UP-NFC)
1994 Deion Sanders, CB, SF (AP, PW): Greg Lloyd, LB, Pit (UP-AFC); Charles Haley, DE, Dal (UP-NFC)
1995 Bryce Paup, LB, Buf (AP, PW, UP-AFC); Reggie White, DE, GB (UP-NFC)
1996 Bruce Smith, DE, Buf (AP, FW, UP-AFC); Kevin Greene, LB, Car (UP-NFC)
1997 Dana Stubblefield, DT, SF (AP, FW)
1998 Reggie White, DE, GB (AP, FW)

Rookie of the Year

1955 Alan Ameche, FB, Bal (UP, SN)
1956 Lenny Moore, HB, Bal (UP); J.C. Caroline, DB, ChiB (SN)
1957 Jim Brown, FB, Cle (UP, AP, SN)
1958 Jimmy Orr, OE, Pit (UP, AP); Bobby Mitchell, HB, Cle (SN)
1959 Nick Pietrosante, FB, Det (AP, SN); Boyd Dowler, OE, GB (UP)
1960 NFL—Gail Cogdill, OE, Det (UP, AP, SN)
1960 AFL—Abner Haynes, HB, DalT (UP, SN)
1961 NFL—Mike Ditka, OE, ChiB (UP, AP, SN)
1961 AFL—Earl Faison, DE, SD (UP, SN)
1962 NFL—Ronnie Bull, HB, ChiB (UP, AP, SN)
1962 AFL—Curtis McClinton, FB, Dal (UP, SN)
1963 NFL—Paul Flatley, OE, Min (UP, AP, SN)
1963 AFL—Billy Joe, FB, Den (UP, SN)
1964 NFL—Charley Taylor, HB, Was (UP, AP, NE, SN)
1964 AFL—Matt Snell, FB, NYJ (UP, SN)
1965 NFL—Gale Sayers, HB, ChiB (UP, AP, NE, SN)
1965 AFL—Joe Namath, QB, NYJ (UP, SN)
1966 NFL—Johnny Roland, HB, StL (UP); Tommy Nobis, LB, Atl (AP, NE, SN)
1966 AFL—Bobby Burnett, HB, Buf (UP, SN)
1967 NFL—Mel Farr, HB, Det (UP, NE, SN)
1967 AFL—George Webster, LB, Hou (UP); Dickie Post, HB, SD (SN)
1968 NFL—Earl McCullouch, OE, Det (UP, NE, SN)
1968 AFL—Paul Robinson, HB, Cin (UP, SN)
1969 NFL—Calvin Hill, HB, Dal (UP, NE, SN)
1969 AFL—Greg Cook, QB, Cin (UP); Carl Garrett, HB, Bos (SN)
1970 Raymond Chester, TE, Oak (NE)
1971 no league-wide selection
1972 Franco Harris, RB, Pit (PW)
1973 Chuck Foreman, RB, Min (PW)
1974 Don Woods, RB, SD (PW)
1975 Steve Bartkowski, QB, Atl (PW)
1976 no league-wide selection
1977 Tony Dorsett, RB, Dal (NE)
1978 Earl Campbell, RB, Hou (FW, NE)
1979 Ottis Anderson, RB, StL (FW, NE)
1980 Billy Sims, RB, Det (FW, NE, SN)
1981 Lawrence Taylor, LB, NYG (NE); George Rogers, RB, NO (FW, SN)
1982 Marcus Allen, RB, LARd (FW, NE, SN)
1983 Eric Dickerson, RB, LARm (FW, NE); Dan Marino, QB, Mia (SN)
1984 Louis Lipps, WR, Pit (FW, NE, SN)
1985 Eddie Brown, WR, Cin (FW, NE, SN)
1986 Reuben Mayes, RB, NO (FW, NE, SN)
1987 Shane Conlan, LB, Buf (FW); Bo Jackson, RB, LARd (NE); Robert Awalt, TE, StL (SN)
1988 John Stephens, RB, NE (FW, NE); Keith Jackson, TE, Phi (SN)
1989 Barry Sanders, RB, Det (FW, NE, SN)
1990 Mark Carrier, S, ChiB (FW); Richmond Webb, OT, Mia (SN)
1991 Mike Croel, LB, Den (FW, SN)
1992 Dale Carter, CB, KC (FW); Santana Dotson, DE, TB (SN)
1993 Jerome Bettis, RB, LARm (FW, SN)
1994 Marshall Faulk, RB, Ind (FW, SN)
1995 Curtis Martin, RB, NE (FW, SN)
1996 Eddie George, RB, Hou (AP, FW, SN)
1997 Warrick Dunn, RB, TB (FW, SN)
1998 Randy Moss, WR, Min (FW, SN)

AFC Rookie of the Year

1970 Dennis Shaw, QB, Buf (UP, SN)
1971 Jim Plunkett, QB, NE (UP, NE, SN)
1972 Franco Harris, RB, Pit (UP, NE, SN)
1973 Boobie Clark, RB, Cin (UP, NE, SN)
1974 Don Woods, RB, SD (UP, NE, SN)
1975 Robert Brazile, LB, Hou (UP, NE, SN)
1976 Mike Haynes, CB, NE (UP, NE, SN)
1977 A.J. Duhe, DE, Mia (UP, SN)
1978 Earl Campbell, RB, Hou (UP, SN)
1979 Jerry Butler, WR, Buf (UP, SN)
1980 Joe Cribbs, RB, Buf (UP)
1981 Joe Delaney, RB, KC (UP)
1982 Marcus Allen, RB, LARd (UP)
1983 Curt Warner, RB, Sea (UP)
1984 Louis Lipps, WR, Pit (UP)
1985 no selection
1986 no selection
1987 no selection
1988 no selection
1989 no selection
1990 Richmond Webb, OT, Mia (UP)
1991 Mike Croel, LB, Den (UP)
1992 Dale Carter, CB, KC (UP)
1993 Rick Mirer, QB, Sea (UP)
1994 Marshall Faulk, RB, Ind (UP)
1995 Curtis Martin, RB, NE (UP)
1996 Terry Glenn, WR, NE (UP)
No more selections

NFC Rookie of the Year

1970 Bruce Taylor, CB, SF (UP, SN)
1971 John Brockington, RB, GB (UP, NE, SN)
1972 Chester Marcol, K, GB (UP, SN); Willie Buchanon, CB, GB (NE)
1973 Charle Young, TE, Phi (UP); Chuck Foreman, RB, Min (NE, SN)
1974 John Hicks, OG, NYG (UP); Wilbur Jackson, RB, SF (NE, SN)
1975 Mike Thomas, RB, Was (UP); Steve Bartkowski, QB, Atl (NE, SN)
1976 Sammy White, WR, Min (UP, NE, SN)
1977 Tony Dorsett, RB, Dal (UP, SN)
1978 Al Baker, DE, Det (UP, SN)
1979 Ottis Anderson, RB, StL (UP, SN)
1980 Billy Sims, RB, Det (UP)
1981 George Rogers, RB, NO (UP)
1982 Jim McMahon, QB, ChiB (UP)
1983 Eric Dickerson, RB, LARm (UP)
1984 Paul McFadden, K, Phi (UP)
1985 no selection

1986 no selection
1987 no selection
1988 no selection
1989 no selection
1990 Mark Carrier, S, ChiB (UP)
1991 Lawrence Dawsey, WR, TB (UP)
1992 Robert Jones, LB, Dal (UP)
1993 Jerome Bettis, RB, LARm (UP)
1994 Bryant Young, DT, SF (UP)
1995 Rashaan Salaam, RB, ChiB (UP)
1996 Simeon Rice, DE, Ariz (UP)
No more selections

Offensive Rookie of the Year

1967 NFL—Mel Farr, HB, Det (AP)
1967 AFL—no selection
1968 NFL—Earl McCullouch, OE, Det (AP)
1968 AFL—no selection
1969 NFL—Calvin Hill, HB, Dal (AP, PW)
1969 AFL—Greg Cook, QB, Cin (PW)
1970 Dennis Shaw, QB, Buf (AP, PW)
1971 John Brockington, RB, GB (AP); Jim Plunkett, QB, NE (PW)
1972 Franco Harris, RB, Pit (AP, PW)
1973 Chuck Foreman, RB, Min (AP, PW)
1974 Don Woods, RB, SD (AP, PW)
1975 Mike Thomas, RB, Was (AP, PWt); Steve Bartkowski, QB, Atl (PWt)
1976 Sammy White, WR, Min (AP, PW)
1977 Tony Dorsett, RB, Dal (AP, PW)
1978 Earl Campbell, RB, Hou (AP, PW)
1979 Ottis Anderson, RB, StL (AP, PW)
1980 Billy Sims, RB, Det (AP, PW)
1981 George Rogers, RB, NO (AP, PW)
1982 Marcus Allen, RB, LARd (AP, PW)
1983 Eric Dickerson, RB, LARm (AP, PW)
1984 Louis Lipps, WR, Pit (AP, PW)
1985 Eddie Brown, WR, Cin (AP)
1986 Reuben Mayes, RB, NO (AP, PW)
1987 Troy Stradford, RB, Mia (AP, PW)
1988 John Stephens, RB, NE (AP, PW*t*); Ickey Woods, RB, Cin (PW*t*)
1989 Barry Sanders, RB, Det (AP, PW)
1990 Emmitt Smith, RB, Dal (AP, PW)
1991 Leonard Russell, RB, NE (AP, PW)
1992 Carl Pickens, WR, Cin (AP); Jason Hanson, K, Det (PW)
1993 Jerome Bettis, RB, LARm (AP, PW)
1994 Marshall Faulk, RB, Ind (AP, PW)
1995 Curtis Martin, RB, NE (AP, PW)
1996 Eddie George, RB, Hou (AP, FW)
1997 Warrick Dunn, RB, TB (AP, FW)
1998 Randy Moss, WR, Min (AP, FW)

Defensive Rookie of the Year

1967 NFL—Lem Barney, CB, Det (AP)
1967 AFL—no selection
1968 NFL—Claude Humphrey, DE, Atl (AP)
1968 AFL—no selection
1969 NFL—Joe Greene, DT, Pit (AP, PW)
1969 AFL—Jim Marsalis, CB, KC (PW)
1970 Bruce Taylor, CB, SF (AP, PW)
1971 Isiah Robertson, LB, LARm (AP, PW)
1972 Sherman White, DE, Cin (PW); Willie Buchanon, CB, GB (AP)
1973 Wally Chambers, DT, ChiB (PW)
1974 Jack Lambert, LB, Pit (AP, PW)
1975 Robert Brazile, LB, Hou (AP, PW)
1976 Mike Haynes, CB, NE (AP, PW)
1977 A.J. Duhe, DE, Mia (AP, PW)
1978 Al Baker, DE, Det (AP, PW)
1979 Jim Haslett, LB, Buf (AP); Jesse Baker, DE, Hou (PW)
1980 Buddy Curry, LB, Atl (APt, PW); Al Richardson, LB, Atl (APt)
1981 Lawrence Taylor, LB, NYG (AP, PW)
1982 Chip Banks, LB, Cle (AP, PW)
1983 Vernon Maxwell, LB, Bal (AP, PW)
1984 Bill Maas, DT, KC (AP); Tom Flynn, S, GB (PW)
1985 Duane Bickett, LB, Ind (AP)
1986 Leslie O'Neal, DE, SD (AP, PW*t*); John Offerdahl, LB, Mia (PW*t*)
1987 Shane Conlan, LB, Buf (AP, PW)
1988 Erik McMillan, S, NYJ (AP, PW)
1989 Derrick Thomas, LB, KC (AP, PW)
1990 Mark Carrier, S, ChiB (AP, PW)
1991 Mike Croel, LB, Den (AP, PW)
1992 Dale Carter, CB, KC (AP, PW)
1993 Dana Stubblefield, DT, SF (AP, PW)
1994 Tim Bowens, DT, Mia (AP, PW)
1995 Hugh Douglas, DE, NYJ (AP, PW)
1996 Simeon Rice, DE, Ariz (AP, FW)
1997 Peter Boulware, LB, Bal (AP, FW)
1998 Charles Woodson, DB, Oak (AP, FW)

Golden Toe Award (PFW)

1971 Garo Yepremian, K, Mia
1972 Don Cockroft, K, Cle
1973 David Ray, K, LARm
1974 Roy Gerela, K, Pit
1975 Ray Guy, P, Oak
1976 Toni Linhart, K, Bal
1977 Mark Moseley, K, Was
1978 Frank Corral, K, LARm
1979 Bob Grupp, P, KC
1980 Fred Steinfort, K, Den
1981 Rafael Septien, K, Dal
1982 Mark Moseley, K, Was
1983 Ali Haji-Sheikh, K, NYG
1984 Norm Johnson, K, Sea
1985 no selection
1986 Morten Andersen, K, NO
1987 Jim Arnold, P, Det
1988 Scott Norwood, K, Buf
1989 Eddie Murray, K, Det
1990 Nick Lowery, K, KC
1991 Jeff Gossett, P, LARd
1992 Rich Camarillo, P, Pho
1993 Norm Johnson, K, Atl
1994 Fuad Reveiz, K, Min
1995 Morten Andersen, K, Atl
1996 Cary Blanchard, K, Ind
1997 Pete Stoyanovich, K, KC
1998 Gary Anderson, K, Min

Comeback Player of the Year (PFW)

1972 Earl Morrall, QB, Mia
1973 Roman Gabriel, QB, Phi
1974 Joe Namath, QB, NYJ
1975 Dave Hampton, RB, Atl
1976 Greg Landry, QB, Det
1977 Craig Morton, QB, Den
1978 John Riggins, RB, Was
1979 Larry Csonka, RB, Mia
1980 Jim Plunkett, QB, Oak
1981 Ken Anderson, QB, Cin
1982 Lyle Alzado, DE, LARd
1983 Billy Johnson, WR-PR, Atl
1984 John Stallworth, WR, Pit
1985 no selection
1986 Tommy Kramer, QB, Min and Joe Montana, QB, SF
1987 Charles White, RB, LARm
1988 Greg Bell, RB, LARm
1989 Ottis Anderson, RB, NYG
1990 Barry Word, RB, KC
1991 Jim McMahon, QB, Phi
1992 Randall Cunningham, QB, Phi
1993 Marcus Allen, RB, KC
1994 Dan Marino, QB, Mia
1995 Jim Harbaugh, QB, Ind
1996 Jerome Bettis, RB, Pit
1997 Robert Brooks, WR, GB
1998 Doug Flutie, QB, Buf

Coach of the Year

1947 NFL—Jimmy Conzelman, ChiC (SN)
1947 AAFC—no selection
1948 NFL—Greasy Neale, Phi (SN)
1948 AAFC—no selection
1949 NFL—no selection
1949 AAFC—Paul Brown, Cl-A (SN)
1950 Steve Owen, NYG (SN)
1951 Paul Brown, Cle (SN)
1952 Hampton Pool, LARm (SN)
1953 Paul Brown, Cle (UP, SN)
1954 no selection
1955 Joe Kuharich, ChiC (UP, SN)
1956 Buddy Parker, Det (UP); Jim Lee Howell, NYG (SN)
1957 Paul Brown, Cle (UP); George Wilson, Det (AP)
1958 Weeb Ewbank, Bal (UP, AP)
1959 Vince Lombardi, GB (UP, AP)
1960 NFL—Buck Shaw, Phi (UP, AP)
1960 AFL—Lou Rymkus, Hou (UP)
1961 NFL—Allie Sherman, NYG (UP, AP); Vince Lombardi, GB (SN)
1961 AFL—Wally Lemm, Hou (UP)
1962 NFL—Allie Sherman, NYG (UP, AP)
1962 AFL—Jack Faulkner, Den (UP)
1963 NFL—George Halas, ChiB (UP, AP, SN)
1963 AFL—Al Davis, Oak (UP)
1964 NFL—Don Shula, Bal (UP, AP, SN)
1964 AFL—Lou Saban, Buf (UP)
1965 NFL—George Halas, ChiB (UP, AP, SN)
1965 AFL—Lou Saban, Buf (UP)
1966 NFL—Tom Landry, Dal (UP, AP, SN)
1966 AFL—Mike Holovak, Bos (UP)
1967 NFL—George Allen, LARm (UP, AP*t*, SN); Don Shula, Bal (AP*t*)
1967 AFL—John Rauch, Oak (UP)
1968 NFL—Don Shula, Bal (UP, AP, SN, PW)
1968 AFL—Hank Stram, KC (UP, PW)
1969 NFL—Bud Grant, Min (UP, AP, SN, PW)
1969 AFL—Paul Brown, Cin (UP); John Madden, Oak (PW)
1970 Paul Brown, Cin (AP); Don Shula, Mia (SN, PW)
1971 George Allen, Was (AP, SN, PW)
1972 Don Shula, Mia (AP, SN, PW)
1973 Chuck Knox, LARm (AP, SN, PW)
1974 Don Coryell, StL (AP, SN, PW)
1975 Ted Marchibroda, Bal (AP, SN, PW)
1976 Forrest Gregg, Cle (AP); Chuck Fairbanks, NE (SN, PW)
1977 Red Miller, Den (AP, SN, FW, PW)
1978 Jack Patera, Sea (AP, SN); Walt Michaels, NYJ (PW)
1979 Jack Pardee, Was (AP); Dick Vermeil, Phi (SN, PW)
1980 Chuck Knox, Buf (AP, SN, PW)
1981 Bill Walsh, SF (AP, SN, PW)
1982 Joe Gibbs, Was (AP, SN, PW)
1983 Joe Gibbs, Was (AP, SN, PW)
1984 Chuck Knox, Sea (AP, SN); Dan Reeves, Den (PW)
1985 Mike Ditka, ChiB (AP, SN)
1986 Bill Parcells, NYG (FW, AP, SN, PW)
1987 Jim Mora, NO (AP, SN, PW)
1988 Mike Ditka, ChiB (AP, PW); Marv Levy, Buf (SN)
1989 Lindy Infante, GB (AP, SN); George Seifert, SF (PW)
1990 Art Shell, LARd (FW, PW); Jimmy Johnson, Dal (AP)
1991 Wayne Fontes, Det (FW, AP, PW); Joe Gibbs, Was (SN)
1992 Bobby Ross, SD (FW, PW); Bill Cowher, Pit (AP, SN)
1993 Dan Reeves, NYG (FW, AP, SN, PW, MX)
1994 Bill Parcells, NE (FW, AP, PW, MX); George Seifert, SF (SN)
1995 Dom Capers, Car (FW, PW); Ray Rhodes, Phi (AP, SN, MX)
1996 Dom Capers, Car (AP, FW, SN)
1997 Jim Fassel, NYG (AP, FW, SN)
1998 Dan Reeves, Atl (AP, FW, SN)

Coach of the Year—AFC

1970 Paul Brown, Cin (UP, FW); Don Shula, Mia (SN)
1971 Don Shula, Mia (UP, FW)
1972 Chuck Noll, Pit (UP); Don Shula, Mia (FW)
1973 John Ralston, Den (UP, FW, PW)
1974 Sid Gillman, Hou (UP, FW, PW)
1975 Ted Marchibroda, Bal (UP, FW)
1976 Chuck Fairbanks, NE (UP, FW)
1977 Red Miller, Den (UP)
1978 Walt Michaels, NYJ (FW, UP)
1979 Sam Rutigliano, Cle (UP); Don Coryell, SD (FW)
1980 Sam Rutigliano, Cle (UP); Chuck Knox, Buf (FW)
1981 Forrest Gregg, Cin (FW, UP)
1982 Tom Flores, LARd (FW, UP)
1983 Chuck Noll, Pit (FW); Chuck Knox, Sea (UP)
1984 Chuck Knox, Sea (FW, UP)
1985 Raymond Berry, NE (FW, UP)
1986 Marty Schottenheimer, Cle (UP)
1987 Ron Meyer, Ind (FW, UP)
1988 Sam Wyche, Cin (FW); Marv Levy, Buf (UP)
1989 Chuck Noll, Pit (FW); Dan Reeves, Den (UP)
1990 Art Shell, LARd (UP)
1991 Dan Reeves, Den (UP)
1992 Bobby Ross, SD (UP)
1993 Marv Levy, Buf (UP)
1994 Bill Parcells, NE (UP)
1995 Marv Levy, Buf (UP)
1996 Tom Coughlin, Jac (UP)
No more selections

Coach of the Year—NFC

1970 Alex Webster, NYG (UP); Dick Nolan, SF (SN, FW)
1971 George Allen, Was (UP, FW)
1972 Dan Devine, GB (UP, FW)
1973 Chuck Knox, LARm (UP, FW)
1974 Don Coryell, StL (UP, FW)
1975 Tom Landry, Dal (UP, FW)
1976 Jack Pardee, ChiB (UP, FW)
1977 Leeman Bennett, Atl (UP)
1978 Dick Vermeil, Phi (FW, UP)
1979 Jack Pardee, Was (UP); Dick Vermeil, Phi (FW)
1980 Leeman Bennett, Atl (FW, UP)
1981 Bill Walsh, SF (FW, UP)
1982 Joe Gibbs, Was (FW, UP)
1983 Joe Gibbs, Was (FW); John Robinson, LARm (UP)
1984 Bill Walsh, SF (FW, UP)
1985 Mike Ditka, ChiB (FW, UP)
1986 Bill Parcells, NYG (UP)
1987 Jim Mora, NO (FW, UP)
1988 Mike Ditka, ChiB (FW, UP)
1989 Lindy Infante, GB (FW, UP)
1990 Jimmy Johnson, Dal (UP)
1991 Wayne Fontes, Det (UP)
1992 Dennis Green, Min (UP)
1993 Dan Reeves, NYG (UP)
1994 Dave Wannstedt, ChiB (UP)
1995 Ray Rhodes, Phi (UP)
1996 Dom Capers (UP)
No more selections

Assistant Coach of the Year (PFW)

1993 Ray Rhodes, GB
1994 Dom Capers, Pit
1995 Pete Carroll, SF
1996 Dave Campo, Dal
1997 John Fox, NYG
1998 Brian Billick, Min

NFL Executive of the Year (PFW)

1993 George Young, NYG
1994 Carmen Policy, SF
1995 Bill Polian, Car
1996 Bill Polian, Car
1997 George Young, NYG
1998 Vikings Front Office

CHAPTER 15

All-Pro Selections

Although sometimes dismissed as "only opinion," all-pro teams are an important source of information in learning how various players were rated by critics of their time. Included here are the most important and respected teams for each season, beginning in 1920. In addition to first-team selections, all available second-team choices are included to make the picture as complete as possible. Player positions are also included.

In 1920, the American Professional Football Association (which became the NFL two years later) was formed. That same year, the first all-pro team was named. The selections were made by Bruce Copeland, the sports editor of the *Rock Island Argus,* and a close follower of the early pro game. In 1921, the *Buffalo Evening News* named a team.

In 1922, two NFL player-coaches, George Halas of the Chicago Bears and Guy Chamberlin of the Canton Bulldogs, named all-pro teams.

An all-pro poll that appeared annually in the *Green Bay Press-Gazette,* where, unlike in many larger metropolitan areas, pro football was covered thoroughly, began in 1923 and received recognition in league cities. The poll ran from 1923-1931 and 1933-35; the voters consisted of, at varying times, sportswriters from league cities, game officials, team coaches, and team owners. Wilfred Smith, a sportswriter with the *Chicago Tribune* who had the benefit of actually having played pro football, picked a team from 1926-29.

Another important team of the 1920s and through the 1930s was named by *Collyer's Eye Magazine,* a sports publication in Chicago, which later merged with *The Baseball World Magazine.* Other sportswriters, coaches, players, and even game officials chose teams in the twenties, but their attempts were so scattered, it is difficult to gauge their validity. For that reason, they are omitted here.

In 1931, the results of the *Press-Gazette* poll gave the league its first official all-pro team. From 1932-39, the NFL's official team was selected by coaches throughout the league. In 1940, the Pro Football Writers of America, which had published teams in 1938-39, named the official team. In 1941-42, a committee of sportswriters picked the official teams. Official NFL teams were discontinued in 1943 in favor of the news-service teams which had actually been around for many years.

United Press chose teams from 1931-1941 and 1943-1957. In 1958, *UP* merged with *International News Service* and *UPI* has published teams ever since. *INS* had named teams intermittently since 1937. The *Associated Press* began picking teams in 1940 and has continued to do so ever since.

Although not a news service, the *New York Daily News* created an important team in 1937 by polling more than 20 football writers in all league cities. The *Daily News* continued presenting interesting teams (with the exception of 1962, when there was a newspaper strike in New York), but in 1970 the writers' poll was discontinued.

Howard Roberts, who later wrote one of the first histories of pro football, chose teams for the *Chicago Daily News* from 1933-36.

During the 1940s, *Pro Football Illustrated,* the first magazine devoted to the game to be published annually, selected teams. Additionally, the *Chicago Herald-American* chose teams in most years during the decade, including the first example of a team with offensive and defensive platoons.

The All-America Football Conference named its official team from 1946-49 and the *AP, UP,* and *New York Daily News* also chose AAFC teams.

The Sporting News, after one shot in 1948, began selecting teams regularly in 1954 as did the Newspaper Enterprise Association.

The AFC official teams were picked by the players in 1960 and from 1962-66; the coaches picked the team in 1961. In 1964, *AP* and *UPI* started picking AFL all-pro teams, joining the players from 1964-66. In 1967, the players stopped their picks and the wire services were the only AFL all-pro teams in 1967 and 1968.

In 1969, the first combined NFL-AFL all-pro team was picked by the Pro Football Hall of Fame. *AP, UPI,* and NEA each picked both an AFL all-pro team and an NFL all-pro team. In 1970-71, the wire services picked all-conference teams; the official all-pro team was chosen by the Professional Football Writers Association (PFWA). From 1972-75, both the PFWA and the NEA picked all-pro teams. Since 1976, the PFWA and AP have picked teams. NEA discontinued choosing teams in 1994. *UPI* and, for most of the period, *The Sporting News* have picked conference teams.

The publication *Pro Football Weekly* has picked both all-NFL and all-conference teams since 1968 with the exception of 1985, when it did not publish. Starting in 1992, *PFW* presented the PFWA selections instead of choosing separately.

Legend:

AP — *Associated Press* 1940-present
BU — *Buffalo Evening News* 1921
CH — Guy Chamberlin, for the *Canton Daily News* 1922-23
CN — *Chicago Daily News* 1933-36

EY — *Collyer's Eye Magazine* 1923-26 & *Collyer's Eye and The Baseball World Magazine* 1929-1941
FW — Professional Football Writers of America 1938-1940, 1966-present
GB — *Green Bay Press-Gazette* 1923-1931, 1933-35
HA — *Chicago Herald-American* 1939-41, 1943, 1945-48
HF — Pro Football Hall of Fame 1969
HS — George Halas, for several newspapers 1922
IN — *International News Service* 1937-1940, 1942-45, 1949
NE — Newspaper Enterprise Association 1954-1992
NY — *New York Daily News* 1937-1961, 1963-69
OA — Official AAFC Team 1946-49
OF — Official NFL Team 1931-1942
OL — Official AFL Team 1960-66
PF — *Pro Football Illustrated* 1943-48
PW — *Pro Football Weekly* 1968-1984, 1986-1991; 1992-present, choices combined with PFWA
RI — *Rock Island Argus* 1920
SM — Wilfrid Smith, for the *Chicago Tribune* 1926-29
SN — *The Sporting News* 1948, 1954-1981, 1983-present
UP — *United Press* 1931-1941, 1943-1957 and *United Press International* 1958-1996

1920

		RI
Guy Chamberlin, Dec	E	1
George Halas, Dec	E	2
Bobby Marshall, RI	E	3
Bob Nash, Akr	E	3
Oke Smith, RI	E	1
Obe Wenig, RI	E	2
Hugh Blacklock, Dec	T	1
Cub Buck, Can	T	2
Walt Buland, RI	T	3
Wilbur Henry, Can	T	1
Burt Ingwerson, Dec	T	3
Ed Shaw, RI	T	2
Alf Cobb, Akr	G	2
Harry Dadmun, Can	G	2
Fred Denfield, RI	G	1
Dewey Lyle, RI	G	1
Ross Petty, Dec	G	3
Brad Tomlin, Akr	G	3
Paul DesJardien, ChiT	C	2
Freeman Fitzgerald, RI	C	3
George Trafton, Dec	C	1
Frank Bacon, Day	B	3
Pete Calac, Can	B	3
Paddy Driscoll, ChiC	B	1
Git Falcon, ChiT	B	2
Milt Ghee, ChiT	B	3
Joe Guyon, Can	B	2
Rip King, Akr	B	1
Al Mahrt, Day	B	2
Eddie Novak, RI	B	1
Fritz Pollard, Akr	B	1
Norb Sacksteder, Day	B	2
Dutch Sternaman, Dec	B	3

1921

		BU
Bob Nash, Buf	E	1
Luke Urban, Buf	E	1
Wilbur Henry, Can	T	1
Belf West, Can	T	1
Bulger Lowe, Cle	G	1
Al Nesser, Akr	G	1
Joe Alexander, Roch	C	1
Benny Boynton, Roch-Was	B	1
Rip King, Akr	B	1
Elmer Oliphant, Buf	B	1
Pete Stinchcomb, Dec	B	1

1922

		HS	CH
Eddie Anderson, Roch-ChiC	E	2	1
Bird Carroll, Can	E	-	1
Guy Chamberlin, Can	E	1	-
Luke Urban, Buf	E	1	-
Tillie Voss, RI	E	2	-
Hugh Blacklock, ChiB	T	1	-
Fred Gillies, ChiC	T	2	-
Russ Hathaway, Day	T	2	-
Wilbur Henry, Can	T	1	1
Steamer Horning, Tol	T	-	1
Hunk Anderson, ChiB	G	2	-
Ed Healey, RI-ChiB	G	1	-
Al Nesser, Akr	G	2	-
Duke Osborn, Can	G	-	1
Herb Stein, Tol	G	1	1
Doc Alexander, Roc	C	1	1
Jim Flower, Akr	C	2	-
Benny Boynton, Roch	B	2	-
Paddy Driscoll, ChiC	B	1	1
Doc Elliott, Can	B	-	1
Tommy Hughitt, Buf	B	1	-
Rip King, Akr	B	1	-
Jim Laird, Buf	B	2	-
Curly Lambeau, GB	B	2	-
Harry Robb, Can	B	-	1
Dutch Sternaman, ChiB	B	2	-
Pete Stinchcomb, ChiB	B	1	1

1923

		GB	EY	CH
Glenn Carberry, Buf	E	-	-	1
Bird Carroll, Can	E	-	-	1
Guy Chamberlin, Can	E	2	1	-
Paul Goebel, Col	E	-	-	1
Duke Hanny, ChiB	E	2	2	-
Dick O'Donnell, Dul	E	3	-	-
Dick Reichle, Mil	E	-	2	-
Gus Tebell, Col	E	1	-	1
Luke Urban, Buf	E	-	1	1
Tillie Voss, Tol	E	3T	-	1
Inky Williams, Ham	E	1	-	-
Ben Winkelman, Mil	E	3	-	-
Cub Buck, GB	T	3	-	-
Russ Hathaway, Day	T	2	-	1
Ed Healey, ChiB	T	1	-	1G
Wilbur Henry, Can	T	1	1	1
Steamer Horning, Tol	T	-	-	1
Link Lyman, Can	T	-	2	1
Elmer McCormick, Buf	T	-	2	-
Ed Sauer, Day	T	-	-	1
Ralph Scott, ChiB	T	-	-	1
Duke Slater, RI	T	2	1	-
Gus Sonnenberg, Col	T	-	-	1
Rudy Comstock, Can	G	-	-	1
Hec Garvey, ChiB	G	2	1	1
Stan Keck, Cle	G	-	2	-
Tom McNamara, Tol	G	3	-	-
Frank Morrissey, Buf	G	2	-	-
Al Nesser, Akr	G	3	-	-
Duke Osborn, Can	G	-	-	1
John Sack, Col	G	-	-	1
Dale Sies, RI	G	-	2	-
Bub Weller, StL	G	1	-	-
Swede Youngstrom, Buf	G	1	1	-
Clyde Zoia, ChiC	G	-	-	1
Larry Conover, Can	C	2	-	1
Charlie Guy, Cle	C	3	-	1
Walt Kreinheder, StL	C	-	1	-
Harry Mehre, Min	C	1	-	-
George Trafton, ChiB	C	-	2	1
Johnny Armstrong, RI	B	3	-	-
Jimmy Conzelman, Mil	B	2	-	1
Jack Crangle, ChiC	B	-	2	-
Dinger Doane, Mil	B	2	-	-
Paddy Driscoll, ChiC	B	1	1	1
Doc Elliott, Can	B	1	-	1
Hal Erickson, Mil	B	3	1	-
Hank Gillo, Rac	B	-	1	-
Tex Grigg, Can	B	-	1	1
Ben Jones, Can	B	-	-	1
John Kyle, Cle	B	3	-	-
Curly Lambeau, GB	B	2	-	-
Al Michaels, Col	B	1	-	-
Goldie Rapp, Col	B	-	-	1
Harry Robb, Can	B	2	2	1
Milt Romney, Rac	B	3	-	-
Dutch Sternaman, ChiB	B	-	-	1
Joe Sternaman, Dul	B	-	2	1
Pete Stinchcomb, ChiB	B	-	2	-

		GB	EY	CH
Lou Smythe, Can	B	-	-	1
Jim Thorpe, Oor	B	1	-	-

1924

		GB	EY
Eddie Anderson, ChiC	E	2	-
Guy Chamberlin, Cle	E	3	1
Oscar Christiansen, Min	E	3	-
Paul Goebel, Col	E	2	2
Duke Hanny, ChiB	E	-	2
Joe Little Twig, RI	E	1	-
Tillie Voss, GB	E	1	-
Mike Wilson, RI	E	-	1
Cub Buck, GB	T	3	-
Mike Gulian, Fra	T	3	-
Ed Healey, ChiB	T	1	2
Link Lyman, Cle	T	2	1
Boni Petcoff, Col	T	1	-
Duke Slater, RI	T	2	-
Olin Smith, Cle	T	-	2
Bub Weller, Mil	T	-	1
George Berry, Akr	G	-	1
Ralph King, Rac	G	3	-
Walt LeJeune, Mil	G	-	2
Jim McMillen, ChiB	G	2	1
Stan Muirhead, Cle-Day	G	1	-
Al Nesser, Akr	G	3	-
Jim Welsh, Fra	G	-	2
Doc Williams, Dul	G	2	-
Swede Youngstrom, Buf	G	1	-
Elmer McCormick, Buf	C	-	1
Andy Nemecek, Col	C	2	-
Len Peterson, KC	C	3	-
Herb Stein, Fra	C	-	2
George Trafton, ChiB	C	1	-
Benny Boynton, Roch-Buf	B	1	1
Wayne Brenkert, Akr	B	3	-
Paddy Driscoll, ChiC	B	2	-
Red Dunn, Mil	B	-	2
Doc Elliott, Cle	B	1	-
Hank Gillo, Rac	B	3	-
Joe Guyon, RI	B	3	-
Tex Hamer, Fra	B	2	1
Ken Huffine, Day	B	-	2
John Hurlburt, ChiC	B	-	2
Curly Lambeau, GB	B	2	-
Dave Noble, Cle	B	2	-
Joe Sternaman, ChiB	B	1	1
Pie Way, Fra	B	1	1
Lin Winters, Col	B	3	-
Hoge Workman, Cle	B	-	2

1925

		GB	EY
Eddie Anderson, ChiC	E	-	2
Charlie Berry, Pott	E	1	1
Lynn Bomar, NYG	E	2	-
Rae Crowther, Fra	E	-	1
Paul Goebel, Col	E	-	3
Duke Hanny, ChiB	E	-	2
Ed Lynch, Roch	E	1	-
Red Maloney, Prov	E	2	-
Tillie Voss, Det	E	-	3
Cub Buck, GB	T	-	3
Norm Harvey, Buf	T	-	3
Ed Healey, ChiB	T	1	1
Link Lyman, Can	T	-	2
Duke Slater, RI	T	2	1
Gus Sonnenberg, Det	T	1	-
Dick Stahlman, GB	T	2	-
Russ Stein, Pott	T	-	2
George Abramson, GB	G	2	-
Willis Brennan, ChiC	G	-	3
Art Carney, NYG	G	1	-
Jim McMillen, ChiB	G	1	2
Century Milstead, NYG	G	-	1
Al Nesser, Akr	G	-	3
Duke Osborn, Pott	G	2	-
Chet Widerquist, RI	G	-	2
Swede Youngstrom, Buf	G	-	1
Ralph Claypool, ChiC	C	1	-
Frank Culver, Can	C	-	2
Dolph Eckstein, Prov	C	2	-
George Trafton, ChiB	C	-	1
Ernie Vick, Det	C	-	3
Heinie Benkert, NYG	B	-	1
Bert Bloodgood, KC	B	-	3
Jimmy Conzelman, Det	B	-	2
Paddy Driscoll, ChiC	B	1	1
Hal Erickson, ChiC	B	-	3

		GB	EY
Walter French, Pott	B	-	1
Hinkey Haines, NYG	B	-	3
Tex Hamer, Fra	B	2	2
Bob Koehler, ChiC	B	-	2
Verne Lewellen, GB	B	2	-
Jack McBride, NYG	B	1	3
Dave Noble, Cle	B	1	-
Jim Robertson, Akr	B	2	-
Joey Sternaman, ChiB	B	1	2
Cy Wentworth, Prov	B	2	-
Barney Wentz, Pott	B	-	1

1926

		GB	EY	SM
Charlie Berry, Pott	E	1	3	-
Fred Bissell, Akr	E	2	3	-
Lavie Dilweg, Mil	E	2	1	1
Ray Flaherty, NY-a	E	-	-	1
Paul Goebel, NY-a	E	-	2	-
Duke Hanny, ChiB	E	-	2	-
Brick Muller, LA	E	1	1	2
George Tully, Ph-a	E	-	-	2
Bull Behman, Ph-a	T	-	-	2
Walt Ellis, ChiC	T	1	-	-
Paul Jappe, Bkn	T	-	3	-
Ed Healey, ChiB	T	1	1	1
Century Milstead, Ph-a	T	-	3	-
Steve Owen, NYG	T	2	-	-
Frank Racis, Pott	T	-	1	-
Duke Slater, RI-a	T	-	2	1
John Thurman, LA	T	2	-	-
Bub Weller, ChiC	T	-	-	2
Jay Berquist, KC	G	2	-	-
Willis Brennan, ChiC	G	-	-	2
Bill Buckler, ChiB	G	2	-	2
Johnny Budd, Fra	G	1	-	1
Rudy Comstock, Fra	G	-	2	-
Jim McMillen, ChiB	G	-	1	1
Gus Sonnenberg, Det	G	1	2T	-
Jim Welsh, Pott	G	-	1	-
Chet Widerquist, ChiC	G	-	3	-
Joe Williams, NYG	G	-	2	-
Joe Alexander, NYG	C	-	3G	2
Ralph Claypool, ChiC	C	-	1	-
O.J. Larson, Ch-a	C	-	3	-
Clyde Smith, KC	C	1	-	-
Herb Stein, Pott	C	2	-	-
George Trafton, ChiB	C	-	2	1
Heinie Benkert, Pott	B	-	3	-
Bert Bloodgood, KC	B	2	1	-
Jim Bradshaw, LA-a	B	-	2	-
Herb DeWitz, KC	B	-	3	-
Paddy Driscoll, ChiB	B	1	1	1
Red Grange, NY-a	B	-	2	-
Hinkey Haines, NYG	B	2	-	-
Tex Hamer, Fra	B	-	-	2
Two-Bits Homan, Fra	B	-	3	-
Tut Imlay, LA	B	1	-	-
Al Kreuz, Ph-a	B	-	-	2
Tony Latone, Pott	B	-	-	1
Verne Lewellen, GB	B	1	-	-
Cully Lidberg, GB	B	-	2	-
Jack McBride, NYG	B	-	3	-
Ernie Nevers, Dul	B	1	1	1
Curly Oden, Prov	B	2	-	-
Joe Sternaman, Ch-a	B	-	-	2
Hust Stockton, Fra	B	2	-	-
Eddie Tryon, NY-a	B	-	1	1
Wildcat Wilson, LA-a	B	-	2	2

1927

		GB	SM
Carl Bacchus, Cle	E	-	1
Lavie Dilweg, GB	E	1	1
Cal Hubbard, NYG	E	1	-
George Kenneally, Pott	E	2	-
Ed Lynch, Prov	E	2	-
Joe Kozlowsky, Prov	T	-	1
Century Milstead, NYG	T	2	1
Duke Slater, ChiC	T	2	-
Gus Sonnenberg, Prov	T	1	-
Ed Weir, Fra	T	1	-
Al Graham, Day	G	2	-
Jim McMillen, ChiB	G	-	1
Mike Michalske, NYY	G	1	1
Steve Owen, NYG	G	1	-
Milt Rehnquist, Cle	G	2	-
Clyde Smith, Cle	C	1	-
George Trafton, ChiB	C	2	1
Paddy Driscoll, ChiB	B	1	1

		GB	SM
Benny Friedman, Cle	B	1	1
Hinkey Haines, NYG	B	2	-
Verne Lewellen, GB-NYY	B	1	1
Jack McBride, NYG	B	2	1
Ernie Nevers, Dul	B	1	-
Bill Senn, ChiB	B	2	-
Eddie Tryon, NYY	B	2	-

1928

		GB	SM
Carl Bacchus, Det	E	2	-
Lavie Dilweg, GB	E	1	1
Ray Flaherty, NYG	E	1	2
Cal Hubbard, NYG	E	2	1
George Kenneally, Pott	E	-	2
Roger Ashmore, GB	T	-	2
Bull Behman, Fra	T	1	2G
Link Lyman, ChiB	T	2	-
Don Murry, ChiB	T	-	2
Bill Owen, Det	T	1	1
Gus Sonnenberg, Prov	T	2	1
Al Graham, Day	G	2	2
Jim McMillen, ChiB	G	1	1
Mike Michalske, NYY	G	1	1
Milt Rehnquist, Prov	G	2	-
Clyde Smith, Prov	C	1	2
Joe Westoupal, Det	C	2	1
Wally Diehl, Fra	B	1	2
Paddy Driscoll, ChiB	B	2	1
Benny Friedman, Det	B	1	1
Ed Kotal, GB	B	2	2
Tony Latone, Pott	B	2	-
Verne Lewellen, GB	B	1	1
Ken Mercer, Fra	B	-	2
Curly Oden, Prov	B	2	2
Wildcat Wilson, Prov	B	1	1

1929

		GB	EY	SM
Lavie Dilweg, GB	E	1	1	1
Ray Flaherty, NYG	E	1	1	1
Luke Johnsos, ChiB	E	2	2	-
Bob Lundell, Min	E	2	-	-
Tom Nash, GB	E	-	-	-
John Spellman, Prov	E	-	2	-
Bob Beattie, Ora	T	1	2	-
Bull Behman, Fra	T	1	1	1
Cal Hubbard, GB	T	-	2	1G
Bill Kern, GB	T	2	-	-
Steve Owen, NYG	T	-	1	-
Duke Slater, ChiC	T	2	-	1
Herb Blumer, ChiC	G	-	2	-
Hal Hanson, Fra	G	2	-	-
Walt Kiesling, ChiC	G	-	1	-
Mike Michalske, GB	G	1	1	1
Frank Racis, Bos	G	2	-	-
Milt Rehnquist, Prov	G	1	2	-
Jugger Earpe, GB	C	2	-	-
Joey Maxwell, Fra	C	-	2	-
Joe Westoupal, NYG	C	1	1	1
Johnny Blood (McNally), GB	B	2	-	-
Wally Diehl, Fra	B	2	-	-
Benny Friedman, NYG	B	1	1	1
Walt Holmer, ChiB	B	-	2	-
Verne Lewellen, GB	B	1	1	1
Ernie Nevers, ChiC	B	1	1	1
George Pease, Ora	B	2	2	-
Tony Plansky, NYG	B	1	1	1
Ken Strong, SI	B	2	2	-
Doug Wycoff, SI	B	-	2	-

1930

		GB	EY
Red Badgro, NYG	E	2	-
Lavie Dilweg, GB	E	1	1
Luke Johnsos, ChiB	E	1	1
Chuck Kassell, ChiC	E	3	2
Tony Kostos, Fra-Min	E	3	-
Tom Nash, GB	E	2	2
Jap Douds, Prov-Port	T	1	2
Cal Hubbard, GB	T	3	-
Bill Kern, GB	T	2	-
Link Lyman, ChiB	T	1	1
Jim Mooney, Nwk-Bkn	T	2	-
Bill Owen, NYG	T	-	1
Duke Slater, ChiC	T	3	2
Zuck Carlson, ChiB	G	-	2
Les Caywood, NYG	G	3	-
Rudy Comstock, NYG	G	2	-
George Gibson, Fra-Min	G	-	2
Al Graham, Prov-Port	G	3	-
Hal Hanson, Fra-Min	G	2	-
Walt Kiesling, ChiC	G	1	1
Mike Michalske, GB	G	1	1
Nate Barrager, Fra-Min	C	3	1
Swede Hagberg, Bkn	C	1	-
Joe Westoupal, NYG	C	2	2
Chuck Bennett, Port	B	3	-
Johnny Blood (McNally), GB	B	3	2
Carl Brumbaugh, ChiB	B	3	-
Red Dunn, GB	B	2	2
Benny Friedman, NYG	B	1	1
Willis Glassgow, Port	B	-	2
Red Grange, ChiB	B	1	1
Father Lumpkin, Port	B	2	-
Jack McBride, Bkn	B	3	-
Bronko Nagurski, ChiB	B	2	2
Ernie Nevers, ChiC	B	1	1
Ken Strong, SI	B	1	1
Stumpy Thomason, Bkn	B	2	-

1931

		OF	UP	EY
Red Badgro, NYG	E	1	-	-
Chuck Braidwood, Cle	E	-	2	-
Lavie Dilweg, GB	E	1	1	2
Ray Flaherty, NYG	E	3	-	-
Luke Johnsos, ChiB	E	2	1	2
Bill McKalip, Port	E	2	2	1
Tom Nash, GB	E	-	-	1
Al Rose, Prov	E	3	-	-
George Christensen, Port	T	1	-	-
Jap Douds, Port	T	2	-	2
Lou Gordon, ChiC-Bkn	T	3	-	-
Len Grant, NYG	T	-	1	2
Cal Hubbard, GB	T	1	1	-
Link Lyman, ChiB	T	-	2	-
Bill Owen, NYG	T	3	2	1
Dick Stahlman, GB	T	2	-	1
Maury Bodenger, Port	G	3	-	-
Zuck Carlson, ChiB	G	3	-	1
Butch Gibson, NYG	G	1	1	1
Al Graham, Prov	G	2	-	-
Walt Kiesling, ChiC	G	2	2	2
Mike Michalske, GB	G	1	1	2
David Myers, Bkn	G	-	2	-
Nate Barrager, Fra-GB	C	3	2	1
Mel Hein, NYG	C	2	-	-
Frank McNally, ChiC	C	1	1	-
Bert Pearson, ChiB	C	-	-	2
Johnny Blood (McNally), GB	B	1	2	2
Carl Brumbaugh, ChiB	B	-	-	2
Dutch Clark, Port	B	1	1	1
Red Dunn, GB	B	2	2	-
Benny Friedman, NYG	B	3	-	-
Red Grange, ChiB	B	1	1	1
Herb Joesting, Fra-ChiB	B	3	-	-
Dutch Kitzmiller, NYG	B	-	2	-
Father Lumpkin, Port	B	3	-	-
Bo Molenda, GB	B	2	-	-
Hap Moran, NYG	B	-	-	2
Bronko Nagurski, ChiB	B	-	-	2
Dick Nesbitt, ChiB	B	3	2	-
Ernie Nevers, ChiC	B	1	1	1
Glenn Presnell, Port	B	2	-	-
Ken Strong, SI	B	2	1	1

1932

		OF	UP	EY
Lavie Dilweg, GB	E	2	2	-
Ray Flaherty, NYG	E	1	1	1
Bill Hewitt, ChiB	E	2	2	1
Luke Johnsos, ChiB	E	1	-	2
Tom Nash, GB	E	-	1	2
George Christensen, Port	T	2	2	2
Turk Edwards, Bos	T	1	-	2
Lou Gordon, ChiC	T	-	2	-
Len Grant, NYG	T	-	1	1
Cal Hubbard, GB	T	1	1	1
Jake Williams, ChiC	T	2	-	-
Maury Bodenger, Port	G	2	-	-
Zuck Carlson, ChiB	G	1	1	1
Ox Emerson, Port	G	-	1	1
Butch Gibson, NYG	G	-	-	2
George Hurley, Bos	G	2	-	-
Walt Kiesling, ChiC	G	1	-	-
Joe Kopcha, ChiB	G	-	2	2
Joe Zeller, GB	G	-	2	-
Nate Barrager, GB	C	1	2	2

		OF	UP	EY
Mel Hein, NYG	C	2	-	-
Tim Moynihan, ChiC	C	h	1	1
Cliff Battles, Bos	B	-	-	1
Bob Campiglio, SI	B	-	2	-
Dutch Clark, Port	B	1	1	1
Red Grange, ChiB	B	2	-	-
Jack Grossman, Bkn	B	2	-	2
Ace Gutowsky, Port	B	-	-	2
Arnie Herber, GB	B	1	1	2
Clarke Hinkle, GB	B	2	2	1
Father Lumpkin, Port	B	1	1	-
Keith Molesworth, ChiB	B	2	2	2
Bronko Nagurski, ChiB	B	1	1	1
Glenn Presnell, Port	B	-	2	-

1933

		OF	UP	CN	GB	EY
Red Badgro, NYG	E	1	-	2	1	-
Lavie Dilweg, GB	E	-	2	-	-	-
Harry Ebding, Port	E	2	1	2	2	-
Ray Flaherty, NYG	E	2	2	1	2	1
Bill Hewitt, ChiB	E	1	1	1	1	1
George Christensen, Port	T	-	1	2	1	1
Turk Edwards, Bos	T	1	2	1	1	-
Lou Gordon, ChiC	T	-	2	-	2	-
Len Grant, NYG	T	2	-	-	2	-
Cal Hubbard, GB	T	1	1	1	1G	1
Link Lyman, ChiB	T	-	-	2	-	-
George Musso, ChiB	T	2	-	-	-	-
Zuck Carlson, ChiB	G	2	2	2	2	-
Ox Emerson, Port	G	-	1	1	-	1
Butch Gibson, NYG	G	2	-	-	-	-
Herman Hickman, Bkn	G	1	2	-	1	-
George Hurley, Bos	G	-	-	2	-	-
Joe Kopcha, ChiB	G	1	1	1	2	1
Mel Hein, NYG	C	1	2	2	2	-
Ookie Miller, ChiB	C	2	1	1	1	1
Cliff Battles, Bos	B	1	1	1	1	1
Benny Friedman, Bkn	B	2	-	-	-	-
Swede Hanson, Phi	B	2	-	2	2	-
Clarke Hinkle, GB	B	-	2	2	2	-
Shipwreck Kelly, Bkn	B	-	2	2	-	-
Jim Musick, Bos	B	2	2	-	2	-
Bronko Nagurski, ChiB	B	1	1	1	1	1
Harry Newman, NYG	B	1	2	2	2	-
Glenn Presnell, Port	B	1	1	1	1	1
Ken Strong, NYG	B	2	1	1	1	1

1934

		OF	UP	CN	GB	EY
Red Badgro, NYG	E	1	-	1	-	-
Harry Ebding, Det	E	2	-	-	-	-
Ray Flaherty, NYG	E	-	2	-	-	1
Bill Hewitt, ChiB	E	1	1	1	1	1
Bill Karr, ChiB	E	-	-	2	2	-
Bill McKalip, Det	E	2	2	2	1	-
Buster Mitchell, Det	E	-	1	-	-	-
Bill Smith, ChiC	E	-	-	-	2	-
George Christensen, Det	T	1	2	-	2	1
Turk Edwards, Bos	T	2	1	1	2	-
Harry Field, ChiC	T	-	2	2	-	-
Link Lyman, ChiB	T	2	1	2	1	1
Bill Morgan, NYG	T	1	-	1	1	-
Zuck Carlson, ChiB	G	-	2	-	-	-
Ox Emerson, Det	G	2	1	1	-	1
Butch Gibson, NYG	G	1	-	-	-	-
Herman Hickman, Bkn	G	-	-	-	2	-
Tom Jones, NYG	G	-	2	2	2	1
Joe Kopcha, ChiB	G	1	1	1	1	-
Mike Michalske, GB	G	2	-	2	1	-
Nate Barrager, GB	C	t2	-	-	-	-
Mel Hein, NYG	C	1	1	1	1	1
Bernie Hughes, ChiC	C	-	2	-	-	-
Ed Kawal, ChiB	C	t2	-	-	2	-
Cap Oehler, Pit	C	-	-	2	-	-
Cliff Battles, Bos	B	2	1	2	2	-
Dutch Clark, Det	B	1	1	1	1	1
Beattie Feathers, ChiB	B	1	1	1	1	1
Ace Gutowsky, Det	B	2	-	-	-	-
Swede Hanson, Phi	B	2	-	-	2	-
Clarke Hinkle, GB	B	-	2	-	2	-
Jack Manders, ChiB	B	-	1U	2	-	-
Bronko Nagurski, ChiB	B	1	1	1	1	1
Harry Newman, NYG	B	2	2	2	2	-
Glenn Presnell, Det	B	-	2	2	-	-
Ken Strong, NYG	B	1	2	1	1	1

U = Honor man

1935

		OF	UP	GB	EY	CN
Joe Carter, Phi	E	-	-	3	-	-
Tod Goodwin, NYG	E	2	2	2	-	-
Don Hutson, GB	E	2	2	3	-	-
Bill Karr, ChiB	E	1	1	1	1	1
Ed Manske, Phi	E	-	-	2	-	-
Bill Smith, ChiC	E	1	1	1	1	1
Tony Blazine, ChiC	T	2	-	-	-	-
George Christensen, Det	T	2	-	-	-	-
Turk Edwards, Bos	T	-	-	1	-	-
Bill Lee, Bkn	T	-	-	2	-	-
Bill Morgan, NYG	T	1	1	1	1	1
George Musso, ChiB	T	1	2	2	1	1
Armand Niccolai, Pit	T	-	2	3	-	-
Ade Schwammel, GB	T	-	1	3	-	-
Rick Concannon, Bos	G	-	-	3	-	-
Bree Cuppoletti, ChiC	G	-	-	2	-	-
Ox Emerson, Det	G	2	1	1	1	1
Lon Evans, GB	G	2	-	-	-	-
Phil Handler, ChiC	G	-	2	-	-	-
Tom Jones, NYG	G	-	-	3	1	-
Joe Kopcha, ChiB	G	1	1	2	-	-
Mike Michalske, GB	G	1	2	1	-	1
Nate Barrager, GB	C	-	-	2	-	-
Frank Bausch, Bos	C	-	-	3	-	-
Mel Hein, NYG	C	1	1	1	1	1
Clare Randolph, Det	C	2	2	-	-	-
Cliff Battles, Bos	B	2	-	3	-	-
Ernie Caddel, Det	B	1	2	-	-	1
Dutch Clark, Det	B	1	1	1	1	1
Ed Danowski, NYG	B	1	1	1	1	1
Arnie Herber, GB	B	2	-	2	1	-
Clarke Hinkle, GB	B	-	1	-	-	-
Ralph Kercheval, Bkn	B	-	-	2	-	-
Jack Manders, ChiB	B	-	-	-	1	1
Mike Mikulak, ChiC	B	1	-	1	-	-
Glenn Presnell, Det	B	-	-	3	-	-
Kink Richards, NYG	B	-	2	-	-	-
Gene Ronzani, ChiB	B	2	1	3	-	-
Phil Sarboe, ChiC	B	2	2	2	-	-
George Sauer, GB	B	-	-	1	-	-
Bill Shepherd, Bos-Det	B	-	2	2	-	-
Ken Strong, NYG	B	-	-	3	-	-

1936

		OF	UP	EY	CN
Joe Carter, Phi	E	-	-	2	2
Milt Gantenbein, GB	E	2	1	2	1
Bill Hewitt, ChiB	E	1	1	1	1
Don Hutson, GB	E	1	2	1	2
Bill Smith, ChiC	E	2	2	-	-
George Christensen, Det	T	2	-	-	1
Turk Edwards, Bos	T	1	1	-	1
Jack Johnson, Det	T	-	-	1	-
Bill Lee, Bkn	T	-	-	-	2
Jim MacMurdo, Bos	T	-	-	2	-
Armand Niccolai, Pit	T	-	2	-	-
Ade Schwammel, GB	T	-	-	2	-
Ernie Smith, GB	T	1	1	-	-
Joe Stydahar, ChiB	T	2	2	1	2
Bree Cuppoletti, ChiC	G	2	2	-	1
Ox Emerson, Det	G	1	1	2	-
Lon Evans, GB	G	1	1	1	1
Danny Fortmann, ChiB	G	2	2	-	-
Eddie Kahn, Bos	G	-	-	2	-
Les Olsson, Bos	G	-	-	-	2
George Rado, Pit	G	-	-	1	2
Frank Bausch, Bos	C	2	1	2	-
Mel Hein, NYG	C	1	2	1	1
Ed Kawal, ChiB	C	-	-	-	2
Cliff Battles, Bos	B	1	1	1	1
Ernie Caddel, Det	B	2	-	-	2
Dutch Clark, Det	B	1	1	1	1
Beattie Feathers, ChiB	B	-	2	2	-
George Grosvenor, ChiC	B	-	2	-	-
Ace Gutowsky, Det	B	-	2	2	2
Arnie Herber, GB	B	2	-	2	1
Clarke Hinkle, GB	B	1	1	-	-
Ralph Kercheval, Bkn	B	-	-	2	-
Tuffy Leemans, NYG	B	1	2	1	2
Bernie Masterson, ChiB	B	-	-	-	2
Bronko Nagurski, ChiB	B	2	1	1	1
Riley Smith, Bos	B	2	-	-	-

1937

		OF	UP	IN	NY	EY
Milt Gantenbein, GB	E	2	-	-	-	-
Bill Hewitt, Phi	E	1	2	1	2	-
Don Hutson, GB	E	2	2	1	1	1
Bill Karr, ChiB	E	-	-	-	2	2

		OF	UP	IN	NY	EY
Ed Klewicki, Det	E	-	1	-	-	2
Wayne Millner, Was	E	-	-	2	-	-
Gaynell Tinsley, ChiC	E	1	1	2	1	1
Turk Edwards, Was	T	1	1	1	1	1
Lou Gordon, ChiC	T	-	2	-	-	2
Ernie Smith, GB	T	2	-	2	2	-
Joe Stydahar, ChiB	T	1	1	2	1	1
Ed Widseth, NYG	T	2	2	1	2	2
John Dell Isola, NYG	G	2	-	-	2	1
Ox Emerson, Det	G	-	-	1	-	-
Lon Evans, GB	G	1	1	-	2	-
Danny Fortmann, ChiB	G	2	2	2	1	2
Russ Letlow, GB	G	-	-	-	-	2
George Musso, ChiB	G	1	1	1	1	1
Les Olsson, Was	G	-	2	-	-	-
Orville Tuttle, NYG	G	-	-	2	-	-
Mike Basrak, Pit	C	-	1	2	-	-
Frank Bausch, ChiB	C	2	-	-	2	1
Mel Hein, NYG	C	1	2	1	1	2
Sammy Baugh, Was	B	1	1	1	1	-
Cliff Battles, Was	B	1	2	1	1	2
Ernie Caddel, Det	B	2	2	-	-	-
Dutch Clark, Det	B	1	1	1	1	1
Ed Danowski, NYG	B	2	-	-	-	2
John Drake, Cle	B	-	2	-	2	-
Johnny Gildea, Pit	B	-	-	2	-	-
Ace Gutowsky, Det	B	-	-	2	-	2
Clarke Hinkle, GB	B	1	1	1	1	1
John Karcis, Pit	B	-	-	-	2	-
Tuffy Leemans, NYG	B	2	-	-	2	-
Jack Manders, ChiB	B	-	1	-	2	1
Bronko Nagurski, ChiB	B	2	-	-	-	1
Ray Nolting, ChiB	B	-	-	2	-	-
Ace Parker, Bkn	B	-	-	2	-	-
Bill Shepherd, Det	B	-	-	-	-	2
Riley Smith, Was	B	-	2	-	-	-

1938

		OF	UP	FW	IN	NY	EY
Don Hutson, GB	E	1	1	1	1	1	-
Gaynell Tinsley, ChiC	E	1	2	1	1	2	1
Joe Carter, Phi	E	-	-	2	-	2	-
Milt Gantenbein, GB	E	2	2	-	-	-	-
Bill Hewitt, Phi	E	2	1	2	2	1	1
Ed Klewicki, Det	E	-	-	-	-	-	2
Jim Poole, NYG	E	-	-	-	2	-	-
Bill Smith, ChiC	E	-	-	-	-	-	2
Conway Baker, ChiC	T	-	2	-	-	-	-
Turk Edwards, Was	T	2	-	2	-	2	1
John Golemgeske, Bkn	T	-	-	-	-	-	2
Jack Johnson, Det	T	-	-	-	2	-	-
Bruiser Kinard, Bkn	T	2	2	1	2	2	-
Joe Stydahar, ChiB	T	1	1	2	1	1	2
Ed Widseth, NYG	T	1	1	1	1	1	1
Ross Carter, ChiC	G	-	-	-	-	-	2
John Dell Isola, NYG	G	-	-	2	2	2	2
Danny Fortmann, ChiB	G	1	1	1	1	1	1
Byron Gentry, Pit	G	-	1	-	-	-	-
Jim Karcher, Was	G	2	-	-	-	-	-
Russ Letlow, GB	G	1	2	1	1	2	1
George Musso, ChiB	G	2	-	-	-	-	-
Les Olsson, Was	G	-	-	-	-	1	-
Orville Tuttle, NYG	G	-	2	2	2	-	-
Mike Basrak, Pit	C	-	-	-	2	-	-
Frank Bausch, ChiB	C	2	2	1	-	2	1
Chuck Cherundolo, Cle	C	-	-	-	-	-	2
Mel Hein, NYG	C	1	1	2	1	1	-
Sammy Baugh, Was	B	-	2	2	-	-	2
Lloyd Cardwell, Det	B	1	-	-	-	2	-
Ward Cuff, NYG	B	-	-	-	2	-	-
Ed Danowski, NYG	B	1	1	1	1	1	1
John Drake, Cle	B	2	-	-	-	-	2
Ace Gutowsky, Det	B	-	2	-	-	-	-
Clarke Hinkle, GB	B	1	1	1	1	1	1
Cecil Isbell, GB	B	2	2	2	2	2	-
Tuffy Leemans, NYG	B	-	2	2	-	2	2
Ace Parker, Bkn	B	1	1	1	1	1	2
Bill Shepherd, Det	B	-	-	2	2	1	1
Riley Smith, Was	B	2	-	-	2	-	-
Whizzer White, Pit	B	2	1	1	1	2	1

1939

		OF	UP	FW	IN	NY	EY	HA
Jim Benton, Cle	E	2	-	-	-	-	-	-
Jim Lee Howell, NYG	E	-	-	-	2	-	-	-
Don Hutson, GB	E	1	1	1	1	1	1	1
Dick Plasman, ChiB	E	-	2	2	-	2	1	2
Jim Poole, NYG	E	1	1	1	1	2	-	1
Perry Schwartz, Bkn	E	2	2	2	2	1	2	2
Bill Smith, ChiC	E	-	-	-	-	-	1	-
Jim Barber, Was	T	1	1	1	-	-	-	2
Turk Edwards, Was	T	-	-	-	1	1	-	-
Jack Johnson, Det	T	-	-	-	2	-	2	-
Bruiser Kinard, Bkn	T	2	2	2	-	-	-	-
John Mellus, NYG	T	-	-	2	2	2	-	1
Baby Ray, GB	T	-	2	-	-	-	1	2
Bo Russell, Was	T	-	-	-	-	-	2	-
Joe Stydahar, ChiB	T	1	1	1	1	1	1	1
Ed Widseth, NYG	T	2	-	-	-	2	-	-
John Dell Isola, NYG	G	1	2	1	-	1	1	-
Danny Fortmann, ChiB	G	1	1	1	1	1	1	1
Byron Gentry, Pit	G	-	-	-	1	-	-	-
Buckets Goldenberg, GB	G	-	-	-	-	-	-	1
Jim Karcher, Was	G	-	-	-	2	-	-	-
Russ Letlow, GB	G	-	-	-	-	2	2	-
Kayo Lunday, NYG	G	-	-	-	2	-	-	-
George Musso, ChiB	G	2	-	2	-	-	-	2
Orville Tuttle, NYG	G	2	2	-	-	-	-	-
John Wiethe, Det	G	-	1	2	-	2	2	2
Ki Aldrich, ChiC	C	2	2	2	2	-	-	2
Mel Hein, NYG	C	1	1	1	1	1	2	-
Alex Wojciechowicz, Det	C	-	-	-	-	2	1	1
Lloyd Cardwell, Det	B	2	-	-	-	-	1	-
Larry Craig, GB	B	-	-	-	-	-	-	1
Ward Cuff, NYG	B	-	-	2	2	-	-	2
John Drake, Cle	B	2	2	2	-	2	2	2
Andy Farkas, Was	B	1	1	1	-	1	1	1
Frank Filchock, Was	B	-	2	-	1	2	-	-
Parker Hall, Cle	B	2	1	1	1	1	2	1
Clarke Hinkle, GB	B	-	2	-	-	-	-	-
Cecil Isbell, GB	B	-	-	-	2	-	-	-
Tuffy Leemans, NYG	B	1	1	2	1	1	2	-
Davey O'Brien, Phi	B	1	2	2	-	2	2	-
Bill Osmanskl, ChiB	B	1	1	1	1	1	1	1
Ace Parker, Bkn	B	2	-	1	2	2	1	2
Fred Vanzo, Det	B	-	-	-	-	-	-	2
Bill Shepherd, Det	B	-	-	-	2	-	-	-

1940

		OF	AP	UP	IN	NY	EY	HA
Chuck Hanneman, Det	E	-	-	-	2	-	-	-
Don Hutson, GB	E	1	1	1	2	1	1	1
Don Looney, Phi	E	2	-	-	-	2	2	2
Carl Mulleneaux, GB	E	-	-	2	-	-	-	-
Jim Poole, NYG	E	2	-	1	1	2	2	2
Perry Schwartz, Bkn	E	1	1	2	1	1	1	1
Chet Adams, Cle	T	-	-	-	2	2	-	-
Lee Artoe, ChiB	T	-	-	-	-	-	-	1
Jim Barber, Was	T	2	-	1	-	2	2	-
Frank Cope, NYG	T	-	-	-	2	-	-	2
Bruiser Kinard, Bkn	T	1	1	1	1	1	1	1
Ed Kolman, ChiB	T	-	-	2	-	-	-	-
John Mellus, NYG	T	2	-	2	-	-	2	-
Joe Stydahar, ChiB	T	1	1	-	1	1	1	2
Dick Bassi, Phi	G	-	-	-	-	-	2	1
Dick Farman, Was	G	-	-	-	2	-	-	-
Danny Fortmann, ChiB	G	1	1	1	1	1	1	1
Russ Letlow, GB	G	-	-	-	-	2	2	2
Doug Oldershaw, NYG	G	2	-	2	-	-	-	-
Steve Slivinski, Was	G	2	-	1	1	2	-	-
Orville Tuttle, NYG	G	-	-	-	2	-	-	-
John Wiethe, Det	G	1	1	2	-	1	1	2
Charley Brock, GB	C	-	-	-	-	-	1	-
Mel Hein, NYG	C	1	1	1	1	1	-	2
Bulldog Turner, ChiB	C	2	-	2	2	2	2	1
Sammy Baugh, Was	B	1	1	1	2	1	1	2
Lloyd Cardwell, Det	B	-	-	-	-	-	1	-
Johnny Drake, Cle	B	1	1	1	2	1	1	1
Gary Famiglietti, ChiB	B	-	-	2	-	-	2	-
Parker Hall, Cle	B	-	-	2	-	2	-	-
Clarke Hinkle, GB	B	2	-	-	1	-	-	2
Cecil Isbell, GB	B	2	-	2	-	2	-	-
Tuffy Leemans, NYG	B	-	-	-	2	-	-	-
Sid Luckman, ChiB	B	-	-	-	2	-	2	1
Pug Manders, Bkn	B	-	-	-	-	-	-	2
George McAfee, ChiB	B	-	-	-	-	2	-	-
Davey O'Brien, Phi	B	2	-	-	-	-	-	-
Ace Parker, Bkn	B	1	1	1	1	1	1	1
Dick Todd, Was	B	2	-	2	1	2	2	-
Fred Vanzo, Det	B	-	-	-	-	-	-	1
Whizzer White, Det	B	1	1	1	1	1	2	2

1941

		OF	AP	UP	NY	EY	HA
Billy Dewell, ChiC	E	-	-	2	2	-	-
Jim Lee Howell, NYG	E	-	2	-	-	-	1
Dick Humbert, Phi	E	-	-	-	2	-	-
Don Hutson, GB	E	1	1	1	1	1	1
Wayne Millner, Was	E	-	-	-	-	2	-
Bob Nowaskey, ChiB	E	-	2	-	-	-	-

		OF	AP	UP	NY	EY	HA
Dick Plasman, ChiB	E	2	-	1	-	2	-
Ray Riddick, GB	E	2	-	-	-	-	-
Perry Schwartz, Bkn	E	1	1	2	1	1	2
George Wilson, ChiB	E	-	-	-	-	-	2
Chet Adams, Cle	T	-	-	-	-	2	-
Lee Artoe, ChiB	T	-	2	-	-	2	2
Bruiser Kinard, Bkn	T	1	2	1	1	-	1
Ed Kolman, ChiB	T	2	-	-	2	-	-
John Mellus, NYG	T	2	1	-	-	1	2
Baby Ray, GB	T	-	-	1	2	1	-
Phil Ragazzo, Phi	T	-	-	2	-	-	-
Willie Wilkin, Was	T	1	1	2	1	-	1
Bill Edwards, NYG	G	2	-	-	-	-	-
Aldo Forte, ChiB	G	-	-	-	-	2	-
Danny Fortmann, ChiB	G	1	1	1	1	1	1
Joe Kuharich, ChiC	G	1	1	2	-	1	1
Augie Lio, Det	G	-	2	-	-	2	2
Riley Matheson, Cle	G	2	-	1	-	-	-
Doug Oldershaw, NYG	G	-	-	-	2	-	-
Bob Suffridge, Phi	G	-	-	-	1	-	-
Pete Tinsley, GB	G	-	2	-	2	-	2
Len Younce, NYG	G	-	-	2	-	-	-
Mel Hein, NYG	C	-	2	-	2	-	2
George Svendsen, GB	C	2	-	2	-	2	-
Bulldog Turner, ChiB	C	1	1	1	1	1	1
Sammy Baugh, Was	B	-	-	2	2	2	-
Ward Cuff, NYG	B	-	-	1	-	2	-
Johnny Drake, Cle	B	-	-	-	-	2	-
Marshall Goldberg, ChiC	B	2	-	2	-	2	2
Clarke Hinkle, GB	B	1	2	-	2	-	-
Cecil Isbell, GB	B	1	1	1	1	1	1
Art Jones, Pit	B	-	2	-	-	-	-
Tuffy Leemans, NYG	B	2	2	-	2	-	2
Sid Luckman, ChiB	B	1	1	2	1	-	1
Pug Manders, Bkn	B	2	1	1	1	1	2
George McAfee, ChiB	B	1	1	1	1	1	1
Bill Osmanski, ChiB	B	-	-	-	-	1	-
Norm Standlee, ChiB	B	-	-	2	-	-	1
Whizzer White, Det	B	2	2	-	2	-	2

1942

		OF	AP	IN	NY
Ed Cifers, Was	E	-	-	1	-
Don Hutson, GB	E	1	1	1	1
Bob Masterson, Was	E	1	2	-	2
Perry Schwartz, Bkn	E	2	2	2	2
George Wilson, ChiB	E	2	1	2	1
Chet Adams, Cle	T	2	2	-	-
Lee Artoe, ChiB	T	1	1	2	1
Bruiser Kinard, Bkn	T	2	2	1	2
Ed Kolman, ChiB	T	-	-	1	2
Joe Stydahar, ChiB	T	-	-	2	-
Willie Wilkin, Was	T	1	1	-	1
Bill Edwards, NYG	G	1	2	1	2
Dick Farman, Was	G	-	-	-	2
Danny Fortmann, ChiB	G	1	1	1	1
Buckets Goldenberg, GB	G	2	2	-	-
Riley Matheson, Cle	G	2	1	-	-
Milt Simington, Pit	G	-	-	2	1
Steve Slivinski, Was	G	-	-	2	-
Chuck Cherundolo, Pit	C	2	2	2	2
Bulldog Turner, ChiB	C	1	1	1	1
Sammy Baugh, Was	B	2	1	1	1
Merle Condit, Bkn	B	2	2	-	2
Bill Dudley, Pit	B	1	1	1	1
Gary Famiglietti, ChiB	B	1	2	1	2
Andy Farkas, Was	B	2	1	-	2
Cecil Isbell, GB	B	1	2	2	1
Tuffy Leemans, NYG	B	-	2	2	-
Sid Luckman, ChiB	B	1	1	1	1
Dante Magnani, Cle	B	2	-	-	-
Ray McLean, ChiB	B	-	-	2	-
Tommy Thompson, Phi	B	-	-	2	2

1943

		AP	UP	NY	PF	IN	HA
Joe Aguirre, Was	E	-	-	1	-	-	-
Bill Fisk, Det	E	-	-	-	2	-	-
Don Hutson, GB	E	1	1	1	1	1	1
Bob Masterson, Was	E	2	2	-	-	1	2
Ed Rucinski, ChiC	E	1	1	2	2	-	1
George Wilson, ChiB	E	2	2	2	1	-	2
Chet Adams, GB	T	2	-	2	-	-	1
Al Blozis, NYG	T	1	1	1	1	1	-
Chet Bulger, ChiC	T	-	2	-	-	-	2
Bruiser Kinard, Bkn	T	1	-	-	2	-	2
Baby Ray, GB	T	-	2	1	1	-	2G
Lou Rymkus, Was	T	-	-	-	-	-	1
Vic Sears, PhPt	T	2	1	2	-	1	-
Frank Cope, NYG	G	-	-	-	2	-	-
Dick Farman, Was	G	1	1	1	-	1	-
Danny Fortmann, ChiB	G	1	1	1	1	-	1
Augie Lio, Det	G	2	2	2	2T	-	1
Riley Matheson, Det	G	-	-	2	2	-	-
Eberle Schultz, PhPt	G	-	-	-	1	-	-
Clyde Shugart, Was	G	-	2	-	-	-	-
Steve Slivinski, Was	G	2	-	-	-	-	2
Len Younce, NYG	G	-	-	-	-	1	-
Charley Brock, GB	C	2	-	-	2	-	2
George Smith, Was	C	-	2	2	-	-	-
Bulldog Turner, ChiB	C	1	1	1	1	1	1
Sammy Baugh, Was	B	1	1	1	1	1	1
Tony Canadeo, GB	B	1	2	1	2	1	2
Harry Clark, ChiB	B	1	1	2	2	-	1
Ward Cuff, NYG	B	2	1	2	1	1	-
Andy Farkas, Was	B	2	-	2	2	-	2
Jack Hinkle, PhPt	B	2	2	-	2	-	2
Sid Luckman, ChiB	B	1	1	1	1	1	1
Wilbur Moore, Was	B	-	-	2	-	-	-
Bill Paschal, NYG	B	-	2	-	1	-	1
Frank Sinkwich, Det	B	-	-	1	-	-	2
Ernie Steele, PhPt	B	-	2	-	-	-	-
Roy Zimmerman, PhPt	B	2	-	-	-	-	-

1944

		AP	UP	IN	NY	PF
Joe Aguirre, Was	E	1	1	1	1	1
Jim Benton, Cle	E	-	2	2	2	-
Don Hutson, GB	E	1	1	1	1	1
George Wilson, ChiB	E	-	2	2	2	-
Chet Bulger, ChPt	T	-	-	-	-	-
Frank Cope, NYG	T	-	1	1	2	1
Bruiser Kinard, Bkn	T	1	2	2	1	-
Baby Ray, GB	T	-	2	2	2	1
Al Wistert, Phi	T	1	1	1	1	-
Pete Gudauskas, ChiB	G	-	-	-	2	-
Augie Lio, Bos	G	-	2	1	2	-
Riley Matheson, Cle	G	1	1	2	1	1
Len Younce, NYG	G	1	1	1	1	1
George Zorich, ChiB	G	-	2	2	-	-
Charley Brock, GB	C	-	2	-	-	-
Mel Hein, NYG	C	-	-	2	2	-
Bulldog Turner, ChiB	C	1	1	1	1	-
Al Wojciechowicz, Det	C	-	-	-	-	1
Ward Cuff, NYG	B	-	1	2	-	1
Frank Filchock, Was	B	-	2	2	2	-
John Grigas, ChPt	B	-	2	1	1	-
Sid Luckman, ChiB	B	1	2	1	1	1
Pug Manders, Bkn	B	-	-	2	2	-
Bill Paschal, NYG	B	1	1	1	1	1
Frank Sinkwich, Det	B	1	1	1	1	1
Steve Van Buren, Phi	B	1	2	-	2	-
Roy Zimmerman, Phi	B	-	1	2	2	-

1945

		AP	UP	IN	NY	PF	HA
Joe Aguirre, Was	E	-	-	1	2	-	1
Jim Benton, Cle	E	1	2	2	1	1	1
Jack Ferrante, Phi	E	-	2	-	2	-	-
Don Hutson, GB	E	1	1	2	1	1	2
Frank Liebel, NYG	E	-	-	-	-	2	-
Steve Pritko, Cle	E	-	1	1	-	2	-
Ed Rucinski, ChiC	E	-	-	-	-	-	2
John Adams, Was	T	-	-	2G	-	1	2
Lee Artoe, ChiB	T	-	-	-	2	-	2
Chet Bulger, ChiC	T	-	-	-	-	2	-
Frank Cope, NYG	T	1	2	-	2	2G	-
Eberle Schultz, Cle	T	-	-	1	-	-	1
Vic Sears, Phi	T	-	2	2	-	-	-
George Sergienko, Bos	T	-	-	2	-	-	-
Emil Uremovich, Det	T	-	1	-	1	2	-
Al Wistert, Phi	T	1	1	1	1	1	1
Bruno Banducci, Phi	G	-	-	-	2	-	-
Stan Batinski, Det	G	-	2	-	-	1	-
Augie Lio, Bos	G	-	2	1	1	2	2
Riley Matheson, Cle	G	1	1	2	1	1	1
Bill Radovich, Det	G	1	1	1	2	-	1
Bob Zimny, ChiC	G	-	-	-	-	-	2
Ki Aldrich, Was	C	-	-	-	2	-	-
Charley Brock, GB	C	1	1	1	1	1	2
Mel Hein, NYG	C	-	-	2	-	-	-
Mike Scarry, Cle	C	-	2	-	-	2	1
Frank Akins, Was	B	-	2	1	2	1	-
Steve Bagarus, Was	B	1	-	-	2	-	2
Sammy Baugh, Was	B	-	1	1	1	2	-
Ted Fritsch, GB	B	-	1	2	2	-	1
Fred Gehrke, Cle	B	-	2	2	-	1	-
Jim Gillette, Cle	B	-	-	1	-	-	-
Don Greenwood, Cle	B	-	-	-	-	-	2
Sid Luckman, ChiB	B	-	2	-	2	2	2
Bob Margarita, ChiB	B	-	2	2	1	2	1

		AP	UP	IN	NY	PF	HA
Bill Paschal, NYG	B	-	-	-	-	-	2
Steve Van Buren, Phi	B	1	1	1	1	1	1
Bob Waterfield, Cle	B	1	1	2	1	1	1
Bob Westfall, Det	B	1	-	-	-	2	-

1946

NFL		ALL-PRO		ALL-LG.		
		AP	HA	UP	NY	PF
Jim Benton, LARm	E	1	1	1	1	1
Billy Dewell, ChiC	E	-	-	2	1	-
Ken Kavanaugh, ChiB	E	-	-	1	2	2
Frank Liebel, NYG	E	-	-	2	-	-
Nolan Luhn, GB	E	-	-	-	-	2
Jim Poole, NYG	E	1	-	-	2	1
John Adams, Was	T	-	-	2	2	1
Frank Cope, NYG	T	-	-	-	2	-
Fred Davis, ChiB	T	-	-	2	-	2
Jim White, NYG	T	2	1	1	1	2
Al Wistert, Phi	T	1	-	1	1	1
Ray Bray, ChiB	G	-	-	-	-	1
Bill Edwards, NYG	G	-	-	-	-	2
Augie Lio, Phi	G	-	-	1	2	-
Riley Matheson, LARm	G	1	1	1	1	1
Buster Ramsey, ChiC	G	-	-	2	2	2
Len Younce, NYG	G	2	-	2	1	-
Vince Banonis, ChiC	C	-	-	-	2	-
Charley Brock, GB	C	-	-	2	-	1
Bulldog Turner, ChiB	C	1	1	1	1	2
Paul Christman, ChiC	QB	-	-	2	-	-
Sid Luckman, ChiB	QB	2	1	2	1	1
Bob Waterfield, LARm	QB	1	-	1	2	2
Steve Bagarus, Was	HB	-	-	-	2	-
Bill Dudley, Pit	HB	2	1	1	1	1
Frank Filchock, NYG	HB	-	-	1	2	-
Hugh Gallarneau, ChiB	HB	-	-	-	2	1
Fred Gehrke, LARm	HB	-	-	-	-	2
Steve Van Buren, Phi	HB	-	-	2	1	2
Ted Fritsch, GB	FB	1	1	1	1	1
Pat Harder, ChiC	FB	-	-	-	-	2
Bill Osmanski, ChiB	FB	-	-	2	-	-

1946

AAFC		ALL-PRO		ALL-LG.		
		AP	HA	UP	NY	OA
Joe Aguirre, LA-A	E	-	-	2	1	-
Alyn Beals, SF-A	E	-	-	1	2	1
Dante Lavelli, CleA	E	2	-	2	2	1
Jack Russell, NY-A	E	2	1	-	-	2
Mac Speedie, CleA	E	-	-	1	1	2
Lee Artoe, LA-A	T	-	-	2	2	2
Lou Groza, CleA	T	-	-	2	-	-
Bruiser Kinard, NY-A	T	1	-	1	1	1
Bob Reinhard, LA-A	T	-	-	-	2	2
Martin Ruby, BknA	T	2	-	1	1	1
Lou Rymkus, CleA	T	-	1	-	-	-
Bruno Banducci, SF-A	G	2	-	1	1	1
Garland Gregory, SF-A	G	-	-	-	2	-
Buddy Jungmichael, MiaA	G	-	-	2	-	2
Bill Radovich, LA-A	G	1	-	1	1	2
Ed Ulinski, CleA	G	-	-	2	2	-
Bill Willis, CleA	G	-	1	-	-	1
Bob Nelson, LA-A	C	2	-	1	2	1
Mike Scarry, CleA	C	-	-	2	1	2
Frank Albert, SF-A	QB	2	-	2	1	2
Otto Graham, CleA	QB	-	-	1	2	1
Ace Parker, NY-A	QB	-	-	2	-	-
Glenn Dobbs, BknA	HB	1	1	1	1	1
Bob Hoernschemeyer, ChiA	HB	-	-	2	2	2
Steve Juzwik, BufA	HB	-	-	-	2	2
Spec Sanders, NY-A	HB	1	-	1	1	1
Marion Motley, CleA	FB	2	-	1	1	1
Norm Standlee, SF-A	FB	-	-	2	2	2

1947

NFL		ALL-PRO	ALL-LG.			
		AP	UP	NY	PF	HA
Jim Benton, LARm	E	-	3	-	-	-
Larry Craig, GB	E	-	3	-	1	1d
Val Jansante, Pit	E	-	2	1	-	-
Ken Kavanaugh, ChiB	E	2	1	1	2	1o
Jim Keane, ChiB	E	-	2	-	-	-
Mal Kutner, ChiC	E	2	1	-	1	1od
Charles Mehelich, Pit	E	-	-	-	-	1d
Pete Pihos, Phi	E	-	-	-	2	-
Gil Bouley, LARm	T	-	-	-	-	1d
Fred Davis, ChiB	T	-	1	1	1	1od
Dick Huffman, LARm	T	1	2	-	-	-
Stan Mauldin, ChiC	T	-	3	-	1	-
Ed Stickel, ChiB	T	-	3	-	-	-
Russ Thomas, Det	T	-	-	-	2	-
Jim White, NYG	T	-	2	-	-	-
Al Wistert, Phi	T	1	1	1	2	1o
John Badaczewski, Bos	G	-	3	-	2	1d
Roger Eason, LARm	G	-	3	-	-	-
Riley Matheson, LARm	G	1	2	1	2	1d
Bill Moore, Pit	G	-	1	-	-	-
Buster Ramsey, ChiC	G	2	-	1	1	1o
Dick Wildung, GB	G	-	2	-	1	1o
Len Younce, NYG	G	-	1	-	-	-
Vince Banonis, ChiC	C	-	1	-	-	-
Chuck Cherundolo, Pit	C	-	2	-	-	-
Fred Naumetz, LARm	C	-	-	-	2	-
Bulldog Turner, ChiB	C	1	3	1	1	1od
Sammy Baugh, Was	QB	2	1	-	2	1o
Paul Christman, ChiC	QB	-	2	-	-	-
Frank Dancewicz, Bos	QB	-	3	-	-	-
Sid Luckman, ChiB	QB	1	1	1	1	-
Elmer Angsman, ChiC	HB	-	-	-	2	1o
Tony Canadeo, GB	HB	-	3	-	-	-
Johnny Clement, Pit	HB	2	2	-	2	-
Bill Dudley, Det	HB	-	3	1	1	1od
Marshall Goldberg, ChiC	HB	-	-	-	-	1d
Charlie Trippi, ChiC	HB	-	2	-	-	-
Steve Van Buren, Phi	HB	1	1	1	1	-
John Cannady, NYG	FB	-	-	-	-	1d
Pat Harder, ChiC	FB	-	1	1	1	-
Walt Schlinkman, GB	FB	-	2	-	2	1o
Camp Wilson, Det	FB	-	3	-	-	-

o=offensive team; d=defensive team

1947

AAFC		ALL-PRO	ALL-LG.	
		AP	NY	OA
Bruce Alford, NY-A	E	1	-	-
Alyn Beals, SF-A	E	-	-	2
Dante Lavelli, CleA	E	-	-	1
Jack Russell, NY-A	E	-	1	2
Mac Speedie, CleA	E	1	1	1
Nate Johnson, NY-A	T	-	1	1
Martin Ruby, BknA	T	2	-	2
Lou Rymkus, CleA	T	-	1	1
John Woudenberg, SF-A	T	2	-	2
Bruno Banducci, SF-A	G	1	1	1
Dick Barwegan, NY-A	G	2	1	2
Len Levy, LA-A	G	-	-	2
Bill Willis, CleA	G	-	-	1
Bob Nelson, LA-A	C	2	1	1
Lou Sossamon, NY-A	C	-	-	2
Frank Albert, SF-A	QB	2	-	-
Otto Graham, CleA	QB	1	1	1
George Ratterman, BufA	QB	-	-	2
Bill Hillenbrand, BalA	HB	-	-	-
Chet Mutryn, BufA	HB	-	1	1
Spec Sanders, NY-A	HB	1	1	1
John Strzykalski, SF-A	HB	-	-	2
Buddy Young, NY-A	HB	-	-	2
Marion Motley, CleA	FB	2	1	1
Norm Standlee, SF-A	FB	-	-	2

1948

NFL		ALL-PRO		ALL-LG.			
		AP	SN	UP	NY	PF	HA
Ed Cifers, ChiB	E	-	-	-	-	-	1d
Tom Fears, LARm	E	-	-	2	2	-	-
Ken Kavanaugh, ChiB	E	-	-	2	2	2	1o
Mal Kutner, ChiC	E	1	1	1	1	1	1o
Pete Pihos, Phi	E	2	2	1	1	1	1d
Bill Swiacki, NYG	E	-	-	-	-	2	-
Gil Bouley, LARm	T	-	-	-	-	-	1d
Chet Bulger, ChiC	T	-	-	-	-	-	1d
Tex Coulter, NYG	T	-	-	2	-	2	-
Fred Davis, ChiB	T	2	2	2	2	2	1o
Dick Huffman, LARm	T	1	1	1	1	1	-
Dick Wildung, GB	T	-	-	-	2	-	-
Al Wistert, Phi	T	-	1	1	1	1	1o
Ray Bray, ChiB	G	-	2	1	1	1	1o
Chuck Drulis, ChiB	G	2	-	2	2	-	-
Don Ettinger, NYG	G	-	-	-	2	-	-
Bucko Kilroy, Phi	G	-	-	2	-	-	-
Milan Lazetich, LARm	G	-	-	-	-	2	1d
Buster Ramsey, ChiC	G	1	1	1	1	1	1o
Wash Serini, ChiB	G	-	-	-	-	2	-
Len Younce, NYG	G	-	-	-	-	-	1d
Vince Banonis, ChiC	C	-	2	2	1	-	1d

NFL		ALL-PRO		ALL-LG.			
		AP	SN	UP	NY	PF	HA
Fred Naumetz, LARm	C	-	-	-	-	2	-
Bulldog Turner, ChiB	C	1	1	1	2	1	1o
Sammy Baugh, Was	QB	2	2	1	1	1	1o
Sid Luckman, ChiB	QB	-	-	-	2	-	-
Johnny Lujack, ChiB	QB	-	-	-	-	-	1d
Tommy Thompson, Phi	QB	2	-	2	2	2	-
Elmer Angsman, ChiC	HB	-	-	-	2	2	1o
Tony Canadeo, GB	HB	-	-	2	-	2	-
Bill Dudley, Det	HB	-	-	-	-	-	1d
George McAfee, ChiB	HB	-	-	2	2	-	1d
Charlie Trippi, ChiC	HB	1	1	1	1	1	1o
Steve Van Buren, Phi	HB	1	1	1	1	1	-
Pat Harder, ChiC	FB	-	2	1	1	1	1o
Joe Muha, Phi	FB	-	-	2	-	2	1d

o=offensive team; d=defensive team

1948

AAFC		ALL-PRO		ALL-LG.		
		AP	SN	UP	NY	OA
Al Baldwin, BufA	E	-	-	2	2	2
Alyn Beals, SF-A	E	2	2	1	1	1
Dante Lavelli, CleA	E	-	-	2	2	2
Mac Speedie, CleA	E	1	1	1	1	1
Bob Reinhard, LA-A	T	1	2	1	1	1
Martin Ruby, BknA	T	-	-	2	-	2
Lou Rymkus, CleA	T	2	-	1	2	1
Arnie Weinmeister, NY-A	T	-	-	-	2	-
John Woudenberg, SF-A	T	-	-	2	1	2
Dick Barwegan, BalA	G	1	1	1	1	1
Weldon Humble, CleA	G	-	-	2	2	-
Riley Matheson, SF-A	G	-	-	-	2	2
Ed Ulinski, CleA	G	-	-	2	-	2
Bill Willis, CleA	G	2	2	1	1	1
Bob Nelson, LA-A	C	-	-	2	2	1
Lou Saban, CleA	C	-	-	1	1	2
George Strohmeyer, BknA	C	2	-	-	-	-
Frank Albert, SF-A	QB	-	1	2	1	2
Otto Graham, CleA	QB	1	2	1	2	1
Glenn Dobbs, LA-A	HB	-	2	2	2	2
Bill Hillenbrand, BalA	HB	-	-	2	2	2
Chet Mutryn, BufA	HB	2	-	1	1	1
Spec Sanders, NY-A	HB	-	-	-	2	-
John Strzykalski, SF-A	HB	2	-	1	1	1
Mickey Colmer, BknA	FB	-	-	2	-	2
Marion Motley, CleA	FB	1	1	1	1	1

1949

NFL		ALL-PRO		ALL-LG.	
		AP	IN	UP	NY
Tom Fears, LARm	E	2	-	1	1
Jack Ferrante, Phi	E	-	-	-	2
Jim Keane, ChiB	E	-	-	2	-
Pete Pihos, Phi	E	1	1d	1	1
Ed Sprinkle, ChiB	E	-	1d	2	2
George Connor, ChiB	T	2	-	2	2
Dick Huffman, LARm	T	1	1d	1	1
Vic Sears, Phi	T	-	-	1	2
Dick Wildung, GB	T	-	-	2	1
Al Wistert, Phi	T	-	1o	-	-
Ray Bray, ChiB	G	2	-	1	1
Charlie DeShane, Det	G	-	-	-	2
Darrell Hogan, Pit	G	-	1d	-	-
Bucko Kilroy, Phi	G	-	-	2	1
Milan Lazetich, LARm	G	-	1d	-	-
Cliff Patton, Phi	G	-	-	2	-
Buster Ramsey, ChiC	G	1	-	1	2
Wash Serini, ChiB	G	-	1o	-	-
Vince Banonis, ChiC	C	-	1o	2	-
Fred Naumetz, LARm	C	1	-	1	1
Bill Walsh, Pit	C	-	-	-	2
Johnny Lujack, ChiB	QB	-	-	-	1
Tommy Thompson, Phi	QB	-	-	2	2
Bob Waterfield, LARm	QB	1	-	1	-
Elmer Angsman, ChiC	HB	2	-	2	2
Tony Canadeo, GB	HB	2	1o	1	2
Don Doll, Det	HB	-	1d	-	-
Gene Roberts, NYG	HB	-	-	2	1
Steve Van Buren, Phi	HB	1	1o	1	1
Emlen Tunnell, NYG	HB	-	1d	-	-
Pat Harder, ChiC	FB	-	-	1	1
Dick Hoerner, LARm	FB	-	-	2	2

o=offensive team; d=defensive team

1949

AAFC		ALL-PRO		ALL-LG.		
		AP	IN	UP	NY	OA
Al Baldwin, BufA	E	-	-	2	-	2
Alyn Beals, SF-A	E	2	1o	1	1	1
Dante Lavelli, CleA	E	-	-	2	2	2
Jack Russell, NY-A	E	-	-	-	2	-
Mac Speedie, CleA	E	1	1o	1	1	1
John Kissell, BufA	T	-	1d	2	1	-
Bob Reinhard, LA-A	T	2	-	-	2	1
Martin Ruby, NY-A	T	-	-	2	2	2
Lou Rymkus, CleA	T	-	1o	1	-	2
Arnie Weinmeister, NY-A	T	1	-	1	1	1
Dick Barwegan, BalA	G	1	-	1	1	1
Visco Grgich, SF-A	G	2	-	1	1	1
Joe Signiago, NY-A	G	-	1o	2	2	2
Bill Willis, CleA	G	-	-	2	2	2
Bob Nelson, LA-A	C	-	-	2	2	-
John Rapacz, ChiA	C	-	-	-	-	2
Lou Saban, CleA	C	2	1d	1	1	1
Frank Albert, SF-A	QB	2	-	2	2	1
Otto Graham, CleA	QB	1	1o	1	1	1
Jim Cason, SF-A	HB	-	1d	-	-	-
Johnny Clement, ChiA	HB	-	-	-	2	-
Bob Hoernschemeyer, ChiA	HB	-	-	2	-	2
Chet Mutryn, BufA	HB	1	1o	1	2	1
George Taliaferro, NY-A	HB	-	-	2	2	2
Herman Wedemeyer, BalA	HB	-	1d	-	-	-
Buddy Young, NY-A	HB	-	-	1	1	2
Marion Motley, CleA	FB	-	-	2	1	2
Joe Perry, SF-A	FB	2	-	1	1	1

1950 ALL-NFL

		AP	UP	NY
Cloyce Box Det	E	2	-	-
Dan Edwards, NYY	E	1	-	-
Tom Fears, LARm	E	1	1	1o
Pete Pihos, Phi	E	-	2	2o
Ray Poole, NYG	E	-	-	1d
Jack Russell, NYY	E	-	-	2d
Bob Shaw, ChiC	E	-	2	2o
Mac Speedie, Cle	E	2	1	1o
Ed Sprinkle, ChiB	E	-	-	1d
Tom Wham, ChiC	E	-	-	2d
George Connor, ChiB	T	1	1	1o
Dick Huffman, LARm	T	2	2	1o
Bob Reinhard, LARm	T	2	2	1d
Lou Rymkus, Cle	T	-	-	2o
Carl Samuelson, Pit	T	-	-	2d
Vic Sears, Phi	T	-	-	2d
Arnie Weinmeister, NYG	T	1	1	1d
Al Wistert, Phi	T	-	-	2o
Dick Barwegan, ChiB	G	1	1	1o
Les Bingaman, Det	G	-	2	2d
Ray Bray, ChiB	G	2	-	1d
Lin Houston, Cle	G	-	-	2o
Bucko Kilroy, Phi	G	-	2	1o
John Mastrangelo, NYG	G	-	-	2o
Ed Neal, GB	G	-	-	2d
Buster Ramsey, ChiC	G	2	-	-
Joe Signiago, NYY	G	1	-	-
Bill Willis, Cle	G	-	1	1d
Tony Adamle, Cle	C	-	-	2d
Chuck Bednarik, Phi	C	1	-	2d
Joe Muha, Phi	C	-	-	1d
Fred Naumetz, LARm	C	-	-	2o
John Rapacz, NYG	C	-	2	1o
Clay Tonnemaker, GB	C	2	1	1d
Otto Graham, Cle	QB	-	2	-
John Lujack, ChiB	QB	1	1	1o
George Ratterman, NYY	QB	-	-	2o
Bob Waterfield, LARm	QB	2	-	-
Don Doll, Det	HB	-	-	1d
Bill Dudley, Was	HB	-	-	2d
Joe Geri, Pit	HB	1	1	1o
Billy Joe Grimes, GB	HB	2	-	1o
Tommy James, Cle	HB	-	-	2d
Spec Sanders, NYY	HB	-	-	1d
Otto Schnellbacher, NYG	HB	-	-	1d
John Strzykalski, SF	HB	2	-	-
Emlen Tunnell, NYG	HB	-	-	2d
Steve Van Buren, Phi	HB	-	2	2o
Doak Walker, Det	HB	1	1	2o
Buddy Young, NYY	HB	-	2	-
Pat Harder, ChiC	FB	-	2	-
Dick Hoerner, LARm	FB	2	-	2o
Marion Motley, Cle	FB	1	1	1o

o=offensive team; d=defensive team

1951

OFFENSE		AP	UP	NY
Tom Fears, LARm	E	-	-	2
Elroy Hirsch, LARm	E	1	1	1
Dante Lavelli, Cle	E	-	1	1
Fran Polsfoot, ChiC	E	-	-	2
Gordy Soltau, SF	E	-	2	-
Bobby Walston, Phi	E	-	2	-
Tex Coulter, NYG	T	-	1	1
Bill Fischer, ChiC	T	-	-	2
Lou Groza, Cle	T	-	1	1
Leo Nomellini, SF	T	1	2	2
Lou Rymkus, Cle	T	-	2	-
Bruno Banducci, SF	G	-	2	-
Dick Barwegan, ChiB	G	1	1	1
Lou Creekmur, Det	G	1	1	1
Abe Gibron, Cle	G	-	-	2
Lin Houston, Cle	G	-	2	-
Al Wistert, Phi	G	-	-	2
Frank Gatski, Cle	C	-	1	1
Vic Lindskog, Phi	C	1	-	-
John Rapacz, NYG	C	-	2	-
Jay Rhodemyre, GB	C	-	-	2
Otto Graham, Cle	QB	1	1	1
Bob Waterfield, LARm	QB	-	2	2
John Dottley, ChiB	RB	-	2	-
Joe Geri, Pit	RB	-	2	2
Bob Hoernschemeyer, Det	RB	-	-	2
Dub Jones, Cle	RB	1	1	1
Ed Price, NYG	RB	1	2	-
Dan Towler, LARm	RB	-	1	1
Doak Walker, Det	RB	1	1	1

DEFENSE		AP	UP	NY
Larry Brink, LARm	DE	1	2	1
Len Ford, Cle	DE	1	1	1
Leon Hart, Det	DE	1o	1	2
Ed Sprinkle, ChiB	DE	-	2	2
George Connor, ChiB	DT	1o	1	1
Al DeRogatis, NYG	DT	1	2	2
John Kissell, Cle	DT	-	-	2
Paul Lipscomb, Was	T	-	-	2
Arnie Weinmeister, NYG	DT	1	1	1
Jon Baker, NYG	MG	-	1	-
Les Bingaman, Det	MG	1	-	2
Bucko Kilroy, Phi	MG	-	-	2
Bob Momsen, Det	MG	-	2	-
Stan West, LARm	MG	-	2	1
Bill Willis, Cle	MG	1	1	1
Tony Adamle, Cle	LB	-	1	1
Chuck Bednarik, Phi	LB	1	1	1
Hardy Brown, SF	LB	-	-	2
John Cannady, NYG	LB	-	2	-
Tommy Thompson, Cle	LB	-	2	-
Tank Younger, LARm	LB	1	-	-
Don Doll, Det	DB	-	2	2
Bill Dudley, Was	DB	-	-	2
Warren Lahr, Cle	DB	-	1	1
Woodley Lewis, LARm	DB	-	2	-
John Lujack, ChiB	DB	-	2	2
Otto Schnellbacher, NYG	DB	1	1	1
Jerry Shipkey, Pit	DB	1	-	2LB
Emlen Tunnell, NYG	DB	1	1	1

o=offensive team; d=defensive team

1952

OFFENSE		AP	UP	NY
Cloyce Box, Det	E	1	-	-
Elroy Hirsch, LARm	E	-	2	2
Billy Howton, GB	E	2	2	1
Gordy Soltau, SF	E	1	1	1
Mac Speedie, Cle	E	2	1	2
Tex Coulter, NYG	T	2	2	-
Lou Groza, Cle	T	1G	1	1
Leo Nomellini, SF	T	1	1	1
Lum Snyder, Phi	T	-	-	2
Bob Toneff, SF	T	2	2	2
Bruno Banducci, SF	G	2	2	1
Dick Barwegan, ChiB	G	-	2	2
Lou Creekmur, Det	G	1	1	1
Bill Fischer, ChiC	G	-	1	2
John Wozniak, Dal	G	2	-	-
Frank Gatski, Cle	C	1	2	1
Bill Johnson, SF	C	2	-	2
Bill Walsh, Pit	C	-	1	-
Otto Graham, Cle	QB	2	1	1
Bobby Layne, Det	QB	1	-	2
Norm Van Brocklin, LARm	QB	-	2	-
Pat Harder, Det	RB	2	-	-
Bob Hoernschemeyer, Det	RB	2	2	1
Ray Mathews, Pit	RB	-	2	2
Hugh McElhenny, SF	RB	1	1	1
Ed Price, NYG	RB	1	1	1
George Taliaferro, Dal	RB	2	-	-
Dan Towler, LARm	RB	1	1	2
Charlie Trippi, ChiC	RB	-	-	2

DEFENSE		AP	UP	NY
Larry Brink, LARm	DE	-	1	-
Len Ford, Cle	DE	1	1	1
Ed Henke, SF	DE	-	2	2
Pete Pihos, Phi	DE	1	2	1
Andy Robustelli, LARm	DE	2	-	2
Ed Sprinkle, ChiB	DE	2	-	-
Al DeRogatis, NYG	DT	-	-	2
Thurm McGraw, Det	DT	1	1	1
Vic Sears, Phi	DT	2	-	2
Ernie Stautner, Pit	DT	2	2	-
Arnie Weinmeister, NYG	DT	1	1	1
Jon Baker, NYG	MG	-	-	2
Les Bingaman, Det	MG	-	1	2
Dale Dodrill, Pit	MG	2	-	-
Bucko Kilroy, Phi	MG	2	2	-
Stan West, LARm	MG	1	1	1
Bill Willis, Cle	MG	1	2	1
Chuck Bednarik, Phi	LB	1	1	-
Hardy Brown, SF	LB	-	-	2
George Connor, ChiB	LB	1oT	1	1
Don Paul, LARm	LB	2	-	-
Jerry Shipkey, Pit	LB	1	2	1
Tommy Thompson, Cle	LB	2	-	2
Tank Younger, LARm	LB	-	2	-
Jack Christiansen, Det	DB	1	2	-
Warren Lahr, Cle	DB	-	2	2
Ollie Matson, ChiC	DB	1	2o	-
Herb Rich, LARm	DB	2	1	1
Jim (Bob) Smith, Det	DB	2	1	1
Emlen Tunnell, NYG	DB	1	1	2
Lowell Wagner, SF	DB	-	-	2
John Williams, Was	DB	2	2	1

o=offensive team

1953

OFFENSE		AP	UP	NY
Elroy Hirsch, LARm	E	1	2	2
Dante Lavelli, Cle	E	-	1	1
Pete Pihos, Phi	E	1	1	1
Gordy Soltau, SF	E	-	2	-
Hugh Taylor, Was	E	-	-	2
Lou Creekmur, Det	T	1G	1	1
Lou Groza, Cle	T	1	1	1
Bob St. Clair, SF	T	-	2	-
Lum Snyder, Phi	T	-	2	-
Clay Tonnemaker, GB	T	-	-	2
Frank Wydo, Phi	T	-	-	2
Bruno Banducci, SF	G	-	1	2
Abe Gibron, Cle	G	-	2	1
Bill Lange, Bal	G	-	-	2
Bud McFadin, LARm	G	-	2	-
Dick Stanfel, Det	G	1	1	1
Brad Ecklund, Bal	C	-	-	2
Frank Gatski, Cle	C	1	1	1
Bill Johnson, SF	C	-	2	-
Otto Graham, Cle	QB	1	1	1
Bobby Layne, Det	QB	-	2	-
Bobby Thomason, Phi	QB	-	-	2
Bob Hoernschemeyer, Det	RB	-	2	1
Chick Jagade, Cle	RB	-	2	-
Hugh McElhenny, SF	RB	1	1	1
John Olszewski, ChiC	RB	-	-	2
Joe Perry, SF	RB	1	1	1
Dan Towler, LARm	RB	-	1	2
Doak Walker, Det	RB	1	2	2

DEFENSE		AP	UP	NY
Larry Brink, LARm	DE	-	-	2
Len Ford, Cle	DE	1	1	1
Bill McPeak, Pit	DE	-	2	-
Andy Robustelli, LARm	DE	1	2	2
Norm Willey, Phi	DE	-	1	1
Don Colo, Cle	DT	-	-	2
Thurm McGraw, Det	DT	-	2	1
Leo Nomellini, SF	DT	1	1	1MG
Ernie Stautner, Pit	DT	-	2	2
Arnie Weinmeister, NYG	DT	1	1	1
Les Bingaman, Det	MG	1	1	1
Dale Dodrill, Pit	MG	-	1	-
Bucko Kilroy, Phi	MG	-	2	2
Art Michalik, SF	MG	-	-	2
Bill Willis, Cle	MG	1	2	-
Chuck Bednarik, Phi	LB	1	2	1

DEFENSE		AP	UP	NY
George Connor, ChiB	LB	1OT	1	1
Don Paul, LARm	LB	1	2	2
Tommy Thompson, Cle	LB	1DB	1	2
Jack Christiansen, Det	DB	1	1	1
Bobby Dillon, GB	DB	-	-	2
Frank Gifford, NYG	DB	-	-	2
Ken Gorgal, Cle	DB	-	1	1
Tommy Keane, Bal	DB	1	1	1
Warren Lahr, Cle	DB	-	2	-
Woodley Lewis, LARm	DB	-	2	-
Bert Rechichar, Bal	DB	-	2	2

1954

OFFENSE		AP	UP	SN	NY
Bob Boyd, LARm	E	1	2	-	1
Dorne Dibble, Det	E	-	-	2	-
Harlon Hill, ChiB	E	2	1	1	1
Pete Pihos, Phi	E	1	1	1	2
Billy Wilson, SF	E	2	2	-	2
Lou Creekmur, Det	T	1	1	1	1
Lou Groza, Cle	T	1	1	1	1
Bob St. Clair, SF	T	2	2	-	2
Ken Snyder, Phi	T	2	2	-	2
Bruno Banducci, SF	G	1	1	1	1
George Connor, ChiBG	G	-	2	-	
Abe Gibron, Cle	G	2	2	-	-
Duane Putnam, LARm	G	2	-	-	-
Dick Stanfel, Det	G	1	1	2	1
Frank Gatski, Cle	C	2	2	2	-
Bill Johnson, SF	C	-	-	-	1
Bill Walsh, Pit	C	1	1	-	2
Otto Graham, Cle	QB	1	1	1	1
Bobby Layne, Det	QB	2	2	2	-
Norm Van Brocklin, LARm	QB	-	-	2	2
Bill Bowman, Det	RB	-	-	-	2
John Henry Johnson, SF	RB	-	2	-	2
Ollie Matson, ChiC	RB	1	1	1	1d
Hugh McElhenny, SF	RB	2	2	2	1
Joe Perry, SF	RB	1	1	1	1
Dan Towler, LARm	RB	2	-	-	-
Doak Walker, Det	RB	1	1	1	1
Billy Wells, Was	RB	-	-	-	2
Tank Younger, LARm	RB	2	2	-	-

DEFENSE		AP	UP	SN	NY
Len Ford, Cle	DE	1	1	2	1
Leon Hart, Det	DE	-	2	-	-
Johh Martinkovic, GB	DE	-	-	-	2
Andy Robustelli, LARm	DE	2	2	-	2
Ed Sprinkle, ChiB	DE	2	-	-	-
Norm Willey, Phi	DE	1	1	-	1
Don Colo, Cle	DT	-	2	-	-
Art Donovan, Bal	DT	1	1	2	2
Ray Krouse, NYG	DT	2	-	-	1
Leo Nomellini, SF	DT	1	1	2	1
Ernie Stautner, Pit	DT	2	2	-	2
Les Bingaman, Det	MG	1	1	1	1
Dale Dodrill, Pit	MG	1	2	-	2
Bucko Kilroy, Phi	MG	2	1	2	-
Mike McCormack, Cle	MG	-	2	-	-
Chuck Bednarik, Phi	LB	1	1	1	1
Tom Catlin, Cle	LB	-	2	-	-
Don Paul, LARm	LB	2	-	-	-
Joe Schmidt, Det	LB	1	2	-	2
Clay Tonnemaker, GB	LB	2	2	-	1
Lavern Torgeson, Det	LB	-	-	-	2
Roger Zatkoff, GB	LB	2MG	1	-	-
Jack Christiansen, Det	DB	1	1	2	1
Jim David, Det	DB	2	1	-	1
Bobby Dillon, GB	DB	1	-	-	2
Tommy James, Cle	DB	-	-	-	2
Warren Lahr, Cle	DB	-	2	-	-
Tom Landry, NYG	DB	1	1	-	2
Night Train Lane, ChiC	DB	2	2	-	2
Emlen Tunnell, NYG	DB	2	-	-	1

1955

OFFENSE		AP	UP	NE	SN	NY
Tom Fears, LARm	E	2	-	-	-	-
Harlon Hill, ChiB	E	1	1	1	1	1
Billy Howton, GB	E	-	-	2	-	2
Pete Pihos, Phi	E	1	2	2	1	2
Kyle Rote, NYG	E	-	2	-	1	-
Billy Wilson, SF	E	2	1	1	1	1
Lou Creekmur, Det	T	2	2	-	-	2
Lou Groza, Cle	T	1	1	1	1	1
Jack Jennings, ChiC	T	-	-	-	1	-
Mike McCormack, Cle	T	-	2	2	1	1
Bob St. Clair, SF	T	2	1	1	-	2
Lum Snyder, Phi	T	-	-	2	-	-
Bill Wightkin, GB	T	1	-	-	-	-
Bill Austin, NYG	G	-	1	-	-	2
Herman Clark, Chi	G	-	-	-	1	-
Abe Gibron, Cle	G	2	1	1	-	1
Stan Jones, ChiB	G	1	2	2	1	2
Duane Putnam, LARm	G	1	2	1	1	1
Harley Sewell, Det	G	-	-	2	-	-
Red Stephens, Was	G	2	-	-	-	-
Frank Gatski, Cle	C	1	1	1	1	1
Bill Johnson, SF	C	-	-	2	-	-
Dick Szymanski, Bal	C	2	2	-	-	2
Otto Graham, Cle	QB	1	1	2	1	1
Tobin Rote, GB	QB	2	-	1	-	2
Norm Van Brocklin, LARm	QB	-	2	-	1	-
Alan Ameche, Bal	RB	1	1	2	1	1
Rick Casares, ChiB	RB	-	-	-	-	1
Howie Ferguson, GB	RB	2	2	1	1	2
Frank Gifford, NYG	RB	1	-	1	1	-
Ollie Matson, ChiC	RB	1	1	1	1	1
Fred Morrison, Cle	RB	-	2	-	1	-
Ray Renfro, Cle	RB	-	-	2	-	-
Ron Waller, LARm	RB	2	1	-	-	-
Doak Walker, Det	RB	-	-	2	1	2
Alex Webster, NYG	RB	2	2	-	-	2

DEFENSE		AP	UP	NE	SN	NY
Gene Brito, Was	DE	1	1	1	-	2
Len Ford, Cle	DE	2	1	1	-	1
Gino Marchetti, Bal	DE	2	-	2	-	2
Andy Robustelli, LARm	DE	1	2	2	1	1
Tom Scott, Phi	DE	-	-	-	1	-
Norm Willey, Phi	DE	-	2	-	-	-
Don Colo, Cle	DT	2	1	1	-	2
Art Donovan, Bal	DT	1	1	1	1	1
Ray Krouse, NYG	DT	-	2	-	-	2DG
Bud McFadin, LARm	DT	2	-	2	-	-
Ernie Stautner, Pit	DT	-	-	-	1	2
Bob Toneff, SF	DT	1	2	2	1	1
Chuck Bednarik, Phi	LB	2	1	1	-	2
George Connor, CHiB	LB	2	1	1	-	1
Dale Dodrill, Pit	LB	2DG	1	1	1	1
Bob Gain, Cle	LB	-	2	-	-	-
Bill George, ChiB	LB	1DG	-	2	-	-
Les Richter, LARm	LB	-	2	-	-	1
Wayne Robinson, Phi	LB	-	-	-	1	-
Joe Schmidt, Det	LB	1	2	1	-	-
Lavern Torgeson, Was	LB	-	-	2	1	-
Roger Zatkoff, GB	LB	1	-	2	1	2
Dick Alban, Was	DB	-	-	-	1	-
Rex Berry, SF	DB	-	-	2	-	-
Jack Christiansen, Det	DB	1	1	1	1	1
Jim David, Det	DB	-	-	2	-	-
Bobby Dillon, GB	DB	1	1	1	1	1
Ken Konz, Cle	DB	2	-	-	-	-
Warren Lahr, Cle	DB	-	2	2	-	2
Tom Landry, NYG	DB	-	-	-	-	2
Night Train Lane, ChiC	DB	-	2	-	-	2
Don Paul, Cle	DB	2	1	-	-	-
Bert Rechichar, Bal	DB	2	2	1	-	1
Joe Scudero, Was	DB	2	-	-	-	-
Will Sherman, LARm	DB	1	1	1	1	1
Emlen Tunnell, NYG	DB	1	2	2	1	2

1956

OFFENSE		ALL-PRO				CONF
		AP	UP	NE	NY	SN
Darrel Brewster, Cle	E	-	-	2	-	-
John Carson, Was	E	-	-	-	-	1
Harlon Hill, ChiB	E	1	1	1	1	1
Elroy Hirsch, LARm	E	-	-	-	2	-
Billy Howton, GB	E	1	1	1	1	1
Kyle Rote, NYG	E	2	2	-	2	1
Billy Wilson, SF	E	2	2	2	-	-
Don Boll, Was	T	2	-	-	-	-
Rosey Brown, NYG	T	1	1	1	1	1
Lou Creekmur, Det	T	1	1	-	2	1
Lou Groza, Cle	T	2	2	-	2	
Mike McCormack, Cle	T	-	-	2	-	1
Bob St. Clair, SF	T	-	-	1	-	-
Bill Wightkin, ChiB	T	-	2	2	1	1
Herman Clark, ChiB	G	2	-	-	2	-
Stan Jones, ChiB	G	1	1	2	1	1
Duane Putnam, LARm	G	2	2	1	1	1
Harley Sewell, Det	G	-	-	2	-	-
Dick Stanfel, Was	G	1	1	1	2	1
Red Stephens, Was	G	-	-	-	-	1
Jack Stroud, NYG	G	-	2	-	-	-
Charley Ane, Det	C	2	1	1	-	-
Larry Strickland, ChiB	C	1	2	2	1	1
Ray Wietecha, NYG	C	-	-	-	2	1

OFFENSE		ALL-PRO				CONF
		AP	UP	NE	NY	SN
Charley Conerly, NYG	QB	-	-	-	-	1
Bobby Layne, Det	QB	1	1	1	1	1
Tobin Rote, GB	QB	2	2	2	2	-
Ollie Matson, ChiC	RB	1	1	1	1	1
Frank Gifford, NYG	RB	1	1	1	1	1
Alan Ameche, Bal	RB	2	-	2	2	1
Preston Carpenter, Cle	RB	-	2	-	-	-
Rick Casares, ChiB	RB	1	1	1	1	1
Leon Hart, Det	RB	-	2	-	-	-
Hugh McElhenny, SF	RB	2	2	2	2	1
Lenny Moore, Bal	RB	-	-	-	2	-
John Olszewski, ChiC	RB	-	-	-	-	1
Ron Waller, LARm	RB	-	-	2	-	-
Alex Webster, NYG	RB	2	-	-	-	-

DEFENSE		ALL-PRO				CONF
		AP	UP	NE	NY	SN
Gene Brito, Was	DE	1	1	1	2	1
Len Ford, Cle	DE	-	-	-	2	-
Bob Gain, Cle	DE	-	2	-	-	-
Gino Marchetti, Bal	DE	2	2	1	2	1
John Martinkovic, GB	DE	-	-	-	-	1
Ed Meadows, ChiB	DE	2	-	-	-	-
Andy Robustelli, NYG	DE	1	1	2	1	1
Tom Scott, Phi	DE	-	-	2	-	-
Don Colo, Cle	DT	2	2	-	-	-
Art Donovan, Bal	DT	1	2	1	2	1
Rosey Grier, NYG	DT	1	1	2	1	1
Ray Krouse, NYG	DT	-	-	-	-	1
Bud McFadin, LARm	DT	-	-	2	2	-
Bob Miller, Det	DT	-	-	-	-	1
Ernie Stautner, Pit	DT	2	1	1	-	-
Chuck Bednarik, Phi	LB	2	1	1	1	-
Dale Dodrill, Pit	LB	-	2	2	2	-
Chuck Drazenovich, Was	LB	2	2	2	-	1
Bill George, ChiB	LB	1	1	1	-	1
Les Richter, LARm	LB	1	-	-	1	1
Wayne Robinson, Phi	LB	-	-	-	-	1
Joe Schmidt, Det	LB	1	1	1	1	1
Bill Svoboda, NYG	LB	2	2	-	2	1
Roger Zatkoff, GB	LB	-	-	2	2	-
Jack Butler, Pit	DB	2	-	2	-	1
J.C. Caroline, ChiB	DB	-	-	-	1	-
Jack Christiansen, Det	DB	1	1	1	1	1
Linden Crow, ChiC	DB	2	-	-	-	-
Jim David, Det	DB	2	2	2	2	-
Bobby Dillon, GB	DB	2	1	1	1	1
Ken Konz, Cle	DB	-	2	-	-	1
Warren Lahr, Cle	DB	-	-	-	-	1
Night Train Lane, ChiC	DB	1	1	1	1	1
Yale Lary, Det	DB	1	2	2	2	1
Dickey Moegle, SF	DB	-	-	-	-	1
Will Sherman, LARm	DB	-	-	2	-	-
Gene Ray Smith, ChiB	DB	-	-	-	2	-
Emlen Tunnell, NYG	DB	1	1	1	2	-

1957

OFFENSE		ALL-PRO				CONF
		AP	UP	NE	NY	SN
Raymond Berry, Bal	E	2	-	-	-	1
Darrel Brewster, Cle	E	2	2	2	-	1
John Carson, Was	E	-	-	-	-	1
Clyde Conner, SF	E	-	-	-	2	-
Billy Howton, GB	E	1	1	1	1	-
Jim Mutscheller, Bal	E	-	2	2	2	-
Billy Wilson, SF	E	1	1	1	1	1
Charley Ane, Det	T	-	-	2	-	-
Rosey Brown, NYG	T	1	1	1	1	1
Lou Creekmur, Det	T	1	2	-	2	1
Lou Groza, Cle	T	2	1	2	1	-
Mike McCormack, Cle	T	2	2	1	-	1
Jim Parker, Bal	T	-	-	-	-	1
Art Spinney, Bal	T	-	-	-	2	-
Stan Jones, ChiB	G	-	-	2	2	-
Duane Putnam, LARm	G	1	1	1	1	1
Harley Sewell, Det	G	2	2	-	-	1
Jim Ray Smith, Cle	G	-	-	-	-	1
Dick Stanfel, Was	G	1	1	1	1	1
Jack Stroud, NYG	G	2	2	2	2	-
Frank Morze, SF	C	-	-	-	-	1
Jim Ringo, GB	C	1	2	1	-	-
Larry Strickland, ChiB	C	2	1	-	1	-
Ray Wietecha, NYG	C	-	-	2	2	1
Charley Conerly, NYG	QB	-	-	-	-	1
Y.A. Tittle, SF	QB	1	1	2	1	1
Johnny Unitas, Bal	QB	2	2	1	2	-
Don Bosseler, Was	RB	2	-	-	-	-

OFFENSE		ALL-PRO				CONF
		AP	UP	NE	NY	SN
Jim Brown, Cle	RB	1	1	1	1	1
Rick Casares, ChiB	RB	2	-	2	2	1
Willie Galimore, ChiB	RB	-	-	-	2	-
Frank Gifford, NYG	RB	1	1	1	1	1
Ollie Matson, ChiC	RB	1	1	1	1	1
Hugh McElhenny, SF	RB	2	-	2	-	-
Lenny Moore, Bal	RB	-	2	2	-	1
Tom Wilson, LARm	RB	2	2	-	2	1

DEFENSE		ALL-PRO				CONF
		AP	UP	NE	NY	SN
Doug Atkins, ChiB	DE	2	-	2	2	-
Gene Brito, Was	DE	1	2	1	2	1
Len Ford, Cle	DE	-	2	-	-	-
Ed Henke, SF	DE	-	-	-	-	1
Gino Marchetti, Bal	DE	1	1	1	1	1
Bill Quinlan, Cle	DE	-	-	-	-	1
Andy Robustelli, NYG	DE	2	1	2	1	-
Don Colo, Cle	DT	2	2	1	1	-
Art Donovan, Bal	DT	1	1	1	1	1
Bob Gain, Cle	DT	-	2	-	1	1
Dave Hanner, GB	DT	-	-	-	-	1
Dick Modzelewski, NYG	DT	-	-	2	-	-
Leo Nomellini, SF	DT	1	1	2	2	-
Ernie Stautner, Pit	DT	2	-	-	2	1
Chuck Bednarik, Phi	LB	2	2	2	1	1
Dick Daugherty, LARm	LB	-	-	-	2	-
Chuck Drazenovich, Was	LB	-	-	2	-	1
Bill George, ChiB	LB	1	1	1	1	-
Sam Huff, NYG	LB	2	-	-	-	1
Marv Matuszak, SF	LB	1	1	1	2	1
Walt Michaels, Cle	LB	-	2	2	-	-
Les Richter, LARm	LB	2	2	-	-	1
Joe Schmidt, Det	LB	1	1	1	1	1
Lavern Torgeson, Was	LB	-	-	-	2	-
Jack Butler, Pit	DB	1	1	1	1	1
Jack Christiansen, Det	DB	1	1	1	1	-
Jim David, Det	DB	-	2	2	2	-
Milt Davis, Bal	DB	1	2	-	2	1
Bobby Dillon, GB	DB	1	1	1	1	1
Ken Konz, Cle	DB	-	-	-	-	1
Night Train Lane, ChiC	DB	-	-	2	2	1
Yale Lary, Det	DB	2	1	1	-	1
Dickey Moegle, SF	DB	2	2	2	1	-
Don Paul, Cle	DB	2	-	-	-	-
Will Sherman, LARm	DB	-	-	-	-	1
Emlen Tunnell, NYG	DB	2	2	2	2	1

1958

OFFENSE		ALL-PRO				CONF
		AP	UP	NE	NY	SN
Raymond Berry, Bal	E	1	1	1	1	1
Woodley Lewis, ChiB	E	-	-	-	-	1
Jimmy Orr, Pit	E	2	2	-	-	-
Pete Retzlaff, Phi	E	2	2	2	2	1
Del Shofner, LARm	E	1	1	1	1	1
Billy Wilson, SF	E	-	-	2	2	-
Rosey Brown, NYG	T	1	1	1	1	1
Lou Creekmur, Det	T	-	2	-	-	1
Mike McCormack, Cle	T	2	2	2	2	1
Jim Parker, Bal	T	1	1	1	1	-
Bob St. Clair, SF	T	2	-	2	-1	
Frank Varrichione, Pit	T	-	-	-	2	-
Duane Putnam, LARm	G	1	1	1	1	1
Harley Sewell, Det	G	-	-	-	2	-
Jim Ray Smith, Cle	G	2	2	2	2	1
Art Spinney, Bal	G	2	2	2	-	1
Dick Stanfel, Was	G	1	1	1	1	1
Jim Ringo, GB	C	2	2	2	1	1
Ray Wietecha, NYG	C	1	1	1	2	1
Bobby Layne, Det-Pit	QB	2	2	2	2	1
Johnny Unitas, Bal	QB	1	1	1	1	1
Alan Ameche, Bal	RB	2	2t	2	2	-
Jon Arnett, LARm	RB	1	1	1	1	1
Jim Brown, Cle	RB	1	1	1	1	1
Rick Casares, ChiB	RB	-	2t	-	-	-
Willie Galimore, ChiB	RB	2	-	-	2	-
Frank Gifford, NYG	RB	2	2	2	-	1
Ollie Matson, ChiC	RB	-	2	2	2	1
Lenny Moore, Bal	RB	1	1	1	1	1
Joe Perry, SF	RB	-	-	-	-	1

DEFENSE		ALL-PRO				CONF
		AP	UP	NE	NY	SN
Doug Atkins, ChiB	DE	2	2	2	1	1
Gene Brito, Was	DE	2	1	1	2	1

DEFENSE		ALL-PRO				CONF
		AP	UP	NE	NY	SN
Gino Marchetti, Bal	DE	1	1	1	1	1
Lou Michaels, Pit	DE	-	-	-	2	-
Andy Robustelli, NYG	DE	1	2	2	-	1
Don Colo, Cle	DT	-	-	-	2	-
Art Donovan, Bal	DT	2	2	2	1	-
Bob Gain, Cle	DT	-	2	1	-	1
Rosey Grier, NYG	DT	2	-	-	-	1
Big Daddy Lipscomb, Bal	DT	1	1	1	1	1
Ernie Stautner, Pit	DT	1	1	2	2	-
Fred Williams, ChiB	DT	-	-	-	-	1
Dale Dodrill, Pit	LB	-	-	-	-	1
Chuck Drazenovich, Was	LB	2	-	-	-	1
Joe Fortunato, ChiB	LB	-	-	-	2	-
Bill George, ChiB	LB	1	1	1	1	-
Sam Huff, NYG	LB	1	1	1	1	-
Walt Michaels, Cle	LB	2	2	2	-	1
Bill Pellington, Bal	LB	-	-	2	-	1
Les Richter, LARm	LB	2	2	2	2	1
Joe Schmidt, Det	LB	1	1	1	1	1
Harland Svare, NYG	LB	-	2	-	-	-
Terry Barr, Det	DB	-	-	-	2	-
Jack Butler, Pit	DB	1	1	1	1	1
Jim David, Det	DB	-	-	2	-	-
Bobby Dillon, GB	DB	1	1	1	1	1
Night Train Lane, ChiC	DB	2	-	2	2	-
Yale Lary, Det	DB	1	1	1	1	-
Andy Nelson, Bal	DB	2	2	2	1	1
Jerry Norton, Phi	DB	-	-	-	-	1
Jim Patton, NYG	DB	1	1	1	2	1
Don Paul, Cle	DB	-	2	-	-	1
Will Sherman, LARm	DB	2	2	2	2	1
Carl Taseff, Bal	DB	2	2	-	-	-
Stan Wallace, ChiB	DB	-	-	-	-	1

1959

OFFENSE		ALL-PRO				CONF
		AP	UP	NE	NY	SN
Raymond Berry, Bal	E	1	1	1	1	1
Bill Howton, Cle	E	-	-	-	2	-
Tommy McDonald, Phi	E	2	2	-	-	1
Jimmy Orr, Pit	E	2	-	-	-	1
Ray Renfro, Cle	E	-	-	-	2	-
Bob Schnelker, NYG	E	-	2	-	-	-
Del Shofner, LARm	E	1	1	1	1	1
Rosey Brown, NYG	T	1	1	1	1	1
Forrest Gregg, GB	T	2	2	-	-	1
Mike McCormack, Cle	T	2	2	-	2	1
Jim Parker, Bal	T	1	1	1	1	1
Frank Varrichione, Pit	T	-	-	-	2	-
Bruce Bosley, SF	G	2	-	-	-	1
Stan Jones, ChiB	G	1	2	-	-	1
John Nisby, Pit	G	-	-	-	-	1
Duane Putnam, LARm	G	-	-	1	2	-
Jim Ray Smith, Cle	G	1	1	1	1	1
Art Spinney, Bal	G	2	1	-	1	-
Jack Stroud, NYG	G	-	2	-	2	-
Jim Ringo, GB	C	1	1	1	1	1
Ray Wietecha, NYG	C	2	2	-	2	1
Charley Conerly, NYG	QB	2t	2	-	2	1
Bobby Layne, Pit	QB	2t	-	-	-	-
Johnny Unitas, Bal	QB	1	1	1	1	1
Alan Ameche, Bal	RB	2	-	-	2	-
Jim Brown, Cle	RB	1	1	1	1	1
John David Crow, ChiC	RB	-	-	-	2	1
Frank Gifford, NYG	RB	1	1	1	1	1
Paul Hornung, GB	RB	2	2	-	-	-
Ollie Matson, LARm	RB	-	2	-	-	1
Bobby Mitchell, Cle	RB	-	-	-	2	-
Lenny Moore, Bal	RB	1	2	1	1	1
J.D. Smith, SF	RB	2	1	-	-	1

DEFENSE		ALL-PRO				CONF
		AP	UP	NE	NY	SN
Doug Atkins, ChiB	DE	2	2	-	2	1
Bob Gain, Cle	DE	-	-	-	-	1
Jim Katcavage, NYG	DE	-	-	-	2	-
Gino Marchetti, Bal	DE	1	1	1	1	1
Lou Michaels, LARm	DE	2	-	-	-	-
Andy Robustelli, NYG	DE	1	1	1	1	1
George Tarasovic, Pit	DE	-	2	-	-	-
Frank Fuller, ChiC	DT	2	-	-	2	-
Rosey Grier, NYG	DT	2	2	-	-	-
Dave Hanner, GB	DT	-	-	-	-	1
Big Daddy Lipscomb, Bal	DT	1	1	-	1	-
Leo Nomellini, SF	DT	1	1	1	1	1
Jess Richardson, Phi	DT	-	-	-	-	1
Ernie Stautner, Pit	DT	-	2	1	2	-
Bob Toneff, Was	DT	-	-	-	-	1
Bill Forrester, GB	LB	-	-	-	2	-
Bill George, ChiB	LB	1	1	1	2	1
Matt Hazeltine, SF	LB	-	-	-	-	1
Sam Huff, NYG	LB	1	1	1	1	1
Walt Michaels, Cle	LB	2	2	-	1	1
John Reger, Pit	LB	2	-	-	2	1
Les Richter, LARm	LB	2	-	-	-	-
Joe Schmidt, Det	LB	1	1	1	1	1
Don Shinnick, Bal	LB	-	2	-	-	-
Erich Barnes, ChiB	DB	2	-	-	-	1
Tom Brookshier, Phi	DB	2	2	1	-	1
Jack Butler, Pit	DB	1	1	-	1	1
Lindon Crow, ChiC	DB	-	-	-	2	-
Milt Davis, Bal	DB	-	2	1	2	-
Dean Derby, Pit	DB	2	1	-	1	-
Bobby Dillon, GB	DB	-	-	-	2	-
Night Train Lane, ChiC	DB	-	-	1	-	-
Yale Lary, Det	DB	2	2	1	-	1
Andy Nelson, Bal	DB	1	2	-	1	1
Jerry Norton, ChiC	DB	-	-	-	-	1
Jim Patton, NYG	DB	1	1	-	1	1
Jess Whittenton, GB	DB	-	-	-	-	1
Abe Woodson, SF	DB	1	1	-	2	-

1960 ALL-NFL

OFFENSE		ALL-NFL				CONF
		AP	UP	NE	NY	SN
Raymond Berry, Bal	E	1	1	1	1	1
Willard Dewveall, ChiB	E	-	-	-	2	-
Tommy McDonald, Phi	E	-	2	1	1	1
R.C. Owens, SF	E	2	-	-	-	-
Jim Philips, LARm	E	2	2	-	-	1
Sonny Randle, StL	E	1	1	2	2	1
Kyle Rote, NYG	E	-	-	2	-	-
Rosey Brown, NYG	T	2	1	2	1	1
Forrest Gregg, GB	T	1	2	2	2	-
Mike McCormack, Cle	T	-	2	-	2	1
Jim Parker, Bal	T	1	1	1	1	1
Bob St. Clair, SF	T	2	-	1	-	1
Bruce Bosley, SF	G	-	2	2	2	-
Stan Jones, ChiB	G	2	1	1	1	1
Jerry Kramer, GB	G	1	2	-	2	-
John Nisby, Pit	G	-	-	-	-	1
Harley Sewell, Det	G	-	-	-	-	1
Jim Ray Smith, Cle	G	1	1	1	1	1
Art Spinney, Bal	G	-	-	2	-	-
Jack Stroud, NYG	G	2	-	-	-	-
Chuck Bednarik, Phi	C	-	-	-	2	-
Art Hunter, LARm	C	2	2	2	-	-
Jim Ringo, GB	C	1	1	1	1	1
Jim Schrader, Was	C	-	-	-	-	1
Milt Plum, Cle	QB	2	-	-	-	-
Johnny Unitas, Bal	QB	-	2	2	2	1
Norm Van Brocklin, Phi	QB	1	1	1	1	1
Jim Brown, Cle	RB	1	1	1	1	1
John David Crow, StL	RB	2	2	-	2	1
Paul Hornung, GB	RB	1	1	1	1	1
Lenny Moore, Bal	RB	1	1	1	1	1
Jim Taylor, GB	RB	2	2	2	2	1
Tom Tracy, Pit	RB	2	-	2	2	1
Bobby Mitchell, Cle	RB	-	2	2	-	-

DEFENSE		ALL-NFL				CONF
		AP	UP	NE	NY	SN
Doug Atkins, ChiB	DE	2	1	1	1	1
Ordell Braase, Bal	DE	-	-	-	2	-
Gene Brito, LARm	DE	-	2	-	-	-
Marion Campbell, Cle	DE	-	-	-	-	1
Bob Gain, Cle	DE	-	2T	-	-	1
Charlie Krueger, SF	DE	2	-	-	-	-
Gino Marchetti, Bal	DE	1	1	1	1	-
John Paluck, Was	DE	-	-	2	-	-
Bill Quinlan, GB	DE	-	-	-	-	1
Andy Robustelli, NYG	DE	1	2	2	2	-
Art Donovan, Bal	DT	2	-	-	-	-
Frank Fuller, StL	DT	-	-	-	-	1
Rosey Grier, NYG	DT	-	-	-	-	1
Henry Jordan, GB	DT	1	1	2	1	-
Alex Karras, Det	DT	1	1	-	2	-
Big Daddy Lipscomb, Bal	DT	-	-	1	1	1
Leo Nomellini, SF	DT	2	-	-	2	1
Jess Richardson, Phi	DT	-	2	-	-	-
Ernie Stautner, Pit	DT	-	-	2	-	-
Bob Toneff, Was	DT	-	-	1	-	-
Chuck Bednarik, Phi	LB	1	1	-	1	1
Bill Forester, GB	LB	1	1	2	2	1

DEFENSE		ALL-NFL				CONF
		AP	UP	NE	NY	SN
Bill George, ChiB	LB	1	1	1	1	1
Sam Huff, NYG	LB	2	2	1	1	1
Walt Michaels, Cle	LB	-	2	-	-	-
Bill Pellington, Bal	LB	-	-	2	-	-
John Reger, Pit	LB	-	2	2	-	1
Les Richter, LARm	LB	2	-	-	-	-
Joe Schmidt, Det	LB	2	-	1	2	1
Wayne Walker, Det	LB	-	-	-	2	-
Erich Barnes, ChiB	CB	-	-	-	-	1
Tom Brookshier, Phi	CB	1	1	1	1	1
Dean Derby, Pit	CB	-	-	-	-	1
Night Train Lane, Det	CB	-	1	1	2	1
Yale Lary, Det	CB	-	-	2	-	-
Eddie Meador, LARm	CB	2	-	-	-	-
John Sample, Bal	CB	-	2S	-	2	-
Jess Whittenton, GB	CB	2	2	-	-	-
Abe Woodson, SF	CB	1	2	2	1	1
Dave Baker, SF	S	2	2	2	2	-
Don Burroughs, Phi	S	2	-	2	2	-
Andy Nelson, Bal	S	-	-	-	-	1
Jerry Norton, StL	S	1	1	1	1	1
Jim Patton, NYG	S	1	1	1	1	1

1960 ALL-AFL

OFFENSE		AP	UP	OL
Howard Clark, LAC	E	-	-	2
Bill Groman, Hou	E	-	1	1
Don Maynard, NYT	E	-	2	2B
Art Powell, NYT	E	1	2	2
Lionel Taylor, Den	E	1	1	1
Jerry Cornelison, DalT	T	-	2	-
Al Jamison, Hou	T	1	-	2
Rich Michael, Hou	T	-	1	1
Ron Mix, LAC	T	1	1	1
Ernie Wright, LAC	T	-	2	2
Ken Adamson, Den	G	-	2	-
Jack Davis, Bos	G	-	1	-
Bill Krisher, DalT	G	1	2	1
Charley Leo, Bos	G	-	-	2
Dan Manoukian, Oak	G	-	-	2
Bob Mischak, NYT	G	1	1	1
Walt Cudzik, Bos	C	-	1	-
Dan McGrew, Buf	C	-	-	2
Jim Otto, Oak	C	1	2	1
Al Dorow, NYT	QB	-	-	2
Jack Kemp, LAC	QB	1	1	1
Frank Tripucka, Den	QB	-	2	-
Billy Cannon, Hou	RB	-	2	2
Wray Carlton, Buf	RB	-	-	2
Elbert Dubenion, Buf	RB	-	2	-
Abner Haynes, DalT	RB	1	1	1
Paul Lowe, LAC	RB	1	1	1
Dave Smith, Hou	RB	1	1	1

DEFENSE		AP	UP	OL
Mel Branch, DalT	DE	1	1	1
Bob Dee, Bos	DE	-	-	2
Paul Miller, DalT	DE	-	2	2
Ron Nery, LAC	DE	-	2	-
Lavern Torczon, Buf	DE	1	1	1
Dick Chorovich, LAC	DT	-	2	-
Bud McFadin, Den	DT	1	1	1
Chuck McMurtry, Buf	DT	1	1	-
Volney Peters, LAC	DT	-	-	1
Orville Trask, Hou	DT	-	2	2
Sid Youngelman, NYT	DT	-	-	2
Tom Addison, Bos	LB	-	-	1
Bob Dougherty, Oak	LB	-	2	-
Mike Dukes, Hou	LB	-	1	-
Larry Grantham, NYT	LB	1	2	2
Sherrill Headrick, DalT	LB	1	2	1
Paul Maguire, LAC	LB	-	1	2
Archie Matsos, Buf	LB	1	1	1
Dennit Morris, Hou	LB	-	-	2
Joe Cannavino, Oak	CB	-	2	-
Goose Gonsoulin, Den	CB	1	2	1
Dick Harris, LAC	CB	1	-	1
Eddie Macon, Oak	CB	-	1	2
Julian Spence, Hou	CB	-	1	-
Dave Webster, DalT	CB	-	-	2
John Bookman, DalT	S	-	1	-
Fred Bruney, Bos	S	-	1	-
Mark Johnston, Hou	S	1	2	2
Richie McCabe, Buf	S	1	2	1
Ross O'Hanley, Bos	S	-	-	1
Jim Wagstaff, Buf	S	-	-	2

1961 ALL-NFL

OFFENSE		ALL-NFL				CONF
		AP	UP	NE	NY	SN
Raymond Berry, Bal	E	-	2	2	-	-
Buddy Dial, Pit	E	-	-	-	2	1
Mike Ditka, ChiB	E	-	2	1	2	1
Jim Phillips, LARm	E	1	1	2	1	1
Del Shofner, NYG	E	1	1	1	1	1
Rosey Brown, NYG	T	1	1	1	1	1
Forrest Gregg, GB	T	-	1	-	2	-
Mike McCormack, Cle	T	-	2	2	2	1
Jim Parker, Bal	T	1	2	1	1	1
Bob St. Clair, SF	T	-	-	2	-	1
Bruce Bosley, SF	G	-	-	2	-	1
Stan Jones, ChiB	G	-	2	-	-	-
Jerry Kramer, GB	G	-	-	-	2	-
John Nisby, Pit	G	-	-	2	-	1
Jim Ray Smith, Cle	G	1	1	1	1	1
Jack Stroud, NYG	G	-	2	-	2	-
Fuzzy Thurston, GB	G	1	1	1	1	1
Chuck Bednarik, Phi	C	-	2	-	-	-
Jim Ringo, GB	C	1	1	1	1	1
Ray Wietecha, NYG	C	-	-	2	2	1
Sonny Jurgensen, Phi	QB	1	1	-	-	1
Bart Starr, GB	QB	-	-	2	2	1
Y.A. Tittle, NYG	QB	-	2	1	1	-
Jon Arnett, LARm	RB	-	2	2	2	-
Jim Brown, Cle	RB	1	1	1	1	1
Paul Hornung, GB	RB	1	1	2	1	1
Tommy McDonald, Phi	RB	-	2	2	2	1
Lenny Moore, Bal	RB	1	1	1	1	1
Don Perkins, Dal	RB	-	-	-	-	1
Jim Taylor, GB	RB	-	2	1	2	1

DEFENSE		ALL-NFL				CONF
		AP	UP	NE	NY	SN
Doug Atkins, ChiB	DE	-	-	1	2	1
Jim Katcavage, NYG	DE	1	1	2	1	-
Gino Marchetti, Bal	DE	1	1	1	1	1
Andy Robustelli, NYG	DE	-	2	2	2	1
Ernie Stautner, Pit	DE	-	-	-	-	1
Leo Sugar, Phi	DE	-	2	-	-	-
Roger Brown, Det	DT	-	2	2	-	-
Bob Gain, Cle	DT	-	2	-	-	-
Rosey Grier, NYG	DT	-	-	-	2	-
Henry Jordan, GB	DT	1	1	1	1	1
Alex Karras, Det	DT	1	1	-	2	1
Big Daddy Lipscomb, Bal	DT	-	-	1	-	-
Dick Modzelewski, NYG	DT	-	-	-	1	-
Leo Nomellini, SF	DT	-	-	2	-	-
Jess Richardson, Phi	DT	-	-	-	-	1
Bob Toneff, Was	DT	-	-	-	-	1
Maxie Baughan, Phi	LB	-	2	-	1	-
Chuck Bednarik, Phi	LB	-	-	-	-	1
Dan Currie, GB	LB	-	1	1	-	-
Bill Forester, GB	LB	1	1	2	1	1
Bill George, ChiB	LB	1	2	1	-	-
Matt Hazeltine, SF	LB	-	-	-	-	1
Sam Huff, NYG	LB	-	-	2	2	-
Cliff Livingston, NYG	LB	-	2	-	2	-
Walt Michaels, Cle	LB	-	-	-	-	1
John Reger, Pit	LB	-	-	2	2	1
Joe Schimdt, Det	LB	1	1	1	1	1
Erich Barnes, NYG	CB	1	1	-	1	1
Don Bishop, Dal	CB	-	-	-	-	1
Jimmy Hill, StL	CB	-	-	1	-	-
Night Train Lane, Det	CB	1S	2	1	2	1
Dick Lynch, NYG	CB	-	2	-	-	-
Eddie Meador, LARm	CB	-	-	-	-	1
Jess Whittenton, GB	CB	1	1	2	2	-
Abe Woodson, SF	CB	-	-	-	1	-
Dave Baker, SF	S	-	-	-	-	1
Don Burroughs, Phi	S	-	2	2	2	-
Ed Dove, SF	S	-	2	-	-	-
Yale Lary, Det	S	-	-	2	-	-
Andy Nelson, Bal	S	-	-	-	-	1
Jerry Norton, StL	S	-	-	1	2	1
Jim Patton, NYG	S	1	1	1	1	1
Johnny Sample, Pit	S	-	1	2	1	-

1961 ALL-AFL

OFFENSE		AP	UP	OL	SN	NY
Gino Cappelletti, Bos	E	-	2B	2	-	2
Bill Groman, Hou	E	1	2	-	1	2
Charley Hennigan, Hou	E	1B	1	1	1	1
Dave Kocourek, SD	E	-	2	2	-	-
Lionel Taylor, Den	E	1	1	1	-	1
Jerry Cornelison, DalT	T	-	2	-	1	-
Jerry DeLucca, Bos	T	-	-	2	-	-

OFFENSE		AP	UP	OL	SN	NY
Al Jamison, Hou	T	1	1	1	1	1
Ron Mix, SD	T	1	1	1	-	1
Ken Rice, Buf	T	-	2	2	-	2
Ernie Wright, SD	T	-	-	-	-	2
Ken Adamson, Den	G	1	2	2	-	2
Wayne Hawkins, Oak	G	-	-	-	1	-
Bill Krisher, DalT	G	-	2	-	-	2
Charley Leo, Bos	G	-	-	1	-	-
Bob Mischak, NYT	G	1	1	1	1	1
Tony Sardisco, Bos	G	-	1	-	-	1
Bob Talamini, Hou	G	-	2	2	-	-
Jim Otto, Oak	C	1	1	1	1	1
Don Rogers, SD	C	-	2	-	-	2
Bob Schmidt, Hou	C	-	-	2	-	-
George Blanda, Hou	QB	1	1	1	1	1
Jack Kemp, SD	QB	-	2	2	-	2
Billy Cannon, Hou	RB	1	1	1	1	1
Larry Garron, Bos	RB	-	-	2	-	-
Abner Haynes, DalT	RB	-	1	1	1	1
Paul Lowe, SD	RB	-	2	2	-	2
Bill Mathis, NYT	RB	1	1	1	1	1
Alan Miller, Oak	RB	-	-	-	-	2
Donnie Stone, Den	RB	-	-	-	-	2
Charley Tolar, Hou	RB	-	2	2	-	-

DEFENSE		AP	UP	OL	SN	NY
Bob Dee, Bos	DE	-	-	2	-	-
Larry Eisenhauer, Bos	DE	-	-	-	-	2
Earl Faison, SD	DE	1	1	1	1	1
Don Floyd, Hou	DE	-	-	1	-	-
Ron Nery, SD	DE	1	2	-	1	2
Lavern Torczon, Buf	DE	-	1	2	-	1
Sid Youngelman, NYT	DE	-	2	-	-	-
Bill Hudson, SD	DT	-	2	-	-	2
Jim Hunt, Bos	DT	-	-	2	-	-
Ed Husmann, Hou	DT	-	2	-	-	2
Ernie Ladd, SD	DT	1	1	2	1	1
Bud McFadin, Den	DT	1	1	1	1	1
Chuck McMurtry, Buf	DT	-	-	1	-	-
Tom Addison, Bos	LB	1	1	2	1	2
Chuck Allen, SD	LB	-	-	1	-	2
Ralph Felton, Buf	LB	-	2	-	-	-
Larry Grantham, NYT	LB	1	1	2	1	1
Sherrill Headrick, DalT	LB	1	1	1	1	1
E.J. Holub, DalT	LB	-	2	2	-	2
Archie Matsos, Buf	LB	-	2	1	-	1
Tony Banfield, Hou	CB	1	1	1	1	2
Dick Felt, NYT	CB	-	-	2	-	-
Claude Gibson, SD	CB	-	2	-	-	2
Dick Harris, SD	CB	1	1	1	1	1
Fred Williamson, Oak	CB	-	2	2	-	-
Billy Atkins, Buf	S	-	1	2	1	1B
Goose Gonsoulin, Den	S	-	2	2	-	-
Mark Johnston, Hou	S	-	-	-	-	1
Charles McNeil, SD	S	1	1	1	1	1
Jim Norton, Hou	S	-	2	-	-	2
Ross O'Hanley, Bos	S	-	-	-	-	2
Dave Webster, DalT	S	1	-	1	-	-

1962 ALL-NFL

OFFENSE		ALL-NFL			CONF
		AP	UP	NE	SN
Gail Cogdill, Det	E	2	2	2	1
Boyd Dowler, GB	E	-	-	-	1
Tommy McDonald, Phi	E	2	-	2	-
Bobby Mitchell, Was	E	1	1	1	1
Sonny Randle, StL	E	-	2	-	-
Del Shofner, NYG	E	1	1	1	1
Preston Carpenter, Pit	TE	-	-	-	1
Mike Ditka, ChiB	TE	2	1	1	1
Ron Kramer, GB	TE	1	2	2	-
Rosey Brown, NYG	T	1	1	2	-
Forrest Gregg, GB	T	1	1	1	1
Mike McCormack, Cle	T	-	-	2	1
Jim Parker, Bal	OT	1G	2	1	1
Bob St. Clair, SF	T	2	-	-	-
Jack Stroud, NYG	T	2	2	-	1
Ted Connelly, SF	G	-	-	-	1
Jerry Kramer, GB	G	1	1	1	-
Ray Lemek, Pit	G	-	-	-	1
Mike Sandusky, Pit	G	-	2	-	-
Harley Sewell, Det	G	-	-	2	-
Jim Ray Smith, Cle	G	2	2	1	1
Fuzzy Thurston, GB	G	2	1	2	1
Buzz Nutter, Pit	C	-	-	2	-
Jim Ringo, GB	C	1	1	1	1
Jim Schrader, Phi	C	-	-	-	1
Ray Wietecha, NYG	C	2	2	-	-
Bart Starr, GB	QB	2	2	2	-
Y.A. Tittle, NYG	QB	1	1	1	1
Billy Wade, ChiB	QB	-	-	-	1
Dick Bass, LARm	RB	2	1	2t	1
Jim Brown, Cle	RB	-	2	-	1
John David Crow, SF	RB	-	-	2t	1
John Henry Johnson, Pit	RB	2	2	2	-
Don Perkins, Dal	RB	1	2	1	-
Jim Taylor, GB	RB	1	1	1	1

DEFENSE		ALL-NFL			CONF
		AP	UP	NE	SN
Doug Atkins, ChiB	DE	-	-	2	1
Willie Davis, GB	DE	1	2	-	-
Bill Glass, Cle	DE	-	-	2	1
Jim Katcavage, NYG	DE	2	1	1	1
Gino Marchetti, Bal	DE	1	1	1	1
Lou Michaels, Pit	DE	-	2t	-	-
Andy Robustelli, NYG	DE	2	2t	-	-
Roger Brown, Det	DT	1	1	1	-
Bob Gain, Cle	DT	2	-	-	-
Rosey Grier, NYG	DT	-	-	-	1
Henry Jordan, GB	DT	1	2	2	1
Alex Karras, Det	DT	2	1	1	1
Leo Nomellini, SF	DT	-	2	-	-
Bob Toneff, Was	DT	-	-	2	1
Ray Nitschke, GB	MLB	2	-	2	-
Bill Pellington, Bal	MLB	-	2	-	-
Joe Schmidt, Det	MLB	1	1	1	1
Jerry Tubbs, Dal	MLB	-	-	-	1
Rod Breedlove, Was	OLB	-	-	-	1
Carl Brettschneider, Det	OLB	-	-	-	1
Dan Currie, GB	OLB	1	1	1	-
Galen Fiss, Cle	OLB	-	2	2	1
Bill Forester, GB	OLB	1	1	1	1
Joe Fortunato, ChiB	OLB	2	-	-	-
Matt Hazeltine, SF	OLB	2	2	2	-
Herb Adderley, GB	CB	1	1	2	-
Erich Barnes, NYG	CB	2	2	-	1
Jimmy Hill, StL	CB	2	-	2	1
Night Train Lane, Det	CB	1	1	1	1
Abe Woodson, SF	CB	-	2	1	1
Don Burroughs, Phi	S	-	-	2	-
Don Fleming, Cle	S	-	-	-	1
Yale Lary, Det	S	1	1	1	1
Jim Patton, NYG	S	1	1	1	1
Rich Petitbon, ChiB	S	2	-	-	-
Clendon Thomas, Pit	S	-	2	-	-
Willie Wood, GB	S	2	2	2	1

1962 ALL-AFL

OFFENSE		AP	UP	OL
Lionel Taylor, Den	E	1	2	-
Charley Hennigan, Hou	E	1	1	1
Chris Burford, DalT	E	1	1	1
Art Powell, NYT	E	-	2	-
Fred Arbanas, DalT	TE	2	2	-
Dave Kocourek, SD	TE	2	1	1
Eldon Danenhauer, Den	T	2	2	1
Al Jamison, Hou	T	1	1	-
Charley Long, Bos	T	2	1	-
Harold Olsen, Buf	T	1	2	-
Jim Tyrer, DalT	T	-	-	1
Bob Mischak, NYT	G	2	-	-
Ron Mix, SD	G	1	1	1
Billy Neighbors, Bos	G	2	2	-
Billy Shaw, Buf	G	1	2	-
Bob Talamini, Hou	G	-	1	1
Jim Otto, Oak	C	1	1	1
Bob Schmidt, Hou	C	2	2	-
George Blanda, Hou	QB	2	2	-
Len Dawson, DalT	QB	1	1	1
Cookie Gilchrist, Buf	RB	1	1	1
Abner Haynes, DalT	RB	1	1	1
Curt McClinton, DalT	RB	-	2	-
Gene Mingo, Den	RB	2	-	-
Charley Tolar, Hou	RB	2	2	-

DEFENSE		AP	UP	OL
Mel Branch, DalT	DE	2	2	1
Bob Dee, Bos	DE	2	-	-
Larry Eisenhauer, Bos	DE	1	1	-
Earl Faison, SD	DE	-	2	-
Don Floyd, Hou	DE	1	1	1
Ed Hussmann, Hou	DT	1	1	-
Jerry Mays, DalT	DT	2	2	1
Bud McFadin, Den	DT	1	1	1
Tom Sestak, Buf	DT	2	2	-
Chuck Allen, SD	MLB	2	-	-
Nick Buoniconti, Bos	MLB	-	2	-
Sherrill Headrick, DalT	MLB	1	1	1

DEFENSE		AP	UP	OL
Tom Addison, Bos	OLB	2	2	-
Doug Cline, Hou	OLB	2	2	-
Larry Grantham, NYT	OLB	1	1	1
E.J. Holub, DalT	OLB	1	1	1
Tony Banfield, Hou	CB	1	1	1
Dick Felt, Bos	CB	2	2	-
Dick Harris, SD	CB	2	2	-
Fred Williamson, Oak	CB	1	1	1
Goose Gonsoulin, Den	S	1	2	1
Jim Norton, Hou	S	2	1	-
Bobby Hunt, DalT	S	1	1	-
Bob Zeman, Den	S	2	2	1

1963 ALL-NFL

OFFENSE		ALL-NFL				CONF
		AP	UP	NE	NY	SN
Terry Barr, Pit	E	2	-	2	-	1
Gail Cogdill, Det	E	2	-	-	-	1
Bobby Joe Conrad, StL	E	1	1	2	1	-
Buddy Dial, Pit	E	-	2	-	-	-
Bobby Mitchell, Was	E	-	2	1	2	1
Sonny Randle, StL	E	-	-	-	2	-
Del Shofner, NYG	E	1	1	1	1	1
Mike Ditka, ChiB	TE	1	1	1	1	1
Ron Kramer, GB	TE	2	2	2	2	-
Pete Retzlaff, Phi	TE	-	-	-	-	1
Charley Bradshaw, Pit	T	2	2	-	2	-
Rosey Brown, NYG	T	2	1	1	1	1
Forrest Gregg, GB	T	1	1	1	1	1
Bob St. Clair, SF	T	-	-	2	-	-
Dick Schafrath, Cle	T	1	2	2	2	1
Bob Wetoska, ChiB	T	-	-	-	-	1
Darrell Dess, NYG	G	2	-	2	2	1
John Gordy, Det	G	-	-	-	-	1
Ken Gray, StL	G	2	1	2	1	1
Jerry Kramer, GB	G	1	1	1	1	1
Jim Parker, Bal	G	1	2	1	2	-
Fuzzy Thurston, GB	G	-	2	-	-	-
Bob DeMarco, StL	C	2	-	2	2	-
Buzz Nutter, Pit	C	-	-	-	-	1
Mike Pyle, ChiB	C	-	2	-	-	1
Jim Ringo, GB	C	1	1	1	1	-
Y.A. Tittle, NYG	QB	1	1	1	1	1
John Unitas, Bal	QB	2	2	2	2	-
Billy Wade, ChiB	QB	-	-	-	-	1
Jim Brown, Cle	RB	1	1	1	1	1
Tim Brown, Phi	RB	-	2	2	2	1
Tommy Mason, Min	RB	1	1	1	1	1
Tom Moore, GB	RB	2	-	-	-	-
Jim Taylor, GB	RB	2	2	2	2	1

DEFENSE		ALL-NFL				CONF
		AP	UP	NE	NY	SN
Doug Atkins, ChiB	DE	1	1	1	1	1
Willie Davis, GB	DE	-	2	2	2	-
Bill Glass, Cle	DE	2	-	-	-	1
Jim Katcavage, NYG	DE	1	1	2	1	1
Gino Marchetti, Bal	DE	2	2	1	2	1
Roger Brown, Det	DT	1	1	1	1	-
Bob Gain, Cle	DT	2	2	-	-	1
Rosey Grier, LARm	DT	-	-	2	-	1
Henry Jordan, GB	DT	1	1	1	1	1
Dick Modzelewski, NYG	DT	-	-	-	-	1
Merlin Olsen, LARm	DT	2	2	2	2	-
Luke Owens, StL	DT	-	-	-	2	-
Bill George, ChiB	MLB	1	1	2	1	1
Sam Huff, NYG	MLB	-	2	-	-	-
Ray Nitschke, GB	MLB	-	-	-	2	-
Myron Pottios, Pit	MLB	2	-	1	-	1
Joe Schmidt, Det	MLB	-	-	1	-	-
Dan Currie, GB	OLB	2	-	1	1	-
Bill Forester, GB	OLB	-	1	2	-	1
Joe Fortunato, ChiB	OLB	1	1	1	1	-
Rip Hawkins, Min	OLB	-	2	-	-	-
Chuck Howley, Dal	OLB	-	-	-	-	1
Bill Koman, StL	OLB	-	-	-	-	1
Larry Morris, ChiB	OLB	2	2	2	2	-
Jack Pardee, LARm	OLB	1	-	-	2	1
Wayne Walker, Det	OLB	-	2	-	-	-
Herb Adderley, GB	CB	1	2	-	2	1
Jim Hill, StL	CB	-	2	-	-	1
Night Train Lane, Det	CB	2	1	2	1	1
Dick Lynch, NYG	CB	1	1	1	1	1
Eddie Meador, LARm	CB	-	-	2	2	-
Abe Woodson, SF	CB	2	-	1	-	-
Yale Lary, Det	S	2	-	-	-	1
Jim Patton, NYG	S	-	-	2	-	-
Richie Petitbon, ChiB	S	1	1	-	1	-
Roosevelt Taylor, ChiB	S	1	2	1	1	1

DEFENSE		ALL-NFL				CONF
		AP	UP	NE	NY	SN
Clendon Thomas, Pit	S	2	-	-	2	1
Larry Wilson, StL	S	-	1	2	2	1
Willie Wood, GB	S	-	2	1	-	-

1963 ALL-AFL

OFFENSE		AP	UP	OL	NE	NY
Lance Alworth, SD	E	1	1	1	1	1
Gino Cappelletti, Bos	E	-	2	-	-	-
Elbert Dubenion, Buf	E	2	-	-	-	2
Charley Hennigan, Hou	E	-	-	-	-	2
Bill Miller, Buf	E	2	-	-	-	-
Art Powell, Oak	E	1	1	1	1	1
Lionel Taylor, Den	E	-	2	-	-	-
Fred Arbanas, KC	TE	1	1	1	-	2
Dave Kocourek, SD	TE	2	2	-	1	1
Stew Barber, Buf	T	1	1	-	-	1
Eldon Danenhauer, Den	T	-	2	-	-	-
Dick Guesman, NYJ	T	-	-	-	-	2
Ron Mix, SD	T	1	1	1	1	1
Jim Tyrer, KC	T	2	2	1	1	2
Wayne Hawkins, Oak	G	2	-	-	-	-
Charley Long, Bos	OG	2T	2	-	-	-
Billy Neighbors, Bos	G	2	1	-	-	2
Billy Shaw, Buf	G	1	1	1	1	1
Bob Talamini, Hou	G	1	2	1	1	1
Jim Otto, Oak	C	1	1	1	1	1
Don Rogers, SD	C	2	-	-	-	2
Bob Schmidt, Hou	C	-	2	-	-	-
George Blanda, Hou	QB	2	-	-	-	2
Jack Kemp, Buf	QB	-	2	-	-	-
Tobin Rote, SD	QB	1	1	1	1	2
Clem Daniels, Oak	RB	1	1	1	1	1
Cookie Gilchrist, Buf	RB	2	2	-	-	1
Billy Joe, Den	RB	-	-	-	-	2
Keith Lincoln, SD	RB	1	1	1	1	2
Paul Lowe, SD	RB	2	2	-	-	-

DEFENSE		AP	UP	OL	NE	NY
Dalva Allen, Oak	DE	2	2	-	1	-
Mel Branch, KC	DE	2	2	-	-	2
Larry Eisenhauer, Bos	DE	1	1	1	1	1
Earl Faison, SD	DE	1	1	1	-	1
Don Floyd, Hou	DE	-	-	-	-	2
Houston Antwine, Bos	DT	1	1	1	1	1
Ed Husmann, Hou	DT	-	2	-	-	-
Jerry Mays, KC	DT	2	2	-	-	2
Bud McFaddin, Den	DT	2	-	-	-	2
Tom Sestak, Buf	DT	1	1	1	1	1
Nick Buoniconti, Bos	MLB	2	2	-	1	2
Archie Matsos, Oak	MLB	1	1	1	-	1
Tom Addison, Bos	OLB	2	2	1	-	2
Doug Cline, Hou	OLB	2	2	-	-	2
Larry Grantham, NYJ	OLB	1	1	-	1	1
E.J. Holub, Dal	OLB	1	1	1	1	1
Tony Banfield, Hou	CB	1	1	-	-	1
Dave Grayson, KC	CB	-	-	1	-	2
Ron Hall, Bos	CB	-	2	-	-	-
Dick Harris, SD	CB	2	-	-	-	-
Dick Westmoreland, SD	CB	2	2	-	1	2
Fred Williamson, Oak	CB	1	1	1	1	1
George Blair, SD	S	2	2	-	-	-
Fred Glick, Hou	S	1	1	1	1	1
Goose Gonsoulin, Den	S	-	-	1	-	-
Bobby Jancik, Hou	S	-	-	-	-	2
Joe Krakoski, Oak	S	2	-	-	-	2
Tom Morrow, Oak	S	1	1	-	1	1
Johnny Robinson, KC	S	-	2	-	-	-

1964 ALL-NFL

OFFENSE		ALL-NFL				CONF
		AP	UP	NE	NY	SN
Gary Ballman, Pit	E	-	-	-	-	1
Frank Clarke, Dal	E	1	2	2	1	-
Gail Cogdill, Det	E	2	-	-	2	-
Bobby Joe Conrad, StL	E	-	2	-	-	-
Max McGee, GB	E	-	-	-	-	1
Bobby Mitchell, Was	E	2	1	2	2	-
Johnny Morris, ChiB	E	1	1	1	1	1
Paul Warfield, Cle	E	-	-	1	-	1
Mike Ditka, ChiB	TE	1	1	1	1	1
Pete Retzlaff, Phi	TE	2	2	2	2	1
Charley Bradshaw, Pit	T	-	2	2	2	1
Bob Brown, Phi	T	2	-	-	-	-
Forrest Gregg, GB	T	1	1	1	1	-
Ernie McMillian, StL	T	-	-	-	2	-
George Preas, Bal	T	2	2	-	-	-
Dick Schafrath, Cle	T	1	1	2	1	1
Frank Varrichione, LARm	T	-	-	-	-	1

OFFENSE		ALL-NFL				CONF
		AP	UP	NE	NY	SN
Bob Vogel, Bal	T	-	-	1	-	-
Bob Wetoska, ChiB	T	-	-	-	-	1
Ed Blaine, Phi	G	-	-	-	-	1
John Gordy, Det	G	2	2	1	-	1
Ken Gray, StL	G	1	1	2	1	1
Gene Hickerson, Cle	G	-	-	2	-	-
Jim Parker, Bal	G	1	1	1	1	1
Alex Sandusky, Bal	G	2	2	-	2	-
Fuzzy Thurston, GB	G	-	-	-	2	-
Bob DeMarco, StL	C	-	-	1	1	1
Jim Ringo, Phi	C	2	2	2	2	-
Mick Tingelhoff, Min	C	1	1	2	-	1
Sonny Jurgensen, Was	QB	-	2	2	2	1
Bart Starr, GB	QB	2	-	-	-	-
John Unitas, Bal	QB	1	1	1	1	1
Bill Brown, Min	RB	2	-	-	-	-
Jim Brown, Cle	RB	1	1	1	1	1
Tommy Mason, Min	RB	-	2	2	-	-
Lenny Moore, Bal	RB	1	1	1	1	1
Charley Taylor, Was	RB	2	-	-	2	1
Jim Taylor, GB	RB	-	2	2	2	1

DEFENSE		ALL-NFL				CONF
		AP	UP	NE	NY	SN
Lionel Aldridge, GB	DE	-	-	-	-	1
Doug Atkins, ChiB	DE	-	-	2	-	-
John Baker, Pit	DE	-	-	-	2	-
Willie Davis, GB	DE	1	1	1	1	-
Bill Glass, Cle	DE	-	-	-	-	1
Deacon Jones, LARm	DE	2	2	2	2	-
Jim Katcavage, NYG	DE	-	-	-	-	1
Gino Marchetti, Bal	DE	1	1	1	1	1
Jim Marshall, Min	DE	-	2	-	-	-
John Paluck, Was	DE	2	-	-	-	-
Roger Brown, Det	DT	-	-	2	-	1
Henry Jordan, GB	DT	1	1	-	1	-
Alex Karras, Det	DT	2	2	2	2	-
Bob Lilly, Dal	DT	1	1	1	1	1
Merlin Olsen, LARm	DT	2	2	1	2	1
Floyd Peters, Phi	DT	-	-	-	-	1
Sam Huff, Was	MLB	-	-	-	-	1
Dale Meinert, StL	MLB	-	2	1	2	-
Ray Nitschke, GB	MLB	1	1	-	1	-
Bill Pellington, Bal	MLB	2	-	2	-	1
Maxie Baughan, Phi	OLB	1	-	-	1	1
Joe Fortunato, ChiB	OLB	1	1	1	1	1
Matt Hazeltine, SF	OLB	2	2	2	-	-
Jim Houston, Cle	OLB	-	-	1	-	-
Bill Koman, StL	OLB	-	-	-	-	1
Steve Stonebreaker, Bal	OLB	-	2	-	2	-
Wayne Walker, Det	OLB	2	1	2	2	1
Herb Adderley, GB	CB	2	2	2	2	1
Erich Barnes, NYG	CB	-	-	1	2	-
Bobby Boyd, Bal	CB	1	1	-	1	-
Pat Fischer, StL	CB	1	1	1	1	1
Jimmy Johnson, SF	CB	-	-	2	-	-
Dick LeBeau, Det	CB	2	2	-	-	-
Bernie Parrish, Cle	CB	2	-	-	-	1
Ed Sharockman, Min	CB	-	-	-	-	1
Paul Krauss, Was	S	1	1	1	1	1
Jerry Logan, Bal	S	-	2	-	-	-
Eddie Meador, LARm	S	-	-	-	-	1
Mel Renfro, Dal	S	2	2	2	1	-
Jim Ridlon, Dal	S	-	-	-	-	1
Roosevelt Taylor, ChiB	S	-	-	2	2	1
Willie Wood, GB	S	1	1	1	2	-

SPECIALISTS		ALL-NFL				CONF
		AP	UP	NE	NY	SN
Bruce Gossett, LARm	K	x	x	x	x	1
Lou Groza, Cle	K	x	x	x	x	1
Don Chandler, NYG	P	x	x	x	x	1
Yale Lary, Det	P	x	x	x	x	1

1964 ALL-AFL

OFFENSE		AP	UP	OL	NE	NY
Lance Alworth, SD	E	1	1	1	1	1
Gino Cappelletti, Bos	E	-	2	-	2	-
Elbert Dubenion, Buf	E	2	-	-	-	2
Charley Hennigan, Hou	E	1	1	1t	1	1
Art Powell, Oak	E	2	2	1t	2	2
Fred Arbanas, KC	TE	1	1	1	1	1
Dave Kocourek, SD	TE	2	2	-	2	2
Stew Barber, Buf	T	1	1	-	1	1
Sonny Bishop, Hou	T	-	2	-	-	-
Eldon Danenhauer, Den	T	2	-	-	-	2
Winston Hill, NYJ	T	-	-	-	2	-
Ron Mix, SD	T	1	1	1	1	1
Jim Tyrer, KC	T	2	2	1	2	2
Wayne Hawkins, Oak	G	2	-	-	-	-
Charley Long, Bos	G	-	2	-	2	2
Bob Mischak, Oak	G	-	-	-	2	-
Billy Neighbors, Bos	G	1	1	-	-	1
Billy Shaw, Buf	G	1	1	1	1	1
Bob Talamini, Hou	G	2	2	1	1	2
Mike Hudock, NYJ	C	-	2	-	-	
Jon Morris, Bos	C	2	-	-	2	2
Jim Otto, Oak	C	1	1	1	1	1
Len Dawson, KC	QB	2	2	-	2	2
Babe Parilli, Bos	QB	1	1	1	1	1
Sid Blanks, Hou	RB	-	2	-	-	-
Clen Daniels, Oak	RB	-	-	-	2	-
Cookie Gilchrist, Buf	RB	1	1	1	1	1
Abner Haynes, KC	RB	2	-	-	-	2
Keith Lincoln, SD	RB	1	1	1	1	1
Matt Snell, NYJ	RB	2	2	-	2	2

DEFENSE		AP	UP	OL	NE	NY
Bobby Bell, KC	DE	2	1	-	2	2
Tom Day, Buf	DE	-	-	-	2	-
Bob Dee, Bos	DE	2	-	-	-	2
Larry Eisenhauer, Bos	DE	1	2	1	1	1
Earl Faison, SD	DE	1	1	1	1	1
Don Floyd, Hou	DE	-	2	-	-	-
Houston Antwine, Bos	DT	-	2	-	-	2
Buck Buchanan, KC	DT	2	2	-	2	2
Ernie Ladd, SD	DT	1	1	-	1	1
Jerry Mays, KC	DT	2	-	1	2	-
Tom Sestak, Buf	DT	1	1	1	1	1
Chuck Allen, SD	MLB	-	2	-	2	-
Nick Buoniconti, Bos	MLB	1	1	1	1	1
Sherrill Headrick, KC	MLB	2	-	-	-	-
Archie Matsos, Oak	MLB	-	-	-	-	2
Tom Addison, Bos	OLB	2	2	1	1	2
Frank Buncom, SD	OLB	2	2	-	-	2
Larry Grantham, NYJ	OLB	1	1	1	1	1
E.J. Holub, KC	OLB	-	-	-	2	-
Mike Stratton, Buf	OLB	1	1	-	2	1
Willie Brown, Den	CB	1	1	1	1	1
Butch Byrd, Buf	CB	-	-	-	2	-
Dave Grayson, KC	CB	1	2	1	2	1
Pete Jaquess, Hou	CB	2	-	-	-	-
Dick Westmoreland, SD	CB	2	2	-	1	2
Fred Williamson, Oak	CB	-	1	-	-	2
Fred Glick, Hou	S	-	-	1	2	-
Goose Gonsoulin, Den	S	-	2	-	-	-
Ron Hall, Bos	S	1	1	-	1	1
Bobby Hunt, KC	S	2	-	-	-	2
Dainard Paulson, NYJ	S	2	1	1	1	2
George Saimes, Buf	S	1	2	-	2	1
Johnny Robinson, KC	S	-	-	2	-	-

1965 ALL-NFL

OFFENSE		ALL-NFL				CONF
		AP	UP	NE	NY	SN
Raymond Berry, Bal	E	2	-	-	2	-
Gary Collins, Cle	E	2	1	-	1	1
Bob Hayes, Dal	E	-	2	-	-	1
Jimmy Orr, Bal	E	1	2	1	2	1
Dave Parks, SF	E	1	1	1	1	1
Mike Ditka, ChiB	TE	2	2	-	2	1
Pete Retzlaff, Phi	TE	1	1	1	1	1
Grady Alderman, Min	T	2	-	-	-	-
Bob Brown, Phi	T	1	-	1	2	-
Rosey Brown, NYG	T	-	-	-	2	1
Forrest Gregg, GB	T	1G	1	-	2	1
Dick Schafrath, Cle	T	1	1	-	1	1
Bob Vogel, Bal	T	2	2	1	1	1
Bob Wetoska, ChiB	T	-	2	-	-	1
John Gordy, Det	G	-	2	1	2	-
Ken Gray, StL	G	2	1	-	1	1
Gene Hickerson, Cle	G	2	2	-	-	-
Jim Parker, Bal	G	1	1	1	1	1
John Wooten, Cle	G	-	-	-	-	1
Bob DeMarco, StL	C	-	2	-	-	1
John Morrow, Cle	C	2	-	-	-	-
Mike Pyle, ChiB	C	-	-	-	2	-
Mick Tingelhoff, Min	C	1	1	1	1	1
John Brodie, SF	QB	2	-	-	-	1
Rudy Bukich, ChiB	QB	-	2	-	2	-
Frank Ryan, Cle	QB	-	-	-	-	1
John Unitas, Bal	QB	1	1	1	1	-
Bill Brown, Min	RB	-	-	-	2	-
Jim Brown, Cle	RB	1	1	1	1	1
Tim Brown, Phi	RB	2	2	-	2	1
Gale Sayers, ChiB	RB	1	1	1	1	1

OFFENSE		ALL-NFL				CONF
		AP	UP	NE	NY	SN
Ken Willard, SF	RB	2	2	-	-	1

DEFENSE		ALL-NFL				CONF
		AP	UP	NE	NY	SN
Doug Atkins, ChiB	DE	2	2	-	-	1
John Baker, Pit	DE	-	-	-	-	1
Ordell Braase, Bal	DE	-	-	-	2	-
Willie Davis, GB	DE	1	1	1	1	1
Bill Glass, Cle	DE	2	2	-	2	1
Deacon Jones, LARm	DE	1	1	1	1	-
Roger Brown, Det	DT	-	2	-	2	1
Alex Karras, Det	DT	1	1	1	1	-
Charlie Krueger, SF	DT	2	-	-	-	-
Bob Lilly, Dal	DT	1	1	1	1	1
Merlin Olsen, LARm	DT	2	2	-	2	1
Sam Silas, StL	DT	-	-	-	-	1
Dick Butkus, ChiB	MLB	1	2	1	1	-
Sam Huff, Was	MLB	-	-	-	-	1
Ray Nitschke, GB	MLB	2	1	-	2	1
Maxie Baughan, Phi	OLB	2	-	-	-	1
Joe Fortunato, ChiB	OLB	1	2	1	2	-
Jim Houston, Cle	OLB	2	1	-	2	1
Steve Stonebreaker, Bal	OLB	-	2	-	1	1
Wayne Walker, Det	OLB	1	1	1	1	1
Herb Adderley, GB	CB	1	1	1	1	-
Bobby Boyd, Bal	CB	1	1	1	1	-
Pat Fischer, StL	CB	-	2	-	2	1
Jimmy Johnson, SF	CB	2	-	-	-	-
Dick LeBeau, Det	CB	2	-	-	-	1
Dick Lynch, NYG	CB	-	-	-	-	1
Bennie McRae, ChiB	CB	-	2	-	-	1
Johnny Sample, Was	CB	-	-	-	2	-
Paul Krause, Was	S	1	1	-	1	1
Eddie Meador, LARm	S	-	-	-	-	1
Mel Renfro, Dal	S	2	2	1	2	1
Roosevelt Taylor, ChiB	S	2	-	-	-	-
Larry Wilson, StL	S	-	2	-	2	-
Willie Wood, GB	S	1	1	1	1	1

SPECIALISTS		ALL-NFL				CONF
		AP	UP	NE	NY	SN
Don Chandler, GB	K	x	x	x	x	1
Lou Groza, Cle	K	x	x	x	x	1
Gary Collins, Cle	P	x	x	x	x	1
Tommy Davis, SF	P	x	x	x	x	1

1965 ALL-AFL

OFFENSE		AP	UP	OL	NE	NY
Lance Alworth, SD	E	1	1	1	1	1
Don Maynard, NYJ	E	2	-	-	-	2
Art Powell, Oak	E	2	2	1t	-	2
Lionel Taylor, Den	E	1	1	1t	1	1
Fred Arbanas, KC	TE	-	2	-	-	-
Willie Frazier, Hou	TE	1	1	1	1	1
Dave Kocourek, SD	TE	2	-	-	-	2
Stew Barber, Buf	T	-	2	-	-	2
Eldon Danenhauer, Den	T	2	2	1	-	2
Ron Mix, SD	T	1	1	-	1	1
Sherman Plunkett, NYJ	T	2	-	-	-	-
Jim Tyrer, KC	T	1	1	1	1	1
Sonny Bishop, Hou	G	-	-	-	-	2
Dan Ficca, NYJ	G	-	2	-	-	-
Wayne Hawkins, Oak	G	2	2	-	1	-
Billy Shaw, Buf	G	1	1	1	1	1
Walt Sweeney, SD	G	2	-	-	-	2
Bob Talamini, Hou	G	1	1	1	-	1
Mike Hudock, NYJ	C	-	-	-	-	2
Jon Morris, Bos	C	2	2	-	-	-
Jim Otto, Oak	C	1	1	1	1	1
John Hadl, SD	QB	2	2	-	-	2
Jack Kemp, Buf	QB	1	1	1	1	1
Ode Burrell, Hou	RB	-	-	-	-	2
Clem Daniels, Oak	RB	-	2	-	-	-
Cookie Gilchrist, Den	RB	1	1	1	1	1
Mack Lee Hill, KC	RB	-	2	-	-	-
Paul Lowe, SD	RB	1	1	1	1	1
Curtis McClinton, KC	RB	2	-	-	-	-
Matt Snell, NYJ	RB	2	-	-	-	2

DEFENSE		AP	UP	OL	NE	NY
Verlon Biggs, NYJ	DE	-	-	-	-	2
Ben Davidson, Oak	DE	2	2	-	-	-
Tom Day, Buf	DE	2	-	-	-	2
Earl Faison, SD	DE	1	1	1	1	1
Jerry Mays, KC	DE	1	2	1	1	1
Ron McDole, Buf	DE	-	1	-	-	-
Buck Buchanan, KC	DT	2	2	-	-	2
Jim Dunaway, Buf	DT	-	2	-	-	2
Ray Jacobs, Den	DT	2	-	-	-	-
Ernie Ladd, SD	DT	1	1	1	1	1
Tom Sestak, Buf	DT	1	1	1	1	1
Nick Buoniconti, Bos	MLB	1	1	1	1	1
John Tracey, Buf	MLB	2	-	-	-	2
Bobby Bell, KC	OLB	1	1	1	1	1
John Bramlett, Den	OLB	-	2	-	-	2
Frank Buncom, SD	OLB	2	-	-	-	-
Larry Grantham, NYJ	OLB	2	2	-	-	2
E.J. Holub, KC	OLB	-	2	-	-	-
Mike Stratton, Buf	OLB	1	1	1	1	1
Willie Brown, Den	CB	-	-	-	-	2
Butch Byrd, Buf	CB	1	2	1	-	1
Speedy Duncan, SD	CB	2	-	-	1	-
Dave Grayson, Oak	CB	1	1	1	1	1
W.K. Hicks, Hou	CB	2	2	-	-	2
Willie Mitchell, KC	CB	-	-	-	-	2
Fred Williamson, KC	CB	-	1	-	-	-
Kenny Graham, SD	S	2	-	-	-	-
Dainard Paulson, NYJ	S	2	1	-	1	1
Johnny Robinson, KC	S	1	2	1	-	2
George Saimes, Buf	S	1	1	1	1	1

SPECIALISTS		AP	UP	OF	NE	NY
Pete Gogolak, Buf	K	x	x	1	x	x
Curly Johnson, NYJ	P	x	x	1	x	x

1966 ALL-NFL

OFFENSE		ALL-NFL					CONF
		AP	UP	NE	FW	NY	SN
Gary Collins, Cle	E	2	2	-	-	2	-
Bob Hayes, Dal	E	1	1	1	1	1	1
Dave Parks, SF	E	2	-	1	-	2	1
Pat Studstill, Det	E	1	1	-	1	1	1
Charley Taylor, Was	E	-	2	-	-	-	1
Mike Ditka, ChiB	TE	2	2	-	-	-	-
John Mackey, Bal	TE	1	1	1	1	1	1
Pete Retzlaff, Phi	TE	-	-	-	-	2	-
Jackie Smith, StL	TE	-	-	-	-	-	1
Bob Brown, Phi	T	1	1	1	1	1	1
Forrest Gregg, GB	T	1	1	1	1	1	-
Ernie McMillan, StL	T	2	2	-	-	-	-
Ralph Neely, Dal	T	2	2	-	-	2	1
Jim Parker, Bal	T	-	-	-	-	2	-
Walt Rock, SF	T	-	-	-	-	-	1
Bob Vogel, Bal	T	-	-	-	-	-	1
John Gordy, Det	G	2	1	-	-	-	1
Ken Gray, StL	G	-	2	-	-	-	1
Gene Hickerson, Cle	G	-	-	1	-	-	1
Jerry Kramer, GB	G	1	1	-	1	1	1
Tony Liscio, Dal	G	2	-	-	-	-	-
John Thomas, SF	G	1	2	1	-	2	-
Fuzzy Thurston, GB	G	-	-	-	-	2	-
John Wooten, Cle	G	-	-	-	1	1	-
Bruce Bosley, SF	C	-	-	-	-	2	-
Bob DeMarco, StL	C	-	2	-	-	-	-
Greg Larson, NYG	C	-	-	-	-	-	1
Jim Ringo, Phi	C	2	-	-	-	-	-
Mick Tingelhoff, Min	C	1	1	1	1	1	1
Sonny Jurgensen, Was	QB	-	-	-	-	-	1
Don Meredith, Dal	QB	2	2	-	-	2	-
Bart Starr, GB	QB	1	1	1	1	1	1
Dick Bass, LARm	RB	2	2	-	-	2	-
Tim Brown, Phi	RB	-	-	-	-	2	-
Leroy Kelly, Cle	RB	1	1	1	1	1	1
Dan Reeves, Dal	RB	2	-	-	-	-	1
Gale Sayers, ChiB	RB	1	1	1	1	1	1
Jim Taylor, GB	RB	-	2	-	-	-	1

DEFENSE		ALL-NFL					CONF
	POS	AP	UP	NE	WA	NY	SN
George Andrie, Dal	DE	-	2	-	-	2	-
Ordell Braase, Bal	DE	2	2	-	-	-	-
Willie Davis, GB	DE	1	1	1	1	1	1
Deacon Jones, LARm	DE	1	1	1	1	1	1
Jim Katcavage, NYG	DE	-	-	-	-	-	1
Ben McGee, Pit	DE	-	-	-	-	-	1
Joe Robb, StL	DE	2	-	-	-	2	-
Roger Brown, Det	DT	-	-	-	-	-	1
Henry Jordan, GB	DT	2	2	-	-	2	-
Alex Karras, Det	DT	2	2	-	-	2	-
Bob Lilly, Dal	DT	1	1	1	1	1	1
Merlin Olsen, LARm	DT	1	1	1	1	1	1
Floyd Peters, Phi	DT	-	-	-	-	-	1
Dick Butkus, ChiB	MLB	2	2	-	-	2	1
Lee Roy Jordan, Dal	MLB	-	-	-	-	-	1

DEFENSE		ALL-NFL					CONF
		AP	UP	NE	WA	NY	SN
Ray Nitschke, GB	MLB	1	1	1	1	1	-
Maxie Baughan, LARm	OLB	2	-	1	-	-	1
Lee Roy Caffey, GB	OLB	1	1	-	-	1	-
John Campbell, Pit	OLB	-	-	-	-	-	1
Joe Fortunato, ChiB	OLB	-	-	-	-	2	-
Jim Houston, Cle	OLB	-	-	-	-	-	1
Chuck Howley, Dal	OLB	1	1	1	1	2	-
Dave Robinson, GB	OLB	-	-	-	-	-	1
Wayne Walker, Det	OLB	2	2	-	1	1	-
Dave Wilcox, SF	OLB	-	2	-	-	-	-
Herb Adderley, GB	CB	1	1	1	1	1	1
Erich Barnes, Cle	CB	-	-	-	-	-	1
Bobby Boyd, Bal	CB	2	1	-	1	2	-
Cornell Green, Dal	CB	1	2	1	-	1	1
Jimmy Johnson, SF	CB	2	2	-	-	-	1
Ross Fichtner, Cle	S	2	-	-	-	2CB	-
Eddie Meador, LARm	S	-	-	-	-	-	1
Richie Petitbon, ChiB	S	-	-	-	-	-	1
Mel Renfro, Dal	S	-	2	-	-	-	-
Jerry Stovall, StL	S	2	2	-	-	2	1
Clendon Thomas, Pit	S	-	-	-	-	2	-
Larry Wilson, StL	S	1	1	1	1	1	1
Willie Wood, GB	S	1	1	1	1	1	-

SPECIALISTS		ALL-NFL					CONF
		AP	UP	NE	WA	NY	SN
Charley Gogolak, Was	K	x	x	x	x	x	1
Bruce Gossett, LARm	K	x	x	x	x	x	1
Sam Baker, Phi	P	x	x	x	x	x	1
David Lee, Bal	P	x	x	x	x	x	1

1966 ALL-AFL

OFFENSE		AP	UP	OL	NE	NY
Lance Alworth, SD	E	1	1	1	1	1
Gino Cappelletti, Bos	E	-	2	-	-	-
Art Powell, Oak	E	2	2	1	2	1
George Sauer, NYJ	E	2	-	2	2	2
Otis Taylor, KC	E	1	1	2	1	2
Fred Arbanas, KC	TE	1	1	1	1	1
Dave Costa, Buf	TE	-	-	-	2	-
Al Denson, Den	TE	2	2	2	-	2
Stew Barber, Buf	T	2	-	2	-	2
Dick Hudson, Buf	T	2	2	-	2	-
Ron Mix, SD	T	1	1	2	1	1
Sherman Plunkett, NYJ	T	-	-	1	-	2
Walter Suggs, Hou	T	-	2	-	2	-
Jim Tyrer, KC	T	1	1	1	1	1
Ed Budde, KC	G	1	-	2	2	2
Sam DeLuca, NYJ	G	2	2	-	-	-
Wayne Hawkins, Oak	G	2	1	2	1	1
Billy Shaw, Buf	G	1	1	1	1	1
Bob Talamini, Hou	G	-	2	1	2	2
Jon Morris, Bos	C	1	2	2	2	2
Jim Otto, Oak	C	2	1	1	1	1
Len Dawson, KC	QB	1	1	1	1	1
John Hadl, SD	QB	-	2	-	-	-
Jack Kemp, Buf	QB	2	-	2	-	2
Joe Namath, NYJ	QB	-	-	-	2	-
Bobby Burnett, Buf	RB	2	2	2	2	1
Wray Carlton, Buf	RB	2	2	2	2	2
Clem Daniels, Oak	RB	1	1	1	1	-
Mike Garrett, KC	RB	-	-	-	-	2
Jim Nance, Bos	RB	1	1	1	1	1

DEFENSE		AP	UP	OL	NE	NY
Verlon Biggs, NYJ	DE	2	1	2	1	2
Ben Davidson, Oak	DE	-	-	-	-	2
Tom Day, Buf	DE	-	-	2	-	-
Larry Eisenhauer, Bos	DE	-	2	1	2	-
Ike Lassiter, Oak	DE	2	-	-	-	-
Jerry Mays, KC	DE	1	1	1	1	1
Ron McDole, Buf	DE	1	2	-	2	1
Houston Antwine, Bos	DT	2	1	1	1t	1
Buck Buchanan, KC	DT	1	1	1	2	2
Jim Dunaway, Buf	DT	1	2	-	-	2
Jim Hunt, Bos	DT	-	-	-	2	-
Tom Keating, Oak	DT	2	2	2	1	-
Tom Sestak, Buf	DT	-	-	2	1t	1
Nick Buoniconti, Bos	MLB	1	1	1	1	1
Sherrill Headrick, KC	MLB	2	-	-	2	2
Harry Jacobs, Buf	MLB	-	2	2	-	-
Johnny Baker, Hou	OLB	-	-	-	2	-
Bobby Bell, KC	OLB	1	1	1	1	1
John Bramlett, Den	OLB	2	2	-	2	-
Frank Buncom, SD	OLB	-	-	2	-	-
Larry Grantham, NYJ	OLB	-	-	-	-	2
E.J. Holub, KC	OLB	2	2	2	-	2
Mike Stratton, Buf	OLB	1	1	1	1	1
Willie Brown, Den	CB	-	-	-	2	-
Butch Byrd, Buf	CB	1	1	1	1	1
Speedy Duncan, SD	CB	2	2	2	-	2
Dave Grayson, Oak	CB	2	2	1	1	1
Kent McCloughan, Oak	CB	1	1	2	2	-
Johnny Sample, NY	CB	-	-	-	-	2
Hagood Clarke, Buf	S	2	-	-	-	2
Kenny Graham, SD	S	1	1	2	1	2
Bobby Hunt, KC	S	2	-	2	2	-
Johnny Robinson, KC	S	1	1	1	1	1
George Saimes, Buf	S	-	2	1	2	1
Willie West, Mia	S	-	2	-	-	-

SPECIALISTS		AP	UP	OL	NE	NY
George Blanda, Hou	K	x	x	2	x	x
Gino Cappelletti, Bos	K	x	x	1	x	x
Bob Scarpitto, Den	P	x	x	1	x	x
Jerrell Wilson, KC	P	x	x	2	x	x

1967 ALL-NFL

OFFENSE		ALL-NFL				CONF
		AP	UP	NE	NY	SN
Boyd Dowler, GB	E	-	-	-	-	1
Bob Hayes, Dal	E	2	2	2	1	1
Homer Jones, NYG	E	2	1	1	1	1
Willie Richardson, Bal	E	1	2	2	2	1
Charley Taylor, Was	E	1	1	1	2	-
John Mackey, Bal	TE	1	2	1	1	1
Jackie Smith, StL	TE	-	-	2	-	-
Jerry Smith, Was	TE	2	1	-	2	1
Bob Brown, Phi	T	2	2	-	-	1
Charlie Cowan, LARm	T	-	2	-	2	-
Forrest Gregg, GB	T	1	1	2	1	1
Ernie McMillan, StL	T	2	-	1	2	-
Ralph Neely, Dal	T	1	1	2	1	1
Bob Vogel, Bal	T	-	-	1	-	1
John Gordy, Det	G	2	2	2	2	-
Ken Gray, StL	G	2	2	-	2	1
Gene Hickerson, Cle	G	1	1	1	1	1
Jerry Kramer, GB	G	1	1	2	1	1
Howard Mudd, SF	G	-	-	1	-	1
Bob DeMarco, StL	C	1	2	2	-	1
Mick Tingelhoff, Min	C	2	1	1	1	1
Sonny Jurgensen, Was	QB	2	2	2	2	1
John Unitas, Bal	QB	1	1	1	1	1
Leroy Kelly, Cle	RB	1	1	1	1	1
Dave Osborn, Min	RB	-	2	2	-	1
Don Perkins, Dal	RB	2	-	-	2	-
Johnny Roland, StL	RB	2	2	2	2	1
Gale Sayers, ChiB	RB	1	1	1	1	1

DEFENSE		ALL-NFL				CONF
		AP	UP	NE	NY	SN
George Andrie, Dal	DE	2	-	-	-	1
Ordell Braase, Bal	DE	2	2	2	2	-
Willie Davis, GB	DE	1	1	1	1	1
Carl Eller, Min	DE	-	2	2	-	-
Bill Glass, Cle	DE	-	-	-	-	1
Deacon Jones, LARm	DE	1	1	1	1	1
Lamar Lundy, LARm	DE	-	-	-	2	-
Henry Jordan, GB	DT	-	-	-	2	-
Alex Karras, Det	DT	2	2	2	2	1
Bob Lilly, Dal	DT	1	1	1	1	1
Fred Miller, Bal	DT	-	-	2	-	-
Floyd Peters, Phi	DT	-	-	-	-	1
Merlin Olsen, LARm	DT	1	1	1	1	1
Chuck Walker, StL	DT	2	2	-	-	-
Dick Butkus, ChiB	MLB	-	1	1	-	-
Dale Meinert, StL	MLB	-	-	-	-	1
Ray Nitschke, GB	MLB	2	-	-	2	-
Tommy Nobis, Atl	MLB	1	2	2	1	1
Maxie Baughan, LARm	OLB	2	1	2	1	1
Chuck Howley, Dal	OLB	1	2	2	2	1
Dave Robinson, GB	OLB	1	1	1	1	1
Andy Russell, Pit	OLB	-	-	-	-	1
Dave Wilcox, SF	OLB	2	2	1	2	-
Herb Adderley, GB	CB	2	-	2	2	1
Lem Barney, Det	CB	-	-	2	2	-
Bobby Boyd, Bal	CB	-	2	-	-	1
Cornell Green, Dal	CB	1	1	1	1	1
Bob Jeter, GB	CB	1	1	1	1	-
Dave Whitsell, NO	CB	2	2	-	-	1
Eddie Meador, LARm	S	2	1	1	2	1
Rich Petitbon, ChiB	S	2	2	2	2	-
Mel Renfro, Dal	S	-	-	-	-	1
Larry Wilson, StL	S	1	2	1	1	1
Willie Wood, GB	S	1	1	2	1	1

SPECIALISTS		ALL-NFL				CONF
		AP	UP	NE	NY	SN
Jim Bakken, StL	K	x	x	x	x	1
Don Chandler, GB	K	x	x	x	x	1
Gary Collins, Cle	P	x	x	x	x	1
Pat Studstill, Det	P	x	x	x	x	1

1967 ALL-AFL

OFFENSE		AP	UP	NE	SN	NY
Lance Alworth, SD	E	1	1	1	1	1
Al Denson, Den	E	2	2	1	2	2
Don Maynard, NYJ	E	2	2	2	-	2
George Sauer, NYJ	E	1	1	2	1	1
Otis Taylor, KC	E	-	-	-	2	-
Fred Arbanas, KC	TE	2	2	1	-	1
Billy Cannon, Oak	TE	1	1	-	2	2
Willie Frazier, SD	TE	-	-	2	1	-
Ron Mix, SD	T	1	1	1	2	1
Sherman Plunkett, NYJ	T	-	-	-	-	2
Harry Schuh, Oak	T	2	1	1	2	2
Walter Suggs, Hou	T	2	2	2	1	-
Jim Tyrer, KC	T	1	2	2	1	1
Ed Budde, KC	G	2	-	2	-	2
Wayne Hawkins, Oak	G	2	2	-	2	2
Dave Herman, NYJ	G	-	-	-	-	1
Walt Sweeney, SD	G	1	1	1	2	1
Bob Talamini, Hou	G	1	1	1	1	-
Gene Upshaw, Oak	G	-	2	2	1	-
Bobby Maples, Hou	C	2	2	-	-	2
Jon Morris, Bos	C	-	-	2	2	-
Jim Otto, Oak	C	1	1	1	1	1
Daryle Lamonica, Oak	QB	1	1	2	1	2
Joe Namath, NYJ	QB	2	2	1	2	1
Emerson Boozer, NYJ	RB	-	-	-	2	-
Hewritt Dixon, Oak	RB	2	2	-	1	2
Mike Garrett, KC	RB	1	1	1	1	1
Hoyle Granger, Hou	RB	2	2	2	-	-
Jim Nance, Bos	RB	1	1	1	2	1
Dickie Post, SD	RB	-	-	2	-	2

DEFENSE		AP	UP	NE	SN	NY
Verlon Biggs, NYJ	DE	-	-	2	2	-
Ben Davidson, Oak	DE	1	1	2	1	1
Pat Holmes, Hou	DE	1	1	1	2	2
Jerry Mays, KC	DE	2	-	-	1	2
Ron McDole, Buf	DE	2	2	1	-	-
Gerry Philbin, NYJ	DE	-	2	-	-	1
Houston Antwine, Bos	DT	2	2	-	2	1
Buck Buchanan, KC	DT	1	1	1	1	1
Dave Costa, Den	DT	2	2	2	-	2
Jim Hunt, Bos	DT	-	-	2	2	-
Tom Keating, Oak	DT	1	1	1	1	2
Nick Buoniconti, Bos	MLB	1	1	2	1	1
Dan Conners, Oak	MLB	2	2	1	2	2
Bobby Bell, KC	OLB	1	1	2	1	1
Frank Buncom, SD	OLB	-	2	-	-	-
Larry Grantham, NYJ	OLB	2	-	-	-	2
Bill Laskey, Oak	OLB	-	-	2	-	-
Gus Otto, Oak	OLB	-	2	-	2	-
Mike Stratton, Buf	OLB	2	-	1	2	2
George Webster, Hou	OLB	1	1	1	1	1
Willie Brown, Oak	CB	2	2	-	2	2
Speedy Duncan, SD	CB	2	-	2	2	2
Miller Farr, Hou	CB	1	1	1	1	1
Kent McCloughan, Oak	CB	1	1	1	1	1
Dick Westmoreland, Mia	CB	-	2	2	-	-
Rodger Bird, Oak	S	2	-	-	-	2
Kenny Graham, SD	S	-	2	2	1	-
Jim Norton, Hou	S	2	2	-	-	2
Johnny Robinson, KC	S	1	1	1	2	1
George Saimes, Buf	S	1	1	1	1	1
Jim Warren, Mia	S	-	-	-	2	-
Don Webb, Bos	S	-	-	2	-	-

SPECIALISTS		AP	UP	NE	SN	NY
George Blanda, Oak	K	x	x	x	1	x
Jan Stenerud, KC	K	x	x	x	2	x
Paul Maguire, Buf	P	x	x	x	2	x
Bob Scarpitto, Den	P	x	x	x	1	x

1968 ALL-NFL

OFFENSE		ALL-PRO	ALL-NFL					CONF
		FW	AP	UP	NE	NY	PW	SN
Carroll Dale, GB	E	-	-	-	2	-	-	1
Bob Hayes, Dal	E	-	1	2	-	1	-	1
Roy Jefferson, Pit	E	-	2	2	2	-	-	1t
Homer Jones, NYG	E	-	-	-	-	2	-	1t
Clifton McNeil, SF	E	1	1	1	1	1	1	1
Lance Rentzel, Dal	E	-	-	-	-	-	-	1t
Willie Richardson, Bal	E	2	-	-	-	-	-	-
Charley Taylor, Was	E	-	-	-	-	2	-	-
Paul Warfield, Cle	E	-	2	1	1	-	1	-
John Mackey, Bal	TE	1	1	1	1	1	*1	1
Milt Morin, Cle	TE	-	-	-	-	-	-	1t
Jackie Smith, StL	TE	-	2	2	2	2	-	1t
Bob Brown, Phi	T	2	1	2	1	2	1	1
Charlie Cowan, LARm	T	-	2	-	-	2	-	1
Ernie McMillan, StL	T	-	-	2	2	-	-	-
Ralph Neely, Dal	T	1	1	1	1	1	*1	1
Bob Vogel, Bal	T	1	2	1	2	1	-	1
Pete Case, NYG	G	2	-	-	-	-	-	-
Gale Gillingham, GB	G	-	-	2	2	-	-	-
Ken Gray, StL	G	-	-	-	-	2	-	1
Gene Hickerson, Cle	G	1	1	1	1	1	*1	1
Jerry Kramer, GB	G	-	2	-	-	-	-	-
Tom Mack, LARm	G	-	-	2	2	-	-	-
Howard Mudd, SF	G	-	1	1	1	1	1	1
Glenn Ressler, Bal	G	-	-	-	-	2	-	-
George Seals, ChiB	G	-	2	-	-	-	-	-
Dan Sullivan, Bal	G	-	-	-	-	-	-	1
Bob DeMarco, StL	C	-	2	2	2	2	-	1
Mick Tingelhoff, Min	C	1	1	1	1	1	1	1
Roman Gabriel, LARm	QB	-	-	-	-	2	-	-
Don Meredith, Dal	QB	-	-	-	2	-	-	-
Earl Morrall, Bal	QB	2	1	1	1	1	1	1
Bill Nelsen, Cle	QB	-	2	2	-	-	-	1
Bill Brown, Min	RB	2	2	2	2	2	-	1
Dick Hoak, Pit	RB	-	-	-	-	-	-	1
Leroy Kelly, Cle	RB	1	1	1	1	1	*1	1
Don Perkins, Dal	RB	-	-	-	2	-	-	-
Gale Sayers ChiB	RB	1	1	1	1	1	*1	1
Ken Willard, SF	RB	-	-	2	-	2	-	-
Tom Woodeshick, Phi	RB	-	2	-	-	-	-	-

DEFENSE		ALL-PRO	ALL-NFL					CONF
		FW	AP	UP	NE	NY	PW	SN
George Andrie, Dal	DE	-	-	2	2	-	-	1
Doug Atkins, NO	DE	-	2	-	2	-	-	1
Carl Eller, Min	DE	1	1	1	1	1	1	1
Deacon Jones, LARm	DE	1	1	1	1	1	*1	1
Jim Marshall, Min	DE	-	-	-	-	2	-	-
Bubba Smith, Bal	DE	2	2	2	-	2	-	-
Walter Johnson, Cle	DT	-	-	-	2	-	-	-
Alex Karras, Det	DT	-	-	-	2	2	-	1
Bob Lilly, Dal	DT	1	1	1	1	1	*1	1
Bob Lurtsema, NYG	DT	-	-	-	-	-	-	1
Fred Miller, Bal	DT	2	-	2	-	2	-	-
Merlin Olsen, LARm	DT	1	1	1	1	1	*1	1
Alan Page, Min	DT	-	-	2	-	-	-	-
Jethro Pugh, Dal	DT	-	2	-	-	-	-	-
Billy Ray Smith, Bal	DT	-	2	-	-	-	-	-
Dick Butkus, ChiB	MLB	1	1	1	1	2	*1	-
Lee Roy Jordan, Dal	MLB	-	-	-	-	-	-	1
Tommy Nobis, Atl	MLB	2	2	2	2	1	-	1
Maxie Baughan, LARm	OLB	-	2	-	-	2	-	1
Mike Curtis, Bal	OLB	1	1	1	2	1	*1	-
Chris Hanburger, Was	OLB	-	-	-	-	-	-	1
Chuck Howley, Dal	OLB	2	1	2	1	2	1	1
Dave Robinson, GB	OLB	2	2	1	1	1	-	1
Andy Russell, Pit	OLB	-	-	2	-	-	-	-
Dave Wilcox, SF	OLB	-	-	-	2	-	-	-
Herb Adderley, GB	CB	-	-	-	-	-	-	1t
Kermit Alexander, SF	CB	-	-	2	-	2	-	-
Erich Barnes, Cle	CB	-	-	-	-	-	-	1t
Lem Barney, Det	CB	1	1	1	1	1	*1	1
Bob Boyd, Bal	CB	1	1	1	-	1	1	1t
Ben Davis, Cle	CB	-	2	-	-	-	-	1t
Pat Fischer, Was	CB	-	-	-	-	-	-	1t
Cornell Green, Dal	CB	2	2	2	1	2	-	1
Bob Jeter, GB	CB	-	-	-	2	-	-	-
Jimmy Johnson, SF	CB	-	-	-	2	-	-	-
Paul Krause, Min	S	-	2	-	-	-	-	-
Carl Lockhart, NYG	S	-	-	-	-	-	-	1t
Jerry Logan, Bal	S	2	-	-	-	-	-	-
Eddie Meador, LARm	S	2	1	2	2	2	-	1
Mel Renfro, Dal	S	-	-	-	-	-	-	1t
Rick Volk, Bal	S	1	-	2	1	-	-	-
Larry Wilson, StL	S	1	1	1	1	1	*1	1
Willie Wood, GB	S	-	2	1	2	1	1	1

SPECIALISTS		ALL-PRO	ALL-NFL					CONF
		FW	AP	UP	NE	NY	PW	SN
Jim Bakken, StL	K	-	x	x	x	x	x	1
Mac Percivel, ChiB	K	-	x	x	x	x	x	1
Bill Lothridge, Atl	P	1	x	x	x	x	x	1
Ron Widby, Dal	P	-	x	x	x	x	x	1

*also named to *PFW* all-pro team

1968 ALL-AFL

OFFENSE		ALL-PRO	ALL-NFL					
		FW	AP	UP	NE	NY	SN	PW
Lance Alworth, SD	E	1	1	1	1	1	1	*1
Gary Garrison, SD	E	-	-	-	-	-	2	-
Don Maynard, NYJ	E	-	2	2	-	1	2	-
Karl Noonan, Mia	E	-	2	2	-	2	-	-
George Sauer, NYJ	E	1	1	1	1	2	1	*1
Billy Cannon, Oak	TE	2	-	-	-	-	-	-
Jacque McKinnon, SD	TE	-	-	-	2	-	2	-
Alvin Reed, Hou	TE	-	2	2	-	1	1	-
Jim Whalen, Bos	TE	-	1	1	1	2	-	1
Stew Barber, Buf	T	-	-	-	-	2	-	-
Winston Hill, NYJ	T	-	-	-	-	2	2	-
Ron Mix, SD	T	2	1	1	1	1	1	*1
Harry Schuh, Oak	T	-	2	2	2	1	-	-
Walter Suggs, Hou	T	-	2	2	2	-	1	-
Jim Tyrer, KC	T	-	1	1	1	-	2	1
Ed Budde, KC	G	-	2	2	2	1	2	-
Dave Herman, NYJ	G	-	-	-	1	2	-	-
Billy Shaw, Buf	G	-	2	-	-	-	2	-
Walt Sweeney, SD	G	-	1	1	1	1	1	*1
Gene Upshaw, Oak	G	2	1	1	2	2	1	1
Bob Johnson, Cin	C	-	-	-	2	-	-	-
Jon Morris, Bos	C	-	-	-	-	-	2	-
Jim Otto, Oak	C	-	1	1	1	2	1	*1
John Schmitt, NYJ	C	-	2	2	-	1	-	-
Len Dawson, KC	QB	-	2	2	-	-	-	-
Bob Griese, Mia	QB	-	-	-	2	-	-	-
John Hadl, SD	QB	-	-	-	-	-	2	-
Daryle Lamonica, Oak	QB	-	-	-	-	2	-	-
Joe Namath, NYJ	QB	1	1	1	1	1	1	*1
Hewritt Dixon, Oak	RB	-	1	1	1	1	1	1
Robert Holmes, KC	RB	-	2	2	2	-	2	-
Dickie Post, SD	RB	-	2	2	2	2	2	-
Paul Robinson, Cin	RB	2	1	1	1	1	1	1
Matt Snell, NYJ	RB	-	-	-	-	2	-	-

DEFENSE		ALL-PRO	ALL-AFL					
		FW	AP	UP	NE	NY	SN	PW
Rich Jackson, Den	DE	-	1	1	-	2	2	1
Ike Lassiter, Oak	DE	-	-	2	2	1	-	-
Jerry Mays, KC	DE	-	2	2	2	-	1	-
Ron McDole, Buf	DE	-	2	-	1	2	2	-
Gerry Philbin, NYJ	DE	2	1	1	1	1	1	*1
Houston Antwine, Bos	DT	-	2	2	1	-	1	-
Dan Birdwell, Oak	DT	-	1	1	2	-	1	1
Buck Buchanan, KC	DT	2	1	1	1	1	2	1
Dave Costa, Den	DT	-	-	-	2	-	2	-
John Elliott, NYJ	DT	-	2	2	-	1	-	-
Jim Hunt, Bos	DT	-	-	-	-	2	-	-
Tom Sestak, Buf	DT	-	-	-	-	2	-	-
Al Atkinson, NYJ	MLB	-	-	-	2t	-	-	-
Nick Buoniconti, Bos	MLB	-	-	2	-	-	1	-
Dan Conners, Oak	MLB	-	2	1	2t	1	-	1
Willie Lanier, KC	MLB	-	1	-	1	2	2	-
Bobby Bell, KC	OLB	-	1	1	1	1	1	1
Frank Buncom, Cin	OLB	-	-	2	-	-	-	-
Larry Grantham, NYJ	OLB	-	2	-	-	2	-	-
Jim Lynch, KC	OLB	-	2	2	2	-	-	-
Gus Otto, Oak	OLB	-	-	-	-	-	2	-
Mike Stratton, Buf	OLB	-	-	-	2	2	2	-
George Webster, Hou	OLB	1	1	1	1	1	1	*1
Willie Brown, Oak	CB	2	1	1	1	-	1	1
Butch Byrd, Buf	CB	-	2	-	2	1	-	-
Miller Farr, Hou	CB	-	1	1	1	1	1	*1
Kent McCloughan, Oak	CB	-	-	-	-	2	2	-
Leroy Mitchell, Bos	CB	-	2	2	-	-	-	-
Johnny Sample, NYJ	CB	-	-	2	-	2	-	-
Jim Warren, Mia	CB	-	-	-	2	-	2	-
Kenny Graham, SD	S	-	2	2	2	2	1	-
Dave Grayson, Oak	S	-	1	1	1	2	2	1
Ken Houston, Hou	S	-	-	-	2	-	-	-
Jim Hudson, NYJ	S	-	2	-	-	1	-	-
Johnny Robinson, KC	S	-	1	1	1	1	1	*1
George Saimes, Buf	S	-	-	2	-	1	2	-

SPECIALISTS		ALL-PRO	ALL-AFL					
		FW	AP	UP	NE	NY	SN	PW
Jan Stenerud, KC	K	2	x	x	x	x	1	-
Jim Turner, NYJ	K	1	x	x	x	x	2	1
Curly Johnson, NYJ	P	-	x	x	x	x	2	-
Jerrell Wilson, KC	P	2	x	x	x	x	1	1

*also named to *PFW* all-pro team

1969 ALL-NFL

OFFENSE		ALL-PRO			ALL-NFL					CONF
		HF	FW	NE	AP	UP	NE	PW	NY	SN
Dan Abramowicz, NO	E	-	-	-	1t	2	-	-	2	1
Gary Collins, Cle	E	-	2	-	1	1	-	-	-	-
Roy Jefferson, Pit	E	-	-	-	1t	1	1	-	1	1
Lance Rentzel, Dal	E	-	-	-	2	-	2	-	-	-
Charley Taylor, Was	E	-	-	2	-	-	2	-	-	-
Paul Warfield, Cle	E	1	2	1	-	-	1	1	2	-
Gene Washington, Min	E	-	-	-	2	2	-	1	1	1
Gene Washington, SF	E	-	-	-	-	-	-	-	-	1
Charlie Sanders, Det	TE	2	-	-	2	2	-	-	-	1
Jackie Smith, StL	TE	-	-	2	-	-	2	-	2	-
Jerry Smith, Was	TE	-	1	1	1	1	1	1	1	1
Grady Alderman, Min	T	-	2	-	2	2	2	-	-	1t
Bob Brown, LARm	T	1	1	1	1	1	1	*1	1	1
Charlie Cowan, LARm	T	-	-	-	2	-	-	-	-	-
Ernie McMillan, StL	T	-	-	-	-	-	-	-	2	-
Ralph Neely, Dal	T	2	2	2	1	1	1	1	1	1
Len Rohde, SF	T	-	-	-	-	-	2	-	-	-
Dick Schafrath, Cle	T	-	-	-	-	-	-	-	-	1
Bob Vogel, Bal	T	-	-	-	-	2	-	-	2	1t
Gale Gillingham, GB	G	2	-	2	1	2	1	-	-	1
Ken Gray, StL	G	-	-	-	-	-	-	-	-	1
Gene Hickerson, Cle	G	1	-	-	1	1	2	*1	1	1
Tom Mack, LARm	G	2	2	2	2	1	1	-	2	1
John Niland, Dal	G	1	-	-	1	2	2	1	1	-
George Seals, ChiB	G	-	-	-	-	-	-	-	2	-
Bill Curry, Bal	C	-	-	-	2	2	-	-	-	-
Bob DeMarco, StL	C	-	-	-	-	-	-	-	-	1
Ed Flanagan, Det	C	-	-	-	-	-	2	-	-	-
Ken Inman, LARm	C	-	-	-	-	-	-	-	2	-
Mick Tingelhoff, Min	C	1	1	1	1	1	1	*1	1	1
Roman Gabriel, LARm	QB	1	2	-	1	1	2	1	1	1
Sonny Jurgensen, Was	QB	-	-	2	2	2	1	-	2	1
Calvin Hill, Dal	RB	1	1	2	1	1	2	1	1	1
Leroy Kelly, Cle	RB	2	2	1	2	2	1	-	2	-
Tom Matte, Bal	RB	-	-	-	-	-	2	-	-	1
Gale Sayers, ChiB	B	1	1	1	1	1	1	*1	1	1
Tom Woodeshick, Phi	RB	-	-	-	2	2	-	-	1	

DEFENSE		ALL-PRO			ALL-NFL					CONF
		HF	FW	NE	AP	UP	NE	PW	NY	SN
George Andrie, Dal	DE	-	-	-	-	2	-	-	-	1
Carl Eller, Min	DE	1	1	1	1	1	1	*1	1	1
Jack Gregory, Cle	DE	-	-	-	-	-	-	-	2	-
Claude Humphrey, Atl	DE	-	-	-	2	-	2	-	-	-
Deacon Jones, LARm	DE	1	1	1	1	1	1	*1	1	1
Jim Marshall, Min	DE	-	-	2	2	2	2	-	2	-
Ron Snidow, Cle	DE	-	-	-	-	-	-	-	-	1t
Chuck Walker, StL	DE	-	-	-	-	-	-	-	-	1t
Joe Greene, Pit	DT	-	-	-	-	-	-	-	2	1
Alex Karras, Det	DT	-	-	-	2	2	2	-	-	-
Bob Lilly, Dal	DT	1	1	1	1	2	1	1	1	1
Merlin Olsen, LARm	DT	1	1	1	1	1	1	*1	1	1
Alan Page, Min	DT	2	2	2	2	1	2	-	2	1
Dick Butkus, ChiB	MLB	1	1	1	1	1	1	*1	1	1
Lee Roy Jordan, Dal	MLB	-	-	-	-	-	-	-	2	1
Mike Lucci, Det	MLB	-	-	-	2	2	-	-	-	-
Ray Nitschke, GB	MLB	-	2	2	-	-	-	-	-	-
Maxie Baughan, LARm	OLB	-	-	-	2	-	-	-	2	1
Mike Curtis, Bal	OLB	-	-	-	-	-	2M	-	2	1
Chris Hanburger, Was	OLB	-	-	-	2	2	2	-	-	1
Chuck Howley, Dal	OLB	1	2	1	1	1	1	*1	1	1
Dave Robinson, GB	OLB	2	2	2	1	1	1	1	1	-
Dave Wilcox, SF	OLB	-	-	-	-	2	2	-	-	-
Herb Adderley, GB	CB	2	2	-	1	-	-	1	2	-
Lem Barney, Det	CB	1	1	1	1	1	1	*1	1	1
Bobby Bryant, Min	CB	-	-	2	2	2	2	-	1	-
Pat Fischer, Was	CB	-	-	-	-	-	-	-	-	1
Cornell Green, Dal	CB	-	-	-	2	1	2	-	-	1
Jimmy Johnson, SF	CB	2	2	2	-	2	1	-	2	1
Mike Howell, Cle	S	-	-	-	-	2	-	-	-	-
Karl Kassulke, Min	S	-	-	-	-	2	-	-	-	-
Ernie Kellerman, Cle	S	-	-	-	-	-	-	-	2	-
Paul Krause, Min	S	-	-	-	2	-	-	-	-	-
Eddie Meador, LARm	S	-	2	-	1	1	-	1	1	1
Mel Renfro, Dal	S	2	2	1	2	-	1	*1	2	1
Rick Volk, Bal	S	-	-	-	-	-	2	-	-	-
Larry Wilson, StL	S	1	1	2	1	1	1	-	1	1
Willie Wood, GB	S	-	-	-	-	-	2	-	-	1

SPECIALISTS		ALL-PRO			ALL-NFL					CONF
		HF	FW	NE	AP	UP	NE	PW	NY	SN
Fred Cox, Min	K	-	-	-	x	x	x	1	x	1
Tom Dempsey, NO	K	-	-	-	x	x	x	-	x	1
David Lee, Bal	P	1	1	1	x	x	x	1	x	1
Ron Widby, Dal	P	-	2	-	x	x	x	-	x	1

*also named to *PFW* all-pro team

1969 ALL-AFL

OFFENSE		ALL-PRO			ALL-AFL					
		HF	FW	NE	AP	UP	NE	SN	NY	PW
Lance Alworth, SD	E	2	1	2	2	1	1	1	2	*1
Fred Biletnikoff, Oak	E	2	1	2	1	2	1	1	1	*1
Al Denson, Den	E	-	-	-	-	-	-	2	2	-
Don Maynard, NYJ	E	1	1	-	1	2	2	2	1	-
Warren Wells, Oak	E	-	-	-	2	1	2	-	-	-
Alvin Reed, Hou	TE	-	-	-	2	2	2	1	2	-
Bob Trumpy, Cin	TE	1	2	-	1	1	1	2	1	*1
Dave Hill, KC	T	-	-	-	-	-	-	2	-	-
Winston Hill, NYJ	T	-	-	-	2	2	1	1	1	-
Harry Schuh, Oak	T	2	-	-	1	1	2	2	2	1
Walter Suggs, Hou	T	-	-	-	2	2	2	-	2	-
Jim Tyrer, KC	T	1	1	2	1	1	1	1	1	*1
Sonny Bishop, Hou	G	-	-	-	-	-	-	2	-	-
Ed Budde, KC	G	-	2	1	1	2	1	1	1	1
Dave Herman, NYJ	G	-	-	-	-	2	-	-	2	-
Mo Moorman, KC	G	-	-	-	2	-	-	2	-	-
Billy Shaw, Buf	G	-	-	-	-	-	2	-	-	-
Walt Sweeney, SD	G	-	-	1	2	1	1	-	2	*1
Gene Upshaw, Oak	G	2	1	-	1	1	2	1	1	-
E.J. Holub, KC	C	-	-	-	2t	-	-	-	-	-
Jon Morris, Bos	C	-	-	-	2t	-	2	-	-	-
Jim Otto, Oak	C	2	2	2	1	1	1	1	1	1
John Schmitt, NYJ	C	-	-	-	2t	2	-	2	2	-
Daryle Lamonica, Oak	QB	2	1	-	1	1	2	1	2	1
Joe Namath, NYJ	QB	-	-	1	2	2	1	2	1	-
Carl Garrett, Bos	RB	-	-	-	-	-	2	-	-	-
Mike Garrett, KC	RB	-	-	-	-	-	2	-	-	-
Floyd Little, Den	RB	2	2	-	1	1	1	1	1	1
Jim Nance, Bos	RB	-	-	-	2	2	-	2	2	-
Dickie Post, SD	RB	-	-	-	2	2	-	2	2	-
Matt Snell, NYJ	RB	-	-	2	1	1	1	1	1	*1

DEFENSE		ALL-PRO			ALL-AFL					
		HF	FW	NE	AP	UP	NE	SN	NY	PW
Elvin Bethea, Hou	DE	-	-	-	-	2	-	-	-	-
Aaron Brown, KC	DE	-	-	-	-	-	-	2	2	-
Steve DeLong, SD	DE	-	-	-	-	-	2	-	-	-
Rich Jackson, Den	DE	2	2	2	1	1	1	1	1	1
Ike Lassiter, Oak	DE	-	-	-	2	2	-	-	2	-
Jerry Mays, KC	DE	-	-	-	2	-	-	2	-	-
Ron McDole, Buf	DE	-	-	-	-	-	1	-	-	-
Gerry Philbin, NYJ	DE	2	2	-	1	1	2	1	1	1
Houston Antwine, Bos	DT	-	-	-	2	-	-	1	-	-
Buck Buchanan, KC	DT	2	-	-	1	1	2	1	1	*1
Dave Costa, Den	DT	-	-	-	-	2	-	2	-	-
Jim Dunaway, Buf	DT	-	-	-	-	-	2	-	2	-
John Elliott, NYJ	DT	-	2	-	1	1	1	2	1	1
Tom Keating, Oak	DT	-	-	2	2	2	1	-	2	-
Nick Buoniconti, Mia	MLB	-	-	-	1	1	1	2t	-	-
Dan Conners, Oak	MLB	-	-	-	2	-	-	1	2	-
Willie Lanier, KC	MLB	2	-	-	-	2	2	2t	1	1
Pete Barnes, SD	OLB	-	-	-	2t	-	-	-	-	-
Bobby Bell, KC	OLB	1	1	1	1	1	1	1	1	*1
Larry Grantham, NYJ	OLB	-	-	-	-	2	-	2	2	-
Jim Lynch, KC	OLB	-	-	-	2	2	2	-	-	-
Gus Otto, Oak	OLB	-	-	-	2t	-	-	2	-	-
Mike Stratton, Buf	OLB	-	-	-	-	-	2	-	2	-
George Webster, Hou	OLB	2	1	2	1	1	1	1	1	1
Willie Brown, Oak	CB	1	1	1	1	1	1	1	1	*1
Butch Byrd, Buf	CB	-	-	-	1	1	1	2	1	1
Booker Edgerson, Buf	CB	-	-	-	-	2	-	-	2	-
Miller Farr, Hou	CB	-	-	-	2	2	2	1	2	-
Emmitt Thomas, KC	CB	-	-	-	-	-	-	2	-	-
Bill Thompson, Den	CB	-	-	-	2	-	2	-	-	-
George Atkinson, Oak	S	-	-	-	-	-	2	-	-	-
Kenny Graham, SD	S	-	-	-	2	2	-	2	2	-
Dave Grayson, Oak	S	2	1	1	1	1	1	1	2	*1
Ken Houston, Hou	S	-	-	-	2	2	2	2	1	-
Johnny Robinson, KC	S	1	-	2	1	1	1	1	1	1

SPECIALISTS		ALL-PRO			ALL-AFL					
		HF	FW	NE	AP	UP	NE	SN	NY	PW
Jan Stenerud, KC	K	1	2	1	x	x	x	1	x	1
Jim Turner, NYJ	K	2	1	-	x	x	x	2	x	-
Paul Maguire, Buf	P	2	-	-	x	x	x	-	x	1
Dennis Partee, SD	P	-	-	-	x	x	x	1	x	-
Larry Seiple, Mia	P	-	-	-	x	x	x	2	x	-

*also named to *PFW* all-pro team

1970 ALL-NFL

OFFENSE		ALL-NFL				ALL-CONF			
		AP	FW	NE	PW	AP	UP	SN	PW
Fred Biletnikoff, Oak	WR	-	2	-	-	1	2	-	-
Marlin Briscoe, Buf	WR	-	2	-	-	1	1	1t	1
Gary Garrison, SD	WR	-	-	-	-	-	2	-	-
Dick Gordon, ChiB	WR	1	1	1	1	1	1	1	1
Clifton McNeil, NYG	WR	-	-	-	-	-	2	-	-
Charley Taylor, Was	WR	-	-	-	-	-	2	-	-
Paul Warfield, Mia	WR	-	-	2	-	-	-	1	-
Gene Washington, SF	WR	1	1	1	1	1	1	1	1
Warren Wells, Oak	WR	-	-	2	-	-	1	1t	1
Raymond Chester, Oak	TE	-	-	-	-	-	2	-	-
Alvin Reed, Hou	TE	-	-	-	-	-	1	-	1
Charlie Sanders, Det	TE	1	1	1	1	1	1	1	1
Jackie Smith, StL	TE	-	-	-	-	-	2	-	-
Bob Trumpy, Cin	TE	-	2	2	-	1	-	1	-
Cas Banaszek, SF	T	-	-	-	-	1	2	-	-
Bob Brown, LARm	T	1	1	1	1	1	1	-	1
Rockne Freitas, Det	T	-	-	-	-	-	2	-	1
Winston Hill, NYJ	T	-	2	2	-	1	1	1	-
Ernie McMillan, StL	T	-	-	2	-	-	1	1	-
Harry Schuh, Oak	T	-	-	-	-	-	2	-	1
Jim Tyrer, KC	T	1	1	1	1	1	1	1	1
Bob Vogel, Bal	T	-	-	-	-	-	2	-	-
Ron Yary, Min	T	-	2	-	-	-	-	1	-
Ed Budde, KC	G	-	-	-	-	-	1	1	-
Gale Gillingham, GB	G	1	2	1	-	1	1	1	1
Irv Goode, StL	G	-	-	2	-	-	2	-	-
Gene Hickerson, Cle	G	-	1	-	-	-	1	-	-
Tom Mack, LARm	G	-	2	2	1	-	1	1	1
John Niland, Dal	G	-	-	-	-	1	2	-	-
Walt Sweeney, SD	G	-	-	1	-	1	2	-	1
Gene Upshaw, Oak	G	1	1	-	1	1	2	1	1
Ed Flanagan, Det	C	-	2	-	-	-	1	1	-
Bob Johnson, Cin	C	-	-	-	-	-	2	-	-
Jim Otto, Oak	C	1	-	1	-	1	1	1	1
Mick Tingelhoff, Min	C	-	1	2	1	1	2	-	1
John Brodie, SF	QB	1	1	1	1	1	1	1	1
Bob Griese, Mia	QB	-	-	2	-	-	-	1	-
Daryle Lamonica, Oak	QB	-	-	-	-	1	1	-	1
Fran Tarkenton, NYG	QB	-	2	-	-	-	2	-	-
John Unitas, Bal	QB	-	-	-	-	-	2	-	-
Larry Brown, Was	RB	1	1	1	1	1	1	1	1
Larry Csonka, Mia	RB	-	-	-	-	-	2	-	1
Hewritt Dixon, Oak	RB	-	-	-	-	1	1	-	-
Mel Farr, Det	RB	-	-	2	-	-	2	-	-
Ron Johnson, NYG	RB	1	1	2	1	1	2	-	1
MacArthur Lane, StL	RB	-	2	1	-	-	1	1	-
Floyd Little, Den	RB	-	2	-	-	1	1	1	1
Jess Phillips, Cin	RB	-	-	-	-	-	-	1	-
Ed Podolak, KC	RB	-	-	-	-	-	2	-	-

DEFENSE		ALL-NFL				ALL-CONF			
		AP	FW	NE	PW	AP	UP	SN	PW
Aaron Brown, KC	DE	-	-	-	-	1	-	-	-
Carl Eller, Min	DE	1	1	1	1	1	1	1	1
Jack Gregory, Cle	DE	-	-	-	-	-	2	-	-
Larry Hand, Det	DE	-	-	-	-	-	2	-	-
Claude Humphrey, Atl	DE	-	-	2	-	1	2	-	1
Rich Jackson, Den	DE	1	1	1	-	1	1	1	1
Deacon Jones, LARm	DE	-	2	2	1	-	1	1	1
Jerry Mays, KC	DE	-	-	-	-	-	2	-	-
Bubba Smith, Bal	DE	-	2	-	-	-	1	1	-
Buck Buchanan, KC	DT	-	-	-	-	1	2	-	-
John Elliott, NYJ	DT	-	2	-	-	1	1	-	1
Manny Fernandez, Mia	DT	-	-	2	-	-	-	-	-
Joe Greene, Pit	DT	-	-	-	-	-	1	1	-
Tom Keating, Oak	DT	-	-	-	-	-	2	1	1
Charlie Krueger, SF	DT	-	-	-	-	-	2	-	-
Bob Lilly, Dal	DT	-	2	2	-	-	2	-	-
Merlin Olsen, LARm	DT	1	1	1	1	1	1	1	1
Alan Page, Min	DT	1	1	1	1	1	1	1	1
Dick Butkus, ChiB	MLB	1	1	1	1	1	1	1	1
Mike Curtis, Bal	MLB	-	-	-	-	-	2	-	-
Willie Lanier, KC	MLB	-	2	2	-	1	1	1	1
Mike Lucci, Det	MLB	-	-	-	-	-	2	-	-
Bobby Bell, KC	OLB	1	1	1	1	1	1	1	1
Fred Carr, GB	OLB	-	-	-	-	-	2	-	-
Paul Guidry, Buf	OLB	-	-	-	-	-	2	-	-
Chris Hanburger, Was	OLB	-	-	-	-	-	-	1	-
Chuck Howley, Dal	OLB	1	1	2	1	1	1	1	1
Paul Naumoff, Det	OLB	-	2	-	-	1	-	-	1
Gus Otto, Oak	OLB	-	2	-	-	-	-	-	-
Ron Pritchard, Hou	OLB	-	-	-	-	-	2	-	-
Andy Russell, Pit	OLB	-	-	2	-	1	1	1	1
Larry Silings, StL	OLB	-	-	-	-	-	1	-	-
Dave Wilcox, SF	OLB	-	-	1	-	-	2	-	-
Lem Barney, Det	CB	-	-	2	-	-	2	-	-
Willie Brown, Oak	CB	-	1	2	-	1	1	1	1
Jimmy Johnson, SF	CB	1	1	1	1	1	1	1	1
Dick LeBeau, Det	CB	-	2	-	-	-	-	-	-

DEFENSE		ALL-NFL				ALL-CONF			
		AP	FW	NE	PW	AP	UP	SN	PW
Jim Marsalis, KC	CB	1	2	-	1	1	1	1	1
Kent McCloughan, Oak	CB	-	-	-	-	-	2	-	-
Mel Renfro, Dal	CB	-	-	-	-	1	-	-	-
Bruce Taylor, SF	CB	-	-	-	-	-	2	-	-
Emmitt Thomas, KC	CB	-	-	-	-	-	2	-	-
Roger Wehrli, StL	CB	-	-	1	-	-	1	1	1
Dave Grayson, Oak	S	-	2	-	-	-	2	-	-
Ken Houston, Hou	S	-	-	2	-	-	2	-	1
Paul Krause, Min	S	-	-	-	-	-	1	-	-
Carl Lockhart, NYG	S	-	2	-	-	1	2	-	1
Jerry Logan, Bal	S	-	-	-	-	1	1	-	-
Johnny Robinson, KC	S	1	1	1	1	1	1	1	1
Rick Volk, Bal	S	-	-	-	-	-	-	1	-
Larry Wilson, StL	S	1	1	1	1	1	1	1	1
Willie Wood, GB	S	-	-	2	-	-	2	1	-

SPECIALISTS		ALL-NFL				ALL-CONF			
		AP	FW	NE	PW	AP	UP	SN	PW
George Blanda, Oak	K	-	2	x	x	-	x	-	x
Fred Cox, Min	K	-	-	x	x	1	x	1	x
Jan Stenerud, KC	K	1	1	x	x	1	x	1	x
Julian Fagan, NO	P	-	-	x	x	1	x	1	x
David Lee, Bal	P	-	2	x	x	-	x	1	x
Dave Lewis, Cin	P	1	1	x	x	1	x	-	x

1971 ALL-NFL

OFFENSE		ALL-NFL				ALL-CONF			
		AP	FW	NE	PW	AP	UP	SN	PW
Fred Biletnikoff, Oak	WR	-	2	2	-	-	2	-	-
Garry Garrison, SD	WR	-	-	-	-	-	2	-	-
Dick Gordon, ChiB	WR	-	-	-	-	-	2	-	-
Bob Grim, Min	WR	-	-	-	-	-	1	1	-
Roy Jefferson, Was	WR	-	-	-	-	1	2	-	1
Otis Taylor, KC	WR	1	1	1	1	1	1	1	1
Paul Warfield, Mia	WR	1	1	1	1	1	1	1	1
Gene Washington, SF	WR	-	2	2	-	1	1	1	1
Raymond Chester, Oak	TE	-	-	-	-	-	2	1	1
Ted Kwalick, SF	TE	-	2	2	-	-	2	-	-
Milt Morin, Cle	TE	-	-	-	-	1	1	-	-
Charlie Sanders, Det	TE	1	1	1	1	1	1	1	1
Cas Banaszek, SF	T	-	-	-	-	-	2	-	1
Bob Brown, Oak	T	-	2	1	-	1	2	1	-
Charlie Cowan, LARm	T	-	-	-	-	-	-	1	-
Winston Hill, NYJ	T	-	-	2	-	-	1	-	-
Ernie McMillan, StL	T	-	-	-	-	-	1	-	-
Jim Tyrer, KC	T	-	2	2	1	1	1	1	1
Bob Vogel, Bal	T	-	-	-	-	-	2	-	1
Rayfield Wright, Dal	T	1	1	-	-	1	2	-	-
Ron Yary, Min	T	1	1	1	1	1	1	1	1
Ed Budde, KC	G	-	-	-	-	-	2	-	-
Gale Gillingham, GB	G	-	2	1	-	-	1	1	1
Larry Little, Mia	G	1	1	-	1	1	1	1	1
Tom Mack, LARm	G	-	2	1	-	1	1	-	-
John Niland, Dal	G	1	1	-	1	1	2	1	1
Woody Peoples, SF	G	-	-	-	-	-	2	-	-
Walt Sweeney, SD	G	-	-	2	-	1	1	-	-
Gene Upshaw, Oak	G	-	-	2	-	-	2	1	1
Forrest Blue, SF	C	1	1	-	1	1	1	-	1
Bill Curry, Bal	C	-	2	2	-	1	1	-	1
Bob DeMarco, Mia	C	-	-	-	-	-	2	-	-
Ed Flanagan, Det	C	-	-	-	-	-	-	1t	-
Len Hauss, Was	C	-	-	-	-	-	2	1t	-
Jim Otto, Oak	C	-	-	1	-	-	-	1	-
Len Dawson, KC	QB	-	-	-	-	-	2	-	-
Bob Griese, Mia	QB	1	1	1	1	1	1	1	1
Greg Landry, Det	QB	-	-	-	-	-	1	-	-
Roger Staubach, Dal	QB	-	2	2	-	1	2	1	1
John Brockington, GB	RB	1	1	1	1	1	1	1	1
Larry Brown, Was	RB	-	-	2	-	-	1	1	1
Norm Bulaich, Bal	RB	-	-	-	-	-	2	-	-
Larry Csonka, Mia	RB	1	1	2	-	1	1	1	1
Willie Ellison, LARm	RB	-	-	-	-	-	2	-	-
Leroy Kelly, Cle	RB	-	2	1	-	-	2	-	-
Floyd Little, Den	RB	-	2	-	1	1	1	1	1
Steve Owens, Det	RB	-	-	-	-	1	2	-	-

DEFENSE		ALL-NFL				ALL-CONF			
		AP	FW	NE	PW	AP	UP	SN	PW
Coy Bacon, LARm	DE	-	-	2	-	-	-	-	-
Elvin Bethea, Hou	DE	-	-	-	-	-	2	-	1
Aaron Brown, KC	DE	-	-	-	-	1	2	-	-
Carl Eller, Min	DE	1	1	1	1	1	1	1	1
Cedrick Hardman, SF	DE	-	2	-	-	-	2	-	-
Claude Humphrey, Atl	DE	-	2	1	-	1	1	1	1
Rich Jackson, Den	DE	-	-	-	-	-	-	1	-
Jim Marshall, Min	DE	-	-	-	-	-	2	-	-

DEFENSE		ALL-NFL				ALL-CONF			
		AP	FW	NE	PW	AP	UP	SN	PW
Bubba Smith, Bal	DE	1	1	2	1	1	1	1	1
Bill Stanfill, Mia	DE	-	-	-	-	-	1	-	-
Bob Brown, GB	DT	-	-	-	-	-	2	-	-
Buck Buchanan, KC	DT	-	-	2	-	-	2	-	1
Curley Culp, KC	DT	-	2	-	-	-	-	-	-
Manny Fernandez, Mia	DT	-	-	-	-	-	2	1t	-
Joe Greene, Pit	DT	-	2	2	-	1	1	1	1
Bob Lilly, Dal	DT	1	1	1	1	1	1	1	1
Merlin Olsen, LARm	DT	-	-	-	-	-	2	-	-
Alan Page, Min	DT	1	1	1	1	1	1	1	1
Mike Reid, Cin	DT	-	-	-	-	1	1	1t	-
Dick Butkus, ChiB	MLB	-	2	2	-	1	1	-	1
Mike Curtis, Bal	MLB	-	-	-	-	-	2	-	-
Willie Lanier, KC	MLB	1	1	1	1	1	1	1	1
Mike Lucci, Det	MLB	-	-	-	-	-	2	1	-
Bobby Bell, KC	OLB	-	2	2	1	1	1	1	1
Larry Grantham, NYJ	OLB	-	-	-	-	-	2	-	-
Ted Hendricks, Bal	OLB	1	1	1	1	1	1	1	1
Chuck Howley, Dal	OLB	-	2	-	-	-	2	-	-
Jack Pardee, Was	OLB	-	-	-	-	1	1	-	1
Ron Pritchard, Hou	OLB	-	-	-	-	-	2	-	-
Isiah Robertson, LARm	OLB	-	-	2	-	-	2	1	-
Dave Wilcox, SF	OLB	1	1	1	-	1	1	1	1
Willie Brown, Oak	CB	1	1	2	1	1	1	1	1
Jimmy Johnson, SF	CB	1	1	1	1	1	1	1	1
Dick LeBeau, Det	CB	-	-	-	-	-	2	-	-
Jim Marsalis, KC	CB	-	-	-	-	-	1	1	-
Mel Renfro, Dal	CB	-	2	1	-	1	2	-	-
Earlie Thomas, NYJ	CB	-	-	-	-	-	2	-	-
Emmitt Thomas, KC	CB	-	2	-	-	1	2	-	1
Roger Wehrli, StL	CB	-	-	2	-	-	1	1	1
Bill Bradley, Phi	S	1	1	-	1	1	1	1t	1
Cornell Green, Dal	S	-	-	-	-	1	-	-	-
Ken Houston, Hou	S	-	2	2	1	-	1	1t	1
Paul Krause, Min	S	-	-	1	-	-	1	1	1
Jerry Logan, Bal	S	-	-	-	-	-	2	1t	-
Richie Petitbon, Was	S	-	-	-	-	-	2	-	-
Johnny Robinson, KC	S	-	-	-	-	-	-	1	-
Jake Scott, Mia	S	-	2	2	-	1	1	-	-
Rick Volk, Bal	S	1	1	1	-	1	2	-	1
Larry Wilson, StL	S	-	-	-	-	-	2	-	-
Willie Wood, GB	S	-	-	-	-	-	-	1t	-

SPECIALISTS		ALL-NFL				ALL-CONF			
		AP	FW	NE	PW	AP	UP	SN	PW
Fred Cox, Min	K	-	-	-	x	-	x	-	1
Curt Knight, Was	K	-	-	1	x	1	x	1	-
Jan Stenerud, KC	K	-	1t	-	x	-	x	-	-
Garo Yepremian, Mia	K	1	1t	2	x	1	x	1	1
Dave Lewis, Cin	P	x	2	x	x	x	x	-	-
Tom McNeill, Phi	P	x	-	x	x	x	x	-	1
Ron Widby, Dal	P	x	-	x	x	x	x	1	-
Jerrel Wilson, KC	P	x	1	x	x	x	x	1	1

1972 ALL-NFL

OFFENSE		ALL-NFL				ALL-CONF			
		AP	FW	NE	PW	AP	UP	SN	PW
Fred Biletnikoff, Oak	WR	1	2	1	1	1	1	1	1
Gary Garrison, SD	WR	-	-	-	-	-	2	-	-
John Gilliam, Min	WR	-	-	-	-	-	2	-	-
Harold Jackson, Phi	WR	2	2	2	-	1	1	1	-
Charley Taylor, Was	WR	-	-	-	-	-	2	-	-
Otis Taylor, KC	WR	-	1	-	-	-	1	-	-
Paul Warfield, Mia	WR	2	-	1	-	1	2	1	-
Gene Washington, SF	WR	1	1	2	1	1	1	1	1
Rich Caster, NYJ	TE	-	-	-	-	-	2	-	-
Raymond Chester, Oak	TE	-	-	-	-	1	1	1	-
Ted Kwalick, SF	TE	1	2	1	-	1	1	-	1
Jim Mitchell, Atl	TE	-	-	2	-	-	-	-	-
Bob Tucker, NYG	TE	2	1	-	-	-	2	1	-
Bob Brown, Oak	T	2	1	-	1	1	1	1	1
Rockne Freitas, Det	T	2	-	-	-	-	2	-	-
Winston Hill, NYJ	T	-	2	2	-	1	1	1	-
George Kunz, Atl	T	-	-	1	-	-	2	-	-
Terry Owens, SD	T	-	-	-	-	-	2	-	-
Art Shell, Oak	T	-	-	-	-	-	2	-	-
Rayfield Wright, Dal	T	1	1	1	1	1	1	1	1
Ron Yary, Min	T	1	2	2	-	1	1	1	-
Larry Little, Mia	G	1	1	1	1	1	1	1	1
Tom Mack, LARm	G	2	-	2	-	1	1	1	-
John Niland, Dal	G	1	2	2	1	1	1	1	1
Blaine Nye, Dal	G	-	-	1	-	-	-	-	-
Woody Peoples, SF	G	-	-	-	-	-	2	-	-
Randy Rasmussen, NYJ	G	-	-	-	-	-	2	-	-
Gene Upshaw, Oak	G	2	1	-	-	1	1	-	-
Bruce Van Dyke, Pit	G	-	2	-	-	-	2	1	-
John Wilbur, Was	G	-	-	-	-	-	2	-	-

OFFENSE		ALL-NFL				ALL-CONF			
		AP	FW	NE	PW	AP	UP	SN	PW
Forrest Blue, SF	C	1	1	2	1	1	1	1	1
Len Hauss, Was	C	-	2	1	-	-	2	-	-
Bob Johnson, Cin	C	-	-	-	-	-	1	-	-
Ray Mansfield, Pit	C	-	-	-	-	-	2	-	-
Jim Otto, Oak	C	2	-	-	-	1	-	1	-
Billy Kilmer, Was	QB	-	-	-	-	1	2	-	-
Daryle Lamonica, Oak	QB	-	2	-	-	-	2	-	-
Earl Morrall, Mia	QB	1	-	2	-	1	-	-	-
Joe Namath, NYJ	QB	2	1	1	1	-	1	1	1
Fran Tarkenton, Min	QB	-	-	-	-	-	1	1	-
John Brockington, GB	RB	-	-	2	-	1	1	1	-
Larry Brown, Was	RB	1	1	1	1	1	1	1	1
Larry Csonka, Mia	RB	2	2	-	1	1	1	1t	1
Dave Hampton, Atl	RB	-	-	-	-	-	2	-	-
Franco Harris, Pit	RB	2	-	2	-	-	2	1	-
Ron Johnson, NYG	RB	-	2	-	-	-	2	-	-
Floyd Little, Den	RB	-	-	-	-	-	2	-	-
O.J. Simpson, Buf	RB	1	1	1	-	1	1	1t	-

DEFENSE		ALL-NFL				ALL-CONF			
		AP	FW	NE	PW	AP	UP	SN	PW
Coy Bacon, LARm	DE	-	2	-	-	-	-	-	-
Elvin Bethea, Hou	DE	-	-	-	-	-	2	1	-
Verlon Biggs, Was	DE	-	2	-	-	-	-	-	-
Vern Den Herder, Mia	DE	-	-	-	-	1	-	-	-
Carl Eller, Min	DE	2	-	-	-	-	2	1	-
Jack Gregory, NYG	DE	2	1	1	1	1	1	-	1
Larry Hand, Det	DE	-	-	2	-	-	-	-	-
Claude Humphrey, Atl	DE	1	1	1	1	1	1	1	1
Deacon Jones, SD	DE	-	-	2	-	-	2	-	-
Bill Stanfill, Mia	DE	1	-	-	-	1	1	1	-
Dwight White, Pit	DE	-	-	-	-	-	1	-	-
John Zook, Atl	DE	-	-	-	-	-	2	-	-
Bob Brown, GB	DT	-	-	-	-	-	2	-	-
Manny Fernandez, Mia	DT	-	-	-	-	-	2	-	-
Joe Greene, Pit	DT	1	1	1	1	1	1	1	1
Bob Lilly, Dal	DT	2	2	2	1	1	1	1	1
Merlin Olsen, LARm	DT	-	-	-	-	-	2	-	-
Alan Page, Min	DT	2	2	2	-	1	1	1	-
Mike Reid, Cin	DT	1	1	1	-	1	1	1	-
Paul Smith, Den	DT	-	-	-	-	-	2	-	-
Nick Buoniconti, Mia	MLB	2	2	-	-	1	2	-	-
Dick Butkus, ChiB	MLB	1	1	1	-	1	1	1	-
Jim Carter, GB	MLB	-	-	-	-	-	2	-	-
Willie Lanier, KC	MLB	-	-	2	1	-	1	1	1
Bobby Bell, KC	OLB	-	-	-	-	-	-	1	-
Fred Carr, GB	OLB	-	-	-	-	-	2	-	-
Jack Ham, Pit	OLB	-	2	-	-	-	2	-	-
Chris Hanburger, Was	OLB	1	1	1	1	1	1	1	1
Ted Hendricks, Bal	OLB	2	-	2	-	1	1	-	-
Isiah Robertson, LARm	OLB	-	-	-	-	-	2	-	-
Andy Russell, Pit	OLB	2	2	2	-	1	1	1	-
Phil Villapiano, Oak	OLB	-	-	-	-	-	2	-	-
Dave Wilcox, SF	OLB	1	1	1	1	1	1	1	1
Lem Barney, Det	CB	-	-	-	-	-	1	1	-
Willie Brown, Oak	CB	2	1	1	1	1	1	1	1
Ken Ellis, GB	CB	1	2	-	-	1	1	-	-
Pat Fischer, Was	CB	-	-	2	-	-	-	-	-
Robert James, Buf	CB	-	-	-	-	1	1	-	-
Jimmy Johnson, SF	CB	1	1	1	1	1	2	1	1
Lemar Parrish, Cin	CB	-	-	-	-	-	-	1	-
Mel Renfro, Dal	CB	2	2	2	-	-	2	-	-
Clarence Scott, Cle	CB	-	-	-	-	-	2	-	-
Emmitt Thomas, KC	CB	-	-	-	-	-	2	-	-
Dick Anderson, Mia	S	1	1	1	-	1	1	1	-
Bill Bradley, Phi	S	1	1	1	1	1	1	1	1
Tommy Casanova, Cin	S	-	-	-	-	-	2	-	-
Dave Elmendorf, LARm	S	-	-	-	-	-	2	-	-
Cornell Green, Dal	S	-	-	-	-	-	2	-	-
Ken Houston, Hou	S	-	2	2	-	-	2	-	-
Paul Krause, Min	S	2	-	-	-	1	1	1	-
Jake Scott, Mia	S	2	2	2	1	1	1	1	1

SPECIALISTS		ALL-NFL				ALL-CONF			
		AP	FW	NE	PW	AP	UP	SN	PW
Roy Gerela, Pit	K	2	2	2	-	1	x	1	-
Chester Marcol, GB	K	1	1	1	1	1	x	1	1
Dave Chapple, LARm	P	x	2	-	-	x	x	1	-
Don Cockroft, Cle	P	x	-	1	-	x	x	-	-
Jerrel Wilson, KC	P	x	1	2	1	x	x	1	1

1973 ALL-NFL

OFFENSE		ALL-NFL				ALL-CONF			
		AP	FW	NE	PW	AP	UP	SN	PW
Fred Biletnikoff, Oak	WR	-	-	-	-	1	2	1	1
Harold Carmichael, Phi	WR	2	1	2	1	1	2	-	1
Issac Curtis, Cin	WR	-	-	-	-	-	2	-	-
John Gilliam, Min	WR	2	2	1	-	-	1	1	-
Harold Jackson, LARm	WR	1	1	1	1	1	1	1	1
Ron Shanklin, Pit	WR	-	-	-	-	-	1	-	-
Charley Taylor, Was	WR	-	-	-	-	-	2	-	-
Paul Warfield, Mia	WR	1	2	2	-	1	1	1	1
Ted Kwalick, SF	TE	-	-	-	-	-	1	1	-
Milt Morin, Cle	TE	-	-	-	-	-	2	-	-
Riley Odoms, Den	TE	2	2	1	-	1	1	1	1
Charle Young, Phi	TE	1	1	2	1	1	2	-	1
Charlie Cowan, LARm	T	2	2	-	-	-	2	-	2
Norm Evans, Mia	T	-	-	-	-	1	2	-	-
Winston Hill, NYJ	T	-	-	-	-	-	1	1	1
George Kunz, Atl	T	2	2	1	1	-	2	-	1
Art Shell, Oak	T	-	-	1	-	1	1	-	1
Russ Washington, SD	T	-	-	-	-	-	2	1	-
Rayfield Wright, Min	T	1	1	2	-	1	1	1	-
Ron Yary, Min	T	1	1	2	1	1	1	1	1
Gale Gillingham, GB	G	-	2	-	-	-	2	-	1
Larry Little, Mia	G	1	1	1	1	1	1	1	1
Tom Mack, LARm	G	2	2	-	1	1	1	1	1
Reggie McKenzie, Buf	G	1	1	2	-	1	1	1	-
John Niland, Dal	G	-	-	-	-	1	1	1	-
Joe Scibelli, LARm	G	-	-	1	-	-	2	-	-
Gene Upshaw, Oak	G	2	-	2	-	-	2	-	1
Bruce Van Dyke, Pit	G	-	-	-	-	-	2	-	-
Forrest Blue, SF	C	2	1	-	1	1	1	1	1
Len Hauss, Was	C	-	2	-	-	-	2	-	-
Bob Johnson, Cin	C	-	-	1	-	-	-	-	-
Jim Langer, Mia	C	1	-	-	-	-	1	1	1
Jack Rudnay, KC	C	-	-	2	-	1	2	-	-
Bob Griese, Mia	QB	-	-	-	-	-	2	1	-
John Hadl, LARm	QB	1	1	2	1	1	1	1	1
Charley Johnson, Den	QB	-	-	-	-	-	1	-	1
Ken Stabler, Oak	QB	-	-	-	-	1	h	-	-
Fran Tarkenton, Min	QB	2	2	1	-	-	2	-	-
John Brockington, GB	RB	2	2	1	-	1	1	1	1
Larry Csonka, Mia	RB	1	2	2	1	1	1	1	1
Dave Hampton, Atl	RB	-	-	-	-	-	2	-	-
Calvin Hill, Dal	RB	2	1	-	-	1	1	1	1
Floyd Little, Den	RB	-	-	-	-	-	2	-	-
Law. McCutcheon, LARm	RB	-	-	2	-	-	2	-	2
Mercury Morris, Mia	RB	-	-	-	-	-	2	-	-
O.J. Simpson, Buf	RB	1	1	1	1	1	1	1	1

DEFENSE		ALL-NFL				ALL-CONF			
		AP	FW	NE	PW	AP	UP	SN	PW
Elvin Bethea, Hou	DE	-	-	2	-	-	2	-	-
Fred Dryer, LARm	DE	-	-	-	-	-	-	-	2
Carl Eller, Min	DE	1	2	-	1	1	1	1	1
L.C. Greenwood, Pit	DE	-	-	-	-	-	2	-	1
Claude Humphrey, Atl	DE	1	1	-	1	1	1	1	1
Bill Stanfill, Mia	DE	2	1	1	-	1	1	1	1
Dwight White, Pit	DE	-	-	-	-	1	1	1	-
Jack Youngblood, LARm	DE	2	2	-	-	-	2	-	2
John Zook, Atl	DE	-	-	2	-	-	2	-	-
Manny Fernandez, Mia	DT	-	-	2	-	-	2	-	-
Joe Greene, Pit	DT	1	1	1	1	1	1	1	1
Bob Lilly, Dal	DT	-	-	-	-	-	2	-	-
Merlin Olsen, LARm	DT	2	-	-	-	1	1	1	1
Alan Page, Min	DT	1	1	1E	1	1	1	1	1
Mike Reid, Cin	DT	2	2	1	-	1	1	1	-
Paul Smith, Den	DT	-	2	2	-	-	2	-	1
Diron Talbert, Was	DT	-	-	-	-	-	2	-	-
Nick Buoniconti, Mia	MLB	-	-	-	-	-	2	-	-
Lee Roy Jordan, Dal	MLB	2	1	1	1	1	1	1	1
Willie Lanier, KC	MLB	1	2	1	-	1	1	1	1
Jeff Siemon, Min	MLB	-	-	-	-	-	2	-	-
Jack Ham, Pit	OLB	2	2	2	-	1	1	1	1
Chris Hanburger, Was	OLB	1	2	1	1	1	1	1	1
Ted Hendricks, Bal	OLB	-	-	2	-	1	2	-	-
Wally Hilgenberg, Min	OLB	-	-	-	-	-	2	-	-
Isiah Robertson, LARm	OLB	1	1	-	-	1	2	-	2
Andy Russell, Pit	OLB	-	-	-	-	-	1	1	1
Phil Villapiano, Oak	OLB	-	-	-	-	-	2	-	-
Dave Wilcox, SF	OLB	2	1	1	1	-	1	1	1
Lem Barney, Det	CB	2	2	2	-	-	2	-	-
Willie Brown, Oak	CB	1	1	1	1	1	2	1	1
Bobby Bryant, Min	CB	-	-	-	-	-	2	-	1
Ken Ellis, GB	CB	-	2	-	-	1	1	1	1
Robert James, Buf	CB	1	-	-	-	1	1	1	-
Lemar Parrish, Cin	CB	-	-	-	-	-	2	-	-
Mel Renfro, Dal	CB	2	1	1	1	1	1	1	1
Clarence Scott, Cle	CB	-	-	2	-	-	1	-	-
Dick Anderson, Mia	S	1	1	1	1	1	1	1	1

DEFENSE		ALL-NFL				ALL-CONF			
		AP	FW	NE	PW	AP	UP	SN	PW
Bill Bradley, Phi	S	2	2	1	-	-	2	-	-
Glen Edwards, Pit	S	-	-	-	-	-	2	-	-
Ken Houston, Was	S	2	2	2	-	1	1	1	1
Paul Krause, Min	S	-	-	-	-	1	1	1	1
Brig Owens, Was	S	-	-	-	-	-	2	-	-
Jake Scott, Mia	S	1	1	2	-	1	1	1	-
Jack Tatum, Oak	S	-	-	-	-	-	-	-	1
Mike Wagner, Pit	S	-	-	-	1	-	2	-	1

SPECIALISTS		ALL-NFL				ALL-CONF			
		AP	FW	NE	PW	AP	UP	SN	PW
George Blanda, Oak	K	-	-	-	-	-	x	1t	-
Roy Gerela, Pit	K	2	2	2	-	-	x	-	-
Bruce Gossett, SF	K	-	-	-	-	-	x	1t	1
Nick Mike-Mayer, Atl	K	-	-	-	-	1	x	1t	-
Garo Yepremian, Mia	K	1	1	1	1	1	x	1t	1
Ray Guy, Oak	P	x	1	1	1	x	x	1	1
Jerrel Wilson, KC	P	x	2	2	-	x	x	-	-
Tom Wittum, SF	P	x	-	-	-	x	x	1	1

1974 ALL-NFL

OFFENSE		ALL-NFL				ALL-CONF			
		AP	FW	NE	PW	AP	UP	SN	PW
Fred Biletnikoff, Oak	WR	-	2	-	-	-	-	-	-
Cliff Branch, Oak	WR	1	1	1	1	1	1	1	1
Harold Carmichael, Phi	WR	-	-	-	-	-	2	-	-
Issac Curtis, Cin	WR	2	2	2	-	1	1	1	-
Mel Gray, StL	WR	-	-	1	-	-	2	-	1
Drew Pearson, Dal	WR	1	1	2	1	1	1	1	1
Ahmad Rashad, Buf	WR	-	-	-	-	-	2	-	-
Charley Taylor, Was	WR	2	-	-	-	1	1	1	-
Paul Warfield, Mia	WR	-	-	-	-	-	2	-	1
Rich Caster, NYJ	TE	-	-	-	-	-	2	-	-
Riley Odoms, Den	TE	1	1	1	1	1	1	1	1
Charlie Sanders, Det	TE	-	-	-	-	-	2	-	-
Charle Young, Phi	TE	2	2	2	-	1	1	1	1
Dan Dierdorf, StL	T	2	2	2	-	-	2	-	-
Norm Evans, Mia	T	-	-	-	-	-	-	1t	-
Winston Hill, NYJ	T	-	-	-	-	-	1	-	1
Jon Kolb, Pit	T	-	-	-	-	-	2	-	-
George Kunz, Atl	T	-	-	-	-	-	2	-	-
Art Shell, Oak	T	1	1	1	1	1	1	1	1
Russ Washington, SD	T	-	-	2	-	1	2	1t	-
Rayfield Wright, Dal	T	2	2	-	-	1	1	1	1
Ron Yary, Min	T	1	1	1	1	1	1	1	1
Joe DeLamiellure, Buf	G	-	-	2	-	-	-	-	-
Gale Gillingham, GB	G	-	-	1	-	1	1	1	-
John Hannah, NE	G	-	-	-	-	-	-	1t	-
Bob Kuechenberg, Mia	G	-	-	-	-	-	2	-	1
Larry Little, Mia	G	1	1	-	-	1	1	1t	-
Tom Mack, LARm	G	2	1	-	1	1	1	1	1
Reggie McKenzie, Buf	G	2	2	-	-	-	1	1	-
John Niland, Dal	G	-	-	-	-	-	2	-	1
Gene Upshaw, Oak	G	1	2	2	1	1	2	-	1
Ed White, Min	G	-	-	1	-	-	2	-	-
Forrest Blue, SF	C	-	-	-	-	-	-	1t	1
Len Hauss, Was	C	2	-	-	-	1	2	1t	-
Bob Johnson, Cin	C	-	-	-	-	-	2	-	-
Jim Langer, Mia	C	1	1	1	-	1	1	1	1
Bobby Maples, Den	C	-	2	-	-	-	-	-	-
Jack Rudnay, KC	C	-	-	2	-	-	-	-	-
Ken Anderson, Cin	QB	-	-	2	-	-	2	-	-
Jim Hart, StL	QB	2	2	-	-	1	1	1	1
Ken Stabler, Oak	QB	1	1	1	1	1	1	1	1
Fran Tarkenton, Min	QB	-	-	-	-	-	2	-	-
Otis Armstrong, Den	RB	1	1	2	1	1	1	1	1
Sam Cunningham, NE	RB	-	-	-	-	-	2	-	-
Chuck Foreman, Min	RB	2	2	2	-	1	1	1	1
Franco Harris, Pit	RB	-	-	-	-	-	2	-	-
Calvin Hill, Dal	RB	-	-	-	-	-	2	-	-
Law. McCutcheon, LARm	RB	2	2	1	-	1	1	1	1
Terry Metcalf, StL	RB	-	-	-	-	-	2	-	-
O.J. Simpson, Buf	RB	1	1	1	1	1	1	1	1

DEFENSE		ALL-NFL				ALL-CONF			
		AP	FW	NE	PW	AP	UP	SN	PW
Elvin Bethea, Hou	DE	-	-	-	-	-	2	-	1
Fred Dryer, LARm	DE	2	-	1	-	-	2	-	-
Carl Eller, Min	DE	-	-	-	-	-	2	-	-
L.C. Greenwood, Pit	DE	1	1	2	1	1	1	1	1
Claude Humphrey, Atl	DE	2	2	1	1	1	1	1	1
Bill Stanfill, Mia	DE	-	2	2	-	1	1	1	-
Dwight White, Pit	DE	-	-	-	-	-	2	-	-
Jack Youngblood, LARm	DE	1	1	-	-	1	1	1	1
Larry Brooks, LARm	DT	-	-	2	-	-	-	-	1
Wally Chambers, ChiB	DT	2	-	-	-	1	2	1	-
Joe Greene, Pit	DT	1	1	1	1	1	1	1	1
Ernie Holmes, Pit	DT	-	-	2	-	-	-	-	-
John Mendenhall, NYG	DT	-	2	-	-	-	1	-	-
Merlin Olsen, LARm	DT	-	2	-	-	-	2	-	-
Alan Page, Min	DT	1	1	1	1	1	1	1	1
Mike Reid, Cin	DT	-	-	-	-	-	2	-	1
Otis Sistrunk, Oak	DT	2	-	-	-	1	1	-	-
Art Thoms, Oak	DT	-	-	-	-	-	2	1	-
Bill Bergey, Phi	MLB	1	1	2	1	1	1	1	1
Mike Curtis, Bal	MLB	-	-	-	-	-	2	-	-
Willie Lanier, KC	MLB	2	2	1	-	1	1	1	1
Jeff Siemon, Min	MLB	-	-	-	-	-	2	-	-
Fred Carr, GB	OLB	-	-	-	-	-	2	-	-
Jack Ham, Pit	OLB	1	1	1	1	1	1	1	1
Chris Hanburger, Was	OLB	2	2	2	-	1	1	1	1
Ted Hendricks, GB	OLB	1	1	1	1	1	1	1	1
Isiah Robertson, LARm	OLB	2	2	2	-	-	2	-	-
Andy Russell, Pit	OLB	-	-	-	-	-	2	-	1
Phil Villapiano, Oak	OLB	-	-	-	-	1	1	1	-
Dave Washington, Buf	OLB	-	-	-	-	-	2	-	-
Mike Bass, Was	CB	2	-	-	-	1	1	1	-
Willie Brown, Oak	CB	-	-	-	-	-	2	-	-
Ken Ellis, GB	CB	-	-	-	-	-	2	-	-
Robert James, Buf	CB	1	1	1	-	1	1	1	1
Jimmy Johnson, SF	CB	-	-	-	-	-	2	-	-
Lemar Parrish, Cin	CB	-	2	2	-	-	2	-	-
Emmitt Thomas, KC	CB	1	1	2	-	1	1	1	1
Roger Wehrli, StL	CB	2	2	1	-	1	1	1	1
Nate Wright, Min	CB	-	-	-	-	-	-	-	1
Dick Anderson, Mia	S	2	2	1	-	-	2	1	-
Bill Bradley, Phi	S	-	-	-	-	-	2	-	-
Ray Brown, Atl	S	-	-	-	-	-	2	-	-
Dave Elmendorf, LARm	S	-	-	-	-	1	-	-	-
Tony Greene, Buf	S	1	1	1	1	1	1	1	1
Cliff Harris, Dal	S	-	-	2	-	-	1	1	1
Ken Houston, Was	S	-	1	2	-	1	1	1	1
Jake Scott, Mia	S	1	2	-	1	1	2	-	1
Jack Tatum, Oak	S	2	-	-	-	-	1	-	-

SPECIALISTS		ALL-NFL				ALL-CONF			
		AP	FW	NE	PW	AP	UP	SN	PW
Jim Bakken, StL	K	-	-	-	-	x	2	-	-
Roy Gerela, Pit	K	2	2	2	-	x	1	1	-
John Leypoldt, Buf	K	-	-	-	-	x	2	-	1
Chester Marcol, GB	K	1	1	-	1	x	1	1	1
Jan Stenerud, KC	K	-	-	1	-	x	-	-	-
Ray Guy, Oak	P	x	1	1	1	x	1	1	1
Billy Van Heusen, Den	P	x	2	-	-	x	-	-	-
Jerrel Wilson, KC	P	x	-	2	-	x	2	-	-
Tom Wittum, SF	P	x	-	-	-	x	1	1	1

1975 ALL-NFL

OFFENSE		ALL-NFL				ALL-CONF			
		AP	FW	NE	PW	AP	UP	SN	PW
Cliff Branch, Oak	WR	1	2	1	-	1	1	-	-
Bob Chandler, Buf	WR	-	-	-	-	-	2	-	-
Isaac Curtis, Cin	WR	2	2	1	1	-	2	1	1
John Gilliam, Min	WR	-	-	-	-	-	2	1	1
Mel Gray, StL	WR	1	1	2	1	1	1	1	1
Ken Payne, GB	WR	-	-	-	-	-	2	-	-
Drew Pearson, Dal	WR	-	-	-	-	-	-	-	1
Lynn Swann, Pit	WR	2	1	2	-	1	1	1	1
Charley Taylor, Was	WR	-	-	-	-	1	1	-	-
Rich Caster, NYJ	TE	-	2	-	-	-	1	-	1
Riley Odoms, Den	TE	1	-	2	-	1	2	1	-
Charlie Sanders, Den	TE	-	-	-	-	-	2	-	-
Charle Young, Phi	TE	2	1	1	1	1	1	1	1
Dan Dierdorf, StL	T	2	1	2	-	1	1	-	1
Vern Holland, Cin	T	-	-	-	-	-	2	-	-
Jon Kolb, Pit	T	-	-	-	-	-	2	-	1
George Kunz, Bal	T	1	2	-	1	1	1	1	1
Ralph Neely, Dal	T	-	-	-	-	-	2	-	-
Art Shell, Oak	T	2	2	2	-	1	1	1	-
Rayfield Wright, Dal	T	-	-	1	-	-	2	1	-
Ron Yary, Min	T	1	1	1	1	1	1	1	1
Joe DeLamielleure, Buf	G	1	1	-	1	1	1	1	1
Conrad Dobler, StL	G	-	-	-	-	-	2	-	1
Bob Keuchenberg, Mia	G	-	2	1	-	-	2	1	-
Larry Little, Mia	G	1	1	2	1	1	1	-	1
Tom Mack, LARm	G	-	2	2	-	1	1	1	1
Reggie McKenzie, Buf	G	2	-	-	-	-	2	-	-
Blaine Nye, Dal	G	-	-	-	-	-	2	-	-
Gene Upshaw, Oak	G	2	-	-	-	-	-	-	-
Ed White, Min	G	-	-	1	-	1	1	1	1
Tom Banks, StL	C	-	-	-	-	-	-	-	1
Len Hauss, Was	C	2	-	-	-	1	1	1	-
Bob Johnson, Cin	C	-	2	-	-	-	-	-	-

OFFENSE		ALL-NFL				ALL-CONF			
		AP	FW	NE	PW	AP	UP	SN	PW
Jim Langer, Mia	C	1	1	1	1	1	1	1	1
Ray Mansfield, Pit	C	-	-	-	-	-	2	-	-
Jack Rudnay, KC	C	-	-	2	-	-	-	-	-
Jeff Van Note, Atl	C	-	-	-	-	-	2	-	-
Ken Anderson, Cin	QB	2	2	2	-	1	1	1	1
Terry Bradshaw, Pit	QB	-	-	-	-	-	2	-	-
Billy Kilmer, Was	QB	-	-	-	-	-	2	-	-
Fran Tarkenton, Min	QB	1	1	1	1	1	1	1	1
Chuck Foreman, Min	RB	1	1	1	1	1	1	1	1
Dave Hampton, Atl	RB	-	-	-	-	-	2	-	-
Franco Harris, Pit	RB	2	2	2	2	1	1	1	1
Law. McCutcheon, LARm	RB	-	-	-	-	-	2	-	-
Terry Metcalf, StL	RB	2	2	2	2	1	1	1	1
Lydell Mitchell, Bal	RB	-	-	-	-	-	2	-	-
John Riggins, NYJ	RB	-	-	-	-	-	2	-	-
O.J. Simpson, Buf	RB	1	1	1	1	1	1	1	1

DEFENSE		ALL-NFL				ALL-CONF			
		AP	FW	NE	PW	AP	UP	SN	PW
Elvin Bethea, Hou	DE	2	-	2	-	-	-	-	-
Fred Dryer, LARm	DE	-	-	-	-	-	2	-	1
John Dutton, Bal	DE	2	2	-	-	1	1	1	-
Carl Eller, Min	DE	-	-	-	-	1	1	-	-
L.C. Greenwood, Pit	DE	1	1	1	1	1	1	1	1
Cedrick Hardman, SF	DE	-	-	2	-	-	2	1	-
Dwight White, Pit	DE	-	2	-	-	-	-	-	1
Jack Youngblood, LARm	DE	1	1	1	1	1	1	1	1
Wally Chambers, ChiB	DT	2	2	1	-	1	1	1	1
Curley Culp, KC-Hou	DT	1	1	1	1	1	1	1	1
Joe Greene, Pit	DT	2	2	2	-	1	1	-	1
Ernie Holmes, Pit	DT	-	-	-	-	-	2	-	-
Merlin Olsen, LARm	DT	-	-	-	-	-	2	-	-
Herb Orvis, Det	DT	-	-	-	-	-	2	-	-
Alan Page, Min	DT	1	1	2	1	1	1	1	1
Jerry Sherk, Cle	DT	-	-	-	-	-	2	1	-
Otis Sistrunk, Oak	DT	-	-	-	-	-	-	-	1
Bill Bergey, Phi	MLB	1	-	2	-	1	1	-	-
Lee Roy Jordan, Dal	MLB	-	-	-	-	-	-	1	1
Jack Lambert, Pit	MLB	2	1	-	1	1	1	1	1
Willie Lanier, KC	MLB	-	2	1	-	-	2	-	-
Jeff Siemon, Min	MLB	-	-	-	-	-	2	-	-
Robert Brazile, Hou	OLB	-	-	-	-	-	2	-	-
Fred Carr, GB	OLB	-	-	2	-	-	2	1	-
Jack Ham, Pit	OLB	1	1	1	1	1	1	1	1
Chris Hanburger, Was	OLB	1	2	2	-	1	1	1	1
Tom MacLeod, Bal	OLB	-	-	-	-	-	-	1	-
Paul Naumoff, Det	OLB	-	-	-	-	-	2	-	-
Isiah Robertson, LARm	OLB	2	2	1	1t	1	1	-	1
Andy Russell, Pit	OLB	-	1	-	-	-	1	-	-
Phil Villapiano, Oak	OLB	2	-	-	1t	1	2	-	1
Lem Barney, Det	CB	-	-	-	-	-	2	-	1
Mel Blount, Pit	CB	1	1	1	1	1	1	1	1
Bobby Bryant, Min	CB	-	2	-	-	-	2	-	-
Pat Fischer, Was	CB	-	-	-	-	1	-	-	-
Rolland Lawrence, Atl	CB	-	-	-	-	-	1	1	-
Lemar Parrish, Cin	CB	-	-	2	-	-	2	-	-
Ken Riley, Cin	CB	2	2	-	-	1	2	1	-
Emmitt Thomas, KC	CB	2	-	1	-	-	1	-	1
Roger Wehrli, StL	CB	1	1	2	1	1	1	1	1
Tom Casanova, Cin	S	-	-	-	-	1	2	-	-
Glen Edwards, Pit	S	-	-	-	-	-	2	-	-
Dave Elmendorf, LARm	S	2	-	2	-	1	2	-	-
Cliff Harris, Dal	S	-	2	1	-	-	2	-	-
Ken Houston, Was	S	1	1	1	1	1	1	1	1
Paul Krause, Min	S	1	1	2	1	1	1	1	1
Jake Scott, Mia	S	2	2	-	-	-	1	1	-
Jack Tatum, Oak	S	-	-	-	-	-	1	1	1
Mike Wagner, Pit	S	-	-	-	-	-	-	-	1

SPECIALISTS		ALL-NFL				ALL-CONF			
		AP	FW	NE	PW	AP	UP	SN	PW
Jim Bakken, StL	K	1	1	1	1	1	1	1	1
Toni Fritsch, Dal	K	-	-	-	-	-	2	-	-
Roy Gerela, Pit	K	-	-	-	-	-	2	-	-
Jan Stenurud, KC	K	2	2	2	-	1	1	1	1
Neal Clabo, Min	P	x	2	-	-	x	-	-	-
Ray Guy, Oak	P	x	1	1	1	x	1	1	1
John James, Atl	P	x	-	-	-	x	1	1	1
Bobby Walden, Pit	P	x	-	-	-	x	2	-	-
Herman Weaver, Det	P	x	-	-	-	x	2	-	-
Jerrel Wilson, KC	P	x	-	2	-	x	-	-	-
Billy Johnson, Hou	KR	x	x	x	1	x	x	x	1
Terry Metcalf, StL	KR	x	x	x	-	x	x	x	1

1976 ALL-NFL

OFFENSE		ALL-NFL				ALL-CONF			
		AP	FW	NE	PW	AP	UP	SN	PW
Cliff Branch, Oak	WR	1	1	1	1	1	1	1	1
Roger Carr, Bal	WR	2	2	2	-	1	2	1	1
Isaac Curtis, Cin	WR	2	2	1	-	-	1	1	-
Frank Grant, Was	WR	-	-	-	-	-	2	-	-
Mel Gray, StL	WR	-	-	-	-	1	-	-	-
Harold Jackson, LARm	WR	-	-	-	-	-	2	-	-
Charle Joiner, SD	WR	-	-	2	-	-	2	-	-
Drew Pearson, Dal	WR	1	1	-	1	1	1	1	1
Sammy White, Min	WR	-	-	-	-	-	1	-	1
Dave Casper, Oak	TE	1	1	1	1	1	1	1	1
Billy Joe DuPree, Dal	TE	-	-	-	-	1	1	-	1
Russ Francis, NE	TE	2	2	2	-	-	2	1	-
Riley Odoms, Den	TE	-	-	-	-	-	2	-	-
Charlie Sanders, Det	TE	-	-	-	-	-	2	-	-
Lionel Antoine, ChiB	T	-	-	-	-	-	2	-	-
Dan Dierdorf, StL	T	1	1	1	1	1	1	1	1
Leon Gray, NE	T	-	-	-	-	-	2	-	-
Jon Kolb, Pit	T	-	-	-	-	-	2	-	-
George Kunz, Bal	T	2	2	2	-	1	1	1	1
Art Shell, Oak	T	-	-	-	1	1	1	1	1
Rayfield Wright, Dal	T	2	2	2	-	-	2	-	-
Ron Yary, Min	T	1	1	1	-	1	1	1	1
Joe DeLamielluere, Buf	G	1	1	1	1	1	1	1	1
Conrad Dobler, StL	G	2	-	1	-	1	1	1	1
John Hannah, NE	G	1	1	2	1	1	1	1	1
Tom Mack, LARm	G	-	-	-	-	-	2	-	-
Reggie McKenzie, Buf	G	-	-	-	-	-	2	-	-
Blaine Nye, Dal	G	-	-	-	-	1	2	-	1
Gene Upshaw, Oak	G	2	2	2	-	-	2	-	-
Ed White, Min	G	-	2	-	-	-	1	1	-
Tom Banks, StL	C	1	2	2	-	1	1	1	1
Len Hauss, Was	C	-	-	-	-	-	2	-	-
Bob Johnson, Cin	C	-	-	-	-	-	2	-	-
Jim Langer, Mia	C	2	1	1	1	1	1	1	1
Bert Jones, Bal	QB	1	1	1	-	1	1	-	-
Ken Stabler, Oak	QB	2	2	2	1	-	2	1	1
Roger Staubach, Dal	QB	-	-	-	-	1	2	1	-
Fran Tarkenton, Min	QB	-	-	-	-	-	1	-	1
Chuck Foreman, Min	RB	2	2	1	-	1	1	1	1
Franco Harris, Pit	RB	-	2	2	-	-	2	-	1
Law. McCutcheon, LARm	RB	-	-	-	-	-	2	-	-
Lydell Mitchell, Bal	RB	2	-	-	-	1	1	1	-
Walter Payton, ChiB	RB	1	1	2	1	1	1	1	1
Greg Pruitt, Cle	RB	-	-	-	-	-	2	-	-
O.J. Simpson, Buf	RB	1	1	1	1	1	1	1	1
Mike Thomas, Was	RB	-	-	-	-	-	2	-	-

DEFENSE		ALL-NFL				ALL-CONF			
		AP	FW	NE	PW	AP	UP	SN	PW
Coy Bacon, Cin	DE	-	2	2	-	1	1	1	1
Fred Cook, Bal	DE	-	-	-	-	-	2	-	-
John Dutton, Bal	DE	1	2	-	-	1	1	1	1
L.C. Greenwood, Pit	DE	-	-	-	-	-	2	-	-
Tommy Hart, SF	DE	2	1	1	1	1	1	1	1
Claude Humphrey, Atl	DE	-	-	2	-	-	2	-	-
Harvey Martin, Dal	DE	2	-	-	-	-	2	-	-
Jack Youngblood, LARm	DE	1	1	1	1	1	1	1	1
Larry Brooks, LARm	DT	-	-	-	-	-	2	-	-
Wally Chambers, ChiB	DT	1	1	1	1	1	1	1	1
Curley Culp, Hou	DT	-	-	-	-	-	2	1	1t
Joe Ehrmann, Bal	DT	-	2	-	-	-	1	-	-
Cleveland Elam, SF	DT	-	-	2	-	-	2	-	-
Joe Greene, Pit	DT	2	-	-	-	1	2	-	1t
Alan Page, Min	DT	2	2	2	-	1	1	1	1
Jerry Sherk, Cle	DT	1	1	1	1	1	1	1	1
Bill Bergey, Phi	MLB	2	2	2	-	1	1	1	1
Randy Gradishar, Den	MLB	-	-	-	-	-	2	-	-
Jack Lambert, Pit	MLB	1	1	1	1	1	1	1	1
Jeff Siemon, Min	MLB	-	-	-	-	-	2	-	-
Robert Brazile, Hou	OLB	2	1	-	-	-	1	1	1
Fred Carr, GB	OLB	-	-	-	-	-	2	-	-
Jack Ham, Pit	OLB	1	1	1	1	1	1	1	1
Chris Hanburger, Was	OLB	-	-	1	1	-	1	1	1
Ted Hendricks, Oak	OLB	2	2	2	-	1	2	-	-
Isiah Robertson, LARm	OLB	1	2	-	-	1	1	1	1
Brad Van Pelt, NYG	OLB	-	-	-	-	1	-	-	-
Phil Villapiano, Oak	OLB	-	-	2	-	-	2	-	-
Charlie Weaver, Det	OLB	-	-	-	-	-	2	-	-
Mel Blount, Pit	CB	-	-	2	1	-	-	1	1
Mike Haynes, NE	CB	2	2	2	-	1	-	1	1
Monte Jackson, LARm	CB	1	1	1	1	1	1	1	1
Joe Lavender, Was	CB	-	-	-	-	-	2	-	-
Lemar Parrish, Cin	CB	-	-	1	-	-	2	-	-
Ken Riley, Cin	CB	2	2	-	-	1	2	-	-
Roger Wehrli, StL	CB	1	1	-	-	1	1	1	1

DEFENSE		ALL-NFL				ALL-CONF			
		AP	FW	NE	PW	AP	UP	SN	PW
Nate Wright, Min	CB	-	-	-	-	-	2	-	-
George Atkinson, Oak	S	-	-	-	-	-	2	-	-
Tom Casanova, Cin	S	1	2	2	-	1	1	-	1
Thom Darden, Cle	S	-	2	-	-	-	-	-	-
Glen Edwards, Pit	S	2	-	2	-	1	2	-	-
Cliff Harris, Dal	S	1	1	1	1	1	1	1	1
Ken Houston, Was	S	-	1	1	1	1	1	1	1
James Hunter, Det	S	-	-	-	-	-	2	-	-
Jack Tatum, Oak	S	-	-	-	-	-	-	1	-
Mark Wagner, Pit	S	2	-	-	-	-	1	1	1
Charlie West, Det	S	-	-	-	-	-	2	-	-

SPECIALISTS		ALL-NFL				ALL-CONF			
		AP	FW	NE	PW	AP	UP	SN	PW
Jim Bakken, StL	K	1	1	1	1	1	1	1	1
Efren Herrera, Dal	K	2	2	-	-	-	2	-	-
Toni Linhart, Bal	K	-	-	-	-	-	1	1	1
Jan Stenerud, KC	K	-	-	2	-	1	-	-	-
Jim Turner, Den	K	-	-	-	-	-	2	-	-
Marv Bateman, Buf	P	-	-	-	-	-	2	-	-
Ray Guy, Oak	P	1	1	1	1	1	1	1	1
John James, Atl	P	2	2	2	-	1	1	1	1
Dave Jennings, NYG	P	-	-	-	-	-	2	-	-
Eddie Brown, Was	KR	2	x	x	-	x	x	x	1P
Cullen Bryant, LARm	KR	x	x	x	-	x	x	x	1K
Duriel Harris, Mia	KR	x	x	x	1K	x	x	x	1K
Rick Upchurch, Den	KR	1	x	x	1P	x	x	x	1P

1977 ALL-NFL

OFFENSE		ALL-NFL				ALL-CONF		
		AP	FW	NE	PW	UP	SN	PW
Cliff Branch, Oak	WR	-	-	1	-	-	-	-
Ken Burrough, Hou	WR	2	-	2	-	2	-	-
Harold Carmichael, Phi	WR	-	-	-	-	2	-	-
Bob Chandler, Buf	WR	-	-	-	-	2	-	-
Harold Jackson, LARm	WR	-	-	2	-	1	1	-
Nat Moore, Mia	WR	1	1	-	-	1	1	1
Drew Pearson, Dal	WR	1	1	1	1	1	1	1
Lynn Swann, Pit	WR	2	-	-	1	1	1	1
Sammy White, Min	WR	-	-	-	-	2	-	1
Dave Casper, Oak	TE	1	1	1	1	1	1	1
Billy Joe DuPree, Dal	TE	-	-	-	-	2	-	-
Russ Francis, NE	TE	-	-	2	-	-	-	-
Jean Fugett, Was	TE	-	-	-	-	1	1	1
Riley Odoms, Den	TE	2	-	-	-	2	-	-
Dan Dierdorf, StL	T	1	1	1	1	1	1	1
Leon Gray, NE	T	-	-	-	-	2	-	-
George Kunz, Bal	T	2	-	2	-	1	1	1
Dennis Lick, ChiB	T	-	-	-	-	2	-	-
Art Shell, Oak	T	1	1	1	1	1	1	1
Stan Walters, Phi	T	-	-	-	-	2	-	-
Russ Washington, SD	T	-	-	-	-	2	-	-
Ron Yary, Min	T	2	-	2	-	1	1	1
Joe DeLamielluere, Buf	G	1	1t	1	1	2	1	1
Conrad Dobler, StL	G	-	-	-	-	2	-	-
John Hannah, NE	G	2	-	1	-	1	-	-
Bob Kuechenberg, Mia	G	-	-	2	-	-	-	-
Larry Little, Mia	G	2	1t	-	-	2	-	-
Tom Mack, LARm	G	-	-	-	-	1	1	1
Revie Sorey, ChiB	G	-	-	-	-	1	-	1
Gene Upshaw, Oak	G	1	1	2	1	1	1	1
Ed White, Min	G	-	-	-	-	2	-	-
Bob Young, StL	G	-	-	-	-	-	1	-
Tom Banks, StL	C	2	-	2	-	1	1	1
Len Hauss, Was	C	-	-	-	-	2	-	-
Jim Langer, Mia	C	1	1	1	1	1	1	1
Mike Webster, Pit	C	-	-	-	-	2	-	-
Bob Griese, Mia	QB	1	1	1	1	1	-	1
Pat Haden, LARm	QB	-	-	-	-	2	-	-
Bert Jones, Bal	QB	2	-	2	-	2	-	-
Craig Morton, Den	QB	-	-	-	-	-	1	-
Roger Staubach, Dal	QB	-	-	-	-	1	1	1
Tony Dorsett, Dal	RB	-	-	-	-	2	-	-
Chuck Foreman, Min	RB	-	-	2	-	2	1	1
Franco Harris, Pit	RB	1	1	1	1	1	1	1
Law. McCutcheon, LARm	RB	-	-	-	-	1	-	-
Lydell Mitchell, Bal	RB	2	-	-	-	1	1	1
Walter Payton, ChiB	RB	1	1	1	1	1	1	1
Greg Pruitt, Cle	RB	-	-	2	-	2	-	-
Mark van Eeghen, Oak	RB	2	-	-	-	2	-	-

DEFENSE		ALL-NFL				ALL-CONF		
		AP	FW	NE	PW	UP	SN	PW
Lyle Alzado, Den	DE	1	1	2	1	1	1	1
Coy Bacon, Cin	DE	-	-	-	-	2	-	-
Fred Cook, Bal	DE	-	-	-	-	2	-	1
Claude Humphrey, Atl	DE	2	-	1	-	2	-	1
Harvey Martin, Dal	DE	1	1	1	1	1	1	1
Lee Roy Selmon, TB	DE	-	-	-	-	2	-	-
Jack Youngblood, LARm	DE	2	-	2	-	1	1	-
Mike Barnes, Bal	DT	-	-	-	-	2	1	-
Larry Brooks, LARm	DT	-	1	2	-	-	1	-
Rubin Carter, Den	DT	2	-	-	-	2	-	-
Curley Culp, Hou	DT	-	-	2	-	-	-	1
Cleveland Elam, SF	DT	1	1	1	1	1	1	1
Joe Greene, Pit	DT	1	-	-	-	1	-	-
Louie Kelcher, SD	DT	2	-	1	-	1	1	1
Alan Page, Min	DT	-	-	-	-	1	-	-
Dave Pear, TB	DT	-	-	-	-	2	-	-
Randy White, Dal	DT	-	-	-	1	2	-	1
Bill Bergey, Phi	MLB	2	1	1	-	1	1	1
Randy Gradishar, Den	MLB	1	-	2	1	1	1	1
Jack Lambert, Pit	MLB	-	-	-	-	2	-	-
Jeff Siemon, Min	MLB	-	-	-	-	2	-	-
Matt Blair, Min	OLB	-	-	-	-	2	1	-
Robert Brazile, Hou	OLB	2	-	1	-	2	-	-
Jack Ham, Pit	OLB	1	1	1	1	1	1	1
Thomas Henderson, Dal	OLB	-	-	-	-	2	-	-
Ted Hendricks, Oak	OLB	-	-	2	-	-	-	-
Tom Jackson, Den	OLB	1	1	-	1	1	1	1
Isiah Robertson, LARm	OLB	2	-	2	-	1	1	1
Brad Van Pelt, NYG	OLB	-	-	-	-	1	-	1
Stan White, Bal	OLB	-	-	-	-	2	-	-
Mel Blount, Pit	CB	-	-	1	-	2	1	-
Allan Ellis, ChiB	CB	-	-	-	-	2	-	-
Mike Haynes, NE	CB	2	-	-	1	1	-	1
Monte Jackson, LARm	CB	2	1	-	-	1	1	1
Rolland Lawrence, Atl	CB	1	1	2	1	1	1	1
Lemar Parrish, Cin	CB	-	-	-	-	2	-	-
Roger Wehrli, StL	CB	1	-	1	-	2	-	-
Louis Wright, Den	CB	-	-	2	-	1	1	1
Lyle Blackwood, Bal	S	2	-	-	-	-	-	-
Tom Casanova, Cin	S	-	-	-	-	-	-	1
Tim Foley, Mia	S	-	-	-	-	2	-	-
Tony Greene, Buf	S	-	-	-	-	2	-	-
Cliff Harris, Dal	S	1	1	1	1	1	1	1
Ken Houston, Was	S	-	-	1	1	1	-	1
Bill Simpson, LARm	S	-	-	-	-	2	1	-
Jack Tatum, Oak	S	-	-	2	-	1	1	-
Bill Thompson, Den	S	1	-	-	-	1	1	1
Charlie Waters, Dal	S	2	1	2	-	2	-	-

SPECIALISTS		ALL-NFL				ALL-CONF		
		AP	FW	NE	PW	UP	SN	PW
Chris Bahr, Cin	K	-	-	-	-	-	1	-
Efren Herrera, Dal	K	1	1	1	1	1	1	1
Toni Linhart, Bal	K	-	-	-	-	2	-	-
Errol Mann, Oak	K	2	-	2	-	1	-	-
Mark Moseley, Was	K	-	-	-	-	2	-	-
Ray Guy, Oak	P	1	1	1	1	1	1	1
John James, Atl	P	2	-	2	-	1	1	1
Pat McInally, Cin	P	-	-	-	-	2	-	-
Bob Parsons, ChiB	P	-	-	-	-	2	-	-
Eddie Brown, Was	KR	-	-	x	-	x	x	1K
Raymond Clayborn, NE	KR	-	-	x	1K	x	x	1K
Bob Hammond, NYG	KR	-	-	x	-	x	x	1P
Billy Johnson, Hou	KR	1	1	x	1P	x	x	1P
Rick Upchurch, Den	KR	2	-	x	-	x	x	-

1978 ALL-NFL

OFFENSE		ALL-NFL				ALL-CONF		
		AP	FW	NE	PW	UP	SN	PW
Harold Carmichael, Phi	WR	-	-	-	-	1	1	1
Tony Hill, Dal	WR	-	-	-	-	-	-	1
John Jefferson, SD	WR	2	-	2	-	2	-	-
Steve Largent, Sea	WR	2	-	2	-	2	1	-
Drew Pearson, Dal	WR	-	-	-	-	2	-	-
Ahmad Rashad, Min	WR	-	-	-	-	2	1	-
Lynn Swann, Pit	WR	1	1	1	1	1	1	1
Wesley Walker, NYJ	WR	1	1	1	1	1	-	1
Sammy White, Min	WR	-	-	-	-	1	-	-
Dave Casper, Oak	TE	1	1	1	1	1	1	1
Henry Childs, NO	TE	-	-	-	-	2	-	-
Billy Joe Dupree, Dal	TE	-	-	-	-	1	1	1
Russ Francis, NE	TE	2	-	2	-	2	-	-
Dan Dierdorf, StL	T	1	1	1	1	1	1	1
Pat Donovan, Dal	T	-	-	-	-	2	-	-
Doug France, LARm	T	2	-	2	-	2	1	1
Leon Gray, NE	T	1	1	2	1	1	1	1
Jon Kolb, Pit	T	-	-	-	-	2	-	1
Greg Sampson, Hou	T	-	-	-	-	2	-	-
Art Shell, Oak	T	2	-	-	-	1	-	-
Stan Walters, Phi	T	-	-	-	-	1	-	-

OFFENSE		ALL-NFL				ALL-CONF		
		AP	FW	NE	PW	UP	SN	PW
Russ Washington, SD	T	-	-	1	-	-	-	-
Joe DeLamielleure, Buf	G	2	1	1	1t	1	1	1t
John Hannah, NE	G	1	1	1	1	1	1	1
Dennis Harrah, LARm	G	-	-	-	-	1	-	1
Bob Kuechenberg, Mia	G	1	-	2	1t	-	1T	1t
Larry Little, Mia	G	2	-	2	-	2	-	-
Tom Lynch, Sea	G	-	-	-	-	2	-	-
Tom Mack, LARm	G	-	-	-	-	2	1	-
Herb Scott, Dal	G	-	-	-	-	1	-	-
Revie Sorey, ChiB	G	-	-	-	-	2	-	-
Bob Young, StL	G	-	-	-	-	-	1	1
Tom Banks, StL	C	-	-	-	-	1	1	1
Jim Clack, NYG	C	-	-	-	-	2	-	-
Jim Langer, Mia	C	2	-	2	-	2	-	-
Mike Webster, Pit	C	1	1	1	1	1	1	1
Terry Bradshaw, Pit	QB	1	1	2	1	1	1	1
Archie Manning, NO	QB	-	-	-	-	1	1	-
Roger Staubach, Dal	QB	-	-	-	-	2	-	1
Jim Zorn, Sea	QB	2	-	1	-	2	-	-
Earl Campbell, Hou	RB	1	1	1	1	1	1	1
Sam Cunningham, NE	RB	-	-	-	-	2	-	-
Tony Dorsett, Dal	RB	-	-	-	-	1	-	-
Franco Harris, Pit	RB	-	-	2	-	2	-	-
Terdell Middleton, GB	RB	-	-	-	-	2	1	-
Wilbert Montgomery, Phi	RB	2	-	-	-	2	-	1
Walter Payton, ChiB	RB	2	1	1	1	1	1	1
Delvin Williams, Mia	RB	1	-	2	-	1	1	1

DEFENSE		ALL-NFL				ALL-CONF		
		AP	FW	NE	PW	UP	SN	PW
Lyle Alzado, Den	DE	2	-	-	-	1	1	1
Bubba Baker, Det	DE	1	1	1	1	2	-	1
Elvin Bethea, Hou	DE	-	-	2	-	1	-	1
L.C. Greenwood, Pit	DE	-	-	-	-	2	1	-
Ed Jones, Dal	DE	-	-	-	-	2	-	-
Joe Klecko, NYJ	DE	-	-	-	-	2	-	-
Lee Roy Selmon, TB	DE	2	-	2	-	1	1	-
Jack Youngblood, LARm	DE	1	1	1	1	1	1	1
Larry Brooks, LARm	DT	2	-	2	-	1	1	1
Curley Culp, Hou	DT	2	-	2	-	2	-	-
Doug English, Det	DT	-	-	-	-	2	-	-
Joe Greene, Pit	DT	-	-	-	-	2	-	1
Louis Kelcher, SD	DT	1	1	1	1	1	1	1
Dave Pear, TB	DT	-	-	-	-	2	-	-
Randy White, Dal	DT	1	1	1	1	1	1	1
Bill Bergey, Phi	MLB	2	-	-	1	1	1	1
Randy Gradishar, Den	MLB	1	1	1	1	1	1	1
Jack Lambert, Pit	MLB	-	-	2	1	1	1	1
Steve Nelson, NE	MLB	-	-	-	-	2	-	-
Matt Blair, Min	OLB	-	-	-	-	1	1	1
Robert Brazile, Hou	OLB	1	1	1	1	1	1	1
Harry Carson, NYG	OLB	2	-	-	-	2M	-	1
Jack Ham, Pit	OLB	1	1	1	1	1	1	1
Ted Hendricks, Oak	OLB	-	-	2	-	2	-	-
Tom Jackson, Den	OLB	2	-	-	-	2	-	-
Fulton Kuykendall, Atl	OLB	-	-	-	-	2	-	1
Brad Van Pelt, NYG	OLB	-	-	2	-	2	1	-
Jim Youngblood, LARm	OLB	-	-	-	-	1	-	-
Mel Blount, Pit	CB	2	-	-	-	2	-	-
Willie Buchanon, GB	CB	1	1t	2	1	1	1	1
Steve Foley, Den	CB	-	-	-	-	2	-	-
Mike Haynes, NE	CB	2	1t	1	-	1	1	1
Rolland Lawrence, Atl	CB	-	-	-	-	2	-	-
Rod Perry, LARm	CB	-	-	-	-	2	1	-
Pat Thomas, LARm	CB	-	-	2	-	1	-	1
Louis Wright, Den	CB	1	1	1	1	1	1	1
Thom Darden, Cle	S	2	1t	1	1	1	1	1
Cliff Harris, Dal	S	1	1t	2	1	1	1	1
Ken Houston, Was	S	1	-	-	-	2	-	-
Donnie Shell, Pit	S	-	-	2	-	2	-	-
Bill Simpson, LARm	S	-	-	-	-	2	-	1
Bill Thompson, Den	S	-	-	-	-	1	1	1
Mike Wagner, Pit	S	-	-	-	-	2	-	-
Charlie Waters, Dal	S	2	1	1	-	1	1	-

SPECIALISTS		ALL-NFL				ALL-CONF		
		AP	FW	NE	PW	UP	SN	PW
Don Cockroft, Cle	K	-	-	-	-	2	-	-
Frank Corral, LARm	K	2	1	1	1	1	1	1
Pat Leahy, NYJ	K	1	-	-	-	1	1	1
Mark Moseley, Was	K	-	-	2	-	2	-	-
Ray Guy, Oak	P	1	1	1	1	1	1	1
Dave Jennings, NYG	P	2	-	2	-	2	-	-
Pat McInally, Cin	P	-	-	-	-	2	-	-
Tom Skladany, Det	P	-	-	-	-	1	1	1
Tony Green, Was	KR	2	x	x	1K	x	x	1K
Rick Upchurch, Den	KR	1	x	x	1P	x	x	1P
Jackie Wallace, LARm	KR	-	x	x	-	x	x	1P
Keith Wright, Cle	KR	-	x	x	-	x	x	1K

1979 ALL-NFL

OFFENSE		ALL-NFL				ALL-CONF		
		AP	FW	NE	PW	UP	SN	PW
Harold Carmichael, Phi	WR	2	-	-	-	1	1	1
Wes Chandler, NO	WR	-	-	2	-	2	-	-
Tony Hill, Dal	WR	-	-	-	-	2	-	-
John Jefferson, SD	WR	1	1	1	1	1	1	1
Steve Largent, Sea	WR	2	-	-	-	2	-	-
Nat Moore, Mia	WR	-	-	-	-	2	-	-
Ahmad Rashad, Min	WR	-	-	2	-	1	1	1
John Stallworth, Pit	WR	1	1	1	1	1	1	1
Dave Casper, Oak	TE	1	-	2	1	-	-	1
Ray Chester, Oak	TE	-	-	1	-	2	-	-
Henry Childs, NO	TE	-	-	-	-	2	-	1
Keith Krepfle, Phi	TE	-	-	-	-	1	1	-
Ozzie Newsome, Cle	TE	2	1	-	-	1	1	-
Pat Donovan, Dal	T	-	-	-	-	1	1	1
Doug France, LARm	T	-	-	-	-	2	-	-
Leon Gray, Hou	T	1	1	1	1	1	1	1
Jon Kolb, Pit	T	-	-	1	-	2	-	-
Marvin Powell, NYJ	T	1	1	2	1	1	1	1
Jerry Sisemore, Phi	T	-	-	-	-	2	-	-
Stan Walters, Phi	T	2	-	-	-	1	1	1
Russ Washington, SD	T	2	-	2	-	2	-	-
Joe DeLamielleure, Buf	G	2	1	1	-	1	1	1
Conrad Dobler, NO	G	-	-	-	-	2	-	-
John Hannah, NE	G	1	1	1	1	1	1	1
Dennis Harrah, LARm	G	-	-	-	-	-	-	1
Gerry Mullins, Pit	G	-	-	2	-	-	-	-
Randy Rasmussen, NYJ	G	-	-	-	-	2	-	-
Herb Scott, Dal	G	-	-	-	-	1	1	-
Revie Sorey, ChiB	G	-	-	-	-	2	-	-
Ed White, SD	G	2	-	-	-	2	-	-
Doug Wilkerson, SD	G	-	-	2	-	-	-	-
Bob Young, StL	G	1	-	-	1	1	1	1
Tom Banks, StL	C	-	-	-	-	1	1	-
Jim Clack, NYG	C	-	-	-	-	2	-	-
Carl Mauck, Hou	C	-	-	-	-	2	-	-
Jack Rudnay, KC	C	-	-	2	-	-	-	-
Rich Saul, LARm	C	-	-	-	-	-	-	1
Jeff Van Note, Atl	C	2	-	-	-	-	-	-
Mike Webster, Pit	C	1	1	1	1	1	1	1
Terry Bradshaw, Pit	QB	-	-	2	-	2	-	-
Dan Fouts, SD	QB	1	1	1	1	1	1	1
Brian Sipe, Cle	QB	2	-	-	-	-	-	-
Roger Staubach, Dal	QB	-	-	-	-	1	1	1
Joe Theismann, Was	QB	-	-	-	-	2	-	-
Ottis Anderson, StL	RB	1	1	2	-	1	1	1
Earl Campbell, Hou	RB	1	1	1	1	1	1	1
Franco Harris, Pit	RB	-	-	2	-	2	-	-
Wilbert Montgomery, Phi	RB	2	-	-	-	2	-	-
Chuck Muncie, NO	RB	-	-	-	-	2	-	-
Walter Payton, ChiB	RB	2	-	1	1	1	1	1
Mike Pruitt, Cle	RB	-	-	-	-	1	1	1
Sherman Smith, Sea	RB	-	-	-	-	2	-	-

DEFENSE		ALL-NFL				ALL-CONF		
		AP	FW	NE	PW	UP	SN	PW
Lyle Alzado, Cle	DE	-	-	-	-	2	-	1
Bubba Baker, Det	DE	-	-	2	-	-	-	-
Elvin Bethea, Hou	DE	2	-	-	-	-	-	-
Fred Dean, SD	DE	-	-	-	-	1	1	1
L.C. Greenwood, Pit	DE	-	-	-	-	1	1	-
Carl Hairston, Phi	DE	-	-	-	-	2	-	-
Harvey Martin, Dal	DE	2	-	2	-	2	-	-
Lee Roy Selmon, TB	DE	1	1	1	1	1	1	1
Art Still, KC	DE	-	-	-	-	2	-	-
Jack Youngblood, LARm	DE	1	1	1	1	1	1	1
Bob Baumhower, Mia	DT	2	-	-	-	-	1	1
Larry Brooks, LARm	DT	1	-	-	-	2	-	-
Dave Butz, Was	DT	-	-	-	-	2	-	-
Curley Culp, Hou	DT	2	-	-	-	2	-	-
Joe Greene, Pit	DT	-	1	2	1	1	1	1
Charles Johnson, Phi	DT	-	-	1	-	1	1	1
Gary Johnson, SD	DT	-	-	2	-	-	-	-
Joe Klecko, NYJ	DT	-	-	-	-	2	-	-
Randy White, Dal	DT	1	1	1	1	1	1	1
Wilbur Young, SD	DT	-	-	-	-	1	-	-
Bob Breunig, Dal	MLB	-	-	-	-	-	-	1
Harry Carson, NYG	MLB	-	-	-	-	1	1	1
Randy Gradishar, Den	MLB	2	1	2	1	2	1	1
Jack Lambert, Pit	MLB	1	-	1	1	1	1	1
Jack Reynolds, LARm	MLB	-	-	-	-	2	1	-
Matt Blair, Min	OLB	-	-	-	-	2	-	1

DEFENSE		ALL-NFL				ALL-CONF		
		AP	FW	NE	PW	UP	SN	PW
Robert Brazile, Hou	OLB	1	1	1	1	1	1	1
Brad Dusek, Was	OLB	-	-	-	-	2	-	-
Jack Ham, Pit	OLB	1	1	1	1	1	1	1
Tom Jackson, Den	OLB	-	-	2	-	-	-	-
David Lewis, TB	OLB	-	-	2	-	1	-	-
Steve Nelson, NE	OLB	-	-	-	-	2	-	-
Dewey Selmon, TB	OLB	2	-	-	-	-	-	-
Bob Swenson, Den	OLB	-	-	-	-	2	-	-
Brad Van Pelt, NYG	OLB	-	-	-	-	1	1	1
Jim Youngblood, LARm	OLB	2	-	-	-	-	1	-
Mel Blount, Pit	CB	2	-	2	-	2	-	-
Lester Hayes, Oak	CB	-	-	-	-	2	-	-
Mike Haynes, NE	CB	2	-	2	-	1	1	1
Joe Lavender, Was	CB	-	-	-	-	2	-	-
Rolland Lawrence, Atl	CB	-	-	-	-	2	-	-
Lemar Parrish, Was	CB	1	1	1	1	1	1	1
Roger Wehrli, StL	CB	-	-	-	-	1	1	1
Louis Wright, Den	CB	1	1	1	1	1	1	1
Thom Darden, Cle	S	2	-	-	-	2	-	1
Gary Fencik, ChiB	S	-	1	-	-	2	1	1
Tim Foley, Mia	S	-	-	2	-	2	-	-
Cliff Harris, Dal	S	-	-	-	-	2	1	-
Ken Houston, Was	S	2	-	-	-	1	-	-
Tom Myers, NO	S	-	-	-	1	1	-	1
Mike Reinfeldt, Hou	S	1	1	1	1	1	1	1
Donnie Shell, Pit	S	1	-	1	-	-	1	-
Bill Thompson, Den	S	-	-	2	-	1	-	-

SPECIALISTS		ALL-NFL				ALL-CONF		
		AP	FW	NE	PW	UP	SN	PW
Tony Franklin, Phi	K	-	-	-	-	2	-	-
Tony Fritsch, Hou	K	1	1	1	-	1	1	1
Efren Herrera, Sea	K	-	-	-	-	2	-	-
Mark Moseley, Was	K	2	-	2	1	1	1	1
Bob Grupp, KC	P	-	1	1	1	1	1	1
Ray Guy, Oak	P	-	-	2	-	2	-	-
Dave Jennings, NYG	P	1	-	-	-	1	1	1
Danny White, Dal	P	-	-	-	-	2	-	-
Roy Green, StL	KR	-	x	x	-	x	1K	1K
Wally Henry, Phi	KR	-	x	x	-	x	1P	1P
Ira Matthews, Oak	KR	-	x	x	1K	x	1K	1K
Tony Nathan, Mia	KR	1	x	x	-	x	1P	-
Rick Upchurch, Den	KR	2	x	x	1P	x	-	1P

1980 ALL-NFL

OFFENSE		ALL-NFL					CONF	
		AP	FW	NE	SN	PW	UP	PW
Jerry Butler, Buf	WR	-	-	-	-	-	2	-
Harold Carmichael, Phi	WR	-	-	2	-	-	2	-
John Jefferson, SD	WR	1	1	1	1	1	1	1
Charlie Joiner, SD	WR	1	-	-	-	-	2	-
James Lofton, GB	WR	2	1	1	1	1	1	1
Stanley Morgan, NE	WR	2	-	2	-	-	1	1
Ahmad Rashad, Min	WR	-	-	-	-	-	1	1
Pat Tilley, StL	WR	-	-	-	-	-	2	-
Russ Francis, NE	TE	-	-	-	-	-	2	-
Jimmie Giles, TB	TE	-	-	-	-	-	2	-
Junior Miller, Atl	TE	2	-	-	-	-	1	1
Ozzie Newsome, Cle	TE	-	-	2	-	-	-	-
Kellen Winslow, SD	TE	1	1	1	1	1	1	1
Doug Dieken, Cle	T	-	-	-	-	-	2	-
Dan Dierdorf, StL	T	2	-	1	-	-	2	-
Pat Donovan, Dal	T	-	-	-	-	-	1	-
Doug France, LARm	T	-	-	-	-	-	2	1
Leon Gray, Hou	T	1	1	2	1	1	1	1
Ken Jones, Buf	T	-	-	-	-	-	2	-
Mike Kenn, Atl	T	1	1	1	1	1	1	1
Marvin Powell, NYJ	T	2	-	2	-	-	1	1
Randy Cross, SF	G	-	-	2	-	-	-	1
Joe Delamielleure, Cle	G	2	1	-	1	-	1	1
John Hannah, NE	G	1	1	1	1	1	1	1
Dennis Harrah, LARm	G	-	-	-	-	-	2	-
Kent Hill, LARm	G	2	-	-	-	1	1	1
Noah Jackson, ChiB	G	-	-	-	-	-	2	-
Reggie McKenzie, Buf	G	-	-	-	-	-	2	-
Herbert Scott, Dal	G	1	-	1	-	-	1	-
Doug Wilkerson, SD	G	-	-	2	-	-	2	-
Tom DeLeone, Cle	C	-	-	-	-	-	2	-
Rich Saul, LARm	C	2	-	2	-	-	2	-
Jeff Van Note, Atl	C	-	-	-	-	-	1	1
Mike Webster, Pit	C	1	1	1	1	1	1	1
Steve Bartkowski, Atl	QB	-	-	-	-	-	-	2
Dan Fouts, SD	QB	2	-	-	-	-	-	2
Ron Jaworski, Phi	QB	-	-	-	-	-	1	1
Brian Sipe, Cle	QB	1	1	1	1	1	1	1
Ottis Anderson, StL	RB	2	-	2	-	-	2	-

OFFENSE		ALL-NFL					CONF	
		AP	FW	NE	SN	PW	UP	PW
William Andrews, Atl	RB	-	-	-	-	-	2	-
Earl Campbell, Hou	RB	1	1	1	1	1	1	1
Joe Cribbs, Buf	RB	-	-	-	-	-	1	1
Kenny King, Oak	RB	-	-	-	-	-	2	-
Walter Payton, ChiB	RB	1	1	1	1	1	1	1
Mike Pruitt, Cle	RB	-	-	-	-	-	2	-
Billy Sims, Det	RB	2	-	2	-	-	1	1

DEFENSE		ALL-NFL					CONF	
		AP	FW	NE	SN	PW	UP	PW
Lyle Alzado, Cle	DE	1	-	-	-	-	1	-
Fred Dean, SD	DE	1	-	-	-	1	2	1
Carl Hairston, Phi	DE	-	-	-	-	-	2	1
Dan Hampton, ChiB	DE	-	-	2	-	-	2	1
Lee Roy Selmon, TB	DE	2	1	1	1	-	1	-
Art Still, KC	DE	2	1	1	1	1	1	1
Ben Williams, Buf	DE	-	-	-	-	-	2	-
Jack Youngblood, LARm	DE	-	-	2	-	-	1	-
Larry Brooks, LARm	DT	-	-	-	-	-	2	-
Charlie Johnson, Phi	DT	1	-	2	-	-	1	1
Gary Johnson, SD	DT	1	1	1	1	1	1	1
Louis Kelcher, SD	DT	2	-	-	-	-	2	1
Reggie Kinlaw, Oak	DT	-	-	-	-	-	2	-
Alan Page, ChiB	DT	-	-	-	-	-	2	1
Fred Smerlas, Buf	DT	-	-	2	-	1	1	1
Randy White, Dal	DT	2	1	1	1	1	1	1
Bill Bergey, Phi	ILB	-	-	-	-	-	2	1
Bob Bruenig, Dal	ILB	2	-	-	-	-	1	-
Buddy Curry, Atl	ILB	-	-	-	-	-	-	1
Randy Gradishar, Den	ILB	-	-	2	1	-	-	-
Jim Haslett, Buf	ILB	-	-	-	-	-	1	-
Jack Lambert, Pit	ILB	1	1	1	-	1	-	1
Steve Nelson, NE	ILB	-	-	-	1	1	2	1
Matt Blair, Min	OLB	1	-	2	-	-	1	1
Robert Brazile, Hou	OLB	2	1	1	1	1	1	1
Jack Ham, Pit	OLB	-	-	2	-	-	2	-
Ted Hendricks, Oak	OLB	1	1	1	1	1	1	1
Woodie Lowe, SD	OLB	-	-	-	-	-	2	-
Al Richardson, Atl	OLB	-	-	-	-	-	2	-
Jerry Robinson, Phi	OLB	2	-	-	-	-	1	1
Brad Van Pelt, NYG	OLB	-	-	-	-	-	2	-
Herm Edwards, Phi	CB	-	-	-	-	-	2	-
Lester Hayes, Oak	CB	1	1	1	1	1	1	1
Mike Haynes, NE	CB	2	-	2	-	-	1	1
Lemar Parrish, Was	CB	2	1	1	1	1	1	1
Rod Perry, LARm	CB	-	-	-	-	-	2	-
Greg Stemrick, Hou	CB	-	-	-	-	-	2	-
Pat Thomas, LARm	CB	1	-	2	-	-	1	1
Louis Wright, Den	CB	-	-	-	-	-	2	-
Gary Barbaro, KC	S	2	-	2	-	-	1	1
Nolan Cromwell, LARm	S	1	1	1	1	1	1	1
Gary Fencik, ChiB	S	-	-	-	-	1	1	1
Bruce Laird, Bal	S	-	-	-	-	-	-	1t
Randy Logan, Phi	S	2	-	2	-	-	2	-
Vernon Perry, Hou	S	-	-	-	-	-	2	-
Mike Reinfeldt, Hou	S	-	-	-	-	-	2	-
Donnie Shell, Pit	S	1	1	1	1	-	1	1t

SPECIALISTS		ALL-NFL					CONF	
		AP	FW	NE	SN	PW	UP	PW
Tim Mazzetti, Atl	K	-	-	-	-	-	2	-
Ed Murray, Det	K	1	1	1	-	-	1	1
John Smith, NE	K	-	-	-	-	1t	2	1t
Fred Steinfort, Den	K	-	-	2	1	1t	1	1t
Ray Guy, Oak	P	-	-	2	-	-	1	1
John James, Atl	P	-	-	-	-	-	2	-
Dave Jennings, NYG	P	1	1	1	1	1	1	1
Luke Prestridge, Den	P	-	-	-	-	-	2	-
Horace Ivory, NE	KR	-	1	x	1K	1K	x	1K
Rich Mauti, NO	KR	-	-	x	-	-	x	1K
J.T. Smith, KC	KR	1	-	x	1P	1P	x	1P
Freddie Solomon, SF	KR	-	-	x	-	x	x	1P

1981 ALL-NFL

OFFENSE		ALL-NFL					CONF	
		AP	FW	NE	SN	PW	UP	PW
Dwight Clark, SF	WR	-	-	-	-	-	2	-
Chris Collinsworth, Cin	WR	2	-	-	-	-	2	-
Alfred Jenkins, Atl	WR	1	1	1	1	1t	1	1
Steve Largent, Sea	WR	-	-	-	-	-	2	-
Frank Lewis, Buf	WR	-	-	2	-	-	1	1
James Lofton, GB	WR	1	1	1	1	1	1	1
Ahmad Rashad, Min	WR	-	-	-	-	-	2	-
Steve Watson, Den	WR	2	-	2	-	1t	1	1
Jimmie Giles, TB	TE	-	-	-	-	-	2	-
Ozzie Newsome, Cle	TE	2	-	-	-	-	-	-
Dan Ross, Cin	TE	-	-	-	-	-	2	-

OFFENSE		ALL-NFL					CONF	
		AP	FW	NE	SN	PW	UP	PW
Joe Senser, Min	TE	-	-	2	-	-	1	1
Kellen Winslow, SD	TE	1	1	1	1	1	1	1
Pat Donovan, Dal	T	2	-	2	-	-	2	1
Keith Dorney, Det	T	-	-	-	-	-	1	-
Leon Gray, Hou	T	-	-	-	-	-	2	-
Mike Kenn, Atl	T	2	-	2	-	-	1	1
Anthony Munoz, Cin	T	1	1	1	1	1	1	1
Marvin Powell, NYJ	T	1	1	1	1	1	1	1
Jerry Sisemore, Phi	T	-	-	-	-	-	2	-
Chris Ward, NYJ	T	-	-	-	-	-	2	-
Randy Cross, SF	G	2	1	1	-	1	1	1
Joe DeLamielleure, Cle	G	-	-	-	-	-	2	-
Wes Hamilton, Min	G	-	-	-	-	-	2	-
John Hannah, NE	G	1	1	1	1	1	1	1
Ed Newman, Mia	G	2	-	2	-	-	2	-
Greg Roberts, TB	G	-	-	-	-	-	2	-
Herbert Scott, Dal	G	1	-	2	1	-	1	1
Doug Wilkerson, SD	G	-	-	-	-	-	1	1
Joe Fields, NYJ	C	2	-	-	-	-	2	-
Larry McCarren, GB	C	-	-	-	-	-	-	1
Guy Morriss, Phi	C	-	-	-	-	-	1	-
Rich Saul, LARm	C	-	-	2	-	-	-	-
Jeff Van Note, Atl	C	-	-	-	-	-	2	-
Mike Webster, Pit	C	1	1	1	1	1	1	1
Ken Anderson, Cin	QB	1	1	1	1	1	1	1
Dan Fouts, SD	QB	-	-	-	-	-	2	-
Joe Montana, SF	QB	2	-	2	-	-	1	1
Danny White, Dal	QB	-	-	-	-	-	2	-
William Andrews, Atl	RB	2	-	-	-	-	2	-
Earl Campbell, Hou	RB	-	-	-	-	-	2	-
Joe Cribbs, Buf	RB	-	-	2	-	-	-	-
Joe Delaney, KC	RB	-	-	-	-	-	1	1
Tony Dorsett, Dal	RB	1	1	1	1	1	1	1
Pete Johnson, Cin	RB	-	-	-	-	-	2	-
Chuck Muncie, SD	RB	-	-	-	-	-	1	1
George Rogers, NO	RB	1	-	2	1	-	1	-
Billy Sims, Det	RB	2	1	1	-	1	2	1

DEFENSE		ALL-NFL					CONF	
		AP	FW	NE	SN	PW	UP	PW
Mike Butler, GB	DE	-	-	-	-	-	2	-
Fred Dean, SD-SF	DE	1	1	2	1	1	1	1
Eddie Edwards, Cin	DE	-	-	-	-	-	2	-
Mark Gastineau, NYJ	DE	2	-	2	-	-	1	1
Carl Hairston, Phi	DE	-	-	-	-	-	2	-
Ed Jones, Dal	DE	2	-	1	-	-	1	1
Joe Klecko, NYJ	DE	1	1	1	1	1	1	1
Ben Williams, Buf	DE	-	-	-	-	-	2	-
Bob Baumhower, Mia	DT	2	-	2	1	-	1	1
Doug English, Det	DT	2	-	1	-	1	2	1
Charley Johnson, Phi	DT	1	-	-	-	-	1	1
Gary Johnson, SD	DT	1	1	-	-	-	2	1
Louis Kelcher, SD	DT	2	-	-	-	-	2	-
Fred Smerlas, Buf	DT	-	-	2	-	-	1	1
Don Smith, Atl	DT	-	-	-	-	-	2	-
Randy White, Dal	DT	1	1	1	1	1	1	1
Harry Carson, NYG	ILB	-	-	-	-	1	1	1
Randy Gradishar, Den	ILB	2	-	2	1	1	1	1
Jack Lambert, Pit	ILB	1	1	1	1	1	2	1
Jack Reynolds, SF	ILB	-	-	-	-	-	2	-
Matt Blair, Min	OLB	-	-	2	-	-	2	1
Robert Brazile, Hou	OLB	2	-	-	-	-	2	-
Mike Douglass, GB	OLB	-	-	-	-	-	2	-
A.J. Duhe, Mia	OLB	-	-	-	-	-	1	-
Ted Hendricks, Oak	OLB	-	-	-	-	-	1	1
Rod Martin, Oak	OLB	-	-	2	-	-	-	-
Jerry Robinson, Phi	OLB	2	1	-	-	-	1	1
Bob Swenson, Den	OLB	1	-	1	1	-	2	1
Lawrence Taylor, NYG	OLB	1	1	1	1	1	1	1
Mel Blount, Pit	CB	1	1	-	-	-	1	1
Mario Clark, Buf	CB	-	-	-	-	-	2t	-
Gary Green, KC	CB	-	-	2	-	-	1	1
Eric Harris, KC	CB	-	-	-	-	-	2t	-
Lester Hayes, Oak	CB	-	-	-	1	-	2	-
Mark Haynes, NYG	CB	2	-	1	-	1	2	1
Ronnie Lott, SF	CB	1	1	1	1	1	1	1
Ken Riley, Cin	CB	-	-	-	-	-	2t	-
Dennis Thurman, Dal	CB	-	-	-	-	-	2	-
Louis Wright, Den	CB	-	-	-	-	-	2t	-
Roynell Young, Phi	CB	2	-	2	-	-	1	-
Gary Barbaro, KC	S	-	1	1	-	-	2	1
Nolan Cromwell, LARm	S	1	1	1	1	1	2	1
Gary Fencik, ChiB	S	1	-	2	1	-	1	-
Dwight Hicks, SF	S	2	-	2	-	1	1	1
Randy Logan, Phi	S	-	-	-	-	-	2	-
Darrol Ray, NYJ	S	-	-	-	-	-	1	1
Donnie Shell, Pit	S	2	-	-	-	-	2	-
Bill Thompson, Den	S	-	-	-	-	-	1	-

SPECIALISTS		ALL-NFL					CONF	
		AP	FW	NE	SN	PW	UP	PW
Pat Leahy, NYJ	K	-	-	-	-	-	2	-
Nick Lowery, KC	K	2	-	1	-	-	1	1
Ed Murray, Det	K	-	-	2	-	-	-	-
Rafael Septien, Dal	K	1	1	-	1	1	1	1
Jan Stenerud, GB	K	-	-	-	-	-	2	-
Ray Guy, Oak	P	-	-	-	-	-	2	-
Dave Jennings, NYG	P	2	-	-	-	-	2	-
Pat McInally, Cin	P	1	1	2	1	-	1	1
Tom Skladany, Det	P	-	-	1	-	1	1	1
LeRoy Irvin, LARm	KR	1	1P	x	1P	1P	x	1P
Mike Nelms, Was	KR	2	1K	x	1K	1K	x	1K
Carl Roaches, Hou	KR	-	-	x	-	-	x	1K
J.T. Smith, KC	KR	-	-	x	-	-	x	1P

1982 ALL-NFL

OFFENSE		ALL-NFL				CONF
		AP	FW	NE	PW	UP
Charlie Brown, Was	WR	-	-	2	-	2
Wes Chandler, SD	WR	1	1	1	1	1
Dwight Clark, SF	WR	1	1	1	1	1
Chris Collinsworth, Cin	WR	2	-	-	-	-
James Lofton, GB	WR	2	-	2	-	1
Wesley Walker, NYJ	WR	-	-	-	-	1
Jimmie Giles, TB	TE	-	-	-	-	1
Ozzie Newsome, Cle	TE	-	-	2	-	-
Dan Ross, Cin	TE	2	-	-	-	2
Kellen Winslow, SD	TE	1	1	1	1	1
Pat Donovan, Dal	T	-	-	-	-	1
Mike Kenn, Atl	T	2	-	2	-	1
Greg Koch, GB	T	-	-	2	-	-
Anthony Munoz, Cin	T	1	1	1	1	1
Marvin Powell, NYJ	T	1	1	1	1	1
Russ Washington, SD	T	2	-	-	-	-
Russ Grimm, Was	G	-	-	-	-	2
John Hannah, NE	G	2	1	2	1	2
Kent Hill, LARd	G	-	-	-	-	1
Ed Newman, Mia	G	2	-	1	-	1
Kurt Peterson, Dal	G	-	-	2	-	-
R.C. Thielemann, Atl	G	1	-	-	-	1
Doug Wilkerson, SD	G	1	1	1	1	1
Joe Fields, NYJ	C	1	-	1	-	2
Larry McCarren, GB	C	-	-	-	-	1
Jeff Van Note, Atl	C	2	-	-	-	-
Mike Webster, Pit	C	-	1	2	1	1
Ken Anderson, Cin	QB	-	-	-	-	2
Dan Fouts, SD	QB	1	1	1	1	1
Joe Thiesmann, Was	QB	-	-	2	-	1
Danny White, Dal	QB	2	-	-	-	2
Marcus Allen, LARd	RB	1	1	1	1	1
William Andrews, Atl	RB	2	-	2	-	1
Tony Dorsett, Dal	RB	2	-	2	-	1
Andra Franklin, Mia	RB	-	-	-	-	2
Freeman McNeil, NYJ	RB	1	1	1	1	1
Chuck Muncie, SD	RB	-	-	-	-	2
George Rogers, NO	RB	-	-	-	-	2
Billy Sims, Det	RB	-	-	-	-	2

DEFENSE		ALL-NFL				CONF
		AP	FW	NE	PW	UP
Lyle Alzado, LARd	DE	-	-	-	-	1
Mark Gastineau, NYJ	DE	1	1	1	1	1
Dennis Harrison, Phi	DE	-	-	-	-	2
Ed Jones, Dal	DE	1	-	2	-	2
Doug Martin, Min	DE	-	-	-	1	1
Harvey Martin, Dal	DE	2	-	-	-	-
Lee Roy Selmon, TB	DE	2	1	1	-	1
Art Still, KC	DE	-	-	-	-	2
Ben Williams, Buf	DE	-	-	2	-	2
Bob Baumhower, Mia	DT	2	-	2	-	1
Doug English, Det	DT	1	-	2	-	-
Dan Hampton, ChiB	DT	2	1	1	1	2
Gary Johnson, SD	DT	2	-	-	-	-
Fred Smerlas, Buf	DT	1	-	-	-	-
Randy White, Dal	DT	1	1	1	1	1
Bob Breunig, Dal	ILB	-	-	-	-	1
Harry Carson, NYG	ILB	2	-	-	-	1
George Cumby, GB	ILB	-	-	2	-	-
Buddy Curry, Atl	ILB	-	-	-	-	2
Mike Douglass, GB	ILB	-	-	-	1	-
Randy Gradishar, Den	ILB	-	-	-	-	1
Jack Lambert, Pit	ILB	1	1	1	1	1
Jim LeClair, Cin	ILB	-	-	-	-	2
Chip Banks, Cle	OLB	-	-	-	-	2
Robert Brazile, Hou	OLB	-	-	-	-	1
Hugh Green, TB	OLB	2	1	2	1	1
Ted Hendricks, LARd	OLB	1	-	-	-	1
Rod Martin, LARd	OLB	-	-	1	-	-

DEFENSE		ALL-NFL				CONF
		AP	FW	NE	PW	UP
Lance Mehl, NYJ	OLB	-	-	-	-	2
Lawrence Taylor, NYG	OLB	1	1	1	1	1
Keena Turner, SF	OLB	-	-	2	-	-
Joel Williams, Atl	OLB	2	-	-	-	-
Louis Breeden, Cin	CB	1	-	1	-	-
Vernon Dean, Was	CB	-	-	-	-	2
Herm Edwards, Phi	CB	-	-	-	-	2
Gary Green, KC	CB	-	-	-	-	2
Lester Hayes, LARd	CB	-	-	2	-	1
Mark Haynes, NYG	CB	1	1	-	1	1
Mike Haynes, NE	CB	2	-	1	-	1
Everson Walls, Dal	CB	2	1	2	1	1
Gary Barbaro, KC	S	-	-	1	-	1
Neal Colzie, TB	S	2	-	-	-	-
Nolan Cromwell, LARm	S	1	1	-	-	1
Kenny Easley, Sea	S	-	-	1	1	1
Gary Fencik, ChiB	S	-	-	-	1	2
Tim Fox, SD	S	2	-	-	-	-
Tony Peters, Was	S	-	-	-	-	1
Darrol Ray, NYJ	S	-	-	2	-	2
Donnie Shell, Pit	S	1	1	2	-	-

SPECIALISTS		ALL-NFL				CONF
		AP	FW	NE	PW	UP
Rolf Benirschke, SD	K	-	-	-	-	1
Nick Lowery, KC	K	-	-	-	-	2
Mark Moseley, Was	K	1	1	1	1	1
Ed Murray, Det	K	-	-	2	-	-
Uwe von Schamann, Mia	K	2	-	-	-	-
Carl Birdsong, StL	P	-	-	-	-	2
Rich Camarillo, NE	P	-	-	2	-	-
Dave Jennings, NYG	P	2	1	1	1	1
Luke Prestridge, Den	P	1	-	-	-	1
Rohn Stark, Bal	P	-	-	-	-	2
LeRoy Irvin, LARm	KR	-	1P	x	-	x
Mike Nelms, Was	KR	2	1K	x	1K	x
Rick Upchurch, Den	KR	1	-	x	1P	x

1983 ALL-NFL

OFFENSE		ALL-NFL					CONF	
		AP	FW	NE	SN	PW	UP	PW
Charlie Brown, Was	WR	-	-	-	-	-	2	-
Carlos Carson, KC	WR	-	-	-	-	-	1	-
Chris Collinsworth, Cin	WR	2	-	2	-	-	1	1
Mark Duper, Mia	WR	-	-	-	-	-	2	-
Roy Green, StL	WR	1	1	1	1	1	1	1
Steve Largent, Sea	WR	-	-	-	1	-	2	-
James Lofton, GB	WR	2	1	2	-	-	2	-
Mike Quick, Phi	WR	1	-	1	-	1	1	1
Tim Smith, Hou	WR	-	-	-	-	-	-	1
Mike Barber, LARm	TE	-	-	-	-	-	2	-
Todd Christensen, LARd	TE	1	1	1	1	1	1	1
Paul Coffman, GB	TE	-	-	-	-	-	1	1
Ozzie Newsome, Cle	TE	2	-	2	-	-	2	-
Pat Donovan, Dal	T	-	-	-	-	-	2	-
Keith Fahnhorst, SF	T	-	-	1	-	-	-	-
Brian Holloway, NE	T	-	-	-	-	-	-	1
Joe Jacoby, Was	T	1	1	1	1	1	1	1
Mike Kenn, Atl	T	2	-	-	-	1	2	1
Eric Laakso, Mia	T	-	-	-	1	-	-	-
Henry Lawrence, LARd	T	-	-	-	-	-	2	-
Anthony Munoz, Cin	T	1	1	-	-	-	1	-
Marvin Powell, NYJ	T	-	-	-	-	-	2	1
Cody Risien, Cle	T	-	-	2	-	-	1	-
Jackie Slater, LARm	T	2	-	2	-	-	1	-
Joe DeLamielleure, Cle	G	2	-	-	-	-	-	-
Russ Grimm, Was	G	1	1	1	-	1	1	1
John Hannah, NE	G	1	1	1	1	1	1	1
Kent Hill, LARm	G	-	-	-	1	-	1	1
Chris Hinton, Bal	G	-	-	-	-	-	2	1
Bob Kuechenberg, Mia	G	-	-	-	-	-	2	-
Mike Munchak, Hou	G	-	-	2	-	-	-	-
Ed Newman, Mia	G	2	-	2	-	-	1	-
Herbert Scott, Dal	G	-	-	-	-	-	2	-
R.C. Thielemann, Atl	G	-	-	-	-	-	2	-
Jeff Bostic, Was	C	-	-	-	-	-	1	1
Larry McCarren, GB	C	-	-	2	-	-	2	-
Dwight Stephenson, Mia	C	2	1	1	-	1	1	1
Mike Webster, Pit	C	1	-	-	1	-	2	-
Lynn Dickey, GB	QB	-	-	-	-	-	2	-
Dan Fouts, SD	QB	-	-	-	-	-	2	-
Dan Marino, Mia	QB	2	-	-	-	-	1	1
Joe Montana, SF	QB	-	-	2	-	-	-	-
Joe Theismann, Was	QB	1	1	1	1	1	1	1
William Andrews, Atl	RB	-	-	1	1	-	-	-
Tony Collins, NE	RB	-	-	-	-	-	2	-
Joe Cribbs, Buf	RB	-	-	-	-	-	1	1
Eric Dickerson, LARm	RB	1	1	1	1	1	1	1
Tony Dorsett, Dal	RB	2	-	-	-	-	2	-
Walter Payton, ChiB	RB	-	-	2	-	-	2	-
Mike Pruitt, Cle	RB	-	-	-	-	-	2	-
John Riggins, Was	RB	1	1	2	-	1	1	1
Curt Warner, Sea	RB	2	-	-	-	-	1	1

DEFENSE		ALL-NFL					CONF	
		AP	FW	NE	SN	PW	UP	PW
Doug Betters, Mia	DE	1	1	1	1	1	1	1
Fred Dean, SF	DE	-	-	-	-	-	2	1
Mark Gastineau, NYJ	DE	1	-	-	-	-	1	-
William Gay, Det	DE	-	-	-	-	-	1	-
Jacob Green, Sea	DE	-	-	2	-	-	2	-
Ed Jones, Dal	DE	2	-	2	-	-	1	1
Howie Long, LARd	DE	2	1	1	1	1	2	1
Lee Roy Selmon, TB	DE	-	-	-	-	-	2	-
Bob Baumhower, Mia	DT	1	-	-	-	1	1	1
Dave Butz, Was	DT	1	-	1	1	1	2	1
Doug English, Det	DT	2	1	2	-	-	-	-
Joe Klecko, NYJ	DT	2	-	-	-	-	-	1
Dave Logan, TB	DT	-	-	-	-	-	-	1
Fred Smerlas, Buf	DT	2	-	1	-	-	2	1
Randy White, Dal	DT	1	1	2	1	1	1	1
Bob Bruenig, Dal	ILB	-	-	-	-	-	1	-
Jim Collins, LARm	ILB	-	-	-	-	-	2	-
Tom Cousineau, Cle	ILB	-	-	2	-	-	1	-
A.J. Duhe, Mia	ILB	-	-	-	-	-	2	-
Randy Gradishar, Den	ILB	2	-	-	-	-	2	-
Jim Kovach, NO	ILB	-	-	-	-	-	2	-
Jack Lambert, Pit	ILB	1	1	1	1	1	1	1
Jerry Robinson, Phi	ILB	-	-	2	-	-	-	-
Mike Singletary, ChiB	ILB	-	-	1	-	1	1	1
Chip Banks, Cle	OLB	1	1	2	-	1	1	1
Hugh Green, TB	OLB	2	-	2	1	-	1	1
Ted Hendricks, LARd	OLB	-	-	-	-	-	2	-
Rickey Jackson, NO	OLB	-	-	-	-	-	-	1
Rod Martin, LARd	OLB	2	-	1	1	-	1	1
Lance Mehl, NYJ	OLB	-	-	-	-	-	2	1
Lawrence Taylor, NYG	OLB	1	1	1	1	1	1	1
Raymond Clayborn, NE	CB	-	-	-	1	-	2	-
Gary Green, KC	CB	-	1	1	-	-	1	-
Lester Hayes, LARd	CB	2	-	2	-	1	1	1
Mark Haynes, NYG	CB	2	-	-	-	-	-	-
Ronnie Lott, SF	CB	-	1	-	-	-	2	1
Johnnie Poe, NO	CB	-	-	2	-	-	1	-
Ken Riley, Cin	CB	1	-	-	1	1	2	1
Everson Walls, Dal	CB	1	-	-	-	-	2	1
Eric Wright, SF	CB	-	-	-	-	-	1	-
Louis Wright, Den	CB	-	-	1	-	-	-	-
Deron Cherry, KC	S	2	-	-	-	-	1	1
Nolan Cromwell, LARm	S	-	-	2	-	-	2	1
Kenny Easley, Sea	S	1	1	1	-	1	1	1
Steve Freeman, Buf	S	-	-	-	1	-	-	-
Russell Gary, NO	S	-	-	-	-	-	1	-
Roland James, NE	S	-	-	-	-	-	2	-
Johnnie Johnson, LARm	S	-	-	1	-	-	2	-
Vann McElroy, LARd	S	2	-	-	-	-	2	-
Mark Murphy, Was	S	1	1	2	1	1	1	1

SPECIALISTS		ALL-NFL					CONF	
		AP	FW	NE	SN	PW	UP	PW
Raul Allegre, Bal	K	-	-	2	-	-	2	-
Gary Anderson, Pit	K	2	-	-	-	-	1	1
Ali Haji-Sheikh, NYG	K	1	1	1	1	1	1	1
Mark Moseley, Was	K	-	-	-	-	-	2	-
Carl Birdsong, StL	P	-	-	-	-	-	1	1
Rich Camarillo, NE	P	2	1	1	1	1	1	1
Frank Garcia, TB	P	-	-	-	-	-	2	-
Rohn Stark, Bal	P	1	-	2	-	-	2	-
Billy Johnson, Atl	KR	2	1P	x	1P	1P	x	1P
Mike Nelms, Was	KR	1	-	x	-	-	x	1K
Greg Pruitt, LARd	KR	-	-	x	-	-	x	1P
Fulton Walker, Mia	KR	-	1K	x	1K	1K	x	1K

1984 ALL-NFL

OFFENSE		ALL-NFL					CONF	
		AP	FW	NE	SN	PW	UP	PW
Mark Clayton, Mia	WR	2	-	-	-	-	2	1
Mark Duper, Mia	WR	-	-	-	-	-	1	-
Roy Green, StL	WR	1	1	1	1	1	1	1
Kevin House, TB	WR	-	-	-	-	-	2	-
Steve Largent, Sea	WR	2	-	-	-	-	2	-
James Lofton, GB	WR	-	-	1	-	-	2	-
Art Monk, Was	WR	1	1	2	1	1	1	1
John Sllworth, Pit	WR	-	-	2	-	-	1	1
Todd Christensen, LARd	TE	2	-	-	-	-	2	-

OFFENSE		ALL-NFL					CONF	
		AP	FW	NE	SN	PW	UP	PW
Paul Coffman, GB	TE	-	-	2	-	-	1	1
Doug Cosbie, Dal	TE	-	-	-	-	-	2	-
Ozzie Newsome, Cle	TE	1	1	1	1	1	1	1
Bill Bain, LARm	T	2	-	-	-	1	-	1
Keith Fahnhorst, SF	T	1	1	1	-	1	1	1
Jon Giesler, Mia	T	-	-	-	-	-	2	-
Brian Holloway, NE	T	-	-	2	-	-	2	1
Joe Jacoby, Was	T	1	1	2	1	-	1	-
Mike Kenn, Atl	T	-	-	-	-	-	2	-
Henry Lawrence, LARd	T	-	-	-	-	-	1	-
Anthony Munoz, Cin	T	2	-	1	1	-	1	1
Luis Sharpe, StL	T	-	-	-	-	-	2	-
John Ayers, SF	G	-	-	-	-	-	-	1
Randy Cross, SF	G	2	-	2	-	1	1	1
Sean Farrell, TB	G	-	-	-	1	-	-	-
Roy Foster, Mia	G	-	-	-	-	-	2	-
Russ Grimm, Was	G	1	1	1	-	-	1	-
John Hannah, NE	G	2	1	1	1	-	1	-
Dennis Harrah, LARm	G	-	-	-	-	-	2	-
Kent Hill, LARm	G	-	-	-	-	-	2	-
Mike Munchak, Hou	G	-	-	2	-	-	2	1
Ed Newman, Mia	G	1	-	-	-	1	1	1
Randy Clark, StL	C	-	-	2	-	-	-	-
Larry McCarren, GB	C	-	-	-	-	-	2	-
Fred Quillan, SF	C	-	-	-	-	-	1	1
Dwight Stephenson, Mia	C	1	1	1	1	1	1	1
Mike Webster, Pit	C	2	-	-	-	-	2	-
Dave Krieg, Sea	QB	-	-	-	-	-	2	-
Neil Lomax, StL	QB	-	-	-	-	-	2	-
Dan Marino, Mia	QB	1	1	1	1	1	1	1
Joe Montana, SF	QB	2	-	2	-	-	1	1
Marcus Allen, LARd	RB	2	-	2	-	-	1	1
Eric Dickerson, LARm	RB	1	1	1	1	1	1	1
Earnest Jackson, SD	RB	-	-	-	-	-	2	1
Freeman McNeil, NYJ	RB	-	-	-	-	-	1	-
Walter Payton, ChiB	RB	1	1	1	1	1	1	1
Gerald Riggs, Atl	RB	-	-	-	-	-	2	-
James Wilder, TB	RB	2	-	2	-	-	2	-
Sammy Winder, Den	RB	-	-	-	-	-	2	-

DEFENSE		ALL-NFL					CONF	
		AP	FW	NE	SN	PW	UP	PW
Jeff Bryant, Sea	DE	-	-	-	-	-	2	-
Richard Dent, ChiB	DE	2	-	-	-	1	1	1
Mark Gastineau, NYJ	DE	1	1	1	1	1	1	1
Jacob Green, Sea	DE	-	-	2	1	-	-	-
Curtis Greer, StL	DE	-	-	-	-	-	2	-
Howie Long, LARd	DE	1	1	1	-	-	1	1
Lee Roy Selmon, TB	DE	-	-	2	-	-	1	1
Art Still, KC	DE	2	-	-	-	-	2	-
Jack Youngblood, LARm	DE	-	-	-	-	-	2	-
Bob Baumhower, Mia	DT	2	-	-	-	-	2	-
Dave Butz, Was	DT	2	-	-	-	-	-	-
Gary Dunn, Pit	DT	-	-	2	-	-	-	-
Doug English, Det	DT	2	-	-	-	-	-	-
Dan Hampton, ChiB	DT	1	-	1	1	1	2	1
Dave Logan, TB	DT	-	-	-	1	-	-	1
Joe Nash, Sea	DT	1	-	2	-	1	1	1
Randy White, Dal	DT	1	1	1	-	1	1	1
Harry Carson, NYG	ILB	-	-	2	1	-	-	-
Robin Cole, Pit	ILB	-	-	-	-	-	2	-
Jim Collins, LARm	ILB	2	-	-	-	1	2	1
Tom Cousineau, Cle	ILB	2	-	-	-	-	1	-
E.J. Junior, StL	ILB	1	1	1	-	-	1	-
Matt Millen, LARd	ILB	-	-	-	-	-	2	-
Steve Nelson, NE	ILB	-	-	2	-	-	1	-
Mike Singletary, ChiB	ILB	1	1	1	1	1	1	1
Scott Studwell, Min	ILB	-	-	-	-	-	2	-
Rickey Jackson, NO	OLB	2	-	2	-	-	1	1
Tom Jackson, Den	OLB	-	-	-	-	-	2	1
Rod Martin, LARd	OLB	1	1	-	-	-	1	-
Clay Matthews, Cle	OLB	2	-	1	1	-	-	1
Mike Merriweather, Pit	OLB	-	-	2	-	1	1	1
Lawrence Taylor, NYG	OLB	1	1	1	1	1	1	1
Andre Tippett, NE	OLB	-	-	-	-	-	2	1
Keena Turner, SF	OLB	-	-	-	-	-	2	-
Otis Wilson, ChiB	OLB	-	-	-	-	-	2	-
Dave Brown, Sea	CB	2	-	-	-	-	2	-
Gary Green, KC	CB	-	-	2	-	-	-	-
Lester Hayes, LARd	CB	-	1	-	-	-	1	-
Mark Haynes, NYG	CB	1	-	1	-	-	1	1
Mike Haynes, LARd	CB	1	1	1	1	1	1	1
Tim Lewis, GB	CB	-	-	-	-	-	2	-
Ronnie Lott, SF	CB	-	-	-	-	-	2	-
Everson Walls, Dal	CB	-	-	-	-	-	1	-
Eric Wright, SF	CB	2	-	-	-	-	-	1
Louis Wright, Den	CB	-	-	2	1	1	2	1
Todd Bell, ChiB	S	2	-	-	1	-	2	1
Deron Cherry, KC	S	1	-	2	-	-	1	-

DEFENSE		ALL-NFL					CONF	
		AP	FW	NE	SN	PW	UP	PW
Michael Downs, Dal	S	2	1	-	-	-	1	-
Kenny Easley, Sea	S	1	1	1	1	1	1	1
Gary Fencik, ChiB	S	-	-	-	-	-	2	-
Dwight Hicks, SF	S	-	-	-	-	-	1	-
Wes Hopkins, Phi	S	-	-	1	-	-	-	1
Vann McElroy, LARd	S	-	-	2	-	-	2	-
Dennis Smith, Den	S	-	-	-	-	1	2	1

SPECIALISTS		ALL-NFL					CONF	
		AP	FW	NE	SN	PW	UP	PW
Gary Anderson, Pit	K	-	-	-	-	-	2	-
Norm Johnson, Sea	K	1	1	2	1	1	1	1
Paul McFadden, Phi	K	-	-	-	-	-	2	-
Jan Stenerud, Min	K	2	-	1	-	-	1	1
Jim Arnold, KC	P	2	-	-	-	-	-	-
Brian Hansen, NO	P	-	-	-	-	-	2	-
Mike Horan, Phi	P	-	-	-	-	-	-	1
Reggie Roby, Mia	P	1	1	1	1	1	1	1
Bucky Scribner, GB	P	-	-	-	-	-	1	-
Rohn Stark, Ind	P	-	-	2	-	-	2	-
Henry Ellard, LARm	KR	1	-	x	1P	-	x	1P
Bobby Humphreys, NYJ	KR	-	1K	x	1K	1K	x	1K
Louis Lipps, Pit	KR	2	1P	x	-	1P	x	1P
Stump Mitchell, StL	KR	-	-	x	-	-	x	1K
Bill Bates, Dal	ST	x	x	x	x	-	x	1
Fredd Young, Sea	ST	x	x	x	x	1	x	1

1985 ALL-NFL

OFFENSE		ALL-NFL				CONF
		AP	FW	NE	SN	UP
Mark Clayton, Mia	WR	-	-	-	-	2
Chris Collinsworth, Cin	WR	-	-	-	-	2
Tony Hill, Dal	WR	-	-	-	-	2
Steve Largent, Sea	WR	1	1	2	-	1
Louis Lipps, Pit	WR	2	1	1	-	1
James Lofton, GB	WR	-	-	2	-	2
Art Monk, Was	WR	2	-	-	1	1
Mike Quick, Phi	WR	1	-	1	1	1
Todd Christensen, LARd	TE	1	1	1	1	1
Doug Cosbie, Dal	TE	-	-	-	-	1
Jimmie Giles, TB	TE	-	-	-	-	2
Ozzie Newsome, Cle	TE	2	-	-	-	2
Mickey Shuler, NYJ	TE	-	-	2	-	-
Jimbo Covert, ChiB	T	1	1	1	1	1
Keith Dorney, Det	T	-	-	-	-	1
Keith Fahnhorst, SF	T	-	-	2	-	-
Chris Hinton, Ind	T	2	-	2	-	1
Brian Holloway, NE	T	2	-	-	-	2
Joe Jacoby, Was	T	-	-	-	-	2
Jim Lachey, SD	T	-	-	-	-	2
Anthony Munoz, Cin	T	1	1	1	1	1
Jackie Slater, LARm	T	-	-	-	-	2
Dan Alexander, NYJ	G	-	-	-	-	2
John Ayers, SF	G	-	-	-	-	2
Randy Cross, SF	G	-	-	1	-	-
Roy Foster, Mia	G	-	-	-	-	1
Russ Grimm, Was	G	1	1	1	1	1
John Hannah, NE	G	1	1	2	1	1
Dennis Harrah, LARm	G	-	-	-	-	1
Kent Hill, LARm	G	2	-	-	-	2
Mike Munchak, Hou	G	2	-	2	-	2
Bill Bryan, Den	C	-	-	2	-	-
Joe Fields, NYJ	C	2	-	-	-	-
Jay Hilgenberg, ChiB	C	-	-	-	-	1
Fred Quillan, SF	C	-	-	-	-	2
Dwight Stephenson, Mia	C	1	1	1	1	1
Mike Webster, Pit	C	-	-	-	-	2
Dan Fouts, SD	QB	2	-	1	-	2
Dan Marino, Mia	QB	1	1	2	1	1
Jim McMahon, ChiB	QB	-	-	-	-	2
Joe Montana, SF	QB	-	-	-	-	1
Marcus Allen, LARd	RB	1	1	1	1	1
Roger Craig, SF	RB	2	-	2	-	2
Lionel James, SD	RB	-	-	-	-	2
Freeman McNeil, NYJ	RB	-	-	2	-	1
Joe Morris, NYG	RB	-	-	-	-	2
Walter Payton, ChiB	RB	1	1	1	1	1
Gerald Riggs, Atl	RB	2	-	-	-	1
Curt Warner Sea	RB	-	-	-	-	2

DEFENSE		ALL-NFL				CONF
		AP	FW	NE	SN	UP
Richard Dent, ChiB	DE	1	1	-	-	1
Mark Gastineau, NYJ	DE	-	-	1	1	2
Jacob Green, Sea	DE	-	-	-	-	2
Ed Jones, Dal	DE	-	-	-	-	2
Rulon Jones, Den	DE	2	-	2	1	1

DEFENSE		ALL-NFL				CONF
		AP	FW	NE	SN	UP
Howie Long, LARd	DE	1	1	1	-	1
Leonard Marshall, NYG	DE	2	-	2	-	1
Michael Carter, SF	DT	2	-	-	-	-
Bob Golic, Cle	DT	2	-	-	1	2
Dan Hampton, ChiB	DT	2	-	2	-	2E
Joe Klecko, NYJ	DT	1	1	1	-	1
Steve McMichael, ChiB	DT	1	-	-	-	2
Joe Nash, Sea	DT	-	-	2	-	-
Randy White, Dal	DT	1	-	1	1	1
Harry Carson, NYG	ILB	2	-	2	-	2
Jim Collins, LARm	ILB	-	-	-	1	2
E.J. Junior, StL	ILB	-	-	-	-	1
Karl Mecklenburg, Den	ILB	1	1	1	-	1
Lance Mehl, NYJ	ILB	2	-	2	-	1
Matt Millen, LARd	ILB	-	-	-	-	2
Steve Nelson, NE	ILB	-	-	-	-	2
Mike Singletary, ChiB	ILB	1	1	1	1	1
Chip Banks, Cle	OLB	-	-	-	-	1
Rickey Jackson, NO	OLB	2	-	-	-	2
Rod Martin, LARd	OLB	-	-	-	-	2
Mike Merriweather, Pit	OLB	-	-	2	-	2
Lawrence Taylor, NYG	OLB	1	1	1	1	1
Andre Tippett, NE	OLB	1	1	1	1	1
Keena Turner, SF	OLB	-	-	2	-	2
Otis Wilson, ChiB	OLB	2	-	-	-	1
Dave Brown, Sea	CB	-	-	-	-	2
Raymond Clayborn, NE	CB	-	-	2	-	2
Gary Green, LARm	CB	-	-	-	-	2
Mike Haynes, LARd	CB	1	1	1	1	1
LeRoy Irvin, LARm	CB	2	-	-	-	2
Everson Walls, Dal	CB	2	1	2	-	1
Eric Wright, SF	CB	1	-	1	1	1
Louis Wright, Den	CB	-	-	-	-	1
Joey Browner, Min	S	-	-	-	-	2
Deron Cherry, KC	S	2	-	2	-	1
Michael Downs, Dal	S	-	-	-	-	1
Ken Easley, Sea	S	1	1	1	1	1
Bo Eason, Hou	S	-	-	2	-	-
Gary Fencik, ChiB	S	2	-	-	-	2
Wes Hopkins, Phi	S	1	1	1	1	1
Fred Marion, NE	S	-	-	-	-	2
Dennis Smith, Den	S	-	-	-	-	2

SPECIALISTS		ALL-NFL				CONF
		AP	FW	NE	SN	UP
Morten Andersen, NO	K	2	-	-	1	1
Gary Anderson, Pit	K	-	1	-	-	1
Kevin Butler, ChiB	K	-	-	2	-	2
Nick Lowery, KC	K	1	-	1	-	2
Dale Hatcher, LARm	P	1	1	-	1	1
Sean Landeta, NYG	P	-	-	-	-	2
Reggie Roby, Mia	P	-	-	2	-	2
Rohn Stark, Ind	P	2	-	1	-	1
Ron Brown, LARm	KR	1	1	x	1K	x
Henry Ellard, LARm	KR	-	-	x	1P	x
Irving Fryar, NE	KR	2	-	x	-	x

1986 ALL-NFL

OFFENSE		ALL-NFL					CONF	
		AP	FW	NE	SN	PW	UP	PW
Gary Clark, Was	WR	2	-	-	-	-	1	1
Steve Largent, Sea	WR	-	-	2	-	-	2	-
Art Monk, Was	WR	-	-	-	-	-	2	-
Stanley Morgan, NE	WR	2	-	2	1	-	1	1
Mike Quick, Phi	WR	-	-	-	-	-	2	-
Jerry Rice, SF	WR	1	1	1	1	1	1	1
Al Toon, NYJ	WR	1	1	1	-	1	1	1
Wesley Walker, NYJ	WR	-	-	-	-	-	2	-
Mark Bavaro, NYG	TE	1	1	2	1	1	1	1
Todd Christensen, LARd	TE	2	-	1	-	-	1	1
Steve Jordan, Min	TE	-	-	-	-	-	2	-
Mickey Shuler, NYJ	TE	-	-	-	-	-	2	-
Brad Benson, NYG	T	2	-	-	-	-	-	-
Jimbo Covert, ChiB	T	1	1	-	1	1	1	1
Jon Giesler, Mia	T	-	-	-	-	-	2	-
Chris Hinton, Ind	T	-	-	-	-	-	1	-
Brian Holloway, NE	T	-	-	1	-	-	-	-
Joe Jacoby, Was	T	-	-	-	-	-	2	-
Anthony Munoz, Cin	T	1	1	1	1	1	1	1
Cody Risien, Cle	T	-	-	-	-	-	2	1
Jackie Slater, LARm	T	2	-	2	-	-	1	1
Gary Zimmerman, Min	T	-	-	2	-	-	2	-
Dan Alexander, NYJ	G	-	-	-	-	-	2	-
Keith Bishop, Den	G	-	-	-	-	-	2	-
Randy Cross, SF	G	2	-	2	-	-	-	-
Dan Fike, Cle	G	-	-	2	-	-	-	-
Roy Foster, Mia	G	-	-	-	-	-	1	1
Bill Fralic, Atl	G	1	-	1	1	1	2	1
Chris Godfrey, NYG	G	-	-	-	-	-	2	-
Russ Grimm, Was	G	2	1	1	-	-	1	-
Dennis Harrah, LARm	G	1	1	-	1	1	1	1
Max Montoya, Cin	G	-	-	-	-	-	1	1
Ray Donaldson, Ind	C	-	-	-	-	-	2	-
Jay Hilgenberg, ChiB	C	2	-	2	-	-	1	1
Doug Smith, LARm	C	-	-	-	-	-	2	-
Dwight Stephenson, Mia	C	1	1	1	1	1	1	1
John Elway, Den	QB	-	-	-	-	-	2	-
Tommy Kramer, Min	QB	2	-	-	-	-	1	1
Dan Marino, Mia	QB	1	1	2	1	1	1	1
Jay Schroeder, Was	QB	-	-	-	-	-	2	-
Phil Simms, NYG	QB	-	-	1	-	-	-	-
Marcus Allen, LARd	RB	-	-	-	-	-	2	-
James Brooks, Cin	RB	-	-	-	-	-	1	1
Eric Dickerson, LARm	RB	1	1	1	1	1	1	1
Rueben Mayes, NO	RB	-	-	-	-	-	2	-
Joe Morris, NYG	RB	1	1	1	1	1	1	1
Walter Payton, ChiB	RB	2	-	2	-	-	2	-
Curt Warner, Sea	RB	2	-	2	-	-	1	1
Gerald Willhite, Den	RB	-	-	-	-	-	2	-

DEFENSE		ALL-NFL					CONF	
		AP	WA	NE	SN	PW	UP	PW
Rick Bryan, Atl	DE	-	-	-	-	-	2	-
Dan Hampton, ChiB	DE	2	-	1	-	-	1	-
Rulon Jones, Den	DE	1	1	2	1	1	1	1
Howie Long, LARd	DE	-	-	2	-	-	-	1
Dexter Manley, Was	DE	1	1	1	1	1	1	1
Leonard Marshall, NYG	DE	2	-	-	-	-	2	-
Bruce Smith, Buf	DE	-	-	-	-	-	2	-
Art Still, KC	DE	-	-	-	-	-	1	-
Lee Williams, SD	DE	-	-	-	-	-	2	-
Jim Burt, NYG	DT	-	-	-	-	-	-	1
Michael Carter, SF	DT	-	-	1	-	-	-	-
Bob Golic, Cle	DT	-	-	2	-	-	-	-
Joe Klecko, NYJ	DT	-	-	-	-	-	2	-
Bill Maas, KC	DT	2	-	-	-	1	-	1
Steve McMichael, ChiB	DT	2	1	-	1	1	2	1
Keith Millard, Min	DT	-	-	2	-	-	-	-
Bill Pickel, LARd	DT	1	-	-	1	-	1	-
Reggie White, Phi	DT	1	1	1	-	-	1	1E
Harry Carson, NYG	ILB	2	-	2	-	-	1	1
Kyle Clifton, NYJ	ILB	-	-	2	-	-	-	-
Carl Ekern, LARm	ILB	-	-	-	-	-	2	-
Mark Jerue, LARm	ILB	-	-	-	-	-	2	-
Karl Mecklenburg, Den	ILB	1	1	1	1	1	1	1
John Offerdahl, Mia	ILB	2	-	-	-	-	1	1
Mike Singletary, ChiB	ILB	1	1	1	1	1	1	1
Billy Ray Smith, SD	ILB	-	-	-	-	-	2	-
Fredd Young, Sea	ILB	-	-	-	-	-	2	-
Chip Banks, Cle	OLB	-	-	-	-	-	1	1
Don Blackmon, NE	OLB	-	-	-	-	-	2	-
Bryan Hinkle, Pit	OLB	-	-	-	-	-	2	-
Rickey Jackson, NO	OLB	2	-	1	-	-	2	-
Wilber Marshall, ChiB	OLB	1	1	2	1	1	1	1
Lawrence Taylor, NYG	OLB	1	1	1	1	1	1	1
Andre Tippett, NE	OLB	2	-	2	-	-	1	1
Keena Turner, SF	OLB	-	-	-	-	-	2	-
Raymond Clayborn, NE	CB	-	-	-	-	1	-	1
Hanford Dixon, Cle	CB	1	1	1	1	1	1	1
Jerry Gray, LARm	CB	2	-	-	-	-	1	1
Darrell Green, Was	CB	2	-	1	-	-	2	1
LeRoy Irvin, LARm	CB	1	1	2	1	-	1	-
Albert Lewis, KC	CB	-	-	2	-	-	2	-
Ronnie Lippett, NE	CB	-	-	-	-	-	1	-
Frank Minnifield, Cle	CB	-	-	-	-	-	2	-
Mike Richardson, ChiB	CB	-	-	-	-	-	2	-
Lloyd Burruss, KC	S	-	-	-	-	-	1	-
Deron Cherry, KC	S	1	-	2	1	-	1	1
Dave Duerson, ChiB	S	2	1	-	1	1	1	1
Kenny Easley, Sea	S	-	-	-	-	-	2	-
Ronnie Lott, SF	S	1	1	1	-	1	1	1
Vann McElroy, LARd	S	-	-	-	-	-	2	-
Vince Newsome, LARm	S	-	-	-	-	-	2	-
Dennis Smith, Den	S	-	-	1	-	-	-	1
Leonard Smith, StL	S	2	-	2	-	-	2	-

SPECIALISTS		ALL-NFL					CONF	
		AP	WA	NE	SN	PW	UP	PW
Morten Andersen, NO	K	1	1	1	1	1	1	1
Tony Franklin, NE	K	2	-	-	-	-	1	1
Pat Leahy, NYJ	K	-	-	2	-	-	-	-
Nick Lowery, KC	K	-	-	-	-	-	2	-
Ray Wersching, SF	K	-	-	-	-	-	2	-
Steve Cox, Was	P	-	-	-	-	-	2	-

SPECIALISTS		ALL-NFL					CONF	
		AP	WA	NE	SN	PW	UP	PW
Sean Landeta, NYG	P	1	1	2	1	1	1	1
Reggie Roby, Mia	P	-	-	-	-	-	2	-
Rohn Stark, Ind	P	2	-	1	-	-	1	1
Bobby Joe Edmonds, Sea	KR	1	1	x	1P	1P	x	1P
Dennis Gentry, ChiB	KR	-	-	x	-	1K	x	1K
Mel Gray, NO	KR	-	-	x	1K	-	x	-
Tim McGee, Cin	KR	-	-	x	-	-	x	1K
Vai Sikahema, StL	KR	2	-	x	-	-	x	1P
Neal Anderson, ChiB	ST	x	x	x	x	-	x	1
Mosi Tatupu, NE	ST	x	x	x	x	1	x	1

1987 ALL-NFL

OFFENSE		ALL-NFL					CONF	
		AP	FW	NE	SN	PW	UP	PW
Chris Burkett, Buf	WR	-	-	-	-	-	2	-
Carlos Carson, KC	WR	-	-	-	-	-	2	-
Anthony Carter, Min	WR	-	-	-	-	-	2	-
Gary Clark, Was	WR	1	-	2	-	-	-	-
Steve Largent, Sea	WR	2	1	2	-	-	1	1
Mike Quick, Phi	WR	-	-	1	-	-	2	-
Jerry Rice, SF	WR	1	1	1	1	1	1	1
J.T. Smith, StL	WR	2	-	-	1	1	1	1
Al Toon, NYJ	WR	-	-	-	-	-	1	1
Robert Awalt, StL	TE	-	-	2	-	-	-	-
Mark Bavaro, NYG	TE	1	1	1	1	1	1	1
Todd Christensen, LARd	TE	-	-	-	-	-	2	1
Steve Jordan, Min	TE	-	-	-	-	-	2	-
Kellen Winslow, SD	TE	2	-	-	-	-	1	-
Jimbo Covert, ChiB	T	-	-	2	-	-	1	-
Chris Hinton, Ind	T	-	-	-	1	-	2	1
Joe Jacoby, Was	T	-	-	1	-	-	-	-
Jim Lachey, SD	T	2	-	-	-	-	1	-
Anthony Munoz, Cin	T	1	1	-	-	1	1	1
Cody Risien, Cle	T	-	-	-	-	-	2	-
Luis Sharpe, StL	T	-	-	-	-	-	2	-
Jackie Slater, LARm	T	2	-	1	-	-	1	1
Gary Zimmerman, Min	T	1	1	2	1	1	2	1
Keith Bishop, Den	G	-	-	2	-	-	2	-
Brad Edelman, NO	G	-	-	-	-	-	2	-
Dan Fike, Cle	G	-	-	-	-	-	2	-
Bill Fralic, Atl	G	1	1	2	1	1	1	1
Dennis Harrah, LARm	G	-	-	-	-	-	2	-
Mike Munchak, Hou	G	1	1	1	1	1	1	1
Tom Newberry, LARm	G	2	-	-	-	-	1	1
Ron Solt, Ind	G	2	-	1	-	-	1	1
Randy Cross, SF	C	-	-	-	-	-	2	-
Ray Donaldson, Ind	C	2	-	2	-	-	2	-
Jay Hilgenberg, ChiB	C	-	-	-	1	-	1	1
Bart Oates, NYG	C	-	-	-	-	-	2	-
Dwight Stephenson, Mia	C	1	1	-	-	1	1	1
Mike Webster, Pit	C	-	-	1	-	-	-	-
John Elway, Den	QB	2	-	1	1	-	1	1
Bernie Kosar, Cle	QB	-	-	-	-	-	2	-
Neil Lomax, StL	QB	-	-	-	-	-	2	-
Joe Montana, SF	QB	1	1	2	-	1	1	1
Earnest Byner, Cle	RB	-	-	-	-	-	2	-
Roger Craig, SF	RB	-	-	-	-	-	2	-
Eric Dickerson, LARm-Ind	RB	1	1	1	1	1	1	1
Rueben Mayes, NO	RB	-	-	-	-	-	1	-
Mike Rozier, Hou	RB	-	-	-	-	-	2	-
Herschel Walker, Dal	RB	2	-	2	-	-	2	1
Curt Warner, Sea	RB	2	-	1	-	-	1	1
Charles White, LARm	RB	1	1	2	1	1	1	1

DEFENSE		ALL-NFL					CONF	
		AP	FW	NE	SN	PW	UP	PW
Bruce Clark, NO	DE	-	-	2	-	-	-	-
Chris Doleman, Min	DE	2	-	1	-	-	1	1
Jacob Green, Sea	DE	-	-	-	-	-	1	1
Carl Hairston, Cle	DE	-	-	-	-	-	2	-
Rulon Jones, Den	DE	-	-	-	-	-	2	-
Dexter Manley, Was	DE	-	-	-	-	-	2	-
Charles Mann, Was	DE	2	-	-	-	-	2	-
Bruce Smith, Buf	DE	1	1	2	1	1	1	1
Reggie White, Phi	DE	1	1	1	1	1	1	1
Michael Carter, SF	DT	1	1	1	1	-	1	1
Tim Krumrie, Cin	DT	2	-	-	-	-	2	-
Bill Maas, KC	DT	-	-	2	-	1	1	1
Steve McMichael, ChiB	DT	1	-	-	1	1	2	1
Keith Millard, Min	DT	2	-	-	-	-	-	-
Shane Conlan, Buf	ILB	2	-	2	-	-	-	-
Vaughan Johnson, NO	ILB	-	-	-	-	-	1	1
Karl Mecklenburg, Den	ILB	2	-	1	-	-	1	1
Brian Noble, GB	ILB	-	-	-	-	-	2	-
John Offerdahl, Mia	ILB	-	-	-	-	-	2	-
Ervin Randle, TB	ILB	-	-	-	-	-	2	-
Mike Singletary, ChiB	ILB	1	1	2	1	1	1	1
Billy Ray Smith, SD	ILB	-	-	-	-	-	2	-
Fredd Young, Sea	ILB	1	1	1	1	1	1	1
Carl Banks, NYG	OLB	1	1	1	1	-	1	-
Chip Banks, SD	OLB	-	-	-	-	-	2	-
Duane Bickett, Ind	OLB	2	-	2	-	-	1	1
Rickey Jackson, NO	OLB	-	-	1	1	-	-	-
Wilber Marshall, ChiB	OLB	-	-	-	-	-	2	1
Mike Merriweather, Pit	OLB	-	-	-	-	-	2	-
Pat Swilling, NO	OLB	-	-	-	-	-	1	-
Lawrence Taylor, NYG	OLB	2	-	-	-	1	2	1
Andre Tippett, NE	OLB	1	1	2	-	1	1	1
Hanford Dixon, Cle	CB	1	1	1	1	1	1	1
Jerry Gray, LARm	CB	-	-	2	-	-	2	1
Darrell Green, Was	CB	-	-	1	-	-	-	-
Don Griffin, SF	CB	-	-	-	-	-	2	-
Albert Lewis, KC	CB	-	-	-	-	-	2	-
Ronnie Lippett, NE	CB	-	-	-	-	-	2	-
Frank Minnifield, Cle	CB	2	1	2	1	1	1	1
Dave Waymer, NO	CB	2	-	-	-	-	1	-
Barry Wilburn, Was	CB	1	-	-	-	-	1	1
Keith Bostic, Hou	S	2	-	1	-	-	1	1
Joey Browner, Min	S	1	1	1	1	1	1	1
Deron Cherry, KC	S	-	-	-	-	-	2	-
Dave Duerson, ChiB	S	2	-	-	-	-	2	-
Kenny Easley, Sea	S	-	-	2	-	-	2	1
Jeff Fuller, SF	S	-	-	-	-	-	-	-
Terry Kinard, NYG	S	-	-	-	-	-	-	-
Ronnie Lott, SF	S	1	1	2	1	1	1	1
Vann McElroy, LARd	S	-	-	-	-	-	1	-
Alvin Walton, Was	S	-	-	-	-	-	2	-

SPECIALISTS		ALL-NFL					CONF	
		AP	FW	NE	SN	PW	UP	PW
Morten Andersen, NO	K	1	1	1	1	1	1	1
Dean Biasucci, Ind	K	2	-	2	-	-	1	1
Pat Leahy, NYJ	K	-	-	-	-	-	2	-
Roger Ruzek, Dal	K	-	-	-	-	-	2	-
Jim Arnold, Det	P	1	1	1	1	1	1	1
Rick Donnelly, Atl	P	-	-	-	-	-	2	-
Ralf Mojsiejenko, SD	P	2	-	2	-	-	1	-
Reggie Roby, Mia	P	-	-	-	-	-	2	1
Dennis Gentry, ChiB	KR	2	1K	x	-	-	x	-
Mel Gray, NO	KR	-	1P	x	1P	1P	x	1P
Lionel James, SD	KR	-	-	x	-	-	x	1P
Paul Palmer, KC	KR	-	-	x	-	-	x	1K
Vai Sikahema, StL	KR	1	-	x	-	-	x	-
Sylvester Stamps, Atl	KR	-	-	x	1K	1K	x	1K
Steve Tasker, Buf	ST	x	x	x	x	-	x	1
Ron Wolfley, StL	ST	x	x	x	x	1	x	1

1988 ALL-NFL

OFFENSE		ALL-NFL					CONF	
		AP	FW	NE	SN	PW	UP	PW
Eddie Brown, Cin	WR	2	-	1	-	-	1	1
Anthony Carter, Min	WR	-	-	-	-	-	2	-
Mark Clayton, Mia	WR	-	-	-	-	-	2	-
Henry Ellard, LARm	WR	1	1	1	1	-	1	1
Drew Hill, Hou	WR	-	-	-	-	-	2	-
Jerry Rice, SF	WR	1	1	2	1	1	1	1
Al Toon, NYJ	WR	2	-	2	-	1	1	1
Rodney Holman, Cin	TE	-	-	-	-	-	2	-
Keith Jackson, Phi	TE	1	1	2	1	1	1	1
Mickey Shuler, NYJ	TE	2	-	1	-	-	1	1
Bruce Armstrong, NE	T	2	-	-	1	-	1	-
Chris Hinton, Ind	T	-	-	2	-	-	2	-
Tunch Ilkin, Pit	T	-	-	-	-	-	2	1
Anthony Munoz, Cin	T	1	1	1	1	1	1	1
Irv Pankey, LARm	T	-	-	1	-	-	-	-
Luis Sharpe, Pho	T	2	-	-	-	-	1	1
Jackie Slater, LARm	T	-	-	-	-	1	2	1
Gary Zimmerman, Min	T	1	1	2	-	-	1	-
Bill Fralic, Atl	G	2	-	1	-	-	1	-
Bruce Matthews, Hou	G	1	1	2	1	1	1	1
Mark May, Was	G	-	-	-	-	-	-	1
Randall McDaniel, Min	G	-	-	-	-	-	2	-
Bryan Millard, Sea	G	-	-	-	-	-	2	-
Max Montoya, Cin	G	-	-	2	-	-	1	-
Mike Munchak, Hou	G	2	-	1	-	-	2	1
Tom Newberry, LARm	G	1	1	-	1	1	1	1
Ray Donaldson, Ind	C	-	-	2	-	-	2	1
Jay Hilgenberg, ChiB	C	1	1	1	1	1	1	1
Kent Hull, Buf	C	2	-	-	-	-	1	-
Randall Cunningham, Phi	QB	2	-	-	-	-	1	1
Boomer Esiason, Cin	QB	1	1	1	1	1	1	1
Jim Everett, LARm	QB	-	-	-	-	-	2	-
Dan Marino, Mia	QB	-	-	2	-	-	-	-
Warren Moon, Hou	QB	-	-	-	-	-	2	-

OFFENSE		ALL-NFL					CONF	
		AP	FW	NE	SN	PW	UP	PW
Neal Anderson, ChiB	RB	-	-	-	-	-	2	-
James Brooks, Cin	RB	-	-	-	-	-	2	-
Roger Craig, SF	RB	1	1	1	1	1	1	1
Eric Dickerson, Ind	RB	1	1	1	1	1	1	1
John Settle, Atl	RB	-	-	-	-	-	-	-
John Stephens, NE	RB	-	-	-	-	-	1	1
Herschel Walker, Dal	RB	2	-	2	-	-	1	1
Ickey Woods, Cin	RB	2	-	2	-	-	2	-

DEFENSE		ALL-NFL					CONF	
		AP	FW	NE	SN	PW	UP	PW
Ray Childress, Hou	DE	2	-	2	-	-	1	1
Richard Dent, ChiB	DE	2	-	2	-	-	1	1
Chris Doleman, Min	DE	-	-	-	-	-	2	-
Freddie Joe Nunn, Pho	DE	-	-	-	-	-	2	-
Bruce Smith, Buf	DE	1	1	1	1	1	1	1
Greg Townsend, LARd	DE	-	-	-	-	-	2	-
Reggie White, Phi	DE	1	1	1	1	1	1	1
Lee Williams, SD	DE	-	-	-	-	-	2	-
Michael Carter, SF	DT	2	-	1	-	-	-	1
Dan Hampton, ChiB	DT	2	-	1	-	1	1	1
Tim Krumrie, Cin	DT	1	1	-	1	1	2	1
Steve McMichael, ChiB	DT	-	-	2	-	-	-	-
Keith Millard, Min	DT	1	1	2	1	-	-	-
Fred Smerlas, Buf	DT	-	-	-	-	-	1	-
Shane Conlan, Buf	ILB	2	1	-	1	1	1	1
Dino Hackett, KC	ILB	-	-	-	-	-	2	-
Vaughan Johnson, NO	ILB	-	-	1	-	-	1	1
John Offerdahl, Mia	ILB	-	-	2	-	-	1	1
Johnny Rembert, NE	ILB	-	-	-	-	-	2	-
Mike Singletary, ChiB	ILB	1	1	1	1	1	1	1
Scott Studwell, Min	ILB	-	-	2	-	-	-	-
Cornelius Bennett, Buf	OLB	1	1	1	1	1	1	1
Duane Bickett, Ind	OLB	-	-	-	-	-	2	-
Mike Cofer, Det	OLB	2t	-	-	-	-	2	-
Charles Haley, SF	OLB	-	-	-	-	-	1	-
Tim Harris, GB	OLB	2t	-	1	-	-	-	1
Clay Matthews, Cle	OLB	-	-	-	-	-	2	-
Lawrence Taylor,NYG	OLB	1	1	2	1	1	1	1
Andre Tippett, NE	OLB	2	-	2	-	-	1	1
Scott Case, Atl	CB	2	-	-	-	-	1	-
Raymond Clayborn, NE	CB	-	-	-	-	-	2	-
Hanford Dixon, Cle	CB	2	-	-	-	-	-	-
Jerry Gray, LARm	CB	-	-	2	-	-	-	1
Carl Lee, Min	CB	1	1	2	1	1	1	1
Albert Lewis, KC	CB	-	-	-	-	-	1	1
Ronnie Lippett, NE	CB	-	-	1	-	-	-	-
Tim McKyer, SF	CB	-	-	-	-	-	2	-
Frank Minnifield, Cle	CB	1	1	1	1	1	1	1
Eric Thomas, Cin	CB	-	-	-	-	-	2	-
Rod Woodson, Pit	CB	-	-	-	-	-	-	-
Bennie Blades, Det	S	-	-	2	-	-	-	-
Joey Browner, Min	S	1	1	1	1	1	1	1
Lloyd Burruss, KC	S	-	-	-	-	-	2	-
Deron Cherry, KC	S	1	1	2	1	1	1	1
Dave Duerson, ChiB	S	-	-	-	-	-	-	1
David Fulcher, Cin	S	2	-	-	-	-	1	1
Terry Hoage, Phi	S	-	-	-	-	-	2	-
Ronnie Lott, SF	S	2	-	1	-	-	1	-
Erik McMillan, NYJ	S	-	-	-	-	-	2	-

SPECIALISTS		ALL-NFL					CONF	
		AP	FW	NE	SN	PW	UP	PW
Morten Andersen, NO	K	-	-	2	-	-	1	-
Dean Biasucci, Ind	K	2	-	-	1	-	-	-
Nick Lowery, KC	K	-	-	1	-	-	2	-
Ed Murray, Det	K	-	-	-	-	-	-	1
Chuck Nelson, Min	K	-	-	-	-	-	2	-
Scott Norwood, Buf	K	1	1	-	-	1	1	1
Jim Arnold, Det	P	2	-	1	-	1	1	1
Rick Donnelly, Atl	P	-	-	-	-	-	2	-
Mike Horan, Den	P	1	1	2	1	-	1	1
Ralf Mojsiejenko, SD	P	-	-	-	-	-	2	-
Tim Brown, LARd	KR	x	1K	x	1K	1K	x	1K
Dennis Gentry, ChiB	KR	x	-	x	-	-	x	1K
John Taylor, SF	KR	x	1P	x	1P	1P	x	1P
Jo Jo Townsell, NYJ	KR	x	-	x	-	-	x	1P
Robert Delpino, LARm	ST	x	x	x	x	-	x	1
Eugene Seale, Hou	ST	x	x	x	x	1	x	1

1989 ALL-NFL

OFFENSE		ALL-NFL					CONF	
		AP	FW	NE	SN	PW	UP	PW
Brian Blades, Sea	WR	-	-	-	-	-	2	-
Mark Carrier, TB	WR	-	-	2	-	-	2	-
Henry Ellard, LARm	WR	-	-	-	-	-	2	-
Anthony Miller, SD	WR	-	-	-	-	-	2	1
Andre Reed, Buf	WR	2	-	2	-	-	1	1
Jerry Rice, SF	WR	1	1	1	1	1	1	1
Sterling Sharpe, GB	WR	1	1	1	1	1	1	1
Webster Slaughter, Cle	WR	2	-	-	-	-	1	-
Ferrell Edmunds, Mia	TE	-	-	-	-	-	2	-
Rodney Holman, Cin	TE	2	-	1	-	1	1	1
Keith Jackson, Phi	TE	1	1	-	1	-	1	1
Steve Jordan, Min	TE	-	-	2	-	-	2	-
John Alt, KC	T	-	-	-	-	-	2	-
Bruce Armstrong, NE	T	-	-	-	-	-	2	-
Lomas Brown, Det	T	-	-	2	-	-	-	-
Paul Gruber, TB	T	-	-	-	-	-	1	-
Chris Hinton, Ind	T	2	-	2	-	-	1	1
Jim Lachey, Was	T	1	-	-	1	1	1	1
Anthony Munoz, Cin	T	1	1	1	1	1	1	1
Jackie Slater, LARm	T	2	-	1	-	-	2	1
Gary Zimmerman, Min	T	-	1	-	-	-	2	-
Roy Foster, Mia	G	-	-	-	-	-	2	-
Bill Fralic, Atl	G	-	-	-	-	-	1	-
Ron Hallstrom, GB	G	-	-	-	-	-	2	-
Bruce Matthews, Hou	G	1	-	2	1	1t	1	1
Randall McDaniel, Min	G	-	-	-	-	-	2	1
Max Montoya, Cin	G	2	-	-	-	-	2	-
Rich Moran, GB	G	-	-	1	-	-	-	-
Mike Munchak, Hou	G	2	1	1	-	1t	1	1
Tom Newberry, LARm	G	1	1	2	1	1	1	1
Ray Donaldson, Ind	C	-	-	-	-	-	2	-
Jay Hilgenberg, ChiB	C	1	1	1	-	1	1	1
Kent Hull, Buf	C	2	-	-	1	-	1	1
Kirk Lowdermilk, Min	C	-	-	2	-	-	2	-
Boomer Esiason, Cin	QB	-	-	-	-	-	2	1
Jim Everett, LARm	QB	-	-	2	-	-	-	-
Don Majkowski, GB	QB	2	-	-	-	-	2	-
Joe Montana, SF	QB	1	1	1	1	1	1	1
Warren Moon, Hou	QB	-	-	-	-	-	1	-
Neal Anderson, ChiB	RB	-	-	-	-	-	1	1
James Brooks, Cin	RB	-	-	-	-	-	2	-
Roger Craig, SF	RB	-	-	-	-	-	2	-
Dalton Hilliard, NO	RB	2	-	2	-	-	2	-
Bo Jackson, LARd	RB	-	-	-	-	-	2	-
Christian Okoye, KC	RB	1	1	1	1	1	1	1
Barry Sanders, Det	RB	1	1	2	1	1	1	1
Thurman Thomas, Buf	RB	2	-	1	-	-	1	1

DEFENSE		ALL-NFL					CONF	
		AP	FW	NE	SN	PW	UP	PW
Chris Doleman, Min	DE	1	1	1	1	1	1	1
Howie Long, LARd	DE	-	-	2	-	-	-	-
Charles Mann, Was	DE	-	-	-	-	-	2	-
Clyde Simmons, Phi	DE	-	-	-	-	-	2	-
Bruce Smith, Buf	DE	2	-	2	-	-	1	1
Greg Townsend, LARd	DE	-	-	-	-	-	2	-
Reggie White, Phi	DE	1	1	1	-	1	1	1
Lee Williams, SD	DE	2	-	-	1	-	1	1
Jerry Ball, Det	DT	-	-	2	-	1	-	1
Jerome Brown, Phi	DT	-	-	2	-	-	-	-
Tony Casillas, Atl	DT	2	-	-	-	-	2	-
Ray Childress, Hou	DT	2	-	-	-	-	2E	-
Greg Kragen, Den	DT	-	-	-	-	-	-	1
Keith Millard, Min	DT	1	1	1	1	1	1	1
Michael Dean Perry, Cle	DT	1	1	1	1	-	1	1
Fred Smerlas, Buf	DT	-	-	-	-	-	2	-
John Grimsley, Hou	ILB	-	-	-	-	-	2	-
Mike Johnson, Cle	ILB	-	-	-	-	-	1	1
Vaughan Johnson, NO	ILB	2	-	1	-	-	1	1
Eugene Lockhart, Dal	ILB	2	-	-	1	-	-	-
Karl Mecklenburg, Den	ILB	1	1	1	-	1	1	1
John Offerdahl, Mia	ILB	-	-	-	-	-	2	-
Mike Singletary, ChiB	ILB	1	1	-	1	1	1	1
Billy Ray Smith, SD	ILB	-	-	2	-	-	-	-
Chris Spielman, Det	ILB	-	-	-	-	-	2	-
Scott Studwell, Min	ILB	-	-	-	-	-	2	-
Michael Walter, SF	ILB	-	-	2	-	-	-	-
Cornelius Bennett, Buf	OLB	-	-	-	-	-	2	-
Kevin Greene, LARm	OLB	2	-	1	1	-	2	-
Tim Harris, GB	OLB	1	1	1	1	1	1	1
Clay Matthews, Cle	OLB	-	-	-	-	-	2	-
Leslie O'Neal, SD	OLB	-	-	-	-	-	1	1
Pat Swilling, NO	OLB	2	-	2	-	-	2	-
Lawrence Taylor, NYG	OLB	1	1	2	-	1	1	1
Derrick Thomas, KC	OLB	-	-	-	-	-	1	1
Eric Allen, Phi	CB	1	-	2	-	1	1	1
Gill Byrd, SD	CB	-	-	-	1	-	-	-
Mark Collins, NYG	CB	-	-	1	-	-	-	-
Jerry Gray, LARm	CB	2	1	-	-	-	2	1
Don Griffin, SF	CB	-	-	-	-	-	1	-
Carl Lee, Min	CB	-	-	-	-	-	2	-
Albert Lewis, KC	CB	1	1	1	1	1	1	1
Frank Minnifield, Cle	CB	2	-	2	-	-	1	-
Nate Odomes, Buf	CB	-	-	-	-	-	2	-
Kevin Ross, KC	CB	-	-	-	-	-	2	-

DEFENSE				ALL-NFL			CONF	
		AP	FW	NE	SN	PW	UP	PW
Rod Woodson, Pit	CB	-	-	-	-	-	-	1
Joey Browner, Min	S	2	-	1	-	-	2	1t
Deron Cherry, KC	S	-	-	-	-	-	2	-
David Fulcher, Cin	S	1	1	2	1	1	1	1
Harry Hamilton, TB	S	-	-	-	1	-	2	-
Ronnie Lott, SF	S	1	1	-	-	1	1	1
Tim McDonald, Pho	S	-	-	1	-	-	1	1t
Erik McMillan, NYJ	S	-	-	2	-	-	1	-
Dennis Smith, Den	S	2	-	-	-	-	2	1

SPECIALISTS				ALL-NFL			CONF	
		AP	FW	NE	SN	PW	UP	PW
Kevin Butler, ChiB	K	-	-	-	-	-	2	-
Mike Cofer, SF	K	1	-	1	-	-	1	-
Mike Lansford, LARm	K	-	-	2	1	-	-	-
Ed Murray, Det	K	2	1	-	-	1	-	1
David Treadwell, Den	K	-	-	-	-	-	1	1
Tony Zendejas, Hou	K	-	-	-	-	-	2	-
Rich Camarillo, Pho	P	2	-	-	-	-	2	-
Sean Landeta, NYG	P	1	1	-	1	1	1	1
Greg Montgomery, Hou	P	-	-	1	-	-	1	1
Reggie Roby, Mia	P	-	-	2	-	-	2	-
Mel Gray, Det	KR	-	-	x	-	-	x	1K
Dave Meggett, NYG	KR	-	1P	x	-	-	x	-
Walter Stanley, Det	KR	-	-	x	1P	1P	x	1P
John Taylor, SF	KR	2	-	x	-	-	x	-
Clarence Verdin, Ind	KR	-	-	x	-	-	x	1P
Rod Woodson, Pit	KR	1	1K	x	1K	1K	x	1K
Rufus Porter, Sea	ST	x	x	x	x	1	x	1
Ron Wolfley, Pho	ST	x	x	x	x	-	x	1

1990 ALL-NFL

OFFENSE				ALL-NFL			CONF	
		AP	FW	NE	SN	PW	UP	PW
Gary Clark, Was	WR	-	-	-	-	-	2	-
Ernest Givins, Hou	WR	2	-	-	-	-	1	-
Drew Hill, Hou	WR	-	-	-	-	-	2	-
Anthony Miller, SD	WR	-	-	-	-	-	2	1
Andre Reed, Buf	WR	2	-	2	-	-	1	1
Jerry Rice, SF	WR	1	1	1	1	1	1	1
Andre Rison, Atl	WR	1	1	1	1	1	1	1
Sterling Sharpe, GB	WR	-	-	2	-	-	2	-
Eric Green, Pit	TE	-	-	-	-	-	2	-
Rodney Holman, Cin	TE	2	-	2	-	-	1	1
Keith Jackson, Phi	TE	1	1	1	1	1	1	1
Jay Novacek, Dal	TE	-	-	-	-	-	2	-
John Alt, KC	T	2	-	-	1	-	1	-
Bruce Armstrong, NE	T	-	-	2	-	-	-	1
Howard Ballard, Buf	T	-	-	-	-	-	2	-
Lomas Brown, Det	T	-	-	2	-	-	1	-
Jimbo Covert, ChiB	T	-	-	-	-	-	2	-
Jim Lachey, Was	T	1	1	1	1	1	1	1
Anthony Munoz, Cin	T	1	1	1	-	1	1	1
Luis Sharpe, Pho	T	2	-	-	-	-	-	-
Jackie Slater, LARm	T	-	-	-	-	-	2	1
Richmond Webb, Mia	T	-	-	-	-	-	2	-
Mark Bortz, ChiB	G	-	-	1	-	-	2	1
Bill Fralic, Atl	G	-	-	-	-	-	-	-
Bruce Matthews, Hou	G	1	1	1	1	1	1	1
Randall McDaniel, Min	G	1	-	2	-	-	1	1
Guy McIntyre, SF	G	-	-	-	-	-	1	-
Mike Munchak, Hou	G	2	-	-	-	-	2	-
Tom Newberry, LARm	G	-	-	-	-	-	2	-
Jim Ritcher, Buf	G	-	-	-	-	-	2	-
Steve Wisniewski, LARd	G	2	1	2	1	1	1	1
Jay Hilgenberg, ChiB	C	2	-	-	-	-	1	1
Kent Hull, Buf	C	1	1	1	1	1	1	1
Don Mosebar, LARd	C	-	-	2	-	-	2	-
Randall Cunningham, Phi	QB	-	1	-	-	1	1	1
Jim Kelly, Buf	QB	-	-	2	-	-	2	-
Joe Montana, SF	QB	1	-	1	-	-	2	-
Warren Moon, Hou	QB	2	-	-	1	-	1	1
Neal Anderson, ChiB	RB	2	-	2	-	-	1	1
James Brooks, Cin	RB	-	-	-	-	-	2	-
Marion Butts, SD	RB	2	-	2	-	-	1	1
Keith Byars, Phi	RB	-	-	-	-	-	2	-
Earnest Byner, Was	RB	-	-	-	-	-	2	-
Bo Jackson, LARd	RB	-	-	-	-	-	2	-
Barry Sanders, Det	RB	1	1	1	1	1	1	1
Thurman Thomas, Buf	RB	1	1	1	1	1	1	1

UPI did not choose a second-team center.

DEFENSE				ALL-NFL			CONF	
		AP	FW	NE	SN	PW	UP	PW
Jeff Cross, Mia	DE	-	-	2	-	-	2	-
Richard Dent, ChiB	DE	2	-	-	-	-	1	1
Chris Doleman, Min	DE	-	-	2	-	-	2	-

DEFENSE				ALL-NFL			CONF	
		AP	FW	NE	SN	PW	UP	PW
Kevin Fagen, SF	DE	-	-	-	-	-	2	-
Howie Long, LARd	DE	-	-	-	-	-	2	-
Bruce Smith, Buf	DE	1	1	1	1	1	1	1
Greg Townsend, LARd	DE	2	-	1	1	-	1	1
Reggie White, Phi	DE	1	1	1T	-	1	1	1
Jerry Ball, Det	DT	2	-	-	-	-	2	1
Jerome Brown, Phi	DT	1	-	-	-	-	1	1
Ray Childress, Hou	DT	2	1	2	1	-	2	-
Michael Dean Perry, Cle	DT	1	1	1	1	1	1	1
Dan Saleaumua, KC	DT	-	-	2	-	1	-	1
Alvin Wright, LARm	DT	-	-	-	-	-	2	-
Shane Conlan, Buf	ILB	2	-	-	-	-	2	-
Byron Evans, Phi	ILB	-	-	2	-	-	-	-
Pepper Johnson, NYG	ILB	1	1	1	1	1	1	1
Vaughan Johnson, NO	ILB	-	-	2	-	-	2	-
David Little, Pit	ILB	-	-	-	-	-	1	1
Eugene Lockhart, Dal	ILB	-	-	-	-	-	2	-
John Offerdahl, Mia	ILB	1	1	1	1	1	1	1
Mike Singletary, ChiB	ILB	2	-	-	-	-	1	1
Cornelius Bennett, Buf	OLB	-	-	-	-	-	1	-
Mike Cofer, Det	OLB	-	-	2	-	-	2	-
Charles Haley, SF	OLB	1	1	1	-	1	1	1
Leslie O'Neal, SD	OLB	-	-	2	-	-	2	-
Pat Swilling, NO	OLB	2	-	-	-	-	2	-
Darryl Talley, Buf	OLB	-	-	-	1	-	2	1
Lawrence Taylor, NYG	OLB	2	-	-	-	-	1	1
Derrick Thomas, KC	OLB	1	1	1	1	1	1	1
Gill Byrd, SD	CB	-	-	2	-	-	-	-
Mark Collins, NYG	CB	-	-	-	-	-	1	-
Darrell Green, Was	CB	2	-	-	-	1	1	1
Don Griffin, SF	CB	-	-	-	-	-	2	-
Wayne Haddix, TB	CB	-	-	-	-	-	-	1
Issiac Holt, Dal	CB	-	-	-	-	-	2	-
Albert Lewis, KC	CB	1	1	1	1	-	1	1
Tim McKyer, Mia	CB	-	-	2	-	-	2	-
Kevin Ross, KC	CB	2	-	-	-	-	2	-
Rod Woodson, Pit	CB	1	1	1	1	1	1	1
Steve Atwater, Den	S	-	-	2	-	-	1	1
Joey Browner, Min	S	1	1	1	1	1	1	1
Mark Carrier, ChiB	S	2	-	-	-	1	1	1
David Fulcher, Cin	S	2	-	-	-	-	1	1
Carnell Lake, Pit	S	-	-	-	-	-	2	-
Ronnie Lott, SF	S	1	1	1	1	-	2	-
Tim McDonald, Pho	S	-	-	2	-	-	2	-
Louis Oliver, Mia	S	-	-	-	-	-	2	-

SPECIALISTS				ALL-NFL			CONF	
		AP	FW	NE	SN	PW	UP	PW
John Carney, SD	K	-	-	2	-	-	-	-
Steve Christie, TB	K	-	-	-	-	-	1	1
Chris Jacke, GB	K	-	-	-	-	-	2	-
Nick Lowery, KC	K	1	1	1	1	1	1	1
Pete Stoyanovich, Mia	K	2	-	-	-	-	2	-
Rich Camarillo, Pho	P	-	-	-	-	-	2	-
Mike Horan, Den	P	-	-	-	-	-	2	-
Sean Landeta, NYG	P	1	1	1	1	1	1	1
Rohn Stark, Ind	P	2	-	2	-	-	1	1
Mel Gray, Det	KR	1	1K	x	1K	1K	1K	1K
Dave Meggett, NYG	KR	2	1P	x	1P	-	1P	1P
Clarence Verdin, Ind	KR	-	-	x	-	1P	1P	1P
Rod Woodson, Pit	KR	-	-	x	-	-	1K	1K
Steve Tasker, Buf	ST	x	x	x	x	-	x	1
Reyna Thompson, NYG	ST	x	x	x	x	1	x	1

1991 ALL-NFL

OFFENSE				ALL-NFL			CONF	
		AP	FW	SN	PW	NE	UP	PW
Gary Clark, Was	WR	2	-	-	-	1	1	-
Michael Irvin, Dal	WR	1	1	1	1	1	1	1
Haywood Jeffires, Hou	WR	1	1	-	-	2	1	1
Andre Reed, Buf	WR	-	-	-	-	2	1	1
Jerry Rice, SF	WR	-	-	1	1	2	-	1
Andre Rison, Atl	WR	2	-	-	-	1	-	-
Marv Cook, NE	TE	1	1	1	1	1	1	1
Jay Novacek, Dal	TE	2	-	-	-	2	1	1
John Alt, KC	T	-	-	-	-	-	1	-
Bruce Armstrong, NE	T	-	-	-	-	-	1	1
Howard Ballard, Buf	T	-	-	-	-	-	-	1
Lomas Brown, Det	T	2	-	-	-	1	-	-
Paul Gruber, TB	T	-	-	-	-	2	-	-
Mike Kenn, Atl	T	1	1	-	1	2	1	1
Jim Lachey, Was	T	1	1	1	1	1	1	1
Anthony Munoz, Cin	T	2	-	1	-	-	-	-
Randall McDaniel, Min	G	2	-	1	-	1	-	1
Guy McIntyre, SF	G	-	-	-	-	-	1	1
Raleigh McKenzie, Was	G	-	-	-	-	-	1	-
Mike Munchak, Hou	G	1	1	-	1	2	1	1

OFFENSE		ALL-NFL					CONF	
		AP	FW	SN	PW	NE	UP	PW
Jim Ritcher, Buf	G	2	-	-	-	2	-	-
Steve Wisniewski, LARd	G	1	1	1	1	1	1	1
Jay Hilgenberg, ChiB	C	-	-	-	-	-	1	1
Kent Hull, Buf	C	1	1	-	-	-	1	-
Bruce Matthews, Hou	C	2	-	-	1	1	-	1
Don Mosebar, LARd	C	-	-	1	-	2	-	-
Jim Kelly, Buf	QB	1	1	1	1	1	1	1
Mark Rypien, Was	QB	2	-	-	-	2	1	1
Earnest Byner, Was	RB	2	-	-	-	-	-	-
Gaston Green, Den	RB	-	-	-	-	-	1	-
Christian Okoye, KC	RB	-	-	-	-	2	-	1
Barry Sanders, Det	RB	1	1	1	1	1	1	1
Emmitt Smith, Dal	RB	2	-	-	-	2	1	1
Thurman Thomas, Buf	RB	1	1	1	1	1	1	1

Note: *NEA* chose three wide receivers.

DEFENSE		ALL-NFL					CONF	
		AP	FW	SN	PW	NE	UP	PW
William Fuller, Hou	DE	-	-	-	-	-	1	1
Jeff Lageman, NYJ	DE	-	-	-	-	2	-	-
Charles Mann, Was	DE	2	-	-	-	-	-	-
Clyde Simmons, Phi	DE	1	1	1	1	1	1	1
Greg Townsend, LARd	DE	2	-	-	-	2	1	1
Reggie White, Phi	DE	1	1	1	1	1	1	1
Jerry Ball, Det	DT	1	1	-	1	1	1	1
Jerome Brown, Phi	DT	1	1	1	1	-	1	1
Ray Childress, Hou	DT	-	-	-	-	1	1	1
Cortez Kennedy, Sea	DT	-	-	-	-	2	-	-
Greg Kragen, Den	DT	-	-	-	-	-	1	-
Steve McMichael, ChiB	DT	2	-	-	-	-	-	-
Michael Dean Perry, Cle	DT	2	-	1	-	2	-	1
Vincent Brown, NE	ILB	2	-	-	-	2	-	1
Vaughn Johnson, NO	ILB	-	-	-	-	-	-	1
Karl Mecklenburg, Den	ILB	-	-	-	-	-	1	-
Sam Mills, NO	ILB	2	1	1	1	2	-	1
Junior Seau, SD	ILB	-	-	-	-	1	-	-
Mike Singletary, ChiB	ILB	1	-	1	-	-	1	-
Al Smith, Hou	ILB	-	1	-	1	-	1	1
Chris Spielman, Det	ILB	1	-	-	-	-	-	-
Jessie Tuggle, Atl	ILB	-	-	-	-	-	1	-
Cornelius Bennett, Buf	OLB	-	-	-	-	1	1	1
Seth Joyner, Phi	OLB	2	1	-	-	1I	-	1
Wilber Marshall, Was	OLB	2	-	-	-	2	1	-
Pat Swilling, NO	OLB	1	1	1	1	1	1	1
Derrick Thomas, KC	OLB	1	-	1	1	2	1	1
Eric Allen, Phi	CB	2	-	-	-	2	-	-
Gill Byrd, SD	CB	-	-	-	-	-	-	1
Cris Dishman, Hou	CB	1	-	-	1	-	1	1
Darrell Green, Was	CB	1	1	1	1	1	1	1
Nate Odomes, Buf	CB	-	-	-	-	-	1	-
Deion Sanders, Atl	CB	2	1	1	-	1	1	1
Rod Woodson, Pit	CB	-	-	-	-	2	-	-
Steve Atwater, Den	S	1	1	-	1	1	1	1
Bennie Blades, Det	S	-	-	-	-	2	1	1
Mark Carrier, ChiB	S	-	-	1	-	1	-	-
Ronnie Lott, LARd	S	1	1	1	1	-	1	1
Tim McDonald, Pho	S	2	-	-	-	2	-	1
Bubba McDowell, Hou	S	2	-	-	-	-	-	-
Andre Waters, Phi	S	-	-	-	-	-	1	-

SPECIALISTS		ALL-NFL					CONF	
		AP	FW	SN	PW	NE	UP	PW
Jeff Jaeger, LARd	K	1	1	-	1	2	1	1
Chip Lohmiller, Was	K	2	-	1	-	-	1	1
Pete Stoyanovich, Mia	K	-	-	-	-	1	-	-
Rich Camarillo, Pho	P	-	-	-	-	-	1	1
Jeff Gossett, LARd	P	1	1	1	1	1	1	1
Reggie Roby, Mia	P	2	-	-	-	2	-	-
Tim Brown, LARd	KR	-	x	-	-	x	x	1P
Mel Gray, Det	KR	1	x	1	1	x	x	1
Nate Lewis, SD	KR	-	x	-	-	x	x	1K
Brian Mitchell, Was	KR	2	x	-	-	x	x	-
Steve Tasker, Buf	ST	x	x	x	1	x	x	1
Bennie Thompson, NO	ST	x	x	x	-	x	x	1

1992 ALL-NFL

OFFENSE		ALL-NFL				CONF	
		AP	FW	SN	NE	UP	PW
Michael Irvin, Dal	WR	2	-	-	2	-	-
Haywood Jeffires, Hou	WR	-	-	-	-	1	1
Anthony Miller, SD	WR	-	-	-	-	1	1
Jerry Rice, SF	WR	1	1	1	1	1	1
Andre Rison, Atl	WR	2	-	-	2	-	-
Sterling Sharpe, GB	WR	1	1	1	1	1	1
Jackie Harris, GB	TE	-	-	-	2	-	-
Keith Jackson, Mia	TE	2	-	-	-	1	1
Brent Jones, SF	TE	-	-	-	1	-	-
Jay Novacek, Dal	TE	1	1	1	-	1	1
Howard Ballard, Buf	T	-	-	-	-	1	1
Harris Barton, SF	T	1	1	1	2	-	1
Lomas Brown, Det	T	-	-	1	-	-	-
Paul Gruber, TB	T	2	-	-	1	-	-
Steve Wallace, SF	T	2	1	-	-	1	1
Richmond Webb, Mia	T	1	-	1	-	1	1
Will Wolford, Buf	T	-	-	-	2	-	-
Gary Zimmerman, Min	T	-	-	-	1	1	-
Carlton Haselrig, Pit	G	-	-	-	-	1	-
Derek Kennard, NO	G	-	-	-	2	-	-
Randall McDaniel, Min	G	1	1	1	1	-	1
Guy McIntyre, SF	G	2	-	-	-	1	1
Mike Munchak, Hou	G	2	-	-	-	1	1
Nate Newton, Dal	G	-	-	-	-	1	-
Dave Richards, SD	G	-	-	-	2	-	-
Steve Wisniewski, LARd	G	1	1	1	-	-	1
Kirk Lowdermilk, Min	C	-	-	-	2	-	-
Bruce Matthews, Hou	C	1	1	1	1G	1	1
Mark Stepnoski, Dal	C	2	-	-	1	1	1
Randall Cunningham, Phi	QB	2t	-	-	-	-	-
Jim Kelly, Buf	QB	2t	-	-	-	-	-
Dan Marino, Mia	QB	-	-	-	2	1	1
Steve Young, SF	QB	1	1	1	1	1	1
Barry Foster, Pit	RB	1	1	1	1	1	1
Barry Sanders, Det	RB	2	-	-	2	1	1
Emmitt Smith, Dal	RB	1	1	1	1	1	1
Thurman Thomas, Buf	RB	2	-	-	2	1	1

DEFENSE		ALL-NFL				CONF	
		AP	FW	SN	NE	UP	PW
Chris Doleman, Min	DE	1	1	1	1	1	1
Leslie O'Neal, SD	DE	-	-	-	2	1	1
Clyde Simmons, Phi	DE	1	-	-	-	-	-
Bruce Smith, Buf	DE	2	-	1	2t	1	1
Neil Smith, KC	DE	-	-	-	2t	-	-
Reggie White, Phi	DE	2	1	-	1	1	1
Ray Childress, Hou	DT	1	1	-	1	-	1
Pierce Holt, SF	DT	2	-	-	2	1	1
Cortez Kennedy, Sea	DT	1	1	1	1	1	1
Greg Kragen, Den	DT	2	-	-	-	-	-
Wayne Martin, NO	DT	-	-	-	2	-	-
Michael Dean Perry, Cle	DT	-	-	1	-	-	-
Henry Thomas, Min	DT	-	-	-	-	-	1
Cornelius Bennett, Buf	ILB	-	-	-	1	-	-
Vincent Brown, NE	ILB	-	-	-	-	1	-
Byron Evans, Phi	ILB	-	-	-	2	-	1
Vaughan Johnson, NO	ILB	-	-	-	-	1	-
Sam Mills, NO	ILB	2	1	1	-	1	1
Junior Seau, SD	ILB	1	1	1	1	1	1
Al Smith, Hou	ILB	1	-	-	2	-	1
Chris Spielman, Det	ILB	2	-	-	-	-	-
Bryan Cox, Mia	OLB	-	-	-	-	1	1
Rickey Jackson, NO	OLB	2	1	-	2	1	1
Seth Joyner, Phi	OLB	2	-	-	2	-	-
Wilber Marshall, Was	OLB	1	1	-	1	1	1
Pat Swilling, NO	OLB	1	-	1	-	-	-
Derrick Thomas, KC	OLB	-	-	1	1	1	1
Eric Allen, Phi	CB	-	-	-	-	1	-
Gill Byrd, SD	CB	2	-	-	-	1	1
Carl Lee, Min	CB	-	-	-	2	-	-
Terry McDaniel, LARd	CB	-	-	-	2	-	-
Audray McMillian, Min	CB	1	1	-	-	1	1
Ricky Reynolds, TB	CB	-	-	-	-	-	1
Deion Sanders, Atl	CB	2	-	1	1	-	-
Rod Woodson, Pit	CB	1	1	1	1	1	1
Steve Atwater, Den	S	1	1	1	1	-	1
Bennie Blades, Det	S	-	-	-	2	-	-
Chuck Cecil, GB	S	-	-	-	-	-	1
Brad Edwards, Was	S	-	-	-	-	1	-
Henry Jones, Buf	S	1	1	1	-	1	1
Carnell Lake, Pit	S	-	-	-	2	-	-
Tim McDonald, Pho	S	2	-	-	1	-	1
Louis Oliver, Mia	S	2	-	-	-	1	-
Todd Scott, Min	S	-	-	-	-	1	-

SPECIALISTS		ALL-NFL				CONF	
		AP	FW	SN	NE	UP	PW
Morten Andersen, NO	K	2	1	-	1	1	1
Pete Stoyanovich, Mia	K	1	-	1	2	1	1
Rich Camarillo, Pho	P	1	1	-	2	1	1
Greg Montgomery, Hou	P	-	-	-	-	1	-
Rohn Stark, Ind	P	2	-	1	1	-	1
John Bailey, Pho	KR	-	-	-	-	1	-
Mel Gray, Det	KR	2	-	1P	1	-	-
Kelvin Martin, Dal	KR	-	1P	-	-	-	1P

SPECIALISTS		ALL-NFL				CONF	
		AP	FW	SN	NE	UP	PW
Deion Sanders, Atl	KR	1	1K	1K	-	-	1K
Vai Sikahema, Phi	KR	-	-	-	2	-	-
Jon Vaughn, NE	KR	-	-	-	-	-	1K
Clarence Verdin, Ind	KR	-	-	-	-	1	1P
Elbert Shelley, Atl	ST	x	-	x	x	x	1
Steve Tasker, Buf	ST	x	1	x	x	x	1

1993 ALL-NFL

OFFENSE		ALL-NFL			CONF	
		AP	FW	SN	UP	PW
Tim Brown, LARd	WR	-	-	-	1	1
Michael Irvin, Dal	WR	2	-	-	-	-
Anthony Miller, SD	WR	-	-	-	1	1
Jerry Rice, SF	WR	1	1	1	1	1
Andre Rison, Atl	WR	2	-	-	-	-
Sterling Sharpe, GB	WR	1	1	1	1	1
Brent Jones, SF	TE	2	-	-	1	1
Shannon Sharpe, Den	TE	1	1	1	1	1
Howard Ballard, Buf	T	-	-	-	1	-
Harris Barton, SF	T	1	1	1	1	1
John Jackson, Pit	T	-	-	-	-	1
Richmond Webb, Mia	T	2	-	-	1	-
Erik Williams, Dal	T	1	1	1	1	1
Gary Zimmerman, Den	T	2	-	-	-	1
Chris Hinton, Atl	G	1	-	-	1	-
Randall McDaniel, Min	G	1	1	1	1	1
Mike Munchak, Hou	G	2	-	-	1	1
Nate Newton, Dal	G	-	-	-	-	1
Steve Wisniewski, LARd	G	2	1	1	1	1
Dermontti Dawson, Pit	C	1	-	-	-	-
Bruce Matthews, Hou	C	2	1	1	1	1
Mark Stepnoski, Dal	C	-	-	-	1	1
Troy Aikman, Dal	QB	-	-	1	-	-
John Elway, Den	QB	2	-	-	1	1
Steve Young, SF	QB	1	1	-	1	1
Marcus Allen, KC	RB	-	-	-	1	1
Jerome Bettis, LARm	RB	1	1	-	1	1
Barry Sanders, Det	RB	2	-	1	-	-
Emmitt Smith, Dal	RB	1	1	1	1	1
Thurman Thomas, Buf	RB	2	-	-	1	1

DEFENSE		ALL-NFL			CONF	
		AP	FW	SN	UP	PW
Richard Dent, ChiB	DE	-	-	-	-	1
Chris Doleman, Min	DE	2	-	-	1	-
Bruce Smith, Buf	DE	1	1	1	1	1
Neil Smith, KC	DE	1	1	-	1	1
Reggie White, GB	DE	2	-	1	1	1
Ray Childress, Hou	DT	2	-	-	1	1
Sean Gilbert, LARm	DT	-	-	-	1	1
Cortez Kennedy, Sea	DT	1	1	1	1	1
Michael Dean Perry, Cle	DT	-	-	1	-	-
John Randle, Min	DT	1	1	-	1	1
Henry Thomas, Min	DT	2	-	-	-	-
Michael Brooks, NYG	ILB	2	-	-	1	1
Vincent Brown, NE	ILB	-	-	-	-	1
Hardy Nickerson, TB	ILB	1	1	1	-	1
Ken Norton, Dal	ILB	2	-	-	-	-
Junior Seau, SD	ILB	1	1	1	1	1
Rickey Jackson, NO	OLB	2	-	1	1	1
Seth Joyner, Phi	OLB	-	1	-	-	1
Greg Lloyd, Pit	OLB	1	1	-	1	1
Darryl Talley, Buf	OLB	-	-	1	-	1
Derrick Thomas, KC	OLB	2	-	-	1	-
Renaldo Turnbull, NO	OLB	1	-	-	1	-
Eric Allen, Phi	CB	2	-	-	1	1
Terry McDaniel, LARd	CB	-	-	-	-	1
Nate Odomes, Buf	CB	2	-	-	1	-
Deion Sanders, Atl	CB	1	1	1	1	1
Rod Woodson, Pit	CB	1	1	1	1	1
Steve Atwater, Den	S	-	-	-	1	-
LeRoy Butler, GB	S	1	1	1	1	1
Tim McDonald, SF	S	2	-	-	1	1
Marcus Robertson, Hou	S	1	-	1	1	1
Eugene Robinson, Sea	S	2	1	-	-	1

SPECIALISTS		ALL-NFL			CONF	
		AP	FW	SN	UP	PW
Gary Anderson, Pit	K	-	-	-	1	1
Jason Hanson, Det	K	-	-	1	-	-
Chris Jacke, GB	K	1	-	-	-	-
Norm Johnson, Atl	K	2	1	-	1	1
Rich Camarillo, Pho	P	2	-	-	1	1
Greg Montgomery, Hou	P	1	1	1	1	1
Mel Gray, Det	KR	-	-	1K	-	-
Tyrone Hughes, NO	KR	2	1K	-	1	1P

SPECIALISTS		ALL-NFL			CONF	
		AP	FW	SN	UP	PW
O.J. McDuffie, Mia	KR	-	-	-	-	1K
Eric Metcalf, Cle	KR	1	1P	1P	1	1P
Elbert Shelley, Atl	ST	x	-	x	x	1
Steve Tasker, Buf	ST	x	1	x	x	1

1994 ALL-NFL

OFFENSE		ALL-NFL			CONF	
		AP	FW	SN	UP	PW
Tim Brown, LARd	WR	-	-	-	2	1
Cris Carter, Min	WR	1	1	1	1	1
Irving Fryar, Mia	WR	2	-	-	1	-
Terance Mathis, Atl	WR	2	-	-	2	-
Carl Pickens, Cin	WR	-	-	-	2	-
Andre Reed, Buf	WR	-	-	-	1	1
Jerry Rice, SF	WR	1	1	1	1	1
Sterling Sharpe, GB	WR	-	-	-	2	-
Ben Coates, NE	TE	1	1	1	1	1
Brent Jones, SF	TE	2	-	-	1	1
Jay Novacek, Dal	TE	-	-	-	2	-
Shannon Sharpe, Den	TE	-	-	-	2	-
Bruce Armstrong, NE	T	-	-	-	1	-
Lomas Brown, Det	T	2	-	-	1	1
Tony Jones, Cle	T	2	-	-	2	1
Willie Roaf, NO	T	1	1	1	1	1
Mark Tuinei, Dal	T	-	-	-	2	-
Steve Wallace, SF	T	-	-	-	2	-
Richmond Webb, Mia	T	1	1	1	1	1
Gary Zimmerman, Den	T	-	-	-	2	-
Bob Kratch, NE	G	-	-	-	2	-
Duval Love, Pit	G	-	-	-	2	-
Randall McDaniel, Min	G	1	1	1	1	1
Nate Newton, Dal	G	1	1	-	1	1
Jesse Sapolu, SF	G	-	-	-	2	-
Keith Sims, Mia	G	2	-	-	1	1
Lance Smith, NYG	G	-	-	-	2	-
Steve Wisniewski, LARd	G	2	-	1	1	1
Dermontti Dawson, Pit	C	1	1	1	1	1
Kevin Glover, Det	C	-	-	-	-	1
Courtney Hall, SD	C	-	-	-	2	-
Bart Oates, SF	C	-	-	-	2	-
Mark Stepnoski, Dal	C	2	-	-	1	-
Troy Aikman, Dal	QB	-	-	-	2	-
Drew Bledsoe, NE	QB	-	-	-	2	-
Dan Marino, Mia	QB	2	-	-	1	1
Steve Young, SF	QB	1	1	1	1	1
Terry Allen, Min	RB	-	-	-	2	-
Marshall Faulk, Ind	RB	2	-	-	1	1
Natrone Means, SD	RB	-	-	-	2	-
Barry Sanders, Det	RB	1	1	1	1	1
Emmitt Smith, Dal	RB	1	1	1	1	1
Thurman Thomas, Buf	RB	-	-	-	2	-
Chris Warren, Sea	RB	2	-	-	1	1
Ricky Watters, SF	RB	-	-	-	2	-

DEFENSE		ALL-NFL			CONF	
		AP	FW	SN	UP	PW
Rob Burnett, Cle	DE	-	-	-	2	-
William Fuller, Phi	DE	-	-	-	2	-
Charles Haley, Dal	DE	1	1	1	1	1
Sean Jones, GB	DE	-	-	-	2	-
Leslie O'Neal, SD	DE	2	-	-	1	1
Bruce Smith, Buf	DE	1	1	1	1	1
Neil Smith, KC	DE	-	-	-	2	-
Reggie White, GB	DE	2	-	-	1	1
Tim Bowens, Mia	DT	-	-	-	2	-
Cortez Kennedy, Sea	DT	1	-	-	1	1
Leon Lett, Dal	DT	-	-	-	1	-
Chester McGlockton, LARd	DT	2	1	1	2	1
Michael Dean Perry, Cle	DT	2	-	-	1	-
John Randle, Min	DT	1	1	1	1	1
Dana Stubblefield, SF	DT	-	-	-	2	1
Henry Thomas, Min	DT	-	-	-	2	-
Bryan Cox, Mia	ILB	-	-	-	-	1
Jack Del Rio, Min	ILB	-	-	-	2	1
Pepper Johnson, Cle	ILB	-	-	-	2	-
Junior Seau, SD	ILB	1	1	1	1	1
Chris Spielman, Det	ILB	2	1	1	1	1
Jessie Tuggle, Atl	ILB	-	-	-	2	-
Cornelius Bennett, Buf	OLB	-	-	-	2	-
Kevin Greene, Pit	OLB	1	1	-	2	1
Ken Harvey, Was	OLB	2	-	-	1	1
Seth Joyner, Ariz	OLB	-	-	-	2	-
Greg Lloyd, Pit	OLB	1	1	1	1	1
Bryce Paup, GB	OLB	-	-	-	1	1
Derrick Thomas, KC	OLB	2	-	-	1	-
Eric Allen, Phi	CB	-	-	-	2	-
Ray Buchanan, Ind	CB	-	-	-	2	-

DEFENSE		ALL-NFL			CONF	
		AP	FW	SN	UP	PW
Dale Carter, KC	CB	-	-	-	2	-
Terry McDaniel, LARd	CB	2	-	-	1	1
Deion Sanders, SF	CB	1	1	1	1	1
Aeneas Williams, Ariz	CB	2	-	-	1	-
Rod Woodson, Pit	CB	1	1	1	1	1
Donnell Woolford, ChiB	CB	-	-	-	2	1
Mark Carrier, ChiB	S	-	-	-	2	-
Merton Hanks, SF	S	2	-	1	1	1
Carnell Lake, Pit	S	2	-	-	1	1
Tim McDonald, SF	S	-	-	-	2	-
Darren Perry, Pit	S	-	-	-	2	-
Stanley Richard, SD	S	-	-	-	2	-
Eric Turner, Cle	S	1	1	-	1	1
Darren Woodson, Dal	S	1	1	1	1	1

SPECIALISTS		ALL-NFL			CONF	
		AP	FW	SN	UP	PW
John Carney, SD	K	1	-	1	1	1
Ed Murray, Phi	K	-	-	-	2	-
Fuad Reveiz, Min	K	2	1	-	1	1
Matt Stover, Cle	K	-	-	-	2	-
Sean Landeta, LARm	P	-	-	-	2	-
Reggie Roby, Was	P	1	1	1	1	1
Tom Rouen, Den	P	-	-	-	2	-
Rick Tuten, Sea	P	2	-	-	1	1
Andre Coleman, SD	KR	-	-	-	x	1K
Darrien Gordon, SD	KR	-	-	-	x	1P
Mel Gray, Det	KR	1	1K	1K	x	1K
Eric Metcalf, Cle	KR	-	-	1P	x	-
Brian Mitchell, Was	KR	2	1P	-	x	1P
Maurice Douglass, ChiB	ST	x	-	x	x	1
Steve Tasker, Buf	ST	x	1	x	x	1

1995 ALL-NFL

OFFENSE		ALL-NFL			CONF	
		AP	FW	SN	UP	PW
Tim Brown, Oak	WR	-	-	-	1	1
Isaac Bruce, StL	WR	-	-	-	2	-
Cris Carter, Min	WR	2	-	-	2	-
Tony Martin, SD	WR	-	-	-	2	-
Herman Moore, Det	WR	1	1	1	1	1
Carl Pickens, Cin	WR	2	-	-	1	1
Jerry Rice, SF	WR	1	1	1	1	1
Yancey Thigpen, Pit	WR	-	-	-	2	-
Mark Chmura, GB	TE	-	-	-	2	1
Ben Coates, NE	TE	1	1	1	1	1
Jay Novacek, Dal	TE	-	-	-	1	-
Shannon Sharpe, Den	TE	2	-	-	2	-
Bruce Armstrong, NE	T	-	-	-	2	1
Lomas Brown, Det	T	1	1	-	1	1
Andy Heck, ChiB	T	-	-	-	2	-
William Roaf, NO	T	1	1	1	1	1
Leon Searcy, Pit	T	-	-	-	2	-
Mark Tuinei, Dal	T	-	-	-	2	-
Richmond Webb, Mia	T	2	-	-	1	1
Erik Williams, Dal	T	-	-	1	-	-
Gary Zimmerman, Den	T	2	-	-	1	-
Larry Allen, Dal	G	2	-	1	2	-
Bruce Matthews, Hou	G	-	-	-	1	1
Randall McDaniel, Min	G	1	1	-	1	1
Nate Newton, Dal	G	1	1	1	1	1
Jesse Sapolu, SF	G	-	-	-	2	-
Keith Sims, Mia	G	-	-	-	2	-
Dave Szott, KC	G	-	-	-	2	-
Steve Wisniewski, Oak	G	2	-	-	1	1
Dermontti Dawson, Pit	C	1	1	1	1	1
Kevin Glover, Det	C	2	-	-	1	1
Kent Hull, Buf	C	-	-	-	2	-
Bart Oates, SF	C	-	-	-	2	-
Troy Aikman, Dal	QB	-	-	-	2	-
Brett Favre, GB	QB	1	1	1	1	1
Jim Harbaugh, Ind	QB	-	-	-	1	1
Dan Marino, Mia	QB	2t	-	-	2	-
Steve Young, SF	QB	2t	-	-	-	-
Terry Allen, Was	RB	-	-	-	2	-
Terrell Davis, Den	RB	-	-	-	2	-
Marshall Faulk, Ind	RB	2	-	-	2	-
Curtis Martin, NE	RB	-	-	-	1	1
Barry Sanders, Det	RB	1	1	1	1	1
Emmitt Smith, Dal	RB	1	1	1	1	1
Chris Warren, Sea	RB	2	-	-	1	1
Ricky Watters, Phi	RB	-	-	-	2	-

DEFENSE		ALL-NFL			CONF	
		AP	FW	SN	UP	PW
William Fuller, Phi	DE	2	-	-	1	1
Charles Haley, Dal	DE	-	-	-	2	-
Sean Jones, GB	DE	-	-	-	2	-
Leslie O'Neal, SD	DE	-	-	-	2	-
Ray Seals, Pit	DE	-	-	-	2	-
Bruce Smith, Buf	DE	1	1	1	1	1
Neil Smith, KC	DE	2	-	-	1	1
Reggie White, GB	DE	1	1	1	1	1
Andy Harmon, Phi	DT	2	-	-	2	-
Cortez Kennedy, Sea	DT	-	-	-	2	-
Chester McGlockton, Oak	DT	1	1	-	1	1
Michael Dean Perry, Den	DT	-	-	-	2	-
John Randle, Min	DT	1	1	1	1	1
Dan Saleaumua, KC	DT	-	-	-	1	1
Dana Stubblefield, SF	DT	2	-	-	1	1
Eric Swann, Ariz	DT	-	-	1	2	-
Bryan Cox, Mia	ILB	-	-	-	2	-
Sam Mills, Car	ILB	-	-	-	2	-
Ken Norton, SF	ILB	1	-	-	1	1
Junior Seau, SD	ILB	2	1	1	1	1
Ken Harvey, Was	OLB	2	-	-	1	1
Greg Lloyd, Pit	OLB	1	1	1	1	1
Bryce Paup, Buf	OLB	1	1	1	1	1
Chris Spielman, Det	OLB	-	-	-	2	-
Pat Swilling, Oak	OLB	-	-	-	2	-
Derrick Thomas, KC	OLB	-	-	-	2	-
William Thomas, Phi	OLB	2	-	-	2	1
Lee Woodall, SF	OLB	-	-	-	1	-
Eric Allen, NO	CB	-	-	-	2	-
Dale Carter, KC	CB	2	-	-	1	1
Eric Davis, SF	CB	1	1	-	1	1
Darryll Lewis, Hou	CB	-	-	-	2	-
Terry McDaniel, Oak	CB	2	-	-	2	1
Deion Sanders, Dal	CB	-	-	1	2	-
Aeneas Williams, Ariz	CB	1	1	1	1	1
Steve Atwater, Den	S	-	-	-	1	-
Blaine Bishop, Hou	S	-	-	-	1	1
Robert Blackmon, Sea	S	-	-	-	2	-
Merton Hanks, SF	S	1	1	1	1	1
Carnell Lake, Pit	S	2	-	-	1C	1
Tim McDonald, SF	S	2	-	-	2	-
Kurt Schulz, Buf	S	-	-	-	2	-
Orlando Thomas, Min	S	-	-	-	2	-
Darren Woodson, Dal	S	1	1	1	1	1

SPECIALISTS		ALL-NFL			CONF	
		AP	FW	SN	UP	PW
Morten Andersen, Atl	K	1	1	1	1	1
Jason Elam, Den	K	2	-	-	1	1
Louie Aguiar, KC	P	2	-	-	-	-
Darren Bennett, SD	P	1	1	1	1	1
Jeff Feagles, Ariz	P	-	-	-	1	1
Andre Coleman, SD	KR	-	-	-	x	1P
Glyn Milburn, Den	KR	2	-	1K	x	1K
Brian Mitchell, Was	KR	1	1	1P	x	1P
Elbert Shelley, Atl	ST	x	-	x	x	1
Steve Tasker, Buf	ST	x	1	x	x	1

1996 ALL-NFL

OFFENSE		ALL-NFL			CONF	
		AP	FW	SN	UP	PW
Tim Brown, Oak	WR	-	-	-	2	-
Isaac Bruce, StL	WR	-	-	-	2	-
Cris Carter, Min	WR	-	-	-	2	-
Terry Glenn, NE	WR	-	-	-	1	-
Tony Martin, SD	WR	2	-	-	2	1
Herman Moore, Det	WR	1	-	1	1	1
Carl Pickens, Cin	WR	2	1	-	1	1
Jerry Rice, SF	WR	1	1	1	1	1
Ben Coates, NE	TE	-	-	-	2	-
Keith Jackson, GB	TE	-	-	-	2	-
Shannon Sharpe, Den	TE	1	1	1	1	1
Wesley Walls, Car	TE	2	-	-	1	1
Bruce Armstrong, NE	OT	2	-	-	1	1
Tony Boselli, Jac	OT	-	-	-	2	-
Lomas Brown, Ariz	OT	-	-	-	1	1
John Jackson, Pit	OT	-	-	-	2	-
William Roaf, NO	OT	2	1	1	1	1
Bob Whitfield, Atl	OT	-	-	-	2	-
Erik Williams, Dal	OT	1	-	-	2	-
Gary Zimmerman, Den	OT	1	1	1	1	1
Larry Allen, Dal	OG	1	1	1	1	1
Bob Dahl, Was	OG	-	-	-	2	-
Bruce Matthews, Hou	OG	2	-	-	1	1
Randall McDaniel, Min	OG	1	1	1	1	1
Nate Newton, Dal	OG	-	-	-	2	-
Will Shields, KC	OG	-	-	-	2	1

OFFENSE		ALL-NFL			CONF	
		AP	FW	SN	UP	PW
Steve Wisniewski, Oak	OG	2	-	-	1	-
Will Wolford, Pit	OG	-	-	-	2	-
Dermontti Dawson, Pit	OC	1	1	1	1	1
Ray Donaldson, Dal	OC	-	-	-	2	-
Mark Glover, Det	OC	-	-	-	1	1
Mark Stepnoski, Hou	OC	2	-	-	2	-
Drew Bledsoe, NE	QB	-	-	-	2	-
Brett Favre, GB	QB	1	1	1	1	1
John Elway, Den	QB	2	-	-	1	1
Steve Young, SF	QB	-	-	-	2	-
Terry Allen, Was	RB	2	-	-	1	1
Jerome Bettis, Pit	RB	1	-	-	1	1
Terrell Davis, Den	RB	1	1	1	1	1
Eddie George, Hou	RB	-	-	-	2	-
Curtis Martin, NE	RB	-	-	-	2	-
Barry Sanders, Det	RB	2	1	1	1	1
Emmitt Smith, Dal	RB	-	-	-	2	-
Ricky Watters, Phi	RB	-	-	-	2	-
Mark Alstott, TB	FB	2	x	x	x	x
Larry Centers, Ariz	FB	1	x	x	x	x

DEFENSE		ALL-NFL			CONF	
		AP	FW	SN	UP	FW
William Fuller, Phi	DE	-	-	-	2	-
Simeon Rice, Ariz	DE	-	-	-	2	-
Michael Sinclair, Sea	DE	-	-	-	2	-
Bruce Smith, Buf	DE	1	1	1	1	1
Neil Smith, KC	DE	-	-	-	2	-
Tony Tolbert, Dal	DE	2	-	-	1	1
Reggie White, GB	DE	2	-	-	1	1
Alfred Williams, Den	DE	1	1	1	1	1
John Jurkovic, Jac	DT	-	-	-	2	-
Cortez Kennedy, Sea	DT	2	-	-	1	1
Charles McGlockton, Oak	DT	2	-	-	1	1
Michael Dean Perry, Den	DT	-	-	-	2	-
John Randle, Min	DT	1	1	1	1	1
Eric Swann, Ariz	DT	-	-	-	2	-
Dana Stubblefield, SF	DT	-	-	-	2	-
Bryant Young, SF	DT	1	1	1	1	1
Levon Kirkland, Pit	IL	2	-	-	2	1
Sam Mills, Car	IL	1	1	-	1	1
Hardy Nickerson, TB	IL	2	-	-	2	-
Junior Seau, SD	IL	1	-	1	1	-
Chad Brown, Pit	OL	1	1	1	1	1
Kevin Greene, Car	OL	1	1	-	1	1
Ken Harvey, Was	OL	-	-	-	2	-
Seth Joyner, Ariz	OL	-	-	-	2	-
Lamar Lathon, Car	OL	2	-	1	1	1
Bryce Paup, NE	OL	-	-	-	2	-
Bill Romanowski, Den	OL	-	-	-	2	-
Derrick Thomas, KC	OL	2	-	-	1	1
Ashley Ambrose, Cin	CB	1	-	-	1	1
Dale Carter, KC	CB	2	-	1	1	1
Mark Collins, KC	CB	-	-	-	2	-
Eric Davis, Car	CB	-	-	-	2	-
Deion Sanders, Dal	CB	1	1	1	1	1
Kevin Smith, Dal	CB	-	-	-	2	-
Aeneas Williams, Ariz	CB	2	1	-	1	1
Rod Woodson, Pit	CB	-	-	-	2	-
Steve Atwater, Den	DS	2	-	-	1	1
Blaine Bishop, Hou	DS	-	-	-	2	-
Tyrone Braxton, Den	DS	-	-	-	2	-
LeRoy Butler, GB	DS	1	1	1	1	1
Merton Hanks, SF	DS	2	-	-	2	-
Carnell Lake, Pit	DS	-	-	-	1	1
Tim McDonald, SF	DS	-	-	-	2	-
Darren Woodson, Dal	DS	1	1	1	1	1

SPECIALISTS		ALL-NFL			CONF	
		AP	FW	SN	UP	FW
Cary Blanchard, Ind	PK	1	1	1	1	1
Chris Bonoil, Dal	PK	-	-	-	2	-
Al Del Greco, Hou	PK	-	-	-	2	-
John Kasay, Car	PK	2	-	-	1	1
Chris Gardocki, Ind	P	1t	1	1	1	1
John Kidd, Mia	P	-	-	-	2	-
Todd Sauerbrun, ChiB	P	-	-	-	2	-
Matt Turk, Was	P	1t	-	-	1	1
Michael Bates, Car	KR	1	1	1	2	1
Dave Meggett, NE	KR	2	-	-	1	-
Tamarick Vanover, KC	KR	-	-	-	-	1
Darrien Gordon, SD	PR	x	-	-	2	1
Desmond Howard, GB	PR	x	1	1	1	1
John Henry Mills, Hou	SP	x	-	x	x	1
Jim Schwantz, Dal	SP	x	1	x	x	1

Note: *AP* chose no second-team punter.

1997 ALL-NFL

OFFENSE		ALL-NFL			CONF
		AP	FW	SN	PW
Herman Moore, Det	WR	1	1	1	1
Rob Moore, Ariz	WR	1	1	-	1
Tim Brown, Oak	WR	2	-	1	1
Yancey Thigpen, Pit	WR	2	-	-	1
Shannon Sharpe, Den	TE	1	1	1	1
Wesley Walls, Car	TE	2	-	-	1
Tony Boselli, Jac	T	1	1	1	1
Jonathan Ogden, Bal	T	1	1	1	1
William Roaf, NO	T	2	-	-	1
Todd Steussie, Min	T	2	-	-	1
Larry Allen, Dal	G	1	1	1	1
Dave Szott, KC	G	1	1	-	1
Randall McDaniel, Min	G	2	-	1	1
Bruce Matthews, Ten	G	-	-	-	1
Will Shields, KC	G	2	-	-	-
Dermontti Dawson, Pit	C	1	1	1	1
Kevin Glover, GB	C	-	-	-	1
Brett Favre, GB	QB	1	1	1	1
John Elway, Den	QB	-	-	-	1
Steve Young, SF	QB	2	-	-	-
Terrell Davis, Den	RB	1	1	1	1
Barry Sanders, Det	RB	1	1	1	1
Jerome Bettis, Pit	RB	2	-	-	1
Dorsey Levens, GB	RB	-	-	-	1
Mike Alstott, TB	FB	1	x	x	x
Charles Way, NYG	FB	2	x	x	x

Notes: Dawson unanimous choice at center (*AP*).
Only three RBs received votes from *AP*.

DEFENSE		ALL-NFL			CONF
		AP	FW	SN	PW
Bruce Smith, Buf	DE	1	1	1	1
Michael Strahan, NYG	DE	1	1	1	1
Chuck Smith, Atl	DE	2	-	-	1t
Robert Porcher, Det	DE	-	-	-	1t
Michael Sinclair, Sea	DE	-	-	-	1
Neil Smith, Den	DE	2t	-	-	-
Reggie White, GB	DE	2t	-	-	-
John Randle, Min	DT	1	1	1	1
Dana Stubblefield, SF	DT	1	1	1	1
Ted Washington, Buf	DT	2	-	-	1
Joel Steed, Pit	DT	-	-	-	1
Warren Sapp, TB	DT	2	-	-	-
Levon Kirkland, Pit	ILB	1	1	1	1
Hardy Nickerson, TB	ILB	1	-	-	1
Junior Seau, SD	ILB	2t	-	-	1
Winfred Tubbs, NO	ILB	2t	-	-	1
Ray Lewis, Bal	ILB	2t	-	-	-
Jessie Armstead, NYG	OLB	1	1	1	1
John Mobley, Den	OLB	1	1	1	1
Derrick Brooks, TB	OLB	2	-	-	1
Chris Slade, NE	OLB	2	-	-	1
Deion Sanders, Dal	CB	1	1	1	1
Aeneas Williams, Ariz	CB	1	1	1	1
James Hasty, KC	CB	2	-	-	1t
Aaron Glenn, NYJ	CB	-	-	-	1
Dale Carter, KC	CB	-	-	-	1t
Cris Dishman, Was	CB	2t	-	-	-
Doug Evans, GB	CB	2t	-	-	-
LeRoy Butler, GB	S	1	1	1	1
Carnell Lake, Pit	S	1	1	1	1
Merton Hanks, SF	S	2	-	-	1
Darryl Williams, Sea	S	2	-	-	1

SPECIALISTS		ALL-NFL			CONF
		AP	FW	SN	UP
Richie Cunningham, Dal	K	1	-	1	-
Jason Hanson, Det	K	2	-	-	1
Pete Stoyanovich, KC	K	-	1	-	1
Bryan Barker, Jac	P	1	1	-	1
Matt Turk, Was	P	2	-	1	1
Michael Bates, Car	KR	2t	1	1	1
Eric Metcalf, SD	KR	1	-	-	-
Tamarick Vanover, KC	KR	-	-	-	1
Darrien Gordon, Den	PR	2t	1	1	1
David Palmer, Min	PR	-	-	-	1
Travis Jervey, GB	ST	x	1	x	1
Larry Whigham, NE	ST	x	-	x	1

1998 ALL-NFL

OFFENSE		ALL-NFL			CONF
		AP	FW	SN	PW
Randy Moss, Min	WR	1	1	1	1
Antonio Freeman, GB	WR	1	1	1	1

OFFENSE		ALL-NFL			CONF
		AP	FW	SN	PW
Eric Moulds, Buf	WR	2t	-	-	1
Keyshawn Johnson, NYJ	WR	-	-	-	1
Ed McCaffrey, Den	WR	2	-	-	-
Jimmy Smith, Jac	WR	2t	-	-	-
Shannon Sharpe, Den	TE	1	1	1	1
Mark Chmura, GB	TE	-	-	-	1
Ben Coates, NE	TE	2	-	-	-
Tony Boselli, Jac	T	1	1	1	1
Larry Allen, Dal	T	1	1	1	1
Todd Steussie, Min	T	2	-	-	1
Jonathan Ogden, Bal	T	2	-	-	1
Randall McDaniel, Min	G	1	1	1	1
Bruce Matthews, Ten	G	1	1	1	1
Ruben Brown, Buf	G	2	-	-	1
Kevin Gogan, SF	G	2	-	-	1
Dermontti Dawson, Pit	C	1	1	1	1
Jeff Christy, Min	C	2t	-	-	1
Kevin Mawae, NYJ	C	2t	-	-	-
Randall Cunningham, Min	QB	1	1	-	1
Steve Young, SF	QB	2	-	1	-
Vinny Testaverde, NYJ	QB	-	-	-	1
Terrell Davis, Den	RB	1	1	1	1
Jamal Anderson, Atl	RB	1	1	1	1
Marshall Faulk, Ind	RB	2	-	-	1
Garrison Hearst, SF	RB	-	-	-	1
Barry Sanders, Det	RB	2	-	-	-
Mike Alstott, TB	FB	1	x	x	x
Sam Gash, Buf	FB	2	x	x	x

DEFENSE		ALL-NFL			CONF
		AP	FW	SN	PW
Reggie White, GB	DE	1	1	1	1
Michael Strahan, NYG	DE	1	1	-	1
Michael McCrary, Sea	DE	-	-	1	1
Michael Sinclair, Sea	DE	2	-	-	1
Bruce Smith, Buf	DE	2	-	-	-
John Randle, Min	DT	1	1	1	1
Darrell Russell, Oak	DT	1	1	-	1
Bryant Young, SF	DT	2t	-	1	-
Ted Washington, Buf	DT	-	-	-	1
Warren Sapp, TB	DT	2t	-	-	1
La'Roi Glover, NO	DT	2	-	-	-
Ray Lewis, Bal	ILB	2	-	1	-
Junior Seau, SD	ILB	1	1	-	-
Zach Thomas, Mia	ILB	1	-	-	-
Jessie Tuggle, Atl	ILB	2	-	-	1
Chad Brown, Sea	OLB	1	1	1	1
Mo Lewis, NYJ	OLB	1	1	-	1
Derrick Brooks, TB	OLB	2	-	-	1
Jessie Armstead, NYG	OLB	-	-	-	1
Dwayne Rudd, Min	OLB	2	-	-	-
Ty Law, NE	CB	1	1	1	1
Deion Sanders, Dal	CB	1	1	1	1
Ray Buchanan, Atl	CB	2	-	-	1
Aaron Glenn, NYJ	CB	-	-	-	1
Sam Madison, Mia	CB	2	-	-	-
Rodney Harrison, SD	S	1	1	1t	1
LeRoy Butler, GB	S	1	1	1	1
Robert Griffith, Min	S	2	-	1t	-
Lawyer Milloy, NE	S	2	-	-	1
Darren Woodson, Dal	S	-	-	1t	-
Eugene Robinson, Atl	S	-	-	-	1

SPECIALISTS		ALL-NFL			CONF
		AP	FW	SN	UP
Gary Anderson, Min	K	1	1	1	1
Jason Elam, Den	K	2	-	-	1
Craig Hentrich, Ten	P	1	1	1	1
Matt Turk, Was	P	2	-	-	1
Terry Fair, Det	KR	-	1t	1	-
Roell Preston, GB	KR	2	1t	-	1
Vaughn Hebron, Den	KR	-	-	-	1
Jermaine Lewis, Bal	PR	1	-	1	1
Deion Sanders, Dal	PR	-	1	-	1
Bennie Thompson, Bal	ST	x	1	x	1
Michael Bates, Car	ST	x	-	x	1

CHAPTER 16

The Pro Bowl

Beau Riffenburgh

The first pro all-star game was played in 1898 when promoter Dave Berry, the Latrobe, Pennsylvania, leader who had originally hired young John Bralier three years earlier, gathered a group of star western Pennsylvania players after the season to take on the Pittsburgh champions—the Duquesne Country and Athletic Club. The game, won by the D.C. & A.C., was not a financial success.

Nevertheless, so-called "all-star" squads continued to appear occasionally on the schedules of various pro teams over the next twenty years. More often than not, the "stars" were simply whatever athletes were available. With little or no practice to give them cohesion, the squads were almost always soundly defeated by the pro teams they faced.

In late 1920, the NFL's first year, a political candidate in Pittsburgh tried to give his campaign a boost by sponsoring a major all-star game between Ohio and Pennsyvania pros at Forbes Field. Few of the promised stars appeared, and those who actually took the field, such as Fritz Pollard, retired early. It is unknown whether the candidate won many votes from the sparse crowd of 3,000.

Several star-teams formed exhibition opponents for Red Grange and the Chicago Bears on his famous barnstorming tours in 1925. Another all-star aggregation made up of former Notre Dame players actually had a bearing on the NFL's championship race when the Pottsville Maroons were suspended by the league for playing the Irish slums at Philadelphia's Shibe Park, within the protected territory of the Frankford Yellow Jackets. A happier result was achieved by an all-star squad of ex-Notre Damers when they raised $115,000 for charity with a game against the New York Giants in 1930.

During the 1930s, preseason all-star games pitting pro teams against squads of graduated collegians were common, with the College All-Star Game played in Chicago by far the best known, best attended, and most prestigious. Postseason all-star games of pro players were regular West Coast events.

The Pro Bowl in its present form was first played after the 1950 season. Peace had been achieved with the All-America Football Conference, and the NFL enjoyed its most successful season up to that point. The expanded league showcased its stars with a game between the cream of the American (Eastern) Conference and the National (Western) Conference. The contest sparked excited interest among fans and has continued to do so down through the years. In 1970, with the NFL-AFL merger, the format was changed slightly in that it became the AFC versus NFC.

Today, selection to the Pro Bowl ranks as one of football's highest honors for a player, and it's common to have bonuses for such selections written into players' contracts. To say a man is a "Pro Bowl player" is to recognize him as one of the very best at his position.

1939 Pro All-Star Game

NEW YORK GIANTS 13, PRO ALL-STARS 10
January 15, 1939, at Los Angeles.
Attendance: 20,000

The NFL-champion Giants scored 10 points in the final quarter, the last three on an 18-yard field goal by Ward Cuff, for a 13-10 victory against an all-star team composed of players from other NFL teams and from two independent pro teams, the Los Angeles Bulldogs and the Hollywood Stars. The game was held at Wrigley Field, a Pacific Coast League baseball stadium in Los Angeles.

N.Y. Giants	0	3	0	10	—	13
Pro All-Stars	0	3	7	0	—	10

NYG—FG Barnum 18
All-Stars—FG E. Smith 25
All-Stars—Cardwell 70 pass from Baugh (Stydahar kick)
NYG—Gelatka 22 pass from Danowski (Cuff kick)
NYG—FG Cuff 18

1940 Pro All-Star Game (January)

GREEN BAY 16, NFL ALL-STARS 7
January 14, 1940, at Los Angeles.
Attendance: 18,000

The Packers defeated an NFL all-star team 16-7 at Gilmore Stadium in Los Angeles. The highlight of the game was a bomb from Cecil Isbell to Don Hutson, who caught the ball in full stride at the All-Stars' 31 and carried the rest of the way to complete a 92-yard scoring play.

Green Bay	3	10	0	3	—	16
NFL All-Stars	0	0	7	0	—	7

GB—FG Hinkle 45
GB—FG Smith 15
GB—Hutson 92 pass from Isbell (Smith kick)
All-Stars—Carter 4 pass from O'Brien (Cuff kick)
GB—FG Smith 7

1940 Pro All-Star Game (December)

CHICAGO BEARS 28, NFL ALL-STARS 14
December 29, 1940, at Los Angeles.
Attendance: 21,624

Sid Luckman threw 2 touchdown passes and ran for another as the Bears won 28-14 in Los Angeles. The score was 14-14 in the third period when Dick Plasman intercepted a pass by Washington's Sammy Baugh and returned it to the All-Stars' 5. Luckman scored from the 1 three plays later.

Chicago Bears	7	7	7	7	—	28
NFL All-Stars	0	14	0	0	—	14

ChiB—Pool 48 lateral from Plasman, who caught 23 pass from Luckman (Martinovich kick)
All-Stars—Livingston 7 interception return (Hinkle kick)
ChiB—Clark 59 pass from Luckman (Snyder kick)
All-Stars—Looney 4 pass from Baugh (Hutson kick)
ChiB—Luckman 1 run (Snyder kick)
ChiB—Maniaci 2 run (Maniaci kick)

1942 Pro All-Star Game (January)

CHICAGO BEARS 35, NFL ALL-STARS 24
January 4, 1942, at New York.
Attendance: 17,725

The Bears ripped open the game with 3 touchdowns in the second period, 2 by George McAfee, en route to defeating the NFL All-Stars 35-24. The game was held at the Polo Grounds in New York because of fears of a Japanese invasion of the West Coast.

Chicago Bears	0	21	7	7	—	35
NFL All-Stars	3	0	14	7	—	24

All-Stars—FG Cuff 19
ChiB—McAfee 3 run (Snyder kick)
ChiB—McAfee 68 punt return (Artoe kick)
ChiB—Swisher 4 run (Stydahar kick)
All-Stars—Schwartz 15 pass from Baugh (Cuff kick)
All-Stars—Dewell 24 pass from Baugh (Cuff kick)
ChiB—McLean 20 pass from Luckman (Snyder kick)
ChiB—Kavanaugh 7 pass from Bussey (Stydahar kick)
All-Stars—Schwartz 26 pass from Baugh (Cuff kick)

1942 Pro All-Star Game (December)

NFL ALL-STARS 17, WASHINGTON 14
December 27, 1942, at Philadelphia.
Attendance: 18,671

Sammy Baugh was not able to catch a plane to Philadelphia for the game, and without him the Redskins were defeated by the NFL All-Stars 17-14. The winning points were scored on a 43-yard field goal by the Bears' Lee Artoe, but the most exciting play came when Pittsburgh's Bill Dudley returned an interception 97 yards for a touchdown.

Washington	7	0	7	0	—	14
NFL All-Stars	0	0	14	3	—	17

Was—Aldrich 30 punt return (Masterson kick)
All-Stars—Dudley 97 interception return (Maznicki kick)
All-Stars—Petty 10 run (Maznicki kick)
Was—Seymour 16 pass from Zimmerman (Masterson kick)
All-Stars—FG Artoe 43

1951 NFL Pro Bowl

AMERICAN CONFERENCE 28,
NATIONAL CONFERENCE 27
January 14, 1951, at Los Angeles.
Attendance: 53,678

In a revival of the Pro Bowl, held at the Memorial Coliseum in Los Angeles, player-of-the-game Otto Graham of Cleveland passed for 1 touchdown and ran for 2 in the third period to lead the American Conference to a 28-27 victory over the National Conference.

American	7	7	14	0	—	28
National	7	13	7	0	—	27

National—Fears 22 pass from Waterfield (Waterfield kick)
American—Dudley 47 punt return (Groza kick)
National—FG Waterfield 30
American—Shaw 49 pass from Graham (Groza kick)
National—FG Waterfield 27
National—Fears 5 pass from Van Brocklin (Waterfield kick)
National—Edwards 65 pass from Waterfield (Waterfield kick)
American—Graham 6 run (Harder kick)
American—Graham 10 run (Harder kick)

1952 NFL Pro Bowl

NATIONAL CONFERENCE 30,
AMERICAN CONFERENCE 13
January 12, 1952, at Los Angeles.
Attendance: 19,400

The National Conference used a series of turnovers by Washington's Sammy Baugh to set up 20 fourth-quarter points and overcome a 13-10 fourth-quarter deficit to win 30-13. Dan Towler, one of three Rams starting in the National Conference's backfield, was named player of the game.

National	3	7	0	20	—	30
American	7	6	0	0	—	13

American—Jones 44 pass from Graham (Graham kick)
National—FG Waterfield 30
American—FG Groza 45
American—FG Groza 11
National—Soltau 1 pass from Van Brocklin (Waterfield kick)
National—Dottley 2 run (kick failed)
National—Nomellini 20 fumble return (Waterfield kick)
National—Hirsch 7 pass from Walker (Lujack kick)

1953 NFL Pro Bowl

NATIONAL CONFERENCE 27,
AMERICAN CONFERENCE 7
January 10, 1953, at Los Angeles.
Attendance: 34,208

Norm Van Brocklin threw a pair of touchdown passes, one of 74 yards to Green Bay's Billy Howton, and Rams teammate Dan Towler added another on a halfback pass to lead the National Conference to a 27-7 victory. Defensive back Don Doll of Detroit was named player of the game.

National	14	0	3	10	—	27
American	0	0	0	7	—	7

National—McElhenny 13 pass from Towler (Harder kick)
National—Howton 74 pass from Van Brocklin (Harder kick)
National—FG Harder 23
American—Graham 1 run (Groza kick)
National—FG Harder 13
National—McElhenny 7 pass from Van Brocklin (Harder kick)

1954 NFL Pro Bowl

EAST 20, WEST 9
January 17, 1954, at Los Angeles.
Attendance: 44,214

Linebacker Chuck Bednarik of Philadelphia was named player of the game after recovering a fumble that led to a field goal and returning an interception 24 yards for a touchdown as the Eastern Conference (renamed from the American Conference) defeated the Western Conference 20-9.

East	3	0	10	7	—	20
West	0	2	0	7	—	9

East—FG Groza 11
West—Safety, Kindt tackled Graham in end zone
East—FG Groza 25
East—Bednarik 24 interception return (Groza kick)
West—Perry 16 run (Walker kick)
East—Renfro 25 run (Groza kick)

1955 NFL Pro Bowl

WEST 26, EAST 19
January 16, 1955, at Los Angeles.
Attendance: 43,972

Y.A. Tittle completed 16 of 26 passes, most of them to San Francisco teammate Billy Wilson, who had 11 receptions for 157 yards and a touchdown, and the West came back from a 19-3 deficit to win 26-19. Wilson was selected player of the game.

West	3	6	7	10	—	26
East	13	6	0	0	—	19

East—Matson 6 pass from Graham (Groza kick)
East—Willey 5 fumble return (kick failed)
West—FG Walker 35
East—Taylor 33 pass from Burk (kick failed)
West—Wilson 14 pass from Tittle (kick failed)
West—Hill 42 pass from Tittle (Walker kick)
West—FG Walker 30
West—Perry 1 run (Walker kick)

1956 NFL Pro Bowl

EAST 31, WEST 30
January 15, 1956, at Los Angeles.
Attendance: 37,667

Player-of-the-game Ollie Matson of the Chicago Cardinals accounted for 286 all-purpose yards, including a 91-yard return of the second-half kickoff for a touchdown, to lead the East to a 31-30 victory. Detroit's Jack Christiansen opened the game with a 103-yard kickoff return for a touchdown.

West	7	7	9	7	—	30
East	7	0	14	10	—	31

West—Christiansen 103 kickoff return (Richter kick)
East—Pihos 12 pass from LeBaron (Groza kick)
West—Howton 73 pass from Brown (Richter kick)
East—Matson 91 kickoff return (Groza kick)
West—Ferguson 1 run (kick blocked)
East—Matson 15 run (Groza kick)
West—FG Rechichar 46
East—FG Groza 50
East—Mathews 20 pass from LeBaron (Groza kick)
West—Waller 3 run (Richter kick)

1957 NFL Pro Bowl

WEST 19, EAST 10
January 13, 1957, at Los Angeles.
Attendance: 44,177

Four field goals by Baltimore's Bert Rechichar were the difference as the West won 19-10. The defenses were so dominant that the two teams combined for only 229 total yards. Rechichar was named the back of the game, and Pittsburgh's Ernie Stautner was the lineman of the game.

West	7	3	3	6	—	19
East	0	7	3	0	—	10

West—Brown 1 run (Layne kick)
East—Rote fumble recovery in end zone (Baker kick)
West—FG Rechichar 41
East—FG Baker 52
West—FG Rechichar 44
West—FG Rechichar 44
West—FG Rechichar 52

1958 NFL Pro Bowl

WEST 26, EAST 7
January 12, 1958, at Los Angeles.
Attendance: 66,634

The West's defense held the East to only 149 yards, while defensive back Bobby Dillon of Green Bay returned an interception 39 yards for a touchdown to lead the West to a 26-7 victory. Halfback Hugh McElhenny of San Francisco was named back of the game and defensive end Gene Brito of Washington was the lineman of the game.

West	6	3	10	7	—	26
East	0	7	0	0	—	7

West—Dillon 39 interception return (kick blocked)
East—Renfro 39 pass from Morrall (Groza kick)
West—FG Rechichar 9
West—FG Rechichar 23
West—Tom Wilson 10 run (Rechichar kick)
West—Ameche 8 pass from Unitas (Rechichar kick)

1959 NFL Pro Bowl

EAST 28, WEST 21
January 11, 1959, at Los Angeles.
Attendance: 72,250

Giants halfback Frank Gifford had 3 receptions and completed 3 of 4 passes for 75 yards and a touchdown to lead the East to a 28-21 victory. Gifford was named the back of the game, and defensive end Doug Atkins of the Bears was the lineman of the game.

East	9	7	0	12	—	28
West	7	7	7	0	—	21

West—Ameche 1 run (Richter kick)
East—FG Groza 25
East—Webster 40 pass from Gifford (kick blocked)
West—McElhenny 20 pass from Wade (Richter kick)
East—Nagler 7 pass from LeBaron (Groza kick)
West—Wade 10 run (Richter kick)
East—FG Groza 25
East—Retzlaff 15 pass from Van Brocklin (Groza kick)
East—Safety, Scott tackled McElhenny in end zone

1960 NFL Pro Bowl

WEST 38, EAST 21
January 17, 1960, at Los Angeles.
Attendance: 56,876

Back-of-the-game Johnny Unitas of Baltimore completed 14 of 22 passes for 187 yards and 3 touchdowns and ran for 43 yards to lead the West to a 38-21 victory. The 49ers' Y.A. Tittle completed 13 of 18 passes for 178 yards and a touchdown for the West. Defensive tackle Gene (Big Daddy) Lipscomb of Pittsburgh was named the lineman of the game.

East	7	7	0	7	—	21
West	10	21	0	7	—	38

East—Patton 22 interception return (Groza kick)
West—Berry 22 pass from Unitas (Hornung kick)
West—FG Hornung 16
East—McDonald 63 pass from Layne (Groza kick)
West—Moore 13 pass from Tittle (Hornung kick)
West—Moore 65 pass from Unitas (Hornung kick)
West—Smith 6 pass from Unitas (Hornung kick)
East—J. Brown 2 pass from Layne (Groza kick)
West—Hornung 2 run (Hornung kick)

1961 NFL Pro Bowl

WEST 35, EAST 31
January 15, 1961, at Los Angeles.
Attendance: 62,971

Johnny Unitas of Baltimore again was voted back of the game after passing for 218 yards and leading the West on 5 touchdown drives in a 35-31 victory. Green Bay's Jim Taylor scored 3 touchdowns for the West to offset 3 touchdown passes by the Eagles' Norm Van Brocklin. Sam Huff of the Giants was voted lineman of the game.

East	3	14	7	7	—	31
West	7	14	7	7	—	35

West—Taylor 2 run (Hornung kick)
East—FG Walston 22
West—Taylor 1 run (Hornung kick)
East—Randle 51 pass from Plum (Walston kick)
East—McDonald 46 pass from Van Brocklin (Walston kick)
West—Moore 44 pass from Unitas (Hornung kick)
West—Taylor 1 run (Hornung kick)
East—Retzlaff 43 pass from Van Brocklin (Walston kick)
West—Arnett 20 run (Hornung kick)
East—Randle 36 pass from Van Brocklin (Walston kick)

1962 AFL All-Star Game

WEST 47, EAST 27
January 7, 1962, at San Diego.
Attendance: 20,973

Cotton Davidson of the Dallas Texans threw 3 touchdown passes to earn player-of-the-game honors as he led the West to a 47-27 victory against the East in the first AFL All-Star Game, held in San Diego. There were a total of 6 touchdown passes in the game, and they went to six different receivers.

East	5	7	7	8	—	27
West	0	21	14	12	—	47

East—FG Blanda 32
East—Safety, Haynes tackled in end zone
West—Stone 45 pass from Davidson (Blair kick)
East—Cannon 34 pass from Blanda (Blanda kick)
West—Haynes 12 run (Blair kick)
West—Kocourek 24 pass from Davidson (Blair kick)
West—Haynes 66 punt return (Blair kick)
West—Norton 10 pass from Davidson (Blair kick)
East—Cappelletti 5 pass from Blanda (Blanda kick)
West—Williamson 53 interception return (kick failed)
East—Hennigan 3 pass from Dorow (Dorow run)
West—Stone 15 run (pass failed)

1962 NFL Pro Bowl

WEST 31, EAST 30
January 14, 1962, at Los Angeles.
Attendance: 57,409

Jon Arnett of the Rams caught a 12-yard touchdown pass from Johnny Unitas of Baltimore with 10 seconds remaining, and Detroit's Jim Martin added the extra point as the West defeated the East 31-30. Cleveland's Jim Brown was named player of the game, and Green Bay's Henry Jordan was lineman of the game.

East	3	7	6	14	—	30
West	14	3	7	7	—	31

East—FG Walston 33
West—Berry 16 pass from Unitas (Martin kick)
West—Lane 42 interception return (Martin kick)
East—Bielski 10 pass from Tittle (Walston kick)
West—FG Martin 27
West—McElhenny 10 pass from Starr (Martin kick)
East—Walston 12 pass from Plum (kick blocked)
East—Webster 2 pass from Tittle (Walston kick)
East—Brown 70 run (Walston kick)
West—Arnett 12 pass from Unitas (Martin kick)

1963 AFL All-Star Game

WEST 21, EAST 14
January 13, 1963, at San Diego.
Attendance: 27,641

Dallas Texans fullback Curtis McClinton, the offensive player of the game, exploded for a 64-yard touchdown run in the first quarter and the West went on to defeat the East 21-14. End Earl Faison of San Diego was named the defensive player of the game.

West	7	7	0	7	—	21
East	0	0	14	0	—	14

West—McClinton 64 run (Mingo kick)
West—Kocourek 11 pass from Dawson (Mingo kick)
East—Hennigan 8 pass from Blanda (Blanda kick)
East—Grantham 29 interception return (Blanda kick)
West—Taylor 20 pass from Tripucka (Mingo kick)

1963 NFL Pro Bowl

EAST 30, WEST 20
January 13, 1963, at Los Angeles.
Attendance: 61,374

Jim Brown of Cleveland was named the back of the game for the second time in a row after rushing for 144 yards and 2 first-quarter touchdowns to lead the East to a 30-20 victory. The West came back for a 20-13 lead, but the East scored 17 points in the final period. Gene (Big Daddy) Lipscomb of Pittsburgh was the lineman of the game.

West	0	3	17	0	—	20
East	13	0	0	17	—	30

East—J. Brown 1 run (Michaels kick)
East—J. Brown 50 run (kick failed)
West—FG Davis 49
West—Bass 1 run (Davis kick)
West—FG Davis 32
West—Ditka 6 pass from Unitas (Davis kick)
East—Carpenter 19 pass from Tittle (Gain kick)
East—FG Michaels 27
East—Bishop 20 fumble return (Michaels kick)

1964 AFL All-Star Game

WEST 27, EAST 24
January 19, 1964, at San Diego.
Attendance: 20,016

Cotton Davidson threw a 25-yard touchdown pass to Oakland teammate Art Powell with 43 seconds left to give the West a 27-24 victory. The East led 24-3 at halftime before offensive-player-of-the-game Keith Lincoln of San Diego began the West's comeback with a 64-yard touchdown run. Oakland's Archie Matsos was named defensive player of the game.

West	0	3	14	10	—	27
East	10	14	0	0	—	24

East—FG Cappelletti 35
East—Gilchrist 1 run (Cappelletti kick)
West—FG Fraser 19
East—Garron 12 pass from Parilli (Cappelletti kick)
East—Mathis 3 pass from Parilli (Cappelletti kick)
West—Lincoln 64 run (Fraser kick)
West—Lowe 5 run (Fraser kick)
West—FG Fraser 7
West—Powell 25 pass from Davidson (Fraser kick)

1964 NFL Pro Bowl

WEST 31, EAST 17
January 12, 1964, at Los Angeles.
Attendance: 67,242

The Colts' Johnny Unitas won honors as back of the game for the third time after throwing 2 touchdown passes and leading the West to a 31-17 victory. Unitas's Baltimore teammate Gino Marchetti was named the lineman of the game.

East	3	0	0	14	—	17
West	7	7	14	3	—	31

East—FG Baker 30
West—Taylor 37 run (T. Davis kick)
West—Berry 4 pass from Unitas (T. Davis kick)
West—Whittenton 26 interception return (T. Davis kick)
West—Cogdill 5 pass from Unitas (T. Davis kick)
East—J. Brown 8 run (Baker kick)
West—FG T. Davis 38
East—J. Brown 3 run (Baker kick)

1965 AFL All-Star Game

WEST 38, EAST 14
January 16, 1965, at Houston.
Attendance: 15,446

San Diego's John Hadl threw 3 touchdown passes in the West's 38-14 victory, but teammate Keith Lincoln was named offensive player of the game after catching a 73-yard touchdown pass and breaking loose on an 80-yard touchdown run. Denver cornerback Willie Brown was the defensive player of the game at Houston's Jeppesen Stadium, in the first AFL All-Star Game played outside San Diego.

West	7	10	14	7	—	38
East	0	14	0	0	—	14

West—Lincoln 73 pass from Dawson (Brooker kick)
West—Daniels 5 pass from Hadl (Brooker kick)
East—Blanks 5 run (Cappelletti kick)
West—FG Brooker 46
East—Buoniconti 17 fumble return (Cappelletti kick)
West—Lincoln 80 run (Brooker kick)
West—Alworth 7 pass from Hadl (Brooker kick)
West—Powell 17 pass from Hadl (Brooker kick)

1965 NFL Pro Bowl

WEST 34, EAST 14
January 10, 1965, at Los Angeles.
Attendance: 60,598

Bill Brown scored twice, the second time on a 2-yard pass from Minnesota teammate and back-of-the-game Fran Tarkenton, to lead the West to a convincing 34-14 victory. Flanker Terry Barr of Detroit was named the lineman of the game.

West	3	14	10	7	—	34
East	0	7	0	7	—	14

West—FG Walker 15
West—B. Brown 2 run (Walker kick)
East—Renfro 47 interception return (Baker kick)
West—B. Brown 2 pass from Tarkenton (Walker kick)
West—Nitschke 42 interception return (Walker kick)
West—FG Walker 28
West—Moore 2 run (Walker kick)
East—J. Brown 27 pass from Jurgensen (Baker kick)

1966 AFL All-Star Game

AFL ALL-STARS 30, BUFFALO 19
January 15, 1966, at Houston.
Attendance: 35,572

Rookie quarterback Joe Namath of the Jets threw 2 touchdown passes to Lance Alworth of San Diego to earn offensive player-of-the-game honors as he led the AFL All-Stars to a 30-19 victory over the champion Buffalo Bills. Chargers linebacker Frank Buncom was the defensive player of the game.

Buffalo	10	3	0	6	—	19
AFL All-Stars	0	6	17	7	—	30

Buf—FG Gogolak 20
Buf—Saimes 61 fumble return (Gogolak kick)
All-Stars—FG Cappelletti 46
Buf—FG Gogolak 11
All-Stars—FG Cappelletti 14
All-Stars—FG Cappelletti 32
All-Stars—Lowe 1 run (Cappelletti kick)
All-Stars—Alworth 43 pass from Namath (Cappelletti kick)
All-Stars—Alworth 10 pass from Namath (Cappelletti kick)
Buf—Carlton 34 pass from Lamonica (run failed)

1966 NFL Pro Bowl

EAST 36, WEST 7
January 16, 1966, at Los Angeles.
Attendance: 60,124

Cleveland fullback Jim Brown ran for 3 touchdowns in his final NFL game to earn back of the game honors for the third time and to lead the East to an easy 36-7 victory. Linebacker Dale Meinert of St Louis was honored as the lineman of the game.

East	10	13	3	10	—	36
West	0	0	0	7	—	7

East—FG Bakken 41
East—J. Brown 2 run (Bakken kick)
East—J. Brown 2 run (Bakken kick)
East—J. Brown 1 run (kick failed)
East—FG Bakken 36
East—FG Bakken 42
East—Renfro 20 interception return (Bakken kick)
West—McDonald 31 pass from Brodie (Walker kick)

1967 AFL All-Star Game

EAST 30, WEST 23
January 21, 1967, at Oakland.
Attendance: 18,876

Babe Parilli of Boston, the offensive player of the game, threw 2 touchdown passes to lead the East to a 30-23 victory in a game the West led 23-2 in the third period. Defensive-player-of-the-game Verlon Biggs of the Jets started the comeback with a 50-yard interception return for a touchdown.

East	0	0	16	14	—	30
West	9	7	7	0	—	23

West—McClinton 31 pass from Dawson (Van Raaphorst kick)
West—Safety, center snap out of end zone
West—Dixon 17 pass from Flores (Van Raaphorst kick)
East—Safety, Dawson tackled in end zone
West—Buchanan 39 fumble return (Van Raaphorst kick)
East—Biggs 50 interception return (Cappelletti kick)
East—Carlton 3 pass from Parilli (Cappelletti kick)
East—Burnett 12 run (Cappelletti kick)
East—Frazier 17 pass from Parilli (Cappelletti kick)

1967 NFL Pro Bowl

EAST 20, WEST 10
January 22, 1967, at Los Angeles.
Attendance: 15,062

The East, with the leadership of lineman-of-the-game Floyd Peters of Philadelphia, defeated the West 20-10 on a muddy field slowed by heavy rains. Back-of-the-game Gale Sayers of the Bears was sensational, running for 110 yards on 11 carries and having plays of 80 and 55 yards negated by penalties.

West	0	0	3	7	—	10
East	6	14	0	0	—	20

East—FG Clark 18
East—FG Clark 17
East—Roland 1 run (Clark kick)
East—Collins 18 pass from Ryan (Clark kick)
West—FG Gossett 27
West—Willard 51 pass from Starr (Gossett kick)

1968 AFL All-Star Game

EAST 25, WEST 24
January 21, 1968, at Jacksonville.
Attendance: 40,103

Joe Namath passed for 2 touchdowns and scored on a 1-yard sneak with 58 seconds left to lead the East to a 25-24 victory. Namath and Jets teammate Don Maynard were co-offensive players of the game, and Leslie (Speedy) Duncan of San Diego was the defensive player of the game.

East	3	10	0	12	—	25
West	7	14	0	3	—	24

East—FG Mercer 10
West—Duncan 90 kickoff return (Blanda kick)
West—Frazier 3 pass from Lamonica (Blanda kick)
East—Lammons 35 pass from Namath (Mercer kick)
West—Alworth 9 pass from Lamonica (Blanda kick)
East—FG Mercer 33
West—FG Blanda 28
East—Maynard 24 pass from Namath (pass failed)
East—Namath 1 run (run failed)

1968 NFL Pro Bowl

WEST 38, EAST 20
January 21, 1968, at Los Angeles.
Attendance: 53,289

The West exploded for 3 touchdowns in the fourth quarter to rally past the East 38-20. Gale Sayers of the Bears, who scored the go-ahead touchdown, was back of the game, and Green Bay linebacker Dave Robinson was lineman of the game.

East	0	13	7	0	—	20
West	10	7	0	21	—	38

West—FG Chandler 26
West—Josephson 4 run (Chandler kick)
East—FG Bakken 45
East—FG Bakken 25
West—Farr 39 pass from Gabriel (Chandler kick)
East—Kelly 1 run (Bakken kick)
East—Taylor 9 pass from Meredith (Bakken kick)
West—Sayers 3 run (Chandler kick)
West—Petitbon 70 interception return (Chandler kick)
West—B. Brown 19 run (Chandler kick)

1969 AFL All-Star Game

WEST 38, EAST 25
January 19, 1969, at Jacksonville.
Attendance: 41,058

Paul Robinson of Cincinnati ran for 2 touchdowns and a 2-point conversion in the fourth quarter to lead the West to a 38-25 victory after trailing 25-13 in the final period. The East built its lead on a record 6 field goals by Jets kicker Jim Turner. Kansas City quarterback Len Dawson won the offensive-player-of-the-game award, and Houston's George Webster was named the game's defensive star.

West	3	0	10	25	—	38
East	3	16	3	3	—	25

East—FG Turner 27
West—FG Stenerud 51
East—Kiick 2 run (Turner kick)
East—FG Turner 16
East—FG Turner 19
East—FG Turner 13
West—Trumpy 6 pass from Dawson (Stenerud kick)
East—FG Turner 18
West—FG Stenerud 30
East—FG Turner 21
West—Dixon 1 run (Stenerud kick)
West—Robinson 1 run (Robinson run)
West—Robinson 1 run (Stenerud kick)
West—FG Stenerud 32

1969 NFL Pro Bowl

WEST 10, EAST 7
January 19, 1969, at Los Angeles.
Attendance: 32,050

The Los Angeles Rams led the way to a 10-7 West victory. The winning coach was the Rams' George Allen, the West's first points were scored by Rams kicker Bruce Gossett, the lineman of the game was Rams defensive tackle Merlin Olsen, and the back of the game was Rams quarterback Roman Gabriel, who directed the winning drive.

East	0	0	7	0	—	7
West	0	3	0	7	—	10

West—FG Gossett 20
East—Warfield 3 pass from Meredith (Baker kick)
West—Brown 1 run (Gossett kick)

1970 AFL All-Star Game

WEST 26, EAST 3
January 17, 1970, at Houston.
Attendance: 30,170

John Hadl of San Diego was named the player of the game after completing 18 of 26 passes for 224 yards and a touchdown to lead the West to a 26-3 victory in the AFL's final contest. The game was played in Houston's Astrodome.

East	0	0	3	0	—	3
West	13	0	3	10	—	26

West—Post 1 run (pass failed)
West—Alworth 21 pass from Hadl (Stenerud kick)
West—FG Stenerud 38
East—FG Turner 44
West—FG Stenerud 30
West—Livingston 11 run (Stenerud kick)

1970 NFL Pro Bowl

WEST 16, EAST 13
January 18, 1970, at Los Angeles.
Attendance: 57,786

Roman Gabriel of the Rams, who earlier had scored on a 1-yard run, threw a 28-yard touchdown pass to Green Bay's Carroll Dale for the winning touchdown in the final minutes of the game. Gale Sayers of Chicago was named back of the game for the third time, and George Andrie of Dallas was voted lineman of the game.

East	7	6	0	0	—	13
West	0	7	0	9	—	16

East—Kelly 10 run (Dempsey kick)
East—FG Dempsey 46
West—Gabriel 1 run (Etter kick)
East—FG Dempsey 27
West—Safety, Brezina tackled Walden in end zone
West—Dale 28 pass from Gabriel (Etter kick)

1971 AFC-NFC Pro Bowl

NFC 27, AFC 6
January 24, 1971, at Los Angeles.
Attendance: 48,222

Mel Renfro of Dallas, voted the outstanding back of the game, returned punts 82 and 56 yards for touchdowns in the final period to break open a close game as the NFC defeated the AFC 27-6 in the first AFC-NFC Pro Bowl. Fred Carr of Green Bay was selected as the game's outstanding lineman.

AFC	0	3	3	0	—	6
NFC	0	3	10	14	—	27

AFC—FG Stenerud 37
NFC—FG Cox 13
NFC—Osborn 23 pass from Brodie (Cox kick)
NFC—FG Cox 35
AFC—FG Stenerud 16
NFC—Renfro 82 punt return (Cox kick)
NFC—Renfro 56 punt return (Cox kick)

1972 AFC-NFC Pro Bowl

AFC 26, NFC 13
January 23, 1972, at Los Angeles.
Attendance: 53,647

Offensive-player-of-the-game Jan Stenerud kicked 4 field goals to help the AFC defeat the NFC 26-13. Linebacker Willie Lanier, Stenerud's Kansas City teammate, was voted the defensive player of the game.

NFC	0	6	0	7	—	13
AFC	0	3	13	10	—	26

NFC—Grim 50 pass from Landry (kick failed)
AFC—FG Stenerud 25
AFC—FG Stenerud 23
AFC—FG Stenerud 48
AFC—Morin 5 pass from Dawson (Stenerud kick)
AFC—FG Stenerud 42
NFC—V. Washington 2 run (Knight kick)
AFC—F. Little 6 run (Stenerud kick)

1973 AFC-NFC Pro Bowl

AFC 33, NFC 28
January 21, 1973, at Irving.
Attendance: 47,879

Player-of-the-game O.J. Simpson of Buffalo rushed for 112 yards to lead the AFC to a 33-14 advantage before 2 NFC touchdowns in the final minute made the score respectable. Green Bay's John Brockington scored 3 touchdowns for the NFC. The game in Irving, Texas, marked the first time since 1942 that the Pro Bowl was played outside Los Angeles.

AFC	0	10	10	13	—	33
NFC	14	0	0	14	—	28

NFC—Brockington 1 run (Marcol kick)
NFC—Brockington 3 pass from Kilmer (Marcol kick)
AFC—Simpson 7 run (Gerela kick)
AFC—FG Gerela 18
AFC—FG Gerela 22
AFC—Hubbard 11 run (Gerela kick)
AFC—Taylor 5 pass from Lamonica (no kick; bad snap)
AFC—Bell 12 interception return (Gerela kick)
NFC—Brockington 1 run (Marcol kick)
NFC—Kwalick 12 pass from Snead (Marcol kick)

1974 AFC-NFC Pro Bowl

AFC 15, NFC 13
January 20, 1974, at Kansas City.
Attendance: 51,482

Garo Yepremian kicked 5 field goals, the last from 42 yards with only 21 seconds left, to account for all of his team's points and give the AFC a 15-13 victory. Miami's kicker was named the player of the game.

NFC	0	10	0	3	—	13
AFC	3	3	3	6	—	15

AFC—FG Yepremian 16
NFC—FG Mike-Mayer 27
NFC—McCutcheon 14 pass from Gabriel (Mike-Mayer kick)
AFC—FG Yepremian 37
AFC—FG Yepremian 27
AFC—FG Yepremian 41
NFC—FG Mike-Mayer 21
AFC—FG Yepremian 42

1975 AFC-NFC Pro Bowl

NFC 17, AFC 10
January 20, 1975, at Miami.
Attendance: 26,484

James Harris of the Rams threw 2 touchdown passes in the fourth quarter to lead the NFC to a 17-10 victory. The touchdown passes by Harris, who was named the player of the game, came only 1:24 apart after he had replaced injured starting quarterback Jim Hart of St Louis.

NFC	0	3	0	14	—	17
AFC	0	0	10	0	—	10

NFC—FG Marcol 33
AFC—Warfield 32 pass from Griese (Gerela kick)
AFC—FG Gerela 33
NFC—Gray 8 pass from J. Harris (Marcol kick)
NFC—Taylor 8 pass from J. Harris (Marcol kick)

1976 AFC-NFC Pro Bowl

NFC 23, AFC 20
January 26, 1976, at New Orleans.
Attendance: 32,108

Mike Boryla of Philadelphia, in the game only because of injuries to other quarterbacks, came off the bench to fire 2 late touchdown passes and lead the NFC to a 23-20 victory. Player-of-the-game Billy (White Shoes) Johnson of Houston had given the AFC a 20-9 lead in the final period with a dazzling 90-yard punt return for a touchdown.

AFC	0	13	0	7	—	20
NFC	0	0	9	14	—	23

AFC—FG Stenerud 20
AFC—FG Stenerud 35
AFC—Burrough 64 pass from Pastorini (Stenerud kick)
NFC—FG Bakken 42
NFC—Foreman 4 pass from Hart (kick blocked)
AFC—Johnson 90 punt return (Stenerud kick)
NFC—Metcalf 14 pass from Boryla (Bakken kick)
NFC—Gray 8 pass from Boryla (Bakken kick)

1977 AFC-NFC Pro Bowl

AFC 24, NFC 14
January 17, 1977, at Seattle.
Attendance: 63,214

With the AFC leading 17-14 in the final period, player-of-the-game Mel Blount of Pittsburgh intercepted a pass by St Louis's Jim Hart in the end zone. Less than three minutes later, Blount again intercepted Hart, returning it to the NFC's 27-yard line to set up the game-clinching touchdown.

NFC	0	14	0	0	—	14
AFC	10	7	0	7	—	24

AFC—Simpson 3 run (Linhart kick)
AFC—FG Linhart 31
NFC—Thomas 15 run (Bakken kick)
AFC—Joiner 12 pass from Anderson (Linhart kick)
NFC—McCutcheon 1 run (Bakken kick)
AFC—Branch 27 pass from Anderson (Linhart kick)

1978 AFC-NFC Pro Bowl

NFC 14, AFC 13
January 23, 1978, at Tampa.
Attendance: 51,337

Trailing 13-0 at halftime, the NFC came back to win 14-13. The Rams' Pat Haden threw a touchdown pass to Terry Metcalf of St. Louis in the third quarter, and then, in the final period, player-of-the-game Walter Payton of Chicago capped a 63-yard drive with a 1-yard touchdown run.

AFC	3	10	0	0	—	13
NFC	0	0	7	7	—	14

AFC—FG Linhart 21
AFC—Branch 10 pass from Stabler (Linhart kick)
AFC—FG Linhart 39
NFC—Metcalf 4 pass from Haden (Herrera kick)
NFC—Payton 1 run (Herrera kick)

1979 AFC-NFC Pro Bowl

NFC 13, AFC 7
January 29, 1979, at Los Angeles.
Attendance: 46,281

Archie Manning of New Orleans and Roger Staubach of Dallas each led a touchdown drive as the NFC edged the AFC 13-7. Ahmad Rashad of Minnesota was named player of the game after catching 5 passes, including 2 on the winning touchdown drive, for 89 yards.

AFC	0	7	0	0	—	7
NFC	0	6	7	0	—	13

NFC—Montgomery 2 run (kick failed)
AFC—Largent 8 pass from Griese (Yepremian kick)
NFC—T. Hill 19 pass from Staubach (Corral kick)

1980 AFC-NFC Pro Bowl

NFC 37, AFC 27
January 27, 1980, at Honolulu.
Attendance: 48,060

Chuck Muncie of New Orleans ran for 2 touchdowns, passed for another, and was named player of the game in the NFC's 37-27 victory. The NFC broke open the game with 20 points in the second quarter. The game was the first Pro Bowl played in Aloha Stadium in Honolulu, Hawaii.

NFC	3	20	7	7	—	37
AFC	3	7	10	7	—	27

NFC—FG Moseley 37
AFC—FG Fritsch 19
NFC—Muncie 1 run (Moseley kick)
AFC—Pruitt 1 pass from Bradshaw (Fritsch kick)
NFC—D. Hill 13 pass from Manning (kick failed)
NFC—T. Hill 25 pass from Muncie (Moseley kick)
NFC—Henry 86 punt return Moseley kick)
AFC—Campbell 2 run (Fritsch kick)
AFC—FG Fritsch 29
NFC—Muncie 11 run (Moseley kick)
AFC—Campbell 1 run (Fritsch kick)

1981 AFC-NFC Pro Bowl

NFC 21, AFC 7
February 1, 1981, at Honolulu.
Attendance: 47,879

Player-of-the-game Eddie Murray kicked 4 field goals and Steve Bartkowski and Alfred Jenkins of Atlanta teamed on a 55-yard touchdown pass to lead the NFC to a 21-7 victory. Detroit's Murray missed a fifth field goal when a 37-yard attempt hit the upright.

AFC	0	7	0	0	—	7
NFC	3	6	0	12	—	21

NFC—FG Murray 31
AFC—Morgan 9 pass from Sipe (J. Smith kick)
NFC—FG Murray 31
NFC—FG Murray 34
NFC—Jenkins 55 pass from Bartkowski (Murray kick)
NFC—FG Murray 36
NFC—Safety, AFC holding penalty in end zone

1982 AFC-NFC Pro Bowl

AFC 16, NFC 13
January 31, 1982, at Honolulu.
Attendance: 50,402

Chargers quarterback Dan Fouts led the AFC 69 yards to set up a 23-yard field goal by Kansas City's Nick Lowery with three seconds left, and the AFC defeated the NFC 16-13. Tight end Kellen Winslow of San Diego and defensive end Lee Roy Selmon of Tampa Bay were co-players of the game.

NFC	0	6	0	7	—	13
AFC	0	0	13	3	—	16

NFC—Giles 4 pass from Montana (kick blocked)
AFC—Muncie 2 run (kick failed)
AFC—Campbell 1 run (Lowery kick)
NFC—Dorsett 4 run (Septien kick)
AFC—FG Lowery 23

1983 AFC-NFC Pro Bowl

NFC 20, AFC 19
February 6, 1983, at Honolulu.
Attendance: 47,201

Danny White of Dallas threw an 11-yard touchdown pass to Green Bay's John Jefferson with 35 seconds left to cap a 20-19 come-from-behind victory for the NFC. Jefferson was named co-player of the game with Dan Fouts of San Diego, who set Pro Bowl records for completions (17) and passing yards (274) for the AFC.

AFC	9	3	7	0	—	19
NFC	0	10	0	10	—	20

AFC—Walker 34 pass from Fouts (Benirschke kick)
AFC—Safety, Still tackled Theismann in end zone
NFC—Andrews 3 run (Moseley kick)
NFC—FG Moseley 35
AFC—FG Benirschke 29
AFC—Allen 1 run (Benirschke kick)
NFC—FG Moseley 41
NFC—Jefferson 11 pass from D. White (Moseley kick)

1984 AFC-NFC Pro Bowl

NFC 45, AFC 3
January 29, 1984, at Honolulu.
Attendance: 50,445

Smarting from a loss in Super Bowl XVIII, Joe Theismann of the Redskins hit 21 of 27 passes for 242 yards and 3 touchdowns to lead the NFC to a smashing 45-3 victory. Theismann, already honored as the Associated Press NFL MVP for his performance during the regular season, was named player of the game.

NFC	3	14	14	14	—	45
AFC	0	3	0	0	—	3

NFC—FG Haji-Sheikh 23
NFC—Andrews 16 pass from Theismann (Haji-Sheikh kick)
NFC—Andrews 2 pass from Montana (Haji-Sheikh kick)
AFC—FG Anderson 43
NFC—Cromwell 44 interception return (Haji-Sheikh kick)
NFC—Lofton 8 pass from Theismann (Haji-Sheikh kick)
NFC—Coffman 6 pass from Theismann (Haji-Sheikh kick)
NFC—Dickerson 14 run (Haji-Sheikh kick)

1985 AFC-NFC Pro Bowl

AFC 22, NFC 14
January 27, 1985, at Honolulu.
Attendance: 50,385

Defensive end Mark Gastineau of the Jets was named player of the game after recording 4 sacks and a safety, but the game's big play was Kansas City defensive end Art Still's 83-yard fumble return for the go-ahead touchdown in the AFC's 22-14 victory.

AFC	0	9	0	13	—	22
NFC	0	0	7	7	—	14

AFC—Safety, Gastineau tackled Dickerson in end zone
AFC—Allen 6 pass from Marino (Johnson kick)
NFC—Lofton 13 pass from Marino (Stenerud kick)
NFC—Payton 1 run (Stenerud kick)
AFC—Still 83 fumble return (Johnson kick)
AFC—FG Johnson 22

1986 AFC-NFC Pro Bowl

NFC 28, AFC 24
February 2, 1986, at Honolulu.
Attendance: 50,101

Giants quarterback Phil Simms was named player of the game after completing 15 of 27 passes for 212 yards and 3 second-half touchdowns as the NFC rebounded from a 24-7 halftime deficit to win 28-24. Marcus Allen of the Raiders helped the AFC build its lead by running and passing for touchdowns.

NFC	0	7	7	14	—	28
AFC	7	17	0	0	—	24

AFC—Allen 2 run (Anderson kick)
NFC—Browner 48 interception return (Andersen kick)
AFC—Chandler 61 pass from Allen (Anderson kick)
AFC—FG Anderson 34
AFC—Lipps 11 pass from O'Brien (Anderson kick)
NFC—Monk 15 pass from Simms (Andersen kick)
NFC—Cosbie 2 pass from Simms (Andersen kick)
NFC—Giles 15 pass from Simms (Andersen kick)

1987 AFC-NFC Pro Bowl

AFC 10, NFC 6
February 1, 1987, at Honolulu.
Attendance: 50,101

John Elway threw a touchdown pass to Todd Christensen, Tony Franklin kicked a field goal, and the AFC defense did the rest, making brilliant stands after the NFC had first downs at the AFC 31-, 7-, 16-, 15-, 5-, and 7-yard lines. The player of the game was Philadelphia defensive end Reggie White, who had 4 sacks.

AFC	7	3	0	0	—	10
NFC	0	0	3	3	—	6

AFC—Christensen 10 pass from Elway (Franklin kick)
AFC—FG Franklin 26
NFC—FG Andersen 38
NFC—FG Andersen 19

1988 AFC-NFC Pro Bowl

AFC 15, NFC 6
February 7, 1988, at Honolulu.
Attendance: 50,113

The AFC defense, led by end Bruce Smith of Buffalo, the player of the game, held the NFC without a touchdown for the second year in a row to win 15-6. The game's lone touchdown came on Buffalo quarterback Jim Kelly's 1-yard run in the second quarter.

NFC	0	6	0	0	—	6
AFC	0	7	6	2	—	15

NFC—FG Andersen 25
AFC—Kelly 1 run (Biasucci kick)
NFC—FG Andersen 36
AFC—FG Biasucci 37
AFC—FG Biasucci 30
AFC—Safety, Montana forced out of end zone

1989 AFC-NFC Pro Bowl

NFC 34, AFC 3
January 29, 1989, at Honolulu.
Attendance: 50,113

The NFC thoroughly dominated the AFC, leading in yards 355-167, forcing 5 turnovers, and holding onto the ball more than 35 minutes en route to a 34-3 victory. Philadelphia's Randall Cunningham completed 10 of 14 passes and ran for 49 yards to earn player-of-the-game honors.

AFC	3	0	0	0	—	3
NFC	7	7	10	10	—	34

AFC—FG Norwood 38
NFC—Walker 4 run (Andersen kick)
NFC—Settle 1 run (Andersen kick)
NFC—FG Andersen 27
NFC—Walker 7 run (Andersen kick)
NFC—FG Andersen 51
NFC—Ellard 8 pass from Wilson (Andersen kick)

1990 AFC-NFC Pro Bowl

NFC 27, AFC 21
February 4, 1990, at Honolulu.
Attendance: 50,445

The NFC defense took over in the third period, scoring twice to defeat the AFC 27-21. Shortly after the NFC went ahead 13-7, player-of-the-game Jerry Gray of the Rams returned an interception 51 yards for a touchdown. Four minutes later, Minnesota's Keith Millard returned a fumble 8 yards for the clinching touchdown.

NFC	3	3	21	0	—	27
AFC	0	7	0	14	—	21

NFC—FG Murray 23
NFC—FG Murray 41
AFC—Okoye 1 run (Treadwell kick)
NFC—Meggett 11 pass from Cunningham (Murray kick)
NFC—Gray 51 interception return (Murray kick)
NFC—Millard 8 fumble recovery return (Murray kick)
AFC—Edmunds 5 pass from Krieg (Treadwell kick)
AFC—M. Johnson 22 interception return (Treadwell kick)

1991 AFC-NFC Pro Bowl

AFC 23, NFC 21
February 3, 1991, at Honolulu.
Attendance: 50,345

Jim Kelly of Buffalo completed 13 of 19 passes for 210 yards and 2 fourth-quarter touchdowns to earn player-of-the-game honors and lead the AFC to a 23-21 victory. Miami's Jeff Cross blocked a field-goal attempt by Morten Andersen of New Orleans with seven seconds left to preserve the victory.

AFC	3	0	3	17	—	23
NFC	0	7	7	7	—	21

AFC—FG Lowery 26
NFC—J. Johnson 1 run (Andersen kick)
AFC—FG Lowery 43
NFC—J. Johnson 9 run (Andersen kick)
AFC—Reed 20 pass from Kelly (Lowery kick)
NFC—Sanders 22 run (Andersen kick)
AFC—FG Lowery 34
AFC—Givins 13 pass from Kelly (Lowery kick)

1992 AFC-NFC Pro Bowl

NFC 21, AFC 15
February 2, 1992, at Honolulu.
Attendance: 50,209

Chris Miller of Atlanta capped an 85-yard drive with an 11-yard touchdown pass to Jerry Rice of San Francisco with 4:04 remaining to lift the NFC to a 21-15 victory. Michael Irvin of Dallas was named player of the game after catching 8 passes for 125 yards and a touchdown.

NFC	7	7	0	7	—	21
AFC	7	5	0	3	—	15

AFC—Clayton 4 pass from Kelly (Jaeger kick)
NFC—Irvin 13 pass from Rypien (Lohmiller kick)
AFC—Safety, Townsend tackled Byner in end zone
AFC—FG Jaeger 48
NFC—Clark 35 pass from Rypien (Lohmiller kick)
AFC—FG Jaeger 27
NFC—Rice 11 pass from Miller (Lohmiller kick)

1993 AFC-NFC Pro Bowl

AFC 23, NFC 20
February 7, 1993, at Honolulu.
Attendance: 50,007

Nick Lowery of the Chiefs kicked a 33-yard field goal after 4:09 of overtime to give the AFC a 23-20 victory. The AFC won despite being dominated by the NFC 471-114 in total yards. Buffalo's special-teams star Steve Tasker was named player of the game after forcing a fumble and blocking a field-goal attempt.

AFC	0	10	3	7	3	—	23
NFC	3	10	0	7	0	—	20

NFC—FG Andersen 27
AFC—Seau 31 interception return (Lowery kick)
NFC—FG Andersen 37
NFC—Irvin 9 pass from Aikman (Andersen kick)
AFC—FG Lowery 42
AFC—FG Lowery 29
AFC—McDaniel 28 blocked field goal return (Lowery kick)
NFC—Hampton 23 pass from Young (Andersen kick)
AFC—FG Lowery 33

1994 AFC-NFC Pro Bowl

NFC 17, AFC 3
February 6, 1994, at Honolulu.
Attendance: 50,026

With the score tied 3-3 late in the third quarter, the NFC used a blocked punt and a fumble recovery to set up 14 points en route to a 17-3 victory. Wide receiver Andre Rison of Atlanta was named player of the game after making 6 catches for 86 yards.

NFC	3	0	7	7	—	17
AFC	0	3	0	0	—	3

NFC—FG Johnson 35
AFC—FG Anderson 25
NFC—Bettis 4 run (Johnson kick)
NFC—Carter 15 pass from Hebert (Johnson kick)

1995 AFC-NFC Pro Bowl

AFC 41, NFC 13
February 5, 1995, at Honolulu.
Attendance: 49,121

The AFC set records for rushing yards (400) and total yards (552) while rolling to a 41-13 victory. Player-of-the-game Marshall Faulk of Indianapolis gained a record 180 yards rushing on only 13 carries, and Chris Warren of Seattle added 127 yards on 14 carries.

AFC	0	17	3	21	—	41
NFC	10	0	3	0	—	13

NFC—FG Reveiz 28
NFC—Carter 51 pass from Young (Reveiz kick)
AFC—Green 22 pass from Elway (Carney kick)
AFC—FG Carney 22
AFC—Hoard 4 run (Carney kick)
NFC—FG Reveiz 49
AFC—FG Carney 23
AFC—Warren 11 run (Carney kick)
AFC—Green 16 pass from Hostetler (Carney kick)
AFC—Faulk 49 run (Carney kick)

1996 AFC-NFC Pro Bowl

NFC 20, AFC 13
February 4, 1996, at Honolulu.
Attendance: 50,034

Jerry Rice had 6 receptions for 82 yards to earn player-of-the-game honors in the NFC's 20-13 victory. The NFC scored 20 first-half points and then hung on to win. The AFC scored first when Jeff Blake completed a Pro Bowl-record 93-yard touchdown pass to Yancey Thigpen.

NFC	3	17	0	0	—	20
AFC	7	0	6	0	—	13

AFC—Thigpen 93 pass from Blake (Elam kick)
NFC—FG Andersen 36
NFC—Rice 1 pass from Favre (Andersen kick)
NFC—Harvey 36 interception return (Andersen kick)
NFC—FG Andersen 24
AFC—Martin 17 pass from Harbaugh (kick failed)

1997 AFC-NFC Pro Bowl

AFC 26, NFC 23
February 2, 1997, at Honolulu.
Attendance: 50,031

MVP Mark Brunell hit Tim Brown with an 80-yard touchdown bomb to tie the game with less than a minute of regulation left, then led the AFC on a 66-yard drive to Cary Blanchard's winning field goal in overtime. The kick of the day was made by investment banker Lance Alstodt who drilled a 35-yarder for a million dollars at halftime as the climax of a nationwide contest by Hershey's.

AFC	0	3	7	13	3	—	26
NFC	9	0	6	8	0	—	23

NFC—FG Kasay 28
NFC—McDaniel 4 pass from Favre (kick failed)
AFC—FG Blanchard 28
NFC—Sanders 6 run (pass failed)
AFC—C.Martin 3 run (Blanchard kick)
AFC—Ambrose 54 interception return (pass failed)
NFC—C.Carter 23 pass from Frerotte (Frerotte to Walls)
AFC—T.Brown 80 passfrom Brunell (Blanchard kick)
AFC—FG Blanchard 37

1998 AFC-NFC Pro Bowl

AFC 29, NFC 24
February 1, 1998, at Honolulu.
Attendance: 49,995

Warren Moon, at 41 the oldest player on the field by four years, came off the bench in the fourth quarter to lead the AFC to 15 points and a comeback victory. The AFC trailed 24-17 late in the game until Moon's 57-yard pass to Tim Brown set up Eddie George's 4-yard touchdown run with 2:31 left. A two-point conversion try failed, but NFC quarterback Chris Chandler fumbled on the next play from scrimmage, and the AFC's Michael Sinclair recovered at the NFC's 16. Three runs by George set up Moon's winning quarterback sneak with 1:49 remaining. Moon, who completed 4 of 8 passes for 89 yards, was named the player of the game.

NFC	7	14	0	3	—	24
AFC	7	0	7	15	—	29

NFC—H. Moore 22 pass from Young (Hanson kick)
AFC—Rison 17 pass from Brunell (Hollis kick)
NFC—R. Moore 36 pass from Young (Hanson kick)
NFC—Levens 12 run (Hanson kick)
AFC—J. Smith 14 pass from Bledsoe (Hollis kick)
NFC—FG Hanson 35
AFC—FG Hollis 48
AFC—George 4 run (pass failed)
AFC—Moon 1 run (pass failed)

1999 AFC-NFC Pro Bowl

AFC 23, NFC 10
February 7, 1999, at Honolulu.
Attendance: 50,075

One week after earning most-valuable-player honors in Super Bowl XXXIII, Denver quarterback John Elway threw a touchdown pass on his only series to give the AFC a lead it would not relinquish en route to its third consecutive Pro Bowl victory. Elway completed 4 of 5 passes for 55 yards on a 61-yard drive the first time the AFC had the ball. He capped the march with a 3-yard touchdown pass to fullback Sam Gash 4:09 into the game. New England's Ty Law, who returned an interception 67 yards for a third-quarter touchdown, and the New York Jets' Keyshawn Johnson, who caught 7 passes for 87 yards, shared player-of-the-game honors. Denver's Jason Elam kicked 3 field goals for the AFC. Each team had 3 interceptions to frustrate the offenses.

AFC	7	3	10	3	—	23
NFC	3	0	7	0	—	10

AFC—Gash 3 pass from Elway (Elam kick)
NFC—FG Anderson 23
AFC—FG Elam 23
AFC—Law 67 interception return (Elam kick)
NFC—E. Smith 2 run (Anderson kick)
AFC—FG Elam 46
AFC—FG Elam 26

Pro Bowl Selections

The year shown refers to the year the game was played, not the season it followed. An asterisk indicates a player was selected but did not play.

Adamle, Tony, FB (2) Cle 1951-52
Adams, Chet, T (2) Cle Jan. 1942, Dec. 1942
Adams, Julius, DE (1) NE 1981
Adamson, Ken, G (1) Den 1962
Adderley, Herb, CB (5) GB 1964-68
Addison, Tom, LB (4) Bos 1962-65
Aikman, Troy, QB (6) Dal 1992-93, 1994*,1995-96, 1997*
Alban, Dick, HB (1) Was 1955
Albert, Frankie, QB (1) SF 1951
Aldrich, Ki, C (2) ChiC Jan. 1940; Was Dec. 1942
Alderman, Grady, T (6) Min 1964-68, 1970
Alexander, Kermit, S (1) SF 1969
Allen, Chuck, LB (2) SD 1964-65
Allen, Eric, CB (6) Phi 1990, 1992-95; NO 1996
Allen, Larry, G-T (4) Dal 1996-1999
Allen, Marcus, RB (6) LARd 1983, 1985-86, 1987*, 1988; KC 1994
Allen, Terry, RB (1) Was 1997
Alstott, Mike, FB (2) TB 1998-99
Alt, John, T (2) KC 1993-94
Alworth, Lance, FL (7) SD 1964-70
Alzado, Lyle, DE (2) Den 1978-79

Ambrose, Ashley, CB Cin 1997
Ameche, Alan, FB (4) Bal 1956-59
Anders, Kimble, FB (3) KC 1996-98
Andersen, Morten, K (7) NO 1986-89, 1991, 1993; Atl 1996
Anderson, Bill, E (2) Was 1960-61
Anderson, Dick, S (3) Mia 1973-75
Anderson, Donny, HB (1) GB 1969
Anderson, Gary, K (4) Pit 1985-86, 1994, Min 1999
Anderson, Gary, RB (1) SD 1987
Anderson, Jamal, RB (1) Atl 1999
Anderson, Ken, QB (4) Cin 1976-77, 1982-83
Anderson, Neal, RB (4) ChiB 1989, 1990*, 1991*, 1992
Anderson, Ottis, RB (2) StL 1980-81
Andrews, William, RB (4) Atl 1981-84
Andrie, George, DE (5) Dal 1966-70
Ane, Charley, T (2) Det 1957, 1959
Angsman, Elmer, HB (1) ChiC 1951
Antwine, Hou, DT (6) Bos 1964*, 1965-69
Apolskis, Ray, C (1) ChiC Jan. 1942
Arbanas, Fred, TE (5) DalT 1963; KC 1964*, 1965*, 1966, 1968
Armstead, Jessie, LB (2) NYG 1998-99
Armstrong, Bruce, T (6) NE 1991-92, 1995-98
Armstrong, Otis, RB (2) Den 1975, 1977
Arnett, Jon, HB (5) LARm 1958-62
Arnold, Jim, P (2) Det 1988-89
Artoe, Lee, T (3) ChiB Dec. 1940; Jan. 1942; Dec. 1942
Atkins, Bill, S (1) Buf 1962
Atkins, Doug, DE (8) ChiB 1958-64, 1966
Atkinson, Al, LB (1) NYJ 1969
Atkinson, George, CB (2) Oak 1969-70
Atwater, Steve, S (8) Den 1991-96, 1997*, 1999
Austin, Bill, G (1) NYG 1955

Bacon, Coy, DE (3) LARm 1973; Cin 1977-78
Bailey, Johnny, KR (1) Ariz 1993
Baisi, Al, G (2) ChiB Dec. 1940; Jan. 1942
Baker, Al, DE (3) Det 1979-81
Baker, Dave, S (1) SF 1960
Baker, Jon, G (2) NYG 1952-53
Baker, Sam, HB-K (4) Was 1957; Dal 1964; Phi 1965, 1969
Baker, Tony, RB (1) NO 1970
Bakken, Jim, K (4) StL 1966, 1968, 1976-77
Balasz, Frank, G B Jan. 1940
Ball, Jerry, DT (3) Det 1990-91, 1992*
Ballard, Howard, T (2) Buf 1993-94
Ballman, Gary, HB-SE (2) Pit 1965-66
Banducci, Bruno, G (1) SF 1955
Banfield, Tony, CB (3) Hou 1962-64
Banks, Carl, LB (1) NYG 1988
Banks, Chip, LB (4) Cle 1983-84, 1986*, 1987
Banks, Tom, C (4) StL 1976-79
Barbaro, Gary, S (3) KC 1981-83
Barber, Jim, T, (1) Was Dec. 1940
Barber, Stew, T (5) Buf 1964-68
Barker, Bryan, K (1) Jac 1998
Barkum, Jerome, WR (1) NYJ 1974
Barnard, Hap, E (1) NYG 1939
Barnes, Billy Ray, FB-HB (3) Phi 1958-60
Barnes, Erich, DB (6) ChiB 1960; NYG 1962-65; Cle 1969
Barnes, Mike, DT (1) Bal 1978
Barnes, Walter (Piggy), G (1) Phi 1951
Barnett, Fred, WR (1) Phi 1993
Barney, Lem, CB (7) Det 1968-70, 1973-74, 1976-77
Barr, Terry, FL (2) Det 1964-65
Bartkowski, Steve, QB (2) Atl 1981-82
Barton, Harris, T (1) SF 1994
Barwegan, Dick, G (4) ChiB 1951-53; Bal 1954
Bass, Dick, HB (3) LARm 1963-64, 1967
Bates, Bill, ST (1) Dal 1985
Bates, Michael, KR-ST (3) Car 1997-99
Baugh, Sammy, QB (5) Was 1939; Dec. 1940; Jan. 1942; Dec. 1942*; 1952
Baughan, Maxie, LB (9) Phi 1961-62, 1964-66; LARm 1967-69, 1970*
Baumhower, Bob, DT-NT (5) Mia 1980, 1982-84, 1985*
Bausch, Frank, C (1) ChiB Dec. 1940
Bavaro, Mark, TE (2) NYG 1987, 1988*

Bednarik, Chuck, LB (8) Phi 1951-55, 1957-58, 1961
Behrman, Dave, LB (1) Buf 1966*
Beinor, Ed, T (1) Was Dec. 1942*
Bierne, Jim, WR (1) Hou 1970
Bell, Bobby, DE-LB (9) KC 1965-73
Bell, Greg, RB (1) ChiB 1985
Bell, Todd, S (1) ChiB 1985
Bemiller, Al, C (1) Buf 1966
Benirschke, Rolf, K (1) SD 1893
Bennett, Cornelius, LB (5) Buf 1989, 1991-94
Bennett, Darren, P (1) SD 1996
Benson, Brad, T (1) NYG 1987
Benton, Jim, E (1) Cle Jan. 1940
Bergey, Bill, LB (5) Cin 1970; Phi 1975, 1977-79
Berry, Bob, QB (1) Atl 1970
Berry, Raymond, SE (5) Bal 1959-60, 1962, 1964-65
Bertelsen, Jim, RB (1) LARm 1974
Bethea, Elvin, DE (8) Hou 1970, 1972-76, 1979-80
Betters, Doug, DE (1) Mia 1984
Bettis, Jerome, RB (4) LARm 1994-95; Pit 1997-98
Biasucci, Dean, K (1) Ind 1988
Bickett, Duane, LB (1) Ind 1988
Bielski, Dick, E (1) Dal 1962
Biggs, Verlon, DE (3) NYJ 1967-69
Biletnikoff, Fred, WR (6) LARd 1968, 1970-72, 1974-75
Bingaman, Les, G (2) Det 1952, 1954
Birdsong, Carl, P (1) StL 1984
Birdwell, Dan, DE (1) LARd 1969
Bishop, Bill, T (1) ChiB 1955
Bishop, Blaine, S (3) Hou 1996, 1997*; Ten 1998
Bishop, Don, CB (1) Dal 1963
Bishop, Keith, G (2) Den 1987-88
Bishop, Sonny, G (1) Hou 1969
Bjork, Del, T (1) ChiB 1939
Blades, Benny, S (1) Det 1992
Blades, Brian, WR (1) Sea 1990
Blair, George, DB (1) SD 1962
Blair, Matt, LB (6) Min 1978-83
Blake, Jeff, QB (1) Cin 1996
Blanchard, Cary, K (1) Ind 1997
Blanda, George, QB-K, (4) Hou 1962-64; LARd 1968
Blanks, Sid, HB (1) Hou 1965
Blazine, Tony, T (1) ChiC Jan. 1940
Bledsoe, Drew, QB (3) NE 1995, 1997-98
Blount, Mel, CB (5) Pit 1976-77, 1979-80, 82
Blozis, Al, T (1) NYG Dec. 1942
Blue, Forrest, C (4) SF 1972-75
Bokamper, Kim, LB (1) Mia 1980
Bono, Steve, QB (1) KC 1996
Boozer, Emerson, HB (2) NYJ 1967, 1969
Bortz, Mark, G (2) ChiB 1989, 1991*
Boryla, Mike, QB (1) Phi 1976
Boselli, Tony, T (3) Jac 1997-99
Bosley, Bruce, G-C (4) SF 1961, 1966-68
Bosseler, Don, FB (1) Was 1960
Bostic, Jeff, C (1) Was 1984
Bostic, Keith, S (1) Hou 1988
Boulware, Peter, LB (1) Bal 1999
Bowens, Tim, DT (1) Mia 1999
Box, Cloyce, E (2) Det 1951, 1953
Boyd, Bob, E (1) LARm 1955
Boyd, Bobby, DB (2) Bal 1965, 1969
Boyette, Garland, LB (2) Hou 1969-70
Braase, Ordell, DE (2) Bal 1967-68
Bradley, Bill, S (3) Phi 1972-74
Bradshaw, Charlie, T (2) Pit 1964-65
Bradshaw, Terry, QB (3) Pit 1976*, 1979-80
Bramlett, John, LB (2) Den 1967; Mia 1968
Branch, Cliff, WR (4) Oak 1975-78
Branch, Mel, DE (3) DalT 1962-63, KC 1964
Braxton, Tyrone, S (1) Den 1997
Bray, Ray, G (4) ChiB Dec 1940, Jan 1942, 1951-52
Brazile, Robert, LB (7) Hou 1977-83
Breedlove, Rod, LB (1) Was 1963
Brenner, Hoby, TE (1) NO 1988
Breunig, Bob, LB (3) Dal 1980-81, 1983
Brewer, Johnny, LB (1) Cle 1967

Brewster, Darrel (Pete), E (2) Cle 1956-57
Brezina, Greg, LB (1) Atl 1970
Brink, Larry, DE (2) LARm 1951-52
Briscoe, Marlin, WR (1) Buf 1971
Brito, Gene, DE (5) Was 1954, 1956-59
Brock, Charlie, C (3) GB Jan. 1940, Dec. 1940, Dec. 1942
Brockington, John, RB (3) GB 1972-74
Brodie, John, QB (2) SF 1966, 1971
Brooker, Tommy, E (1) KC 1965
Brooks, James, RB (4) Cin 1987, 1989-91
Brooks, Derrick, LB (2) TB 1998-99
Brooks, Larry, DT (5) LARm 1977-78, 1979*, 1980-81
Brooks, Leo, DT (1) StL 1977
Brooks, Michael, LB (1) Den 1993
Brookshier, Tom, CB (2) Phi 1960-61
Brown, Bill, FB (4) Min 1965-66, 1968-69
Brown, Bob, T, (6) Phi 1966-67, 1969; LARm 1970*, 1971*; Oak 1972*
Brown, Bob, DT (1) GB 1973
Brown, Chad, LB (2) Pit 1997; Sea 1999
Brown, Charlie, WR (2) Was 1983-84
Brown, Dave, CB (1) Sea 1985
Brown, Ed, QB (2) ChiB 1956-57
Brown, Eddie, KR (2) Was 1977-78
Brown, Eddie, WR (1) Cin 1989
Brown, Hardy, LB (1) SF 1953
Brown, Jerome, DT (2) Phi 1991*, 1992
Brown, Jim, FB (9) Cle 1958-66
Brown, Larry, RB (4) Was 1970-72, 1973*
Brown, Larry, T (1) Pit 1983
Brown, Lomas, T (7) Det 1991-96, Ariz 1997
Brown, Roger, DT (6) Det 1963-67; LARm 1968
Brown, Ron, KR (1) LARm 1986
Brown, Roosevelt, T (9) NYG 1956-61, 1963, 1965-66
Brown, Ruben, G (3) Buf 1997-99
Brown, Tim, KR-WR (7) LARd 1989, 1992, 1994-95; Oak 1996-98
Brown, Timmy, HB (3) Phi 1963-64, 1966
Brown, Willie, CB (9) Den 1965-66; Oak 1968-74
Browner, Joey, ST-S (6) Min 1986-91
Bruce, Isaac, WR (1) StL 1997
Bruder, Hank, QB (1) GB Jan. 1940
Brumm, Don, DE (1) StL 1969
Brunell, Mark, QB (2) Jac 1997-98
Bruney, Fred, S (2) Bos 1962-63
Bryant, Bobby, CB (2) Min 1976, 1977*
Buchanan, Buck, DT (8) KC 1965-72
Buchanan, Ray, CB (1) Atl 1999
Buchanon, Willie, CB (3) GB 1974*, 1975, 1979
Budde, Ed, G (7) KC 1964, 1967-72
Buhler, Larry, FB (1) GB Jan. 1940
Bulaich, Norm, RB (1) Bal 1972*
Buncom, Frank, LB (3) SD 1965-66, 1968
Buoniconti, Nick, LB (8) Bos 1964-68; Mia 1970, 1973*, 1974
Burford, Chris, E (1) DalT 1962
Burk, Adrian, QB (2) Phi 1955-56
Burnett, Bobby, HB (1) Buf 1967
Burnett, Dale, HB (1) NYG 1939
Burnett, Rob, DE (1) Cle 1995
Burrell, Ode, HB (1) Hou 1966
Burrough, Ken, WR (2) Hou 1976, 1978
Burrus, Lloyd, S (1) KC 1987
Burt, Jim, T (1) NYG 1987
Bussey, Young, QB (2) ChiB Jan. 1942, Dec. 1942
Butkus, Dick, LB (8) ChiB 1966-73
Butler, Jack, DB (4) Pit 1956-59
Butler, Jerry, WR (1) Buf 1981
Butler, Jim, RB (1) Atl 1970
Butler, LeRoy, S (4) GB 1994, 1997-99
Butts, Marion, RB (2) SD 1991*, 1992
Butz, Dave, DT (1) Was 1984
Byars, Keith, RB (1) Mia 1994
Byner, Earnest, RB (2) Was 1991-92
Byrd, Butch, CB (5) Buf 1965-1967, 1969-70
Byrd, Gill, CB (1) SD 1992

Caffey, Lee Roy, LB (1) GB 1966
Camarillo, Rich, P (5) NE 1984; Ariz 1990, 1992-94
Campbell, Earl, RB (5) Hou 1979-82, 1984
Campbell, Marion, DT (2) Phi 1960-61
Campbell, Woodie, HB (1) Hou 1968*
Canady, John, C (2) NYG 1951, 1953
Cannon, Billy, HB-TE (2) Hou, 1962; LARd, 1970
Cappelletti, Gino, E (5) Bos 1962, 1964-67
Carapella, Al, T (1) SF 1955
Cardwell, Lloyd, HB (1) Det 1939
Carlton, Wray, FB (1) Buf 1967
Carmichael, Harold, WR (4) Phi 1974, 1979-81
Carney, John, K (1) SD 1995
Carolan, Reg, E (1) DalT 1963
Caroline, J.C., HB (1) ChiB 1957
Carollo, Joe, T (1) LARm 1969
Carpenter, Ken, HB (1) Cle 1952
Carpenter, Preston, E (1) Pit 1963
Carr, Fred, LB (3) GB 1971, 1973, 1976
Carr, Roger, WR (1) Bal 1977
Carrier, Mark, S (3) ChiB 1991-92, 1994
Carrier, Mark, WR (1) TB 1990
Carroll, Vic, G (1) Was Dec. 1942
Carson, Carlos, WR (1) KC 1988
Carson, Harry, LB (9) NYG 1979*, 1980, 1982, 1986-88
Carson, Johnny, E (1) Was 1958
Carter, Anthony, WR (2) Min 1988-89
Carter, Cris, WR (6) Min 1994-99
Carter, Dale, CB (4) KC 1995-96, 1997*, 1998
Carter, Jim, LB (1) GB 1974
Carter, Joe, E (2) Phi 1939; Jan. 1940
Carter, Michael, NT-DT (3) SF 1986, 1988-89
Casanova, Tommy, S (3) Cin 1975, 1977-78
Casares, Rick, FB-HB (5) ChiB 1956-60
Case, Scott, CB (1) Atl 1989
Casey, Bernie, FL (1) LARm 1968
Cason, Jim, HB (2) SF 1952, 1955
Casper, Dave, TE (5) LARd 1977-80; Hou 1981
Caster, Rich, TE (3) NYJ 1973, 1975-76
Cecil, Chuck, S (1) GB 1993
Centers, Larry, FB (2) Ariz 1996*, 1997
Chambers, Wally, DT (3) ChiB 1974, 1976-77
Chandler, Chris, QB (2) Atl 1998-99
Chandler, Don, K (1) GB 1968
Chandler, Wes, WR (4) NO 1980; SD 1983-84, 1986
Chandnois, Lynn, HB (2) Pit 1953-54
Chapple, Dave, P (1) LARm 1973
Cherry, Deron, S (6) KC 1984-89
Cherundolo, Chuck, C (2) Pit Jan. 1942, Dec. 1942
Chesney, Chester, (1) ChiB Dec. 1940
Chester, Raymond, TE (4) LARd 1971-73, 1980
Childress, Ray, DE-DT-NT (5) Hou 1989, 1991, 1992*, 1993-94
Childs, Henry, TE (1) NO 1980
Chmura, Mark, TE (3) GB 1996, 1998-99
Christensen, Todd, TE (5) LARd 1984-88
Christiansen, Jack, S (5) Det 1954-58
Christy, Dick, HB (1) NYT 1963
Christy, Jeff, C Min 1999
Cifers, Ed, E, (1) Was Dec. 1940
Clancy, Jack, SE (1) Mia 1968
Clark, Bruce, DE (1) NO 1985
Clark, Dwight, WR (2) SF 1982-83
Clark, Gary, WR (4) Was 1987-88, 1991-92
Clark, Harry, HB (2) ChiB Dec. 1940, Jan. 1942
Clark, Mike, K (1) Pit 1967
Clarke, Hagood, DB (1) Buf 1966
Clarke, Leon, E (2) LARm 1956-57
Clayborn, Raymond, CB (3) NE 1984, 1986-87
Clayton, Mark, WR (5) Mia 1985-87, 1989, 1992
Coates, Ben, TE (5) NE 1995-99
Cofer, Mike, LB (1) Det 1989
Coffman, Paul, TE (3) GB 1983-85
Cogdill, Gail, SE (3) Det 1961, 1963-64
Colclough, Jim, E (1) Bos 1963*
Cole, Pete, G (1) NYG 1939
Cole, Robin, LB (1) Pit 1985
Collett, Elmer, G (1) SF 1970
Collins, Gary, FL (2) Cle 1966-67

Collins, Jim, LB (1) LARm 1986
Collins, Kerry, QB (1) Car 1997
Collins, Ray, G (1) SF 1952
Collins, Tony, RB (1) NE 1984
Collinsworth, Cris, WR (3) Cin 1982-84
Colo, Don, T (3) Cle 1955-56, 1959
Condit, Merlyn, HB (2) Pit Dec. 1940, Bkn Dec. 1942
Conerly, Charlie, QB (2) NYG 1951*, 1957
Conlan, Shane, LB (3) Buf 1989*, 1990-91
Conners, Dan, LB (3) Oak 1967-69
Connolly, Ted, G (1) SF 1962
Connor, George, T (4) ChiB 1951-54
Conrad, Bobby Joe, FL (1) StL 1965
Conti, Enio, G (1) Phi Dec. 1942
Cook, Marv, TE (2) NE 1992-93
Cooke, Ed, DE (1) Mia 1967
Coomer, Joe, T (1) Pit Jan. 1942
Cope, Frank, T (2) NYG 1939, Dec. 1940
Cordill, Olie, HB (1) Cle Dec. 1940
Corey, Walt, LB (1) KC 1964
Cornelison, Jerry, T (1) DalT 1963
Corral, Frank, K (1) LARm 1979
Cosbie, Doug, TE (3) Dal 1984-86
Costa, Dave, DT (4) Oak 1964; Den 1968-70
Costa, Paul, TE (2) Buf 1966-67
Coulter, DeWitt (Tex), T (2) NYG 1952-53
Covert, Jim, T (2) ChiB 1986-87
Cowan, Charlie, T (3) LARm 1969-71
Cox, Bryan, LB (3) Mia 1993, 1995-96
Cox, Fred, K (1) Min 1971
Craft, Russ, HB (2) Phi 1952-53
Craig, Larry, QB-E (3) GB Jan. 1940, Jan. 1942, Dec. 1942
Craig, Roger, RB (4) SF 1986, 1988-89, 1990*
Creekmur, Lou, T (8) Det 1951-58
Cribbs, Joe, RB (3) Buf 1981, 1982*, 1984
Cromwell, Nolan, S (4) LARm 1981-84
Cross, Irv, CB (2) Phi 1965-66
Cross, Jeff, DE (1) Mia 1991
Cross, Randy, G (3) SF 1982-83, 1985
Crow, John David, HB (4) ChiC 1960; StL 1961, 1963; SF 1966
Crow, Lindon, DB (3) ChiC 1957-58; NYG 1960
Csonka, Larry, RB (5) Mia 1971-72, 1973*, 1974*, 1975
Cuff, Ward, HB (3) NYG 1939, Jan. 1940, Jan. 1942
Culp, Curley, DT (6) KC 1970, 1972; Hou 1976-79
Cunningham, Randall, QB (4) Phi 1989-91; Min 1999
Cunningham, Sam, RB (1) NE 1979
Current, Mike, T (1) Den 1970
Currie, Dan, LB (1) GB 1961
Curry, Bill, C (2) Bal 1972-73
Curtis, Isaac, WR (4) Cin 1974-77
Curtis, Mike, LB (4) Bal 1959, 1971-72, 1975

Dalby, Dave, C (1) Oak 1978
Dale, Carroll, WR (3) GB 1969-71
Danenhauer, Eldon, T (2) Den 1963, 1966
Daniels, Clem, HB (4) Oak 1964-67
Danowski, Ed, FB (1) NYG 1939
Darden, Thom, S (1) Cle 1979
Daughtery, Dick, LB (1) LARm 1958
David, Jim, DB (6) Det 1955-60
Davidson, Ben, DE (3) Oak 1967-69
Davidson, Cotton, QB (2) DalT 1962; Oak 1964
Davis, Ben, CB (1) Cle (1) 1973
Davis, Eric, CB (1) SF 1996
Davis, Fred, T (2) Was Dec. 1942; ChiB 1951
Davis, Glenn, HB (1) LARm 1951
Davis, Terrell, RB (3) Den 1997-98, 1999*
Davis, Tommy, K (2) SF 1963-64
Davis, Willie, DE (5) GB 1964-68
Dawson, Dermontti, C (7) Pit 1993-99
Dawson, Len, QB (7) DalT 1963; KC 1965, 1967-69, 1970*, 1972
Day, Tom, DE (1) Buf 1966
Deal, Rufus, FB (1) Was Dec. 1942
Dean, Fred, DE (4) SD 1980-81; SF 1982, 1984
Dean, Ted, HB (1) Phi 1962
Dee, Bob, DE (4) Bos 1962, 1964-66
DeLamielleure, Joe, G (6) Buf 1976-80; Cle 1981
Delaney, Joe, RB (1) KC 1982
DeLeone, Tom, C (2) Cle 1980-81
DeLong, Steve, DE (1) SD 1970
Del Rio, Jack, LB (1) Min 1995
DeMarco, Bob, C (3) StL 1964, 1966, 1968*
Dempsey, Tom, K (1) NO 1970
Denson, Al, FL (2) Den 1968, 1970
Dent, Richard, DE (4) ChiB 1985-86, 1991, 1994
Derby, Dean, DB (1) Pit 1960
DeRogatis, Al, T (2) NYG 1951-52
Dess, Darrell, G (2) NYG 1963-64
Dewell, Bill, E (1) ChiC Jan. 1940
Dewveall, Willard, E (1) Hou 1963
Dial, Buddy, FL (2) Pit 1962, 1964*
Dickerson, Eric, RB (6) LARm 1984-85, 1987; Ind 1988-90
Dieken, Doug, T (1) Cle 1981
Dierdorf, Dan, T (6) StL 1975-79, 1981
Dilfer, Trent, QB (1) TB 1998
Dillon, Bobby, HB (4) GB 1956-59
Dishman, Cris, CB (2) Hou 1992; Was 1998
Ditka, Mike, TE (5) ChiB 1962-66
Dixon, Hanford, CB (3) Cle 1987-89
Dixon, Hewritt, FB (4) Oak 1967-69, 1971
Dobler, Conrad, G (3) StL 1976-78
Dodrill, Dale, G (4) Pit 1954-56, 1958
Doleman, Chris, DE (8) Min 1988-91, 1993-94; Atl 1996; SF 1998
Doll, Don, HB (4) Det 1951-53; Was 1954
Donaldson, Ray, C (6) Ind 1987-90; Dal 1996*, 1997*
Donovan, Art, DT (5) Bal 1954-58
Donovan, Pat, T (4) Dal 1980-83
Doran, Jim, E (1) Dal 1961
Dorney, Keith, T (1) Det 1983
Dorow, Al, QB (2) Was 1957; NY Titans 1962
Dorsett, Tony, RB (4) Dal 1979, 1982-84
Dottley, John, FB (1) ChiB 1952
Dougherty, Phil, C (1) ChiC 1939
Dove, Bob, E (1) ChiC 1951
Dove, Eddie, S (1) SF 1962
Dowler, Boyd, FL (2) GB 1966, 1968
Drake, Johnny, FB (3) Cle 1939, Jan. 1940, Dec. 1940
Drazenovich, Chuck, LB (4) Was 1956-59
Drulis, Chuck, G (1) ChiB Dec. 1942
Dryer, Fred, DE (1) LARm 1976
Dubenion, Elbert, FL (1) Buf 1965
Dudley, Bill, HB (3) Pit Dec 1942; Was 1951-52
Duerson, Dave, S (4) ChiB 1986-89
Duhe, A.J., LB (1) Mia 1985
Dunaway, Jim, DT (4) Buf 1966-69
Duncan, Curtis, WR (1) Hou 1993
Duncan, Leslie (Speedy), DB-KR (4) SD 1966-68; Was 1972
Dunn, Warrick, RB (1) TB 1998
Duper, Mark, WR (3) Mia 1984-85, 1987*
DuPree, Billy Joe, TE (3) Dal 1977-79
Dutton, John, DE (3) Bal 1976-78

Easley, Kenny, S (5) Sea 1983-86, 1988
Ecklund, Brad, C (2) NYY 1951-52
Edelman, Brad, G (1) NO 1988
Edgerson, Booker, DB (1) Buf 1966
Edmonds, Bobby Joe, KR (1) Sea 1987
Edmunds, Ferrell, TE (2) Mia 1990-91
Edwards, Dan, E (1) NYG 1951
Edwards, Glen (Turk), T (1) Was Jan. 1940
Edwards, Glen, S (2) Pit 1976-77
Eisenhauer, Larry, DE (4) Bos 1963-65, 1967
Ekern, Carl, LB (1) LARm 1987
Elam, Cleveland, DT (2) SF 1977-78
Elam, Jason, K (2) Den 1996, 1999
Ellard, Henry, KR-WR (3) LARm 1985, 1989-90
Eller, Carl, DE (6) Min 1969-72, 1974*, 1975
Elliott, John, DT (3) NYJ 1969-71
Elliott, Jumbo, T (1) NYG 1994*
Ellis, Allan, CB (1) ChiB 1978
Ellis, Ken, CB (2) GB 1974-75
Ellison, Willie, RB (1) LARm 1972*
Elter, Leo, HB (1) Was 1957

Elway, John, QB (9) Den 1987-88, 1990*, 1992*, 1994-95, 1997*, 1998*, 1999
Engebretsen, Paul (Tiny) G (1) GB Jan. 1940
English, Doug, DT (4) Det 1979, 1982-84
Erlandson, Tom, LB (1) Mia 1967
Esiason, Boomer, QB (4) Cin 1987, 1989*, 1990*; NYJ 1994
Etter, Bob, K (1) Atl 1970
Evans, Norm, T (2) Mia 1973, 1975
Everett, Jim, QB (1) LARm 1991
Everett, Thomas, S (1) Dal 1994

Fahnhorst, Keith, T (1) SF 1985
Faison, Earl, DE (5) SD 1962-66
Falaschi, Nello, QB (2) NYG 1939; Jan. 1940
Famiglietti, Gary, HB (3) ChiB Dec. 1940, Jan. 1942, Dec. 1942
Farkas, Andy, FB (2) Was Jan. 1940, Dec. 1942
Farman, Dick, G (1) Was Dec. 1942
Farr, Mel, RB (2) Det 1968, 1971
Farr, Miller, CB (3) Hou 1968-70
Farragut, Ken, C (1) Phi 1954
Faulk, Marshall, RB (3) Ind 1995-96, 1999
Favre, Brett, QB (5) GB 1993-94, 1996-97, 1998*
Feagles, Jeff, P (1) Ariz 1996
Fears, Tom, E (1) LARm 1951
Federovich, John, T (1) ChiB Jan. 1942
Felt, Dick, CB (2) NYT 1962; Bos 1963
Fencik, Gary, S (2) ChiB 1981-82
Ferguson, Charley, E (1) Buf 1966
Ferguson, Howie, FB (1) GB 1956
Fields, Joe, C (2) NYJ 1982-83
Filchock, Frank, HB (2) Was Jan. 1940, Jan. 1942
Finks, Jim, QB (1) Pit 1953
Fischer, Bill, G (3) ChiC 1951-53
Fischer, Pat, CB (3) StL 1965-66; Was 1970
Fiss, Galen, LB (2) Cle 1963-64
Flanagan, Ed, C (4) Det 1970-72, 1974
Flatley, Paul, SE (1) Min 1967
Flint, George, G (1) Buf 1966
Flores, Tom, QB (1) Oak 1967
Floyd, Don, DE (2) Hou 1962-63
Flutie, Doug, QB (1) Buf 1999
Foley, Dave, T (1) Buf 1974
Foley, Tim, S (1) Mia 1980
Folkins, Lee, TE (1) Dal 1964
Ford, Len, DE (4) Cle 1952-55
Foreman, Chuck, RB (5) Min 1974-76, 1977*, 1978
Forester, Bill, LB (4) GB 1960-63
Forte, Aldo, G (2) ChiB Dec. 1940, Jan. 1942
Fortmann, Dan, G (3) ChiB dec. 1940, Jan. 1942, Dec. 1942
Fortunato, Joe, LB (5) ChiB 1959, 1963-66
Foster, Barry, RB (1) Pit 1993
Foster, Roy, G (2) Mia 1986-87
Fouts, Dan, QB (6) SD 1980-84, 1986
Fox, Tim, S (1) NE 1981
Fralic, Bill, G (4) Atl 1987-88, 1989*, 1990
France, Doug, T (2) LARm 1978-79
Francis, Russ, TE (1) NE 1981
Franklin, Andra, RB (1) Mia 1983
Franklin, Tony, K (1) NE 1987
Fraser, Jim, LB (3) Den 1963-65
Frazier, Charlie (1) TE, Hou 1967
Frazier, Willie, TE (3) SD 1966, 1968, 1970
Frederickson, Tucker, FB (1) NYG 1966
Freeman, Antonio, WR (1) GB 1999
Freitas, Rockne (Rocky), T (1) Det 1973*
Frerotte, Gus, QB (1) Was 1997
Fritsch, Toni, K (1) Hou 1980
Fryar, Irving, KR-WR (5) NE 1986; Mia 1994-95, Phi 1997-98
Fugett, Jean, TE (1) Was 1978
Fulcher, David, S (3) Cin 1989-91
Fuller, Frank, T (1) ChiC 1960
Fuller, William, DE (4) Hou 1992; Phi 1995-97
Fullwood, Brent, RB (1) GB 1990

Gabriel, Roman, QB (4) LARm 1968-70; Phi 1974
Gain, Bob, DT-DE (5) Cle 1958-60, 1962-63
Galazin, Stan, C (1) NYG 1939
Galimore, Willie, HB (1) ChiB 1959
Gallarneau, Hugh, HB (1) ChiB Jan. 1942
Gardocki, Chris, P (1) Ind 1997
Garrett, Carl, RB (1) Bos 1970
Garrett, Mike, HB (2) KC 1967-68
Garrison, Gary, WR (4) SD 1969, 1971*, 1972-73
Garrison, Walt, RB (1) Dal 1973
Garron, Larry, HB (4) Bos 1962, 1964-65, 1968
Gash, Sam, FB (1) Buf 1999
Gastineau, Mark, DE (5) NYJ 1982-86
Gatski, Frank, C (1) Cle 1956
Gayle, Shaun, S (1) ChiB 1992
Gelatka, Chuck, E (1) NYG 1939
Gentry, Byron, G (2) Pit 1939, Jan. 1940
George, Bill, MG-LB (8) ChiB 1955-1962
George, Eddie, RB (2) Ten 1998-99
George, Ray, T (1) Det Jan. 1940
Gerela, Roy, K (2) Pit 1973, 1975
Geri, Joe, HB (2) Pit 1951-52
Gibbons, Jim, TE (3) Det 1961-62, 1965
Gibron, Abe, G (4) Cle 1953-56
Gifford, Frank, HB (7) NYG 1954-57, 1959-60, 1964
Gilbert, Kline, T (1) ChiB 1958
Gilbert, Sean, DT (1) LARm 1994
Gilchrist, Cookie, FB (4) Buf 1963-65; Den 1966
Gildea, Johnny, QB (1) NYG 1939
Giles, Jimmie, TE (4) TB 1981-83, 1986
Gilliam, John, WR (4) Min 1973-76
Gilliam, Jon, C-LB (1) DalT 1962
Gillingham, Gale, G (5) GB 1970-72, 1974*, 1975
Gillom, Horace, E (1) Cle 1953
Gilmer, Harry, QB (2) Was 1951, 1953
Givins, Ernest, WR (2) Hou 1991, 1993
Glass, Bill, DE (4) Cle 1963-65, 1968
Glenn, Aaron, CB (2) NYJ 1998, 1999*
Glick, Fred, DB (3) Hou 1963-65
Glover, Kevin, C (3) Det 1996-98
Goddard, Ed, QB (1) Cle 1939
Goeddeke, George, G (1) Den 1970
Gogan, Kevin, G (3) LARd 1995, SF 1998-99
Gogolak, Pete, K (1) Buf 1966
Goldenberg, Charles (Buckets), G (1) GB Jan. 1940
Golic, Bob, NT (2) Cle 1986-87
Gonsoulin, Austin (Goose), S (5) Den 1962-65, 1967
Goode, Rob, FB (2) Was 1952, 1955
Goode, Irv, G (2) StL 1965, 1968
Goode, Tom, C (1) Mia 1970
Gordon, Dick, WR (2) ChiB 1971*, 1972
Gordy, John, G (3) Det 1964-66
Gore, Gordon, HB (1) LA Bulldogs 1939
Gossett, Bruce, K (2) LARm 1967, 1969
Gossett, Jeff, P (1) LARd 1992
Gradishar, Randy, LB (7) Den 1976, 1978-80, 1982-84
Graham, Kenny, S (4) SD 1966, 1968-70
Graham, Otto, QB (5) Cle 1951-55
Granger, Hoyle, FB (2) Hou 1968-69
Grantham, Larry, LB (5) NYT 1963; NYJ 1964-65, 1967, 1970
Gray, Jerry, CB (4) LARm 1987-90
Gray, Ken, G (6) StL 1962, 1964-65, 1967-69
Gray, Leon, T (4) NE 1977, 1979; Hou 1980, 1982
Gray, Mel, KR (4) Det 1991-92, 1993*, 1995
Gray, Mel, WR (4) StL 1975-78
Grayson, Dave, CB-S (6) DalT 1963; KC 1964-65; Oak 1966-67, 1970
Green, Bobby Joe, P (1) ChiB 1971
Green, Cornell, CB (5) Dal 1966-68, 1972-73
Green, Darrell, CB (7) Was 1985, 1987-88, 1991-92, 1997-98
Green, Eric, TE (2) Pit 1994-95
Green, Ernie, FB (2) Cle 1967-68
Green, Gary, CB (4) KC 1982-84; LARm 1986
Green, Gaston, RB (1) Den 1992
Green, Harold, RB (1) Cin 1993
Green, Hugh, LB (2) TB 1983-84
Green, Jacob, DE (2) Sea 1987-88
Green, John, E (1) Phi 1951
Green, Roy, WR (2) StL 1984-85
Green, Tony, KR (1) Was 1979

Greene, Joe, DT (10) Pit 1970-77, 1979-80
Greene, Kevin, LB (5) LARm 1990; Pit 1995-96; Car 1997, 1999
Greene, Tony, S (1) Buf 1978
Greenfield, Tom, C (1) GB Jan. 1940
Greenwood, L.C., DE (6) Pit 1974-77, 1979-80
Gregg, Forrest, T (9) GB 1960-65, 1967-69
Gregory, Jack, DE (2) Cle 1970; NYG 1973
Grgich, Visco, G (1) SF 1951
Grier, Roosevelt, DT (3) NYG 1954*, 1957, 1961
Griese, Bob, QB (8) Mia 1968-69, 1971-72, 1974-75, 1978-79
Grim, Bob, WR (1) Min 1972
Grimes, Billy, HB (2) GB 1951-52
Grimm, Russ, G (4) Was 1984-87
Grimsley, John, LB (1) Hou 1989
Groom, Jerry, T (1) ChiC 1955
Groza, Lou, T (9) Cle 1951-56, 1958-60
Grupp, Bob, P (1) KC 1980
Guy, Ray, P (7) Oak 1974-79, 1981

Hackett, Dino, LB (1) KC 1989*
Haddix, Wayne, CB (1) TB 1991
Haden, Jack, T (1) NYG 1939
Haden, Pat, QB (1) LARm 1978
Hadl, John, QB (6) SD 1965-66, 1969-70, 1973; LARm 1974
Haji-Sheikh, Ali, K (1) NYG 1984
Haley, Charles, LB-DE (5) SF 1989, 1991-92; Dal 1995-96
Hall, Parker, HF (1) Cle Jan. 1940
Hall, Ron, DB (1) Bos 1964
Ham, Jack, LB (8) Pit 1974*, 1975-79, 1980*, 1981
Hampton, Dan, DE-DT-NT (4) ChiB 1981, 1983, 1985-86
Hampton, Rodney, RB (2) NYG 1993-94
Hanburger, Chris, LB (9) Was 1967-70, 1973-76, 1977*
Hanken, Ray, E (1) NYG 1939
Hanks, Merton, S (4) SF 1995-98
Hannah, John, G (9) NE 1977, 1979-83, 1984*, 1985-86
Hanner, Dave, DT (2) GB 1954-55
Hansen, Brian, P (1) NO 1985
Hansen, Owen, HB (1) Hollywood 1939
Hanson, Jason, K (1) Det 1998
Harbaugh, Jim, QB (1) Ind 1996
Harder, Pat, FB (2) ChiC 1951; Det 1953
Hardman, Cedrick, DE (2) SF 1972, 1976
Hardy, Jim, QB (1) ChiC 1951
Hare, Cecil, HB (2) Was Jan. 1942, Dec. 1942
Hare, Ray, QB (1) Was Dec. 1942
Harmon, Ronnie, RB (1) SD 1993
Harrah, Dennis, G (6) LARm 1979-81, 1986-88
Harris, Cliff, S (5) Dal 1975-76, 1978-80
Harris, Dick, CB (1) SD 1962
Harris, Franco, RB (9) Pit 1973-76, 1977*, 1978-81
Harris, James, QB (1) LARm 1975
Harris, Tim, LB (1) GB 1990
Harrison, Dennis, DE (1) Phi 1983
Harrison, Rodney, S (1) SD 1999
Hart, Jim, QB (4) StL 1975-78
Hart, Leon, E (1) Det 1952*
Hart, Tommy, DE (1) SF 1977
Harvey, Ken, LB (4) Was 1995-97, 1998*
Haselrig, Carlton, G (1) Pit 1993
Hasty, James, CB (1) KC 1998
Hatcher, Dale, P (1) LARm 1986
Hauss, Len, C (5) Was 1967, 1969-71, 1973
Hawkins, Rip, LB (1) Min 1964
Hawkins, Wayne, G (5) Oak 1964-68
Hayes, Bob, SE (3) Dal 1966-68
Hayes, Lester, CB (5) Oak 1981-82; LARd 1983-85
Haynes, Abner, HB (3) DalT 1962-63; KC 1965
Haynes, Mark, CB (3) NYG 1983-84, 1985*
Haynes, Mike, CB (9) NE 1977*, 1978-81, 1983; LARd 1985-87
Hazeltine, Matt, LB (2) SF 1963, 1965
Headrick, Sherrill, LB (4) DalT 1962-63, KC 1966-67
Hearst, Garrison, RB (1) SF 1999*
Hebert, Bobby, QB (1) Atl 1994
Hein, Mel, C (4) NYG 1939, Jan. 1940, Dec. 1940, Jan. 1942
Henderson, Thomas, LB (1) Dal 1979
Hendricks, Ted, LB (8) Bal 1972-74; GB 1975; Oak 1981-82; LARd 1983-84
Henke, Ed, E (1) SF 1953
Hennigan, Charley, E (5) Hou 1962-66
Henry, Wally, KR (1) Phi 1980
Hentrich, Craig, P (1) Ten 1999
Herber, Arnie, QB (1) GB Jan. 1940
Herman, Dave, G (2) NYJ 1969-70
Herrera, Efren, K (1) Dal 1978
Heyward, Craig, RB (1) Atl 1996
Hickerson, Gene, G (6) Cle 1966-71
Hicks, Dwight, S (4) SF 1982-85
Hicks, W.K., CB (1) Hou 1967
Hilgenberg, Jay, C (7) ChiB 1986-92
Hilgenberg, Joel, C (1) NO 1993
Hill, Calvin, RB (4) Dal 1970*, 1973, 1974*, 1975
Hill, David, TE (2) Det 1979-80
Hill, Drew, WR (2) Hou 1989*, 1991
Hill, Harlon, E (3) ChiB 1955-57
Hill, J.D., WR (1) Buf 1973
Hill, Jimmy, DB (3) StL 1961-63
Hill, Kent, G (5) LARm 1981, 1983-86
Hill, Mack Lee, FB (1) KC 1965
Hill, Tony, WR (3) Dal 1979-80, 1986
Hill, Winston, G-T (8) NYJ 1965, 1968-74
Hilliard, Dalton, RB (1) NO 1990
Hines, Glen Ray, T (2) Hou 1969-70
Hinkle, Clarke, FB (3) GB 1939, Jan. 1940, Dec. 1940
Hinton, Chris, G-T (7) Bal 1984; Ind 1986-90; Atl 1992
Hirsch, Elroy (Crazylegs), E (3) LARm 1952-54
Hoaglin, Fred, C (1) Cle 1970
Hoak, Dick, HB (1) Pit 1959
Hoard, Leroy, RB (1) Cle 1995
Hock, John, G (1) LARm 1957
Hoerner, Dick, FB (1) LARm 1951
Hoernschemeyer, Bob (Hunchy), HB (2) Det 1952-53
Hoffman, John, HB-E (2) ChiB 1954, 1956
Hollis, Mike, K (1) Jac 1998
Holloway, Brian, T (3) NE 1984-86
Holman, Rodney, TE (3) Cin 1989-91
Holmes, Pat, DE (2) Hou 1968-69
Holmes, Robert, RB (1) KC 1970
Holt, Pierce, DT (1) SF 1993
Holub, E.J., LB (5) DalT 1962, 1963*; KC 1965*, 1966-67
Hopkins, Wes, S (1) Phi 1986
Hopp, Harry, FB (1) Det Dec. 1942
Horan, Mike, P (1) Den 1989
Hornung, Paul, HB (2) GB 1960-61
Horton, Ethan, TE (1) LARd 1992
Hostetler, Jeff, QB (1) LARd 1995
Houston, Ken, S (12) Hou 1969-73; Was 1974-79, 1980*
Houton, Jim, LB (4) Cle 1965-66, 1970-71
Howard, Erik, DT (1) NYG 1991
Howell, Jim Lee, E (1) NYG 1939
Howley, Chuck, LB (6) Dal 1966-70, 1972
Howton, Billy, E (4) GB 1953, 1956-58
Hubbard, Marv, RB (3) Oak 1972-74
Hubbert, Brad, FB (1) SD 1968
Hudson, Bill, DT (1) SD 1962
Hudson, Dick, T (1) Buf 1966
Huff, Sam, LB (5) NYG 1959-62; Was 1965
Huffman, Dick, T (1) LARm 1951
Hughes, Bill, C (1) ChiB Jan. 1942
Hughes, George, G (2) Pit 1952, 1954
Hughes, Tyrone, KR (1) NO 1994
Hull, Kent, C (3) Buf 1989-91
Humbert, Dick, E (1) Phi Jan. 1942
Humble, Weldon, G (1) Cle 1951
Humphrey, Bobby, RB (1) Den 1991
Humphrey, Claude, DE (6) Atl 1971-75, 1978
Hunt, Bobby, DB (1) KC 1965
Hunt, Jim, DT (4) Bos 1962*, 1967-68, 1970
Hunter, Art, C (1) Cle 1960
Husmann, Ed, DT (3) Hou 1962-64
Hutson, Don, E (4) GB Jan. 1940, Dec. 1940, Jan. 1942, Dec. 1942*

Ilkin, Tunch, T (2) Pit 1989-90
Irvin, LeRoy, CB (2) LARm 1986-87

Irvin, Michael, WR (5) Dal 1992-96
Isbell, Cecil, QB (4) GB 1939, Jan. 1940, Jan. 1942, Dec. 1942*
Ivy, Frank (Pop), E (1) ChiC Dec. 1942

Jackson, Bo, RB (1) LARd 1991*
Jackson, Earnest, RB (2) SD 1985; Pit 1987
Jackson, Frank, SE (1) KC 1966
Jackson, Harold, WR (5) Phi 1970, 1973; LARm 1974, 1976, 1978
Jackson, Keith, TE (5) Phi 1989-91; Mia 1993*; GB 1997
Jackson, Monte, CB (2) LARm 1977, 1978*
Jackson, Rich, DE (3) Den 1969-71
Jackson, Rickey, LB (6) NO 1984-87, 1993-94
Jackson, Tom, LB (3) Den 1978-80
Jacobs, Harry, LB (2) Buf 1966, 1970
Jacoby, Joe, T (4) Was 1984-87
Jacunski, Harry, E (1) GB Jan. 1940
Jaeger, Jeff, K (1) LARd 1992
Jagade, Harry (Chick), FB (1) Cle 1954
James, Craig, RB (1) NE 1986
James, Dick, HB (1) Was 1962
James, John, P (3) Atl 1976-78
James, Robert, CB (3) Buf 1973-75
James, Tommy, HB (1) Cle 1954
Jamison, Al, T (2) Hou 1962-63
Janik, Tom, DB (2) Buf 1966, 1968
Jankowski, Eddie, HB (1) GB Jan. 1940
Jaquess, Pete, DB (1) Hou 1965
Jarmoluk, Mike, T (1) Phi 1952
Jauron, Dick, KR (1) Det 1975
Jaworski, Ron, QB (1) Phi 1981
Jefferson, John, WR (4) SD 1979-81; GB 1983
Jefferson, Roy, WR (3) Pit 1969-70; Was 1972
Jeffires, Haywood, WR (3) Hou 1992-94
Jenkins, Alfred, WR (2) Atl 1981-82
Jennings, Dave, P (4) NYG 1979-81, 1983
Jervey, Travis, ST (1) GB 1998
Jessie, Ron, WR (1) LARm 1977
Jeter, Bob, DB (2) GB 1968, 1970
Joe, Billy, FB (1) Buf 1966
Johnson, Bill, C (2) SF 1953-54
Johnson, Billy (White Shoes), KR (3) Hou 1976, 1978; Atl 1984
Johnson, Bob, C (1) Cin 1969
Johnson, Charley, QB (1) StL 1964
Johnson, Charlie, DT (3) Phi 1980-82
Johnson, Curley, P (1) NYJ 1966
Johnson, Ezra, DE (1) GB 1979
Johnson, Gary, DT (4) SD 1980-83
Johnson, Jimmy, CB (5) SF 1970*, 1971-73, 1975*
Johnson, Joe, DE (1) NO 1999
Johnson, John, T (1) Det Jan. 1940
Johnson, John Henry, FB-HB (4) SF 1955; Pit 1963-65
Johnson, Johnny, RB (1) Ariz 1991
Johnson, Keyshawn, WR (1) NYJ 1999
Johnson, Larry, C (1) NYG 1939
Johnson, Mike, LB (2) Cle 1990-91
Johnson, Norm, K (2) Sea 1985; Atl 1994
Johnson, Pepper, LB (2) NYG 1991; Cle 1995
Johnson, Pete, RB (1) Cin 1982
Johnson, Ron, RB (2) NYG 1971, 1973
Johnson, Vaughan, LB (4) NO 1990-93
Johnson, Walter, DT (3) Cle 1968-70
Johnston, Daryl, RB (2) Dal 1994-95
Johnston, Mark, DB (1) Hou 1962
Joiner, Charlie, WR (3) SD 1977, 1980-81
Jones, Art, HB (1) Pit Jan. 1942
Jones, Bert, QB (1) Bal 1977
Jones, Brent, TE (4) SF 1993-96
Jones, Cody, DT (1) LARm 1979
Jones, David (Deacon), DE (8) LARm 1965-71; SD 1973
Jones, Dub, HB (1) Cle 1952
Jones, Ed (Too Tall), DE (3) Dal 1982-84
Jones, Henry, S (1) Buf 1993
Jones, Homer, SE (2) NYG 1968-69
Jones, Rulon, DE (2) Den 1986-87
Jones, Sean, DE (1) Hou 1994
Jones, Stan, G (7) ChiB 1956-62
Jones, Tony, T (1) Den 1999
Jordan, Henry, DT (4) GB 1961-62, 1964, 1967
Jordan, Lee Roy, LB (5) Dal 1968-69, 1970*, 1974*, 1975
Jordan, Steve, TE (6) Min 1987-92
Josephson, Les, HB (1) LARm 1968
Joyce, Don, DE (1) Bal 1959
Joyner, Seth, LB (3) Phi 1992, 1994; Ariz 1995
Junior, E.J., LB (2) StL 1985-86
Jurgensen, Sonny, QB (5) Phi 1962*; Was 1965, 1967*, 1968*, 1970*
Justice, Ed, HB (1) Was Dec. 1942

Kaminski, Larry, C (1) Den 1968
Kapp, Joe, QB (1) Min 1970*
Karas, Emil, LB (3) SD 1962-64
Karcis, John, FB (1) NYG 1939
Karras, Alex, DT (4) Det 1961-63, 1966
Kasey, John, K (1) Car 1997
Kassulke, Karl, S (1) Min 1971
Katcavage, Jim, DE (3) NYG 1962-64
Kavanaugh, Ken, E (2) ChiB Dec. 1940, Jan. 1942
Keane, Tom, HB (1) Bal 1954
Keating, Tom, DT (2) Oak 1967-68
Kelcher, Louie, DT (3) SD 1978-79, 1981
Kell, Paul, T (1) GB Jan. 1940
Kellerman, Ernie, DB (1) Cle 1969
Kelly, Jim, QB (4) Buf 1988, 1991-92, 1993*
Kelly, Leroy, HB (6) Cle 1967-72
Kemp, Jack, QB (7) SD 1962; Buf 1963, 1964*, 1965-67, 1970
Kenn, Mike, T (5) Atl 1981-85
Kennedy, Cortez, T-DT (7) Sea 1992-97, 1999
Kenney, Bill, QB (1) KC 1984
Keys, Brady, DB (1) Pit 1967
Khayat, Bob, G-K (1) Was 1973
Kiick, Jim, RB (2) Mia 1969-70
Kilmer, Billy, QB (1) Was 1973
Kilroy, Frank (Bucko), G (3) Phi 1953-55
Kinard, Frank (Bruiser), T (5) Bkn 1939, Jan. 1940, Dec. 1940, Jan. 1942, Dec. 1942
Kinard, Terry, S (1) NYG 1989
Kindt, Don, HB (1) ChiB 1954
King, Kenny, RB (1) Oak 1981*
Kirkland, Levon, LB (2) Pit 1997-98
Klecko, Joe, DE-DT-NT (4) NYJ 1982, 1984-1986
Klein, Dick, E (1) Bos 1963
Knight, Curt, K (1) Was 1972
Kocourek, Dave, TE (4) SD 1962-65
Kolman, Ed, T (3) ChiB Dec. 1940, Jan. 1942, Dec. 1942
Koman, Bill, DE (2) StL 1963, 1965
Konz, Kenny, HB (1) Cle 1956
Kosar, Bernie, QB (1) Cle 1988
Koy, Ernie, HB (1) NYG 1968
Kragen, Greg, NT (1) Den 1990
Kramer, Jerry, G (3) GB 1963-64, 1968
Kramer, Ron, TE (1) GB 1963
Kramer, Tommy, QB (1) Min 1987
Krause, Paul, S (8) Was 1965-66; Min 1970, 1972-76
Krieg, Dave, QB (3) Sea 1985, 1989-90
Krisher, Bill, G (1) DalT 1962
Krouse, Ray, T (1) NYG 1955
Krueger, Al, E (1) Was Dec. 1942*
Krueger, Charlie, DT (2) SF 1961, 1965
Krumrie, Tim, NT (2) Cin 1988, 1989*
Krupa, Joe, DT (1) Pit 1964
Kuechenberg, Bob, G (6) Mia 1975-76, 1978-79, 1983-84
Kuharich, Joe, G (1) ChiC Jan. 1942
Kunz, George, T (8) Atl 1970, 1972-74; Bal 1975-78
Kupp, Jake, G (1) NO 1970
Kwalick, Ted, TE (3) SF 1972-74

Lachey, Jim, T (3) SD 1988; Was 1991-92
Ladd, Ernie, DT (4) SD 1963-66
Lahar, Harold, G (1) ChiB Jan. 1942
Laird, Bruce, CB (1) Bal 1973
Lake, Carnell, S (4) Pit 1995-98
Lambert, Jack, LB (9) Pit 1976-84
Lammons, Pete, TE (1) NYJ 1968

Lamonica, Daryle, QB (5) Buf 1966; Oak 1968, 1970*, 1971, 1973
Landeta, Sean, P (2) NYG 1987, 1991
Landry, Greg, QB (1) Det 1972
Landry, Tom, DB (1) NYG 1955
Lane, Dick (Night Train), DB (7) ChiC 1955-57, 1959; Det 1961-63
Lane, MacArthur, RB (1) StL 1971
Langer, Jim, C (6) Mia 1974-79
Lanier, Willie, LB (8) KC 1969-75, 1976*
Lansford, Buck, G (1) Phi 1957
Largent, Steve, WR (7) Sea 1979, 1980*, 1982, 1985-88
Larsen, Gary, DT (2) Min 1970-71
Larson, Greg, C (1) NYG 1969
Lary, Yale, S (9) Det 1954, 1957-63, 1965
Laskey, Bill, LB (1) Buf 1966
Lassiter, Isaac, DE (1) Oak 1967
Lathon, Lamar, LB (1) Car 1997
Lattner, Johnny, HB (1) Pit 1955
Lavelli, Dante, E (3) Cle 1952, 1954-55
Lavender, Joe, CB (2) Was 1980-81
Law, Ty, CB (1) NE 1999
Lawrence, Henry, T (2) LARd 1984-85
Lawrence, Jimmy, HB (1) GB Jan. 1940
Lawrence, Rolland, CB (1) Atl 1978
Laws, Joe, HB (1) GB Jan. 1940
Layne, Bobby, QB (5) Det 1952-54, 1957; Pit 1960
LeBaron, Eddie, QB (4) Was 1956, 1958-59; Dal 1963
LeBeau, Dick, DB (3) Det 1965-67
LeClair, Jim, LB (1) Cin 1977
Lee, Bill, T (1) GB Jan. 1940
Lee, Carl, CB (3) Min 1989-91
Leemans, Alphonse (Tuffy), HB (2) NYG 1939, Jan. 1942
LeMaster, Frank, LB (1) Phi 1982
Lemek, Ray, T (1) Was 1962
Leo, Charlie, G (1) Bos 1962
Letlow, Russ, G (2) GB 1939, Jan. 1940
Lett, Leon, DT (2) Dal 1995, 1999
Levens, Dorsey, RB (1) GB 1998
LeVias, Jerry, WR (1) Hou 1970*
Lewis, Albert, CB (4) KC 1988, 1989*, 1990-91
Lewis, Darryll, CB (1) Hou 1996
Lewis, David, LB (1) TB 1981
Lewis, Frank, WR (1) Buf 1982
Lewis, Jermaine, KR (1) Bal 1999
Lewis, Mo, LB (1) NYJ 1999
Lewis, Ray, LB (2) Bal 1998-99
Lewis, Woodley, HB (1) LARm 1951
Lilly, Bob, DT (11) Dal 1963, 1965-72, 1973*, 1974*
Lincoln, Keith, HB-FB (5) SD 1963-66; Buf 1968
Linhart, Toni, K (2) Bal 1977-78
Lio, Augie, G (2) Det Jan. 1942, Dec. 1942
Lipps, Louis, KR-WR (2) Pit 1985-86
Lipscomb, Gene (Big Daddy), DT (3) Bal 1959-60; Pit 1963
Lipscomb, Paul, T (4) Was 1951-54
Little, David, LB (1) Pit 1991
Little, Floyd, RB (5) Den 1969-72, 1974
Little, Larry, G (5) Mia 1970, 1972-75
Livingston, Andy, RB (1) NO 1970
Livingston, Mike, QB (1) KC 1970
Livingston, Ted, G (1) Cle Dec. 1940
Lloyd, Dave, LB (1) Phi 1970
Lloyd, Greg, LB (5) Pit 1992-96
Lockhart, Carl (Spider), DB (2) NYG 1967, 1969
Lofton, James, WR (8) GB 1979, 1981-86; Buf 1992
Logan, Jerry, S (3) Bal 1966, 1971-72
Lohmiller, Chip, K (1) Was 1992
Lomax, Neil, QB (2) StL 1985, 1988
Long, Charley, T-G (2) Bos 1963-64
Long, Howie, DE (8) LARd 1984-88, 1990, 1993-94
Looney, Don, E (1) Phi Dec. 1940
Lott, Ronnie, CB-S (10) SF 1982-85, 1987-91; LARd 1992
Love, Duval, G (1) Pit 1995
LoVetere, John, DT (1) NYG 1964
Lowe, Paul, HB (2) SD 1964, 1966
Lowery, Nick, K (3) KC 1982, 1991, 1993
Lucci, Mike, LB (1) Det 1982
Luckman, Sid, QB (3) ChiB Dec. 1940, Jan. 1942, Dec. 1942
Lujack, Johnny, QB (2) ChiB 1951-52
Lunday, Kenneth (Kayo), G (1) NYG 1939
Lundy, Lamar, DE (1) LARm 1960
Lyles, Lenny, DB (1) Bal 1967
Lynch, Dick, CB (1) NYG 1964
Lynch, Jim, LB (1) KC 1969
Lynch, John, S (1) TB 1998

Maas, Bill, NT (2) KC 1987-88
Mack, Kevin, RB (2) Cle 1986, 1988
Mack, Tom, G (11) LARm 1968-76, 1978-79
Mackey, John, TE (5) Bal 1964, 1966-69
MacKinnon, Jacque, TE (2) SD 1967, 1969
Magnani, Dante, HB (1) Cle Dec. 1942
Maguire, Paul, LB (2) SD 1963; Buf 1966
Majkowski, Don, QB (1) GB 1990*
Malone, Charley, E (1) Was Dec. 1942*
Manders, Clarence (Pug), FB (3) Bkn Jan. 1940, Dec. 1940, Jan. 1942
Manders, Dave, C (1) Dal 1967
Maniaci, Joe, FB (2) ChiB Dec. 1940, Jan. 1942
Manley, Dexter, DE (1) Was 1987
Mann, Charles, DE (4) Was 1988-90, 1992
Manning, Archie, QB (2) NO 1979-80
Manske, Edgar (Eggs), E (1) ChiB Dec. 1940
Maples, Bobby, C (1) Hou 1969
Marchetti, Gino, DE (10) Bal 1955-58, 1960-65
Marcol, Chester, K (2) GB 1973, 1975
Marconi, Joe, FB (1) ChiB 1964
Marino, Dan, QB (9) Mia 1984*, 1985, 1986*, 1987*, 1988*, 1992*, 1993, 1995*, 1996*
Marion, Fred, S (1) NE 1986
Marsalis, Jim, CB (2) KC 1970-71
Marshall, Jim, DE (2) Min 1969-70
Marshall, Leonard, DE (2) NYG 1986-87
Marshall, Wilber, LB (3) ChiB 1987-88; Was 1993
Martin, Curtis, RB (3) NE 1996-97; NYJ 1999
Martin, Eric, WR (1) NO 1989
Martin, Harvey, DE (4) Dal 1977-78, 1979*, 1980
Martin, Jim, K (1) Det 1962
Martin, Rod, LB (2) LARd 1984-85
Martin, Tony, WR (1) SD 1997
Martin, Wayne, DE (1) NO 1995
Martinkovic, John, E (3) GB 1954-56
Martinovich, Phil, G (1) ChiB Dec. 1940
Maryland, Russell, T (1) Dal 1994
Mason, Tommy, HB (3) Min 1963-65
Massey, Carlton, E (1) Cle 1956
Massey, Robert, CB (1) Ariz 1993
Masterson, Bernie, QB (1) ChiB Dec. 1940
Masterson, Bob, E (1) Was Dec. 1942
Mathews, Ray, HB (2) Pit 1953, 1956
Mathis, Bill, FB-HB (2) NYT 1962; NYJ 1964
Mathis, Terance, WR (1) Atl 1995
Matson, Ollie, HB (5) ChiC 1953, 1955-58
Matsos, Archie, LB (3) Buf 1962-63; Oak 1964
Matte, Tom, HB (2) Bal 1969-70
Matthews, Bruce, G-C (11) Hou 1989-95, 1996*, 1997; Ten 1998*, 1999*
Matthews, Clay, LB (4) Cle 1986, 1988-90
Matuszak, Marv, G-LB (3) Pit 1954, SF 1958; Buf 1963
Matuza, Al, C (1) ChiB Jan. 1942
May, Mark, G (1) Was 1989
Mayberry, Tony, C (2) TB 1998-99
Mayes, Rueben, RB (2) NO 1987*, 1988*
Maynard, Don, FL (4) NYJ 1966, 1968-69, 1970*
Mays, Jerry, DE-DT (7) DalT 1963; KC 1965-69, 1971
Maznicki, Frank, HB (1) ChiB Dec. 1942
McAfee, George, HB (1) ChiB Jan. 1942
McCaffrey, Ed, WR (1) Den 1999
McCardell, Keenan, WR (1) Jac 1997 McCarren, Larry, C (2) GB 1983-84
McChesney, Bob, E (2) Was 1939, Dec. 1942
McClairen, Jack, E (1) Pit 1958
McClinton, Curtis, FB (3) DalT 1963; KC 1967-68
McCloughan, Kent, CB (2) Oak 1967, 1968*

McCord, Darris, T-E (1) Det 1958
McCormack, Mike, T (6) NYY 1952; Cle 1957-58, 1961-63
McCrary, Michael, DE (1) Bal 1999
McCutcheon, Lawrence, RB (5) LARm 1974-78
McDaniel, Ed, LB (1) Min 1999*
McDaniel, Randall, G (10) Min 1990-99
McDaniel, Terry, CB (5) LARd 1993-95; Oak 1996-97
McDole, Ron, DE (2) Buf 1966, 1968
McDonald, Tim, S (6) Ariz 1990, 1992*, 1993; SF 1994-96
McDonald, Tommy, HB-E (6) Phi 1959-63; LARm 1966
McElhenny, Hugh, HB (6) SF 1953-54, 1957-59; Min 1962
McElroy, Vann, S (2) LARd 1984-85
McFadin, Bud, T-DT (5) LARm 1956-57; Den 1962-64
McGee, Ben, DE (2) Pit 1967, 1969
McGee, Max, E (1) GB 1962
McGinest, Willie, DE (1) NE 1997
McGlockton, Chester, DT (4) LARd 1995; Oak 1996-98
McGraw, Thurman, T (1) Det 1951
McInally, Pat, P (1) Cin 1982
McIntyre, Guy, G (5) SF 1990-94
McKeever, Marlin, TE (1) LARm 1967
McLaughlin, Leon, C (1) LARm 1955
McLean, Ray (Scooter), HB (2) ChiB Dec. 1940, Jan. 1942
McLeod, Bob, E (1) Hou 1962
McMahon, Jim, QB (1) ChiB 1986
McMichael, Steve, NT (2) ChiB 1987-88
McMillan, Erik, S (2) NYJ 1989-90
McMillan, Ernie, T (4) StL 1966, 1968, 1970-71
McMillian, Audray, CB (1) Min 1993*
McMurtry, Chuck, DT (1) Buf 1962
McNeil, Charlie, S (1) SD 1962
McNeil, Clifton, FL (1) SF 1969
McNeil, Freeman, RB (3) NYJ 1983, 1985-86
McNeil, Gerald, KR (1) Cle 1988
McPeak, Bill, E (3) Pit 1953-54, 1957
Meador, Eddie, DB (5) LARm 1961, 1965-67, 1967
Means, Natrone, RB (1) SD 1995
Mecklenburg, Karl, LB (6) Den 1986-88, 1990*, 1992, 1994
Meggett, Dave, KR (2) NYG 1990; NE 1997
Mehl, Lance, LB (1) NYJ 1986
Mehringer, Pete, G (1) LA Bulldogs 1939
Meinert, Dale, LB (3) StL 1964, 1966, 1968
Mellus, John, T (2) NYG 1939, Jan. 1942
Mercer, Mike, K (1) Buf 1968
Meredith, Don, QB (3) Dal 1967-69
Meredith, Dudley, DT (1) Buf 1966
Merriweather, Mike, LB (3) Pit 1985-87
Mertens, Jerry, HB (1) SF 1959
Metcalf, Eric, KR (3) Cle 1994-95; SD 1998
Metcalf, Terry, RB (3) StL 1975-76, 1978
Michael, Rich, T (2) Hou 1963-64
Michaels, Lou, DE-K (2) Pit 1963-64
Michaels, Walt, MG-LB (5) Cle 1956-60
Michalik, Art, G (1) SF 1954
Middleton, Terdell, RB (1) GB 1979
Mihal, Joe, T (2) ChiB Dec. 1940, Jan. 1942
Mike-Mayer, Nick, K (1) Atl 1974
Milburn, Glyn, KR (1) Den 1996
Millard, Keith, DT (2) Min 1989-90
Millen, Matt, LB (1) Oak 1989
Miller, Alan, FB (1) Oak 1962
Miller, Anthony, WR (5) SD 1990-91, 1993-94; Den 1996
Miller, Chris, QB (1) Atl 1992
Miller, Fred, DT (3) Bal 1968-69, 1970*
Miller, Junior, TE (2) Atl 1981-82
Miller, Paul, DE (2) LARm 1956-57
Milloy, Lawyer, S (1) NE 1999
Mills, John Henry, ST (1) Hou 1997
Mills, Pete, DE (1) Buf 1966
Mills, Sam, LB (5) NO 1988-89, 1992-93; Car 1997
Mingo, Gene, HB (1) Den 1963
Minnifield, Frank, CB (4) Cle 1987-90
Mishak, Bob, G (2) NYT 1962-63
Mitchell, Bobby, HB-FL (4) Cle 1961; Was 1963-65
Mitchell, Brian, KR (1) Was 1996
Mitchell, Jim, TE (2) Atl 1970, 1973
Mitchell, Leroy, DB (1) Bos 1969
Mitchell, Lydell, RB (3) Bal 1976-78
Mix, Ron, T-G (8) SD 1962-69
Modzelewski, Dick, DT (1) Cle 1965
Moegle, Dickie, HB (1) SF 1956
Mojsiejenko, Ralf, P (1) SD 1988
Monk, Art, WR (3) Was 1985-87
Montana, Joe, QB (8) SF 1982, 1984-85, 1986*, 1988, 1990*, 1991*; KC 1994*
Montgomery, Greg, P (1) Hou 1994
Montgomery, Wilbert, RB (2) Phi 1979-80
Montoya, Max, G (4) Cin 1987, 1989-90; Oak 1994
Moon, Warren, QB (9) Hou 1989-94; Min 1995-96; Sea 1998
Moore, Al, E (1) GB Jan. 1940
Moore, Bill, E (1) LA Bulldogs, 1939
Moore, Herman, WR (4) Det 1995-98
Moore, Lenny, HB (7) Bal 1957, 1959-63, 1965
Moore, Nat, WR (1) Mia 1978
Moore, Rob, WR (2) NYJ 1995; Ariz 1998
Moore, Tom, HB (1) GB 1963
Moore, Wayne, T (1) Mia 1974*
Moore, Wilbur, HB (1) Was Dec. 1942
Moore, Zeke, CB (2) Hou 1970-71
Morgan, Stanley, WR (4) NE 1980-81, 1987-88
Morin, Milt, TE (2) Cle 1969, 1972
Morrall, Earl, QB (2) Pit 1958; Bal 1969
Morris, Dennit, LB (1) Hou 1962
Morris, Eugene (Mercury), RB-KR (3) Mia 1972-73, 1974*
Morris, Joe, RB (2) NYG 1986-87
Morris, Johnny, FL (1) ChiB 1961
Morris, Jon, C (7) Bos 1965-71
Morrison, Fred (Curly), FB (1) Cle 1956
Morrow, John, C (2) Cle 1962, 1964
Mosebar, Don, C (3) Oak 1987, 1991-92
Moseley, Mark, K (2) Was 1980, 1983
Moses, Haven, WR (2) Buf 1970; Den 1974
Moss, Randy, WR (1) Min 1999
Motley, Marion, FB (1) Cle 1951
Moulds, Eric, WR (1) Buf 1999
Mudd, Howard, G (3) SF 1967-69
Mul-Key, Herb, KR (1) Was 1974
Mulleneaux, Carl, E (2) GB Jan. 1940, Dec. 1940
Munchak, Mike, G (9) Hou 1985-86, 1988-93, 1994*
Muncie, Chuck, RB (3) NO 1980; SD 1982-83
Munoz, Anthony, T (11) Cin 1982-87, 1988* 1989-90, 1991*, 1992
Murphy, Mark, S (1) Was 1984
Murray, Ed, K (2) Det 1981, 1990
Musso, George, G (3) ChiB Jan. 1940, Dec. 1940, Jan. 1942
Mutscheller, Jim, E (1) Bal 1958
Myers, Chip, WR (1) Cin 1973
Myers, Tommy, S (1) NO 1980

Nagler, Gern, E (1) ChiC 1959
Nalen, Tom, C (2) Den 1998-99
Namath, Joe, QB (5) NYJ 1966, 1968-69, 1970*, 1973*
Nance, Jim, FB (2) Bos 1967*, 1968
Nash, Joe, NT (1) Sea 1985
Naumoff, Paul, LB (1) Det 1971
Neal, Ed, C (1) GB 1951
Neely, Ralph, T (2) Dal 1968, 1970
Neighbors, Billy, G (1) Bos 1964
Nelms, Mike, KR (3) Was 1981-83
Nelsen, Bill, QB (1) Cle 1970
Nelson, Andy, S (1) Bal 1961
Nelson, Steve, LB (3) NE 1981, 1985-86
Neville, Tom, T-C (1) Bos 1967
Newberry, Tom, G (2) LARm 1989, 1990*
Newman, Ed, G (4) Mia 1982, 1983*, 1984-85
Newsome, Ozzie, TE (3) Cle 1982, 1985-86
Newton, Nate, G (6) Dal 1993-97, 1999
Nickel, Elbie, E (3) Pit 1953-54, 1957
Nickerson, Hardy, LB (4) TB 1994, 1997-99
Niemi, Laurie, T (2) Was 1952-53
Niland, John, G (6) Dal 1969-74
Nisby, John, G (3) Pit 1960, 1962; Was 1963
Nitschke, Ray, LB (1) GB 1965
Nobis, Tommy, LB (5) Atl 1967-69, 1971, 1973

Nolting, Ray, HB (2) ChiB Dec. 1940, Jan. 1942
Nomellini, Leo, DT (10) SF 1951-54, 1957-62
Noonan, Karl, FL (1) Mia 1969
Norton, Don, E (2) SD 1962, 1963*
Norton, Jerry S (5) Phi 1958-59; ChiC 1960; StL 1961-62
Norton, Jim, S (3) Hou 1963-64, 1968
Norton, Ken, LB (3) Dal 1994; SF 1996, 1998
Norwood, Scott, D-K (1) Buf 1989
Novacek, Jay, TE (5) Dal 1992-95, 1996*
Nowaskey, Bob, E (2) ChiB Dec. 1940, Jan. 1942
Nutter, Madison (Buzz), C (1) Pit 1963
Nye, Blaine, G (2) Dal 1975, 1977

Oakes, Don, T (1) Bos 1968
Oates, Bart, C (5) NYG 1991-92, 1994; SF 1995-96
O'Brien, Davey, QB (1) Phi Jan. 1940
O'Brien, Ken, QB (2) NYJ 1986, 1992
Odom, Steve, WR (1) GB 1976
Odomes, Nate, CB (2) Buf 1993-94
Odoms, Riley, TE (4) Den 1974-76, 1979
O'Donnell, Joe, T (1) Buf 1966
O'Donnell, Neil, QB (1) Pit 1993
Offerdahl, John, LB (5) Mia 1987-88, 1989*, 1990, 1991*
Ogden, Jonathan, T (2) Bal 1998-99
Okoye, Christian, RB (2) KC 1990, 1992*
Oldershaw, Doug, G (1) NYG Dec. 1940
Olsen, Merlin, DT (14) LARm 1963-70, 1971*, 1972-76
Olson, Harold, T (1) Buf 1962
Olszewski, Johnny, FB (2) ChiC 1954, 1956
O'Neal, Leslie, LB-DE (6) SD 1990-91, 1993-96
Orr, Jimmy, FL (2) Pit 1960; Bal 1966
Osborn, Dave, RB (1) Min 1971
Osmanski, Bill, FB (2) ChiB Dec. 1940, Jan. 1942
Otis, Jim, RB (1) StL 1976
Otto, Gus, LB (1) Oak 1970
Otto, Jim, C (12) Oak 1962-73
Owens, Steve, RB (1) Det 1972

Page, Alan, DT (9) Min 1969-76, 1977*
Paluck, John, DE (1) Was 1965
Panfil, Ken, T (1) ChiC 1960
Pardee, Jack, LB (1) LARm 1964
Parilli, Vito (Babe), QB (3) Bos 1964-65, 1967
Parker, Jim, T-G (8) Bal 1959-66
Parks, Dave, E (3) SF 1965-67
Parrish, Bernie, DB (2) Cle 1961, 1964
Parrish, Lemar, CB-KR (8) Cin 1971-72, 1975-78; Was 1980-81
Parry, Owen (Ox), T (1) NYG 1939
Pastorini, Dan, QB (1) Hou 1976
Patton, Jim, S (5) NYG 1959-63
Paul, Don, C (3) LARm 1952-54
Paul, Don, HB-S (4) ChiC 1954; Cle 1957-59
Paulson, Dainard, DB (2) NYJ 1965-66
Paup, Bryce, LB (4) GB 1995; Buf 1996-98
Payton, Walter, RB (9) ChiB 1977-81, 1984-87
Pear, Dave, DT (1) TB 1979
Pearson, Drew, WR (3) Dal 1975, 1977-78
Peoples, Woody, G (2) SF 1973-74
Perkins, Don, HB-FB (6) Dal 1962-64, 1967-69
Perry, Joe, FB (3) SF 1953-55
Perry, Michael Dean, DT (6) Cle 1990-92, 1994-95; Den 1997
Perry, Rod, CB (2) LARm 1979, 1981*
Peters, Floyd, DT (3) Phi 1965, 1967-68
Peters, Tony, S (1) Was 1983
Peters, Volney, T (1) Was 1956
Petitbon, Richie, S (4) ChiB 1963-64, 1967-68
Petty, John, FB (1) ChiB Dec. 1942
Philbin, Gerry, DE (2) NYJ 1969-70
Phillips, Jim, E (3) LARm 1961-63
Pickens, Carl, WR (2) Cin 1996-97
Pietrosante, Nick, FB (2) Det 1961-62
Pihos, Pete, E (6) Phi 1951-56
Pinckert, Erny, QB (2) Was 1939, Jan. 1940
Plasman, Dick, E (2) ChiB Dec. 1940, Jan. 1942
Plum, Milt, QB (2) Cle 1961-62
Plunkett, Sherman, T (2) NYJ 1965, 1967
Podoley, Jim, HB (1) Was 1958
Poillon, Dick, HB (1) Was Dec. 1942
Polsfoot, Fran, E (1) ChiC 1952
Pool, Hampton, E (2) ChiB Dec. 1940, Jan. 1942
Poole, Jim, E (3) NYG 1939, Jan. 1940, Dec. 1940
Porcher, Robert, DE (1) Det 1998
Porter, Rufus, ST (2) Sea 1989-90
Post, Dickie, HB (2) SD 1968*, 1970
Pottios, Myron, LB (3) Pit 1962, 1964-65
Powell, Art, WR (4) Oak 1964-67
Powell, Marvin, T (5) NYJ 1980-83, 1984*
Preston, Roell, KR (1) GB 1999
Prestridge, Luke, P (1) Den 1983
Price, Charles (Cotton), QB (1) Det Dec. 1940
Price, Eddie, FB (3) NYG 1952-53, 1955
Pritchard, Bosh, HB (1) Phi Dec. 1942
Promuto, Vince, G (2) Was 1964-65
Pruitt, Greg, KR-RB (5) Cle 1974-75, 1977-78; LARd 1984
Pruitt, Mike, RB (2) Cle 1980-81
Putnam, Duane, G (4) LARm 1955-56, 1958-59
Pyle, Mike, C (1) ChiB 1964

Quick, Mike, WR (5) Phi 1984-86, 1987*, 1988
Quillan, Fred, C (2) SF 1985-86
Quinlan, Volney (Skeet), HB (1) LARm 1955

Radovich, Bill, G (1) Det 1939
Randle, John, DT (6) Min 1994-99
Randle, Sonny, WR (4) StL 1961-63, 1966
Rashad, Ahmad, WR (4) Min 1979-82
Ray, Buford (Baby), T (1) GB Jan. 1940
Reaves, Ken, CB (1) Atl 1970
Rechichar, Bert, HB (3) Bal 1956-58
Redman, Rick, LB (1) SD 1968
Reed, Alvin, TE (2) Hou 1969-70
Reed, Andre, WR (7) Buf 1989-91, 1992*, 1993, 1994*, 1995
Reger, John, LB (3) Pit 1960-62
Reichow, Jerry, E (1) Min 1962
Reid, Mike, DT (2) Cin 1973, 1974*
Reinfeldt, Mike, S (1) Hou 1980
Rembert, Johnny, LB (2) NE 1989-90
Renfro, Mel, CB-S (10) Dal 1965-72, 1973*, 1974
Renfro, Ray, HB (3) Cle 1954, 1958, 1961
Retzlaff, Pete, E (5) Phi 1959, 1961, 1964-66
Reveiz, Fuad, K (1) Min 1995
Reynolds, Bob, T (3) StL 1967, 1969-70
Reynolds, Jack, LB (2) LARm 1976, 1981
Rice, Jerry, WR (11) SF 1987-88, 1989*, 1990-94, 1996, 1997*, 1999
Rice, Ken, T (1) Buf 1962
Richards, Elvin (Kink), FB-HB (2) NYG 1939, Dec. 1940
Richardson, Jess, T (1) Phi 1960
Richardson, Willie, FL (2) Bal 1968-69
Richter, Les, LB (8) LARm 1955-62
Riffle, Dick, HB (1) Pit Jan. 1942
Riggins, John, RB (1) NYJ 1976
Riggs, Gerald, RB (3) Atl 1986-88
Ringo, Jim, C (10) GB 1958-64; Phi 1965-66, 1968
Risien, Cody, T (2) Cle 1987-88
Rison, Andre, WR (5) Atl 1991-94; KC 1998
Ritcher, Jim, G (2) Buf 1992-93
Roaches, Carl, KR (1) Hou 1982
Roaf, William, T (5) NO 1995-98, 1999*
Robb, Joe, DE (1) StL 1967
Roberson, Bo, SE (1) Buf 1966
Roberts, Gene, HB (1) NYG 1951
Roberts, William, G (1) NYG 1991
Robertson, Isiah, LB (6) LARm 1972, 1974-78
Robinson, Dave, LB (3) GB 1967-68, 1970
Robinson, Eugene, S (3) Sea 1993-94; Atl 1999
Robinson, Jerry, LB (1) Phi 1982
Robinson, Johnny, S (7) KC 1964, 1965*, 1966-69, 1971
Robinson, Paul, RB (2) Cin 1969-70
Robinson, Wayne, LB (2) Phi 1955-56
Robustelli, Andy, DE (7) LARm 1954, 1956; NYG 1957-58, 1960-62
Roby, Reggie, P (3) Mia 1985, 1990; Was 1995
Rochester, Paul, DT (1) DalT 1962

Rock, Walter, T (1) SF 1966
Rogel, Fran, FB (1) Pit 1957
Rogers, George, RB (2) NO 1982-83
Rohde, Len, T (1) SF 1971
Roland, Johnny, HB (2) StL 1967, 1968*
Romanowski, Bill, LB (2) Den 1997, 1999
Ross, Dan, TE (1) Cin 1983
Ross, Kevin, CB (2) KC 1990-91
Rossovich, Tim, LB (1) Phi 1970
Rote, Kyle, HB-E (4) NYG 1954*, 1955-57
Rote, Tobin, QB (2) GB 1957; SD 1964
Rowe, Bob, DT (1) StL 1969
Rozier, Mike, RB (2) Hou 1988-89
Rucinski, Eddie, E (1) Bkn Dec. 1942
Rudnay, Jack, C (4) KC 1974-77
Russell, Andy, LB (7) Pit 1969, 1971-76
Russell, Darrell, DT (1) Oak 1999
Rutgens, Joe, DT (2) Was 1964, 1966
Rutkowski, Ed, FL (1) Buf 1966
Ryan, Frank, QB (3) Cle 1965-67
Rypien, Mark, QB (2) Was 1990, 1992

Saimes, George, S (5) Buf 1965-69
St. Clair, Bob, T (5) SF 1957, 1959-62
St. Jean, Len, G (1) Bos 1967
Saleaumua, Dan, DT (1) KC 1996
Sanders, Barry, RB (10) Det 1990-93, 1994* 1995-98, 1999*
Sanders, Charlie, TE (7) Det 1969-72, 1975-77
Sanders, Deion, CB (7) Atl 1992-94; SF 1995, Dal 1997*, 1998*, 1999
Sanders, Orban (Spec), DB (1) NY Yanks 1951
Sandusky, Mike, G (1) Pit 1961
Sanford, Leo, LB-C (2) ChiC 1957-58
Sapolu, Jesse, C-G (2) SF 1994-95
Sapp, Warren, DT (2) TB 1998-99
Sauer, George, SE (4) NYJ 1967-70
Saul, Rich, C (6) LARm 1977-82
Sayers, Gale, HB (4) ChiB 1966-68, 1970
Scarpitto, Bob, E (1) Den 1967
Schafrath, Dick, T (6) Cle 1964-69
Schlereth, Mark, G (2) Was 1992; Den 1999
Schmidt, Bob, C (3) Hou 1962-64
Schmidt, Henry, DT (1) Buf 1966
Schmidt, Joe, LB (9) Det 1955-63
Schnelker, Bob, E (2) NYG 1959-60
Schnellbacher, Otto, HB (2) NYG 1951-52
Schottenheimer, Marty, LB (1) Buf 1966
Schrader, Jim, C (3) Was 1959-60, 1962
Schroeder, Gene, E (1) ChiB 1953
Schroeder, Jay, QB (1) Was 1987
Schuh, Harry, T (3) Oak 1968, 1970-71
Schultz, Charles, T (1) GB Jan. 1940
Schwantz, Jim, ST (1) Dal 1997
Schwartz, Perry, E (4) Bkn 1939, Jan. 1940, Jan. 1942, Dec. 1942
Scibelli, Joe, G (1) LARm 1969
Scott, Clarence, CB (1) Cle 1974
Scott, Herbert, G (3) Dal 1980-82
Scott, Jake, S (5) Mia 1972*, 1973-74, 1975*, 1976
Scott, Todd, S (1) Min 1993
Scott, Tom, E (2) Phi 1958-59
Scudero, Joe (Scooter), HB (1) Was 1965
Seau, Junior, LB (8) SD 1992-99
Sellers, Ron, WR (1) Bos 1970
Selmon, Lee Roy, DE (6) TB 1980*, 1981-85
Senser, Joe, TE (1) Min 1982*
Septien, Rafael, K (1) Dal 1982
Sestak, Tom, DT (4) Buf 1963-65, 1966*
Settle, John, RB (1) Atl 1989
Sewell, Harley, G (4) Det 1958-60, 1963
Seymour, Bob, HB (1) Was Dec. 1942
Shaffer, Lelan, QB (1) NYG 1939
Shanklin, Ron, WR (1) Pit 1974*
Sharpe, Luis, T (3) StL 1988; Ariz 1989-90
Sharpe, Shannon, TE (7) Den 1993-94, 1995*, 1996-98, 1999*
Sharpe, Sterling, WR (5) GB 1990-91, 1993, 1994*, 1995*
Shaw, Billy, G (8) Buf 1963-70
Shaw, Bob, E (1) ChiC 1951
Shell, Art, T (8) Oak 1973-79, 1981
Shell, Donnie, S (5) Pit 1979-83
Shelley, Elbert, ST (4) Atl 1993-96
Sherk, Jerry, DT (4) Cle 1974-77
Sherman, Saul, QB (1) ChiB Dec. 1940*
Sherman, Will, S (2) LARm 1956, 1959
Shields, Will, G (4) KC 1996-99
Shipkey, Jerry, FB (3) Pit 1951-53
Shirk, John, E (1) ChiC Dec. 1940
Shofner, Del, SE (5) LARm 1959-60; NYG 1962-64
Shonta, Chuck, DB (1) Bos 1967
Shugart, Clyde, G (2) Was Jan. 1942, Dec. 1942*
Shuler, Mickey, TE (2) NYJ 1987, 1989
Siegal, John, E (3) ChiB Dec. 1940, Jan. 1942, Dec. 1942
Siemon, Jeff, LB (4) Min 1974, 1976-78
Sikahema, Vai, KR (2) StL 1987-88
Silas, Sam, DT (1) StL 1966
Simington, Milt, G (1) Pit Dec. 1942*
Simmons, Clyde, DE (2) Phi 1992-93
Simmons, Jack, C (1) ChiC 1957
Simms, Phil, QB (2) NYG 1986, 1994*
Simpson, O.J., RB (6) Buf 1970, 1973-77
Sims, Billy, RB (3) Det 1981-83
Sims, Keith, G (3) Mia 1994-96
Sinclair, Michael, DE (3) Sea 1997-99
Singletary, Mike, LB (10) ChiB 1984-93
Sipe, Brian, QB (1) Cle 1981
Sisemore, Jerry, T (2) Phi 1980, 1982
Sistrunk, Otis, DT (1) Oak 1975
Sivell, Jim, G (1) Bkn Jan. 1942
Skladany, Tom, P (1) Det 1982
Skoronski, Bob, T (1) GB 1967
Slade, Chris, LB (1) NE 1998
Slater, Jackie, T (7) LARm 1984, 1986-91
Slaughter, Webster, WR (2) Cle 1990; Hou 1994*
Slivinski, Steve, G (1) Was Dec. 1942
Smerlas, Fred, DT (5) Buf 1981-84, 1989
Smith, Al, LB (2) Hou 1992-93
Smith, Bill, E (1) ChiC Jan. 1940
Smith, Bob, HB (1) Det 1953
Smith, Bob, HB (1) Buf 1966
Smith, Bruce, DE (11) Buf 1988-91, 1993*, 1994*, 1995-96, 1997*, 1998-99
Smith, Bubba, DE (2) Bal 1971-72
Smith, Dennis, S (6) Den 1986-87, 1990-92, 1994
Smith, Doug, C (6) LARm 1985, 1986*, 1987-90
Smith, Emmitt, RB (7) Dal 1991-93, 1994*, 1995*, 1996, 1999
Smith, Ernie, T (2) Hollywood 1939; GB Jan. 1940
Smith, George, C (1) Was Dec. 1942
Smith, Harry, G (1) Det Dec. 1940
Smith, J.D., FB (2) SF 1960, 1963
Smith, J.D., T (1) Phi 1962*
Smith, J.T., WR-KR (2) KC 1981; Pho 1989
Smith, Jackie, TE (5) StL 1967-71
Smith, Jerry, TE (2) Was 1968, 1970
Smith, Jimmy, WR (2) Jac 1998-99
Smith, Jim Ray, G (5) Cle 1959, 1960*, 1961-63
Smith, John, K (1) NE 1981
Smith, Neil, DE (6) KC 1992-94, 1995*, 1996; Den 1998
Smith, Paul, DT (2) Den 1973-74
Smith, Robert, RB (1) Min 1999
Smith, Ron, KR (1) ChiB 1973
Smith, Stu, QB (1) Pit 1939
Snead, Norm, QB (3) Was 1964; Phi 1966; NYG 1973
Snell, Matt, FB (3) NYJ 1965*, 1967, 1970
Snow, Jack, SE (1) LARm 1968*
Snyder, Bob, QB (2) ChiB Dec. 1940, Jan. 1942
Snyder, Ken, T (2) Phi 1954-55
Soar, Hank, HB (1) NYG 1939
Sochia, Brian, DT (1) Mia 1989
Solt, Ron, G (1) Ind 1988
Soltau, Gordy, E (3) SF 1952-54
Spadaccini, Vic, QB (1) Cle 1940
Speedie, Mac, E (1) Cle 1951
Spielman, Chris, LB (4) Det 1990-92, 1995
Spinney, Art, G (2) Bal 1960-61

Springs, Shawn, CB (1) Sea 1999
Sprinkle, Ed, E (4) ChiB 1951-53, 1955
Stabler, Ken, QB (4) Oak 1974-75, 1977*, 1978
Stacy, Billy, DB (1) StL 1962
Stallings, Larry, LB (1) StL 1971
Stallworth, John, WR (4) Pit 1980, 1983-85
Standlee, Norm, FB (2) ChiB Jan. 1942; SF 1951
Stanfel, Dick, G (5) Det 1954; Was 1956-59
Stanfill, Bill, DE (5) Mia 1970, 1972, 1973*, 1974*, 1975
Stark, Rohn, P (4) Ind 1986-87, 1991, 1993
Starr, Bart, QB (4) GB 1961-63, 1967
Staubach, Roger, QB (6) Dal 1972, 1976*, 1977, 1978*, 1979-80
Stautner, Ernie, T-DE (9) Pit 1953-54, 1956-62
Steed, Joel, DT (1) Pit 1998
Stemrick, Greg, CB (1) Hou 1981
Stenerud, Jan, K (6) KC 1969-72, 1976; Min 1985
Stephens, John, RB (1) NE 1989
Stephenson, Dwight, C (5) Mia 1984-86, 1987*, 1988*
Stepnoski, Mark, C (5) Dal 1993, 1994*, 1995; Hou 1996-97
Steussie, Todd, T (2) Min 1998-99
Still, Art, DE (4) KC 1981-83, 1985
Stits, Bill, HB (1) Det 1955
Stone, Donnie, HB (1) Den 1962
Stovall, Jerry, DB (3) StL 1967-68, 1970
Strahan, Michael, DE (2) NYG 1998-99
Stralka, Clem, G (1) Was Dec. 1942
Stratton, Mike, LB (6) Buf 1964-69
Strickland, Larry, C (1) ChiB 1957
Stroud, Jack, G (3) NYG 1956, 1958, 1961
Stryzkalski, Johnny (Strike), HB (1) SF 1951
Stubblefield, Dana, DT (3) SF 1995-96, 1998
Studstill, Pat, FL-P (2) Det 1966-67
Studwell, Scott, LB (2) Min 1988-89
Sturm, Jerry, G-C (2) Den 1965, 1967
Stydahar, Joe, T (4) ChiB 1939, Jan. 1940, Dec. 1940, Jan. 1942
Sugar, Leo, DE (2) ChiC 1959; StL 1961
Suggs, Walt, T (2) Hou 1968-69
Sunde, Milt, G (1) Min 1967
Svendsen, Bud, C (1) GB Jan. 1940
Svoboda, Bill, HB (1) ChiC 1954
Swann, Eric, DT (2) Ariz 1996-97
Swann, Lynn, WR (3) Pit 1976, 1978-79
Sweeney, Walt, G (9) SD 1965-73
Swenson, Bob, LB (1) Den 1982
Swilling, Pat, LB (5) NO 1990-93; Det 1994
Swisher, Bob, HB (2) ChiB Dec. 1940, Jan. 1942
Szymanski, Dick, C (3) Bal 1956, 1963, 1965

Talamini, Bob, G (6) Hou 1963-68
Talbert, Diron, DT (1) Was 1975
Taliaferro, George, HB (3) NYY 1952; DalT 1953; Bal 1954
Taliaferro, Mike, QB (1) Bos 1970
Talley, Darryl, LB (2) Buf 1991-92
Tarkenton, Fran, QB (9) Min 1965-66, 1975*, 1976*, 1977*; NYG 1968-71
Tasker, Steve, ST (7) Buf 1988, 1991-96
Tatum, Jack, S (3) Oak 1974-75, 1976*
Tatupu, Mosi, ST (1) NE 1987
Taylor, Bruce, CB (1) SF 1972*
Taylor, Charley, HB-WR (8) Was 1965-68, 1973-76
Taylor, Hugh (Bones), E (2) Was 1953, 1955
Taylor, Jim, FB (5) GB 1961-62, 1963*, 1964-65
Taylor, John, WR (2) SF 1989, 1990*
Taylor, Lawrence, LB (10) NYG 1982-91
Taylor, Lionel, E (3) Den 1962-63, 1966*
Taylor, Otis, WR (3) KC 1967, 1972-73
Taylor, Roosevelt, S (2) ChiB 1964, 1969
Terrell, Marvin, G (1) DalT 1963
Testaverde, Vinny, QB (2) Bal 1997; NYJ 1999
Teteak, Deral, G (1) GB 1953
Theismann, Joe, QB (2) Was 1983-84
Thielemann, R.C., G (3) Atl 1982-84
Thigpen, Yancey, WR (2) Pit 1996, 1998
Thomas, Aaron, E (1) NYG 1965
Thomas, Clendon, S (1) Pit 1964
Thomas, Derrick, LB (9) KC 1990-98
Thomas, Emmitt, CB (5) KC 1969, 1972-73, 1975-76
Thomas, Eric, CB (1) Cin 1989
Thomas, Henry, DE-DT (2) Min 1992-93
Thomas, J.T., CB (1) Pit 1977
Thomas, John, G (1) SF 1967
Thomas, Mike, RB (1) Was 1977
Thomas, Pat, CB (2) LARm 1979, 1981
Thomas, Thurman, RB (5) Buf 1990-92, 1993*, 1994
Thomas, William, LB (2) Phi 1996-97
Thomason, Bobby, QB (3) Phi 1954, 1956-57
Thompson, Bennie, ST (2) NO 1992; Bal 1999
Thompson, Billy, S (3) Den 1978-79, 1982
Thompson, Reyna, S (1) NYG 1991
Thompson, Tommy, QB (1) Phi Dec. 1942
Tilley, Pat, WR (1) StL 1981*
Tingelhoff, Mick, C (6) Min 1965-70
Tinsley, Gaynell, E (1) ChiC 1939
Tinsley, Pete, G (1) GB Jan. 1940
Tippett, Andre, LB (5) NE 1985-89
Titchenal, Bob, C (1) Was Dec. 1942
Tittle, Y.A., QB (6) SF 1954-55, 1958, 1960; NYG 1962-63
Todd, Dick, HB (2) Was Dec. 1940, Dec. 1942*
Tolar, Charlie, FB (2) Hou 1962-63
Tolbert, Tony, DE (1) Dal 1997
Toneff, Bob, DT (4) SF 1956; Was 1960-62
Tonnemaker, Clayton, LB (1) GB 1954
Toon, Al, WR (3) NYJ 1987-89
Torczon, Laverne, DE (1) Buf 1962
Torgeson, LaVern, C-LB (3) Det 1955; Was 1956-57
Torrance, Jack, T (1) ChiB Dec. 1940
Toth, Zollie, FB (1) NYY 1951
Towler, Dan, FB-HB (4) LARm 1952-55
Townsend, Greg, DE (2) LARd 1991-92
Tracey, John, LB (2) Buf 1966-67
Tracy, Tom (The Bomb), FB (2) Pit 1959, 1961
Treadwell, David, K (1) Den 1990
Trippi, Charley, QB-HB (2) ChiC 1953-54
Tripson, John, E (1) Det Jan. 1942
Tripucka, Frank, QB (1) Den 1963
Trumpy, Bob, TE (4) Cin 1969, 1970*, 1971, 1974
Tubbs, Jerry, LB (1) Dal 1963
Tubbs, Winfred, LB (1) SF 1999
Tuggle, Jessie, LB (5) Atl 1993, 1995-96, 1998-99
Tuinei, Mark, T (2) Dal 1995-96
Tunnell, Emlen, S (9) NYG 1951-58; GB 1960
Turk, Matt, P (3) Was 1997-99
Turnbull, Renaldo, LB (1) NO 1994
Turner, Bake, SE (1) NYJ 1964
Turner, Cecil, KR (1) ChiB 1971
Turner, Clyde (Bulldog), C (4) ChiB Dec. 1940, Jan. 1942, 1951-52
Turner, Eric, S (2) Cle 1995; Bal 1997
Turner, Jim, K (2) NYJ 1969-70
Turner, Keena, LB (1) SF 1985
Tuten, Rick, P (1) Sea 1995
Tuttle, Orville, G (2) NYG 1939, Jan. 1940
Tyler, Wendell, RB (1) SF 1985
Tyrer, Jim, T (9) DalT 1963; KC 1964-67, 1969-72

Ulinski, Harry, C (1) Was 1956
Unitas, Johnny, QB (10) Bal 1958-65, 1967-68
Upchurch, Rick, KR (4) Den 1977, 1979-80, 1983
Upshaw, Gene, G (7) Oak 1969, 1973-78
Uram, Andy, HB (1) GB Jan. 1940

Van Brocklin, Norm, QB (9) LARm 1951-56; Phi 1959, 1960*, 1961
Van Dyke, Bruce, G (1) Pit 1974
van Eeghen, Mark, RB (1) Oak 1978
Van Note, Jeff, C (5) Atl 1975-76, 1981-83
Van Pelt, Brad, LB (5) NYG 1977-81
Van Raaphorst, Dick, K (1) 1967
Vanzo, Fred, QB (1) Det Jan. 1940
Varrichione, Frank, T (5) Pit 1956, 1958-59, 1961; LARm 1963
Verdin, Clarence, KR (2) Ind 1991, 1993
Villapiano, Phil, LB (4) Oak 1974-77
Vogel, Bob, T (5) Bal 1965-66, 1968, 1969*, 1972
Volk, Rick, DB (3) Bal 1968, 1970, 1972

Wade, Bill, QB (2) LARm 1959; ChiB 1964
Wagner, Mike, S (2) Pit 1976-77
Walden, Bobby, P (1) Pit 1970
Walker, Chuck, DT (1) StL 1967
Walker, Doak, HB (5) Det 1951-52, 1954-56
Walker, Herschel, RB (2) Dal 1988-89
Walker, Wayne, LB-K (3) Det 1964-66
Walker, Wesley, WR (2) NYJ 1979, 1983
Wallace, Steve, T (1) SF 1993
Waller, Ron, HB (1) LARm 1956
Wallner, Fred, G (1) ChiC 1956
Walls, Everson, CB (4) Dal 1982-84, 1986
Walls, Wesley, TE (3) Car 1997-99
Walsh, Bill, C (2) Pit 1951-52
Walston, Bobby, E-K (2) Phi 1961-62
Walters, Stan, T (2) Phi 1979-80
Warfield, Paul, WR (8) Cle 1965, 1969-70; Mia 1971-72, 1973*, 1974*, 1975
Warlick, Ernie, E (4) Buf 1963-66
Warner, Charley, DB (1) Buf 1966
Warner, Curt, RB (3) Sea 1984, 1987*, 1988*
Warren, Chris, RB (3) Sea 1994-96
Warren, Jim, DB (1) Mia 1967
Washington, Dave, LB (1) SF 1977
Washington, Gene, WR (2) Min 1970-71
Washington, Gene, WR (4) SF 1970-73
Washington, Joe, RB (1) Bal 1980
Washington, Russ, T (5) SD 1975-76, 1978-80
Washington, Ted, DT (2) Buf 1998-99
Washington, Vic, RB (1) SF 1972
Waterfield, Bob, QB (2) LARm 1951-52
Waters, Charlie, S (3) Dal 1977-79
Watson, Steve, WR (1) Den 1982
Watters, Ricky, RB (5) SF 1993-95; Phi 1996-97
Watts, George, T (1) Was Dec. 1942*
Waymer, Dave, CB (1) NO 1988
Weatherall, Jim, T (2) Phi 1956-57
Webb, Don, S (1) Bos 1970
Webb, Richmond, T (7) Mia 1991-97
Webster, Alex, FB (2) NYG 1959, 1962
Webster, David, S (1) DalT 1962
Webster, George, LB (3) Hou 1968*, 1969, 1970*
Webster, Mike, C (9) Pit 1979-86, 1988
Wehrli, Roger, CB (7) StL 1971-72, 1975-78, 1980
Weinmeister, Arnie, T (4) NYG 1951-54
Weisgerber, Dick, QB (1) GB Jan. 1940
Wells, Billy, HB (1) Was 1955
Wells, Warren, WR (2) Oak 1969, 1971
West, Stan, G (2) LARm 1952-53
West, Willie, S (2) Buf 1964; Mia 1967
Westmoreland, Dick, CB (1) Mia 1968
Wham, Tom, E (1) ChiC 1952
Whigham, Larry, ST (1) NE 1998
White, Arthur (Tarzan), G (1) NYG 1939
White, Charles, RB (1) LARm 1988
White, Danny, QB (1) Dal 1983
White, Dwight, DE (2) Pit 1973-74
White, Ed, G (4) Min 1976-78; SD 1980
White, Lorenzo, RB (1) Hou 1993
White, Randy, DT-NT (9) Dal 1978-86
White, Reggie, DE (13) Phi 1987-93; GB 1994, 1995*, 1996-99
White, Sammy, WR (2) Min 1977-78
Whited, Marv, QB (1) Was Dec. 1942*
Whitfield, Bob, T (1) Atl 1999
Whitsell, Dave, DB (1) NO 1968
Whittenton, Jesse, DB (2) GB 1962, 1964
Wiatrak, John, C (1) LA Bulldogs 1939
Widby, Ron, P (1) Dal 1972
Widseth, Ed, T (1) NYG 1939
Wietecha, Ray, C (4) NYG 1958-59, 1961, 1963
Wiggin, Paul, DE (2) Cle 1966, 1968
Wightkin, Bill, T (1) ChiB 1956
Wilcox, Dave, LB (7) SF 1967, 1969-70, 1971*, 1972-74
Wilder, James, RB (1) TB 1985
Wildung, Dick, T (1) GB 1952
Wilkerson, Doug, G (3) 1981-83
Wilkin, Willie, T (3) Was Dec. 1940, Jan. 1942, Dec. 1942
Willard, Ken, FB (4) SF 1966-67, 1969-70
Willey, Norm, E (2) Phi 1955-56
Williams, Aeneas, CB (5) Ariz 1995-99
Williams, Ben, DE (1) Buf 1983
Williams, Darryl, S (1) Sea 1998
Williams, Delvin, RB (2) SF 1977; Mia 1979
Williams, Erik, T (3) Dal 1994, 1997-98
Williams, Fred, T (4) ChiB 1953-54, 1959-60
Williams, John L., RB (2) Sea 1991-92
Williams, Johnny, HB (1) Was 1953
Williams, Lee, DE (2) SD 1989-90
Williams, Willie, DB (1) NYG 1970
Williamson, Carlton, S (2) SF 1985-86
Williamson, Fred, CB (3) Oak 1962-64
Willis, Bill, G (3) Cle 1951-53
Wilson, Billy, E (6) SF 1955-60
Wilson, George, E (3) ChiB Dec. 1940, Jan. 1942, Dec. 1942
Wilson, Jerrel, P (3) KC 1971-73
Wilson, Larry, S (8) StL 1963-64, 1966-71
Wilson, Nemiah, CB (1) Oak 1968
Wilson, Otis, LB (1) ChiB 1986
Wilson, Tom, HB (1) LARm 1958
Wilson, Wade, QB (1) Min 1989
Wimberly, Abner, E (1) GB 1953
Winder, Sammy, RB (2) Den 1985, 1987
Winkler, Jim, T (1) LARm 1953
Winslow, Kellen, TE (5) SD 1981-84, 1988
Winters, Frank, C (1) GB 1997
Wisniewski, Steve, G (7) LARd 1991-92, 1993*, 1994, 1995*; Oak 1996, 1998
Wistert, Al, T (1) Phi 1951
Wittum, Tom, P (2) SF 1974-75
Wolfe, Hugh, FB (1) NYG 1939
Wolfley, Ron, ST-RB (4) StL 1987-88; Ariz 1989-90
Wolford, Will, T (3) Buf 1991, 1993*; Ind 1996
Wood, Duane, DB (1) KC 1964
Wood, Willie, S (8) GB 1963, 1965-71
Woodall, Lee, LB (2) SF 1996, 1998
Woodeshick, Tom, FB (1) Phi 1969
Woodson, Abe, DB (5) SF 1960-64
Woodson, Charles, CB (1) Oak 1999
Woodson, Darren, S (5) Dal 1995-97, 1998*, 1999
Woodson, Marv, DB (1) Pit 1968
Woodson, Rod, KR-CB (7) Pit 1990-96
Woolford, Donnell, CB (1) ChiB 1994
Wooten, John, G (2) Cle 1966-67
Woudenberg, John, T (1) Pit Dec. 1942
Wozniak, John, G (1) DalT 1953
Wright, Eric, CB (2) SF 1985, 1986*
Wright, Ernie, T (3) SD 1962, 1964, 1966
Wright, Louis, CB (5) Den 1978-80, 1984, 1986
Wright, Rayfield, T (6) Dal 1972-77
Wycheck, Frank, TE (1) Ten 1999

Yary, Ron, T (7) Min 1972-78
Yepremian, Garo, K (2) Mia 1974, 1979
Young, Bill, T (1) Was Dec. 1942
Young, Bob, G (2) StL 1979-80
Young, Bryant, DL (1) SF 1997
Young, Buddy, HB (1) Bal 1955
Young, Charle, TE (3) Phi 1974-76
Young, Fredd, ST-LB (4) Sea 1985-88
Young, Roynell, CB (1) Phi 1982
Young, Steve, QB (7) SF 1993-96, 1997*, 1998-99
Youngblood, Jack, DE (7) LARm 1974-80
Youngblood, Jim, LB (1) LARm 1980
Younger, Paul (Tank), FB-HB (4) LARm 1952-54, 1956*

Zarnas, Gust, G (1) GB Jan. 1940
Zatkoff, Roger, LB (3) GB 1955-57
Zeman, Bob, DB (1) Den 1963
Zeno, Joe, G (1) Was Dec. 1942*
Zimmerman, Gary, T (7) Min 1988-90, 1993; Den 1995, 1996*, 1997*
Zimmerman, Roy, QB (1) Was Dec. 1942
Zook, John, DE (1) Atl 1974

STRATEGY: THE INSIDE GAME

CHAPTER 17

The Evolution of Strategy

Kevin Lamb

No matter how casually people toss "genius" and "coach" into the same sentence, pro football coaches are not artists creating masterpieces on their chalkboards. They're pragmatists trying to win next week's game. The Washington Redskins didn't come up with their one-back offense [See figure 13 in the Playbook chapter, which follows; all succeeding references are to figures in that chapter.] in the early 1980s to be new and different. They did it to keep from getting their brains beat in by the New York Giants' Lawrence Taylor. The Chicago Bears' widely imitated 46 Defense started out as a ploy for an undermanned team to subdue the much-admired passing game of Don Coryell's San Diego Chargers. Thirty years earlier, the 4-3 defense was popularized in an urgent reaction to the Cleveland Browns' passing success. It turned out to be the defense everyone used from the mid-1950s to the mid-1970s.

Football strategy does not hatch from doodlings on playbooks or cocktail napkins so much as it evolves out of necessities that keep changing. An offense does something successfully, other offenses copy it, a defense finds a way to stop it, other defenses copy that, some offenses adjust to the new defensive tactic, and so it goes. To make those adjustments, coaches draw from the vast, but finite, universe of things that can be done with 11 players at one time. The creative coaches—the ones remembered as innovative geniuses—are those who do the best job of applying old principles to new circumstances.

Washington's "Counter Gap," for example, was the signature running play for the Redskins' one-back offense in their Super Bowl seasons of 1982 and 1983. The ball carrier took a step before the handoff, then ran the other direction behind a pulling guard and tackle. It was pretty much the same play the Oakland Raiders called "counter trey" and ran from two-back sets in the 1960s. It was pretty much the same play Forrest Evashevski ran from the Wing T in the late 1950s at Iowa and the same Single-Wing play [See figure 2.] that was popular among NFL teams in the 1930s.

"There are new ideas that come up, but most often you would have seen them at some point in the history of football," Bill Walsh said late in his career as the San Francisco 49ers' head coach. Walsh developed what became the offense of the 1990s, but he admitted to borrowing heavily from both the Packers' Vince Lombardi and the Chargers' Sid Gillman, whose respective offenses dominated the NFL and AFL in the 1960s.

"The basic Green Bay sweep [See figure 10.] is still our basic play," Walsh said. The 49ers just made some small blocking adjustments for the different defenses they faced. "Some of the most effective plays that are utilized in the NFL are plays that originated in the 1950s. They have become very common plays. They are extremely effective for a time, and then people begin to account for them. And you go to other things and then come back with them again a few years later."

The Shotgun formation [See figure 12.] unveiled by Dallas in 1975 was not remembered for its similarity to the Double Wing of the early 1900s [See figure 3.] but as a more recently failed experiment from 1961, when San Francisco coach Howard (Red) Hickey planned to run all the 49ers' plays from the Shotgun. He traded slow-footed quarterback Y.A. Tittle and shuttled in three younger quarterbacks who could run and pass. After five games, the 49ers were 4-1, including victories by 49-0 and 35-0.

San Francisco's next opponent was the Bears. Chicago defensive coach Clark Shaughnessy had helped George Halas develop the modern T-formation [See figure 8.] during the 1930s. The Bears had ample institutional memory. "We got out some of the old playbooks we had used against the Single Wing," Halas said. Bill George moved up from his middle linebacker spot in the Bears' 4-3 defense to play middle guard, right on top of the center. With the longer snap, the center couldn't react quickly, and George kept beating him to one side or the other. Chicago won 31-0, and that was that for the Shotgun the first time around.

Even of his vaunted T-formation with men in motion, Bears founder Halas said, "We weren't doing anything that we hadn't done in the twenties." What Halas did, with considerable help from Shaughnessy and Ralph Jones, was assemble some old concepts into a new package that dominated the forties.

Walsh developed the West Coast Offense much the same way from the work of Lombardi, Gillman, Coryell, and others. It was an ongoing project for 20 years of Walsh's career, from his 1968-1975 stint as Paul Brown's assistant to his NFL retirement in 1989, and it was still evolving in the mid-1990s. Coaches tinkered with it all over the league. Some were Walsh's former assistants, others picked it up by observation. The offense's most distinctive characteristic is the quick, precisely timed pass that is thrown before the receiver breaks toward the ball. People called them "spot passes" when Washington ran timing routes for quarterback Sammy Baugh in the thirties.

As defenses became increasingly aggressive in the 1980s and 1990s, quick passes became increasingly attractive.

Most strategy changes reflect the actions and reactions of offenses and defenses, but standout players, equipment changes, and new rules can affect strategy more suddenly. The 4-3 defense, for example, didn't really catch on until the Giants' Sam Huff and the Lions' Joe Schmidt started playing middle linebacker in 1956. Lawrence Taylor redefined both his position and the 3-4 defense [See figure 37.], just as landmark tight ends Mike Ditka and Kellen Winslow stimulated use of the pro-set and one-back offenses, respectively. The facemask changed the way players blocked and tackled, and it's doubtful that anything has affected strategy more than changes in the shape of the football.

When Defense Dominated

Passing had passed the gimmick stage by the time the colleges streamlined their football in 1912. It went from 27 inches around the middle to 23, still an inch-and-a-half thicker than today's ball. The next year, when Notre Dame beat Army with Gus Dorais throwing to Knute Rockne, the pass began gaining recognition as a legitimate tactic, but still didn't work much better than a foam facemask. Offenses tried to protect the passer with run-blocking techniques. Pass plays often consisted of a deep snap to a player who quickly threw the ball up for grabs. That's what they called the pass then: "Throwing it up for grabs." Most razzle-dazzle plays were running plays, with laterals but not forward passes. It was rare for a team to throw as many as 10 times a game in the early twenties.

Yet it was an era of offensive experimentation. The scores didn't show it, but teams tried to find something—anything—to break the stranglehold that defenses had on the game. The dominant teams scored little more than half what they would score in the 1980s and 1990s, and the bad teams rarely scored at all.

Most of this experimenting went on at the college level, even after the NFL was formed in 1920. The colleges had more time. Pro players in the twenties worked day jobs and practiced a few nights a week. Pro football would not generate innovation until it could pay a living wage.

By 1920, Halas's Illinois coach, Bob Zuppke, already used the flea-flicker, where the passer first hands off and then receives a lateral before throwing downfield. He had a hook-and-ladder play where a receiver caught a pass and lateraled to a teammate trailing behind. And Zuppke was relatively conservative. He stayed with the tight T-formation—three backs and two tight ends—when other teams were starting to spread players out a bit.

Glenn (Pop) Warner began developing the Single Wing and Double Wing on Jim Thorpe's Carlisle (Pennsylvania) Indian teams around 1908. Warner's wing formations both used an unbalanced line, with two linemen on one side of the center and four on the other, and both started plays with a snap to the tailback about four yards behind the center.

The tailback was the primary runner and passer. The quarterback was a blocking back, in a gap just behind two interior linemen. The wingback was just behind and outside the strongside end, and the fullback was a few steps from the tailback toward the strong side. For the Double Wing, the fullback moved up to a weakside wingback position.

This was still power football, but the Single Wing added some deception with the tailback doing a lot of spinning and faking. There were laterals and reverses, draw plays and delayed passes, counters and traps. The Single Wing was the NFL's prevailing offense by the mid-twenties.

Another popular formation, the Notre Dame Box [See figure 6.] that Knute Rockne developed, used the balanced line of the T-formation and the snap to the tailback of the Single Wing. The Box was really a parallelogram, with players spread out more than in the Single Wing—a deeper tailback, wider wingback (called a halfback), and slightly split ends. Some T-formations already were splitting backs to the outside, running off spinning quarterbacks and sending men in motion, too.

One problem for offenses was that their players were too close together. Even when the eligible receivers spread out a bit, the linemen practically shared footprints when they lined up. They were afraid to give defenders any space between them, but in so doing they enabled defenders to play closer than cards in a sealed deck.

Offenses didn't stretch defenses at the perimeters, either. They didn't want to get too close to the sideline. If a player was tackled two yards from the sideline, the next play had to start there. Hash marks were several years away.

Perhaps the biggest problem for offenses was that shedding blocks and tackling were more natural activities than blocking. There weren't many blocking techniques other than lowering your head and driving your shoulder into the other guy. Halas later recalled the first reverse body block he saw with the kind of awe an archaeologist might feel on finding a 9-volt battery in a 4,000-year-old village.

It was 1922. Rookie guard Heartley (Hunk) Anderson was to take on Paul Robeson, the future singer, actor and political activist who had been All-America at Rutgers. Robeson was a bigger man whose response to a shoulder in the chest wouldn't be much different from that of an oak. So Anderson blocked Robeson by pivoting on his foot so his hip swung around into the bigger man's side and knocked him off balance.

The T Inside

In 1930, Halas took a three-year break from coaching to concentrate on drumming up fan interest in his game. The coach he hired was Ralph Jones, a suburban high school athletic director who had been Halas's freshman football and varsity basketball coach at Illinois. The Bears weren't the only team advancing offensive strategy in the thirties, but Halas lived to be 88, and survivors are the ones who get to tell the stories of history.

Besides, Halas clearly was a coaching innovator whose offense was one of the best of the thirties and would enable the Bears to be the most dominant team in NFL history in the early forties. He was a more significant pioneer in the areas of marketing and league management, but as a coach, he was the first to have his players practice daily, and to have his coaches study game films and communicate from the press box during games.

Halas credited Jones with conceiving the modern T-formation with men in motion, probably the most significant strategic development ever in the NFL. Clark Shaughnessy refined it in the late thirties, and other coaches have been improving it ever since. Halas himself was more than a curious spectator. The basic T-formation was in use in the nineteenth century, but Halas said Jones was the architect who drew the first diagrams of the bridge that took the T from a power package to a versatile vehicle for both passes and runs.

One of the first things Jones did was spread out his linemen. Instead of standing one foot apart in the interior gaps and two feet at the ends, they tripled those distances. The wider splits gave defensive linemen more room to shoot into the backfield, but they also gave the Bears' linemen and backs more room to maneuver. The Bears featured quick-opening run plays, where Halas said, "The idea was not to flatten the defender but to knock him out of the way."

Ever since Walter Camp introduced the T in the 1880s, the quarterback had taken a short toss from the center. With the direct snap, the quarterback had the ball sooner, he was better hidden from the defense and the center could block quicker, especially when George Trafton introduced the one-handed snap. The quarterback was able to hand or toss the ball away quicker, and the ball carrier could reach the hole before the defense could convene to stop him.

The Bears' quick-opening plays didn't use lead-blocking backs, which touched off the kind of eye-rolling controversy that the Run-and-Shoot offense would ignite 60 years later by eliminating tight ends. It helped that Chicago's Bronko Nagurski, their rookie fullback in 1930, was bigger than many linemen. Sheer power still had a role in Jones's offense. It just wasn't the only role.

"Football became a game of brains," Halas said. When the left halfback went in motion to the right side, he wound up in position to catch a lateral, receive a short pass or long pass, or block on an outside run. If the defensive halfback followed him, it left an opening for a run to the other side.

This new T-formation with a man in motion [See figure 7.] didn't exactly set the football world on its ear. It was 1934 before the Bears broke their team record of 14.0 points per game, shattering it with 22.0. In 1932, the Bears began the season with three scoreless ties and a 2-0 defeat. But they averaged 16.8 points the rest of the way, for a 6-1-6 record that tied the Portsmouth Spartans' 6-1-4 for the league championship. The accounting method back then simply ignored ties as if they had never happened. So Portsmouth and Chicago scheduled a playoff for the championship.

They played indoors at Chicago Stadium on December 18, 1932, because a blizzard had buried Wrigley Field under 19 inches of snow. Chicago Stadium's cement floor was covered with dirt from a circus, but the field was 20 yards shorter and 15 yards narrower than regulation.

The teams agreed to stretch the field to 100 yards by moving the offensive team back 20 yards whenever it crossed midfield, but the ceiling and sideboards posed tougher problems. They made special kicking rules to deal with the ceiling, and they introduced something called in-bounds lines that called for every play to start at least 10 yards from the sidelines and the hockey boards.

Chicago won 9-0 on a controversial third-and-goal play from Portsmouth's 2-yard line. Nagurski took a handoff and started toward the line, then backpedaled and passed the ball to Red Grange, who was wide open in the end zone. The Spartans howled. The rule then said no forward pass could be thrown within five yards of the line of scrimmage. They said Nagurski didn't backpedal far enough. But the touchdown counted.

"After Nagurski's pass, I figured we were on to something," Halas recalled. "Why not just let a back throw the ball from anywhere behind the line of scrimmage?"

Hutson, Baugh, and Higher Scores

The NFL had been content to follow college rules until 1932, when it established its own rules committee with Halas as chairman. The Depression left fans with less money to spend on entertainment, and the NFL's low scoring gave them less entertainment for their dollar. Ten of the league's 48 games in 1932 ended in ties. The league made three significant changes from the college rules on February 25, 1933.

"We hoped the new rules would open up the game," Halas would recall. From 1933 on, increasing offense became the most prominent of the three major reasons for changing the NFL's rules, the others being safety and fairness.

The big changes all arose from that Chicago Stadium game. The NFL owners moved the goal posts from end lines to the goal lines, making field-goal attempts 10 yards shorter. They made passing legal from anywhere behind the line of scrimmage. And they established in-bounds lines, later known as hashmarks, located 10 yards from each sideline. No longer would a team have to waste a down moving the ball away from the sideline.

The results were not immediately dramatic in the 1933 season, but the first scheduled championship game showed that the best teams could be daring and successful with their razzle-dazzle plays. The Giants scored on a flea-flicker, and the Bears scored on Zuppke's old hook-and-ladder play. The Giants used a center-eligible play, making the center an end by dropping the only player on one side of him into the backfield. The winning Bears also scored on a halfback pass to the quarterback, and with an option pass from Nagurski that, this time, was planned.

Once the owners got a taste of revising the rule book, they couldn't stop. They streamlined the football again in 1934, to today's specifications of between 21¼ and 21½ inches around the middle. They moved the hashmarks another five yards away from each sideline in 1935. Soon they encouraged passing by dropping the rule that an incomplete pass in the end zone was a touchback. They also began a work that is still in progress—rules designed to protect the passer after he threw the ball.

Running still ruled the NFL, though. It would be 45 years before passing achieved full partnership, and at least

10 before it became a reliable winning strategy. Most passers were Single-Wing tailbacks whose running and kicking abilities were valued at least as much as their passing.

Don Hutson and Sammy Baugh were the NFL's first superstars in the passing game. Hutson joined Green Bay as a receiver in 1935, and Baugh joined Washington as a Single-Wing passing tailback in 1937. Hutson's career record of 99 touchdown catches lasted 44 years, and Hutson and Baugh still hold the records for most times leading the league in catches and receiving yards (Hutson), and pass attempts, pass completions, and passing efficiency (Baugh).

With 34 catches in 1936 and 41 the next year, Hutson raised the NFL single-season record for receptions by 15. The Packers played for three of the four NFL championships of 1936-39 and won two of them.

Hutson was a special receiver the way Einstein was a special physicist. Hutson ran the first option routes, using signals to let quarterback Arnie Herber know where he was going, and he developed the technique of hooking back for the ball and dropping to his knees for a low pass that only the receiver could catch. But he also was fortunate to be playing for Earl (Curly) Lambeau.

Lambeau was the Packers' founder and coach, and their tailback through the twenties. He made Green Bay the NFL's most venturesome passing team. Lambeau appreciated the value of an end who could catch passes.

It wasn't so apparent back then. A player who came out of the game had to stay out for the rest of the quarter, so offensive ends also were defensive ends. One reason Hutson was a rare receiver was that 185-pound greyhounds didn't make very good defensive ends. Lambeau adjusted. He used his blocking back at end on defense so Hutson could play defensive back.

Pass attempts crept up to an average of 15 a game for each team by 1936, but still it apparently didn't put much fear into defenses. Their only tactical change through the thirties was to drop the center off the line, creating a 6-2-2-1, with the tailback playing a deep safety on defense. The limited substitution rule would have discouraged passing even if receivers weren't expected to play defensive end.

College teams still were setting the tactical trends, and the Southwest Conference was the place for passing. Texas Christian built an offense around passes timed to arrive at a specific spot just as a receiver got there. TCU's Baugh led the NFL in passing as a rookie in '37, but it wasn't his regular season that made other teams reconsider the pros and cons of passing. It was his performance in the championship game; Washington beat Chicago 28-21 with Baugh throwing 35 passes—more than twice the league average. He completed 17 for 335 yards and 3 touchdowns, all for at least 35 yards for the team with the league-leading rusher, Cliff Battles.

From 1937 to 1939, National Football League scoring jumped dramatically. The average team's pass attempts per game rose from 15 in 1936 to 20 in 1939. The league's completion percentage soared from .365 in 1936 to .443 in 1941. Someone broke the individual record for passing yards every year from 1939 through 1943, and Don Hutson's record for catches rose to 74 in 1942.

Move and Counter

The only team that could score with Green Bay and Washington in the late thirties was Chicago, still fiddling with that oddball T-formation. Clark Shaughnessy had replaced Amos Alonzo Stagg as the University of Chicago's coach in 1933, and he took an interest in what the Bears were doing a few miles to the north. He started helping Halas analyze other teams in scouting reports in 1935, and before long he was adding new twists to the T with a man in motion.

Shaughnessy split an end toward one side and sent a back in motion to the other side, giving the Bears two wide receivers and a tight end—the first pro-set offense more than 20 years before it became the NFL standard. They added outside passes to their quick-hitting run plays and developed more sophisticated traps and counters to their game plan.

When Sid Luckman joined the Bears in 1939, he didn't pass nearly as often as Baugh, but the Bears averaged 12.5 yards whenever he did. Still the only team using the T, they scored 27.1 points a game, breaking their own record by five points.

Shaughnessy took the T to Stanford University in 1940 and produced an undefeated season and a Rose Bowl victory. The Bears struggled a little without him. On November 17, the Redskins beat them 7-3 with a 5-3-2-1 defense, dropping another lineman off the line to stop the quick passes and misdirection runs.

But Chicago scored 78 points in its next two games to earn a rematch with Washington in the championship game. Shaughnessy took a few days off from Rose Bowl preparation to help the Bears fine-tune their offense. For a psychological edge, Halas posted newspaper clippings in the locker room with derogatory quotes from the Redskins. For a physical edge, he had the Bears wear low-cut shoes, better suited for speed than the high-tops everyone else wore.

Less than a minute into that championship game on December 8, 1940, fullback Bill Osmanski ran 68 yards for a touchdown, and the Bears never looked back. They won 73-0.

The Bears won three of four championships from 1940-43, with a four-year record of 37-5-1 that was the best in NFL history. Their per-game scoring averages of 36.0 in 1941 and 34.2 in 1942 trail only the 1950 Los Angeles Rams and the 1961 Houston Oilers. And the Bears piled up their numbers in a league where 16.2 was the average.

When players and coaches returned from World War II in 1946, Luckman later said, "The other teams had started figuring out how to stop our T-formation offense." So Halas had him changing plays at the line of scrimmage—calling audibles. Then as now, the idea was to abandon a play if the defense was ready for it. Luckman said he called audibles to run away from a shifted defense or to pass away from double coverage. The Bears called doubles often enough so they became quite adept at last-minute changes in plays.

"We used audibles twenty or twenty-five percent of the time after the war," Luckman said. "I'd look for some sort of tipoff, and if I saw what I was looking for, I'd shout

'Red,' which would mean danger to the whole team. You couldn't audible every time you called 'Red.' The defense would figure it out. So sometimes in the huddle I'd say 'Ignore red,' and that meant I was going to say 'Red' at the line but it wouldn't mean anything."

There hadn't been any need for audibles when defenses ruled the NFL. For most of the league's first 25 seasons, a defense would line up the same way down after down and dare the offense to get past them. That worked just fine until the passing game gave offenses some versatility. Then defenses had to start guessing the next play and moving their defenders to stop whatever they expected.

The 1938-39 scoring explosion was the first of three big scoring leaps in 10 years. A second came in 1943, when the wartime free-substitution rule enabled teams to throw passes to well-rested specialists. Then scoring surged again in 1947-48. The 1947 season was the first when more than 40 percent of NFL plays were passes.

It was time for coaches to take their defenses back to the chalkboard. Philadelphia had the best results with a new defense that helped it win the Eastern Division in 1947 and the NFL championships of 1948-49. To stop the new passing onslaught, Eagles coach Earle (Greasy) Neale used four defensive backs. He replaced the middle linebacker with a second safety and turned the defensive halfbacks into today's cornerbacks.

The 5-3-2-1 became a 5-2-4, which eventually became the modern 3-4 defense. The ends in Philadelphia's defense later became the 3-4's outside linebackers, who could either rush the passer or drop into coverage. The bigger difference was on the interior line. The Eagles put their defensive linemen over the center and in the guard-tackle gaps, with the linebackers outside of them.

After their first championship, the Eagles played the annual College All-Star game and won 38-0. The All-Stars' coach was Oklahoma's Bud Wilkinson, who took Neale's defense back to the Big Eight and tinkered with it. Eventually, Wilkinson's 5-2 had the ends standing up like linebackers. [See figure 32.] He moved the defensive tackles outside, opposite the offensive tackles and brought the linebackers inside, across from the offensive guards.

Wilkinson's defense was appropriated by the NFL in the mid-1970s and called the 3-4. The first NFL coach to use it on every down was New England's Chuck Fairbanks, Wilkinson's successor at Oklahoma. Meanwhile, coaches called Neale's version of the 5-2 the Eagle Defense [See figure 33.] and made it the prevailing NFL defense into the mid-1950s. Thirty years later, the alignment resurfaced as the 46 Defense that helped Chicago win Super Bowl XX.

Systems and Signals

Halas credited Ralph Jones with making the first game plans. Jones and his assistants made a list of about 12 running plays and 12 pass plays on Monday, gave the list to the players on Tuesday, and concentrated on those plays all week in practice.

Jones also developed the first rudimentary "system of terminology." The foundation of Jones's system was his use of numbers for the backs and for the running gaps on the line of scrimmage [See figure 1.]. The "0" gap was between the center and left guard, "1" between the center and right guard, and so on, with "9" being wide around the right side. So "24, 43" meant the left halfback (2) was to run outside the left tackle (4) with the right halfback (4) in motion, on a snap count of three.

When Luckman and other quarterbacks called audibles in the forties, it wasn't the bold flash of independence that it became in the 1980s and 1990s. In fact, it was an early way for coaches to program their quarterbacks: "When you see that, you have to do this." Otherwise, the quarterback called the play himself.

The first coach to call all his team's offensive plays was Paul Brown with the Cleveland Browns.

"Paul Brown brought organization into pro football," Sid Gillman said. "He brought a practice routine. I always felt before Paul Brown, coaches just rolled the ball out onto the field.

"He broke down practice into individual areas. Before him, everything was eleven-on-eleven. Paul was an organizational genius. Everybody knew, when they hit the field, what they were going to do. He had position coaches. I don't know that anyone had position coaches before Paul Brown."

Nobody had year-round coaches, certainly. "We didn't sell automobiles in the offseason," was how Brown put it. "We did what we called the statistical study. We rated every player on every play. We took every play we had and analyzed it as to how well it worked. We did it from motion pictures."

Movies had been in football from as early as 1932, when Halas had a photographer shooting Bears games from the Wrigley Field roof with a hand-held 16-millimeter camera. But Brown was the first coach to use film for systematically grading players. And Gillman eventually bred the modern computerized breakdowns that became a basic element in devising strategy. Gillman studied film to learn tendencies—an opponent's preferred plays on third-and-long or second-and-short—and planned accordingly.

Gillman had grown up in a family that owned theaters. He was as comfortable with celluloid as a baker with dough. He hired the NFL's first full-time team photographer in 1956, his second year as the Rams' coach. He copied, spliced, and edited film into the first game-preparation reels. Every strongside sweep of the season, for example, went on one reel. Other reels did the same for the Rams' defense, and for each opponent's offense and defense.

When Halas used film in the thirties and forties, it was mainly for scouting individuals. He studied an opposing lineman's stance to see if it signaled whether the upcoming play was a pass or a run. He'd see if a back took a different stance when he was going to get the ball or search for clues by looking at the way opposing players held their hands and where they looked and where they moved their feet.

Teams still look for individual tendencies as well as strategic tendencies, and sometimes they hit paydirt. When the 1979 Houston Oilers were getting ready to play San Diego in the playoffs, they noticed something odd on the film of San Diego's previous game, against Denver.

"Every time they ran the ball, Denver's linebackers

raised their hands up in the air before the play," said Wade Phillips, Houston's defensive coordinator at the time. "We knew they had something." A Houston coach talked to a Denver player and found out San Diego quarterback Dan Fouts was standing with his feet squared before runs but with one foot behind the other for passes. Houston upset San Diego 17-14 with safety Vernon Perry intercepting 4 passes.

In the forties, Halas said, NFL teams began exchanging films on the sly. If Chicago was playing Philadelphia and Washington was playing Detroit, the Bears would trade their earlier game against Detroit to Washington for Washington's earlier game against Philadelphia. Eventually, the league office stopped discouraging the practice and standardized it. Each team was required to provide its next opponent with its previous three games, and most teams used the underground market to land even more games. Much later, in the mid-1980s, the league converted all its surveillance from film to videotape.

The NFL also wound up standardizing the phone lines from coaches in the press box to coaches on the sideline. The first coach to watch a game from above field level might have been Chicago assistant Luke Johnsos, who went into the Wrigley Field stands to watch a Brooklyn Dodgers game in 1937. Johnsos found he could see plays develop better than the sideline coaches, so he used messengers that day to shuttle his intelligence down to the bench.

Brown was widely credited with instituting press-box coaches and inventing the playbook, but what he really did was modernize them. He established the process by which strategy is developed even today. "There isn't any question that he was absolutely the most capable man in the league administratively," said Walsh, his former assistant.

Under Brown, coaches became teachers and players became students. Before him, it was assumed the players learned all the fundamentals they needed in college. Halas had shown film to his quarterbacks, but Brown showed it to everyone. His scouting reports were detailed. His playbooks were dynamic textbooks in which players were expected to take notes.

Brown was the first coach to build an extensive college scouting network. He was the first to use intelligence and psychological tests, the first to seriously scout black players, the first to time players in the 40-yard dash. "I figured that was about what you had to run to cover a kickoff or a punt," he said, and 40-yard times became the most recognizable standard for a player's speed.

But more than anything else, Brown was known—and criticized—for calling all the offensive plays. "Nobody says anything about coaches making the defensive calls," Brown said.

In order to call plays, Brown had to decide how to transmit them to the quarterback. Hand signals could be stolen. Wide receivers needed continuity with the passer. Brown decided to alternate guards, he said, "because they weren't involved in touching the football or in the quarterback's cadence, the more intricate aspects." When coaches' play calling caught on throughout the league, though, signals became the preferred transmitters. Guards had grown too big for the 50-yard sprints.

Brown tried putting a radio transmitter in the quarterback's helmet long before the NFL adopted it in the 1990s. In 1956, Brown got the league to approve a wireless earphone for George Ratterman, the Browns' quarterback after Otto Graham retired. The experiment lasted less than a year. "People had fun with it, if you know what I mean," Brown said. An opposing coach with a citizen's band radio could easily learn the Browns' next play.

The Browns had a more lasting impact on helmets in 1955, when Graham popularized the single-bar facemask. After the last holdout, quarterback Bobby Layne, retired in 1962, facemasks were on everyone's helmet.

Cage-like facemasks were used as early as the thirties, but they were impractical for backs and receivers. When plastic helmets became standard in 1949, plastic bars and masks began to appear. Facemasks, plastic helmets, and free substitution had the unintended consequences of making the game more violent. With facemasks, players kept their heads up when blocking and tackling. Wearing plastic helmets, tacklers launched themselves as head-first missiles at ball carriers until the most dangerous "spearing" techniques were outlawed in the 1970s. With free substitution, players lost the best incentive for avoiding dirty play because they didn't have to worry about retaliation.

Postwar Explosions

In much the same way that Brown was Halas's descendant administratively, he also built on Halas's strategic foundation from the thirties. "We concentrated on speed," Brown said. "Even in the offensive linemen."

Brown developed the draw play [See figure 29.] for 238-pound fullback Marion Motley, "so any time you rushed the passer, you were in danger of getting hurt," he said. Motley averaged an astounding 8.2 yards per carry in the AAFC in 1946, and 5.7 for his AAFC-NFL career. (The NFL didn't absorb AAFC records, so the Browns' later fullback, Jim Brown, holds the league record of 5.2 yards per carry.)

"Paul ran trapping plays [See figure 30.] and a quick-toss play to [Jim] Brown and [Bobby] Mitchell," Walsh said, "and that toss-trap series was unique to the game, really. It had been seen prior to that, but what he did—what everyone successful does—was utilize his personnel."

With the Browns leading the way, AAFC rushing skyrocketed from 3.4 yards a carry in 1946 to 4.6 two years later. NFL teams noticed, too. From 1946-48, their averages leaped from 126 to 151 yards per game and 3.2 to 4.0 yards per carry, both figures setting league records.

But Brown left an even more distinctive signature on the passing game. He invented the pass pocket. Before Brown, linemen tried to push pass blockers away much as they did on running plays. If a defensive lineman sidestepped a block on a running play, the ball carrier would go past him. But on passes, a defensive lineman wanted to step around his blocker, so he could shoot through a gap and head for the passer.

Brown taught his pass blockers to shield defenders out of the way instead of trying to move them. The best way to do that was for the blockers to drop back into a semicircle and stay between the pass rushers and the quarterback. AAFC teams, again following the Browns' lead, had better completion percentages and fewer pass attempts than the NFL in all four AAFC seasons—just the opposite of what the AFL did in the 1960s.

The AAFC folded after the 1949 season, with the Browns, San Francisco 49ers, and a moribund Baltimore franchise moving to the NFL. The 1950 season opened with a special Saturday night game between the Browns and Philadelphia, the defending NFL champion, the most eagerly anticipated regular-season game in league history to that point. Cleveland won 35-10 by mixing passes to the outside with draw plays up the middle.

Sure, they could win with fancy passing stuff, Philadelphia coach Neale said, but could they slug it out with the Eagles? Brown gave a resounding answer in the rematch later that season, a 13-7 Cleveland victory in which the Browns were the last NFL team to go a whole game without officially throwing a pass (a single attempt disappeared because of a penalty.) They wound up playing in all six NFL championship games from 1950-55, and winning three of them.

The brief wartime era of free substitution ended in 1946, but it was back again three years later, and back to stay. Now players could specialize on offense or defense, and the first to do so were passers and receivers. No longer did they have to wear themselves out playing defensive back, too.

Clark Shaughnessy returned to the NFL in 1948 as the Los Angeles Rams' coach. He reinstated his occasional formation from the thirties, with two backs, two wide receivers, and one tight end—the modern pro set. Shaughnessy's offense still featured backs in motion and receivers with speed, stretching the defense from sideline to sideline.

He lasted just two seasons, but the Rams won the Western Conference in 1949 and in 1950 under Joe Stydahar. Tom Fears caught 77 and then 84 passes for the Rams, a record that lasted 10 years. Sometimes the Rams split a back wide to one side and sent the tight end in motion to the other side, the first regular alignment with four wide receivers [See figure 14.]. When they sent the single back wide on occasion, they had five wide receivers and no backs [See figure 15.].

The 1950 team beat Baltimore 70-27 and Detroit 65-24 on successive weekends, still two of the four highest scoring games by one team. The Rams' 12-game average of 38.8 points per game is the NFL's best ever, and their per-game passing yardage of 309.1 ranks second to Miami in 1984, the year Dan Marino set yardage and touchdown records.

The 1951 Rams, also coached by Stydahar, set a per-game record with 458.8 yards of total offense. To give defenses a change of pace from their brisk passing game, Stydahar liked to use three fullbacks at the same time in the original Bull Elephant backfield. The Rams used two quarterbacks almost equally from 1950-52. Bob Waterfield and Norm Van Brocklin alternated. Each passed for more than 1,500 yards in 1951, even though Waterfield didn't play in the season opener because of an injury. Van Brocklin passed for 554 yards in that game, and the team gained 735. Both figures are NFL records, although the 54-14 romp over the New York Yanks that night was one of five games in which the Rams exceeded 40 points in 1951.

The Umbrella Opens

The 1950 Browns entered an NFL where defenses used either the 5-2-4 Eagle or the older 5-3-3. With 66 points in their first two games, Cleveland demonstrated that both defenses were vulnerable to sideline passes downfield and flare-outs to the backs. New York Giants coach Steve Owen devised something different when his team faced the Browns in the third game of the 1950 season.

Owen used a fourth defensive back to defend against longer passes and spread out his front seven across the scrimmage line instead of stacking linebackers behind linemen. His middle linebacker across from the center could rush or drop back, unlike a middle guard on the center's nose. His ends were outside linebackers, stationed on the line but standing up so they could drop back into pass coverage.

Owen called it his Umbrella Defense [See figuure 34.] because the secondary opened up into a dome shape when the outside linebackers retreated. It came to be called simply the 4-3, and it became the basis of virtually all NFL defenses from the mid-1950s to the mid-1970s. On October 1, 1950, New York beat Cleveland 6-0, the first time a Paul Brown team had been shut out.

But the new defense took a while to catch on. Some teams went to the 4-3 by dropping their middle guards in the 5-2 back off the line. But Detroit won the 1952 and '53 championships with 350-pound middle guard Les Bingaman anchoring a 5-2 defense, and Cleveland won the next two championships with the 5-2.

The 4-3 defense, built for pass coverage with linebackers and defensive backs strung across the field and four full-time pass-rushing linemen, came of age in 1956. The Giants drafted Sam Huff to play middle linebacker and made the 4-3 their base alignment. Bingaman retired in Detroit, and the Lions eventually moved Joe Schmidt from left linebacker to middle linebacker in their new 4-3.

Daylight, Gaps, and Nickels

When Jim Lee Howell became Giants head coach in 1954, he hired two new coordinators: Vince Lombardi from Earl (Red) Blaik's Army staff to run the offense and defensive back Tom Landry to run the defense.

Lombardi's teams would become known for power football, but his innovations were in following the path of least resistance. He introduced a system that stopped asking blockers and pass receivers to defeat defenders positioned smack in the way of the offense's play.

His passing offense was one of the first to give receivers optional reads. If a defensive back was shading a receiver to the inside, for example, the quarterback and receiver would read that coverage, and the receiver would automatically change his slant over the middle to a sideline route.

His blocking schemes were the most significant way Lombardi changed offensive strategy. When Lombardi entered the NFL in 1954, everyone blocked man-to-man. For every play, each offensive lineman was assigned a defender to block. But multiple defenses—shifting among the Eagle, 4-3, and 5-3 defenses—meant blockers had to learn several assignments for each play. Besides, letting defensive alignments determine blocking assignments was, as Lombardi put it, "a defensive approach to offensive football." He created something he called "rule blocking." Offensive linemen were responsible for sealing off areas, regardless of which defender was there.

Option blocking came at the point of attack, where Lombardi had a blocker move the defender whichever way he was going. The ball carrier would read the block, cut the other way, and run to daylight.

Most NFL teams emphasized power running up the middle—one reason the 4-3 defense was slow in displacing defenses that had middle guards. So Lombardi widened the splits between his offensive linemen. Then he pulled his guards to lead running plays to the outside, a play still widely called the Lombardi Sweep, although he freely admitted he was using an old Single-Wing concept.

While Lombardi was creating an offense based on running to daylight, Landry was basing the Giants' defense on recognition and reaction. Instead of attacking the blockers and sorting the ball carrier out of the crowd, Landry had his defenders try to recognize the play as quickly as possible, avoid their blockers, and swarm to the ball. "A recognition defense," he called it. The goal was for the defense to flow to daylight and blot it out.

Landry's defense in New York made middle linebacker Sam Huff the first defensive glamour player. The middle linebacker was in a desirable position anyway, midway between the flanks of the offense and able to follow the play without a blocker breathing on his facemask. Eventually, Landry obliged him even more. He slid the defensive tackles inside to the center-guard gaps and assigned them to keep the blockers from reaching Huff, whose job was to fill any holes the runner might find.

That was the first true gap defense with a four-man line. Instead of neutralizing blockers, the linemen and linebackers were responsible for plugging gaps. But, while Landry's defensive linemen delayed their first steps to read and react to where the play was going, the most notorious gap defenses featured quick, aggressive lines that disrupted the run by charging between the blockers every time as if they were rushing the passer. That was how Pittsburgh in the 1970s and Chicago in the 1980s played the most feared defense of their times.

Landry left New York a year after Lombardi to coach the expansion Dallas Cowboys, where he turned his creativity to offense. The result was multiple formations, with lots of shifting before the snap, so defenses had little time to anticipate the play from the way the offense lined up. Landry had men still in motion when the ball was snapped and even had his offensive linemen stand up momentarily from their stances to block the defenders' view of the shifting.

"I was really attacking my own defense to a certain extent," Landry explained. "The defense we built in New York in the late 1950s was a recognition defense almost 100 percent of the time. So if we were going to attack it, we were going to have to find out a way to slow down the recognition."

The emphasis on recognition was a natural outgrowth of film study. Like Landry's defense, offenses also learned to anticipate what the other team had up its sleeve by seeing how the defense lined up and moved at the snap. Quarterbacks read a defense's alignment to see which receiver might be open, and defenses disguised their coverages to make the reading more difficult.

This was a gradual process. The use of five defensive backs, for example, goes back as far as forward passes on third-and-long, and it started becoming popular against the Rams of the early 1950s. By 1960, although the 4-3 was the prevailing base defense, teams often used five or six defensive alignments depending on the opponent and the situation, especially on short-yardage or obvious passing downs.

George Allen did not invent either disguised coverages or the Nickel defense (with five defensive backs). He just took them "a step further," said Dave Whitsell, a cornerback for the Bears when Allen became defensive coordinator in 1962. "George probably refined the Nickel defense [See figure 53.] more than anyone. He would use it on second down, sometimes first down. He would give the quarterback a hell of a lot more looks than he was used to."

The Nickel substituted a defensive back for the weakside linebacker. With five defensive backs, a defense could double cover both outside receivers and still leave the weakside safety free in the middle. Or it could double cover the best two receivers, whoever they were. "If you took those two out, you could get the matchups you wanted, and not take what you were forced to do by the offense," said Jack Pardee, who played linebacker seven years for Allen.

New Wrinkles with the Pass

Tight ends became fairly common in the late 1950s, but they hadn't been part of the base offensive formations except for Clark Shaughnessy's dablings with Chicago in the late thirties and Los Angeles in the late forties. Ends were just ends, usually lined up a few steps from the tackles.

When Lombardi joined Green Bay in 1959, Ron Kramer became one of the first true tight ends who lined up next to a tackle and was expected to block and catch passes equally well [See figure 27.]. Then in 1961, Chicago drafted Mike Ditka, a 6-3, 230-pounder who became the prototype tight end with 56 catches as a rookie for a flanker-like average of 19.2 yards.

The AFL is remembered for wide-open games featuring long bombs with only occasional runs, sort of a full-contact version of backyard touch football. That stretches the truth a little, but doesn't pop its seams. AFL teams did pass more than they ran in each of the league's 10 seasons, and they outscored the NFL in 9 of them. Statistics say the NFL passed more efficiently in those years, but the AFL was a big-play league.

Like the AAFC, the AFL made a substantial contribution to pass-blocking techniques. While NFL linemen still kept their fists to their chests and their elbows out, wing-like, AFL blockers started using their hands to push the pass rushers away. To pass the ball farther downfield, they had to block better upfield.

The new leagues that periodically challenged the NFL nurtured innovation, partly because they were willing to hire coaches like Sid Gillman, who challenged conventional thinking. Two of Gillman's early assistants were Al Davis and Chuck Noll, and he conferred regularly with Don Coryell, the creative San Diego State coach at the time.

Gillman pioneered stretching the defense vertically, which later characterized the winning Raider teams of Davis and his successors. He also cultivated the shorter game of passes to backs and timed passes to wide receivers, which characterized the West Coast Offense that Bill Walsh developed. And he added a wrinkle to multiple formations by shifting his tight end from side to side, changing the strongside of the offense.

Gillman kept a diagram of the football field in his office, and the basis of his offense was: use the whole thing. "We're going to spread you out horizontally and stretch that perimeter, and we're going to stretch the perimeter vertically by establishing the deep pass," he said. If the defense had to respect the deep pass, the shorter passes would be there all day.

"They say if you run well, you can throw well, but I think it's the reverse," Gillman said. "If you can throw well, you're going to be able to run. The pass creates a degree of looseness that enables you to run."

Seven the Hard Way

Defensively, it followed that Gillman's philosophy was to shrink the field—keep the other guys from getting outside on the run and crowd their receivers on the pass. Gillman coached the bump-and-run coverage that the Raiders popularized, with cornerbacks standing up on the line where they could hit the receiver and run with him.

When other AFL coaches applied the bumping principle to their defenses, they had the double zone that Kansas City used so effectively. Each cornerback beat on his wide receiver until the receiver slipped past, at which point a safety was waiting to pick him up.

The AFL also stacked linebackers directly behind defensive linemen, [See figure 45.] a practice that had left defenses of the forties vulnerable to attacks on the flanks. But with AFL defensive backs and linemen more spread out, stacking the linebackers shielded them even more securely from blockers than Landry had done for Sam Huff.

While Hank Stram's 1969 Chiefs were preparing for the Super Bowl against Minnesota, he made headlines by predicting that offenses of the 1970s would use more multiple formations, more of the fairly new I-formation [See figure 11.], more men in motion, and more moving pass pockets, with the quarterback rolling one way or another behind pulling linemen.

The Chiefs were already doing those things, so when they won the Super Bowl, the media anointed them the Offense of the 1970s. But what beat Minnesota in Super Bowl IV was really the Defense of the 1970s: odd fronts, big linemen, quick linebackers, and zone pass coverage.

Odd fronts were a common changeup NFL defense in the 1960s called the Frisco Defense. Instead of using a symmetrical line, the Frisco moved the weakside defensive tackle over the center in an overshift or "over." [See figure 38.] In the late 1960s and early 1970s, the overshift became a transitional missing link in the evolution from the 4-3 to the 3-4 defenses. Twenty years later, when defenses changed their focus from the run to the pass, the undershift (away from the strongside) became a transitional defense as the NFL evolved back from the 3-4 to the 4-3. [See figure 39.]

Halfway through the 1972 exhibition season, the Miami Dolphins had only two defensive ends still healthy. They had a big, young linebacker who had played some defensive end at Cleveland the year before, so defensive coordinator Bill Arnsparger moved the kid to the line that week. But when Bob Matheson played defensive end, he stood up like a linebacker.

Lining up outside the weakside offensive tackle, Matheson had 2 sacks in that game. The Dolphins used him in his hybrid end-backer position throughout that undefeated season. They called it the 53 Defense, after Matheson's number, but it was really the first regular use of a 3-4 defense.

"We used it primarily against the pass, to give us a dimension of disguise," Matheson said. At first, he stayed on the weakside and either joined a four-man rush or dropped into eight-man coverage. Then he started moving around, to the strongside or over the middle. Later on, the Dolphins tried keeping Matheson back in coverage but rushing a different linebacker.

The 3-4 became an every-down defense in 1974 for Chuck Fairbanks at New England and for Gillman's former defensive coordinator O.A. (Bum) Phillips at Houston. In the next 15 years, every team except Dallas, Chicago, and Washington used the 3-4 as a base defense for at least a while. One reason: linebackers were more plentiful than linemen. A 225-pound defensive end in college was well-suited to play outside linebacker in a 3-4.

Another reason for the 3-4's popularity was its flexibility. It could use eight in coverage, send the normal four-man rush without identifying the four rush men, or blitz with five or six pass rushers. As offenses kept shifting formations and spreading players from sideline to sideline in the 1980s, the 3-4 had an extra man standing up who could move with the offense.

The 3-4 spelled the end for small centers quick enough to cut off linebackers. Now they had to be big enough to handle the nose tackles across from them. In Super Bowl IV, Kansas City obliterated Minnesota's 235-pound all-pro center Mick Tingelhoff by putting him head-to-head with its defensive tackles, 275-pound Buck Buchanan or 260-pound Curley Culp. The Oilers traded for Culp in 1974 specifically to become their first nose tackle, and his strength and quickness made him the prototype.

Nearly all 3-4 defenses played the old two-gap style of defense, where the linemen and inside linebackers were supposed to stand up the blockers across from them so they could plug the gaps to either side, essentially blocking the blockers so outside linebackers were free to make plays. While the 4-3 made stars of its linemen and middle linebackers, the 3-4 shone the spotlight on outside linebackers.

But the teams that stayed with the 4-3 tended to play one-gap defenses, with defenders responsible for spaces between the blockers, and linemen getting the glory. Nobody did it better than Pittsburgh. The Steelers, with L.C. Greenwood outside and Joe Greene inside, were winning Super Bowls. In 1976, Pittsburgh had a nine-game winning streak that looked like something out of the twenties: five shutouts and 28 points allowed.

Let's Change the Rules

By the early 1970s, zone coverages [See figure 50.] had pretty much choked off the long passing game. NFL scoring reached an 11-year low in 1968, and a 24-year low in 1970. Stram's moving pocket was a reaction to the damage a defense could cause a stationary quarterback. So were shorter, quicker passes. There wasn't much point having the quarterback drop back seven steps to throw if hardly anyone could get open far downfield.

The NFL had fewer passes in 1971 than at any time since 1959, and this was only two years after absorbing the "pass-happy" AFL. Miami won the AFC while throwing fewer than 21 passes a game.

So the owners took matters into their own hands in 1972 and changed the rules. By trying to open up the passing game, they created some unintended consequences. Their main change was moving the hash marks closer together, lining them up with the goal-post uprights. That left no narrow side of the field that defenses could almost disregard. But it turned out to help the running game more than the pass. In fact, it might have hurt the pass. Pass defenders didn't have to commit to the wide side of the field, so it was easier for defenses to disguise their coverages.

In 1972, Miami went undefeated with 2.2 runs for every pass in the regular season, and 2.9 in three playoff games. Then in 1973, O.J. Simpson ran for a record 2,003 yards, and his Buffalo team made the playoffs with 4 touchdown passes all year. Simpson did most of his running from the I-formation, starting seven yards behind the line with an ideally placed lead blocker [See figure 21.] and plenty of room to look for daylight. It was a bad formation for passing, with neither back shaded toward the outside, but Buffalo rarely passed.

Zone defenses had the deep passes covered, and quicker pass rushers weren't giving outside receivers time to get open. Backs became the most practical pass receivers and, for many teams, passes became the most effective way to spring backs loose for runs. They were handy for dump-off passes against the blitz [See figures 41, 42, 43.], and they were catching what Minnesota coach Bud Grant called "sort of an off-tackle pass" on designed plays.

When Lydell Mitchell caught 72 passes for Baltimore in 1974, he was the first running back to lead the NFL in catches, and the first of six in a row. In 1977, Dallas made Preston Pearson the first receiving specialist at running back. He went into the game on passing downs. Before long, teams were drafting small, quick backs in the first three rounds to use primarily as pass receivers.

Aside from running backs, the biggest beneficiaries of the 1972 hashmark change were kickers, who some felt already were overrunning the game. As defenses became more dominant and points more precious, field goals [See figure 59.] became more significant. And with artificial turf, soccer-style kickers, and kicking specialists more common, kicking became more efficient.

Green Bay's Don Chandler became the first full-time kicker to lead the NFL in scoring in 1963, Hungarian-born Pete Gogolak joined the Buffalo Bills in 1964 as American football's first soccer-style kicker, and the Kansas City Chief's Jan Stenerud was the first soccer-style scoring leader in 1970.

But in 1974, a year after the per-game rate of field-goal attempts reached an all-time peak, the owners moved the goal posts back 10 yards from the goal line to the end line. With far fewer field goals in 1974, NFL scoring fell to its lowest since 1944. Deeper goal posts didn't help the deep-passing game. For the first time since 1934, fewer than 4 percent of all pass attempts went for touchdowns.

By 1978, offense was fading fast. Net rushing yards exceeded net passing yards in 1977 for the first time since 1956, and 1977 scoring was the NFL's lowest since 1942, 17.2 points per game for a team. The rules were in for a major rewrite.

Let's Change the Rules, Part 2

Ideally, a passer has at least a 1½-second window between the time his receivers get open and the pass rush closes in on him. By 1977, that window had shrunk to a peephole, so the NFL passed landmark rule changes that extended it on both ends.

The illegal chuck rule prohibited defenders from initiating contact with a receiver more than five yards from the line of scrimmage. And the liberalized holding rule helped pass blockers by allowing them to open their hands and fully extend their arms. The league also added a seventh official to monitor contact downfield.

One year later, the league added another rule to help quarterbacks stay healthy. It instructed referees to blow the whistle when the quarterback was "clearly in the grasp and control of a tackler," instead of waiting for him to be knocked down.

Rule makers clearly were encouraging coaches to make more use of the pass. Quarterback coaches, virtually nonexistent in 1977, became almost essential within 10 years. Receivers had the freedom to go deep or across the field unimpeded, and passers had time to wait for them. With speed more important than size, small receivers who wouldn't have been able to withstand the pre-1978 beatings downfield reappeared. In fact, as the chuck rule encouraged contact at the line, smaller wide receivers had the advantage of being smaller targets.

Even tight ends became smaller and faster. Ozzie Newsome was considered too small for the position when Cleveland drafted him in 1978, but the Browns played in Pittsburgh's division and figured they could nullify the

Steelers' double zone with a third deep threat in the middle. When the new rules no longer allowed linebackers to take turns jostling Newsome on his way downfield, other teams wanted their own greyhound tight ends.

Defenses, handicapped both on the pass rush and in coverage, had to concentrate on one or the other. The previous few years had seen heavy blitzing, so at first many teams tried beating the pass by sending extra rush men. Next, many teams tried playing 3-4 defenses and keeping eight men back in zone coverage.

In the secondary, a variety of coverages began surfacing in 1978 and grew steadily through the next two decades. By the mid-1980s, some coaches boasted of 50 or more different coverage schemes. Most were combinations of man-for-man and zone. [See figure 51.] Zone on the strongside, man on the weakside. Or zone on the sidelines, man in the middle. Or four defenders covering three receivers on one side, three covering two on the other.

The most popular combination coverage was called man under, with zone coverage deep and man-for-man underneath—in front of the deep zones. Defenses were trying for the best of both worlds. Zone was more effective stopping the run and preventing big plays, and man [See figure 49.] was more effective covering quick passes. Even full zone coverage often meant a defender would latch on to the first receiver through his zone and cover him man-for-man.

At first, defensive coaches tried a lot of jamming right at the line, the one place defenders could hit receivers. Offenses often sidestepped the jam by having a receiver in motion as the ball was snapped, so the purpose of jamming changed from flattening a receiver to channeling him in one direction. The defensive back would "tailgate" the receiver, staying between him and the ball. (Cornerbacks had to be quicker to play these new defenses, and the best ones were chosen earlier and earlier in the draft.)

The rules' effects showed up gradually on scoreboards and statistical sheets. NFL pass completions reached an all-time high of 54.1 percent in 1979 and haven't been that low since. The 1980 season was the first time since 1969 that pass plays exceeded running plays. In 1981, Dan Fouts averaged 300 passing yards a game for San Diego, and NFL sacks were down to 6.7 percent of pass plays, the lowest since the league started counting them in 1963. Touchdown passes exceeded interceptions in consecutive years for the first time in 1983-84. In 1983, the NFL scored its most points since 1965.

A 1981 rule meant to keep the ball clean actually helped receivers. It outlawed stickum, the gooey substance that helped attach footballs to fingers and even forearms. Before long, though, many receivers were wearing gloves even in domed stadiums. The gloves had tacky surfaces, which served the same purpose as stickum.

Most equipment changes in the 1970s and 1980s met the increasing demand for quickness and speed. Air-cushioned helmets were lighter and more comfortable. Rounded shoulder pads and skin-tight jerseys with slicker material made it harder for defensive linemen to grab pass blockers and toss them aside. Offensive linemen also started wearing gloves and, for the brief time it was legal, chose colors that matched opponents' jerseys so that holding would be harder to detect.

Flak jackets protected quarterbacks and receivers with injured ribs. Weighing only a few ounces, with air-filled pockets as shock absorbers, the vests led to air-cushioned shoulder pads that weighed less and better dispersed the force of a blow than foam-cushioned pads.

Old Positions, New Uses

The 1981 San Francisco 49ers won Super Bowl XVI after going 10-38 the previous three seasons—showing how quickly the pass could propel a team up the standings. While running backs either were great or they weren't, 49ers coach Bill Walsh contended passers and receivers could be taught what to look for and how to respond in a successful passing game.

In Walsh's offense, every down was a passing down. [See figure 28.] He emphasized high-percentage passes, timed precisely, that could control the ball as well as running plays. He used myriad formations and motion to move defenders where he wanted them, and he could go a whole game without repeating a play. While winning four Super Bowls in the 1980s, the 49ers of Walsh and George Seifert laid the groundwork for the offense that came to characterize the 1990s.

The 49ers' pass patterns were timed, Walsh said, to one-tenth of a second. That meant coordinating the split (or width) of the wide receiver and the depth of his route and the drop of the quarterback. Walsh would work for hours with a quarterback on just his drop.

The 49ers often kept their receivers closer to the ball, in tighter splits, enabling slightly quicker timing. It also made it easier for them to attack an area as a group. Flooding a zone with more than one receiver was an old strategy, but the 49ers also used congestion to their advantage against man-for-man coverage. Two receivers would run routes that crossed, so that one might obstruct his teammates' defender. Soon everyone was doing it.

Besides using a play list well into the hundreds each week, Walsh used 150 formations in the games that Washington scouted in preparing for the NFC Championship Game after the 1983 season. The 49ers put wide receivers in the backfield and tight ends and backs on the sideline. And a single play might have had 20 variations, depending on what the defense did. San Francisco took Lombardi's "sight adjustment" concept to a new level, adapting most of its pass plays to defensive reactions.

While offenses were burning out scoreboard lights, the clearest defensive trends were a gravitation toward 3-4 defenses and liberal substitution. George Allen may have been the first coach to switch between run-stuffing and pass-rushing specialists on the defensive line. Rookie Jimmie Jones was his designated pass rusher at Washington in 1971. The 49ers did the same thing in 1981 with Fred Dean, a smallish defensive end who could still beat pass blockers with his quickness. Soon, designated pass rusher was a definite roster spot. Extra defensive backs often replaced linebackers on likely pass plays.

As was the case when free substitution became legal, the number of all-around great players decreased while the number of players who accomplished one thing very well increased. And, while middle linebackers became part-timers, the spotlight shifted to outside linebackers who could stop the run and sack the passer.

The position was a product of 3-4 defenses. The Houston Oilers' Robert Brazile and Oakland Raiders' Ted Hendricks were early designated blitzers, both in 1975. But the player who defined the position of outside linebacker was the New York Giants' Lawrence Taylor, a spectacular rookie in 1981.

Before Taylor, most 3-4 defenses were passive units that clogged the secondary with people and, above all, did not give up big plays. Taylor, at 6-3 and 237 pounds, offered a more aggressive way to play the 3-4. He could be the fourth pass rusher or the fourth linebacker or the decoy while another linebacker rushed the passer. By the mid-1980s everyone had one of those big linebackers/small defensive ends.

A bit earlier, San Diego's Kellen Winslow redefined the tight end position. He caught at least 88 passes in 1980, '81, and '83 playing what Chargers coach Don Coryell called H-back. Eric Sievers was the tight end next to a tackle. Winslow was the motion tight end who lined up in the slot inside a wide receiver, wide toward the sideline, tight across the line from Sievers, at wingback behind Sievers, or in the backfield—almost anywhere. Within a few years, more than half the teams were using the second tight end in some situations. The 1982 Washington Redskins won Super Bowl XVII with a base offense of two tight ends and one back.

Washington coach Joe Gibbs, Coryell's former assistant, was the first to make the one-back a run-oriented offense. The Redskins introduced it after an 0-5 start in 1981 and promptly beat Chicago with 227 yards rushing. The Redskins passed plenty, but they reversed the old formula of jabbing with the run to soften up a defense with a knockout pass. They jabbed with the pass, wearing out a defense by making it pass rush, then burying the opponent with a heavy dose of running back John Riggins. As a result, close games quickly became blowouts.

Gibbs said he embraced the one-back offense to keep Taylor out of his backfield, and it worked. The Redskins won their next six games against the Giants by putting the extra tight end in Taylor's face and double-teaming him with a tackle. The balanced offense also caused problems for secondaries accustomed to playing the strongside and weakside differently. There was no strongside. Washington didn't use a lot of different plays, but its many formations gave multiple looks to each play.

Even as full-time one-back offenses petered out in the late 1980s, the concept of a single feature back prevailed. Fullback became a block-and-catch position, just like H-back. The one-back offense's legacy endured in blocking backs, multiple formations, spread passing formations, and zone blocking with huge linemen.

Zone blocking had been the cornerstone of Lombardi's run-to-daylight offense. "We think of zone blocking as a snowplow effect," said former Washington line coach Joe Bugel. With defenses shifting in and out of so many formations before the snap, and blitzing at odd angles after the snap, the Redskins blockers' job was to occupy space and keep defenders in front of them, to act as shields more than battering rams.

The 46 Defense

To stop the one-back offense with two strong sides, Chicago tried a defense with two strong sides. The Bears were 1-6 in 1981, with a loss in Washington's watershed one-back debut, when San Diego came to town with a 5-2 record. Chicago played most of the game in a 5-1-5 alignment that it had used sporadically since 1978. The Bears called it their 46 Defense because free safety Doug Plank, number 46, played middle linebacker. It had been designed as a pass defense that was more effective against the run than a regular Nickel defense. It added an extra lineman to the weak side of a 4-3. Winslow spent most of the day blocking the fifth pass rusher, and Fouts had his worst day as a pro. Later that season, Cincinnati used five-man lines in beating San Diego twice, the second time in the AFC Championship Game.

At that point in the offensive resurgence, some defenses laid back in zone coverage and some attacked with frequent blitzes, but there weren't many in between. Both kinds of defenses consciously looked for turnovers—an easier way to get the ball back than stopping an offense on downs.

Zone teams had coverage men facing the line and breaking to the ball. Blitzing teams forced turnovers by disrupting and hurrying the play. Many felt defenses might as well gamble more because they had less to lose. Touchdowns weren't that hard to come by anyway.

The Bears were a blitzing team, and their 46 Defense came of age in 1984, when the Bears started shifting in and out of it without making substitutions. They set the league record with 72 sacks that season and won the Super Bowl the next year, when they allowed only 10 points in three playoff games and, in one regular-season stretch of five games, their defense scored 25 points and gave up 20.

Although the original personnel in the 46 was a 5-1-5, its alignment always was a 4-4-3. Three defensive linemen were across from the center and guards, making it impossible to double-team the man on the center. That was where Bears defensive coordinator Buddy Ryan, the coach who developed the 46, put his best pass rushers—Dan Hampton in Chicago and Reggie White in Philadelphia after Ryan became the Eagles' coach. With NFL quarterbacks dropping into shallower pockets, a strong inside pass rush became essential for keeping them from stepping up away from the outside rush.

There were no defenders across from the offensive tackles, who were generally the offense's best pass blockers but also the linemen least likely to have an open space in front of them. The weakside defensive end lined up outside the offensive tackle, and the strongside linebacker, as in most defenses, lined up across from the tight end. But the weakside linebacker moved over to the strongside in a blitzing lane just outside the tight end. The two inside linebackers—one a nominal strong safety—were off the line and across from the offensive tackles, giving the 46 an eight-man front. Ryan also used a slew of pass coverages and had his cornerbacks covering wide receivers closely. "If you drop back in a zone, they can unload the ball before you get there" with the pass rush, he said. Time was the key to the 46: Rush the quarterback quickly and delay his ability to throw the ball.

The 46, with its blitzes of five to eight rush men, took away the offense's time. Instead of stopping a player, the 46 tried to stop the play from beginning.

Here Comes the Blitz!

By 1986, nearly every defense was blitzing wholeheartedly, and NFL offenses needed a counter-stroke to keep defenses from tossing quarterbacks around like the littlest kid's hat at the bus stop. They had to make their plays happen quicker.

Sight adjusting grew in popularity. If a receiver saw a blitz, he redirected his route to the area the blitzer had left, so the quarterback could get him the ball before the blitzer got the quarterback. The problem was, once defenses learned the sight adjustment to a certain blitz was a 5-yard route, they'd call that blitz on third-and-7. Another problem was that even when quarterbacks completed their passes, they were getting clobbered by unblocked blitzers as they threw.

There are two ways to beat a blitzing pass defense. One is to throw the ball where the blitzers would have been if they hadn't blitzed. The other is to block all the blitzers. Against an eight-man front, that meant designating eight blockers, which left only two available receivers instead of the usual four.

This "maximum-protection" approach was popular, too, not only for keeping blitzers and doctors away from the quarterback, but also for giving receivers a chance to get far downfield. It was difficult to sustain a 10-play drive against an aggressive defense bent on forcing mistakes, so big plays were the best way to beat it.

The long-term solution to beating blitzes was quick, timed passes from formations stretched across the field. Denver and Washington both had three wide receivers in their base offense for the Super Bowl after the 1987 season.

Dallas had re-introduced the Shotgun formation in 1975, snapping the ball to the quarterback five yards deep and spreading three wide receivers across the field. It was widely ridiculed at first because it announced to the defense that a pass was coming, but Landry reasoned, who was kidding whom on third-and-8?

When Mike Ditka left Landry's staff to coach Chicago in 1982, he couldn't wait to use the Shotgun on first down. Why wait until the defense put in six defensive backs and its pass-rush specialists? The Shotgun became just another look for a multiple-formation offense. About half the NFL teams used it at times through much of the 1980s.

The most extreme of the spread offenses was the Run-and-Shoot, exclusively a four-wide-receiver offense. Several teams used Run-and-Shoot plays on passing downs, but when Detroit adopted it in 1989 and Houston in 1990, they emptied their rosters of tight ends. The leading Run-and-Shoot proponent was Detroit offensive coordinator Darrel (Mouse) Davis, who helped introduce and refine it.

The quarterback always sprinted out to one side or another. The four wide receivers always started with two on each side, but one went in motion the other way. Quickness was so much more important than size that 6-foot wide receivers were a rarity. All routes were adjusted to defensive reactions. The idea was that the formations would spread a defense so thin that there had to be a weakness somewhere, and then a receiver would adjust to find it.

But the Oilers fulfilled the Run-and-Shoot critics' prophecies when they lost 1991 and 1992 playoff games by first blowing a late lead to Denver, then blowing a huge 35-3 lead to Buffalo. By 1995, only Atlanta was using the offense even sporadically.

Another way to wrestle control back from the defense was the No-Huddle offense, which caused defensive substituting problems. Cincinnati operated frequently without a huddle in 1985, although plays were signaled from the coaches just as in ordinary offenses. The Bengals seldom went into a hurry-up tempo, although that was always an option. They sometimes let the play clock run down while the defensive players had to stay in their stances, ready for the snap at any instant.

Other teams stopped huddling from time-to-time, too, but when the Buffalo Bills went to their No-Huddle offense in 1990, they upped the ante by using it all the time and doing it in hurry-up mode. Quarterback Jim Kelly called most of the plays, and the selection was relatively conservative. For the first time in recent memory, a strategic innovation featured less instead of more. Bills' games had fewer formations, fewer specialists, fewer substitutions, fewer defensive stunts and blitzes and coverages, and fewer blocking combinations.

Buffalo's Super Bowl opponent after that 1990 season was the New York Giants, with an offense that was both diametrically opposed to Buffalo's and the perfect counterstroke. They pounded the ball in a low-risk offense behind huge linemen. By reducing each teams' possessions in a game from, say, 12 to 10, the Giants made each possession more valuable and each turnover more important. They weren't the first team to stop a strong offense by keeping it off the field, but they were the first to win a Super Bowl against a team that almost never huddled.

Coach Bill Parcells's slow-down offense put a premium on avoiding turnovers, while their Taylor-led defense forced turnovers with an aggressive pass rush and zone coverage. Conventional wisdom said a blitzing team had to play man-for-man because fewer than seven people couldn't cover the zones. But the Giants showed that six zones were plenty—if the pass rush didn't give the receivers time to spread out.

The Defense Struggles Back

From jumbo to Run-and-Shoot, the late 1980s and early 1990s were an offensive laboratory just as the early 1980s had been rife with defensive experimentation. The 1978 rule changes backfired in the sense that by making it easier to pass, they forced the defense into tactics that made it harder to keep the passer healthy. But they speeded up the evolution of strategy. Offenses and defenses adjusted to each other's innovations in a matter of weeks.

Offenses learned to block blitzes by sliding their lines toward the direction of the blitz. Blocking styles put even more emphasis on offensive linemen's size. In 1990, the Dallas line averaged 296 pounds. The Giants' Super Bowl victory that season made 300-pound blockers even more popular. The NFL had only eight 300-pounders in 1986 but had 179 only 10 years later, most of them on the offensive line.

To beat the ever-growing blockers, pass rushers become ever-quicker. Blockers reached the point where virtually no pass rusher could overpower them, and rush men were so quick that the only way to stop them was to cut off their angles with sheer size, so offensive linemen kept growing and defensive linemen kept shrinking.

The blitz never fell entirely out of favor. Throughout NFL history, blitzing periods have been brief and furious until offenses reacted by beating them with long passes. But offenses were more apt to beat the 1980s blitzing with short passes, so defenses re-tooled their blitzes instead of abandoning them. They disguised blitzes by lining up in eight-man fronts and dropped different players into coverage. Sometimes three linemen and two linebackers rushed, and a lineman dropped back. Many teams tried to confuse blockers with stunts that sent players every which way even when only four men rushed.

The Rams played the 1989 season with two down linemen and five linebackers, at least two of whom rushed on every play. They called it their Eagle Defense because, although it looked like a knock-off of the 46 through contemporary eyes, it put players in the same spots where Greasy Neale had put them in his 5-2 Eagle Defense.

Other teams practically abandoned the traditional run-stopping notion that linemen had to see where the play was going before they took off running. Floyd Peters's Minnesota Vikings front four looked as if it would pass rush on every down, disrupting the run by infiltrating the backfield. Passes were so pervasive, nearly every down was considered a passing down. The quick linemen of choice weren't much bigger than the linebackers of 10 years earlier. Only 12 of the 28 teams played a base 3-4 defense in 1993, and just three of 30 used it three years later.

The same pass-rush schemes that were outlandishly aggressive a few years earlier became the norm by 1990, defensive necessities to keep up with improved blocking and quicker passes The lingering legacy of the 46 Defense was that an eight-man front was the best way to stop the run. To stop the pass, teams shifted from all-out, aggressive pass rush to aggressive coverage. Instead of hurrying the play so defensive backs didn't have to cover for long, defenses more often tried to slow down the play to give the pass rush more time.

Defenses disguised their coverage more than ever to confuse quarterbacks. The double zone made a comeback with a new twist. Instead of two deep zones, it had four. The four-across coverage was especially effective against four wide receivers, and, with six defensive backs, the defense still had a cornerback to bump a receiver on each side.

The double zone also made an imposing picket line on goal-line stands. For years, it was almost a league rule that defenses played man-for-man near the goal line because it was too risky to let anyone run unattended that close to the end zone. But there wasn't so much empty space between zones anymore when quarterbacks tried to unload the ball in two seconds, and a defense backed up to the goal line especially could keep its zones bunched together. Moreover, those crossing routes that picked off man-for-man defenders didn't faze a zone defense.

The variety of zone and combo coverage finally brought the upper hand back to the defense when scoring dropped significantly in 1991 and again in 1993, down 12 percent from its 1990 level and 22 percent from the 1983 peak. So the rules changed again in 1994. Illegal contact downfield, which had gradually been tolerated again, was once more outlawed, and quarterbacks' safety further was protected. Scoring shot back up to 1990 levels in 1994, one of the best seasons ever for passing. Sacks were an all-time low of 5.9 percent of pass plays. Defenses had to find a new way to confuse offenses.

Their solution was the zone blitz, a term that sounded as self-contradicting as a symphony for banjos and accordions. Football coaches grew up believing a team that rushed more than four men didn't have enough left over to play zone coverage. But pass plays took more time to execute back then.

The zone blitz wasn't new. Lombardi used it sporadically in the 1960s. Peters used it a few times a game at Minnesota in the late 1980s. They'd send a linebacker, the offense would adjust its play for the blitz, but a defensive lineman would drop into coverage and the offense would throw a man-for-man pass play at a zone defense. That wasn't technically a blitz, though, because only four men rushed.

The 1990s zone blitzes were true blitzes. Two or three linebackers came from the same side and maybe a cornerback, too. Defensive linemen dropped five yards back, and 330-pound offensive linemen wound up trying to block sprinters. Where the 3-4 defense had confused quarterbacks by not identifying the fourth pass rusher, these zone blitzes weren't identifying any of the pass rushers, or how many there would be.

It was the logical extension of a 12-year cycle where defenses forced faster passes, offenses beat them by designing faster passes, defenses countered by forcing pass plays to take more time, and offenses beat those strategies by designing still faster passes from spread-out formations. For roughly the second half of that cycle, people were forecasting the return of power offenses that shifted the focus back from time to space—either with longer passes or stronger running games.

By the 1990s, specialization was giving new legs to the running game. Most teams had running backs, who rarely blocked, and blocking backs, who rarely ran. The clubs weren't wearing down their star runners by making them block, and they were helping create daylight for them by hiring full-time blockers to deal with the oppressive variety of defensive schemes.

"You can't just put a guy back there and say, 'Okay, go get number fifty-one,' " Green Bay offensive coordinator

Sherm Lewis said. In one instance, his Packers more than quadrupled a player's rushing yardage by taking him out of the starting lineup. After gaining 120 as the starting fullback, Dorsey Levens ran for 566 yards in 1996 as the number-two running back as the Packers won their first Super Bowl in almost three decades.

So if Pro Football Hall of Fame members Jim Taylor and Paul Hornung had played for Green Bay in the nineties instead of the fifties and sixties, they probably would have split time instead of starting together in the backfield. Jim Brown, Larry Csonka, and Franco Harris wouldn't have been fullbacks. In 1998, only three teams had a fullback among their top two ground gainers, down from 18 in 1986.

And a lot of teams didn't bother splitting the running-back job. Team-leading rushers accounted for 59 percent of NFL yardage in 1998, up from 47 percent 12 years earlier. Most important, the rushing averages per carry and per game rose back to pre-1990s levels.

But no matter how creative the coaches are, their strategy is always dependent on the players available to carry it out. The most lasting innovations generally have a Sid Luckman or Sam Huff or Mike Ditka or Kellen Winslow or Lawrence Taylor to make the impossible become probable.

"Football goes in cycles," NFL quarterback Archie Manning said in the early 1980s. "Wide ties keep coming back again. So will the running game."

CHAPTER 18

The Playbook

By Rick Korch

No other team sport depends nearly so much on teamwork as football, which involves 11 players on each team working together to achieve one goal—either scoring or keeping the other team from scoring.

Vince Lombardi once said football is nothing more than running and jumping, blocking and tackling, throwing and catching. But then comes the rest of the game—the strategy and the formations, the tactics and techniques, shotguns and blitzes, overs and unders, bombs and flares, H-backs and Nickel backs, dimes and quarters, zones and gadgets, T-formations, I-formations, and pro sets.

The offense comes out of its huddle. It lines up in its normal formation. The quarterback yells out a few signals. The center snaps the ball. The quarterback hands off the ball to the halfback, who runs around right end behind the blocks of two guards, a tackle, and the fullback. He goes about 4 yards before he is tackled by the opponent's middle linebacker and safety.

Simple, isn't it?

Not really. Here's what actually happens. After the previous play, the center sets the huddle 7 yards behind the ball. Ten players put their hands on their knees and look at the quarterback's mouth. Only the quarterback talks, unless he asks someone a question.

In a typical pro set, the quarterback calls:

1. The formation;
2. Whether the tight end is to be on the left or right side;
3. The play;
4. The snap count. Then he says "Break."

Here's a typical play call: "Red right. Eighteen. Bob odd oh. On three."

Here's what it means: "Red Right" tells the players where to line up (it is the most common offensive formation in professional football). "Eighteen" means the halfback will carry the ball on a sweep around the right end. "Bob" tells the fullback to block the linebacker outside the right end. "Odd" tells the linemen which way to block and for the right guard to pull and lead the way for the halfback. "Oh" tells the left guard to follow the right guard. "Three" is the snap count.

Then the offense breaks its huddle and goes into a formation, but the formations often change several times as players shift and go in motion before the snap. The only limitations are the 40 seconds between plays and the rule calling for seven men on the line of scrimmage. Offenses like to shift players before the snap of the football because shifting just one player on offense can change the assignments for all 11 players on defense.

At the line of scrimmage, the quarterback calls out more signals:

1. The defense the opponent is playing;
2. a color and a number;
3. the color and number again;
4. "Down!";
5. a series of huts.

For example, the quarterback might yell out, "Pro. Blue 32. Blue 32. Down. Hut! (pause) Hut! Hut!

Here's what that means: The color and the number are so important that they are usually repeated. An offense changes its "live" color each week. If the quarterback calls out the "live" color and a new play, he has called an audible—meaning he has changed the play he called in the huddle to a new one. If any color other than the "live" color is called first, the play is a "dummy" call, designed to throw off the defense. On an audible, the ball usually is snapped on the second hut. The huts are non-rhythmic to keep the defense off balance. The shifting of the backs and the man in motion takes place after the quarterback calls "Down!"

At the same time, the center is making line calls to help the offensive line cope with the defense's shifts. He tells the line whether to block "even" (the man in front of you) or "odd" (angle blocking by the center and the guard or cross-blocking by the guard and the tackle). "Jet" might be the code word for even, and "pizza" could be the code word for odd. Whether the lineman gets a "call" or not, he has a contingency plan for every block. That's called "rule blocking."

While all this is happening on the offensive side of the ball, the defensive captain, usually a middle or inside linebacker, calls defensive signals. The defensive coordinator can send in a defense from the sideline before the play, but the defensive captain has to make adjustments based on the offensive formation he sees. The defense mixes things up by going into zone coverage, man-for-man coverage, or a combination of both, to keep the offense from knowing what to expect. The coordinator might call out "Pro. Tom. Right. Cover 4."

Here's what that means:

1. The linemen and linebackers play a "pro" front, the standard 4-3 defense;
2. "Tom" is a stunt by the defensive end and the defensive tackle;
3. "Right" tells the defensive player where the of-

fense's tight end will most likely be. (Right on defense means strongside left on offense. If the offense comes out strongside right, the defense will shift.)

4. "Cover 4" tells the deep backs to play coverage number 4, man-for-man, double-teaming the flanker and split end.

Every offensive player has to be set for a full second before the snap. Finally, the center hikes the ball, and the halfback runs for a 4-yard gain. That gain wouldn't reflect much of what's in a pro football team's playbook. What's the difference between Sam and Will and Mac and Mike? Which is the three hole, and where are the gaps? What's the difference between stunts and stacks? And, what are the keys for pluggers to blitz?

There's a common misconception that all it takes to play football is speed and size. But it takes brains, too, as is quickly apparent if you ever glance at an NFL team's playbook. Most playbooks look basically the same, but they differ greatly in terminology, philosophy, strategy, and game plan. Playbooks are dull reading because there's very little to read; they're mostly squares, triangles, and circles and a bunch of lines.

Nearly every offensive scheme, in one form or another, has been used before. Today's one-back formation is similar to the double-wing formation developed 50 years ago by famed Cleveland Browns coach Paul Brown.

And the 3-4 defense that was used by nearly every NFL team in the 1980s was almost the same as the Oklahoma defense devised in the 1940s by legendary University of Oklahoma football coach Bud Wilkinson. Now almost all NFL teams have gone back to the 4-3 defense that was a staple in the 1960s.

Teams have separate playbooks for their offense and defense. The offensive playbook includes quarterback calls, terminology, the play-numbering system, the numbering of the backs, formations (both offensive and defensive, so the offensive players can learn to recognize defenses), the two-minute drill, the automatic or checkoff system at the line, and the means of calling signals. The playbook also lists hundreds of plays and alternate plays for each play. The defensive playbook addresses things such as the prevent-scoring theory, pass-defense theory (which concerns man-for-man or zone preferences), and the theory of blitzing.

NFL coaches who stick to the basics might have only about 60 to 75 running plays in their books and about the same number of passes. Teams that run more diversified offenses have many more. Altogether, there are only about 500 possible plays.

What factors determine which play to call?

Teams try to use their strengths against their opponents' weaknesses. Coaches use statistics, computers, down-and-distance tendencies from frequency charts (such as what the opponent is most likely to do on third-and-short), scouting reports, and film of previous games. Frequency charts also tell a defense what formation the offense most likely will use in a particular situation. Before each game, coaches try to determine which plays will have the greater success potential both offensively and defensively. This is the game plan.

Down and distance dictates to the greatest extent what kind of play is going to be called. For example, teams usually can expect a run between the tackles on third-and-1, and, almost always, a pass on third-and 10. Motion by a running back or a tight end also can be a tipoff that a running play is coming because the motion is usually going in the direction the run is headed.

Whatever the down, the alignment of the tight end always determines the strength of the formation. On running plays, the side with the tight end is the strongside because he gives the offense an extra blocker to the right or left of the center. (If there are two tight ends, the coach designates one of them as the strongside.) On passing plays, the number of receivers determines the strongside. The side with the greater number of receivers is strong, and it may or may not be the tight end's side.

On the other hand, every defensive formation is both strong and weak, and here's the reason why: To provide support against the run, a team exposes its defensive backs to the pass. To overprotect one side of the field, it must underman another side.

The play called in the huddle is a combination of the series plus the hole in the line. In the old days, when there were four players in the backfield, the quarterback was number 1, the two halfbacks were numbers 2 and 4, and the fullback was number 3. Today, since there are only one or two running backs, they are numbered by the space they are set in, regardless of whether they are halfbacks or fullbacks—2 to the left, 3 behind the quarterback, and 4 to the right.

The second digit refers to the hole in the line. Odd numbers usually are to the left of the center and even numbers are to the right.

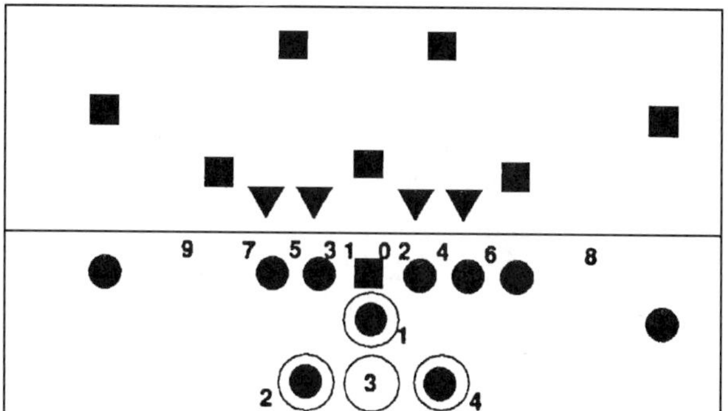

Figure 1. *Holes and Numbers*

Here's an example. The Green Bay Packers' famed Power Sweep was the most dominant play in the 1960s. Today, the formation and play is usually called "Red Right 38." Red Right is the basic formation. The play is the 3 back running into the 8 hole. It's a simple formation and a simple play.

The Offense and Offensive Formations

The pro set has been the basic formation in the NFL for more than 30 years. It is easy to distinguish because it has two running backs, two wide receivers, and a tight end. But it took nearly 50 years to develop. Many offensive formations that are no longer in use laid the framework for today's diversified sets, as follows:

Single Wing—Invented around 1906 by Glenn (Pop) Warner, the Single Wing enabled the offense to trick the defense with a lot of spins and reverses, but its greatest value was in concentrating great power at the point of attack on running plays. It is very similar to the Green Bay Packers' power sweep of the 1960s. (See below.)

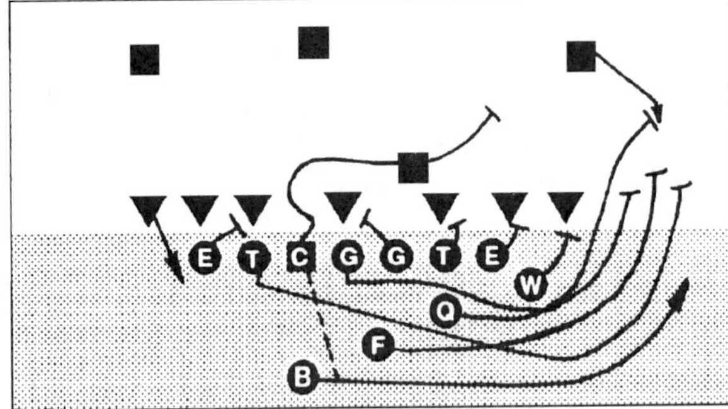

Figure 2. *Single Wing*

Double Wing—The Double Wing laid the foundation for spread formations such as the Shotgun that became popular almost 50 years later because it put two receivers to one side.

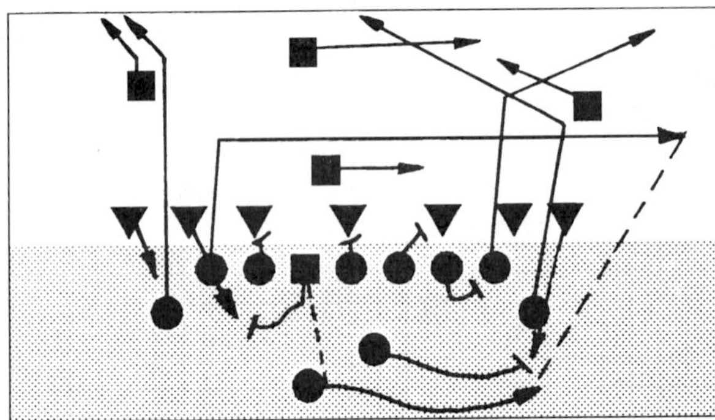

Figure 3. *Double Wing*

Triple Wing—The Triple Wing is similar to the Double Wing, but it placed three receivers to one side of the center.

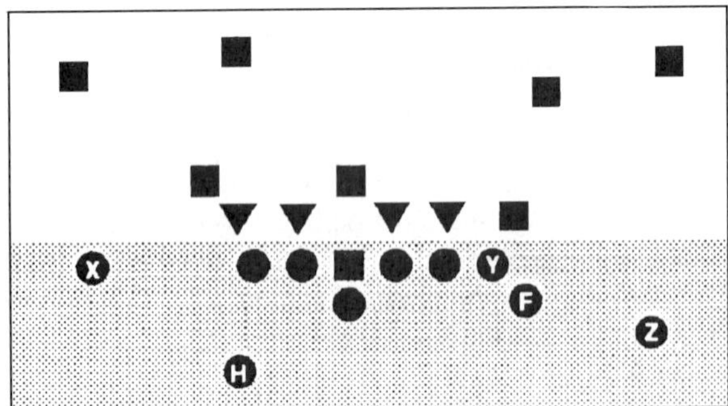

Figure 4. *Triple Wing*

A-Formation—Steve Owen, coach of the New York Giants from 1931-1953, developed the A-formation, which had: 1) unusual line splits; 2) the line strong to one side and the backfield strong to the other; and, 3) a direct snap to the left halfback rather than to a T-quarterback.

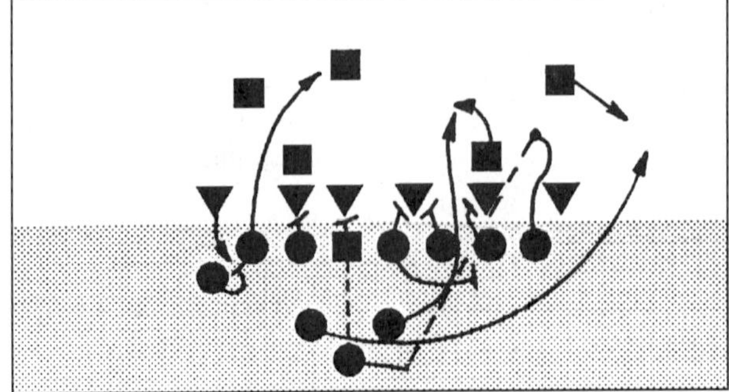

Figure 5. *A-Formation*

Notre Dame Box—Legendary Notre Dame coach Knute Rockne devised this play about 1920. The Fighting Irish would shift from a T-formation to their Box and then take off on an end run, practically all in one motion, with the ball being snapped to a halfback. (Rules eventually were changed that required offensive players to be still for a full second before the snap.)

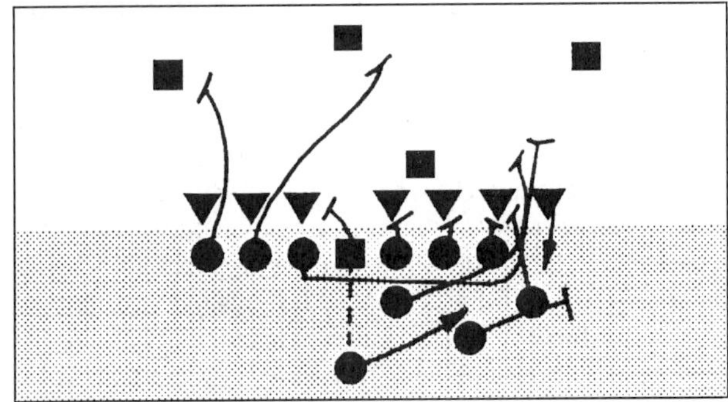

Figure 6. *Notre Dame Box*

Man in Motion—All but one offensive player must be stationary at the time the ball is snapped. The player (wide receiver, tight end, or running back) who runs across the field behind the line of scrimmage is the man in motion. Putting a man in motion allows the offense to put a running back closer to the outside before the play begins, after which he can take a quick pitchout, or serve as a lead blocker. Putting a man in motion also forces the defense to make adjustments.

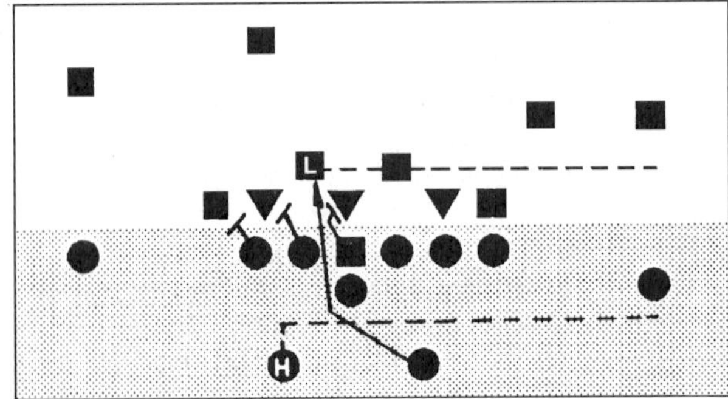

Figure 7. *Man in Motion Wing*

T-Formation—Now the dominant formation, the "T," as it is called, was first used by the Chicago Bears in 1930. It put the quarterback under center for the first time and spread the defense by putting smaller, faster players out wide where they could get more running room or go downfield for passes. The T-formation was popularized after the Chicago Bears used it to defeat the Washington Redskins 73-0 in the 1940 NFL Championship Game. It is the basis for all offensive strategies in the last 55 years.

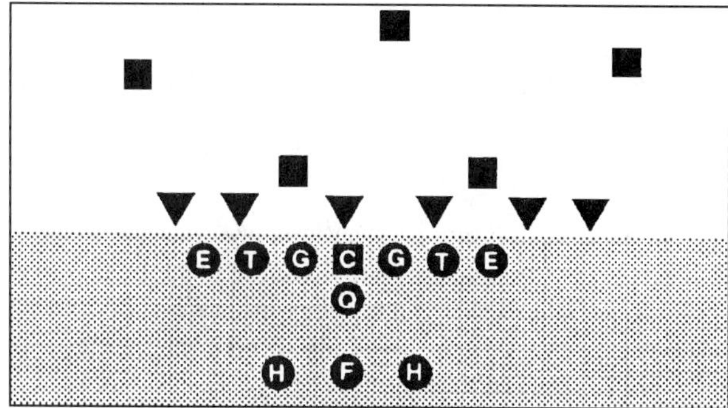

Figure 8. *T-Formation*

Slot-T—The Bears had started man-in-motion in the 1930s, which removed one player from the backfield. By the late 1940s, that player was positioned to either side of the formation, rather than going in motion. He became the flanker and usually was positioned between the tackle and the split end. Eventually, the flanker came to be seen not as a halfback removed from the backfield, but rather as a third receiver. Later, the terms wide receiver and tight end were adopted to designate the three ends.

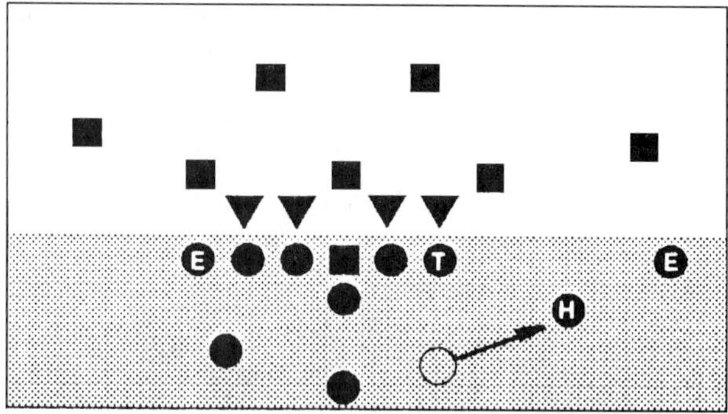

Figure 9. *Slot-T Formation*

Green Bay Power Sweep—Vince Lombardi was a master at teaching running and blocking, and he had great players to run his signature play. The Packers used the power sweep as often as a dozen times a game. Both guards pulled to lead, the tight end blocked the outside linebacker, and the lead running back blocked the end. (Note how similar Green Bay's power sweep is to the Single Wing and the Notre Dame Box.)

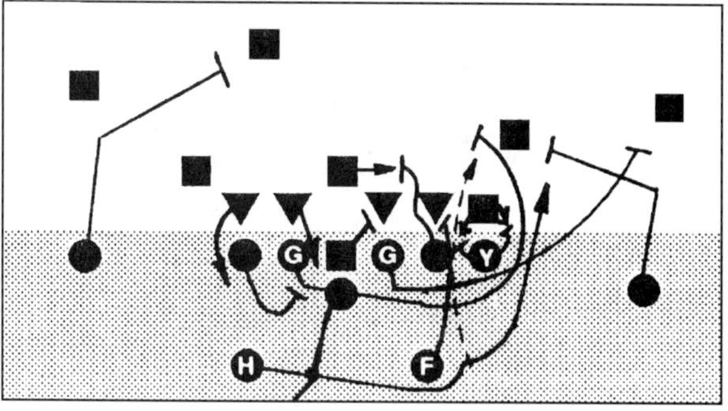

Figure 10. *Green Bay Power Sweep*

I-Formation—The I-formation was created in the 1950s by a college coach named Tom Nugent. Hank Stram, who coached the Kansas City Chiefs in two of the first four Super Bowls, was one of the first to use it in pro football, and later it became the trademark formation for Earl Campbell and Eric Dickerson. The ball carrier sets up deep, which allows him to "read" the blocks ahead of him and pick the hole he wants to run to. A wide variety of fakes can be used in the "I" because the ball is screened until the last second. It's particularly effective on running plays up the middle or off tackle.

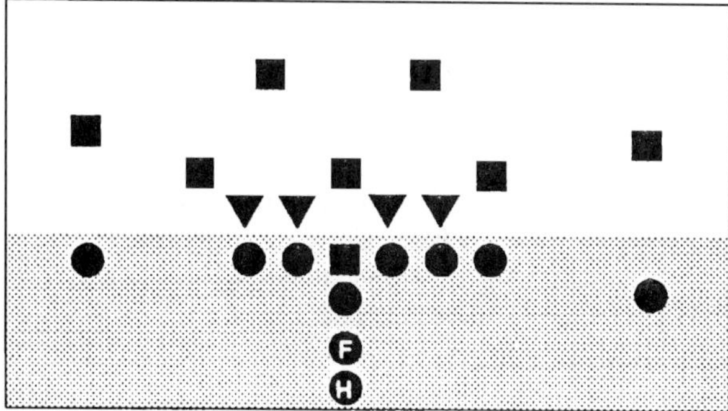

Figure 11. *I-Formation*

Shotgun—The modern Shotgun was designed for the passing game, but not all teams use it. The Dallas Cowboys started using it in 1975 and won the NFC championship that season. Rather than taking the snap direct from the center, the quarterback sets up about 4 yards behind the center, which allows him to see more of the field and gives him more time to read the zones because he doesn't have to drop back. It first came into being in 1960, when Red Hickey used it with the San Francisco 49ers.

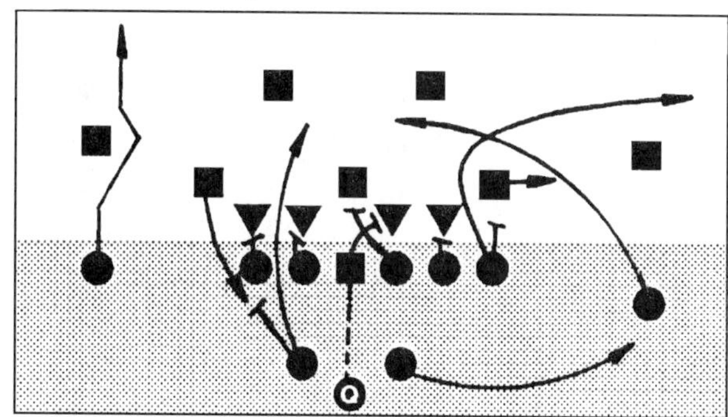

Figure 12. *Shotgun Formation*

One-Back Offense—This formation, devised in the last decade, uses two tight ends and only one running back. The second tight end is usually called the H-back, and really is just a relocated fullback. The advantages are that there is no weakside of the field, another blocker is set closer to the line, and there is a second tight end (or third wide receiver) instead of a back who can get downfield quicker for passes. The one-back formation helps the running game because it creates better running lanes, and it creates them from passing formations because it scatters the defense across the field. If the second tight end is lined up next to the tackle, it is a variation of the old T-formation. (The halfbacks have moved outside to become wide receivers.) If the tight end is away from the tackle, it's a variation of the I-formation. (The blocking back has moved out from behind the quarterback and becomes a receiver.)

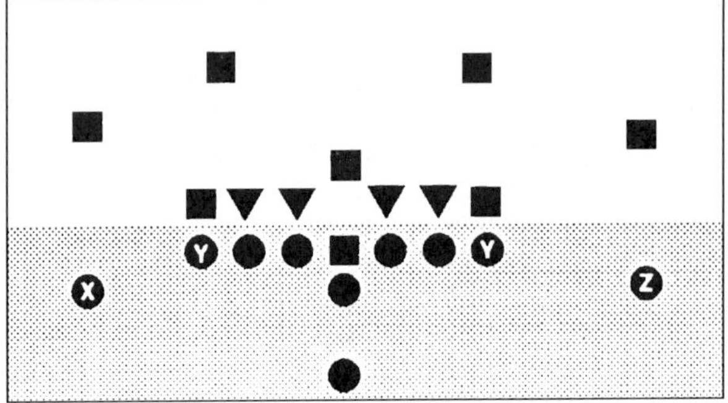

Figure 13. *One-Back Formation*

Multiple-Receiver Formations—Most offenses now use three or four wide receivers in passing situations, substituting for slower tight ends and running backs. Often they won't even have any backs in the backfield. With three or four wide receivers, someone should be able to get open every time—if the quarterback has time to pass the ball. These formations were spurred by Run-and-Shoot offense, which was popular with the Detroit Lions, Houston Oilers, and Atlanta Falcons in the early 1990s. In the Run-and-Shoot, the routes of the receivers are determined by the coverage (man or zone). By 1999, the Run-and-Shoot virtually was extinct in the NFL, a gimmick offense that failed to take hold. However, the use of four and even five receivers was around to stay.

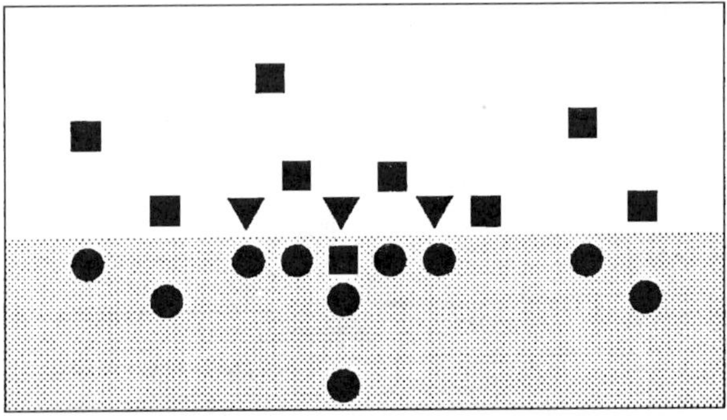

Figure 14. *Four Wide Receivers*

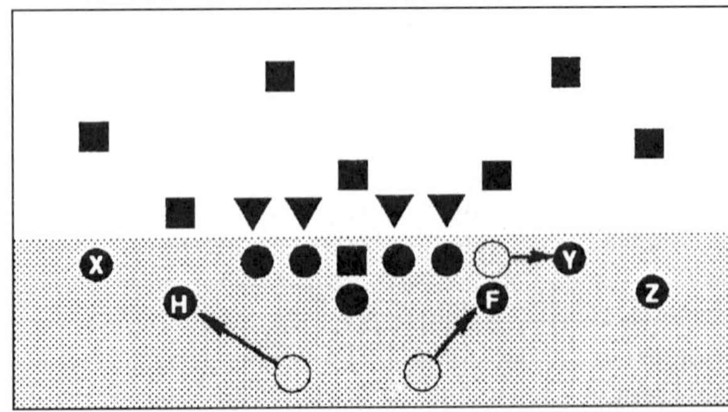

Figure 15. *No-Back Formation*

When a coach talks about his "system," he really is talking about how he names his formations. Take, for example, three great coaches—Paul Brown, Sid Gillman, and Tom Landry. If the running backs were split behind the quarterback, and the fullback was on the same side as the tight end, Brown called that "split right," Gillman called it "full," and Landry called it "red." If the backs were split behind the quarterback and the halfback was on the same side as the tight end, Brown called it "split left," Gillman called that "half," and Landry called it "green." If the backs were not split but the fullback was behind the quarterback and the halfback was opposite the tight end, Brown called it "opposite," Gillman called that "far," and Landry called it "brown."

Whatever the naming conventions are, the game starts with blocking. Offensive linemen are the unsung heroes of football, the faceless players who are rarely noticed—unless they get called for a penalty or blow an assignment that causes a play to lose yardage. Nevertheless, they do a job just as important as anyone else on the field. It's the offensive linemen who make the blocks that open the holes for running backs to run through.

Pass rushers charge across the line of scrimmage in "lanes," up the middle and from the sides. They want to pressure the quarterback from the front and squeeze him from the sides. And they have a variety of routes—through the blocker, past his inside shoulder, around his outside shoulder, or faking one way and going the other.

Blockers read the angle of the rush as they set up, trying to anticipate moves. When pass blocking, offensive linemen stand at the snap of the ball and retreat to set up a "pocket" for the quarterback. When pass blocking, offensive linemen can use their hands; defenders always can. In run blocking, offensive linemen "fire out" across the line. They can extend their arms, but cannot hold defenders.

There are many kinds of blocking patterns:

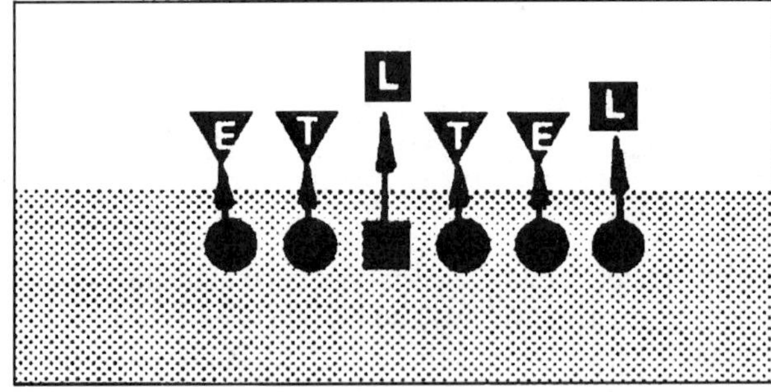

Figure 16. *Power Blocking*

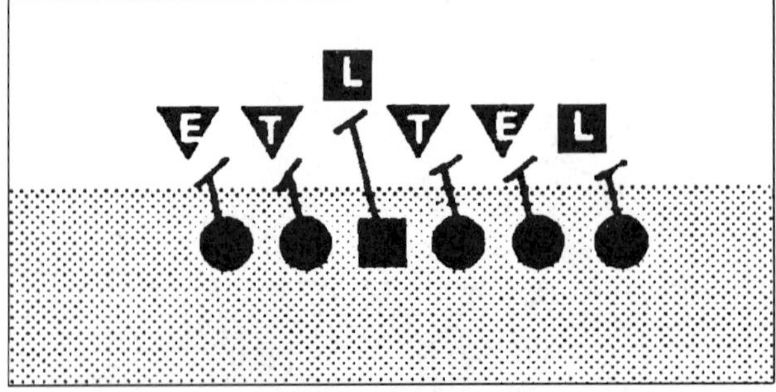

Figure 17. *Angle Blocking*

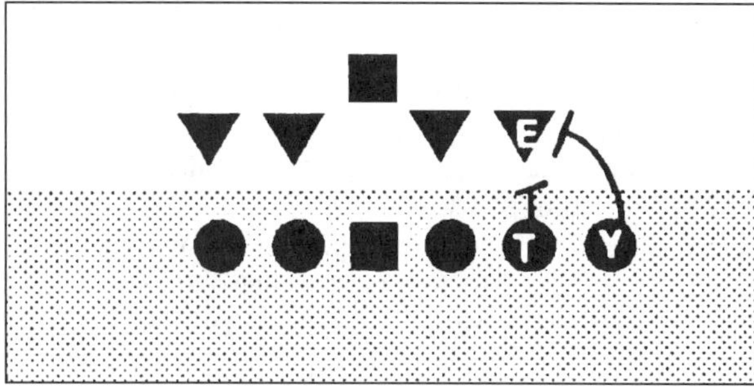

Figure 18. *Double-Teaming*

Figure 19. *Wedge Blocking*

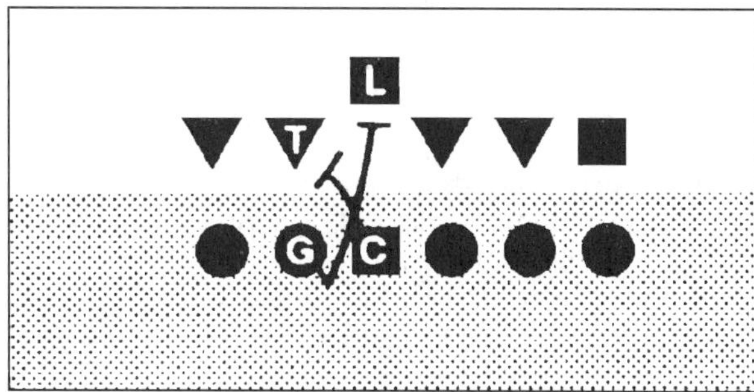

Figure 20. *Cross Blocking*

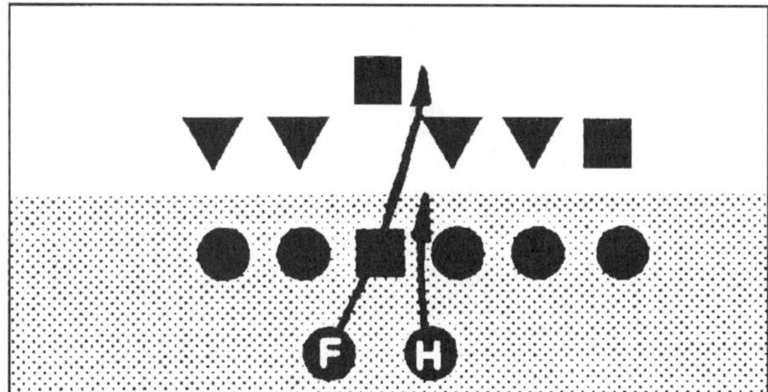

Figure 21. *Lead Blocking*

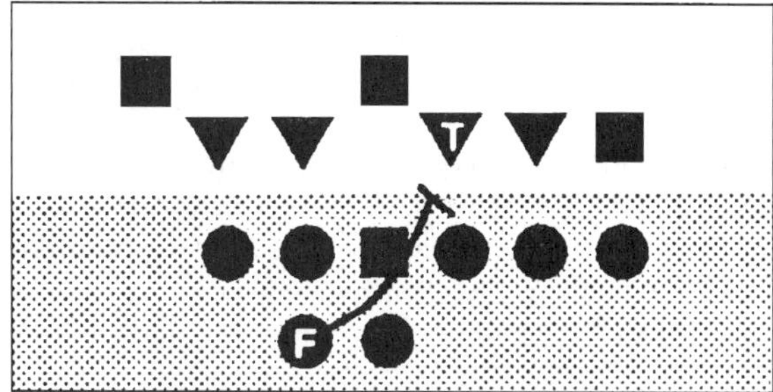

Figure 22. *Isolation Blocking*

The Passing Tree

These different kinds of blocks allow the offense to set up for either a run or a pass. Just as there are many different running plays for a coach to choose from, there are even more passing plays. Different pass patterns are required for wide receivers, tight ends, and running backs. Every team has what is called a passing tree, but not all trees are the same.

Here is a typical one for wide receivers: When it is drawn on a blackboard, it looks like a leafless tree, with every branch a numbered pass route. The odd numbers are the outside routes and the even numbers are the inside routes.

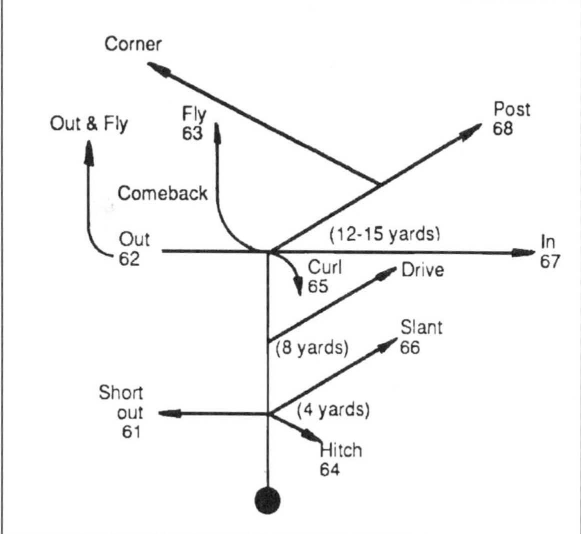

Figure 23. *Passing Tree - Wide Receivers*

What the receiver needs to know on every play is:

1. the formation (where he lines up);
2. the snap count (when he releases);
3. a single digit number (the route he runs).

The X receiver's route is the first number called, the Y tight end is the second number, and the Z receiver is the third. Thus on a "976" for example, the split end runs an up (straight up the field), the tight end executes a deep corner, and the flanker runs an in pattern. Some teams use only a two-digit play call, depending on whether the wide receiver or tight end is the primary receiver.

Just as a quarterback reads a certain key or keys as he is setting up, the receiver has keys to read to tell him if he is to break the route into a specific area or to run away from the coverage. True coordination between the quarterback and his receivers occurs when they read the same thing and are in a situation in which they know, before the pass is thrown, to whom it will be thrown.

Thus, every pass pattern has a contingency, a set of automatic adjustments, or "breakoffs," for the receivers. For example, if the defensive back plays one way, the receiver breaks off the pattern and goes to the option.

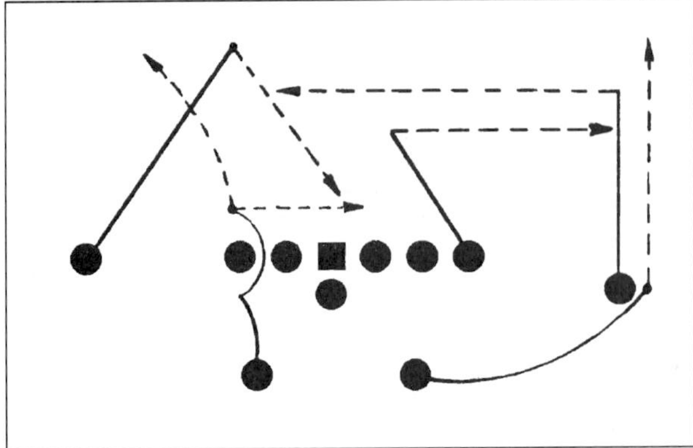

Figure 24. *Breakoff Patterns*

Here are some of the most common pass routes:

Slant—Used when the defensive back is playing off the line. The receiver charges out, takes two or three steps, then cuts to the middle, in front of the defender.

Quick out—Take a couple of steps, cut to the sidelines.

Out—Break toward the sidelines at an angle, coming back toward the line of scrimmage. That keeps the defender from being able to get to the ball.

Curl—Run downfield, then come back to the line of scrimmage (the easiest way to complete a pass).

Post—Break to the defensive back's inside shoulder, like a curl, get him going the wrong way, then cut upfield toward the goal post.

Fly—Give the defensive back a quick stutter step, as if running a post, then go straight upfield.

Corner—Run the stem—the first 5-8 yards of any pass pattern—then run the post for 5-6 yards, and break to the corner.

Running backs also have a passing tree, and they have breakoff patterns.

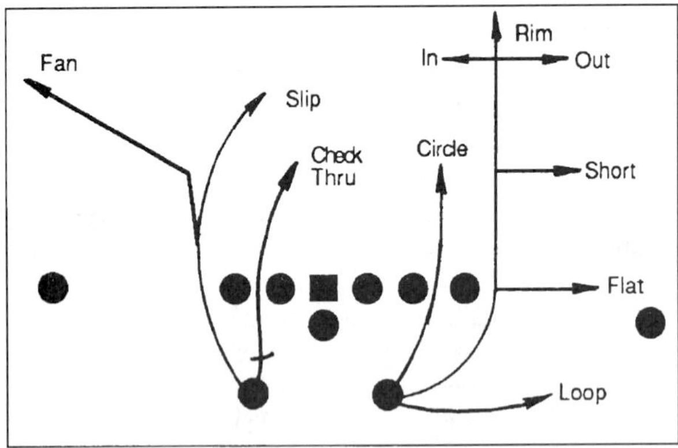

Figure 25. *Passing Tree - Running Backs*

Pass Plays

Most passes are thrown no more than 15 yards, and they usually are based on the theory of moving running backs into certain areas to force linebackers to move with them—which often leaves a receiver uncovered. On longer passes, the receiver's job is simple; he just has to "get open." To do so, he uses a variety of moves and patterns to shake off his defender.

But the best way to attack a good pass defense is to use the whole field, spreading it out with short, medium, and long passes.

Play Action—The idea of play action is to make the play appear to be a run, when it really is a pass. In this diagram, the quarterback fakes to the fullback before dropping back and throwing to one of two targets on the left, either the running back short or the wide receiver looping deep and toward the sideline. The pulling guard also helps to make the play appear to be a run, as do the rest of the linemen, who carry out their run-blocking assignments. This is the most widely used method of controlling the linebackers, who often step forward to try to make a tackle that isn't there, or freeze in their tracks for a second, and are out of position to cover the pass.

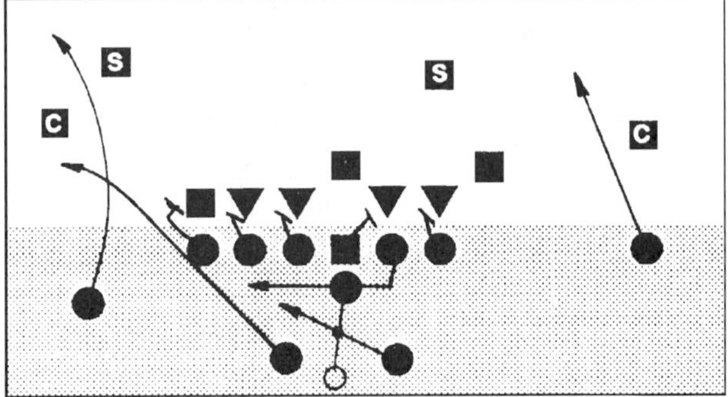

Figure 26. *Play Action Pass*

Screen Pass—The screen is used when the defense expects a pass, and it works well against a zone defense because if the linebackers drop too deeply into coverage they will be out of position to tackle the receiver. The quarterback drops to his regular passing position, and the offensive linemen set up a pass block, trying to get the defensive linemen to charge. The receivers run downfield, faking a deep pass. The backs set up as they do on a pass. As the pass rushers hit the "pocket," the quarterback retreats a little deeper, then throws a pass to a running back who has released in the flat.

Option Screen Pass—On the option screen pass, the primary receiver is the flanker, who runs a quick route along the sideline. The quarterback either throws immediately to a spot ahead of the receiver or keeps the ball momentarily if the receiver is covered. Then the quarterback drops back into his "pocket" and waits for a normal screen pass to develop, which gives the secondary receiver a wall of blockers.

Rollout Pass—Rollout passes are very effective if the wide receiver can get open. They get the quarterback out on the edge of the formation, giving him a good view of the field. (A "waggle" is the opposite of rolling out, setting up away from the flow.) In the first diagram, the quarterback rolls to his right behind the pulling center, while the halfback, slotted right, goes in motion left to draw some pressure off the quarterback. The Z receiver runs an out, trying to keep the cornerback inside. In the second diagram, the tight end is the intended receiver.

Deep Flood—Nothing is more spectacular and nothing puts points up on the scoreboard faster than the bomb. The quarterback takes a seven-step drop, while the receivers normally fake a short pattern, then go deep.

Inside Deep—One way to beat a zone defense is to flood one of the zones with several receivers. In this play, the Y receiver (tight end) does a down-and-in in front of the weak safety, the Z flanker runs a deeper down-and-in away from the cornerback, and the X receiver goes deep on a fly route. The outlet receivers are the halfback and fullback running flare patterns to the outside.

Combination—In combination patterns, teams try to use all of their receivers to strike deep, medium, and short at the same time. The quarterback takes a seven-step drop and looks for an open receiver.

Tight End as Receiver—Tight ends are being used more and more as receiving threats, especially on long passes. One of today's biggest plays is a tight end running deep between the two zones in a two-deep zone defense. In the diagram, the tight end is the primary receiver and runs a corner route.

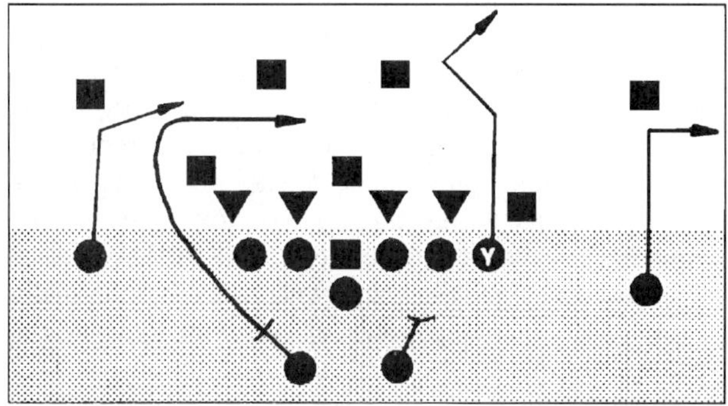

Figure 27. *Tight End as Receiver*

Short Passing Game/West Coast Offense—Offenses want to maintain ball control, and they can do that with a short passing game. The short game sends out wide receivers as decoys to draw defensive backs away from the line of scrimmage, then it floods the running backs and tight ends with high-percentage passes, most traveling no more than 10 yards beyond the line of scrimmage. Many teams, in a trend led by the San Francisco 49ers, use a short passing game that features a running back as a frequent receiver after the wide receivers have cleared out his short area by running longer routes. In the West Coast offense, wide receivers often are used as primary targets in a short passing game by running crossing routes while a running back and tight end go farther downfield. By 1999, about half of the NFL teams predominantly were using the West Coast offense.

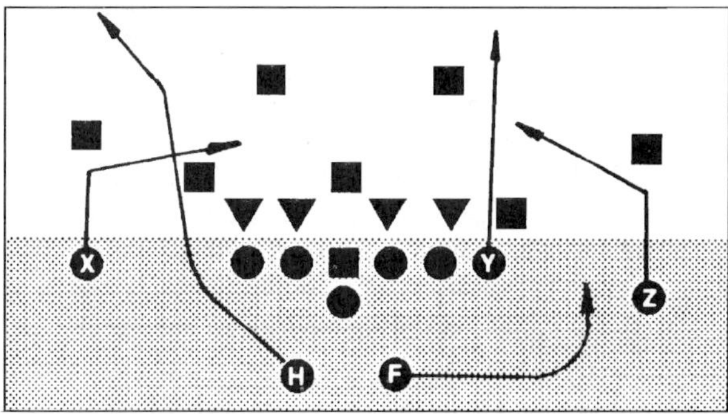

Figure 28. *49ers Short Pass*

Deception/Halfback Option—These are passes by a running back, who can either run or pass; it is his option. Walter Payton, the NFL's all-time leading rusher, threw 8 touchdown passes during his career. Option passes put a great deal of pressure on linebackers and defensive backs. Halfback-option passes usually are thrown from a sweep.

Flea-flicker—The quarterback, who usually lines up in the Shotgun, takes the snap and makes a short lateral to the lone running back, who heads toward the strongside behind the pulling weak tackle. Before he turns the corner, the halfback stops, pivots and laterals the ball to the quarterback, who has run into the left flat while the defense shifts toward the expected run. In other variations of the flea-flicker, the halfback almost immediately laterals back to the quarterback who throws to a wide receiver running a post pattern.

Running Plays

Teams try to mix their ball carriers and blocking schemes because keeping a defense off balance is as important for a good running game as it is for the passing game. Here are some of the many different running plays that are used the most.

Sweep—The ball carrier takes a handoff from the quarterback and runs parallel to the line of scrimmage while allowing his blockers (the guards and sometimes a tackle) to get in front before he turns upfield. The play is aimed at the defensive end, the outside linebacker, and the cornerback who comes up to force. The play is set up by the other running back faking into the line and looking to block a defensive lineman.

Dive—Every team's playbook has a dive. The running back takes a quick handoff and hits the hole between tackle and guard. He often has the other running back as a lead blocker, with the middle linebacker as his target.

Pitch—The quarterback fakes to one running back who heads up the middle, then tosses a short lateral to the other set back who has begun his move to the outside.

Veer—This is another quick-hitting play, in which the ball can be handed off to either back whose route is determined by the reaction of the defensive linemen.

Slant—The running back runs at an angle, or slant, toward the hole. The other back also runs at that same angle to lead interference.

Draw—The draw begins as a simulated pass, like a screen, then suddenly develops into a run. The offensive linemen retreat, as if they are pass blocking, inviting the defense to charge. The quarterback drops back, too, almost to normal passing depth. Then he suddenly turns and hands the ball to a running back. The defensive linemen, in their anxiety to rush the quarterback, may leave a fairly big unprotected area at the line of scrimmage. As the running back bursts toward the line, the offensive linemen turn the rushers to the side. It's the opposite of play-action, because the offensive players act as if it is a pass, and it turns into a run.

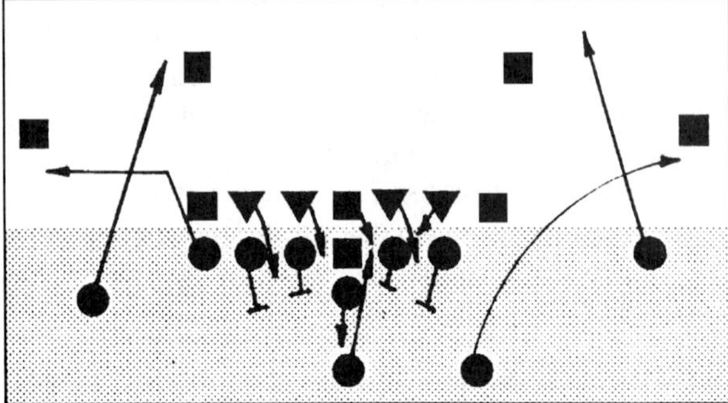

Figure 29. *Draw Play*

Trap—This is football's best sucker play. It takes advantage of the enthusiastic or reckless charge of a defensive lineman and turns his quick reactions against him. To trap this player, a guard vacates his normal blocking area and allows the defensive lineman to penetrate the line so he has a clear shot to the backfield. Then he's blocked by the guard from the opposite side who pulls and hits him from the side. The ball carrier cuts behind the trap block.

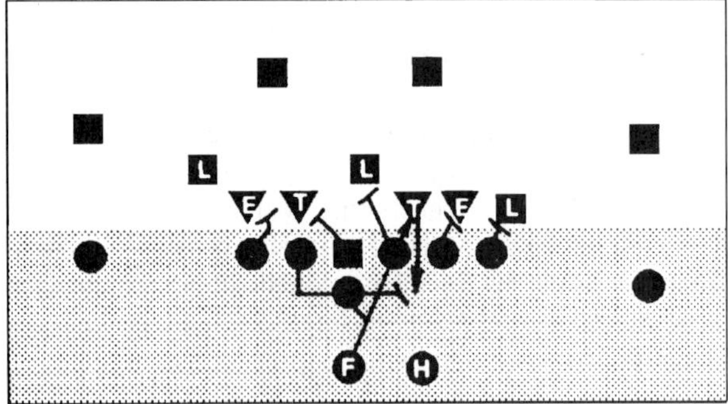

Figure 30. *Trap Play*

Long Trap—This play is run from Shotgun formation and has an extra advantage because it comes from a passing formation on a passing down (usually with three wide receivers). In this diagram, the pass-rushing defensive left end takes himself out of the play by going after the quarterback, which frees the offensive right tackle to help the ball carrier farther downfield by blocking the strong safety. The defensive left tackle is the victim of the trap block.

Off Tackle—This is one of the oldest plays in football, and is reminiscent of the days of the Single Wing. On this play, the running back dives through the hole opened by the blocks of the tight end, the pulling guard and the fullback. It attacks the defense where it is weakest, at strongside linebacker.

One-Back Run—Depending on the motion, the play can be run from any of several formations. The blocks at the point of attack are very important, especially the left tackle on the defensive right end, the left guard needing some movement on the right inside linebacker, and the center cutting off the nose tackle. Notice the H-back, the second tight end, who blocks the weak outside linebacker to the outside. The running back has three lanes to choose from: over tackle, cut back over guard, or outside tackle.

Counter Play (Misdirection)—When a running play looks as if it is going in one direction and ends up going in another, it is called a counter. In the play diagrammed, the quarterback fakes a lateral to the halfback, who decoys around right end. The fullback takes a handoff and hits up the middle behind the center, who changes blocking assignments with the weakside guard.

I-Formation Run—This play makes use of a tailback's power and quickness, especially if the block on the strong safety is accurately read, and the outside lane opens up. On this play, the strongside guard pulls and blocks the strongside linebacker; the tight end and strongside tackle double-team the defensive end; the weakside guard assists with the block on the left inside linebacker; the center blocks the nose tackle; the fullback blocks the strong safety; the flanker takes the cornerback. Finally, the tailback takes the toss from the quarterback and reads the block by the strongside guard and the fullback's containment of the strong safety.

Quarterback Sneak—This is a popular play when a team needs only a yard for a first down or a touchdown.

Bootleg—This play is rarely used because coaches are hesitant to use their quarterbacks as ball carriers. In the bootleg, the quarterback has the option of either running or passing, depending on what the defense does. On a weakside bootleg, the backs fake to the strongside and the quarterback fakes the ball to them. If the defense rushes the quarterback, he'll throw to a wide receiver who usually is running a square-out route or a turn-in route. If the linebacker drops on the weakside, then the quarterback will run the ball. He usually has a blocker in front of him.

End Reverse—The strongside flanker runs in motion to and from the formation before taking on the left cornerback; the fullback blocks the weak outside linebacker; the strongside linemen slant downfield toward the weakside; the weakside guard blocks the weak inside backer; the quarterback reverses out and tosses the ball to the halfback. The wide receiver pulls and heads toward the halfback, who hands him the ball. Running away from the flow of the play, the wide receiver reads the block on the cornerback before cutting upfield.

Fake Reverse—On this play, the quarterback takes a couple of steps back and pitches the ball to the running back swinging left; the running back turns to the wide receiver coming around and gives him the handoff on a reverse. The wide receiver fakes a run with a couple of steps, then drops back and throws downfield to the other wide receiver, who has had a lot of time to put on a move to get past the cornerback.

The Defense

In football, the offense gets the most of the glamour and the glory, but defense wins championships. Rarely will a high-scoring offense with a mediocre defense win a Super Bowl.

Defense is simple: Stop the other team and get the ball back.

Defensive coaches spend their time trying to anticipate what the offense is going to do, how to arrange their defense so it can't be blocked effectively, and how to load it one way or the other to stop the offense. The defensive playbook is just as big as that of the offense, but it is as much technique as it is tactics. Remember, defense is reaction to the offense's action, so it is hard to diagram plays, although today's defenses often try to attack the offense before it is able to get going.

Defense needs coordination between individuals on the team. For example, there must be coordination between the middle linebacker and the two defensive tackles, just as there has to be coordination between the outside linebackers and the defensive ends, and the end, outside linebacker, and cornerback on either side.

There are only two or three elements in a defensive call:

1. The front, which indicates a specific arrangement of linemen and linebackers and everyone's responsibility against the run;
2. The pass coverage, the style of defense to be played by the linebackers and deep backs;
3. The kind of blitz, if there is one.

After the snap of the ball, each defensive player reacts to a particular offensive player, his key. A linebacker's key usually would be the fullback. Because the fullback is a likely blocker for the halfback, and because offenses run to the strongside more often than not, simple logic tells you that keying the fullback in that situation probably will lead the linebacker to the ball.

Defensive linemen key the man across from them. On any given play, the offensive linemen will do one of the following: drive toward the defensive lineman, pull left, pull right, back up in pass protection, or try to slip inside the defensive lineman. Whatever the offensive linemen do tells the defensive linemen the type of play being run and where the offensive players will go.

On pass plays, defensive linemen want to avoid blockers so they can rush the passer. If defensive linemen do that on running plays, they might take themselves out of position to make a tackle or funnel the ball carrier toward a teammate. Defenses are also set up differently on runs than on passes. Defensive linemen might make their initial charge at an angle that makes them difficult to pass block but easy to block for a run. So, sometimes doing the right thing to stop a pass might be the wrong thing to do to stop a run.

The Evolution Of Defensive Formations

In the early days of football, teams used a nine-man line. Then came lines with eight, seven, six, five, four and, finally, just three players. Because three-man lines couldn't generate enough of a pass rush, teams finally evolved back into the four-man lines that dominate pro football today. The biggest changes in the secondary occurred because of so many multiple-receiver formations on offense; defenses now play five, six, or seven defensive backs at a time with linebackers coming out of the game, not linemen.

5-3 Defense—To reduce that number of players on the defensive line to five, which put more players back into pass protection, was a bold move. It probably was first used in the NFL by the New York Giants in 1934, and it became the standard pro defense for a decade.

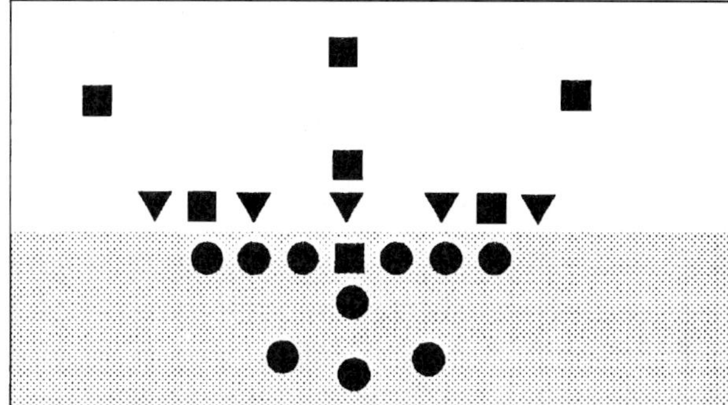

Figure 31. *5-3 Defense*

Oklahoma Defense—The legendary Bud Wilkinson created this defense at the University of Oklahoma in the late 1940s. It soon became the dominant defense in college football and strongly influenced pro defenses; however, it was mostly scoffed at until the Miami Dolphins adopted it in 1972, went undefeated, and won the Super Bowl. The 3-4 defense dominated the NFL in the late 1970s and most of the 1980s.

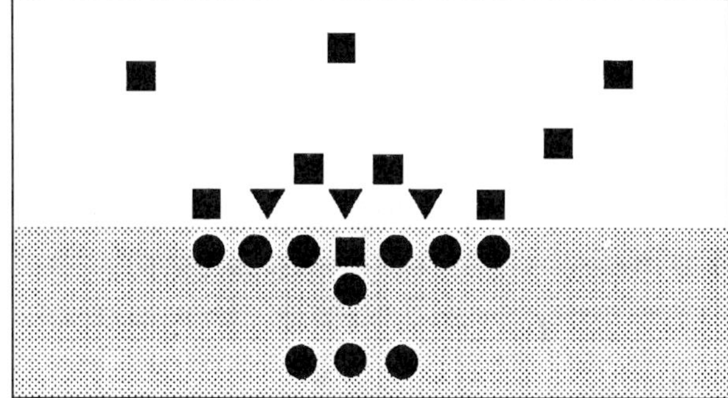

Figure 32. *Oklahoma Defense*

Eagle Defense—The Eagle defense was devised by Philadelphia coach Earle (Greasy) Neale in the 1940s to stop the T-formation. He set the defense in a 5-2-4 alignment, putting the linebackers a step or two off the line of scrimmage. The outside linebackers didn't have to cover deep passes, but they did delay receivers and covered short passes. This was the first use of a four-player secondary. Although the Eagles won NFL championships in 1948 and 1949, the defense was weak in the middle because there was no middle linebacker. In 1950, Cleveland's Paul Brown beat the Eagles by splitting his ends wide and either throwing sideline passes to them or running his big fullback, Marion Motley, up the middle on the draw play, an innovation at the time.

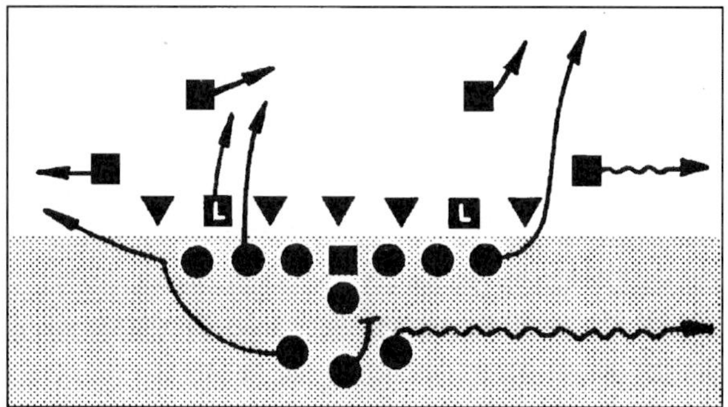

Figure 33. *Eagle Defense*

Umbrella Defense—To stop fast receivers from coming out of the backfield, New York coach Steve Owen and his defensive captain Tom Landry devised the Umbrella defense in 1950, with the defensive backs arranged in an umbrella-like shape and the defensive ends either rushing or dropping off the line to cover passes in the manner of later outside linebackers.

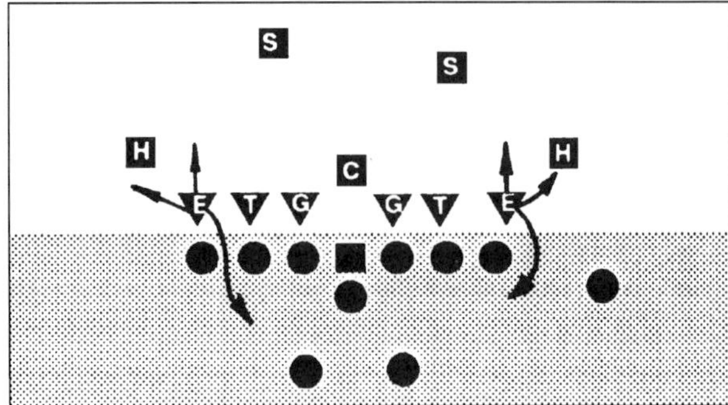

Figure 34. *Umbrella Defense*

4-3 Defense—Outside linebackers grew out of the Umbrella defense, and eventually the middle guard dropped off the line of scrimmage to become a middle linebacker. One of the outside linebackers usually plays on the line of scrimmage across from the tight end in the 4-3. It is a balanced defense that can meet most of the challenges of the offense, and it allows defenses to put maximum pressure on the quarterback.

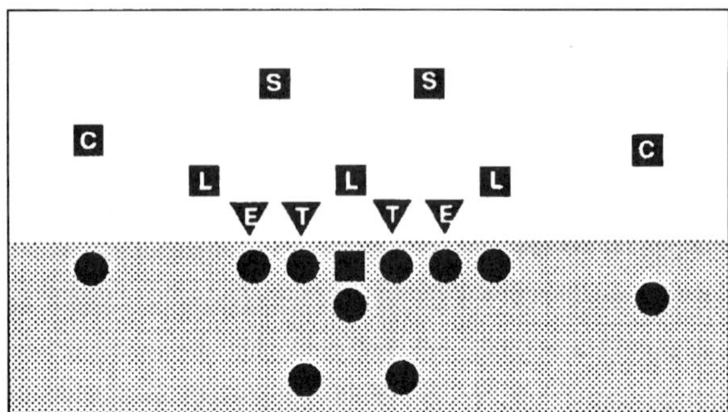

Figure 35. *4-3 Defense*

Stunt 4-3 Defense—Pittsburgh would put defensive tackle Joe Greene at a 45-degree angle in the gap between a guard and center and put middle linebacker Jack Lambert behind Greene. This tactic helped the Steelers win four Super Bowls in the 1970s.

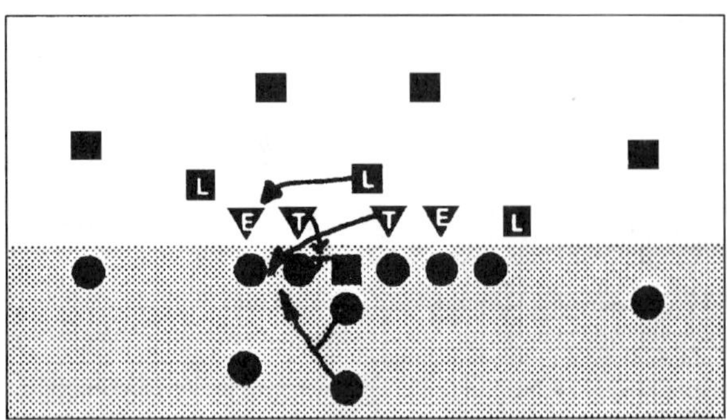

Figure 36. *Stunt 4-3 Defense*

3-4 Defense—The 3-4 defense can be traced back to the University of Oklahoma, but it is also an offspring of the 5-2 Eagle defense of the 1940s and 1950s, except that the ends have become stand-up linebackers so they can cover passes. In the 3-4, three linemen rush the passer, and a linebacker is kept in reserve as a potential designated blitzer. A fourth linebacker gives more flexibility near the line of scrimmage, providing greater potential for both stopping the run and better pass coverage. However, the 3-4 generally puts less pressure on the quarterback.

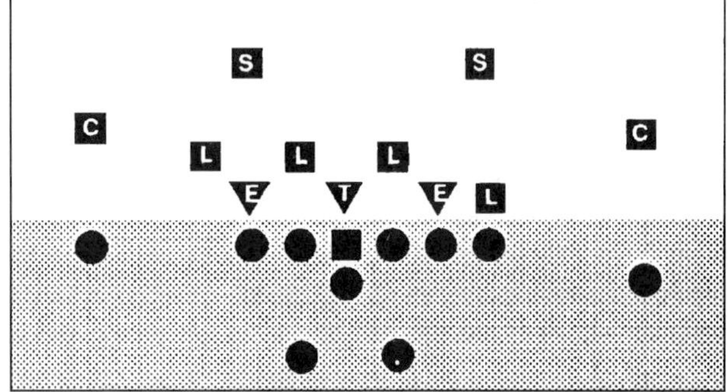

Figure 37. *3-4 Defense*

Over and Under Defenses—Defenses often try to put more defensive linemen near the expected point of attack. So, in an over defense, all four members of the defensive front shift one position over toward the strongside of the offensive formation. An undershift is exactly the opposite because the defensive line shifts away from the strongside. There are other variations in which only some of the linemen shift positions.

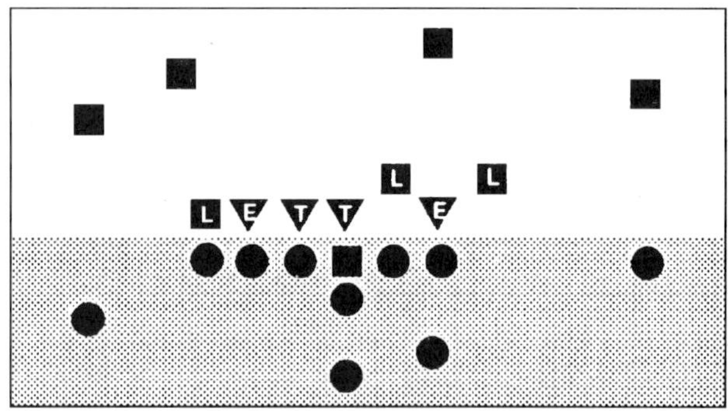

Figure 38. *4-3 Over Defense*

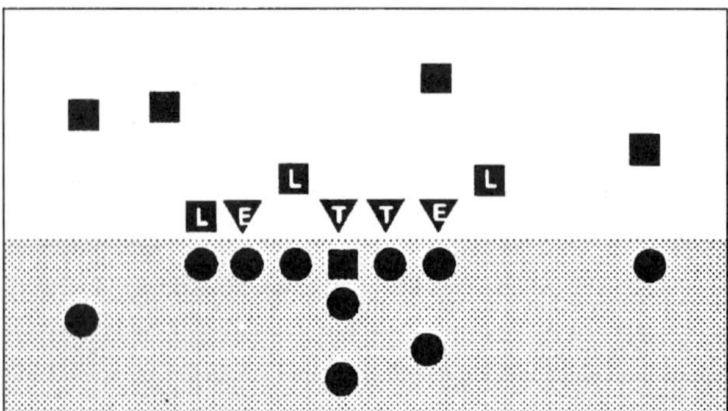

Figure 39. *4-3 Under Defense*

Flex Defense—The Flex defense was pioneered by Tom Landry's Dallas Cowboys and rarely was used by any other team. The Flex set two linemen off the line of scrimmage two or three yards and was geared toward stopping runs. The two offset linemen would read the combinations of blocks, while the other linemen attacked and clogged up the blocking patterns.

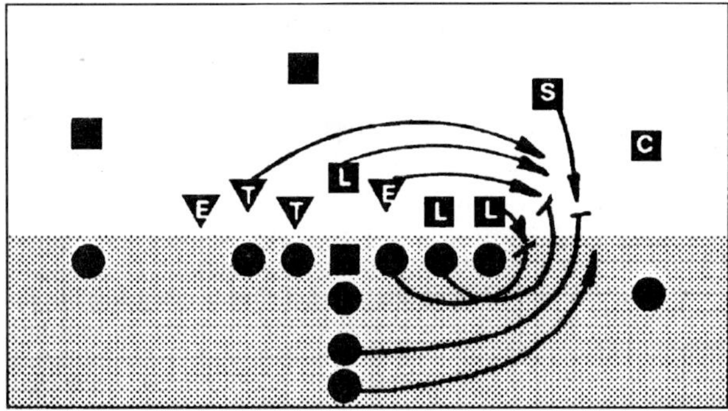

Figure 40. *Flex Defense*

Taking the Offensive

Modern defenses often try to force offenses to react before they have a chance to act. There are a lot of things defenses can do to force the action, and one favorite tactic is the blitz.

The Blitz—The blitz was first seen in the 1950s, when teams were passing so much the defense had to come up with an innovation to rush the passer. Thus, the blitz (originally called "red dog") was born.

In a blitz, defenders generally play man-for-man coverage. The defensive goal is to spring someone free for a sack or get one-on-one blocking for all the rushers. The blitzer doesn't have to reach the quarterback for the blitz to work. The idea is to disrupt the timing of the offense and confuse its blocking. The blitz can be effective against both the run and pass, and even the threat of a blitz can be as effective as the real thing. A defense can fake a blitz, then drop back at the hike of the ball.

There are two ways for offenses to beat a blitz: block all the blitzers or throw the ball before defenders can reach the quarterback. Teams usually try to do the latter.

Outside Linebacker Blitz—Disaster often occurs when a team assigns its remaining back to block one of the top weak outside linebackers. Getting to the quarterback on this play means the outside linebacker has to get by only the fullback. The Giants' Lawrence Taylor was a master at this play.

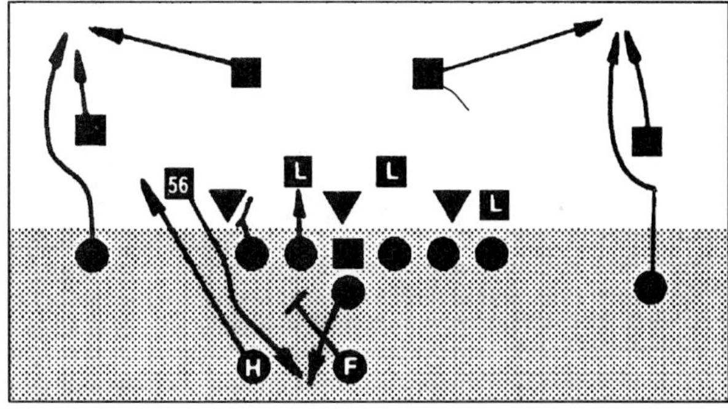

Figure 41. *Outside Linebacker Blitz*

Middle Linebacker Blitz—In a blitz by the middle linebacker, the blitz usually is in coordination with one of the defensive tackles. For example, the middle linebacker can blitz to the strongside with the defensive tackle taking the inside, or he can blitz to the weakside with the weakside defensive tackle taking the inside. He can also blitz right up the middle with both defensive tackles taking the outside.

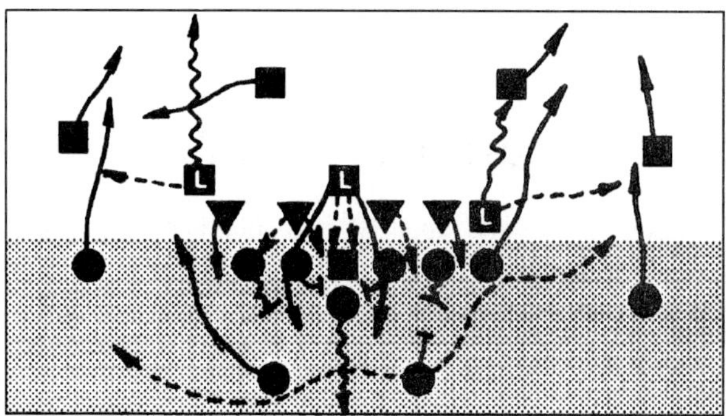

Figure 42. *Middle Linebacker Blitz*

Safety Blitz—The free safety blitzes more often than does the strong safety. In this diagram, even if the offense keeps a back in to pick up the rush, the pressure is severe because a blitz by the safety is usually not anticipated.

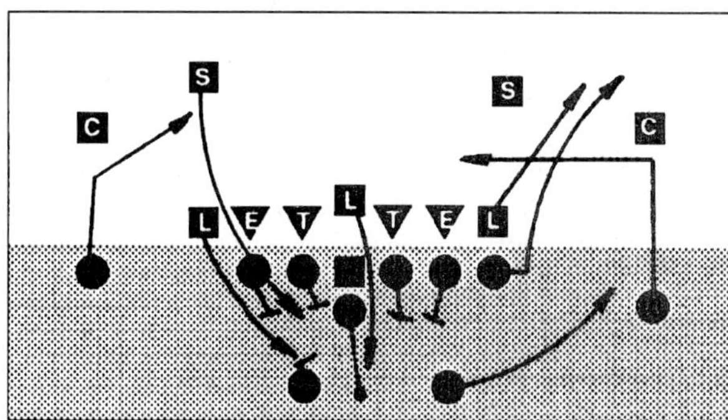

Figure 43. *Safety Blitz*

Zone Blitz — The zone blitz was popularized in the mid- and late-1990s by teams such as Pittsburgh, Cincinnati, and Carolina. The zone blitz, at its most basic level, involves a 3-4 defense rushing players the quarterback is not expecting (usually cornerbacks and safeties) and dropping back a couple of players he is expecting to rush (usually linemen).

On a typical zone blitz, two defensive linemen will start upfield toward the quarterback. The offensive linemen will brace to stop them, and then the defensive linemen will stop and backpedal into short zones, leaving two offensive linemen with nobody to block, while the offense is under siege at another point. However, the latest defensive stratagem may be past its prime already: As familiarity with it has grown, its potency has been reduced.

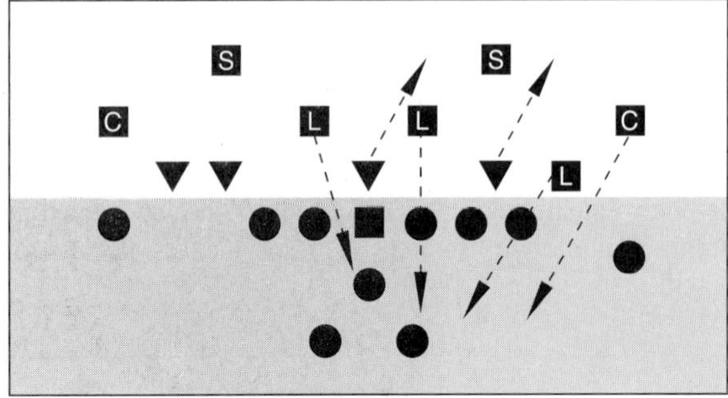

Defensive Games

Stunts, stacks and slants are effective tactics in which defensive linemen use unexpected moves to get past blockers to the runner or quarterback. During a game, defensive linemen constantly move around, setting up in different positions. They're trying to expose and take advantage of weaknesses found in the offense.

Stunts—Stunts change the responsibility of two or more players. Stunts confuse blocking assignments, exert pressure at the point of attack, and break up the offense's timing. The simplest stunt is a change stunt, in which defensive tackle and a linebacker change positions. The hope is that blockers will lose track of one of them, or run into each other trying to follow them (like setting a pick in basketball). There are end-tackle stunts, in which the end pinches in and tries to contain two men and the tackle loops around him; tackle-end stunts, which are the reverse; tackle-tackle stunts; and deep loops, in which a player might swoop in from two positions away. There are also all kinds of stunts with the linebackers. Offenses have solved the problem of stunting somewhat by zone blocking—blocking any defender who comes into a given area.

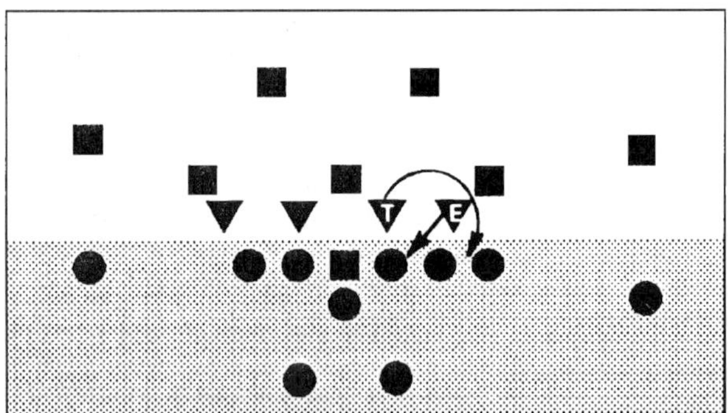

Figure 44. *Stunt*

Stacks—Stacking is lining up one or more of the linebackers directly behind the linemen, essentially hiding them, to keep offensive linemen away from them. Kansas City beat Minnesota in Super Bowl IV using this tactic, as did Baltimore when it beat Dallas the next year.

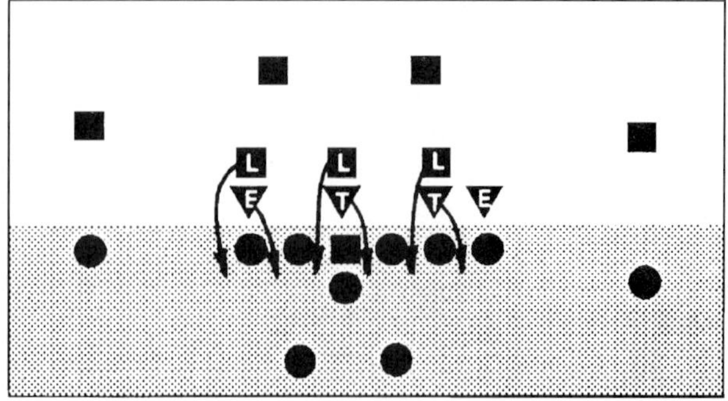

Figure 45. *Stack*

Slants—A slant is a charge by a defensive lineman to the left or right instead of straight ahead.

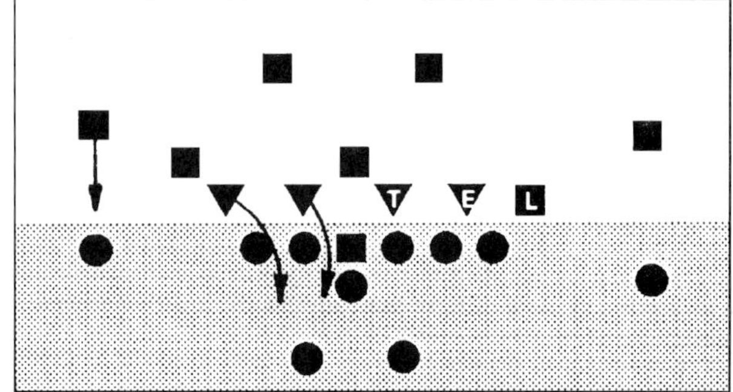

Figure 46. *Slant*

Force—There are certain areas of the field that a defense must protect. One of these is the outside on a running play. A cornerback or safety must not let a ball carrier get outside him because he might be the last defender between the runner and the goal line. The defender has to force the runner back toward the middle of the field and contain the play. Determining which defensive player is the force man depends on the split of the wide receiver. The strong safety usually calls out who will force and who will stay back in pass coverage. (Linebackers also occasionally force.)

Cornerback Force—If the wide receiver is set in close, less than 10 yards wide, the cornerback usually has force responsibilities.

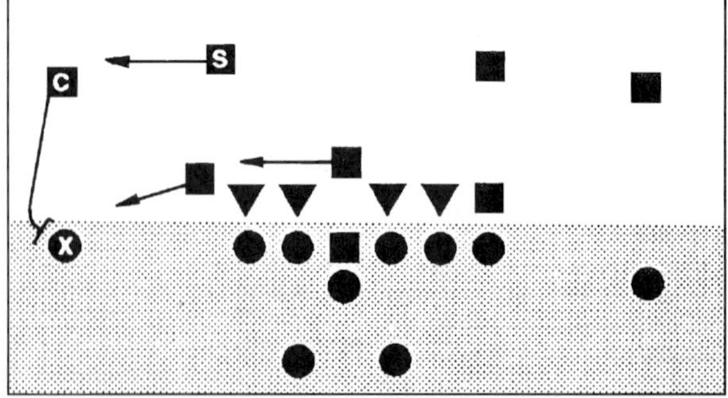

Figure 47. *Cornerback Force*

Safety Force—The safety becomes the force man when the wide receiver is split outside more than 10 yards.

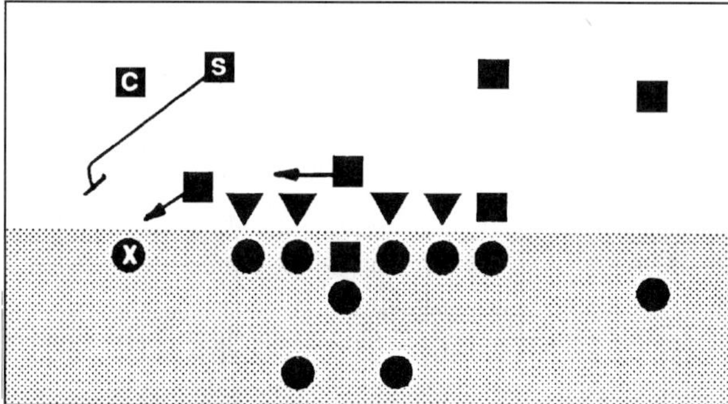

Figure 48. *Safety Force*

Pass Defense

There are two main pass coverages: man-for-man and zone.

Man-for-Man Coverage—This is the simplest defense. Linebackers and defensive backs cover the running back or receiver to whom they have been assigned. They hook up with the receiver as he leaves the line of scrimmage and stay with him until the play is over. In man-for-man, cornerbacks cover the wide receivers and the strong safety usually covers the tight end. The free safety either helps out or covers the halfback, and the linebackers key the fullback.

The weaknesses of man-for-man coverage are that it puts a great deal of pressure on the cornerbacks and the strong safety, and it is vulnerable to post routes (bombs down the middle) because there is little help on the inside.

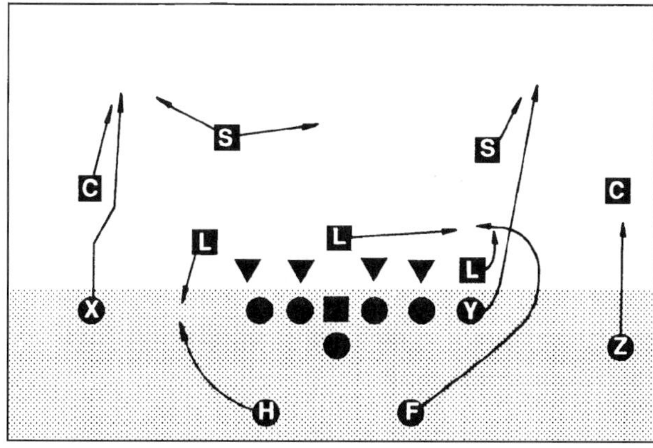

Figure 49. *Man-to-Man Coverage*

Zone Coverage—Zone defenses started to be used a lot in the late 1960s, although they date back to the 1940s and 1950s. Zone defense is simply covering an area of the field, rather than a specific receiver, and it works best in stopping long passes. Zone defense reverses the saying that, "Offense acts and defense reacts." Rather than following the receiver's initiative, as in man-for-man coverage, the defensive backs in a zone cover certain parts of the field and can dictate where the offense runs its routes.

The basic theory is to get every area, or zone, covered, and to create movement so that the quarterback and receivers are working against a constantly shifting scene. Zone defenses are further broken down into strongside and weakside rotations, double zones and half-zones.

Here's how a zone works: At the snap, the strongside cornerback steps forward into the teeth of the strongside, or "rolls up," where the fullback, the flanker, and the tight end might be running their patterns. As he's rotating up, everybody else is "taking drops," moving back to the deepest and widest boundaries of their zones. Then they wait for the play to unfold. As the receivers begin to enter the zones, the defenders start to move together, tightening the amount of open territory.

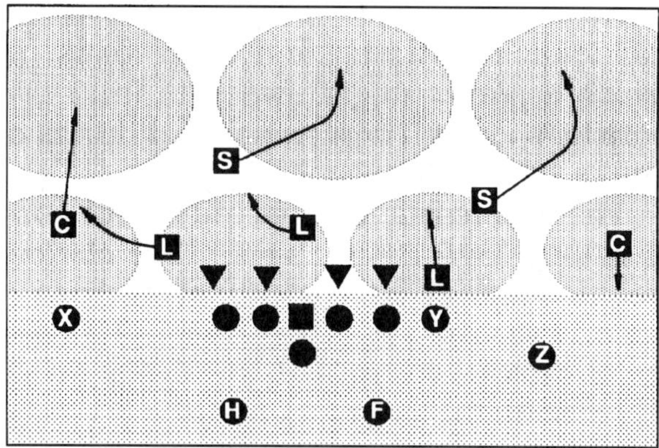

Figure 50. *Zone Defense*

The main weakness of zone defenses is that a short passing game can pick them apart because the quarterback is throwing underneath the linebackers (especially over the middle) and to the sides (the "seams"). There are open seams between the zones, and a good passer can hit a receiver in these cracks. That's why a team with a strong pass rush uses the zone the most, because they can keep the passer under pressure so he doesn't have time to "read" the coverage and figure out where the openings are.

Zone defenses can be stretched horizontally (deep) with a fast receiver, or vertically with patterns to the sidelines or in the flats to running backs (which is one reason why running backs catch so many passes today). Offenses can also "flood" a zone with two or more receivers. Zone defenses also leave gaping holes for running plays.

Zone defenses sometimes are combined with other coverages. In a half-zone, one side of the secondary plays man while the other side plays zone, or a combination of man coverage shallow and zone coverage deep. In some instances, defenders read predesigned keys, and switch from zone to man, or vice versa. There could also be zone coverage on the strongside and man on the weakside, or zone coverage outside and man coverage inside.

There are seven zones in a 4-3 defense and eight zones in 3-4 defense. The weakness of a combination defense, which involves double coverage, is that in order to cover one man with two, defenses leave themselves open for flares by the fullback, screens to the halfback, and post patterns by the wide receiver on the strongside.

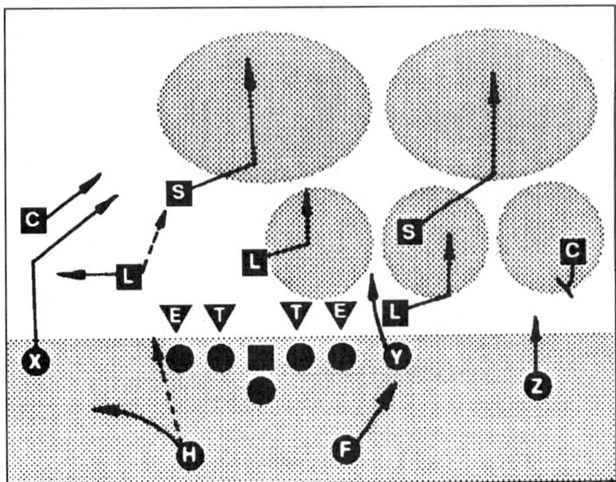

Figure 51. *Combination Zone*

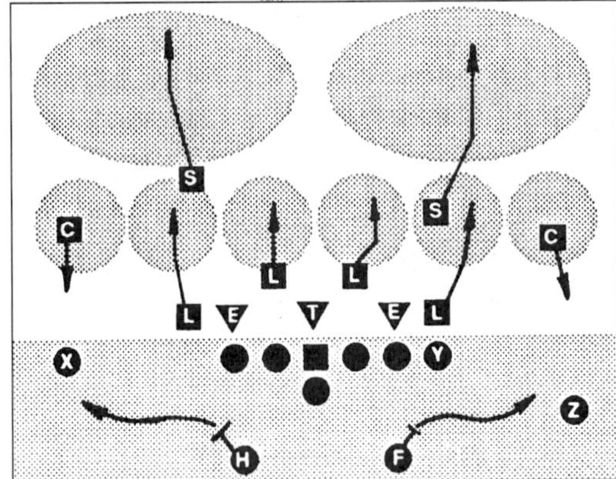

Figure 52. *3-4 Zone*

Multiple Defensive Backs—A fifth defensive back usually is used in situations when the offense is likely to pass. The fifth defensive back, called the Nickel back, can be placed anywhere in the secondary. He usually covers the third wide receiver, usually the slot man, man-for-man with deep help from a safety. At other times, the Nickel back will drop back and play centerfield like a free safety.

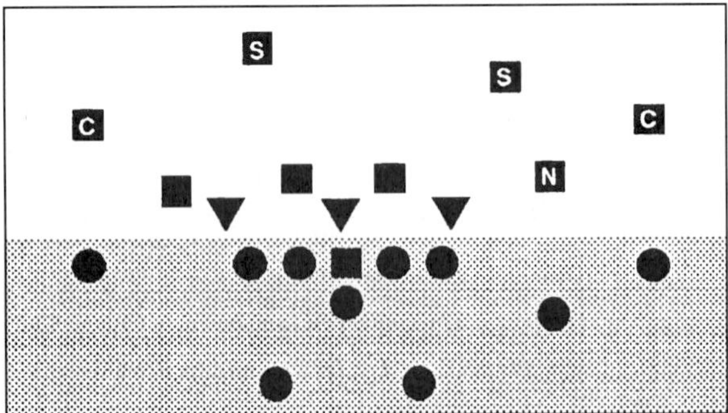

Figure 53. *Nickel Defense*

The Dime defensive back, a sixth defensive back replacing another linebacker, is used when the defense is certain the offense will pass. A seventh defensive back, usually called the quarter or seven penny, is used quite often these days. A few teams have, on occasion, used as few as two down linemen and as many as nine backs. The biggest weakness of having seven defensive backs is that such a defense is very easy to run against.

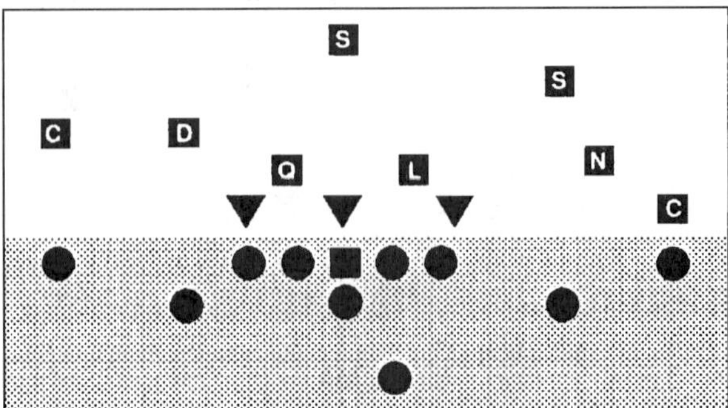

Figure 54. *Quarter Defense*

In a variation better known as a "prevent defense," generally employed to protect a lead late in the game, the defense might rush as few as three people and drop eight defenders into pass coverage. The defense usually will line up in a four-deep zone, with the corners covering the sideline routes and the linebackers, who usually are defensive backs who have moved inside, worrying about screens, draws, and quarterback scrambles. The theory is to allow short passes and tackle receivers before they can get out of bounds to stop the clock. Teams with a big enough lead can afford the luxury of giving up yards in exchange for time. The prevent can backfire, however, if there is too much time or too small of a lead.

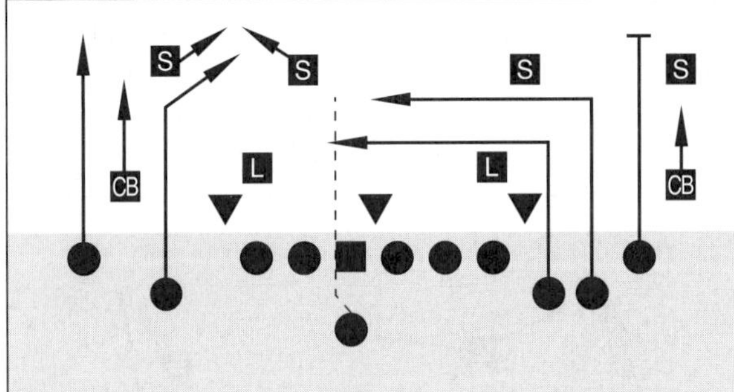

Special Teams

Special teams get the least attention from coaches and fans, but one out of every seven plays involves the special teams, and nearly a third of all points are scored by special teams. Special-teams players work from diagrams in playbooks just as the offensive and defensive players do and are involved in plays with more total yards gained per game than is compiled by both offenses.

At least one of three things takes place on all kicks: 1) a large amount of yardage is involved, usually 40 yards or more; 2) there is a change of possession; and 3) there's a specific attempt to score points.

Kickoffs—Members of this special team have one responsibility: Contain the ball and the man carrying it. Everyone is assigned a lane of coverage. The players race downfield careful to keep their lane of attack covered; otherwise, a weak spot can be created. Along the two outside lanes are the two force men, whose job is to turn the ball carrier back in to the center of the field where he can be tackled by the other players. Coaches demand gang tackling to increase the chances of a fumble and recovery.

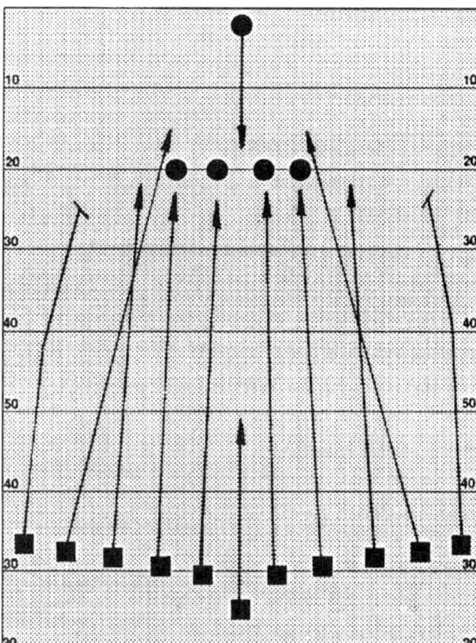

Figure 55. *Kickoff*

Kickoff Return—There are three separate groups of players on a kickoff-return team. The first wave is five blockers, the second is the four-man wedge, and the third is the two returners. There also are three types of kickoff returns: middle, left, and right. At the time of the kickoff, the wedge of blockers begins its retreat, falling back to escort the returner. The wedge blocker must be ready to meet the onslaught of rushing tacklers. The returner follows the wedge until he sees an opening; then he is on his own.

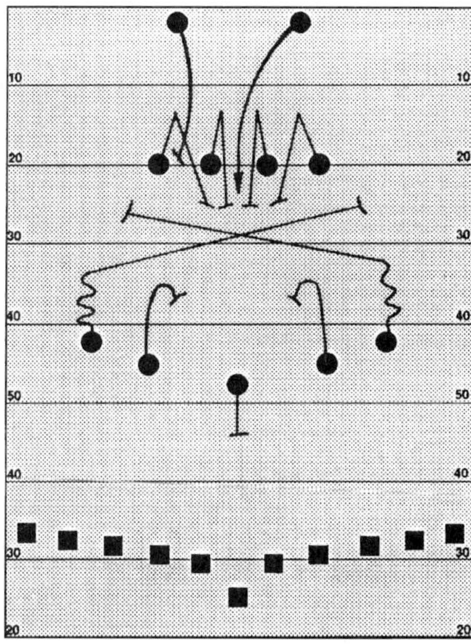

Figure 56. *Kickoff Return*

Punting—Punting teams want to drive their opponents in the other direction as far as possible. Ideally, the snap should take eight-tenths of a second and the punter should get the ball off in another 1.2 seconds. Any punt that takes longer than two seconds is in risk of being blocked. A punter should have at least four seconds of hang time (the length of time a punt is in the air). Punters don't want to outkick their coverage, so a punter who gets a lot of hang time is valuable. The goal of the punt-coverage team is to stop the return man as quickly as possible after he has caught the ball.

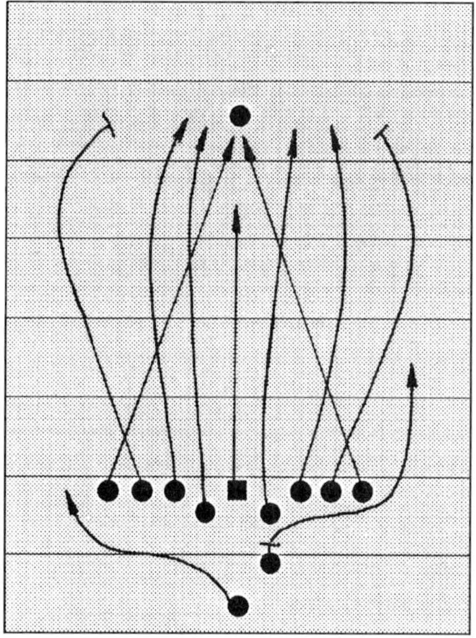

Figure 57. *Punt*

Punt Return—Punt returns are supposed to go to either the left or the right. Punt returners are seldom able to run up the middle because the hang time allows the kicking team to get downfield. Blockers then set up a wall to either side of the field for the runner to run behind. If the return team wants to try to block the punt, it usually masses a large number of players against one part of the offensive line in an all-out effort to get to the punter. Punt blockers are instructed to aim for a point 2 yards in front of the expected impact of the punter's foot and the football, so they do not rough the punter and get penalized.

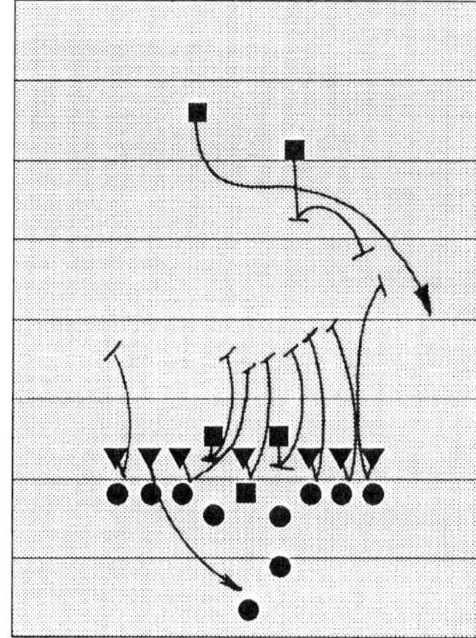

Figure 58. *Punt Return*

Field-Goal and Extra-Point Attempts—Both field goals and extra points are kicked in the same basic manner. The holder and kicker work together to make sure they get the kick off in 1.3 seconds. Taking any longer risks a blocked kick.

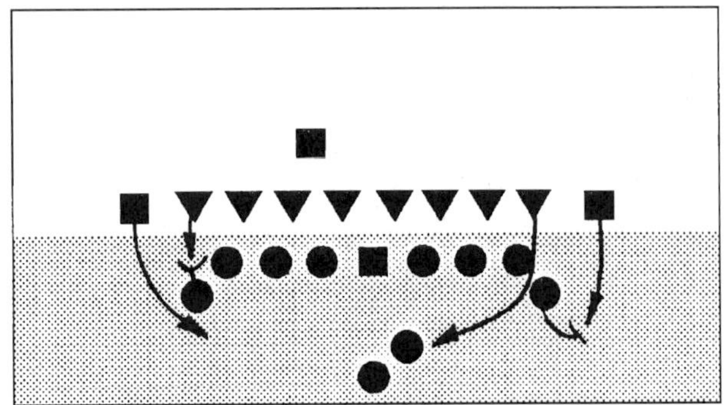

Figure 59. *Field Goal Attempt*

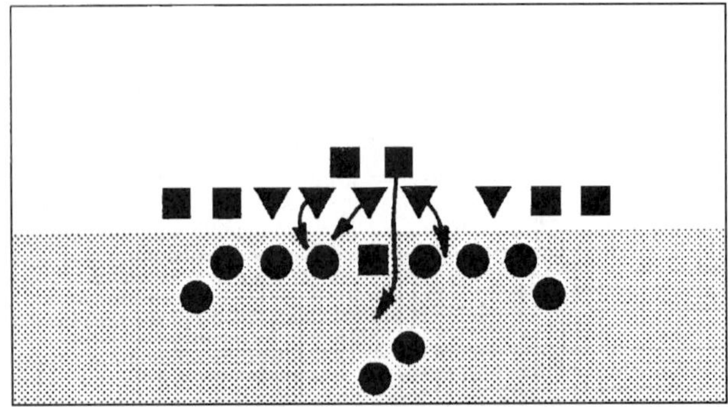

Figure 60. *Field Goal Block*

Blocking Kicks—Blocking a field goal can turn around a game because it reverses the momentum. Tall linemen fill the middle and either try to break through the offensive line to block the kick or leap high in the air to bat down a low kick. The players on the outside have a direct angle to blocking the kick—if they get there in time.

That's an overview of the basic NFL playbook. Almost every coach uses the same plays, and the talent level in football is fairly even. It's the execution of the plays that nearly always spells the difference between losing and winning.

CHAPTER 19

The West Coast Offense

Ted Brock

The West Coast offense, the darling of offensive coordinators around the National Football League, got its start not in San Francisco but across the Bay. Its seeds—which were planted in Oakland, sprouted in Cincinnati, and flourished in San Francisco—actually originated with a washed-up defensive coordinator, influenced by three Pro Football Hall of Fame members.

Bill Walsh, the father of the West Coast offense, spent the early part of his coaching career devising ways to stop teams—and failing at it. But he stuck with coaching, finding his niche on offense in the mid-1960s and eventually transforming pro football, just as Walsh's college coach had predicted.

"Bill Walsh is destined to be among the best teachers and coaches San Jose State has ever graduated," Bob Bronzan wrote in a 1956 recommendation letter. "His ability and knowledge and interest leave nothing to be desired."

More than four decades later, Walsh has coached and taught his way into the Pro Football Hall of Fame. He tutored several great quarterbacks (including Steve Young and Joe Montana, the two top-rated passers in NFL history) and changed the way an entire league moves the ball.

Walsh's introduction to football gave no indication of his future brilliance. As a player, Walsh showed promise as a coach; in other words, he wasn't much. The former high school sprinter had been robbed of his speed by a torn quadriceps. He played two seasons at running back for San Mateo Junior College, then two at end for Bronzan at San Jose State.

After a stint in the Army, he earned his master's degree from San Jose State. (His master's thesis: "How to Stop the Pro Spread Offense.") Walsh first coached at the high school level, then joined Marv Levy's staff at California in 1960, though more as a recruiter than a defensive coordinator. He spent three seasons there, then moved to Stanford, also as a defensive coach and recruiter.

So far, he had not enjoyed much success stopping offenses, pro spread or otherwise. That point became moot in 1966, when Walsh joined the Raiders' staff as an offensive assistant. Walsh quickly became indoctrinated in Oakland's passing attack, which was based on the theories of a pair of Hall of Fame members: Chargers coach Sid Gillman, who had revolutionized the passing game in the 1950s and 1960s, and the Raiders' Al Davis, who had been Gillman's assistant for three seasons and had installed a similar system in Oakland.

Walsh credits Davis as the biggest influence on his development. "The Raiders had everybody catching the ball," Walsh said, describing an element that would become a trademark of his teams.

The expansion Cincinnati Bengals began play in 1968, with Walsh serving as quarterbacks and receivers coach. Working with passers gave him an opportunity to test another theory, about molding a quarterback through extensive training and film work. Walsh helped make Greg Cook a rookie wonder in 1969, and when Cook suffered a career-ending injury, Walsh helped turn career backup Virgil Carter into the league's most accurate passer in 1971.

A License to Drive an Offense

Those success stories had helped Walsh gain the confidence of Cincinnati's head coach, the legendary Paul Brown. So much so that in 1971, the Bengals drafted a player solely on Walsh's recommendation—quarterback Ken Anderson of tiny Augustana College in Illinois.

Only Walsh had scouted Anderson, and the only film he could find was so washed out that the Bengals' brass could not see anything. But the Bengals trusted Walsh's instincts and drafted Anderson in the third round.

Anderson did not appear to be a classic pro quarterback. He had a decent arm and size (6 feet 2 inches, 212 pounds), but he had been a sprint-out passer in college. That began to change almost immediately. The Bengals drafted Anderson in late January; by February he and Walsh were working together almost every day, starting from scratch. Walsh taught Anderson how to drop back, set up, and cradle the ball.

Anderson became the Bengals' starter in 1972 and the NFL's leading passer in 1974 and 1975. By the end of their five-year run together, Anderson had become so technically proficient that Walsh had taken to videotaping their training sessions. "Everything Kenny did was perfect, the way I see it," Walsh explained later.

"Bill always utilizes his quarterback's strong points, going with whatever it is each one can do best," Anderson said before Super Bowl XVI in January, 1982. "The things he did with Cook and Carter and me were very different because we were different. But he always emphasizes not throwing interceptions."

Out of this emerged a high-percentage, low-risk passing attack that could control the ball like the running game.

("Nickel and diming, they called it," Walsh said. "The pass just wasn't used that way.") The Bengals' pass catchers—receivers, running backs, and tight ends—turned the field into a horizontal playground. They would cross underneath an opponent's defensive backs and flood zones, giving linebackers fits. Fullbacks would take short passes and rumble forward. Wide receivers had thc liberty to read and react to the defensive alignment, and the quarterbacks were taught to choose receivers according to a set progression, going down the line until they found an open man.

For example, Anderson would drop back to pass and look first to the primary receiver; if he was not open, then Anderson would look to the number-two receiver, and so on. The precision timing meant that each receiver would be finishing his route just as Anderson would be looking to him.

"What he does is make you aware of all the receivers on all plays, so you know who has to be open," Anderson said of Walsh.

Walsh's teams honed their timing in practice. One of their drills involved mastering every play against every possible defense. Soon this evolved into variations on the play, and then new plays. Sometimes Walsh would think of a play on Saturday and put it in Sunday. "Credit Paul Brown for giving me the latitude to explore," Walsh said later.

Eventually the playbook became encyclopedic, so Walsh took to scripting the first 20-25 plays of a game. The team practiced the script during the week, and by Sunday, they had the timing down perfectly.

The West Coast offense had been born—on the banks of the Ohio River.

The West Coast Offense Goes West

The Bengals passed over Walsh to select former 49ers center Bill Johnson as Brown's successor in 1976. That prompted Walsh to return to California as an assistant on Tommy Prothro's staff in San Diego. He brought to the Chargers his ideas and his playbook—along with film of his workouts with Anderson.

All would prove invaluable to Dan Fouts. In his first three seasons, the Chargers' quarterback had thrown 36 interceptions and only 16 touchdowns. Watching those sessions on film and working with Walsh—even for just one season—helped put Fouts on the road to the Hall of Fame.

Walsh became the head coach at Stanford in 1977 and continued in his role as the quarterback's best friend. Cardinal passers led the NCAA in each of Walsh's seasons at Stanford (Guy Benjamin in 1977 and Steve Dils in 1978) while the school posted a 17-7 mark and won a bowl game each season.

In between those two seasons, the Los Angeles Rams almost hired Walsh. Rams owner Carroll Rosenbloom dithered, however, and Walsh committed to Stanford for another year. But for Rosenbloom's hesitancy, the West Coast offense might have started 400 miles to the south and as a result, the NFL would have been a lot different in the 1980s.

The Ultimate West Coast Quarterback

In 1979, the San Francisco 49ers hired Walsh as their head coach. He chose Joe Montana, a spindly but mobile Notre Dame quarterback with an arm most pro scouts could take or leave, in the third round of that year's draft. Walsh used Montana sparingly as an understudy to Steve DeBerg, and coached a team that had gone 2-14 in 1978 to a 1979 record of 2-14. By 1981, Montana and a roster that Walsh had revamped according to his needs were on their way to Super Bowl XVI. The 49ers won that game and two more Super Bowls (XIX and XXIII) with Walsh calling the shots and Montana at the controls. Montana added a fourth Super Bowl (XXIV) under George Seifert.

In the decade and a half following the 49ers' turnaround, the Bill Walsh offense has spread its seed across the NFL landscape and become the West Coast Offense as other teams grabbed Walsh's assistants. Paul Hackett, the son of a scientist, had been a record-breaking passer for the University of California at Davis, under the tutelage of Jim Sochor. He served as Walsh's quarterbacks and receivers coach from 1983-85, arguably the height of the Walsh-Montana reign and the period of San Francisco's second NFL championship in Super Bowl XIX. Hackett had been an assistant at Cleveland, and later served as head coach at the University of Pittsburgh and offensive coordinator for the Kansas City Chiefs. In 1998, Hackett became head coach at the University of Southern California.

"All of us who grew up in passing games learned that the defense would tell us where to throw the ball," said Hackett, who was to Walsh in San Francisco what Walsh was to Paul Brown in Cincinnati. "Until I met Bill, I thought that way. Then I met him, and he said, 'Let's have the quarterback use a progression read: primary receiver, secondary, etc. We'll coach offense first and (worry about) defense second.' Bill would say to a quarterback, 'Just look at the receiver and throw to him if he's open.' It gives you less to think about as a quarterback. I thought that was absolutely marvelous.

"Bill and Paul Brown got more than they ever thought they would out of Virgil Carter and Kenny Anderson. Here, you're getting maximum performance out of guys who are not stars. In San Diego, Bill did the same thing with Dan Fouts. Steve DeBerg [Montana's predecessor] was awesome in Bill's system."

The quarterback had to work harder, but the hard work paid off. The more he knew about a defense, the more he knew about what his progression of reads would be. It helped make average quarterbacks good and make good quarterbacks great. As Hackett said, "He is doing a great job all these years, and all of a sudden he gets a talented guy [Montana] who takes the 49ers to a world championship—plus Dwight Clark and Freddie Solomon, and Earl Cooper."

Not that Clark, Solomon, and Cooper, or even Dan Audick, the quintessential West Coast offense tackle, were ordinary athletes. They fit the Walsh system.

"I need intelligent people, people without hang-ups that make it difficult to communicate," Walsh said. "I don't mean players must have genius IQs. But they need quick, resourceful minds."

Everyone on the 49ers' 1981 squad had a role to play and had the intelligence to adapt to Walsh's specifications. Walsh's insistence on high-percentage, low-risk passes, thrown out of a number of formations, was the key to controlling the football. Like game pieces, defenders went where Walsh wanted them to go, lost in a whirl of crossing receivers and obstructed sight lines. He liked to boast that he timed his pass patterns to a tenth of a second.

The way Montana dropped, set up, and threw to a receiver who understood the width and depth of his pattern might have looked relaxed, but only because 49ers practice sessions were crisp, tidy affairs devoted mostly to the demands of a special geometry. The 49ers' wide receivers often lined up closer to the ball than most and got off the line of scrimmage quicker than most.

The Perfect Go-To Receiver

Then in 1985, two Super Bowl champions into the revolution, came The Man. "The West Coast offense exploded with one person: number eighty," Hackett says. "When Jerry Rice arrived the West Coast offense became also a vertical game, which kept it alive.

"We [the 49ers teams of the early 1980s] didn't have speed and the vertical element, so we relied on Montana's mobility," Hackett says. "When Jerry got there, on every third and fourth play they're throwing post-and-go [a deep pattern with a 45-degree cut], and all of a sudden that becomes the featured element of the offense. Now we combine the greatest quarterback in the history of football with the greatest receiver in history."

And still, there had to be break-in time. In Rice's rookie year with the 49ers, most of the exploding was going on inside Rice's head. "I came into the league wanting to be an impact player from the start, but it didn't work out," Rice said. "I was totally confused. They handed me this big playbook that was very complex. I had to learn to pick up so much in different situations. The thing I forgot was to catch the football."

Rice was dropping the ball with regularity—at one point, 11 times in 11 games—yet Walsh kept him on the field more often than the veteran Freddie Solomon. Late in the season, Rice's Hall of Fame career took off with a 10-catch, 241-yard day against the Los Angeles Rams.

Rice may have transformed the Bill Walsh offense, but a constant thread since Walsh's arrival in 1979 had been line play, as taught by assistant Bobb McKittrick. McKittrick, who worked with Walsh in San Diego, remembers Walsh's infatuation with the passing game. Walsh liked the fact that the Chargers' running game was built around the Wing-T, with split backs, rather than the power-oriented I-formation which was just then coming into vogue.

"I played Single-Wing football," McKittrick said of his days as a player under Tommy Prothro at Oregon State. "We had so few plays, you could count them on one hand. It was fundamental. You double-teamed, trapped, did a lot of things where you had angle advantages.

"Coach Walsh's offense became a blend of my fundamental technique—bend the knees, get low, that kind of thing—and his technique with the quarterback," McKittrick said. "Coach Prothro would have said, 'Jeez, we can't have that many plays,' and when I first saw it I said the same thing. It was like going from basic math to algebra. But then I thought, if you can put a man on the moon, develop fiber optics, and make computer chips, you can learn more plays in football. Our offense became more complex and larger than anybody else's."

It All Starts at the Line

Hackett credits McKittrick for bringing Walsh's approach to the line—with great success. "Bobb has always taken care of all the little nuances of pass protection. In the offensive line, there were so many progressions, the offensive line could do all sorts of things in progression, then let the defense react.

"You have to have good tackles," Hackett says. "The best example of this was when the zone blitz arrived, and the West Coast offense was able to find a way to solve all the zone blitz issues. The coaches and the linemen in the West Coast Offense were able to pick and choose the kind of protection they would execute. The zone blitz is very similar to the 46 defense Buddy Ryan used with the Chicago Bears. Part of the Bobb McKittrick legacy is the multiple approach to protecting the quarterback against that kind of an attack."

Before McKittrick, Walsh, or the rest of the NFL ever dreamed of Ryan's 46 defense of the mid-1980s or the zone blitz of the 1990s, there was the business of rounding out an offensive line in the early 1980s. The 49ers had Randy Cross at right guard, John Ayers at left guard, Fred Quillan at center, and Keith Fahnhorst at right tackle, but they weren't done yet.

"When I was with the Chargers," McKittrick recalls, "we brought Dan Audick in from St. Louis, where he'd played for Don Coryell. I'd known him since the '78 season. He was very athletic and intelligent, a classic overachiever who got the job done. I look for things other people don't look for. Size is not a big thing to me. You have to have some size, sure, but intelligence and the ability to move are the key things."

At 6 feet 3 inches, 252 pounds, Audick was hardly a behemoth by NFL standards, but he became the final piece in the 49ers' Super Bowl mosaic. Five athletic players across the line meant crisper trap blocking, and well-timed counters. With speed at the guards to lead the sweeps and keep Montana protected well into his third or fourth read, and with the tackles protecting the perimeter in Montana's variety of three- and five-step drops, Walsh's gang had a winner. The next step was sustaining success.

Audick's stay was shortened when the 49ers drafted All-America tackle Bubba Paris from Michigan. Credit McKittrick with rounding the 300-pound Paris into the West Coast offense. The other four linemen "were together through the '86 season," McKittrick says. "In about 133 games, none of those four missed more than four starts. Bubba was a regular from '83 to '86. What a remarkable time to have so many good players in that offense."

McKittrick's extension on the field was Cross at right guard. Cross's command of the Walsh offense and background as a center both at UCLA and in his first three seasons in San Francisco made him indispensable, especially in 1987 (when Quillan was injured) and 1988 (when Quillan retired).

Through two decades of the West Coast offense and a myriad of players, McKittrick remains a constant in San Francisco. He stayed with the 49ers under Walsh's successor, George Seifert, and he remains part of Steve Mariucci's coaching staff.

Disciples On Both Coasts and In Between

While the most proficient practitioners of the West Coast offense have come from San Francisco, a new group of coaches has emerged, Mariucci included, who are the disciples of disciples of the West Coast offense. A list of those using the offense reads like a who's who of the most successful coaches in the NFL: Seattle, with new head coach, Mike Holmgren, a former 49ers offensive coordinator; Green Bay, with new head coach Ray Rhodes, who played and coached for Walsh in San Francisco and formerly served as Holmgren's defensive coordinator with the Packers; Minnesota, coached by Dennis Green, a former receivers coach under Walsh; and Denver, coached by Mike Shanahan, an offensive coordinator under Seifert.

There also are the teams who pick and choose elements of the system. Finally in 1998, the Raiders came on board, abandoning their vertical passing game and hiring 34-year-old Jon Gruden, a West Coast offense trainee under Seifert, Holmgren, and Rhodes, as head coach.

Hiring the coach and signing the skill position players are not enough, though.

"I always thought McKittrick was the missing link for all these other teams that want to run this offense," says Cross, now a television commentator. "People talk about the organization and the players, but if you look at the [49ers'] staff since 1979, he's the one who's been there throughout. You talk about those tackles being so important? The first three championships were won with three different left tackles [Audick, Paris, and Steve Wallace]. It's not like you have Art Shell in there for fifteen years.

"This offense is about using your head, actually using what you have and trying to get over your ego. In the NFL there's so much of the . . . 'I'm going to get you and let's go downtown' attitude. In the West Coast offense, there's a high premium on patience, not just on the quarterback but on everybody."

Cross notes that the much of the yardage in "The Drive," which led to "The Catch" by Dwight Clark in the 1981 NFC Championship Game, was eaten up on the ground. Patience. And don't forget, Cross says, for all the attention given to Walsh's intricate passing schemes, "His teams always had a 1,000-yard rusher." Cross couldn't agree more with McKittrick's affinity for athletic, intelligent offensive linemen and reckons this is the wave of the future. "It did my heart good to work on the Super Bowl [XXXII] telecast and to look at the Green Bay and Denver offensive lines. Every one of the offensive linemen out there could stand up straight and see their feet."

McKittrick sees it as an integral part of his collaboration with Walsh. "In Coach Walsh's offense [offensive linemen] double-read," McKittrick says. "We released one of the backs [in the pass pattern] most of the time, so linemen had to take the middle linebacker and an outside linebacker. To get linemen adept at picking up both of them took niftier, more alert athletes. Most coaches never thought about coaching them that way. That was in the early years."

Now that McKittrick has carried the torch through the Seifert years and the beginning of the Mariucci years, he thinks he knows the heart of the Bill Walsh legacy: organizational principles.

"One of the big things all the [West Coast offense] head coaches have used is the way we practice. We wear pads less than most teams," McKittrick says. "It's come right back to us; coach Mariucci got his organizing mode from Holmgren, who got it from coach Walsh.

"You see it in the way Mariucci's practices are scripted. There's a base offense period. For example, we'll use these ten plays against these defenses. There's a card for each one—red zone, goal line; it's probably true for Shanahan, Rhodes, and Gruden. Sam Wyche [an assistant under Walsh in San Francisco] used this [as a head coach] at Cincinnati and Tampa."

As McKittrick's career winds down, the 49ers' legacy is secure. Walsh saw to that, videotaping the coaches' meetings to build an institutional library that continues to influence the staff today.

Cross's future will be full of seasons spent in the broadcast booth, where his experience as a West Coast offensive lineman informs his natural wit. "It was fun. It was great. With that system and the players that we had, it got so that in the ten years I was playing it really wasn't fair. In 1984, for instance, outside of the one game we lost, we came out of the tunnel every Sunday or Monday night, and it wasn't a matter of whether—it was how much. We knew it, the fans knew it, and, most important, the guys we were playing knew it."

CHAPTER 20

Quarterbacks: A History

Beau Riffenburgh

During professional football's early days, quarterbacks did not exist. In fact, neither did the forward pass. That all changed at the instigation of President Theodore Roosevelt. Horrified by a college sport that resulted in 18 deaths and 149 major injuries in 1905 alone, the President stated, "Brutality and foul play should receive the same summary punishment given to a man who cheats at cards." T.R. threatened to ban the sport by presidential decree if those in charge did not clean it up.

In December, 1905, the Intercollegiate Athletic Association of the United States (later renamed the National Collegiate Athletic Association) was organized to govern intercollegiate athletics, particularly football. At a meeting on January 12, 1906, the association's new rules committee dramatically changed the focus of the sport from a plodding, brutal, and unimaginative attack featuring popular but dangerous mass formations, such as the flying wedge, to one with more daring and offensive potential. The changes included:

- legalizing the forward pass;
- reducing the game from 70 to 60 minutes;
- establishing a neutral zone separating the teams by the length of the ball;
- increasing the distance to be gained for a first down from 5 to 10 yards;
- requiring six (later changed to seven) men to be on the line of scrimmage.

The new rules, which also affected the pro sport because it had not yet developed any rules of its own, eliminated the mass plays, forced the development of outside running attacks, and led to the popularization of the first of the modern offensive formations, the T. In the early years of the century, Amos Alonzo Stagg used the T-formation at the University of Chicago. In the next decade, Bob Zuppke at the University of Illinois utilized the T while serving as the mentor to George Halas and Ralph Jones. Elsewhere, Glenn (Pop) Warner developed the Single-Wing, which soon became the most popular formation.

The passing game, however, didn't immediately catch on, largely because of severe restrictions. For example, a pass could not be thrown to a receiver within five yards of either side of where the ball was put in play (that is, the center). In addition, a passer had to be at least five yards behind the line of scrimmage. Thus, the new passing game was confined to simple corner routes. Nevertheless, on October 27, 1906, in a game against a combined team from Benwood and Moundsville, West Virginia, George (Peggy) Parratt, the quarterback of the Massillon Tigers, completed a forward pass to end (Bullet) Dan Riley. It was the first authenticated pass completion in pro football history.

Still, passes remained few and far between in the professional game, until Green Bay's Earl (Curly) Lambeau began throwing out of his Notre Dame Box formation during the 1920s. But even the success of Lambeau and the Packers' other passers—halfback Verne Lewellen and tailback Red Dunn—didn't cause the real acceptance of the passing game. That was accomplished by former Michigan All-America Benny Friedman, who entered the NFL in 1927 with the Cleveland Bulldogs and immediately eclipsed Lambeau's passing records. Friedman also shocked fans and players alike by calling passes on first down, previously a rarity.

The next year the passing game made another important stride forward when Pop Warner's Stanford team easily defeated Army in New York, causing Warner's Double-Wing formation to be widely imitated. With two backs spread out and close to the line of scrimmage, the Double-Wing laid the foundation for the spread formations used today. It also provided the basis of many of the first formations built around the passing game.

T for Eleven

Two developments in the 1930s—the renewed popularity of the T-formation and the appearance of pro football's first great receiver—paved the way for the emergence of the modern quarterback and today's passing game.

Although the T had been used since the turn of the century, most coaches considered it a moribund formation by 1930. But the most popular formations—the Notre Dame Box and the Single-Wing—never were effective for the passing game, and the T, with its quarterback dropping straight back, ultimately proved ideal for reading defenses and picking up receivers.

In 1930, George Halas took a three-year break from coaching the Bears to concentrate on running the club and drumming up fan interest. His replacement was Ralph Jones, who immediately started tinkering with the Bears' T-formation. Jones widened the splits between Chicago's interior offensive linemen, giving them and the backs more room to maneuver. Jones also moved the ends out wide, spaced the halfbacks wider, and placed one of the halfbacks in motion.

With these splits and his man in motion, Jones not only spread the game horizontally, but also vertically, because players were out wide they could easily get downfield for passes. Moreover, the man in motion initially gave tremendous problems to the defenses, which were not nearly as sophisticated as the offenses of the time. The back could turn in and make a crack-back block on the defensive end, lure a linebacker out of position—opening up a running lane—or pull a defensive back out of position, opening up areas to pass.

By 1932, Jones's efforts paid dividends. That year the Bears finished 6-1-6, tying the Portsmouth Spartans (6-1-4) for first place (ties did not count). For the NFL's first 12 seasons, the team with the best winning percentage has been declared champion. Since this was the first time teams had tied in winning percentage, a special playoff game was set up to determine the champion. Because of snowstorms, it was played indoors at Chicago Stadium, and the Bears won 9-0, with the big play being a 2-yard touchdown pass from Bronko Nagurski to Red Grange.

That "special" game spawned a host of changes in the NFL, most notably the creation of two divisions in order to have a postseason championship game every year. It also produced a host of new rules that were the NFL's first real breakaway from the college game. Among the new rules were the use of inbounds lines (now called hashmarks), placed 10 yards from each sideline; the legalization of passing from anywhere behind the line of scrimmage; moving the goal posts from the back of the end zone to the goal line; and slimming the ball down to facilitate passing.

These changes not only opened up the passing game, they proved to be the first of many revisions. In the next several years, the football was again streamlined, the hashmarks were moved another five yards from the sideline, passing was encouraged by dropping the rule that an incomplete pass into the end zone was a touchback, and rules to protect the passer were implemented.

Hutson and Baugh

The Packers, coached by Lambeau (his playing career ended in 1929), were the first team to take full advantage of these rules. Green Bay had two outstanding passers in tailback Arnie Herber and his successor Cecil Isbell, but the key to the Packers' success was Don Hutson, a slim, lightning-fast end who had moves that were vastly ahead of any others in the game. Hutson was, and remains, the most dominant player at one position in football history. When he entered the NFL in 1935, the record for receptions in a season was 24 (which increased to 26 that year). He caught 34 in 1936, increased the record to 41 the next year, made 58 catches in 1941, and broke that mark with 74 in 1942.

Hutson also increased the yardage mark for a single season from 432 yards in 1935 to 1,211 and improved the touchdown reception record from 5 to 17.

What Hutson did for receiving, Sammy Baugh did for passing. Not only was Baugh arguably the best overall player in the history of pro football, he was far ahead of his contemporaries as a passer. As a rookie in 1937, "Slingin' Sammy" led the Redskins to the NFL Championship Game, where he passed for 354 yards and 3 touchdowns in a 28-21 victory over the Bears. He set an NFL record that season with 81 completions, a mark he eventually raised to 210. Baugh helped make the forward pass an integral part of the pro game. He was one of the first advocates of the short passing game, and, with his ability to see the entire field, to comprehend defensive reactions instantly, and to fire the ball without hesitation, he made the primitive defenses of his day obsolete.

"He would cock the ball, bring it down, and drift off as if about to run, cock again, make a mock throw to one side, and shoot a touchdown to the other," New York Giants head coach Steve Owen wrote of Baugh. "He was never committed until he was flat on the ground and the ball with him. I have seen him make bullet-like throws with his tremendous wrist action as he was nailed by a hard tackle and falling."

After eight years as a tailback in the Double-Wing, in 1945 Baugh made the transition to a T-formation quarterback, and he proved to be even more devastating. He immediately broke his own NFL completion percentage record of 62.7 by hitting 70.3 percent, a mark that lasted until 1982.

Shaughnessy Shows the Way

Baugh's move was symbolic of a shift to the T-formation in the 1940s. The focal point in this shift was the Chicago Bears, with Clark Shaughnessy and Sid Luckman leading the way. By 1939, the Bears' T had grown more complex, to counter teams such as the Lions and Packers, who had solved it by rotating their defensive backs to the side of the motion. All that complexity required a special quarterback, and the Bears found one that year in Luckman, an All-America tailback at Columbia and the club's top pick. In Chicago, he came under the tutelage of Shaughnessy, who was the head coach at the University of Chicago and a volunteer assistant for the Bears.

Luckman was one of the great technicians of the game. He was a masterful ball-handler and an excellent passer, but, most importantly, he was perfect for the new system that Shaughnessy had installed. Luckman spun from under center and faked, handed off, or pitched on quick-opening plays, quite a contrast from the slowly developing plays of the traditional Single-Wing. Because of Luckman's speed, double-team blocking was no longer necessary, so linemen could move out fast, brush block their opponents, and move downfield to block someone else.

Shaughnessy also put in the same system at Stanford, where he became head coach in 1940, and his team went 10-0 behind another wizard of the T, Frankie Albert. But during the break before Stanford played in the Rose Bowl, Shaughnessy returned to Chicago to revamp the Bears' offense before the 1940 NFL Championship Game. His major change was to add a counter play, in which the Bears split one man wide, sent another man in motion to the opposite side, and then ran back to the side of the spread end. The counter was as old as football itself, but Shaughnessy realized that it would be devastatingly effective against the Washington defense, which predictably shifted its linebackers toward the man in motion.

"I drew up the entire offense," Shaughnessy said later. "I threw out all the junk that wasn't working. Then I looked at the pictures of the Redskins-Bears game of two weeks earlier [the Redskins had won 7-3]. It was obvious that Washington was going to use a certain defense and wasn't going to change."

On the first play of the game, Bears halfback George McAfee went in motion. Washington's linebackers moved with him, just as Shaughnessy knew they would. The Bears ran the same motion on the next play, but fullback Bill Osmanski swept around end in the opposite direction and ran 68 yards for a touchdown that started Chicago's 73-0 rout, which is still the biggest margin of victory in NFL history.

Several weeks later, when Stanford defeated Nebraska in the Rose Bowl, the T was hailed as the offensive wave of the future. Indeed, in the span of the next eight years, every NFL team except Pittsburgh went to the T full time. Modern football—and the modern quarterback—had arrived.

Shaughnessy wasn't done refining the T-formation, however. In 1948, he became head coach of the Los Angeles Rams. The next year, the Rams acquired halfback Elroy (Crazylegs) Hirsch. Shaughnessy wanted to get Hirsch into the lineup, but he was concerned about whether he could take the pounding a halfback received. So, despite having two outstanding ends in NFL receiving leader Tom Fears and Bob Shaw, Shaughnessy split Hirsch out wide as a flanker, creating the first full-time player at that position.

The result was devastating. By combining with star quarterback Bob Waterfield and rookie Norm Van Brocklin, Fears broke Hutson's NFL record with 77 receptions, while the Rams roared into the NFL Championship Game. However, on a rain-soaked, muddy field that nullified their superior speed, the Rams lost to the Eagles. A power struggle within the organization claimed Shaughnessy, who was fired.

Shaughnessy's replacement was Joe Stydahar, who hired Hamp Pool as his offensive coach. Pool further refined Shaughnessy's offense, benefiting from working with four future Hall of Fame members: Fears, Hirsch, Waterfield, and Van Brocklin.

"We had all kinds of formations," Pool later said. "We used quite a lot of slot formation—with the halfback just outside the linemen and off the line of scrimmage. Then we'd put the other halfback in motion the other way. This would leave us only one setback, the fullback, to block on pass protection. But we would get four men into deep patterns in a hurry, and we would just eat them up. The defenses we were facing were exclusively man-to-man, and no one person could stay with Hirsch or Fears."

With perhaps the most electrifying offense the NFL has ever seen, the Rams scored an amazing 38.8 points per game in 1950. Fears broke his own record with 84 catches. But the Rams again lost in the NFL title game, with the Cleveland Browns winning on a last-minute field goal. The next year, the Rams were back again, as it was Hirsch who led the league with 66 receptions for a record 1,495 yards and 17 touchdowns. And the big-play attack finally carried through the postseason, as Los Angeles defeated the Browns 24-17 in the NFL Championship Game when Fears scored on a 73-yard pass from Van Brocklin in the fourth quarter.

Professor Brown

The Browns might not have been as exciting as the Rams, but no team has ever put together a decade like Cleveland did from 1946 to 1955. With Paul Brown as head coach and Otto Graham at quarterback, they appeared in 10 consecutive championship games—four in the All-America Football Conference and six in the NFL—winning seven times.

Brown was the first coach to bring a true sense of science to professional football. Many routine parts of the pro game today—full-time coaching staffs, the study of game films, calling plays via messengers, classroom study, intelligence testing, using playbooks, and extensive college scouting—were either Brown's innovations or were brought to a new level of efficiency by him.

"I don't think it's stretching the truth to say Paul Brown redesigned the game," Graham said. "He was the first to make football a year-round job for his coaches and players. He was the first to take his players to a hotel the night before a game in their hometown, to get them away from the kids and the noise and neighbors and distractions.

"We were the first team to carry notebooks. We'd start off each year talking about the most basic fundamentals. He'd dictate to us, and we'd write it down, things like how to do your calisthenics, the right way to touch your toes, how to form a huddle. After ten years I was still writing it all down. It was like being in the Navy and hearing the same lecture on how to make hospital corners on your bed sheets. But you remembered.

"And Paul was an innovator on the field. He took advantage of the fact that the defenses of the time were pretty basic and non-mobile. There were no blitzes, no stunts, no zones. So he took advantage of the defenses by developing the draw play for Marion Motley and the sideline pass—break to the side and come back for the ball—for [Mac] Speedie, [Dante] Lavelli, and myself."

Brown's insistence on running precise pass routes rather than the somewhat sloppy routes of the time may have been his most important innovation.

"We had never seen such a spot-passing program as they had," Philadelphia defensive back Russ Craft later said when recalling how the Browns made their NFL debut by picking apart the 1949 NFL champion Eagles. "We would be on top of the receivers, but they caught the ball anyway because the pass was so well timed."

It helped that the Browns possessed one of the best pairs of receivers ever—Speedie and Lavelli—catching those passes, but even more important was "Mr. Automatic," Otto Graham. The finest passing technician of his time, Graham led either the AAFC or the National Football League in passing five times, while finishing second three more times in his 10 years.

"Otto Graham was the key to the whole team," Brown later said. "He had the finest peripheral vision I've ever witnessed, and that is a very big factor in a quarterback. He had total composure on the field, the ability to find whatever receiver was going to come open, and the arm and athletic ability to get the ball to him. His hand-eye coordination was most unusual, and he was bigger than you'd think and faster than you'd think.

"Otto was my greatest player because he played the most important position, and he played it to perfection. He was the crux of how we got things done. I don't discount Marion Motley, Dante Lavelli, or Jim Brown. But the guy who was the engineer, the guy with the touch that pulled us out of so many situations, was Otto Graham. To put it simply, find me another quarterback who took his team to as many championships."

Not Just a Sideline

If there was one area where the Brown-Graham partnership lost a little of its sparkle, it was over another of Brown's contributions to quarterbacking: calling the plays from the sidelines. "When Paul began calling the plays from the bench, I disagreed, but the whole thing was exaggerated over the years," Graham once said. "I didn't like it, but I didn't resent it.

"Calling a play is nothing more than a guess. You see those movies where the quarterback raises up from the huddle, looks at the defense, then ducks down and calls the play. Well, that's baloney. Paul could see as much or more from the sideline than I could from the huddle. My complaint was that he didn't want me to audible. He did let me check off now and then, but I had to be right. The rest of the time, Paul called the plays, and the record shows he called 'em pretty good."

Brown was firm in his views about this issue. "Otto was one of the brightest players you could imagine," he said. "But nobody under pressure of performing can give as much thought to play selection as he should. We were feeding in information from all our coaches in the press box—and we always had a coach sitting in the end zone. I was a quarterback myself—not a very good one—and in those days when you couldn't think of anything else, you'd run off tackle. What does a quarterback see when he makes a handoff? What part of the defense does he see? He doesn't see much. Field level is the worst vantage point in the stadium.

"Besides, a coach calling the plays takes a lot of heat off the quarterback—and a lot of coaches don't want this responsibility. I didn't care. The players perform and get the credit. If people wanted to blast me for a dumb call, I could take it."

Pass First

While Brown and Graham were enjoying their greatest success, on the other side of the country another coach who never received the same level of acclaim was developing the passing game in a different way. Chuck Taylor had been a little-known offensive lineman for Shaughnessy's 1940 Stanford team before serving as the school's freshman coach for several years. He then moved on to the San Francisco 49ers, where he coached under Buck Shaw, before returning to Stanford as head coach in 1951. That very year, he led Stanford to the Rose Bowl.

"I learned fast that Stanford wasn't going to run over anybody," Taylor later said. "But passing could keep us in almost every game, and could allow us to upset a team that was physically stronger than we were. So we made the decision to go to a style of passing that was unique at the time. We would establish the passing game first. We wouldn't run to establish the pass, but the other way around. It was the real start of that strategy in football."

Not only was Taylor's pass-first philosophy the forerunner of today's playbooks, but he also added sophistication to what had been rather primitive concepts.

"The traditional passing game had had the receiver run down ten yards and turn around," Taylor remarked. "There never was any deviation from the pattern. But we changed that. We divided the field up into nine zones and called zone patterns instead of specific routes. That way, it was up to the receivers to get open, and it was the quarterback's responsibility to be able to read the defense and his own receiver."

Taylor not only allowed for deviation on a play, but before the play. His adoption of a sophisticated set of audibles, and his quarterbacks' success with them, helped popularize the practice of changing of plays at the line of scrimmage. Meanwhile, in the huddle, most professional quarterbacks called their own plays during the 1960s. However, that began to change in the following decade when the Cowboys made five Super Bowl appearances during the 1970's, with coach Tom Landry calling the plays. This system is still in use for most NFL teams today; virtually all teams send in the plays from the sidelines—now via radio waves instead of sending in substitutes or wig-wagging signals—although quarterbacks usually have permission to change the play at the line of scrimmage if the situation necessitates.

The Master

One of the more vitriolic debates over play-calling occurred in Los Angeles, where one of the best quarterbacks ever, Norm Van Brocklin, linked up with one of the great offensive coaching minds, Sid Gillman. Though Gillman had posted an impressive record at Miami of Ohio and the University of Cincinnati, he had not yet developed all of the theories and nuances that later earned him selection to the Pro Football Hall of Fame. When he joined Los Angeles in 1955, his intermittent calling of plays quickly soured his relationship with his all-pro quarterback.

"The coach really shouldn't call the plays," Van Brocklin later said. "It is not good for the quarterback because he becomes an automaton. He stops thinking. He comes to depend upon the coach and can't depend upon himself. Then, when a coach who has been calling all the plays starts doing it in fits and starts, it makes the whole situation difficult. I never objected to taking a suggestion from the bench, but I did object to play-calling becoming a divisive force on the team."

Despite this conflict, the Rams won the Western Conference in Gillman's first season, before being thrashed by the Browns in the 1955 NFL Championship Game, Graham's last game. But more importantly, the season served as a training ground for Gillman, who would go on to be a leader in the use of the short-passing game.

"At that point, it wasn't a question of innovations," Gillman said. "We simply had great talent—we had Dutch Van Brocklin and Tom Fears and Elroy Hirsch and Ron

Waller. The main thing was Fears. We were just beginning to understand how moves are made by a receiver. Fears was one of the greatest 'move' men in the history of the game. He didn't have much speed, but he could turn 'em on their heads. We studied Fears and we began coaching what he was doing."

But it was Gillman's association with Van Brocklin that helped Gillman develop the theories that would alter the passing philosophy for many quarterbacks to come. "Just watching what Van Brocklin did in practice was a learning experience," Gillman said. "How he played and how he thought helped contribute enormously to the development of the passing game." In later years, Gillman helped develop an enormous range of successful quarterbacks—Bill Wade, Zeke Bratkowski, Frank Ryan, Jack Kemp, John Hadl, and Ron Jaworski—with theories gleaned at least in part from his association with Van Brocklin.

In 1960, Gillman became the head coach of the Los Angeles Chargers of the new American Football League. Not only did he lend the AFL a certain amount of credibility, he developed one of pro football's most explosive offenses. In fact, Gillman's teams epitomized "AFL-style" football, which mixed deep passes to speedy wide receivers with short, safe passes to tight ends and backs.

Gillman had truly talented receivers with great speed—such as Lance Alworth and Gary Garrison—and turned them into all-pro pass-catchers, or, in Alworth's case, a Hall of Fame receiver. Gillman also started training other football minds, including Jack Faulkner, Chuck Noll, and Don Klosterman.

But none of Gillman's assistants added more to the passing game than Al Davis, who became head coach of the Oakland Raiders in 1963. Davis became a major influence in the passing game of the 1960s and early 1970s. His "vertical passing game" emphasized huge offensive lines that could protect quarterbacks for a long time, and deep passing to speedy wide receivers, such as Warren Wells and Cliff Branch. Of course, having Fred Biletnikoff constantly open short helped the Raiders' deep passing game, but Davis's scheme helped make Daryle Lamonica and Kenny Stabler among the most feared passers in pro football.

Meanwhile, Van Brocklin moved into the coaching ranks, taking over the expansion Minnesota Vikings in 1961, and he immediately found out what a coach-quarterback disagreement looked like from the other side. Van Brocklin had earlier commented that a quarterback should run the ball only if his life were in immediate danger. Who should be Van Brocklin's first quarterback at Minnesota but Fran Tarkenton, a rookie in 1961. Tarkenton, of course, went on to play 18 years and establish numerous NFL passing records, but it was his scrambling that so distressed Van Brocklin.

"With Tarkenton," Van Brocklin said after they had been together several seasons, "you need to have an exceptionally good third-and-forty offense." At a time when NFL quarterbacks did not run the ball a great deal, Tarkenton started the swing in the other direction. Within the next decade, youngsters such as Greg Landry and Bobby Douglass were breaking quarterback running marks left and right. But while Douglass and Landry did their thing, the passing game followed Tarkenton's lead and reversed upon itself.

Air Coryell

The coach most responsible for the shift to the ball-control passing attack was Don Coryell. Coryell had made previously little-known San Diego State a national power, while developing a host of quarterbacks who would play in the NFL: Rod Dowhower, Don Horn, Dennis Shaw, Brian Sipe, and Jesse Freitas. When he joined the St Louis Cardinals in 1973, they had not made the playoffs in 25 years. But after one rebuilding year, with Coryell masterminding the offense and Jim Hart leading it on the field, the Cardinals won two division titles in a row. Coryell then moved to San Diego, where he joined with Dan Fouts to produce an era of aerial success even greater than the Chargers had enjoyed under Gillman.

"It was the system," Fouts later said. "If you check back through Don Coryell's history as a coach, you'll find he had success throwing the ball wherever he went. We believed in his system, and that's what was most important. From the head man down to the waterboys, everybody knew we were going to throw the ball and be successful doing it."

Coryell's system relied on spot passes and mismatches, which made it unique at the time. Coryell's quarterbacks—and both Hart and Fouts were great ones—didn't throw to where receivers were, but to where the receiver figured to end up. They threw to spots. That allowed them to deliver the ball quickly, using two- and three-step drops rather than the common five- or seven-step drops. The ball was put in the air so quickly that the defensive line did not have the time to pressure the quarterback nor did the linebackers or defensive backs have time to react, which cut down on the number of interceptions, increased the number of short passes, and fashioned a new offensive dimension: the ball-control passing game.

Coryell became the first coach to extensively use two tight ends in a one-back offense, a formation that became popular throughout football after Washington won Super Bowl XVII using it. This formation forced the defense to give single coverage to either a wide receiver or to San Diego's Hall of Fame tight end Kellen Winslow, who possessed the speed and receiving talents of a wide receiver.

"We like to line up two tight ends and work over the middle," Dan Fouts observed while he was still playing for Coryell. "That forces teams to cover a tight end with a safety or linebacker. Our tight ends should have a speed advantage against linebackers and a size advantage against safeties, so we should get a completion. We can also get an advantage in numbers. We'll flood zones or overload zones. We'll put two guys in an area where there is one defender or three guys in an area where there are two defenders.

"We're tough to defend. If you play us zone, you can't blitz and the quarterback has time to throw. If you play us man-to-man, you might get beat long. There's always the threat that someone's going deep in our offense. We look to him first."

It was Coryell's system, but he was fortunate to have a man perfectly suited to it. Fouts was virtually a machine, able to make three, four, even five reads before deciding on his target. And that choice also had to take into account decisions by the receivers, a concept initiated by Chuck Taylor but perfected by Coryell.

"Not only is a receiver at liberty to make adjustments in his route, he is expected to," Fouts continued with his explanation. "I have my reads and the receiver has his—and we're both reading the same thing. I'm expecting the adjustment to come. If the defense is in zone coverage, I know what's coming from my receiver. Guys like Charlie Joiner, Wes Chandler, and Kellen Winslow have instant recognition. That's what separates the great ones from the guys selling cars."

Fouts and Coryell—and all other recent offensive coaches and personnel—benefited greatly from the rules changes that were adopted to open up the passing game and make pro football more exciting. In 1974, defensive players were limited to bumping or chucking a pass receiver only once, and rolling blocks by wide receivers were made illegal.

Four years later, National Football League rules changes permitted a defender to maintain contact with a receiver within five yards of the line of scrimmage, but outlawed contact beyond that point.

League officials also interpreted the pass-blocking rule to permit the extending of arms and open hands, which allowed the offensive line to better protect the quarterback.

The West Coast Offense Arrives

These new rules particularly favored the creative, and none more so than Bill Walsh during his 10 years as head coach of San Francisco. A former assistant to both Paul Brown in Cincinnati (Brown founded the Bengals after leaving Cleveland) and Coryell in San Diego, Walsh popularized the ball-control passing game even more than Coryell because Walsh's teams went one step further: they won three Super Bowls.

In Walsh's rookie season as an NFL coach in 1979—after having tutored Guy Benjamin and Steve Dils at Stanford, each of whom led the nation in passing as a senior—Steve DeBerg set NFL records for pass attempts and completions for the 49ers.

But the next year, DeBerg lost his job to second-year pro Joe Montana, who proved to be the perfect operative for Walsh's theories. Montana's pinpoint passing, timely running, and ability to pull out wins when all seemed lost helped make the 49ers the team of the decade in the 1980s. Montana's magic continued even after Walsh as the 49ers won a fourth Super Bowl after the 1989 season under Walsh's successor, George Seifert.

"Unlike the Steelers, who won their first two Super Bowls with a magnificent defense, the 49ers won primarily because of Montana," said former New York Jets personnel director Mike Hickey. "He was the key to their team all along. As a guy who can get the job done that a quarterback is supposed to do—win—Montana is one of the two or three best ever."

Remarkably, despite Montana's success, some people called for his removal in favor of Steve Young as early as 1988. One of the greatest physical talents to play quarterback in the NFL, Young had to wait his turn until 1991 and 1992, when Montana missed most of two successive seasons with injuries. But Young made the most of his chances, leading the NFL in passing both years, as he did again in 1993 (after Montana was traded to Kansas City), 1994, 1996, and 1997. Young shares Sammy Baugh's record of six league passing titles.

"Young is clearly one of the greatest quarterbacks ever," Seifert said while he was still coaching the 49ers. "It is not just that he is such a phenomenal athlete and one of the best runners ever from his position, but he is also statistically the most proficient passer in league history.

"He has suffered some by popular comparisons to Montana, but on an individual level he has produced even more than Joe did. Certainly no other player has led the league in passing five times in six years. They were different stylistically, but it would be hard to take one over the other. Either could make a claim as the best ever."

The Best Ever

The same could be said about a number of other quarterbacks. A survey was done several years ago of personnel directors and scouts—men who had been around professional football for up to 50 years and had therefore seen virtually all of the greats—attempting to determine the finest quarterback ever.

At that time, five different quarterbacks received mention as the best ever. Then, in 1994, four quarterbacks were put on the NFL's 75th Anniversary All-Time Team, voted on by media and NFL personnel. Three players received the nod from just one of these panels—Montana, the master of the come-from-behind victory; Layne, the greatest leader; and Sonny Jurgensen, the best pure passer ever.

Three other quarterbacks received mention from both—Baugh, arguably the most complete football player ever; Graham, the greatest winner; and Johnny Unitas, who had been elected as the all-time choice in 1969 on the National Football League's 50th Anniversary Team.

"Sammy Baugh might be the best overall football player in NFL history," one of the scouts said at the time of the voting. "But Johnny Unitas stands alone as a quarterback. He was cool, he was daring, he was flawless. He had perfect passing form. He was the ultimate thinker and leader. He could fire up a team or keep them cold and calculating. He could do anything and everything. I don't think there will be another like him."

Each of these six, established himself as a ferocious competitor, a superior athlete, a leader with a drive to win. Each worked to succeed in that most vital, most glamorous, and most difficult of positions—NFL quarterback.

CHAPTER 21

What Makes Quarterbacks Great

Beau Riffenburgh

Football is a team game that rewards teamwork. Thus, a team that is weak at any one position still can win on a consistent basis. At any position, that is, except quarterback. The quarterback is the central element of the game, the most glamorous player, the one in the public spotlight. Comparisons of Dan Marino and John Elway can be heard in stadiums, bars, and offices every week during the season. You don't hear similar discussions about other, less glamorous positions.

Quarterback also is the most demanding position in pro football. As legendary coach and innovator Paul Brown summed it up: "Playing quarterback in the NFL is so tough it is almost impossible. The basic reason is that there is a degree of excellence required that is so high it is virtually unimaginable to outsiders." No other position in any sport requires such a consistently high level of performance. Thus, fans focus on quarterbacks, and they create the excitement and the long-term memories. They get the biggest acclaim, or attract the most bad-mouthing.

"The praise and the criticism are both blown totally out of proportion," former NFL quarterback Bert Jones said. "In my career, I received both sides of it, and usually neither the credit nor the criticism was totally justified. But if you want to play the position, if you want to be the focal position of the team, you have to put up with the pressure that goes along with the job. There have been a lot of talented young quarterbacks in the NFL who have not made the grade, not through any physical or on-the-field failing, but because they couldn't handle the pressure."

"I don't think the job has ever been created that is more difficult than being a quarterback in the NFL," Pro Football Hall of Fame quarterback Sonny Jurgensen said. "It requires more time, work, and dedication than any other profession I know.

"Its demands are both physical and mental. If there's a weakness anywhere in the quarterback's preparations, he lets down not only himself but his teammates, coaches, and fans. The pressures are simply overwhelming, especially today when the entire NFL schedule is televised. It takes a special kind of person to really make it as a successful NFL quarterback."

Those people have come in all shapes and sizes, and with all temperaments. There was Johnny Unitas, whose composure and play calling gave new meaning to the terms poise and cool, and Norm Van Brocklin, whose fiery behavior belied his controlled approach to the game. Mobility has been a large part of the game of Steve Young, but Dan Marino would no sooner run the ball than sit on the sideline. John Elway has a rocket launcher for an arm and can throw a tight spiral 70 yards, while Jim McMahon threw wounded ducks that sometimes looked like they would fly out of the stadium.

Freewheeling, hell-raising Bobby Layne, who was known to draw game-winning plays in the dirt on the field, was an explosive leader about whom teammate Yale Lary once commented, "When Bobby said block, you blocked. When Bobby said drink, you drank."

Compare that description with Layne's counterpart in three consecutive NFL Championship Games from 1952-54—Cleveland quarterback Otto Graham. Graham was a stoic who neither interfered with coach Paul Brown's play calling nor broke training rules the night before a game, and who, when he became a coach himself, carried on most of his mentor's strict rules and regulations.

Quarterbacks are like fingerprints; no two are alike. Some have been magnificent physical specimens, such as Randall Cunningham; some had to virtually reconstruct themselves physically, such as Bill Kilmer; some were supremely cerebral, such as Frank Ryan; some were unfairly accused of not being bright enough, such as Terry Bradshaw, and some were marvelously gifted in every facet of the game, such as Sammy Baugh.

Other quarterbacks didn't seem to have the classic abilities, but they became champions, such as Jeff Hostetler; some were intensely dedicated, such as Bart Starr; and some were simply unwilling to take "no" for an answer, in a game, such as Roger Staubach or Joe Montana, or in a career, such as Len Dawson or Earl Morrall.

These mysterious components that form the successful quarterback make the position and the people who play it so difficult to classify. Ask a dozen personnel directors in the NFL what they want in a quarterback, and you will get a dozen different answers. Yet, while all those answers would be accurate, they would only begin to define what it takes to be an NFL quarterback.

Any good offensive coach can train a player with all of these qualities to function as a solid quarterback. It is the other aspects of playing the position—the intangibles—

that make the difference between mediocrity and stardom. Ultimately, a quarterback will be measured by the most important yardstick of all: winning. The good ones can be the best passers or the most outstanding athletes, but the great ones are the winners.

"People ask me about the great quarterbacks, and I'll start with Otto Graham," said Howard (Red) Hickey, the former head coach of the San Francisco 49ers and one of the most innovative thinkers in NFL history. "He won a lot of championships. Then I mention Layne and [Bob] Waterfield and Van Brocklin, and, before I can get to Unitas or Starr, they'll say, 'But you left out Y.A. Tittle.' And I'll say, 'But Tittle never won a championship.' That's what a championship quarterback does—wins championships.

"Now Layne, as bad as he looked throwing the ball, was a winner. You'd want him in your huddle. Players feel that way about a quarterback. When a leader is in there, they'll perform, they'll go."

"When you talk about the greatest quarterbacks, you talk first about the winners," agreed Hall of Fame coach Tom Landry. "That list necessarily starts with Otto Graham. Ten championship game appearances in ten years—and seven of them for titles—make him the greatest winner in pro football history. There have been a number of others—Bobby Layne, John Unitas, Bart Starr, Roger Staubach, Joe Montana, and now Troy Aikman—but Graham set a standard that has not been matched by any of them. And to many people, that one thing is the ultimate proof of the quality of the quarterback, indeed what the position is all about."

Of course, some of the greatest quarterbacks have not won titles: Jurgensen, Tittle, and Dan Fouts never won "the big one." Montana's success helped deprive Marino and Ken Anderson of Super Bowl rings. Likewise, Fran Tarkenton was thrice denied a Super Bowl ring by three of the top winning quarterbacks of the 1970s: Bob Griese, Terry Bradshaw, and Ken Stabler.

Leading the Way

"Being a leader, that is, having total control of your team, is, above all, the one asset a quarterback must have," Vince Lombardi, the Hall of Fame coach of the Green Bay Packers and Washington Redskins, once said. "A coach would like a skilled play caller, a slick ball handler, and an accurate passer, but the one thing that is a must is having a person who can control any situation he is presented with. This requires a player with confidence, a forceful personality, and the ability to make his teammates believe in him as much as he does himself.

"If you look at the great quarterbacks through the years—Graham, Layne, Unitas, Starr—they have all had that in common. In the final moments of a close game, they could take total control of their own team, which usually meant taking control of—and winning—the game."

Nothing on that front has changed since Lombardi's Packers dominated the game. More than anything, a quarterback still must lead by example.

No one is a bigger believer in the leadership qualities of a quarterback than St. Louis Rams offensive coordinator Jerry Rhome. Rhome is one of the game's great teachers of quarterbacks, as demonstrated by a roll call of former pupils that includes Jim Zorn, Dave Krieg, Joe Theismann, Doug Williams, Troy Aikman, and Warren Moon.

"Leadership is one of the areas that separates the greats from the guys," said Rhome, a former All-America passer at Tulsa. "And you cannot train someone to be a leader; it is natural or not. Leadership comes from within the man himself. He has to be tough-minded, confident, even a little cocky at times.

"Just how he talks in the huddle can make a difference. It's going to show if he doubts himself. Players around him will feel it. He has to let it be known that he intends to keep plugging away right to the bitter end of the game, regardless of the situation. You can't expect the others to live and die out there with you if you don't project that.

"To a certain extent, given enough time and commitment, coaches can build a player at almost any position. Sure, you have to have some basics; a certain amount of speed helps for a receiver, and you need to have a frame that you can build up for a lineman. But within general parameters, if the coaches and players want to work hard enough and long enough, players can generally be developed. Even most of the talents that are called natural can be trained if the player has the potential.

"This is much less true of quarterbacks because so much of what they do is innate, is part of their personality, part of what makes them an individual, rather than something strictly athletic or mental. These things are already ingrained long before we see them.

"Of course, you can train a quarterback in a lot of areas. You can make sure that he understands all manner of defenses and that he will know how to break them down. And you can train him to read what kind of zone the defense will be sitting in and to adjust accordingly. But you cannot make a quarterback confident. You can nurture his confidence, but you can't instill it. It is either going to grow from everything the quarterback does and the way he works with the coaches and the players, or it isn't. That's one reason so many of the top quarterbacks seem brash. Heck, if they didn't know they could accomplish whatever they wanted to, they would have been weeded out of pro football a long time ago."

It took years for Lombardi to nurture that kind of confidence in Bart Starr. "Confidence comes from success, and when I went to Green Bay, I had come off a year in which I had no success at all, my senior year at Alabama when I sat on the bench," Starr once recalled.

Indeed, Starr's entire college career had been up-and-down, and he wasn't selected by the Packers until the seventeenth round of the 1956 NFL draft.

"My first couple of years I knew I wasn't playing well, and I began to wonder if I was able to," he said. "I didn't often consider getting out of football, but I frequently wondered why I was wasting my time in it. That changed under Lombardi."

Midway through the 1959 season, Lombardi's first in Green Bay, the coach made it clear that Starr was his starting quarterback. He slowly built the young man's confidence while he tutored him in quarterbacking skills.

The result was a new Starr, who led the Packers to the

NFL Championship Game in his second season under Lombardi. He went on to lead the Packers to five NFL titles, plus victories (and most-valuable-player awards) in the first two Super Bowls, and Starr led the NFL in passing three times.

Starr's performance in the 1967 NFL Championship Game, forever known as the Ice Bowl, epitomized the confidence that Lombardi valued so highly. Battling a powerful Dallas defense and arctic conditions with a backfield full of substitutes, Starr led the Packers 68 yards to the winning touchdown, which he scored with only 13 seconds left on a now-famous quarterback sneak.

"Bart was at his peak today," flanker Carroll Dale said after the game. "When we went into the huddle to start that final drive, there was never any doubt about what was going to happen. Bart just let it be known that we were going to win that game. He didn't have to say anything. We just knew it from the way he acted."

Those words were echoed 19 years later by Cleveland linebacker Clay Matthews after John Elway took over in the 1986 AFC Championship Game. Starting at his 2 with less than six minutes left, Elway drove the Broncos 98 yards in 15 plays, completing 9 passes and running twice himself. He threw a 5-yard touchdown pass to Mark Jackson with 37 seconds left in regulation to send the game into overtime. Denver ultimately won and advanced to Super Bowl XXI.

"When they only got the kickoff out to the two, some of our guys felt we were out of the woods," Matthews said of Elway's fourth-quarter charge, which became known as "The Drive." "But you could see looking at Elway across the line that he had no doubt that they were going to score. I have never seen such confidence, such competitiveness, such desire."

Courage Under Fire

"Certainly one trait that all the top quarterbacks have is competitiveness," said Tom Flores, a former quarterback himself and later head coach of both the Raiders and Seahawks. "They are tenacious and brave. And they have a lot of pride in themselves and what they can accomplish. They always want one last chance at getting the ball because they feel that they can win any game at the last moment if they need to."

Another quality that is required to be a successful quarterback is courage. Anyone willing to take the punishment that comes with the job must possess a large amount of physical courage. But to be a quarterback one has to have mental courage as well, and that comes in two varieties.

"A quarterback must have the courage to throw without fear in any situation from any place on the field," Allie Sherman, the former head coach of the New York Giants, once said. "I don't mean fear of being intercepted or throwing incomplete. He must have absolute faith that each pass will connect, and he must transmit this faith to his teammates. No one ever had more courage in this respect than Y.A. Tittle, who, going into every single game he ever played, knew he was going to have a perfect day."

There is a second kind of mental courage. "A quarterback simply must have the courage to maintain confidence in himself despite the lack of it shown in him by the front office, coaches, fans, or the press," said Joe Gibbs, the Hall of Fame coach for the Washington Redskins (1981-1992). "He has to tune out all the negatives and continue to work, continue to strive, continue to believe in himself.

"One of my players had to fight through such difficulties one year, and it was never harder than when we finally made him the starter late in the season. And the result of this kind of courage? Well, after a year in which he started only twice in the regular season and in which the fans were calling for him to be yanked in the conference championship game, Doug Williams threw four touchdown passes in one quarter to lead us to a victory over Denver in Super Bowl XXII."

Like Williams, Montana and Staubach were both involved in occasional quarterback controversies, but both men had the confidence and courage to come through, and both led their teams to multiple Super Bowl victories. Montana and Staubach also had plenty of other tools to work with. That is not uncommon. In addition to their intangible qualities, all of the top quarterbacks have been blessed with a combination of outstanding mental and physical skills.

"There are certain quantifiable things the top quarterbacks all have," said Dick Steinberg, the late general manager of the New York Jets. "The obvious ones are size, speed, native intelligence, and a quick release. There are also a number of other things that can't be measured, but that have to be there. The most important of these, to me, is arm strength.

"A quarterback has to have the ability to throw the fifteen-yard out pattern—that's a damn long pass—and it has to be on a line. For that pass he needs the ability to drive the ball into the zones and keep it away from the defenders who are reacting to it. The top quarterbacks also should have leadership, poise, anticipation of the receiver, touch, mobility, and good overall athletic ability."

The Dominant Trait

Of course, not all quarterbacks have all of these talents in equal proportion. But they frequently can make up for less of one by excellence in another area.

Jurgensen, for example, was not the most mobile quarterback, but no one could boast a quicker release, and few have been calmer under pressure. In 1961, his first year as a regular with the Eagles, Jurgensen dropped back to pass, but one of the Redskins' defensive linemen grabbed his right arm before he could throw the ball. Jurgensen simply snatched the ball from his right hand with his left, and completed a left-handed pass to halfback Billy Ray Barnes for a 27-yard gain.

"Quarterbacks have to be composed at all times," Flores said. "If the quarterback panics, the whole team panics. The rest of the team must have confidence in him. Kenny Stabler didn't yell much. But when he did, they listened. On the other hand, Bert Jones was very demonstrative. He used to go around throwing up his arms and making all kinds of gestures. But it worked for him."

Jones, who played for the Baltimore Colts and Los

Angeles Rams, was one of those physically talented quarterbacks mentioned by Steinberg. On the physical side, quarterbacks have always had to be able to pass, fake, pivot, hand off, and run if necessary, but in recent years several other attributes have become increasingly important.

As offensive and defensive linemen have gotten bigger, quarterbacks have had to follow suit so they can to see over them when passing. Strength, speed, and mobility likewise have become more important. Mobile quarterbacks such as Elway or Montana keep pressure on defenses by rolling out or scrambling. In Super Bowl XIX, Montana's 59 rushing yards were instrumental in four of San Francisco's touchdown drives as the 49ers cruised to a 38-16 victory against Miami. Dan Marino of the Dolphins actually set Super Bowl passing records for attempts and completions, but the 49ers' defense exploited his lack of mobility and his team's lack of a running attack.

On the other hand, few players have had a release as quick as Marino's. "Only Sonny Jurgensen and Joe Namath have been able to get rid of the ball as quickly as Marino," former Miami head coach Don Shula said.

"That quick release is important because you won't always have time to drop back, set up, find your receiver, and throw the ball with a perfect passing motion and follow-through. There simply are times when you have to put it in a certain spot before that defensive lineman grinds you into the ground. Marino can do that."

As important as the release is having quick feet. Despite his bad knees, Namath had incredibly quick feet; he could drop back so quickly that he could get rid of the ball before the pass rush could reach him. He could also sidestep a fast rush. But the quickness with which a quarterback gets rid of the ball and his ability to avoid the rush aren't the ultimate passing requirements.

"More important than anything else, the quarterback has to be able to throw the ball," said Hall of Fame coach Sid Gillman, one of the most innovative and progressive offensive minds in the history of football.

"That isn't as easy as it sounds. A lot of people can drop back and hurl a football fifty or sixty yards, but the quarterback has to be able to put it in a precise spot; if it is six inches shorter, longer, or to either side, it will be intercepted. And he has to be able to do that while moving away from four monsters who are trying to dismember him.

"Passing takes not only strength but amazing accuracy. The keys to that accuracy are coordination, depth perception, the ability to project where players will be on the field before they have gotten there, and utter self-confidence. Some of that, of course, is trainable, but some isn't. It is a God-given talent, a natural, instinctive thing that you have or you don't. No coach can help you with it.

"As a matter of fact, coaches can sometimes hurt players by overcoaching them. There are certain fundamentals that every passer should have, but the most important issue is if he completes the pass. There was talk about having to work on Dan Marino's delivery when he first came into the NFL. He was regarded as a quarterback who forced the ball too much, releasing it a little too early in his throw for maximum velocity and the best guidance, and waiting until the receiver got open rather than anticipating. But Don Shula didn't try to drastically change Marino, and his first year he led the AFC in passing, and the next he shattered all of the single-season passing marks."

Just as Shula believed in Marino, Green Bay general manager Ron Wolf showed total confidence in the league's current phenom, Green Bay's Brett Favre. Hugely impressed with Favre's talents in college, in 1992 Wolf offered the Falcons a first-round draft choice for him after a rookie year in which he threw only 5 passes. (Atlanta had only expended a second-round pick to draft Favre in 1991.) In the six years since, Favre has passed for more than 3,200 yards each season, has passed for 33 or more touchdowns four years in a row, and has been named National Football League's most valuable player by the Associated Press three consecutive times.

"Favre might not have your classic passing style," said a former NFL quarterback who is now a scout. "He tends to wind up a little more than he should, slowing his delivery of the ball, and, as with Marino, he likes to try to force the ball into zones, just trying to throw it past the defenders. There are aspects of his game that, on the surface, could be worked on, but although you can argue with his style, you can't argue with his results."

Everyone is Different

Passing styles vary significantly among great quarterbacks, but they share one thing in common—all of them have worked. A roll call of some of football's greatest quarterbacks and their throwing tendencies proves that whatever works, works:

- Graham used an overhand grip and a three-quarter motion. He threw a soft, floating pass that seemed to descend slowly and gently, but almost always reached his receiver.
- Layne threw the ball with his hands on or off the laces and with the ball coming from behind the ear or in a three-quarter motion. He threw a hard pass that got to its target quickly but frequently was wobbly and difficult to handle.
- Unitas had the classic throwing style, with his fingers on the laces, his arm coming through in a perfect behind-the-ear delivery, and a complete arm and body follow-through. His passing was arguably the best of them all.
- Jurgensen dropped the ball from his ear a little, although not always to a three-quarter motion. His release was so quick that it almost seemed impossible to get it on film, and he could throw from either foot, while off-balance, or with an entire defensive line on him. He never had much of an offensive line; otherwise, Jurgensen might be regarded as the best quarterback of all-time, rather than just the best pure passer.
- Marino fires an extremely fast pass with a release similar to Jurgensen's and with his fingers always on the laces. Early in his career, he relied on the aggressiveness of his receivers, particularly Mark Clayton and Mark Duper, but he has forced the ball less as the years have gone by.

- Elway throws a perfect spiral so hard that players talk about the Elway cross—the little mark made by the end of the football hitting a receiver's chest if he doesn't catch it with his hands. Elway has uncommon arm strength that allows him to throw a blazing pass even while backpedaling.

Although different in style and athletic ability, these quarterbacks all had one thing in common—intelligence. A successful quarterback must know his team's entire offense, including what each player on the team is supposed to do on every play. He also must be able to judge both the talent and the desire of his teammates because he needs to know how they will react in specific situations. He needs to know each opponent, so that he will know how to attack them in different situations. The quarterback also must possess the ability to read the defense when he goes to the line of scrimmage and to change his play accordingly. And he must be able to do this correctly and consistently.

"The great ones are consistent," said Starr, who himself was one of the most consistent passers ever and is the top-rated passer in NFL postseason history. "They aren't hot one Sunday and cold the next. You don't want the roller-coaster effect."

"The play that an NFL quarterback has to make consistently, the one that separates the real quarterback from the would-be, is the third-and-long play," said Jurgensen. "On third-and-long, you have to throw the ball and the defense knows it. In fact, everybody in the stands or watching on TV knows it. Your teammates know it, too, of course, and they are depending on you to make the call that will get the first down. If you can't make that call and come through under that pressure consistently, you'll be sitting with the other fans pretty soon."

THE GAME OFF THE FIELD

CHAPTER 22

Blitzing the English Language

Ted Brock

The average Joe woke up this morning, got into his car, found a seam in the northbound lane of the freeway, and drove to work. At his desk, he huddled with his co-workers, went over his game plan for the day, and suddenly realized just how much football has penetrated the English language.

The NFL has had a phenomenal impact on the way we speak. Moreover, the constant use of "footspeak" on the front page, not the sports page, demonstrates just how accepted the usages have become. One example: The widow of the Shah of Iran, interviewed on National Public Radio, said Iranians have been "Monday-morning quarterbacking" since the 1979 Iranian revolution.

Dale Herbeck, chair of the Department of Communications at Boston College, says, "People tend to think of sports as just something we do. But if you look at it, sports have become such a part of our national culture."

That culture generally has different subsets of language for different professions. However, Tim Green, the former Atlanta Falcons defensive end, goes back and forth among many roles—television sportscaster, radio commentator, writer, and lawyer. He still uses metaphors he picked up 20 years ago in the locker room.

"As somebody closely associated with the game, I try to use analogies outside the game," Green says. "But I find that in board rooms, universities, and certainly in the world of TV, football analogies are very much in vogue. 'We fumbled that.' 'We had to punt.' 'Sometimes you have to take a loss.' 'We got sacked on that one.' "

Purists may point out that "sacked" comes from the vernacular of war. Random House senior editor Jesse Sheidlower, who directs professor-author A.E. Lighter's three-volume *Random House Dictionary of American Slang,* notes that, "Many aspects of life involve some sort of competition. Metaphors from many different sports are used in military or government contexts."

In 1997 and '98 Herbeck took part in a symposium at the Pro Football Hall of Fame titled "Pro Football and American Life." Part of his research sent him on a Lexis Nexis computer search. "I just started whipping through football terms as they were used during the Gulf War," Herbeck says. Among his discoveries was a banner displayed outside an air base that read, "Iraq has won the toss and has elected to receive." Herbeck also notes that expressions such as "the ground game" came up during a press conference with General Norman Schwarzkopf, and commanders even attached the code name "Hail Mary" to the Allied ground offensive that liberated Kuwait from Iraqi forces.

Roy I. Mumme, a professor in the School of Education at Florida Gulf Coast University and also a contributor to the Hall of Fame's symposium, takes the Schwarzkopf "Hail Mary" a step further. "As Americans were confronting Saddam Hussein's army in the east, General Schwarzkopf had another army to the west," he says. "They were on an end run."

Another of Mumme's war-football nuggets dates to the origin of football's oldest, most recognizable method of attack, the T-formation.

"A German tank general named Heinz Guderian published a book about the blitzkrieg, which basically was an end run on France, around the Maginot Line. Coach Clark Shaughnessy read that book and used it to reinvent the T-formation for the Chicago Bears."

Though the football-war connection is strong, *Sports Illustrated* senior editor Frank Deford notes the football vernacular's versatility over time.

"You used to hear during Vietnam that football was analogous to war," Deford says. "Now we're not in a martial era but a business era, so now it's perfectly applicable to business uses. Football's a tough game; business is a tough world."

Tim Green's experience straddles both worlds.

"I think a lot of business people get into the more visceral, violent terms," Green says. " 'They're trying to ram the ball down our throat.' 'Let's take them out at the knees.' People in business, when I start to talk about what it's like in the locker room, the trenches, they get this glow around their faces. When we start bantering football analogies back and forth, people love it."

Geraldine Moyle, who teaches in the writing program at UCLA, says, "Football metaphor seems to be part of male bonding. When I'm in class, I make it clear that I love certain sports, pro football included. Some students look at me as if this woman is invading their domain. They get into it when they realize they have a writing teacher who says things like 'I'll punt on that one' or 'You're facing third and long.' "

It happens when she's among her colleagues, with similar effect. In my experience, if a woman uses that kind of metaphor, it gives men permission to talk about sports," she says. "A lot of the men I know academically wouldn't use that kind of language. It would have been . . . out of bounds."

Moyle, who was born and raised in England, has steeped herself in the history of American football. She says her enthusiasm for football metaphor occasionally dates her.

"I might say, when time is running out in a class session, 'I think we'd better drop-kick that subject into next week,' and they look at me as if I'd just used the term 'carbon paper' or 'E ticket at Disneyland,' " she says. (For the record, the last dropkick in the NFL was made by Ray [Scooter] McLean of the Chicago Bears on December 21, 1941.)

Herbeck sometimes hears a chorus of objection to the use of football expressions in everyday speech.

"Sports metaphor can be a way of belonging," he says. "Women's studies people make the argument that sports metaphor disempowers and pushes a person out. If you can't speak the language, they argue, you can't play.

"That one doesn't cut too much ice with me. Football does have a healthy female fan base. Some of these metaphors have become so much a part of the vernacular that people outside sports can still appreciate what the metaphor means."

Green's attempts to keep his football metaphors in check continue to fail under outside pressure. The clincher came during a meeting with his book editor.

"She and I usually talk about dialogue and scenes and vocabulary," Green says. "She knows absolutely nothing about sports. But one day she said, 'I'm really just your position coach. I'm going to have to defer to your head coach,' meaning my acquiring editor. It's funny when people assume you want to be talked to in football terms."

There are other phrases that are mistaken for "footspeak" but really come from other areas of life. One of the best-known is "the whole nine yards."

"You can take my word for it," Deford says. "It had nothing to do with football."

Mumme takes a crack at it: "One theory is that in World War II, the heavily armed P-51 aircraft measured twenty-seven feet from the machine guns on one wing to the machine guns on the other wing. According to this theory, when an airman had exhausted his ammunition, his phrase was 'I used the whole nine yards.' "

Who knows where this expression came from? "No one does," Sheidlower says. "This has been discussed at extreme length. You talk to ten people, you'll get ten stories. 'Cement trucks carry a load of nine cubic yards' is one you hear pretty often, but that's not true."

Herbeck has a simple explanation for the popularity of football language in everyday speech.

"The reason football metaphors are used," he says, "is that they work."

* * *

In the Pocket (Dictionary)
by Bob Carroll

Football lingo long ago invaded the real world, but, sometimes, the results can be disastrous. Corporate types, mere role players, make rookie mistakes and wind up in third-and-long situations.

An anecdote on the Internet described an executive who said his company was "in the red zone." Investors, believing the business was on the verge of a breakthrough, bought stock—only to discover that what the executive meant was the red *ink* zone.

To prepare you for handling the Xs and Os of real-world communication, here's a mini-camp of football terms and how they fit into real-life commentary.

Blue-chip – adj. Of high value, as in a "blue-chip prospect." Originally from poker, the designation has spread from football to other sports to just about anything that can be ranked.

Breakaway – v., adj. To suddenly outdistance competitors, as in "Pringle's Purple Peppermints experienced breakaway sales this quarter."

Bring in the chains – v. To take a closer look, as in "Let's bring in the chains on this proposal." You might say in this article we're "bringing in the chains" on football terms.

Chip shot – n. A task easy to accomplish, as in "Doing this report will be a chip shot." The term originally came from a golf term for a short shot to the green; it now is also thought of as an easy field goal.

Clothesline – v. To stop an opponent in his tracks, as in "Our new, lower-priced model will clothesline the field." Technically this is an illegal tackle made by holding one's arm out stiffly at shoulder level and allowing an opponent to run into it with his head above the arm.

Dump off – v. To get rid of an unwanted or unpleasant task to an underling, as in "Mr. Bigbucks dumped off his speech before the Podunk Reading Circle to his VP." In a football game, a quarterback about to be sacked dumps off the ball to a nearby player in hopes of exchanging an imminent long loss for a shorter one—or even a gain. In the real world, we spend half our working time being dumped off on and the other half looking for "dumpees" that we can dump off on.

Flag – v. To call attention to an error, often resulting in punishment, as in "Old Lady Glutz flagged Timmy for chewing gum in class." When one is flagged, of course, the proper response is an equal mix of shame, remorse, and fierce determination not to be caught again.

Hearing footsteps – v. Betraying nervousness at the possible outcome of an impending situation. Originally what a wide receiver imagines when he goes over the middle.

Playbook – n. The choices available in making one's game plan. One should always be careful to distinguish between a game plan, which is a selection of those options that will help achieve a goal, and a playbook, which has every possible option but no thoughtful distinction between what will work, and, what will work in this particular situation.

Pocket – n. A comfortable place, one not to be abandoned abruptly for some wild idea, as in "Interesting suggestion, Fitzdrummond, but I think we'll stay in the pocket on this one and pass on your suggestion of painting the horses blue."

Ring bell of – v. To put in a dazed condition, as in "The new commercials really rang Acme's bell." Ringing the bell – good; getting one's bell rung – bad. If one's bell is rung too often, one tends to hear bells when no one is ringing them.

Super Bowl – n. The ultimate contest. "The Pillsbury Bakeoff is the Super Bowl of cooking." Saddam Hussein didn't understand this when he spoke of "the Mother of all Battles." General Norman Schwartzkopf wisely avoided motherhood metaphors and stuck with football; you see who won.

Swivel-hip – v. To dazzle, usually as a way to avoid or hide a pitfall. An example: "Ann Marie's plan swivel-hipped the board with predicted benefits while she didn't reveal the costs until the end, when everyone had fallen asleep."

Triple-threat – n. Originally, someone who could run, pass, and kick. Now, someone with many talents, as in "da Vinci was a real triple threat, but, in perspective, Raphael was just one-dimensional."

CHAPTER 23

The NFL on TV

Tom Barnidge

Television was in its infancy and the NFL in the throes of adolescence when the first pro football game was telecast live in 1939. It was a time when only an estimated 1,000 New York homes were equipped with TV sets, and NFL games (average attendance: 19,476) played to more empty seats than fans. Accordingly, the arrival of cameras and broadcast equipment at Ebbets Field on October 22 of that year seemed to qualify more as a novelty than as an historic event. The grainy black-and-white images that flickered on local TV screens showed the Brooklyn Dodgers defeating the Philadelphia Eagles 23-14 before 13,057 people who probably knew they were watching teams headed for losing seasons.

Hindsight affords a more eloquent perspective on the occasion. That romantic first meeting between the NFL and TV marked the beginning of one of the most successful marriages in entertainment history.

Television was destined to explode into the marketplace, invading living rooms far and near, as network broadcast signals linked all corners of the country. Pro football ideally suited for television and destined to become a programming staple, happily reaped the benefits of frequent and widespread exposure.

One force propelled the other like energetic kids on a teeter-totter. The NFL attracted larger and larger television audiences; the networks allocated more and more broadcast hours for games. The ultimate product of this relationship would be the Super Bowl, the most-watched program on American television. NFL clubs would receive annual rights fees that, by 1999, were worth more than $70 million per team.

As successful as the pairing of football and TV has been, it did not happen overnight.

In the NFL's earliest television days, every franchise looked out for itself. A club's success in securing a broadcast package and negotiating its asking price usually hinged on the size of the local market and the on-field success of its team.

One barometer of the frontier-TV climate was the 1947 Chicago Bears, who played in the country's second-largest city and kicked off the schedule as the defending NFL champion. Owner-coach George Halas sold the TV rights for that season for a paltry $900 per game. Even in 1956, nearly a decade later, the Green Bay Packers were able to attract only $35,000 for broadcast rights for the entire season.

In 1950, the Los Angeles Rams contracted through an understandably interested sponsor, Admiral Television, a manufacturer of TV sets, to televise their entire schedule. Because only road games had been televised previously, Admiral agreed to reimburse the Rams for lost ticket sales on home games as part of this unprecedented deal. Under this arrangement, attendance figures for 1949 were used as a basis of comparison. When that amount was translated into dollars, it turned out to be $307,000. The experiment ended quickly.

If the NFL and television sensed their common destiny, they remained at arm's length, unsure at this stage how to maximize their relationship. The league's 12 franchises negotiated individual contracts and televised road games to local markets, but seldom could any club command more than $100,000 in rights fees for a season.

Telecasts were limited to road games, according to league policy—successfully defended several times in court—from the 1950s until 1973, when Congress adopted experimental legislation requiring any NFL game that had been declared a sellout 72 hours prior to kickoff to be made available for local TV. That the Redskins happened at the time to be the hottest ticket in Washington was surely coincidental.

The Turning Point

The spark that ignited a budding love affair arrived in 1958, after a 12-game season in which the 9-3 Baltimore Colts and the 9-3 New York Giants distinguished themselves as the NFL's two best teams. In a showcase championship game broadcast by NBC from New York's Yankee Stadium, a national television audience tuned in to watch some of the greatest players in history.

The Colts featured Johnny Unitas, Gino Marchetti, Art Donovan, and Lenny Moore. The Giants were led by Charlie Conerly, Sam Huff, and Frank Gifford. All told, 15 future Pro Football Hall of Fame members were involved as coaches or players in a game that kept fans on the edges of their seats from start to finish.

When the score was tied 17-17 at the end of regulation time, a nation huddled around TV screens to watch NFL teams in the first sudden-death overtime that mattered. A preseason game played in Portland, Oregon, in 1955 had seen the Giants and Los Angeles Rams play into overtime, but that was only a forgotten experiment. This was the Main Event.

"I think the NFL as a national entity first came alive on television with the Giants-Colts championship game in 1958," says Dennis Lewin, NFL senior vice president of broadcasting and network television. "That exposure on a national level, with one of the greatest games ever played, launched pro football into the American consciousness."

After 8 minutes 15 seconds of overtime, in the early evening chill of December 28, 1958, the Colts' Alan Ameche bulled into the end zone at the end of a heart-pounding 80-yard drive. Baltimore had won 23-17. More importantly, a budding television star—the National Football League—had arrived and realized its initial promise.

"I was lucky enough to be a participant in that game," says announcer Pat Summerall, then a defensive end and kicker for the Giants. "The magnitude of what that game did to bring football to the attention of the country never has diminished."

The "Greatest Game Ever Played," as the 1958 championship game often has been described, opened the eyes of television executives to the marketability of the NFL. Traditional rivalries, gifted athletes, and dramatic confrontations were packaged neatly on Sunday afternoons when competitive programming was its weakest.

From the visionary perspective of Commissioner Pete Rozelle, newly elected in 1960, two obstacles remained before the NFL could capitalize on its good fortune. First of all, the league needed the blessings of club owners to package all their games into a single national contract, rather than piecemeal through local-market outlets. Secondly, it needed congressional approval for a single-network, league-wide television contract in order to avoid antitrust violations.

Rozelle went about lobbying on both fronts and demonstrated his powers of persuasion. On September 30, 1961, President John F. Kennedy signed into law a single-network, sports-league bill introduced by Representative Emanuel Celler (D-New York). On January 10, 1962, club owners entered into an agreement with CBS that called for the televising of all regular-season NFL games for $4.65 million annually.

It soon became clear that the format of pro football games was suited perfectly to a television broadcast. A sustained burst of action was followed by a sustained break when teams huddled or left the field. Announcers had time to discuss strategy and anticipate play calling. Advertisers had time to deliver their commercial messages.

"I've often discussed this with the people I work with," says Summerall, a broadcaster for more than 30 years. "It's almost as if when the game was invented, it was invented for television.

"You've got four quarters and obvious time outs. The field is like a stage on which you can see all twenty-two actors, plus the supporting cast on the sidelines. Then the action comes to a stop, and the team goes back into the huddle, which gives you a chance to talk with your buddy and think about what might happen next."

Technology's Role

Football games also were perfect showcases for television's technological advances. More camera angles permitted viewers to examine the subtleties of each play. Instant replay allowed the audience to thrill to acrobatic moves again and again. Split-screen technology isolated passer and receiver at the same time. Slow-motion playback helped demonstrate why a key play succeeded or failed.

The nature of the schedule was another factor that added to pro football's appeal. With each game separated by a week's worth of anticipation, an air of drama preceded each kickoff.

"We play one game a week, and, therefore, each one is an event," says Art Modell, owner of the Baltimore Ravens and former chairman of the NFL's Broadcast Committee. "That's the distinction between the NFL and the other pro sports. The infrequency of play makes each Sunday something special, whether you're in front of your TV set or at the stadium."

Increasing rights fees reflected the network's enthusiasm for the NFL. For the 1964-65 seasons, CBS agreed to pay $14.1 million per year. For 1966-69, the figure had increased to $18.1 million. By 1970, it was $46.25 million.

And there is no question that television fees enabled the American Football League to become the first league successfully to challenge the NFL. The AFL's first modest pact, signed with ABC in 1960 before the newcomers had kicked a ball, was its key to survival during its first five years. When the young league signed a five-year, $36 million pact with NBC in 1965, the NFL knew the AFL was here to stay. An agreement to merge came the next year.

With the arrival of the 1966 NFL-AFL merger, which went into effect in 1970, the league not only increased its number of teams, it also expanded its television exposure. CBS, which had carried NFL games, became the official network for the new National Football Conference. NBC was given rights to show games of the American Football Conference.

Both networks broadcast the initial Super Bowl (then known as the AFL-NFL World Championship Game) on January 15, 1967. For the next 17 seasons, until ABC entered the rotation, CBS and NBC alternated the assignment, beginning with CBS in Super Bowl II.

The first Super Bowl was the only Super Bowl that did not sell out at the gate, but it was clearly a television ratings success. The combined Nielsen rating of both networks was 40.8, with their broadcasts reaching an audience of 85 million.

But there was more to come. The event that signaled the NFL's pre-eminence in sports television arrived in 1970, when ABC accepted Rozelle's innovative proposal for weekly prime-time football programming. *Monday Night Football* was born.

Interestingly, both CBS and NBC, the NFL's regular broadcast partners, had been approached with this concept earlier. Each of the established networks rejected the notion of allocating three hours of prime-time television for weekly NFL games.

"There was a reluctance on the part of television executives to pre-empt regular programming," says Val Pinchbeck, formerly the NFL's senior vice president of broadcasting and network television. "CBS had the *Doris Day Show* in a certain time slot, and it would not alter that. NBC had the *Monday Night Movies.*"

ABC, with the weakest Nielsen ratings of the networks, was a logical third choice. But even ABC expressed some doubts about the project until Rozelle bluntly explained his alternative plan: If no network was interested in televising Monday night games, the NFL would arrange to syndicate the programming.

ABC Makes Its Move

Fearful that many of its affiliates would drop the ABC network feed in order to broadcast an NFL game, ABC reconsidered the offer and made a deal. That decision marked the beginning of television's second-longest running prime-time television series, which celebrates its twenty-ninth season in 1999. (Only *60 Minutes* has been on the air longer.)

"I don't think anybody dreamed what it would become," Lewin says. "I don't think there was any way to anticipate it. The other networks passed, so there obviously was some skepticism."

The distinctive members of ABC's broadcast team contributed profoundly to its early success. Howard Cosell, opinionated and outspoken, considered himself a professional journalist and objective critic. Former quarterback Don Meredith, unassuming and blessed with homespun wit, counterbalanced Cosell's life-and-death seriousness. Hall-of-Fame halfback Frank Gifford, who replaced Keith Jackson in the program's second year, was the smooth-spoken, charismatic play-by-play announcer. The prime-time telecasts, produced with show-biz flair, attracted an enormous audience, which came as no surprise to Rozelle.

"There are more TV sets in use on Monday night than on Sunday afternoon," he explained. "We're undoubtedly getting a lot of new fans."

ABC, CBS, and NBC jointly shared NFL rights until 1987, when cable network ESPN was added to the mix. Concerned about oversaturating the market with their product, NFL executives limited ESPN to eight Sunday night telecasts over the last half of the season.

The fears were unfounded. The ESPN experiment was so well received that when a new contract was negotiated in 1990, cable network TNT was allowed to purchase rights to Sunday night games for the first eight weeks of the season. It marked the first time that any sports league had simultaneous contracts with five different networks.

Escalating rights fees reflected the increasing popularity of pro football. The NFL television package climbed by leaps and bounds:

Years	Amount (in millions) Per Year
1982-86	$ 420
1987-89	$ 473
1990-93	$ 900
1994-97	$1,100
1998-2005	$2,200

The 1994 package marked a milestone. It heralded the addition of the FOX network as a national broadcast partner and the absence of CBS for the first time since the first single-network contract in 1962. But CBS would be back. In 1998, when the NFL negotiated a record-setting television package—$17.6 billion for eight years—CBS outbid NBC for the rights to AFC games. In addition, ESPN won the rights to a season-long cable package.

If the price for NFL games is high, their appeal as entertainment programming is unmistakable. The three most-watched shows in TV history are Super Bowl games. But how important has television been to the NFL? "I think it's been integral to the game's success," Pinchbeck says. "In a given week, you could have close to a million people watching games from the stands and a hundred million or more watching on TV.

"All of our teams are on TV in the regular season, and people across the country can get to know each team, which is why a kid in Long Island can grow up rooting for Terry Bradshaw, or a youngster in Philadelphia can be a fan of Dan Marino. Television is the engine that drives the train."

CHAPTER 24

Super Bowl Commercials

Phil Barber

In the third quarter of Super Bowl XVIII, 60 seconds would change history and burn a lasting image into American consciousness. No, it was not Marcus Allen's 74-yard, reverse-field touchdown run, which cemented the Raiders' 38-9 victory over Washington. The defining moment in question occurred during a time out, when an athletic-looking young woman charged into a darkly ominous gathering and smashed the towering image of Big Brother with a mighty heave of her hammer.

This was "1984," the only commercial Apple Computer, Inc., would run during that Orwellian year. America still feels its effects. As Street & Smith's *Sports Business Journal* pointed out in a report on Super Bowl advertising, Apple's timing, as it turns out, was impeccable. The next decade would witness financial explosions in two industries: sports marketing and new technology. It also would raise the first MTV generation, nourished with quick visual cuts and sensory bombardment (i.e., the aesthetics of the television commercial). Furthermore, Super Bowl XVIII would be the last AFC victory for 14 years; a long string of NFC-dominated blowouts occasionally had viewers' minds wandering.

All of these factors combined to make "1984" a revelation. (*Advertising Age* later named Chiat/Day's creation the TV ad of the decade.) Apple, still reeling from the massive failure of its $10,000 Lisa computer, would sell 50,000 Macintosh units in 100 days following Super Bowl XVIII, fueling a high-tech revolution.

The landmark commercial signaled a breakthrough in Super Bowl advertising. Today, the list of sponsors almost is as hotly anticipated as the two teams' starting lineups. Eisner & Associates, a Baltimore ad agency, found that approximately 7 percent of all Super Bowl viewers tune in solely to watch the commercials. The ads are previewed and reviewed in the national media, including *USA Today*. The newspaper's Ad Meter, which is based on fans' reactions to the commercials, has become the newspaper's largest annual project.

Nike's "Hare Jordan," the Budweiser frogs and lizards, Pepsi's tattletale security camera, and the Tabasco-ingesting, spontaneously combusting mosquito nearly are as indelible as Joe Montana-to-John Taylor and Desmond Howard's kick returns.

"It's not just the Super Bowl of football," says Jerry Solomon, who buys commercial time for clients of SFM Media, "it's the Super Bowl of advertising."

Or as Bink Garrison, chairman of Ingalls Advertising, puts it: "The Super Bowl is like the space shuttle of advertising—it's the launch vehicle for the industry."

Is it any wonder major advertisers and their agency representatives now sit in the Super Bowl broadcast booth, ready to trouble-shoot any glitches that might beset their commercials? Not when you consider how much they pay for the right to sing and dance in front of the Super Bowl audience. Advertisers paid an average of $42,500 for a 30-second spot in Super Bowl I (called the AFL-NFL World Championship Game at the time). When "1984" hit the airwaves, the price was $485,000 for 30 seconds. At Super Bowl XXXIII in January, 1999, it had vaulted to $1.6 million. That was about three times as much as that season's next-most-expensive, prime-time advertising.

Besides its in-game commercial units, FOX was able to charge top dollar for its pregame and postgame spots last January 31, and even for the ads that ran during two subsequent sitcoms (see chart).

FOX Network's Super Bowl XXXIII Ad Rates
Per 30 Seconds

11 A.M. to 2 P.M.	$35,000-$75,000
2 P.M. to 5 P.M.	$120,000-$175,000
5 P.M. to 6:23 P.M. (kickoff)	$375,000-$1,000,000
During game (on average)	$1,600,000
Postgame	$750,000-$800,000
Family Guy and *The Simpsons*	$700,000-$800,000

Add another $45 million garnered by FOX's 22 owned-and-operated affiliates, and the network's total take was close to $200 million—the greatest single-day income in the history of television.

A Giant Imprint

Super Bowl advertisers tend to be entrenched, deep-pocketed corporations such as Anheuser-Busch, American Express, and Oldsmobile. But the lineup for XXXIII included upstarts such as HotJobs.com, a small Internet job-search company that never before had advertised on TV. HotJobs reportedly spent more than $2.5 million to produce and air a 30-second commercial during the third quarter, though the company made less than $5 million in 1998. Co-founder Richard Johnson even dipped into personal assets to get it done.

Why would anyone risk his, or his employer's, financial well-being for 30 seconds of air time—about as long as it took Dallas defensive tackle Leon Lett to return a fumble 64 yards in Super Bowl XXVII?

You can start with the stark numbers of Super Bowl viewership. More than 800 million people around the globe watched Super Bowl XXXIII on television in January 1999. Stateside, some 127 million Americans—nearly half the population—tuned in to Denver's victory over Atlanta. The top five most-watched television programs of all time (total number of viewers) are Super Bowls.

"There's no other way—on TV or any other medium—in which you can reach a bigger audience," says George Rosenbaum, chief executive officer of Leo J. Shapiro & Associates, a Chicago-based market research firm. "In one day you can make a giant imprint on the nation."

Hallmark Cards reports that the Super Bowl has become the nation's top at-home party occasion, overtaking New Year's Eve. It doesn't hurt that the game falls soon after the holiday season, when, according to *MediaSport* author Lawrence Wenner, "We're still stuck inside with bad weather and we're looking for excuses to get together and celebrate something."

A massive, captive audience always has been golden to TV marketers. But the Super Bowl has become even more important in the 1990s as the Big Three networks have been challenged by FOX, UPN, WB, and 500 cable channels. The advent of digital television only will increase the number of viewing options. In effect, the American TV audience continually is being chopped and splintered, and the Super Bowl is one of the few events that retains the power to glue it back together.

"I see football as vitally important," says David Hill, chairman of the FOX network. "In the year 2005, it's going to look like a giant in a sea of pygmies."

The NFL's impact goes beyond Nielsen ratings. Viewers consistently describe Super Bowl ads as more interesting than those on regular prime-time programming, and they are able to recall more of the content. Fifty-two percent of viewers polled by Starcom Media Services reported discussing Super Bowl XXXIII commercials the day after the game.

Perhaps more important, advertisers agree that the Super Bowl audience is not a typical group. First Union Corporation chose to run a 60-second commercial during Super Bowl XXXIII because, as a spokeswoman explained, the company wanted to get its message in front of corporate executives and other decision-makers. Part of the message is implied: "We've got enough money to advertise during the Super Bowl."

"Wall Street is easily impressed with Super Bowl ads, which everyone knows cost a bundle," says Joann O'Brien, Intel's media relations manager. "If you have the means to advertise during it, then that says to everyone the company is healthy. That alone may boost the company stock a few points or sway an analyst."

Wall Street isn't the only corridor that pays close attention to Super Bowl ads. The commercials also can serve to pump up retailers, especially when the commercials are tied to merchandise, point-of-purchase promotions, or sweepstakes. As name-brand producers have learned, nothing boosts worker morale like running a Super Bowl ad.

"This is the Super Bowl, and game day is Anheuser-Busch-owned," said Tony Ponturo, the beer giant's vice president of corporate media and sports marketing (Anheuser-Busch is the Super Bowl's exclusive beer advertiser through 2002). "Our employees expect it, our wholesaler system expects it, I think the retailer expects it, and we hope our consumer expects it as well."

"We got pretty big bang for the buck," says Pete Ellis, whose Internet car dealership, Auto-by-tel.com Inc., drummed up so much traffic with a 1997 ad that it bought time again in 1998.

During Super Bowl XXXI, Intel ran an ad that encouraged viewers to log on to the computer-chip company's Web site and vote for the outcome of a follow-up spot. They got more than 388,761 "hits." The popularity of "Hare Jordan" actually spawned a feature-length movie, *Space Jam.* And Anheuser-Busch says that for the last decade, its beer sales annually have spiked in late January.

Even supermodels can attest to the Super Bowl's star power. It was a Pepsi ad in 1992 that boosted the career of Cindy Crawford. And Ali Landry's phone rang off the hook after she delighted the couch potatoes by catching a Doritos puff in her mouth in 1998. "I had to change my number," she says. "The job offers were amazing."

Airplane Banners and Web Sites

With testimonials arriving from so many different directions, you can see why advertisers go to extremes to promote their spots. Many companies make their commercials available to outlets such as *Entertainment Tonight* as the big game approaches. Before Super Bowl XXXIII, Frito-Lay actually sent newspapers a videotape detailing the making of its Smokey Red Barbecue Doritos commercial. And Anheuser-Busch executives called a press conference in Manhattan to outline their long-term Super Bowl game plan, brandishing rough and finished versions of commercials they were considering for their nine slots during XXXIII.

Heavy promotion doesn't heat up until the playoffs, but the jockeying for ad space starts immediately after the previous Super Bowl concludes. Traditionally, 25 percent of Super Bowl ad space is purchased immediately after the previous edition; 50 percent is bought during the spring; and the remaining 25 percent goes between September and mid-January.

"Usually the big sponsors buy early and pay the rate card," says Neil Pilson, the former president of CBS Sports.

Smaller, less-conventional companies often wait it out, hoping to find a late bargain. Occasionally, the commercials themselves are made in the eleventh hour. After firing one agency, HotJobs hired a replacement, McCann-Erickson Detroit, just six weeks before its Super Bowl XXXIII ad was due. (The networks generally want to receive all Super Bowl ads a week before the game, earlier than for other sporting events.) CompuServe's 1997 ad was conceived 10 days before the game.

Usually, however, a great deal of time goes into planning a Super Bowl commercial, which can make or break a company's advertising plan for the year. With animation to create, celebrities to sign, and corporate approvals to be secured, even a year can seem like a squeeze.

"James Cameron took forever to get *Titanic* done," says Tony Weisman, senior vice president at Leo Burnett Company in Chicago. "That's the difference. If we miss it, we miss it. They're not going to postpone the Super Bowl for us."

Cameron has yet to direct a Super Bowl ad, but other major Hollywood directors have. Ridley Scott (*Blade Runner, Alien*) did the "1984" spot. George Lucas (the *Star Wars* trilogy) directed the recent ad for First Union, and the edgy Coen Brothers (*Fargo, The Big Lebowski*) did one for Honda Odyssey.

Still, not every Super Bowl advertiser opts for a Hollywood-sized epic. Some offer scaled-down commercials, either to offset the high purchase price or simply to stand out in a glitzy crowd. "It's enough for them to be at the party," says Melanie Wells, advertising reporter for *USA Today*. "They don't have to wear a black tie."

While national television ads form the centerpiece of Super Bowl advertising, TV money trickles down to the local stations that broadcast the game. FOX's New York affiliate reportedly sold its last package of five pregame spots for a local record of $600,000 in January, 1999. Radio is a factor, too. CBS/Westwood One charged between $4,000 and $7,500—roughly twice the regular-season rate—for radio spots at Super Bowl XXXIII.

And now you can throw Web sites into the advertising mix. Jaan Janes, senior director of programming and marketing for NFL Interactive, estimates that "a few-thousand sites" ran some sort of Super Bowl coverage last January. SuperBowl.com, a joint project of the NFL and the portal service Lycos, drew close to 5 million distinct Internet users before, during, and after Super Bowl XXXIII.

Other methods of advertising remain decidedly low-tech. Last January, an "aerial ad man" charged about $12,000 for a 15-hour package of flying a commercial message over Super Bowl-related events (but not the game) in South Florida.

Thanks, Mean Joe

Lest we forget, the NFL is an advertising vehicle in months other than January. Though they pale next to the Super Bowl, the AFC and NFC Championship Games usually place in the top four of the year's highest-rated TV programs, cementing the league's media stature.

And disguised in the overall NFL ratings is a demographic considered critical to the modern TV industry: It's a guy thing. Women generally watch more television than men and are therefore exposed to more advertising. But reaching men (especially those in the 21-35 age group) is harder. Nothing entices them like NFL football.

"When we didn't have football, we were looked upon as a second-rate network," says Leslie Moonves, president of CBS Television. "The twenty-eight-year-old media buyer in New York probably never watched a show on CBS. Now he watches football, and he's going to realize we have some other shows he's interested in."

That certainly was the case when FOX heavily promoted its new animated series, *The PJs,* during the Vikings-Cardinals playoff game last season. The target audience, young men, responded in such numbers that *The PJs* preview was FOX's top-rated program before the Super Bowl. That's a lucid example of why CBS was willing to join FOX and ABC/ESPN in offering up record-setting rights fees for NFL games in 1998. All three NFL-affiliated networks showed slight increases in male viewership (2-3 percent) during the 1998 fall season, while the exile, NBC, was down a whopping 26 percent.

"The NFL is insurance," says Dean Bonham, the head of Bonham Group, a firm that specializes in analyzing financial deals for sports properties. "For these networks, whether they lose money on the deal or not, the NFL is not part of the problem. It's part of the solution."

Of course, you don't have to advertise only during a football game to tap into the NFL's selling power. Over the years, Madison Avenue has been infatuated with football types: Joe Namath rubbing Noxzema shaving cream onto his legs; Walt Garrison sticking a pinch of Skoal between his cheek and gums; Mean Joe Greene downing an awe-struck kid's Coke (that one captured a Clio award); O.J. Simpson running through airports in lieu of renting a car from Hertz; John Madden bursting through every wall in sight to pitch Lite Beer from Miller, while his cohorts shout "Tastes great!" or "Less filling!"

Other well-known football ads never were intended to sell a single bottle or box of any product. They are the more than 1,000 United Way of America spots directed by Mario Pellegrini. Bills guard Reggie McKenzie did the first in 1974, for a Buffalo-area medical clinic. NFL Commissioner Pete Rozelle was so convinced of the ad's positive appeal that he immediately ordered one for every NFL team. Since then the images have included everything from Gary Jeter with his legless father, to Lomas Brown holding out a massive finger to a newborn crack baby, to Don Shula's emotional request for donations to fight breast cancer, the disease that claimed his first wife, Dorothy.

No player, coach, or executive ever has accepted a dime for the spots, but most wind up feeling rewarded. Roger Staubach, the great Cowboys quarterback, made one of the first United Way ads in 1974. He appeared with Gayla Vaughn, a little girl who had undergone heart surgery. Vaughn recovered, and Pellegrini later made commercials in which Staubach visited her (re-created) high school prom and wedding. Former 49ers tackle Steve Wallace and his wife were so touched by the ad they did for the Bay Shore Foster Child Care Service that they wound up adopting two young girls.

The series is the longest-running of its kind in television history. It's impossible to gauge how much money the United Way's 1,400 local chapters have garnered directly through the ads. We do know the umbrella organization's annual collection has gone from $800 million to $3.4 billion since 1974, and that the 40 seconds of free air time the United Way receives during every NFL game amount to a precious donation.

"We could never afford to buy that time," says Betty Stanley Beene, president of the United Way of America. "It amounts to sixty-five million dollars annually. More people see our Super Bowl spots than vote in a presidential election."

Thanks to the NFL and its stars, advertising works—for all of us.

CHAPTER 25

Three Reels and a Cloud of Dust

Bob Carroll and Michael Gershman

Movies have been far friendlier to professional football players than to pro football itself. The number of athletes whose names once were found in NFL lineups but now can be seen in cast listings far outstrips former baseball or basketball players. A few NFL graduates have achieved stardom; many more work steadily in supporting roles.

Although pro players have been a popular presence on the silver screen since before talkies, on those rare occasions when Hollywood made movies about pro football, the films have been less than realistic. In the days when movie cameras were hand-cranked, films with college football as a background and the Big Game as the climactic scene were cranked out with monotonous regularity. A few old-timers such as Harold Lloyd's *The Freshman* and the Marx Brothers' *Horse Feathers* still are great fun. But most of the "football films" made in the first half of the century were tiresomely predictable: Boy wins both Big Game and girl by overcoming crooks, cheaters, gamblers, or rich opponents. About the only pre-World War II pro football film Hollywood made was, literally, *Pro Football* (1934), a short subject featuring Red Grange, Bronko Nagurski, George Halas, and other legends. Not surprisingly, it never made the Oscar cut. Grange had made *One Minute to Play* (1926) and six other films but the football depicted in them wasn't the professional brand.

Pro football fans may decry the relative absence of their favorite sport at the Bijou, but there are logical reasons. For one thing, college football was more popular than the pro game in the 1920s and 1930s. Movie moguls like making money even more than making movies. Naturally, they set their football films in the more popular college milieu.

Pro football also was limited geographically to the Northeast and Midwest through the 1930s. That made selling a pro football movie across the entire nation a dicey proposition.

The climate began to change after World War II. Pro football began its steady climb to overtake and eventually pass college football in popularity. In 1946, the Cleveland Rams moved to Los Angeles, opening up the West Coast to the NFL. The league became truly national. Filmmakers in Hollywood began to consider pro football as a new, popular, and lucrative source of material for the silver screen.

The First Real Pro Football Movie

A breakthrough of sorts came in 1953 when a film about a real pro football player was released. Elroy (Crazylegs) Hirsch was one of the greatest stars in the NFL at the time—a sure-handed receiver with an odd and recognizable gait. His story, *Crazylegs,* made a surprisingly good film, thanks in no small part to the actor who played the lead, one Elroy Hirsch. Two years later, Hirsch again showed himself to be an accomplished actor in a prison movie called *Unchained.* In addition to Hirsch, the film contained one of the greatest musical themes of all time in "Unchained Melody," but apparently the public preferred watching Hirsch score on the playing field rather than on the silver screen. His movie career petered out.

Perhaps the most surprising football-field-to-films transition came in 1966 when Jim Brown gave up his football career to become a movie star. At the time, Cleveland's great fullback held most of the NFL's rushing records and was coming off a season in which he'd led the league in rushing for the eighth time in nine seasons. But instead of reporting to training camp, Brown announced his retirement to remain in England to finish a film in which he had a featured role, *The Dirty Dozen.*

It turned out to be a good career move. Brown quickly moved from featured roles in such films as *Ice Station Zebra* to leads in *tick . . . tick . . . tick* and *100 Rifles.* Although his roles usually entailed some degree of athleticism, Brown proved a competent actor and had a strong screen presence.

The practice of boosting the box-office by casting a big name athlete was nothing new in Hollywood. Nevertheless, Brown's success was a spur to other former NFL stars. Since the 1960s, luminaries such as Joe Namath, Fred Williamson, O.J. Simpson, Fred Dryer, Merlin Olsen, Carl Weathers, Alex Karras, Howie Long, and Bernie Casey have had some success on the screen.

It also is telling that Olsen and Long, and, to a lesser extent, Namath and Simpson, had success on television as analysts on NFL game broadcasts. Many former players get on-camera experience during games, but there seems to be almost no predictability about which former players will shine on the screen. Dan Marino and Brett Favre have been featured in major films in the last few years, but their reviews suggest they keep their day jobs. Terry Bradshaw played a part in *Hooper* (1978) but has been more successful building a TV career, as have Dryer, Olsen, and Karras—all of whom played leads in TV series.

A recognizable name might get a former player a part or two, but long-term success requires a different kind of talent. Although few fans remember that the late Woody Strode spent a year as a reserve end with the Los Angeles Rams in 1946, he had a long and successful career in movies. Two of his best roles came in *Sergeant Rutledge* (1960) and *The Man Who Shot Liberty Valence* (1962).

Two former football players who achieved the highest ranks of stardom never played professionally and, indeed, had negligible college football careers. Marion Morrison was a nonentity tackle at USC before he metamorphosed into John Wayne. Burt Reynolds once was an obscure running back at Florida State.

A number of movie and TV stars also had their brief moments on the football field. Dean Cain, who portrayed Superman in the *Lois & Clark* TV show, was a defensive back who went to training camp with the Buffalo Bills before a knee injury ended his pro career. Others, such as Robert Urich (Florida State), James Caan (Michigan State), and Jock (*Yancy Derringer*) Mahoney (Iowa), starred in college.

Why So Few Good Football Movies?

Although Hollywood has discovered that featuring the football player-turned-actor could be big box office, it seldom has been able to translate the sport itself successfully to the screen. One reason is strictly technical. Staged scrimmages tend to look staged. Even when actors with football training are used, it is difficult for them to make blocking and tackling look real when they must follow the dictates of a script. Try telling an NFL linebacker he must let an actor block him so another actor can win the game with a 50-yard run. Game scenes in recent movies have benefited from fast cuts and clever angles, but the best football footage is taken from real game films. (Of course, if you're looking for realistic football, you can always rent one of NFL Films' superb efforts.)

A more fatal flaw with football movies is one that dooms all sports movies. The suspense of real games never can be duplicated in a scripted film. We usually know as we set out for the theater that the hero's team will win or at least achieve a moral victory.

Because no football movie can give us the same football thrills as the real thing, football movies usually are about anything but football. Scriptwriters take a love story, a coming-of-age epic, a murder mystery, a courage-overcomes-handicap tear-jerker, or any of the other basic plots and slap it into a football setting. As a result, some rather strange choices end up classified as "football movies." Where do we draw the line at defining the term?

Knute Rockne: All-American is a football movie, but not a *pro* football movie. *The Longest Yard* is a *prison* football movie. *All the Right Moves* is a *high school* football movie. Only movies with an emphasis on *pro* football apply here. (We're also ruling out *Jerry Maguire,* because it's more about love and money than pro football.)

Cat on a Hot Tin Roof is not a pro football movie just because Paul Newman's character supposedly was a halfback at one time. *Black Sunday* is a football movie because the plot revolves around a terrorist attack on the stadium in which the Super Bowl is being played, and actual Steelers-Cowboys game film helps build suspense before the final shootout. The difference is that Newman's character could have been a shoe salesman without destroying *Cat's* story line, but, with *Black Sunday,* a sports setting was an absolute necessity, and not even a World Series game would have had the same impact.

Armed with such distinctions, we present our choices as the best and worst pro football films ever made.

The Best

1. *Brian's Song* (1970). The true story of the Bears' Brian Piccolo (James Caan) and his friendship with Gale Sayers (Billy Dee Williams) during Piccolo's unsuccessful fight with cancer. Watch it with someone you love and for months you'll be able to bring them to tears by humming the theme song. Despite its tragic subject, this is a life-affirming gem.
2. *North Dallas Forty* (1979). Like Pete Gent's book on which it was based, this is an unflattering portrait of the business of football. Nevertheless, good performances by Nick Nolte and others, plus some surprises, make it worth watching.
3. *Black Sunday* (1977). An excellent thriller, with Robert Shaw heroic and Bruce Dern scary. You won't soon forget the killer blimp swooping in on the Super Bowl. The intercut Pittsburgh-Dallas footage is a real bonus.
4. *The Guy Who Came Back* (1951). Paul Douglas plays a fullback whose excesses ruin his career, but he ends up as the title character. Very loosely based on Bronko Nagurski's return to the Bears from his wrestling career because of World War II manpower shortages, the plot is predictable, but Douglas makes it entertaining.
5. *Fighting Back* (1980). Not to be confused with the other movies of the same name, this is the one in which Robert Ulrich plays Rocky Bleier, who fought back from a serious wound in Vietnam to help Pittsburgh win four Super Bowls. Includes good game footage.
6. *Crazylegs* (1953). Another good "biopic." Although Elroy Hirsch's story isn't as compelling as Bleier's, his play on the field was more spectacular.
7. *Paper Lion* (1968). Once you get past the ridiculous-though-true premise—famous writer goes to Detroit training camp masquerading as a prospect—you can enjoy Alan Alda masquerading as George Plimpton masquerading as a quarterback and seeing all those old Lions. Alex Karras steals the picture.
8. *Semi-Tough* (1977). You'll laugh (but not often), you'll cry (at a missed opportunity), and you'll forget the details quicker than Barry Sanders can slip though a seam in the defense. A Burt Reynolds comedy on a par with one of the later Bandit breed. Good actual game film, though.
9. *Trouble Along the Way* (1953). Sort of a pro football film. Down-and-out college coach John Wayne pays play-

ers to come in to give him a string of victories. Of course, Wayne eventually learns that honesty is indeed the best policy. He does get to mouth the words, usually attributed to Vince Lombardi: "Winning isn't everything; it's the only thing."

10. *Easy Living* (1949). Routine melodrama redeemed by the absence of the usual cliches. Aging star Victor Mature would (and should) retire, but shrewish wife Lizabeth Scott wants him to remain a money machine. Lucille Ball is excellent in a straight role. Former Rams star Kenny Washington has one line.

The Worst

In reverse order from the merely bad to the absolutely abysmal:

5. *Triple Threat* (1934). You know your movie's in trouble when the poster advertising it has pictures of 11 NFL players and none of the actors and actresses. Considering that the cast included Hall of Famers Sammy Baugh, Bill Dudley, Steve Van Buren, and Bob Waterfield, the producers were clearly playing the wrong game.

4. *Jim Thorpe: All-American* (1951). If you can buy Burt Lancaster as a Native American, you might enjoy some of this. At least Burt, who was an athlete, makes a better Jim Thorpe than William Bendix, who wasn't, made a Babe Ruth.

3. *Two-Minute Warning* (1976). There's a sniper at the big game and Charlton Heston is going to get him. You'll soon find yourself caring more about who won the football game. After Merv Griffin sings the National Anthem, it's all downhill.

2. *Superdome (*1978). The poor man's Two-Minute Warning. This one is so bad that when they showed it on TV they added nearly an hour and a whole new plot!

1. *Number One* (1969). Poor Charlton Heston should have stuck with racing chariots; football isn't his game. Here he pretends to be an aging quarterback (older than even Steve DeBerg, we think) who doesn't know when to quit. *North Dallas Forty* handled this kind of story well; this dull and dull-witted mess is the direct opposite. If we were handing out sacks instead of stars, this one would get five.

* * *

Selected Filmography of Movies Featuring NFL Players

Frankie Albert — *The Spirit of Stanford*
Doug Atkins — *Breakheart Pass*
Ernie Barnes — *Number One*
Sammy Baugh — *Texas Rangers*
Brian Bosworth — *Stone Cold*
Jim Brown — *Black Gunn; Dark of the Sun; The Dirty Dozen; The Grasshopper; I'm Gonna Get You, Sucka; 100 Rifles; Rio Conchos; The Running Man; Slaughter; The Split; Three the Hard Way; tick . . . tick . . . tick.*
Timmy Brown — *M*A*S*H*
Dick Butkus — *Gus; The Last Boy Scout*
Bernie Casey — *Revenge of the Nerds; Swamp Thing*
Ben Davidson — *M*A*S*H*
Fred Dryer — *Death Before Dishonor*
Carl Eller — *Busting*
Brett Favre — *There's Something About Mary*
Tom Fears — *Easy Living*
Frank Gifford — *The All-American; Darby's Rangers; That's My Boy; Two Minute Warning*
Mean Joe Greene — *Pop Goes the Weasel*
Elroy (Crazylegs) Hirsch — *Crazylegs; Unchained*
Paul Hornung — *Semi-Tough*
Ed (Too Tall) Jones — *Semi-Tough*
Joe Kapp — *Two Minute Warning; The Longest Yard*
Alex Karras — *Blazing Saddles; Paper Lion; Against All Odds*
Jim Kelly — *Three the Hard Way*
Tommy Kramer — *North Dallas Forty*
Howie Long — *Broken Arrow, That Thing You Do*
Ed Marinaro — *Dead Aim; Queen's Logic*
Dan Marino — *Ace Ventura, Pet Detective*
John Matuszak — *North Dallas Forty*
Jim McMahon — *Johnny Be Good*
Dandy Don Meredith — *Kate Bliss and the Ticker Tape Kid*
Ray Nitschke — *The Longest Yard*
Merlin Olsen — *The Undefeated*
Tim Rossovich — *The Long Riders*
O. J. Simpson — *Capricorn One; The Cassandra Crossing; Fire Power; Killer Force; The Naked Gun series; The Towering Inferno*
Bubba Smith — *Police Academy series*
Lynn Swann — *The Program, The Last Boy Scout*
Johnny Unitas — *Gus*
Kenny Washington — *Easy Living; While Thousands Cheer*
Bob Waterfield — *Jungle Manhunt*
Carl Weathers — *Action Jackson; Close Encounters of the Third Kind; Force Ten From Navarone; Predator; the Rocky series*
Fred Williamson — *Adios Amigo; Black Caesar; Breakheart Pass; The Hammer; The Longest Yard; M*A*S*H; Tell Me You Love Me, Junie Moon; Two-Minute Warning.*
Jack Youngblood — *North Dallas Forty*

Ensemble Films

A number of films have featured NFL players and coaches in job lots. They include:

Ace Ventura: Pet Detective — Kim Bokamper, Marco Coleman, Dan Marino, Scott Mitchell, Pete Stoyanovich, Dwight Stephenson.

The Black Six — Lem Barney, Mean Joe Greene, Carl Eller, Willie Lanier, Mercury Morris, Gene Washington.

Brian's Song — Dick Butkus, Bernie Casey, Abe Gibron, Jack Concannon, Ed O'Bradovich.

Crazylegs — Tom Fears, Dick (Night Train) Lane, Don Paul, Norm Van Brocklin, Bob Waterfield, Paul (Tank) Younger.

Heaven Can Wait — Al De Rogatis. Deacon Jones, Les Josephson, Jack Snow.
Jerry Maguire — Troy Aikman, Drew Bledsoe, Ki-Jana Carter, Kerry Collins, Dan Dierdorf, Wayne Fontes, Frank Gifford, Rich Kotite, Tim McDonald, Rick Mirer, Warren Moon, Art Monk, Herman Moore, Rob Moore.
Little Giants — Tim Brown, Steve Emtman, John Madden, Bruce Smith, Emmitt Smith.
The Longest Yard — Pervis Atkins, Joe Kapp, Ray Nitschke, Ernie Wheelright.
*M*A*S*H* — Tim Brown, Buck Buchanan, Jack Concannon, Ben Davidson, Noland Smith, Fran Tarkenton, Fred Williamson, Tom Woodeschick.
Necessary Roughness — Dick Butkus, Earl Campbell, Roger Craig, Ben Davidson, Tony Dorsett, Ed (Too Tall) Jones, Jim Kelly, Jerry Rice, Herschel Walker, Randy White.
Paper Lion — Lem Barney, Carl Brettschneider, Roger Brown, Jim David, Frank Gifford, John Gordy, Alex Karras, Chuck Knox, Ron Kramer, Vince Lombardi, Mike Lucci, Bill McPeak, Jim Martin, Joe Schmidt, Pat Studstill, Karl Sweetan.
Reggie's Prayer — Brett Favre, Roosevelt Grier, Mike Holmgren, Keith Jackson, Bryce Paup, William Roaf, Gale Sayers. Reggie White.
Triple Threat — Sammy Baugh, Paul Christman, Bill Dudley, Sid Luckman, Charlie Trippi, Steve Van Buren, Bob Waterfield.
The Waterboy — Bill Cowher, Dan Fouts, Jimmy Johnson, Lynn Swann, Lawrence Taylor.

OTHER LEAGUES

CHAPTER 26

The Early AFLs

Rick Korch

The American Football League. Len Dawson. George Blanda. Jack Kemp. Lance Alworth. Jim Otto. And Joe Namath. Those are the players everybody thinks of when the American Football League is mentioned, but there actually have been *four* different American Football Leagues. They were the leagues of Red Grange and C.C. Pyle, Al Kreuz, Ken Strong, and Hank Soar. They didn't last long, but they deeply affected professional football, and each had a unique tale to tell.

Throughout the history of the NFL, the league has faced competition from upstart leagues. Some were no better than minor-league level. Others were quite formidable. Three of them in the early days of pro football were called the American Football League.

1926 American Football League

Red Grange was the star and savior of the National Football League in 1925. In 1926, he became the NFL's competitor.

Grange's barnstorming tour with the Chicago Bears lasted until late January, 1926. His contract expired, and it did not include a reserve clause; thus, he became a free agent. Grange's agent, C.C. Pyle, offered Grange's services to the Bears for a five-figure contract and one-third ownership in the Bears, but he was turned down.

A few weeks after the tour ended, Pyle requested a New York franchise for Grange and himself. Pyle had, in fact, already taken out a five-year lease on Yankee Stadium. With the nation's marquee stadium and the biggest star in pro football, Pyle reasoned that every team figured to profit greatly. But Tim Mara, the owner of the New York Giants, which had just begun play the year before, refused to go along. Not only did he want the huge New York market for himself, but he also disliked Pyle.

Most of the 20 owners of NFL teams seemed to favor Pyle's plan, but Mara had a written contract that gave him exclusive rights to New York. When the NFL owners finally backed Mara and turned Pyle down, Pyle announced the formation of the American Football League, a competing organization whose main attraction would be Grange of the New York Yankees.

Nine clubs made up the new league. In addition to New York, teams were placed in Boston, Brooklyn, Chicago, Cleveland, Newark and Philadelphia; the Rock Island Independents, a charter member of the NFL, jumped to the new league. The ninth team was a road team that nominally represented Los Angeles. After famed sportswriter Grantland Rice turned down an offer to lead the AFL, Big Bill Edwards, a star athlete at Princeton in the 1890s, was named league president.

In addition to Grange, the AFL had other star players, mostly young glamour backs who had just graduated from college. Brooklyn signed Harry Stuhldreher of the famed Four Horsemen of Notre Dame; Los Angeles had George (Wildcat) Wilson of Washington; Newark had Doug Wycoff from Georgia Tech; and Philadelphia signed Al Kreuz from Pennsylvania.

Some NFL veterans also jumped to the new league, including seven members of the 1925 Cleveland Bulldogs who went to the AFL's Cleveland team. Joey Sternaman, the brother of Bears co-owner Dutch Sternaman, was induced to go into direct competition with his brother as owner, coach, and quarterback of the Chicago Bulls. Sternaman gained the right to play in Comiskey Park, exiling the NFL's Cardinals to play in much smaller Normal Park.

Pyle was the owner of the New York franchise, but apparently he also helped out the Los Angeles club and may have even backed Sternaman's Chicago team. In other words, he probably owned one-third of the league. The public thought of the AFL as Grange's league; in reality, it was Pyle's.

The NFL fought back by adding a few teams—including one in Brooklyn—and by signing bigger-name players, including some West Coast stars. But the AFL had its own big-name players. Grange scored 8 touchdowns in 15 games, but the league's leading scorer was his teammate, Eddie Tryon, who also had 8 touchdowns but scored 72 points because he kicked extra points and field goals.

The first AFL started play on September 26 with three games. The league counted on the well-known backs to draw fans, but attendance was lacking from the start. By the end of October, the Newark and Cleveland franchises folded, and the Brooklyn team went under a few weeks later (though it was merged into the NFL's Brooklyn team). Then Boston quit playing, and Rock Island, which had become a road team after its first three games, gave up in mid-November. At the end of the schedule in December, only New York, Philadelphia, Chicago, and Wilson's traveling Los Angeles squad still were playing. (Three of those four, remember, were underwritten by Pyle.)

The Yankees were the class of the league, scoring 212 points, more than twice the number scored by any other

AFL team. But because they played 15 games, finishing 10-5, they ended up in second place behind the Philadelphia Quakers, who were 8-2 (despite scoring just 93 points).

The race for the AFL's first—and, as it turned out, only—championship came down to two late November games between the high-scoring Yankees and the low-scoring Quakers. The Yankees were then 8-3, just behind the 6-2 Quakers. One of Philadelphia's losses was a 23-0 trouncing by New York on October 30.

The two teams met again on Thanksgiving Day at Yankee Stadium in front of 22,000 fans. Grange injured his hip, but New York had built a 10-6 lead. Then the Quakers' Pie Way, the smallest but fastest man on the field, caught a 40-yard touchdown pass from Johnny Scott, and Philadelphia had the victory.

Two days later, the same two teams had a rematch in Shibe Park. Again, the attendance was reported at 22,000, though it was probably closer to 15,000. Grange was unable to play, and Al Kreuz was knocked out early for Philadelphia. Bob Dinsmore filled in for Kreuz and kicked a pair of field goals, Scott threw another touchdown pass, and Philadelphia clinched the league title with a 13-6 victory.

The Yankees went on a postseason tour of the West and South in a vain effort to recapture the magic of the previous winter's Grange tour. But the rest of the AFL—what was left of it—meekly folded. In a final move, the champion Quakers met the NFL's New York Giants, a seventh-place team, in a snowstorm on December 12 at the Polo Grounds. Before 5,000 shivering spectators, the Quakers were thrashed soundly, 31-0.

The AFL teams were undercapitalized, and a lack of fans meant club owners couldn't cover promised salaries. Most of the teams weren't very good because they had been assembled hastily, lacked competent linemen, and were poorly coached. And, despite the star backs in the league, scoring was rare. In 41 league games, the AFL teams scored just 42 touchdowns. Only the Yankees averaged 2 a game. The champion Quakers scored 33 of their 93 points on field goals.

1926 Final Standings	W	L	T	Pct	PF	PA
Philadelphia Quakers	8	2	0	.800	93	52
New York Yankees	10	5	0	.667	212	82
Cleveland Panthers	3	2	0	.600	62	46
Los Angeles Wildcats	6	6	2	.500	105	83
Chicago Bulls	5	6	3	.455	88	69
Boston Bulldogs	2	4	0	.333	20	81
Rock Island Independents	2	6	1	.250	21	126
Brooklyn Horsemen	1	3	0	.250	25	68
Newark Bears	0	3	2	.000	7	26

A particularly rainy autumn held down crowds in most cities, but, more than anything, the AFL's chances for survival were predicated on the popularity of Grange and his Yankees. The league's other teams counted on two big paydays—one when Grange visited the town, and the second when they visited Yankee Stadium.

Thus the first and best of the early American Football Leagues lasted only one year. Through it all, Grange retained the respect and affection of the NFL, which is why Grange's team, the New York Yankees, was accepted into the NFL for 1927.

1936-37 American Football League

Fifteen cities applied for membership into the second American Football League, and plans were announced on November 15, 1935. The league was the brain child of Dr. Harry March, who, for many years, had been the personnel director for the New York Giants and an executive in the NFL office.

March designed his league as a players' league, and NFL veterans played prominent roles in the organization and administration of all the teams. Eight franchises were awarded on April 11, 1936: Boston, Cleveland, Jersey City, New York, Philadelphia, Pittsburgh, Providence, and Syracuse. By August, Jersey City, Philadelphia, and Providence were out, and Rochester was in. Then, in early September, Rochester was out and Brooklyn was in, though it started as a team without a stadium.

The second AFL had some big-name players and coaches: Jack McBride was the coach of the New York Yankees, and Ken Strong was their star player; the Syracuse Braves had Red Badgro as player-coach.

On the field, the 1936 AFL had major-league status among some fans, with Boston, Cleveland, New York, and Pittsburgh all fielding strong teams. However, the Syracuse franchise was a flop from the start both on the field and at the gate, and Badgro left after three games to return to the NFL. A week later, March resigned as league president and was replaced by James Bush, president of the New York Yankees.

Three days later, after suffering their fifth straight loss, the Syracuse Braves moved to Rochester. They played two more games and folded, leaving the AFL with only five teams. Strange begat stranger. The still-homeless Brooklyn team then moved to Rochester in mid-November, though it failed to win a game all season.

The Boston Shamrocks won the league's first championship with an 8-3 record. The Shamrocks defeated the Cleveland Rams and the New York Yankees—the league's next two best teams—in the final weeks of the season to take the title.

1936 Final Standings	W	L	T	Pct	PF	PA
Boston Shamrocks	8	3	0	.727	133	97
Cleveland Rams	5	2	2	.714	123	77
New York Yankees	5	3	2	.625	75	74
Pittsburgh Americans	3	2	1	.600	78	65
Syracuse/Rochester Braves	1	6	0	.143	41	113
Brooklyn/Rochester Tigers	0	6	1	.000	58	82

In 1937, the Cleveland Rams were accepted into the NFL on February 12. Jilted in their attempt to join the NFL, the Los Angeles Bulldogs joined the AFL. The first so-called major league team to play home games on the West Coast, the Bulldogs had compiled a 3-2-1 record against NFL teams in 1936. They were to prove to be the class of the AFL in 1937. One other new franchise was the Cincinnati Bengals, who, although this version of the AFL lasted only one more year, managed to survive through 1941 in other minor leagues also called AFL.

J.J. Schafer took over as AFL president, and the league's advisory board included heavyweight champ Jack Dempsey and singer Bing Crosby. The 1937 AFL suffered from the loss of several star players to the NFL, most notably Hank Soar, Bob Snyder, and Don Irwin.

The Los Angeles Bulldogs may have hurt the league more than they helped it. Sweeping to a 9-0 record and outscoring their opponents 233-72, the Bulldogs won the championship, and none of the other five teams finished over .500. In fact, for the second year in a row, only five of the six AFL teams lasted the season.

1937 Final Standings	W	L	T	Pct	PF	PA
Los Angeles Bulldogs	9	0	0	1.000	233	72
Rochester Tigers	3	3	1	.500	94	115
New York Yankees	2	3	1	.400	57	115
Cincinnati Bengals	2	4	2	.333	105	103
Boston Shamrocks	2	5	0	.286	76	98
Pittsburgh Americans	0	3	0	.000	7	69

The lack of star attractions and the lack of a title chase made the league less attractive than it had been the year before. This time, the league didn't make it through the offseason. Although three of its teams continued to operate in 1938, they did so as independents. This version of the American Football League was finished.

1940-41 American Football League

A league called the AFL actually continued in minor-league fashion in 1938 and 1939. By 1940, a new American Football League announced itself as major and ready to compete against the NFL.

On July 13, six teams formed the new league: Boston, Buffalo, Columbus, Cincinnati, Milwaukee, and New York. Two incumbent teams in the 1939 minor league AFL—St. Louis and Kenosha—were turned down for membership.

Though recognized as a major league, the AFL of 1940 was not a strong league. Headed by president William D. Griffith, it tried raiding the NFL for players but had little success.

The league's two strongest teams were Columbus and Milwaukee, two holdovers from the 1939 minor league. The league's top runner, halfback Al (Obbie) Novakofski led Milwaukee to a 7-0 start, but the Chiefs then lost their last two games of the season. Columbus, meanwhile, dropped its opener, but didn't lose again and finished 8-1-1. The Boston Bears were the other team above .500, and the New York Yankees had the league's best passing combination in Bill Hutchinson to Harlan Gustafson. But 2-8 Buffalo and 1-7 Cincinnati scored only 44 and 53 points, respectively, for the entire season.

1940 Final Standings	W	L	T	Pct	PF	PA
Columbus Bullies	8	1	1	.889	134	69
Milwaukee Chiefs	7	2	0	.778	180	59
Boston Bears	5	4	1	.556	120	79
New York Yankees	4	5	0	.444	137	138
Buffalo Indians	2	8	0	.200	44	137
Cincinnati Bengals	1	7	0	.125	53	186

On December 8, the AFL started plans on the 1941 season, announcing a draft of 50 college stars, giving the players the added incentive of choosing their teams. However, the draft proved unsuccessful and no players of note signed with the league.

Franchise moves were the offseason news, and several cities applied for membership, such as Baltimore, Detroit, and Philadelphia. As it turned out, the league barely was able to field five teams. The Boston Bears dropped out before the new season commenced, and Buffalo was unable to make a go at it before being acquired by new ownership.

The most interesting news of the offseason was in New York, where the Yankees signed Texas A&M All-America fullback John Kimbrough. However, the league office suspended Yankees owner Douglas Hertz and then revoked his franchise. A syndicate headed by William Cox (who later owned baseball's Philadelphia Phillies) took over the New York team and renamed it the Americans, but Kimbrough wasn't among the assets inherited by the new owners. That deal eventually was worked out, and then, on October 10, the Americans signed Michigan All-America Tom Harmon—the first time the AFL found itself a major story on sports pages across the country.

Nine days later, a crowd of 25,000—more than the NFL's New York Giants and Brooklyn Dodgers drew that day—saw Kimbrough and Harmon make their pro debut against the Columbus Bullies in Yankee Stadium. The game was a 7-7 tie with Harmon running for New York's touchdown. However, Harmon left the team after that game to enter military service.

Columbus won the league title with a 5-1-2 record, edging New York, which went 5-2-1, and Milwaukee, which finished 4-3-1.

1941 Final Standings	W	L	T	Pct	PF	PA
Columbus Bullies	5	1	2	.833	142	55
New York Americans	5	2	1	.714	116	73
Milwaukee Chiefs	4	3	1	.571	115	84
Buffalo Tigers	2	6	0	.333	72	172
Cincinnati Bengals	1	5	2	.167	69	120

Playing with only five teams, the 1941 AFL seemed to be on fairly solid ground, and a Detroit franchise was set to enter in 1942. But those plans received a major setback with the Japanese attack on Pearl Harbor in December 1941 and America's entry into World War II. On September 1, New York owner William Cox announced the AFL would close shop for the duration of the war. The league never was revived.

1926 American Football League Rosters

*—also played in NFL (see Player Register)

BOSTON BULLDOGS
Coleman, Ned - G-E - Holy Cross
Corrigan, Phil - BB-WB - E - Boston College
*Cronin, Bill - TB - Boston College
*Etelman, Carl - BB-WB - Boston U., Harvard, Tufts
Gehrke, Erwin - FB-WB-BB - Harvard
*Gilroy, Johnny - TB-WB - Georgetown
Gilroy, Ralph - TB-FB-E - Princeton
*Hagenbuckle, Vern - G - Dartmouth
Johnson, Oscar - FB-WB - Vermont
*Lowe, Bull - E - Lafayette, Fordham
Murphy, Bill - E - Boston U.
*McGlone, Joe - BB - Harvard
McManus, Art - G - Boston College [*from Newark*]
Morrison, Charlie - E-G-T - none
O'Brien, Tom - T - Boston College
Paten, Ray - G - Boston College
*Pierotti, Al - C - Washington & Lee
Ray, Art - G - Holy Cross
Smith, Pete - C-E - Holy Cross
Stephens, Bill - T-G-C - Bucknell
Surabian, Zeke - T - Williams
Treat, Herb - T - Boston College, Princeton
Wallis, Jim - WB-BB-FB - Holy Cross

BROOKLYN HORSEMEN
Bingham, Shep - E - Yale
Bolger, Jim - WB-TB - St. Mary's (Cal.), St. Bonaventure
Brennan, Paul - C-G - Fordham
*Britton, Earl - FB-TB - Illinois
*Drews, Ted - E - Princeton
Fitzgerald, Jim - BB - St. John's (N.Y.)
*Flaherty, Jim - WB - Georgetown
*Frugone, Jim - TB - Syracuse
*Garvey, Hec - T - Notre Dame [*to New York Yankees*]
*Harrison, Ed - E - Boston College
*Howard, Red - G - New Hampshire, Princeton
Hummell, Charlie - T - Lafayette
Hunsinger, Ed - E - Notre Dame
Koslick, Bill - T - none
Layden, Elmer - FB - Notre Dame [*from Rhode Island*]
Olsen, Swede - G - none
Nicholas, Bob - T - Oglethorpe
*Plumridge, Ted - C - Colgate, St. John's (N.Y.)
Pollock, Sheldon - C - Lafayette
Prendergast, Leo - T-C - Lafayette
Sehres, Dave - WB-G - New York U.
*Share, Nate - T - Tufts
Sheehy, Jack - G-C - New York U.
Smith, Ray - TB-WB-BB - Lebanon Valley
*Stuhldreher, Harry - BB - Notre Dame
*Taylor, Tarzan - G - Ohio State

CHICAGO BULLS
*Anderson, Eddie - E - Notre Dame
Blackwood, Hal - G - Chicago, Northwestern
Boyle, Jack - E - Loras
*Buckeye, Garland - G - none
*Connell, Ward - WB-E - Notre Dame
*Crawford, Mush - G-T - Beloit, Lake Forest, Illinois
*Fahay, John - E - St. Thomas, Marquette
*Giaver, Bill - WB - Georgia Tech
*Goodman, Aubrey - T-E - Baylor, Chicago
*Graham, Fred - E - Indiana State, West Virginia
*Hall, Harry - BB-TB - Chicago, Illinois
*Larson, Ojay - C - Notre Dame
*Mahan, Red - G - West Virginia
McMullan, John - T - Notre Dame
*Mohardt, Johnny - TB - Notre Dame
Richerson, Doss - G-E-T - Missouri
Romey, Dick - E - Iowa
*Stahlman, Dick - T-G - DePaul, Northwestern [*from Rhode Island*]
*Sternaman, Joey - BB - Illinois
*Strader, Red - WB-FB - St. Mary's (Cal.)
Swenson, Swede - G - Chicago, Dartmouth
*Tays, Jim - TB - Penn State, Chicago
*White, Buck - FB - Howard Payne, Valparaiso
Whiteman, Sam - WB-TB-FB - Missouri

CLEVELAND PANTHERS
Behm, Norty - E-FB - Iowa State
*Cunningham, Cookie - E - Ohio State
Dean, - T
*Elliott, Doc - FB - Lafayette [*to Philadelphia*]
Evans, Mike - T - Ohio Wesleyan
Gribben, Billy - TB - Case Western Reserve
Kregenow, Ed - E - Akron
*Michaels, Al - TB - Heidelberg, Ohio State
*Nesser, Al - G-E - none
*Noble, Dave - WB - Nebraska
Otterbacher, John - G - Ohio State
*Roberts, Guy - FB-WB-BB - Iowa State
*Roberts, Red - T - Centre
*Sack, Jack - G - Pittsburgh
*Spiers, Bob - T-G - Ohio State
Thornburg, Al - C - Iowa State
*Vince, Ralph - G - Washington & Jefferson
Virant, Leo - G - Dayton
*Weaver, Red - C - Centre
*Winters, Jay - BB - Ohio Wesleyan
*Wolf, Dick - BB - Miami (Ohio)

LOS ANGELES WILDCATS
*Bradshaw, Jim - BB - Illinois, Nevada-Reno
*Bross, Mal - BB-TB-WB - Gonzaga
*Bucklin, Ted - FB-BB - Idaho
Busch, Nick - G - Gonzaga, Georgetown
Carey, Dana - G - California
*Erickson, Waldon - T - Washington
*Flaherty, Ray - E - Gonzaga
*Illman, Ted - WB-TB-BB - Montana
Johnston, Charlie - T-G - Stanford
*Lawson, Jim - E - Stanford
McRae, Ed - G - Washington
Morrison, Duke - FB-WB - California
Morrison, Ram - WB-T - Oklahoma
Reed, Dick - E-T - Oregon
Shipkey, Harry - T - Stanford
*Stephens, Ray - C - Idaho
*Vesser, John - E - Idaho
Walters, Chal - C - Washington
*Wilson, Abe - G - Washington
*Wilson, Wildcat - TB - Washington

NEWARK BEARS
Black, Eddie - E - Muhlenberg
Brewster, Jim - BB - Georgia Tech
Clark, Russ - T-G - Muhlenberg
Connelly, Vaughn - FB-WB - Georgia Tech
*Davis, Carl - T - Michigan, West Virginia
Goldstein, Goldy - G - Florida
*Hansen, Hal - FB-E - Minnesota
*Kerr, George - G - Catholic
King, Ken - E - Kentucky
Manella, Dom - G - none
Maurer, Adrian - WB - Oglethorpe
McManus, Art - G - Boston College [*to Bos*]
Murray, John - C - Georgia Tech
Newton, Ark - WB-TB - Florida
Rice, Orian - C-G - Syracuse, Muhlenberg
Rives, Bob - T-E - Vanderbilt
*Stein, Sammy - E - none
Tursi, Silvio - E - Muhlenberg
*Williams, Cy - T - Florida
*Williams, Ike - FB-BB - Georgia Tech
*Wycoff, Doug - TB - Georgia Tech

NEW YORK YANKEES
*Baker, Bullet - TB-BB-FB - USC
Coglizer, Art - E - Missouri
*Fry, Wes - FB-WB - Iowa
*Garvey, Hec - G - Notre Dame [*from Brooklyn*]
*Goebel, Paul - E - Michigan
*Goetz, Gus - T - Michigan
*Grange, Red - TB-BB - Illinois
*Griffen, Hal - C - Iowa
*Hall, Dick - T - Butler, Illinois
Hubert, Pooley - FB - Alabama
Kearney, Frank - T - Cornell
Kriz, Leo - G-T - Iowa, George Washington
*Maloney, Red - E-WB - Dartmouth
*Marks, Larry - WB-E - Indiana
*Michalske, Mike - G-T - Penn State
*Minick, Paul - G - Iowa
*Oliver, Bill - G - Alabama
*Otte, Lowell - E-T - Iowa
*Pease, George - BB - Columbia
*Scott, Ralph - T-G - Wisconsin
Schimititisch, Steve - C-G - Columbia
*Tryon, Eddie - WB - Colgate

PHILADELPHIA QUAKERS
*Asplundh, Les - FB-BB-WB - Swarthmore
*Beattie, Bob - WB-T - Princeton
*Behman, Bull - T - Dickinson
*Cartin, Charlie - T-C - Holy Cross
Coleman, Bill - G - Penn
*Crowther, Saville - G - Penn State, Colgate
Dinsmore, Bob - BB-TB-WB- Princeton
*Elliott, Doc - TB-FB - Lafayette [*from Cleveland*]
Fay, Jerry - T-G - Grove City
*Ford, Adrian - WB-E - Lafayette
Gebhardt, Lou - WB - Lafayette
Johnson, Knute - E - Muhlenberg
*Killinger, Glenn - TB - Penn State
Kostos, Joe - E - Bucknell
Kreuz, Al - FB - Penn
Marhefka, Joe - TB - Penn State, Lafayette
*Milstead, Century - T - Wabash, Yale
Robinson, Karl - C Penn
*Scott, Johnny - BB - Lafayette
*Spagna, Butch - G - Brown, Lehigh
*Sullivan, George - TB - Penn
*Thomas, Whitey - E - Penn State
*Tully, George - E - Dartmouth
*Way, Charlie - WB-TB - Penn State

ROCK ISLAND INDEPENDENTS
*Armstrong, Johnny - BB - Dubuque
*Biggs, Riley - C-G - Baylor
*Bradshaw, Wes - TB-BB -Trinity (Tex.), Baylor
Coyle, Frank - E - St. Ambrose, Detroit
*Hartzog, Bug - G-T - Baylor
*Hill, Chuck - FB-E - Iowa State
*Kaplan, Ave - TB-WB-BB - Hamline
*Kolls, Louis - C - St. Ambrose
Layden, Elmer - FB - Notre Dame [*to Brooklyn*]
*McCarthy, Vince - WB - St. Viator
*Norton, Marty - TB-WB - none
*Novak, Eddie - FB-BB - none
Rohrabaugh, Ray - WB-TB - Franklin (Ind.)
Scarpino, Bill - E - Des Moines
*Slater, Duke - T - Iowa (to Chicago Cardinals)
*Stahlman, Dick - T - DePaul, Northwestern [*to Chicago Rockets*]
Truckenmiller, Ken - G - Cornell College
Urban , Frank - E - M.I.T.
Walker, Homer - E - Baylor
*Widerquist, Chet - G - Northwestern, Washington & Jefferson
*Widick, Ralph - C-T - Emporia State
*Wilson, Mike - E - Lehigh

CHAPTER 27

The All-America Football Conference

Phil Barber

Arch Ward, who organized baseball's All-Star Game and football's College All-Star Game, also was the man responsible for launching the All-America Football Conference. On June 4, 1944, Ward, the sports editor of the *Chicago Tribune,* met in St. Louis with representatives from Buffalo, Chicago, Los Angeles, New York, and San Francisco. He already had power of attorney for Arthur McBride of Cleveland. The six parties arrived at few conclusions that day, but they did come away with a name: the All-America Football Conference.

If the name was catchy, it also was significant. The AAFC planned to be the first truly national U.S. sports league, with teams in New York, Chicago, Los Angeles, and San Francisco. That part of the experiment succeeded, as did others. Though the four seasons (1946-49) of the All-America Football Conference have faded into obscurity, the league had a lasting impact on the NFL.

Three of its teams—the Cleveland Browns, San Francisco 49ers, and Baltimore Colts—were adopted by the older league in 1950. Thirteen AAFC players are members of the Pro Football Hall of Fame. Many of the new league's innovations—such as the 14-game schedule, consistent air travel, and widespread use of zone defenses—lived beyond 1949. And, when the Rams' Kenny Washington and Woody Strode re-integrated the NFL in 1946, they had to share recognition with Marion Motley and Bill Willis of the AAFC's Browns.

Jim Crowley, like reigning NFL Commissioner Elmer Layden (and not coincidentally) one of the legendary Four Horsemen of Notre Dame, was named commissioner of the AAFC in November, 1944. Lou Gehrig's widow, Eleanor, was named secretary and treasurer.

A Brooklyn franchise was added, and when Miami was accepted into the league in 1945, it rounded out the eight-team lineup. All that were missing at that point were headlines, and Layden inadvertently supplied those in August, 1945. In a prepared statement, Layden suggested that the new league "first get a ball, then make a schedule, and then play a game."

For months afterward, the statement lived as paraphrase: "Tell them to get a ball first." It became the AAFC's rallying cry.

The ownership of the eight AAFC franchises was a varied lot. In aggregate, they were short on pro football experience but long on finances. The press referred to their meetings as "the millionaires' coffee klatch." Some of the prospective owners—actor Don Ameche, oilman James Brueil, and lumber baron Anthony Morabito—had been lobbying unsuccessfully for years to obtain an NFL franchise.

Brueil's Buffalo Bisons prepared to play in Civic Stadium, Morabito's San Francisco 49ers in Kezar Stadium. Ameche's ownership group, which included movie producer Louis B. Mayer, lined up the gigantic Los Angeles Memorial Coliseum for the Dons. William D. Cox operated the Brooklyn Dodgers, which, like their baseball counterparts, would play in Ebbets Field. John Keeshin, a trucking magnate and racetrack owner, headed the Chicago Rockets, who would play in Soldier Field. In Miami, owner Harvey Hester called his team the Seahawks and contracted to play in the Orange Bowl.

Dan Topping, owner of the NFL's Brooklyn Dodgers, left the older league and joined the AAFC. Topping purchased an interest in baseball's New York Yankees and gave his new AAFC team the same name. The other conference owners were so eager to embrace Topping (and Yankee Stadium) that each paid him $75,000, plus a promise of $25,000 from gate receipts.

The other principal owner in the conference was Arthur (Mickey) McBride, who had sold newspapers in Chicago at age 6 and went on to make a fortune in real estate and taxicabs. McBride, who was passionate about his team, asked John Dietrich of the *Cleveland Press,* "Who is the best football coach in America?"

"Paul Brown," Dietrich answered.

Brown was an Ohio legend who had built winning programs at Massillon High School, Ohio State, and the Great Lakes Naval Training Center. He brought an active mind, unmatched organizational skills, and capable assistants such as Blanton Collier and Weeb Ewbank to the Browns. McBride was so optimistic he rented out 80,000-seat Municipal Stadium, and then set to work promoting the Browns on billboards, radio, and, of course, his taxis. He even hired a staff of fetching women to attend the phone banks for ticket orders.

The 1946 Season

The talent level in the AAFC was unquestionably high from the start. The new league signed more than 100 players with NFL experience, and only three wound up on the first all-conference team. The Yankees (nee Dodgers) started with two future members of the Pro Football Hall of Fame in tailback Clarence (Ace) Parker and tackle Frank (Bruiser) Kinard, then added triple-threat Frank Sinkwich, the NFL's most valuable player in 1944. The Dons picked up quarterback Charlie O'Rourke and all-pro tackle Lee Artoe, the Seahawks grabbed end Hampton Pool, and the 49ers got fullback Norm Standlee—all former Chicago Bears.

Forty of the 66 College All-Stars signed with the AAFC. Like the NFL, the new league also capitalized on the scores of athletes returning from military duty, and those who had played at Fleet City and March Field in California, Randolph Field in Texas, and Sampson Naval Training Center in New York. The Rockets' coach, Dick Hanley, and their biggest star, Elroy (Crazylegs) Hirsch, along with many of their other players had lined up together on the team at El Toro Marine Air Base in southern California.

The AAFC played its first league game on September 6, 1946. In one sense, it was a rousing success—60,135 fans were on hand for the event. But the Browns' 44-0 pasting of Miami also was a harbinger of failure for the Seahawks. Harvey Hester had filled his roster with young men from south of the Mason-Dixon Line, but his hopes were dashed by a 3-11 record and financial insolvency. Miami played its games on Monday nights, and two were washed out by hurricanes. After the season, the AAFC owners chipped in roughly $80,000 to pay off the Seahawks' debts to their players and to United Air Lines; then they expelled the franchise from the league.

The Browns, on the other hand, were a booming success. They lost only twice, and their home attendance of better than 57,000 per game more than doubled any other team's. Quarterback Otto Graham was the best pure passer in the league, and he had two dominant ends to throw to in Dante Lavelli and Mac Speedie. Fullback Marion Motley (who, like Graham, would be selected to the NFL's 75th Anniversary Team) kept defenses off balance with his punishing runs.

Between Cleveland and Miami, there was a spectrum of performances. The Yankees, powered by Orban (Spec) Sanders, the AAFC's leading rusher, were the second-best team in the league. The 49ers, featuring the potent passing combination of Frankie Albert to Alyn Beals, and the Dons, with a strong line built around center Bob Nelson, had their moments. But Chicago, Brooklyn, and Buffalo struggled. Brooklyn averaged fewer than 14,000 fans per game despite the presence of sensational tailback Glenn Dobbs, who passed, ran, and punted his way to the AAFC's first most-valuable-player award.

When a team mutiny threatened in Chicago, the Rockets replaced Hanley, the stern Marine colonel, early in the season, and gave the job to, of all things, a committee of players—Bob Dove, Ned Matthews, and Willie Wilkin. The *Chicago Tribune* reported a Rockets' practice session at which assistant coach Ernie Nevers stripped to the waist to take a sun bath. After two more games, Pat Boland was named head coach.

All in all, the AAFC's inaugural season was a strong start. The conference had presented a wide-open style of play, had made inroads in New York, Los Angeles, and Chicago, and could hold up the Browns as a team to compete with any in the NFL.

1946 Standings

Eastern Division	W	L	T	Pct	PF	PA
New York Yankees	10	3	1	.769	270	192
Brooklyn Dodgers	3	10	1	.250	226	339
Buffalo Bisons	3	10	1	.250	249	370
Miami Seahawks	3	11	0	.214	167	378
Western Division						
Cleveland Browns	12	2	0	.857	423	137
San Francisco 49ers	9	5	0	.643	307	189
Los Angeles Dons	7	5	2	.583	305	290
Chicago Rockets	5	6	3	.455	263	315

Championship: Cleveland 14, New York 9

The 1947 Season

Though the AAFC would see more coaches fired, more front offices shaken up, and more one-sided games in 1947, that season can be viewed as the conference's pinnacle. The Browns continued to attract widespread attention, and the AAFC franchises in New York and Los Angeles did better than their NFL rivals—both on the field and at the gate.

Jim Crowley resigned as commissioner of the league to become vice president, general manager, and head coach of the Chicago Rockets. Crowley's replacement was Jonas Ingram, former commander of the U.S. Navy's Atlantic Fleet. As deputy commissioner, Ingram appointed his long-time Navy associate, O.O. (Scrappy) Kessing, who had a lengthy history of military bravery. "Junior officer Kessing was twice led out to be shot by the enemy as a highlight of his duty against Mexico in 1916," his AAFC biography read. "He volunteered as a balloon pilot in World War I, duty which involved eight-hour watches in a cold, tiny basket."

Ingram moved the league offices from Chicago to New York, right into the Empire State Building. Across town, Dan Topping's co-owners of the baseball Yankees—Larry MacPhail and Del Webb—bought into his football team, lending further credibility to the league.

The expulsion of the Seahawks had left a hole in the Eastern Division, but it quickly was filled by the Baltimore Colts, owned by a group led by Robert Rodenberg. The Colts moved into Municipal Stadium and hired NFL notable Cecil Isbell as head coach.

Tony Morabito, the 49ers' owner, was unsuccessful in his bid to sign Glenn Davis and Felix (Doc) Blanchard, "Mr. Inside and Mr. Outside" from Army's celebrated 1944-45-46 backfield. The AAFC also pursued other stars, including Illinois scatback Buddy Young and Notre Dame quarterback George Ratterman, who had combined to lead the College All-Stars to a 16-0 victory over the Chicago Bears. Young signed with the Yankees, Ratterman with the Bills (as the Buffalo team was now called).

The Browns again were the class of the AAFC, with the Yankees in close pursuit. Graham passed for 2,753 yards and 25 touchdowns (against only 11 interceptions), with end Speedie catching 67 passes for 1,146 yards. New York's Spec Sanders ran wild, rushing for 1,432 yards and 18 touchdowns, and passing for 1,442 yards and 14 touchdowns.

When the two teams met at Yankee Stadium on November 23, the Browns were 10-1, the Yankees 9-2. The crowd of 70,060 was tremendous, though not as big as the pro-record 82,576 who watched New York beat the Dons in the Los Angeles Coliseum on September 12. The Yankees shocked Cleveland by taking a 28-0 lead in the first half, but Otto Graham brought his Cleveland Browns roaring back in the second half, and the game ended in a 28-28 tie. It stands as the most memorable game in the four-year history of the AAFC.

Three weeks later, the two teams vied for the conference championship and the Browns won 14-3 to take their second consecutive title. At the other end of the league were the Chicago Rockets, who went 1-13, the Baltimore Colts (2-11-1), and the Brooklyn Dodgers, who finished 3-10-1 and attracted only 11,000 fans per game.

1947 Standings

Eastern Division	W	L	T	Pct	PF	PA
New York Yankees	11	2	1	.846	378	239
Buffalo Bills	8	4	2	.667	320	288
Brooklyn Dodgers	3	10	1	.231	181	340
Baltimore Colts	2	11	1	.154	167	377
Western Division						
Cleveland Browns	12	1	1	.923	410	185
San Francisco 49ers	8	4	2	.667	327	264
Los Angeles Dons	7	7	0	.500	328	256
Chicago Rockets	1	13	0	.071	263	425
Championship: Cleveland 14, New York 3						

The 1948 Season

As the 1948 season approached, the executives of the AAFC saw a wide gulf between the haves and have-nots of their league. Ingram issued a drastic directive to the eight teams, ordering the strongest among them to make players available to the weakest. But even the most farsighted of owners, such as McBride and Los Angeles's Ben Lindheimer, who had spent hundreds of thousands of dollars propping up the AAFC, were reluctant to comply. Only the Yankees followed the order in good faith; their reward was a watered-down team that fell to 6-8. The Browns traded the rights to rookie quarterback Y.A. Tittle to Baltimore and were hurt in the long run.

There were administrative shakeups all around the AAFC: Robert Embry headed a group that assumed control of the Colts; Branch Rickey, the famed president of baseball's Brooklyn Dodgers, took over the wobbly Dodgers football team; and the Rockets also changed hands, going to a Chicago community group fronted by R. Edward Garn.

On the field, the action was just as furious. Cleveland upgraded from dominant to invincible, going 14-0, then smashing the Bills 49-7 in the 1948 championship game. Graham again was phenomenal, very nearly matching his statistics of the year before, and Motley ran for a conference-best 964 yards. The Browns' might was demonstrated best when they won three games in an eight-day span. Branch Rickey had convinced AAFC owners that football players could play more frequently than once a week.

The Browns' capper was a 31-28 victory at San Francisco, the most important game of the season. Lawrence (Buck) Shaw's 49ers fielded an explosive offense, with Frankie Albert passing for 29 touchdowns, 14 of them to Alyn Beals. Their only two losses were to the Cleveland Browns.

Chicago again was horrible, epitomized by a humiliating turnover differential of minus-32. The Rockets lost their last 11 games and finished 1-13 (again). Brooklyn sank to 2-12, and its attendance fell, too, to less than 10,400 per game. However, Cleveland, San Francisco, and Los Angeles all outdrew every NFL team.

1948 Standings

Eastern Division	W	L	T	Pct	PF	PA
Buffalo Bills	7	7	0	.500	360	358
Baltimore Colts	7	7	0	.500	333	327
New York Yankees	6	8	0	.429	265	301
Brooklyn Dodgers	2	12	0	.143	253	387
Western Division						
Cleveland Browns	14	0	0	1.000	389	190
San Francisco 49ers	12	2	0	.857	495	248
Los Angeles Dons	7	7	0	.500	258	305
Chicago Rockets	1	13	0	.071	202	439
Division Playoff: Buffalo 28, Baltimore 17						
Championship: Cleveland 49, Buffalo 7						

The 1949 Season

The worst teams were draining money from the AAFC, but the conference got some hope when the NFL agreed to form a committee to meet with AAFC officials. It was the first time the established league had publicly acknowledged its junior rival. The groups met in Philadelphia in December and vowed to end the "pro football war." But talks broke down, and both leagues made plans to renew the withering fight in 1949.

"I firmly believe in the future of the conference," Scrappy Kessing said in the 1949 AAFC media guide. He was commissioner now, having filled the shoes of Jonas Ingram, who had resigned in January.

Whether Kessing believed his own words or not is debatable, but the owners of the AAFC's team were justified in harboring doubts. The schedule was reduced from 14 to 12 games. Brooklyn finally succumbed to its lack of support and merged with the Yankees. Six former Dodgers were assigned to Brooklyn-New York, the rest to Chicago. Topping served as president of the hybrid, Rickey as chairman of the board.

Baltimore listed its third president in three years, Walter Driskill, while a group led by James C. Thompson purchased the Rockets and renamed them the Hornets. Money was so short in Chicago that players from the Browns and Rockets had to act as grounds crew before a game in the snow. Lindheimer philanthropically traded star tailback Herman Wedemeyer to the Colts; when they couldn't fulfill Wedemeyer's $12,000 contract, Lindheimer floated half of it. In September, the Dons' chairman of the board suffered a severe heart attack, and his doctors convinced him to leave the sport.

Rather than carry a three-team division, the AAFC lumped all of its seven teams together in 1949. The story was much the same as it had been in '48, with Cleveland finishing 9-1-2 and San Francisco just a step behind at 9-3. Graham, Speedie, and Albert had typically stellar seasons, and 49ers fullback Joe Perry—with a league-best 783 rushing yards—emerged as a future great.

The two stubborn leagues continued to be hurt at the ticket office. The NFL's Green Bay Packers, Pittsburgh Steelers, and Detroit Lions all were in dire straits. Finally, lines of communication led to a meeting between NFL Commissioner Bert Bell and J. Arthur Friedlund, the AAFC's legal counsel. After three days of grueling give-and-take, they emerged from Bell's Philadelphia office on December 10 and announced a merger agreement. The next day, Cleveland beat San Francisco 21-7 in the last AAFC Championship Game.

1949 Standings

Eastern Division	W	L	T	Pct	PF	PA
Cleveland Browns	9	1	2	.900	339	171
San Francisco 49ers	9	3	0	.750	416	227
Brooklyn-N.Y. Yankees	8	4	0	.667	196	206
Buffalo Bills	5	5	2	.500	236	256
Chicago Hornets	4	8	0	.333	179	268
Los Angeles Dons	4	8	0	.333	253	322
Baltimore Colts	1	11	0	.083	172	341

Playoff: Cleveland 31, Buffalo 21

Playoff: San Francisco 17, Brooklyn-N.Y. 7

Championship: Cleveland 21, San Francisco 7

Merged

Under the terms of agreement, the Browns, 49ers, and Colts were absorbed into the NFL. Baltimore was the only surprise. The Colts had finished a dismal 1-11, but Washington Redskins owner George Preston Marshall, long a vocal opponent of a merger, reversed himself and decided the Colts could become a natural rival. So Marshall waived his 75-mile territorial rights—for $150,000.

Bills owner James Brueil received a 25-percent interest in the Browns, who were awarded three Buffalo players—halfback Rex Bumgardner, tackle John Kissell, and guard Abe Gibron. Six Brooklyn-New York Yankees were assigned to the New York Giants, including four who would form the nucleus of the Giants' great defensive teams of the fifties—backs Tom Landry, Otto Schnellbacher, and Harmon Rowe, and tackle Arnie Weinmeister.

Many other AAFC stars dropped into the open arms of NFL teams. Spec Sanders, Buddy Young, and Dons tailback George Taliaferro went to the New York Yanks; end Len Ford went to the Browns; tailback Bob (Hunchy) Hoernschmeyer went from the Hornets to the Detroit Lions; halfback Chet Mutryn went from Buffalo to the Colts; tackle Bob Reinhard went to the Rams.

All-time statistical leaders of the AAFC included Graham (10,085 passing yards), Albert (88 touchdown passes), Motley (3,024 rushing yards), Speedie (211 pass receptions), Beals (278 points on 46 touchdown receptions and 2 extra points), and Cleveland's Cliff Lewis (24 interceptions).

For about two months after the merger, the new entity was referred to as the National-American Football League in newspaper stories and press releases. In March, it reverted to the National Football League.

CHAPTER 28

The World Football League, 1974-75

Ray Didinger

The World Football League was an ambitious but ill-fated endeavor that lasted less than two full seasons before folding on October 22, 1975. The league was the brain child of Gary L. Davidson, who earlier had launched the American Basketball Association and the World Hockey Association, along with a group of young investor sportsmen who felt they could compete successfully against the National Football League, just as the upstart American Football League had done a decade earlier.

Davidson, the WFL's original commissioner, predicted the league "would eventually encompass the entire world." Davidson's reign as commissioner encompassed only one season and the league itself was out of business in 22 months.

The WFL took an aggressive approach, signing a number of NFL stars—including Larry Csonka, Paul Warfield, and Jim Kiick of the Super Bowl-champion Miami Dolphins—to big-money contracts, but losses in the millions and dwindling fan support in most cities doomed the league.

Davidson blamed bad timing for the WFL's quick demise.

"[President] Nixon was about to leave office, the prime rate went to about twelve percent, and the [Dow Jones Industrial Average] went down to 600," Davidson said. "Every day there was some new scandal out of Washington. People were dissatisfied and scared. The economy was really hurt and [the WFL] was a victim of that."

The league had some novel ideas, such as beginning the season in July, when NFL teams were still in training camp, and playing most of its games on Wednesday nights to avoid conflicts with the colleges and the NFL on weekends. Still, the new league could not find an audience.

The WFL was plagued by financial instability almost from the outset. Owners bailed out, bills went unpaid. Two teams, the Detroit Wheels and Jacksonville Sharks, went bankrupt after 14 games and did not even finish the first season.

Two other teams were forced to move during the inaugural season. The New York Stars, who were drawing fewer than 8,000 people for games at Downing Stadium on Randall's Island, moved to Charlotte after two months. The Houston Texans could not afford the rent in the Astrodome, so they moved to Shreveport, Louisiana.

The WFL owners were, for the most part, guilty of underestimating the start-up costs for their franchises and greatly overestimating the amount of revenue they would generate. Many of the owners did not have the means to withstand losses, such as the $2.5 million debt run up in Detroit.

"Some [owners] paid ridiculous bonuses," said John Bosacco, who owned the Philadelphia Bell. "They thought they could stockpile assets, then sell them at a profit. But they overpaid everybody right from the start, then couldn't find buyers. It was a mess."

The 1974 Season

The league began on an optimistic note as it kicked off its first season on July 10, 1974, with six games. The announced attendance of 258,624, an average of 43,104 per game, far exceeded expectations. *Sports Illustrated,* in its coverage of the first week, wrote: "The World Football League could be a gilt-edged investment for owners and players."

However, the Bell was forced to admit its attendance figures for the first two home games—55,534 for the opener and 64,719 for the next game—were padded. The actual paid attendance was 13,800 for the first game, 6,200 for the second. The other tickets were giveaways.

The revelation deflated the WFL's claims of large paying crowds and badly damaged the league's credibility. Soon, people were calling the WFL the "World Freebie League." It was a public relations blow the new league could not afford.

For all of its mismanagement, the WFL had some quality coaches in its first season, including Jack Pardee (Florida), John McVay (Memphis), and Tom Fears (Southern California). It also had a few "name" players, including former Heisman Trophy winner John Huarte, who quarterbacked Memphis, and future Pro Football Hall of Fame member Leroy Kelly, who played halfback for Chicago.

The World Bowl, the WFL's first championship game, was played December 5 in Birmingham. The game matched the Birmingham Americans, who had not been paid in five weeks, against the Florida Blazers, who had not been paid in more than three months. Things were so bad with the Blazers that Pardee and his coaches bought the toilet paper for the locker room.

The Americans won the title game 22-21 behind the quarterbacking of ex-49er George Mira. After the game, the Americans uniforms were impounded by sheriff's deputies and later sold at a sporting goods store to cover a portion of the team's debt.

1974 Standings

Eastern Division	W	L	T	Pct	PF	PA
Florida Blazers	14	6	0	.700	419	280
N.Y. Stars/Charlotte Hornets	10	10	0	.500	467	350
Philadelphia Bell	9	11	0	.450	493	413
Jacksonville Sharks	4	10	0	.286	258	358
Central Division						
Memphis Southmen	17	3	0	.850	629	365
Birmingham Americans	15	5	0	.750	503	394
Chicago Fire	7	13	0	.350	446	622
Detroit Wheels	1	13	0	.071	209	358
Western Division						
Southern California Sun	13	7	0	.650	486	441
Hawaiians	9	11	0	.450	413	425
Portland Storm	7	12	1	.375	264	426
Houston Texans/ Shreveport Steamer	7	12	1	.375	240	415

Divisional playoffs: Florida 18, Philadelphia 3
Hawaii 32, So. California 14

Semifinals: Florida 18, Memphis 15
Birmingham 22, Hawaii 19

World Bowl: Birmingham 22, Florida 21

The 1975 Season

In 1975, the league reinvented itself as the New World Football League, with some new owners, a new commissioner (Chris Hemmeter, owner of the Hawaiians franchise), and a new business approach. The WFL's idea, called "The Hemmeter Plan," was a profit-sharing concept in which most of the players would be paid one percent of their team's income. If there was no income, the players would be paid the minimum salary: $500 a game for 20 games.

The Hemmeter Plan did not apply to the star players, such as Csonka, Warfield, and Kiick, who had come over from the NFL. They were guaranteed their large salaries. The three ex-Dolphins earned a combined $3.5 million for their one season with the Memphis Southmen.

The league brought in several other name players from the NFL, including receiver John Gilliam (Minnesota, signed with Chicago), tight end Ted Kwalick (49ers, signed with Philadelphia) and running back Calvin Hill (Dallas, signed with Hawaii). Southern California added Anthony Davis, the former star halfback from USC, who led the league with 1,200 yards rushing and 16 touchdowns.

"I feel like the Pilgrims when they sighted the Statue of Liberty, not knowing what to expect," Hill said at an April, 1975, press conference launching the new season.

The WFL also courted New York Jets quarterback Joe Namath with a $4 million offer to sign with the Chicago Winds. The Jets' signing of Namath had put the AFL on the map in 1965. The WFL brass felt luring Namath to its league, even though he was a fading and gimpy-kneed 32-year-old, would give them the same kind of credibility. However, when Namath decided to re-sign with the Jets—after the Winds had all but assured his deliverance—it made the WFL look foolish. The Chicago franchise sold fewer than 2,000 season tickets, and the team folded just five weeks into the 1975 season.

The WFL tried some new ideas, but most were laughed at. For example, the league wanted players to wear pants color-coded by position: blue for defensive linemen; red for linebackers; yellow for defensive backs; purple for offensive linemen, etc. The players refused to wear them.

"I've spent eleven years trying to build a serious image," Warfield said. "I'm too far along in my career to begin playing Emmett Kelly."

Assessing the caliber of player he found in the WFL, Warfield said: "There are definitely people here who can play in the NFL and there also are definitely some who cannot. The yardstick has been the old AFL, which I watched on TV and didn't think that much of. I saw some better football last year in the WFL."

Warfield had 25 catches for Memphis and scored 3 touchdowns in 1975. Csonka rushed for 421 yards. The lowest paid of the three, Kiick, was the most productive, scoring 10 touchdowns as the Southmen went 7-4.

The ex-Dolphins also helped the Memphis team at the gate. The Southmen led the league with 9,000 season tickets sold and averaged 20,000 for seven home dates. The other teams struggled, however, with Philadelphia drawing fewer than 4,000 for four of its five games at Franklin Field (capacity 60,000).

As more teams ran into financial trouble, embarrassments multiplied. The Charlotte team was evicted from its practice field because it failed to pay the rent. In Jacksonville, the blocking sleds and tackling dummies were impounded. In San Antonio, players were asked to take pay cuts so the team could meet its expenses.

The Philadelphia Bell tried to save money by renting an old school bus on a trip to Southern California. When the team arrived at Anaheim Stadium for a practice, the security guard refused to admit them because he didn't believe they were the real team. One of the players had to open his jacket and show the guard his Bell T-shirt to convince him to open the gate.

The next night, the Bell and the Southern California Sun played the highest-scoring game in the league's brief history, with the Sun winning 58-39 behind 3 touchdown passes by quarterback Pat Haden. Only 17,811 fans turned out on a night when the Sun was giving away free 10-speed bicycles. The game lasted three and one-half hours. The TV station carrying the game in Philadelphia signed off at 1:30 A.M. even though there still were 10 minutes left to play.

The WFL had bad luck with some of its marquee players. Csonka missed part of the season with a torn muscle in his abdomen. Hill was sidelined with a bad knee. Daryle Lamonica, the former Oakland quarterback who signed with the Sun, was injured and decided to retire.

In October, with only two teams (Memphis and Birmingham) showing signs of economic life, the WFL folded. Hemmeter's announcement came on October 22, with seven weeks left in the regular season. Birmingham had the distinction of owning the best record at the time, 9-3.

"[The league] was on the operating table for two years, this was merely a form of euthanasia," said Bosacco, who estimated his losses with the Bell at $2 million.

"I feel like a big balloon that somebody just stuck a pin in," said Ron Holliday, a receiver with the Bell.

1975 Standings

Eastern Division	W	L	T	Pct	PF	PA
Birmingham Vulcans	9	3	0	.750	257	186
Memphis Southmen (Grizzlies)	7	4	0	.636	254	206
Charlotte Hornets	6	5	0	.545	225	199
Jacksonville Express	6	5	0	.545	227	247
Philadelphia Bell	4	7	0	.364	195	237
Western Division						
Southern California Sun	7	5	0	.583	354	341
San Antonio Wings	7	6	0	.538	364	268
Shreveport Steamer	5	7	0	.417	276	313
Portland Thunder	4	7	0	.364	213	239
Hawaiians	4	7	0	.364	210	281
Chicago Winds	1	4	0	.200	67	125

About 380 players were left without jobs. A few stars, notably Gilliam and Kwalick, immediately jumped back to the NFL. Csonka, Kiick, Warfield, and Hill rejoined the NFL in 1976.

Even in folding the league, Hemmeter contended his revenue-sharing plan worked. He said the competition from the NFL was just too much for the new league to overcome.

"[The plan] was never intended to develop a market," Hemmeter said. "What we needed was a strong marketing plan. You can have an exciting product, but if it doesn't have customer appeal on the shelf, it's worthless."

Aftermath

The WFL sank in a sea of red ink, but some of its survivors prospered in the NFL. John McVay, head coach of the Memphis Southmen, helped the San Francisco 49ers win five Super Bowls as general manager and vice president. Coaches Jack Pardee (Florida Blazers), Lindy Infante (assistant, Charlotte Hornets), and Marty Schottenheimer (assistant, Portland Storm) became NFL coaches.

Several players, the most prominent of them Danny White, used the WFL as a training ground into the NFL. White, a third-round draft choice of the Dallas Cowboys, signed instead as a punter and backup quarterback with Memphis. He took the quarterback job away from John Huarte in 1975. The former Arizona State star finally signed with the Cowboys in 1976 and succeeded another former Heisman Trophy winner, Roger Staubach, at quarterback in 1980.

Vince Papale, a wide receiver with the Philadelphia Bell, signed with the Eagles and played three seasons. Papale never would have seen the inside of an NFL locker room had it not been for the WFL. With no college experience (he attended St. Joseph's University, which had no football team), he was a 28-year-old rookie from a rough-touch league when he caught the coach's eye during a Bell tryout in 1974. He contributed as a receiver and special teams player until the league's demise.

The Eagles signed him as a free agent, and the Philadelphia native made the roster in 1976, the same year the film *Rocky* was released. The parallels between the two stories—Philly guys battling the odds, going the distance—made Papale a crowd favorite at Veterans Stadium, which was more than you could say for the league.

CHAPTER 29

The United States Football League

John Hogrogian

The United States Football League (USFL) began as a marketing idea and ended as a lawsuit. The marketing idea was that the American sports fan wanted more football than he or she could consume during the traditional September-to-January season. The USFL intended to play a February-to-July season to tap into that supposedly insatiable appetite. Thus the new league also would avoid direct conflict with the powerful NFL.

United States Football League officials unveiled their new league at a press conference on May 11, 1982. In short order, the USFL signed a two-year contract (worth $18 million) with the ABC television network to broadcast a game of the week. On June 14, 1982, Chet Simmons was named the commissioner of the USFL. He had been the president of the ESPN cable television network, and the fledgling league quickly signed a two-year contract (worth $12 million) with ESPN for the broadcast of two games per week.

On August 31, 1982, the new league announced that it would begin play in 1983 with 12 teams in three divisions. The teams stocked their rosters mostly with players released by NFL clubs. The USFL commissioner's office suggested that each team limit its player payroll to about $1.2 million in salaries, with competitive balance to make up for the obvious absence of star appeal. The league office also stated that USFL teams would not sign college players who had not completed their amateur eligibility. Of the college seniors who did sign with USFL teams, 10 might have been early round selections in the NFL draft that April.

The 12 United States Football League teams opened their training camps in early February. On February 23, the new league simultaneously captured headlines and trashed several principles it previously had embraced. On that day, Heisman Trophy winner Herschel Walker, a star running back from the University of Georgia, signed a contract to play for the New Jersey Generals. Only a junior, Walker forfeited his last year of college eligibility, signing a three-year contract for $5 million, approximately double the salary of Chicago Bears halfback Walter Payton. The suggested team salary limit of $1.2 million abruptly went out the window just a few days before the start of its inaugural season.

The 1983 Season

The USFL entered its first season with 12 teams, three divisions, two television contracts, and major-league stadiums as homes for most of its teams. Most of the players were unknown to the average fan and were beginning their second football season within a one-year period. Each team scheduled 18 games, with no preseason games. The three divisional winners and one wild- card team would go on to the playoffs.

The novelty of spring football drew high television ratings at the start of the season. For the opening six games on March 6-7, the average attendance was 40,512. As spring turned into early summer, however, attendance fell, and so did television ratings.

In the Atlantic Division, the Philadelphia Stars posted a 15-3 record with a ground-oriented offense and an effective Doghouse Defense. The focal point of the offense was rookie halfback Kelvin Bryant, the league's second-best rusher and winner of the MVP award. The key player on defense was linebacker Sam Mills, a fireplug rookie from Montclair State College.

Despite a winning record, the Stars drew an average of only 18,860 fans to their home games, including a playoff game. With the league's marquee player in Herschel Walker, the New Jersey Generals averaged 33,822. Walker led the USFL in rushing with 1,812 yards, but a porous defense doomed the Generals to a losing record.

In the Central Division, Michigan and Chicago made the playoffs, with Tampa Bay just missing out. Coach George Allen stocked the Chicago Blitz with a mix of NFL veterans and promising youngsters such as halfback Tim Spencer and wide receiver Trumaine Johnson. Even with a winning team, the Blitz mostly was ignored by Chicago sports fans.

In contrast, the Tampa Bay Bandits had the league's second-best average home attendance—39,896. The Bandits won their first four games and signed rookie halfback Gary Anderson in mid-May after the NFL's San Diego Chargers had made him their first draft pick. By losing three of their final four games, however, the Bandits missed a playoff spot.

Overtaking Chicago and Tampa Bay were the late-blooming Michigan Panthers, who lost four of their first five games, then battled back to finish first in the division. Rookies Bobby Hebert and Anthony Carter formed the USFL's top passing combination. A strong line featured Pittsburgh Steelers' alumni Ray Pinney, Tyrone McGriff, and Thom Dornbrook. The Michigan defense was built around veteran linebacker John Corker, who led the USFL with 28½ sacks. The Birmingham Stallions finished last in the division with a 9-9 record.

Coincidentally, the Oakland Invaders, led by quarterback Fred Besana and tight end Raymond Chester, finished first in the Pacific Division with a 9-9 record. The Los Angeles Express hovered around the .500 mark all season and played before small crowds in the vast Los Angeles Memorial Coliseum. The Denver Gold led the league with an average home attendance of 41,736, but the team lost six of its last nine games. The Arizona Wranglers were even worse, dropping their last 10 games.

The Michigan Panthers and Philadelphia Stars won in the first round of playoffs. On July 17, the Panthers faced the Stars in the USFL Championship Game before 50,906 fans in Denver. Michigan built a 17-3 lead in the first three quarters on 2 touchdown passes from Bobby Hebert to Derek Holloway, then withstood Philadelphia's fourth-quarter comeback to win 24-22. Hebert was voted the game's MVP.

Even with the two network television contracts, the USFL lost almost $40 million, an average of about $3.3 million per team. The average attendance at a USFL game was 25,000 fans, about what had been expected. The financial losses were higher than anticipated because several teams exceeded the recommended salary cap of $1.2 million. The league directors were undiscouraged and planned on bigger things in 1984.

1983 Standings

Atlantic Division	W	L	T	Pct	PF	PA
Philadelphia Stars	15	3	0	.833	379	204
Boston Breakers	11	7	0	.611	399	334
New Jersey Generals	6	12	0	.333	314	437
Washington Federals	4	14	0	.222	297	442
Central Division						
Michigan Panthers	12	6	0	.667	451	337
Chicago Blitz	12	6	0	.667	456	271
Tampa Bay Bandits	11	7	0	.611	363	378
Birmingham Stallions	9	9	0	.500	343	326
Pacific Division						
Oakland Invaders	9	9	0	.500	319	317
Los Angeles Express	8	10	0	.444	296	370
Denver Gold	7	11	0	.389	284	304
Arizona Wranglers	4	14	0	.222	261	442

Division Playoffs: Philadelphia 44, Chicago 38 (OT) Michigan 37, Oakland 21

Championship: Michigan 24, Philadelphia 22

The 1984 Season

The original USFL team owners suddenly were in the minority. Six of the charter teams were sold to new owners, each reportedly at a profit. The owners of the 1983 Chicago franchise purchased the Arizona franchise and brought its coach and players with them to the desert. A new owner took over the Chicago franchise, but the league itself would end up running that team when the new owner walked away. The Boston team moved to New Orleans. In addition, the USFL added six expansion teams—San Antonio, Houston, Tulsa, Memphis, Jacksonville, and Pittsburgh. With membership up to 18 teams, the league restructured itself into four divisions, two each in the Eastern and Western Conferences.

Several veteran NFL players joined the USFL this year. Most prominent were Birmingham running back Joe Cribbs, New Orleans tight end Dan Ross, and quarterbacks Doug Williams of Oklahoma and Brian Sipe of New Jersey. USFL teams also signed a number of college players who arguably were the best new players at their positions. Among them were quarterbacks Jim Kelly of Houston and Steve Young of Los Angeles, running backs Mike Rozier (the 1983 Heisman Trophy winner) of Pittsburgh and Marcus Dupree of New Orleans, offensive lineman Gary Zimmerman of Los Angeles, and defensive lineman Reggie White of Memphis.

Despite all the new talent, however, the USFL had little depth and uneven performances.

The best record in the league belonged to the Philadelphia Stars, who won the Atlantic Division with a 16-2 mark. Coached by Jim Mora, the Stars had the best defense in the league and a versatile offense featuring quarterback Chuck Fusina and running back Kelvin Bryant.

Philadelphia's only two losses were to the New Jersey Generals, greatly improved under new owner Donald Trump and new head coach Walt Michaels. A 14-4 record earned the Generals a wild-card playoff spot. Sipe quarterbacked a ground-oriented offense that featured Herschel Walker (1,339 yards).

In the Southern Division, both the Birmingham Stallions and the Tampa Bay Bandits made the playoffs with 14-4 records. The Stallions were vastly improved. Joe Cribbs led the USFL with 1,467 rushing yards. Tampa Bay's star was halfback Gary Anderson, who ran for 19 touchdowns and caught passes for 2 more. The Bandits drew an average of 46,158 fans to their home games, second best in the league. Jacksonville had a losing team but led the USFL with an average home attendance of 46,736.

In the Central Division, the defending champion Michigan Panthers slumped when star wide receiver Anthony Carter went out of action with a broken left arm. They barely salvaged a wild-card berth by winning three games in June. Sweeping past the Panthers to win the divisional title were the expansion Houston Gamblers. With four wide receivers, no tight end, and one running back, the Run-and-Shoot offense relied on rookie quarterback Jim Kelly both to run and pass on sprint-out plays. Kelly thrived in the open offense, passing for 5,219 yards and 44 touchdowns, and winning the league's MVP award. Wide receiver Richard Johnson caught 115 passes and Ricky Sanders 101.

In the Pacific Division, both the Los Angeles Express and the Arizona Wranglers rebounded from slow starts to win playoff spots with 10-8 records. The Express signed quarterback Steve Young to a lucrative contract after the season had started, then won 9 of 13 games. George Allen's Wranglers boasted a tough defense and the running of Tim Spencer.

In the first round of the playoffs, Los Angeles beat Michigan 27-21 in three overtimes before only 7,964 fans in Los Angeles. It was the longest game in pro football history.

The championship game saw Philadelphia beat Arizona 23-3 before 52,862 spectators in Tampa. Chuck Fusina, voted game MVP, completed 12 of 17 passes. It was George Allen's final game as a pro head coach.

For the season, the average attendance at USFL games was about 27,000, a small increase over 1983. Poor crowds in Chicago, Washington, and Los Angeles held that figure down. Television ratings were respectable, but both the attendance and the ratings fell off after May 1. With player salaries rising, the USFL lost approximately $40 million this season.

1984 Standings

Eastern Conference						
Atlantic Division	**W**	**L**	**T**	**Pct**	**PF**	**PA**
Philadelphia Stars	16	2	0	.889	479	225
New Jersey Generals	14	4	0	.778	430	312
Pittsburgh Maulers	3	15	0	.167	259	379
Washington Federals	3	15	0	.167	270	492
Southern Division						
Birmingham Stallions	14	4	0	.778	539	316
Tampa Bay Bandits	14	4	0	.778	498	347
New Orleans Breakers	8	10	0	.444	348	395
Memphis Showboats	7	11	0	.389	320	455
Jacksonville Bulls	6	12	0	.333	327	455
Western Conference						
Western Division						
Houston Gamblers	13	5	0	.722	618	400
Michigan Panthers	10	8	0	.556	400	382
San Antonio Gunslingers	7	11	0	.389	309	325
Oklahoma Outlaws	6	12	0	.333	251	459
Chicago Blitz	5	13	0	.278	340	466
Pacific Division						
Los Angeles Express	10	8	0	.556	338	373
Arizona Wranglers	10	8	0	.556	502	284
Denver Gold	9	9	0	.500	356	413
Oakland Invaders	7	11	0	.389	242	348

Quarterfinals: Philadelphia 28, New Jersey 7
Los Angeles 27, Michigan 21 (OT)
Birmingham 36, Tampa Bay 17
Arizona 17, Houston 16.

Semifinals: Arizona 35, Los Angeles 23
Philadelphia 20, Birmingham 10

Championship: Philadelphia 23, Arizona 3

The 1985 Season

On August 22, 1984, Commissioner Chet Simmons announced that the USFL would shift its playing schedule from the spring to the fall in 1986. Simmons pointed to the greater revenues and fan interest in football in the fall. Some experts speculated that the USFL owners wanted to force a merger with the NFL by moving to the fall. A third and final spring season would be played in 1985.

A chain reaction of franchise moves for 1985 followed the announcement. The Pittsburgh and Chicago teams disbanded. The Michigan Panthers were merged into the Oakland Invaders, while the Oklahoma Outlaws joined the Arizona Wranglers to form the Arizona Outlaws. Washington moved to Orlando, New Orleans moved to Portland, and Philadelphia moved to Baltimore. For its lame-duck spring season, the USFL would have 14 teams in two divisions, with eight teams making the playoffs.

On October 18, 1984, the USFL sued the NFL on antitrust grounds. The new league sought more than $500 million, and, if successful, could have received nearly $1.7 billion because antitrust damages are trebled under federal law. One month after the lawsuit was commenced, Commissioner Chet Simmons resigned and was replaced by Harry Usher, an attorney who had been vice president of the 1984 Los Angeles Olympic Organizing Committee.

The 1985 spring season had an anticlimactic feel to it from the start. The only prominent rookies joining the league were Heisman Trophy-winning quarterback Doug Flutie with New Jersey and defensive lineman Keith Millard of Jacksonville. Television ratings fell about 30 percent from 1984, and attendance was down everywhere but in New Jersey and Memphis. The league itself had to fund the ownerless Los Angeles team. Birmingham, San Antonio, Portland, Tampa Bay, and Houston all were late in paying their bills. The league's financial losses continued to mount at an accelerated rate.

On the field, five Eastern Division teams made the playoffs. The Birmingham Stallions had a good offense featuring NFL veterans Cliff Stoudt, Joe Cribbs, and Jim Smith. Safety Chuck Clanton led the league with 16 interceptions. The New Jersey Generals traveled on the broad shoulders of Herschel Walker, who ran for 2,411 yards. The Memphis Showboats won seven of their last nine games, relying on a good defense built around second-year tackle Reggie White.

The transplanted Baltimore Stars stumbled in the early going and had to win five of their last six games to squeeze into the playoffs. Also just making the cut were the Tampa Bay Bandits. Jacksonville missed the playoffs but again had the USFL's best home attendance, averaging 45,806.

1985 Standings

Eastern Conference	**W**	**L**	**T**	**Pct**	**PF**	**PA**
Birmingham Stallions	13	5	0	.722	436	299
New Jersey Generals	11	7	0	.611	418	377
Memphis Showboats	11	7	0	.611	428	337
Baltimore Stars	10	7	1	.583	368	260
Tampa Bay Bandits	10	8	0	.556	405	422
Jacksonville Bulls	9	9	0	.500	407	402
Orlando Renegades	5	13	0	.278	308	481
Western Conference	**W**	**L**	**T**	**Pct**	**PF**	**PA**
Oakland Invaders	13	4	1	.750	473	359
Denver Gold	11	7	0	.611	433	389
Houston Gamblers	10	8	0	.556	544	388
Arizona Wranglers	8	10	0	.444	376	405
Portland Breakers	6	12	0	.333	275	422
San Antonio Gunslingers	5	13	0	.278	296	436
Los Angeles Express	3	15	0	.167	266	456

Quarterfinals: Birmingham 22, Houston 20
Memphis 48, Denver 7
Oakland 48, Tampa Bay 27
Baltimore 20, New Jersey 17

Semifinals: Baltimore 28, Birmingham 14
Oakland 28, Memphis 19

Championship: Baltimore 28, Oakland 24

Only three teams made the playoffs in the West. The Oakland Invaders won eight of their last nine games to post a 13-4-1 mark for the league's best record. Quarterback Bobby Hebert, running back Albert Bentley, wide receiver Anthony Carter, and lineman Ray Pinney all came from Michigan in the merger to star in Oakland's offense. The Denver Gold hired Houston Gamblers offensive coordinator Darrel (Mouse) Davis as head coach and installed the Run-and-Shoot offense. In Houston, the USFL's original

Run-and-Shoot offense continued to shine with quarterback Jim Kelly (4,623 yards, 39 touchdown passes). The Gamblers survived a late-season slump caused by a knee injury to Kelly. Knee injuries hampered Los Angeles quarterback Steve Young and ended the season for Portland running back Marcus Dupree.

In the championship game in Giants Stadium on July 14, the Stars beat the Invaders 28-24 to retain the USFL title before an audience of 49,263 fans. Baltimore halfback Kelvin Bryant ran for 103 yards and 3 touchdowns, earning the game's MVP award.

Afterwards

A few days after the 1985 USFL Championship Game, NFL teams opened their training camps. A substantial number of prominent USFL players signed NFL contracts and turned up in those camps. Bobby Hebert, Anthony Carter, Steve Young, Mike Rozier, Reggie White, Gary Anderson, and Bart Oates led this first talent drain from the new league.

The USFL planned an 18-game schedule in the fall of 1986 for its eight surviving teams: New Jersey, Baltimore, Tampa Bay, Jacksonville, Orlando, Birmingham, Memphis, and Arizona. The Houston Gamblers were merged into the New Jersey Generals. Most of the 1985 Western Division teams simply disbanded.

The USFL's most important battle, however, was in the courtroom. Beginning in May of 1986, the USFL presented its antitrust case to a jury in the federal court in New York City. The USFL attempted to prove that the NFL had monopoly power in the realm of pro football and had used that power to try to drive the new league out of business.

The USFL argued primarily that the NFL pressured the three major television networks (all of which broadcast NFL games) into refusing to show USFL games in the fall of 1986. The new league sought monetary damages and an injunction prohibiting the NFL from having contracts with all three television networks. On July 29, the jury delivered a verdict that devastated the USFL.

The jury found that the NFL had monopoly power in the area of pro football. However, the jury rejected all of the USFL's television-related claims, which were the self-proclaimed heart of the USFL's case. The jury apparently believed that most of the USFL's problems arose from its own mismanagement. It awarded to the USFL only $1 in damages, which was trebled. The award of only $3 was a bitter pill for the USFL.

On August 4, 1986, Commissioner Usher announced that the USFL team owners had decided to cancel the impending 1986 season. Without either a television contract or a substantial award from the antitrust case, the league did not have the financial means to go on. Usher stated that the league hoped to succeed on appeal in its antitrust case and to play a 1987 fall schedule. With the 1986 season scratched, the remaining USFL stars fled to the NFL. Herschel Walker, Kelvin Bryant, Jim Kelly, Doug Flutie, Gary Zimmerman, and numerous other USFL stalwarts played with NFL teams in 1986.

With its legal appeal still pending and with no players under contract, Commissioner Usher announced on January 8, 1987, that the USFL would stay dormant in 1987.

On March 10, 1988, a federal appeals court in New York City affirmed the jury's award of $1, rejecting the USFL's claims of procedural flaws in the trial. Although some legal skirmishing remained, the decision by the appeals court ended any faint hope that the USFL would return to action. It would be remembered as only a footnote, the short-lived spring league with the expensive stars.

CHAPTER 30

NFL Europe

Rick Korch

Miami of Ohio is known as the Cradle of Coaches. Penn State is renowned for its stellar linebackers. Southern California is known for its great running backs. And the NFL Europe League rapidly is becoming known for sending top quarterbacks to the NFL.

Three quarterbacks who are alumni of the NFL Europe League—Brad Johnson (Washington), Jon Kitna (Seattle), and Doug Pederson (Philadelphia)—could start in the NFL in 1999, and that number is sure to grow in future years.

Baseball, basketball, and hockey are international sports, played all over the world. Football is an American sport. Or is it?

Football certainly is the most popular sport in the United States. But since 1991, professional football also has been played overseas, where it is drawing an increasing number of fans every year.

The NFL had talked about "globalizing" the sport since the mid-1980s, and, in 1989, the league assigned former Dallas Cowboys president Tex Schramm to do a feasibility study for a European league. On July 1 of that year, the NFL voted to start the World League of American Football in the spring of 1991. It didn't take long for the league to negotiate network television contracts with both ABC and the USA Network (as well as in several European countries).

For its first year, the league had 10 charter franchises in three divisions playing a 50-game regular-season schedule (10 games per team):

North American East—Montreal, New York/New Jersey, Orlando, and Raleigh-Durham

North American West—Birmingham, Sacramento, and San Antonio

European—Barcelona, Spain; Frankfurt, Germany; and London, England

London finished first in the league in average attendance (40,841) and all three European clubs were ranked in the top five in attendance. The league set a record with an average of 35,035 in its final weekend. The World League concluded its first season with the World Bowl before a sellout crowd of 61,108 in London's Wembley Stadium, with the hometown Monarchs defeating the Barcelona Dragons 21-0.

The World League had several firsts: the use of electronic radio communication in players' helmets, a "helmet cam"— a small television camera in the helmet of a few players—and 40 foreign players (four per team) on rosters.

In its second season, Columbus, Ohio, replaced Raleigh-Durham in the North American East Division. The Sacramento Surge defeated the Orlando Thunder 21-17 before 43,789 in Montreal for the second World Bowl title.

In the fall of 1992, the NFL clubs that funded and essentially owned the World League decided to concentrate solely on the league's European popularity. They suspended play for 1993, and, late that year, voted to form a six-team, all-European league to begin play in 1995.

In the spring of 1995, the World League became a joint venture between the NFL and FOX Sports and returned. Barcelona, Frankfurt, and London were joined by Amsterdam, Dusseldorf, and Scotland.

Nearly every NFL team contributed to an allocation of 37 players to the World League, which started again on April 8, 1995, with teams in Frankfurt and Rhein, Germany; Amsterdam, The Netherlands; London, England; Barcelona, Spain; and Scotland. On June 17, the Frankfurt Galaxy beat the Amsterdam Admirals 26-22 to win the World Bowl before 23,847 in Amsterdam's Olympic Stadium, an impressive figure for a country that had never seen professional football before that year.

Fan support was enough to continue the globalization of American football. In 1996, the same six teams played 10-game schedules, and 72 NFL players were allocated to World League teams. The Scottish Claymores defeated the Frankfurt Galaxy 32-27 in World Bowl '96 before 38,982 in Edinburgh, Scotland. The game was broadcast in 126 countries.

In 1997, 122 NFL players—including 13 quarterbacks—from 28 teams were sent to the World League. Jon Kitna passed for 401 yards to lead the Barcelona Dragons to a 38-24 victory over the Rhein Fire in the World Bowl. That fall, a record 118 players with World League experience were on NFL rosters.

In 1998, the league changed its name to NFL Europe. The league's sixth season kicked off with its 200th game on April 4, and three teams tied for first place during the regular season. A tiebreaker sent the Frankfurt Galaxy and the Rhein Fire to the World Bowl, where the Fire, led by Jim Arellanes's 3 touchdown passes, won 34-10 before 48,000 fans.

In 1999, the England Monarchs dropped out of NFL Europe and were replaced by the Berlin Thunder, leaving a six-team league. A record 152 current NFL players headed to Europe from 29 of the 31 teams. Fifteen of those players were quarterbacks.

"I think quarterbacks are among the players with the most to gain from competing in our league," Amsterdam head coach Al Luginbill says. "It is probably the toughest position to play in our sport. Those players can really benefit by being tested in game situations on a weekly basis."

NFL Europe basically is a developmental league for the NFL, and it has contributed a number of good players. Darren Bennett, an Australian rules football player, was an all-league selection in the World League in 1995 and was the AFC's punter in the Pro Bowl six months later. In 1998, 43 players with NFL Europe experience were on NFL postseason rosters. In fact, the 1998 Super Bowl champion Denver Broncos had seven players who played in the NFL Europe League.

"The NFL Europe League is an outstanding developmental league," Broncos head coach Mike Shanahan says. "The experience those players gained by playing in Europe has served them well in the NFL."

"Any time you can give developing players a chance to play against top competition, it's a big plus," Vikings coach Dennis Green says. "The NFL Europe League has helped us in that we've gotten a chance to see some of our young players perform under game conditions."

Kitna finished 1998 as the Seahawks' starting quarterback.

"I would not have had the opportunities I have had in the NFL if I had not played in Europe," he says. "In Barcelona, I proved that I could be starting quarterback of a pro football team.

"The opportunity to play and gain actual game experience was very important for my growth as a player. Quarterbacks need to get their game repetitions and take some hits. It's the only way to learn. You learn how to read pro defenses and how to react to specific situations in a game.

"Along with the game experience, the Dragons helped to raise my confidence level to the point where there was no doubt in my mind I belonged on an NFL squad. And when it was time for me to step in and take over at the Seahawks, I was ready both mentally and physically. It's the best competition outside of the NFL."

1991 World League Standings

European Division	W	L	T	Pct	PF	PA
London Monarchs*	9	1	0	.900	310	121
Barcelona Dragons	8	2	0	.800	206	126
Frankfurt Galaxy	7	3	0	.700	155	139
North American East						
New York/New Jersey Knights*	5	5	0	.500	257	155
Orlando Thunder	5	5	0	.500	242	286
Montreal Machine	4	6	0	.400	145	244
Raleigh-Durham Skyhawks	0	10	0	.000	123	300
North America West						
Birmingham Fire*	5	5	0	.500	140	140
Sacramento Surge	4	6	0	.400	176	196
San Antonio Riders	3	7	0	.300	179	229

**Division winner*
***Wild Card qualifier for playoffs*

Playoffs
Barcelona 10 at Birmingham 3
London 42 at New York/New Jersey 26

World Bowl '91
London 21 Barcelona 0 at London, England

1992 World League Standings

European Division	W	L	T	Pct	PF	PA
Barcelona Dragons*	5	5	0	.500	104	161
Frankfurt Galaxy	3	7	0	.300	150	257
London Monarchs	2	7	1	.250	178	203
North American East						
Orlando Thunder*	8	2	0	.800	247	127
New York/New Jersey Knights	6	4	0	.600	284	188
Montreal Machine	2	8	0	.200	175	274
Ohio Glory	1	9	0	.100	132	230
North America West						
Sacramento Surge*	8	2	0	.800	250	152
Birmingham Fire**	7	2	1	.750	192	165
San Antonio Riders	7	3	0	.700	195	150

**Division winner*
***Wild Card qualifier for playoffs*

Playoffs
Birmingham 7 at Orlando 45
Barcelona 21 at Sacramento 17

World Bowl '92
Sacramento 21 Orlando 17 at Montreal, Quebec

1995 World League Standings

First Half Standings	W	L	T	Pct	PF	PA
Amsterdam Admirals*	5	0	0	1.000	109	45
Barcelona Dragons	3	2	0	.600	114	102
Frankfurt Galaxy	2	3	0	.400	115	97
London Monarchs	2	3	0	.400	90	118
Rhein Fire	2	3	0	.400	87	122
Scottish Claymores	1	4	0	.200	54	85
Second Half Standings						
Amsterdam Admirals*	4	1	0	.800	137	107
Frankfurt Galaxy*	4	1	0	.800	114	102
Barcelona Dragons	3	2	0	.600	115	97
London Monarchs	2	3	0	.400	90	118
Rhein Fire	2	3	0	.400	87	122
Scottish Claymores	1	4	0	.200	54	85
Overall Final Standings						
Amsterdam Admirals*	9	1	0	.900	246	152
Frankfurt Galaxy*	6	4	0	.600	279	202
Barcelona Dragons	5	5	0	.500	237	247
London Monarchs	4	6	0	.400	174	220
Rhein Fire	4	6	0	.400	221	279
Scottish Claymores	2	8	0	.200	153	210

*Clinched World Bowl '95 playoff berth

World Bowl '95
Frankfurt 26 Amsterdam 22 at Amsterdam, The Netherlands

1996 World League Standings

Overall Final Standings	W	L	T	Pct	PF	PA
Scottish Claymores*	7	3	0	.700	233	190
Frankfurt Galaxy#	6	4	0	.600	221	220
Amsterdam Admirals	5	5	0	.500	250	210
Barcelona Dragons	5	5	0	.500	192	230
London Monarchs	4	6	0	.400	161	192
Rhein Fire	3	7	0	.300	176	191

**Qualified to host World Bowl as first-half champions*
***Qualified for World Bowl on overall record*

World Bowl '96
Scotland 32 Frankfurt 22 at Murrayfield, Scotland

1997 NFL Europe Standings

Overall Final Standings	W	L	T	Pct	PF	PA
Rhein Fire	7	3	0	.700	206	146
Barcelona Dragons*	5	5	0	.500	236	209
Scottish Claymores	5	5	0	.500	134	154
Amsterdam Admirals	5	5	0	.500	156	160
Frankfurt Galaxy	4	6	0	.400	147	142
London Monarchs	4	6	0	.400	116	184

World Bowl
Barcelona 38, Rhein 24
**First-half champion*

1998 NFL Europe Standings

Overall Final Standings	W	L	T	Pct	PF	PA
Frankfurt Galaxy	7	3	0	.700	167	164
Rhein Fire	7	3	0	.700	198	174
Amsterdam Admirals	7	3	0	.700	205	174
Barcelona Dragons	4	6	0	.400	185	200
London Monarchs	3	7	0	.300	161	200
Scottish Claymores	2	8	0	.200	153	182

World Bowl
Rhein 34, Frankfurt 10

THE REGISTER, ROSTERS, AND LEADERS

The Player Register

The Player Register includes the record of every player who has appeared in a National Football League game, as well as players from the All-America Football Conference (AAFC) from 1946-49. NFL records include games played in the American Football League, 1960-69, but do not include games played in any other professional league. However, records of men who played in the AAFC are presented in the Player Register as a point of information. No AAFC achievements (single-game or single-season records) are included, nor are AAFC career totals merged into any NFL career totals.

In compiling this register of more than 17,000 players, the editors and the Elias Sports Bureau used official game sheets whenever possible. For the early years where no game sheets exist, we were able to find at least two lineups from postgame newspaper stories. For many games, we checked a half dozen stories or more.

If a player did not actually play in an official regular-season game, he is not listed. Many players have appeared in preseason games, and some have been on rosters during the regular season but did not actually play.

An exception to this "must-have-played" rule is applied to reserve quarterbacks. It is common for a team's third quarterback and, occasionally, even the second quarterback to go through an entire season waiting on the sideline with a clipboard. The most famous example of this is Cliff Stoudt, who "stood" enough seasons to earn his pension before he ever got into a regular-season game. Because they contribute to their team's success simply by providing a safety net in case the regular quarterback is injured, we have included all reserve quarterbacks' seasons in the register.

The players are listed alphabetically by surname (last name), and, when more than one player bears the same name, they are listed alphabetically by given name—not by "use name." By use name we mean the name that was or may have been applied to a player during his playing career. This is the standard method of alphabetizing used in biographical reference works. In the case of pro football, it makes it easier to find a lesser-known player. On the whole, we have been conservative in ascribing nicknames, doing so only when the player generally was known by that name during his playing days.

A finding aid tops each page of the Player Register. Readers will find, in capital letters, the surname of the player whose entry heads up the page and the player whose entry concludes it. Another finding aid is the use of bold-face numerals to indicate league-leading performance in a given statistical category. Condensed type appears occasionally throughout this section; it has no special significance but is designed to accommodate unusually wide "fields," such as the team field when a man has appeared for two or more teams in a given year.

Each player entry is made up of two parts: demographic information and statistical information, which may have numerous components. We'll consider the demographic part of the player's entry first.

Demographics

The player's USE NAME begins his entry. It is set:

1. in larger type than any other part of the entry;
2. in capital letters;
3. bold faced.

The player's use name is printed with the given name or, if one exists, nickname first, followed by his surname. In other words, RED GRANGE, not GRANGE, RED.

Next on the first line is the player's full name, printed in this order: surname, first name, middle name. The surname is given first because the Player Register is alphabetized by full name rather than use name. Here you will find Grange, Harold Edward, and near him Grant, Harold Peter, Jr., better known by his use name of Bud.

If no middle name is listed, the player may not have had one. As we sometimes found, he often would not admit to having one. On the other hand, some players were better known by their middle names. Ewell Walker might be unfamiliar to fans, but Doak Walker is in the Pro Football Hall of Fame.

The next first-line entry is the player's height and weight. Occasionally, when the player's name is unusually long (see Theodore Stanislaus Andrulewicz), this information is carried over into the second line.

In researching heights and weights, we often found that retired players remembered themselves as being an inch or more taller and considerably heavier than the information printed in programs during their playing days. Program heights and weights often have been unreliable. The New York Giants listed tackle John Alexander as 6 feet 1 inch. He actually was 6-4. Les Bingaman, the Lions' famous middle guard, was listed in programs at 272 pounds, but according to legend, he often squashed the scales at 350.

Unless we found convincing evidence to the contrary, we have listed the most likely published height and weight for a player. We were able to verify John Alexander's actual height, but we could not prove that Bingaman weighed more than his published pounds. Secondly, the published weights of players with long careers tend to increase during their careers. In such cases, we averaged the weight over a whole career in order to give a single figure.

At the far right of each first line, again in bold face, you will find the player's position or positions given in the common abbreviations that all football fans know, plus some less familiar ones; see below. His most-played position is listed first.

Position Abbreviations:

BB = Blocking back
C = Center
DB = Defensive back
DE = Defensive end
DG = Defensive guard
DT = Defensive tackle
NT = Nose tackle
FB = Fullback
FL = Flanker
G = Offensive and defensive guard
HB = Halfback
K = Punter or placekicker (and did not play any other position in a particular year.
LB = Linebacker
MG = Middle guard
OG = Offensive guard
OE = Offensive end
OT = Offensive tackle
QB = Quarterback
RB = Running back
T = Offensive and defensive tackle
TB = Tailback
TE = Tight end
WB = Wingback
WR = Wide receiver

If a player had a well-known nickname that is not his use name, that nickname is given in parentheses at the beginning of the second line. In cases where a name was changed (see Karim Abdul-Jabbar) or, if for any other reason a player was known by a different name during his career, the change is in parentheses, here preceded by AKA, for "also known as."

For most players, the second line of their entries begin with Col: in italics. This indicates a college, university, junior college (marked JC) or community college (CC) attended by the player. It does not indicate graduation or even that he lettered in football. For example, a few former college trackmen and basketball players who did not play football in college have appeared in NFL games. If a player did not attend college, this will be entered as no college. If the abbreviation *Col:* does not appear, as is the case for a few mystery men of the 1920s, we simply do not know whether the player attended college or not.

More common is the multi-college entry, indicating the player attended more than one school. Here the schools are given chronologically in the order attended. When a school has changed its name, the current name is given. Therefore, players who attended Carnegie Tech years ago will find themselves listed as having attended Carnegie-Mellon.

The next entry is the player's high school (*HS:*) or high schools. This is a unique feature of *Total Football* and an important one. If a player is born in Massachusetts, attends high school in Indiana, and then goes on to play for San Diego State, where is he from? Rather than try to answer the question arbitrarily, we simply present the options. Of course, including this information allows the browser to discover players from his or her old high school (or its bitter rival) who went on to NFL careers. However, unlike colleges, we have given the name of the high school as it was known when the player attended school. There have been so many consolidations, closings, and re-openings that the current name of a high school, if it still exists, often would be meaningless or misleading.

If the high school has the same name as the city or town in which it is located, the name is given followed by the postal abbreviation for the state in brackets. If the high school's name is different from its city, the name of the city and state are in brackets. If we couldn't find the high school, there is no *HS:* and no entry for that information.

A B: announces birth information. The birthdate is given in number form. The day of the month follows the slash, and, after another slash, the year is given in all four digits. Birthplace is one of the most difficult pieces of demographic information to find, given that both colleges and pro team media guides often opt for the ambiguous "hometown." Death dates and places are handled similarly except for the occasional entry of "Deceased," when it is known that the player has died but no date or place is available. Sadly, many players of the past have passed on with their deaths being noted only by friends, relatives, and a single small-town newspaper.

If the player was drafted by the NFL, that information follows the notation *Drafted:* in his entry. The year of the draft, round in which he was drafted, and the team that drafted him are given in that order. A very few players have an additional note of interest. An entry such as *HOF:* 1980 means the player was enshrined in the Pro Football Hall of Fame in 1980.

Statistical Information

Individual football statistics vary. While most offensive linemen accumulate no statistics except their number of games played, a back or receiver may rush, pass, catch passes, kick extra points and field goals, punt, return punts, return kickoffs, intercept passes, and even (since 1982) register sacks. Most backs will register at least two of these events during their careers, and many may tally five or more. There are 128 possible combinations of statistical categories. Accordingly, to present all statistics across a single page would require a book that is two feet wide!

Even more to the point, the vast majority of most lines would be taken up with empty space or zero after zero. Defensive linemen nowadays seldom catch passes, modern kickers intercept few passes, and several statistical categories were not kept until dates as far apart as 1932 and 1982.

To keep the statistics contained in *Total Football* easy to locate, we decided on two formats:

1. Categories in which a player accumulated significant totals are given in tabular form.

2. When there are relatively few entries, they are given in linear (or paragraph) form immediately after the player's

demographic information and always commence with a "new paragraph" at flush left.

Linear Information

If a player appeared in the All-America Football Conference of 1946-49, any statistics from that league are given first after the letters AAFC. Statistics from the AAFC are not NFL statistics, although there is a tendency to lump them together. We present them here separately because that is historically accurate. The NFL did not incorporate AAFC statistics into its records when that league collapsed, but it did incorporate American Football League records after that merger.

If a player appeared in both the AAFC and the NFL, his AAFC statistics are given first even if he began his career in the NFL. NFL statistics are given in a new paragraph with NFL as the beginning notation. If a player appeared only in the NFL, no league identification is given.

Each year of the player's career is given in boldface, followed by the team for which he played in that year. In the case of a player appearing for more than one NFL team during a season, his combined record is given followed by his record for each team in the order in which he played for them. (AAFC records are given only in their combined form because, at present, it is not possible to separate the records by team.)

If part of a player's record appears in tabular form, his games played will be given in the table. If there is no table, the games played in a season will be given immediately after his team and followed by G. For example, **1964** ChiB: 7 G means the man played in seven games with the Chicago Bears in 1964.

The abbreviations for categories in the linear text, though fairly obvious, should be explained. Rush = rushing, Pass = passing, Rec = pass receiving, Int = interceptions, Punt = punting, Scor = scoring, PR = punt returns, KR = kickoff returns, Sac = sacks. (Internal abbreviations will be dealt with below in Tabular Information.)

In order to give the linear information as succinctly and clearly as possible, we have used a simplified form. An entry after Rush might read 3-12 4.0. This means the player had 3 rushing attempts, gained 12 yards, and averaged 4 yards per attempt. A player who registered negative yardage would have an entry such as 2-(-4) -2.0, meaning 2 attempts for a total of minus-4 yards and an average of minus -2 yards per attempt. A notation of 1 TD following the average means he scored a rushing touchdown. This same system is followed for Rec (with the first number being the number of passes caught), PR, and KR.

Pass statistics in the linear form are given with attempts-completions, completion percentage, yards gained, average gain per attempt, and touchdowns and interceptions where applicable.

When kicking is involved in scoring statistics, the total points are given first, followed by field goals-field-goal attempts and the percentage of successful attempts followed by the notation FG. Then come extra points-attempts, percentage, and the notation XK (extra points kicked). Finally, any touchdowns scored are noted. When no kicks are involved, only the points and touchdowns are noted. Punt records give the attempts-yards punted and the average. With Int, no average gain is given. Sacks are always noted in the linear section.

In years for which a statistical category is unavailable (such as all categories except scoring from 1920-1931 or interceptions 1920-1939), a player's touchdowns in that category still are listed. An entry such as **1927** GB 8 G, Int 1 TD, 6 Pt means that a Packer played in 8 games in 1927, intercepted one pass for a touchdown, and scored 6 points. It does not mean that he intercepted one pass all season: He may well have intercepted several, but, unfortunately, we only have an official record of the one he ran back for a touchdown.

Totals and averages that led the league in a given year are bold faced.

The final part of the linear record gives the career totals and averages for any player whose career was longer than a single year. These totals do not, of course, include any statistical categories dealt with in tabular form.

Tabular Information

Tables of individual statistical categories are labeled in bold at the top, and a line below the name of the category shows which subheads are encompassed in that category. In naming the categories in tables, the name of the category is spelled out, not abbreviated as in the linear section. Most tables show only one statistical category, but, in some cases, when the player's statistics merit it, two categories appear side by side. Examples include Rushing and Receiving as well as Punt Returns and Kickoff Returns.

The first line of a table begins at flush left with the notations Year Team G. This means that in the columns below these notations will be the teams for which the men played, the seasons (chronologically), and the number of games he appeared in each season. (Note: If the player has more than one table covering the same period, his games played will be given in the first table only.) The rest of the line is devoted to the statistical category presented using the following abbreviations:

Rushing:

Att = rushing attempts
Yds = yards gained
Avg = average gain per attempt
TD = rushing touchdowns

Passing:

Att = passing attempts
Comp = completions
Comp% = completion percentage
Yds = yards gained
YPA = yards gained per attempt
TD = touchdown passes
INT = interceptions

Rating = the player's efficiency rating, according to the NFL's passer rating system, which ranks passers on a scale based upon a formula derived from their completion percentage, yards gained per attempt, touchdown percentage, and interception percentage.

Receiving:

Rec = pass receptions
Yds = yards gained
Avg = average gain per reception
TD = touchdowns

Scoring:

Pt = points scored
FG = field goals made
FGA = field goals attempted
FG% = field-goal percentage
XK = extra points kicked
XKA = extra points attempted
XK% = extra-point percentage
TD = touchdowns
Saf. = safeties

Interceptions:

INT = interceptions
YDS = yards returned
TD = touchdowns

Punting:

Punt = punts
Yds = yardage kicked (measured from the line of scrimmage to where the ball is caught or downed)
Avg = average yards per punt

Punt Returns:

Ret = punts returned
Yds = yards returned
Avg = average yards per punt return
TD = touchdowns

Kickoff Returns:

Ret = kickoffs returned
Yds = yards returned
Avg = average yards per kickoff return
TD = touchdowns

When Fumbles (Fum) or Total Touchdowns (Tot TD) are included in a table, they do not necessarily apply to the statistical category denoted in that table. For example, a player's rushing record might be given, but of the 2 fumbles and 3 total touchdowns at the right of his 1955 rushing record, 1 fumble and 1 touchdown may have come as the result of pass receptions.

Here is a sample player record, which illustrates the differences between minimal statistics (handled in paragraph form) and substantial numbers (presented in tables).

LOU LEADFOOT Leadfoot, Eugene Louis, Jr. 6′2″, 205 **RB-LB-G**
(Butterfingers) *Col:* Mudwallow JC; West Liberty State College; Michigan
HS: Harwood [Wheeling, WV] B: 10/19/1947, Bilgewater, DE
D: 8/6/1995, Teeming Fen, OK *Drafted:* 1967 Round 7 LARm HOF: 1991
1967 LARm: Punt 2-44 22.0; PR 3-47; Int 3-(-4). 1968 LARm: Int 1-10 1 TD. 1969 Cle-ChiB: Punt 5-211 42.2. Cle: Punt 2-90 45.0. ChiB: Punt 3-121 40.3. 1974 Det: PR 1-5. Total: Punt 8-255 31.9; PR 4-49; Int 4-6 1 TD.

	Passing								
Year Team	**G**	**Att**	**Comp**	**Comp%**	**Yds**	**YPA**	**TD**	**Int**	**Rating**
1967 LARm	2	11	4	36.4	96	8.73	1	3	59.5
1968 LARm	6	48	21	43.8	348	7.25	3	4	54.9
1969 Cle-ChiB	10	74	26	35.1	333	4.50	2	6	25.3
1969 Cle	1	2	1	50.0	10	5.00	0	1	60.2
1969 ChiB	9	72	25	34.7	323	4.49	2	5	24.1
1970 ChiB	14	312	161	51.6	1992	6.38	7	17	56.5
1971 Det	12	55	19	34.5	260	4.73	0	10	11.0
1972 Det	14	368	207	56.3	2915	7.92	28	20	84.7
1973 Det	3	96	53	55.2	518	5.40	6	9	52.3
1974 Det	1	1	1	100.0	7	7.00	0	0	85.5
NFL Total	62	965	493	51.1	6469	6.70	47	69	61.3

		Rushing				Receiving					Tot
Year Team	**G**	**Att**	**Yds**	**Avg**	**TD**	**Rec**	**Yds**	**Avg**	**TD**	**Fum**	**TD**
1967 LARm	10	45	4.5	0	3	28	9.3	0	2	0	5
1968 LARm	33	361	10.9	4	5	130	26.0	2	3	7	8
1969 Cle-ChiB	8	44	5.5	0	3	20	6.7	1	0	1	3
1969 Cle	1	-2	-2.0	0	2	18	9.0	0	0	1	2
1969 ChiB	7	46	6.6	0	1	2	2.0	1	0	1	1
1970 ChiB	150	874	5.8	9	24	312	13.0	2	6	11	30
1971 Det	57	184	3.2	2	8	74	9.3	0	4	2	12
1972 Det	68	312	4.6	1	2	0	—	0	2	1	4
1973 Det	2	0	0.0	0	3	14	4.7	0	1	0	4
1974 Det	—	—	—	—	1	1	7.0	0	0	1	
NFL Total	328	1820	5.5	16	52	585	11.9	5	18	22	70

Conclusion

The statistics in the Player Register were provided by the Elias Sports Bureau, the official record keeper of the NFL since 1961. Not only does Elias keep each season's statistics, but its statisticians also have gone back to seasons long ago before they began keeping watch to review the statistics from those years. Therefore, some previously published statistics between 1920-1960 have been corrected in this volume. Such changes were made only after careful research and examination of all pertinent data. Scoring records from the 1920s, researched by David Neft, Joel Bussert, and Bob Carroll, have been accepted as official. In all cases, the league itself was consulted.

Demographic information for individual players never has been kept as meticulously as their playing statistics, and there are still many gaps, particularly from the early years of the league. We ask any readers with information to write to the Pro Football Researchers Association, 12870 Rt. 30, N. Huntingdon, PA 15642.

JOE ABBEY Abbey, Joseph Reed 6′1″, 202 **OE-DE**
Col: Texas; North Texas *HS:* Denton [TX] B: 3/21/1925, Denton, TX
1948 ChiB: 12 G; Rec 5-67 13.4; 1 Fum. **1949** NYB: 6 G; Rec 8-110 13.8.
Total: 18 G; Rec 13-177 13.6; 1 Fum.

FAYE ABBOTT Abbott, Lafayette 5′8″, 182 **BB-QB-FB-TB**
(Hack) *Col:* Syracuse *HS:* Lancaster [NY] B: 8/16/1895, Clearport, OH D: 1/21/1965, Dayton, OH
1921 Day: 9 G; Rec 1 TD; 6 Pt. **1922** Day: 6 G. **1923** Day: 8 G; Rush 1 TD; 6 Pt. **1924** Day: 7 G. **1925** Day: 8 G; Scor 3, 1 FG. **1926** Day: 6 G.
1927 Day: 7 G. **1928** Day: 5 G; Scor 3, 1 FG. **1929** Day: 1 G. **Total:** 57 G; Rush 1 TD; Rec 1 TD; Scor 18, 2 FG; Tot TD 2.

VINCE ABBOTT Abbott, Vincent Steven 5′11″, 207 **K**
Col: Washington; Cal State-Fullerton *HS:* Tsawwassen [Vancouver, Canada] B: 5/31/1958, London, England
1987 SD: 12 G; Scor 61, 13-22 59.1% FG, 22-23 95.7% XK. **1988** SD: 11 G; Scor 39, 8-12 66.7% FG, 15-15 100.0% XK. **Total:** 23 G; Scor 100, 21-34 61.8% FG, 37-38 97.4% XK.

DUKE ABBRUZZI Abbruzzi, Louis John 5′10″, 175 **HB-DB**
Col: Rhode Island *HS:* Warren [RI] B: 8/3/1917, Warren, RI
D: 12/6/1982, Newport, RI
1946 Bos: 3 G; Pass 1-1 100.0%, 11 11.00; Rush 6-26 4.3; Rec 2-55 27.5; PR 1-1 1.0; KR 8-147 18.4; 3 Fum.

KARIM ABDUL-JABBAR Abdul-Jabbar, Karim 5′10″, 205 **RB**
(AKA Sharmon Shah) *Col:* UCLA *HS:* Susan Miller Dorsey [Los Angeles, CA] B: 6/28/1974, Los Angeles, CA *Drafted:* 1996 Round 3 Mia

		Rushing				Receiving					Tot
Year Team	**G**	**Att**	**Yds**	**Avg**	**TD**	**Rec**	**Yds**	**Avg**	**TD**	**Fum**	**TD**
1996 Mia	16	307	1116	3.6	11	23	139	6.0	0	4	11
1997 Mia	16	283	892	3.2	**15**	29	261	9.0	1	3	**16**
1998 Mia	15	270	960	3.6	6	21	102	4.9	0	2	6
NFL Total	47	860	2968	3.5	32	73	502	6.9	1	9	33

FRED ABEL Abel, Fred K 5′10″, 170 **BB-FB**
Col: Washington *HS:* Montesanto [WA] B: 7/17/1903, Lincoln, NE
D: 8/2/1980, Port Townsend, WA
1926 Mil: 3 G.

BUD ABELL Abell, Harry Everett 6′3″, 220 **LB**
Col: Missouri *HS:* Southeast [Kansas City, MO] B: 12/21/1940, Kansas City, MO *Drafted:* 1964 Round 23 KC
1966 KC: 14 G. **1967** KC: 14 G. **1968** KC: 12 G; KR 1-0; Int 2-14.
Total: 40 G; KR 1-0; Int 2-14.

WALTER ABERCROMBIE Abercrombie, Walter Augustus 6′0″, 207 **RB**
Col: Baylor *HS:* University [Waco, TX] B: 9/26/1959, Waco, TX
Drafted: 1982 Round 1 Pit
1982 Pit: KR 7-139 19.9. **1988** Phi: KR 5-87 17.4. **Total:** KR 12-226 18.8.

		Rushing				Receiving					Tot
Year Team	**G**	**Att**	**Yds**	**Avg**	**TD**	**Rec**	**Yds**	**Avg**	**TD**	**Fum**	**TD**
1982 Pit	6	21	100	4.8	2	1	14	14.0	0	0	2
1983 Pit	15	112	446	4.0	4	26	391	15.0	3	2	7
1984 Pit	14	145	610	4.2	1	16	135	8.4	0	0	1
1985 Pit	16	227	851	3.7	7	24	209	8.7	2	5	9
1986 Pit	16	214	877	4.1	6	47	395	8.4	2	4	8
1987 Pit	12	123	459	3.7	2	24	209	8.7	0	4	2
1988 Phi	5	5	14	2.8	0	1	-2	-2.0	0	0	0
NFL Total	84	847	3357	4.0	22	139	1351	9.7	7	15	29

CLIFF ABERSON Aberson, Clifford Alexander 6′0″, 195 **TB-DB**
Col: No College *HS:* Nicholas Senn [Chicago, IL] B: 8/28/1921, Chicago, IL D: 6/23/1973, Vallejo, CA
1946 GB: Pass 41-14 34.1%, 184 4.49 5 Int; KR 3-69 23.0; Int 3-53.

		Rushing				
Year Team	**G**	**Att**	**Yds**	**Avg**	**TD**	**Fum**
1946 GB	10	48	161	3.4	0	2

CLIFTON ABRAHAM Abraham, Clifton Eugene 5′9″, 185 **DB**
Col: Florida State *HS:* David W. Carter [Dallas, TX] B: 12/9/1971, Dallas, TX *Drafted:* 1995 Round 5 TB
1995 TB: 6 G. **1996** ChiB: 2 G. **1997** Car: 1 G. **Total:** 9 G.

DONNIE ABRAHAM Abraham, Nathaniel Donnell 5′10″, 190 **DB**
Col: East Tennessee State *HS:* Orangeburg-Wilkinson [Orangeburg, SC]
B: 10/8/1973, Orangeburg, SC *Drafted:* 1996 Round 3 TB

		Interceptions		
Year Team	**G**	**Int**	**Yds**	**TD**
1996 TB	16	5	27	0
1997 TB	16	5	16	0
1998 TB	13	1	3	0
NFL Total	45	11	46	0

ROBERT ABRAHAM Abraham, Robert Eugene 6′1″, 228 **LB**
Col: North Carolina State *HS:* Myrtle Beach [SC] B: 7/13/1960, Myrtle Beach, SC *Drafted:* 1982 Round 3 Hou
1982 Hou: 9 G. **1983** Hou: 14 G; Int 1-0; 1 Sac. **1984** Hou: 16 G; Int 1-1.
1985 Hou: 16 G; 1 Sac. **1986** Hou: 16 G; 2 Sac. **1987** Hou: 2 G.
Total: 73 G; Int 2-1; 4 Sac.

DANNY ABRAMOWICZ Abramowicz, Daniel Stanley 6′1″, 195 **WR**
Col: Xavier (Ohio) *HS:* Central Catholic [Steubenville, OH]
B: 7/13/1945, Steubenville, OH *Drafted:* 1967 Round 17 NO
1968 NO: Rush 2-27 13.5. **1969** NO: Rush 3-61 20.3. **1970** NO: Rush 1-7 7.0. **1971** NO: PR 1-0. **1974** SF: Pass 1-1 100.0%, 41 41.00.
Total: Pass 1-1 100.0%, 41 41.00; Rush 6-95 15.8; PR 1-0.

		Receiving				
Year Team	**G**	**Rec**	**Yds**	**Avg**	**TD**	**Fum**
1967 NO	14	50	721	14.4	6	0
1968 NO	14	54	890	16.5	7	0
1969 NO	14	**73**	1015	13.9	7	0
1970 NO	14	55	906	16.5	5	2
1971 NO	14	37	657	17.8	5	1
1972 NO	13	38	668	17.6	7	1
1973 NO-SF	14	37	460	12.4	1	0
1973 NO	2	2	18	9.0	0	0
1973 SF	12	35	442	12.6	1	0
1974 SF	14	25	369	14.8	1	1
NFL Total	111	369	5686	15.4	39	5

SID ABRAMOWITZ Abramowitz, Sidney H 6′6″, 280 **OT**
Col: Air Force; Tulsa *HS:* Leavenworth [KS] B: 5/21/1960, Culver City, CA *Drafted:* 1983 Round 5 Bal
1983 Bal: 14 G. **1984** Sea: 4 G. **1985** NYJ: 1 G. **1987** Ind: 3 G.
Total: 22 G.

KEVIN ABRAMS Abrams, Kevin R 5′8″, 175 **DB**
Col: Syracuse *HS:* Hillsborough [Tampa, FL] B: 2/28/1974, Tampa, FL
Drafted: 1997 Round 2 Det
1997 Det: 15 G; Int 1-29; 2 Sac. **1998** Det: 16 G; PR 2-12 6.0; 3 Sac.
Total: 31 G; PR 2-12 6.0; Int 1-29; 5 Sac.

NATE ABRAMS Abrams, Nathan 5′4″, 145 **OE**
Col: No College *HS:* Green Bay East [WI] B: 12/25/1897, Green Bay, WI D: 4/30/1941, Green Bay, WI
1921 GB: 1 G; Int **1** TD; 6 Pt.

BOBBY ABRAMS Abrams, Robert Jr. 6′3″, 240 **LB**
Col: Michigan *HS:* Henry Ford [Detroit, MI] B: 4/12/1967, Detroit, MI
1990 NYG: 16 G. **1991** NYG: 16 G. **1992** Dal-Cle-NYG: 8 G. Dal: 4 G. Cle: 3 G. NYG: 1 G. **1993** Dal-Min: 9 G. Dal: 5 G. Min: 4 G. **1994** Min: 16 G.
1995 NE: 9 G. **Total:** 74 G.

GEORGE ABRAMSON Abramson, George N 5′7″, 198 **G-T**
Col: Minnesota *HS:* Virginia [MN] B: 5/13/1903, Eveleth, MN
D: 3/15/1985, Beverly Hills, CA
1925 GB: 10 G; Scor 8, 2 FG, 2 XK.

DICK ABRELL Abrell, Richard Thompson 5′10″, 172 **BB-WB**
(Abe) *Col:* Purdue *HS:* Linton [IN] B: 5/18/1892, Linton, IN
D: 5/5/1973, West Orange, NJ
1920 Day: 6 G.

RAY ABRUZZESE Abruzzese, Raymond Lewis Jr. 5′11″, 194 **DB**
Col: Hinds CC MS; Alabama *HS:* South Philadelphia [Philadelphia, PA]
B: 10/27/1937, Philadelphia, PA *Drafted:* 1962 Round 23 Buf
1962 Buf: PR 3-17 5.7; KR 10-194 19.4. **1963** Buf: PR 17-152 8.9; KR 6-118 19.7. **1965** NYJ: KR 1-16 16.0. **Total:** PR 20-169 8.5; KR 17-328 19.3.

		Interceptions		
Year Team	**G**	**Int**	**Yds**	**TD**
1962 Buf	12	3	44	0
1963 Buf	14	3	9	0
1964 Buf	9	0	0	0
1965 NYJ	12	2	13	0
1966 NYJ	14	2	9	0
NFL Total	61	10	75	0

FRANK ABRUZZINO Abruzzino, Frank Marion Jr. 6′0″, 193 **LB-BB-C-G**
Col: Colgate *HS:* Lincoln [Shinnston, WV] B: 1/22/1908, Shinnston, WV D: 6/13/1986, Ft. Lauderdale, FL
1931 Bkn: 14 G. **1933** Cin: 9 G. **Total:** 23 G.

DICK ABSHER Absher, Richard Alfred Jr. 6′4″, 230 **LB-K**
Col: Maryland *HS:* Bullis Prep [Potomac, MD] B: 4/19/1944, Washington, DC *Drafted:* 1967 Round 5 Phi
1967 Was-Atl: 2 G; Scor 4, 0-1 FG, 4-4 100.0% XK. Was: 1 G; Scor 4, 0-1 FG, 4-4 100.0% XK. Atl: 1 G. **1968** Atl: 10 G. **1969** NO: 14 G; Int 1-7.
1970 NO: 10 G. **1971** NO: 14 G; KR 1-3 3.0; Int 1-21. **1972** Phi: 8 G; Int 1-7. **Total:** 58 G; KR 1-3 3.0; Int 3-35; Scor 4, 0-1 FG, 4-4 100.0% XK.

STEVE ACHE Ache, Stephen 6′3″, 229 **LB**
Col: Coffeyville CC KS; Triton CC IL; Southwest Missouri State
B: 3/16/1962, Syracuse, NY
1987 Min: 3 G.

GEORGE ACHICA Achica, George 6′5″, 260 **DT**
Col: USC *HS:* Andrew Hill [San Jose, CA] B: 12/19/1960, American Samoa *Drafted:* 1983 Round 3 Bal
1985 Ind: 4 G.

SNEEZE ACHIU Achiu, Walter Tin Kit 5′8″, 169 **WB-TB-OE-BB**
(Chink) *Col:* Dayton; Hawaii *HS:* St. Louis [Honolulu, HI] B: 8/3/1902, Honolulu, HI D: 3/21/1989, Eugene, OR
1927 Day: 7 G. **1928** Day: 4 G. **Total:** 11 G.

BILL ACKER Acker, William Berry Jr. 6′3″, 255 **NT**
Col: Texas *HS:* Freer [TX] B: 11/7/1956, Freer, TX *Drafted:* 1980 Round 6 StL
1980 StL: 16 G. **1981** StL: 8 G. **1982** KC: 3 G. **1983** Buf: 11 G. **1984** Buf: 15 G. **1987** KC: 2 G. **Total:** 55 G.

RICK ACKERMAN Ackerman, Richard Carl 6′4″, 258 **DT**
Col: Memphis *HS:* Glenbard North [Carol Stream, IL] B: 6/16/1959, La Grange, IL
1982 SD: 9 G; 3 Sac. **1983** SD: 15 G; 1.5 Sac. **1984** SD-LARd: 15 G; 2 Sac. SD: 9 G; 1 Sac. LARd: 6 G; 1 Sac. **1987** LARd: 3 G; 1 Sac.
Total: 42 G; 7.5 Sac.

TOM ACKERMAN Ackerman, Thomas Michael 6′3″, 290 **OG**
Col: Eastern Washington *HS:* Nooksack [WA] B: 9/6/1972, Bellingham, WA *Drafted:* 1996 Round 5 NO
1996 NO: 2 G. **1997** NO: 14 G. **1998** NO: 15 G. **Total:** 31 G.

RON ACKS Acks, Ronald William 6′2″, 214 **LB**
Col: Illinois *HS:* Carbondale [IL] B: 10/3/1944, Herrin, IL
Drafted: 1966 Round 4 Min
1968 Atl: 1 G. **1969** Atl: 14 G; Int 0-15; 6 Pt. **1970** Atl: 8 G. **1971** Atl: 14 G; Int 1-0. **1972** NE: 14 G. **1973** NE: 14 G; Int 1-11. **1974** GB: 13 G.
1975 GB: 14 G. **1976** GB: 13 G. **Total:** 105 G; Int 2-26; 6 Pt.

FRED ACORN Acorn, Frederick Earl 5′10″, 185 **CB**
Col: Texas *HS:* Rotan [TX] B: 3/17/1961, Rotan, TX *Drafted:* 1984 Round 3 TB
1984 TB: 16 G; Int 1-14.

ED ADAMCHIK Adamchik, Edward James 6′2″, 235 **C**
Col: Pittsburgh *HS:* Johnstown [PA] B: 11/2/1941, Johnstown, PA
Drafted: 1963 Round 12 NYG
1965 NYG-Pit: 4 G. NYG: 2 G. Pit: 2 G. **Total:** 4 G.

TONY ADAMLE Adamle, Anthony 6′0″, 215 **LB-FB**
Col: Ohio State *HS:* Collinwood [Cleveland, OH] B: 5/15/1924, Fairmont, WV *Drafted:* 1947 Round 10 ChiB
AAFC **1947** CleA: Rec 1-22 22.0; PR 0-36; KR 1-22 22.0; Int 1-25.
1949 CleA: Rec 1-13 13.0; Int 4-42. **Total:** Rec 2-35 17.5; PR 0-36; KR 1-22 22.0; Int 5-67.

		Rushing			
Year Team	**G**	**Att**	**Yds**	**Avg**	**TD**
1947 CleA	14	23	95	4.1	1
1948 CleA	14	17	88	5.2	1
1949 CleA	12	17	64	3.8	0
AAFC Total	40	57	247	4.3	2

NFL **1950** Cle: 12 G; Rush 3-8 2.7; KR 4-53 13.3; Int 1-17; 2 Fum.
1951 Cle: 12 G; Int 1-12. **1954** Cle: 11 G. **Total:** 35 G; Rush 3-8 2.7; KR 4-53 13.3; Int 2-29; 2 Fum.

MIKE ADAMLE Adamle, Michael David 5′9″, 197 **RB**
Col: Northwestern *HS:* Theodore Roosevelt [Kent, OH] B: 10/4/1949, Kent, OH *Drafted:* 1971 Round 5 KC
1975 ChiB: Pass 2-2 100.0%, 57 28.50. **1976** ChiB: PR 1-2 2.0; Scor **1** Saf. **Total:** Pass 2-2 100.0%, 57 28.50; PR 1-2 2.0; Scor 1 Saf.

		Rushing				Receiving			
Year Team	**G**	**Att**	**Yds**	**Avg**	**TD**	**Rec**	**Yds**	**Avg**	**TD**
1971 KC	8	13	43	3.3	0	1	6	6.0	1
1972 KC	14	73	303	4.2	1	15	76	5.1	0
1973 NYJ	14	67	264	3.9	0	9	63	7.0	0
1974 NYJ	12	28	93	3.3	2	9	84	9.3	0
1975 ChiB	14	94	353	3.8	1	15	111	7.4	0
1976 ChiB	14	33	93	2.8	0	4	28	7.0	1
NFL Total	76	308	1149	3.7	4	53	368	6.9	2

	Kickoff Returns					Tot
Year Team	**Ret**	**Yds**	**Avg**	**TD**	**Fum**	**TD**
1971 KC	7	149	21.3	0	0	1
1972 KC	8	185	23.1	0	3	1
1973 NYJ	5	79	15.8	0	5	0
1974 NYJ	2	17	8.5	0	0	2
1975 ChiB	1	27	27.0	0	4	1
1976 ChiB	11	179	16.3	0	0	1
NFL Total	34	636	18.7	0	12	6

TONY ADAMS Adams, Anthony Lee 6′0″, 198 **QB**
Col: Texas; Utah State *HS:* Ramona [Riverside, CA] B: 3/9/1950, San Antonio, TX *Drafted:* 1973 Round 14 SD
1975 KC: Rec 1-(-7) -7.0. **Total:** Rec 1-(-7) -7.0.

		Passing							
Year Team	**G**	**Att**	**Comp**	**Comp%**	**Yds**	**YPA**	**TD**	**Int**	**Rating**
1975 KC	6	77	36	46.8	445	5.78	2	4	52.1
1976 KC	14	71	36	50.7	575	8.10	3	4	68.7
1977 KC	14	92	47	51.1	691	7.51	2	11	43.6
1978 KC	16	79	44	55.7	415	5.25	2	3	63.0
1987 Min	3	89	49	55.1	607	6.82	3	5	64.2
NFL Total	53	408	212	52.0	2733	6.70	12	27	55.5

	Rushing				
Year Team	**Att**	**Yds**	**Avg**	**TD**	**Fum**
1975 KC	8	42	5.3	0	4
1976 KC	5	46	9.2	0	1
1977 KC	5	21	4.2	0	1
1978 KC	9	15	1.7	0	0
1987 Min	11	31	2.8	0	3
NFL Total	38	155	4.1	0	9

CHET ADAMS Adams, Chester Frank 6′3″, 233 **DT-OT-OE-DE**
Col: Ohio U. *HS:* South [Cleveland, OH] B: 10/24/1915, Cleveland, OH
D: 10/28/1990, Cleveland, OH
AAFC **1946** CleA: 14 G; Int 1-4 1 TD; Scor 17, 5-5 100.0% XK; 1 Fum TD; Tot TD 2. **1947** CleA: 13 G; Scor 4, 1-1 100.0% FG, 1-2 50.0% XK.
1948 CleA: 14 G. **1949** BufA: 12 G; Scor 44, 4-11 36.4% FG, 32-32 100.0% XK. **Total:** 53 G; Int 1-4 1 TD; Scor 65, 5-12 41.7% FG, 38-39 97.4% XK; 1 Fum TD; Tot TD 2.

NFL **1939** Cle: 9 G; Scor 5, 5-5 100.0% XK. **1940** Cle: 11 G; Rec 3-28 9.3; Scor 10, 1-5 20.0% FG, 7-9 77.8% XK. **1941** Cle: 11 G; Scor 16, 1-2 50.0% FG, 13-14 92.9% XK. **1942** Cle: 11 G; Scor 23, 3-6 50.0% FG, 14-15 93.3% XK. **1943** GB: 10 G; Scor 3, 1-6 16.7% FG. **1950** NYY: 12 G; Scor 51, 2-9 22.2% FG, 45-48 93.8% XK. **Total:** 64 G; Rec 3-28 9.3; Scor 108, 8-28 28.6% FG, 84-91 92.3% XK.

CURTIS ADAMS Adams, Curtis Ladonn 5′11″, 198 **RB**
Col: Central Michigan *HS:* Orchard View [Muskegon, MI]
B: 4/30/1962, Muskegon, MI *Drafted:* 1985 Round 8 SD
1985 SD: Rec 1-12 12.0; KR 2-50 25.0. **1986** SD: Rec 4-26 6.5; KR 5-100 20.0. **1987** SD: Rec 4-38 9.5; KR 4-32 8.0. **1988** SD: KR 1-13 13.0.
Total: Rec 9-76 8.4; KR 12-195 16.3.

		Rushing				
Year Team	**G**	**Att**	**Yds**	**Avg**	**TD**	**Fum**
1985 SD	1	16	49	3.1	1	0
1986 SD	7	118	366	3.1	4	3
1987 SD	12	90	343	3.8	1	1
1988 SD	7	38	149	3.9	1	1
NFL Total	27	262	907	3.5	7	5

BRENT ADAMS Adams, David Brent 6′5″, 256 **OT**
Col: Tennessee *HS:* Elbert Co. [Elberton, GA] B: 6/26/1952, Elberton, GA *Drafted:* 1975 Round 8 Atl
1975 Atl: 13 G. **1976** Atl: 14 G. **1977** Atl: 14 G. **Total:** 41 G.

DAVID ADAMS Adams, David Delaney 5′6″, 168 **RB**
Col: Arizona *HS:* Sunnyside [Tucson, AZ] B: 6/24/1964, Tucson, AZ
Drafted: 1987 Round 12 Ind
1987 Dal: 3 G; Rush 7-49 7.0 1 TD; Rec 1-8 8.0; KR 6-113 18.8; 6 Pt; 2 Fum.

DOUG ADAMS Adams, Douglas 0 6′1″, 225 **LB**
Col: Ohio State *HS:* Xenia [OH] B: 11/3/1949, Xenia, OH
D: 8/9/1997, Macon, OH *Drafted:* 1971 Round 7 Den
1971 Cin: 11 G. **1972** Cin: 14 G; Int 3-44. **1973** Cin: 12 G. **1974** Cin: 12 G.
Total: 49 G; Int 3-44.

EARNEST ADAMS Adams, Earnest 6′2″, 226 **LB**
Col: Illinois *HS:* Dillard [Fort Lauderdale, FL] B: 3/12/1959, Fort Lauderdale, FL
1987 Det: 3 G.

FLOZELL ADAMS Adams, Flozell Jootin 6′7″, 335 **OG-TE**
(Flo) *Col:* Michigan State *HS:* Proviso West [Hillside, IL]
B: 5/10/1975, Bellwood, FL *Drafted:* 1998 Round 2 Dal
1998 Dal: 16 G.

GEORGE ADAMS Adams, George Wallace 6′1″, 225 **RB**
Col: Kentucky *HS:* Lafayette [Lexington, KY] B: 12/22/1962, Lexington, KY *Drafted:* 1985 Round 1 NYG
1985 NYG: Pass 1-0; KR 14-241 17.2. **1987** NYG: KR 9-166 18.4.
1990 NE: KR 1-7 7.0. **Total:** Pass 1-0; KR 24-414 17.3.

		Rushing				Receiving					Tot
Year Team	G	Att	Yds	Avg	TD	Rec	Yds	Avg	TD	Fum	TD
1985 NYG	16	128	498	3.9	2	31	389	12.5	2	7	4
1987 NYG	12	61	169	2.8	1	35	298	8.5	1	3	2
1988 NYG	16	29	76	2.6	0	27	174	6.4	0	0	0
1989 NYG	14	9	29	3.2	0	2	7	3.5	0	0	0
1990 NE	16	28	111	4.0	0	16	146	9.1	1	1	1
1991 NE	2	2	3	1.5	0	0	0	—	0	0	0
NFL Total	76	257	886	3.4	3	111	1014	9.1	4	11	7

HENRY ADAMS Adams, Henry 6′1″, 190 **C**
(Heinie) *Col:* Pittsburgh *HS:* California [Coal Center, PA]
B: 12/24/1915, California, PA
1939 ChiC: 3 G.

NEAL ADAMS Adams, Howard O'Neale 6′3″, 195 **OE**
Col: Arkansas *HS:* Beebe [AR] B: 1/21/1919, El Paso, AR
D: 10/27/1998, Sand Springs, OK
AAFC **1946** BknA: 13 G; Rec 15-225 15.0 2 TD; 12 Pt. **1947** BknA: 1 G.
Total: 14 G; Rec 15-225 15.0 2 TD; 12 Pt.

NFL **1942** NYG: Int 1-66 **1** TD. **1943** NYG: KR 1-8 8.0. **1944** NYG: KR 2-29 14.5. **Total:** KR 3-37 12.3; Int 1-66 1 TD.

		Receiving				Tot
Year Team	G	Rec	Yds	Avg	TD	TD
1942 NYG	11	6	87	14.5	3	4
1943 NYG	8	8	65	8.1	1	2
1944 NYG	10	14	342	**24.4**	1	1
1945 NYG	9	0	0	—	0	0
NFL Total	38	28	494	17.6	5	7

JOHN ADAMS Adams, John Albert 6′3″, 235 **FB-OE**
Col: Santa Monica Coll. CA (J.C.); UCLA; Los Angeles State
HS: Herbert Hoover [San Diego, CA] B: 11/28/1937, San Diego, CA
D: 8/8/1995, Helendale, CA *Drafted:* 1959 Round 5 ChiB
1960 ChiB: Rec 2-(-20) -10.0. **1961** ChiB: Pass 1-1 100.0%, 11 11.00; Rec 5-80 16.0; Punt 2-56 28.0. **1962** ChiB: Rec 5-111 22.2 3 TD. **1963** LARm: Rec 9-93 10.3; Punt 4-121 30.3. **Total:** Pass 1-1 100.0%, 11 11.00; Rec 21-264 12.6 3 TD; Punt 6-177 29.5.

		Rushing					Tot
Year Team	G	Att	Yds	Avg	TD	Fum	TD
1959 ChiB	12	4	-13	-3.3	0	0	0
1960 ChiB	12	23	114	5.0	0	0	0
1961 ChiB	13	14	-2	-0.1	1	1	1
1962 ChiB	14	0	0	—	0	0	3
1963 LARm	13	0	0	—	0	0	0
NFL Total	64	41	99	2.4	1	1	4

JOHN ADAMS Adams, John William 6′7″, 242 **T**
(Tree) *Col:* Notre Dame *HS:* Subiaco Acad. [AR] B: 9/22/1921, Charleston, AR D: 8/20/1969, Bethesda, MD *Drafted:* 1945 Round 2 Was
1945 Was: 10 G. **1946** Was: 11 G. **1947** Was: 10 G. **1948** Was: 12 G. **1949** Was: 12 G. **Total:** 55 G.

JULIUS ADAMS Adams, Julius Thomas Jr. 6′3″, 270 **DE**
Col: Texas Southern *HS:* Ballard [Macon, GA] B: 4/26/1948, Macon, GA *Drafted:* 1971 Round 2 NE
1971 NE: 14 G. **1972** NE: 11 G. **1973** NE: 14 G. **1974** NE: 14 G. **1975** NE: 9 G. **1976** NE: 14 G. **1977** NE: 14 G. **1978** NE: 1 G. **1979** NE: 16 G. **1980** NE: 16 G. **1981** NE: 16 G. **1982** NE: 9 G; 2 Sac. **1983** NE: 16 G; 8 Sac. **1984** NE: 16 G; 4 Sac. **1985** NE: 16 G; 5 Sac. **1987** NE: 10 G. **Total:** 206 G; 19 Sac.

MIKE ADAMS Adams, Michael Christopher 5′11″, 185 **WR**
Col: Texas *HS:* Sam Houston [Arlington, TX] B: 3/25/1974, Dallas, TX
Drafted: 1997 Round 7 Pit
1997 Pit: 6 G; Rec 1-39 39.0; KR 10-215 21.5; 1 Fum.

MICHAEL ADAMS Adams, Michael Glendale 5′10″, 195 **DB**
Col: Mississippi Delta CC; Arkansas State *HS:* Broad Street [Shelby, MS] B: 4/5/1964, Shelby, MS *Drafted:* 1987 Round 3 NO
1987 NO: 7 G; KR 4-52 13.0; 1 Fum. **1988** NO: 5 G. **1989** Pho: 3 G. **Total:** 15 G; KR 4-52 13.0; 1 Fum.

PETE ADAMS Adams, Peter Anthony 6′4″, 260 **OG**
Col: USC *HS:* University [San Diego, CA] B: 5/4/1951, San Diego, CA
Drafted: 1973 Round 1 Cle
1974 Cle: 12 G. **1976** Cle: 13 G. **Total:** 25 G.

BOB ADAMS Adams, Robert Bruce 6′2″, 225 **TE-OT**
Col: U. of Pacific *HS:* San Mateo [CA] B: 8/15/1946, Stockton, CA
1973 NE: Rush 2-7 3.5. **1976** Atl: KR 1-21 21.0. **Total:** Rush 2-7 3.5; KR 1-21 21.0.

		Receiving				
Year Team	G	Rec	Yds	Avg	TD	Fum
1969 Pit	14	6	80	13.3	0	0
1970 Pit	14	3	36	12.0	0	0
1971 Pit	14	20	160	8.0	0	1
1973 NE	12	14	197	14.1	0	0
1974 NE	13	17	244	14.4	0	0
1975 Den	2	0	0	—	0	0
1976 Atl	13	1	15	15.0	0	0
NFL Total	82	61	732	12.0	0	1

SAM ADAMS Adams, Samuel Aaron 6′3″, 295 **DT**
Col: Texas A&M *HS:* Cypress Creek [Houston, TX] B: 6/13/1973, Houston, TX *Drafted:* 1994 Round 1 Sea
1994 Sea: 12 G; 4 Sac. **1995** Sea: 16 G; Scor **1** Saf; 2 Pt; 3.5 Sac. **1996** Sea: 16 G; 5.5 Sac. **1997** Sea: 16 G; 7 Sac. **1998** Sea: 16 G; Int 1-25 1 TD; 6 Pt; 2 Sac. **Total:** 76 G; Int 1-25 1 TD; Scor 1 Saf; 8 Pt; 22 Sac.

SAM ADAMS Adams, Samuel Edward 6′3″, 256 **OG**
Col: Prairie View A&M *HS:* Jasper [TX] B: 9/20/1948, Jasper, TX
1972 NE: 6 G. **1973** NE: 12 G. **1974** NE: 14 G. **1975** NE: 13 G. **1976** NE: 14 G. **1977** NE: 14 G. **1978** NE: 16 G. **1979** NE: 15 G. **1980** NE: 15 G. **1981** NO: 16 G. **Total:** 135 G.

SCOTT ADAMS Adams, Scott Alexander 6′5″, 301 **OT-OG**
Col: Georgia *HS:* Columbia [Lake City, FL] B: 9/28/1966, Lake City, FL
1992 Min: 15 G; KR 1-0; 1 Fum. **1993** Min: 15 G. **1994** NO: 11 G. **1995** ChiB: 4 G. **1996** TB: 7 G. **1997** Atl: 6 G. **Total:** 58 G; KR 1-0; 1 Fum.

STAN ADAMS Adams, Stanley Earl 6′2″, 215 **LB**
Col: Memphis *HS:* Marion [AR] B: 5/22/1960, Marion, AR
1984 LARd: 4 G.

STEFON ADAMS Adams, Stefon Lee 5′10″, 189 **DB**
Col: East Carolina *HS:* Southwest Guilford [High Point, NC]
B: 8/11/1963, High Point, NC *Drafted:* 1985 Round 3 LARd
1986 LARd: Int 1-32. **1987** LARd: Int 1-8. **1989** LARd: Scor **1** Saf.
Total: Int 2-40; Scor 1 Saf.

		Punt Returns				Kickoff Returns				
Year Team	G	Ret	Yds	Avg	TD	Ret	Yds	Avg	TD	Fum
1986 LARd	16	0	0	—	0	27	573	21.2	0	0
1987 LARd	9	5	39	7.8	0	3	61	20.3	0	0
1988 LARd	14	6	45	7.5	0	8	132	16.5	0	0
1989 LARd	14	19	156	8.2	0	22	425	19.3	0	2
1990 Cle-Mia	12	13	81	6.2	0	5	49	9.8	0	2
1990 Cle	10	13	81	6.2	0	3	33	11.0	0	2
1990 Mia	2	0	0	—	0	2	16	8.0	0	0
NFL Total	65	43	321	7.5	0	65	1240	19.1	0	4

THEO ADAMS Adams, Theo P 6′4″, 300 **OT**
Col: Hawaii *HS:* McKinley [Honolulu, HI] B: 4/24/1966, San Francisco, CA
1992 Sea: 10 G. **1993** TB: 7 G. **Total:** 17 G.

TOM ADAMS Adams, Thomas Frank 6′4″, 215 **WR**
Col: Minnesota-Duluth *HS:* Keewatin [MN] B: 4/26/1940, Keewatin, MN
1962 Min: 6 G; Rec 3-51 17.0.

VASHONE ADAMS Adams, Vashone LaRey 5′10″, 197 **DB**
Col: Butte Coll. CA (J.C.); Fort Hays State; Eastern Michigan
HS: Overland [KS] B: 9/12/1973, Aurora, CO
1995 Cle: 8 G. **1996** Bal: 16 G; Int 1-16. **1997** NO: 5 G. **Total:** 29 G; Int 1-16.

VERLIN ADAMS Adams, Verlin T 6′0″, 205 **DE-T-G-OE**
(Sparky) *Col:* Charleston (WV) B: 7/14/1918, Burnwell, KY
D: 4/30/1985, Charleston, WV *Drafted:* 1943 Round 29 NYG
1943 NYG: 4 G. **1944** NYG: 7 G; Rec 1-12 12.0. **1945** NYG: 1 G; Int 1-3.
Total: 12 G; Rec 1-12 12.0; Int 1-3.

BILL ADAMS Adams, William Joseph 6′2″, 255 **OG-OT**
Col: Holy Cross *HS:* Swampscott [MA] B: 2/4/1950, Lynn, MA
Drafted: 1972 Round 7 Mia
1972 Buf: 6 G. **1974** Buf: 8 G. **1975** Buf: 6 G. **1976** Buf: 11 G. **1977** Buf: 9 G. **1978** Buf: 6 G. **Total:** 46 G.

WILLIE ADAMS Adams, Willie James 6′2″, 235 **DE-LB**
Col: New Mexico State *HS:* Roy Miller [Corpus Christi, TX]
B: 12/12/1941, Corpus Christi, TX *Drafted:* 1965 Round 11 Was
1965 Was: 14 G. **1966** Was: 14 G. **Total:** 28 G.

WILLIS ADAMS Adams, Willis Dean 6′2″, 194 **WR**
Col: Navarro Coll. TX (J.C.); Houston *HS:* Schulenburg [TX]
B: 8/22/1956, Weimar, TX *Drafted:* 1979 Round 1 Cle
1979 Cle: Rush 2-4 2.0. **1980** Cle: Rush 2-7 3.5. **1983** Cle: Rush 1-2 2.0.
Total: Rush 5-13 2.6.

		Receiving				
Year Team	G	Rec	Yds	Avg	TD	Fum
1979 Cle	16	1	6	6.0	0	1
1980 Cle	16	8	165	20.6	0	0
1981 Cle	7	1	24	24.0	0	0
1982 Cle	1	0	0	—	0	0
1983 Cle	16	20	374	18.7	2	1
1984 Cle	16	21	261	12.4	0	1

1985 Cle	3	10	132	13.2	0	0
NFL Total	75	61	962	15.8	2	3

KEN ADAMSON Adamson, Kenneth Marshall 6′2″, 235 **OG**
Col: Notre Dame *HS:* Marist [Atlanta, GA] B: 10/12/1938, Phoenix, AZ
1960 Den: 14 G. **1961** Den: 14 G. **1962** Den: 4 G. **Total:** 32 G.

ABE ADDAMS Addams, Abraham Buchanan 6′2″, 220 **DE**
Col: Indiana *HS:* Male [Louisville, KY] B: 7/12/1926, Louisville, KY
1949 Det: 5 G.

HERB ADDERLEY Adderley, Herbert A 6′0″, 205 **DB**
Col: Michigan State *HS:* Northeast [Philadelphia, PA] B: 6/8/1939, Philadelphia, PA *Drafted:* 1961 Round 1 GB *HOF:* 1980
1965 GB: PR 1-0. **Total:** PR 1-0.

		Kickoff Returns				Interceptions				Tot
Year Team	**G**	**Ret**	**Yds**	**Avg**	**TD**	**Int**	**Yds**	**TD**	**Fum**	**TD**
1961 GB	14	18	478	26.6	0	1	9	0	1	0
1962 GB	14	15	418	27.9	**1**	7	132	**1**	2	2
1963 GB	14	20	597	29.9	1	5	86	0	1	1
1964 GB	13	19	508	26.7	0	4	56	0	1	0
1965 GB	14	10	221	22.1	0	6	**175**	**3**	1	3
1966 GB	14	14	320	22.9	0	4	125	1	1	1
1967 GB	14	10	207	20.7	0	4	16	1	0	1
1968 GB	14	14	331	23.6	0	3	27	0	2	0
1969 GB	14	0	0	—	0	5	**169**	1	0	1
1970 Dal	14	0	0	—	0	3	69	0	0	0
1971 Dal	12	0	0	—	0	6	182	0	0	0
1972 Dal	13	0	0	—	0	0	0	0	0	0
NFL Total	164	120	3080	25.7	2	48	1046	7	9	9

TOM ADDISON Addison, Thomas Marion 6′2″, 230 **LB**
Col: South Carolina *HS:* Lancaster [SC] B: 4/12/1936, Lancaster, SC
Drafted: 1958 Round 12 Bal

		Interceptions		
Year Team	**G**	**Int**	**Yds**	**TD**
1960 Bos	11	0	0	0
1961 Bos	14	4	17	0
1962 Bos	14	5	42	**1**
1963 Bos	14	4	27	0
1964 Bos	14	2	4	0
1965 Bos	14	1	13	0
1966 Bos	14	0	0	0
1967 Bos	11	0	0	0
NFL Total	106	16	103	1

NICK ADDUCI Adduci, Nicholas Frank 5′10″, 207 **LB**
(Bull) *Col:* Nebraska *HS:* Pullman Tech [Chicago, IL] B: 7/12/1929, Chicago, IL
1954 Was: 10 G. **1955** Was: 12 G; PR 1-10 10.0. **Total:** 22 G; PR 1-10 10.0.

JOHN ADICKES Adickes, John Matthew 6′3″, 264 **C**
Col: Baylor *HS:* Killeen [TX] B: 6/29/1964, Queens, NY *Drafted:* 1987 Round 6 ChiB
1987 ChiB: 6 G. **1988** ChiB: 16 G; 1 Fum. **1989** Min: 1 G. **Total:** 23 G; 1 Fum.

MARK ADICKES Adickes, Mark Stephen 6′4″, 278 **OG**
Col: Baylor *HS:* Killeen [TX] B: 4/22/1961, Badconstadt, Germany
Drafted: 1984 Supplemental Round 1 KC
1986 KC: 15 G. **1987** KC: 12 G; Rec 1-3 3.0 1 TD; 6 Pt. **1988** KC: 10 G. **1989** KC: 16 G. **1990** Was: 8 G. **1991** Was: 16 G. **Total:** 77 G; Rec 1-3 3.0 1 TD; 6 Pt.

KEVIN ADKINS Adkins, James Kevin 6′1″, 250 **DB**
Col: Oklahoma *HS:* Midwest City [OK] B: 8/27/1965, Midwest City, OK
1987 KC: 2 G.

MARGENE ADKINS Adkins, Margene 5′10″, 183 **WR**
Col: Trinity Valley CC TX; Wichita State *HS:* Kirkpatrick [Fort Worth, TX]
B: 4/30/1947, Fort Worth, TX *Drafted:* 1970 Round 2 Dal
1970 Dal: PR 4-44 11.0. **1971** Dal: Rec 4-53 13.3; PR 4-5 1.3. **1972** NO: Rec 9-96 10.7; PR 7-0. **1973** NYJ: Rec 6-109 18.2. **Total:** Rec 19-258 13.6; PR 15-49 3.3.

		Kickoff Returns				
Year Team	**G**	**Ret**	**Yds**	**Avg**	**TD**	**Fum**
1970 Dal	5	7	149	21.3	0	1
1971 Dal	3	0	0	—	0	0
1972 NO	14	**43**	**1020**	23.7	0	4
1973 NYJ	13	31	615	19.8	0	2
NFL Total	35	81	1784	22.0	0	7

BOB ADKINS Adkins, Robert Grant 6′1″, 213 **BB-DE-G-LB**
Col: Marshall *HS:* Point Pleasant [WV] B: 2/7/1917, Letart, WV
D: 12/6/1997, Pleasant Valley, WV
1940 GB: 10 G; Rush 1-5 5.0; Rec 4-73 18.3 1 TD; Int 2-35 **1** TD; Scor 13, 0-1 FG, 1-2 50.0% XK; Tot TD 2. **1941** GB: 6 G; Int 2-79; Scor 3, 3-3 100.0% XK. **1945** GB: 4 G; 1 Fum. **Total:** 20 G; Rush 1-5 5.0; Rec 4-73 18.3 1 TD; Int 4-114 1 TD; Scor 16, 0-1 FG, 4-5 80.0% XK; Tot TD 2; 1 Fum.

ROY ADKINS Adkins, Roy S 5′7″, 180 **G**
Col: Millikin; Bethany (W.V.) *HS:* Stephen Decatur [Decatur, IL]
B: 10/5/1898, Bement, IL D: 2/10/1975, Montclair, NJ
1920 Sta: 4 G.

SAM ADKINS Adkins, Samuel Alan 6′2″, 214 **QB**
Col: Wichita State *HS:* Grover Cleveland [Los Angeles, CA]
B: 5/21/1955, Van Nuys, CA *Drafted:* 1977 Round 10 Sea
1977 Sea: 1 G; Rush 3-6 2.0; 1 Fum. **1979** Sea: 3 G; Pass 3-0; Rush 2-11 5.5. **1980** Sea: 4 G; Pass 23-10 43.5%, 136 5.91 1 TD 3 Int; Rush 6-18 3.0. **1981** Sea: 3 G; Pass 13-7 53.8%, 96 7.38 1 TD 1 Int; Rush 3-28 9.3. **Total:** 11 G; Pass 39-17 43.6%, 232 5.95 2 TD 4 Int; Rush 14-63 4.5; 1 Fum.

ERIK AFFHOLTER Affholter, Erik Konrad 6′0″, 187 **WR**
Col: USC *HS:* Oak Park [Agoura Hills, CA] B: 4/10/1966, Detroit, MI
Drafted: 1989 Round 4 Was
1991 GB: 4 G; Rec 7-68 9.7.

DICK AFFLIS Afflis, William Richard 6′0″, 251 **OT-DG-OG**
(Bruiser) *Col:* Purdue; Nevada-Reno *HS:* Shortridge [Indianapolis, IN]
B: 6/27/1929, Lafayette, IN D: 11/10/1991, Lafayette, IN
Drafted: 1951 Round 16 GB
1951 GB: 12 G. **1952** GB: 12 G. **1953** GB: 12 G. **1954** GB: 12 G; Int 1-3. **Total:** 48 G; Int 1-3.

BEN AGAJANIAN Agajanian, Benjamin James 6′0″, 215 **K**
(Aggie; Bootin') *Col:* Compton CC CA; New Mexico *HS:* San Pedro [CA] B: 8/28/1919, Santa Ana, CA
AAFC **1947** LA-A: 13 G; Scor 84, 15-24 62.5% FG, 39-40 97.5% XK. **1948** LA-A: 13 G; Scor 46, 5-15 33.3% FG, 31-32 96.9% XK. **Total:** 26 G; Scor 130, 20-39 51.3% FG, 70-72 97.2% XK.

NFL Statistics

		Scoring						
Year Team	**G**	**Pts**	**FG**	**FGA**	**FG%**	**XK**	**XKA**	**XK%**
1945 Phi-Pit	6	13	4	4	100.0	1	2	50.0
1945 Phi	1	0	0	0	—	0	0	—
1945 Pit	5	13	4	4	100.0	1	2	50.0
1949 NYG	12	59	8	13	**61.5**	35	36	**97.2**
1953 LARm	10	66	10	24	41.7	36	37	97.3
1954 NYG	12	74	13	**25**	52.0	35	35	100.0
1955 NYG	12	62	10	15	66.7	32	33	97.0
1956 NYG	10	38	5	13	38.5	23	23	100.0
1957 NYG	12	62	10	18	55.6	32	32	100.0
1960 LAC	14	85	13	24	54.2	46	47	97.9
1961 DalT-GB	6	27	4	11	36.4	15	15	100.0
1961 DalT	3	16	3	9	33.3	7	7	100.0
1961 GB	3	11	1	2	50.0	8	8	100.0
1962 Oak	6	25	5	14	35.7	10	11	90.9
1964 SD	3	14	2	4	50.0	8	8	100.0
NFL Total	103	525	84	165	50.9	273	279	97.8

ALEX AGASE Agase, Alexander Arrasi 5′10″, 212 **LB-OG**
Col: Purdue; Illinois *HS:* Evanston Twp. [Evanston, IL] B: 3/27/1922, Chicago, IL *Drafted:* 1944 Round 6 GB
AAFC **1947** LA-A-ChiA: 14 G; Int 1-4. **1948** CleA: 13 G. **1949** CleA: 11 G; Int 3-31. **Total:** 38 G; Int 4-35.

NFL **1950** Cle: 11 G; Int 1-14. **1951** Cle: 11 G; Int 2-7. **1953** Bal: 10 G; Int 1-5. **Total:** 32 G; Int 4-26.

LOUIS AGE Age, Louis Theodore III 6′7″, 350 **OT**
Col: Southwestern Louisiana *HS:* St. Augustine [New Orleans, LA]
B: 2/1/1970, New Orleans, LA *Drafted:* 1992 Round 11 ChiB
1992 ChiB: 6 G.

MEL AGEE Agee, Melvin 6′5″, 300 **DE-DT**
Col: Illinois *HS:* George Washington [Chicago, IL] B: 11/22/1968, Chicago, IL *Drafted:* 1991 Round 6 Ind
1991 Ind: 16 G. **1992** Ind: 1 G. **1993** Atl: 11 G; 2.5 Sac. **1994** Atl: 16 G. **1995** Atl: 10 G. **Total:** 54 G; 2.5 Sac.

SAM AGEE Agee, Samuel Webster 6′1″, 218 **FB**
(Steamroller) *Col:* Vanderbilt *HS:* Columbia Mil. Acad. [TN]
B: 10/21/1915, Courtland, AL
1938 ChiC: Pass 2-2 100.0%, 27 13.50; Rec 2-5 2.5. **1939** ChiC: Pass 3-0; Rec 1-6 6.0. **Total:** Pass 5-2 40.0%, 27 5.40; Rec 3-11 3.7.

		Rushing			
Year Team	**G**	**Att**	**Yds**	**Avg**	**TD**
1938 ChiC	10	48	178	3.7	1
1939 ChiC	11	44	133	3.0	1
NFL Total	21	92	311	3.4	2

TOMMIE AGEE Agee, Thomas Lee 6'0", 225 RB
Col: Auburn *HS:* Maplesville [AL] B: 2/22/1964, Chilton, AL
Drafted: 1987 Round 5 Sea
1988 Sea: Pass 1-0, 1 Int. **Total:** Pass 1-0, 1 Int.

		Rushing				Receiving				Tot
Year Team	G	Att	Yds	Avg	TD	Rec	Yds	Avg	TD	TD
1988 Sea	16	1	2	2.0	0	3	31	10.3	0	0
1989 KC	9	1	3	3.0	0	0	0	—	0	0
1990 Dal	16	53	213	4.0	0	30	272	9.1	1	1
1991 Dal	16	9	20	2.2	1	7	43	6.1	0	1
1992 Dal	16	16	54	3.4	0	3	18	6.0	0	0
1993 Dal	12	6	13	2.2	0	0	0	—	0	0
1994 Dal	15	5	4	0.8	0	1	2	2.0	0	0
NFL Total	100	91	309	3.4	1	44	366	8.3	1	2

BOB AGLER Agler, Robert 6'1", 208 HB-DB-FB-LB
(Moe) *Col:* Otterbein *HS:* Mifflin [Columbus, OH] B: 3/13/1924, Columbus, OH
1948 LARm: 8 G; Rush 8-41 5.1. **1949** LARm: 8 G; Rush 4-7 1.8.
Total: 16 G; Rush 12-48 4.0.

RAY AGNEW Agnew, Raymond Mitchell Jr. 6'3", 285 DE-DT
Col: North Carolina State *HS:* Carver [Winston-Salem, NC]
B: 12/9/1967, Winston-Salem, NC *Drafted:* 1990 Round 1 NE
1990 NE: 12 G; 2.5 Sac. **1991** NE: 13 G; 2 Sac. **1992** NE: 14 G; 1 Sac.
1993 NE: 16 G; 1.5 Sac. **1994** NE: 11 G; 0.5 Sac. **1995** NYG: 16 G; 1 Sac.
1996 NYG: 13 G; Int 1-34 1 TD; 6 Pt; 0.5 Sac. **1997** NYG: 15 G; 2 Sac.
1998 StL: 16 G; Int 1-0; 5 Sac. **Total:** 126 G; Int 2-34 1 TD; 6 Pt; 16 Sac.

LOUIE AGUIAR Aguiar, Louis Raymond 6'2", 215 P
Col: Utah State *HS:* Granada [Livermore, CA] B: 6/30/1966, Livermore, CA
1991 NYJ: Rush 1-18 18.0; Scor 3, 1-2 50.0% FG. **1993** NYJ: Pass 2-0, 1 Int; Rush 3-(-27) -9.0. **1997** KC: Pass 1-1 100.0%, 35 35.00; Rush 2-11 5.5. **Total:** Pass 3-1 33.3%, 35 11.67 1 Int; Rush 6-2 0.3; Scor 3, 1-2 50.0% FG.

		Punting			
Year Team	G	Punts	Yds	Avg	Fum
1991 NYJ	16	64	2521	39.4	0
1992 NYJ	16	73	2993	41.0	0
1993 NYJ	16	73	2806	38.4	2
1994 KC	16	85	3582	42.1	0
1995 KC	16	91	3990	43.8	0
1996 KC	16	88	3667	41.7	0
1997 KC	16	82	3465	42.3	0
1998 KC	16	75	3226	43.0	0
NFL Total	128	631	26250	41.6	2

JOE AGUIRRE Aguirre, Joseph 6'4", 225 OE-DE
Col: St. Mary's (Cal.) *HS:* Ogden [UT] B: 10/17/1918, Rock Springs, WY *Drafted:* 1941 Round 9 Was
AAFC **1946** LA-A: Pass 1-0; Rush 2-(-5) -2.5; Punt 2-91 45.5; Scor 55, 4-11 36.4% FG, 31-32 96.9% XK. **1948** LA-A: KR 1-10 10.0; Scor 56, 2-3 66.7% XK. **Total:** Pass 1-0; Rush 2-(-5) -2.5; KR 1-10 10.0; Punt 2-91 45.5; Scor 141, 4-11 36.4% FG, 33-35 94.3% XK.

		Receiving			
Year Team	G	Rec	Yds	Avg	TD
1946 LA-A	14	14	246	17.6	2
1947 LA-A	12	8	158	19.8	4
1948 LA-A	13	38	599	15.8	9
1949 LA-A	4	3	37	12.3	1
AAFC Total	43	63	1040	16.5	16

NFL **1941** Was: Scor 26, 2-5 40.0% FG, 8-9 88.9% XK. **1943** Was: Rush 1-21 21.0; KR 3-21 7.0; Scor 48, 0-2 FG, 6-9 66.7% XK. **1944** Was: Punt 2-87 43.5; Scor 51, 4-8 **50.0**% FG, 15-18 **83.3**% XK. **1945** Was: Scor 44, **7-13** 53.8% FG, 23-23 100.0% XK. **Total:** Rush 1-21 21.0; KR 3-21 7.0; Punt 2-87 43.5; Scor 169, 13-28 46.4% FG, 52-59 88.1% XK.

		Receiving				
Year Team	G	Rec	Yds	Avg	TD	Fum
1941 Was	10	10	103	10.3	2	0
1943 Was	10	37	420	11.4	7	0
1944 Was	10	34	410	12.1	4	0
1945 Was	10	16	189	11.8	0	1
NFL Total	40	97	1122	11.6	13	1

CHIDI AHANOTU Ahanotu, Chidi Obioma 6'2", 283 DE-DT
Col: California *HS:* Berkeley [CA] B: 10/11/1970, Modesto, CA
Drafted: 1993 Round 6 TB
1993 TB: 16 G; 1.5 Sac. **1994** TB: 16 G; 1 Sac. **1995** TB: 16 G; 3 Sac. **1996** TB: 13 G; 5.5 Sac. **1997** TB: 16 G; 10 Sac. **1998** TB: 4 G.
Total: 81 G; 21 Sac.

DAN AHERN Ahern, Daniel Francis 6'2", 200 T
Col: Georgetown *HS:* Manchester Central [NH] B: 2/15/1898, Manchester, NH D: 8/31/1963, Washington DC
1921 Was: 3 G.

DAVE AHRENS Ahrens, David Iver 6'3", 238 LB
Col: Wisconsin *HS:* Oregon [WI] B: 12/5/1958, Cedar Falls, IA
Drafted: 1981 Round 6 StL
1981 StL: 16 G; Int 1-14 1 TD; 6 Pt. **1982** StL: 9 G; KR 1-5 5.0. **1983** StL: 16 G; Rec 1-4 4.0. **1984** StL: 16 G. **1985** Ind: 16 G. **1986** Ind: 16 G; 2 Sac. **1987** Ind: 12 G; PR 1-0. **1988** Det: 8 G. **1989** Mia: 11 G; KR 1-10 10.0; 1 Sac. **1990** Sea: 10 G. **Total:** 130 G; Rec 1-4 4.0; PR 1-0; KR 2-15 7.5; Int 1-14 1 TD; 6 Pt; 3 Sac.

TONY AIELLO Aiello, Anthony Samuel 5'6", 165 WB-BB
Col: Youngstown State *HS:* Brookfield [OH] B: 4/29/1921, Monongahela, PA
1944 Det-Bkn: 5 G; Rush 6-22 3.7; PR 1-9 9.0. Det: 4 G; Rush 6-22 3.7; PR 1-9 9.0. Bkn: 1 G. **Total:** 5 G; Rush 6-22 3.7; PR 1-9 9.0.

CARL AIKENS Aikens, Carl Kenneth Jr. 6'1", 185 WR
Col: Northern Illinois *HS:* Curie [Chicago, IL] B: 6/5/1962, Great Lakes, IL
1987 LARd: 3 G; Rush 1-1 1.0; Rec 8-134 16.8 3 TD; 18 Pt.

TROY AIKMAN Aikman, Troy Kenneth 6'4", 219 QB
Col: Oklahoma; UCLA *HS:* Henryetta [OK] B: 11/21/1966, West Covina, CA *Drafted:* 1989 Round 1 Dal
1989 Dal: Rec 1-(-13) -13.0. **1991** Dal: Rec 1-(-6) -6.0. **Total:** Rec 2-(-19) -9.5.

		Passing							
Year Team	G	Att	Comp	Comp%	Yds	YPA	TD	Int	Rating
1989 Dal	11	293	155	52.9	1749	5.97	9	18	55.7
1990 Dal	15	399	226	56.6	2579	6.46	11	18	66.6
1991 Dal	12	363	237	65.3	2754	7.59	11	10	86.7
1992 Dal	16	473	302	63.8	3445	7.28	23	14	89.5
1993 Dal	14	392	271	**69.1**	3100	7.91	15	6	99.0
1994 Dal	14	361	233	64.5	2676	7.41	13	12	84.9
1995 Dal	16	432	280	64.8	3304	7.65	16	7	93.6
1996 Dal	15	465	296	63.7	3126	6.72	12	13	80.1
1997 Dal	16	518	292	56.4	3283	6.34	19	12	78.0
1998 Dal	11	315	187	59.4	2330	7.40	12	5	88.5
NFL Total	140	4011	2479	61.8	28346	7.07	141	115	82.8

	Rushing				
Year Team	Att	Yds	Avg	TD	Fum
1989 Dal	38	302	7.9	0	6
1990 Dal	40	172	4.3	1	5
1991 Dal	16	5	0.3	1	4
1992 Dal	37	105	2.8	1	4
1993 Dal	32	125	3.9	0	7
1994 Dal	30	62	2.1	1	2
1995 Dal	21	32	1.5	1	5
1996 Dal	35	42	1.2	1	6
1997 Dal	25	79	3.2	0	6
1998 Dal	22	69	3.1	2	3
NFL Total	296	993	3.4	8	48

JIM AILINGER Ailinger, James Joseph 5'11", 185 G
Col: Buffalo *HS:* Hutchinson [Buffalo, NY] B: 7/10/1901, Buffalo, NY
1924 Buf: 8 G.

CHARLES AIU Aiu, Charles Kahoalii 6'2", 251 OG
Col: Hawaii *HS:* Damien [Honolulu, HI] B: 5/22/1954, Honolulu, HI
1976 SD: 12 G. **1977** SD: 14 G. **1978** SD-Sea: 7 G. SD: 6 G. Sea: 1 G.
Total: 33 G.

DAVID AKERS Akers, David Roy 5'10", 180 K
Col: Louisville *HS:* Tates Creek [Lexington, KY] B: 12/9/1974, Lexington, KY
1998 Was: 1 G; Scor 2, 0-2 FG, 2-2 100.0% XK.

HAROLD AKIN Akin, Harold Dwayne 6'5", 260 OT
Col: Oklahoma State *HS:* Putnam City [Oklahoma City, OK]
B: 1/11/1945, McAlester, OK *Drafted:* 1967 Round 3 SD
1967 SD: 3 G. **1968** SD: 10 G. **Total:** 13 G.

LEN AKIN Akin, Leonard Rosser 5'11", 207 G-LB
(Tex) *Col:* Baylor *HS:* Woodrow Wilson [Dallas, TX] B: 4/8/1916, McKinney, TX D: 3/5/1987, Irving, TX *Drafted:* 1940 Round 5 ChiB
1942 ChiB: 11 G; Int 1-0.

AL AKINS Akins, Albert George 6'1", 199 HB-DB
Col: Washington; Washington State *HS:* John R. Rogers [Spokane, WA]
B: 6/13/1921, Spokane, WA D: 8/29/1995, Reno, NV
AAFC **1946** CleA: 4 G; Rush 5-42 8.4 1 TD; KR 2-74 37.0; Int 1-7; 6 Pt.
1947 BknA: 13 G; Rush 15-79 5.3 1 TD; Rec 6-101 16.8 1 TD; PR 1-17 17.0; KR 5-131 26.2; Int 1-31; Tot TD 2; 12 Pt. **1948** BknA-BufA: 8 G; Rush 4-(-9) -2.3; Rec 3-12 4.0. **Total:** 25 G; Rush 24-112 4.7 2 TD; Rec 9-113 12.6 1 TD; PR 1-17 17.0; KR 7-205 29.3; Int 2-38; Tot TD 3; 18 Pt.

FRANK AKINS Akins, Frank Scott 5'10", 208 **FB**
Col: Washington State *HS:* John R. Rogers [Spokane, WA]
B: 3/31/1919, John, MT D: 7/6/1992, Redding, CA *Drafted:* 1943 Round 28 Was
1943 Was: Rec 1-51 51.0; Punt 3-54 18.0. **1944** Was: Rec 5-27 5.4; KR 1-14 14.0; Punt 1-39 39.0. **1945** Was: Rec 8-57 7.1; KR 1-21 21.0. **1946** Was: Rec 2-15 7.5. **Total:** Rec 16-150 9.4; KR 2-35 17.5; Punt 4-93 23.3.

		Rushing				
Year Team	**G**	**Att**	**Yds**	**Avg**	**TD**	**Fum**
1943 Was	6	10	25	2.5	0	0
1944 Was	6	46	154	3.3	1	0
1945 Was	10	**147**	797	5.4	6	3
1946 Was	8	41	166	4.0	0	1
NFL Total	30	244	1142	4.7	7	4

MIKE AKIU Akiu, Karl Michael 5'9", 182 **WR**
Col: Washington State; Hawaii *HS:* Kalahoe [Kailua, HI] B: 2/12/1962, Kailua, HI *Drafted:* 1985 Round 7 Hou
1985 Hou: 9 G; Rec 2-32 16.0; 6 Pt. **1986** Hou: 11 G; Rec 4-67 16.8. **Total:** 20 G; Rec 6-99 16.5; 6 Pt.

DICK ALBAN Alban, Richard Herbert 6'0", 193 **DB**
Col: Northwestern *HS:* La Porte [IN] B: 6/17/1929, Hanover, PA
Drafted: 1952 Round 9 Was
1955 Was: PR 3-0. **1957** Pit: KR 2-33 16.5. **Total:** PR 3-0; KR 2-33 16.5.

		Interceptions			
Year Team	**G**	**Int**	**Yds**	**TD**	**Fum**
1952 Was	12	1	27	0	0
1953 Was	12	4	13	0	0
1954 Was	12	9	81	0	1
1955 Was	12	2	48	0	0
1956 Pit	12	2	21	0	0
1957 Pit	12	1	35	0	2
1958 Pit	12	5	25	0	0
1959 Pit	12	6	119	0	0
NFL Total	96	30	369	0	3

DOM ALBANESE Albanese, Dominic 5'9", 190 **BB-OE-FB**
Col: Ohio Dominican *HS:* Aquinas [Columbus, OH] B: 9/9/1903
D: 3/17/1992, Millersport, OH
1925 Col: 3 G; Pass 1 TD.

VANNIE ALBANESE Albanese, Vincent Michelo 6'0", 184 **FB-DB-BB-LB**
Col: Syracuse *HS:* Manlius [NY] B: 12/2/1912, Syracuse, NY
D: 9/2/1984, Canandaigua, NY
1937 Bkn: Pass 2-1 50.0%, 5 2.50. **1938** Bkn: Pass 1-0. **Total:** Pass 3-1 33.3%, 5 1.67.

		Rushing			
Year Team	**G**	**Att**	**Yds**	**Avg**	**TD**
1937 Bkn	10	21	53	2.5	0
1938 Bkn	8	27	97	3.6	0
NFL Total	18	48	150	3.1	0

TOM ALBERGHINI Alberghini, Thomas Joseph 5'10", 200 **G**
Col: Holy Cross *HS:* Peabody [MA] B: 10/27/1920, Peabody, MA
1945 Pit: 1 G.

FRANKIE ALBERT Albert, Frank Cullen 5'10", 166 **QB-DB**
Col: Stanford *HS:* Glendale [CA] B: 1/27/1920, Chicago, IL
Drafted: 1942 Round 1 ChiB
AAFC **1946** SF-A: PR 1-6 6.0; KR 4-74 18.5. **1947** SF-A: KR 1-23 23.0; Scor 30, 0-2 XK. **1948** SF-A: Rec 1-1 1.0; Scor 49, 1-2 50.0% XK. **1949** SF-A: Scor 18, 0-1 XK. **Total:** Rec 1-1 1.0; PR 1-6 6.0; KR 5-97 19.4; Scor 121, 1-5 20.0% XK.

		Passing							
Year Team	**G**	**Att**	**Comp**	**Comp%**	**Yds**	**YPA**	**TD**	**Int**	**Rating**
1946 SF-A	14	197	104	52.8	1404	7.13	14	14	69.8
1947 SF-A	14	242	128	52.9	1692	6.99	18	15	74.3
1948 SF-A	14	264	154	58.3	1990	7.54	29	10	102.9
1949 SF-A	12	260	129	49.6	1862	7.16	27	16	82.2
AAFC Total	54	963	515	53.5	6948	7.21	88	55	83.4

	Rushing				Punting		
Year Team	**Att**	**Yds**	**Avg**	**TD**	**Punts**	**Yds**	**Avg**
1946 SF-A	69	-10	-0.1	4	54	2214	41.0
1947 SF-A	46	179	3.9	5	40	1759	44.0
1948 SF-A	69	349	5.1	8	35	1568	44.8
1949 SF-A	35	249	7.1	3	31	1495	48.2
AAFC Total	219	767	3.5	20	160	7036	44.0

NFL Statistics

		Passing							
Year Team	**G**	**Att**	**Comp**	**Comp%**	**Yds**	**YPA**	**TD**	**Int**	**Rating**
1950 SF	12	306	155	50.7	1767	5.77	14	23	52.3
1951 SF	12	166	90	54.2	1116	6.72	5	10	60.2
1952 SF	12	129	71	55.0	964	7.47	8	10	67.5
NFL Total	36	601	316	52.6	3847	6.40	27	43	57.7

	Rushing				Punting			
Year Team	**Att**	**Yds**	**Avg**	**TD**	**Punts**	**Yds**	**Avg**	**Fum**
1950 SF	53	272	5.1	3	37	1424	38.5	4
1951 SF	35	146	4.2	3	34	1507	44.3	0
1952 SF	22	87	4.0	1	68	2899	42.6	3
NFL Total	110	505	4.6	7	139	5830	41.9	7

SERGIO ALBERT Albert, Sergio 6'3", 195 **K**
Col: Anahuac (Mexico); U.S. International *HS:* (in Mexico City)
B: 10/28/1951, Mexico City, Mexico *Drafted:* 1974 Round 8 StL
1974 StL: 12 G.

TREV ALBERTS Alberts, Trev Kendall 6'4", 245 **LB**
Col: Nebraska *HS:* U. of Northern Iowa [Cedar Falls, IA] B: 8/8/1970, Cedar Falls, IA *Drafted:* 1994 Round 1 Ind
1994 Ind: 5 G; 2 Sac. **1995** Ind: 15 G; 2 Sac. **1996** Ind: 9 G; Int 1-19. **Total:** 29 G; Int 1-19; 4 Sac.

ART ALBRECHT Albrecht, Arthur Walter 6'1", 203 **T-C-LB**
Col: Wisconsin *HS:* Lincoln [Manitowoc, WI] B: 2/24/1921, Manitowoc, WI
1942 Pit: 3 G. **1943** ChiC: 5 G. **1944** Bos: 6 G. **Total:** 14 G.

TED ALBRECHT Albrecht, Theodore Carl 6'4", 253 **OT-OG**
Col: California *HS:* Vallejo [CA] B: 10/8/1954, Harvey, IL
Drafted: 1977 Round 1 ChiB
1977 ChiB: 14 G. **1978** ChiB: 15 G. **1979** ChiB: 16 G. **1980** ChiB: 16 G. **1981** ChiB: 16 G. **Total:** 77 G.

IRA ALBRIGHT Albright, Ira Ladol 6'0", 285 **NT-RB**
Col: Tyler JC TX; Northeastern State (Okla.) *HS:* South Oak Cliff [Dallas, TX] B: 1/2/1959, Dallas, TX
1987 Buf: 3 G.

ETHAN ALBRIGHT Albright, Laurence Ethan 6'5", 283 **OG-C-OT**
Col: North Carolina *HS:* Grimsley [Greensboro, NC] B: 5/1/1971, Greensboro, NC
1995 Mia: 10 G. **1996** Buf: 16 G. **1997** Buf: 16 G. **1998** Buf: 16 G. **Total:** 58 G.

BILL ALBRIGHT Albright, William Charles 6'1", 233 **OG-OT-DT**
Col: Wisconsin *HS:* Horlick [Racine, WI] B: 4/4/1929, Racine, WI
Drafted: 1951 Round 20 NYG
1951 NYG: 11 G. **1952** NYG: 12 G. **1953** NYG: 12 G; **1** Fum TD; 6 Pt. **1954** NYG: 12 G. **Total:** 47 G; 1 Fum TD; 6 Pt.

VINCE ALBRITTON Albritton, Vince Denader 6'2", 215 **DB**
Col: Washington *HS:* McClymonds [Oakland, CA] B: 7/23/1962, Oakland, CA
1984 Dal: 16 G; 1 Sac. **1985** Dal: 7 G. **1986** Dal: 16 G. **1987** Dal: 11 G. **1988** Dal: 6 G; 2 Sac. **1989** Dal: 16 G; Int 1-3. **1990** Dal: 8 G. **1991** Dal: 6 G. **Total:** 86 G; Int 1-3; 3 Sac.

GRADY ALDERMAN Alderman, Grady Charles 6'2", 247 **OT-OG**
Col: Detroit Mercy *HS:* Madison [Madison Heights, MI] B: 12/10/1938, Detroit, MI *Drafted:* 1960 Round 10 Det
1960 Det: 11 G. **1961** Min: 14 G. **1962** Min: 14 G. **1963** Min: 14 G. **1964** Min: 14 G; Rush 0-22. **1965** Min: 13 G. **1966** Min: 14 G. **1967** Min: 14 G. **1968** Min: 14 G; KR 1-0. **1969** Min: 14 G; KR 1-0. **1970** Min: 14 G. **1971** Min: 13 G. **1972** Min: 14 G. **1973** Min: 14 G. **1974** Min: 13 G. **Total:** 204 G; Rush 0-22; KR 2-0.

JOHN ALDERTON Alderton, John 6'1", 200 **DE**
Col: Maryland *HS:* Fort Hill [Cumberland, MD] B: 9/5/1931
Drafted: 1953 Round 7 Pit
1953 Pit: 10 G.

KI ALDRICH Aldrich, Charles Collins 6'0", 207 **C-LB-G**
Col: Texas Christian *HS:* Temple [TX] B: 6/1/1916, Rodgers, TX
D: 3/12/1983, Temple, TX *Drafted:* 1939 Round 1 ChiC
1939 ChiC: 11 G. **1940** ChiC: 11 G; Int 1-34. **1941** Was: 11 G; Int 2-46; Scor 7, 1-3 33.3% FG, 4-5 80.0% XK. **1942** Was: 11 G; KR 1-8 8.0; 6 Pt. **1945** Was: 6 G. **1946** Was: 11 G; Int 3-31 **1** TD; 6 Pt. **1947** Was: 12 G; Int 2-9. **Total:** 73 G; KR 1-8 8.0; Int 8-120 1 TD; Scor 19, 1-3 33.3% FG, 4-5 80.0% XK; Tot TD 2.

ALLEN ALDRIDGE Aldridge, Allen Ray Jr. 6'1", 247 **LB**
Col: Tyler JC TX; Houston *HS:* Willowridge [Sugar Land, TX]
B: 5/30/1972, Houston, TX *Drafted:* 1994 Round 2 Den
1994 Den: 16 G. **1995** Den: 16 G; 1.5 Sac. **1996** Den: 16 G. **1997** Den: 16 G. **1998** Det: 16 G; 3 Sac. **Total:** 80 G; 4.5 Sac.

ALLEN ALDRIDGE Aldridge, Allen Ray Sr. 6'6", 250 **DE**
Col: Prairie View A&M *HS:* E.H. Henry [Eagle Lake, TX] B: 4/27/1945, Eagle Lake, TX
1971 Hou: 13 G; 1 Fum. **1972** Hou: 8 G; 1 Fum. **1974** Cle: 14 G. **Total:** 35 G; 2 Fum.

BENNIE ALDRIDGE Aldridge, Bennie Leo 6'0", 195 **DB-HB**
(Lefty) *Col:* Oklahoma State *HS:* Velma-Alma [OK] B: 10/24/1926, Velma, OK D: 1956
1950 NYY: Rec 4-56 14.0; PR 2-17 8.5. **1951** NYY: PR 1-0. **1952** Dal-SF: Rec 4-22 5.5 1 TD. SF: Rec 4-22 5.5 1 TD. **1953** GB: PR 1-0. **Total:** Rec 8-78 9.8 1 TD; PR 4-17 4.3.

		Rushing				Interceptions			
Year Team	**G**	**Att**	**Yds**	**Avg**	**TD**	**Int**	**Yds**	**TD**	**Fum**
1950 NYY	11	16	69	4.3	0	1	0	0	0
1951 NYY	12	0	0	—	0	5	57	0	0
1952 Dal-SF	12	13	36	2.8	0	0	0	0	1
1952 Dal	1	0	0	—	0	0	0	0	0
1952 SF	11	13	36	2.8	0	0	0	0	1
1953 GB	8	0	0	—	0	5	85	0	0
NFL Total	43	29	105	3.6	0	11	142	0	1

JERRY ALDRIDGE Aldridge, Jerry Charles 6'2", 220 **RB**
Col: Angelo State *HS:* Jacksonville [TX] B: 9/17/1956, Jacksonville, TX
Drafted: 1979 Round 5 SF
1980 SF: 1 G.

LIONEL ALDRIDGE Aldridge, Lionel 6'3", 254 **DE**
Col: Utah State *HS:* Pittsburg [CA] B: 2/14/1941, Evergreen, LA
D: 2/12/1998, Shorewood, WI *Drafted:* 1963 Round 4 GB
1963 GB: 14 G. **1964** GB: 14 G; 1 Fum TD; 6 Pt. **1965** GB: 14 G. **1966** GB: 13 G. **1967** GB: 12 G. **1968** GB: 14 G; 1 Fum. **1969** GB: 14 G. **1970** GB: 14 G. **1971** GB: 14 G. **1972** SD: 14 G. **1973** SD: 10 G. **Total:** 147 G; 1 Fum TD; 6 Pt; 1 Fum.

MELVIN ALDRIDGE Aldridge, Melvin Keith 6'2", 195 **DB**
Col: Tyler JC TX; Murray State *HS:* Pittsburg [TX] B: 7/22/1970, Pittsburg, TX
1993 Hou: 1 G. **1995** Ariz: 2 G. **Total:** 3 G.

ARNOLD ALE Ale, Arnold Tauese 6'2", 234 **LB**
Col: Notre Dame; UCLA *HS:* Carson [CA] B: 6/17/1970, San Pedro, CA
1994 KC: 2 G. **1996** SD: 7 G. **Total:** 9 G.

INK ALEAGA Aleaga, Ink A 6'1", 225 **LB**
Col: Washington *HS:* Maryknoll [Honolulu, HI] B: 4/4/1973, Honolulu, HI
1997 NO: 3 G. **1998** NO: 15 G; 1 Sac. **Total:** 18 G; 1 Sac.

KEITH ALEX Alex, Hiram Keith 6'4", 307 **OG**
Col: Texas A&M *HS:* Central [Beaumont, TX] B: 6/9/1969, Kountze, TX
Drafted: 1992 Round 9 Atl
1993 Atl: 14 G.

STEVE ALEXAKOS Alexakos, Steven Theodore 6'2", 260 **OG**
Col: Diablo Valley Coll. CA (J.C.); San Jose State *HS:* Las Lomas [Walnut Creek, CA] B: 12/15/1946, Lowell, MA *Drafted:* 1969 Round 9 Bos
1970 Den: 8 G. **1971** NYG: 10 G. **Total:** 18 G.

BRENT ALEXANDER Alexander, Brent 5'11", 189 **DB**
Col: Tennessee State *HS:* Gallatin [TN] B: 7/10/1971, Gallatin, TN
1994 Ariz: 16 G. **1995** Ariz: 16 G; Int 2-14; 0.5 Sac. **1996** Ariz: 16 G; Int 2-3. **1997** Ariz: 16 G. **1998** Car: 16 G. **Total:** 80 G; Int 4-17; 0.5 Sac.

BRUCE ALEXANDER Alexander, Bruce Edward 5'9", 170 **DB**
Col: Stephen F. Austin St. *HS:* Lufkin [TX] B: 9/17/1965, Lufkin, TX
1989 Det: 8 G; KR 5-100 20.0. **1990** Det: 1 G. **1991** Det: 9 G; Int 1-0. **1992** Mia: 12 G; Int 1-0. **1993** Mia: 14 G; 1 Sac. **Total:** 44 G; KR 5-100 20.0; Int 2-0; 1 Sac.

CHARLES ALEXANDER Alexander, Charles Fred Jr. 6'1", 224 **RB**
Col: Louisiana State *HS:* Ball [Galveston, TX] B: 7/28/1957, Galveston, TX *Drafted:* 1979 Round 1 Cin

		Rushing				Receiving					Tot
Year Team	**G**	**Att**	**Yds**	**Avg**	**TD**	**Rec**	**Yds**	**Avg**	**TD**	**Fum**	**TD**
1979 Cin	16	88	286	3.3	1	11	91	8.3	0	0	1
1980 Cin	16	169	702	4.2	2	36	192	5.3	0	2	2
1981 Cin	15	98	292	3.0	2	28	262	9.4	1	0	3
1982 Cin	9	64	207	3.2	1	14	85	6.1	1	1	2
1983 Cin	14	153	523	3.4	3	32	187	5.8	0	1	3
1984 Cin	16	132	479	3.6	2	29	203	7.0	0	2	2
1985 Cin	16	44	156	3.5	2	15	110	7.3	0	0	2
NFL Total	102	748	2645	3.5	13	165	1130	6.8	2	6	15

DAN ALEXANDER Alexander, Daniel Lamarr 6'4", 260 **OG-OT**
Col: Louisiana State *HS:* Mirabeau B. Lamar [Houston, TX]
B: 6/17/1955, Houston, TX *Drafted:* 1977 Round 8 NYJ
1977 NYJ: 14 G. **1978** NYJ: 16 G. **1979** NYJ: 16 G. **1980** NYJ: 16 G. **1981** NYJ: 16 G. **1982** NYJ: 9 G. **1983** NYJ: 16 G. **1984** NYJ: 16 G. **1985** NYJ: 16 G. **1986** NYJ: 16 G. **1987** NYJ: 12 G. **1988** NYJ: 14 G. **1989** NYJ: 15 G. **Total:** 192 G.

DAVID ALEXANDER Alexander, David Franklin 6'3", 275 **C-OT-OG**
Col: Tulsa *HS:* Broken Arrow [OK] B: 7/28/1964, Silver Spring, MD
Drafted: 1987 Round 5 Phi
1987 Phi: 12 G; KR 1-6 6.0. **1988** Phi: 16 G. **1989** Phi: 16 G; 1 Fum. **1990** Phi: 16 G. **1991** Phi: 16 G. **1992** Phi: 16 G. **1993** Phi: 16 G. **1994** Phi: 16 G; Rec 2-1 0.5. **1996** NYJ: 7 G. **Total:** 131 G; Rec 2-1 0.5; KR 1-6 6.0; 1 Fum.

DERRICK ALEXANDER Alexander, Derrick Laborn 6'4", 277 **DE**
Col: Florida State *HS:* William M. Raines [Jacksonville, FL]
B: 11/13/1973, Jacksonville, FL *Drafted:* 1995 Round 1 Min
1995 Min: 15 G; 2 Sac. **1996** Min: 12 G; 3.5 Sac. **1997** Min: 14 G; 4.5 Sac. **1998** Min: 16 G; 7.5 Sac. **Total:** 57 G; 17.5 Sac.

DERRICK ALEXANDER Alexander, Derrick Scott 6'2", 195 **WR**
Col: Michigan *HS:* Benedictine [Detroit, MI] B: 11/6/1971, Detroit, MI
Drafted: 1994 Round 1 Cle
1994 Cle: Rush 4-38 9.5; Scor 1 2XP. **1995** Cle: Rush 1-29 29.0; PR 9-122 13.6 **1** TD; KR 21-419 20.0. **1996** Bal: Rush 3-0; PR 1-15 15.0; KR 1-13 13.0; Scor 1 2XP. **1997** Bal: Rush 1-0; PR 1-34 34.0. **Total:** Rush 9-67 7.4; PR 11-171 15.5 1 TD; KR 22-432 19.6; Scor 2 2XP.

		Receiving					Tot
Year Team	**G**	**Rec**	**Yds**	**Avg**	**TD**	**Fum**	**TD**
1994 Cle	14	48	828	17.3	2	2	2
1995 Cle	14	15	216	14.4	0	3	1
1996 Bal	15	62	1099	17.7	9	0	9
1997 Bal	15	65	1009	15.5	9	1	9
1998 KC	15	54	992	18.4	4	0	4
NFL Total	73	244	4144	17.0	24	6	25

ELIJAH ALEXANDER Alexander, Elijah Alfred III 6'2", 233 **LB**
Col: Kansas State *HS:* Dunbar [Fort Worth, TX] B: 8/2/1970, Fort Worth, TX *Drafted:* 1992 Round 10 TB
1992 TB: 12 G. **1993** Den: 16 G. **1994** Den: 16 G; Int 1-2; 1 Sac. **1995** Den: 9 G; Int 2-5; 0.5 Sac. **1996** Ind: 14 G; 1 Sac. **1997** Ind: 13 G; Int 1-43 1 TD; 6 Pt; 1 Sac. **1998** Ind: 13 G; Int 1-12. **Total:** 93 G; Int 5-62 1 TD; 6 Pt; 3.5 Sac.

GLENN ALEXANDER Alexander, Glenn Elliott 6'3", 205 **WR**
Col: Grambling State *HS:* St. Augustine [New Orleans, LA]
B: 6/3/1947, New Orleans, LA *Drafted:* 1970 Round 3 Buf
1970 Buf: 13 G; Rec 4-51 12.8; PR 1-2 2.0; KR 12-204 17.0.

HAROLD ALEXANDER Alexander, Harold Donald II 6'2", 224 **P**
Col: Appalachian State *HS:* Pickens [SC] B: 10/20/1970, Pickens, SC
Drafted: 1993 Round 3 Atl
1993 Atl: Rush 2-(-7) -3.5. **1994** Atl: Rush 1-0. **Total:** Rush 3-(-7) -2.3.

		Punting		
Year Team	**G**	**Punts**	**Yds**	**Avg**
1993 Atl	16	72	3114	43.3
1994 Atl	15	71	2836	39.9
NFL Total	31	143	5950	41.6

JEFF ALEXANDER Alexander, Jeffrey O'Neal 6'0", 232 **RB**
Col: Southern University *HS:* Baker [LA] B: 1/15/1965, Baton Rouge, LA
1989 Den: Rec 8-84 10.5. **Total:** Rec 8-84 10.5.

		Rushing			
Year Team	**G**	**Att**	**Yds**	**Avg**	**TD**
1989 Den	14	45	146	3.2	2
1992 Den	7	0	0	—	0
NFL Total	21	45	146	3.2	2

JOHN ALEXANDER Alexander, John 6'4", 234 **T**
Col: Rutgers; Fordham *HS:* South Side [Newark, NJ] B: 7/4/1896, New York, NY D: 8/5/1986, Edison, NJ
1922 Mil: 8 G. **1926** NYG: 9 G; 1 Fum TD; 6 Pt. **Total:** 17 G; 1 Fum TD; 6 Pt.

JOHN ALEXANDER Alexander, John Wesley 6'2", 250 **DE**
Col: Rutgers *HS:* Plainfield [NJ] B: 11/12/1955, Hattiesburg, MS
Drafted: 1977 Round 11 Mia
1977 Mia: 4 G. **1978** Mia: 8 G. **Total:** 12 G.

DOC ALEXANDER Alexander, Joseph A 5'11", 220 **C-G-T-OE**
(Goliath) *Col:* Syracuse *HS:* Central [Syracuse, NY] B: 4/1/1898, Silver Creek, NY D: 9/12/1975, New York, NY
1921 Roch: 4 G. **1922** Roch: 4 G. **1924** Roch: 2 G. **1925** NYG: 13 G; Int 1 TD; 6 Pt. **1926** NYG: 13 G; Int **1** TD; 1 Fum TD; Tot TD 2; 12 Pt. **1927** NYG: 4 G; 1 Fum TD; 6 Pt. **Total:** 40 G; Int 2 TD; 2 Fum TD; Tot TD 4; 24 Pt.

KERMIT ALEXANDER Alexander, Kermit Joseph 5'11", 187 **DB**
Col: UCLA *HS:* Mount Carmel [Los Angeles, CA] B: 1/4/1941, New Iberia, LA *Drafted:* 1963 Round 1 SF
1966 SF: **1** Fum TD. **Total:** 1 Fum TD.

Year Team	G	Punt Returns Ret	Yds	Avg	TD	Kickoff Returns Ret	Yds	Avg	TD
1963 SF	14	0	0	—	0	24	638	26.6	0
1964 SF	14	21	189	9.0	1	20	483	24.2	0
1965 SF	14	35	262	7.5	0	**32**	**741**	23.2	0
1966 SF	14	30	198	6.6	**1**	37	984	26.6	0
1967 SF	13	6	64	10.7	0	1	18	18.0	0
1968 SF	14	24	87	3.6	0	20	360	18.0	0
1969 SF	11	4	-18	-4.5	0	3	47	15.7	0
1970 LARm	14	7	38	5.4	0	7	126	18.0	0
1971 LARm	14	1	5	5.0	0	0	0	—	0
1972 Phi	7	0	0	—	0	0	0	—	0
1973 Phi	14	5	10	2.0	0	9	189	21.0	0
NFL Total	143	133	835	6.3	2	153	3586	23.4	0

Year Team	Interceptions Int	Yds	TD	Fum	Tot TD
1963 SF	5	72	0	2	0
1964 SF	5	65	0	3	1
1965 SF	3	23	0	7	0
1966 SF	4	73	0	4	2
1967 SF	5	72	0	0	0
1968 SF	9	155	1	4	1
1969 SF	5	39	0	3	0
1970 LARm	4	47	1	1	1
1971 LARm	3	122	1	0	1
1973 Phi	0	0	0	5	0
NFL Total	43	668	3	29	6

KEVIN ALEXANDER Alexander, Kevin John 5'9", 185 **WR**
Col: Utah State *HS:* Valencia [Placentia, CA] B: 1/23/1975, Baton Rouge, LA
1996 NYG: 4 G; Rec 4-88 22.0; KR 2-27 13.5. **1997** NYG: 14 G; Rec 18-276 15.3 1 TD; KR 3-30 10.0; 6 Pt. **Total:** 18 G; Rec 22-364 16.5 1 TD; KR 5-57 11.4; 6 Pt.

PATRISE ALEXANDER Alexander, Liyongo Patrise 6'1", 244 **LB**
Col: Southwestern Louisiana *HS:* Ball [Galveston, TX] B: 10/23/1972, Galveston, TX
1996 Was: 16 G. **1997** Was: 16 G. **1998** Was: 1 G. **Total:** 33 G.

MIKE ALEXANDER Alexander, Michael Fitzgerald 6'3", 195 **WR**
Col: Nassau CC NY; Penn State *HS:* Piscataway [NJ] B: 3/19/1965, New York, NY *Drafted:* 1988 Round 8 LARd
1989 LARd: 16 G; Rec 15-295 19.7 1 TD; 6 Pt. **1991** Buf: 3 G; Rec 1-7 7.0. **Total:** 19 G; Rec 16-302 18.9 1 TD; 6 Pt.

ROBERT ALEXANDER Alexander, Robert Alan 6'0", 185 **RB**
Col: West Virginia *HS:* South Charleston [WV] B: 4/21/1958, Charleston, WV *Drafted:* 1981 Round 10 LARm
1982 LARm: 9 G; Rush 1-3 3.0; Rec 1-(-7) -7.0; KR 8-139 17.4; 2 Fum. **1983** LARm: 15 G; Rush 7-28 4.0; Rec 1-10 10.0; KR 13-222 17.1; 2 Fum. **Total:** 24 G; Rush 8-31 3.9; Rec 2-3 1.5; KR 21-361 17.2; 4 Fum.

ROGERS ALEXANDER Alexander, Rogers Bernard 6'3", 222 **LB**
Col: Penn State *HS:* DeMatha [Hyattsville, MD] B: 8/11/1964, Washington, DC *Drafted:* 1986 Round 4 NYJ
1986 NYJ: 1 G. **1987** NE: 3 G; KR 1-4 4.0. **Total:** 4 G; KR 1-4 4.0.

STEPHEN ALEXANDER Alexander, Stephen 6'4", 246 **TE**
Col: Oklahoma *HS:* Chickasha [OK] B: 11/7/1975, Chickasha, OK
Drafted: 1998 Round 2 Was

Year Team	G	Receiving Rec	Yds	Avg	TD	Fum
1998 Was	15	37	383	10.4	4	2

RAY ALEXANDER Alexander, Vernest Raynard 6'4", 195 **WR**
Col: Florida A&M *HS:* John S. Shaw [Mobile, AL] B: 1/8/1962, Miami, FL

Year Team	G	Receiving Rec	Yds	Avg	TD
1984 Den	8	8	132	16.5	1
1988 Dal	16	54	788	14.6	6
1989 Dal	2	1	16	16.0	0
NFL Total	26	63	936	14.9	7

VINCENT ALEXANDER Alexander, Vincent Leon 5'10", 205 **RB**
Col: Southern Mississippi *HS:* Covington [LA] B: 3/11/1964, St. Tammany, LA
1987 NO: 1 G; Rush 21-71 3.4 1 TD; Rec 2-15 7.5; 6 Pt; 2 Fum.

WILLIE ALEXANDER Alexander, Willie James 6'2", 194 **DB**
Col: Alcorn State *HS:* George Washington Carver [Montgomery, AL] B: 9/21/1949, Montgomery, AL *Drafted:* 1971 Round 6 Hou

Year Team	G	Interceptions Int	Yds	TD	Fum
1971 Hou	14	4	74	0	0
1972 Hou	14	1	16	0	0
1973 Hou	11	3	3	0	1
1974 Hou	14	2	56	0	0
1975 Hou	14	3	41	0	0
1976 Hou	12	0	0	0	0
1977 Hou	14	3	111	**1**	0
1978 Hou	16	5	51	0	0
1979 Hou	13	2	27	0	0
NFL Total	122	23	379	1	1

ALTON ALEXIS Alexis, Alton 6'0", 184 **WR**
Col: Tulane *HS:* New Iberia [LA] B: 11/16/1957, New Iberia, LA
Drafted: 1980 Round 11 Cin
1980 Cin: 1 G.

TED ALFLEN Alflen, Theodore Thomas 6'0", 195 **RB**
Col: Springfield *HS:* Massapequa [NY] B: 1/3/1947, Dunsmuir, CA
1969 Den: 4 G.

JULIE ALFONSE Alfonse, Julius 5'8", 180 **WB-DB-TB**
Col: Minnesota *HS:* Cumberland [WI] B: 10/12/1911, Cumberland, WI
Drafted: 1937 Round 2 Cle
1937 Cle: Pass 10-4 40.0%, 48 4.80; Rec 5-113 22.6. **1938** Cle: Pass 2-2 100.0%, 19 9.50; Rec 2-47 23.5; Int **1** TD. **Total:** Pass 12-6 50.0%, 67 5.58; Rec 7-160 22.9; Int 1 TD.

Year Team	G	Rushing Att	Yds	Avg	TD	Tot TD
1937 Cle	10	33	60	1.8	0	0
1938 Cle	10	16	16	1.0	0	2
NFL Total	20	49	76	1.6	0	2

BRIAN ALFORD Alford, Brian Wayne 6'1", 190 **WR**
Col: Purdue *HS:* Oak Park [MI] B: 6/7/1975, Detroit, MI
Drafted: 1998 Round 3 NYG
1998 NYG: 2 G; Rec 1-11 11.0.

GENE ALFORD Alford, Eugene Morris 5'9", 180 **WB-DB-BB-FB**
Col: Sul Ross State; Texas Tech *HS:* Rising Star [TX]; Daniel Baker Acad. [Eastland, TX] B: 4/3/1905, Rising Star, TX D: 12/1975, Ada, OK
1931 Port: Rec 1 TD. **1932** Port: Rec 2-15 7.5. **1933** Port: Pass 6-0, 1 Int; Rec 2-76 38.0 1 TD. **1934** Cin-StL: Pass 7-1 14.3%, 4 0.57 1 Int; Rec 1-7 7.0; Scor 6, 1 FG, 3 XK. StL: Pass 7-1 14.3%, 4 0.57 1 Int; Rec 1-7 7.0; Scor 6, 1 FG, 3 XK. **Total:** Pass 13-1 7.7%, 4 0.31 2 Int; Rec 5-98 19.6 2 TD; Scor 24, 1 FG, 3 XK.

Year Team	G	Rushing Att	Yds	Avg	TD	Tot TD
1931 Port	14	—	—	—	1	2
1932 Port	10	13	50	3.8	0	0
1933 Port	10	18	59	3.3	0	1
1934 Cin-StL	4	9	27	3.0	0	0
1934 Cin	1	2	7	3.5	0	0
1934 StL	3	7	20	2.9	0	0
NFL Total	38	40	136	3.4	1	3

BRUCE ALFORD Alford, Herbert Bruce Jr. 6'0", 190 **K**
Col: Texas Christian *HS:* R.L. Paschal [Fort Worth, TX] B: 4/21/1945, Forth Worth, TX *Drafted:* 1967 Round 5 ChiB

Year Team	G	Scoring Pts	FG	FGA	FG%	XK	XKA	XK%
1967 Was	2	3	0	2	0.0	3	4	75.0
1968 Buf	11	57	14	24	58.3	15	15	100.0
1969 Buf	14	74	17	26	65.4	23	24	95.8
NFL Total	27	134	31	52	59.6	41	43	95.3

BRUCE ALFORD Alford, Herbert Bruce Sr. 6'0", 190 **OE-DB**
Col: Texas Christian *HS:* Waco [TX] B: 9/12/1922, Waco, TX
AAFC **1946** NY-A: KR 1-62 62.0. **1947** NY-A: PR 1-34 34.0 1 TD; KR 2-90 45.0 1 TD; Int 1-1. **1949** NY-A: KR 2-31 15.5. **Total:** PR 1-34 34.0 1 TD; KR 5-183 36.6 1 TD; Int 1-1.

Year Team	G	Receiving Rec	Yds	Avg	TD	Tot TD
1946 NY-A	13	13	173	13.3	0	0
1947 NY-A	13	20	298	14.9	5	7
1948 NY-A	14	32	578	18.1	3	3
1949 NY-A	11	11	213	19.4	1	1
AAFC Total	51	76	1262	16.6	9	11

NFL **1950** NYY: 12 G; Rec 1-14 14.0; 6 Pt. **1951** NYY: 12 G; Rec 4-65 16.3. **Total:** 24 G; Rec 5-79 15.8; 6 Pt.

LYNWOOD ALFORD Alford, Lynwood A 6'3", 220 **LB**
Col: Coffeyville CC KS; Syracuse *HS:* Aliquippa [PA] B: 8/22/1963
1987 NYJ: 1 G.

MIKE ALFORD Alford, Michael Deal 6'3", 230 **C**
Col: Auburn *HS:* Choctawhatchee [Fort Walton Beach, FL]
B: 6/19/1943, DeFuniak Springs, FL *Drafted:* 1965 Round 14 StL
1965 StL: 13 G. **1966** Det: 12 G; KR 1-0; 1 Fum. **Total:** 25 G; KR 1-0; 1 Fum.

WARREN ALFSON Alfson, Warren Frank 6'0", 198 **G-LB**
Col: Nebraska *HS:* Wisner [NE] B: 5/10/1915, Wisner, NE
Drafted: 1941 Round 14 Bkn
1941 Bkn: 11 G; Int 2-49.

TUINEAU ALIPATE Alipate, Tuineau 6'1", 245 **LB**
Col: Washington State *HS:* James Logan [Union City, CA]
B: 8/21/1967, Tonga
1994 NYJ: 8 G. **1995** Min: 16 G. **Total:** 24 G.

DON ALLARD Allard, Donald 6'1", 188 **QB**
Col: Boston College *HS:* Somerville [MA] B: 4/1936 *Drafted:* 1959 Round 1 Was
1961 NYT: 1 G. **1962** Bos: 4 G. **Total:** 5 G.

RAUL ALLEGRE Allegre, Raul Enrique 5'9", 165 **K**
Col: Montana; Texas *HS:* Shelton [WA] B: 6/15/1959, Torreon, Mexico

		Scoring						
Year Team	**G**	**Pts**	**FG**	**FGA**	**FG%**	**XK**	**XKA**	**XK%**
1983 Bal	16	112	30	35	85.7	22	24	91.7
1984 Ind	12	47	11	18	61.1	14	14	100.0
1985 Ind	16	84	16	26	61.5	36	39	92.3
1986 NYG	13	105	24	32	75.0	33	33	100.0
1987 NYG	12	76	17	27	63.0	25	26	96.2
1988 NYG	6	44	10	11	90.9	14	14	100.0
1989 NYG	10	83	20	26	76.9	23	24	95.8
1990 NYG	3	21	4	5	80.0	9	9	100.0
1991 NYG-NYJ	4	22	5	6	83.3	7	7	100.0
1991 NYG	3	11	2	2	100.0	5	5	100.0
1991 NYJ	1	11	3	4	75.0	2	2	100.0
NFL Total	92	594	137	186	73.7	183	190	96.3

ANTHONY ALLEN Allen, Anthony Derrick 5'11", 180 **WR**
Col: Washington *HS:* James A. Garfield [Seattle, WA] B: 6/29/1959, McComb, MS *Drafted:* 1983 Round 6 Atl
1985 Atl: KR 8-140 17.5. **Total:** KR 8-140 17.5.

		Receiving				Punt Returns				
Year Team	**G**	**Rec**	**Yds**	**Avg**	**TD**	**Ret**	**Yds**	**Avg**	**TD**	**Fum**
1985 Atl	16	14	207	14.8	2	21	141	6.7	0	0
1986 Atl	5	10	156	15.6	2	2	10	5.0	0	1
1987 Was	3	13	337	25.9	3	0	0	—	0	0
1988 Was	14	5	48	9.6	1	10	62	6.2	0	2
1989 SD	7	2	19	9.5	0	2	3	1.5	0	0
NFL Total	45	44	767	17.4	8	35	216	6.2	0	3

CARL ALLEN Allen, Carl Blanchard 6'0", 175 **RB-DB**
Col: Ouachita Baptist *HS:* Magnolia [AR] B: 6/25/1920, Haskell, OK
D: 7/3/1996, Portland, OR
AAFC **1948** BknA: 13 G; Rush 1-9 9.0; PR 1-17 17.0; Int 2-45 1 TD; 6 Pt.

CHUCK ALLEN Allen, Charles Richard 6'1", 225 **LB**
Col: Washington *HS:* Cle Elum [WA] B: 9/7/1939, Cle Elum, WA
Drafted: 1961 Round 28 SD
1963 SD: **1** Fum TD. **Total:** 1 Fum TD.

		Interceptions			Tot
Year Team	**G**	**Int**	**Yds**	**TD**	**TD**
1961 SD	9	5	111	1	1
1962 SD	14	1	7	0	0
1963 SD	14	5	37	0	1
1964 SD	14	4	75	0	0
1965 SD	14	1	0	0	0
1966 SD	5	1	8	0	0
1967 SD	13	2	2	0	0
1968 SD	11	1	4	0	0
1969 SD	14	0	0	0	0
1970 Pit	14	4	48	0	0
1971 Pit	10	3	45	0	0
1972 Phi	12	1	15	0	0
NFL Total	144	28	352	1	2

DALVA ALLEN Allen, Dalva Ray 6'4", 245 **DE**
Col: Houston *HS:* Gonzales [TX] B: 1/13/1935, Gonzales, TX
Drafted: 1957 Round 23 LARm
1960 Hou: 14 G; Int 1-0. **1961** Hou: 14 G. **1962** Oak: 14 G. **1963** Oak: 14 G. **1964** Oak: 14 G. **Total:** 70 G; Int 1-0.

DEREK ALLEN Allen, Derek Scott 6'4", 290 **OG**
Col: Illinois *HS:* J.D. Darnell [Milan, IL]; Naval Academy Prep [Newport, RI] B: 1/30/1971, Genesco, IL
1995 NYG: 1 G.

DON ALLEN Allen, Donald Ray 6'0", 200 **FB**
(Redbird) *Col:* Texas *HS:* New London [TX] B: 8/20/1939, Leon Co., TX
1960 Den: Rec 5-34 6.8; KR 5-72 14.4.

		Rushing				
Year Team	**G**	**Att**	**Yds**	**Avg**	**TD**	**Fum**
1960 Den	10	30	18	0.6	1	2

DOUG ALLEN Allen, Douglas Ferguson 6'2", 228 **LB**
Col: Penn State *HS:* Corning-Painted Post West [Painted Post, NY]
B: 11/13/1951, Tampa, FL *Drafted:* 1974 Round 2 Buf
1974 Buf: 14 G; Int 1-16. **1975** Buf: 14 G. **Total:** 28 G; Int 1-16.

DUANE ALLEN Allen, Duane Douglas 6'4", 225 **TE**
Col: Mount San Antonio Coll. CA (J.C.); Rancho Santiago Coll. CA (J.C.)
HS: Alhambra [CA] B: 10/21/1937, Alhambra, CA *Drafted:* 1961 Round 9 LARm
1961 LARm: 10 G; Rec 2-80 40.0 2 TD; 12 Pt. **1962** LARm: 7 G; Rec 3-90 30.0 2 TD; 12 Pt. **1963** LARm: 7 G. **1964** LARm: 7 G; Rec 2-29 14.5 1 TD; 6 Pt. **1965** Pit: 2 G. **1966** ChiB: 11 G; Rec 3-28 9.3. **1967** ChiB: 5 G.
Total: 49 G; Rec 10-227 22.7 5 TD; 30 Pt.

EARL ALLEN Allen, Earl Edward 5'11", 193 **DB**
Col: Michigan; Houston *HS:* Westbury [Houston, TX] B: 10/24/1961, Houston, TX
1987 Hou: 1 G.

ED ALLEN Allen, Edmund Joseph 5'8", 175 **OE**
Col: Creighton *HS:* Dixon [IL] B: 6/5/1901, Dixon, IL Deceased
1928 ChiC: 2 G.

EDDIE ALLEN Allen, Edward Bostwic Jr. 6'1", 200 **FB-LB**
Col: Pennsylvania *HS:* Batavia [NY] B: 5/5/1920, Dansville, NY
Drafted: 1946 Round 11 ChiB
1947 ChiB: 9 G; Rush 12-16 1.3; Punt 8-299 37.4; 2 Fum.

EGYPT ALLEN Allen, Egypt Tyrone 6'0", 203 **DB**
Col: Texas Christian *HS:* South Oak Cliff [Dallas, TX] B: 7/28/1964, Dallas, TX
1987 ChiB: 6 G.

BUDDY ALLEN Allen, Elihu 5'11", 193 **HB**
Col: Utah State *HS:* McClymonds [Oakland, CA] B: 7/11/1937
Drafted: 1960 Round 1 Bos
1961 Den: 1 G; Rush 3-(-4) -1.3; 1 Fum.

ERIC ALLEN Allen, Eric Andre 5'10", 184 **DB**
Col: Arizona State *HS:* Point Loma [San Diego, CA] B: 11/22/1965, San Diego, CA *Drafted:* 1988 Round 2 Phi
1990 Phi: KR 1-2 2.0. **1993** Phi: 2 Sac. **Total:** KR 1-2 2.0; 2 Sac.

		Interceptions			
Year Team	**G**	**Int**	**Yds**	**TD**	**Fum**
1988 Phi	16	5	76	0	0
1989 Phi	15	8	38	0	1
1990 Phi	16	3	37	1	0
1991 Phi	16	5	20	0	0
1992 Phi	16	4	49	0	0
1993 Phi	16	6	**201**	**4**	0
1994 Phi	16	3	61	0	0
1995 NO	16	2	28	0	0
1996 NO	16	1	33	0	0
1997 NO	16	2	27	0	0
1998 Oak	10	5	59	0	0
NFL Total	169	44	629	5	1

ERMAL ALLEN Allen, Ermal Glen 5'11", 165 **QB-DB**
(Flip) *Col:* Kentucky *HS:* Morristown [TN] B: 12/25/1918, Kyles Ford, TN D: 2/9/1988, Dallas, TX
AAFC **1947** CleA: 12 G; Pass 13-4 30.8%, 88 6.77; Rush 7-11 1.6; PR 4-28 7.0; Int 4-63; Punt 4-135 33.8.

GARY ALLEN Allen, Gary Eugene 5'10", 183 **RB**
Col: Hawaii *HS:* Baldwin Park [CA] B: 4/23/1960, Baldwin Park, CA
Drafted: 1982 Round 6 Hou
1982 Hou: Rush 2-2 1.0; Rec 2-35 17.5 1 TD. **1983** Hou-Dal: Rush 1-5 5.0. Hou: Rush 1-5 5.0. **Total:** Rush 3-7 2.3; Rec 2-35 17.5 1 TD.

		Punt Returns				Kickoff Returns					Tot
Year Team	**G**	**Ret**	**Yds**	**Avg**	**TD**	**Ret**	**Yds**	**Avg**	**TD**	**Fum**	**TD**
1982 Hou	7	0	0	—	0	15	292	19.5	0	1	1
1983 Hou-Dal	7	9	153	17.0	**1**	8	178	22.3	0	0	1
1983 Hou	1	0	0	—	0	0	0	—	0	0	0
1983 Dal	6	9	153	17.0	1	8	178	22.3	0	0	1
1984 Dal	16	54	446	8.3	0	33	666	20.2	0	2	0
NFL Total	30	63	599	9.5	1	56	1136	20.3	0	3	2

GEORGE ALLEN Allen, George Robert 6'7", 270 **OT**
Col: West Texas A&M *HS:* Mary C. Womack [Longview, TX]
B: 4/4/1944, Longview, TX *Drafted:* 1966 Round 4 Hou
1966 Hou: 9 G.

JERRY ALLEN Allen, Gerald 6′1″, 200 **RB**
Col: Nebraska-Omaha *HS:* Washington [Massillon, OH] B: 6/26/1941, Canton, OH *Drafted:* 1966 Round 8 Bal
1966 Bal: PR 1-0; KR 3-53 17.7. **1967** Was: KR 1-13 13.0. **Total:** PR 1-0; KR 4-66 16.5.

		Rushing				Receiving					Tot
Year Team	G	Att	Yds	Avg	TD	Rec	Yds	Avg	TD	Fum	TD
1966 Bal	4	0	0	—	0	0	0	—	0	1	0
1967 Was	11	77	262	3.4	3	11	101	9.2	1	1	4
1968 Was	11	123	399	3.2	4	21	294	14.0	1	3	5
1969 Was	2	1	3	3.0	0	1	5	5.0	0	0	0
NFL Total	28	201	664	3.3	7	33	400	12.1	2	5	9

GRADY ALLEN Allen, Grady Lynn 6′3″, 225 **LB**
Col: Texas A&M *HS:* Nacogdoches [TX] B: 1/1/1946, St. Augustine, TX
1968 Atl: 14 G; KR 1-0. **1969** Atl: 14 G; Int 1-6. **1970** Atl: 14 G; Int 1-0. **1971** Atl: 3 G. **1972** Atl: 14 G. **Total:** 59 G; KR 1-0; Int 2-6.

GREG ALLEN Allen, Gregory W 5′11″, 200 **RB**
Col: Florida State *HS:* Milton [FL] B: 6/4/1963, Milton, FL *Drafted:* 1985 Round 2 Cle
1985 Cle: 7 G; Rush 8-32 4.0; KR 1-4 4.0; 1 Fum. **1986** TB: 2 G; Rush 1-3 3.0; KR 1-21 21.0. **Total:** 9 G; Rush 9-35 3.9; KR 2-25 12.5; 1 Fum.

HARVEY ALLEN Allen, Harvey James Jr. 6′3″, 215 **DB**
Col: Nevada-Las Vegas *HS:* John C. Fremont [Los Angeles, CA] B: 10/2/1964
1987 Sea: 2 G.

JACKIE ALLEN Allen, Jack Franklin 6′1″, 190 **DB**
Col: Baylor *HS:* South Oak Cliff [Dallas, TX] B: 9/24/1947, Lawton, OK *Drafted:* 1969 Round 6 Oak
1969 Oak: 5 G; PR 1-(-2) -2.0; KR 3-67 22.3; 1 Fum. **1970** Buf: 14 G; PR 2-10 5.0; 1 Fum. **1971** Buf: 14 G; 1 Fum. **1972** Phi: 1 G. **Total:** 34 G; PR 3-8 2.7; KR 3-67 22.3; 3 Fum.

JAMES ALLEN Allen, James 5′10″, 212 **RB**
Col: Oklahoma *HS:* Wynnewood [OK] B: 3/28/1975
1998 ChiB: Rec 8-77 9.6 1 TD.

		Rushing					Tot
Year Team	G	Att	Yds	Avg	TD	Fum	TD
1998 ChiB	6	58	270	4.7	1	1	2

JIMMY ALLEN Allen, James Lee 6′2″, 194 **DB**
Col: Pierce Coll. CA (J.C.); UCLA *HS:* Los Angeles [CA] B: 3/6/1952, Clearwater, FL *Drafted:* 1974 Round 4 Pit
1974 Pit: KR 1-7 7.0. **1978** Det: 1 Fum TD. **Total:** KR 1-7 7.0; 1 Fum TD.

		Interceptions			
Year Team	G	Int	Yds	TD	Fum
1974 Pit	14	0	0	0	1
1975 Pit	14	2	0	0	0
1976 Pit	10	0	0	0	0
1977 Pit	12	5	76	0	2
1978 Det	14	5	70	0	1
1979 Det	16	4	0	0	0
1980 Det	15	6	38	0	0
1981 Det	15	9	123	0	0
NFL Total	110	31	307	0	4

JEFF ALLEN Allen, Jeffery 5′11″, 190 **DB**
Col: Central Coll. (Iowa); Iowa State *HS:* Wendell Phillips [Chicago, IL] B: 8/27/1948, Chicago, IL *Drafted:* 1971 Round 13 StL
1971 StL: 1 G.

JEFFREY ALLEN Allen, Jeffrey 5′11″, 190 **DB**
Col: California-Davis *HS:* Cordova [Rancho Cordova, CA] B: 7/18/1957, Richmond, IN *Drafted:* 1980 Round 8 Mia
1980 Mia: 16 G; KR 1-0. **1982** SD: 9 G; Int 1-0. **Total:** 25 G; KR 1-0; Int 1-0.

JOHNNY ALLEN Allen, John Mckee 6′2″, 224 **C-LB**
Col: Purdue *HS:* Ross [Fremont, OH] B: 6/4/1933, Monmouth, IL *Drafted:* 1955 Round 8 Was
1955 Was: 12 G. **1956** Was: 12 G. **1957** Was: 12 G. **1958** Was: 12 G. **Total:** 48 G.

CARL ALLEN Allen, Joseph Carl 6′0″, 185 **DB**
Col: Southern Mississippi *HS:* Rowan [Hattiesburg, MS]; Blair HS [Hattiesburg, MS] B: 12/21/1955, Hattiesburg, MS *Drafted:* 1977 Round 11 Cin
1980 StL: PR 1-0. **Total:** PR 1-0.

		Interceptions			
Year Team	G	Int	Yds	TD	Fum
1977 StL	14	1	22	0	0
1978 StL	15	6	54	0	0
1979 StL	15	5	126	0	0
1980 StL	16	3	104	1	1
1981 StL	10	0	0	0	0
1982 StL	9	1	0	0	0
NFL Total	79	16	306	1	1

KEVIN ALLEN Allen, Kevin Eugene 6′5″, 285 **OT**
Col: Indiana *HS:* Northwest [Cincinnati, OH] B: 6/21/1963, Cincinnati, OH *Drafted:* 1985 Round 1 Phi
1985 Phi: 16 G.

LARRY ALLEN Allen, Larry Christopher 6′3″, 325 **OG**
Col: Butte Coll. CA (J.C.); Sonoma State *HS:* Centennial [Compton, CA]; Vintage HS [Napa, CA] B: 11/27/1971, Los Angeles, CA *Drafted:* 1994 Round 2 Dal
1994 Dal: 16 G. **1995** Dal: 16 G. **1996** Dal: 16 G. **1997** Dal: 16 G. **1998** Dal: 16 G. **Total:** 80 G.

PATRICK ALLEN Allen, Lloyd Patrick 5′10″, 180 **DB**
Col: Utah State *HS:* James A. Garfield [Seattle, WA] B: 8/26/1961, Seattle, WA *Drafted:* 1984 Round 4 Hou
1984 Hou: 16 G; KR 11-210 19.1; Int 1-2. **1985** Hou: 16 G. **1986** Hou: 16 G; Int 3-20. **1987** Hou: 11 G; Int 1-37. **1988** Hou: 15 G; Int 1-23. **1989** Hou: 16 G. **1990** Hou: 16 G; Int 1-27. **Total:** 106 G; KR 11-210 19.1; Int 7-109.

LOU ALLEN Allen, Louis Eugene 6′3″, 215 **OT**
Col: Duke *HS:* Greensboro [NC] B: 7/12/1924, Gadsden., AL *Drafted:* 1950 Round 5 Pit
1950 Pit: 12 G. **1951** Pit: 12 G. **Total:** 24 G.

LYNN ALLEN Allen, Lynn **WB**
Col: Detroit Mercy Deceased
1920 Det: 2 G.

MARCUS ALLEN Allen, Marcus LeMarr 6′2″, 210 **RB**
Col: USC *HS:* Abraham Lincoln [San Diego, CA] B: 3/26/1960, San Diego, CA *Drafted:* 1982 Round 1 LARd
1982 LARd: Pass 4-1 25.0%, 47 11.75. **1983** LARd: Pass 7-4 57.1%, 111 15.86 3 TD; 1 Fum TD. **1984** LARd: Pass 4-1 25.0%, 38 9.50. **1985** LARd: Pass 2-1 50.0%, 16 8.00. **1987** LARd: Pass 2-1 50.0%, 23 11.50. **1988** LARd: Pass 2-1 50.0%, 21 10.50. **1990** LARd: Pass 1-0, 1 Int. **1991** LARd: Pass 2-1 50.0%, 11 5.50 1 TD. **1994** KC: Scor 1 2XP. **1996** KC: Pass 1-0. **1997** KC: Pass 2-2 100.0%, 15 7.50 2 TD. **Total:** Pass 27-12 44.4%, 282 10.44 6 TD 1 Int; Scor 1 2XP; 1 Fum TD.

		Rushing				Receiving					Tot
Year Team	G	Att	Yds	Avg	TD	Rec	Yds	Avg	TD	Fum	TD
1982 LARd	9	160	697	4.4	**11**	38	401	10.6	3	5	**14**
1983 LARd	16	266	1014	3.8	9	68	590	8.7	2	**14**	12
1984 LARd	16	275	1168	4.2	13	64	758	11.8	5	8	**18**
1985 LARd	16	380	**1759**	4.6	11	67	555	8.3	3	3	14
1986 LARd	13	208	759	3.6	5	46	453	9.8	2	7	7
1987 LARd	12	200	754	3.8	5	51	410	8.0	0	3	5
1988 LARd	15	223	831	3.7	7	34	303	8.9	1	5	8
1989 LARd	8	69	293	4.2	2	20	191	9.6	0	2	2
1990 LARd	16	179	682	3.8	12	15	189	12.6	1	1	13
1991 LARd	8	63	287	4.6	2	15	131	8.7	0	1	2
1992 LARd	16	67	301	4.5	2	28	277	9.9	1	1	3
1993 KC	16	206	764	3.7	**12**	34	238	7.0	3	4	15
1994 KC	13	189	709	3.8	7	42	349	8.3	0	3	7
1995 KC	16	207	890	4.3	5	27	210	7.8	0	2	5
1996 KC	16	206	830	4.0	9	27	270	10.0	0	2	9
1997 KC	16	124	505	4.1	11	11	86	7.8	0	4	11
NFL Total	222	3022	12243	4.1	123	587	5411	9.2	21	65	145

MARVIN ALLEN Allen, Marvin Ray 5′10″, 215 **RB**
Col: Tulane *HS:* Hirschi [Wichita Falls, TX] B: 11/23/1965, Wichita Falls, TX *Drafted:* 1988 Round 11 NE
1990 NE: Rec 6-48 8.0. **1991** NE: Rec 1-9 9.0. **Total:** Rec 7-57 8.1.

		Rushing				Kickoff Returns				
Year Team	G	Att	Yds	Avg	TD	Ret	Yds	Avg	TD	Fum
1988 NE	11	7	40	5.7	0	18	391	21.7	0	0
1989 NE	3	11	51	4.6	1	6	124	20.7	0	0
1990 NE	8	63	237	3.8	1	11	168	15.3	0	1
1991 NE	15	13	50	3.8	0	8	161	20.1	0	0
NFL Total	37	94	378	4.0	2	43	844	19.6	0	1

NATE ALLEN Allen, Nathaniel Sheraldton 5′10″, 170 **DB**
Col: Texas Southern *HS:* Georgetown [SC] B: 5/13/1948, Georgetown, SC *Drafted:* 1971 Round 11 KC
1971 KC: 4 G. **1972** KC: 14 G; Rec 1-20 20.0; Int 1-4. **1973** KC: 14 G; Int 1-8. **1974** KC: 12 G; Int 1-52. **1975** SF: 14 G; Int 1-37 1 TD; 6 Pt. **1976** Min: 12 G; Int 3-44; 6 Pt. **1977** Min: 14 G; Int 1-0. **1978** Min: 16 G. **1979** Min-Det: 8 G; PR 1-(-1) -1.0; Int 1-0. Min: 5 G; PR 1-(-1) -1.0; Int 1-0. Det: 3 G. **Total:** 108 G; Rec 1-20 20.0; PR 1-(-1) -1.0; Int 9-145 1 TD; Tot TD 2; 12 Pt.

TAJE ALLEN Allen, Taje LaQuane 5′10″, 185 **DB**
Col: Texas *HS:* Estacado [Lubbock, TX] B: 11/6/1973, Lubbock, TX *Drafted:* 1997 Round 5 StL
1997 StL: 14 G. **1998** StL: 16 G. **Total:** 30 G.

TERRY ALLEN Allen, Terry Thomas Jr. 5'10", 204 RB
Col: Clemson *HS:* Banks Co. [Homer, GA] B: 2/21/1968, Commerce, GA *Drafted:* 1990 Round 9 Min
1991 Min: KR 1-14 14.0. **1994** Min: Scor 1 2XP. **Total:** KR 1-14 14.0; Scor 1 2XP.

		Rushing				Receiving					Tot
Year Team	G	Att	Yds	Avg	TD	Rec	Yds	Avg	TD	Fum	TD
1991 Min	15	120	563	4.7	2	6	49	8.2	1	4	3
1992 Min	16	266	1201	4.5	13	49	478	9.8	2	9	15
1994 Min	16	255	1031	4.0	8	17	148	8.7	0	3	8
1995 Was	16	338	1309	3.9	10	31	232	7.5	1	6	11
1996 Was	16	347	1353	3.9	**21**	32	194	6.1	0	4	**21**
1997 Was	10	210	724	3.4	4	20	172	8.6	1	2	5
1998 Was	10	148	700	4.7	2	17	128	7.5	0	4	2
NFL Total	99	1684	6881	4.1	60	172	1401	8.1	5	32	65

TREMAYNE ALLEN Allen, Tremayne Aubrey 6'2", 234 TE
Col: Florida *HS:* Brentwood Acad. [TN] B: 8/9/1974, Nashville, TN
1997 ChiB: 2 G; Rec 1-9 9.0.

KURT ALLERMAN Allerman, Kurt Daniel 6'3", 222 LB
Col: Penn State *HS:* Kinnelon [NJ] B: 8/30/1955, Glen Ridge, NJ *Drafted:* 1977 Round 3 StL
1977 StL: 14 G; KR 2-39 19.5. **1978** StL: 15 G. **1979** StL: 16 G; KR 2-16 8.0. **1980** GB: 13 G. **1981** GB: 16 G. **1982** StL: 9 G. **1983** StL: 16 G; KR 1-11 11.0. **1984** StL: 16 G. **1985** Det: 10 G. **Total:** 125 G; KR 5-66 13.2.

TY ALLERT Allert, Ty Hunter 6'2", 233 LB
Col: Texas *HS:* Northbrook [Houston, TX] B: 7/23/1963, Rosenberg, TX *Drafted:* 1986 Round 4 SD
1986 SD: 16 G. **1987** SD-Phi: 10 G. SD: 3 G. Phi: 7 G. **1988** Phi: 10 G. **1989** Phi: 7 G. **1990** Den-Sea: 8 G. Den: 7 G. Sea: 1 G. **Total:** 51 G.

DON ALLEY Alley, Donald Wayne 6'2", 200 WR
Col: Adams State *HS:* Wheat Ridge [CO] B: 4/21/1945, Cheyenne, WY *Drafted:* 1967 Round 16 Bal
1967 Bal: 10 G; Rec 1-11 11.0. **1969** Pit: 8 G; Rec 1-16 16.0. **Total:** 18 G; Rec 2-27 13.5.

HANK ALLISON Allison, Henry Henderson 6'3", 255 OG-OT
Col: Coll. of the Sequoias CA (J.C.); San Diego State *HS:* South [Akron, OH] B: 2/11/1947, Stevenson, AL *Drafted:* 1971 Round 2 Phi
1971 Phi: 14 G. **1972** Phi: 6 G. **1975** StL: 14 G. **1976** StL: 10 G. **1977** StL-Den: 11 G. StL: 8 G. Den: 3 G. **Total:** 55 G.

NEELY ALLISON Allison, James Nealy 6'0", 190 E
Col: Texas A&M B: 5/14/1902, Ballinger, TX D: 2/21/1970, Houston, TX
1926 Buf: 9 G; Rec 1 TD; 6 Pt. **1927** Buf: 2 G. **1928** NYG: 13 G. **Total:** 24 G; Rec 1 TD; 6 Pt.

JIM ALLISON Allison, James Russell 6'0", 215 RB
Col: El Camino Coll. CA (J.C.); San Diego State *HS:* Redondo [Redondo Beach, CA] B: 3/2/1943, Richmond, CA *Drafted:* 1965 Round 12 SD
1965 SD: Rec 8-109 13.6; KR 4-80 20.0; Punt 2-72 36.0. **1966** SD: Rec 12-99 8.3. **1968** SD: Pass 1-1 100.0%, 23 23.00 1 TD; Rec 2-22 11.0; KR 7-121 17.3. **Total:** Pass 1-1 100.0%, 23 23.00 1 TD; Rec 22-230 10.5; KR 11-201 18.3; Punt 2-72 36.0.

		Rushing				
Year Team	G	Att	Yds	Avg	TD	Fum
1965 SD	14	29	100	3.4	0	0
1966 SD	14	31	213	6.9	2	1
1967 SD	3	10	34	3.4	0	0
1968 SD	12	23	31	1.3	0	0
NFL Total	43	93	378	4.1	2	1

BUDDY ALLISTON Alliston, Vaughn Samuel Jr. 6'0", 218 LB
Col: Mississippi *HS:* Florence [MS] B: 12/14/1933, Jackson, MS *Drafted:* 1956 Round 15 GB
1960 Den: 11 G; Int 1-65.

BOB ALLMAN Allman, Robert M 6'0", 198 OE-DE
Col: Michigan State *HS:* Central [Bay City, MI] B: 2/28/1913 D: 8/14/1995, Springfield, MI *Drafted:* 1936 Round 4 ChiB
1936 ChiB: 1 G.

BRIAN ALLRED Allred, Brian McCray 5'10", 175 DB
Col: Allan Hancock Coll. CA (J.C.); Sacramento State *HS:* Hammond [Columbia, MD] B: 3/16/1969, Washington, DC
1993 Sea: 4 G.

JOHN ALLRED Allred, John 6'4", 249 TE
Col: USC *HS:* Torrey Pines [Encinitas, CA] B: 9/9/1974, Del Mar, CA *Drafted:* 1997 Round 2 ChiB
1997 ChiB: 15 G; Rec 8-70 8.8; KR 2-21 10.5. **1998** ChiB: 4 G. **Total:** 19 G; Rec 8-70 8.8; KR 2-21 10.5.

JOE ALLTON Allton, Joseph J 6'2", 235 T
Col: Oklahoma *HS:* Claremore [OK] B: 9/7/1920, Claremore, OK D: 2/26/1989, Claremore, OK
1942 ChiC: 11 G; Int 1-24.

JEFF ALM Alm, Jeffrey Lawrence 6'6", 284 DT
Col: Notre Dame *HS:* Carl Sandburg [Orland Park, IL] B: 3/31/1968, New York, NY D: 12/14/1993 *Drafted:* 1990 Round 2 Hou
1990 Hou: 16 G; 0.5 Sac. **1991** Hou: 12 G; 1 Sac. **1992** Hou: 14 G; 1 Sac. **1993** Hou: 2 G. **Total:** 44 G; 2.5 Sac.

BEAU ALMODOBAR Almodobar, Beau 5'9", 180 WR
Col: Norwich B: 10/25/1962
1987 NYG: 2 G.

GERALD ALPHIN Alphin, Gerald Alan 6'3", 220 WR
Col: Kansas State *HS:* St. Louis University [MO] B: 5/21/1964, Portland, OR
1990 NO: 11 G; Rec 4-57 14.3. **1991** NO: 5 G. **Total:** 16 G; Rec 4-57 14.3.

LYNEAL ALSTON Alston, Lyneal 6'1", 205 WR
Col: Southern Mississippi *HS:* Theodore [AL] B: 7/23/1964, Mobile, AL
1987 Pit: 3 G; Rec 3-84 28.0 2 TD; 12 Pt.

MACK ALSTON Alston, Mack C Jr. 6'2", 230 TE
Col: Maryland East. Shore *HS:* Howard [Georgetown, SC] B: 4/27/1947, Georgetown, SC *Drafted:* 1970 Round 11 Was
1973 Hou: Rush 1-13 13.0. **1974** Hou: Rush 1-(-3) -3.0. **Total:** Rush 2-10 5.0.

		Receiving				
Year Team	G	Rec	Yds	Avg	TD	Fum
1970 Was	8	0	0	—	0	0
1971 Was	12	5	87	17.4	0	1
1972 Was	14	2	53	26.5	0	0
1973 Hou	14	19	195	10.3	4	0
1974 Hou	13	17	249	14.6	3	1
1975 Hou	13	18	165	9.2	4	0
1976 Hou	14	19	174	9.2	1	1
1977 Bal	14	0	0	—	0	0
1978 Bal	16	18	210	11.7	2	0
1979 Bal	14	10	114	11.4	1	0
1980 Bal	13	0	0	—	0	0
NFL Total	145	108	1247	11.5	15	3

O'BRIEN ALSTON Alston, O'Brien Darwin 6'6", 246 LB
Col: Maryland *HS:* Oxon Hill [MD] B: 12/21/1965, New Haven, CT *Drafted:* 1988 Round 10 Ind
1988 Ind: 15 G; 3 Sac. **1989** Ind: 4 G; 1 Sac. **Total:** 19 G; 4 Sac.

MIKE ALSTOTT Alstott, Michael Joseph 6'1", 248 RB
Col: Purdue *HS:* Joliet Catholic [IL] B: 12/21/1973, Joliet, IL *Drafted:* 1996 Round 2 TB
1996 TB: KR 1-14 14.0. **1997** TB: KR 1-0. **1998** TB: Pass 1-0; KR 1-8 8.0. **Total:** Pass 1-0; KR 3-22 7.3.

		Rushing				Receiving					Tot
Year Team	G	Att	Yds	Avg	TD	Rec	Yds	Avg	TD	Fum	TD
1996 TB	16	96	377	3.9	3	65	557	8.6	3	4	6
1997 TB	15	176	665	3.8	7	23	178	7.7	3	5	10
1998 TB	16	215	846	3.9	8	22	152	6.9	1	5	9
NFL Total	47	487	1888	3.9	18	110	887	8.1	7	14	25

JOHN ALT Alt, John Michael 6'8", 298 OT
Col: Iowa *HS:* Columbia Heights [MN] B: 5/30/1962, Stuttgart, Germany *Drafted:* 1984 Round 1 KC
1984 KC: 15 G. **1985** KC: 13 G. **1986** KC: 7 G. **1987** KC: 9 G. **1988** KC: 14 G. **1989** KC: 16 G. **1990** KC: 16 G. **1991** KC: 16 G. **1992** KC: 16 G. **1993** KC: 16 G. **1994** KC: 13 G. **1995** KC: 16 G. **1996** KC: 12 G. **Total:** 179 G.

JIM ALTHOFF Althoff, James 6'3", 278 DT
Col: Winona State *HS:* McHenry [IL] B: 9/27/1961, McHenry, IL
1987 ChiB: 4 G; 3.5 Sac.

WILSON ALVAREZ Alvarez, Wilson 6'0", 165 K
Col: New Mexico Mil. Inst. (J.C.); Coll. of the Sequoias CA (J.C.); Southeastern Loui *HS:* Dr. Domingo Leigue [Santa Cruz, Bolivia] B: 3/22/1957, Santa Cruz, Bolivia
1981 Sea: 4 G; Scor 23, 3-7 42.9% FG, 14-15 93.3% XK.

STEVE ALVERS Alvers, Steven Dean 6'4", 240 TE-C
Col: Taft Coll. CA (J.C.); Miami (Fla.) *HS:* North Miami Beach [FL] B: 4/4/1957, Palm Beach, FL *Drafted:* 1979 Round 7 NYG
1981 Buf: 16 G. **1982** NYJ: 3 G. **Total:** 19 G.

STEVE ALVORD Alvord, Steven Lee 6'4", 272 DT
Col: Washington *HS:* Bellingham [WA] B: 10/2/1964, Bellingham, WA *Drafted:* 1987 Round 8 StL
1987 StL: 12 G; 1.5 Sac. **1988** Pho: 15 G; 2 Sac. **Total:** 27 G; 3.5 Sac.

TOM ALWARD Alward, Thomas Lavern 6'4", 255 **OG**
Col: Nebraska *HS:* Bendle [Burton, MI] B: 10/13/1952, Flint, MI
Drafted: 1975 Round 6 NYJ
1976 TB: 14 G.

LANCE ALWORTH Alworth, Lance Dwight 6'0", 184 **WR**
(Bambi) *Col:* Arkansas *HS:* Brookhaven [MS] B: 8/3/1940, Houston, TX *Drafted:* 1962 Round 2 SD *HOF:* 1978
1962 SD: Rush 1-17 17.0. **1963** SD: Rush 2-14 7.0; KR 10-216 21.6. **1964** SD: Pass 1-1 100.0%, -11 -11.00; Rush 3-60 20.0 2 TD. **1965** SD: Rush 3-(-12) -4.0. **1966** SD: Rush 3-10 3.3. **1967** SD: Pass 1-0; Rush 1-5 5.0. **1968** SD: Rush 3-18 6.0; Scor **1** 2XP. **1969** SD: Rush 5-25 5.0. **1971** Dal: Rush 2-(-10) -5.0. **1972** Dal: Rush 1-2 2.0. **Total:** Pass 2-1 50.0%, -11 5.50; Rush 24-129 5.4 2 TD; KR 10-216 21.6; Scor 1 2XP.

		Receiving				Punt Returns					Tot
Year Team	**G**	**Rec**	**Yds**	**Avg**	**TD**	**Ret**	**Yds**	**Avg**	**TD**	**Fum**	**TD**
1962 SD	4	10	226	22.6	3	0	0	—	0	0	3
1963 SD	14	61	1205	19.8	11	11	120	10.9	0	0	11
1964 SD	12	61	1235	20.2	**13**	18	189	10.5	0	3	**15**
1965 SD	14	69	**1602**	**23.2**	**14**	0	0	—	0	2	**14**
1966 SD	13	**73**	**1383**	18.9	**13**	0	0	—	0	0	**13**
1967 SD	11	52	1010	19.4	9	0	0	—	0	0	9
1968 SD	14	**68**	**1312**	19.3	10	0	0	—	0	0	10
1969 SD	14	**64**	1003	15.7	4	0	0	—	0	0	4
1970 SD	14	35	608	17.4	4	0	0	—	0	0	4
1971 Dal	12	34	487	14.3	2	0	0	—	0	0	2
1972 Dal	14	15	195	13.0	2	0	0	—	0	0	2
NFL Total	136	542	10266	18.9	85	29	309	10.7	0	5	87

LYLE ALZADO Alzado, Lyle Martin 6'3", 255 **DE-DT**
Col: Yankton *HS:* Lawrence [Cedarhurst, NY] B: 4/3/1949, Brooklyn, NY D: 5/14/1992, Portland, OR *Drafted:* 1971 Round 4 Den
1971 Den: 12 G. **1972** Den: 14 G. **1973** Den: 14 G. **1974** Den: 14 G. **1975** Den: 14 G. **1976** Den: 1 G. **1977** Den: 14 G. **1978** Den: 16 G; Scor **1** Saf; 2 Pt. **1979** Cle: 15 G. **1980** Cle: 16 G. **1981** Cle: 15 G. **1982** LARd: 9 G; 7 Sac. **1983** LARd: 15 G; Scor 1 Saf; 2 Pt; 7 Sac. **1984** LARd: 16 G; 6 Sac. **1985** LARd: 11 G; Scor 1 Saf; **1** Fum TD; 8 Pt; 3 Sac. **Total:** 196 G; Scor 3 Saf; 1 Fum TD; 12 Pt; 23.0 Sac.

JOHN AMBERG Amberg, John McCaslin 5'11", 195 **DB-HB**
Col: Kansas *HS:* Shawnee Mission [KS] B: 3/6/1929, Johnson County, KS
1951 NYG: 12 G; Rush 7-35 5.0; Int 3-38. **1952** NYG: 12 G; Rush 7-27 3.9; Rec 3-40 13.3; Int 2-18. **Total:** 24 G; Rush 14-62 4.4; Rec 3-40 13.3; Int 5-56.

ASHLEY AMBROSE Ambrose, Ashley Avery 5'10", 185 **DB**
Col: Mississippi Valley State *HS:* Alcee Fortier [New Orleans, LA] B: 9/17/1970, New Orleans, LA *Drafted:* 1992 Round 2 Ind
1992 Ind: KR 8-126 15.8. **1997** Cin: 1 Sac. **Total:** KR 8-126 15.8; 1 Sac.

		Interceptions			
Year Team	**G**	**Int**	**Yds**	**TD**	**Fum**
1992 Ind	10	0	0	0	2
1993 Ind	14	0	0	0	0
1994 Ind	16	2	50	0	0
1995 Ind	16	3	12	0	0
1996 Cin	16	8	63	1	0
1997 Cin	16	3	56	0	0
1998 Cin	15	2	0	0	0
NFL Total	103	18	181	1	2

JOHN AMBROSE Ambrose, John Vincent 6'0", 185 **C**
(Whitey) *Col:* Catholic *HS:* Commerce [Worcester, MA] B: 3/24/1910, Three Rivers, MA D: 11/7/1995, Shrewsbury, MA
1932 Bkn: 6 G.

DICK AMBROSE Ambrose, Richard John 6'0", 235 **LB**
(Bam Bam) *Col:* Virginia *HS:* Iona Prep [New Rochelle, NY] B: 1/17/1953, New Rochelle, NY *Drafted:* 1975 Round 12 Cle
1975 Cle: 14 G; KR 1-3 3.0. **1976** Cle: 10 G; KR 1-16 16.0. **1977** Cle: 14 G; KR 1-20 20.0. **1978** Cle: 16 G; Int 2-46. **1979** Cle: 15 G; Int 1-0. **1980** Cle: 16 G. **1981** Cle: 16 G; Int 1-0. **1982** Cle: 9 G; Int 1-0. **1983** Cle: 6 G. **Total:** 116 G; KR 3-39 13.0; Int 5-46.

WALT AMBROSE Ambrose, Walter L 5'11", 210 **G**
Col: Carroll (Wis.) *HS:* Portage [WI] B: 8/7/1905, Portage, WI D: Portage, WI
1930 Port: 1 G.

ALAN AMECHE Ameche, Alan Dante 6'0", 218 **FB**
(The Horse AKA Lino Dante Ameche) *Col:* Wisconsin *HS:* Mary Bradford [Kenosha, WI] B: 6/1/1933, Kenosha, WI D: 8/8/1988, Houston, TX *Drafted:* 1955 Round 1 Bal
1955 Bal: KR 4-60 15.0. **1956** Bal: KR 2-38 19.0. **Total:** KR 6-98 16.3.

		Rushing				Receiving					Tot
Year Team	**G**	**Att**	**Yds**	**Avg**	**TD**	**Rec**	**Yds**	**Avg**	**TD**	**Fum**	**TD**
1955 Bal	12	**213**	**961**	4.5	**9**	27	141	5.2	0	3	**9**
1956 Bal	12	178	858	4.8	8	26	189	7.3	0	3	8
1957 Bal	12	144	493	3.4	5	15	137	9.1	2	3	7
1958 Bal	12	171	791	4.6	8	13	81	6.2	1	1	9
1959 Bal	12	178	679	3.8	7	13	129	9.9	1	3	8
1960 Bal	10	80	263	3.3	3	7	56	8.0	0	0	3
NFL Total	70	964	4045	4.2	40	101	733	7.3	4	13	44

GLEN AMERSON Amerson, Glen Douglas 6'1", 186 **DB**
(Amo) *Col:* Texas Tech *HS:* Munday [TX] B: 11/24/1938, Munday, TX
1961 Phi: 14 G.

DAVE AMES Ames, David Randolph 6'0", 185 **HB-DB**
Col: Richmond *HS:* Woodrow Wilson [Portsmouth, VA] B: 1/16/1937, Portsmouth, VA *Drafted:* 1960 Round 2 Bos
1961 NYT-Den: 12 G; Rush 19-114 6.0; Rec 6-20 3.3; PR 2-17 8.5; KR 12-240 20.0; Int 1-0; 2 Fum. NYT: 5 G; Int 1-0. Den: 7 G; Rush 19-114 6.0; Rec 6-20 3.3; PR 2-17 8.5; KR 12-240 20.0; 2 Fum. **Total:** 12 G; Rush 19-114 6.0; Rec 6-20 3.3; PR 2-17 8.5; KR 12-240 20.0; Int 1-0; 2 Fum.

VINCENT AMEY Amey, Vincent Wayne 6'2", 289 **DE**
Col: Arizona State *HS:* James Logan [Union City, CA] B: 2/9/1975, Los Angeles, CA *Drafted:* 1998 Round 7 Oak
1998 Oak: 4 G; KR 1-0.

DICK AMMAN Amman, Richard Dale 6'5", 245 **DE-DT**
Col: Florida State *HS:* Cocoa Beach [FL] B: 9/21/1950, Seattle, WA *Drafted:* 1972 Round 10 Dal
1972 Bal: 14 G. **1973** Bal: 14 G. **Total:** 28 G.

MARTY AMSLER Amsler, Charles Martin 6'5", 255 **DE**
Col: Indiana; Ivy Tech State-SW IN (J.C.) *HS:* Benjamin Bosse [Evansville, IN] B: 10/26/1942, Evansville, IN *Drafted:* 1965 Round 18 Dal
1967 ChiB: 14 G; Int 1-0. **1969** ChiB: 11 G. **1970** Cin-GB: 12 G. Cin: 3 G. GB: 9 G. **Total:** 37 G; Int 1-0.

JOE AMSTUTZ Amstutz, Gerald Joseph 6'5", 264 **C**
Col: Indiana *HS:* Central Catholic [Toledo, OH] B: 10/12/1934, Toledo, OH *Drafted:* 1957 Round 6 Cle
1957 Cle: 11 G.

NORM AMUNDSEN Amundsen, Norman Robert 5'11", 245 **OG**
Col: Wisconsin *HS:* Kelvyn Park [Chicago, IL] B: 9/28/1932, Chicago, IL *Drafted:* 1955 Round 6 GB
1957 GB: 12 G.

GEORGE AMUNDSON Amundson, George Arthur 6'3", 215 **RB**
Col: Iowa State *HS:* Central [Aberdeen, SD] B: 3/31/1951, Pendleton, OR *Drafted:* 1973 Round 1 Hou
1974 Hou: Pass 1-0, 1 Int; KR 2-17 8.5. **Total:** Pass 1-0, 1 Int; KR 2-17 8.5.

		Rushing				Receiving					Tot
Year Team	**G**	**Att**	**Yds**	**Avg**	**TD**	**Rec**	**Yds**	**Avg**	**TD**	**Fum**	**TD**
1973 Hou	9	15	56	3.7	0	7	60	8.6	0	1	0
1974 Hou	14	59	138	2.3	4	18	152	8.4	1	1	5
1975 Phi	6	0	0	—	0	0	0	—	0	0	0
NFL Total	29	74	194	2.6	4	25	212	8.5	1	2	5

VITO ANANIS Ananis, Vito Francis 5'10", 195 **HB-DB**
Col: Boston College *HS:* Rindge Technical [Cambridge, MA]; Worcester Acad. [MA] B: 1/25/1915, Cambridge, MA D: 9/3/1994, Wayland, MA
1945 Was: 1 G; Rush 3-8 2.7.

RUDY ANDABAKER Andabaker, Rudolph Edward 5'11", 196 **OG**
Col: Pittsburgh *HS:* Donora [PA] B: 8/1/1928, Donora, PA
1952 Pit: 6 G. **1954** Pit: 4 G. **Total:** 10 G.

KIMBLE ANDERS Anders, Kimble Lynard 5'11", 225 **RB**
Col: Houston *HS:* Ball [Galveston, TX] B: 9/10/1966, Galveston, TX
1992 KC: KR 1-20 20.0. **1993** KC: KR 1-47 47.0. **1994** KC: KR 2-36 18.0. **1996** KC: KR 2-37 18.5. **1997** KC: KR 1-0. **1998** KC: KR 1-16 16.0. **Total:** KR 8-156 19.5.

		Rushing				Receiving					Tot
Year Team	**G**	**Att**	**Yds**	**Avg**	**TD**	**Rec**	**Yds**	**Avg**	**TD**	**Fum**	**TD**
1991 KC	2	0	0	—	0	2	30	15.0	0	0	0
1992 KC	11	1	1	1.0	0	5	65	13.0	0	1	0
1993 KC	16	75	291	3.9	0	40	326	8.2	1	1	1
1994 KC	16	62	231	3.7	2	67	525	7.8	1	1	3
1995 KC	16	58	398	6.9	2	55	349	6.3	1	1	3
1996 KC	16	54	201	3.7	2	60	529	8.8	2	0	4
1997 KC	15	79	397	5.0	0	59	453	7.7	2	3	2
1998 KC	16	58	230	4.0	1	64	462	7.2	2	6	3
NFL Total	108	387	1749	4.5	7	352	2739	7.8	9	13	16

MORTEN ANDERSEN Andersen, Morten 6'2", 218 **K**
Col: Michigan State *HS:* Ben Davis [Indianapolis, IN] B: 8/19/1960, Struer, Denmark *Drafted:* 1982 Round 4 NO

		Scoring						
Year Team	**G**	**Pts**	**FG**	**FGA**	**FG%**	**XK**	**XKA**	**XK%**
1982 NO	8	12	2	5	40.0	6	6	100.0

1983 NO	16	91	18	24	75.0	37	38	97.4
1984 NO	16	94	20	27	74.1	34	34	100.0
1985 NO	16	120	31	35	88.6	27	29	93.1
1986 NO	16	108	26	30	**86.7**	30	30	**100.0**
1987 NO	12	121	**28**	**36**	77.8	37	37	100.0
1988 NO	16	110	26	36	72.2	32	33	97.0
1989 NO	16	104	20	29	69.0	44	45	97.8
1990 NO	16	92	21	27	77.8	29	29	100.0
1991 NO	16	113	25	32	78.1	38	38	100.0
1992 NO	16	120	29	34	85.3	33	34	97.1
1993 NO	16	117	28	35	80.0	33	33	100.0
1994 NO	16	116	28	**39**	71.8	32	32	100.0
1995 Atl	16	122	31	37	83.8	29	30	96.7
1996 Atl	16	97	22	29	75.9	31	31	100.0
1997 Atl	16	104	23	27	85.2	35	35	100.0
1998 Atl	16	120	23	28	82.1	51	52	98.1
NFL Total	260	1761	401	510	78.6	558	566	98.6

STAN ANDERSEN Andersen, Stanley 6′2″, 218 **T-OE-DE**
Col: Stanford *HS:* Kingsburg [CA] B: 9/14/1917, Portland, OR
Drafted: 1940 Round 12 ChiC
1940 Cle: 11 G. **1941** Cle-Det: 11 G; Rec 7-79 11.3; KR 1-14 14.0. Cle: 5 G; Rec 2-20 10.0. Det: 6 G; Rec 5-59 11.8; KR 1-14 14.0. **Total:** 22 G; Rec 7-79 11.3; KR 1-14 14.0.

ANDERSON Anderson **WB**
Col: No College Deceased
1922 Ham: 1 G.

ALEC ANDERSON Anderson, Alexander Aloysius 5′8″, 166 **G**
Col: Boston College; Holy Cross; Georgetown *HS:* Somerville [MA]
B: 6/17/1893 D: 11/14/1953
1921 Was: 1 G.

ALFRED ANDERSON Anderson, Alfred Anthony 6′1″, 219 **RB**
Col: Baylor *HS:* Richfield [Waco, TX] B: 8/4/1961, Waco, TX
Drafted: 1984 Round 3 Min
1984 Min: Pass 7-3 42.9%, 95 13.57 2 TD 1 Int. **1986** Min: Pass 2-1 50.0%, 17 8.50. **Total:** Pass 9-4 44.4%, 112 12.44 2 TD 1 Int.

		Rushing				Receiving			
Year Team	**G**	**Att**	**Yds**	**Avg**	**TD**	**Rec**	**Yds**	**Avg**	**TD**
1984 Min	16	201	773	3.8	2	17	102	6.0	1
1985 Min	12	50	121	2.4	4	16	175	10.9	1
1986 Min	16	83	347	4.2	2	17	179	10.5	2
1987 Min	10	68	319	4.7	2	7	69	9.9	0
1988 Min	16	87	300	3.4	7	23	242	10.5	1
1989 Min	11	52	189	3.6	2	20	193	9.7	0
1990 Min	11	59	207	3.5	2	13	80	6.2	0
1991 Min	16	26	118	4.5	1	1	2	2.0	0
NFL Total	108	626	2374	3.8	22	114	1042	9.1	5

	Kickoff Returns					Tot
Year Team	**Ret**	**Yds**	**Avg**	**TD**	**Fum**	**TD**
1984 Min	30	639	21.3	0	8	3
1985 Min	0	0	—	0	0	5
1986 Min	3	38	12.7	0	3	4
1987 Min	0	0	—	0	1	2
1988 Min	0	0	—	0	3	8
1989 Min	5	75	15.0	0	3	2
1990 Min	3	44	14.7	0	1	2
1991 Min	1	7	7.0	0	0	1
NFL Total	42	803	19.1	0	19	27

ANTHONY ANDERSON Anderson, Anthony Eugeen 6′0″, 197 **RB**
Col: Temple *HS:* Thomas McKean [Wilmington, DE] B: 9/27/1956, Wilmington, DE
1979 Pit: 16 G; Rush 18-118 6.6 1 TD; KR 13-200 15.4; 6 Pt; 1 Fum.
1980 Atl: 16 G; Rush 6-5 0.8; KR 7-97 13.9. **Total:** 32 G; Rush 24-123 5.1 1 TD; KR 20-297 14.9; 6 Pt; 1 Fum.

ANTHONY ANDERSON Anderson, Anthony Ray 6′2″, 205 **DB**
Col: Grambling State *HS:* Jonesboro-Hodge [Jonesboro, LA]
B: 10/24/1964, Ruston, LA *Drafted:* 1987 Round 10 SD
1987 SD: 3 G; 0.5 Sac.

ANTONIO ANDERSON Anderson, Antonio Kenneth 6′6″, 311 **DE**
Col: Syracuse *HS:* Midwood [Brooklyn, NY]; Milford Acad. [CT]
B: 6/4/1973, Brooklyn, NY *Drafted:* 1997 Round 4 Dal
1997 Dal: 16 G; 2 Sac. **1998** Dal: 5 G. **Total:** 21 G; 2 Sac.

ARIC ANDERSON Anderson, Aric Howard 6′2″, 220 **LB**
Col: Millikin *HS:* William Fremd [Palatine, IL] B: 4/9/1965, Waverly, IA
1987 GB: 3 G.

ART ANDERSON Anderson, Arthur Anthony 6′3″, 244 **OT**
Col: Idaho *HS:* Wahpeton [ND] B: 10/9/1936, Breckenridge, MN
1961 ChiB: 14 G. **1962** ChiB: 14 G; Rush 1-7 7.0. **1963** Pit: 13 G.
Total: 41 G; Rush 1-7 7.0.

BILLY ANDERSON Anderson, Billy Guy 6′1″, 195 **QB**
Col: Tulsa *HS:* Ferris [TX] B: 2/17/1941, Palme, TX D: 4/11/1996, Houston, TX *Drafted:* 1965 Redshirt Round 1 Hou
1967 Hou: 8 G.

BRAD ANDERSON Anderson, Bradley Stewart 6′2″, 196 **WR**
Col: Brigham Young; Arizona *HS:* Alhambra [Phoenix, AZ]
B: 1/12/1961, Glendale, AZ *Drafted:* 1984 Round 8 ChiB
1984 ChiB: 13 G; Rec 3-77 25.7 1 TD; 6 Pt. **1985** ChiB: 14 G; Rec 1-6 6.0.
Total: 27 G; Rec 4-83 20.8 1 TD; 6 Pt.

BRUCE ANDERSON Anderson, Bruce Albert 6′4″, 250 **DE-DT**
(Spider) *Col:* Willamette *HS:* Marshfield [Coos Bay, OR]
B: 1/18/1944, Coos Bay, OR *Drafted:* 1966 Round 6 LARm
1966 LARm: 7 G. **1967** NYG: 14 G. **1968** NYG: 14 G. **1969** NYG: 10 G.
1970 Was: 14 G. **Total:** 59 G.

CHARLIE ANDERSON Anderson, Charles Edward 6′0″, 230 **DE-OE**
Col: Louisiana Tech *HS:* Plain Dealing [LA] B: 9/2/1933, Atlanta, AR
Drafted: 1956 Round 15 ChiC
1956 ChiC: 2 G.

NEAL ANDERSON Anderson, Charles Neal 5′11″, 210 **RB**
Col: Florida *HS:* Graceville [FL] B: 8/14/1964, Graceville, FL
Drafted: 1986 Round 1 ChiB
1986 ChiB: KR 4-26 6.5. **1988** ChiB: Pass 1-0. **1991** ChiB: Pass 1-0.
1993 ChiB: Pass 1-0. **Total:** Pass 3-0; KR 4-26 6.5.

		Rushing				Receiving					Tot
Year Team	**G**	**Att**	**Yds**	**Avg**	**TD**	**Rec**	**Yds**	**Avg**	**TD**	**Fum**	**TD**
1986 ChiB	14	35	146	4.2	0	4	80	20.0	1	1	1
1987 ChiB	11	129	586	4.5	3	47	467	9.9	3	2	6
1988 ChiB	16	249	1106	4.4	12	39	371	9.5	0	8	12
1989 ChiB	16	274	1275	4.7	11	50	434	8.7	4	5	15
1990 ChiB	15	260	1078	4.1	10	42	484	11.5	3	2	13
1991 ChiB	13	210	747	3.6	6	47	368	7.8	3	5	9
1992 ChiB	16	156	582	3.7	5	42	399	9.5	6	6	11
1993 ChiB	15	202	646	3.2	4	31	160	5.2	0	2	4
NFL Total	116	1515	6166	4.1	51	302	2763	9.1	20	31	71

CHET ANDERSON Anderson, Chester Leonard Jr. 6′3″, 245 **TE**
Col: Minnesota *HS:* Central [Duluth, MN] B: 3/14/1945, Duluth, MN
Drafted: 1967 Round 14 Pit
1967 Pit: 14 G; Rec 8-141 17.6 2 TD; 12 Pt.

CLIFF ANDERSON Anderson, Clifton Junior 6′2″, 215 **OE**
(Doc) *Col:* Indiana *HS:* Cape May [NJ] B: 11/25/1929, Cape May, NJ
D: 3/16/1979, Princess Anne, MD *Drafted:* 1952 Round 25 ChiC
1952 ChiC: KR 1-8 8.0. **Total:** KR 1-8 8.0.

		Receiving			
Year Team	**G**	**Rec**	**Yds**	**Avg**	**TD**
1952 ChiC	12	11	191	17.4	2
1953 ChiC-NYG	9	17	266	15.6	0
1953 ChiC	1	1	8	8.0	0
1953 NYG	8	16	258	16.1	0
NFL Total	21	28	457	16.3	2

CURTIS ANDERSON Anderson, Curtis Lee 6′6″, 250 **DE**
Col: Central State (Ohio) *HS:* Withrow [Cincinnati, OH] B: 5/16/1957, Cincinnati, OH *Drafted:* 1979 Round 5 Dal
1979 KC: 6 G.

DARREN ANDERSON Anderson, Darren Hunter 5′10″, 185 **DB**
Col: Toledo *HS:* Walnut Hills [Cincinnati, OH] B: 1/11/1969, Cincinnati, OH *Drafted:* 1992 Round 4 NE
1992 NE-TB: 2 G. NE: 1 G. TB: 1 G. **1993** TB: 14 G; Int 1-6. **1994** KC: 15 G. **1995** KC: 16 G. **1996** KC: 11 G. **1997** KC: 11 G; Int 1-55 1 TD; 6 Pt; 2 Sac. **1998** Atl: 5 G. **Total:** 74 G; Int 2-61 1 TD; 6 Pt; 2 Sac.

DON ANDERSON Anderson, Donald Cortez 5′10″, 196 **DB**
Col: Purdue *HS:* Cody [Detroit, MI] B: 7/8/1963, Detroit, MI
Drafted: 1985 Round 2 Ind
1985 Ind: 5 G; Int 1-1; 1 Fum. **1987** TB: 11 G. **Total:** 16 G; Int 1-1; 1 Fum.

SCOTT ANDERSON Anderson, Donald Scott 6′4″, 242 **C**
Col: Missouri *HS:* Hannibal [IL] B: 2/13/1951, Denton, IL
Drafted: 1974 Round 3 Min
1974 Min: 5 G. **1976** Min: 2 G. **Total:** 7 G.

DUNSTAN ANDERSON Anderson, Dunstan Evrette 6′3″, 260 **DE**
Col: Tulsa *HS:* O.D. Wyatt [Fort Worth, TX] B: 12/31/1970, Fort Worth, TX
1994 Atl: 1 G. **1997** Mia: 9 G. **Total:** 10 G.

DWAYNE ANDERSON Anderson, Dwayne Everett 6′0″, 205 **DB**
Col: Southern Methodist *HS:* Roosevelt [St. Louis, MO] B: 12/7/1961, St. Louis, MO
1987 StL: 1 G.

EDDIE ANDERSON Anderson, Eddie Lee Jr. 6'1", 210 **DB**
Col: Fort Valley State *HS:* Warner Robins [GA] B: 7/22/1963, Warner Robins, GA *Drafted:* 1986 Round 6 Sea
1992 LARd: 1 Sac. **1993** LARd: 1 Sac. **1994** LARd: 2 Sac. **Total:** 4 Sac.

		Interceptions		
Year Team	G	Int	Yds	TD
1986 Sea	5	0	0	0
1987 LARd	13	1	58	0
1988 LARd	16	2	-6	0
1989 LARd	15	5	**233**	**2**
1990 LARd	16	3	49	0
1991 LARd	16	2	14	0
1992 LARd	16	3	131	1
1993 LARd	16	2	52	0
1994 LARd	14	0	0	0
1995 Oak	14	1	0	0
1996 Oak	7	0	0	0
1997 Oak	11	0	0	0
NFL Total	159	19	531	3

EDDIE ANDERSON Anderson, Edward Nicholas 5'10", 176 **E**
Col: Notre Dame *HS:* Mason City [IA] B: 11/13/1900, Oskaloosa, IA D: 4/26/1974, Clearwater, FL
1922 Roch-ChiC: 10 G. Roch: 3 G. ChiC: 7 G. **1923** ChiC: 11 G; Rec 1 TD; 6 Pt. **1924** ChiC: 9 G. **1925** ChiC: 13 G; Rec 1 TD; 6 Pt. **Total:** 43 G; Rec 2 TD; 12 Pt.

ERICK ANDERSON Anderson, Erick Scott 6'1", 240 **LB**
Col: Michigan *HS:* Glenbrook South [Glenview, IL] B: 10/7/1968, Long Beach, CA *Drafted:* 1992 Round 7 KC
1993 KC: 8 G. **1994** Was: 2 G. **Total:** 10 G.

SUGARFOOT ANDERSON Anderson, Ezzret 6'4", 215 **OE-DE**
Col: Kentucky State *HS:* Langston [Hot Springs, AR] B: 2/10/1920, Nashville, AR
AAFC **1947** LA-A: 13 G; Rush 3-24 8.0; Rec 11-126 11.5 1 TD; 6 Pt.

FRED ANDERSON Anderson, Fredell Lamont 6'4", 238 **DE-DT**
Col: Oregon State; Prairie View A&M *HS:* Toppenish [WA] B: 10/30/1954, Toppenish, WA
1978 Pit: 16 G. **1980** Sea: 7 G. **1981** Sea: 14 G. **1982** Sea: 1 G. **Total:** 38 G.

DONNY ANDERSON Anderson, Garry Don 6'2", 215 **RB**
Col: Texas Tech *HS:* Stinnett [TX] B: 5/16/1943, Borger, TX *Drafted:* 1965 Round 1 GB
1966 GB: PR 6-124 20.7 **1** TD. **1967** GB: Pass 2-1 50.0%, 19 9.50; PR 9-98 10.9. **1968** GB: Pass 3-1 33.3%, 12 4.00 1 TD. **1970** GB: Pass 1-0. **1971** GB: Pass 4-2 50.0%, 9 2.25 1 TD. **1972** StL: Pass 3-2 66.7%, 71 23.67. **Total:** Pass 13-6 46.2%, 111 8.54 2 TD; PR 15-222 14.8 1 TD.

		Rushing				Receiving			
Year Team	G	Att	Yds	Avg	TD	Rec	Yds	Avg	TD
1966 GB	14	25	104	4.2	2	2	33	16.5	0
1967 GB	14	97	402	4.1	6	22	331	15.0	3
1968 GB	14	170	761	4.5	5	25	333	13.3	1
1969 GB	14	87	288	3.3	1	14	308	22.0	1
1970 GB	14	222	853	3.8	5	36	414	11.5	0
1971 GB	14	186	757	4.1	5	26	306	11.8	1
1972 StL	14	153	536	3.5	4	28	298	10.6	2
1973 StL	14	167	679	4.1	10	41	409	10.0	3
1974 StL	14	90	316	3.5	3	15	116	7.7	3
NFL Total	126	1197	4696	3.9	41	209	2548	12.2	14

	Kickoff Returns				Punting				Tot
Year Team	Ret	Yds	Avg	TD	Punts	Yds	Avg	Fum	TD
1966 GB	23	533	23.2	0	2	89	44.5	3	3
1967 GB	11	226	20.5	0	65	2378	36.6	3	9
1968 GB	0	0	—	0	59	2359	40.0	7	6
1969 GB	0	0	—	0	58	2329	40.2	4	2
1970 GB	0	0	—	0	81	3302	40.8	8	5
1971 GB	0	0	—	0	50	2022	40.4	6	6
1972 StL	0	0	—	0	72	2847	39.5	6	6
1973 StL	0	0	—	0	0	0	—	7	13
1974 StL	0	0	—	0	0	0	—	2	6
NFL Total	34	759	22.3	0	387	15326	39.6	46	56

GARY ANDERSON Anderson, Gary Allan 5'11", 176 **K**
Col: Syracuse *HS:* Brettonwood [Durban, South Africa] B: 7/16/1959, Durban, South Africa *Drafted:* 1982 Round 7 Buf
1994 Pit: Rush 1-3 3.0. **Total:** Rush 1-3 3.0.

		Scoring						
Year Team	G	Pts	FG	FGA	FG%	XK	XKA	XK%
1982 Pit	9	52	10	12	83.3	22	22	100.0
1983 Pit	16	119	27	31	87.1	38	39	97.4
1984 Pit	16	117	24	32	75.0	45	45	100.0
1985 Pit	16	139	**33**	**42**	78.6	40	40	100.0
1986 Pit	16	95	21	32	65.6	32	32	100.0
1987 Pit	12	87	22	27	81.5	21	21	100.0
1988 Pit	16	118	28	36	77.8	34	35	97.1
1989 Pit	16	91	21	30	70.0	28	28	100.0
1990 Pit	16	92	20	25	80.0	32	32	100.0
1991 Pit	16	100	23	33	69.7	31	31	100.0
1992 Pit	16	113	28	36	77.8	29	31	93.5
1993 Pit	16	116	28	30	93.3	32	32	100.0
1994 Pit	16	104	24	29	82.8	32	32	100.0
1995 Phi	16	98	22	30	73.3	32	33	97.0
1996 Phi	16	115	25	29	86.2	40	40	100.0
1997 SF	16	125	29	36	80.6	38	38	100.0
1998 Min	16	**164**	35	35	**100.0**	**59**	**59**	**100.0**
NFL Total	261	1845	**420**	525	80.0	585	590	99.2

GARY ANDERSON Anderson, Gary Allan 6'3", 253 **OG**
Col: Stanford *HS:* Placer [Auburn, CA] B: 9/22/1955, Fairfield, CA *Drafted:* 1977 Round 10 Det
1977 Det: 13 G. **1978** Det-NO: 3 G. Det: 1 G. NO: 2 G. **1980** Was: 5 G; KR 1-0. **Total:** 21 G; KR 1-0.

GARY ANDERSON Anderson, Gary Wayne 6'0", 185 **RB-WB**
Col: Arkansas *HS:* Hickman [Columbia, MO] B: 4/18/1961, Columbia, MO *Drafted:* 1983 Round 1 SD
1986 SD: Pass 1-1 100.0%, 4 4.00 1 TD. **Total:** Pass 1-1 100.0%, 4 4.00 1 TD.

		Rushing				Receiving			
Year Team	G	Att	Yds	Avg	TD	Rec	Yds	Avg	TD
1985 SD	12	116	429	3.7	4	35	422	12.1	2
1986 SD	16	127	442	3.5	1	80	871	10.9	8
1987 SD	12	80	260	3.3	3	47	503	10.7	2
1988 SD	14	225	1119	5.0	3	32	182	5.7	0
1990 TB	16	166	646	3.9	3	38	464	12.2	2
1991 TB	16	72	263	3.7	1	25	184	7.4	0
1992 TB	15	55	194	3.5	1	34	284	8.4	0
1993 TB-Det	10	28	56	2.0	0	11	89	8.1	1
1993 TB	6	28	56	2.0	0	11	89	8.1	1
1993 Det	4	0	0	—	0	0	0	—	0
NFL Total	111	869	3409	3.9	16	302	2999	9.9	15

	Punt Returns				Kickoff Returns					Tot
Year Team	Ret	Yds	Avg	TD	Ret	Yds	Avg	TD	Fum	TD
1985 SD	0	0	—	0	13	302	23.2	1	5	7
1986 SD	25	227	9.1	0	24	482	20.1	0	5	9
1987 SD	0	0	—	0	22	433	19.7	0	4	5
1988 SD	0	0	—	0	0	0	—	0	5	3
1990 TB	0	0	—	0	6	123	20.5	0	7	5
1991 TB	0	0	—	0	34	643	18.9	0	4	1
1992 TB	6	45	7.5	0	29	564	19.4	0	3	1
1993 TB-Det	17	113	6.6	0	15	232	15.5	0	4	1
1993 TB	17	113	6.6	0	12	181	15.1	0	3	1
1993 Det	0	0	—	0	3	51	17.0	0	1	0
NFL Total	48	385	8.0	0	143	2779	19.4	1	37	32

HUNK ANDERSON Anderson, Heartley William 5'11", 191 **G-C**
Col: Notre Dame *HS:* Calumet [MI] B: 9/22/1898, Calumet, MI D: 4/24/1978, West Palm Beach, FL
1922 ChiB: 10 G. **1923** Cle-ChiB: 12 G. Cle: 1 G. ChiB: 11 G. **1924** ChiB: 10 G. **1925** ChiB: 8 G. **Total:** 40 G.

HERBIE ANDERSON Anderson, Herbert James 5'9", 183 **DB**
Col: Texas A&M–Kingsville *HS:* Thomas Jefferson [Port Arthur, TX] B: 11/19/1968, Port Arthur, TX *Drafted:* 1991 Round 10 Pho
1991 Hou: 1 G.

JAMAL ANDERSON Anderson, Jamal Sharif 5'11", 237 **RB**
Col: Utah *HS:* El Camino Real [Woodland Hills, CA] B: 9/30/1972, Woodland Hills, CA *Drafted:* 1994 Round 7 Atl
1997 Atl: Pass 4-1 25.0%, 27 6.75 1 TD 1 Int. **1998** Atl: Pass 2-0; Scor 1 2XP. **Total:** Pass 6-1 16.7%, 27 4.50 1 TD 1 Int; Scor 1 2XP.

		Rushing				Receiving			
Year Team	G	Att	Yds	Avg	TD	Rec	Yds	Avg	TD
1994 Atl	3	2	-1	-0.5	0	0	0	—	0
1995 Atl	16	39	161	4.1	1	4	42	10.5	0
1996 Atl	16	232	1055	4.5	5	49	473	9.7	1
1997 Atl	16	290	1002	3.5	7	29	284	9.8	3
1998 Atl	16	**410**	1846	4.5	14	27	319	11.8	2
NFL Total	67	973	4063	4.2	27	109	1118	10.3	6

	Kickoff Returns					Tot
Year Team	Ret	Yds	Avg	TD	Fum	TD
1994 Atl	1	11	11.0	0	0	0
1995 Atl	24	541	22.5	0	0	1
1996 Atl	4	80	20.0	0	4	6
1997 Atl	0	0	—	0	4	10
1998 Atl	0	0	—	0	5	16
NFL Total	29	632	21.8	0	13	33

CURTIS ANDERSON Anderson, Jerome Curtis 6'0", 193 DB
Col: Pittsburgh *HS:* E.C. Glass [Lynchburg, VA] B: 9/29/1973, Lynchburg, VA
1997 Jac: 9 G.

JERRY ANDERSON Anderson, Jerry 0 5'11", 198 DB
Col: Northeastern Oklahoma A&M (J.C.); Oklahoma *HS:* Murfreesboro [TN] B: 10/27/1953, Murfreesboro, TN D: 5/27/1989, Murfreesboro, TN *Drafted:* 1977 Round 4 Cin
1977 Cin: 14 G; PR 1-0; KR 8-129 16.1; 1 Fum. **1978** TB: 2 G. **Total:** 16 G; PR 1-0; KR 8-129 16.1; 1 Fum.

PRESTON ANDERSON Anderson, Jerry Preston 6'1", 183 DB
Col: Rice *HS:* Bonham [TX] B: 9/30/1951, Bonham, TX *Drafted:* 1974 Round 16 Cle
1974 Cle: 14 G.

JESSE ANDERSON Anderson, Jesse Lemond 6'2", 245 TE
Col: Mississippi State *HS:* West Point [MS] B: 7/26/1966, West Point, MS *Drafted:* 1990 Round 4 TB
1990 TB: 16 G; Rec 5-77 15.4. **1991** TB: 15 G; Rec 6-73 12.2 2 TD; 12 Pt. **1992** TB-Pit: 3 G. TB: 1 G. Pit: 2 G. **1993** NO: 1 G. **Total:** 35 G; Rec 11-150 13.6 2 TD; 12 Pt.

KEN ANDERSON Anderson, Kenneth Allan 6'2", 212 QB
(Kenny) *Col:* Augustana (Ill.) *HS:* Batavia [IL] B: 2/15/1949, Batavia, IL *Drafted:* 1971 Round 3 Cin

		Passing							
Year Team	G	Att	Comp	Comp%	Yds	YPA	TD	Int	Rating
1971 Cin	11	131	72	55.0	777	5.93	5	4	72.6
1972 Cin	13	301	171	56.8	1918	6.37	7	7	74.0
1973 Cin	14	329	179	54.4	2428	7.38	18	12	81.2
1974 Cin	13	328	**213**	**64.9**	**2667**	**8.13**	18	10	**95.7**
1975 Cin	13	377	228	60.5	**3169**	8.41	21	11	**93.9**
1976 Cin	14	338	179	53.0	2367	7.00	19	14	76.9
1977 Cin	14	323	166	51.4	2145	6.64	11	11	69.7
1978 Cin	12	319	173	54.2	2219	6.96	10	22	58.0
1979 Cin	15	339	189	55.8	2340	6.90	16	10	80.7
1980 Cin	13	275	166	60.4	1778	6.47	6	13	66.9
1981 Cin	16	479	300	62.6	3754	7.84	29	10	**98.4**
1982 Cin	9	309	**218**	**70.6**	2495	8.07	12	9	**95.3**
1983 Cin	13	297	198	**66.7**	2333	7.86	12	13	85.6
1984 Cin	11	275	175	63.6	2107	7.66	10	12	81.0
1985 Cin	3	32	16	50.0	170	5.31	2	0	86.7
1986 Cin	8	23	11	47.8	171	7.43	1	2	51.2
NFL Total	192	4475	2654	59.3	32838	7.34	197	160	81.9

	Rushing				
Year Team	Att	Yds	Avg	TD	Fum
1971 Cin	22	125	5.7	1	5
1972 Cin	22	94	4.3	3	5
1973 Cin	26	97	3.7	0	5
1974 Cin	43	314	7.3	2	3
1975 Cin	49	188	3.8	2	4
1976 Cin	31	134	4.3	1	3
1977 Cin	26	128	4.9	2	5
1978 Cin	29	167	5.8	1	8
1979 Cin	28	235	8.4	2	1
1980 Cin	16	122	7.6	0	1
1981 Cin	46	320	7.0	1	5
1982 Cin	25	85	3.4	4	1
1983 Cin	22	147	6.7	1	4
1984 Cin	11	64	5.8	0	1
1985 Cin	1	0	0.0	0	1
NFL Total	397	2220	5.6	20	52

KIM ANDERSON Anderson, Kim Sherwood 5'11", 183 DB
Col: Pasadena City Coll. CA (J.C.); Arizona State *HS:* Pasadena [CA] B: 7/19/1957, Pasadena, CA *Drafted:* 1979 Round 3 Bal
1980 Bal: PR 3-1 0.3; Int 2-35. **1981** Bal: Rush 1-0; PR 2-6 3.0; Int 1-49. **1982** Bal: Int 2-25. **1983** Bal: Int 2-81 1 TD; 0.5 Sac. **Total:** Rush 1-0; PR 5-7 1.4; Int 7-190 1 TD; 0.5 Sac.

		Kickoff Returns				
Year Team	G	Ret	Yds	Avg	TD	Fum
1980 Bal	16	20	386	19.3	0	4
1981 Bal	14	20	393	19.7	0	2
1982 Bal	9	0	0	—	0	0
1983 Bal	16	0	0	—	0	0
1984 Ind	1	0	0	—	0	0
NFL Total	56	40	779	19.5	0	6

LARRY ANDERSON Anderson, Lawrence Andrew 5'11", 183 DB
Col: Louisiana Tech *HS:* Neville [Monroe, LA] B: 9/25/1956, West Monore, LA *Drafted:* 1978 Round 4 Pit
1979 Pit: Int 1-19. **1983** Bal: Int 1-0; 1 Fum TD. **Total:** Int 2-19; 1 Fum TD.

		Punt Returns				Kickoff Returns					Tot
Year Team	G	Ret	Yds	Avg	TD	Ret	Yds	Avg	TD	Fum	TD
1978 Pit	16	0	0	—	0	37	930	25.1	**1**	2	1
1979 Pit	16	0	0	—	0	34	732	21.5	0	4	0
1980 Pit	4	0	0	—	0	14	379	27.1	0	0	0
1981 Pit	16	20	208	10.4	0	37	825	22.3	0	1	0
1982 Bal	9	8	54	6.8	0	27	517	19.1	0	2	0
1983 Bal	9	20	138	6.9	0	18	309	17.2	0	1	1
1984 Ind	12	27	182	6.7	0	22	525	23.9	0	4	0
NFL Total	82	75	582	7.8	0	189	4217	22.3	1	14	2

MARCUS ANDERSON Anderson, Marcus James 5'11", 178 WR
Col: Tulane *HS:* La Grange [Lake Charles, LA] B: 6/12/1959, Port Arthur, TX
1981 ChiB: 12 G; Rec 9-243 27.0 2 TD; KR 1-(-5) -5.0; 12 Pt; 1 Fum.

MAX ANDERSON Anderson, Max Arthur 5'8", 180 RB
Col: Trinity Valley CC TX; Arizona State *HS:* Mary A. Brown [Smithville, TX] B: 6/6/1945, Stockton, CA *Drafted:* 1968 Round 5 Buf
1968 Buf: Pass 1-0. **1969** Buf: PR 19-142 7.5. **Total:** Pass 1-0; PR 19-142 7.5.

		Rushing				Receiving			
Year Team	G	Att	Yds	Avg	TD	Rec	Yds	Avg	TD
1968 Buf	14	147	525	3.6	2	22	140	6.4	0
1969 Buf	11	13	74	5.7	1	7	65	9.3	0
NFL Total	25	160	599	3.7	3	29	205	7.1	0

	Kickoff Returns					Tot
Year Team	Ret	Yds	Avg	TD	Fum	TD
1968 Buf	**39**	**971**	24.9	**1**	3	3
1969 Buf	4	86	21.5	0	1	1
NFL Total	43	1057	24.6	1	4	4

MEL ANDERSON Anderson, Melvin Anthony 5'11", 175 WR
Col: Minnesota *HS:* Steel Valley [Munhall, PA] B: 8/29/1965
1987 Pit: 2 G; PR 7-38 5.4; KR 1-8 8.0.

OCKIE ANDERSON Anderson, Oscar Carl 5'9", 165 TB-BB-WB
Col: Colgate *HS:* Erie Central [PA] B: 10/15/1894, Erie, PA D: 1/25/1962, Buffalo, NY
1920 Buf: 11 G. **1921** Buf: 11 G; Pass 1 TD; Rush 5 TD; Rec 1 TD; PR **1** TD; Tot TD **7**; 42 Pt. **1922** Buf: 7 G; Rec 1 TD; 6 Pt. **Total:** 29 G; Pass 1 TD; Rush 5 TD; Rec 2 TD; PR 1 TD; Tot TD 8; 48 Pt.

OTTIS ANDERSON Anderson, Ottis Jerome 6'2", 220 RB
(O.J.) *Col:* Miami (Fla.) *HS:* Forest Hill [West Palm Beach, FL] B: 1/19/1957, West Palm Beach, FL *Drafted:* 1979 Round 1 StL
1979 StL: Pass 1-0. **Total:** Pass 1-0.

		Rushing				Receiving					Tot
Year Team	G	Att	Yds	Avg	TD	Rec	Yds	Avg	TD	Fum	TD
1979 StL	16	331	1605	4.8	8	41	308	7.5	2	10	10
1980 StL	16	301	1352	4.5	9	36	308	8.6	0	5	9
1981 StL	16	328	1376	4.2	9	51	387	7.6	0	13	9
1982 StL	8	145	587	4.0	3	14	106	7.6	0	2	3
1983 StL	15	296	1270	4.3	5	54	459	8.5	1	10	6
1984 StL	15	289	1174	4.1	6	70	611	8.7	2	8	8
1985 StL	9	117	479	4.1	4	23	225	9.8	0	3	4
1986 StL-NYG	12	75	237	3.2	3	19	137	7.2	0	2	3
1986 StL	4	51	156	3.1	2	10	91	9.1	0	2	2
1986 NYG	8	24	81	3.4	1	9	46	5.1	0	0	1
1987 NYG	4	2	6	3.0	0	2	16	8.0	0	0	0
1988 NYG	16	65	208	3.2	8	9	57	6.3	0	0	8
1989 NYG	16	325	1023	3.1	14	28	268	9.6	0	2	14
1990 NYG	16	225	784	3.5	11	18	139	7.7	0	1	11
1991 NYG	10	53	141	2.7	1	11	41	3.7	0	0	1
1992 NYG	13	10	31	3.1	0	0	0	—	0	0	0
NFL Total	182	2562	10273	4.0	81	376	3062	8.1	5	56	86

PAUL ANDERSON Anderson, Paul Theodore 6'0", 200 G
(Andy) *Col:* Illinois *HS:* Rock Island [IL] B: 2/6/1902, Rock Island, IL D: 11/30/1970, Berryville, AR
1925 RI: 1 G.

RALPH ANDERSON Anderson, Ralph Edward 6'2", 180 DB
(Sticks) *Col:* West Texas A&M *HS:* Lincoln [Dallas, TX] B: 4/3/1949, Dalls, TX *Drafted:* 1971 Round 5 Pit
1971 Pit: 7 G; Int 1-14. **1972** Pit: 14 G; Int 3-68; Scor **1** Saf; 2 Pt. **1973** NE: 13 G; Int 2-3. **Total:** 34 G; Int 6-85; Scor 1 Saf; 2 Pt.

RALPH ANDERSON Anderson, Ralph M 6'4", 223 OE
Col: Santa Monica Coll. CA (J.C.); Los Angeles State *HS:* Alexander Hamilton [Los Angeles, CA] B: 1/1/1937, Long Beach, CA D: 11/26/1960, Los Angeles, CA *Drafted:* 1958 Round 9 ChiB

		Receiving				
Year Team	G	Rec	Yds	Avg	TD	Fum
1958 ChiB	12	11	177	16.1	1	1

1960 LAC	10	44	614	14.0	5	0
NFL Total	22	55	791	14.4	6	1

RICHIE ANDERSON Anderson, Richard Darnoll 6′2″, 223 **RB**
Col: Penn State *HS:* Sherwood [Sandy Spring, MD] B: 9/13/1971, Sandy Spring, MD *Drafted:* 1993 Round 6 NYJ
1993 NYJ: KR 4-66 16.5. **1994** NYJ: KR 3-43 14.3. **1995** NYJ: Pass 1-0.
Total: Pass 1-0; KR 7-109 15.6.

		Rushing				Receiving					Tot
Year Team	**G**	**Att**	**Yds**	**Avg**	**TD**	**Rec**	**Yds**	**Avg**	**TD**	**Fum**	**TD**
1993 NYJ	7	0	0	—	0	0	0	—	0	1	0
1994 NYJ	13	43	207	4.8	1	25	212	8.5	1	1	2
1995 NYJ	10	5	17	3.4	0	5	26	5.2	0	2	0
1996 NYJ	16	47	150	3.2	1	44	385	8.8	0	0	1
1997 NYJ	16	21	70	3.3	0	26	150	5.8	1	2	1
1998 NYJ	8	1	2	2.0	0	3	12	4.0	0	0	0
NFL Total	70	117	446	3.8	2	103	785	7.6	2	6	4

DICK ANDERSON Anderson, Richard Joseph 6′5″, 245 **OT**
Col: Ohio State *HS:* Lodi [OH] B: 1/26/1944, Massillon, OH
1967 NO: 2 G; Scor **1** Saf; 2 Pt.

DICK ANDERSON Anderson, Richard Paul 6′2″, 196 **DB**
Col: Colorado *HS:* Boulder [CO] B: 2/10/1946, Midland, MI
Drafted: 1968 Round 3 Mia
1968 Mia: KR 6-106 17.7. **1969** Mia: Rec 1-8 8.0; Punt 5-188 37.6.
1970 Mia: KR 1-8 8.0. **1972** Mia: Punt 4-147 36.8; **1** Fum TD.
Total: Rec 1-8 8.0; KR 7-114 16.3; Punt 9-335 37.2; 1 Fum TD.

		Punt Returns				Interceptions				Tot
Year Team	**G**	**Ret**	**Yds**	**Avg**	**TD**	**Int**	**Yds**	**TD**	**Fum**	**TD**
1968 Mia	14	5	18	3.6	0	8	**230**	1	1	1
1969 Mia	14	12	82	6.8	0	3	106	0	1	0
1970 Mia	14	1	6	6.0	0	8	**191**	0	1	0
1971 Mia	14	8	114	14.3	0	2	33	0	1	0
1972 Mia	14	5	19	3.8	0	3	34	0	1	1
1973 Mia	14	6	52	8.7	0	**8**	163	**2**	0	2
1974 Mia	14	3	9	3.0	0	1	3	0	0	0
1976 Mia	9	2	21	10.5	0	1	32	0	0	0
1977 Mia	14	4	3	0.8	0	0	0	0	0	0
NFL Total	121	46	324	7.0	0	34	792	3	5	4

RICKEY ANDERSON Anderson, Rickey Recardo 6′1″, 211 **RB**
Col: South Carolina State *HS:* Kingsland [GA] B: 3/21/1953, Kingsland, GA *Drafted:* 1978 Round 3 SD
1978 SD: 16 G; Rush 3-11 3.7; Rec 1-(-3) -3.0; KR 6-83 13.8.

BOBBY ANDERSON Anderson, Robert Conrad 6′0″, 208 **RB**
Col: Colorado *HS:* Boulder [CO] B: 10/11/1947, Midland, MI
Drafted: 1970 Round 1 Den
1970 Den: Pass 7-4 57.1%, 59 8.43. **1971** Den: Pass 3-1 33.3%, 48 16.00. **1972** Den: Pass 3-1 33.3%, 14 4.67 1 TD. **1973** Den: Pass 3-2 66.7%, 47 15.67. **1975** NE-Was: Pass 1-0. Was: Pass 1-0.
Total: Pass 17-8 47.1%, 168 9.88 1 TD.

		Rushing				Receiving			
Year Team	**G**	**Att**	**Yds**	**Avg**	**TD**	**Rec**	**Yds**	**Avg**	**TD**
1970 Den	14	83	368	4.4	4	9	140	15.6	0
1971 Den	13	139	533	3.8	3	37	353	9.5	1
1972 Den	9	72	319	4.4	1	23	215	9.3	1
1973 Den	12	19	61	3.2	1	15	153	10.2	0
1975 NE-Was	6	1	1	1.0	0	0	0	—	0
1975 NE	5	1	1	1.0	0	0	0	—	0
1975 Was	1	0	0	—	0	0	0	—	0
NFL Total	54	314	1282	4.1	9	84	861	10.3	2

	Kickoff Returns					Tot
Year Team	**Ret**	**Yds**	**Avg**	**TD**	**Fum**	**TD**
1970 Den	21	520	24.8	0	1	4
1971 Den	8	187	23.4	0	6	4
1972 Den	1	13	13.0	0	2	2
1973 Den	0	0	—	0	0	1
NFL Total	30	720	24.0	0	9	11

BOB ANDERSON Anderson, Robert Paul 6′2″, 215 **HB**
Col: Army *HS:* Cocoa [FL] B: 3/31/1938, Elizabeth, NJ *Drafted:* 1960 Round 9 NYG
1963 NYG: 1 G; Rush 1-(-2) -2.0.

ROGER ANDERSON Anderson, Roger Cole 6′5″, 265 **DT-OT**
(Big Red) *Col:* Virginia Union *HS:* Oxford [NC] B: 11/11/1942, Bedford, VA *Drafted:* 1964 Round 7 NYG
1964 NYG: 11 G. **1965** NYG: 8 G. **1967** NYG: 4 G. **1968** NYG: 14 G; Int 1-0. **Total:** 37 G; Int 1-0.

JOHN ANDERSON Anderson, Roger John 6′3″, 226 **LB**
Col: Michigan *HS:* South [Waukesha, WI] B: 2/14/1956, Waukesha, WI
Drafted: 1978 Round 1 GB
1979 GB: Scor 4, 1-1 100.0% FG, 1-2 50.0% XK. **1982** GB: 0.5 Sac.
1983 GB: 4.5 Sac. **1984** GB: 3.5 Sac. **1985** GB: KR 1-14 14.0; 6 Sac.
1987 GB: 4 Sac. **1988** GB: 1 Sac. **Total:** KR 1-14 14.0; Scor 10, 1-1 100.0% FG, 1-2 50.0% XK; 19.5 Sac.

		Interceptions		
Year Team	**G**	**Int**	**Yds**	**TD**
1978 GB	13	5	27	0
1979 GB	7	0	0	0
1980 GB	9	0	0	0
1981 GB	16	3	12	0
1982 GB	9	3	22	0
1983 GB	16	5	54	1
1984 GB	16	3	24	0
1985 GB	16	2	2	0
1986 GB	4	1	3	0
1987 GB	12	2	22	0
1988 GB	14	0	0	0
1989 GB	14	1	1	0
NFL Total	146	25	167	1

RONNIE ANDERSON Anderson, Ronnie Derrell 6′1″, 189 **WR**
Col: Allegheny *HS:* University School [Hunting Valley, OH]
B: 2/27/1974, Cleveland, OH
1998 Ariz: 4 G; Rec 1-8 8.0.

STEVIE ANDERSON Anderson, Stevie 6′5″, 215 **WR**
Col: Grambling State *HS:* Jonesboro-Hodge [Jonesboro, LA]
B: 5/12/1970, Monroe, LA *Drafted:* 1993 Round 8 Pho
1994 NYJ: 10 G; Rec 9-90 10.0. **1995** Ariz: 5 G; Rec 3-34 11.3 1 TD; KR 1-17 17.0; Scor 2 2XP; 10 Pt. **1996** Ariz: 8 G; Rec 4-64 16.0.
Total: 23 G; Rec 16-188 11.8 1 TD; KR 1-17 17.0; Scor 2 2XP; 10 Pt.

STUART ANDERSON Anderson, Stuart Noel 6′1″, 238 **LB**
Col: Virginia *HS:* Cardinal [Mathews, VA] B: 12/25/1959, Mathews, VA
Drafted: 1982 Round 4 KC
1982 Was: 2 G; KR 1-7 7.0. **1983** Was: 16 G. **1984** Was-Cle: 6 G. Was: 2 G. Cle: 4 G. **1985** Was: 16 G. **Total:** 40 G; KR 1-7 7.0.

TAZ ANDERSON Anderson, Tazwell Leigh Jr. 6′2″, 220 **TE**
Col: Georgia Tech *HS:* Savannah [GA] B: 11/15/1938, Savannah, GA
Drafted: 1960 Round 7 Cle
1961 StL: Rush 15-39 2.6 1 TD. **1962** StL: KR 1-6 6.0. **Total:** Rush 15-39 2.6 1 TD; KR 1-6 6.0.

		Receiving					Tot
Year Team	**G**	**Rec**	**Yds**	**Avg**	**TD**	**Fum**	**TD**
1961 StL	14	22	399	18.1	2	1	3
1962 StL	14	35	535	15.3	3	0	3
1963 StL	5	5	47	9.4	0	0	0
1964 StL	13	7	60	8.6	0	0	0
1966 Atl	8	10	195	19.5	3	0	3
1967 Atl	8	8	99	12.4	1	0	1
NFL Total	62	87	1335	15.3	9	1	10

TERRY ANDERSON Anderson, Terry C 5′9″, 182 **WR**
Col: Bethune-Cookman *HS:* Dorchester [Boston, MA] B: 1/10/1955, Eastover, SC *Drafted:* 1977 Round 12 Mia
1977 Mia: 11 G; Rush 1-11 11.0; PR 1-6 6.0; KR 7-167 23.9.
1978 Mia-Was: 14 G; Rec 1-56 56.0; PR 5-47 9.4; KR 10-227 22.7. Mia: 4 G; KR 7-157 22.4. Was: 10 G; Rec 1-56 56.0; PR 5-47 9.4; KR 3-70 23.3. **1980** SF: 4 G; KR 6-104 17.3; 2 Fum. **Total:** 29 G; Rush 1-11 11.0; Rec 1-56 56.0; PR 6-53 8.8; KR 23-498 21.7; 2 Fum.

VICKEY RAY ANDERSON Anderson, Vickey Ray 6′0″, 205 **RB**
Col: Oklahoma *HS:* Classen [Oklahoma City, OK] B: 5/3/1956, Oklahoma City, OK
1980 GB: 7 G; Rush 4-5 1.3; Rec 2-2 1.0; 1 Fum.

BILL ANDERSON Anderson, Walter William 6′3″, 211 **OE-TE**
Col: Tennessee *HS:* Manatee [Bradenton, FL] B: 7/16/1936, Hendersonville, NC *Drafted:* 1958 Round 3 Was
1960 Was: Rush 1-6 6.0. **1961** Was: Rush 3-5 1.7. **1962** Was: Punt 7-235 33.6. **1963** Was: Pass 1-0, 1 Int. **Total:** Pass 1-0, 1 Int; Rush 4-11 2.8; Punt 7-235 33.6.

		Receiving				
Year Team	**G**	**Rec**	**Yds**	**Avg**	**TD**	**Fum**
1958 Was	12	18	396	22.0	2	0
1959 Was	11	35	734	21.0	6	2
1960 Was	12	38	488	12.8	3	1
1961 Was	14	40	637	15.9	0	1
1962 Was	12	23	386	16.8	2	1
1963 Was	13	14	288	20.6	1	0
1965 GB	14	8	105	13.1	1	0
1966 GB	10	2	14	7.0	0	0
NFL Total	98	178	3048	17.1	15	5

WARREN ANDERSON Anderson, Warren 6′2″, 195 **WR**
Col: West Virginia State *HS:* James Blair [Williamsburg, VA]
B: 7/3/1955, Williamsburg, VA *Drafted:* 1977 Round 4 Hou
1977 Hou: 8 G; KR 8-182 22.8. **1978** StL: 2 G. **Total:** 10 G; KR 8-182 22.8.

WILL ANDERSON Anderson, Willard August 5'10", 173 **FB-BB-TB**
Col: Syracuse *HS:* Muskegon [MI] B: 5/5/1897, Muskegon, MI
D: 4/24/1982, Hinsdale, IL
1923 Roch: 1 G. **1924** Roch: 3 G. **Total:** 4 G.

BILLY ANDERSON Anderson, William 6'0", 198 **HB-DB**
Col: Compton CC CA *HS:* Susan Miller Dorsey [Los Angeles, CA]
B: 3/3/1929, Los Angeles, CA *Drafted:* 1953 Round 1 ChiB
1953 ChiB: 12 G; Rec 3-33 11.0; PR 1-7 7.0; KR 5-127 25.4; Punt 1-46 46.0. **1954** ChiB: 7 G; Rush 3-8 2.7; KR 1-15 15.0; 1 Fum. **Total:** 19 G; Rush 3-8 2.7; Rec 3-33 11.0; PR 1-7 7.0; KR 6-142 23.7; Punt 1-46 46.0; 1 Fum.

BILL ANDERSON Anderson, William H 6'2", 190 **DE**
Col: West Virginia *HS:* Triadelphia [Wheeling, WV] B: 1/6/1921, Triadelphia, WV D: 4/1984, Wheeling, WV
1945 Bos: 6 G.

WILLIAM ANDERSON Anderson, William Tim 6'0", 205 **DB**
Col: Ohio State *HS:* Follansbee [WV] B: 8/1/1949, Colliers, WV
Drafted: 1971 Round 1 SF
1975 SF: 13 G. **1976** Buf: 2 G. **Total:** 15 G.

WILLIE ANDERSON Anderson, Willie Aaron 6'5", 340 **OT**
Col: Auburn *HS:* C.F. Vigor [Prichard, AL] B: 7/11/1975, Whistler, AL
Drafted: 1996 Round 1 Cin
1996 Cin: 16 G. **1997** Cin: 16 G. **1998** Cin: 16 G. **Total:** 48 G.

FLIPPER ANDERSON Anderson, Willie Lee Jr. 6'0", 175 **WR**
Col: UCLA *HS:* Paulsboro [NJ] B: 3/7/1965, Paulsboro, NJ
Drafted: 1988 Round 2 LARm
1989 LARm: Rush 1-(-1) -1.0. **1990** LARm: Rush 1-13 13.0. **1992** LARm: KR 1-9 9.0. **1994** LARm: Rush 1-11 11.0. **Total:** Rush 3-23 7.7; KR 1-9 9.0.

		Receiving				
Year Team	G	Rec	Yds	Avg	TD	Fum
1988 LARm	16	11	319	29.0	0	0
1989 LARm	16	44	1146	**26.0**	5	0
1990 LARm	16	51	1097	**21.5**	4	0
1991 LARm	12	32	530	16.6	1	2
1992 LARm	15	38	657	17.3	7	1
1993 LARm	15	37	552	14.9	4	0
1994 LARm	16	46	945	20.5	5	0
1995 Ind	2	8	111	13.9	2	0
1996 Was	2	0	0	—	0	0
1997 Den	4	0	0	—	0	0
NFL Total	114	267	5357	20.1	28	3

WINNIE ANDERSON Anderson, Winston Donley 6'0", 185 **OE-DE**
Col: Colgate *HS:* Manlius [NY] B: 11/10/1909, Charleston, WV
D: 11/11/1950, Columbus, OH
1936 NYG: 5 G; Rec 7-74 10.6.

ERIC ANDOLSEK Andolsek, Eric Thomas 6'2", 284 **OG**
Col: Louisiana State *HS:* Thibodaux [LA] B: 8/22/1966, Thibodaux, LA
D: 6/23/1992, Thibodaux, LA *Drafted:* 1988 Round 5 Det
1988 Det: 13 G; KR 1-3 3.0. **1989** Det: 16 G. **1990** Det: 16 G; KR 1-12 12.0. **1991** Det: 16 G. **Total:** 61 G; KR 2-15 7.5.

STEVE ANDRAKO Andrako, Stephen Francis 6'0", 210 **C-LB**
Col: Ohio State *HS:* North Braddock [PA] B: 9/11/1915, Braddock, PA
D: 11/30/1980, Half Moon Bay, CA *Drafted:* 1940 Round 15 Was
1940 Was: 5 G.

AL ANDREWS Andrews, Alvin Wayne 6'3", 216 **LB**
Col: Laney Coll. CA (J.C.); New Mexico State *HS:* Oakland Technical [CA] B: 7/10/1945, Oakland, CA
1970 Buf: 8 G; KR 1-16 16.0. **1971** Buf: 14 G; Int 1-0. **Total:** 22 G; KR 1-16 16.0; Int 1-0.

GEORGE ANDREWS Andrews, George Eldon II 6'3", 226 **LB**
Col: Nebraska *HS:* Harry A. Burke [Omaha, NE] B: 11/28/1955, Omaha, NE *Drafted:* 1979 Round 1 LARm
1979 LARm: 16 G; Rec 1-2 2.0. **1980** LARm: 13 G. **1981** LARm: 15 G. **1982** LARm: 9 G; 3 Sac. **1983** LARm: 16 G; Int 1-22; 3 Sac. **1984** LARm: 11 G; 6 Sac. **Total:** 80 G; Rec 1-2 2.0; Int 1-22; 12 Sac.

J.B. ANDREWS Andrews, J.B. 208 **WB-DB**
Col: Texas-El Paso B: 5/10/1912, Dallas, TX
1934 StL: 2 G; Pass 19-8 42.1%, 97 5.11 1 Int; Rush 10-52 5.2.

JOHN ANDREWS Andrews, John Milton 6'3", 227 **TE-RB**
Col: Indiana *HS:* Shortridge [Indianapolis, IN] B: 11/2/1948, Indianapolis, IN *Drafted:* 1971 Round 5 Bal
1972 SD: 1 G. **1973** Bal: 8 G; Rec 1-1 1.0 1 TD; KR 1-13 13.0; 6 Pt. **1974** Bal: 14 G; Rush 5-6 1.2; KR 1-18 18.0. **Total:** 23 G; Rush 5-6 1.2; Rec 1-1 1.0 1 TD; KR 2-31 15.5; 6 Pt.

JOHN ANDREWS Andrews, John V Jr. 6'5", 251 **DE-DT**
Col: Morgan State *HS:* Mumford [Detroit, MI] B: 11/7/1951, Detroit, MI
Drafted: 1973 Round 7 Det
1975 Mia: 14 G. **1976** Mia: 14 G. **Total:** 28 G.

ROY ANDREWS Andrews, Leroy B 6'0", 226 **G-BB-T-OE**
(Bull) *Col:* Pittsburg State B: 1898 Deceased
1923 StL: 5 G. **1924** KC: 8 G; Pass 1 TD; Scor 4, 1 FG, 1 XK. **1925** KC: 7 G; Scor 4, 1 FG, 1 XK. **1926** KC: 8 G; Scor 1, 1 XK. **1927** Cle: 2 G. **Total:** 30 G; Pass 1 TD; Scor 9, 2 FG, 3 XK.

MITCH ANDREWS Andrews, Mitchell Dean 6'2", 239 **TE**
Col: Louisiana State *HS:* H.L. Bourgeois [Gray, LA] B: 3/4/1964, Houma, LA
1987 Den: 8 G; Rec 4-53 13.3.

RICKY ANDREWS Andrews, Richard Guy 6'2", 236 **LB**
Col: Washington *HS:* University [Mililani, HI] B: 4/14/1966, Western Samoa *Drafted:* 1989 Round 10 SD
1990 Sea: 15 G.

TOM ANDREWS Andrews, Thomas Edward 6'4", 265 **OT-C**
Col: Louisville *HS:* Padua Franciscan [Parma, OH] B: 1/11/1962, Parma, OH *Drafted:* 1984 Round 4 ChiB
1984 ChiB: 7 G. **1985** ChiB: 14 G. **1987** Sea: 2 G. **Total:** 23 G.

BILLY ANDREWS Andrews, William Doughty Jr. 6'0", 220 **LB**
Col: Southeastern Louisiana *HS:* Clinton [LA] B: 6/14/1945, Clinton, LA *Drafted:* 1967 Round 13 Cle
1967 Cle: 14 G. **1968** Cle: 14 G; KR 1-0; 1 Fum. **1969** Cle: 14 G. **1970** Cle: 14 G; Int 1-25 1 TD; 6 Pt. **1971** Cle: 14 G; Int 3-34. **1972** Cle: 14 G; Int 1-4. **1973** Cle: 5 G. **1974** Cle: 11 G; Int 1-18. **1975** SD: 14 G; KR 6-93 15.5. **1976** KC: 14 G; PR 1-38 38.0; Int 1-11. **1977** KC: 14 G. **Total:** 142 G; PR 1-38 38.0; KR 7-93 13.3; Int 7-92 1 TD; 6 Pt; 1 Fum.

WILLIAM ANDREWS Andrews, William L 6'0", 206 **RB**
Col: Auburn *HS:* Thomasville [GA] B: 12/25/1955, Thomasville, GA
Drafted: 1979 Round 3 Atl
1983 Atl: Pass 1-0. **1986** Atl: KR 4-71 17.8. **Total:** Pass 1-0; KR 4-71 17.8.

		Rushing				Receiving					Tot
Year Team	G	Att	Yds	Avg	TD	Rec	Yds	Avg	TD	Fum	TD
1979 Atl	15	239	1023	4.3	3	39	309	7.9	2	5	5
1980 Atl	16	265	1308	4.9	4	51	456	8.9	1	6	5
1981 Atl	16	289	1301	4.5	10	81	735	9.1	2	12	12
1982 Atl	9	139	573	4.1	5	42	503	12.0	2	1	7
1983 Atl	16	331	1567	4.7	7	59	609	10.3	4	6	11
1986 Atl	15	52	214	4.1	1	5	35	7.0	0	0	1
NFL Total	87	1315	5986	4.6	30	277	2647	9.6	11	30	41

GEORGE ANDRIE Andrie, George Joseph 6'6", 250 **DE**
Col: Marquette *HS:* Catholic Central [Grand Rapids, MI] B: 4/20/1940, Grand Rapids, MI *Drafted:* 1962 Round 6 Dal
1962 Dal: 14 G. **1963** Dal: 12 G. **1964** Dal: 14 G. **1965** Dal: 14 G; **1** Fum TD; 6 Pt. **1966** Dal: 14 G; Int 1-6 1 TD; 6 Pt. **1967** Dal: 14 G. **1968** Dal: 14 G. **1969** Dal: 14 G; Scor **1** Saf; 2 Pt. **1970** Dal: 14 G. **1971** Dal: 14 G. **1972** Dal: 3 G. **Total:** 141 G; Int 1-6 1 TD; Scor 1 Saf; 1 Fum TD; Tot TD 2; 14 Pt.

PLATO ANDROS Andros, Plato Gus 6'0", 240 **OG-DG-OT**
Col: Oklahoma *HS:* Central [Oklahoma City, OK] B: 11/28/1921, Oklahoma City, OK
1947 ChiC: 12 G. **1948** ChiC: 12 G. **1949** ChiC: 12 G. **1950** ChiC: 9 G. **Total:** 45 G.

TEDDY ANDRULEWICZ Andrulewicz, Theodore Stanislaus 5'11", 175 **WB**
(Tuffy) *Col:* Villanova *HS:* Mount Carmel [PA] B: 1/1/1905, Mount Carmel, PA D: 1/3/1996, Whitehall, PA
1930 Nwk: 11 G; Rec 1 TD; 6 Pt.

LOU ANDRUS Andrus, Louis John 6'6", 230 **LB**
Col: Brigham Young *HS:* Granite [Salt Lake City, UT] B: 7/10/1943, Murray, UT *Drafted:* 1967 Round 11 Den
1967 Den: 8 G.

SHELDON ANDRUS Andrus, Sheldon James Jr. 6'2", 271 **DT**
Col: Nicholls State *HS:* Port Barre [LA] B: 10/5/1962, Lafayette, LA
1986 NO: 1 G. **1987** NO: 3 G. **Total:** 4 G.

SIG ANDRUSKING Andrusking, Sigmond 5'8", 187 **G**
Col: Detroit Mercy *HS:* East [Erie, PA] B: 1914, Erie, PA
1937 Bkn: 7 G.

ZENON ANDRUSYSHYN Andrusyshyn, Zenon 6'2", 210 **P-K**
Col: UCLA *HS:* Oakville-Trafalgar [Oakville, Canada] B: 2/25/1947, Gunzburg, Germany *Drafted:* 1970 Round 9 Dal
1978 KC: Rush 1-0.

		Punting			
Year Team	G	Punts	Yds	Avg	Fum
1978 KC	16	79	3247	41.1	1

JOSEPH ANDRUZZI Andruzzi, Joseph Dominick 6'3", 310 **OG**
Col: Southern Connecticut State *HS:* Tottenville [Staten Island, NY]
B: 8/23/1975, Brooklyn, NY
1998 GB: 15 G.

CHARLIE ANE Ane, Charles Teetai III 6'1", 233 **C**
Col: Michigan State *HS:* Punahou School [Honolulu, HI] B: 8/12/1952, Los Angeles, CA
1975 KC: 14 G. **1976** KC: 14 G. **1977** KC: 14 G. **1978** KC: 16 G; 1 Fum. **1979** KC: 16 G. **1980** KC: 16 G. **1981** GB: 15 G. **Total:** 105 G; 1 Fum.

CHARLIE ANE Ane, Charles Teetai Jr. 6'2", 260 **OT-C**
Col: Compton CC CA; USC *HS:* Punahou School [Honolulu, HI] B: 1/25/1931, Honolulu, HI *Drafted:* 1953 Round 4 Det
1953 Det: 12 G. **1954** Det: 12 G. **1955** Det: 12 G. **1956** Det: 12 G; KR 1-19 19.0. **1957** Det: 12 G. **1958** Det: 12 G. **1959** Det: 11 G; Rush 0-10. **Total:** 83 G; Rush 0-10; KR 1-19 19.0.

JIM ANGELO Angelo, James Anthony 6'3", 275 **OG**
Col: Indiana (Pa.) *HS:* Indiana [PA] B: 8/23/1963, Pittsburgh, PA
1987 Phi: 1 G.

ELMER ANGSMAN Angsman, Elmer Joseph Jr. 5'11", 200 **HB**
(Bud) *Col:* Notre Dame *HS:* Mount Carmel [Chicago, IL] B: 12/11/1925, Chicago, IL *Drafted:* 1946 Round 3 ChiC
1946 ChiC: Pass 1-0; KR 1-13 13.0. **1947** ChiC: KR 2-17 8.5. **1949** ChiC: Pass 1-0; KR 5-66 13.2. **1951** ChiC: KR 2-51 25.5. **Total:** Pass 2-0; KR 10-147 14.7.

		Rushing				Receiving					Tot
Year Team	G	Att	Yds	Avg	TD	Rec	Yds	Avg	TD	Fum	TD
1946 ChiC	11	48	328	6.8	2	2	44	22.0	0	2	2
1947 ChiC	12	110	412	3.7	7	5	138	27.6	1	5	8
1948 ChiC	12	131	638	4.9	8	9	142	15.8	1	5	9
1949 ChiC	12	125	674	5.4	6	5	57	11.4	0	4	6
1950 ChiC	12	102	362	3.5	1	7	56	8.0	1	3	2
1951 ChiC	12	121	380	3.1	3	9	195	21.7	1	6	4
1952 ChiC	12	46	114	2.5	0	4	22	5.5	1	1	1
NFL Total	83	683	2908	4.3	27	41	654	16.0	5	26	32

SCOTT ANKROM Ankrom, Scott Randall 6'1", 194 **WR**
Col: Texas Christian *HS:* John Jay [San Antonio, TX] B: 1/4/1966, San Antonio, TX *Drafted:* 1989 Round 12 Dal
1989 Dal: 10 G; KR 2-6 3.0; 1 Fum.

DUNC ANNAN Annan, Duncan Colin 5'10", 178 **WB-TB-FB-BB**
Col: Brown; Chicago *HS:* Hyde Park [Chicago, IL]; Keewatin Acad.[Chicago, IL]; Univ. HS [Chicago, IL] B: 8/10/1895, Chicago, IL D: 6/21/1981, Palm Beach, FL
1920 ChiT: 8 G. **1922** Tol: 9 G; Rush 2 TD; Rec **2** TD; Int 1 TD; Scor **1** 1XP; Tot TD 5; 31 Pt. **1923** Ham: 2 G. **1924** Ham: 5 G. **1925** Ham-Akr: 12 G. Ham: 2 G. Akr: 10 G; Rush 1 TD; 6 Pt. **1926** Ham-Akr: 7 G. Ham: 3 G. Akr: 4 G. **Total:** 43 G; Rush 3 TD; Rec 2 TD; Int 1 TD; Scor 1 1XP; Tot TD 6; 37 Pt.

SAM ANNO Anno, Samuel Scott-Griffin 6'2", 236 **LB**
Col: USC *HS:* Santa Monica [CA] B: 1/26/1965, Silver Spring, MD
1987 LARm-Min: 9 G. LARm: 3 G. Min: 6 G. **1988** Min: 13 G. **1989** TB: 16 G. **1990** TB: 16 G. **1991** TB: 16 G. **1992** SD: 16 G. **1993** SD: 16 G. **Total:** 102 G.

CHARLES ANTHONY Anthony, Charles Raymond 6'1", 230 **LB**
Col: USC *HS:* Edison [Fresno, CA] B: 7/10/1952, Houston, TX *Drafted:* 1974 Round 15 SD
1974 SD: 13 G; Int 1-23.

EDWARD ANTHONY Anthony, Edward Tyrone 5'11", 212 **RB**
Col: North Carolina *HS:* West Forsyth [Clemmons, NC] B: 3/3/1962, Winston-Salem, NC *Drafted:* 1984 Round 3 NO

		Rushing				Receiving			
Year Team	G	Att	Yds	Avg	TD	Rec	Yds	Avg	TD
1984 NO	15	20	105	5.3	1	12	113	9.4	0
1985 NO	16	17	65	3.8	0	28	185	6.6	0
NFL Total	31	37	170	4.6	1	40	298	7.5	0

	Kickoff Returns				
Year Team	Ret	Yds	Avg	TD	Fum
1984 NO	22	490	22.3	0	1
1985 NO	23	476	20.7	0	0
NFL Total	45	966	21.5	0	1

REIDEL ANTHONY Anthony, Reidel Clarence 5'11", 178 **WR**
Col: Florida *HS:* Glades Central [Belle Glade, FL] B: 10/20/1976, Pahokee, FL *Drafted:* 1997 Round 1 TB
1997 TB: Rush 5-84 16.8. **1998** TB: Rush 4-43 10.8; Scor 1 2XP. **Total:** Rush 9-127 14.1; Scor 1 2XP.

		Receiving				Kickoff Returns			
Year Team	G	Rec	Yds	Avg	TD	Ret	Yds	Avg	TD
1997 TB	16	35	448	12.8	4	25	592	23.7	0
1998 TB	15	51	708	13.9	7	46	1118	24.3	0
NFL Total	31	86	1156	13.4	11	71	1710	24.1	0

TERRY ANTHONY Anthony, Terrence 6'0", 200 **WR**
Col: Florida State *HS:* Mainland [Daytona Beach, FL] B: 3/9/1968, Daytona Beach, FL *Drafted:* 1990 Round 11 TB
1990 TB: 1 G. **1991** TB: 9 G; Rec 4-51 12.8. **Total:** 10 G; Rec 4-51 12.8.

TERRENCE ANTHONY Anthony, Terrence Everett 5'10", 183 **DB**
Col: Iowa State *HS:* Assumption [East St. Louis, IL] B: 1/17/1965, East St. Louis, IL *Drafted:* 1987 Round 9 Atl
1987 StL: 1 G.

LIONEL ANTOINE Antoine, Lionel Sylvester 6'6", 262 **OT**
Col: Southern Illinois *HS:* M.F. Nichols [Biloxi MS] B: 8/31/1950, Biloxi, MS *Drafted:* 1972 Round 1 ChiB
1972 ChiB: 5 G. **1973** ChiB: 13 G. **1974** ChiB: 14 G. **1975** ChiB: 14 G. **1976** ChiB: 13 G. **1978** ChiB: 9 G. **Total:** 68 G.

GLENN ANTRUM Antrum, Glenn 5'11", 175 **WR**
Col: Connecticut *HS:* Ansonia [CT] B: 2/3/1966, Derby, CT
1989 NE: 1 G.

HOUSTON ANTWINE Antwine, Houston 6'0", 270 **DT**
Col: Southern Illinois *HS:* Manassas [Memphis, TN] B: 4/11/1939, Louise, MS *Drafted:* 1961 Round 8 Hou
1961 Bos: 14 G. **1962** Bos: 14 G. **1963** Bos: 14 G. **1964** Bos: 14 G. **1965** Bos: 14 G; Int 1-2. **1966** Bos: 14 G. **1967** Bos: 13 G. **1968** Bos: 14 G. **1969** Bos: 14 G. **1970** Bos: 14 G. **1971** NE: 3 G. **1972** Phi: 14 G. **Total:** 156 G; Int 1-2.

STEVE APKE Apke, Steven James 6'1", 222 **LB**
Col: Pittsburgh *HS:* Moeller [Cincinnati, OH] B: 8/3/1965, Cincinnati, OH
1987 Pit: 3 G.

CHUCK APOLSKIS Apolskis, Charles Casimir 6'2", 207 **OE**
Col: DePaul *HS:* Fenger [Chicago, IL] B: 12/18/1914, Cicero, IL Deceased
1938 ChiB: 1 G. **1939** ChiB: 1 G. **Total:** 2 G.

RAY APOLSKIS Apolskis, Raymond Edward 5'11", 206 **LB-OG-C**
Col: Marquette *HS:* Fenger [Chicago, IL] B: 10/19/1918, Cicero, IL *Drafted:* 1941 Round 5 ChiC
1941 ChiC: 11 G; Int 1-4. **1942** ChiC: 11 G; Int 2-15. **1945** ChiC: 5 G. **1946** ChiC: 6 G; Int 1-20. **1947** ChiC: 12 G. **1948** ChiC: 12 G. **1949** ChiC: 8 G; Int 1-16. **1950** ChiC: 9 G; Int 1-6. **Total:** 74 G; Int 6-61.

JIM APPLE Apple, James Dunbar 6'0", 200 **HB**
Col: Upsala B: 7/14/1938
1961 NYT: 3 G; Rush 7-2 0.3; PR 2-12 6.0; KR 1-16 16.0; 1 Fum.

CLARENCE APPLEGRAN Applegran, Clarence Oliver 6'2", 200 **G**
Col: Illinois *HS:* Lake View [Chicago, IL] B: 11/1893, Chicago, IL D: 5/6/1960, Chicago, IL
1920 Det: 4 G.

SCOTT APPLETON Appleton, Gordon Scott 6'3", 260 **DT**
Col: Texas *HS:* Brady [TX] B: 2/20/1942, Brady, TX D: 3/2/1992, Austin, TX *Drafted:* 1964 Round 1 Hou
1964 Hou: 14 G; Int 2-11. **1965** Hou: 14 G. **1966** Hou: 14 G. **1967** SD: 14 G; **1** Fum TD; 6 Pt. **1968** SD: 14 G. **Total:** 70 G; Int 2-11; 1 Fum TD; 6 Pt.

MARGER APSIT Apsit, Marger 5'11", 200 **BB-LB-DB-TB**
(Megs) *Col:* USC *HS:* Aurora West [IL] B: 6/5/1909, Aurora, IL D: 12/22/1988, Bakersfield, CA
1931 Fra-Bkn: 9 G. Fra: 6 G. Bkn: 3 G. **1932** GB: 2 G; Rush 4-6 1.5. **1933** Bos: 12 G; Pass 5-1 20.0%, 25 5.00 2 Int; Rush 7-35 5.0; Rec 1-24 24.0. **Total:** 23 G; Pass 5-1 20.0%, 25 5.00 2 Int; Rush 11-41 3.7; Rec 1-24 24.0.

BEN APUNA Apuna, Benjamin Clavin 6'1", 222 **LB**
Col: Mesa CC AZ; Arizona State *HS:* Waipahu [HI] B: 6/26/1957, Honolulu, HI *Drafted:* 1980 Round 7 StL
1980 NYG: 10 G.

LEO ARAGUZ Araguz, Leobardo Jaime 5'11", 190 **P**
Col: Stephen F. Austin St. *HS:* Harlingen [TX] B: 1/18/1970, Pharr, TX
1996 Oak: Rush 1-0. **1997** Oak: Rush 1-0. **1998** Oak: Pass 1-1 100.0%, -1 -1.00; Rush 1-(-12) -12.0. **Total:** Pass 1-1 100.0%, -1 1.00; Rush 3-(-12) -4.0.

		Punting			
Year Team	G	Punts	Yds	Avg	Fum
1996 Oak	3	13	534	41.1	0
1997 Oak	16	93	4189	45.0	1
1998 Oak	16	98	4256	43.4	0
NFL Total	35	204	8979	44.0	1

EVAN ARAPOSTATHIS Arapostathis, Evan Anthony 5'9", 160 **P**
Col: Grossmont Coll. CA (J.C.); Eastern Illinois *HS:* Helix [La Mesa, CA] B: 10/30/1963, San Diego, CA
1986 StL: 5 G; Pass 1-0; Punt 30-1140 38.0.

FRED ARBANAS Arbanas, Frederick Vincent 6'3", 240 **TE**
(Fritz) *Col:* Michigan State *HS:* St. Mary's of Redford [Detroit, MI]
B: 1/14/1939, Detroit, MI *Drafted:* 1961 Round 7 DalT
1966 KC: Scor **1** 2XP. **1968** KC: Rush 3-14 4.7. **1969** KC: Rush 1-1 1.0.
Total: Rush 4-15 3.8; Scor 1 2XP.

		Receiving				
Year Team	G	Rec	Yds	Avg	TD	Fum
1962 DalT	14	29	469	16.2	6	2
1963 KC	14	34	373	11.0	6	2
1964 KC	14	34	686	20.2	8	0
1965 KC	14	24	418	17.4	4	0
1966 KC	14	22	305	13.9	4	0
1967 KC	14	20	295	14.8	5	0
1968 KC	14	11	189	17.2	0	0
1969 KC	14	16	258	16.1	0	0
1970 KC	6	8	108	13.5	1	0
NFL Total	118	198	3101	15.7	34	4

HASSON ARBUBAKRR Arbubakrr, Hasson 6'4", 250 **DE**
Col: Pasadena City Coll. CA (J.C.); Texas Tech *HS:* Weequahic [Newark, NJ] B: 12/9/1960, Newark, NJ *Drafted:* 1983 Round 9 TB
1983 TB: 16 G; 1 Sac. **1984** Min: 4 G; 0.5 Sac. **Total:** 20 G; 1.5 Sac.

CHARLES ARBUCKLE Arbuckle, Charles Edward 6'3", 248 **TE**
Col: UCLA *HS:* Willowridge [Sugar Land, TX] B: 9/13/1968, Beaumont, TX *Drafted:* 1990 Round 5 NO

		Receiving				
Year Team	G	Rec	Yds	Avg	TD	Fum
1992 Ind	16	13	152	11.7	1	0
1993 Ind	16	15	90	6.0	0	1
1994 Ind	7	1	7	7.0	0	0
1995 Ind	3	4	33	8.3	0	0
NFL Total	42	33	282	8.5	1	1

LESTER ARCHAMBEAU Archambeau, Lester Milward III 6'5", 275 **DE**
Col: Stanford *HS:* Montville [NJ] B: 6/27/1967, Montville, NJ
Drafted: 1990 Round 7 GB
1990 GB: 4 G. **1991** GB: 16 G; 4.5 Sac. **1992** GB: 16 G; 1 Sac. **1993** Atl: 15 G. **1994** Atl: 16 G; 2 Sac. **1995** Atl: 16 G; 3 Sac. **1996** Atl: 15 G; 2 Sac. **1997** Atl: 16 G; Int 1-0; 8.5 Sac. **1998** Atl: 15 G; 10 Sac. **Total:** 129 G; Int 1-0; 31.0 Sac.

DAN ARCHER Archer, Daniel G 6'5", 245 **OG-OT**
Col: Oregon *HS:* Thomas Downey [Modesto, CA] B: 9/29/1944, Grand Rapids, MI *Drafted:* 1966 Redshirt Round 6 Oak
1967 Oak: 14 G. **1968** Cin: 8 G. **Total:** 22 G.

DAVID ARCHER Archer, David Mark 6'2", 207 **QB**
Col: Snow Coll. UT (J.C.); Iowa State *HS:* Soda Springs [ID]
B: 2/15/1962, Fayetteville, NC

		Passing							
Year Team	G	Att	Comp	Comp%	Yds	YPA	TD	Int	Rating
1984 Atl	2	18	11	61.1	181	10.06	1	1	90.3
1985 Atl	16	312	161	51.6	1992	6.38	7	17	56.5
1986 Atl	11	294	150	51.0	2007	6.83	10	9	71.6
1987 Atl	9	23	9	39.1	95	4.13	0	2	15.7
1988 Was	1	2	0	0.0	0	0.00	0	0	39.6
1989 SD	16	12	5	41.7	62	5.17	0	1	23.6
NFL Total	55	661	336	50.8	4337	6.56	18	30	61.9

	Rushing				
Year Team	Att	Yds	Avg	TD	Fum
1984 Atl	6	38	6.3	0	1
1985 Atl	70	347	5.0	2	9
1986 Atl	52	298	5.7	0	8
1987 Atl	2	8	4.0	0	0
1988 Was	3	1	0.3	0	0
1989 SD	2	14	7.0	0	0
NFL Total	135	706	5.2	2	18

TROY ARCHER Archer, James Troy 6'4", 250 **DT-DE**
Col: Rio Hondo Coll. CA (J.C.); Colorado *HS:* California [Whittier, CA]
B: 1/16/1955, Glendale, CA D: 6/22/1979, North Bergen, NJ
Drafted: 1976 Round 1 NYG
1976 NYG: 14 G. **1977** NYG: 14 G. **1978** NYG: 10 G; 1 Fum TD; 6 Pt.
Total: 38 G; 1 Fum TD; 6 Pt.

MIKE ARCHIE Archie, Michael Lamont 5'8", 205 **RB**
Col: Penn State *HS:* Sharon [PA] B: 10/14/1972, Sharon, PA
Drafted: 1996 Round 7 Hou
1997 Ten: PR 1-5 5.0. **1998** Ten: Pass 2-1 50.0%, 18 9.00 1 TD; Rush 6-24 4.0 1 TD; Rec 5-25 5.0; PR 7-52 7.4. **Total:** Pass 2-1 50.0%, 18 9.00 1 TD; Rush 6-24 4.0 1 TD; Rec 5-25 5.0; PR 8-57 7.1.

		Kickoff Returns				
Year Team	G	Ret	Yds	Avg	TD	Fum
1996 Hou	2	2	24	12.0	0	0
1997 Ten	5	2	24	12.0	0	0
1998 Ten	16	42	913	21.7	0	3
NFL Total	23	46	961	20.9	0	3

JULIE ARCHOSKA Archoska, Julius 5'11", 180 **E**
Col: Syracuse *HS:* Classical [Lynn, MA] B: 3/13/1905, Lynn, MA
D: 3/18/1972, Lynn, MA
1930 SI: 4 G.

BILLY ARD Ard, William Donovan 6'3", 265 **OG**
Col: Wake Forest *HS:* Watchung [NJ] B: 3/12/1959, East Orange, NJ
Drafted: 1981 Round 8 NYG
1981 NYG: 13 G. **1982** NYG: 9 G. **1983** NYG: 16 G. **1984** NYG: 15 G. **1985** NYG: 16 G. **1986** NYG: 16 G. **1987** NYG: 12 G. **1988** NYG: 16 G. **1989** GB: 15 G. **1990** GB: 15 G. **1991** GB: 5 G. **Total:** 148 G.

TONY ARDIZZONE Ardizzone, Anthony Allen 6'3", 240 **C**
Col: Northwestern *HS:* St. Joseph [Westchester, IL] B: 12/19/1956, La Grange, IL *Drafted:* 1978 Round 6 Det
1979 ChiB: 16 G.

TONY ARENA Arena, Anthony Gerald 6'0", 200 **C-LB**
Col: Michigan State *HS:* Northwestern [Detroit, MI] B: 7/2/1918, Detroit, MI *Drafted:* 1942 Round 13 Det
1942 Det: 1 G.

JOE ARENAS Arenas, Lupe Joseph 5'11", 180 **HB-DB**
Col: Nebraska-Omaha *HS:* Lincoln [NE] B: 12/12/1925, Cedar Rapids, IA *Drafted:* 1951 Round 8 SF
1952 SF: Pass 1-0. **1953** SF: Pass 1-0; Int 2-29. **1954** SF: Int 3-26. **1955** SF: Pass 1-0; Int 1-0. **1957** SF: Pass 3-3 100.0%, 92 30.67 2 TD.
Total: Pass 6-3 50.0%, 92 15.33 2 TD; Int 6-55.

		Rushing				Receiving			
Year Team	G	Att	Yds	Avg	TD	Rec	Yds	Avg	TD
1951 SF	12	34	183	5.4	3	1	12	12.0	1
1952 SF	12	44	183	4.2	0	5	47	9.4	1
1953 SF	12	72	380	5.3	6	10	113	11.3	1
1954 SF	12	11	77	7.0	0	2	12	6.0	0
1955 SF	12	37	150	4.1	0	13	255	19.6	2
1956 SF	12	0	0	—	0	14	226	16.1	1
1957 SF	12	5	14	2.8	1	1	10	10.0	0
NFL Total	84	203	987	4.9	10	46	675	14.7	6

	Punt Returns				Kickoff Returns					Tot
Year Team	Ret	Yds	Avg	TD	Ret	Yds	Avg	TD	Fum	TD
1951 SF	21	272	13.0	0	21	542	25.8	0	1	4
1952 SF	7	40	5.7	0	11	291	26.5	0	3	1
1953 SF	8	93	11.6	0	16	551	**34.4**	0	5	7
1954 SF	23	117	5.1	0	16	362	22.6	0	3	0
1955 SF	21	55	2.6	0	24	594	24.8	0	4	2
1956 SF	19	117	6.2	**1**	27	801	29.7	**1**	1	3
1957 SF	25	80	3.2	0	24	657	27.4	0	3	1
NFL Total	124	774	6.2	1	139	3798	27.3	1	20	18

ARNIE ARENZ Arenz, Arnold Henry 6'2", 215 **BB-LB**
Col: St. Louis *HS:* Flat River [MO] B: 10/13/1911, Flat River, MO
D: 1/31/1985, Olympia, WA
1934 Bos: 3 G; Pass 5-1 20.0%, 8 1.60 1 Int; Rush 4-11 2.8; Rec 2-16 8.0.

BOB ARGUS Argus, Robert 5'10", 193 **WB-FB-TB-BB**
Col: No College *HS:* West Side [Rochester, NY]; Corning Acad. [NY]
B: 1/1894, Hammondsport, NY Deceased
1920 Roch: 10 G. **1921** Roch: 5 G. **1922** Roch: 5 G; Rush 1 TD; 6 Pt. **1923** Roch: 4 G. **1924** Roch: 7 G. **1925** Roch: 5 G. **Total:** 36 G; Rush 1 TD; 6 Pt.

GUMP ARIAIL Ariail, David William 5'11", 205 **E**
Col: Auburn *HS:* Phillips [Birmingham, AL] B: 12/29/1910, Birmingham, AL
1934 Bkn-Cin: 2 G. Bkn: 1 G. Cin: 1 G. **Total:** 2 G.

MIKE ARIEY Ariey, Michael August 6'5", 285 **OT**
Col: San Diego State *HS:* Garces Memorial [Bakersfield, CA]
B: 3/12/1964, Bakersfield, CA
1989 GB: 1 G.

OBED ARIRI Ariri, Obed Chukwuma 5'8", 170 **K**
Col: Clemson *HS:* Holy Ghost Coll. [Owerri, Nigeria] B: 4/7/1956, Owerri, Nigeria *Drafted:* 1981 Round 7 Bal
1984 TB: 16 G; Scor 95, 19-26 73.1% FG, 38-40 95.0% XK. **1987** Was: 2 G; Scor 15, 3-5 60.0% FG, 6-6 100.0% XK. **Total:** 18 G; Scor 110, 22-31 71.0% FG, 44-46 95.7% XK.

JUSTIN ARMOUR Armour, Justin Hugh 6'4", 210 **WR**
Col: Stanford *HS:* Manitou Springs [CO] B: 1/1/1973, Colorado Springs, CO *Drafted:* 1995 Round 4 Buf
1995 Buf: Pass 1-0; Rush 4-(-5) -1.3. **Total:** Pass 1-0; Rush 4-(-5) -1.3.

Year Team	G	Receiving Rec	Yds	Avg	TD	Fum
1995 Buf	15	26	300	11.5	3	1
1997 Phi	1	0	0	—	0	0
1998 Den	8	1	23	23.0	0	0
NFL Total	24	27	323	12.0	3	1

LOYD ARMS Arms, Lloyd 6′1″, 215 **G**
Col: Oklahoma State *HS:* Sulphur [OK] B: 9/24/1919, Sulphur, OK
Drafted: 1943 Round 12 ChiB
1946 ChiC: 8 G. **1947** ChiC: 12 G. **1948** ChiC: 7 G. **Total:** 27 G.

JESSIE ARMSTEAD Armstead, Jessie Willard 6′1″, 236 **LB**
Col: Miami (Fla.) *HS:* David W. Carter [Dallas, TX] B: 10/26/1970, Dallas, TX *Drafted:* 1993 Round 8 NYG
1993 NYG: 16 G; Int 1-0. **1994** NYG: 16 G; Int 1-0; 3 Sac. **1995** NYG: 16 G; Int 1-58 1 TD; 6 Pt; 0.5 Sac. **1996** NYG: 16 G; Int 2-23; 1 Fum; 3 Sac. **1997** NYG: 16 G; Int 2-57 1 TD; 6 Pt; 3.5 Sac. **1998** NYG: 16 G; Int 2-4; 5 Sac. **Total:** 96 G; Int 9-142 2 TD; 12 Pt; 1 Fum; 15 Sac.

ADGER ARMSTRONG Armstrong, Adger Jr. 6′0″, 213 **RB**
Col: Texas A&M *HS:* Cyfair [Houston, TX]; Jersey Village HS [Houston, TX] B: 6/21/1957, Houston, TX
1981 Hou: KR 3-36 12.0. **1983** TB: KR 1-10 10.0. **Total:** KR 4-46 11.5.

Year Team	G	Rushing Att	Yds	Avg	TD	Receiving Rec	Yds	Avg	TD	Fum	Tot TD
1980 Hou	16	0	0	—	0	0	0	—	0	0	0
1981 Hou	16	31	146	4.7	0	29	278	9.6	1	2	1
1982 Hou	6	8	15	1.9	0	12	75	6.3	0	0	0
1983 TB	11	7	30	4.3	0	15	173	11.5	2	0	2
1984 TB	15	10	34	3.4	2	22	180	8.2	3	1	5
1985 TB	16	2	6	3.0	0	2	4	2.0	1	0	1
NFL Total	80	58	231	4.0	2	80	710	8.9	7	3	9

ANTONIO ARMSTRONG Armstrong, Antonio Donnell 6′1″, 235 **LB**
Col: Texas A&M *HS:* Kashmere [Houston, TX] B: 10/15/1973, Houston, TX *Drafted:* 1995 Round 6 SF
1995 Mia: 4 G.

BRUCE ARMSTRONG Armstrong, Bruce Charles 6′4″, 295 **OT-OG**
Col: Louisville *HS:* Miami Central [FL] B: 9/7/1965, Miami, FL
Drafted: 1987 Round 1 NE
1987 NE: 12 G. **1988** NE: 16 G. **1989** NE: 16 G. **1990** NE: 16 G. **1991** NE: 16 G. **1992** NE: 8 G. **1993** NE: 16 G. **1994** NE: 16 G. **1995** NE: 16 G. **1996** NE: 16 G. **1997** NE: 16 G. **1998** NE: 16 G. **Total:** 180 G.

QUINCY ARMSTRONG Armstrong, Carl Quince Jr. 6′3″, 230 **C**
Col: North Texas *HS:* Pascal [Fort Worth, TX] B: 11/22/1928, Clyde, TX
1954 Cle: 2 G.

CHARLIE ARMSTRONG Armstrong, Charles Andrew 5′10″, 180 **DB-TB**
Col: Mississippi College *HS:* Newton [MS] B: 4/20/1919, Hickory, MS
AAFC **1946** BknA: 10 G; Pass 21-9 42.9%, 126 6.00 1 TD 2 Int; Rush 22-78 3.5; PR 6-97 16.2; KR 3-93 31.0; Int 2-54; Punt 6-231 38.5.

GRAHAM ARMSTRONG Armstrong, Graham Leo 6′4″, 230 **T**
Col: John Carroll *HS:* Cathedral Latin [Cleveland, OH] B: 5/30/1918, Cleveland, OH D: 1985
AAFC **1947** BufA: 14 G; Scor 8, 0-1 FG, 8-10 80.0% XK. **1948** BufA: 13 G; Rec 1-0; KR 1-9 9.0; Scor 15, 0-1 FG, 15-17 88.2% XK.
Total: 27 G; Rec 1-0; KR 1-9 9.0; Scor 23, 0-2 FG, 23-27 85.2% XK.

NFL **1941** Cle: 7 G. **1945** Cle: 1 G. **Total:** 8 G.

HARVEY ARMSTRONG Armstrong, Harvey Lee 6′3″, 265 **NT**
Col: Southern Methodist *HS:* Kashmere [Houston, TX] B: 12/29/1959, Houston, TX *Drafted:* 1982 Round 7 Phi
1982 Phi: 8 G. **1983** Phi: 16 G; 3.5 Sac. **1984** Phi: 16 G; 3 Sac. **1986** Ind: 16 G; Int 1-4; 3.5 Sac. **1987** Ind: 11 G. **1988** Ind: 16 G; 2 Sac. **1989** Ind: 16 G; 1 Sac. **1990** Ind: 12 G. **Total:** 111 G; Int 1-4; 13 Sac.

JIMMY ARMSTRONG Armstrong, James Berton 5′8″, 166 **DB**
Col: Appalachian State *HS:* Lucy Ragsdale [Jamestown, NC]
B: 6/18/1962
1987 Dal: 2 G.

JOHN ARMSTRONG Armstrong, John A 5′8″, 170 **BB**
Col: Dubuque *HS:* Hutchinson [KS] B: 1894 Deceased
1923 RI: 8 G; Pass 3 TD; Rush 2 TD; 12 Pt. **1924** RI: 9 G; Pass 1 TD; Rush 1 TD; Scor 7, 1 XK. **1925** RI: 11 G; Pass 3 TD; Rec 3 TD; KR **1** TD; Int 1 TD; Scor 31, 1 XK; Tot TD 5. **Total:** 28 G; Pass 7 TD; Rush 3 TD; Rec 3 TD; KR 1 TD; Int 1 TD; Tot TD 8.

JOHN ARMSTRONG Armstrong, John Earl 5′9″, 190 **DB**
Col: Northwest Mississippi CC; Richmond *HS:* Bruce [MS]
B: 7/7/1963, Calhoun City, MS
1987 Buf: 3 G; KR 2-25 12.5; 1 Fum; 2 Sac.

NEILL ARMSTRONG Armstrong, Neill Ford 6′2″, 189 **OE-DB**
(Bird; Felix) *Col:* Oklahoma State *HS:* Tishomingo [OK] B: 3/9/1926, Tishomingo, OK *Drafted:* 1947 Round 1 Phi
1947 Phi: KR 3-38 12.7. **1948** Phi: Int 2-30. **1950** Phi: Int 3-4. **1951** Phi: Int 4-18. **Total:** KR 3-38 12.7; Int 9-52.

Year Team	G	Receiving Rec	Yds	Avg	TD	Fum
1947 Phi	12	17	197	11.6	2	1
1948 Phi	12	24	325	13.5	3	0
1949 Phi	12	24	271	11.3	5	0
1950 Phi	12	8	124	15.5	1	0
1951 Phi	6	3	44	14.7	0	0
NFL Total	54	76	961	12.6	11	1

OTIS ARMSTRONG Armstrong, Otis 5′10″, 196 **RB**
Col: Purdue *HS:* David Farragut [Chicago, IL] B: 11/15/1950, Chicago, IL *Drafted:* 1973 Round 1 Den

Year Team	G	Rushing Att	Yds	Avg	TD	Receiving Rec	Yds	Avg	TD
1973 Den	14	26	90	3.5	0	2	43	21.5	1
1974 Den	14	263	**1407**	**5.3**	9	38	405	10.7	3
1975 Den	4	31	155	5.0	0	1	10	10.0	0
1976 Den	14	247	1008	4.1	5	39	457	11.7	1
1977 Den	10	130	489	3.8	4	18	128	7.1	0
1978 Den	16	112	381	3.4	1	12	98	8.2	1
1979 Den	15	108	453	4.2	2	14	138	9.9	1
1980 Den	9	106	470	4.4	4	7	23	3.3	0
NFL Total	96	1023	4453	4.4	25	131	1302	9.9	7

Year Team	Kickoff Returns Ret	Yds	Avg	TD	Fum	Tot TD
1973 Den	20	472	23.6	0	1	1
1974 Den	16	386	24.1	0	6	12
1975 Den	0	0	—	0	2	0
1976 Den	0	0	—	0	4	6
1977 Den	0	0	—	0	2	4
1978 Den	0	0	—	0	1	2
1979 Den	1	21	21.0	0	2	3
1980 Den	0	0	—	0	1	4
NFL Total	37	879	23.8	0	19	32

NORRIS ARMSTRONG Armstrong, Phillip Norris 5′10″, 165 **T**
(Army) *Col:* Centre *HS:* Fort Smith [AR] B: 9/15/1898, Fort Smith, AR
D: 10/11/1981, Danville, KY
1922 Mil: 1 G.

RAY ARMSTRONG Armstrong, Ramon Lee 6′1″, 235 **DT**
Col: Texas Christian *HS:* Ennis [TX] B: 10/6/1937, Ennis, TX
Drafted: 1960 Round 2 NYT
1960 Oak: 14 G.

TRACE ARMSTRONG Armstrong, Raymond Lester 6′4″, 267 **DE**
Col: Arizona State; Florida *HS:* John Carroll [Birmingham, AL]
B: 10/5/1965, Bethesda, MD *Drafted:* 1989 Round 1 ChiB
1989 ChiB: 15 G; 5 Sac. **1990** ChiB: 16 G; 10 Sac. **1991** ChiB: 12 G; 1.5 Sac. **1992** ChiB: 14 G; 6.5 Sac. **1993** ChiB: 16 G; 11.5 Sac. **1994** ChiB: 15 G; 7.5 Sac. **1995** Mia: 15 G; 4.5 Sac. **1996** Mia: 16 G; 12 Sac. **1997** Mia: 16 G; 5.5 Sac. **1998** Mia: 16 G; 10.5 Sac. **Total:** 151 G; 74.5 Sac.

BOB ARMSTRONG Armstrong, Robert Alva Jr. 5′11″, 221 **T-G-C**
Col: Rice; Missouri *HS:* Oak Cliff [Dallas, TX] B: 2/16/1909, Dallas, TX
D: 2/28/1990, San Antonio, TX
1931 Port: 14 G. **1932** Port: 6 G. **Total:** 20 G.

TYJI ARMSTRONG Armstrong, Tyji Donrapheal 6′4″, 259 **TE**
Col: Central Coll. (Iowa); Mississippi *HS:* Robichaud [Dearborn Heights, MI] B: 10/3/1970, Inkster, MI *Drafted:* 1992 Round 3 TB
1993 TB: Rush 2-5 2.5. **1994** TB: Rush 1-(-1) -1.0; KR 1-6 6.0. **1995** TB: KR 1-6 6.0. **Total:** Rush 3-4 1.3; KR 2-12 6.0.

Year Team	G	Receiving Rec	Yds	Avg	TD	Fum
1992 TB	15	7	138	19.7	1	0
1993 TB	12	9	86	9.6	1	0
1994 TB	16	22	265	12.0	1	2
1995 TB	16	7	68	9.7	0	1
1996 Dal	16	2	10	5.0	0	0
1998 StL	12	6	54	9.0	0	0
NFL Total	87	53	621	11.7	3	3

BILL ARMSTRONG Armstrong, William Wright 6′1″, 210 **G**
Col: UCLA *HS:* Hollywood [Los Angeles, CA] B: 1920
1943 Bkn: 4 G.

AL ARNDT Arndt, Alfred Herman 5′11″, 205 **G**
Col: South Dakota State *HS:* New Ulm [MN] B: 7/15/1911, Comfrey, MN Deceased
1935 Pit: 7 G; Rush 1-21 21.0.

DICK ARNDT Arndt, Richard Lee 6′5″, 265 **DT**
(Herman) *Col:* Stanford; Idaho *HS:* Sandpoint [ID] B: 3/12/1944, Bonners Ferry, ID *Drafted:* 1966 Round 5 LARm
1967 Pit: 14 G. **1968** Pit: 3 G. **1969** Pit: 3 G. **1970** Pit: 14 G. **Total:** 34 G.

JIM ARNESON Arneson, James Arnold 6′3″, 247 **OG-C**
Col: Arizona *HS:* Palo Verde [Tucson, AZ] B: 1/7/1951, Iowa City, IA
Drafted: 1973 Round 12 Dal
1973 Dal: 12 G. **1974** Dal: 14 G. **1975** Was: 7 G. **Total:** 33 G.

MARK ARNESON Arneson, Mark Edward 6′2″, 220 **LB**
Col: Arizona *HS:* Palo Verde [Tucson, AZ] B: 9/9/1949, Iowa City, IA
Drafted: 1972 Round 2 StL
1972 StL: 14 G. **1973** StL: 14 G; Int 1-13. **1974** StL: 14 G. **1975** StL: 14 G; Int 1-6. **1976** StL: 14 G; Int 1-0. **1977** StL: 14 G; Int 2-23. **1978** StL: 16 G. **1979** StL: 11 G; **1** Fum TD; 6 Pt. **1980** StL: 16 G. **Total:** 127 G; Int 5-42; 1 Fum TD; 6 Pt.

JON ARNETT Arnett, Jon Dwayne 5′11″, 197 **HB-OE**
(Jaguar Jon) *Col:* USC *HS:* Manual Arts [Los Angeles, CA]
B: 4/20/1934, Los Angeles, CA *Drafted:* 1957 Round 1 LARm
1958 LARm: Pass 1-0. **1959** LARm: Pass 5-1 20.0%, 13 2.60. **1960** LARm: Pass 1-0. **1961** LARm: Pass 13-3 23.1%, 47 3.62 1 Int. **1962** LARm: Pass 5-3 60.0%, 28 5.60 1 TD. **1963** LARm: Pass 1-0, 1 Int. **1964** ChiB: Pass 4-0. **1965** ChiB: Pass 2-1 50.0%, 59 29.50 1 TD. **1966** ChiB: Pass 1-0. **Total:** Pass 33-8 24.2%, 147 4.45 2 TD 2 Int.

		Rushing				Receiving			
Year Team	**G**	**Att**	**Yds**	**Avg**	**TD**	**Rec**	**Yds**	**Avg**	**TD**
1957 LARm	12	86	347	4.0	2	18	322	17.9	3
1958 LARm	12	133	683	5.1	6	35	494	14.1	1
1959 LARm	12	73	371	5.1	2	38	419	11.0	1
1960 LARm	12	104	436	4.2	2	29	226	7.8	2
1961 LARm	14	158	609	3.9	4	28	194	6.9	0
1962 LARm	10	76	238	3.1	2	12	137	11.4	0
1963 LARm	9	58	208	3.6	1	15	119	7.9	1
1964 ChiB	14	119	400	3.4	1	25	223	8.9	2
1965 ChiB	14	102	363	3.6	5	12	114	9.5	0
1966 ChiB	14	55	178	3.2	1	10	42	4.2	0
NFL Total	123	964	3833	4.0	26	222	2290	10.3	10

	Punt Returns				Kickoff Returns					Tot
Year Team	**Ret**	**Yds**	**Avg**	**TD**	**Ret**	**Yds**	**Avg**	**TD**	**Fum**	**TD**
1957 LARm	14	85	6.1	0	18	504	**28.0**	**1**	5	6
1958 LARm	18	**223**	**12.4**	0	16	331	20.7	0	4	7
1959 LARm	17	184	10.8	1	14	320	22.9	0	5	4
1960 LARm	10	60	6.0	0	17	416	24.5	0	1	4
1961 LARm	10	75	7.5	0	25	653	26.1	**1**	3	5
1962 LARm	5	49	9.8	0	2	87	43.5	0	1	2
1963 LARm	1	7	7.0	0	12	279	23.3	0	1	2
1964 ChiB	19	188	9.9	0	15	331	22.1	0	5	3
1965 ChiB	11	52	4.7	0	5	150	30.0	0	3	5
1966 ChiB	15	58	3.9	0	2	39	19.5	0	3	1
NFL Total	120	981	8.2	1	126	3110	24.7	2	31	39

DAVID ARNOLD Arnold, David Paul 6′3″, 208 **DB**
Col: Michigan *HS:* Warren G. Harding [Warren, OH] B: 11/21/1966, Warren, OH *Drafted:* 1989 Round 5 Pit
1989 Pit: 15 G.

JAHINE ARNOLD Arnold, Jahine Amid 6′0″, 187 **WR**
Col: De Anza Coll. CA (J.C.); Fresno State *HS:* Homestead [Cupertino, CA] B: 6/19/1973, Rockville, CT *Drafted:* 1996 Round 4 Pit
1996 Pit: 9 G; Rush 1-(-3) -3.0; Rec 6-76 12.7; PR 2-6 3.0; KR 19-425 22.4; 1 Fum. **1998** Pit: 3 G; PR 4-19 4.8; KR 3-78 26.0. **Total:** 12 G; Rush 1-(-3) -3.0; Rec 6-76 12.7; PR 6-25 4.2; KR 22-503 22.9; 1 Fum.

JIM ARNOLD Arnold, James Edward 6′2″, 215 **P**
Col: Vanderbilt *HS:* Dalton [GA] B: 1/31/1961, Dalton, GA
Drafted: 1983 Round 5 KC
1984 KC: Rush 1-0. **1988** Det: Pass 1-0. **1991** Det: Rush 2-42 21.0. **Total:** Pass 1-0; Rush 3-42 14.0.

		Punting			
Year Team	**G**	**Punts**	**Yds**	**Avg**	**Fum**
1983 KC	16	93	3710	39.9	0
1984 KC	16	**98**	**4397**	**44.9**	1
1985 KC	16	**93**	3827	41.2	0
1986 Det	7	36	1533	42.6	0
1987 Det	11	46	2007	43.6	0
1988 Det	16	97	**4110**	42.4	0
1989 Det	16	82	3538	43.1	0
1990 Det	16	63	2560	40.6	0
1991 Det	16	75	3092	41.2	0
1992 Det	16	65	2846	43.8	0
1993 Det	16	72	3207	44.5	0
1994 Mia	12	46	1810	39.3	0
NFL Total	174	866	36637	42.3	1

JAY ARNOLD Arnold, Jay Lawrence 6′1″, 210 **HB-DB-BB-WB**
(Bird) *Col:* Texas *HS:* Greenville [TX] B: 9/9/1912, Rogers, TX
D: 4/8/1982, Houston, TX
1938 Phi: Int **1** TD; Scor 27, 0-1 FG, 3-3 100.0% XK; **1** Fum TD. **1939** Phi: Punt 1-42 42.0. **1940** Phi: Int 1-4. **1941** Pit: Int 1-0. **Total:** Int 2-4 1 TD; Punt 1-42 42.0; Scor 39, 0-1 FG, 3-3 100.0% XK; 1 Fum TD.

		Rushing				Receiving				Tot
Year Team	**G**	**Att**	**Yds**	**Avg**	**TD**	**Rec**	**Yds**	**Avg**	**TD**	**TD**
1937 Phi	10	5	7	1.4	0	8	142	17.8	0	0
1938 Phi	11	19	22	1.2	0	6	74	12.3	2	4
1939 Phi	10	8	1	0.1	0	13	207	15.9	1	2
1940 Phi	9	3	9	3.0	0	7	145	20.7	0	0
1941 Pit	10	2	4	2.0	0	1	5	5.0	0	0
NFL Total	50	37	43	1.2	0	35	573	16.4	3	6

JOHN ARNOLD Arnold, John Richard 5′10″, 175 **WR**
Col: Wyoming *HS:* Washington [Tacoma, WA] B: 10/5/1955, Shizuoka, Japan

		Punt Returns				Kickoff Returns				
Year Team	**G**	**Ret**	**Yds**	**Avg**	**TD**	**Ret**	**Yds**	**Avg**	**TD**	**Fum**
1979 Det	7	19	164	8.6	0	23	539	23.4	0	0
1980 Det	10	28	204	7.3	0	9	145	16.1	0	1
NFL Total	17	47	368	7.8	0	32	684	21.4	0	1

LEFRANCIS ARNOLD Arnold, LeFrancis 6′3″, 245 **OG**
Col: Oregon *HS:* Compton [CA] B: 11/24/1952, Los Angeles, CA
1974 Den: 2 G.

WALT ARNOLD Arnold, Walter Henslee 6′3″, 228 **TE**
Col: New Mexico *HS:* Los Alamos [NM] B: 8/31/1958, Galveston, TX
1985 KC: KR 2-9 4.5. **1986** KC: **1** Fum TD. **Total:** KR 2-9 4.5; 1 Fum TD.

		Receiving				Tot
Year Team	**G**	**Rec**	**Yds**	**Avg**	**TD**	**TD**
1980 LARm	16	5	75	15.0	1	1
1981 LARm	16	20	212	10.6	2	2
1982 Hou	9	0	0	—	0	0
1983 Hou	13	12	137	11.4	1	1
1984 Was-KC	14	11	95	8.6	1	1
1984 Was	4	0	0	—	0	0
1984 KC	10	11	95	8.6	1	1
1985 KC	16	28	339	12.1	1	1
1986 KC	16	20	169	8.5	1	2
1987 KC	5	3	26	8.7	0	0
NFL Total	105	99	1053	10.6	7	8

DOUG ARONSON Aronson, Douglas 6′3″, 293 **OG**
Col: San Diego State *HS:* South San Francisco [CA] B: 8/14/1964, San Francisco, CA
1987 Cin: 2 G.

JOHN ARP Arp, John Allen 6′5″, 275 **OT**
Col: Lincoln (Mo.) B: 8/15/1965
1987 ChiB: 2 G.

RICK ARRINGTON Arrington, Richard Cameron 6′2″, 200 **QB**
Col: Tulsa *HS:* Myers Park [Charlotte, NC] B: 2/26/1947, Charlotte, NC
1970 Phi: Rush 4-33 8.3 1 TD. **1971** Phi: Rush 5-23 4.6. **1972** Phi: Rush 1-2 2.0. **Total:** Rush 10-58 5.8 1 TD.

		Passing								
Year Team	**G**	**Att**	**Comp**	**Comp%**	**Yds**	**YPA**	**TD**	**Int**	**Rating**	**Fum**
1970 Phi	6	73	37	50.7	328	4.49	1	3	50.5	0
1971 Phi	10	118	55	46.6	576	4.88	2	5	49.3	1
1972 Phi	1	13	5	38.5	46	3.54	0	1	16.8	1
NFL Total	17	204	97	47.5	950	4.66	3	9	47.6	2

CHUCK ARROBIO Arrobio, Charles Augustus 6′4″, 250 **OT**
Col: USC *HS:* Glendale [CA] B: 7/9/1944, Los Angeles, CA
1966 Min: 11 G.

ARROWHEAD Arrowhead 5′7″, 160 **E**
Col: No College Deceased
1923 Oor: 4 G; Rec 2 TD; 12 Pt.

ELMER ARTERBURN Arterburn, Elmer Forrest Jr. 5′10″, 175 **DB**
(Junior) *Col:* Ranger Coll. TX (J.C.); Texas Tech *HS:* Ranger [TX]
B: 6/15/1929, Drumright, OK
1954 ChiC: 1 G.

GARY ARTHUR Arthur, Gary Patrick 6′5″, 250 **TE**
Col: Miami (Ohio) *HS:* Chaminade [Dayton, OH] B: 1/9/1948, Dayton, OH *Drafted:* 1970 Round 5 NYJ
1970 NYJ: 7 G. **1971** NYJ: 14 G; Rec 1-12 12.0. **Total:** 21 G; Rec 1-12 12.0.

MIKE ARTHUR Arthur, Michael Scott 6'3", 280 **C**
Col: Texas A&M *HS:* Spring Woods [Houston, TX] B: 5/7/1968, Minneapolis, MN *Drafted:* 1991 Round 5 Cin
1991 Cin: 7 G. **1992** Cin: 16 G; 4 Fum. **1993** NE: 13 G. **1994** NE: 12 G; 1 Fum. **1995** GB: 11 G; KR 1-10 10.0. **1996** GB: 5 G; 1 Fum. **Total:** 64 G; KR 1-10 10.0; 6 Fum.

CORRIE ARTMAN Artman, Corwin Walter 6'2", 238 **T**
(Chang; Whitey) *Col:* Stanford *HS:* Long Beach Polytechnic [CA] B: 1/8/1907, Santa Monica, CA D: 3/9/1970, Long Beach, CA
1931 NYG: 12 G. **1932** Bos: 1 G. **1933** Pit: 10 G. **Total:** 23 G.

LEE ARTOE Artoe, Lee Robert Reno 6'3", 234 **T**
(Jelly) *Col:* Santa Clara; California *HS:* Lincoln [Tacoma, WA] B: 3/2/1916, Tacoma, WA *Drafted:* 1940 Round 9 ChiB
AAFC **1946** LA-A: 14 G; KR 1-13 13.0; Scor 1, 1-2 50.0% XK. **1947** LA-A: 14 G; KR 1-16 16.0. **1948** BalA: 14 G. **Total:** 42 G; KR 2-29 14.5; Scor 1, 1-2 50.0% XK.

NFL **1940** ChiB: 11 G; Scor 4, 1-1 100.0% FG, 1-2 50.0% XK. **1941** ChiB: 11 G; Scor 6, 1-7 14.3% FG, 3-4 75.0% XK. **1942** ChiB: 11 G; Scor 20, 0-1 FG, 20-22 90.9% XK. **1945** ChiB: 9 G; Scor 0-1 FG. **Total:** 42 G; Scor 30, 2-10 20.0% FG, 24-28 85.7% XK.

HERMAN ARVIE Arvie, Herman Joseph 6'4", 312 **OT**
Col: Grambling State *HS:* Opelousas [LA] B: 10/12/1970, Opelousas, LA *Drafted:* 1993 Round 5 Cle
1993 Cle: 16 G. **1994** Cle: 16 G. **1995** Cle: 16 G. **1996** Bal: 14 G; Rec 1-1 1.0 1 TD; 6 Pt. **Total:** 62 G; Rec 1-1 1.0 1 TD; 6 Pt.

DOUG ASAD Asad, Douglas Samuel 6'2", 205 **TE**
Col: Northwestern *HS:* Fairview [Fairview Park, OH] B: 8/27/1938, Fairview Park, OH
1960 Oak: KR 3-66 22.0. **1961** Oak: KR 1-10 10.0. **Total:** KR 4-76 19.0.

		Receiving			
Year Team	**G**	**Rec**	**Yds**	**Avg**	**TD**
1960 Oak	13	14	197	14.1	1
1961 Oak	14	42	592	14.1	2
NFL Total	27	56	789	14.1	3

WILLIE ASBURY Asbury, William Wesley 6'1", 226 **RB**
Col: Kent State *HS:* Princeton [Cincinnati, OH] B: 2/22/1943, Crawfordsville, GA *Drafted:* 1966 Round 4 Atl
1966 Pit: Pass 1-0. **Total:** Pass 1-0.

		Rushing				Receiving					Tot
Year Team	**G**	**Att**	**Yds**	**Avg**	**TD**	**Rec**	**Yds**	**Avg**	**TD**	**Fum**	**TD**
1966 Pit	14	169	544	3.2	7	19	228	12.0	2	6	9
1967 Pit	12	80	315	3.9	4	3	52	17.3	0	4	4
1968 Pit	7	4	9	2.3	0	3	27	9.0	0	0	0
NFL Total	33	253	868	3.4	11	25	307	12.3	2	10	13

DARREL ASCHBACHER Aschbacher, Darrel Godsil 6'1", 220 **OG**
Col: Boise State; Oregon *HS:* Crook Co. [Pineville, OR] B: 6/2/1935, Pineville, OR
1959 Phi: 11 G.

FRANK ASCHENBRENNER Aschenbrenner, Francis Xavier 5'10", 188 **RB**
Col: Marquette; North Carolina; Northwestern *HS:* North Division [Milwaukee, WI] B: 7/12/1925, Haibuehl, Germany
AAFC **1949** ChiA: 6 G; Rush 8-14 1.8; Rec 2-(-4) -2.0; KR 2-35 17.5.

JUDDY ASH Ash, Julian Samuel 6'2", 205 **G**
Col: Oregon State *HS:* La Grande [OR] B: 7/12/1900, San Francisco, CA D: 10/30/1965, Newport, OR
1926 LA: 2 G.

BILL ASHBAUGH Ashbaugh, William D 5'10", 175 **FB-WB**
Col: Pittsburgh *HS:* Washington [PA]; Bellefonte Acad. [PA] B: 9/24/1899, Hartsville, NY D: 7/1971, Olean, NY
1924 RI: 1 G. **1925** KC: 1 G. **Total:** 2 G.

CLIFF ASHBURN Ashburn, Clifford L 5'11", 190 **G-T-OE**
Col: Nebraska *HS:* Tilden [NE] B: 11/21/1905, Tilden, NE D: 11/9/1989, Scottsbluff, NE
1929 NYG: 13 G.

RICHARD ASHE Ashe, Richard Anthony 6'4", 260 **TE**
Col: Humboldt State *HS:* Birmingham [Moreno Valley, CA] B: 3/14/1967, Chicago, IL
1990 LARm: 1 G.

JAMIE ASHER Asher, Jamie Allem 6'3", 245 **TE**
Col: Louisville *HS:* Warren Central [Indianapolis, IN]; Clay Co. HS [Clay, KY] B: 10/31/1972, Indianapolis, IN *Drafted:* 1995 Round 5 Was
1995 Was: KR 1-13 13.0. **1996** Was: KR 1-13 13.0. **1997** Was: KR 1-17 17.0. **1998** Was: KR 1-8 8.0. **Total:** KR 4-51 12.8.

		Receiving			
Year Team	**G**	**Rec**	**Yds**	**Avg**	**TD**
1995 Was	7	14	172	12.3	0
1996 Was	16	42	481	11.5	4
1997 Was	16	49	474	9.7	1
1998 Was	9	28	294	10.5	0
NFL Total	48	133	1421	10.7	5

BOB ASHER Asher, Robert Dabney 6'5", 250 **OT-OG**
Col: Vanderbilt *HS:* Bishop Dennis J. O'Connell [Arlington, VA] B: 6/13/1948, Arlington, VA *Drafted:* 1970 Round 2 Dal
1970 Dal: 6 G. **1972** ChiB: 14 G. **1973** ChiB: 13 G. **1974** ChiB: 14 G. **1975** ChiB: 11 G. **Total:** 58 G.

WALKER LEE ASHLEY Ashley, Walker Lee 6'0", 234 **LB**
Col: Penn State *HS:* Henry Snyder [Jersey City, NJ] B: 7/28/1960, Bayonne, NJ *Drafted:* 1983 Round 3 Min
1983 Min: 15 G. **1984** Min: 15 G. **1986** Min: 16 G. **1987** Min: 12 G. **1988** Min: 16 G; Int 1-94 1 TD; 6 Pt. **1989** KC: 16 G; Int 1-0. **1990** Min: 4 G. **Total:** 94 G; Int 2-94 1 TD; 6 Pt.

DARRYL ASHMORE Ashmore, Darryl Allan 6'7", 310 **OT**
Col: Northwestern *HS:* Peoria [IL] B: 11/1/1969, Peoria, IL *Drafted:* 1992 Round 7 LARm
1993 LARm: 9 G. **1994** LARm: 11 G. **1995** StL: 16 G. **1996** StL-Was: 11 G. StL: 6 G. Was: 5 G. **1997** Was: 11 G. **1998** Oak: 15 G; 1 Fum TD; 6 Pt. **Total:** 73 G; 1 Fum TD; 6 Pt.

ROGER ASHMORE Ashmore, Marion Roger 6'0", 215 **T**
(Bert) *Col:* Gonzaga *HS:* J.M. Weatherwax [Aberdeen, WA] B: 1903 Deceased
1926 Mil: 9 G; Scor 2, 2 XK. **1927** Dul: 9 G. **1928** GB: 13 G. **1929** GB: 8 G. **Total:** 39 G.

JOSH ASHTON Ashton, Joshua Jr. 6'1", 205 **RB**
Col: Tulsa *HS:* Eagle Lake [TX] B: 8/24/1949, Eagle Lake, TX D: 11/1/1993, Eagle Lake, TX *Drafted:* 1971 Round 9 NE
1972 NE: KR 15-309 20.6. **Total:** KR 15-309 20.6.

		Rushing				Receiving					Tot
Year Team	**G**	**Att**	**Yds**	**Avg**	**TD**	**Rec**	**Yds**	**Avg**	**TD**	**Fum**	**TD**
1972 NE	14	128	546	4.3	3	22	207	9.4	1	3	4
1973 NE	12	93	305	3.3	0	11	113	10.3	0	4	0
1974 NE	12	26	99	3.8	0	0	0	—	0	0	0
1975 StL	2	10	44	4.4	0	0	0	—	0	1	0
NFL Total	40	257	994	3.9	3	33	320	9.7	1	8	4

JOE ASKA Aska, Joe 5'11", 236 **RB**
Col: Coffeyville CC KS; Cisco JC TX; Central Oklahoma *HS:* Putnam City [Oklahoma City, OK] B: 7/14/1972, St. Croix, Virgin Islands *Drafted:* 1995 Round 3 Oak
1996 Oak: Rec 8-63 7.9; KR 1-17 17.0. **1997** Oak: KR 2-46 23.0. **Total:** Rec 8-63 7.9; KR 3-63 21.0.

		Rushing				
Year Team	**G**	**Att**	**Yds**	**Avg**	**TD**	**Fum**
1995 Oak	1	0	0	—	0	0
1996 Oak	15	62	326	5.3	1	1
1997 Oak	7	12	10	0.8	0	0
NFL Total	23	74	336	4.5	1	1

MIKE ASKEA Askea, Michael Vaughn 6'4", 260 **OT**
Col: Stanford *HS:* Visalia [CA] B: 1/7/1951, Visalia, CA *Drafted:* 1973 Round 7 Den
1973 Den: 4 G.

BERT ASKSON Askson, Bert 6'3", 223 **DE-TE**
Col: Texas Southern *HS:* Kashmere [Houston, TX] B: 12/16/1945, Houston, TX *Drafted:* 1970 Round 14 Pit
1971 Pit: 11 G. **1973** NO: 1 G. **1975** GB: 14 G; Rec 2-25 12.5. **1976** GB: 14 G; Rec 1-2 2.0 1 TD; 6 Pt. **1977** GB: 14 G; Rec 2-51 25.5. **Total:** 54 G; Rec 5-78 15.6 1 TD; 6 Pt.

JIM ASMUS Asmus, James Victor Daniel 6'2", 195 **K**
Col: Mount San Antonio Coll. CA (J.C.); Hawaii *HS:* La Puente [CA] B: 12/2/1958, Meppal, Holland
1987 SF: 3 G; Punt 12-384 32.0.

ED ASPATORE Aspatore, Edward Charles 6'1", 220 **T-G**
Col: Marquette *HS:* Fond Du Lac [WI] B: 6/23/1909, Fond Du Lac, WI D: 3/14/1986, Louisville, KY
1934 Cin: 6 G.

LES ASPLUNDH Asplundh, Lester 6'3", 213 **FB-BB-WB**
Col: Swarthmore *HS:* Bryn Athyn Acad. [PA] B: 5/3/1901, Bryn Athyn, PA D: 5/3/1984, Philadelphia, PA
1925 Buf: 1 G.

JACK ATCHASON Atchason, Jack Dean 6′4″, 215 **OE**
Col: Western Illinois *HS:* Phelps Career [Washington, DC]
B: 11/16/1936, Springfield, IL *Drafted:* 1960 Round 1 DalT
1960 Bos-Hou: 3 G; Rec 5-48 9.6 1 TD; 6 Pt. Bos: 1 G; Rec 2-22 11.0. Hou: 2 G; Rec 3-26 8.7 1 TD; 6 Pt. **Total:** 3 G; Rec 5-48 9.6 1 TD; 6 Pt.

BURL ATCHESON Atcheson, Burl M.K. **OE**
Col: No College *HS:* East [Columbus, OH] B: 1902, Columbus, OH
Deceased
1922 Col: 1 G.

BILL ATESSIS Atessis, William James 6′3″, 240 **DE-DT**
Col: Texas *HS:* Jesse H. Jones [Houston, TX] B: 7/16/1949, Houston, TX *Drafted:* 1971 Round 2 Bal
1971 NE: 5 G.

PETE ATHAS Athas, Peter Garrett 5′11″, 185 **DB-WR**
Col: Miami-Dade CC FL; Tennessee *HS:* Miami Edison [FL]
B: 9/15/1946, Hackensack, NJ *Drafted:* 1970 Round 10 Dal
1971 NYG: Rush 1-3 3.0. **1975** Cle-Min: KR 6-95 15.8. Cle: KR 6-95 15.8.
1976 NO: KR 2-68 34.0. **Total:** Rush 1-3 3.0; KR 8-163 20.4.

		Punt Returns				Interceptions			
Year Team	**G**	**Ret**	**Yds**	**Avg**	**TD**	**Int**	**Yds**	**TD**	**Fum**
1971 NYG	13	3	21	7.0	0	2	52	1	1
1972 NYG	14	8	95	11.9	0	4	11	0	1
1973 NYG	14	20	153	7.7	0	5	52	0	5
1974 NYG	14	20	180	9.0	0	2	0	0	1
1975 Cle-Min	11	6	37	6.2	0	1	0	0	4
1975 Cle	6	5	36	7.2	0	0	0	0	3
1975 Min	5	1	1	1.0	0	1	0	0	1
1976 NO	13	35	332	9.5	0	2	22	0	3
NFL Total	79	92	818	8.9	0	16	137	1	15

DALE ATKESON Atkeson, Dale Wayne 6′2″, 211 **FB**
Col: No College *HS:* Nathaniel Narbonne [Los Angeles, CA]
B: 12/24/1930, Kansas City, MO
1954 Was: Rec 4-75 18.8; PR 4-29 7.3. **1955** Was: Rec 9-81 9.0 1 TD.
1956 Was: Rec 6-28 4.7; PR 1-12 12.0. **Total:** Rec 19-184 9.7 1 TD; PR 5-41 8.2.

		Rushing				Kickoff Returns					Tot
Year Team	**G**	**Ret**	**Yds**	**Avg**	**TD**	**Ret**	**Yds**	**Avg**	**TD**	**Fum**	**TD**
1954 Was	10	68	176	2.6	2	24	623	26.0	1	5	3
1955 Was	11	77	300	3.9	1	4	106	26.5	0	2	2
1956 Was	5	63	163	2.6	1	1	25	25.0	0	1	1
NFL Total	26	208	639	3.1	4	29	754	26.0	1	8	6

DAVE ATKINS Atkins, David Charles 6′1″, 205 **RB**
Col: New Mexico Mil. Inst. (J.C.); Texas-El Paso *HS:* Victoria [TX]
B: 5/18/1949, Victoria, TX *Drafted:* 1973 Round 8 SF
1973 SF: 5 G; Rush 4-19 4.8 1 TD; Rec 1-(-3) -3.0; KR 3-93 31.0; 6 Pt.
1974 SF: 1 G. **1975** SD: 3 G; Rush 1-4 4.0. **Total:** 9 G; Rush 5-23 4.6 1 TD; Rec 1-(-3) -3.0; KR 3-93 31.0; 6 Pt.

DOUG ATKINS Atkins, Douglas Leon 6′8″, 257 **DE**
Col: Tennessee *HS:* Humboldt [TN] B: 5/8/1930, Humboldt, TN
Drafted: 1953 Round 1 Cle *HOF:* 1982
1953 Cle: 8 G. **1954** Cle: 12 G. **1955** ChiB: 12 G. **1956** ChiB: 6 G; KR 1-0.
1957 ChiB: 12 G. **1958** ChiB: 12 G. **1959** ChiB: 12 G. **1960** ChiB: 12 G.
1961 ChiB: 14 G. **1962** ChiB: 14 G. **1963** ChiB: 14 G; Int 1-0; Scor **1** Saf; 2 Pt. **1964** ChiB: 12 G. **1965** ChiB: 14 G; Int 1-0. **1966** ChiB: 12 G; Int 1-3.
1967 NO: 14 G. **1968** NO: 11 G. **1969** NO: 14 G. **Total:** 205 G; KR 1-0; Int 3-3; Scor 1 Saf; 2 Pt.

GENE ATKINS Atkins, Gene Reynard 5′11″, 201 **DB**
Col: Florida A&M *HS:* James S. Rickards [Tallahassee, FL]
B: 11/22/1964, Tallahassee, FL *Drafted:* 1987 Round 7 NO
1990 NO: 3 Sac. **1991** NO: 3 Sac. **1993** NO: 1 Sac. **1994** Mia: 1 Sac.
Total: 8 Sac.

		Kickoff Returns				Interceptions			
Year Team	**G**	**Ret**	**Yds**	**Avg**	**TD**	**Int**	**Yds**	**TD**	**Fum**
1987 NO	13	0	0	—	0	3	12	0	0
1988 NO	16	20	424	21.2	0	4	42	0	1
1989 NO	14	12	245	20.4	0	1	-2	0	1
1990 NO	16	19	471	24.8	0	2	15	0	1
1991 NO	16	20	368	18.4	0	5	**198**	0	0
1992 NO	16	0	0	—	0	3	0	0	0
1993 NO	16	0	0	—	0	3	59	0	0
1994 Mia	15	0	0	—	0	3	24	0	0
1995 Mia	16	0	0	—	0	1	0	0	0
1996 Mia	5	0	0	—	0	0	0	0	0
NFL Total	143	71	1508	21.2	0	25	348	0	3

GEORGE ATKINS Atkins, George Arthur 6′1″, 210 **OG**
Col: Auburn *HS:* Shades Valley [Birmingham, AL] B: 4/10/1932, Birmingham, AL *Drafted:* 1955 Round 15 Det
1955 Det: 12 G.

JAMES ATKINS Atkins, James Curtis 6′6″, 306 **OT**
Col: Southwestern Louisiana *HS:* Woodland [Amite, LA] B: 1/28/1970, Amite, LA
1994 Sea: 4 G. **1995** Sea: 16 G. **1996** Sea: 16 G. **1997** Sea: 13 G.
1998 Bal: 9 G; Rec 1-0. **Total:** 58 G; Rec 1-0.

KELVIN ATKINS Atkins, Kelvin Lamar 6′3″, 235 **LB**
(Kal) *Col:* Illinois *HS:* Evans [Orlando, FL] B: 7/3/1960, Orlando, FL
Drafted: 1982 Round 8 TB
1983 ChiB: 13 G.

PERVIS ATKINS Atkins, Pervis R Jr. 6′1″, 230 **HB-WR**
(Afterburner) *Col:* Rancho Santiago Coll. CA (J.C.); San Francisco State; New Mexico State *HS:* Oakland Technical [CA] B: 11/24/1935, Ruston, LA *Drafted:* 1960 Round 3 LARm

		Rushing				Receiving			
Year Team	**G**	**Att**	**Yds**	**Avg**	**TD**	**Rec**	**Yds**	**Avg**	**TD**
1961 LARm	14	5	19	3.8	0	5	67	13.4	0
1962 LARm	14	7	19	2.7	0	35	393	11.2	1
1963 LARm	14	5	11	2.2	0	14	174	12.4	1
1964 Was	13	25	98	3.9	1	8	35	4.4	0
1965 Was-Oak	9	18	44	2.4	0	2	6	3.0	0
1965 Was	4	18	44	2.4	0	1	0	0.0	0
1965 Oak	5	0	0	—	0	1	6	6.0	0
1966 Oak	14	14	10	0.7	0	0	0	—	0
NFL Total	78	74	201	2.7	1	64	675	10.5	2

	Punt Returns				Kickoff Returns					Tot
Year Team	**Ret**	**Yds**	**Avg**	**TD**	**Ret**	**Yds**	**Avg**	**TD**	**Fum**	**TD**
1961 LARm	0	0	—	0	4	77	19.3	0	1	0
1962 LARm	11	94	8.5	0	28	676	24.1	0	4	1
1963 LARm	12	36	3.0	0	19	429	22.6	0	3	1
1964 Was	13	138	10.6	0	14	319	22.8	0	3	1
1965 Was-Oak	3	11	3.7	0	1	15	15.0	0	2	0
1965 Was	3	11	3.7	0	1	15	15.0	0	2	0
1966 Oak	1	13	13.0	0	29	608	21.0	0	2	0
NFL Total	40	292	7.3	0	95	2124	22.4	0	15	3

BOB ATKINS Atkins, Robert Lee Jr. 6′3″, 215 **DB**
Col: Grambling State *HS:* Luther Judson Price [Atlanta, GA]
B: 4/2/1946, Atlanta, GA *Drafted:* 1968 Round 2 StL

		Interceptions			
Year Team	**G**	**Int**	**Yds**	**TD**	**Fum**
1968 StL	14	2	0	0	1
1969 StL	13	3	74	0	0
1970 Hou	14	1	7	0	0
1971 Hou	12	1	25	1	0
1972 Hou	14	2	37	0	0
1973 Hou	5	0	0	0	0
1974 Hou	14	6	85	0	0
1975 Hou	14	4	133	0	0
1976 Hou	14	0	0	0	0
NFL Total	114	19	361	1	1

STEVE ATKINS Atkins, Steven Elwood 6′0″, 216 **RB**
Col: Maryland *HS:* Spotsylvania [VA] B: 6/22/1956, Spotsylvania, VA
Drafted: 1979 Round 2 GB
1979 GB: Rec 10-89 8.9. **1980** GB: Rec 7-47 6.7 1 TD. **1981** GB-Phi: Rec 1-2 2.0; KR 1-15 15.0. GB: Rec 1-2 2.0. Phi: KR 1-15 15.0.
Total: Rec 18-138 7.7 1 TD; KR 1-15 15.0.

		Rushing					Tot
Year Team	**G**	**Att**	**Yds**	**Avg**	**TD**	**Fum**	**TD**
1979 GB	7	42	239	5.7	1	1	1
1980 GB	9	67	216	3.2	1	1	2
1981 GB-Phi	4	12	33	2.8	0	1	0
1981 GB	3	11	12	1.1	0	1	0
1981 Phi	1	1	21	21.0	0	0	0
NFL Total	20	121	488	4.0	2	3	3

BILLY ATKINS Atkins, William Ellis 6′1″, 196 **DB-HB**
Col: Auburn *HS:* Millport [AL] B: 11/19/1934, Millport, AL
D: 11/5/1991, El Paso, TX *Drafted:* 1958 Round 5 SF
1958 SF: Rush 1-5 5.0. **1960** Buf: Rush 2-47 23.5; Scor 45, 6-13 46.2% FG, 27-33 81.8% XK. **1961** Buf: Rush 2-87 43.5 1 TD; PR 2-30 15.0; Scor 41, 2-6 33.3% FG, 29-31 93.5% XK. **Total:** Rush 5-139 27.8 1 TD; PR 2-30 15.0; Scor 86, 8-19 42.1% FG, 56-64 87.5% XK.

		Interceptions			Punting			
Year Team	**G**	**Int**	**Yds**	**TD**	**Punts**	**Yds**	**Avg**	**Fum**
1958 SF	12	1	6	0	25	983	39.3	0
1959 SF	11	0	0	0	0	0	—	0
1960 Buf	14	5	23	0	**89**	**3468**	39.0	1
1961 Buf	14	**10**	158	0	**85**	**3783**	**44.5**	0
1962 NYT	7	4	30	0	22	969	44.0	0
1963 NYJ-Buf	3	0	0	0	0	0	—	0
1963 NYJ	2	0	0	0	0	0	—	0
1963 Buf	1	0	0	0	0	0	—	0

1964 Den	3	0	0	0	0	0	—	0
NFL Total	64	20	217	0	221	9203	41.6	1

AL ATKINSON Atkinson, Allen Edward 6'2", 230 **LB**
(Hombre) *Col:* Villanova *HS:* Monsignor Bonner [Upper Darby, PA]
B: 7/28/1943, Philadelphia, PA *Drafted:* 1965 Round 3 Buf

		Interceptions		
Year Team	**G**	**Int**	**Yds**	**TD**
1965 NYJ	14	1	2	0
1966 NYJ	14	4	48	0
1967 NYJ	14	5	59	0
1968 NYJ	12	2	24	0
1969 NYJ	10	2	4	0
1970 NYJ	14	3	50	0
1971 NYJ	10	2	19	0
1972 NYJ	13	1	7	0
1973 NYJ	5	1	11	0
1974 NYJ	14	0	0	0
NFL Total	120	21	224	0

FRANK ATKINSON Atkinson, Franklyn Rhem 6'3", 240 **DT**
Col: Stanford *HS:* Menlo-Atherton [Atherton, CA] B: 12/13/1941
Drafted: 1963 Round 8 Pit
1963 Pit: 14 G. **1964** Den: 3 G. **Total:** 17 G.

BUTCH ATKINSON Atkinson, George Henry 6'0", 180 **DB**
Col: Morris Brown *HS:* Sol C. Johnson [Savannah, GA] B: 1/4/1947, Savannah, GA *Drafted:* 1968 Round 7 Oak
1971 Oak: **1** Fum TD. **1973** Oak: **1** Fum TD. **Total:** 2 Fum TD.

		Punt Returns				Kickoff Returns			
Year Team	**G**	**Ret**	**Yds**	**Avg**	**TD**	**Ret**	**Yds**	**Avg**	**TD**
1968 Oak	14	**36**	**490**	13.6	**2**	32	802	**25.1**	0
1969 Oak	14	25	153	6.1	0	16	382	23.9	0
1970 Oak	14	4	12	3.0	0	23	574	25.0	0
1971 Oak	14	20	159	8.0	0	0	0	—	0
1972 Oak	14	10	33	3.3	0	3	75	25.0	0
1973 Oak	14	**41**	336	8.2	1	0	0	—	0
1974 Oak	14	4	31	7.8	0	0	0	—	0
1975 Oak	14	8	33	4.1	0	2	60	30.0	0
1976 Oak	14	0	0	—	0	0	0	—	0
1977 Oak	12	0	0	—	0	0	0	—	0
1979 Den	6	0	0	—	0	0	0	—	0
NFL Total	144	148	1247	8.4	3	76	1893	24.9	0

	Interceptions				Tot
Year Team	**Int**	**Yds**	**TD**	**Fum**	**TD**
1968 Oak	4	66	1	7	3
1969 Oak	2	38	1	0	1
1970 Oak	3	35	0	0	0
1971 Oak	4	70	0	0	1
1972 Oak	4	37	0	2	0
1973 Oak	3	48	0	1	2
1974 Oak	4	39	0	1	0
1975 Oak	4	77	0	1	0
1977 Oak	2	38	0	0	0
NFL Total	30	448	2	12	7

JESS ATKINSON Atkinson, Jesse Gerald 5'9", 165 **K**
Col: Maryland *HS:* Crossland [Temple Hills, MD] B: 12/11/1961, Ann Arbor, MI
1985 NYG-StL: 8 G; Rush 1-14 14.0 1 TD; Scor 53, 10-18 55.6% FG, 17-18 94.4% XK. NYG: 6 G; Rush 1-14 14.0 1 TD; Scor 50, 10-15 66.7% FG, 14-15 93.3% XK. StL: 2 G; Scor 3, 0-3 FG, 3-3 100.0% XK. **1986** Was: 1 G; Scor 3, 3-3 100.0% XK. **1987** Was: 1 G; Scor 4, 1-1 100.0% FG, 1-1 100.0% XK. **1988** Ind: 1 G. **Total:** 11 G; Rush 1-14 14.0 1 TD; Scor 60, 11-19 57.9% FG, 21-22 95.5% XK.

RICKY ATKINSON Atkinson, Richard E Jr. 6'0", 175 **DB**
Col: Southern Connecticut State *HS:* Valley Regional [Deep River, CT]
B: 8/28/1965, Middletown, CT
1987 NE: 1 G.

REGGIE ATTACHE Attache, Reginald 5'7", 195 **WB-FB**
Col: Sherman Indian Deceased
1922 Oor: 8 G.

ALEX ATTY Atty, Alexander George 5'8", 216 **G**
(Blacky) *Col:* West Virginia *HS:* Johnstown [PA] B: 12/8/1916, Johnstown, PA D: 5/2/1973, Pottsville, PA *Drafted:* 1939 Round 18 Cle
1939 Cle: 3 G.

STEVE ATWATER Atwater, Stephen Dennis 6'3", 218 **DB**
Col: Arkansas *HS:* Lutheran North [St. Louis, MO] B: 10/28/1966, Chicago, IL *Drafted:* 1989 Round 1 Den
1990 Den: KR 1-0; 1 Sac. **1991** Den: 1 Sac. **1992** Den: 1 Sac. **1993** Den: 1 Sac. **1997** Den: 1 Sac. **Total:** KR 1-0; 5 Sac.

		Interceptions			
Year Team	**G**	**Int**	**Yds**	**TD**	**Fum**
1989 Den	16	3	34	0	0
1990 Den	15	2	32	0	0
1991 Den	16	5	104	0	0
1992 Den	15	2	22	0	0
1993 Den	16	2	81	0	0
1994 Den	14	1	24	0	0
1995 Den	16	3	54	0	0
1996 Den	16	3	11	0	1
1997 Den	15	2	42	1	0
1998 Den	16	1	4	0	0
NFL Total	155	24	408	1	1

JOHN ATWOOD Atwood, John Horton 5'11", 195 **HB-WB-DB**
Col: Wisconsin *HS:* Delavan-Darien [Delavan, WI] B: 1/27/1923, Janesville, WI
1948 NYG: 8 G; Rush 9-6 0.7; Rec 10-141 14.1 1 TD; PR 4-32 8.0; KR 3-58 19.3; Int 1-0; 6 Pt; 2 Fum.

EARL AUDET Audet, Earl Toussaint 6'2", 252 **T**
Col: Georgetown; USC *HS:* Lockwood [Warwick, RI] B: 5/14/1921, Providence, RI *Drafted:* 1944 Round 2 Was
AAFC **1946** LA-A: 13 G. **1947** LA-A: 14 G. **1948** LA-A: 14 G. **Total:** 41 G.

NFL **1945** Was: 10 G.

DAN AUDICK Audick, Daniel James Bartholomew 6'3", 252 **OT-OG**
Col: Hawaii *HS:* Wasson [Colorado Springs, CO] B: 11/15/1954, San Bernardino, CA *Drafted:* 1977 Round 4 Pit
1977 StL: 2 G. **1978** SD: 1 G. **1979** SD: 16 G. **1980** SD: 15 G. **1981** SF: 16 G. **1982** SF: 7 G. **1983** StL: 12 G. **1984** StL: 7 G. **Total:** 76 G.

HOWIE AUER Auer, Howard Joseph 6'1", 205 **T**
Col: Michigan *HS:* Central [Bay City, MI] B: 1/9/1908, Detroit, MI
D: 11/12/1985, Venice, FL
1933 Phi: 2 G.

JIM AUER Auer, James Robert 6'7", 275 **DE**
Col: Georgia *HS:* Washington Twp. [Sewell, NJ] B: 1/4/1962, Philadelphia, PA
1987 Phi: 1 G; 0.5 Sac.

JOE AUER Auer, Joseph 6'1", 200 **RB**
Col: Miami (Fla.); Georgia Tech *HS:* Coral Gables [FL] B: 10/11/1941, Trenton, NJ *Drafted:* 1963 Round 15 KC
1964 Buf: **1** Fum TD. **1966** Mia: PR 5-99 19.8. **1967** Mia: PR 9-42 4.7. **Total:** PR 14-141 10.1; 1 Fum TD.

		Rushing				Receiving			
Year Team	**G**	**Att**	**Yds**	**Avg**	**TD**	**Rec**	**Yds**	**Avg**	**TD**
1964 Buf	12	63	191	3.0	2	11	166	15.1	0
1965 Buf	5	3	19	6.3	0	0	0	—	0
1966 Mia	14	121	416	3.4	4	22	263	12.0	4
1967 Mia	13	44	128	2.9	1	18	218	12.1	2
1968 Atl	7	3	19	6.3	0	0	0	—	0
NFL Total	51	234	773	3.3	7	51	647	12.7	6

	Kickoff Returns					Tot
Year Team	**Ret**	**Yds**	**Avg**	**TD**	**Fum**	**TD**
1964 Buf	0	1	—	0	2	3
1966 Mia	28	698	24.9	1	7	9
1967 Mia	21	441	21.0	0	7	3
1968 Atl	2	31	15.5	0	0	0
NFL Total	51	1171	23.0	1	16	15

SCOTT AUER Auer, Scott Eugene 6'5", 255 **OT-OG**
Col: Michigan State *HS:* Elmhurst [Fort Wayne, IN] B: 10/4/1961, Fort Wayne, IN *Drafted:* 1984 Round 9 KC
1984 KC: 16 G. **1985** KC: 7 G. **Total:** 23 G.

TODD AUER Auer, Todd M 6'1", 230 **LB**
Col: Western Illinois *HS:* Gale-Ettrick-Trempealeau [Galesville, WI]
B: 1/8/1965, Winona, MN
1987 GB: 3 G.

DOWE AUGHTMAN Aughtman, Lorenzo Dowe 6'2", 260 **DT**
Col: Auburn *HS:* T.R. Miller [Brewton, AL] B: 1/28/1961, Brewton, AL
Drafted: 1984 Round 11 Dal
1984 Dal: 7 G.

SKY AUGUST August, Edward W 5'10", 180 **TB-WB**
Col: Villanova *HS:* Mahanoy City [PA] B: 8/5/1904, Mahanoy City, PA
D: 10/15/1993, Mahanoy City, PA
1931 Prov: 7 G.

STEVE AUGUST August, Steven Paul 6'4", 255 **OT**
Col: Tulsa *HS:* Jeannette [PA] B: 9/4/1954, Jeannette, PA
Drafted: 1977 Round 1 Sea
1977 Sea: 6 G. **1978** Sea: 14 G. **1979** Sea: 16 G. **1980** Sea: 16 G. **1981** Sea: 16 G; Rec 1-9 9.0. **1982** Sea: 8 G. **1983** Sea: 15 G. **1984** Sea-Pit: 11 G. Sea: 6 G. Pit: 5 G. **Total:** 102 G; Rec 1-9 9.0.

GENE AUGUSTERFER Augusterfer, Eugene Francis 5'9", 180 **BB-DB**
Col: Catholic *HS:* St. John's [Washington, DC] B: 10/4/1914, Washington, DC Deceased
1935 Pit: 1 G.

MIKE AUGUSTYNIAK Augustyniak, Michael Eugene 5'11", 225 **RB**
Col: Purdue *HS:* Leo [IN] B: 7/17/1956, Fort Wayne, IN

		Rushing				Receiving					Tot
Year Team	G	Att	Yds	Avg	TD	Rec	Yds	Avg	TD	Fum	TD
1981 NYJ	10	85	339	4.0	1	18	144	8.0	0	3	1
1982 NYJ	9	50	178	3.6	4	24	189	7.9	0	2	4
1983 NYJ	8	18	50	2.8	2	10	71	7.1	1	0	3
NFL Total	27	153	567	3.7	7	52	404	7.8	1	5	8

CHALMERS AULT Ault, Chalmers Augustus 5'9", 195 **T**
Col: West Virginia Wesleyan *HS:* Moundsville [WV] B: 7/10/1900, Jacobsburg, OH D: 5/18/1979, Buckhannon, WV
1924 Cle: 2 G. **1925** Cle: 1 G. **Total:** 3 G.

DAVID AUPIU Aupiu, Lotupue David 6'2", 235 **LB**
Col: Brigham Young *HS:* Carson [CA] B: 2/10/1961, Honolulu, HI
1987 LARm: 1 G.

CLIFF AUSTIN Austin, Clifford 6'0", 203 **RB**
Col: Clemson *HS:* Avondale [Avondale Estates, GA] B: 3/2/1960, Atlanta, GA *Drafted:* 1983 Round 3 NO
1983 NO: Rec 2-25 12.5. **1985** Atl: Rec 1-21 21.0. **1986** Atl: Rec 3-21 7.0. **1987** TB: Rec 5-51 10.2. **Total:** Rec 11-118 10.7.

		Rushing				Kickoff Returns					Tot
Year Team	G	Ret	Yds	Avg	TD	Ret	Yds	Avg	TD	Fum	TD
1983 NO	11	4	16	4.0	0	7	112	16.0	0	0	0
1984 Atl	15	4	7	1.8	0	4	77	19.3	0	0	0
1985 Atl	14	20	110	5.5	0	39	838	21.5	1	0	1
1986 Atl	15	62	280	4.5	1	7	120	17.1	0	1	1
1987 TB	3	19	32	1.7	1	0	0	—	0	0	1
NFL Total	58	109	445	4.1	2	57	1147	20.1	1	1	3

ERIC AUSTIN Austin, Eric Dewayne 5'10", 217 **DB**
Col: Jackson State *HS:* Moss Point [MS] B: 6/7/1973, Moss Point, MS *Drafted:* 1996 Round 4 TB
1996 TB: 2 G.

HISE AUSTIN Austin, Hise 6'4", 191 **DB**
Col: Prairie View A&M *HS:* M.C. Williams [Houston, TX] B: 9/8/1950, Houston, TX *Drafted:* 1973 Round 8 GB
1973 GB: 9 G. **1975** KC: 3 G. **Total:** 12 G.

JIM AUSTIN Austin, James L 6'2", 199 **E**
Col: St. Mary's (Cal.) *HS:* Hollywood [Los Angeles, CA] B: 9/10/1913, Omaha, NE D: 10/1975, La Jolla, CA

		Receiving			
Year Team	G	Rec	Yds	Avg	TD
1937 Bkn	7	13	185	14.2	0
1938 Bkn	11	14	180	12.9	1
1939 Det	10	5	102	20.4	0
NFL Total	28	32	467	14.6	1

DARRELL AUSTIN Austin, Kenneth Darrell 6'4", 250 **OG-C-OT**
Col: South Carolina *HS:* Union [SC] B: 11/6/1951, Union, SC *Drafted:* 1974 Round 16 Den
1975 NYJ: 12 G. **1976** NYJ: 11 G. **1977** NYJ: 9 G. **1978** NYJ: 13 G. **1979** TB: 16 G. **1980** TB: 8 G. **Total:** 69 G.

OCIE AUSTIN Austin, Ocie Moore 6'3", 200 **DB**
Col: Utah State *HS:* Berkeley [CA] B: 1/8/1947, Norfolk, VA *Drafted:* 1968 Round 10 Bal
1968 Bal: 14 G. **1969** Bal: 14 G; Int 2-10. **1970** Pit: 7 G; Int 1-22. **1971** Pit: 14 G. **Total:** 49 G; Int 3-32.

RAYMOND AUSTIN Austin, Raymond Demont 5'11", 190 **DB**
Col: Tennessee *HS:* Eisenhower [Lawton, OK] B: 12/21/1974, Greensboro, NC *Drafted:* 1997 Round 5 NYJ
1997 NYJ: 16 G. **1998** ChiB: 12 G. **Total:** 28 G.

KENT AUSTIN Austin, Richard Kent 6'1", 195 **QB**
Col: Mississippi *HS:* Brentwood [TN] B: 6/25/1963, Natick, MA *Drafted:* 1986 Round 12 StL
1986 StL: 16 G; Rush 1-0.

BILLY AUSTIN Austin, William Dominic 5'10", 195 **DB**
Col: New Mexico *HS:* Kempner [Houston, TX] B: 3/8/1975, Washington, DC
1998 Ind: 1 G.

BILL AUSTIN Austin, William Lee 6'1", 223 **OG-OT**
Col: Oregon State *HS:* Woodburn [OR] B: 10/18/1928, San Pedro, CA *Drafted:* 1949 Round 13 NYG
1949 NYG: 9 G; Int 1-0. **1950** NYG: 12 G. **1953** NYG: 12 G. **1954** NYG: 11 G. **1955** NYG: 12 G. **1956** NYG: 8 G. **1957** NYG: 11 G. **Total:** 75 G; Int 1-0.

BILLY AUTREY Autrey, William Rex 6'3", 220 **C**
Col: Stephen F. Austin St. *HS:* Marquez [TX] B: 1/17/1933, Ridge, TX
1953 ChiB: 7 G.

DARNELL AUTRY Autry, Huntington Darnell 5'10", 210 **RB**
Col: Northwestern *HS:* Tempe [AZ] B: 6/19/1976, Weisbaden, Germany *Drafted:* 1997 Round 4 ChiB
1997 ChiB: Rec 9-59 6.6; Scor 1 2XP.

		Rushing				
Year Team	G	Att	Yds	Avg	TD	Fum
1997 ChiB	13	112	319	2.8	1	2

HANK AUTRY Autry, Melvin Henry 6'3", 240 **C**
Col: Southern Mississippi *HS:* Hattiesburg [MS] B: 5/2/1947, Hattiesburg, MS *Drafted:* 1969 Round 17 Hou
1969 Hou: 14 G; 1 Fum. **1970** Hou: 14 G. **Total:** 28 G; 1 Fum.

TROY AUZENNE Auzenne, Troy Anthony 6'7", 293 **OT**
Col: California *HS:* Bishop Amat [La Puente, CA] B: 6/26/1969, El Monte, CA *Drafted:* 1992 Round 2 ChiB
1992 ChiB: 16 G. **1993** ChiB: 11 G. **1994** ChiB: 11 G. **1995** ChiB: 11 G. **1996** Ind: 12 G. **Total:** 61 G.

CHUCK AVEDISIAN Avedisian, Charles Toros 5'9", 203 **G-LB**
Col: Providence *HS:* Pawtucket [RI] B: 9/19/1917, West Hoboken, NJ D: 8/26/1983, New Britain, CT
1942 NYG: 10 G. **1943** NYG: 10 G; 6 Pt. **1944** NYG: 10 G; Int 1-48 1 TD; 6 Pt. **Total:** 30 G; Int 1-48 1 TD; Tot TD 2; 12 Pt.

BOB AVELLINI Avellini, Robert Hayden 6'2", 208 **QB**
Col: Maryland *HS:* Memorial [New Hyde Park, NY] B: 8/28/1953, Queens, NY *Drafted:* 1975 Round 6 ChiB

		Passing							
Year Team	G	Att	Comp	Comp%	Yds	YPA	TD	Int	Rating
1975 ChiB	8	126	67	53.2	942	7.48	6	11	57.0
1976 ChiB	14	271	118	43.5	1580	5.83	8	15	49.4
1977 ChiB	14	293	154	52.6	2004	6.84	11	18	61.3
1978 ChiB	13	264	141	53.4	1718	6.51	5	16	54.8
1979 ChiB	7	51	27	52.9	310	6.08	2	3	60.1
1981 ChiB	9	32	15	46.9	185	5.78	1	3	36.6
1982 ChiB	2	20	8	40.0	84	4.20	0	0	52.9
1983 ChiB	2	0	0	—	0	—	0	0	—
1984 ChiB	4	53	30	56.6	288	5.43	0	3	48.3
NFL Total	73	1110	560	50.5	7111	6.41	33	69	54.8

	Rushing				
Year Team	Att	Yds	Avg	TD	Fum
1975 ChiB	4	-3	-0.8	1	2
1976 ChiB	18	58	3.2	1	3
1977 ChiB	37	109	2.9	1	8
1978 ChiB	34	54	1.6	2	5
1979 ChiB	3	10	3.3	0	0
1981 ChiB	5	2	0.4	0	0
1984 ChiB	3	-5	-1.7	0	2
NFL Total	104	225	2.2	5	20

JOHN AVENI Aveni, John Patrick 6'3", 212 **K-DE**
Col: Indiana *HS:* Glassboro [NJ] B: 3/17/1935, Glassboro, NJ *Drafted:* 1959 Round 27 ChiB
1959 ChiB: 12 G; Scor 58, 10-19 52.6% FG, 28-32 87.5% XK. **1960** ChiB: 12 G; Scor 44, 7-16 43.8% FG, 23-25 92.0% XK. **1961** Was: 14 G; Pass 1-0; Rec 6-84 14.0 1 TD; Scor 42, 5-28 17.9% FG, 21-23 91.3% XK; 2 Fum. **Total:** 38 G; Pass 1-0; Rec 6-84 14.0 1 TD; Scor 144, 22-63 34.9% FG, 72-80 90.0% XK; 2 Fum.

SISTO AVERNO Averno, Sisto Joseph 5'11", 235 **OG-LB**
Col: Muhlenberg *HS:* Paterson [NJ] B: 5/12/1925, Paterson, NJ
1950 Bal: 12 G. **1951** NYY: 12 G; KR 3-28 9.3. **1952** Dal: 12 G. **1953** Bal: 12 G. **1954** Bal: 3 G. **Total:** 51 G; KR 3-28 9.3.

DON AVERY Avery, Donald Lee 6'4", 254 **T**
Col: Alabama; USC *HS:* John Marshall [Los Angeles, CA] B: 2/10/1921, Los Angeles, CA
AAFC **1948** LA-A: 1 G.

NFL **1946** Was: 11 G. **1947** Was: 10 G; KR 2-24 12.0; 1 Fum. **Total:** 21 G; KR 2-24 12.0; 1 Fum.

JIM AVERY Avery, James 6'2", 235 **TE**
Col: Northern Illinois B: 7/11/1944, Grand Rapids, MI
1966 Was: 1 G.

JOHN AVERY Avery, John Edward 5'9", 190 **RB**
Col: Northwest Mississippi CC; Mississippi *HS:* Asheville [NC] B: 1/11/1976, Richmond, VA *Drafted:* 1998 Round 1 Mia
1998 Mia: Rec 10-67 6.7 1 TD.

		Rushing				Kickoff Returns					Tot
Year Team	G	Ret	Yds	Avg	TD	Ret	Yds	Avg	TD	Fum	TD
1998 Mia	16	143	503	3.5	2	43	1085	25.2	0	5	3

KEN AVERY Avery, Kenneth William 6′0″, 227 **LB**
Col: Southern Mississippi *HS:* South Dade [Homestead, FL]
B: 5/23/1944, New York, NY *Drafted:* 1966 Round 12 NYG
1967 NYG: 13 G. **1968** NYG: 14 G. **1969** Cin: 14 G. **1970** Cin: 14 G; Int 1-5. **1971** Cin: 14 G. **1972** Cin: 13 G. **1973** Cin: 14 G; Int 1-15. **1974** Cin: 13 G. **1975** KC: 14 G. **Total:** 123 G; Int 2-20.

STEVE AVERY Avery, Steven George 6′2″, 233 **RB**
Col: Northern Michigan *HS:* Central [Brookfield, WI] B: 8/18/1966, Milwaukee, WI
1989 Hou: 1 G. **1991** GB: 1 G. **1993** Pit: Postseason only. **1994** Pit: 14 G; Rush 2-4 2.0; Rec 1-2 2.0. **1995** Pit: 11 G; Rush 1-3 3.0; Rec 11-82 7.5 1 TD; 6 Pt. **Total:** 27 G; Rush 3-7 2.3; Rec 12-84 7.0 1 TD; 6 Pt.

JOE AVEZZANO Avezzano, Joseph William 6′2″, 235 **C**
Col: Florida State *HS:* Andrew Jackson [Jacksonville, FL]
B: 11/17/1943, Yonkers, NY *Drafted:* 1966 Redshirt Round 6 Bos
1966 Bos: 3 G.

BUTCH AVINGER Avinger, Clarence Edmund 6′1″, 215 **FB**
Col: Alabama *HS:* Sidney Lanier [Montgomery, AL] B: 12/15/1928, Beatrice, AL *Drafted:* 1951 Round 1 Pit
1953 NYG: Rush 5-6 1.2; Rec 2-8 4.0.

		Punting			
Year Team	**G**	**Punts**	**Yds**	**Avg**	**Fum**
1953 NYG	12	42	1597	38.0	1

ROB AWALT Awalt, Robert Mitchell 6′5″, 258 **TE**
Col: Sacramento City Coll. CA (J.C.); Nevada-Reno; San Diego State
HS: Valley [Sacramento, CA] B: 4/9/1964, Landsthul, Germany
Drafted: 1987 Round 3 StL
1987 StL: Rush 2-(-9) -4.5. **1989** Pho: Pass 1-0, 1 Int. **Total:** Pass 1-0, 1 Int; Rush 2-(-9) -4.5.

		Receiving				
Year Team	**G**	**Rec**	**Yds**	**Avg**	**TD**	**Fum**
1987 StL	12	42	526	12.5	6	0
1988 Pho	16	39	454	11.6	4	1
1989 Pho	16	33	360	10.9	0	0
1990 Dal	13	13	133	10.2	0	1
1991 Dal	12	5	57	11.4	0	1
1992 Buf	14	4	34	8.5	0	0
1993 Buf	12	2	19	9.5	0	0
NFL Total	95	138	1583	11.5	10	3

OBAFEMI AYANBADEJO Ayanbadejo, Obafemi 6′2″, 230 **RB**
Col: Cabrillo Coll. CA (J.C.); San Diego State *HS:* Santa Cruz [CA]
B: 3/5/1975, Chicago, IL
1998 Min: 1 G.

BUDDY AYDELETTE Aydelette, William Leslie 6′4″, 256 **OT**
Col: Alabama *HS:* S.S. Murphy [Mobile, AL] B: 8/19/1956, Mobile, AL
Drafted: 1980 Round 7 GB
1980 GB: 9 G. **1987** Pit: 12 G. **Total:** 21 G.

JOHN AYERS Ayers, John Milton 6′5″, 258 **OG-OT**
Col: Texas; West Texas A&M *HS:* Carrizo Springs [TX] B: 4/14/1953, Carrizo Springs, TX D: 10/2/1995, Canyon, TX *Drafted:* 1976 Round 8 SF
1977 SF: 14 G. **1978** SF: 16 G. **1979** SF: 16 G. **1980** SF: 16 G. **1981** SF: 16 G. **1982** SF: 8 G. **1983** SF: 16 G. **1984** SF: 16 G. **1985** SF: 16 G. **1986** SF: 14 G. **1987** Den: 9 G. **Total:** 157 G.

MARVIN AYERS Ayers, Marvin Lee 6′5″, 265 **DE**
Col: Southern Methodist; Grambling State *HS:* South Oak Cliff [Dallas, TX] B: 9/12/1963, Dallas, TX
1987 Phi: 2 G.

JOE AZELBY Azelby, Joseph K 6′1″, 225 **LB**
Col: Harvard *HS:* Bergen Catholic [Oradell, NJ] B: 3/5/1962, New York, NY *Drafted:* 1984 Round 10 Buf
1984 Buf: 14 G.

MIKE BAAB Baab, Michael James 6′4″, 270 **C**
Col: Tarrant Co. JC TX; Austin CC TX; Texas *HS:* Trinity [Euless, TX]
B: 12/6/1959, Fort Worth, TX *Drafted:* 1982 Round 5 Cle
1982 Cle: 7 G. **1983** Cle: 15 G. **1984** Cle: 16 G; 1 Fum. **1985** Cle: 16 G; Rush 1-0; 1 Fum. **1986** Cle: 16 G. **1987** Cle: 12 G. **1988** NE: 15 G. **1989** NE: 16 G. **1990** Cle: 16 G. **1991** Cle: 16 G. **1992** KC: 3 G. **Total:** 148 G; Rush 1-0; 2 Fum.

STEVE BAACK Baack, Steven William 6′4″, 264 **NT-OG-DE-DT**
Col: Oregon *HS:* Grant [John Day, OR] B: 11/16/1960, Ames, IA
Drafted: 1984 Round 3 Det
1984 Det: 16 G. **1985** Det: 16 G; 2 Sac. **1986** Det: 16 G. **1987** Det: 7 G. **Total:** 55 G; 2 Sac.

AL BABARTSKY Babartsky, Albert John 6′0″, 225 **T**
Col: Fordham *HS:* Shenandoah Valley [Shenandoah, PA]
B: 4/19/1915, Shenandoah, PA *Drafted:* 1938 Round 3 ChiC
1938 ChiC: 6 G. **1939** ChiC: 11 G; **1** Fum TD; 6 Pt. **1941** ChiC: 10 G; KR 3-57 19.0. **1943** ChiB: 9 G. **1944** ChiB: 10 G. **1945** ChiB: 8 G. **Total:** 54 G; KR 3-57 19.0; 1 Fum TD; 6 Pt.

CHARLIE BABB Babb, Charles David 6′0″, 190 **DB**
Col: Memphis *HS:* Charleston [MO] B: 2/4/1950, Sikeston, MO
Drafted: 1972 Round 5 Mia
1974 Mia: PR 2-29 14.5; KR 1-0. **1975** Mia: PR 7-95 13.6. **1976** Mia: PR 3-38 12.7. **1977** Mia: PR 2-10 5.0. **1978** Mia: PR 9-57 6.3. **1979** Mia: PR 1-0. **Total:** PR 24-229 9.5; KR 1-0.

		Interceptions		
Year Team	**G**	**Int**	**Yds**	**TD**
1972 Mia	14	1	24	0
1973 Mia	14	0	0	0
1974 Mia	14	0	0	0
1975 Mia	14	4	18	0
1976 Mia	14	2	20	0
1977 Mia	6	1	15	0
1978 Mia	16	3	61	0
1979 Mia	5	1	3	0
NFL Total	97	12	141	0

GENE BABB Babb, Eugene Walter 6′3″, 216 **FB-LB**
(Duke) *Col:* Austin *HS:* Odessa [TX] B: 12/27/1934, El Paso, TX
Drafted: 1957 Round 19 SF
1957 SF: KR 1-0. **1958** SF: KR 2-30 15.0. **1960** Dal: KR 3-46 15.3. **1961** Dal: KR 2-34 17.0. **1962** Hou: Int 2-31 **1** TD. **1963** Hou: Int 2-24. **Total:** KR 8-110 13.8; Int 4-55 1 TD.

		Rushing				Receiving					Tot
Year Team	**G**	**Att**	**Yds**	**Avg**	**TD**	**Rec**	**Yds**	**Avg**	**TD**	**Fum**	**TD**
1957 SF	12	102	330	3.2	3	20	141	7.1	0	4	3
1958 SF	12	7	9	1.3	0	0	0	—	0	0	0
1960 Dal	10	39	115	2.9	0	13	140	10.8	1	0	1
1961 Dal	14	0	0	—	0	0	0	—	0	0	0
1962 Hou	14	3	0	0.0	0	0	0	—	0	0	1
1963 Hou	14	1	7	7.0	0	0	0	—	0	0	0
NFL Total	76	152	461	3.0	3	33	281	8.5	1	4	5

HARRY BABCOCK Babcock, Harry Lewis 6′2″, 193 **OE-DE**
Col: Georgia *HS:* Pearl River [NY] B: 8/12/1930, West Nyack, NY
Drafted: 1953 Round 1 SF
1953 SF: 10 G; Rec 7-59 8.4; KR 2-3 1.5. **1954** SF: 12 G; Rec 6-91 15.2. **1955** SF: 8 G; Rec 3-31 10.3; 1 Fum. **Total:** 30 G; Rec 16-181 11.3; KR 2-3 1.5; 1 Fum.

SAM BABCOCK Babcock, Samuel Lyle 5′6″, 168 **WB-FB-BB**
Col: Syracuse *HS:* Suffield Acad. [CT] B: 11/5/1901, Gray, IA
D: 7/28/1970, National City, CA
1926 Can: 8 G.

BOB BABICH Babich, Robert 6′2″, 231 **LB**
Col: Miami (Ohio) *HS:* Memorial [Campbell, OH] B: 5/5/1947, Youngstown, OH *Drafted:* 1969 Round 1 SD
1970 SD: 14 G. **1971** SD: 14 G; **1** Fum TD; 6 Pt. **1972** SD: 14 G; Int 2-9. **1973** Cle: 14 G; Int 1-48. **1974** Cle: 14 G; Int 1-4. **1975** Cle: 11 G. **1976** Cle: 14 G; Int 2-29. **1977** Cle: 14 G; KR 1-14 14.0. **1978** Cle: 16 G. **Total:** 125 G; KR 1-14 14.0; Int 6-90; 1 Fum TD; 6 Pt.

JOHN BABINECZ Babinecz, John Michael 6′1″, 222 **LB**
Col: Villanova *HS:* Central Catholic [Pittsburgh, PA] B: 7/27/1950, Pittsburgh, PA *Drafted:* 1972 Round 2 Dal
1972 Dal: 14 G. **1973** Dal: 12 G. **1975** ChiB: 14 G; Int 1-15. **Total:** 40 G; Int 1-15.

MARTY BACCAGLIO Baccaglio, Martin H 6′3″, 245 **DE**
Col: Coll. of Marin CA (J.C.); San Jose State *HS:* Novato [CA]
B: 9/28/1944, San Francisco, CA *Drafted:* 1967 Round 14 SD
1968 SD-Cin: 12 G; KR 2-0. SD: 9 G; KR 2-0. Cin: 3 G. **1969** Cin: 14 G. **1970** Cin: 14 G. **Total:** 40 G; KR 2-0.

CARL BACCHUS Bacchus, Robert Carl 6′0″, 205 **OE**
Col: Missouri *HS:* Central [Kansas City, MO] B: 7/31/1904, Pine Bluff, AR D: 3/2/1985, Kansas City, MO
1927 Cle: 10 G; Rec 3 TD; 18 Pt. **1928** Det: 9 G; Rec 4 TD; 24 Pt. **Total:** 19 G; Rec 7 TD; 42 Pt.

JOE BACHMAIER Bachmaier, Joseph William 5′9″, 175 **G-C-T-OE**
Col: No College *HS:* None B: 3/10/1895, Rochester, NY
D: 1/14/1974, Rochester, NY
1920 Roch: 9 G. **1921** Roch: 4 G. **1922** Roch: 3 G. **1923** Roch: 1 G. **1924** Roch: 4 G. **Total:** 21 G.

JAY BACHMAN Bachman, Jay Lance 6′3″, 250 **C**
Col: Cincinnati *HS:* Ross [Hamilton, OH] B: 12/8/1945, Hamilton, OH
Drafted: 1967 Round 5 GB
1968 Den: 6 G. **1969** Den: 14 G. **1970** Den: 11 G. **1971** Den: 14 G; KR 2-20 10.0. **Total:** 45 G; KR 2-20 10.0.

TED BACHMAN Bachman, Theodore Lewis Jr. 6′0″, 190 **DB**
Col: Porterville Coll. CA (J.C.); New Mexico State *HS:* Burroughs [Ridgecrest, CA] B: 1/19/1952, Pensacola, FL
1976 Sea-Mia: 13 G. Sea: 5 G. Mia: 8 G. **Total:** 13 G.

RIP BACHOR Bachor, Ludwig A 6′0″, 215 **T**
(Elmo) *Col:* Detroit Mercy *HS:* Western [Detroit, MI] B: 12/10/1901, Calumet, MI D: 12/11/1959, Lansing, MI
1928 Det: 1 G.

BACKNOR Backnor **C**
Col: No College Deceased
1921 Ton: 1 G.

FRANK BACON Bacon, Francis William 5′11″, 182 **WB-TB-E**
Col: Wabash *HS:* South Bend Central [IN]; Princeton Prep [IN]
B: 1/11/1894, South Bend, IN D: 8/31/1977, Port Clinton, OH
1920 Day: 9 G. **1921** Day: 9 G; Rush 5 TD; Rec 1 TD; Tot TD 6; 36 Pt. **1922** Day: 6 G; Pass 1 TD; Rush 1 TD; 6 Pt. **1923** Day-Akr: 9 G. Day: 8 G. Akr: 1 G. **1924** Day: 8 G; 1 Fum TD; 6 Pt. **1925** Day: 6 G. **Total:** 47 G; Pass 1 TD; Rush 6 TD; Rec 1 TD; 1 Fum TD; Tot TD 8; 48 Pt.

COY BACON Bacon, Lander McCoy 6′4″, 270 **DE-DT**
Col: Jackson State *HS:* Ironton [OH] B: 8/30/1942, Cadiz, KY
1968 LARm: 7 G. **1969** LARm: 14 G. **1970** LARm: 14 G; 1 Fum TD; 6 Pt. **1971** LARm: 14 G; Int 1-0. **1972** LARm: 14 G. **1973** SD: 12 G; Int 1-80 1 TD; 6 Pt. **1974** SD: 14 G. **1975** SD: 14 G. **1976** Cin: 14 G; Scor **1** Saf; 2 Pt. **1977** Cin: 12 G. **1978** Was: 16 G. **1979** Was: 16 G. **1980** Was: 16 G. **1981** Was: 3 G. **Total:** 180 G; Int 2-80 1 TD; Scor 1 Saf; 1 Fum TD; Tot TD 2; 14 Pt.

JOHN BADACZEWSKI Badaczewski, John Walter 6′1″, 239 **OG-DG**
(Baddie) *Col:* Case Western Reserve *HS:* Windber [PA] B: 1/27/1922, Johnstown, PA
1946 Bos: 11 G. **1947** Bos: 12 G. **1948** Bos-ChiC: 11 G. Bos: 6 G. ChiC: 5 G. **1949** Was: 12 G. **1950** Was: 12 G. **1951** Was: 12 G. **1953** ChiB: 12 G. **Total:** 82 G.

RICK BADANJEK Badanjek, Richard Alan 5′8″, 217 **RB**
Col: Maryland *HS:* Chalker [Southington, OH] B: 3/25/1962, Warren, OH *Drafted:* 1986 Round 7 Was
1987 Atl: Rec 6-35 5.8; KR 2-27 13.5. **Total:** Rec 6-35 5.8; KR 2-27 13.5.

		Rushing				
Year Team	**G**	**Att**	**Yds**	**Avg**	**TD**	**Fum**
1986 Was	6	0	0	—	0	0
1987 Atl	2	29	87	3.0	1	1
1988 Atl	6	0	0	—	0	0
NFL Total	14	29	87	3.0	1	1

RICHIE BADAR Badar, Richard Chester 6′1″, 190 **QB**
Col: Indiana *HS:* St. Stanislaus [Cleveland, OH] B: 3/8/1943, Cleveland, OH
1967 Pit: 1 G.

BRAD BADGER Badger, Bradley Thomas 6′4″, 298 **OG**
Col: Snow Coll. UT (J.C.); Stanford *HS:* Corvallis [OR] B: 1/11/1975, Corvallis, OR *Drafted:* 1997 Round 5 Was
1997 Was: 12 G. **1998** Was: 16 G. **Total:** 28 G.

RED BADGRO Badgro, Morris Hiram 6′0″, 191 **OE-DE**
Col: USC *HS:* Kent [WA] B: 12/1/1902, Kent, WA D: 7/13/1998, Kent, WA *HOF:* 1981
1930 NYG: Pass 1 TD. **1933** NYG: **1** Fum TD. **Total:** Pass 1 TD; 1 Fum TD.

		Receiving				Tot
Year Team	**G**	**Rec**	**Yds**	**Avg**	**TD**	**TD**
1927 NYY	12	—	—	—	1	1
1928 NYY	1	—	—	—	0	0
1930 NYG	17	—	—	—	3	3
1931 NYG	13	—	—	—	0	0
1932 NYG	12	6	106	17.7	0	0
1933 NYG	12	9	176	19.6	2	3
1934 NYG	13	**16**	206	12.9	1	1
1935 NYG	5	1	13	13.0	0	0
1936 Bkn	9	3	59	19.7	0	0
NFL Total	94	35	560	16.0	7	8

STEVE BAGARUS Bagarus, Stephen Michael Jr. 6′0″, 173 **HB-DB**
Col: Notre Dame *HS:* Michael Washington [South Bend, IN]
B: 6/19/1919, South Bend, IN D: 10/17/1981, Gaithersburg, MD
1946 Was: Int 4-66. **1947** LARm: Int 1-31. **Total:** Int 5-97.

		Rushing				Receiving			
Year Team	**G**	**Att**	**Yds**	**Avg**	**TD**	**Rec**	**Yds**	**Avg**	**TD**
1945 Was	10	39	154	3.9	1	34	617	18.1	5
1946 Was	11	53	168	3.2	0	31	438	14.1	3
1947 LARm	2	3	15	5.0	0	0	0	—	0
1948 Was	5	3	6	2.0	0	15	100	6.7	1
NFL Total	28	98	343	3.5	1	80	1155	14.4	9

	Punt Returns				Kickoff Returns					Tot
Year Team	**Ret**	**Yds**	**Avg**	**TD**	**Ret**	**Yds**	**Avg**	**TD**	**Fum**	**TD**
1945 Was	**21**	**251**	12.0	0	12	325	27.1	0	2	6
1946 Was	18	192	10.7	0	13	332	25.5	0	6	3
1947 LARm	2	18	9.0	0	1	11	11.0	0	1	0
1948 Was	0	0	—	0	1	15	15.0	0	0	1
NFL Total	41	461	11.2	0	27	683	25.3	0	9	10

HERM BAGBY Bagby, Herman 5′9″, 175 **WB-TB-FB-BB**
Col: Arkansas *HS:* Pine Bluff [AR] B: 2/21/1903, Lake Village, AR D: 2/29/1980, Lake Village, AR
1926 Bkn: 8 G; Rec 1 TD; Int **1** TD; 1 Fum TD; Tot TD 3; 18 Pt. **1927** Cle: 4 G. **Total:** 12 G; Rec 1 TD; Int 1 TD; 1 Fum TD; Tot TD 3; 18 Pt.

ED BAGDON Bagdon, Edward 5′10″, 204 **OG-LB**
Col: Michigan State *HS:* Fordson [Dearborn, MI] B: 4/30/1926, Dearborn, MI D: 10/25/1990, Hesperia, CA *Drafted:* 1950 Round 7 ChiC
1950 ChiC: 11 G; Rec 1-19 19.0; KR 1-11 11.0. **1951** ChiC: 12 G. **1952** Was: 3 G; Scor 7, 1-3 33.3% FG, 4-6 66.7% XK. **Total:** 26 G; Rec 1-19 19.0; KR 1-11 11.0; Scor 7, 1-3 33.3% FG, 4-6 66.7% XK.

BILLY BAGGETT Baggett, William Boyce 5′11″, 175 **HB-DB**
Col: Louisiana State *HS:* South Park [Beaumont, TX] B: 6/2/1929, Greenville, TX *Drafted:* 1951 Round 22 LARm
1952 Dal: 11 G; Rush 19-65 3.4; Rec 3-41 13.7 1 TD; PR 12-102 8.5; KR **23**-567 24.7; Int 1-10; 6 Pt; 4 Fum.

CURT BAHAM Baham, Roy Curtis 5′11″, 180 **DB**
Col: Tulane *HS:* Covington [LA] B: 3/2/1963, Covington, LA
1987 Sea: 3 G.

PETE BAHAN Bahan, Leonard Finlan 5′9″, 165 **BB-TB-FB**
Col: Notre Dame; Detroit Mercy *HS:* Somerset [KY] B: 2/18/1898, Colegrove, PA D: 5/1/1977, Fort Worth, TX
1923 Cle-Buf: 9 G; Pass 1 TD. Cle: 7 G; Pass 1 TD. Buf: 2 G. **Total:** 9 G; Pass 1 TD.

KEN BAHNSEN Bahnsen, Kenneth Antone 5′10″, 200 **FB**
Col: Tyler JC TX; North Texas *HS:* Vinton [LA] B: 2/19/1930, Vinton, LA *Drafted:* 1953 Round 21 SF
1953 SF: 7 G; Rush 1-1 1.0; KR 1-21 21.0.

CHRIS BAHR Bahr, Christopher Kurt 5′10″, 170 **K**
Col: Penn State *HS:* Neshaminy [Langhorne, PA] B: 2/3/1953, State College, PA *Drafted:* 1976 Round 2 Cin
1977 Cin: Punt 2-88 44.0. **1978** Cin: Punt 4-108 27.0. **1981** Oak: Punt 2-43 21.5. **Total:** Punt 8-239 29.9.

		Scoring						
Year Team	**G**	**Pts**	**FG**	**FGA**	**FG%**	**XK**	**XKA**	**XK%**
1976 Cin	14	81	14	27	51.9	39	42	92.9
1977 Cin	14	82	19	27	70.4	25	26	96.2
1978 Cin	16	74	16	30	53.3	26	29	89.7
1979 Cin	16	79	13	23	56.5	40	42	95.2
1980 Oak	16	98	19	37	51.4	41	44	93.2
1981 Oak	16	69	14	24	58.3	27	33	81.8
1982 LARd	9	62	10	16	62.5	**32**	33	97.0
1983 LARd	16	114	21	27	77.8	51	53	96.2
1984 LARd	16	100	20	27	74.1	40	42	95.2
1985 LARd	16	100	20	32	62.5	40	42	95.2
1986 LARd	16	99	21	28	75.0	36	36	100.0
1987 LARd	13	84	19	29	65.5	27	28	96.4
1988 LARd	16	91	18	29	62.1	37	39	94.9
1989 SD	16	80	17	25	68.0	29	30	96.7
NFL Total	210	1213	241	381	63.3	490	519	94.4

MATT BAHR Bahr, Matthew David 5′10″, 175 **K**
Col: Penn State *HS:* Neshaminy [Langhorne, PA] B: 7/6/1956, Philadelphia, PA *Drafted:* 1979 Round 6 Pit
1988 Cle: Rush 1-(-8) -8.0. **1995** NE: Punt 1-29 29.0. **Total:** Rush 1-(-8) -8.0; Punt 1-29 29.0.

		Scoring						
Year Team	**G**	**Pts**	**FG**	**FGA**	**FG%**	**XK**	**XKA**	**XK%**
1979 Pit	16	104	18	30	60.0	**50**	**52**	96.2
1980 Pit	16	96	19	28	67.9	39	42	92.9
1981 SF-Cle	15	79	15	26	57.7	34	34	100.0
1981 SF	4	18	2	6	33.3	12	12	100.0
1981 Cle	11	61	13	20	65.0	22	22	100.0
1982 Cle	9	38	7	15	46.7	17	17	100.0
1983 Cle	16	101	21	24	**87.5**	38	40	**95.0**
1984 Cle	16	97	24	32	75.0	25	25	100.0
1985 Cle	16	77	14	18	77.8	35	35	100.0
1986 Cle	12	90	20	26	76.9	30	30	100.0
1987 Cle	3	21	4	5	80.0	9	10	90.0
1988 Cle	16	104	24	29	82.8	32	33	97.0
1989 Cle	16	88	16	24	66.7	40	40	100.0
1990 NYG	13	80	17	23	73.9	29	30	96.7
1991 NYG	13	90	22	29	75.9	24	25	96.0
1992 NYG	12	77	16	21	76.2	29	29	100.0

1993 Phi-NE	14	67	13	18	72.2	28	29	96.6
1993 Phi	11	42	8	13	61.5	18	19	94.7
1993 NE	3	25	5	5	100.0	10	10	100.0
1994 NE	16	117	27	34	79.4	36	36	100.0
1995 NE	16	96	23	33	69.7	27	27	100.0
NFL Total	235	1422	300	415	72.3	522	534	97.8

AARON BAILEY Bailey, Aaron Duane 5′10″, 185 **WR**
Col: Coll. of DuPage IL (J.C.); Louisville *HS:* Pioneer [Ann Arbor, MI]
B: 10/24/1971, Ann Arbor, MI
1995 Ind: Rush 1-34 34.0. **1997** Ind: Rush 3-20 6.7; PR 1-19 19.0.
1998 Ind: PR 19-176 9.3. **Total:** Rush 4-54 13.5; PR 20-195 9.8.

		Receiving				Kickoff Returns					Tot
Year Team	**G**	**Rec**	**Yds**	**Avg**	**TD**	**Ret**	**Yds**	**Avg**	**TD**	**Fum**	**TD**
1994 Ind	13	2	30	15.0	0	0	0	—	0	0	0
1995 Ind	15	21	379	18.0	3	21	495	23.6	1	0	4
1996 Ind	14	18	302	16.8	0	43	1041	24.2	1	3	1
1997 Ind	13	26	329	12.7	3	55	1206	21.9	0	2	3
1998 Ind	9	0	0	—	0	34	759	22.3	0	2	0
NFL Total	64	67	1040	15.5	6	153	3501	22.9	2	7	8

BYRON BAILEY Bailey, Byron Ledare 5′10″, 192 **HB**
Col: Washington State *HS:* West Seattle [Seattle, WA] B: 10/12/1930, Omaha, NE *Drafted:* 1952 Round 25 Det
1952 Det: Rec 2-28 14.0; KR 1-23 23.0. **1953** GB: Rec 8-119 14.9; KR 2-34 17.0. **Total:** Rec 10-147 14.7; KR 3-57 19.0.

		Rushing				
Year Team	**G**	**Att**	**Yds**	**Avg**	**TD**	**Fum**
1952 Det	8	19	74	3.9	2	0
1953 GB	10	13	29	2.2	0	1
NFL Total	18	32	103	3.2	2	1

CARLTON BAILEY Bailey, Carlton Wilson 6′3″, 242 **LB**
Col: North Carolina *HS:* Woodlawn [Baltimore, MD] B: 12/15/1964, Baltimore, MD *Drafted:* 1988 Round 9 Buf
1988 Buf: 6 G. **1989** Buf: 16 G; Int 1-16. **1990** Buf: 16 G; 2 Sac. **1991** Buf: 16 G. **1992** Buf: 16 G; 1 Sac. **1993** NYG: 16 G; 1 Fum; 1.5 Sac.
1994 NYG: 16 G. **1995** Car: 16 G; 3 Sac. **1996** Car: 16 G; 2.5 Sac.
1997 Car: 8 G. **Total:** 142 G; Int 1-16; 1 Fum; 10 Sac.

CLARENCE BAILEY Bailey, Clarence J 5′11″, 220 **RB**
Col: Wesley; Hampton *HS:* Milford [DE] B: 3/7/1963, Milford, DE
1987 Mia: 3 G; Rush 10-55 5.5.

MONK BAILEY Bailey, Claron Everett 6′2″, 180 **DB**
Col: Utah *HS:* Moab [UT] B: 4/22/1938, Moab, UT
1964 StL: 12 G. **1965** StL: 11 G. **Total:** 23 G.

DAVID BAILEY Bailey, David 6′4″, 240 **DE**
Col: Oklahoma State *HS:* U.S. Grant [Oklahoma City, OK] B: 9/3/1965, Coatesville, PA
1990 Phi: 13 G.

BILL BAILEY Bailey, Edgar Lee 6′3″, 213 **OE-DE**
Col: Duke *HS:* Lexington [NC] B: 4/12/1916, Thomasville, NC
D: 4/9/1990, Winston-Salem, NC *Drafted:* 1940 Round 4 Bkn
1940 Bkn: 10 G; Rec 1-12 12.0. **1941** Bkn: 5 G; Rec 1-14 14.0.
Total: 15 G; Rec 2-26 13.0.

EDWIN BAILEY Bailey, Edwin Raymond 6′4″, 271 **OG**
Col: South Carolina State *HS:* Tompkins [Savannah, GA]
B: 5/15/1959, Savannah, GA *Drafted:* 1981 Round 5 Sea
1981 Sea: 16 G. **1982** Sea: 9 G. **1983** Sea: 16 G. **1984** Sea: 12 G.
1985 Sea: 16 G. **1986** Sea: 12 G; Rec 1-3 3.0. **1987** Sea: 12 G. **1988** Sea: 16 G. **1989** Sea: 16 G. **1990** Sea: 11 G. **1991** Sea: 3 G. **Total:** 139 G; Rec 1-3 3.0.

ELMER BAILEY Bailey, Elmer Francis 6′0″, 196 **WR**
Col: Lincoln (Mo.); Minnesota *HS:* Mechanic Arts [St. Paul, MN]
B: 12/13/1957, Evanston, IL *Drafted:* 1980 Round 4 Mia
1980 Mia: 14 G; Rec 4-105 26.3. **1981** Mia: 16 G. **1982** Bal: 1 G.
Total: 31 G; Rec 4-105 26.3.

ERIC BAILEY Bailey, Eric Renard 6′5″, 240 **TE**
Col: Kansas State *HS:* Dunbar [Fort Worth, TX] B: 5/12/1963, Fort Worth, TX
1987 Phi: 3 G; Rec 8-69 8.6.

TOM BAILEY Bailey, George Thomas 6′2″, 211 **RB**
Col: Florida State *HS:* Coral Gables [FL] B: 2/7/1949, Gainesville, FL
Drafted: 1971 Round 10 Phi
1973 Phi: KR 2-18 9.0. **1974** Phi: KR 1-14 14.0. **Total:** KR 3-32 10.7.

		Rushing				Receiving					Tot
Year Team	**G**	**Att**	**Yds**	**Avg**	**TD**	**Rec**	**Yds**	**Avg**	**TD**	**Fum**	**TD**
1971 Phi	13	23	41	1.8	1	7	55	7.9	0	0	1
1972 Phi	14	7	22	3.1	0	5	32	6.4	0	1	0
1973 Phi	12	20	91	4.6	0	10	80	8.0	1	1	1
1974 Phi	11	10	32	3.2	0	6	27	4.5	0	1	0
NFL Total	50	60	186	3.1	1	28	194	6.9	1	3	2

HAROLD BAILEY Bailey, Harold Craig 6′2″, 195 **WR**
Col: Oklahoma State *HS:* Jack Yates [Houston, TX] B: 4/12/1957, Houston, TX *Drafted:* 1980 Round 8 Hou
1982 Hou: Rush 1-13 13.0. **Total:** Rush 1-13 13.0.

		Receiving			
Year Team	**G**	**Rec**	**Yds**	**Avg**	**TD**
1981 Hou	11	0	0	—	0
1982 Hou	9	26	367	14.1	0
NFL Total	20	26	367	14.1	0

HENRY BAILEY Bailey, Henry Charles Jr. 5′8″, 176 **WR**
Col: Nevada-Las Vegas *HS:* John F. Kennedy [Chicago, IL]; George W. Collins HS [Chicago, IL] B: 2/28/1973, Suffolk, VA *Drafted:* 1995 Round 7 Pit
1996 NYJ: 8 G; Rush 1-(-4) -4.0; Rec 5-65 13.0; KR 24-470 19.6.

HOWARD BAILEY Bailey, Howard Henry 6′0″, 205 **T**
(Screeno) *Col:* Tennessee *HS:* Knoxville [TN] B: 1/10/1912, Birmingham, AL D: 8/1966
1935 Phi: 1 G.

JIM BAILEY Bailey, James Arrelaus 6′2″, 215 **G**
Col: West Virginia State *HS:* East [Columbus, OH] B: 1927
AAFC **1949** ChiA: 7 G.

JIM BAILEY Bailey, James Randall 6′4″, 253 **DT-DE**
Col: Kansas *HS:* Central [Kansas City, MO] B: 6/9/1948, Kansas City, MO *Drafted:* 1970 Round 2 Bal
1970 Bal: 10 G. **1971** Bal: 13 G. **1972** Bal: 14 G. **1973** Bal: 14 G.
1974 Bal: 14 G. **1975** NYJ: 14 G; Int 1-8. **1976** Atl: 7 G. **1977** Atl: 14 G.
1978 Atl: 16 G. **Total:** 116 G; Int 1-8.

JOHNNY BAILEY Bailey, Johnny Lee 5′8″, 190 **RB**
Col: Texas A&M–Kingsville *HS:* Jack Yates [Houston, TX]
B: 3/17/1967, Houston, TX *Drafted:* 1990 Round 9 ChiB
1990 ChiB: Pass 1-1 100.0%, 22 22.00. **1995** StL: Scor 1 2XP.
Total: Pass 1-1 100.0%, 22 22.00; Scor 1 2XP.

		Rushing				Receiving			
Year Team	**G**	**Att**	**Yds**	**Avg**	**TD**	**Rec**	**Yds**	**Avg**	**TD**
1990 ChiB	16	26	86	3.3	0	0	0	—	0
1991 ChiB	14	15	43	2.9	1	0	0	—	0
1992 Pho	12	52	233	4.5	1	33	331	10.0	1
1993 Pho	13	49	253	5.2	1	32	243	7.6	0
1994 LARm	14	11	35	3.2	1	58	516	8.9	0
1995 StL	12	36	182	5.1	2	38	265	7.0	0
NFL Total	81	189	832	4.4	6	161	1355	8.4	1

	Punt Returns				Kickoff Returns					Tot
Year Team	**Ret**	**Yds**	**Avg**	**TD**	**Ret**	**Yds**	**Avg**	**TD**	**Fum**	**TD**
1990 ChiB	36	399	11.1	**1**	23	363	15.8	0	8	1
1991 ChiB	36	281	7.8	0	16	311	19.4	0	4	1
1992 Pho	20	263	**13.2**	0	28	690	24.6	0	2	2
1993 Pho	35	282	8.1	1	31	699	22.5	0	4	2
1994 LARm	19	153	8.1	0	12	260	21.7	0	2	1
1995 StL	2	42	21.0	0	5	97	19.4	0	1	2
NFL Total	148	1420	9.6	2	115	2420	21.0	0	21	9

LARRY BAILEY Bailey, Lawrence 6′4″, 238 **DT**
Col: U. of Pacific *HS:* Palo Alto [CA] B: 5/10/1952, San Mateo, CA
Drafted: 1974 Round 9 Atl
1974 Atl: 1 G.

MARK BAILEY Bailey, Mark 6′3″, 237 **RB**
Col: California; Long Beach State *HS:* El Rancho [Pico Rivera, CA]
B: 12/13/1954, Lynwood, CA *Drafted:* 1977 Round 4 KC
1977 KC: Rec 17-206 12.1 1 TD; KR 3-46 15.3. **1978** KC: Rec 5-13 2.6.
Total: Rec 22-219 10.0 1 TD; KR 3-46 15.3.

		Rushing					Tot
Year Team	**G**	**Att**	**Yds**	**Avg**	**TD**	**Fum**	**TD**
1977 KC	14	66	266	4.0	2	4	3
1978 KC	13	83	298	3.6	0	0	0
NFL Total	27	149	564	3.8	2	4	3

ROBERT BAILEY Bailey, Robert Martin Luther 5′9″, 176 **DB**
Col: Miami (Fla.) *HS:* Miami Southridge [FL] B: 9/3/1968, Barbados
Drafted: 1991 Round 4 LARm
1991 LARm: 6 G. **1992** LARm: 16 G; Int 3-61 1 TD; 6 Pt. **1993** LARm: 9 G; Int 2-41. **1994** LARm: 16 G; PR 1-103 103.0 1 TD; 6 Pt. **1995** Was-Dal: 13 G. Was: 4 G. Dal: 9 G. **1996** Mia: 14 G; 1 Sac. **1997** Det: 15 G; Int 1-0; 2 Sac. **1998** Det: 16 G. **Total:** 105 G; PR 1-103 103.0 1 TD; Int 6-102 1 TD; Tot TD 2; 12 Pt; 3 Sac.

RUSS BAILEY Bailey, Russell Brooks 5′11″, 183 **C**
Col: West Virginia *HS:* Weston [WV] B: 10/17/1897, Weston, WV
D: 9/15/1949, Shawnee Hills, WV
1920 Akr: 11 G. **1921** Akr: 12 G. **Total:** 23 G.

STACEY BAILEY Bailey, Stacey Dwayne 6′0″, 162 **WR**
Col: San Jose State *HS:* Terra Linda [San Rafael, CA] B: 2/10/1960, San Rafael, CA *Drafted:* 1982 Round 3 Atl
1983 Atl: Rush 2-(-5) -2.5. **1985** Atl: Rush 1-(-3) -3.0. **1986** Atl: Rush 1-6 6.0. **Total:** Rush 4-(-2) -0.5.

		Receiving				
Year Team	G	Rec	Yds	Avg	TD	Fum
1982 Atl	5	2	24	12.0	1	1
1983 Atl	14	55	881	16.0	6	1
1984 Atl	16	67	1138	17.0	6	1
1985 Atl	15	30	364	12.1	0	1
1986 Atl	6	3	39	13.0	0	0
1987 Atl	7	20	325	16.3	3	1
1988 Atl	10	17	437	25.7	2	0
1989 Atl	15	8	170	21.3	0	0
1990 Atl	3	4	44	11.0	0	0
NFL Total	91	206	3422	16.6	18	5

THOMAS BAILEY Bailey, Thomas James Jr. 6′0″, 196 **WR**
Col: Auburn *HS:* Enterprise [AL] B: 12/6/1971, Dallas, TX
1995 Cin: 1 G.

VICTOR BAILEY Bailey, Victor 6′2″, 196 **WR**
Col: Texas-El Paso; Missouri *HS:* Dunbar [Fort Worth, TX] B: 7/3/1970, Ft. Worth, TX *Drafted:* 1993 Round 2 Phi

		Receiving			
Year Team	G	Rec	Yds	Avg	TD
1993 Phi	16	41	545	13.3	1
1994 Phi	16	20	311	15.6	1
1996 KC	2	1	12	12.0	0
NFL Total	34	62	868	14.0	2

DON BAILEY Bailey, William Donald 6′4″, 264 **C**
Col: Miami (Fla.) *HS:* Hialeah-Miami Lakes [Hialeah, FL] B: 3/24/1961, Miami, FL *Drafted:* 1983 Round 11 Den
1984 Ind: 10 G; 2 Fum. **1985** Ind: 10 G. **Total:** 20 G; 2 Fum.

TEDDY BAILEY Bailey, William Theodore 6′1″, 225 **RB**
Col: Cincinnati *HS:* Withrow [Cincinnati, OH] B: 8/12/1944, Cincinnati, OH
1967 Buf: 1 G. **1969** Bos: 2 G. **Total:** 3 G.

BILL BAIN Bain, William Ernest 6′4″, 279 **OG-OT**
Col: San Diego City Coll. CA (J.C.); Colorado; USC *HS:* St. Paul [Santa Fe Springs, CA] B: 8/9/1952, Los Angeles, CA *Drafted:* 1975 Round 2 GB
1975 GB: 14 G; KR 1-10 10.0. **1976** Den: 14 G. **1978** Den: 1 G. **1979** LARm: 8 G. **1980** LARm: 16 G. **1981** LARm: 16 G. **1982** LARm: 9 G. **1983** LARm: 16 G. **1984** LARm: 16 G. **1985** LARm: 15 G. **1986** NYJ-NE: 7 G. NYJ: 4 G. NE: 3 G. **Total:** 132 G; KR 1-10 10.0.

BILL BAIRD Baird, William Arthur 5′10″, 180 **DB-HB**
Col: San Francisco State *HS:* Lindsay [CA] B: 3/1/1939, Lindsay, CA
1964 NYJ: Rush 1-8 8.0; KR 11-240 21.8. **1965** NYJ: KR 2-50 25.0. **Total:** Rush 1-8 8.0; KR 13-290 22.3.

		Punt Returns				Interceptions				Tot
Year Team	G	Ret	Yds	Avg	TD	Int	Yds	TD	Fum	TD
1963 NYJ	14	4	143	35.8	1	6	31	0	0	1
1964 NYJ	14	18	170	9.4	0	8	130	**1**	0	1
1965 NYJ	14	14	88	6.3	0	3	9	0	2	0
1966 NYJ	14	5	35	7.0	0	5	76	1	0	1
1967 NYJ	14	25	219	8.8	0	3	27	0	3	0
1968 NYJ	14	18	111	6.2	0	4	74	0	0	0
1969 NYJ	14	4	21	5.3	0	5	10	0	0	0
NFL Total	98	88	787	8.9	1	34	357	2	5	3

AL BAISI Baisi, Albert Frank 6′0″, 217 **G**
Col: West Virginia *HS:* Elkins [WV] B: 9/6/1917, Norton, WV
1940 ChiB: 7 G. **1941** ChiB: 9 G. **1946** ChiB: 4 G. **1947** Phi: 2 G. **Total:** 22 G.

ART BAKER Baker, Arthur Ray 6′0″, 220 **FB**
Col: Syracuse *HS:* Erie Acad. [PA] B: 12/31/1937, Erie, PA
Drafted: 1961 Round 3 Buf
1961 Buf: Rec 6-73 12.2; KR 12-281 23.4. **1962** Buf: Rec 3-12 4.0; KR 7-220 31.4 **1** TD. **Total:** Rec 9-85 9.4; KR 19-501 26.4 1 TD.

		Rushing					Tot
Year Team	G	Att	Yds	Avg	TD	Fum	TD
1961 Buf	14	152	498	3.3	3	7	3
1962 Buf	3	2	9	4.5	0	0	1
NFL Total	17	154	507	3.3	3	7	4

CHARLES BAKER Baker, Charles Edward 6′2″, 226 **LB**
Col: New Mexico *HS:* Ector [TX] B: 9/26/1957, Mount Pleasant, TX
Drafted: 1980 Round 3 StL
1980 StL: 16 G; KR 0-27. **1981** StL: 14 G. **1982** StL: 9 G. **1983** StL: 16 G. **1984** StL: 9 G. **1985** StL: 15 G. **1986** StL: 16 G; 3.5 Sac. **1987** StL: 14 G. **Total:** 109 G; KR 0-27; 3.5 Sac.

CONWAY BAKER Baker, Conway Oscar 5′11″, 228 **T-G**
Col: Centenary *HS:* C.E. Byrd [Shreveport, LA] B: 9/9/1911, Marlin, TX
D: 5/28/1997, Shreveport, LA
1936 ChiC: 9 G. **1937** ChiC: 6 G; Scor 6, 6 XK. **1938** ChiC: 11 G; Scor 0-1 FG. **1939** ChiC: 11 G. **1940** ChiC: 11 G. **1941** ChiC: 10 G. **1942** ChiC: 11 G. **1943** ChiC: 10 G; Scor 14, 1-2 50.0% FG, 5-6 83.3% XK; **1** Fum TD. **1944** ChPt: 9 G; Scor 11, 11-15 73.3% XK. **1945** ChiC: 8 G; Scor 0-1 FG, 0-1 XK. **Total:** 96 G; Scor 31, 1-4 25.0% FG, 22-22 72.7% XK; 1 Fum TD.

DAVE BAKER Baker, David Lee 6′0″, 192 **DB**
Col: Oklahoma *HS:* Bartlesville [OK] B: 7/30/1937, Coffeyville, KS
Drafted: 1959 Round 1 SF
1960 SF: Punt 3-143 47.7. **Total:** Punt 3-143 47.7.

		Interceptions			
Year Team	G	Int	Yds	TD	Fum
1959 SF	12	5	75	0	1
1960 SF	12	**10**	96	0	1
1961 SF	14	6	123	0	0
NFL Total	38	21	294	0	2

ED BAKER Baker, Edward Everett 6′2″, 200 **QB**
Col: Lafayette *HS:* West Essex [North Caldwell, NJ] B: 5/29/1948, East Orange, NJ
1972 Hou: 1 G; Pass 10-4 40.0%, 47 4.70 4 Int; Rush 1-9 9.0.

FRANK BAKER Baker, Frank Louis 6′2″, 182 **E**
Col: Northwestern *HS:* George Washington [Cedar Rapids, IA]
B: 7/23/1909, Madison, WI D: 9/1985, Richmond, CA
1931 GB: 2 G; Rec 1 TD; 6 Pt.

AL BAKER Baker, James Albert London 6′6″, 265 **DE**
(Bubba) *Col:* Colorado State *HS:* Weequahic [Newark, NJ]
B: 12/9/1956, Jacksonville, FL *Drafted:* 1978 Round 2 Det
1978 Det: 16 G. **1979** Det: 16 G. **1980** Det: 15 G; Int 1-0. **1981** Det: 11 G; Int 1-9. **1982** Det: 9 G; 8.5 Sac. **1983** StL: 16 G; Int 2-24; 13 Sac. **1984** StL: 15 G; 10 Sac. **1985** StL: 16 G; 4 Sac. **1986** StL: 16 G; 10.5 Sac. **1987** Cle: 12 G; 3.5 Sac. **1988** Min: 14 G; 5.5 Sac. **1989** Cle: 16 G; 7.5 Sac. **1990** Cle: 9 G; 3 Sac. **Total:** 181 G; Int 4-33; 65.5 Sac.

JERRY BAKER Baker, Jerry Eugene 6′2″, 297 **NT**
Col: Coffeyville CC KS; Marion Mil. Inst. AL (J.C.); Tulane *HS:* Fort Meade [FL] B: 3/6/1960, Bartow, FL
1983 Den: 5 G.

JESSE BAKER Baker, Jesse Lewis 6′5″, 269 **DE**
Col: Jacksonville State *HS:* Rockdale Co. [Conyers, GA] B: 7/10/1957, Conyers, GA *Drafted:* 1979 Round 2 Hou
1979 Hou: 16 G; **1** Fum TD; 6 Pt. **1980** Hou: 16 G. **1981** Hou: 16 G. **1982** Hou: 9 G; 7.5 Sac. **1983** Hou: 16 G; 5.5 Sac. **1984** Hou: 16 G; 11 Sac. **1985** Hou: 16 G; 5.5 Sac. **1986** Dal-Hou: 14 G; 3 Sac. Dal: 3 G; 1 Sac. Hou: 11 G; 2 Sac. **1987** Hou: 9 G; Scor **1** Saf; 2 Pt; 2.5 Sac. **Total:** 128 G; Scor 1 Saf; 1 Fum TD; 8 Pt; 35 Sac.

JOHN BAKER Baker, John Haywood Jr. 6′6″, 279 **DE-DT-OT**
(Big John) *Col:* North Carolina Central *HS:* Washington [Raleigh, NC]; Ligon HS [Raleigh, NC] B: 6/10/1935, Raleigh, NC *Drafted:* 1958 Round 5 LARm
1958 LARm: 12 G. **1959** LARm: 12 G. **1960** LARm: 12 G; Int 1-62. **1961** LARm: 13 G. **1962** Phi: 7 G. **1963** Pit: 14 G. **1964** Pit: 14 G; PR 1-0. **1965** Pit: 14 G. **1966** Pit: 7 G. **1967** Pit: 13 G; Int 1-0. **1968** Det: 13 G. **Total:** 131 G; PR 1-0; Int 2-62.

JOHNNY BAKER Baker, John Hendrix III 6′3″, 230 **LB-DE**
Col: Mississippi State *HS:* Meridian [MS] B: 3/15/1941, Coy, AL
Drafted: 1963 Round 7 Hou
1963 Hou: 6 G. **1964** Hou: 14 G; Rec 2-18 9.0; Int 1-17 **1** TD; 6 Pt. **1965** Hou: 7 G. **1966** Hou: 14 G; Int 1-0. **1967** SD: 10 G. **Total:** 51 G; Rec 2-18 9.0; Int 2-17 1 TD; 6 Pt.

JOHN BAKER Baker, John Willey Alexander Jr. 6′5″, 260 **DE**
Col: Virginia Union; Norfolk State *HS:* I.C. Norcom [Portsmouth, VA]
B: 8/15/1942, Detroit, MI
1970 NYG: 14 G.

JON BAKER Baker, Jonathan 6′2″, 214 **LB-DG-OG**
Col: California *HS:* Polytech [San Francisco, CA] B: 6/14/1923, San Francisco, CA D: 11/26/1992, San Rafael, CA *Drafted:* 1949 Round 7 LARm
1949 NYG: 10 G; 1 Fum. **1950** NYG: 12 G. **1951** NYG: 12 G. **1952** NYG: 12 G. **Total:** 46 G; 1 Fum.

JON BAKER Baker, Jonathan David 6′1″, 170 **K**
Col: Bakersfield Coll. CA (J.C.); Arizona State *HS:* Foothill [Bakersfield, CA] B: 8/13/1972, Orange, CA
1995 Dal: 3 G.

KEITH BAKER Baker, Keith Leonard 5′10″, 187 **WR**
Col: Texas A&M; Texas Southern *HS:* Franklin D. Roosevelt [Dallas, TX] B: 6/4/1957, Dallas, TX
1985 Phi: 8 G; Rec 2-25 12.5.

LARRY BAKER Baker, Lawrence Joe 6′2″, 240 **OT**
Col: Bowling Green State *HS:* Shelby [OH] B: 3/9/1937
Drafted: 1959 Round 27 Cle
1960 NYT: 2 G; KR 1-18 18.0; 1 Fum.

SAM BAKER Baker, Loris Hoskins 6′2″, 217 **FB-K**
Col: Oregon State *HS:* Stadium [Tacoma, WA]; Corvallis HS [OR] B: 11/12/1929, San Francisco, CA *Drafted:* 1952 Round 11 LARm
1953 Was: Rec 2-21 10.5; KR 9-186 20.7. **1956** Was: Rec 4-35 8.8; PR 1-0. **1961** Cle: KR 3-57 19.0. **1962** Dal: Pass 1-0. **1968** Phi: Pass 1-1 100.0%, 58 58.00 1 TD; Rec 1-3 3.0. **Total:** Pass 2-1 50.0%, 58 29.00 1 TD; Rec 7-59 8.4; PR 1-0; KR 12-243 20.3.

		Rushing				Punting		
Year Team	**G**	**Att**	**Yds**	**Avg**	**TD**	**Punts**	**Yds**	**Avg**
1953 Was	11	17	72	4.2	1	17	614	36.1
1956 Was	12	25	117	4.7	0	59	2510	42.5
1957 Was	12	2	23	11.5	1	50	2139	42.8
1958 Was	12	0	0	—	0	48	2181	**45.4**
1959 Was	12	2	3	1.5	0	49	2229	45.5
1960 Cle	12	1	-11	-11.0	0	55	2309	42.0
1961 Cle	14	0	0	—	0	53	2296	43.3
1962 Dal	14	0	0	—	0	57	2589	45.4
1963 Dal	14	1	15	15.0	0	71	3138	44.2
1964 Phi	14	0	0	—	0	49	2073	42.3
1965 Phi	12	0	0	—	0	37	1551	41.9
1966 Phi	14	1	15	15.0	0	42	1726	41.1
1967 Phi	14	0	0	—	0	61	2335	38.3
1968 Phi	14	0	0	—	0	55	2248	40.9
1969 Phi	14	0	0	—	0	0	0	—
NFL Total	195	49	234	4.8	2	703	29938	42.6

	Scoring							
Year Team	**Pts**	**FG**	**FGA**	**FG%**	**XK**	**XKA**	**XK%**	**Fum**
1953 Was	0	0	0	—	0	0	—	2
1956 Was	67	**17**	25	68.0	16	19	84.2	3
1957 Was	**77**	14	23	60.9	29	30	96.7	0
1958 Was	64	13	26	50.0	25	25	100.0	0
1959 Was	51	10	22	45.5	21	22	95.5	0
1960 Cle	80	12	20	60.0	**44**	**46**	95.7	0
1962 Dal	92	14	27	51.9	**50**	**51**	98.0	0
1963 Dal	65	9	20	45.0	38	38	100.0	0
1964 Phi	84	16	26	61.5	36	37	97.3	0
1965 Phi	65	9	23	39.1	38	40	95.0	0
1966 Phi	92	18	25	**72.0**	38	39	**97.4**	0
1967 Phi	81	12	19	63.2	45	45	100.0	0
1968 Phi	74	19	30	63.3	17	21	81.0	0
1969 Phi	79	16	30	53.3	31	31	100.0	0
NFL Total	977	179	316	56.6	428	444	96.4	5

MELVIN BAKER Baker, Melvin Clyde 6′0″, 189 **WR**
Col: Texas Southern *HS:* Elmore [Houston, TX] B: 8/12/1950, Beaumont, TX *Drafted:* 1974 Round 8 Mia
1974 Mia: 9 G; Rec 4-121 30.3 2 TD; KR 1-22 22.0; 12 Pt; 1 Fum. **1975** NO-NE-SD: 4 G; Rush 1-21 21.0; Rec 2-26 13.0. NO: 2 G; Rush 1-21 21.0; Rec 2-26 13.0. NE: 1 G. SD: 1 G. **1976** Hou: 8 G; Rush 1-2 2.0; Rec 3-32 10.7; KR 1-15 15.0. **Total:** 21 G; Rush 2-23 11.5; Rec 9-179 19.9 2 TD; KR 2-37 18.5; 12 Pt; 1 Fum.

MYRON BAKER Baker, Myron Tobias 6′1″, 232 **LB**
Col: Louisiana Tech *HS:* Haughton [LA] B: 1/6/1971, Haughton, LA
Drafted: 1993 Round 4 ChiB
1993 ChiB: 16 G; 1 Fum TD; Tot TD 2; 12 Pt. **1994** ChiB: 16 G. **1995** ChiB: 16 G. **1996** Car: 16 G; KR 1-11 11.0. **1997** Car: 2 G. **Total:** 66 G; KR 1-11 11.0; 1 Fum TD; Tot TD 2; 12 Pt.

RALPH BAKER Baker, Ralph Robert 6′3″, 228 **LB**
Col: Penn State *HS:* Lewistown [PA] B: 8/25/1942, Lewistown, PA
Drafted: 1964 Round 6 NYJ
1964 NYJ: Scor 1 Saf. **1971** NYJ: Scor **1** 1XP. **Total:** Scor 1 Saf, 1 1XP.

		Interceptions		
Year Team	**G**	**Int**	**Yds**	**TD**
1964 NYJ	14	2	17	0
1965 NYJ	14	2	24	0
1966 NYJ	11	0	0	0
1967 NYJ	14	1	0	0
1968 NYJ	14	3	31	0
1969 NYJ	11	1	0	0
1970 NYJ	14	2	8	0
1971 NYJ	12	0	0	0
1972 NYJ	10	2	0	0
1973 NYJ	14	4	51	1
1974 NYJ	14	2	87	1
NFL Total	142	19	218	2

RON BAKER Baker, Ronald 6′4″, 260 **OG**
Col: Oklahoma State *HS:* Emerson [Gary, IN] B: 11/19/1954, Gary, IN
Drafted: 1977 Round 10 Bal
1978 Bal: 16 G. **1979** Bal: 16 G. **1980** Phi: 16 G; KR 1-6 6.0. **1981** Phi: 16 G. **1982** Phi: 9 G. **1983** Phi: 16 G. **1984** Phi: 16 G. **1985** Phi: 15 G. **1986** Phi: 16 G. **1987** Phi: 10 G. **1988** Phi: 9 G. **Total:** 155 G; KR 1-6 6.0.

BULLET BAKER Baker, Roy Marlon 5′8″, 180 **BB-TB-HB-WB**
(Bullet; Snow) *Col:* Santa Clara; USC *HS:* Long Beach Polytechnic [CA] B: 11/4/1900, Casper, WY D: Long Beach, CA
1927 NYY: 14 G; Pass 1 TD; Rush 1 TD; 6 Pt. **1928** GB: 11 G. **1929** GB-ChiC: 6 G. GB: 2 G. ChiC: 4 G. **1930** ChiC: 10 G. **1931** SI: 9 G; Pass 1 TD. **Total:** 50 G; Pass 2 TD; Rush 1 TD; 6 Pt.

SHANNON BAKER Baker, Shannon Maurice 5′9″, 185 **WR**
Col: Florida State *HS:* Lakeland [FL] B: 7/20/1971, Bartow, FL
Drafted: 1993 Round 8 Atl
1994 Ind: 4 G; Rec 2-15 7.5.

STEPHEN BAKER Baker, Stephen Edward 5′8″, 160 **WR**
(The Touchdown Maker) *Col:* West Los Angeles Coll. CA (J.C.); Fresno State *HS:* Alexander Hamilton [Los Angeles, CA] B: 8/30/1964, San Antonio, TX *Drafted:* 1987 Round 3 NYG
1987 NYG: Rush 1-18 18.0; PR 3-16 5.3. **1988** NYG: PR 5-34 6.8. **1990** NYG: Rush 1-3 3.0. **Total:** Rush 2-21 10.5; PR 8-50 6.3.

		Receiving				
Year Team	**G**	**Rec**	**Yds**	**Avg**	**TD**	**Fum**
1987 NYG	12	15	277	18.5	2	1
1988 NYG	16	40	656	16.4	7	0
1989 NYG	15	13	255	19.6	2	0
1990 NYG	16	26	541	20.8	4	0
1991 NYG	15	30	525	17.5	4	0
1992 NYG	16	17	333	19.6	2	0
NFL Total	90	141	2587	18.3	21	1

TERRY BAKER Baker, Terry Wayne 6′3″, 200 **QB-HB**
Col: Oregon State *HS:* Ockley Green School [Portland, OR]; Jefferson [Portland, OR] B: 5/5/1941, Pine River, MN *Drafted:* 1963 Round 1 LARm
1963 LARm: Pass 19-11 57.9%, 140 7.37 4 Int. **1964** LARm: Pass 1-0. **1965** LARm: Pass 1-1 100.0%, 14 14.00. **Total:** Pass 21-12 57.1%, 154 7.33 4 Int.

		Rushing				Receiving					Tot
Year Team	**G**	**Att**	**Yds**	**Avg**	**TD**	**Rec**	**Yds**	**Avg**	**TD**	**Fum**	**TD**
1963 LARm	4	9	46	5.1	0	0	0	—	0	1	0
1964 LARm	5	24	82	3.4	0	8	92	11.5	0	0	0
1965 LARm	9	25	82	3.3	1	22	210	9.5	2	3	3
NFL Total	18	58	210	3.6	1	30	302	10.1	2	4	3

TONY BAKER Baker, Tony Ferrino 5′10″, 182 **RB**
Col: East Carolina *HS:* T. Wingate Andrews [High Point, NC] B: 6/11/1964, High Point, NC *Drafted:* 1986 Round 10 Atl
1986 Atl-Cle: 4 G; Rush 1-3 3.0. Atl: 2 G; Rush 1-3 3.0. Cle: 2 G. **1988** Cle: 4 G; Rush 3-19 6.3. **1989** Pho: 10 G; Rush 20-31 1.6; Rec 2-18 9.0; KR 11-245 22.3; 1 Fum. **Total:** 18 G; Rush 24-53 2.2; Rec 2-18 9.0; KR 11-245 22.3; 1 Fum.

TONY BAKER Baker, Vernon Anthony 5′11″, 229 **RB**
Col: Iowa State *HS:* Burlington [IA] B: 2/16/1945, Fort Madison, IA D: 8/9/1998, Mediapolis, IA

		Rushing				Receiving					Tot
Year Team	**G**	**Att**	**Yds**	**Avg**	**TD**	**Rec**	**Yds**	**Avg**	**TD**	**Fum**	**TD**
1968 NO	1	4	2	0.5	0	0	0	—	0	0	0
1969 NO	14	134	642	**4.8**	1	34	352	10.4	1	2	2
1970 NO	8	82	337	4.1	1	12	47	3.9	0	1	1
1971 NO-Phi	9	46	174	3.8	0	10	80	8.0	1	2	1
1971 NO	4	29	125	4.3	0	6	44	7.3	1	1	1
1971 Phi	5	17	49	2.9	0	4	36	9.0	0	1	0
1972 Phi	13	90	322	3.6	0	16	114	7.1	0	2	0
1973 LARm	14	85	344	4.0	7	0	0	—	0	0	7
1974 LARm	14	53	135	2.5	5	4	65	16.3	0	0	5
1975 SD	13	42	131	3.1	1	6	27	4.5	0	1	1
NFL Total	86	536	2087	3.9	15	82	685	8.4	2	8	17

WAYNE BAKER Baker, Wayne Mitchell 6′6″, 270 **DT**
Col: Brigham Young *HS:* Plains [MT] B: 7/7/1953, Sandpoint, ID
Drafted: 1975 Round 3 SF
1975 SF: 14 G; KR 4-45 11.3.

JIM BAKKEN Bakken, James Leroy 5′11″, 200 **K**
Col: Wisconsin *HS:* West [Madison, WI] B: 11/2/1940, Madison, WI
Drafted: 1962 Round 7 LARm
1965 StL: Rush 1-28 28.0. **Total:** Rush 1-28 28.0.

Year Team	G	Punting Punts	Yds	Avg
1962 StL	8	0	0	—
1963 StL	14	0	0	—
1964 StL	14	0	0	—
1965 StL	14	26	1098	42.2
1966 StL	14	29	961	33.1
1967 StL	14	0	0	—
1968 StL	14	0	0	—
1969 StL	14	0	0	—
1970 StL	14	0	0	—
1971 StL	14	5	207	41.4
1972 StL	14	1	26	26.0
1973 StL	14	0	0	—
1974 StL	14	0	0	—
1975 StL	14	0	0	—
1976 StL	14	0	0	—
1977 StL	14	0	0	—
1978 StL	16	4	147	36.8
NFL Total	234	65	2439	37.5

	Scoring							
Year Team	Pts	FG	FGA	FG%	XK	XKA	XK%	Fum
1962 StL	0	0	1	0.0	0	0	—	0
1963 StL	77	11	21	52.4	44	44	100.0	0
1964 StL	115	**25**	**38**	65.8	40	40	100.0	0
1965 StL	96	21	31	**67.7**	33	33	**100.0**	1
1966 StL	96	23	40	57.5	27	28	96.4	0
1967 StL	**117**	**27**	39	**69.2**	36	36	**100.0**	0
1968 StL	85	15	24	62.5	40	40	100.0	0
1969 StL	74	12	24	50.0	38	40	95.0	0
1970 StL	97	20	32	62.5	37	38	97.4	0
1971 StL	87	21	32	65.6	24	24	100.0	0
1972 StL	61	14	22	63.6	19	21	90.5	0
1973 StL	100	23	32	71.9	31	31	100.0	0
1974 StL	69	13	22	59.1	30	36	83.3	0
1975 StL	97	19	24	79.2	40	41	97.6	0
1976 StL	93	20	27	74.1	33	35	94.3	0
1977 StL	56	7	16	43.8	35	36	97.2	0
1978 StL	60	11	22	50.0	27	30	90.0	0
NFL Total	1380	282	447	63.1	534	553	96.6	1

FRANK BALASZ Balasz, Frank Steve 6′2″, 212 **FB-LB-DB**
Col: Iowa *HS:* Albert G. Lane Tech [Chicago, IL] B: 1/23/1918, Chicago, IL Deceased *Drafted:* 1939 Round 16 GB
1939 GB: Rec 1-11 11.0; Punt 1-35 35.0. **1940** GB: Pass 1-0, 1 Int; Rec 1-7 7.0; Int 1-11. **1941** GB-ChiC: Pass 4-0, 2 Int; Rec 2-17 8.5; KR 1-21 21.0; Punt 7-259 37.0; Scor 1, 1-1 100.0% XK. GB: Scor 1, 1-1 100.0% XK. ChiC: Pass 4-0, 2 Int; Rec 2-17 8.5; KR 1-21 21.0; Punt 7-259 37.0. **1945** ChiC: Rec 1-15 15.0. **Total:** Pass 5-0, 3 Int; Rec 5-50 10.0; KR 1-21 21.0; Int 1-11; Punt 8-294 36.8; Scor 7, 1-1 100.0% XK.

		Rushing			
Year Team	G	Att	Yds	Avg	TD
1939 GB	5	11	41	3.7	0
1940 GB	7	25	107	4.3	1
1941 GB-ChiC	10	23	81	3.5	0
1941 GB	1	2	-1	-0.5	0
1941 ChiC	9	21	82	3.9	0
1945 ChiC	2	1	-1	-1.0	0
NFL Total	24	60	228	3.8	1

ED BALATTI Balatti, Edward T 6′1″, 195 **E-DB**
Col: No College *HS:* Oakland Technical [CA] B: 4/8/1924, Los Banos, CA D: 8/27/1990, Novato, CA
AAFC **1946** SF-A: 14 G; Rec 4-15 3.8; Int 0-22 1 TD; Scor 8, 2-2 100.0% XK. **1947** SF-A: 14 G; Rec 8-98 12.3 1 TD; PR 2-8 4.0 1 TD; KR 1-16 16.0; Scor 13, 1-1 100.0% XK; Tot TD 2. **1948** SF-A-NY-A-BufA: 10 G. **Total:** 38 G; Rec 12-113 9.4 1 TD; PR 2-8 4.0 1 TD; KR 1-16 16.0; Int 0-22 1 TD; Scor 21, 3-3 100.0% XK; Tot TD 3.

LOU BALDACCI Baldacci, Louis Granville 6′2″, 200 **HB**
Col: Michigan *HS:* St. Vincent [Akron, OH] B: 12/17/1934, Richmond, VA *Drafted:* 1956 Round 10 Pit
1956 Pit: Pass 1-0; Rec 5-62 12.4; Punt 26-1010 38.8.

		Rushing				
Year Team	G	Att	Yds	Avg	TD	Fum
1956 Pit	10	31	140	4.5	0	1

MIKE BALDASSIN Baldassin, Michael Robert 6′1″, 218 **LB**
Col: Washington *HS:* Woodrow Wilson [Tacoma, WA] B: 7/26/1955, Tacoma, WA
1977 SF: 14 G; PR 1-0; 6 Pt; 1 Fum. **1978** SF: 16 G. **Total:** 30 G; PR 1-0; 6 Pt; 1 Fum.

BRIAN BALDINGER Baldinger, Brian David 6′4″, 278 **OG-OT-C**
Col: Nassau CC NY; Duke *HS:* Massapequa [NY] B: 1/7/1960, Pittsburgh, PA
1982 Dal: 4 G. **1983** Dal: 16 G. **1984** Dal: 16 G. **1986** Dal: 16 G. **1987** Dal: 3 G. **1988** Ind: 16 G; Rec 1-37 37.0. **1989** Ind: 16 G. **1990** Ind: 16 G. **1991** Ind: 16 G; 3 Fum. **1992** Phi: 12 G. **1993** Phi: 12 G. **Total:** 143 G; Rec 1-37 37.0; 3 Fum.

GARY BALDINGER Baldinger, Gary Thomas 6′3″, 264 **DE-NT**
Col: Wake Forest *HS:* Massapequa [NY] B: 10/4/1963, Philadelphia, PA *Drafted:* 1986 Round 9 KC
1986 KC: 5 G. **1987** KC: 7 G. **1988** KC: 11 G. **1990** Buf-Ind: 10 G. Buf: 9 G. Ind: 1 G. **1991** Buf: 7 G. **1992** Buf: 4 G. **Total:** 44 G.

RICH BALDINGER Baldinger, Richard L 6′4″, 285 **OT-OG**
Col: Wake Forest *HS:* Massapequa [NY] B: 12/31/1959, Camp Lejeune, NC *Drafted:* 1982 Round 10 NYG
1982 NYG: 1 G. **1983** NYG-KC: 8 G. NYG: 2 G. KC: 6 G. **1984** KC: 14 G. **1985** KC: 16 G. **1986** KC: 16 G. **1987** KC: 12 G. **1988** KC: 14 G. **1989** KC: 16 G. **1990** KC: 16 G. **1991** KC: 16 G. **1992** KC: 13 G. **1993** NE: 15 G. **Total:** 157 G.

KARL BALDISCHWILER Baldischwiler, John Karl 6′5″, 265 **OT**
Col: Oklahoma *HS:* Okmulgee [OK] B: 1/19/1956, Okmulgee, OK *Drafted:* 1978 Round 7 Mia
1978 Det: 16 G. **1979** Det: 16 G. **1980** Det: 16 G. **1981** Det: 16 G. **1982** Det: 9 G. **1983** Bal: 14 G. **1985** Ind: 16 G. **1986** Ind: 15 G. **Total:** 118 G.

AL BALDWIN Baldwin, Alton 6′2″, 201 **OE-DB**
Col: Arkansas *HS:* Hot Springs [AR] B: 3/21/1923, Hot Springs, AR D: 5/23/1994, Hot Springs, AR *Drafted:* 1947 Round 4 Bos
AAFC **1947** BufA: KR 1-6 6.0; Int 2-90. **1948** BufA: Scor 48, 0-1 XK. **1949** BufA: Rush 2-1 0.5. **Total:** Rush 2-1 0.5; KR 1-6 6.0; Int 2-90; Scor 132, 0-1 XK.

		Receiving			
Year Team	G	Rec	Yds	Avg	TD
1947 BufA	14	25	468	18.7	7
1948 BufA	13	54	916	17.0	8
1949 BufA	12	53	719	13.6	7
AAFC Total	39	132	2103	15.9	22

NFL **1950** GB: Int 5-35.

		Receiving				
Year Team	G	Rec	Yds	Avg	TD	Fum
1950 GB	12	28	555	19.8	3	3

BURR BALDWIN Baldwin, Burr Browning 6′1″, 197 **OE-DE**
Col: UCLA *HS:* Bakersfield [CA] B: 6/13/1922, Bakersfield, CA
AAFC **1947** LA-A: 13 G; Rec 12-275 22.9 1 TD; 6 Pt. **1948** LA-A: 12 G; Rec 10-96 9.6. **1949** LA-A: 9 G; Rush 1-1 1.0; Rec 2-26 13.0; Int 2-4. **Total:** 34 G; Rush 1-1 1.0; Rec 24-397 16.5 1 TD; Int 2-4; 6 Pt.

CLIFF BALDWIN Baldwin, Clifford W 5′9″, 170 **WB-BB**
(Kip) *Col:* No College B: 9/22/1900, Muncie, IN D: 1/25/1979, Muncie, IN
1920 Mun: 1 G. **1921** Mun: 2 G. **Total:** 3 G.

DON BALDWIN Baldwin, Donald Wayne 6′3″, 263 **DE**
Col: Purdue *HS:* West [St. Charles, MO] B: 7/9/1964, St. Charles, MO
1987 NYJ: 8 G.

GEORGE BALDWIN Baldwin, George Whitfield Evans 5′11″, 190 **OE-T**
Col: Virginia *HS:* Upper Montclair [NJ] B: 5/3/1902, Washington, DC D: 6/13/1971, Neptune, NJ
1925 Cle: 9 G.

JACK BALDWIN Baldwin, John David 6′3″, 223 **C-LB**
Col: Centenary *HS:* Gladewater [TX] B: 7/31/1921, Clyde, TX D: 9/13/1989, Kerrville, TX
AAFC **1946** NY-A: 7 G. **1947** NY-A-SF-A: 5 G. **1948** BufA: 3 G. **Total:** 15 G.

KEITH BALDWIN Baldwin, Keith Manning 6′4″, 263 **DE**
Col: Texas A&M *HS:* M.B. Smiley [Houston, TX] B: 10/13/1960, Houston, TX *Drafted:* 1982 Round 2 Cle
1982 Cle: 9 G; 1 Sac. **1983** Cle: 16 G; 1 Sac. **1984** Cle: 16 G; 4.5 Sac. **1985** Cle: 10 G; 1 Sac. **1987** SD: 6 G. **1988** SD: 6 G. **Total:** 63 G; 7.5 Sac.

RANDY BALDWIN Baldwin, Randy Chadwick 5′10″, 220 **RB**
Col: Holmes CC MS; Mississippi *HS:* Griffin [GA] B: 8/19/1967, Griffin, GA *Drafted:* 1991 Round 4 Min
1992 Cle: Rec 2-30 15.0. **1993** Cle: Rec 1-5 5.0 1 TD. **1994** Cle: Rec 3-15 5.0. **Total:** Rec 6-50 8.3 1 TD.

		Rushing				Kickoff Returns					Tot
Year Team	G	Ret	Yds	Avg	TD	Ret	Yds	Avg	TD	Fum	TD
1991 Min	4	0	0	—	0	1	14	14.0	0	0	0
1992 Cle	15	10	31	3.1	0	30	675	22.5	0	1	0
1993 Cle	14	18	61	3.4	0	24	444	18.5	0	2	1

1994 Cle	16	23	78	3.4	0	28	753	26.9	1	1	1
1995 Car	7	23	61	2.7	0	14	316	22.6	0	1	0
1996 Bal	9	0	0	—	0	20	405	20.3	0	1	0
NFL Total	65	74	231	3.1	0	117	2607	22.3	1	6	2

BOB BALDWIN Baldwin, Robert Manuel 6′1″, 225 **FB-HB**
Col: Clemson *HS:* Baltimore City College [MD] B: 7/7/1943, Baltimore, MD
1966 Bal: 9 G; KR 2-18 9.0.

TOM BALDWIN Baldwin, Thomas Burke 6′4″, 274 **DT-NT-DE**
Col: Thornton CC IL; Wisconsin; Tulsa *HS:* Thornton Fractional South [Lansing, IL] B: 5/13/1961, Evergreen Park, IL *Drafted:* 1984 Round 9 NYJ
1984 NYJ: 16 G; 1.5 Sac. **1985** NYJ: 16 G; **1** Fum TD; 6 Pt. **1986** NYJ: 16 G; KR 2-3 1.5; 1 Fum; 1 Sac. **1988** NYJ: 16 G; 1 Sac. **Total:** 64 G; KR 2-3 1.5; 1 Fum TD; 6 Pt; 1 Fum; 3.5 Sac.

ERIC BALL Ball, Eric Clinton 6′2″, 218 **RB**
Col: UCLA *HS:* Ypsilanti [MI] B: 7/1/1966, Cleveland, OH
Drafted: 1989 Round 2 Cin
1989 Cin: Rec 6-44 7.3. **1990** Cin: Rec 2-46 23.0 1 TD. **1991** Cin: Rec 3-17 5.7. **1992** Cin: Rec 6-66 11.0 2 TD. **1993** Cin: Rec 4-39 9.8. **1994** Cin: Rec 1-4 4.0. **Total:** Rec 22-216 9.8 3 TD.

		Rushing				Kickoff Returns					Tot
Year Team	G	Ret	Yds	Avg	TD	Ret	Yds	Avg	TD	Fum	TD
1989 Cin	15	98	391	4.0	3	1	19	19.0	0	3	3
1990 Cin	13	22	72	3.3	1	16	366	22.9	0	1	2
1991 Cin	6	10	21	2.1	1	13	262	20.2	0	1	1
1992 Cin	16	16	55	3.4	2	20	411	20.6	0	1	4
1993 Cin	15	8	37	4.6	1	23	501	21.8	0	0	1
1994 Cin	16	2	0	0.0	0	42	915	21.8	0	1	0
1995 Oak	16	2	10	5.0	0	0	0	—	0	0	0
NFL Total	97	158	586	3.7	8	115	2474	21.5	0	7	11

JERRY BALL Ball, Jerry Lee 6′1″, 312 **NT-DT**
Col: Southern Methodist *HS:* Westbrook [Beaumont, TX]
B: 12/15/1964, Beaumont, TX *Drafted:* 1987 Round 3 Det
1987 Det: 12 G; KR 2-23 11.5; 1 Sac. **1988** Det: 16 G; 2 Sac. **1989** Det: 16 G; 9 Sac. **1990** Det: 15 G; 2 Sac. **1991** Det: 13 G; Scor 1 Saf; 2 Pt; 2 Sac. **1992** Det: 12 G; 1 Fum TD; 6 Pt; 2.5 Sac. **1993** Cle: 16 G; 3 Sac. **1994** LARd: 16 G; 3 Sac. **1995** Oak: 15 G; 3 Sac. **1996** Oak: 16 G; Int 1-66 1 TD; 6 Pt; 3 Sac. **1997** Min: 12 G. **1998** Min: 16 G. **Total:** 175 G; KR 2-23 11.5; Int 1-66 1 TD; Scor 1 Saf; 1 Fum TD; Tot TD 2; 14 Pt; 30.5 Sac.

LARRY BALL Ball, Larry Lavern 6′6″, 232 **LB**
Col: Louisville *HS:* Rushville [IL] B: 9/27/1949, Iowa City, IA
Drafted: 1972 Round 4 Mia
1972 Mia: 10 G. **1973** Mia: 14 G; Int 1-2. **1974** Mia: 14 G. **1975** Det: 14 G; 6 Pt. **1976** TB: 13 G; Int 1-2. **1977** Mia: 8 G. **1978** Mia: 6 G. **Total:** 79 G; Int 2-4; 6 Pt.

MICHAEL BALL Ball, Michael Jr. 6′0″, 216 **DB**
Col: Southern University *HS:* Booker T. Washington [New Orleans, LA]
B: 8/5/1964, New Orleans, LA *Drafted:* 1988 Round 4 Ind
1988 Ind: 16 G. **1989** Ind: 16 G; Int 1-5. **1990** Ind: 16 G; KR 1-0. **1991** Ind: 15 G; 1 Sac. **1992** Ind: 16 G. **1993** Ind: 5 G. **Total:** 84 G; KR 1-0; Int 1-5; 1 Sac.

SAM BALL Ball, Samuel Davis 6′4″, 250 **OT**
(Foot; Dancing Bear) *Col:* Kentucky *HS:* Henderson Co. [Henderson, KY] B: 6/1/1944, Henderson, KY *Drafted:* 1966 Round 1 Bal
1966 Bal: 7 G. **1967** Bal: 14 G. **1968** Bal: 14 G. **1969** Bal: 14 G. **1970** Bal: 12 G. **Total:** 61 G.

PAT BALLAGE Ballage, Patrick Fitzgerald 6′1″, 202 **DB**
Col: Notre Dame *HS:* South [Pueblo, CO] B: 4/8/1964, Fort Hood, TX
1986 Ind: 2 G. **1987** Ind: 3 G. **Total:** 5 G.

HOWARD BALLARD Ballard, Howard Louis 6′6″, 325 **OT**
(House) *Col:* Alabama A&M *HS:* Clay Co. [Ashland, AL]
B: 11/3/1963, Ashland, AL *Drafted:* 1987 Round 11 Buf
1988 Buf: 16 G. **1989** Buf: 16 G. **1990** Buf: 16 G. **1991** Buf: 16 G. **1992** Buf: 16 G. **1993** Buf: 16 G. **1994** Sea: 16 G. **1995** Sea: 16 G. **1996** Sea: 16 G. **1997** Sea: 10 G. **1998** Sea: 16 G. **Total:** 170 G.

QUINTON BALLARD Ballard, Quinton McCoy 6′3″, 289 **DT**
Col: Elon *HS:* Gates Co. [Gatesville, NC] B: 11/18/1960, Ahoskie, NC
1983 Bal: 15 G; 2 Sac.

GARY BALLMAN Ballman, Gary John 6′1″, 215 **WR-HB**
Col: Michigan State *HS:* East Detroit [Eastpointe, MI] B: 7/6/1940, Detroit, MI *Drafted:* 1962 Round 8 Pit
1964 Pit: Pass 1-0, 1 Int. **1970** Phi: Pass 1-0. **Total:** Pass 2-0, 1 Int.

		Rushing				Receiving			
Year Team	G	Att	Yds	Avg	TD	Rec	Yds	Avg	TD
1962 Pit	3	3	7	2.3	0	0	0	—	0
1963 Pit	14	8	59	7.4	0	26	492	18.9	5
1964 Pit	13	11	43	3.9	0	47	935	19.9	7
1965 Pit	14	17	46	2.7	3	40	859	21.5	5
1966 Pit	13	0	0	—	0	41	663	16.2	5
1967 Phi	12	1	17	17.0	1	36	524	14.6	6
1968 Phi	12	1	30	30.0	0	30	341	11.4	4
1969 Phi	14	0	0	—	0	31	492	15.9	2
1970 Phi	14	0	0	—	0	47	601	12.8	3
1971 Phi	6	0	0	—	0	13	238	18.3	0
1972 Phi	8	0	0	—	0	9	183	20.3	0
1973 NYG-Min	8	0	0	—	0	3	38	12.7	0
1973 NYG	5	0	0	—	0	1	16	16.0	0
1973 Min	3	0	0	—	0	2	22	11.0	0
NFL Total	131	41	202	4.9	4	323	5366	16.6	37

	Kickoff Returns					Tot
Year Team	Ret	Yds	Avg	TD	Fum	TD
1963 Pit	22	698	31.7	1	2	6
1964 Pit	14	386	27.6	0	2	7
1965 Pit	8	150	18.8	0	2	8
1966 Pit	20	477	23.9	0	2	5
1967 Phi	2	43	21.5	0	2	7
1968 Phi	0	0	—	0	0	4
1969 Phi	0	0	—	0	0	2
1970 Phi	0	0	—	0	1	3
1971 Phi	0	0	—	0	1	0
NFL Total	66	1754	26.6	1	12	42

MIKE BALLOU Ballou, Mikell Randolph 6′3″, 238 **LB**
Col: Santa Monica Coll. CA (J.C.); UCLA *HS:* Los Angeles [CA]
B: 9/11/1947, Los Angeles, CA *Drafted:* 1970 Round 3 Bos
1970 Bos: 14 G.

BOB BALOG Balog, Robert Steven 6′2″, 225 **C-LB**
Col: Georgia; Denver *HS:* Chaney [Youngstown, OH] B: 11/2/1924
1949 Pit: 7 G. **1950** Pit: 9 G. **Total:** 16 G.

VIC BALTZELL Baltzell, Victor Leroy 5′11″, 205 **WB-DB**
(Dick) *Col:* Southwestern (Ks) *HS:* Hebron [NE] B: 6/20/1912, Soda Springs, ID D: 4/25/1986, Omaha, NE
1935 Bos: 2 G; Rush 1-0.

STEVE BANAS Banas, Stephen Peter 6′0″, 190 **BB-DB**
Col: Notre Dame *HS:* Catholic Central [Hammond, IN] B: 4/30/1907, Bridgeport, CT D: 5/10/1974, Gardena, CA
1935 Det-Phi: 3 G; Pass 2-0; Rush 8-3 0.4. Det: 1 G; Rush 3-0. Phi: 2 G; Pass 2-0; Rush 5-3 0.6. **Total:** 3 G; Pass 2-0; Rush 8-3 0.4.

JOHN BANASZAK Banaszak, John Arthur 6′3″, 242 **DT-DE**
Col: Eastern Michigan *HS:* Holy Name [Cleveland, OH] B: 8/24/1950, Cleveland, OH
1975 Pit: 14 G. **1976** Pit: 13 G. **1977** Pit: 8 G. **1978** Pit: 16 G. **1979** Pit: 16 G; Int 1-3. **1980** Pit: 12 G. **1981** Pit: 12 G. **Total:** 91 G; Int 1-3.

PETE BANASZAK Banaszak, Peter Andrew 5′11″, 210 **RB**
Col: Miami (Fla.) *HS:* Crivitz [WI] B: 5/21/1944, Crivitz, WI
Drafted: 1966 Round 5 Oak
1968 Oak: Pass 1-0, 1 Int. **1971** Oak: KR 1-0. **1973** Oak: KR 3-48 16.0. **1974** Oak: KR 8-137 17.1. **1975** Oak: KR 2-24 12.0. **1976** Oak: KR 2-23 11.5. **1977** Oak: KR 7-119 17.0. **Total:** Pass 1-0, 1 Int; KR 23-351 15.3.

		Rushing				Receiving					Tot
Year Team	G	Att	Yds	Avg	TD	Rec	Yds	Avg	TD	Fum	TD
1966 Oak	14	4	18	4.5	0	1	11	11.0	0	0	0
1967 Oak	10	68	376	5.5	1	16	192	12.0	1	0	2
1968 Oak	13	91	362	4.0	4	15	182	12.1	1	6	5
1969 Oak	12	88	377	4.3	0	17	119	7.0	3	0	3
1970 Oak	10	21	75	3.6	2	1	2	2.0	0	1	2
1971 Oak	14	137	563	4.1	8	13	128	9.8	0	3	8
1972 Oak	14	30	138	4.6	1	9	63	7.0	0	1	1
1973 Oak	14	34	198	5.8	0	6	31	5.2	0	0	0
1974 Oak	14	80	272	3.4	5	9	64	7.1	0	1	5
1975 Oak	14	187	672	3.6	**16**	10	64	6.4	0	1	16
1976 Oak	14	114	370	3.2	5	15	74	4.9	0	2	5
1977 Oak	14	67	214	3.2	5	2	14	7.0	0	2	5
1978 Oak	16	43	137	3.2	0	7	78	11.1	0	1	0
NFL Total	173	964	3772	3.9	47	121	1022	8.4	5	18	52

CAS BANASZEK Banaszek, Casimir Joseph II 6′3″, 254 **OT**
Col: Northwestern *HS:* Gordon Tech [Chicago, IL] B: 10/24/1945, Chicago, IL *Drafted:* 1967 Round 1 SF
1968 SF: 14 G; KR 1-15 15.0. **1969** SF: 14 G. **1970** SF: 13 G. **1971** SF: 14 G. **1972** SF: 13 G. **1973** SF: 9 G. **1974** SF: 14 G. **1975** SF: 14 G. **1976** SF: 9 G. **1977** SF: 6 G. **Total:** 120 G; KR 1-15 15.0.

HUGH BANCROFT Bancroft, Hugh Norman **OE**
Col: No College *HS:* Warsaw [NY] B: 8/4/1894, Wethersfield Springs, NY D: 10/31/1974, Dunedin, FL
1923 Roch: 2 G.

ROMEO BANDISON Bandison, Romeo 6′5″, 290 **DT**
Col: Oregon *HS:* Tamalpais [Mill Valley, CA] B: 2/12/1971, The Hague, Netherlands *Drafted:* 1994 Round 3 Cle
1995 Was: 4 G. **1996** Was: 10 G. **Total:** 14 G.

BRUNO BANDUCCI Banducci, Bruno 5'11", 216 **OG-DG**
Col: Stanford *HS:* Richmond [CA] B: 11/11/1920, Tasignano, Italy D: 9/15/1985, Sonoma, CA *Drafted:* 1943 Round 6 Phi
AAFC **1946** SF-A: 14 G. **1947** SF-A: 10 G; PR 1-19 19.0; KR 1-27 27.0. **1948** SF-A: 8 G. **1949** SF-A: 12 G. **Total:** 44 G; PR 1-19 19.0; KR 1-27 27.0.

NFL **1944** Phi: 10 G. **1945** Phi: 9 G. **1950** SF: 12 G; Rec 0-11 1 TD; 6 Pt. **1951** SF: 12 G; KR 1-3 3.0. **1952** SF: 12 G; Rec 1-(-4) -4.0. **1953** SF: 12 G. **1954** SF: 11 G. **Total:** 78 G; Rec 1-7 7.0 1 TD; KR 1-3 3.0; 6 Pt.

JOHN BANDURA Bandura, John Parker 6'0", 206 **OE-DE**
Col: Southwestern Louisiana B: 8/7/1919, Hammond, IN D: 5/25/1983, Hawthorne, CA
1943 Bkn: 1 G.

DON BANDY Bandy, Donald Stewart 6'3", 255 **OG**
Col: Compton CC CA; Tulsa *HS:* Lynwood [CA] B: 7/1/1945, South Gate, CA *Drafted:* 1967 Round 6 Was
1967 Was: 14 G. **1968** Was: 12 G. **Total:** 26 G.

JOEY BANES Banes, Bobby Joe Jr. 6'7", 282 **OT**
Col: Houston *HS:* Klein [TX] B: 4/7/1967, Houston, TX *Drafted:* 1990 Round 11 Hou
1990 Ind: 1 G.

HERB BANET Banet, Herbert Charles 6'2", 200 **TB-HB-DB**
Col: Manchester *HS:* South Side [Fort Wayne, IN] B: 10/17/1913, Ft. Wayne, IN
1937 GB: 7 G; Pass 7-1 14.3%, 2 0.29 2 Int; Rush 9-29 3.2; Rec 1-6 6.0.

TONY BANFIELD Banfield, James Anthony 6'1", 185 **DB**
Col: Oklahoma State *HS:* Broken Arrow [OK] B: 12/18/1937, Independence, KS
1962 Hou: PR 2-71 35.5 1 TD. **Total:** PR 2-71 35.5 1 TD.

		Interceptions		
Year Team	G	Int	Yds	TD
1960 Hou	11	3	22	0
1961 Hou	14	8	136	0
1962 Hou	14	6	17	0
1963 Hou	14	7	21	0
1965 Hou	14	3	28	0
NFL Total	67	27	224	0

BEN BANGS Bangs, Benton M Jr. 5'10", 180 **WB**
(Biff) *Col:* Coll. of Southern Idaho (J.C.); Washington State *HS:* Moscow [ID] B: 9/5/1893, Moscow, ID D: 6/7/1970, Wenatchee, WA
1926 LA: 1 G.

EMIL BANJAVIC Banjavic, Emil Thomas 6'1", 194 **WB-DB**
(Banji) *Col:* Arizona *HS:* Staunton [IL] B: 9/19/1918, Staunton, IL D: 12/1/1995, Las Vegas, NV *Drafted:* 1942 Round 9 Det
1942 Det: 10 G; Rush 11-67 6.1; Rec 5-50 10.0 1 TD; PR 2-29 14.5; KR 4-69 17.3; Int 1-15; Punt 5-235 47.0; 6 Pt.

TED BANKER Banker, Theodore William 6'2", 270 **OG-C-OT**
Col: Southeast Missouri State *HS:* Altoff [Belleville, IL] B: 2/17/1961, Belleville, IL
1984 NYJ: 4 G; KR 1-5 5.0. **1985** NYJ: 16 G. **1986** NYJ: 15 G. **1987** NYJ: 13 G. **1988** NYJ: 11 G. **1989** Cle: 16 G. **Total:** 75 G; KR 1-5 5.0.

TONY BANKS Banks, Anthony Lamar 6'4", 215 **QB**
Col: Mesa CC AZ; Michigan State *HS:* Herbert Hoover [San Diego, CA] B: 4/5/1973, San Diego, CA *Drafted:* 1996 Round 2 StL
1996 StL: Scor 1 2XP. **1998** StL: Scor 1 2XP. **Total:** Scor 2 2XP.

		Passing							
Year Team	G	Att	Comp	Comp%	Yds	YPA	TD	Int	Rating
1996 StL	14	368	192	52.2	2544	6.91	15	15	71.0
1997 StL	16	487	252	51.7	3254	6.68	14	13	71.5
1998 StL	14	408	241	59.1	2535	6.21	7	14	68.6
NFL Total	44	1263	685	54.2	8333	6.60	36	42	70.4

	Rushing				
Year Team	Att	Yds	Avg	TD	Fum
1996 StL	61	212	3.5	0	**21**
1997 StL	47	186	4.0	1	15
1998 StL	40	156	3.9	3	10
NFL Total	148	554	3.7	4	46

ANTONIO BANKS Banks, Antonio Dontral 5'10", 203 **DB**
Col: Virginia Tech *HS:* Warwick [Newport News, VA] B: 3/12/1973, Ivor, VA *Drafted:* 1997 Round 4 Min
1998 Min: 4 G.

CARL BANKS Banks, Carl 6'4", 235 **LB**
Col: Michigan State *HS:* Beecher [Flint, MI] B: 8/29/1962, Flint, MI *Drafted:* 1984 Round 1 NYG
1984 NYG: 16 G; 3 Sac. **1985** NYG: 12 G; 3 Sac. **1986** NYG: 16 G; 6.5 Sac. **1987** NYG: 12 G; Int 1-0; 9 Sac. **1988** NYG: 14 G; Int 1-15 1 TD; 6 Pt; 1.5 Sac. **1989** NYG: 16 G; Rec 1-22 22.0 1 TD; Int 1-6; 6 Pt; 4 Sac. **1990** NYG: 9 G; 1 Sac. **1991** NYG: 16 G; 4 Sac. **1992** NYG: 15 G; 4 Sac. **1993** Was: 15 G; 1 Sac. **1994** Cle: 16 G; 1.5 Sac. **1995** Cle: 16 G; 1 Sac. **Total:** 173 G; Rec 1-22 22.0 1 TD; Int 3-21 1 TD; Tot TD 2; 12 Pt; 39.5 Sac.

CHUCK BANKS Banks, Charles Edward 6'2", 225 **RB**
Col: Ferrum; West Virginia Tech *HS:* Northwestern [Hyattsville, MD] B: 1/4/1964, Baltimore, MD *Drafted:* 1986 Round 12 Hou
1986 Hou: Rec 7-71 10.1. **1987** Ind: Rec 9-50 5.6. **Total:** Rec 16-121 7.6.

		Rushing				
Year Team	G	Att	Yds	Avg	TD	Fum
1986 Hou	13	29	80	2.8	0	1
1987 Ind	3	50	245	4.9	0	1
NFL Total	16	79	325	4.1	0	2

ESTES BANKS Banks, Estes McLeod 6'3", 215 **RB**
Col: Colorado *HS:* George Washington [Los Angeles, CA] B: 12/18/1945, Los Angeles, CA *Drafted:* 1967 Round 8 Oak
1968 Cin: Rec 4-15 3.8 1 TD; KR 6-106 17.7. **Total:** Rec 4-15 3.8 1 TD; KR 6-106 17.7.

		Rushing				
Year Team	G	Att	Yds	Avg	TD	Fum
1967 Oak	9	10	26	2.6	0	0
1968 Cin	14	34	131	3.9	0	2
NFL Total	23	44	157	3.6	0	2

FRED BANKS Banks, Frederick Ray 5'10", 177 **WR**
Col: Chowan Coll. NC; Liberty *HS:* Baker [Columbus, GA] B: 5/26/1962, Columbus, GA *Drafted:* 1985 Round 8 Cle
1990 Mia: Rush 1-3 3.0. **Total:** Rush 1-3 3.0.

		Receiving				
Year Team	G	Rec	Yds	Avg	TD	Fum
1985 Cle	10	5	62	12.4	2	0
1987 Mia	3	1	10	10.0	1	0
1988 Mia	11	23	430	18.7	2	0
1989 Mia	15	30	520	17.3	1	1
1990 Mia	8	13	131	10.1	0	0
1991 Mia	7	9	119	13.2	1	0
1992 Mia	16	22	319	14.5	3	0
1993 Mia-ChiB	10	2	45	22.5	0	0
1993 Mia	2	1	26	26.0	0	0
1993 ChiB	8	1	19	19.0	0	0
NFL Total	80	105	1636	15.6	10	1

GORDON BANKS Banks, Gordon Gerard 5'10", 175 **WR**
Col: Stanford *HS:* Loyola [Los Angeles, CA] B: 3/12/1958, Los Angeles, CA
1980 NO: Rush 1-(-5) -5.0. **1981** NO: KR 1-9 9.0. **1985** Dal: Rush 1-(-1) -1.0. **1986** Dal: KR 1-56 56.0. **Total:** Rush 2-(-6) -3.0; KR 2-65 32.5.

		Receiving				Punt Returns				
Year Team	G	Rec	Yds	Avg	TD	Ret	Yds	Avg	TD	Fum
1980 NO	7	1	7	7.0	0	0	0	—	0	0
1981 NO	6	2	18	9.0	0	2	0	0.0	0	2
1985 Dal	2	0	0	—	0	3	27	9.0	0	0
1986 Dal	16	17	202	11.9	0	27	160	5.9	0	4
1987 Dal	5	15	231	15.4	1	5	33	6.6	0	1
NFL Total	36	35	458	13.1	1	37	220	5.9	0	7

ROBERT BANKS Banks, Robert Nathan 6'5", 259 **DE**
Col: Notre Dame *HS:* Peninsula Catholic [Newport News, VA]; Hampton HS [VA] B: 12/10/1963, Williamsburg, VA *Drafted:* 1987 Round 7 Hou
1988 Hou: 14 G. **1989** Cle: 15 G; 4 Sac. **1990** Cle: 15 G. **Total:** 44 G; 4 Sac.

ROY BANKS Banks, Roy Fitzpatrick 5'10", 190 **WR**
Col: Eastern Illinois *HS:* Martin Luther King [Detroit, MI] B: 11/29/1965, Detroit, MI *Drafted:* 1987 Round 5 Ind
1987 Ind: 1 G. **1988** Ind: 14 G; KR 4-56 14.0. **Total:** 15 G; KR 4-56 14.0.

TAVIAN BANKS Banks, Tavian Remond 5'9", 203 **RB**
Col: Iowa *HS:* Bettendorf [IA] B: 2/17/1974, Moline, IL *Drafted:* 1998 Round 4 Jac
1998 Jac: Rec 4-20 5.0; KR 5-133 26.6.

		Rushing				
Year Team	G	Att	Yds	Avg	TD	Fum
1998 Jac	6	26	140	5.4	1	2

TOM BANKS Banks, Thomas Sidney Jr. 6'1", 245 **C-OG**
Col: Auburn *HS:* John Carroll [Birmingham, AL] B: 8/20/1948, Birmingham, AL *Drafted:* 1970 Round 8 StL
1971 StL: 9 G. **1972** StL: 14 G; 2 Fum. **1973** StL: 14 G. **1974** StL: 1 G. **1975** StL: 14 G. **1976** StL: 14 G; 1 Fum. **1977** StL: 14 G. **1978** StL: 16 G. **1979** StL: 14 G; 1 Fum. **1980** StL: 6 G. **Total:** 116 G; 4 Fum.

CHRIS BANKS Banks, Warren Christopher 6'1", 300 **OG**
Col: Kansas *HS:* Lexington [MO] B: 4/4/1973, Lexington, MO
Drafted: 1996 Round 7 Den
1998 Den: 4 G.

CHIP BANKS Banks, William 6'4", 243 **LB**
Col: USC *HS:* Lucy Craft Laney [Augusta, GA] B: 9/18/1959, Fort Lawton, OK *Drafted:* 1982 Round 1 Cle
1982 Cle: 9 G; Int 1-14; 5.5 Sac. **1983** Cle: 16 G; Int 3-95 1 TD; 6 Pt; 4 Sac. **1984** Cle: 16 G; Int 1-8; 2.5 Sac. **1985** Cle: 16 G; 11 Sac. **1986** Cle: 16 G; 4.5 Sac. **1987** SD: 12 G; Int 1-20; 3 Sac. **1989** Ind: 10 G; Int 2-13; 1 Sac. **1990** Ind: 16 G; 4.5 Sac. **1991** Ind: 11 G; 1 Sac. **1992** Ind: 16 G; Int 1-3; 9 Sac. **Total:** 138 G; Int 9-153 1 TD; 6 Pt; 46.0 Sac.

WILLIE BANKS Banks, Willie Green 6'2", 250 **OG**
Col: Alcorn State *HS:* N.C. O'Bannon [Greenville, MS] B: 3/17/1946, Greenville, MS D: 7/2/1989, Brentwood, MD *Drafted:* 1968 Round 6 Was
1968 Was: 10 G. **1969** Was: 9 G. **1970** NYG: 5 G. **1973** NE: 13 G. **Total:** 37 G.

MICHAEL BANKSTON Bankston, Michael Kane 6'5", 285 **DE-DT-NT**
Col: Sam Houston State *HS:* East Bernard [TX] B: 3/12/1970, Eagle Lake, TX *Drafted:* 1992 Round 4 Pho
1992 Pho: 16 G; 2 Sac. **1993** Pho: 16 G; 3 Sac. **1994** Ariz: 16 G; 7 Sac. **1995** Ariz: 16 G; Int 1-28; 1 Fum; 2 Sac. **1996** Ariz: 16 G; 0.5 Sac. **1997** Ariz: 16 G; 2 Sac. **1998** Cin: 16 G; 4.5 Sac. **Total:** 112 G; Int 1-28; 1 Fum; 21 Sac.

WARREN BANKSTON Bankston, Warren Stephen 6'4", 235 **RB-TE**
Col: Tulane *HS:* Hammond [LA] B: 7/22/1947, Baton Rouge, LA
Drafted: 1969 Round 2 Pit
1969 Pit: KR 4-89 22.3. **1971** Pit: KR 5-76 15.2. **1972** Pit: KR 1-20 20.0. **1973** Oak: KR 1-12 12.0. **1974** Oak: KR 1-10 10.0. **1975** Oak: KR 1-19 19.0. **1976** Oak: KR 2-27 13.5. **1977** Oak: KR 1-0. **Total:** KR 16-253 15.8.

		Rushing				Receiving					Tot
Year Team	**G**	**Att**	**Yds**	**Avg**	**TD**	**Rec**	**Yds**	**Avg**	**TD**	**Fum**	**TD**
1969 Pit	14	62	259	4.2	1	6	6	1.0	0	6	1
1970 Pit	4	26	122	4.7	2	7	30	4.3	0	1	2
1971 Pit	14	70	274	3.9	0	17	148	8.7	0	5	0
1972 Pit	7	7	20	2.9	0	1	5	5.0	0	0	0
1973 Oak	11	0	0	—	0	0	0	—	0	0	0
1974 Oak	14	1	6	6.0	0	0	0	—	0	0	0
1975 Oak	14	0	0	—	0	2	21	10.5	1	0	1
1976 Oak	14	1	3	3.0	0	5	73	14.6	1	0	1
1977 Oak	14	0	0	—	0	0	0	—	0	0	0
1978 Oak	8	0	0	—	0	0	0	—	0	0	0
NFL Total	114	167	684	4.1	3	38	283	7.4	2	12	5

BRUCE BANNON Bannon, Bruce Patrick 6'3", 225 **LB**
Col: Penn State *HS:* Morris Hills [Rockaway, NJ] B: 3/11/1951, Rockaway, NJ *Drafted:* 1973 Round 5 NYJ
1973 Mia: 14 G; KR 1-10 10.0; 1 Fum. **1974** Mia: 14 G. **Total:** 28 G; KR 1-10 10.0; 1 Fum.

VINCE BANONIS Banonis, Vincent Joseph 6'1", 230 **C-LB**
Col: Detroit Mercy *HS:* Catholic Central [Redford, MI] B: 4/9/1921, Detroit, MI *Drafted:* 1942 Round 4 ChiC
1947 ChiC: 1 Fum TD. **Total:** 1 Fum TD.

		Interceptions			Tot
Year Team	**G**	**Int**	**Yds**	**TD**	**TD**
1942 ChiC	11	2	22	0	0
1944 ChPt	2	0	0	0	0
1946 ChiC	11	2	1	0	0
1947 ChiC	12	3	55	0	1
1948 ChiC	12	2	32	0	0
1949 ChiC	12	4	66	1	1
1950 ChiC	12	0	0	0	0
1951 Det	12	1	12	0	0
1952 Det	12	0	0	0	0
1953 Det	12	0	0	0	0
NFL Total	108	14	188	1	2

AL BANSAVAGE Bansavage, Albert Anthony 6'2", 220 **LB**
Col: The Citadel; USC *HS:* Union City [NJ] B: 1/9/1938, Jersey City, NJ *Drafted:* 1960 Round 2 Oak
1960 LAC: 3 G. **1961** Oak: 14 G. **Total:** 17 G.

BRAD BANTA Banta, Dennis Bradford 6'6", 260 **TE**
Col: USC *HS:* University [Baton Rouge, LA] B: 12/14/1970, Baton Rouge, LA *Drafted:* 1994 Round 4 Ind
1994 Ind: 16 G. **1995** Ind: 16 G; Rec 1-6 6.0. **1996** Ind: 13 G. **1997** Ind: 15 G. **1998** Ind: 16 G; Rec 1-7 7.0. **Total:** 76 G; Rec 2-13 6.5.

JACK BANTA Banta, Herbert Jack 5'11", 191 **HB-DB**
Col: USC *HS:* Los Angeles [CA] B: 11/19/1917, Los Angeles, CA D: 2/22/1977, Newport Beach, CA *Drafted:* 1941 Round 10 Was
1941 Was-Phi: Punt 9-412 45.8. Phi: Punt 9-412 45.8. **1944** Phi: PR 7-81 11.6; KR 3-54 18.0; Int 1-34; Punt 9-398 44.2. **1945** Phi: PR 4-74 18.5; KR 2-37 18.5. **1946** LARm: PR 2-26 13.0; KR 8-142 17.8; Int 2-44; Punt 1-44 44.0. **1947** LARm: PR 2-19 9.5; KR 2-50 25.0; Int 2-13; Punt 3-125 41.7. **1948** LARm: PR 1-14 14.0; KR 6-119 19.8; Punt 17-639 37.6. **Total:** PR 16-214 13.4; KR 21-402 19.1; Int 5-91; Punt 39-1618 41.5.

		Rushing				Receiving					Tot
Year Team	**G**	**Att**	**Yds**	**Avg**	**TD**	**Rec**	**Yds**	**Avg**	**TD**	**Fum**	**TD**
1941 Was-Phi	7	29	93	3.2	1	2	42	21.0	0	0	1
1941 Was	1	2	1	0.5	0	0	0	—	0	0	0
1941 Phi	6	27	92	3.4	1	2	42	21.0	0	0	1
1944 Phi	7	38	198	5.2	3	1	8	8.0	0	0	3
1945 Phi	5	15	49	3.3	1	1	10	10.0	0	1	1
1946 LARm	10	44	209	4.8	0	8	81	10.1	1	4	1
1947 LARm	12	40	193	4.8	1	14	198	14.1	0	1	1
1948 LARm	12	32	105	3.3	0	4	34	8.5	0	1	0
NFL Total	53	198	847	4.3	6	30	373	12.4	1	7	7

GARY BARBARO Barbaro, Gary Wayne 6'4", 203 **DB**
Col: Nicholls State *HS:* East Jefferson [Metairie, LA] B: 2/11/1954, New Orleans, LA *Drafted:* 1976 Round 3 KC

		Interceptions		
Year Team	**G**	**Int**	**Yds**	**TD**
1976 KC	14	3	27	0
1977 KC	14	8	**165**	**1**
1978 KC	16	3	92	0
1979 KC	16	7	142	1
1980 KC	16	10	163	0
1981 KC	16	5	134	0
1982 KC	9	3	48	**1**
NFL Total	101	39	771	3

ROLAND BARBAY Barbay, Roland Anthony Jr. 6'4", 260 **NT**
Col: Louisiana State *HS:* Holy Cross [New Orleans, LA] B: 10/1/1964, New Orleans, LA *Drafted:* 1987 Round 7 Sea
1987 Sea: 5 G.

JOE BARBEE Barbee, Joseph Adams 6'3", 250 **DT**
Col: Kent State *HS:* Twinsburg [OH] B: 8/30/1933, Cleveland, OH D: 8/12/1969
1960 Oak: 1 G.

TIKI BARBER Barber, Atiim Kiambu 5'10", 205 **RB**
Col: Virginia *HS:* Cave Spring [Roanoke, VA] B: 4/7/1975, Montgomery County, VA *Drafted:* 1997 Round 2 NYG
1997 NYG: Scor 1 2XP. **1998** NYG: KR 14-250 17.9. **Total:** KR 14-250 17.9; Scor 1 2XP.

		Rushing				Receiving					Tot
Year Team	**G**	**Att**	**Yds**	**Avg**	**TD**	**Rec**	**Yds**	**Avg**	**TD**	**Fum**	**TD**
1997 NYG	12	136	511	3.8	3	34	299	8.8	1	3	4
1998 NYG	16	52	166	3.2	0	42	348	8.3	3	1	3
NFL Total	28	188	677	3.6	3	76	647	8.5	4	4	7

BEN BARBER Barber, Benjamin 6'3", 235 **T-G**
Col: No College Deceased
1925 Buf: 9 G.

CHRIS BARBER Barber, Christopher Edgar 6'0", 187 **DB**
Col: North Carolina A&T *HS:* Parkland [Winston-Salem, NC]
B: 1/15/1964, Fort Bragg, NC
1987 Cin: 3 G. **1989** Cin: 8 G. **1992** TB: 3 G. **Total:** 14 G.

ERNIE BARBER Barber, Ernest C 6'1", 225 **C-LB**
Col: San Francisco *HS:* Manteca [CA] B: 1/14/1915, Manteca, CA D: 6/5/1989, Manteca, CA
1945 Was: 3 G.

RONDE BARBER Barber, Jamael Oronde 5'10", 186 **DB**
Col: Virginia *HS:* Cave Spring [Roanoke, VA] B: 4/7/1975, Montgomery County, VA *Drafted:* 1997 Round 3 TB
1997 TB: 1 G. **1998** TB: 16 G; PR 1-23 23.0 1 TD; Int 2-67; 6 Pt; 3 Sac. **Total:** 17 G; PR 1-23 23.0 1 TD; Int 2-67; 6 Pt; 3 Sac.

JIM BARBER Barber, James Patrick 6'3", 223 **T**
Col: San Francisco *HS:* Manteca [CA] B: 7/21/1912, Murfreesboro, TN D: 1/30/1998, Spokane, WA
1935 Bos: 10 G. **1936** Bos: 12 G. **1937** Was: 11 G. **1938** Was: 11 G. **1939** Was: 10 G. **1940** Was: 11 G. **1941** Was: 11 G. **Total:** 76 G.

KURT BARBER Barber, Kurt 6'4", 245 **LB-DE**
Col: USC *HS:* Tilghman [Paducah, KY] B: 1/5/1969, Paducah, KY
Drafted: 1992 Round 2 NYJ
1992 NYJ: 16 G; 0.5 Sac. **1993** NYJ: 13 G. **1994** NYJ: 15 G; 1 Sac. **1995** NYJ: 6 G; 2 Sac. **Total:** 50 G; 3.5 Sac.

MARION BARBER Barber, Marion Sylvester 6'3", 224 **RB**
Col: Minnesota *HS:* Chadsey [Detroit, MI] B: 12/6/1959, Fort Lauderdale, FL *Drafted:* 1981 Round 2 NYJ
1983 NYJ: KR 1-9 9.0. **1987** NYJ: KR 2-5 2.5. **1988** NYJ: KR 1-11 11.0. **Total:** KR 4-25 6.3.

Year Team	G	Rushing Att	Yds	Avg	TD	Receiving Rec	Yds	Avg	TD	Fum	Tot TD
1982 NYJ	6	8	24	3.0	0	0	0	—	0	0	0
1983 NYJ	14	15	77	5.1	1	7	48	6.9	1	0	2
1984 NYJ	14	31	148	4.8	2	10	79	7.9	0	3	2
1985 NYJ	8	9	41	4.6	0	3	46	15.3	0	0	0
1986 NYJ	15	11	27	2.5	0	5	36	7.2	0	1	0
1987 NYJ	12	0	0	—	0	0	0	—	0	0	0
1988 NYJ	16	0	0	—	0	0	0	—	0	0	0
NFL Total	85	74	317	4.3	3	25	209	8.4	1	4	4

MARK BARBER Barber, Mark Ernest 5′11″, 192 **FB-LB**
Col: South Dakota State *HS:* Alpena [SD] B: 5/19/1915, Alpena, SD D: 2/24/1975
1937 Cle: 5 G; Pass 3-1 33.3%, 7 2.33; Rush 14-35 2.5.

MICHAEL BARBER Barber, Michael Dale Jr. 5′10″, 172 **WR**
Col: Marshall *HS:* Winfield [WV] B: 6/19/1967, Winfield, WV *Drafted:* 1989 Round 4 SF
1990 Cin: Rush 1-(-13) -13.0; KR 1-14 14.0. **1991** Cin: PR 13-70 5.4; KR 1-7 7.0. **Total:** Rush 1-(-13) -13.0; PR 13-70 5.4; KR 2-21 10.5.

Year Team	G	Receiving Rec	Yds	Avg	TD
1989 SF	8	0	0	—	0
1990 Cin	16	14	196	14.0	1
1991 Cin	15	23	255	11.1	1
1992 TB	2	1	32	32.0	0
NFL Total	41	38	483	12.7	2

MIKE BARBER Barber, Michael Dwayne 6′3″, 235 **TE-WR**
Col: Louisiana Tech *HS:* White Oak [TX] B: 6/4/1953, Marshall, TX *Drafted:* 1976 Round 2 Hou
1978 Hou: Rush 2-14 7.0. **1979** Hou: Rush 2-4 2.0. **1980** Hou: Rush 1-1 1.0; KR 1-12 12.0. **Total:** Rush 5-19 3.8; KR 1-12 12.0.

Year Team	G	Receiving Rec	Yds	Avg	TD	Fum
1976 Hou	2	0	0	—	0	0
1977 Hou	13	9	94	10.4	1	0
1978 Hou	16	32	513	16.0	3	4
1979 Hou	15	27	377	14.0	3	1
1980 Hou	16	59	712	12.1	5	0
1981 Hou	16	13	190	14.6	1	0
1982 LARm	9	18	166	9.2	1	0
1983 LARm	16	55	657	11.9	3	1
1984 LARm	11	7	42	6.0	0	1
1985 LARm-Den	15	2	37	18.5	0	0
1985 LARm	5	1	29	29.0	0	0
1985 Den	10	1	8	8.0	0	0
NFL Total	129	222	2788	12.6	17	7

MIKE BARBER Barber, Michael Lanard 6′0″, 246 **LB**
Col: Clemson *HS:* Lewisville [Richburg, SC] B: 11/9/1971, Edgemore, SC
1995 Sea: 2 G. **1996** Sea: 13 G; KR 1-12 12.0. **1997** Sea: 8 G. **1998** Ind: 12 G; Int 1-0; 2 Sac. **Total:** 35 G; KR 1-12 12.0; Int 1-0; 2 Sac.

BOB BARBER Barber, Robert J 6′3″, 240 **DE**
Col: Grambling State *HS:* Ferriday [LA] B: 12/26/1951, Ferriday, LA *Drafted:* 1975 Round 2 Pit
1976 GB: 14 G. **1977** GB: 14 G. **1978** GB: 16 G. **1979** GB: 16 G. **Total:** 60 G.

RUDY BARBER Barber, Rudolph 6′1″, 255 **LB**
Col: Bethune-Cookman B: 12/24/1944, Auburndale, FL
1968 Mia: 2 G.

SHAWN BARBER Barber, Shawn William 6′1″, 224 **LB**
Col: Richmond *HS:* Hermitage [Richmond, VA] B: 1/14/1975, Richmond, VA *Drafted:* 1998 Round 4 Was
1998 Was: 16 G; Int 1-0.

STEW BARBER Barber, Stewart Clair 6′2″, 250 **OT-LB**
Col: Penn State *HS:* Bradford [PA] B: 6/14/1939, Bradford, PA *Drafted:* 1961 Round 4 Buf
1961 Buf: 14 G; Int 3-30 1 TD; 6 Pt. **1962** Buf: 14 G. **1963** Buf: 14 G; KR 1-9 9.0; 1 Fum. **1964** Buf: 14 G; KR 2-0. **1965** Buf: 14 G. **1966** Buf: 14 G. **1967** Buf: 14 G. **1968** Buf: 14 G; KR 1-0. **1969** Buf: 13 G. **Total:** 125 G; KR 4-9 2.3; Int 3-30 1 TD; 6 Pt; 1 Fum.

PETE BARBOLAK Barbolak, Peter M 6′3″, 235 **T**
Col: Purdue *HS:* J. Sterling Morton [Cicero, IL] B: 4/1/1926, Chicago, IL *Drafted:* 1948 Round 17 Pit
1949 Pit: 10 G.

ELMER BARBOUR Barbour, Wesley Elmer 6′1″, 200 **BB-LB**
Col: Wake Forest *HS:* Durham [NC] B: 2/2/1919, Rocky Mount, NC D: 2/10/1993, Norfolk, VA *Drafted:* 1945 Round 1 NYG
1945 NYG: 3 G.

JOHN BAREFIELD Barefield, John Glen 6′2″, 224 **LB**
Col: Texas A&M–Kingsville *HS:* Stroman [Victoria, TX] B: 3/23/1955, Victoria, TX *Drafted:* 1978 Round 2 StL
1978 StL: 9 G. **1979** StL: 15 G; KR 3-62 20.7. **1980** StL: 6 G. **Total:** 30 G; KR 3-62 20.7.

KEN BAREFOOT Barefoot, Kenneth David 6′4″, 230 **TE**
Col: Virginia Tech *HS:* Great Bridge [Chesapeake, VA] B: 10/11/1945, Portsmouth, VA *Drafted:* 1968 Round 5 Was
1968 Was: 8 G; 6 Pt.

KEN BARFIELD Barfield, Kenneth Alfred 6′2″, 238 **OT-DT**
Col: Mississippi *HS:* Sunnyside [GA]; Griffin HS [GA] B: 7/19/1929, Sunnyside, GA *Drafted:* 1952 Round 23 Was
1954 Was: 8 G.

ADRIAN BARIL Baril, George Adrian 5′11″, 210 **T-G**
(Barrel) *Col:* St. Thomas B: 6/4/1898, Red Lake Falls, MN Deceased
1923 Min: 9 G. **1924** Min: 5 G. **1925** Mil: 2 G. **Total:** 16 G.

CARL BARISICH Barisich, Carl John 6′4″, 258 **NT-DT**
Col: Princeton *HS:* Bergen Catholic [Oradell, NJ] B: 7/12/1951, Jersey City, NJ *Drafted:* 1973 Round 11 Cle
1973 Cle: 14 G. **1974** Cle: 13 G. **1975** Cle: 14 G. **1976** Sea: 14 G. **1977** Mia: 3 G. **1978** Mia: 16 G. **1979** Mia: 11 G. **1980** Mia: 15 G; 1 Fum. **1981** NYG: 2 G. **Total:** 102 G; 1 Fum.

TONY BARKER Barker, Anthony Ray 6′2″, 230 **LB**
Col: Rice *HS:* Northwest [Wichita, KS] B: 9/9/1968, Wichita, KS *Drafted:* 1992 Round 10 Was
1992 Was: 8 G.

BRYAN BARKER Barker, Bryan Christopher 6′2″, 189 **P**
Col: Santa Clara *HS:* Miramonte [Orinda, CA] B: 6/28/1964, Jacksonville Beach, FL
1997 Jac: Pass 1-1 100.0%, 22 22.00; Rush 1-0. **Total:** Pass 1-1 100.0%, 22 22.00; Rush 1-0.

Year Team	G	Punting Punts	Yds	Avg	Fum
1990 KC	13	64	2479	38.7	0
1991 KC	16	57	2303	40.4	0
1992 KC	15	75	3245	43.3	0
1993 KC	16	76	3240	42.6	0
1994 Phi	11	66	2696	40.8	0
1995 Jac	16	82	3591	43.8	0
1996 Jac	16	69	3016	43.7	0
1997 Jac	16	66	2964	44.9	1
1998 Jac	16	85	3824	45.0	0
NFL Total	135	640	27358	42.7	1

ED BARKER Barker, Edward Ross 6′3″, 196 **OE**
Col: Washington State *HS:* Sunnyside [WA] B: 5/31/1931, Dillon, MT *Drafted:* 1953 Round 1 LARm

Year Team	G	Receiving Rec	Yds	Avg	TD
1953 Pit	6	17	172	10.1	1
1954 Was	12	23	353	15.3	3
NFL Total	18	40	525	13.1	4

HUBERT BARKER Barker, Hubert Lyle 5′10″, 193 **BB-LB**
(Deadeye) *Col:* Arkansas *HS:* Welch [OK] B: 11/12/1918, Welch, OK D: 4/6/1994, Tulsa, OK
1942 NYG: 1 G. **1943** NYG: 2 G. **1944** NYG: 9 G; Rush 1-3 3.0; Rec 3-34 11.3. **1945** NYG: 4 G. **Total:** 16 G; Rush 1-3 3.0; Rec 3-34 11.3.

LEO BARKER Barker, Leonardo 6′2″, 226 **LB**
Col: New Mexico State *HS:* Cristobal [Panama Canal Zone] B: 11/7/1959, Cristobal, Panama Canal Zone *Drafted:* 1984 Round 7 Cin
1984 Cin: 16 G. **1985** Cin: 16 G. **1986** Cin: 16 G; Int 2-7. **1987** Cin: 12 G. **1988** Cin: 16 G; **1** Fum TD; 6 Pt; 3 Sac. **1989** Cin: 16 G. **1990** Cin: 14 G. **1991** Cin: 16 G; Int 1-29. **Total:** 122 G; Int 3-36; 1 Fum TD; 6 Pt; 3 Sac.

DICK BARKER Barker, Richard William Jr. 5′9″, 180 **G**
Col: Iowa State *HS:* Central [Oklahoma City, OK] B: 1/6/1897, Sedalia, MO D: 12/17/1964, State College, PA
1921 Sta-RI: 5 G. Sta: 2 G. RI: 3 G. **Total:** 5 G.

ROY BARKER Barker, Roy 6′5″, 287 **DT-DE**
Col: North Carolina *HS:* Central Islip [NY] B: 2/14/1969, New York, NY *Drafted:* 1992 Round 4 Min
1992 Min: 8 G. **1993** Min: 16 G; 6 Sac. **1994** Min: 16 G; 3.5 Sac. **1995** Min: 16 G; Int 1-(-2); 3 Sac. **1996** SF: 16 G; 12.5 Sac. **1997** SF: 13 G; 5.5 Sac. **1998** SF: 16 G; Int 1-(-4); 12 Sac. **Total:** 101 G; Int 2-(-6); 42.5 Sac.

RALPH BARKMAN Barkman, Ralph 5′8″, 165 **WB-TB**
(Mose) *Col:* Schuylkill *HS:* Roxbury [Succasunna, NJ] B: 1907, NJ Deceased
1929 Ora: 8 G; Scor **1** 1XP; 1 Pt.

ROD BARKSDALE Barksdale, Rodney Dean 6'1", 189 **WR**
Col: Arizona *HS:* Compton [CA] B: 9/8/1962, Los Angeles, CA

		Receiving				
Year Team	G	Rec	Yds	Avg	TD	Fum
1986 LARd	16	18	434	24.1	2	1
1987 Dal	12	12	165	13.8	1	0
NFL Total	28	30	599	20.0	3	1

JEROME BARKUM Barkum, Jerome Phillip 6'3", 218 **TE-WR**
Col: Jackson State *HS:* 33rd Avenue [Gulfport, MS] B: 7/18/1950, Gulfport, MS *Drafted:* 1972 Round 1 NYJ
1972 NYJ: KR 1-0. **1973** NYJ: Rush 1-2 2.0. **1974** NYJ: Rush 1-2 2.0. **1975** NYJ: Rush 1-(-7) -7.0. **Total:** Rush 3-(-3) -1.0; KR 1-0.

		Receiving				
Year Team	G	Rec	Yds	Avg	TD	Fum
1972 NYJ	14	16	304	19.0	2	1
1973 NYJ	14	44	810	18.4	6	0
1974 NYJ	14	41	524	12.8	3	0
1975 NYJ	13	36	549	15.3	5	0
1976 NYJ	4	5	54	10.8	1	0
1977 NYJ	14	26	450	17.3	6	0
1978 NYJ	16	28	391	14.0	3	0
1979 NYJ	13	27	401	14.9	4	1
1980 NYJ	16	13	244	18.8	1	0
1981 NYJ	16	39	495	12.7	7	0
1982 NYJ	9	19	182	9.6	1	0
1983 NYJ	15	32	385	12.0	1	2
NFL Total	158	326	4789	14.7	40	4

LOU BARLE Barle, Louis Peter 6'1", 205 **BB-DB-LB**
(Fats) *Col:* Minnesota-Duluth *HS:* Gilbert [MN] B: 6/23/1916, Gilbert, MN
1938 Det: 1 G. **1939** Cle: 3 G; Rec 2-16 8.0. **Total:** 4 G; Rec 2-16 8.0.

COREY BARLOW Barlow, Corey Antonio 5'9", 182 **DB**
Col: Auburn *HS:* Fulton [Atlanta, GA] B: 11/1/1970, Atlanta, GA
Drafted: 1992 Round 5 Phi
1993 Phi: 10 G.

REGGIE BARLOW Barlow, Reggie Devon 6'0", 195 **WR**
Col: Alabama State *HS:* Sidney Lanier [Montgomery, AL]
B: 1/22/1973, Montgomery, AL *Drafted:* 1996 Round 4 Jac
1997 Jac: Rec 5-74 14.8. **1998** Jac: Rec 11-168 15.3. **Total:** Rec 16-242 15.1.

		Punt Returns				Kickoff Returns					Tot
Year Team	G	Ret	Yds	Avg	TD	Ret	Yds	Avg	TD	Fum	TD
1996 Jac	7	0	0	—	0	0	0	—	0	0	0
1997 Jac	16	36	412	11.4	0	10	267	26.7	1	2	1
1998 Jac	16	43	**555**	12.9	1	30	747	24.9	0	1	1
NFL Total	39	79	967	12.2	1	40	1014	25.4	1	3	2

GEORGE BARNA Barna, George J 6'1", 198 **OE**
Col: Hobart *HS:* Somerville [NJ] B: 3/23/1908 D: 11/24/1972, Royalton, NY
1929 Fra: 17 G; 1 Fum TD; 6 Pt.

CHARLES BARNARD Barnard, William Charles 6'2", 190 **OE**
(Hap) *Col:* Central Oklahoma *HS:* Happy [TX] B: 3/3/1915, Ovalo, TX
1938 NYG: 5 G; Rec 1-33 33.0.

TOM BARNDT Barndt, Thomas Allen 6'3", 301 **DT-OG-C**
Col: Pittsburgh *HS:* Mentor [OH] B: 3/14/1972, Mentor, OH
Drafted: 1995 Round 6 KC
1996 KC: 13 G. **1997** KC: 16 G; 2 Sac. **1998** KC: 16 G; 3.5 Sac.
Total: 45 G; 5.5 Sac.

AL BARNES Barnes, Allen Marvin 6'1", 170 **WR**
Col: New Mexico State *HS:* Pasadena [CA] B: 7/4/1949, Los Angeles, CA
1972 Det: 9 G; Rec 4-58 14.5 1 TD; 6 Pt. **1973** Det: 11 G; Rec 3-43 14.3 1 TD; KR 1-0; 6 Pt; 1 Fum. **Total:** 20 G; Rec 7-101 14.4 2 TD; KR 1-0; 12 Pt; 1 Fum.

BENNY BARNES Barnes, Benny Jewell 6'1", 190 **DB**
Col: Stanford *HS:* Lufkin [TX] B: 3/3/1951, Lufkin, TX
1973 Dal: Scor **2** Saf. **1974** Dal: Rec 1-37 37.0. **1976** Dal: Rec 1-43 43.0.
1979 Dal: **1** Fum TD. **1981** Dal: 1 Fum TD. **1982** Dal: 1 Sac.
Total: Rec 2-80 40.0; Scor 2 Saf; 2 Fum TD; 1 Sac.

		Interceptions			
Year Team	G	Int	Yds	TD	Fum
1972 Dal	4	0	0	0	0
1973 Dal	14	1	1	0	0
1974 Dal	14	0	0	0	0
1975 Dal	14	0	0	0	0
1976 Dal	14	1	23	0	0
1977 Dal	14	0	0	0	0
1978 Dal	14	5	72	0	0
1979 Dal	15	2	20	0	0
1980 Dal	11	1	30	0	0
1981 Dal	16	1	24	0	1
1982 Dal	9	0	0	0	0
NFL Total	139	11	170	0	1

BILLY BARNES Barnes, Billy Ray 5'11", 201 **HB**
(Bullet) *Col:* Wake Forest *HS:* Landis [NC] B: 5/14/1935, Landis, NC
Drafted: 1957 Round 2 Phi
1957 Phi: Pass 1-0. **1958** Phi: Pass 6-4 66.7%, 104 17.33 3 TD. **1959** Phi: Pass 7-0, 2 Int. **1960** Phi: Pass 3-0, 2 Int. **1962** Was: Pass 4-3 75.0%, 48 12.00. **1963** Was: Pass 4-3 75.0%, 81 20.25 1 TD; PR 1-0. **1965** Min: KR 3-37 12.3. **Total:** Pass 25-10 40.0%, 233 9.32 4 TD 4 Int; PR 1-0; KR 3-37 12.3.

		Rushing				Receiving					Tot
Year Team	G	Att	Yds	Avg	TD	Rec	Yds	Avg	TD	Fum	TD
1957 Phi	12	143	529	3.7	1	19	212	11.2	1	8	2
1958 Phi	12	156	551	3.5	7	35	423	12.1	0	10	7
1959 Phi	12	181	687	3.8	7	32	314	9.8	2	7	9
1960 Phi	12	117	315	2.7	4	19	132	6.9	2	2	6
1961 Phi	12	92	309	3.4	1	15	194	12.9	3	4	4
1962 Was	10	159	492	3.1	3	14	220	15.7	0	4	3
1963 Was	12	93	374	4.0	5	15	256	17.1	1	3	6
1965 Min	14	48	148	3.1	0	3	15	5.0	0	1	0
1966 Min	2	5	16	3.2	1	1	20	20.0	0	0	1
NFL Total	98	994	3421	3.4	29	153	1786	11.7	9	39	38

BRUCE BARNES Barnes, Bruce Francis 5'11", 215 **P**
Col: UCLA *HS:* Sanger [CA] B: 6/21/1951, Coshocton, OH
Drafted: 1973 Round 12 NE

		Punting		
Year Team	G	Punts	Yds	Avg
1973 NE	14	55	2134	38.8
1974 NE	9	45	1604	35.6
NFL Total	23	100	3738	37.4

CHARLIE BARNES Barnes, Charles Edward 6'5", 230 **OE**
Col: Northeast Louisiana *HS:* Eudora [AR] B: 10/5/1939, Eudora, AR
Drafted: 1961 Round 19 Buf
1961 DalT: 4 G; Rec 1-13 13.0; 1 Fum.

DERRICK BARNES Barnes, Derrick Carnelious 6'0", 261 **LB**
Col: Oregon *HS:* Saratoga [CA] B: 9/11/1974, Hattiesburg, MS
1997 NO: 1 G.

EARNEST BARNES Barnes, Earnest Earl 6'4", 262 **DE**
Col: Mississippi State *HS:* Moss Point [MS] B: 2/10/1961, Moss Point, MS
1983 Bal: 7 G.

EMERY BARNES Barnes, Emery Oakland 6'6", 235 **DE**
Col: Oregon *HS:* Jefferson [Portland, OR] B: 12/15/1929, New Orleans, LA D: 7/1/1998, Port Moody, Canada *Drafted:* 1954 Round 18 GB
1956 GB: 2 G.

ERICH BARNES Barnes, Erich Theodore 6'2", 201 **DB**
(E) *Col:* Purdue *HS:* Elkhart Central [IN] B: 7/4/1935, Elkhart, IN
Drafted: 1958 Round 4 ChiB
1958 ChiB: KR 1-0. **1961** NYG: Rec 2-74 37.0 1 TD. **1964** NYG: PR 1-0; 1 Fum TD. **1968** Cle: KR 1-0. **Total:** Rec 2-74 37.0 1 TD; PR 1-0; KR 2-0; 1 Fum TD.

		Interceptions				Tot
Year Team	G	Int	Yds	TD	Fum	TD
1958 ChiB	12	4	90	1	0	2
1959 ChiB	12	5	67	0	0	0
1960 ChiB	12	0	0	0	0	0
1961 NYG	14	7	**195**	**2**	0	3
1962 NYG	14	6	61	0	0	0
1963 NYG	14	3	0	0	0	0
1964 NYG	14	2	26	1	0	2
1965 Cle	13	1	35	0	0	0
1966 Cle	14	4	128	0	0	0
1967 Cle	13	4	47	0	0	0
1968 Cle	14	3	64	1	0	1
1969 Cle	14	1	55	1	1	1
1970 Cle	14	5	85	1	0	1
1971 Cle	3	0	0	0	0	0
NFL Total	177	45	853	7	1	10

ERNIE BARNES Barnes, Ernest Eugene Jr. 6'3", 247 **OG-OT**
Col: North Carolina Central *HS:* Hillside [Durham, NC] B: 7/15/1938, Durham, NC *Drafted:* 1960 Round 10 Bal
1960 NYT: 5 G. **1961** SD: 10 G. **1962** SD: 3 G. **1963** Den: 14 G; Rush 0-2.
1964 Den: 11 G. **Total:** 43 G; Rush 0-2.

GARY BARNES Barnes, Gary Marshall 6'4", 200 **WR**
(Bama) *Col:* Clemson *HS:* Valley [AL] B: 9/13/1939, Fairfax, AL
Drafted: 1962 Round 3 GB

Year Team	G	Receiving Rec	Yds	Avg	TD	Fum
1962 GB	13	0	0	—	0	0
1963 Dal	12	15	195	13.0	0	0
1964 ChiB	13	4	61	15.3	0	0
1966 Atl	9	12	173	14.4	1	1
1967 Atl	13	10	154	15.4	1	1
NFL Total	60	41	583	14.2	2	2

JEFF BARNES Barnes, Jeffrey Keith 6′2″, 223 **LB**
Col: Chabot Coll. CA (J.C.); California *HS:* Hayward [CA] B: 3/1/1955, Philadelphia, PA *Drafted:* 1977 Round 5 Oak
1977 Oak: 14 G. **1978** Oak: 16 G. **1979** Oak: 16 G; Int 1-8. **1980** Oak: 16 G. **1981** Oak: 15 G. **1982** LARd: 9 G; 1.5 Sac. **1983** LARd: 16 G. **1984** LARd: 16 G; Int 1-15; 1 Sac. **1985** LARd: 16 G; Int 1-0; 2 Sac. **1986** LARd: 16 G; Int 2-7; 1 Fum; 2 Sac. **1987** LARd: 7 G. **Total:** 157 G; Int 5-30; 1 Fum; 6.5 Sac.

JOHNNIE BARNES Barnes, Johnnie Darnell 6′1″, 185 **WR**
Col: Hampton *HS:* John F. Kennedy [Suffolk, VA] B: 7/21/1968, Suffolk, VA *Drafted:* 1992 Round 9 SD
1992 SD: 1 G. **1993** SD: 14 G; Rec 10-137 13.7. **1994** SD: 11 G; Rec 1-6 6.0. **1995** Pit: 3 G; Rec 3-48 16.0. **Total:** 29 G; Rec 14-191 13.6.

JOE BARNES Barnes, Joseph William 5′11″, 205 **QB**
Col: Texas Tech *HS:* Reagan [Big Lake, TX] B: 12/8/1951, Fort Worth, TX *Drafted:* 1974 Round 13 ChiB
1974 ChiB: 3 G; Pass 9-2 22.2%, 29 3.22 1 Int; Rush 1-19 19.0; Punt 1-27 27.0.

LARRY BARNES Barnes, Larry Edward 6′1″, 228 **FB-DE**
Col: Colorado State *HS:* Sterling [CO] B: 10/6/1931, Sterling, CO *Drafted:* 1956 Round 7 SF
1957 SF: 10 G; Pass 1-1 100.0%, -2 -2.00; Rush 20-78 3.9; Rec 1-1 1.0; Punt 19-894 47.1; 2 Fum. **1960** Oak: 14 G; Scor 55, 6-25 24.0% FG, 37-39 94.9% XK. **Total:** 24 G; Pass 1-1 100.0%, -2 2.00; Rush 20-78 3.9; Rec 1-1 1.0; Punt 19-894 47.1; Scor 55, 6-25 24.0% FG, 37-39 94.9% XK; 2 Fum.

LARRY BARNES Barnes, Lawrence 5′11″, 220 **RB**
Col: Tennessee State *HS:* Jess Lanier [Birmingham, AL] B: 7/17/1954, Bessemer, AL
1977 SD: Rec 1-10 10.0. **1978** SD-StL-Phi: Rec 2-13 6.5; KR 2-22 11.0. SD: Rec 2-13 6.5. Phi: KR 2-22 11.0. **1979** Phi: Rec 1-6 6.0; KR 1-23 23.0. **Total:** Rec 4-29 7.3; KR 3-45 15.0.

Year Team	G	Rushing Att	Yds	Avg	TD	Fum
1977 SD	5	24	70	2.9	0	0
1978 SD-StL-Phi	13	4	12	3.0	1	0
1978 SD	4	3	8	2.7	0	0
1978 StL	2	0	0	—	0	0
1978 Phi	7	1	4	4.0	1	0
1979 Phi	16	25	74	3.0	1	3
NFL Total	34	53	156	2.9	2	3

LEW BARNES Barnes, Lew Eric 5′8″, 163 **WR**
Col: San Diego Mesa Coll. CA (J.C.); Oregon *HS:* Abraham Lincoln [San Diego, CA] B: 12/27/1962, Long Beach, CA *Drafted:* 1986 Round 5 ChiB
1986 ChiB: Rec 4-54 13.5; KR 3-94 31.3 **1** TD. **1988** Atl: KR 6-142 23.7. **Total:** Rec 4-54 13.5; KR 9-236 26.2 1 TD.

Year Team	G	Punt Returns Ret	Yds	Avg	TD	Fum
1986 ChiB	16	**57**	482	8.5	0	5
1988 Atl	13	34	307	9.0	0	4
1989 KC	2	2	41	20.5	0	0
NFL Total	31	93	830	8.9	0	9

MIKE BARNES Barnes, Michael Howard 6′3″, 205 **DB**
Col: Murray State Coll. OK (J.C.); Texas-Arlington *HS:* Denison [TX] B: 12/30/1944, Denison, TX *Drafted:* 1967 Round 4 StL
1967 StL: 3 G; KR 1-0. **1968** StL: 14 G. **Total:** 17 G; KR 1-0.

MIKE BARNES Barnes, Michael Joseph 6′6″, 255 **DT-DE**
Col: Miami (Fla.) *HS:* Peabody [Pittsburgh, PA] B: 12/24/1950, Pittsburgh, PA *Drafted:* 1973 Round 2 Bal
1973 Bal: 14 G. **1974** Bal: 11 G. **1975** Bal: 14 G. **1976** Bal: 14 G. **1977** Bal: 14 G. **1978** Bal: 10 G. **1979** Bal: 14 G. **1980** Bal: 16 G. **1981** Bal: 6 G. **Total:** 113 G.

PETE BARNES Barnes, Peter G 6′1″, 239 **LB**
Col: Southern University *HS:* Mary C. Womack [Longview, TX] B: 8/31/1945, Keatchie, LA *Drafted:* 1967 Round 6 Hou

Year Team	G	Interceptions Int	Yds	TD
1967 Hou	8	0	0	0
1968 Hou	14	0	0	0
1969 SD	13	5	64	0
1970 SD	14	3	22	0
1971 SD	14	2	57	1
1972 SD	14	1	9	0
1973 StL	12	1	0	0
1974 StL	14	0	0	0
1975 StL	14	2	26	0
1976 NE	13	0	0	0
1977 NE	12	1	13	0
NFL Total	142	15	191	1

REGGIE BARNES Barnes, Reginald Keith 6′1″, 235 **LB**
Col: Oklahoma *HS:* South Grand Prairie [Grand Prairie, TX] B: 10/23/1969, Arlington, TX
1993 Pit: 16 G. **1995** Dal: 7 G. **Total:** 23 G.

RODRIGO BARNES Barnes, Rodrigo De Triana 6′1″, 215 **LB**
Col: Rice *HS:* George Washington Carver [Waco, TX] B: 2/10/1950, Waco, TX *Drafted:* 1973 Round 7 Dal
1973 Dal: 14 G. **1974** Dal-NE: 7 G. Dal: 2 G. NE: 5 G. **1975** NE-Mia: 6 G. NE: 1 G. Mia: 5 G. **1976** Oak: 5 G. **Total:** 32 G.

ROOSEVELT BARNES Barnes, Roosevelt Jr. 6′2″, 224 **LB**
Col: Purdue *HS:* Wayne [Fort Wayne, IN] B: 8/3/1958, Fort Wayne, IN *Drafted:* 1982 Round 10 Det
1982 Det: 9 G. **1983** Det: 16 G; Int 2-70; 1 Sac. **1984** Det: 16 G. **1985** Det: 16 G; Int 1-(-1). **Total:** 57 G; Int 3-69; 1 Sac.

TOMUR BARNES Barnes, Tomur 5′10″, 188 **DB**
Col: Cisco JC TX; North Texas *HS:* Ross S. Sterling [Houston, TX] B: 9/8/1970, McNair, TX
1994 Hou: 1 G. **1995** Hou: 15 G; KR 1-(-4) -4.0; Int 2-6. **1996** Hou-Min-Was: 10 G. Hou: 5 G. Min: 2 G. Was: 3 G. **1997** Ten: 3 G. **Total:** 29 G; KR 1-(-4) -4.0; Int 2-6.

WALT BARNES Barnes, Walter Charles 6′3″, 245 **DT-DE**
Col: Nebraska *HS:* St. Mel's [Chicago, IL] B: 1/19/1944, Chicago, IL *Drafted:* 1966 Round 2 Was
1966 Was: 14 G; KR 1-14 14.0. **1967** Was: 14 G. **1968** Was: 14 G; KR 1-0. **1969** Den: 9 G; KR 1-16 16.0. **1970** Den: 6 G. **1971** Den: 4 G. **Total:** 61 G; KR 3-30 10.0.

WALT BARNES Barnes, Walter Lee 6′1″, 238 **OG-DG**
(Piggy) *Col:* Louisiana State *HS:* Parkersburg [WV] B: 1/26/1918, Parkersburg, WV D: 1/6/1998, Woodland Hills, CA
1948 Phi: 11 G; Scor **1** Saf; 2 Pt. **1949** Phi: 12 G. **1950** Phi: 12 G. **1951** Phi: 12 G; KR 1-15 15.0. **Total:** 47 G; KR 1-15 15.0; Scor 1 Saf; 2 Pt.

BUSTER BARNETT Barnett, Buster 6′5″, 228 **TE**
Col: Jackson State *HS:* Noxubee Co. [Macon, MS] B: 11/24/1958, Macon, MS *Drafted:* 1981 Round 11 Buf

Year Team	G	Receiving Rec	Yds	Avg	TD
1981 Buf	16	4	36	9.0	1
1982 Buf	9	4	39	9.8	0
1983 Buf	15	10	94	9.4	0
1984 Buf	16	8	67	8.4	0
NFL Total	56	26	236	9.1	1

DEAN BARNETT Barnett, Donald Dean 6′2″, 225 **TE**
Col: Fullerton Coll. CA (J.C.); Nevada-Las Vegas *HS:* Lowell [San Francisco, CA] B: 6/6/1957, Long Beach, CA
1983 Den: 8 G.

DOUG BARNETT Barnett, Douglas Shirl Jr. 6′3″, 253 **DE-C**
Col: Azusa Pacific *HS:* Edgewood [West Covina, CA] B: 4/12/1960, Montebello, CA *Drafted:* 1982 Round 5 LARm
1982 LARm: 9 G. **1983** LARm: 16 G; KR 1-0. **1985** Was: 2 G. **1987** Atl: 10 G. **Total:** 37 G; KR 1-0.

FRED BARNETT Barnett, Fred Lee Jr. 6′0″, 204 **WR**
Col: Arkansas State *HS:* Rosedale [MS] B: 6/17/1966, Shelby, MS *Drafted:* 1990 Round 3 Phi
1990 Phi: Rush 2-13 6.5; KR 4-65 16.3. **1991** Phi: Rush 1-0. **1992** Phi: Rush 1-(-15) -15.0. **1995** Phi: Scor 1 2XP. **Total:** Rush 4-(-2) -0.5; KR 4-65 16.3; Scor 1 2XP.

Year Team	G	Receiving Rec	Yds	Avg	TD	Fum
1990 Phi	16	36	721	20.0	8	0
1991 Phi	15	62	948	15.3	4	2
1992 Phi	16	67	1083	16.2	6	1
1993 Phi	4	17	170	10.0	0	1
1994 Phi	16	78	1127	14.4	5	1
1995 Phi	14	48	585	12.2	5	0
1996 Mia	9	36	562	15.6	3	1
1997 Mia	6	17	166	9.8	1	1
NFL Total	96	361	5362	14.9	32	7

HARLON BARNETT Barnett, Harlon T 5′11″, 203 DB
Col: Michigan State *HS:* Princeton [Cincinatti, OH] B: 1/2/1967, Cincinnati, OH *Drafted:* 1990 Round 4 Cle
1990 Cle: 6 G; KR 1-15 15.0. **1991** Cle: 16 G; 1 Sac. **1992** Cle: 16 G. **1993** NE: 14 G; Int 1-40. **1994** NE: 16 G; Int 3-51. **1995** Min: 15 G. **1996** Min: 16 G; 1 Sac. **Total:** 99 G; KR 1-15 15.0; Int 4-91; 2 Sac.

STEVE BARNETT Barnett, Jerry Stephen 6′2″, 255 OT
Col: Oregon *HS:* Washington [Fremont, CA] B: 6/4/1941, Sand Springs, OK *Drafted:* 1963 Round 2 ChiB
1963 ChiB: 13 G. **1964** Was: 14 G. **Total:** 27 G.

OLIVER BARNETT Barnett, Oliver Wesley 6′3″, 285 DE-DT-NT
Col: Kentucky *HS:* Jefferson Co. [Louisville, KY] B: 4/9/1966, Louisville, KY *Drafted:* 1990 Round 3 Atl
1990 Atl: 15 G. **1991** Atl: 15 G; 1 Fum TD; 6 Pt; 1 Sac. **1992** Atl: 16 G; KR 1-13 13.0. **1993** Buf: 16 G; 2 Sac. **1994** Buf: 16 G; 1 Sac. **1995** SF: 7 G; 1 Sac. **Total:** 85 G; KR 1-13 13.0; 1 Fum TD; 6 Pt; 5 Sac.

SOLON BARNETT Barnett, Solon S Jr. 6′1″, 235 T-G
Col: Southwestern (Tex.); Baylor *HS:* Livingston [TX] B: 3/30/1921, New Willard, TX *Drafted:* 1943 Round 8 GB
1945 GB: 4 G. **1946** GB: 1 G. **Total:** 5 G.

TOM BARNETT Barnett, Thomas George 5′11″, 190 HB-DB
Col: Purdue *HS:* Alliance [OH] B: 7/11/1937, Alliance, OH
Drafted: 1959 Round 8 Pit
1959 Pit: Rec 7-52 7.4 1 TD; KR 2-24 12.0. **Total:** Rec 7-52 7.4 1 TD; KR 2-24 12.0.

		Rushing					Tot
Year Team	G	Att	Yds	Avg	TD	Fum	TD
1959 Pit	12	75	238	3.2	1	3	2
1960 Pit	12	6	25	4.2	0	0	0
NFL Total	24	81	263	3.2	1	3	2

TIM BARNETT Barnett, Tim Andre 6′1″, 209 WR
Col: Jackson State *HS:* Rosedale [MS] B: 4/19/1968, Gunnison, MS
Drafted: 1991 Round 3 KC
1993 KC: Rush 1-3 3.0. **Total:** Rush 1-3 3.0.

		Receiving				
Year Team	G	Rec	Yds	Avg	TD	Fum
1991 KC	16	41	564	13.8	5	0
1992 KC	12	24	442	18.4	4	1
1993 KC	16	17	182	10.7	1	0
NFL Total	44	82	1188	14.5	10	1

TROY BARNETT Barnett, Troy Anthony 6′4″, 289 DE
Col: North Carolina *HS:* Southwest [Jacksonville, NC] B: 5/24/1971, Jacksonville, NC
1994 NE: 14 G; 1 Sac. **1995** NE: 16 G; 2 Sac. **1996** NE-Was: 4 G. NE: 1 G. Was: 3 G. **Total:** 34 G; 3 Sac.

VINCENT BARNETT Barnett, Vincent Crawford 6′1″, 200 DB
Col: Mississippi Delta CC; Arkansas State *HS:* Nugent Center [Benoit, MS] B: 2/19/1965, Mound Bayou, MS
1987 Cle: 3 G.

BILL BARNETT Barnett, William Perry 6′4″, 258 DE-NT
Col: Nebraska *HS:* Stillwater [MN] B: 5/10/1956, St. Paul, MN
Drafted: 1980 Round 3 Mia
1980 Mia: 16 G; KR 1-7 7.0. **1981** Mia: 9 G. **1982** Mia: 5 G; 0.5 Sac. **1983** Mia: 15 G. **1984** Mia: 16 G; 2 Sac. **1985** Mia: 16 G. **Total:** 77 G; KR 1-7 7.0; 2.5 Sac.

EPPIE BARNEY Barney, Eppie 6′0″, 204 WR
Col: Iowa State *HS:* Collinwood [Cleveland, OH] B: 3/20/1944, Birmingham, AL *Drafted:* 1967 Round 3 Cle
1967 Cle: 14 G; Rec 1-3 3.0; KR 1-11 11.0. **1968** Cle: 12 G; Rush 0-8 1 TD; Rec 18-189 10.5 1 TD; Tot TD 2; 12 Pt. **Total:** 26 G; Rush 0-8 1 TD; Rec 19-192 10.1 1 TD; KR 1-11 11.0; Tot TD 2; 12 Pt.

LEM BARNEY Barney, Lemuel Jackson 6′0″, 188 DB
(Stroll) *Col:* Jackson State *HS:* 33rd Avenue [Gulfport, MS]
B: 9/8/1945, Gulfport, MS *Drafted:* 1967 Round 2 Det *HOF:* 1992
1969 Det: Rush 3-36 12.0. **1973** Det: Rush 2-9 4.5. **Total:** Rush 5-45 9.0.

		Punt Returns				Kickoff Returns			
Year Team	G	Ret	Yds	Avg	TD	Ret	Yds	Avg	TD
1967 Det	14	4	14	3.5	0	5	87	17.4	0
1968 Det	14	13	79	6.1	0	25	670	26.8	1
1969 Det	13	9	191	21.2	**1**	7	154	22.0	0
1970 Det	13	25	259	10.4	**1**	2	96	48.0	0
1971 Det	9	14	122	8.7	0	9	222	24.7	0
1972 Det	14	15	108	7.2	0	1	17	17.0	0
1973 Det	14	27	231	8.6	0	1	28	28.0	0
1974 Det	13	5	37	7.4	0	0	0	—	0
1975 Det	10	8	80	10.0	0	0	0	—	0
1976 Det	14	23	191	8.3	0	0	0	—	0
1977 Det	12	0	0	—	0	0	0	—	0
NFL Total	140	143	1312	9.2	2	50	1274	25.5	1

	Interceptions			Punting				Tot
Year Team	Int	Yds	TD	Punts	Yds	Avg	Fum	TD
1967 Det	**10**	**232**	**3**	47	1757	37.4	2	3
1968 Det	7	82	0	0	0	—	5	2
1969 Det	8	126	0	66	2249	34.1	3	1
1970 Det	7	168	**2**	0	0	—	2	3
1971 Det	3	78	1	0	0	—	5	1
1972 Det	3	88	0	0	0	—	1	0
1973 Det	4	130	0	0	0	—	3	0
1974 Det	4	61	0	0	0	—	0	0
1975 Det	5	23	0	0	0	—	0	0
1976 Det	2	62	1	0	0	—	4	1
1977 Det	3	27	0	0	0	—	0	0
NFL Total	56	1077	7	113	4006	35.5	25	11

MILTON BARNEY Barney, Milton 5′9″, 156 WR
Col: Alcorn State *HS:* Gulfport [MS] B: 12/23/1963
1987 Atl: 3 G; Rec 10-175 17.5 2 TD; PR 5-28 5.6; 12 Pt; 1 Fum.

TOMMY BARNHARDT Barnhardt, John Thomas Ray 6′2″, 213 P
Col: East Carolina; North Carolina *HS:* South Rowan [China Grove, NC]
B: 6/11/1963, Salisbury, NC *Drafted:* 1986 Round 9 TB
1987 NO-ChiB: Rush 1-(-13) -13.0. NO: Rush 1-(-13) -13.0. **1991** NO: Rush 1-0. **1992** NO: Rush 4-(-2) -0.5. **1993** NO: Pass 1-1 100.0%, 7 7.00; Rush 1-18 18.0. **1994** NO: Pass 1-0; Rush 1-21 21.0. **1996** TB: Rush 2-27 13.5. **1997** TB: Pass 1-1 100.0%, 25 25.00. **Total:** Pass 3-2 66.7%, 32 10.67; Rush 10-51 5.1.

		Punting			
Year Team	G	Punts	Yds	Avg	Fum
1987 NO-ChiB	5	17	719	42.3	0
1987 NO	3	11	483	43.9	0
1987 ChiB	2	6	236	39.3	0
1988 Was	4	15	628	41.9	0
1989 NO	11	55	2179	39.6	0
1990 NO	16	70	2990	42.7	0
1991 NO	16	86	**3743**	43.5	0
1992 NO	16	67	2947	44.0	2
1993 NO	16	77	3356	43.6	0
1994 NO	16	67	2920	43.6	0
1995 Car	16	95	3906	41.1	0
1996 TB	16	70	3015	43.1	0
1997 TB	6	29	1304	45.0	0
1998 TB	16	81	3340	41.2	0
NFL Total	154	729	31047	42.6	2

DAN BARNHART Barnhart, Daniel High 6′0″, 200 TB-DB
(Chief) *Col:* St. Mary's (Cal.); Centenary *HS:* Brownsville [TX]
B: 6/27/1912, Chickasha, OK D: 6/16/1965, Los Angeles Co., CA
1934 Phi: 1 G; Pass 1-1 100.0%, 4 4.00 1 TD.

ROY BARNI Barni, Roy Bruno 5′11″, 185 DB
Col: San Francisco *HS:* Galileo [San Francisco, CA] B: 2/15/1927, San Francisco, CA D: 7/22/1957, San Francisco, CA
1952 ChiC: PR 2-17 8.5. **1954** Phi: PR 1-0. **1955** Phi-Was: KR 1-0; **1** Fum TD. Was: KR 1-0; 1 Fum TD. **Total:** PR 3-17 5.7; KR 1-0; 1 Fum TD.

		Interceptions		
Year Team	G	Int	Yds	TD
1952 ChiC	12	6	70	0
1953 ChiC	8	0	0	0
1954 Phi	10	2	0	0
1955 Phi-Was	12	1	0	0
1955 Phi	4	0	0	0
1955 Was	8	1	0	0
1956 Was	12	2	47	0
NFL Total	54	11	117	0

EDDIE BARNIKOW Barnikow, Edward John 1 FB
Col: No College *HS:* Suffield [CT] B: 12/18/1897, Meriden, CT
D: 12/1/1953, Schenectady, NY
1926 Har: 2 G.

LEN BARNUM Barnum, Leonard Warner 6′0″, 200 QB-DB-FB-WB
(Feets; Bear Tracks) *Col:* West Virginia Wesleyan *HS:* Parkersburg [WV] B: 9/18/1912, Parkersburg, WV D: 11/24/1998, Columbia City, IN *Drafted:* 1936 Round 2 Pit
1938 NYG: Rec 3-37 12.3. **1939** NYG: Rec 3-50 16.7; Scor 24, 3-7 42.9% FG, 3-3 100.0% XK. **1940** NYG: Rec 1-15 15.0; Int 2-48; Scor 9, 1-4 25.0% FG, 6-7 85.7% XK. **1941** Phi: Rec 1-11 11.0; KR 3-58 19.3; Int 2-20; Scor 8, 2-6 33.3% FG, 2-2 100.0% XK. **1942** Phi: Rec 3-54 18.0; PR 1-44 44.0; KR 1-16 16.0; Int 1-11; Scor 16, 3-7 42.9% FG, 7-8 87.5% XK. **Total:** Rec 11-167 15.2; PR 1-44 44.0; KR 4-74 18.5; Int 5-79; Scor 63, 9-24 37.5% FG, 18-20 90.0% XK.

		Passing							
Year Team	G	Att	Comp	Comp%	Yds	YPA	TD	Int	Rating
1938 NYG	10	6	1	16.7	45	7.50	0	1	18.8
1939 NYG	11	27	8	29.6	141	5.22	3	1	70.4

1940 NYG	10	23	9	39.1	150	6.52	3	2	65.2
1941 Phi	11	55	19	34.5	260	4.73	0	10	11.0
1942 Phi	10	9	1	11.1	6	0.67	0	1	0.0
NFL Total	52	120	38	31.7	602	5.02	6	15	26.5

	Rushing				Punting		
Year Team	**Att**	**Yds**	**Avg**	**TD**	**Punts**	**Yds**	**Avg**
1938 NYG	35	97	2.8	1	—	—	—
1939 NYG	91	237	2.6	2	29	1181	40.7
1940 NYG	48	128	2.7	0	39	1571	40.3
1941 Phi	35	64	1.8	0	41	1788	43.6
1942 Phi	30	64	2.1	0	50	2106	42.1
NFL Total	239	590	2.5	3	159	6646	41.8

PETE BARNUM Barnum, Robert Leroy 5'10", 195 **TB-FB**
Col: West Virginia *HS:* Parkersburg [WV] B: 1901, PA D: Baltimore, MD
1926 Col: 6 G; Int **1** TD; 6 Pt.

MALCOLM BARNWELL Barnwell, Malcolm 5'11", 184 **WR**
Col: Virginia Union *HS:* Burke [Charleston, SC] B: 6/28/1958, Charleston, SC *Drafted:* 1980 Round 7 Oak
1981 Oak: KR 15-265 17.7. **1982** LARd: Rush 2-18 9.0. **1983** LARd: Rush 1-12 12.0. **Total:** Rush 3-30 10.0; KR 15-265 17.7.

		Receiving				
Year Team	**G**	**Rec**	**Yds**	**Avg**	**TD**	**Fum**
1981 Oak	16	9	190	21.1	1	2
1982 LARd	9	23	387	16.8	0	0
1983 LARd	16	35	513	14.7	1	0
1984 LARd	16	45	851	18.9	2	1
1985 Was-NO	9	3	28	9.3	0	0
1985 Was	7	3	28	9.3	0	0
1985 NO	2	0	0	—	0	0
NFL Total	66	115	1969	17.1	4	3

DAVE BARR Barr, David Hoover Jr. 6'3", 210 **QB**
Col: California *HS:* Concord [CA] B: 5/9/1972, Oakland, CA
Drafted: 1995 Round 4 Phi
1995 StL: 2 G; Pass 9-5 55.6%, 42 4.67; Rush 1-5 5.0.

TERRY BARR Barr, Terry Albert 6'0", 189 **FL-DB-HB**
Col: Michigan *HS:* Central [Grand Rapids, MI] B: 8/10/1935, Grand Rapids, MI *Drafted:* 1957 Round 3 Det
1957 Det: Int 1-0. **1958** Det: Int 3-62. **1959** Det: Pass 1-0; Int 1-29. **1960** Det: Pass 1-0. **1964** Det: Pass 1-0. **Total:** Pass 3-0; Int 5-91.

		Rushing				Receiving			
Year Team	**G**	**Att**	**Yds**	**Avg**	**TD**	**Rec**	**Yds**	**Avg**	**TD**
1957 Det	12	0	0	—	0	0	0	—	0
1958 Det	12	0	0	—	0	0	0	—	0
1959 Det	11	5	57	11.4	1	10	180	18.0	0
1960 Det	12	17	74	4.4	1	5	26	5.2	1
1961 Det	14	6	-8	-1.3	0	40	630	15.8	6
1962 Det	6	0	0	—	0	25	425	17.0	3
1963 Det	14	1	9	9.0	0	66	1086	16.5	**13**
1964 Det	14	2	31	15.5	0	57	1030	18.1	9
1965 Det	7	1	-12	-12.0	0	24	433	18.0	3
NFL Total	102	32	151	4.7	2	227	3810	16.8	35

	Punt Returns				Kickoff Returns					Tot
Year Team	**Ret**	**Yds**	**Avg**	**TD**	**Ret**	**Yds**	**Avg**	**TD**	**Fum**	**TD**
1957 Det	9	33	3.7	0	9	153	17.0	0	1	0
1958 Det	11	23	2.1	0	4	197	49.3	1	2	1
1959 Det	16	102	6.4	0	9	224	24.9	0	2	1
1960 Det	14	104	7.4	0	4	81	20.3	0	0	2
1961 Det	0	0	—	0	0	0	—	0	0	6
1962 Det	0	0	—	0	0	0	—	0	0	3
1963 Det	0	0	—	0	0	0	—	0	4	13
1964 Det	0	0	—	0	0	0	—	0	1	9
1965 Det	0	0	—	0	0	0	—	0	0	3
NFL Total	50	262	5.2	0	26	655	25.2	1	10	38

SHORTY BARR Barr, Wallace Andre 5'8", 201 **BB-TB-FB**
Col: Wisconsin *HS:* South Division [Milwaukee, WI] B: 11/30/1897, Milwaukee, WI Deceased
1923 Rac: 10 G; Pass 5 TD; Rush 1 TD; 6 Pt. **1924** Rac: 9 G. **1925** Mil: 4 G. **1926** Rac: 3 G; Pass 1 TD. **Total:** 26 G; Pass 6 TD; Rush 1 TD; 6 Pt.

BOB BARRABEE Barrabee, Robert Sidney 5'9", 190 **OE**
Col: New York U. *HS:* Malden [MA]; Cushing Acad. [Ashburnham, MA] B: 7/23/1905, Malden, MA D: 6/1984, Elberon Park, NJ
1931 SI: 10 G.

NATE BARRAGAR Barragar, Nathan R 6'0", 212 **C-LB-G**
Col: USC *HS:* San Fernando [CA] B: 6/3/1907, KS D: 8/10/1985, Santa Monica, CA
1930 Min-Fra: 13 G. Min: 8 G. Fra: 5 G. **1931** Fra: 6 G. GB: 7 G. **1932** GB: 12 G. **1934** GB: 12 G. **1935** GB: 10 G. **Total:** 60 G.

NAPOLEON BARREL Barrel, Napoleon Paul 5'8", 200 **C-BB**
Col: Carlisle B: 12/25/1885, Richwood, MN D: 12/1964, MI
1923 Oor: 7 G.

REGGIE BARRETT Barrett, Aaron Reginald 6'3", 214 **WR**
Col: Texas-El Paso *HS:* Roy Miller [Corpus Christi, TX] B: 8/14/1969, Corpus Christi, TX *Drafted:* 1991 Round 3 Det
1991 Det: 2 G. **1992** Det: 8 G; Rec 4-67 16.8 1 TD; 6 Pt. **Total:** 10 G; Rec 4-67 16.8 1 TD; 6 Pt.

DAVE BARRETT Barrett, David Earl 6'0", 230 **RB**
Col: Houston *HS:* Roy Miller [Corpus Christi, TX] B: 9/9/1959, Corpus Christi, TX *Drafted:* 1982 Round 4 TB
1982 TB: 7 G.

EMMETT BARRETT Barrett, Emmett Edward 6'2", 192 **C-LB**
Col: Portland *HS:* Trinity [Sioux City, IA] B: 11/7/1918, Sioux City, IA
1942 NYG: 10 G.

JAN BARRETT Barrett, Jan M 6'3", 230 **TE**
Col: Fresno State *HS:* Santa Ynez [CA] B: 11/13/1939, Santa Barbara, CA D: 10/7/1973, Bakersfield, CA *Drafted:* 1963 Round 6 GB
1963 GB-Oak: 6 G; Rec 1-9 9.0. GB: 3 G. Oak: 3 G; Rec 1-9 9.0.
1964 Oak: 14 G; Rec 12-212 17.7 2 TD; 12 Pt. **Total:** 20 G; Rec 13-221 17.0 2 TD; 12 Pt.

JEAN BARRETT Barrett, Jean Martin Jr. 6'6", 253 **OT-C-OG**
Col: Tulsa *HS:* W.T. White [Dallas, TX] B: 5/24/1951, Fort Worth, TX
Drafted: 1972 Round 2 SF
1973 SF: 14 G. **1974** SF: 14 G. **1975** SF: 9 G. **1976** SF: 14 G. **1977** SF: 14 G. **1979** SF: 13 G; KR 1-5 5.0. **1980** SF: 15 G. **Total:** 93 G; KR 1-5 5.0.

JOHNNY BARRETT Barrett, John Francis 5'9", 195 **TE-OE-WB**
Col: Washington & Lee *HS:* Oak Park [IL]; Keewatin Acad. [Prarie du Chien, WI] B: 8/29/1895 D: 3/1974, Montvale, NJ
1920 ChiT: 6 G.

JOHN BARRETT Barrett, John Patrick 5'6", 170 **C-T-OE**
(Bunny) *Col:* Detroit Mercy *HS:* Holyoke [MA] B: 2/25/1899, Holyoke, MA D: 9/1966, Detroit, MI
1924 Akr: 5 G; 6 Pt. **1925** Akr: 8 G. **1926** Det: 11 G; 1 Fum TD; 6 Pt.
1927 Pott: 5 G. **1928** Det: 5 G. **Total:** 34 G; 1 Fum TD; Tot TD 2; 12 Pt.

BOB BARRETT Barrett, Robert Patrick 6'3", 200 **OE**
Col: Baldwin-Wallace *HS:* Lakewood [OH] B: 11/18/1935, Cleveland, OH
1960 Buf: 2 G.

JEFF BARRETT Barrett, Warren Jefferson 6'1", 182 **OE-DE**
Col: Louisiana State B: 2/8/1913, San Antonio, TX D: 2/15/1970, Corpus Christi, TX
1937 Bkn: Rush 1-8 8.0. **1938** Bkn: Rush 2-3 1.5. **Total:** Rush 3-11 3.7.

		Receiving			
Year Team	**G**	**Rec**	**Yds**	**Avg**	**TD**
1936 Bkn	12	14	268	19.1	1
1937 Bkn	11	20	461	**23.1**	3
1938 Bkn	11	13	205	15.8	2
NFL Total	34	47	934	19.9	6

SEBASTIAN BARRIE Barrie, Sebastian J L 6'2", 275 **DE-DT**
Col: Prairie View A&M; Liberty *HS:* Lincoln [Dallas, TX] B: 5/26/1970, Dallas, TX
1992 GB: 3 G. **1994** Ariz: 10 G. **1995** SD: 7 G. **Total:** 20 G.

TOM BARRINGTON Barrington, George Thomas 6'1", 213 **RB**
Col: Ohio State *HS:* Lima [OH] B: 1/29/1944, Lima, OH
Drafted: 1966 Round 3 Was
1966 Was: Pass 1-0. **1967** NO: Pass 2-0. **1968** NO: Pass 6-2 33.3%, 42 7.00. **1969** NO: Pass 2-1 50.0%, 15 7.50; PR 1-8 8.0. **Total:** Pass 11-3 27.3%, 57 5.18; PR 1-8 8.0.

		Rushing				Receiving			
Year Team	**G**	**Att**	**Yds**	**Avg**	**TD**	**Rec**	**Yds**	**Avg**	**TD**
1966 Was	6	10	37	3.7	0	2	23	11.5	0
1967 NO	14	34	121	3.6	0	4	50	12.5	0
1968 NO	14	45	111	2.5	0	9	33	3.7	1
1969 NO	11	7	33	4.7	1	4	42	10.5	0
1970 NO	12	72	228	3.2	2	22	130	5.9	0
NFL Total	57	168	530	3.2	3	41	278	6.8	1

	Kickoff Returns					Tot
Year Team	**Ret**	**Yds**	**Avg**	**TD**	**Fum**	**TD**
1966 Was	2	39	19.5	0	1	0
1967 NO	7	113	16.1	0	2	0
1968 NO	0	0	—	0	0	1
1969 NO	17	394	23.2	0	0	1
1970 NO	6	129	21.5	0	3	2
NFL Total	32	675	21.1	0	6	4

JIM BARRON Barron, James Martin 6'0", 195 **T**
(Botchy) *Col:* Georgetown *HS:* Boston College [MA] B: 11/10/1890, South Boston, MA D: 2/6/1936, Boston, MA
1921 Roch: 4 G; Int **1** TD; 6 Pt.

MICHEAL BARROW Barrow, Micheal Calvin 6'2", 236 **LB**
Col: Miami (Fla.) *HS:* Homestead [FL] B: 4/19/1970, Homestead, FL
Drafted: 1993 Round 2 Hou
1993 Hou: 16 G; 1 Sac. **1994** Hou: 16 G; 2.5 Sac. **1995** Hou: 13 G; 3 Sac. **1996** Hou: 16 G; 6 Sac. **1997** Car: 16 G; 8.5 Sac. **1998** Car: 16 G; Int 1-10; 4 Sac. **Total:** 93 G; Int 1-10; 25.0 Sac.

SCOTT BARROWS Barrows, Scott Marvin 6'2", 278 **OG-C**
Col: West Virginia *HS:* Marietta [OH] B: 3/31/1963, Marietta, OH
1986 Det: 16 G. **1987** Det: 12 G. **1988** Det: 16 G. **Total:** 44 G.

AL BARRY Barry, Allan 6'2", 238 **OG**
Col: USC *HS:* Beverly Hills [CA] B: 12/24/1930, Los Angeles, CA
Drafted: 1953 Round 30 GB
1954 GB: 12 G. **1957** GB: 12 G. **1958** NYG: 12 G. **1959** NYG: 12 G. **1960** LAC: 5 G. **Total:** 53 G.

FRED BARRY Barry, Frederick 5'10", 184 **DB**
Col: Boston U. *HS:* Washington [PA] B: 7/31/1948, Washington, PA
Drafted: 1970 Round 8 KC
1970 Pit: 9 G.

NORM BARRY Barry, Norman Christopher 5'10", 170 **BB-WB**
Col: Notre Dame *HS:* Notre Dame Prep [South Bend, IN]
B: 12/25/1897, Chicago, IL D: 10/13/1988, Chicago, IL
1921 ChiC-GB: 11 G. ChiC: 3 G. GB: 8 G; Rush 1 TD; 6 Pt. **1922** Mil: 1 G. **Total:** 12 G; Rush 1 TD; 6 Pt.

ODELL BARRY Barry, Odell Carl 5'10", 180 **WR**
Col: Findlay *HS:* V. W. Scott [Toledo, OH] B: 10/10/1941, Memphis, TN *Drafted:* 1964 Round 19 Den
1964 Den: Rush 3-7 2.3; Rec 4-31 7.8. **1965** Den: Rush 2-19 9.5; Rec 2-11 5.5. **Total:** Rush 5-26 5.2; Rec 6-42 7.0.

		Punt Returns				Kickoff Returns				
Year Team	**G**	**Ret**	**Yds**	**Avg**	**TD**	**Ret**	**Yds**	**Avg**	**TD**	**Fum**
1964 Den	14	16	149	9.3	**1**	**47**	**1245**	26.5	0	6
1965 Den	12	21	210	10.0	0	26	611	23.5	0	1
NFL Total	26	37	359	9.7	1	73	1856	25.4	0	7

PAUL BARRY Barry, Paul F 6'0", 208 **HB**
Col: Tulsa *HS:* Ysleta [El Paso, TX] B: 8/7/1926, El Paso, TX
1950 LARm: Rec 7-122 17.4. **1952** LARm: Rec 2-43 21.5 1 TD. **1953** Was: Rec 8-70 8.8; KR 6-112 18.7. **1954** ChiC: Rec 7-29 4.1; KR 5-80 16.0. **Total:** Rec 24-264 11.0 1 TD; KR 11-192 17.5.

		Rushing					Tot
Year Team	**G**	**Att**	**Yds**	**Avg**	**TD**	**Fum**	**TD**
1950 LARm	12	50	231	4.6	2	0	2
1952 LARm	6	3	-1	-0.3	0	0	1
1953 Was	12	56	218	3.9	0	2	0
1954 ChiC	12	50	156	3.1	0	4	0
NFL Total	42	159	604	3.8	2	6	3

JOHN BARSHA Barsha, John F **FB**
(AKA Abraham Barshofsky) *Col:* Syracuse *HS:* Boys [Brooklyn, NY]
B: 12/25/1898, Russia D: 2/18/1976, New York, NY
1920 Roch: 3 G.

STEVE BARTALO Bartalo, Stephen James 5'9", 200 **RB**
Col: Colorado State *HS:* Thomas B. Doherty [Colorado Springs, CO]
B: 7/15/1964, Limestone, ME *Drafted:* 1987 Round 6 TB
1987 TB: 9 G; Pass 1-0, 1 Int; Rush 9-30 3.3 1 TD; Rec 1-5 5.0; KR 1-15 15.0; 6 Pt.

SAM BARTHOLOMEW Bartholomew, Samuel Wilson 5'11", 188 **FB-LB-BB-DB**
(Bart) *Col:* Tennessee *HS:* Greenbrier [Hillsboro, WV] B: 4/10/1917, Charleston, WV D: 2/15/1998, Johnson City, TN *Drafted:* 1940 Round 11 Was
1941 Phi: 9 G; Rush 21-69 3.3; Rec 3-15 5.0; PR 1-1 1.0; KR 2-56 28.0; Int 1-5.

STEVE BARTKOWSKI Bartkowski, Steven Joseph 6'4", 213 **QB**
Col: California *HS:* Buchser [Santa Clara, CA] B: 11/12/1952, Des Moines, IA *Drafted:* 1975 Round 1 Atl

		Passing							
Year Team	**G**	**Att**	**Comp**	**Comp%**	**Yds**	**YPA**	**TD**	**Int**	**Rating**
1975 Atl	11	255	115	45.1	1662	6.52	13	15	59.3
1976 Atl	5	120	57	47.5	677	5.64	2	9	39.5
1977 Atl	8	136	64	47.1	796	5.85	5	13	38.4
1978 Atl	14	369	187	50.7	2489	6.75	10	18	61.1
1979 Atl	14	380	204	53.7	2505	6.59	17	20	67.3
1980 Atl	16	463	257	55.5	3544	7.65	**31**	16	88.2
1981 Atl	16	533	297	55.7	3829	7.18	30	23	79.2
1982 Atl	9	262	166	63.4	1905	7.27	8	11	77.9
1983 Atl	14	432	274	63.4	3167	7.33	22	**5**	**97.6**
1984 Atl	11	269	181	**67.3**	2158	8.02	11	10	89.7
1985 Atl	5	111	69	62.2	738	6.65	5	1	92.8
1986 LARm	6	126	61	48.4	654	5.19	2	3	59.4
NFL Total	129	3456	1932	55.9	24124	6.98	156	144	75.4

	Rushing				
Year Team	**Att**	**Yds**	**Avg**	**TD**	**Fum**
1975 Atl	14	15	1.1	2	6
1976 Atl	8	-10	-1.3	1	2
1977 Atl	18	13	0.7	0	5
1978 Atl	33	60	1.8	2	7
1979 Atl	14	36	2.6	2	4
1980 Atl	25	35	1.4	2	6
1981 Atl	11	2	0.2	0	4
1982 Atl	13	4	0.3	1	7
1983 Atl	16	38	2.4	1	7
1984 Atl	15	34	2.3	0	7
1985 Atl	5	9	1.8	0	3
1986 LARm	6	3	0.5	0	4
NFL Total	178	239	1.3	11	62

DOUG BARTLETT Bartlett, Douglas William 6'2", 250 **LB**
Col: Northern Illinois *HS:* Griffin [Springfield, IL] B: 5/22/1963, Springfield, IL *Drafted:* 1987 Round 4 LARm
1988 Phi: 10 G; 1 Sac.

EARL BARTLETT Bartlett, Earl Elburn 6'0", 200 **HB-DB**
(Cowboy) *Col:* Centre *HS:* Purcell [OK] B: 12/16/1908, Purcell, OK
D: 1/26/1987, Danville, KY
1939 Pit: 1 G.

RICH BARTLEWSKI Bartlewski, Richard Stanley Jr. 6'5", 250 **TE**
Col: Fresno State *HS:* Chowchilla [CA] B: 8/15/1967, Butler, PA
1990 LARd: 4 G. **1991** Atl: 1 G. **Total:** 5 G.

EPHESIANS BARTLEY Bartley, Ephesians Alexander Jr. 6'2", 213 **LB**
Col: Florida *HS:* Duncan U. Fletcher [Neptune Beach, FL] B: 8/9/1969, Jacksonville, FL *Drafted:* 1992 Round 9 Phi
1992 Phi: 6 G.

DON BARTON Barton, Donald Reid 5'11", 175 **HB-DB**
Col: Texas *HS:* Longview [TX]; Kemper Mil. Acad. [Boonville, MO]
B: 5/29/1930, Cisco, TX
1953 GB: 5 G; Rush 7-40 5.7; Rec 2-51 25.5 1 TD; PR 2-13 6.5; KR 1-14 14.0; 6 Pt.

GREG BARTON Barton, Gregory Lee 6'2", 195 **QB**
Col: Long Beach City Coll. CA (J.C.); Tulsa *HS:* R.A. Millikan [Long Beach, CA] B: 7/14/1946, Denver, CO *Drafted:* 1968 Round 9 Det
1969 Det: 1 G; Pass 1-0.

HARRIS BARTON Barton, Harris Scott 6'4", 283 **C**
Col: North Carolina *HS:* Dunwoody [GA] B: 4/19/1964, Atlanta, GA
Drafted: 1987 Round 1 SF
1987 SF: 12 G. **1988** SF: 16 G. **1989** SF: 16 G. **1990** SF: 16 G. **1991** SF: 16 G. **1992** SF: 13 G. **1993** SF: 15 G. **1994** SF: 9 G. **1995** SF: 12 G. **1996** SF: 13 G. **Total:** 138 G.

JIM BARTON Barton, James Edward 6'5", 250 **C**
Col: Marshall *HS:* Wahama [Mason, WV] B: 6/12/1935, Kirbyville, PA
1960 DalT: 14 G. **1961** Den: 14 G. **1962** Den: 14 G. **Total:** 42 G.

HANK BARTOS Bartos, Henry 6'1", 216 **G**
Col: North Carolina *HS:* Vandergrift [PA] B: 5/20/1913, Brooklyn, NY
D: 12/28/1987 *Drafted:* 1938 Round 10 Was
1938 Was: 7 G.

JOE BARTOS Bartos, Joseph Stephen Jr. 6'2", 194 **HB**
Col: Navy *HS:* Lorain [OH] B: 11/18/1926, Lorain, OH D: 3/11/1989, Bridgeport, CT
1950 Was: 12 G; Rush 9-36 4.0; 1 Fum.

MIKE BARTRUM Bartrum, Michael Weldon 6'5", 242 **TE**
Col: Marshall *HS:* Meigs [Pomeroy, OH] B: 6/23/1970, Gallipolis, OH
1993 KC: 3 G. **1995** GB: 4 G. **1996** NE: 16 G; Rec 1-1 1.0 1 TD; 6 Pt. **1997** NE: 9 G. **1998** NE: 16 G. **Total:** 48 G; Rec 1-1 1.0 1 TD; 6 Pt.

DICK BARWEGAN Barwegan, Richard James 6'1", 227 **OG-DG-LB**
Col: Purdue *HS:* Fenger [Chicago, IL] B: 12/25/1921, Chicago, IL
D: 9/3/1966, Baltimore, MD *Drafted:* 1945 Round 6 Bkn
AAFC **1947** NY-A: 14 G. **1948** BalA: 12 G; Int 1-0. **1949** BalA: 12 G. **Total:** 38 G; Int 1-0.

NFL **1950** ChiB: 11 G. **1951** ChiB: 12 G. **1952** ChiB: 11 G. **1953** Bal: 11 G. **1954** Bal: 9 G. **Total:** 54 G.

CARL BARZILAUSKAS Barzilauskas, Carl Joseph 6'6", 280 **DT**
Col: Indiana *HS:* John F. Kennedy [Waterbury, CT] B: 3/19/1951, Waterbury, CT *Drafted:* 1974 Round 1 NYJ
1974 NYJ: 14 G. **1975** NYJ: 14 G. **1976** NYJ: 12 G. **1977** NYJ: 9 G. **1978** GB: 16 G; Int 1-5. **1979** GB: 5 G. **Total:** 70 G; Int 1-5.

FRITZ BARZILAUSKAS Barzilauskas, Francis Daniel 6'1", 230 **OG-DG**
Col: Holy Cross; Yale *HS:* Crosby [Waterbury, CT]; Cheshire Acad. [CT]
B: 6/13/1920, Waterbury, CT D: 11/30/1990, North Haven, CT
Drafted: 1947 Round 1 Bos
1947 Bos: 5 G. **1948** Bos: 12 G. **1949** NYB: 12 G. **1951** NYG: 7 G.
Total: 36 G.

NICK BASCA Basca, Michael Martin 5'8", 170 **HB-DB**
Col: Villanova *HS:* Phoenixville [PA]; Pennington Prep [NJ]
B: 12/4/1916, Phoenixville, PA D: 11/11/1944, France
1941 Phi: 11 G; Pass 4-0, 1 Int; Rush 15-44 2.9 1 TD; Rec 2-45 22.5; PR 1-8 8.0; KR 1-22 22.0; Int 3-27; Punt 10-348 34.8; Scor 18, 1-2 50.0% FG, 9-9 100.0% XK.

BRIAN BASCHNAGEL Baschnagel, Brian Dale 5'11", 187 **WR-DB**
Col: Ohio State *HS:* North Allegheny [Wexford, PA] B: 1/8/1954, Kingston, NY *Drafted:* 1976 Round 3 ChiB
1976 ChiB: Rush 1-(-12) -12.0; PR 2-2 1.0. **1977** ChiB: Pass 1-0; Rush 1-0; PR 3-54 18.0. **1978** ChiB: Rush 2-0; PR 1-2 2.0. **1979** ChiB: Pass 1-0. **1981** ChiB: Pass 1-1 100.0%, 18 18.00; Rush 1-10 10.0. **1982** ChiB: Pass 1-0. **1983** ChiB: Rush 2-2 1.0. **1984** ChiB: Pass 2-1 50.0%, 7 3.50; Rush 1-0. **Total:** Pass 6-2 33.3%, 25 4.17; Rush 8-0; PR 6-58 9.7.

		Receiving				Kickoff Returns					Tot
Year Team	**G**	**Rec**	**Yds**	**Avg**	**TD**	**Ret**	**Yds**	**Avg**	**TD**	**Fum**	**TD**
1976 ChiB	14	13	226	17.4	0	29	754	26.0	0	1	0
1977 ChiB	10	4	50	12.5	0	23	557	24.2	1	1	1
1978 ChiB	16	2	29	14.5	0	20	455	22.8	0	1	0
1979 ChiB	16	30	452	15.1	2	12	260	21.7	0	0	2
1980 ChiB	16	28	396	14.1	2	0	0	—	0	0	2
1981 ChiB	16	34	554	16.3	3	2	34	17.0	0	2	3
1982 ChiB	9	12	194	16.2	2	0	0	—	0	0	2
1983 ChiB	16	5	70	14.0	0	3	42	14.0	0	1	0
1984 ChiB	16	6	53	8.8	0	0	0	—	0	1	0
NFL Total	129	134	2024	15.1	9	89	2102	23.6	1	7	10

MOSE BASHAW Bashaw, Moses J 5'9", 200 **T**
HS: Overland Aviation [St. Paul, MN] B: 1/1888 Deceased
1920 Ham: 7 G.

MYRT BASING Basing, Myrton Nathan 5'9", 190 **HB-FB-OE-TB**
(Biff) *Col:* Lawrence *HS:* Appleton [WI] B: 10/29/1900, Appleton, WI
D: 4/29/1957, Colorado Springs, CO
1923 GB: 9 G; Rush 2 TD; 12 Pt. **1924** GB: 11 G. **1925** GB: 13 G; Rush 4 TD; Rec 2 TD; Tot TD 6; 36 Pt. **1926** GB: 5 G; Rush 1 TD; 6 Pt. **1927** GB: 3 G. **Total:** 41 G; Rush 7 TD; Rec 2 TD; Tot TD 9; 54 Pt.

MICHAEL BASINGER Basinger, Michael 6'3", 258 **DT**
Col: California-Riverside B: 12/11/1951, Merced, CA
1974 GB: 1 G.

RICH BASKA Baska, Richard Paul 6'3", 225 **LB**
Col: UCLA *HS:* Carson [CA] B: 2/19/1952, Bismarck, ND
1976 Den: 14 G. **1977** Den: 4 G. **Total:** 18 G.

MIKE BASRAK Basrak, Michael J 6'2", 220 **C-LB**
Col: Duquesne *HS:* Bellaire [OH] B: 11/23/1912, Bellaire, OH
D: 12/18/1973, Skokie, IL *Drafted:* 1937 Round 1 Pit
1937 Pit: 10 G. **1938** Pit: 5 G. **Total:** 15 G.

GLENN BASS Bass, Alden Glenn 6'2", 205 **WR-HB**
Col: East Carolina *HS:* Wilson [NC] B: 4/12/1939, Wilson, NC
Drafted: 1961 Round 23 SD
1961 Buf: Rush 2-8 4.0; PR 8-75 9.4. **1963** Buf: Rush 14-59 4.2.
Total: Rush 16-67 4.2; PR 8-75 9.4.

		Receiving				
Year Team	**G**	**Rec**	**Yds**	**Avg**	**TD**	**Fum**
1961 Buf	14	50	765	15.3	3	2
1962 Buf	14	32	555	17.3	4	0
1963 Buf	9	9	153	17.0	1	0
1964 Buf	14	43	897	20.9	7	1
1965 Buf	4	18	299	16.6	1	1
1966 Buf	14	10	130	13.0	0	1
1967 Hou	7	5	42	8.4	1	0
1968 Hou	3	0	0	—	0	0
NFL Total	79	167	2841	17.0	17	5

ANTHONY BASS Bass, Anthony Emmanole 6'1", 192 **DB**
Col: Bethune-Cookman *HS:* South Charleston [WV] B: 3/26/1975, St. Albans, WV
1998 Min: 3 G.

DON BASS Bass, Donald Wayne 6'2", 218 **TE-WR**
Col: Houston *HS:* Fort Worth Polytechnic [TX] B: 3/11/1956, Fort Worth, TX D: 10/26/1989, Waxahachie, TX *Drafted:* 1978 Round 3 Cin
1978 Cin: Rush 1-(-4) -4.0; PR 3-8 2.7; KR 7-138 19.7; 1 Fum TD.
1979 Cin: Rush 4-35 8.8. **1981** Cin: Rush 1-9 9.0. **Total:** Rush 6-40 6.7; PR 3-8 2.7; KR 7-138 19.7; 1 Fum TD.

		Receiving					Tot
Year Team	**G**	**Rec**	**Yds**	**Avg**	**TD**	**Fum**	**TD**
1978 Cin	16	27	447	16.6	4	1	5
1979 Cin	16	58	724	12.5	3	0	3
1980 Cin	14	32	409	12.8	6	0	6
1981 Cin	6	0	0	—	0	0	0
1982 NO	3	0	0	—	0	0	0
NFL Total	55	117	1580	13.5	13	1	14

MIKE BASS Bass, Michael Thomas 6'0", 190 **DB**
Col: Michigan *HS:* Ypsilanti [MI] B: 3/31/1945, Ypsilanti, MI
Drafted: 1967 Round 12 GB
1970 Was: KR 1-0. **1971** Was: KR 4-61 15.3. **1972** Was: KR 2-22 11.0.
1974 Was: KR 1-22 22.0. **Total:** KR 8-105 13.1.

		Interceptions				Tot
Year Team	**G**	**Int**	**Yds**	**TD**	**Fum**	**TD**
1967 Det	2	0	0	0	0	0
1969 Was	14	3	31	0	0	0
1970 Was	14	4	37	0	1	0
1971 Was	14	8	78	1	0	1
1972 Was	14	3	53	0	0	1
1973 Was	14	5	161	1	0	1
1974 Was	14	3	33	1	0	1
1975 Was	14	4	85	0	0	0
NFL Total	100	30	478	3	1	4

NORM BASS Bass, Norman Delaney 6'3", 210 **DB**
Col: U. of Pacific *HS:* Vallejo [CA] B: 1/21/1939, Laurel, MS
1964 Den: 1 G.

DICK BASS Bass, Richard Lee 5'10", 200 **FB-HB**
Col: U. of Pacific *HS:* Vallejo [CA] B: 3/15/1937, Georgetown, MS
Drafted: 1959 Round 1 LARm
1960 LARm: PR 11-62 5.6. **1961** LARm: PR 4-109 27.3 1 TD.
1962 LARm: Pass 3-1 33.3%, 22 7.33; PR 6-81 13.5. **1963** LARm: Pass 1-0; PR 1-11 11.0. **1964** LARm: PR 1-0. **1965** LARm: PR 1-0.
Total: Pass 4-1 25.0%, 22 5.50; PR 24-263 11.0 1 TD.

		Rushing				Receiving			
Year Team	**G**	**Att**	**Yds**	**Avg**	**TD**	**Rec**	**Yds**	**Avg**	**TD**
1960 LARm	12	31	153	4.9	0	13	92	7.1	0
1961 LARm	14	98	608	6.2	4	16	145	9.1	0
1962 LARm	14	196	1033	5.3	6	30	262	8.7	2
1963 LARm	12	143	520	3.6	5	30	348	11.6	0
1964 LARm	9	72	342	4.8	2	9	83	9.2	0
1965 LARm	12	121	549	4.5	2	21	230	11.0	2
1966 LARm	14	248	1090	4.4	8	31	274	8.8	0
1967 LARm	14	187	627	3.4	6	27	212	7.9	1
1968 LARm	10	121	494	4.1	1	27	195	7.2	2
1969 LARm	1	1	1	1.0	0	0	0	—	0
NFL Total	112	1218	5417	4.4	34	204	1841	9.0	7

	Kickoff Returns					Tot
Year Team	**Ret**	**Yds**	**Avg**	**TD**	**Fum**	**TD**
1960 LARm	11	246	22.4	0	3	0
1961 LARm	23	698	**30.3**	0	6	5
1962 LARm	19	446	23.5	0	7	8
1963 LARm	0	0	—	0	2	5
1964 LARm	1	25	25.0	0	4	2
1965 LARm	0	0	—	0	7	4
1966 LARm	0	0	—	0	5	8
1967 LARm	0	0	—	0	6	7
1968 LARm	0	0	—	0	3	3
NFL Total	54	1415	26.2	0	43	42

ROBERT BASS Bass, Robert Shawn 6'1", 239 **LB**
Col: Nassau CC NY; Miami (Fla.) *HS:* Samuel J. Tilden [Brooklyn, NY]
B: 11/10/1970, Brooklyn, NY
1995 ChiB: 2 G.

BILL BASS Bass, William T 5'10", 180 **RB-DB**
Col: Tennessee State; Nevada-Reno *HS:* Monongahela [PA] B: 1922, Greensboro, NC
AAFC **1947** ChiA: Pass 1-1 100.0%, 14 14.00; Rec 8-79 9.9 1 TD; PR 10-85 8.5; KR 12-264 22.0; Int 2-104 1 TD.

		Rushing				Tot
Year Team	**G**	**Att**	**Yds**	**Avg**	**TD**	**TD**
1947 ChiA	14	28	44	1.6	0	2

HENRY BASSETT Bassett, Henry Herbert 6'2", 215 **T**
Col: Nebraska *HS:* Falls City [NE] B: 9/1/1899, Atchison, KS
D: 2/1973, Tulsa, OK
1924 KC: 7 G.

MO BASSETT Bassett, Maurice LaFrancis 6'1", 230 **FB**
Col: Langston *HS:* Lincoln [Chickasha, OK] B: 4/26/1931, Chickasha, OK D: 5/24/1991, Springfield, OH *Drafted:* 1954 Round 3 Cle
1954 Cle: KR 1-20 20.0. **1955** Cle: KR 7-151 21.6. **Total:** KR 8-171 21.4.

		Rushing				Receiving					Tot
Year Team	G	Att	Yds	Avg	TD	Rec	Yds	Avg	TD	Fum	TD
1954 Cle	12	144	588	4.1	6	20	205	10.3	0	4	6
1955 Cle	12	38	174	4.6	3	9	83	9.2	0	3	3
1956 Cle	12	41	129	3.1	1	4	29	7.3	1	0	2
NFL Total	36	223	891	4.0	10	33	317	9.6	1	7	11

DICK BASSI Bassi, Richard Joseph 5′11″, 214 **G-LB**
Col: Santa Clara *HS:* Mission [San Francisco, CA] B: 1/1/1915, San Luis Obispo, CA D: 8/12/1973, San Francisco, CA *Drafted:* 1937 Round 4 Was
AAFC **1946** SF-A: 8 G; Int 1-2. **1947** SF-A: 8 G. **Total:** 16 G; Int 1-2.

NFL **1938** ChiB: 9 G; **1** Fum TD; 6 Pt. **1939** ChiB: 10 G. **1940** Phi: 11 G. **1941** Pit: 11 G; Rec 1-6 6.0. **Total:** 41 G; Rec 1-6 6.0; 1 Fum TD; 6 Pt.

REDS BASSMAN Bassman, Herman 5′11″, 180 **TB-HB-DB**
Col: Ursinus *HS:* Central Philadelphia [Philadelphia, PA] B: 2/25/1913, Philadelphia, PA
1936 Phi: 8 G; Pass 3-1 33.3%, 3 1.00 1 Int; Rush 4-19 4.8; Rec 2-38 19.0.

BERT BASTON Baston, Albert Preston 6′1″, 170 **E**
Col: Minnesota *HS:* St. Louis Park [MN] B: 12/3/1894, St. Louis Park, MN D: 11/16/1979, St. Cloud, MN
1920 Cle: 8 G.

CHARLIE BATCH Batch, Charles D'Donte 6′2″, 216 **QB**
Col: Eastern Michigan *HS:* Steel Valley [Munhall, PA] B: 12/5/1974, Homestead, PA *Drafted:* 1998 Round 2 Det

		Passing							
Year Team	G	Att	Comp	Comp%	Yds	YPA	TD	Int	Rating
1998 Det	12	303	173	57.1	2178	7.19	11	6	83.5

	Rushing				
Year Team	Att	Yds	Avg	TD	Fum
1998 Det	41	229	5.6	1	2

DON BATCHELOR Batchelor, Donald G 6′3″, 225 **T**
Col: Ohio Northern; Grove City *HS:* Hicksville [OH] B: 6/15/1895, Hicksville, OH D: 9/24/1971, Grand Blanc, MI
1922 Can: 1 G. **1923** Tol: 2 G. **Total:** 3 G.

MARV BATEMAN Bateman, Marvin Fredrich 6′4″, 213 **P**
Col: Utah *HS:* Highland [Salt Lake City, UT] B: 4/5/1950, Salt Lake City, UT *Drafted:* 1972 Round 3 Dal
1973 Dal: Scor 1, 1-1 100.0% XK. **1977** Buf: Rush 1-0. **Total:** Rush 1-0; Scor 1, 1-1 100.0% XK.

		Punting		
Year Team	G	Punts	Yds	Avg
1972 Dal	14	51	1949	38.2
1973 Dal	13	55	2290	41.6
1974 Dal-Buf	7	67	2712	40.5
1974 Dal	2	33	1218	36.9
1974 Buf	5	34	1494	43.9
1975 Buf	14	61	2536	41.6
1976 Buf	14	86	3678	**42.8**
1977 Buf	14	81	3229	39.9
NFL Total	76	401	16394	40.9

MARIO BATES Bates, Mario Doniel 6′1″, 217 **RB**
Col: Arizona State *HS:* Amphitheater [Tucson, AZ] B: 1/16/1973, Tucson, AZ *Drafted:* 1994 Round 2 NO
1994 NO: KR 1-20 20.0. **1997** NO: Pass 1-1 100.0%, 21 21.00 1 TD. **Total:** Pass 1-1 100.0%, 21 21.00 1 TD; KR 1-20 20.0.

		Rushing				Receiving				
Year Team	G	Att	Yds	Avg	TD	Rec	Yds	Avg	TD	Fum
1994 NO	11	151	579	3.8	6	8	62	7.8	0	3
1995 NO	16	244	951	3.9	7	18	114	6.3	0	2
1996 NO	14	164	584	3.6	4	13	44	3.4	0	4
1997 NO	12	119	440	3.7	4	5	42	8.4	0	2
1998 Ariz	16	60	165	2.8	6	1	14	14.0	0	0
NFL Total	69	738	2719	3.7	27	45	276	6.1	0	11

MICHAEL BATES Bates, Michael Dion 5′10″, 189 **WR**
Col: Arizona *HS:* Amphitheater [Tucson, AZ] B: 12/19/1969, Tucson, AZ *Drafted:* 1992 Round 6 Sea
1993 Sea: Rush 2-12 6.0; Rec 1-6 6.0. **1994** Sea: Rush 2-(-4) -2.0; Rec 5-112 22.4 1 TD. **1997** Car: PR 1-8 8.0. **Total:** Rush 4-8 2.0; Rec 6-118 19.7 1 TD; PR 1-8 8.0.

		Kickoff Returns					Tot
Year Team	G	Ret	Yds	Avg	TD	Fum	TD
1993 Sea	16	30	603	20.1	0	1	0
1994 Sea	15	26	508	19.5	0	3	1
1995 Cle	13	9	176	19.6	0	0	0
1996 Car	14	33	998	**30.2**	1	2	1
1997 Car	16	47	1281	**27.3**	0	4	0
1998 Car	14	59	1480	25.1	1	1	1
NFL Total	88	204	5046	24.7	2	11	3

PATRICK BATES Bates, Patrick James 6′3″, 220 **DB**
Col: Texas A&M *HS:* Ball [Galveston, TX] B: 11/27/1970, Galveston, TX *Drafted:* 1993 Round 1 LARd
1993 LARd: 13 G; Int 1-0. **1994** LARd: 16 G. **1996** Atl: 15 G. **Total:** 44 G; Int 1-0.

TED BATES Bates, Ted Douglas 6′3″, 219 **LB**
Col: Oregon State *HS:* Manual Arts [Los Angeles, CA] B: 9/22/1936, Baytown, TX *Drafted:* 1959 Round 5 ChiC
1959 ChiC: 12 G. **1960** StL: 12 G; KR 1-6 6.0. **1961** StL: 14 G. **1962** StL: 8 G. **1963** NYJ: 8 G. **Total:** 54 G; KR 1-6 6.0.

BILL BATES Bates, William Frederick 6′1″, 204 **DB**
Col: Tennessee *HS:* Farragut [Knoxville, TN] B: 6/6/1961, Knoxville, TN
1983 Dal: 4 Sac. **1984** Dal: 5 Sac. **1985** Dal: PR 22-152 6.9; 1 Sac. **1986** Dal: 2.5 Sac. **1987** Dal: 3 Sac. **1988** Dal: 0.5 Sac. **1989** Dal: Rush 1-0. **1990** Dal: Rush 1-4 4.0. **1994** Dal: 1 Sac. **1997** Dal: 1 Sac. **Total:** Rush 2-4 2.0; PR 22-152 6.9; 18 Sac.

		Interceptions			
Year Team	G	Int	Yds	TD	Fum
1983 Dal	16	1	29	0	1
1984 Dal	12	1	3	0	0
1985 Dal	16	4	15	0	0
1986 Dal	15	0	0	0	0
1987 Dal	12	3	28	0	0
1988 Dal	16	1	0	0	0
1989 Dal	16	1	18	0	0
1990 Dal	16	1	4	0	0
1991 Dal	16	0	0	0	0
1992 Dal	5	0	0	0	0
1993 Dal	16	2	25	0	0
1994 Dal	15	0	0	0	0
1995 Dal	16	0	0	0	0
1996 Dal	14	0	0	0	0
1997 Dal	16	0	0	0	0
NFL Total	217	14	122	0	1

STAN BATINSKI Batinski, Stanley Charles 5′10″, 215 **G**
(Bull) *Col:* Temple *HS:* Greenfield [MA] B: 3/4/1917, Greenfield, MA D: 1/29/1990, Greenfield, MA
1941 Det: 8 G. **1943** Det: 7 G. **1944** Det: 9 G. **1945** Det: 10 G. **1946** Det: 11 G. **1947** Det: 12 G. **1948** Bos: 12 G. **1949** NYB: 12 G. **Total:** 81 G.

MICHAEL BATISTE Batiste, Michael 6′3″, 315 **OG-DT**
Col: Tulane *HS:* Westbrook [Beaumont, TX] B: 12/24/1970, Beaumont, TX
1995 Dal: 2 G. **1998** Was: 6 G. **Total:** 8 G.

JOHN BATORSKI Batorski, John Michael Jr. 6′2″, 238 **OE-DE**
(Bat) *Col:* Colgate *HS:* Lackawanna [NY] B: 9/27/1920, Lackawanna, NY D: 11/16/1982, Old Field, NY
AAFC **1946** BufA: 8 G; Rec 2-27 13.5.

MARCO BATTAGLIA Battaglia, Marco Antonio 6′3″, 252 **TE**
Col: Rutgers *HS:* St. Francis Prep [Queens, NY] B: 1/25/1973, Queens, NY *Drafted:* 1996 Round 2 Cin
1996 Cin: KR 1-8 8.0. **1998** Cin: KR 1-5 5.0. **Total:** KR 2-13 6.5.

		Receiving				
Year Team	G	Rec	Yds	Avg	TD	Fum
1996 Cin	16	8	79	9.9	0	0
1997 Cin	16	12	149	12.4	1	2
1998 Cin	16	10	47	4.7	1	1
NFL Total	48	30	275	9.2	2	3

MATT BATTAGLIA Battaglia, Matthew Martin 6′2″, 225 **LB**
Col: Louisville *HS:* Lithonia [GA] B: 9/25/1965, Tallahassee, FL
1987 Phi: 3 G; 1 Sac.

PAT BATTEN Batten, Patrick Ward 6′2″, 225 **FB**
Col: Hardin-Simmons *HS:* Eldora [IA] B: 12/5/1941, Indianola, IA *Drafted:* 1964 Round 3 Det
1964 Det: 3 G.

JIM BATTLE Battle, James 6′5″, 235 **OT**
Col: Southern University *HS:* Booker T. Washington [Shreveport, LA] B: 9/18/1941, Shreveport, LA *Drafted:* 1966 Round 6 Cle
1966 Cle: 6 G.

JIM BATTLE Battle, James 6′1″, 255 **OG**
(J.B.) *Col:* Southern Illinois *HS:* Union Acad. [Bartow, FL] B: 2/20/1938, Bartow, FL
1963 Min: 14 G.

MIKE BATTLE Battle, Michael Leonard 6'1", 180 **DB**
(Blade) *Col:* Long Beach City Coll. CA (J.C.); USC *HS:* Lawndale [CA]; El Segundo HS [CA] B: 7/9/1946, South Gate, CA *Drafted:* 1969 Round 12 NYJ
1969 NYJ: Int 1-25. **1970** NYJ: Rec 1-2 2.0. **Total:** Rec 1-2 2.0; Int 1-25.

		Punt Returns				Kickoff Returns				
Year Team	G	Ret	Yds	Avg	TD	Ret	Yds	Avg	TD	Fum
1969 NYJ	14	34	235	6.9	0	31	750	24.2	0	3
1970 NYJ	14	19	117	6.2	0	**40**	891	22.3	0	2
NFL Total	28	53	352	6.6	0	71	1641	23.1	0	5

RALPH BATTLE Battle, Ralph Keith 6'2", 205 **DB**
Col: Jacksonville State *HS:* J.O. Johnson [Huntsville, AL]
B: 6/15/1961, Huntsville, AL
1984 Cin: 3 G.

RON BATTLE Battle, Ronald Jerome 6'3", 220 **TE**
Col: North Texas *HS:* Southwood [Shreveport, LA] B: 3/27/1959, Shreveport, LA *Drafted:* 1981 Round 7 LARm
1981 LARm: 4 G. **1982** LARm: 9 G; Rush 1-1 1.0; Rec 2-62 31.0 1 TD; 6 Pt. **Total:** 13 G; Rush 1-1 1.0; Rec 2-62 31.0 1 TD; 6 Pt.

CLIFF BATTLES Battles, Clifford Franklin 6'1", 195 **TB-DB-WB-FB**
(Gyp) *Col:* West Virginia Wesleyan *HS:* Kenmore [Akron, OH]
B: 5/1/1910, Akron, OH D: 4/28/1981, Clearwater, FL *HOF:* 1968
1933 Bos: PR 1 TD; Scor 27, 1 FG. **1934** Bos: Scor 43, 1 XK. **1935** Bos: KR **1** TD. **1936** Bos: PR **1** TD. **1937** Was: Int 1 TD. **Total:** PR 2 TD; KR 1 TD; Int 1 TD; Scor 190, 1 FG, 1 XK.

		Passing							
Year Team	G	Att	Comp	Comp%	Yds	YPA	TD	Int	Rating
1932 Bos	8	20	2	10.0	42	2.10	0	2	0.0
1933 Bos	12	21	5	23.8	65	3.10	0	3	0.4
1934 Bos	12	9	1	11.1	7	0.78	0	0	39.6
1935 Bos	7	22	5	22.7	92	4.18	0	1	25.6
1936 Bos	11	52	18	34.6	242	4.65	1	6	17.1
1937 Was	10	33	13	39.4	142	4.30	0	3	15.0
NFL Total	60	157	44	28.0	590	3.76	1	15	5.3

	Rushing				Receiving				Tot
Year Team	Att	Yds	Avg	TD	Rec	Yds	Avg	TD	TD
1932 Bos	**148**	**576**	3.9	3	4	60	15.0	1	4
1933 Bos	136	737	**5.4**	3	11	185	16.8	0	4
1934 Bos	96	480	5.0	6	5	95	19.0	1	7
1935 Bos	67	230	3.4	1	3	22	7.3	0	2
1936 Bos	176	614	3.5	5	6	103	17.2	1	7
1937 Was	**216**	**874**	4.0	**5**	9	81	9.0	1	**7**
NFL Total	839	3511	4.2	23	38	546	14.4	4	31

BOBBY BATTON Batton, Robert Joseph 5'11", 190 **RB**
Col: Santa Rosa JC CA; Nevada-Las Vegas *HS:* Mission [San Francisco, CA] B: 3/17/1957, Yazoo City, MS *Drafted:* 1980 Round 7 NYJ
1980 NYJ: 8 G; Rush 3-4 1.3.

GREG BATY Baty, Gregory James 6'5", 241 **TE**
Col: Stanford *HS:* Sparta [NJ] B: 8/28/1964, Hastings, MI
Drafted: 1986 Round 8 NE
1993 Mia: KR 1-7 7.0. **1994** Mia: KR 1-0. **Total:** KR 2-7 3.5.

		Receiving				
Year Team	G	Rec	Yds	Avg	TD	Fum
1986 NE	16	37	331	8.9	2	0
1987 NE-LARm	9	18	175	9.7	2	0
1987 NE	5	15	138	9.2	2	0
1987 LARm	4	3	37	12.3	0	0
1988 Pho	1	0	0	—	0	0
1990 Mia	12	0	0	—	0	0
1991 Mia	16	20	269	13.5	1	1
1992 Mia	16	3	19	6.3	1	0
1993 Mia	16	5	78	15.6	1	0
1994 Mia	16	2	11	5.5	1	1
NFL Total	102	85	883	10.4	8	2

A.C. BAUER Bauer, A.C. 6'2", 210 **T**
B: 1900 Deceased
1923 Rac: 1 G.

HANK BAUER Bauer, Henry John 5'10", 200 **RB**
Col: California Lutheran *HS:* Magnolia [Anaheim, CA] B: 7/15/1954, Scottsbluff, NE
1977 SD: Rec 1-15 15.0 1 TD. **1978** SD: Rec 10-78 7.8 1 TD. **1979** SD: KR 4-92 23.0. **1980** SD: KR 2-37 18.5. **1981** SD: Rec 1-4 4.0 1 TD; PR 1-7 7.0; KR 1-14 14.0. **1982** SD: KR 2-24 12.0. **Total:** Rec 12-97 8.1 3 TD; PR 1-7 7.0; KR 9-167 18.6.

		Rushing					Tot
Year Team	G	Att	Yds	Avg	TD	Fum	TD
1977 SD	13	4	4	1.0	0	1	1
1978 SD	16	85	304	3.6	8	2	9
1979 SD	16	22	28	1.3	8	1	8
1980 SD	16	10	34	3.4	1	0	1
1981 SD	16	2	7	3.5	0	0	1
1982 SD	9	0	0	—	0	0	0
NFL Total	86	123	377	3.1	17	4	20

HERB BAUER Bauer, Herbert Frank 5'10", 190 **OE**
Col: Baldwin-Wallace *HS:* Lakewood [OH] B: 10/13/1906, Cleveland, OH D: 7/30/1980, Ann Arbor, MI
1925 Cle: 2 G.

JOHN BAUER Bauer, John Richard 6'3", 235 **OG**
(Buckwheat) *Col:* Illinois *HS:* Benton [IL] B: 3/11/1932, Benton, IL
Drafted: 1954 Round 1 Cle
1954 NYG: 2 G.

SAMMY BAUGH Baugh, Samuel Adrian 6'2", 182 **QB-TB-DB**
(Slingin' Sam) *Col:* Texas Christian *HS:* Temple [TX]; Sweetwater HS [TX] B: 3/17/1914, Temple, TX *Drafted:* 1937 Round 1 Was
HOF: 1963
1942 Was: PR 5-63 12.6. **1943** Was: PR 2-13 6.5. **1944** Was: Rec 1-0; PR 4-23 5.8. **1945** Was: Scor 1, 0-1 XK, 1 1XP. **Total:** Rec 1-0; PR 11-99 9.0; Scor 55, 0-1 XK, 1 1XP.

		Passing							
Year Team	G	Att	Comp	Comp%	Yds	YPA	TD	Int	Rating
1937 Was	11	**171**	**81**	47.4	**1127**	6.59	8	14	50.5
1938 Was	9	128	63	49.2	853	6.66	5	11	48.1
1939 Was	9	96	53	55.2	518	5.40	6	9	52.3
1940 Was	11	177	111	**62.7**	**1367**	7.72	**12**	10	85.6
1941 Was	11	193	106	54.9	1236	6.40	10	19	52.2
1942 Was	11	225	132	**58.7**	1524	6.77	16	11	82.5
1943 Was	10	**239**	**133**	**55.6**	1754	7.34	23	19	78.0
1944 Was	8	146	82	56.2	849	5.82	4	8	59.4
1945 Was	8	182	**128**	**70.3**	1669	9.17	11	4	109.9
1946 Was	11	161	87	54.0	1163	7.22	8	17	54.2
1947 Was	12	**354**	**210**	**59.3**	**2938**	8.30	**25**	15	92.0
1948 Was	12	**315**	**185**	**58.7**	**2599**	8.25	22	23	78.3
1949 Was	12	255	145	**56.9**	1903	7.46	18	14	81.2
1950 Was	11	166	90	54.2	1130	6.81	10	11	68.1
1951 Was	12	154	67	43.5	1104	7.17	7	17	43.8
1952 Was	7	33	20	60.6	152	4.61	2	1	79.4
NFL Total	165	2995	1693	56.5	21886	7.31	187	203	72.2

	Rushing				Interceptions		
Year Team	Att	Yds	Avg	TD	Int	Yds	TD
1937 Was	86	240	2.8	1	—	—	0
1938 Was	21	35	1.7	0	—	—	0
1939 Was	14	46	3.3	0	—	—	0
1940 Was	20	16	0.8	0	3	84	0
1941 Was	27	14	0.5	0	4	83	0
1942 Was	20	61	3.1	1	5	77	0
1943 Was	19	-43	-2.3	0	**11**	112	0
1944 Was	19	-38	-2.0	0	4	21	0
1945 Was	19	-71	-3.7	0	4	114	0
1946 Was	18	-76	-4.2	1	0	0	0
1947 Was	25	47	1.9	2	0	0	0
1948 Was	4	4	1.0	1	0	0	0
1949 Was	13	67	5.2	2	0	0	0
1950 Was	7	27	3.9	1	0	0	0
1951 Was	11	-5	-0.5	0	0	0	0
1952 Was	1	1	1.0	0	0	0	0
NFL Total	324	325	1.0	9	31	491	0

	Punting			
Year Team	Punts	Yds	Avg	Fum
1939 Was	26	998	38.4	0
1940 Was	35	1799	**51.4**	0
1941 Was	30	1462	**48.7**	0
1942 Was	37	1785	**48.2**	0
1943 Was	**50**	**2295**	45.9	0
1944 Was	44	1787	40.6	0
1945 Was	33	1429	**43.3**	5
1946 Was	33	1488	45.1	7
1947 Was	35	1528	43.7	**15**
1948 Was	0	0	—	7
1949 Was	1	53	53.0	0
1950 Was	9	352	39.1	6
1951 Was	4	221	55.3	6
1952 Was	1	48	48.0	1
NFL Total	338	15245	**45.1**	47

TOM BAUGH Baugh, Thomas Anthony 6'3", 274 **C**
Col: Southern Illinois *HS:* Riverside-Brookfield Twp. [Riverside, IL]
B: 12/1/1963, Chicago, IL *Drafted:* 1986 Round 4 KC
1986 KC: 5 G. **1987** KC: 12 G; 1 Fum. **1988** KC: 12 G; 1 Fum. **1989** Cle: 16 G. **Total:** 45 G; 2 Fum.

MAXIE BAUGHAN Baughan, Maxie Calloway 6'1", 230 **LB**
Col: Georgia Tech *HS:* Bessemer [AL] B: 8/3/1938, Forkland, AL
Drafted: 1960 Round 2 Phi
1960 Phi: KR 2-18 9.0. **1961** Phi: PR 1-11 11.0. **1962** Phi: KR 3-9 3.0.
Total: PR 1-11 11.0; KR 5-27 5.4.

		Interceptions			
Year Team	**G**	**Int**	**Yds**	**TD**	**Fum**
1960 Phi	12	3	50	0	0
1961 Phi	14	1	22	0	0
1962 Phi	14	1	0	0	0
1963 Phi	14	1	9	0	0
1964 Phi	14	0	0	0	0
1965 Phi	12	1	33	1	0
1966 LARm	14	2	3	0	1
1967 LARm	14	4	69	0	0
1968 LARm	14	4	29	0	0
1969 LARm	13	0	0	0	0
1970 LARm	10	1	3	0	0
1974 Was	2	0	0	0	0
NFL Total	147	18	218	1	1

HARRY BAUJAN Baujan, Harry Clifford 5'8", 170 **E**
Col: Notre Dame *HS:* Beardstown [IL]; Notre Dame Prep [South Bend, IN] B: 5/24/1894, Beardstown, IL D: 12/30/1976, Dayton, OH
1920 Cle: 6 G. **1921** Cle: 5 G. **Total:** 11 G.

ALF BAUMAN Bauman, Alfred Ernest 6'2", 228 **DT-OT**
Col: Northwestern *HS:* Austin [Chicago, IL] B: 1/3/1920, Chicago, IL D: 3/2/1979, Pacifica, CA *Drafted:* 1942 Round 2 Det
AAFC **1947** ChiA: 3 G.

NFL **1947** Phi: 2 G. **1948** ChiB: 5 G. **1949** ChiB: 12 G. **1950** ChiB: 12 G; KR 1-9 9.0. **Total:** 31 G; KR 1-9 9.0.

CHARLIE BAUMANN Baumann, Bruce Charles 6'1", 203 **K**
Col: West Virginia *HS:* Cathedral Prep [Erie, PA] B: 8/25/1967, Erie, PA
1991 Mia: 2 G; Scor 12, 2-2 100.0% FG, 6-6 100.0% XK. NE: 7 G; Scor 30, 7-10 70.0% FG, 9-10 90.0% XK. **1992** NE: 16 G; Scor 55, 11-17 64.7% FG, 22-24 91.7% XK. **Total:** 25 G; Scor 97, 20-29 69.0% FG, 37-40 92.5% XK.

BUDDY BAUMANN Baumann, Carl 6'1", 190 **T-G**
Col: No College B: 1900, WI Deceased
1922 Rac: 4 G.

JOE BILLY BAUMGARDNER Baumgardner, Joseph William 6'1", 198 **HB**
Col: Texas *HS:* Austin [TX] B: 2/16/1925, Wheeler, TX
1948 Det: 2 G.

STEVE BAUMGARTNER Baumgartner, Steven John 6'7", 256 **DE-LB-DT**
Col: Purdue *HS:* Benet Acad. [Lisle, IL] B: 3/26/1951, Chicago, IL
Drafted: 1973 Round 2 NO
1973 NO: 14 G. **1974** NO: 14 G. **1975** NO: 14 G. **1976** NO: 14 G.
1977 NO-Hou: 11 G. NO: 5 G. Hou: 6 G. **1978** Hou: 16 G. **1979** Hou: 12 G. **Total:** 95 G.

BILL BAUMGARTNER Baumgartner, William R 6'3", 202 **OE-DE**
Col: Minnesota *HS:* Denfeld [Duluth, MN] B: 4/17/1921, Duluth, MN D: 9/1981
AAFC **1947** BalA: 2 G.

BOB BAUMHOWER Baumhower, Robert Glenn 6'5", 261 **NT**
Col: Alabama *HS:* Palm Beach Gardens [Palm Beach, FL]; Tuscaloosa HS [AL] B: 8/4/1955, Portsmouth, VA *Drafted:* 1977 Round 2 Mia
1977 Mia: 14 G. **1978** Mia: 16 G; Int 1-0; 1 Fum TD; 6 Pt. **1979** Mia: 16 G. **1980** Mia: 16 G. **1981** Mia: 16 G. **1982** Mia: 9 G; 3.5 Sac. **1983** Mia: 16 G; 8 Sac. **1984** Mia: 15 G; **1** Fum TD; 6 Pt; 2 Sac. **1986** Mia: 12 G; 1 Sac.
Total: 130 G; Int 1-0; 2 Fum TD; 12 Pt; 14.5 Sac.

FRANK BAUSCH Bausch, Frank Joseph 6'3", 220 **C-LB**
(Pete) *Col:* Kansas *HS:* Cathedral [Wichita, KS] B: 6/14/1908, Marion, SD D: 4/6/1976, Wichita, KS
1934 Bos: 11 G; Rush 1-3 3.0. **1935** Bos: 10 G. **1936** Bos: 12 G.
1937 ChiB: 9 G. **1938** ChiB: 11 G. **1939** ChiB: 11 G. **1940** ChiB: 10 G.
1941 Phi: 4 G. **Total:** 78 G; Rush 1-3 3.0.

JIM BAUSCH Bausch, James Aloysius Bernard 6'1", 208 **TB-FB-DB-LB**
(Jarrin' Jim) *Col:* Wichita State; Kansas *HS:* Cathedral [Wichita, KS] B: 3/29/1906, Marion, SD D: 7/9/1974, Hot Springs, AR
1933 ChiC-Cin: Pass 26-6 23.1%, 60 2.31 3 Int. ChiC: Pass 4-2 50.0%, 19 4.75 1 Int. Cin: Pass 22-4 18.2%, 41 1.86 2 Int. **Total:** Pass 26-6 23.1%, 60 2.31 3 Int.

		Rushing			
Year Team	**G**	**Att**	**Yds**	**Avg**	**TD**
1933 ChiC-Cin	7	36	70	1.9	0
1933 ChiC	2	7	13	1.9	0
1933 Cin	5	29	57	2.0	0
NFL Total	7	36	70	1.9	0

DAVID BAVARO Bavaro, David Anthony 6'0", 234 **LB**
Col: Syracuse *HS:* Danvers [MA] B: 3/27/1967, Danvers, MA
Drafted: 1990 Round 9 Pho
1990 Pho: 14 G. **1991** Buf: 2 G. **1992** Min: 5 G. **1993** NE: 12 G. **1994** NE: 9 G. **Total:** 42 G.

MARK BAVARO Bavaro, Mark Anthony 6'4", 245 **TE**
Col: Notre Dame *HS:* Danvers [MA] B: 4/28/1963, Winthrop, MA
Drafted: 1985 Round 4 NYG
1987 NYG: KR 1-16 16.0. **Total:** KR 1-16 16.0.

		Receiving				
Year Team	**G**	**Rec**	**Yds**	**Avg**	**TD**	**Fum**
1985 NYG	16	37	511	13.8	4	0
1986 NYG	16	66	1001	15.2	4	3
1987 NYG	12	55	867	15.8	8	2
1988 NYG	16	53	672	12.7	4	1
1989 NYG	7	22	278	12.6	3	0
1990 NYG	15	33	393	11.9	5	0
1992 Cle	16	25	315	12.6	2	0
1993 Phi	16	43	481	11.2	6	0
1994 Phi	12	17	215	12.6	3	0
NFL Total	126	351	4733	13.5	39	6

BIBBLES BAWEL Bawel, Edward Ray 6'1", 185 **DB-OE**
Col: Evansville *HS:* Boonville [IN] B: 11/21/1930, Boonville, IN
1952 Phi: Rec 2-60 30.0. **1955** Phi: Rec 1-6 6.0; KR 8-169 21.1. **1956** Phi: KR 1-25 25.0. **Total:** Rec 3-66 22.0; KR 9-194 21.6.

		Punt Returns				Interceptions				Tot
Year Team	**G**	**Ret**	**Yds**	**Avg**	**TD**	**Int**	**Yds**	**TD**	**Fum**	**TD**
1952 Phi	12	**34**	261	7.7	1	8	121	0	2	1
1955 Phi	12	15	32	2.1	0	9	**168**	**2**	2	2
1956 Phi	12	0	0	—	0	1	33	0	0	0
NFL Total	36	49	293	6.0	1	18	322	2	4	3

CARL BAX Bax, Carl William 6'4", 290 **OG-OT**
Col: Missouri *HS:* St. Charles [MO] B: 1/5/1966, St. Charles, MO
Drafted: 1989 Round 8 TB
1989 TB: 6 G. **1990** TB: 9 G. **Total:** 15 G.

ROB BAXLEY Baxley, Robert R 6'5", 285 **OT**
Col: Iowa *HS:* Oswego [IL] B: 3/14/1969, Oswego, IL *Drafted:* 1992 Round 11 Pho
1992 Pho: 6 G.

FRED BAXTER Baxter, Frederick Denard 6'3", 260 **TE**
Col: Auburn *HS:* Pike Co. [Brundige, AL] B: 6/14/1971, Brundige, AL
Drafted: 1993 Round 5 NYJ
1994 NYJ: KR 1-20 20.0. **1995** NYJ: KR 6-36 6.0. **1997** NYJ: KR 1-0.
1998 NYJ: KR 1-8 8.0. **Total:** KR 9-64 7.1.

		Receiving				
Year Team	**G**	**Rec**	**Yds**	**Avg**	**TD**	**Fum**
1993 NYJ	7	3	48	16.0	1	0
1994 NYJ	11	3	11	3.7	1	0
1995 NYJ	15	18	222	12.3	1	1
1996 NYJ	16	7	114	16.3	0	1
1997 NYJ	16	27	276	10.2	3	1
1998 NYJ	14	3	50	16.7	0	0
NFL Total	79	61	721	11.8	6	3

BRAD BAXTER Baxter, Herman Bradley 6'1", 235 **RB**
Col: Alabama State *HS:* Slocomb [AL] B: 5/5/1967, Dothan, AL
Drafted: 1989 Round 11 Min

		Rushing				Receiving				
Year Team	**G**	**Att**	**Yds**	**Avg**	**TD**	**Rec**	**Yds**	**Avg**	**TD**	**Fum**
1989 NYJ	1	0	0	—	0	0	0	—	0	0
1990 NYJ	16	124	539	4.3	6	8	73	9.1	0	4
1991 NYJ	16	184	666	3.6	11	12	124	10.3	0	6
1992 NYJ	15	152	698	4.6	6	4	32	8.0	0	3
1993 NYJ	16	174	559	3.2	7	20	158	7.9	0	3
1994 NYJ	15	60	170	2.8	4	10	40	4.0	0	0
1995 NYJ	15	85	296	3.5	1	26	160	6.2	0	0
NFL Total	94	779	2928	3.8	35	80	587	7.3	0	16

JIMMY BAXTER Baxter, James 5'7", 173 **WB-OE**
Col: No College B: 10/1892, OH Deceased
1923 Rac: 1 G. **1924** Ken: 4 G. **Total:** 5 G.

LLOYD BAXTER Baxter, Lloyd Thomas 6'2", 210 **C**
Col: Louisiana Tech; Southern Methodist *HS:* Sherman [TX]
B: 1/18/1923, Howe, TX *Drafted:* 1945 Round 22 GB
1948 GB: 11 G.

MARTIN BAYLESS Bayless, Martin Ashley 6′2″, 210 DB
Col: Bowling Green State *HS:* Belmont [Dayton, OH] B: 10/11/1962, Dayton, OH *Drafted:* 1984 Round 4 StL
1986 Buf: 1 Sac. **1987** SD: 2.5 Sac. **1988** SD: 1 Sac. **1989** SD: 1 Sac. **1990** SD: 3 Sac. **1993** KC: 1 Sac. **1994** Was: 1 Fum TD. **1995** KC: 1 Sac. **1996** KC: 1 Sac. **Total:** 1 Fum TD; 11.5 Sac.

		Interceptions		
Year Team	**G**	**Int**	**Yds**	**TD**
1984 StL-Buf	16	0	0	0
1984 StL	3	0	0	0
1984 Buf	13	0	0	0
1985 Buf	12	2	10	0
1986 Buf	16	1	0	0
1987 SD	12	0	0	0
1988 SD	15	0	0	0
1989 SD	16	1	0	0
1990 SD	14	1	0	0
1991 SD	16	1	0	0
1992 KC	16	1	0	0
1993 KC	16	2	14	0
1994 Was	16	3	38	0
1995 KC	11	0	0	0
1996 KC	16	0	0	0
NFL Total	192	12	62	0

RICK BAYLESS Bayless, Richard Allen 6′0″, 202 RB
Col: Iowa *HS:* Forest Lake [MN] B: 10/15/1964, Hugo, MN
1989 Min: 1 G.

TOM BAYLESS Bayless, Thomas McDowell 6′4″, 240 OG
Col: Purdue *HS:* East St. Louis [IL] B: 12/17/1947, Knob Lick, MO *Drafted:* 1970 Round 15 NYJ
1970 NYJ: 2 G.

JOHN BAYLEY Bayley, John Merrill 5′11″, 185 T
Col: Syracuse *HS:* Massena [NY] B: 11/10/1903, Massena, NY D: 4/5/1969, Massena, NY
1927 NYY: 7 G.

JOHN BAYLOR Baylor, John Martin 6′0″, 203 DB
Col: Southern Mississippi *HS:* Meridian [MS] B: 3/5/1965, Meridian, MS *Drafted:* 1988 Round 5 Ind
1989 Ind: 16 G. **1990** Ind: 10 G. **1991** Ind: 16 G; Int 4-50; 1 Sac. **1992** Ind: 16 G; Int 1-1; 3 Sac. **1993** Ind: 16 G; Int 3-11. **Total:** 74 G; Int 8-62; 4 Sac.

RAYMOND BAYLOR Baylor, Raymond 6′5″, 263 DE
Col: Texas Southern *HS:* Evan E. Worthing [Houston, TX] B: 3/7/1947, Houston, TX
1974 SD: 1 G.

TIM BAYLOR Baylor, Timothy 6′6″, 195 DB
Col: Morgan State *HS:* Cardozo [Washington, DC] B: 5/23/1954, Washington, DC *Drafted:* 1976 Round 10 Bal
1976 Bal: 14 G. **1977** Bal: 13 G. **1978** Bal: 16 G. **1979** Min: 16 G. **Total:** 59 G.

CHRIS BAYNE Bayne, Christopher Oliver 6′1″, 205 DB
Col: San Bernardino Valley Coll. CA (J.C.); Fresno State *HS:* John W. North [Riverside, CA] B: 3/22/1975, Riverside, CA *Drafted:* 1997 Round 7 Atl
1997 Atl: 13 G. **1998** Atl: 10 G. **Total:** 23 G.

CRAIG BAYNHAM Baynham, Gordon Craig 6′1″, 203 RB
Col: Georgia Tech *HS:* North Augusta [SC] B: 7/24/1944, Casper, WY *Drafted:* 1966 Round 12 Dal
1968 Dal: Pass 1-0. **Total:** Pass 1-0.

		Rushing				Receiving			
Year Team	**G**	**Att**	**Yds**	**Avg**	**TD**	**Rec**	**Yds**	**Avg**	**TD**
1967 Dal	14	3	6	2.0	1	3	13	4.3	0
1968 Dal	14	103	438	4.3	5	29	380	13.1	3
1969 Dal	10	3	-2	-0.7	0	0	0	—	0
1970 ChiB	5	26	68	2.6	0	12	43	3.6	0
1972 StL	7	17	43	2.5	0	1	10	10.0	0
NFL Total	50	152	553	3.6	6	45	446	9.9	3

	Kickoff Returns					Tot
Year Team	**Ret**	**Yds**	**Avg**	**TD**	**Fum**	**TD**
1967 Dal	12	331	27.6	0	0	1
1968 Dal	23	590	25.7	0	**8**	8
1969 Dal	6	114	19.0	0	1	0
1972 StL	0	0	—	0	2	0
NFL Total	41	1035	25.2	0	11	9

REAVES BAYSINGER Baysinger, Reaves Henry 6′0″, 180 OE
(Ribs) *Col:* Syracuse *HS:* Central [Akron, OH] B: 2/22/1902, Akron, OH D: 12/4/1994, Hilton, NY
1924 Roch: 1 G.

WINNIE BAZE Baze, Winford Eason 5′11″, 200 WB-TB-DB-FB
Col: Schreiner Coll.; Texas Tech *HS:* Robert Lee [TX] B: 7/14/1914, Robert Lee, TX
1937 Phi: 10 G; Pass 3-0; Rush 3-14 4.7; Rec 1-2 2.0.

FRED BEACH Beach, Fred Cantrell 180 G
Col: California B: 2/8/1897 D: 9/24/1981, Loma Linda, CA
1926 LA: 1 G.

PAT BEACH Beach, Patrick Jesse 6′4″, 247 TE
Col: Washington State *HS:* Pullman [WA] B: 12/28/1959, Grants Pass, OR *Drafted:* 1982 Round 6 Bal
1983 Bal: KR 1-0. **1988** Ind: KR 1-35 35.0. **Total:** KR 2-35 17.5.

		Receiving				
Year Team	**G**	**Rec**	**Yds**	**Avg**	**TD**	**Fum**
1982 Bal	9	4	45	11.3	1	0
1983 Bal	16	5	56	11.2	1	0
1985 Ind	16	36	376	10.4	6	3
1986 Ind	16	25	265	10.6	1	2
1987 Ind	12	28	239	8.5	0	0
1988 Ind	16	26	235	9.0	0	1
1989 Ind	16	14	87	6.2	2	1
1990 Ind	16	12	124	10.3	1	0
1991 Ind	12	5	56	11.2	0	0
1992 Phi	16	8	75	9.4	2	0
1993 Pho	15	0	0	—	0	0
NFL Total	160	163	1558	9.6	14	7

SANJAY BEACH Beach, Sanjay Ragiv 6′0″, 189 WR
Col: Colorado State *HS:* Chandler [AZ] B: 2/21/1966, Clark AFB, Philippines
1991 SF: PR 10-53 5.3; KR 2-37 18.5. **Total:** PR 10-53 5.3; KR 2-37 18.5.

		Receiving				
Year Team	**G**	**Rec**	**Yds**	**Avg**	**TD**	**Fum**
1989 NYJ	1	0	0	—	0	0
1991 SF	16	4	43	10.8	0	1
1992 GB	16	17	122	7.2	1	1
1993 SF	9	5	59	11.8	1	0
NFL Total	42	26	224	8.6	2	2

WALTER BEACH Beach, Walter III 6′0″, 190 DB-RB
Col: Central Michigan *HS:* Pontiac Central [MI] B: 1/31/1935, Pontiac, MI *Drafted:* 1960 Round 2 Oak
1960 Bos: 6 G; Rush 6-(-4) -0.7; Rec 9-132 14.7 1 TD; PR 1-21 21.0; KR 7-146 20.9; 6 Pt; 2 Fum. **1961** Bos: 12 G; PR 1-21 21.0; KR 2-38 19.0; Int 1-37. **1963** Cle: 1 G. **1964** Cle: 14 G; Int 4-81 1 TD; 6 Pt. **1965** Cle: 10 G; Int 0-2. **1966** Cle: 5 G; Int 1-0. **Total:** 48 G; Rush 6-(-4) -0.7; Rec 9-132 14.7 1 TD; PR 2-42 21.0; KR 9-184 20.4; Int 6-120 1 TD; Tot TD 2; 12 Pt; 2 Fum.

NORM BEAL Beal, Norman Lewis 5′11″, 170 DB
Col: Missouri *HS:* Normandy [St. Louis, MO] B: 6/16/1940, St. Louis, MO
1962 StL: 7 G; PR 7-46 6.6; KR 16-394 24.6; 1 Fum.

BILL BEALLES Bealles, William John 6′7″, 290 OT
Col: Northern Illinois; Northern Iowa *HS:* Victor Andrew [Tinley Park, IL] B: 6/11/1963, Steubenville, OH
1987 Mia: 3 G.

ALYN BEALS Beals, Alyn Richard 6′0″, 188 OE-DE
Col: Santa Clara *HS:* San Francisco Polytechnic [CA] B: 4/27/1921, Marysville, CA D: 8/11/1993, Redwood City, CA *Drafted:* 1943 Round 6 ChiB
AAFC **1946** SF-A: Rush 2-(-7) -3.5; Scor 61, 1-1 100.0% XK. **1947** SF-A: Rush 5-48 9.6; Int 1-0. **1949** SF-A: Rush 4-32 8.0; Scor 73, 1-1 100.0% XK. **Total:** Rush 11-73 6.6; Int 1-0; Scor 278, 2-2 100.0% XK.

		Receiving			
Year Team	**G**	**Rec**	**Yds**	**Avg**	**TD**
1946 SF-A	14	40	586	14.7	10
1947 SF-A	13	47	655	13.9	10
1948 SF-A	14	46	591	12.8	14
1949 SF-A	12	44	678	15.4	12
AAFC Total	53	177	2510	14.2	46

NFL Statistics

		Receiving			
Year Team	**G**	**Rec**	**Yds**	**Avg**	**TD**
1950 SF	12	22	315	14.3	3
1951 SF	12	12	126	10.5	0
NFL Total	24	34	441	13.0	3

SHAWN BEALS Beals, Shawn E 5′10″, 178 WR
Col: Idaho State *HS:* Pittsburg [CA] B: 8/16/1966, Walnut Creek, CA

Year Team	G	Ret	Yds	Avg	TD	Fum
		Kickoff Returns				
1988 Phi	13	34	625	18.4	0	1

TIM BEAMER Beamer, Timothy Carl 5′11″, 190 **DB**
(Houdini) *Col:* Johnson C. Smith; Illinois *HS:* Galax [VA] B: 4/6/1948, Galax, VA *Drafted:* 1971 Round 5 Buf
1971 Buf: 12 G; PR 7-22 3.1; KR 20-394 19.7; 5 Fum.

AUTRY BEAMON Beamon, Autry Jr. 6′1″, 190 **DB**
Col: Texas A&M-Commerce *HS:* Kaufman [TX] B: 11/12/1953, Terrell, TX *Drafted:* 1975 Round 12 Min
1975 Min: PR 1-0; Scor **1** Saf. **1976** Min: PR 7-19 2.7. **Total:** PR 8-19 2.4; Scor 1 Saf.

Year Team	G	Int	Yds	TD	Fum
		Interceptions			
1975 Min	14	1	0	0	1
1976 Min	14	1	41	0	1
1977 Sea	14	6	36	0	0
1978 Sea	16	4	17	0	0
1979 Sea	15	1	38	0	0
1980 Cle	13	0	0	0	0
1981 Cle	14	0	0	0	0
NFL Total	100	13	132	0	2

WILLIE BEAMON Beamon, Willie Rufus 5′11″, 173 **DB**
Col: Northern Iowa *HS:* Sun Coast [Riviera Beach, FL] B: 6/14/1970, Belle Glade, FL
1993 NYG: 13 G; Int 1-0. **1994** NYG: 15 G; 1 Sac. **1995** NYG: 16 G. **1996** NYG: 5 G; Int 1-20. **Total:** 49 G; Int 2-20; 1 Sac.

BYRON BEAMS Beams, Byron Donnell 6′6″, 248 **OT-DT**
Col: Notre Dame *HS:* Ada [OK] B: 9/8/1929, Konawa, OK D: 11/14/1992 *Drafted:* 1957 Round 20 LARm
1959 Pit: 6 G. **1960** Pit: 3 G. **1961** Hou: 7 G. **Total:** 16 G.

BUBBA BEAN Bean, Earnest Ray 5′11″, 195 **RB**
Col: Texas A&M *HS:* Kirbyville [TX] B: 1/26/1954, Kirbyville, TX *Drafted:* 1976 Round 1 Atl
1976 Atl: Pass 1-1 100.0%, 49 49.00 1 TD; KR 2-38 19.0. **1978** Atl: Pass 1-0, 1 Int. **Total:** Pass 2-1 50.0%, 49 24.50 1 TD 1 Int; KR 2-38 19.0.

Year Team	G	Att	Yds	Avg	TD	Rec	Yds	Avg	TD	Fum	Tot TD
		Rushing				Receiving					
1976 Atl	14	124	428	3.5	2	16	148	9.3	1	4	3
1978 Atl	15	193	707	3.7	3	31	209	6.7	1	7	4
1979 Atl	11	88	393	4.5	1	12	137	11.4	0	0	1
NFL Total	40	405	1528	3.8	6	59	494	8.4	2	11	8

ED BEARD Beard, Edward Leroy 6′1″, 226 **LB**
Col: Tennessee *HS:* Oscar F. Smith [Chesapeake, VA] B: 12/9/1939, Fredericksburg, VA *Drafted:* 1964 Round 14 SF
1965 SF: 12 G. **1966** SF: 12 G. **1967** SF: 14 G. **1968** SF: 14 G; Int 2-93. **1969** SF: 3 G. **1970** SF: 14 G; KR 2-8 4.0; 1 Fum. **1971** SF: 14 G; KR 1-21 21.0. **1972** SF: 14 G; KR 2-(-1) -0.5; Int 1-10. **Total:** 97 G; KR 5-28 5.6; Int 3-103; 1 Fum.

TOM BEARD Beard, Thomas LeRoy 6′6″, 280 **C**
Col: Michigan State *HS:* Battle Creek Central [MI] B: 6/10/1948, Findlay, OH *Drafted:* 1971 Round 8 Den
1972 Buf: 12 G.

AARON BEASLEY Beasley, Aaron Bruce 6′0″, 202 **DB**
Col: West Virginia *HS:* Pottstown [PA]; Valley Forge Mil. Acad. [Wayne, PA] B: 7/7/1973, Pottstown, PA *Drafted:* 1996 Round 3 Jac
1996 Jac: 9 G; Int 1-0; 1 Sac. **1997** Jac: 9 G; Int 1-5. **1998** Jac: 16 G; Int 3-35; 1 Fum TD; 6 Pt. **Total:** 34 G; Int 5-40; 1 Fum TD; 6 Pt; 1 Sac.

FRED BEASLEY Beasley, Frederick Jerome 6′0″, 220 **RB**
Col: Auburn *HS:* Robert E. Lee [Montgomery, AL] B: 9/18/1974, Montgomery, AL *Drafted:* 1998 Round 6 SF
1998 SF: 16 G; Rec 1-11 11.0.

JOHN BEASLEY Beasley, John H 6′3″, 230 **G**
Col: Earlham B: 4/7/1897, Terre Haute, IN D: 11/1964, Franklin, IN
1923 Day: 6 G.

JOHN BEASLEY Beasley, John Walter 6′3″, 228 **TE**
Col: California *HS:* Buena Park [CA] B: 4/6/1945, Pasadena, CA *Drafted:* 1967 Round 8 Min
1969 Min: **1** Fum TD. **Total:** 1 Fum TD.

Year Team	G	Rec	Yds	Avg	TD	Fum	Tot TD
		Receiving					
1967 Min	14	13	120	9.2	4	0	4
1968 Min	14	23	289	12.6	0	0	0
1969 Min	14	33	361	10.9	4	1	5
1970 Min	14	17	237	13.9	2	0	2
1972 Min	14	28	232	8.3	1	0	1
1973 Min-NO	13	32	283	8.8	2	0	2
1973 Min	5	1	3	3.0	1	0	1
1973 NO	8	31	280	9.0	1	0	1
1974 NO	14	5	85	17.0	0	0	0
NFL Total	97	151	1607	10.6	13	1	14

TERRY BEASLEY Beasley, Terry Paul 5′11″, 186 **WR**
Col: Auburn *HS:* Robert E. Lee [Montgomery, AL] B: 2/5/1950, Montgomery, AL *Drafted:* 1972 Round 1 SF
1974 SF: Rush 1-(-3) -3.0. **1975** SF: Rush 1-5 5.0. **Total:** Rush 2-2 1.0.

Year Team	G	Rec	Yds	Avg	TD	Fum
		Receiving				
1972 SF	8	1	20	20.0	0	0
1974 SF	13	17	253	14.9	3	0
1975 SF	8	20	297	14.9	0	1
NFL Total	29	38	570	15.0	3	1

TOM BEASLEY Beasley, Thomas Lynn 6′5″, 253 **DE-DT-NT**
Col: Virginia Tech *HS:* Northfork [WV] B: 8/11/1954, Bluefield, WV *Drafted:* 1977 Round 3 Pit
1978 Pit: 15 G. **1979** Pit: 13 G. **1980** Pit: 15 G. **1981** Pit: 13 G. **1982** Pit: 7 G; 6 Sac. **1983** Pit: 16 G; 2.5 Sac. **1984** Was: 13 G; 2 Sac. **1985** Was: 12 G; 1 Sac. **1986** Was: 1 G. **Total:** 105 G; 11.5 Sac.

PETE BEATHARD Beathard, Peter Frank 6′1″, 200 **QB**
Col: USC *HS:* El Segundo [CA] B: 3/7/1942, Hermosa Beach, CA *Drafted:* 1964 Round 1 Det
1965 KC: Scor 1 2XP. **Total:** Scor 1 2XP.

Year Team	G	Att	Comp	Comp%	Yds	YPA	TD	Int	Rating
		Passing							
1964 KC	14	9	4	44.4	50	5.56	1	2	59.7
1965 KC	14	89	36	40.4	632	7.10	1	6	41.0
1966 KC	14	90	39	43.3	578	6.42	4	4	61.3
1967 KC-Hou	11	231	94	40.7	1114	4.82	9	**14**	43.8
1967 KC	1	2	0	0.0	0	0.00	0	0	39.6
1967 Hou	10	229	94	41.0	1114	4.86	9	14	44.2
1968 Hou	9	223	105	47.1	1559	6.99	7	16	51.0
1969 Hou	12	370	180	48.6	2455	6.64	10	21	55.6
1970 StL	4	17	7	41.2	114	6.71	2	1	79.0
1971 StL	9	141	60	42.6	1030	7.30	6	12	46.7
1972 LARm	14	48	19	39.6	255	5.31	1	7	24.6
1973 KC	9	64	31	48.4	389	6.08	2	1	71.7
NFL Total	110	1282	575	44.9	8176	6.38	43	84	49.9

Year Team	Att	Yds	Avg	TD	Fum
	Rushing				
1964 KC	4	43	10.8	0	1
1965 KC	25	138	5.5	4	3
1966 KC	20	152	7.6	1	3
1967 KC-Hou	32	133	4.2	1	4
1967 KC	0	0	—	0	1
1967 Hou	32	133	4.2	1	3
1968 Hou	18	79	4.4	2	2
1969 Hou	19	89	4.7	2	2
1970 StL	2	2	1.0	0	1
1971 StL	4	29	7.3	0	2
1972 LARm	1	-1	-1.0	0	1
1973 KC	6	16	2.7	1	1
NFL Total	131	680	5.2	11	20

BOB BEATTIE Beattie, Robert Wetherson 6′3″, 230 **T**
Col: Princeton *HS:* Manual Training [Brooklyn, NY] B: 10/16/1902, New York, NY D: 6/3/1983, Orangeburg, NY
1927 NYY: 1 G. **1929** Ora: 11 G. **1930** Nwk: 5 G. **Total:** 17 G.

CHUCK BEATTY Beatty, Charles 6′2″, 200 **DB**
(Hatchet) *Col:* North Texas *HS:* Turner [Waxahachie, TX] B: 2/8/1946, Waxahachie, TX *Drafted:* 1969 Round 7 Pit
1969 Pit: 7 G. **1970** Pit: 12 G; Int 2-49 1 TD; 6 Pt. **1971** Pit: 3 G. **1972** Pit-StL: 12 G; Int 2-16. Pit: 8 G; Int 2-16. StL: 4 G. **Total:** 34 G; Int 4-65 1 TD; 6 Pt.

ED BEATTY Beatty, Edward Marshall Jr. 6′3″, 229 **C**
Col: Mississippi *HS:* Tiptonville [TN] B: 4/6/1932, Clarksdale, MS *Drafted:* 1954 Round 1 LARm
1955 SF: 9 G. **1956** SF: 12 G. **1957** Pit: 12 G. **1958** Pit: 12 G. **1959** Pit: 12 G. **1960** Pit: 12 G. **1961** Pit-Was: 11 G. Pit: 6 G. Was: 5 G. **Total:** 80 G.

AL BEAUCHAMP Beauchamp, Alfred 6′2″, 237 **LB**
Col: Southern University *HS:* Baton Rouge [LA] B: 6/25/1944, Baton Rouge, LA *Drafted:* 1968 Round 5 Cin
1970 Cin: 1 Fum TD. **Total:** 1 Fum TD.

Year Team	G	Int	Yds	TD	Fum	Tot TD
		Interceptions				
1968 Cin	14	2	35	1	0	1
1969 Cin	13	1	8	0	0	0
1970 Cin	14	1	2	0	0	1
1971 Cin	14	6	53	1	0	1
1972 Cin	14	1	8	0	1	0
1973 Cin	14	3	4	0	1	0

1974 Cin	14	1	34	0	0	0
1975 Cin	14	0	0	0	0	0
1976 StL	14	0	0	0	0	0
NFL Total	125	15	144	2	2	3

JOE BEAUCHAMP Beauchamp, Joseph Scott 6'0", 188 **DB**
(Beau) *Col:* Northwestern Coll. OH (J.C.); Iowa State *HS:* Rufus King [Milwaukee, WI] B: 4/11/1944, Chicago, IL *Drafted:* 1966 Redshirt Round 6 SD
1966 SD: KR 4-64 16.0. **1970** SD: KR 1-0. **1972** SD: KR 1-0.
Total: KR 6-64 10.7.

		Interceptions			
Year Team	**G**	**Int**	**Yds**	**TD**	**Fum**
1966 SD	8	2	24	0	1
1967 SD	14	3	44	0	0
1968 SD	14	5	114	**2**	0
1969 SD	14	0	0	0	0
1970 SD	13	1	25	0	0
1971 SD	13	4	95	0	1
1972 SD	14	6	96	1	0
1973 SD	9	0	0	0	0
1974 SD	10	1	35	0	0
1975 SD	8	1	0	0	0
NFL Total	117	23	433	3	2

DOUG BEAUDOIN Beaudoin, Douglas Lee 6'1", 193 **DB**
Col: Minnesota *HS:* Jamestown [ND] B: 5/15/1954, Dickinson, ND
Drafted: 1976 Round 9 NE
1976 NE: 9 G; PR 2-18 9.0; KR 6-134 22.3; 1 Fum. **1977** NE: 11 G; PR 1-0; KR 4-73 18.3. **1978** NE: 15 G; Int 3-25. **1979** NE: 10 G; Int 1-30. **1980** Mia: 10 G. **1981** SD: 4 G; KR 1-31 31.0. **Total:** 59 G; PR 3-18 6.0; KR 11-238 21.6; Int 4-55; 1 Fum.

CLAYTON BEAUFORD Beauford, Clayton Maurice 5'11", 190 **WR**
Col: Auburn *HS:* Palatka [FL] B: 3/1/1963, Palatka, FL
1987 Cle: 1 G; KR 1-22 22.0.

JIM BEAVER Beaver, James Edward 6'1", 235 **DT**
Col: Florida *HS:* Palm Beach [West Palm Beach, FL] B: 5/18/1938, Miami, FL *Drafted:* 1961 Round 8 Phi
1962 Phi: 1 G.

AUBREY BEAVERS Beavers, Aubrey Tod 6'3", 231 **LB**
Col: Oklahoma *HS:* Jack Yates [Houston, TX] B: 8/30/1971, Houston, TX *Drafted:* 1994 Round 2 Mia
1994 Mia: 16 G; Int 2-0. **1995** Mia: 16 G; Int 1-8. **1996** NYJ: 7 G.
Total: 39 G; Int 3-8.

SCOTT BEAVERS Beavers, Scott Travis 6'4", 277 **OG**
Col: Georgia Tech *HS:* Campbell [Smyrna, GA] B: 2/17/1967, Atlanta, GA
1990 Den: 2 G.

GARY BEBAN Beban, Gary Joseph 6'1", 195 **QB-RB-WR**
Col: UCLA *HS:* Sequoia [Redwood City, CA] B: 8/5/1946, San Francisco, CA *Drafted:* 1968 Round 2 LARm
1968 Was: 4 G; Pass 1-0; Rush 5-18 3.6; Rec 1-12 12.0. **1969** Was: 1 G.
Total: 5 G; Pass 1-0; Rush 5-18 3.6; Rec 1-12 12.0.

NICK BEBOUT Bebout, Nicholas 6'5", 261 **OT**
Col: Wyoming *HS:* Shoshoni [WY] B: 5/5/1951, Riverton, WY
Drafted: 1973 Round 6 Atl
1973 Atl: 13 G. **1974** Atl: 13 G. **1975** Atl: 14 G. **1976** Sea: 14 G. **1977** Sea: 13 G. **1978** Sea: 16 G. **1979** Sea: 13 G. **1980** Min: 1 G. **Total:** 97 G.

BRETT BECH Bech, Brett Lamar 6'1", 184 **WR**
Col: Louisiana State *HS:* Slidell [LA] B: 8/20/1971, Slidell, LA
1997 NO: 10 G; Rec 3-50 16.7; KR 3-47 15.7. **1998** NO: 16 G; Rec 14-264 18.9 3 TD; KR 1-20 20.0; 18 Pt. **Total:** 26 G; Rec 17-314 18.5 3 TD; KR 4-67 16.8; 18 Pt.

HUB BECHTOL Bechtol, Hubert Edwin 6'3", 202 **DE-OE**
(Big Boy) *Col:* Texas; Texas Tech *HS:* Lubbock [TX] B: 4/20/1926, Amarillo, TX
AAFC **1947** BalA: 14 G; Rush 2-(-1) -0.5; Rec 17-167 9.8 1 TD; KR 1-13 13.0; Int 1-7; 6 Pt. **1948** BalA: 12 G; Rec 2-25 12.5; KR 0-4. **1949** BalA: 12 G; Int 1-6. **Total:** 38 G; Rush 2-(-1) -0.5; Rec 19-192 10.1 1 TD; KR 1-17 17.0; Int 2-13; 6 Pt.

BRADEN BECK Beck, Braden William 6'2", 200 **K**
Col: Stanford *HS:* Baton Rouge [LA] B: 1/12/1944, Oakland, CA
1971 Hou: 2 G; Scor 4, 1-2 50.0% FG, 1-2 50.0% XK.

CARL BECK Beck, Carl 5'11", 180 **TB-FB-WB-T**
Col: West Virginia *HS:* Harrisburg Tech [PA] B: 1900, Harrisburg, PA
D: Harrisburg, PA
1921 Buf: 6 G.

CLARENCE BECK Beck, Clarence Robert 5'11", 200 **T-G**
Col: Penn State *HS:* Harrisburg Tech [PA] B: 10/3/1894, Harrisburg, PA D: 10/1970, Grampian, PA
1925 Pott: 7 G.

KEN BECK Beck, Kenneth L 6'2", 245 **DT-DE**
Col: Texas A&M *HS:* Minden [LA] B: 9/3/1935, Minden, LA
Drafted: 1959 Round 4 ChiC
1959 GB: 12 G. **1960** GB: 12 G. **Total:** 24 G.

MARTY BECK Beck, Martin J 5'9", 175 **WB-FB-BB-TB**
Col: No College *HS:* Fordham Prep [Bronx, NY] B: 1/2/1900, New York, NY D: 6/15/1968, New York, NY
1921 Akr: 8 G. **1922** Akr: 1 G. **1924** Akr: 1 G. **1926** Akr: 1 G. **Total:** 11 G.

RAY BECK Beck, Ray Merrill 6'2", 224 **OG-DG**
Col: Georgia Tech *HS:* Cedartown [GA] B: 3/7/1931, Bowden, GA
Drafted: 1952 Round 2 NYG
1952 NYG: 12 G; KR 0-7. **1955** NYG: 12 G. **1956** NYG: 10 G; Int 1-2; 1 Fum. **1957** NYG: 12 G. **Total:** 46 G; KR 0-7; Int 1-2; 1 Fum.

DAVE BECKER Becker, David Paul 6'2", 190 **DB**
Col: Iowa *HS:* Atlantic [IA] B: 1/15/1957, Atlantic, IA *Drafted:* 1979 Round 12 ChiB
1980 ChiB: 11 G.

DOUG BECKER Becker, Douglas James 6'0", 220 **LB**
Col: Notre Dame *HS:* Badin [Hamilton, OH] B: 6/27/1956, Hamilton, OH *Drafted:* 1978 Round 10 Pit
1978 ChiB-Buf: 9 G. ChiB: 1 G. Buf: 8 G. **Total:** 9 G.

JOHNNIE BECKER Becker, John W 5'11", 208 **T-E-G-WB**
Col: Dayton; Denison *HS:* Steele [Dayton, OH] B: 2/10/1903
D: 9/17/1947
1926 Day: 6 G. **1927** Day: 7 G. **1928** Day: 5 G. **1929** Day: 1 G. **Total:** 19 G.

KURT BECKER Becker, Kurt Frank 6'5", 271 **OG**
Col: Michigan *HS:* Aurora East [IL] B: 12/22/1958, Aurora, IL
Drafted: 1982 Round 6 ChiB
1982 ChiB: 5 G. **1983** ChiB: 16 G. **1984** ChiB: 16 G. **1985** ChiB: 3 G. **1986** ChiB: 14 G. **1987** ChiB: 12 G. **1988** ChiB: 16 G. **1989** LARm: 2 G. **1990** ChiB: 10 G. **Total:** 94 G.

WAYLAND BECKER Becker, Wayland Herman 6'0", 198 **OE-DE**
Col: Marquette *HS:* Green Bay East [WI] B: 11/2/1910, Soporton, WI
D: 12/1984, Lena, WI
1935 Bkn: Pass 4-3 75.0%, 37 9.25; Rush 1-(-3) -3.0. **1937** GB: Rush 2-5 2.5. **Total:** Pass 4-3 75.0%, 37 9.25; Rush 3-2 0.7.

		Receiving			
Year Team	**G**	**Rec**	**Yds**	**Avg**	**TD**
1934 ChiB-Bkn	11	4	46	11.5	0
1934 ChiB	2	1	18	18.0	0
1934 Bkn	9	3	28	9.3	0
1935 Bkn	11	10	131	13.1	1
1936 GB	9	5	66	13.2	1
1937 GB	10	2	13	6.5	0
1938 GB	11	7	166	23.7	0
1939 Pit	2	0	0	—	0
NFL Total	54	28	422	15.1	2

JACK BECKETT Beckett, John Wesley 6'1", 200 **T**
Col: Oregon *HS:* Eugene [OR] B: 1/5/1892, Eight Mile, OR
D: 7/26/1981, San Diego, CA
1920 Buf: 2 G. **1922** Col: 1 G. **Total:** 3 G.

IAN BECKLES Beckles, Ian Harold 6'1", 300 **OG**
Col: Waldorf Coll. IA (J.C.); Indiana *HS:* Lindsay Place [Montreal, Canada] B: 7/20/1967, Montreal, Canada *Drafted:* 1990 Round 5 TB
1990 TB: 16 G. **1991** TB: 16 G. **1992** TB: 11 G. **1993** TB: 14 G. **1994** TB: 16 G. **1995** TB: 15 G. **1996** TB: 13 G. **1997** Phi: 9 G. **1998** Phi: 16 G.
Total: 126 G.

ART BECKLEY Beckley, Arthur K 5'10", 180 **BB-WB**
Col: Michigan State *HS:* Central [Bay City, MI] B: 9/1/1901 D: 1965
1926 Day: 6 G; Scor 3, 1 FG.

BRAD BECKMAN Beckman, Bradley Scott 6'3", 236 **TE**
Col: Nebraska-Omaha *HS:* Omaha Northwest [NE] B: 12/31/1964, Lincoln, NE D: 12/18/1989, Suwanee, GA *Drafted:* 1988 Round 7 Min
1988 NYG: 9 G; KR 1-7 7.0. **1989** Atl: 15 G; Rec 11-102 9.3 1 TD; KR 2-15 7.5; 6 Pt. **Total:** 24 G; Rec 11-102 9.3 1 TD; KR 3-22 7.3; 6 Pt.

ED BECKMAN Beckman, Edwin Jay 6'4", 229 **TE**
Col: Florida State *HS:* South Miami [Miami, FL] B: 1/2/1955, Key West, FL
1977 KC: 14 G; Rec 1-3 3.0. **1978** KC: 16 G; KR 3-74 24.7; Scor **1** Saf; 2 Pt. **1979** KC: 9 G; Rec 2-21 10.5. **1980** KC: 16 G; KR 3-38 12.7. **1981** KC: 15 G. **1982** KC: 9 G. **1983** KC: 15 G; Rec 13-130 10.0; 1 Fum. **1984** KC: 13 G; Rec 7-44 6.3 1 TD; 6 Pt. **Total:** 107 G; Rec 23-198 8.6 1 TD; KR 6-112 18.7; Scor 1 Saf; 8 Pt; 1 Fum.

TOM BECKMAN Beckman, Thomas Clare 6'5", 250 **DE**
Col: Michigan *HS:* Chesaning [MI] B: 9/21/1950, Saginaw, MI
Drafted: 1972 Round 3 StL
1972 StL: 2 G.

BECKWITH Beckwith 150 **TB**
Col: No College B: 1895 Deceased
1920 Col: 3 G.

VANCE BEDFORD Bedford, Vance Juano 5′11″, 170 **DB**
Col: Texas *HS:* Hebert [Beaumont, TX] B: 8/20/1958, Houston, TX
Drafted: 1982 Round 5 StL
1982 StL: Postseason only.

GENE BEDFORD Bedford, William Eugene 5′9″, 165 **OE**
(Blink) *Col:* Centre; Southern Methodist B: 12/2/1896, Dallas, TX
D: 10/6/1977, San Antonio, TX
1925 Roch: 2 G. **1926** Ham: 1 G. **Total:** 3 G.

CHUCK BEDNARIK Bednarik, Charles Philip 6′3″, 233 **C-LB**
(Concrete Charlie) *Col:* Pennsylvania *HS:* Bethlehem Catholic [PA]; Liberty HS [Bethlehem, PA] B: 5/1/1925, Bethlehem, PA
Drafted: 1949 Round 1 Phi *HOF:* 1967
1953 Phi: Punt 12-483 40.3. **1954** Phi: PR 2-26 13.0; KR 3-40 13.3. **1956** Phi: KR 1-17 17.0. **Total:** PR 2-26 13.0; KR 4-57 14.3; Punt 12-483 40.3.

		Interceptions			
Year Team	**G**	**Int**	**Yds**	**TD**	**Fum**
1949 Phi	10	0	0	0	0
1950 Phi	12	1	9	0	0
1951 Phi	12	0	0	0	0
1952 Phi	12	2	14	0	0
1953 Phi	12	6	116	**1**	1
1954 Phi	12	1	9	0	0
1955 Phi	12	1	36	0	0
1956 Phi	12	2	0	0	0
1957 Phi	11	3	51	0	0
1958 Phi	12	0	0	0	0
1959 Phi	12	0	0	0	0
1960 Phi	12	2	0	0	0
1961 Phi	14	2	33	0	0
1962 Phi	14	0	0	0	0
NFL Total	169	20	268	1	1

AL BEDNER Bedner, Albert Leon 5′10″, 195 **G-T**
Col: Lafayette *HS:* Wilkes-Barre [PA] B: 7/9/1898, Wilkes-Barre, PA
D: 7/12/1988, Wilkes-Barre, PA
1924 Fra: 6 G. **1925** NYG: 9 G. **1926** NYG: 8 G. **Total:** 23 G.

TOM BEDORE Bedore, Thomas 5′11″, 193 **G-LB**
Col: Pepperdine *HS:* Tupper Lake [NY] B: 11/17/1925, Faust, NY
1944 Was: 2 G.

HAL BEDSOLE Bedsole, Harold Jay 6′5″, 236 **TE**
Col: Pierce Coll. CA (J.C.); USC *HS:* Reseda [Los Angeles, CA]
B: 12/21/1941, Chicago, IL *Drafted:* 1964 Round 2 Min

		Receiving			
Year Team	**G**	**Rec**	**Yds**	**Avg**	**TD**
1964 Min	14	18	295	16.4	5
1965 Min	9	8	123	15.4	3
1966 Min	1	0	0	—	0
NFL Total	24	26	418	16.1	8

DON BEEBE Beebe, Donald Lee 5′11″, 185 **WR**
Col: Western Illinois; Aurora; Chadron State *HS:* Kaneland [Maple Park, IL] B: 12/18/1964, Aurora, IL *Drafted:* 1989 Round 3 Buf
1990 Buf: Rush 1-23 23.0. **1992** Buf: Rush 1-(-6) -6.0. **1994** Buf: Rush 2-11 5.5. **1996** GB: **1** Fum TD. **Total:** Rush 4-28 7.0; 1 Fum TD.

		Receiving				Kickoff Returns					Tot
Year Team	**G**	**Rec**	**Yds**	**Avg**	**TD**	**Ret**	**Yds**	**Avg**	**TD**	**Fum**	**TD**
1989 Buf	14	17	317	18.6	2	16	353	22.1	0	1	2
1990 Buf	12	11	221	20.1	1	6	119	19.8	0	0	1
1991 Buf	11	32	414	12.9	6	7	121	17.3	0	3	6
1992 Buf	12	33	554	16.8	2	0	0	—	0	1	2
1993 Buf	14	31	504	16.3	3	10	160	16.0	0	1	3
1994 Buf	13	40	527	13.2	4	12	230	19.2	0	3	4
1995 Car	14	14	152	10.9	1	9	215	23.9	0	0	1
1996 GB	16	39	699	17.9	4	15	403	26.9	1	1	6
1997 GB	10	2	28	14.0	0	6	134	22.3	0	0	0
NFL Total	116	219	3416	15.6	23	81	1735	21.4	1	10	25

KEITH BEEBE Beebe, Hiram Keith 5′9″, 180 **BB-DB**
Col: Occidental *HS:* Anaheim [CA] B: 3/16/1921, Anaheim, CA
Drafted: 1943 Round 22 NYG
1944 NYG: 5 G; Pass 3-1 33.3%, 9 3.00 1 Int; Rush 8-12 1.5; Int 3-26; Punt 7-206 29.4.

EARL BEECHAM Beecham, Earl F 5′8″, 180 **RB**
Col: Bucknell *HS:* Great Neck South [NY] B: 9/8/1965, Brooklyn, NY
1987 NYG: 1 G; Rush 5-22 4.4; KR 3-70 23.3.

WILLIE BEECHER Beecher, William Wiegel 5′10″, 170 **K**
Col: Utah State *HS:* James Logan [Logan, UT] B: 4/14/1963, El Paso, TX
1987 Mia: 3 G; Scor 21, 3-4 75.0% FG, 12-12 100.0% XK.

FRANK BEEDE Beede, Frank McNulty 6′4″, 292 **OG-C**
Col: Oklahoma Panhandle State *HS:* Antioch [CA] B: 5/1/1973, Antioch, CA
1996 Sea: 14 G. **1997** Sea: 16 G; KR 1-0; 1 Fum. **Total:** 30 G; KR 1-0; 1 Fum.

BRUCE BEEKLEY Beekley, Bruce Edward 6′2″, 225 **LB**
Col: Oregon *HS:* Woodside [CA] B: 12/15/1956, Cincinatti, OH
Drafted: 1979 Round 10 Atl
1980 GB: 15 G.

FERRIS BEEKLEY Beekley, Ferris Eugene 5′8″, 185 **G-BB**
(M.D.) *Col:* Miami (Ohio) *HS:* Lockland [OH] B: 2/27/1897, Butler Co., OH D: 6/15/1986, Cincinnati, OH
1921 Cin: 3 G.

BOB BEEMER Beemer, Robert Lester 6′5″, 231 **DE**
Col: Toledo *HS:* Concord [MI] B: 5/14/1963, Jackson, MI
1987 Det: 2 G.

TOM BEER Beer, Thomas E 6′1″, 237 **LB-RB**
Col: Saginaw Valley State; Wayne State (Mich.) B: 3/27/1969, Bay Port, MI *Drafted:* 1994 Round 7 Det
1994 Det: 9 G. **1995** Det: 16 G. **1996** Det: 16 G. **Total:** 41 G.

TOM BEER Beer, Thomas John 6′4″, 235 **TE-OG**
Col: Detroit Mercy; Houston *HS:* Grosse Pointe [MI]; St. Ambrose HS [Detroit, MI] B: 12/21/1944, Detroit, MI *Drafted:* 1967 Round 2 Den
1967 Den: KR 1-10 10.0. **1970** Bos: KR 1-4 4.0. **1972** NE: KR 1-15 15.0. **Total:** KR 3-29 9.7.

		Receiving				
Year Team	**G**	**Rec**	**Yds**	**Avg**	**TD**	**Fum**
1967 Den	14	11	155	14.1	0	0
1968 Den	14	20	276	13.8	1	0
1969 Den	9	9	200	22.2	0	0
1970 Bos	14	11	150	13.6	0	1
1971 NE	14	12	191	15.9	3	0
1972 NE	14	2	40	20.0	0	0
NFL Total	79	65	1012	15.6	4	1

TERRY BEESON Beeson, Terry Eugene 6′3″, 240 **LB**
Col: Kansas *HS:* Coffeyville [KS] B: 9/19/1955, Coffeyville, KS
Drafted: 1977 Round 2 Sea
1977 Sea: 14 G. **1978** Sea: 16 G. **1979** Sea: 16 G; Int 1-3. **1980** Sea: 16 G. **1981** Sea: 15 G. **1982** SF: 5 G. **Total:** 82 G; Int 1-3.

CHUCK BEHAN Behan, Charles Edward 6′3″, 195 **OE-DE**
Col: Northern Illinois *HS:* Crystal Lake [IL] B: 8/4/1920, Crystal Lake, IL D: 5/18/1945, Okinawa
1942 Det: 9 G; Rec 4-63 15.8.

BULL BEHMAN Behman, Russell K 5′10″, 215 **T**
Col: Lebanon Valley; Dickinson *HS:* Steelton [PA] B: 1/15/1900, Steelton, PA D: 3/24/1950, Harrisburg, PA
1924 Fra: 14 G. **1925** Fra: 16 G; Int 1 TD; Scor 39, 5 FG, 12 XK; Tot TD 2. **1927** Fra: 11 G. **1928** Fra: 16 G. **1929** Fra: 18 G. **1930** Fra: 7 G. **1931** Fra: 8 G. **Total:** 90 G; Int 1 TD; Scor 39, 5 FG, 12 XK; Tot TD 2.

MARK BEHNING Behning, Mark Gerald 6′6″, 290 **OT**
Col: Nebraska *HS:* Denton [TX] B: 9/26/1961, Alpena, MI
Drafted: 1985 Round 2 Pit
1986 Pit: 16 G.

DAVE BEHRMAN Behrman, David Wesley 6′5″, 260 **OT-C**
Col: Michigan State *HS:* Dowagiac [MI] B: 11/9/1941, Dowagiac, MI
Drafted: 1963 Round 1 Buf
1963 Buf: 14 G. **1965** Buf: 14 G. **1967** Den: 11 G. **Total:** 39 G.

TOM BEIER Beier, Thomas Eugene 5′11″, 195 **DB**
Col: Detroit Mercy; Miami (Fla.) *HS:* St. Joseph's [Bay City, MI]
B: 6/23/1945, Fremont, OH *Drafted:* 1967 Round 10 Mia
1967 Mia: 14 G; Rec 1-19 19.0; Int 1-7. **1969** Mia: 14 G; PR 5-8 1.6; KR 4-58 14.5; Int 1-7; 1 Fum. **Total:** 28 G; Rec 1-19 19.0; PR 5-8 1.6; KR 4-58 14.5; Int 2-14; 1 Fum.

LARRY BEIL Beil, Lawrence J 6′2″, 235 **T**
Col: Portland *HS:* Jefferson [Portland, OR] B: 8/31/1921
1948 NYG: 9 G.

ED BEINOR Beinor, Joseph Edward 6′2″, 222 **T-DE**
(Beefy) *Col:* Notre Dame *HS:* Thornton Twp. [Harvey, IL]
B: 11/16/1917, Harvey, IL D: 1/6/1991, Edwardsville, IL *Drafted:* 1939 Round 4 Bkn
1940 ChiC: 11 G. **1941** ChiC-Was: 11 G. ChiC: 3 G. Was: 8 G. **1942** Was: 11 G. **Total:** 33 G.

JIM BEIRNE Beirne, James Patrick 6′2″, 206 **WR-TE**
Col: Purdue *HS:* McKeesport [PA] B: 10/15/1946, McKeesport, PA
Drafted: 1968 Round 4 Hou
1968 Hou: Rush 1-3 3.0. **1969** Hou: Scor **1** 2XP. **1970** Hou: PR 1-1 1.0. **1974** SD: PR 1-7 7.0. **1976** Hou: KR 1-12 12.0. **Total:** Rush 1-3 3.0; PR 2-8 4.0; KR 1-12 12.0; Scor 1 2XP.

		Receiving			
Year Team	**G**	**Rec**	**Yds**	**Avg**	**TD**
1968 Hou	14	31	474	15.3	4
1969 Hou	14	42	540	12.9	4
1970 Hou	14	16	216	13.5	1
1971 Hou	14	38	550	14.5	1
1972 Hou	10	7	95	13.6	1
1973 Hou	1	0	0	—	0
1974 SD	14	7	121	17.3	0
1975 Hou	6	1	15	15.0	0
1976 Hou	7	0	0	—	0
NFL Total	94	142	2011	14.2	11

RANDY BEISLER Beisler, Randall Lee 6′5″, 250 **OG-OT-DE-DT**
Col: Indiana *HS:* William A. Wirt [Gary, IN] B: 10/24/1944, Gary, IN
Drafted: 1966 Round 1 Phi
1966 Phi: 14 G; KR 1-17 17.0. **1967** Phi: 14 G; KR 1-0. **1968** Phi: 8 G; Int 1-12. **1969** SF: 14 G. **1970** SF: 14 G. **1971** SF: 14 G. **1972** SF: 14 G. **1973** SF: 14 G. **1974** SF: 9 G. **1975** KC: 3 G. **Total:** 118 G; KR 2-17 8.5; Int 1-12.

BILL BELANICH Belanich, Frank George 6′0″, 205 **T-OE**
Col: Dayton *HS:* Cathedral Latin [Cleveland, OH] B: 5/19/1903, Euclid, OH D: 8/12/1960
1927 Day: 8 G; 1 Fum TD; 6 Pt. **1928** Day: 7 G. **1929** Day: 4 G. **Total:** 19 G; 1 Fum TD; 6 Pt.

KEVIN BELCHER Belcher, Kevin 6′3″, 266 **OG**
Col: Texas-El Paso *HS:* Redford [Detroit, MI] B: 2/23/1961, Detroit, MI
Drafted: 1983 Round 6 NYG
1983 NYG: 16 G. **1984** NYG: 16 G; Rec 1-4 4.0. **Total:** 32 G; Rec 1-4 4.0.

KEVIN BELCHER Belcher, Kevin Leander 6′5″, 280 **OT**
Col: Wisconsin B: 11/9/1961, Bridgeport, CT D: 4/12/1997, Howard, WI *Drafted:* 1985 Round 7 LARd
1985 LARd: 4 G. **1987** Den: 1 G. **Total:** 5 G.

BUNNY BELDEN Belden, Charles William 5′8″, 173 **WB-BB-OE-FB**
Col: St. Mary's (Cal.) *HS:* Visalia [CA] B: 12/7/1900, Chicago, IL
D: 11/1976, Skokie, IL
1927 Dul: 6 G. **1930** ChiC: 12 G; Rush 1 TD; Rec 2 TD; Tot TD 3; 18 Pt. **1931** ChiC: 8 G; Rush 2 TD; 12 Pt. **Total:** 26 G; Rush 3 TD; Rec 2 TD; Tot TD 5; 30 Pt.

LES BELDING Belding, Lester Coit 5′11″, 195 **E-WB**
Col: Upper Iowa; Iowa *HS:* Mason City [IA] B: 12/5/1900, Mason City, IA D: 1965
1925 RI: 1 G.

STEVE BELICHICK Belichick, Stephen Nicholos 5′9″, 190 **FB-LB**
Col: Case Western Reserve *HS:* Struthers [OH] B: 1/7/1919, Monessen, PA
1941 Det: Rec 1-13 13.0; PR 1-77 77.0 **1** TD; KR 1-36 36.0; Int 1-10.

		Rushing				Tot
Year Team	**G**	**Att**	**Yds**	**Avg**	**TD**	**TD**
1941 Det	6	28	118	4.2	2	3

CHUCK BELIN Belin, Charles Edward 6′2″, 312 **OG**
Col: Wisconsin *HS:* Vincent [Milwaukee, WI] B: 10/27/1970, Milwaukee, WI *Drafted:* 1993 Round 5 LARm
1994 LARm: 14 G. **1995** StL: 6 G. **1996** StL: 1 G. **Total:** 21 G.

ROCKY BELK Belk, Anthony Lovett 6′0″, 187 **WR**
Col: Miami (Fla.) *HS:* Fort Hunt [Alexandria, VA] B: 6/20/1960, Alexandria, VA *Drafted:* 1983 Round 7 Cle
1983 Cle: 10 G; Rush 1-(-5) -5.0; Rec 5-141 28.2 2 TD; 12 Pt.

VENO BELK Belk, Veno Luzon 6′3″, 233 **TE**
Col: Michigan State *HS:* Northwestern [Flint, MI] B: 3/7/1963, Tifton, GA
1987 Buf: 2 G; Rec 1-7 7.0.

BILL BELK Belk, William Arthur 6′3″, 253 **DE**
Col: Maryland East. Shore *HS:* Barr St. [Lancaster, SC] B: 2/19/1946, Lancaster, SC *Drafted:* 1968 Round 6 SF
1968 SF: 10 G; Int 1-6 1 TD; 6 Pt. **1969** SF: 14 G. **1970** SF: 14 G; KR 1-7 7.0. **1971** SF: 8 G. **1972** SF: 14 G. **1973** SF: 13 G. **1974** SF: 14 G; 1 Fum TD; 6 Pt. **Total:** 87 G; KR 1-7 7.0; Int 1-6 1 TD; 1 Fum TD; Tot TD 2; 12 Pt.

ALBERT BELL Bell, Albert II 6′0″, 170 **WR**
Col: Coffeyville CC KS; Alabama *HS:* Crenshaw [Los Angeles, CA]
B: 4/23/1964, Birmingham, AL
1988 GB: 5 G.

ANTHONY BELL Bell, Anthony Dewitt 6′3″, 235 **LB**
Col: Michigan State *HS:* Boyd H. Anderson [Lauderdale Lakes, FL]
B: 7/2/1964, Miami, FL *Drafted:* 1986 Round 1 StL
1986 StL: 16 G; 4 Sac. **1987** StL: 12 G; Int 1-13; 1 Fum; 1 Sac. **1988** Pho: 16 G; 1 Sac. **1989** Pho: 16 G; 2 Sac. **1990** Pho: 16 G; Int 1-0; 3 Sac. **1991** Det: 10 G; KR 1-0. **1992** LARd: 16 G. **Total:** 102 G; KR 1-0; Int 2-13; 1 Fum; 11 Sac.

BILLY BELL Bell, Billy Ray 5′10″, 170 **DB**
Col: Lamar *HS:* Dayton [TX] B: 1/16/1961, Dayton, TX
1989 Hou: 4 G. **1991** KC: 8 G; Int 1-4. **Total:** 12 G; Int 1-4.

BOBBY BELL Bell, Bobby Lee Jr. 6′3″, 217 **LB**
Col: Missouri *HS:* Lee's Summit [MO] B: 2/7/1962, St. Paul, MN
Drafted: 1984 Round 4 NYJ
1984 NYJ: 15 G. **1987** ChiB: 3 G; 3.5 Sac. **Total:** 18 G; 3.5 Sac.

CARLOS BELL Bell, Carlos R 6′5″, 238 **TE**
Col: South Texas J.C.; Houston *HS:* Clinton [OK] B: 9/21/1947, Clinton, OK *Drafted:* 1971 Round 4 NO
1971 NO: 1 G.

COLEMAN BELL Bell, Coleman Bernard II 6′2″, 243 **TE**
Col: Miami (Fla.) *HS:* Thomas Jefferson [Tampa, FL] B: 4/22/1970, Tampa, FL
1995 Was: 11 G; Rec 14-166 11.9 1 TD; 6 Pt; 1 Fum.

ED BELL Bell, Edward 6′1″, 227 **G-T**
Col: Indiana *HS:* Austin [Chicago, IL] B: 9/20/1921, Chicago, IL
D: 12/6/1990, South Bend, IN
AAFC **1946** MiaA: 7 G.

NFL **1947** GB: 11 G. **1948** GB: 12 G. **1949** GB: 12 G. **Total:** 35 G.

EDDIE BELL Bell, Edward Allen 5′10″, 160 **WR**
(The Flea) *Col:* Compton CC CA; Idaho State *HS:* George Washington Carver [Waco, TX] B: 9/13/1946, Waco, TX *Drafted:* 1970 Round 9 NYJ
1970 NYJ: Pass 1-0, 1 Int; Rush 2-(-7) -3.5; PR 7-33 4.7; KR 3-61 20.3. **1971** NYJ: PR 1-(-3) -3.0. **1972** NYJ: Rush 1-(-5) -5.0. **1975** NYJ: PR 2-42 21.0. **1976** SD: PR 7-31 4.4; KR 1-18 18.0. **Total:** Pass 1-0, 1 Int; Rush 3-(-12) -4.0; PR 17-103 6.1; KR 4-79 19.8.

		Receiving				
Year Team	**G**	**Rec**	**Yds**	**Avg**	**TD**	**Fum**
1970 NYJ	14	21	246	11.7	2	0
1971 NYJ	14	5	110	22.0	1	1
1972 NYJ	13	35	629	18.0	2	1
1973 NYJ	13	24	319	13.3	2	0
1974 NYJ	13	13	126	9.7	1	0
1975 NYJ	14	20	344	17.2	4	0
1976 SD	5	0	0	—	0	0
NFL Total	86	118	1774	15.0	12	2

EDDIE BELL Bell, Edward B 6′1″, 212 **DB**
Col: Pennsylvania *HS:* West Philadelphia [Philadelphia, PA]
B: 3/25/1931, Philadelphia, PA *Drafted:* 1953 Round 5 Phi
1957 Phi: KR 1-7 7.0. **Total:** KR 1-7 7.0.

		Interceptions			
Year Team	**G**	**Int**	**Yds**	**TD**	**Fum**
1955 Phi	12	1	30	0	0
1956 Phi	12	4	61	1	0
1957 Phi	12	2	38	0	0
1958 Phi	12	2	33	0	0
1960 NYT	14	2	20	0	1
NFL Total	62	11	182	1	1

JERRY BELL Bell, Gerald Alfred 6′5″, 230 **TE**
Col: Arizona State *HS:* El Cerrito [CA] B: 3/7/1959, Derby, CT
Drafted: 1982 Round 3 TB

		Receiving				
Year Team	**G**	**Rec**	**Yds**	**Avg**	**TD**	**Fum**
1982 TB	9	1	5	5.0	0	0
1983 TB	16	18	200	11.1	1	2
1984 TB	16	29	397	13.7	4	0
1985 TB	9	43	496	11.5	2	2
1986 TB	10	10	120	12.0	0	0
NFL Total	60	101	1218	12.1	7	4

GORDON BELL Bell, Gordon Granville 5′9″, 180 **RB**
Col: Michigan *HS:* Troy [OH] B: 12/25/1953, Troy, OH *Drafted:* 1976 Round 4 NYG
1976 NYG: PR 1-1 1.0. **1977** NYG: PR 1-0. **1978** StL: PR 14-101 7.2. **Total:** PR 16-102 6.4.

		Rushing				Receiving			
Year Team	**G**	**Att**	**Yds**	**Avg**	**TD**	**Rec**	**Yds**	**Avg**	**TD**
1976 NYG	14	67	233	3.5	2	25	198	7.9	0
1977 NYG	10	16	63	3.9	0	4	33	8.3	0

1978 StL	6	7	23	3.3	0	3	28	9.3	0
NFL Total	30	90	319	3.5	2	32	259	8.1	0

	Kickoff Returns				
Year Team	**Ret**	**Yds**	**Avg**	**TD**	**Fum**
1976 NYG	18	352	19.6	0	2
1977 NYG	12	235	19.6	0	0
1978 StL	8	177	22.1	0	3
NFL Total	38	764	20.1	0	5

GREG BELL Bell, Gregory Leon 5'10", 210 **RB**
Col: Notre Dame *HS:* South [Columbus, OH] B: 8/1/1962, Columbus, OH *Drafted:* 1984 Round 1 Buf
1984 Buf: KR 1-15 15.0. **1985** Buf: Pass 1-0. **Total:** Pass 1-0; KR 1-15 15.0.

		Rushing				Receiving					Tot
Year Team	**G**	**Att**	**Yds**	**Avg**	**TD**	**Rec**	**Yds**	**Avg**	**TD**	**Fum**	**TD**
1984 Buf	16	262	1100	4.2	7	34	277	8.1	1	5	8
1985 Buf	16	223	883	4.0	8	58	576	9.9	1	8	9
1986 Buf	6	90	377	4.2	4	12	142	11.8	2	2	6
1987 Buf-LARm	4	22	86	3.9	0	9	96	10.7	1	1	1
1987 Buf	2	14	60	4.3	0	4	37	9.3	0	0	0
1987 LARm	2	8	26	3.3	0	5	59	11.8	1	1	1
1988 LARm	16	288	1212	4.2	**16**	24	124	5.2	2	6	**18**
1989 LARm	16	272	1137	4.2	**15**	19	85	4.5	0	7	15
1990 LARd	6	47	164	3.5	1	1	7	7.0	0	0	1
NFL Total	80	1204	4959	4.1	51	157	1307	8.3	7	29	58

NICK BELL Bell, H. Nickolas 6'2", 255 **RB**
Col: Iowa *HS:* Clark [Las Vegas, NV] B: 8/19/1968, Las Vegas, NV *Drafted:* 1991 Round 2 LARd
1991 LARd: Rec 6-62 10.3. **1992** LARd: Rec 4-40 10.0; KR 1-16 16.0. **1993** LARd: Rec 11-111 10.1. **Total:** Rec 21-213 10.1; KR 1-16 16.0.

		Rushing				
Year Team	**G**	**Att**	**Yds**	**Avg**	**TD**	**Fum**
1991 LARd	9	78	307	3.9	3	2
1992 LARd	16	81	366	4.5	3	2
1993 LARd	10	67	180	2.7	1	2
NFL Total	35	226	853	3.8	7	6

HENRY BELL Bell, Henry 5'10", 210 **HB**
B: 1937
1960 Den: Rec 2-13 6.5; KR 2-60 30.0.

		Rushing				
Year Team	**G**	**Att**	**Yds**	**Avg**	**TD**	**Fum**
1960 Den	10	43	238	5.5	0	1

JOE BELL Bell, Joseph 6'3", 250 **DE**
Col: Norfolk State B: 4/20/1956
1979 Oak: 1 G.

KAY BELL Bell, Kay Dee 6'2", 220 **T-G**
Col: Washington State *HS:* Lincoln [Seattle, WA] B: 10/14/1914, Hoquiam, WA D: 10/27/1994, Redmond, WA *Drafted:* 1937 Round 10 Det
1937 ChiB: 10 G. **1942** NYG: 11 G. **Total:** 21 G.

KEN BELL Bell, Kenneth Shawn 5'10", 190 **RB-WR**
Col: Boston College *HS:* Greenwich [CT] B: 11/16/1964, Greenwich, CT
1986 Den: Rec 2-10 5.0. **1987** Den: Rec 1-8 8.0. **1988** Den: PR 1-4 4.0. **1989** Den: PR 21-143 6.8. **Total:** Rec 3-18 6.0; PR 22-147 6.7.

		Rushing				Kickoff Returns				
Year Team	**G**	**Att**	**Yds**	**Avg**	**TD**	**Ret**	**Yds**	**Avg**	**TD**	**Fum**
1986 Den	16	9	17	1.9	0	23	531	23.1	0	1
1987 Den	12	13	43	3.3	0	15	323	21.5	0	2
1988 Den	16	9	36	4.0	0	36	762	21.2	0	2
1989 Den	15	0	0	—	0	30	602	20.1	0	5
NFL Total	59	31	96	3.1	0	104	2218	21.3	0	10

KERWIN BELL Bell, Kerwin Douglas 6'3", 207 **QB**
Col: Florida *HS:* Lafayette [Mayo, FL] B: 6/15/1965, Live Oak, FL *Drafted:* 1988 Round 7 Mia
1996 Ind: 1 G; Pass 5-5 100.0%, 75 15.00 1 TD; Rush 1-(-1) -1.0.

KEVIN BELL Bell, Kevin Abraham 5'10", 180 **WR**
Col: Lamar *HS:* South Park [Beaumont, TX] B: 3/14/1955, Beaumont, TX *Drafted:* 1978 Round 12 SD
1978 NYJ: 9 G; KR 2-66 33.0.

LEN BELL Bell, Leonard Charles 5'11", 201 **DB**
Col: Indiana *HS:* Thomas Jefferson [Rockford, IL] B: 3/14/1964, Rockford, IL *Drafted:* 1987 Round 3 Cin
1987 Cin: 1 G.

MARK BELL Bell, Mark Elvin 6'5", 241 **DE**
Col: Colorado State *HS:* Bishop Carroll [Wichita, KS] B: 8/30/1957, Wichita, KS *Drafted:* 1979 Round 4 Sea
1979 Sea: 16 G; Rec 2-20 10.0; 1 Fum. **1980** Sea: 16 G; Rec 1-13 13.0. **1982** Sea: 9 G; 1 Sac. **1983** Bal: 7 G. **1984** Ind: 16 G. **Total:** 64 G; Rec 3-33 11.0; 1 Fum; 1 Sac.

MARK BELL Bell, Mark Ricardo 5'9", 175 **WR-KR**
Col: Colorado State *HS:* Lynwood [CA] B: 6/14/1957, Jamestown, OH *Drafted:* 1979 Round 5 StL
1980 StL: 11 G; Rec 8-123 15.4; PR 21-195 9.3; 1 Fum. **1981** StL: 1 G. **Total:** 12 G; Rec 8-123 15.4; PR 21-195 9.3; 1 Fum.

MIKE BELL Bell, Mike J 6'4", 255 **DE**
Col: Colorado State *HS:* Bishop Carroll [Wichita, KS] B: 8/30/1957, Wichita, KS *Drafted:* 1979 Round 1 KC
1979 KC: 11 G. **1980** KC: 2 G. **1981** KC: 16 G. **1982** KC: 6 G. **1983** KC: 16 G; 10 Sac. **1984** KC: 15 G; 1 Fum; 13.5 Sac. **1985** KC: 11 G; 6 Sac. **1987** KC: 12 G; 6.5 Sac. **1988** KC: 12 G; 2 Sac. **1989** KC: 15 G; 1 Sac. **1990** KC: 16 G; 1 Sac. **1991** KC: 3 G. **Total:** 135 G; 1 Fum; 40 Sac.

MYRON BELL Bell, Myron Corey 5'11", 203 **DB**
Col: Michigan State *HS:* Macomber-Whitney [Toledo, OH] B: 9/15/1971, Toledo, OH *Drafted:* 1994 Round 5 Pit
1994 Pit: 15 G. **1995** Pit: 16 G; Int 2-4. **1996** Pit: 16 G; 2 Sac. **1997** Pit: 16 G; Int 1-10; 1.5 Sac. **1998** Cin: 16 G; 1 Sac. **Total:** 79 G; Int 3-14; 4.5 Sac.

RICHARD BELL Bell, Richard Aaron 6'0", 200 **RB**
Col: Nebraska *HS:* John Muir [Pasadena, CA] B: 5/3/1967, Los Angeles, CA *Drafted:* 1990 Round 12 Pit
1990 Pit: 16 G; Rush 5-18 3.6; Rec 12-137 11.4 1 TD; 6 Pt.

RICKY BELL Bell, Richard Jr. 5'10", 194 **DB**
Col: North Carolina State *HS:* Eau Claire [Columbia, SC] B: 10/2/1974, Columbia, SC
1996 Jac: 12 G; KR 6-119 19.8; 1 Fum. **1997** ChiB: 5 G. **1998** ChiB: 14 G. **Total:** 31 G; KR 6-119 19.8; 1 Fum.

RICKY BELL Bell, Richard Thomas 6'0", 205 **RB**
Col: St. John's (Minn.) *HS:* Rocori [Cold Spring, MN] B: 10/18/1960, St. Cloud, MN
1983 Min: 14 G; KR 1-14 14.0.

RICKY BELL Bell, Ricky Lynn 6'2", 220 **RB**
Col: USC *HS:* John C. Fremont [Los Angeles, CA] B: 4/8/1955, Houston, TX D: 11/28/1984, Los Angeles, CA *Drafted:* 1977 Round 1 TB
1982 SD: KR 1-10 10.0. **Total:** KR 1-10 10.0.

		Rushing				Receiving					Tot
Year Team	**G**	**Att**	**Yds**	**Avg**	**TD**	**Rec**	**Yds**	**Avg**	**TD**	**Fum**	**TD**
1977 TB	11	148	436	2.9	1	11	88	8.0	0	4	1
1978 TB	12	185	679	3.7	6	15	122	8.1	0	1	6
1979 TB	16	283	1263	4.5	7	25	248	9.9	2	6	9
1980 TB	14	174	599	3.4	2	38	292	7.7	1	3	3
1981 TB	7	30	80	2.7	0	8	92	11.5	0	1	0
1982 SD	4	2	6	3.0	0	0	0	—	0	0	0
NFL Total	64	822	3063	3.7	16	97	842	8.7	3	15	19

BOB BELL Bell, Robert Francis Jr. 6'4", 250 **DT-DE**
Col: Cincinnati *HS:* West [Philadelphia, PA]; Bordertown Mil. Inst. [NJ] B: 1/25/1948, Philadelphia, PA *Drafted:* 1971 Round 1 Det
1971 Det: 14 G; **1** Fum TD; 6 Pt. **1972** Det: 14 G. **1973** Det: 13 G. **1974** StL: 9 G. **1975** StL: 14 G. **1976** StL: 14 G. **1977** StL: 7 G. **1978** StL: 15 G. **Total:** 100 G; 1 Fum TD; 6 Pt.

BOBBY BELL Bell, Robert Lee Jr. 6'4", 228 **LB**
Col: Minnesota *HS:* Cleveland [Shelby, NC] B: 6/17/1940, Shelby, NC *Drafted:* 1963 Round 7 KC *HOF:* 1983
1964 KC: **1** Fum TD. **1966** KC: **1** Fum TD. **1969** KC: KR 1-53 53.0 **1** TD. **Total:** KR 1-53 53.0 1 TD; 2 Fum TD.

		Interceptions				Tot
Year Team	**G**	**Int**	**Yds**	**TD**	**Fum**	**TD**
1963 KC	14	1	20	0	0	0
1964 KC	14	1	4	0	0	1
1965 KC	14	4	73	1	1	1
1966 KC	14	2	14	0	0	1
1967 KC	14	4	82	1	0	1
1968 KC	14	5	95	0	0	0
1969 KC	14	0	0	0	0	1
1970 KC	14	3	57	1	0	1
1971 KC	14	1	26	1	0	1
1972 KC	14	3	56	1	0	1
1973 KC	14	1	24	0	0	0
1974 KC	14	1	28	1	0	1
NFL Total	168	26	479	6	1	9

THEO BELL Bell, Theopolis Jr. 6'0", 185 **WR**
Col: Arizona *HS:* Bakersfield [CA] B: 12/21/1953, Bakersfield, CA
Drafted: 1976 Round 4 Pit
1976 Pit: Rush 1-5 5.0. **1980** Pit: KR 3-50 16.7. **1981** TB: Rush 1-7 7.0. **Total:** Rush 2-12 6.0; KR 3-50 16.7.

		Receiving				Punt Returns				
Year Team	G	Rec	Yds	Avg	TD	Ret	Yds	Avg	TD	Fum
1976 Pit	13	3	43	14.3	1	39	390	10.0	0	5
1978 Pit	16	6	53	8.8	1	21	152	7.2	0	0
1979 Pit	13	3	61	20.3	0	45	378	8.4	0	1
1980 Pit	14	29	748	25.8	2	34	339	10.0	0	1
1981 TB	16	21	318	15.1	2	27	132	4.9	0	1
1982 TB	9	15	203	13.5	0	9	62	6.9	0	0
1983 TB	16	25	410	16.4	2	10	48	4.8	0	0
1984 TB	15	22	350	15.9	0	4	10	2.5	0	1
1985 TB	15	12	189	15.8	0	0	0	—	0	0
NFL Total	127	136	2375	17.5	8	189	1511	8.0	0	9

TODD BELL Bell, Todd Anthony 6'1", 207 **DB**
Col: Ohio State *HS:* Middletown [OH] B: 11/28/1958, Middletown, OH
Drafted: 1981 Round 4 ChiB
1981 ChiB: 16 G; Int 1-92 1 TD; 6 Pt. **1982** ChiB: 9 G; KR 1-14 14.0; 1 Sac. **1983** ChiB: 15 G; KR 2-18 9.0; 3 Sac. **1984** ChiB: 16 G; KR 2-33 16.5; Int 4-46 1 TD; 6 Pt; 4.5 Sac. **1986** ChiB: 15 G; Int 1-(-1). **1987** ChiB: 12 G; KR 1-18 18.0; 1 Fum; 1 Sac. **1988** Phi: 16 G; Int 0-24; 0.5 Sac. **1989** Phi: 4 G; Int 1-13. **Total:** 103 G; KR 6-83 13.8; Int 7-174 2 TD; 12 Pt; 1 Fum; 10 Sac.

WILLIAM BELL Bell, William 5'11", 214 **RB**
Col: Georgia Tech *HS:* Miami Edison [FL] B: 7/22/1971, Miami, FL
1994 Was: 7 G; KR 2-43 21.5. **1995** Was: 16 G; Rush 4-13 3.3; KR 8-121 15.1. **1996** Was: 16 G; Rec 3-23 7.7; KR 8-130 16.3. **Total:** 39 G; Rush 4-13 3.3; Rec 3-23 7.7; KR 18-294 16.3.

BILL BELL Bell, William Stephen 6'0", 192 **K**
Col: Kansas *HS:* Falls Church [VA] B: 12/9/1947, Fort Knox, KY
Drafted: 1970 Round 17 Atl
1971 Atl: Punt 16-577 36.1. **1972** Atl: Rush 1-(-3) -3.0. **Total:** Rush 1-(-3) -3.0; Punt 16-577 36.1.

		Scoring						
Year Team	G	Pts	FG	FGA	FG%	XK	XKA	XK%
1971 Atl	14	68	13	21	61.9	29	33	87.9
1972 Atl	14	79	16	30	53.3	31	31	100.0
1973 NE	3	7	1	4	25.0	4	5	80.0
NFL Total	31	154	30	55	54.5	64	69	92.8

JAY BELLAMY Bellamy, John Lee 5'11", 198 **SAF**
Col: Rutgers *HS:* Matawan [NJ] B: 7/8/1972, Perth Amboy, NJ
1994 Sea: 3 G. **1995** Sea: 15 G. **1996** Sea: 16 G; Int 3-18. **1997** Sea: 16 G; Int 1-13; 2 Sac. **1998** Sea: 16 G; Int 3-40; 1 Sac. **Total:** 66 G; Int 7-71; 3 Sac.

MIKE BELLAMY Bellamy, Michael Sinclair II 6'0", 195 **WR**
Col: Coll. of DuPage IL (J.C.); Illinois *HS:* Kenwood Acad. [Chicago, IL] B: 6/28/1966, New York, NY *Drafted:* 1990 Round 2 Phi
1990 Phi: 6 G; PR 2-22 11.0; KR 1-17 17.0; 1 Fum.

VIC BELLAMY Bellamy, Victor K 6'1", 195 **DB**
Col: Syracuse *HS:* Central Philadelphia [Philadelphia, PA] B: 6/2/1963, Philadelphia, PA
1987 Phi: 3 G.

BOB BELLINGER Bellinger, Robert F 5'11", 216 **G**
Col: Gonzaga *HS:* Seattle Prep [WA] B: 1/20/1913, Spokane, WA
D: 5/8/1985, Lansing, MI
1934 NYG: 9 G. **1935** NYG: 9 G. **Total:** 18 G.

RODNEY BELLINGER Bellinger, Rodney Carwell 5'8", 186 **DB**
Col: Miami (Fla.) *HS:* Coral Gables [FL] B: 6/4/1962, Miami, FL
Drafted: 1984 Round 3 Buf
1984 Buf: 10 G; Int 1-0. **1985** Buf: 16 G; Int 2-64. **1986** Buf: 16 G; KR 2-32 16.0; Int 1-14; **1** Fum TD; 6 Pt. **Total:** 42 G; KR 2-32 16.0; Int 4-78; 1 Fum TD; 6 Pt.

MARK BELLINI Bellini, Mark Joseph 5'11", 185 **WR**
Col: Brigham Young *HS:* San Leandro [CA] B: 1/19/1964, San Leandro, CA *Drafted:* 1987 Round 7 Ind
1987 Ind: 10 G; Rec 5-69 13.8. **1988** Ind: 15 G; Rec 5-64 12.8. **Total:** 25 G; Rec 10-133 13.3.

JOE BELLINO Bellino, Joseph Michael 5'9", 185 **HB-WR**
Col: Navy *HS:* Winchester [MA] B: 3/13/1938, Winchester, MA
Drafted: 1961 Round 19 Bos
1965 Bos: Rec 5-74 14.8. **1966** Bos: Rec 6-77 12.8 1 TD; PR 4-19 4.8. **1967** Bos: PR 15-129 8.6. **Total:** Rec 11-151 13.7 1 TD; PR 19-148 7.8.

		Rushing				Kickoff Returns				
Year Team	G	Att	Yds	Avg	TD	Ret	Yds	Avg	TD	Fum
1965 Bos	10	24	49	2.0	0	7	138	19.7	0	0
1966 Bos	11	0	0	—	0	18	410	22.8	0	1
1967 Bos	14	6	15	2.5	0	18	357	19.8	0	0
NFL Total	35	30	64	2.1	0	43	905	21.0	0	1

GREG BELLISARI Bellisari, Greg Ernest 6'0", 236 **LB**
Col: Ohio State *HS:* Boca Raton [FL] B: 6/21/1975, Boynton Beach, FL
1997 TB: 14 G. **1998** TB: 2 G. **Total:** 16 G.

GEORGE BELOTTI Belotti, George D 6'4", 250 **C**
Col: USC *HS:* Oxnard [CA] B: 11/29/1934, Los Angeles, CA
Drafted: 1957 Round 8 GB
1960 Hou: 14 G. **1961** Hou-SD: 4 G. Hou: 2 G. SD: 2 G. **Total:** 18 G.

CEASAR BELSER Belser, Ceasar Edward 6'0", 205 **DB**
Col: Arkansas-Pine Bluff *HS:* George Washington Carver [Montgomery, AL] B: 9/13/1944, Montgomery, AL *Drafted:* 1966 Round 10 Was
1968 KC: 14 G; KR 4-38 9.5; 4 Fum. **1969** KC: 14 G. **1970** KC: 14 G. **1971** KC: 14 G; PR 1-2 2.0. **1974** SF: 4 G. **Total:** 60 G; PR 1-2 2.0; KR 4-38 9.5; 4 Fum.

JASON BELSER Belser, Jason Daks 5'9", 188 **DB**
Col: Oklahoma *HS:* South [Raytown, MO] B: 5/28/1970, Kansas City, MO *Drafted:* 1992 Round 8 Ind
1995 Ind: KR 1-15 15.0. **1996** Ind: 1 Sac. **1997** Ind: 1 Sac. **1998** Ind: PR 1-53 53.0; 1 Sac. **Total:** PR 1-53 53.0; KR 1-15 15.0; 3 Sac.

		Interceptions			
Year Team	G	Int	Yds	TD	Fum
1992 Ind	16	3	27	0	1
1993 Ind	16	1	14	0	0
1994 Ind	13	1	31	0	0
1995 Ind	16	1	0	0	0
1996 Ind	16	4	81	**2**	0
1997 Ind	16	2	121	1	0
1998 Ind	16	1	19	0	0
NFL Total	109	13	293	3	1

HORACE BELTON Belton, Horace 5'8", 200 **RB**
Col: Southeastern Louisiana *HS:* Scotlandville [Baton Rouge, LA] B: 7/16/1955, Baton Rouge, LA
1978 KC: Rec 11-88 8.0. **1979** KC: Rec 4-44 11.0. **1980** KC: Rec 5-94 18.8. **Total:** Rec 20-226 11.3.

		Rushing				Kickoff Returns				
Year Team	G	Att	Yds	Avg	TD	Ret	Yds	Avg	TD	Fum
1978 KC	16	24	79	3.3	0	9	227	25.2	0	1
1979 KC	16	44	134	3.0	1	22	463	21.0	0	1
1980 KC	14	68	273	4.0	2	6	110	18.3	0	3
NFL Total	46	136	486	3.6	3	37	800	21.6	0	5

WILLIE BELTON Belton, Willie Davis 5'11", 207 **RB**
Col: Maryland East. Shore *HS:* Washington [Greenville, SC]
B: 12/12/1948, Greenville, SC D: 12/5/1992, Greenville, SC
1971 Atl: Rec 3-22 7.3. **1972** Atl: Rec 1-(-1) -1.0. **Total:** Rec 4-21 5.3.

		Rushing				Punt Returns			
Year Team	G	Att	Yds	Avg	TD	Ret	Yds	Avg	TD
1971 Atl	14	56	237	4.2	1	30	163	5.4	0
1972 Atl	14	10	20	2.0	0	17	110	6.5	0
1973 StL	3	0	0	—	0	1	2	2.0	0
1974 StL	5	12	49	4.1	0	4	8	2.0	0
NFL Total	36	78	306	3.9	1	52	283	5.4	0

	Kickoff Returns				
Year Team	Ret	Yds	Avg	TD	Fum
1971 Atl	28	706	25.2	0	9
1972 Atl	21	441	21.0	0	5
1973 StL	3	83	27.7	0	0
1974 StL	5	111	22.2	0	1
NFL Total	57	1341	23.5	0	15

BRIAN BELWAY Belway, Brian P 6'6", 265 **DE**
Col: Calgary (Canada) *HS:* St. Francis Sec. School [Calgary, Canada] B: 5/28/1963, Ottawa, Canada
1987 LARd: 1 G.

AL BEMILLER Bemiller, Albert Delane 6'3", 243 **C-OG**
(Tombstone) *Col:* Syracuse *HS:* Hanover [PA] B: 4/18/1938, Hanover, PA *Drafted:* 1961 Round 7 Buf
1961 Buf: 14 G. **1962** Buf: 14 G. **1963** Buf: 14 G. **1964** Buf: 14 G. **1965** Buf: 14 G. **1966** Buf: 14 G. **1967** Buf: 14 G. **1968** Buf: 14 G; Rec 1-0. **1969** Buf: 14 G. **Total:** 126 G; Rec 1-0.

CAREY BENDER Bender, Carey Wayne 5'8", 185 **RB**
Col: Coe *HS:* Marion [IA] B: 1/28/1972, Marion, IA
1996 Buf: 1 G.

WES BENDER Bender, Wes Todd 5'10", 242 **RB**
Col: Glendale CC CA; USC *HS:* Burbank [CA]; John Burroughs HS [Burbank, CA] B: 8/2/1970, Van Nuys, CA
1994 LARd: 9 G; Rec 2-14 7.0. **1997** NO: 11 G; Rush 5-9 1.8; 1 Fum. **Total:** 20 G; Rush 5-9 1.8; Rec 2-14 7.0; 1 Fum.

JESSE BENDROSS Bendross, Jesse James 6′0″, 196 **WR**
Col: Alabama *HS:* Miramar [FL] B: 7/19/1962, Hollywood, FL
Drafted: 1984 Round 7 SD
1985 SD: KR 1-2 2.0. **Total:** KR 1-2 2.0.

		Receiving				
Year Team	**G**	**Rec**	**Yds**	**Avg**	**TD**	**Fum**
1984 SD	16	16	213	13.3	0	1
1985 SD	16	11	156	14.2	2	0
1987 Phi	3	0	0	—	0	0
NFL Total	35	27	369	13.7	2	1

DAVED BENEFIELD Benefield, Daved 6′4″, 231 **LB**
Col: Cal State-Northridge *HS:* Marantha [Sierra Madre, CA]
B: 2/16/1968, Los Angeles, CA
1996 SF: 15 G.

LOU BENFATTI Benfatti, Lewis Vincent 6′4″, 285 **DT**
Col: Penn State *HS:* Morris Knolls [Rockaway, NJ] B: 3/9/1971, Green Pond, NJ *Drafted:* 1994 Round 3 NYJ
1994 NYJ: 7 G. **1995** NYJ: 12 G; KR 1-25 25.0. **Total:** 19 G; KR 1-25 25.0.

BRANT BENGEN Bengen, Brant Wayne 5′8″, 172 **WR**
Col: British Columbia (Canada); Idaho *HS:* Bellingham [WA]
B: 3/30/1964
1987 Sea: 3 G; Rec 2-33 16.5; KR 2-47 23.5.

ROLF BENIRSCHKE Benirschke, Rolf Joachim 6′0″, 171 **K**
Col: California-Davis *HS:* La Jolla [CA] B: 2/7/1955, Boston, MA
Drafted: 1977 Round 12 Oak

		Scoring						
Year Team	**G**	**Pts**	**FG**	**FGA**	**FG%**	**XK**	**XKA**	**XK%**
1977 SD	14	72	17	23	73.9	21	24	87.5
1978 SD	15	91	18	22	81.8	37	43	86.0
1979 SD	4	24	4	4	100.0	12	13	92.3
1980 SD	16	118	24	36	66.7	46	48	95.8
1981 SD	16	112	19	26	73.1	**55**	**61**	90.2
1982 SD	9	80	16	22	72.7	**32**	**34**	94.1
1983 SD	16	88	15	24	62.5	43	45	95.6
1984 SD	14	92	17	26	65.4	41	41	100.0
1985 SD	1	2	0	0	—	2	2	100.0
1986 SD	16	87	16	25	64.0	39	41	95.1
NFL Total	121	766	146	208	70.2	328	352	93.2

DAN BENISH Benish, Daniel James 6′5″, 273 **DT**
Col: Clemson *HS:* Hubbard [OH] B: 11/21/1960, Youngstown, OH
1983 Atl: 16 G; 1 Sac. **1984** Atl: 15 G; 1 Sac. **1985** Atl: 16 G; 3.5 Sac.
1986 Atl: 5 G. **1987** Was: 3 G; 2 Sac. **Total:** 55 G; 7.5 Sac.

TONY BENJAMIN Benjamin, Anthony Lee 6′3″, 225 **RB**
Col: Duke *HS:* Monessen [PA] B: 10/27/1955, Monnesen, PA
Drafted: 1977 Round 6 Sea
1977 Sea: 6 G; Rush 13-48 3.7; Rec 4-27 6.8. **1978** Sea: 6 G; Rush 1-7 7.0; Rec 1-9 9.0. **1979** Sea: 16 G; Rush 5-13 2.6; Rec 1-6 6.0; KR 2-33 16.5. **Total:** 28 G; Rush 19-68 3.6; Rec 6-42 7.0; KR 2-33 16.5.

GUY BENJAMIN Benjamin, Guy Emory 6′4″, 210 **QB**
Col: Stanford *HS:* James Monroe [Los Angeles, CA] B: 6/27/1955, Los Angles, CA *Drafted:* 1978 Round 2 Mia
1978 Mia: Rush 1-(-2) -2.0. **1981** SF: Rush 1-1 1.0. **1983** SF: Rush 1-1 1.0. **Total:** Rush 3-0.

		Passing								
Year Team	**G**	**Att**	**Comp**	**Comp%**	**Yds**	**YPA**	**TD**	**Int**	**Rating**	**Fum**
1978 Mia	3	8	6	75.0	91	11.38	1	1	112.0	0
1979 Mia	4	4	3	75.0	28	7.00	0	0	93.8	0
1980 NO	2	17	7	41.2	28	1.65	0	1	24.4	0
1981 SF	4	26	15	57.7	171	6.58	1	1	74.4	0
1982 SF	2	1	1	100.0	10	10.00	0	0	108.3	0
1983 SF	4	12	7	58.3	111	9.25	1	0	117.0	1
NFL Total	19	68	39	57.4	439	6.46	3	3	73.1	1

RYAN BENJAMIN Benjamin, Ryan Lamont 5′7″, 183 **RB**
Col: Coll. of the Sequoias CA (J.C.); U. of Pacific *HS:* Tulare [CA]
B: 4/23/1970, Pixley, CA
1993 Cin: 1 G; Rush 3-5 1.7; Rec 1-16 16.0; KR 4-78 19.5.

BILL BENJAMIN Benjamin, William Joseph 6′3″, 226 **LB**
Col: San Jose State *HS:* San Fernando [CA] B: 9/14/1958, Indianapolis, IN
1987 Ind: 2 G; 1 Sac.

HEINIE BENKERT Benkert, Henry Marvin 5′9″, 168 **WB-TB-BB**
Col: Rutgers *HS:* East Side [Newark, NJ] B: 6/30/1901, Newark, NJ
D: 7/15/1972, Orange, NJ
1925 NYG: 11 G. **1926** Pott: 8 G. **1929** Ora: 8 G. **1930** Nwk: 5 G.
Total: 32 G.

FRED BENNERS Benners, Frederick Hagaman 6′3″, 195 **QB**
Col: University of the South (TN); Southern Methodist *HS:* Highland Park [Dallas, TX] B: 6/22/1930, Dallas, TX *Drafted:* 1951 Round 8 NYG
1952 NYG: Rush 5-16 3.2.

		Passing								
Year Team	**G**	**Att**	**Comp**	**Comp%**	**Yds**	**YPA**	**TD**	**Int**	**Rating**	**Fum**
1952 NYG	6	58	25	43.1	320	5.52	0	5	25.1	1

BEN BENNETT Bennett, Allen Beverly 6′1″, 200 **QB**
Col: Duke *HS:* Peterson [Sunnyvale, CA] B: 5/5/1962, Greensboro, NC
Drafted: 1984 Round 6 Atl
1987 Cin: 1 G; Pass 6-2 33.3%, 25 4.17 1 Int; Rush 2-17 8.5.

ANTOINE BENNETT Bennett, Antoine 5′11″, 185 **DB**
Col: Florida A&M *HS:* Miami Edison [FL] B: 11/29/1967, Miami, FL
Drafted: 1991 Round 12 Cin
1991 Cin: 3 G. **1992** Cin: 11 G. **Total:** 14 G.

BARRY BENNETT Bennett, Barry Martin 6′4″, 257 **DT-DE-NT**
Col: Concordia (Minn.) *HS:* North [North St. Paul, MN] B: 12/10/1955, St. Paul, MN *Drafted:* 1978 Round 3 NO
1978 NO: 16 G. **1979** NO: 16 G. **1980** NO: 15 G. **1981** NO: 3 G.
1982 NYJ: 7 G; 1 Sac. **1983** NYJ: 13 G; 1 Sac. **1984** NYJ: 15 G; 4 Sac.
1985 NYJ: 16 G; 7.5 Sac. **1986** NYJ: 16 G; 3.5 Sac. **1987** NYJ: 13 G; 1.5 Sac. **1988** NYJ-Min: 2 G. NYJ: 1 G. Min: 1 G. **Total:** 132 G; 18.5 Sac.

BRANDON BENNETT Bennett, Brandon Purrell 5′10″, 201 **RB**
Col: South Carolina *HS:* Riverside [Taylors, SC] B: 2/3/1973, Greenville, SC
1998 Cin: Rec 8-153 19.1; KR 3-61 20.3.

		Rushing				
Year Team	**G**	**Att**	**Yds**	**Avg**	**TD**	**Fum**
1998 Cin	14	77	243	3.2	2	1

CHARLES BENNETT Bennett, Charles Anthony 6′5″, 257 **DE**
Col: Mississippi Delta CC; Southwestern Louisiana *HS:* Coahoma Co. [Clarksdale, MS] B: 2/9/1963, Alligator, MS *Drafted:* 1985 Round 7 ChiB
1987 Mia: 3 G.

CHUCK BENNETT Bennett, Charles Henry 5′9″, 193 **WB-DB-BB**
Col: Indiana *HS:* Linton [IN] B: 8/9/1907, Linton, IN D: 6/9/1973, Countryside, IL
1930 Port: 14 G; Rush 5 TD; Rec 1 TD; Int 1 TD; Tot TD 7; 42 Pt.
1931 Port: 1 G. **1933** ChiC: 2 G; Rush 2-(-1) -0.5. **Total:** 17 G; Rush 2-(-1) -0.5 5 TD; Rec 1 TD; Int 1 TD; Tot TD 7; 42 Pt.

CORNELIUS BENNETT Bennett, Cornelius O'Landa 6′2″, 237 **LB**
Col: Alabama *HS:* Ensley [Birmingham, AL] B: 8/25/1965, Birmingham, AL *Drafted:* 1987 Round 1 Ind
1987 Buf: 8 G; 8.5 Sac. **1988** Buf: 16 G; Int 2-30; 9.5 Sac. **1989** Buf: 12 G; Int 2-5; 5.5 Sac. **1990** Buf: 16 G; 6 Pt; 4 Sac. **1991** Buf: 16 G; 1 Fum TD; 6 Pt; 9 Sac. **1992** Buf: 15 G; 4 Sac. **1993** Buf: 16 G; Int 1-5; 1 Fum; 5 Sac.
1994 Buf: 16 G; 5 Sac. **1995** Buf: 14 G; Int 1-69 1 TD; 6 Pt; 2 Sac.
1996 Atl: 13 G; Int 1-3; 3 Sac. **1997** Atl: 16 G; 7 Sac. **1998** Atl: 16 G; 1 Sac. **Total:** 174 G; Int 7-112 1 TD; 1 Fum TD; Tot TD 3; 18 Pt; 1 Fum; 63.5 Sac.

DARREN BENNETT Bennett, Darren Leslie 6′5″, 235 **P**
Col: No College *HS:* Applecross [Australia] B: 1/9/1965, Sydney, Australia

		Punting			
Year Team	**G**	**Punts**	**Yds**	**Avg**	**Fum**
1995 SD	16	72	3221	44.7	0
1996 SD	16	87	3967	45.6	0
1997 SD	16	89	3972	44.6	0
1998 SD	16	95	4174	43.9	1
NFL Total	64	343	15334	44.7	1

DONNELL BENNETT Bennett, Donnell Jr. 6′0″, 242 **RB**
Col: Miami (Fla.) *HS:* Cardinal Gibbons [Fort Lauderdale, FL]
B: 9/14/1972, Ft. Lauderdale, FL *Drafted:* 1994 Round 2 KC
1994 KC: KR 1-12 12.0. **Total:** KR 1-12 12.0.

		Rushing				Receiving					Tot
Year Team	**G**	**Att**	**Yds**	**Avg**	**TD**	**Rec**	**Yds**	**Avg**	**TD**	**Fum**	**TD**
1994 KC	15	46	178	3.9	2	7	53	7.6	0	2	2
1995 KC	3	7	11	1.6	0	1	12	12.0	0	0	0
1996 KC	16	36	166	4.6	0	8	21	2.6	0	0	0
1997 KC	14	94	369	3.9	1	7	5	0.7	0	0	1
1998 KC	16	148	527	3.6	5	16	91	5.7	1	4	6
NFL Total	64	331	1251	3.8	8	39	182	4.7	1	6	9

JUG BENNETT Bennett, Earl Clinton Jr. 5′8″, 188 **G-LB**
Col: Hardin-Simmons *HS:* Graham [TX] B: 2/27/1920, Skiatock, OK
1946 GB: 3 G.

EDGAR BENNETT Bennett, Edgar III 6'0", 221 **RB**
Col: Florida State *HS:* Robert E. Lee [Jacksonville, FL] B: 2/15/1969, Jacksonville, FL *Drafted:* 1992 Round 4 GB
1992 GB: KR 5-104 20.8. **1996** GB: Scor 2 2XP. **1998** ChiB: Pass 2-1 50.0%, 18 9.00 1 TD. **Total:** Pass 2-1 50.0%, 18 9.00 1 TD; KR 5-104 20.8; Scor 2 2XP.

		Rushing				Receiving					Tot
Year Team	G	Att	Yds	Avg	TD	Rec	Yds	Avg	TD	Fum	TD
1992 GB	16	61	214	3.5	0	13	93	7.2	0	2	0
1993 GB	16	159	550	3.5	9	59	457	7.7	1	0	10
1994 GB	16	178	623	3.5	5	78	546	7.0	4	1	9
1995 GB	16	316	1067	3.4	3	61	648	10.6	4	2	7
1996 GB	16	222	899	4.0	2	31	176	5.7	1	2	3
1998 ChiB	16	173	611	3.5	2	28	209	7.5	0	2	2
NFL Total	96	1109	3964	3.6	21	270	2129	7.9	10	9	31

LEWIS BENNETT Bennett, Lewis Bonaparte II 5'11", 175 **WR**
Col: Florida A&M *HS:* William M. Raines [Jacksonville, FL] B: 8/4/1963, Jacksonville, FL
1987 NYG: 3 G; Rec 10-184 18.4 1 TD; 6 Pt.

MONTE BENNETT Bennett, Monte Lewis 6'3", 265 **NT-DE**
Col: Kansas State *HS:* Sterling [KS] B: 4/27/1959, Sterling, KS
1981 NO: 16 G. **1987** SD: 3 G. **Total:** 19 G.

PHIL BENNETT Bennett, Philip 6'3", 225 **LB**
Col: Miami (Fla.) *HS:* Carrick [Pittsburgh, PA] B: 2/14/1935 *Drafted:* 1957 Round 19 Pit
1960 Bos: 2 G.

ROY BENNETT Bennett, Roy Mitchell 6'2", 195 **DB**
Col: Jackson State *HS:* West End [Birmingham, AL] B: 7/5/1961, Birmingham, AL
1988 SD: 16 G; Int 1-21; 6 Pt. **1989** SD: 16 G; Int 3-4. **Total:** 32 G; Int 4-25; 6 Pt.

SID BENNETT Bennett, Sydney Chisholm 5'10", 192 **T-G**
Col: Northwestern *HS:* Geneva [IL] B: 2/2/1895, Geneva, IL D: 12/30/1971, Elgin, IL
1920 ChiT: 6 G. **1922** Mil: 2 G. **Total:** 8 G.

TOMMY BENNETT Bennett, Tommy 6'2", 219 **DB**
Col: UCLA *HS:* Samuel F.B. Morse [San Diego, CA] B: 2/19/1973, Las Vegas, NV
1996 Ariz: 16 G. **1997** Ariz: 13 G; Int 1-0; 6 Pt. **1998** Ariz: 16 G; Int 2-100 1 TD; 6 Pt. **Total:** 45 G; Int 3-100 1 TD; Tot TD 2; 12 Pt.

TONY BENNETT Bennett, Tony Lydell 6'2", 250 **LB**
Col: Mississippi *HS:* Coahoma Co. [Clarksdale, MS] B: 7/1/1967, Alligator, MS *Drafted:* 1990 Round 1 GB
1990 GB: 14 G; 3 Sac. **1991** GB: 16 G; 13 Sac. **1992** GB: 16 G; 1 Fum TD; 6 Pt; 13.5 Sac. **1993** GB: 10 G; 6.5 Sac. **1994** Ind: 16 G; 1 Fum TD; 6 Pt; 9 Sac. **1995** Ind: 16 G; Scor **1** Saf; **1** Fum TD; 8 Pt; 10.5 Sac. **1996** Ind: 14 G; 6 Sac. **1997** Ind: 6 G; 3 Sac. **Total:** 108 G; Scor 1 Saf; 3 Fum TD; 20 Pt; 64.5 Sac.

WOODY BENNETT Bennett, Woodrow Jr. 6'2", 227 **RB**
Col: Arizona Western Coll. (J.C.); Miami (Fla.) *HS:* William Penn [York, PA] B: 3/24/1955, York, PA
1979 NYJ: KR 1-7 7.0. **1980** NYJ-Mia: KR 6-88 14.7. NYJ: KR 6-88 14.7. **1983** Mia: KR 1-6 6.0. **Total:** KR 8-101 12.6.

		Rushing				Receiving					Tot
Year Team	G	Att	Yds	Avg	TD	Rec	Yds	Avg	TD	Fum	TD
1979 NYJ	15	2	4	2.0	1	1	9	9.0	0	1	1
1980 NYJ-Mia	14	46	200	4.3	0	3	26	8.7	1	2	1
1980 NYJ	10	3	13	4.3	0	0	0	—	0	1	0
1980 Mia	4	43	187	4.3	0	3	26	8.7	1	1	1
1981 Mia	3	28	104	3.7	0	4	22	5.5	0	1	0
1982 Mia	1	9	15	1.7	0	0	0	—	0	0	0
1983 Mia	16	49	197	4.0	2	6	35	5.8	0	1	2
1984 Mia	16	144	606	4.2	7	6	44	7.3	1	4	8
1985 Mia	16	54	256	4.7	0	10	101	10.1	1	0	1
1986 Mia	16	36	162	4.5	0	4	33	8.3	0	1	0
1987 Mia	12	25	102	4.1	0	4	18	4.5	0	0	0
1988 Mia	16	31	115	3.7	0	2	16	8.0	0	1	0
NFL Total	125	424	1761	4.2	10	40	304	7.6	3	11	13

BRAD BENSON Benson, Bradley William 6'3", 262 **OT-OG-C**
Col: Penn State *HS:* Altoona [PA] B: 11/25/1955, Altoona, PA *Drafted:* 1977 Round 8 NE
1978 NYG: 16 G. **1979** NYG: 10 G. **1980** NYG: 15 G. **1981** NYG: 11 G. **1982** NYG: 9 G. **1983** NYG: 16 G. **1984** NYG: 16 G. **1985** NYG: 16 G. **1986** NYG: 16 G. **1987** NYG: 12 G. **Total:** 137 G.

CHARLES BENSON Benson, Charles Henry 6'3", 267 **DE**
Col: Baylor *HS:* Aldine [Houston, TX] B: 11/21/1960, Houston, TX *Drafted:* 1983 Round 3 Mia
1983 Mia: 8 G. **1984** Mia: 16 G; 1 Sac. **1985** Ind: 1 G. **1987** Det: 3 G; Int 1-2; 1 Sac. **Total:** 28 G; Int 1-2; 2 Sac.

CLIFF BENSON Benson, Clifford Anthony 6'4", 238 **TE**
Col: Purdue *HS:* Alan B. Shepard [Palos Heights, IL] B: 8/28/1961, Chicago, IL *Drafted:* 1984 Round 5 Atl
1984 Atl: Rush 3-8 2.7. **Total:** Rush 3-8 2.7.

		Receiving			
Year Team	G	Rec	Yds	Avg	TD
1984 Atl	16	26	244	9.4	0
1985 Atl	16	10	37	3.7	0
1987 Was-NO	10	2	11	5.5	0
1987 Was	2	0	0	—	0
1987 NO	8	2	11	5.5	0
1988 NO	7	1	5	5.0	0
NFL Total	49	39	297	7.6	0

DARREN BENSON Benson, Darren 6'7", 308 **DT**
Col: Trinity Valley CC TX *HS:* Craigmont [Memphis, TN] B: 8/25/1974, Memphis, TN
1995 Dal: 6 G. **1997** Dal: 6 G. **Total:** 12 G.

DUANE BENSON Benson, Dean Duane 6'2", 215 **LB**
Col: Hamline *HS:* Grand Meadow [MN] B: 8/5/1945, Belmond, IA *Drafted:* 1967 Round 11 Oak
1967 Oak: 8 G; KR 1-0. **1968** Oak: 12 G. **1969** Oak: 14 G; KR 1-0. **1970** Oak: 14 G; Int 1-14. **1971** Oak: 14 G. **1972** Atl: 14 G. **1973** Atl: 14 G; KR 3-20 6.7. **1974** Hou: 13 G; Int 2-0. **1975** Hou: 4 G. **1976** Hou: 14 G. **Total:** 121 G; KR 5-20 4.0; Int 3-14.

GEORGE BENSON Benson, George Nathan 6'1", 205 **HB-DB-FB**
Col: Northwestern *HS:* Hammond [IN] B: 5/7/1919, Madison, IN
AAFC **1947** BknA: 1 G; Rush 2-5 2.5.

HARRY BENSON Benson, Harry Hartley 5'10", 218 **G**
Col: Western Maryland *HS:* Baltimore City College [MD] B: 1910, Baltimore, MD D: 5/17/1943, Attu Island, AK
1935 Phi: 6 G.

MITCHELL BENSON Benson, Mitchell Oswell 6'4", 302 **NT-DT**
Col: Texas Christian *HS:* Eastern Hills [Fort Worth, TX] B: 5/30/1967, Fort Worth, TX *Drafted:* 1989 Round 3 Ind
1989 Ind: 16 G. **1990** Ind: 9 G. **1991** SD: 16 G; KR 1-2 2.0; 1 Fum; 1 Sac. **Total:** 41 G; KR 1-2 2.0; 1 Fum; 1 Sac.

THOMAS BENSON Benson, Thomas Carl 6'2", 238 **LB**
Col: Oklahoma *HS:* Ardmore [OK] B: 9/6/1961, Ardmore, OK *Drafted:* 1984 Round 2 Atl
1984 Atl: 16 G; 2 Sac. **1985** Atl: 16 G; 1.5 Sac. **1986** SD: 16 G; 5 Sac. **1987** SD: 11 G; 1 Sac. **1988** NE: 12 G. **1989** LARd: 16 G; Int 2-36; 2 Sac. **1990** LARd: 16 G. **1991** LARd: 16 G; Int 1-25; 1 Sac. **1992** LARd: 1 G. **Total:** 120 G; Int 3-61; 12.5 Sac.

TROY BENSON Benson, Troy B 6'2", 235 **LB**
Col: Pittsburgh *HS:* Altoona [PA] B: 7/30/1963, Altoona, PA *Drafted:* 1985 Round 5 NYJ
1986 NYJ: 15 G. **1987** NYJ: 11 G. **1988** NYJ: 16 G; Int 1-2; 2 Sac. **1989** NYJ: 16 G. **Total:** 58 G; Int 1-2; 2 Sac.

ALBERT BENTLEY Bentley, Albert Timothy 5'11", 213 **RB**
Col: Miami (Fla.) *HS:* Immokalee [FL] B: 8/15/1960, Naples, FL *Drafted:* 1984 Supplemental Round 2 Ind
1985 Ind: Pass 1-1 100.0%, 6 6.00. **1988** Ind: Pass 1-0. **1989** Ind: Pass 1-0. **Total:** Pass 3-1 33.3%, 6 2.00.

		Rushing				Receiving			
Year Team	G	Att	Yds	Avg	TD	Rec	Yds	Avg	TD
1985 Ind	15	54	288	5.3	2	11	85	7.7	0
1986 Ind	12	73	351	4.8	3	25	230	9.2	0
1987 Ind	12	142	631	4.4	7	34	447	13.1	2
1988 Ind	16	45	230	5.1	2	26	252	9.7	1
1989 Ind	16	75	299	4.0	1	52	525	10.1	3
1990 Ind	16	137	556	4.1	4	71	664	9.4	2
1991 Ind	1	0	0	—	0	7	42	6.0	0
1992 Pit	2	0	0	—	0	0	0	—	0
NFL Total	90	526	2355	4.5	19	226	2245	9.9	8

	Kickoff Returns					Tot
Year Team	Ret	Yds	Avg	TD	Fum	TD
1985 Ind	27	674	25.0	0	1	2
1986 Ind	32	687	21.5	0	2	3
1987 Ind	22	500	22.7	0	3	9
1988 Ind	39	775	19.9	0	2	3
1989 Ind	17	328	19.3	0	3	5
1990 Ind	11	211	19.2	0	2	6
1992 Pit	1	17	17.0	0	0	0
NFL Total	149	3192	21.4	0	13	28

RAY BENTLEY Bentley, Ray Russell 6'2", 240 **LB**
Col: Central Michigan *HS:* Hudsonville [MI] B: 11/25/1960, Grand Rapids, MI
1986 Buf: 13 G. **1987** Buf: 9 G; 1 Sac. **1988** Buf: 16 G; Int 1-0; 1 Sac. **1989** Buf: 15 G. **1990** Buf: 16 G; Int 1-13. **1991** Buf: 16 G; Int 1-58.

1992 Cin: 2 G; 1 Fum TD; 6 Pt. **Total:** 87 G; Int 3-71; 1 Fum TD; 6 Pt; 2 Sac.

SCOTT BENTLEY Bentley, Scott L 6'0", 203 **K**
Col: Florida State *HS:* Overland [Aurora, CO] B: 4/10/1974, Dallas, TX
1997 Den-Atl: 3 G; Scor 10, 2-3 66.7% FG, 4-4 100.0% XK. Den: 1 G; Scor 10, 2-3 66.7% FG, 4-4 100.0% XK. Atl: 2 G. **Total:** 3 G; Scor 10, 2-3 66.7% FG, 4-4 100.0% XK.

JIM BENTON Benton, James Warren 6'3", 200 **OE-DE**
(Big Jim) *Col:* Arkansas *HS:* Carthage [AR]; Pine Bluff HS [AR]; Fordyce HS [AR] B: 9/25/1916, Carthage, AR *Drafted:* 1938 Round 1 Cle
1938 Cle: **1** Fum TD. **1939** Cle: Rush 7-19 2.7. **1940** Cle: Rush 1-0. **1944** Cle: KR 2-4 2.0; 1 Fum TD. **1945** Cle: KR 3-16 5.3. **Total:** Rush 8-19 2.4; KR 5-20 4.0; 2 Fum TD.

		Receiving					Tot
Year Team	**G**	**Rec**	**Yds**	**Avg**	**TD**	**Fum**	**TD**
1938 Cle	11	21	418	19.9	5	0	6
1939 Cle	11	27	388	14.4	**7**	0	8
1940 Cle	10	22	351	16.0	3	0	3
1942 Cle	9	23	345	15.0	1	0	1
1943 ChiB	9	13	235	18.1	3	0	3
1944 Cle	10	39	505	12.9	6	0	7
1945 Cle	9	45	**1067**	23.7	8	2	8
1946 LARm	11	**63**	**981**	15.6	6	1	6
1947 LARm	11	35	511	14.6	6	1	6
NFL Total	91	288	4801	16.7	45	4	48

CHRIS BENTZ Bentz, Christian 6'4", 215 **T**
Col: Northern State; Montana *HS:* Central [Aberdeen, SD]
B: 12/20/1891, SD D: 1/1981, Spokane, WA
1920 Det: 2 G.

ROMAN BENTZ Bentz, Roman Walter 6'2", 230 **G-T**
(Grizz) *Col:* Tulane *HS:* Horicon [WI] B: 9/1/1919, Iron Ridge, WI D: 6/24/1996, Tomahawk, WI
AAFC **1946** NY-A: 12 G. **1947** NY-A: 13 G. **1948** NY-A-SF-A: 9 G. **Total:** 34 G.

AL BENTZIN Bentzin, Alfred Ernest 6'0", 188 **G**
(Mike) *Col:* Marquette *HS:* Watertown [WI]; Marquette Acad. [Milwaukee, WI] B: 3/7/1902, Watertown, WI D: 1/1979, Watertown, WI
1924 Rac: 10 G.

GEORGE BENYOLA Benyola, George 5'10", 195 **K**
Col: Kilgore Coll. TX (J.C.); Louisiana Tech *HS:* Allen [TX]
B: 9/17/1964, Perth Amboy, NJ
1987 NYG: 3 G; Scor 12, 3-5 60.0% FG, 3-3 100.0% XK.

EDDIE BENZ Benz, Edward G 5'7", 155 **OE**
(AKA Edward Bentz) *Col:* No College B: 2/11/1892, Buffalo, NY
D: 7/13/1971, Hamburg, NY
1922 Roch: 1 G.

LARRY BENZ Benz, Larry Walker 5'11", 185 **DB**
Col: Northwestern *HS:* Cleveland Heights [OH] B: 1/28/1941, Chattanooga, TN
1963 Cle: KR 1-0. **Total:** KR 1-0.

		Interceptions			
Year Team	**G**	**Int**	**Yds**	**TD**	**Fum**
1963 Cle	14	7	114	0	1
1964 Cle	13	4	67	0	0
1965 Cle	14	5	78	0	0
NFL Total	41	16	259	0	1

PETE BERCICH Bercich, Peter James 6'1", 240 **LB**
Col: Notre Dame *HS:* Providence [New Lenox, IL] B: 12/23/1971, Joliet, IL *Drafted:* 1994 Round 7 Min
1995 Min: 9 G. **1996** Min: 15 G. **1997** Min: 16 G. **1998** Min: 15 G. **Total:** 55 G.

BOB BERCICH Bercich, Robert Edward 6'1", 198 **DB**
Col: Michigan State *HS:* Argo [Summit, IL] B: 11/9/1936, Chicago, IL
Drafted: 1960 Round 1 LAC
1960 Dal: 12 G; Int 2-27. **1961** Dal: 6 G; Int 3-48. **Total:** 18 G; Int 5-75.

PAUL BEREZNEY Berezney, Paul Lawrence 6'2", 221 **T**
Col: Fordham *HS:* William L. Dickinson [Jersey City, NJ] B: 9/25/1915, Jersey City, NJ D: 3/29/1990, Columbus, GA
AAFC **1946** MiaA: 1 G.

NFL **1942** GB: 11 G; KR 1-7 7.0. **1943** GB: 10 G. **1944** GB: 10 G. **Total:** 31 G; KR 1-7 7.0.

PETE BEREZNEY Berezney, Peter John Jr. 6'2", 240 **T**
Col: Notre Dame *HS:* William L. Dickinson [Jersey City, NJ]
B: 11/14/1923, Jersey City, NJ
AAFC **1947** LA-A: 12 G. **1948** BalA: 13 G. **Total:** 25 G.

MITCH BERGER Berger, Mitchell Shannon 6'2", 224 **P**
Col: Tyler JC TX; Colorado *HS:* North Delta [Vancouver, Canada]
B: 6/24/1972, Kamloops, Canada *Drafted:* 1994 Round 6 Phi
1997 Min: Rush 1-0. **Total:** Rush 1-0.

		Punting			
Year Team	**G**	**Punts**	**Yds**	**Avg**	**Fum**
1994 Phi	5	25	951	38.0	0
1996 Min	16	88	3616	41.1	0
1997 Min	14	73	3133	42.9	1
1998 Min	16	55	2458	44.7	0
NFL Total	51	241	10158	42.1	1

RON BERGER Berger, Ronald C 6'8", 290 **DE**
Col: Wayne State (Neb.) *HS:* Edwin Denby [Detroit, MI] B: 9/30/1943, Detroit, MI
1969 Bos: 7 G; KR 1-20 20.0. **1970** Bos: 14 G. **1971** NE: 14 G. **1972** NE: 6 G. **Total:** 41 G; KR 1-20 20.0.

GIL BERGERSON Bergerson, Charles Gilbert 6'6", 245 **G-T**
Col: Oregon State *HS:* Vernonia [OR] B: 7/19/1910, Vernonia, OR
D: 9/18/1987, Corvallis, OR
1932 ChiB: 13 G. **1933** ChiB-ChiC: 10 G. ChiB: 2 G. ChiC: 8 G. **1935** Bkn: 12 G. **1936** Bkn: 5 G. **Total:** 40 G.

ERIC BERGESON Bergeson, Eric Scott 5'11", 192 **DB**
Col: Brigham Young *HS:* Timpview [Provo, UT] B: 1/1/1966, Salt Lake City, UT
1990 Atl: 13 G.

BRUCE BERGEY Bergey, Bruce Gene 6'4", 240 **DE**
Col: Glendale CC CA; UCLA *HS:* Pine Valley [South Dayton, NY]
B: 8/8/1946, South Dayton, NY *Drafted:* 1971 Round 14 KC
1971 KC-Hou: 7 G; KR 1-15 15.0. KC: 6 G; KR 1-15 15.0. Hou: 1 G. **Total:** 7 G; KR 1-15 15.0.

BILL BERGEY Bergey, William Earl 6'2", 243 **LB**
Col: Arkansas State *HS:* South Dayton [NY] B: 2/9/1945, South Dayton, NY *Drafted:* 1969 Round 2 Cin

		Interceptions		
Year Team	**G**	**Int**	**Yds**	**TD**
1969 Cin	14	2	62	0
1970 Cin	14	3	35	0
1971 Cin	14	1	16	0
1972 Cin	12	0	0	0
1973 Cin	14	3	50	0
1974 Phi	14	5	57	0
1975 Phi	14	3	48	0
1976 Phi	14	2	48	0
1977 Phi	14	2	4	0
1978 Phi	16	4	70	0
1979 Phi	3	1	0	0
1980 Phi	16	1	7	0
NFL Total	159	27	397	0

SCOTT BERGOLD Bergold, Scott M 6'7", 263 **OT**
Col: Wisconsin *HS:* West [Wauwatosa, WI] B: 11/19/1961, Milwaukee, WI *Drafted:* 1985 Round 2 StL
1985 StL: 16 G.

CHUCK BERNARD Bernard, Charles Jospeh 6'3", 225 **C-LB**
Col: Michigan *HS:* Benton Harbor [MI] B: 8/29/1911, Chicago, IL
D: 3/30/1962, Detroit, MI
1934 Det: 10 G.

DAVE BERNARD Bernard, David Edgar 5'10", 194 **LB-BB**
(King) *Col:* Mississippi *HS:* Central [Sioux City, IA] B: 9/26/1912, Jefferson, SD D: 7/17/1973, Montgomery, AL
1944 Cle: 8 G; Pass 4-0, 2 Int; Rush 1-6 6.0. **1945** Cle: 7 G; 1 Fum. **Total:** 15 G; Pass 4-0, 2 Int; Rush 1-6 6.0; 1 Fum.

GEORGE BERNARD Bernard, George **G-T**
Col: No College
1926 Rac: 4 G.

KARL BERNARD Bernard, Gregory Karl 5'11", 205 **RB**
Col: Louisiana State; Southwestern Louisiana *HS:* Baton Rouge Catholic [LA] B: 10/12/1964, New Orleans, LA
1987 Det: Rec 13-91 7.0; KR 4-54 13.5.

		Rushing				
Year Team	**G**	**Att**	**Yds**	**Avg**	**TD**	**Fum**
1987 Det	8	45	187	4.2	2	3

FRANK BERNARDI Bernardi, Frank Dominic 5'9", 181 **DB-HB**
Col: Colorado *HS:* Austin [Chicago, IL] B: 6/17/1933, Highwood, IL
Drafted: 1955 Round 4 ChiC
1955 ChiC: Rush 8-17 2.1; Rec 4-77 19.3 1 TD; Int 1-18. **1956** ChiC: Rush 14-4 0.3; Rec 4-56 14.0; KR 4-101 25.3; Int 1-2. **1957** ChiC: Pass 1-0; Rush 1-4 4.0; Rec 1-13 13.0; Int 2-40. **Total:** Pass 1-0; Rush 23-25 1.1; Rec 9-146 16.2 1 TD; KR 4-101 25.3; Int 4-60.

		Punt Returns					Tot
Year Team	**G**	**Ret**	**Yds**	**Avg**	**TD**	**Fum**	**TD**
1955 ChiC	11	19	163	8.6	0	2	1
1956 ChiC	12	18	217	12.1	**1**	0	1
1957 ChiC	12	2	12	6.0	0	0	0
1960 Den	6	0	0	—	0	0	0
NFL Total	41	39	392	10.1	1	2	2

MIL BERNER Berner, Milford C 6′2″, 204 **C-LB**
Col: Syracuse *HS:* St. Joseph's [Kenmore, NY] B: 7/8/1906
D: 12/17/1993, Schaumburg, IL
1933 Cin: 1 G.

ED BERNET Bernet, Edward Nelson 6′3″, 203 **OE**
Col: Southern Methodist *HS:* Highland Park [Dallas, TX]
B: 10/24/1933, Dallas, TX *Drafted:* 1955 Round 3 Pit

		Receiving				
Year Team	**G**	**Rec**	**Yds**	**Avg**	**TD**	**Fum**
1955 Pit	12	22	276	12.5	1	1
1960 DalT	9	4	49	12.3	0	0
NFL Total	21	26	325	12.5	1	1

LEE BERNET Bernet, Lee Anthony III 6′2″, 250 **OT**
Col: Wisconsin *HS:* Morgan Park [Chicago, IL] B: 1/24/1944, Chicago, IL
1965 Den: 14 G. **1966** Den: 14 G. **Total:** 28 G.

GEORGE BERNHARDT Bernhardt, George W 5′10″, 213 **G**
Col: Illinois *HS:* Riverside [IL]; Brookfield HS [IL] B: 6/15/1920
D: 12/1987
AAFC **1946** BknA: 14 G; KR 1-13 13.0. **1947** BknA: 2 G. **1948** BknA-ChiA: 14 G. **Total:** 30 G; KR 1-13 13.0.

ROGER BERNHARDT Bernhardt, Roger Ernest 6′4″, 244 **OG**
Col: Butler County CC KS; Kansas *HS:* Lyons [NY] B: 10/14/1949, Lyons, NY *Drafted:* 1973 Round 3 Pit
1974 NYJ: 14 G. **1975** KC: 4 G. **Total:** 18 G.

KENNETH BERNICH Bernich, Kenneth Overton 6′2″, 250 **LB**
Col: Auburn *HS:* Archbishop Shaw [Marrero, LA] B: 9/6/1951, Biloxi, MS *Drafted:* 1975 Round 4 SD
1975 NYJ: 5 G.

DAN BERNOSKE Bernoske, Daniel Gabriel 5′10″, 190 **G**
Col: Indiana *HS:* Michigan City [IN] B: 7/20/1905, Michigan City, IN
D: 6/29/1979, Indianapolis, IN
1926 Lou: 2 G.

RICK BERNS Berns, Richard Ricky 6′2″, 205 **RB**
Col: Nebraska *HS:* Wichita Falls [TX] B: 2/5/1956, Kadina AFB, Okinawa *Drafted:* 1979 Round 3 TB
1979 TB: Rec 5-40 8.0; KR 1-6 6.0. **1980** TB: Rec 1-6 6.0; KR 1-19 19.0. **Total:** Rec 6-46 7.7; KR 2-25 12.5.

		Rushing				
Year Team	**G**	**Att**	**Yds**	**Avg**	**TD**	**Fum**
1979 TB	16	23	102	4.4	0	0
1980 TB	16	39	131	3.4	0	2
1982 LARd	2	0	0	—	0	0
1983 LARd	16	6	22	3.7	0	0
NFL Total	50	68	255	3.8	0	2

BOBBY BERNS Berns, William Jennings 6′1″, 200 **G-T**
Col: Purdue B: 12/10/1895, Linton, IN D: 7/22/1980, Greenwood, IN
1920 Mun: 1 G. **1922** Day: 6 G. **1923** Day: 8 G. **1924** Day: 1 G. **Total:** 16 G.

JOE BERNSTEIN Bernstein, Joseph G 6′0″, 210 **FB-G-T**
(AKA Joe Burten) *Col:* Louisiana State; Tulsa B: 11/23/1893, Elmira, NY D: 3/28/1967, Orange, NJ
1921 NYG: 1 G. **1923** RI: 5 G. **1924** RI: 5 G. **Total:** 11 G.

ROD BERNSTINE Bernstine, Rod Earl 6′3″, 238 **RB-TE**
Col: Texas A&M *HS:* Bryan [TX] B: 2/8/1965, Fairfield, CA
Drafted: 1987 Round 1 SD
1987 SD: KR 1-13 13.0. **1991** SD: Pass 1-1 100.0%, 11 11.00 1 TD; KR 1-7 7.0. **Total:** Pass 1-1 100.0%, 11 11.00 1 TD; KR 2-20 10.0.

		Rushing				Receiving					Tot
Year Team	**G**	**Att**	**Yds**	**Avg**	**TD**	**Rec**	**Yds**	**Avg**	**TD**	**Fum**	**TD**
1987 SD	10	1	9	9.0	0	10	76	7.6	1	0	1
1988 SD	14	2	7	3.5	0	29	340	11.7	0	0	0
1989 SD	5	15	137	9.1	1	21	222	10.6	1	0	2
1990 SD	12	124	589	4.8	4	8	40	5.0	0	1	4
1991 SD	13	159	766	4.8	8	11	124	11.3	0	1	8
1992 SD	9	106	499	4.7	4	12	86	7.2	0	2	4
1993 Den	15	223	816	3.7	4	44	372	8.5	0	3	4
1994 Den	3	17	91	5.4	0	9	70	7.8	0	0	0
1995 Den	3	23	76	3.3	1	5	54	10.8	0	0	1
NFL Total	84	670	2990	4.5	22	149	1384	9.3	2	7	24

JAY BERQUIST Berquist, Jay Theodore John 6′3″, 235 **G**
Col: Nebraska *HS:* Lincoln [NE]; Holdrege HS [NE] B: 7/30/1901, Loomis, NE
1924 KC: 9 G. **1926** KC: 9 G. **1927** ChiC: 1 G. **Total:** 19 G.

TIM BERRA Berra, Timothy Thomas 5′11″, 185 **WR**
Col: Massachusetts *HS:* Montclair [NJ]; Seton Hall Prep [South Orange, NJ] B: 9/23/1951, Montclair, NJ *Drafted:* 1974 Round 17 Bal
1974 Bal: 14 G; PR 16-114 7.1; KR 13-259 19.9; 2 Fum.

ED BERRANG Berrang, Edward Patrick 6′2″, 206 **DE-OE**
Col: Villanova *HS:* Blythe Twp. [New Philadelphia, PA]; N.Y. Mil. Acad. [Cornwall-on-Hudson, NY] B: 10/14/1922, Philadelphia, PA
D: 7/3/1992, Kensington, MD *Drafted:* 1949 Round 5 Was
1949 Was: 11 G; Rec 1-5 5.0. **1950** Was: 11 G; Rec 1-14 14.0. **1951** Was-Det: 12 G; Int 1-14. Was: 2 G. Det: 10 G; Int 1-14. **1952** GB-Was: 8 G; Int 2-4. GB: 1 G. Was: 7 G; Int 2-4. **Total:** 42 G; Rec 2-19 9.5; Int 3-18.

BILL BERREHSEM Berrehsem, William Stewart 5′10″, 195 **T-E**
Col: Washington & Jefferson *HS:* Linsly Mil. Inst. [Wheeling, WV]
B: 4/25/1903 D: 11/6/1968, Baldwin, PA
1926 Col: 6 G.

BERT BERRY Berry, Bertrand Demond 6′2″, 248 **LB**
Col: Notre Dame *HS:* Humble [TX] B: 8/15/1975, Houston, TX
Drafted: 1997 Round 3 Ind
1997 Ind: 10 G. **1998** Ind: 16 G; 4 Sac. **Total:** 26 G; 4 Sac.

CHARLIE BERRY Berry, Charles Francis 6′0″, 185 **OE**
Col: Lafayette *HS:* Phillipsburg [NJ] B: 10/18/1902, Phillipsburg, NJ
D: 9/6/1972, Evanston, IL
1925 Pott: 10 G; Rec **4** TD; Scor **74**, 3 FG, **29** XK; Tot TD 6. **1926** Pott: 10 G; Rec 2 TD; 1 Fum TD; Tot TD 3; 18 Pt. **Total:** 20 G; Rec 6 TD; Scor 92, 3 FG, 29 XK; 1 Fum TD; Tot TD 9.

REX BERRY Berry, Charles Rex 5′11″, 190 **DB-HB**
(Carbon Comet) *Col:* Coll. of Eastern Utah (J.C.); Brigham Young
HS: Carbon [Price, UT] B: 9/9/1924, Moab, UT *Drafted:* 1951 Round 14 SF
1951 SF: Rec 1-12 12.0. **1952** SF: Rush 1-7 7.0. **1953** SF: PR 7-42 6.0; KR 1-37 37.0. **1955** SF: PR 1-11 11.0. **Total:** Rush 1-7 7.0; Rec 1-12 12.0; PR 8-53 6.6; KR 1-37 37.0.

		Interceptions			
Year Team	**G**	**Int**	**Yds**	**TD**	**Fum**
1951 SF	10	4	77	0	0
1952 SF	12	2	27	0	0
1953 SF	12	7	142	**1**	1
1954 SF	8	3	69	1	0
1955 SF	12	3	69	1	0
1956 SF	12	3	20	0	1
NFL Total	66	22	404	3	2

CONNIE MACK BERRY Berry, Connie Mack 6′3″, 215 **DE-OE**
(Warhouse) *Col:* North Carolina State *HS:* Parker [Spartanburg, SC]
B: 4/19/1915, Spartanburg, SC D: 6/24/1980, Fayetteville, NC
AAFC **1947** ChiA: 1 G.

NFL **1942** ChiB: **1** Fum TD. **Total:** 1 Fum TD.

		Receiving				Tot
Year Team	**G**	**Rec**	**Yds**	**Avg**	**TD**	**TD**
1939 Det	3	0	0	—	0	0
1940 GB-Cle	4	1	17	17.0	0	0
1940 GB	1	1	17	17.0	0	0
1940 Cle	3	0	0	—	0	0
1942 ChiB	10	4	29	7.3	0	2
1943 ChiB	10	4	99	24.8	2	2
1944 ChiB	10	21	378	18.0	6	6
1945 ChiB	7	12	202	16.8	0	0
1946 ChiB	6	4	58	14.5	0	0
NFL Total	50	46	783	17.0	8	10

ED BERRY Berry, Edward Jr. 5′10″, 183 **DB**
Col: Utah State *HS:* Carlmont [Belmont, CA] B: 9/28/1963, San Francisco, CA *Drafted:* 1986 Round 7 GB
1986 GB: 16 G; KR 1-16 16.0. **1987** SD: 2 G. **Total:** 18 G; KR 1-16 16.0.

GEORGE BERRY Berry, George W 5′11″, 203 **G-T-C**
Col: No College B: 2/18/1900, Milwaukee, WI D: 3/25/1986, Half Moon Bay, CA
1922 Rac-Ham: 6 G. Rac: 2 G. Ham: 4 G. **1923** Ham: 7 G. **1924** Ham-Akr: 8 G. Ham: 5 G. Akr: 3 G. **1925** Akr: 5 G; Int 1 TD; 6 Pt. **1926** Akr-Ham: 9 G. Akr: 8 G. Ham: 1 G. **Total:** 35 G; Int 1 TD; 6 Pt.

GIL BERRY Berry, Gilbert Irwin 5′10″, 178 **TB-DB**
Col: Illinois *HS:* Abingdon [IL] B: 3/21/1911, Lewistown, IL
D: 4/20/1974, Indianapolis., IN
1935 ChiC: Pass 4-0, 1 Int.

Year Team	G	Rushing Att	Yds	Avg	TD
1935 ChiC	6	44	77	1.8	0

HOWARD BERRY Berry, Joseph Howard Jr. 5'11", 165 **TB-WB**
(Nig) *Col:* Muhlenberg *HS:* Northeast [Philadelphia, PA]
B: 12/31/1894, Philadelphia, PA D: 4/29/1976, Philadelphia, PA
1921 Roch: 4 G; Rec 1 TD; Int **1** TD; Scor 20, 2 FG, 2 XK; Tot TD 2.

LATIN BERRY Berry, Latin Dafonso 5'10", 196 **DB**
Col: Oregon *HS:* Milwaukie [OR] B: 1/13/1967, Lakeview Terrace, CA
Drafted: 1990 Round 3 LARm
1990 LARm: 16 G; KR 17-315 18.5. **1991** Cle: 15 G. **1992** Cle: 1 G.
Total: 32 G; KR 17-315 18.5.

LOUIS BERRY Berry, Louis Albert 6'0", 193 **P**
Col: Florida State *HS:* A. Crawford Mosley [Lynn Haven, FL]
B: 7/21/1965, Hattiesburg, MS
1987 Atl: 2 G; Punt 7-258 36.9.

RAYMOND BERRY Berry, Raymond Emmett 6'2", 187 **OE**
Col: Schreiner Coll.; Southern Methodist *HS:* Paris [TX] B: 2/27/1933, Corpus Christi, TX *Drafted:* 1954 Round 20 Bal *HOF:* 1973
1955 Bal: KR 2-27 13.5. **Total:** KR 2-27 13.5.

Year Team	G	Receiving Rec	Yds	Avg	TD	Fum	Tot TD
1955 Bal	12	13	205	15.8	0	0	0
1956 Bal	12	37	601	16.2	2	0	2
1957 Bal	12	47	**800**	17.0	6	0	6
1958 Bal	12	**56**	794	14.2	**9**	0	9
1959 Bal	12	**66**	**959**	14.5	**14**	0	**14**
1960 Bal	12	**74**	**1298**	17.5	10	0	10
1961 Bal	12	75	873	11.6	0	0	0
1962 Bal	14	51	687	13.5	3	1	3
1963 Bal	9	44	703	16.0	3	0	3
1964 Bal	12	43	663	15.4	6	0	6
1965 Bal	14	58	739	12.7	7	0	7
1966 Bal	14	56	786	14.0	7	0	7
1967 Bal	7	11	167	15.2	1	0	1
NFL Total	154	631	9275	14.7	68	1	68

RAY BERRY Berry, Raymond Lenn 6'2", 227 **LB**
Col: Baylor *HS:* Cooper [Abilene, TX] B: 10/28/1963, Lovington, NM
Drafted: 1987 Round 2 Min
1987 Min: 11 G. **1988** Min: 15 G. **1989** Min: 16 G; Scor **1** Saf; 2 Pt; 3 Sac. **1990** Min: 16 G. **1991** Min: 16 G; Int 1-11; 1 Sac. **1992** Min: 8 G. **1993** Sea: 7 G. **Total:** 89 G; Int 1-11; Scor 1 Saf; 2 Pt; 4 Sac.

REGGIE BERRY Berry, Reginald Dennis 6'0", 190 **DB**
Col: Arizona Western Coll. (J.C.); Long Beach State *HS:* Central [Minneapolis, MN] B: 3/13/1950, Minneapolis, MN
1972 SD: 9 G; KR 7-138 19.7; 1 Fum. **1973** SD: 8 G. **1974** SD: 13 G.
Total: 30 G; KR 7-138 19.7; 1 Fum.

BOB BERRY Berry, Robert Chadwick 5'11", 185 **QB**
Col: Oregon *HS:* San Jose [CA] B: 3/10/1942, San Jose, CA
Drafted: 1964 Round 11 Phi
1972 Atl: Rec 1-(-9) -9.0. **1976** Min: Postseason only. **Total:** Rec 1-(-9) -9.0.

Year Team	G	Passing Att	Comp	Comp%	Yds	YPA	TD	Int	Rating
1965 Min	2	2	0	0.0	0	0.00	0	0	39.6
1966 Min	3	37	13	35.1	215	5.81	1	5	25.0
1967 Min	2	7	3	42.9	43	6.14	0	0	63.4
1968 Atl	10	153	81	52.9	1433	9.37	7	13	65.1
1969 Atl	7	124	71	57.3	1087	8.77	10	2	106.5
1970 Atl	12	269	156	58.0	1806	6.71	16	13	78.1
1971 Atl	11	226	136	60.2	2005	8.87	11	16	75.9
1972 Atl	14	277	154	55.6	2158	7.79	13	12	78.5
1973 Min	6	24	10	41.7	121	5.04	1	2	37.0
1974 Min	10	48	34	70.8	305	6.35	5	1	113.6
1975 Min	1	6	3	50.0	24	4.00	0	0	60.4
NFL Total	78	1173	661	56.4	9197	7.84	64	64	77.2

Year Team	Rushing Att	Yds	Avg	TD	Fum
1966 Min	3	12	4.0	0	0
1967 Min	0	0	—	0	1
1968 Atl	26	139	5.3	2	5
1969 Atl	20	68	3.4	0	6
1970 Atl	13	60	4.6	0	6
1971 Atl	19	31	1.6	0	4
1972 Atl	24	86	3.6	2	7
1973 Min	2	5	2.5	0	0
1974 Min	1	8	8.0	0	0
1975 Min	1	0	0.0	0	1
NFL Total	109	409	3.8	4	30

ROYCE BERRY Berry, Royce Elmer 6'4", 250 **DE**
Col: Houston *HS:* Odessa [TX] B: 4/14/1946, Odessa, TX
Drafted: 1969 Round 7 Cin
1969 Cin: 13 G. **1970** Cin: 14 G; **2** Fum TD; 12 Pt. **1971** Cin: 14 G. **1972** Cin: 14 G. **1973** Cin: 14 G. **1974** Cin: 13 G. **1976** ChiB: 12 G.
Total: 94 G; 2 Fum TD; 12 Pt.

WAYNE BERRY Berry, Wayne Chandler 6'0", 175 **HB-DB**
Col: Washington State *HS:* La Grande [OR] B: 8/2/1931, LaGrande, OR *Drafted:* 1954 Round 7 NYG
1954 NYG: 10 G; Rush 1-30 30.0.

MARV BERSCHET Berschet, Marvin Walter 6'2", 220 **OG-DE**
(Moose) *Col:* Illinois *HS:* Arlington [Arlington Heights, IL]
B: 12/28/1929, Arlington Hgts, IL *Drafted:* 1952 Round 16 Was
1954 Was: 12 G. **1955** Was: 4 G. **Total:** 16 G.

LIBBY BERTAGNOLLI Bertagnolli, Libero Lorenz 5'9", 189 **G-LB**
(Bert) *Col:* Washington-St. Louis *HS:* Benld [IL] B: 11/13/1914, Benld, IL D: 9/14/1992, Bloomington, IL
1942 ChiC: 10 G. **1945** ChiC: 1 G. **Total:** 11 G.

ANGELO BERTELLI Bertelli, Angelo Bortolo **QB**
(Springfield Rifle) *Col:* Notre Dame *HS:* Cathedral [Springfield, MA]
B: 6/18/1921, West Springfield, MA
AAFC **1946** LA-A: Rush 11-(-16) -1.5 1 TD; Punt 2-76 38.0. **1947** ChiA: Rush 1-2 2.0; Scor 0-1 FG. **1948** ChiA: Rush 2-(-1) -0.5.
Total: Rush 14-(-15) -1.1 1 TD; Punt 2-76 38.0; Scor 6, 0-1 FG.

Year Team	G	Passing Att	Comp	Comp%	Yds	YPA	TD	Int	Rating
1946 LA-A	12	127	67	52.8	917	7.22	7	14	54.9
1947 ChiA	1	7	2	28.6	-5	-0.71	0	2	0.0
1948 ChiA	3	32	7	21.9	60	1.88	1	3	10.9
AAFC Total	16	166	76	45.8	972	5.86	8	19	41.1

JIM BERTELSEN Bertelsen, James Allen 5'11", 205 **RB**
Col: Texas *HS:* Hudson [WI] B: 2/26/1950, St. Paul, MN
Drafted: 1972 Round 2 LARm
1972 LARm: KR 4-88 22.0. **1973** LARm: KR 1-15 15.0. **1975** LARm: KR 1-17 17.0. **Total:** KR 6-120 20.0.

Year Team	G	Rushing Att	Yds	Avg	TD	Receiving Rec	Yds	Avg	TD
1972 LARm	14	123	581	4.7	5	29	331	11.4	1
1973 LARm	14	206	854	4.1	4	19	267	14.1	1
1974 LARm	13	127	419	3.3	2	20	175	8.8	0
1975 LARm	13	116	457	3.9	3	14	208	14.9	0
1976 LARm	14	42	155	3.7	2	6	33	5.5	0
NFL Total	68	614	2466	4.0	16	88	1014	11.5	2

Year Team	Punt Returns Ret	Yds	Avg	TD	Fum	Tot TD
1972 LARm	16	232	14.5	0	4	6
1973 LARm	26	259	10.0	0	4	5
1974 LARm	11	132	12.0	0	4	2
1975 LARm	11	143	13.0	0	2	3
1976 LARm	10	55	5.5	0	3	2
NFL Total	74	821	11.1	0	17	18

BILL BERTHUSEN Berthusen, William Scott 6'5", 290 **NT**
Col: Iowa State *HS:* Marshalltown [IA] B: 6/26/1964, Grinnell, IA
Drafted: 1987 Round 12 NYG
1987 Cin-NYG: 4 G; 2.5 Sac. Cin: 3 G; 2.5 Sac. NYG: 1 G. **Total:** 4 G; 2.5 Sac.

TONY BERTI Berti, Charles Anton Jr. 6'6", 300 **OT**
Col: Colorado *HS:* Skyview [Thorton, CO] B: 6/21/1972, Rock Springs, WY *Drafted:* 1995 Round 6 SD
1995 SD: 1 G. **1996** SD: 16 G. **1997** SD: 16 G. **Total:** 33 G.

JIM BERTOGLIO Bertoglio, James Emory 5'9", 187 **FB-WB**
Col: Creighton *HS:* Butte [MT] B: 9/1/1905, Meaderville, MT
D: 1/14/1976, Salt Lake City, UT
1926 Col: 7 G; Rush 1 TD; 6 Pt.

TONY BERTUCA Bertuca, Anthony Francis 6'2", 225 **LB**
Col: Wenatchee Valley Coll. WA (J.C.); Cal State-Chico *HS:* St. Patrick [Chicago, IL] B: 1/4/1950, Chicago, IL
1974 Bal: 14 G; PR 1-0.

ED BERWICK Berwick, Edwin J 6'0", 185 **C-OE**
Col: Loyola (Chicago) Deceased
1926 Lou: 4 G.

WILL BERZINSKI Berzinski, Willis John 6'2", 195 **HB**
Col: Wis.-La Crosse *HS:* Arcadia [WI] B: 7/18/1934, Arcadia, WI
D: 3/4/1994, Rochester, MN *Drafted:* 1956 Round 4 LARm
1956 Phi: 4 G; Rush 15-72 4.8; Rec 3-35 11.7; 1 Fum.

WARREN BESON Beson, Warren Lawson 6'0", 205 **C**
Col: Minnesota *HS:* West [Minneapolis, MN] B: 11/16/1923, Minneapolis, MN D: 10/25/1959, Northfield, MN
AAFC **1949** BalA: 3 G.

GERALD BESS Bess, Gerald D 6'0", 188 **DB**
Col: Tuskegee B: 5/24/1958, Pensacola, FL
1987 Buf: 2 G.

RUFUS BESS Bess, Rufus T Jr. 5'9", 184 **DB**
Col: South Carolina State *HS:* Butler [Hartsville, SC] B: 9/13/1956, Darlington, SC
1982 Min: 0.5 Sac. **1984** Min: 1 Sac. **1985** Min: 1 Sac. **Total:** 2.5 Sac.

		Punt Returns				Kickoff Returns			
Year Team	**G**	**Ret**	**Yds**	**Avg**	**TD**	**Ret**	**Yds**	**Avg**	**TD**
1979 Oak	16	0	0	—	0	0	0	—	0
1980 Buf	16	0	0	—	0	0	0	—	0
1981 Buf	16	0	0	—	0	1	6	6.0	0
1982 Min	8	2	17	8.5	0	0	0	—	0
1983 Min	14	21	158	7.5	0	2	44	22.0	0
1984 Min	16	2	9	4.5	0	3	47	15.7	0
1985 Min	11	0	0	—	0	2	33	16.5	0
1986 Min	16	23	162	7.0	0	31	705	22.7	0
1987 Min	3	7	86	12.3	0	10	169	16.9	0
NFL Total	116	55	432	7.9	0	49	1004	20.5	0

	Interceptions			
Year Team	**Int**	**Yds**	**TD**	**Fum**
1979 Oak	1	0	0	0
1981 Buf	1	12	0	0
1983 Min	3	38	0	2
1984 Min	3	7	0	1
1985 Min	2	27	0	0
1986 Min	1	12	0	3
1987 Min	0	0	0	4
NFL Total	11	96	0	10

DON BESSILLIEU Bessillieu, Donald Andrew 6'1", 200 **DB**
Col: Georgia Tech *HS:* Kendrick [Columbus, GA] B: 5/4/1956, Fort Benning, GA *Drafted:* 1979 Round 5 Mia
1980 Mia: PR 1-0; Int 4-13; **1** Fum TD. **1981** Mia: PR 1-12 12.0; Int 1-0. **Total:** PR 2-12 6.0; Int 5-13; 1 Fum TD.

		Kickoff Returns				
Year Team	**G**	**Ret**	**Yds**	**Avg**	**TD**	**Fum**
1979 Mia	16	0	20	—	0	0
1980 Mia	16	40	890	22.3	0	4
1981 Mia	16	7	114	16.3	0	1
1982 StL	3	0	0	—	0	0
1983 LARd	4	0	0	—	0	0
1985 LARd	4	0	0	—	0	0
NFL Total	59	47	1024	21.8	0	5

ART BEST Best, Arthur Robie 6'1", 205 **RB**
Col: Notre Dame; Kent State *HS:* Bishop Hartley [Columbus, OH] B: 3/18/1953, Camden, NJ *Drafted:* 1977 Round 6 LARm
1977 ChiB: 14 G; Rush 6-20 3.3; KR 6-127 21.2; 2 Fum. **1978** ChiB: 16 G; Rush 2-11 5.5. **1980** NYG: 1 G. **Total:** 31 G; Rush 8-31 3.9; KR 6-127 21.2; 2 Fum.

GREG BEST Best, Gregory Lee 5'10", 185 **DB**
Col: Kansas State *HS:* Black Hawk [Beaver Falls, PA] B: 1/14/1960, New Brighton, PA
1983 Pit: 13 G; 1 Fum TD; 6 Pt. **1984** Cle: 5 G. **Total:** 18 G; 1 Fum TD; 6 Pt.

KEITH BEST Best, Keith Alan 6'3", 220 **LB**
Col: Kansas State *HS:* McKinley [Canton, OH] B: 8/21/1950, Canton, OH
1972 KC: 6 G.

TEDDY BESTA Besta, Theodore James **WB**
Col: No College *HS:* Crane Tech [Chicago, IL]; Harrison HS [Chicago, IL] B: 9/25/1899, Chicago, IL D: 7/1965, IL
1922 Ham: 1 G. **1924** Ham: 2 G. **Total:** 3 G.

ELVIN BETHEA Bethea, Elvin Lamont 6'2", 260 **DE**
Col: North Carolina A&T *HS:* Trenton Central [NJ] B: 3/1/1946, Trenton, NJ *Drafted:* 1968 Round 3 Hou
1968 Hou: 14 G. **1969** Hou: 14 G; Scor **1** Saf; 2 Pt. **1970** Hou: 14 G. **1971** Hou: 14 G. **1972** Hou: 14 G. **1973** Hou: 14 G. **1974** Hou: 14 G; 1 Fum TD; 6 Pt. **1975** Hou: 14 G; Scor **1** Saf; 2 Pt. **1976** Hou: 14 G. **1977** Hou: 9 G. **1978** Hou: 16 G. **1979** Hou: 14 G. **1980** Hou: 14 G. **1981** Hou: 15 G. **1982** Hou: 9 G; 1 Sac. **1983** Hou: 7 G. **Total:** 210 G; Scor 2 Saf; 1 Fum TD; 10 Pt; 1 Sac.

LARRY BETHEA Bethea, Larry 6'5", 251 **DT-DE**
Col: Michigan State *HS:* Ferguson [Newport News, VA] B: 7/21/1956, Florence, SC D: 4/23/1987, Newport News, VA *Drafted:* 1978 Round 1 Dal
1978 Dal: 16 G. **1979** Dal: 16 G. **1980** Dal: 11 G. **1981** Dal: 16 G. **1982** Dal: 8 G; 2 Sac. **1983** Dal: 14 G; 3 Sac. **Total:** 81 G; 5 Sac.

BOBBY BETHUNE Bethune, Bobby Wayne 5'11", 190 **DB**
Col: Mississippi State *HS:* Leeds [AL] B: 12/10/1938, Leeds, AL *Drafted:* 1961 Round 9 ChiB
1962 SD: 10 G; KR 12-251 20.9; Int 3-6.

GEORGE BETHUNE Bethune, George Edward 6'4", 238 **LB**
Col: Alabama *HS:* Choctawhatchee [Fort Walton Beach, FL] B: 3/30/1967, Fort Walton Beach, FL *Drafted:* 1989 Round 7 LARm
1989 LARm: 16 G; 2 Sac. **1990** LARm: 16 G; 2 Sac. **Total:** 32 G; 4 Sac.

LARRY BETTENCOURT Bettencourt, Lawrence Joseph 5'11", 205 **C-LB**
Col: St. Mary's (Cal.) *HS:* Washington Union [Centerville, CA] B: 9/22/1905, Newark, CA D: 9/15/1978, New Orleans, LA
1933 GB: 2 G.

DOUG BETTERS Betters, Douglas Lloyd 6'7", 262 **DE**
Col: Montana; Nevada-Reno *HS:* Arlington [Arlington Heights, IL] B: 6/11/1956, Lincoln, NE *Drafted:* 1978 Round 6 Mia
1978 Mia: 16 G. **1979** Mia: 16 G. **1980** Mia: 16 G. **1981** Mia: 15 G. **1982** Mia: 9 G; 4 Sac. **1983** Mia: 16 G; 16 Sac. **1984** Mia: 16 G; 14 Sac. **1985** Mia: 14 G; 5.5 Sac. **1986** Mia: 16 G; 4 Sac. **1987** Mia: 12 G. **Total:** 146 G; 43.5 Sac.

JAMES BETTERSON Betterson, James Thomas 6'0", 210 **RB**
Col: North Carolina *HS:* High Point Central [NC] B: 8/20/1954, Blackshear, GA *Drafted:* 1976 Round 8 Den
1977 Phi: Rec 4-41 10.3; KR 1-13 13.0. **1978** Phi: Rec 2-8 4.0; KR 7-185 26.4. **Total:** Rec 6-49 8.2; KR 8-198 24.8.

		Rushing				
Year Team	**G**	**Att**	**Yds**	**Avg**	**TD**	**Fum**
1977 Phi	14	62	233	3.8	1	2
1978 Phi	9	11	32	2.9	0	1
NFL Total	23	73	265	3.6	1	3

MIKE BETTIGA Bettiga, Michael John 6'3", 193 **WR**
Col: Coll of the Redwoods CA (J.C.); Humboldt State *HS:* Fortuna Union [CA] B: 9/10/1950, Scotia, CA *Drafted:* 1973 Round 15 SF
1974 SF: 10 G.

JEROME BETTIS Bettis, Jerome Abram 5'11", 243 **RB**
(The Bus) *Col:* Notre Dame *HS:* MacKenzie [Detroit, MI] B: 2/16/1972, Detroit, MI *Drafted:* 1993 Round 1 LARm
1994 LARm: Scor 2 2XP. **Total:** Scor 2 2XP.

		Rushing				Receiving					Tot
Year Team	**G**	**Att**	**Yds**	**Avg**	**TD**	**Rec**	**Yds**	**Avg**	**TD**	**Fum**	**TD**
1993 LARm	16	294	1429	4.9	7	26	244	9.4	0	4	7
1994 LARm	16	319	1025	3.2	3	31	293	9.5	1	5	4
1995 StL	15	183	637	3.5	3	18	106	5.9	0	4	3
1996 Pit	16	320	1431	4.5	11	22	122	5.5	0	7	11
1997 Pit	15	**375**	1665	4.4	7	15	110	7.3	2	6	9
1998 Pit	15	316	1185	3.8	3	16	90	5.6	0	2	3
NFL Total	93	1807	7372	4.1	34	128	965	7.5	3	28	37

TOM BETTIS Bettis, William Thomas 6'2", 228 **LB**
Col: Purdue *HS:* St. Mel's [Chicago, IL] B: 3/17/1933, Chicago, IL *Drafted:* 1955 Round 1 GB
1955 GB: 12 G. **1956** GB: 12 G. **1957** GB: 12 G. **1958** GB: 12 G. **1959** GB: 12 G; Int 1-0. **1960** GB: 12 G. **1961** GB: 12 G. **1962** Pit: 11 G. **1963** ChiB: 14 G. **Total:** 109 G; Int 1-0.

ED BETTRIDGE Bettridge, Edward N 6'1", 235 **LB**
Col: Bowling Green State *HS:* Sandusky [OH] B: 9/16/1940, Sandusky, OH
1964 Cle: 3 G.

JOHN BETTRIDGE Bettridge, John William 5'10", 188 **FB-LB**
Col: Ohio State *HS:* Sandusky [OH] B: 3/19/1910, Sandusky, OH D: 12/10/1975, Sandusky, OH
1937 ChiB-Cle: 9 G; Rush 22-35 1.6; Rec 1-17 17.0. ChiB: 3 G; Rush 1-0. Cle: 6 G; Rush 21-35 1.7; Rec 1-17 17.0. **Total:** 9 G; Rush 22-35 1.6; Rec 1-17 17.0.

STEVE BEUERLEIN Beuerlein, Stephen Taylor 6'3", 210 **QB**
Col: Notre Dame *HS:* Servite [Anaheim, CA] B: 3/7/1965, Hollywood, CA *Drafted:* 1987 Round 4 LARd
1988 LARd: Rec 1-21 21.0. **Total:** Rec 1-21 21.0.

		Passing							
Year Team	**G**	**Att**	**Comp**	**Comp%**	**Yds**	**YPA**	**TD**	**Int**	**Rating**
1988 LARd	10	238	105	44.1	1643	6.90	8	**7**	66.6
1989 LARd	10	217	108	49.8	1677	7.73	13	9	78.4
1991 Dal	8	137	68	49.6	909	6.64	5	2	77.2

1992 Dal	16	18	12	66.7	152	8.44	0	1	69.7
1993 Pho	16	418	258	61.7	3164	7.57	18	17	82.5
1994 Ariz	9	255	130	51.0	1545	6.06	5	9	61.6
1995 Jac	7	142	71	50.0	952	6.70	4	7	60.5
1996 Car	8	123	69	56.1	879	7.15	8	2	93.5
1997 Car	7	153	89	58.2	1032	6.75	6	3	83.6
1998 Car	12	343	216	63.0	2613	7.62	17	12	88.2
NFL Total	103	2044	1126	55.1	14566	7.13	84	69	77.3

	Rushing				
Year Team	**Att**	**Yds**	**Avg**	**TD**	**Fum**
1988 LARd	30	35	1.2	0	6
1989 LARd	16	39	2.4	0	6
1991 Dal	7	-14	-2.0	0	0
1992 Dal	4	-7	-1.8	0	0
1993 Pho	22	45	2.0	0	8
1994 Ariz	22	39	1.8	1	8
1995 Jac	5	32	6.4	0	3
1996 Car	12	17	1.4	0	9
1997 Car	4	32	8.0	0	1
1998 Car	22	26	1.2	0	13
NFL Total	144	244	1.7	1	54

TOM BEUTLER Beutler, Thomas Joseph 6′1″, 234 **LB**
(Bullets) *Col:* Toledo *HS:* Central Catholic [Toledo, OH] B: 9/29/1946, Bluffton, OH *Drafted:* 1968 Round 12 Cle
1970 Cle: 4 G. **1971** Bal: 4 G. **Total:** 8 G.

DAVID BEVERLY Beverly, David Edward 6′2″, 180 **P**
Col: Auburn *HS:* Sweet Water [AL] B: 8/19/1950, Selma, AL
1974 Hou: Rush 1-4 4.0. **1976** GB: Pass 1-1 100.0%, 18 18.00. **1977** GB: Rush 2-(-3) -1.5. **1978** GB: Pass 2-2 100.0%, 88 44.00; Rush 1-0. **1979** GB: Pass 2-1 50.0%, 23 11.50. **1980** GB: Pass 1-0; Rush 6-21 3.5. **Total:** Pass 6-4 66.7%, 129 21.50; Rush 10-22 2.2.

		Punting			
Year Team	**G**	**Punts**	**Yds**	**Avg**	**Fum**
1974 Hou	14	79	3100	39.2	0
1975 Hou-GB	12	78	2941	37.7	0
1975 Hou	2	12	459	38.3	0
1975 GB	10	66	2482	37.6	0
1976 GB	14	83	3074	37.0	0
1977 GB	14	85	3391	39.9	1
1978 GB	16	106	3759	35.5	1
1979 GB	16	69	2785	40.4	0
1980 GB	16	86	3294	38.3	1
NFL Total	102	586	22344	38.1	3

DWIGHT BEVERLY Beverly, Dwight Anthony 5′11″, 205 **RB**
Col: Illinois *HS:* Alain Leroy Locke [Los Angeles, CA] B: 12/5/1961, Long Beach, CA
1987 NO: Rec 1-8 8.0; KR 3-46 15.3.

		Rushing				
Year Team	**G**	**Att**	**Yds**	**Avg**	**TD**	**Fum**
1987 NO	3	62	217	3.5	2	1

ED BEVERLY Beverly, Edward Louis Jr. 5′11″, 172 **WR**
Col: Arizona State *HS:* John Harris [Harrisburg, PA] B: 9/27/1949, Harrisburg, PA *Drafted:* 1973 Round 5 SF
1973 SF: 2 G.

ERIC BEVERLY Beverly, Eric Raymonde 6′3″, 279 **C**
Col: Miami (Ohio) *HS:* Bedford [Bedford Heights, OH] B: 3/28/1974, Cleveland, OH
1998 Det: 16 G.

RANDY BEVERLY Beverly, Randolph Ray 5′11″, 190 **DB**
Col: Trinidad State JC CO; Colorado State *HS:* Wildwood [NJ]
B: 4/3/1944, Wildwood, NJ
1970 Bos: KR 1-0. **Total:** KR 1-0.

		Interceptions		
Year Team	**G**	**Int**	**Yds**	**TD**
1967 NYJ	14	4	54	0
1968 NYJ	13	4	127	1
1969 NYJ	13	2	37	0
1970 Bos	13	0	0	0
1971 NE	8	2	19	0
NFL Total	61	12	237	1

GEORGE BEYERS Beyers, George 168 **WB**
Deceased
1921 Was: 3 G.

TIM BIAKABUTUKA Biakabutuka, Tshimanga 6′0″, 215 **RB**
Col: Michigan *HS:* Rousseau [Longuevil, Canada]; Vanier Coll. [Montreal, Canada] B: 1/24/1974, Kinshasa, Zaire *Drafted:* 1996 Round 1 Car
1998 Car: Rec 8-138 17.3 1 TD. **Total:** Rec 8-138 17.3 1 TD.

		Rushing					Tot
Year Team	**G**	**Att**	**Yds**	**Avg**	**TD**	**Fum**	**TD**
1996 Car	4	71	229	3.2	0	0	0
1997 Car	8	75	299	4.0	2	1	2
1998 Car	10	101	427	4.2	3	1	4
NFL Total	22	247	955	3.9	5	2	6

FRANK BIANCHINI Bianchini, Frank 5′8″, 190 **RB**
Col: Hofstra B: 5/27/1961
1987 NE: 1 G.

JOHNNY BIANCONE Biancone, John L 5′6″, 165 **TB-DB-QB**
Col: Oregon State *HS:* Benson Polytechnic [Portland, OR]
B: 12/5/1911, Portland, OR D: 9/6/1996, Portland, OR
1936 Bkn: 5 G; Pass 3-1 33.3%, 29 9.67; Rush 8-34 4.3.

DEAN BIASUCCI Biasucci, Dean 6′0″, 190 **K**
Col: Western Carolina *HS:* Miramar [FL] B: 7/25/1962, Niagara Falls, NY

		Scoring						
Year Team	**G**	**Pts**	**FG**	**FGA**	**FG%**	**XK**	**XKA**	**XK%**
1984 Ind	15	22	3	5	60.0	13	14	92.9
1986 Ind	16	65	13	25	52.0	26	27	96.3
1987 Ind	12	96	24	27	**88.9**	24	24	**100.0**
1988 Ind	16	114	25	32	78.1	39	40	97.5
1989 Ind	16	94	21	27	77.8	31	32	96.9
1990 Ind	16	83	17	24	70.8	32	33	97.0
1991 Ind	16	59	15	26	57.7	14	14	100.0
1992 Ind	16	72	16	29	55.2	24	24	100.0
1993 Ind	16	93	26	31	83.9	15	16	93.8
1994 Ind	16	85	16	24	66.7	37	37	100.0
1995 StL	8	40	9	12	75.0	13	14	92.9
NFL Total	163	823	185	262	70.6	268	275	97.5

DUANE BICKETT Bickett, Duane Clair 6′5″, 251 **LB**
Col: USC *HS:* Glendale [CA] B: 12/1/1962, Los Angeles, CA
Drafted: 1985 Round 1 Ind
1985 Ind: 16 G; Int 1-0; 6 Sac. **1986** Ind: 16 G; Int 2-10; 5 Sac. **1987** Ind: 12 G; 1 Fum; 8 Sac. **1988** Ind: 16 G; Int 3-7; 3.5 Sac. **1989** Ind: 16 G; Int 1-6; 8 Sac. **1990** Ind: 15 G; Int 1-9; 4.5 Sac. **1991** Ind: 16 G; 5 Sac. **1992** Ind: 15 G; Int 1-14; 6.5 Sac. **1993** Ind: 15 G; 3.5 Sac. **1994** Sea: 7 G. **1995** Sea: 15 G; 1 Sac. **1996** Car: 16 G; KR 1-12 12.0; 2 Sac. **Total:** 175 G; KR 1-12 12.0; Int 9-46; 1 Fum; 53.0 Sac.

ADOLPH BIEBERSTEIN Bieberstein, Adolph Joseph 5′10″, 205 **G**
Col: Wisconsin *HS:* Phillips [WI] B: 12/17/1902, Phillips, WI
D: 12/31/1981, Madison, WI
1926 Rac-GB: 6 G. Rac: 5 G. GB: 1 G. **Total:** 6 G.

LEO BIEDERMANN Biedermann, Leo George 6′7″, 254 **OT**
Col: Diablo Valley Coll. CA (J.C.); California *HS:* Westmoor [Daly City, CA] B: 10/19/1955, Omaha, NE *Drafted:* 1978 Round 12 Cle
1978 Cle: 16 G.

GREG BIEKERT Biekert, Gregory Scott 6′2″, 238 **LB**
Col: Colorado *HS:* Longmont [CO] B: 3/14/1969, Iowa City, IA
Drafted: 1993 Round 7 LARd
1993 LARd: 16 G. **1994** LARd: 16 G; Int 1-11; 1.5 Sac. **1995** Oak: 16 G; 1 Sac. **1996** Oak: 16 G. **1997** Oak: 16 G; KR 1-16 16.0; 2.5 Sac. **1998** Oak: 16 G; 3 Sac. **Total:** 96 G; KR 1-16 16.0; Int 1-11; 8 Sac.

DICK BIELSKI Bielski, Richard Adam 6′1″, 224 **OE-FB**
Col: Maryland *HS:* Patterson [Baltimore, MD] B: 9/7/1932, Maple Shade, NJ *Drafted:* 1955 Round 1 Phi
1957 Phi: KR 2-11 5.5. **1958** Phi: KR 5-66 13.2. **1960** Dal: KR 1-4 4.0. **1963** Bal: KR 1-0. **Total:** KR 9-81 9.0.

		Rushing				Receiving			
Year Team	**G**	**Att**	**Yds**	**Avg**	**TD**	**Rec**	**Yds**	**Avg**	**TD**
1955 Phi	12	28	67	2.4	1	8	48	6.0	0
1956 Phi	12	52	162	3.1	1	8	63	7.9	0
1957 Phi	12	0	0	—	0	8	81	10.1	2
1958 Phi	12	0	0	—	0	23	234	10.2	1
1959 Phi	12	0	0	—	0	15	264	17.6	1
1960 Dal	12	0	0	—	0	4	38	9.5	1
1961 Dal	14	0	0	—	0	26	377	14.5	3
1962 Bal	14	0	0	—	0	15	200	13.3	2
1963 Bal	14	0	0	—	0	0	0	—	0
NFL Total	114	80	229	2.9	2	107	1305	12.2	10

	Scoring								Tot
Year Team	**Pts**	**FG**	**FGA**	**FG%**	**XK**	**XKA**	**XK%**	**Fum**	**TD**
1955 Phi	56	9	23	39.1	23	24	95.8	1	1
1956 Phi	6	0	1	0.0	0	0	—	1	1
1957 Phi	12	0	2	0.0	0	0	—	0	2
1958 Phi	0	0	0	—	0	0	—	1	1
1959 Phi	6	0	5	0.0	0	0	—	0	1
1960 Dal	0	0	0	—	0	0	—	0	1
1961 Dal	46	6	9	66.7	10	10	100.0	0	3

1962 Bal	70	11	25	44.0	25	28	89.3	0	2
NFL Total	208	26	65	40.0	58	62	93.5	3	12

TOM BIENEMANN Bienemann, Thomas Jerome 6′3″, 221 **DE-OE-LB**
(Beans) *Col:* Drake *HS:* Kenosha [WI] B: 1/28/1928, Kenosha, WI
Drafted: 1951 Round 11 ChiC
1951 ChiC: 12 G; Rec 1-8 8.0; KR 2-34 17.0; Int 1-5; 1 Fum. **1952** ChiC: 12 G. **1953** ChiC: 12 G. **1954** ChiC: 11 G. **1955** ChiC: 10 G; Int 2-8. **1956** ChiC: 8 G; Int 1-2. **Total:** 65 G; Rec 1-8 8.0; KR 2-34 17.0; Int 4-15; 1 Fum.

ERIC BIENIEMY Bieniemy, Eric Jr. 5′7″, 207 **RB**
Col: Colorado *HS:* Bishop Amat [La Puente, CA] B: 8/15/1969, New Orleans, LA *Drafted:* 1991 Round 2 SD
1995 Cin: Pass 2-0. **Total:** Pass 2-0.

		Rushing				Receiving			
Year Team	**G**	**Att**	**Yds**	**Avg**	**TD**	**Rec**	**Yds**	**Avg**	**TD**
1991 SD	15	3	17	5.7	0	0	0	—	0
1992 SD	15	74	264	3.6	3	5	49	9.8	0
1993 SD	16	33	135	4.1	1	1	0	0.0	0
1994 SD	16	73	295	4.0	0	5	48	9.6	0
1995 Cin	16	98	381	3.9	3	43	424	9.9	0
1996 Cin	16	56	269	4.8	2	32	272	8.5	0
1997 Cin	16	21	97	4.6	1	31	249	8.0	0
1998 Cin	16	17	56	3.3	0	27	153	5.7	0
NFL Total	126	375	1514	4.0	10	144	1195	8.3	0

	Punt Returns				Kickoff Returns					Tot
Year Team	**Ret**	**Yds**	**Avg**	**TD**	**Ret**	**Yds**	**Avg**	**TD**	**Fum**	**TD**
1992 SD	30	229	7.6	0	15	257	17.1	0	4	3
1993 SD	0	0	—	0	7	110	15.7	0	1	1
1994 SD	0	0	—	0	0	0	—	0	1	0
1995 Cin	7	47	6.7	0	8	168	21.0	0	1	3
1996 Cin	0	0	—	0	0	0	—	0	1	2
1997 Cin	0	0	—	0	34	789	23.2	1	2	2
1998 Cin	0	0	—	0	5	87	17.4	0	1	0
NFL Total	37	276	7.5	0	69	1411	20.4	1	11	11

SCOTTY BIERCE Bierce, Bruce W 5′9″, 164 **E**
Col: Akron *HS:* Cuyahoga Falls [OH] B: 9/3/1896, Kearney, NE
D: 4/26/1982, Valley City, OH
1920 Akr: 10 G. **1921** Akr: 12 G; Rec 1 TD; 1 Fum TD; Tot TD 2; 12 Pt. **1922** Akr: 4 G; Rec **2** TD; 12 Pt. **1923** Cle-Buf: 10 G; Pass 1 TD; Rush 1 TD; Rec 2 TD; Tot TD 3; 18 Pt. Cle: 7 G; Rec 2 TD; 12 Pt. Buf: 3 G; Pass 1 TD; Rush 1 TD; 6 Pt. **1924** Cle: 4 G. **1925** Akr: 8 G. **Total:** 48 G; Pass 1 TD; Rush 1 TD; Rec 5 TD; 1 Fum TD; Tot TD 7; 42 Pt.

BIG BEAR Big Bear 6′4″, 215 **T**
Col: No College Deceased
1922 Oor: 1 G. **1923** Oor: 5 G. **Total:** 6 G.

LYLE BIGBEE Bigbee, Lyle Randolph 6′0″, 180 **OE**
Col: Oregon *HS:* Albany [OR] B: 8/22/1893, Sweet Home, OR
D: 8/5/1942, Portland, OR
1922 Mil: 3 G.

KEIRON BIGBY Bigby, Keiron 5′10″, 177 **WR**
Col: Brown *HS:* St. Anthony's [Smithtown, NY] B: 2/27/1966
1987 Was: 1 G.

RILEY BIGGS Biggs, Riley Edgar 6′2″, 230 **C-G**
Col: Baylor *HS:* Southampton [NY] B: 3/24/1900, Montgomery Co., TX
D: 11/24/1971, Liberty, TX
1926 NYG: 3 G. **1927** NYG: 10 G. **Total:** 13 G.

VERLON BIGGS Biggs, Verlon Marion 6′4″, 275 **DE**
Col: Jackson State *HS:* Moss Point [MS] B: 3/16/1943, Moss Point, MS D: 6/7/1994, Moss Point, MS *Drafted:* 1965 Round 3 NYJ
1965 NYJ: 14 G; Int 1-44. **1966** NYJ: 14 G; Scor **1** Saf; 2 Pt. **1967** NYJ: 14 G. **1968** NYJ: 13 G. **1969** NYJ: 12 G. **1970** NYJ: 13 G. **1971** Was: 13 G. **1972** Was: 14 G; **1** Fum TD; 6 Pt. **1973** Was: 14 G; **1** Fum TD; 6 Pt. **1974** Was: 14 G. **Total:** 135 G; Int 1-44; Scor 1 Saf; 2 Fum TD; 14 Pt.

JACK BIGHEAD Bighead, John 6′3″, 215 **DE-OE**
Col: Pepperdine *HS:* Los Angeles Polytechnic [CA] B: 4/23/1930, Beggs, OK D: 4/28/1993, Parker, AZ *Drafted:* 1952 Round 15 Dal
1954 Bal: 11 G; Rec 6-89 14.8. **1955** LARm: 2 G. **Total:** 13 G; Rec 6-89 14.8.

JONATHAN BILBO Bilbo, Jonathan Payne 6′0″, 195 **T-G**
(Ode; Yoppie) *Col:* Mississippi *HS:* Picayune Memorial [MS]
B: 10/17/1914, Talisheek, LA
1938 ChiC: 8 G. **1939** ChiC: 1 G. **Total:** 9 G.

DICK BILDA Bilda, Richard Francis 6′2″, 210 **TB-DB**
Col: Marquette *HS:* Marquette Acad. [Milwaukee, WI] B: 5/17/1919, Milwaukee, WI
1944 GB: 3 G; Pass 1-0; Int 1-25.

FRED BILETNIKOFF Biletnikoff, Frederick S 6′1″, 190 **WR**
Col: Florida State *HS:* Erie Tech [PA] B: 2/23/1943, Erie, PA
Drafted: 1965 Round 2 Oak *HOF:* 1988
1968 Oak: **1** Fum TD. **Total:** 1 Fum TD.

		Receiving					Tot
Year Team	**G**	**Rec**	**Yds**	**Avg**	**TD**	**Fum**	**TD**
1965 Oak	14	24	331	13.8	0	0	0
1966 Oak	10	17	272	16.0	3	2	3
1967 Oak	14	40	876	**21.9**	5	1	5
1968 Oak	14	61	1037	17.0	6	0	7
1969 Oak	14	54	837	15.5	12	1	12
1970 Oak	14	45	768	17.1	7	0	7
1971 Oak	14	**61**	929	15.2	9	1	9
1972 Oak	14	58	802	13.8	7	0	7
1973 Oak	14	48	660	13.8	4	0	4
1974 Oak	14	42	593	14.1	7	0	7
1975 Oak	11	43	587	13.7	2	0	2
1976 Oak	13	43	551	12.8	7	0	7
1977 Oak	14	33	446	13.5	5	1	5
1978 Oak	16	20	285	14.3	2	0	2
NFL Total	190	589	8974	15.2	76	6	77

RON BILLINGSLEY Billingsley, Ronald Smith 6′8″, 290 **DT-DE**
Col: Wyoming *HS:* Carver [Gadsden, AL] B: 4/6/1945, Florence, AL
Drafted: 1967 Round 1 SD
1967 SD: 13 G. **1968** SD: 13 G. **1969** SD: 9 G. **1970** SD: 9 G. **1971** Hou: 13 G. **1972** Hou: 4 G. **Total:** 61 G.

JOHN BILLMAN Billman, John Arthur 6′1″, 202 **G-LB-T**
Col: Minnesota *HS:* Central [Minneapolis, MN] B: 12/1/1919, Minneapolis, MN
AAFC **1946** BknA: 3 G. **1947** ChiA: 2 G. **Total:** 5 G.

FRANK BILLOCK Billock, Francis 6′0″, 230 **T**
Col: St. Mary's (Minn.) *HS:* Grand Rapids [MN] B: 5/20/1912, Grand Rapids, MI D: 10/1964
1937 Pit: 2 G.

LEWIS BILLUPS Billups, Lewis Kenneth 5′11″, 190 **DB**
Col: North Alabama *HS:* Niceville [FL] B: 10/10/1963, Tampa, FL
D: 4/9/1994, Orlando, FL *Drafted:* 1986 Round 2 Cin
1986 Cin: 12 G; 1 Sac. **1987** Cin: 11 G. **1988** Cin: 16 G; Int 4-47; **1** Fum TD; 6 Pt. **1989** Cin: 16 G; Int 2-0. **1990** Cin: 15 G; Int 3-39. **1991** Cin: 13 G; 1 Sac. **1992** GB: 5 G. **Total:** 88 G; Int 9-86; 1 Fum TD; 6 Pt; 2 Sac.

TERRY BILLUPS Billups, Terry Michael 5′9″, 180 **DB**
Col: North Carolina *HS:* Oak Ridge [Orlando, FL] B: 2/9/1975, Weisbaden, Germany
1998 Dal: 1 G.

LES BINGAMAN Bingaman, Lester Alonza 6′3″, 272 **DG-OG**
Col: Illinois *HS:* Lew Wallace [Gary, IN] B: 2/3/1926, McKenzie, TN
D: 11/20/1970, Miami, FL *Drafted:* 1948 Round 3 Det
1948 Det: 12 G. **1949** Det: 12 G. **1950** Det: 12 G. **1951** Det: 6 G. **1952** Det: 12 G; Int 1-8. **1953** Det: 12 G; KR 1-3 3.0; Int 1-1. **1954** Det: 12 G. **Total:** 78 G; KR 1-3 3.0; Int 2-9.

CRAIG BINGHAM Bingham, Craig Marlon 6′2″, 218 **LB**
Col: Syracuse *HS:* Stamford [CT] B: 9/26/1959, Kingston, Jamaica
Drafted: 1982 Round 6 Pit
1982 Pit: 6 G. **1983** Pit: 12 G; KR 1-15 15.0. **1984** Pit: 11 G. **1985** SD: 8 G. **1987** Pit: 3 G. **Total:** 40 G; KR 1-15 15.0.

DON BINGHAM Bingham, Donald Dean 6′0″, 185 **HB**
Col: Sul Ross State *HS:* Odessa [TX] B: 11/7/1929, Shattuck, OK
Drafted: 1953 Round 7 ChiB
1956 ChiB: 12 G; Rush 7-36 5.1; Rec 1-7 7.0; PR 13-7 0.5; KR 17-444 26.1 **1** TD; 6 Pt; 1 Fum.

DWIGHT BINGHAM Bingham, Dwight Nottis 6′6″, 265 **DE**
Col: Mississippi *HS:* Stamford [CT] B: 8/5/1961, Kingston, Jamaica
1987 Atl: 3 G.

GREGG BINGHAM Bingham, Gregory Raleigh 6′1″, 227 **LB**
Col: Purdue *HS:* Gordon Tech [Chicago, IL] B: 3/13/1951, Evanston, IL
Drafted: 1973 Round 4 Hou
1977 Hou: 1 Fum TD. **1980** Hou: KR 1-0. **1982** Hou: 3 Sac. **1984** Hou: 2 Sac. **Total:** KR 1-0; 1 Fum TD; 5 Sac.

		Interceptions			
Year Team	**G**	**Int**	**Yds**	**TD**	**Fum**
1973 Hou	14	2	22	0	0
1974 Hou	14	4	36	0	0
1975 Hou	14	4	57	0	0
1976 Hou	14	2	18	0	0
1977 Hou	14	2	36	0	1
1978 Hou	16	0	0	0	0
1979 Hou	16	3	78	0	0
1980 Hou	16	0	0	0	1
1981 Hou	16	2	20	0	0

1982 Hou	7	1	8	0	0
1983 Hou	16	1	4	0	0
1984 Hou	16	0	0	0	0
NFL Total	173	21	279	0	2

GUY BINGHAM Bingham, Guy Richard 6'3", 255 **C-OG-OT**
Col: Montana *HS:* J.M. Weatherwax [Aberdeen, WA] B: 2/25/1958, Koiaumi Gumma Ken, Japan *Drafted:* 1980 Round 10 NYJ
1980 NYJ: 16 G; KR 1-19 19.0. **1981** NYJ: 16 G. **1982** NYJ: 7 G. **1983** NYJ: 16 G. **1984** NYJ: 16 G. **1985** NYJ: 16 G. **1986** NYJ: 16 G. **1987** NYJ: 12 G. **1988** NYJ: 10 G. **1989** Atl: 16 G. **1990** Atl: 16 G. **1991** Atl: 13 G. **1992** Was: 15 G. **1993** Was: 14 G; 1 Fum. **Total:** 199 G; KR 1-19 19.0; 1 Fum.

DAVID BINN Binn, David Aaron 6'3", 240 **TE**
Col: California *HS:* San Mateo [CA] B: 2/6/1972, San Mateo, CA
1994 SD: 16 G. **1995** SD: 16 G. **1996** SD: 16 G. **1997** SD: 16 G. **1998** SD: 15 G. **Total:** 79 G.

JOHN BINOTTO Binotto, John 5'10", 185 **HB-DB**
Col: Duquesne *HS:* Cecil [PA] B: 11/24/1919, Lawrence, PA
1942 Pit-Phi: 9 G; Rush 17-47 2.8; PR 2-25 12.5. Pit: 7 G; Rush 16-57 3.6; PR 2-25 12.5. Phi: 2 G; Rush 1-(-10) -10.0. **Total:** 9 G; Rush 17-47 2.8; PR 2-25 12.5.

DENNY BIODROWSKI Biodrowski, Dennis James 6'1", 250 **OG**
(Bid) *Col:* Memphis *HS:* William A. Wirt [Gary, IN] B: 6/27/1940, Gary, IN *Drafted:* 1962 Round 18 SD
1963 KC: 2 G. **1964** KC: 1 G. **1965** KC: 6 G. **1966** KC: 14 G. **1967** KC: 7 G. **Total:** 30 G.

JOHN BIOLO Biolo, John Robert 5'10", 191 **G**
Col: Lake Forest *HS:* Iron Mountain [MI] B: 2/8/1916, Iron Mountain, MI
1939 GB: 1 G.

RODGER BIRD Bird, Rodger Paul 6'0", 200 **DB**
Col: Kentucky *HS:* Corbin [KY] B: 7/2/1943, Corbin, KY
Drafted: 1966 Round 1 Oak
1966 Oak: Int 4-48. **1967** Oak: Int 1-0. **1968** Oak: Int 3-62 1 TD.
Total: Int 8-110 1 TD.

		Punt Returns				Kickoff Returns				
Year Team	**G**	**Ret**	**Yds**	**Avg**	**TD**	**Ret**	**Yds**	**Avg**	**TD**	**Fum**
1966 Oak	14	**37**	**323**	8.7	0	19	390	20.5	0	0
1967 Oak	14	**46**	**612**	13.3	0	6	143	23.8	0	1
1968 Oak	10	11	128	11.6	0	0	0	—	0	1
NFL Total	38	94	1063	11.3	0	25	533	21.3	0	2

STEVE BIRD Bird, Steven L 5'11", 171 **WR**
Col: Eastern Kentucky *HS:* Corbin [KY] B: 10/20/1960, Indianapolis, IN *Drafted:* 1983 Round 5 StL
1983 StL: 14 G; PR 14-76 5.4; KR 9-194 21.6; 1 Fum. **1984** StL-SD: 9 G; PR 6-60 10.0; KR 11-205 18.6; 1 Fum. StL: 8 G; PR 5-56 11.2; KR 9-190 21.1. SD: 1 G; PR 1-4 4.0; KR 2-15 7.5; 1 Fum. **Total:** 23 G; PR 20-136 6.8; KR 20-399 20.0; 2 Fum.

J.J. BIRDEN Birden, LaJourdain J 5'9", 180 **WR**
Col: Oregon *HS:* Lakeridge [Lake Oswego, OR] B: 6/16/1965, Portland, OR *Drafted:* 1988 Round 8 Cle
1990 KC: PR 10-72 7.2; KR 1-14 14.0. **1993** KC: PR 5-43 8.6. **1994** KC: Scor 1 2XP. **Total:** PR 15-115 7.7; KR 1-14 14.0; Scor 1 2XP.

		Receiving				
Year Team	**G**	**Rec**	**Yds**	**Avg**	**TD**	**Fum**
1990 KC	11	15	352	23.5	3	1
1991 KC	15	27	465	17.2	2	1
1992 KC	16	42	644	15.3	3	3
1993 KC	16	51	721	14.1	2	1
1994 KC	13	48	637	13.3	4	1
1995 Atl	10	31	303	9.8	1	0
1996 Atl	12	30	319	10.6	2	2
NFL Total	93	244	3441	14.1	17	9

CRAIG BIRDSONG Birdsong, Gary Craig 6'2", 217 **DB**
Col: North Texas *HS:* Kaufman [TX] B: 8/16/1964, Kaufman, TX
1987 Hou: 3 G.

CARL BIRDSONG Birdsong, George Carlisle 6'0", 192 **P**
Col: Southwestern Oklahoma State *HS:* Amarillo [TX] B: 1/1/1959, Kaufman, TX
1981 StL: Rush 1-(-2) -2.0. **1983** StL: Pass 1-1 100.0%, 11 11.00. **1985** StL: Pass 1-0. **Total:** Pass 2-1 50.0%, 11 5.50; Rush 1-(-2) -2.0.

		Punting		
Year Team	**G**	**Punts**	**Yds**	**Avg**
1981 StL	16	69	2883	41.8
1982 StL	9	54	2365	43.8
1983 StL	16	85	3529	41.5
1984 StL	16	67	2594	38.7
1985 StL	16	85	3545	41.7
NFL Total	73	360	14916	41.4

DAN BIRDWELL Birdwell, Daniel Lee 6'4", 250 **DT-DE**
Col: Houston *HS:* Big Spring [TX] B: 10/14/1940, Big Spring, TX
D: 2/14/1978, Huntington Beach, CA *Drafted:* 1962 Round 6 Oak
1962 Oak: 14 G; Scor 0-1 FG. **1963** Oak: 10 G; KR 1-7 7.0. **1964** Oak: 14 G; Int 2-21; 1 Fum. **1965** Oak: 14 G. **1966** Oak: 14 G; Int 1-2. **1967** Oak: 14 G; Scor **1** Saf; 2 Pt. **1968** Oak: 14 G. **1969** Oak: 2 G. **Total:** 96 G; KR 1-7 7.0; Int 3-23; Scor 2, 0-1 FG, 1 Saf; 2 Pt; 1 Fum.

MATT BIRK Birk, Matthew Robert 6'4", 315 **OT**
Col: Harvard *HS:* Cretin-Derham Hall [St. Paul, MN] B: 7/23/1976, St. Paul, MN *Drafted:* 1998 Round 6 Min
1998 Min: 7 G.

KEITH BIRLEM Birlem, Keith 5'11", 198 **DB-OE-WB**
Col: San Jose State B: 5/4/1915, San Jose, CA D: 5/7/1943, Berlin, Germany
1939 ChiC-Was: 9 G; Rec 2-17 8.5. ChiC: 6 G; Rec 2-17 8.5. Was: 3 G. **Total:** 9 G; Rec 2-17 8.5.

TOM BIRNEY Birney, Thomas Francis 6'4", 220 **K**
Col: Michigan State *HS:* J.M. Weatherwax [Aberdeen, WA]
B: 8/11/1956, Bellshill, Scotland
1979 GB: 6 G; Scor 28, 7-9 77.8% FG, 7-10 70.0% XK. **1980** GB: 7 G; Scor 32, 6-12 50.0% FG, 14-18 77.8% XK. **Total:** 13 G; Scor 60, 13-21 61.9% FG, 21-28 75.0% XK.

JOE BISCAHA Biscaha, Joseph Daniel 6'1", 190 **OE**
Col: Richmond *HS:* Pope Pius XII [Passaic, NJ] B: 6/1/1937, Passaic, NJ *Drafted:* 1959 Round 27 NYG
1959 NYG: 8 G; Rec 1-5 5.0. **1960** Bos: 1 G. **Total:** 9 G; Rec 1-5 5.0.

BLAINE BISHOP Bishop, Blaine Elwood 5'9", 197 **CB**
Col: St. Joseph's (Ind.); Ball State *HS:* Cathedral [Indianapolis, IN]
B: 7/24/1970, Indianapolis, IN *Drafted:* 1993 Round 8 Hou
1993 Hou: 16 G; Int 1-1; 1 Fum; 1 Sac. **1994** Hou: 16 G; KR 2-18 9.0; Int 1-21; 1.5 Sac. **1995** Hou: 16 G; Int 1-62 1 TD; 6 Pt; 1.5 Sac. **1996** Hou: 15 G; Int 1-6. **1997** Ten: 14 G; 1.5 Sac. **1998** Ten: 13 G; Int 1-13; 3 Sac. **Total:** 90 G; KR 2-18 9.0; Int 5-103 1 TD; 6 Pt; 1 Fum; 8.5 Sac.

DON BISHOP Bishop, Donald William 6'2", 209 **DB-FL-HB**
Col: Los Angeles City Coll. CA (J.C.) *HS:* Thomas Jefferson [Los Angeles, CA] B: 7/1/1934, Los Angeles, CA
1958 Pit: Rec 3-57 19.0. **1959** Pit-ChiB: PR 4-10 2.5. Pit: PR 4-10 2.5. **1962** Dal: **1** Fum TD. **Total:** Rec 3-57 19.0; PR 4-10 2.5; 1 Fum TD.

		Interceptions		
Year Team	**G**	**Int**	**Yds**	**TD**
1958 Pit	12	0	0	0
1959 Pit-ChiB	3	0	0	0
1959 Pit	2	0	0	0
1959 ChiB	1	0	0	0
1960 Dal	12	3	13	0
1961 Dal	14	8	172	0
1962 Dal	14	6	134	0
1963 Dal	13	5	45	0
1964 Dal	14	0	0	0
1965 Dal	14	0	0	0
NFL Total	96	22	364	0

SONNY BISHOP Bishop, Erwin Wilfred 6'2", 245 **OG**
Col: Riverside CC CA; Fresno State *HS:* El Cajon Valley [CA]
B: 10/1/1939, Winner, SD *Drafted:* 1962 Round 11 SD
1962 DalT: 14 G. **1963** Oak: 14 G. **1964** Hou: 14 G; Rec 1-0. **1965** Hou: 14 G. **1966** Hou: 14 G. **1967** Hou: 12 G. **1968** Hou: 14 G. **1969** Hou: 14 G. **Total:** 110 G; Rec 1-0.

GREG BISHOP Bishop, Gregory Lawrence 6'5", 305 **OG**
Col: U. of Pacific *HS:* Lodi [CA] B: 5/2/1971, Stockton, CA
Drafted: 1993 Round 4 NYG
1993 NYG: 8 G. **1994** NYG: 16 G. **1995** NYG: 16 G. **1996** NYG: 16 G. **1997** NYG: 16 G. **1998** NYG: 16 G. **Total:** 88 G.

HAROLD BISHOP Bishop, Harold Lucius Jr. 6'4", 254 **TE**
Col: Louisiana State *HS:* Central East [Tuscaloosa, AL] B: 4/8/1970, Boonville, MS *Drafted:* 1994 Round 3 TB
1994 TB: 6 G. **1995** Cle: 13 G; Rec 16-135 8.4. **1996** Bal: 8 G; Rec 2-22 11.0. **1998** Pit: 7 G; Rec 1-4 4.0. **Total:** 34 G; Rec 19-161 8.5.

KEITH BISHOP Bishop, Keith Bryan 6'3", 260 **OG-C**
Col: Nebraska; Baylor *HS:* Robert E. Lee [Midland, TX] B: 3/10/1957, San Diego, CA *Drafted:* 1980 Round 6 Den
1980 Den: 16 G. **1982** Den: 9 G. **1983** Den: 16 G. **1984** Den: 16 G. **1985** Den: 14 G. **1986** Den: 16 G. **1987** Den: 12 G. **1988** Den: 16 G; 1 Fum. **1989** Den: 14 G. **Total:** 129 G; 1 Fum.

RICHARD BISHOP Bishop, Richard Allen 6'1", 275 **NT-DE**
Col: Marshalltown CC IA; Louisville *HS:* Glenville [Cleveland, OH]
B: 3/23/1950, Cleveland, OH *Drafted:* 1974 Round 5 Cin
1976 NE: 14 G. **1977** NE: 12 G. **1978** NE: 16 G; Scor **1** Saf; 2 Pt. **1979** NE: 14 G. **1980** NE: 13 G. **1981** NE: 16 G. **1982** Mia: 2 G. **1983** LARm: 2 G. **Total:** 89 G; Scor 1 Saf; 2 Pt.

BILL BISHOP Bishop, William Eugene 6′4″, 248 **DT-OT**
Col: North Texas *HS:* Borger [TX] B: 5/8/1931, Borger, TX
D: 5/14/1998, Geneva, IL *Drafted:* 1952 Round 8 ChiB
1952 ChiB: 12 G. **1953** ChiB: 12 G; Int 1-30. **1954** ChiB: 12 G. **1955** ChiB: 12 G; Int 1-5. **1956** ChiB: 12 G. **1957** ChiB: 11 G. **1958** ChiB: 12 G; **1** Fum TD; 6 Pt. **1959** ChiB: 12 G. **1960** ChiB: 12 G. **1961** Min: 10 G.
Total: 117 G; Int 2-35; 1 Fum TD; 6 Pt.

FRANK BISSELL Bissell, Franklin H.P. 6′1″, 180 **OE**
(Monk; Doc) *Col:* Fordham *HS:* West [Akron, OH] B: 8/15/1902, Oberlin, OH D: 1/1/1983, Salina, KS
1925 Akr: 8 G. **1926** Akr: 8 G. **Total:** 16 G.

DON BITTERLICH Bitterlich, Donald R 5′7″, 166 **K**
Col: Temple *HS:* William Tennent [Warminster, PA] B: 1/5/1954, Warminster, PA *Drafted:* 1976 Round 3 Sea
1976 Sea: 3 G; Scor 10, 1-4 25.0% FG, 7-7 100.0% XK.

CHARLIE BIVINS Bivins, Charles Louis 6′1″, 212 **HB-TE**
Col: Morris Brown *HS:* Luther Judson Price [Atlanta, GA]
B: 10/16/1938, Atlanta, GA D: 3/11/1994 *Drafted:* 1960 Round 7 ChiB

		Rushing				Receiving			
Year Team	**G**	**Att**	**Yds**	**Avg**	**TD**	**Rec**	**Yds**	**Avg**	**TD**
1960 ChiB	12	1	-11	-11.0	0	0	0	—	0
1961 ChiB	14	43	188	4.4	1	4	-9	-2.3	0
1962 ChiB	12	14	44	3.1	1	3	52	17.3	0
1963 ChiB	14	44	104	2.4	0	3	22	7.3	0
1964 ChiB	11	29	92	3.2	0	11	59	5.4	1
1965 ChiB	14	0	0	—	0	4	108	27.0	2
1966 ChiB	14	0	0	—	0	2	6	3.0	0
1967 Pit-Buf	11	22	81	3.7	1	1	24	24.0	0
1967 Pit	2	7	23	3.3	1	1	24	24.0	0
1967 Buf	9	15	58	3.9	0	0	0	—	0
NFL Total	102	153	498	3.3	3	28	262	9.4	3

	Kickoff Returns					Tot
Year Team	**Ret**	**Yds**	**Avg**	**TD**	**Fum**	**TD**
1960 ChiB	15	362	24.1	0	1	0
1961 ChiB	25	668	26.7	0	1	1
1962 ChiB	12	243	20.3	0	1	1
1963 ChiB	2	40	20.0	0	0	0
1964 ChiB	8	218	27.3	0	1	1
1965 ChiB	0	0	—	0	0	2
1966 ChiB	0	0	—	0	1	0
1967 Pit-Buf	16	380	23.8	0	0	1
1967 Pit	0	0	—	0	0	1
1967 Buf	16	380	23.8	0	0	0
NFL Total	78	1911	24.5	0	5	6

HERB BIZER Bizer, Herbert 0 5′11″, 205 **E-FB**
Col: Carroll (Wis.) B: 8/3/1906, WI D: 12/4/1974, East Kingsford, MI
1929 Buf: 9 G.

DEL BJORK Bjork, Delbert Leonard 6′1″, 218 **T**
Col: Oregon *HS:* Astoria [OR] B: 6/27/1914, Astoria, OR
D: 8/26/1988, Astoria, OR *Drafted:* 1937 Round 6 ChiB
1937 ChiB: 10 G. **1938** ChiB: 10 G. **Total:** 20 G.

HANK BJORKLUND Bjorklund, John Henry 6′1″, 200 **RB**
Col: Princeton *HS:* Glen Head [NY] B: 6/5/1950, Glen Head, NY
Drafted: 1972 Round 12 NYJ
1972 NYJ: Rec 4-54 13.5; KR 7-150 21.4. **1973** NYJ: Rec 2-15 7.5; KR 9-175 19.4. **1974** NYJ: Rec 2-15 7.5; KR 4-73 18.3. **Total:** Rec 8-84 10.5; KR 20-398 19.9.

		Rushing				
Year Team	**G**	**Att**	**Yds**	**Avg**	**TD**	**Fum**
1972 NYJ	7	15	42	2.8	0	0
1973 NYJ	10	22	72	3.3	0	1
1974 NYJ	13	23	57	2.5	0	2
NFL Total	30	60	171	2.9	0	3

BOB BJORKLUND Bjorklund, Robert John 6′2″, 225 **C-LB-E**
Col: Minnesota *HS:* North [Minneapolis, MN] B: 6/12/1918, Minneapolis, MN D: 1/27/1994, Hopkins, MN *Drafted:* 1941 Round 18 Pit
1941 Phi: 7 G.

ERIC BJORNSON Bjornson, Eric Thomas 6′4″, 236 **TE**
Col: Washington *HS:* Bishop O'Dowd [Oakland, CA] B: 12/15/1971, San Francisco, CA *Drafted:* 1995 Round 4 Dal
1996 Dal: Scor 1 2XP. **1997** Dal: Scor 1 2XP. **1998** Dal: Rush 1-7 7.0 1 TD. **Total:** Rush 1-7 7.0 1 TD; Scor 2 2XP.

		Receiving					Tot
Year Team	**G**	**Rec**	**Yds**	**Avg**	**TD**	**Fum**	**TD**
1995 Dal	14	7	53	7.6	0	0	0
1996 Dal	14	48	388	8.1	3	1	3
1997 Dal	14	47	442	9.4	0	2	0
1998 Dal	16	15	218	14.5	1	0	2
NFL Total	58	117	1101	9.4	4	3	5

BARRY BLACK Black, Barry Gordon 6′2″, 280 **OG**
Col: Santa Rosa JC CA; Boise State *HS:* Santa Rosa [CA] B: 3/7/1965
1987 LARd: 3 G.

CHARLIE BLACK Black, Charles Terrence 5′9″, 160 **E**
Col: Kansas *HS:* Alton [IL] B: 1/5/1901, Alton, IL D: 12/14/1988, Citrus Heights, CA
1925 Dul: 2 G.

JAMES BLACK Black, James 5′11″, 198 **RB**
Col: Akron *HS:* Dover [OH] B: 4/3/1962, Lima, OH
1984 Cle: 2 G.

JAMES BLACK Black, James R III 6′4″, 280 **DE**
Col: South Carolina State *HS:* West Side [Gary, IN] B: 11/4/1956, Xenia, OH
1987 KC: 1 G.

BLONDY BLACK Black, John Thomas 5′11″, 195 **RB-DB**
Col: Mississippi State *HS:* Philadelphia [MS] B: 8/20/1920, Philadelphia, MS
AAFC **1946** BufA: 4 G; Rush 1-10 10.0; Rec 1-21 21.0; PR 2-58 29.0; Int 1-18. **1947** BalA: 5 G; Rush 5-39 7.8; Rec 1-7 7.0. **Total:** 9 G; Rush 6-49 8.2; Rec 2-28 14.0; PR 2-58 29.0; Int 1-18.

MEL BLACK Black, Melvin 6′2″, 228 **LB**
Col: Rancho Santiago Coll. CA (J.C.); Eastern Illinois *HS:* West Haven [CT] B: 2/2/1962, New Haven, CT
1986 NE: 3 G. **1987** NE: 3 G. **Total:** 6 G.

MIKE BLACK Black, Michael David 6′4″, 285 **OT**
Col: Sacramento State *HS:* Del Oro [Loomis, CA] B: 8/24/1964, Auburn, CA *Drafted:* 1986 Round 9 Sea
1986 Phi: 1 G. **1987** NYG: 2 G. **Total:** 3 G.

MIKE BLACK Black, Peter Michael 6′1″, 197 **P**
Col: Arizona State *HS:* Glendale [CA] B: 1/18/1961, Glendale, CA
Drafted: 1983 Round 7 Det
1983 Det: Pass 1-0, 1 Int; Rush 2-(-10) -5.0. **1984** Det: Rush 3-(-6) -2.0. **1985** Det: Rush 1-0. **1986** Det: Rush 1-(-8) -8.0. **1987** Det: Rush 1-0.
Total: Pass 1-0, 1 Int; Rush 8-(-24) -3.0.

		Punting			
Year Team	**G**	**Punts**	**Yds**	**Avg**	**Fum**
1983 Det	16	71	2911	41.0	1
1984 Det	16	76	3164	41.6	0
1985 Det	16	73	3054	41.8	1
1986 Det	9	46	1819	39.5	1
1987 Det	1	6	233	38.8	1
NFL Total	58	272	11181	41.1	4

STAN BLACK Black, Stanley Ross 6′0″, 196 **DB**
Col: Mississippi State *HS:* Heritage Acad. Columbus [MS]
B: 11/12/1955, Greenville, MS *Drafted:* 1977 Round 4 SF
1977 SF: 13 G; PR 13-38 2.9; 1 Fum.

TIM BLACK Black, Timothy A 6′2″, 215 **LB**
Col: Baylor *HS:* Palo Duro [Amarillo, TX] B: 1/3/1955, Midland, TX
Drafted: 1977 Round 7 Det
1977 StL: 4 G.

TODD BLACK Black, Todd Mitchell 5′11″, 174 **WR**
Col: Concordia (Minn.) B: 4/12/1964
1987 ChiB: 1 G.

PETER BLACKBEAR Blackbear, Coowee Scoorice 6′0″, 190 **OE**
Col: No College B: 10/11/1899, OK D: 7/1976, Salina, OK
1923 Oor: 2 G.

BILL BLACKBURN Blackburn, William Whitford Jr. 6′6″, 228 **LB-C**
Col: Southwestern Louisiana; Rice *HS:* Stephen F. Austin [Houston, TX]
B: 2/5/1923, Weleetka, OK *Drafted:* 1944 Round 5 ChiC
1946 ChiC: Rush 1-10 10.0; Punt 35-1465 41.9; Scor **1** Saf. **1947** ChiC: Punt 1-19 19.0. **1949** ChiC: KR 1-4 4.0. **1950** ChiC: PR 1-2 2.0.
Total: Rush 1-10 10.0; PR 1-2 2.0; KR 1-4 4.0; Punt 36-1484 41.2; Scor 1 Saf.

		Interceptions				Tot
Year Team	**G**	**Int**	**Yds**	**TD**	**Fum**	**TD**
1946 ChiC	11	3	56	0	1	1
1947 ChiC	12	3	35	0	0	0
1948 ChiC	12	2	58	**2**	0	2
1949 ChiC	12	3	34	1	0	1
1950 ChiC	12	0	0	0	0	0
NFL Total	59	11	183	3	1	4

TODD BLACKLEDGE Blackledge, Todd Alan 6′3″, 225 **QB**
Col: Penn State *HS:* Hoover [North Canton, OH] B: 2/25/1961, Canton, OH *Drafted:* 1983 Round 1 KC

Year Team	G	Passing Att	Comp	Comp%	Yds	YPA	TD	Int	Rating
1983 KC	4	34	20	58.8	259	7.62	3	0	112.3
1984 KC	11	294	147	50.0	1707	5.81	6	11	59.2
1985 KC	12	172	86	50.0	1190	6.92	6	14	50.3
1986 KC	10	211	96	45.5	1200	5.69	10	6	67.6
1987 KC	3	31	15	48.4	154	4.97	1	1	60.4
1988 Pit	3	79	38	48.1	494	6.25	2	3	60.8
1989 Pit	3	60	22	36.7	282	4.70	1	3	36.9
NFL Total	46	881	424	48.1	5286	6.00	29	38	60.2

Year Team	Rushing Att	Yds	Avg	TD	Fum
1983 KC	1	0	0.0	0	1
1984 KC	18	102	5.7	1	8
1985 KC	17	97	5.7	0	3
1986 KC	23	60	2.6	0	5
1987 KC	5	21	4.2	0	2
1988 Pit	8	25	3.1	1	4
1989 Pit	9	20	2.2	0	3
NFL Total	81	325	4.0	2	26

HUGH BLACKLOCK Blacklock, Hugh M 6′0″, 220 **T-C-G**
(Chief) *Col:* Michigan State *HS:* Grand Rapids Union [MI] B: 1/1893, East Grand Rapids, MI D: 5/18/1954, Grand Rapids, MI
1920 Sta: 13 G. **1921** Sta: 11 G; Scor 2, 2 XK. **1922** ChiB: 12 G. **1923** ChiB: 4 G. **1924** ChiB: 11 G. **1925** ChiB: 3 G. **1926** Bkn: 5 G. **Total:** 59 G.

STUB BLACKMAN Blackman, Harold Lennon 5′11″, 195 **FB**
Col: Tulsa *HS:* Abilene [TX]; Claremore HS [OK] B: 1/15/1908 D: 10/30/1994, Corsicana, TX
1930 ChiB: 1 G.

KEN BLACKMAN Blackman, Kenneth Blake 6′6″, 320 **OG**
Col: Illinois *HS:* Wylie [Abilene, TX] B: 11/8/1972, Brunswick, GA *Drafted:* 1996 Round 3 Cin
1996 Cin: 14 G. **1997** Cin: 13 G. **1998** Cin: 8 G. **Total:** 35 G.

DON BLACKMON Blackmon, Donald Kirk 6′3″, 235 **LB**
Col: Tulsa *HS:* Boyd H. Anderson [Lauderdale Lakes, FL] B: 3/14/1958, Pompano, FL *Drafted:* 1981 Round 4 NE
1981 NE: 16 G. **1982** NE: 9 G; Int 2-7; 4.5 Sac. **1983** NE: 15 G; Int 1-39; 3.5 Sac. **1984** NE: 16 G; Int 1-3; 5 Sac. **1985** NE: 14 G; Int 1-14; Scor **2** Saf; 4 Pt; 8 Sac. **1986** NE: 15 G; 7.5 Sac. **1987** NE: 4 G; 1 Sac. **Total:** 89 G; Int 5-63; Scor 2 Saf; 4 Pt; 29.5 Sac.

ROBERT BLACKMON Blackmon, Robert James 6′0″, 208 **DB**
Col: Baylor *HS:* Van Vleck [TX] B: 5/12/1967, Bay City, TX *Drafted:* 1990 Round 2 Sea
1991 Sea: 1 Sac. **1992** Sea: 3.5 Sac. **1993** Sea: 1 Fum TD. **1995** Sea: 1 Sac. **1996** Sea: 1 Sac. **1997** Ind: 1 Fum TD; 3 Sac. **1998** Ind: 1 Sac. **Total:** 2 Fum TD; 10.5 Sac.

Year Team	G	Interceptions Int	Yds	TD	Tot TD
1990 Sea	15	0	0	0	0
1991 Sea	16	3	59	0	0
1992 Sea	15	1	69	0	0
1993 Sea	16	2	0	0	1
1994 Sea	15	1	24	0	0
1995 Sea	13	5	46	0	0
1996 Sea	16	3	48	0	1
1997 Ind	14	1	2	0	1
1998 Ind	15	1	14	0	0
NFL Total	135	17	262	0	3

ROOSEVELT BLACKMON Blackmon, Roosevelt III 6′1″, 185 **DB**
(Tadpole) *Col:* Morris Brown *HS:* Glades Central [Belle Glade, FL] B: 9/10/1974, Pahokee, FL *Drafted:* 1998 Round 4 GB
1998 GB-Cin: 15 G. GB: 3 G. Cin: 12 G. **Total:** 15 G.

RICHARD BLACKMORE Blackmore, Richard Earl 5′10″, 174 **DB**
Col: Mississippi State *HS:* Vicksburg [MS] B: 8/14/1956, Vicksburg, MS
1979 Phi: 16 G; PR 1-0. **1980** Phi: 16 G; Int 2-0. **1981** Phi: 16 G; Int 2-43. **1982** Phi: 9 G; Int 1-20 **1** TD; 6 Pt. **1983** SF: 11 G. **Total:** 68 G; PR 1-0; Int 5-63 1 TD; 6 Pt.

JEFF BLACKSHEAR Blackshear, Jeffrey Leon 6′6″, 323 **OG**
Col: Northeast Mississippi CC; Northeast Louisiana *HS:* Fort Pierce Westwood [FL] B: 3/29/1969, Ft. Pierce, FL *Drafted:* 1993 Round 8 Sea
1993 Sea: 15 G. **1994** Sea: 16 G. **1995** Sea: 16 G. **1996** Bal: 16 G. **1997** Bal: 16 G. **1998** Bal: 16 G. **Total:** 95 G.

ALOIS BLACKWELL Blackwell, Alois Sterling 5′10″, 195 **RB**
Col: Houston *HS:* Cuero [TX] B: 11/12/1954, Cuero, TX *Drafted:* 1978 Round 4 Dal
1978 Dal: 13 G; Rush 9-37 4.1; KR 3-70 23.3. **1979** Dal: 6 G. **Total:** 19 G; Rush 9-37 4.1; KR 3-70 23.3.

HAL BLACKWELL Blackwell, Harold 6′1″, 205 **HB-DB**
Col: South Carolina B: 5/12/1919 D: 1/6/1994, Bronx, NY
1945 ChiC: 2 G; Punt 17-661 38.9.

KELLY BLACKWELL Blackwell, Kelly Reardon 6′1″, 255 **TE**
Col: Texas Christian *HS:* Richland [North Richland Hills, TX] B: 2/13/1969, Blytheville, TX
1992 ChiB: 16 G; Rec 5-54 10.8. **1993** Dal: 2 G. **Total:** 18 G; Rec 5-54 10.8.

KORY BLACKWELL Blackwell, Kory 5′11″, 185 **DB**
Col: Massachusetts *HS:* Adlai E. Stevenson [Bronx, NY] B: 8/3/1972, New York, NY
1998 NYG: 5 G.

WILL BLACKWELL Blackwell, William Herman Jr. 6′0″, 185 **WR**
Col: San Diego State *HS:* Skyline [Oakland, CA] B: 7/9/1975, Texarkana, TX *Drafted:* 1997 Round 2 Pit
1997 Pit: Rush 2-14 7.0. **1998** Pit: Scor 1 2XP. **Total:** Rush 2-14 7.0; Scor 1 2XP.

Year Team	G	Receiving Rec	Yds	Avg	TD	Punt Returns Ret	Yds	Avg	TD
1997 Pit	14	12	168	14.0	1	23	149	6.5	0
1998 Pit	16	32	297	9.3	1	4	22	5.5	0
NFL Total	30	44	465	10.6	2	27	171	6.3	0

Year Team	Kickoff Returns Ret	Yds	Avg	TD	Fum	Tot TD
1997 Pit	32	791	24.7	1	3	2
1998 Pit	20	382	19.1	0	1	1
NFL Total	52	1173	22.6	1	4	3

GLENN BLACKWOOD Blackwood, Glenn Allen 6′0″, 187 **DB**
Col: Texas *HS:* Winston Churchill [San Antonio, TX] B: 2/23/1957, San Antonio, TX *Drafted:* 1979 Round 8 Mia
1980 Mia: PR 1-0. **1981** Mia: PR 2-8 4.0. **1982** Mia: PR 2-2 1.0; 2 Sac. **1983** Mia: PR 1-10 10.0; 1 Sac. **1985** Mia: PR 3-20 6.7. **1986** Mia: PR 1-0. **1987** Mia: PR 1-1 1.0. **Total:** PR 11-41 3.7; 3 Sac.

Year Team	G	Interceptions Int	Yds	TD	Fum
1979 Mia	11	0	0	0	0
1980 Mia	16	3	0	0	0
1981 Mia	16	4	124	0	0
1982 Mia	9	2	42	**1**	1
1983 Mia	16	3	0	0	0
1984 Mia	16	6	169	0	0
1985 Mia	14	6	36	0	0
1986 Mia	10	2	10	0	2
1987 Mia	10	3	17	0	0
NFL Total	118	29	398	1	3

LYLE BLACKWOOD Blackwood, Lyle Vernon 6′1″, 190 **DB**
Col: Blinn Coll. TX (J.C.); Texas Christian *HS:* Winston Churchill [San Antonio, TX] B: 5/2/1951, San Antonio, TX *Drafted:* 1973 Round 9 Den
1974 Cin: KR 1-17 17.0. **1976** Sea: Rec 1-8 8.0; KR 10-230 23.0. **1977** Bal: KR 1-24 24.0. **1978** Bal: KR 1-18 18.0. **1979** Bal: KR 3-41 13.7. **1980** Bal: KR 2-41 20.5. **1982** Mia: 1 Sac. **1985** Mia: KR 2-32 16.0. **Total:** Rec 1-8 8.0; KR 20-403 20.2; 1 Sac.

Year Team	G	Punt Returns Ret	Yds	Avg	TD	Interceptions Int	Yds	TD	Fum
1973 Cin	7	4	12	3.0	0	0	0	0	0
1974 Cin	13	10	29	2.9	0	0	0	0	0
1975 Cin	14	23	123	5.3	0	2	44	0	1
1976 Sea	11	19	132	6.9	0	0	0	0	1
1977 Bal	14	7	22	3.1	0	**10**	163	0	3
1978 Bal	16	1	2	2.0	0	4	146	2	0
1979 Bal	16	4	-1	-0.3	0	4	63	0	0
1980 Bal	11	0	0	—	0	1	0	0	0
1981 Mia	12	0	0	—	0	3	12	0	0
1982 Mia	9	0	0	—	0	2	41	0	0
1983 Mia	16	0	0	—	0	4	77	0	0
1984 Mia	16	0	0	—	0	3	29	0	0
1985 Mia	16	0	0	—	0	1	0	0	0
1986 Mia	5	1	0	0.0	0	1	14	0	1
NFL Total	176	69	319	4.6	0	35	589	2	6

BRIAN BLADES Blades, Brian Keith 5′11″, 189 **WR**
Col: Miami (Fla.) *HS:* Piper [Sunrise, FL] B: 7/24/1965, Ft. Lauderdale, FL *Drafted:* 1988 Round 2 Sea
1988 Sea: Rush 5-24 4.8. **1989** Sea: Rush 1-3 3.0. **1990** Sea: Rush 3-19 6.3. **1991** Sea: Rush 2-17 8.5. **1992** Sea: Rush 1-5 5.0. **1993** Sea: Rush 5-52 10.4. **1994** Sea: Rush 2-32 16.0; Scor 1 2XP. **1995** Sea: Rush 2-4 2.0. **Total:** Rush 21-156 7.4; Scor 1 2XP.

Year Team	G	Receiving Rec	Yds	Avg	TD	Fum
1988 Sea	16	40	682	17.1	8	1

1989 Sea	16	77	1063	13.8	5	3
1990 Sea	16	49	525	10.7	3	0
1991 Sea	16	70	1003	14.3	2	1
1992 Sea	6	19	256	13.5	1	1
1993 Sea	16	80	945	11.8	3	1
1994 Sea	16	81	1086	13.4	4	1
1995 Sea	16	77	1001	13.0	4	0
1996 Sea	11	43	556	12.9	2	1
1997 Sea	11	30	319	10.6	2	1
1998 Sea	16	15	184	12.3	0	1
NFL Total	156	581	7620	13.1	34	11

BENNIE BLADES Blades, Horatio Benedict 6′0″, 221 **DB**
Col: Miami (Fla.) *HS:* Piper [Sunrise, FL] B: 9/3/1966, Ft. Lauderdale, FL *Drafted:* 1988 Round 1 Det
1988 Det: 1 Sac. **1990** Det: 1 Sac. **1994** Det: 1 Sac. **1995** Det: Scor **1** Saf; 1 Sac. **1997** Sea: 1 Sac. **Total:** Scor 1 Saf; 5 Sac.

		Interceptions			Tot
Year Team	G	Int	Yds	TD	TD
1988 Det	15	2	12	0	0
1989 Det	16	0	0	0	0
1990 Det	12	2	25	0	0
1991 Det	16	1	14	0	0
1992 Det	16	3	56	0	1
1993 Det	4	0	0	0	0
1994 Det	16	1	0	0	0
1995 Det	16	1	0	0	0
1996 Det	15	2	112	1	1
1997 Sea	10	2	11	0	0
NFL Total	136	14	230	1	2

BRIAN BLADOS Blados, Brian Timothy 6′5″, 300 **OT**
Col: North Carolina *HS:* Washington Lee [Arlington, VA] B: 1/11/1962, Arlington, VA *Drafted:* 1984 Round 1 Cin
1984 Cin: 16 G. **1985** Cin: 16 G; Rec 1-4 4.0. **1986** Cin: 16 G. **1987** Cin: 11 G. **1988** Cin: 16 G. **1989** Cin: 13 G. **1990** Cin: 4 G. **1991** Cin-Ind: 13 G. Cin: 6 G. Ind: 7 G. **1992** TB: 2 G. **Total:** 107 G; Rec 1-4 4.0.

JOE BLAHAK Blahak, Joseph Phillip 5′9″, 187 **DB**
Col: Nebraska *HS:* Scotus Central Catholic [Columbus, NE]
B: 8/29/1950, Columbus, NE *Drafted:* 1973 Round 8 Hou
1973 Hou: 12 G; KR 2-41 20.5; Int 2-120. **1974** Min: 7 G. **1975** Min: 9 G; Int 1-16; Scor **1** Saf; 2 Pt. **1976** TB-NE: 4 G. TB: 2 G. NE: 2 G. **1977** Min: 12 G. **Total:** 44 G; KR 2-41 20.5; Int 3-136; Scor 1 Saf; 2 Pt.

RUSS BLAILOCK Blailock, William Russell Jr. 5′10″, 230 **T-G**
Col: Baylor *HS:* McGregor [TX] B: 6/29/1902, McGregor, TX
D: 1/20/1972, Dallas, TX
1923 Mil: 12 G; Rush 1 TD; 6 Pt. **1925** Akr: 8 G; Scor 5, 1 FG, 2 XK. **Total:** 20 G; Rush 1 TD; Scor 11, 1 FG, 2 XK.

ED BLAINE Blaine, Edward Homer 6′1″, 240 **OG**
Col: Missouri *HS:* Farmington [MO] B: 1/30/1940, Farmington, MO
Drafted: 1962 Round 2 GB
1962 GB: 14 G. **1963** Phi: 14 G; 1 Fum. **1964** Phi: 14 G. **1965** Phi: 14 G. **1966** Phi: 14 G. **Total:** 70 G; 1 Fum.

GEORGE BLAIR Blair, George Leroy 5′11″, 195 **DB-K**
Col: Mississippi *HS:* Pascagoula [MS] B: 5/10/1938, Pascagoula, MS
Drafted: 1960 Round 2 LAC
1961 SD: KR 1-2 2.0; Int 2-4. **1962** SD: Int 2-36. **1963** SD: Int 1-40. **Total:** KR 1-2 2.0; Int 5-80.

		Scoring						
Year Team	G	Pts	FG	FGA	FG%	XK	XKA	XK%
1961 SD	14	81	13	27	48.1	42	47	89.4
1962 SD	14	82	17	20	**85.0**	31	34	**91.2**
1963 SD	14	95	17	28	**60.7**	44	**48**	**91.7**
1964 SD	4	14	3	5	60.0	5	6	83.3
NFL Total	46	272	50	80	62.5	122	135	90.4

MATT BLAIR Blair, Matthew Albert 6′5″, 232 **LB**
Col: Northeastern Oklahoma A&M (J.C.); Iowa State *HS:* Colonel White [Dayton, OH] B: 9/20/1950, Hilo, HI *Drafted:* 1974 Round 2 Min
1975 Min: PR 2-(-2) -1.0. **1976** Min: KR 1-0. **1978** Min: 1 Fum TD. **1981** Min: KR 1-0. **1982** Min: 1.5 Sac. **1983** Min: 4.5 Sac. **1984** Min: 1 Sac. **1985** Min: 1 Sac. **Total:** PR 2-(-2) -1.0; KR 2-0; 1 Fum TD; 8 Sac.

		Interceptions				Tot
Year Team	G	Int	Yds	TD	Fum	TD
1974 Min	14	1	-3	0	0	0
1975 Min	14	1	18	0	1	0
1976 Min	14	2	25	0	0	0
1977 Min	14	1	18	0	0	1
1978 Min	16	3	28	0	0	1
1979 Min	16	3	32	0	0	0
1980 Min	14	3	0	0	0	0
1981 Min	16	1	1	0	1	0
1982 Min	9	0	0	0	0	0
1983 Min	16	1	0	0	0	0
1984 Min	11	0	0	0	0	0
1985 Min	6	0	0	0	0	0
NFL Total	160	16	119	0	2	2

MICHAEL BLAIR Blair, Michael Angelo Christopher 5′11″, 245 **RB**
Col: Ball State *HS:* Thornwood [South Holland, IL] B: 11/26/1974, Chicago, IL
1998 Cin-GB: 13 G; Rush 3-7 2.3; Rec 3-20 6.7; 1 Fum. Cin: 2 G; Rush 1-4 4.0; Rec 1-7 7.0; 1 Fum. GB: 11 G; Rush 2-3 1.5; Rec 2-13 6.5. **Total:** 13 G; Rush 3-7 2.3; Rec 3-20 6.7; 1 Fum.

PAUL BLAIR Blair, Paul Kevin 6′4″, 295 **OT**
Col: Oklahoma State *HS:* Edmond Memorial [OK] B: 8/3/1963, Edmond, OK *Drafted:* 1986 Round 4 ChiB
1986 ChiB: 14 G. **1987** ChiB: 10 G. **1990** Min: 2 G. **Total:** 26 G.

STANLEY BLAIR Blair, Stanley R 6′0″, 190 **DB**
Col: Oklahoma State; Southeastern Oklahoma State *HS:* Dollarway [Pine Bluff, AR] B: 7/4/1964, Pine Bluff, AR
1990 Pho: 5 G.

THOMAS BLAIR Blair, Thomas Calvin 6′4″, 220 **TE**
Col: Tulsa *HS:* East Lansing [MI] B: 8/4/1951, Ann Arbor, MI
Drafted: 1974 Round 11 Det
1974 Det: 11 G.

JEFF BLAKE Blake, Jeffery Bertrand 6′0″, 203 **QB**
Col: East Carolina *HS:* Seminole [Sanford, FL] B: 12/4/1970, Sanford, FL *Drafted:* 1992 Round 6 NYJ
1994 Cin: Scor 1 2XP. **1995** Cin: Scor 1 2XP. **Total:** Scor 2 2XP.

		Passing							
Year Team	G	Att	Comp	Comp%	Yds	YPA	TD	Int	Rating
1992 NYJ	3	9	4	44.4	40	4.44	0	1	18.1
1994 Cin	10	306	156	51.0	2154	7.04	14	9	76.9
1995 Cin	16	567	326	57.5	3822	6.74	28	17	82.1
1996 Cin	16	549	308	56.1	3624	6.60	24	14	80.3
1997 Cin	11	317	184	58.0	2125	6.70	8	7	77.6
1998 Cin	8	93	51	54.8	739	7.95	3	3	78.2
NFL Total	64	1841	1029	55.9	12504	6.79	77	51	79.4

	Rushing				
Year Team	Att	Yds	Avg	TD	Fum
1992 NYJ	2	-2	-1.0	0	1
1994 Cin	37	204	5.5	1	6
1995 Cin	53	309	5.8	2	10
1996 Cin	72	317	4.4	2	7
1997 Cin	45	234	5.2	3	7
1998 Cin	15	103	6.9	0	1
NFL Total	224	1165	5.2	8	32

RICKY BLAKE Blake, Ricky Darnell 6′2″, 244 **RB**
Col: Alabama A&M *HS:* Lincoln Co. [Fayetteville, TN] B: 7/15/1967, Fayetteville, TN
1991 Dal: 2 G; Rush 15-80 5.3 1 TD; Rec 1-5 5.0; 6 Pt.

TOM BLAKE Blake, Thomas Clinton 6′2″, 220 **T**
Col: Tennessee; Cincinnati *HS:* Middletown [OH] B: 7/19/1927, Bushton, IL
1949 NYB: 5 G; PR 1-6 6.0.

ROBERT BLAKELY Blakely, Robert Ervin 6′0″, 190 **WR**
Col: North Dakota State *HS:* Central [St. Paul, MN] B: 9/20/1959, St. Paul, MN
1982 KC: 2 G.

DICK BLANCHARD Blanchard, Richard L 6′3″, 225 **LB**
Col: Tulsa *HS:* Rich Central [Olympia Fields, IL] B: 1/17/1949, Waukesha, WI
1972 NE: 14 G; Int 1-20.

CARY BLANCHARD Blanchard, Robert Cary 6′1″, 227 **K**
Col: Oklahoma State *HS:* L.D. Bell [Hurst, TX] B: 11/5/1968, Fort Worth, TX
1998 Was: Punt 3-113 37.7. **Total:** Punt 3-113 37.7.

		Scoring						
Year Team	G	Pts	FG	FGA	FG%	XK	XKA	XK%
1992 NYJ	11	65	16	22	72.7	17	17	**100.0**
1993 NYJ	16	82	17	26	65.4	31	31	100.0
1995 Ind	12	82	19	24	79.2	25	25	100.0
1996 Ind	16	135	36	40	**90.0**	27	27	**100.0**
1997 Ind	16	117	32	**41**	78.0	21	21	100.0
1998 Was	13	63	11	17	64.7	30	31	96.8
NFL Total	84	544	131	170	77.1	151	152	99.3

TOM BLANCHARD Blanchard, Thomas Richard 6′0″, 190 **P**
Col: Oregon *HS:* Grants Pass [OR] B: 5/28/1948, Grants Pass, OR
Drafted: 1971 Round 12 NYG
1971 NYG: Pass 1-1 100.0%, 18 18.00. **1972** NYG: Pass 1-0; Rush 1-17 17.0. **1977** NO: Pass 3-1 33.3%, 3 1.00 1 TD 1 Int. **1978** NO: Rush 2-0.

1979 TB: Rush 1-0. **1981** TB: Rush 1-0. **Total:** Pass 5-2 40.0%, 21 4.20 1 TD 1 Int; Rush 5-17 3.4.

		Punting			
Year Team	G	Punts	Yds	Avg	Fum
1971 NYG	14	66	2681	40.6	1
1972 NYG	14	47	2006	42.7	0
1973 NYG	14	56	2347	41.9	0
1974 NO	13	88	3704	42.1	0
1975 NO	14	92	**3776**	41.0	0
1976 NO	14	**101**	3974	39.3	0
1977 NO	14	82	3474	42.4	0
1978 NO	16	84	3532	42.0	0
1979 TB	16	93	3679	39.6	1
1980 TB	16	88	3722	42.3	0
1981 TB	3	22	899	40.9	1
NFL Total	148	819	33794	41.3	3

TONY BLAND Bland, Anthony 6′3″, 213 **WR**
Col: Florida A&M *HS:* Pinellas Park [Largo, FL] B: 12/12/1972, St. Petersburg, FL
1997 Min: 2 G. **1998** Min: 1 G. **Total:** 3 G.

CARL BLAND Bland, Carl Nathaniel 5′11″, 182 **WR**
Col: Virginia Union *HS:* Thomas Jefferson [Richmond, VA]
B: 8/17/1961, Fluvanna Co., VA
1988 Det: Rush 1-4 4.0; PR 5-59 11.8. **1989** GB: 1 Fum TD.
Total: Rush 1-4 4.0; PR 5-59 11.8; 1 Fum TD.

		Receiving				Kickoff Returns					Tot
Year Team	G	Rec	Yds	Avg	TD	Ret	Yds	Avg	TD	Fum	TD
1984 Det	3	0	0	—	0	0	0	—	0	0	0
1985 Det	8	12	157	13.1	0	0	0	—	0	0	0
1986 Det	16	44	511	11.6	2	6	114	19.0	0	1	2
1987 Det	10	2	14	7.0	1	2	44	22.0	0	0	1
1988 Det	16	21	307	14.6	2	8	179	22.4	0	1	2
1989 GB	16	11	164	14.9	1	13	256	19.7	0	0	2
1990 GB	14	0	0	—	0	7	104	14.9	0	0	0
NFL Total	83	90	1153	12.8	6	36	697	19.4	0	2	7

GEORGE BLANDA Blanda, George Frederick 6′2″, 215 **QB-K**
Col: Kentucky *HS:* Youngwood [PA] B: 9/17/1927, Youngwood, PA
Drafted: 1949 Round 12 ChiB *HOF:* 1981
1949 ChiB: Punt 19-746 39.3. **1950** Bal-ChiB: Punt 2-30 15.0. ChiB: Punt 2-30 15.0. **1951** ChiB: KR 2-19 9.5; Int 1-13. **1953** ChiB: Rec 0-7. **1954** ChiB: Scor 1 1XP. **1956** ChiB: Punt 1-33 33.0. **1961** Hou: Rec 1-(-16) -16.0. **Total:** Rec 1-(-16) -16.0; KR 2-19 9.5; Int 1-13; Punt 22-809 36.8; Scor 1 1XP.

		Passing							
Year Team	G	Att	Comp	Comp%	Yds	YPA	TD	Int	Rating
1949 ChiB	12	21	9	42.9	197	9.38	0	5	37.3
1950 Bal-ChiB	12	1	0	0.0	0	0.00	0	0	39.6
1950 Bal	1	0	0	—	0	—	0	0	—
1950 ChiB	11	1	0	0.0	0	0.00	0	0	39.6
1951 ChiB	12	0	0	—	0	—	0	0	—
1952 ChiB	12	131	47	35.9	664	5.07	8	11	38.5
1953 ChiB	12	**362**	**169**	46.7	2164	5.98	14	23	52.3
1954 ChiB	8	281	131	46.6	1929	6.86	15	17	62.1
1955 ChiB	12	97	42	43.3	459	4.73	4	7	41.6
1956 ChiB	12	69	37	53.6	439	6.36	7	4	82.9
1957 ChiB	12	19	8	42.1	65	3.42	0	3	11.8
1958 ChiB	12	7	2	28.6	19	2.71	0	0	39.6
1960 Hou	14	363	169	46.6	2413	6.65	24	22	65.4
1961 Hou	14	362	187	51.7	**3330**	**9.20**	**36**	22	91.3
1962 Hou	14	418	197	47.1	2810	6.72	27	42	51.3
1963 Hou	14	**423**	**224**	53.0	**3003**	7.10	24	25	70.1
1964 Hou	14	**505**	**262**	51.9	3287	6.51	17	27	61.4
1965 Hou	14	**442**	**186**	42.1	2542	5.75	20	30	47.9
1966 Hou	14	271	122	45.0	1764	6.51	17	21	55.3
1967 Oak	14	38	15	39.5	285	7.50	3	3	59.6
1968 Oak	14	49	30	61.2	522	10.65	6	2	120.1
1969 Oak	14	13	6	46.2	73	5.62	2	1	71.5
1970 Oak	14	55	29	52.7	461	8.38	6	5	79.4
1971 Oak	14	58	32	55.2	378	6.52	4	6	58.6
1972 Oak	14	15	5	33.3	77	5.13	1	0	73.5
1973 Oak	14	0	0	—	0	—	0	0	—
1974 Oak	14	4	1	25.0	28	7.00	1	0	95.8
1975 Oak	14	3	1	33.3	11	3.67	0	1	5.6
NFL Total	340	4007	1911	47.7	26920	6.72	236	277	60.6

	Rushing			
Year Team	Att	Yds	Avg	TD
1949 ChiB	2	9	4.5	1
1952 ChiB	20	104	5.2	1
1953 ChiB	24	62	2.6	0
1954 ChiB	19	41	2.2	0
1955 ChiB	15	54	3.6	2
1956 ChiB	6	47	7.8	0
1957 ChiB	5	-5	-1.0	1
1960 Hou	16	16	1.0	4
1961 Hou	7	12	1.7	0
1962 Hou	3	6	2.0	0
1963 Hou	4	1	0.3	0
1964 Hou	4	-2	-0.5	0
1965 Hou	4	-6	-1.5	0
1966 Hou	3	1	0.3	0
1969 Oak	1	0	0.0	0
1970 Oak	2	4	2.0	0
NFL Total	135	344	2.5	9

	Scoring							
Year Team	Pts	FG	FGA	FG%	XK	XKA	XK%	Fum
1949 ChiB	27	7	15	46.7	0	0	—	0
1950 Bal-ChiB	18	6	15	40.0	0	0	—	0
1950 ChiB	18	6	15	40.0	0	0	—	0
1951 ChiB	44	6	17	35.3	26	26	100.0	0
1952 ChiB	54	6	25	24.0	30	30	100.0	0
1953 ChiB	48	7	20	35.0	27	27	100.0	3
1954 ChiB	47	8	16	50.0	22	22	100.0	3
1955 ChiB	82	11	16	**68.8**	37	37	**100.0**	0
1956 ChiB	81	12	**28**	42.9	**45**	**47**	95.7	2
1957 ChiB	71	14	**26**	53.8	23	23	100.0	0
1958 ChiB	69	11	23	47.8	36	37	97.3	0
1960 Hou	115	15	**33**	45.5	46	47	97.9	8
1961 Hou	112	16	26	**61.5**	**64**	**65**	**98.5**	3
1962 Hou	81	11	26	42.3	**48**	**49**	98.0	2
1963 Hou	66	9	22	40.9	39	39	100.0	8
1964 Hou	76	13	29	44.8	37	38	97.4	7
1965 Hou	61	11	21	52.4	28	28	100.0	2
1966 Hou	87	16	30	53.3	39	40	97.5	3
1967 Oak	**116**	20	30	**66.7**	**56**	**57**	**98.2**	0
1968 Oak	117	21	34	61.8	**54**	**54**	100.0	1
1969 Oak	105	20	37	54.1	**45**	**45**	100.0	1
1970 Oak	84	16	29	55.2	36	36	100.0	1
1971 Oak	86	15	22	68.2	41	42	97.6	1
1972 Oak	95	17	26	65.4	**44**	44	100.0	1
1973 Oak	100	23	33	69.7	31	31	100.0	0
1974 Oak	77	11	17	64.7	**44**	**46**	95.7	0
1975 Oak	83	13	21	61.9	44	48	91.7	1
NFL Total	**2002**	335	**637**	52.6	**942**	**958**	98.3	47

ERNIE BLANDIN Blandin, Ernest Elmer 6′4″, 248 **DT-OT**
Col: Tulane *HS:* Leon [KS] B: 6/21/1919, Augusta, KS D: 9/16/1968, Randallstown, MD *Drafted:* 1942 Round 5 Phi
AAFC **1946** CleA: 14 G. **1947** CleA: 12 G; Rush 1-(-6) -6.0. **1948** BalA: 14 G. **1949** BalA: 10 G. **Total:** 50 G; Rush 1-(-6) -6.0.

NFL **1950** Bal: 12 G; Rec 1-16 16.0; KR 3-31 10.3; 2 Fum. **1953** Bal: 9 G. **Total:** 21 G; Rec 1-16 16.0; KR 3-31 10.3; 2 Fum.

BRIAN BLANKENSHIP Blankenship, Brian Patrick 6′1″, 286 **OG**
Col: Nebraska-Omaha; Nebraska *HS:* Daniel J. Gross [Omaha, NE]
B: 4/7/1963, Omaha, NE
1987 Pit: 13 G. **1988** Pit: 13 G; KR 1-5 5.0. **1989** Pit: 16 G. **1990** Pit: 16 G; 1 Fum. **1991** Pit: 3 G. **Total:** 61 G; KR 1-5 5.0; 1 Fum.

GREG BLANKENSHIP Blankenship, Gregory 6′1″, 212 **LB**
Col: Cal State-Hayward *HS:* Vallejo [CA] B: 3/24/1954, Vallejo, CA
1976 Oak-Pit: 10 G. Oak: 4 G. Pit: 6 G. **Total:** 10 G.

SID BLANKS Blanks, Sidney 6′1″, 200 **RB**
Col: Texas A&M–Kingsville *HS:* San Felipe [Del Rio, TX] B: 4/29/1941, Del Rio, TX *Drafted:* 1964 Round 5 Hou
1964 Hou: Pass 1-1 100.0%, 8 8.00 1 TD. **Total:** Pass 1-1 100.0%, 8 8.00 1 TD.

		Rushing				Receiving			
Year Team	G	Att	Yds	Avg	TD	Rec	Yds	Avg	TD
1964 Hou	14	145	756	5.2	**6**	56	497	8.9	1
1966 Hou	14	71	235	3.3	0	19	234	12.3	2
1967 Hou	13	66	206	3.1	1	11	93	8.5	1
1968 Hou	14	63	169	2.7	0	13	184	14.2	0
1969 Bos	14	7	30	4.3	0	2	16	8.0	0
1970 Bos	14	13	44	3.4	0	5	49	9.8	0
NFL Total	83	365	1440	3.9	7	106	1073	10.1	4

	Punt Returns				Kickoff Returns					Tot
Year Team	Ret	Yds	Avg	TD	Ret	Yds	Avg	TD	Fum	TD
1964 Hou	0	0	—	0	9	207	23.0	0	5	7
1966 Hou	0	0	—	0	21	487	23.2	0	2	2
1967 Hou	0	0	—	0	0	0	—	0	2	2
1968 Hou	22	179	8.1	0	0	0	—	0	3	0
1969 Bos	5	10	2.0	0	6	131	21.8	0	1	0
1970 Bos	9	83	9.2	0	7	152	21.7	0	0	0
NFL Total	36	272	7.6	0	43	977	22.7	0	13	11

JERRY BLANTON Blanton, Gerald 6'1", 231 LB
Col: Kentucky *HS:* Thomas DeVilbiss [Toledo, OH] B: 12/20/1956, Toledo, OH *Drafted:* 1978 Round 11 Buf
1979 KC: 16 G. **1980** KC: 16 G. **1981** KC: 9 G. **1982** KC: 9 G; 1 Sac. **1983** KC: 16 G. **1984** KC: 10 G; Int 1-14; 0.5 Sac. **1985** KC: 16 G; 0.5 Sac. **Total:** 92 G; Int 1-14; 2 Sac.

SCOTT BLANTON Blanton, Robert Scott 6'2", 221 K
Col: Oklahoma *HS:* Norman [OK] B: 7/1/1973, Norman, OK
1996 Was: Punt 2-84 42.0. **Total:** Punt 2-84 42.0.

		Scoring						
Year Team	G	Pts	FG	FGA	FG%	XK	XKA	XK%
1996 Was	16	118	26	32	81.3	40	40	100.0
1997 Was	15	82	16	24	66.7	34	34	100.0
1998 Was	2	10	2	4	50.0	4	4	100.0
NFL Total	33	210	44	60	73.3	78	78	100.0

ANTHONY BLAYLOCK Blaylock, Anthony Darius 5'10", 190 DB
Col: Winston-Salem State *HS:* Garner [NC] B: 2/21/1965, Raleigh, NC *Drafted:* 1988 Round 4 Cle
1988 Cle: 12 G. **1989** Cle: 16 G; 4 Sac. **1990** Cle: 16 G; Int 2-45; 1 Fum TD; 6 Pt; 1 Sac. **1991** Cle-SD: 7 G. Cle: 5 G. SD: 2 G. **1992** SD: 11 G; Int 2-0. **1993** ChiB: 9 G; Int 2-3. **Total:** 71 G; Int 6-48; 1 Fum TD; 6 Pt; 5 Sac.

PHIL BLAZER Blazer, Philip Paul 6'1", 235 OG
Col: North Carolina *HS:* Munhall [PA] B: 2/25/1936 *Drafted:* 1958 Round 8 Det
1960 Buf: 14 G.

TONY BLAZINE Blazine, Anthony Abraham Jr. 6'0", 232 T
Col: Illinois Wesleyan *HS:* Johnston City [IL] B: 1/2/1912, Canton, IL D: 7/3/1963
1935 ChiC: 12 G. **1936** ChiC: 11 G. **1937** ChiC: 11 G; Rec 1-2 2.0. **1938** ChiC: 11 G; **1** Fum TD; 6 Pt. **1939** ChiC: 11 G. **1940** ChiC: 7 G. **1941** NYG: 10 G. **Total:** 73 G; Rec 1-2 2.0; 1 Fum TD; 6 Pt.

JEFF BLEAMER Bleamer, Jeffrey Harrison 6'4", 253 OT-OG
Col: Penn State *HS:* Louis E. Dieruff [Allentown, PA] B: 6/22/1953, Allentown, PA *Drafted:* 1975 Round 8 Phi
1975 Phi: 14 G. **1976** Phi: 10 G; KR 1-0. **1977** NYJ: 8 G. **Total:** 32 G; KR 1-0.

CURTIS BLEDSOE Bledsoe, Curtis Kemp 5'11", 215 RB
Col: Chabot Coll. CA (J.C.); San Diego State *HS:* Mount Eden [Hayward, CA] B: 3/19/1957, Odessa, TX
1981 KC: Rec 3-27 9.0; KR 6-117 19.5. **1982** KC: Rec 1-5 5.0. **Total:** Rec 4-32 8.0; KR 6-117 19.5.

		Rushing				
Year Team	G	Att	Yds	Avg	TD	Fum
1981 KC	13	20	65	3.3	0	4
1982 KC	3	10	20	2.0	0	2
NFL Total	16	30	85	2.8	0	6

DREW BLEDSOE Bledsoe, Drew McQueen 6'5", 233 QB
Col: Washington State *HS:* Walla Walla [WA] B: 2/14/1972, Ellensburg, WA *Drafted:* 1993 Round 1 NE
1995 NE: Rec 1-(-9) -9.0. **Total:** Rec 1-(-9) -9.0.

		Passing							
Year Team	G	Att	Comp	Comp%	Yds	YPA	TD	Int	Rating
1993 NE	13	429	214	49.9	2494	5.81	15	15	65.0
1994 NE	16	**691**	**400**	57.9	**4555**	6.59	25	27	73.6
1995 NE	15	**636**	323	50.8	3507	5.51	13	16	63.7
1996 NE	16	**623**	**373**	59.9	4086	6.56	27	15	83.7
1997 NE	16	522	314	60.2	3706	7.10	28	15	87.7
1998 NE	14	481	263	54.7	3633	7.55	20	14	80.9
NFL Total	90	3382	1887	55.8	21981	6.50	128	102	75.7

	Rushing				
Year Team	Att	Yds	Avg	TD	Fum
1993 NE	32	82	2.6	0	8
1994 NE	44	40	0.9	0	9
1995 NE	20	28	1.4	0	11
1996 NE	24	27	1.1	0	9
1997 NE	28	55	2.0	0	4
1998 NE	28	44	1.6	0	9
NFL Total	176	276	1.6	0	50

MAL BLEEKER Bleeker, Malcolm S 6'0", 205 G-C
Col: Columbia *HS:* Flushing [Queens, NY]; Mercerburg Acad. [PA] B: 1907
1930 Bkn: 3 G.

MEL BLEEKER Bleeker, Melvin Wallace 5'11", 189 HB-DB
Col: USC *HS:* John C. Fremont [Los Angeles, CA] B: 8/20/1920, Los Angeles, CA D: 4/24/1996, Mission Viejo, CA
1944 Phi: Rec 8-299 37.4 4 TD; PR 1-3 3.0; Int 1-0. **1945** Phi: Rec 3-32 10.7; PR 4-37 9.3. **1946** Phi: Rec 3-29 9.7. **1947** LARm: KR 3-50 16.7; Int 1-0; 1 Fum TD. **Total:** Rec 14-360 25.7 4 TD; PR 5-40 8.0; KR 3-50 16.7; Int 2-0; 1 Fum TD.

		Rushing					Tot
Year Team	G	Att	Yds	Avg	TD	Fum	TD
1944 Phi	9	60	315	5.3	4	0	8
1945 Phi	4	50	167	3.3	2	2	2
1946 Phi	4	6	-7	-1.2	0	1	0
1947 LARm	11	23	111	4.8	0	3	1
NFL Total	28	139	586	4.2	6	6	11

TOM BLEICK Bleick, Thomas Ward 6'2", 200 DB
Col: Georgia Tech *HS:* Talladega [AL] B: 3/21/1943, Talladega, AL *Drafted:* 1965 Round 9 Bal
1966 Bal: 7 G. **1967** Atl: 2 G. **Total:** 9 G.

JOHNNY BLEIER Bleier, John Ludwig 160 WB-BB
Col: No College B: 8/25/1892, Reading, OH D: 4/13/1981, Hyattsville, MD
1921 Was: 3 G.

BOB BLEIER Bleier, John Robert 6'3", 210 QB
Col: Richmond *HS:* St. Thomas Aquinas [Rochester, NY] B: 6/1/1964, Rochester, NY
1987 NE: 3 G; Pass 39-14 35.9%, 181 4.64 1 TD 1 Int; Rush 5-(-5) -1.0 1 TD; 6 Pt; 2 Fum.

ROCKY BLEIER Bleier, Robert Patrick 5'11", 210 RB
Col: Notre Dame *HS:* Xavier [Appleton, WI] B: 3/5/1946, Appleton, WI *Drafted:* 1968 Round 16 Pit
1968 Pit: PR 2-13 6.5; KR 6-119 19.8. **1971** Pit: KR 1-21 21.0. **1972** Pit: PR 2-1 0.5; KR 2-40 20.0. **1973** Pit: KR 3-47 15.7. **1974** Pit: KR 3-67 22.3. **Total:** PR 4-14 3.5; KR 15-294 19.6.

		Rushing				Receiving					Tot
Year Team	G	Att	Yds	Avg	TD	Rec	Yds	Avg	TD	Fum	TD
1968 Pit	10	6	39	6.5	0	3	68	22.7	0	0	0
1971 Pit	6	0	0	—	0	0	0	—	0	0	0
1972 Pit	14	1	17	17.0	0	0	0	—	0	1	0
1973 Pit	12	3	0	0.0	0	0	0	—	0	2	0
1974 Pit	12	88	373	4.2	2	7	87	12.4	0	2	2
1975 Pit	11	140	528	3.8	2	15	65	4.3	0	7	2
1976 Pit	14	220	1036	4.7	5	24	294	12.3	0	4	5
1977 Pit	13	135	465	3.4	4	18	161	8.9	0	6	4
1978 Pit	16	165	633	3.8	5	17	168	9.9	1	6	6
1979 Pit	16	92	434	4.7	4	31	277	8.9	0	4	4
1980 Pit	16	78	340	4.4	1	21	174	8.3	1	0	2
NFL Total	140	928	3865	4.2	23	136	1294	9.5	2	32	25

PAUL BLESSING Blessing, Paul Theodore 6'4", 215 OE-DE
Col: Nebraska-Kearney *HS:* Ord, [NE] B: 1/6/1919, Tilden, NE D: 5/6/1990, Englewood, CO
1944 Det: 8 G.

TONY BLEVINS Blevins, Tony 6'0", 165 DB
Col: Kansas *HS:* Rockhurst [Kansas City, MO] B: 1/29/1975, Rockford, IL
1998 SF-Ind: 5 G. SF: 2 G. Ind: 3 G. **Total:** 5 G.

DENNIS BLIGEN Bligen, Dennis 5'11", 215 RB
Col: St. John's (N.Y.) *HS:* Murray Bergtraum [New York, NY] B: 3/3/1962, New York, NY
1985 NYJ: Rec 5-43 8.6. **1986** NYJ-TB: Rec 2-6 3.0. NYJ: Rec 2-6 3.0. **1987** NYJ: Rec 11-81 7.4. **Total:** Rec 18-130 7.2.

		Rushing				
Year Team	G	Att	Yds	Avg	TD	Fum
1984 NYJ	1	0	0	—	0	0
1985 NYJ	9	22	107	4.9	1	1
1986 NYJ-TB	5	20	65	3.3	1	2
1986 NYJ	4	20	65	3.3	1	2
1986 TB	1	0	0	—	0	0
1987 NYJ	6	31	128	4.1	1	1
NFL Total	21	73	300	4.1	3	4

STAN BLINKA Blinka, Stanley John 6'2", 230 LB
Col: Sam Houston State *HS:* Rockdale [TX] B: 4/29/1957, Columbus, OH *Drafted:* 1979 Round 5 NYJ
1979 NYJ: 16 G; Int 2-12. **1980** NYJ: 16 G. **1981** NYJ: 16 G; Int 1-15. **1982** NYJ: 8 G. **1983** NYJ: 16 G. **Total:** 72 G; Int 3-27.

HARRY BLISS Bliss, Harold W 5'8", 155 BB-TB-WB
Col: Ohio State *HS:* Butler [PA] B: 1897 Deceased
1921 Col: 9 G; Scor 1, 1 XK.

HOMER BLISS Bliss, Homer Clisson 5'11", 195 G
Col: Washington & Jefferson *HS:* Northwestern [Detroit, MI] B: 8/16/1904 D: 4/1970, Detroit, MI
1928 ChiC: 1 G.

GREG BLOEDORN Bloedorn, Gregory S 6'6", 278 **C**
Col: Cornell *HS:* Glenbard South [Glen Ellyn, IL] B: 11/15/1972, Elmhurst, IL
1997 Sea: 2 G.

TOM BLONDIN Blondin, Thomas Albert 6'0", 195 **G**
Col: West Virginia Wesleyan *HS:* Williamstown [WV] B: 10/25/1910, Marietta, OH D: 12/15/1978, Parkersburg, WV
1933 Cin: 3 G.

JOHNNY BLOOD McNally, John Victor (Blood) 6'1", 188 **HB-WB-DB-TB**
Col: Wis.-River Falls; St. John's (Minn.); Notre Dame *HS:* New Richmond [WI] B: 11/27/1903, New Richmond, WI D: 11/28/1985, Palm Springs, CA *HOF:* 1963
1928 Pott: Int **1** TD; Scor **1** 1XP. **1929** GB: PR **1** TD. **1931** GB: Int **1** TD. **1932** GB: Int **1** TD. **1933** GB: Scor 1 1XP. **1935** GB: Int **1** TD. **1936** GB: Int 1 TD; Scor 19, 1 XK. **1937** Pit: KR **1** TD. **Total:** PR 1 TD; KR 1 TD; Int 5 TD; Scor 2 1XP.

		Passing							
Year Team	**G**	**Att**	**Comp**	**Comp%**	**Yds**	**YPA**	**TD**	**Int**	**Rating**
1925 Mil	6	—	—	—	—	—	0	—	—
1926 Dul	13	—	—	—	—	—	0	—	—
1927 Dul	9	—	—	—	—	—	0	—	—
1928 Pott	10	—	—	—	—	—	0	—	—
1929 GB	12	—	—	—	—	—	1	—	—
1930 GB	10	—	—	—	—	—	0	—	—
1931 GB	14	—	—	—	—	—	1	—	—
1932 GB	13	3	0	0.0	0	0.00	0	0	39.6
1933 GB	9	2	0	0.0	0	0.00	0	0	39.6
1934 Pit	5	1	0	0.0	0	0.00	0	0	39.6
1935 GB	9	33	11	33.3	164	4.97	0	3	12.7
1936 GB	8	6	3	50.0	20	3.33	1	0	97.2
1937 Pit	9	25	10	40.0	115	4.60	1	2	34.6
1938 Pit	10	0	0	—	0	—	0	0	—
NFL Total	137	70	24	34.3	299	4.27	4	5	37.7

	Rushing				Receiving				Tot
Year Team	**Att**	**Yds**	**Avg**	**TD**	**Rec**	**Yds**	**Avg**	**TD**	**TD**
1926 Dul	—	—	—	1	—	—	—	1	2
1927 Dul	—	—	—	0	—	—	—	1	1
1928 Pott	—	—	—	0	—	—	—	2	3
1929 GB	—	—	—	2	—	—	—	2	5
1930 GB	—	—	—	0	—	—	—	**5**	5
1931 GB	—	—	—	2	—	—	—	**11**	**14**
1932 GB	37	130	3.5	0	14	168	12.0	3	4
1933 GB	14	41	2.9	0	8	215	26.9	**3**	3
1934 Pit	3	3	1.0	0	1	10	10.0	0	0
1935 GB	42	115	2.7	0	25	404	16.2	3	4
1936 GB	13	65	5.0	0	7	147	21.0	2	3
1937 Pit	9	37	4.1	0	10	168	16.8	4	5
1938 Pit	2	-5	-2.5	0	2	5	2.5	0	0
NFL Total	120	386	3.2	5	67	1117	16.7	37	49

AL BLOODGOOD Bloodgood, Elbert Lorraine 5'8", 153 **BB-TB-WB**
Col: DePauw; Nebraska *HS:* Beatrice [NE] B: 9/5/1901, Beatrice, NE D: 1947
1925 KC: 6 G; Scor 7, 2 FG, 1 XK. **1926** KC: 11 G; Rush 2 TD; Rec 1 TD; Scor 47, 8 FG, 5 XK; Tot TD 3. **1927** Cle: 10 G; Rush 4 TD; Rec 1 TD; Scor 45, 1 FG, 6 XK; 1 Fum TD; Tot TD **6**. **1928** NYG: 5 G; PR **1** TD; 6 Pt. **1930** GB: 3 G. **Total:** 35 G; Rush 6 TD; Rec 2 TD; PR 1 TD; Scor 105, 11 FG, 12 XK; 1 Fum TD; Tot TD 10.

ALVIN BLOUNT Blount, Alvin Wilbert 5'9", 197 **RB**
Col: Maryland *HS:* Eleanor Roosevelt [Greenbelt, MD] B: 2/12/1965, Washington, DC *Drafted:* 1987 Round 9 Dal
1987 Dal: Rec 1-5 5.0.

		Rushing				
Year Team	**G**	**Att**	**Yds**	**Avg**	**TD**	**Fum**
1987 Dal	2	46	125	2.7	3	1

TONY BLOUNT Blount, Anthony Urban 6'1", 195 **DB**
Col: Virginia *HS:* Frederick Douglass [Atlanta, GA] B: 11/5/1958, Atlanta, GA *Drafted:* 1980 Round 5 NYG
1980 NYG: 3 G.

ED BLOUNT Blount, Edward Cleo 6'0", 195 **QB**
Col: Washington State *HS:* Blair [Pasadena, CA] B: 2/26/1964, Los Angeles, CA
1987 SF: 1 G; Rush 1-0; 1 Fum.

ERIC BLOUNT Blount, Eric Lamont 5'9", 192 **WR**
Col: North Carolina *HS:* Ayden-Grifton [Ayden, NC] B: 9/22/1970, Ayden, NC *Drafted:* 1992 Round 8 Pho
1992 Pho: 4 G; Rush 1-(-1) -1.0; Rec 3-18 6.0; PR 13-101 7.8; KR 11-251 22.8. **1993** Pho: 6 G; Rush 5-28 5.6 1 TD; Rec 5-36 7.2; PR 9-90 10.0; KR 8-163 20.4; 6 Pt. **Total:** 10 G; Rush 6-27 4.5 1 TD; Rec 8-54 6.8; PR 22-191 8.7; KR 19-414 21.8; 6 Pt.

JEB BLOUNT Blount, John Eugene 6'3", 200 **QB**
Col: Tulsa *HS:* Longview [TX] B: 7/12/1954, Tyler, TX *Drafted:* 1976 Round 2 Oak
1977 TB: Rush 5-26 5.2.

		Passing								
Year Team	**G**	**Att**	**Comp**	**Comp%**	**Yds**	**YPA**	**TD**	**Int**	**Rating**	**Fum**
1977 TB	5	89	37	41.6	522	5.87	0	7	28.4	2

LAMAR BLOUNT Blount, Lloyd Lamar 6'1", 190 **OE-DB-HB**
(Pappy) *Col:* Duke; Mississippi State *HS:* Philadelphia [MS] B: 4/11/1920, Decatur, MS
AAFC **1946** MiaA: 12 G; Rec 13-218 16.8 1 TD; 6 Pt. **1947** BufA-BalA: 10 G; Rush 4-5 1.3; Rec 8-148 18.5. **Total:** 22 G; Rush 4-5 1.3; Rec 21-366 17.4 1 TD; 6 Pt.

MEL BLOUNT Blount, Melvin Cornell 6'3", 205 **DB**
Col: Southern University *HS:* Lyons [GA] B: 4/10/1948, Vidalia, GA *Drafted:* 1970 Round 3 Pit *HOF:* 1989
1970 Pit: PR 1-52 52.0. **1972** Pit: **1** Fum TD. **1983** Pit: 1 Fum TD. **Total:** PR 1-52 52.0; 2 Fum TD.

		Kickoff Returns				Interceptions				Tot
Year Team	**G**	**Ret**	**Yds**	**Avg**	**TD**	**Int**	**Yds**	**TD**	**Fum**	**TD**
1970 Pit	14	18	535	29.7	0	1	4	0	0	0
1971 Pit	14	4	76	19.0	0	2	16	0	1	0
1972 Pit	14	0	0	—	0	3	75	0	0	1
1973 Pit	14	0	0	—	0	4	82	0	0	0
1974 Pit	13	5	152	30.4	0	2	74	1	0	1
1975 Pit	14	8	139	17.4	0	**11**	121	0	1	0
1976 Pit	14	0	0	—	0	6	75	0	1	0
1977 Pit	14	0	0	—	0	6	65	0	0	0
1978 Pit	16	0	0	—	0	4	55	0	0	0
1979 Pit	16	0	0	—	0	3	1	0	0	0
1980 Pit	16	1	9	9.0	0	4	28	0	0	0
1981 Pit	16	0	0	—	0	6	106	1	0	1
1982 Pit	9	0	0	—	0	1	2	0	0	0
1983 Pit	16	0	0	—	0	4	32	0	0	1
NFL Total	200	36	911	25.3	0	57	736	2	3	4

AL BLOZIS Blozis, Alfred Charles 6'6", 250 **T**
(Big Bertha) *Col:* Georgetown *HS:* William L. Dickinson [Jersey City, NJ] B: 1/5/1919, Garfield, NJ D: 1/31/1945, Colmar, France *Drafted:* 1942 Round 3 NYG
1942 NYG: 11 G. **1943** NYG: 10 G; Rec 1-15 15.0; 6 Pt. **1944** NYG: 2 G. **Total:** 23 G; Rec 1-15 15.0; 6 Pt.

TONY BLUE Blue, Anthony Allen 5'9", 185 **DB**
Col: Nevada-Las Vegas *HS:* Morningside [Inglewood, CA] B: 9/19/1964, Inglewood, CA
1987 Sea: 3 G.

FORREST BLUE Blue, Forrest Murrell Jr. 6'6", 261 **C-OT**
Col: Auburn *HS:* Chamberlain [Tampa, FL] B: 9/7/1944, Marfa, TX *Drafted:* 1968 Round 1 SF
1968 SF: 14 G. **1969** SF: 14 G; 1 Fum. **1970** SF: 14 G. **1971** SF: 14 G; **1** Fum TD; 6 Pt. **1972** SF: 14 G. **1973** SF: 14 G. **1974** SF: 12 G. **1975** Bal: 11 G. **1976** Bal: 14 G. **1977** Bal: 14 G. **1978** Bal: 13 G. **Total:** 148 G; 1 Fum TD; 6 Pt; 1 Fum.

LUTHER BLUE Blue, Luther 5'11", 185 **WR**
Col: Iowa State *HS:* Valdosta [GA] B: 10/21/1954, Valdosta, GA *Drafted:* 1977 Round 4 Det
1977 Det: Rush 1-(-6) -6.0; PR 1-0; KR 1-24 24.0. **1978** Det: Rush 5-9 1.8; PR 7-59 8.4; KR 7-170 24.3. **1979** Det: Rush 1-(-8) -8.0; KR 1-26 26.0. **1980** Phi: KR 1-16 16.0. **Total:** Rush 7-(-5) -0.7; PR 8-59 7.4; KR 10-236 23.6.

		Receiving				
Year Team	**G**	**Rec**	**Yds**	**Avg**	**TD**	**Fum**
1977 Det	14	8	90	11.3	1	1
1978 Det	16	31	350	11.3	2	2
1979 Det	9	8	102	12.8	1	0
1980 Phi	3	0	0	—	0	0
NFL Total	42	47	542	11.5	4	3

JIM BLUMENSTOCK Blumenstock, James A 5'11", 190 **FB-DB**
(Blackie) *Col:* Fordham *HS:* Rutherford [NJ] B: 4/28/1918, Rutherford, NJ D: 7/31/1963, Passaic, NJ *Drafted:* 1942 Round 19 NYG
1947 NYG: Pass 8-4 50.0%, 48 6.00 1 Int; Rec 4-15 3.8; PR 1-8 8.0; KR 2-77 38.5.

		Rushing				
Year Team	**G**	**Att**	**Yds**	**Avg**	**TD**	**Fum**
1947 NYG	10	54	168	3.1	2	2

HERB BLUMER Blumer, Herbert George 6′1″, 200 **E-DE-T-G**
Col: Missouri *HS:* Webster Groves [MO] B: 3/7/1900, St. Louis, MO D: 4/13/1987, Danville, CA
1925 ChiC: 10 G; Rec 2 TD; 12 Pt. **1926** ChiC: 12 G. **1927** ChiC: 9 G. **1928** ChiC: 6 G. **1929** ChiC: 10 G. **1930** ChiC: 11 G. **1933** ChiC: 1 G. **Total:** 59 G; Rec 2 TD; 12 Pt.

MATT BLUNDIN Blundin, Matthew Brent 6′3″, 233 **QB**
Col: Virginia *HS:* Ridley [Folsom, PA] B: 3/7/1969, Darby, PA
Drafted: 1992 Round 2 KC
1993 KC: 1 G; Pass 3-1 33.3%, 2 0.67. **1994** KC: 1 G; Pass 5-1 20.0%, 13 2.60 1 Int. **1997** Det: 1 G; Pass 1-0, 1 Int. **Total:** 3 G; Pass 9-2 22.2%, 15 1.67 2 Int.

RONNIE BLYE Blye, Ronald Jerry 6′1″, 202 **RB**
(AKA Ronald Jerry Bliey) *Col:* Notre Dame; Florida A&M *HS:* Pinellas Park [Largo, FL]; Samuel J. Tilden HS [Brooklyn, NY] B: 12/29/1943, Clearwater, FL
1968 NYG: Rec 10-91 9.1. **1969** Phi: Rec 2-(-6) -3.0. **Total:** Rec 12-85 7.1.

		Rushing				Kickoff Returns				
Year Team	G	Att	Yds	Avg	TD	Ret	Yds	Avg	TD	Fum
1968 NYG	13	53	243	4.6	1	35	734	21.0	0	2
1969 Phi	14	8	25	3.1	0	19	370	19.5	0	0
NFL Total	27	61	268	4.4	1	54	1104	20.4	0	2

STEVE BOADWAY Boadway, Steven Troy 6′4″, 240 **LB**
Col: Arizona *HS:* Lompoc [CA] B: 6/20/1962, Bakersfield, CA
1987 Det: 2 G.

DWAINE BOARD Board, Dwaine P 6′5″, 248 **DE**
Col: North Carolina A&T *HS:* Franklin Co. [Rocky Mount, VA] B: 11/29/1956, Union Hall, VA *Drafted:* 1979 Round 5 Pit
1979 SF: 16 G. **1980** SF: 3 G. **1981** SF: 16 G. **1982** SF: 1 G; 0.5 Sac. **1983** SF: 16 G; 1 Fum TD; 6 Pt; 13 Sac. **1984** SF: 16 G; 10 Sac. **1985** SF: 16 G; 11.5 Sac. **1986** SF: 16 G; 8 Sac. **1987** SF: 14 G; 2 Sac. **1988** SF-NO: 7 G. SF: 3 G. NO: 4 G. **Total:** 121 G; 1 Fum TD; 6 Pt; 45 Sac.

MACK BOATNER Boatner, Mack Ernest 6′0″, 220 **RB**
Col: Southeastern Louisiana *HS:* White Castle [LA] B: 10/4/1958, White Castle, LA *Drafted:* 1982 Round 9 Mia
1986 TB: 7 G; KR 1-2 2.0.

HARRY BOATSWAIN Boatswain, Harry Kwane 6′4″, 295 **OT**
Col: New Haven *HS:* James Madison [Brooklyn, NY] B: 6/26/1969, Brooklyn, NY *Drafted:* 1991 Round 5 SF
1992 SF: 16 G. **1993** SF: 16 G. **1994** SF: 13 G. **1995** Phi: 13 G. **1996** NYJ: 16 G. **Total:** 74 G.

BON BOATWRIGHT Boatwright, Bon Lovell 6′5″, 262 **DT**
Col: Oklahoma State *HS:* West Rusk [New London, TX] B: 10/28/1951, Henderson, TX *Drafted:* 1974 Round 8 SD
1974 SD: 10 G.

ADAM BOB Bob, Adam Jr. 6′2″, 240 **LB**
Col: Texas A&M *HS:* Northside [Lafayette, LA] B: 10/30/1967, Milwaukee, WI *Drafted:* 1989 Round 10 NYJ
1989 NYJ: 5 G.

E. BOBADASH Bobadash, E. **E**
Col: No College Deceased
1922 Oor: 1 G.

HUBERT BOBO Bobo, Hubert Lee 6′0″, 220 **LB**
Col: Ohio State *HS:* Dover [Chauncey, OH] B: 7/2/1934, Athens, OH
Drafted: 1957 Round 13 Phi
1960 LAC: 3 G. **1961** NYT: 14 G; Int 4-57. **1962** NYT: 14 G; Int 1-14. **Total:** 31 G; Int 5-71.

ORLANDO BOBO Bobo, Orlando 6′3″, 301 **OG**
Col: East Mississippi CC; Northeast Louisiana *HS:* West Point [MS] B: 2/9/1974, West Point, MS
1997 Min: 5 G. **1998** Min: 4 G. **Total:** 9 G.

JOHN BOCK Bock, John Matthew 6′3″, 290 **C-OG**
Col: Louisville; Indiana State *HS:* Crystal Lake Central [IL] B: 2/11/1971, Chicago, IL
1995 NYJ: 10 G; 1 Fum. **1996** Mia: 2 G. **1997** Mia: 14 G. **1998** Mia: 16 G. **Total:** 42 G; 1 Fum.

JOE BOCK Bock, Joseph Alan 6′4″, 256 **C**
Col: Virginia *HS:* East [Rochester, NY] B: 7/21/1959, Rochester, NY
1987 StL-Buf: 2 G. StL: 1 G. Buf: 1 G. **Total:** 2 G.

WAYNE BOCK Bock, Wayne R Jr. 6′4″, 265 **DT**
Col: Illinois *HS:* Argo [Summit, IL] B: 5/28/1934, Third River Twp., MN
Drafted: 1957 Round 5 ChiC
1957 ChiC: 4 G.

TONY BODDIE Boddie, Dominec Leanthony 5′11″, 195 **RB**
Col: Montana State *HS:* Bremerton [WA] B: 11/11/1960, Portsmith, WA
1986 Den: 1 G; Rush 1-2 2.0. **1987** Den: 5 G; Rush 3-7 2.3 1 TD; Rec 9-85 9.4; 6 Pt. **Total:** 6 G; Rush 4-9 2.3 1 TD; Rec 9-85 9.4; 6 Pt.

LYNN BODEN Boden, Lynn Ray 6′5″, 270 **OG-OT**
Col: South Dakota State *HS:* Osceola [NE] B: 6/5/1953, Stromburg, NE *Drafted:* 1975 Round 1 Det
1975 Det: 14 G. **1976** Det: 14 G. **1977** Det: 13 G; KR 1-14 14.0. **1978** Det: 16 G. **1979** ChiB: 10 G. **Total:** 67 G; KR 1-14 14.0.

MAURY BODENGER Bodenger, Morris 5′10″, 214 **G**
(Bodie) *Col:* Tulane *HS:* Jackson [New Orleans, LA]; Gulf Coast Mil. Acad. [MS] B: 7/31/1909, New Orleans, LA D: 2/9/1960, Cleveland, OH
1931 Port: 13 G. **1932** Port: 12 G. **1933** Port: 11 G. **1934** Det: 12 G. **Total:** 48 G.

PING BODIE Bodie, M. Risso **FB**
Col: No College B: 5/10/1897, Italy D: 12/14/1981, Stockton, CA
1921 ChiC: 1 G.

BILL BOEDEKER Boedeker, William Henry Jr. 5′11″, 192 **HB-DB**
Col: DePaul *HS:* North Side [Fort Wayne, IN] B: 3/7/1924, Milwaukee, WI
AAFC **1946** ChiA: PR 2-29 14.5; KR 2-84 42.0; Int 1-26. **1947** CleA: PR 3-82 27.3; KR 6-133 22.2. **1948** CleA: PR 2-8 4.0; KR 4-61 15.3. **1949** CleA: KR 9-189 21.0. **Total:** PR 7-119 17.0; KR 21-467 22.2; Int 1-26.

		Rushing				Receiving				Tot
Year Team	G	Att	Yds	Avg	TD	Rec	Yds	Avg	TD	TD
1946 ChiA	12	6	8	1.3	0	5	82	16.4	1	1
1947 CleA	12	31	194	6.3	4	8	175	21.9	1	5
1948 CleA	14	78	254	3.3	3	13	237	18.2	2	5
1949 CleA	12	50	269	5.4	1	11	371	33.7	2	3
AAFC Total	50	165	725	4.4	8	37	865	23.4	6	14

NFL **1950** GB-Phi: 10 G; Rush 8-16 2.0; Rec 1-10 10.0; PR 5-49 9.8; KR 1-20 20.0. GB: 9 G; Rush 8-16 2.0; Rec 1-10 10.0; PR 5-49 9.8; KR 1-20 20.0. Phi: 1 G. **Total:** 10 G; Rush 8-16 2.0; Rec 1-10 10.0; PR 5-49 9.8; KR 1-20 20.0.

JIM BOEKE Boeke, James Frederick 6′5″, 255 **OT**
Col: Heidelberg *HS:* Cuyahoga Falls [OH] B: 9/11/1938, Akron, OH
Drafted: 1960 Round 19 LARm
1960 LARm: 12 G. **1961** LARm: 14 G. **1962** LARm: 14 G. **1963** LARm: 14 G. **1964** Dal: 14 G. **1965** Dal: 14 G. **1966** Dal: 10 G. **1967** Dal: 14 G. **1968** NO: 13 G. **Total:** 119 G.

FRED BOENSCH Boensch, Frederick Maximilian 6′4″, 228 **G-LB**
Col: California; Stanford *HS:* San Mateo [CA] B: 9/27/1920, Portland, OR *Drafted:* 1944 Round 7 Cle
1947 Was: 12 G; Int 1-0; 1 Fum. **1948** Was: 12 G. **Total:** 24 G; Int 1-0; 1 Fum.

CHUCK BOERIO Boerio, Charles 6′0″, 205 **LB**
Col: Illinois *HS:* Kincaid [IL] B: 3/9/1930, Kincaid, IL *Drafted:* 1952 Round 20 GB
1952 GB: 1 G.

CHAMP BOETTCHER Boettcher, Raymond Edward 5′10″, 193 **FB-TB-BB**
Col: Lawrence *HS:* Watertown [WI] B: 9/18/1900, Reeseville, WI D: 12/20/1965, Watertown, WI
1926 Rac: 4 G.

REX BOGGAN Boggan, Rex Reed 6′3″, 245 **DT**
Col: Mississippi *HS:* Tech [Memphis, TN] B: 3/27/1930, Tupelo, MS D: 12/8/1985, Spartanburg, SC *Drafted:* 1952 Round 20 NYG
1955 NYG: 11 G.

MARK BOGGS Boggs, Mark Allen 6′5″, 301 **OT**
Col: Ball State *HS:* Bradley-Bourbonnais [Bradley, IL] B: 5/7/1964, Kankakee, IL
1987 Ind: 1 G.

GEORGE BOGUE Bogue, George Richardson 6′0″, 210 **FB-WB**
Col: Stanford *HS:* San Mateo [CA] B: 2/10/1906, Omaha, NE D: 10/13/1972, Pasadena, CA
1930 ChiC-Nwk: 7 G; Scor 1, 1 XK. ChiC: 4 G; Scor 1, 1 XK. Nwk: 3 G. **Total:** 7 G.

FRED BOHANNON Bohannon, Frederick Jerome 6′0″, 201 **CB-KR**
Col: Mississippi Valley State *HS:* Woodlawn [Birmingham, AL] B: 5/31/1958, Birmingham, AL
1982 Pit: 7 G; KR 14-329 23.5; 3 Fum.

DEWEY BOHLING Bohling, Dewey Arthur 5′11″, 190 **HB**
Col: Hardin-Simmons *HS:* Highland [Albuquerque, NM] B: 8/22/1938, Hebron, NE *Drafted:* 1959 Round 13 Pit
1960 NYT: Pass 5-0. **1961** NYT-Buf: Pass 1-0; PR 4-0; KR 10-246 24.6. Buf: Pass 1-0; PR 4-0; KR 10-246 24.6. **Total:** Pass 6-0; PR 4-0; KR 10-246 24.6.

		Rushing				Receiving					Tot
Year Team	**G**	**Att**	**Yds**	**Avg**	**TD**	**Rec**	**Yds**	**Avg**	**TD**	**Fum**	**TD**
1960 NYT	14	123	431	3.5	2	30	268	8.9	4	4	6
1961 NYT-Buf	12	55	153	2.8	2	13	217	16.7	1	1	3
1961 NYT	5	13	19	1.5	0	3	34	11.3	0	0	0
1961 Buf	7	42	134	3.2	2	10	183	18.3	1	1	3
NFL Total	26	178	584	3.3	4	43	485	11.3	5	5	9

ROB BOHLINGER Bohlinger, Robert Paul 6′8″, 310 **OT**
Col: Wyoming *HS:* Totino Grace [Maple Grove, MN] B: 6/14/1975, Minneapolis, MN
1998 Car: 13 G.

FRANK BOHLMANN Bohlmann, Frank Henry 5′11″, 212 **G**
Col: Marquette *HS:* North Division [Milwaukee, WI] B: 1/26/1917, Milwaukee, WI
1942 ChiC: 5 G.

RON BOHM Bohm, Ronald Leland 6′3″, 250 **DT**
Col: Illinois *HS:* Walnut [IL] B: 9/3/1964, Princeton, IL
1987 StL: 3 G.

REED BOHOVICH Bohovich, George Reed 6′1″, 260 **OG-OT**
Col: Lehigh *HS:* St. Joseph's [Kenmore, NY] B: 11/18/1941, Buffalo, NY *Drafted:* 1962 Round 9 NYG
1962 NYG: 10 G.

KARL BOHREN Bohren, Karl W 5′8″, 180 **WB-FB**
(Jake) *Col:* Pittsburgh *HS:* Reynoldsville [PA] B: 5/26/1902
D: 3/11/1987, Jefferson, PA
1927 Buf: 3 G.

NOVO BOJOVIC Bojovic, Novo 5′10″, 172 **K**
Col: Central Michigan *HS:* Hamtramck [MI] B: 11/2/1959, Titograd, Yugoslavia
1985 StL: 6 G; Scor 20, 3-7 42.9% FG, 11-12 91.7% XK.

KIM BOKAMPER Bokamper, Kim E 6′6″, 245 **DE-LB**
Col: San Jose City Coll. CA (J.C.); Concordia (Minn.); San Jose State *HS:* Milpitas [CA] B: 9/25/1954, San Diego, CA *Drafted:* 1976 Round 1 Mia
1977 Mia: 14 G. **1978** Mia: 16 G; Int 1-2; Scor **1** Saf; 2 Pt. **1979** Mia: 14 G; Int 1-3. **1980** Mia: 16 G; Int 1-6. **1981** Mia: 16 G. **1982** Mia: 9 G; Int 1-1; 3.5 Sac. **1983** Mia: 15 G; Int 2-43 1 TD; 6 Pt; 1 Fum; 2 Sac. **1984** Mia: 11 G; 4 Sac. **1985** Mia: 16 G; 2.5 Sac. **Total:** 127 G; Int 6-55 1 TD; Scor 1 Saf; 8 Pt; 1 Fum; 12 Sac.

GEORGE BOLAN Bolan, George Henry 5′11″, 203 **FB-HB**
Col: Purdue *HS:* Deerfield [IL] B: 4/1897, Lake Forest, IL
D: 1/17/1940, New York, NY
1921 Sta: 5 G. **1922** ChiB: 10 G; Rush 2 TD; 12 Pt. **1923** ChiB: 11 G. **1924** ChiB: 1 G. **Total:** 27 G; Rush 2 TD; 12 Pt.

NED BOLCAR Bolcar, Ned Francis 6′1″, 240 **LB**
Col: Notre Dame *HS:* Phillipsburg [NJ] B: 1/12/1967, Phillipsburg, NJ *Drafted:* 1990 Round 6 Sea
1990 Sea: 5 G; Int 1-0. **1991** Mia: 8 G. **Total:** 13 G; Int 1-0.

GARY BOLDEN Bolden, Gary Lonnell 6′1″, 275 **DT**
(The Mule) *Col:* Southwestern Oklahoma State *HS:* Clinton [OK]
B: 2/13/1962, Clinton, OK
1987 Phi: 2 G.

JURAN BOLDEN Bolden, Juran 6′2″, 201 **DB**
Col: Mississippi Delta CC *HS:* Hillsborough [Tampa, FL] B: 6/27/1974, Tampa, FL *Drafted:* 1996 Round 4 Atl
1996 Atl: 9 G. **1997** Atl: 14 G; KR 5-106 21.2. **1998** Atl-GB-Car: 12 G. Atl: 3 G. GB: 3 G. Car: 6 G. **Total:** 35 G; KR 5-106 21.2.

LEROY BOLDEN Bolden, Leroy Jr. 5′8″, 170 **HB**
Col: Michigan State *HS:* Northern [Flint, MI] B: 8/24/1932, Wabash, AR *Drafted:* 1955 Round 6 Cle
1958 Cle: 11 G; Rush 15-55 3.7; KR 14-362 25.9 1 TD; 6 Pt. **1959** Cle: 12 G; Rush 4-11 2.8; KR 9-170 18.9; 1 Fum. **Total:** 23 G; Rush 19-66 3.5; KR 23-532 23.1 1 TD; 6 Pt; 1 Fum.

RICKEY BOLDEN Bolden, Rickey Allen 6′6″, 274 **TE-OT**
Col: Southern Methodist *HS:* Hillcrest [Dallas, TX] B: 9/8/1961, Dallas, TX *Drafted:* 1984 Round 4 Cle
1984 Cle: 12 G; Rec 1-19 19.0; 1 Fum. **1985** Cle: 16 G. **1986** Cle: 7 G. **1987** Cle: 5 G. **1988** Cle: 16 G; Rec 1-3 3.0 1 TD; 6 Pt. **1989** Cle: 6 G. **Total:** 62 G; Rec 2-22 11.0 1 TD; 6 Pt; 1 Fum.

CHASE BOLDT Boldt, Stephen Chase 5′7″, 145 **BB-OE-FB**
Col: No College *HS:* Male [Louisville, KY] B: 5/7/1900, Louisville, KY
D: 5/16/1973, Louisville, KY
1921 Lou: 2 G. **1922** Lou: 4 G; Rush 1 TD; 6 Pt. **1923** Lou: 2 G. **Total:** 8 G; Rush 1 TD; 6 Pt.

BOOKIE BOLIN Bolin, Treva Gene 6′2″, 240 **OG**
Col: Mississippi *HS:* Okolona [MS] B: 6/17/1940, Hamilton, AL
Drafted: 1962 Round 5 NYG
1962 NYG: 9 G. **1963** NYG: 13 G. **1964** NYG: 14 G. **1965** NYG: 14 G. **1966** NYG: 14 G. **1967** NYG: 13 G. **1968** Min: 6 G. **1969** Min: 6 G. **Total:** 89 G.

RUSS BOLINGER Bolinger, Russell Dean 6′5″, 255 **OG-OT**
Col: California-Riverside; Long Beach State *HS:* Lompoc [CA]
B: 9/10/1954, Wichita, KS *Drafted:* 1976 Round 3 Det
1976 Det: 12 G. **1977** Det: 14 G. **1979** Det: 16 G; Rec 1-(-1) -1.0. **1980** Det: 16 G. **1981** Det: 16 G. **1982** Det: 9 G. **1983** LARm: 16 G. **1984** LARm: 16 G. **1985** LARm: 6 G. **Total:** 121 G; Rec 1-(-1) -1.0.

NICK BOLKOVAC Bolkovac, Nicholas Frank 6′1″, 230 **DT-OT**
Col: Pittsburgh *HS:* Woodrow Wilson [Youngstown, OH] B: 3/20/1928, McKees Rocks, PA *Drafted:* 1951 Round 30 Was
1953 Pit: 12 G; Scor 45, 4-12 33.3% FG, 27-28 96.4% XK; **1** Fum TD. **1954** Pit: 5 G; Scor 12, 3-4 75.0% FG, 3-3 100.0% XK. **Total:** 17 G; Scor 57, 7-16 43.8% FG, 30-31 96.8% XK; 1 Fum TD.

DON BOLL Boll, Donald Elroy 6′2″, 270 **OT-OG**
Col: Nebraska *HS:* Scribner [NE] B: 7/16/1927, Scribner, NE
Drafted: 1953 Round 4 Was
1953 Was: 12 G; KR 1-11 11.0. **1954** Was: 12 G. **1955** Was: 12 G. **1956** Was: 12 G. **1957** Was: 12 G. **1958** Was: 9 G. **1959** Was: 12 G. **1960** NYG: 11 G. **Total:** 92 G; KR 1-11 11.0.

BRIAN BOLLINGER Bollinger, Brian Reid 6′5″, 285 **OG**
Col: North Carolina *HS:* Melbourne [FL] B: 11/21/1968, Indiatlantic, FL
Drafted: 1992 Round 3 SF
1992 SF: 16 G. **1993** SF: 16 G. **1994** SF: 7 G. **Total:** 39 G.

EDDIE BOLLINGER Bollinger, Edward Ebbert Jr. 6′1″, 215 **T**
Col: Bucknell *HS:* Youngwood [PA] B: 7/9/1906, Nothumberland, PA
D: 7/14/1984, Lancaster, PA
1930 Fra: 4 G.

ANDY BOLTON Bolton, Andrew 6′1″, 205 **RB**
Col: Fisk *HS:* Northside [Memphis, TN] B: 5/23/1954, Memphis, TN
Drafted: 1976 Round 4 Sea
1976 Sea-Det: 12 G; Rush 15-71 4.7; KR 15-280 18.7; 2 Fum. Sea: 5 G; Rush 13-44 3.4; KR 15-280 18.7; 2 Fum. Det: 7 G; Rush 2-27 13.5. **1977** Det: 14 G; Rush 3-4 1.3; Rec 1-6 6.0; KR 6-86 14.3. **1978** Det: 6 G; Rush 2-5 2.5. **Total:** 32 G; Rush 20-80 4.0; Rec 1-6 6.0; KR 21-366 17.4; 2 Fum.

HARRY BOLTON Bolton, Harry Ernest 6′3″, 280 **T**
Col: Oklahoma State B: 3/24/1919, Gray Horse, OK D: 7/1986, Fairfax, OK
1944 Det: 1 G.

RON BOLTON Bolton, Ronald Clifton 6′2″, 180 **DB**
Col: Norfolk State *HS:* Peabody [Petersburg, VA] B: 4/16/1950, Petersburg, VA *Drafted:* 1972 Round 5 NE

		Interceptions		
Year Team	**G**	**Int**	**Yds**	**TD**
1972 NE	14	0	0	0
1973 NE	14	6	65	0
1974 NE	14	7	18	0
1975 NE	13	5	33	0
1976 Cle	14	3	76	1
1977 Cle	14	3	50	0
1978 Cle	10	0	0	0
1979 Cle	16	3	20	0
1980 Cle	16	6	62	0
1981 Cle	16	1	3	0
1982 Cle	4	1	0	0
NFL Total	145	35	327	1

SCOTT BOLTON Bolton, Scott Allen 6′0″, 188 **WR**
Col: Auburn *HS:* Theodore [AL] B: 1/4/1965, Mobile, AL
Drafted: 1988 Round 12 GB
1988 GB: 4 G; Rec 2-33 16.5.

LYNN BOMAR Bomar, Robert Lynn 6′1″, 210 **E**
Col: Vanderbilt *HS:* Fitzgerald Clark [Tullahoma, TN] B: 1/21/1901, Gallatin, TN D: 6/11/1964, Nashville, TN
1925 NYG: 12 G; Rec 3 TD; 18 Pt. **1926** NYG: 8 G; Rec 2 TD; 12 Pt. **Total:** 20 G; Rec 5 TD; 30 Pt.

JACK BONADIES Bonadies, John A 208 **G-T**
Col: No College B: 12/2/1892, Corleto Perticara, Italy D: 10/13/1965, Hartford, CT
1926 Har: 5 G.

CHUCK BOND Bond, Charles Eishmel 6'2", 236 **T**
Col: Washington *HS:* Hoquiam [WA] B: 11/5/1914, Fairland, OK
D: 9/24/1989, Puyallup, WA *Drafted:* 1937 Round 5 Was
1937 Was: 11 G. **1938** Was: 11 G. **Total:** 22 G.

JIM BOND Bond, James D Jr. 5'9", 200 **G**
Col: Pittsburgh *HS:* Central [Pittsburgh, PA] B: 2/1894, Pittsburgh, PA
Deceased
1926 Bkn: 2 G.

RINK BOND Bond, Randall Earl 5'10", 200 **BB-LB**
Col: Washington *HS:* Hoquiam [WA] B: 6/3/1917, Fairland, OK
1938 Was: 1 G. **1939** Pit: 11 G; Rush 1-4 4.0. **Total:** 12 G; Rush 1-4 4.0.

BOURBON BONDURANT Bondurant, Bourbon Patch 6'1", 202 **T-E**
(Sandy) *Col:* DePauw *HS:* Meade Co. [Bradenburg, KY]
B: 2/18/1898, Brandenburg, KY D: 9/4/1971, Scottsdale, AZ
1921 Eva: 5 G; Scor 6, 6 XK. **1922** ChiB-Eva: 3 G. ChiB: 1 G. Eva: 2 G.
Total: 8 G.

WARREN BONE Bone, Warren James 6'4", 260 **DE**
Col: Texas Southern *HS:* Fairfield [AL] B: 11/4/1964, Fairfield, AL
1987 GB: 1 G.

ERNIE BONELLI Bonelli, Ernest Bernard 5'11", 194 **FB-LB-HB-DB**
(Wizard; Bull) *Col:* Pittsburgh *HS:* Aspinwall [PA] B: 7/27/1919,
Russellton, PA
1945 ChiC: Rec 3-9 3.0; PR 3-37 12.3; KR 2-45 22.5; Int 1-23. **1946** Pit:
Rec 1-26 26.0. **Total:** Rec 4-35 8.8; PR 3-37 12.3; KR 2-45 22.5; Int 1-23.

		Rushing				
Year Team	**G**	**Att**	**Yds**	**Avg**	**TD**	**Fum**
1945 ChiC	7	32	93	2.9	0	4
1946 Pit	3	6	7	1.2	0	0
NFL Total	10	38	100	2.6	0	4

SHANE BONHAM Bonham, Steven Shane 6'2", 272 **DT**
Col: Air Force; Tennessee *HS:* Lathrop [Fairbanks, AK] B: 10/18/1970,
Fairbanks, AK *Drafted:* 1994 Round 3 Det
1994 Det: 15 G. **1995** Det: 16 G; 1 Sac. **1996** Det: 15 G; 2 Sac. **1997** Det:
16 G; 1 Sac. **1998** SF: 8 G. **Total:** 70 G; 4 Sac.

CHRIS BONIOL Boniol, Christopher Donald 5'11", 169 **K**
Col: Louisiana Tech *HS:* Alexandria [LA] B: 12/9/1971, Alexandria, LA
1995 Dal: Punt 2-77 38.5. **Total:** Punt 2-77 38.5.

		Scoring						
Year Team	**G**	**Pts**	**FG**	**FGA**	**FG%**	**XK**	**XKA**	**XK%**
1994 Dal	16	114	22	29	75.9	48	48	100.0
1995 Dal	16	127	27	28	**96.4**	46	**48**	**95.8**
1996 Dal	16	120	32	36	88.9	24	25	96.0
1997 Phi	16	99	22	31	71.0	33	33	100.0
1998 Phi	16	57	14	21	66.7	15	17	88.2
NFL Total	80	517	117	145	80.7	166	171	97.1

BRIAN BONNER Bonner, Brian 6'2", 225 **LB**
Col: Wisconsin; Minnesota *HS:* Washburn [Minneapolis, MN]
B: 10/9/1965, Minneapolis, MN *Drafted:* 1988 Round 9 SF
1989 Was: 6 G.

GLEN BONNER Bonner, Glen Lee 6'2", 202 **RB**
Col: Yakima Valley CC WA; Washington *HS:* Davis [Yakima, WA]
B: 5/5/1952, Bremerton, WA
1974 SD: Rec 11-101 9.2 1 TD. **1975** SD: Rec 2-8 4.0. **Total:** Rec 13-109
8.4 1 TD.

		Rushing					Tot
Year Team	**G**	**Att**	**Yds**	**Avg**	**TD**	**Fum**	**TD**
1974 SD	12	66	199	3.0	3	3	4
1975 SD	10	28	120	4.3	0	0	0
NFL Total	22	94	319	3.4	3	3	4

MELVIN BONNER Bonner, Melvin O'Neal 6'3", 207 **WR**
Col: Baylor *HS:* Van Vleck [TX] B: 2/18/1970, Hempstead, TX
Drafted: 1993 Round 6 Den
1993 Den: 3 G.

RIK BONNESS Bonness, Richard Kyes 6'3", 220 **LB**
Col: Nebraska *HS:* Bellevue [NE] B: 3/20/1954, Borger, TX
Drafted: 1976 Round 3 Oak
1976 Oak: 14 G. **1977** TB: 13 G. **1978** TB: 16 G. **1979** TB: 16 G.
Total: 59 G.

STEVE BONO Bono, Steven Christopher 6'4", 215 **QB**
Col: UCLA *HS:* Norristown [PA] B: 5/11/1962, Norristown, PA
Drafted: 1985 Round 6 Min
1987 Pit: Rec 1-2 2.0. **1998** StL: Scor 1 2XP. **Total:** Rec 1-2 2.0;
Scor 1 2XP.

		Passing							
Year Team	**G**	**Att**	**Comp**	**Comp%**	**Yds**	**YPA**	**TD**	**Int**	**Rating**
1985 Min	1	10	1	10.0	5	0.50	0	0	39.6
1986 Min	1	1	1	100.0	3	3.00	0	0	79.2
1987 Pit	3	74	34	45.9	438	5.92	5	2	76.3
1988 Pit	2	35	10	28.6	110	3.14	1	2	25.9
1989 SF	1	5	4	80.0	62	12.40	1	0	157.9
1991 SF	9	237	141	59.5	1617	6.82	11	**4**	88.5
1992 SF	16	56	36	64.3	463	8.27	2	2	87.1
1993 SF	8	61	39	63.9	416	6.82	0	1	76.9
1994 KC	7	117	66	56.4	796	6.80	4	4	74.6
1995 KC	16	520	293	56.3	3121	6.00	21	10	79.5
1996 KC	13	438	235	53.7	2572	5.87	12	13	68.0
1997 GB	2	10	5	50.0	29	2.90	0	0	56.3
1998 StL	6	136	69	50.7	807	5.93	5	4	69.1
NFL Total	85	1700	934	54.9	10439	6.14	62	**42**	75.3

	Rushing				
Year Team	**Att**	**Yds**	**Avg**	**TD**	**Fum**
1987 Pit	8	27	3.4	1	5
1991 SF	17	46	2.7	0	7
1992 SF	15	23	1.5	0	2
1993 SF	12	14	1.2	1	0
1994 KC	4	-1	-0.3	0	0
1995 KC	28	113	4.0	5	10
1996 KC	26	27	1.0	0	5
1997 GB	3	-3	-1.0	0	1
1998 StL	10	13	1.3	0	4
NFL Total	123	259	2.1	7	34

ELLIOTT BONOWITZ Bonowitz, Elliott 6'1", 190 **G-BB-T-E**
Col: Wilmington (Del.) B: 1903 Deceased
1923 Col: 6 G. **1924** Day: 8 G. **1925** Day: 6 G. **Total:** 20 G.

MICHAEL BOOKER Booker, Michael Allen Jr. 6'2", 203 **DB**
Col: Nebraska *HS:* El Camino [Oceanside, CA] B: 4/27/1975,
Cincinnati, OH *Drafted:* 1997 Round 1 Atl
1997 Atl: 15 G; Int 3-16. **1998** Atl: 14 G; Int 1-27; 1 Fum. **Total:** 29 G;
Int 4-43; 1 Fum.

VAUGHN BOOKER Booker, Vaughn Jamel 6'5", 290 **DE**
Col: Cincinnati *HS:* Robert A. Taft [Cincinnati, OH] B: 2/24/1968,
Cincinnati, OH
1994 KC: 13 G; KR 2-10 5.0. **1995** KC: 16 G; **1** Fum TD; 6 Pt; 1.5 Sac.
1996 KC: 14 G; 1 Sac. **1997** KC: 13 G; 4 Sac. **1998** GB: 16 G; 3 Sac.
Total: 72 G; KR 2-10 5.0; 1 Fum TD; 6 Pt; 9.5 Sac.

JOHNNY BOOKMAN Bookman, John Dolan Jr. 5'11", 182 **DB**
Col: Miami (Fla.) *HS:* Baton Rouge [LA] B: 9/6/1932, Baton Rouge, LA
D: 10/23/1995, Baton Rouge, LA *Drafted:* 1957 Round 8 NYG
1957 NYG: KR 4-102 25.5. **Total:** KR 4-102 25.5.

		Interceptions		
Year Team	**G**	**Int**	**Yds**	**TD**
1957 NYG	11	3	54	1
1960 DalT	14	4	0	0
1961 NYT	8	6	33	0
NFL Total	33	13	87	1

BILLY BOOKOUT Bookout, Billy Paul 5'11", 180 **DB**
Col: Oklahoma; Austin *HS:* Wichita Falls [TX] B: 1/1/1932, Choice, TX
1955 GB: 12 G; Int 2-39. **1956** GB: 7 G; Int 1-4. **Total:** 19 G; Int 3-43.

BOB BOOKS Books, Robert C 5'11", 190 **TB-FB**
Col: Dickinson *HS:* Mercersburg Acad. [PA] B: 1902 Deceased
1926 Fra: 4 G.

GREG BOONE Boone, Gregory Joel 5'9", 196 **RB**
Col: Duke *HS:* Bel Air [MD] B: 1/8/1962, Aberdeen, MD
1987 TB: 2 G; Rush 1-2 2.0.

DAVE BOONE Boone, Humphrey David Jr. 6'3", 248 **DE**
Col: Eastern Michigan *HS:* Cass Tech [Detroit, MI] B: 10/30/1951,
Detroit, MI *Drafted:* 1974 Round 11 Min
1974 Min: 5 G.

J.R. BOONE Boone, J.R. 5'8", 162 **HB-DB**
(Jack Rabbit) *Col:* Tulsa *HS:* Sand Springs [OK] B: 7/29/1921,
Clinton, OK *Drafted:* 1948 Round 20 ChiB
1948 ChiB: Pass 1-1 100.0%, 4 4.00; KR 2-31 15.5; Int 1-12. **1949** ChiB:
Int 1-21. **1953** GB: Pass 1-1 100.0%, -2 -2.00. **Total:** Pass 2-2 100.0%, 2
1.00; KR 2-31 15.5; Int 2-33.

		Rushing				Receiving			
Year Team	**G**	**Att**	**Yds**	**Avg**	**TD**	**Rec**	**Yds**	**Avg**	**TD**
1948 ChiB	11	48	266	5.5	5	10	143	14.3	2
1949 ChiB	12	35	111	3.2	0	14	336	24.0	3
1950 ChiB	10	13	15	1.2	0	8	139	17.4	0
1951 ChiB	10	3	9	3.0	0	6	117	19.5	0
1952 SF	12	24	72	3.0	0	25	461	18.4	1
1953 GB	8	7	24	3.4	0	6	55	9.2	1
NFL Total	63	130	497	3.8	5	69	1251	18.1	7

Year Team	Punt Returns Ret	Yds	Avg	TD	Fum	Tot TD
1948 ChiB	11	137	12.5	0	5	7
1949 ChiB	14	170	12.1	0	5	3
1950 ChiB	17	215	12.6	0	0	0
1951 ChiB	14	113	8.1	0	0	0
1952 SF	11	66	6.0	0	1	1
1953 GB	5	24	4.8	0	1	1
NFL Total	72	725	10.1	0	12	12

JACK BOONE Boone, Robert Lee 5′11″, 175 **WB-DB-HB-QB**
Col: Elon *HS:* Woodrow Wilson [Portsmouth, VA] B: 5/28/1918, Roanoke Rapids, NC D: 2/6/1984, Greenville, NC
1942 Cle: 2 G; Rush 3-(-1) -0.3; Rec 2-58 29.0 1 TD; PR 1-5 5.0; Int 1-4; 6 Pt.

DORIAN BOOSE Boose, Dorian Alexander 6′5″, 292 **DE**
Col: Walla Walla CC WA; Washington State *HS:* Henry Foss [Tacoma, WA] B: 1/29/1974, Frankfurt, Germany *Drafted:* 1998 Round 2 NYJ
1998 NYJ: 12 G.

CLARENCE BOOTH Booth, Clarence E 6′0″, 223 **T**
Col: Southern Methodist B: 9/4/1919, Childress, TX *Drafted:* 1943 Round 18 ChiC
1943 ChiC: 6 G. **1944** ChPt: 5 G. **Total:** 11 G.

ISSAC BOOTH Booth, Issac Ramoun 6′3″, 190 **DB**
Col: Sacramento City Coll. CA (J.C.); California *HS:* Perry Meridian [Indianapolis, IN] B: 5/23/1971, Indianapolis, IN *Drafted:* 1994 Round 5 Cle
1994 Cle: 16 G; Int 1-4. **1995** Cle: 8 G; Int 1-11. **1996** Bal: 11 G. **Total:** 35 G; Int 2-15.

DICK BOOTH Booth, Richard Thomas 6′1″, 190 **WB-DB**
Col: Case Western Reserve *HS:* East Liverpool [OH] B: 7/13/1918, Newell, WV
1941 Det: Pass 8-5 62.5%, 135 16.88 2 TD 1 Int; Rec 7-103 14.7; KR 4-122 30.5; Int 1-18; Punt 1-25 25.0. **1945** Det: Rec 3-90 30.0 1 TD; PR 2-8 4.0; KR 1-26 26.0. **Total:** Pass 8-5 62.5%, 135 16.88 2 TD 1 Int; Rec 10-193 19.3 1 TD; PR 2-8 4.0; KR 5-148 29.6; Int 1-18; Punt 1-25 25.0.

Year Team	G	Rushing Att	Yds	Avg	TD	Fum	Tot TD
1941 Det	11	29	80	2.8	1	0	1
1945 Det	4	4	20	5.0	0	1	1
NFL Total	15	33	100	3.0	1	1	2

JOHN BOOTY Booty, John Fitzgerald 6′0″, 185 **DB**
Col: Cisco JC TX; Texas Christian *HS:* Carthage [TX] B: 10/9/1965, DeBerry, TX *Drafted:* 1988 Round 10 NYJ
1991 Phi: 1 Sac. **1992** Phi: KR 1-11 11.0. **1993** Pho: 3 Sac. **1995** TB: Rec 1-48 48.0. **Total:** Rec 1-48 48.0; KR 1-11 11.0; 4 Sac.

Year Team	G	Interceptions Int	Yds	TD
1988 NYJ	16	3	0	0
1989 NYJ	9	1	13	0
1990 NYJ	13	0	0	0
1991 Phi	13	1	24	0
1992 Phi	16	3	22	0
1993 Pho	12	2	24	0
1994 NYG	16	3	95	0
1995 TB	7	1	21	0
NFL Total	102	14	199	0

EMERSON BOOZER Boozer, Emerson Jr. 5′11″, 195 **RB**
Col: Maryland East. Shore *HS:* Lucy Craft Laney [Augusta, GA] B: 7/4/1943, Augusta, GA *Drafted:* 1966 Round 6 NYJ

Year Team	G	Rushing Att	Yds	Avg	TD	Receiving Rec	Yds	Avg	TD
1966 NYJ	14	97	455	4.7	5	8	133	16.6	0
1967 NYJ	8	119	442	3.7	**10**	12	205	17.1	3
1968 NYJ	12	143	441	3.1	5	12	101	8.4	0
1969 NYJ	14	130	604	4.6	4	20	222	11.1	0
1970 NYJ	10	139	581	4.2	5	28	258	9.2	0
1971 NYJ	14	188	618	3.3	5	11	120	10.9	1
1972 NYJ	11	120	549	4.6	11	11	142	12.9	3
1973 NYJ	13	182	831	4.6	3	22	130	5.9	3
1974 NYJ	13	153	563	3.7	4	14	161	11.5	1
1975 NYJ	9	20	51	2.6	0	1	16	16.0	1
NFL Total	118	1291	5135	4.0	52	139	1488	10.7	12

Year Team	Kickoff Returns Ret	Yds	Avg	TD	Fum	Tot TD
1966 NYJ	26	659	25.3	1	0	6
1967 NYJ	11	213	19.4	0	1	**13**
1968 NYJ	0	0	—	0	5	5
1969 NYJ	0	0	—	0	3	4
1970 NYJ	0	0	—	0	2	5
1971 NYJ	0	0	—	0	6	6
1972 NYJ	0	0	—	0	3	**14**
1973 NYJ	0	0	—	0	6	6
1974 NYJ	0	0	—	0	3	5
1975 NYJ	0	0	—	0	0	1
NFL Total	37	872	23.6	1	29	65

FRED BORAK Borak, Fred Aloisius 6′1″, 195 **DE**
Col: Creighton B: 5/4/1913, Kenosha, WI D: 4/1966
1938 GB: 1 G.

JON BORCHARDT Borchardt, Jon L 6′5″, 260 **OG-OT**
Col: Montana State *HS:* Park Center [Brooklyn Park, MN] B: 8/13/1957, Minneapolis, MN *Drafted:* 1979 Round 3 Buf
1979 Buf: 16 G. **1980** Buf: 16 G. **1981** Buf: 16 G. **1982** Buf: 9 G. **1983** Buf: 16 G. **1984** Buf: 16 G. **1985** Sea: 13 G. **1986** Sea: 16 G. **1987** Sea: 12 G. **Total:** 130 G.

DENNIS BORCKY Borcky, Dennis Michael 6′4″, 285 **NT**
Col: Memphis *HS:* Chichester [Boothwyn, PA] B: 9/14/1964, Chester, PA
1987 NYG: 2 G.

CHRIS BORDANO Bordano, Chris 6′1″, 241 **LB**
Col: Southern Methodist *HS:* Southwest [San Antonio, TX] B: 12/30/1974, San Antonio, TX *Drafted:* 1998 Round 6 NO
1998 NO: 16 G; 1 Sac.

BEN BORDELON Bordelon, Benjamin Gerald 6′5″, 301 **OT**
Col: Louisiana State *HS:* Central Lafourche [Mathews, LA] B: 4/9/1974, Mathews, LA
1997 SD: 16 G; KR 2-0.

KEN BORDELON Bordelon, Kenneth Patrick 6′4″, 228 **LB**
Col: Louisiana State *HS:* Brother Martin [New Orleans, LA] B: 8/26/1954, New Orleans, LA *Drafted:* 1976 Round 5 LARm
1976 NO: 12 G. **1977** NO: 14 G. **1979** NO: 16 G; Int 2-24 1 TD; 6 Pt. **1980** NO: 16 G. **1981** NO: 15 G; Int 1-3. **1982** NO: 9 G; 1 Sac. **Total:** 82 G; Int 3-27 1 TD; 6 Pt; 1 Sac.

LES BORDEN Borden, Lester Dewis 6′0″, 185 **OE-DE**
Col: Fordham *HS:* Hebron Academy [ME] B: 4/8/1910, Everett, MA D: 5/19/1981, Gulph Mills, PA
1935 NYG: 1 G.

NATE BORDEN Borden, Nathaniel 6′0″, 234 **DE**
Col: Indiana *HS:* William L. Dickinson [Jersey City, NJ] B: 9/22/1931, Union, SC D: 9/30/1992, Las Vegas, NV *Drafted:* 1955 Round 25 GB
1955 GB: 12 G. **1956** GB: 12 G; KR 1-0. **1957** GB: 9 G. **1958** GB: 12 G. **1959** GB: 12 G. **1960** Dal: 12 G. **1961** Dal: 14 G. **1962** Buf: 9 G. **Total:** 92 G; KR 1-0.

NATE BORDERS Borders, Nathan Wayne 5′10″, 190 **DB**
Col: Indiana *HS:* Riverside [Ellwood City, PA] B: 6/11/1963, Ellwood City, PA
1987 Cin: 3 G.

NICK BORELLI Borelli, Nicholas Charles 5′10″, 175 **FB-WB-TB-BB**
(Nick Borrell) *Col:* Muhlenberg *HS:* Cliffside Park [NJ] B: 3/2/1905, Cliffside Park, NJ D: 12/12/1992, Cliffside Park, NJ
1930 Nwk: 10 G.

JOCELYN BORGELLA Borgella, Jocelyn Kenza 5′10″, 180 **DB**
Col: Cincinnati *HS:* Miami Edison [FL] B: 8/26/1971, Nassau, Bahamas *Drafted:* 1994 Round 6 Det
1994 Det: 4 G. **1996** Det: 11 G. **Total:** 15 G.

DIRK BORGOGNONE Borgognone, Dirk Ronald 6′2″, 221 **K**
Col: Truckee Meadows CC NV; Tennessee; U. of Pacific *HS:* Reno [NV] B: 1/9/1968, Elko, NV
1995 GB: 2 G.

KYLE BORLAND Borland, Kyle Craig 6′3″, 232 **LB**
Col: Wisconsin *HS:* Fort Atkinson [WI] B: 7/5/1961, Denison, IA
1987 LARm: 2 G; 2 Sac.

RICH BORRESEN Borresen, Richard David 6′5″, 252 **TE**
Col: Nassau CC NY; Northwestern *HS:* Valley Stream North [Franklin Square, NY] B: 3/16/1964, Queens, NY
1987 Dal: 3 G; KR 1-5 5.0.

JOHN BORTON Borton, John Robert 6′0″, 208 **QB**
Col: Ohio State *HS:* Alliance [OH] B: 12/14/1932, Alliance, OH *Drafted:* 1955 Round 13 Cle
1957 Cle: 5 G; Pass 6-3 50.0%, 22 3.67 1 Int.

MARK BORTZ Bortz, Mark Steven 6′6″, 282 **OG**
Col: Iowa *HS:* Pardeeville [WI] B: 2/12/1961, Pardeeville, WI *Drafted:* 1983 Round 8 ChiB
1983 ChiB: 16 G. **1984** ChiB: 15 G. **1985** ChiB: 16 G. **1986** ChiB: 15 G; Rec 1-8 8.0. **1987** ChiB: 12 G. **1988** ChiB: 16 G. **1989** ChiB: 16 G. **1990** ChiB: 16 G. **1991** ChiB: 9 G. **1992** ChiB: 12 G. **1993** ChiB: 16 G. **1994** ChiB: 12 G. **Total:** 171 G; Rec 1-8 8.0.

MIKE BORYLA Boryla, Michael Jay 6′3″, 200 **QB**
Col: Stanford *HS:* Regis [Denver, CO] B: 3/6/1951, Rockville Centre, NY *Drafted:* 1974 Round 4 Cin

		Passing							
Year Team	G	Att	Comp	Comp%	Yds	YPA	TD	Int	Rating
1974 Phi	4	102	60	58.8	580	5.69	5	3	78.9
1975 Phi	7	166	87	52.4	996	6.00	6	12	52.7
1976 Phi	11	246	123	50.0	1247	5.07	9	14	53.4
1978 TB	1	5	2	40.0	15	3.00	0	0	47.9
NFL Total	23	519	272	52.4	2838	5.47	20	29	58.1

	Rushing				
Year Team	Att	Yds	Avg	TD	Fum
1974 Phi	6	25	4.2	0	2
1975 Phi	8	33	4.1	0	1
1976 Phi	29	166	5.7	2	3
1978 TB	0	0	—	0	1
NFL Total	43	224	5.2	2	7

JOHN BOSA Bosa, John Wilfred 6′4″, 270 **DE**
Col: Boston College *HS:* Keene [NH] B: 1/10/1964, Keene, NH *Drafted:* 1987 Round 1 Mia
1987 Mia: 12 G; 3 Sac. **1988** Mia: 6 G; 2 Sac. **1989** Mia: 13 G; 2 Sac. **Total:** 31 G; 7 Sac.

WADE BOSARGE Bosarge, Wade 5′10″, 175 **DB**
Col: Tulsa *HS:* Peter F. Alba [Bayou La Batre, AL] B: 9/14/1955, Bayou La Batre, AL
1977 Mia-NO: 10 G. Mia: 5 G. NO: 5 G. **Total:** 10 G.

FRANK BOSCH Bosch, Frank William 6′4″, 255 **DT**
Col: Colorado *HS:* Boise [ID] B: 10/24/1945, Bremerton, WA *Drafted:* 1968 Round 17 Was
1968 Was: 14 G. **1969** Was: 14 G. **1970** Was: 11 G. **Total:** 39 G.

JOHN BOSDETT Bosdett, John A 1 **OE**
Col: No College *HS:* Evanston Tech [Evanston, IL] B: 11/4/1895, Cook Co., IL D: 9/1980, Oklahoma City, OK
1920 ChiT: 6 G.

TONY BOSELLI Boselli, Don Anthony Jr. 6′7″, 324 **OT**
Col: USC *HS:* Fairview [Boulder, CO] B: 4/17/1972, Modesto, CA *Drafted:* 1995 Round 1 Jac
1995 Jac: 13 G. **1996** Jac: 16 G. **1997** Jac: 12 G. **1998** Jac: 15 G. **Total:** 56 G.

BRUCE BOSLEY Bosley, Bruce Lee 6′2″, 241 **OG-C-DE**
Col: West Virginia *HS:* Green Bank [WV] B: 11/5/1933, Fresno, CA D: 4/26/1995, San Francisco, CA *Drafted:* 1956 Round 2 SF
1956 SF: 12 G. **1957** SF: 6 G. **1958** SF: 12 G. **1959** SF: 12 G. **1960** SF: 12 G. **1961** SF: 12 G. **1962** SF: 13 G. **1963** SF: 14 G. **1964** SF: 14 G. **1965** SF: 14 G. **1966** SF: 14 G. **1967** SF: 14 G. **1968** SF: 14 G. **1969** Atl: 12 G. **Total:** 175 G.

KEITH BOSLEY Bosley, Myron Keith 6′5″, 320 **OT**
Col: Eastern Kentucky *HS:* Madison [Richmond, KY] B: 6/19/1963, Richmond, KY
1987 Cle: 3 G.

CAP BOSO Boso, Casper N 6′4″, 232 **TE**
Col: Joliet JC IL; Illinois *HS:* Bishop Chatard [Indianapolis, IN] B: 9/10/1962, Kansas City, MO *Drafted:* 1986 Round 8 Pit

		Receiving			
Year Team	G	Rec	Yds	Avg	TD
1986 StL	2	0	0	—	0
1987 ChiB	12	17	188	11.1	2
1988 ChiB	6	6	50	8.3	0
1989 ChiB	16	17	182	10.7	1
1990 ChiB	13	11	135	12.3	1
1991 ChiB	6	3	36	12.0	0
NFL Total	55	54	591	10.9	4

DON BOSSELER Bosseler, Donald John 6′1″, 212 **FB**
(Bull) *Col:* Miami (Fla.) *HS:* Batavia [NY] B: 1/24/1936, Weathersfield, NY *Drafted:* 1957 Round 1 Was
1958 Was: PR 1-2 2.0. **1959** Was: Pass 1-0. **Total:** Pass 1-0; PR 1-2 2.0.

		Rushing				Receiving					Tot
Year Team	G	Att	Yds	Avg	TD	Rec	Yds	Avg	TD	Fum	TD
1957 Was	12	167	673	4.0	7	19	152	8.0	0	3	7
1958 Was	10	109	475	4.4	4	14	101	7.2	0	0	4
1959 Was	12	119	644	5.4	3	11	47	4.3	0	1	3
1960 Was	11	109	428	3.9	2	13	86	6.6	0	0	2
1961 Was	12	77	220	2.9	2	16	94	5.9	1	2	3
1962 Was	14	93	336	3.6	2	32	258	8.1	0	3	2
1963 Was	14	79	290	3.7	2	25	289	11.6	0	0	2
1964 Was	11	22	46	2.1	0	6	56	9.3	0	0	0
NFL Total	96	775	3112	4.0	22	136	1083	8.0	1	9	23

JAMES BOSTIC Bostic, James Edward 5′11″, 230 **RB**
Col: Auburn *HS:* Dillard [Fort Lauderdale, FL] B: 3/13/1972, Ft. Lauderdale, FL *Drafted:* 1994 Round 3 LARm
1998 Phi: 2 G.

JEFF BOSTIC Bostic, Jeff Lynn 6′2″, 268 **C**
Col: Clemson *HS:* Ben L. Smith [Greensboro, NC] B: 9/18/1958, Greensboro, NC
1980 Was: 16 G. **1981** Was: 16 G; Rec 1-(-4) -4.0. **1982** Was: 9 G. **1983** Was: 16 G. **1984** Was: 8 G. **1985** Was: 10 G. **1986** Was: 16 G. **1987** Was: 12 G. **1988** Was: 13 G. **1989** Was: 16 G. **1990** Was: 16 G. **1991** Was: 16 G; 1 Fum. **1992** Was: 4 G; 1 Fum. **1993** Was: 16 G. **Total:** 184 G; Rec 1-(-4) -4.0; 2 Fum.

JOE BOSTIC Bostic, Joe Earl Jr. 6′3″, 265 **OG-OT**
Col: Clemson *HS:* Ben L. Smith [Greensboro, NC] B: 4/20/1957, Greensboro, NC *Drafted:* 1979 Round 3 StL
1979 StL: 16 G. **1980** StL: 16 G. **1981** StL: 14 G. **1982** StL: 8 G. **1983** StL: 14 G. **1984** StL: 16 G. **1985** StL: 16 G. **1986** StL: 13 G. **1987** StL: 9 G. **1988** Pho: 10 G. **Total:** 132 G.

JOHN BOSTIC Bostic, Jonathan Earl 5′10″, 176 **DB**
Col: Bethune-Cookman *HS:* Astronaut [Titusville, FL] B: 10/6/1962, Titusville, FL *Drafted:* 1985 Round 6 KC
1985 Det: 13 G. **1986** Det: 13 G; Int 1-8. **1987** Det: 3 G. **Total:** 29 G; Int 1-8.

KEITH BOSTIC Bostic, William Keith 6′1″, 216 **DB**
Col: Michigan *HS:* Pioneer [Ann Arbor, MI] B: 1/17/1961, Ann Arbor, MI *Drafted:* 1983 Round 2 Hou
1983 Hou: 3 Sac. **1984** Hou: **1** Fum TD; 2 Sac. **1985** Hou: 5 Sac. **1986** Hou: 2 Sac. **1987** Hou: 3 Sac. **1988** Hou: 2 Sac. **Total:** 1 Fum TD; 17 Sac.

		Interceptions			
Year Team	G	Int	Yds	TD	Fum
1983 Hou	16	2	0	0	0
1984 Hou	16	0	0	0	0
1985 Hou	16	3	28	0	0
1986 Hou	16	1	0	0	0
1987 Hou	12	6	-14	0	1
1988 Hou	16	1	7	0	0
1990 Cle	4	0	0	0	0
NFL Total	96	13	21	0	1

LEW BOSTICK Bostick, Lewis Townley 6′0″, 197 **G**
Col: Alabama *HS:* Ramsey [Birmingham, AL] B: 10/3/1916, Birmingham, AL *Drafted:* 1939 Round 9 Cle
1939 Cle: 7 G; Punt 1-55 55.0; Scor 2, 2-2 100.0% XK. **1942** Cle: 1 G. **Total:** 8 G; Punt 1-55 55.0; Scor 2, 2-2 100.0% XK.

MCKINLEY BOSTON Boston, McKinley Jr. 6′2″, 250 **DE-LB**
Col: Minnesota *HS:* P.W. Moore [Elizabeth City, NC] B: 11/5/1945, Elizabeth City, NC *Drafted:* 1968 Round 15 NYG
1968 NYG: 13 G. **1969** NYG: 14 G. **Total:** 27 G.

BEN BOSWELL Boswell, Benjamin F 6′0″, 245 **T**
Col: Texas Christian B: 3/4/1910, Fort Worth, TX
1933 Port: 1 G. **1934** Bos: 11 G. **Total:** 12 G.

BRIAN BOSWORTH Bosworth, Brian Keith 6′2″, 248 **LB**
(Boz) *Col:* Oklahoma *HS:* MacArthur [Irving, TX] B: 3/9/1965, Oklahoma City, OK *Drafted:* 1987 Supplemental Round 1 Sea
1987 Sea: 12 G; 4 Sac. **1988** Sea: 10 G. **1989** Sea: 2 G. **Total:** 24 G; 4 Sac.

RON BOTCHAN Botchan, Ronald Leslie 6′1″, 238 **LB**
Col: Occidental *HS:* Belmont [Los Angeles, CA] B: 2/15/1935, Brooklyn, NY
1960 LAC: 14 G; Int 2-8. **1961** Hou: 14 G. **Total:** 28 G; Int 2-8.

KIRK BOTKIN Botkin, Kirk Randal 6′3″, 245 **TE**
Col: Arkansas *HS:* Robert E. Lee [Baytown, TX] B: 3/19/1971, Baytown, TX
1994 NO: 3 G. **1995** NO: 16 G; Rec 1-8 8.0. **1996** Pit: 16 G; Rec 4-36 9.0. **1997** Pit: 13 G; Rec 1-11 11.0. **Total:** 48 G; Rec 6-55 9.2.

SCOTT BOUCHER Boucher, Scott Allen 6′3″, 260 **OG**
Col: Blinn Coll. TX (J.C.); Northeast Louisiana *HS:* Eisenhower [Houston, TX] B: 9/15/1958, Houston, TX
1987 Hou: 2 G.

JIM BOUDREAUX Boudreaux, James Lee 6′4″, 260 **OT-DE**
Col: Louisiana Tech *HS:* Plaquemine [LA] B: 10/11/1944, Ville Platte, LA *Drafted:* 1966 Round 2 Bos
1966 Bos: 4 G. **1967** Bos: 5 G. **1968** Bos: 3 G. **Total:** 12 G.

LEE BOUGGESS Bouggess, Lee Edward 6′2″, 210 **RB**
Col: Louisville *HS:* Shawnee [Louisville, KY] B: 1/18/1948, Louisville, KY *Drafted:* 1970 Round 3 Phi
1970 Phi: Pass 1-0. **Total:** Pass 1-0.

Year Team	G	Rushing Att	Yds	Avg	TD	Receiving Rec	Yds	Avg	TD	Fum	Tot TD
1970 Phi	14	159	401	2.5	2	50	401	8.0	2	6	4
1971 Phi	10	97	262	2.7	2	24	170	7.1	1	1	3
1973 Phi	8	15	34	2.3	1	4	18	4.5	0	0	1
NFL Total	32	271	697	2.6	5	78	589	7.6	3	7	8

KEVIN BOUIE Bouie, Kevin Lamont 6′1″, 230 **RB**
Col: Garden City CC KS; Mississippi State *HS:* Pahokee [FL]
B: 8/18/1971, Pahokee, FL *Drafted:* 1995 Round 7 Phi
1996 SD: 1 G. **1997** Ariz: 5 G; Rush 11-26 2.4; KR 6-136 22.7. **Total:** 6 G; Rush 11-26 2.4; KR 6-136 22.7.

TONY BOUIE Bouie, Tony Vanderson 5′10″, 188 **DB**
Col: Arizona *HS:* Holy Cross [New Orleans, LA] B: 8/7/1972, New Orleans, LA
1995 TB: 9 G; Int 1-19. **1996** TB: 16 G. **1997** TB: 16 G; Rec 1-25 25.0. **1998** TB: 16 G. **Total:** 57 G; Rec 1-25 25.0; Int 1-19.

GIL BOULEY Bouley, Gilbert Joseph 6′2″, 235 **DT-OT**
Col: Boston College *HS:* Norwich Acad. [CT] B: 11/15/1921, Plainfield, CT *Drafted:* 1944 Round 2 Cle
1945 Cle: 6 G. **1946** LARm: 11 G. **1947** LARm: 12 G; Rec 1-15 15.0; PR 1-24 24.0; 1 Fum TD; 6 Pt. **1948** LARm: 12 G; Rec 1-15 15.0; KR 1-8 8.0; 1 Fum. **1949** LARm: 12 G. **1950** LARm: 11 G; Rec 1-11 11.0. **Total:** 64 G; Rec 3-41 13.7; PR 1-24 24.0; KR 1-8 8.0; 1 Fum TD; 6 Pt; 1 Fum.

PETER BOULWARE Boulware, Peter Nicholas 6′4″, 255 **LB**
Col: Florida State *HS:* Spring Valley [Columbia, SC] B: 12/18/1974, Columbia, SC *Drafted:* 1997 Round 1 Bal
1997 Bal: 16 G; 11.5 Sac. **1998** Bal: 16 G; 8.5 Sac. **Total:** 32 G; 20 Sac.

EMIL BOURES Boures, Emil Nicholas 6′1″, 259 **C-OG**
Col: Pittsburgh *HS:* Bishop Kenric [Lake Charles, LA] B: 1/29/1960, Bridgeport, PA *Drafted:* 1982 Round 7 Pit
1982 Pit: 5 G. **1983** Pit: 16 G; 1 Fum. **1984** Pit: 8 G. **1985** Pit: 6 G. **Total:** 35 G; 1 Fum.

MARC BOUTTE Boutte, Marc Anthony 6′4″, 307 **DT**
Col: Louisiana State *HS:* William Oscar Boston [Lake Charles, LA] B: 7/25/1969, Lake Charles, LA *Drafted:* 1992 Round 3 LARm
1992 LARm: 16 G; 1 Sac. **1993** LARm: 16 G; 1 Sac. **1994** Was: 9 G. **1995** Was: 16 G; 2 Sac. **1996** Was: 10 G; Int 1-0. **1997** Was: 16 G; Int 1-10; 2 Sac. **1998** Was: 13 G; Scor **1** Saf; 2 Pt; 2 Sac. **Total:** 96 G; Int 2-10; Scor 1 Saf; 2 Pt; 8 Sac.

LO BOUTWELL Boutwell, Leon A 5′7″, 188 **BB-WB-FB**
Col: Carlisle *HS:* Mercersburg Acad. [PA] B: 10/3/1892, Orr, ND D: 10/4/1969, Mechanicsburg, OH
1922 Oor: 8 G. **1923** Oor: 7 G. **Total:** 15 G.

TOMMY BOUTWELL Boutwell, Thomas Mitchell 6′2″, 200 **WR-QB**
Col: Mississippi Gulf Coast CC; Southern Mississippi *HS:* Hattiesburg [MS] B: 12/31/1946, Bluffton, OH *Drafted:* 1969 Round 13 Cle
1969 Mia: 5 G; Rec 4-29 7.3.

SHAWN BOUWENS Bouwens, Shawn Michael 6′4″, 293 **OG**
Col: Nebraska Wesleyan *HS:* Lincoln Northeast [NE] B: 5/25/1968, Lincoln, NE *Drafted:* 1990 Round 9 NE
1991 Det: 16 G. **1992** Det: 16 G. **1993** Det: 15 G. **1994** Det: 16 G; 1 Fum. **1995** Jac: 10 G. **Total:** 73 G; 1 Fum.

WILLIE BOUYER Bouyer, Willie Louis 6′3″, 200 **WR**
Col: Michigan State *HS:* Chadsey [Detroit, MI] B: 9/24/1966, Detroit, MI
1989 Sea: 1 G; Rec 1-9 9.0.

MATT BOUZA Bouza, Matthew Kyle 6′3″, 211 **WR**
Col: California *HS:* Jesuit [Sacramento, CA] B: 4/8/1958, San Jose, CA
1982 Bal: PR 2-0; KR 3-31 10.3. **1983** Bal: KR 1-(-4) -4.0. **1984** Ind: PR 3-17 5.7. **1986** Ind: Rush 1-12 12.0. **Total:** Rush 1-12 12.0; PR 5-17 3.4; KR 4-27 6.8.

Year Team	G	Receiving Rec	Yds	Avg	TD	Fum
1981 SF	1	0	0	—	0	0
1982 Bal	9	22	287	13.0	2	1
1983 Bal	11	25	385	15.4	0	1
1984 Ind	16	22	270	12.3	0	1
1985 Ind	12	27	381	14.1	2	0
1986 Ind	16	71	830	11.7	5	0
1987 Ind	12	42	569	13.5	4	2
1988 Ind	15	25	342	13.7	4	0
1989 Ind	2	0	0	—	0	0
NFL Total	94	234	3064	13.1	17	5

TONY BOVA Bova, Anthony J 6′1″, 190 **OE-DB-DE-QB**
Col: St. Francis (Pa.) *HS:* Kiski School [Saltsburg, PA] B: 8/21/1917, Pittsburgh, PA D: 10/15/1973, O'Hara Twp., Allegheny Co., PA
1942 Pit: KR 1-2 2.0; Int 1-16. **1943** PhPt: Rush 1-11 11.0. **1944** ChPt: Pass 30-6 20.0%, 96 3.20 **1** Int; Rush 14-(-22) -1.6. **1945** Pit: Pass 1-0; Rush 6-11 1.8; KR 1-24 24.0. **1947** Pit: KR 1-16 16.0; Scor **1** Saf. **Total:** Pass 31-6 19.4%, 96 3.10 1 Int; Rush 21-0; KR 3-42 14.0; Int 1-16; Scor 1 Saf.

Year Team	G	Receiving Rec	Yds	Avg	TD	Fum
1942 Pit	11	3	37	12.3	0	0
1943 PhPt	10	17	419	**24.6**	5	0
1944 ChPt	9	19	287	15.1	2	0
1945 Pit	10	15	215	14.3	0	1
1946 Pit	11	6	171	28.5	0	1
1947 Pit	10	0	0	—	0	0
NFL Total	61	60	1129	18.8	7	2

PETER BOVE Bove, Peter Anthony Jr. 5′10″, 187 **G**
Col: Holy Cross *HS:* Rutland [VT]; Somerville HS [MA] B: 9/21/1906, VT D: 6/11/1974, Christiansted, St.Croix, Virgin Islands
1930 Nwk: 3 G.

GORDON BOWDELL Bowdell, Gordon Bennett III 6′2″, 203 **WR**
Col: Michigan State *HS:* Cabrini [Allen Park, MI] B: 10/9/1948, Detroit, MI *Drafted:* 1971 Round 7 Bal
1971 Den: 2 G; Rec 1-19 19.0.

JOE BOWDEN Bowden, Joseph Tarrod 5′11″, 230 **LB**
Col: Oklahoma *HS:* North Mesquite [Mesquite, TX] B: 2/25/1970, Dallas, TX *Drafted:* 1992 Round 5 Hou
1992 Hou: 14 G. **1993** Hou: 16 G; 1 Sac. **1994** Hou: 14 G. **1995** Hou: 16 G; KR 1-6 6.0; 1 Sac. **1996** Hou: 16 G; 3 Sac. **1997** Ten: 16 G; Int 1-9; 2.5 Sac. **1998** Ten: 16 G; Int 1-1 1 TD; 1 Fum TD; Tot TD 2; 12 Pt; 1.5 Sac. **Total:** 108 G; KR 1-6 6.0; Int 2-10 1 TD; 1 Fum TD; Tot TD 2; 12 Pt; 9 Sac.

JIM BOWDOIN Bowdoin, James L 6′1″, 227 **G**
(Goofy) *Col:* Alabama *HS:* Elba [AL] B: 1/15/1904, Coffee Springs, AL D: 5/11/1969, Chickasaw., AL
1928 GB: 11 G. **1929** GB: 12 G. **1930** GB: 9 G. **1931** GB: 13 G. **1932** Bkn-NYG: 12 G. Bkn: 6 G. NYG: 6 G. **1933** Port: 7 G. **1934** Bkn: 11 G. **Total:** 75 G.

KEN BOWEN Bowen, Kenneth Edgar 6′1″, 220 **LB**
Col: East Tennessee State *HS:* St. Thomas Aquinas [Fort Lauderdale, FL] B: 11/15/1962, Columbus, GA
1987 Atl: 1 G.

TIM BOWENS Bowens, Timothy L 6′4″, 315 **DT**
Col: Itawamba CC MS; Mississippi *HS:* Okolona [MS] B: 2/7/1973, Okolona, MS *Drafted:* 1994 Round 1 Mia
1994 Mia: 16 G; 3 Sac. **1995** Mia: 16 G; 2 Sac. **1996** Mia: 16 G; 3 Sac. **1997** Mia: 16 G; 1 Fum TD; 6 Pt; 5 Sac. **1998** Mia: 16 G. **Total:** 80 G; 1 Fum TD; 6 Pt; 13 Sac.

PHIL BOWER Bower, James Philip 5′8″, 160 **BB-WB**
(Brainy) *Col:* Middlebury; Dartmouth B: 10/22/1894, Richmond, VA D: 7/17/1975, Vergennes, VT
1921 Cle: 5 G.

SAM BOWERS Bowers, Samuel Tyrone 6′4″, 250 **TE**
Col: Westchester CC NY; Fordham *HS:* White Plains [NY] B: 12/22/1957, White Plains, NY
1987 ChiB: 3 G; Rec 1-6 6.0.

BILL BOWERS Bowers, William James 6′0″, 198 **DB**
Col: USC *HS:* Canoga Park [CA] B: 10/31/1928, Kansas City, MO
1954 LARm: 8 G.

TONY BOWICK Bowick, Vantonio Bernard 6′2″, 265 **NT**
Col: Tennessee-Chattanooga *HS:* Slocomb [AL] B: 10/3/1966, Dothan, AL *Drafted:* 1989 Round 12 Atl
1989 Atl: 12 G.

LARRY BOWIE Bowie, Larry Darnell 6′0″, 249 **RB**
Col: Northeastern Oklahoma A&M (J.C.); Georgia *HS:* Anniston [AL] B: 3/21/1973, Anniston, AL
1997 Was: KR 1-15 15.0. **Total:** KR 1-15 15.0.

Year Team	G	Rushing Att	Yds	Avg	TD	Receiving Rec	Yds	Avg	TD	Fum	Tot TD
1996 Was	3	0	0	—	0	3	17	5.7	0	0	0
1997 Was	15	28	100	3.6	2	34	388	11.4	2	2	4
1998 Was	5	4	8	2.0	0	7	53	7.6	1	0	1
NFL Total	23	32	108	3.4	2	44	458	10.4	3	2	5

LARRY BOWIE Bowie, Lawrence Glen 6′2″, 245 **OG**
Col: Purdue *HS:* Ravenna [OH] B: 10/13/1939, Pike, WV *Drafted:* 1962 Round 6 Min
1962 Min: 14 G; KR 2-7 3.5. **1963** Min: 14 G; KR 1-0. **1964** Min: 14 G. **1965** Min: 14 G. **1966** Min: 14 G. **1967** Min: 14 G. **1968** Min: 8 G. **Total:** 92 G; KR 3-7 2.3.

TODD BOWLES Bowles, Todd Robert 6′2″, 203 **DB**
Col: Temple *HS:* Elizabeth [NJ] B: 11/18/1963, Elizabeth, NJ
1989 Was: 1 Sac. **1990** Was: KR 1-0; 1 Sac. **1993** Was: KR 1-27 27.0. **Total:** KR 2-27 13.5; 2 Sac.

Year Team	G	Int	Yds	TD
		Interceptions		
1986 Was	15	2	0	0
1987 Was	12	4	24	0
1988 Was	16	1	20	0
1989 Was	16	3	25	0
1990 Was	16	3	74	0
1991 SF	16	1	0	0
1992 Was	16	1	65	0
1993 Was	10	0	0	0
NFL Total	117	15	208	0

ANDY BOWLING Bowling, Andrew Walter 6′2″, 235 **LB**
Col: Virginia Tech *HS:* E.C. Glass [Lynchburg, VA] B: 9/25/1945, Lynchburg, VA *Drafted:* 1967 Round 4 StL
1967 Atl: 6 G.

BARRY BOWMAN Bowman, Barry D 5′11″, 180 **P**
Col: Louisiana Tech *HS:* Spring Hill [Longview, TX] B: 12/18/1964
1987 Sea: 1 G; Punt 3-104 34.7.

JIM BOWMAN Bowman, James Edwin 6′2″, 210 **DB**
Col: Central Michigan *HS:* Cadillac [MI] B: 10/26/1963, Cadillac, MI
Drafted: 1985 Round 2 NE
1985 NE: 16 G; PR 1-(-3) -3.0. **1986** NE: 16 G. **1987** NE: 12 G; Int 2-3; 0.5 Sac. **1988** NE: 16 G; Int 1-0. **1989** NE: 13 G. **Total:** 73 G; PR 1-(-3) -3.0; Int 3-3; 0.5 Sac.

KEN BOWMAN Bowman, Kenneth Brian 6′3″, 230 **C**
Col: Wisconsin *HS:* Rock Island [IL] B: 12/15/1942, Milan, IL
Drafted: 1964 Round 8 GB
1964 GB: 14 G. **1965** GB: 14 G. **1966** GB: 4 G. **1967** GB: 13 G. **1968** GB: 14 G. **1969** GB: 12 G. **1970** GB: 10 G; 1 Fum. **1971** GB: 14 G. **1972** GB: 14 G. **1973** GB: 14 G; 1 Fum. **Total:** 123 G; 2 Fum.

KEVIN BOWMAN Bowman, Kevin Gerard 6′3″, 205 **WR**
Col: Sacramento City Coll. CA (J.C.); Colorado; San Jose State
HS: Luther Burbank [Sacramento, CA] B: 2/23/1962, Sacramento, CA
1987 Phi: 3 G; Rec 6-127 21.2 1 TD; PR 4-43 10.8; KR 7-153 21.9; 6 Pt; 1 Fum.

STEVE BOWMAN Bowman, Steven Ellis 6′0″, 195 **HB**
Col: Alabama *HS:* Pascagoula [MS] B: 11/30/1944, Pascagoula, MS
Drafted: 1966 Round 15 NYG
1966 NYG: 4 G.

BILL BOWMAN Bowman, William Ekron Jr. 6′2″, 215 **FB**
Col: William & Mary *HS:* Riverside Mil. Acad. [VA]; Emporia [VA]
B: 9/22/1931, Birmingham, AL *Drafted:* 1954 Round 3 Det
1954 Det: KR 6-178 29.7 1 TD. **1956** Det: KR 1-24 24.0. **Total:** KR 7-202 28.9 1 TD.

		Rushing				Receiving					Tot
Year Team	G	Att	Yds	Avg	TD	Rec	Yds	Avg	TD	Fum	TD
1954 Det	12	96	397	4.1	2	34	288	8.5	2	8	5
1956 Det	6	20	84	4.2	1	5	34	6.8	1	0	2
1957 Pit	5	28	76	2.7	0	11	107	9.7	0	2	0
NFL Total	23	144	557	3.9	3	50	429	8.6	3	10	7

FABIEN BOWNES Bownes, Fabien Alfranso 5′11″, 185 **WR**
Col: Western Illinois *HS:* Waubonsie Valley [Aurora, IL] B: 2/29/1972, Aurora, IL
1995 ChiB: 1 G. **1997** ChiB: 16 G; Rec 12-146 12.2; KR 19-396 20.8. **1998** ChiB: 16 G; Rec 5-69 13.8 1 TD; KR 1-19 19.0; 6 Pt. **Total:** 33 G; Rec 17-215 12.6 1 TD; KR 20-415 20.8; 6 Pt.

ARDA BOWSER Bowser, Arda Crawford 6′2″, 210 **FB-WB-TB**
Col: Bethany (W.V.); Bucknell *HS:* Ford City [PA] B: 1/9/1899, Danville, PA D: 9/7/1996, Winter Park, FL
1922 Can: 5 G; Rush 2 TD; Scor 14, 2 XK. **1923** Cle: 3 G. **Total:** 8 G; Rush 2 TD.

CHARLES BOWSER Bowser, Charles Emanuel 6′3″, 231 **LB**
Col: Duke *HS:* Plymouth [NC] B: 10/2/1959, Plymouth, NC
Drafted: 1982 Round 4 Mia
1982 Mia: 9 G; 2 Sac. **1983** Mia: 16 G; 6.5 Sac. **1984** Mia: 15 G; 9 Sac. **1985** Mia: 2 G; 2.5 Sac. **Total:** 42 G; 20 Sac.

WALT BOWYER Bowyer, Walter Nathaniel Jr. 6′4″, 254 **DE**
Col: Arizona State *HS:* Wilkinsburg [PA] B: 9/8/1960, Pittsburgh, PA
Drafted: 1983 Round 10 Den
1983 Den: 14 G; 2 Sac. **1984** Den: 16 G; 3 Sac. **1987** Den: 15 G; 0.5 Sac. **1988** Den: 16 G; Int 1-1; 1 Sac. **Total:** 61 G; Int 1-1; 6.5 Sac.

CLOYCE BOX Box, Cloyce Kennedy 6′4″, 220 **OE-HB**
Col: Louisiana Tech; West Texas A&M *HS:* Waco [TX] B: 8/24/1923, Hamilton, TX D: 10/24/1993, Frisco, TX *Drafted:* 1948 Round 18 Was
1949 Det: KR 3-50 16.7. **Total:** KR 3-50 16.7.

		Rushing				Receiving					Tot
Year Team	G	Att	Yds	Avg	TD	Rec	Yds	Avg	TD	Fum	TD
1949 Det	10	30	62	2.1	0	15	276	18.4	4	2	4
1950 Det	12	0	0	—	0	50	1009	20.2	11	0	11
1952 Det	12	0	0	—	0	42	924	22.0	**15**	0	**15**
1953 Det	12	0	0	—	0	16	403	25.2	2	0	2
1954 Det	11	1	20	20.0	0	6	53	8.8	0	0	0
NFL Total	57	31	82	2.6	0	129	2665	20.7	32	2	32

JERRY BOYARSKY Boyarsky, Gerard Mark Joseph 6′3″, 290 **NT**
Col: Pittsburgh *HS:* Lakeland [Jermyn, PA] B: 5/15/1959, Scranton, PA
Drafted: 1981 Round 5 NO
1981 NO: 11 G. **1982** Cin: 2 G. **1983** Cin: 15 G; 1.5 Sac. **1984** Cin: 15 G. **1985** Cin: 16 G; 1 Sac. **1986** Buf-GB: 12 G. Buf: 10 G. GB: 2 G. **1987** GB: 12 G; 2 Sac. **1988** GB: 2 G; 0.5 Sac. **1989** GB: 13 G. **Total:** 98 G; 5 Sac.

BRENT BOYD Boyd, Brent Varner 6′3″, 268 **OG**
Col: UCLA *HS:* Lowell [La Habra, CA] B: 3/23/1957, Downey, CA
Drafted: 1980 Round 3 Min
1980 Min: 16 G; KR 1-20 20.0. **1981** Min: 3 G. **1982** Min: 4 G. **1983** Min: 16 G. **1985** Min: 15 G. **1986** Min: 5 G. **Total:** 59 G; KR 1-20 20.0.

DENNIS BOYD Boyd, Dennis James 6′6″, 255 **DE-DT-OT-C**
Col: Oregon State *HS:* Douglas [Winston, OR] B: 11/5/1955, Washington, DC *Drafted:* 1977 Round 3 Sea
1977 Sea: 14 G. **1978** Sea: 16 G; KR 1-6 6.0. **1979** Sea: 11 G. **1981** Sea: 16 G; Rec 1-3 3.0 1 TD; 6 Pt. **1982** Sea: 2 G. **Total:** 59 G; Rec 1-3 3.0 1 TD; KR 1-6 6.0; 6 Pt.

ELMO BOYD Boyd, Elmo David 6′0″, 188 **WR**
Col: Eastern Kentucky *HS:* Troy [OH] B: 6/15/1954, Muleshoe, TX
Drafted: 1977 Round 3 SF
1978 SF-GB: 11 G; Rec 9-115 12.8 1 TD; 6 Pt; 1 Fum. SF: 9 G; Rec 9-115 12.8 1 TD; 6 Pt; 1 Fum. GB: 2 G. **Total:** 11 G; Rec 9-115 12.8 1 TD; 6 Pt; 1 Fum.

GREG BOYD Boyd, Gregory Earl 6′6″, 274 **DE**
Col: Fresno City Coll. CA (J.C.); San Diego State *HS:* Edison [Fresno, CA] B: 9/15/1952, Merced, CA *Drafted:* 1976 Round 6 NE
1977 NE: 13 G. **1978** NE: 10 G. **1980** Den: 16 G. **1981** Den: 15 G. **1982** Den: 9 G; Scor 1 Saf; 2 Pt. **1983** GB: 12 G; Scor 1 Saf; 2 Pt; 2 Sac. **1984** SF-LARd: 7 G. SF: 2 G. LARd: 5 G. **Total:** 82 G; Scor 2 Saf; 4 Pt; 2 Sac.

GREG BOYD Boyd, Gregory Paul 6′2″, 201 **DB**
Col: Arizona *HS:* Saguaro [Scottsdale, AZ] B: 12/30/1950, Scottsdale, AZ *Drafted:* 1973 Round 14 Mia
1973 NE: 2 G. **1974** NO: 4 G. **Total:** 6 G.

JEROME BOYD Boyd, Jerome Anthony 6′2″, 225 **LB**
Col: Santa Monica Coll. CA (J.C.); Oregon State *HS:* Crenshaw [Los Angeles, CA] B: 9/18/1961, Los Angeles, CA
1983 Sea: 5 G.

MALIK BOYD Boyd, Malik A 5′10″, 175 **DB**
Col: Southern University *HS:* M.B. Smiley [Houston, TX] B: 11/5/1970, Houston, TX
1994 Min: 16 G; Int 1-22.

BOB BOYD Boyd, Robert B 6′2″, 201 **OE-DB**
(Sea Biscuit) *Col:* Riverside CC CA; Compton CC CA; Loyola Marymount *HS:* Riverside Polytechnic [CA] B: 3/7/1928, Riverside, CA
1950 LARm: Rush 1-(-2) -2.0. **1951** LARm: Int 2-3. **1953** LARm: PR 5-26 5.2; KR 3-42 14.0; Int 1-35. **1956** LARm: Rush 1-(-7) -7.0; KR 4-62 15.5. **Total:** Rush 2-(-9) -4.5; PR 5-26 5.2; KR 7-104 14.9; Int 3-38.

		Receiving				
Year Team	G	Rec	Yds	Avg	TD	Fum
1950 LARm	12	9	220	24.4	4	0
1951 LARm	12	9	128	14.2	1	0
1953 LARm	12	24	548	**22.8**	4	0
1954 LARm	12	53	**1212**	22.9	6	2
1955 LARm	7	22	383	17.4	3	0
1956 LARm	12	30	586	19.5	7	3
1957 LARm	12	29	534	18.4	3	2
NFL Total	79	176	3611	20.5	28	7

BOBBY BOYD Boyd, Robert Dean 5′11″, 195 **DB-HB**
Col: Oklahoma *HS:* Garland [TX] B: 12/3/1937, Garland, TX
Drafted: 1960 Round 10 Bal
1961 Bal: Pass 1-0; PR 18-173 9.6. **1962** Bal: Rush 2-13 6.5; PR 3-23 7.7. **1963** Bal: **1** Fum TD. **1964** Bal: Rush 1-25 25.0; KR 1-0. **Total:** Pass 1-0; Rush 3-38 12.7; PR 21-196 9.3; KR 1-0; 1 Fum TD.

		Interceptions				Tot
Year Team	G	Int	Yds	TD	Fum	TD
1960 Bal	11	7	132	0	0	0
1961 Bal	14	2	0	0	0	0
1962 Bal	14	7	163	0	1	0
1963 Bal	12	3	17	0	0	1
1964 Bal	14	9	**185**	0	0	0
1965 Bal	14	**9**	78	1	1	1
1966 Bal	14	6	114	1	0	1
1967 Bal	14	6	145	1	0	1

1968 Bal	14	8	160	1	0	1
NFL Total	121	57	994	4	2	5

SAM BOYD Boyd, Sam Bradford 6′1″, 188 **OE-DE**
Col: Baylor *HS:* Cleburne [TX] B: 8/12/1914, Rockwall, TX
Drafted: 1939 Round 6 Pit
1939 Pit: 11 G; Rec 21-423 20.1 2 TD; 12 Pt. **1940** Pit: 3 G. **Total:** 14 G; Rec 21-423 20.1 2 TD; 12 Pt.

SEAN BOYD Boyd, Sean Lefell 6′2″, 206 **DB**
Col: North Carolina *HS:* Ashbrook [Gastonia, NC] B: 12/19/1972, Gastonia, NC *Drafted:* 1996 Round 5 Min
1996 Atl: 2 G.

STEPHEN BOYD Boyd, Stephen Gerard 6′0″, 247 **LB**
Col: Boston College *HS:* Valley Stream [NY] B: 8/22/1972, Valley Stream, NY *Drafted:* 1995 Round 5 Det
1995 Det: 16 G; 1 Sac. **1996** Det: 8 G. **1997** Det: 16 G; Int 1-4; 1 Fum TD; 6 Pt. **1998** Det: 13 G; 4 Sac. **Total:** 53 G; Int 1-4; 1 Fum TD; 6 Pt; 5 Sac.

TOM BOYD Boyd, Thomas Barton 6′3″, 210 **LB**
Col: Alabama *HS:* Robert E. Lee [Huntsville, AL] B: 11/24/1959, Huntsville, AL *Drafted:* 1982 Round 8 GB
1987 Det: 4 G; 1 Sac.

TOMMIE BOYD Boyd, Tomie Leeshay 6′0″, 195 **WR**
Col: Toledo *HS:* Eastern [Lansing, MI] B: 12/21/1971, Lansing, MI
1997 Det: 16 G; Rec 10-142 14.2. **1998** Det: 9 G; Rec 4-52 13.0 1 TD; PR 4-11 2.8; KR 8-163 20.4; 6 Pt. **Total:** 25 G; Rec 14-194 13.9 1 TD; PR 4-11 2.8; KR 8-163 20.4; 6 Pt.

BILL BOYD Boyd, Walter Alvin Jr. 5′11″, 175 **WB-BB**
Col: Westminster (Mo.) *HS:* Louisiana [MO] B: 1907, Louisiana, MO
1930 ChiC: 12 G; Rush 1 TD; Rec 1 TD; Tot TD 2; 12 Pt. **1931** ChiC: 4 G. **Total:** 16 G; Rush 1 TD; Rec 1 TD; Tot TD 2; 12 Pt.

MIKE BOYDA Boyda, Michael Bartholomew 6′1″, 205 **LB-FB**
Col: Washington & Lee *HS:* Elders Ridge [PA] B: 11/28/1921, Jenners, PA D: 7/16/1984, Overland Park, KS *Drafted:* 1949 Round 5 NYB
1949 NYB: Pass 1-0; Int 1-25.

		Punting		
Year Team	**G**	**Punts**	**Yds**	**Avg**
1949 NYB	9	56	2475	44.2

MAX BOYDSTON Boydston, Max Ray 6′2″, 210 **OE**
Col: Oklahoma *HS:* Muskogee [OK] B: 1/22/1932, Ardmore, OK
Drafted: 1955 Round 1 ChiC

		Receiving			
Year Team	**G**	**Rec**	**Yds**	**Avg**	**TD**
1955 ChiC	9	3	79	26.3	1
1956 ChiC	12	6	116	19.3	2
1957 ChiC	12	14	193	13.8	0
1958 ChiC	10	3	42	14.0	1
1960 DalT	14	29	357	12.3	3
1961 DalT	11	12	167	13.9	1
1962 Oak	14	30	374	12.5	0
NFL Total	82	97	1328	13.7	8

BRANT BOYER Boyer, Brant T 6′1″, 234 **LB**
Col: Snow Coll. UT (J.C.); Arizona *HS:* North Summit [Coalville, UT] B: 6/27/1971, Ogden, UT *Drafted:* 1994 Round 6 Mia
1994 Mia: 14 G. **1995** Jac: 2 G. **1996** Jac: 12 G. **1997** Jac: 16 G; 1.5 Sac. **1998** Jac: 11 G; 1 Sac. **Total:** 55 G; 2.5 Sac.

MARK BOYER Boyer, Mark Hearn 6′4″, 233 **TE-RB**
Col: USC *HS:* Edison [Huntington Beach, CA] B: 9/16/1962, Huntington Beach, CA *Drafted:* 1985 Round 9 Ind
1990 NYJ: KR 1-14 14.0. **1991** NYJ: KR 1-0. **Total:** KR 2-14 7.0.

		Receiving				
Year Team	**G**	**Rec**	**Yds**	**Avg**	**TD**	**Fum**
1985 Ind	16	25	274	11.0	0	0
1986 Ind	16	22	237	10.8	1	1
1987 Ind	7	10	73	7.3	0	0
1988 Ind	16	27	256	9.5	2	0
1989 Ind	16	11	58	5.3	2	1
1990 NYJ	16	40	334	8.4	1	1
1991 NYJ	11	16	153	9.6	0	0
1992 NYJ	16	19	149	7.8	0	0
NFL Total	114	170	1534	9.0	6	3

VERDI BOYER Boyer, Verdi Emerson Jr. 5′10″, 195 **T**
(Blister) *Col:* UCLA *HS:* Huntington Park [CA] B: 9/2/1911, San Francisco, CA
1936 Bkn: 11 G.

LON BOYETT Boyett, Lon 6′6″, 240 **TE**
Col: Cal State-Northridge *HS:* Antelope Valley [Lancaster, CA] B: 12/24/1953, Lancaster, CA
1978 SF: 3 G.

GARLAND BOYETTE Boyette, Garland Dean 6′1″, 238 **LB**
Col: Grambling State *HS:* Orange [TX] B: 3/22/1940, Rayville, LA
1962 StL: 14 G. **1963** StL: 9 G. **1966** Hou: 14 G; KR 3-42 14.0. **1967** Hou: 14 G. **1968** Hou: 14 G; Int 1-0. **1969** Hou: 14 G. **1970** Hou: 13 G; Int 1-18. **1971** Hou: 14 G; **1** Fum TD; 6 Pt. **1972** Hou: 14 G. **Total:** 120 G; KR 3-42 14.0; Int 2-18; 1 Fum TD; 6 Pt.

DERAL BOYKIN Boykin, Deral Lamont 5′11″, 196 **DB**
Col: Kansas; Louisville *HS:* Theodore Roosevelt [Kent, OH] B: 9/2/1970, Kent, OH *Drafted:* 1993 Round 6 LARm
1993 LARm: 16 G; KR 13-216 16.6; 1 Fum TD; 6 Pt; 1 Fum. **1994** Was: 12 G. **1995** Jac: 5 G. **1996** Phi: 10 G. **Total:** 43 G; KR 13-216 16.6; 1 Fum TD; 6 Pt; 1 Fum.

GREG BOYKIN Boykin, Gregory Alan 6′0″, 225 **RB**
Col: Northwestern *HS:* Theodore Roosevelt [Kent, OH] B: 12/8/1953, Ravenna, OH *Drafted:* 1977 Round 7 NO
1977 NO: Rec 3-21 7.0; KR 5-76 15.2. **1978** SF: Rec 19-112 5.9; KR 3-37 12.3. **Total:** Rec 22-133 6.0; KR 8-113 14.1.

		Rushing				
Year Team	**G**	**Att**	**Yds**	**Avg**	**TD**	**Fum**
1977 NO	14	5	-9	-1.8	0	0
1978 SF	16	102	361	3.5	2	3
NFL Total	30	107	352	3.3	2	3

JIM BOYLAN Boylan, James Owen 6′1″, 185 **WR**
Col: Washington State *HS:* Birmingham [Van Nuys, CA] B: 3/19/1939, Washington, DC
1963 Min: 3 G; Rec 6-78 13.0 1 TD; 6 Pt.

JIM BOYLE Boyle, James Robert 6′5″, 270 **OT**
Col: Tulane *HS:* Moeller [Cincinnati, OH] B: 7/27/1961, Cincinnati, OH
Drafted: 1984 Round 9 Mia
1987 Pit: 3 G; Rec 1-0. **1988** Pit: 6 G; KR 1-19 19.0. **Total:** 9 G; Rec 1-0; KR 1-19 19.0.

KNUCKLES BOYLE Boyle, William 5′11″, 232 **T**
Col: Albright *HS:* Harrisburg Tech [PA]; New York Mil. Acad. [Cornwall-on-Hudson, NY] B: 1909
1934 NYG: 1 G.

BENNY BOYNTON Boynton, Ben Lee 5′9″, 170 **TB-BB-WB**
(The Purple Streak) *Col:* Williams *HS:* Waco [TX] B: 12/6/1898, Waco, TX D: 1/23/1963, Dallas, TX
1921 Roch-Was: 5 G; Pass 5 TD; Rush 3 TD; Scor 32, 1 FG, 11 XK. Roch: 3 G; Pass 3 TD; Rush 2 TD; Scor 23, 1 FG, 8 XK. Was: 2 G; Pass 2 TD; Rush 1 TD; Scor 9, 3 XK. **1922** Roch: 1 G. **1924** Roch-Buf: 10 G; Pass 6 TD; Rush 2 TD; Rec 3 TD; PR **1** TD; Scor 59, 4 FG, 11 XK; Tot TD 6. Roch: 1 G. Buf: 9 G; Pass 6 TD; Rush 2 TD; Rec 3 TD; PR 1 TD; Scor 59, 4 FG, 11 XK; Tot TD 6. **Total:** 16 G; Pass 11 TD; Rush 5 TD; Rec 3 TD; PR 1 TD; Scor 91, 5 FG, 22 XK; Tot TD 9.

GEORGE BOYNTON Boynton, George Douglas 5′11″, 190 **DB**
Col: Ranger Coll. TX (J.C.); Eastern New Mexico; Texas A&M-Commerce *HS:* Quanah [TX] B: 7/6/1937, Los Angeles, CA *Drafted:* 1960 Round 16 Bal
1962 Oak: 3 G.

JOHN BOYNTON Boynton, John Alden 6′4″, 255 **OT**
Col: Tennessee *HS:* Bledsoe Co. [Pikeville, TN] B: 3/28/1946, Pikeville, TN *Drafted:* 1968 Round 7 Mia
1969 Mia: 14 G.

ORDELL BRAASE Braase, Ordell Wayne 6′4″, 245 **DE**
Col: South Dakota *HS:* Mitchell [SD] B: 3/13/1932, Mitchell, SD
Drafted: 1954 Round 14 Bal
1957 Bal: 12 G. **1958** Bal: 12 G. **1959** Bal: 12 G. **1960** Bal: 12 G. **1961** Bal: 13 G. **1962** Bal: 14 G; **1** Fum TD; 6 Pt. **1963** Bal: 14 G. **1964** Bal: 14 G. **1965** Bal: 12 G. **1966** Bal: 14 G. **1967** Bal: 14 G; **1** Fum TD; 6 Pt. **1968** Bal: 14 G. **Total:** 157 G; 2 Fum TD; 12 Pt.

TOM BRAATZ Braatz, Thomas Myron 6′1″, 216 **LB-OE**
(Bubble) *Col:* Marquette *HS:* Mary Bradford [Kenosha, WI] B: 5/12/1933, Kenosha, WI *Drafted:* 1955 Round 14 Was
1957 Was: 10 G; Rec 2-52 26.0. **1958** Was-LARm: 4 G; KR 1-8 8.0. Was: 3 G; KR 1-8 8.0. LARm: 1 G. **1959** Was: 12 G; Int 1-17. **1960** Dal: 12 G; Int 1-4. **Total:** 38 G; Rec 2-52 26.0; KR 1-8 8.0; Int 2-21.

DANNY BRABHAM Brabham, Daniel Edward 6′4″, 235 **LB**
Col: Arkansas *HS:* St. Helena Central [Greensburg, LA] B: 2/25/1941, Magnolia, MS *Drafted:* 1963 Round 1 Hou
1963 Hou: 14 G; Int 1-1. **1964** Hou: 13 G. **1965** Hou: 14 G. **1966** Hou: 3 G. **1967** Hou: 12 G. **1968** Cin: 9 G. **Total:** 65 G; Int 1-1.

CARY BRABHAM Brabham, James Cary 6′0″, 195 **DB**
Col: Southern Methodist *HS:* Hughes Springs [TX] B: 8/11/1970, Longview, TX
1994 LARd: 7 G.

BILL BRACE Brace, George Wells 6′0″, 180 **G-C**
(Bus) *Col:* Brown *HS:* Dunkirk [NY] B: 11/19/1895, Sheridan, NY D: 1/7/1972, Jamestown, NY
1920 Buf: 10 G. **1921** Buf: 11 G. **1922** Buf: 10 G. **Total:** 31 G.

GREG BRACELIN Bracelin, Gregory Lee 6′1″, 214 LB
Col: California *HS:* De Anza [Richmond, CA] B: 4/16/1957, Lawrence, KS *Drafted:* 1980 Round 9 Den
1980 Den: 12 G. **1981** Oak: 15 G. **1982** Bal: 9 G; Int 1-31; 2 Sac. **1983** Bal: 16 G; Int 2-19; 5.5 Sac. **1984** Ind: 16 G; 2 Sac. **Total:** 68 G; Int 3-50; 9.5 Sac.

DON BRACKEN Bracken, Donald Craig 6′1″, 214 P
Col: Michigan *HS:* Hot Springs Co. [Thermopolis, WY] B: 2/16/1962, Coalinga, CA

		Punting		
Year Team	G	Punts	Yds	Avg
1985 GB	7	26	1052	40.5
1986 GB	13	55	2203	40.1
1987 GB	12	72	2947	40.9
1988 GB	16	85	3287	38.7
1989 GB	16	66	2682	40.6
1990 GB	16	64	2431	38.0
1992 LARm	16	76	3122	41.1
1993 LARm	3	17	651	38.3
NFL Total	99	461	18375	39.9

TONY BRACKENS Brackens, Tony Lynn Jr. 6′4″, 260 DE
Col: Texas *HS:* Fairfield [TX] B: 12/26/1974, Fairfield, TX
Drafted: 1996 Round 2 Jac
1996 Jac: 16 G; Int 1-27; 7 Sac. **1997** Jac: 15 G; 7 Sac. **1998** Jac: 12 G; 3.5 Sac. **Total:** 43 G; Int 1-27; 17.5 Sac.

M.L. BRACKETT Brackett, M.L. 6′5″, 248 DE-DT-LB
Col: Auburn *HS:* Etowah [Attalla, AL] B: 7/4/1933, Etowah Co., AL
Drafted: 1956 Round 2 ChiB
1956 ChiB: 12 G; Int 1-24. **1957** ChiB: 8 G; KR 3-5 1.7. **1958** NYG: 12 G. **Total:** 32 G; KR 3-5 1.7; Int 1-24.

CHARLIE BRACKINS Brackins, Charles 6′2″, 202 QB
Col: Prairie View A&M *HS:* Lincoln [Dallas, TX] B: 1/12/1932, Dallas, TX *Drafted:* 1955 Round 16 GB
1955 GB: 7 G; Pass 2-0.

DAVE BRADEN Braden, David E. Thomas 6′0″, 210 G-LB
Col: Marquette *HS:* St. John's Cathedral [Milwaukee, WI]
B: 9/27/1917, Milwaukee, WI D: 8/2/1980, Milwaukee, WI
1945 ChiC: 1 G.

COREY BRADFORD Bradford, Corey Lamon 6′0″, 197 WR
Col: Hinds CC MS; Jackson State *HS:* Clinton [LA] B: 12/8/1975, Baton Rouge, LA *Drafted:* 1998 Round 5 GB
1998 GB: 8 G; Rec 3-27 9.0; KR 2-33 16.5; 1 Fum.

PAUL BRADFORD Bradford, Paul 5′9″, 185 DB
Col: Coll. of San Mateo CA (J.C.); Portland State *HS:* Carlmont [Belmont, CA] B: 4/20/1974, East Palo Alto, CA *Drafted:* 1997 Round 5 SD
1997 SD: 15 G; Int 2-56 1 TD; 1 Fum TD; Tot TD 2; 12 Pt.

RONNIE BRADFORD Bradford, Ronnie Lee 5′10″, 188 DB
Col: Colorado *HS:* Adams City [Commerce, OK] B: 10/1/1970, Minot, ND *Drafted:* 1993 Round 4 Mia
1993 Den: 10 G; PR 1-0; Int 1-0; 1 Fum. **1994** Den: 12 G; 1 Sac. **1995** Den: 4 G. **1996** Ariz: 15 G; Int 1-0. **1997** Atl: 16 G; Int 4-9. **1998** Atl: 14 G; Int 3-11 1 TD; Scor **1** Saf; 8 Pt. **Total:** 71 G; PR 1-0; Int 9-20 1 TD; Scor 1 Saf; 8 Pt; 1 Fum; 1 Sac.

BYRON BRADFUTE Bradfute, Byron Gilbert 6′3″, 243 OT
Col: Southern Mississippi *HS:* Jones [Beeville, TX] B: 12/12/1937, Beeville, TX *Drafted:* 1960 Round 1 LAC
1960 Dal: 12 G. **1961** Dal: 5 G. **Total:** 17 G.

CARLOS BRADLEY Bradley, Carlos Humberto 6′0″, 224 LB
Col: Wake Forest *HS:* Germantown [Philadelphia, PA] B: 4/27/1960, Philadelphia, PA *Drafted:* 1981 Round 11 SD
1981 SD: 8 G. **1982** SD: 9 G. **1983** SD: 16 G; 0.5 Sac. **1984** SD: 8 G. **1985** SD: 10 G; Int 2-36; 2 Sac. **1987** Phi: 3 G. **Total:** 54 G; Int 2-36; 2.5 Sac.

CHUCK BRADLEY Bradley, Charles John 6′6″, 243 TE
Col: Oregon *HS:* Atherton [CA] B: 10/13/1950, Hinsdale, IL
Drafted: 1973 Round 2 Mia
1975 SD: 4 G; Rec 1-42 42.0. **1976** SD: 7 G; Rec 1-7 7.0. **1977** SD-ChiB: 8 G. SD: 1 G. ChiB: 7 G. **Total:** 19 G; Rec 2-49 24.5.

CHUCK BRADLEY Bradley, Charles Warren II 6′5″, 296 OT
Col: Kentucky *HS:* Fern Creek [KY] B: 4/9/1970, Covington, KY
Drafted: 1993 Round 6 Hou
1993 Cin: 1 G.

DANNY BRADLEY Bradley, Daniel Louis 5′9″, 175 RB
Col: Oklahoma *HS:* Pine Bluff [AR] B: 3/2/1963, Pine Bluff, AR
Drafted: 1985 Round 7 LARm
1987 Det: 3 G; Rec 7-50 7.1 2 TD; PR 12-53 4.4; KR 9-188 20.9; 12 Pt; 2 Fum.

DAVE BRADLEY Bradley, David Earl 6′4″, 245 OG
Col: Penn State *HS:* Chief Logan [Burnham, PA] B: 2/13/1947, Burnham, PA *Drafted:* 1969 Round 2 GB
1969 GB: 4 G. **1970** GB: 4 G. **1971** GB: 7 G. **1972** StL: 1 G. **Total:** 16 G.

ED BRADLEY Bradley, Edward William II 6′0″, 212 G
Col: Wake Forest *HS:* Warren G. Harding [Bridgeport, CT]; Stratford HS [CT] B: 9/16/1926, Stratford, CT *Drafted:* 1950 Round 16 ChiB
1950 ChiB: 4 G. **1952** ChiB: 8 G. **Total:** 12 G.

ED BRADLEY Bradley, Edward William III 6′2″, 239 LB
Col: Wake Forest *HS:* Stratford [CT] B: 4/22/1950, Bridgeport, CT
Drafted: 1972 Round 4 Pit
1972 Pit: 12 G. **1973** Pit: 14 G. **1974** Pit: 10 G. **1975** Pit: 13 G. **1976** Sea: 14 G; Int 1-29. **1977** SF: 14 G. **1978** SF: 16 G. **Total:** 93 G; Int 1-29.

HAL BRADLEY Bradley, Eugene Hal 6′4″, 205 OE
Col: Elon *HS:* Lafayette [Kipling, NC] B: 11/23/1913, Winston-Salem, NC D: 6/14/1981, Durham, NC
1938 Was: 7 G; Rec 1-14 14.0. **1939** Was-ChiC: 4 G; Rec 3-29 9.7. Was: 1 G. ChiC: 3 G; Rec 3-29 9.7. **Total:** 11 G; Rec 4-43 10.8.

FREDDIE BRADLEY Bradley, Freddie Lee Jr. 5′10″, 208 RB
Col: Moorpark Coll. CA (J.C.); Arkansas; Sonoma State *HS:* Hueneme [Oxnard, CA] B: 6/12/1970, Helena, AR *Drafted:* 1996 Round 7 SD
1996 SD: Rec 1-20 20.0.

		Rushing			
Year Team	G	Att	Yds	Avg	TD
1996 SD	10	32	109	3.4	0

HAL BRADLEY Bradley, Harold Willard 185 G
Col: Iowa *HS:* Englewood [Chicago, IL] B: 9/27/1905, KS Deceased
1928 ChiC: 2 G.

HAROLD BRADLEY Bradley, Harold Willard Jr. 6′2″, 230 OG
Col: Iowa *HS:* Englewood [Chicago, IL] B: 10/13/1929, Chicago, IL
1954 Cle: 12 G. **1955** Cle: 12 G. **1956** Cle: 11 G. **1958** Phi: 12 G. **Total:** 47 G.

HENRY BRADLEY Bradley, Henry Averson 6′2″, 261 NT-DT
Col: Alcorn State *HS:* Davidson [St. Joseph, LA] B: 9/4/1953, St. Joesph, LA *Drafted:* 1978 Round 9 SD
1979 Cle: 5 G. **1980** Cle: 16 G. **1981** Cle: 16 G. **1982** Cle: 6 G. **Total:** 43 G.

LUTHER BRADLEY Bradley, Luther Alexander 6′2″, 195 DB
Col: Notre Dame *HS:* Muncie Northside [IN] B: 5/7/1955, Florence, SC
Drafted: 1978 Round 1 Det
1978 Det: 16 G; Int 3-85 1 TD; 6 Pt. **1979** Det: 16 G; Int 4-11. **1980** Det: 8 G; Int 1-0. **1981** Det: 16 G; Int 1-0. **Total:** 56 G; Int 9-96 1 TD; 6 Pt.

STEVE BRADLEY Bradley, Steven Carl 6′2″, 216 QB
Col: Valparaiso; Indiana *HS:* Knox [IL] B: 7/16/1963 *Drafted:* 1986 Round 12 Cin
1987 ChiB: 1 G; Pass 18-6 33.3%, 77 4.28 2 TD 3 Int; Rush 1-(-3) -3.0.

BILL BRADLEY Bradley, William Calvin 5′11″, 190 DB
Col: Texas *HS:* Palestine [TX] B: 1/24/1947, Palestine, TX
Drafted: 1969 Round 3 Phi
1969 Phi: Pass 1-0; Rush 1-5 5.0. **1970** Phi: Rush 1-14 14.0. **1973** Phi: Rush 1-0. **Total:** Pass 1-0; Rush 3-19 6.3.

		Punt Returns				Kickoff Returns			
Year Team	G	Ret	Yds	Avg	TD	Ret	Yds	Avg	TD
1969 Phi	14	28	181	6.5	0	21	467	22.2	0
1970 Phi	12	0	0	—	0	0	0	—	0
1971 Phi	14	18	118	6.6	0	0	0	—	0
1972 Phi	14	22	155	7.0	0	2	22	11.0	0
1973 Phi	14	8	106	13.3	0	0	0	—	0
1974 Phi	14	22	248	11.3	0	0	0	—	0
1975 Phi	14	4	4	1.0	0	0	0	—	0
1976 Phi	14	9	64	7.1	0	0	0	—	0
1977 StL	4	11	77	7.0	0	4	75	18.8	0
NFL Total	114	122	953	7.8	0	27	564	20.9	0

	Interceptions			Punting			
Year Team	Int	Yds	TD	Punts	Yds	Avg	Fum
1969 Phi	1	56	1	74	2942	39.8	2
1970 Phi	0	0	0	61	2246	36.8	0
1971 Phi	**11**	**248**	0	2	76	38.0	2
1972 Phi	**9**	73	0	56	2250	40.2	1
1973 Phi	4	21	0	18	735	40.8	2
1974 Phi	2	19	0	2	67	33.5	0
1975 Phi	5	56	0	0	0	—	0
1976 Phi	2	63	0	0	0	—	0
NFL Total	34	536	1	213	8316	39.0	7

CHARLIE BRADSHAW Bradshaw, Charles Marvin 6′6″, 260 **OT**
Col: Baylor *HS:* Center [TX] B: 3/13/1936, Center, TX *Drafted:* 1957 Round 8 LARm
1958 LARm: 12 G. **1959** LARm: 12 G. **1960** LARm: 12 G. **1961** Pit: 12 G; 1 Fum. **1962** Pit: 14 G. **1963** Pit: 14 G. **1964** Pit: 14 G. **1965** Pit: 14 G. **1966** Pit: 14 G. **1967** Det: 14 G. **1968** Det: 13 G. **Total:** 145 G; 1 Fum.

JIM BRADSHAW Bradshaw, James Alfred 6′2″, 205 **DB**
Col: Tennessee-Chattanooga *HS:* St. Clairsville [OH] B: 1/13/1939, St. Clairsville, OH *Drafted:* 1963 Round 18 Pit
1963 Pit: Punt 2-70 35.0. **1964** Pit: PR 1-2 2.0; **2** Fum TD. **1965** Pit: PR 5-73 14.6. **1966** Pit: PR 2-3 1.5. **1967** Pit: PR 16-97 6.1. **Total:** PR 24-175 7.3; Punt 2-70 35.0; 2 Fum TD.

		Interceptions				Tot
Year Team	**G**	**Int**	**Yds**	**TD**	**Fum**	**TD**
1963 Pit	14	1	0	0	0	0
1964 Pit	14	1	39	0	1	2
1965 Pit	12	5	117	1	0	1
1966 Pit	9	4	82	1	0	1
1967 Pit	13	0	0	0	2	0
NFL Total	62	11	238	2	3	4

JIM BRADSHAW Bradshaw, James W 5′6″, 150 **WB**
(Rabbit) *Col:* Illinois; Nevada-Reno B: 6/23/1898, Greene Co., MO D: 7/6/1987, Monterey, CA
1924 KC: 1 G.

MORRIS BRADSHAW Bradshaw, Morris C Jr. 6′1″, 195 **WR**
Col: Ohio State *HS:* Edwardsville [IL] B: 10/19/1952, Highland, IL *Drafted:* 1974 Round 4 Oak
1974 Oak: KR 1-0. **1975** Oak: Rush 1-(-5) -5.0. **1976** Oak: Rush 1-4 4.0. **1978** Oak: Rush 1-5 5.0. **Total:** Rush 3-4 1.3; KR 1-0.

		Receiving				
Year Team	**G**	**Rec**	**Yds**	**Avg**	**TD**	**Fum**
1974 Oak	12	0	0	—	0	0
1975 Oak	14	7	180	25.7	4	0
1976 Oak	14	1	25	25.0	1	0
1977 Oak	14	5	90	18.0	0	0
1978 Oak	16	40	552	13.8	2	1
1979 Oak	3	3	28	9.3	0	0
1980 Oak	16	6	132	22.0	1	0
1981 Oak	15	22	298	13.5	3	0
1982 NE	8	6	111	18.5	1	1
NFL Total	112	90	1416	15.7	12	2

TERRY BRADSHAW Bradshaw, Terry Paxton 6′3″, 215 **QB**
Col: Louisiana Tech *HS:* Woodlawn [Shreveport, LA] B: 9/2/1948, Shreveport, LA *Drafted:* 1970 Round 1 Pit *HOF:* 1989
1970 Pit: Punt 3-52 17.3. **1978** Pit: Rec 0-1. **1980** Pit: Punt 5-173 34.6. **Total:** Rec 0-1; Punt 8-225 28.1.

		Passing							
Year Team	**G**	**Att**	**Comp**	**Comp%**	**Yds**	**YPA**	**TD**	**Int**	**Rating**
1970 Pit	13	218	83	38.1	1410	6.47	6	24	30.4
1971 Pit	14	373	203	54.4	2259	6.06	13	22	59.7
1972 Pit	14	308	147	47.7	1887	6.13	12	12	64.1
1973 Pit	10	180	89	49.4	1183	6.57	10	15	54.5
1974 Pit	8	148	67	45.3	785	5.30	7	8	55.2
1975 Pit	14	286	165	57.7	2055	7.19	18	9	88.0
1976 Pit	10	192	92	47.9	1177	6.13	10	9	65.4
1977 Pit	14	314	162	51.6	2523	**8.04**	17	19	71.4
1978 Pit	16	368	207	56.3	2915	**7.92**	**28**	20	84.7
1979 Pit	16	472	259	54.9	3724	7.89	26	25	77.0
1980 Pit	15	424	218	51.4	3339	7.88	24	22	75.0
1981 Pit	14	370	201	54.3	2887	7.80	22	14	83.9
1982 Pit	9	240	127	52.9	1768	7.37	**17**	11	81.4
1983 Pit	1	8	5	62.5	77	9.63	2	0	133.9
NFL Total	168	3901	2025	51.9	27989	7.17	212	210	70.9

	Rushing				
Year Team	**Att**	**Yds**	**Avg**	**TD**	**Fum**
1970 Pit	32	233	7.3	1	3
1971 Pit	53	247	4.7	5	7
1972 Pit	58	346	6.0	7	4
1973 Pit	34	145	4.3	3	3
1974 Pit	34	224	6.6	2	1
1975 Pit	35	210	6.0	3	6
1976 Pit	31	219	7.1	3	7
1977 Pit	31	171	5.5	3	10
1978 Pit	32	93	2.9	1	8
1979 Pit	21	83	4.0	0	10
1980 Pit	36	111	3.1	2	13
1981 Pit	38	162	4.3	2	7
1982 Pit	8	10	1.3	0	5
1983 Pit	1	3	3.0	0	0
NFL Total	444	2257	5.1	32	84

WES BRADSHAW Bradshaw, Wesley Walker 5′8″, 175 **BB-TB-WB**
Col: Trinity (Tex.); Baylor *HS:* Athens [TX] B: 11/26/1897, Athens, TX D: 4/10/1960, Athens, TX
1924 RI: 7 G. **1926** Buf: 1 G. **Total:** 8 G.

CRAIG BRADSHAW Bradshaw, William Craig 6′5″, 215 **QB**
Col: Louisiana Tech; Utah State *HS:* Southwood [Shreveport, LA] B: 8/14/1957, Shreveport, LA *Drafted:* 1980 Round 7 Hou
1980 Hou: 2 G.

DONNY BRADY Brady, Donald Maynard 6′2″, 195 **DB**
Col: Nassau CC NY; Wisconsin *HS:* Mepham [Bellmore, NY] B: 11/26/1973, North Bellmore, NY
1995 Cle: 2 G. **1996** Bal: 16 G; 0.5 Sac. **1997** Bal: 16 G. **1998** Bal: 13 G; 1 Sac. **Total:** 47 G; 1.5 Sac.

ED BRADY Brady, Edward John 6′2″, 238 **LB**
Col: Illinois *HS:* Morris [IL] B: 6/17/1962, Morris, IL *Drafted:* 1984 Round 8 LARm
1984 LARm: 16 G. **1985** LARm: 16 G. **1986** Cin: 16 G; 1 Fum. **1987** Cin: 12 G. **1988** Cin: 16 G. **1989** Cin: 16 G. **1990** Cin: 16 G. **1991** Cin: 16 G. **1992** TB: 16 G. **1993** TB: 16 G. **1994** TB: 16 G. **1995** TB: 16 G; 1 Fum. **Total:** 188 G; 2 Fum.

JEFF BRADY Brady, Jeffrey Thomas 6′1″, 235 **LB**
Col: Kentucky *HS:* Newport Central Catholic [KY] B: 11/9/1968, Cincinnati, OH *Drafted:* 1991 Round 12 Pit
1991 Pit: 16 G. **1992** GB: 8 G. **1993** LARm-SD: 9 G. LARm: 6 G. SD: 3 G. **1994** TB: 16 G. **1995** Min: 16 G; Int 2-7; 3 Sac. **1996** Min: 16 G; Int 3-20; 1.5 Sac. **1997** Min: 15 G; 1 Fum TD; 6 Pt. **1998** Car: 16 G; KR 1-8 8.0; Int 4-85; 1 Fum; 4 Sac. **Total:** 112 G; KR 1-8 8.0; Int 9-112; 1 Fum TD; 6 Pt; 1 Fum; 8.5 Sac.

KERRY BRADY Brady, Kerry Patrick 6′1″, 205 **K**
Col: Portland CC OR; Hawaii *HS:* Hudson's Bay [Vancouver, WA] B: 8/27/1963, Vancouver, WA
1987 Dal: 1 G; Scor 1, 1-1 100.0% XK. **1988** Ind: 2 G. **1989** Buf: 3 G. **Total:** 6 G; Scor 1, 1-1 100.0% XK.

KYLE BRADY Brady, Kyle James 6′6″, 264 **TE**
Col: Penn State *HS:* Cedar Cliff [Camp Hill, PA] B: 1/14/1972, New Cumberland, PA *Drafted:* 1995 Round 1 NYJ
1995 NYJ: KR 2-25 12.5. **1996** NYJ: KR 2-26 13.0; Scor 1 2XP. **1998** NYJ: KR 1-20 20.0. **Total:** KR 5-71 14.2; Scor 1 2XP.

		Receiving				
Year Team	**G**	**Rec**	**Yds**	**Avg**	**TD**	**Fum**
1995 NYJ	15	26	252	9.7	2	0
1996 NYJ	16	15	144	9.6	1	1
1997 NYJ	16	22	238	10.8	2	1
1998 NYJ	16	30	315	10.5	5	1
NFL Total	63	93	949	10.2	10	3

PAT BRADY Brady, Patrick Thomas 6′1″, 195 **QB-K**
Col: Bradley; Nevada-Reno *HS:* Bishop O'Dea [Seattle, WA] B: 9/7/1926, Seattle, WA *Drafted:* 1952 Round 13 NYG
1952 Pit: Pass 3-1 33.3%, 14 4.67. **1953** Pit: Pass 1-0. **Total:** Pass 4-1 25.0%, 14 3.50.

		Punting		
Year Team	**G**	**Punts**	**Yds**	**Avg**
1952 Pit	12	77	3328	43.2
1953 Pit	12	**80**	**3752**	**46.9**
1954 Pit	12	66	2852	**43.2**
NFL Total	36	223	9932	44.5

PHIL BRADY Brady, Philip Alonzo 6′3″, 210 **DB**
Col: Brigham Young *HS:* Scottsdale [AZ] B: 4/22/1943, Tempe, AZ
1969 Den: 4 G.

RICKEY BRADY Brady, Rickey Lee Jr. 6′4″, 246 **TE**
Col: Oklahoma *HS:* Putnam City West [Oklahoma City, OK] B: 11/19/1971, Oklahoma City, OK *Drafted:* 1994 Round 6 LARm
1994 LARm: 1 G.

MIKE BRAGG Bragg, Michael Edward 5′11″, 186 **P**
Col: Richmond *HS:* J.E.B. Stuart [Falls Church, VA]; Staunton Mil. Acad. [VA] B: 9/26/1946, Richmond, VA *Drafted:* 1968 Round 5 Was
1968 Was: Rush 1-(-3) -3.0. **1969** Was: Rush 1-3 3.0. **1970** Was: Pass 1-0; Rush 2-25 12.5. **1974** Was: Scor 10, 1-1 100.0% FG, 7-8 87.5% XK. **1978** Was: Pass 2-2 100.0%, 69 34.50. **Total:** Pass 3-2 66.7%, 69 23.00; Rush 4-25 6.3; Scor 10, 1-1 100.0% FG, 7-8 87.5% XK.

		Punting			
Year Team	**G**	**Punts**	**Yds**	**Avg**	**Fum**
1968 Was	14	76	3288	43.3	2
1969 Was	14	70	2957	42.2	0
1970 Was	14	61	2493	40.9	0
1971 Was	14	58	2348	40.5	0
1972 Was	14	59	2273	38.5	0
1973 Was	14	64	2581	40.3	0
1974 Was	14	74	2823	38.1	0

1975 Was	14	72	2924	40.6	0
1976 Was	14	90	3503	38.9	0
1977 Was	14	91	3502	38.5	0
1978 Was	16	103	4056	39.4	0
1979 Was	16	78	2998	38.4	0
1980 Bal	16	82	3203	39.1	0
NFL Total	188	978	38949	39.8	2

BYRON BRAGGS Braggs, Byron Charles 6′4″, 290 **DE**
Col: Alabama *HS:* George Washington Carver [Montgomery, AL] B: 10/10/1959, Montgomery, AL *Drafted:* 1981 Round 5 GB
1981 GB: 16 G; KR 1-0. **1982** GB: 9 G. **1983** GB: 16 G; 5.5 Sac. **1984** TB: 14 G. **Total:** 55 G; KR 1-0; 5.5 Sac.

STEPHEN BRAGGS Braggs, Stephen 5′9″, 178 **DB**
Col: Texas *HS:* M.B. Smiley [Houston, TX] B: 8/29/1965, Houston, TX *Drafted:* 1987 Round 6 Cle
1987 Cle: 12 G. **1988** Cle: 16 G; KR 1-27 27.0. **1989** Cle: 7 G; KR 2-20 10.0. **1990** Cle: 15 G; Int 2-13; 2.5 Sac. **1991** Cle: 16 G; Int 3-15; 1 Sac. **1992** Mia: 6 G; 1 Sac. **1993** Mia: 11 G. **Total:** 83 G; KR 3-47 15.7; Int 5-28; 4.5 Sac.

DENNIS BRAGONIER Bragonier, Dennis John 6′0″, 186 **DB**
Col: Chabot Coll. CA (J.C.); Stanford *HS:* Hayward [CA] B: 1/22/1951, Hayward, CA
1974 SF: 2 G.

RICH BRAHAM Braham, Richard Lee Jr. 6′4″, 292 **OT-OG-C**
Col: West Virginia *HS:* University [Morgantown, WV] B: 11/6/1970, Morgantown, WV *Drafted:* 1994 Round 3 Ariz
1994 Cin: 3 G. **1996** Cin: 16 G. **1997** Cin: 16 G. **1998** Cin: 12 G. **Total:** 47 G.

TOM BRAHANEY Brahaney, Thomas Frank 6′2″, 245 **C**
Col: Oklahoma *HS:* Midland [TX] B: 10/23/1951, Midland, TX *Drafted:* 1973 Round 5 StL
1973 StL: 14 G. **1974** StL: 14 G. **1975** StL: 14 G; 1 Fum. **1976** StL: 14 G; 2 Fum. **1977** StL: 14 G. **1978** StL: 16 G; 1 Fum. **1979** StL: 16 G; 1 Fum. **1980** StL: 16 G. **1981** StL: 16 G. **Total:** 134 G; 5 Fum.

LARRY BRAHM Brahm, Lawrence 5′10″, 204 **G-LB**
Col: Temple *HS:* Blair Acad. [Blairstown, NJ] B: 8/12/1916, Bayonne, NJ D: 7/16/1959, Yonkers, NY
1942 Cle: 10 G; Int 1-15.

CHUCK BRAIDWOOD Braidwood, Charles 6′0″, 199 **OE-DE**
Col: Loyola (Chicago); Tennessee-Chattanooga B: 10/15/1903 D: 1944, South Pacific
1930 Port: 10 G. **1931** Cle: 8 G. **1932** ChiC: 1 G. **1933** Cin: 6 G; Rec 2-29 14.5. **Total:** 25 G; Rec 2-29 14.5.

ART BRAMAN Braman, Arthur Henry 5′11″, 215 **T**
(Bull) *Col:* Yale *HS:* Phillips Exeter Acad. [Exeter, NH] B: 8/4/1897, Torrington, CT D: 8/12/1967, Carmel Highlands, CA
1922 Rac: 8 G. **1923** Rac: 6 G. **Total:** 14 G.

DON BRAMLETT Bramlett, Donald Kirk 6′2″, 270 **DT**
Col: Memphis; Carson-Newman *HS:* Evangelical Christian School [Cordova, TN] B: 10/5/1962, Memphis, TN
1987 Min: 3 G.

JOHN BRAMLETT Bramlett, John Cameron 6′1″, 220 **LB**
(Bull) *Col:* Memphis *HS:* Humes [Memphis, TN] B: 7/7/1941, Memphis, TN
1965 Den: **1** Fum TD. **Total:** 1 Fum TD.

		Interceptions			Tot
Year Team	**G**	**Int**	**Yds**	**TD**	**TD**
1965 Den	14	1	25	1	2
1966 Den	14	1	12	0	1
1967 Mia	14	4	35	0	0
1968 Mia	13	2	14	0	0
1969 Bos	12	1	26	0	0
1970 Bos	12	1	16	0	0
1971 Atl	7	0	0	0	0
NFL Total	86	10	128	1	3

MARK BRAMMER Brammer, Mark Dewitt 6′3″, 238 **TE**
Col: Michigan State *HS:* Traverse City [MI] B: 5/3/1958, Traverse City, MI *Drafted:* 1980 Round 3 Buf
1980 Buf: Rush 1-8 8.0. **1981** Buf: Rush 2-17 8.5. **Total:** Rush 3-25 8.3.

		Receiving				
Year Team	**G**	**Rec**	**Yds**	**Avg**	**TD**	**Fum**
1980 Buf	16	26	283	10.9	4	0
1981 Buf	16	33	365	11.1	2	3
1982 Buf	9	25	225	9.0	2	0
1983 Buf	12	25	215	8.6	2	0
1984 Buf	12	7	49	7.0	0	0
NFL Total	65	116	1137	9.8	10	3

GEORGE BRANCATO Brancato, George A 5′9″, 177 **HB-DB**
Col: Rancho Santiago Coll. CA (J.C.); Louisiana State *HS:* Lafayette [Brooklyn, NY] B: 5/27/1931, Brooklyn, NY
1954 ChiC: 5 G; Rush 2-26 13.0; Rec 3-28 9.3.

CALVIN BRANCH Branch, Calvin Stanley 5′11″, 195 **DB**
Col: Colorado State *HS:* Klein Oak [Spring, TX] B: 5/8/1974, Versailles, KY *Drafted:* 1997 Round 6 Oak
1997 Oak: 6 G. **1998** Oak: 16 G; KR 5-70 14.0; 1 Fum. **Total:** 22 G; KR 5-70 14.0; 1 Fum.

CLIFF BRANCH Branch, Clifford Jr. 5′11″, 170 **WR**
Col: Wharton Co. JC TX; Colorado *HS:* Evan E. Worthing [Houston, TX] B: 8/1/1948, Houston, TX *Drafted:* 1972 Round 4 Oak
1972 Oak: Rush 1-5 5.0; PR 12-21 1.8; KR 9-191 21.2. **1975** Oak: Rush 2-18 9.0. **1976** Oak: Rush 3-12 4.0. **1979** Oak: Rush 1-4 4.0. **1980** Oak: Rush 1-1 1.0. **1982** LARd: Rush 2-10 5.0. **1983** LARd: Rush 1-20 20.0. **Total:** Rush 11-70 6.4; PR 12-21 1.8; KR 9-191 21.2.

		Receiving				
Year Team	**G**	**Rec**	**Yds**	**Avg**	**TD**	**Fum**
1972 Oak	14	3	41	13.7	0	2
1973 Oak	13	19	290	15.3	3	0
1974 Oak	14	60	**1092**	18.2	**13**	1
1975 Oak	14	51	893	17.5	9	0
1976 Oak	14	46	1111	24.2	**12**	0
1977 Oak	13	33	540	16.4	6	0
1978 Oak	16	49	709	14.5	1	2
1979 Oak	14	59	844	14.3	6	1
1980 Oak	16	44	858	19.5	7	0
1981 Oak	16	41	635	15.5	1	0
1982 LARd	9	30	575	19.2	4	0
1983 LARd	12	39	696	17.8	5	0
1984 LARd	14	27	401	14.9	0	0
1985 LARd	4	0	0	—	0	0
NFL Total	183	501	8685	17.3	67	6

MEL BRANCH Branch, Melvin Leroy 6′2″, 230 **DE**
Col: Louisiana State *HS:* DeRidder [LA] B: 2/15/1937, Leesville, LA *Drafted:* 1960 Round 2 Den
1960 DalT: 14 G. **1961** DalT: 14 G. **1962** DalT: 14 G. **1963** KC: 14 G. **1964** KC: 14 G. **1965** KC: 14 G. **1966** Mia: 14 G; KR 1-15 15.0. **1967** Mia: 14 G. **1968** Mia: 14 G. **Total:** 126 G; KR 1-15 15.0.

REGGIE BRANCH Branch, Reginald Etoy 5′11″, 232 **RB**
Col: West Virginia State; East Carolina *HS:* Seminole [Sanford, FL] B: 10/22/1962, Sanford, FL
1985 Was: 8 G. **1986** Was: 1 G. **1987** Was: 12 G; Rush 4-9 2.3 1 TD; KR 4-61 15.3; 6 Pt. **1988** Was: 7 G. **1989** Was: 10 G; KR 1-6 6.0. **Total:** 38 G; Rush 4-9 2.3 1 TD; KR 5-67 13.4; 6 Pt.

ART BRANDAU Brandau, Arthur Albert 6′2″, 210 **C-LB**
Col: Tennessee *HS:* Baltimore City College [MD] B: 6/23/1922, Baltimore, MD *Drafted:* 1945 Round 10 Pit
1945 Pit: 1 G. **1946** Pit: 5 G. **Total:** 6 G.

BUTCH BRANDAU Brandau, Arthur Frank 192 **TB-FB-WB**
Col: No College *HS:* East Detroit [Eastpointe, MI] B: 12/5/1897 D: 7/1973, Detroit, MI
1921 Det: 4 G.

DAN BRANDENBURG Brandenburg, Daniel James 6′2″, 240 **LB**
Col: Indiana State *HS:* Central [Rensselaer, IN] B: 2/16/1973, Rensselaer, IN *Drafted:* 1996 Round 7 Buf
1997 Buf: 12 G. **1998** Buf: 16 G. **Total:** 28 G.

JOHN BRANDES Brandes, John Wesley 6′2″, 249 **TE**
Col: Cameron *HS:* Lamar [Arlington, TX] B: 4/2/1964, Fort Riley, KS
1987 Ind: 12 G; Rec 5-35 7.0. **1988** Ind: 16 G. **1989** Ind: 16 G. **1990** Was: 16 G. **1991** Was: 16 G. **1992** Was-NYG: 5 G; 1 Fum. Was: 1 G. NYG: 4 G; 1 Fum. **1993** SF: 9 G; KR 1-10 10.0; 1 Fum. **Total:** 90 G; Rec 5-35 7.0; KR 1-10 10.0; 2 Fum.

DAVID BRANDON Brandon, David Sherrod 6′4″, 234 **LB**
Col: Memphis *HS:* Mitchell [Memphis, TN] B: 2/9/1965, Memphis, TN *Drafted:* 1987 Round 3 Buf
1987 SD: 8 G; 6 Pt. **1988** SD: 8 G. **1989** SD: 13 G. **1991** Cle: 16 G; Int 2-70 1 TD; 6 Pt; 3 Sac. **1992** Cle: 16 G; Int 2-123 1 TD; 1 Fum TD; Tot TD 2; 12 Pt; 1 Sac. **1993** Cle-Sea: 13 G. Cle: 6 G. Sea: 7 G. **1994** Sea: 13 G. **1995** SD: 16 G; 1 Sac. **1996** Atl: 16 G; 1 Sac. **1997** Atl: 4 G; 1 Sac. **Total:** 123 G; Int 4-193 2 TD; 1 Fum TD; Tot TD 4; 24 Pt; 7 Sac.

MICHAEL BRANDON Brandon, Michael Breon 6′4″, 290 **DE**
Col: Florida *HS:* Taylor Co. [Perry, FL] B: 7/30/1968, Daytona Beach, FL *Drafted:* 1992 Round 12 Ind
1993 Ind: 15 G. **1994** Ariz: 1 G. **1995** SF: 11 G. **1996** SF: 4 G. **Total:** 31 G.

JIM BRANDT Brandt, James Richard 6′1″, 205 **HB-DB**
(Popcorn) *Col:* St. Thomas *HS:* Bold [Olivia, MN] B: 5/19/1929, Fargo, ND *Drafted:* 1951 Round 12 Pit
1952 Pit: KR 1-24 24.0. **1953** Pit: Pass 1-0; Rec 2-15 7.5; PR 6-34 5.7; KR 6-135 22.5. **1954** Pit: Rec 1-9 9.0. **Total:** Pass 1-0; Rec 3-24 8.0; PR 6-34 5.7; KR 7-159 22.7.

Year Team	G	Rushing Att	Yds	Avg	TD	Fum
1952 Pit	9	0	0	—	0	0
1953 Pit	12	42	106	2.5	3	1
1954 Pit	12	19	82	4.3	1	0
NFL Total	33	61	188	3.1	4	1

SPEED BRANEY Braney, Joseph P 6'0", 188 **G-T**
(Joseph P. Breheney) *Col:* Syracuse; Fordham *HS:* Dean Acad. [Franklin, MA] B: 1894, Johnston, RI D: 12/1/1949, Providence, RI
1925 Prov: 6 G. **1926** Prov: 7 G. **Total:** 13 G.

SOLOMON BRANNAN Brannan, Solomon Embra 6'1", 188 **DB-HB**
Col: Morris Brown *HS:* Tompkins [Savannah, GA] B: 9/5/1942, Savannah, GA
1965 KC: 10 G; PR 5-10 2.0; KR 9-226 25.1; 2 Fum. **1966** KC: 3 G; KR 1-24 24.0. **1967** NYJ: 12 G; KR 9-204 22.7. **Total:** 25 G; PR 5-10 2.0; KR 19-454 23.9; 2 Fum.

ROBERT BRANNON Brannon, Robert Lee 6'7", 245 **DE**
Col: Crowder College MO (J.C.); Kent State; Arkansas *HS:* A.C. Flora [Columbia, SC] B: 3/26/1961, Charleston, SC
1987 Cle-NO: 2 G. Cle: 1 G. NO: 1 G. **Total:** 2 G.

PHIL BRANON Branon, Philip James 6'0", 200 **T**
(Rev.) *Col:* Holy Cross *HS:* Edmunds [Burlington, VT] B: 9/27/1898, Fairbanks, VT D: 11/22/1970, Montego Bay, Jamaica
1925 Cle: 1 G.

KENT BRANSTETTER Branstetter, Kent Wayne 6'3", 260 **OT**
Col: Tyler JC TX; Houston *HS:* La Marque [TX] B: 2/3/1949, Galveston, TX *Drafted:* 1972 Round 9 NO
1973 GB: 9 G.

CHRIS BRANTLEY Brantley, Christopher Charles 5'10", 180 **WR**
Col: Rutgers *HS:* Teaneck [NJ] B: 12/12/1970, Rahway, NJ
Drafted: 1994 Round 4 LARm
1994 LARm: 15 G; Rec 4-29 7.3; PR 3-18 6.0; KR 7-150 21.4. **1996** Buf: 10 G; Rec 5-47 9.4 1 TD; 6 Pt. **Total:** 25 G; Rec 9-76 8.4 1 TD; PR 3-18 6.0; KR 7-150 21.4; 6 Pt.

JOHN BRANTLEY Brantley, John Phillip 6'2", 243 **LB**
Col: Georgia *HS:* Wildwood [FL] B: 10/23/1965, Ocala, FL
Drafted: 1988 Round 12 Hou
1989 Hou: 8 G. **1992** Was: 12 G. **Total:** 20 G.

SCOT BRANTLEY Brantley, Scot Eugene 6'1", 230 **LB**
Col: Florida *HS:* Forest [Ocala, FL] B: 2/24/1958, Chester, SC
Drafted: 1980 Round 3 TB
1980 TB: 16 G; Int 1-6. **1981** TB: 16 G; KR 1-0; Int 1-2. **1982** TB: 9 G; 2 Sac. **1983** TB: 16 G; Int 1-0; 2 Sac. **1984** TB: 16 G; Int 3-55; 1 Sac. **1985** TB: 13 G. **1986** TB: 16 G; Int 2-65. **1987** TB: 12 G. **Total:** 114 G; KR 1-0; Int 8-128; 5 Sac.

GENE BRANTON Branton, Rheugene James 6'4", 223 **WR**
Col: Texas Southern *HS:* C. Leon King [Tampa, FL] B: 11/23/1960, Tampa, FL *Drafted:* 1983 Round 6 TB
1983 TB: 1 G. **1985** TB: 3 G. **Total:** 4 G.

ZEKE BRATKOWSKI Bratkowski, Edmund Raymond 6'2", 210 **QB**
Col: Georgia *HS:* Schlarman [Danville, IL] B: 10/20/1931, Danville, IL
Drafted: 1953 Round 2 ChiB

Year Team	G	Passing Att	Comp	Comp%	Yds	YPA	TD	Int	Rating
1954 ChiB	12	130	67	51.5	1087	8.36	8	17	60.8
1957 ChiB	12	80	37	46.3	527	6.59	1	9	32.7
1958 ChiB	12	90	41	45.6	571	6.34	7	6	64.6
1959 ChiB	12	62	31	50.0	403	6.50	2	5	48.0
1960 ChiB	11	175	87	49.7	1051	6.01	6	21	40.4
1961 LARm	13	230	124	53.9	1547	6.73	8	13	63.1
1962 LARm	13	219	110	50.2	1541	7.04	9	16	56.5
1963 LARm-GB	6	93	49	52.7	567	6.10	4	9	46.1
1963 LARm	4	82	45	54.9	471	5.74	3	6	53.5
1963 GB	2	11	4	36.4	96	8.73	1	3	59.5
1964 GB	5	36	19	52.8	277	7.69	1	1	75.8
1965 GB	6	48	21	43.8	348	7.25	3	4	54.9
1966 GB	8	64	36	56.3	569	8.89	4	2	93.8
1967 GB	6	94	53	56.4	724	7.70	5	9	59.3
1968 GB	10	126	68	54.0	835	6.63	3	7	59.5
1971 GB	6	37	19	51.4	298	8.05	4	3	80.7
NFL Total	132	1484	762	51.3	10345	6.97	65	122	54.3

Year Team	Rushing Att	Yds	Avg	TD	Punting Punts	Yds	Avg	Fum
1954 ChiB	15	35	2.3	1	39	1599	41.0	2
1957 ChiB	12	83	6.9	0	16	617	38.6	3
1958 ChiB	3	0	0.0	0	14	555	39.6	1
1959 ChiB	7	86	12.3	0	0	0	—	0
1960 ChiB	8	20	2.5	0	7	252	36.0	2
1961 LARm	12	36	3.0	3	12	458	38.2	4
1962 LARm	7	14	2.0	0	0	0	—	4
1963 LARm-GB	4	-3	-0.8	0	0	0	—	2
1963 LARm	3	-1	-0.3	0	0	0	—	2
1963 GB	1	-2	-2.0	0	0	0	—	0
1964 GB	2	0	0.0	0	0	0	—	2
1965 GB	4	-1	-0.3	0	0	0	—	1
1966 GB	4	7	1.8	0	0	0	—	0
1967 GB	5	6	1.2	0	0	0	—	2
1968 GB	8	24	3.0	0	0	0	—	4
1971 GB	1	1	1.0	1	0	0	—	1
NFL Total	92	308	3.3	5	88	3481	39.6	28

EDDIE BRATT Bratt, Edwin John 190 **OE**
Col: No College *HS:* Cathedral [Duluth, MN] B: 3/6/1898, Foreston, MN D: 9/23/1970, Minneapolis, MN
1924 Dul: 1 G.

JASON BRATTON Bratton, Jason Edward 6'1", 252 **RB**
Col: Grambling State *HS:* Pine Tree [Longview TX] B: 10/19/1972, Longview, TX
1996 Buf: 2 G; Rush 4-8 2.0.

MEL BRATTON Bratton, Melvin Torrence 6'1", 225 **RB**
Col: Miami (Fla.) *HS:* Miami Northwestern [FL] B: 2/2/1965, Miami, FL
Drafted: 1989 Round 7 Den
1989 Den: KR 2-19 9.5. **1990** Den: KR 3-37 12.3. **Total:** KR 5-56 11.2.

Year Team	G	Rushing Att	Yds	Avg	TD	Receiving Rec	Yds	Avg	TD	Fum	Tot TD
1989 Den	16	30	108	3.6	1	10	69	6.9	3	0	4
1990 Den	16	27	82	3.0	3	29	276	9.5	1	3	4
NFL Total	32	57	190	3.3	4	39	345	8.8	4	3	8

CHAD BRATZKE Bratzke, Chad Allen 6'4", 275 **DE**
Col: Eastern Kentucky *HS:* Bloomingdale [Valrico, FL] B: 9/15/1971, Brandon, FL *Drafted:* 1994 Round 5 NYG
1994 NYG: 2 G. **1995** NYG: 6 G. **1996** NYG: 16 G; 5 Sac. **1997** NYG: 10 G; 3.5 Sac. **1998** NYG: 16 G; 11 Sac. **Total:** 50 G; 19.5 Sac.

ALEX BRAVO Bravo, Alexander 6'0", 190 **DB**
Col: Cal Poly-S.L.O. *HS:* Santa Barbara [CA] B: 7/27/1930, Tucson, AZ *Drafted:* 1954 Round 9 LARm
1957 LARm: 12 G. **1958** LARm: 3 G. **1960** Oak: 14 G; Int 4-64; 1 Fum. **1961** Oak: 14 G; Int 2-0. **Total:** 43 G; Int 6-64; 1 Fum.

JACK BRAVYAK Bravyak, John 6'3", 255 **DE**
Col: Luzerne Co. CC PA; Temple B: 9/10/1959
1987 Buf: 1 G.

ED BRAWLEY Brawley, Edward Michael 5'9", 175 **G**
Col: Holy Cross *HS:* Medford [MA] B: 7/17/1888, Boston, MA
D: 5/1/1956, Peabody, MA
1921 NYG-Cle: 6 G. NYG: 1 G. Cle: 5 G. **Total:** 6 G.

DAVID BRAXTON Braxton, David Harold 6'2", 240 **LB**
Col: Wake Forest *HS:* Jacksonville [NC] B: 5/25/1965, Omaha, NE
Drafted: 1989 Round 2 Min
1989 Min: 3 G. **1990** Min-Pho: 12 G. Min: 1 G. Pho: 11 G. **1991** Pho: 16 G; 1 Sac. **1992** Pho: 15 G. **1993** Pho: 16 G. **1994** Cin: 9 G. **Total:** 71 G; 1 Sac.

HEZ BRAXTON Braxton, Hezekiah Ezekial III 6'2", 227 **FB**
Col: Virginia Union *HS:* Frederick Douglass [Baltimore, MD]
B: 4/11/1936, Baltimore, MD *Drafted:* 1961 Round 12 SD
1962 SD: 8 G; Rush 17-35 2.1 1 TD; Rec 4-17 4.3; PR 1-0; Scor **1** 2XP; 8 Pt. **1963** Buf: 1 G. **Total:** 9 G; Rush 17-35 2.1 1 TD; Rec 4-17 4.3; PR 1-0; Scor 1 2XP; 8 Pt.

JIM BRAXTON Braxton, James Robert 6'1", 243 **RB**
Col: West Virginia *HS:* Connellsville [PA] B: 5/23/1949, Vanderbilt, PA
D: 7/28/1986, Buffalo, NY *Drafted:* 1971 Round 3 Buf
1971 Buf: Pass 3-1 33.3%, 49 16.33; KR 5-90 18.0. **1972** Buf: KR 1-12 12.0. **1973** Buf: KR 1-0. **Total:** Pass 3-1 33.3%, 49 16.33; KR 7-102 14.6.

Year Team	G	Rushing Att	Yds	Avg	TD	Receiving Rec	Yds	Avg	TD	Fum	Tot TD
1971 Buf	13	21	84	4.0	0	18	141	7.8	0	2	0
1972 Buf	14	116	453	3.9	5	24	232	9.7	1	2	6
1973 Buf	6	108	494	4.6	4	6	101	16.8	0	2	4
1974 Buf	12	146	543	3.7	4	18	171	9.5	0	5	4
1975 Buf	14	186	823	4.4	9	26	282	10.8	4	7	13
1976 Buf	1	1	0	0.0	0	0	0	—	0	0	0
1977 Buf	14	113	372	3.3	1	43	461	10.7	1	7	2
1978 Buf-Mia	16	50	121	2.4	2	9	85	9.4	0	1	2
1978 Buf	6	30	73	2.4	0	5	38	7.6	0	1	0
1978 Mia	10	20	48	2.4	2	4	47	11.8	0	0	2
NFL Total	90	741	2890	3.9	25	144	1473	10.2	6	26	31

TYRONE BRAXTON Braxton, Tyrone Scott 5'11", 185 **DB**
Col: North Dakota State *HS:* James Madison Memorial [Madison, WI]
B: 12/17/1964, Madison, WI *Drafted:* 1987 Round 12 Den
1988 Den: 1 Sac. **1991** Den: 1 Sac. **1994** Mia: KR 1-34 34.0. **1997** Den: 0.5 Sac. **Total:** KR 1-34 34.0; 2.5 Sac.

Year Team	G	Interceptions Int	Yds	TD	Fum
1987 Den	2	0	0	0	0
1988 Den	16	2	6	0	0
1989 Den	16	6	103	1	0
1990 Den	3	1	10	0	0
1991 Den	16	4	55	1	1
1992 Den	16	2	54	0	0
1993 Den	16	3	37	0	0
1994 Mia	16	2	3	0	0
1995 Den	16	2	36	0	0
1996 Den	16	**9**	128	1	0
1997 Den	16	4	113	1	0
1998 Den	16	1	72	0	0
NFL Total	165	36	617	4	1

MAURY BRAY Bray, Andrew Maurice 6'2", 220 **T**
(Mule) *Col:* Southern Methodist *HS:* Abilene [TX] B: 8/27/1909, Paducah, TX D: 12/9/1966, Tahoka, TX
1935 Pit: 12 G. **1936** Pit: 12 G. **Total:** 24 G.

RAY BRAY Bray, Raymond Robert 6'0", 237 **DG-OG**
(Muscles) *Col:* Western Michigan; North Carolina *HS:* Vulcan [MI] B: 2/1/1917, Caspian, MI D: 12/26/1993, Mesa, AZ *Drafted:* 1939 Round 7 ChiB
1939 ChiB: 11 G. **1940** ChiB: 6 G. **1941** ChiB: 11 G. **1942** ChiB: 11 G. **1946** ChiB: 10 G. **1947** ChiB: 12 G. **1948** ChiB: 12 G; KR 1-8 8.0. **1949** ChiB: 12 G. **1950** ChiB: 12 G. **1951** ChiB: 12 G. **1952** GB: 12 G. **Total:** 121 G; KR 1-8 8.0.

CARL BRAZELL Brazell, Carl L 5'10", 195 **BB-DB**
Col: Baylor *HS:* Barbers Hill [Mont Belvieu, TX] B: 7/20/1917 D: 5/30/1978, Zanesville, OH
1938 Cle: 11 G; Rush 4-14 3.5; Rec 7-100 14.3.

LARRY BRAZIEL Braziel, Lawrence 6'0", 188 **DB**
(Bobo) *Col:* Compton CC CA; USC *HS:* Dunbar [Fort Worth, TX] B: 9/25/1954, Fort Worth, TX *Drafted:* 1979 Round 5 Bal

Year Team	G	Interceptions Int	Yds	TD	Fum	Tot TD
1979 Bal	16	4	49	1	0	2
1980 Bal	15	2	87	0	0	0
1981 Bal	16	3	35	0	1	0
1982 Cle	6	0	0	0	0	0
1983 Cle	13	0	0	0	0	0
1984 Cle	13	0	0	0	0	0
1985 Cle	16	2	40	0	0	0
NFL Total	95	11	211	1	1	2

ROBERT BRAZILE Brazile, Robert Lorenzo Jr. 6'4", 241 **LB**
(Dr. Doom) *Col:* Jackson State *HS:* C.F. Vigor [Prichard, AL] B: 2/7/1953, Mobile, AL *Drafted:* 1975 Round 1 Hou
1982 Hou: 6.5 Sac. **1983** Hou: 2.5 Sac. **1984** Hou: 2 Sac. **Total:** 11 Sac.

Year Team	G	Interceptions Int	Yds	TD
1975 Hou	14	0	0	0
1976 Hou	14	1	8	0
1977 Hou	14	3	40	0
1978 Hou	16	1	30	0
1979 Hou	16	2	45	0
1980 Hou	16	2	38	0
1981 Hou	16	2	7	0
1982 Hou	9	1	31	0
1983 Hou	16	0	0	0
1984 Hou	16	1	2	0
NFL Total	147	13	201	0

SAM BRAZINSKY Brazinsky, Samuel Joseph 6'1", 215 **C-LB**
Col: Villanova *HS:* Kulpmont [PA] B: 1/9/1921, Kulpmont, PA
AAFC **1946** BufA: 5 G; Int 2-7.

CARL BRAZLEY Brazley, Carl Eugene 6'0", 180 **DB**
Col: Western Kentucky *HS:* Seneca [KY] B: 9/5/1957, Louisville, KY
1987 SD: 2 G; Int 1-0.

DON BREAUX Breaux, Donald Carl 6'1", 205 **QB**
Col: McNeese State *HS:* La Grange [Lake Charles, LA] B: 8/3/1940, Jennings, LA
1963 Den: Rush 11-50 4.5. **1965** SD: Rush 1-(-1) -1.0. **Total:** Rush 12-49 4.1.

Year Team	G	Passing Att	Comp	Comp%	Yds	YPA	TD	Int	Rating	Fum
1963 Den	9	138	70	50.7	935	6.78	7	6	71.4	7
1965 SD	14	43	22	51.2	404	9.40	2	4	60.6	2
NFL Total	23	181	92	50.8	1339	7.40	9	10	68.8	9

BILL BREDDE Bredde, William M 6'1", 195 **HB-DB**
Col: Oklahoma State *HS:* Pawnee [OK] B: 12/31/1932, Winterhaven, CA *Drafted:* 1954 Round 4 ChiC
1954 ChiC: 12 G; Rush 13-57 4.4 1 TD; Rec 3-44 14.7; KR 1-19 19.0; Int 2-44; 6 Pt; 2 Fum.

JOHN BREDICE Bredice, John Joseph 6'1", 213 **OE**
Col: Boston U. *HS:* Notre Dame [West Haven, CT] B: 6/23/1934, Waterbury, CT *Drafted:* 1956 Round 9 Phi
1956 Phi: 12 G; Rec 10-146 14.6 1 TD; 6 Pt.

ED BREDING Breding, Edward Vincent 6'4", 235 **LB**
Col: Texas A&M *HS:* Jacksboro [TX] B: 11/3/1944, Billings, MT *Drafted:* 1967 Round 15 Was
1967 Was: 14 G; Scor **1** Saf; 2 Pt. **1968** Was: 14 G. **Total:** 28 G; Scor 1 Saf; 2 Pt.

JIM BREECH Breech, James Thomas 5'6", 161 **K**
Col: California *HS:* Sacramento [CA] B: 4/11/1956, Sacramento, CA *Drafted:* 1978 Round 8 Det
1980 Cin: Punt 2-67 33.5. **1985** Cin: Punt 5-153 30.6. **1988** Cin: Punt 3-64 21.3. **1989** Cin: Punt 2-58 29.0. **1990** Cin: Punt 1-34 34.0. **1991** Cin: Punt 1-33 33.0. **1992** Cin: Pass 1-1 100.0%, 12 12.00. **Total:** Pass 1-1 100.0%, 12 12.00; Punt 14-409 29.2.

Year Team	G	Scoring Pts	FG	FGA	FG%	XK	XKA	XK%	Fum
1979 Oak	16	95	18	27	66.7	41	45	91.1	0
1980 Cin	4	23	4	7	57.1	11	12	91.7	0
1981 Cin	16	115	22	32	68.8	49	51	96.1	0
1982 Cin	9	67	14	18	77.8	25	26	96.2	0
1983 Cin	16	87	16	23	69.6	39	41	95.1	1
1984 Cin	16	103	22	31	71.0	37	37	100.0	0
1985 Cin	16	120	24	33	72.7	48	50	96.0	0
1986 Cin	16	101	17	32	53.1	50	51	98.0	0
1987 Cin	12	97	24	30	80.0	25	27	92.6	0
1988 Cin	16	89	11	16	68.8	**56**	**59**	94.9	0
1989 Cin	12	73	12	14	85.7	37	38	97.4	0
1990 Cin	16	92	17	21	81.0	41	44	93.2	0
1991 Cin	16	96	23	29	79.3	27	27	100.0	0
1992 Cin	16	88	19	27	70.4	31	31	100.0	0
NFL Total	197	1246	243	340	71.5	517	539	95.9	1

LOUIS BREEDEN Breeden, Louis Everett 5'11", 185 **DB**
Col: Richmond CC NC; North Carolina Central *HS:* Hamlet [NC] B: 10/26/1953, Hamlet, NC *Drafted:* 1977 Round 7 Cin
1978 Cin: PR 6-(-12) -2.0; KR 1-12 12.0. **1982** Cin: 1 Sac. **1983** Cin: 1 Sac. **1985** Cin: 1 Sac. **Total:** PR 6-(-12) -2.0; KR 1-12 12.0; 3 Sac.

Year Team	G	Interceptions Int	Yds	TD	Fum
1978 Cin	16	3	25	0	2
1979 Cin	10	0	0	0	0
1980 Cin	16	7	91	0	0
1981 Cin	16	4	145	1	0
1982 Cin	6	2	9	0	1
1983 Cin	14	2	47	0	0
1984 Cin	16	4	96	0	1
1985 Cin	16	2	24	0	0
1986 Cin	16	7	72	1	0
1987 Cin	8	2	49	0	0
NFL Total	134	33	558	2	4

BILL BREEDEN Breeden, William John 6'1", 210 **HB-OE-DB**
Col: Oklahoma *HS:* Central [Oklahoma City, OK] B: 11/7/1913, Haskell, OK D: 12/16/1982, Dallas, TX *Drafted:* 1937 Round 3 Pit
1937 Pit: 9 G; Rush 10-25 2.5; Rec 6-59 9.8.

ROD BREEDLOVE Breedlove, Rodney Winston 6'2", 230 **LB**
Col: Maryland *HS:* Allegany [Cumberland, MD] B: 3/10/1938, Cumberland, MD *Drafted:* 1960 Round 3 SF

Year Team	G	Interceptions Int	Yds	TD
1960 Was	11	3	67	0
1961 Was	11	2	31	0
1962 Was	14	3	27	0
1963 Was	14	1	0	0
1964 Was	12	0	0	0
1965 Pit	14	0	0	0
1966 Pit	11	2	10	0
1967 Pit	14	0	0	0
NFL Total	101	11	135	0

ADRIAN BREEN Breen, Adrian Owen 6'4", 183 **QB**
Col: Morehead State *HS:* Roger Bacon [Cincinnati, OH] B: 1/11/1965, Bronxville, NY
1987 Cin: 2 G; Pass 8-3 37.5%, 9 1.13 1 TD; Rush 6-18 3.0; 1 Fum.

GENE BREEN Breen, Joseph Eugene 6′2″, 230 **LB**
Col: Virginia Tech *HS:* Mount Lebanon [PA] B: 6/21/1941, Crafton, PA
Drafted: 1963 Round 15 GB
1964 GB: 6 G. **1965** Pit: 14 G. **1966** Pit: 2 G. **1967** LARm: 7 G. **1968** LARm: 3 G. **Total:** 32 G.

JEFF BREGEL Bregel, Jeffery Bryan 6′4″, 280 **OG**
Col: USC *HS:* John F. Kennedy [Los Angeles, CA] B: 5/1/1964, Redondo Beach, CA *Drafted:* 1987 Round 2 SF
1987 SF: 5 G. **1988** SF: 13 G. **1989** SF: 3 G. **Total:** 21 G.

BOB BREITENSTEIN Breitenstein, Robert Corr 6′3″, 265 **OT-OG**
Col: Tulsa *HS:* Farmington [NM] B: 4/8/1943, Buenos Aires, Argentina
Drafted: 1965 Round 5 Den
1965 Den: 14 G. **1966** Den: 14 G. **1967** Den-Min: 13 G. Den: 2 G. Min: 11 G. **1969** Atl: 10 G. **1970** Atl: 7 G. **Total:** 58 G.

WAYNE BRENKERT Brenkert, Wayne Dewey 5′10″, 170 **TB-BB-WB**
Col: Detroit J.C.; Washington & Jefferson *HS:* Central [Detroit, MI]
B: 3/5/1898, Highland Park, MI D: 8/1/1979, Eustis, FL
1923 Akr: 7 G; Rush 2 TD; 12 Pt. **1924** Akr: 8 G; Rush 3 TD; 18 Pt.
Total: 15 G; Rush 5 TD; 30 Pt.

BRIAN BRENNAN Brennan, Brian Michael 5′9″, 178 **WR**
Col: Boston College *HS:* Brother Rice [Birmingham, MI] B: 2/15/1962, Bloomfield, MI *Drafted:* 1984 Round 4 Cle
1985 Cle: Pass 1-1 100.0%, 33 33.00 1 TD. **1986** Cle: Pass 1-1 100.0%, 35 35.00; **1** Fum TD. **1992** Cin-SD: KR 1-10 10.0. SD: KR 1-10 10.0.
Total: Pass 2-2 100.0%, 68 34.00 1 TD; KR 1-10 10.0; 1 Fum TD.

		Receiving				Punt Returns					Tot
Year Team	G	Rec	Yds	Avg	TD	Ret	Yds	Avg	TD	Fum	TD
1984 Cle	15	35	455	13.0	3	25	199	8.0	0	1	3
1985 Cle	12	32	487	15.2	0	19	153	8.1	1	3	1
1986 Cle	16	55	838	15.2	6	0	0	—	0	1	7
1987 Cle	13	43	607	14.1	6	0	0	—	0	1	6
1988 Cle	16	46	579	12.6	1	0	0	—	0	0	1
1989 Cle	14	28	289	10.3	0	0	0	—	0	1	0
1990 Cle	16	45	568	12.6	2	9	72	8.0	0	1	2
1991 Cle	15	31	325	10.5	1	2	11	5.5	0	1	1
1992 Cin-SD	15	19	188	9.9	1	1	3	3.0	0	0	1
1992 Cin	9	16	166	10.4	1	0	0	—	0	0	1
1992 SD	6	3	22	7.3	0	1	3	3.0	0	0	0
NFL Total	132	334	4336	13.0	20	56	438	7.8	1	9	22

JACK BRENNAN Brennan, John Carter 6′1″, 204 **G**
Col: Michigan *HS:* Carl Schurz [Chicago, IL] B: 9/28/1913, Racine, WI
D: 3/1975 *Drafted:* 1939 Round 17 GB
1939 GB: 2 G.

LEO BRENNAN Brennan, Leo Francis 6′0″, 210 **T**
Col: Holy Cross *HS:* Brighton Acad. [MA] B: 9/19/1919, Boston, MA
1942 Phi: 11 G.

MATT BRENNAN Brennan, Matthew William 6′1″, 190 **BB-TB**
Col: Villanova; Fordham; Lafayette *HS:* Fordham Prep [Bronx, NY]
B: 10/3/1897, Stamford, CT D: 1/3/1963, PA
1925 NYG: 6 G; Scor 3, 1 FG. **1926** Bkn: 10 G; Pass 1 TD; Rush 1 TD; Scor 11, 1 FG, 2 XK. **Total:** 16 G; Pass 1 TD; Rush 1 TD; Scor 14, 2 FG, 2 XK.

MIKE BRENNAN Brennan, Michael Sean 6′5″, 274 **OT**
Col: Notre Dame *HS:* Mount St. Joseph [Baltimore, MD] B: 3/22/1967, Los Angeles, CA *Drafted:* 1990 Round 4 Cin
1990 Cin: 16 G. **1991** Cin: 3 G. **Total:** 19 G.

PHIL BRENNAN Brennan, Philip 5′11″, 165 **E**
Col: Loyola (Chicago) *HS:* Hyde Park [Chicago, IL] B: 8/20/1902
D: 9/24/1994, Park Ridge, IL
1930 Nwk: 1 G.

WILLIS BRENNAN Brennan, Willis 6′0″, 214 **G-T**
(Willie) *Col:* No College B: 2/12/1893, Chicago, IL Deceased
1920 ChiC: 9 G. **1921** ChiC: 6 G. **1922** ChiC: 8 G. **1923** ChiC: 10 G. **1924** ChiC: 10 G; 1 Fum TD; 6 Pt. **1925** ChiC: 13 G. **1926** ChiC: 11 G. **1927** ChiC: 11 G. **Total:** 78 G; 1 Fum TD; 6 Pt.

AL BRENNER Brenner, Allen Ray 6′1″, 200 **DB**
Col: Michigan State *HS:* Niles [MI] B: 11/13/1947, Benton Harbor, MI
Drafted: 1969 Round 7 NYG
1969 NYG: 6 G; PR 2-6 3.0; KR 2-39 19.5. **1970** NYG: 1 G; PR 1-5 5.0.
Total: 7 G; PR 3-11 3.7; KR 2-39 19.5.

HOBY BRENNER Brenner, Hoby F.J. 6′4″, 240 **TE**
Col: USC *HS:* Fullerton [CA] B: 6/2/1959, Linwood, CA
Drafted: 1981 Round 3 NO

		Receiving				
Year Team	G	Rec	Yds	Avg	TD	Fum
1981 NO	9	7	143	20.4	0	1
1982 NO	8	16	171	10.7	0	1
1983 NO	16	41	574	14.0	3	0
1984 NO	16	28	554	19.8	6	0
1985 NO	16	42	652	15.5	3	1
1986 NO	15	18	286	15.9	0	0
1987 NO	12	20	280	14.0	2	0
1988 NO	10	5	67	13.4	0	0
1989 NO	16	34	398	11.7	4	1
1990 NO	16	17	213	12.5	2	0
1991 NO	16	16	179	11.2	0	0
1992 NO	15	12	161	13.4	0	0
1993 NO	10	11	171	15.5	1	0
NFL Total	175	267	3849	14.4	21	4

RAY BRENNER Brenner, Raymond H 5′5″, 145 **WB**
Col: No College B: 3/18/1898, East Greenville, OH D: 6/14/1975, Massillon, OH
1925 Can: 2 G.

MONTE BRETHAUER Brethauer, Monte Leon 6′1″, 178 **DB-OE**
Col: Oregon *HS:* Jefferson [Portland, OR] B: 4/8/1931, Portland, OR
D: 10/14/1994, Portland, OR *Drafted:* 1953 Round 24 Bal
1953 Bal: Rec 10-133 13.3; Int 1-17. **Total:** Rec 10-133 13.3; Int 1-17.

		Punting			
Year Team	G	Punts	Yds	Avg	Fum
1953 Bal	12	0	0	—	1
1955 Bal	12	55	2161	39.3	2
NFL Total	24	55	2161	39.3	3

JEEP BRETT Brett, Edwin Darrah 6′2″, 205 **OE-DE**
Col: Washington State *HS:* Lewiston [ID] B: 3/20/1914, Lewiston, ID
D: 5/17/1989, Edmonds, WA *Drafted:* 1936 Round 4 ChiC
1936 ChiC-Pit: 9 G; Rec 7-139 19.9. ChiC: 1 G. Pit: 8 G; Rec 7-139 19.9.
1937 Pit: 10 G; Rec 8-135 16.9 1 TD; 6 Pt. **Total:** 19 G; Rec 15-274 18.3 1 TD; 6 Pt.

CARL BRETTSCHNEIDER Brettschneider, Carl Eugene 6′1″, 223 **LB**
Col: Iowa State *HS:* Dundee [IL] B: 12/2/1931, Dundee, IL
1956 ChiC: 12 G. **1957** ChiC: 12 G. **1958** ChiC: 10 G. **1959** ChiC: 12 G; Int 1-2. **1960** Det: 12 G. **1961** Det: 12 G. **1962** Det: 14 G; Int 2-15.
1963 Det: 5 G. **Total:** 89 G; Int 3-17.

BOB BREUNIG Breunig, Robert Paul 6′2″, 226 **LB**
Col: Arizona State *HS:* Alhambra [Phoenix, AZ] B: 7/4/1953, Inglewood, CA *Drafted:* 1975 Round 3 Dal
1975 Dal: 10 G; Rec 1-21 21.0; KR 2-13 6.5. **1976** Dal: 14 G. **1977** Dal: 14 G; Int 1-15. **1978** Dal: 16 G; Int 1-2. **1979** Dal: 16 G. **1980** Dal: 16 G; Int 3-34. **1981** Dal: 16 G; Int 2-8. **1982** Dal: 9 G; Int 1-1; 1.5 Sac. **1983** Dal: 16 G; Int 1-0. **1984** Dal: 8 G. **Total:** 135 G; Rec 1-21 21.0; KR 2-13 6.5; Int 9-60; 1.5 Sac.

DORIAN BREW Brew, Dorian Culbert 5′10″, 182 **DB**
Col: Kansas *HS:* McCluer North [Florissant, MO] B: 7/19/1974, St. Louis, MO *Drafted:* 1996 Round 3 Mia
1996 Bal: 7 G. **1997** Bal-SD: 9 G; KR 5-88 17.6. Bal: 3 G; KR 5-88 17.6. SD: 6 G. **Total:** 16 G; KR 5-88 17.6.

BILLY BREWER Brewer, Billy Ervin 6′0″, 190 **DB**
Col: Mississippi *HS:* Stephen D. Lee [Columbus, MS] B: 10/8/1934, Columbus, MS *Drafted:* 1960 Round 2 Bos
1960 Was: 11 G.

CHRIS BREWER Brewer, Christopher 6′1″, 203 **RB**
Col: Arizona *HS:* George Washington [Denver, CO] B: 1/23/1962, Denver, CO *Drafted:* 1984 Round 9 Den
1984 Den: Rec 2-20 10.0. **1987** ChiB: Rec 5-56 11.2 1 TD.
Total: Rec 7-76 10.9 1 TD.

		Rushing					Tot
Year Team	G	Att	Yds	Avg	TD	Fum	TD
1984 Den	13	10	28	2.8	0	1	0
1987 ChiB	3	24	55	2.3	2	0	3
NFL Total	16	34	83	2.4	2	1	3

DEWELL BREWER Brewer, Dewell Lerome 5′8″, 201 **RB**
Col: Oklahoma *HS:* Lawton [OK] B: 5/22/1970, Lawton, OK
1994 Ind: KR 18-358 19.9.

		Punt Returns				
Year Team	G	Ret	Yds	Avg	TD	Fum
1994 Ind	16	**42**	339	8.1	1	3

UNTZ BREWER Brewer, Edward Brooke 5′6″, 160 **WB-TB**
Col: Maryland *HS:* Western [Washington, DC]; St. Albans HS [Washington, DC] B: 11/21/1894, Washington, DC D: Rockville, MD
1922 Akr: 8 G; Rush 1 TD; 6 Pt.

JOHN BREWER Brewer, John Edward Jr. 6′4″, 230 **FB**
Col: Louisville *HS:* Iaeger [WV] B: 8/26/1928, Twin Branch, WV
D: 7/28/1983, Louisville, KY *Drafted:* 1952 Round 28 Phi
1952 Phi: Rec 5-19 3.8. **1953** Phi: Rec 4-43 10.8. **Total:** Rec 9-62 6.9.

Year Team	G	Rushing Att	Yds	Avg	TD	Fum
1952 Phi	12	50	188	3.8	2	3
1953 Phi	6	17	85	5.0	1	1
NFL Total	18	67	273	4.1	3	4

JOHNNY BREWER Brewer, John Mills 6′0″, 185 **WB**
Col: Georgia Tech *HS:* Griffin [GA] B: 4/6/1906, Griffin, GA
D: 5/2/1980, New Port Richey, FL
1929 Day: 6 G.

JOHNNY BREWER Brewer, Johnny Lee 6′4″, 230 **TE-LB-DE**
(Tonto) *Col:* Mississippi *HS:* Redwood [MS] B: 3/8/1937, Vicksburg, MS *Drafted:* 1960 Round 4 Cle
1961 Cle: KR 1-2 2.0. **1966** Cle: Int 1-0. **1967** Cle: Int 2-75 1 TD.
Total: KR 1-2 2.0; Int 3-75 1 TD.

Year Team	G	Receiving Rec	Yds	Avg	TD	Tot TD
1961 Cle	14	0	0	—	0	0
1962 Cle	14	22	290	13.2	2	2
1963 Cle	14	29	454	15.7	0	0
1964 Cle	14	25	338	13.5	3	3
1965 Cle	14	13	174	13.4	1	1
1966 Cle	14	0	0	—	0	0
1967 Cle	14	0	0	—	0	1
1968 NO	14	0	0	—	0	0
1969 NO	14	0	0	—	0	0
1970 NO	9	0	0	—	0	0
NFL Total	135	89	1256	14.1	6	7

JIM BREWINGTON Brewington, James Wilson Jr. 6′6″, 280 **OT**
Col: North Carolina Central *HS:* C.M. Eppes [Greenville, NC]
B: 2/25/1939, Greenville, NC *Drafted:* 1961 Round 17 GB
1961 Oak: 14 G.

PETE BREWSTER Brewster, Darrel Burton 6′3″, 210 **OE**
Col: Purdue *HS:* Portland [IN] B: 9/1/1930, Adams City, IN
Drafted: 1952 Round 2 ChiC
1952 Cle: KR 1-11 11.0. **Total:** KR 1-11 11.0.

Year Team	G	Receiving Rec	Yds	Avg	TD	Fum
1952 Cle	12	4	117	29.3	1	1
1953 Cle	12	32	632	19.8	4	1
1954 Cle	12	42	676	16.1	4	3
1955 Cle	12	34	622	18.3	6	1
1956 Cle	12	28	417	14.9	1	0
1957 Cle	12	30	614	20.5	2	0
1958 Cle	11	16	294	18.4	1	1
1959 Pit	9	22	360	16.4	2	0
1960 Pit	12	2	26	13.0	0	0
NFL Total	104	210	3758	17.9	21	7

WALT BREWSTER Brewster, Walter S 6′1″, 195 **T**
Col: West Virginia *HS:* Greenbrier Mil. Acad. [Lewisburg, WV]
B: 11/11/1907, Lewisburg, WV D: 5/1957
1929 Buf: 8 G.

GREG BREZINA Brezina, Gregory 6′0″, 226 **LB**
Col: Houston *HS:* Louise [TX] B: 1/7/1946, Sinton, TX *Drafted:* 1968 Round 11 Atl
1969 Atl: Rec 1-9 9.0. **1971** Atl: Rec 1-3 3.0. **Total:** Rec 2-12 6.0.

Year Team	G	Interceptions Int	Yds	TD
1968 Atl	10	0	0	0
1969 Atl	14	1	2	0
1971 Atl	14	3	22	0
1972 Atl	14	0	0	0
1973 Atl	14	3	51	0
1974 Atl	14	1	9	0
1975 Atl	14	4	11	0
1976 Atl	11	0	0	0
1977 Atl	14	0	0	0
1978 Atl	16	0	0	0
1979 Atl	16	0	0	0
NFL Total	151	12	95	0

BOBBY BREZINA Brezina, Robert Paul 6′0″, 200 **HB**
Col: Houston *HS:* Louise [TX] B: 4/28/1941, Sinton, TX *Drafted:* 1963 Round 20 GB
1963 Hou: 1 G.

HARRY BRIAN Brian, Harold William 6′0″, 180 **WB-TB**
(AKA Harold Hite) *Col:* Grove City *HS:* Kendall Acad. [Tulsa, OK]
B: 9/25/1896, Lincoln, NE D: 3/14/1985, Fort Worth, TX
1926 Har: 4 G; Rec 1 TD; 6 Pt.

BILL BRIAN Brian, William Lawson 6′2″, 210 **T-C-LB**
Col: Gonzaga *HS:* Vancouver [WA] B: 10/12/1912, Lincoln, NE
1935 Phi: 9 G; Rush 1-2 2.0. **1936** Phi: 11 G. **Total:** 20 G; Rush 1-2 2.0.

FRANK BRIANTE Briante, Francis Xavier 5′10″, 185 **TB-FB-HB-BB**
(Bullet) *Col:* New York U. *HS:* White Plains [NY] B: 3/5/1905, White Plains, NY D: 5/26/1996, White Plains, NY
1929 SI: 9 G; Rush 1 TD; 6 Pt. **1930** Nwk: 4 G; Int 1 TD; 6 Pt. **Total:** 13 G; Rush 1 TD; Int 1 TD; Tot TD 2; 12 Pt.

ALUNDIS BRICE Brice, Alundis Marcell 5′10″, 178 **DB**
Col: Mississippi *HS:* Brookhaven [MS] B: 5/1/1970, Brookhaven, MS
Drafted: 1995 Round 4 Dal
1995 Dal: 10 G; Int 1-2. **1996** Dal: 14 G. **Total:** 24 G; Int 1-2.

WILL BRICE Brice, William Jamison 6′4″, 227 **P**
Col: Virginia *HS:* Lancaster [SC] B: 10/24/1974, Lancaster, SC

Year Team	G	Punting Punts	Yds	Avg
1997 StL	6	41	1713	41.8

SHIRLEY BRICK Brick, Shirley Eclipse 5′8″, 165 **E**
Col: Rice *HS:* North Side [Fort Worth, TX] B: 1898 D: 1929
1920 Buf: 1 G.

GEORGE BRICKLEY Brickley, George Vincent 5′10″, 190 **TB-FB-BB**
Col: Trinity (Conn.) *HS:* Everett [MA] B: 7/19/1894, Everett, MA
D: 2/23/1947, Everett, MA
1920 Cle: 5 G. **1921** NYG: 2 G. **Total:** 7 G.

LANE BRIDGFORD Bridgford, Lane 5′10″, 180 **FB-WB-BB-TB**
Col: Knox B: 8/11/1898, Joy, IL D: 7/12/1973, Los Angeles, CA
1921 RI: 5 G. **1922** RI: 3 G. **Total:** 8 G.

TOM BRIEHL Briehl, Thomas Michael 6′3″, 247 **LB**
Col: Stanford *HS:* Gerard Catholic [Phoenix, AZ] B: 9/8/1962, Phoenix, AZ *Drafted:* 1985 Round 4 Hou
1985 Hou: 16 G; KR 1-5 5.0. **1987** Hou: 3 G. **Total:** 19 G; KR 1-5 5.0.

DOUG BRIEN Brien, Douglas Robert Zachariah 6′0″, 180 **K**
Col: California *HS:* De La Salle [Concord, CA] B: 11/24/1970, Bloomfield, NJ *Drafted:* 1994 Round 3 SF
1998 NO: Punt 2-72 36.0. **Total:** Punt 2-72 36.0.

Year Team	G	Scoring Pts	FG	FGA	FG%	XK	XKA	XK%
1994 SF	16	105	15	20	75.0	**60**	**62**	96.8
1995 SF-NO	14	92	19	29	65.5	35	35	100.0
1995 SF	6	40	7	12	58.3	19	19	100.0
1995 NO	8	52	12	17	70.6	16	16	100.0
1996 NO	16	81	21	25	84.0	18	18	100.0
1997 NO	16	91	23	27	85.2	22	22	100.0
1998 NO	16	91	20	22	90.9	31	31	100.0
NFL Total	78	460	98	123	79.7	166	168	98.8

O.J. BRIGANCE Brigance, Orenthial James 6′0″, 236 **LB**
Col: Rice *HS:* Willowridge [Sugar Land, TX] B: 9/29/1969, Houston, TX
1996 Mia: 12 G. **1997** Mia: 16 G. **1998** Mia: 16 G. **Total:** 44 G.

GREGG BRIGGS Briggs, Gregg 6′3″, 214 **DB**
Col: Copiah-Lincoln CC MS; Arkansas-Pine Bluff; Texas Southern
HS: Franklin [Meadville, MS] B: 10/19/1968, Meadville, MS
Drafted: 1992 Round 5 Dal
1995 Dal: 11 G. **1996** ChiB: 14 G. **1997** Min: 14 G. **1998** Min: Postseason only. **Total:** 39 G.

PAUL BRIGGS Briggs, Paul Leonard 6′4″, 248 **T**
Col: Colorado *HS:* Grand Junction [CO] B: 4/18/1920, Providence, RI
Drafted: 1944 Round 7 Det
1948 Det: 12 G.

BOB BRIGGS Briggs, Robert James 6′4″, 258 **DT-DE**
Col: Heidelberg *HS:* Brighton [Rochester, NY] B: 4/28/1945, Toledo, OH D: 5/5/1997, Sanibel Island, FL *Drafted:* 1967 Round 9 SF
1968 SD: 14 G. **1969** SD: 14 G; KR 1-0; **1** Fum TD; 6 Pt. **1970** SD: 10 G. **1971** Cle: 14 G. **1972** Cle: 13 G; Int 1-16; **1** Fum TD; 6 Pt. **1973** Cle: 12 G. **1974** KC: 7 G. **Total:** 84 G; KR 1-0; Int 1-16; 2 Fum TD; 12 Pt.

BOB BRIGGS Briggs, Robert Louis 6′1″, 228 **FB**
Col: Central Oklahoma *HS:* George Washington Carver [Amarillo, TX]
B: 1/12/1941, Amarillo, TX *Drafted:* 1965 Round 10 Was
1965 Was: 7 G; Rush 6-10 1.7; Rec 3-40 13.3; KR 2-8 4.0; 2 Fum.

WALTER BRIGGS Briggs, Walter Robert 6′1″, 205 **QB**
Col: Montclair State *HS:* Hackensack [NJ] B: 8/6/1965, Elmira, NY
1987 NYJ: 1 G; Pass 2-0, 1 Int; Rush 1-4 4.0.

BILL BRIGGS Briggs, William John 6′3″, 245 **DE**
(Big Cat) *Col:* Iowa *HS:* Hackensack [NJ] B: 12/25/1943, Sanford, NC *Drafted:* 1966 Round 5 NYG
1966 Was: 9 G. **1967** Was: 14 G; KR 1-1 1.0. **Total:** 23 G; KR 1-1 1.0.

HI BRIGHAM Brigham, Haven Alva 5′11″, 185 **G**
Col: Ohio State *HS:* Bowling Green [OH] B: 7/13/1892, Toledo, OH D: 10/6/1987, Toledo, OH
1920 Col: 3 G.

JEREMY BRIGHAM Brigham, Jeremy Paul 6′6″, 255 **TE**
Col: Washington *HS:* Saguaro [Scottsdale, AZ] B: 3/22/1975, Boston, MA *Drafted:* 1998 Round 5 Oak
1998 Oak: 2 G.

GREG BRIGHT Bright, Gregory Keith 6′0″, 208 **DB**
Col: Morehead State *HS:* Butler [Louisville, KY] B: 8/2/1957, Fort Campbell, KY *Drafted:* 1980 Round 9 Cin
1980 Cin: 16 G; PR 1-0; Int 1-5. **1981** Cin: 4 G. **Total:** 20 G; PR 1-0; Int 1-5.

LEON BRIGHT Bright, Leon Jr. 5′9″, 192 **RB**
Col: Florida State *HS:* Merritt Island [FL] B: 5/19/1955, Starke, FL

		Rushing				Receiving			
Year Team	**G**	**Att**	**Yds**	**Avg**	**TD**	**Rec**	**Yds**	**Avg**	**TD**
1981 NYG	15	51	197	3.9	2	28	291	10.4	0
1982 NYG	8	1	5	5.0	0	2	19	9.5	0
1983 NYG	7	1	2	2.0	0	2	33	16.5	0
1984 TB	12	0	0	—	0	0	0	—	0
1985 TB	8	0	0	—	0	0	0	—	0
NFL Total	50	53	204	3.8	2	32	343	10.7	0

	Punt Returns				Kickoff Returns				
Year Team	**Ret**	**Yds**	**Avg**	**TD**	**Ret**	**Yds**	**Avg**	**TD**	**Fum**
1981 NYG	52	410	7.9	0	25	481	19.2	0	3
1982 NYG	**37**	**325**	8.8	0	4	72	18.0	0	0
1983 NYG	17	117	6.9	0	21	475	22.6	0	2
1984 TB	23	173	7.5	0	16	303	18.9	0	2
1985 TB	12	124	10.3	0	11	213	19.4	0	4
NFL Total	141	1149	8.1	0	77	1544	20.1	0	11

HAL BRILL Brill, Harold Edwin 5′10″, 175 **TB-DB**
Col: Wichita State *HS:* Norton [KS] B: 3/26/1914 D: 9/2/1980, Wichita, KS
1939 Det: 2 G.

DARRICK BRILZ Brilz, Darrick Joseph 6′3″, 287 **OG-C**
Col: Oregon State *HS:* Pinole Valley [Pinole, CA] B: 2/14/1964, Richmond, CA
1987 Was: 7 G. **1988** SD: 14 G. **1989** Sea: 14 G. **1990** Sea: 16 G. **1991** Sea: 16 G. **1992** Sea: 16 G. **1993** Sea: 16 G. **1994** Cin: 15 G. **1995** Cin: 16 G. **1996** Cin: 13 G. **1997** Cin: 16 G. **1998** Cin: 16 G. **Total:** 175 G.

JIM BRIM Brim, James Hamilton 6′3″, 187 **WR**
Col: Wake Forest *HS:* Mount Airy [NC] B: 2/28/1963, Mount Airy, NC
1987 Min: 3 G; Rush 2-36 18.0 1 TD; Rec 18-282 15.7 2 TD; Tot TD 3; 18 Pt.

MICHAEL BRIM Brim, Michael Anthony 6′0″, 192 **DB**
Col: Virginia Union *HS:* George Washington [Danville, VA] B: 1/23/1966, Danville, VA *Drafted:* 1988 Round 4 Pho
1991 NYJ: 1 Sac. **Total:** 1 Sac.

		Interceptions		
Year Team	**G**	**Int**	**Yds**	**TD**
1988 Pho	4	0	0	0
1989 Det-Min	9	0	0	0
1989 Det	2	0	0	0
1989 Min	7	0	0	0
1990 Min	16	2	11	0
1991 NYJ	16	4	52	0
1992 NYJ	16	6	139	1
1993 Cin	16	3	74	1
1994 Cin	16	2	72	0
1995 Cin	1	0	0	0
NFL Total	94	17	348	2

WALT BRINDLEY Brindley, Walter C 5′8″, 153 **BB-TB**
Col: Drake *HS:* West [Des Moines, IA] B: 5/24/1895 D: 8/13/1959
1921 RI: 2 G. **1922** RI: 3 G. **Total:** 5 G.

LARRY BRINK Brink, Lawrence Raymond 6′5″, 235 **DE-OE**
Col: Northern Illinois *HS:* Foley [MN] B: 9/12/1923, Milaca, MN *Drafted:* 1948 Round 15 LARm
1948 LARm: 11 G; Rush 1-(-3) -3.0; Rec 4-36 9.0. **1949** LARm: 11 G. **1950** LARm: 12 G; Scor **1** Saf; 2 Pt. **1951** LARm: 12 G. **1952** LARm: 12 G; Int 1-0. **1953** LARm: 12 G. **1954** ChiB: 12 G; **1** Fum TD; 6 Pt. **Total:** 82 G; Rush 1-(-3) -3.0; Rec 4-36 9.0; Int 1-0; Scor 1 Saf; 1 Fum TD; 8 Pt.

LESTER BRINKLEY Brinkley, Lester L 6′6″, 270 **DE**
Col: Mississippi *HS:* Drew [MS] B: 5/13/1965, Ruleville, MS
1990 Dal: 6 G.

CHARLIE BRINKMAN Brinkman, Charles William 6′2″, 208 **WR**
(Cookie) *Col:* Louisville *HS:* Roger Bacon [Cincinnati, OH] B: 5/26/1949, Cincinnati, OH
1972 Cle: 1 G.

DANA BRINSON Brinson, Dana Demone 5′9″, 167 **WR**
Col: Nebraska *HS:* Valdosta [GA] B: 4/10/1965, Valdosta, GA *Drafted:* 1989 Round 8 SD
1989 SD: 10 G; Rush 17-64 3.8; Rec 12-71 5.9; PR 11-112 10.2; 3 Fum.

LARRY BRINSON Brinson, Lawrence Sylvesta 6′0″, 214 **RB**
Col: Florida *HS:* Miami Northwestern [FL] B: 6/6/1954, Opalocka, FL
1980 Sea: Rec 1-9 9.0. **Total:** Rec 1-9 9.0.

		Rushing				Kickoff Returns				
Year Team	**G**	**Att**	**Yds**	**Avg**	**TD**	**Ret**	**Yds**	**Avg**	**TD**	**Fum**
1977 Dal	14	8	28	3.5	1	17	409	24.1	0	2
1978 Dal	10	18	96	5.3	2	6	93	15.5	0	1
1979 Dal	14	14	48	3.4	0	2	23	11.5	0	1
1980 Sea	7	16	57	3.6	1	0	0	—	0	1
NFL Total	45	56	229	4.1	4	25	525	21.0	0	5

VINCENT BRISBY Brisby, Vincent Cole 6′3″, 190 **WR**
Col: Northeast Louisiana *HS:* Washington-Marion [Lake Charles, LA] B: 1/25/1971, Houston, TX *Drafted:* 1993 Round 2 NE

		Receiving				
Year Team	**G**	**Rec**	**Yds**	**Avg**	**TD**	**Fum**
1993 NE	16	45	626	13.9	2	1
1994 NE	14	58	904	15.6	5	1
1995 NE	16	66	974	14.8	3	0
1996 NE	3	0	0	—	0	0
1997 NE	16	23	276	12.0	2	0
1998 NE	6	7	96	13.7	2	0
NFL Total	71	199	2876	14.5	14	2

MARLIN BRISCOE Briscoe, Marlin Oliver 5′11″, 178 **WR-QB**
Col: Nebraska-Omaha *HS:* Omaha South [NE] B: 9/10/1945, Oakland, CA *Drafted:* 1968 Round 14 Den
1972 Mia: KR 1-0. **Total:** KR 1-0.

		Passing							
Year Team	**G**	**Att**	**Comp**	**Comp%**	**Yds**	**YPA**	**TD**	**Int**	**Rating**
1968 Den	11	224	93	41.5	1589	7.09	14	13	62.9
1969 Buf	13	1	0	0.0	0	0.00	0	1	0.0
1970 Buf	14	0	0	—	0	—	0	0	—
1971 Buf	14	2	1	50.0	36	18.00	0	0	95.8
1972 Mia	10	3	3	100.0	72	24.00	0	0	118.8
1973 Mia	14	0	0	—	0	—	0	0	—
1974 Mia	4	1	0	0.0	0	0.00	0	0	39.6
1975 SD-Det	11	2	0	0.0	0	0.00	0	0	39.6
1975 SD	3	0	0	—	0	—	0	0	—
1975 Det	8	2	0	0.0	0	0.00	0	0	39.6
1976 NE	14	0	0	—	0	—	0	0	—
NFL Total	105	233	97	41.6	1697	7.28	14	14	62.1

	Rushing				Receiving					Tot
Year Team	**Att**	**Yds**	**Avg**	**TD**	**Rec**	**Yds**	**Avg**	**TD**	**Fum**	**TD**
1968 Den	41	308	7.5	3	0	0	—	0	3	3
1969 Buf	0	0	—	0	32	532	16.6	5	1	5
1970 Buf	3	19	6.3	0	57	1036	18.2	8	3	8
1971 Buf	0	0	—	0	44	603	13.7	5	0	5
1972 Mia	0	0	—	0	16	279	17.4	4	0	4
1973 Mia	2	-5	-2.5	0	30	447	14.9	2	0	2
1974 Mia	1	17	17.0	0	11	132	12.0	1	0	1
1975 SD-Det	2	-3	-1.5	0	24	372	15.5	4	1	4
1975 SD	0	0	—	0	2	25	12.5	0	0	0
1975 Det	2	-3	-1.5	0	22	347	15.8	4	1	4
1976 NE	0	0	—	0	10	136	13.6	1	0	1
NFL Total	49	336	6.9	3	224	3537	15.8	30	8	33

BUBBY BRISTER Brister, Walter Andrew III 6′3″, 205 **QB**
Col: Tulane; Northeast Louisiana *HS:* Neville [Monroe, LA] B: 8/15/1962, Alexandria, LA *Drafted:* 1986 Round 3 Pit
1989 Pit: Rec 1-(-10) -10.0. **1995** NYJ: Rec 1-2 2.0. **Total:** Rec 2-(-8) -4.0.

		Passing							
Year Team	**G**	**Att**	**Comp**	**Comp%**	**Yds**	**YPA**	**TD**	**Int**	**Rating**
1986 Pit	2	60	21	35.0	291	4.85	0	2	37.6
1987 Pit	2	12	4	33.3	20	1.67	0	3	2.8
1988 Pit	13	370	175	47.3	2634	7.12	11	14	65.3
1989 Pit	14	342	187	54.7	2365	6.92	9	10	73.1
1990 Pit	16	387	223	57.6	2725	7.04	20	14	81.6
1991 Pit	8	190	103	54.2	1350	7.11	9	9	72.9
1992 Pit	6	116	63	54.3	719	6.20	2	5	61.0
1993 Phi	10	309	181	58.6	1905	6.17	14	5	84.9
1994 Phi	7	76	51	67.1	507	6.67	2	1	89.1
1995 NYJ	9	170	93	54.7	726	4.27	4	8	53.7
1997 Den	1	9	6	66.7	48	5.33	0	0	79.9

1998 Den	7	131	78	59.5	986	7.53	10	3	99.0
NFL Total	95	2172	1185	54.6	14276	6.57	81	74	73.2

	Rushing				
Year Team	**Att**	**Yds**	**Avg**	**TD**	**Fum**
1986 Pit	6	10	1.7	1	1
1988 Pit	45	209	4.6	6	8
1989 Pit	27	25	0.9	0	4
1990 Pit	25	64	2.6	0	9
1991 Pit	11	17	1.5	0	4
1992 Pit	10	16	1.6	0	2
1993 Phi	20	39	2.0	0	3
1994 Phi	1	7	7.0	0	0
1995 NYJ	16	18	1.1	0	4
1997 Den	4	2	0.5	0	0
1998 Den	19	102	5.4	1	2
NFL Total	184	509	2.8	8	37

WILLIE BRISTER Brister, Willie Jerry 6′4″, 236 **TE**
Col: Southern University *HS:* Baton Rouge [LA] B: 1/28/1952, Tylertown, MS *Drafted:* 1974 Round 15 NYJ
1974 NYJ: 12 G; Rec 5-90 18.0. **1975** NYJ: 12 G; Rec 1-3 3.0; **1** Fum TD; 6 Pt. **Total:** 24 G; Rec 6-93 15.5; 1 Fum TD; 6 Pt.

JOHN BRISTOR Bristor, John Rollins 6′0″, 188 **CB**
Col: California (Pa.); Waynesburg *HS:* West Greene [Rogersville, PA] B: 11/25/1955, Waynesburg, PA
1979 SF: 1 G.

OBIE BRISTOW Bristow, Jessie Gordon 6′2″, 210 **FB-BB-TB-WB**
Col: Central Oklahoma; Oklahoma *HS:* Pryor [OK] B: 4/17/1900, Pryor, OK D: 12/22/1969, Big Spring, TX
1925 KC-Cle: 9 G; Pass 2 TD. KC: 8 G; Pass 2 TD. Cle: 1 G. **1926** KC: 8 G. **Total:** 17 G; Pass 2 TD.

GENE BRITO Brito, Genaro Herman 6′1″, 226 **DE-OE**
Col: Loyola Marymount *HS:* Abraham Lincoln [Los Angeles, CA] B: 10/23/1925, Huntington Park, CA D: 6/8/1965, Duarte, CA
Drafted: 1951 Round 17 Was
1951 Was: KR 4-39 9.8. **1952** Was: KR 2-5 2.5. **1953** Was: KR 1-6 6.0. **1956** Was: Int 1-6. **Total:** KR 7-50 7.1; Int 1-6.

		Receiving			
Year Team	**G**	**Rec**	**Yds**	**Avg**	**TD**
1951 Was	12	24	313	13.0	0
1952 Was	12	21	270	12.9	2
1953 Was	12	2	35	17.5	0
1955 Was	12	0	0	—	0
1956 Was	12	0	0	—	0
1957 Was	12	0	0	—	0
1958 Was	12	0	0	—	0
1959 LARm	2	0	0	—	0
1960 LARm	11	0	0	—	0
NFL Total	97	47	618	13.1	2

RANKIN BRITT Britt, Alton Rankin 6′2″, 205 **OE**
Col: Texas A&M B: 1915 *Drafted:* 1939 Round 9 Phi
1939 Phi: 1 G.

CHARLEY BRITT Britt, Charles William 6′2″, 180 **DB**
(Cash) *Col:* Georgia *HS:* North Augusta [SC] B: 3/20/1938, Augusta, GA D: 10/2/1981, GA *Drafted:* 1960 Round 3 LARm

		Interceptions		
Year Team	**G**	**Int**	**Yds**	**TD**
1960 LARm	12	5	117	1
1961 LARm	11	5	29	0
1962 LARm	11	3	50	0
1963 LARm	10	1	45	0
1964 Min	5	0	0	0
NFL Total	49	14	241	1

EDDIE BRITT Britt, Edward Joseph 6′2″, 205 **DB-FB-TB**
Col: Holy Cross *HS:* Lexington [MA] B: 7/19/1912, Lexington, MA D: 11/21/1978, Pelham, NH
1936 Bos: Pass 44-18 40.9%, 294 6.68 3 TD 5 Int; Rec 6-106 17.7. **Total:** Pass 44-18 40.9%, 294 6.68 3 TD 5 Int; Rec 6-106 17.7.

		Rushing			
Year Team	**G**	**Att**	**Yds**	**Avg**	**TD**
1936 Bos	10	72	180	2.5	0
1937 Was	4	7	21	3.0	0
1938 Bkn	1	0	0	—	0
NFL Total	15	79	201	2.5	0

JIM BRITT Britt, James Earl 6′0″, 185 **DB**
Col: Louisiana State *HS:* Minden [LA] B: 9/12/1960, Minden, LA
Drafted: 1983 Round 2 Atl
1983 Atl: 14 G. **1984** Atl: 16 G; Int 1-10. **1985** Atl: 2 G; Int 1-8. **1986** Atl: 16 G; **1** Fum TD; 6 Pt. **1987** Atl: 12 G; Int 1-(-1). **Total:** 60 G; Int 3-17; 1 Fum TD; 6 Pt.

RALPH BRITT Britt, James Ralph Jr. 6′3″, 240 **TE**
Col: North Carolina State *HS:* North Duplin [Calypso, NC]
B: 3/18/1965, Goldsboro, NC
1987 Pit: 3 G; KR 2-9 4.5; 1 Fum.

JESSIE BRITT Britt, Jessie Loftin Jr. 6′4″, 198 **WR**
Col: North Carolina A&T *HS:* Gates Co. [Gatesville, NC] B: 3/3/1963, Suffolk, VA
1986 Pit: 8 G.

MAURICE BRITT Britt, Maury Lee Jr. 6′4″, 210 **OE-DE**
(Footsie) *Col:* Arkansas *HS:* Lonoke [AR] B: 6/29/1919, Carlisle, AR D: 11/26/1995, Little Rock, AR *Drafted:* 1941 Round 13 Det
1941 Det: 9 G; Rec 1-45 45.0 1 TD; 6 Pt.

OSCAR BRITT Britt, Oscar Lee 5′11″, 193 **G**
(Honey) *Col:* Mississippi *HS:* Lincoln Co. [Wesson, MS]
B: 6/18/1919, Brookhaven, MS D: 12/13/1992, Ontario, CA
Drafted: 1943 Round 12 Was
1946 Was: 1 G.

JON BRITTENUM Brittenum, Jon Roger 6′0″, 185 **QB**
Col: Arkansas *HS:* Brinkley [AR] B: 5/27/1944, Brinkley, AR
Drafted: 1966 Redshirt Round 8 Mia
1968 SD: 14 G; Pass 17-9 52.9%, 125 7.35 1 TD 1 Int; Rush 2-(-4) -2.0.

EARL BRITTON Britton, Earl Tanner 6′3″, 212 **FB-BB-TB**
Col: Illinois *HS:* Elgin [IL] B: 7/15/1903, Elgin, IL D: 10/24/1973, Elgin, IL
1925 ChiB: 5 G. **1926** Bkn: 3 G. **1927** Day-Fra: 14 G; Scor 3, 1 FG. Day: 8 G; Scor 3, 1 FG. Fra: 6 G. **1928** Day: 7 G. **1929** ChiC: 2 G. **Total:** 31 G; Scor 3, 1 FG.

MAX BROADHURST Broadhurst, Arthur 6′0″, 220 **T**
Col: No College B: 8/9/1886, WI D: 10/1964, OR
1920 Day: 1 G.

KARL BROADLEY Broadley, Karl T 6′4″, 250 **G**
Col: Bethany (W.V.) B: 11/10/1895, Fort Worth, TX D: 4/13/1967, St. Petersburg, FL
1925 Cle: 4 G.

JERRY BROADNAX Broadnax, Jerry Lee 6′2″, 225 **TE**
Col: Southern University *HS:* L.G. Pinkston [Dallas, TX] B: 8/19/1951, Dallas, TX
1974 Hou: 8 G; Rec 3-69 23.0.

MARION BROADSTONE Broadstone, Marion Glenn 6′2″, 210 **T-G**
Col: Nebraska *HS:* Norfolk [NE] B: 6/24/1906, Pender, NE
D: 4/10/1972, San Jose, CA
1931 NYG: 3 G.

CHARLEY BROCK Brock, Charles Jacob 6′2″, 207 **C-LB**
(Ears) *Col:* Nebraska *HS:* Kramer [Columbus, NE] B: 3/15/1916, Columbus, NE D: 5/25/1987, Green Bay, WI *Drafted:* 1939 Round 2 GB
1942 GB: **1** Fum TD. **Total:** 1 Fum TD.

		Interceptions			Tot
Year Team	**G**	**Int**	**Yds**	**TD**	**TD**
1939 GB	10	—	—	**1**	1
1940 GB	11	3	7	0	0
1941 GB	11	0	0	0	0
1942 GB	11	6	25	0	1
1943 GB	6	4	61	0	0
1944 GB	10	1	1	0	0
1945 GB	10	4	**122**	**2**	2
1946 GB	11	0	0	0	0
1947 GB	12	2	14	0	0
NFL Total	92	20	230	3	4

CLYDE BROCK Brock, Clyde V 6′5″, 268 **OT**
Col: Utah State *HS:* Ogden [UT] B: 8/30/1940, Los Angeles, CA
Drafted: 1962 Round 2 ChiB
1962 Dal: 14 G. **1963** Dal-SF: 11 G. Dal: 4 G. SF: 6 G. **Total:** 24 G.

FRED BROCK Brock, Fred 5′11″, 181 **WR**
Col: Southern Mississippi *HS:* Jefferson Davis [Montgomery, AL]
B: 11/15/1974, Montgomery, AL
1997 Ariz: 2 G; Rec 1-29 29.0. **1998** Ariz: 12 G; Rec 2-12 6.0. **Total:** 14 G; Rec 3-41 13.7.

LOU BROCK Brock, James Lewis 6′0″, 195 **HB-DB-FB-TB**
Col: Purdue *HS:* Stafford [KS] B: 12/9/1917, Stafford, KS
D: 5/7/1989, Stafford, KS *Drafted:* 1940 Round 2 GB
1941 GB: KR 4-94 23.5. **1942** GB: KR 9-179 19.9; Scor 20, 0-1 FG, 2-2 100.0% XK. **1943** GB: KR 5-112 22.4. **1944** GB: KR 2-41 20.5. **1945** GB: KR 1-12 12.0. **Total:** KR 21-438 20.9; Scor 98, 0-1 FG, 2-2 100.0% XK.

		Passing							
Year Team	**G**	**Att**	**Comp**	**Comp%**	**Yds**	**YPA**	**TD**	**Int**	**Rating**
1940 GB	11	2	0	0.0	0	0.00	0	0	39.6
1941 GB	11	0	0	—	0	—	0	0	—

1942 GB	11	0	0	—	0	—	0	0	—
1943 GB	10	22	9	40.9	274	12.45	3	1	108.7
1944 GB	5	21	5	23.8	94	4.48	2	0	77.5
1945 GB	10	22	5	22.7	151	6.86	2	3	46.4
NFL Total	58	67	19	28.4	519	7.75	7	4	69.3

	Rushing				Receiving			
Year Team	Att	Yds	Avg	TD	Rec	Yds	Avg	TD
1940 GB	18	60	3.3	0	5	97	19.4	0
1941 GB	14	44	3.1	0	22	307	14.0	2
1942 GB	95	237	2.5	2	20	139	7.0	1
1943 GB	45	67	1.5	2	4	57	14.3	1
1944 GB	36	200	5.6	3	4	74	18.5	2
1945 GB	46	196	4.3	3	4	87	21.8	0
NFL Total	254	804	3.2	10	59	761	12.9	6

	Punt Returns				Interceptions		
Year Team	Ret	Yds	Avg	TD	Int	Yds	TD
1940 GB	—	—	—	0	5	116	0
1941 GB	15	153	10.2	0	2	3	0
1942 GB	8	86	10.8	0	2	32	0
1943 GB	8	126	15.8	0	1	9	0
1944 GB	4	36	9.0	0	0	0	0
1945 GB	4	37	9.3	0	3	33	0
NFL Total	39	438	11.2	0	13	193	0

	Punting				Tot
Year Team	Punts	Yds	Avg	Fum	TD
1940 GB	3	125	41.7	0	0
1941 GB	3	128	42.7	0	2
1942 GB	32	1218	38.1	0	3
1943 GB	32	1164	36.4	0	3
1944 GB	14	491	35.1	0	5
1945 GB	0	0	—	1	3
NFL Total	84	3126	37.2	1	16

LOU BROCK Brock, Louis Clark Jr. 5'10", 175 **DB**
Col: USC *HS:* Ladue Horton Watkins [St. Louis, MO] B: 5/8/1964, Chicago, IL *Drafted:* 1987 Round 2 SD
1987 SD: 1 G. **1988** Sea-Det: 3 G. Sea: 1 G. Det: 2 G. **Total:** 4 G.

MATT BROCK Brock, Matthew Lee 6'5", 290 **DE-DT**
Col: Oregon *HS:* University City [San Diego, CA] B: 1/14/1966, Ogden, UT *Drafted:* 1989 Round 3 GB
1989 GB: 7 G. **1990** GB: 16 G; 4 Sac. **1991** GB: 16 G; 2.5 Sac. **1992** GB: 16 G; 4 Sac. **1993** GB: 16 G; Int 1-0; 2 Sac. **1994** GB: 5 G. **1995** NYJ: 16 G; Int 1-9; **1** Fum TD; 6 Pt; 5 Sac. **1996** NYJ: 16 G; 2 Sac.
Total: 108 G; Int 2-9; 1 Fum TD; 6 Pt; 19.5 Sac.

PETE BROCK Brock, Peter Anthony 6'5", 267 **C-OG-OT-TE**
Col: Colorado *HS:* Jesuit [Beaverton, OR] B: 7/14/1954, Portland, OR *Drafted:* 1976 Round 1 NE
1976 NE: 14 G; Rec 1-6 6.0 1 TD; 6 Pt. **1977** NE: 14 G. **1978** NE: 15 G. **1979** NE: 16 G; 2 Fum. **1980** NE: 16 G. **1981** NE: 16 G. **1982** NE: 9 G. **1983** NE: 13 G. **1984** NE: 12 G. **1985** NE: 9 G. **1986** NE: 16 G; 1 Fum. **1987** NE: 4 G. **Total:** 154 G; Rec 1-6 6.0 1 TD; 6 Pt; 3 Fum.

DIETER BROCK Brock, Ralph Dieter 6'0", 195 **QB**
Col: Jacksonville State; Auburn *HS:* Jones Valley [Birmingham, AL] B: 2/12/1951, Birmingham, AL
1985 LARm: Rush 20-38 1.9.

		Passing								
Year Team	G	Att	Comp	Comp%	Yds	YPA	TD	Int	Rating	Fum
1985 LARm	15	365	218	59.7	2658	7.28	16	13	82.0	6

STAN BROCK Brock, Stanley James 6'6", 288 **OT**
Col: Colorado *HS:* Jesuit [Beaverton, OR] B: 6/8/1958, Portland, OR *Drafted:* 1980 Round 1 NO
1980 NO: 16 G. **1981** NO: 16 G; KR 2-18 9.0. **1982** NO: 9 G. **1983** NO: 16 G; KR 1-15 15.0. **1984** NO: 14 G. **1985** NO: 16 G. **1986** NO: 16 G. **1987** NO: 12 G; KR 1-11 11.0. **1988** NO: 7 G. **1989** NO: 16 G. **1990** NO: 16 G. **1991** NO: 16 G. **1992** NO: 16 G. **1993** SD: 16 G. **1994** SD: 16 G. **1995** SD: 16 G. **Total:** 234 G; KR 4-44 11.0.

WILLIE BROCK Brock, Willis Arthur 6'3", 250 **C**
Col: Mount Hood CC OR; Colorado *HS:* Jesuit [Beaverton, OR] B: 9/20/1955, Portland, OR *Drafted:* 1978 Round 12 KC
1978 Det: 4 G.

BLAKE BROCKERMEYER Brockermeyer, Blake Weeks 6'4", 301 **OT**
Col: Texas *HS:* Arlington Heights [Fort Worth, TX] B: 4/11/1973, Fort Worth, TX *Drafted:* 1995 Round 1 Car
1995 Car: 16 G. **1996** Car: 12 G. **1997** Car: 16 G. **1998** Car: 14 G. **Total:** 58 G.

JEFF BROCKHAUS Brockhaus, Jeffery Jerome 6'2", 218 **K**
Col: Missouri *HS:* Brentwood [MO] B: 4/15/1959, Fort Lauderdale, FL
1987 SF: 3 G; Scor 20, 3-6 50.0% FG, 11-13 84.6% XK.

JOHN BROCKINGTON Brockington, John Stanley 6'1", 225 **RB**
Col: Ohio State *HS:* Thomas Jefferson [Brooklyn, NY] B: 9/7/1948, Brooklyn, NY *Drafted:* 1971 Round 1 GB
1973 GB: Pass 1-0. **Total:** Pass 1-0.

		Rushing				Receiving					Tot
Year Team	G	Att	Yds	Avg	TD	Rec	Yds	Avg	TD	Fum	TD
1971 GB	14	216	1105	5.1	4	14	98	7.0	1	4	5
1972 GB	14	274	1027	3.7	8	19	243	12.8	1	4	9
1973 GB	14	265	1144	4.3	3	16	128	8.0	0	4	3
1974 GB	14	266	883	3.3	5	43	314	7.3	0	6	5
1975 GB	14	144	434	3.0	7	33	242	7.3	1	2	8
1976 GB	14	117	406	3.5	2	11	49	4.5	0	3	2
1977 GB-KC	11	65	186	2.9	1	21	223	10.6	1	0	2
1977 GB	1	11	25	2.3	0	2	1	0.5	0	0	0
1977 KC	10	54	161	3.0	1	19	222	11.7	1	0	2
NFL Total	95	1347	5185	3.8	30	157	1297	8.3	4	23	34

HAL BRODA Broda, Harold Albert 6'1", 180 **E**
Col: Brown *HS:* McKinley [Canton, OH] B: 7/27/1905, Canton, OH D: 2/13/1989, Canton, OH
1927 Cle: 3 G.

BOB BRODHEAD Brodhead, Robert Edgar 6'2", 207 **QB**
Col: Duke *HS:* Kittanning [PA] B: 12/20/1936, Kittanning, PA *Drafted:* 1958 Round 12 Cle
1960 Buf: 4 G; Pass 25-7 28.0%, 75 3.00 3 Int; Rush 15-100 6.7; Scor 1 2XP; 2 Pt.

JOHN BRODIE Brodie, John Riley 6'1", 198 **QB**
Col: Stanford *HS:* Oakland Technical [CA] B: 8/14/1935, Menlo Park, CA *Drafted:* 1957 Round 1 SF

		Passing							
Year Team	G	Att	Comp	Comp%	Yds	YPA	TD	Int	Rating
1957 SF	5	21	11	52.4	160	7.62	2	3	69.6
1958 SF	12	172	103	**59.9**	1224	7.12	6	13	61.8
1959 SF	12	64	30	46.9	354	5.53	2	7	35.0
1960 SF	11	207	103	49.8	1111	5.37	6	9	57.5
1961 SF	14	283	155	54.8	2588	**9.14**	14	12	84.7
1962 SF	14	304	175	57.6	2272	7.47	18	16	79.0
1963 SF	3	61	30	49.2	367	6.02	3	4	57.2
1964 SF	14	392	193	49.2	2498	6.37	14	16	64.6
1965 SF	13	**391**	**242**	**61.9**	**3112**	7.96	**30**	16	95.3
1966 SF	14	427	232	54.3	2810	6.58	16	22	65.8
1967 SF	14	349	168	48.1	2013	5.77	11	16	57.6
1968 SF	14	**404**	**234**	57.9	**3020**	7.48	22	21	78.0
1969 SF	13	347	194	55.9	2405	6.93	16	15	74.9
1970 SF	14	378	**223**	59.0	**2941**	7.78	**24**	10	93.8
1971 SF	14	387	208	53.7	2642	6.83	18	24	65.0
1972 SF	6	110	70	63.6	905	8.23	9	8	86.4
1973 SF	14	194	98	50.5	1126	5.80	3	12	47.7
NFL Total	201	4491	2469	55.0	31548	7.02	214	224	72.3

	Rushing				
Year Team	Att	Yds	Avg	TD	Fum
1957 SF	2	0	0.0	0	0
1958 SF	11	-12	-1.1	1	6
1959 SF	5	6	1.2	0	0
1960 SF	18	171	9.5	1	1
1961 SF	28	90	3.2	2	1
1962 SF	37	258	7.0	4	8
1963 SF	7	63	9.0	0	1
1964 SF	27	135	5.0	2	11
1965 SF	15	60	4.0	1	4
1966 SF	5	18	3.6	3	4
1967 SF	20	147	7.4	1	3
1968 SF	18	71	3.9	0	4
1969 SF	11	62	5.6	0	1
1970 SF	9	29	3.2	2	1
1971 SF	14	45	3.2	3	3
1972 SF	3	8	2.7	1	0
1973 SF	5	16	3.2	1	0
NFL Total	235	1167	5.0	22	48

J.W. BRODNAX Brodnax, John Willis Jr. 6'0", 208 **FB**
(Red) *Col:* Louisiana State *HS:* Bastrop [LA] B: 3/6/1936 *Drafted:* 1959 Round 15 Pit
1960 Den: 14 G; Rush 15-18 1.2; Rec 5-39 7.8 1 TD; KR 5-117 23.4; 6 Pt.

CHUCK BRODNICKI Brodnicki, Charles T 6'2", 218 **G**
Col: Villanova *HS:* St. Rita [Chicago, IL] B: 11/2/1908 D: 8/1986, Chicago, IL
1934 Bkn: 1 G.

JEFF BROHM Brohm, Jeffery Scott 6'1", 205 **QB**
Col: Louisville *HS:* Trinity [Louisville, KY] B: 4/24/1971, Louisville, KY
1996 SF: Rush 16-43 2.7. **1997** SF: Rush 4-11 2.8. **Total:** Rush 20-54 2.7.

Year Team	G	Passing Att	Comp	Comp%	Yds	YPA	TD	Int	Rating	Fum
1996 SF	3	34	21	61.8	189	5.56	1	0	86.5	1
1997 SF	5	24	16	66.7	164	6.83	0	1	68.8	3
NFL Total	8	58	37	63.8	353	6.09	1	1	79.2	4

FRED BROKER Broker, Frederick 5′9″, 175 **T**
Col: Carlisle *HS:* Carlisle Indian School [PA] B: 1/17/1893
D: 12/1971, Park Rapids, MN
1922 Oor: 1 G.

LORENZO BROMELL Bromell, Lorenzo Alexis 6′6″, 266 **DE**
Col: Clemson *HS:* Choppee [Georgetown, SC] B: 9/23/1975, Georgetown, SC *Drafted:* 1998 Round 4 Mia
1998 Mia: 14 G; 8 Sac.

BEN BRONSON Bronson, Benjamin James 5′10″, 165 **WR**
Col: Tyler JC TX; Baylor *HS:* Jasper [TX] B: 9/9/1972, Jasper, TX
1995 Ind: 9 G; PR 13-79 6.1; KR 1-31 31.0; 2 Fum.

ZACK BRONSON Bronson, Robert Zachary 6′1″, 191 **DB**
Col: McNeese State *HS:* Jasper [TX] B: 1/28/1974, Jasper, TX
1997 SF: 16 G; Int 1-22. **1998** SF: 11 G; Int 4-34. **Total:** 27 G; Int 5-56.

TOMMY BROOKER Brooker, William Thomas 6′2″, 235 **OE-K**
Col: Alabama *HS:* Demopolis [AL] B: 10/31/1939, Demopolis, AL
Drafted: 1962 Round 17 DalT
1962 DalT: Rec 4-138 34.5 3 TD. **1963** KC: Rec 2-32 16.0.
Total: Rec 6-170 28.3 3 TD.

Year Team	G	Scoring Pts	FG	FGA	FG%	XK	XKA	XK%
1962 DalT	14	87	12	22	54.5	33	33	100.0
1963 KC	9	38	6	14	42.9	20	20	100.0
1964 KC	14	70	8	17	47.1	**46**	**46**	100.0
1965 KC	14	76	13	30	43.3	37	37	100.0
1966 KC	4	19	2	2	100.0	13	13	100.0
NFL Total	55	290	41	85	48.2	149	149	100.0

KEITH BROOKING Brooking, Keith Howard 6′2″, 244 **LB**
Col: Georgia Tech *HS:* East Coweta [Sharpsburg, GA] B: 10/30/1975, Senoia, GA *Drafted:* 1998 Round 1 Atl
1998 Atl: 15 G; Int 1-12.

MITCHELL BROOKINS Brookins, Mitchell Eugene 5′11″, 196 **WR**
Col: Illinois *HS:* Wendell Phillips [Chicago, IL] B: 12/10/1960, Chicago, IL *Drafted:* 1984 Round 4 Buf
1984 Buf: 16 G; Rush 2-27 13.5; Rec 18-318 17.7 1 TD; 6 Pt. **1985** Buf: 5 G; Rec 3-71 23.7; KR 6-152 25.3. **Total:** 21 G; Rush 2-27 13.5; Rec 21-389 18.5 1 TD; KR 6-152 25.3; 6 Pt.

BARRETT BROOKS Brooks, Barrett Charles 6′4″, 312 **OT**
Col: Kansas State *HS:* McCluer North [Florissant, MO] B: 5/5/1972, St. Louis, MO *Drafted:* 1995 Round 2 Phi
1995 Phi: 16 G. **1996** Phi: 16 G; KR 1-0. **1997** Phi: 16 G. **1998** Phi: 16 G; KR 1-7 7.0. **Total:** 64 G; KR 2-7 3.5.

BOBBY BROOKS Brooks, Bobby Daniel 6′1″, 195 **DB**
Col: Bishop *HS:* I.M. Terrell [Dallas, TX] B: 2/24/1951, Dallas, TX
Drafted: 1974 Round 11 NYG
1974 NYG: 14 G; PR 1-9 9.0; KR 5-106 21.2. **1975** NYG: 14 G; Int 4-38.
1976 NYG: 4 G; Int 1-9. **Total:** 32 G; PR 1-9 9.0; KR 5-106 21.2; Int 5-47.

CARLOS BROOKS Brooks, Carlos Taron 6′0″, 200 **DB**
Col: Bowling Green State *HS:* Middletown [OH] B: 5/8/1971, Hamilton, OH
1995 Ariz: 7 G.

CLIFF BROOKS Brooks, Clifford Jr. 6′1″, 190 **DB**
Col: Tennessee State *HS:* Dunbar [TX] B: 6/21/1949, Pineland, TX
Drafted: 1972 Round 2 Cle
1972 Cle: 14 G. **1973** Cle: 14 G. **1974** Cle: 13 G. **1975** Phi: 14 G.
1976 Phi-NYJ-Buf: 3 G. Phi: 1 G. NYJ: 1 G. Buf: 1 G. **Total:** 58 G.

DERRICK BROOKS Brooks, Derrick Dewan 6′0″, 232 **LB**
Col: Florida State *HS:* Booker T. Washington [Pensacola, FL]
B: 4/18/1973, Pensacola, FL *Drafted:* 1995 Round 1 TB
1995 TB: 16 G; 1 Sac. **1996** TB: 16 G; Int 1-6. **1997** TB: 16 G; Int 2-13; 1 Fum; 1.5 Sac. **1998** TB: 16 G; Int 1-25. **Total:** 64 G; Int 4-44; 1 Fum; 2.5 Sac.

ETHAN BROOKS Brooks, Ethan 6′6″, 299 **OT**
Col: Williams *HS:* Westminster [Simsbury, CT] B: 4/27/1972, Simsbury, CT *Drafted:* 1996 Round 7 Atl
1996 Atl: 2 G. **1998** StL: 15 G. **Total:** 17 G.

JAMES BROOKS Brooks, James Robert 5′10″, 180 **RB**
Col: Auburn *HS:* Warner Robins [GA] B: 12/28/1958, Warner Robins, GA *Drafted:* 1981 Round 1 SD
1985 Cin: Pass 1-1 100.0%, 8 8.00 1 TD. **1986** Cin: Pass 1-0.
Total: Pass 2-1 50.0%, 8 4.00 1 TD.

Year Team	G	Rushing Att	Yds	Avg	TD	Receiving Rec	Yds	Avg	TD
1981 SD	14	109	525	4.8	3	46	329	7.2	3
1982 SD	9	87	430	4.9	6	13	66	5.1	0
1983 SD	15	127	516	4.1	3	25	215	8.6	0
1984 Cin	15	103	396	3.8	2	34	268	7.9	2
1985 Cin	16	192	929	4.8	7	55	576	10.5	5
1986 Cin	16	205	1087	**5.3**	5	54	686	12.7	4
1987 Cin	9	94	290	3.1	1	22	272	12.4	2
1988 Cin	15	182	931	5.1	8	29	287	9.9	6
1989 Cin	16	221	1239	5.6	7	37	306	8.3	2
1990 Cin	16	195	1004	5.1	5	26	269	10.3	4
1991 Cin	15	152	571	3.8	2	40	348	8.7	2
1992 Cle-TB	6	18	44	2.4	0	2	-1	-0.5	0
1992 Cle	4	13	38	2.9	0	2	-1	-0.5	0
1992 TB	2	5	6	1.2	0	0	0	—	0
NFL Total	162	1685	7962	4.7	49	383	3621	9.5	30

Year Team	Punt Returns Ret	Yds	Avg	TD	Kickoff Returns Ret	Yds	Avg	TD	Fum	Tot TD
1981 SD	22	290	13.2	0	40	949	23.7	0	7	6
1982 SD	12	138	11.5	0	**33**	**749**	22.7	0	4	6
1983 SD	18	137	7.6	0	32	607	19.0	0	8	3
1984 Cin	0	0	—	0	7	144	20.6	0	4	4
1985 Cin	0	0	—	0	3	38	12.7	0	7	12
1986 Cin	0	0	—	0	0	0	—	0	2	9
1987 Cin	0	0	—	0	2	42	21.0	0	0	3
1988 Cin	0	0	—	0	1	-6	-6.0	0	1	14
1989 Cin	0	0	—	0	0	0	—	0	9	9
1990 Cin	0	0	—	0	0	0	—	0	3	9
1991 Cin	0	0	—	0	11	190	17.3	0	5	4
1992 Cle-TB	0	0	—	0	3	49	16.3	0	1	0
1992 TB	0	0	—	0	3	49	16.3	0	1	0
NFL Total	52	565	10.9	0	132	2762	20.9	0	51	79

JON BROOKS Brooks, Jonathan 6′2″, 215 **LB**
Col: Clemson *HS:* Saluda [SC] B: 6/22/1957, Saluda, SC
Drafted: 1979 Round 4 Det
1979 Det: 15 G. **1980** Atl-StL: 5 G. Atl: 4 G. StL: 1 G. **Total:** 20 G.

KEVIN BROOKS Brooks, Kevin Craig 6′6″, 277 **DE-DT**
Col: Michigan *HS:* MacKenzie [Detroit, MI] B: 2/9/1963, Detroit, MI
Drafted: 1985 Round 1 Dal
1985 Dal: 11 G; 2 Sac. **1986** Dal: 9 G; 2.5 Sac. **1987** Dal: 13 G; 3 Sac. **1988** Dal: 15 G; 5 Sac. **1989** Det: 15 G; 1 Fum; 2 Sac. **1990** Det: 6 G; 1 Sac. **Total:** 69 G; 1 Fum; 15.5 Sac.

LARRY BROOKS Brooks, Larry Lee 6′3″, 255 **DT**
Col: Virginia State *HS:* Prince George [VA] B: 6/10/1950, Prince George, VA *Drafted:* 1972 Round 14 LARm
1972 LARm: 8 G. **1973** LARm: 14 G. **1974** LARm: 13 G. **1975** LARm: 8 G. **1976** LARm: 14 G. **1977** LARm: 14 G. **1978** LARm: 14 G. **1979** LARm: 16 G. **1980** LARm: 16 G. **1981** LARm: 8 G. **1982** LARm: 6 G. **Total:** 131 G.

LEE BROOKS Brooks, Leonard Leo Jr. 6′5″, 261 **DT**
Col: Texas *HS:* Kermit [TX] B: 12/7/1947, Shidler, OK *Drafted:* 1970 Round 2 Hou
1970 Hou: 13 G. **1971** Hou: 11 G; Int 1-14. **1972** Hou: 12 G. **1973** StL: 13 G. **1974** StL: 14 G. **1975** StL: 8 G. **1976** StL: 8 G. **Total:** 79 G; Int 1-14.

MICHAEL BROOKS Brooks, Michael 6′1″, 236 **LB**
Col: Louisiana State *HS:* Ruston [LA] B: 9/2/1964, Ruston, LA
Drafted: 1987 Round 3 Den
1987 Den: 12 G; 1 Sac. **1988** Den: 16 G. **1989** Den: 16 G; Scor **1** Saf; 2 Pt; 1 Sac. **1990** Den: 16 G; 2 Sac. **1991** Den: 14 G; Int 2-7. **1992** Den: 15 G; Int 1-17; 1 Fum TD; 6 Pt. **1993** NYG: 13 G; 1 Sac. **1994** NYG: 16 G; Int 1-10; 1 Fum; 1 Sac. **1995** NYG: 16 G; 1 Sac. **1996** Det: 4 G.
Total: 138 G; Int 4-34; Scor 1 Saf; 1 Fum TD; 8 Pt; 1 Fum; 7 Sac.

MICHAEL BROOKS Brooks, Michael Antonio 6′0″, 195 **DB**
Col: North Carolina State *HS:* Walter H. Page [Greensboro, NC]
B: 3/12/1967, Greensboro, NC
1989 SD: 1 G. **1990** SD-Dal: 4 G. SD: 1 G. Dal: 3 G. **Total:** 5 G.

PERRY BROOKS Brooks, Perry 6′3″, 264 **DT**
Col: Southern University *HS:* Wesley Ray [Angie, LA] B: 12/4/1954, Bogalusa, LA *Drafted:* 1976 Round 7 NE
1978 Was: 16 G. **1979** Was: 12 G. **1980** Was: 12 G. **1981** Was: 15 G. **1982** Was: 5 G; 1 Sac. **1983** Was: 16 G; 2.5 Sac. **1984** Was: 16 G; 5.5 Sac. **Total:** 92 G; 9 Sac.

TONY BROOKS Brooks, Raymond Anthony 6′0″, 230 **RB**
Col: Holy Cross (Ind.); Notre Dame *HS:* Booker T. Washington [Tulsa, OK] B: 8/17/1969, Tulsa, OK *Drafted:* 1992 Round 4 Phi
1992 Phi: 5 G; KR 1-11 11.0.

REGGIE BROOKS Brooks, Reginald Arthur 5′8″, 211 **RB**
Col: Notre Dame *HS:* Booker T. Washington [Tulsa, OK] B: 1/19/1971, Tulsa, OK *Drafted:* 1993 Round 2 Was
1993 Was: KR 1-12 12.0. **Total:** KR 1-12 12.0.

Year Team	G	Rushing Att	Yds	Avg	TD	Receiving Rec	Yds	Avg	TD	Fum
1993 Was	16	223	1063	4.8	3	21	186	8.9	0	4
1994 Was	13	100	297	3.0	2	13	68	5.2	0	3
1995 Was	1	2	-2	-1.0	0	0	0	—	0	0
1996 TB	11	112	368	3.3	2	3	13	4.3	0	1
NFL Total	41	437	1726	3.9	7	37	267	7.2	0	8

BOB BROOKS Brooks, Robert Arthur 6′0″, 215 **FB**
Col: Ohio U. *HS:* George Rogers Clark [Winchester, KY] B: 5/3/1938
Drafted: 1961 Round 21 NYT
1961 NYT: 14 G; Rush 15-55 3.7; KR 8-111 13.9; 1 Fum.

ROBERT BROOKS Brooks, Robert Darren 6′0″, 177 **WR**
(Shoo-in) *Col:* South Carolina *HS:* Greenwood [SC] B: 6/23/1970, Greenwood, SC *Drafted:* 1992 Round 3 GB
1992 GB: Rush 2-14 7.0. **1993** GB: Rush 3-17 5.7. **1994** GB: Rush 1-0. **1995** GB: Rush 4-21 5.3. **1996** GB: Rush 4-2 0.5. **1997** GB: Rush 2-19 9.5. **1998** GB: Rush 1-2 2.0. **Total:** Rush 17-75 4.4.

Year Team	G	Receiving Rec	Yds	Avg	TD	Punt Returns Ret	Yds	Avg	TD
1992 GB	16	12	126	10.5	1	11	102	9.3	0
1993 GB	14	20	180	9.0	0	16	135	8.4	0
1994 GB	16	58	648	11.2	4	40	352	8.8	1
1995 GB	16	102	1497	14.7	13	0	0	—	0
1996 GB	7	23	344	15.0	4	0	0	—	0
1997 GB	15	60	1010	16.8	7	0	0	—	0
1998 GB	12	31	420	13.5	3	0	0	—	0
NFL Total	96	306	4225	13.8	32	67	589	8.8	1

Year Team	Kickoff Returns Ret	Yds	Avg	TD	Fum	Tot TD
1992 GB	18	338	18.8	0	0	1
1993 GB	23	611	**26.6**	**1**	1	1
1994 GB	9	260	28.9	1	4	6
1995 GB	1	28	28.0	0	0	13
1996 GB	0	0	—	0	0	4
1997 GB	0	0	—	0	0	7
1998 GB	0	0	—	0	0	3
NFL Total	51	1237	24.3	2	5	35

STEVE BROOKS Brooks, Steven Edward 6′5″, 245 **TE**
Col: Occidental *HS:* Buena [Ventura, CA] B: 6/2/1971, Detroit, MI
1996 Det: 1 G.

CHET BROOKS Brooks, Terrance Donnell 5′11″, 191 **DB**
Col: Texas A&M *HS:* David W. Carter [Dallas, TX] B: 1/1/1966, Midland, TX *Drafted:* 1988 Round 11 SF
1988 SF: 10 G. **1989** SF: 15 G; Int 3-31; 1 Sac. **1990** SF: 8 G. **Total:** 33 G; Int 3-31; 1 Sac.

BUD BROOKS Brooks, William 6′0″, 210 **OG**
Col: Arkansas B: 9/6/1930 *Drafted:* 1955 Round 5 Det
1955 Det: 1 G.

BUCKY BROOKS Brooks, William Eldridge Jr. 6′0″, 192 **DB**
Col: North Carolina *HS:* Millbrook [Raleigh, NC] B: 1/22/1971, Raleigh, NC *Drafted:* 1994 Round 2 Buf
1998 KC-Oak: PR 1-0. Oak: PR 1-0. **Total:** PR 1-0.

Year Team	G	Kickoff Returns Ret	Yds	Avg	TD	Fum
1994 Buf	3	9	162	18.0	0	1
1996 GB-Jac	8	17	412	24.2	0	0
1996 GB	2	0	0	—	0	0
1996 Jac	6	17	412	24.2	0	0
1997 Jac-GB-KC	9	0	0	—	0	0
1997 Jac	3	0	0	—	0	0
1997 GB	3	0	0	—	0	0
1997 KC	3	0	0	—	0	0
1998 KC-Oak	12	0	0	—	0	1
1998 KC	6	0	0	—	0	0
1998 Oak	6	0	0	—	0	1
NFL Total	32	26	574	22.1	0	2

BILL BROOKS Brooks, William Jr. 6′0″, 192 **WR**
Col: Boston U. *HS:* North [Framingham, MA] B: 4/6/1964, Boston, MA *Drafted:* 1986 Round 4 Ind
1986 Ind: Rush 4-5 1.3; KR 8-143 17.9. **1987** Ind: Rush 2-(-2) -1.0. **1988** Ind: Rush 5-62 12.4. **1989** Ind: Rush 2-(-3) -1.5. **1992** Ind: Rush 2-14 7.0. **1993** Buf: Rush 3-30 10.0. **1995** Buf: Rush 3-7 2.3. **Total:** Rush 21-113 5.4; KR 8-143 17.9.

Year Team	G	Receiving Rec	Yds	Avg	TD	Punt Returns Ret	Yds	Avg	TD	Fum
1986 Ind	16	65	1131	17.4	8	18	141	7.8	0	2
1987 Ind	12	51	722	14.2	3	22	136	6.2	0	3
1988 Ind	16	54	867	16.1	3	3	15	5.0	0	1
1989 Ind	16	63	919	14.6	4	0	0	—	0	1
1990 Ind	16	62	823	13.3	5	0	0	—	0	0
1991 Ind	16	72	888	12.3	4	0	0	—	0	0
1992 Ind	14	44	468	10.6	1	0	0	—	0	0
1993 Buf	16	60	714	11.9	5	1	3	3.0	0	0
1994 Buf	16	42	482	11.5	2	0	0	—	0	1
1995 Buf	15	53	763	14.4	11	6	35	5.8	0	0
1996 Was	16	17	224	13.2	0	0	0	—	0	0
NFL Total	169	583	8001	13.7	46	50	330	6.6	0	8

BILLY BROOKS Brooks, William McKinley III 6′3″, 204 **WR**
Col: Oklahoma *HS:* Lyndon B. Johnson [Austin, TX] B: 8/20/1953, Houston, TX *Drafted:* 1976 Round 1 Cin
1976 Cin: Rush 1-(-13) -13.0. **1977** Cin: Rush 2-(-4) -2.0. **Total:** Rush 3-(-17) -5.7.

Year Team	G	Receiving Rec	Yds	Avg	TD	Fum
1976 Cin	12	16	191	11.9	0	2
1977 Cin	14	39	772	19.8	4	3
1978 Cin	15	30	506	16.9	2	0
1979 Cin	4	8	214	26.8	1	0
1981 SD-Hou	10	3	37	12.3	0	0
1981 SD	7	1	21	21.0	0	0
1981 Hou	3	2	16	8.0	0	0
NFL Total	55	96	1720	17.9	7	5

TOM BROOKSHIER Brookshier, Thomas Jefferson 6′0″, 196 **DB**
(Brookie) *Col:* Colorado *HS:* Roswell [NM] B: 12/16/1931, Roswell, NM *Drafted:* 1953 Round 10 Phi

Year Team	G	Interceptions Int	Yds	TD	Fum
1953 Phi	11	8	41	0	1
1956 Phi	11	1	31	0	0
1957 Phi	12	4	74	0	0
1958 Phi	11	1	0	0	1
1959 Phi	12	3	13	0	0
1960 Phi	12	1	14	0	0
1961 Phi	7	2	20	0	0
NFL Total	76	20	193	0	2

JAY BROPHY Brophy, James Jay 6′3″, 233 **LB**
Col: Miami (Fla.) *HS:* John R. Buchtel [Akron, OH] B: 7/27/1960, Akron, OH *Drafted:* 1984 Round 2 Mia
1984 Mia: 11 G. **1985** Mia: 16 G; Int 1-41; 1 Sac. **1986** Mia: 4 G. **1987** NYJ: 3 G; 1 Sac. **Total:** 34 G; Int 1-41; 2 Sac.

AL BROSKY Brosky, Alfred Edward 5′11″, 175 **DB**
Col: Illinois *HS:* Harrison [Chicago, IL] B: 6/9/1930, Chicago, IL
Drafted: 1951 Round 27 LARm
1954 ChiC: 9 G; Int 2-11.

MAL BROSS Bross, Matthew A 5′9″, 170 **BB-HB-TB-WB**
Col: Gonzaga B: 12/7/1903 D: 2/8/1989, Seattle, WA
1927 GB: 2 G.

BERN BROSTEK Brostek, Bern Orion 6′3″, 300 **C-OG**
Col: Washington *HS:* Iolani [Honolulu, HI] B: 9/11/1966, Honolulu, HI
Drafted: 1990 Round 1 LARm
1990 LARm: 16 G. **1991** LARm: 14 G. **1992** LARm: 16 G. **1993** LARm: 16 G; 1 Fum. **1994** LARm: 10 G. **1995** StL: 16 G. **1996** StL: 16 G. **1997** StL: 1 G. **Total:** 105 G; 1 Fum.

BOB BROTZKI Brotzki, Robert John 6′5″, 281 **OT**
Col: Syracuse *HS:* St. Mary's Central Catholic [Sandusky, OH]
B: 12/24/1962, Sandusky, OH *Drafted:* 1986 Round 9 Ind
1986 Ind: 2 G. **1987** Ind: 11 G. **1988** Ind-Dal: 5 G. Ind: 1 G. Dal: 4 G. **Total:** 18 G.

LUTHER BROUGHTON Broughton, Luther Rashard Jr. 6′2″, 248 **TE**
Col: Furman *HS:* Cainhoy [Huger, SC] B: 11/30/1974, Charleston, SC
Drafted: 1997 Round 5 Phi
1998 Car: 16 G; Rec 6-142 23.7 1 TD; 6 Pt; 1 Fum.

WALTER BROUGHTON Broughton, Walter Craig 5′10″, 180 **WR**
Col: Jacksonville State *HS:* T.R. Miller [Brewton, AL] B: 10/20/1962, Brewton, AL
1986 Buf: 8 G; Rush 1-(-6) -6.0; Rec 3-71 23.7; PR 12-53 4.4; KR 11-243 22.1; 5 Fum. **1987** Buf: 9 G; Rec 5-90 18.0 1 TD; 6 Pt. **1988** Buf: 1 G. **Total:** 18 G; Rush 1-(-6) -6.0; Rec 8-161 20.1 1 TD; PR 12-53 4.4; KR 11-243 22.1; 6 Pt; 5 Fum.

WILLIE BROUGHTON Broughton, Willie Lee 6′5″, 280 **DE-DT**
Col: Miami (Fla.) *HS:* Fort Pierce Central [FL] B: 9/9/1964, Fort Pierce, FL *Drafted:* 1985 Round 4 Ind
1985 Ind: 15 G; 1 Sac. **1986** Ind: 15 G; 1 Sac. **1989** Dal: 16 G; 3 Sac. **1990** Dal: 4 G. **1992** LARd: 16 G; 1 Sac. **1993** LARd: 15 G; 1 Sac. **1995** NO: 16 G; 2 Sac. **1996** NO: 14 G; 2 Sac. **Total:** 111 G; 11 Sac.

FRED BROUSSARD Broussard, Frederick E 6′3″, 235 **C**
Col: Texas A&M; Northwestern State-Louisiana *HS:* De Quincy [LA]
B: 4/29/1933 *Drafted:* 1955 Round 4 Pit
1955 Pit-NYG: 7 G. Pit: 6 G. NYG: 1 G. **1960** Den: 1 G. **Total:** 8 G.

STEVE BROUSSARD Broussard, John Steven 6′0″, 200 **P**
Col: Marion Mil. Inst. AL (J.C.); Auburn; Southern Mississippi *HS:* Notre Dame [Biloxi, MS] B: 7/19/1947, McComb, MS
1975 GB: 4 G; Punt 29-922 31.8.

STEVE BROUSSARD Broussard, Steven Nelson 5′7″, 201 **RB-WR**
Col: Washington State *HS:* Manual Arts [Los Angeles, CA]
B: 2/22/1967, Los Angeles, CA *Drafted:* 1990 Round 1 Atl
1994 Cin: Pass 1-0; Scor 1 2XP. **Total:** Pass 1-0; Scor 1 2XP.

		Rushing				Receiving			
Year Team	G	Att	Yds	Avg	TD	Rec	Yds	Avg	TD
1990 Atl	13	126	454	3.6	4	24	160	6.7	0
1991 Atl	14	99	449	4.5	4	12	120	10.0	1
1992 Atl	15	84	363	4.3	1	11	96	8.7	1
1993 Atl	8	39	206	5.3	1	1	4	4.0	0
1994 Cin	13	94	403	4.3	2	34	218	6.4	0
1995 Sea	15	46	222	4.8	1	10	94	9.4	0
1996 Sea	12	15	106	7.1	1	6	26	4.3	0
1997 Sea	16	70	418	6.0	5	24	143	6.0	1
1998 Sea	15	5	4	0.8	0	4	21	5.3	0
NFL Total	121	578	2625	4.5	19	126	882	7.0	3

	Kickoff Returns					Tot
Year Team	Ret	Yds	Avg	TD	Fum	TD
1990 Atl	3	45	15.0	0	6	4
1991 Atl	0	0	—	0	1	5
1992 Atl	0	0	—	0	3	2
1993 Atl	0	0	—	0	0	1
1994 Cin	7	115	16.4	0	5	2
1995 Sea	43	1064	24.7	0	4	1
1996 Sea	43	979	22.8	0	2	1
1997 Sea	50	1076	21.5	0	0	6
1998 Sea	29	781	26.9	1	1	1
NFL Total	175	4060	23.2	1	22	23

ANGIE BROVELLI Brovelli, Angelo Augustine 6′0″, 193 **DB-TB-FB-HB**
(Dark Angel) *Col:* St. Mary's (Cal.) B: 8/21/1910, Porterville, CA
D: 8/5/1995, Acampo, CA
1933 Pit: Pass 25-8 32.0%, 114 4.56 3 Int; Rec 6-137 22.8; Scor 13, 1 XK. **Total:** Pass 25-8 32.0%, 114 4.56 3 Int; Rec 6-137 22.8.

		Rushing			
Year Team	G	Att	Yds	Avg	TD
1933 Pit	8	60	236	3.9	2
1934 Pit	5	37	112	3.0	1
NFL Total	13	97	348	3.6	3

AARON BROWN Brown, Aaron Cedric 6′2″, 235 **LB**
Col: Ohio State *HS:* Western Reserve Acad. [Hudson, OH]
B: 1/13/1956, Warren, OH *Drafted:* 1978 Round 10 TB
1978 TB: 16 G; Int 1-10. **1979** TB: 12 G. **1980** TB: 16 G. **1985** Phi: 7 G.
1986 Atl: 16 G. **1987** Atl: 6 G. **Total:** 73 G; Int 1-10.

AARON BROWN Brown, Aaron Lewis Jr. 6′5″, 255 **DE**
Col: Minnesota *HS:* Lincoln [Port Arthur, TX] B: 11/16/1943, Port Arthur, TX D: 11/15/1997, Houston, TX *Drafted:* 1966 Round 1 KC
1966 KC: 14 G; PR 1-43 43.0; KR 1-6 6.0. **1968** KC: 14 G. **1969** KC: 14 G.
1970 KC: 11 G. **1971** KC: 13 G; Int 1-68 1 TD; 6 Pt. **1972** KC: 12 G.
1973 GB: 8 G; KR 3-26 8.7. **1974** GB: 2 G. **Total:** 88 G; PR 1-43 43.0; KR 4-32 8.0; Int 1-68 1 TD; 6 Pt.

ALLEN BROWN Brown, Allen 6′5″, 235 **TE**
(Red) *Col:* Mississippi *HS:* Natchez [MS] B: 3/2/1943, Natchez, MS
Drafted: 1965 Round 3 GB
1966 GB: 5 G. **1967** GB: 14 G; Rec 3-43 14.3; KR 1-13 13.0. **Total:** 19 G; Rec 3-43 14.3; KR 1-13 13.0.

ANDRE BROWN Brown, Andre Lamont 6′3″, 210 **WR**
Col: Miami (Fla.) *HS:* Fenger [Chicago, IL] B: 8/21/1966, Chicago, IL
1989 Mia: KR 2-9 4.5. **Total:** KR 2-9 4.5.

		Receiving				
Year Team	G	Rec	Yds	Avg	TD	Fum
1989 Mia	16	24	410	17.1	5	1
1990 Mia	6	3	49	16.3	0	0
NFL Total	22	27	459	17.0	5	1

TONY BROWN Brown, Anthony Brewster 6′5″, 285 **OT**
Col: Pittsburgh *HS:* Stamford Catholic [CT] B: 7/11/1964, Stamford, CT
1987 Buf: 2 G.

A.B. BROWN Brown, Anthony James 5′9″, 210 **RB**
Col: Pittsburgh; West Virginia *HS:* Salem [NJ] B: 12/4/1965, Salem, NJ
Drafted: 1989 Round 8 NYJ
1989 NYJ: Rec 4-10 2.5. **1990** NYJ: KR 1-63 63.0. **1991** NYJ: KR 10-100 10.0. **1992** NYJ: Rec 4-30 7.5. **Total:** Rec 8-40 5.0; KR 11-163 14.8.

		Rushing				
Year Team	G	Att	Yds	Avg	TD	Fum
1989 NYJ	16	12	63	5.3	0	0
1990 NYJ	1	1	8	8.0	0	0
1991 NYJ	9	3	4	1.3	1	2
1992 NYJ	7	24	42	1.8	0	1
NFL Total	33	40	117	2.9	1	3

TONY BROWN Brown, Anthony Lamar 5′9″, 183 **DB**
Col: Fresno State *HS:* John F. Kennedy [Los Angeles, CA]
B: 5/15/1970, Bangkok, Thailand *Drafted:* 1992 Round 5 Hou
1992 Hou: 12 G. **1993** Hou: 16 G. **1994** Sea: 13 G. **1995** Sea: 16 G.
Total: 57 G.

ANTHONY BROWN Brown, Anthony Quantrell 6′5″, 315 **OT-OG**
Col: Mesa CC AZ; Utah *HS:* American [Wurzburg, Germany]
B: 11/6/1972, Okinawa
1995 Cin: 7 G. **1996** Cin: 7 G. **1997** Cin: 6 G. **1998** Cin: 16 G. **Total:** 36 G.

ARNOLD BROWN Brown, Arnold Lee 5′11″, 185 **DB**
Col: North Carolina Central *HS:* Emsley A. Laney [Wilmington, NC]
B: 8/27/1962, Wilmington, NC *Drafted:* 1985 Round 5 Sea
1985 Det: 7 G. **1987** Sea: 2 G. **Total:** 9 G.

BOOKER BROWN Brown, Booker Taylor 6′2″, 257 **OT-OG**
Col: Santa Barbara City Coll. CA (J.C.); USC *HS:* Santa Barbara [CA]
B: 9/25/1952, Desson, MS *Drafted:* 1974 Round 6 Hou
1975 SD: 11 G. **1977** SD: 6 G. **Total:** 17 G.

BOYD BROWN Brown, Boyd 6′4″, 222 **TE**
Col: Alcorn State *HS:* Wilkinson Co. [Woodville, MS] B: 5/24/1952, Crosby, MS *Drafted:* 1974 Round 17 Den
1974 Den: 14 G; KR 3-56 18.7. **1975** Den: 12 G; Rec 1-14 14.0.
1976 Den: 14 G; KR 3-41 13.7. **1977** NYG: 6 G. **Total:** 46 G; Rec 1-14 14.0; KR 6-97 16.2.

STAN BROWN Brown, Byron Stanley 5′11″, 185 **WR**
Col: Purdue *HS:* Salesian [Richmond, CA] B: 8/4/1949, Martinez, CA
Drafted: 1971 Round 5 Cle
1971 Cle: 6 G; KR 7-157 22.4; 1 Fum.

CARLOS BROWN Brown, Carlos Allen 6′3″, 210 **QB**
Col: U. of Pacific *HS:* Riverdale [CA] B: 7/31/1952, Shreveport, LA
Drafted: 1975 Round 12 GB
1976 GB: Rush 12-49 4.1. **Total:** Rush 12-49 4.1.

		Passing								
Year Team	G	Att	Comp	Comp%	Yds	YPA	TD	Int	Rating	Fum
1975 GB	13	4	3	75.0	63	15.75	1	0	156.3	1
1976 GB	13	74	26	35.1	333	4.50	2	6	25.3	2
NFL Total	26	78	29	37.2	396	5.08	3	6	35.0	3

CEDRIC BROWN Brown, Cedric Wallace Jr. 6′1″, 199 **DB**
Col: Kent State *HS:* Linden-McKinley [Columbus, OH] B: 5/6/1954, Columbus, OH *Drafted:* 1976 Round 12 Oak
1978 TB: PR 2-9 4.5. **1980** TB: **1** Fum TD. **Total:** PR 2-9 4.5; 1 Fum TD.

		Interceptions				Tot
Year Team	G	Int	Yds	TD	Fum	TD
1976 TB	1	0	0	0	0	0
1977 TB	14	2	66	0	1	0
1978 TB	14	6	110	0	1	0
1979 TB	16	3	79	0	0	0
1980 TB	13	1	0	0	0	1
1981 TB	16	9	215	2	1	2
1982 TB	9	3	31	0	0	0
1983 TB	8	4	78	0	0	0
1984 TB	9	1	14	0	0	0
NFL Total	100	29	593	2	3	3

CEDRICK BROWN Brown, Cedrick David 5′10″, 178 **DB**
Col: Washington State *HS:* Compton [CA] B: 9/6/1964, Compton, CA
1987 Phi: 12 G; PR 1-(-1) -1.0; KR 1-13 13.0; Int 1-9; 1 Sac.

CHAD BROWN Brown, Chadrick Chico 6′7″, 265 **DE**
Col: Mississippi *HS:* Thomasville [GA] B: 7/9/1971, Thomasville, GA
Drafted: 1993 Round 8 Pho
1993 Pho: 5 G. **1994** Ariz: 8 G. **1995** Ariz: 5 G; 0.5 Sac. **Total:** 18 G; 0.5 Sac.

CHAD BROWN Brown, Chadwick Everett 6′2″, 240 **LB**
Col: Colorado *HS:* John Muir [Pasadena, CA] B: 7/12/1970, Pasadena, CA *Drafted:* 1993 Round 2 Pit
1993 Pit: 16 G; 3 Sac. **1994** Pit: 16 G; Int 1-9; 8.5 Sac. **1995** Pit: 10 G; 5.5 Sac. **1996** Pit: 14 G; Int 2-20; 1 Fum; 13 Sac. **1997** Sea: 15 G;

2 Fum TD; 12 Pt; 6.5 Sac. **1998** Sea: 16 G; Int 1-11; 7.5 Sac. **Total:** 87 G; Int 4-40; 2 Fum TD; 12 Pt; 1 Fum; 44 Sac.

CHARLIE BROWN Brown, Charles 5′10″, 182 **WR**
Col: South Carolina State *HS:* St. John's [John's Island, SC]
B: 10/29/1958, Charleston, SC *Drafted:* 1981 Round 8 Was
1983 Was: Rush 4-53 13.3. **Total:** Rush 4-53 13.3.

		Receiving				
Year Team	**G**	**Rec**	**Yds**	**Avg**	**TD**	**Fum**
1982 Was	9	32	690	**21.6**	8	1
1983 Was	15	78	1225	15.7	8	0
1984 Was	9	18	200	11.1	3	0
1985 Atl	13	24	412	17.2	2	0
1986 Atl	16	63	918	14.6	4	1
1987 Atl	6	5	103	20.6	0	0
NFL Total	68	220	3548	16.1	25	2

ED BROWN Brown, Charles Edward 6′2″, 200 **QB-DB**
Col: Hartnell Coll. CA (J.C.); San Francisco *HS:* San Luis Obispo [CA]
B: 10/26/1928, San Luis Obispo, CA *Drafted:* 1952 Round 6 ChiB
1954 ChiB: Int 1-18. **1956** ChiB: **1** Fum TD. **1960** ChiB: Rec 1-(-6) -6.0.
1961 ChiB: Scor 4, 1-2 50.0% FG, 1-1 100.0% XK. **Total:** Rec 1-(-6) -6.0; Int 1-18; Scor 94, 1-2 50.0% FG, 1-1 100.0% XK; 1 Fum TD.

		Passing							
Year Team	**G**	**Att**	**Comp**	**Comp%**	**Yds**	**YPA**	**TD**	**Int**	**Rating**
1954 ChiB	12	17	10	58.8	283	16.65	3	1	118.3
1955 ChiB	12	164	85	51.8	1307	7.97	9	10	71.4
1956 ChiB	12	168	96	**57.1**	1667	**9.92**	11	12	83.1
1957 ChiB	12	185	84	45.4	1321	7.14	6	16	44.4
1958 ChiB	12	218	102	46.8	1418	6.50	10	17	51.0
1959 ChiB	12	247	125	50.6	1881	7.62	13	10	76.7
1960 ChiB	12	149	59	39.6	1079	7.24	7	11	50.2
1961 ChiB	14	98	46	46.9	742	7.57	4	11	46.8
1962 Pit	14	84	43	51.2	726	8.64	5	6	70.8
1963 Pit	14	362	168	46.4	2982	8.24	21	20	71.4
1964 Pit	14	272	121	44.5	1990	7.32	12	19	55.2
1965 Pit-Bal	14	23	10	43.5	204	8.87	1	5	50.2
1965 Pit	13	18	7	38.9	123	6.83	0	5	23.4
1965 Bal	1	5	3	60.0	81	16.20	1	0	143.8
NFL Total	154	1987	949	47.8	15600	7.85	102	138	62.8

	Rushing				Punting				Tot
Year Team	**Att**	**Yds**	**Avg**	**TD**	**Punts**	**Yds**	**Avg**	**Fum**	**TD**
1954 ChiB	9	36	4.0	0	18	684	38.0	0	0
1955 ChiB	43	203	4.7	2	44	1766	40.1	4	2
1956 ChiB	40	164	4.1	1	42	1644	39.1	3	2
1957 ChiB	31	129	4.2	1	34	1365	40.1	5	1
1958 ChiB	32	94	2.9	3	27	1140	42.2	4	3
1959 ChiB	33	108	3.3	1	**64**	2634	41.2	7	1
1960 ChiB	19	89	4.7	2	56	2231	39.8	2	2
1961 ChiB	13	18	1.4	0	58	2448	42.2	1	0
1962 Pit	2	-8	-4.0	0	60	2400	40.0	1	0
1963 Pit	15	20	1.3	2	57	2256	39.6	5	2
1964 Pit	26	110	4.2	2	31	1346	43.4	5	2
1965 Pit-Bal	2	-3	-1.5	0	2	80	40.0	3	0
1965 Pit	1	-1	-1.0	0	0	0	—	2	0
1965 Bal	1	-2	-2.0	0	2	80	40.0	1	0
NFL Total	265	960	3.6	14	493	19994	40.6	40	15

CHARLIE BROWN Brown, Charles Edward 6′2″, 220 **DB-HB**
Col: Syracuse *HS:* Washington [Massillon, OH] B: 9/13/1942, Heflin, AL *Drafted:* 1966 Round 2 ChiB
1966 ChiB: 14 G; KR 0-28. **1967** ChiB: 8 G; KR 2-34 17.0; Int 1-23.
1968 Buf: 8 G; Rush 3-39 13.0; KR 12-274 22.8; 1 Fum. **Total:** 30 G; Rush 3-39 13.0; KR 14-336 24.0; Int 1-23; 1 Fum.

CHARLIE BROWN Brown, Charles Edwin 6′4″, 245 **OT**
Col: Houston *HS:* Mount Vernon [TX] B: 8/1/1936
1962 Oak: 14 G.

CHUCK BROWN Brown, Charles Edwin Jr. 6′1″, 235 **C-OG**
Col: Houston *HS:* John Foster Dulles [Sugar Land, TX] B: 3/15/1957, Houston, TX
1979 StL: 4 G.

CHARLIE BROWN Brown, Charles Kelly 6′2″, 195 **WR**
Col: Merritt Coll. CA (J.C.); Northern Arizona *HS:* Castlemont [Oakland, CA] B: 10/13/1948, Oakland, CA *Drafted:* 1970 Round 14 Det
1970 Det: 14 G; Rec 2-38 19.0.

BUD BROWN Brown, Charles Lee 6′0″, 194 **DB**
Col: Southern Mississippi *HS:* Kemper Co. [DeKalb, MS]
B: 4/19/1961, DeKalb, MS *Drafted:* 1984 Round 11 Mia
1984 Mia: 16 G; Int 1-53. **1985** Mia: 16 G; Int 2-40. **1986** Mia: 16 G; Int 1-3; 1 Fum. **1987** Mia: 9 G; PR 2-8 4.0; Int 1-0; 1 Fum. **1988** Mia: 16 G. **Total:** 73 G; PR 2-8 4.0; Int 5-96; 2 Fum.

CHARLIE BROWN Brown, Charles Robert 5′10″, 195 **RB**
(Choo-Choo) *Col:* Missouri *HS:* Jefferson City [MO] B: 10/16/1945, Jefferson City, MO *Drafted:* 1967 Round 10 NO
1967 NO: 3 G; Rush 8-16 2.0 2 TD; Rec 3-23 7.7; PR 3-1 0.3; KR 5-103 20.6; 12 Pt. **1968** NO: 3 G; PR 8-60 7.5 1 TD; KR 8-137 17.1; 6 Pt.
Total: 6 G; Rush 8-16 2.0 2 TD; Rec 3-23 7.7; PR 11-61 5.5 1 TD; KR 13-240 18.5; Tot TD 3; 18 Pt.

CHRIS BROWN Brown, Christopher 6′1″, 295 **OT**
Col: New York Tech; Lamar *HS:* Canarsie [Brooklyn, NY] B: 7/16/1963
1987 NYJ: 1 G.

CHRIS BROWN Brown, Christopher Duke 6′0″, 200 **DB**
Col: Notre Dame *HS:* Owensboro Catholic [KY] B: 4/11/1962, Owensboro, KY *Drafted:* 1984 Round 6 Pit
1984 Pit: 16 G; KR 1-11 11.0; Int 1-31. **1985** Pit: 6 G. **Total:** 22 G; KR 1-11 11.0; Int 1-31.

CLAY BROWN Brown, Clayton Lee 6′3″, 223 **TE**
Col: Brigham Young *HS:* San Gabriel [CA] B: 9/20/1958, Los Angeles, CA *Drafted:* 1981 Round 2 Den
1982 Atl: 1 G. **1983** Den: 3 G. **Total:** 4 G.

SONNY BROWN Brown, Clifton D 6′2″, 200 **DB**
Col: Oklahoma *HS:* Alice [TX] B: 11/12/1963, Tinker AFB, OK
1987 Hou: 2 G.

CORNELL BROWN Brown, Cornell Desmond 6′0″, 240 **LB**
Col: Virginia Tech *HS:* E.C. Glass [Lynchburg, VA] B: 3/15/1975, Englewood, NJ *Drafted:* 1997 Round 6 Bal
1997 Bal: 16 G; Int 1-21; 0.5 Sac. **1998** Bal: 16 G. **Total:** 32 G; Int 1-21; 0.5 Sac.

CORWIN BROWN Brown, Corwin Alan 6′1″, 200 **DB**
Col: Michigan *HS:* Percy L. Julian [Chicago, IL] B: 4/25/1970, Chicago, IL *Drafted:* 1993 Round 4 NE
1993 NE: 15 G. **1994** NE: 16 G. **1995** NE: 16 G. **1996** NE: 14 G; **1** Fum TD; 6 Pt. **1997** NYJ: 16 G; Rec 1-26 26.0. **1998** NYJ: 16 G; Int 1-0.
Total: 93 G; Rec 1-26 26.0; Int 1-0; 1 Fum TD; 6 Pt.

CURTIS BROWN Brown, Curtis Jerome 5′10″, 203 **RB**
Col: Fort Scott CC KS; Missouri *HS:* St. Charles [MO] B: 12/7/1954, St. Louis, MO *Drafted:* 1977 Round 3 Buf
1978 Buf: PR 1-0. **Total:** PR 1-0.

		Rushing				Receiving			
Year Team	**G**	**Att**	**Yds**	**Avg**	**TD**	**Rec**	**Yds**	**Avg**	**TD**
1977 Buf	7	8	34	4.3	0	5	20	4.0	1
1978 Buf	15	128	591	4.6	4	18	130	7.2	0
1979 Buf	15	172	574	3.3	1	39	401	10.3	3
1980 Buf	16	153	559	3.7	3	27	137	5.1	0
1981 Buf	14	62	226	3.6	0	7	46	6.6	1
1982 Buf	9	41	187	4.6	0	6	38	6.3	0
1983 Hou	2	3	0	0.0	1	0	0	—	0
NFL Total	78	567	2171	3.8	9	102	772	7.6	5

	Kickoff Returns					Tot
Year Team	**Ret**	**Yds**	**Avg**	**TD**	**Fum**	**TD**
1977 Buf	3	66	22.0	0	0	1
1978 Buf	17	428	25.2	**1**	7	5
1979 Buf	3	42	14.0	0	10	4
1980 Buf	10	181	18.1	0	4	3
1981 Buf	7	140	20.0	0	4	1
1982 Buf	1	17	17.0	0	1	0
1983 Hou	0	0	—	0	0	1
NFL Total	41	874	21.3	1	26	15

CYRON BROWN Brown, Cyron DeAndre 6′5″, 265 **DE**
Col: Western Illinois *HS:* Albert G. Lane Tech [Chicago, IL]
B: 6/28/1975, Chicago, IL
1998 Den: 4 G.

DAN BROWN Brown, Daniel Joseph 6′1″, 200 **DE**
Col: Villanova *HS:* West Catholic [Philadelphia, PA] B: 8/26/1925, Philadelphia, PA D: 6/17/1995, Havertown, PA *Drafted:* 1950 Round 11 Was
1950 Was: 11 G; KR 1-6 6.0; 1 Fum.

DAVE BROWN Brown, David Alexander 5′11″, 190 **HB**
Col: Alabama *HS:* Ensley [Birmingham, AL] B: 2/14/1920, Birmingham, AL *Drafted:* 1943 Round 23 NYG
1943 NYG: Rec 5-29 5.8; PR 7-106 15.1; Int 6-64. **1946** NYG: PR 1-0.
1947 NYG: Rec 1-5 5.0; PR 4-22 5.5; KR 1-30 30.0. **Total:** Rec 6-34 5.7; PR 12-128 10.7; KR 1-30 30.0; Int 6-64.

		Rushing				
Year Team	**G**	**Att**	**Yds**	**Avg**	**TD**	**Fum**
1943 NYG	10	32	131	4.1	0	0
1946 NYG	7	9	5	0.6	0	1
1947 NYG	7	6	5	0.8	0	2
NFL Total	24	47	141	3.0	0	3

DAVE BROWN Brown, David Dwayne 6'2", 215 **LB**
Col: Miami (Ohio) *HS:* John H. Patterson [Dayton, OH] B: 1/17/1964, Dayton, OH
1987 Phi: 1 G.

DAVE BROWN Brown, David Michael 6'5", 220 **QB**
Col: Duke *HS:* Westfield [NJ] B: 2/25/1970, Summit, NJ
Drafted: 1992 Supplemental Round 1 NYG
1994 NYG: Punt 2-57 28.5. **1995** NYG: Punt 1-15 15.0. **Total:** Punt 3-72 24.0.

		Passing							
Year Team	G	Att	Comp	Comp%	Yds	YPA	TD	Int	Rating
1992 NYG	2	7	4	57.1	21	3.00	0	0	62.2
1993 NYG	1	0	0	—	0	—	0	0	—
1994 NYG	15	350	201	57.4	2536	7.25	12	16	72.5
1995 NYG	16	456	254	55.7	2814	6.17	11	10	73.1
1996 NYG	16	398	214	53.8	2412	6.06	12	20	61.3
1997 NYG	7	180	93	51.7	1023	5.68	5	3	71.1
1998 Ariz	1	5	2	40.0	31	6.20	0	0	61.3
NFL Total	58	1396	768	55.0	8837	6.33	40	49	69.2

	Rushing				
Year Team	Att	Yds	Avg	TD	Fum
1992 NYG	2	-1	-0.5	0	0
1993 NYG	3	-4	-1.3	0	0
1994 NYG	60	196	3.3	2	11
1995 NYG	45	228	5.1	4	10
1996 NYG	50	170	3.4	0	9
1997 NYG	17	29	1.7	1	1
1998 Ariz	1	2	2.0	0	0
NFL Total	178	620	3.5	7	31

DAVE BROWN Brown, David Steven 6'1", 190 **DB**
Col: Michigan *HS:* Garfield [Akron, OH] B: 1/16/1953, Akron, OH
Drafted: 1975 Round 1 Pit
1975 Pit: KR 6-126 21.0. **1976** Sea: Scor **1** Saf. **Total:** KR 6-126 21.0; Scor 1 Saf.

		Punt Returns				Interceptions			
Year Team	G	Ret	Yds	Avg	TD	Int	Yds	TD	Fum
1975 Pit	13	22	217	9.9	0	0	0	0	1
1976 Sea	14	11	74	6.7	0	4	70	0	0
1977 Sea	14	0	0	—	0	4	68	**1**	0
1978 Sea	16	0	0	—	0	3	44	0	0
1979 Sea	16	0	0	—	0	5	46	0	0
1980 Sea	16	0	0	—	0	6	32	0	0
1981 Sea	10	0	0	—	0	2	2	0	0
1982 Sea	9	0	0	—	0	1	3	0	0
1983 Sea	16	0	0	—	0	6	83	0	1
1984 Sea	16	0	0	—	0	8	179	**2**	0
1985 Sea	16	0	0	—	0	6	58	**1**	0
1986 Sea	16	0	0	—	0	5	58	1	0
1987 GB	12	0	0	—	0	3	16	0	0
1988 GB	16	0	0	—	0	3	27	0	0
1989 GB	16	0	0	—	0	6	12	0	0
NFL Total	216	33	291	8.8	0	62	698	5	2

DEAN BROWN Brown, Dean Venor 5'10", 175 **DB**
Col: Fort Valley State *HS:* Henry Co. Training School [GA]
B: 11/6/1945, McDonough, GA
1969 Cle: 5 G; KR 2-45 22.5. **1970** Mia: 5 G; KR 1-0; Int 1-32. **Total:** 10 G; KR 3-45 15.0; Int 1-32.

DEAUNTAE BROWN Brown, DeAuntae 5'11", 195 **DB**
Col: Central State (Ohio) *HS:* Osborne [Detroit, MI] B: 4/28/1974, Detroit, MI *Drafted:* 1997 Round 7 Phi
1997 Phi: 1 G.

DENNIS BROWN Brown, Dennis Trammel 6'4", 290 **DE**
Col: Washington *HS:* Jordan [Long Beach, CA] B: 11/6/1967, Los Angeles, CA *Drafted:* 1990 Round 2 SF
1990 SF: 15 G; 6 Sac. **1991** SF: 16 G; 3 Sac. **1992** SF: 16 G; Int 1-0; 3.5 Sac. **1993** SF: 16 G; 5.5 Sac. **1994** SF: 16 G; Int 1-0; 3 Sac. **1995** SF: 16 G; 1.5 Sac. **1996** SF: 15 G; 2 Sac. **Total:** 110 G; Int 2-0; 24.5 Sac.

DEREK BROWN Brown, Derek Darnell 5'9", 201 **RB**
Col: Nebraska *HS:* Servite [Anaheim, CA] B: 4/15/1971, Banning, CA
Drafted: 1993 Round 4 NO
1993 NO: KR 3-58 19.3. **1994** NO: KR 1-3 3.0. **1996** NO: KR 1-10 10.0. **Total:** KR 5-71 14.2.

		Rushing				Receiving					Tot
Year Team	G	Att	Yds	Avg	TD	Rec	Yds	Avg	TD	Fum	TD
1993 NO	13	180	705	3.9	2	21	170	8.1	1	1	3
1994 NO	16	146	489	3.3	3	44	428	9.7	1	4	4
1995 NO	16	49	159	3.2	1	35	266	7.6	1	0	2
1996 NO	11	13	30	2.3	0	8	54	6.8	0	0	0
NFL Total	56	388	1383	3.6	6	108	918	8.5	3	5	9

DEREK BROWN Brown, Derek Vernon 6'6", 259 **TE**
Col: Notre Dame *HS:* Merritt Island [FL] B: 3/31/1970, Fairfax, VA
Drafted: 1992 Round 1 NYG
1994 NYG: KR 1-1 1.0. **Total:** KR 1-1 1.0.

		Receiving			
Year Team	G	Rec	Yds	Avg	TD
1992 NYG	16	4	31	7.8	0
1993 NYG	16	7	56	8.0	0
1994 NYG	13	0	0	—	0
1996 Jac	16	17	141	8.3	0
1997 Jac	13	8	84	10.5	1
1998 Oak	16	7	89	12.7	0
NFL Total	90	43	401	9.3	1

DONALD BROWN Brown, Donald 5'11", 189 **DB**
(Turkey) *Col:* Oklahoma; Maryland *HS:* Annapolis [MD]
B: 11/28/1963, Annapolis, MD *Drafted:* 1986 Round 5 SD
1986 SD-Mia: 15 G; Int 1-23. SD: 13 G; Int 1-23. Mia: 2 G. **1987** NYG: 3 G; Int 1-4. **Total:** 18 G; Int 2-27.

DON BROWN Brown, Donald Albert 6'1", 205 **HB**
Col: Houston *HS:* Dayton [TX] B: 8/30/1937, Dayton, TX
Drafted: 1959 Round 2 LARm
1960 Hou: 3 G.

DON BROWN Brown, Donald Colby 6'6", 262 **OT**
Col: Santa Clara *HS:* Camden [San Jose, CA] B: 4/2/1959, San Jose, CA
1983 SD: 13 G.

DOUG BROWN Brown, Douglas Gordon 6'7", 290 **DT**
Col: Simon Fraser (Canada) *HS:* Port Moody Secondary School [Canada] B: 9/29/1974, Vancouver, Canada
1998 Was: 10 G.

DOUG BROWN Brown, Douglas Pat 6'4", 250 **DT**
Col: Fresno State *HS:* Woodrow Wilson [Long Beach, CA]
B: 5/31/1938, Long Beach, CA *Drafted:* 1960 Round 12 LARm
1962 LARm: 1 G. **1964** Oak: 12 G. **Total:** 13 G.

EDDIE BROWN Brown, Eddie Lee 6'0", 185 **WR**
Col: Navarro Coll. TX (J.C.); Miami (Fla.) *HS:* Miami Senior [FL]
B: 12/18/1962, Miami, FL *Drafted:* 1985 Round 1 Cin
1985 Cin: KR 1-6 6.0. **1988** Cin: PR 10-48 4.8. **Total:** PR 10-48 4.8; KR 1-6 6.0.

		Rushing				Receiving				
Year Team	G	Att	Yds	Avg	TD	Rec	Yds	Avg	TD	Fum
1985 Cin	16	14	129	9.2	0	53	942	17.8	8	2
1986 Cin	16	8	32	4.0	0	58	964	16.6	4	0
1987 Cin	12	1	0	0.0	0	44	608	13.8	3	3
1988 Cin	16	1	-5	-5.0	0	53	1273	**24.0**	9	1
1989 Cin	15	0	0	—	0	52	814	15.7	6	0
1990 Cin	14	0	0	—	0	44	706	16.0	9	0
1991 Cin	13	1	8	8.0	0	59	827	14.0	2	0
NFL Total	102	25	164	6.6	0	363	6134	16.9	41	6

ERIC BROWN Brown, Eric 5'11", 177 **DB**
Col: Savannah State *HS:* Savannah [GA] B: 4/12/1967
1989 Dal: 1 G.

ERIC BROWN Brown, Eric 6'2", 180 **WR**
Col: Tulsa *HS:* Mercy [St. Louis, MO] B: 9/7/1964
1987 KC: 2 G; Rec 5-69 13.8.

ERIC BROWN Brown, Eric Jon 6'0", 210 **DB**
Col: Blinn Coll. TX (J.C.); Mississippi State *HS:* Judson [Converse, TX]
B: 3/20/1975, San Antonio, TX *Drafted:* 1998 Round 2 Den
1998 Den: 11 G.

FRED BROWN Brown, Fred Richert 6'4", 240 **LB-TE**
Col: American River Coll. CA (J.C.); Miami (Fla.) *HS:* La Sierra [Carmichael, CA] B: 5/4/1943, Honolulu, HI *Drafted:* 1965 Round 3 LARm
1965 LARm: 14 G. **1967** Phi: 13 G; KR 1-17 17.0; Int 2-29. **1968** Phi: 7 G. **1969** Phi: 6 G; Rec 1-20 20.0. **Total:** 40 G; Rec 1-20 20.0; KR 1-17 17.0; Int 2-29.

FRED BROWN Brown, Frederick 5'11", 185 **HB**
Col: Georgia *HS:* Northside [Atlanta, GA] B: 12/22/1938, Atlanta, GA
1961 Buf: Rec 1-11 11.0; PR 2-14 7.0; KR 2-105 52.5 **1** TD. **1963** Buf: Rec 3-7 2.3; KR 2-40 20.0. **Total:** Rec 4-18 4.5; PR 2-14 7.0; KR 4-145 36.3 1 TD.

		Rushing					Tot
Year Team	G	Att	Yds	Avg	TD	Fum	TD
1961 Buf	5	53	192	3.6	1	1	2
1963 Buf	4	6	18	3.0	1	0	1
NFL Total	9	59	210	3.6	2	1	3

GARY BROWN Brown, Gary Lee 6′4″, 307 **OT**
Col: Nassau CC NY; Georgia Tech *HS:* Brentwood [NY] B: 6/25/1971, Amityville, NY *Drafted:* 1994 Round 5 Pit
1994 GB: 1 G. **1995** GB: 16 G. **1996** GB: 8 G. **Total:** 25 G.

GARY BROWN Brown, Gary Leroy 5′11″, 230 **RB**
Col: Penn State *HS:* Williamsport [PA] B: 7/1/1969, Williamsport, PA *Drafted:* 1991 Round 8 Hou
1991 Hou: KR 3-30 10.0. **1992** Hou: KR 1-15 15.0. **1993** Hou: KR 2-29 14.5. **Total:** KR 6-74 12.3.

		Rushing				Receiving					Tot
Year Team	**G**	**Att**	**Yds**	**Avg**	**TD**	**Rec**	**Yds**	**Avg**	**TD**	**Fum**	**TD**
1991 Hou	11	8	85	10.6	1	2	1	0.5	0	0	1
1992 Hou	16	19	87	4.6	1	1	5	5.0	0	0	1
1993 Hou	16	195	1002	5.1	6	21	240	11.4	2	4	8
1994 Hou	12	169	648	3.8	4	18	194	10.8	1	6	5
1995 Hou	10	86	293	3.4	0	6	16	2.7	0	2	0
1997 SD	15	253	945	3.7	4	21	137	6.5	0	2	4
1998 NYG	16	247	1063	4.3	5	13	36	2.8	0	1	5
NFL Total	96	977	4123	4.2	21	82	629	7.7	3	15	24

GEORGE BROWN Brown, George T 190 **T**
Col: No College B: 7/13/1894, Millport, OH D: 3/24/1973, Youngstown, OH
1923 Akr: 3 G.

GEORGE BROWN Brown, George William 6′2″, 222 **OG-DG**
Col: Texas Christian *HS:* North Side [Fort Worth, TX] B: 9/23/1923, Boyd, TX
AAFC **1949** NY-A: 8 G.

NFL **1950** NYY: 12 G.

GILBERT BROWN Brown, Gilbert Jesse 6′2″, 333 **NT-DT**
Col: Kansas *HS:* MacKenzie [Detroit, MI] B: 2/22/1971, Farmington, MI *Drafted:* 1993 Round 3 Min
1993 GB: 2 G. **1994** GB: 13 G; 3 Sac. **1995** GB: 13 G. **1996** GB: 16 G; 1 Sac. **1997** GB: 12 G; 3 Sac. **1998** GB: 16 G. **Total:** 72 G; 7 Sac.

GORDON BROWN Brown, Gordon S 5′11″, 220 **RB**
Col: Hutchinson CC KS; Tulsa *HS:* Denbigh [Newport News, VA] B: 3/19/1963, Philadelphia, PA
1987 Ind: 3 G; Rush 19-85 4.5 1 TD; 6 Pt; 1 Fum.

GREG BROWN Brown, Gregory Lee 6′5″, 254 **DE-DT**
Col: Kansas State; Eastern Illinois *HS:* Howard D. Woodson [Washington, DC] B: 1/5/1957, Washington, DC
1981 Phi: 16 G; 1 Fum TD; 6 Pt. **1982** Phi: 9 G; 1 Fum TD; 6 Pt; 4 Sac. **1983** Phi: 16 G; 8.5 Sac. **1984** Phi: 16 G; 16 Sac. **1985** Phi: 16 G; 13 Sac. **1986** Phi: 16 G; Scor **1** Saf; 2 Pt; 9 Sac. **1987** Atl: 12 G; 2 Sac. **1988** Atl: 16 G. **Total:** 117 G; Scor 1 Saf; 2 Fum TD; 14 Pt; 52.5 Sac.

GUY BROWN Brown, Guy III 6′4″, 223 **LB**
Col: Houston *HS:* Palestine [TX] B: 6/1/1955, Palestine, TX *Drafted:* 1977 Round 4 Dal
1977 Dal: 14 G. **1978** Dal: 15 G. **1979** Dal: 15 G. **1980** Dal: 16 G. **1981** Dal: 16 G; Int 1-28. **1982** Dal: 9 G. **Total:** 85 G; Int 1-28.

HARDY BROWN Brown, Hardy 6′0″, 193 **LB-DB-FB**
(Thumper) *Col:* Southern Methodist; Tulsa *HS:* Masonic Home School [Fort Worth, TX] B: 5/8/1924, Quanah, TX D: 11/8/1991, Stockton, CA *Drafted:* 1947 Round 10 NYG
AAFC **1948** BknA: 11 G; Rush 6-23 3.8 1 TD; Rec 3-36 12.0 1 TD; Int 1-0; Scor 37, 0-1 FG, 25-29 86.2% XK; Tot TD 2. **1949** ChiA: 12 G; Rush 1-2 2.0; Rec 1-10 10.0; Int 3-59; Punt 10-397 39.7. **Total:** 23 G; Rush 7-25 3.6 1 TD; Rec 4-46 11.5 1 TD; Int 4-59; Punt 10-397 39.7; Scor 37, 0-1 FG, 25-29 86.2% XK; Tot TD 2.

NFL **1950** Was-Bal: 12 G; KR 2-15 7.5; Int 1-16; Scor 0-1 XK; 1 Fum. Was: 8 G; KR 2-15 7.5; 1 Fum. Bal: 4 G; Int 1-16; Scor 0-1 XK. **1951** SF: 12 G; Int 1-5. **1952** SF: 12 G; KR 2-31 15.5; Int 1-16. **1953** SF: 12 G; KR 1-3 3.0; Int 1-7. **1954** SF: 11 G; Int 3-42 1 TD; Punt 10-384 38.4; 6 Pt. **1955** SF: 12 G; Int 2-28. **1956** ChiC: 8 G. **1960** Den: 13 G. **Total:** 92 G; KR 5-49 9.8; Int 9-114 1 TD; Punt 10-384 38.4; Scor 6, 0-1 XK; 6 Pt; 1 Fum.

HOWIE BROWN Brown, Howard Kenneth 5′11″, 215 **OG-DG-OT-DT**
(Goon) *Col:* Indiana *HS:* Fairview [Dayton, OH] B: 1/26/1922, Dayton, OH D: 4/4/1975, Bloomington, IL *Drafted:* 1946 Round 20 GB
1948 Det: 12 G. **1949** Det: 12 G. **1950** Det: 12 G; KR 1-0. **Total:** 36 G; KR 1-0.

IVORY LEE BROWN Brown, Ivory Lee 6′2″, 245 **RB**
Col: Tyler JC TX; Arkansas-Pine Bluff *HS:* Palestine [TX] B: 8/17/1969, Palestine, TX *Drafted:* 1991 Round 7 Pho
1992 Pho: Rec 7-54 7.7.

		Rushing			
Year Team	**G**	**Att**	**Yds**	**Avg**	**TD**
1992 Pho	7	68	194	2.9	2

J.B. BROWN Brown, James Harold 6′0″, 193 **DB**
Col: Maryland *HS:* DeMatha [Hyattsville, MD] B: 1/5/1967, Washington, DC *Drafted:* 1989 Round 12 Mia
1990 Mia: 1 Sac. **Total:** 1 Sac.

		Interceptions			
Year Team	**G**	**Int**	**Yds**	**TD**	**Fum**
1989 Mia	16	0	0	0	0
1990 Mia	16	0	0	0	0
1991 Mia	15	1	0	0	0
1992 Mia	16	4	119	1	0
1993 Mia	16	5	43	0	1
1994 Mia	16	3	82	0	0
1995 Mia	13	2	20	0	1
1996 Mia	14	1	29	0	0
1997 Pit	13	0	0	0	0
1998 Ariz	15	0	0	0	0
NFL Total	150	16	293	1	2

JAMES BROWN Brown, James Lamont 6′6″, 330 **OT**
Col: Virginia State *HS:* Jules E. Mastbaum Area Vo-Tech [Philadelphia, PA] B: 11/30/1970, Philadelphia, PA *Drafted:* 1992 Round 3 Dal
1993 NYJ: 14 G. **1994** NYJ: 16 G. **1995** NYJ: 14 G. **1996** Mia: 16 G. **1997** Mia: 16 G. **1998** Mia: 16 G. **Total:** 92 G.

JIM BROWN Brown, James Nathaniel 6′2″, 232 **FB**
Col: Syracuse *HS:* Manhasset [NY] B: 2/17/1936, St. Simons Island, GA *Drafted:* 1957 Round 1 Cle *HOF:* 1971
1961 Cle: Pass 3-1 33.3%, 37 12.33 1 TD. **1962** Cle: Pass 2-1 50.0%, 28 14.00. **1963** Cle: Pass 4-0. **1964** Cle: Pass 1-1 100.0%, 13 13.00 1 TD. **1965** Cle: Pass 2-1 50.0%, 39 19.50 1 TD. **Total:** Pass 12-4 33.3%, 117 9.75 3 TD.

		Rushing				Receiving			
Year Team	**G**	**Att**	**Yds**	**Avg**	**TD**	**Rec**	**Yds**	**Avg**	**TD**
1957 Cle	12	202	**942**	4.7	**9**	16	55	3.4	1
1958 Cle	12	**257**	**1527**	5.9	**17**	16	138	8.6	1
1959 Cle	12	**290**	**1329**	4.6	**14**	24	190	7.9	0
1960 Cle	12	215	**1257**	5.8	9	19	204	10.7	2
1961 Cle	14	**305**	**1408**	4.6	8	46	459	10.0	2
1962 Cle	14	230	996	4.3	13	47	517	11.0	5
1963 Cle	14	**291**	**1863**	**6.4**	**12**	24	268	11.2	3
1964 Cle	14	**280**	**1446**	**5.2**	7	36	340	9.4	2
1965 Cle	14	**289**	**1544**	5.3	**17**	34	328	9.6	4
NFL Total	118	2359	12312	**5.2**	106	262	2499	9.5	20

	Kickoff Returns					Tot
Year Team	**Ret**	**Yds**	**Avg**	**TD**	**Fum**	**TD**
1957 Cle	6	136	22.7	0	7	10
1958 Cle	3	74	24.7	0	5	**18**
1959 Cle	4	88	22.0	0	2	**14**
1960 Cle	14	300	21.4	0	9	11
1961 Cle	2	50	25.0	0	6	10
1962 Cle	0	0	—	0	9	18
1963 Cle	0	0	—	0	7	**15**
1964 Cle	0	0	—	0	6	9
1965 Cle	0	0	—	0	6	21
NFL Total	29	648	22.3	0	57	126

JAMIE BROWN Brown, Jamie Shepard II 6′8″, 320 **OT**
Col: Florida A&M *HS:* Miami Killian [FL] B: 4/24/1972, Miami, FL *Drafted:* 1995 Round 4 Den
1995 Den: 6 G. **1996** Den: 12 G. **1997** Den: 11 G. **1998** SF: 8 G. **Total:** 37 G.

JEROME BROWN Brown, Jerome 6′2″, 292 **DT**
Col: Miami (Fla.) *HS:* Hernando [Brooksville, FL] B: 2/4/1965, Brooksville, FL D: 6/25/1992, Brooksville, FL *Drafted:* 1987 Round 1 Phi
1987 Phi: 12 G; Int 2-7; 4 Sac. **1988** Phi: 16 G; Int 1-(-5); 5 Sac. **1989** Phi: 16 G; 10.5 Sac. **1990** Phi: 16 G; 1 Sac. **1991** Phi: 16 G; 9 Sac. **Total:** 76 G; Int 3-2; 29.5 Sac.

JESSE BROWN Brown, Jesse J 5′10″, 180 **TB**
Col: Pittsburgh *HS:* Nichols School [Buffalo, NY] B: 1903 Deceased
1926 Pott: 14 G; Pass 3 TD.

JOHN BROWN Brown, John Calvin Jr. 6′2″, 248 **OT**
Col: Syracuse *HS:* Camden [NJ] B: 6/9/1939, Camden, NJ *Drafted:* 1961 Round 4 Cle
1962 Cle: 14 G. **1963** Cle: 14 G. **1964** Cle: 11 G. **1965** Cle: 14 G. **1966** Cle: 14 G. **1967** Pit: 14 G. **1968** Pit: 13 G. **1969** Pit: 14 G. **1970** Pit: 14 G. **1971** Pit: 14 G. **Total:** 136 G.

JOHN BROWN Brown, John Edward 6′4″, 230 **LB-C**
Col: North Carolina Central *HS:* Theodore Roosevelt [Gary, IN] B: 4/9/1922, Belen, MS
AAFC **1947** LA-A: 14 G; Int 1-4. **1948** LA-A: 14 G; Int 1-1. **1949** LA-A: 12 G; Int 3-46; 12 Pt. **Total:** 40 G; Int 5-51; 12 Pt.

JACK BROWN Brown, John Roman 6'0", 191 **C-G-T**
Col: Dayton B: 10/24/1902, Dayton, OH D: 11/25/1987, Dayton, OH
1926 Day: 2 G. **1927** Day: 3 G. **1928** Day: 5 G. **1929** Day: 6 G. **Total:** 16 G.

JONATHAN BROWN Brown, Jonathan Bernard 6'4", 270 **DE**
Col: Tennessee *HS:* Booker T. Washington [Tulsa, OK] B: 11/28/1975, Chickasha, OK *Drafted:* 1998 Round 3 GB
1998 GB: 4 G.

BARRY BROWN Brown, Joseph Barry 6'3", 230 **LB-TE**
Col: Florida *HS:* Ann Arbor [MI] B: 4/17/1943, Boston, MA
Drafted: 1965 Round 19 Bal
1966 Bal: 10 G; KR 2-14 7.0; Int 1-7. **1967** Bal: 14 G. **1968** NYG: 12 G. **1969** Bos: 7 G; Rec 6-69 11.5. **1970** Bos: 14 G; Rec 15-145 9.7; KR 1-0. **Total:** 57 G; Rec 21-214 10.2; KR 3-14 4.7; Int 1-7.

KEN BROWN Brown, Kenneth Anderson 6'1", 235 **LB**
Col: Virginia Tech *HS:* Monacan [Richmond, VA]; Fork Union Mil. Acad. [VA] B: 5/5/1971, Wiesbaden, Germany *Drafted:* 1995 Round 4 Den
1995 Den: 2 G.

KEN BROWN Brown, Kenneth Bernard 5'8", 175 **WR**
Col: Southern Arkansas *HS:* Pine Bluff [AR] B: 3/10/1965, Monroe, LA
1987 Cin: 3 G; PR 5-16 3.2; KR 3-45 15.0.

KEN BROWN Brown, Kenneth Eugene 6'1", 245 **C**
Col: New Mexico *HS:* Ganesha [Pomona, CA] B: 4/19/1954, Saginaw, MI
1979 Den: 16 G. **1980** GB: 7 G; 1 Fum. **Total:** 23 G; 1 Fum.

KEN BROWN Brown, Kenneth J 5'10", 203 **RB**
Col: No College *HS:* Frederick Douglass [Oklahoma City, OK]
B: 11/8/1945, Holdenville, OK

		Rushing				Receiving			
Year Team	**G**	**Att**	**Yds**	**Avg**	**TD**	**Rec**	**Yds**	**Avg**	**TD**
1970 Cle	11	1	-8	-8.0	0	0	0	—	0
1971 Cle	10	11	47	4.3	0	0	0	—	0
1972 Cle	14	32	114	3.6	2	5	64	12.8	0
1973 Cle	14	161	537	3.3	0	22	187	8.5	0
1974 Cle	14	125	458	3.7	4	29	194	6.7	2
1975 Cle	14	16	45	2.8	1	2	23	11.5	0
NFL Total	77	346	1193	3.4	7	58	468	8.1	2

	Kickoff Returns					Tot
Year Team	**Ret**	**Yds**	**Avg**	**TD**	**Fum**	**TD**
1970 Cle	2	44	22.0	0	0	0
1971 Cle	15	330	22.0	0	3	0
1972 Cle	20	473	23.7	0	4	2
1973 Cle	0	0	—	0	5	0
1974 Cle	1	9	9.0	0	1	6
1975 Cle	7	126	18.0	0	0	1
NFL Total	45	982	21.8	0	13	9

KEVIN BROWN Brown, Kevin Don 6'2", 178 **P**
Col: Amarillo Coll. TX (J.C.); West Texas A&M *HS:* Panhandle [TX]
B: 1/11/1963, Panhandle, TX
1987 ChiB: 3 G; Rush 1-0; Punt 18-742 41.2; 1 Fum.

LANCE BROWN Brown, Lance Allen 6'2", 200 **DB**
Col: Indiana *HS:* Terry Parker [Jacksonville, FL] B: 2/2/1972, Jacksonville, FL *Drafted:* 1995 Round 5 Pit
1995 Ariz: 11 G. **1996** Ariz: 1 G. **1998** Pit: 16 G. **Total:** 28 G.

LARON BROWN Brown, Laron Gregg 5'9", 172 **WR**
Col: Tennessee; Texas *HS:* Nettie Lee Roth [Dayton, OH]
B: 11/10/1963, Dayton, OH *Drafted:* 1987 Round 11 Was
1987 Den: 3 G; Rec 4-40 10.0; KR 3-57 19.0.

LARRY BROWN Brown, Larry Donell 6'5", 260 **OT**
Col: Miami (Fla.) *HS:* William M. Raines [Jacksonville, FL] B: 6/4/1955, Jacksonville, FL *Drafted:* 1978 Round 9 KC
1978 KC: 1 G. **1979** KC: 4 G. **Total:** 5 G.

LARRY BROWN Brown, Larry Jr. 5'11", 186 **DB**
Col: Los Angeles Southwest Coll. CA (J.C.); Texas Christian *HS:* Los Angeles [CA] B: 11/30/1969, Miami, FL *Drafted:* 1991 Round 12 Dal

		Interceptions		
Year Team	**G**	**Int**	**Yds**	**TD**
1991 Dal	16	2	31	0
1992 Dal	16	1	30	0
1993 Dal	16	0	0	0
1994 Dal	15	4	21	0
1995 Dal	16	6	124	**2**
1996 Oak	8	1	4	0
1997 Oak	4	0	0	0
1998 Dal	4	0	0	0
NFL Total	95	14	210	2

LARRY BROWN Brown, Lawrence 5'11", 180 **WR**
Col: Mankato State *HS:* American Senior [Hialeah, FL] B: 9/4/1963, Miami, FL
1987 Min: 1 G.

LARRY BROWN Brown, Lawrence 6'4", 246 **OT-TE**
Col: Kansas *HS:* Bradford [Starke, FL] B: 6/16/1949, Jacksonville, FL
Drafted: 1971 Round 5 Pit

		Receiving				
Year Team	**G**	**Rec**	**Yds**	**Avg**	**TD**	**Fum**
1971 Pit	13	1	3	3.0	1	0
1972 Pit	9	1	13	13.0	1	0
1973 Pit	14	5	88	17.6	0	0
1974 Pit	14	17	190	11.2	1	0
1975 Pit	14	16	244	15.3	1	2
1976 Pit	13	7	97	13.9	0	0
1977 Pit	14	0	0	—	0	0
1978 Pit	8	0	0	—	0	0
1979 Pit	15	1	1	1.0	1	0
1980 Pit	16	0	0	—	0	0
1981 Pit	14	0	0	—	0	0
1982 Pit	8	0	0	—	0	0
1983 Pit	8	0	0	—	0	0
1984 Pit	7	0	0	—	0	0
NFL Total	167	48	636	13.3	5	2

LARRY BROWN Brown, Lawrence Jr. 5'11", 195 **RB**
Col: Dodge City CC KS; Kansas State *HS:* Schenley [Pittsburgh, PA]
B: 9/19/1947, Clairton, PA *Drafted:* 1969 Round 8 Was
1974 Was: Pass 1-1 100.0%, 16 16.00. **Total:** Pass 1-1 100.0%, 16 16.00.

		Rushing				Receiving					Tot
Year Team	**G**	**Att**	**Yds**	**Avg**	**TD**	**Rec**	**Yds**	**Avg**	**TD**	**Fum**	**TD**
1969 Was	14	202	888	4.4	4	34	302	8.9	0	6	4
1970 Was	13	237	**1125**	4.7	5	37	341	9.2	2	6	7
1971 Was	13	253	948	3.7	4	16	176	11.0	2	6	6
1972 Was	12	285	1216	4.3	8	32	473	14.8	4	9	12
1973 Was	14	273	860	3.2	8	40	482	12.1	6	7	**14**
1974 Was	11	163	430	2.6	3	37	388	10.5	4	2	7
1975 Was	14	97	352	3.6	3	25	225	9.0	2	2	5
1976 Was	11	20	56	2.8	0	17	98	5.8	0	2	0
NFL Total	102	1530	5875	3.8	35	238	2485	10.4	20	40	55

RAY BROWN Brown, Leonard Ray Jr. 6'5", 295 **OT-OG**
Col: Memphis; Arizona State; Arkansas State *HS:* Marion [AR]
B: 12/12/1962, West Memphis, AR *Drafted:* 1986 Round 8 StL
1986 StL: 11 G. **1987** StL: 7 G. **1988** Pho: 15 G. **1989** Was: 7 G. **1990** Was: Postseason only. **1992** Was: 16 G. **1993** Was: 16 G. **1994** Was: 16 G. **1995** Was: 16 G. **1996** SF: 16 G. **1997** SF: 15 G. **1998** SF: 16 G. **Total:** 151 G.

LOMAS BROWN Brown, Lomas Jr. 6'4", 282 **OT**
Col: Florida *HS:* Miami Springs [FL] B: 3/30/1963, Miami, FL
Drafted: 1985 Round 1 Det
1985 Det: 16 G. **1986** Det: 16 G. **1987** Det: 11 G. **1988** Det: 16 G. **1989** Det: 16 G; Rush 1-3 3.0. **1990** Det: 16 G. **1991** Det: 15 G. **1992** Det: 16 G. **1993** Det: 11 G. **1994** Det: 16 G. **1995** Det: 15 G. **1996** Ariz: 16 G. **1997** Ariz: 14 G. **1998** Ariz: 16 G. **Total:** 210 G; Rush 1-3 3.0.

MARC BROWN Brown, Marc Stacy 6'2", 195 **WR**
Col: Westchester CC NY; Towson State *HS:* Nyack [Upper Nyack, NY]
B: 5/7/1961, Nyack, NY
1987 Buf: 3 G; Rec 9-120 13.3 1 TD; KR 2-35 17.5; 6 Pt.

MARK BROWN Brown, Mark Anthony 6'2", 230 **LB**
Col: Los Angeles Southwest Coll. CA (J.C.); Purdue *HS:* Inglewood [CA]
B: 7/18/1961, New Brunswick, NJ *Drafted:* 1983 Round 9 Mia
1983 Mia: 14 G; KR 1-0; Int 1-0; 2 Sac. **1984** Mia: 16 G; 1 Sac. **1985** Mia: 15 G; Int 1-5; 1 Sac. **1986** Mia: 14 G; 5 Sac. **1987** Mia: 12 G; 1 Sac. **1988** Mia: 13 G; Int 2-13; 0.5 Sac. **1989** Det: 6 G. **1990** Det: 15 G. **1991** Det: 2 G. **Total:** 107 G; KR 1-0; Int 4-18; 10.5 Sac.

MARV BROWN Brown, Marvin Clifford 5'8", 150 **HB**
Col: Tarleton State; Texas A&M-Commerce *HS:* Waco [TX]; Alice HS [TX] B: 8/15/1930, Marshall, TX
1957 Det: 4 G; Rush 2-6 3.0; PR 3-16 5.3; KR 6-106 17.7.

MATT BROWN Brown, Matthew 5'10", 170 **HB**
(Buster) *Col:* Syracuse Deceased
1920 Akr: 1 G.

MONTY BROWN Brown, Montague N.Gai 6'0", 228 **LB**
Col: Ferris State *HS:* Bridgeport [Saginaw, MI] B: 4/13/1970, Bridgeport, MI
1993 Buf: 13 G. **1994** Buf: 3 G. **1995** Buf: 16 G. **1996** NE: 11 G. **Total:** 43 G.

OMAR BROWN Brown, Omar Lamont 5′10″, 200 **DB**
Col: North Carolina *HS:* William Penn [York, PA] B: 3/28/1975, York, PA *Drafted:* 1998 Round 4 Atl
1998 Atl: 2 G.

ORLANDO BROWN Brown, Orlando Claude 6′7″, 341 **OT**
Col: Central State (Ohio); South Carolina State *HS:* Howard D. Woodson [Washington, DC] B: 12/12/1970, Washington, DC
1994 Cle: 14 G. **1995** Cle: 16 G. **1996** Bal: 16 G. **1997** Bal: 16 G. **1998** Bal: 13 G. **Total:** 75 G.

OTTO BROWN Brown, Otto 6′1″, 188 **DB**
Col: Prairie View A&M *HS:* Florida A & M University [Tallahassee, FL] B: 1/12/1947, Tallahassee, FL
1969 Dal: 14 G; Int 1-31. **1970** NYG: 13 G. **1971** NYG: 12 G; 6 Pt. **1972** NYG: 13 G; Int 1-2. **1973** NYG: 11 G. **Total:** 63 G; Int 2-33; 6 Pt.

EDDIE BROWN Brown, Paul Edward 5′11″, 187 **DB**
Col: Tennessee *HS:* Marion Co. [Jasper, TN] B: 2/19/1952, Jasper, TN *Drafted:* 1974 Round 8 Cle
1974 Cle: Int 2-24. **1975** Cle-Was: Int 1-33. Was: Int 1-33. **1976** Was: Int 1-8. **1977** Was: Int 1-0. **1979** LARm: Int 3-32. **Total:** Int 8-97.

		Punt Returns				Kickoff Returns				
Year Team	G	Ret	Yds	Avg	TD	Ret	Yds	Avg	TD	Fum
1974 Cle	13	2	0	0.0	0	6	138	23.0	0	0
1975 Cle-Was	14	8	68	8.5	0	6	126	21.0	0	0
1975 Cle	3	2	16	8.0	0	6	126	21.0	0	0
1975 Was	11	6	52	8.7	0	0	0	—	0	0
1976 Was	14	48	**646**	13.5	1	30	738	24.6	0	4
1977 Was	14	**57**	452	7.9	0	34	852	25.1	0	2
1978 LARm	1	1	13	13.0	0	0	0	—	0	0
1979 LARm	16	56	332	5.9	0	5	103	20.6	0	3
NFL Total	72	172	1511	8.8	1	81	1957	24.2	0	9

PRESTON BROWN Brown, Preston Melville 5′10″, 184 **WR**
Col: Vanderbilt *HS:* Maplewood [Nashville, TN] B: 3/2/1958, Nashville, TN *Drafted:* 1980 Round 6 NE
1980 NE: PR 10-42 4.2. **1982** NE: Rec 4-114 28.5 1 TD. **Total:** Rec 4-114 28.5 1 TD; PR 10-42 4.2.

		Kickoff Returns				
Year Team	G	Ret	Yds	Avg	TD	Fum
1980 NE	5	9	156	17.3	0	1
1982 NE	9	0	0	—	0	0
1983 NYJ	16	29	645	22.2	0	3
1984 Cle	2	8	136	17.0	0	0
NFL Total	32	46	937	20.4	0	4

RAY BROWN Brown, Raymond Lloyd 6′2″, 195 **DB-QB**
Col: Mississippi *HS:* Greenville [MS] B: 9/7/1936, Clarksdale, MS *Drafted:* 1958 Round 5 Bal
1958 Bal: Pass 2-1 50.0%, -1 -0.50; Rush 1-(-9) -9.0. **1959** Bal: Pass 4-1 25.0%, 14 3.50; Rush 2-4 2.0. **1960** Bal: Pass 13-6 46.2%, 65 5.00 1 TD; Rush 2-25 12.5. **Total:** Pass 19-8 42.1%, 78 4.11 1 TD; Rush 5-20 4.0.

		Interceptions			Punting			
Year Team	G	Int	Yds	TD	Punts	Yds	Avg	Fum
1958 Bal	12	8	149	0	41	1635	39.9	1
1959 Bal	12	5	89	0	2	97	48.5	0
1960 Bal	12	0	0	0	52	2001	38.5	0
NFL Total	36	13	238	0	95	3733	39.3	1

RAY BROWN Brown, Raymond Madison 6′1″, 208 **DB**
Col: West Texas A&M *HS:* Trimble Tech [Fort Worth, TX] B: 1/12/1949, Fort Worth, TX *Drafted:* 1971 Round 6 Atl

		Punt Returns				Interceptions			
Year Team	G	Ret	Yds	Avg	TD	Int	Yds	TD	Fum
1971 Atl	10	1	0	0.0	0	3	32	0	0
1972 Atl	14	8	71	8.9	0	2	46	0	1
1973 Atl	14	40	360	9.0	0	6	99	0	4
1974 Atl	14	9	96	10.7	0	8	164	1	0
1975 Atl	14	2	12	6.0	0	4	119	1	0
1976 Atl	14	0	0	—	0	3	58	0	0
1977 Atl	14	0	0	—	0	5	56	0	1
1978 NO	16	0	0	—	0	4	50	0	0
1979 NO	12	0	0	—	0	1	2	0	0
1980 NO	15	0	0	—	0	2	31	0	0
NFL Total	137	60	539	9.0	0	38	657	2	6

RAY BROWN Brown, Raynard Albert 5′9″, 185 **WR**
Col: South Carolina *HS:* Ben L. Smith [Greensboro, NC] B: 7/25/1965, Bronx, NY *Drafted:* 1987 Round 10 Det
1987 SF: 1 G.

REGGIE BROWN Brown, Regilyn DeWayne 6′0″, 244 **RB**
Col: Coll. of the Desert CA (J.C.); Ohio U.; Fresno State *HS:* Henry Ford [Detroit, MI] B: 6/26/1973, Detroit, MI *Drafted:* 1996 Round 3 Sea
1996 Sea: 7 G; KR 4-51 12.8. **1997** Sea: 11 G; KR 1-16 16.0. **1998** Sea: 15 G; Rush 1-2 2.0; KR 4-44 11.0. **Total:** 33 G; Rush 1-2 2.0; KR 9-111 12.3.

REGGIE BROWN Brown, Reginald Alonzo 6′1″, 195 **WR**
Col: Alabama State *HS:* Miami Central [FL] B: 5/5/1970, Miami, FL
1993 Hou: 4 G; Rec 2-30 15.0. **1994** Hou: 4 G; Rec 4-34 8.5; Scor 1 2XP; 2 Pt. **Total:** 8 G; Rec 6-64 10.7; Scor 1 2XP; 2 Pt.

REGGIE BROWN Brown, Reginald Dwayne 6′2″, 241 **LB**
Col: Texas A&M *HS:* Reagan [Austin, TX] B: 9/28/1974, Austin, TX *Drafted:* 1996 Round 1 Det
1996 Det: 10 G. **1997** Det: 16 G; Int 2-83 2 TD; 12 Pt; 2.5 Sac. **Total:** 26 G; Int 2-83 2 TD; 12 Pt; 2.5 Sac.

REGGIE BROWN Brown, Reginald Van 5′11″, 211 **RB**
Col: Pasadena City Coll. CA (J.C.); Oregon *HS:* Malcolm X Shabazz [Newark, NJ] B: 3/12/1960, Dendron, VA *Drafted:* 1982 Round 4 Atl
1987 Phi: Rec 8-53 6.6. **Total:** Rec 8-53 6.6.

		Rushing				Kickoff Returns				
Year Team	G	Att	Yds	Avg	TD	Ret	Yds	Avg	TD	Fum
1982 Atl	8	0	0	—	0	24	466	19.4	0	0
1983 Atl	2	0	0	—	0	0	0	—	0	0
1987 Phi	3	39	136	3.5	0	1	20	20.0	0	2
NFL Total	13	39	136	3.5	0	25	486	19.4	0	2

RICHARD BROWN Brown, Richard McClure 6′1″, 220 **C**
Col: Iowa *HS:* Cedar Rapids [IA] B: 5/27/1907, Waverly, IA
1930 Port: 11 G.

RICHARD BROWN Brown, Richard Solomon 6′3″, 240 **LB**
Col: San Diego State *HS:* Westminster [CA] B: 9/21/1965, Western Samoa
1987 LARm: 8 G; KR 1-15 15.0. **1989** LARm: 13 G. **1990** SD: 11 G. **1991** Cle: 16 G; Int 1-19; 0.5 Sac. **1992** Cle: 10 G; 1 Sac. **1994** Min: 3 G. **1995** Min: 16 G. **1996** Min: 14 G; KR 3-35 11.7. **Total:** 91 G; KR 4-50 12.5; Int 1-19; 1.5 Sac.

ROBERT BROWN Brown, Robert Earl 6′2″, 225 **TE**
Col: Alcorn State *HS:* East Side [Cleveland, MS] B: 1/1/1943, Pace, MS
1970 StL: Rush 1-8 8.0. **Total:** Rush 1-8 8.0.

		Receiving			
Year Team	G	Rec	Yds	Avg	TD
1969 StL	12	0	0	—	0
1970 StL	14	0	0	—	0
1971 Min	8	6	141	23.5	0
1972 NO	14	11	175	15.9	1
1973 NO	5	11	132	12.0	0
NFL Total	53	28	448	16.0	1

ROBERT BROWN Brown, Robert Eddie 6′5″, 260 **DT-DE**
Col: Arkansas-Pine Bluff *HS:* Morehouse [Bastrop, LA] B: 2/22/1940, Bonita, LA *Drafted:* 1964 Round 13 SF
1966 GB: 14 G. **1967** GB: 14 G. **1968** GB: 6 G. **1969** GB: 14 G. **1970** GB: 14 G. **1971** GB: 14 G. **1972** GB: 14 G; Scor **1** Saf; 2 Pt. **1973** GB: 14 G. **1974** SD: 14 G. **1975** Cin: 14 G. **1976** Cin: 14 G. **Total:** 146 G; Scor 1 Saf; 2 Pt.

ROBERT BROWN Brown, Robert Lee 6′2″, 268 **DE**
Col: Chowan Coll. NC; Virginia Tech *HS:* John A. Holmes [Edenton, NC] B: 5/21/1960, Edenton, NC *Drafted:* 1982 Round 4 GB
1982 GB: 8 G. **1983** GB: 16 G. **1984** GB: 16 G; Int 1-5 1 TD; 6 Pt; 5 Sac. **1985** GB: 16 G; Scor 1 Saf; 2 Pt; 3 Sac. **1986** GB: 16 G; 2 Sac. **1987** GB: 12 G; 3 Sac. **1988** GB: 16 G; 1.5 Sac. **1989** GB: 16 G; 3 Sac. **1990** GB: 16 G; 3 Sac. **1991** GB: 16 G; Int 1-37; 4 Sac. **1992** GB: 16 G; 1 Sac. **Total:** 164 G; Int 2-42 1 TD; Scor 1 Saf; 8 Pt; 25.5 Sac.

BOB BROWN Brown, Robert Stanford 6′4″, 280 **OT**
(The Boomer) *Col:* Nebraska *HS:* East Tech [Cleveland, OH] B: 12/8/1941, Cleveland, OH *Drafted:* 1964 Round 1 Phi
1964 Phi: 14 G. **1965** Phi: 14 G. **1966** Phi: 14 G. **1967** Phi: 8 G. **1968** Phi: 14 G. **1969** LARm: 14 G. **1970** LARm: 14 G. **1971** Oak: 10 G. **1972** Oak: 14 G. **1973** Oak: 10 G. **Total:** 126 G.

ROGER BROWN Brown, Roger 6′0″, 196 **DB**
Col: Virginia Tech *HS:* Cardinal Gibbons [Baltimore, MD] B: 12/16/1966, Baltimore, MD *Drafted:* 1990 Round 8 GB
1990 NYG: 5 G. **1991** NYG: 16 G. **1992** NE: 16 G. **Total:** 37 G.

ROGER BROWN Brown, Roger Lee 6′5″, 300 **DT**
Col: Maryland East. Shore *HS:* Nyack [Upper Nyack, NY] B: 5/1/1937, Surrey Co., VA *Drafted:* 1960 Round 4 Det
1960 Det: 12 G. **1961** Det: 14 G; Int 1-10. **1962** Det: 14 G; Scor **2** Saf; 4 Pt. **1963** Det: 14 G; Int 1-20. **1964** Det: 14 G. **1965** Det: 14 G; Scor **1** Saf; 2 Pt. **1966** Det: 14 G. **1967** LARm: 14 G. **1968** LARm: 14 G. **1969** LARm: 14 G. **Total:** 138 G; Int 2-30; Scor 3 Saf; 6 Pt.

RON BROWN Brown, Ronald 6′4″, 225 **LB**
Col: USC *HS:* Bishop Amat [La Puente, CA] B: 4/28/1964, Oroville, CA
Drafted: 1987 Round 8 SD
1987 LARd: 3 G; 2 Sac. **1988** LARd: 16 G. **Total:** 19 G; 2 Sac.

RON BROWN Brown, Ronald James 5′11″, 181 **WR-DB**
Col: Arizona State *HS:* Baldwin Park [CA] B: 3/31/1961, Los Angeles, CA *Drafted:* 1983 Round 2 Cle
1984 LARm: Rush 2-25 12.5. **1985** LARm: Rush 2-13 6.5. **1986** LARm: Rush 4-5 1.3. **1987** LARm: Rush 2-22 11.0. **1988** LARm: Rush 3-24 8.0. **1989** LARm: Rush 6-27 4.5. **1991** LARm: Rush 2-11 5.5.
Total: Rush 21-127 6.0.

		Receiving				Kickoff Returns					Tot
Year Team	G	Rec	Yds	Avg	TD	Ret	Yds	Avg	TD	Fum	TD
1984 LARm	16	23	478	20.8	4	0	0	—	0	0	4
1985 LARm	13	14	215	15.4	3	28	918	**32.8**	**3**	2	6
1986 LARm	14	25	396	15.8	3	36	794	22.1	0	1	3
1987 LARm	12	26	521	20.0	2	27	581	21.5	1	2	3
1988 LARm	7	2	16	8.0	0	19	401	21.1	0	1	0
1989 LARm	16	5	113	22.6	1	**47**	968	20.6	0	3	1
1990 LARd	16	0	0	—	0	30	575	19.2	0	1	0
1991 LARm	6	3	52	17.3	0	12	256	21.3	0	0	0
NFL Total	100	98	1791	18.3	13	199	4493	22.6	4	10	17

RON BROWN Brown, Ronald William 5′10″, 186 **WR**
Col: Pasadena City Coll. CA (J.C.); Colorado *HS:* John Muir [Pasadena, CA] B: 1/11/1963, Queens, NY *Drafted:* 1986 Round 6 NYG
1987 StL: 3 G; Rush 1-9 9.0; Rec 2-16 8.0; KR 1-40 40.0.

ROSEY BROWN Brown, Roosevelt Jr. 6′3″, 255 **OT**
Col: Morgan State *HS:* Jefferson [Charlottesville, VA] B: 10/20/1932, Charlottesville, VA *Drafted:* 1953 Round 27 NYG *HOF:* 1975
1953 NYG: 12 G. **1954** NYG: 12 G. **1955** NYG: 12 G; KR 1-14 14.0; 1 Fum. **1956** NYG: 12 G. **1957** NYG: 12 G. **1958** NYG: 11 G; KR 1-0. **1959** NYG: 12 G; KR 1-18 18.0. **1960** NYG: 12 G; KR 1-0. **1961** NYG: 14 G. **1962** NYG: 13 G. **1963** NYG: 13 G. **1964** NYG: 13 G. **1965** NYG: 14 G; KR 1-0. **Total:** 162 G; KR 5-32 6.4; 1 Fum.

RUBEN BROWN Brown, Ruben Pernell 6′3″, 304 **OG**
Col: Pittsburgh *HS:* E.C. Glass [Lynchburg, VA] B: 2/13/1972, Lynchburg, VA *Drafted:* 1995 Round 1 Buf
1995 Buf: 16 G. **1996** Buf: 14 G. **1997** Buf: 16 G. **1998** Buf: 13 G.
Total: 59 G.

RUFUS BROWN Brown, Rufus Bernard 6′2″, 295 **OG**
Col: Florida A&M *HS:* Plant City [FL] B: 6/19/1962, Bartow, FL
1987 TB: 2 G.

RUSH BROWN Brown, Rush Jr. 6′2″, 257 **DT-DE-NT**
Col: Ball State *HS:* Scotland [Laurinburg, NC] B: 6/27/1954, Laurinburg, NC *Drafted:* 1980 Round 10 StL
1980 StL: 16 G; Int 1-9. **1981** StL: 16 G. **1982** StL: 9 G; 3 Sac. **1983** StL: 6 G; 1 Sac. **Total:** 47 G; Int 1-9; 4 Sac.

PETE BROWN Brown, Samuel Morris 6′2″, 210 **C-LB**
Col: Georgia Tech *HS:* Rossville [GA] B: 12/19/1930, Rossville, GA
1954 SF: Pass 1-1 100.0%, 19 19.00; Rush 1-(6) -6.0; Int 1-47.
Total: Pass 1-1 100.0%, 19 19.00; Rush 1-(6) -6.0; Int 1-47.

		Punting		
Year Team	G	Punts	Yds	Avg
1953 SF	12	0	0	—
1954 SF	12	49	1837	37.5
NFL Total	24	49	1837	37.5

SELWYN BROWN Brown, Selwyn G 5′11″, 205 **DB**
Col: Miami (Fla.) *HS:* Northeast [St. Petersburg, FL] B: 9/28/1965, St. Petersburg, FL
1988 TB: 4 G.

SIDNEY BROWN Brown, Sidney Louis 6′0″, 186 **DB**
Col: Oklahoma *HS:* St. Augustine [New Orleans, LA] B: 1/27/1956, New Orleans, LA *Drafted:* 1977 Round 3 NE
1978 NE: 16 G.

STEVE BROWN Brown, Steven Douglas 5′11″, 189 **DB**
Col: Oregon *HS:* C.K. McClatchy [Sacramento, CA] B: 5/20/1960, Sacramento, CA *Drafted:* 1983 Round 3 Hou
1985 Hou: 1 Sac. **1986** Hou: 1 Sac. **1989** Hou: 3 Sac. **Total:** 5 Sac.

		Kickoff Returns				Interceptions				Tot
Year Team	G	Ret	Yds	Avg	TD	Int	Yds	TD	Fum	TD
1983 Hou	16	31	795	25.6	**1**	1	16	0	2	1
1984 Hou	16	3	17	5.7	0	1	26	0	1	0
1985 Hou	15	2	45	22.5	0	5	41	0	1	0
1986 Hou	16	0	0	—	0	2	34	0	0	0
1987 Hou	10	0	0	—	0	2	45	0	1	0
1988 Hou	14	0	0	—	0	2	48	1	0	1
1989 Hou	16	0	0	—	0	5	54	0	0	0
1990 Hou	16	0	0	—	0	0	0	0	0	0
NFL Total	119	36	857	23.8	1	18	264	1	5	2

TERRY BROWN Brown, Terry Lynn 6′0″, 205 **DB**
Col: Oklahoma State *HS:* Marlow [OK] B: 1/9/1947, Walters, OK
Drafted: 1969 Round 3 StL
1969 StL: 14 G; Rec 1-7 7.0; PR 6-39 6.5; KR 15-320 21.3; Int 1-21; 2 Fum. **1970** StL: 10 G; KR 2-32 16.0. **1972** Min: 8 G. **1973** Min: 14 G; Int 1-63 1 TD; 6 Pt. **1974** Min: 14 G; Int 2-15. **1975** Min: 13 G; Int 2-33; **1** Fum TD; 6 Pt. **1976** Cle: 12 G; Int 1-24. **Total:** 85 G; Rec 1-7 7.0; PR 6-39 6.5; KR 17-352 20.7; Int 7-156 1 TD; 1 Fum TD; Tot TD 2; 12 Pt; 2 Fum.

THEOTIS BROWN Brown, Theotis II 6′2″, 225 **RB**
Col: UCLA *HS:* Skyline [Oakland, CA] B: 4/20/1957, Chicago, IL
Drafted: 1979 Round 2 StL
1980 StL: KR 2-26 13.0. **1982** Sea: KR 2-33 16.5. **1983** Sea-KC: Pass 1-1 100.0%, 11 11.00; KR 15-301 20.1. KC: Pass 1-1 100.0%, 11 11.00; KR 15-301 20.1. **Total:** Pass 1-1 100.0%, 11 11.00; KR 19-360 18.9.

		Rushing				Receiving					Tot
Year Team	G	Att	Yds	Avg	TD	Rec	Yds	Avg	TD	Fum	TD
1979 StL	16	73	318	4.4	7	25	191	7.6	0	3	7
1980 StL	16	40	186	4.7	1	21	290	13.8	1	2	2
1981 StL-Sea	14	156	583	3.7	8	29	328	11.3	0	8	8
1981 StL	4	15	52	3.5	2	4	60	15.0	0	2	2
1981 Sea	10	141	531	3.8	6	25	268	10.7	0	6	6
1982 Sea	9	53	141	2.7	2	12	95	7.9	0	3	2
1983 Sea-KC	15	130	481	3.7	8	47	418	8.9	2	4	10
1983 Sea	3	6	14	2.3	0	0	0	—	0	1	0
1983 KC	12	124	467	3.8	8	47	418	8.9	2	3	10
1984 KC	14	97	337	3.5	4	38	236	6.2	0	2	4
NFL Total	84	549	2046	3.7	30	172	1558	9.1	3	22	33

TIMMY BROWN Brown, Thomas Allen 5′11″, 198 **RB**
Col: Ball State *HS:* Indiana Soldiers and Sailors Children's Home [Knightstown, IN] B: 5/24/1937, Knightstown, IN *Drafted:* 1959 Round 27 GB
1963 Phi: Pass 3-1 33.3%, 11 3.67 1 TD 1 Int. **1964** Phi: Pass 2-0, 1 Int.
1965 Phi: Pass 1-0. **Total:** Pass 6-1 16.7%, 11 1.83 1 TD 2 Int.

		Rushing				Receiving			
Year Team	G	Att	Yds	Avg	TD	Rec	Yds	Avg	TD
1959 GB	1	0	0	—	0	0	0	—	0
1960 Phi	12	9	35	3.9	2	9	247	27.4	2
1961 Phi	13	50	338	6.8	1	14	264	18.9	2
1962 Phi	14	137	545	4.0	5	52	849	16.3	6
1963 Phi	14	192	841	4.4	6	36	487	13.5	4
1964 Phi	10	90	356	4.0	5	15	244	16.3	5
1965 Phi	13	158	861	**5.4**	6	50	682	13.6	3
1966 Phi	13	161	548	3.4	3	33	371	11.2	3
1967 Phi	7	53	179	3.4	1	22	202	9.2	1
1968 Bal	11	39	159	4.1	2	4	53	13.3	0
NFL Total	108	889	3862	4.3	31	235	3399	14.5	26

	Punt Returns				Kickoff Returns					Tot
Year Team	Ret	Yds	Avg	TD	Ret	Yds	Avg	TD	Fum	TD
1960 Phi	10	47	4.7	0	11	295	26.8	0	3	4
1961 Phi	8	125	15.6	1	**29**	**811**	28.0	**1**	4	5
1962 Phi	6	81	13.5	0	30	831	27.7	**1**	7	13
1963 Phi	16	152	9.5	0	**33**	**945**	28.6	1	8	11
1964 Phi	10	96	9.6	0	30	692	23.1	0	4	10
1965 Phi	4	13	3.3	0	3	46	15.3	0	8	9
1966 Phi	1	0	0.0	0	20	562	28.1	**2**	4	8
1967 Phi	0	0	—	0	13	301	23.2	0	1	2
1968 Bal	16	125	7.8	0	15	298	19.9	0	2	2
NFL Total	71	639	9.0	1	184	4781	26.0	5	41	64

TED BROWN Brown, Thomas Edward 5′10″, 206 **RB**
Col: North Carolina State *HS:* T. Wingate Andrews [High Point, NC]
B: 2/15/1957, High Point, NC *Drafted:* 1979 Round 1 Min
1979 Min: KR 8-186 23.3. **1981** Min: Pass 1-0, 1 Int. **1985** Min: KR 1-7 7.0. **1986** Min: KR 2-18 9.0. **Total:** Pass 1-0, 1 Int; KR 11-211 19.2.

		Rushing				Receiving					Tot
Year Team	G	Att	Yds	Avg	TD	Rec	Yds	Avg	TD	Fum	TD
1979 Min	14	130	551	4.2	1	31	197	6.4	0	6	1
1980 Min	16	219	912	4.2	8	62	623	10.0	2	6	10
1981 Min	16	274	1063	3.9	6	83	694	8.4	2	3	8
1982 Min	8	120	515	4.3	1	31	207	6.7	2	0	3
1983 Min	10	120	476	4.0	10	41	357	8.7	1	2	11
1984 Min	13	98	442	4.5	3	46	349	7.6	3	2	6
1985 Min	14	93	336	3.6	7	30	291	9.7	3	1	10
1986 Min	13	63	251	4.0	4	15	132	8.8	0	0	4
NFL Total	104	1117	4546	4.1	40	339	2850	8.4	13	20	53

TOM BROWN Brown, Thomas Martin 6′1″, 223 **RB**
Col: Pittsburgh *HS:* Burrell [Lower Burrell, PA] B: 11/20/1964, Ridgway, PA *Drafted:* 1987 Round 7 Mia
1987 Mia: 1 G; Rush 3-3 1.0; Rec 1-6 6.0. **1989** Mia: 9 G; Rush 13-26 2.0; Rec 13-117 9.0; 1 Fum. **Total:** 10 G; Rush 16-29 1.8; Rec 14-123 8.8; 1 Fum.

TOM BROWN Brown, Thomas McClaren 6′2″, 216 **E**
Col: William & Mary *HS:* Butler [PA] B: 5/22/1921, Pittsburgh, PA
1942 Pit: 9 G; Rec 4-69 17.3; 6 Pt.

THOMAS BROWN Brown, Thomas Wayne 6′4″, 247 **DE-NT**
Col: Baylor *HS:* Ball [Galveston, TX] B: 7/8/1957, Galveston, TX
Drafted: 1980 Round 11 Phi
1980 Phi: 16 G. **1981** Cle: 16 G; KR 2-17 8.5. **1983** Cle: 16 G. **Total:** 48 G; KR 2-17 8.5.

TOM BROWN Brown, Thomas William 6′4″, 190 **WR**
Col: Augustana (S.D.) *HS:* Milaca [MN] B: 12/24/1963, Princeton, MN
1987 Cin: 2 G.

TOM BROWN Brown, Thomas William 6′1″, 192 **DB**
Col: Maryland *HS:* Montgomery Blair [Silver Spring, MD]
B: 12/12/1940, Laureldale, PA *Drafted:* 1963 Round 2 GB
1964 GB: KR 7-167 23.9. **1968** GB: **1** Fum TD. **Total:** KR 7-167 23.9; 1 Fum TD.

		Punt Returns				Interceptions			Tot
Year Team	**G**	**Ret**	**Yds**	**Avg**	**TD**	**Int**	**Yds**	**TD**	**TD**
1964 GB	14	0	0	—	0	1	30	0	0
1965 GB	14	0	0	—	0	3	42	0	0
1966 GB	14	2	0	0.0	0	4	21	0	0
1967 GB	14	9	40	4.4	0	1	51	0	0
1968 GB	14	16	111	6.9	1	4	66	0	2
1969 Was	1	0	0	—	0	0	0	0	0
NFL Total	71	27	151	5.6	1	13	210	0	2

TIM BROWN Brown, Timothy Donell 6′0″, 195 **WR**
Col: Notre Dame *HS:* Woodrow Wilson [Dallas, TX] B: 7/22/1966, Dallas, TX *Drafted:* 1988 Round 1 LARd
1997 Oak: Scor 1 2XP. **Total:** Scor 1 2XP.

		Rushing				Receiving			
Year Team	**G**	**Att**	**Yds**	**Avg**	**TD**	**Rec**	**Yds**	**Avg**	**TD**
1988 LARd	16	14	50	3.6	1	43	725	16.9	5
1989 LARd	1	0	0	—	0	1	8	8.0	0
1990 LARd	16	0	0	—	0	18	265	14.7	3
1991 LARd	16	5	16	3.2	0	36	554	15.4	5
1992 LARd	15	3	-4	-1.3	0	49	693	14.1	7
1993 LARd	16	2	7	3.5	0	80	1180	14.8	7
1994 LARd	16	0	0	—	0	89	1309	14.7	9
1995 Oak	16	0	0	—	0	89	1342	15.1	10
1996 Oak	16	6	35	5.8	0	90	1104	12.3	9
1997 Oak	16	5	19	3.8	0	**104**	1408	13.5	5
1998 Oak	16	1	-7	-7.0	0	81	1012	12.5	9
NFL Total	160	36	116	3.2	1	680	9600	14.1	69

	Punt Returns				Kickoff Returns					Tot
Year Team	**Ret**	**Yds**	**Avg**	**TD**	**Ret**	**Yds**	**Avg**	**TD**	**Fum**	**TD**
1988 LARd	49	444	9.1	0	**41**	**1098**	**26.8**	**1**	5	7
1989 LARd	4	43	10.8	0	3	63	21.0	0	1	0
1990 LARd	34	295	8.7	0	0	0	—	0	3	3
1991 LARd	29	330	11.4	1	1	29	29.0	0	1	6
1992 LARd	37	383	10.4	0	2	14	7.0	0	6	7
1993 LARd	40	465	11.6	1	0	0	—	0	1	8
1994 LARd	40	**487**	12.2	0	0	0	—	0	3	9
1995 Oak	36	364	10.1	0	0	0	—	0	0	10
1996 Oak	32	272	8.5	0	1	24	24.0	0	3	9
1997 Oak	0	0	—	0	1	7	7.0	0	1	5
1998 Oak	3	23	7.7	0	0	0	—	0	3	9
NFL Total	304	3106	10.2	2	49	1235	25.2	1	27	73

TROY BROWN Brown, Troy Fitzgerald 5′10″, 190 **WR**
Col: Marshall *HS:* Hilda [Blackville, SC] B: 7/2/1971, Blackville, SC
Drafted: 1993 Round 8 NE
1995 NE: **1** Fum TD. **1997** NE: Rush 1-(-18) -18.0. **Total:** Rush 1-(-18) -18.0; 1 Fum TD.

		Receiving				Punt Returns			
Year Team	**G**	**Rec**	**Yds**	**Avg**	**TD**	**Ret**	**Yds**	**Avg**	**TD**
1993 NE	12	2	22	11.0	0	25	224	9.0	0
1994 NE	9	0	0	—	0	24	202	8.4	0
1995 NE	16	14	159	11.4	0	0	0	—	0
1996 NE	16	21	222	10.6	0	0	0	—	0
1997 NE	16	41	607	14.8	6	0	0	—	0
1998 NE	10	23	346	15.0	1	17	225	13.2	0
NFL Total	79	101	1356	13.4	7	66	651	9.9	0

	Kickoff Returns					Tot
Year Team	**Ret**	**Yds**	**Avg**	**TD**	**Fum**	**TD**
1993 NE	15	243	16.2	0	2	0
1994 NE	1	14	14.0	0	2	0
1995 NE	31	672	21.7	0	1	1
1996 NE	29	634	21.9	0	0	0
1997 NE	0	0	—	0	0	6
1998 NE	0	0	—	0	0	1
NFL Total	76	1563	20.6	0	5	8

TYRONE BROWN Brown, Tyrone Berry 5′11″, 168 **WR**
Col: Toledo *HS:* Withrow [Cincinnati, OH] B: 1/3/1973, Cincinnati, OH

		Receiving				
Year Team	**G**	**Rec**	**Yds**	**Avg**	**TD**	**Fum**
1995 Atl	6	17	198	11.6	0	1
1996 Atl	9	28	325	11.6	1	0
NFL Total	15	45	523	11.6	1	1

VINCENT BROWN Brown, Vincent Bernard 6′2″, 245 **LB**
Col: Mississippi Valley State *HS:* Walter F. George [Atlanta, GA]
B: 1/9/1965, Atlanta, GA *Drafted:* 1988 Round 2 NE
1989 NE: 4 Sac. **1990** NE: 2.5 Sac. **1991** NE: 3 Sac. **1992** NE: 1 Fum TD; 0.5 Sac. **1993** NE: 1 Sac. **1994** NE: 1.5 Sac. **1995** NE: 4 Sac.
Total: 1 Fum TD; 16.5 Sac.

		Interceptions			Tot
Year Team	**G**	**Int**	**Yds**	**TD**	**TD**
1988 NE	16	0	0	0	0
1989 NE	14	1	-1	0	0
1990 NE	16	0	0	0	0
1991 NE	16	0	0	0	0
1992 NE	13	1	49	1	2
1993 NE	16	1	24	0	0
1994 NE	16	3	22	0	0
1995 NE	16	4	1	0	0
NFL Total	123	10	95	1	2

FRED BROWN Brown, W. Frederick 6′2″, 195 **G**
Col: New York U. *HS:* Dedham [MA] B: 12/9/1905 D: 7/3/1973, Brooklyn, NY
1930 SI: 7 G.

BUDDY BROWN Brown, William Brightie 6′1″, 220 **OG**
Col: Arkansas *HS:* Wynne [AR] B: 10/19/1926, Wynne, AR
Drafted: 1951 Round 19 Was
1951 Was: 12 G. **1952** Was: 12 G. **1953** GB: 11 G. **1954** GB: 12 G; KR 1-0. **1955** GB: 12 G. **1956** GB: 12 G. **Total:** 71 G; KR 1-0.

BILL BROWN Brown, William Dorsey 5′11″, 228 **RB**
(Boom-Boom) *Col:* Illinois *HS:* Mendota Twp. [Mendota, IL]
B: 6/29/1938, Mendota, IL *Drafted:* 1961 Round 2 ChiB
1961 ChiB: KR 4-54 13.5. **1963** Min: KR 3-105 35.0 1 TD. **1964** Min: KR 5-68 13.6. **1966** Min: Pass 1-0. **1968** Min: Pass 1-1 100.0%, 3 3.00. **1972** Min: KR 3-37 12.3. **1973** Min: KR 3-35 11.7. **1974** Min: KR 3-19 6.3.
Total: Pass 2-1 50.0%, 3 1.50; KR 21-318 15.1 1 TD.

		Rushing				Receiving					Tot
Year Team	**G**	**Att**	**Yds**	**Avg**	**TD**	**Rec**	**Yds**	**Avg**	**TD**	**Fum**	**TD**
1961 ChiB	14	22	81	3.7	0	2	6	3.0	0	2	0
1962 Min	14	34	103	3.0	0	10	124	12.4	1	1	1
1963 Min	14	128	445	3.5	5	17	109	6.4	2	7	8
1964 Min	14	226	866	3.8	7	48	703	14.6	9	9	16
1965 Min	14	160	699	4.4	6	41	503	12.3	1	9	7
1966 Min	14	**251**	829	3.3	6	37	359	9.7	0	4	6
1967 Min	14	185	610	3.3	5	22	263	12.0	0	3	5
1968 Min	14	222	805	3.6	11	31	329	10.6	3	6	14
1969 Min	12	126	430	3.4	3	21	183	8.7	0	3	3
1970 Min	14	101	324	3.2	0	15	149	9.9	2	3	2
1971 Min	14	46	136	3.0	2	10	94	9.4	0	0	2
1972 Min	14	82	263	3.2	4	22	298	13.5	4	4	8
1973 Min	14	47	206	4.4	3	5	22	4.4	1	2	4
1974 Min	14	19	41	2.2	0	5	41	8.2	0	3	0
NFL Total	194	1649	5838	3.5	52	286	3183	11.1	23	56	76

BILL BROWN Brown, William Evans 6′1″, 230 **LB**
Col: Bridgeport; Syracuse *HS:* Yorktown [Yorktown Heights, NY]
B: 4/25/1936 D: 4/18/1989, Hempstead, NY
1960 Bos: 14 G; Int 1-8.

WILLIE BROWN Brown, William Ferdie 6′1″, 195 **DB**
Col: Grambling State *HS:* Yazoo Training [MS] B: 12/2/1940, Yazoo City, MS *HOF:* 1984
1963 Den: PR 3-29 9.7; KR 3-70 23.3. **1964** Den: Scor 1 Saf.
Total: PR 3-29 9.7; KR 3-70 23.3; Scor 1 Saf.

		Interceptions		
Year Team	**G**	**Int**	**Yds**	**TD**
1963 Den	8	1	0	0
1964 Den	14	9	140	0
1965 Den	14	2	18	0
1966 Den	14	3	37	0
1967 Oak	14	7	33	1
1968 Oak	14	2	27	1
1969 Oak	14	5	111	0
1970 Oak	8	3	0	0
1971 Oak	14	2	2	0
1972 Oak	14	4	26	0
1973 Oak	14	3	-1	0
1974 Oak	9	1	31	0

1975 Oak	12	4	-1	0
1976 Oak	14	3	25	0
1977 Oak	14	4	24	0
1978 Oak	13	1	0	0
NFL Total	204	54	472	2

BILL BROWN Brown, William Lewis Jr. 6'0", 202 **QB-DB**
Col: Texas Tech *HS:* McKeesport [PA] B: 6/1/1917, McKeesport, PA
1943 Bkn: 5 G; Rec 4-42 10.5. **1944** Bkn: 10 G; Pass 3-1 33.3%, 11 3.67; Rush 4-10 2.5; Rec 2-10 5.0; PR 2-16 8.0; KR 1-12 12.0; Int 1-6. **Total:** 15 G; Pass 3-1 33.3%, 11 3.67; Rush 4-10 2.5; Rec 6-52 8.7; PR 2-16 8.0; KR 1-12 12.0; Int 1-6.

WILLIE BROWN Brown, Willie F 6'0", 188 **WR-HB**
Col: USC *HS:* Long Beach Polytechnic [CA] B: 3/21/1942, Tuscaloosa, AL *Drafted:* 1964 Round 3 LARm
1964 LARm: Rec 1-19 19.0; PR 4-23 5.8. **1965** LARm: Rec 4-91 22.8 1 TD; PR 9-63 7.0. **1966** Phi: PR 5-(-1) -0.2. **Total:** Rec 5-110 22.0 1 TD; PR 18-85 4.7.

		Rushing				Kickoff Returns				
Year Team	**G**	**Att**	**Yds**	**Avg**	**TD**	**Ret**	**Yds**	**Avg**	**TD**	**Fum**
1964 LARm	9	0	0	—	0	6	122	20.3	0	2
1965 LARm	14	44	133	3.0	0	24	615	25.6	0	3
1966 Phi	7	0	0	—	0	4	58	14.5	0	0
NFL Total	30	44	133	3.0	0	34	795	23.4	0	5

NORRIS BROWN Brown, Willie Norris 6'3", 220 **TE**
Col: Georgia *HS:* Laurens [SC] B: 7/10/1961, Laurens, SC
Drafted: 1983 Round 8 Min
1983 Min: 2 G.

GORDIE BROWNE Browne, Gordon Wayland 6'5", 265 **OT**
Col: Boston College *HS:* Chambersburg [PA]; Millis HS [Medfield, MA] B: 12/5/1951, Franklin, MA *Drafted:* 1974 Round 2 NYJ
1974 NYJ: 10 G. **1975** NYJ: 13 G. **Total:** 23 G.

JIM BROWNE Browne, James Christopher 6'1", 215 **RB**
Col: Northwestern; Boston College *HS:* Brother Rice [Birmingham, MI] B: 3/16/1962, Pontiac, MI
1987 LARd: 2 G; Rush 2-1 0.5; Rec 2-8 4.0.

JIM BROWNER Browner, Jimmie Lee 6'1", 209 **DB**
Col: Notre Dame *HS:* Western Reserve Acad. [Hudson, OH] B: 12/4/1955, Warren, OH *Drafted:* 1979 Round 12 Cin
1979 Cin: 16 G; KR 6-87 14.5; Int 1-15. **1980** Cin: 2 G; KR 2-10 5.0. **Total:** 18 G; KR 8-97 12.1; Int 1-15.

JOEY BROWNER Browner, Joey Matthew 6'2", 221 **DB**
Col: USC *HS:* Western Reserve Acad. [Hudson, OH]; Southwest [Atlanta, GA] B: 5/15/1960, Warren, OH *Drafted:* 1983 Round 1 Min
1983 Min: 2 Sac. **1984** Min: **1** Fum TD; 1 Sac. **1985** Min: KR 1-0; 1 Sac. **1986** Min: 0.5 Sac. **1987** Min: 1 Sac. **1989** Min: 1 Sac. **1990** Min: 3 Sac. **Total:** KR 1-0; 1 Fum TD; 9.5 Sac.

		Interceptions				Tot
Year Team	**G**	**Int**	**Yds**	**TD**	**Fum**	**TD**
1983 Min	16	2	0	0	1	0
1984 Min	16	1	20	0	0	1
1985 Min	16	2	17	**1**	1	1
1986 Min	16	4	62	1	0	1
1987 Min	12	6	67	0	0	0
1988 Min	16	5	29	0	0	0
1989 Min	16	5	70	0	0	0
1990 Min	16	7	103	1	0	1
1991 Min	14	5	97	0	0	0
1992 TB	7	0	0	0	0	0
NFL Total	145	37	465	3	2	4

KEITH BROWNER Browner, Keith Tellus 6'6", 245 **LB**
Col: USC *HS:* Western Reserve Acad. [Hudson, OH]; Southwest [Atlanta, GA] B: 1/24/1962, Warren, OH *Drafted:* 1984 Round 2 TB
1984 TB: 16 G; 2 Sac. **1985** TB: 16 G; Int 1-25; 1 Fum; 1.5 Sac. **1986** TB: 15 G; Int 1-16; 4 Sac. **1987** SF-LARd: 2 G; 0.5 Sac. SF: 1 G; 0.5 Sac. LARd: 1 G. **1988** SD: 16 G; Int 2-65 1 TD; 6 Pt; 2.5 Sac. **Total:** 65 G; Int 4-106 1 TD; 6 Pt; 1 Fum; 10.5 Sac.

ROSS BROWNER Browner, Ross Dean 6'3", 262 **DE**
Col: Notre Dame *HS:* Western Reserve Acad. [Hudson, OH] B: 3/22/1954, Warren, OH *Drafted:* 1978 Round 1 Cin
1978 Cin: 11 G. **1979** Cin: 16 G; KR 2-29 14.5. **1980** Cin: 15 G. **1981** Cin: 16 G. **1982** Cin: 9 G; Int 1-29; 3 Sac. **1983** Cin: 12 G; Scor **1** 1XP; 1 Pt; 3 Sac. **1984** Cin: 16 G; 8 Sac. **1985** Cin: 16 G; Scor 1 Saf; 2 Pt; 9 Sac. **1986** Cin: 16 G; 6.5 Sac. **1987** GB: 11 G; 1 Sac. **Total:** 138 G; KR 2-29 14.5; Int 1-29; Scor 1 Saf, 1 1XP; 3 Pt; 30.5 Sac.

CHARLIE BROWNING Browning, Charles A 6'2", 200 **HB**
Col: Washington *HS:* Stockton [CA] B: 7/28/1943 *Drafted:* 1965 Round 17 NYJ
1965 NYJ: 1 G; KR 1-31 31.0.

DAVE BROWNING Browning, David Scott 6'5", 245 **DE**
Col: Spokane CC WA; Washington *HS:* Liberty [Fairfield, WA] B: 8/18/1956, Spokane, WA *Drafted:* 1978 Round 2 Oak
1978 Oak: 12 G. **1979** Oak: 16 G. **1980** Oak: 16 G. **1981** Oak: 16 G; Int 1-8. **1982** LARd: 5 G; 1 Sac. **1983** NE: 12 G; 2 Sac. **Total:** 77 G; Int 1-8; 3 Sac.

GREGG BROWNING Browning, Gregg Jr. 6'0", 190 **OE**
Col: Denver *HS:* Trinidad [CO] B: 1/12/1922, Trinidad, CO
Drafted: 1945 Round 6 Pit
1947 NYG: 3 G; Rec 1-12 12.0; 1 Fum.

JOHN BROWNING Browning, John 6'4", 284 **DE**
Col: West Virginia *HS:* North Miami [FL] B: 9/30/1973, Miami, FL
Drafted: 1996 Round 3 KC
1996 KC: 13 G; 2 Sac. **1997** KC: 14 G; 4 Sac. **1998** KC: 8 G. **Total:** 35 G; 6 Sac.

CLAUDE BROWNLEE Brownlee, Claude 6'4", 265 **DT**
Col: Benedict *HS:* William H. Spencer [Columbus, GA] B: 4/8/1944, Columbus, GA
1967 Mia: 3 G.

DARRICK BROWNLOW Brownlow, Darrick Dewayne 5'10", 241 **LB**
Col: Illinois *HS:* Cathedral [Indianapolis, IN] B: 12/28/1968, Indianapolis, IN *Drafted:* 1991 Round 5 Dal
1991 Dal: 16 G; PR 1-0. **1992** TB: 16 G. **1993** TB: 15 G. **1994** Dal: 16 G. **1995** Was: 16 G; Scor **1** Saf; 2 Pt. **1996** Was: 16 G. **Total:** 95 G; PR 1-0; Scor 1 Saf; 2 Pt.

DICK BRUBAKER Brubaker, Carl Richard 6'0", 202 **OE-DE**
Col: Ohio Wesleyan; Ohio State *HS:* Shaker Heights [OH] B: 1/2/1932, Cleveland, OH D: 6/14/1978 *Drafted:* 1955 Round 15 ChiC
1955 ChiC: 10 G; Rec 6-125 20.8. **1957** ChiC: 3 G. **1960** Buf: 9 G; Rec 7-75 10.7 1 TD; 6 Pt. **Total:** 22 G; Rec 13-200 15.4 1 TD; 6 Pt.

AUNDRAY BRUCE Bruce, Aundray 6'5", 265 **LB-TE-DE**
Col: Auburn *HS:* George Washington Carver [Montgomery, AL] B: 4/30/1966, Montgomery, AL *Drafted:* 1988 Round 1 Atl
1988 Atl: 16 G; Int 2-10; 6 Sac. **1989** Atl: 16 G; KR 1-15 15.0; Int 1-0; 6 Sac. **1990** Atl: 16 G; 4 Sac. **1991** Atl: 14 G; Rec 1-11 11.0. **1992** LARd: 16 G; 3.5 Sac. **1993** LARd: 16 G; 2 Sac. **1994** LARd: 16 G. **1995** Oak: 14 G; Int 1-1 1 TD; 6 Pt; 5.5 Sac. **1996** Oak: 16 G; 4 Sac. **1997** Oak: 10 G; 1 Sac. **1998** Oak: 1 G. **Total:** 151 G; Rec 1-11 11.0; KR 1-15 15.0; Int 4-11 1 TD; 6 Pt; 32 Sac.

GAIL BRUCE Bruce, Gail Robert 6'1", 206 **DE-OE**
Col: Washington *HS:* Puyallup [WA] B: 9/29/1923, Puyallup, WA
Drafted: 1946 Round 30 Pit
AAFC **1948** SF-A: 14 G; Rush 1-1 1.0; Rec 5-49 9.8. **1949** SF-A: 12 G; Rec 1-9 9.0; KR 1-8 8.0; Int 1-5. **Total:** 26 G; Rush 1-1 1.0; Rec 6-58 9.7; KR 1-8 8.0; Int 1-5.

NFL **1950** SF: 12 G; Rec 1-10 10.0; Int 1-4. **1951** SF: 12 G; Scor **1** 1XP; 1 Pt. **Total:** 24 G; Rec 1-10 10.0; Int 1-4; Scor 1 1XP; 1 Pt.

ISAAC BRUCE Bruce, Isaac Isidore 6'0", 184 **WR**
Col: Santa Monica Coll. CA (J.C.); Memphis *HS:* Dillard [Fort Lauderdale, FL] B: 11/10/1972, Ft. Lauderdale, FL *Drafted:* 1994 Round 2 LARm
1994 LARm: Rush 1-2 2.0. **1995** StL: Rush 3-17 5.7; PR 0-52; Scor 1 2XP. **1996** StL: Pass 2-1 50.0%, 15 7.50 1 Int; Rush 1-4 4.0. **1998** StL: Rush 1-30 30.0. **Total:** Pass 2-1 50.0%, 15 7.50 1 Int; Rush 6-53 8.8; PR 0-52; Scor 1 2XP.

		Receiving				
Year Team	**G**	**Rec**	**Yds**	**Avg**	**TD**	**Fum**
1994 LARm	12	21	272	13.0	3	0
1995 StL	16	119	1781	15.0	13	2
1996 StL	16	84	**1338**	15.9	7	1
1997 StL	12	56	815	14.6	5	1
1998 StL	5	32	457	14.3	1	0
NFL Total	61	312	4663	14.9	29	4

LES BRUCKNER Bruckner, Leslie Charles 6'1", 195 **FB-LB**
(Bruck) *Col:* Michigan State *HS:* Milan [MI] B: 4/16/1918, Milan, MI
1945 ChiC: 2 G; KR 1-13 13.0; 1 Fum.

NICK BRUCKNER Bruckner, Nicholas P Jr. 5'11", 185 **WR**
Col: Nassau CC NY; Syracuse *HS:* Newfield [NY] B: 5/19/1961, Queens, NY
1983 NYJ: 7 G. **1984** NYJ: 16 G; Rec 1-11 11.0; PR 2-25 12.5; KR 1-17 17.0. **1985** NYJ: 9 G. **Total:** 32 G; Rec 1-11 11.0; PR 2-25 12.5; KR 1-17 17.0.

HANK BRUDER Bruder, Henry George Jr. 6'0", 199 **BB-DB-LB-TB**
Col: Northwestern *HS:* Pekin [IL] B: 11/22/1907, Pekin, IL
D: 6/29/1970, Matoon, IL
1931 GB: Pass 1 TD. **1932** GB: Pass 4-1 25.0%, 23 5.75 1 Int. **1933** GB: Pass 7-3 42.9%, 14 2.00. **1934** GB: Pass 6-2 33.3%, 22 3.67; Int **1** TD; Scor 22, 4 XK. **1935** GB: Pass 1-1 100.0%, 17 17.00; Int **1** TD. **1937** GB: Pass 6-0, 2 Int. **Total:** Pass 24-7 29.2%, 76 3.17 1 TD 3 Int; Int 2 TD.

Year Team	G	Rushing Att	Yds	Avg	TD	Receiving Rec	Yds	Avg	TD	Tot TD
1931 GB	13	—	—	—	1	—	—	—	2	3
1932 GB	14	75	209	2.8	2	8	143	17.9	2	4
1933 GB	9	77	250	3.2	2	4	69	17.3	0	2
1934 GB	13	48	106	2.2	1	7	104	14.9	1	3
1935 GB	10	44	158	3.6	0	4	67	16.8	0	1
1936 GB	11	4	-7	-1.8	0	2	25	12.5	0	0
1937 GB	10	15	56	3.7	1	0	0	—	0	1
1938 GB	8	2	6	3.0	0	2	14	7.0	0	0
1939 GB	10	0	0	—	0	4	65	16.3	1	1
1940 Pit	8	0	0	—	0	5	49	9.8	0	0
NFL Total	106	265	778	2.9	7	36	536	14.9	6	15

DOC BRUDER Bruder, Woodruff Harlan 5′11″, 178 **WB-TB-BB-FB**
(Woody) *Col:* Pittsburgh; West Virginia *HS:* Heights [Houston, TX] B: 2/5/1901, Houston, TX D: 11/13/1952, Houston, TX
1925 Buf-Fra: 11 G; Rush 1 TD; Scor 8, 2 XK. Buf: 6 G; Rush 1 TD; 6 Pt. Fra: 5 G; Scor 2, 2 XK. **1926** Fra: 13 G; Rush 2 TD; PR 1 TD; Scor 19, 1 XK; Tot TD 3. **Total:** 24 G; Rush 3 TD; PR 1 TD; Tot TD 4.

BOB BRUDZINSKI Brudzinski, Robert Louis 6′4″, 230 **LB**
Col: Ohio State *HS:* Ross [Fremont, OH] B: 1/1/1955, Fremont, OH
Drafted: 1977 Round 1 LARm
1977 LARm: 14 G; Int 2-24. **1978** LARm: 16 G; Int 1-31 1 TD; 6 Pt. **1979** LARm: 16 G; Int 1-26. **1980** LARm: 9 G. **1981** Mia: 16 G; Int 2-35. **1982** Mia: 9 G; Int 1-5; 4.5 Sac. **1983** Mia: 16 G; 1 Sac. **1984** Mia: 16 G; Int 1-0; 3 Sac. **1985** Mia: 14 G; Int 1-6; **1** Fum TD; 6 Pt; 3 Sac. **1986** Mia: 16 G; 2 Sac. **1987** Mia: 12 G; 1 Sac. **1988** Mia: 16 G. **1989** Mia: 10 G; KR 1-6 6.0. **Total:** 180 G; KR 1-6 6.0; Int 9-127 1 TD; 1 Fum TD; Tot TD 2; 12 Pt; 14.5 Sac.

CHARLIE BRUECKMAN Brueckman, Charles William 6′2″, 223 **LB**
Col: Pittsburgh *HS:* Sto-Rox [McKees Rocks, PA] B: 11/23/1935, McKees Rocks, PA *Drafted:* 1957 Round 9 SF
1958 Was: 9 G. **1960** LAC: 14 G. **Total:** 23 G.

MARK BRUENER Bruener, Mark Frederick 6′4″, 258 **TE**
Col: Washington *HS:* J.M. Weatherwax [Aberdeen, WA] B: 9/16/1972, Olympia, WA *Drafted:* 1995 Round 1 Pit
1995 Pit: KR 2-19 9.5. **1996** Pit: Scor 1 2XP. **Total:** KR 2-12 6.0; Scor 1 2XP.

Year Team	G	Receiving Rec	Yds	Avg	TD	Fum
1995 Pit	16	26	238	9.2	3	0
1996 Pit	12	12	141	11.8	0	0
1997 Pit	16	18	117	6.5	6	1
1998 Pit	16	19	157	8.3	2	0
NFL Total	60	75	653	8.7	11	1

BOB BRUER Bruer, Robert Anthony 6′5″, 235 **TE**
Col: Mankato State *HS:* Montello [WI] B: 5/22/1953, Madison, WI
Drafted: 1975 Round 9 Hou
1979 SF: Rush 5-(-4) -0.8; KR 1-20 20.0. **1980** SF-Min: KR 2-20 10.0. Min: KR 2-20 10.0. **Total:** Rush 5-(-4) -0.8; KR 3-40 13.3.

Year Team	G	Receiving Rec	Yds	Avg	TD	Fum
1979 SF	16	26	254	9.8	1	1
1980 SF-Min	13	0	0	—	0	0
1980 SF	1	0	0	—	0	0
1980 Min	12	0	0	—	0	0
1981 Min	15	7	38	5.4	3	1
1982 Min	8	8	102	12.8	2	0
1983 Min	16	31	315	10.2	2	0
NFL Total	68	72	709	9.8	8	2

BOB BRUGGERS Bruggers, Robert Eugene 6′1″, 230 **LB**
Col: Minnesota *HS:* Danube [MN] B: 4/20/1944, Lincoln, NE
1966 Mia: 14 G; KR 1-3 3.0. **1967** Mia: 4 G; Int 1-20. **1968** Mia-SD: 11 G. Mia: 6 G. SD: 5 G. **1969** SD: 12 G; Int 1-5. **1970** SD: 13 G. **1971** SD: 3 G. **Total:** 57 G; KR 1-3 3.0; Int 2-25.

JOHN BRUHIN Bruhin, John Glenn 6′3″, 280 **OG**
Col: Tennessee *HS:* Powell [TN] B: 12/9/1964, Knoxville, TN
Drafted: 1988 Round 4 TB
1988 TB: 16 G. **1989** TB: 9 G. **1990** TB: 14 G. **1991** TB: 10 G. **Total:** 49 G.

CARL BRUMBAUGH Brumbaugh, Carl Lowry 5′10″, 170 **QB-DB-BB**
Col: Ohio State; Florida *HS:* West Milton [OH] B: 9/22/1906, West Milton, OH D: 10/25/1969, West Milton, OH
1930 ChiB: Scor **1** 1XP. **1934** ChiB: Scor 14, 2 XK. **Total:** Scor 1 1XP.

Year Team	G	Passing Att	Comp	Comp%	Yds	YPA	TD	Int	Rating
1930 ChiB	14	—	—	—	—	—	0	—	—
1931 ChiB	12	—	—	—	—	—	2	—	—
1932 ChiB	13	7	3	42.9	71	10.14	0	0	80.1
1933 ChiB	13	29	8	27.6	101	3.48	1	6	13.5
1934 ChiB	13	35	8	22.9	232	6.63	2	**2**	49.9
1936 ChiB	12	28	8	28.6	140	5.00	3	3	44.0
1937 Cle-Bkn-ChiB	10	18	5	27.8	87	4.83	0	3	7.6
1937 Cle	5	2	1	50.0	20	10.00	0	0	85.4
1937 Bkn	4	16	4	25.0	67	4.19	0	3	4.9
1937 ChiB	1	0	0	—	0	—	0	0	—
1938 ChiB	9	4	2	50.0	25	6.25	0	0	69.8
NFL Total	96	121	34	28.1	656	5.42	8	14	32.1

Year Team	Rushing Att	Yds	Avg	TD	Receiving Rec	Yds	Avg	TD	Tot TD
1930 ChiB	—	—	—	1	—	—	—	0	1
1931 ChiB	—	—	—	1	—	—	—	0	1
1932 ChiB	17	14	0.8	0	9	129	14.3	0	0
1933 ChiB	20	39	2.0	0	5	82	16.4	0	0
1934 ChiB	7	-9	-1.3	0	5	84	16.8	2	2
1936 ChiB	9	-1	-0.1	0	5	39	7.8	2	2
1937 Cle-Bkn-ChiB	7	-3	-0.4	0	0	0	—	0	0
1937 Cle	2	8	4.0	0	0	0	—	0	0
1937 Bkn	5	-11	-2.2	0	0	0	—	0	0
1938 ChiB	3	-15	-5.0	0	1	23	23.0	0	0
NFL Total	63	25	0.4	2	25	357	14.3	4	6

JUSTIN BRUMBAUGH Brumbaugh, Justin Jay 6′0″, 205 **TB-BB**
Col: Bucknell *HS:* Tarentum [PA] B: 3/2/1905, Springdale, PA
D: 7/3/1951, Rochester, MN
1931 Fra: 8 G.

BOYD BRUMBAUGH Brumbaugh, Urban Boyd 5′11″, 195 **FB-TB-HB**
Col: Duquesne *HS:* Steel Valley [Munhall, PA] B: 8/24/1915, Springdale, PA D: 4/5/1988, Homestead, PA *Drafted:* 1938 Round 1 Bkn
1938 Bkn: Rec 1-5 5.0 1 TD. **1939** Bkn-Pit: Rec 5-95 19.0 1 TD; Punt 1-34 34.0. Bkn: Rec 1-5 5.0. Pit: Rec 4-90 22.5 1 TD; Punt 1-34 34.0. **1940** Pit: Rec 1-0; Punt 6-194 32.3. **1941** Pit: Rec 1-1 1.0; PR 7-60 8.6; KR 11-271 24.6. **Total:** Rec 8-101 12.6 2 TD; PR 7-60 8.6; KR 11-271 24.6; Punt 7-228 32.6.

Year Team	G	Passing Att	Comp	Comp%	Yds	YPA	TD	Int	Rating
1938 Bkn	7	0	0	—	0	—	0	0	—
1939 Bkn-Pit	11	9	3	33.3	121	13.44	2	1	81.9
1939 Bkn	5	2	0	0.0	0	0.00	0	0	39.6
1939 Pit	6	7	3	42.9	121	17.29	2	1	89.9
1940 Pit	8	7	2	28.6	46	6.57	0	1	14.9
1941 Pit	10	41	13	31.7	260	6.34	2	8	31.6
NFL Total	36	57	18	31.6	427	7.49	4	10	43.4

Year Team	Rushing Att	Yds	Avg	TD	Tot TD
1938 Bkn	45	191	4.2	0	1
1939 Bkn-Pit	111	343	3.1	2	3
1939 Bkn	25	61	2.4	0	0
1939 Pit	86	282	3.3	2	3
1940 Pit	32	79	2.5	0	0
1941 Pit	68	114	1.7	2	2
NFL Total	256	727	2.8	4	6

JACK BRUMFIELD Brumfield, Jackson Louis 6′2″, 215 **DE**
Col: Southern Mississippi *HS:* Franklinton [LA] B: 5/1/1931, Franklinton, LA
1954 SF: 12 G.

JIM BRUMFIELD Brumfield, James I 6′1″, 195 **RB**
Col: Indiana State *HS:* Elizabeth [PA] B: 9/4/1947, Osyka, MS
1971 Pit: 14 G; KR 12-271 22.6; 1 Fum.

SCOTT BRUMFIELD Brumfield, Scott Wheeler 6′8″, 321 **OT-OG**
Col: Dixie Coll. UT (J.C.); Brigham Young *HS:* Spanish Fork [UT] B: 8/19/1970, Salt Lake City, UT
1993 Cin: 16 G. **1994** Cin: 2 G. **1995** Cin: 14 G. **1996** Cin: 9 G. **1997** Cin: 15 G. **Total:** 56 G.

BOB BRUMLEY Brumley, Robert Lee 6′0″, 200 **WB-DB**
Col: Rice B: 9/24/1919 *Drafted:* 1942 Round 8 Cle
1945 Det: 1 G; Rush 5-18 3.6; Rec 2-27 13.5; 1 Fum.

DON BRUMM Brumm, Donald Dwain 6′3″, 245 **DE**
Col: Purdue *HS:* Hammond [IN] B: 10/4/1941, Chicago Heights, IL
Drafted: 1963 Round 1 StL
1963 StL: 11 G. **1964** StL: 14 G. **1965** StL: 14 G; **1** Fum TD; 6 Pt. **1966** StL: 14 G. **1967** StL: 10 G. **1968** StL: 14 G; **1** Fum TD; 6 Pt. **1969** StL: 4 G. **1970** Phi: 7 G. **1971** Phi: 9 G. **1972** StL: 14 G. **Total:** 111 G; 2 Fum TD; 12 Pt.

FRED BRUMM Brumm, Frederick Jr. **T-C**
Col: Union (N.Y.) B: 11/1887, Tonawanda, NY Deceased
1921 Ton: 1 G.

ROMAN BRUMM Brumm, Roman Henry 6′0″, 182 **E-G-T-C**
Col: Wis.-La Crosse; Wis.-Eau Claire; Wisconsin *HS:* James Madison Memorial [Madison, WI] B: 3/5/1898, Madison, WI D: 9/2/1981
1924 Rac: 9 G. **1925** Mil: 5 G. **1926** Rac: 4 G. **Total:** 18 G.

DEWEY BRUNDAGE Brundage, Jean Dewey 6′3″, 210 **DE**
Col: Brigham Young *HS:* El Monte [CA] B: 10/1/1931, Alhambra, CA
Drafted: 1954 Round 22 Det
1954 Pit: 11 G.

BILL BRUNDIGE Brundige, William Glenn 6′5″, 270 **DT-DE**
Col: Colorado *HS:* Haxtun [CO] B: 11/13/1948, Holyoke, CO
Drafted: 1970 Round 2 Was
1970 Was: 14 G; KR 1-1 1.0. **1971** Was: 14 G. **1972** Was: 11 G. **1973** Was: 14 G. **1974** Was: 14 G. **1975** Was: 14 G. **1976** Was: 14 G. **1977** Was: 12 G. **Total:** 107 G; KR 1-1 1.0.

LARRY BRUNE Brune, Lawrence Dee 6′2″, 202 **DB**
Col: Rice *HS:* C.E. King [Houston, TX] B: 5/4/1953, San Diego, CA
Drafted: 1976 Round 7 Min
1980 Min: 16 G; Int 2-68.

MARK BRUNELL Brunell, Mark Allen 6′1″, 218 **QB**
Col: Washington *HS:* St. Joseph [Santa Maria, CA] B: 9/17/1970, Los Angeles, CA *Drafted:* 1993 Round 5 GB
1996 Jac: Scor 2 2XP. **Total:** Scor 2 2XP.

		Passing							
Year Team	**G**	**Att**	**Comp**	**Comp%**	**Yds**	**YPA**	**TD**	**Int**	**Rating**
1994 GB	2	27	12	44.4	95	3.52	0	0	53.8
1995 Jac	13	346	201	58.1	2168	6.27	15	7	82.6
1996 Jac	16	557	353	63.4	**4367**	**7.84**	19	20	84.0
1997 Jac	14	435	264	60.7	3281	7.54	18	7	91.2
1998 Jac	13	354	208	58.8	2601	7.35	20	9	89.9
NFL Total	58	1719	1038	60.4	12512	7.28	72	43	86.3

	Rushing				
Year Team	**Att**	**Yds**	**Avg**	**TD**	**Fum**
1994 GB	6	7	1.2	1	1
1995 Jac	67	480	7.2	4	5
1996 Jac	80	396	5.0	3	14
1997 Jac	48	257	5.4	2	4
1998 Jac	49	192	3.9	0	3
NFL Total	250	1332	5.3	10	27

SAM BRUNELLI Brunelli, Samuel Aldino 6′2″, 270 **OT-OG**
Col: Colorado State *HS:* Weldon Valley [Weldona, CO] B: 12/13/1943, Fort Morgan, CO
1966 Den: 2 G. **1967** Den: 12 G. **1968** Den: 14 G. **1969** Den: 14 G. **1970** Den: 13 G. **1971** Den: 5 G. **Total:** 60 G.

BOB BRUNET Brunet, Robert Paul 6′1″, 205 **RB**
Col: Louisiana Tech *HS:* Cut Off [Larose, LA] B: 7/29/1946, Larose, LA
Drafted: 1968 Round 7 Was
1968 Was: Rec 18-160 8.9 1 TD. **1970** Was: Rec 3-28 9.3. **1971** Was: Rec 2-4 2.0. **1972** Was: Rec 1-8 8.0; KR 8-190 23.8. **1975** Was: KR 5-83 16.6. **1976** Was: KR 4-85 21.3. **1977** Was: KR 2-40 20.0.
Total: Rec 24-200 8.3 1 TD; KR 19-398 20.9.

		Rushing					Tot
Year Team	**G**	**Att**	**Yds**	**Avg**	**TD**	**Fum**	**TD**
1968 Was	7	71	227	3.2	0	7	1
1970 Was	6	9	37	4.1	0	0	0
1971 Was	7	10	27	2.7	0	1	0
1972 Was	14	30	82	2.7	2	1	2
1973 Was	14	2	4	2.0	0	0	0
1975 Was	14	6	23	3.8	1	0	1
1976 Was	14	0	0	—	0	0	0
1977 Was	5	3	6	2.0	0	0	0
NFL Total	81	131	406	3.1	3	9	4

FRED BRUNEY Bruney, Frederick Karl 5′10″, 184 **DB**
Col: Ohio State *HS:* Martins Ferry [OH] B: 12/30/1931, Martins Ferry, OH *Drafted:* 1953 Round 3 Cle
1953 SF: KR 2-46 23.0. **1956** SF-Pit: KR 9-235 26.1. Pit: KR 9-235 26.1. **1957** Pit: KR 5-101 20.2. **1960** Bos: KR 2-39 19.5. **Total:** KR 18-421 23.4.

		Punt Returns				Interceptions			
Year Team	**G**	**Ret**	**Yds**	**Avg**	**TD**	**Int**	**Yds**	**TD**	**Fum**
1953 SF	12	1	11	11.0	0	5	59	0	0
1956 SF-Pit	10	5	20	4.0	0	1	39	0	0
1956 SF	5	0	0	—	0	0	0	0	0
1956 Pit	5	5	20	4.0	0	1	39	0	0
1957 Pit	12	17	86	5.1	0	1	0	0	1
1958 LARm	3	0	0	—	0	0	0	0	0
1960 Bos	12	4	31	7.8	0	3	35	0	0
1961 Bos	14	**23**	109	4.7	0	2	20	0	0
1962 Bos	14	3	8	2.7	0	3	70	**1**	1
NFL Total	77	53	265	5.0	0	15	223	1	2

AUSTIN BRUNKLACHER Brunklacher, N. Austin 193 **G**
Col: No College B: 1898, KY Deceased
1921 Lou: 1 G. **1922** Lou: 4 G. **1923** Lou: 2 G. **Total:** 7 G.

SCOTT BRUNNER Brunner, Scott Lee 6′5″, 205 **QB**
Col: Delaware *HS:* Henderson [West Chester, PA]; Lawrenceville School [NJ] B: 3/24/1957, Sellersville, PA *Drafted:* 1980 Round 6 NYG

		Passing							
Year Team	**G**	**Att**	**Comp**	**Comp%**	**Yds**	**YPA**	**TD**	**Int**	**Rating**
1980 NYG	16	112	52	46.4	610	5.45	4	6	53.1
1981 NYG	16	190	79	41.6	978	5.15	5	11	42.8
1982 NYG	9	298	161	54.0	2017	6.77	10	9	73.9
1983 NYG	16	386	190	49.2	2516	6.52	9	22	54.3
1985 StL	16	60	30	50.0	336	5.60	1	6	33.1
NFL Total	73	1046	512	48.9	6457	6.17	29	54	56.3

	Rushing				
Year Team	**Att**	**Yds**	**Avg**	**TD**	**Fum**
1980 NYG	10	18	1.8	0	3
1981 NYG	14	20	1.4	0	6
1982 NYG	19	27	1.4	1	5
1983 NYG	26	64	2.5	0	8
1985 StL	3	8	2.7	0	3
NFL Total	72	137	1.9	1	25

DAVE BRUNO Bruno, David 6′1″, 235 **P**
Col: Gavilan Coll. CA (J.C.); Moraine Valley CC IL B: 3/19/1963, Chicago, IL
1987 Min: 2 G; Punt 13-464 35.7.

JOHN BRUNO Bruno, John Currie Jr. 6′2″, 190 **P**
Col: Penn State *HS:* Upper St. Clair [Pittsburgh, PA] B: 9/10/1964, Jeannette, PA *Drafted:* 1987 Round 5 StL
1987 Pit: 3 G; Punt 16-619 38.7.

LARRY BRUNSON Brunson, Larry Rudolph 5′11″, 180 **WR**
Col: Mesa; Colorado *HS:* Montezuma-Cortez [Cortez, CO]
B: 8/11/1949, Little Rock, AR *Drafted:* 1972 Round 11 Den
1974 KC: Rush 5-(-33) -6.6. **1975** KC: Rush 2-89 44.5. **1976** KC: Rush 3-(-1) -0.3. **1977** KC: Rush 2-8 4.0. **Total:** Rush 12-63 5.3.

		Receiving				Punt Returns			
Year Team	**G**	**Rec**	**Yds**	**Avg**	**TD**	**Ret**	**Yds**	**Avg**	**TD**
1974 KC	14	22	374	17.0	2	19	111	5.8	0
1975 KC	14	23	398	17.3	2	1	4	4.0	0
1976 KC	14	33	656	19.9	1	31	387	12.5	0
1977 KC	11	20	295	14.8	0	20	108	5.4	0
1978 Oak	2	0	0	—	0	0	0	—	0
1979 Oak	11	5	49	9.8	1	2	8	4.0	0
1980 Den	13	1	15	15.0	0	2	12	6.0	0
NFL Total	79	104	1787	17.2	6	75	630	8.4	0

	Kickoff Returns				
Year Team	**Ret**	**Yds**	**Avg**	**TD**	**Fum**
1974 KC	12	280	23.3	0	3
1975 KC	1	8	8.0	0	0
1976 KC	0	0	—	0	2
1977 KC	11	216	19.6	0	1
1978 Oak	6	154	25.7	0	0
1979 Oak	17	441	**25.9**	0	1
1980 Den	40	923	23.1	0	0
NFL Total	87	2022	23.2	0	7

MIKE BRUNSON Brunson, Michael Sanders 6′1″, 190 **RB**
Col: Mesa; Arizona State *HS:* Montezuma-Cortez [Cortez, CO]
B: 7/30/1947, Little Rock, AR *Drafted:* 1970 Round 11 Atl
1970 Atl: 8 G; Rush 1-9 9.0; KR 4-54 13.5.

BRUNSWICK Brunswick 5′10″, 182 **G**
Col: No College
1920 Ham: 1 G.

ROSS BRUPBACHER Brupbacher, Ross Alan 6′3″, 215 **LB**
Col: Texas A&M *HS:* Lafayette [LA] B: 4/7/1948, Lafayette, LA
Drafted: 1970 Round 4 ChiB
1971 ChiB: **1** Fum TD. **Total:** 1 Fum TD.

		Interceptions				Tot
Year Team	**G**	**Int**	**Yds**	**TD**	**Fum**	**TD**
1970 ChiB	14	2	17	0	0	0
1971 ChiB	14	2	34	0	1	1
1972 ChiB	14	1	11	0	0	1
1976 ChiB	14	7	49	0	1	0
NFL Total	56	12	111	0	2	2

TEDY BRUSCHI Bruschi, Tedy Lacap 6′1″, 245 **LB**
Col: Arizona *HS:* Roseville [CA] B: 6/9/1973, San Francisco, CA
Drafted: 1996 Round 3 NE
1996 NE: 16 G; 6 Pt; 4 Sac. **1997** NE: 16 G; 4 Sac. **1998** NE: 16 G; KR 1-4 4.0; 2 Sac. **Total:** 48 G; KR 1-4 4.0; 6 Pt; 10 Sac.

JIM BRUTZ Brutz, James Charles 6′0″, 230 **T**
Col: Notre Dame *HS:* Warren G. Harding [Warren, OH] B: 2/12/1919, Niles, OH
AAFC **1946** ChiA: 14 G. **1948** ChiA: 9 G. **Total:** 23 G.

JOHNNY BRYAN Bryan, John Frederick 5′8″, 170 **HB-QB-TB-WB**
(Red) *Col:* Dartmouth; Chicago *HS:* Lyons Twp. [La Grange, IL]
B: 2/28/1897, Chicago, IL D: 7/1/1966, Fort Collins, CO
1922 ChiC: 10 G. **1923** ChiB: 13 G; Pass 2 TD; Rush 4 TD; 24 Pt. **1924** ChiB: 11 G; Rush 2 TD; Rec 1 TD; Tot TD 3; 18 Pt. **1925** Mil-ChiB: 11 G; Rec 1 TD; 6 Pt. Mil: 5 G. ChiB: 6 G; Rec 1 TD; 6 Pt. **1926** Mil-ChiB: 12 G. Mil: 9 G; Rush 1 TD; 6 Pt. ChiB: 3 G. **1927** ChiB: 1 G. **Total:** 58 G; Pass 2 TD; Rush 7 TD; Rec 2 TD; Tot TD 9; 54 Pt.

RICK BRYAN Bryan, Rick Don 6′4″, 265 **DT-DE-NT-LB**
Col: Oklahoma *HS:* Coweta [OK] B: 3/20/1962, Tulsa, OK
Drafted: 1984 Round 1 Atl
1984 Atl: 16 G; Scor **1** Saf; 2 Pt; 2 Sac. **1985** Atl: 16 G; Scor **1** 1XP; 1 Pt; 7.5 Sac. **1986** Atl: 16 G; 7 Sac. **1987** Atl: 9 G; 2.5 Sac. **1988** Atl: 16 G; 5 Sac. **1989** Atl: 2 G; 1 Sac. **1990** Atl: 16 G; 1 Sac. **1991** Atl: 16 G; 3 Sac. **1993** Atl: 2 G. **Total:** 109 G; Scor 1 Saf, 1 1XP; 3 Pt; 29.0 Sac.

STEVE BRYAN Bryan, Steven Ray 6′2″, 256 **DE-NT-LB**
Col: Oklahoma *HS:* Coweta [OK] B: 5/6/1964, Wagoner, OK
Drafted: 1987 Round 5 ChiB
1987 Den: 4 G. **1988** Den: 8 G. **Total:** 12 G.

WALTER BRYAN Bryan, Walter Dean 6′1″, 185 **DB-HB**
(Jo Jo) *Col:* Tarleton State; Texas Tech *HS:* Olney [TX]
B: 12/23/1933, Olney, TX *Drafted:* 1955 Round 9 Bal
1955 Bal: 10 G; Rush 2-4 2.0; Int 1-4.

BILLY BRYAN Bryan, William Kirby 6′2″, 251 **C-OG**
Col: Duke *HS:* Walter M. Williams [Burlington, NC] B: 6/21/1955, Burlington, NC *Drafted:* 1977 Round 4 Den
1977 Den: 1 G. **1978** Den: 13 G. **1979** Den: 16 G. **1980** Den: 16 G; 2 Fum. **1981** Den: 14 G; 1 Fum. **1982** Den: 9 G. **1983** Den: 16 G. **1984** Den: 16 G; 1 Fum. **1985** Den: 16 G. **1986** Den: 16 G. **1987** Den: 4 G. **1988** Den: 16 G. **Total:** 153 G; 4 Fum.

BOBBY BRYANT Bryant, Bobby Lee 6′1″, 170 **DB**
(Bones) *Col:* South Carolina *HS:* Willingham [Macon, GA]
B: 1/24/1944, Macon, GA *Drafted:* 1967 Round 7 Min
1968 Min: KR 19-373 19.6. **1971** Min: KR 1-23 23.0. **1972** Min: KR 2-41 20.5; **1** Fum TD. **Total:** KR 22-437 19.9; 1 Fum TD.

		Punt Returns				Interceptions				Tot
Year Team	**G**	**Ret**	**Yds**	**Avg**	**TD**	**Int**	**Yds**	**TD**	**Fum**	**TD**
1968 Min	14	10	49	4.9	0	2	60	1	2	1
1969 Min	10	2	9	4.5	0	8	97	0	0	0
1970 Min	11	0	0	—	0	3	40	1	0	1
1971 Min	13	2	26	13.0	0	3	51	0	2	0
1972 Min	14	10	48	4.8	0	4	82	0	1	1
1973 Min	14	25	140	5.6	0	7	105	1	1	1
1974 Min	1	0	0	—	0	0	0	0	0	0
1975 Min	14	19	125	6.6	0	6	111	0	6	0
1976 Min	12	0	0	—	0	2	30	0	0	0
1977 Min	14	0	0	—	0	4	44	0	0	0
1978 Min	16	0	0	—	0	7	69	0	1	0
1979 Min	14	1	7	7.0	0	2	50	0	0	0
1980 Min	14	0	0	—	0	3	10	0	0	0
NFL Total	161	69	404	5.9	0	51	749	3	13	4

CHARLIE BRYANT Bryant, Charles Limar 6′0″, 207 **RB**
Col: Allen *HS:* Columbus [Lakeview, SC] B: 3/7/1941, Lakeview, SC
Drafted: 1966 Round 9 StL
1968 Atl: Rec 1-11 11.0. **1969** Atl: Rec 2-15 7.5. **Total:** Rec 3-26 8.7.

		Rushing				Kickoff Returns				
Year Team	**G**	**Att**	**Yds**	**Avg**	**TD**	**Ret**	**Yds**	**Avg**	**TD**	**Fum**
1966 StL	4	5	31	6.2	0	2	70	35.0	0	0
1967 StL	14	3	16	5.3	0	14	324	23.1	0	1
1968 Atl	2	9	29	3.2	0	5	112	22.4	0	2
1969 Atl	14	50	246	4.9	0	21	407	19.4	0	2
NFL Total	34	67	322	4.8	0	42	913	21.7	0	5

CHUCK BRYANT Bryant, Charles S 6′2″, 220 **OE**
Col: Ohio State *HS:* Zanesville [OH] B: 9/12/1940 *Drafted:* 1962 Round 3 StL
1962 StL: 13 G.

DOMINGO BRYANT Bryant, Domingo Garcia 6′4″, 178 **DB**
Col: Texas A&M *HS:* Garrison [TX] B: 12/8/1963, Nacogodoches, TX
Drafted: 1986 Round 6 Pit
1987 Hou: 13 G; Int 4-75. **1988** Hou: 14 G; Int 3-56 1 TD; 6 Pt. **Total:** 27 G; Int 7-131 1 TD; 6 Pt.

JUNIOR BRYANT Bryant, Edward Ethan Jr. 6′4″, 278 **DE-DT**
Col: Notre Dame *HS:* Creighton Prep [Omaha, NE] B: 1/16/1971, Omaha, NE
1995 SF: 16 G; 1 Sac. **1996** SF: 16 G; 0.5 Sac. **1997** SF: 16 G; 2.5 Sac. **1998** SF: 16 G; 5 Sac. **Total:** 64 G; 9 Sac.

HUBIE BRYANT Bryant, Hubert Lavann 5′10″, 170 **WR**
Col: Minnesota *HS:* Penn Hills [Pittsburgh, PA] B: 2/10/1946, Pittsburgh, PA
1970 Pit: Rush 3-25 8.3; Rec 8-154 19.3. **1971** NE: Rush 4-1 0.3; Rec 14-212 15.1 1 TD; KR 10-252 25.2. **Total:** Rush 7-26 3.7; Rec 22-366 16.6 1 TD; KR 10-252 25.2.

		Punt Returns				
Year Team	**G**	**Ret**	**Yds**	**Avg**	**TD**	**Fum**
1970 Pit	14	37	159	4.3	0	3
1971 NE	11	10	24	2.4	0	1
1972 NE	2	0	0	—	0	0
NFL Total	27	47	183	3.9	0	4

JIM BRYANT Bryant, James Gorman 5′6″, 156 **BB-WB**
Col: George Washington; Pennsylvania B: 7/12/1894, Toronto, Canada
D: 4/18/1972, Sacramento, CA
1920 Cle: 3 G.

JEFF BRYANT Bryant, Jeffrey Dwight 6′5″, 276 **DE**
Col: Clemson *HS:* Gordon [Decatur, GA] B: 5/22/1960, Atlanta, GA
Drafted: 1982 Round 1 Sea
1982 Sea: 9 G; 3 Sac. **1983** Sea: 16 G; 8 Sac. **1984** Sea: 16 G; Int 1-1; Scor **1** Saf; 2 Pt; 14.5 Sac. **1985** Sea: 16 G; 8.5 Sac. **1986** Sea: 12 G; 4 Sac. **1987** Sea: 12 G; 4 Sac. **1988** Sea: 16 G; 3.5 Sac. **1989** Sea: 15 G; 3.5 Sac. **1990** Sea: 15 G; 5.5 Sac. **1991** Sea: 16 G; 3 Sac. **1992** Sea: 16 G; 4.5 Sac. **1993** Sea: 16 G; 1 Sac. **Total:** 175 G; Int 1-1; Scor 1 Saf; 2 Pt; 63.0 Sac.

KELVIN BRYANT Bryant, Kelvin Leroy 6′2″, 195 **RB**
Col: North Carolina *HS:* Tarboro [NC] B: 9/26/1960, Tarboro, NC
Drafted: 1983 Round 7 Was
1987 Was: Pass 1-0. **Total:** Pass 1-0.

		Rushing				Receiving					Tot
Year Team	**G**	**Att**	**Yds**	**Avg**	**TD**	**Rec**	**Yds**	**Avg**	**TD**	**Fum**	**TD**
1986 Was	10	69	258	3.7	4	43	449	10.4	3	2	7
1987 Was	11	77	406	5.3	1	43	490	11.4	5	4	6
1988 Was	10	108	498	4.6	1	42	447	10.6	5	3	6
1990 Was	15	6	24	4.0	0	26	248	9.5	1	0	1
NFL Total	46	260	1186	4.6	6	154	1634	10.6	14	9	20

BOB BRYANT Bryant, Robert Earl 6′5″, 230 **OE**
Col: Texas *HS:* Plainview [TX] B: 5/19/1937
1960 DalT: 10 G; Rec 5-43 8.6.

BOB BRYANT Bryant, Robert R 6′3″, 226 **T**
Col: Rancho Santiago Coll. CA (J.C.); Texas Tech *HS:* Olton [TX]
B: 6/14/1919, Frederick, OK
AAFC **1946** SF-A: 14 G. **1947** SF-A: 14 G. **1948** SF-A: 14 G; PR 1-14 14.0. **1949** SF-A: 5 G. **Total:** 47 G; PR 1-14 14.0.

STEVE BRYANT Bryant, Stephen Theodore 6′2″, 195 **WR**
Col: Los Angeles Southwest Coll. CA (J.C.); Purdue *HS:* George Washington [Los Angeles, CA] B: 10/10/1959, Los Angeles, CA
Drafted: 1982 Round 4 Hou
1983 Hou: Pass 1-1 100.0%, 24 24.00 1 TD. **Total:** Pass 1-1 100.0%, 24 24.00 1 TD.

		Receiving				
Year Team	**G**	**Rec**	**Yds**	**Avg**	**TD**	**Fum**
1982 Hou	7	0	0	—	0	0
1983 Hou	16	16	211	13.2	0	0
1984 Hou	14	19	278	14.6	0	1
1985 Hou	4	0	0	—	0	0
1987 Ind	1	1	12	12.0	0	0
NFL Total	42	36	501	13.9	0	1

TIM BRYANT Bryant, Timothy Craig 6′1″, 217 **LB**
Col: Vanderbilt; Southern Mississippi *HS:* Mount Juliet [TN]
B: 5/5/1962, Nashville, TN
1987 Min: 1 G.

TRENT BRYANT Bryant, Trent Baron 5′10″, 180 **DB**
Col: Arkansas *HS:* Arkadelphia [AR] B: 8/14/1959, Arkadelphia, AR
Drafted: 1981 Round 10 Bal
1981 Was: 4 G. **1982** KC: 9 G. **1983** KC: 16 G; Int 1-19. **1987** KC: 3 G; Int 1-0. **Total:** 32 G; Int 2-19.

WARREN BRYANT Bryant, Warren 6′6″, 273 **OT**
Col: Kentucky *HS:* Miami Edison [FL] B: 11/11/1955, Miami, FL
Drafted: 1977 Round 1 Atl
1977 Atl: 14 G. **1978** Atl: 13 G. **1979** Atl: 16 G. **1980** Atl: 16 G. **1981** Atl: 11 G. **1982** Atl: 9 G. **1983** Atl: 16 G. **1984** Atl-LARd: 9 G. Atl: 4 G. LARd: 5 G. **Total:** 104 G.

WAYMOND BRYANT Bryant, Waymond 6′4″, 236 **LB**
Col: Tennessee State *HS:* Franklin D. Roosevelt [Dallas, TX]
B: 7/28/1952, Dallas, TX *Drafted:* 1974 Round 1 ChiB
1974 ChiB: 13 G; Int 2-11. **1975** ChiB: 13 G. **1976** ChiB: 14 G; Int 2-6. **1977** ChiB: 13 G. **Total:** 53 G; Int 4-17.

CULLEN BRYANT Bryant, William Cullen 6′1″, 234 **RB**
Col: Colorado *HS:* General William Mitchell [Colorado Springs, CO]
B: 5/20/1951, Fort Sill, OK *Drafted:* 1973 Round 2 LARm

		Rushing				Receiving			
Year Team	**G**	**Att**	**Yds**	**Avg**	**TD**	**Rec**	**Yds**	**Avg**	**TD**
1973 LARm	13	0	0	—	0	0	0	—	0
1974 LARm	14	10	24	2.4	0	2	14	7.0	0
1975 LARm	14	117	467	4.0	2	20	229	11.5	0
1976 LARm	14	21	64	3.0	2	2	28	14.0	0
1977 LARm	14	6	42	7.0	0	4	28	7.0	0
1978 LARm	16	178	658	3.7	7	8	76	9.5	0
1979 LARm	16	177	619	3.5	5	31	227	7.3	0
1980 LARm	16	183	807	4.4	3	53	386	7.3	3
1981 LARm	13	109	436	4.0	1	22	160	7.3	0
1982 LARm	1	0	0	—	0	0	0	—	0
1983 Sea	10	27	87	3.2	0	3	8	2.7	0
1984 Sea	9	20	58	2.9	0	3	20	6.7	0
1987 LARm	3	1	2	2.0	0	0	0	—	0
NFL Total	153	849	3264	3.8	20	148	1176	7.9	3

	Punt Returns				Kickoff Returns					Tot
Year Team	**Ret**	**Yds**	**Avg**	**TD**	**Ret**	**Yds**	**Avg**	**TD**	**Fum**	**TD**
1973 LARm	0	0	—	0	13	369	28.4	1	0	1
1974 LARm	17	171	10.1	0	23	617	26.8	**1**	0	1
1975 LARm	2	47	23.5	0	12	280	23.3	0	4	2
1976 LARm	29	321	11.1	0	16	459	28.7	**1**	2	3
1977 LARm	20	141	7.1	0	2	35	17.5	0	1	0
1978 LARm	3	27	9.0	0	0	0	—	0	0	7
1979 LARm	0	0	—	0	0	0	—	0	2	5
1980 LARm	0	0	—	0	0	0	—	0	1	6
1981 LARm	0	0	—	0	0	0	—	0	1	1
1984 Sea	0	0	—	0	3	53	17.7	0	0	0
NFL Total	71	707	10.0	0	69	1813	26.3	3	11	26

BILL BRYANT Bryant, William Jr. 5′11″, 195 **DB**
(Boone) *Col:* Grambling State *HS:* Webster [Minden, LA]
B: 2/24/1951, Shreveport, LA *Drafted:* 1974 Round 6 Cin
1976 NYG: 14 G. **1977** NYG: 14 G; Int 3-54 **1** TD; 6 Pt. **1978** NYG-Phi: 14 G. NYG: 11 G. Phi: 3 G. **Total:** 42 G; Int 3-54 1 TD; 6 Pt.

BENO BRYANT Bryant, Wilson G 5′9″, 175 **RB**
Col: Washington *HS:* Susan Miller Dorsey [Los Angeles, CA]
B: 1/1/1971, Los Angeles, CA
1994 Sea: 2 G; Rush 1-6 6.0; PR 1-31 31.0; KR 7-136 19.4.

MARK BUBEN Buben, Mark Michael 6′3″, 260 **DE-NT**
Col: Tufts *HS:* Metheun [MA] B: 3/23/1957, Auburn, MA
1979 NE: 16 G. **1981** NE: 16 G; Int 1-49. **1982** Cle: 3 G. **Total:** 35 G; Int 1-49.

MIKE BUCCHIANERI Bucchianeri, Amadeo Roger 5′10″, 212 **G**
Col: Indiana *HS:* Monongahela [PA] B: 1/9/1917, Van Voorhis, PA
D: 2/19/1992, Ocala, FL
1941 GB: 1 G. **1944** GB: 8 G. **1945** GB: 5 G. **Total:** 14 G.

RAY BUCEK Bucek, Felix A 6′0″, 186 **G-LB**
Col: Texas A&M *HS:* Schulenburg [TX] B: 1/31/1922, Schulenburg, TX
D: 8/13/1965, Cape Girardeau, MO *Drafted:* 1943 Round 17 Pit
1946 Pit: 11 G.

CHARLES BUCHANAN Buchanan, Charles Harrison 6′3″, 245 **DE**
Col: Tennessee State *HS:* Hamilton [Memphis, TN] B: 9/20/1964, Memphis, TN *Drafted:* 1987 Round 8 Pit
1988 Cle: 9 G; Scor 1 Saf; 2 Pt; 5 Sac.

BUCK BUCHANAN Buchanan, Junious 6′7″, 270 **DT**
Col: Grambling State *HS:* A.H. Parker [Birmingham, AL] B: 9/10/1940, Gainesville, AL D: 7/16/1992, Kansas City, MO *Drafted:* 1963 Round 1 KC *HOF:* 1990
1963 KC: 14 G. **1964** KC: 14 G. **1965** KC: 14 G. **1966** KC: 14 G. **1967** KC: 14 G; KR 1-0. **1968** KC: 14 G; Int 1-11; Scor **1** Saf; 2 Pt. **1969** KC: 14 G. **1970** KC: 14 G. **1971** KC: 14 G; Int 1-9. **1972** KC: 14 G. **1973** KC: 14 G; Int 1-17. **1974** KC: 14 G. **1975** KC: 14 G. **Total:** 182 G; KR 1-0; Int 3-37; Scor 1 Saf; 2 Pt.

RAY BUCHANAN Buchanan, Raymond Louis 5′9″, 195 **DB**
(Big Play) *Col:* Louisville *HS:* Proviso East [Maywood, IL]
B: 9/29/1971, Chicago, IL *Drafted:* 1993 Round 3 Ind
1994 Ind: 1 Sac. **1995** Ind: KR 1-22 22.0; 1 Sac. **1996** Ind: KR 1-20 20.0; 0.5 Sac. **Total:** KR 2-42 21.0; 2.5 Sac.

		Punt Returns				Interceptions			
Year Team	**G**	**Ret**	**Yds**	**Avg**	**TD**	**Int**	**Yds**	**TD**	**Fum**
1993 Ind	16	0	0	—	0	4	45	0	0
1994 Ind	16	0	0	—	0	8	221	**3**	0
1995 Ind	16	16	113	7.1	0	2	60	0	1
1996 Ind	13	12	201	16.8	0	2	32	0	0
1997 Atl	16	0	37	—	0	5	49	0	0
1998 Atl	16	1	4	4.0	0	7	102	0	0
NFL Total	93	29	355	12.2	0	28	509	3	1

RICHARD BUCHANAN Buchanan, Richard Lawrence Jr. 5′10″, 178 **WR**
Col: Northwestern *HS:* Proviso East [Maywood, IL] B: 5/8/1969, Chicago, IL
1993 LARm: 5 G; PR 8-41 5.1. **1994** LARm: 3 G; Rec 5-60 12.0.
Total: 8 G; Rec 5-60 12.0; PR 8-41 5.1.

STEVE BUCHANAN Buchanan, Stephen Talmadge 5′8″, 160 **TB-BB**
Col: Miami (Ohio) *HS:* Steele [Dayton, OH] B: 3/4/1903
D: 11/21/1992, Dayton, OH
1929 Day: 6 G.

TIM BUCHANAN Buchanan, Timothy 6′1″, 230 **LB**
Col: Arizona State; Hawaii *HS:* John Muir [Pasadena, CA]
B: 5/26/1946, Pasadena, CA *Drafted:* 1969 Round 8 Cin
1969 Cin: 14 G.

WILLIE BUCHANON Buchanon, Willie James 6′0″, 190 **DB**
Col: Mira Costa Coll. CA (J.C.); San Diego State *HS:* Oceanside [CA]
B: 11/4/1950, Oceanside, CA *Drafted:* 1972 Round 1 GB

		Interceptions				Tot
Year Team	**G**	**Int**	**Yds**	**TD**	**Fum**	**TD**
1972 GB	14	4	62	0	0	1
1973 GB	6	0	0	0	0	0
1974 GB	14	4	10	0	0	0
1975 GB	2	0	0	0	0	0
1976 GB	14	2	28	0	0	0
1977 GB	14	2	41	**1**	1	1
1978 GB	16	9	93	1	0	1
1979 SD	16	0	0	0	0	0
1980 SD	16	2	13	0	0	0
1981 SD	16	5	31	0	0	0
1982 SD	9	0	0	0	0	0
NFL Total	137	28	278	2	1	3

FRANK BUCHER Bucher, Frank H 5′11″, 190 **E**
(Butcher) *Col:* Detroit Mercy *HS:* Fairport [NY]; East Rochester HS [NY] B: 12/19/1900, Fairport, NY D: 3/20/1971, Brighton, MI
1925 Pott: 10 G; Rec 2 TD; 12 Pt. **1926** Pott: 13 G. **Total:** 23 G; Rec 2 TD; 12 Pt.

BILL BUCHER Bucher, William George 5′10″, 180 **OE**
Col: Clarkson *HS:* Jamestown [NY] B: 4/23/1903 D: 5/29/1976, Detroit, MI
1925 Det: 1 G.

CUB BUCK Buck, Howard 6′0″, 259 **T**
Col: Wisconsin *HS:* Eau Claire [WI] B: 8/7/1892, Eau Claire Co., WI
D: 6/14/1966, Rock Island, IL
1920 Can: 11 G. **1921** GB: 6 G. **1922** GB: 10 G; Scor 6, 1 FG, 3 XK. **1923** GB: 10 G; Scor 23, 6 FG, 5 XK. **1924** GB: 11 G; Pass 1 TD; Scor 17, 3 FG, 8 XK. **1925** GB: 12 G; Scor 8, 8 XK. **Total:** 60 G; Pass 1 TD; Scor 54, 10 FG, 24 XK.

JASON BUCK Buck, Jason Ogden 6′5″, 268 **DE**
Col: Ricks Coll. ID (J.C.); Brigham Young *HS:* South Fremont [St. Anthony, ID] B: 7/27/1963, Moses Lake, WA *Drafted:* 1987 Round 1 Cin
1987 Cin: 12 G; 2 Sac. **1988** Cin: 16 G; 6 Sac. **1989** Cin: 16 G; 6 Sac. **1990** Cin: 16 G; 0.5 Sac. **1991** Was: 8 G; 1.5 Sac. **1992** Was: 16 G; 3 Sac. **1993** Was: 13 G; KR 1-15 15.0. **Total:** 97 G; KR 1-15 15.0; 19 Sac.

MIKE BUCK Buck, Michael Eric 6′3″, 227 **QB**
Col: Maine *HS:* Sayville [NY] B: 4/22/1967, Queens, NY
Drafted: 1990 Round 6 NO
1992 NO: Rush 3-(-4) -1.3. **1993** NO: Rush 1-0. **1995** Ariz: Rush 1-0.
Total: Rush 5-(-4) -0.8.

		Passing								
Year Team	**G**	**Att**	**Comp**	**Comp%**	**Yds**	**YPA**	**TD**	**Int**	**Rating**	**Fum**
1991 NO	2	2	1	50.0	61	30.50	0	1	56.3	0
1992 NO	2	4	2	50.0	10	2.50	0	0	56.3	0
1993 NO	4	54	32	59.3	448	8.30	4	3	87.6	2
1995 Ariz	4	32	20	62.5	271	8.47	1	0	99.9	1
NFL Total	12	92	55	59.8	790	8.59	5	4	87.7	3

VINCE BUCK Buck, Vincent Lamont 6′0″, 198 **DB**
Col: Central State (Ohio) *HS:* Owensboro [KY] B: 1/12/1968, Owensboro, KY *Drafted:* 1990 Round 2 NO
1990 NO: KR 3-38 12.7. **1992** NO: 0.5 Sac. **1993** NO: 3 Sac. **1994** NO: 1 Sac. **Total:** KR 3-38 12.7; 4.5 Sac.

		Punt Returns				Interceptions			
Year Team	**G**	**Ret**	**Yds**	**Avg**	**TD**	**Int**	**Yds**	**TD**	**Fum**
1990 NO	16	37	305	8.2	0	0	0	0	2
1991 NO	13	31	260	8.4	0	5	12	0	0
1992 NO	10	2	4	2.0	0	2	51	1	0
1993 NO	16	0	0	—	0	2	28	0	0
1994 NO	16	0	0	—	0	1	0	0	0
1995 NO	13	0	0	—	0	0	0	0	1
NFL Total	84	70	569	8.1	0	10	91	1	3

DON BUCKEY Buckey, Donald Charles 5′11″, 180 **WR**
Col: North Carolina State *HS:* Kenmore [Akron, OH] B: 11/9/1953, Akron, OH *Drafted:* 1976 Round 12 NYJ
1976 NYJ: 4 G; Rec 5-36 7.2.

JEFF BUCKEY Buckey, Jeffery Michael 6′5″, 305 **OG**
Col: Stanford *HS:* Bakersfield [CA] B: 8/7/1974, Bakersfield, CA *Drafted:* 1996 Round 7 Mia
1996 Mia: 15 G. **1997** Mia: 16 G. **1998** Mia: 7 G. **Total:** 38 G.

GARLAND BUCKEYE Buckeye, Garland Maiers 6′0″, 238 **G-C**
(Gob) *Col:* No College *HS:* Joliet Central [IL] B: 10/16/1897, Heron Lake, MN D: 11/14/1975, Stone Lake, WI
1920 ChiT: 6 G. **1921** ChiC: 5 G. **1922** ChiC: 11 G. **1923** ChiC: 10 G. **1924** ChiC: 8 G. **Total:** 40 G.

BILL BUCKLER Buckler, William Earl 6′0″, 224 **G-T-OE-DE**
Col: Alabama B: 4/29/1901, St. Paul, MN D: 6/20/1979, Wood River, IL
1926 ChiB: 15 G; Scor 1, 1 XK. **1927** ChiB: 12 G. **1928** ChiB: 13 G. **1931** ChiB: 13 G. **1932** ChiB: 14 G; Scor 1, 1 XK. **1933** ChiB: 11 G. **Total:** 78 G.

PHIL BUCKLEW Bucklew, Philip Hinkle 6′1″, 205 **OE-DE**
Col: Xavier (Ohio) B: 12/18/1914, Columbus, OH D: 12/30/1992, Fairfax, VA
1937 Cle: 11 G; Rec 3-51 17.0. **1938** Cle: 1 G; Rec 1-14 14.0. **Total:** 12 G; Rec 4-65 16.3.

CURTIS BUCKLEY Buckley, Curtis LaDonn 6′0″, 186 **DB-WR**
Col: Kilgore Coll. TX (J.C.); Texas A&M-Commerce *HS:* Silsbee [TX] B: 9/25/1970, Oakdale, CA
1993 TB: 10 G. **1994** TB: 13 G; KR 8-177 22.1; 1 Fum. **1995** TB: 15 G; KR 2-29 14.5. **1996** SF: 15 G. **1997** SF: 15 G. **1998** SF-NYG: 14 G. SF: 8 G. NYG: 6 G. **Total:** 82 G; KR 10-206 20.6; 1 Fum.

TERRELL BUCKLEY Buckley, Douglas Terrell 5′10″, 177 **DB**
Col: Florida State *HS:* Pascagoula [MS] B: 6/7/1971, Pascagoula, MS *Drafted:* 1992 Round 1 GB
1995 Mia: KR 1-16 16.0. **1996** Mia: KR 1-48 48.0. **1997** Mia: 1 Fum TD. **Total:** KR 2-64 32.0; 1 Fum TD.

		Punt Returns				Interceptions				Tot
Year Team	**G**	**Ret**	**Yds**	**Avg**	**TD**	**Int**	**Yds**	**TD**	**Fum**	**TD**
1992 GB	14	21	211	10.0	1	3	33	1	7	2
1993 GB	16	11	76	6.9	0	2	31	0	1	0
1994 GB	16	0	0	—	0	5	38	0	0	0
1995 Mia	16	0	0	—	0	1	0	0	0	0
1996 Mia	16	3	24	8.0	0	6	**164**	1	1	1
1997 Mia	16	4	58	14.5	0	4	26	0	0	1
1998 Mia	16	29	354	12.2	0	8	157	1	1	1
NFL Total	110	68	723	10.6	1	29	449	3	10	5

MARCUS BUCKLEY Buckley, Marcus Wayne 6′3″, 240 **LB**
Col: Texas A&M *HS:* Eastern Hills [Fort Worth, TX] B: 2/3/1971, Fort Worth, TX *Drafted:* 1993 Round 3 NYG
1993 NYG: 16 G. **1994** NYG: 16 G. **1995** NYG: 16 G. **1996** NYG: 15 G. **1997** NYG: 12 G. **1998** NYG: 14 G; Int 1-0; 1.5 Sac. **Total:** 89 G; Int 1-0; 1.5 Sac.

RALPH BUCKLEY Buckley, Ralph Joseph 5′8″, 175 **BB-HB**
Col: Fordham *HS:* Washington [Meriden, CT] B: 3/18/1907, Meriden, CT D: 7/13/1979, Dunedin, FL
1930 SI: 7 G; Rec 1 TD; 6 Pt.

TED BUCKLIN Bucklin, Theodore Harry 6′0″, 197 **FB-BB-G**
Col: Idaho *HS:* James Logan [Logan, UT] D: 10/1945
1927 ChiC: 9 G; Rush 1 TD; 6 Pt. **1931** NYG: 5 G. **Total:** 14 G; Rush 1 TD; 6 Pt.

TOM BUCKMAN Buckman, Thomas Harry 6′4″, 230 **TE**
Col: Texas A&M *HS:* Amon-Carter Riverside [Fort Worth, TX] B: 3/7/1947, Fort Worth, TX *Drafted:* 1969 Round 12 GB
1969 Den: 7 G; Rec 4-48 12.0 1 TD; 6 Pt.

BRENTSON BUCKNER Buckner, Brentson Andre 6′2″, 305 **DE**
Col: Clemson *HS:* Carver [Columbus, GA] B: 9/30/1971, Columbus, GA *Drafted:* 1994 Round 2 Pit
1994 Pit: 13 G; 2 Sac. **1995** Pit: 16 G; **1** Fum TD; 6 Pt; 3 Sac. **1996** Pit: 15 G; 1 Fum; 3 Sac. **1997** Cin: 14 G. **1998** SF: 13 G; 0.5 Sac. **Total:** 71 G; 1 Fum TD; 6 Pt; 1 Fum; 8.5 Sac.

BOB BUCZKOWSKI Buczkowski, John Robert 6′5″, 260 **DE**
Col: Pittsburgh *HS:* Gateway [Monroeville, PA] B: 5/5/1964, Pittsburgh, PA *Drafted:* 1986 Round 1 LARd
1987 LARd: 2 G; 1 Sac. **1989** Pho: 4 G. **1990** Cle: 15 G; 0.5 Sac. **Total:** 21 G; 1.5 Sac.

CARL BUDA Buda, Carl Joseph 5′11″, 220 **G**
Col: Creighton; Tulsa *HS:* Omaha South [NE] B: 2/22/1919, Omaha, NE D: 6/22/1994, Omaha, NE *Drafted:* 1944 Round 11 Pit
1945 Pit: 3 G.

FRANK BUDD Budd, Francis Joseph 5′10″, 187 **WR**
Col: Villanova *HS:* Asbury Park [NJ] B: 7/20/1939, Long Branch, NJ *Drafted:* 1962 Round 7 Phi
1962 Phi: 13 G; Rec 5-130 26.0 1 TD; 6 Pt. **1963** Was: 14 G; Rec 5-106 21.2; KR 10-252 25.2; 1 Fum. **Total:** 27 G; Rec 10-236 23.6 1 TD; KR 10-252 25.2; 6 Pt; 1 Fum.

JOHNNY BUDD Budd, John Walter 5′11″, 246 **T-G**
Col: Lafayette *HS:* Blair Acad. [Blairstown, NJ] B: 1/14/1899, Newton, NJ D: 12/26/1963, Fountain Hill, PA
1926 Fra: 17 G; Scor 30, 6 FG, 12 XK. **1927** Pott: 13 G. **1928** Pott: 10 G; Scor 3, 3 XK. **Total:** 40 G; Scor 33, 6 FG, 15 XK.

BRAD BUDDE Budde, Brad Edward 6′4″, 262 **OG**
Col: USC *HS:* Rockhurst [Kansas City, MO] B: 5/9/1958, Detroit, MI *Drafted:* 1980 Round 1 KC
1980 KC: 16 G; KR 3-28 9.3. **1981** KC: 16 G. **1982** KC: 9 G. **1983** KC: 12 G. **1984** KC: 16 G. **1985** KC: 7 G. **1986** KC: 16 G. **Total:** 92 G; KR 3-28 9.3.

ED BUDDE Budde, Edward Leon 6′5″, 265 **OG**
Col: Michigan State *HS:* Edwin Denby [Detroit, MI] B: 11/2/1940, Highland Park, MI *Drafted:* 1963 Round 1 KC
1963 KC: 14 G. **1964** KC: 14 G. **1965** KC: 14 G. **1966** KC: 14 G. **1967** KC: 14 G. **1968** KC: 14 G. **1969** KC: 14 G. **1970** KC: 14 G. **1971** KC: 14 G. **1972** KC: 13 G. **1973** KC: 12 G. **1974** KC: 14 G. **1975** KC: 1 G. **1976** KC: 11 G. **Total:** 177 G.

FRANK BUDKA Budka, Frank Charles 6′0″, 194 **DB**
Col: Notre Dame *HS:* Pompano [Pompano Beach, FL] B: 3/20/1942, Cleveland, OH *Drafted:* 1964 Round 4 ChiB
1964 LARm: 14 G; Int 2-18.

BILL BUDNESS Budness, William Walter 6′2″, 218 **LB**
Col: Boston College *HS:* Chicopee [MA] B: 1/30/1943, Chicopee, MA *Drafted:* 1964 Round 4 Oak
1964 Oak: 9 G; Int 2-29. **1965** Oak: 14 G; Int 1-0; 1 Fum. **1966** Oak: 14 G. **1967** Oak: 13 G. **1968** Oak: 14 G. **1969** Oak: 14 G. **1970** Oak: 14 G. **Total:** 92 G; Int 3-29; 1 Fum.

TOM BUDREWICZ Budrewicz, Thomas Paul 6′2″, 245 **OG**
Col: Brown *HS:* Greenfield [MA] B: 5/27/1938, Greenfield, MA *Drafted:* 1960 Round 2 NYT
1961 NYT: 2 G; KR 1-0.

GEORGE BUEHLER Buehler, George Siegrist Jr. 6′2″, 260 **OG**
Col: Stanford *HS:* Whittier [CA] B: 8/10/1947, Whittier, CA *Drafted:* 1969 Round 2 Oak
1969 Oak: 2 G. **1970** Oak: 14 G. **1971** Oak: 14 G. **1972** Oak: 14 G. **1973** Oak: 14 G. **1974** Oak: 14 G. **1975** Oak: 14 G. **1976** Oak: 14 G. **1977** Oak: 14 G. **1978** Oak-Cle: 12 G. Oak: 1 G. Cle: 11 G. **1979** Cle: 11 G. **Total:** 137 G.

BART BUETOW Buetow, Barton Max 6′5″, 250 **OT**
(The Mad Scientist) *Col:* Minnesota *HS:* Mounds View [Arden Hills, MN] B: 10/28/1950, Minneapolis, MN *Drafted:* 1972 Round 3 Min
1973 NYG: 7 G. **1976** Min: 2 G. **Total:** 9 G.

TED BUFFALO Buffalo, William Francis 6′0″, 190 **T-OE-G**
Col: Haskell Indian B: 11/5/1901, WI D: 8/19/1969, Washburn, WI
1923 Oor: 9 G; 1 Fum TD; 6 Pt.

HARRY BUFFINGTON Buffington, Harry Webster 6′0″, 206 **G-LB-BB**
(Buff) *Col:* Oklahoma State *HS:* Pryor [OK] B: 8/27/1919, Pryor, OK
AAFC **1946** BknA: 12 G. **1947** BknA: 14 G. **1948** BknA: 10 G. **Total:** 36 G.

NFL **1942** NYG: 9 G; Int 1-10.

DOUG BUFFONE Buffone, Douglas John 6′3″, 230 **LB**
Col: Louisville *HS:* Shannock Valley [Rural Valley, PA] B: 6/27/1944, Yatesboro, PA *Drafted:* 1966 Round 4 ChiB
1967 ChiB: **1** Fum TD. **1971** ChiB: Rush 1-19 19.0. **1979** ChiB: Rush 1-14 14.0; Rec 1-22 22.0. **Total:** Rush 2-33 16.5; Rec 1-22 22.0; 1 Fum TD.

		Interceptions			
Year Team	**G**	**Int**	**Yds**	**TD**	**Fum**
1966 ChiB	14	0	0	0	0
1967 ChiB	14	3	39	0	0
1968 ChiB	14	1	21	0	0
1969 ChiB	14	2	12	0	0
1970 ChiB	14	4	33	0	0
1971 ChiB	14	2	27	0	0
1972 ChiB	14	1	0	0	0
1973 ChiB	14	3	22	0	0
1974 ChiB	14	1	0	0	0
1975 ChiB	14	1	12	0	0
1976 ChiB	2	0	0	0	0
1977 ChiB	13	1	12	0	0
1978 ChiB	15	3	22	0	1
1979 ChiB	16	2	11	0	0
NFL Total	186	24	211	0	1

TONY BUFORD Buford, Anthony D 6'2", 222 LB
Col: Tulsa *HS:* Lutheran North [St. Louis, MO] B: 4/21/1964, St. Louis, MO
1987 StL: 2 G.

MAURY BUFORD Buford, Maury Anthony 6'1", 191 P
Col: Texas Tech *HS:* Mount Pleasant [TX] B: 2/18/1960, Mount Pleasant, TX *Drafted:* 1982 Round 8 SD
1983 SD: Pass 1-0. **1985** ChiB: Pass 1-1 100.0%, 5 5.00. **1986** ChiB: Rush 1-(-13) -13.0. **1989** ChiB: Rush 1-6 6.0. **1990** ChiB: Rush 1-(-9) -9.0. **Total:** Pass 2-1 50.0%, 5 2.50; Rush 3-(-16) -5.3.

		Punting			
Year Team	G	Punts	Yds	Avg	Fum
1982 SD	9	21	868	41.3	0
1983 SD	16	63	2763	43.9	0
1984 SD	16	66	2773	42.0	0
1985 ChiB	16	68	2870	42.2	0
1986 ChiB	16	69	2850	41.3	1
1988 NYG	15	73	3012	41.3	0
1989 ChiB	16	72	2844	39.5	0
1990 ChiB	16	76	3073	40.4	1
1991 ChiB	16	69	2814	40.8	0
NFL Total	136	577	23867	41.4	2

GARY BUGENHAGEN Bugenhagen, Gary Alan 6'2", 240 OG-OT
Col: Syracuse *HS:* Clarence [NY] B: 2/6/1945, Buffalo, NY *Drafted:* 1967 Round 4 Buf
1967 Buf: 14 G. **1970** Bos: 10 G. **Total:** 24 G.

DANNY BUGGS Buggs, Daniel 6'2", 188 WR
(Lightning) *Col:* West Virginia *HS:* Avondale [Avondale Estates, GA] B: 4/22/1953, Duluth, GA *Drafted:* 1975 Round 3 NYG
1975 NYG: Rush 1-0; PR 19-93 4.9; KR 16-353 22.1. **1977** Was: KR 0-17. **Total:** Rush 1-0; PR 19-93 4.9; KR 16-370 23.1.

		Receiving				
Year Team	G	Rec	Yds	Avg	TD	Fum
1975 NYG	14	0	0	—	0	5
1976 NYG-Was	11	2	25	12.5	0	0
1976 NYG	5	0	0	—	0	0
1976 Was	6	2	25	12.5	0	0
1977 Was	14	26	341	13.1	1	0
1978 Was	13	36	575	16.0	2	0
1979 Was	16	46	631	13.7	1	0
NFL Total	68	110	1572	14.3	4	5

LARRY BUHLER Buhler, Lawrence Abraham 6'2", 210 FB-HB-BB-DB
Col: Minnesota *HS:* Windom [MN] B: 5/28/1917, Mountain Lake, MN D: 8/21/1990, Rochester, MN *Drafted:* 1939 Round 1 GB
1940 GB: Int 2-58. **1941** GB: KR 1-10 10.0. **Total:** KR 1-10 10.0; Int 2-58.

		Rushing			
Year Team	G	Att	Yds	Avg	TD
1939 GB	3	5	3	0.6	0
1940 GB	7	36	118	3.3	0
1941 GB	11	0	0	—	0
NFL Total	21	41	121	3.0	0

DREW BUIE Buie, Leslie Drew 6'0", 185 WR
Col: Catawba *HS:* N.C. Griffith [Winston-Salem, NC] B: 7/12/1947, Council, NC *Drafted:* 1969 Round 9 Oak
1969 Oak: 14 G; Rec 1-37 37.0. **1970** Oak: 14 G; Rec 2-52 26.0. **1971** Oak: 14 G; Rush 2-32 16.0; Rec 5-133 26.6 2 TD; 12 Pt. **1972** Cin: 4 G; Rec 1-5 5.0. **Total:** 46 G; Rush 2-32 16.0; Rec 9-227 25.2 2 TD; 12 Pt.

RAY BUIVID Buivid, Raymond Vincent 6'1", 195 QB-HB-DB
(Buzz) *Col:* Marquette *HS:* Port Washington [WI] B: 8/15/1915, Sheboygan, WI D: 7/5/1972, Cherry Hill, NJ *Drafted:* 1937 Round 1 ChiC
1937 ChiB: Rec 1-4 4.0 1 TD. **1938** ChiB: Rec 1-8 8.0. **Total:** Rec 2-12 6.0 1 TD.

		Passing							
Year Team	G	Att	Comp	Comp%	Yds	YPA	TD	Int	Rating
1937 ChiB	6	35	17	48.6	205	5.86	6	**2**	82.7
1938 ChiB	11	48	17	35.4	295	6.15	5	**2**	74.6
NFL Total	17	83	34	41.0	500	6.02	11	4	80.8

	Rushing			
Year Team	Att	Yds	Avg	TD
1937 ChiB	19	24	1.3	0
1938 ChiB	32	65	2.0	0
NFL Total	51	89	1.7	0

GLENN BUJNOCH Bujnoch, Glenn David 6'5", 260 OG
Col: Texas A&M *HS:* Mount Carmel [Houston, TX] B: 12/20/1953, Houston, TX *Drafted:* 1976 Round 2 Cin
1976 Cin: 14 G. **1977** Cin: 13 G; Rush 1-4 4.0 1 TD; 6 Pt. **1978** Cin: 16 G. **1979** Cin: 15 G. **1980** Cin: 16 G. **1981** Cin: 6 G. **1982** Cin: 9 G. **1983** TB: 6 G. **1984** TB: 8 G. **Total:** 103 G; Rush 1-4 4.0 1 TD; 6 Pt.

JOE BUKANT Bukant, Joseph 6'0", 216 FB-TB-HB-LB
(Buckin' Joe) *Col:* Washington-St. Louis *HS:* Divernon Twp. [IL] B: 10/31/1915, Divernon, IL *Drafted:* 1938 Round 2 Phi
1939 Phi: Punt 1-54 54.0. **1940** Phi: Rec 1-13 13.0; Int 1-10; Punt 15-568 37.9. **1943** ChiC: Rec 1-0; Punt 5-181 36.2. **Total:** Rec 2-13 6.5; Int 1-10; Punt 21-803 38.2.

		Passing							
Year Team	G	Att	Comp	Comp%	Yds	YPA	TD	Int	Rating
1938 Phi	11	1	1	100.0	14	14.00	0	0	118.8
1939 Phi	11	1	0	0.0	0	0.00	0	0	39.6
1940 Phi	11	0	0	—	0	—	0	0	—
1942 ChiC	10	15	4	26.7	56	3.73	0	2	3.1
1943 ChiC	8	40	14	35.0	109	2.73	1	5	12.5
NFL Total	51	57	19	33.3	179	3.14	1	7	9.2

	Rushing			
Year Team	Att	Yds	Avg	TD
1938 Phi	48	119	2.5	0
1939 Phi	59	136	2.3	3
1940 Phi	18	50	2.8	1
1942 ChiC	17	34	2.0	0
1943 ChiC	42	87	2.1	0
NFL Total	184	426	2.3	4

FRED BUKATY Bukaty, Frederick Francis 5'11", 195 FB
Col: Kansas *HS:* Bishop Hogan [Kansas City, KS] B: 2/13/1936, Kansas City, KS
1961 Den: Rec 14-94 6.7; KR 3-41 13.7; Scor 1 2XP.

		Rushing				
Year Team	G	Att	Yds	Avg	TD	Fum
1961 Den	14	76	187	2.5	5	3

RUDY BUKICH Bukich, Rudolph Andrew 6'1", 195 QB
(Rifle) *Col:* Iowa; USC *HS:* Roosevelt [St. Louis, MO] B: 3/15/1932, St.Louis, MO *Drafted:* 1953 Round 2 LARm

		Passing							
Year Team	G	Att	Comp	Comp%	Yds	YPA	TD	Int	Rating
1953 LARm	8	32	14	43.8	169	5.28	0	3	21.5
1956 LARm	3	23	10	43.5	130	5.65	1	3	36.8
1957 Was	7	28	6	21.4	103	3.68	0	3	2.8
1958 Was-ChiB	4	23	8	34.8	166	7.22	1	1	57.5
1958 Was	3	22	8	36.4	166	7.55	1	1	60.0
1958 ChiB	1	1	0	0.0	0	0.00	0	0	39.6
1959 ChiB	5	0	0	—	0	—	0	0	—
1960 Pit	12	51	25	49.0	358	7.02	2	3	60.7
1961 Pit	11	156	89	57.1	1253	8.03	11	16	67.0
1962 ChiB	5	13	3	23.1	79	6.08	1	4	38.5
1963 ChiB	6	43	29	67.4	369	8.58	3	2	97.9
1964 ChiB	9	160	99	**61.9**	1099	6.87	12	7	89.0
1965 ChiB	14	312	176	56.4	2641	8.46	20	9	93.7
1966 ChiB	14	309	147	47.6	1858	6.01	10	21	49.3
1967 ChiB	3	33	18	54.5	185	5.61	0	2	45.6
1968 ChiB	2	7	2	28.6	23	3.29	0	0	40.8
NFL Total	103	1190	626	52.6	8433	7.09	61	74	66.6

	Rushing				
Year Team	Att	Yds	Avg	TD	Fum
1953 LARm	14	28	2.0	1	4
1956 LARm	1	8	8.0	0	0
1957 Was	8	-2	-0.3	0	1
1958 Was-ChiB	2	16	8.0	0	0
1958 Was	1	23	23.0	0	0
1958 ChiB	1	-7	-7.0	0	0
1959 ChiB	1	0	0.0	0	0
1960 Pit	3	-8	-2.7	0	3
1961 Pit	14	4	0.3	2	7
1963 ChiB	7	1	0.1	1	0
1964 ChiB	12	28	2.3	0	3
1965 ChiB	28	33	1.2	3	**12**
1966 ChiB	18	14	0.8	2	8
1967 ChiB	4	-13	-3.3	0	2
NFL Total	112	109	1.0	9	40

GEORGE BUKSAR Buksar, George Benjamin 6'0", 206 LB-FB
Col: Purdue; San Francisco *HS:* George Rogers Clark [Whiting, IN] B: 8/12/1926, St.Joseph, MI
AAFC **1949** ChiA: 6 G; Pass 1-0; Rush 13-16 1.2 1 TD; 6 Pt.

NFL **1950** Bal: 9 G; Rush 12-44 3.7; Rec 2-2 1.0; Int 6-79. **1951** Was: 11 G; PR 1-0; KR 4-56 14.0; Int 1-20. **1952** Was: 10 G; Rush 3-3 1.0;

Rec 2-3 1.5; KR 4-43 10.8; Scor 24, 3-7 42.9% FG, 15-18 83.3% XK.
Total: 30 G; Rush 15-47 3.1; Rec 4-5 1.3; PR 1-0; KR 8-99 12.4; Int 7-99; Scor 24, 3-7 42.9% FG, 15-18 83.3% XK.

NORM BULAICH Bulaich, Norman Batton 6′1″, 218 **RB**
Col: Texas Christian *HS:* La Marque [TX] B: 12/25/1946, Galveston, TX
Drafted: 1970 Round 1 Bal
1972 Bal: KR 1-62 62.0. **Total:** KR 1-62 62.0.

		Rushing				Receiving					Tot
Year Team	G	Att	Yds	Avg	TD	Rec	Yds	Avg	TD	Fum	TD
1970 Bal	12	139	426	3.1	3	11	123	11.2	0	6	3
1971 Bal	13	152	741	4.9	8	25	229	9.2	2	4	10
1972 Bal	6	27	109	4.0	1	9	55	6.1	0	2	1
1973 Phi	14	106	436	4.1	1	42	403	9.6	3	8	4
1974 Phi	11	50	152	3.0	0	28	204	7.3	0	3	0
1975 Mia	14	78	309	4.0	5	32	276	8.6	5	2	10
1976 Mia	11	122	540	4.4	4	28	151	5.4	0	1	4
1977 Mia	14	91	416	4.6	4	25	180	7.2	0	3	4
1978 Mia	16	40	196	4.9	2	16	92	5.8	0	0	2
1979 Mia	9	9	37	4.1	2	8	53	6.6	1	1	3
NFL Total	120	814	3362	4.1	30	224	1766	7.9	11	30	41

WALT BULAND Buland, Walter 6′1″, 213 **T-G**
(Big Boy) *Col:* No College *HS:* None B: 1892, MN Deceased
1920 RI: 5 G. **1921** RI: 6 G. **1924** GB-RI: 6 G. GB: 1 G. RI: 5 G. **1926** Dul: 2 G. **Total:** 19 G.

CHET BULGER Bulger, Chester Noyes 6′3″, 260 **OT-DT**
Col: Auburn *HS:* Stevens [Rumford, ME] B: 9/18/1917, Rumford, ME
1942 ChiC: 5 G. **1943** ChiC: 10 G; Scor 1, 1-1 100.0% XK. **1944** ChPt: 10 G; KR 1-5 5.0. **1945** ChiC: 10 G; **1** Fum TD; 6 Pt. **1946** ChiC: 6 G. **1947** ChiC: 12 G. **1948** ChiC: 12 G. **1949** ChiC: 9 G. **1950** Det: 12 G.
Total: 86 G; KR 1-5 5.0; Scor 7, 1-1 100.0% XK; 1 Fum TD.

SCOTT BULL Bull, John Scott 6′5″, 211 **QB**
Col: Arkansas *HS:* Jonesboro [AR] B: 6/8/1953, Camden, AR
Drafted: 1976 Round 6 SF

		Passing							
Year Team	G	Att	Comp	Comp%	Yds	YPA	TD	Int	Rating
1976 SF	14	48	21	43.8	252	5.25	2	4	39.6
1977 SF	6	24	7	29.2	89	3.71	0	2	7.8
1978 SF	16	121	48	39.7	651	5.38	1	11	22.4
NFL Total	36	193	76	39.4	992	5.14	3	17	24.8

	Rushing				
Year Team	Att	Yds	Avg	TD	Fum
1976 SF	15	66	4.4	2	2
1977 SF	5	20	4.0	0	2
1978 SF	29	100	3.4	1	6
NFL Total	49	186	3.8	3	10

RONNIE BULL Bull, Ronald David 6′0″, 200 **RB**
Col: Baylor *HS:* Bishop [TX] B: 2/2/1940, Kingsville, TX
Drafted: 1962 Round 1 ChiB
1962 ChiB: Pass 3-0; KR 9-235 26.1. **1963** ChiB: Pass 3-0; KR 7-105 15.0. **1964** ChiB: Pass 3-1 33.3%, 13 4.33; KR 2-44 22.0. **1965** ChiB: Pass 3-2 66.7%, 63 21.00. **1966** ChiB: Pass 1-1 100.0%, 21 21.00. **1968** ChiB: Pass 1-0. **1969** ChiB: Pass 1-0. **1970** ChiB: Pass 4-2 50.0%, 46 11.50 1 TD 1 Int. **1971** Phi: Pass 1-1 100.0%, 15 15.00.
Total: Pass 20-7 35.0%, 158 7.90 1 TD 1 Int; KR 18-384 21.3.

		Rushing				Receiving					Tot
Year Team	G	Att	Yds	Avg	TD	Rec	Yds	Avg	TD	Fum	TD
1962 ChiB	14	113	363	3.2	1	31	331	10.7	0	5	1
1963 ChiB	13	117	404	3.5	1	19	132	6.9	2	0	3
1964 ChiB	13	86	320	3.7	1	15	35	2.3	0	1	1
1965 ChiB	13	91	417	4.6	3	16	186	11.6	1	2	4
1966 ChiB	14	100	318	3.2	0	20	174	8.7	0	4	0
1967 ChiB	12	61	176	2.9	0	18	250	13.9	1	0	1
1968 ChiB	13	107	472	4.4	3	17	145	8.5	0	3	3
1969 ChiB	6	44	187	4.3	0	14	91	6.5	0	1	0
1970 ChiB	12	68	214	3.1	0	13	60	4.6	0	1	0
1971 Phi	13	94	351	3.7	0	9	75	8.3	1	2	1
NFL Total	123	881	3222	3.7	9	172	1479	8.6	5	19	14

KENDRICKE BULLARD Bullard, Kendricke Bernard 6′1″, 183 **WR**
Col: Arkansas State *HS:* Dollarway [Pine Bluff, AR] B: 4/30/1972, San Diego, CA
1996 Jac: 12 G; KR 7-157 22.4; 1 Fum.

LOUIS BULLARD Bullard, Louis Eugene 6′6″, 265 **OT**
Col: Jackson State *HS:* Horn Lake [MS] B: 5/6/1956, Hernando, MS
Drafted: 1978 Round 5 Sea
1978 Sea: 16 G. **1979** Sea: 3 G. **1980** Sea: 16 G. **Total:** 35 G.

GALE BULLMAN Bullman, Delmar Gale 6′0″, 182 **E**
Col: West Virginia Wesleyan *HS:* Marietta [OH] B: 8/18/1901, Lesterville, WV D: 6/24/1977, Rolla, MO
1925 Col: 3 G.

AMOS BULLOCKS Bullocks, Amos Lee 6′1″, 202 **HB**
Col: Southern Illinois *HS:* Dunbar [Chicago, IL] B: 2/7/1939, Chicago, IL *Drafted:* 1962 Round 20 Dal
1962 Dal: Rec 3-46 15.3 1 TD. **1963** Dal: Rec 7-70 10.0. **1966** Pit: Pass 1-0; Rec 5-64 12.8 1 TD. **Total:** Pass 1-0; Rec 15-180 12.0 2 TD.

		Rushing				Kickoff Returns					Tot
Year Team	G	Ret	Yds	Avg	TD	Ret	Yds	Avg	TD	Fum	TD
1962 Dal	11	33	196	5.9	2	14	265	18.9	0	3	3
1963 Dal	14	96	341	3.6	2	19	453	23.8	0	4	2
1964 Dal	1	0	0	—	0	1	19	19.0	0	0	0
1966 Pit	8	29	83	2.9	1	0	0	—	0	1	2
NFL Total	34	158	620	3.9	5	34	737	21.7	0	8	7

CHUCK BULLOUGH Bullough, Charles George 6′1″, 238 **LB**
Col: Michigan State *HS:* Orchard Park [NY] B: 3/3/1969, Lansing, MI
Drafted: 1992 Round 8 Phi
1993 Mia: 3 G. **1994** Mia: 1 G. **Total:** 4 G.

HANK BULLOUGH Bullough, Henry Charles 6′0″, 230 **OG-LB**
Col: Michigan State *HS:* Timkin [Canton, OH] B: 1/24/1934, Scranton, PA *Drafted:* 1955 Round 5 GB
1955 GB: 12 G. **1958** GB: 8 G. **Total:** 20 G.

BRIAN BULLUCK Bulluck, Brian Jay 6′3″, 236 **LB**
Col: North Carolina State *HS:* E.E. Smith [Fayetteville, NC]
B: 10/29/1965, Roanoke Rapids, NC
1987 Ind: 2 G; 1 Sac.

ART BULTMAN Bultman, Arthur Frank 6′2″, 201 **C-LB-T**
(Red) *Col:* Indiana; Marquette *HS:* Green Bay West [WI]
B: 9/16/1907, Green Bay, WI D: 2/1967
1931 Bkn: 12 G. **1932** GB: 13 G. **1933** GB: 13 G. **1934** GB: 11 G.
Total: 49 G.

MAX BUMGARDNER Bumgardner, Max Andrew 6′2″, 190 **DE**
Col: Texas *HS:* Wichita Falls [TX] B: 5/13/1923, Wichita Falls, TX
Drafted: 1948 Round 1 ChiB
1948 Det: 11 G.

REX BUMGARDNER Bumgardner, Rex Keith 5′11″, 193 **HB-DB**
Col: West Virginia *HS:* Victory [Clarksburg, WV] B: 9/6/1923, Clarksburg, WV
AAFC **1948** BufA: Rec 1-63 63.0; PR 16-336 21.0 2 TD; KR 9-141 15.7; Int 2-7. **1949** BufA: Rec 7-168 24.0 4 TD; PR 4-35 8.8; KR 9-163 18.1.
Total: Rec 8-231 28.9 4 TD; PR 20-371 18.6 2 TD; KR 18-304 16.9; Int 2-7.

		Rushing				Tot
Year Team	G	Att	Yds	Avg	TD	TD
1948 BufA	13	14	82	5.9	0	2
1949 BufA	10	101	391	3.9	1	5
AAFC Total	23	115	473	4.1	1	7

NFL **1950** Cle: Rec 9-112 12.4 1 TD. **1951** Cle: Rec 5-61 12.2 1 TD; KR 3-75 25.0. **1952** Cle: PR 4-24 6.0; KR 5-89 17.8; Int 2-33.
Total: Rec 14-173 12.4 2 TD; PR 4-24 6.0; KR 8-164 20.5; Int 2-33.

		Rushing					Tot
Year Team	G	Att	Yds	Avg	TD	Fum	TD
1950 Cle	10	67	231	3.4	2	1	3
1951 Cle	10	45	126	2.8	1	1	2
1952 Cle	11	9	38	4.2	0	0	0
NFL Total	31	121	395	3.3	3	2	5

DEREK BUNCH Bunch, Derek Carl 6′3″, 215 **LB**
Col: Michigan State *HS:* Meadowdale [Dayton, OH] B: 10/28/1961, Fort Sill, OK
1987 Was: 3 G.

JARROD BUNCH Bunch, Jarrod Glenn 6′2″, 250 **FB**
Col: Michigan *HS:* Ashtabula [OH] B: 8/9/1968, Ashtabula, OH
Drafted: 1991 Round 1 NYG
1992 NYG: KR 2-27 13.5. **Total:** KR 2-27 13.5.

		Rushing				Receiving					Tot
Year Team	G	Att	Yds	Avg	TD	Rec	Yds	Avg	TD	Fum	TD
1991 NYG	16	1	0	0.0	0	2	8	4.0	0	1	0
1992 NYG	16	104	501	4.8	3	11	50	4.5	1	3	4
1993 NYG	13	33	128	3.9	2	13	98	7.5	1	2	3
1994 LARd	3	0	0	—	0	0	0	—	0	0	0
NFL Total	48	138	629	4.6	5	26	156	6.0	2	6	7

FRANK BUNCOM Buncom, Frank James Jr. 6′2″, 235 **LB**
Col: East Los Angeles Coll. CA (J.C.); USC *HS:* Susan Miller Dorsey [Los Angeles, CA] B: 11/2/1939, Shreveport, LA D: 9/14/1969, Cincinnati, OH *Drafted:* 1962 Round 6 SD
1962 SD: 14 G; Int 4-49. **1963** SD: 14 G. **1964** SD: 14 G; Int 1-11. **1965** SD: 14 G. **1966** SD: 14 G. **1967** SD: 14 G. **1968** Cin: 12 G.
Total: 96 G; Int 5-60.

MIKE BUNDRA Bundra, Michael P 6'3", 255 **DT**
Col: Bakersfield Coll. CA (J.C.); USC *HS:* Catasauqua [PA]
B: 6/24/1939, Coplay, PA *Drafted:* 1962 Round 6 Det
1962 Det: 12 G. **1963** Det: 14 G. **1964** Min-Cle: 13 G. Min: 4 G. Cle: 9 G. **1965** NYG: 9 G. **Total:** 48 G.

KEN BUNGARDA Bungarda, Kestutis John 6'6", 270 **OT**
Col: Arizona Western Coll. (J.C.); Missouri *HS:* Livingston [Berkeley, CA]
B: 1/25/1957, Hartford, CT *Drafted:* 1979 Round 11 Cin
1980 SF: 15 G.

JOHN BUNTING Bunting, John Stephen 6'1", 220 **LB**
Col: North Carolina *HS:* Springbrook [Silver Spring, MD] B: 7/15/1950, Portland, ME *Drafted:* 1972 Round 10 Phi
1972 Phi: 14 G; Int 1-45. **1973** Phi: 7 G. **1974** Phi: 14 G; Int 2-23. **1975** Phi: 14 G; Int 1-6. **1976** Phi: 14 G. **1977** Phi: 14 G. **1978** Phi: 6 G; Int 1-9. **1979** Phi: 15 G; Int 2-13. **1980** Phi: 16 G. **1981** Phi: 9 G. **1982** Phi: 9 G; Int 1-0; 3 Sac. **Total:** 132 G; Int 8-96; 3 Sac.

JOHN BUNYAN Bunyan, John J 5'10", 215 **G-C**
(Bunny; Moose) *Col:* New York U. *HS:* Williston Northampton School [Easthampson, MA] B: 1906
1929 SI: 5 G. **1930** SI: 11 G. **1932** SI-Bkn: 7 G. SI: 6 G. Bkn: 1 G. **Total:** 23 G.

DAN BUNZ Bunz, Daniel 6'4", 226 **LB**
Col: California-Riverside; Long Beach State *HS:* Oakmont [Roseville, CA] B: 10/7/1955, Roseville, CA *Drafted:* 1978 Round 1 SF
1978 SF: 16 G; Int 1-13. **1979** SF: 14 G; Int 1-2; 1 Fum. **1980** SF: 16 G. **1981** SF: 14 G. **1982** SF: 1 G. **1983** SF: 9 G. **1984** SF: 16 G; Int 1-2; 1 Sac. **1985** Det: 2 G; Int 1-17. **Total:** 88 G; Int 4-34; 1 Fum; 1 Sac.

NICK BUONICONTI Buoniconti, Nicholas Anthony 5'11", 220 **LB**
Col: Notre Dame *HS:* Cathedral [Springfield, MA] B: 12/15/1940, Springfield, MA *Drafted:* 1962 Round 13 Bos
1962 Bos: PR 1-8 8.0. **1963** Bos: **1** Fum TD. **1967** Bos: Scor **1** Saf. **1973** Mia: **1** Fum TD. **Total:** PR 1-8 8.0; Scor 1 Saf; 2 Fum TD.

		Interceptions			
Year Team	**G**	**Int**	**Yds**	**TD**	**Fum**
1962 Bos	14	2	3	0	0
1963 Bos	14	3	42	0	0
1964 Bos	14	5	75	0	0
1965 Bos	14	3	31	0	0
1966 Bos	14	4	43	0	0
1967 Bos	13	4	7	0	0
1968 Bos	8	3	22	0	0
1969 Mia	13	3	27	0	0
1970 Mia	14	0	0	0	0
1971 Mia	14	1	16	0	1
1972 Mia	14	2	17	0	0
1973 Mia	13	0	0	0	0
1974 Mia	13	2	29	0	0
1976 Mia	11	0	0	0	0
NFL Total	183	32	312	0	1

CORNELL BURBAGE Burbage, Cornell Rodney 5'10", 186 **WR**
Col: Kentucky *HS:* Bryan Station [Lexington, KY] B: 2/22/1965, Lexington, KY
1987 Dal: PR 5-29 5.8. **1988** Dal: KR 20-448 22.4. **1989** Dal: PR 3-5 1.7; KR 3-55 18.3. **Total:** PR 8-34 4.3; KR 23-503 21.9.

		Receiving				
Year Team	**G**	**Rec**	**Yds**	**Avg**	**TD**	**Fum**
1987 Dal	3	7	168	24.0	2	0
1988 Dal	10	2	50	25.0	0	1
1989 Dal	10	17	134	7.9	0	0
NFL Total	23	26	352	13.5	2	1

JERRY BURCH Burch, Gerald Thomas 6'1", 195 **WR-P**
Col: Georgia Tech *HS:* McGill Inst. [Mobile, AL] B: 12/13/1939
Drafted: 1961 Round 13 Oak
1961 Oak: 14 G; Rec 18-235 13.1 1 TD; Punt 12-315 26.3; 6 Pt.

DON BURCHFIELD Burchfield, Donald Lee 6'3", 233 **TE**
Col: Ball State *HS:* Southport [Indianapolis, IN] B: 3/17/1949, Indianapolis, IN *Drafted:* 1971 Round 13 NO
1971 NO: 14 G; Rec 3-36 12.0; KR 1-5 5.0.

LLOYD BURDICK Burdick, Lloyd Sumner 6'4", 248 **T**
(Tiny; Shorty) *Col:* Illinois *HS:* Morgan Park Mil. Acad. [IL]
B: 8/8/1908, Assumption, IL D: 8/9/1945, Michigan, ND
1931 ChiB: 9 G. **1932** ChiB: 13 G. **1933** Cin: 10 G. **Total:** 32 G.

CHRIS BURFORD Burford, Christopher William III 6'3", 220 **WR**
Col: Stanford *HS:* Oakland [CA] B: 1/31/1938, Oakland, CA
Drafted: 1960 Round 1 DalT
1961 DalT: Rush 1-(-13) -13.0. **1962** DalT: Rush 1-13 13.0. **1963** KC: Rush 1-10 10.0; Scor **1** 2XP. **Total:** Rush 3-10 3.3; Scor 1 2XP.

		Receiving				
Year Team	**G**	**Rec**	**Yds**	**Avg**	**TD**	**Fum**
1960 DalT	14	46	789	17.2	5	1
1961 DalT	14	51	850	16.7	5	1
1962 DalT	11	45	645	14.3	**12**	0
1963 KC	14	68	824	12.1	9	0
1964 KC	12	51	675	13.2	7	0
1965 KC	11	47	575	12.2	6	0
1966 KC	14	58	758	13.1	8	1
1967 KC	13	25	389	15.6	3	0
NFL Total	103	391	5505	14.1	55	3

GLENN BURGEIS Burgeis, M. Glenn 6'1", 220 **T**
Col: Tulsa *HS:* Central [Tulsa, OK] B: 10/7/1921, Ballard, TX
D: 6/1/1998 *Drafted:* 1945 Round 5 ChiB
1945 ChiB: 3 G.

TODD BURGER Burger, Todd Richard 6'3", 303 **OG**
Col: Penn State *HS:* Arthur L. Johnson Regional [Clark, NJ]
B: 3/20/1970, Clark, NJ
1994 ChiB: 4 G. **1995** ChiB: 16 G. **1996** ChiB: 11 G. **1997** ChiB: 15 G. **1998** NYJ: 16 G. **Total:** 62 G.

CHARLIE BURGESS Burgess, Charles 6'0", 230 **LB**
Col: Carson-Newman B: 12/29/1962
1987 NYG: 2 G.

FERNANZA BURGESS Burgess, Fernanza 6'1", 210 **WR**
Col: Morris Brown *HS:* South Miami [Miami, FL] B: 3/6/1960, Miami, FL
1984 Mia-NYJ: 14 G. Mia: 3 G. NYJ: 11 G. **Total:** 14 G.

JAMES BURGESS Burgess, James Paul 6'0", 230 **LB**
Col: Miami (Fla.) *HS:* Homestead [FL] B: 3/31/1974, Miami, FL
1997 SD: 15 G. **1998** SD: 16 G. **Total:** 31 G.

MARVELL BURGESS Burgess, Marvell Jr. 6'3", 195 **DB**
Col: Henderson State *HS:* Hialeah-Miami Lakes [Hialeah, FL]
B: 10/7/1965, Miami, FL
1987 Mia: 1 G.

RONNIE BURGESS Burgess, Ronald K 5'11", 174 **DB**
Col: Wake Forest *HS:* Sumter [SC] B: 3/7/1963, Sumter, SC
Drafted: 1985 Round 10 GB
1985 GB: 7 G.

AL BURGIN Burgin, Albert E 6'0", 200 **G**
Col: No College B: 4/13/1894, Toledo, OH D: 7/28/1978, San Francisco, CA
1922 Tol: 1 G.

TED BURGMEIER Burgmeier, Ted Joseph 5'10", 185 **DB-KR**
Col: Notre Dame *HS:* Wahlert Catholic [Dubuque, IA] B: 11/8/1955, Dubuque, IA *Drafted:* 1978 Round 5 Mia
1978 KC: 8 G; PR 4-59 14.8; 1 Fum.

EARL BURGNER Burgner, Earl William 5'6", 165 **BB-WB**
(Puss) *Col:* Wittenberg *HS:* South [Akron, OH] B: 5/19/1900, Akron, OH D: 1/11/1970, Dayton, OH
1923 Day: 2 G.

ADRIAN BURK Burk, Adrian Matthew 6'2", 190 **QB**
(Abe) *Col:* Kilgore Coll. TX (J.C.); Baylor *HS:* Gaston [Joinerville, TX]
B: 12/14/1927, Mexia, TX *Drafted:* 1950 Round 1 Bal

		Passing							
Year Team	**G**	**Att**	**Comp**	**Comp%**	**Yds**	**YPA**	**TD**	**Int**	**Rating**
1950 Bal	12	119	43	36.1	798	6.71	6	12	37.4
1951 Phi	12	218	92	42.2	1329	6.10	14	23	44.5
1952 Phi	12	82	37	45.1	561	6.84	4	5	59.0
1953 Phi	10	119	56	47.1	788	6.62	4	9	48.6
1954 Phi	12	231	123	53.2	1740	7.53	**23**	17	80.4
1955 Phi	12	228	110	48.2	1359	5.96	9	17	49.2
1956 Phi	12	82	39	47.6	426	5.20	1	6	36.9
NFL Total	82	1079	500	46.3	7001	6.49	61	89	52.2

	Rushing				Punting			
Year Team	**Att**	**Yds**	**Avg**	**TD**	**Punts**	**Yds**	**Avg**	**Fum**
1950 Bal	11	19	1.7	1	**81**	**3243**	40.0	3
1951 Phi	28	12	0.4	1	67	2646	39.5	5
1952 Phi	7	28	4.0	0	**83**	3335	40.2	1
1953 Phi	8	54	6.8	3	41	1765	43.0	7
1954 Phi	15	18	1.2	0	**73**	2918	40.0	7
1955 Phi	36	132	3.7	2	61	2615	42.9	4
1956 Phi	17	61	3.6	0	**68**	**2843**	41.8	2
NFL Total	122	324	2.7	7	474	19365	40.9	29

SCOTT BURK Burk, Marshall Scott 6'2", 193 **DB**
Col: Oklahoma State *HS:* Cherry Creek [Englewood, CO] B: 8/2/1956, Houston, TX *Drafted:* 1979 Round 9 Cin
1979 Cin: 16 G; PR 1-0; 1 Fum.

ANTHONY BURKE Burke, Anthony Howard 6'3", 262 **DT**
Col: Minnesota *HS:* Hopkins [MN] B: 9/2/1964, Kankakee, IL
1987 StL: 1 G.

CHICK BURKE Burke, Charles Framcis 5'9", 166 **WB**
Col: Dartmouth *HS:* Natick [MA] B: 9/30/1901, Natick, MA
D: 5/20/1973, Keene, NH
1925 Prov: 5 G.

DON BURKE Burke, Donald 6'0", 235 **LB-OG**
Col: Hartnell Coll. CA (J.C.); USC *HS:* Oakland [CA] B: 2/7/1926, Chico, CA *Drafted:* 1950 Round 12 SF
1950 SF: 6 G. **1951** SF: 9 G. **1952** SF: 12 G; KR 1-25 25.0; Int 1-35 1 TD; 6 Pt. **1953** SF: 10 G. **1954** SF: 2 G. **Total:** 39 G; KR 1-25 25.0; Int 1-35 1 TD; 6 Pt.

JOHN BURKE Burke, John Richard 6'3", 248 **TE**
Col: Virginia Tech *HS:* Holmdel [NJ] B: 9/7/1971, Elizabeth, NJ
Drafted: 1994 Round 4 NE
1994 NE: KR 3-11 3.7. **1995** NE: KR 1-7 7.0. **1998** SD: KR 1-5 5.0.
Total: KR 5-23 4.6.

		Receiving			
Year Team	**G**	**Rec**	**Yds**	**Avg**	**TD**
1994 NE	16	9	86	9.6	0
1995 NE	16	15	136	9.1	0
1996 NE	11	1	19	19.0	0
1997 NYJ	7	0	0	—	0
1998 SD	10	3	32	10.7	0
NFL Total	60	28	273	9.8	0

JOE BURKE Burke, Joseph Richard 6'0", 200 **RB**
Col: Rutgers *HS:* Bishop Maginn [Albany, NY] B: 2/9/1961, Albany, NY
1987 NYJ: 2 G.

MARK BURKE Burke, Mark Allen 6'1", 175 **DB**
Col: West Virginia *HS:* Marietta [OH] B: 6/10/1954, Marietta, OH
1976 Phi: 1 G; PR 1-14 14.0.

MIKE BURKE Burke, Michael Dennis 5'10", 188 **P**
Col: Chabot Coll. CA (J.C.); Oregon State; Miami (Fla.) *HS:* Amador Valley [Pleasanton, CA] B: 7/28/1950, Sacramento, CA
1974 LARm: Pass 1-0; Scor 1, 1-3 33.3% XK.

		Punting		
Year Team	**G**	**Punts**	**Yds**	**Avg**
1974 LARm	8	46	1701	37.0

RANDY BURKE Burke, Randall William 6'2", 190 **WR**
Col: Kentucky *HS:* Southwest Miami [Miami, FL] B: 5/26/1955, Miami, FL *Drafted:* 1977 Round 1 Bal
1978 Bal: PR 1-0; KR 1-2 2.0; Scor **1** Saf. **Total:** PR 1-0; KR 1-2 2.0; Scor 1 Saf.

		Receiving			
Year Team	**G**	**Rec**	**Yds**	**Avg**	**TD**
1978 Bal	15	0	0	—	0
1979 Bal	16	6	151	25.2	0
1980 Bal	10	14	185	13.2	3
1981 Bal	16	10	153	15.3	0
NFL Total	57	30	489	16.3	3

VERN BURKE Burke, Vernon Eugene 6'4", 215 **TE**
Col: Bakersfield Coll. CA (J.C.); Oregon State *HS:* North [Bakersfield, CA] B: 4/30/1941, San Luis Obispo, CA *Drafted:* 1963 Round 5 SF

		Receiving			
Year Team	**G**	**Rec**	**Yds**	**Avg**	**TD**
1965 SF	3	2	38	19.0	1
1966 Atl	14	28	348	12.4	1
1967 NO	7	8	84	10.5	0
NFL Total	24	38	470	12.4	2

CHRIS BURKETT Burkett, Christopher 6'4", 205 **WR**
Col: Jackson State *HS:* Collins [MS] B: 8/21/1962, Laurel, MS
Drafted: 1985 Round 2 Buf
1989 Buf-NYJ: Rush 1-(-4) -4.0. NYJ: Rush 1-(-4) -4.0. **1991** NYJ: Rush 1-(-2) -2.0. **Total:** Rush 2-(-6) -3.0.

		Receiving					Tot
Year Team	**G**	**Rec**	**Yds**	**Avg**	**TD**	**Fum**	**TD**
1985 Buf	16	21	371	17.7	0	0	0
1986 Buf	14	34	778	**22.9**	4	1	4
1987 Buf	12	56	765	13.7	4	1	4
1988 Buf	11	23	354	15.4	1	0	1
1989 Buf-NYJ	15	24	298	12.4	1	0	1
1989 Buf	2	3	20	6.7	0	0	0
1989 NYJ	13	21	278	13.2	1	0	1
1990 NYJ	16	14	204	14.6	0	0	0
1991 NYJ	15	23	327	14.2	4	0	5
1992 NYJ	16	57	724	12.7	1	1	1
1993 NYJ	16	40	531	13.3	4	1	4
NFL Total	131	292	4352	14.9	19	4	20

JEFF BURKETT Burkett, Jefferson Davis 6'1", 190 **OE-DB**
Col: Louisiana State *HS:* Laurel [MS] B: 7/15/1921, Hattiesburg, MS
D: 10/24/1947, Bryce Canyon, UT
1947 ChiC: 3 G; Rush 1-11 11.0; Rec 2-44 22.0 1 TD; Int 1-25; Punt 11-521 47.4; 6 Pt.

JACKIE BURKETT Burkett, Walter Jackson 6'4", 230 **LB-C**
Col: Auburn *HS:* Choctawhatchee [Fort Walton Beach, FL]
B: 12/16/1936, Thorsby, AL *Drafted:* 1959 Round 1 Bal

		Interceptions		
Year Team	**G**	**Int**	**Yds**	**TD**
1961 Bal	14	1	23	0
1962 Bal	14	2	21	0
1963 Bal	14	0	0	0
1964 Bal	12	0	0	0
1965 Bal	11	0	0	0
1966 Bal	14	0	0	0
1967 NO	14	3	57	0
1968 Dal	3	0	0	0
1969 Dal	11	0	0	0
1970 NO	14	4	36	0
NFL Total	121	10	137	0

JOE BURKS Burks, Joseph 5'10", 171 **C**
(Flyweight) *Col:* Washington State *HS:* Walla Walla [WA] B: 7/8/1899
D: 11/1969, Chicago, IL
1926 Mil: 9 G.

RANDY BURKS Burks, Randall James 5'11", 170 **WR**
Col: Southeastern Oklahoma State; Oklahoma State *HS:* Gray [Idabel, OK] B: 8/22/1953, Idabel, OK *Drafted:* 1976 Round 8 StL
1976 ChiB: 1 G; Rec 1-55 55.0 1 TD; 6 Pt.

RAY BURKS Burks, Raymond Charles Jr. 6'3", 217 **LB**
Col: UCLA *HS:* Gardena [CA] B: 3/9/1955, Gardena, CA
Drafted: 1977 Round 12 KC
1977 KC: 13 G; Rush 1-51 51.0; KR 1-15 15.0.

SHAWN BURKS Burks, Shawn Spencer 6'1", 230 **LB**
Col: Louisiana State *HS:* Central [Baton Rouge, LA] B: 2/10/1963, Baton Rouge, LA
1986 Was: 15 G.

STEVE BURKS Burks, Steven Bruce 6'5", 211 **WR**
Col: Arkansas State *HS:* Cabot [AR] B: 8/6/1953, Little Rock, AR
Drafted: 1975 Round 4 NE
1975 NE: 13 G; Rec 6-158 26.3; KR 4-65 16.3. **1976** NE: 8 G; Rush 1-2 2.0; Rec 2-27 13.5. **1977** NE: 13 G; Rec 5-79 15.8. **Total:** 34 G; Rush 1-2 2.0; Rec 13-264 20.3; KR 4-65 16.3.

ALEX BURL Burl, Alex Jr. 5'10", 165 **HB**
Col: Colorado State *HS:* Manual [Denver, CO] B: 8/8/1931, Warren, AR *Drafted:* 1954 Round 30 ChiC
1956 ChiC: 8 G; Rush 1-2 2.0; Rec 2-24 12.0 1 TD; KR 3-59 19.7; 6 Pt.

JOHN BURLESON Burleson, John Charles 6'2", 237 **T-G**
(Tex) *Col:* Southern Methodist *HS:* Albany [TX] B: 8/21/1909, Albany, TX D: 10/6/1983, Abilene, TX
1933 Port-Pit-Cin: 6 G. Port: 1 G. Pit: 3 G. Cin: 2 G. **Total:** 6 G.

GARY BURLEY Burley, Gary Steven 6'3", 272 **DE**
Col: Wharton Co. JC TX; Pittsburgh *HS:* Grove City [OH]
B: 12/8/1952, Urbancrest, OH *Drafted:* 1975 Round 3 Cin
1976 Cin: 14 G. **1977** Cin: 14 G. **1978** Cin: 16 G; Scor **1** Saf; 2 Pt.
1979 Cin: 16 G. **1980** Cin: 11 G. **1981** Cin: 16 G. **1982** Cin: 4 G. **1983** Cin: 14 G; 2 Sac. **1984** Atl: 12 G; 5 Sac. **Total:** 117 G; Scor 1 Saf; 2 Pt; 7 Sac.

GEORGE BURMAN Burman, George Robert 6'3", 255 **C-OG-OT**
Col: Northwestern *HS:* Whiting [IN] B: 12/1/1942, Chicago, IL
Drafted: 1964 Round 15 ChiB
1964 ChiB: 14 G. **1967** LARm: 14 G. **1968** LARm: 1 G. **1969** LARm: 14 G; KR 1-11 11.0. **1970** LARm: 14 G. **1971** Was: 14 G. **1972** Was: 14 G.
Total: 85 G; KR 1-11 11.0.

DANNY BURMEISTER Burmeister, Daniel Joseph 6'2", 201 **DB**
Col: North Carolina *HS:* Oakton [Vienna, VA] B: 9/13/1963
1987 Was: 3 G.

FORREST BURMEISTER Burmeister, Forrest Barth 6'3", 215 **G-T**
Col: Purdue *HS:* Central [Davenport, IA] B: 8/18/1913, Stockton, IA
1937 Cle: 11 G. **1938** Cle: 1 G. **Total:** 12 G.

MAX BURNELL Burnell, Herman Joseph 5'11", 180 **HB-DB**
Col: Notre Dame *HS:* Cathedral [Duluth, MN] B: 5/7/1915, Duluth, MN
1944 ChiB: 2 G.

CHESTER BURNETT Burnett, Chester Dean 5'10", 224 **LB**
Col: Arizona *HS:* J.K. Mullen [Denver, CO] B: 4/15/1975, Denver, CO
Drafted: 1998 Round 7 Min
1998 Was: 5 G; KR 1-5 5.0.

DALE BURNETT Burnett, Dale Metz 6'1", 187 **WB-DB-FB-BB**
Col: Emporia State *HS:* Dodge City [KS] B: 1/23/1908, Larned, KS D: 4/17/1997, Emporia, KS
1930 NYG: Scor 40, 4 XK. **1933** NYG: Pass 1-0; Int **1** TD. **1935** NYG: **1** Fum TD. **Total:** Pass 1-0; Int 1 TD; 1 Fum TD.

		Rushing				Receiving				Tot
Year Team	G	Att	Yds	Avg	TD	Rec	Yds	Avg	TD	TD
1930 NYG	14	—	—	—	4	—	—	—	2	6
1931 NYG	14	—	—	—	1	—	—	—	2	3
1932 NYG	12	28	75	2.7	0	11	125	11.4	1	1
1933 NYG	14	17	34	2.0	0	12	212	17.7	**3**	4
1934 NYG	10	4	6	1.5	0	10	166	16.6	2	2
1935 NYG	8	6	32	5.3	0	12	209	17.4	4	6
1936 NYG	12	10	0	0.0	0	16	246	15.4	3	3
1937 NYG	9	7	4	0.6	0	10	121	12.1	1	1
1938 NYG	11	6	13	2.2	0	13	145	11.2	1	1
1939 NYG	11	1	3	3.0	0	8	86	10.8	0	0
NFL Total	115	79	167	2.1	5	92	1310	14.2	19	27

RAY BURNETT Burnett, James Raymond 6'4", 205 **HB**
(Rabbit) *Col:* Arkansas Tech; Central Arkansas *HS:* Atkins [AR] B: 1/29/1914, Russellville, AR D: 7/19/1996, North Little Rock, AR
1938 ChiC: 1 G; Pass 2-1 50.0%, 19 9.50; Rush 1-(-10) -10.0.

LEN BURNETT Burnett, Leonard Everett 6'1", 195 **DB**
Col: Oregon *HS:* Abraham Lincoln [San Diego, CA] B: 8/29/1939, San Diego, CA
1961 Pit: 4 G.

ROB BURNETT Burnett, Robert Barry 6'4", 280 **DE**
Col: Syracuse *HS:* Newfield [NY] B: 8/27/1967, Livingston, NJ *Drafted:* 1990 Round 5 Cle
1990 Cle: 16 G; 2 Sac. **1991** Cle: 13 G; 3 Sac. **1992** Cle: 16 G; 9 Sac. **1993** Cle: 16 G; 9 Sac. **1994** Cle: 16 G; 10 Sac. **1995** Cle: 16 G; 7.5 Sac. **1996** Bal: 6 G; 3 Sac. **1997** Bal: 15 G; 4 Sac. **1998** Bal: 16 G; Scor **1** Saf; 2 Pt; 2.5 Sac. **Total:** 130 G; Scor 1 Saf; 2 Pt; 50.0 Sac.

BOBBY BURNETT Burnett, Robert Clell 6'3", 210 **RB**
Col: Arkansas *HS:* Smackover [AR] B: 1/4/1943, Clinton, AR *Drafted:* 1966 Round 4 Buf

		Rushing				Receiving					Tot
Year Team	G	Att	Yds	Avg	TD	Rec	Yds	Avg	TD	Fum	TD
1966 Buf	14	187	766	4.1	4	34	419	12.3	4	3	8
1967 Buf	8	45	96	2.1	0	11	114	10.4	0	4	0
1969 Den	3	5	9	1.8	0	0	0	—	0	0	0
NFL Total	25	237	871	3.7	4	45	533	11.8	4	7	8

VICTOR BURNETT Burnett, Victor 6'5", 250 **DE**
Col: Long Beach City Coll. CA (J.C.); Texas Tech; Fresno State *HS:* Compton [CA] B: 10/5/1962, Los Angeles, CA
1987 StL: 3 G.

DAVE BURNETTE Burnette, David Lynn 6'6", 278 **OT**
Col: Central Arkansas; Arkansas *HS:* Parkin [AR] B: 3/24/1961, Parkin, AR *Drafted:* 1985 Round 12 Ind
1987 Dal: 1 G.

REGGIE BURNETTE Burnette, Reginald 6'2", 240 **LB**
Col: Houston *HS:* Rayville [LA] B: 10/4/1968, Rayville, LA *Drafted:* 1991 Round 7 GB
1991 GB: 3 G. **1992** TB: 15 G. **1993** TB: 5 G. **Total:** 23 G.

TOM BURNETTE Burnette, Thomas Denmark 6'1", 194 **BB-LB**
Col: North Carolina B: 7/29/1915, Fremont, NC D: 9/9/1994, Martinsville, VA *Drafted:* 1938 Round 6 Pit
1938 Pit-Phi: 14 G; Pass 1-0; Rush 1-0; Rec 1-3 3.0; Scor 0-1 FG. Pit: 6 G; Pass 1-0; Rush 1-0; Rec 1-3 3.0; Scor 0-1 FG. Phi: 8 G. **Total:** 14 G; Pass 1-0; Rush 1-0; Rec 1-3 3.0; Scor 0-1 FG.

LEM BURNHAM Burnham, Lemuel 6'4", 236 **DE**
Col: Rancho Santiago Coll. CA (J.C.); U.S. International *HS:* Jewett [Winter Haven, FL] B: 8/30/1947, Winter Haven, FL *Drafted:* 1974 Round 15 KC
1977 Phi: 14 G. **1978** Phi: 15 G. **1979** Phi: 16 G. **Total:** 45 G.

STANLEY BURNHAM Burnham, Stanley 5'10", 175 **TB-BB**
Col: Harvard *HS:* Gloucester [MA] B: 3/2/1897, Ipswich, MA D: 7/10/1949
1925 Fra: 5 G.

TIM BURNHAM Burnham, Timothy Scott 6'5", 280 **OT**
Col: Washington *HS:* Anderson [CA] B: 5/6/1963, Redding, CA
1987 Sea: 3 G; 1 Fum.

HANK BURNINE Burnine, Harold Henry 6'2", 188 **OE**
Col: Missouri *HS:* Richmond [MO] B: 11/9/1932, Henrietta, MO *Drafted:* 1955 Round 12 NYG
1956 NYG-Phi: 10 G; Rec 10-208 20.8 2 TD; 12 Pt. NYG: 3 G. Phi: 7 G; Rec 10-208 20.8 2 TD; 12 Pt. **1957** Phi: 7 G; Rec 7-63 9.0. **Total:** 17 G; Rec 17-271 15.9 2 TD; 12 Pt.

ED BURNS Burns, Edward Joseph 6'3", 210 **QB**
Col: Nebraska *HS:* Archbishop Rummel [Omaha, NE] B: 12/7/1954, Council Bluffs, IA
1979 NO: 16 G. **1980** NO: 2 G. **Total:** 18 G.

JASON BURNS Burns, Jason Michael 5'7", 195 **RB**
Col: Wisconsin *HS:* Percy L. Julian [Chicago, IL] B: 11/27/1972, Chicago, IL
1995 Cin: 1 G; Rush 1-1 1.0.

KEITH BURNS Burns, Keith Bernard 6'2", 245 **LB**
Col: Navarro Coll. TX (J.C.); Oklahoma State *HS:* T.C. Williams [Alexandria, VA] B: 5/16/1972, Greeleyville, SC *Drafted:* 1994 Round 7 Den
1994 Den: 11 G. **1995** Den: 16 G; KR 1-5 5.0; 1.5 Sac. **1996** Den: 16 G. **1997** Den: 16 G; KR 4-45 11.3. **1998** Den: 16 G; KR 2-17 8.5; 1 Fum. **Total:** 75 G; KR 7-67 9.6; 1 Fum; 1.5 Sac.

LAMONT BURNS Burns, Lamont Antonio 6'4", 300 **OG**
Col: East Carolina *HS:* Walter H. Page [Greensboro, NC] B: 3/16/1974, Greensboro, NC *Drafted:* 1997 Round 5 NYJ
1997 NYJ: 4 G.

LEON BURNS Burns, Leon Keith 6'2", 228 **RB**
Col: Laney Coll. CA (J.C.); Long Beach State *HS:* St. Mary's Prep [Berkeley, CA] B: 9/15/1940, Oakland, CA D: 12/22/1984, Los Angeles, CA *Drafted:* 1971 Round 1 SD
1971 SD: Rec 3-22 7.3; KR 2-19 9.5. **1972** StL: Rec 6-24 4.0; KR 1-7 7.0. **Total:** Rec 9-46 5.1; KR 3-26 8.7.

		Rushing				
Year Team	G	Att	Yds	Avg	TD	Fum
1971 SD	14	61	223	3.7	1	2
1972 StL	14	26	69	2.7	2	0
NFL Total	28	87	292	3.4	3	2

MIKE BURNS Burns, Michael Wayne 6'0", 181 **DB**
Col: Contra Costa Coll. CA (J.C.); USC *HS:* El Cerrito [CA] B: 4/6/1954, Oakland, CA *Drafted:* 1977 Round 6 SF
1977 SF: 14 G. **1978** Det: 15 G; Int 1-0. **Total:** 29 G; Int 1-0.

BOB BURNS Burns, Robert Henry 6'3", 212 **RB**
Col: Georgia *HS:* Chamberlain [Tampa, FL] B: 1/12/1952, Tampa, FL *Drafted:* 1974 Round 9 NYJ
1974 NYJ: Rec 11-83 7.5 1 TD; KR 3-52 17.3.

		Rushing				
Year Team	G	Att	Yds	Avg	TD	Fum
1974 NYJ	14	40	158	4.0	0	2

GEORGE BURNSIDE Burnside, George Harrison 5'9", 160 **BB**
Col: Wisconsin; South Dakota *HS:* Neenah [WI] B: 1/21/1899, Oconto Falls, WI D: 11/1962, WA
1926 Rac: 2 G.

CLINTON BURRELL Burrell, Clinton Blane 6'1", 192 **DB**
Col: Louisiana State *HS:* Franklin [LA] B: 9/4/1956, Franklin, LA *Drafted:* 1979 Round 6 Cle
1979 Cle: 16 G; 1 Fum. **1980** Cle: 15 G; Int 5-51. **1981** Cle: 2 G. **1982** Cle: 9 G; Int 1-14 **1** TD; 6 Pt; 2 Sac. **1983** Cle: 12 G; Int 2-0. **1984** Cle: 13 G. **Total:** 67 G; Int 8-65 1 TD; 6 Pt; 1 Fum; 2 Sac.

GEORGE BURRELL Burrell, George Reed Jr. 5'10", 180 **DB**
Col: Pennsylvania *HS:* Kingsway Regional [Swedesboro, NJ] B: 1/1/1948, Camden, NJ
1969 Den: 14 G; PR 5-56 11.2; KR 6-108 18.0; Int 2-65 1 TD; 6 Pt.

JOHN BURRELL Burrell, Johnny Buster 6'3", 185 **WR**
Col: Rice *HS:* Fort Worth Polytechnic [TX] B: 11/22/1940, Fort Worth, TX *Drafted:* 1962 Round 7 SF
1962 Pit: Rush 6-38 6.3. **1964** Pit: KR 2-0. **1967** Was: KR 1-2 2.0. **Total:** Rush 6-38 6.3; KR 3-2 0.7.

		Receiving				
Year Team	G	Rec	Yds	Avg	TD	Fum
1962 Pit	14	8	193	24.1	0	0
1963 Pit	14	2	27	13.5	0	0
1964 Pit	14	6	113	18.8	0	0
1966 Was	4	1	9	9.0	0	0
1967 Was	10	9	95	10.6	0	1
NFL Total	56	26	437	16.8	0	1

ODE BURRELL Burrell, Ode Jr. 6'0", 190 **RB-P-WR**
Col: Holmes CC MS; Mississippi State *HS:* Durant [MS] B: 9/15/1939, Goodman, MS *Drafted:* 1964 Round 4 Hou
1964 Hou: PR 1-0. **1965** Hou: PR 3-39 13.0; Scor **2** 2XP. **1966** Hou: Pass 1-1 100.0%, 9 9.00; PR 8-78 9.8. **1968** Hou: PR 2-26 13.0. **1969** Hou: PR 1-6 6.0; Punt 29-1066 36.8. **Total:** Pass 1-1 100.0%, 9 9.00; PR 15-149 9.9; Punt 29-1066 36.8; Scor 2 2XP.

Year Team	G	Rushing Att	Yds	Avg	TD	Receiving Rec	Yds	Avg	TD
1964 Hou	7	8	10	1.3	0	5	73	14.6	0
1965 Hou	14	130	528	4.1	3	55	650	11.8	4
1966 Hou	14	122	406	3.3	0	33	400	12.1	5
1967 Hou	10	3	-3	-1.0	0	12	193	16.1	0
1968 Hou	1	0	0	—	0	2	35	17.5	0
1969 Hou	13	41	147	3.6	0	5	28	5.6	0
NFL Total	59	304	1088	3.6	3	112	1379	12.3	9

Year Team	Kickoff Returns Ret	Yds	Avg	TD	Fum	Tot TD
1964 Hou	17	449	26.4	**1**	3	1
1965 Hou	8	202	25.3	0	6	7
1966 Hou	1	16	16.0	0	3	5
1967 Hou	0	0	—	0	1	0
1968 Hou	2	70	35.0	0	0	0
1969 Hou	5	101	20.2	0	2	0
NFL Total	33	838	25.4	1	15	13

BO BURRIS Burris, James England Jr. 6′3″, 195 **DB**
Col: Houston *HS:* Brazosport [Freeport, TX] B: 10/16/1944, Luling, TX
Drafted: 1967 Round 2 NO
1967 NO: 14 G. **1968** NO: 14 G; Int 3-129 1 TD; 6 Pt. **1969** NO: 12 G; Int 1-24. **Total:** 40 G; Int 4-153 1 TD; 6 Pt.

JEFF BURRIS Burris, Jeffrey Lamar 6′0″, 201 **DB**
Col: Notre Dame *HS:* Northwestern [Rock Hill, SC] B: 6/7/1972, York, SC *Drafted:* 1994 Round 1 Buf
1994 Buf: Int 2-24. **1995** Buf: Int 1-19. **1996** Buf: Int 1-28. **1997** Buf: KR 1-10 10.0; Int 2-19. **1998** Ind: Int 1-0. **Total:** KR 1-10 10.0; Int 7-90.

Year Team	G	Punt Returns Ret	Yds	Avg	TD	Fum
1994 Buf	16	32	332	10.4	0	2
1995 Buf	9	20	229	11.5	0	0
1996 Buf	15	27	286	10.6	0	1
1997 Buf	14	21	198	9.4	0	3
1998 Ind	14	0	0	—	0	0
NFL Total	68	100	1045	10.5	0	6

BUDDY BURRIS Burris, Paul Buddy 5′11″, 215 **LB-OG**
Col: Tulsa; Oklahoma *HS:* Muskogee [OK] B: 1/20/1923, Rogers Co., OK *Drafted:* 1947 Round 3 GB
1949 GB: 10 G; Int 1-0. **1950** GB: 12 G; KR 3-18 6.0. **1951** GB: 7 G. **Total:** 29 G; KR 3-18 6.0; Int 1-0.

JOHN BURROUGH Burrough, John Leslie 6′5″, 275 **DT-DE**
Col: Washington State; Wyoming *HS:* Pinedale [WY] B: 5/17/1972, Laramie, WY *Drafted:* 1995 Round 7 Atl
1995 Atl: 16 G. **1996** Atl: 16 G. **1997** Atl: 16 G; KR 1-6 6.0; 1 Sac. **1998** Atl: 16 G; 0.5 Sac. **Total:** 64 G; KR 1-6 6.0; 1.5 Sac.

KEN BURROUGH Burrough, Kenneth Othell 6′3″, 215 **WR**
Col: Texas Southern *HS:* William M. Raines [Jacksonville, FL]
B: 7/14/1948, Jacksonville, FL *Drafted:* 1970 Round 1 NO
1970 NO: Rush 1-4 4.0; KR 15-298 19.9. **1971** Hou: KR 8-157 19.6. **1973** Hou: Rush 5-38 7.6 1 TD. **1974** Hou: Rush 1-0. **1976** Hou: Rush 3-22 7.3. **1977** Hou: Pass 1-0; Rush 4-10 2.5. **1978** Hou: Pass 1-0; Rush 3-(-11) -3.7. **1979** Hou: Pass 1-0. **Total:** Pass 3-0; Rush 17-63 3.7 1 TD; KR 23-455 19.8.

Year Team	G	Receiving Rec	Yds	Avg	TD	Fum	Tot TD
1970 NO	12	13	196	15.1	2	3	2
1971 Hou	13	25	370	14.8	1	0	1
1972 Hou	14	26	521	20.0	4	0	4
1973 Hou	14	43	577	13.4	2	2	3
1974 Hou	11	36	492	13.7	2	1	2
1975 Hou	14	53	**1063**	20.1	8	1	8
1976 Hou	14	51	932	18.3	7	0	7
1977 Hou	14	43	816	19.0	8	4	8
1978 Hou	16	47	624	13.3	2	0	2
1979 Hou	16	40	752	18.8	6	1	6
1980 Hou	2	4	91	22.8	0	0	0
1981 Hou	16	40	668	16.7	7	1	7
NFL Total	156	421	7102	16.9	49	13	50

DERRICK BURROUGHS Burroughs, Derrick D'wayne 6′1″, 180 **DB**
Col: Memphis *HS:* Mattie T. Blount [Prichard, AL] B: 5/18/1962, Mobile, AL *Drafted:* 1985 Round 1 Buf
1985 Buf: 14 G; Int 2-7. **1986** Buf: 15 G; Int 2-49. **1987** Buf: 12 G; Int 2-11. **1988** Buf: 14 G. **1989** Buf: 3 G; 1 Sac. **Total:** 58 G; Int 6-67; 1 Sac.

DON BURROUGHS Burroughs, Donald Edward 6′4″, 190 **DB**
(Blade) *Col:* Ventura Coll. CA (J.C.); Pasadena City Coll. CA (J.C.); Colorado State *HS:* Fillmore [CA] B: 8/19/1931, Los Angeles, CA
1957 LARm: PR 1-11 11.0. **1959** LARm: PR 1-0. **Total:** PR 2-11 5.5.

Year Team	G	Interceptions Int	Yds	TD	Fum
1955 LARm	12	9	103	0	0
1956 LARm	12	2	9	0	0
1957 LARm	12	3	29	0	0
1958 LARm	12	7	72	0	1
1959 LARm	10	0	0	0	0
1960 Phi	12	9	124	0	0
1961 Phi	13	7	90	0	0
1962 Phi	12	7	96	0	0
1963 Phi	13	4	36	0	0
1964 Phi	14	2	5	0	1
NFL Total	122	50	564	0	2

JAMES BURROUGHS Burroughs, James Edward 6′1″, 190 **DB**
Col: Michigan State *HS:* Pahokee [FL] B: 1/21/1958, Pahokee, FL
Drafted: 1982 Round 3 Bal
1982 Bal: 8 G; Int 1-94 **1** TD; 6 Pt. **1983** Bal: 16 G; Int 2-8. **1984** Ind: 6 G; Int 3-9. **Total:** 30 G; Int 6-111 1 TD; 6 Pt.

SAMMIE BURROUGHS Burroughs, Sammie Lee 6′0″, 227 **LB**
Col: Mount San Antonio Coll. CA (J.C.); Portland State *HS:* Pomona [CA] B: 6/21/1973, Pomona, CA
1996 Ind: 16 G. **1997** Ind: 16 G; 1 Sac. **Total:** 32 G; 1 Sac.

CURTIS BURROW Burrow, Curtis D 5′11″, 185 **K**
Col: Central Arkansas *HS:* Brinkley [AR] B: 12/11/1962, Brinkley, AR
1988 GB: 1 G; Scor 2, 0-1 FG, 2-4 50.0% XK.

JIM BURROW Burrow, James Arthur Jr. 5′11″, 181 **DB**
Col: Nebraska *HS:* Amory [MS] B: 11/29/1953, Hampton, VA
Drafted: 1976 Round 8 GB
1976 GB: 3 G.

KEN BURROW Burrow, Kenneth Robert 6′0″, 191 **WR**
Col: Utah State; San Diego State *HS:* De Aniza [El Sobrante, CA]
B: 3/29/1948, Richmond, CA *Drafted:* 1971 Round 2 Atl
1971 Atl: Rush 1-5 5.0. **1972** Atl: Rush 3-3 1.0. **1973** Atl: Rush 2-17 8.5. **Total:** Rush 6-25 4.2.

Year Team	G	Receiving Rec	Yds	Avg	TD	Fum
1971 Atl	14	33	741	22.5	6	1
1972 Atl	14	29	492	17.0	5	1
1973 Atl	9	31	567	18.3	7	1
1974 Atl	14	34	545	16.0	1	0
1975 Atl	13	25	323	12.9	2	1
NFL Total	64	152	2668	17.6	21	4

HARRY BURRUS Burrus, Harry Clifton Jr. 6′1″, 195 **E-DB**
Col: Hardin-Simmons *HS:* Bald Spring [TX] B: 4/6/1921, Slaton, TX
AAFC **1946** NY-A: Rush 1-3 3.0; Int 2-37. **1947** NY-A: Rush 1-5 5.0; Int 1-11. **1948** ChiA-BknA: Rush 1-(-3) -3.0; Int 3-82; Scor 8, 2-3 66.7% XK. **Total:** Rush 3-5 1.7; Int 6-130; Scor 26, 2-3 66.7% XK.

Year Team	G	Receiving Rec	Yds	Avg	TD
1946 NY-A	11	10	251	25.1	1
1947 NY-A	14	8	192	24.0	2
1948 ChiA-BknA	13	10	227	22.7	1
AAFC Total	38	28	670	23.9	4

LLOYD BURRUSS Burruss, Lloyd Earl Jr. 6′0″, 204 **DB**
Col: Maryland *HS:* Charlottesville [VA] B: 10/31/1957, Charlottesville, VA *Drafted:* 1981 Round 3 KC
1981 KC: KR 5-91 18.2. **1983** KC: 0.5 Sac. **1985** KC: 2 Sac. **Total:** KR 5-91 18.2; 2.5 Sac.

Year Team	G	Interceptions Int	Yds	TD	Fum	Tot TD
1981 KC	16	4	75	1	1	1
1982 KC	9	1	25	0	0	0
1983 KC	12	4	46	0	0	0
1984 KC	16	2	16	0	0	0
1985 KC	15	1	0	0	0	0
1986 KC	15	5	**193**	**3**	0	4
1987 KC	11	0	0	0	0	0
1988 KC	10	2	57	0	0	0
1989 KC	9	1	0	0	0	0
1990 KC	16	1	14	0	0	0
1991 KC	16	1	83	0	0	0
NFL Total	145	22	509	4	1	5

TONY BURSE Burse, Tony Lee 6′0″, 220 **RB**
Col: Middle Tennessee State *HS:* La Fayette [GA] B: 4/4/1965, Lafayette, GA *Drafted:* 1987 Round 12 Sea
1987 Sea: 12 G; Rush 7-36 5.1; KR 1-1 1.0; 1 Fum.

JIMMY BURSON Burson, James Oertell 6′0″, 175 **DB**
Col: Auburn *HS:* La Grange [GA] B: 10/13/1940, La Grange, GA
Drafted: 1963 Round 11 StL
1964 StL: PR 12-125 10.4 1 TD; KR 2-38 19.0. **1965** StL: PR 1-0.
1968 Atl: PR 11-56 5.1. **Total:** PR 24-181 7.5 1 TD; KR 2-38 19.0.

		Interceptions				Tot
Year Team	**G**	**Int**	**Yds**	**TD**	**Fum**	**TD**
1963 StL	1	0	0	0	0	0
1964 StL	14	3	53	0	2	1
1965 StL	12	5	113	0	0	0
1966 StL	11	2	20	0	0	0
1967 StL	13	2	0	0	0	0
1968 Atl	14	4	100	1	0	1
NFL Total	65	16	286	1	2	2

HAL BURT Burt, Harold Allen 5′10″, 175 **G**
Col: Kansas *HS:* Eureka [KS] B: 9/11/1900, Eureka, KS
D: 4/17/1979, Kerrville, TX
1924 Cle: 2 G.

JIM BURT Burt, James P 6′1″, 260 **NT-DT**
Col: Miami (Fla.) *HS:* Orchard Park [NY] B: 6/7/1959, Buffalo, NY
1981 NYG: 13 G. **1982** NYG: 4 G; 1 Sac. **1983** NYG: 7 G. **1984** NYG: 16 G; 7 Sac. **1985** NYG: 16 G; 4 Sac. **1986** NYG: 13 G; 1 Sac. **1987** NYG: 8 G; 2 Sac. **1988** NYG: 16 G; **1** Fum TD; 6 Pt; 3 Sac. **1989** SF: 8 G. **1990** SF: 13 G; 2 Sac. **1991** SF: 4 G. **Total:** 118 G; 1 Fum TD; 6 Pt; 20 Sac.

RUSS BURT Burt, Russell Edward 5′8″, 170 **WB-FB**
(Peanuts) *Col:* Canisius *HS:* Tech [Buffalo, NY] B: 12/15/1900, Buffalo, NY D: 4/7/1978, Orlando, FL
1924 Buf: 1 G; Rec 1 TD; Scor 7, 1 XK. **1925** Buf: 1 G. **Total:** 2 G; Rec 1 TD.

ALBERT BURTON Burton, Albert III 6′5″, 267 **DE**
Col: Bethune-Cookman *HS:* Mainland [Daytona Beach, FL]
B: 3/30/1952, Daytona Beach, FL
1976 Hou: 12 G. **1977** Hou: 6 G. **Total:** 18 G.

DEREK BURTON Burton, Derek L 6′2″, 270 **OT**
Col: Oklahoma State *HS:* Okmulgee [OK] B: 8/10/1963, Seattle, WA
1987 Min: 3 G.

SHANE BURTON Burton, Franklin Shane 6′6″, 305 **DT**
Col: Tennessee *HS:* Bandys [Catawba, NC] B: 1/18/1974, Logan, WV
Drafted: 1996 Round 5 Mia
1996 Mia: 16 G; 3 Sac. **1997** Mia: 16 G; 4 Sac. **1998** Mia: 15 G; 2 Sac.
Total: 47 G; 9 Sac.

JAMES BURTON Burton, James Terrell 5′9″, 184 **DB**
Col: Hawaii; Fresno State *HS:* Long Beach Polytechnic [CA]
B: 4/27/1971, Torrance, CA *Drafted:* 1994 Round 5 KC
1994 ChiB: 13 G. **1995** ChiB: 11 G. **1996** ChiB: 16 G; Int 1-11. **1997** ChiB: 5 G. **Total:** 45 G; Int 1-11.

KENDRICK BURTON Burton, Kendrick Duran 6′5″, 288 **DE**
Col: Alabama *HS:* Hartselle [AL] B: 9/7/1974, Decatur, AL
Drafted: 1996 Round 4 Hou
1996 Hou: 4 G.

LARRY BURTON Burton, Lawrence Godfrey Jr. 6′1″, 192 **WR**
Col: Purdue *HS:* Mary Nottingham Smith [Accomack, VA]
B: 12/15/1951, Northampton, VA *Drafted:* 1975 Round 1 NO
1975 NO: Rush 2-8 4.0. **1976** NO: Rush 3-(-4) -1.3. **Total:** Rush 5-4 0.8.

		Receiving				
Year Team	**G**	**Rec**	**Yds**	**Avg**	**TD**	**Fum**
1975 NO	13	16	305	19.1	2	0
1976 NO	14	18	297	16.5	2	0
1977 NO	1	1	13	13.0	0	0
1978 SD	3	5	127	25.4	3	1
1979 SD	12	4	62	15.5	0	0
NFL Total	43	44	804	18.3	7	1

LEONARD BURTON Burton, Leonard Bernard 6′3″, 275 **C**
Col: Northwest Mississippi CC; South Carolina *HS:* Oakhaven [Memphis, TN] B: 6/18/1964, Memphis, TN *Drafted:* 1986 Round 3 Buf
1986 Buf: 14 G. **1987** Buf: 12 G. **1988** Buf: 16 G. **1989** Buf: 16 G.
1992 Det: 2 G. **Total:** 60 G.

LYLE BURTON Burton, Lyle Ralph 6′1″, 195 **G-T-FB**
(Liz) *Col:* DePauw *HS:* Hoopeston Area [IL] B: 5/21/1900, Sullivan, IL
D: 2/8/1962, Peoria, IL
1924 Ham: 1 G. **1925** RI: 7 G. **Total:** 8 G.

RON BURTON Burton, Ronald Eugene 5′10″, 190 **HB**
Col: Northwestern *HS:* Springfield [OH] B: 7/25/1936, Springfield, OH
Drafted: 1960 Round 1 Bos
1961 Bos: Pass 1-0, 1 Int. **1963** Bos: Postseason only. **Total:** Pass 1-0, 1 Int.

		Rushing				Receiving			
Year Team	**G**	**Att**	**Yds**	**Avg**	**TD**	**Rec**	**Yds**	**Avg**	**TD**
1960 Bos	13	66	280	4.2	1	21	196	9.3	0
1961 Bos	14	82	260	3.2	2	13	115	8.8	0
1962 Bos	14	134	548	4.1	2	40	461	11.5	4
1964 Bos	14	102	340	3.3	3	27	306	11.3	2
1965 Bos	14	45	108	2.4	1	10	127	12.7	2
NFL Total	69	429	1536	3.6	9	111	1205	10.9	8

	Punt Returns				Kickoff Returns					Tot
Year Team	**Ret**	**Yds**	**Avg**	**TD**	**Ret**	**Yds**	**Avg**	**TD**	**Fum**	**TD**
1960 Bos	1	0	0.0	0	4	161	40.3	0	2	1
1961 Bos	8	128	16.0	0	15	401	26.7	**1**	3	3
1962 Bos	**21**	122	5.8	0	13	238	18.3	0	7	7
1964 Bos	11	78	7.1	0	7	131	18.7	0	1	5
1965 Bos	15	61	4.1	0	7	188	26.9	0	6	3
NFL Total	56	389	6.9	0	46	1119	24.3	1	19	19

RON BURTON Burton, Ronald Leon 6′1″, 250 **LB**
Col: North Carolina *HS:* Highland Springs [VA] B: 5/2/1964, Richmond, VA
1987 Dal: 12 G. **1988** Dal: 16 G; 2 Sac. **1989** Dal-Pho: 16 G; Int 1-0. Dal: 6 G; Int 1-0. Pho: 10 G. **1990** LARd: 5 G. **Total:** 49 G; Int 1-0; 2 Sac.

LEON BURTON Burton, Walter Leon 5′9″, 172 **HB**
Col: Charles Stewart Mott CC MI; Arizona State *HS:* Northern [Flint, MI]
B: 3/13/1935, Flint, MI *Drafted:* 1958 Round 8 SF
1960 NYT: Rush 16-119 7.4 1 TD; Rec 3-8 2.7; PR 12-93 7.8.

		Kickoff Returns					Tot
Year Team	**G**	**Ret**	**Yds**	**Avg**	**TD**	**Fum**	**TD**
1960 NYT	14	**30**	**862**	28.7	**2**	6	3

SHERRILL BUSBY Busby, Shelby 6′2″, 200 **DE**
Col: Troy State B: 6/17/1916, Florala, AL D: 6/26/1986, Pensacola, FL
1940 Bkn: 2 G.

ELMER BUSCH Busch, Elmer E 5′10″, 210 **G-C**
(Pete) *Col:* Sherman Indian; Carlisle B: 1890, CA Deceased
1922 Oor: 9 G.

MIKE BUSCH Busch, Michael Paul 6′4″, 214 **QB**
Col: Idaho State; South Dakota State *HS:* Huron [SD] B: 2/8/1962, Huron, SD
1987 NYG: 2 G; Pass 47-17 36.2%, 278 5.91 3 TD 2 Int.

BLAIR BUSH Bush, Blair Walter 6′3″, 268 **C**
Col: Washington *HS:* Palos Verdes [Rolling Hills Estates, CA]
B: 11/25/1956, Fort Hood, TX *Drafted:* 1978 Round 1 Cin
1978 Cin: 16 G. **1979** Cin: 12 G. **1980** Cin: 16 G. **1981** Cin: 16 G.
1982 Cin: 8 G. **1983** Sea: 16 G. **1984** Sea: 16 G. **1985** Sea: 16 G.
1986 Sea: 7 G. **1987** Sea: 11 G. **1988** Sea: 16 G. **1989** GB: 16 G.
1990 GB: 16 G. **1991** GB: 16 G. **1992** LARm: 16 G. **1993** LARm: 16 G.
1994 LARm: 16 G. **Total:** 246 G.

DEVIN BUSH Bush, Devin Marquese 5′11″, 210 **DB**
Col: Florida State *HS:* Hialeah-Miami Lakes [Hialeah, FL] B: 7/3/1973, Miami, FL *Drafted:* 1995 Round 1 Atl
1995 Atl: 11 G; Int 1-0. **1996** Atl: 16 G; Int 1-2. **1997** Atl: 16 G; Int 1-4.
1998 Atl: 13 G. **Total:** 56 G; Int 3-6.

FRANK BUSH Bush, Frank Everett 6′1″, 218 **LB**
Col: North Carolina State *HS:* Clarke Central [Athens, GA]
B: 1/10/1963, Athens, GA *Drafted:* 1985 Round 5 Hou
1985 Hou: 16 G; 3 Sac. **1986** Hou: 3 G; 1 Sac. **Total:** 19 G; 4 Sac.

LEWIS BUSH Bush, Lewis Fitzgerald 6′2″, 245 **LB**
Col: Washington State *HS:* Washington [Tacoma, WA] B: 12/2/1969, Atlanta, GA *Drafted:* 1993 Round 4 SD
1993 SD: 16 G. **1994** SD: 16 G. **1995** SD: 16 G; Int 1-0. **1996** SD: 16 G; 1 Sac. **1997** SD: 14 G. **1998** SD: 10 G; 1 Sac. **Total:** 88 G; Int 1-0; 2 Sac.

RAY BUSH Bush, Raymond M 5′8″, 180 **E**
Col: Loyola (Chicago) B: 1903
1926 Lou: 4 G.

STEVE BUSH Bush, Steven Jack 6′3″, 258 **TE**
Col: Arizona State *HS:* Paradise Valley [Phoenix, AZ] B: 7/4/1974, Phoenix, AZ
1997 Cin: 16 G. **1998** Cin: 12 G; Rec 4-39 9.8. **Total:** 28 G; Rec 4-39 9.8.

TOM BUSHBY Bushby, Thomas Bateman 5′10″, 200 **WB-DB**
(Tom-Tom) *Col:* Kansas State B: 12/30/1911, Munden, KS
D: 10/1983, Northridge, CA
1934 Cin: 6 G; Rush 7-9 1.3; Rec 1-4 4.0. **1935** Phi: 2 G. **Total:** 8 G; Rush 7-9 1.3; Rec 1-4 4.0.

SAM BUSICH Busich, Samuel 6′3″, 189 **OE-DE**
Col: Ohio State *HS:* Lorain [OH] B: 11/17/1913, Lorain, OH
D: 2/1/1991
1936 Bos: 11 G; Rec 6-57 9.5 1 TD; Scor 10, 1 FG, 1 XK. **1937** Cle: 10 G; Rec 13-136 10.5. **1943** Det: 1 G; Scor 1, 1-1 100.0% XK. **Total:** 22 G; Rec 19-193 10.2 1 TD; Scor 11, 1 FG, 2-1 100.0% XK.

STEVE BUSICK Busick, Steven Ray 6'4", 227 **LB**
Col: USC *HS:* Temple City [CA] B: 12/10/1958, Los Angeles, CA
Drafted: 1981 Round 7 Den
1981 Den: 16 G. **1982** Den: 9 G. **1983** Den: 16 G; 2 Sac. **1984** Den: 16 G; Int 2-21; 1 Sac. **1985** Den: 16 G. **1986** LARm: 4 G. **1987** SD: 1 G.
Total: 78 G; Int 2-21; 3 Sac.

RAY BUSLER Busler, Raymond Albert 6'1", 222 **T**
Col: Marquette *HS:* Watertown [WI] B: 1/16/1914, Watertown, WI
D: 10/9/1969, Granite City, IL
1940 ChiC: 11 G. **1941** ChiC: 8 G. **1945** ChiC: 1 G. **Total:** 20 G.

ART BUSS Buss, Arthur 6'3", 219 **T**
Col: Michigan State *HS:* Benton Harbor [MI] B: 7/14/1911, St. Joseph, MI
1934 ChiB: 13 G. **1935** ChiB: 9 G. **1936** Phi: 12 G. **1937** Phi: 11 G.
Total: 45 G.

GERRY BUSSELL Bussell, Gerald Wheeler 6'0", 190 **DB**
Col: Georgia Tech *HS:* Englewood [Jacksonville, FL] B: 9/7/1943, Middlesboro, KY *Drafted:* 1965 Round 9 Den
1965 Den: 6 G; PR 2-24 12.0; KR 5-103 20.6; 1 Fum.

BARNEY BUSSEY Bussey, Barney Albert 6'0", 210 **DB-LB**
Col: South Carolina State *HS:* Lincoln Co. [Lincolnton, GA]
B: 5/20/1962, Lincolnton, GA *Drafted:* 1984 Round 5 Cin
1986 Cin: 1 Sac. **1987** Cin: 2 Sac. **1988** Cin: 4 Sac. **1989** Cin: 2.5 Sac.
1990 Cin: 1 Fum TD; 2 Sac. **1994** TB: 1.5 Sac. **Total:** 1 Fum TD; 13 Sac.

		Kickoff Returns				Interceptions				Tot
Year Team	G	Ret	Yds	Avg	TD	Int	Yds	TD	Fum	TD
1986 Cin	16	0	0	—	0	1	19	0	0	0
1987 Cin	12	21	406	19.3	0	1	0	0	1	0
1988 Cin	16	7	83	11.9	0	0	0	0	1	0
1989 Cin	16	0	0	—	0	1	0	0	0	1
1990 Cin	16	0	0	—	0	4	37	0	0	1
1991 Cin	12	0	0	—	0	2	18	0	0	0
1992 Cin	16	1	18	18.0	0	1	3	0	0	0
1993 TB	16	0	0	—	0	0	0	0	0	0
1994 TB	16	0	0	—	0	0	0	0	0	0
1995 TB	8	0	0	—	0	0	0	0	0	0
NFL Total	144	29	507	17.5	0	10	77	0	2	2

DEXTER BUSSEY Bussey, Dexter Manley 6'1", 195 **RB**
Col: Oklahoma; Texas-Arlington *HS:* John F. Kennedy [Dallas, TX]
B: 3/11/1952, Dallas, TX *Drafted:* 1974 Round 3 Det
1974 Det: KR 5-59 11.8. **1975** Det: KR 2-38 19.0. **1976** Det: KR 1-14 14.0.
Total: KR 8-111 13.9.

		Rushing				Receiving					Tot
Year Team	G	Att	Yds	Avg	TD	Rec	Yds	Avg	TD	Fum	TD
1974 Det	11	9	22	2.4	0	4	24	6.0	0	1	0
1975 Det	13	157	696	4.4	2	14	175	12.5	2	7	4
1976 Det	14	196	858	4.4	3	28	218	7.8	0	6	3
1977 Det	8	85	338	4.0	4	11	116	10.5	1	2	5
1978 Det	16	225	924	4.1	5	31	275	8.9	1	9	6
1979 Det	16	144	625	4.3	1	15	102	6.8	0	3	1
1980 Det	16	145	720	5.0	3	39	364	9.3	0	2	3
1981 Det	16	105	446	4.2	0	18	92	5.1	0	3	0
1982 Det	9	48	136	2.8	0	16	138	8.6	0	2	0
1983 Det	15	57	249	4.4	0	8	49	6.1	1	1	1
1984 Det	16	32	91	2.8	0	9	63	7.0	0	0	0
NFL Total	150	1203	5105	4.2	18	193	1616	8.4	5	36	23

YOUNG BUSSEY Bussey, Ruey Young 5'9", 184 **DB-QB**
Col: Louisiana State *HS:* San Jacinto [Houston, TX] B: 10/4/1917, Timpson, TX D: 1/11/1945, Lingayen Gulf, Philipines *Drafted:* 1940 Round 18 ChiB
1941 ChiB: 10 G; Pass 40-13 32.5%, 353 8.83 5 TD 3 Int; Rush 13-(-27) -2.1; PR 1-40 40.0; Int 2-5; Punt 2-74 37.0.

PAUL BUTCHER Butcher, Paul Martin 6'0", 230 **LB**
Col: Wayne State (Mich.) *HS:* St. Alphonsus [Dearborn, MI]
B: 11/8/1963, Detroit, MI
1986 Det: 12 G. **1987** Det: 12 G. **1988** Det: 16 G. **1989** LARm: Postseason only. **1990** LARm: 16 G. **1991** LARm: 16 G. **1992** LARm: 1 G.
1993 Ind: 16 G; KR 2-2 1.0. **1994** Ind: 13 G. **1995** Car: 16 G; KR 1-5 5.0.
1996 Oak: 16 G. **Total:** 134 G; KR 3-7 2.3.

WENDELL BUTCHER Butcher, Wendell Ralph 6'1", 197 **BB-LB-FB**
Col: Gustavus Adolphus *HS:* Worthington [MN] B: 3/28/1914, Worthington, MN D: 12/18/1988, Memphis, TN
1938 Bkn: Rec 3-44 14.7. **1939** Bkn: Rec 9-73 8.1. **1940** Bkn: Rec 2-21 10.5. **1942** Bkn: Rec 1-16 16.0. **Total:** Rec 15-154 10.3.

		Rushing			
Year Team	G	Att	Yds	Avg	TD
1938 Bkn	9	30	99	3.3	1
1939 Bkn	10	2	2	1.0	0
1940 Bkn	5	0	0	—	0
1941 Bkn	9	1	2	2.0	0
1942 Bkn	11	0	0	—	0
NFL Total	44	33	103	3.1	1

CARL BUTKUS Butkus, Carl John 6'1", 245 **T**
Col: George Washington *HS:* Scranton [PA] B: 12/26/1922, Scranton, PA D: 8/3/1978, Washington, DC
AAFC **1948** NY-A: 4 G.

NFL **1948** Was: 9 G. **1949** NYG: 11 G. **Total:** 20 G.

DICK BUTKUS Butkus, Richard Marvin 6'3", 245 **LB**
Col: Illinois *HS:* Chicago Vocational [IL] B: 12/9/1942, Chicago, IL
Drafted: 1965 Round 1 ChiB *HOF:* 1979
1966 ChiB: KR 3-32 10.7. **1968** ChiB: KR 2-30 15.0. **1969** ChiB: KR 3-28 9.3; Scor **1** Saf. **1970** ChiB: KR 1-0. **1971** ChiB: KR 2-15 7.5; Scor **1** 1XP.
1972 ChiB: Rush 1-28 28.0; KR 1-15 15.0; Scor **1** 1XP. **1973** ChiB: **1** Fum TD. **Total:** Rush 1-28 28.0; KR 12-120 10.0; Scor 1 Saf, 2 1XP; 1 Fum TD.

		Interceptions		
Year Team	G	Int	Yds	TD
1965 ChiB	14	5	84	0
1966 ChiB	14	1	3	0
1967 ChiB	14	1	24	0
1968 ChiB	13	3	14	0
1969 ChiB	13	2	13	0
1970 ChiB	14	3	0	0
1971 ChiB	14	4	9	0
1972 ChiB	14	2	19	0
1973 ChiB	9	1	0	0
NFL Total	119	22	166	0

CHUCK BUTLER Butler, Charles Wallace 6'0", 220 **LB**
Col: Chabot Coll. CA (J.C.); Utah State; Boise State *HS:* Bishop O'Dowd [Oakland, CA] B: 12/18/1961, New Haven, CT
1984 Sea: 8 G.

DAVE BUTLER Butler, David Michael 6'4", 225 **LB**
Col: Notre Dame *HS:* St. John's [Toledo, OH] B: 7/17/1965, Ridgewood, NJ
1987 Cle: 1 G.

DUANE BUTLER Butler, Duane M 6'1", 211 **DB**
Col: Eastern Michigan; Illinois State *HS:* Trotwood-Madison [Trotwood, OH] B: 11/29/1973
1997 Min: 3 G. **1998** Min: 14 G. **Total:** 17 G.

SOL BUTLER Butler, Edward Solomon 5'8", 181 **WB-TB-FB-BB**
Col: Dubuque *HS:* Hutchinson [KS] B: 7/26/1897 D: 11/6/1988, Chicago, IL
1923 RI-Ham: 6 G. RI: 3 G. Ham: 3 G. **1924** Ham-Akr: 6 G; Rush 2 TD; 12 Pt. Ham: 5 G; Rush 1 TD; 6 Pt. Akr: 1 G; Rush 1 TD; 6 Pt. **1925** Ham: 2 G. **1926** Can-Ham: 9 G. Can: 8 G. Ham: 1 G. **Total:** 23 G; Rush 2 TD; 12 Pt.

FRANK BUTLER Butler, Frank John 6'3", 237 **C-LB-T**
(Butts) *Col:* Notre Dame; Michigan State *HS:* Tilden [Chicago, IL]
B: 5/3/1907, Bloomington, IL D: 11/1979, Glenwood, IL
1934 GB: 3 G. **1935** GB: 6 G. **1936** GB: 9 G. **1938** GB: 8 G. **Total:** 26 G.

GARY BUTLER Butler, Gary Bernard 6'3", 235 **TE**
Col: Rice *HS:* Conroe [TX] B: 1/11/1951, Houston, TX *Drafted:* 1973 Round 2 KC
1973 KC: 14 G; Rush 2-10 5.0; Rec 8-124 15.5 2 TD; 12 Pt; 1 Fum.
1975 ChiB: 8 G. **1977** TB: 3 G; Rec 1-21 21.0. **Total:** 25 G; Rush 2-10 5.0; Rec 9-145 16.1 2 TD; 12 Pt; 1 Fum.

HILLARY BUTLER Butler, Hillary 6'2", 240 **LB**
Col: Washington *HS:* Lakes [Tacoma, WA] B: 1/5/1971, San Francisco, CA
1998 Sea: 7 G.

CANNONBALL BUTLER Butler, James 5'9", 194 **RB**
Col: Edward Waters *HS:* Carver [Delray Beach, FL] B: 5/4/1943, Quincy, FL *Drafted:* 1965 Round 14 Pit

		Rushing				Receiving			
Year Team	G	Att	Yds	Avg	TD	Rec	Yds	Avg	TD
1965 Pit	14	46	108	2.3	0	9	117	13.0	1
1966 Pit	14	46	114	2.5	2	4	93	23.3	1
1967 Pit	11	90	293	3.3	0	4	23	5.8	0
1968 Atl	12	94	365	3.9	2	15	127	8.5	0
1969 Atl	14	163	655	4.0	3	17	297	17.5	2
1970 Atl	14	166	636	3.8	0	24	151	6.3	1
1971 Atl	13	186	594	3.2	2	15	143	9.5	2
1972 StL	5	6	3	0.5	0	1	8	8.0	0
NFL Total	97	797	2768	3.5	9	89	959	10.8	7

	Kickoff Returns					Tot
Year Team	Ret	Yds	Avg	TD	Fum	TD
1965 Pit	25	509	20.4	0	7	1
1966 Pit	17	454	26.7	1	4	4

1967 Pit	10	223	22.3	0	1	0
1968 Atl	37	799	21.6	0	1	2
1969 Atl	13	405	31.2	0	3	5
1970 Atl	14	284	20.3	0	**10**	1
1971 Atl	13	372	28.6	0	7	4
1972 StL	4	85	21.3	0	1	0
NFL Total	133	3131	23.5	1	34	17

JERRY BUTLER Butler, Jerry Kenneth 5′11″, 193 **RB**
Col: Tennessee Mil. Acad. (J.C.); East Tennessee State *HS:* Avondale [Avondale Estates, GA] B: 12/7/1961, Smyrna, TN
1987 Atl: 1 G; Rush 1-1 1.0; Rec 2-7 3.5; PR 2-10 5.0; KR 1-13 13.0.

JERRY BUTLER Butler, Jerry O'Dell 6′0″, 178 **WR**
Col: Clemson *HS:* Ware Shoals [SC] B: 10/12/1957, Ware Shoals, SC
Drafted: 1979 Round 1 Buf
1979 Buf: Rush 2-13 6.5. **1980** Buf: Rush 1-18 18.0. **1981** Buf: Rush 1-1 1.0. **Total:** Rush 4-32 8.0.

		Receiving				
Year Team	**G**	**Rec**	**Yds**	**Avg**	**TD**	**Fum**
1979 Buf	13	48	834	17.4	4	1
1980 Buf	16	57	832	14.6	6	0
1981 Buf	16	55	842	15.3	8	2
1982 Buf	7	26	336	12.9	4	0
1983 Buf	9	36	385	10.7	3	1
1985 Buf	16	41	770	18.8	2	0
1986 Buf	11	15	302	20.1	2	0
NFL Total	88	278	4301	15.5	29	4

JACK BUTLER Butler, John Bradshaw 6′1″, 200 **DB**
Col: St. Bonaventure *HS:* Mount Carmel [Niagara Falls, Canada]
B: 11/12/1927, Pittsburgh, PA
1951 Pit: PR 1-2 2.0. **1952** Pit: Rec 3-37 12.3 2 TD. **1953** Pit: Rec 2-43 21.5 1 TD; PR 1-5 5.0. **1954** Pit: Rec 1-12 12.0. **1956** Pit: Rec 1-10 10.0 1 TD; **1** Fum TD. **1957** Pit: PR 1-10 10.0. **Total:** Rec 7-102 14.6 4 TD; PR 3-17 5.7; 1 Fum TD.

		Interceptions			Tot
Year Team	**G**	**Int**	**Yds**	**TD**	**TD**
1951 Pit	12	5	142	1	1
1952 Pit	12	7	168	0	2
1953 Pit	12	9	147	**1**	2
1954 Pit	12	4	75	**2**	2
1955 Pit	12	0	0	0	0
1956 Pit	12	6	113	0	2
1957 Pit	12	**10**	85	0	0
1958 Pit	12	9	81	0	0
1959 Pit	7	2	16	0	0
NFL Total	103	52	827	4	9

JOHN BUTLER Butler, John Damon 6′1″, 200 **DB**
Col: Principia *HS:* Palos Verdes [Rolling Hills Estates, CA]
B: 4/13/1965, San Diego, CA
1987 SF: 3 G.

KEITH BUTLER Butler, John Keith 6′4″, 230 **LB**
Col: Memphis *HS:* Robert E. Lee [Huntsville, AL] B: 5/16/1956, Anniston, AL *Drafted:* 1978 Round 2 Sea
1978 Sea: 16 G. **1979** Sea: 14 G; Int 1-4. **1980** Sea: 16 G; Int 2-11. **1981** Sea: 16 G; Int 2-0; 1 Fum. **1982** Sea: 8 G; 2 Sac. **1983** Sea: 16 G; Int 1-0. **1984** Sea: 16 G; 1 Sac. **1985** Sea: 16 G; Int 2-31. **1986** Sea: 16 G; 1 Sac. **1987** Sea: 12 G. **Total:** 146 G; Int 8-46; 1 Fum; 4 Sac.

JOHNNY BUTLER Butler, John William 5′10″, 185 **HB**
Col: Tennessee *HS:* Knoxville [TN] B: 9/14/1918, Knoxville, TN
D: 4/1963 *Drafted:* 1942 Round 7 Pit
1943 PhPt: Pass 13-6 46.2%, 84 6.46 1 Int; Rec 3-63 21.0; PR 13-108 8.3; KR 6-92 15.3; Punt 11-407 37.0. **1944** ChPt-Bkn: Pass 23-8 34.8%, 107 4.65 1 Int; Rec 3-109 36.3 2 TD; PR 9-99 11.0; KR 4-92 23.0; Int 3-16; Punt 13-485 37.3. ChPt: Rec 3-109 36.3 2 TD; PR 3-22 7.3; KR 3-72 24.0; Int 2-16. Bkn: Pass 23-8 34.8%, 107 4.65 1 Int; PR 6-77 12.8; KR 1-20 20.0; Int 1-0; Punt 13-485 37.3. **1945** Phi: Rec 2-14 7.0; KR 1-21 21.0; Int 1-32. **Total:** Pass 36-14 38.9%, 191 5.31 2 Int; Rec 8-186 23.3 2 TD; PR 22-207 9.4; KR 11-205 18.6; Int 4-48; Punt 24-892 37.2.

		Rushing				Tot
Year Team	**G**	**Att**	**Yds**	**Avg**	**TD**	**TD**
1943 PhPt	10	87	362	4.2	3	3
1944 ChPt-Bkn	9	60	94	1.6	0	2
1944 ChPt	3	20	48	2.4	0	2
1944 Bkn	6	40	46	1.2	0	0
1945 Phi	7	21	61	2.9	1	1
NFL Total	26	168	517	3.1	4	6

KEVIN BUTLER Butler, Kevin Gregory 6′0″, 215 **K**
Col: Georgia *HS:* Redan [Stone Mountain, GA] B: 7/24/1962, Savannah, GA *Drafted:* 1985 Round 4 ChiB

		Scoring						
Year Team	**G**	**Pts**	**FG**	**FGA**	**FG%**	**XK**	**XKA**	**XK%**
1985 ChiB	16	**144**	31	37	83.8	51	51	100.0
1986 ChiB	16	120	28	**41**	68.3	36	37	97.3
1987 ChiB	12	85	19	28	67.9	28	30	93.3
1988 ChiB	16	82	15	19	78.9	37	38	97.4
1989 ChiB	16	88	15	19	78.9	43	45	95.6
1990 ChiB	16	114	26	37	70.3	36	37	97.3
1991 ChiB	16	89	19	29	65.5	32	34	94.1
1992 ChiB	16	91	19	26	73.1	34	34	100.0
1993 ChiB	16	102	27	36	75.0	21	22	95.5
1994 ChiB	15	87	21	29	72.4	24	24	100.0
1995 ChiB	16	114	23	31	74.2	45	45	100.0
1996 Ariz	7	59	14	17	82.4	17	19	89.5
1997 Ariz	6	33	8	12	66.7	9	10	90.0
NFL Total	184	1208	265	361	73.4	413	426	96.9

LEROY BUTLER Butler, LeRoy III 6′0″, 197 **DB**
Col: Florida State *HS:* Robert E. Lee [Jacksonville, FL] B: 7/19/1968, Jacksonville, FL *Drafted:* 1990 Round 2 GB
1993 GB: 1 Fum TD; 1 Sac. **1994** GB: 1 Sac. **1995** GB: 1 Sac. **1996** GB: 6.5 Sac. **1997** GB: 3 Sac. **1998** GB: 1 Fum TD; 4 Sac. **Total:** 2 Fum TD; 16.5 Sac.

		Interceptions			Tot
Year Team	**G**	**Int**	**Yds**	**TD**	**TD**
1990 GB	16	3	42	0	0
1991 GB	16	3	6	0	0
1992 GB	15	1	0	0	0
1993 GB	16	6	131	0	1
1994 GB	13	3	68	0	0
1995 GB	16	5	105	0	0
1996 GB	16	5	149	1	1
1997 GB	16	5	4	0	0
1998 GB	16	3	3	0	1
NFL Total	140	34	508	1	3

MIKE BUTLER Butler, Michael Anthony 6′5″, 265 **DE**
Col: Kansas *HS:* Calvin Coolidge [Washington, DC] B: 4/4/1954, Washington, DC *Drafted:* 1977 Round 1 GB
1977 GB: 14 G. **1978** GB: 16 G. **1979** GB: 14 G; **1** Fum TD; 6 Pt. **1980** GB: 16 G. **1981** GB: 16 G. **1982** GB: 9 G; 2 Sac. **1985** GB: 10 G; 2 Sac. **Total:** 95 G; 1 Fum TD; 6 Pt; 4 Sac.

RAY BUTLER Butler, Raymond Leonard 6′3″, 200 **WR**
Col: Wharton Co. JC TX; USC *HS:* Sweeny [TX] B: 6/28/1956, Port Lavaca, TX *Drafted:* 1980 Round 4 Bal
1982 Bal: Rush 3-10 3.3. **1985** Ind-Sea: Rush 1-(-1) -1.0. Ind: Rush 1-(-1) -1.0. **Total:** Rush 4-9 2.3.

		Receiving				
Year Team	**G**	**Rec**	**Yds**	**Avg**	**TD**	**Fum**
1980 Bal	16	34	574	16.9	2	0
1981 Bal	16	46	832	18.1	9	0
1982 Bal	9	17	268	15.8	2	0
1983 Bal	11	10	207	20.7	3	0
1984 Ind	16	43	664	15.4	6	0
1985 Ind-Sea	13	19	345	18.2	2	0
1985 Ind	11	19	345	18.2	2	0
1985 Sea	2	0	0	—	0	0
1986 Sea	16	19	351	18.5	4	0
1987 Sea	12	33	465	14.1	5	1
1988 Sea	11	18	242	13.4	4	0
NFL Total	120	239	3948	16.5	37	1

BOBBY BUTLER Butler, Robert Calvin 5′11″, 174 **DB**
Col: Florida State *HS:* Atlantic [Delray Beach, FL] B: 5/28/1959, Boynton Beach, FL *Drafted:* 1981 Round 1 Atl
1983 Atl: KR 1-17 17.0. **1989** Atl: 1 Fum TD. **1990** Atl: 1 Fum TD.
Total: KR 1-17 17.0; 2 Fum TD.

		Interceptions			Tot
Year Team	**G**	**Int**	**Yds**	**TD**	**TD**
1981 Atl	16	5	86	0	0
1982 Atl	9	2	0	0	0
1983 Atl	16	4	12	0	0
1984 Atl	15	2	25	0	0
1985 Atl	16	5	-4	0	0
1986 Atl	7	1	33	1	1
1987 Atl	12	4	48	0	0
1988 Atl	16	1	22	0	0
1989 Atl	16	0	0	0	1
1990 Atl	16	3	0	0	2
1991 Atl	15	0	0	0	0
1992 Atl	15	0	0	0	0
NFL Total	169	27	222	1	4

BOB BUTLER Butler, Robert Douglas 6′1″, 230 **OG**
Col: Kentucky *HS:* Madisonville [KY] B: 10/27/1940, Madisonville, KY
Drafted: 1962 Round 9 Phi
1962 Phi: 3 G. **1963** NYJ: 1 G. **Total:** 4 G.

BILL BUTLER Butler, William Edward 6′0″, 218 **RB**
Col: Kansas State *HS:* Escambia [Pensacola, FL] B: 8/12/1950, Leaksville, NC *Drafted:* 1972 Round 5 NO
1972 NO: KR 1-14 14.0. **1974** NO: KR 1-12 12.0. **Total:** KR 2-26 13.0.

		Rushing				Receiving					Tot
Year Team	**G**	**Att**	**Yds**	**Avg**	**TD**	**Rec**	**Yds**	**Avg**	**TD**	**Fum**	**TD**
1972 NO	14	54	233	4.3	0	25	226	9.0	2	3	2
1973 NO	13	87	348	4.0	1	19	125	6.6	2	5	3
1974 NO	14	21	74	3.5	0	2	3	1.5	0	2	0
NFL Total	41	162	655	4.0	1	46	354	7.7	4	10	5

SKIP BUTLER Butler, William Foster 6′1″, 201 **K**
Col: Texas-Arlington *HS:* Gladewater [TX] B: 10/21/1947, Gladewater, TX *Drafted:* 1970 Round 4 GB
1976 Hou: Rush 1-0. **Total:** Rush 1-0.

		Punting		
Year Team	**G**	**Punts**	**Yds**	**Avg**
1971 NO-NYG	3	0	0	—
1971 NO	2	0	0	—
1971 NYG	1	0	0	—
1972 Hou	13	3	105	35.0
1973 Hou	14	36	1344	37.3
1974 Hou	14	0	0	—
1975 Hou	14	0	0	—
1976 Hou	14	11	370	33.6
1977 Hou	1	0	0	—
NFL Total	73	50	1819	36.4

	Scoring						
Year Team	**Pts**	**FG**	**FGA**	**FG%**	**XK**	**XKA**	**XK%**
1971 NO-NYG	8	1	5	20.0	5	6	83.3
1971 NO	8	1	5	20.0	5	6	83.3
1972 Hou	51	12	19	63.2	15	16	93.8
1973 Hou	66	15	24	62.5	21	21	100.0
1974 Hou	56	9	19	47.4	29	29	100.0
1975 Hou	85	18	30	60.0	31	34	91.2
1976 Hou	72	16	27	59.3	24	24	100.0
1977 Hou	2	0	3	0.0	2	3	66.7
NFL Total	340	71	127	55.9	127	133	95.5

BILL BUTLER Butler, William M 6′4″, 226 **LB**
Col: Cal State-Northridge *HS:* Reseda [Los Angeles, CA] B: 8/4/1947, Los Angeles, CA
1970 Den: 14 G.

BILL BUTLER Butler, William R 5′10″, 189 **DB-HB**
Col: Tennessee-Chattanooga B: 7/10/1937, Berlin, WI *Drafted:* 1959 Round 19 GB
1959 GB: Rec 1-(-2) -2.0. **1963** Min: Rec 4-39 9.8. **1964** Min: Rec 1-58 58.0. **Total:** Rec 6-95 15.8.

		Rushing				Punt Returns			
Year Team	**G**	**Att**	**Yds**	**Avg**	**TD**	**Ret**	**Yds**	**Avg**	**TD**
1959 GB	11	7	49	7.0	0	18	163	9.1	1
1960 Dal	12	0	0	—	0	13	131	10.1	0
1961 Pit	10	0	0	—	0	2	11	5.5	0
1962 Min	14	0	0	—	0	12	169	14.1	0
1963 Min	14	17	48	2.8	0	21	220	10.5	**1**
1964 Min	14	5	11	2.2	0	22	156	7.1	0
NFL Total	75	29	108	3.7	0	88	850	9.7	2

	Kickoff Returns				Interceptions				Tot
Year Team	**Ret**	**Yds**	**Avg**	**TD**	**Int**	**Yds**	**TD**	**Fum**	**TD**
1959 GB	21	472	22.5	0	0	0	0	1	1
1960 Dal	20	399	20.0	0	1	0	0	2	0
1961 Pit	6	117	19.5	0	3	103	1	1	1
1962 Min	26	588	22.6	0	5	80	**1**	3	1
1963 Min	**33**	713	21.6	0	0	0	0	8	1
1964 Min	26	597	23.0	0	2	15	0	4	0
NFL Total	132	2886	21.9	0	11	198	2	19	4

HARRY BUTSKO Butsko, Harry 6′3″, 225 **LB**
Col: Maryland *HS:* Minersville Area [Pottsville, PA] B: 2/2/1941, Pottsville, PA *Drafted:* 1963 Round 15 Was
1963 Was: 4 G.

GREG BUTTLE Buttle, Gregory Ellis 6′3″, 235 **LB**
Col: Penn State *HS:* Mainland Regional [Linwood, NJ] B: 6/20/1954, Atlantic City, NJ *Drafted:* 1976 Round 3 NYJ
1976 NYJ: Rush 1-26 26.0; **1** Fum TD. **1981** NYJ: Scor **1** Saf. **1983** NYJ: 1.5 Sac. **1984** NYJ: **1** Fum TD. **Total:** Rush 1-26 26.0; Scor 1 Saf; 2 Fum TD; 1.5 Sac.

		Interceptions				Tot
Year Team	**G**	**Int**	**Yds**	**TD**	**Fum**	**TD**
1976 NYJ	14	2	20	0	1	1
1977 NYJ	13	2	54	**1**	0	1
1978 NYJ	8	2	34	0	0	0
1979 NYJ	16	2	27	0	0	0
1980 NYJ	14	1	15	0	0	0
1981 NYJ	15	2	34	0	0	0
1982 NYJ	7	1	9	0	0	0
1983 NYJ	9	1	17	0	0	0
1984 NYJ	14	2	5	0	0	1
NFL Total	110	15	215	1	1	3

EDDIE BUTTS Butts, Edward Carmack 190 **BB-WB**
Col: Cal State-Chico *HS:* Chico [CA] B: 8/18/1903 D: 6/15/1994, Billings, MT
1929 ChiC: 9 G.

MARION BUTTS Butts, Marion Stevenson Jr. 6′1″, 248 **RB**
Col: Northeastern Oklahoma A&M (J.C.); Florida State *HS:* Worth Academy [Sylvester, GA] B: 8/1/1966, Sylvester, GA *Drafted:* 1989 Round 7 SD
1991 SD: KR 1-0. **1995** Hou: KR 2-14 7.0. **Total:** KR 3-14 4.7.

		Rushing				Receiving					Tot
Year Team	**G**	**Att**	**Yds**	**Avg**	**TD**	**Rec**	**Yds**	**Avg**	**TD**	**Fum**	**TD**
1989 SD	15	170	683	4.0	9	7	21	3.0	0	2	9
1990 SD	14	265	1225	4.6	8	16	117	7.3	0	0	8
1991 SD	16	193	834	4.3	6	10	91	9.1	1	3	7
1992 SD	15	218	809	3.7	4	9	73	8.1	0	4	4
1993 SD	16	185	746	4.0	4	15	105	7.0	0	0	4
1994 NE	16	243	703	2.9	8	9	54	6.0	0	1	8
1995 Hou	12	71	185	2.6	4	2	10	5.0	0	0	4
NFL Total	104	1345	5185	3.9	43	68	471	6.9	1	10	44

DAVE BUTZ Butz, David Roy 6′7″, 291 **DT-DE**
Col: Purdue *HS:* Maine South [Park Ridge, IL] B: 6/23/1950, Lafayette, AL *Drafted:* 1973 Round 1 StL
1973 StL: 12 G; KR 1-23 23.0. **1974** StL: 1 G. **1975** Was: 14 G. **1976** Was: 14 G. **1977** Was: 12 G. **1978** Was: 16 G; Int 1-3. **1979** Was: 15 G. **1980** Was: 16 G. **1981** Was: 16 G; Int 1-26. **1982** Was: 9 G; 4.5 Sac. **1983** Was: 16 G; 11.5 Sac. **1984** Was: 15 G; 4.5 Sac. **1985** Was: 16 G; 5 Sac. **1986** Was: 16 G; 6 Sac. **1987** Was: 12 G; 3 Sac. **1988** Was: 16 G; 1 Sac. **Total:** 216 G; KR 1-23 23.0; Int 2-29; 35.5 Sac.

RICH BUZIN Buzin, Richard Lawrence 6′5″, 255 **OT**
Col: Penn State *HS:* Woodrow Wilson [Youngstown, OH]
B: 1/25/1946, Youngstown, OH *Drafted:* 1968 Round 2 NYG
1968 NYG: 14 G. **1969** NYG: 14 G. **1970** NYG: 14 G. **1971** LARm: 5 G. **1972** ChiB: 2 G. **Total:** 49 G.

BERNARD BUZYNISKI Buzyniski, Bernard J 6′3″, 228 **LB**
(Buz) *Col:* Holy Cross *HS:* DeSales [Lockport, NY] B: 5/3/1938, Lockport, NY
1960 Buf: 14 G; Int 1-5.

KEITH BYARS Byars, Keith Alan 6′1″, 245 **RB-TE**
Col: Ohio State *HS:* Nettie Lee Roth [Dayton, OH] B: 10/14/1963, Dayton, OH *Drafted:* 1986 Round 1 Phi
1986 Phi: Pass 2-1 50.0%, 55 27.50 1 TD; KR 2-47 23.5. **1988** Phi: Pass 2-0; KR 2-20 10.0. **1989** Phi: KR 1-27 27.0. **1990** Phi: Pass 4-4 100.0%, 53 13.25 4 TD. **1991** Phi: Pass 2-0, 1 Int. **1992** Phi: Pass 1-0. **1993** Mia: Pass 2-1 50.0%, 11 5.50 1 TD. **1996** Mia-NE: Scor 1 2XP. NE: Scor 1 2XP. **Total:** Pass 13-6 46.2%, 119 9.15 6 TD 1 Int; KR 5-94 18.8; Scor 1 2XP.

		Rushing				Receiving					Tot
Year Team	**G**	**Att**	**Yds**	**Avg**	**TD**	**Rec**	**Yds**	**Avg**	**TD**	**Fum**	**TD**
1986 Phi	16	177	577	3.3	1	11	44	4.0	0	3	1
1987 Phi	10	116	426	3.7	3	21	177	8.4	1	3	4
1988 Phi	16	152	517	3.4	6	72	705	9.8	4	5	10
1989 Phi	16	133	452	3.4	5	68	721	10.6	0	4	5
1990 Phi	16	37	141	3.8	0	81	819	10.1	3	4	3
1991 Phi	16	94	383	4.1	1	62	564	9.1	3	5	4
1992 Phi	15	41	176	4.3	1	56	502	9.0	2	1	3
1993 Mia	16	64	269	4.2	3	61	613	10.0	3	3	6
1994 Mia	9	19	64	3.4	2	49	418	8.5	5	0	7
1995 Mia	16	15	44	2.9	1	51	362	7.1	2	0	3
1996 Mia-NE	14	2	2	1.0	0	32	289	9.0	2	0	2
1996 Mia	4	0	0	—	0	5	40	8.0	0	0	0
1996 NE	10	2	2	1.0	0	27	249	9.2	2	0	2
1997 NE	16	11	24	2.2	0	20	189	9.5	3	1	3
1998 NYJ	13	4	34	8.5	0	26	258	9.9	3	0	3
NFL Total	189	865	3109	3.6	23	610	5661	9.3	31	29	54

RICK BYAS Byas, Richard Reese Jr. 5′9″, 180 **DB**
Col: Eastern Michigan; Wayne State (Mich.) *HS:* MacKenzie [Detroit, MI]
B: 10/19/1950, Detroit, MI
1974 Atl: 14 G; KR 5-136 27.2. **1975** Atl: 14 G; KR 5-94 18.8. **1976** Atl: 14 G; PR 1-8 8.0; KR 12-270 22.5; 2 Fum. **1977** Atl: 14 G; PR 1-10 10.0; Int 3-122 **1** TD; 6 Pt. **1978** Atl: 16 G; PR 2-12 6.0; Int 2-37; 6 Pt. **1979** Atl:

16 G; KR 1-19 19.0; Int 1-34; **1** Fum TD; 6 Pt. **1980** Atl: 15 G. **Total:** 103 G; PR 4-30 7.5; KR 23-519 22.6; Int 6-193 1 TD; 1 Fum TD; Tot TD 3; 18 Pt; 2 Fum.

KEN BYERS Byers, Kenneth Vernon Jr. 6′1″, 240 **OG**
Col: Cincinnati *HS:* Linden-McKinley [Columbus, OH] B: 4/6/1940, Logan, OH *Drafted:* 1962 Round 7 NYG
1962 NYG: 14 G. **1963** NYG: 14 G. **1964** NYG-Min: 14 G. NYG: 8 G. Min: 6 G. **1965** Min: 14 G. **Total:** 56 G.

SCOTT BYERS Byers, Norman Scott 5′11″, 170 **DB**
Col: Southwestern Coll. CA (J.C.); Long Beach State *HS:* Abraham Lincoln [San Diego, CA] B: 7/3/1958, Bayonne, NJ
1984 SD: 6 G.

FRANK BYKOWSKI Bykowski, Frank Peter 6′0″, 205 **G**
Col: Purdue *HS:* South Bend Central [IN] B: 3/24/1915, South Bend, IN D: 4/1/1985, Bradenton, FL *Drafted:* 1940 Round 6 Pit
1940 Pit: 1 G.

JOE BYLER Byler, Joseph Edward 6′5″, 240 **T**
Col: Nebraska *HS:* Alma [NE] B: 8/25/1922, Republican City, NE D: 5/5/1994, Des Moines, IA
1946 NYG: 7 G.

EARNEST BYNER Byner, Earnest Alexander 5′10″, 215 **RB**
Col: East Carolina *HS:* Baldwin [Milledgeville, GA] B: 9/15/1962, Milledgeville, GA *Drafted:* 1984 Round 10 Cle
1984 Cle: **1** Fum TD. **1989** Was: Pass 1-0. **1990** Was: Pass 2-1 50.0%, 31 15.50 1 TD. **1991** Was: Pass 4-1 25.0%, 18 4.50 1 TD. **1992** Was: Pass 3-1 33.3%, 41 13.67 1 TD. **1997** Bal: Scor 1 2XP. **Total:** Pass 10-3 30.0%, 90 9.00 3 TD; Scor 1 2XP; 1 Fum TD.

		Rushing				Receiving			
Year Team	G	Att	Yds	Avg	TD	Rec	Yds	Avg	TD
1984 Cle	16	72	426	5.9	2	11	118	10.7	0
1985 Cle	16	244	1002	4.1	8	45	460	10.2	2
1986 Cle	7	94	277	2.9	2	37	328	8.9	2
1987 Cle	12	105	432	4.1	8	52	552	10.6	2
1988 Cle	16	157	576	3.7	3	59	576	9.8	2
1989 Was	16	134	580	4.3	7	54	458	8.5	2
1990 Was	16	**297**	1219	4.1	6	31	279	9.0	1
1991 Was	16	274	1048	3.8	5	34	308	9.1	0
1992 Was	16	262	998	3.8	6	39	338	8.7	1
1993 Was	16	23	105	4.6	1	27	194	7.2	0
1994 Cle	16	75	219	2.9	2	11	102	9.3	0
1995 Cle	16	115	432	3.8	2	61	494	8.1	2
1996 Bal	16	159	634	4.0	4	30	270	9.0	1
1997 Bal	16	84	313	3.7	0	21	128	6.1	0
NFL Total	211	2095	8261	3.9	56	512	4605	9.0	15

	Kickoff Returns					Tot
Year Team	Ret	Yds	Avg	TD	Fum	TD
1984 Cle	22	415	18.9	0	3	3
1985 Cle	0	0	—	0	5	10
1986 Cle	0	0	—	0	1	4
1987 Cle	1	2	2.0	0	5	10
1988 Cle	0	0	—	0	5	5
1989 Was	0	0	—	0	2	9
1990 Was	0	0	—	0	2	7
1991 Was	0	0	—	0	3	5
1992 Was	0	0	—	0	1	7
1993 Was	0	0	—	0	0	1
1994 Cle	0	0	—	0	0	2
1995 Cle	5	98	19.6	0	1	4
1996 Bal	4	61	15.3	0	1	5
1997 Bal	1	0	0.0	0	2	0
NFL Total	33	576	17.5	0	31	72

BUTLER BY'NOT'E By'Not'e, Butler III 5′9″, 190 **RB**
Col: Ohio State *HS:* Vashon [St. Louis, MO] B: 9/29/1972, St. Louis, MO *Drafted:* 1994 Round 7 Den

		Kickoff Returns			
Year Team	G	Ret	Yds	Avg	TD
1994 Den	9	24	545	22.7	0
1995 Car	7	18	335	18.6	0
NFL Total	16	42	880	21.0	0

KENNY BYNUM Bynum, Kenneth Bernard 5′11″, 191 **RB**
Col: South Carolina State *HS:* Gainesville [FL] B: 5/29/1974, Gainesville, FL *Drafted:* 1997 Round 5 SD
1997 SD: Rec 2-4 2.0. **1998** SD: Rec 4-27 6.8. **Total:** Rec 6-31 5.2.

		Rushing				Kickoff Returns				
Year Team	G	Att	Yds	Avg	TD	Ret	Yds	Avg	TD	Fum
1997 SD	13	30	97	3.2	0	38	814	21.4	0	0
1998 SD	10	11	23	2.1	0	19	345	18.2	0	3
NFL Total	23	41	120	2.9	0	57	1159	20.3	0	3

REGGIE BYNUM Bynum, Reginald Deshain 6′1″, 185 **WR**
Col: Oregon State *HS:* Independence [San Jose, CA] B: 2/10/1964, Greenville, MS *Drafted:* 1986 Round 9 Buf
1987 Buf: 1 G; Rec 2-24 12.0.

BORIS BYRD Byrd, Boris Kaelin 6′0″, 210 **DB**
Col: Austin Peay State *HS:* American [Kaiserlauten, Germany] B: 4/15/1962, Warren Co., KY
1987 NYG: 3 G; KR 4-99 24.8.

DARRYL BYRD Byrd, Darryl Terrence 6′1″, 220 **LB**
Col: Chabot Coll. CA (J.C.); Illinois *HS:* James Logan [Union City, CA] B: 9/3/1960, San Diego, CA
1983 LARd: 16 G. **1984** LARd: 16 G. **1987** LARd: 3 G. **Total:** 35 G.

DENNIS BYRD Byrd, Dennis DeWayne 6′5″, 270 **DE-DT**
Col: Tulsa *HS:* Mustang [OK] B: 10/5/1966, Marion, NC *Drafted:* 1989 Round 2 NYJ
1989 NYJ: 16 G; KR 1-1 1.0; 7 Sac. **1990** NYJ: 16 G; Scor **1** Saf; 2 Pt; 13 Sac. **1991** NYJ: 16 G; 7 Sac. **1992** NYJ: 9 G; 1 Sac. **Total:** 57 G; KR 1-1 1.0; Scor 1 Saf; 2 Pt; 28.0 Sac.

DENNIS BYRD Byrd, Dennis Wayne 6′4″, 260 **DE**
Col: North Carolina State *HS:* Lincolnton [NC] B: 8/31/1946, Marion, NC *Drafted:* 1968 Round 1 Bos
1968 Bos: 14 G.

BUTCH BYRD Byrd, George Edward Jr. 6′0″, 211 **DB**
Col: Boston U. *HS:* La Salle Inst. [Troy, NY] B: 9/20/1941, Watervliet, NY *Drafted:* 1964 Round 4 Buf
1965 Buf: KR 1-4 4.0. **Total:** KR 1-4 4.0.

		Punt Returns				Interceptions				Tot
Year Team	G	Ret	Yds	Avg	TD	Int	Yds	TD	Fum	TD
1964 Buf	14	2	4	2.0	0	7	178	**1**	0	1
1965 Buf	14	22	220	10.0	0	5	119	0	3	0
1966 Buf	14	23	186	8.1	**1**	6	110	1	3	2
1967 Buf	14	30	142	4.7	0	5	25	0	3	0
1968 Buf	14	2	11	5.5	0	6	76	1	0	1
1969 Buf	14	7	37	5.3	0	7	95	1	1	1
1970 Buf	14	0	0	—	0	4	63	1	0	1
1971 Den	14	0	0	—	0	0	0	0	0	0
NFL Total	112	86	600	7.0	1	40	666	5	10	6

GILL BYRD Byrd, Gill Arnette 5′11″, 195 **DB**
Col: San Jose State *HS:* Lowell [San Francisco, CA] B: 2/20/1961, San Francisco, CA *Drafted:* 1983 Round 1 SD

		Interceptions			
Year Team	G	Int	Yds	TD	Fum
1983 SD	14	1	0	0	0
1984 SD	13	4	157	**2**	0
1985 SD	16	1	25	0	0
1986 SD	15	5	45	0	0
1987 SD	12	0	0	0	0
1988 SD	16	7	82	0	1
1989 SD	16	7	38	0	0
1990 SD	16	7	63	0	0
1991 SD	15	6	48	0	0
1992 SD	16	4	88	0	0
NFL Total	149	42	546	2	1

ISAAC BYRD Byrd, Isaac III 6′1″, 188 **WR**
Col: Kansas *HS:* Parkway Central [Chesterfield, MO] B: 11/16/1974, St. Louis, MO *Drafted:* 1997 Round 6 KC
1997 Ten: 2 G. **1998** Ten: 4 G; Rec 6-71 11.8. **Total:** 6 G; Rec 6-71 11.8.

ISRAEL BYRD Byrd, Israel Fabian 5′11″, 184 **DB**
Col: Allan Hancock Coll. CA (J.C.); Utah State *HS:* Parkway Central [Chesterfield, MO] B: 2/1/1971, St. Louis, MO
1994 NO: 3 G. **1995** NO: 4 G. **Total:** 7 G.

MAC BYRD Byrd, McArthur N Jr. 6′0″, 215 **LB**
Col: USC *HS:* Xavier Prep [New Orleans, LA] B: 5/28/1942, New Orleans, LA
1965 LARm: 2 G.

RICHARD BYRD Byrd, Richard Ellen 6′3″, 264 **DE**
Col: Southern Mississippi *HS:* Jim Hill [Jackson, MS] B: 3/20/1962, Natchez, MS *Drafted:* 1985 Round 2 Hou
1985 Hou: 15 G; 1 Sac. **1986** Hou: 16 G; 3 Sac. **1987** Hou: 12 G; 1 Sac. **1988** Hou: 16 G; Int 1-1. **1989** Hou: 16 G. **Total:** 75 G; Int 1-1; 5 Sac.

SYLVESTER BYRD Byrd, Sylvester Carl 6′2″, 225 **TE**
Col: Kansas *HS:* Ward [Kansas City, KS]; Kansas U. HS [Lawrence, KS] B: 5/1/1963, Kansas City, KS
1987 Atl: 3 G; Rec 7-125 17.9.

BILL BYRNE Byrne, William Joseph 6′0″, 240 **OG**
Col: Boston College *HS:* Montclair [NJ] B: 11/19/1940, New York, NY *Drafted:* 1962 Round 4 Phi
1963 Phi: 12 G.

CARL BYRUM Byrum, Carl Edward 6'0", 232 **RB**
Col: Mississippi Valley State *HS:* Southhaven [MS] B: 6/29/1963, Olive Branch, MS *Drafted:* 1986 Round 5 Buf
1986 Buf: Rec 13-104 8.0 1 TD. **1987** Buf: Rec 3-23 7.7. **1988** Buf: Rec 2-0; KR 2-9 4.5. **Total:** Rec 18-127 7.1 1 TD; KR 2-9 4.5.

		Rushing				
Year Team	**G**	**Att**	**Yds**	**Avg**	**TD**	**Fum**
1986 Buf	13	38	156	4.1	0	0
1987 Buf	13	66	280	4.2	0	4
1988 Buf	15	28	91	3.3	0	1
NFL Total	41	132	527	4.0	0	5

BRIAN CABRAL Cabral, Kealiihaaheo Brian David 6'1", 233 **LB**
(AKA Brian David Kealiihaaheo) *Col:* Colorado *HS:* St. Louis [Honolulu, HI] B: 6/23/1956, Fort Benning, GA *Drafted:* 1978 Round 4 Atl
1979 Atl: 3 G. **1980** GB: 7 G. **1981** ChiB: 16 G. **1982** ChiB: 8 G. **1983** ChiB: 16 G; KR 2-11 5.5; 1 Sac. **1984** ChiB: 16 G; Rec 1-7 7.0. **1985** ChiB: 1 G. **1986** ChiB: 3 G. **Total:** 70 G; Rec 1-7 7.0; KR 2-11 5.5; 1 Sac.

LARRY CABRELLI Cabrelli, Lawrence Andrew 5'11", 194 **OE-DE-DB**
Col: Colgate *HS:* Barringer [Newark, NJ] B: 3/28/1917, Newark, NJ D: 6/5/1974, Bryn Mawr, PA
1943 PhPt: Int 1-24 **1** TD. **1944** Phi: Rush 1-(-2) -2.0. **1945** Phi: KR 2-25 12.5; Int 1-1. **Total:** Rush 1-(-2) -2.0; KR 2-25 12.5; Int 2-25 1 TD.

		Receiving				Tot
Year Team	**G**	**Rec**	**Yds**	**Avg**	**TD**	**TD**
1941 Phi	7	4	90	22.5	1	1
1942 Phi	11	15	229	15.3	1	1
1943 PhPt	10	12	199	16.6	1	2
1944 Phi	9	14	169	12.1	1	1
1945 Phi	10	15	140	9.3	0	0
1946 Phi	8	8	98	12.3	1	1
1947 Phi	6	0	0	—	0	0
NFL Total	61	68	925	13.6	5	6

AUGIE CABRINHA Cabrinha, August Hermengilde 5'9", 170 **WB-DB**
Col: Dayton *HS:* St. Louis [Honolulu, HI] B: 4/13/1902, Honomu, HI D: 3/8/1979, Honolulu, HI
1927 Day: 3 G.

ERNIE CADDEL Caddel, Ernest Wiley Jr. 6'2", 199 **WB-DB**
(Blonde Antelope) *Col:* Stanford *HS:* Tulare [CA]; Corcoran HS [CA] B: 3/12/1911, Granite, OK D: 3/28/1992, Roseville, CA
1934 Det: Pass 13-5 38.5%, 106 8.15 1 TD 1 Int; Int **1** TD. **1935** Det: Pass 6-4 66.7%, 169 28.17 2 TD 1 Int. **1936** Det: Pass 4-1 25.0%, 30 7.50 2 Int. **1937** Det: Pass 4-0. **1938** Det: Pass 2-2 100.0%, 45 22.50. **Total:** Pass 29-12 41.4%, 350 12.07 3 TD 4 Int; Int 1 TD.

		Rushing				Receiving				Tot
Year Team	**G**	**Att**	**Yds**	**Avg**	**TD**	**Rec**	**Yds**	**Avg**	**TD**	**TD**
1933 Port	11	70	286	4.1	2	6	107	17.8	**3**	5
1934 Det	12	105	528	5.0	4	9	127	14.1	1	6
1935 Det	12	87	450	**5.2**	**6**	10	171	17.1	0	6
1936 Det	11	91	580	**6.4**	4	19	150	7.9	1	5
1937 Det	11	76	429	**5.6**	3	9	80	8.9	0	3
1938 Det	7	14	38	2.7	1	1	6	6.0	0	1
NFL Total	64	443	2311	5.2	20	54	641	11.9	5	26

EDDIE CADE Cade, Eddie Ray 6'1", 206 **DB**
Col: Arizona State *HS:* Santa Cruz Valley Union [Eloy, AZ] B: 8/4/1973, Casa Grande, AZ
1995 NE: 10 G.

MOSSY CADE Cade, Tomories 6'1", 197 **DB**
Col: Texas *HS:* Santa Cruz Valley Union [Eloy, AZ] B: 12/26/1961, Casa Grande, AZ *Drafted:* 1984 Round 1 SD
1985 GB: 14 G; Int 1-0. **1986** GB: 16 G; Int 4-26; 1 Sac. **Total:** 30 G; Int 5-26; 1 Sac.

DAVE CADIGAN Cadigan, David Patrick 6'4", 285 **OT-OG**
Col: USC *HS:* Newport Harbor [Newport Beach, CA] B: 4/6/1965, Needham, MA *Drafted:* 1988 Round 1 NYJ
1988 NYJ: 5 G. **1989** NYJ: 13 G. **1990** NYJ: 5 G. **1991** NYJ: 15 G. **1992** NYJ: 15 G. **1993** NYJ: 16 G. **1994** Cin: 13 G. **Total:** 82 G.

JIM CADILE Cadile, James Dee 6'4", 240 **OG-OT**
Col: San Jose State *HS:* San Jose [CA] B: 7/16/1940, San Jose, CA *Drafted:* 1962 Round 4 ChiB
1962 ChiB: 4 G. **1963** ChiB: 13 G. **1964** ChiB: 14 G. **1965** ChiB: 14 G. **1966** ChiB: 14 G. **1967** ChiB: 10 G. **1968** ChiB: 14 G. **1969** ChiB: 14 G. **1970** ChiB: 12 G. **1971** ChiB: 13 G. **1972** ChiB: 6 G. **Total:** 128 G.

GLENN CADREZ Cadrez, Glenn E 6'3", 240 **LB**
Col: Chaffey Coll. CA (J.C.); Houston *HS:* Central [El Centro, CA] B: 1/2/1970, El Centro, CA *Drafted:* 1992 Round 6 NYJ
1992 NYJ: 16 G. **1993** NYJ: 16 G. **1994** NYJ: 16 G; KR 1-10 10.0. **1995** NYJ-Den: 11 G; 2 Sac. NYJ: 1 G. Den: 10 G; 2 Sac. **1996** Den: 16 G. **1997** Den: 16 G. **1998** Den: 16 G; Int 2-11; 4 Sac. **Total:** 107 G; KR 1-10 10.0; Int 2-11; 6 Sac.

JOHN CADWELL Cadwell, John 6'3", 230 **OG**
Col: Oregon State *HS:* Acalanes [Lafayette, CA] B: 9/16/1930, Oakland, CA
1961 DalT: 4 G.

IVAN CAESAR Caesar, Ivan Orsen II 6'1", 241 **LB**
Col: Boston College *HS:* Dorchester [Boston, MA] B: 1/7/1967, St. Thomas, Virgin Islands *Drafted:* 1991 Round 11 Min
1991 Min: 14 G.

GEORGE CAFEGO Cafego, George 5'10", 169 **QB-TB-DB-HB**
(Bad News) *Col:* Tennessee *HS:* Oak Hill [WV] B: 8/30/1915, Whipple, WV D: 2/8/1998, Knoxville, TN *Drafted:* 1940 Round 1 ChiC
1940 Bkn: Rec 9-105 11.7. **1943** Bkn-Was: PR 6-52 8.7; KR 9-218 24.2. Bkn: PR 2-12 6.0; KR 6-134 22.3. Was: PR 4-40 10.0; KR 3-84 28.0. **1944** Bos: Rec 2-8 4.0; PR 4-49 12.3; KR 3-48 16.0; Int 1-39. **1945** Bos: Rec 2-20 10.0; PR 1-0; KR 2-47 23.5; Int 1-2. **Total:** Rec 13-133 10.2; PR 11-101 9.2; KR 14-313 22.4; Int 2-41.

		Passing							
Year Team	**G**	**Att**	**Comp**	**Comp%**	**Yds**	**YPA**	**TD**	**Int**	**Rating**
1940 Bkn	10	17	7	41.2	105	6.18	1	2	42.2
1943 Bkn-Was	9	45	22	48.9	258	5.73	1	3	46.3
1943 Bkn	5	36	17	47.2	209	5.81	0	3	30.9
1943 Was	4	9	5	55.6	49	5.44	1	0	108.1
1944 Bos	9	73	35	47.9	454	6.22	3	7	42.1
1945 Bos	7	26	13	50.0	149	5.73	0	4	28.0
NFL Total	35	161	77	47.8	966	6.00	5	16	37.7

	Rushing				Punting			
Year Team	**Att**	**Yds**	**Avg**	**TD**	**Punts**	**Yds**	**Avg**	**Fum**
1940 Bkn	41	109	2.7	0	1	18	18.0	0
1943 Bkn-Was	34	-12	-0.4	0	21	719	34.2	0
1943 Bkn	19	-46	-2.4	0	10	307	30.7	0
1943 Was	15	34	2.3	0	11	412	37.5	0
1944 Bos	61	31	0.5	1	16	582	36.4	0
1945 Bos	19	-51	-2.7	0	6	213	35.5	2
NFL Total	155	77	0.5	1	44	1532	34.8	2

LEE ROY CAFFEY Caffey, Lee Roy 6'4", 240 **LB**
Col: Texas A&M *HS:* Thorndale [TX] B: 6/3/1941, Thorndale, TX D: 1/18/1994, Houston, TX *Drafted:* 1963 Round 7 Phi
1963 Phi: KR 1-6 6.0. **1964** GB: KR 1-0. **Total:** KR 2-6 3.0.

		Interceptions		
Year Team	**G**	**Int**	**Yds**	**TD**
1963 Phi	14	1	87	1
1964 GB	14	1	44	0
1965 GB	14	1	42	1
1966 GB	14	3	62	1
1967 GB	13	2	28	0
1968 GB	14	0	0	0
1969 GB	14	2	1	0
1970 ChiB	14	0	0	0
1971 Dal	6	0	0	0
1972 SD	12	1	4	0
NFL Total	129	11	268	3

CHRIS CAGLE Cagle, Christian Keener 5'10", 174 **DB-FB-TB-WB**
(Red) *Col:* Southwestern Louisiana; Army *HS:* Merrysville [LA] B: 5/1/1905, De Ridder, LA D: 12/23/1942, Queens, NY
1932 NYG: Rec 8-135 16.9 2 TD; PR **1** TD. **1933** Bkn: Rec 5-59 11.8. **Total:** Rec 13-194 14.9 2 TD; PR 1 TD.

		Passing							
Year Team	**G**	**Att**	**Comp**	**Comp%**	**Yds**	**YPA**	**TD**	**Int**	**Rating**
1930 NYG	4	—	—	—	—	—	0	—	—
1931 NYG	14	—	—	—	—	—	1	—	—
1932 NYG	10	7	3	42.9	68	9.71	0	1	38.7
1933 Bkn	10	74	31	41.9	457	6.18	2	10	32.2
1934 Bkn	10	60	14	23.3	224	3.73	3	7	19.7
NFL Total	48	141	48	34.0	749	5.31	6	18	27.2

	Rushing				Tot
Year Team	**Att**	**Yds**	**Avg**	**TD**	**TD**
1931 NYG	—	—	—	1	1
1932 NYG	73	205	2.8	1	4
1933 Bkn	49	135	2.8	0	0
1934 Bkn	22	51	2.3	0	0
NFL Total	144	391	2.7	2	5

JIM CAGLE Cagle, James Colquitt 6'5", 255 **DT**
Col: Georgia *HS:* Marietta [GA] B: 1/15/1952, Jacksonville, FL *Drafted:* 1974 Round 5 Phi
1974 Phi: 14 G.

JOHNNY CAGLE Cagle, John Link 6'3", 260 **DE**
(Bull) *Col:* Clemson *HS:* Brookland Cayce [Cayce, SC] B: 3/26/1947, Anderson, SC *Drafted:* 1969 Round 14 Bos
1969 Bos: 6 G.

DAVE CAHILL Cahill, David Allen 6'3", 245 **DT-DE**
Col: Northern Arizona *HS:* Tempe [AZ] B: 7/26/1942, Stanley, WI
1966 Phi: 14 G. **1967** LARm: 14 G. **1969** Atl: 11 G; PR 1-0. **Total:** 39 G; PR 1-0.

RONNIE CAHILL Cahill, Ronald Maurice 5'8", 170 **TB-DB**
(Butch) *Col:* Holy Cross *HS:* Mann [Leominster [MA] B: 4/25/1915, Leominster, MA D: 9/6/1992, Leominster, MA
1943 ChiC: PR 1-19 19.0; KR 3-56 18.7; Punt 3-88 29.3.

		Passing							
Year Team	G	Att	Comp	Comp%	Yds	YPA	TD	Int	Rating
1943 ChiC	10	109	50	45.9	608	5.58	3	21	33.1

	Rushing			
Year Team	Att	Yds	Avg	TD
1943 ChiC	62	-11	-0.2	0

BILL CAHILL Cahill, William Blackburn 5'11", 180 **DB**
Col: Washington *HS:* Bellevue [WA] B: 5/2/1951, Bellevue, WA
Drafted: 1973 Round 7 NO
1973 Buf: 5 G; PR 4-73 18.3 1 TD; KR 2-42 21.0; 6 Pt. **1974** Buf: 14 G; PR 10-62 6.2; KR 1-26 26.0. **Total:** 19 G; PR 14-135 9.6 1 TD; KR 3-68 22.7; 6 Pt.

DENNY CAHILL Cahill, William Dennis 225 **G**
Col: No College *HS:* Nichols School [Buffalo, NY] Deceased
1920 Roch: 2 G.

TINY CAHOON Cahoon, Ivan Wells 6'2", 235 **T**
Col: Montana; Gonzaga *HS:* Baraboo [WI] B: 5/22/1900, Baraboo, WI D: 2/3/1973, Concord, CA
1926 GB: 11 G. **1927** GB: 8 G; 6 Pt. **1928** GB: 10 G. **1929** GB: 2 G. **Total:** 31 G; 6 Pt.

JIM CAIN Cain, James Edgar 6'1", 202 **DE-OE**
Col: Alabama *HS:* Eudora [AL] B: 10/1/1927, Eudora, AL
Drafted: 1949 Round 7 ChiC
1949 ChiC: 12 G. **1950** Det: 12 G; Rec 1-8 8.0; KR 1-10 10.0; **1** Fum TD; 6 Pt. **1953** Det: 12 G. **1954** Det: 12 G. **1955** Det: 12 G. **Total:** 60 G; Rec 1-8 8.0; KR 1-10 10.0; 1 Fum TD; 6 Pt.

J.V. CAIN Cain, James Victor 6'4", 224 **WR-TE**
Col: Colorado *HS:* Booker T. Washington [Houston, TX] B: 7/22/1951, Houston, TX D: 7/22/1979, St. Charles, MO *Drafted:* 1974 Round 1 StL
1974 StL: KR 1-5 5.0. **Total:** KR 1-5 5.0.

		Receiving				
Year Team	G	Rec	Yds	Avg	TD	Fum
1974 StL	14	13	152	11.7	1	0
1975 StL	14	12	134	11.2	1	2
1976 StL	14	26	400	15.4	5	0
1977 StL	13	25	328	13.1	2	0
NFL Total	55	76	1014	13.3	9	2

JOE CAIN Cain, Joseph Harrison Jr. 6'1", 242 **LB**
Col: Stanford; Oregon Tech *HS:* Compton [CA] B: 6/11/1965, Los Angeles, CA *Drafted:* 1988 Round 8 Min
1989 Sea: 9 G. **1990** Sea: 16 G. **1991** Sea: 16 G; Int 1-5. **1992** Sea: 16 G; Int 2-3. **1993** ChiB: 15 G. **1994** ChiB: 16 G. **1995** ChiB: 16 G. **1996** ChiB: 16 G; 1 Sac. **1997** Sea: 11 G. **Total:** 131 G; Int 3-8; 1 Sac.

LYNN CAIN Cain, Lynn Dwight 6'1", 205 **RB**
Col: East Los Angeles Coll. CA (J.C.); USC *HS:* Theodore Roosevelt [Los Angeles, CA] B: 10/16/1955, Los Angeles, CA *Drafted:* 1979 Round 4 Atl
1979 Atl: KR 7-149 21.3. **1983** Atl: KR 11-200 18.2. **1985** LARm: KR 6-115 19.2. **Total:** KR 24-464 19.3.

		Rushing				Receiving					Tot
Year Team	G	Att	Yds	Avg	TD	Rec	Yds	Avg	TD	Fum	TD
1979 Atl	10	63	295	4.7	2	15	181	12.1	2	2	4
1980 Atl	16	235	914	3.9	8	24	223	9.3	1	6	9
1981 Atl	16	156	542	3.5	4	55	421	7.7	2	3	6
1982 Atl	9	54	173	3.2	1	13	101	7.8	1	2	2
1983 Atl	16	19	63	3.3	1	3	24	8.0	0	1	1
1984 Atl	15	77	276	3.6	3	12	87	7.3	0	2	3
1985 LARm	7	11	46	4.2	0	5	24	4.8	0	0	0
NFL Total	89	615	2309	3.8	19	127	1061	8.4	6	16	25

PATRICK CAIN Cain, Patrick James 6'2", 260 **C-OG**
Col: Cal Poly-Pomona; Wichita State *HS:* Pomona [Arvada, CO] B: 10/1/1962, Denver, CO
1987 Det: 3 G.

PETE CALAC Calac, Peter 5'10", 190 **FB-E-WB-TB**
Col: Carlisle; West Virginia Wesleyan *HS:* Sherman Indian [Redlands, CA] B: 5/13/1892, Valley Center, CA D: 1/13/1968, Canton, OH
1920 Can: 13 G. **1921** Cle-Was: 9 G. Cle: 8 G; Rush 3 TD; 18 Pt. Was: 1 G. **1922** Oor: 9 G; Rush 2 TD; 12 Pt. **1923** Oor: 10 G; Rush 1 TD; 6 Pt. **1924** Buf: 11 G; Rush 2 TD; 12 Pt. **1925** Can: 7 G. **1926** Can: 10 G. **Total:** 69 G; Rush 8 TD; 48 Pt.

RALPH CALCAGNI Calcagni, Ralph Cleo 6'3", 230 **T**
Col: Cornell; Pennsylvania *HS:* Connellsville [PA] B: 2/6/1922, Smithton, PA D: 8/29/1948, Meadeville, PA *Drafted:* 1944 Round 29 Bos
1946 Bos: 11 G. **1947** Pit: 9 G; Scor **1** Saf; 2 Pt. **Total:** 20 G; Scor 1 Saf; 2 Pt.

ALAN CALDWELL Caldwell, Alan Lorenzo 6'0", 176 **DB**
Col: North Carolina *HS:* East Foryth [Kernerville, NC] B: 5/22/1956, Winston-Salem, NC
1979 NYG: 16 G; Int 2-2; 1 Fum.

TONY CALDWELL Caldwell, Anthony L 6'1", 225 **LB**
Col: Washington *HS:* Carson [CA] B: 4/1/1961, Los Angeles, CA
Drafted: 1983 Round 3 LARd
1983 LARd: 16 G. **1984** LARd: 16 G. **1985** LARd: 3 G. **1987** Sea: 1 G; Int 1-4. **Total:** 36 G; Int 1-4.

BRUCE CALDWELL Caldwell, Bruce 6'0", 190 **TB-FB**
Col: Brown; Yale *HS:* Cumberland [RI] B: 2/8/1906, Ashton, RI D: 2/15/1959, New Haven, CT
1928 NYG: 10 G; Rush 1 TD; Scor 9, 1 FG.

BRYAN CALDWELL Caldwell, Bryan Craig 6'4", 248 **DE**
Col: Mesa CC AZ; Arizona State *HS:* Fountain Valley [CA] B: 5/6/1960, Oakland, CA *Drafted:* 1983 Round 3 Dal
1984 Hou: 8 G.

SCOTT CALDWELL Caldwell, Craig Scott 5'10", 196 **RB**
Col: Texas-Arlington *HS:* Sam Houston [Arlington, TX] B: 2/8/1963, Dallas, TX *Drafted:* 1985 Round 8 Det
1987 Den: 3 G; Rush 16-53 3.3; Rec 4-34 8.5.

DARRYL CALDWELL Caldwell, Darryl 6'5", 245 **OT**
Col: Tennessee State *HS:* C.W. Hayes [Birmingham, AL] B: 2/2/1960, Birmingham, AL
1983 Buf: 14 G.

DAVID CALDWELL Caldwell, David Anthony 6'1", 261 **NT**
Col: Texas Christian *HS:* Highlands [San Antonio, TX] B: 2/28/1965, Bay City, TX
1987 GB: 3 G; 0.5 Sac.

KNUTE CALDWELL Caldwell, Harold Paul 6'1", 210 **T**
(AKA Knute Cauldwell) *Col:* Wabash B: 1/1897, Rockville, IN Deceased
1925 Akr: 5 G; Scor 5, 5 XK. **1926** Akr: 7 G. **Total:** 12 G.

MIKE CALDWELL Caldwell, Isaiah Michael 6'2", 232 **LB**
Col: Middle Tennessee State *HS:* Oak Ridge [TN] B: 8/31/1971, Oak Ridge, TN *Drafted:* 1993 Round 3 Cle
1993 Cle: 15 G. **1994** Cle: 16 G; PR 1-2 2.0; Int 1-0. **1995** Cle: 16 G; Int 2-24 1 TD; 6 Pt. **1996** Bal: 9 G; Int 1-45 1 TD; 6 Pt; 4.5 Sac. **1997** Ariz: 16 G; Int 1-5; 2 Sac. **1998** Phi: 16 G; Int 1-33; 1 Sac. **Total:** 88 G; PR 1-2 2.0; Int 6-107 2 TD; 12 Pt; 7.5 Sac.

MIKE CALDWELL Caldwell, Michael Todd 6'2", 200 **WR**
Col: California *HS:* San Ramon Valley [Danville, CA] B: 3/28/1971, Cleveland, OH
1995 SF: 2 G; KR 2-40 20.0. **1996** SF: 1 G; Rec 2-9 4.5. **Total:** 3 G; Rec 2-9 4.5; KR 2-40 20.0.

RAVIN CALDWELL Caldwell, Ravin Jr. 6'3", 233 **LB**
Col: Arkansas *HS:* Northside [Fort Smith, AR] B: 8/4/1963, Port Arthur, TX *Drafted:* 1986 Round 5 Was
1987 Was: 12 G. **1988** Was: 16 G; PR 1-0; Scor 1 Saf; 2 Pt; 4 Sac. **1989** Was: 15 G; 3.5 Sac. **1990** Was: 16 G; 1 Sac. **1991** Was: 16 G. **1992** Was: 4 G. **1993** SF: Postseason only. **Total:** 79 G; PR 1-0; Scor 1 Saf; 2 Pt; 8.5 Sac.

JAMIE CALEB Caleb, Jamie 6'1", 210 **HB-FB**
Col: Grambling State *HS:* Carroll [Monroe, LA] B: 10/29/1936, Calhoun, LA *Drafted:* 1959 Round 16 Cle
1960 Cle: Rush 8-60 7.5 1 TD; Rec 5-(-18) -3.6. **1961** Min: Pass 1-0; Rush 3-11 3.7; Rec 2-(-8) -4.0; PR 1-8 8.0. **Total:** Pass 1-0; Rush 11-71 6.5 1 TD; Rec 7-(-26) -3.7; PR 1-8 8.0.

		Kickoff Returns				
Year Team	G	Ret	Yds	Avg	TD	Fum
1960 Cle	12	5	90	18.0	0	2
1961 Min	10	22	504	22.9	0	0
1965 Cle	5	0	0	—	0	0
NFL Total	27	27	594	22.0	0	2

DON CALHOUN Calhoun, Donald Clevester 6'0", 206 **RB**
Col: Kansas State *HS:* North [Wichita, KS] B: 4/29/1952, Muskogee, OK *Drafted:* 1974 Round 10 Buf
1974 Buf: KR 6-90 15.0. **1975** Buf-NE: KR 1-17 17.0. NE: KR 1-17 17.0. **1976** NE: KR 9-183 20.3. **1981** NE: KR 2-38 19.0. **Total:** KR 18-328 18.2.

Year Team	G	Rushing Att	Yds	Avg	TD	Receiving Rec	Yds	Avg	TD	Fum	Tot TD
1974 Buf	14	21	88	4.2	0	2	10	5.0	0	0	0
1975 Buf-NE	11	42	184	4.4	1	5	111	22.2	1	3	2
1975 Buf	6	19	80	4.2	0	0	0	—	0	1	0
1975 NE	5	23	104	4.5	1	5	111	22.2	1	2	2
1976 NE	14	129	721	**5.6**	1	12	56	4.7	0	4	1
1977 NE	14	198	727	3.7	4	13	152	11.7	0	3	4
1978 NE	14	76	391	5.1	1	3	29	9.7	0	1	1
1979 NE	16	137	456	3.3	5	15	66	4.4	1	2	6
1980 NE	16	200	787	3.9	9	27	129	4.8	0	2	9
1981 NE	14	57	205	3.6	2	7	71	10.1	0	1	2
1982 Phi	1	0	0	—	0	0	0	—	0	0	0
NFL Total	114	860	3559	4.1	23	84	624	7.4	2	16	25

ERIC CALHOUN Calhoun, Eric V 5′9″, 210 **T-G**
(Enoch) *Col:* Denison *HS:* East Liverpool [OH] B: 8/1/1900
D: 9/23/1974, South Euclid, OH
1926 Day: 6 G.

RICK CALHOUN Calhoun, James Ricky 5′7″, 190 **RB**
Col: Cal State-Fullerton *HS:* John W. North [Riverside, CA]
B: 5/30/1963, Montgomery, AL *Drafted:* 1987 Round 9 Det
1987 LARd: 3 G; Rush 7-36 5.1; Rec 1-17 17.0; PR 8-92 11.5 1 TD; KR 9-217 24.1; 6 Pt.

MIKE CALHOUN Calhoun, Michael Edward 6′4″, 260 **DT-DE**
Col: Notre Dame *HS:* Fitch [Austintown, OH] B: 5/6/1957, Youngstown, OH *Drafted:* 1979 Round 10 Dal
1980 TB-SF: 7 G. TB: 3 G. SF: 4 G. **Total:** 7 G.

LONNY CALICCHIO Calicchio, Lawrence Robert 6′3″, 249 **P**
Col: Northwest Mississippi CC; Mississippi *HS:* South Plantation [Plantation, FL] B: 10/24/1972, Plantation, FL
1997 Phi: 2 G.

DEAN CALIGUIRE Caliguire, Dean Patrick 6′2″, 280 **OG-C**
Col: Pittsburgh *HS:* Montour [McKees Rocks, PA] B: 3/2/1967, Pittsburgh, PA *Drafted:* 1990 Round 4 SF
1991 SF-Pit: 9 G. SF: 2 G. Pit: 7 G. **Total:** 9 G.

JACK CALL Call, John Arthur 6′1″, 200 **HB**
Col: Colgate *HS:* Cortland [NY] B: 7/30/1935, Cortland, NY
Drafted: 1957 Round 13 Bal
1957 Bal: Rec 4-18 4.5; KR 14-329 23.5. **1958** Bal: Rec 4-28 7.0; KR 2-48 24.0. **1959** Pit: Rec 1-0; KR 6-146 24.3. **Total:** Rec 9-46 5.1; KR 22-523 23.8.

Year Team	G	Rushing Att	Yds	Avg	TD	Fum
1957 Bal	12	33	145	4.4	0	0
1958 Bal	12	37	154	4.2	0	3
1959 Pit	4	3	9	3.0	0	0
NFL Total	28	73	308	4.2	0	3

KEVIN CALL Call, Kevin Bradley 6′7″, 302 **OT**
Col: Colorado State *HS:* Fairview [Boulder, CO] B: 11/13/1961, Boulder, CO *Drafted:* 1984 Round 5 Ind
1984 Ind: 15 G. **1985** Ind: 14 G. **1986** Ind: 16 G. **1987** Ind: 12 G. **1988** Ind: 8 G. **1989** Ind: 15 G. **1990** Ind: 8 G. **1991** Ind: 16 G. **1992** Ind: 16 G. **1993** Ind: 10 G. **Total:** 130 G.

DAN CALLAHAN Callahan, Dan Earl 6′0″, 230 **OG**
Col: Wooster *HS:* East [Akron, OH] B: 7/11/1938, Akron, OH
1960 NYT: 9 G.

JIM CALLAHAN Callahan, James Ross 5′11″, 185 **TB-DB**
Col: Texas; Texas Tech *HS:* Wink [TX] B: 12/19/1920, El Paso, TX
D: 3/27/1978, El Paso, TX
1946 Det: PR 6-71 11.8; KR 8-174 21.8; Int 2-8; Punt 4-182 45.5.

Year Team	G	Passing Att	Comp	Comp%	Yds	YPA	TD	Int	Rating
1946 Det	9	67	22	32.8	359	5.36	2	7	22.1

Year Team	Rushing Att	Yds	Avg	TD	Fum
1946 Det	52	86	1.7	2	4

BOB CALLAHAN Callahan, Robert Francis 6′0″, 205 **C-LB**
Col: Missouri; Michigan *HS:* Beaumont [St. Louis, MO] B: 9/26/1923, St. Louis, MO
AAFC **1948** BufA: 7 G.

BILL CALLAHAN Callahan, William Timothy 6′0″, 200 **DB**
Col: Pittsburgh *HS:* Valley [New Kensington, PA] B: 4/11/1964, Natrona Heights, PA *Drafted:* 1986 Round 4 Pit
1987 Buf: 1 G.

LEE CALLAND Calland, Arthur Lee 6′0″, 190 **DB**
(Sweet Lee) *Col:* Louisville *HS:* Central [Louisville, KY] B: 9/14/1941, Louisville, KY
1963 Min: KR 2-45 22.5. **1970** Pit: KR 1-0. **Total:** KR 3-45 15.0.

Year Team	G	Interceptions Int	Yds	TD	Fum
1963 Min	14	0	0	0	1
1964 Min	1	0	0	0	0
1965 Min	5	0	0	0	0
1966 Atl	14	3	6	0	0
1967 Atl	14	3	106	1	0
1968 Atl	7	2	34	0	0
1969 ChiB-Pit	12	2	0	0	0
1969 ChiB	4	0	0	0	0
1969 Pit	8	2	0	0	0
1970 Pit	14	7	38	0	0
1971 Pit	13	2	0	0	0
1972 Pit	7	0	0	0	0
NFL Total	101	19	184	1	1

KEN CALLICUTT Callicutt, Kenneth Byron 6′0″, 190 **RB**
Col: Clemson *HS:* Chester [SC] B: 8/20/1955, Chester, SC
1979 Det: Rush 3-6 2.0; Rec 2-16 8.0; PR 4-25 6.3. **1980** Det: Rec 1-19 19.0; PR 1-0. **1981** Det: Rec 2-24 12.0. **Total:** Rush 3-6 2.0; Rec 5-59 11.8; PR 5-25 5.0.

Year Team	G	Kickoff Returns Ret	Yds	Avg	TD	Fum
1978 Det	13	2	12	6.0	0	1
1979 Det	16	24	406	16.9	0	2
1980 Det	13	16	301	18.8	0	5
1981 Det	16	2	23	11.5	0	0
1982 Det	8	0	0	—	0	0
NFL Total	66	44	742	16.9	0	8

LEN CALLIGARO Calligaro, Leonard John 5′11″, 190 **BB-LB**
Col: Wisconsin *HS:* Hurley [WI] B: 6/4/1921, Hurley, WI
1944 NYG: 10 G; Rush 3-4 1.3 1 TD; Rec 2-11 5.5; 6 Pt.

BILL CALLIHAN Callihan, William Earl 6′3″, 217 **BB-DB-LB-FB**
Col: Nebraska *HS:* Grand Island [NE] B: 5/15/1916, Paxton, NE
D: 8/23/1986, Columbus, NE *Drafted:* 1939 Round 7 Det
1940 Det: Int 2-18. **1942** Det: Pass 1-0, 1 Int; Int 3-29; Punt 1-44 44.0. **1943** Det: Pass 2-0, 1 Int; PR 2-5 2.5; Int 1-7. **1944** Det: KR 3-46 15.3. **1945** Det: Pass 5-3 60.0%, 34 6.80 1 TD 2 Int; Int 2-8; Scor 31, 25-27 92.6% XK. **Total:** Pass 8-3 37.5%, 34 4.25 1 TD 4 Int; PR 2-5 2.5; KR 3-46 15.3; Int 8-62; Punt 1-44 44.0; Scor 55, 25-27 92.6% XK.

Year Team	G	Rushing Att	Yds	Avg	TD	Receiving Rec	Yds	Avg	TD	Fum	Tot TD
1940 Det	10	0	0	—	0	4	42	10.5	0	0	0
1941 Det	11	0	0	—	0	4	34	8.5	0	0	0
1942 Det	11	0	0	—	0	4	48	12.0	0	0	0
1943 Det	10	5	17	3.4	1	8	108	13.5	3	0	4
1944 Det	10	1	3	3.0	0	8	67	8.4	0	0	0
1945 Det	10	27	85	3.1	0	4	88	22.0	1	2	1
NFL Total	62	33	105	3.2	1	32	387	12.1	4	2	5

CHRIS CALLOWAY Calloway, Christopher Fitzpatrick 5′10″, 188 **WR**
Col: Michigan *HS:* Mount Carmel [Chicago, IL] B: 3/29/1968, Chicago, IL *Drafted:* 1990 Round 4 Pit
1992 NYG: KR 2-29 14.5. **1993** NYG: KR 6-89 14.8. **1994** NYG: Rush 8-77 9.6. **1995** NYG: Rush 2-(-9) -4.5. **1996** NYG: Rush 1-2 2.0. **1997** NYG: Rush 1-(-1) -1.0. **Total:** Rush 12-69 5.8; KR 8-118 14.8.

Year Team	G	Receiving Rec	Yds	Avg	TD	Fum
1990 Pit	16	10	124	12.4	1	0
1991 Pit	12	15	254	16.9	1	0
1992 NYG	16	27	335	12.4	1	0
1993 NYG	16	35	513	14.7	3	0
1994 NYG	16	43	666	15.5	2	1
1995 NYG	16	56	796	14.2	3	0
1996 NYG	16	53	739	13.9	4	1
1997 NYG	16	58	849	14.6	8	0
1998 NYG	16	62	812	13.1	6	1
NFL Total	140	359	5088	14.2	29	3

ERNIE CALLOWAY Calloway, Ernest Henry 6′6″, 255 **DT-DE**
Col: Texas Southern *HS:* Jones [Orlando, FL] B: 1/1/1948, Orlando, FL
Drafted: 1969 Round 2 Phi
1969 Phi: 14 G. **1970** Phi: 14 G. **1971** Phi: 14 G. **1972** Phi: 5 G. **Total:** 47 G.

TONY CALVELLI Calvelli, Anthony J 5′10″, 189 **C-LB-G**
Col: Coll. of San Mateo CA (J.C.); Stanford *HS:* Stockton [CA]
B: 7/16/1915, Stockton, CA D: 5/17/1979, San Francisco, CA
Drafted: 1939 Round 9 Det
AAFC **1947** SF-A: 13 G; Int 1-2.

NFL **1939** Det: 7 G. **1940** Det: 11 G; Int 2-51 **1** TD; 6 Pt. **Total:** 18 G; Int 2-51 1 TD; 6 Pt.

TOM CALVIN Calvin, Thomas Marvin 6′0″, 200 **HB**
Col: Alabama *HS:* Athens [AL] B: 6/13/1926, Athens, AL
Drafted: 1951 Round 25 Pit
1952 Pit: Rec 2-4 2.0; PR 2-12 6.0; KR 5-120 24.0. **1953** Pit: Rec 4-28 7.0. **1954** Pit: Rec 1-19 19.0; KR 1-15 15.0. **Total:** Rec 7-51 7.3; PR 2-12 6.0; KR 6-135 22.5.

		Rushing				
Year Team	**G**	**Att**	**Yds**	**Avg**	**TD**	**Fum**
1952 Pit	12	7	14	2.0	0	2
1953 Pit	10	13	65	5.0	0	0
1954 Pit	6	12	57	4.8	0	1
1955 Pit	2	0	0	—	0	0
NFL Total	30	32	136	4.3	0	3

RICH CAMARILLO Camarillo, Richard Jon 5′11″, 196 **K-P**
Col: Washington *HS:* El Rancho [Pico Rivera, CA] B: 11/29/1959, Whittier, CA
1987 NE: Rush 1-0. **1989** Pho: Pass 1-1 100.0%. **1990** Pho: Rush 1-(-11) -11.0. **1991** Pho: Pass 1-0. **1992** Pho: Scor 0-1 XK. **1993** Pho: Rush 1-0. **1994** Hou: Pass 1-0. **1995** Hou: Pass 1-0. **Total:** Pass 4-1 25.0%; Rush 3-(-11) -3.7; Scor 0-1 XK.

		Punting			
Year Team	**G**	**Punts**	**Yds**	**Avg**	**Fum**
1981 NE	9	47	1959	41.7	1
1982 NE	9	49	2140	43.7	0
1983 NE	16	81	3615	44.6	0
1984 NE	7	48	2020	42.1	0
1985 NE	16	92	**3953**	43.0	0
1986 NE	16	89	3746	42.1	0
1987 NE	12	62	2489	40.1	0
1988 LARm	9	40	1579	39.5	0
1989 Pho	15	76	3298	**43.4**	0
1990 Pho	16	67	2865	42.8	1
1991 Pho	16	76	3445	45.3	0
1992 Pho	15	54	2317	42.9	0
1993 Pho	16	73	3189	43.7	0
1994 Hou	16	96	**4115**	42.9	1
1995 Hou	16	77	3165	41.1	1
1996 Oak	1	0	0	—	0
NFL Total	205	1027	43895	42.7	4

DENNIS CAMBAL Cambal, Dennis Hayden 6′2″, 225 **TE**
Col: William & Mary *HS:* Phillips Andover Acad. [Andover, MA]
B: 1/27/1949, Waltham, MA *Drafted:* 1972 Round 14 Oak
1973 NYJ: 8 G.

GLENN CAMERON Cameron, Glenn Scott 6′2″, 225 **LB**
Col: Florida *HS:* Coral Gables [FL] B: 2/21/1953, Miami, FL
Drafted: 1975 Round 1 Cin
1975 Cin: 14 G. **1976** Cin: 14 G. **1977** Cin: 14 G. **1978** Cin: 15 G. **1979** Cin: 15 G. **1980** Cin: 14 G; Int 3-43. **1981** Cin: 16 G; Int 1-0. **1982** Cin: 9 G. **1983** Cin: 16 G; 2 Sac. **1984** Cin: 16 G; Int 1-15; 1 Sac. **1985** Cin: 16 G. **Total:** 159 G; Int 5-58; 3 Sac.

JACK CAMERON Cameron, Jack Lyndon 6′0″, 182 **WR**
Col: Winston-Salem State *HS:* Person [Roxboro, NC] B: 11/5/1961, Durham, NC
1984 ChiB: Rec 1-13 13.0.

		Kickoff Returns			
Year Team	**G**	**Ret**	**Yds**	**Avg**	**TD**
1984 ChiB	16	26	485	18.7	0

JOHN CAMERON Cameron, John James 175 **G**
Col: Kalamazoo; Central Michigan *HS:* Central Lake [MI] B: 7/13/1900
Deceased
1926 Det: 8 G.

PAUL CAMERON Cameron, Paul Leslie 6′0″, 185 **DB**
Col: UCLA *HS:* Burbank [CA] B: 10/4/1932, Burbank, CA
Drafted: 1954 Round 8 Pit
1954 Pit: 12 G; PR 2-19 9.5; Int 7-118; 1 Fum.

JIM CAMP Camp, James Vernon 6′0″, 162 **QB-WB**
Col: Randolph-Macon; North Carolina *HS:* Schofield [Danville, VA]
B: 8/8/1924, Union, SC
AAFC **1948** BknA: 12 G; Rush 8-43 5.4; Rec 1-43 43.0; KR 1-12 12.0; Int 1-69.

REGGIE CAMP Camp, Reginald Louis 6′4″, 274 **DE**
Col: California *HS:* Jefferson [Daly City, CA] B: 2/28/1961, San Francisco, CA *Drafted:* 1983 Round 3 Cle
1983 Cle: 16 G; 4.5 Sac. **1984** Cle: 16 G; 14 Sac. **1985** Cle: 16 G; 8.5 Sac. **1986** Cle: 16 G; 7 Sac. **1987** Cle: 6 G; 1 Sac. **1988** Atl: 4 G. **Total:** 74 G; 35 Sac.

AL CAMPANA Campana, Albert Louis 5′11″, 180 **HB-DB**
Col: Youngstown State *HS:* Hubbard [OH] B: 2/25/1926, Hubbard, OH
1950 ChiB: Rec 5-58 11.6; KR 4-54 13.5; Int 1-0. **1952** ChiB: Rec 1-3 3.0. **1953** ChiC: KR 3-56 18.7. **Total:** Rec 6-61 10.2; KR 7-110 15.7; Int 1-0.

		Rushing				
Year Team	**G**	**Att**	**Yds**	**Avg**	**TD**	**Fum**
1950 ChiB	9	45	134	3.0	1	2
1951 ChiB	2	2	3	1.5	0	0
1952 ChiB	12	9	14	1.6	0	0
1953 ChiC	8	2	-5	-2.5	0	1
NFL Total	31	58	146	2.5	1	3

JOE CAMPANELLA Campanella, Joseph Arthur 6′2″, 242 **LB-DT-OT**
Col: Ohio State *HS:* Cathedral Latin [Cleveland, OH] B: 9/3/1930, Cleveland, OH D: 2/15/1967, Baltimore, MD *Drafted:* 1952 Round 3 Cle
1952 Dal: 12 G; KR 3-40 13.3. **1953** Bal: 12 G; KR 2-13 6.5. **1954** Bal: 12 G; Int 1-0. **1955** Bal: 11 G; Int 2-35. **1956** Bal: 10 G. **1957** Bal: 11 G. **Total:** 68 G; KR 5-53 10.6; Int 3-35.

ARNOLD CAMPBELL Campbell, Arnold Rene 6′3″, 260 **DE**
Col: Alcorn State *HS:* Charleston [MS] B: 11/13/1962, Charleston, MS
1987 Buf: 3 G.

CARTER CAMPBELL Campbell, Carter Bradford 6′4″, 240 **LB-DE**
Col: Treasure Valley CC OR; Weber State *HS:* Vanden [Travis AFB, CA]
B: 9/29/1947, Mobile, AL *Drafted:* 1970 Round 8 SF
1970 SF: 1 G. **1971** Den: 14 G. **1972** NYG: 14 G. **1973** NYG: 14 G. **Total:** 43 G.

DON CAMPBELL Campbell, Donald C 6′0″, 225 **T**
(Pop) *Col:* Carnegie Mellon B: 11/25/1916 D: 9/1/1991, Philadelphia, PA
1939 Pit: 11 G. **1940** Pit: 11 G. **Total:** 22 G.

EARL CAMPBELL Campbell, Earl Christian 5′11″, 232 **RB**
Col: Texas *HS:* John Tyler [Tyler, TX] B: 3/29/1955, Tyler, TX
Drafted: 1978 Round 1 Hou *HOF:* 1991
1980 Hou: Pass 2-1 50.0%, 57 28.50 1 TD. **1982** Hou: Pass 1-0, 1 Int. **Total:** Pass 3-1 33.3%, 57 19.00 1 TD 1 Int.

		Rushing				Receiving					Tot
Year Team	**G**	**Att**	**Yds**	**Avg**	**TD**	**Rec**	**Yds**	**Avg**	**TD**	**Fum**	**TD**
1978 Hou	15	302	**1450**	4.8	13	12	48	4.0	0	9	13
1979 Hou	16	368	**1697**	4.6	**19**	16	94	5.9	0	8	**19**
1980 Hou	15	**373**	**1934**	**5.2**	**13**	11	47	4.3	0	4	13
1981 Hou	16	361	1376	3.8	10	36	156	4.3	0	10	10
1982 Hou	9	157	538	3.4	2	18	130	7.2	0	2	2
1983 Hou	14	322	1301	4.0	12	19	216	11.4	0	4	12
1984 Hou-NO	14	146	468	3.2	4	3	27	9.0	0	2	4
1984 Hou	6	96	278	2.9	4	3	27	9.0	0	2	4
1984 NO	8	50	190	3.8	0	0	0	—	0	0	0
1985 NO	16	158	643	4.1	1	6	88	14.7	0	4	1
NFL Total	115	2187	9407	4.3	74	121	806	6.7	0	43	74

MARION CAMPBELL Campbell, Francis Marion 6′3″, 250 **DT-DE-OT**
Col: Georgia *HS:* Chester [SC] B: 5/25/1929, Chester, SC
Drafted: 1952 Round 4 SF
1954 SF: 12 G. **1955** SF: 11 G; Int 1-0. **1956** Phi: 12 G; Int 1-1; 1 Fum. **1957** Phi: 10 G. **1958** Phi: 11 G. **1959** Phi: 12 G; Int 1-0. **1960** Phi: 12 G. **1961** Phi: 14 G. **Total:** 94 G; Int 3-1; 1 Fum.

GARY CAMPBELL Campbell, Gary Kalani 6′1″, 218 **LB**
Col: Colorado *HS:* St. Louis [Honolulu, HI] B: 3/4/1952, Honolulu, HI
Drafted: 1976 Round 10 Pit
1977 ChiB: 14 G. **1978** ChiB: 16 G. **1979** ChiB: 16 G; Int 1-32. **1980** ChiB: 16 G; Int 3-36. **1981** ChiB: 16 G. **1982** ChiB: 9 G; 1 Sac. **1983** ChiB: 6 G; 1 Sac. **Total:** 93 G; Int 4-68; 2 Sac.

TOMMY CAMPBELL Campbell, George Thomas 6′0″, 188 **DB**
Col: Monroe CC NY; Iowa State *HS:* Uniondale [NY] B: 12/30/1947, New York, NY *Drafted:* 1973 Round 7 Atl
1976 Phi: 14 G.

GLENN CAMPBELL Campbell, Glenn Rex 5′11″, 199 **OE-DE**
(Turtle; Flash) *Col:* Emporia State B: 4/20/1904, Thayer, KS
D: 9/16/1973, Topeka, KS
1929 NYG: 15 G; Rec 1 TD; 6 Pt. **1930** NYG: 17 G; Rec 2 TD; Tot TD 4; 24 Pt. **1931** NYG: 14 G; Rec 2 TD; 12 Pt. **1932** NYG: 10 G; Rec 5-44 8.8. **1933** NYG: 12 G; Rec 8-129 16.1 1 TD; 6 Pt. **1935** Phi-Pit: 2 G; Pass 5-2 40.0%, 38 7.60; Rush 1-6 6.0; Rec 1-2 2.0. Phi: 1 G; Rec 1-2 2.0. Pit: 1 G; Pass 5-2 40.0%, 38 7.60; Rush 1-6 6.0. **Total:** 70 G; Pass 5-2 40.0%, 38 7.60; Rush 1-6 6.0; Rec 14-175 12.5 6 TD; Tot TD 8; 48 Pt.

JIM CAMPBELL Campbell, James Ray 6′2″, 232 **LB**
Col: West Texas A&M *HS:* Ector [TX] B: 1/16/1946, Coleman, TX
Drafted: 1968 Round 14 SD
1969 SD: 1 G; Int 1-0.

JEFF CAMPBELL Campbell, Jeffrey Thomas 5'8", 167 **WR**
Col: Colorado *HS:* Battle Mountain [Minturn, CO] B: 3/29/1968, Denver, CO *Drafted:* 1990 Round 5 Det
1990 Det: PR 1-0. **1992** Det: PR 3-15 5.0. **1994** Den: Rush 2-6 3.0. **Total:** Rush 2-6 3.0; PR 4-15 3.8.

		Receiving				Kickoff Returns				
Year Team	G	Rec	Yds	Avg	TD	Ret	Yds	Avg	TD	Fum
1990 Det	16	19	236	12.4	2	12	238	19.8	0	1
1991 Det	14	2	49	24.5	0	9	85	9.4	0	1
1992 Det	12	8	155	19.4	1	4	61	15.3	0	1
1993 Det	10	7	55	7.9	0	0	0	—	0	0
1994 Den	16	1	22	22.0	1	3	24	8.0	0	0
NFL Total	68	37	517	14.0	4	28	408	14.6	0	3

JESSE CAMPBELL Campbell, Jesse Gilbert Jr. 6'1", 211 **DB**
Col: North Carolina State *HS:* West Craven [Vanceboro, NC] B: 4/11/1969, Washington, DC *Drafted:* 1991 Round 2 Phi
1992 NYG: 11 G. **1993** NYG: 16 G; Int 1-0. **1994** NYG: 14 G; Int 2-3. **1995** NYG: 16 G. **1996** NYG: 16 G; Int 2-14. **1997** Was: 16 G; Int 1-7. **1998** Was: 3 G; Int 1-4; 1 Fum. **Total:** 92 G; Int 7-28; 1 Fum.

JACK CAMPBELL Campbell, John Carter 6'5", 277 **OT**
Col: USC; Utah *HS:* West [Torrance, CA] B: 12/16/1958, Los Angeles, CA *Drafted:* 1982 Round 6 Sea
1982 Sea: 1 G.

JOHN CAMPBELL Campbell, John William 6'3", 225 **LB**
Col: Minnesota *HS:* Wadena [MN] B: 10/7/1938, Wadena, MN *Drafted:* 1963 Round 11 Min
1963 Min: 14 G; KR 1-8 8.0; 1 Fum. **1964** Min: 14 G. **1965** Pit: 14 G; 1 Fum TD; 6 Pt. **1966** Pit: 13 G; KR 1-15 15.0; Int 2-6. **1967** Pit: 14 G; KR 1-25 25.0; Int 2-52. **1968** Pit: 8 G; Int 1-20. **1969** Pit-Bal: 11 G. Pit: 3 G. Bal: 8 G. **Total:** 88 G; KR 3-48 16.0; Int 5-78; 1 Fum TD; 6 Pt; 1 Fum.

JOSEPH CAMPBELL Campbell, Joseph Jr. 6'4", 245 **DE**
Col: New Mexico State *HS:* Verbum Dei [Los Angeles, CA]; Morningside HS [Inglewood, CA]; Tempe HS [AZ] B: 12/28/1966, Chandler, AZ *Drafted:* 1988 Round 4 SD
1988 SD: 16 G; 3 Sac. **1989** SD: 9 G. **Total:** 25 G; 3 Sac.

JOE CAMPBELL Campbell, Joseph Patrick 6'6", 254 **DE-NT**
Col: Maryland *HS:* Salesianum [Wilmington, DE] B: 5/8/1955, Wilmington, DE *Drafted:* 1977 Round 1 NO
1977 NO: 14 G; KR 2-33 16.5. **1978** NO: 16 G. **1979** NO: 10 G. **1980** NO-Oak: 15 G. NO: 5 G. Oak: 10 G. **1981** Oak-TB: 10 G. Oak: 3 G. TB: 7 G. **Total:** 65 G; KR 2-33 16.5.

KEN CAMPBELL Campbell, Kenneth 6'1", 213 **OE**
Col: West Chester *HS:* Columbia [PA] B: 1939
1960 NYT: 1 G.

LAMAR CAMPBELL Campbell, Lamar 5'11", 182 **DB**
Col: Wisconsin *HS:* Strath Haven [Chester, PA] B: 8/29/1976, Chester, PA
1998 Det: 12 G.

LEON CAMPBELL Campbell, Leon 6'0", 199 **FB**
(Muscles) *Col:* Arkansas *HS:* Bauxite [AR] B: 7/1/1927, Bauxite, AR *Drafted:* 1950 Round 2 Bal
1950 Bal: Rec 1-5 5.0. **1952** ChiB: Rec 2-1 0.5. **1953** ChiB: Rec 5-74 14.8. **1954** ChiB: Rec 3-0. **1955** Pit: Rec 9-76 8.4. **Total:** Rec 20-156 7.8.

		Rushing				Kickoff Returns				
Year Team	G	Att	Yds	Avg	TD	Ret	Yds	Avg	TD	Fum
1950 Bal	3	20	93	4.7	0	0	0	—	0	2
1952 ChiB	8	24	76	3.2	0	2	106	53.0	1	3
1953 ChiB	12	22	130	5.9	0	19	455	23.9	0	3
1954 ChiB	6	18	38	2.1	0	3	77	25.7	0	0
1955 Pit	12	18	42	2.3	0	4	133	33.3	0	1
NFL Total	41	102	379	3.7	0	28	771	27.5	1	9

MARK CAMPBELL Campbell, Mark Anthony 6'1", 290 **DT**
Col: Florida *HS:* Miami Sunset [FL] B: 9/12/1972, Jamaica *Drafted:* 1996 Round 3 Den
1997 Ariz: 5 G.

MATT CAMPBELL Campbell, Matthew Thomas 6'4", 284 **OT-OG-TE**
Col: South Carolina *HS:* North Augusta [SC] B: 7/14/1972, North Augusta, SC
1995 Car: 10 G; Rec 3-32 10.7; 1 Fum. **1996** Car: 9 G. **1997** Car: 16 G. **1998** Car: 10 G. **Total:** 45 G; Rec 3-32 10.7; 1 Fum.

MIKE CAMPBELL Campbell, Michael Linwood 5'11", 200 **RB**
Col: Lenoir-Rhyne *HS:* Altavista [VA] B: 5/29/1945, Altavista, VA *Drafted:* 1967 Round 6 StL
1968 Det: 3 G; Rush 7-24 3.4; Rec 2-15 7.5; 1 Fum.

MILT CAMPBELL Campbell, Milton Gray 6'3", 217 **HB**
Col: Indiana *HS:* Plainfield [NJ] B: 12/9/1933, Plainfield, NJ *Drafted:* 1957 Round 5 Cle
1957 Cle: 9 G; Pass 1-0; Rush 7-23 3.3; Rec 1-25 25.0 1 TD; KR 11-263 23.9; 6 Pt.

DICK CAMPBELL Campbell, Raymond Richard 6'1", 227 **LB**
Col: Marquette *HS:* Green Bay West [WI] B: 7/17/1935, Green Bay, WI *Drafted:* 1958 Round 10 Pit
1958 Pit: 12 G; Int 1-58. **1959** Pit: 12 G; Int 1-6. **1960** Pit: 12 G; Int 1-5. **Total:** 36 G; Int 3-69.

RICH CAMPBELL Campbell, Richard Delano 6'4", 224 **QB**
Col: California *HS:* Santa Teresa [San Jose, CA] B: 12/22/1958, Miami, FL *Drafted:* 1981 Round 1 GB
1984 GB: Rush 2-2 1.0. **Total:** Rush 2-2 1.0.

		Passing								
Year Team	G	Att	Comp	Comp%	Yds	YPA	TD	Int	Rating	Fum
1981 GB	2	30	15	50.0	168	5.60	0	4	27.5	0
1982 GB	1	0	0	—	0	—	0	0	—	0
1983 GB	1	0	0	—	0	—	0	0	—	0
1984 GB	3	38	16	42.1	218	5.74	3	5	47.8	1
NFL Total	7	68	31	45.6	386	5.68	3	9	38.8	1

SCOTT CAMPBELL Campbell, Robert Scott 6'0", 196 **QB**
Col: Purdue *HS:* Milton S. Hershey [Hershey, PA] B: 4/15/1962, Hershey, PA *Drafted:* 1984 Round 7 Pit

		Passing							
Year Team	G	Att	Comp	Comp%	Yds	YPA	TD	Int	Rating
1984 Pit	5	15	8	53.3	109	7.27	1	1	71.3
1985 Pit	16	96	43	44.8	612	6.38	4	6	53.8
1986 Pit-Atl	4	7	1	14.3	7	1.00	0	0	39.6
1986 Pit	3	4	0	0.0	0	0.00	0	0	39.6
1986 Atl	1	3	1	33.3	7	2.33	0	0	42.4
1987 Atl	12	260	136	52.3	1728	6.65	11	14	65.0
1989 Atl	1	0	0	—	0	—	0	0	—
1990 Atl	7	76	36	47.4	527	6.93	3	4	61.7
NFL Total	45	454	224	49.3	2983	6.57	19	25	61.6

	Rushing				
Year Team	Att	Yds	Avg	TD	Fum
1984 Pit	3	-5	-1.7	0	1
1985 Pit	9	28	3.1	0	3
1986 Pit-Atl	1	7	7.0	0	0
1986 Atl	1	7	7.0	0	0
1987 Atl	21	102	4.9	2	4
1990 Atl	9	38	4.2	0	1
NFL Total	43	170	4.0	2	9

BOB CAMPBELL Campbell, Robert Thomas 6'0", 195 **WR**
Col: Penn State *HS:* Vestal [NY] B: 4/18/1947, Johnson City, NY *Drafted:* 1969 Round 4 Pit
1969 Pit: Rush 1-5 5.0; Rec 1-32 32.0.

		Punt Returns				Kickoff Returns				
Year Team	G	Ret	Yds	Avg	TD	Ret	Yds	Avg	TD	Fum
1969 Pit	14	28	133	4.8	0	26	522	20.1	0	5

RUSS CAMPBELL Campbell, Russell Lee 6'5", 259 **TE**
Col: Kansas State *HS:* North [Wichita, KS] B: 4/2/1969, Columbus, OH *Drafted:* 1992 Round 7 Pit
1992 Pit: 7 G; KR 1-0.

STAN CAMPBELL Campbell, Stanley Hugh 6'0", 226 **OG**
Col: Iowa State *HS:* Rochelle Twp. [Rochelle, IL] B: 8/26/1930, Rochelle, IL *Drafted:* 1952 Round 18 Det
1952 Det: 3 G. **1955** Det: 7 G. **1956** Det: 7 G. **1957** Det: 12 G. **1958** Det: 12 G. **1959** Phi: 12 G. **1960** Phi: 12 G. **1961** Phi: 13 G. **1962** Oak: 14 G. **Total:** 92 G.

SONNY CAMPBELL Campbell, Thee Arthur 5'11", 192 **RB**
Col: Northern Arizona *HS:* Marana [Tucson, AZ] B: 3/5/1948, Marana, AZ
1970 Atl: Rec 7-92 13.1; KR 10-230 23.0. **1971** Atl: Rec 3-40 13.3; KR 4-95 23.8. **Total:** Rec 10-132 13.2; KR 14-325 23.2.

		Rushing				
Year Team	G	Att	Yds	Avg	TD	Fum
1970 Atl	11	28	116	4.1	2	1
1971 Atl	14	29	79	2.7	0	1
NFL Total	25	57	195	3.4	2	2

BILL CAMPBELL Campbell, William Roscoe 6'0", 195 **LB-C-DB**
Col: Oklahoma *HS:* Pawhuska [OK] B: 8/6/1920, Pawhuska, OK D: 10/1974 *Drafted:* 1943 Round 17 ChiC
1945 ChiC: 6 G. **1946** ChiC: 11 G; KR 1-17 17.0. **1947** ChiC: 4 G. **1948** ChiC: 7 G. **1949** NYB-ChiC: 10 G. NYB: 4 G. ChiC: 6 G. **Total:** 38 G; KR 1-17 17.0.

WOODY CAMPBELL Campbell, Woodrow Lamar 5'10", 204 **RB**
Col: Northwestern *HS:* Carter-Parramore [Quincy, FL] B: 9/26/1944, Mount Pleasant, FL *Drafted:* 1967 Round 10 Hou
1967 Hou: Pass 1-0; KR 1-19 19.0. **1971** Hou: Pass 2-2 100.0%, 34 17.00 2 TD. **Total:** Pass 3-2 66.7%, 34 11.33 2 TD; KR 1-19 19.0.

Year Team	G	Rushing Att	Yds	Avg	TD	Receiving Rec	Yds	Avg	TD	Fum	Tot TD
1967 Hou	14	110	511	4.6	4	17	136	8.0	2	0	6
1968 Hou	14	115	436	3.8	6	21	234	11.1	0	4	6
1969 Hou	4	28	98	3.5	1	7	82	11.7	0	1	1
1970 Hou	6	59	189	3.2	1	15	78	5.2	0	0	1
1971 Hou	12	96	259	2.7	1	20	179	9.0	0	0	1
NFL Total	50	408	1493	3.7	13	80	709	8.9	2	5	15

JAMES CAMPEN Campen, James Frederick 6′3″, 269 **C**
Col: Sacramento City Coll. CA (J.C.); Tulane *HS:* Ponderosa [Shingle Springs, CA] B: 6/11/1964, Sacramento, CA
1987 NO: 3 G. **1988** NO: 3 G. **1989** GB: 15 G. **1990** GB: 16 G; 2 Fum. **1991** GB: 13 G. **1992** GB: 13 G. **1993** GB: 4 G. **Total:** 67 G; 2 Fum.

BILLY CAMPFIELD Campfield, William 5′11″, 200 **RB**
Col: Kansas *HS:* Derby [KS] B: 8/20/1956, Las Vegas, NV
Drafted: 1978 Round 11 Phi

Year Team	G	Rushing Att	Yds	Avg	TD	Receiving Rec	Yds	Avg	TD
1978 Phi	16	61	247	4.0	0	15	101	6.7	0
1979 Phi	16	30	165	5.5	3	16	115	7.2	0
1980 Phi	15	44	120	2.7	1	26	275	10.6	2
1981 Phi	16	31	115	3.7	1	36	326	9.1	3
1982 Phi	6	1	2	2.0	0	14	141	10.1	1
1983 NYG	4	2	21	10.5	0	1	12	12.0	0
NFL Total	73	169	670	4.0	5	108	970	9.0	6

Year Team	Kickoff Returns Ret	Yds	Avg	TD	Fum	Tot TD
1978 Phi	18	368	20.4	0	3	0
1979 Phi	7	251	35.9	**1**	1	4
1980 Phi	26	540	20.8	0	4	3
1981 Phi	12	223	18.6	0	3	4
1982 Phi	2	30	15.0	0	1	1
1983 NYG	9	154	17.1	0	1	0
NFL Total	74	1566	21.2	1	13	12

BOB CAMPIGLIO Campiglio, Robert Fulton 6′1″, 183 **DB-TB-WB-BB**
Col: West Liberty State *HS:* Milton [PA]; Mercersburg Acad. [PA]
B: 1908, Milton, PA
1932 SI: Pass 20-7 35.0%, 109 5.45; Rec 3-59 19.7 1 TD. **1933** Bos: Pass 1-0, 1 Int. **Total:** Pass 21-7 33.3%, 109 5.19 1 Int; Rec 3-59 19.7 1 TD.

Year Team	G	Rushing Att	Yds	Avg	TD	Tot TD
1932 SI	11	104	504	**4.8**	2	3
1933 Bos	6	10	30	3.0	0	0
NFL Total	17	114	534	4.7	2	3

T.J. CAMPION Campion, Thomas J 6′2″, 235 **T**
(Turk) *Col:* Southeastern Louisiana B: 11/14/1918 D: 2/8/1996, Louisville, KY *Drafted:* 1947 Round 17 Phi
1947 Phi: 5 G.

NICK CAMPOFREDA Campofreda, Nicholas William 6′1″, 240 **C-T**
Col: Western Maryland *HS:* Baltimore City College [MD] B: 1/14/1914, Baltimore, MD D: 5/23/1959, Towson, MD
1944 Was: 3 G.

DON CAMPORA Campora, Don Carlo 6′3″, 268 **DT**
Col: U. of Pacific *HS:* Linden [CA]; Stockton HS [CA] B: 8/30/1927, Trenton, UT D: 6/5/1978, San Bernardino, CA *Drafted:* 1950 Round 2 SF
1950 SF: 12 G. **1952** SF: 8 G. **1953** Was: 5 G. **Total:** 25 G.

ALAN CAMPOS Campos, Alan Raul 6′3″, 236 **LB**
Col: Louisville *HS:* Miami Palmetto [FL] B: 3/3/1973, Miami, FL
Drafted: 1996 Round 5 Dal
1996 Dal: 15 G.

LARRY CANADA Canada, Lawrence L 6′2″, 233 **RB**
Col: Wisconsin *HS:* Austin [Chicago, IL] B: 12/16/1954, Chicago, IL
1978 Den: Rec 6-37 6.2. **1979** Den: Rec 3-36 12.0; KR 3-31 10.3. **1981** Den: Rec 3-37 12.3 1 TD; KR 2-19 9.5. **Total:** Rec 12-110 9.2 1 TD; KR 5-50 10.0.

Year Team	G	Rushing Att	Yds	Avg	TD	Fum	Tot TD
1978 Den	16	79	365	4.6	3	1	3
1979 Den	16	36	143	4.0	0	2	0
1981 Den	16	33	113	3.4	3	1	4
NFL Total	48	148	621	4.2	6	4	7

TONY CANADEO Canadeo, Anthony Robert 5′11″, 190 **HB-DB-TB-FB**
(The Gray Ghost) *Col:* Gonzaga *HS:* Steinmetz [Chicago, IL]
B: 5/5/1919, Chicago, IL *Drafted:* 1941 Round 7 GB *HOF:* 1974
1941 GB: Int 2-30. **1942** GB: Int 1-35. **1943** GB: Int 2-15. **1946** GB: Int 1-23. **1948** GB: Int 3-26. **Total:** Int 9-129.

Year Team	G	Passing Att	Comp	Comp%	Yds	YPA	TD	Int	Rating
1941 GB	9	16	4	25.0	54	3.38	2	0	80.7
1942 GB	11	59	24	40.7	310	5.25	3	4	46.6
1943 GB	10	129	56	43.4	875	6.78	9	12	51.0
1944 GB	3	20	9	45.0	89	4.45	0	0	58.1
1946 GB	11	27	7	25.9	189	7.00	1	3	29.0
1947 GB	12	8	3	37.5	101	12.63	1	1	85.4
1948 GB	12	8	2	25.0	24	3.00	0	0	39.6
1949 GB	12	0	0	—	0	—	0	0	—
1950 GB	12	0	0	—	0	—	0	0	—
1951 GB	12	0	0	—	0	—	0	0	—
1952 GB	12	1	0	0.0	0	0.00	0	0	39.6
NFL Total	116	268	105	39.2	1642	6.13	16	20	49.1

Year Team	Rushing Att	Yds	Avg	TD	Receiving Rec	Yds	Avg	TD
1941 GB	43	137	3.2	3	0	0	—	0
1942 GB	89	272	3.1	3	10	66	6.6	0
1943 GB	94	489	5.2	3	3	31	10.3	2
1944 GB	31	149	4.8	0	1	12	12.0	0
1946 GB	122	476	3.9	0	2	25	12.5	0
1947 GB	103	464	4.5	2	0	0	—	0
1948 GB	123	589	4.8	4	9	81	9.0	0
1949 GB	208	1052	5.1	4	3	-2	-0.7	0
1950 GB	93	247	2.7	4	10	54	5.4	0
1951 GB	54	131	2.4	1	22	226	10.3	2
1952 GB	65	191	2.9	2	9	86	9.6	1
NFL Total	1025	4197	4.1	26	69	579	8.4	5

Year Team	Punt Returns Ret	Yds	Avg	TD	Kickoff Returns Ret	Yds	Avg	TD
1941 GB	4	26	6.5	0	4	110	27.5	0
1942 GB	7	76	10.9	0	6	137	22.8	0
1943 GB	8	93	11.6	0	10	242	24.2	0
1944 GB	1	4	4.0	0	1	12	12.0	0
1946 GB	6	76	12.7	0	6	163	27.2	0
1947 GB	10	111	11.1	0	15	312	20.8	0
1948 GB	4	55	13.8	0	9	166	18.4	0
1949 GB	0	0	—	0	2	20	10.0	0
1950 GB	5	68	13.6	0	16	411	25.7	0
1951 GB	0	0	—	0	4	101	25.3	0
1952 GB	1	4	4.0	0	2	62	31.0	0
NFL Total	46	513	11.2	0	75	1736	23.1	0

Year Team	Punting Punts	Yds	Avg	Fum	Tot TD
1941 GB	10	405	40.5	0	3
1942 GB	18	645	35.8	0	3
1943 GB	3	102	34.0	0	5
1944 GB	13	479	36.8	0	0
1946 GB	0	0	—	3	0
1947 GB	0	0	—	0	2
1948 GB	1	38	38.0	5	4
1949 GB	0	0	—	6	4
1950 GB	0	0	—	4	4
1951 GB	0	0	—	2	3
1952 GB	0	0	—	4	3
NFL Total	45	1669	37.1	24	31

JIM CANADY Canady, James Maurice 5′10″, 178 **DB-HB-BB**
Col: Texas *HS:* Stephen F. Austin [Austin, TX] B: 1/14/1926, Austin, TX
Drafted: 1947 Round 3 ChiB
1948 ChiB: PR 1-37 37.0. **1949** ChiB-NYB: Rec 5-80 16.0; PR 4-36 9.0; KR 10-233 23.3; Int 5-58. ChiB: Int 3-22. NYB: Rec 5-80 16.0; PR 4-36 9.0; KR 10-233 23.3; Int 2-36. **Total:** Rec 5-80 16.0; PR 5-73 14.6; KR 10-233 23.3; Int 5-58.

Year Team	G	Rushing Att	Yds	Avg	TD	Fum
1948 ChiB	3	2	8	4.0	0	0
1949 ChiB-NYB	12	23	91	4.0	0	3
1949 ChiB	5	6	8	1.3	0	0
1949 NYB	7	17	83	4.9	0	3
NFL Total	15	25	99	4.0	0	3

WHIT CANALE Canale, John Whitfield 6′3″, 245 **DE-DT**
Col: Tennessee *HS:* Memphis Catholic [TN] B: 12/27/1941, Sarasota, FL *Drafted:* 1965 Round 17 Pit
1966 Mia: 3 G. **1968** Bos: 13 G. **Total:** 16 G.

JUSTIN CANALE Canale, Justin Dominic 6′2″, 250 **OG**
Col: Mississippi State *HS:* Memphis Catholic [TN] B: 4/11/1943, Memphis, TN *Drafted:* 1965 Round 6 Bos
1965 Bos: 14 G; KR 2-0. **1966** Bos: 14 G. **1967** Bos: 14 G; Scor 1, 1-1 100.0% XK. **1968** Bos: 14 G; Rec 1-0. **1969** Cin: 8 G. **Total:** 64 G; Rec 1-0; KR 2-0; Scor 1, 1-1 100.0% XK.

ROCCO CANALE Canale, Rocco P 5'11", 240 **T-G**
(Walking Billboard) *Col:* Boston College *HS:* Watertown [NY]
B: 5/1/1917, Boston, MA D: 11/1/1995, Watertown, NY *Drafted:* 1943 Round 9 Phi
1943 PhPt: 5 G. **1944** Phi: 9 G. **1945** Phi: 3 G. **1946** Bos: 11 G. **1947** Bos: 10 G. **Total:** 38 G.

PHIL CANCIK Cancik, Phillip 6'1", 228 **LB**
Col: Northern Arizona *HS:* Scottsdale [AZ] B: 4/19/1957, South Bend, IN
1980 NYG: 5 G. **1981** KC: 16 G. **Total:** 21 G.

SHELDON CANLEY Canley, Sheldon Lavell 5'9", 195 **RB**
Col: Allan Hancock Coll. CA (J.C.); San Jose State *HS:* Lompoc [CA]
B: 4/19/1968, Santa Barbara, CA *Drafted:* 1991 Round 7 SF
1992 NYJ: 1 G; Rush 4-9 2.3.

JOHN CANNADY Cannady, John Hanley 6'2", 227 **LB-C-BB**
Col: Indiana *HS:* Spartanburg [SC]; Owensboro HS [KY] B: 5/9/1923, Charleston, SC *Drafted:* 1947 Round 2 NYG
1947 NYG: Rush 1-14 14.0. **Total:** Rush 1-14 14.0.

		Interceptions			
Year Team	**G**	**Int**	**Yds**	**TD**	**Fum**
1947 NYG	11	1	0	0	0
1948 NYG	12	2	62	0	0
1949 NYG	12	1	15	0	0
1950 NYG	11	2	23	0	0
1951 NYG	12	3	52	0	0
1952 NYG	12	2	2	0	1
1953 NYG	12	1	33	0	0
1954 NYG	10	2	16	0	0
NFL Total	92	14	203	0	1

PAT CANNAMELA Cannamela, Patterson N 6'0", 195 **LB**
Col: Ventura Coll. CA (J.C.); USC *HS:* Chapman Tech [New London, CT]
B: 4/27/1929, New London, CT D: 1/28/1973, Los Angeles, CA
Drafted: 1952 Round 11 Dal
1952 Dal: 12 G; Scor 8, 0-1 FG, 8-10 80.0% XK.

AL CANNAVA Cannava, Anthony Louis 5'10", 180 **HB-DB**
Col: Notre Dame; Boston College *HS:* Medford [MA] B: 5/24/1924, Boston, MA
1950 GB: 1 G; Rush 1-2 2.0; Rec 1-28 28.0; PR 2-9 4.5; KR 1-10 10.0; 1 Fum.

JOE CANNAVINO Cannavino, Joseph Patrick 5'11", 185 **DB**
Col: Ohio State *HS:* Collinwood [Cleveland, OH] B: 1/20/1935, Cleveland, OH *Drafted:* 1957 Round 16 Bal
1960 Oak: PR 1-4 4.0. **1962** Buf: PR 1-3 3.0. **Total:** PR 2-7 3.5.

		Interceptions		
Year Team	**G**	**Int**	**Yds**	**TD**
1960 Oak	14	4	45	0
1961 Oak	14	5	14	0
1962 Buf	4	1	19	0
NFL Total	32	10	78	0

JOHN CANNELLA Cannella, John Matthew 6'1", 199 **G-C-LB-T**
(Jack) *Col:* Fordham *HS:* William L. Dickinson [Jersey City, NJ]
B: 2/8/1908, New York, NY D: 10/31/1996, Glen Cove, NY
1933 NYG: 9 G. **1934** NYG: 2 G. **Total:** 11 G.

JAMES CANNIDA Cannida, James Thomas II 6'2", 275 **DT**
Col: Nevada-Reno *HS:* American [Fremont, CA] B: 1/3/1975, Savannah, GA *Drafted:* 1998 Round 6 TB
1998 TB: 10 G.

JOHN CANNON Cannon, John Raymond 6'5", 260 **DE-NT**
Col: William & Mary *HS:* Holmdel [NJ] B: 7/30/1960, Long Branch, NJ
Drafted: 1982 Round 3 TB
1982 TB: 9 G. **1983** TB: 14 G; 5 Sac. **1984** TB: 16 G; Int 1-0; 3.5 Sac. **1985** TB: 16 G; 4.5 Sac. **1986** TB: 9 G; 2 Sac. **1987** TB: 11 G; 2 Sac. **1988** TB: 16 G; 3 Sac. **1989** TB: 16 G; 1 Sac. **1990** TB: 15 G; 1 Sac. **Total:** 122 G; Int 1-0; 22 Sac.

MARK CANNON Cannon, Mark Maida 6'3", 258 **C**
Col: Texas-Arlington *HS:* Stephen F. Austin [Austin, TX] B: 6/14/1962, Whittier, CA *Drafted:* 1984 Round 11 GB
1984 GB: 16 G. **1985** GB: 16 G. **1986** GB: 7 G. **1987** GB: 12 G; 1 Fum. **1988** GB: 16 G; 2 Fum. **1989** GB-KC: 12 G. GB: 1 G. KC: 11 G. **1991** Ind: 4 G. **Total:** 83 G; 3 Fum.

BILLY CANNON Cannon, William Abb Jr. 6'4", 231 **LB**
Col: Texas A&M *HS:* Broadmoor [Baton Rouge, LA] B: 10/8/1961, Baton Rouge, LA *Drafted:* 1984 Round 1 Dal
1984 Dal: 8 G.

BILLY CANNON Cannon, William Abb Sr. 6'1", 207 **HB-TE**
Col: Louisiana State *HS:* Istrouma [Baton Rouge, LA] B: 8/2/1937, Philadelphia, MS *Drafted:* 1960 Round 1 Hou
1960 Hou: Pass 3-0; PR 4-96 24.0. **1961** Hou: Pass 5-0, 1 Int; PR 9-70 7.8. **1962** Hou: Pass 3-2 66.7%, 46 15.33 1 TD; Scor **1** 2XP. **1963** Hou: Pass 1-0. **1966** Oak: PR 1-12 12.0. **Total:** Pass 12-2 16.7%, 46 3.83 1 TD 1 Int; PR 14-178 12.7; Scor 1 2XP.

		Rushing				Receiving			
Year Team	**G**	**Att**	**Yds**	**Avg**	**TD**	**Rec**	**Yds**	**Avg**	**TD**
1960 Hou	14	152	644	4.2	1	15	187	12.5	5
1961 Hou	14	200	**948**	**4.7**	6	43	586	13.6	9
1962 Hou	14	147	474	3.2	7	32	451	14.1	6
1963 Hou	6	13	45	3.5	0	5	39	7.8	0
1964 Oak	14	89	338	3.8	3	37	454	12.3	5
1965 Oak	10	0	0	—	0	7	127	18.1	0
1966 Oak	14	0	0	—	0	14	436	31.1	2
1967 Oak	14	0	0	—	0	32	629	19.7	10
1968 Oak	14	0	0	—	0	23	360	15.7	6
1969 Oak	13	0	0	—	0	21	262	12.5	2
1970 KC	6	1	6	6.0	0	7	125	17.9	2
NFL Total	133	602	2455	4.1	17	236	3656	15.5	47

	Kickoff Returns					Tot
Year Team	**Ret**	**Yds**	**Avg**	**TD**	**Fum**	**TD**
1960 Hou	8	266	33.3	1	3	7
1961 Hou	18	439	24.4	0	5	15
1962 Hou	18	442	24.6	0	5	13
1963 Hou	2	39	19.5	0	2	0
1964 Oak	21	518	24.7	0	5	8
1966 Oak	0	0	—	0	0	2
1967 Oak	0	0	—	0	1	10
1968 Oak	0	0	—	0	0	6
1969 Oak	0	0	—	0	0	2
1970 KC	0	0	—	0	0	2
NFL Total	67	1704	25.4	1	21	65

LEO CANTOR Cantor, Leo 6'0", 195 **DB-HB-FB**
Col: UCLA *HS:* Theodore Roosevelt [Los Angeles, CA] B: 2/28/1919, Chicago, IL D: 6/4/1995, San Fernando, CA
1942 NYG: Pass 29-12 41.4%, 155 5.34 1 TD 1 Int; PR 5-69 13.8; KR 1-24 24.0; Int 2-46; Punt 20-763 38.2. **1945** ChiC: Pass 18-3 16.7%, 116 6.44 4 Int; Rec 15-159 10.6; PR 5-59 11.8; KR 6-123 20.5; Int 5-70; Punt 5-166 33.2. **Total:** Pass 47-15 31.9%, 271 5.77 1 TD 5 Int; Rec 15-159 10.6; PR 10-128 12.8; KR 7-147 21.0; Int 7-116; Punt 25-929 37.2.

		Rushing				
Year Team	**G**	**Att**	**Yds**	**Avg**	**TD**	**Fum**
1942 NYG	10	67	124	1.9	2	0
1945 ChiC	10	83	291	3.5	5	2
NFL Total	20	150	415	2.8	7	2

CHRIS CANTY Canty, Christopher Patrick 5'9", 185 **DB**
Col: Kansas State *HS:* Eastern [Vorhees, NJ] B: 3/30/1976, Voorhees, NJ *Drafted:* 1997 Round 1 NE
1997 NE: 16 G; KR 4-115 28.8; 2 Sac. **1998** NE: 16 G; PR 16-170 10.6; KR 11-198 18.0; Int 1-12; 2 Fum; 1 Sac. **Total:** 32 G; PR 16-170 10.6; KR 15-313 20.9; Int 1-12; 2 Fum; 3 Sac.

BILL CAPECE Capece, William George 5'7", 170 **K**
Col: Florida State *HS:* Chaminade [Hollywood, FL] B: 4/1/1959, Maimi, FL *Drafted:* 1981 Round 12 Hou

		Scoring						
Year Team	**G**	**Pts**	**FG**	**FGA**	**FG%**	**XK**	**XKA**	**XK%**
1981 TB	13	75	15	24	62.5	30	32	93.8
1982 TB	9	68	18	23	78.3	14	14	100.0
1983 TB	15	53	10	23	43.5	23	26	88.5
NFL Total	37	196	43	70	61.4	67	72	93.1

JAMES CAPERS Capers, James O 6'4", 232 **LB**
Col: Central Michigan *HS:* Loy Norrix [Kalamazoo, MI] B: 6/14/1958, Kalamazoo, MI
1987 Cle: 3 G.

WAYNE CAPERS Capers, Wayne Erwin 6'2", 198 **WR**
Col: Kansas *HS:* South Miami [Miami, FL] B: 5/17/1961, Miami, FL
Drafted: 1983 Round 2 Pit
1984 Pit: Rush 1-(-3) -3.0. **1985** Ind: Rush 3-18 6.0 1 TD. **1986** Ind: Rush 1-11 11.0. **Total:** Rush 5-26 5.2 1 TD.

		Receiving				Tot
Year Team	**G**	**Rec**	**Yds**	**Avg**	**TD**	**Fum**	**TD**
1983 Pit	11	10	185	18.5	1	0	1
1984 Pit	16	7	81	11.6	0	1	0
1985 Ind	14	25	438	17.5	4	1	5
1986 Ind	6	9	118	13.1	0	0	0
NFL Total	47	51	822	16.1	5	2	6

WARREN CAPONE Capone, Warren Samuel 6'1", 218 **LB**
Col: Louisiana State *HS:* Baton Rouge Catholic [LA] B: 8/14/1951, Baton Rouge, LA
1975 Dal: 5 G. **1976** NO: 7 G; KR 2-0; **1** Fum TD; 6 Pt; 2 Fum. **Total:** 12 G; KR 2-0; 1 Fum TD; 6 Pt; 2 Fum.

DICK CAPP Capp, Richard Francis 6′4″, 240 **TE-LB**
Col: Boston College *HS:* Deering [Portland, ME] B: 4/9/1942, Portland, ME *Drafted:* 1966 Round 17 Bos
1967 GB: 2 G. **1968** Pit: 14 G. **Total:** 16 G.

BOB CAPPADONA Cappadona, Robert Joseph 6′1″, 225 **RB**
(Cappy) *Col:* Notre Dame; Northeastern *HS:* Watertown [MA] B: 12/13/1942, Watertown, MA *Drafted:* 1965 Redshirt Round 3 Bos
1966 Bos: KR 3-46 15.3; Scor **1** 2XP. **1967** Bos: Rec 6-104 17.3 1 TD; KR 3-26 8.7. **1968** Buf: Rec 18-92 5.1 2 TD; Scor **1** 2XP.
Total: Rec 24-196 8.2 3 TD; KR 6-72 12.0; Scor 2 2XP.

		Rushing					Tot
Year Team	G	Att	Yds	Avg	TD	Fum	TD
1966 Bos	14	22	88	4.0	1	0	1
1967 Bos	13	28	100	3.6	0	3	1
1968 Buf	14	73	272	3.7	1	3	3
NFL Total	41	123	460	3.7	2	6	5

GINO CAPPELLETTI Cappelletti, Gino Raymond Michael 6′0″, 190 **WR-K-DB**
Col: Minnesota *HS:* Keewatin [MN] B: 3/26/1934, Keewatin, MN
1960 Bos: PR 1-3 3.0; KR 4-100 25.0; Int 4-68; Scor **3** 2XP. **1961** Bos: Pass 1-1 100.0%, 27 27.00 1 TD. **1962** Bos: Rush 1-(-5) -5.0. **1963** Bos: Rush 1-2 2.0. **1964** Bos: Rush 1-7 7.0; Scor 1 2XP. **1968** Bos: Rush 1-2 2.0. **Total:** Pass 1-1 100.0%, 27 27.00 1 TD; Rush 4-6 1.5; PR 1-3 3.0; KR 4-100 25.0; Int 4-68; Scor 4 2XP.

		Receiving			
Year Team	G	Rec	Yds	Avg	TD
1960 Bos	14	1	28	28.0	0
1961 Bos	14	45	768	17.1	8
1962 Bos	14	34	479	14.1	5
1963 Bos	14	34	493	14.5	2
1964 Bos	14	49	865	17.7	7
1965 Bos	14	37	680	18.4	9
1966 Bos	14	43	676	15.7	6
1967 Bos	14	35	397	11.3	3
1968 Bos	14	13	182	14.0	2
1969 Bos	14	1	21	21.0	0
1970 Bos	13	0	0	—	0
NFL Total	153	292	4589	15.7	42

	Scoring							
Year Team	Pts	FG	FGA	FG%	XK	XKA	XK%	Fum
1960 Bos	60	8	21	38.1	30	32	93.8	1
1961 Bos	**147**	**17**	**32**	53.1	48	50	96.0	1
1962 Bos	128	20	37	54.1	38	40	95.0	0
1963 Bos	**113**	**22**	**38**	57.9	35	36	97.2	1
1964 Bos	**155**	**25**	**39**	64.1	36	36	100.0	0
1965 Bos	**132**	17	27	**63.0**	27	27	**100.0**	0
1966 Bos	**119**	16	32	50.0	35	36	97.2	0
1967 Bos	95	16	31	51.6	29	30	96.7	1
1968 Bos	83	15	27	55.6	26	26	100.0	0
1969 Bos	68	14	34	41.2	26	27	96.3	0
1970 Bos	30	6	15	40.0	12	13	92.3	0
NFL Total	1130	176	333	52.9	342	353	96.9	4

JOHN CAPPELLETTI Cappelletti, John Raymond 6′1″, 215 **RB**
Col: Penn State *HS:* Monsignor Bonner [Upper Darby, PA] B: 6/9/1952, Philadelphia, PA *Drafted:* 1974 Round 1 LARm
1974 LARm: KR 2-17 8.5. **1975** LARm: KR 3-39 13.0. **1980** SD: KR 1-0. **Total:** KR 6-56 9.3.

		Rushing				Receiving					Tot
Year Team	G	Att	Yds	Avg	TD	Rec	Yds	Avg	TD	Fum	TD
1974 LARm	14	55	198	3.6	0	6	35	5.8	0	2	0
1975 LARm	13	48	158	3.3	6	0	0	—	0	2	6
1976 LARm	14	177	688	3.9	1	30	302	10.1	1	3	2
1977 LARm	14	178	598	3.4	5	28	228	8.1	1	5	6
1978 LARm	14	174	604	3.5	3	41	382	9.3	1	4	4
1980 SD	10	101	364	3.6	5	13	112	8.6	0	1	5
1981 SD	16	68	254	3.7	4	10	126	12.6	1	3	5
1982 SD	9	22	82	3.7	0	7	48	6.9	0	1	0
1983 SD	1	1	5	5.0	0	0	0	—	0	0	0
NFL Total	105	824	2951	3.6	24	135	1233	9.1	4	21	28

BILL CAPPLEMAN Cappleman, George William 6′3″, 210 **QB**
Col: Florida State *HS:* Dunedin [FL] B: 3/12/1947, Brooksville, FL
Drafted: 1970 Round 2 Min
1970 Min: 1 G; Pass 7-4 57.1%, 49 7.00. **1973** Det: 7 G; Pass 11-5 45.5%, 33 3.00 1 Int; Rush 1-(-2) -2.0. **Total:** 8 G; Pass 18-9 50.0%, 82 4.56 1 Int; Rush 1-(-2) -2.0.

BILL CAPPS Capps, Thomas Willburn 6′1″, 233 **T-G**
Col: East Central (OK) *HS:* Randlett [OK]; Horace Mann HS [Ada, OK]
B: 3/27/1904, Coalville, OK D: 2/1979, Weatherford, OK
1929 Fra: 5 G. **1930** Fra-Min: 10 G. Fra: 9 G. Min: 1 G. **Total:** 15 G.

CARL CAPRIA Capria, Carl Daniel 6′3″, 185 **DB**
Col: Purdue *HS:* H. Frank Carey [Franklin Square, NY] B: 6/8/1952, Bronx, NY *Drafted:* 1974 Round 5 Det
1974 Det: 12 G; PR 1-12 12.0. **1975** NYJ: 1 G. **Total:** 13 G; PR 1-12 12.0.

RALPH CAPRON Capron, Ralph Earl 5′11″, 165 **WB**
Col: Minnesota *HS:* South [Minneapolis, MN]; Mercersburg Acad. [PA]
B: 6/16/1889, Minneapolis, MN D: 9/18/1980, Los Angeles, CA
1920 ChiT: 1 G.

JIM CAPUZZI Capuzzi, Camillo James 6′0″, 190 **DB-QB**
Col: Marquette; Cincinnati *HS:* McKinley [Niles, OH] B: 3/12/1932, Niles, OH
1955 GB: 2 G. **1956** GB: 7 G; Int 2-65. **Total:** 9 G; Int 2-65.

MAC CARA Cara, Dominic Anthony 5′10″, 193 **OE-DE**
Col: North Carolina State *HS:* Bellaire [OH] B: 11/11/1914, Reggio di Calabria, Italy D: 4/16/1993, Steubenville, OH *Drafted:* 1937 Round 10 Was
1937 Pit: 10 G; Rec 2-36 18.0. **1938** Pit: 9 G; Rush 1-(-1) -1.0; Rec 4-18 4.5. **Total:** 19 G; Rush 1-(-1) -1.0; Rec 6-54 9.0.

ROLAND CARANCI Caranci, Roland 6′1″, 227 **T**
Col: Colorado *HS:* Boulder [CO] B: 3/4/1921, Marshall, CO
1944 NYG: 2 G.

GLENN CARANO Carano, Glenn Thomas 6′3″, 201 **QB**
Col: Nevada-Las Vegas *HS:* Earl Wooster [Reno, NV] B: 11/18/1955, San Pedro, CA *Drafted:* 1977 Round 2 Dal
1980 Dal: Rush 4-6 1.5. **1981** Dal: Rush 8-9 1.1. **Total:** Rush 12-15 1.3.

		Passing								
Year Team	G	Att	Comp	Comp%	Yds	YPA	TD	Int	Rating	Fum
1978 Dal	2	0	0	—	0	—	0	0	—	0
1979 Dal	3	0	0	—	0	—	0	0	—	0
1980 Dal	3	12	5	41.7	69	5.75	2	0	100.3	0
1981 Dal	5	45	16	35.6	235	5.22	1	1	51.6	3
1982 Dal	7	0	0	—	0	—	0	0	—	0
1983 Dal	16	0	0	—	0	—	0	0	—	0
NFL Total	36	57	21	36.8	304	5.33	3	1	65.2	3

AL CARAPELLA Carapella, Alfred Richard 6′0″, 235 **DT-OT-LB**
(Big Al) *Col:* Miami (Fla.) *HS:* Tuckahoe [NY] B: 4/26/1927, Tuckahoe, NY
1951 SF: 12 G; Int 1-11. **1952** SF: 12 G. **1953** SF: 12 G. **1954** SF: 12 G; Int 2-40. **1955** SF: 12 G; PR 1-0. **Total:** 60 G; PR 1-0; Int 3-51.

JOE CARAVELLO Caravello, Joseph John 6′3″, 270 **TE**
Col: El Camino Coll. CA (J.C.); Tulane *HS:* El Segundo [CA]
B: 6/6/1963, Santa Monica, CA
1987 Was: 11 G; Rec 2-29 14.5. **1988** Was: 12 G; Rec 2-15 7.5. **1989** SD: 12 G; Rush 1-0; Rec 10-95 9.5. **1990** SD: 7 G; Rec 2-21 10.5 1 TD; 6 Pt.
Total: 42 G; Rush 1-0; Rec 16-160 10.0 1 TD; 6 Pt.

GLEN CARBERRY Carberry, Glen Michael 6′0″, 190 **E**
(Judge) *Col:* Army; Notre Dame *HS:* St.Ignatius [Chicago, IL]
B: 4/10/1896, Ames, IA D: 2/19/1976, Bronx, NY
1923 Buf: 10 G. **1924** Buf: 2 G. **1925** Cle: 1 G. **Total:** 13 G.

HARPER CARD Card, J. Harper 6′1″, 183 **T**
Col: No College *HS:* Male [Louisville, KY] B: 1903 Deceased
1921 Lou: 1 G. **1922** Lou: 4 G. **Total:** 5 G.

CARL CARDARELLI Cardarelli, Carl 1 **C**
(Squash) *Col:* No College *HS:* Central [Akron, OH] B: 9/1896, Akron, OH Deceased
1924 Akr: 2 G. **1925** Cle: 1 G. **Total:** 3 G.

FRED CARDINAL Cardinal, Frederick 5′11″, 220 **LB**
(Tank; Blitz) *Col:* Notre Dame; Baldwin-Wallace *HS:* Washington [Massillon, OH] B: 2/12/1925, Dover, OH
AAFC **1947** NY-A: 1 G.

JOHN CARDWELL Cardwell, John R 5′9″, 170 **HB**
Col: No College B: 7/28/1893 D: 5/13/1974, Wilmington, DE
1923 StL: 2 G.

JOE CARDWELL Cardwell, Joseph Thomas 6′3″, 235 **T-DE**
Col: Duke *HS:* Great Bridge [Chesapeake, VA] B: 1/31/1912, Montgomery, AL D: 7/6/1957, Norfolk, VA
1937 Pit: 7 G. **1938** Pit: 11 G. **Total:** 18 G.

LLOYD CARDWELL Cardwell, Lloyd Raymond 6′2″, 195 **WB-DB-FB**
(Wild Hoss) *Col:* Nebraska *HS:* Seward [NE] B: 4/19/1913, Republic, KS D: 11/9/1997, Omaha, NE *Drafted:* 1937 Round 1 Det
1938 Det: Pass 1-1 100.0%, 35 35.00. **1940** Det: Pass 1-0; Int 4-17.
1941 Det: PR 3-25 8.3; KR 1-22 22.0. **1942** Det: PR 2-45 22.5; KR 1-13 13.0; Int 2-40. **1943** Det: PR 2-21 10.5; KR 3-56 18.7. **Total:** Pass 2-1 50.0%, 35 17.50; PR 7-91 13.0; KR 5-91 18.2; Int 6-57.

		Rushing				Receiving				Tot
Year Team	G	Att	Yds	Avg	TD	Rec	Yds	Avg	TD	TD
1937 Det	9	36	181	5.0	0	3	51	17.0	1	1

1938 Det	10	73	294	4.0	4	9	138	15.3	1	5
1939 Det	10	29	141	4.9	1	13	250	19.2	2	3
1940 Det	10	48	186	3.9	2	20	349	17.5	1	3
1941 Det	4	10	19	1.9	0	0	0	—	0	0
1942 Det	7	6	78	13.0	1	5	135	27.0	0	1
1943 Det	7	3	6	2.0	0	1	9	9.0	0	0
NFL Total	57	205	905	4.4	8	51	932	18.3	5	13

BRIAN CAREY Carey, Brian Richard 6′0″, 200 **WR**
Col: American International *HS:* Gloucester [MA] B: 11/6/1963, Woburn, MA
1987 NE: 2 G.

JOE CAREY Carey, Joseph 6′2″, 195 **G-T**
Col: Illinois Tech *HS:* Lake View [Chicago, IL] B: 11/14/1895, Chicago, IL D: 7/22/1962
1920 ChiC: 7 G. **1921** GB: 6 G. **Total:** 13 G.

RICHARD CAREY Carey, Richard Andre 5′9″, 185 **DB**
Col: Idaho *HS:* James A. Garfield [Seattle, WA] B: 5/6/1968, Seattle, WA
1989 Cin: 7 G; PR 3-29 9.7; KR 6-104 17.3; Int 1-5; 1 Fum. **1990** Buf: 3 G. **Total:** 10 G; PR 3-29 9.7; KR 6-104 17.3; Int 1-5; 1 Fum.

BOB CAREY Carey, Robert Winfield 6′5″, 219 **OE**
Col: Michigan State *HS:* Charlevoix [MI] B: 2/8/1930, Charlevoix, MI D: 10/25/1988, Cincinnati, OH *Drafted:* 1952 Round 1 LARm
1952 LARm: Scor 12, 0-1 FG; 1 Fum TD. **1954** LARm: Scor 5, 1-1 100.0% FG, 2-2 100.0% XK. **Total:** Scor 23, 1-2 50.0% FG, 2-2 100.0% XK; 1 Fum TD.

		Receiving					Tot
Year Team	G	Rec	Yds	Avg	TD	Fum	TD
1952 LARm	12	36	539	15.0	1	1	2
1954 LARm	2	5	49	9.8	0	0	0
1956 LARm	7	5	60	12.0	1	0	1
1958 ChiB	11	1	15	15.0	0	0	0
NFL Total	32	47	663	14.1	2	1	3

HARLAND CARL Carl, Harland Irvin 6′0″, 195 **HB**
Col: Wisconsin *HS:* Greenwood [WI] B: 10/1/1931, Greenwood, WI *Drafted:* 1953 Round 14 ChiB
1956 ChiB: Rec 2-31 15.5; KR 4-102 25.5.

		Rushing				
Year Team	G	Att	Yds	Avg	TD	Fum
1956 ChiB	9	29	66	2.3	1	1

DEAN CARLSON Carlson, Dean Paul 6′3″, 210 **QB**
Col: Iowa State *HS:* Rushford [MN] B: 8/1/1950, Rushford, MN *Drafted:* 1972 Round 7 KC
1974 KC: 1 G; Pass 15-7 46.7%, 116 7.73 1 Int; Rush 2-17 8.5.

OKE CARLSON Carlson, Eugene 6′0″, 206 **T-G-C**
Col: No College *HS:* Two Harbors [MN]
1924 Dul: 4 G. **1925** Dul: 3 G. **1926** Dul: 11 G. **Total:** 18 G.

HAL CARLSON Carlson, Harold Erwin 6′3″, 220 **G**
Col: Northwestern; DePaul *HS:* Bowen [Chicago, IL] B: 1/22/1915, Chicago, IL D: 6/6/1981, Scottsdale, AZ
1937 ChiC: 1 G.

IRV CARLSON Carlson, Irvin G 5′8″, 170 **WB-TB**
Col: St. John's (Minn.); Wisconsin B: 8/1896, St. Cloud, MN Deceased
1924 Ken: 2 G.

JEFF CARLSON Carlson, Jeffrey Allen 6′3″, 215 **QB**
Col: Weber State *HS:* Pacifica [Garden Grove, CA] B: 5/23/1966, Long Beach, CA *Drafted:* 1989 Round 4 LARm
1990 TB: Rush 1-0. **1991** TB: Rush 5-25 5.0. **1992** NE: Rush 11-32 2.9. **Total:** Rush 17-57 3.4.

		Passing								
Year Team	G	Att	Comp	Comp%	Yds	YPA	TD	Int	Rating	Fum
1990 TB	1	0	0	—	0	—	0	0	—	1
1991 TB	3	65	31	47.7	404	6.22	1	6	34.4	2
1992 NE	3	49	18	36.7	232	4.73	1	3	33.7	2
NFL Total	7	114	49	43.0	636	5.58	2	9	34.1	5

ZUCK CARLSON Carlson, Jules Ed 6′0″, 208 **G-T-C-LB**
Col: Oregon State *HS:* The Dalles [OR] B: 11/12/1904, Isaca, ID D: 1/21/1986, Chicago, IL
1929 ChiB: 14 G. **1930** ChiB: 13 G. **1931** ChiB: 11 G. **1932** ChiB: 13 G. **1933** ChiB: 11 G. **1934** ChiB: 12 G. **1935** ChiB: 12 G. **1936** ChiB: 9 G. **Total:** 95 G.

MARK CARLSON Carlson, Mark 6′6″, 284 **OT**
Col: Southern Connecticut State *HS:* The Morgan School [Clinton, CT] B: 6/6/1963, Milford, CT
1987 Was: 3 G.

CODY CARLSON Carlson, Matthew Cody 6′3″, 202 **QB**
(Commander) *Col:* Baylor *HS:* Winston Churchill [San Antonio, TX] B: 11/5/1963, Dallas, TX *Drafted:* 1987 Round 3 Hou

		Passing							
Year Team	G	Att	Comp	Comp%	Yds	YPA	TD	Int	Rating
1988 Hou	6	112	52	46.4	775	6.92	4	6	59.2
1989 Hou	6	31	15	48.4	155	5.00	0	1	49.8
1990 Hou	6	55	37	67.3	383	6.96	4	2	96.3
1991 Hou	3	12	7	58.3	114	9.50	1	0	118.1
1992 Hou	11	227	149	65.6	1710	7.53	9	11	81.2
1993 Hou	8	90	51	56.7	605	6.72	2	4	66.2
1994 Hou	5	132	59	44.7	727	5.51	1	4	52.2
NFL Total	45	659	370	56.1	4469	6.78	21	28	70.0

	Rushing				
Year Team	Att	Yds	Avg	TD	Fum
1988 Hou	12	36	3.0	1	5
1989 Hou	3	-3	-1.0	0	1
1990 Hou	11	52	4.7	0	0
1991 Hou	4	-3	-0.8	0	1
1992 Hou	27	77	2.9	1	8
1993 Hou	14	41	2.9	2	3
1994 Hou	10	17	1.7	0	6
NFL Total	81	217	2.7	4	24

ROY CARLSON Carlson, Roy Harold 5′9″, 178 **E-G**
Col: Bradley B: 5/8/1906, Chicago, IL D: 9/10/1984, Phoenix, AZ
1928 ChiB: 10 G; Rec 1 TD; 6 Pt. **1929** Day: 6 G. **Total:** 16 G; Rec 1 TD; 6 Pt.

WES CARLSON Carlson, Wesley C 6′1″, 210 **G-T**
Col: Detroit Mercy B: MI Deceased
1926 GB: 4 G.

DARRYL CARLTON Carlton, Darryl Marvin 6′6″, 271 **OT**
Col: Tampa *HS:* Fort Meade [FL] B: 6/24/1953, Bartow, FL *Drafted:* 1975 Round 1 Mia
1975 Mia: 14 G. **1976** Mia: 14 G. **1977** TB: 14 G. **1978** TB: 13 G. **1979** TB: 16 G. **Total:** 71 G.

WRAY CARLTON Carlton, Linwood Wray 6′2″, 225 **HB-FB**
Col: Duke *HS:* Wallace [NC] B: 6/18/1937, Wallace, NC *Drafted:* 1959 Round 3 Phi
1961 Buf: Pass 2-0; KR 4-60 15.0. **Total:** Pass 2-0; KR 4-60 15.0.

		Rushing				Receiving					Tot
Year Team	G	Att	Yds	Avg	TD	Rec	Yds	Avg	TD	Fum	TD
1960 Buf	14	137	533	3.9	7	29	477	16.4	4	7	11
1961 Buf	14	101	311	3.1	4	17	193	11.4	0	5	4
1962 Buf	11	94	530	5.6	2	7	54	7.7	0	5	2
1963 Buf	4	29	125	4.3	0	1	9	9.0	0	1	0
1964 Buf	4	39	114	2.9	1	2	23	11.5	0	2	1
1965 Buf	14	156	592	3.8	**6**	24	196	8.2	1	2	7
1966 Buf	14	156	696	4.5	6	21	280	13.3	0	4	6
1967 Buf	12	107	467	4.4	3	9	97	10.8	0	3	3
NFL Total	87	819	3368	4.1	29	110	1329	12.1	5	29	34

ED CARMAN Carman, Edmund Ralph 5′11″, 199 **T-E**
(Zeb) *Col:* Purdue B: 1/21/1894, Joliet, IL D: 4/9/1964, West Lafayette, IN
1922 Ham: 6 G. **1925** Buf-Ham: 6 G; Scor 1, 1 XK. Buf: 1 G. Ham: 5 G; Scor 1, 1 XK. **Total:** 12 G.

CHARLIE CARMAN Carman, William Charlies 5′10″, 215 **G**
(Chili) *Col:* Vanderbilt *HS:* Marvin University [Clinton, KY] B: 1/6/1897 D: 11/1975, McAllen, TX
1920 Det: 1 G. **1921** Det: 6 G. **Total:** 7 G.

AL CARMICHAEL Carmichael, Albert Rienhold 6′1″, 200 **HB**
(Hoagy) *Col:* Rancho Santiago Coll. CA (J.C.); USC *HS:* Gardena [CA] B: 11/10/1928, Boston, MA *Drafted:* 1953 Round 1 GB
1960 Den: Pass 1-1 100.0%, 26 26.00. **Total:** Pass 1-1 100.0%, 26 26.00.

		Rushing				Receiving			
Year Team	G	Att	Yds	Avg	TD	Rec	Yds	Avg	TD
1953 GB	12	49	199	4.1	1	12	131	10.9	0
1954 GB	10	33	130	3.9	0	18	251	13.9	0
1955 GB	10	6	45	7.5	0	16	222	13.9	1
1956 GB	12	32	199	6.2	0	13	180	13.8	1
1957 GB	12	37	118	3.2	1	13	184	14.2	0
1958 GB	12	9	21	2.3	0	3	26	8.7	1
1960 Den	10	41	211	5.1	2	32	616	19.3	5
1961 Den	6	15	24	1.6	0	5	23	4.6	0
NFL Total	84	222	947	4.3	4	112	1633	14.6	8

	Punt Returns				Kickoff Returns					Tot
Year Team	Ret	Yds	Avg	TD	Ret	Yds	Avg	TD	Fum	TD
1953 GB	20	199	10.0	0	26	641	24.7	0	3	1

1954 GB	9	43	4.8	0	20	531	26.6	0	2	0
1955 GB	10	89	8.9	0	14	418	**29.9**	**1**	0	2
1956 GB	21	165	7.9	0	**33**	**927**	28.1	**1**	6	2
1957 GB	25	190	7.6	0	**31**	**690**	22.3	0	3	1
1958 GB	15	67	4.5	0	29	700	24.1	0	2	1
1960 Den	**15**	101	6.7	0	22	581	26.4	0	3	7
1961 Den	7	58	8.3	0	16	310	19.4	0	4	0
NFL Total	122	912	7.5	0	191	4798	25.1	2	23	14

HAROLD CARMICHAEL Carmichael, Lee Harold 6′8″, 225 **WR**
Col: Southern University *HS:* William M. Raines [Jacksonville, FL]
B: 9/22/1949, Jacksonville, FL *Drafted:* 1971 Round 7 Phi
1973 Phi: Rush 3-42 14.0. **1974** Phi: Pass 1-0; Rush 2-(-6) -3.0. **1975** Phi: Rush 1-6 6.0. **1976** Phi: Pass 2-0. **1978** Phi: Rush 1-21 21.0. **1979** Phi: Rush 1-0. **1981** Phi: Rush 1-1 1.0. **1983** Phi: Pass 1-1 100.0%, 45 45.00 1 TD. **Total:** Pass 4-1 25.0%, 45 11.25 1 TD; Rush 9-64 7.1.

		Receiving				
Year Team	G	Rec	Yds	Avg	TD	Fum
1971 Phi	9	20	288	14.4	0	2
1972 Phi	13	20	276	13.8	2	1
1973 Phi	14	**67**	**1116**	16.7	9	3
1974 Phi	14	56	649	11.6	8	1
1975 Phi	14	49	639	13.0	7	2
1976 Phi	14	42	503	12.0	5	0
1977 Phi	14	46	665	14.5	7	0
1978 Phi	16	55	1072	19.5	8	1
1979 Phi	16	52	872	16.8	11	0
1980 Phi	16	48	815	17.0	9	1
1981 Phi	16	61	1028	16.9	6	3
1982 Phi	9	35	540	15.4	4	3
1983 Phi	15	38	515	13.6	3	0
1984 Dal	2	1	7	7.0	0	0
NFL Total	182	590	8985	15.2	79	17

PAUL CARMICHAEL Carmichael, Paul Harold 6′0″, 200 **HB**
Col: El Camino Coll. CA (J.C.) *HS:* Inglewood [CA] B: 8/28/1944, Inglewood, CA
1965 Den: 3 G; KR 1-15 15.0.

RAY CARNELLY Carnelly, Raymond Harry 6′2″, 187 **TB-HB-DB-QB**
Col: Carnegie Mellon *HS:* Beaver Falls [PA] B: 8/11/1916, Beaver Falls, PA *Drafted:* 1939 Round 14 Bkn
1939 Bkn: 9 G; Pass 14-3 21.4%, 35 2.50 3 Int; Rush 15-64 4.3; Rec 1-5 5.0; Scor 0-1 FG.

ART CARNEY Carney, Arthur Gerald 6′2″, 230 **G-E**
Col: Navy *HS:* Alexander Hamilton [Brooklyn, NY] B: 9/23/1900, New York, NY D: 3/24/1962, Bronxville, NY
1925 NYG: 9 G. **1926** NYG: 8 G. **Total:** 17 G.

CHUCK CARNEY Carney, Charles Roslyn 6′1″, 190 **T-G**
Col: Illinois *HS:* Evanston Twp. [Evanston, IL] B: 8/25/1900, Chicago, IL D: 9/5/1984, Manchester, MA
1922 Col: 3 G.

JOHN CARNEY Carney, John Michael 5′11″, 170 **K**
Col: Notre Dame *HS:* Cardinal Newman [West Palm Beach, FL]
B: 4/20/1964, Hartford, CT
1993 SD: Punt 4-155 38.8. **Total:** Punt 4-155 38.8.

		Scoring						
Year Team	G	Pts	FG	FGA	FG%	XK	XKA	XK%
1988 TB	4	12	2	5	40.0	6	6	100.0
1989 TB	1	0	0	0	—	0	0	—
1990 LARm-SD	13	84	19	21	90.5	27	28	96.4
1990 LARm	1	0	0	0	—	0	0	—
1990 SD	12	84	19	21	90.5	27	28	96.4
1991 SD	16	88	19	29	65.5	31	31	100.0
1992 SD	16	113	26	32	81.3	35	35	100.0
1993 SD	16	124	31	40	77.5	31	33	93.9
1994 SD	16	**135**	**34**	38	89.5	33	33	100.0
1995 SD	16	95	21	26	80.8	32	33	97.0
1996 SD	16	118	29	36	80.6	31	31	100.0
1997 SD	4	26	7	7	100.0	5	5	100.0
1998 SD	16	97	26	30	86.7	19	19	100.0
NFL Total	134	892	214	264	81.1	250	254	98.4

BRETT CAROLAN Carolan, Brett H 6′3″, 241 **TE**
Col: Washington State *HS:* San Marin [Novato, CA] B: 3/16/1971, San Rafael, CA
1994 SF: 4 G; Rec 2-10 5.0. **1995** SF: 14 G; Rec 1-3 3.0. **1996** Mia: 6 G; Rec 4-48 12.0 1 TD; 6 Pt. **Total:** 24 G; Rec 7-61 8.7 1 TD; 6 Pt.

REGGIE CAROLAN Carolan, Reginald Howard 6′6″, 236 **TE**
Col: Idaho *HS:* Sir Francis Drake [San Anselmo, CA] B: 10/25/1939, San Rafael, CA D: 1/2/1983, San Rafael, CA *Drafted:* 1961 Round 17 SD
1962 SD: 14 G; Rec 3-39 13.0 1 TD; 6 Pt. **1963** SD: 4 G. **1964** KC: 6 G; Rec 3-54 18.0 1 TD; 6 Pt. **1965** KC: 14 G; Rec 6-65 10.8; Scor 1 2XP; 2 Pt. **1966** KC: 14 G; Rec 7-154 22.0 3 TD; 18 Pt. **1967** KC: 14 G; Rec 2-26 13.0; KR 1-2 2.0; Punt 1-42 42.0; Scor 1 2XP; 2 Pt. **1968** KC: 14 G; Rec 2-26 13.0; Punt 2-101 50.5. **Total:** 80 G; Rec 23-364 15.8 5 TD; KR 1-2 2.0; Punt 3-143 47.7; Scor 2 2XP; 34 Pt.

JAMES CAROLINE Caroline, James C 6′0″, 185 **DB-HB**
(J.C.) *Col:* Illinois *HS:* Booker T. Washington [Columbia, SC]
B: 1/17/1933, Warrenton, GA *Drafted:* 1956 Round 7 ChiB
1956 ChiB: PR 2-29 14.5; KR 2-32 16.0. **1957** ChiB: Rec 1-33 33.0; PR 6-20 3.3; KR 4-77 19.3. **1958** ChiB: Rec 5-78 15.6 1 TD; KR 6-123 20.5. **1960** ChiB: **1** Fum TD. **Total:** Rec 6-111 18.5 1 TD; PR 8-49 6.1; KR 12-232 19.3; 1 Fum TD.

		Rushing				Interceptions				Tot
Year Team	G	Att	Yds	Avg	TD	Int	Yds	TD	Fum	TD
1956 ChiB	12	34	141	4.1	2	6	182	**2**	0	4
1957 ChiB	12	1	1	1.0	0	2	22	0	0	0
1958 ChiB	12	33	121	3.7	0	0	0	0	3	1
1959 ChiB	12	0	0	—	0	5	14	0	1	0
1960 ChiB	12	0	0	—	0	3	31	0	0	1
1961 ChiB	14	0	0	—	0	3	48	0	0	0
1962 ChiB	14	0	0	—	0	2	21	0	0	0
1963 ChiB	14	0	0	—	0	1	3	0	0	0
1964 ChiB	14	0	0	—	0	2	84	0	0	0
1965 ChiB	2	0	0	—	0	0	0	0	0	0
NFL Total	118	68	263	3.9	2	24	405	2	4	6

JOE CAROLLO Carollo, Joseph Paul 6′2″, 265 **OT**
Col: Notre Dame *HS:* Roosevelt [Wyandotte, MI] B: 3/25/1940, Wyandotte, MI *Drafted:* 1962 Round 2 LARm
1962 LARm: 13 G. **1963** LARm: 14 G. **1964** LARm: 14 G. **1965** LARm: 14 G. **1966** LARm: 14 G. **1967** LARm: 14 G. **1968** LARm: 14 G. **1969** Phi: 14 G. **1970** Phi: 14 G. **1971** LARm: 11 G. **1972** Cle: 2 G. **1973** Cle: 12 G. **Total:** 150 G.

ROGER CARON Caron, Roger Eugene 6′5″, 282 **OT**
Col: Harvard *HS:* Norwell [MA] B: 6/3/1962, Boston, MA
Drafted: 1985 Round 5 Ind
1985 Ind: 7 G. **1986** Ind: 3 G. **Total:** 10 G.

DON CAROTHERS Carothers, Donald E 6′5″, 225 **OE**
Col: Bradley *HS:* Moline [IL] B: 5/13/1934, Moline, IL *Drafted:* 1957 Round 10 ChiC
1960 Den: 3 G; Rec 2-25 12.5.

JOE CARPE Carpe, Joseph A 6′0″, **T-OE-C**
Col: Millikin *HS:* Westville [IL] B: 1/23/1903, Westville, IL
D: 11/3/1977, Quincy, MA
1926 Fra: 6 G. **1927** Pott: 4 G. **1928** Pott: 9 G. **1929** Bost: 6 G. **1933** Phi: 2 G. **Total:** 27 G.

BRIAN CARPENTER Carpenter, Brian Milton 5′10″, 167 **DB**
Col: Michigan *HS:* Southwestern [Flint, MI] B: 11/27/1960, Flint, MI
Drafted: 1982 Round 4 Dal
1982 NYG: 4 G. **1983** Was: 15 G; Int 1-2. **1984** Was-Buf: 16 G; Int 3-11. Was: 3 G. Buf: 13 G; Int 3-11. **Total:** 35 G; Int 4-13.

JACK CARPENTER Carpenter, Jack Chrisman 6′0″, 240 **T**
Col: Missouri; Michigan *HS:* Northeast [Kansas City, MO]
B: 7/29/1923
AAFC **1947** BufA: 13 G. **1948** BufA: 12 G. **1949** BufA-SF-A: 11 G; Rec 2-20 10.0. **Total:** 36 G; Rec 2-20 10.0.

KEN CARPENTER Carpenter, Kenneth Leroy 6′0″, 195 **HB-OE**
Col: Oregon State *HS:* Seaside [OR] B: 2/26/1926, Seaside, OR
Drafted: 1950 Round 1 Cle
1950 Cle: Pass 1-0, 1 Int. **Total:** Pass 1-0, 1 Int.

		Rushing				Receiving			
Year Team	G	Att	Yds	Avg	TD	Rec	Yds	Avg	TD
1950 Cle	12	35	181	5.2	1	5	45	9.0	0
1951 Cle	11	85	402	4.7	4	12	183	15.3	2
1952 Cle	8	72	408	5.7	3	16	136	8.5	1
1953 Cle	12	46	195	4.2	3	9	109	12.1	2
1960 Den	6	4	13	3.3	0	29	350	12.1	1
NFL Total	49	242	1199	5.0	11	71	823	11.6	6

	Punt Returns				Kickoff Returns					Tot
Year Team	Ret	Yds	Avg	TD	Ret	Yds	Avg	TD	Fum	TD
1950 Cle	4	58	14.5	0	5	98	19.6	0	4	1
1951 Cle	14	173	12.4	0	9	196	21.8	0	2	6
1952 Cle	10	139	13.9	1	11	234	21.3	0	5	5
1953 Cle	6	0	0.0	0	16	367	22.9	0	2	5
1960 Den	0	0	—	0	0	0	—	0	0	1
NFL Total	34	370	10.9	1	41	895	21.8	0	13	18

LEW CARPENTER Carpenter, Lewis Glenn 6′1″, 220 **HB-FB-FL-OE**
Col: Arkansas *HS:* West Memphis [AR] B: 1/12/1932, Hayti, MO
Drafted: 1953 Round 8 Det
1953 Det: Int 1-73 **1** TD. **Total:** Int 1-73 1 TD.

Year Team	G	Rushing Att	Yds	Avg	TD	Receiving Rec	Yds	Avg	TD
1953 Det	12	7	24	3.4	0	0	0	—	0
1954 Det	11	104	476	4.6	3	16	145	9.1	2
1955 Det	12	137	543	4.0	6	44	312	7.1	2
1957 Cle	10	83	315	3.8	4	5	65	13.0	0
1958 Cle	12	73	308	4.2	2	5	47	9.4	0
1959 GB	12	60	322	5.4	1	5	47	9.4	0
1960 GB	12	1	24	24.0	0	1	21	21.0	0
1961 GB	14	1	5	5.0	0	3	29	9.7	0
1962 GB	14	0	0	—	0	7	104	14.9	0
1963 GB	14	2	8	4.0	0	1	12	12.0	0
NFL Total	123	468	2025	4.3	16	87	782	9.0	4

Year Team	Punt Returns Ret	Yds	Avg	TD	Kickoff Returns Ret	Yds	Avg	TD	Fum	Tot TD
1953 Det	0	0	—	0	8	172	21.5	0	1	1
1954 Det	0	0	—	0	2	46	23.0	0	1	5
1955 Det	0	0	—	0	4	78	19.5	0	6	8
1957 Cle	0	0	—	0	1	24	24.0	0	3	4
1958 Cle	0	0	—	0	1	18	18.0	0	3	2
1959 GB	13	150	11.5	0	1	24	24.0	0	3	1
1960 GB	9	59	6.6	0	12	249	20.8	0	4	0
1961 GB	6	130	21.7	0	0	0	—	0	0	0
1963 GB	0	0	—	0	5	75	15.0	0	1	0
NFL Total	28	339	12.1	0	34	686	20.2	0	22	21

ROB CARPENTER Carpenter, Robert Gordon 6′2″, 215 **WR**
Col: Notre Dame; Syracuse *HS:* Amityville Memorial [NY] B: 8/1/1968, Amityville, NY *Drafted:* 1991 Round 4 Cin
1992 NYJ: Pass 1-0; Rush 1-2 2.0. **Total:** Pass 1-0; Rush 1-2 2.0.

Year Team	G	Receiving Rec	Yds	Avg	TD	Punt Returns Ret	Yds	Avg	TD	Fum
1991 NE	9	3	45	15.0	0	0	0	—	0	0
1992 NYJ	16	13	161	12.4	1	28	208	7.4	0	3
1993 NYJ	16	6	83	13.8	0	0	0	—	0	0
1994 NYJ	3	0	0	—	0	0	0	—	0	0
1995 Phi	16	29	318	11.0	0	12	79	6.6	0	2
NFL Total	60	51	607	11.9	1	40	287	7.2	0	5

ROB CARPENTER Carpenter, Robert Joseph Jr. 6′1″, 224 **RB**
Col: Miami (Ohio) *HS:* Lancaster [OH] B: 4/20/1955, Lancaster, OH
Drafted: 1977 Round 3 Hou
1978 Hou: KR 1-11 11.0. **1979** Hou: KR 2-34 17.0. **1980** Hou: KR 1-7 7.0. **1986** LARm: KR 2-19 9.5. **Total:** KR 6-71 11.8.

Year Team	G	Rushing Att	Yds	Avg	TD	Receiving Rec	Yds	Avg	TD	Fum	Tot TD
1977 Hou	11	144	652	4.5	1	23	156	6.8	0	3	1
1978 Hou	11	82	348	4.2	5	17	150	8.8	0	0	5
1979 Hou	16	92	355	3.9	3	16	116	7.3	1	3	4
1980 Hou	15	97	359	3.7	3	43	346	8.0	0	4	3
1981 Hou-NYG	14	208	822	4.0	5	37	281	7.6	1	3	6
1981 Hou	4	18	74	4.1	0	13	80	6.2	1	1	1
1981 NYG	10	190	748	3.9	5	24	201	8.4	0	2	5
1982 NYG	5	67	204	3.0	1	7	29	4.1	0	0	1
1983 NYG	10	170	624	3.7	4	26	258	9.9	2	2	6
1984 NYG	16	250	795	3.2	7	26	209	8.0	1	2	8
1985 NYG	14	60	201	3.4	0	20	162	8.1	0	0	0
1986 LARm	6	2	3	1.5	0	0	0	—	0	0	0
NFL Total	118	1172	4363	3.7	29	215	1707	7.9	5	17	34

RON CARPENTER Carpenter, Ronald Allen 6′1″, 189 **DB**
Col: Miami (Ohio) *HS:* Princeton [Cincinatti, OH] B: 1/20/1970, Cincinnati, OH

Year Team	G	Kickoff Returns Ret	Yds	Avg	TD	Fum
1993 Min-Cin	13	0	0	—	0	0
1993 Min	7	0	0	—	0	0
1993 Cin	6	0	0	—	0	0
1995 NYJ	13	20	553	**27.7**	0	2
1996 NYJ	2	6	107	17.8	0	0
1998 StL	6	0	0	—	0	0
NFL Total	34	26	660	25.4	0	2

RON CARPENTER Carpenter, Ronald Nelson 6′4″, 261 **DT-DE**
Col: North Carolina State *HS:* Thomasville [NC] B: 6/24/1948, High Point, NC *Drafted:* 1970 Round 2 Cin
1970 Cin: 14 G. **1971** Cin: 14 G. **1972** Cin: 14 G. **1973** Cin: 13 G. **1974** Cin: 14 G; Scor **1** Saf; 2 Pt. **1975** Cin: 14 G. **1976** Cin: 14 G. **Total:** 97 G; Scor 1 Saf; 2 Pt.

RON CARPENTER Carpenter, Ronnie Dean 6′2″, 230 **LB**
Col: Texas A&M *HS:* Marshall [TX] B: 9/2/1941, Marshall, TX
Drafted: 1964 Round 12 SD
1964 SD: 12 G; KR 1-15 15.0; Int 1-29. **1965** SD: 6 G. **Total:** 18 G; KR 1-15 15.0; Int 1-29.

STEVE CARPENTER Carpenter, Steven 6′2″, 195 **DB**
Col: Western Illinois *HS:* Edwardsville [IL] B: 1/22/1958, Staunton, IL
1980 NYJ: 3 G. **1981** StL: 1 G. **Total:** 4 G.

PRESTON CARPENTER Carpenter, Verda Preston 6′2″, 190 **OE-HB**
Col: Arkansas *HS:* West Memphis [AR] B: 1/24/1934, Hayti, MO
Drafted: 1956 Round 1 Cle
1960 Pit: Pass 2-1 50.0%, 2 1.00. **1964** Was: Pass 1-0. **Total:** Pass 3-1 33.3%, 2 0.67.

Year Team	G	Rushing Att	Yds	Avg	TD	Receiving Rec	Yds	Avg	TD
1956 Cle	12	188	756	4.0	0	16	124	7.8	0
1957 Cle	12	3	86	28.7	1	27	398	14.7	2
1958 Cle	12	3	2	0.7	0	29	474	16.3	1
1959 Cle	12	1	4	4.0	0	24	372	15.5	2
1960 Pit	12	17	36	2.1	0	29	495	17.1	2
1961 Pit	13	7	9	1.3	0	33	460	13.9	4
1962 Pit	13	1	-3	-3.0	0	36	492	13.7	4
1963 Pit	14	1	-3	-3.0	0	17	233	13.7	1
1964 Was	14	1	7	7.0	0	31	466	15.0	3
1965 Was	9	0	0	—	0	23	298	13.0	0
1966 Was-Min	13	1	-10	-10.0	0	30	518	17.3	4
1966 Was	1	0	0	—	0	3	31	10.3	0
1966 Min	12	1	-10	-10.0	0	27	487	18.0	4
1967 Mia	13	0	0	—	0	10	127	12.7	0
NFL Total	149	223	884	4.0	1	305	4457	14.6	23

Year Team	Punt Returns Ret	Yds	Avg	TD	Kickoff Returns Ret	Yds	Avg	TD	Fum	Tot TD
1956 Cle	1	18	18.0	0	15	381	25.4	0	5	0
1957 Cle	0	0	—	0	0	0	—	0	2	3
1958 Cle	0	0	—	0	0	0	—	0	0	1
1959 Cle	0	0	—	0	0	0	—	0	0	2
1960 Pit	13	120	9.2	0	10	255	25.5	0	2	2
1961 Pit	3	18	6.0	0	0	0	—	0	1	4
1962 Pit	7	109	15.6	0	1	29	29.0	0	0	4
1963 Pit	0	0	—	0	0	0	—	0	0	1
1964 Was	2	19	9.5	0	0	0	—	0	1	3
1966 Was-Min	0	0	—	0	0	0	—	0	0	4
1966 Min	0	0	—	0	0	0	—	0	0	4
1967 Mia	0	0	—	0	3	87	29.0	0	1	0
NFL Total	26	284	10.9	0	29	752	25.9	0	12	24

CARL CARR Carr, Carl Edward 6′3″, 230 **LB**
Col: North Carolina *HS:* T.C. Williams [Alexandria, VA] B: 3/26/1964, South Boston, VA *Drafted:* 1986 Round 10 NYJ
1987 Det: 3 G; 2 Sac.

CHETTI CARR Carr, Chester L 5′9″, 185 **DB**
Col: Central Oklahoma; Northwestern Okla. State *HS:* Enid [OK]
B: 1/1/1963, Enid, OK
1987 LARd: 2 G.

CHARLEY CARR Carr, Clytus Henry 5′10″, 175 **WB-BB**
Col: Western Michigan *HS:* Otsego [MI] B: 1/21/1904, Otsego, MI
D: 11/1/1976, Marshall, MI
1926 Ham: 2 G.

EARL CARR Carr, Earl 6′0″, 224 **RB**
Col: Florida *HS:* Oak Ridge [Orlando, FL] B: 1/22/1955, Tallahassee, FL *Drafted:* 1978 Round 5 StL
1978 SF: 14 G; Rush 1-2 2.0. **1979** Phi: 1 G; Rush 1-(-1) -1.0; Rec 1-2 2.0. **Total:** 15 G; Rush 2-1 0.5; Rec 1-2 2.0.

EDDIE CARR Carr, Edwin Forrest 6′0″, 185 **DB-HB**
Col: No College *HS:* Olney [Philadelphia, PA]; Valley Forge Mil. Acad. [Wayne, PA] B: 4/27/1923
AAFC **1947** SF-A: Rec 4-41 10.3; PR 1-20 20.0; KR 2-42 21.0.
1948 SF-A: Rec 3-40 13.3; KR 1-16 16.0. **1949** SF-A: Rec 7-165 23.6 3 TD; PR 1-6 6.0. **Total:** Rec 14-246 17.6 3 TD; PR 2-26 13.0; KR 3-58 19.3.

Year Team	G	Rushing Att	Yds	Avg	TD	Interceptions Int	Yds	TD	Tot TD
1947 SF-A	10	11	42	3.8	0	2	59	0	0
1948 SF-A	13	14	121	8.6	1	7	144	1	2
1949 SF-A	7	19	120	6.3	2	7	87	1	7
AAFC Total	30	44	283	6.4	3	16	290	2	9

FRED CARR Carr, Freddie Alton 6′5″, 238 **LB**
Col: Phoenix Coll. AZ (J.C.); Texas-El Paso *HS:* Phoenix Union [AZ]
B: 8/19/1946, Phoenix, AZ *Drafted:* 1968 Round 1 GB
1968 GB: 14 G. **1969** GB: 14 G. **1970** GB: 14 G; Int 2-45. **1971** GB: 14 G. **1972** GB: 14 G. **1973** GB: 14 G. **1974** GB: 14 G; Int 1-0. **1975** GB: 14 G; Int 3-28. **1976** GB: 14 G; Int 1-10 1 TD; 6 Pt. **1977** GB: 14 G; Int 1-15. **Total:** 140 G; Int 8-98 1 TD; 6 Pt.

GREGG CARR Carr, Gregg Kevin 6′2″, 219 **LB**
Col: Auburn *HS:* Woodlawn [Birmingham, AL] B: 3/31/1962, Birmingham, AL *Drafted:* 1985 Round 6 Pit
1985 Pit: 16 G; 1 Sac. **1986** Pit: 16 G. **1987** Pit: 12 G; Scor **1** Saf; 2 Pt; 3 Sac. **1988** Pit: 13 G; Int 1-27; 3.5 Sac. **Total:** 57 G; Int 1-27; Scor 1 Saf; 2 Pt; 7.5 Sac.

HARLAN CARR Carr, Harlan Bradley 5′10″, 165 **QB**
(Whippet; Gotch) *Col:* Syracuse *HS:* Auburn [NY] B: 4/30/1903, Union Springs, NY D: 10/24/1970, Auburn, NY
1927 Buf-Pott: 10 G; Rush 2 TD; Rec 1 TD; Tot TD 3; 18 Pt. Buf: 5 G; Rush 1 TD; 6 Pt. Pott: 5 G; Rush 1 TD; Rec 1 TD; Tot TD 2; 12 Pt. **Total:** 10 G; Rush 2 TD; Rec 1 TD; Tot TD 3; 18 Pt.

HENRY CARR Carr, Henry Joseph 6′3″, 190 **DB**
Col: Burlington Co. Coll. NJ (J.C.); Arizona State *HS:* Northwestern [Detroit, MI] B: 11/27/1942, Detroit, MI *Drafted:* 1965 Round 4 NYG
1965 NYG: 14 G; PR 4-13 3.3; Int 2-19; 1 Fum. **1966** NYG: 14 G; Int 4-110 1 TD; 6 Pt. **1967** NYG: 9 G; Int 1-13. **Total:** 37 G; PR 4-13 3.3; Int 7-142 1 TD; 6 Pt; 1 Fum.

JIMMY CARR Carr, James Henry 6′1″, 206 **DB-LB-HB**
(Gummy) *Col:* Charleston (WV) *HS:* East Bank [WV] B: 3/25/1933, Kayford, WV
1955 ChiC: Rec 9-157 17.4; PR 1-0; KR 4-93 23.3. **1957** ChiC: KR 2-39 19.5. **1960** Phi: KR 1-5 5.0; **1** Fum TD. **1964** Was: PR 1-0; KR 1-0. **Total:** Rec 9-157 17.4; PR 2-0; KR 8-137 17.1; 1 Fum TD.

		Rushing				Interceptions			
Year Team	**G**	**Att**	**Yds**	**Avg**	**TD**	**Int**	**Yds**	**TD**	**Fum**
1955 ChiC	12	30	115	3.8	0	0	0	0	1
1957 ChiC	6	0	0	—	0	0	0	0	1
1959 Phi	12	0	0	—	0	5	65	0	0
1960 Phi	10	0	0	—	0	2	4	0	0
1961 Phi	13	0	0	—	0	2	20	0	0
1962 Phi	14	0	0	—	0	3	59	0	0
1963 Phi	14	0	0	—	0	1	25	0	0
1964 Was	14	0	0	—	0	2	13	0	0
1965 Was	13	0	0	—	0	0	0	0	0
NFL Total	108	30	115	3.8	0	15	186	0	2

LEVERT CARR Carr, Levert F 6′2″, 272 **OT-DT-OG**
Col: Independence CC KS; North Central *HS:* John R. Buchtel [Akron, OH] B: 6/30/1944, Birmingham, AL
1969 SD: 7 G. **1970** Buf: 7 G. **1971** Buf: 14 G. **1972** Hou: 14 G. **1973** Hou: 13 G. **Total:** 55 G.

LYDELL CARR Carr, Lydell 6′1″, 226 **RB**
Col: Oklahoma *HS:* Enid [OK] B: 5/27/1965, Enid, OK *Drafted:* 1988 Round 4 NO
1989 Pho: 5 G; KR 1-15 15.0.

PAUL CARR Carr, Paul Howard Jr. 6′0″, 205 **DB-LB**
(Rock) *Col:* Citrus Coll. CA (J.C.); Houston *HS:* Citrus [Azusa, CA] B: 9/4/1931, Los Angeles, CA *Drafted:* 1953 Round 7 SF
1955 SF: 10 G; Int 1-11. **1956** SF: 12 G; KR 1-11 11.0; Int 2-18. **1957** SF: 8 G; KR 1-10 10.0; 1 Fum. **Total:** 30 G; KR 2-21 10.5; Int 3-29; 1 Fum.

REGGIE CARR Carr, Reginald S 6′3″, 300 **DE**
Col: Jackson State *HS:* Meridian [MS] B: 2/17/1963, Meridian, MS
1987 NYG: 3 G.

ROGER CARR Carr, Roger Dale 6′3″, 200 **WR**
Col: Louisiana Tech *HS:* Enid [OK]; Cotton Valley HS [LA] B: 7/1/1952, Seminole, OK *Drafted:* 1974 Round 1 Bal
1980 Bal: Rush 1-(-8) -8.0. **Total:** Rush 1-(-8) -8.0.

		Receiving			
Year Team	**G**	**Rec**	**Yds**	**Avg**	**TD**
1974 Bal	11	21	405	19.3	0
1975 Bal	14	23	517	22.5	2
1976 Bal	14	43	**1112**	**25.9**	11
1977 Bal	7	11	199	18.1	1
1978 Bal	16	30	629	21.0	6
1979 Bal	9	27	400	14.8	1
1980 Bal	16	61	924	15.1	5
1981 Bal	15	38	584	15.4	3
1982 Sea	9	15	265	17.7	2
1983 SD	4	2	36	18.0	0
NFL Total	115	271	5071	18.7	31

TOM CARR Carr, Thomas Winther 6′4″, 264 **DT**
Col: Morgan State *HS:* Overbrook [Philadelphia, PA] B: 4/6/1942, Philadelphia, PA
1968 NO: 4 G.

ALPHONSO CARREKER Carreker, Alphonso 6′6″, 268 **DE**
Col: Florida State *HS:* Marion-Franklin [Columbus, OH] B: 5/25/1962, Columbus, OH *Drafted:* 1984 Round 1 GB
1984 GB: 14 G; 3 Sac. **1985** GB: 16 G; 9 Sac. **1986** GB: 16 G; 2.5 Sac. **1987** GB: 12 G; Int 1-6; 4 Sac. **1988** GB: 14 G. **1989** Den: 16 G; 5.5 Sac. **1991** Den: 6 G. **Total:** 94 G; Int 1-6; 24.0 Sac.

VINCE CARREKER Carreker, Vincent Lewis 6′0″, 183 **DB**
Col: Columbus State CC OH; Central State (Ohio); Cincinnati *HS:* Marion-Franklin [Columbus, OH] B: 8/21/1963, Columbus, OH
1987 Cle: 2 G.

DUANE CARRELL Carrell, Duane Blore 5′10″, 185 **P**
Col: Florida State *HS:* Woodrow Wilson [Washington, DC] B: 10/3/1949, Washington, DC
1974 Dal: Pass 1-1 100.0%, 37 37.00. **1976** NYJ: Rush 2-0. **1977** NYJ-StL: Rush 2-(-15) -7.5. NYJ: Rush 2-(-15) -7.5. **Total:** Pass 1-1 100.0%, 37 37.00; Rush 4-(-15) -3.8.

		Punting			
Year Team	**G**	**Punts**	**Yds**	**Avg**	**Fum**
1974 Dal	7	40	1591	39.8	0
1975 LARm	14	73	2874	39.4	0
1976 NYJ	14	81	3218	39.7	2
1977 NYJ-StL	12	63	2314	36.7	1
1977 NYJ	2	14	557	39.8	1
1977 StL	10	49	1757	35.9	0
NFL Total	47	257	9997	38.9	3

JOHN CARRELL Carrell, John Harvey 6′3″, 227 **LB**
Col: New Mexico Mil. Inst. (J.C.); Texas Tech *HS:* Lovington [NM] B: 12/19/1942, Amarillo, TX *Drafted:* 1965 Round 15 Pit
1966 Hou: 8 G.

MARK CARRIER Carrier, John Mark 6′0″, 186 **WR**
Col: Nicholls State *HS:* Church Point [LA] B: 10/28/1965, Lafayette, LA *Drafted:* 1987 Round 3 TB
1987 TB: KR 1-0. **1993** Cle: Rush 4-26 6.5 1 TD; PR 6-92 15.3 1 TD. **1994** Cle: Rush 1-14 14.0 1 TD; PR 9-112 12.4. **1995** Car: Rush 3-(-4) -1.3; PR 6-25 4.2. **Total:** Rush 8-36 4.5 2 TD; PR 21-229 10.9 1 TD; KR 1-0.

		Receiving					Tot
Year Team	**G**	**Rec**	**Yds**	**Avg**	**TD**	**Fum**	**TD**
1987 TB	10	26	423	16.3	3	0	3
1988 TB	16	57	970	17.0	5	2	5
1989 TB	16	86	1422	16.5	9	1	9
1990 TB	16	49	813	16.6	4	0	4
1991 TB	16	47	698	14.9	2	2	2
1992 TB	14	56	692	12.4	4	1	4
1993 Cle	16	43	746	17.3	3	0	5
1994 Cle	16	29	452	15.6	5	1	6
1995 Car	16	66	1002	15.2	3	0	3
1996 Car	16	58	808	13.9	6	0	6
1997 Car	9	33	436	13.2	2	1	2
1998 Car	16	19	301	15.8	2	0	2
NFL Total	177	569	8763	15.4	48	8	51

MARK CARRIER Carrier, Mark Anthony 6′1″, 192 **DB**
Col: USC *HS:* Long Beach Polytechnic [CA] B: 4/28/1968, Lake Charles, LA *Drafted:* 1990 Round 1 ChiB
1997 Det: PR 1-0. **Total:** PR 1-0.

		Interceptions			
Year Team	**G**	**Int**	**Yds**	**TD**	**Fum**
1990 ChiB	16	**10**	39	0	0
1991 ChiB	16	2	54	0	0
1992 ChiB	16	0	0	0	0
1993 ChiB	16	4	94	1	0
1994 ChiB	16	2	10	0	0
1995 ChiB	16	0	0	0	0
1996 ChiB	13	2	0	0	0
1997 Det	16	5	94	0	1
1998 Det	13	3	33	0	1
NFL Total	138	28	324	1	2

DARREN CARRINGTON Carrington, Darren Russell 6′2″, 200 **DB**
Col: Northern Arizona *HS:* James Monroe [Bronx, NY] B: 10/10/1966, Bronx, NY *Drafted:* 1989 Round 5 Den
1989 Den: PR 1-0; KR 6-152 25.3. **1991** SD: KR 0-24. **1993** SD: 1 Sac. **Total:** PR 1-0; KR 6-176 29.3; 1 Sac.

		Interceptions			
Year Team	**G**	**Int**	**Yds**	**TD**	**Fum**
1989 Den	16	1	2	0	1
1990 Det	12	0	0	0	0
1991 SD	16	3	30	0	0
1992 SD	16	6	152	1	0
1993 SD	16	7	104	0	1
1994 SD	16	3	51	0	0
1995 Jac	6	1	17	0	0
1996 Oak	14	1	21	0	0
NFL Total	112	22	377	1	2

ED CARRINGTON Carrington, Edward Codrington Jr. 6'4", 225 **TE**
Col: Virginia *HS:* Episcopal [Alexandria, VA] B: 9/1/1944, Beaumont, TX *Drafted:* 1967 Round 7 Hou
1968 Hou: 1 G. **1969** Hou: 14 G. **Total:** 15 G.

RUSS CARROCCIO Carroccio, Russell B 6'1", 235 **OG-OT-DG-DT**
Col: Virginia *HS:* Clifton [NJ] B: 4/28/1931 D: 6/28/1994, Wayne, NJ
1954 NYG: 9 G. **1955** NYG-Phi: 12 G; Int 1-7. NYG: 5 G; Int 1-7. Phi: 7 G. **Total:** 21 G; Int 1-7.

BART CARROLL Carroll, Bart J 5'11", 180 **T**
Col: Colgate *HS:* Massena [NY] B: 12/29/1893, Massena, NY D: 4/1/1967, Schenectady, NY
1920 Roch: 2 G.

BIRD CARROLL Carroll, Elmer Ellsworth 5'8", 185 **OE**
Col: Washington & Jefferson *HS:* Scottdale [PA] B: 7/25/1896, Scottdale, PA D: 8/6/1982, Winter Park, FL
1921 Can: 6 G; Rec 1 TD; 6 Pt. **1922** Can: 12 G; Rec 1 TD; Scor 7, 1 XK. **1923** Can: 9 G; Rec 2 TD; Scor **1** 1XP; 13 Pt. **1925** Can: 7 G. **Total:** 34 G; Rec 4 TD; Scor 1 1XP.

GENE CARROLL Carroll, Harry Eugene 5'10", 190 **OE-G**
(Harry) *Col:* Marietta; Waynesburg *HS:* St. Marys [WV] B: 10/16/1896, St. Mary's, WV D: 2/17/1968, West Chester, PA
1922 Col: 4 G.

HERMAN CARROLL Carroll, Herman Jr. 6'4", 265 **DE**
Col: Mississippi State *HS:* North [Natchez, MS] B: 6/20/1971, Natchez, MS *Drafted:* 1994 Round 5 NO
1994 NO: 4 G.

JIM CARROLL Carroll, James Samuel 6'2", 230 **LB**
Col: Notre Dame *HS:* Marist [Atlanta, GA] B: 5/6/1943, Jonesboro, AR *Drafted:* 1965 Round 12 NYG
1965 NYG: 14 G; Int 1-3. **1966** NYG-Was: 13 G; Int 1-36. NYG: 1 G. Was: 12 G; Int 1-36. **1967** Was: 14 G; Int 1-0. **1968** Was: 14 G. **1969** NYJ: 6 G; KR 1-0; 1 Fum. **Total:** 61 G; KR 1-0; Int 3-39; 1 Fum.

JAY CARROLL Carroll, Jay Timothy 6'4", 230 **TE**
Col: Minnesota *HS:* Cotter [Winona, MN] B: 11/8/1961, Winona, MN *Drafted:* 1984 Round 7 TB
1984 TB: 16 G; Rec 5-50 10.0 1 TD; 6 Pt. **1985** Min: 16 G; Rec 1-8 8.0. **Total:** 32 G; Rec 6-58 9.7 1 TD; 6 Pt.

JOE CARROLL Carroll, Joseph Walker 6'1", 220 **LB**
Col: Pittsburgh *HS:* Warren G. Harding [Warren, OH] B: 5/29/1950, Warren, OH *Drafted:* 1972 Round 11 Oak
1972 Oak: 13 G. **1973** Oak: 9 G. **Total:** 22 G.

LEO CARROLL Carroll, Leo H 6'7", 250 **DE**
Col: Glendale CC CA; Tulsa; San Diego State *HS:* Alhambra [CA] B: 2/16/1944, Alhambra, CA *Drafted:* 1967 Round 2 Atl
1968 GB: 6 G. **1969** Was: 14 G. **1970** Was: 7 G. **Total:** 27 G.

RONNIE CARROLL Carroll, Ronald Dean 6'2", 265 **OG**
Col: Arkansas; Sam Houston State *HS:* Spring Woods [Houston, TX] B: 4/11/1949, Galveston, TX *Drafted:* 1973 Round 12 Buf
1974 Hou: 14 G.

VICTOR CARROLL Carroll, Victor E 6'3", 235 **T-C-G-LB**
Col: Pasadena City Coll. CA (J.C.); Nevada-Reno *HS:* Alhambra [CA] B: 11/9/1912, Alhambra, CA D: 7/6/1986, Mission Viejo, CA
1936 Bos: 5 G; Int 1 TD; 6 Pt. **1937** Was: 10 G. **1938** Was: 10 G. **1939** Was: 11 G. **1940** Was: 11 G. **1941** Was: 10 G; Rec 1-31 31.0; Int 2-38 **1** TD; 6 Pt. **1942** Was: 6 G. **1943** NYG: 10 G. **1944** NYG: 10 G; PR 1-28 28.0 **1** TD; Int 1-8; Scor **1** Saf; 8 Pt. **1945** NYG: 2 G. **1946** NYG: 6 G; KR 1-11 11.0. **1947** NYG: 11 G; Rec 7-123 17.6 2 TD; Int 1-31; 12 Pt. **Total:** 102 G; Rec 8-154 19.3 2 TD; PR 1-28 28.0 1 TD; KR 1-11 11.0; Int 4-77 2 TD; Scor 1 Saf; Tot TD 5; 32 Pt.

WESLEY CARROLL Carroll, Wesley Byron 6'0", 183 **WR**
Col: Miami (Fla.) *HS:* John Hay [Cleveland, OH] B: 9/6/1967, Cleveland, OH *Drafted:* 1991 Round 2 NO

		Receiving				
Year Team	**G**	**Rec**	**Yds**	**Avg**	**TD**	**Fum**
1991 NO	12	18	184	10.2	1	0
1992 NO	16	18	292	16.2	2	1
1993 Cin	12	6	81	13.5	0	0
NFL Total	40	42	557	13.3	3	1

PAUL OTT CARRUTH Carruth, Paul Ott 6'1", 220 **RB**
Col: Alabama *HS:* Parklane [McComb, MS] B: 7/22/1961, Hattiesburg, MS
1986 GB: KR 4-40 10.0. **1987** GB: Pass 1-1 100.0%, 3 3.00 1 TD; KR 1-8 8.0. **1988** GB: Pass 2-0. **Total:** Pass 3-1 33.3%, 3 1.00 1 TD; KR 5-48 9.6.

		Rushing				Receiving					Tot
Year Team	**G**	**Att**	**Yds**	**Avg**	**TD**	**Rec**	**Yds**	**Avg**	**TD**	**Fum**	**TD**
1986 GB	16	81	308	3.8	2	24	134	5.6	2	1	4
1987 GB	12	64	192	3.0	3	10	78	7.8	1	0	4
1988 GB	15	49	114	2.3	0	24	211	8.8	0	4	0
1989 KC	2	0	0	—	0	1	3	3.0	0	0	0
NFL Total	45	194	614	3.2	5	59	426	7.2	3	5	8

RAE CARRUTH Carruth, Rae Lamar 5'11", 194 **WR**
Col: Colorado *HS:* Valley [Sacramento, CA] B: 1/20/1974, Sacramento, CA *Drafted:* 1997 Round 1 Car
1997 Car: Rush 6-23 3.8. **Total:** Rush 6-23 3.8.

		Receiving				
Year Team	**G**	**Rec**	**Yds**	**Avg**	**TD**	**Fum**
1997 Car	15	44	545	12.4	4	2
1998 Car	2	4	59	14.8	0	0
NFL Total	17	48	604	12.6	4	2

CARLOS CARSON Carson, Carlos Andre 5'11", 180 **WR**
Col: Louisiana State *HS:* John I. Leonard [Lake Worth, FL] B: 12/28/1958, Lake Worth, FL *Drafted:* 1980 Round 5 KC
1980 KC: Rush 2-41 20.5. **1981** KC: Rush 1-(-1) -1.0. **1983** KC: Pass 1-1 100.0%, 48 48.00 1 TD; Rush 2-20 10.0. **1984** KC: Rush 1-(-8) -8.0. **1985** KC: Rush 3-25 8.3. **1987** KC: Rush 1-(-7) -7.0. **1988** KC: Rush 1-1 1.0. **1989** KC-Phi: Rush 1-(-9) -9.0. Phi: Rush 1-(-9) -9.0. **Total:** Pass 1-1 100.0%, 48 48.00 1 TD; Rush 12-62 5.2.

		Receiving				Kickoff Returns				
Year Team	**G**	**Rec**	**Yds**	**Avg**	**TD**	**Ret**	**Yds**	**Avg**	**TD**	**Fum**
1980 KC	16	5	68	13.6	0	40	917	22.9	0	1
1981 KC	5	7	179	25.6	1	10	227	22.7	0	1
1982 KC	9	27	494	18.3	2	0	0	—	0	1
1983 KC	16	80	1351	16.9	7	1	12	12.0	0	2
1984 KC	16	57	1078	18.9	4	1	2	2.0	0	0
1985 KC	15	47	843	17.9	4	0	0	—	0	0
1986 KC	10	21	497	23.7	4	5	88	17.6	0	1
1987 KC	12	55	1044	19.0	7	0	0	—	0	1
1988 KC	14	46	711	15.5	3	0	0	—	0	0
1989 KC-Phi	13	8	107	13.4	1	0	0	—	0	0
1989 KC	7	7	95	13.6	1	0	0	—	0	0
1989 Phi	6	1	12	12.0	0	0	0	—	0	0
NFL Total	126	353	6372	18.1	33	57	1246	21.9	0	7

HARRY CARSON Carson, Harold Donald 6'2", 237 **LB**
Col: South Carolina State *HS:* McClenaghan [Florence, SC] B: 11/26/1953, Florence, SC *Drafted:* 1976 Round 4 NYG
1976 NYG: KR 1-5 5.0. **1979** NYG: **1** Fum TD. **1982** NYG: 3 Sac. **1983** NYG: 1 Sac. **1985** NYG: 1 Sac. **1986** NYG: Rec 1-13 13.0 1 TD; 2 Sac. **1987** NYG: 1 Sac. **Total:** Rec 1-13 13.0 1 TD; KR 1-5 5.0; 1 Fum TD; 8 Sac.

		Interceptions			Tot
Year Team	**G**	**Int**	**Yds**	**TD**	**TD**
1976 NYG	12	0	0	0	0
1977 NYG	14	0	0	0	0
1978 NYG	16	3	86	0	0
1979 NYG	16	3	28	0	1
1980 NYG	8	0	0	0	0
1981 NYG	16	0	0	0	0
1982 NYG	9	1	6	0	0
1983 NYG	10	0	0	0	0
1984 NYG	16	1	6	0	0
1985 NYG	16	0	0	0	0
1986 NYG	16	1	20	0	1
1987 NYG	12	0	0	0	0
1988 NYG	12	2	66	0	0
NFL Total	173	11	212	0	2

HOWARD CARSON Carson, Hueland Howard 6'2", 233 **LB**
Col: Howard Payne *HS:* Grapevine [TX] B: 2/11/1957, Hico, TX
1981 LARm: 10 G. **1982** LARm: 2 G. **1983** LARm: 16 G. **Total:** 28 G.

JOHNNY CARSON Carson, John Richard 6'3", 202 **OE**
(Big John) *Col:* Georgia *HS:* Roosevelt [Atlanta, GA] B: 1/31/1930, Atlanta, GA *Drafted:* 1953 Round 15 Cle

		Receiving				
Year Team	**G**	**Rec**	**Yds**	**Avg**	**TD**	**Fum**
1954 Was	12	12	139	11.6	0	0
1955 Was	12	23	443	19.3	3	1
1956 Was	12	39	504	12.9	3	0
1957 Was	12	34	583	17.1	3	0
1958 Was	4	14	244	17.4	2	0
1959 Was	5	6	74	12.3	0	0
1960 Hou	14	45	604	13.4	4	1
NFL Total	71	173	2591	15.0	15	2

KERN CARSON Carson, Kern 6'1", 200 **HB**
Col: San Diego State *HS:* Abraham Lincoln [San Diego, CA] B: 1/29/1941, Hope, AR *Drafted:* 1963 Round 29 Den
1965 SD-NYJ: 13 G; Rush 7-25 3.6 2 TD; PR 1-7 7.0; KR 17-355 20.9; 12 Pt; 3 Fum. SD: 3 G; KR 3-44 14.7. NYJ: 10 G; Rush 7-25 3.6 2 TD; PR 1-7 7.0; KR 14-311 22.2; 12 Pt; 3 Fum. **Total:** 13 G; Rush 7-25 3.6 2 TD; PR 1-7 7.0; KR 17-355 20.9; 12 Pt; 3 Fum.

MALCOLM CARSON Carson, Malcolm Darryl 6'2", 260 **OG**
Col: Tennessee-Chattanooga *HS:* C.W. Hayes [Birmingham, AL]
B: 11/1/1959, Birmingham, AL
1984 Min: 1 G.

DWAYNE CARSWELL Carswell, Dwayne 6'3", 260 **TE**
Col: Liberty *HS:* Temple [Jacksonville, FL]; University Christian HS [Jacksonville, FL] B: 1/18/1972, Jacksonville, FL
1994 Den: KR 1-0. **Total:** KR 1-0.

		Receiving			
Year Team	**G**	**Rec**	**Yds**	**Avg**	**TD**
1994 Den	4	0	0	—	0
1995 Den	9	3	37	12.3	0
1996 Den	16	15	85	5.7	0
1997 Den	16	12	96	8.0	1
1998 Den	16	4	51	12.8	0
NFL Total	61	34	269	7.9	1

ALEX CARTER Carter, Alexander 6'3", 255 **DE**
Col: Tennessee State *HS:* South Miami [Miami, FL] B: 9/6/1963, Miami, FL
1987 Cle: 3 G; 1 Sac.

ANTHONY CARTER Carter, Anthony 5'11", 181 **WR**
Col: Michigan *HS:* Sun Coast [Riviera Beach, FL] B: 9/17/1960, Riviera Beach, FL *Drafted:* 1983 Round 12 Mia
1985 Min: PR 9-117 13.0. **1987** Min: PR 3-40 13.3. **1988** Min: PR 1-3 3.0; KR 1-0. **1989** Min: PR 1-2 2.0; KR 1-19 19.0. **1992** Min: Pass 1-0. **1995** Det: PR 1-3 3.0; KR 2-46 23.0. **Total:** Pass 1-0; PR 15-165 11.0; KR 4-65 16.3.

		Rushing				Receiving					Tot
Year Team	**G**	**Att**	**Yds**	**Avg**	**TD**	**Rec**	**Yds**	**Avg**	**TD**	**Fum**	**TD**
1985 Min	16	0	0	—	0	43	821	19.1	8	1	8
1986 Min	12	1	12	12.0	0	38	686	18.1	7	1	7
1987 Min	12	0	0	—	0	38	922	**24.3**	7	0	7
1988 Min	16	4	41	10.3	0	72	1225	17.0	6	1	6
1989 Min	16	3	18	6.0	0	65	1066	16.4	4	0	4
1990 Min	15	3	16	5.3	0	70	1008	14.4	8	2	8
1991 Min	15	13	117	9.0	1	51	553	10.8	5	0	6
1992 Min	16	16	66	4.1	1	41	580	14.1	2	1	3
1993 Min	15	7	19	2.7	0	60	775	12.9	5	1	5
1994 Det	4	0	0	—	0	8	97	12.1	3	0	3
1995 Det	3	0	0	—	0	0	0	—	0	0	0
NFL Total	140	47	289	6.1	2	486	7733	15.9	55	7	57

TONY CARTER Carter, Antonio Marcus 6'0", 230 **RB**
Col: Minnesota *HS:* South [Columbus, OH] B: 8/23/1972, Columbus, OH
1994 ChiB: KR 6-99 16.5. **1995** ChiB: KR 3-24 8.0. **1997** ChiB: KR 2-34 17.0. **Total:** KR 11-157 14.3.

		Rushing				Receiving				
Year Team	**G**	**Att**	**Yds**	**Avg**	**TD**	**Rec**	**Yds**	**Avg**	**TD**	**Fum**
1994 ChiB	14	0	0	—	0	1	24	24.0	0	0
1995 ChiB	16	10	34	3.4	0	40	329	8.2	1	1
1996 ChiB	16	11	43	3.9	0	41	233	5.7	0	1
1997 ChiB	16	9	56	6.2	0	24	152	6.3	0	0
1998 NE	11	2	3	1.5	0	18	166	9.2	0	0
NFL Total	73	32	136	4.3	0	124	904	7.3	1	2

BLANCHARD CARTER Carter, Blanchard 6'4", 250 **OT**
Col: Nevada-Las Vegas *HS:* Edison [Stockton, CA] B: 6/3/1955, Stockton, CA *Drafted:* 1977 Round 7 Bal
1977 TB: 13 G.

CARL CARTER Carter, Carl Anthony 5'11", 180 **DB**
Col: Texas Tech *HS:* O.D. Wyatt [Fort Worth, TX] B: 3/7/1964, Fort Worth, TX *Drafted:* 1986 Round 4 StL
1986 StL: 14 G; PR 1-0; KR 2-21 10.5; Int 2-12; 1 Fum. **1987** StL: 12 G; Int 1-0. **1988** Pho: 16 G; Int 3-0. **1989** Pho: 15 G; Int 1-0. **1990** Cin: 15 G. **1991** TB: 11 G; PR 1-1 1.0; Int 1-4. **1992** GB: 7 G. **Total:** 90 G; PR 2-1 0.5; KR 2-21 10.5; Int 8-16; 1 Fum.

CHRIS CARTER Carter, Christopher Cary 6'1", 201 **DB**
Col: Texas *HS:* John Tyler [Tyler, TX] B: 9/27/1974, Tyler, TX
Drafted: 1997 Round 3 NE
1997 NE: 16 G. **1998** NE: 16 G; 1 Sac. **Total:** 32 G; 1 Sac.

CRIS CARTER Carter, Christopher D 6'3", 202 **WR**
Col: Ohio State *HS:* Middletown [OH] B: 11/25/1965, Troy, OH
Drafted: 1987 Supplemental Round 4 Phi
1987 Phi: Pass 1-0; KR 12-241 20.1. **1988** Phi: Rush 1-1 1.0; **1** Fum TD. **1989** Phi: Rush 2-16 8.0. **1990** Min: Rush 2-6 3.0. **1992** Min: Rush 5-15 3.0. **1994** Min: Scor 2 2XP. **1995** Min: Rush 1-0. **1996** Min: KR 1-3 3.0. **1997** Min: Scor **3** 2XP. **1998** Min: Rush 1-(-1) -1.0. **Total:** Pass 1-0; Rush 12-37 3.1; KR 13-244 18.8; Scor 5 2XP; 1 Fum TD.

		Receiving					Tot
Year Team	**G**	**Rec**	**Yds**	**Avg**	**TD**	**Fum**	**TD**
1987 Phi	9	5	84	16.8	2	0	2
1988 Phi	16	39	761	19.5	6	0	7
1989 Phi	16	45	605	13.4	11	1	11
1990 Min	16	27	413	15.3	3	0	3
1991 Min	16	72	962	13.4	5	1	5
1992 Min	12	53	681	12.8	6	1	6
1993 Min	16	86	1071	12.5	9	0	9
1994 Min	16	**122**	1256	10.3	7	4	7
1995 Min	16	122	1371	11.2	**17**	0	17
1996 Min	16	96	1163	12.1	10	1	10
1997 Min	16	89	1069	12.0	**13**	3	13
1998 Min	16	78	1011	13.0	12	0	12
NFL Total	181	834	10447	12.5	101	11	102

DALE CARTER Carter, Dale Lavelle 6'1", 188 **DB**
Col: Ellsworth CC IA; Tennessee *HS:* Newton Co. [Covington, GA]
B: 11/28/1969, Covington, GA *Drafted:* 1992 Round 1 KC
1992 KC: KR 11-190 17.3. **1993** KC: Rush 1-2 2.0. **1996** KC: Rush 1-3 3.0; Rec 6-89 14.8 1 TD. **Total:** Rush 2-5 2.5; Rec 6-89 14.8 1 TD; KR 11-190 17.3.

		Punt Returns				Interceptions				Tot
Year Team	**G**	**Ret**	**Yds**	**Avg**	**TD**	**Int**	**Yds**	**TD**	**Fum**	**TD**
1992 KC	16	38	398	10.5	**2**	7	65	1	7	3
1993 KC	15	27	247	9.1	0	1	0	0	4	0
1994 KC	16	16	124	7.8	0	2	24	0	1	0
1995 KC	16	0	0	—	0	4	45	0	0	0
1996 KC	14	2	18	9.0	0	3	17	0	1	1
1997 KC	16	0	0	—	0	2	9	0	0	0
1998 KC	11	0	0	—	0	2	23	0	0	0
NFL Total	104	83	787	9.5	2	21	183	1	13	4

DARYL CARTER Carter, Daryl 6'2", 222 **LB**
Col: Wisconsin *HS:* Washington [Milwaukee, WI] B: 2/24/1975
1997 ChiB: 1 G.

DAVID CARTER Carter, David C 6'2", 250 **C-OG**
Col: Western Kentucky *HS:* Lincoln [Vincennes, IN] B: 11/27/1953, Vincennes, IN *Drafted:* 1977 Round 6 Hou
1977 Hou: 14 G. **1978** Hou: 16 G. **1979** Hou: 16 G. **1980** Hou: 16 G. **1981** Hou: 16 G. **1982** Hou: 9 G. **1983** Hou: 16 G; 1 Fum. **1984** Hou-NO: 14 G. Hou: 7 G. NO: 7 G. **1985** NO: 4 G. **Total:** 121 G; 1 Fum.

DEXTER CARTER Carter, Dexter Anthony 5'9", 175 **RB**
Col: Florida State *HS:* Appling Co. [Baxley, GA] B: 9/15/1967, Baxley, GA *Drafted:* 1990 Round 1 SF

		Rushing				Receiving			
Year Team	**G**	**Att**	**Yds**	**Avg**	**TD**	**Rec**	**Yds**	**Avg**	**TD**
1990 SF	16	114	460	4.0	1	25	217	8.7	0
1991 SF	16	85	379	4.5	2	23	253	11.0	1
1992 SF	3	4	9	2.3	0	1	43	43.0	1
1993 SF	16	10	72	7.2	1	3	40	13.3	0
1994 SF	16	8	34	4.3	0	7	99	14.1	0
1995 NYJ-SF	17	7	22	3.1	0	2	4	2.0	0
1995 NYJ	10	0	0	—	0	1	0	0.0	0
1995 SF	7	7	22	3.1	0	1	4	4.0	0
1996 SF	16	19	66	3.5	1	0	0	—	0
NFL Total	100	247	1042	4.2	5	61	656	10.8	2

	Punt Returns				Kickoff Returns					Tot
Year Team	**Ret**	**Yds**	**Avg**	**TD**	**Ret**	**Yds**	**Avg**	**TD**	**Fum**	**TD**
1990 SF	0	0	—	0	41	783	19.1	0	8	1
1991 SF	0	0	—	0	37	839	22.7	**1**	5	4
1992 SF	0	0	—	0	2	55	27.5	0	0	1
1993 SF	34	411	12.1	1	25	494	19.8	0	5	2
1994 SF	38	321	8.4	0	48	1105	23.0	1	2	1
1995 NYJ-SF	30	309	10.3	**1**	56	1227	21.9	0	8	1
1995 NYJ	21	145	6.9	0	33	705	21.4	0	7	0
1995 SF	9	164	18.2	1	23	522	22.7	0	1	1
1996 SF	36	317	8.8	0	41	909	22.2	0	5	1
NFL Total	138	1358	9.8	2	250	5412	21.6	2	33	11

BERNARD CARTER Carter, Edward Bernard 6'3", 238 **LB**
Col: East Carolina *HS:* Lincoln [Tallahassee, FL] B: 8/22/1971, Miami, FL *Drafted:* 1994 Round 6 TB
1995 Jac: 5 G.

GERALD CARTER Carter, Gerald Louis 6'1", 190 **WR**
Col: Tyler JC TX; Texas A&M *HS:* Bryan [TX] B: 6/19/1957, Bryan, TX
Drafted: 1980 Round 9 TB
1980 NYJ: KR 1-12 12.0. **1983** TB: Rush 1-0. **1984** TB: Rush 1-16 16.0. **1985** TB: Rush 1-13 13.0. **1986** TB: Rush 1-(-5) -5.0. **Total:** Rush 4-24 6.0; KR 1-12 12.0.

		Receiving				
Year Team	**G**	**Rec**	**Yds**	**Avg**	**TD**	**Fum**
1980 NYJ	3	0	0	—	0	1

1981 TB	16	1	10	10.0	0	0
1982 TB	9	10	140	14.0	0	0
1983 TB	16	48	694	14.5	2	3
1984 TB	16	60	816	13.6	5	1
1985 TB	16	40	557	13.9	3	1
1986 TB	15	42	640	15.2	2	2
1987 TB	12	38	586	15.4	5	0
NFL Total	103	239	3443	14.4	17	8

JIM CARTER Carter, James Charles 6′3″, 235 **LB-OG**
Col: Minnesota *HS:* South St. Paul [MN] B: 10/18/1948, St. Paul, MN
Drafted: 1970 Round 3 GB
1970 GB: 11 G. **1971** GB: 13 G; KR 1-5 5.0; Int 1-16. **1972** GB: 14 G; Int 1-0. **1973** GB: 14 G; Int 3-44 1 TD; 6 Pt. **1974** GB: 14 G; Int 1-0. **1975** GB: 12 G. **1977** GB: 14 G. **1978** GB: 14 G. **Total:** 106 G; KR 1-5 5.0; Int 6-60 1 TD; 6 Pt.

JIMMIE CARTER Carter, Jimmie Renerd 6′1″, 220 **LB**
Col: New Mexico *HS:* Reagan [Austin, TX] B: 7/26/1961, Weimar, TX
1987 StL: 1 G.

JON CARTER Carter, Jon Stacy 6′4″, 273 **DT**
Col: Pittsburgh *HS:* Varnado [LA] B: 3/12/1965, Los Angeles, CA
Drafted: 1988 Round 5 NYG
1989 Dal: 13 G.

JOE CARTER Carter, Joseph Thomas 5′11″, 198 **RB**
Col: Alabama *HS:* Starkville [MS] B: 6/23/1962, Starkville, MS
Drafted: 1984 Round 4 Mia
1984 Mia: Rec 8-53 6.6. **1985** Mia: Rec 2-7 3.5; KR 4-82 20.5. **1986** Mia: Rec 1-6 6.0; KR 9-133 14.8. **Total:** Rec 11-66 6.0; KR 13-215 16.5.

		Rushing				
Year Team	**G**	**Att**	**Yds**	**Avg**	**TD**	**Fum**
1984 Mia	13	100	495	5.0	1	3
1985 Mia	10	14	76	5.4	0	2
1986 Mia	7	4	18	4.5	0	2
NFL Total	30	118	589	5.0	1	7

KI-JANA CARTER Carter, Kenneth Leonard 5′10″, 226 **RB**
Col: Penn State *HS:* Westerville South [OH] B: 9/12/1973, Westerville, OH *Drafted:* 1995 Round 1 Cin
1997 Cin: Pass 1-0; KR 1-9 9.0. **Total:** Pass 1-0; KR 1-9 9.0.

		Rushing				Receiving					Tot
Year Team	**G**	**Att**	**Yds**	**Avg**	**TD**	**Rec**	**Yds**	**Avg**	**TD**	**Fum**	**TD**
1996 Cin	16	91	264	2.9	8	22	169	7.7	1	2	9
1997 Cin	15	128	464	3.6	7	21	157	7.5	0	3	7
1998 Cin	1	2	4	2.0	0	6	25	4.2	0	0	0
NFL Total	32	221	732	3.3	15	49	351	7.2	1	5	16

KENT CARTER Carter, Kent Alexander 6′3″, 235 **LB**
Col: Los Angeles City Coll. CA (J.C.); USC *HS:* Cathedral [Los Angeles, CA] B: 5/25/1950, Los Angeles, CA *Drafted:* 1972 Round 17 StL
1974 NE: 2 G.

KEVIN CARTER Carter, Kevin Louis 6′5″, 280 **DE**
Col: Florida *HS:* Lincoln [Tallahassee, FL] B: 9/21/1973, Miami, FL
Drafted: 1995 Round 1 StL
1995 StL: 16 G; Scor **1** Saf; 2 Pt; 6 Sac. **1996** StL: 16 G; 9.5 Sac. **1997** StL: 16 G; 7.5 Sac. **1998** StL: 16 G; 12 Sac. **Total:** 64 G; Scor 1 Saf; 2 Pt; 35 Sac.

LOUIS CARTER Carter, Louis Edward 5′11″, 207 **RB**
Col: Maryland *HS:* Arundel [Gambrills, MD] B: 2/6/1953, Laurel, MD
Drafted: 1975 Round 3 Oak
1975 Oak: KR 1-13 13.0. **1976** TB: Pass 5-2 40.0%, 24 4.80 1 TD; KR 15-300 20.0. **1977** TB: Pass 2-0. **1978** TB: Pass 5-2 40.0%, 87 17.40; KR 6-97 16.2. **Total:** Pass 12-4 33.3%, 111 9.25 1 TD; KR 22-410 18.6.

		Rushing				Receiving				
Year Team	**G**	**Att**	**Yds**	**Avg**	**TD**	**Rec**	**Yds**	**Avg**	**TD**	**Fum**
1975 Oak	8	11	27	2.5	0	2	39	19.5	0	0
1976 TB	14	171	521	3.0	1	20	135	6.8	0	2
1977 TB	14	59	117	2.0	2	10	65	6.5	0	2
1978 TB	16	81	275	3.4	1	19	139	7.3	0	6
NFL Total	52	322	940	2.9	4	51	378	7.4	0	10

MARTY CARTER Carter, Marty LaVincent 6′1″, 209 **DB**
Col: Middle Tennessee State *HS:* La Grange [GA] B: 12/17/1969, La Grange, GA *Drafted:* 1991 Round 8 TB
1992 TB: 2 Sac. **1994** TB: Rec 1-21 21.0; KR 1-0; 1 Sac. **1997** ChiB: 1 Sac. **Total:** Rec 1-21 21.0; KR 1-0; 4 Sac.

		Interceptions		
Year Team	**G**	**Int**	**Yds**	**TD**
1991 TB	14	1	5	0
1992 TB	16	3	1	0
1993 TB	16	1	0	0
1994 TB	16	0	0	0
1995 ChiB	16	2	20	0
1996 ChiB	16	3	34	0
1997 ChiB	15	1	14	0
1998 ChiB	16	0	0	0
NFL Total	125	11	74	0

MICHAEL CARTER Carter, Michael D'Andrea 6′2″, 285 **NT**
Col: Southern Methodist *HS:* Thomas Jefferson [Dallas, TX]
B: 10/29/1960, Dallas, TX *Drafted:* 1984 Round 5 SF
1984 SF: 16 G; 4 Sac. **1985** SF: 12 G; 7 Sac. **1986** SF: 15 G; 2 Sac. **1987** SF: 12 G; 1 Sac. **1988** SF: 16 G; Int 1-0; 6.5 Sac. **1989** SF: 8 G. **1990** SF: 15 G; 1 Sac. **1991** SF: 15 G. **1992** SF: 12 G; 1 Sac. **Total:** 121 G; Int 1-0; 22.5 Sac.

MIKE CARTER Carter, Michael Norman 6′1″, 210 **WR**
Col: San Francisco City Coll. CA (J.C.); Sacramento State *HS:* Lowell [San Francisco, CA] B: 2/18/1948, Little Rock, AR
1970 GB: 2 G. **1972** SD: 5 G; Rush 1-25 25.0; Rec 2-24 12.0. **Total:** 7 G; Rush 1-25 25.0; Rec 2-24 12.0.

M.L. CARTER Carter, Milton Louis 5′9″, 173 **DB**
Col: Monterey Peninsula Coll. CA (J.C.); Cal State-Fullerton; San Jose State *HS:* Monterey [CA] B: 12/9/1955, Beaufort, SC
1979 KC: 16 G; Int 3-33. **1980** KC: 7 G. **1981** KC: 10 G. **Total:** 33 G; Int 3-33.

PERRY CARTER Carter, Perry Lynn 6′0″, 194 **DB**
Col: Southern Mississippi *HS:* McComb [MS] B: 8/5/1971, McComb, MS *Drafted:* 1994 Round 4 Ariz
1995 KC: 2 G. **1996** Oak: 4 G. **1997** Oak: 16 G. **1998** Oak: 6 G. **Total:** 28 G.

RODNEY CARTER Carter, Rodney Carl 6′0″, 218 **RB**
Col: Purdue *HS:* Elizabeth [NJ] B: 10/30/1964, Elizabeth, NJ
Drafted: 1986 Round 7 Pit
1988 Pit: Pass 3-2 66.7%, 56 18.67. **1989** Pit: Pass 1-1 100.0%, 15 15.00. **Total:** Pass 4-3 75.0%, 71 17.75.

		Rushing				Receiving				Tot
Year Team	**G**	**Att**	**Yds**	**Avg**	**TD**	**Rec**	**Yds**	**Avg**	**TD**	**TD**
1987 Pit	11	5	12	2.4	0	16	180	11.3	3	3
1988 Pit	14	36	216	6.0	3	32	363	11.3	2	5
1989 Pit	15	11	16	1.5	1	38	267	7.0	3	4
NFL Total	40	52	244	4.7	4	86	810	9.4	8	12

ROSS CARTER Carter, Ross Challis 6′0″, 238 **G-C-LB**
(Timber Beast) *Col:* Southwestern Oregon CC; Oregon *HS:* Lakeview [OR] B: 3/10/1914, Republic, MO *Drafted:* 1936 Round 8 ChiC
1936 ChiC: 10 G. **1937** ChiC: 11 G. **1938** ChiC: 11 G. **1939** ChiC: 10 G. **Total:** 42 G.

RUBIN CARTER Carter, Rubin 6′0″, 256 **NT-DT**
Col: Miami (Fla.) *HS:* Stranahan [Fort Lauderdale, FL] B: 12/12/1952, Pompano Beach, FL *Drafted:* 1975 Round 5 Den
1975 Den: 14 G. **1976** Den: 14 G. **1977** Den: 14 G. **1978** Den: 16 G. **1979** Den: 15 G; **1** Fum TD; 6 Pt. **1980** Den: 16 G. **1981** Den: 16 G. **1982** Den: 9 G. **1983** Den: 16 G; 1 Sac. **1984** Den: 15 G; 3 Sac. **1985** Den: 16 G; 1 Sac. **1986** Den: 5 G. **Total:** 166 G; 1 Fum TD; 6 Pt; 5 Sac.

RUSSELL CARTER Carter, Russell Edmonds Jr. 6′2″, 195 **DB**
Col: Southern Methodist *HS:* Lower Merion [Ardmore, PA]
B: 2/10/1962, Philadelphia, PA *Drafted:* 1984 Round 1 NYJ
1984 NYJ: 11 G; Int 4-26; 3 Sac. **1985** NYJ: 8 G; 1 Sac. **1986** NYJ: 13 G. **1987** NYJ: 8 G. **1988** LARd: 15 G; KR 1-14 14.0; 2 Sac. **1989** LARd: 9 G. **Total:** 64 G; KR 1-14 14.0; Int 4-26; 6 Sac.

STEVE CARTER Carter, Stephen Edward 5′10″, 170 **WR**
Col: Albany State (Ga.) *HS:* Southeastern [Detroit, MI] B: 9/12/1962, New York, NY
1987 TB: 3 G; Rec 1-12 12.0.

TOM CARTER Carter, Thomas III 6′0″, 185 **DB**
Col: Notre Dame *HS:* Lakewood [St. Petersburg, FL] B: 9/5/1972, St. Petersburg, FL *Drafted:* 1993 Round 1 Was

		Interceptions		
Year Team	**G**	**Int**	**Yds**	**TD**
1993 Was	14	6	54	0
1994 Was	16	3	58	0
1995 Was	16	4	116	1
1996 Was	16	5	24	0
1997 ChiB	16	3	12	0
1998 ChiB	4	2	20	0
NFL Total	82	23	284	1

VIRGIL CARTER Carter, Virgil R 6′1″, 192 **QB**
Col: Brigham Young *HS:* Folsom [CA] B: 11/9/1945, Anabella, UT
Drafted: 1967 Round 6 ChiB
1971 Cin: Scor **1** 1XP. **Total:** Scor 1 1XP.

		Passing							
Year Team	**G**	**Att**	**Comp**	**Comp%**	**Yds**	**YPA**	**TD**	**Int**	**Rating**
1968 ChiB	7	122	55	45.1	769	6.30	4	5	59.8

Year Team									
1969 ChiB	3	71	36	50.7	343	4.83	2	5	44.5
1970 Cin	13	278	143	51.4	1647	5.92	9	9	66.9
1971 Cin	10	222	138	**62.2**	1624	7.32	10	7	86.2
1972 Cin	10	82	47	57.3	579	7.06	3	4	71.1
1975 SD	1	5	3	60.0	24	4.80	0	1	32.5
1976 ChiB	8	5	3	60.0	77	15.40	1	0	143.8
NFL Total	52	785	425	54.1	5063	6.45	29	31	69.9

	Rushing				
Year Team	Att	Yds	Avg	TD	Fum
1968 ChiB	48	265	5.5	4	3
1969 ChiB	4	19	4.8	0	0
1970 Cin	34	246	7.2	2	5
1971 Cin	8	42	5.3	0	5
1972 Cin	12	57	4.8	2	2
1975 SD	2	11	5.5	0	0
1976 ChiB	1	0	0.0	0	0
NFL Total	109	640	5.9	8	15

WALTER CARTER Carter, Walter Burke 6′4″, 276 **DE**
Col: Florida State *HS:* Maggie L. Walker [Richmond, VA]
B: 12/19/1957, Richmond, VA *Drafted:* 1980 Round 10 Oak
1987 TB: 2 G.

ALLEN CARTER Carter, Wayne Allen 5′11″, 208 **RB**
Col: USC *HS:* Bonita [La Verne, CA] B: 12/12/1952, Pomona, CA
Drafted: 1975 Round 4 NE
1975 NE: Rush 22-95 4.3; Rec 2-39 19.5. **Total:** Rush 22-95 4.3; Rec 2-39 19.5.

		Kickoff Returns				
Year Team	G	Ret	Yds	Avg	TD	Fum
1975 NE	14	32	879	27.5	**1**	2
1976 NE	1	1	19	19.0	0	0
NFL Total	15	33	898	27.2	1	2

PAT CARTER Carter, Wendell Patrick 6′4″, 256 **TE**
Col: Florida State *HS:* Riverview [Sarasota, FL] B: 8/1/1966, Sarasota, FL *Drafted:* 1988 Round 2 Det
1991 LARm: KR 1-18 18.0. **Total:** KR 1-18 18.0.

		Receiving				
Year Team	G	Rec	Yds	Avg	TD	Fum
1988 Det	15	13	145	11.2	0	0
1989 LARm	16	0	0	—	0	0
1990 LARm	16	8	58	7.3	0	0
1991 LARm	16	8	69	8.6	2	1
1992 LARm	16	20	232	11.6	3	0
1993 LARm	11	14	166	11.9	1	0
1994 Hou	16	11	74	6.7	1	0
1995 StL	16	0	0	—	0	0
1996 Ariz	16	26	329	12.7	1	0
1997 Ariz	16	7	44	6.3	1	0
NFL Total	154	107	1117	10.4	9	1

JOE CARTER Carter, William Joseph 6′1″, 201 **OE-DE**
Col: Austin; Southern Methodist *HS:* North Dallas [Dallas, TX]
B: 7/23/1910, Dalhart, TX
1933 Phi: Scor 13, 1 XK. **1935** Phi: Rush 7-19 2.7. **1938** Phi: **1** Fum TD. **1939** Phi: Rush 1-4 4.0. **1940** Phi: Rush 1-(-3) -3.0. **1944** Bkn: Punt 9-325 36.1. **1945** ChiC: KR 1-44 44.0. **Total:** Rush 9-20 2.2; KR 1-44 44.0; Punt 9-325 36.1; 1 Fum TD.

		Receiving				Tot
Year Team	G	Rec	Yds	Avg	TD	TD
1933 Phi	9	5	109	21.8	2	2
1934 Phi	11	**16**	238	14.9	4	4
1935 Phi	11	11	260	**23.6**	2	2
1936 Phi	9	4	42	10.5	1	1
1937 Phi	10	15	282	18.8	3	3
1938 Phi	11	27	386	14.3	7	8
1939 Phi	11	24	292	12.2	2	2
1940 Phi	6	12	201	16.8	0	0
1942 GB	11	2	19	9.5	1	1
1944 Bkn	10	13	143	11.0	0	0
1945 ChiC	10	3	17	5.7	0	0
NFL Total	109	132	1989	15.1	22	23

WILLIE CARTER Carter, Willie Lee 5′11″, 198 **HB-DB**
Col: Tennessee State *HS:* Central [Louisville, KY] B: 2/2/1931, Louisville, KY D: 6/6/1986, Lousville, KY
1953 ChiC: 8 G; Rush 2-(-3) -1.5; PR 4-20 5.0; KR 8-178 22.3; 2 Fum.

JASON CARTHEN Carthen, Jason 6′3″, 255 **LB**
Col: Ohio U. *HS:* V. W. Scott [Toledo, OH] B: 11/16/1970, Toledo, OH
1993 NE: 5 G. **1994** NE: 1 G. **Total:** 6 G.

MILT CARTHENS Carthens, Milton 6′4″, 305 **OT**
Col: Michigan *HS:* Lahser [Bloomfield Hills, MI] B: 12/22/1960
1987 Ind: 1 G.

MAURICE CARTHON Carthon, Maurice 6′1″, 225 **RB**
Col: Arkansas State *HS:* Osceola [AR] B: 4/24/1961, Chicago, IL

		Rushing				Receiving					Tot
Year Team	G	Att	Yds	Avg	TD	Rec	Yds	Avg	TD	Fum	TD
1985 NYG	16	27	70	2.6	0	8	81	10.1	0	1	0
1986 NYG	16	72	260	3.6	0	16	67	4.2	0	1	0
1987 NYG	11	26	60	2.3	0	8	71	8.9	0	0	0
1988 NYG	16	46	146	3.2	2	19	194	10.2	1	0	3
1989 NYG	16	57	153	2.7	0	15	132	8.8	0	1	0
1990 NYG	16	36	143	4.0	0	14	151	10.8	0	1	0
1991 NYG	16	32	109	3.4	0	7	39	5.6	0	1	0
1992 Ind	16	4	9	2.3	0	3	10	3.3	0	0	0
NFL Total	123	300	950	3.2	2	90	745	8.3	1	5	3

CHARLIE CARTON Carton, Charles Peter 5′10″, 195 **E-T-C-G**
Col: Holy Cross *HS:* Roman Catholic [Philadelphia, PA] B: 3/6/1901, Philadelphia, PA D: 6/9/1951, Queens, NY
1925 Fra: 13 G; Rec 1 TD; 6 Pt.

DALE CARVER Carver, Dale Keith 6′2″, 225 **LB**
Col: Georgia *HS:* Palm Bay [FL] B: 3/5/1961, Melbourne, FL
1983 Cle: 16 G.

MEL CARVER Carver, Melvin 5′11″, 221 **RB**
Col: Laney Coll. CA (J.C.); Nevada-Las Vegas *HS:* Encinal [Alameda, CA] B: 7/14/1959, Pensacola, FL
1982 TB: KR 3-62 20.7. **1983** TB: KR 2-24 12.0. **Total:** KR 5-86 17.2.

		Rushing				Receiving					Tot
Year Team	G	Att	Yds	Avg	TD	Rec	Yds	Avg	TD	Fum	TD
1982 TB	9	70	229	3.3	1	4	46	11.5	1	2	2
1983 TB	16	114	348	3.1	0	32	262	8.2	1	6	1
1984 TB	5	11	44	4.0	0	3	27	9.0	0	1	0
1985 TB	2	0	0	—	0	0	0	—	0	0	0
1987 Ind	1	2	3	1.5	0	0	0	—	0	0	0
NFL Total	33	197	624	3.2	1	39	335	8.6	2	9	3

SHANTE CARVER Carver, Shante Ebony 6′5″, 250 **DE**
Col: Arizona State *HS:* Lincoln [Stockton, CA] B: 2/12/1971, Stockton, CA *Drafted:* 1994 Round 1 Dal
1994 Dal: 10 G. **1995** Dal: 16 G; 2.5 Sac. **1996** Dal: 10 G; 3 Sac. **1997** Dal: 16 G; 6 Sac. **Total:** 52 G; 11.5 Sac.

LARRY CARWELL Carwell, Lawrence Neil 6′1″, 188 **DB**
Col: Iowa State *HS:* Memorial [Campbell, OH] B: 8/5/1944, Vada, GA
D: 1/10/1984, Bahamas *Drafted:* 1967 Round 3 Hou

		Punt Returns				Kickoff Returns			
Year Team	G	Ret	Yds	Avg	TD	Ret	Yds	Avg	TD
1967 Hou	9	9	154	17.1	0	8	164	20.5	0
1968 Hou	14	27	227	8.4	0	15	335	22.3	0
1969 Bos	13	5	43	8.6	0	1	28	28.0	0
1970 Bos	10	3	48	16.0	0	1	30	30.0	0
1971 NE	14	0	0	—	0	0	0	—	0
1972 NE	14	5	2	0.4	0	0	0	—	0
NFL Total	74	49	474	9.7	0	25	557	22.3	0

	Interceptions				Tot
Year Team	Int	Yds	TD	Fum	TD
1967 Hou	0	31	0	1	0
1968 Hou	4	81	1	4	1
1969 Bos	4	114	0	0	0
1971 NE	5	72	1	0	1
1972 NE	1	0	0	1	1
NFL Total	14	298	2	6	3

KEN CASANEGA Casanega, Kenneth Thomas 5′11″, 175 **DB-HB**
Col: Santa Clara *HS:* Castlemont [Oakland, CA] B: 2/18/1921, CA
AAFC **1946** SF-A: Rec 5-102 20.4 1 TD; PR 18-248 13.8; KR 3-61 20.3; Int 8-146. **Total:** Rec 5-102 20.4 1 TD; PR 18-248 13.8; KR 3-61 20.3; Int 8-146.

		Rushing				Tot
Year Team	G	Att	Yds	Avg	TD	TD
1946 SF-A	14	29	90	3.1	1	2
1948 SF-A	1	0	0	—	0	0
AAFC Total	15	29	90	3.1	1	2

TOMMY CASANOVA Casanova, Thomas Henry III 6′2″, 202 **DB**
Col: Louisiana State *HS:* Notre Dame [Crowley, LA] B: 8/29/1950, New Orleans, LA *Drafted:* 1972 Round 2 Cin
1972 Cin: KR 1-34 34.0. **1974** Cin: KR 1-48 48.0. **1976** Cin: **1** Fum TD. **1977** Cin: Rush 1-20 20.0. **Total:** Rush 1-20 20.0; KR 2-82 41.0; 1 Fum TD.

		Punt Returns				Interceptions				Tot
Year Team	G	Ret	Yds	Avg	TD	Int	Yds	TD	Fum	TD
1972 Cin	14	30	289	9.6	**1**	5	108	0	0	1
1973 Cin	10	15	119	7.9	0	4	33	0	0	0

1974 Cin	14	24	265	11.0	0	2	26	0	3	0
1975 Cin	11	11	60	5.5	0	0	0	0	1	0
1976 Cin	11	10	45	4.5	0	5	109	2	2	3
1977 Cin	11	1	6	6.0	0	1	0	0	0	0
NFL Total	71	91	784	8.6	1	17	276	2	6	4

RICK CASARES Casares, Ricardo Jose 6′2″, 226 **FB**
Col: Florida *HS:* Thomas Jefferson [Tampa, FL] B: 7/4/1931, Tampa, FL *Drafted:* 1954 Round 2 ChiB
1955 ChiB: Pass 3-2 66.7%, 27 9.00 1 TD 1 Int. **1956** ChiB: Pass 3-0, 1 Int; KR 3-95 31.7; Punt 1-51 51.0. **1957** ChiB: Pass 2-1 50.0%, 32 16.00; KR 1-0; Punt 2-67 33.5. **1958** ChiB: Pass 4-1 25.0%, 13 3.25 1 TD. **1959** ChiB: Pass 1-0, 1 Int; Punt 3-139 46.3. **1960** ChiB: Punt 1-60 60.0. **1962** ChiB: Pass 2-1 50.0%, 35 17.50 1 TD. **1963** ChiB: KR 2-18 9.0. **Total:** Pass 15-5 33.3%, 107 7.13 3 TD 3 Int; KR 6-113 18.8; Punt 7-317 45.3.

		Rushing				Receiving					Tot
Year Team	**G**	**Att**	**Yds**	**Avg**	**TD**	**Rec**	**Yds**	**Avg**	**TD**	**Fum**	**TD**
1955 ChiB	12	125	672	**5.4**	4	16	136	8.5	1	3	5
1956 ChiB	12	**234**	**1126**	4.8	**12**	23	203	8.8	2	5	**14**
1957 ChiB	12	**204**	700	3.4	6	25	225	9.0	0	2	6
1958 ChiB	12	176	651	3.7	2	32	290	9.1	1	5	3
1959 ChiB	12	177	699	3.9	10	27	273	10.1	2	7	12
1960 ChiB	12	160	566	3.5	5	8	64	8.0	0	5	5
1961 ChiB	13	135	588	4.4	8	8	69	8.6	0	1	8
1962 ChiB	13	75	255	3.4	2	10	71	7.1	1	4	3
1963 ChiB	10	65	277	4.3	0	19	94	4.9	1	2	1
1964 ChiB	13	35	123	3.5	0	14	113	8.1	2	1	2
1965 Was	3	2	5	2.5	0	1	5	5.0	0	0	0
1966 Mia	6	43	135	3.1	0	8	45	5.6	1	0	1
NFL Total	130	1431	5797	4.1	49	191	1588	8.3	11	35	60

CHAD CASCADDEN Cascadden, Chad Stevens 6′1″, 235 **LB**
Col: Wisconsin *HS:* Chippewa Falls [WI] B: 5/14/1972, Chippewa Falls, WI
1995 NYJ: 12 G. **1996** NYJ: 16 G; 3 Sac. **1997** NYJ: 15 G. **1998** NYJ: 13 G; 1 Fum TD; 6 Pt; 5 Sac. **Total:** 56 G; 1 Fum TD; 6 Pt; 8 Sac.

ERNIE CASE Case, Ernest Francis 5′10″, 170 **QB-DB**
Col: UCLA *HS:* John C. Fremont [Los Angeles, CA] B: 11/23/1919, Case, TX D: 12/13/1995, Palos Verdes Estates, CA
AAFC **1947** BalA: 14 G; Pass 11-4 36.4%, 49 4.45 1 Int; Rush 1-0; PR 2-18 9.0; KR 4-104 26.0; Int 2-56; Punt 5-152 30.4; Scor 4, 1-1 100.0% FG, 1-1 100.0% XK.

FRANK CASE Case, Francis 6′4″, 243 **DE**
Col: Penn State *HS:* Central Bucks West [Doylestown, PA] B: 8/14/1958, Jacksonville, NC *Drafted:* 1981 Round 11 KC
1981 KC: 7 G.

SCOTT CASE Case, Jeffrey Scott 6′1″, 183 **DB**
Col: Northeastern Oklahoma A&M (J.C.); Oklahoma *HS:* Alva [OK]; Memorial HS [Edmond, OK] B: 5/17/1962, Waynoka, OK *Drafted:* 1984 Round 2 Atl
1984 Atl: Scor **1** Saf. **1985** Atl: 1 Sac. **1988** Atl: 1 Sac. **1989** Atl: 1 Sac. **1990** Atl: KR 1-13 13.0; 3 Sac. **1993** Atl: 1.5 Sac. **Total:** KR 1-13 13.0; Scor 1 Saf; 7.5 Sac.

		Interceptions		
Year Team	**G**	**Int**	**Yds**	**TD**
1984 Atl	16	0	0	0
1985 Atl	14	4	78	0
1986 Atl	16	4	41	0
1987 Atl	11	1	12	0
1988 Atl	16	**10**	47	0
1989 Atl	14	2	13	0
1990 Atl	16	3	38	1
1991 Atl	16	2	23	0
1992 Atl	12	2	0	0
1993 Atl	16	0	3	0
1994 Atl	15	2	12	0
1995 Dal	16	0	0	0
NFL Total	178	30	267	1

PETE CASE Case, Ronald Lee 6′3″, 245 **OG**
Col: Georgia *HS:* Decatur [GA] B: 12/27/1940, Dayton, OH *Drafted:* 1962 Round 2 Phi
1962 Phi: 14 G. **1963** Phi: 12 G. **1964** Phi: 14 G. **1965** NYG: 14 G. **1966** NYG: 14 G. **1967** NYG: 14 G; Rush 0-16. **1968** NYG: 14 G. **1969** NYG: 14 G. **1970** NYG: 7 G. **Total:** 117 G; Rush 0-16.

STONEY CASE Case, Stoney Jarrod 6′3″, 204 **QB**
Col: New Mexico *HS:* Permian [Odessa, TX] B: 7/7/1972, Odessa, TX *Drafted:* 1995 Round 3 Ariz
1995 Ariz: Rush 1-4 4.0. **1997** Ariz: Rush 7-8 1.1 1 TD. **Total:** Rush 8-12 1.5 1 TD.

		Passing								
Year Team	**G**	**Att**	**Comp**	**Comp%**	**Yds**	**YPA**	**TD**	**Int**	**Rating**	**Fum**
1995 Ariz	2	2	1	50.0	19	9.50	0	1	43.8	0
1997 Ariz	3	55	29	52.7	316	5.75	0	2	54.8	3
NFL Total	5	57	30	52.6	335	5.88	0	3	48.5	3

PETE CASEY Casey, Albert R 180 **HB**
Col: No College *HS:* Potosi [MO] B: 12/2/1895, Potosi, MO D: 8/25/1976, St. Louis, MO
1923 StL: 7 G; Rec 1 TD; 1 Fum TD; Tot TD 2; 12 Pt.

ALVRO CASEY Casey, Alvro E 6′0″, 215 **T**
(Running Wolf) *Col:* Haskell Indian; Northeastern Oklahoma A&M (J.C.) *HS:* Muskogee [OK] B: 3/29/1903, Muskogee, OK D: 10/22/1971, Big Spring, TX
1926 Akr: 4 G.

BERNIE CASEY Casey, Bernard Terry 6′4″, 215 **WR**
Col: Bowling Green State *HS:* East [Columbus, OH] B: 6/8/1939, Wyco, WV *Drafted:* 1961 Round 1 SF
1966 SF: Rush 1-23 23.0. **Total:** Rush 1-23 23.0.

		Receiving				
Year Team	**G**	**Rec**	**Yds**	**Avg**	**TD**	**Fum**
1961 SF	12	10	185	18.5	1	1
1962 SF	13	53	819	15.5	6	1
1963 SF	14	47	762	16.2	7	0
1964 SF	13	58	808	13.9	4	0
1965 SF	14	59	765	13.0	8	0
1966 SF	13	50	669	13.4	1	1
1967 LARm	14	53	871	16.4	8	0
1968 LARm	12	29	565	19.5	5	0
NFL Total	105	359	5444	15.2	40	3

EDDIE CASEY Casey, Edward Lawrence 5′10″, 161 **WB**
(Natick Eddie) *Col:* Harvard *HS:* Natick [MA]; Phillips Exeter Acad. [Exeter, NH] B: 5/16/1894, Natick, MA D: 7/26/1966, Boston, MA
1920 Buf: 1 G.

TOM CASEY Casey, Thomas Ray 5′11″, 175 **TB-DB**
Col: Hampton *HS:* Westinghouse [Pittsburgh, PA] B: 7/30/1924, Wellsville, OH
AAFC **1948** NY-A: 11 G; Pass 5-2 40.0%, 31 6.20 1 TD; Rush 18-75 4.2; PR 9-229 25.4 1 TD; KR 7-170 24.3; Punt 6-242 40.3; 6 Pt.

TIM CASEY Casey, Timothy Michael 6′1″, 225 **LB**
(Cobra) *Col:* Oregon *HS:* Jesuit [Portland, OR] B: 2/29/1944, Portland, OR
1969 ChiB-Den: 5 G. ChiB: 3 G. Den: 2 G. **Total:** 5 G.

JOHN CASH Cash, John Lewis 6′3″, 240 **DE**
Col: Allen *HS:* Risley [GA] B: 8/5/1936, Brunswick, GA
1961 Den: 14 G. **1962** Den: 14 G; Int 1-5. **Total:** 28 G; Int 1-5.

KEITH CASH Cash, Keith Lovell 6′4″, 242 **TE**
Col: Texas *HS:* Holmes [San Antonio, TX] B: 8/7/1969, San Antonio, TX *Drafted:* 1991 Round 7 Was
1991 Pit: PR 1-6 6.0. **1992** KC: KR 1-36 36.0. **1993** KC: Rush 1-0. **Total:** Rush 1-0; PR 1-6 6.0; KR 1-36 36.0.

		Receiving				
Year Team	**G**	**Rec**	**Yds**	**Avg**	**TD**	**Fum**
1991 Pit	5	7	90	12.9	1	0
1992 KC	15	12	113	9.4	2	0
1993 KC	15	24	242	10.1	4	1
1994 KC	6	19	192	10.1	2	0
1995 KC	14	42	419	10.0	1	0
1996 KC	9	14	80	5.7	0	1
NFL Total	64	118	1136	9.6	10	2

KERRY CASH Cash, Kerry Lenard 6′4″, 250 **TE**
Col: Texas *HS:* Holmes [San Antonio, TX] B: 8/7/1969, San Antonio, TX *Drafted:* 1991 Round 5 Ind
1993 Ind: KR 1-11 11.0. **Total:** KR 1-11 11.0.

		Receiving				
Year Team	**G**	**Rec**	**Yds**	**Avg**	**TD**	**Fum**
1991 Ind	4	1	18	18.0	0	0
1992 Ind	16	43	521	12.1	3	0
1993 Ind	16	43	402	9.3	3	2
1994 Ind	16	16	190	11.9	1	1
1995 Oak	16	25	254	10.2	2	2
1996 ChiB	4	4	42	10.5	0	0
NFL Total	72	132	1427	10.8	9	5

RICK CASH Cash, Richard Francis 6′5″, 248 **DT-DE**
(Thumper) *Col:* Missouri; Northeast Missouri State *HS:* Webster Groves [MO] B: 7/1/1945, St. Louis, MO *Drafted:* 1968 Round 10 GB
1968 Atl: 14 G. **1969** LARm: 14 G. **1970** LARm: 8 G. **1972** NE: 14 G. **1973** NE: 14 G. **Total:** 64 G.

TONY CASILLAS Casillas, Tony Steven 6′3″, 278 **NT-DT**
Col: Oklahoma *HS:* East Central [Tulsa, OK] B: 10/26/1963, Tulsa, OK
Drafted: 1986 Round 1 Atl
1986 Atl: 16 G; 1 Sac. **1987** Atl: 9 G; 2 Sac. **1988** Atl: 16 G; 2 Sac. **1989** Atl: 16 G; 2 Sac. **1990** Atl: 9 G; 1 Sac. **1991** Dal: 16 G; 2.5 Sac. **1992** Dal: 15 G; 3 Sac. **1993** Dal: 15 G; 2 Sac. **1994** NYJ: 12 G; 1.5 Sac. **1995** NYJ: 11 G; 3 Sac. **1996** Dal: 16 G. **1997** Dal: 15 G; 3 Sac.
Total: 166 G; 23.0 Sac.

KEN CASNER Casner, Kenneth Wayne 6′2″, 245 **DT**
Col: Baylor *HS:* Scott [KS]; Waco HS [TX] B: 1/23/1930, Fort Scott, KS
1952 LARm: 11 G; 1 Fum TD; 6 Pt.

JIM CASON Cason, James Allnut Jr. 6′0″, 171 **DB-HB**
Col: Louisiana State *HS:* Patti Welder Victoria [TX] B: 7/25/1927, Sondheimer, LA *Drafted:* 1948 Round 5 ChiC
AAFC **1948** SF-A: Rec 4-99 24.8 1 TD; KR 10-212 21.2. **1949** SF-A: Pass 2-1 50.0%, 38 19.00 1 TD; Rec 5-38 7.6; KR 11-247 22.5.
Total: Pass 2-1 50.0%, 38 19.00 1 TD; Rec 9-137 15.2 1 TD; KR 21-459 21.9.

		Rushing				Punt Returns			
Year Team	G	Att	Yds	Avg	TD	Ret	Yds	Avg	TD
1948 SF-A	13	20	146	7.3	2	22	309	14.0	0
1949 SF-A	12	21	70	3.3	1	21	351	16.7	0
AAFC Total	25	41	216	5.3	3	43	660	15.3	0

	Interceptions			Tot
Year Team	Int	Yds	TD	TD
1948 SF-A	5	46	0	3
1949 SF-A	9	152	0	1
AAFC Total	14	198	0	4

NFL **1950** SF: PR 11-173 15.7; KR 2-48 24.0. **1951** SF: PR 13-115 8.8; KR 10-196 19.6. **1954** SF: Pass 13-7 53.8%, 40 3.08 1 Int.
Total: Pass 13-7 53.8%, 40 3.08 1 Int; PR 24-288 12.0; KR 12-244 20.3.

		Rushing				Receiving			
Year Team	G	Att	Yds	Avg	TD	Rec	Yds	Avg	TD
1950 SF	9	38	129	3.4	1	30	374	12.5	3
1951 SF	12	1	5	5.0	0	1	8	8.0	0
1952 SF	10	0	0	—	0	0	0	—	0
1954 SF	9	2	1	0.5	0	0	0	—	0
1955 LARm	12	0	0	—	0	0	0	—	0
1956 LARm	12	0	0	—	0	0	0	—	0
NFL Total	64	41	135	3.3	1	31	382	12.3	3

	Interceptions				Tot
Year Team	Int	Yds	TD	Fum	TD
1950 SF	1	22	0	3	4
1951 SF	8	147	1	1	1
1952 SF	2	4	0	0	0
1954 SF	0	0	0	1	0
1955 LARm	5	41	1	0	1
1956 LARm	4	63	0	0	0
NFL Total	20	277	2	5	6

WENDELL CASON Cason, Wendell B 5′11″, 191 **DB**
Col: Oregon *HS:* Carson [CA] B: 1/22/1963, Lakewood, CA
1985 Atl: 14 G; Int 3-30. **1986** Atl: 16 G; Int 1-10. **1987** Atl: 3 G.
Total: 33 G; Int 4-40.

CY CASPER Casper, Charles Andrew 6′0″, 190 **TB-DB-BB-WB**
Col: Texas Christian *HS:* Harlandale [San Antonio, TX] B: 5/28/1912, Memphis, TX D: 3/7/1968, Fort Worth, TX
1934 GB-StL: Pass 4-1 25.0%, 29 7.25; Rec 5-70 14.0. StL: Pass 4-1 25.0%, 29 7.25; Rec 5-70 14.0. **1935** Pit: Pass 4-1 25.0%, 3 0.75; Rec 5-94 18.8 1 TD. **Total:** Pass 8-2 25.0%, 32 4.00; Rec 10-164 16.4 1 TD.

		Rushing				Tot
Year Team	G	Att	Yds	Avg	TD	TD
1934 GB-StL	4	27	99	3.7	0	0
1934 GB	1	4	19	4.8	0	0
1934 StL	3	23	80	3.5	0	0
1935 Pit	9	56	102	1.8	1	3
NFL Total	13	83	201	2.4	1	3

DAVE CASPER Casper, David John 6′4″, 240 **TE**
(The Ghost) *Col:* Notre Dame *HS:* Chilton [WI] B: 9/26/1951, Bemidji, MN *Drafted:* 1974 Round 2 Oak
1976 Oak: Rush 1-5 5.0. **1978** Oak: Pass 1-0; Rush 1-5 5.0; 1 Fum TD. **1980** Oak-Hou: Rush 2-8 4.0. Hou: Rush 2-8 4.0. **1982** Hou: Rush 2-9 4.5. **Total:** Pass 1-0; Rush 6-27 4.5; 1 Fum TD.

		Receiving					Tot
Year Team	G	Rec	Yds	Avg	TD	Fum	TD
1974 Oak	14	4	26	6.5	3	0	3
1975 Oak	14	5	71	14.2	1	0	1
1976 Oak	13	53	691	13.0	10	0	10
1977 Oak	14	48	584	12.2	6	1	6
1978 Oak	16	62	852	13.7	9	1	10
1979 Oak	15	57	771	13.5	3	1	3
1980 Oak-Hou	16	56	796	14.2	4	3	4
1980 Oak	6	22	270	12.3	1	1	1
1980 Hou	10	34	526	15.5	3	2	3
1981 Hou	16	33	572	17.3	8	0	8
1982 Hou	9	36	573	15.9	6	1	6
1983 Hou-Min	13	20	251	12.6	0	0	0
1983 Hou	3	7	79	11.3	0	0	0
1983 Min	10	13	172	13.2	0	0	0
1984 LARd	7	4	29	7.3	2	0	2
NFL Total	147	378	5216	13.8	52	7	53

CRAIG CASSADY Cassady, Craig Howard 5′11″, 175 **DB**
Col: Ohio State *HS:* Whetstone [Columbus, OH] B: 12/21/1953, Columbus, OH *Drafted:* 1976 Round 8 NO
1977 NO: 12 G.

HOPALONG CASSADY Cassady, Howard Albert 5′10″, 183 **HB-FL**
Col: Ohio State *HS:* Central [Columbus, OH] B: 3/2/1934, Columbus, OH *Drafted:* 1956 Round 1 Det
1956 Det: Pass 2-0, 1 Int. **1961** Det: Pass 1-0. **Total:** Pass 3-0, 1 Int.

		Rushing				Receiving			
Year Team	G	Att	Yds	Avg	TD	Rec	Yds	Avg	TD
1956 Det	12	97	413	4.3	0	9	83	9.2	0
1957 Det	12	73	250	3.4	3	25	325	13.0	3
1958 Det	10	45	198	4.4	0	23	406	17.7	7
1959 Det	12	52	203	3.9	1	15	316	21.1	4
1960 Det	12	17	28	1.6	1	20	238	11.9	1
1961 Det	14	31	131	4.2	1	5	45	9.0	1
1962 Cle-Phi	10	1	6	6.0	0	14	188	13.4	2
1962 Cle	5	0	0	—	0	0	0	—	0
1962 Phi	5	1	6	6.0	0	14	188	13.4	2
1963 Det	2	0	0	—	0	0	0	—	0
NFL Total	84	316	1229	3.9	6	111	1601	14.4	18

	Punt Returns				Kickoff Returns					Tot
Year Team	Ret	Yds	Avg	TD	Ret	Yds	Avg	TD	Fum	TD
1956 Det	13	83	6.4	0	16	382	23.9	0	2	0
1957 Det	0	0	—	0	10	232	23.2	0	3	6
1958 Det	3	4	1.3	0	6	126	21.0	0	3	7
1959 Det	1	14	14.0	0	8	163	20.4	0	2	5
1960 Det	1	25	25.0	0	4	82	20.5	0	0	2
1961 Det	16	159	9.9	0	9	127	14.1	0	2	2
1962 Cle-Phi	8	49	6.1	0	24	482	20.1	0	1	2
1962 Cle	7	47	6.7	0	10	233	23.3	0	0	0
1962 Phi	1	2	2.0	0	14	249	17.8	0	1	2
1963 Det	1	7	7.0	0	0	0	—	0	0	0
NFL Total	43	341	7.9	0	77	1594	20.7	0	13	24

FRANK CASSARA Cassara, Frank 6′0″, 215 **FB-LB**
Col: St. Mary's (Cal.) *HS:* San Fernando [CA] B: 3/22/1928, San Fernando, CA
1954 SF: 6 G; Rush 3-17 5.7; Rec 1-12 12.0; 1 Fum.

TOM CASSESE Cassese, Thomas Lee 6′1″, 198 **DB-HB**
Col: C.W. Post *HS:* Holy Cross [Queens, NY] B: 4/7/1946, Queens, NY
Drafted: 1967 Round 8 Den
1967 Den: 14 G; Rush 1-5 5.0; PR 3-14 4.7; KR 1-19 19.0; Int 1-24; 1 Fum.

DICK CASSIANO Cassiano, Richard Peter 5′11″, 175 **TB-HB-DB**
Col: Pittsburgh B: 10/7/1917, Albany, NY D: 5/28/1980, Guilderland, NY *Drafted:* 1940 Round 4 GB
1940 Bkn: Pass 30-9 30.0%, 128 4.27 1 TD **2** Int; Rec 2-67 33.5 2 TD.

		Rushing			
Year Team	G	Att	Yds	Avg	TD
1940 Bkn	10	35	84	2.4	0

CASSIDY Cassidy **BB**
Col: No College Deceased
1921 Ton: 1 G.

RON CASSIDY Cassidy, Ronald Gene 6′0″, 184 **WR**
Col: Fullerton Coll. CA (J.C.); Utah State *HS:* Los Alamitos [CA]
B: 7/23/1957, Ventura, CA *Drafted:* 1979 Round 8 GB
1979 GB: 8 G; Rec 6-102 17.0. **1980** GB: 15 G; Rec 5-109 21.8; PR 17-139 8.2; 1 Fum. **1981** GB: 10 G; Rec 1-6 6.0; PR 2-0; 1 Fum. **1983** GB: 12 G. **1984** GB: 15 G; Rec 2-16 8.0. **Total:** 60 G; Rec 14-233 16.6; PR 19-139 7.3; 2 Fum.

WALT CASSIDY Cassidy, Walter 5′10″, 200 **E**
Col: Detroit Mercy *HS:* Morrison R. Waite [Toledo, OH] B: 12/16/1899 D: 10/1974, Cleveland, OH
1924 Ken: 5 G.

MIKE CASTEEL Casteel, Miles Webster 5′11″, 175 **BB-TB-WB**
Col: Kalamazoo *HS:* St. Johns [MI] B: 12/30/1895, Elmira, NY
D: 3/27/1977, Phoenix, AZ
1922 RI: 6 G; Rush 1 TD; 6 Pt.

RICH CASTER Caster, Richard C 6′5″, 228 **TE-WR**
Col: Jackson State *HS:* Lillie B. Williamson [Mobile, AL]
B: 10/16/1948, Mobile, AL *Drafted:* 1970 Round 2 NYJ
1970 NYJ: KR 1-0. **1971** NYJ: Rush 2-10 5.0. **1972** NYJ: Rush 2-6 3.0. **1973** NYJ: Rush 1-(-9) -9.0. **1976** NYJ: Rush 6-73 12.2. **1977** NYJ: Rush 2-(-15) -7.5. **1978** Hou: Rush 5-32 6.4. **1979** Hou: Rush 4-25 6.3; KR 1-0. **1981** NO-Was: Rush 1-(-3) -3.0. NO: Rush 1-(-3) -3.0.
Total: Rush 23-119 5.2; KR 2-0.

		Receiving				
Year Team	G	Rec	Yds	Avg	TD	Fum
1970 NYJ	14	19	393	20.7	3	0
1971 NYJ	14	26	454	17.5	6	0
1972 NYJ	14	39	833	21.4	10	0
1973 NYJ	14	35	593	16.9	4	1
1974 NYJ	13	38	745	19.6	7	2
1975 NYJ	14	47	820	17.4	4	0
1976 NYJ	14	31	391	12.6	1	1
1977 NYJ	10	10	205	20.5	1	1
1978 Hou	14	20	316	15.8	5	1
1979 Hou	16	18	239	13.3	1	1
1980 Hou	16	27	341	12.6	3	1
1981 NO-Was	7	12	185	15.4	0	2
1981 NO	4	7	108	15.4	0	2
1981 Was	3	5	77	15.4	0	0
1982 Was	1	0	0	—	0	0
NFL Total	161	322	5515	17.1	45	10

JESSE CASTETE Castete, Jesse Joseph 5′11″, 180 **DB**
Col: McNeese State *HS:* Marion [Lake Charles, LA] B: 9/3/1933, St. Landry, LA *Drafted:* 1956 Round 24 ChiB
1956 ChiB-LARm: 11 G; Int 2-26. ChiB: 8 G; Int 2-26. LARm: 3 G.
1957 LARm: 11 G. **Total:** 22 G; Int 2-26.

JIM CASTIGLIA Castiglia, James Vincent 5′11″, 208 **FB-LB**
Col: Georgetown *HS:* Passaic [NJ] B: 9/30/1918, Passaic, NJ
Drafted: 1941 Round 19 Pit
AAFC **1947** BalA: 2 G; Rush 9-18 2.0; Rec 1-10 10.0.

NFL **1941** Phi: Pass 7-0, 1 Int; KR 7-199 28.4; Int 1-0. **1946** Phi: KR 1-17 17.0. **1947** Was: KR 1-10 10.0. **1948** Was: KR 1-18 18.0. **Total:** Pass 7-0, 1 Int; KR 10-244 24.4; Int 1-0.

		Rushing				Receiving					Tot
Year Team	G	Att	Yds	Avg	TD	Rec	Yds	Avg	TD	Fum	TD
1941 Phi	11	60	183	3.1	4	4	24	6.0	0	0	4
1945 Phi	1	13	29	2.2	0	0	0	—	0	0	0
1946 Phi	11	39	87	2.2	1	11	51	4.6	0	2	1
1947 Was	7	104	426	4.1	5	11	88	8.0	0	1	5
1948 Was	10	97	330	3.4	0	7	73	10.4	2	2	2
NFL Total	40	313	1055	3.4	10	33	236	7.2	2	5	12

JEREMIAH CASTILLE Castille, Jeremiah 5′10″, 175 **DB**
Col: Alabama *HS:* Central [Phenix City, AL] B: 1/15/1961, Columbus, GA *Drafted:* 1983 Round 3 TB

		Interceptions			
Year Team	G	Int	Yds	TD	Fum
1983 TB	15	1	69	1	0
1984 TB	16	3	38	0	0
1985 TB	16	7	49	0	1
1986 TB	13	0	0	0	0
1987 Den	11	0	0	0	0
1988 Den	16	3	51	0	0
NFL Total	87	14	207	1	1

ERIC CASTLE Castle, Eric Dean 6′3″, 212 **DB**
Col: Oregon *HS:* Lebanon Union [OR] B: 3/15/1970, Longview, WA
Drafted: 1993 Round 6 SD
1993 SD: 5 G. **1994** SD: 16 G. **1995** SD: 16 G. **1996** SD: 16 G.
Total: 53 G.

TOBY CASTON Caston, Sebastian Tobias 6′1″, 235 **LB**
Col: Louisiana State *HS:* Neville [Monroe, LA] B: 7/17/1965, Monroe, LA D: 10/2/1994, Dallas, TX *Drafted:* 1987 Round 6 Hou
1987 Hou: 6 G. **1988** Hou: 16 G. **1989** Det: 16 G. **1990** Det: 12 G.
1991 Det: 16 G. **1992** Det: 15 G. **1993** Det: 9 G. **Total:** 90 G.

CHRIS CASTOR Castor, Christopher David 6′0″, 170 **WR**
Col: Duke *HS:* Cary [NC] B: 8/13/1960, Burlington, NC *Drafted:* 1983 Round 5 Sea
1983 Sea: 8 G. **1984** Sea: 15 G; Rec 8-89 11.1. **Total:** 23 G; Rec 8-89 11.1.

TONY CATALANO Catalano, Anthony Emil **G**
Col: No College *HS:* Salida [CO] B: 4/13/1895, Indianapolis, IN
D: 7/25/1980, Boise, ID
1920 Ham: 1 G.

ALCIDES CATANHO Catanho, Alcides 6′3″, 223 **LB**
Col: Rutgers *HS:* Elizabeth [NJ] B: 1/20/1972, Elizabeth, NJ
1995 NE: 12 G. **1996** Was: 15 G. **Total:** 27 G.

MARK CATANO Catano, Mark R 6′3″, 265 **OG**
Col: Valdosta State *HS:* Hendrick Hudson [Montrose, NY]
B: 1/26/1962, Yonkers, NY
1984 Pit: 16 G; KR 1-0. **1985** Pit: 15 G; 3 Sac. **1986** Buf: 1 G. **Total:** 32 G; KR 1-0; 3 Sac.

TONEY CATCHINGS Catchings, Toney Bruce 6′3″, 236 **LB**
Col: Copiah-Lincoln CC MS; Cincinnati *HS:* Crystal Springs [MS]
B: 8/11/1965, Jackson, MS
1987 Cin: 3 G; 2.5 Sac.

GREG CATER Cater, Gregory Wayne 6′0″, 191 **P**
Col: Tennessee-Chattanooga *HS:* La Grange [GA] B: 4/17/1957, La Grange, GA *Drafted:* 1980 Round 10 Buf
1980 Buf: Pass 1-1 100.0%, 15 15.00; Rush 2-(-10) -5.0. **1987** StL: Rush 2-3 1.5. **Total:** Pass 1-1 100.0%, 15 15.00; Rush 4-(-7) -1.8.

		Punting		
Year Team	G	Punts	Yds	Avg
1980 Buf	16	73	2828	38.7
1981 Buf	16	80	3175	39.7
1982 Buf	9	35	1328	37.9
1983 Buf	16	89	3533	39.7
1986 StL	11	61	2271	37.2
1987 StL	9	39	1470	37.7
NFL Total	77	377	14605	38.7

MIKE CATERBONE Caterbone, Michael Thomas 5′11″, 175 **WR**
Col: Franklin & Marshall *HS:* J.P. McCaskey [Lancaster, PA]
B: 2/17/1962, Lancaster, PA
1987 Mia: 3 G; Rec 2-46 23.0; PR 9-78 8.7; 1 Fum.

TOM CATERBONE Caterbone, Thomas Paul 5′8″, 175 **DB**
Col: Franklin & Marshall *HS:* Lancaster Catholic [PA] B: 6/29/1964, Lancaster, PA
1987 Phi: 2 G; PR 2-13 6.5.

ROYAL CATHCART Cathcart, Royal Jenesen 6′0″, 185 **HB**
Col: Compton CC CA; California-Santa Barbara *HS:* Long Beach Polytechnic [CA] B: 4/8/1926, Canute, OK
1950 SF: 2 G; Rush 3-5 1.7.

SAM CATHCART Cathcart, Samuel Woodrow 6′0″, 175 **DB-HB**
Col: Long Beach City Coll. CA (J.C.); California-Santa Barbara
HS: Long Beach Polytechnic [CA] B: 7/7/1924, Canute, OK
AAFC **1949** SF-A: Rec 12-182 15.2; PR 18-306 17.0; KR 7-138 19.7; Int 1-0.

		Rushing			
Year Team	G	Att	Yds	Avg	TD
1949 SF-A	12	69	412	6.0	1

NFL **1950** SF: Rec 7-99 14.1; PR 16-185 11.6; KR 13-311 23.9; Int 3-58. **1952** SF: Pass 1-0, 1 Int; Rec 2-15 7.5; PR 1-23 23.0; KR 1-20 20.0; Int 3-64. **Total:** Pass 1-0, 1 Int; Rec 9-114 12.7; PR 17-208 12.2; KR 14-331 23.6; Int 6-122.

		Rushing				
Year Team	G	Att	Yds	Avg	TD	Fum
1950 SF	12	33	76	2.3	0	6
1952 SF	12	6	21	3.5	0	0
NFL Total	24	39	97	2.5	0	6

TOM CATLIN Catlin, Thomas Allen 6′1″, 213 **LB-C**
Col: Oklahoma *HS:* Ponca City [OK] B: 9/8/1931, Ponca City, OK
1953 Cle: 12 G; Int 1-16. **1954** Cle: 11 G; Int 1-6. **1957** Cle: 4 G. **1958** Cle: 12 G. **1959** Phi: 12 G. **Total:** 51 G; Int 2-22.

DARYL CATO Cato, Ralph Daryl 6′2″, 195 **C-LB**
(Pete) *Col:* Arkansas *HS:* Lonoke [AR] B: 1/8/1920, Lonoke, AR
D: 10/3/1970
AAFC **1946** MiaA: 12 G; Rush 0-3; Int 1-29.

CARMEN CAVALLI Cavalli, Carmen Anthony Jr. 6′4″, 245 **DE**
Col: Richmond *HS:* St. Thomas More [Philadelphia, PA] B: 6/11/1937, Philadelphia, PA *Drafted:* 1960 Round 1 Oak
1960 Oak: 14 G.

MATT CAVANAUGH Cavanaugh, Matthew Andrew 6′2″, 212 **QB**
Col: Pittsburgh *HS:* Chaney [Youngstown, OH] B: 10/27/1956, Youngstown, OH *Drafted:* 1978 Round 2 NE
1981 NE: Rec 1-9 9.0. **1990** NYG: Postseason only. **Total:** Rec 1-9 9.0.

Year Team	G	Passing Att	Comp	Comp%	Yds	YPA	TD	Int	Rating
1979 NE	13	1	1	100.0	10	10.00	0	0	108.3
1980 NE	16	105	63	60.0	885	8.43	9	5	95.9
1981 NE	16	219	115	52.5	1633	7.46	5	13	59.8
1982 NE	7	60	27	45.0	490	8.17	5	5	66.7
1983 SF	5	0	0	—	0	—	0	0	—
1984 SF	8	61	33	54.1	449	7.36	4	0	99.7
1985 SF	16	54	28	51.9	334	6.19	1	1	69.5
1986 Phi	10	58	28	48.3	397	6.84	2	4	53.6
1987 Phi	3	0	0	—	0	—	0	0	—
1988 Phi	5	16	7	43.8	101	6.31	1	1	59.6
1989 Phi	9	5	3	60.0	33	6.60	1	1	79.6
1991 NYG	4	0	0	—	0	—	0	0	—
NFL Total	112	579	305	52.7	4332	7.48	28	30	71.7

Year Team	Rushing Att	Yds	Avg	TD	Fum
1979 NE	1	-2	-2.0	0	0
1980 NE	19	97	5.1	0	1
1981 NE	17	92	5.4	3	2
1982 NE	2	3	1.5	0	1
1983 SF	1	8	8.0	0	0
1984 SF	4	-11	-2.8	0	0
1985 SF	4	5	1.3	0	0
1986 Phi	9	26	2.9	0	2
1987 Phi	1	-2	-2.0	0	0
1989 Phi	2	-3	-1.5	0	1
NFL Total	60	213	3.6	3	7

RONNIE CAVENESS Caveness, Ronald Glen 6′1″, 225 **LB**
Col: Arkansas *HS:* M.B. Smiley [Houston, TX] B: 3/6/1943, Houston, TX *Drafted:* 1965 Round 2 KC
1965 KC: 7 G. **1966** Hou: 14 G; Int 1-6. **1967** Hou: 14 G. **1968** Hou: 11 G. **Total:** 46 G; Int 1-6.

JAMES CAVER Caver, James Jr. 5′9″, 175 **DB**
Col: Missouri *HS:* Waynesville [MO] B: 9/28/1960, Birmingham, AL
1983 Det: 2 G; KR 4-71 17.8; 1 Fum.

BEN CAVIL Cavil, Ben Anthony 6′2″, 310 **OG**
(Big Ben) *Col:* Oklahoma *HS:* La Marque [TX] B: 1/31/1972, Galveston, TX
1997 Bal: 15 G. **1998** Bal: 16 G. **Total:** 31 G.

GRADY CAVNESS Cavness, Grady Crayton 5′11″, 187 **DB**
Col: Texas-El Paso *HS:* Jack Yates [Houston, TX] B: 3/1/1947, Houston, TX *Drafted:* 1969 Round 2 Den
1969 Den: 14 G; Int 2-30. **1970** Atl: 4 G; KR 3-61 20.3. **Total:** 18 G; KR 3-61 20.3; Int 2-30.

JOHN CAVOSIE Cavosie, John Clement 6′0″, 207 **FB-LB-DB-WB**
(Cutz; Nag) *Col:* Wisconsin; Butler *HS:* Ironwood [MI] B: 1/6/1908, Shenandoah, PA D: 3/16/1995, Indianapolis, IN
1932 Port: Pass 12-5 41.7%, 66 5.50 2 TD; Int 1 TD. **1933** Port: Pass 3-1 33.3%, 8 2.67; Rec 6-148 24.7 1 TD; Scor 10, 1 FG, 1 XK.
Total: Pass 15-6 40.0%, 74 4.93 2 TD; Rec 6-148 24.7 1 TD; Int 1 TD; Scor 28, 1 FG, 1 XK.

Year Team	G	Rushing Att	Yds	Avg	TD	Tot TD
1931 Port	13	—	—	—	0	0
1932 Port	11	62	184	3.0	2	3
1933 Port	9	7	8	1.1	0	1
NFL Total	33	69	192	2.8	2	4

LOWELL CAYLOR Caylor, Lowell Howard 6′3″, 205 **DB**
Col: Miami (Ohio) *HS:* Roosevelt [Dayton, OH] B: 6/17/1941, Dayton, OH *Drafted:* 1963 Round 16 ChiB
1964 Cle: 13 G.

LESTER CAYWOOD Caywood, Lester Les 6′0″, 230 **G-T**
(Wimpy) *Col:* St. John's (N.Y.) *HS:* Sapulpa [OK] B: 8/18/1903, Sapulpa, OK D: 2/1986, Oakwood, OK
1926 Buf: 6 G. **1927** Pott-NYG-Cle: 8 G. Pott: 5 G. NYG: 1 G. Cle: 2 G. **1928** Det: 9 G. **1929** NYG: 12 G. **1930** NYG: 16 G; Int 1 TD; 6 Pt. **1931** ChiC-NYG: 12 G. ChiC: 1 G. NYG: 11 G. **1932** NYG-Bkn: 8 G. NYG: 7 G. Bkn: 1 G. **1933** Cin: 10 G. **1934** Cin: 8 G. **Total:** 89 G; Int 1 TD; 6 Pt.

LLOYD CEARING Cearing, Lloyd 185 **BB-WB-TB**
(Speed) *Col:* Valparaiso *HS:* Hammond [IN] B: 11/3/1900, Monon, IN Deceased
1922 Ham: 6 G. **1923** Ham: 7 G. **Total:** 13 G.

CURTIS CEASER Ceaser, Curtis 6′2″, 190 **WR**
Col: Grambling State *HS:* Westbrook [Beaumont, TX] B: 8/11/1972, Lincoln, NE *Drafted:* 1995 Round 7 NYJ
1995 NYJ: 4 G.

CHUCK CECIL Cecil, Charles Douglas 6′0″, 184 **DB**
Col: Arizona *HS:* Helix [La Mesa, CA] B: 11/8/1964, Red Bluff, CA *Drafted:* 1988 Round 4 GB
1992 GB: PR 1-0. **Total:** PR 1-0.

Year Team	G	Interceptions Int	Yds	TD	Fum
1988 GB	16	4	56	0	0
1989 GB	9	1	16	0	0
1990 GB	9	1	0	0	0
1991 GB	16	3	76	0	0
1992 GB	16	4	52	0	1
1993 Pho	15	0	0	0	0
1995 Hou	14	3	35	1	0
NFL Total	95	16	235	1	1

JIMMY CEFALO Cefalo, James Carmen 5′11″, 190 **WR**
Col: Penn State *HS:* Pittston [PA] B: 10/6/1956, Pittston, PA
Drafted: 1978 Round 3 Mia
1978 Mia: KR 2-40 20.0. **Total:** KR 2-40 20.0.

Year Team	G	Receiving Rec	Yds	Avg	TD	Punt Returns Ret	Yds	Avg	TD	Fum
1978 Mia	16	6	145	24.2	3	28	232	8.3	0	3
1979 Mia	16	12	223	18.6	3	2	10	5.0	0	0
1980 Mia	16	11	199	18.1	1	0	0	—	0	0
1981 Mia	16	29	631	21.8	3	0	0	—	0	0
1982 Mia	9	17	356	20.9	1	0	0	—	0	1
1983 Mia	1	0	0	—	0	0	0	—	0	0
1984 Mia	16	18	185	10.3	2	0	0	—	0	1
NFL Total	90	93	1739	18.7	13	30	242	8.1	0	5

BOB CELERI Celeri, Robert Lavern 5′10″, 180 **QB**
Col: California *HS:* Fort Bragg [CA] B: 6/1/1927, Ft. Bragg, CA D: 3/9/1975, Buffalo, NY *Drafted:* 1950 Round 10 SF
1951 NYY: Rec 2-71 35.5 1 TD; Punt 5-224 44.8. **1952** Dal: Rec 4-37 9.3 1 TD; Punt 21-876 41.7. **Total:** Rec 6-108 18.0 2 TD; Punt 26-1100 42.3.

Year Team	G	Passing Att	Comp	Comp%	Yds	YPA	TD	Int	Rating
1951 NYY	11	238	102	42.9	1797	7.55	12	15	59.8
1952 Dal	8	75	31	41.3	490	6.53	3	3	60.4
NFL Total	19	313	133	42.5	2287	7.31	15	18	60.0

Year Team	Rushing Att	Yds	Avg	TD	Fum
1951 NYY	36	107	3.0	0	3
1952 Dal	17	135	7.9	0	6
NFL Total	53	242	4.6	0	9

MARIO CELOTTO Celotto, Mario Raymond 6′3″, 228 **LB**
Col: USC *HS:* St. Bernard's [Manhattan Beach, CA] B: 8/23/1956, Los Angeles, CA *Drafted:* 1978 Round 7 Buf
1978 Buf: 4 G. **1980** Oak: 11 G. **1981** Oak-Bal-LARm: 10 G. Oak: 7 G. LARm: 3 G. **Total:** 25 G.

TONY CEMORE Cemore, Anthony Salvatore 6′0″, 210 **G**
Col: Creighton *HS:* Omaha Tech [NE] B: 8/8/1917, Omaha, NE D: 3/28/1981, Omaha, NE
1941 Phi: 10 G; Int 1-6.

JOHN CENCI Cenci, John Richard 6′0″, 215 **C**
Col: Pittsburgh *HS:* Schenley [Pittsburgh, PA] B: 1/4/1934, Pittsburgh, PA
1956 Pit: 7 G.

LARRY CENTERS Centers, Larry Eugene 6′0″, 215 **RB**
Col: Stephen F. Austin St. *HS:* Tatum [TX] B: 6/1/1968, Tatum, TX
Drafted: 1990 Round 5 Pho
1991 Pho: PR 5-30 6.0. **1995** Ariz: Pass 1-0, 1 Int. **Total:** Pass 1-0, 1 Int; PR 5-30 6.0.

Year Team	G	Rushing Att	Yds	Avg	TD	Receiving Rec	Yds	Avg	TD
1990 Pho	6	0	0	—	0	0	0	—	0
1991 Pho	9	14	44	3.1	0	19	176	9.3	0
1992 Pho	16	37	139	3.8	0	50	417	8.3	2
1993 Pho	16	25	152	6.1	0	66	603	9.1	3
1994 Ariz	16	115	336	2.9	5	77	647	8.4	2
1995 Ariz	16	78	254	3.3	2	101	962	9.5	2
1996 Ariz	16	116	425	3.7	2	99	766	7.7	7
1997 Ariz	15	101	276	2.7	1	54	409	7.6	1
1998 Ariz	16	31	110	3.5	0	69	559	8.1	2
NFL Total	126	517	1736	3.4	10	535	4539	8.5	19

Year Team	Kickoff Returns Ret	Yds	Avg	TD	Fum	Tot TD
1990 Pho	16	272	17.0	0	1	0
1991 Pho	16	330	20.6	0	4	0
1992 Pho	0	0	—	0	1	2

1993 Pho	0	0	—	0	1	3
1994 Ariz	0	0	—	0	2	7
1995 Ariz	1	15	15.0	0	2	4
1996 Ariz	0	0	—	0	1	9
1997 Ariz	0	0	—	0	1	2
1998 Ariz	0	0	—	0	1	2
NFL Total	33	617	18.7	0	14	29

FRANK CEPHOUS Cephous, Frank III 5′10″, 205 **RB**
Col: UCLA *HS:* St. Mark's [Wilmington, DE] B: 7/4/1961, Philadelphia, PA *Drafted:* 1984 Round 11 NYG
1984 NYG: 16 G; Rush 3-2 0.7; KR 9-178 19.8.

GENE CEPPETELLI Ceppetelli, Eugene C 6′2″, 245 **C**
Col: Villanova *HS:* Cooper Cliff [Canada] B: 7/28/1942, Sudbury, Canada
1968 Phi: 14 G. **1969** Phi-NYG: 13 G. Phi: 7 G. NYG: 6 G. **Total:** 27 G.

GORDY CERESINO Ceresino, Gordon Joseph 6′0″, 224 **LB**
Col: Stanford *HS:* Notre Dame [Los Angeles, CA] B: 10/26/1957, Thunder Bay, Canada
1979 SF: 16 G.

JOE CERNE Cerne, Joseph 6′2″, 240 **C**
Col: Northwestern *HS:* Mary Bradford [Kenosha, WI] B: 4/26/1942, Chrnomlj, Yugoslavia *Drafted:* 1965 Round 2 SF
1965 SF: 11 G; KR 1-0. **1966** SF: 14 G. **1967** SF: 14 G. **1968** Atl: 6 G; KR 1-0. **Total:** 45 G; KR 2-0.

BILLY CESARE Cesare, William Joseph 5′11″, 190 **DB**
Col: Memphis; Miami (Fla.) *HS:* Miami Beach [FL] B: 6/2/1955, New York, NY
1978 TB: 10 G. **1979** TB: 16 G. **1980** Mia: 2 G. **1981** TB: 16 G. **1982** Det: 2 G. **Total:** 46 G.

SAL CESARIO Cesario, Salvatore J 6′4″, 255 **OT**
Col: Cal Poly-S.L.O. *HS:* Bellarmine Prep [San Jose, CA] B: 7/4/1963, Stockton, CA *Drafted:* 1986 Round 12 NYJ
1987 Dal: 3 G.

JEFF CHADWICK Chadwick, Jeffrey Allan 6′3″, 190 **WR**
Col: Grand Valley State *HS:* Divine Child [Dearborn, MI]
B: 12/16/1960, Detroit, MI
1984 Det: Rush 1-12 12.0 1 TD. **1987** Det: Rush 1-(-6) -6.0. **1990** Sea: Rush 1-(-3) -3.0. **Total:** Rush 3-3 1.0 1 TD.

		Receiving					Tot
Year Team	**G**	**Rec**	**Yds**	**Avg**	**TD**	**Fum**	**TD**
1983 Det	16	40	617	15.4	4	0	4
1984 Det	16	37	540	14.6	2	0	3
1985 Det	7	25	478	19.1	3	0	3
1986 Det	15	53	995	18.8	5	1	5
1987 Det	8	30	416	13.9	0	0	0
1988 Det	10	20	304	15.2	3	0	3
1989 Det-Sea	12	9	104	11.6	0	0	0
1989 Det	1	1	9	9.0	0	0	0
1989 Sea	11	8	95	11.9	0	0	0
1990 Sea	16	27	478	17.7	4	1	4
1991 Sea	12	22	255	11.6	3	0	3
1992 LARm	14	29	362	12.5	3	1	3
NFL Total	126	292	4549	15.6	27	3	28

PAT CHAFFEY Chaffey, Patrick Lowell 6′1″, 220 **RB**
Col: Oregon State *HS:* North Marion [Aurora, OR] B: 4/19/1967, McMinnville, OR *Drafted:* 1990 Round 5 ChiB
1991 Atl: KR 1-14 14.0. **1992** NYJ: Rec 7-56 8.0. **1993** NYJ: Rec 4-55 13.8 1 TD. **Total:** Rec 11-111 10.1 1 TD; KR 1-14 14.0.

		Rushing					Tot
Year Team	**G**	**Att**	**Yds**	**Avg**	**TD**	**Fum**	**TD**
1991 Atl	14	29	127	4.4	1	1	1
1992 NYJ	14	27	186	6.9	1	0	1
1993 NYJ	3	5	17	3.4	0	0	1
NFL Total	31	61	330	5.4	2	1	3

MIKE CHALENSKI Chalenski, Michael Alan 6′5″, 279 **DE-DT**
Col: Pittsburgh; UCLA *HS:* David Brearly Regional [Kenilworth, NJ]
B: 1/28/1970, Elizabeth, NJ
1993 Phi: 15 G. **1995** Phi: 9 G. **1996** NYJ: 15 G; 0.5 Sac. **1997** Mia: 8 G. **1998** Det: 8 G. **Total:** 55 G; 0.5 Sac.

GEORGE CHALMERS Chalmers, George B 6′0″, 196 **C-LB**
Col: New York U. *HS:* Medford [MA] B: 10/19/1908 D: 8/7/1988, Los Angeles, CA
1933 Bkn: 7 G.

BYRON CHAMBERLAIN Chamberlain, Byron Daniel 6′1″, 240 **TE-WR**
Col: Missouri; Wayne State (Neb.) *HS:* Eastern Hills [Fort Worth, TX]
B: 10/17/1971, Honolulu, HI *Drafted:* 1995 Round 7 Den
1995 Den: 5 G; Rec 1-11 11.0. **1996** Den: 11 G; Rec 12-129 10.8; KR 3-49 16.3; 1 Fum. **1997** Den: 10 G; Rec 2-18 9.0; KR 1-13 13.0; 1 Fum. **1998** Den: 16 G; Rec 3-35 11.7. **Total:** 42 G; Rec 18-193 10.7; KR 4-62 15.5; 2 Fum.

DAN CHAMBERLAIN Chamberlain, Daniel 6′3″, 200 **OE-HB**
Col: Sacramento State *HS:* Placerville [CA] B: 8/26/1937, Grand Rapids, MI *Drafted:* 1959 Round 25 Det
1960 Buf: 12 G; Rec 17-279 16.4 4 TD; KR 1-24 24.0; 24 Pt. **1961** Buf: 3 G; Rec 1-16 16.0. **Total:** 15 G; Rec 18-295 16.4 4 TD; KR 1-24 24.0; 24 Pt.

GARTH CHAMBERLAIN Chamberlain, Garth G 6′0″, 215 **G**
Col: Brigham Young *HS:* Jordan [Sandy, UT] B: 5/20/1920, Alton, UT
D: 12/21/1988, Chandler, AZ *Drafted:* 1942 Round 17 Pit
1945 Pit: 3 G.

GUY CHAMBERLIN Chamberlin, Berlin Guy 6′2″, 196 **E-WB**
Col: Nebraska Wesleyan; Nebraska *HS:* Blue Springs [NE]
B: 1/16/1894, Blue Springs, NE D: 4/4/1967, Lincoln, NE *HOF:* 1965
1920 Sta: 12 G. **1921** Sta: 11 G; Rec 2 TD; Int **1** TD; Tot TD 3; 18 Pt. **1922** Can: 12 G; Rush 3 TD; Rec 1 TD; Int **2** TD; Tot TD **7**; 42 Pt. **1923** Can: 11 G; Rec 2 TD; 12 Pt. **1924** Cle: 9 G; Rec 2 TD; 12 Pt. **1925** Fra: 14 G; Rec 1 TD; Tot TD 2; 12 Pt. **1926** Fra: 17 G; 1 Fum TD; 6 Pt. **1927** ChiC: 6 G. **Total:** 92 G; Rush 3 TD; Rec 8 TD; Int 3 TD; 1 Fum TD; Tot TD 17; 102 Pt.

RUSTY CHAMBERS Chambers, Russell Francis 6′1″, 218 **LB**
Col: Tulane *HS:* Loranger [LA] B: 11/10/1953, Amite, LA D: 7/1/1981, Hammond, LA
1975 NO: 12 G; KR 1-15 15.0; **1** Fum TD; 6 Pt. **1976** NO-Mia: 14 G. NO: 4 G. Mia: 10 G. **1977** Mia: 14 G. **1978** Mia: 16 G; Int 1-49; 1 Fum. **1979** Mia: 16 G; Int 1-4. **1980** Mia: 16 G. **Total:** 88 G; KR 1-15 15.0; Int 2-53; 1 Fum TD; 6 Pt; 1 Fum.

WALLY CHAMBERS Chambers, Wallace Hassim 6′6″, 250 **DE**
Col: Eastern Kentucky *HS:* Mount Clemens [MI] B: 5/15/1951, Phenix City, AL *Drafted:* 1973 Round 1 ChiB
1973 ChiB: 14 G. **1974** ChiB: 14 G. **1975** ChiB: 14 G. **1976** ChiB: 14 G; Int 1-8. **1977** ChiB: 4 G. **1978** TB: 12 G. **1979** TB: 16 G. **Total:** 88 G; Int 1-8.

BILL CHAMBERS Chambers, William Joseph 6′2″, 230 **G**
Col: Alabama; Georgia Tech; UCLA *HS:* Loyola [Los Angeles, CA]
B: 1923
AAFC **1948** NY-A: 13 G. **1949** NY-A: 12 G. **Total:** 25 G.

AL CHAMBLEE Chamblee, Aldric Doran 6′1″, 240 **LB**
Col: Virginia Tech *HS:* Green Run [Virginia Beach, VA] B: 11/17/1968, Virginia Beach, VA *Drafted:* 1991 Round 12 TB
1991 TB: 9 G; 1 Sac. **1992** TB: 13 G; KR 1-9 9.0; 1 Sac. **Total:** 22 G; KR 1-9 9.0; 2 Sac.

ED CHAMPAGNE Champagne, Edward J 6′3″, 236 **DT-OT**
Col: Louisiana State *HS:* St. Peter's [New Orleans, LA] B: 12/4/1922, New Orleans, LA *Drafted:* 1947 Round 16 LARm
1947 LARm: 4 G. **1948** LARm: 12 G. **1949** LARm: 12 G. **1950** LARm: 11 G; Rec 4-52 13.0 1 TD; 6 Pt. **Total:** 39 G; Rec 4-52 13.0 1 TD; 6 Pt.

JIM CHAMPION Champion, James Henry 6′0″, 238 **OT-DT-LB**
Col: Mississippi State *HS:* Charleston [MS] B: 1/11/1926, Tillatoba, MS
1950 NYY: 7 G; Scor **1** Saf; 2 Pt. **1951** NYY: 12 G. **Total:** 19 G; Scor 1 Saf; 2 Pt.

ROBERT CHANCEY Chancey, Robert Dewayne 6′0″, 250 **RB**
Col: No College *HS:* Stanhope-Elmore [Millbrook, AL] B: 9/7/1972, Macon, AL
1998 ChiB: Rec 11-102 9.3; KR 2-18 9.0. **Total:** Rec 11-102 9.3; KR 2-18 9.0.

		Rushing				
Year Team	**G**	**Att**	**Yds**	**Avg**	**TD**	**Fum**
1997 SD	6	0	0	—	0	0
1998 ChiB	16	29	122	4.2	2	2
NFL Total	22	29	122	4.2	2	2

AL CHANDLER Chandler, Albert Morris 6′2″, 233 **TE**
Col: Oklahoma *HS:* Frederick Douglass [Oklahoma City, OK]
B: 11/18/1950, Oklahoma City, OK *Drafted:* 1973 Round 2 Cin

		Receiving			
Year Team	**G**	**Rec**	**Yds**	**Avg**	**TD**
1973 Cin	13	0	0	—	0
1974 Cin	14	1	9	9.0	0
1976 NE	14	5	49	9.8	3
1977 NE	14	7	68	9.7	0
1978 StL-NE	15	16	190	11.9	4
1978 StL	11	16	190	11.9	4
1978 NE	4	0	0	—	0
1979 StL-NE	15	6	51	8.5	2
1979 StL	8	5	49	9.8	2
1979 NE	7	1	2	2.0	0
NFL Total	85	35	367	10.5	9

CHRIS CHANDLER Chandler, Christopher Mark 6'4", 220 **QB**
Col: Washington *HS:* Everett [WA] B: 10/12/1965, Everett, WA
Drafted: 1988 Round 3 Ind
1995 Hou: Scor 1 2XP. **1998** Atl: Rec 1-22 22.0. **Total:** Rec 1-22 22.0; Scor 1 2XP.

		Passing							
Year Team	G	Att	Comp	Comp%	Yds	YPA	TD	Int	Rating
1988 Ind	15	233	129	55.4	1619	6.95	8	12	67.2
1989 Ind	3	80	39	48.8	537	6.71	2	3	63.4
1990 TB	7	83	42	50.6	464	5.59	1	6	41.4
1991 TB-Pho	9	154	78	50.6	846	5.49	5	10	50.9
1991 TB	6	104	53	51.0	557	5.36	4	8	47.6
1991 Pho	3	50	25	50.0	289	5.78	1	2	57.8
1992 Pho	15	413	245	59.3	2832	6.86	15	15	77.1
1993 Pho	4	103	52	50.5	471	4.57	3	2	64.8
1994 LARm	12	176	108	61.4	1352	7.68	7	2	93.8
1995 Hou	13	356	225	63.2	2460	6.91	17	10	87.8
1996 Hou	12	320	184	57.5	2099	6.56	16	11	79.7
1997 Atl	14	342	202	59.1	2692	7.87	20	7	95.1
1998 Atl	14	327	190	58.1	3154	9.65	25	12	100.9
NFL Total	118	2587	1494	57.8	18526	7.16	119	90	80.9

	Rushing				
Year Team	Att	Yds	Avg	TD	Fum
1988 Ind	46	139	3.0	3	8
1989 Ind	7	57	8.1	1	0
1990 TB	13	71	5.5	1	5
1991 TB-Pho	26	111	4.3	0	6
1991 TB	18	79	4.4	0	3
1991 Pho	8	32	4.0	0	3
1992 Pho	36	149	4.1	1	9
1993 Pho	3	2	0.7	0	2
1994 LARm	18	61	3.4	1	3
1995 Hou	28	58	2.1	2	12
1996 Hou	28	113	4.0	0	8
1997 Atl	43	158	3.7	0	9
1998 Atl	36	121	3.4	2	6
NFL Total	284	1040	3.7	11	68

DON CHANDLER Chandler, Donald Gene 6'2", 215 **K**
(Babe) *Col:* Florida *HS:* Will Rogers [Tulsa, OK] B: 9/5/1934, Council Bluffs, IA *Drafted:* 1956 Round 5 NYG
1956 NYG: Rush 1-7 7.0; Rec 1-5 5.0. **1957** NYG: Pass 2-2 100.0%, 40 20.00; Rush 1-2 2.0. **1958** NYG: Pass 1-1 100.0%, 27 27.00; Rush 1-15 15.0. **1959** NYG: Rush 1-24 24.0. **1960** NYG: Rush 2-19 9.5. **1961** NYG: Rush 3-30 10.0. **1962** NYG: Rush 1-(-11) -11.0. **1963** NYG: Rush 1-0. **1965** GB: Rush 1-27 27.0. **1966** GB: Rush 1-33 33.0. **Total:** Pass 3-3 100.0%, 67 22.33; Rush 13-146 11.2; Rec 1-5 5.0.

		Punting		
Year Team	G	Punts	Yds	Avg
1956 NYG	12	59	2473	41.9
1957 NYG	12	60	2673	**44.6**
1958 NYG	12	**65**	**2859**	44.0
1959 NYG	12	55	2565	46.6
1960 NYG	8	31	1256	40.5
1961 NYG	14	68	2984	43.9
1962 NYG	14	55	2233	40.6
1963 NYG	14	59	2648	44.9
1964 NYG	14	73	3328	45.6
1965 GB	14	74	3176	42.9
1966 GB	14	60	2452	40.9
1967 GB	14	1	31	31.0
NFL Total	154	660	28678	43.5

	Scoring							
Year Team	Pts	FG	FGA	FG%	XK	XKA	XK%	Fum
1956 NYG	3	0	0	—	3	3	100.0	0
1959 NYG	2	0	1	0.0	2	2	100.0	0
1961 NYG	0	0	0	—	0	0	—	2
1962 NYG	104	19	28	**67.9**	47	48	**97.9**	0
1963 NYG	**106**	18	29	62.1	**52**	**56**	92.9	0
1964 NYG	54	9	20	45.0	27	29	93.1	2
1965 GB	88	17	26	65.4	37	38	97.4	0
1966 GB	77	12	28	42.9	41	43	95.3	0
1967 GB	96	19	29	65.5	39	39	100.0	0
NFL Total	530	94	161	58.4	248	258	96.1	4

EDGAR CHANDLER Chandler, Edgar Thomas Jr. 6'3", 225 **LB**
Col: Georgia *HS:* Cedartown [GA] B: 8/31/1946, Cedartown, GA
D: 10/17/1992, Rome, GA *Drafted:* 1968 Round 4 Buf
1968 Buf: 13 G. **1969** Buf: 14 G. **1970** Buf: 14 G; Int 1-59 1 TD; 6 Pt. **1971** Buf: 14 G; Int 1-13; Scor 1 Saf; 2 Pt. **1972** Buf: 1 G. **1973** NE: 12 G; 1 Fum. **Total:** 68 G; Int 2-72 1 TD; Scor 1 Saf; 8 Pt; 1 Fum.

KARL CHANDLER Chandler, Karl Victor 6'5", 250 **C-OG**
Col: Princeton *HS:* Marple Newtown [Newtown Square, PA]
B: 2/15/1952, Delaware Co., PA
1974 NYG: 14 G. **1975** NYG: 14 G. **1976** NYG: 12 G; 1 Fum. **1977** NYG: 14 G; 2 Fum. **1978** Det: 11 G. **1979** Det: 1 G. **Total:** 66 G; 3 Fum.

BOB CHANDLER Chandler, Robert Donald 6'0", 180 **WR**
Col: USC *HS:* Whittier [CA] B: 4/24/1949, Long Beach, CA
D: 1/27/1995, Los Angeles, CA *Drafted:* 1971 Round 7 Buf
1972 Buf: Rush 3-27 9.0. **1973** Buf: Pass 1-0; Rush 5-(-14) -2.8; PR 2-5 2.5; Scor **1** 1XP. **1975** Buf: Rush 2-5 2.5. **1976** Buf: Rush 1-0.
Total: Pass 1-0; Rush 11-18 1.6; PR 2-5 2.5; Scor 1 1XP.

		Receiving				
Year Team	G	Rec	Yds	Avg	TD	Fum
1971 Buf	13	5	60	12.0	0	0
1972 Buf	14	33	528	16.0	5	1
1973 Buf	14	30	427	14.2	3	2
1974 Buf	14	7	88	12.6	1	0
1975 Buf	14	55	746	13.6	6	0
1976 Buf	14	61	824	13.5	10	3
1977 Buf	14	60	745	12.4	4	0
1978 Buf	16	44	581	13.2	5	1
1979 Buf	3	0	0	—	0	0
1980 Oak	16	49	786	16.0	10	1
1981 Oak	11	26	458	17.6	4	2
1982 LARd	2	0	0	—	0	0
NFL Total	145	370	5243	14.2	48	10

THORNTON CHANDLER Chandler, Thornton Greene 6'5", 243 **TE**
Col: Florida A&M; Alabama *HS:* William M. Raines [Jacksonville, FL]
B: 11/27/1963, Jacksonville, FL *Drafted:* 1986 Round 6 Dal
1987 Dal: KR 1-7 7.0. **1989** Dal: KR 1-8 8.0. **Total:** KR 2-15 7.5.

		Receiving				
Year Team	G	Rec	Yds	Avg	TD	Fum
1986 Dal	15	6	57	9.5	2	1
1987 Dal	12	5	25	5.0	1	0
1988 Dal	16	18	186	10.3	1	0
1989 Dal	6	0	0	—	0	0
NFL Total	49	29	268	9.2	4	1

WES CHANDLER Chandler, Wesley Sandy 6'0", 186 **WR**
Col: Florida *HS:* New Smyrna Beach [FL] B: 8/22/1956, New Smyrna Beach, FL *Drafted:* 1978 Round 1 NO
1978 NO: Rush 2-10 5.0. **1979** NO: Punt 8-248 31.0. **1980** NO: Pass 1-1 100.0%, 43 43.00; Rush 1-9 9.0. **1981** NO-SD: Pass 2-0; Rush 5-(-1) -0.2. SD: Pass 2-0; Rush 5-(-1) -0.2. **1982** SD: Rush 5-32 6.4. **1983** SD: Rush 2-25 12.5. **1985** SD: Rush 1-9 9.0. **1986** SD: Punt 5-167 33.4.
Total: Pass 3-1 33.3%, 43 14.33; Rush 16-84 5.3; Punt 13-415 31.9.

		Receiving				Punt Returns			
Year Team	G	Rec	Yds	Avg	TD	Ret	Yds	Avg	TD
1978 NO	16	35	472	13.5	2	34	233	6.9	0
1979 NO	16	65	1069	16.4	6	3	13	4.3	0
1980 NO	16	65	975	15.0	6	8	36	4.5	0
1981 NO-SD	16	69	1142	16.6	6	5	79	15.8	0
1981 NO	4	17	285	16.8	1	0	0	—	0
1981 SD	12	52	857	16.5	5	5	79	15.8	0
1982 SD	8	49	**1032**	21.1	**9**	0	0	—	0
1983 SD	16	58	845	14.6	5	8	26	3.3	0
1984 SD	15	52	708	13.6	6	0	0	—	0
1985 SD	15	67	1199	17.9	10	0	0	—	0
1986 SD	16	56	874	15.6	4	3	13	4.3	0
1987 SD	12	39	617	15.8	2	0	0	—	0
1988 SF	4	4	33	8.3	0	6	28	4.7	0
NFL Total	150	559	8966	16.0	56	67	428	6.4	0

	Kickoff Returns				
Year Team	Ret	Yds	Avg	TD	Fum
1978 NO	32	760	23.8	0	1
1979 NO	7	136	19.4	0	0
1980 NO	0	0	—	0	2
1981 NO-SD	8	125	15.6	0	1
1981 SD	8	125	15.6	0	1
1983 SD	0	0	—	0	3
1985 SD	0	0	—	0	1
1986 SD	1	11	11.0	0	2
1987 SD	0	0	—	0	1
NFL Total	48	1032	21.5	0	11

LYNN CHANDNOIS Chandnois, Lynn Everett 6'2", 198 **HB-TB**
Col: Michigan State *HS:* Central [Flint, MI] B: 2/24/1925, Fayette, MI
Drafted: 1950 Round 1 Pit

		Passing							
Year Team	G	Att	Comp	Comp%	Yds	YPA	TD	Int	Rating
1950 Pit	12	6	1	16.7	5	0.83	0	2	0.0
1951 Pit	12	43	16	37.2	256	5.95	2	4	34.6
1952 Pit	12	2	0	0.0	0	0.00	0	0	39.6

1953 Pit	12	3	1	33.3	11	3.67	0	0	45.1
1954 Pit	11	3	1	33.3	13	4.33	0	0	47.9
1955 Pit	8	1	0	0.0	0	0.00	0	1	0.0
1956 Pit	5	1	0	0.0	0	0.00	0	0	39.6
NFL Total	72	59	19	32.2	285	4.83	2	7	20.8

	Rushing				Receiving			
Year Team	**Att**	**Yds**	**Avg**	**TD**	**Rec**	**Yds**	**Avg**	**TD**
1950 Pit	71	216	3.0	0	7	158	22.6	0
1951 Pit	108	332	3.1	2	28	440	15.7	4
1952 Pit	97	298	3.1	1	28	370	13.2	2
1953 Pit	123	470	3.8	3	43	412	9.6	0
1954 Pit	45	147	3.3	1	22	176	8.0	0
1955 Pit	105	353	3.4	5	27	385	14.3	0
1956 Pit	44	118	2.7	4	7	71	10.1	1
NFL Total	593	1934	3.3	16	162	2012	12.4	7

	Punt Returns				Kickoff Returns					Tot
Year Team	**Ret**	**Yds**	**Avg**	**TD**	**Ret**	**Yds**	**Avg**	**TD**	**Fum**	**TD**
1950 Pit	3	33	11.0	0	12	351	29.3	0	3	0
1951 Pit	12	55	4.6	0	12	390	**32.5**	0	7	6
1952 Pit	17	111	6.5	0	17	599	**35.2**	**2**	3	5
1953 Pit	26	101	3.9	0	21	610	29.0	**1**	9	4
1954 Pit	8	12	1.5	0	13	256	19.7	0	4	1
1955 Pit	0	0	—	0	9	223	24.8	0	2	5
1956 Pit	0	0	—	0	8	291	36.4	0	0	5
NFL Total	66	312	4.7	0	92	2720	29.6	3	28	26

TOM CHANTILES Chantiles, Thomas James 5'10", 225 **T**
Col: USC *HS:* William Penn [York, PA] B: 7/2/1916, York, PA
1942 Det: 2 G.

CLARENCE CHAPMAN Chapman, Clarence Earl 5'10", 185 **DB**
Col: Eastern Michigan *HS:* Redford [Detroit, MI] B: 12/10/1953, Detroit, MI *Drafted:* 1976 Round 7 Oak
1977 NO: Int 1-16. **1978** NO: Int 2-(-4). **1979** NO: Int 2-12. **Total:** Int 5-24.

		Kickoff Returns			
Year Team	**G**	**Ret**	**Yds**	**Avg**	**TD**
1976 NO	1	3	63	21.0	0
1977 NO	14	15	385	25.7	1
1978 NO	14	9	149	16.6	0
1979 NO	16	0	0	—	0
1980 NO	12	0	0	—	0
1981 Cin	5	8	171	21.4	0
1985 Det	3	0	0	—	0
NFL Total	65	35	768	21.9	1

TED CHAPMAN Chapman, Edward Arthur 6'3", 260 **DE**
Col: Maryland *HS:* Parkside [Salisbury, MD] B: 4/5/1964, Philadelphia, PA
1987 LARd: 2 G.

GIL CHAPMAN Chapman, Gil 5'9", 180 **WR**
Col: Michigan *HS:* Thomas Jefferson [Elizabeth, NJ] B: 8/23/1953, Elizabeth, NJ *Drafted:* 1975 Round 7 Buf
1975 NO: Rec 1-7 7.0; PR 17-207 12.2.

		Kickoff Returns				
Year Team	**G**	**Ret**	**Yds**	**Avg**	**TD**	**Fum**
1975 NO	9	28	614	21.9	0	1

MIKE CHAPMAN Chapman, Michael George 6'4", 250 **C-OG**
Col: Texas *HS:* Lyndon B. Johnson [Austin, TX] B: 2/10/1961, Laredo, TX
1984 Atl: 4 G.

LEON CHAPPELL Chappell, Leonidas Marion 6'2", 205 **G**
(AKA Leon Shappell) *Col:* No College *HS:* Oak Park [IL]
B: 12/24/1898, Neota, IL D: 5/28/1978, Carmel Valley, CA
1920 ChiC: 8 G. **1921** ChiC: 1 G. **Total:** 9 G.

DAVE CHAPPLE Chapple, David T 6'1", 184 **P**
Col: California-Santa Barbara *HS:* Arcadia [CA] B: 3/30/1947, Arcadia, CA *Drafted:* 1969 Round 10 SF
1973 LARm: Rush 1-0. **Total:** Rush 1-0.

		Punting			
Year Team	**G**	**Punts**	**Yds**	**Avg**	**Fum**
1971 Buf	1	3	101	33.7	0
1972 LARm	14	53	2344	44.2	0
1973 LARm	14	51	2079	40.8	2
1974 LARm-NE	11	55	1995	36.3	0
1974 LARm	6	29	1028	35.4	0
1974 NE	5	26	967	37.2	0
NFL Total	40	162	6519	40.2	2

JACK CHAPPLE Chapple, John Louis 6'1", 225 **LB**
Col: New Mexico Mil. Inst. (J.C.); Stanford *HS:* Coronado [CA]
B: 7/23/1943, Daytona Beach, FL D: 10/19/1979 *Drafted:* 1965 Round 3 SF
1965 SF: 14 G; **1** Fum TD; 6 Pt.

BOB CHAPPUIS Chappuis, Robert Richard 6'0", 190 **TB-DB**
Col: Michigan *HS:* Thomas DeVilbiss [Toledo, OH] B: 2/24/1923, Toledo, OH
AAFC **1948** BknA: PR 1-8 8.0; KR 3-55 18.3. **Total:** PR 1-8 8.0; KR 3-55 18.3.

		Passing							
Year Team	**G**	**Att**	**Comp**	**Comp%**	**Yds**	**YPA**	**TD**	**Int**	**Rating**
1948 BknA	13	213	100	46.9	1402	6.58	8	15	51.8
1949 ChiA	6	14	2	14.3	40	2.86	0	4	0.0
AAFC Total	19	227	102	44.9	1442	6.35	8	19	42.9

	Rushing			
Year Team	**Att**	**Yds**	**Avg**	**TD**
1948 BknA	52	310	6.0	1
1949 ChiA	4	13	3.3	0
AAFC Total	56	323	5.8	1

DICK CHAPURA Chapura, Richard Harry Jr. 6'3", 277 **DT**
Col: Missouri *HS:* Riverview [Sarasota, FL] B: 6/15/1964, Sarasota, FL
Drafted: 1987 Round 10 ChiB
1987 ChiB: 2 G. **1988** ChiB: 15 G; 2 Sac. **1989** ChiB: 16 G; KR 1-8 8.0; 3 Sac. **1990** Phi-Pho: 10 G; 1 Sac. Phi: 7 G; 1 Sac. Pho: 3 G. **Total:** 43 G; KR 1-8 8.0; 6 Sac.

JOHN CHARLES Charles, John James 6'0", 205 **DB**
(J.C.) *Col:* Purdue *HS:* Linden [NJ] B: 5/9/1944, Newark, NJ
Drafted: 1967 Round 1 Bos

		Interceptions		
Year Team	**G**	**Int**	**Yds**	**TD**
1967 Bos	14	1	35	1
1968 Bos	12	1	29	0
1969 Bos	13	4	46	1
1970 Min	8	1	25	0
1971 Hou	14	5	94	0
1972 Hou	13	2	6	0
1973 Hou	4	2	74	0
1974 Hou	1	0	0	0
NFL Total	79	16	309	2

MIKE CHARLES Charles, Michael William 6'4", 292 **NT-DT**
Col: Syracuse *HS:* Central [Newark, NJ] B: 9/23/1962, Newark, NJ
Drafted: 1983 Round 2 Mia
1983 Mia: 16 G; Scor 1 Saf; 2 Pt; 3 Sac. **1984** Mia: 10 G; 3 Sac. **1985** Mia: 16 G; 7 Sac. **1986** Mia: 9 G; Int 1-2. **1987** SD: 11 G; 1 Sac. **1988** SD: 16 G. **1989** SD: 6 G. **1990** LARd: 10 G. **1991** LARm: 7 G. **Total:** 101 G; Int 1-2; Scor 1 Saf; 2 Pt; 14 Sac.

WIN CHARLES Charles, Winston Holt 5'9", 160 **TB-BB**
(Speed) *Col:* William & Mary B: 1904 D: 1/29/1949
1928 Day: 5 G.

CLIFFORD CHARLTON Charlton, Clifford Tyrone 6'3", 240 **LB**
Col: Florida *HS:* Leon [Tallahassee, FL] B: 2/16/1965, Tallahassee, FL
Drafted: 1988 Round 1 Cle
1988 Cle: 16 G. **1989** Cle: 15 G; 1 Sac. **Total:** 31 G; 1 Sac.

CARL CHARON Charon, Carl Henry 5'10", 202 **DB**
Col: Michigan State *HS:* Boyne City [MI] B: 3/17/1940, Boyne City, MI
Drafted: 1962 Round 18 Was
1962 Buf: 14 G; Int 7-131 **1** TD; Tot TD 2; 12 Pt. **1963** Buf: 12 G; **1** Fum TD; 6 Pt. **Total:** 26 G; Int 7-131 1 TD; 1 Fum TD; Tot TD 3; 18 Pt.

LEN CHARPIER Charpier, Leonard Louis 5'10", 235 **FB**
(Tank) *Col:* Illinois *HS:* Curtis [Chicago, IL] B: 2/17/1897, Washington Heights, IL D: 10/3/1947, Chicago, IL
1920 ChiC: 1 G.

BEN CHASE Chase, Benjamin Semple III 6'3", 235 **G**
Col: Navy *HS:* Herbert Hoover [San Diego, CA] B: 3/18/1923, Bisbee, AZ
1947 Det: 11 G.

RALPH CHASE Chase, Ralph E 6'3", 220 **T**
(Horse) *Col:* Pittsburgh *HS:* Wyoming Seminary [Kingston, PA]
Deceased
1926 Ham-Akr: 5 G. Ham: 1 G. Akr: 4 G. **Total:** 5 G.

CLIFF CHATMAN Chatman, Clifford 6'2", 225 **RB**
Col: Oklahoma; Central Oklahoma *HS:* Clinton [OK] B: 3/13/1959, Clinton, OK *Drafted:* 1981 Round 4 NYG
1982 NYG: 6 G; Rush 22-80 3.6 2 TD; Rec 1-13 13.0; 12 Pt.

RICKY CHATMAN Chatman, Ricky Lynn 6'2", 230 **LB**
Col: Louisiana State *HS:* Winnfield [LA] B: 1/4/1962, Jonesboro, LA
1987 Ind: 3 G; 1 Sac.

LAZ CHAVEZ Chavez, Lazarus Emmanuel 6'0", 220 **LB**
Col: Iona *HS:* Port Chester [NY] B: 12/20/1963, Port Chester, NY
1987 Mia: 3 G.

EDDIE CHAVIS Chavis, Edward L 6'0", 182 **WR**
Col: Montclair State *HS:* Plainfield [NJ] B: 7/12/1963, Plainfield, NJ
1987 Mia: 3 G; Rec 7-108 15.4.

BARNEY CHAVOUS Chavous, Barney Lewis 6'3", 252 **DE**
Col: South Carolina State *HS:* Schofield [Aiken, SC] B: 3/22/1951, Aiken, SC *Drafted:* 1973 Round 2 Den
1973 Den: 14 G. **1974** Den: 14 G. **1975** Den: 9 G. **1976** Den: 14 G. **1977** Den: 13 G. **1978** Den: 16 G. **1979** Den: 16 G. **1980** Den: 16 G. **1981** Den: 16 G. **1982** Den: 9 G; Scor **1** Saf; 2 Pt; 5 Sac. **1983** Den: 15 G; 1 Fum TD; 6 Pt; 4.5 Sac. **1984** Den: 15 G; 7.5 Sac. **1985** Den: 16 G; 6 Sac. **Total:** 183 G; Scor 1 Saf; 1 Fum TD; 8 Pt; 23.0 Sac.

COREY CHAVOUS Chavous, Corey 6'0", 204 **DB**
Col: Vanderbilt *HS:* Silver Bluff [Aiken, SC] B: 1/15/1976, Aiken, SC
Drafted: 1998 Round 2 Ariz
1998 Ariz: 16 G; Int 2-0.

ERNIE CHEATHAM Cheatham, Ernest Clifford Jr. 6'4", 255 **DT**
Col: Loyola Marymount *HS:* St. Anthony's [Long Beach, CA]
B: 7/26/1929, Long Beach, CA *Drafted:* 1951 Round 21 Pit
1954 Pit-Bal: 6 G. Pit: 4 G. Bal: 2 G. **Total:** 6 G.

LLOYD CHEATHAM Cheatham, Hilliard Lloyd 6'2", 211 **BB-LB-DB-WB**
Col: Auburn *HS:* Carbon Hill [AL] B: 3/20/1919, Nantes, OK
D: 6/11/1989, Charlotte, NC *Drafted:* 1942 Round 2 ChiC
AAFC **1946** NY-A: 13 G; Rush 3-2 0.7; Rec 4-54 13.5 1 TD; PR 1-26 26.0; KR 1-7 7.0; Int 1-3; 6 Pt. **1947** NY-A: 14 G; Rush 1-(-2) -2.0; Rec 4-124 31.0 2 TD; 12 Pt. **1948** NY-A: 12 G; Rush 2-1 0.5; Rec 7-76 10.9; KR 1-18 18.0. **Total:** 39 G; Rush 6-1 0.2; Rec 15-254 16.9 3 TD; PR 1-26 26.0; KR 2-25 12.5; Int 1-3; 18 Pt.

NFL **1942** ChiC: 11 G; Rush 1-1 1.0; Rec 6-29 4.8 1 TD; PR 3-32 10.7; KR 2-37 18.5; Int 1-4; 6 Pt.

COONIE CHECKAYE Checkaye, Severin Joseph 5'9", 185 **BB**
Col: No College *HS:* Muncie Central [IN] B: 1/6/1893, Muncie, IN
D: 11/18/1970, Muncie, IN
1920 Mun: 1 G. **1921** Mun: 2 G. **Total:** 3 G.

RICHARD CHEEK Cheek, Donald Richard 6'3", 266 **OG**
Col: Auburn *HS:* Bay [Panama City, FL] B: 1/19/1948, Panama City, FL *Drafted:* 1970 Round 8 Buf
1970 Buf: 14 G.

LOUIS CHEEK Cheek, Louis Ray Jr. 6'6", 295 **OT-OG**
Col: Texas A&M *HS:* Fairfield [TX] B: 10/6/1964, Galveston, TX
Drafted: 1988 Round 8 Mia
1988 Mia: 15 G. **1989** Mia: 13 G. **1990** Dal-Phi: 5 G. Dal: 4 G. Phi: 1 G. **1991** GB: 12 G. **Total:** 45 G.

B.W. CHEEKS Cheeks, Will Jr. 6'1", 229 **HB**
Col: Texas Southern *HS:* Phillis Wheatley [Houston, TX] B: 8/1/1941, Hearne, TX
1965 Hou: 2 G; KR 1-19 19.0; 1 Fum.

MICHAEL CHEEVER Cheever, Michael John 6'4", 293 **C**
Col: Georgia Tech *HS:* Newnan [GA] B: 6/24/1973, Newnan, GA
Drafted: 1996 Round 2 Jac
1996 Jac: 11 G. **1997** Jac: 6 G. **Total:** 17 G.

DON CHELF Chelf, Donald Richard 6'3", 235 **OT-OG**
Col: Iowa *HS:* West Liberty [IA] B: 3/25/1933, West Liberty, IA
Drafted: 1954 Round 12 Bal
1960 Buf: 14 G. **1961** Buf: 14 G. **Total:** 28 G.

RED CHENOWETH Chenoweth, Fred Myer 5'6", 150 **TB**
Col: West Virginia *HS:* Philippi [WV]; Broaddus Acad. [Philippi, WV]
B: 8/26/1893, Marion Co., WV D: 6/24/1965, Weston, WV
1921 Lou: 1 G.

HAROLD CHERNE Cherne, Harold Thomas 6'0", 230 **T-G**
Col: DePaul *HS:* Hyde Park [Chicago, IL]; YMCA HS [Chicago, IL];Mount Carmel HS [Chicago, IL] B: 3/7/1907, La Salle, IL
D: 1/31/1983, Salinas, CA
1933 Bos: 4 G.

GEORGE CHEROKE Cheroke, George 5'9", 195 **G**
Col: Ohio State *HS:* Shadyside [OH] B: 1/2/1921, Jenners, PA
AAFC **1946** CleA: 14 G.

TONY CHERRY Cherry, Anthony Earl 5'7", 187 **RB**
Col: Riverside CC CA; Oregon *HS:* Victor Valley [Victorville, CA]
B: 2/8/1963, Tripoli, Libya *Drafted:* 1986 Round 9 SF
1986 SF: 5 G; Rush 11-42 3.8; KR 2-29 14.5; 2 Fum. **1987** SF: 1 G; Rush 13-65 5.0 1 TD; 6 Pt. **Total:** 6 G; Rush 24-107 4.5 1 TD; KR 2-29 14.5; 6 Pt; 2 Fum.

DERON CHERRY Cherry, Deron Leigh 5'11", 197 **DB**
Col: Rutgers *HS:* Palmyra [NJ] B: 9/12/1959, Riverside, NJ
1981 KC: KR 3-52 17.3. **1982** KC: KR 1-39 39.0. **1983** KC: KR 2-54 27.0; 1.5 Sac. **1984** KC: KR 1-0. **1986** KC: 1 Sac. **1989** KC: 1 Sac.
Total: KR 7-145 20.7; 3.5 Sac.

		Interceptions				Tot
Year Team	**G**	**Int**	**Yds**	**TD**	**Fum**	**TD**
1981 KC	13	1	4	0	0	0
1982 KC	7	0	0	0	0	0
1983 KC	16	7	100	0	2	0
1984 KC	16	7	140	0	0	0
1985 KC	16	7	87	**1**	0	1
1986 KC	16	9	150	0	0	2
1987 KC	8	3	58	0	0	0
1988 KC	16	7	51	0	0	0
1989 KC	15	2	27	0	0	0
1990 KC	9	3	40	0	0	0
1991 KC	16	4	31	0	0	0
NFL Total	148	50	688	1	2	3

ED CHERRY Cherry, Edgar Franklin 6'0", 208 **FB-DB**
Col: Amarillo Coll. TX (J.C.); Hardin-Simmons *HS:* Shamrock [TX]
B: 7/16/1913, Wellington, TX D: 11/11/1985, San Angelo, TX
Drafted: 1938 Round 5 ChiC
1938 ChiC: 2 G; Rush 6-18 3.0. **1939** ChiC-Pit: 6 G; Rush 10-30 3.0. ChiC: 4 G; Rush 10-30 3.0. Pit: 2 G. **Total:** 8 G; Rush 16-48 3.0.

JE'ROD CHERRY Cherry, Je'Rod L 6'1", 210 **DB**
Col: California *HS:* Berkeley [CA] B: 5/30/1973, Charlotte, NC
Drafted: 1996 Round 2 NO
1996 NO: 13 G. **1997** NO: 16 G. **1998** NO: 14 G; 2 Sac. **Total:** 43 G; 2 Sac.

MIKE CHERRY Cherry, Mike 6'3", 226 **QB**
Col: Arkansas; Murray State *HS:* Arkansas [Texarkana, AR]
B: 12/15/1973, Texarkana, AR *Drafted:* 1997 Round 6 NYG
1997 NYG: 1 G; Rush 1-(-2) -2.0. **1998** NYG: 1 G; Pass 1-0; Rush 3-(-3) -1.0. **Total:** 2 G; Pass 1-0; Rush 4-(-5) -1.3.

RAPHEL CHERRY Cherry, Raphel Jerome 6'0", 194 **DB**
Col: Hawaii *HS:* George Washington [Los Angeles, CA] B: 12/19/1961, Little Rock, AR *Drafted:* 1985 Round 5 Was
1985 Was: 16 G; Rec 1-11 11.0; PR 4-22 5.5; KR 1-9 9.0; Int 2-29. **1987** Det: 10 G; Int 1-2. **1988** Det: 16 G; Int 2-0. **Total:** 42 G; Rec 1-11 11.0; PR 4-22 5.5; KR 1-9 9.0; Int 5-31.

STAN CHERRY Cherry, Stanley D 6'5", 200 **LB**
Col: Morgan State *HS:* Edmondson [Baltimore, MD] B: 11/2/1950, Baltimore, MD D: 2/10/1993, Baltimore, MD
1973 Bal: 3 G.

BILL CHERRY Cherry, William Kimble 6'4", 275 **C-OG**
Col: Middle Tennessee State *HS:* Stewart Co. [Dover, TN] B: 1/5/1961, De Land, FL
1986 GB: 16 G; 1 Fum. **1987** GB: 12 G; KR 1-0. **Total:** 28 G; KR 1-0; 1 Fum.

CHUCK CHERUNDOLO Cherundolo, Charles James 6'1", 215 **C-LB**
Col: Penn State *HS:* Old Forge [PA] B: 8/8/1916, Old Forge, PA
1937 Cle: 11 G. **1938** Cle: 11 G. **1939** Cle: 10 G. **1940** Phi: 11 G; Int 1-0. **1941** Pit: 11 G; Int 1-13. **1942** Pit: 11 G; Int 1-3. **1945** Pit: 6 G; Int 1-17. **1946** Pit: 11 G; Int 1-0. **1947** Pit: 12 G. **1948** Pit: 12 G. **Total:** 106 G; Int 5-33.

RED CHESBRO Chesbro, Marcel Marcus 5'11", 190 **G**
Col: Colgate *HS:* Hamilton [NY] B: 8/22/1914, Brookfield, NY
D: 4/11/1970, Hamilton, NY *Drafted:* 1938 Round 5 Cle
1938 Cle: 8 G.

AL CHESLEY Chesley, Albert Cornell 6'3", 240 **LB**
Col: Pittsburgh *HS:* Eastern [Washington, DC] B: 8/23/1957, Washington, DC *Drafted:* 1979 Round 11 Phi
1979 Phi: 16 G; Int 2-39. **1980** Phi: 16 G. **1981** Phi: 16 G; Int 2-66. **1982** Phi-ChiB: 8 G. Phi: 4 G. ChiB: 4 G. **Total:** 56 G; Int 4-105.

FRANK CHESLEY Chesley, Francis Michael 6'3", 219 **LB**
Col: Wyoming *HS:* Eastern [Washington, DC] B: 7/14/1955, Washington, DC *Drafted:* 1978 Round 6 NO
1978 GB: 1 G.

JOHN CHESLEY Chesley, John Kenneth 6'5", 225 **TE**
Col: Oklahoma State *HS:* Eastern [Washington, DC] B: 7/2/1962, Washington, DC *Drafted:* 1984 Round 10 Mia
1984 Mia: 1 G.

CHET CHESNEY Chesney, Chester Anton 6'2", 227 **C-LB**
Col: DePaul *HS:* St. Hyacinth [Chicago, IL]; Albert G. Lane Tech HS [Chicago, IL] B: 3/9/1916, Chicago, IL D: 9/20/1986, Marco Island, FL
1939 ChiB: 7 G. **1940** ChiB: 3 G. **Total:** 10 G.

GEORGE CHESSER Chesser, George Allen 6'2", 220 **RB-P**
Col: Mississippi; Delta State *HS:* Starkville [MS] B: 9/11/1942, Starkville, MS
1966 Mia: 14 G; Rush 16-74 4.6; Rec 1-4 4.0; Punt 7-233 33.3. **1967** Mia: 4 G; Rush 2-3 1.5. **Total:** 18 G; Rush 18-77 4.3; Rec 1-4 4.0; Punt 7-233 33.3.

WES CHESSON Chesson, Wesley Merritt III 6'2", 195 **WR**
Col: Duke *HS:* John A. Holmes [Edenton, NC] B: 1/15/1949, Edenton, NC *Drafted:* 1971 Round 7 Atl
1971 Atl: Rush 1-(-4) -4.0. **1972** Atl: KR 1-0. **1974** Phi: KR 1-1 1.0. **Total:** Rush 1-(-4) -4.0; KR 2-1 0.5.

		Receiving			
Year Team	**G**	**Rec**	**Yds**	**Avg**	**TD**
1971 Atl	14	20	224	11.2	0
1972 Atl	13	18	338	18.8	1
1973 Atl-Phi	4	2	36	18.0	1
1973 Atl	2	2	36	18.0	1
1973 Phi	2	0	0	—	0
1974 Phi	12	0	0	—	0
NFL Total	43	40	598	15.0	2

LARRY CHESTER Chester, Larry 6'2", 305 **DT**
Col: Temple B: 10/17/1975
1998 Ind: 14 G; 3 Sac.

RAYMOND CHESTER Chester, Raymond Thomas 6'3", 232 **TE**
Col: Morgan State *HS:* Frederick Douglass [Baltimore, MD] B: 6/28/1948, Cambridge, MD *Drafted:* 1970 Round 1 Oak
1971 Oak: Rush 3-5 1.7. **1972** Oak: Rush 1-3 3.0. **1973** Bal: Rush 1-1 1.0. **1978** Oak: KR 2-27 13.5. **Total:** Rush 5-9 1.8; KR 2-27 13.5.

		Receiving				
Year Team	**G**	**Rec**	**Yds**	**Avg**	**TD**	**Fum**
1970 Oak	14	42	556	13.2	7	1
1971 Oak	14	28	442	15.8	7	0
1972 Oak	13	34	576	16.9	8	0
1973 Bal	13	18	181	10.1	1	1
1974 Bal	14	37	461	12.5	1	3
1975 Bal	14	38	457	12.0	3	1
1976 Bal	14	24	467	19.5	3	0
1977 Bal	14	31	556	17.9	3	1
1978 Oak	16	13	146	11.2	2	0
1979 Oak	14	58	712	12.3	8	0
1980 Oak	16	28	366	13.1	4	1
1981 Oak	16	13	93	7.2	1	0
NFL Total	172	364	5013	13.8	48	8

JOE CHETTI Chetti, Joseph Salvatore 5'9", 205 **RB**
Col: C.W. Post *HS:* North Babylon [NY] B: 11/19/1963, Bay Shore, NY
1987 Buf: 2 G; Rec 1-9 9.0.

GEORGE CHEVERKO Cheverko, George Francis 6'1", 197 **DB-WB-HB**
Col: Fordham *HS:* Hazleton [PA] B: 7/29/1920, Beaver Meadows, PA D: 11/1977 *Drafted:* 1944 Round 5 Cle
1947 NYG: 9 G; Rush 19-63 3.3; Rec 17-300 17.6 3 TD; PR 5-88 17.6; KR 7-135 19.3; Int 3-54; 18 Pt; 2 Fum. **1948** NYG-Was: 10 G; Rush 3-10 3.3; Rec 1-41 41.0; PR 1-5 5.0; KR 3-80 26.7; Int 6-168. NYG: 8 G; Rush 3-10 3.3; Rec 1-41 41.0; PR 1-5 5.0; KR 3-80 26.7; Int 5-144. Was: 2 G; Int 1-24. **Total:** 19 G; Rush 22-73 3.3; Rec 18-341 18.9 3 TD; PR 6-93 15.5; KR 10-215 21.5; Int 9-222; 18 Pt; 2 Fum.

JIM CHEYUNSKI Cheyunski, James Michael 6'1", 225 **LB**
Col: Syracuse *HS:* West Bridgewater [MA] B: 12/29/1945, Bridgewater, MA *Drafted:* 1968 Round 12 Bos
1968 Bos: 13 G; KR 1-0; Int 1-21. **1969** Bos: 14 G; Int 1-37. **1970** Bos: 11 G. **1971** NE: 14 G; Int 1-24. **1972** NE: 14 G. **1973** Buf: 13 G; Int 3-31. **1974** Buf: 14 G; Int 1-6. **1975** Bal: 14 G; Int 2-8. **1976** Bal: 14 G. **Total:** 121 G; KR 1-0; Int 9-127.

FRED CHICKEN Chicken, Fred S 5'10", 185 **TB**
Col: No College *HS:* North [Minneapolis, MN] B: 4/5/1888, Minneapolis, MN D: 11/24/1968, La Crosse, WI
1920 RI: 6 G.

JOHN CHICKERNEO Chickerneo, John Louis 6'1", 205 **BB-LB**
(Chick) *Col:* Pittsburgh *HS:* Warren G. Harding [Warren, OH] B: 3/13/1917, Gary, IN D: 10/3/1995, Deerfield, IL *Drafted:* 1939 Round 2 NYG
1942 NYG: 4 G; Int 1-2; Punt 8-302 37.8.

TONY CHICKILLO Chickillo, Anthony Paul 6'3", 262 **NT-DE-OG**
Col: Miami (Fla.) *HS:* Southwest Miami [Miami, FL] B: 7/8/1960, Miami, FL *Drafted:* 1983 Round 5 TB
1984 SD: 1 G. **1985** SD: 4 G. **1987** NYJ: 2 G. **Total:** 7 G.

NICK CHICKILLO Chickillo, Nicholas Angelo 5'11", 220 **LB-OG**
Col: Miami (Fla.) *HS:* West Scranton [Scranton, PA] B: 10/17/1930, Scranton, PA *Drafted:* 1953 Round 15 ChiC
1953 ChiC: 12 G.

FREDDIE CHILDRESS Childress, Freddie Lee 6'4", 331 **OG-OT**
Col: Arkansas *HS:* Central [West Helena, AR] B: 9/17/1966, Little Rock, AR *Drafted:* 1989 Round 2 Cin
1991 NE: 15 G; 1 Fum TD; 6 Pt. **1992** Cle: 16 G. **Total:** 31 G; 1 Fum TD; 6 Pt.

JOE CHILDRESS Childress, Joseph 6'0", 202 **HB-FB**
Col: Auburn *HS:* Robertsdale [AL] B: 10/26/1933, Robertsdale, AL D: 5/5/1986, Kingwood, TX *Drafted:* 1956 Round 1 ChiC
1956 ChiC: KR 1-0. **1957** ChiC: Pass 2-1 50.0%, 43 21.50 1 Int. **1958** ChiC: Pass 1-0. **1962** StL: KR 3-19 6.3. **Total:** Pass 3-1 33.3%, 43 14.33 1 Int; KR 4-19 4.8.

		Rushing				Receiving					Tot
Year Team	**G**	**Att**	**Yds**	**Avg**	**TD**	**Rec**	**Yds**	**Avg**	**TD**	**Fum**	**TD**
1956 ChiC	11	43	203	4.7	0	6	82	13.7	1	1	1
1957 ChiC	12	41	168	4.1	1	10	146	14.6	0	3	1
1958 ChiC	10	50	170	3.4	0	35	406	11.6	4	3	4
1959 ChiC	9	30	59	2.0	0	4	73	18.3	1	1	1
1960 StL	12	34	240	7.1	0	11	202	18.4	2	2	2
1962 StL	14	37	162	4.4	0	15	207	13.8	1	2	1
1963 StL	14	174	701	4.0	2	25	354	14.2	2	2	4
1964 StL	9	102	413	4.0	0	12	203	16.9	2	0	2
1965 StL	5	19	94	4.9	0	3	27	9.0	0	0	0
NFL Total	96	530	2210	4.2	3	121	1700	14.0	13	14	16

RAY CHILDRESS Childress, Raymond Clay Jr. 6'6", 272 **DE-DT-NT**
Col: Texas A&M *HS:* J.J. Pearce [Richardson, TX] B: 10/20/1962, Memphis, TN *Drafted:* 1985 Round 1 Hou
1985 Hou: 16 G; 3.5 Sac. **1986** Hou: 16 G; 5 Sac. **1987** Hou: 13 G; 6 Sac. **1988** Hou: 16 G; 8.5 Sac. **1989** Hou: 14 G; 8.5 Sac. **1990** Hou: 16 G; Scor **1** Saf; 2 Pt; 8 Sac. **1991** Hou: 15 G; 7 Sac. **1992** Hou: 16 G; 1 Fum TD; 6 Pt; 13 Sac. **1993** Hou: 16 G; 1 Fum TD; 6 Pt; 9 Sac. **1994** Hou: 16 G; 6 Sac. **1995** Hou: 6 G; 1 Sac. **1996** Dal: 3 G; 1 Sac. **Total:** 163 G; Scor 1 Saf; 2 Fum TD; 14 Pt; 76.5 Sac.

CLARENCE CHILDS Childs, Clarence Norris 5'11", 186 **DB-HB**
Col: Florida A&M *HS:* Rochelle [Lakeland, FL] B: 1/13/1938, Lakeland, FL *Drafted:* 1961 Round 20 Bos
1964 NYG: Rec 11-97 8.8; PR 6-40 6.7. **1966** NYG: Int 2-32. **Total:** Rec 11-97 8.8; PR 6-40 6.7; Int 2-32.

		Rushing				Kickoff Returns				
Year Team	**G**	**Att**	**Yds**	**Avg**	**TD**	**Ret**	**Yds**	**Avg**	**TD**	**Fum**
1964 NYG	13	40	102	2.6	0	34	987	**29.0**	**1**	7
1965 NYG	14	0	0	—	0	29	718	24.8	0	2
1966 NYG	14	0	0	—	0	34	855	25.1	1	1
1967 NYG	14	0	0	—	0	29	603	20.8	0	2
1968 ChiB	4	0	0	—	0	8	291	36.4	0	0
NFL Total	59	40	102	2.6	0	134	3454	25.8	2	12

HENRY CHILDS Childs, Henry 6'2", 223 **TE**
Col: Kansas State *HS:* Douglass [Thomasville, GA] B: 4/16/1951, Thomasville, GA *Drafted:* 1974 Round 5 Atl
1974 Atl-NO: KR 1-0. Atl: KR 1-0. **1976** NO: Rush 1-16 16.0 1 TD; KR 1-6 6.0. **1978** NO: Rush 2-(-4) -2.0. **1981** LARm: Rush 1-0. **Total:** Rush 4-12 3.0 1 TD; KR 2-6 3.0.

		Receiving					Tot
Year Team	**G**	**Rec**	**Yds**	**Avg**	**TD**	**Fum**	**TD**
1974 Atl-NO	7	0	0	—	0	0	0
1974 Atl	6	0	0	—	0	0	0
1974 NO	1	0	0	—	0	0	0
1975 NO	14	10	179	17.9	0	0	0
1976 NO	14	26	349	13.4	3	0	4
1977 NO	13	33	518	15.7	9	0	9
1978 NO	16	53	869	16.4	4	1	4
1979 NO	16	51	846	16.6	5	1	5
1980 NO	13	34	463	13.6	6	1	6
1981 LARm	7	12	145	12.1	1	1	1
1984 GB	3	4	32	8.0	0	0	0
NFL Total	103	223	3401	15.3	28	4	29

JIMMY CHILDS Childs, James Joe 6'2", 194 **WR**
Col: Cal Poly-S.L.O. *HS:* La Puente [CA] B: 8/9/1956, El Dorado, AR *Drafted:* 1978 Round 4 StL
1978 StL: 8 G; Rec 4-50 12.5 1 TD; KR 4-77 19.3; 6 Pt. **1979** StL: 13 G; Rec 8-93 11.6. **Total:** 21 G; Rec 12-143 11.9 1 TD; KR 4-77 19.3; 6 Pt.

RON CHILDS Childs, Ron Lee 5'11", 212 **LB**
Col: Washington State *HS:* Kamiaken [Kennewick, WA] B: 9/18/1971, South Kennewick, WA
1995 NO: 9 G.

GENE CHILTON Chilton, Gene Alan 6'3", 281 **C-OT**
Col: Texas *HS:* Memorial [Houston, TX] B: 3/27/1964, Houston, TX *Drafted:* 1986 Round 3 StL
1986 StL: 16 G. **1987** StL: 11 G. **1989** KC: 16 G. **1990** NE: 4 G. **1991** NE: 16 G; Rush 1-0; 1 Fum. **1992** NE: 16 G; 1 Fum. **Total:** 79 G; Rush 1-0; 2 Fum.

BILL CHIPLEY Chipley, William Allen 6′3″, 199 **OE-DB**
Col: Clemson; Washington & Lee *HS:* E.C. Glass [Lynchburg, VA]
B: 7/2/1920, Lynchburg, VA *Drafted:* 1947 Round 8 Bos
1947 Bos: Rush 1-3 3.0. **1948** Bos: Int 3-52 1 TD. **1949** NYB: KR 1-7 7.0.
Total: Rush 1-3 3.0; KR 1-7 7.0; Int 3-52 1 TD.

Year Team	G	Receiving Rec	Yds	Avg	TD	Tot TD
1947 Bos	6	5	105	21.0	1	1
1948 Bos	12	13	131	10.1	1	2
1949 NYB	12	57	631	11.1	2	2
NFL Total	30	75	867	11.6	4	5

JOHN CHIRICO Chirico, John J 6′0″, 220 **RB**
Col: Columbia *HS:* Chaminade [Mineola, NY] B: 8/15/1965, Brooklyn, NY
1987 NYJ: 3 G; Rush 12-22 1.8 1 TD; Rec 4-18 4.5; 6 Pt; 1 Fum.

ANDY CHISICK Chisick, Andrew Bernard 6′1″, 207 **C-LB**
Col: Villanova *HS:* Good Counsel [Newark, NJ] B: 6/10/1916, Sagamore, PA D: 3/13/1986, Somerset, KY *Drafted:* 1940 Round 7 ChiC
1940 ChiC: 11 G. **1941** ChiC: 11 G; Int 1-7. **Total:** 22 G; Int 1-7.

ED CHLEBEK Chlebek, Edward 5′11″, 175 **QB**
Col: Western Michigan *HS:* Western [Detroit, MI] B: 2/9/1940
1963 NYJ: 2 G; Pass 4-2 50.0%, 5 1.25; 1 Fum.

MARK CHMURA Chmura, Mark William 6′5″, 248 **TE**
Col: Boston College *HS:* Frontier Regional [South Deerfield, MA]
B: 2/22/1969, Deerfield, MA *Drafted:* 1992 Round 6 GB
1993 GB: KR 1-0. **1995** GB: Scor 1 2XP. **Total:** KR 1-0; Scor 1 2XP.

Year Team	G	Receiving Rec	Yds	Avg	TD	Fum
1993 GB	14	2	13	6.5	0	1
1994 GB	14	14	165	11.8	0	0
1995 GB	16	54	679	12.6	7	0
1996 GB	13	28	370	13.2	0	0
1997 GB	15	38	417	11.0	6	1
1998 GB	15	47	554	11.8	4	1
NFL Total	87	183	2198	12.0	17	3

PUTT CHOATE Choate, Mark Putnam 6′0″, 225 **LB**
Col: Southern Methodist *HS:* Coahoma [TX] B: 12/11/1956, Big Spring, TX
1987 GB: 2 G.

BOB CHOATE Choate, Robert M 6′1″, 225 **G**
Col: Haskell Indian *HS:* Pryor [OK] B: 12/2/1893, Pryor, OK
D: 7/1985, Antioch, CA
1924 KC: 1 G.

MAX CHOBOIAN Choboian, Max John 6′4″, 215 **QB**
Col: Oregon; Cal State-Northridge *HS:* Tulare [CA] B: 3/17/1942, Tulare, CA D: 1/2/1977, Fresno, CA
1966 Den: Rush 21-45 2.1 2 TD.

Year Team	G	Passing Att	Comp	Comp%	Yds	YPA	TD	Int	Rating	Fum
1966 Den	14	163	82	50.3	1110	6.81	4	12	49.9	4

JOHN CHOMA Choma, John Gregory 6′5″, 261 **OG-C-OT**
Col: Virginia *HS:* Normandy [Parma, OH] B: 2/9/1955, Cleveland, OH
Drafted: 1978 Round 5 SD
1981 SF: 14 G. **1982** SF: 7 G. **1983** SF: 6 G. **Total:** 27 G.

STEVE CHOMYSZAK Chomyszak, Stephen John 6′6″, 265 **DT**
Col: Syracuse *HS:* Johnson City [NY] B: 2/27/1944, Johnson City, NY
D: 1/25/1988, Johnson City, NY *Drafted:* 1966 Round 12 NYJ
1966 NYJ: 2 G. **1968** Cin: 10 G. **1969** Cin: 14 G. **1970** Cin: 14 G.
1971 Cin: 14 G. **1972** Cin: 13 G. **1973** Cin: 12 G. **Total:** 79 G.

JASON CHORAK Chorak, Jason 6′4″, 256 **DE**
Col: Washington *HS:* Vashon [WA] B: 9/23/1974, Vashon, WA
Drafted: 1998 Round 7 StL
1998 Ind: 8 G; 1 Sac.

DICK CHOROVICH Chorovich, Richard Milan 6′4″, 260 **DT**
(Animal) *Col:* Miami (Ohio) *HS:* St. Clairsville [OH] B: 11/29/1933, St. Clairsville, OH D: 8/1997, St. Clairsville, OH *Drafted:* 1955 Round 12 Bal
1955 Bal: 11 G. **1956** Bal: 3 G. **1960** LAC: 14 G. **Total:** 28 G.

JOSEPH CHRAPE Chrape, Joseph 210 **G-T**
Col: Hibbing CC MN *HS:* Greenway [Coleraine, MN] B: 1910, MN
1929 Min: 9 G.

WAYNE CHREBET Chrebet, Wayne John 5′10″, 185 **WR**
Col: Hofstra *HS:* Garfield [NJ] B: 8/14/1973, Garfield, NJ
1995 NYJ: Rush 1-1 1.0. **1997** NYJ: KR 1-5 5.0. **Total:** Rush 1-1 1.0; KR 1-5 5.0.

Year Team	G	Receiving Rec	Yds	Avg	TD	Punt Returns Ret	Yds	Avg	TD	Fum
1995 NYJ	16	66	726	11.0	4	0	0	—	0	1
1996 NYJ	16	84	909	10.8	3	28	139	5.0	0	5
1997 NYJ	16	58	799	13.8	3	0	0	—	0	0
1998 NYJ	16	75	1083	14.4	8	0	0	—	0	0
NFL Total	64	283	3517	12.4	18	28	139	5.0	0	6

ERIK CHRISTENSEN Christensen, Erik Robert Jr. 6′3″, 235 **DE**
Col: Richmond *HS:* Woodbridge [NJ]; Fork Union Mil. Acad. [VA]
B: 10/30/1931, Elizabeth, NJ *Drafted:* 1955 Round 7 Was
1956 Was: 2 G.

FRANK CHRISTENSEN Christensen, Frank Langton 6′1″, 199 **BB-DB-FB-LB**
Col: Utah *HS:* Granite [Salt Lake City, UT] B: 6/1/1910, Salt Lake City, UT
1934 Det: Pass 8-3 37.5%, 23 2.88; Rec 1-43 43.0. **1935** Det: Pass 21-6 28.6%, 92 4.38 3 Int; Rec 5-57 11.4 1 TD; Scor 8, 2 XK. **1936** Det: Pass 6-2 33.3%, 22 3.67 1 Int; Rec 2-58 29.0 1 TD. **Total:** Pass 35-11 31.4%, 137 3.91 4 Int; Rec 8-158 19.8 2 TD.

Year Team	G	Rushing Att	Yds	Avg	TD	Tot TD
1934 Det	11	96	304	3.2	2	2
1935 Det	12	11	6	0.5	0	1
1936 Det	11	2	-2	-1.0	0	1
1937 Det	8	0	0	—	0	0
NFL Total	42	109	308	2.8	2	4

GEORGE CHRISTENSEN Christensen, George Washington 6′2″, 238 **T-G**
(Chris; Tarzan) *Col:* Oregon *HS:* Pendleton [OR]; Weatherwax HS [Aberdeen, WA] B: 12/13/1909, Pendleton, OR D: 7/1/1968, Detroit, MI
1931 Port: 14 G. **1932** Port: 12 G. **1933** Port: 11 G. **1934** Det: 13 G.
1935 Det: 12 G. **1936** Det: 12 G. **1937** Det: 10 G. **1938** Det: 11 G.
Total: 95 G.

JEFF CHRISTENSEN Christensen, Jeffrey Bruce 6′3″, 202 **QB**
Col: Eastern Illinois *HS:* Gibson City [IL] B: 1/8/1960, Gibson City, IL
Drafted: 1983 Round 5 Cin
1983 Cin: Rush 1-(-2) -2.0. **1987** Cle: Rush 11-41 3.7. **Total:** Rush 12-39 3.3.

Year Team	G	Passing Att	Comp	Comp%	Yds	YPA	TD	Int	Rating	Fum
1983 Cin	1	0	0	—	0	—	0	0	—	0
1987 Cle	3	58	24	41.4	297	5.12	1	3	42.1	3
NFL Total	4	58	24	41.4	297	5.12	1	3	42.1	3

KOESTER CHRISTENSEN Christensen, Koester L 5′10″, 195 **E**
Col: Michigan State *HS:* Escanaba [MI] B: 1905 D: 1946
1930 Port: 1 G.

TODD CHRISTENSEN Christensen, Todd Jay 6′3″, 230 **TE-FB**
Col: Brigham Young *HS:* Henry D. Sheldon [Eugene, OR] B: 8/3/1956, Bellefonte, PA *Drafted:* 1978 Round 2 Dal
1980 Oak: KR 1-10 10.0; **1** Fum TD. **1981** Oak: KR 4-54 13.5; Scor **1** Saf.
1982 LARd: Rush 1-(-6) -6.0. **Total:** Rush 1-(-6) -6.0; KR 5-64 12.8; Scor 1 Saf; 1 Fum TD.

Year Team	G	Receiving Rec	Yds	Avg	TD	Fum	Tot TD
1979 NYG-Oak	13	0	0	—	0	0	0
1979 NYG	1	0	0	—	0	0	0
1979 Oak	12	0	0	—	0	0	0
1980 Oak	16	0	0	—	0	0	1
1981 Oak	16	8	115	14.4	2	0	2
1982 LARd	9	42	510	12.1	4	3	4
1983 LARd	16	**92**	1247	13.6	12	1	12
1984 LARd	16	80	1007	12.6	7	1	7
1985 LARd	16	82	987	12.0	6	0	6
1986 LARd	16	**95**	1153	12.1	8	1	8
1987 LARd	12	47	663	14.1	2	0	2
1988 LARd	7	15	190	12.7	0	0	0
NFL Total	137	461	5872	12.7	41	6	42

BOB CHRISTIAN Christian, Robert Douglas 5′11″, 226 **RB**
Col: Northwestern *HS:* McCluer North [Florissant, MO] B: 11/14/1968, St. Louis, MO *Drafted:* 1991 Round 12 Atl
1995 Car: Scor 1 2XP. **Total:** Scor 1 2XP.

Year Team	G	Rushing Att	Yds	Avg	TD	Receiving Rec	Yds	Avg	TD	Fum	Tot TD
1992 ChiB	2	0	0	—	0	0	0	—	0	0	0
1993 ChiB	14	8	19	2.4	0	16	160	10.0	0	0	0
1994 ChiB	12	7	29	4.1	0	2	30	15.0	0	0	0
1995 Car	14	41	158	3.9	0	29	255	8.8	1	1	1
1997 Atl	16	7	8	1.1	0	22	154	7.0	1	3	1

1998 Atl	14	8	21	2.6	2	19	214	11.3	1	1	3
NFL Total	72	71	235	3.3	2	88	813	9.2	3	5	5

JACK CHRISTIANSEN Christiansen, John LeRoy 6′1″, 205 **DB-HB**
Col: Colorado State *HS:* Odd Fellows Orphanage [Canon City, CO]
B: 12/20/1928, Sublette, KS D: 6/29/1986, Stanford, CA
Drafted: 1951 Round 6 Det *HOF:* 1970
1952 Det: Rush 19-148 7.8 2 TD; Rec 3-32 10.7. **Total:** Rush 19-143 7.5 2 TD; Rec 3-32 10.7.

		Punt Returns				Kickoff Returns			
Year Team	**G**	**Ret**	**Yds**	**Avg**	**TD**	**Ret**	**Yds**	**Avg**	**TD**
1951 Det	12	18	343	19.1	**4**	11	270	24.5	0
1952 Det	11	15	322	**21.5**	**2**	16	409	25.6	0
1953 Det	12	8	22	2.8	0	10	183	18.3	0
1954 Det	11	23	225	9.8	**1**	5	102	20.4	0
1955 Det	9	12	87	7.3	0	7	169	24.1	0
1956 Det	12	6	73	12.2	**1**	6	116	19.3	0
1957 Det	12	3	12	4.0	0	4	80	20.0	0
1958 Det	10	0	0	—	0	0	0	—	0
NFL Total	89	85	1084	12.8	8	59	1329	22.5	0

	Interceptions				Tot
Year Team	**Int**	**Yds**	**TD**	**Fum**	**TD**
1951 Det	2	53	0	1	4
1952 Det	2	47	0	2	4
1953 Det	**12**	**238**	**1**	3	1
1954 Det	8	84	1	1	2
1955 Det	3	49	0	2	0
1956 Det	8	109	0	0	1
1957 Det	**10**	137	1	0	1
1958 Det	1	0	0	0	0
NFL Total	46	717	3	9	13

MARTY CHRISTIANSEN Christiansen, Martin A 6′0″, 200 **FB**
Col: Minnesota *HS:* Washburn [Minneapolis, MN] B: 8/30/1917, Minneapolis, MN D: 4/27/1984, El Cajon, CA *Drafted:* 1940 Round 5 ChiC

		Rushing			
Year Team	**G**	**Att**	**Yds**	**Avg**	**TD**
1940 ChiC	6	32	71	2.2	1

BOB CHRISTIANSEN Christiansen, Robert Scott 6′4″, 230 **DT**
Col: UCLA *HS:* Reseda [Los Angeles, CA] B: 5/8/1949, Marshalltown, IA *Drafted:* 1972 Round 5 LARm
1972 Buf: 4 G.

OSCAR CHRISTIANSON Christianson, Oscar 5′10″, 186 **E-TB**
(Bully) *Col:* No College *HS:* Two Harbors [MN] B: 4/2/1899
D: 5/1972, St. Anthony, MN
1921 Min: 4 G; Rush 1 TD; 6 Pt. **1922** Min: 4 G. **1923** Min: 6 G. **1924** Min: 6 G. **Total:** 20 G; Rush 1 TD; 6 Pt.

STEVE CHRISTIE Christie, Geoffrey Stephen 6′0″, 185 **K**
Col: William & Mary *HS:* Trafalgar [Oakville, Canada] B: 11/13/1967, Hamilton, Canada

		Scoring						
Year Team	**G**	**Pts**	**FG**	**FGA**	**FG%**	**XK**	**XKA**	**XK%**
1990 TB	16	96	23	27	85.2	27	27	100.0
1991 TB	16	67	15	20	75.0	22	22	100.0
1992 Buf	16	115	24	30	80.0	43	44	97.7
1993 Buf	16	105	23	32	71.9	36	37	97.3
1994 Buf	16	110	24	28	85.7	38	38	100.0
1995 Buf	16	126	31	40	77.5	33	35	94.3
1996 Buf	16	105	24	29	82.8	33	33	100.0
1997 Buf	16	93	24	30	80.0	21	21	100.0
1998 Buf	16	140	33	**41**	80.5	41	41	100.0
NFL Total	144	957	221	277	79.8	294	298	98.7

FLOYD CHRISTMAN Christman, Floyd F 5′11″, 180 **WB-TB**
Col: Thiel *HS:* Greenville [PA] B: 10/14/1902, Greenville, PA
D: 1/24/1971, Rock Creek, OH
1925 Buf: 9 G; Rec 1 TD; 6 Pt.

PAUL CHRISTMAN Christman, Paul Joseph 6′0″, 210 **QB**
(Pitchin' Paul) *Col:* Missouri *HS:* Maplewood [MO] B: 3/5/1918, St. Louis, MO D: 3/2/1970, Lake Forest, IL *Drafted:* 1941 Round 2 ChiC
1945 ChiC: KR 1-44 44.0. **Total:** KR 1-44 44.0.

		Passing							
Year Team	**G**	**Att**	**Comp**	**Comp%**	**Yds**	**YPA**	**TD**	**Int**	**Rating**
1945 ChiC	8	**219**	89	40.6	1147	5.24	5	12	42.6
1946 ChiC	11	229	100	43.7	1656	7.23	13	18	54.8
1947 ChiC	12	301	138	45.8	2191	7.28	17	22	59.0
1948 ChiC	7	114	51	44.7	740	6.49	5	4	66.4
1949 ChiC	12	151	75	49.7	1015	6.72	11	13	59.9
1950 GB	11	126	51	40.5	545	4.33	7	**7**	49.2
NFL Total	61	1140	504	44.2	7294	6.40	58	76	54.8

	Rushing				
Year Team	**Att**	**Yds**	**Avg**	**TD**	**Fum**
1945 ChiC	30	-34	-1.1	1	**12**
1946 ChiC	28	-61	-2.2	3	**15**
1947 ChiC	8	11	1.4	2	3
1948 ChiC	8	6	0.8	1	1
1949 ChiC	4	34	8.5	0	2
1950 GB	7	18	2.6	1	2
NFL Total	85	-26	-0.3	8	35

HERB CHRISTOPHER Christopher, Herbert 5′10″, 195 **CB**
Col: Morris Brown *HS:* Magnolia [Thomasville, GA] B: 4/7/1954, Thomasville, GA
1979 KC: 9 G; Int 2-1. **1980** KC: 16 G; Int 2-25. **1981** KC: 16 G. **1982** KC: 9 G. **Total:** 50 G; Int 4-26.

JIM CHRISTOPHERSON Christopherson, James Monroe 6′0″, 218 **LB-K**
Col: Concordia (Minn.) *HS:* Henning [MN] B: 2/17/1938, Wadena, MN
1962 Min: 14 G; Int 1-32; Scor 61, 11-20 55.0% FG, 28-28 100.0% XK.

RYAN CHRISTOPHERSON Christopherson, Ryan Ray 5′11″, 237 **RB**
Col: Wyoming *HS:* Cactus [Glendale, AZ] B: 7/26/1972, Sioux Falls, SD *Drafted:* 1995 Round 5 Jac
1995 Jac: 11 G; Rush 16-16 1.0 1 TD; Rec 1-(-1) -1.0; 6 Pt; 1 Fum.
1996 Jac-Ariz: 8 G. Jac: 2 G. Ariz: 6 G. **Total:** 19 G; Rush 16-16 1.0 1 TD; Rec 1-(-1) -1.0; 6 Pt; 1 Fum.

EARL CHRISTY Christy, Earl Oliver 5′10″, 195 **HB-DB**
(Speedy) *Col:* Maryland East. Shore *HS:* Havre de Grace [MD]
B: 3/19/1943, Perryman, MD
1968 NYJ: Int 1-16. **Total:** Int 1-16.

		Punt Returns				Kickoff Returns				
Year Team	**G**	**Ret**	**Yds**	**Avg**	**TD**	**Ret**	**Yds**	**Avg**	**TD**	**Fum**
1966 NYJ	6	5	23	4.6	0	10	203	20.3	0	1
1967 NYJ	10	16	83	5.2	0	23	521	22.7	0	0
1968 NYJ	14	13	116	8.9	0	25	599	24.0	0	2
NFL Total	30	34	222	6.5	0	58	1323	22.8	0	3

GREG CHRISTY Christy, Gregory Alan 6′4″, 285 **OT**
Col: Pittsburgh *HS:* Freeport [PA] B: 4/29/1962, Natrona Heights, PA
1985 Buf: 7 G.

JEFF CHRISTY Christy, Jeffrey Allen 6′3″, 284 **C**
Col: Pittsburgh *HS:* Freeport [PA] B: 2/3/1969, Natrona Heights, PA
Drafted: 1992 Round 4 Pho
1993 Min: 9 G. **1994** Min: 16 G. **1995** Min: 16 G. **1996** Min: 16 G.
1997 Min: 12 G. **1998** Min: 16 G. **Total:** 85 G.

DICK CHRISTY Christy, Richard Joseph 5′10″, 191 **HB**
Col: North Carolina State *HS:* St. James [Chester, PA] B: 11/24/1935, Philadelphia, PA D: 8/7/1966, Chester, PA *Drafted:* 1958 Round 3 GB
1960 Bos: Pass 11-6 54.5%, 94 8.55 2 TD 2 Int. **1961** NYT: Pass 1-0.
1962 NYT: Pass 6-0. **Total:** Pass 18-6 33.3%, 94 5.22 2 TD 2 Int.

		Rushing				Receiving			
Year Team	**G**	**Att**	**Yds**	**Avg**	**TD**	**Rec**	**Yds**	**Avg**	**TD**
1958 Pit	12	38	101	2.7	0	7	73	10.4	0
1960 Bos	13	78	363	4.7	3	26	268	10.3	2
1961 NYT	14	81	180	2.2	2	29	521	18.0	1
1962 NYT	14	114	535	4.7	3	62	538	8.7	3
1963 NYJ	11	26	88	3.4	1	8	73	9.1	0
NFL Total	64	337	1267	3.8	9	132	1473	11.2	6

	Punt Returns				Kickoff Returns					Tot
Year Team	**Ret**	**Yds**	**Avg**	**TD**	**Ret**	**Yds**	**Avg**	**TD**	**Fum**	**TD**
1958 Pit	17	153	9.0	0	16	384	24.0	0	4	0
1960 Bos	8	73	9.1	0	24	617	25.7	0	9	5
1961 NYT	18	**383**	**21.3**	**2**	15	360	24.0	0	7	5
1962 NYT	15	**250**	**16.7**	**2**	**38**	**824**	21.7	0	8	8
1963 NYJ	9	46	5.1	0	24	585	24.4	0	2	1
NFL Total	67	905	13.5	4	117	2770	23.7	0	30	19

PETE CHRYPLEWICZ Chryplewicz, Peter Gerald 6′5″, 253 **TE**
Col: Notre Dame *HS:* Adlai Stevenson [Sterling Heights, MI]
B: 4/27/1974, Detroit, MI *Drafted:* 1997 Round 5 Det
1997 Det: 10 G; Rec 3-27 9.0 1 TD; 6 Pt. **1998** Det: 16 G; Rec 4-20 5.0 2 TD; 12 Pt; 1 Fum. **Total:** 26 G; Rec 7-47 6.7 3 TD; 18 Pt; 1 Fum.

EUGENE CHUNG Chung, Yon Eugene 6′4″, 301 **OG-OT**
Col: Virginia Tech *HS:* Oakton [Vienna, VA] B: 6/14/1969, Prince Georges Co., MD *Drafted:* 1992 Round 1 NE
1992 NE: 15 G. **1993** NE: 16 G. **1994** NE: 3 G. **1995** Jac: 11 G. **1997** Ind: 10 G. **Total:** 55 G.

RICKY CHURCHMAN Churchman, Richard Cecil 6′1″, 195 **DB**
Col: Texas *HS:* Pearland [TX] B: 3/14/1958, Pearland, TX
Drafted: 1980 Round 4 SF
1980 SF: 16 G; PR 2-16 8.0; Int 4-7; 1 Fum. **1981** SF: 3 G. **Total:** 19 G; PR 2-16 8.0; Int 4-7; 1 Fum.

DON CHURCHWELL Churchwell, Donnis Hanson 6′1″, 253 **OT-DT**
(Bull) *Col:* Mississippi *HS:* George Co. [Lucedale, MS] B: 5/11/1936, Leaksville, MS *Drafted:* 1959 Round 5 Bal
1959 Was: 10 G. **1960** Oak: 1 G. **Total:** 11 G.

DON CHUY Chuy, Donald John 6′0″, 260 **OG**
Col: Clemson *HS:* Nutley [NJ] B: 7/20/1941, Newark, NJ
Drafted: 1963 Round 5 LARm
1963 LARm: 14 G. **1964** LARm: 12 G. **1965** LARm: 11 G. **1966** LARm: 9 G. **1967** LARm: 14 G. **1968** LARm: 14 G. **1969** Phi: 8 G. **Total:** 82 G.

JOE CIBULAS Cibulas, Joseph James 6′0″, 220 **T**
Col: Duquesne *HS:* Mount Pleasasnt [PA] B: 5/31/1921, Whitney, PA
D: 5/15/1998, Pittsburgh, PA *Drafted:* 1943 Round 23 Pit
1945 Pit: 5 G.

MIKE CICCOLELLA Ciccolella, Michael Eugene 6′0″, 225 **LB**
Col: Dayton *HS:* St. Anthony's [Follansbee, WV] B: 10/19/1943, Follansbee, WV *Drafted:* 1965 Round 18 NYG
1966 NYG: 14 G. **1967** NYG: 7 G. **1968** NYG: 14 G; Int 1-7. **Total:** 35 G; Int 1-7.

BEN CICCONE Ciccone, Benjamin M 5′10″, 297 **C-LB**
(Scaggie) *Col:* Duquesne *HS:* New Castle [PA] B: 10/10/1909, New Castle, PA D: 7/7/1990, New Castle, PA
1934 Pit: 11 G; Rush 1-(-5) -5.0. **1935** Pit: 12 G. **1942** ChiC: 2 G.
Total: 25 G; Rush 1-(-5) -5.0.

CHICK CICHOWSKI Cichowski, Eugene Walter 6′0″, 195 **DB**
Col: Indiana *HS:* Albert G. Lane Tech [Chicago, IL] B: 5/20/1934, Chicago, IL *Drafted:* 1957 Round 21 Pit
1957 Pit: 12 G. **1958** Was: 1 G. **1959** Was: 1 G. **Total:** 14 G.

TOM CICHOWSKI Cichowski, Thomas John 6′4″, 250 **OT**
Col: Maryland *HS:* Southington [CT] B: 6/13/1944, New Britain, CT
Drafted: 1966 Redshirt Round 2 Oak
1967 Den: 11 G. **1968** Den: 2 G. **Total:** 13 G.

GUS CIFELLI Cifelli, August Blaze 6′4″, 244 **OT**
Col: Notre Dame *HS:* La Salle Prep [Philadelphia, PA] B: 2/3/1926, Philadelphia, PA *Drafted:* 1950 Round 19 Det
1950 Det: 12 G. **1951** Det: 12 G. **1952** Det: 12 G. **1953** GB: 12 G.
1954 Phi-Pit: 12 G; PR 1-0. Phi: 7 G; PR 1-0. Pit: 5 G. **Total:** 60 G; PR 1-0.

ED CIFERS Cifers, Edward Clifton 6′2″, 227 **OE-DE**
Col: Tennessee *HS:* Kingsport [TN] B: 7/18/1916, Church Hill, TN
Drafted: 1941 Round 4 Was
1942 Was: KR 2-0; **1** Fum TD. **1947** ChiB: KR 2-33 16.5; Int 1-20 1 TD.
1948 ChiB: Rush 1-5 5.0. **Total:** Rush 1-5 5.0; KR 4-33 8.3; Int 1-20 1 TD; 1 Fum TD.

		Receiving					Tot
Year Team	G	Rec	Yds	Avg	TD	Fum	TD
1941 Was	11	10	94	9.4	1	0	1
1942 Was	11	18	196	10.9	1	0	3
1946 Was	11	6	61	10.2	0	0	0
1947 ChiB	11	3	48	16.0	1	1	2
1948 ChiB	12	0	0	—	0	0	0
NFL Total	56	37	399	10.8	3	1	6

BOB CIFERS Cifers, Robert Gale 5′11″, 201 **HB-DB-BB**
Col: Tennessee *HS:* Kingsport [TN] B: 9/5/1920, Church Hill, TN
Drafted: 1944 Round 2 Det
1946 Det: Pass 6-2 33.3%, 24 4.00 1 Int; Rec 4-178 44.5 4 TD; PR 1-3 3.0. **1947** Pit: Pass 3-2 66.7%, 28 9.33; Rec 3-58 19.3; KR 2-30 15.0; Int 1-32. **1948** Pit: Pass 4-0, 1 Int; Rec 4-55 13.8; PR 1-8 8.0; KR 9-245 27.2. **1949** GB: Rec 1-5 5.0. **Total:** Pass 13-4 30.8%, 52 4.00 2 Int; Rec 12-296 24.7 4 TD; PR 2-11 5.5; KR 11-275 25.0; Int 1-32.

		Rushing				Punting				Tot
Year Team	G	Att	Yds	Avg	TD	Punts	Yds	Avg	Fum	TD
1946 Det	11	8	18	2.3	0	30	1369	**45.6**	2	4
1947 Pit	10	87	356	4.1	0	68	2796	41.1	3	0
1948 Pit	12	112	361	3.2	1	62	2454	39.6	4	1
1949 GB	9	23	52	2.3	0	1	49	49.0	0	0
NFL Total	42	230	787	3.4	1	161	6668	41.4	9	5

RALPH CINDRICH Cindrich, Ralph Edward 6′1″, 228 **LB**
Col: Pittsburgh *HS:* Avella [PA] B: 10/29/1949, Washington, PA
Drafted: 1972 Round 5 Atl
1972 NE: 12 G. **1973** Hou: 13 G. **1974** Hou-Den: 7 G. Hou: 6 G. Den: 1 G.
1975 Hou: 4 G. **Total:** 36 G.

LARRY CIPA Cipa, Lawrence Andre 6′3″, 209 **QB**
Col: Michigan *HS:* McNicholas [Cincinnati, OH] B: 10/5/1951, Detroit, MI *Drafted:* 1974 Round 15 NO
1974 NO: Rush 12-35 2.9 1 TD. **1975** NO: Rush 6-2 0.3.
Total: Rush 18-37 2.1 1 TD.

		Passing								
Year Team	G	Att	Comp	Comp%	Yds	YPA	TD	Int	Rating	Fum
1974 NO	4	55	20	36.4	242	4.40	0	0	50.7	2
1975 NO	4	37	14	37.8	182	4.92	1	3	29.3	3
NFL Total	8	92	34	37.0	424	4.61	1	3	42.1	5

STEVE CISOWSKI Cisowski, Steven James 6′5″, 275 **OT**
Col: Santa Clara *HS:* Westmont [Campbell, CA] B: 1/16/1963, Campbell, CA *Drafted:* 1986 Round 8 NYG
1987 Dal: 3 G.

FRANK CIVILETTO Civiletto, Frank Jerry 5′9″, 180 **WB**
(Civy) *Col:* Case Western Reserve; Springfield *HS:* Central [Cleveland, OH] B: 9/11/1900, Buffalo, NY D: 2/9/1970, Cleveland, OH
1923 Cle: 4 G.

NEIL CLABO Clabo, William Neil 6′2″, 200 **P**
Col: Tennessee *HS:* Farragut [Knoxville, TN] B: 11/18/1952, Miami Beach, FL *Drafted:* 1975 Round 10 Min

		Punting		
Year Team	G	Punts	Yds	Avg
1975 Min	14	73	2997	41.1
1976 Min	13	69	2678	38.8
1977 Min	14	83	3302	39.8
NFL Total	41	225	8977	39.9

DARRYL CLACK Clack, Darryl Earl 5′10″, 219 **RB**
Col: Arizona State *HS:* Widefield [Colorado Springs, CO]
B: 10/29/1963, San Antonio, TX *Drafted:* 1986 Round 2 Dal
1986 Dal: Rec 1-18 18.0. **1988** Dal: Rec 17-126 7.4 1 TD. **1989** Dal: Rec 4-69 17.3. **Total:** Rec 22-213 9.7 1 TD.

		Rushing				Kickoff Returns					Tot
Year Team	G	Ret	Yds	Avg	TD	Ret	Yds	Avg	TD	Fum	TD
1986 Dal	16	4	19	4.8	0	19	421	22.2	0	3	0
1987 Dal	12	0	0	—	0	29	635	21.9	0	1	0
1988 Dal	15	11	54	4.9	0	32	690	21.6	0	0	1
1989 Dal	8	14	40	2.9	2	3	56	18.7	0	1	2
NFL Total	51	29	113	3.9	2	83	1802	21.7	0	5	3

JIM CLACK Clack, James Thomas 6′3″, 250 **C-OG**
Col: Wake Forest *HS:* Rocky Mount [NC] B: 10/26/1947, Rocky Mount, NC
1971 Pit: 14 G; KR 1-12 12.0; 1 Fum. **1972** Pit: 14 G. **1973** Pit: 12 G.
1974 Pit: 13 G. **1975** Pit: 14 G. **1976** Pit: 11 G; KR 1-0; 1 Fum. **1977** Pit: 14 G. **1978** NYG: 16 G. **1979** NYG: 16 G. **1980** NYG: 16 G. **1981** NYG: 6 G. **Total:** 146 G; KR 2-12 6.0; 2 Fum.

WALT CLAGO Clago, Walter 6′0″, 195 **E**
Col: Detroit Mercy *HS:* Cass Tech [Detroit, MI] B: 6/1899, Detroit, MI Deceased
1921 Det: 6 G. **1922** RI: 7 G. **Total:** 13 G.

ROBERT CLAIBORNE Claiborne, Robert Cardell 5′10″, 175 **WR**
Col: Grossmont Coll. CA (J.C.); Southwestern Coll. CA (J.C.); San Diego State *HS:* Mount Miguel [Spring Valley, CA] B: 7/10/1967, New Orleans, LA *Drafted:* 1990 Round 12 Det
1992 SD: 9 G; Rec 1-15 15.0. **1993** TB: 5 G; Rec 5-61 12.2; PR 6-32 5.3; KR 4-57 14.3; 2 Fum. **Total:** 14 G; Rec 6-76 12.7; PR 6-32 5.3; KR 4-57 14.3; 2 Fum.

FRANK CLAIR Clair, Frank James 6′1″, 204 **OE-DE**
Col: Ohio State *HS:* Hamilton [OH] B: 5/12/1917, Hamilton, OH
1941 Was: 10 G; Rec 2-12 6.0.

RICKEY CLAITT Claitt, Rickey 5′10″, 206 **RB**
Col: Bethune-Cookman *HS:* Avon Park [FL] B: 4/12/1957, Sylvester, GA
1980 Was: Rec 3-34 11.3 1 TD; KR 2-18 9.0. **1981** Was: KR 1-14 14.0.
Total: Rec 3-34 11.3 1 TD; KR 3-32 10.7.

		Rushing					Tot
Year Team	G	Att	Yds	Avg	TD	Fum	TD
1980 Was	15	57	215	3.8	1	3	2
1981 Was	13	3	19	6.3	0	0	0
NFL Total	28	60	234	3.9	1	3	2

JACK CLANCY Clancy, John David 6′2″, 195 **WR**
Col: Michigan *HS:* St. Mary's of Redford [Detroit, MI] B: 6/18/1944, Humboldt, IA *Drafted:* 1966 Redshirt Round 3 Mia
1967 Mia: Pass 1-1 100.0%, 17 17.00; Rush 3-(-4) -1.3. **Total:** Pass 1-1 100.0%, 17 17.00; Rush 3-(-4) -1.3.

		Receiving				
Year Team	G	Rec	Yds	Avg	TD	Fum
1967 Mia	14	67	868	13.0	2	2
1969 Mia	8	21	289	13.8	1	0
1970 GB	14	16	244	15.3	2	0
NFL Total	36	104	1401	13.5	5	2

SAM CLANCY Clancy, Samuel 6′7″, 288 **DE-DT**
Col: Pittsburgh *HS:* Brashear [Pittsburgh, PA] B: 5/29/1958, Pittsburgh, PA *Drafted:* 1982 Round 11 Sea
1983 Sea: 13 G. **1985** Cle: 14 G; 1 Sac. **1986** Cle: 16 G; 6.5 Sac. **1987** Cle: 13 G; 2 Sac. **1988** Cle: 16 G; 4.5 Sac. **1989** Ind: 16 G; 0.5 Sac. **1990** Ind: 16 G; 7.5 Sac. **1991** Ind: 16 G; 2.5 Sac. **1992** Ind: 16 G; 4.5 Sac. **1993** Ind: 16 G; 1 Sac. **Total:** 152 G; 30.0 Sac.

SEAN CLANCY Clancy, Sean Matthew 6′4″, 218 **LB**
Col: Amherst *HS:* Chaminade [Mineola, NY] B: 10/22/1956, Manhasset, NY *Drafted:* 1978 Round 8 Mia
1978 Mia: 16 G. **1979** StL: 10 G. **Total:** 26 G.

STU CLANCY Clancy, Stuart Joseph 5′10″, 189 **DB-FB-TB-WB**
Col: Holy Cross *HS:* Branford [CT]; St.John's Prep [Brooklyn, NY] B: 6/6/1906, Branford, CT D: 9/24/1965, Branford, CT
1932 SI-NYG: Pass 13-2 15.4%, 45 3.46 4 Int; Rec 4-58 14.5 1 TD. SI: Pass 13-2 15.4%, 45 3.46 4 Int; Rec 1-15 15.0. NYG: Rec 3-43 14.3 1 TD. **1933** NYG: Pass 3-1 33.3%, 35 11.67; Rec 2-14 7.0. **Total:** Pass 16-3 18.8%, 80 5.00 4 Int; Rec 6-72 12.0 1 TD.

		Rushing				Tot
Year Team	**G**	**Att**	**Yds**	**Avg**	**TD**	**TD**
1930 Nwk	2	—	—	—	0	0
1931 SI	11	—	—	—	1	1
1932 SI-NYG	12	54	181	3.4	0	1
1932 SI	9	18	25	1.4	0	0
1932 NYG	3	36	156	4.3	0	1
1933 NYG	11	44	136	3.1	2	2
1934 NYG	9	17	60	3.5	0	0
1935 NYG	5	13	32	2.5	1	1
NFL Total	50	128	409	3.2	4	5

CHUCK CLANTON Clanton, Cleveland Edward III 5′11″, 192 **DB**
Col: Auburn *HS:* Pine Forest [Pensacola, FL] B: 7/15/1962, Richmond, VA *Drafted:* 1984 Supplemental Round 2 GB
1985 GB: 3 G.

SAM CLAPHAN Claphan, Samuel Jack 6′6″, 285 **OT-OG**
Col: Oklahoma *HS:* Stillwell [OK] B: 10/10/1956, Tahlequah, OK *Drafted:* 1979 Round 2 Cle
1981 SD: 16 G. **1982** SD: 2 G. **1983** SD: 16 G. **1984** SD: 16 G. **1985** SD: 12 G. **1986** SD: 16 G. **1987** SD: 9 G. **Total:** 87 G.

DENNIS CLARIDGE Claridge, Dennis Bert 6′2″, 220 **QB**
Col: Nebraska *HS:* Robbinsdale [MN] B: 8/18/1941, Phoenix, AZ *Drafted:* 1963 Round 3 GB
1965 GB: Rush 2-(-3) -1.5. **1966** Atl: Rush 5-15 3.0. **Total:** Rush 7-12 1.7.

		Passing								
Year Team	**G**	**Att**	**Comp**	**Comp%**	**Yds**	**YPA**	**TD**	**Int**	**Rating**	**Fum**
1965 GB	1	1	1	100.0	13	13.00	0	0	118.8	1
1966 Atl	7	70	40	57.1	471	6.73	2	2	75.4	1
NFL Total	8	71	41	57.7	484	6.82	2	2	76.3	2

AL CLARK Clark, Al 6′0″, 185 **DB**
Col: Grambling State; Northern Arizona; Eastern Michigan *HS:* Greenville Park [Hammond, LA] B: 2/29/1948, Bogalusa, LA *Drafted:* 1971 Round 3 Det
1971 Det: 9 G; KR 8-216 27.0; 2 Fum. **1972** LARm: 14 G; KR 3-59 19.7; Int 1-18; 1 Fum. **1973** LARm: 14 G; KR 2-80 40.0; Int 1-5. **1974** LARm: 14 G. **1975** LARm: 4 G. **1976** Phi: 14 G; PR 4-57 14.3; Int 1-0. **Total:** 69 G; PR 4-57 14.3; KR 13-355 27.3; Int 3-23; 3 Fum.

POTS CLARK Clark, Alfred F 5′7″, 180 **HB**
Col: Nevada-Reno B: 12/11/1900 D: 9/18/1973, Ontario, CA
1927 Fra-Dul: 7 G. Fra: 1 G. Dul: 6 G. **Total:** 7 G.

ALLAN CLARK Clark, Allan Vincent 5′10″, 186 **RB**
Col: Northern Arizona *HS:* San Marcos [Santa Barbara, CA] B: 6/8/1957, Grand Rapids, MN *Drafted:* 1979 Round 10 NE
1979 NE: Rec 2-35 17.5. **1980** NE: **1** Fum TD. **Total:** Rec 2-35 17.5; 1 Fum TD.

		Rushing				Kickoff Returns					Tot
Year Team	**G**	**Ret**	**Yds**	**Avg**	**TD**	**Ret**	**Yds**	**Avg**	**TD**	**Fum**	**TD**
1979 NE	16	19	84	4.4	2	37	816	22.1	0	0	2
1980 NE	11	9	56	6.2	1	3	21	7.0	0	0	2
1982 Buf-GB	6	0	0	—	0	4	75	18.8	0	1	0
1982 Buf	1	0	0	—	0	0	0	—	0	0	0
1982 GB	5	0	0	—	0	4	75	18.8	0	1	0
NFL Total	33	28	140	5.0	3	44	912	20.7	0	1	4

BERNARD CLARK Clark, Bernard 6′2″, 248 **LB**
Col: Miami (Fla.) *HS:* Leto [Tampa, FL] B: 1/12/1967, Tampa, FL *Drafted:* 1990 Round 3 Cin
1990 Cin: 14 G. **1991** Sea-Cin: 14 G. Sea: 2 G. Cin: 12 G. **Total:** 28 G.

BERYL CLARK Clark, Beryl Leon 6′0″, 200 **TB-DB**
Col: Oklahoma *HS:* Cherokee [OK] B: 10/13/1917, Cherokee, OK *Drafted:* 1940 Round 16 ChiC
1940 ChiC: Rec 1-20 20.0; Int 2-58; Punt 28-914 32.6; Scor 3, 3-3 100.0% XK.

		Passing							
Year Team	**G**	**Att**	**Comp**	**Comp%**	**Yds**	**YPA**	**TD**	**Int**	**Rating**
1940 ChiC	9	58	25	43.1	316	5.45	2	6	32.6

	Rushing			
Year Team	**Att**	**Yds**	**Avg**	**TD**
1940 ChiC	39	9	0.2	0

BRET CLARK Clark, Bret 6′3″, 198 **DB**
Col: Nebraska *HS:* Nebraska City [NE] B: 2/24/1961, Nebraska City, NE *Drafted:* 1985 Round 7 LARd
1986 Atl: 16 G; Rush 2-8 4.0; Int 5-94; 1 Sac. **1987** Atl: 1 G. **1988** Atl: 12 G; Int 4-40; 1 Fum. **Total:** 29 G; Rush 2-8 4.0; Int 9-134; 1 Fum; 1 Sac.

BRIAN CLARK Clark, Brian Matthew 6′2″, 190 **K**
Col: Florida *HS:* Sarasota [FL] B: 6/28/1958, Canton, OH *Drafted:* 1982 Round 10 NE
1982 TB: 1 G.

BRUCE CLARK Clark, Bruce M 6′3″, 273 **DT**
Col: Penn State *HS:* New Castle [PA] B: 3/31/1958, New Castle, PA *Drafted:* 1980 Round 1 GB
1982 NO: 9 G; 5.5 Sac. **1983** NO: 15 G; 4.5 Sac. **1984** NO: 15 G; Int 1-9; 10.5 Sac. **1985** NO: 16 G; 8.5 Sac. **1986** NO: 16 G; 6 Sac. **1987** NO: 15 G; Scor **1** Saf; 2 Pt; 4.5 Sac. **1988** NO: 16 G. **1989** KC: 11 G. **Total:** 113 G; Int 1-9; Scor 1 Saf; 2 Pt; 39.5 Sac.

CHARLIE CLARK Clark, Charles Arthur Jr. 5′10″, 205 **G**
Col: Harvard *HS:* Milton Acad. [MA] B: 2/15/1898, Somerville, MA D: 5/31/1960, New York, NY
1924 ChiC: 4 G.

BOOBIE CLARK Clark, Charles Lee 6′2″, 245 **RB**
Col: Bethune-Cookman *HS:* New Stanton [Jacksonville, FL] B: 11/8/1949, Jacksonville, FL D: 10/25/1988, Jacksonville, FL *Drafted:* 1973 Round 12 Cin
1978 Cin: KR 1-11 11.0. **Total:** KR 1-11 11.0.

		Rushing				Receiving					Tot
Year Team	**G**	**Att**	**Yds**	**Avg**	**TD**	**Rec**	**Yds**	**Avg**	**TD**	**Fum**	**TD**
1973 Cin	14	254	988	3.9	8	45	347	7.7	0	8	8
1974 Cin	8	99	312	3.2	5	23	194	8.4	1	3	6
1975 Cin	14	167	594	3.6	4	42	334	8.0	0	5	4
1976 Cin	13	151	671	4.4	7	23	158	6.9	1	3	8
1977 Cin	10	68	226	3.3	1	7	33	4.7	0	2	1
1978 Cin	14	40	187	4.7	0	11	73	6.6	0	1	0
1979 Hou	15	22	51	2.3	0	6	58	9.7	0	0	0
1980 Hou	6	1	3	3.0	0	0	0	—	0	0	0
NFL Total	94	802	3032	3.8	25	157	1197	7.6	2	22	27

DAN CLARK Clark, Dan Lee 6′2″, 233 **LB**
Col: Rancho Santiago Coll. CA (J.C.); San Jose State *HS:* Saddleback [Santa Ana, CA] B: 5/21/1964, Toma, Japan
1987 LARm: 1 G.

DARRYL CLARK Clark, Darryl Wade 5′11″, 204 **RB**
Col: Texas *HS:* Jeff Davis [Houston, TX] B: 8/9/1961, Houston, TX
1987 ChiB: 3 G; Rush 5-11 2.2.

DERRICK CLARK Clark, Derrick 6′1″, 235 **RB**
Col: Garden City CC KS; Florida State; Evangel *HS:* Apopka [FL] B: 5/4/1971, Apopka, FL
1994 Den: Rec 9-47 5.2; KR 3-34 11.3.

		Rushing				
Year Team	**G**	**Att**	**Yds**	**Avg**	**TD**	**Fum**
1994 Den	16	56	168	3.0	3	1

DEXTER CLARK Clark, Dexter Dewayne 6′0″, 190 **DB**
Col: Toledo *HS:* Central [Flint, MI] B: 5/5/1964, Dermott, AR
1987 Det: 2 G.

DON CLARK Clark, Donald Rex 5′11″, 197 **LB-G**
Col: USC *HS:* George Washington [Los Angeles, CA] B: 12/22/1923, Shurdan, IA D: 8/6/1989, Huntington Beach, CA
AAFC **1948** SF-A: 14 G; Int 1-12. **1949** SF-A: 12 G; Int 1-16. **Total:** 26 G; Int 2-28.

DWIGHT CLARK Clark, Dwight Edward 6′4″, 212 **WR**
Col: Clemson *HS:* Garinger [Charlotte, NC] B: 1/8/1957, Kinston, NC *Drafted:* 1979 Round 10 SF
1981 SF: Pass 1-0; Rush 3-32 10.7. **1983** SF: Pass 1-0; Rush 3-18 6.0. **1984** SF: Pass 1-0. **Total:** Pass 3-0; Rush 6-50 8.3.

Year Team	G	Receiving Rec	Yds	Avg	TD	Fum
1979 SF	16	18	232	12.9	0	0
1980 SF	16	82	991	12.1	8	2
1981 SF	16	85	1105	13.0	4	0
1982 SF	9	**60**	913	15.2	5	1
1983 SF	16	70	840	12.0	8	0
1984 SF	16	52	880	16.9	6	0
1985 SF	16	54	705	13.1	10	0
1986 SF	16	61	794	13.0	2	0
1987 SF	13	24	290	12.1	5	1
NFL Total	134	506	6750	13.3	48	4

DUTCH CLARK Clark, Earl Harry 6′0″, 185 **TB-DB**
Col: Colorado College *HS:* Central [Pueblo, CO] B: 10/11/1906, Fowler, CO D: 8/5/1978, Canon City, CO *HOF:* 1963
1931 Port: Scor 60, 6 XK. **1932** Port: Scor **55**, **3** FG, **10** XK. **1934** Det: Scor 73, 4 FG, 13 XK. **1935** Det: Scor **55**, 1 FG, **16** XK. **1936** Det: Scor **73**, 4 FG, **19** XK. **1937** Det: Scor 45, 1 FG, 6 XK. **1938** Det: Scor 8, 2-2 100.0% FG, 2-2 100.0% XK. **Total:** Scor 369, 15-2 100.0% FG, 72-2 100.0% XK.

Year Team	G	Passing Att	Comp	Comp%	Yds	YPA	TD	Int	Rating
1931 Port	11	—	—	—	—	—	1	—	—
1932 Port	11	52	17	32.7	272	5.23	2	8	24.4
1934 Det	12	50	23	46.0	383	**7.66**	0	3	47.3
1935 Det	12	26	11	42.3	133	5.12	2	4	44.7
1936 Det	12	71	38	**53.5**	467	6.58	4	6	57.7
1937 Det	11	39	19	48.7	202	5.18	1	3	40.8
1938 Det	6	12	6	50.0	50	4.17	1	2	49.3
NFL Total	75	250	114	45.6	1507	6.03	11	26	40.3

Year Team	Rushing Att	Yds	Avg	TD	Receiving Rec	Yds	Avg	TD	Tot TD
1931 Port	—	—	—	**9**	—	—	—	0	9
1932 Port	137	461	3.4	3	10	107	10.7	3	6
1934 Det	123	763	6.2	**8**	6	72	12.0	0	8
1935 Det	120	427	3.6	4	9	124	13.8	2	6
1936 Det	123	628	5.1	**7**	1	5	5.0	0	7
1937 Det	96	468	4.9	**5**	2	33	16.5	1	6
1938 Det	7	25	3.6	0	0	0	—	0	0
NFL Total	606	2772	4.6	36	28	341	12.2	6	42

ERNIE CLARK Clark, Ernest Robert 6′1″, 220 **LB**
Col: Michigan State *HS:* Medina [NY] B: 8/11/1937, Arcadia, FL *Drafted:* 1963 Round 13 Det
1963 Det: 14 G; KR 1-13 13.0. **1964** Det: 14 G; KR 2-29 14.5. **1965** Det: 14 G; Int 1-7. **1966** Det: 14 G; Int 1-7. **1967** Det: 12 G; Int 1-0; 1 Fum. **1968** StL: 14 G; Int 1-15. **Total:** 82 G; KR 3-42 14.0; Int 4-29; 1 Fum.

GAIL CLARK Clark, Gail Allen 6′2″, 226 **LB**
Col: Michigan State *HS:* Bellefontaine [OH] B: 4/14/1951, Bellefontaine, OH *Drafted:* 1973 Round 4 Pit
1973 ChiB: 11 G. **1974** NE: 8 G. **Total:** 19 G.

GARY CLARK Clark, Gary C 5′9″, 175 **WR**
Col: James Madison *HS:* Pulaski Co. [Dublin, VA] B: 5/1/1962, Radford, VA *Drafted:* 1984 Supplemental Round 2 Was
1985 Was: Rush 2-10 5.0. **1986** Was: PR 1-14 14.0. **1987** Was: Rush 1-0. **1988** Was: Rush 2-6 3.0; PR 8-48 6.0. **1989** Was: Rush 2-19 9.5. **1990** Was: Rush 1-1 1.0. **1991** Was: Rush 1-0. **1992** Was: Rush 2-18 9.0. **Total:** Rush 11-54 4.9; PR 9-62 6.9.

Year Team	G	Receiving Rec	Yds	Avg	TD	Fum
1985 Was	16	72	926	12.9	5	0
1986 Was	15	74	1265	17.1	7	1
1987 Was	12	56	1066	19.0	7	3
1988 Was	16	59	892	15.1	7	2
1989 Was	15	79	1229	15.6	9	1
1990 Was	16	75	1112	14.8	8	0
1991 Was	16	70	1340	19.1	10	0
1992 Was	16	64	912	14.3	5	1
1993 Pho	14	63	818	13.0	4	1
1994 Ariz	15	50	771	15.4	1	0
1995 Mia	16	37	525	14.2	2	0
NFL Total	167	699	10856	15.5	65	9

GREG CLARK Clark, Gregory Jay 6′4″, 251 **TE**
Col: Ricks Coll. ID (J.C.); Stanford *HS:* Viewmont [Bountiful, UT] B: 4/7/1972, Bountiful, UT *Drafted:* 1997 Round 3 SF
1997 SF: 15 G; Rec 8-96 12.0 1 TD; 6 Pt. **1998** SF: 13 G; Rec 12-124 10.3 1 TD; Scor 1 2XP; 8 Pt. **Total:** 28 G; Rec 20-220 11.0 2 TD; Scor 1 2XP; 14 Pt.

GREG CLARK Clark, Gregory Klondike 6′0″, 228 **LB**
Col: Arizona State *HS:* North [Torrance, CA] B: 3/5/1965, Los Angeles, CA *Drafted:* 1988 Round 12 ChiB
1988 ChiB: 15 G. **1989** Mia: 16 G. **1990** LARm: 11 G. **1991** GB-SD: 16 G. GB: 2 G. SD: 14 G. **1992** Sea: 12 G. **Total:** 70 G.

HAL CLARK Clark, Harold E asdf 5′10″, 195 **E-BB**
(Fuss; Butch) *Col:* No College *HS:* Cathedral [Rochester, NY] B: 10/25/1893, NY D: 7/9/1973, Rochester, NY
1920 Roch: 8 G. **1922** Roch: 3 G. **1923** Roch: 4 G; Rec 1 TD; 6 Pt. **1924** Roch: 7 G. **1925** Roch: 5 G. **Total:** 27 G; Rec 1 TD; 6 Pt.

HERMAN CLARK Clark, Herman Piikea 6′3″, 256 **OG-LB**
(Buddy) *Col:* Oregon State *HS:* Punahou School [Honolulu, HI] B: 11/30/1930, Honolulu, HI D: 11/9/1989, Molokai, HI *Drafted:* 1952 Round 4 ChiB
1952 ChiB: 12 G; Int 1-8. **1954** ChiB: 5 G. **1955** ChiB: 11 G. **1956** ChiB: 12 G. **1957** ChiB: 12 G. **Total:** 52 G; Int 1-8.

HOWARD CLARK Clark, Howard Morris 6′2″, 215 **TE**
Col: Tennessee-Chattanooga *HS:* Dalton [GA] B: 8/23/1935, Dalton, GA

Year Team	G	Receiving Rec	Yds	Avg	TD	Fum
1960 LAC	13	27	431	16.0	0	1
1961 SD	10	11	182	16.5	0	0
NFL Total	23	38	613	16.1	0	1

JAMES CLARK Clark, James A 5′9″, 170 **FB-HB-DB**
(Bo) *Col:* Pittsburgh *HS:* Greensburg [PA]; Kiski School [Saltsburg, PA] B: 1909 Deceased
1934 Pit: Pass 1-0; Rec 1-28 28.0 1 TD. **Total:** Pass 1-0; Rec 1-28 28.0 1 TD.

Year Team	G	Rushing Att	Yds	Avg	TD
1933 Pit	10	76	192	2.5	0
1934 Pit	9	31	84	2.7	0
NFL Total	19	107	276	2.6	0

JIM CLARK Clark, James Kalaeone 6′1″, 230 **OG-OT-DT-LB**
Col: Oregon State *HS:* Punahou School [Honolulu, HI] B: 7/18/1929, Honolulu, HI *Drafted:* 1952 Round 5 Was
1952 Was: 12 G. **1953** Was: 12 G. **Total:** 24 G.

JESSIE CLARK Clark, Jessie Lee 6′0″, 231 **RB**
Col: Arkansas; Louisiana Tech *HS:* Crossett [AR] B: 1/3/1960, Thebes, AR *Drafted:* 1983 Round 7 GB
1988 Det-Pho: KR 2-10 5.0. Pho: KR 2-10 5.0. **1989** Pho-Min: KR 2-6 3.0. Pho: KR 1-0. Min: KR 1-6 6.0. **Total:** KR 4-16 4.0.

Year Team	G	Rushing Att	Yds	Avg	TD	Receiving Rec	Yds	Avg	TD	Fum	Tot TD
1983 GB	16	71	328	4.6	0	18	279	15.5	1	2	1
1984 GB	11	87	375	4.3	4	29	234	8.1	2	2	6
1985 GB	16	147	633	4.3	5	24	252	10.5	2	4	7
1986 GB	5	18	41	2.3	0	6	41	6.8	0	1	0
1987 GB	12	56	211	3.8	0	22	119	5.4	1	0	1
1988 Det-Pho	9	0	0	—	0	0	0	—	0	0	0
1988 Det	5	0	0	—	0	0	0	—	0	0	0
1988 Pho	4	0	0	—	0	0	0	—	0	0	0
1989 Pho-Min	14	20	99	5.0	0	2	14	7.0	0	2	0
1989 Pho	11	10	42	4.2	0	0	0	—	0	1	0
1989 Min	3	10	57	5.7	0	2	14	7.0	0	1	0
1990 Min	5	16	49	3.1	0	1	4	4.0	0	0	0
NFL Total	88	415	1736	4.2	9	102	943	9.2	6	11	15

JON CLARK Clark, Jon 6′6″, 345 **OT**
Col: Temple *HS:* John Bartram [Philadelphia, PA] B: 4/11/1973, Philadelphia, PA *Drafted:* 1996 Round 6 ChiB
1996 ChiB: 1 G. **1997** ChiB: 1 G. **1998** Ariz: 6 G. **Total:** 8 G.

KELVIN CLARK Clark, Kelvin Wayne 6′3″, 260 **OT-OG**
Col: Nebraska *HS:* Odessa [TX] B: 1/30/1956, Odessa, TX *Drafted:* 1979 Round 1 Den
1979 Den: 15 G. **1980** Den: 14 G. **1981** Den: 16 G. **1982** NO: 9 G. **1983** NO: 16 G; 1 Fum TD; 6 Pt. **1984** NO: 16 G. **1985** NO: 2 G. **Total:** 88 G; 1 Fum TD; 6 Pt.

KEN CLARK Clark, Kenneth Lawrence 6′2″, 197 **P**
Col: St. Mary's (Canada) *HS:* New Toronto [Toronto, Canada] B: 5/26/1948, Southampton, England
1979 LARm: Pass 2-2 100.0%, 32 16.00; Rush 1-3 3.0.

Year Team	G	Punting Punts	Yds	Avg	Fum
1979 LARm	16	93	3731	40.1	1

KEN CLARK Clark, Kenneth R 5′9″, 201 **RB**
Col: Nebraska *HS:* Bryan [Omaha, NE] B: 6/11/1966, Evergreen, AL
Drafted: 1990 Round 8 Ind
1992 Ind: KR 3-54 18.0. **Total:** KR 3-54 18.0.

		Rushing				Receiving				
Year Team	G	Att	Yds	Avg	TD	Rec	Yds	Avg	TD	Fum
1990 Ind	5	7	10	1.4	0	5	23	4.6	0	0
1991 Ind	16	114	366	3.2	0	33	245	7.4	0	4
1992 Ind	13	40	134	3.4	0	5	46	9.2	0	0
NFL Total	34	161	510	3.2	0	43	314	7.3	0	4

KEVIN CLARK Clark, Kevin Randall 5′10″, 185 **DB**
(K.C.) *Col:* San Jose State *HS:* C.K. McClatchy [Sacramento, CA]
B: 6/8/1964, Sacramento, CA
1987 Den: KR 2-33 16.5; Int 3-105. **1990** Den: KR 20-505 **25.3**. **1991** Den: KR 2-45 22.5. **Total:** KR 24-583 24.3; Int 3-105.

		Punt Returns				
Year Team	G	Ret	Yds	Avg	TD	Fum
1987 Den	11	18	233	12.9	1	1
1988 Den	3	13	115	8.8	0	0
1990 Den	8	21	159	7.6	0	0
1991 Den	4	7	67	9.6	0	1
NFL Total	26	59	574	9.7	1	2

LEROY CLARK Clark, Leroy Darnell 5′11″, 202 **P**
Col: Prairie View A&M *HS:* College Station [TX] B: 1/16/1950, College Station, TX
1976 Hou: 1 G; Punt 10-335 33.5.

LOUIS CLARK Clark, Louis Steven 6′0″, 193 **WR**
Col: Mississippi State *HS:* Shannon [MS] B: 7/3/1964, Shannon, MS
Drafted: 1987 Round 10 Sea
1989 Sea: KR 1-31 31.0. **Total:** KR 1-31 31.0.

		Receiving				
Year Team	G	Rec	Yds	Avg	TD	Fum
1987 Sea	2	0	0	—	0	0
1988 Sea	7	1	20	20.0	1	0
1989 Sea	16	25	260	10.4	1	1
1990 Sea	4	0	0	—	0	0
1991 Sea	16	21	228	10.9	2	0
1992 Sea	10	20	290	14.5	1	0
NFL Total	55	67	798	11.9	5	1

MARIO CLARK Clark, Mario Sean 6′2″, 194 **DB**
Col: Oregon *HS:* Pasadena [CA] B: 3/29/1954, Pasadena, CA
Drafted: 1976 Round 1 Buf
1984 SF: 1 Sac. **Total:** 1 Sac.

		Interceptions		
Year Team	G	Int	Yds	TD
1976 Buf	14	2	21	0
1977 Buf	14	7	151	0
1978 Buf	16	5	29	0
1979 Buf	16	5	95	0
1980 Buf	16	1	0	0
1981 Buf	16	5	142	0
1982 Buf	9	0	0	0
1983 Buf	14	0	0	0
1984 SF	11	1	0	0
NFL Total	126	26	438	0

MIKE CLARK Clark, Michael Hugh 6′4″, 253 **DE**
Col: Florida *HS:* Graceville [FL] B: 3/30/1959, Dothan, AL
Drafted: 1981 Round 7 LARm
1981 Was: 5 G. **1982** SF: 6 G. **1987** TB: 3 G; 1 Sac. **Total:** 14 G; 1 Sac.

SPARK CLARK Clark, Michael Keith 5′7″, 182 **RB**
Col: Akron *HS:* St. Joseph [Cleveland, OH] B: 5/22/1965, Jackson, MS
1987 Pit: 1 G; KR 1-18 18.0.

MIKE CLARK Clark, Michael Vincent 6′1″, 205 **K**
Col: Texas A&M *HS:* Longview [TX] B: 11/7/1940, Marshall, TX
1967 Pit: Pass 1-0. **Total:** Pass 1-0.

		Scoring						
Year Team	G	Pts	FG	FGA	FG%	XK	XKA	XK%
1963 Phi	14	50	7	15	46.7	29	32	90.6
1964 Pit	14	67	13	25	52.0	28	31	90.3
1965 Pit	14	52	11	19	57.9	19	24	79.2
1966 Pit	14	97	21	32	65.6	34	34	100.0
1967 Pit	14	71	12	22	54.5	35	35	100.0
1968 Dal	14	105	17	29	58.6	**54**	**54**	100.0
1969 Dal	14	103	20	36	55.6	43	44	97.7
1970 Dal	14	89	18	27	66.7	35	35	100.0
1971 Dal	12	86	13	25	52.0	**47**	**47**	100.0
1973 Dal	4	4	1	2	50.0	1	2	50.0
NFL Total	128	724	133	232	57.3	325	338	96.2

BRYAN CLARK Clark, Monte Bryan 6′2″, 198 **QB**
Col: Michigan State *HS:* Los Altos [Hacienda Heights, CA]
B: 7/27/1960, Redwood City, CA
1984 Cin: 1 G.

MONTE CLARK Clark, Monte Dale 6′6″, 265 **OT-DT-DE**
Col: USC *HS:* Kingsburg [CA] B: 1/24/1937, Fillmore, CA
Drafted: 1959 Round 4 SF
1959 SF: 12 G. **1960** SF: 12 G; KR 1-15 15.0. **1961** SF: 12 G. **1962** Dal: 14 G. **1963** Cle: 8 G. **1964** Cle: 14 G; KR 1-0. **1965** Cle: 14 G. **1966** Cle: 12 G. **1967** Cle: 13 G. **1968** Cle: 14 G. **1969** Cle: 14 G. **Total:** 139 G; KR 2-15 7.5.

ALGY CLARK Clark, Myers Arden 5′10″, 190 **DB-BB-HB-WB**
Col: Ohio State B: 1904
1930 Bkn: 10 G. **1931** Cle: 8 G; Rush 1 TD; Rec 1 TD; Tot TD 2; 12 Pt. **1932** Bos: 9 G; Rec 1-25 25.0; **1** Fum TD; 6 Pt. **1933** Cin: 10 G; Pass 4-2 50.0%, 13 3.25 1 Int; Rush 6-13 2.2; Rec 5-82 16.4; Scor 15, 4 FG, 3 XK. **1934** Cin-Phi: 10 G; Pass 10-4 40.0%, 28 2.80 2 Int; Rush 1-0; Rec 2-18 9.0; Scor 3, 1 FG. Cin: 7 G; Pass 10-4 40.0%, 28 2.80 2 Int; Rush 1-0; Rec 2-18 9.0; Scor 3, 1 FG. Phi: 3 G. **Total:** 47 G; Pass 14-6 42.9%, 41 2.93 3 Int; Rush 7-13 1.9 1 TD; Rec 8-125 15.6 1 TD; Scor 36, 5 FG, 3 XK; 1 Fum TD; Tot TD 3.

BABE CLARK Clark, Otho 5′8″, 170 **FB-C-T**
Col: No College *HS:* East [Rochester, NY] Deceased
1920 Roch: 8 G.

PHIL CLARK Clark, Philip Eugene 6′3″, 208 **DB**
(P.C.) *Col:* Northwestern *HS:* Taylor [North Bend, OR] B: 4/28/1945, Burlington, KY *Drafted:* 1967 Round 3 Dal
1967 Dal: 11 G; Int 1-6. **1968** Dal: 12 G; 1 Fum. **1969** Dal: 14 G; Int 2-2. **1970** ChiB: 13 G; Int 1-32. **1971** NE: 2 G. **Total:** 52 G; Int 4-40; 1 Fum.

RANDY CLARK Clark, Randall Byron 6′3″, 260 **C-OT-OG**
Col: Northern Illinois *HS:* Prospect [Mount Prospect, IL] B: 7/27/1957, Chicago, IL *Drafted:* 1980 Round 8 ChiB
1980 StL: 8 G; KR 2-14 7.0. **1981** StL: 16 G. **1982** StL: 9 G. **1983** StL: 14 G; 1 Fum. **1984** StL: 16 G. **1985** StL: 16 G. **1986** StL: 12 G. **1987** Atl: 3 G. **Total:** 94 G; KR 2-14 7.0; 1 Fum.

RANDY CLARK Clark, Randall Charles 6′0″, 195 **DB**
Col: Florida *HS:* Venice [FL] B: 2/18/1962, Marshall, MI
Drafted: 1984 Round 8 KC
1984 TB: 2 G.

REGGIE CLARK Clark, Reggie Boice 6′2″, 238 **LB**
Col: North Carolina *HS:* Providence [Charlotte, NC] B: 10/17/1967, Charlotte, NC
1994 Pit: 5 G. **1995** Jac: 5 G. **1996** Jac: 5 G. **Total:** 15 G.

RICO CLARK Clark, Rico Cornell 5′10″, 181 **DB**
Col: Louisville *HS:* Lakeside [Atlanta, GA] B: 6/6/1974, Atlanta, GA
1997 Ind: 4 G; Int 1-14. **1998** Ind: 16 G; KR 3-38 12.7; Int 1-30. **Total:** 20 G; KR 3-38 12.7; Int 2-44.

ROBERT CLARK Clark, Robert James 5′11″, 175 **WR**
Col: North Carolina Central *HS:* Marshall-Walker [Richmond, VA]
B: 8/6/1965, Brooklyn, NY *Drafted:* 1987 Round 10 NO
1991 Det: KR 1-0. **Total:** KR 1-0.

		Receiving				
Year Team	G	Rec	Yds	Avg	TD	Fum
1987 NO	2	3	38	12.7	0	0
1988 NO	16	19	245	12.9	2	1
1989 Det	16	41	748	18.2	2	2
1990 Det	16	52	914	17.6	8	0
1991 Det	14	47	640	13.6	6	0
1992 Mia	3	3	59	19.7	0	0
NFL Total	67	165	2644	16.0	18	3

SEDRIC CLARK Clark, Sedric C 6′2″, 245 **LB**
Col: Tulsa *HS:* Willowridge [Sugar Land, TX] B: 1/28/1973, Missouri City, TX *Drafted:* 1996 Round 7 Oak
1996 Bal: 6 G.

STEVE CLARK Clark, Stephen Spence 6′4″, 255 **NT-OG**
Col: Utah *HS:* Skyline [Salt Lake City, UT] B: 8/2/1960, Salt Lake City, UT *Drafted:* 1982 Round 9 Mia
1982 Mia: 2 G. **1983** Mia: 11 G. **1984** Mia: 12 G. **1985** Mia: 16 G. **Total:** 41 G.

STEVEN CLARK Clark, Stevan Dion 6′5″, 258 **DE**
Col: Kansas State *HS:* Mifflin [Columbus, OH] B: 10/29/1959, Chattanooga, TN *Drafted:* 1981 Round 5 NE
1981 NE: 7 G.

STEVE CLARK Clark, Steven 6′2″, 190 **DB**
Col: Liberty *HS:* Falls Church [VA] B: 12/14/1962, Arlington, VA
1987 Buf: 3 G; Int 1-23.

TORIN CLARK Clark, Torin 6′1″, 175 **DB**
Col: West Virginia State B: 12/31/1963
1987 TB: 2 G.

VINNIE CLARK Clark, Vincent Eugene 6′0″, 194 **DB**
Col: Ohio State *HS:* Cincinnati Academy of Physical Education [Cincinnati, OH] B: 1/22/1969, Cincinnati, OH *Drafted:* 1991 Round 1 GB
1992 GB: PR 1-0. **1993** Atl: PR 1-0; 1 Fum TD. **Total:** PR 2-0; 1 Fum TD.

		Interceptions			
Year Team	**G**	**Int**	**Yds**	**TD**	**Fum**
1991 GB	16	2	42	0	0
1992 GB	16	2	70	0	0
1993 Atl	15	2	59	0	1
1994 Atl-NO	16	5	149	0	0
1994 Atl	11	4	119	0	0
1994 NO	5	1	30	0	0
1995 Jac	16	1	0	0	0
1996 Jac	4	1	15	0	0
NFL Total	83	13	335	0	1

WAYNE CLARK Clark, Wayne Joseph 6′3″, 210 **OE-DE**
Col: Utah B: 4/13/1918, Los Angeles, CA Deceased
1944 Det: 8 G; Rec 2-27 13.5.

WAYNE CLARK Clark, Wayne Maurice 6′2″, 203 **QB**
Col: U.S. International *HS:* Buckeye Union [AZ] B: 5/30/1947, Oskaloosa, IA *Drafted:* 1970 Round 8 SD
1972 SD: Rush 2-(-8) -4.0. **1973** SD: Rush 13-86 6.6. **1974** Cin: Rush 1-8 8.0 1 TD. **Total:** Rush 16-86 5.4 1 TD.

		Passing								
Year Team	**G**	**Att**	**Comp**	**Comp%**	**Yds**	**YPA**	**TD**	**Int**	**Rating**	**Fum**
1970 SD	1	2	1	50.0	48	24.00	0	0	95.8	0
1972 SD	13	6	2	33.3	67	11.17	0	2	36.8	2
1973 SD	11	90	40	44.4	532	5.91	0	9	24.2	1
1974 Cin	14	22	9	40.9	98	4.45	0	3	15.2	0
1975 KC	1	0	0	—	0	—	0	0	—	1
NFL Total	40	120	52	43.3	745	6.21	0	14	24.5	4

BILL CLARK Clark, William 6′1″, 190 **C-G**
Col: No College *HS:* Wendell Phillips [Chicago, IL] Deceased
1920 ChiC: 3 G.

BILL CLARK Clark, William D 5′11″, 194 **G-C**
Col: No College B: 1891, IN Deceased
1920 Day: 2 G.

WILLIE CLARK Clark, Willie Calvin Jr. 5′10″, 186 **DB**
Col: Notre Dame *HS:* American [Madrid, Spain]; Wheatland HS [CA] B: 1/6/1972, New Haven, CT *Drafted:* 1994 Round 3 SD
1994 SD: 6 G. **1995** SD: 16 G; Int 2-14. **1996** SD: 16 G; Int 2-83 1 TD; 6 Pt. **1997** Phi: 16 G; KR 1-39 39.0 1 TD; 6 Pt. **1998** SD: 5 G. **Total:** 59 G; KR 1-39 39.0 1 TD; Int 4-97 1 TD; Tot TD 2; 12 Pt.

FRANK CLARKE Clarke, Frank Delano 6′1″, 215 **OE**
Col: Trinidad State JC CO; Colorado *HS:* Beloit [WI] B: 2/7/1934, Beloit, WI *Drafted:* 1956 Round 5 Cle
1957 Cle: KR 2-22 11.0. **1964** Dal: Pass 1-0. **Total:** Pass 1-0; KR 2-22 11.0.

		Rushing				Receiving					Tot
Year Team	**G**	**Att**	**Yds**	**Avg**	**TD**	**Rec**	**Yds**	**Avg**	**TD**	**Fum**	**TD**
1957 Cle	12	0	0	—	0	4	77	19.3	0	2	0
1958 Cle	12	0	0	—	0	3	91	30.3	0	0	0
1959 Cle	12	0	0	—	0	3	44	14.7	0	0	0
1960 Dal	8	1	-6	-6.0	0	9	290	32.2	3	0	3
1961 Dal	14	0	0	—	0	41	919	**22.4**	9	1	9
1962 Dal	12	0	0	—	0	47	1043	**22.2**	**14**	2	14
1963 Dal	14	1	12	12.0	0	43	833	19.4	10	3	10
1964 Dal	14	10	46	4.6	0	65	973	15.0	5	1	5
1965 Dal	14	8	58	7.3	0	41	682	16.6	4	2	4
1966 Dal	14	8	49	6.1	0	26	355	13.7	4	0	4
1967 Dal	14	4	72	18.0	1	9	119	13.2	1	0	2
NFL Total	140	32	231	7.2	1	291	5426	18.6	50	11	51

FRED CLARKE Clarke, Fred **E**
Col: No College Deceased
1920 Roch: 1 G.

HAGOOD CLARKE Clarke, Hagood III 6′0″, 205 **DB**
Col: Florida *HS:* Baylor Prep [Chatanooga, TN] B: 6/14/1942, Atlanta, GA *Drafted:* 1964 Round 18 Buf
1964 Buf: KR 16-330 20.6. **Total:** KR 16-330 20.6.

		Punt Returns				Interceptions				Tot
Year Team	**G**	**Ret**	**Yds**	**Avg**	**TD**	**Int**	**Yds**	**TD**	**Fum**	**TD**
1964 Buf	14	**33**	317	9.6	**1**	0	0	0	3	1
1965 Buf	14	1	13	13.0	0	7	60	0	0	0
1966 Buf	14	2	12	6.0	0	5	118	1	1	1
1967 Buf	11	0	0	—	0	0	0	0	0	0
1968 Buf	14	29	241	8.3	1	0	0	0	1	1
NFL Total	67	65	583	9.0	2	12	178	1	5	3

HARRY CLARKE Clarke, Harry Charles 6′0″, 186 **HB-DB**
(Flash) *Col:* West Virginia *HS:* Uniontown [PA] B: 12/1/1916, Cumberland, MD *Drafted:* 1940 Round 11 ChiB
AAFC **1946** LA-A: Rec 10-123 12.3 2 TD; PR 2-24 12.0; KR 2-48 24.0; Int 2-7. **1947** LA-A: Rec 3-54 18.0; PR 3-38 12.7; KR 8-225 28.1. **1948** LA-A-ChiA: Rec 4-38 9.5; PR 2-27 13.5; KR 4-96 24.0. **Total:** Rec 17-215 12.6 2 TD; PR 7-89 12.7; KR 14-369 26.4; Int 2-7.

		Rushing				Tot
Year Team	**G**	**Att**	**Yds**	**Avg**	**TD**	**TD**
1946 LA-A	14	62	250	4.0	0	2
1947 LA-A	12	44	173	3.9	2	2
1948 LA-A-ChiA	7	22	79	3.6	0	0
AAFC Total	33	128	502	3.9	2	4

NFL **1940** ChiB: Pass 3-0, 2 Int; Punt 1-30 30.0. **1941** ChiB: PR 4-56 14.0; KR 5-158 31.6; Scor 1, 1-1 100.0% XK. **1942** ChiB: PR 5-76 15.2; KR 5-159 31.8. **1943** ChiB: Pass 1-0, 1 Int; PR 10-158 15.8; KR 13-326 25.1; **1** Fum TD. **Total:** Pass 4-0, 3 Int; PR 19-290 15.3; KR 23-643 28.0; Punt 1-30 30.0; Scor 115, 1-1 100.0% XK; 1 Fum TD.

		Rushing				Receiving			
Year Team	**G**	**Att**	**Yds**	**Avg**	**TD**	**Rec**	**Yds**	**Avg**	**TD**
1940 ChiB	11	56	258	4.6	2	3	80	26.7	0
1941 ChiB	10	28	122	4.4	0	2	61	30.5	0
1942 ChiB	10	58	273	4.7	4	6	131	21.8	2
1943 ChiB	10	120	556	4.6	2	23	535	23.3	7
NFL Total	41	262	1209	4.6	8	34	807	23.7	9

	Interceptions			Tot
Year Team	**Int**	**Yds**	**TD**	**TD**
1940 ChiB	4	62	**1**	3
1941 ChiB	2	62	0	0
1942 ChiB	0	0	0	6
1943 ChiB	5	32	0	10
NFL Total	11	156	1	19

KEN CLARKE Clarke, Kenneth Maurice 6′2″, 268 **NT-DT**
Col: Syracuse *HS:* Boston English [MA] B: 8/28/1956, Savannah, GA
1978 Phi: 16 G. **1979** Phi: 16 G. **1980** Phi: 16 G; KR 1-0; 1 Fum. **1981** Phi: 16 G; KR 1-0; Scor **1** Saf; 2 Pt. **1982** Phi: 9 G; 4.5 Sac. **1983** Phi: 16 G; 1 Sac. **1984** Phi: 16 G; 10.5 Sac. **1985** Phi: 16 G; 7 Sac. **1986** Phi: 16 G; 8 Sac. **1987** Phi: 11 G; 1.5 Sac. **1988** Sea: 16 G; 2 Sac. **1989** Min: 11 G; 2 Sac. **1990** Min: 12 G; 7 Sac. **1991** Min: 16 G. **Total:** 203 G; KR 2-0; Scor 1 Saf; 2 Pt; 1 Fum; 43.5 Sac.

LEON CLARKE Clarke, Leon T 6′4″, 232 **OE-FL**
Col: USC *HS:* Venice [Los Angeles, CA] B: 1/10/1933, Los Angeles, CA *Drafted:* 1956 Round 2 LARm
1957 LARm: Rush 1-(-4) -4.0. **Total:** Rush 1-(-4) -4.0.

		Receiving					Tot
Year Team	**G**	**Rec**	**Yds**	**Avg**	**TD**	**Fum**	**TD**
1956 LARm	12	36	650	18.1	4	1	4
1957 LARm	9	23	442	19.2	4	0	4
1958 LARm	11	18	135	7.5	4	0	5
1959 LARm	11	29	453	15.6	0	2	0
1960 Cle	9	11	184	16.7	4	0	4
1961 Cle	13	11	211	19.2	2	0	2
1962 Cle	11	10	106	10.6	0	1	0
1963 Min	3	3	34	11.3	0	0	0
NFL Total	79	141	2215	15.7	18	4	19

BILL CLARKIN Clarkin, William C 5′10″, 210 **T-G**
Col: No College *HS:* St. Benedict's Prep [Newark, NJ] B: 9/11/1898, Hartford, CT D: 12/7/1982, Altoona, FL
1929 Ora: 5 G.

CONRAD CLARKS Clarks, Conrad 5′10″, 200 **DB**
Col: Pearl River CC MS; Northeast Louisiana *HS:* Franklin [LA] B: 4/21/1969, Franklin, LA
1995 Ind: 6 G.

STU CLARKSON Clarkson, Stuart Lenox 6′2″, 217 **LB-C**
Col: Texas A&M–Kingsville *HS:* Corpus Christi [TX] B: 7/4/1919, Corpus Christi, TX D: 10/25/1957, Hitchcock, TX *Drafted:* 1942 Round 20 ChiB

		Interceptions			
Year Team	**G**	**Int**	**Yds**	**TD**	**Fum**
1942 ChiB	7	0	0	0	0
1946 ChiB	11	3	79	**1**	0
1947 ChiB	12	2	10	0	1
1948 ChiB	10	2	14	0	0
1949 ChiB	12	2	9	0	0

1950 ChiB	11	0	0	0	0
1951 ChiB	11	1	0	0	0
NFL Total	74	10	112	1	1

BOB CLASBY Clasby, Robert James 6′5″, 260 **DE-DT**
Col: Notre Dame *HS:* Boston College [MA] B: 9/28/1960, Detroit, MI
Drafted: 1983 Round 9 Sea
1986 StL: 16 G; 3 Sac. **1987** StL: 12 G; 4.5 Sac. **1988** Pho: 16 G; Int 1-7; 5 Sac. **1989** Pho: 4 G; 2 Sac. **1990** Pho: 1 G. **Total:** 49 G; Int 1-7; 14.5 Sac.

CORWIN CLATT Clatt, Corwin Samuel 6′0″, 210 **DB-FB-LB**
(Corny) *Col:* Notre Dame *HS:* East Peoria [IL] B: 2/5/1924, West Des Moines, IA *Drafted:* 1945 Round 6 ChiC
1948 ChiC: 12 G; Rush 6-38 6.3; Int 1-20. **1949** ChiC: 12 G; PR 1-22 22.0; Int 2-39. **Total:** 24 G; Rush 6-38 6.3; PR 1-22 22.0; Int 3-59.

BOBBY CLATTERBUCK Clatterbuck, Bobby Dean 6′3″, 195 **QB**
Col: Houston *HS:* San Angelo [TX] B: 7/3/1932, Columbia, MO
Drafted: 1954 Round 27 NYG

		Passing							
Year Team	**G**	**Att**	**Comp**	**Comp%**	**Yds**	**YPA**	**TD**	**Int**	**Rating**
1954 NYG	10	101	50	49.5	781	7.73	6	**7**	66.5
1955 NYG	3	16	6	37.5	46	2.88	0	0	45.8
1956 NYG	2	7	4	57.1	54	7.71	0	1	42.3
1957 NYG	1	2	2	100.0	39	19.50	1	0	158.3
1960 LAC	2	23	15	65.2	112	4.87	1	1	73.1
NFL Total	18	149	77	51.7	1032	6.93	8	9	66.7

	Rushing				
Year Team	**Att**	**Yds**	**Avg**	**TD**	**Fum**
1954 NYG	19	-21	-1.1	1	5
1955 NYG	1	-3	-3.0	0	1
1957 NYG	3	3	1.0	0	0
1960 LAC	3	11	3.7	0	1
NFL Total	26	-10	-0.4	1	7

SHANNON CLAVELLE Clavelle, Shannon Lynn 6′2″, 287 **DE**
Col: Colorado *HS:* Walker [New Orleans, LA] B: 10/12/1973, Lafayette, LA *Drafted:* 1995 Round 6 Buf
1995 GB: 1 G. **1996** GB: 8 G; 0.5 Sac. **1997** GB-KC: 7 G. GB: 6 G. KC: 1 G. **Total:** 16 G; 0.5 Sac.

BOYD CLAY Clay, Boyd Davis 6′1″, 220 **T**
(Preacher) *Col:* Tennessee *HS:* Dupont [Nashville, TN] B: 5/6/1915, Hahenwald, TN D: 6/22/1978, Mt. Juliet, TN *Drafted:* 1940 Round 11 Cle
1940 Cle: 11 G; Scor 0-1 FG. **1941** Cle: 11 G; Scor 4, 1-2 50.0% FG, 1-1 100.0% XK. **1942** Cle: 8 G; Scor 4, 4-4 100.0% XK. **1944** Cle: 4 G. **Total:** 34 G; Scor 8, 1-3 33.3% FG, 5-5 100.0% XK.

HAYWARD CLAY Clay, Hayward John 6′3″, 260 **TE**
Col: Texas A&M *HS:* Snyder [TX] B: 7/5/1973, Snyder, TX
Drafted: 1996 Round 6 StL
1996 StL: 11 G; Rec 4-51 12.8. **1998** Dal: 3 G; Rec 1-27 27.0. **Total:** 14 G; Rec 5-78 15.6.

JOHN CLAY Clay, John Gregory 6′5″, 300 **OT**
Col: Missouri *HS:* Northwest [St. Louis, MO] B: 5/1/1964, St. Louis, MO *Drafted:* 1987 Round 1 LARd
1987 LARd: 10 G. **1988** SD: 2 G. **Total:** 12 G.

RANDY CLAY Clay, Oscar Randall 6′0″, 188 **HB-DB**
Col: Texas *HS:* Pampa [TX] B: 5/30/1928, Pampa, TX *Drafted:* 1950 Round 3 NYG
1950 NYG: Rec 7-69 9.9; KR 1-25 25.0; Int 2-42; Scor 15, 1-1 100.0% FG, 0-1 XK. **1953** NYG: Rec 5-51 10.2 1 TD; KR 1-20 20.0; Int 2-22; Scor 32, 2-7 28.6% FG, 20-22 90.9% XK. **Total:** Rec 12-120 10.0 1 TD; KR 2-45 22.5; Int 4-64; Scor 47, 3-8 37.5% FG, 20-23 87.0% XK.

		Rushing					Tot
Year Team	**G**	**Att**	**Yds**	**Avg**	**TD**	**Fum**	**TD**
1950 NYG	12	74	254	3.4	2	5	2
1953 NYG	12	16	26	1.6	0	0	1
NFL Total	24	90	280	3.1	2	5	3

OZZIE CLAY Clay, Oswald 6′0″, 190 **WR**
Col: Iowa State *HS:* Ridgeview [Hickory, NC] B: 9/10/1941, Hickory, NC *Drafted:* 1964 Round 17 Was
1964 Was: 14 G; PR 4-5 1.3; KR 19-482 25.4; 2 Fum.

ROY CLAY Clay, Roy Harvey 6′0″, 185 **WB-DB**
Col: Colorado State B: 1/10/1920 D: 4/18/1996, Watsonville, CA
Drafted: 1944 Round 8 NYG
1944 NYG: 1 G.

WALT CLAY Clay, Walter Earl 5′11″, 196 **DB-HB-TB**
(Hatchet) *Col:* Colorado *HS:* Longmont [CO] B: 1/8/1924, Erie, CO
AAFC **1946** ChiA: Pass 27-12 44.4%, 140 5.19 2 TD 3 Int; Rec 4-48 12.0; PR 8-70 8.8; KR 2-43 21.5; Int 6-72; Punt 1-45 45.0. **1947** ChiA-LA-A: Rec 1-52 52.0; Int 1-20. **1948** LA-A: Rec 10-118 11.8 1 TD; KR 4-48 12.0; Int 2-33. **1949** LA-A: Pass 1-1 100.0%, 8 8.00. **Total:** Pass 28-13 46.4%, 148 5.29 2 TD 3 Int; Rec 15-218 14.5 1 TD; PR 8-70 8.8; KR 6-91 15.2; Int 9-125; Punt 1-45 45.0.

		Rushing				Tot
Year Team	**G**	**Att**	**Yds**	**Avg**	**TD**	**TD**
1946 ChiA	13	65	283	4.4	1	1
1947 ChiA-LA-A	11	9	42	4.7	0	0
1948 LA-A	13	86	293	3.4	3	4
1949 LA-A	10	9	34	3.8	0	0
AAFC Total	47	169	652	3.9	4	5

BILLY CLAY Clay, William Frank 6′1″, 195 **DB**
Col: Mississippi *HS:* Enterprise [MS]; Pearl HS [MS] B: 4/28/1944, Oxford, MS *Drafted:* 1966 Round 4 Was
1966 Was: 6 G; Int 1-0.

WILLIE CLAY Clay, Willie James 5′10″, 193 **DB**
(Big Play) *Col:* Georgia Tech *HS:* Linsly [Wheeling, WV] B: 9/5/1970, Pittsburgh, PA *Drafted:* 1992 Round 8 Det
1993 Det: KR 2-34 17.0; **2** Fum TD; 1 Sac. **1994** Det: PR 3-20 6.7. **1995** Det: PR 5-49 9.8. **Total:** PR 8-69 8.6; KR 2-34 17.0; 2 Fum TD; 1 Sac.

		Interceptions			Tot
Year Team	**G**	**Int**	**Yds**	**TD**	**TD**
1992 Det	6	0	0	0	0
1993 Det	16	0	0	0	2
1994 Det	16	3	54	1	1
1995 Det	16	8	**173**	0	0
1996 NE	16	4	50	0	0
1997 NE	16	6	109	1	1
1998 NE	16	3	19	0	0
NFL Total	102	24	405	2	4

RAYMOND CLAYBORN Clayborn, Raymond Dean 6′0″, 186 **DB**
Col: Texas *HS:* Trimble Tech [Fort Worth, TX] B: 1/2/1955, Fort Worth, TX *Drafted:* 1977 Round 1 NE
1977 NE: Scor 1 Saf. **Total:** Scor 1 Saf.

		Kickoff Returns				Interceptions				Tot
Year Team	**G**	**Ret**	**Yds**	**Avg**	**TD**	**Int**	**Yds**	**TD**	**Fum**	**TD**
1977 NE	14	28	869	**31.0**	**3**	0	0	0	1	3
1978 NE	16	27	636	23.6	0	4	72	0	0	0
1979 NE	16	2	33	16.5	0	5	56	0	0	0
1980 NE	16	0	0	—	0	5	87	0	0	0
1981 NE	16	0	0	—	0	2	39	0	0	0
1982 NE	9	0	0	—	0	1	26	0	0	0
1983 NE	16	0	0	—	0	0	0	0	0	0
1984 NE	16	0	0	—	0	3	102	0	0	0
1985 NE	16	0	0	—	0	6	80	**1**	0	1
1986 NE	16	0	0	—	0	3	4	0	0	0
1987 NE	10	0	0	—	0	2	24	0	0	1
1988 NE	16	0	0	—	0	4	65	0	0	0
1989 NE	14	0	0	—	0	1	0	0	0	0
1990 Cle	16	0	0	—	0	0	0	0	0	0
1991 Cle	1	0	0	—	0	0	0	0	0	0
NFL Total	208	57	1538	27.0	3	36	555	1	1	5

RALPH CLAYPOOL Claypool, Ralph LeClaire 5′9″, 191 **C**
Col: Purdue *HS:* Central [Davenport, IA] B: 12/15/1898, Blue Grass, IA D: 11/17/1969, Webster Groves, MO
1925 ChiC: 13 G. **1926** ChiC: 11 G. **1927** ChiC: 2 G. **1928** ChiC: 4 G. **Total:** 30 G.

HARVEY CLAYTON Clayton, Harvey Jerome 5′9″, 179 **DB**
Col: Florida State *HS:* South Dade [Homestead, FL] B: 4/4/1961, Kendall, FL
1983 Pit: 14 G; Int 1-70 1 TD; 6 Pt; 2 Sac. **1984** Pit: 14 G; PR 1-0; Int 1-0; 1 Sac. **1985** Pit: 14 G. **1986** Pit: 15 G; Int 3-18. **1987** NYG: 2 G. **Total:** 59 G; PR 1-0; Int 5-88 1 TD; 6 Pt; 3 Sac.

MARK CLAYTON Clayton, Mark Gregory 5′9″, 177 **WR**
Col: Louisville *HS:* Cathedral [Indianapolis, IN] B: 4/8/1961, Indianapolis, IN *Drafted:* 1983 Round 8 Mia
1983 Mia: Pass 1-1 100.0%, 48 48.00 1 TD; Rush 2-9 4.5; KR 1-25 25.0. **1984** Mia: Pass 1-0, 1 Int; Rush 3-35 11.7; KR 2-15 7.5. **1985** Mia: Rush 1-10 10.0. **1986** Mia: Rush 2-33 16.5. **1987** Mia: Rush 2-8 4.0. **1988** Mia: Rush 1-4 4.0. **1989** Mia: Rush 3-9 3.0. **Total:** Pass 2-1 50.0%, 48 24.00 1 TD 1 Int; Rush 14-108 7.7; KR 3-40 13.3.

		Receiving				Punt Returns					Tot
Year Team	**G**	**Rec**	**Yds**	**Avg**	**TD**	**Ret**	**Yds**	**Avg**	**TD**	**Fum**	**TD**
1983 Mia	14	6	114	19.0	1	41	392	9.6	**1**	3	2
1984 Mia	15	73	1389	19.0	**18**	8	79	9.9	0	2	**18**
1985 Mia	16	70	996	14.2	4	2	14	7.0	0	2	4
1986 Mia	15	60	1150	19.2	10	1	0	0.0	0	1	10
1987 Mia	12	46	776	16.9	7	0	0	—	0	0	7
1988 Mia	16	86	1129	13.1	**14**	0	0	—	0	0	14

1989 Mia	15	64	1011	15.8	9	0	0	—	0	1	9
1990 Mia	10	32	406	12.7	3	0	0	—	0	1	3
1991 Mia	16	70	1053	15.0	12	0	0	—	0	0	12
1992 Mia	13	43	619	14.4	3	0	0	—	0	1	3
1993 GB	16	32	331	10.3	3	0	0	—	0	0	3
NFL Total	158	582	8974	15.4	84	52	485	9.3	1	11	85

RALPH CLAYTON Clayton, Ralph Darrell 6′3″, 222 **WR-FB**
Col: Michigan *HS:* Redford [Detroit, MI] B: 9/29/1958, Highland Park, MI *Drafted:* 1980 Round 2 NYJ
1981 StL: 7 G.

STAN CLAYTON Clayton, Stanley David 6′3″, 265 **OT-OG**
Col: Penn State *HS:* Cherry Hill-East [NJ] B: 1/31/1965, Philadelphia, PA *Drafted:* 1988 Round 10 Atl
1988 Atl: 2 G. **1989** Atl: 13 G. **1990** NE: 11 G. **Total:** 26 G.

PAUL CLEARY Cleary, Paul Hanson 6′1″, 196 **DE-OE**
Col: Rancho Santiago Coll. CA (J.C.); USC *HS:* Santa Ana [CA] B: 2/7/1922, North Loop, NE D: 1/8/1996, South Laguna, CA
AAFC **1948** NY-A: 13 G; Rec 4-37 9.3; KR 1-8 8.0. **1949** ChiA: 10 G. **Total:** 23 G; Rec 4-37 9.3; KR 1-8 8.0.

CAMERON CLEELAND Cleeland, Cameron 6′4″, 272 **TE**
Col: Washington *HS:* Sedro Woolley [WA] B: 4/15/1975, Sedro Wooley, WA *Drafted:* 1998 Round 2 NO

		Receiving				
Year Team	**G**	**Rec**	**Yds**	**Avg**	**TD**	**Fum**
1998 NO	16	54	684	12.7	6	1

CAL CLEMENS Clemens, Charles Calvin Jr. 6′1″, 195 **BB-DB**
Col: USC *HS:* Central [Oklahoma City, OK] B: 7/7/1909, Oklahoma City, OK D: 5/1966
1936 GB: 9 G; Pass 1-0; Rush 3-(-8) -2.7; Rec 1-18 18.0; Scor 1, 1 XK.

BOB CLEMENS Clemens, Robert Norwood 6′2″, 200 **FB**
Col: Georgia *HS:* Scottsboro [AL] B: 8/3/1933, Scottsboro, AL
Drafted: 1955 Round 7 GB
1955 GB: 2 G.

BOB CLEMENS Clemens, Robert William 6′1″, 208 **FB**
Col: Pittsburgh *HS:* Munhall [PA] B: 8/27/1939, North Braddock, PA
Drafted: 1961 Round 10 Bal
1962 Bal: 9 G; Rush 2-9 4.5.

ALEX CLEMENT Clement, Alexander Mitchell 5′10″, 170 **WB**
Col: Williams *HS:* Chicopee [MA]; Phillips Exeter Acad. [Exeter, NH] B: 2/11/1904, Plymouth, MA D: 1/13/1970, Plymouth, MA
1925 Fra: 4 G.

ANTHONY CLEMENT Clement, Anthony 6′7″, 355 **OT**
Col: Southwestern Louisiana *HS:* Cecilia [LA] B: 4/10/1976, Lafayette, LA *Drafted:* 1998 Round 2 Ariz
1998 Ariz: 1 G.

HENRY CLEMENT Clement, Henry Littlefield Jr. 6′3″, 195 **TE**
(Skip) *Col:* North Carolina *HS:* Westbury [NY] B: 6/15/1939, New York, NY *Drafted:* 1961 Round 11 Pit
1961 Pit: 14 G; Rec 5-65 13.0.

JOHNNY CLEMENT Clement, John Louis 6′0″, 189 **TB-DB**
(Mr. Zero) *Col:* Southern Methodist B: 10/31/1919, Stonebluff, OK D: 12/1969 *Drafted:* 1941 Round 4 ChiC
AAFC.

		Passing							
Year Team	**G**	**Att**	**Comp**	**Comp%**	**Yds**	**YPA**	**TD**	**Int**	**Rating**
1949 ChiA	12	114	58	50.9	906	7.95	6	13	55.6

	Rushing			
Year Team	**Att**	**Yds**	**Avg**	**TD**
1949 ChiA	106	388	3.7	5

NFL **1941** ChiC: PR 13-113 8.7; KR 2-42 21.0; Punt 4-125 31.3. **1946** Pit: Rec 1-22 22.0; PR 3-26 8.7; KR 3-66 22.0; Punt 9-314 34.9. **1947** Pit: Rec 1-6 6.0; KR 1-24 24.0. **Total:** Rec 2-28 14.0; PR 16-139 8.7; KR 6-132 22.0; Punt 13-439 33.8.

		Passing							
Year Team	**G**	**Att**	**Comp**	**Comp%**	**Yds**	**YPA**	**TD**	**Int**	**Rating**
1941 ChiC	9	100	48	48.0	690	6.90	3	7	51.7
1946 Pit	11	47	16	34.0	345	7.34	1	3	41.5
1947 Pit	10	123	52	42.3	1004	8.16	7	9	59.8
1948 Pit	5	58	18	31.0	281	4.84	3	7	25.8
NFL Total	35	328	134	40.9	2320	7.07	14	26	46.8

	Rushing				
Year Team	**Att**	**Yds**	**Avg**	**TD**	**Fum**
1941 ChiC	61	94	1.5	1	0
1946 Pit	43	60	1.4	1	4
1947 Pit	129	670	5.2	4	7
1948 Pit	67	261	3.9	2	5
NFL Total	300	1085	3.6	8	16

CHUCK CLEMENTS Clements, Chad 6′3″, 214 **QB**
Col: Houston *HS:* Huntsville [TX] B: 9/29/1973, Kingsville, TX
Drafted: 1997 Round 6 NYJ
1997 NYJ: 1 G; Rush 2-(-3) -1.5.

CHASE CLEMENTS Clements, George Chase 6′2″, 205 **T**
Col: Washington & Jefferson *HS:* Mount Vernon [OH] B: 12/31/1901 D: 8/8/1971, Toledo, OH
1925 Akr-Cle: 3 G. Akr: 2 G. Cle: 1 G. **Total:** 3 G.

TOM CLEMENTS Clements, Thomas Albert 6′0″, 183 **QB**
Col: Notre Dame *HS:* Canevin [Pittsburgh, PA] B: 6/18/1953, McKees Rocks, PA
1980 KC: 1 G; Pass 12-7 58.3%, 77 6.42; Rush 2-0; 2 Fum.

VINCE CLEMENTS Clements, Vincent Anthony Jr. 6′3″, 210 **RB**
Col: Connecticut *HS:* Southington [CT] B: 1/4/1949, Southington, CT
Drafted: 1971 Round 4 Min
1972 NYG: Rec 9-118 13.1. **1973** NYG: Rec 15-129 8.6 1 TD.
Total: Rec 24-247 10.3 1 TD.

		Rushing					Tot
Year Team	**G**	**Att**	**Yds**	**Avg**	**TD**	**Fum**	**TD**
1972 NYG	4	46	221	4.8	0	2	0
1973 NYG	12	57	214	3.8	1	0	2
NFL Total	16	103	435	4.2	1	2	2

CHARLIE CLEMONS Clemons, Charlie Fitzgerald 6′2″, 255 **LB**
Col: Northeastern Oklahoma A&M (J.C.); Georgia *HS:* Griffin [GA] B: 7/4/1972, Griffin, GA
1997 StL: 5 G. **1998** StL: 16 G; KR 1-0; 2 Sac. **Total:** 21 G; KR 1-0; 2 Sac.

CRAIG CLEMONS Clemons, Craig Lynn 5′11″, 195 **DB**
Col: Iowa *HS:* Piqua [OH] B: 6/1/1949, Sidney, OH *Drafted:* 1972 Round 1 ChiB
1972 ChiB: 14 G; PR 2-15 7.5; KR 2-53 26.5; 1 Fum. **1973** ChiB: 14 G; Int 2-30. **1974** ChiB: 14 G; Int 4-84. **1975** ChiB: 14 G; Int 2-109 1 TD; 6 Pt. **1976** ChiB: 14 G; Int 1-28. **1977** ChiB: 12 G. **Total:** 82 G; PR 2-15 7.5; KR 2-53 26.5; Int 9-251 1 TD; 6 Pt; 1 Fum.

DUANE CLEMONS Clemons, Duane Anthony 6′5″, 273 **DE-LB**
Col: California *HS:* John W. North [Riverside, CA] B: 5/23/1974, Riverside, CA *Drafted:* 1996 Round 1 Min
1996 Min: 13 G. **1997** Min: 13 G; 7 Sac. **1998** Min: 16 G; 2.5 Sac.
Total: 42 G; 9.5 Sac.

MIKE CLEMONS Clemons, Michael Lutrell 5′5″, 166 **RB**
Col: William & Mary *HS:* Dunedin [FL] B: 1/15/1965, Clearwater, FL
Drafted: 1987 Round 8 KC
1987 KC: 8 G; Rush 2-7 3.5; PR 19-162 8.5; KR 1-3 3.0; 3 Fum.

RAY CLEMONS Clemons, Norville Raymond 6′0″, 215 **G**
Col: Central Oklahoma *HS:* Duke [OK] B: 6/4/1912 D: 12/11/1980, Detroit, MI
1939 Det: 6 G; Rec 1-5 5.0; Punt 15-640 42.7.

TOPPER CLEMONS Clemons, Orman Wendell 5′11″, 205 **RB**
Col: Wake Forest *HS:* Cinnaminson [NJ]; Fork Union Mil. Acad. [VA] B: 9/16/1963, Riverside, NJ
1987 Phi: 3 G; Rush 3-0; Rec 1-13 13.0 1 TD; KR 1-0; 6 Pt.

RAY CLEMONS Clemons, Raymond Gordon 5′10″, 220 **G**
Col: St. Mary's (Cal.) *HS:* Fremont [Oakland, CA] B: 4/2/1921, Roseville, CA
1947 GB: 9 G.

MIKE CLENDENEN Clendenen, Michael Dean 5′11″, 191 **K**
Col: Houston *HS:* La Porte [TX] B: 6/12/1963, Dallas, TX
1987 Den: 3 G; Scor 16, 3-4 75.0% FG, 7-7 100.0% XK.

AINER CLEVE Cleve, Ainer Martin 5′9″, 175 **WB-BB-TB-OE**
Col: No College *HS:* South [Minneapolis, MN] B: 11/27/1897, Minneapolis, MN D: 3/23/1990, Edina, MN
1921 Min: 3 G. **1922** Min: 4 G; Rec 1 TD; 6 Pt. **1923** Min: 8 G; Rec 1 TD; 6 Pt. **1924** Min: 4 G. **Total:** 19 G; Rec 2 TD; 12 Pt.

GREG CLEVELAND Cleveland, Gregory Leon 6′5″, 295 **NT**
Col: Florida *HS:* Edgewater [Orlando, FL] B: 8/19/1964, Winter Park, FL
1987 Mia: 2 G.

GREG CLIFTON Clifton, Gregory 5′11″, 175 **WR**
Col: Johnson C. Smith; Virginia Military *HS:* Independence [Charlotte, NC] B: 2/6/1968, Charlotte, NC
1993 Was: 2 G; Rec 2-15 7.5.

KYLE CLIFTON Clifton, Ronald Kyle 6′4″, 236 **LB**
Col: Texas Christian *HS:* Bridgeport [TX] B: 8/23/1962, Olney, TX
Drafted: 1984 Round 3 NYJ
1989 NYJ: 2 Sac. **1990** NYJ: 0.5 Sac. **1991** NYJ: 1 Sac. **1992** NYJ: 1 Sac. **1993** NYJ: 1 Sac. **1994** NYJ: KR 1-13 13.0. **Total:** KR 1-13 13.0; 5.5 Sac.

Year Team	G	Interceptions Int	Yds	TD
1984 NYJ	16	1	0	0
1985 NYJ	16	3	10	0
1986 NYJ	16	2	8	0
1987 NYJ	12	0	0	0
1988 NYJ	16	0	0	0
1989 NYJ	16	0	0	0
1990 NYJ	16	3	49	0
1991 NYJ	16	1	3	0
1992 NYJ	16	1	1	0
1993 NYJ	16	1	3	0
1994 NYJ	16	0	0	0
1995 NYJ	16	0	0	0
1996 NYJ	16	0	0	0
NFL Total	204	12	74	0

BEN CLIME Clime, Benjamin Sidney 5′11″, 190 **G-OE-WB**
Col: Swarthmore *HS:* Philadelphia Central [PA] B: 10/14/1891, Philadelphia, PA D: 1/13/1973, Fort Lauderdale, FL
1920 Roch: 6 G. **1921** Roch: 1 G. **Total:** 7 G.

TONY CLINE Cline, Anthony Francis Jr. 6′4″, 247 **TE**
Col: Stanford *HS:* Davis [CA] B: 11/24/1971, Davis, CA
Drafted: 1995 Round 4 Buf
1995 Buf: KR 1-11 11.0. **1997** Buf: KR 1-0. **Total:** KR 2-11 5.5.

Year Team	G	Receiving Rec	Yds	Avg	TD
1995 Buf	16	8	64	8.0	0
1996 Buf	16	19	117	6.2	1
1997 Buf	10	1	29	29.0	0
NFL Total	42	28	210	7.5	1

TONY CLINE Cline, Anthony Francis Sr. 6′3″, 244 **DE**
Col: Miami (Fla.) *HS:* Michigan City [IN] B: 7/25/1948, Michigan, IN
Drafted: 1970 Round 4 Oak
1970 Oak: 14 G; Int 1-0. **1971** Oak: 13 G; Int 1-0. **1972** Oak: 14 G; Int 1-11. **1973** Oak: 14 G. **1974** Oak: 5 G. **1975** Oak: 12 G. **1976** SF: 7 G. **1977** SF: 14 G; Rec 1-15 15.0. **Total:** 93 G; Rec 1-15 15.0; Int 3-11.

DOUG CLINE Cline, Charles Douglas 6′2″, 230 **LB-RB**
Col: Clemson *HS:* Valdese [NC] B: 3/22/1938, Valdese, NC
D: 10/10/1995, Rutherford College, NC *Drafted:* 1960 Round 1 Hou
1960 Hou: Rec 4-15 3.8; KR 3-42 14.0. **1961** Hou: KR 1-24 24.0; Int 1-24; Scor **1** Saf; **2** Fum TD. **1962** Hou: Int 2-14. **1963** Hou: Int 3-16.
1966 Hou-SD: Int 1-23; **1** Fum TD. Hou: Int 1-23; 1 Fum TD.
Total: Rec 4-15 3.8; KR 4-66 16.5; Int 7-77; Scor 1 Saf; 3 Fum TD.

Year Team	G	Rushing Att	Yds	Avg	TD	Fum	Tot TD
1960 Hou	14	37	105	2.8	2	2	2
1961 Hou	14	0	0	—	0	0	2
1962 Hou	14	0	0	—	0	0	0
1963 Hou	14	0	0	—	0	0	0
1964 Hou	14	0	0	—	0	0	0
1965 Hou	14	0	0	—	0	0	0
1966 Hou-SD	11	0	0	—	0	0	1
1966 Hou	9	0	0	—	0	0	1
1966 SD	2	0	0	—	0	0	0
NFL Total	95	37	105	2.8	2	2	5

JACKIE CLINE Cline, Jackie Wayne 6′5″, 279 **DE-NT**
Col: Alabama *HS:* McAdory [McCalla, AL] B: 3/13/1960, Kansas City, KS
1987 Pit-Mia: 8 G. Pit: 1 G. Mia: 7 G. **1988** Mia: 14 G; 4 Sac. **1989** Mia: 15 G; 1 Sac. **1990** Det: 5 G; 1 Sac. **Total:** 42 G; 6 Sac.

OLLIE CLINE Cline, Oliver Monroe 6′0″, 200 **FB-LB**
Col: Ohio State *HS:* Fredericktown [OH] B: 12/31/1925, Mt. Vernon, OH *Drafted:* 1948 Round 12 ChiB
AAFC **1948** CleA: KR 3-55 18.3. **1949** BufA: Rec 15-110 7.3; KR 1-21 21.0. **Total:** Rec 15-110 7.3; KR 4-76 19.0.

Year Team	G	Rushing Att	Yds	Avg	TD
1948 CleA	11	29	129	4.4	0
1949 BufA	11	125	518	4.1	3
AAFC Total	22	154	647	4.2	3

NFL **1950** Det: Rec 7-18 2.6; KR 1-20 20.0. **1951** Det: KR 3-48 16.0. **1952** Det: Rec 2-45 22.5. **1953** Det: Rec 10-126 12.6 1 TD; KR 1-0. **Total:** Rec 19-189 9.9 1 TD; KR 5-68 13.6.

Year Team	G	Rushing Att	Yds	Avg	TD	Fum	Tot TD
1950 Det	10	69	227	3.3	2	7	2
1951 Det	12	3	15	5.0	0	0	0
1952 Det	8	13	36	2.8	1	0	1
1953 Det	12	42	169	4.0	0	1	1
NFL Total	42	127	447	3.5	3	8	4

DEXTOR CLINKSCALE Clinkscale, Frederick Dextor 5′11″, 192 **DB**
Col: South Carolina State *HS:* J.L. Mann [Greenville, SC]
B: 4/13/1958, Greenville, SC
1980 Dal: 16 G. **1982** Dal: 9 G; Int 1-0; 2 Sac. **1983** Dal: 15 G; Int 2-68 1 TD; 6 Pt; 2 Sac. **1984** Dal: 15 G; Int 3-32; 1 Sac. **1985** Dal: 16 G; Int 3-16; 2 Sac. **1986** Ind: 5 G. **Total:** 76 G; Int 9-116 1 TD; 6 Pt; 7 Sac.

JOEY CLINKSCALES Clinkscales, William Joseph 6′0″, 199 **WR**
Col: Tennessee *HS:* Austin-East [Knoxville, TN] B: 5/21/1964, Asheville, NC *Drafted:* 1987 Round 9 Pit
1987 Pit: 7 G; Rec 13-240 18.5 1 TD; 6 Pt. **1988** Pit-TB: 7 G. Pit: 4 G. TB: 3 G. **Total:** 14 G; Rec 13-240 18.5 1 TD; 6 Pt.

CHARLES CLINTON Clinton, Charles 5′8″, 170 **DB**
Col: Long Beach City Coll. CA (J.C.); San Jose State *HS:* Long Beach Polytechnic [CA] B: 1/29/1962
1987 Hou: 2 G.

JACK CLOUD Cloud, Jack Martin 5′10″, 220 **FB-LB**
Col: William & Mary *HS:* Maury [Norfolk, VA] B: 1/1/1925, Britton, OK
Drafted: 1950 Round 6 GB
1950 GB: Rec 3-19 6.3. **1951** GB: Rec 3-16 5.3 1 TD. **1952** Was: KR 1-18 18.0. **1953** Was: KR 4-68 17.0; Int 2-39 **1** TD. **Total:** Rec 6-35 5.8 1 TD; KR 5-86 17.2; Int 2-39 1 TD.

Year Team	G	Rushing Att	Yds	Avg	TD	Fum	Tot TD
1950 GB	9	18	52	2.9	3	1	3
1951 GB	4	29	61	2.1	1	2	2
1952 Was	8	7	21	3.0	0	0	0
1953 Was	12	3	7	2.3	0	0	1
NFL Total	33	57	141	2.5	4	3	6

DAVE CLOUTIER Cloutier, David Lee 6′0″, 195 **DB**
Col: South Carolina; Maine *HS:* Gardiner [ME] B: 11/22/1938, Gardiner, ME *Drafted:* 1962 Round 18 Dal
1964 Bos: 12 G; PR 20-136 6.8; KR 1-46 46.0; 1 Fum.

HERBERT CLOW Clow, Herbert W 5′4″, 180 **FB**
Col: Wis.-Superior *HS:* Central [Duluth, MN] B: 5/7/1899, MN
D: 11/24/1977, Duluth, MN
1924 Dul: 1 G.

JOHN CLOWES Clowes, John Alexander 6′1″, 240 **DT-OT-OG**
Col: William & Mary *HS:* Matthew Whaley [Williamsburg, VA]
B: 12/15/1921, Williamsburg, VA D: 2/13/1978, Norfolk, VA
AAFC **1948** BknA: 14 G. **1949** ChiA: 12 G. **Total:** 26 G.

NFL **1950** NYY: 11 G. **1951** NYY: 12 G. **Total:** 23 G.

DON CLUNE Clune, Donald Andrew 6′3″, 195 **WR**
Col: Pennsylvania *HS:* Cardinal O'Hara [Havertown, PA] B: 7/31/1952, Havertown, PA *Drafted:* 1974 Round 5 NYG
1974 NYG: 4 G. **1975** NYG: 14 G; Rec 5-97 19.4. **1976** Sea: 10 G; Rec 4-67 16.8. **Total:** 28 G; Rec 9-164 18.2.

RICH COADY Coady, Richard Joseph Jr. 6′3″, 245 **C-TE**
Col: Memphis *HS:* Taft [Chicago, IL] B: 12/17/1944, Chicago, IL
Drafted: 1968 Round 11 ChiB
1970 ChiB: 14 G; Rec 6-44 7.3 1 TD; 6 Pt. **1971** ChiB: 14 G; 1 Fum. **1972** ChiB: 14 G; 2 Fum. **1973** ChiB: 14 G; 4 Fum. **1974** ChiB: 11 G; 1 Fum. **Total:** 67 G; Rec 6-44 7.3 1 TD; 6 Pt; 8 Fum.

JOHNNY COAKER Coaker, John F **T-G**
Col: No College B: 1902, NY Deceased
1924 Roch: 5 G.

DEXTER COAKLEY Coakley, William Dexter 5′10″, 228 **LB**
Col: Appalachian State *HS:* Waldo [Mount Pleasant, SC]; Fork Union Mil. Acad. [VA] B: 10/20/1972, Charleston, SC *Drafted:* 1997 Round 3 Dal
1997 Dal: 16 G; Int 1-6; 1 Fum TD; 6 Pt; 2.5 Sac. **1998** Dal: 16 G; Int 1-18; 2 Sac. **Total:** 32 G; Int 2-24; 1 Fum TD; 6 Pt; 4.5 Sac.

BERT COAN Coan, Elroy Bert III 6′5″, 220 **HB**
Col: Texas Christian; Kansas *HS:* Pasadena [TX] B: 7/2/1940, Timpson, TX *Drafted:* 1962 Round 14 SD
1966 KC: Pass 1-1 100.0%, 18 18.00 1 TD. **Total:** Pass 1-1 100.0%, 18 18.00 1 TD.

Year Team	G	Rushing Att	Yds	Avg	TD	Receiving Rec	Yds	Avg	TD
1962 SD	4	12	10	0.8	0	1	52	52.0	0
1963 KC	8	18	100	5.6	0	2	35	17.5	0
1964 KC	8	11	56	5.1	2	2	8	4.0	0
1965 KC	14	45	137	3.0	1	9	85	9.4	2
1966 KC	14	96	521	5.4	7	18	131	7.3	2
1967 KC	12	63	275	4.4	4	5	41	8.2	0
1968 KC	12	40	160	4.0	1	2	15	7.5	0
NFL Total	72	285	1259	4.4	15	39	367	9.4	4

Year Team	Kickoff Returns Ret	Yds	Avg	TD	Fum	Tot TD
1962 SD	2	31	15.5	0	0	0
1963 KC	0	0	—	0	1	0
1964 KC	5	124	24.8	0	0	2
1965 KC	19	479	25.2	0	2	3
1966 KC	1	22	22.0	0	3	9
1967 KC	1	29	29.0	0	2	4
1968 KC	5	100	20.0	0	1	1
NFL Total	33	785	23.8	0	9	19

BEN COATES Coates, Ben Terence Jr. 6'5", 245 **TE**
Col: Livingstone *HS:* Greenwood [SC] B: 8/16/1969, Greenwood, SC
Drafted: 1991 Round 5 NE
1991 NE: Rush 1-(-6) -6.0; KR 1-6 6.0. **1992** NE: Rush 1-2 2.0. **1994** NE: Rush 1-0. **1996** NE: Scor 1 2XP. **1997** NE: KR 1-20 20.0.
Total: Rush 3-(-4) -1.3; KR 2-26 13.0; Scor 1 2XP.

Year Team	G	Receiving Rec	Yds	Avg	TD	Fum
1991 NE	16	10	95	9.5	1	0
1992 NE	16	20	171	8.6	3	1
1993 NE	16	53	659	12.4	8	0
1994 NE	16	96	1174	12.2	7	2
1995 NE	16	84	915	10.9	6	4
1996 NE	16	62	682	11.0	9	1
1997 NE	16	66	737	11.2	8	0
1998 NE	14	67	668	10.0	6	0
NFL Total	126	458	5101	11.1	48	8

RAY COATES Coates, Rayford Jerald 6'1", 195 **HB-DB**
Col: Louisiana State *HS:* Jesuit [New Orleans [LA] B: 5/8/1924, New Orleans, LA *Drafted:* 1948 Round 8 NYG
1948 NYG: Pass 2-1 50.0%, 26 13.00 1 TD; KR 6-107 17.8. **1949** NYG: Rec 8-152 19.0 1 TD; PR 6-78 13.0; Int 1-11. **Total:** Pass 2-1 50.0%, 26 13.00 1 TD; Rec 8-152 19.0 1 TD; PR 6-78 13.0; KR 6-107 17.8; Int 1-11.

Year Team	G	Rushing Att	Yds	Avg	TD	Fum	Tot TD
1948 NYG	9	50	176	3.5	3	1	3
1949 NYG	12	27	55	2.0	0	3	1
NFL Total	21	77	231	3.0	3	4	4

ALF COBB Cobb, Alfred R 5'11", 210 **G-T**
(Ty) *Col:* Syracuse *HS:* Waltham [MA] B: 6/7/1892, Athol, MA
D: 9/7/1974, West Hartford, CT
1920 Akr: 11 G. **1921** Akr: 1 G. **1925** Cle: 9 G. **Total:** 21 G.

GARRY COBB Cobb, Garry Wilbert 6'2", 227 **LB**
Col: USC *HS:* Stamford [CT] B: 3/16/1957, Carthage, NC
Drafted: 1979 Round 9 Dal
1981 Det: Rec 1-19 19.0. **1982** Det: Rec 1-25 25.0. **1983** Det: 1 Sac. **1984** Det: 3 Sac. **1985** Phi: 5 Sac. **1986** Phi: 6 Sac. **1987** Phi: 1 Sac. **1988** Dal: 7.5 Sac. **Total:** Rec 2-44 22.0; 23.5 Sac.

Year Team	G	Interceptions Int	Yds	TD
1979 Det	8	0	0	0
1980 Det	16	0	0	0
1981 Det	16	3	32	0
1982 Det	6	2	12	0
1983 Det	15	4	19	0
1984 Det	16	0	0	0
1985 Phi	16	0	0	0
1986 Phi	16	1	3	0
1987 Phi	12	0	0	0
1988 Dal	16	0	0	0
1989 Dal	3	0	0	0
NFL Total	140	10	66	0

MARVIN COBB Cobb, Marvin Lawrence 6'0", 189 **DB**
Col: USC *HS:* Notre Dame [Riverside, CA] B: 8/6/1953, Detroit, MI
Drafted: 1975 Round 11 Cin
1975 Cin: PR 1-1 1.0. **1976** Cin: PR 3-14 4.7. **1977** Cin: Pass 1-0; Rush 1-0; PR 1-4 4.0; KR 1-15 15.0. **1980** Pit-Min: PR 3-19 6.3; KR 1-19 19.0. Pit: PR 3-19 6.3; KR 1-19 19.0. **Total:** Pass 1-0; Rush 1-0; PR 8-38 4.8; KR 2-34 17.0.

Year Team	G	Interceptions Int	Yds	TD	Fum
1975 Cin	13	4	116	1	0
1976 Cin	14	3	55	0	0
1977 Cin	14	2	37	0	1
1978 Cin	16	1	13	0	0
1979 Cin	14	3	19	0	0
1980 Pit-Min	8	0	0	0	1
1980 Pit	6	0	0	0	1
1980 Min	2	0	0	0	0
NFL Total	79	13	240	1	2

MIKE COBB Cobb, Michael 6'5", 244 **TE**
Col: Michigan State *HS:* North [Youngstown, OH] B: 12/10/1955, Youngstown, OH *Drafted:* 1977 Round 1 Cin
1977 Cin: 13 G. **1978** ChiB: 13 G; Rec 1-7 7.0. **1979** ChiB: 16 G; Rec 6-91 15.2. **1980** ChiB: 4 G; Rec 2-16 8.0. **1981** ChiB: 16 G; Rec 2-20 10.0.
Total: 62 G; Rec 11-134 12.2.

REGGIE COBB Cobb, Reginald John 6'1", 220 **RB**
Col: Tennessee *HS:* Central [Knoxville, TX] B: 7/7/1968, Knoxville, TN
Drafted: 1990 Round 2 TB

Year Team	G	Rushing Att	Yds	Avg	TD	Receiving Rec	Yds	Avg	TD
1990 TB	16	151	480	3.2	2	39	299	7.7	0
1991 TB	16	196	752	3.8	7	15	111	7.4	0
1992 TB	16	310	1171	3.8	9	21	156	7.4	0
1993 TB	12	221	658	3.0	3	9	61	6.8	1
1994 GB	16	153	579	3.8	3	35	299	8.5	1
1995 Jac	1	9	18	2.0	0	0	0	—	0
1996 NYJ	15	25	85	3.4	1	4	23	5.8	0
NFL Total	92	1065	3743	3.5	25	123	949	7.7	2

Year Team	Kickoff Returns Ret	Yds	Avg	TD	Fum	Tot TD
1990 TB	11	223	20.3	0	8	2
1991 TB	2	15	7.5	0	3	7
1992 TB	0	0	—	0	3	9
1993 TB	0	0	—	0	5	4
1994 GB	0	0	—	0	1	4
1995 Jac	0	0	—	0	1	0
1996 NYJ	23	488	21.2	0	0	1
NFL Total	36	726	20.2	0	21	27

BOB COBB Cobb, Robert Lewis 6'4", 248 **DE**
Col: Cincinnati; Arizona *HS:* Aiken [Cincinnati, OH] B: 10/12/1957, Cincinnati, OH *Drafted:* 1981 Round 3 LARm
1981 LARm: 6 G. **1982** TB: 3 G. **1984** Min: 2 G; 1 Sac. **Total:** 11 G; 1 Sac.

TOM COBB Cobb, Thomas 5'11", 250 **T-G**
Col: St. John's (N.Y.) *HS:* Wagoner [OK] B: 11/29/1903 D: 12/1978, East Prarie, MO
1926 KC: 11 G. **1927** Cle: 12 G. **1928** Det: 9 G. **1931** ChiC: 5 G.
Total: 37 G.

TREVOR COBB Cobb, Trevor Sebastian 5'9", 209 **RB**
Col: Rice *HS:* J. Frank Dobie [Pasadena, TX] B: 11/20/1970, Houston, TX
1994 ChiB: 1 G.

LYRON COBBINS Cobbins, Lyron Duryea 5'11", 240 **LB**
Col: Notre Dame *HS:* Wyandotte [Kansas City, KS] B: 9/17/1974, Kansas City, KS
1997 Ariz: 6 G.

ERIC COBBLE Cobble, Eric Neal 5'10", 205 **RB**
Col: Southwest Texas State B: 4/11/1964
1987 Hou: 3 G; Rush 9-23 2.6.

DUFFY COBBS Cobbs, Robert S 5'11", 178 **DB**
Col: Penn State *HS:* Groveton [Alexadria, VA] B: 1/17/1964
1987 NE: 3 G.

RED COCHRAN Cochran, John Thurman Jr. 6'0", 193 **DB-HB-FB**
(Snort) *Col:* Wake Forest *HS:* Hueytown [AL] B: 8/2/1922, Fairfield, AL *Drafted:* 1944 Round 8 ChiC
1947 ChiC: Pass 1-0; Rec 1-7 7.0 1 TD. **1949** ChiC: Pass 1-0; Rec 7-107 15.3 1 TD. **Total:** Pass 2-0; Rec 8-114 14.3 2 TD.

Year Team	G	Rushing Att	Yds	Avg	TD	Punt Returns Ret	Yds	Avg	TD
1947 ChiC	12	14	36	2.6	1	10	147	14.7	0
1948 ChiC	12	3	15	5.0	0	8	122	15.3	0
1949 ChiC	12	20	87	4.4	1	15	314	**20.9**	**2**
NFL Total	36	37	138	3.7	2	33	583	17.7	2

Year Team	Kickoff Returns Ret	Yds	Avg	TD	Interceptions Int	Yds	TD
1947 ChiC	4	46	11.5	0	8	122	0
1948 ChiC	1	6	6.0	0	7	111	0
1949 ChiC	20	410	20.5	0	0	0	0
NFL Total	25	462	18.5	0	15	233	0

Year Team	Punting Punts	Yds	Avg	Fum	Tot TD
1947 ChiC	1	25	25.0	1	2
1948 ChiC	6	229	38.2	1	0
1949 ChiC	52	2186	42.0	1	4
NFL Total	59	2440	41.4	3	6

LEON COCHRAN Cochran, Leon Thomas 6′0″, 209 **FB**
(Bull) *Col:* Auburn *HS:* Woodlawn [Birmingham, AL] B: 4/13/1924, Birmingham, AL
1949 Was: Rec 7-82 11.7.

Year Team	G	Rushing Att	Yds	Avg	TD
1949 Was	11	34	135	4.0	1

MARK COCHRAN Cochran, Mark Donald 6′5″, 284 **OT**
Col: Baylor *HS:* Sam Rayburn [Pasadena, TX] B: 5/6/1963, Pasadena, TX
1987 SF: 3 G.

MOOSE COCHRAN Cochran, Stuart W 6′0″, 195 **OE**
Col: Chicago B: 6/6/1897 D: 5/10/1979, Wheaton, IL
1922 Mil: 2 G.

GENE COCKRELL Cockrell, Gene Oliver 6′4″, 247 **OT-DE**
(Bud) *Col:* Oklahoma; Hardin-Simmons *HS:* Pampa [TX]
B: 6/10/1934, Pampa, TX *Drafted:* 1957 Round 28 Cle
1960 NYT: 14 G. **1961** NYT: 14 G; PR 1-2 2.0. **1962** NYT: 14 G.
Total: 42 G; PR 1-2 2.0.

DON COCKROFT Cockroft, Donald Lee 6′2″, 195 **K**
Col: Adams State *HS:* Fort Carson [Fountain, CO] B: 2/6/1945, Cheyenne, WY *Drafted:* 1967 Round 3 Cle
1971 Cle: Rush 1-12 12.0. **1973** Cle: Rush 1-(-3) -3.0. **1974** Cle: Pass 1-1 100.0%, 27 27.00. **1975** Cle: Pass 2-2 100.0%. **1976** Cle: Pass 1-0.
Total: Pass 4-3 75.0%, 27 6.75; Rush 2-9 4.5.

Year Team	G	Punting Punts	Yds	Avg
1968 Cle	14	61	2297	37.7
1969 Cle	14	57	2138	37.5
1970 Cle	14	71	3023	42.6
1971 Cle	14	62	2508	40.5
1972 Cle	14	81	**3498**	43.2
1973 Cle	14	**82**	3321	40.5
1974 Cle	14	90	3643	40.5
1975 Cle	14	82	3317	40.5
1976 Cle	14	64	2487	38.9
1977 Cle	14	1	30	30.0
1978 Cle	16	0	0	—
1979 Cle	16	0	0	—
1980 Cle	16	0	0	—
NFL Total	188	651	26262	40.3

Year Team	Scoring Pts	FG	FGA	FG%	XK	XKA	XK%	Fum
1968 Cle	100	18	24	**75.0**	46	48	**95.8**	0
1969 Cle	81	12	23	52.2	**45**	**45**	100.0	0
1970 Cle	70	12	22	54.5	34	35	97.1	0
1971 Cle	79	15	28	53.6	34	34	100.0	0
1972 Cle	94	22	27	**81.5**	28	29	**96.6**	0
1973 Cle	90	22	31	71.0	24	24	100.0	0
1974 Cle	71	14	16	**87.5**	29	30	**96.7**	1
1975 Cle	72	17	23	73.9	21	24	87.5	0
1976 Cle	72	15	28	53.6	27	30	90.0	0
1977 Cle	81	17	23	73.9	30	31	96.8	0
1978 Cle	94	19	28	67.9	37	40	92.5	0
1979 Cle	89	17	29	58.6	38	43	88.4	0
1980 Cle	87	16	26	61.5	39	44	88.6	0
NFL Total	1080	216	328	65.9	432	457	94.5	1

JOE COCOZZO Cocozzo, Joseph Ramond 6′4″, 300 **OG**
Col: Michigan *HS:* Mechanicville [NY] B: 8/7/1970, Mechanicville, NY
Drafted: 1993 Round 3 SD
1993 SD: 16 G. **1994** SD: 13 G. **1995** SD: 16 G. **1996** SD: 16 G. **1997** SD: 16 G. **Total:** 77 G.

SHERMAN COCROFT Cocroft, Sherman Carlson 6′1″, 195 **DB**
Col: Cabrillo Coll. CA (J.C.); San Jose State *HS:* Watsonville [CA]
B: 8/29/1961, Watsonville, CA
1985 KC: 16 G; Int 3-27. **1986** KC: 16 G; KR 1-23 23.0; Int 3-32. **1987** KC: 12 G; PR 1-0. **1988** Buf: 13 G; Int 1-17. **1989** TB: 10 G; Scor **1** Saf; 2 Pt.
Total: 67 G; PR 1-0; KR 1-23 23.0; Int 7-76; Scor 1 Saf; 2 Pt.

RON CODER Coder, Ronald William 6′4″, 250 **OG-OT**
Col: Penn State *HS:* Yamoto [Tokyo, Japan] B: 5/24/1954, Savannah, GA *Drafted:* 1976 Round 3 Pit
1976 Sea: 13 G. **1977** Sea: 14 G. **1979** Sea: 15 G. **1980** StL: 11 G.
Total: 53 G.

ED CODY Cody, Edward Joseph 5′10″, 191 **DB-FB**
(Catfoot) *Col:* Purdue *HS:* New Britain [CT] B: 2/27/1923, Newington, CT D: 10/16/1994, Santa Ana, CA *Drafted:* 1946 Round 3 GB
1947 GB: Rec 1-2 2.0; PR 2-30 15.0; KR 10-269 26.9. **1948** GB: KR 2-31 15.5; Scor 11, 11-13 84.6% XK. **1949** ChiB: PR 1-4 4.0; KR 8-181 22.6; Int 2-50 1 TD. **Total:** Rec 1-2 2.0; PR 3-34 11.3; KR 20-481 24.1; Int 2-50 1 TD; Scor 29, 11-13 84.6% XK.

Year Team	G	Rushing Att	Yds	Avg	TD	Fum	Tot TD
1947 GB	10	56	263	4.7	2	2	2
1948 GB	10	26	58	2.2	0	2	0
1949 ChiB	8	11	25	2.3	0	4	1
1950 ChiB	10	0	0	—	0	0	0
NFL Total	38	93	346	3.7	2	8	3

BILL CODY Cody, William Eugene 6′2″, 230 **LB**
(Wild Bill) *Col:* Auburn *HS:* William R. Boone [Orlando, FL]
B: 8/2/1944, Greenwood, MS *Drafted:* 1966 Round 5 Det
1966 Det: 1 G. **1967** NO: 9 G. **1968** NO: 14 G. **1969** NO: 3 G. **1970** NO: 14 G. **1972** Phi: 11 G. **Total:** 52 G.

STAN COFALL Cofall, Stanley Bingham 5′11″, 190 **TB-BB**
Col: Notre Dame *HS:* East Tech [Cleveland, OH]; East HS [Cleveland, OH] B: 5/5/1894, Cleveland, OH D: 9/21/1961, Cleveland, OH
1920 Cle: 3 G.

MIKE COFER Cofer, James Michael 6′1″, 192 **K**
Col: North Carolina State *HS:* Country Day [Charlotte, NC]
B: 2/19/1964, Columbia, SC

Year Team	G	Scoring Pts	FG	FGA	FG%	XK	XKA	XK%
1987 NO	2	8	1	1	100.0	5	7	71.4
1988 SF	16	121	27	**38**	71.1	40	41	97.6
1989 SF	16	**136**	29	36	80.6	49	**51**	96.1
1990 SF	16	111	24	36	66.7	39	39	100.0
1991 SF	16	91	14	28	50.0	49	50	98.0
1992 SF	16	107	18	27	66.7	**53**	**54**	98.1
1993 SF	16	107	16	26	61.5	**59**	**61**	96.7
1995 Ind	4	21	4	9	44.4	9	9	100.0
NFL Total	102	702	133	201	66.2	303	312	97.1

JOE COFER Cofer, Joseph Louis 6′0″, 200 **DB**
Col: Tennessee *HS:* Rule [Knoxville, TN] B: 3/5/1963, Knoxville, TN
1987 Was: 3 G; 2 Sac.

MIKE COFER Cofer, Michael Lynn 6′5″, 245 **LB-DE**
Col: Tennessee *HS:* Rule [Knoxville, TN] B: 4/7/1960, Knoxville, TN
Drafted: 1983 Round 3 Det
1983 Det: 16 G; 4.5 Sac. **1984** Det: 16 G; 7 Sac. **1985** Det: 7 G; 1 Sac. **1986** Det: 16 G; 7.5 Sac. **1987** Det: 11 G; 8.5 Sac. **1988** Det: 16 G; 12 Sac. **1989** Det: 15 G; 9 Sac. **1990** Det: 16 G; Int 1-0; 10 Sac. **1991** Det: 2 G; 1 Sac. **1992** Det: 8 G; 2 Sac. **Total:** 123 G; Int 1-0; 62.5 Sac.

PAT COFFEE Coffee, James Lilburn 5′11″, 183 **TB-DB**
Col: Louisiana State *HS:* Minden [LA] B: 8/3/1915, Deann, AR
D: 1/25/1986, Baton Rouge, LA

Year Team	G	Passing Att	Comp	Comp%	Yds	YPA	TD	Int	Rating
1937 ChiC	9	119	52	43.7	824	6.92	4	11	40.0
1938 ChiC	10	39	16	41.0	200	5.13	0	4	18.1
NFL Total	19	158	68	43.0	1024	6.48	4	15	33.8

Year Team	Rushing Att	Yds	Avg	TD
1937 ChiC	55	157	2.9	1
1938 ChiC	40	169	4.2	2
NFL Total	95	326	3.4	3

DON COFFEY Coffey, Donald Eugene 6′4″, 190 **WR**
Col: Memphis *HS:* Morristown [TN] B: 8/18/1939, Burnsville, NC
1963 Den: 3 G.

JUNIOR COFFEY Coffey, Junior Lee 6′2″, 215 **RB**
Col: Washington *HS:* Dimmitt [TX] B: 3/21/1942, Kyle, TX
Drafted: 1965 Round 7 GB
1965 GB: KR 1-9 9.0. **1966** Atl: KR 1-18 18.0. **Total:** KR 2-27 13.5.

Year Team	G	Rushing Att	Yds	Avg	TD	Receiving Rec	Yds	Avg	TD	Fum	Tot TD
1965 GB	13	3	12	4.0	0	0	0	—	0	0	0
1966 Atl	14	199	722	3.6	4	15	182	12.1	1	4	5
1967 Atl	14	180	722	4.0	4	30	196	6.5	1	3	5
1969 Atl-NYG	12	131	511	3.9	2	14	89	6.4	3	4	5
1969 Atl	6	49	168	3.4	1	8	64	8.0	2	0	3
1969 NYG	6	82	343	4.2	1	6	25	4.2	1	4	2
1971 NYG	6	22	70	3.2	0	5	20	4.0	0	2	0
NFL Total	59	535	2037	3.8	10	64	487	7.6	5	13	15

KEN COFFEY Coffey, Kenneth Eugene 6'0", 193 **DB**
Col: Tyler JC TX; Southwest Texas State *HS:* Big Spring [TX]
B: 11/7/1960, Rantoul, IL *Drafted:* 1982 Round 9 Was
1983 Was: 13 G; Int 4-62; 1 Sac. **1984** Was: 12 G; PR 1-6 6.0; Int 1-15. **1986** Was: 16 G; Int 2-0. **Total:** 41 G; PR 1-6 6.0; Int 7-77; 1 Sac.

WAYNE COFFEY Coffey, Wayne Everett 5'7", 158 **WR**
Col: Cisco JC TX; Southwest Texas State *HS:* Abilene [TX]
B: 5/30/1964, Rantoul, IL
1987 NE: 3 G; Rec 3-66 22.0.

RANDY COFFIELD Coffield, Randall Steven 6'4", 215 **LB**
Col: Florida State *HS:* Hialeah [FL] B: 12/12/1953, Miami, FL
Drafted: 1976 Round 10 Sea
1976 Sea: 13 G. **1978** NYG: 2 G. **1979** NYG: 9 G; KR 1-12 12.0. **Total:** 24 G; KR 1-12 12.0.

PAUL COFFMAN Coffman, Paul Randolph 6'3", 222 **TE**
Col: Kansas State *HS:* Chase [KS] B: 3/29/1956, St. Louis, MO
1980 GB: Rush 1-3 3.0. **1981** GB: KR 3-77 25.7. **Total:** Rush 1-3 3.0; KR 3-77 25.7.

		Receiving				
Year Team	**G**	**Rec**	**Yds**	**Avg**	**TD**	**Fum**
1978 GB	16	0	0	—	0	0
1979 GB	16	56	711	12.7	4	4
1980 GB	16	42	496	11.8	3	0
1981 GB	16	55	687	12.5	4	1
1982 GB	9	23	287	12.5	2	0
1983 GB	16	54	814	15.1	11	1
1984 GB	14	43	562	13.1	9	1
1985 GB	16	49	666	13.6	6	1
1986 KC	15	12	75	6.3	2	1
1987 KC	12	5	42	8.4	1	0
1988 Min	8	0	0	—	0	0
NFL Total	154	339	4340	12.8	42	9

TIM COFIELD Cofield, Tim Lee 6'2", 243 **LB**
Col: Elizabeth City State *HS:* Murfreesboro [NC] B: 5/18/1963, Murfreesboro, NC
1986 KC: 15 G; 5 Sac. **1987** KC: 12 G. **1988** KC: 16 G; Int 1-0; 3.5 Sac. **1989** NYJ-Buf: 11 G; 1 Sac. NYJ: 6 G. Buf: 5 G; 1 Sac. **Total:** 54 G; Int 1-0; 9.5 Sac.

GAIL COGDILL Cogdill, Gail Ross 6'3", 200 **WR**
Col: Washington State *HS:* Lewis and Clark [Spokane, WA]
B: 4/7/1937, Worland, WY *Drafted:* 1960 Round 6 Det
1962 Det: Rush 1-2 2.0; KR 1-4 4.0; **1** Fum TD. **1964** Det: Rush 1-(-4) -4.0; 1 Fum TD. **Total:** Rush 2-(-2) -1.0; KR 1-4 4.0; 2 Fum TD.

		Receiving					Tot
Year Team	**G**	**Rec**	**Yds**	**Avg**	**TD**	**Fum**	**TD**
1960 Det	12	43	642	14.9	1	0	1
1961 Det	14	45	956	21.2	6	0	6
1962 Det	14	53	991	18.7	7	2	8
1963 Det	14	48	945	19.7	10	1	10
1964 Det	11	45	665	14.8	2	2	3
1965 Det	9	20	247	12.4	0	0	0
1966 Det	14	47	411	8.7	1	0	1
1967 Det	12	21	322	15.3	1	0	1
1968 Det-Bal	8	3	42	14.0	0	0	0
1968 Det	3	3	42	14.0	0	0	0
1968 Bal	5	0	0	—	0	0	0
1969 Atl	13	24	374	15.6	5	0	5
1970 Atl	6	7	101	14.4	1	0	1
NFL Total	127	356	5696	16.0	34	5	36

GEORGE COGHILL Coghill, George 6'0", 210 **DB**
Col: Wake Forest *HS:* James Monroe [Fredericksburg, VA]
B: 3/30/1970, Fredericksburg, VA
1998 Den: 9 G; PR 3-20 6.7; Int 1-20.

ABE COHEN Cohen, Abraham 6'0", 230 **OG**
Col: Tennessee-Chattanooga B: 3/23/1933 *Drafted:* 1955 Round 26 NYG
1960 Bos: 14 G.

ANGELO COIA Coia, Angelo Anthony 6'3", 195 **WR**
Col: USC *HS:* Northeast [Philadelphia, PA] B: 4/21/1938, Philadelphia, PA *Drafted:* 1960 Round 20 ChiB
1960 ChiB: Rush 3-(-4) -1.3; PR 2-2 1.0. **1963** ChiB: Rush 2-2 1.0. **Total:** Rush 5-(-2) -0.4; PR 2-2 1.0.

		Receiving				
Year Team	**G**	**Rec**	**Yds**	**Avg**	**TD**	**Fum**
1960 ChiB	12	25	478	19.1	4	0
1961 ChiB	11	12	249	20.8	3	0
1962 ChiB	9	22	361	16.4	4	0
1963 ChiB	12	11	116	10.5	1	0
1964 Was	14	29	500	17.2	5	0
1965 Was	13	18	240	13.3	3	0
1966 Atl	6	4	93	23.3	0	1
NFL Total	77	121	2037	16.8	20	1

WILL COKELEY Cokeley, Will Harlin 6'2", 220 **LB**
Col: Coffeyville CC KS; Kansas State *HS:* Washburn Rural [Topeka, KS]
B: 12/6/1960, Topeka, KS
1987 Buf: 3 G; Int 1-4.

JACK COLAHAN Colahan, John Roland 6'3", 212 **T**
Col: Colorado Mines *HS:* Moorhead [MN] B: 2/5/1905, MN
D: 7/2/1973, Las Vegas, NV
1928 NYY: 2 G.

STEVE COLAVITO Colavito, Steven Michael 6'0", 225 **LB**
Col: Wesley; Wake Forest *HS:* Cardinal Hayes [Bronx, NY]
B: 8/9/1951, New York, NY
1975 Phi: 4 G.

DANNY COLBERT Colbert, Danny Joel 5'11", 175 **DB**
Col: Texas Christian; Tulsa *HS:* South Oak Cliff [Dallas, TX]
B: 12/15/1950, Corsicana, TX *Drafted:* 1974 Round 9 SD
1974 SD: 6 G; PR 15-128 8.5; KR 10-215 21.5. **1975** SD: 13 G; PR 2-32 16.0; KR 5-91 18.2; Int 2-10; 1 Fum. **1976** SD: 13 G. **Total:** 32 G; PR 17-160 9.4; KR 15-306 20.4; Int 2-10; 1 Fum.

DARRELL COLBERT Colbert, Darrell Ray 5'10", 174 **WR**
Col: Texas Southern *HS:* Westbrook [Beaumont, TX] B: 11/16/1964, Beaumont, TX
1987 KC: 12 G; Rec 3-21 7.0; PR 1-11 11.0; KR 1-18 18.0. **1988** KC: 3 G; Rec 1-(-3) -3.0; 1 Fum. **Total:** 15 G; Rec 4-18 4.5; PR 1-11 11.0; KR 1-18 18.0; 1 Fum.

LEWIS COLBERT Colbert, Lewis Welton 5'11", 182 **P**
Col: Auburn *HS:* Glenwood Acad. [Phenix City, AL] B: 8/23/1963, Phenix City, AL *Drafted:* 1986 Round 8 KC

		Punting		
Year Team	**G**	**Punts**	**Yds**	**Avg**
1986 KC	16	99	4033	40.7
1987 KC	2	10	377	37.7
1989 SD	2	8	266	33.3
NFL Total	20	117	4676	40.0

RONDY COLBERT Colbert, Rondy Estes 5'9", 185 **DB**
Col: Lamar *HS:* Ross C. Sterling [Houston, TX] B: 1/7/1954, Corsicana, TX *Drafted:* 1975 Round 17 NYG
1975 NYG: KR 17-408 24.0. **1976** NYG: KR 2-42 21.0. **Total:** KR 19-450 23.7.

		Punt Returns				
Year Team	**G**	**Ret**	**Yds**	**Avg**	**TD**	**Fum**
1975 NYG	14	27	238	8.8	1	6
1976 NYG	14	13	72	5.5	0	4
1977 StL	4	0	0	—	0	0
NFL Total	32	40	310	7.8	1	10

DANIEL COLCHICO Colchico, Daniel Mametta 6'5", 245 **DE**
Col: Diablo Valley Coll. CA (J.C.); San Jose State *HS:* Mount Diablo [Concord, CA] B: 5/27/1935, Berkeley, CA *Drafted:* 1959 Round 7 SF
1960 SF: 12 G; KR 5-68 13.6. **1961** SF: 14 G. **1962** SF: 14 G. **1963** SF: 14 G. **1964** SF: 12 G. **1965** SF: 1 G. **1969** NO: 9 G. **Total:** 76 G; KR 5-68 13.6.

JIM COLCLOUGH Colclough, James Michael 6'1", 185 **WR**
Col: Boston College *HS:* Quincy [MA] B: 3/31/1936, Medford, MA
Drafted: 1959 Round 30 Was
1961 Bos: Rush 3-37 12.3. **1962** Bos: Rush 1-14 14.0. **1964** Bos: Scor **2** 2XP. **1966** Bos: KR 1-2 2.0. **Total:** Rush 4-51 12.8; KR 1-2 2.0; Scor 2 2XP.

		Receiving				
Year Team	**G**	**Rec**	**Yds**	**Avg**	**TD**	**Fum**
1960 Bos	14	49	666	13.6	9	3
1961 Bos	14	42	757	18.0	9	1
1962 Bos	14	40	868	**21.7**	10	1
1963 Bos	14	42	693	16.5	3	1
1964 Bos	14	32	657	20.5	5	0
1965 Bos	14	40	677	16.9	3	0
1966 Bos	14	16	284	17.8	0	1
1967 Bos	14	14	263	18.8	0	0
1968 Bos	14	8	136	17.0	0	0
NFL Total	126	283	5001	17.7	39	7

EDDIE COLE Cole, Edward Lee 6'2", 235 **LB**
Col: Mississippi *HS:* Clarkside [MS] B: 12/16/1956, Clarkside, MS
Drafted: 1979 Round 11 Det
1979 Det: 15 G. **1980** Det: 13 G; Scor 1 Saf; 2 Pt. **Total:** 28 G; Scor 1 Saf; 2 Pt.

EMERSON COLE Cole, Emerson Elvin 6'2", 215 **FB-DB-LB**
Col: Toledo *HS:* Swanton [OH] B: 12/10/1927, Carrier Mills, IL
Drafted: 1950 Round 12 Cle
1950 Cle: KR 1-22 22.0. **1951** Cle: Rec 4-30 7.5; KR 2-28 14.0.
1952 Cle-ChiB: KR 5-99 19.8. Cle: KR 4-71 17.8. ChiB: KR 1-28 28.0.
Total: Rec 4-30 7.5; KR 8-149 18.6.

		Rushing				
Year Team	G	Att	Yds	Avg	TD	Fum
1950 Cle	12	26	105	4.0	0	0
1951 Cle	12	46	252	5.5	1	2
1952 Cle-ChiB	7	0	0	—	0	0
1952 Cle	6	0	0	—	0	0
1952 ChiB	1	0	0	—	0	0
NFL Total	31	72	357	5.0	1	2

FRED COLE Cole, Frederick Michael 6'0", 226 **OG**
(Fireplug) *Col:* Maryland *HS:* West Side [Newark, NJ] B: 6/14/1937, Newark, NJ *Drafted:* 1959 Round 6 ChiB
1960 LAC: 14 G.

PETE COLE Cole, Garth Peter 5'11", 222 **G**
Col: Trinity (Tex.) *HS:* Stamford [TX] B: 5/5/1916, Stamford, TX
D: 9/7/1971
1937 NYG: 2 G. **1938** NYG: 9 G. **1939** NYG: 10 G. **1940** NYG: 9 G.
Total: 30 G.

JOHN COLE Cole, John 5'9", 197 **FB-LB-BB**
(King) *Col:* St. Joseph's (Pa) B: 1915 Deceased
1938 Phi: Rec 2-9 4.5. **1940** Phi: Rec 2-11 5.5; Punt 10-336 33.6; Scor 6, 1-1 100.0% FG, 3-4 75.0% XK. **Total:** Rec 4-20 5.0; Punt 10-336 33.6; Scor 6, 1-1 100.0% FG, 3-4 75.0% XK.

		Rushing			
Year Team	G	Att	Yds	Avg	TD
1938 Phi	11	1	4	4.0	0
1940 Phi	7	26	75	2.9	0
NFL Total	18	27	79	2.9	0

LARRY COLE Cole, Lawrence Rudolph 6'5", 252 **DE-DT**
Col: Air Force; Hawaii *HS:* Granite Falls [MN] B: 11/15/1946, Clarkfield, MN *Drafted:* 1968 Round 16 Dal
1968 Dal: 14 G; Int 1-5 1 TD; **1** Fum TD; Tot TD 2; 12 Pt. **1969** Dal: 14 G; Int 1-41 1 TD; 6 Pt. **1970** Dal: 10 G. **1971** Dal: 14 G. **1972** Dal: 9 G. **1973** Dal: 14 G. **1974** Dal: 14 G. **1975** Dal: 13 G. **1976** Dal: 14 G. **1977** Dal: 12 G. **1978** Dal: 16 G; Int 1-13. **1979** Dal: 16 G. **1980** Dal: 16 G; Int 1-43 1 TD; 6 Pt. **Total:** 176 G; Int 4-102 3 TD; 1 Fum TD; Tot TD 4; 24 Pt.

LEE COLE Cole, Lee 5'11", 188 **DB**
Col: San Bernardino Valley Coll. CA (J.C.); Arizona State *HS:* San Gorgonio [San Bernardino, CA] B: 6/25/1974, Riverside, CA
1996 Hou: 3 G.

LINZY COLE Cole, Linzy Jr. 5'11", 172 **WR**
Col: Trinity Valley CC TX; Texas Christian *HS:* James Madison [Dallas, TX] B: 4/21/1948, Dallas, TX *Drafted:* 1970 Round 9 ChiB
1970 ChiB: Rec 3-47 15.7. **Total:** Rec 3-47 15.7.

		Punt Returns				Kickoff Returns				
Year Team	G	Ret	Yds	Avg	TD	Ret	Yds	Avg	TD	Fum
1970 ChiB	7	14	83	5.9	0	0	0	—	0	1
1971 Hou	14	14	107	7.6	0	32	834	26.1	0	2
1972 Hou-Buf	10	7	35	5.0	0	18	456	25.3	0	1
1972 Hou	2	0	0	—	0	2	41	20.5	0	0
1972 Buf	8	7	35	5.0	0	16	415	25.9	0	1
NFL Total	31	35	225	6.4	0	50	1290	25.8	0	4

ROBIN COLE Cole, Robin 6'2", 220 **LB-DE**
Col: New Mexico *HS:* Compton [CA] B: 9/11/1955, Los Angeles, CA
Drafted: 1977 Round 1 Pit
1977 Pit: 8 G. **1978** Pit: 16 G. **1979** Pit: 13 G; KR 1-3 3.0. **1980** Pit: 14 G; Int 1-34. **1981** Pit: 14 G; Int 1-29. **1982** Pit: 9 G; 5 Sac. **1983** Pit: 16 G; 5 Sac. **1984** Pit: 16 G; Int 1-12; 2 Sac. **1985** Pit: 16 G; Int 1-4; 3 Sac. **1986** Pit: 16 G; 0.5 Sac. **1987** Pit: 12 G; Int 1-0; 1 Sac. **1988** NYJ: 16 G; 3 Sac. **Total:** 166 G; KR 1-3 3.0; Int 5-79; 19.5 Sac.

TERRY COLE Cole, Terry Philip 6'2", 220 **RB**
(T Bear) *Col:* Indiana *HS:* Mitchell [IN] B: 7/7/1945, Dallas, TX
Drafted: 1968 Round 9 Bal
1968 Bal: KR 5-123 24.6. **Total:** KR 5-123 24.6.

		Rushing				Receiving					Tot
Year Team	G	Att	Yds	Avg	TD	Rec	Yds	Avg	TD	Fum	TD
1968 Bal	14	104	418	4.0	3	13	75	5.8	0	4	3
1969 Bal	9	73	204	2.8	2	9	65	7.2	1	2	3
1970 Pit	10	9	8	0.9	0	3	31	10.3	0	1	0
1971 Mia	4	3	11	3.7	0	0	0	—	0	0	0
NFL Total	37	189	641	3.4	5	25	171	6.8	1	7	6

TOM COLELLA Colella, Thomas Anthony 6'0", 187 **DB-HB-TB**
Col: Canisius *HS:* Albion [NY] B: 7/3/1918, Albion, NY D: 5/15/1992, Hamburg, NY *Drafted:* 1942 Round 7 Det
AAFC **1946** CleA: Rec 1-12 12.0 1 TD; PR 8-172 21.5; KR 1-29 29.0.
1947 CleA: Rec 4-63 15.8 1 TD; PR 5-113 22.6 1 TD; KR 1-13 13.0.
1948 CleA: Rec 1-7 7.0; PR 5-60 12.0. **1949** BufA: Rec 2-6 3.0; PR 5-42 8.4; KR 7-107 15.3. **Total:** Rec 8-88 11.0 2 TD; PR 23-387 16.8 1 TD; KR 9-149 16.6.

		Rushing				Interceptions		
Year Team	G	Att	Yds	Avg	TD	Int	Yds	TD
1946 CleA	14	30	118	3.9	2	10	110	0
1947 CleA	14	11	77	7.0	1	6	130	1
1948 CleA	13	14	60	4.3	1	2	34	0
1949 BufA	11	7	-9	-1.3	0	3	49	0
AAFC Total	52	62	246	4.0	4	21	323	1

	Punting			Tot
Year Team	Punts	Yds	Avg	TD
1946 CleA	47	1895	40.3	3
1947 CleA	1	36	36.0	4
1948 CleA	49	1716	35.0	1
1949 BufA	44	1554	35.3	0
AAFC Total	141	5201	36.9	8

NFL **1942** Det: PR 2-14 7.0; KR 4-74 18.5; Int 1-10. **1943** Det: Rec 1-(-1) -1.0; PR 2-11 5.5. **1944** Cle: Rec 2-64 32.0 1 TD; PR 4-65 16.3; KR 10-241 24.1; Int 4-53; Scor 21, 1-1 100.0% FG. **1945** Cle: Rec 7-64 9.1 2 TD; PR 1-10 10.0; KR 3-79 26.3. **Total:** Rec 10-127 12.7 3 TD; PR 9-100 11.1; KR 17-394 23.2; Int 5-63; Scor 45, 1-1 100.0% FG.

		Passing							
Year Team	G	Att	Comp	Comp%	Yds	YPA	TD	Int	Rating
1942 Det	9	41	18	43.9	178	4.34	0	4	17.2
1943 Det	8	31	11	35.5	103	3.32	0	4	5.9
1944 Cle	10	75	27	36.0	336	4.48	4	10	28.9
1945 Cle	10	1	0	0.0	0	0.00	0	0	39.6
NFL Total	37	148	56	37.8	617	4.17	4	18	20.4

	Rushing				Punting				Tot
Year Team	Att	Yds	Avg	TD	Punts	Yds	Avg	Fum	TD
1942 Det	23	51	2.2	0	16	609	38.1	0	0
1943 Det	15	24	1.6	0	7	315	45.0	0	0
1944 Cle	53	208	3.9	2	33	1247	37.8	0	3
1945 Cle	46	224	4.9	2	0	0	—	4	4
NFL Total	137	507	3.7	4	56	2171	38.8	4	7

AL COLEMAN Coleman, Alvin M 6'1", 183 **DB**
(Cat) *Col:* Jackson State; Tennessee State *HS:* Jim Hill [Jackson, MS]
B: 12/27/1944, Gulfport, MS *Drafted:* 1967 Round 4 Min
1967 Min: 2 G. **1969** Cin: 14 G; PR 1-0. **1970** Cin: 11 G. **1971** Cin: 4 G; Int 1-15. **1972** Phi: 12 G; Scor **1** Saf; 2 Pt. **1973** Phi: 14 G; KR 2-24 12.0; 1 Fum. **Total:** 57 G; PR 1-0; KR 2-24 12.0; Int 1-15; Scor 1 Saf; 2 Pt; 1 Fum.

ANDRE COLEMAN Coleman, Andre Clintonian 5'9", 165 **WR**
Col: Kansas State *HS:* Hickory [Hermitage, PA] B: 9/19/1972, Charlotte, NC *Drafted:* 1994 Round 3 SD
1996 SD: Rush 2-0. **Total:** Rush 2-0.

		Receiving				Punt Returns			
Year Team	G	Rec	Yds	Avg	TD	Ret	Yds	Avg	TD
1994 SD	13	0	0	—	0	0	0	—	0
1995 SD	15	3	67	22.3	0	28	326	11.6	**1**
1996 SD	16	36	486	13.5	2	0	0	—	0
1997 Sea-Pit	10	0	0	—	0	5	5	1.0	0
1997 Sea	2	0	0	—	0	0	0	—	0
1997 Pit	8	0	0	—	0	5	5	1.0	0
1998 Pit	4	4	49	12.3	1	10	53	5.3	0
NFL Total	58	43	602	14.0	3	43	384	8.9	1

	Kickoff Returns					Tot
Year Team	Ret	Yds	Avg	TD	Fum	TD
1994 SD	49	1293	26.4	2	3	2
1995 SD	62	1411	22.8	**2**	10	3
1996 SD	55	1210	22.0	0	4	2
1997 Sea-Pit	27	552	20.4	0	2	0
1997 Sea	3	65	21.7	0	1	0
1997 Pit	24	487	20.3	0	1	0
1998 Pit	0	0	—	0	1	1
NFL Total	193	4466	23.1	4	20	8

ANTHONY COLEMAN Coleman, Anthony Quinn 6'0", 185 **DB**
Col: Baylor *HS:* Lufkin [TX] B: 8/20/1964, Henderson, TX
1987 Dal: 3 G.

BEN COLEMAN Coleman, Benjamin Leon 6'5", 330 **OG-OT**
Col: Wake Forest *HS:* Park View [South Hill, VA] B: 5/18/1971, South Hill, VA *Drafted:* 1993 Round 2 Pho
1993 Pho: 12 G. **1994** Ariz: 15 G. **1995** Ariz-Jac: 13 G. Ariz: 3 G. Jac: 10 G. **1996** Jac: 16 G. **1997** Jac: 16 G. **1998** Jac: 16 G. **Total:** 88 G.

CHARLES COLEMAN Coleman, Charles Edward 6'4", 222 **TE**
Col: Alcorn State *HS:* West Marion School [Foxworth, MS] B: 9/16/1963, Kokomo, MS
1987 NYG: 3 G; Rec 1-5 5.0; KR 1-20 20.0.

DANIEL COLEMAN Coleman, Daniel 6'4", 249 **DE**
Col: Murray State *HS:* Chester Co. [Henderson, TN] B: 8/14/1962, Lansing, MI
1987 Min: 3 G; 2 Sac.

DENNIS COLEMAN Coleman, Dennis Franklin 6'4", 225 **LB**
Col: Mississippi *HS:* Aberdeen [MS] B: 12/19/1948, Aberdeen, MS
1971 NE: 9 G.

DON COLEMAN Coleman, Donald Alvin 6'2", 222 **LB**
Col: Michigan *HS:* St. John's [Toledo, OH] B: 1/11/1952, Toledo, OH *Drafted:* 1974 Round 16 NO
1974 NO: 14 G; KR 2-13 6.5. **1975** NO: 13 G. **Total:** 27 G; KR 2-13 6.5.

ERIC COLEMAN Coleman, Eric Gerard 6'0", 190 **DB**
Col: Wyoming *HS:* Thomas Jefferson [Denver, CO] B: 12/27/1966, Denver, CO *Drafted:* 1989 Round 2 NE
1989 NE: 8 G; Int 1-1. **1990** NE: 7 G. **Total:** 15 G; Int 1-1.

FRED COLEMAN Coleman, Frederick 6'4", 240 **TE**
Col: Northeast Louisiana *HS:* Leland [MS] B: 6/26/1953, Greenville, MS *Drafted:* 1976 Round 5 Buf
1976 Buf: 7 G.

GREG COLEMAN Coleman, Gregory Jerome 6'0", 185 **P**
Col: Florida A&M *HS:* William M. Raines [Jacksonville, FL] B: 9/9/1954, Jacksonville, FL *Drafted:* 1976 Round 14 Cin
1977 Cle: Rush 1-(-3) -3.0. **1978** Min: Rush 2-22 11.0. **1982** Min: Rush 1-15 15.0. **1983** Min: Rush 1-(-9) -9.0. **1984** Min: Pass 1-0; Rush 2-11 5.5. **1985** Min: Rush 2-0. **1986** Min: Rush 2-46 23.0. **1988** Was: Pass 1-0; Rush 2-(-13) -6.5. **Total:** Pass 2-0; Rush 13-69 5.3.

		Punting			
Year Team	**G**	**Punts**	**Yds**	**Avg**	**Fum**
1977 Cle	14	61	2389	39.2	0
1978 Min	9	51	1991	39.0	0
1979 Min	16	90	3551	39.5	0
1980 Min	16	81	3139	38.8	0
1981 Min	15	88	3646	41.4	0
1982 Min	9	**58**	2384	41.1	0
1983 Min	16	91	3780	41.5	0
1984 Min	16	82	3473	42.4	0
1985 Min	16	67	2867	42.8	1
1986 Min	16	67	2774	41.4	0
1987 Min	9	45	1786	39.7	0
1988 Was	10	39	1505	38.6	1
NFL Total	162	820	33285	40.6	2

HERB COLEMAN Coleman, Herbert Edward 6'0", 200 **C-LB**
Col: Notre Dame *HS:* Chester [WV] B: 6/18/1923, Chester, WV D: 1/1/1985, Northville, MI
AAFC **1946** ChiA: 14 G; KR 1-20 20.0; Int 1-25. **1947** ChiA: 13 G. **1948** ChiA-BalA: 10 G. **Total:** 37 G; KR 1-20 20.0; Int 1-25.

KEO COLEMAN Coleman, Keombani M 6'1", 255 **LB**
Col: Navarro Coll. TX (J.C.); Mississippi State *HS:* Milwaukee Tech [WI] B: 5/1/1970, Los Angeles, CA *Drafted:* 1992 Round 4 NYJ
1992 NYJ: 6 G. **1993** GB: 12 G. **Total:** 18 G.

LEONARD COLEMAN Coleman, Leonard David 6'2", 203 **DB**
Col: Vanderbilt *HS:* Lake Worth [FL] B: 1/30/1962, Boynton Beach, FL *Drafted:* 1984 Round 1 Ind
1985 Ind: 12 G. **1986** Ind: 16 G; Int 4-36. **1987** Ind: 4 G. **1988** SD: 16 G; Int 2-0. **1989** SD: 1 G. **Total:** 49 G; Int 6-36.

LINCOLN COLEMAN Coleman, Lincoln Cales 6'1", 249 **FB**
Col: Notre Dame; Baylor *HS:* Bryan Adams [Dallas, TX] B: 8/12/1969, Dallas, TX
1993 Dal: Rec 4-24 6.0. **1994** Dal: Rec 8-46 5.8. **Total:** Rec 12-70 5.8.

		Rushing				
Year Team	**G**	**Att**	**Yds**	**Avg**	**TD**	**Fum**
1993 Dal	7	34	132	3.9	2	1
1994 Dal	11	64	180	2.8	1	2
NFL Total	18	98	312	3.2	3	3

MARCO COLEMAN Coleman, Marco Darnell 6'3", 267 **DE-LB**
Col: Georgia Tech *HS:* Patterson Cooperative [Dayton, OH] B: 12/18/1969, Dayton, OH *Drafted:* 1992 Round 1 Mia
1992 Mia: 16 G; 6 Sac. **1993** Mia: 15 G; 5.5 Sac. **1994** Mia: 16 G; 6 Sac. **1995** Mia: 16 G; 6.5 Sac. **1996** SD: 16 G; 4 Sac. **1997** SD: 16 G; Int 1-2; 2 Sac. **1998** SD: 16 G; 3.5 Sac. **Total:** 111 G; Int 1-2; 33.5 Sac.

MARCUS COLEMAN Coleman, Marcus Le'Shan 6'2", 210 **DB**
Col: Texas Tech *HS:* Lake Highlands [Dallas, TX] B: 5/24/1974, Dallas, TX *Drafted:* 1996 Round 5 NYJ
1996 NYJ: 13 G; Int 1-23. **1997** NYJ: 16 G; Int 1-24. **1998** NYJ: 14 G. **Total:** 43 G; Int 2-47.

MONTE COLEMAN Coleman, Monte Leon 6'2", 242 **LB**
Col: Central Arkansas *HS:* Pine Bluff [AR] B: 11/4/1957, Pine Bluff, AR *Drafted:* 1979 Round 11 Was
1980 Was: Rec 1-12 12.0. **1983** Was: 2 Sac. **1984** Was: PR 0-27; 10.5 Sac. **1985** Was: 1 Sac. **1986** Was: 3 Sac. **1987** Was: 4 Sac. **1988** Was: 3 Sac. **1989** Was: Rush 1-(-1) -1.0; 4 Sac. **1990** Was: 3 Sac. **1991** Was: 3.5 Sac. **1992** Was: 3 Sac. **1993** Was: 1 Fum TD; 6 Sac. **1994** Was: 0.5 Sac. **Total:** Rush 1-(-1) -1.0; Rec 1-12 12.0; PR 0-27; 1 Fum TD; 43.5 Sac.

		Interceptions				Tot
Year Team	**G**	**Int**	**Yds**	**TD**	**Fum**	**TD**
1979 Was	16	1	13	0	0	0
1980 Was	16	3	92	0	0	0
1981 Was	12	3	52	1	0	1
1982 Was	8	0	0	0	0	0
1983 Was	10	0	0	0	0	0
1984 Was	16	1	49	1	0	1
1985 Was	10	0	0	0	0	0
1986 Was	11	0	0	0	0	0
1987 Was	12	2	53	0	0	0
1988 Was	13	1	11	0	0	0
1989 Was	15	2	24	1	1	1
1990 Was	15	1	0	0	0	0
1991 Was	16	1	0	0	0	0
1992 Was	15	0	0	0	1	0
1993 Was	14	2	27	0	0	1
1994 Was	16	0	0	0	0	0
NFL Total	215	17	321	3	2	4

PAT COLEMAN Coleman, Patrick Darryl 5'7", 176 **WR**
Col: Mississippi *HS:* Cleveland [MS] B: 4/8/1967, Cleveland, MS *Drafted:* 1990 Round 9 Hou
1993 Hou: Rush 1-1 1.0. **1994** Hou: Rush 1-2 2.0. **Total:** Rush 2-3 1.5.

		Receiving				Punt Returns			
Year Team	**G**	**Rec**	**Yds**	**Avg**	**TD**	**Ret**	**Yds**	**Avg**	**TD**
1990 NE	1	0	0	—	0	0	0	—	0
1991 Hou	14	11	138	12.5	1	22	138	6.3	0
1992 Hou	14	2	10	5.0	0	7	35	5.0	0
1993 Hou	13	9	129	14.3	0	0	0	—	0
1994 Hou	10	20	298	14.9	1	2	13	6.5	0
NFL Total	52	42	575	13.7	2	31	186	6.0	0

	Kickoff Returns				
Year Team	**Ret**	**Yds**	**Avg**	**TD**	**Fum**
1990 NE	2	18	9.0	0	0
1991 Hou	13	256	19.7	0	3
1992 Hou	14	290	20.7	0	0
1993 Hou	3	37	12.3	0	0
NFL Total	32	601	18.8	0	3

RALPH COLEMAN Coleman, Ralph Donnell 6'4", 216 **LB**
Col: North Carolina A&T *HS:* Carver [Spartanburg, SC] B: 8/31/1950, Spartanburg, SC *Drafted:* 1972 Round 8 Dal
1972 Dal: 1 G.

RONNIE COLEMAN Coleman, Ronald L 5'10", 195 **RB**
Col: Alabama A&M *HS:* Walker [Jasper, AL] B: 7/9/1951, Jasper, AL
1974 Hou: Pass 2-0. **1975** Hou: Pass 1-0. **1976** Hou: Pass 1-0, 1 Int. **1977** Hou: Pass 3-1 33.3%, 44 14.67 1 TD. **Total:** Pass 7-1 14.3%, 44 6.29 1 TD 1 Int.

		Rushing				Receiving			
Year Team	**G**	**Att**	**Yds**	**Avg**	**TD**	**Rec**	**Yds**	**Avg**	**TD**
1974 Hou	13	52	193	3.7	1	4	9	2.3	0
1975 Hou	14	175	790	4.5	5	18	129	7.2	0
1976 Hou	13	171	684	4.0	2	40	247	6.2	3
1977 Hou	14	185	660	3.6	5	22	115	5.2	1
1978 Hou	15	61	188	3.1	1	19	246	12.9	1
1979 Hou	14	21	81	3.9	0	12	114	9.5	1
1980 Hou	14	14	82	5.9	1	16	168	10.5	0
1981 Hou	16	21	91	4.3	1	19	211	11.1	0
NFL Total	113	700	2769	4.0	16	150	1239	8.3	6

	Punt Returns				Kickoff Returns					Tot
Year Team	**Ret**	**Yds**	**Avg**	**TD**	**Ret**	**Yds**	**Avg**	**TD**	**Fum**	**TD**
1974 Hou	0	0	—	0	3	91	30.3	0	1	1
1975 Hou	1	0	0.0	0	8	149	18.6	0	6	5
1976 Hou	7	91	13.0	1	0	0	—	0	8	6
1977 Hou	0	0	—	0	0	0	—	0	7	6
1978 Hou	16	142	8.9	0	2	40	20.0	0	4	2
1979 Hou	1	-5	-5.0	0	16	321	20.1	0	2	1
1980 Hou	0	0	—	0	0	0	—	0	1	1

1981 Hou	0	0	—	0	0	0	—	0	2	1
NFL Total	25	228	9.1	1	29	601	20.7	0	31	23

SIDNEY COLEMAN Coleman, Sidney 6′2″, 250 **LB**
Col: Southern Mississippi *HS:* Harrison Central [Gulfport, MS]
B: 1/14/1964, Gulfport, MS
1988 TB: 16 G. **1989** TB: 4 G. **1990** TB: 16 G; KR 1-9 9.0. **1991** Pho: 16 G. **1992** TB: 1 G. **Total:** 53 G; KR 1-9 9.0.

STEVE COLEMAN Coleman, Steven 6′5″, 252 **DE**
Col: Delaware State *HS:* Germantown [Philadelphia, PA] B: 8/8/1950, Philadelphia, PA
1974 Den: 2 G.

JAMES COLEY Coley, James Lester 6′3″, 270 **TE**
Col: Clemson *HS:* Robert E. Lee [Jacksonville, FL] B: 4/13/1967, Jacksonville, FL
1990 ChiB: 16 G; Rec 1-7 7.0. **1991** Ind: 7 G; Rec 1-13 13.0. **Total:** 23 G; Rec 2-20 10.0.

JAKE COLHOUER Colhouer, Jacob C 6′1″, 225 **G**
Col: Oklahoma State *HS:* Warren [OK] B: 1/15/1922, Altus, OK
D: 4/14/1998, Lake Oswego, OR *Drafted:* 1946 Round 9 ChiC
1946 ChiC: 9 G. **1947** ChiC: 12 G; KR 2-16 8.0. **1948** ChiC: 11 G. **1949** NYG: 8 G. **Total:** 40 G; KR 2-16 8.0.

STALIN COLINET Colinet, Stalin 6′6″, 281 **DE**
Col: Boston College *HS:* Cardinal Hayes [Bronx, NY] B: 7/19/1974, New York, NY *Drafted:* 1997 Round 3 Min
1997 Min: 10 G. **1998** Min: 11 G; 1 Sac. **Total:** 21 G; 1 Sac.

ELMER COLLETT Collett, Charles Elmer 6′6″, 244 **OG**
Col: San Francisco State *HS:* Tamalpais [Mill Valley, CA] B: 11/7/1944, Oakland, CA *Drafted:* 1966 Round 14 SF
1967 SF: 14 G. **1968** SF: 14 G. **1969** SF: 14 G. **1970** SF: 14 G. **1971** SF: 14 G. **1972** SF: 14 G. **1973** Bal: 14 G. **1974** Bal: 14 G. **1975** Bal: 14 G. **1976** Bal: 14 G. **1977** Bal: 5 G. **Total:** 145 G.

BRUCE COLLIE Collie, Bruce Stokes 6′6″, 275 **OT-OG**
Col: Texas-Arlington *HS:* Robert E. Lee [San Antonio, TX]
B: 6/27/1962, Nuremberg, Germany *Drafted:* 1985 Round 5 SF
1985 SF: 16 G. **1986** SF: 16 G. **1987** SF: 11 G. **1988** SF: 15 G. **1989** SF: 16 G. **1990** Phi: 12 G. **1991** Phi: 5 G. **Total:** 91 G.

BOBBY COLLIER Collier, Bobby Frank 6′3″, 230 **OT-DT**
Col: Southern Methodist *HS:* Longview [TX] B: 12/11/1929, Stephens, AR *Drafted:* 1950 Round 18 LARm
1951 LARm: 11 G; KR 1-8 8.0.

FLOYD COLLIER Collier, Floyd Lee 6′1″, 215 **T**
Col: San Jose State; Fresno State; USC *HS:* Exeter [CA] B: 5/20/1924, Fresno, CA
AAFC **1948** SF-A: 12 G.

JIM COLLIER Collier, James Richard 6′3″, 205 **TE**
Col: Arkansas *HS:* Van Buren [AR] B: 5/8/1939, Van Buren, AR
Drafted: 1961 Round 7 NYG
1962 NYG: 13 G; Rec 1-27 27.0; KR 1-0. **1963** Was: 14 G. **Total:** 27 G; Rec 1-27 27.0; KR 1-0.

MIKE COLLIER Collier, Michael J 5′11″, 200 **RB**
Col: Morgan State *HS:* Edmondson [Baltimore, MD] B: 9/21/1953, Baltimore, MD *Drafted:* 1975 Round 14 Pit
1975 Pit: Rec 1-7 7.0. **1977** Buf: Rec 3-23 7.7. **1979** Buf: Rec 7-43 6.1. **Total:** Rec 11-73 6.6.

		Rushing				Kickoff Returns					Tot
Year Team	**G**	**Ret**	**Yds**	**Avg**	**TD**	**Ret**	**Yds**	**Avg**	**TD**	**Fum**	**TD**
1975 Pit	14	21	124	5.9	3	22	523	23.8	**1**	2	4
1977 Buf	6	31	116	3.7	0	4	55	13.8	0	1	0
1979 Buf	16	34	130	3.8	2	7	129	18.4	0	3	2
NFL Total	36	86	370	4.3	5	33	707	21.4	1	6	6

REGGIE COLLIER Collier, Reginald C 6′3″, 207 **QB**
Col: Southern Mississippi *HS:* D'Iberville [MS] B: 5/14/1961, Biloxi, MS *Drafted:* 1983 Round 6 Dal
1986 Dal: 4 G; Pass 15-8 53.3%, 96 6.40 1 TD 2 Int; Rush 6-53 8.8; 2 Fum. **1987** Pit: 2 G; Pass 7-4 57.1%, 110 15.71 2 TD 1 Int; Rush 4-20 5.0. **Total:** 6 G; Pass 22-12 54.5%, 206 9.36 3 TD 3 Int; Rush 10-73 7.3; 2 Fum.

STEVE COLLIER Collier, Steven Andre 6′7″, 342 **OT**
Col: Garden City CC KS; Illinois; Bethune-Cookman
HS: Whitney-Young [Chicago, IL] B: 4/19/1963, Chicago, IL
1987 GB: 10 G.

TIM COLLIER Collier, Timothy Jr. 6′0″, 172 **DB**
Col: Texas A&M-Commerce *HS:* South Oak Cliff [Dallas, TX]
B: 5/31/1954, Terrell, TX *Drafted:* 1976 Round 9 KC
1979 KC: KR 1-0. **Total:** KR 1-0.

		Interceptions			
Year Team	**G**	**Int**	**Yds**	**TD**	**Fum**
1976 KC	13	2	10	0	0
1977 KC	9	2	134	**1**	0
1978 KC	15	3	38	0	0
1979 KC	15	2	45	0	1
1980 StL	12	2	22	0	0
1981 StL	14	1	17	0	0
1982 StL-SF	6	0	0	0	0
1982 StL	4	0	0	0	0
1982 SF	2	0	0	0	0
1983 SF	10	3	32	1	0
NFL Total	94	15	298	2	1

RIP COLLINS Collins, Albin Harrell 6′0″, 190 **HB-FB**
Col: Louisiana State *HS:* Baton Rouge [LA] B: 11/9/1926, Baton Rouge, LA *Drafted:* 1949 Round 6 NYB
AAFC **1949** ChiA: Pass 1-0; Rec 6-161 26.8; KR 2-23 11.5; Int 1-0.

		Rushing				Punting		
Year Team	**G**	**Att**	**Yds**	**Avg**	**TD**	**Punts**	**Yds**	**Avg**
1949 ChiA	12	28	88	3.1	0	41	1725	42.1

NFL **1950** Bal: Rec 19-295 15.5; KR 2-33 16.5; Int 1-7; Punt 2-91 45.5. **1951** GB: Rec 1-5 5.0; KR 1-40 40.0; Int 2-0; Punt 2-81 40.5. **Total:** Rec 20-300 15.0; KR 3-73 24.3; Int 3-7; Punt 4-172 43.0.

		Rushing				
Year Team	**G**	**Att**	**Yds**	**Avg**	**TD**	**Fum**
1950 Bal	12	69	101	1.5	0	4
1951 GB	7	5	4	0.8	0	0
NFL Total	19	74	105	1.4	0	4

SONNY COLLINS Collins, Alfred Eugene 6′1″, 196 **RB**
Col: Kentucky *HS:* Madisonville [KY] B: 1/17/1953, Madisonville, KY
Drafted: 1976 Round 2 Atl
1976 Atl: Rec 4-37 9.3; KR 7-141 20.1.

		Rushing				
Year Team	**G**	**Att**	**Yds**	**Avg**	**TD**	**Fum**
1976 Atl	11	91	319	3.5	0	1

RAY COLLINS Collins, Alvin Raymond 5′11″, 238 **DT-OT**
(Socks) *Col:* Louisiana State *HS:* Fair Park [Shreveport, LA]
B: 8/4/1927, Shreveport, LA
1950 SF: 12 G. **1951** SF: 12 G; KR 1-6 6.0. **1952** SF: 8 G. **1954** NYG: 12 G. **1960** DalT: 14 G. **1961** DalT: 13 G. **Total:** 71 G; KR 1-6 6.0.

ANDRE COLLINS Collins, Andre Pierre 6′1″, 237 **LB**
Col: Penn State *HS:* Cinnaminson [NJ] B: 5/4/1968, Riverside, NJ
Drafted: 1990 Round 2 Was
1990 Was: 6 Sac. **1991** Was: 3 Sac. **1992** Was: 2 Sac. **1993** Was: 6 Sac. **1994** Was: KR 1-0; 1.5 Sac. **1995** Cin: KR 1-(-3) -3.0; 4 Sac. **1997** Cin: 3 Sac. **Total:** KR 2-(-3) -1.5; 25.5 Sac.

		Interceptions			
Year Team	**G**	**Int**	**Yds**	**TD**	**Fum**
1990 Was	16	0	0	0	0
1991 Was	16	2	33	1	1
1992 Was	14	1	59	0	0
1993 Was	13	1	5	0	0
1994 Was	16	4	150	2	0
1995 Cin	16	2	3	0	0
1996 Cin	14	0	0	0	0
1997 Cin	16	0	0	0	0
1998 ChiB	16	3	29	0	0
NFL Total	137	13	279	3	1

TONY COLLINS Collins, Anthony 5′11″, 208 **RB**
Col: East Carolina *HS:* Penn Yan Acad. [NY] B: 5/27/1959, Sanford, FL
Drafted: 1981 Round 2 NE
1981 NE: Pass 1-0; PR 3-15 5.0. **Total:** Pass 1-0; PR 3-15 5.0.

		Rushing				Receiving			
Year Team	**G**	**Att**	**Yds**	**Avg**	**TD**	**Rec**	**Yds**	**Avg**	**TD**
1981 NE	16	204	873	4.3	7	26	232	8.9	0
1982 NE	9	164	632	3.9	1	19	187	9.8	2
1983 NE	16	219	1049	4.8	10	27	257	9.5	0
1984 NE	16	138	550	4.0	5	16	100	6.3	0
1985 NE	16	163	657	4.0	3	52	549	10.6	2
1986 NE	16	156	412	2.6	3	77	684	8.9	5
1987 NE	13	147	474	3.2	3	44	347	7.9	3
1990 Mia	1	0	0	—	0	0	0	—	0
NFL Total	103	1191	4647	3.9	32	261	2356	9.0	12

	Kickoff Returns					Tot
Year Team	**Ret**	**Yds**	**Avg**	**TD**	**Fum**	**TD**
1981 NE	39	773	19.8	0	8	7
1982 NE	0	0	—	0	5	3
1983 NE	0	0	—	0	10	10
1984 NE	25	544	21.8	0	3	5
1985 NE	0	0	—	0	6	5
1986 NE	0	0	—	0	4	8

1987 NE	1	18	18.0	0	6	6
1990 Mia	2	30	15.0	0	0	0
NFL Total	67	1365	20.4	0	42	44

BRETT COLLINS Collins, Brett William 6′1″, 226 **LB**
Col: Washington *HS:* Glencoe [Hillsboro, OR] B: 10/8/1968, Sheridan, WY *Drafted:* 1992 Round 12 GB
1992 GB: 11 G. **1993** GB-LARm: 14 G. GB: 4 G. LARm: 10 G. **1994** LARm: 2 G. **Total:** 27 G.

CALVIN COLLINS Collins, Calvin Lewis 6′2″, 307 **C**
Col: Texas A&M *HS:* West Brook [Beaumont, TX] B: 1/5/1974, Beaumont, TX *Drafted:* 1997 Round 6 Atl
1997 Atl: 15 G. **1998** Atl: 16 G. **Total:** 31 G.

CLARENCE COLLINS Collins, Clarence Robert 6′1″, 180 **WR**
Col: Illinois State *HS:* Hazelwood East [St. Louis, MO] B: 2/1/1962, St. Louis, MO
1987 StL: 1 G.

MO COLLINS Collins, Damon Jamal 6′4″, 325 **OT**
Col: Florida *HS:* West Charlotte [Charlotte, NC] B: 9/22/1976, Charlotte, NC *Drafted:* 1998 Round 1 Oak
1998 Oak: 16 G.

LARRY COLLINS Collins, Daniel Larry 5′11″, 189 **RB**
Col: Texas A&M–Kingsville *HS:* Thomas Edison [San Antonio, TX] B: 8/8/1955, San Antonio, TX *Drafted:* 1978 Round 3 Cle
1978 Cle: Rush 22-64 2.9 1 TD; Rec 1-4 4.0. **Total:** Rush 22-64 2.9 1 TD; Rec 1-4 4.0.

		Kickoff Returns				
Year Team	**G**	**Ret**	**Yds**	**Avg**	**TD**	**Fum**
1978 Cle	15	32	709	22.2	0	4
1980 NO	8	0	0	—	0	0
NFL Total	23	32	709	22.2	0	4

DWIGHT COLLINS Collins, Dwight Dean 6′1″, 208 **WR**
Col: Pittsburgh *HS:* Beaver Falls [PA] B: 8/23/1961, Rochester, NY *Drafted:* 1984 Round 6 Min
1984 Min: 16 G; Rush 3-(-14) -4.7; Rec 11-143 13.0 1 TD; 6 Pt.

KIRK COLLINS Collins, Edward Kirk 5′11″, 182 **DB**
Col: Blinn Coll. TX (J.C.); Baylor *HS:* Sam Houston [San Antonio, TX] B: 7/18/1958, San Antonio, TX D: 2/22/1984, Anaheim, CA *Drafted:* 1980 Round 7 LARm
1981 LARm: 16 G. **1982** LARm: 9 G. **1983** LARm: 4 G; Int 5-113. **Total:** 29 G; Int 5-113.

FABRAY COLLINS Collins, Fabray R 6′2″, 215 **LB**
Col: Southern Illinois *HS:* Paul Robeson [Chicago, IL] B: 9/16/1961, Chicago, IL
1987 Min: 3 G.

GARY COLLINS Collins, Gary James 6′5″, 215 **WR-P**
Col: Maryland *HS:* Williamstown [PA] B: 8/20/1940, Williamstown, PA *Drafted:* 1962 Round 1 Cle
1962 Cle: KR 1-0. **1965** Cle: Rush 1-16 16.0. **1966** Cle: Rush 2-38 19.0. **1967** Cle: Rush 1-6 6.0. **Total:** Rush 4-60 15.0; KR 1-0.

		Receiving				Punting			
Year Team	**G**	**Rec**	**Yds**	**Avg**	**TD**	**Punts**	**Yds**	**Avg**	**Fum**
1962 Cle	14	11	153	13.9	2	45	1926	42.8	0
1963 Cle	14	43	674	15.7	**13**	54	2160	40.0	0
1964 Cle	14	35	544	15.5	8	48	2016	42.0	0
1965 Cle	14	50	884	17.7	10	65	3035	**46.7**	0
1966 Cle	14	56	946	16.9	12	57	2223	39.0	0
1967 Cle	13	32	500	15.6	7	57	2078	36.5	1
1968 Cle	5	9	230	25.6	0	2	52	26.0	0
1969 Cle	14	54	786	14.6	11	3	112	37.3	0
1970 Cle	12	26	351	13.5	4	0	0	—	1
1971 Cle	13	15	231	15.4	3	5	162	32.4	0
NFL Total	127	331	5299	16.0	70	336	13764	41.0	2

GEORGE COLLINS Collins, George Francis III 6′2″, 257 **OG-OT**
Col: Georgia *HS:* Warner Robins [GA] B: 12/9/1955, Macon, GA
1978 StL: 13 G. **1979** StL: 15 G. **1980** StL: 16 G; KR 1-0; 1 Fum. **1981** StL: 16 G. **1982** StL: 9 G. **Total:** 69 G; KR 1-0; 1 Fum.

GERALD COLLINS Collins, Gerald Michael 6′2″, 250 **LB**
Col: Vanderbilt *HS:* Roosevelt [St. Louis, MO] B: 2/13/1971, St. Louis, MO
1995 Cin: 3 G.

GLEN COLLINS Collins, Glen Leon 6′6″, 265 **DE**
Col: Mississippi State *HS:* Jim Hill [Jackson, MS] B: 7/10/1959, Jackson, MS *Drafted:* 1982 Round 1 Cin
1982 Cin: 7 G; 1 Sac. **1983** Cin: 16 G; 5 Sac. **1984** Cin: 16 G; 3 Sac. **1985** Cin: 16 G. **1987** SF: 3 G; 2 Sac. **Total:** 58 G; 11 Sac.

GREG COLLINS Collins, Gregory Vincent 6′3″, 228 **LB**
Col: Notre Dame *HS:* Brother Rice [Birmingham, MI] B: 12/8/1952, Troy, MI *Drafted:* 1975 Round 2 SF
1975 SF: 14 G. **1976** Sea: 13 G. **1977** Buf: 11 G. **Total:** 38 G.

HARRY COLLINS Collins, Harry 5′11″, 190 **G**
Col: Canisius B: 1/18/1900, England D: 1/16/1983, Fort Myers, FL
1924 Buf: 11 G.

JIM COLLINS Collins, James Brian 6′2″, 230 **LB**
Col: Syracuse *HS:* Mendham [NJ] B: 6/11/1958, Orange, NJ *Drafted:* 1981 Round 2 LARm
1981 LARm: 7 G. **1982** LARm: 6 G. **1983** LARm: 16 G; Int 2-46; 1 Sac. **1984** LARm: 16 G; Int 2-43; 1 Fum; 0.5 Sac. **1985** LARm: 16 G; Int 2-8; 2 Sac. **1987** LARm: 15 G; 1 Sac. **1988** LARm: 4 G. **1989** SD: 13 G. **Total:** 93 G; Int 6-97; 1 Fum; 4.5 Sac.

JERALD COLLINS Collins, Jerald Ezra 6′2″, 220 **LB**
Col: Western Michigan *HS:* Muskegon [MI] B: 2/1/1947, Muskegon, MI
1969 Buf: 9 G; KR 2-14 7.0. **1970** Buf: 3 G; KR 2-17 8.5. **1971** Buf: 2 G. **Total:** 14 G; KR 4-31 7.8.

KERRY COLLINS Collins, Kerry Michael 6′5″, 240 **QB**
Col: Penn State *HS:* Wilson [West Lawn, PA] B: 12/30/1972, West Lawn, PA *Drafted:* 1995 Round 1 Car
1996 Car: Scor 1 2XP. **1998** Car-NO: Rec 1-(-11) -11.0; Scor 1 2XP. Car: Rec 1-(-11) -11.0; Scor 1 2XP. **Total:** Rec 1-(-11) -11.0; Scor 2 2XP.

		Passing							
Year Team	**G**	**Att**	**Comp**	**Comp%**	**Yds**	**YPA**	**TD**	**Int**	**Rating**
1995 Car	15	433	214	49.4	2717	6.27	14	19	61.9
1996 Car	13	364	204	56.0	2454	6.74	14	9	79.4
1997 Car	13	381	200	52.5	2124	5.57	11	**21**	55.7
1998 Car-NO	11	353	170	48.2	2213	6.27	12	15	62.0
1998 Car	4	162	76	46.9	1011	6.24	8	5	70.8
1998 NO	7	191	94	49.2	1202	6.29	4	10	54.5
NFL Total	52	1531	788	51.5	9508	6.21	51	64	64.5

	Rushing				
Year Team	**Att**	**Yds**	**Avg**	**TD**	**Fum**
1995 Car	42	74	1.8	3	13
1996 Car	32	38	1.2	0	6
1997 Car	26	65	2.5	1	8
1998 Car-NO	30	153	5.1	1	13
1998 Car	7	40	5.7	0	5
1998 NO	23	113	4.9	1	8
NFL Total	130	330	2.5	5	40

MARK COLLINS Collins, Mark Anthony 5′10″, 196 **DB**
Col: Cal State-Fullerton *HS:* Pacific [San Bernardino, CA] B: 1/16/1964, San Bernardino, CA *Drafted:* 1986 Round 2 NYG
1986 NYG: PR 3-11 3.7; KR 11-204 18.5. **1987** NYG: 1.5 Sac. **1988** NYG: KR 4-67 16.8; Scor 1 Saf. **1989** NYG: KR 1-0; 1 Sac. **1993** NYG: 1 Sac. **1994** KC: 2 Sac. **1995** KC: **1** Fum TD. **1996** KC: 1 Sac. **1998** Sea: 1.5 Sac. **Total:** PR 3-11 3.7; KR 16-271 16.9; Scor 1 Saf; 1 Fum TD; 8 Sac.

		Interceptions				Tot
Year Team	**G**	**Int**	**Yds**	**TD**	**Fum**	**TD**
1986 NYG	15	1	0	0	2	0
1987 NYG	11	2	28	0	0	0
1988 NYG	11	1	13	0	0	0
1989 NYG	16	2	12	0	0	0
1990 NYG	13	2	0	0	0	0
1991 NYG	16	4	77	0	0	0
1992 NYG	14	1	0	0	0	0
1993 NYG	16	4	77	1	0	1
1994 KC	14	2	83	1	0	1
1995 KC	16	1	8	0	1	1
1996 KC	16	6	45	0	0	0
1997 GB	1	0	0	0	0	0
1998 Sea	9	1	0	0	0	0
NFL Total	168	27	343	2	3	3

PATRICK COLLINS Collins, Patrick Norman 5′9″, 177 **RB**
Col: Oklahoma *HS:* Booker T. Washington [Tulsa, OK] B: 8/4/1966, Okmulgee, OK *Drafted:* 1988 Round 8 GB
1988 GB: 5 G; Rush 2-2 1.0; Rec 2-17 8.5.

PAUL COLLINS Collins, Paul Andrew 6′2″, 203 **OE-DE**
(Rip) *Col:* Pittsburgh *HS:* Trinity [Sioux City, IA] B: 10/31/1907, Danbury, IA D: 9/25/1988, Largo, FL
1932 Bos: 10 G; Rec 1-7 7.0. **1933** Bos: 12 G; Rec 3-32 10.7. **1934** Bos: 12 G. **1935** Bos: 9 G; Rec 3-47 15.7. **Total:** 43 G; Rec 7-86 12.3.

PAUL COLLINS Collins, Paul Reagan 5′11″, 178 **QB**
Col: Missouri *HS:* Hickman [Columbia, MO] B: 9/28/1922 *Drafted:* 1945 Round 2 ChiC
1945 ChiC: 3 G; Pass 17-3 17.6%, 43 2.53 2 Int; Rush 10-13 1.3; 3 Fum.

ROOSEVELT COLLINS Collins, Roosevelt Jr. 6′4″, 235 **LB**
Col: Texas Christian *HS:* Booker T. Washington [Shreveport, LA]
B: 1/25/1968, Shreveport, LA *Drafted:* 1992 Round 6 Mia
1992 Mia: 10 G.

SHANE COLLINS Collins, Shane William 6′3″, 267 **DE**
Col: Arizona State *HS:* Bozeman [MT] B: 4/11/1969, Roundup, MT
Drafted: 1992 Round 2 Was
1992 Was: 16 G; 1 Sac. **1993** Was: 7 G. **1994** Was: 7 G. **Total:** 30 G; 1 Sac.

SHAWN COLLINS Collins, Shawn 6′2″, 207 **WR**
Col: Northern Arizona *HS:* Kearny [San Diego, CA] B: 2/20/1967, San Diego, CA *Drafted:* 1989 Round 1 Atl

		Receiving				
Year Team	G	Rec	Yds	Avg	TD	Fum
1989 Atl	16	58	862	14.9	3	0
1990 Atl	16	34	503	14.8	2	1
1991 Atl	4	3	37	12.3	0	0
1992 Cle	9	3	31	10.3	0	0
1993 GB	4	0	0	—	0	0
NFL Total	49	98	1433	14.6	5	1

TODD COLLINS Collins, Todd Franklin 6′2″, 248 **LB**
Col: Georgia; Tennessee; Carson-Newman *HS:* Jefferson Co. [Dandridge, TN] B: 5/27/1970, New Market, TN *Drafted:* 1992 Round 3 NE
1992 NE: 10 G. **1993** NE: 16 G; Int 1-8; 1 Sac. **1994** NE: 7 G. **1996** NE: 16 G; Int 1-7. **1997** NE: 15 G; 1.5 Sac. **1998** NE: 12 G. **Total:** 76 G; Int 2-15; 2.5 Sac.

TODD COLLINS Collins, Todd Steven 6′4″, 224 **QB**
Col: Michigan *HS:* Walpole [MA] B: 11/5/1971, Walpole, MA
Drafted: 1995 Round 2 Buf

		Passing							
Year Team	G	Att	Comp	Comp%	Yds	YPA	TD	Int	Rating
1995 Buf	7	29	14	48.3	112	3.86	0	1	44.0
1996 Buf	7	99	55	55.6	739	7.46	4	5	71.9
1997 Buf	14	391	215	55.0	2367	6.05	12	13	69.5
NFL Total	28	519	284	54.7	3218	6.20	16	19	68.5

	Rushing				
Year Team	Att	Yds	Avg	TD	Fum
1995 Buf	9	23	2.6	0	0
1996 Buf	21	43	2.0	0	3
1997 Buf	30	77	2.6	0	10
NFL Total	60	143	2.4	0	13

TRENT COLLINS Collins, Trent John 6′1″, 187 **DB**
Col: Coll. of the Sequoias CA (J.C.); San Diego State *HS:* John Ehret [Marrero, LA] B: 5/18/1961, New Orleans, LA
1987 NYJ: 3 G; PR 1-0; 1 Fum.

BILL COLLINS Collins, William Harold 5′8″, 195 **G**
(Spot) *Col:* Southwestern (Tex.); Texas *HS:* G. W. Brackenridge [San Antonio, TX] B: 3/4/1922, Breckenridge, TX D: 3/26/1996, Temple, TX
1947 Bos: 12 G.

BILL COLLINS Collins, William Kinney 5′8″, 160 **OE**
Col: Wisconsin *HS:* James Madison Memorial [Madison, WI]
B: 10/20/1901, Madison, WI D: 1/24/1976, Corpus Christi, TX
1922 Mil: 3 G.

CRIS COLLINSWORTH Collinsworth, Anthony Cris 6′5″, 192 **WR**
Col: Florida *HS:* Astronaut [Titusville, FL] B: 1/27/1959, Dayton, OH
Drafted: 1981 Round 2 Cin
1982 Cin: Rush 1-(-11) -11.0. **1983** Cin: Rush 2-2 1.0. **1984** Cin: Rush 1-7 7.0. **1985** Cin: Pass 1-0, 1 Int; Rush 1-3 3.0. **1986** Cin: Rush 2-(-16) -8.0.
Total: Pass 1-0, 1 Int; Rush 7-(-15) -2.1.

		Receiving				
Year Team	G	Rec	Yds	Avg	TD	Fum
1981 Cin	16	67	1009	15.1	8	3
1982 Cin	9	49	700	14.3	1	1
1983 Cin	14	66	1130	17.1	5	2
1984 Cin	15	64	989	15.5	6	0
1985 Cin	16	65	1125	17.3	5	1
1986 Cin	16	62	1024	16.5	10	1
1987 Cin	8	31	494	15.9	0	0
1988 Cin	13	13	227	17.5	1	1
NFL Total	107	417	6698	16.1	36	9

FERRIC COLLONS Collons, Ferric Jason 6′7″, 290 **DE**
Col: California *HS:* Jesuit [Sacramento, CA] B: 12/4/1969, Belleville, IL
1995 NE: 16 G; 4 Sac. **1996** NE: 15 G; 0.5 Sac. **1997** NE: 5 G; 1 Sac.
1998 NE: 14 G. **Total:** 50 G; 5.5 Sac.

DOUG COLMAN Colman, Douglass Clayton 6′2″, 250 **LB**
Col: Nebraska *HS:* Ocean City [NJ] B: 6/4/1973, Somers Point, NJ
Drafted: 1996 Round 6 NYG
1996 NYG: 13 G. **1997** NYG: 14 G. **1998** NYG: 16 G. **Total:** 43 G.

WAYNE COLMAN Colman, Wayne Charles 6′2″, 230 **LB**
Col: Temple *HS:* Atlantic City [NJ] B: 4/13/1946, Ventnor, NJ
1968 Phi: 14 G. **1969** Phi-NO: 9 G; Int 1-11. Phi: 5 G; Int 1-11. NO: 4 G.
1970 NO: 14 G. **1971** NO: 14 G; Int 1-0. **1972** NO: 14 G. **1973** NO: 12 G.
1974 NO: 14 G; Int 1-17. **1976** NO: 7 G. **Total:** 98 G; Int 3-28.

MICKEY COLMER Colmer, John Francis 6′2″, 219 **FB-LB-BB**
Col: Miramonte J.C. (GA) *HS:* Redondo [Redondo Beach, CA]
B: 10/23/1918, CA
AAFC **1946** BknA: PR 1-9 9.0; KR 1-9 9.0; Int 1-0. **1947** BknA: Pass 3-1 33.3%, 20 6.67; KR 3-77 25.7. **1948** BknA: Pass 1-0; KR 8-163 20.4.
1949 NY-A: Pass 1-0; KR 1-16 16.0. **Total:** Pass 5-1 20.0%, 20 4.00; PR 1-9 9.0; KR 13-265 20.4; Int 1-0.

		Rushing				Receiving			
Year Team	G	Att	Yds	Avg	TD	Rec	Yds	Avg	TD
1946 BknA	12	46	155	3.4	0	22	327	14.9	1
1947 BknA	14	152	578	3.8	9	18	190	10.6	1
1948 BknA	14	164	704	4.3	6	21	372	17.7	4
1949 NY-A	8	36	100	2.8	0	2	10	5.0	0
AAFC Total	48	398	1537	3.9	15	63	899	14.3	6

	Punting			Tot
Year Team	Punts	Yds	Avg	TD
1946 BknA	0	0	—	1
1947 BknA	56	2504	44.7	10
1948 BknA	56	2382	42.5	10
1949 NY-A	5	232	46.4	0
AAFC Total	117	5118	43.7	21

DON COLO Colo, Donald Richard 6′3″, 252 **DT**
Col: Brown *HS:* East Bridgewater [MA] B: 1/5/1925, East Bridgewater, MA *Drafted:* 1950 Round 3 Bal
1950 Bal: 12 G. **1951** NYY: 12 G. **1952** Dal: 4 G; Int 1-11. **1953** Cle: 12 G.
1954 Cle: 12 G. **1955** Cle: 12 G. **1956** Cle: 12 G; Int 1-0. **1957** Cle: 12 G.
1958 Cle: 12 G. **Total:** 100 G; Int 2-11.

HARRY COLON Colon, Harry 6′0″, 203 **DB**
Col: Missouri *HS:* Washington [Kansas City, KS] B: 2/14/1969, Kansas City, KS *Drafted:* 1991 Round 8 NE
1991 NE: 16 G. **1992** Det: 16 G. **1993** Det: 15 G; Int 2-28; 1 Sac.
1994 Det: 16 G; Int 1-3. **1995** Jac: 16 G; Int 3-46. **1997** Det: 8 G.
Total: 87 G; Int 6-77; 1 Sac.

TONY COLORITO Colorito, Anthony Ivor 6′5″, 260 **NT**
Col: USC *HS:* Midwood [Brooklyn, NY] B: 9/8/1964, Brooklyn, NY
Drafted: 1986 Round 5 Den
1986 Den: 15 G.

JIMMY COLQUITT Colquitt, James Michael 6′4″, 209 **P**
Col: Tennessee *HS:* Doyle [Knoxville, TN] B: 1/17/1963, Knoxville, TN
1985 Sea: 2 G; Punt 12-481 40.1.

CRAIG COLQUITT Colquitt, Joseph Craig 6′1″, 182 **P**
Col: Cleveland State CC TN; Tennessee *HS:* South [Knoxville, TN]
B: 6/9/1954, Knoxville, TN *Drafted:* 1978 Round 3 Pit
1980 Pit: Rush 1-17 17.0. **1981** Pit: Rush 1-8 8.0. **1984** Pit: Rush 1-0.
Total: Rush 3-25 8.3.

		Punting			
Year Team	G	Punts	Yds	Avg	Fum
1978 Pit	16	66	2642	40.0	0
1979 Pit	16	68	2733	40.2	0
1980 Pit	16	61	2483	40.7	1
1981 Pit	16	84	3641	43.3	0
1983 Pit	16	80	3352	41.9	0
1984 Pit	16	70	2883	41.2	0
1987 Ind	1	2	61	30.5	0
NFL Total	97	431	17795	41.3	1

TIM COLSTON Colston, Timothy Maurice 6′0″, 275 **DE**
Col: Kansas State *HS:* C. Leon King [Tampa, FL] B: 12/18/1973, Tampa, FL
1996 Car: 2 G.

JEFF COLTER Colter, Jeffrey 5′10″, 171 **DB**
Col: Eastern Arizona Coll. (J.C.); Kansas *HS:* Amphitheater [Tucson, AZ]
B: 4/23/1961, Tucson, AZ
1984 Min: 16 G. **1987** KC: 1 G. **Total:** 17 G.

LLOYD COLTERYAHN Colteryahn, Lloyd Kenneth 6′2″, 220 **OE**
(Colt) *Col:* Maryland *HS:* Brentwood [Pittsburgh, PA] B: 8/26/1931, Brentwood, PA *Drafted:* 1953 Round 4 Pit

		Receiving			
Year Team	G	Rec	Yds	Avg	TD
1954 Bal	12	30	384	12.8	0

1955 Bal	12	21	251	12.0	3
1956 Bal	3	3	29	9.7	0
NFL Total	27	54	664	12.3	3

GEORGE COLTON Colton, George Curtis 6′4″, 279 **OG**
Col: Maryland *HS:* Lindenhurst [NY] B: 7/28/1963, Lindenhurst, NY
Drafted: 1986 Round 9 NE
1987 NE: 3 G.

JIM COLVIN Colvin, James R 6′3″, 252 **DT-DE-OG**
Col: Houston *HS:* Lutcher Stark [Orange, TX] B: 11/30/1937, Monahans, TX *Drafted:* 1960 Round 8 Bal
1960 Bal: 12 G. **1961** Bal: 13 G. **1962** Bal: 14 G. **1963** Bal: 14 G; Scor **1** Saf; 2 Pt. **1964** Dal: 14 G. **1965** Dal: 14 G. **1966** Dal: 14 G. **1967** NYG: 8 G. **Total:** 103 G; Scor 1 Saf; 2 Pt.

NEAL COLZIE Colzie, Cornelius Connie 6′2″, 200 **DB**
Col: Ohio State *HS:* Coral Gables [FL] B: 2/28/1953, Fitzgerald, GA
Drafted: 1975 Round 1 Oak
1976 Oak: KR 6-115 19.2. **1978** Oak: KR 1-15 15.0; 1 Fum TD. **1982** TB: 2 Sac. **Total:** KR 7-130 18.6; 1 Fum TD; 2 Sac.

		Punt Returns				Interceptions				Tot
Year Team	G	Ret	Yds	Avg	TD	Int	Yds	TD	Fum	TD
1975 Oak	13	48	**655**	13.6	0	4	38	0	4	0
1976 Oak	14	41	448	10.9	0	0	0	0	2	0
1977 Oak	13	32	334	10.4	0	3	13	0	2	0
1978 Oak	16	47	310	6.6	0	3	62	0	3	1
1979 Mia	16	0	0	—	0	5	86	0	0	0
1980 TB	16	0	0	—	0	1	39	0	0	0
1981 TB	16	2	12	6.0	0	6	110	1	1	1
1982 TB	9	0	0	—	0	3	64	0	0	0
1983 TB	5	0	0	—	0	0	0	0	0	0
NFL Total	118	170	1759	10.3	0	25	412	1	12	2

CHRIS COMBS Combs, Christopher Allen 6′4″, 238 **TE-OT**
Col: New Mexico *HS:* National [Sweetwater, CA] B: 3/17/1958, San Diego, CA *Drafted:* 1980 Round 4 Hou
1980 StL: 16 G; Rec 2-52 26.0 1 TD; 6 Pt. **1981** StL: 16 G; Rec 5-54 10.8. **Total:** 32 G; Rec 7-106 15.1 1 TD; 6 Pt.

BILL COMBS Combs, Loyal William 5′11″, 183 **OE-DB**
Col: Purdue *HS:* Lowell [IN] B: 6/29/1920, Holden, IL D: 10/27/1998, West Lafayette, IN
1942 Phi: 10 G; Rec 4-44 11.0 1 TD; 6 Pt.

DARREN COMEAUX Comeaux, Darren 6′1″, 227 **LB**
Col: Arizona State *HS:* San Diego [CA] B: 4/15/1960, San Diego, CA
1982 Den: 3 G. **1983** Den: 14 G. **1984** Den: 16 G; Int 1-5; 1 Sac. **1985** Den: 11 G. **1986** Den: 16 G; 1 Sac. **1987** SF: 8 G. **1988** Sea: 9 G; Int 1-18; 1 Fum. **1989** Sea: 16 G; KR 1-9 9.0; Int 1-0. **1990** Sea: 9 G; 1 Sac. **1991** Sea: 16 G; 0.5 Sac. **Total:** 118 G; KR 1-9 9.0; Int 3-23; 1 Fum; 3.5 Sac.

GREG COMELLA Comella, Greg 6′1″, 240 **RB**
Col: Stanford *HS:* Xaverian Brothers [Westwood, MA] B: 7/29/1975, Wellesley, MA
1998 NYG: 16 G; Rush 1-6 6.0; Rec 1-3 3.0; KR 1-12 12.0.

HOOK COMER Comer, John S Jr. 180 **FB**
Col: No College *HS:* Toronto [OH] B: 10/1898, Cass Twp. Muskingum Co., OH Deceased
1926 Can: 1 G.

MARTY COMER Comer, Martin F 6′0″, 203 **DE-OE**
Col: Tulane *HS:* Horace Mann School [Gary, IN] B: 10/28/1917, Indianapolis, IN D: 3/22/1998, New Orleans, LA
AAFC **1946** BufA: 6 G; Rec 2-17 8.5; 6 Pt. **1947** BufA: 14 G; Rec 2-75 37.5 1 TD; 6 Pt. **1948** BufA: 7 G; Rec 5-66 13.2 1 TD; 6 Pt. **Total:** 27 G; Rec 9-158 17.6 2 TD; Tot TD 3; 18 Pt.

ULYSSES COMIER Comier, Adonis 5′10″, 195 **FB**
Col: No College B: 1905 Deceased
1929 Buf: 3 G.

VINCE COMMISA Commisa, Vincent John 5′9″, 190 **G**
Col: Notre Dame *HS:* Barringer [Newark, NJ] B: 11/1/1921, Newark, NJ D: 3/5/1990, Orange, NJ
1944 Bos: 1 G.

CHUCK COMMISKEY Commiskey, Charles Edward 6′4″, 290 **OG**
Col: Mississippi *HS:* Pascagoula [MS] B: 3/2/1958, Killeen, TX
Drafted: 1981 Round 9 Phi
1986 NO: 16 G. **1987** NO: 12 G. **1988** NO: 6 G. **Total:** 34 G.

IRV COMP Comp, Irvin Henry Jr. 6′2″, 204 **DB-TB-QB**
Col: Benedictine *HS:* Bay View [Milwaukee, WI] B: 5/17/1919, Milwaukee, WI D: 7/11/1989, Woodruff, WI *Drafted:* 1943 Round 2 GB
1943 GB: PR 1-20 20.0; KR 4-81 20.3; Punt 12-453 37.8. **1944** GB: Rec 2-16 8.0 1 TD; PR 2-32 16.0; KR 2-35 17.5. **1945** GB: Rec 1-50 50.0 1 TD; PR 4-36 9.0; KR 5-110 22.0. **1946** GB: KR 1-29 29.0. **1947** GB: PR 1-0. **1948** GB: PR 3-35 11.7. **Total:** Rec 3-66 22.0 2 TD; PR 11-123 11.2; KR 12-255 21.3; Punt 12-453 37.8.

		Passing							
Year Team	G	Att	Comp	Comp%	Yds	YPA	TD	Int	Rating
1943 GB	9	92	46	50.0	662	7.20	7	4	81.0
1944 GB	10	**177**	80	45.2	**1159**	6.55	12	21	50.0
1945 GB	9	106	44	41.5	865	8.16	7	11	53.1
1946 GB	11	94	27	28.7	333	3.54	1	8	9.9
1947 GB	12	1	0	0.0	0	0.00	0	1	0.0
1948 GB	11	49	16	32.7	335	6.84	1	7	25.0
1949 GB	7	0	0	—	0	—	0	0	—
NFL Total	69	519	213	41.0	3354	6.46	28	52	41.6

	Rushing				Interceptions				Tot
Year Team	Att	Yds	Avg	TD	Int	Yds	TD	Fum	TD
1943 GB	77	182	2.4	3	10	149	**1**	0	4
1944 GB	52	134	2.6	2	6	54	0	0	3
1945 GB	57	92	1.6	1	2	67	1	5	3
1946 GB	61	62	1.0	1	2	38	0	6	1
1947 GB	5	46	9.2	0	6	65	0	2	0
1948 GB	3	3	1.0	0	5	86	0	3	0
1949 GB	0	0	—	0	3	24	0	0	0
NFL Total	255	519	2.0	7	34	483	2	16	11

TONY COMPAGNO Compagno, Anthony 5′11″, 199 **FB-DB**
Col: St. Mary's (Cal.) *HS:* Jefferson [Daly City, CA] B: 1/29/1921, Daly City, CA D: 4/8/1971, San Mateo Co., CA *Drafted:* 1943 Round 19 Pit
1946 Pit: Rec 8-101 12.6; KR 1-27 27.0. **1947** Pit: Rec 9-190 21.1 1 TD; KR 2-32 16.0. **1948** Pit: Rec 1-4 4.0; PR 4-21 5.3. **Total:** Rec 18-295 16.4 1 TD; PR 4-21 5.3; KR 3-59 19.7.

		Rushing				Interceptions				Tot
Year Team	G	Att	Yds	Avg	TD	Int	Yds	TD	Fum	TD
1946 Pit	10	67	217	3.2	1	1	40	0	7	1
1947 Pit	12	34	126	3.7	2	4	163	**2**	6	5
1948 Pit	12	24	101	4.2	0	7	179	1	5	1
NFL Total	34	125	444	3.6	3	12	382	3	18	7

CHUCK COMPTON Compton, Charles 5′10″, 190 **DB**
Col: Merced Coll. CA (J.C.); Boise State B: 1/13/1965, Atwater, CA
1987 GB: 2 G.

MIKE COMPTON Compton, Michael Eugene 6′6″, 297 **OG-OT-C**
Col: West Virginia *HS:* Richlands [VA] B: 9/18/1970, Richlands, VA
Drafted: 1993 Round 3 Det
1993 Det: 8 G. **1994** Det: 2 G. **1995** Det: 16 G. **1996** Det: 15 G; 1 Fum. **1997** Det: 16 G. **1998** Det: 16 G. **Total:** 73 G; 1 Fum.

OGDEN COMPTON Compton, Ogden Bingham 6′1″, 180 **QB**
Col: Hardin-Simmons *HS:* North Dallas [Dallas, TX] B: 8/25/1932, Ithaca, NY
1955 ChiC: Rush 6-(-8) -1.3.

		Passing							
Year Team	G	Att	Comp	Comp%	Yds	YPA	TD	Int	Rating
1955 ChiC	9	61	22	36.1	339	5.56	1	6	21.2

DICK COMPTON Compton, Richard Lee 6′2″, 190 **WR-DB-HB**
Col: McMurry *HS:* Colorado [Colorado City, TX] B: 4/16/1940, Colorado City, TX
1962 Det: Rush 1-3 3.0. **1963** Det: PR 2-11 5.5; KR 1-13 13.0; Int 1-23; Punt 2-85 42.5. **1964** Det: Rush 3-2 0.7; KR 0-42. **1965** Hou: Rush 1-2 2.0; KR 4-68 17.0. **1967** Pit: Rush 1-1 1.0. **Total:** Rush 6-8 1.3; PR 2-11 5.5; KR 5-123 24.6; Int 1-23; Punt 2-85 42.5.

		Receiving				
Year Team	G	Rec	Yds	Avg	TD	Fum
1962 Det	10	0	0	—	0	0
1963 Det	13	2	41	20.5	0	1
1964 Det	12	0	0	—	0	0
1965 Hou	3	3	140	46.7	2	0
1967 Pit	12	42	507	12.1	1	1
1968 Pit	7	5	45	9.0	1	0
NFL Total	57	52	733	14.1	4	2

ED COMSTOCK Comstock, Elwyn C 6′2″, 208 **G-T**
Col: West Virginia Wesleyan; Washington-St. Louis B: 7/12/1903 D: 8/1980, Belle Meade, NJ
1929 Buf: 8 G. **1930** Bkn: 6 G. **1931** SI: 9 G. **Total:** 23 G.

RUDY COMSTOCK Comstock, Rudolph S 5′10″, 209 **G-T**
Col: Georgetown *HS:* Pawhuska [OK] B: 9/23/1900, OK D: 11/1975, Penn Yan, NY
1923 Can: 12 G. **1924** Cle: 9 G. **1925** Can: 8 G. **1926** Fra: 17 G. **1927** Fra: 18 G. **1928** Fra: 16 G. **1929** Fra: 17 G. **1930** NYG: 15 G. **1931** GB: 14 G. **1932** GB: 13 G. **1933** GB: 13 G. **Total:** 152 G.

BILL CONATY Conaty, William Buckley 6′2″, 306 **C**
Col: Virginia Tech *HS:* Camden Catholic [NJ]; Milford Acad. [CT]
B: 3/8/1973, Baltimore, MD
1997 Buf: 1 G. **1998** Buf: 15 G. **Total:** 16 G.

RICK CONCANNON Concannon, Ernest Raymond 6'0", 217 **G-T**
Col: New York U. *HS:* Waltham [MA]; Dean Acad. [Franklin, MA]
B: 1/12/1908, Waltham, MA D: 6/17/1986, Bradenton, FL
1932 SI: 1 G. **1934** Bos: 10 G. **1935** Bos: 11 G. **1936** Bos: 3 G.
Total: 25 G.

JACK CONCANNON Concannon, John Joseph Jr. 6'3", 205 **QB**
Col: Boston College *HS:* Matignon [Cambridge, MA] B: 2/25/1943, Boston, MA *Drafted:* 1964 Round 2 Phi
1966 Phi: Rec 1-7 7.0; PR 2-3 1.5. **Total:** Rec 1-7 7.0; PR 2-3 1.5.

		Passing							
Year Team	G	Att	Comp	Comp%	Yds	YPA	TD	Int	Rating
1964 Phi	4	23	12	52.2	199	8.65	2	1	92.5
1965 Phi	3	29	12	41.4	176	6.07	1	3	33.8
1966 Phi	11	51	21	41.2	262	5.14	1	4	31.7
1967 ChiB	13	186	92	49.5	1260	6.77	6	14	50.9
1968 ChiB	7	143	71	49.7	715	5.00	5	9	49.7
1969 ChiB	14	160	87	54.4	783	4.89	4	8	55.3
1970 ChiB	14	385	194	50.4	2130	5.53	16	18	61.5
1971 ChiB	3	77	42	54.5	334	4.34	0	3	49.4
1974 GB	14	54	28	51.9	381	7.06	1	3	57.7
1975 Det	7	2	1	50.0	30	15.00	0	0	95.8
NFL Total	90	1110	560	50.5	6270	5.65	36	63	54.8

	Rushing				
Year Team	Att	Yds	Avg	TD	Fum
1964 Phi	16	134	8.4	1	1
1965 Phi	9	104	11.6	0	0
1966 Phi	25	195	7.8	2	2
1967 ChiB	67	279	4.2	3	4
1968 ChiB	28	104	3.7	2	1
1969 ChiB	22	62	2.8	1	2
1970 ChiB	42	136	3.2	2	6
1971 ChiB	5	5	1.0	0	1
1974 GB	3	7	2.3	1	0
NFL Total	217	1026	4.7	12	17

MERL CONDIT Condit, Merlyn Edwin 5'11", 187 **HB-DB**
(The Magician) *Col:* Carnegie Mellon *HS:* Charleston [WV]
B: 3/21/1917, Belle Vernon, PA D: 10/18/1992, Wexford, PA
Drafted: 1940 Round 2 Cle
1940 Pit: Pass 15-2 13.3%, 33 2.20 2 Int; Punt 12-453 37.8. **1941** Bkn: Pass 6-1 16.7%, 3 0.50 1 Int; Punt 1-38 38.0; Scor 41, 2-11 18.2% FG, 11-12 91.7% XK. **1942** Bkn: Pass 17-5 29.4%, 27 1.59 2 Int; Punt 7-315 45.0; Scor 37, 3-6 50.0% FG, 10-10 100.0% XK. **1943** Bkn: Pass 6-0, 1 Int; Punt 19-725 38.2; Scor 12, 0-3 FG. **1945** Was: Scor 19, 1-1 100.0% XK. **1946** Pit: Pass 4-2 50.0%, 89 22.25 1 TD; Scor 10, 0-2 FG, 4-4 100.0% XK. **Total:** Pass 48-10 20.8%, 152 3.17 1 TD 6 Int; Punt 39-1531 39.3; Scor 125, 5-22 22.7% FG, 26-27 96.3% XK.

		Rushing				Receiving			
Year Team	G	Att	Yds	Avg	TD	Rec	Yds	Avg	TD
1940 Pit	10	52	205	3.9	0	4	30	7.5	1
1941 Bkn	11	91	357	3.9	4	5	32	6.4	0
1942 Bkn	11	129	647	5.0	2	9	111	12.3	0
1943 Bkn	8	67	190	2.8	1	7	101	14.4	1
1945 Was	5	36	173	4.8	3	3	16	5.3	0
1946 Pit	9	46	141	3.1	1	4	33	8.3	0
NFL Total	54	421	1713	4.1	11	32	323	10.1	2

	Punt Returns				Kickoff Returns			
Year Team	Ret	Yds	Avg	TD	Ret	Yds	Avg	TD
1941 Bkn	5	44	8.8	0	8	178	22.3	0
1942 Bkn	20	196	9.8	0	8	172	21.5	0
1943 Bkn	6	47	7.8	0	6	178	29.7	0
1946 Pit	3	31	10.3	0	3	19	6.3	0
NFL Total	34	318	9.4	0	25	547	21.9	0

	Interceptions				Tot
Year Team	Int	Yds	TD	Fum	TD
1940 Pit	2	7	0	0	1
1941 Bkn	3	15	0	0	4
1942 Bkn	6	**117**	**1**	0	3
1943 Bkn	1	0	0	0	2
1945 Was	0	0	0	1	3
1946 Pit	0	0	0	6	1
NFL Total	12	139	1	7	14

TOM CONDON Condon, Thomas Joseph 6'3", 255 **OG**
Col: Boston College *HS:* Notre Dame [West Haven, CT]
B: 10/26/1952, Derby, CT *Drafted:* 1974 Round 10 KC
1974 KC: 14 G. **1975** KC: 9 G. **1976** KC: 14 G. **1977** KC: 14 G. **1978** KC: 16 G. **1979** KC: 16 G. **1980** KC: 16 G. **1981** KC: 16 G. **1982** KC: 7 G. **1983** KC: 9 G. **1984** KC: 16 G. **1985** NE: 1 G. **Total:** 148 G.

GLEN CONDREN Condren, Glen Paige 6'4", 251 **DT-DE**
Col: Oklahoma *HS:* Muldrow [OK] B: 6/10/1942, Fort Smith, AR
Drafted: 1964 Round 11 NYG
1965 NYG: 8 G. **1966** NYG: 13 G. **1967** NYG: 13 G. **1969** Atl: 9 G. **1970** Atl: 14 G. **1971** Atl: 12 G. **1972** Atl: 10 G. **Total:** 79 G.

FRED CONE Cone, Fred 5'11", 199 **FB-K**
Col: Clemson *HS:* Moore Acad. [Pineapple, AL] B: 6/21/1926, Pineapple, AL *Drafted:* 1951 Round 3 GB
1951 GB: KR 1-20 20.0; Punt 1-47 47.0. **1952** GB: KR 2-23 11.5. **1954** GB: KR 1-22 22.0. **1957** GB: KR 5-83 16.6. **Total:** KR 9-148 16.4; Punt 1-47 47.0.

		Rushing				Receiving			
Year Team	G	Att	Yds	Avg	TD	Rec	Yds	Avg	TD
1951 GB	12	56	190	3.4	1	28	315	11.3	0
1952 GB	10	70	276	3.9	2	8	98	12.3	1
1953 GB	12	92	301	3.3	5	18	165	9.2	1
1954 GB	12	15	18	1.2	0	4	19	4.8	0
1955 GB	12	12	25	2.1	0	1	7	7.0	0
1956 GB	12	49	211	4.3	2	12	218	18.2	2
1957 GB	12	53	135	2.5	2	4	30	7.5	0
1960 Dal	12	0	0	—	0	0	0	—	0
NFL Total	94	347	1156	3.3	12	75	852	11.4	4

	Scoring								Tot
Year Team	Pts	FG	FGA	FG%	XK	XKA	XK%	Fum	TD
1951 GB	50	5	7	71.4	29	35	82.9	1	1
1952 GB	53	1	1	100.0	32	34	94.1	6	3
1953 GB	74	5	16	31.3	23	25	92.0	2	6
1954 GB	54	9	16	56.3	27	29	93.1	1	0
1955 GB	78	**16**	**24**	66.7	30	30	100.0	0	0
1956 GB	72	5	8	62.5	33	36	91.7	2	4
1957 GB	74	12	17	70.6	26	26	100.0	2	2
1960 Dal	39	6	13	46.2	21	23	91.3	0	0
NFL Total	494	59	102	57.8	221	238	92.9	14	16

CHARLIE CONERLY Conerly, Charles Albert Jr. 6'1", 185 **QB**
(Chuck) *Col:* Mississippi *HS:* Clarksdale [MS] B: 9/19/1921, Clarksdale, MS D: 2/13/1996, Memphis, TN *Drafted:* 1945 Round 11 Was
1948 NYG: KR 4-72 18.0. **1952** NYG: Scor 2, 1-1 100.0% XK, 1 1XP. **1954** NYG: Scor 7, 1-1 100.0% XK. **1955** NYG: Scor 1, 1-1 100.0% XK. **Total:** KR 4-72 18.0; Scor 64, 3-3 100.0% XK, 1 1XP.

		Passing							
Year Team	G	Att	Comp	Comp%	Yds	YPA	TD	Int	Rating
1948 NYG	12	299	162	54.2	2175	7.27	22	13	84.0
1949 NYG	12	305	152	49.8	2138	7.01	17	20	64.1
1950 NYG	11	132	56	42.4	1000	7.58	8	**7**	67.1
1951 NYG	12	189	93	49.2	1277	6.76	10	22	49.3
1952 NYG	11	169	82	48.5	1090	6.45	13	10	70.4
1953 NYG	12	303	143	47.2	1711	5.65	13	25	44.9
1954 NYG	10	210	103	49.0	1439	6.85	17	11	76.7
1955 NYG	12	202	98	48.5	1310	6.49	13	13	64.2
1956 NYG	12	174	90	51.7	1143	6.57	10	**7**	75.0
1957 NYG	12	232	128	55.2	1712	7.38	11	11	74.9
1958 NYG	10	184	88	47.8	1199	6.52	10	9	66.8
1959 NYG	10	194	113	58.2	1706	**8.79**	14	**4**	102.7
1960 NYG	12	134	66	49.3	954	7.12	8	7	70.9
1961 NYG	13	106	44	41.5	634	5.98	7	8	52.2
NFL Total	161	2833	1418	50.1	19488	6.88	173	167	68.2

	Rushing				Punting			
Year Team	Att	Yds	Avg	TD	Punts	Yds	Avg	Fum
1948 NYG	40	160	4.0	5	17	678	39.9	5
1949 NYG	23	42	1.8	0	2	70	35.0	4
1950 NYG	23	22	1.0	1	20	760	38.0	2
1951 NYG	17	65	3.8	1	72	2856	39.7	4
1952 NYG	27	115	4.3	0	0	0	—	1
1953 NYG	24	91	3.8	0	0	0	—	5
1954 NYG	24	107	4.5	1	0	0	—	3
1955 NYG	12	10	0.8	0	0	0	—	4
1956 NYG	11	11	1.0	0	1	33	33.0	0
1957 NYG	15	24	1.6	1	0	0	—	11
1958 NYG	12	-17	-1.4	0	0	0	—	3
1959 NYG	15	38	2.5	1	0	0	—	2
1960 NYG	14	1	0.1	0	18	665	36.9	6
1961 NYG	13	16	1.2	0	0	0	—	4
NFL Total	270	685	2.5	10	130	5062	38.9	54

MEL CONGER Conger, Melvin Reese 6'2", 225 **DE-OE**
Col: Georgia *HS:* Boys [Atlanta, GA] B: 6/4/1919, Atlanta, GA
D: 7/21/1996, Atlanta, GA
AAFC **1946** NY-A: 7 G; Rec 3-61 20.3. **1947** BknA: 2 G. **Total:** 9 G; Rec 3-61 20.3.

LARRY CONJAR Conjar, Lawrence Wayne 6′1″, 214 **RB**
Col: Notre Dame *HS:* Bishop McDevitt [Harrisburg, PA] B: 10/28/1945, Harrisburgh, PA *Drafted:* 1967 Round 2 Cle
1967 Cle: Rec 6-68 11.3. **1968** Phi: Scor **1** Saf. **Total:** Rec 6-68 11.3; Scor 1 Saf.

		Rushing				
Year Team	**G**	**Att**	**Yds**	**Avg**	**TD**	**Fum**
1967 Cle	12	20	78	3.9	0	3
1968 Phi	14	8	21	2.6	0	0
1969 Bal	6	1	0	0.0	0	0
1970 Bal	3	1	3	3.0	0	0
NFL Total	35	30	102	3.4	0	3

CARY CONKLIN Conklin, Cary Lee 6′4″, 220 **QB**
Col: Washington *HS:* Eisenhower [Yakima, WA] B: 2/29/1968, Yakima, WA *Drafted:* 1990 Round 4 Was
1992 Was: Rush 3-(-4) -1.3. **1993** Was: Rush 2-(-2) -1.0. **Total:** Rush 5-(-6) -1.2.

		Passing								
Year Team	**G**	**Att**	**Comp**	**Comp%**	**Yds**	**YPA**	**TD**	**Int**	**Rating**	**Fum**
1992 Was	1	2	2	100.0	16	8.00	1	0	139.6	0
1993 Was	4	87	46	52.9	496	5.70	4	3	70.9	1
1995 SF	2	12	4	33.3	48	4.00	0	0	46.5	0
NFL Total	7	101	52	51.5	560	5.54	5	3	72.2	1

BILL CONKRIGHT Conkright, William Franklin 6′1″, 203 **C-LB-OE-DE**
(Red) *Col:* Oklahoma *HS:* Central [Tulsa, OK] B: 4/17/1914, Beggs, OK D: 10/27/1980, Houston, TX *Drafted:* 1937 Round 5 ChiB
1937 ChiB: 8 G. **1938** ChiB: 9 G; Rec 1-2 2.0 1 TD; 6 Pt. **1939** Cle: 11 G. **1940** Cle: 2 G; Int 1-0. **1941** Cle: 11 G; Int 1-0. **1942** Cle: 11 G; Int 2-10. **1943** Bkn-Was: 9 G; Int 1-12. Bkn: 7 G; Int 1-12. Was: 2 G. **1944** Cle: 1 G. **Total:** 62 G; Rec 1-2 2.0 1 TD; Int 5-22; 6 Pt.

SHANE CONLAN Conlan, Shane Patrick 6′3″, 235 **LB**
Col: Penn State *HS:* Frewsburg [NY] B: 3/4/1964, Frewsburg, NY *Drafted:* 1987 Round 1 Buf
1987 Buf: 12 G; 0.5 Sac. **1988** Buf: 13 G; Int 1-0; 1.5 Sac. **1989** Buf: 10 G; Int 1-0; 1 Sac. **1990** Buf: 16 G; 1 Sac. **1991** Buf: 16 G. **1992** Buf: 13 G; Int 1-7; 2 Sac. **1993** LARm: 12 G; Int 1-28. **1994** LARm: 15 G; 1 Sac. **1995** StL: 13 G; Int 1-1. **Total:** 120 G; Int 5-36; 7 Sac.

GERRY CONLEE Conlee, Gerry Russell 5′11″, 203 **C-LB**
Col: St. Mary's (Cal.) *HS:* Chico [CA] B: 8/22/1914, Porterville, CA
AAFC **1946** SF-A: 10 G. **1947** SF-A: 13 G; PR 1-1 1.0. **Total:** 23 G; PR 1-1 1.0.

NFL **1938** Cle: 8 G. **1943** Det: 10 G; KR 1-15 15.0; Int 1-2. **Total:** 18 G; KR 1-15 15.0; Int 1-2.

STEVEN CONLEY Conley, Donald Steven 6′5″, 235 **LB**
(Shinky) *Col:* Arkansas *HS:* Luther South [Chicago, IL] B: 1/18/1972, Chicago, IL *Drafted:* 1996 Round 3 Pit
1996 Pit: 2 G. **1997** Pit: 16 G; Int 1-(-3); 4 Sac. **1998** Ind-Pit: 3 G. Ind: 1 G. Pit: 2 G. **Total:** 21 G; Int 1-(-3); 4 Sac.

JOHN CONLEY Conley, John 6′1″, 220 **T-G**
Col: No College B: 1890 Deceased
1922 Col: 6 G. **1926** Col: 4 G. **Total:** 10 G.

STEVE CONLEY Conley, Stephen Craig 6′2″, 225 **LB-RB**
Col: Arizona Western Coll. (J.C.); Kansas *HS:* Arlington [Arlington Heights, IL] B: 3/9/1949, Chicago, IL *Drafted:* 1972 Round 7 Cin
1972 Cin-StL: 8 G; Rush 3-8 2.7. Cin: 1 G; Rush 3-8 2.7. StL: 7 G. **Total:** 8 G; Rush 3-8 2.7.

CHRIS CONLIN Conlin, Christopher Howard 6′4″, 290 **OG**
Col: Penn State *HS:* Bishop McDevitt [Wyncote, PA] B: 6/7/1965, Philadelphia, PA *Drafted:* 1987 Round 5 Mia
1987 Mia: 3 G. **1990** Ind: 16 G. **1991** Ind: 8 G. **Total:** 27 G.

RAY CONLIN Conlin, Raymond Mario 6′2″, 258 **DT**
Col: Ohio State *HS:* Washington Twp. [Sewell, NJ] B: 6/7/1962, Philadelphia, PA
1987 Phi: 1 G.

TUFFY CONN Conn, George Washington 5′6″, 155 **WB-TB-FB**
Col: Oregon State *HS:* Pasadena [CA] B: 2/22/1895, Helron, IL D: 8/2/1973, Laguna Beach, CA
1920 Akr-Cle: 9 G. Akr: 3 G. Cle: 6 G. **Total:** 9 G.

DICK CONN Conn, Richard Raymond 6′0″, 185 **DB**
Col: Georgia *HS:* Lakeside [Atlanta, GA] B: 1/9/1951, Louisville, KY
1974 Pit: 12 G; PR 10-69 6.9; KR 1-34 34.0. **1975** NE: 3 G. **1976** NE: 13 G; KR 2-29 14.5. **1977** NE: 14 G. **1978** NE: 15 G; PR 1-2 2.0; KR 1-26 26.0; Int 1-24. **1979** NE: 1 G. **Total:** 58 G; PR 11-71 6.5; KR 4-89 22.3; Int 1-24.

BABE CONNAUGHTON Connaughton, Harry Aloysius 6′2″, 285 **G**
(Pud; Gunboat) *Col:* Georgetown *HS:* St. Joseph's Prep [Philadelphia, PA] B: 6/6/1905, Philadelphia, PA D: 8/11/1969, Braham, MN
1927 Fra: 16 G.

ALBERT CONNELL Connell, Gene Anthony 6′0″, 179 **WR**
Col: Texas A&M *HS:* Piper [Sunrise, FL] B: 5/13/1974, Fort Lauderdale, FL *Drafted:* 1997 Round 4 Was
1997 Was: Rush 1-3 3.0. **Total:** Rush 1-3 3.0.

		Receiving			
Year Team	**G**	**Rec**	**Yds**	**Avg**	**TD**
1997 Was	5	9	138	15.3	2
1998 Was	14	28	451	16.1	2
NFL Total	19	37	589	15.9	4

MIKE CONNELL Connell, Michael C 6′1″, 200 **P**
Col: Cincinnati *HS:* Sharon [PA] B: 3/15/1956, Sharon, PA *Drafted:* 1978 Round 10 SF
1981 Was: Rush 1-0. **Total:** Rush 1-0.

		Punting			
Year Team	**G**	**Punts**	**Yds**	**Avg**	**Fum**
1978 SF	16	96	3583	37.3	0
1980 Was	16	85	3331	39.2	0
1981 Was	16	73	2923	40.0	2
NFL Total	48	254	9837	38.7	2

WARD CONNELL Connell, Ward Thomas 5′10″, 173 **FB-WB-OE**
(Doc) *Col:* Notre Dame *HS:* Beloit [WI]; Notre Dame Prep [South Bend, IN] B: 5/1899, Menominee Falls, WI Deceased
1926 ChiC: 2 G.

BILL CONNELL Connell, William Joseph 181 **WB**
Col: No College *HS:* West [Rochester, NY] B: 10/19/1893, Rochester, NY D: 3/1/1976, Canandaigua, NY
1920 Roch: 1 G.

MIKE CONNELLY Connelly, Michael James 6′4″, 247 **C-OG-OT**
Col: Washington State; Utah State *HS:* Pasadena [CA] B: 10/16/1935, Monrovia, CA *Drafted:* 1960 Round 1 Buf
1960 Dal: 12 G. **1961** Dal: 14 G. **1962** Dal: 14 G. **1963** Dal: 14 G. **1964** Dal: 14 G. **1965** Dal: 10 G. **1966** Dal: 14 G. **1967** Dal: 14 G; 1 Fum. **1968** Pit: 14 G. **Total:** 120 G; 1 Fum.

CLYDE CONNER Conner, Clyde Raymond 6′2″, 193 **OE**
Col: Coll. of San Mateo CA (J.C.); U. of Pacific *HS:* South San Francisco [CA] B: 5/18/1933, Tuttle, OK

		Receiving				
Year Team	**G**	**Rec**	**Yds**	**Avg**	**TD**	**Fum**
1956 SF	12	22	362	16.5	1	1
1957 SF	8	30	412	13.7	4	0
1958 SF	12	49	512	10.4	5	1
1959 SF	9	13	162	12.5	1	0
1960 SF	10	38	531	14.0	2	0
1961 SF	5	11	177	16.1	1	0
1962 SF	13	24	240	10.0	4	0
1963 SF	11	16	247	15.4	0	1
NFL Total	80	203	2643	13.0	18	3

DARION CONNER Conner, Darion 6′2″, 250 **LB**
Col: Jackson State *HS:* Noxubee Co. [Macon, MS] B: 9/28/1967, Macon, MS *Drafted:* 1990 Round 2 Atl
1990 Atl: 16 G; 2 Sac. **1991** Atl: 15 G; 1 Fum; 3.5 Sac. **1992** Atl: 16 G; 7 Sac. **1993** Atl: 14 G; 1.5 Sac. **1994** NO: 16 G; Int 1-56; 10.5 Sac. **1995** Car: 16 G; 7 Sac. **1996** Phi: 7 G. **1997** Phi: 14 G; 1.5 Sac. **Total:** 114 G; Int 1-56; 1 Fum; 33 Sac.

DAN CONNERS Conners, Daniel Joseph 6′2″, 230 **LB**
Col: Miami (Fla.) *HS:* St. Mary's [PA] B: 2/6/1941, St. Mary's, PA *Drafted:* 1964 Round 2 Oak
1964 Oak: KR 1-0. **1967** Oak: **1** Fum TD. **1969** Oak: **1** Fum TD. **Total:** KR 1-0; 2 Fum TD.

		Interceptions			Tot
Year Team	**G**	**Int**	**Yds**	**TD**	**TD**
1964 Oak	5	0	0	0	0
1965 Oak	14	0	0	0	0
1966 Oak	14	2	55	1	1
1967 Oak	14	3	42	1	2
1968 Oak	14	2	5	0	0
1969 Oak	14	1	75	1	2
1970 Oak	10	0	0	0	0
1971 Oak	14	3	36	0	0
1972 Oak	14	1	0	0	0
1973 Oak	14	0	0	0	0
1974 Oak	14	3	19	0	0
NFL Total	141	15	232	3	5

HARRY CONNOLLY Connolly, Harry William 5′11″, 190 **TB-DB**
(Mickey) *Col:* Boston College *HS:* Norwalk [CT] B: 7/16/1920, Norwalk, CT
AAFC **1946** BknA: 3 G; Pass 8-2 25.0%, 29 3.63 1 Int; Rush 8-18 2.3; PR 1-6 6.0; KR 2-41 20.5.

TED CONNOLLY Connolly, Theodore William 6'3", 240 **OG**
(Rollo) *Col:* Santa Clara; Tulsa *HS:* Piedmont [CA] B: 12/5/1931, Oakland, CA *Drafted:* 1954 Round 9 SF
1954 SF: 12 G. **1956** SF: 5 G. **1957** SF: 10 G. **1958** SF: 12 G; KR 1-0. **1959** SF: 12 G. **1960** SF: 4 G. **1961** SF: 14 G. **1962** SF: 13 G. **1963** Cle: 10 G. **Total:** 92 G; KR 1-0.

GEORGE CONNOR Connor, George Leo 6'3", 240 **OT-LB-DT-OG**
(Moose) *Col:* Holy Cross; Notre Dame *HS:* De La Salle Inst. [Chicago, IL] B: 1/21/1925, Chicago, IL *Drafted:* 1946 Round 1 NYG
HOF: 1975
1948 ChiB: 11 G; KR 1-5 5.0. **1949** ChiB: 12 G; Rec 3-51 17.0. **1950** ChiB: 11 G; Rec 1-21 21.0; KR 0-9; Int 1-8. **1951** ChiB: 12 G; KR 1-9 9.0; Int 2-21. **1952** ChiB: 12 G; Int 2-31. **1953** ChiB: 12 G; Rec 1-17 17.0; KR 1-21 21.0. **1954** ChiB: 8 G; KR 2-32 16.0; Int 1-6. **1955** ChiB: 12 G; Int 1-0; **1** Fum TD; 6 Pt. **Total:** 90 G; Rec 5-89 17.8; KR 5-76 15.2; Int 7-66; 1 Fum TD; 6 Pt.

DUTCH CONNOR Connor, Stafford Joseph 5'10", 190 **FB-WB**
(AKA Stanislaus Josef Kosczarek) *Col:* New Hampshire *HS:* Exeter [NH] B: 4/16/1894, Poland D: 11/24/1978, San Antonio, TX
1925 Prov: 3 G; Scor 2, 2 XK. **1926** Bkn: 1 G. **Total:** 4 G.

BILL CONNOR Connor, William Joseph 6'1", 240 **G-T**
Col: Rhode Island; Providence; Catholic *HS:* Bulkeley [New London, CT] B: 4/8/1899, Providence, RI D: 12/14/1980, Norwich, CT
1929 Bost: 7 G. **1930** Nwk: 1 G. **Total:** 8 G.

HAM CONNORS Connors, Hamilton C 190 **E**
Col: No College *HS:* East Rochester [NY] B: 2/22/1898, Pittsburgh, PA D: 2/27/1967, East Rochester, NY
1925 Roch: 1 G.

ZUEHL CONOLY Conoly, William Zuehl 6'0", 227 **G**
Col: Southwestern (Tex.); Texas B: 9/13/1920, San Antonio, TX
Drafted: 1943 Round 10 Phi
1946 ChiC: 9 G.

FRANK CONOVER Conover, Frank Jr. 6'5", 317 **DT**
Col: Syracuse *HS:* Manalapan [Englishtown, NJ] B: 4/6/1968, Manalapan, NJ *Drafted:* 1991 Round 8 Cle
1991 Cle: 4 G; 1 Sac.

SCOTT CONOVER Conover, Kelsey Scott 6'4", 285 **OG-OT**
Col: Purdue *HS:* Freehold [NJ] B: 9/27/1968, Neptune, NJ
Drafted: 1991 Round 5 Det
1991 Det: 16 G. **1992** Det: 15 G. **1993** Det: 1 G. **1994** Det: 11 G; Rec 1-1 1.0 1 TD; 6 Pt. **1995** Det: 14 G. **1996** Det: 10 G. **Total:** 67 G; Rec 1-1 1.0 1 TD; 6 Pt.

LARRY CONOVER Conover, Lamer S.G. 5'10", 190 **C**
(Atlantic City) *Col:* Penn State *HS:* Atlantic City [NJ] B: 3/1894, Atlantic City, NJ D: 8/4/1955, Atlantic City, NJ
1921 Can: 1 G. **1923** Can: 12 G; Scor 1, 1 XK. **1925** Cle: 11 G. **Total:** 24 G.

CHRIS CONRAD Conrad, Christopher Lee 6'6", 301 **OT**
Col: Fresno State *HS:* Brea-Olinda [Brea, CA] B: 5/27/1975, Fullerton, CA *Drafted:* 1998 Round 3 Pit
1998 Pit: 6 G.

J.R. CONRAD Conrad, James Robert 6'4", 300 **OG**
Col: Oklahoma *HS:* Fairland [OK] B: 2/2/1974, Fairland, OK
Drafted: 1996 Round 7 NE
1997 NYJ: 12 G.

MARTY CONRAD Conrad, Martin Henry 6'1", 240 **C-G-E**
(Pudge) *Col:* Kalamazoo *HS:* Hartford [MI] B: 11/30/1895 Deceased
1922 Tol: 8 G. **1923** Tol: 8 G. **1924** Ken: 3 G. **1925** Akr: 3 G. **Total:** 22 G.

BOBBY JOE CONRAD Conrad, Robert Joseph 6'2", 194 **WR-K**
Col: Penn State *HS:* Clifton [TX] B: 11/17/1935, Clifton, TX
Drafted: 1958 Round 5 NYG
1958 ChiC: Int 4-46; Scor 51, 6-17 35.3% FG, 33-35 94.3% XK. **1959** ChiC: Pass 3-2 66.7%, 82 27.33 1 TD 1 Int; Scor 84, 6-9 66.7% FG, 30-31 96.8% XK. **1960** StL: Scor 34, 2-5 40.0% FG, 28-29 96.6% XK. **1961** StL: Pass 1-1 100.0%, 5 5.00; Scor 22, 0-1 FG, 4-4 100.0% XK. **1962** StL: Scor 24, 0-1 FG. **Total:** Pass 4-3 75.0%, 87 21.75 1 TD 1 Int; Int 4-46; Scor 389, 14-33 42.4% FG, 95-99 96.0% XK.

		Rushing				Receiving			
Year Team	**G**	**Att**	**Yds**	**Avg**	**TD**	**Rec**	**Yds**	**Avg**	**TD**
1958 ChiC	12	0	0	—	0	0	0	—	0
1959 ChiC	12	74	328	4.4	2	14	142	10.1	3
1960 StL	12	23	91	4.0	0	7	103	14.7	0
1961 StL	14	20	22	1.1	0	30	499	16.6	2
1962 StL	14	0	0	—	0	62	954	15.4	4
1963 StL	14	1	0	0.0	0	**73**	967	13.2	10
1964 StL	14	0	0	—	0	61	780	12.8	6
1965 StL	14	0	0	—	0	58	909	15.7	5
1966 StL	14	0	0	—	0	34	388	11.4	2
1967 StL	14	0	0	—	0	47	637	13.6	2
1968 StL	14	0	0	—	0	32	449	14.0	4
1969 Dal	8	0	0	—	0	4	74	18.5	0
NFL Total	156	118	441	3.7	2	422	5902	14.0	38

	Punt Returns				Kickoff Returns					Tot
Year Team	**Ret**	**Yds**	**Avg**	**TD**	**Ret**	**Yds**	**Avg**	**TD**	**Fum**	**TD**
1958 ChiC	19	129	6.8	0	1	33	33.0	0	2	0
1959 ChiC	16	133	8.3	1	18	388	21.6	0	10	6
1960 StL	8	86	10.8	0	12	338	28.2	0	4	0
1961 StL	5	103	20.6	1	1	28	28.0	0	2	3
1962 StL	2	10	5.0	0	0	0	—	0	1	4
1963 StL	1	1	1.0	0	0	0	—	0	2	10
1964 StL	0	0	—	0	1	26	26.0	0	2	6
1965 StL	0	0	—	0	0	0	—	0	0	5
1966 StL	0	0	—	0	0	0	—	0	1	2
1967 StL	0	0	—	0	0	0	—	0	0	2
1968 StL	0	0	—	0	0	0	—	0	0	4
NFL Total	51	462	9.1	2	33	813	24.6	0	24	42

IRV CONSTANTINE Constantine, C. Irving 5'9", 200 **HB**
(Murphy) *Col:* Syracuse *HS:* Curtis [Staten Island, NY] B: 1/18/1907, New York, NY D: 5/14/1966, New Hyde Park, NY
1931 SI: 1 G.

ED CONTI Conti, Enio Edward 5'11", 204 **G**
Col: Arkansas; Bucknell *HS:* New Utrecht [Brooklyn, NY]
B: 2/15/1913, Naples, Italy
1941 Phi: 9 G; Rush 1-(-1) -1.0. **1942** Phi: 11 G. **1943** PhPt: 10 G; Int 1-0. **1944** Phi: 8 G. **1945** Phi: 2 G. **Total:** 40 G; Rush 1-(-1) -1.0; Int 1-0.

JOHN CONTOULIS Contoulis, John James 6'5", 260 **DT**
Col: Connecticut *HS:* New London [CT] B: 10/9/1939, New London, CT *Drafted:* 1962 Round 16 Min
1964 NYG: 12 G.

BILL CONTZ Contz, Julius William 6'5", 268 **OT**
Col: Penn State *HS:* Belle Vernon [PA] B: 12/5/1961, Belle Veron, PA
Drafted: 1983 Round 5 Cle
1983 Cle: 16 G; KR 1-3 3.0. **1984** Cle: 15 G; KR 1-10 10.0. **1985** Cle: 4 G. **1986** Cle-NO: 14 G. Cle: 1 G. NO: 13 G. **1987** NO: 3 G. **1988** NO: 11 G. **Total:** 63 G; KR 2-13 6.5.

BRETT CONWAY Conway, Brett Alan 6'2", 192 **K**
Col: Penn State *HS:* Parkview [Lilburn, GA] B: 3/8/1975, Atlanta, GA
Drafted: 1997 Round 3 GB
1998 Was: 6 G.

CURTIS CONWAY Conway, Curtis LaMont 6'0", 190 **WR**
Col: El Camino Coll. CA (J.C.); USC *HS:* Hawthorne [CA]
B: 3/13/1971, Los Angeles, CA *Drafted:* 1993 Round 1 ChiB
1994 ChiB: Pass 1-1 100.0%, 23 23.00 1 TD; PR 8-63 7.9; Scor 1 2XP. **1995** ChiB: Pass 1-0. **1996** ChiB: Pass 1-1 100.0%, 33 33.00 1 TD. **1997** ChiB: Pass 1-0. **1998** ChiB: Pass 1-0. **Total:** Pass 5-2 40.0%, 56 11.20 2 TD; PR 8-63 7.9; Scor 1 2XP.

		Rushing				Receiving			
Year Team	**G**	**Att**	**Yds**	**Avg**	**TD**	**Rec**	**Yds**	**Avg**	**TD**
1993 ChiB	16	5	44	8.8	0	19	231	12.2	2
1994 ChiB	13	6	31	5.2	0	39	546	14.0	2
1995 ChiB	16	5	77	15.4	0	62	1037	16.7	12
1996 ChiB	16	8	50	6.3	0	81	1049	13.0	7
1997 ChiB	7	3	17	5.7	0	30	476	15.9	1
1998 ChiB	15	5	48	9.6	0	54	733	13.6	3
NFL Total	83	32	267	8.3	0	285	4072	14.3	27

	Kickoff Returns				
Year Team	**Ret**	**Yds**	**Avg**	**TD**	**Fum**
1993 ChiB	21	450	21.4	0	1
1994 ChiB	10	228	22.8	0	2
1996 ChiB	0	0	—	0	1
1998 ChiB	0	0	—	0	1
NFL Total	31	678	21.9	0	5

DAVE CONWAY Conway, David Alexander Jr. 6'0", 195 **K**
Col: Texas *HS:* Robert E. Lee [Baytown, TX] B: 1/6/1945, Baytown, TX
Drafted: 1967 Round 7 SD
1971 GB: 1 G; Scor 5, 0-1 FG, 5-5 100.0% XK.

ERNIE CONWELL Conwell, Ernest Harold 6'1", 265 **TE**
Col: Washington *HS:* Kentwood [Kent, WA] B: 8/17/1972, Renton, WA
Drafted: 1996 Round 2 StL

		Receiving			
Year Team	**G**	**Rec**	**Yds**	**Avg**	**TD**
1996 StL	10	15	164	10.9	0
1997 StL	16	38	404	10.6	4
1998 StL	7	15	105	7.0	0
NFL Total	33	68	673	9.9	4

JOE CONWELL Conwell, Joseph Stanislaus 6'5", 275 **OT**
Col: North Carolina *HS:* Lower Merion [Ardmore, PA] B: 2/24/1961, Philadelphia, PA *Drafted:* 1984 Supplemental Round 2 SF
1986 Phi: 16 G. **1987** Phi: 12 G. **Total:** 28 G.

JIMMY CONZELMAN Conzelman, James Good 6'0", 175 **BB-TB-HB-OE**
Col: Washington-St. Louis *HS:* McKinley [St. Louis, MO] B: 3/6/1898, St. Louis, MO D: 7/31/1970, St. Louis, MO *HOF:* 1964
1920 Sta: 11 G. **1921** RI: 7 G; Pass 2 TD; Rush 1 TD; Scor 15, 1 FG; 1 Fum TD; Tot TD 2. **1922** RI-Mil: 10 G; Pass **3** TD; Rush **7** TD; Scor 48, 2 FG; Tot TD **7**. RI: 7 G; Pass 2 TD; Rush 7 TD; Scor 48, 2 FG. Mil: 3 G; Pass 1 TD. **1923** Mil: 13 G; Pass 2 TD; Rush 3 TD; Rec 1 TD; Scor 26, 2 XK; Tot TD 4. **1924** Mil: 13 G; Pass 3 TD; Int **1** TD; 6 Pt. **1925** Det: 12 G; Rec 3 TD; 18 Pt. **1926** Det: 12 G; Rush 1 TD; Rec 1 TD; Scor 13, 1 XK; Tot TD 2. **1927** Prov: 14 G; Rush 1 TD; Rec 3 TD; Tot TD 4; 24 Pt. **1928** Prov: 4 G; Rec 2 TD; Scor **1** 1XP; 13 Pt. **1929** Prov: 6 G; Rec 1 TD; 6 Pt. **Total:** 102 G; Pass 10 TD; Rush 13 TD; Rec 11 TD; Int 1 TD; Scor 169, 3 FG, 3 XK, 1 1XP; 1 Fum TD; Tot TD 26.

ANTHONY COOK Cook, Anthony Andrew 6'3", 295 **DE-DT**
Col: South Carolina State *HS:* Marlboro Co. [Bennettsville, SC] B: 5/30/1972, Bennettsville, SC *Drafted:* 1995 Round 2 Hou
1995 Hou: 10 G; Scor **1** Saf; 2 Pt; 4.5 Sac. **1996** Hou: 12 G; 7.5 Sac. **1997** Ten: 16 G. **1998** Ten: 13 G; 2 Sac. **Total:** 51 G; Scor 1 Saf; 2 Pt; 14 Sac.

CHARLES COOK Cook, Charles McKinley 6'3", 255 **DE**
Col: Miami (Fla.) *HS:* F.W. Buchholz [Gainesville, FL] B: 5/13/1959, Gainesville, FL
1983 NYG: 4 G.

CLAIR COOK Cook, Clair 5'9", 170 **WB**
Col: No College *HS:* Muskegon [MI]
1928 Day: 4 G.

DAVE COOK Cook, David Fouts 6'2", 203 **DB-WB-FB**
Col: Illinois *HS:* Soldan [St. Louis, MO] B: 1/1/1912, Elgin, IL D: 12/19/1949, St. Louis, MO
1934 ChiC: Rec 2-9 4.5; Scor 4, 1 FG, 1 XK. **1935** ChiC: Pass 1-1 100.0%, 7 7.00. **1936** ChiC-Bkn: Rec 1-2 2.0. ChiC: Rec 1-2 2.0. **Total:** Pass 1-1 100.0%, 7 7.00; Rec 3-11 3.7; Scor 10, 1 FG, 1 XK.

		Rushing			
Year Team	**G**	**Att**	**Yds**	**Avg**	**TD**
1934 ChiC	9	23	112	4.9	0
1935 ChiC	10	31	121	3.9	1
1936 ChiC-Bkn	5	10	24	2.4	0
1936 ChiC	2	3	15	5.0	0
1936 Bkn	3	7	9	1.3	0
NFL Total	24	64	257	4.0	1

ED COOK Cook, Edward Joseph 6'2", 245 **OT-OG**
(Hank) *Col:* Notre Dame *HS:* Southeast Catholic [Philadelphia, PA] B: 6/29/1932, Philadelphia, PA
1958 ChiC: 8 G. **1959** ChiC: 12 G. **1960** StL: 11 G. **1961** StL: 14 G. **1962** StL: 7 G. **1963** StL: 13 G. **1964** StL: 14 G. **1965** StL: 14 G. **1966** Atl: 14 G. **1967** Atl: 4 G. **Total:** 111 G.

GENE COOK Cook, Eugene 6'3", 215 **OE**
Col: Toledo *HS:* West Tech [Cleveland, OH] B: 1/11/1934, Greenfield, TN
1959 Det: 1 G; Rec 1-43 43.0.

FRED COOK Cook, Frederick Harrison III 6'4", 244 **DE**
Col: Southern Mississippi *HS:* Our Lady of Victory [Pascagoula, MS] B: 4/15/1952, Pascagoula, MS *Drafted:* 1974 Round 2 Bal
1974 Bal: 14 G. **1975** Bal: 14 G; Int 1-8; **1** Fum TD; 6 Pt. **1976** Bal: 14 G; Int 1-1. **1977** Bal: 14 G. **1978** Bal: 16 G. **1979** Bal: 16 G. **1980** Bal: 16 G. **Total:** 104 G; Int 2-9; 1 Fum TD; 6 Pt.

GREG COOK Cook, Gregory Lynn 6'4", 220 **QB**
(The Blond Bomber) *Col:* Cincinnati *HS:* Chillicothe [OH] B: 11/20/1946, Dayton, OH *Drafted:* 1969 Round 1 Cin

		Passing							
Year Team	**G**	**Att**	**Comp**	**Comp%**	**Yds**	**YPA**	**TD**	**Int**	**Rating**
1969 Cin	11	197	106	53.8	1854	**9.41**	15	11	88.3
1973 Cin	1	3	1	33.3	11	3.67	0	0	45.1
NFL Total	12	200	107	53.5	1865	9.33	15	11	87.6

	Rushing				
Year Team	**Att**	**Yds**	**Avg**	**TD**	**Fum**
1969 Cin	25	148	5.9	1	**10**
NFL Total	25	148	5.9	1	10

JAMES COOK Cook, Jim C 6'3", 220 **G**
Col: Notre Dame *HS:* Green Bay East [WI] B: 11/27/1888, Green Bay, WI D: 8/21/1979, Green Bay, WI
1921 GB: 2 G.

KELLY COOK Cook, Kelly Edward 5'11", 225 **RB**
Col: Oklahoma State *HS:* Midwest City [OK] B: 8/20/1962, Cushing, OK
1987 GB: 11 G; Rush 2-3 1.5; KR 10-147 14.7.

LEON COOK Cook, Leon Spencer 6'0", 245 **T**
Col: Northwestern *HS:* Enid [OK] B: 3/27/1920, Enid, OK D: 5/1983, Minneapolis, MN
1942 Phi: 2 G.

MARV COOK Cook, Marvin Eugene 6'4", 234 **TE**
Col: Iowa *HS:* West Branch [IA] B: 2/24/1966, Iowa City, IA
Drafted: 1989 Round 3 NE
1993 NE: KR 1-8 8.0. **Total:** KR 1-8 8.0.

		Receiving				
Year Team	**G**	**Rec**	**Yds**	**Avg**	**TD**	**Fum**
1989 NE	16	3	13	4.3	0	0
1990 NE	16	51	455	8.9	5	2
1991 NE	16	82	808	9.9	3	2
1992 NE	16	52	413	7.9	2	3
1993 NE	16	22	154	7.0	1	1
1994 ChiB	16	21	212	10.1	1	0
1995 StL	16	26	135	5.2	1	1
NFL Total	112	257	2190	8.5	13	9

TED COOK Cook, Theodore Walter 6'2", 195 **OE-DB**
Col: Alabama *HS:* Woodlawn [AL]; West End HS [AL] B: 2/6/1922, Birmingham, AL D: 5/2/1990, Birmingham, AL
1947 Det: PR 1-10 10.0; KR 2-14 7.0. **1948** GB: PR 2-18 9.0. **1949** GB: KR 1-7 7.0. **Total:** PR 3-28 9.3; KR 3-21 7.0.

		Receiving				Interceptions			
Year Team	**G**	**Rec**	**Yds**	**Avg**	**TD**	**Int**	**Yds**	**TD**	**Fum**
1947 Det	11	7	111	15.9	1	2	0	0	0
1948 GB	12	13	156	12.0	0	6	81	0	1
1949 GB	11	25	442	17.7	1	5	52	0	0
1950 GB	12	16	182	11.4	3	0	0	0	1
NFL Total	46	61	891	14.6	5	13	133	0	2

TOI COOK Cook, Toi Fitzgerald 5'11", 188 **DB**
Col: Stanford *HS:* Montclair Prep [Canoga Park, CA] B: 12/3/1964, Chicago, IL *Drafted:* 1987 Round 8 NO
1987 NO: PR 1-3 3.0. **1989** NO: Rec 1-8 8.0; 1 Sac. **1990** NO: 1 Sac. **1992** NO: 1 Sac. **1993** NO: 1 Sac. **1996** Car: 4 Sac. **1997** Car: 1 Sac. **Total:** Rec 1-8 8.0; PR 1-3 3.0; 9 Sac.

		Interceptions			
Year Team	**G**	**Int**	**Yds**	**TD**	**Fum**
1987 NO	7	0	0	0	0
1988 NO	16	1	0	0	0
1989 NO	16	3	81	1	1
1990 NO	16	2	55	0	0
1991 NO	14	3	54	0	0
1992 NO	16	6	90	1	0
1993 NO	16	1	0	0	0
1994 SF	16	1	18	0	0
1995 SF	2	0	0	0	0
1996 Car	15	3	28	0	0
1997 Car	16	0	0	0	0
NFL Total	150	20	326	2	1

ED COOKE Cooke, Edward Grey 6'4", 250 **DE**
Col: Maryland *HS:* Granby [Norfolk, VA] B: 5/3/1935, Pilot Mountain, NC *Drafted:* 1958 Round 3 ChiB
1958 ChiB-Phi: 10 G; 1 Fum. ChiB: 3 G; 1 Fum. Phi: 7 G. **1959** Bal: 4 G. **1960** NYT: 11 G. **1961** NYT: 14 G; Int 3-46. **1962** NYT: 14 G; Int 1-20; 6 Pt. **1963** NYJ: 9 G. **1964** Den: 14 G; **1** Fum TD; 6 Pt. **1965** Den: 14 G; Int 3-36. **1966** Mia: 14 G. **1967** Mia: 13 G. **Total:** 117 G; Int 7-102; 1 Fum TD; Tot TD 2; 12 Pt; 1 Fum.

BILL COOKE Cooke, William Morrill 6'5", 249 **DT-DE-OT**
Col: Connecticut; Massachusetts *HS:* Worcester Acad. [MA] B: 2/26/1951, Lowell, MA *Drafted:* 1975 Round 10 GB
1975 GB: 5 G. **1976** SF: 9 G. **1977** SF: 14 G. **1978** Sea-Det: 16 G. Sea: 4 G. Det: 12 G. **1979** Sea: 15 G. **1980** Sea: 16 G. **Total:** 75 G.

JOHNIE COOKS Cooks, Johnie Earl 6'4", 247 **LB**
Col: Mississippi State *HS:* Leland [MS] B: 11/23/1958, Leland, MS
Drafted: 1982 Round 1 Bal
1982 Bal: 9 G; 1.5 Sac. **1983** Bal: 16 G; Int 1-15; 1 Fum TD; 6 Pt; 1 Fum; 5 Sac. **1984** Ind: 16 G; 11.5 Sac. **1985** Ind: 16 G; Int 1-7; 5 Sac. **1986** Ind: 15 G; Int 1-1; 1 Sac. **1987** Ind: 10 G; Int 1-2; 1 Fum; 5 Sac. **1988** Ind-NYG: 14 G; 1 Sac. Ind: 1 G. NYG: 13 G; 1 Sac. **1989** NYG: 16 G; 1 Sac. **1990** NYG: 14 G; 1 Sac. **1991** Cle: 2 G. **Total:** 128 G; Int 4-25; 1 Fum TD; 6 Pt; 2 Fum; 32 Sac.

KERRY COOKS Cooks, Kerry George 5'11", 204 **DB**
Col: Iowa *HS:* Nimitz [Irving, TX] B: 3/28/1974, Dallas, TX
Drafted: 1998 Round 5 Min
1998 GB: 9 G.

RAYFORD COOKS Cooks, Rayford Earl 6′3″, 245 **DE**
Col: North Texas *HS:* L.G. Pinkston [Dallas, TX] B: 8/25/1962, Dallas, TX
1987 Hou: 10 G; 2 Sac.

TERRENCE COOKS Cooks, Terrence Kenneth 6′0″, 230 **LB**
Col: Nicholls State *HS:* Assumption [Napoleonville, LA] B: 10/25/1966, New Orleans, LA
1989 NE: 3 G.

BOB COOLBAUGH Coolbaugh, Irwin Robert 6′4″, 200 **WR**
Col: Richmond *HS:* Franklin Monroe [Dallas, PA] B: 7/5/1939, Kingston, PA *Drafted:* 1961 Round 15 Oak
1961 Oak: KR 1-15 15.0; Scor 1 2XP.

		Receiving			
Year Team	**G**	**Rec**	**Yds**	**Avg**	**TD**
1961 Oak	14	32	435	13.6	4

LARRY COOMBS Coombs, Lawrence Mahlon 6′4″, 260 **OG-C**
Col: Idaho *HS:* Timberline [Lacey, WA] B: 8/9/1957, Arcata, CA
1980 NO: 1 G.

TOM COOMBS Coombs, Thomas Barton 6′3″, 236 **TE**
Col: Puget Sound; Idaho *HS:* Capitol [Olympia, WA] B: 5/31/1959, Eureka, CA *Drafted:* 1982 Round 7 NYJ
1982 NYJ: 3 G. **1983** NYJ: 12 G; Rec 1-1 1.0. **Total:** 15 G; Rec 1-1 1.0.

JOE COOMER Coomer, Joe David 6′6″, 281 **T-G**
Col: Austin *HS:* Greenville [TX] B: 9/11/1918, Greenville, TX
D: 10/18/1979, Whitehouse, TX
1941 Pit: 10 G. **1945** Pit: 9 G; Scor 0-1 FG. **1946** Pit: 7 G. **1947** ChiC: 12 G; KR 1-0; 1 Fum. **1948** ChiC: 12 G. **1949** ChiC: 12 G. **Total:** 62 G; KR 1-0; Scor 0-1 FG; 1 Fum.

TY COON Coon, Edward Howard Jr. 6′0″, 215 **G**
Col: North Carolina State B: 7/26/1915, White Plains, NY D: 1/9/1992, Watertown, CT *Drafted:* 1940 Round 7 Bkn
1940 Bkn: 9 G.

MARK COONEY Cooney, Mark Joseph 6′4″, 230 **LB**
Col: Colorado *HS:* St. Anthony Seminary [San Antonio, TX]
B: 6/2/1951, Denver, CO *Drafted:* 1974 Round 16 GB
1974 GB: 13 G.

ROBERT COONS Coons, Robert Allan 6′5″, 249 **TE**
(Bob) *Col:* Fullerton Coll. CA (J.C.); Pittsburgh *HS:* El Dorado [Placentia, CA] B: 9/18/1969, Brea, CA
1995 Buf: 4 G; Rec 3-28 9.3. **1996** Buf: 16 G; Rec 1-12 12.0. **1997** Buf: 12 G; KR 1-12 12.0. **Total:** 32 G; Rec 4-40 10.0; KR 1-12 12.0.

ADRIAN COOPER Cooper, Adrian 6′5″, 268 **TE**
Col: Oklahoma *HS:* South [Denver, CO] B: 4/27/1968, Denver, CO
Drafted: 1991 Round 4 Pit
1992 Pit: KR 1-8 8.0. **1993** Pit: KR 1-2 2.0. **Total:** KR 2-10 5.0.

		Receiving				
Year Team	**G**	**Rec**	**Yds**	**Avg**	**TD**	**Fum**
1991 Pit	16	11	147	13.4	2	0
1992 Pit	16	16	197	12.3	3	1
1993 Pit	14	9	112	12.4	0	1
1994 Min	12	32	363	11.3	0	2
1995 Min	13	18	207	11.5	0	0
1996 SF	6	1	11	11.0	0	1
NFL Total	77	87	1037	11.9	5	5

LOUIS COOPER Cooper, Alexander Louis 6′2″, 240 **LB**
Col: Western Carolina *HS:* Marion [SC] B: 8/5/1963, Marion, SC
Drafted: 1985 Round 11 Sea
1985 KC: 8 G. **1986** KC: 16 G; 4.5 Sac. **1987** KC: 12 G; Int 1-0. **1988** KC: 11 G. **1989** KC: 16 G; 1 Sac. **1990** KC: 16 G; 2 Sac. **1991** Mia: 12 G. **1993** Phi: 11 G. **Total:** 102 G; Int 1-0; 7.5 Sac.

BERT COOPER Cooper, Bertram Genard 6′1″, 242 **LB**
Col: Florida State *HS:* Florida [Tallahassee, FL] B: 8/24/1952, Tallahassee, FL *Drafted:* 1975 Round 12 NYJ
1976 TB: 12 G; KR 1-22 22.0.

EVAN COOPER Cooper, Evan 5′11″, 185 **DB**
Col: Michigan *HS:* Miami Killian [FL] B: 6/25/1962, Miami, FL
Drafted: 1984 Round 4 Phi
1985 Phi: 1 Sac. **1986** Phi: 1 Sac. **Total:** 2 Sac.

		Punt Returns				Kickoff Returns			
Year Team	**G**	**Ret**	**Yds**	**Avg**	**TD**	**Ret**	**Yds**	**Avg**	**TD**
1984 Phi	16	40	250	6.3	0	17	299	17.6	0
1985 Phi	16	43	364	8.5	0	3	32	10.7	0
1986 Phi	16	16	139	8.7	0	2	42	21.0	0
1987 Phi	12	0	0	—	0	5	86	17.2	0
1988 Atl	9	2	10	5.0	0	16	331	20.7	0
1989 Atl	16	0	0	—	0	0	0	—	0
NFL Total	85	101	763	7.6	0	43	790	18.4	0

	Interceptions			
Year Team	**Int**	**Yds**	**TD**	**Fum**
1985 Phi	2	13	0	1
1986 Phi	3	20	0	2
1987 Phi	2	0	0	1
1988 Atl	0	0	0	1
1989 Atl	4	54	0	0
NFL Total	11	87	0	5

GEORGE COOPER Cooper, George Junious 6′2″, 225 **LB**
Col: Michigan State *HS:* Northern [Detroit, MI] B: 12/24/1958, Detroit, MI
1987 SF: 10 G.

HAL COOPER Cooper, Harold W 5′10″, 207 **G**
Col: Detroit Mercy *HS:* Western [Detroit, MI] B: 1914 Deceased
1937 Det: 7 G.

JIM COOPER Cooper, James Albert 6′5″, 262 **OT-C-OG**
Col: Temple *HS:* Cardinal Dougherty [Philadelphia, PA] B: 9/28/1955, Philadelphia, PA *Drafted:* 1977 Round 6 Dal
1977 Dal: 14 G. **1978** Dal: 14 G. **1979** Dal: 15 G. **1980** Dal: 15 G. **1981** Dal: 16 G. **1982** Dal: 9 G. **1983** Dal: 16 G. **1984** Dal: 7 G. **1985** Dal: 15 G. **1986** Dal: 12 G. **Total:** 133 G.

JIM COOPER Cooper, James Paul 6′0″, 205 **C-LB**
Col: Texas Christian; North Texas *HS:* Colorado [Colorado City, TX]
B: 6/28/1924, Colorado City, TX
AAFC **1948** BknA: 1 G.

JOE COOPER Cooper, Joseph Donald 5′10″, 175 **K**
Col: California *HS:* Bullard [Fresno, CA] B: 10/30/1960, Fresno, CA
1984 Hou: 7 G; Rush 1-(-2) -2.0; Scor 46, 11-13 84.6% FG, 13-13 100.0% XK. **1986** NYG: 2 G; Scor 10, 2-4 50.0% FG, 4-4 100.0% XK. **Total:** 9 G; Rush 1-(-2) -2.0; Scor 56, 13-17 76.5% FG, 17-17 100.0% XK.

KEN COOPER Cooper, Kenneth Rousseau 6′1″, 205 **OG-DG**
Col: Vanderbilt *HS:* Lauderdale Co. [Rogersville, AL]; Morgan Prep [Petersburg, TN] B: 2/26/1923, Rogersville, AL *Drafted:* 1949 Round 15 GB
AAFC **1949** BalA: 12 G.

NFL **1950** Bal: 12 G.

EARL COOPER Cooper, Marion Earl 6′2″, 227 **RB-TE**
Col: Rice *HS:* Lincoln [Lexington, TX] B: 9/17/1957, Giddings, TX
Drafted: 1980 Round 1 SF
1983 SF: KR 3-45 15.0. **1984** SF: KR 1-0. **Total:** KR 4-45 11.3.

		Rushing				Receiving					Tot
Year Team	**G**	**Att**	**Yds**	**Avg**	**TD**	**Rec**	**Yds**	**Avg**	**TD**	**Fum**	**TD**
1980 SF	16	171	720	4.2	5	83	567	6.8	4	8	9
1981 SF	16	98	330	3.4	1	51	477	9.4	0	3	1
1982 SF	9	24	77	3.2	0	19	153	8.1	1	1	1
1983 SF	16	0	0	—	0	15	207	13.8	3	1	3
1984 SF	16	3	13	4.3	0	41	459	11.2	4	0	4
1985 SF	15	2	12	6.0	0	4	45	11.3	0	0	0
1986 LARd	5	0	0	—	0	0	0	—	0	0	0
NFL Total	93	298	1152	3.9	6	213	1908	9.0	12	13	18

MARK COOPER Cooper, Mark Samuel 6′5″, 270 **OT**
Col: Miami (Fla.) *HS:* Miami Killian [FL] B: 2/14/1960, Camden, NJ
Drafted: 1983 Round 2 Den
1983 Den: 10 G. **1984** Den: 15 G. **1985** Den: 15 G; Rec 1-13 13.0. **1986** Den: 8 G. **1987** Den-TB: 9 G. Den: 5 G. TB: 4 G. **1988** TB: 15 G. **1989** TB: 6 G. **Total:** 78 G; Rec 1-13 13.0.

NORM COOPER Cooper, Norman Tellons 6′4″, 210 **C-LB**
Col: Samford *HS:* Lauderdale Co. [Rogersville, AL] B: 8/8/1913, Rogersville, AL D: 12/26/1994, Birmingham, AL
1937 Bkn: 10 G. **1938** Bkn: 10 G. **Total:** 20 G.

REGGIE COOPER Cooper, Reginald John 6′2″, 214 **LB**
Col: Nebraska *HS:* Slidell [LA] B: 7/11/1968, Bogalusa, LA
1991 Dal: 2 G.

RICHARD COOPER Cooper, Richard Warren 6′5″, 290 **OT**
Col: Tennessee *HS:* Melrose [Memphis, TN] B: 11/1/1964, Memphis, TN
1990 NO: 2 G. **1991** NO: 15 G. **1992** NO: 16 G; Rec 0-20. **1993** NO: 16 G. **1994** NO: 14 G. **1995** NO: 14 G. **1996** Phi: 16 G. **1998** Phi: 15 G. **Total:** 108 G; Rec 0-20.

SAM COOPER Cooper, Samuel VanVoorhis 6′0″, 200 **T**
Col: Geneva *HS:* Mars [PA] B: 2/1/1909, Venetia, PA D: 8/22/1998, Green Tree, PA
1933 Pit: 1 G.

THURLOW COOPER Cooper, Sheldon Thurlow 6′5″, 228 **TE-DE**
Col: Maine *HS:* Cony [Augusta, ME]; Maine Central Inst. [Pittsfield, ME] B: 3/18/1933, Augusta, ME *Drafted:* 1956 Round 16 Cle
1960 NYT: KR 1-0; Scor 1 2XP. **1961** NYT: KR 1-0; Scor 24, 0-1 FG. **1962** NYT: KR 1-3 3.0; Scor **1** 2XP. **Total:** KR 3-3 1.0; Scor 52, 0-1 FG, 2 2XP.

		Receiving			
Year Team	G	Rec	Yds	Avg	TD
1960 NYT	13	9	161	17.9	3
1961 NYT	14	15	208	13.9	4
1962 NYT	14	12	122	10.2	1
NFL Total	41	36	491	13.6	8

BILL COOPER Cooper, William Albert 6′3″, 215 **FB-LB**
Col: Muskingum *HS:* New Philadelphia [OH] B: 7/12/1939, Carrollton, OH *Drafted:* 1961 Round 3 SF
1961 SF: 12 G; Rush 8-17 2.1 1 TD; KR 3-44 14.7; 6 Pt. **1962** SF: 10 G; Rush 2-(-2) -1.0; KR 1-17 17.0. **1963** SF: 14 G; KR 2-8 4.0; 1 Fum. **1964** SF: 2 G. **Total:** 38 G; Rush 10-15 1.5 1 TD; KR 6-69 11.5; 6 Pt; 1 Fum.

BUD COOPER Cooper, William Gordon 6′1″, 204 **TB-FB-DB**
Col: Penn State *HS:* Milton [PA] B: 4/14/1913, Buffalo, NY
1937 Cle: 5 G; Pass 5-2 40.0%, 21 4.20 1 Int; Rush 19-45 2.4; Rec 1-14 14.0.

FRANK COPE Cope, Francis Wallace 6′2″, 225 **T**
Col: Santa Clara *HS:* Hayward [CA] B: 11/19/1915, Anaconda, MT D: 10/8/1990, San Jose, CA
1938 NYG: 9 G. **1939** NYG: 11 G. **1940** NYG: 11 G. **1941** NYG: 11 G; 6 Pt. **1942** NYG: 11 G. **1943** NYG: 10 G. **1944** NYG: 10 G. **1945** NYG: 9 G. **1946** NYG: 11 G. **1947** NYG: 5 G. **Total:** 98 G; 6 Pt.

JIM COPE Cope, James Charles 6′1″, 235 **LB**
Col: Ohio State *HS:* South Allegheny [McKeesport, PA] B: 6/23/1953, Oil City, PA *Drafted:* 1975 Round 5 Cle
1976 Atl: 6 G.

ANTHONY COPELAND Copeland, Anthony Lamar 6′2″, 250 **LB**
Col: Wichita State; Louisville *HS:* Walter F. George [Atlanta, GA] B: 4/14/1963
1987 Was: 3 G.

DANNY COPELAND Copeland, Danny Lamar 6′2″, 210 **DB**
Col: Eastern Kentucky *HS:* Central [Thomasville, GA] B: 1/24/1966, Camilla, GA *Drafted:* 1988 Round 9 Cle
1991 Was: Int 1-0. **1992** Was: 1 Fum TD; 1 Sac. **1993** Was: Int 1-0. **Total:** Int 2-0; 1 Fum TD; 1 Sac.

		Kickoff Returns				
Year Team	G	Ret	Yds	Avg	TD	Fum
1989 KC	16	26	466	17.9	0	1
1990 KC	14	0	0	—	0	0
1991 Was	16	0	0	—	0	0
1992 Was	13	0	0	—	0	0
1993 Was	14	0	0	—	0	0
NFL Total	73	26	466	17.9	0	1

HORACE COPELAND Copeland, Horace Cornellius 6′3″, 200 **WR**
Col: Miami (Fla.) *HS:* Maynard Evans [Orlando, FL] B: 1/2/1971, Orlando, FL *Drafted:* 1993 Round 4 TB
1993 TB: Rush 3-34 11.3. **1994** TB: Scor 1 2XP. **Total:** Rush 3-34 11.3; Scor 1 2XP.

		Receiving				
Year Team	G	Rec	Yds	Avg	TD	Fum
1993 TB	14	30	633	21.1	4	0
1994 TB	16	17	308	18.1	0	0
1995 TB	15	35	605	17.3	2	0
1997 TB	13	33	431	13.1	1	3
1998 Mia	2	0	0	—	0	0
NFL Total	60	115	1977	17.2	7	3

JOHN COPELAND Copeland, John Anthony 6′3″, 285 **NT-DE**
Col: Hinds CC MS; Alabama *HS:* Valley [AL] B: 9/20/1970, Lanett, AL *Drafted:* 1993 Round 1 Cin
1993 Cin: 14 G; 3 Sac. **1994** Cin: 12 G; 1 Sac. **1995** Cin: 16 G; 9 Sac. **1996** Cin: 13 G; 3 Sac. **1997** Cin: 15 G; 1 Fum TD; 6 Pt; 3 Sac. **1998** Cin: 5 G; Int 1-3. **Total:** 75 G; Int 1-3; 1 Fum TD; 6 Pt; 19 Sac.

RON COPELAND Copeland, Ronald Wayne 6′5″, 196 **WR**
Col: East Los Angeles Coll. CA (J.C.); UCLA *HS:* Susan Miller Dorsey [Los Angeles, CA] B: 10/3/1946, Los Angeles, CA D: 5/22/1975, Walnut, CA *Drafted:* 1969 Round 7 ChiB
1969 ChiB: 6 G.

RUSSELL COPELAND Copeland, Russell Samoan 6′0″, 200 **WR**
Col: Memphis *HS:* Tupelo [MS] B: 11/4/1971, Tupelo, MS *Drafted:* 1993 Round 4 Buf
1994 Buf: Rush 1-(-7) -7.0. **1995** Buf: Rush 1-(-1) -1.0. **Total:** Rush 2-(-8) -4.0.

		Receiving				Punt Returns			
Year Team	G	Rec	Yds	Avg	TD	Ret	Yds	Avg	TD
1993 Buf	16	13	242	18.6	0	31	274	8.8	1
1994 Buf	15	21	255	12.1	1	1	11	11.0	0
1995 Buf	16	42	646	15.4	1	2	8	4.0	0
1996 Buf	11	7	85	12.1	0	14	119	8.5	0
1998 Phi-GB	14	20	232	11.6	0	0	0	—	0
1998 Phi	11	18	221	12.3	0	0	0	—	0
1998 GB	3	2	11	5.5	0	0	0	—	0
NFL Total	72	103	1460	14.2	2	48	412	8.6	1

	Kickoff Returns					Tot
Year Team	Ret	Yds	Avg	TD	Fum	TD
1993 Buf	24	436	18.2	0	1	1
1994 Buf	12	232	19.3	0	0	1
1995 Buf	0	0	—	0	1	1
1996 Buf	6	136	22.7	0	2	0
1998 Phi-GB	3	52	17.3	0	1	0
1998 Phi	3	52	17.3	0	1	0
NFL Total	45	856	19.0	0	5	3

JIM COPELAND Copeland, Wyatte James Jr. 6′3″, 243 **OG-C**
Col: Virginia *HS:* Lane [Charlottesville, VA] B: 3/5/1945, Charlottesville, VA *Drafted:* 1967 Round 10 Cle
1967 Cle: 14 G. **1968** Cle: 14 G; KR 1-0; 1 Fum. **1969** Cle: 8 G. **1970** Cle: 14 G. **1971** Cle: 14 G. **1972** Cle: 1 G. **1973** Cle: 14 G. **1974** Cle: 2 G. **Total:** 81 G; KR 1-0; 1 Fum.

CHARLIE COPLEY Copley, Charles Francis 5′9″, 191 **T-OE**
Col: Muhlenberg; Missouri-Rolla *HS:* Mahanoy City [PA] B: 9/1887, Mahanoy City, PA D: 5/29/1944, Reading, PA
1920 Akr: 11 G. **1921** Akr: 12 G; Scor 10, 10 XK. **1922** Akr-Mil: 7 G; Scor 1, 1 XK. Akr: 3 G. Mil: 4 G; Scor 1, 1 XK. **Total:** 30 G.

AL COPPAGE Coppage, Alton Minor 6′1″, 195 **OE-DE-DB**
Col: Oklahoma *HS:* Hollis [OK] B: 2/9/1916, Pilot Point, TX D: 1/9/1992, Hollis, OK *Drafted:* 1940 Round 13 ChiC
AAFC **1946** CleA: 14 G; Rec 2-34 17.0. **1947** BufA: 13 G; Rec 20-226 11.3 2 TD; KR 2-28 14.0; 12 Pt. **Total:** 27 G; Rec 22-260 11.8 2 TD; KR 2-28 14.0; 12 Pt.

NFL **1942** ChiC: KR 1-11 11.0. **Total:** KR 1-11 11.0.

		Receiving			
Year Team	G	Rec	Yds	Avg	TD
1940 ChiC	11	15	163	10.9	1
1941 ChiC	9	8	117	14.6	0
1942 ChiC	11	20	196	9.8	0
NFL Total	31	43	476	11.1	1

GUS COPPENS Coppens, August Richard 6′5″, 270 **OT**
Col: UCLA *HS:* Sunny Hills [Fullerton, CA] B: 2/7/1955, Lynwood, CA *Drafted:* 1978 Round 12 LARm
1979 NYG: 9 G.

GEORGE CORBETT Corbett, George Burdette 5′9″, 179 **QB-HB-DB**
Col: Millikin *HS:* Arthur [IL] B: 6/14/1908, Dix, IL D: 10/11/1990, Springfield, IL
1932 ChiB: Pass 3-2 66.7%, 61 20.33; Rec 7-164 23.4 1 TD; Scor 1 1XP. **1933** ChiB: Pass 12-4 33.3%, 31 2.58 2 Int. **1934** ChiB: Pass 3-1 33.3%, 36 12.00 1 TD; Rec 1-2 2.0. **1935** ChiB: Pass 7-1 14.3%, 9 1.29; Rec 2-5 2.5; Scor 3, 1 FG. **1936** ChiB: Pass 13-5 38.5%, 64 4.92 1 Int; Rec 3-69 23.0 1 TD. **1938** ChiB: Pass 9-3 33.3%, 32 3.56 1 TD 3 Int; Rec 1-10 10.0; Int **1** TD. **Total:** Pass 47-16 34.0%, 233 4.96 2 TD 6 Int; Rec 14-250 17.9 2 TD; Int 1 TD; Scor 22, 1 FG, 1 1XP.

		Rushing				Tot
Year Team	G	Att	Yds	Avg	TD	TD
1932 ChiB	12	52	178	3.4	0	1
1933 ChiB	6	25	54	2.2	0	0
1934 ChiB	7	30	119	4.0	0	0
1935 ChiB	4	9	0	0.0	0	0
1936 ChiB	9	13	45	3.5	0	1
1937 ChiB	1	0	0	—	0	0
1938 ChiB	7	7	29	4.1	0	1
NFL Total	46	136	425	3.1	0	3

JAMES CORBETT Corbett, James B 6′4″, 218 **TE**
Col: Pittsburgh *HS:* McDowell [Erie, PA] B: 2/22/1955, Brockton, MA *Drafted:* 1977 Round 7 Cin
1977 Cin: Rush 1-(-1) -1.0. **1978** Cin: KR 1-15 15.0. **Total:** Rush 1-(-1) -1.0; KR 1-15 15.0.

		Receiving				
Year Team	G	Rec	Yds	Avg	TD	Fum
1977 Cin	14	7	127	18.1	1	1
1978 Cin	16	12	187	15.6	0	0
1979 Cin	10	3	34	11.3	0	0
1980 Cin	4	3	28	9.3	0	0
NFL Total	44	25	376	15.0	1	1

STEVE CORBETT Corbett, Stephen Paul 6'4", 250 **OG**
Col: Boston College *HS:* St. Thomas Aquinas [Dover, NH]
B: 8/11/1951, Dover, NH *Drafted:* 1974 Round 2 NE
1975 NE: 14 G.

DON CORBITT Corbitt, Donald Oliver 6'4", 224 **C-LB**
Col: Arizona *HS:* Prescott [AZ] B: 4/1/1924, Creston, IA D: 9/3/1993, Phoenix, AZ *Drafted:* 1948 Round 26 Was
1948 Was: 3 G.

TOM CORBO Corbo, Thomas Joseph 5'11", 210 **G-LB**
(T.J.) *Col:* Duquesne *HS:* Altoona [PA] B: 1/11/1918, Altoona, PA
1944 Cle: 10 G; Int 1-0.

BUNNY CORCORAN Corcoran, Arthur Andrew 5'11", 185 **OE-WB-TB**
(Buddy) *Col:* Georgetown; Fordham B: 11/23/1894, Boston, MA
D: 7/27/1958, Chelsea, MA
1920 Can: 11 G. **1921** Akr-Cle: 9 G; Rec 1 TD; 6 Pt. Akr: 1 G. Cle: 8 G; Rec 1 TD; 6 Pt. **1922** Akr: 9 G; Pass 1 TD. **1923** Buf; 1 G. **Total:** 30 G; Pass 1 TD; Rec 1 TD; 6 Pt.

KING CORCORAN Corcoran, James P 6'0", 200 **QB**
Col: Maryland *HS:* Dickinson [Jersey City, NJ]; Cony HS [Augusta, ME]
B: 7/6/1943, Jersey City, NJ
1968 Bos: 2 G; Pass 7-3 42.9%, 33 4.71 2 Int; Rush 1-(-1) -1.0.

JACK CORCORAN Corcoran, John Waldon 180 **C-G**
Col: St. Thomas; St. Louis *HS:* Mechanic Arts [St. Paul, MN]
B: 6/13/1904, St. Paul, MN D: 1/8/1987, Encinitas, CA
1930 Min: 5 G.

LOU CORDILEONE Cordileone, Louis Anthony 6'1", 250 **DT-DE-OG**
Col: Clemson *HS:* St. Michael's [Union City, NJ] B: 8/4/1937, Jersey City, NJ *Drafted:* 1960 Round 1 NYG
1960 NYG: 11 G. **1961** SF: 12 G. **1962** LARm-Pit: 14 G. LARm: 2 G. Pit: 12 G. **1963** Pit: 14 G; KR 1-18 18.0. **1967** NO: 11 G. **1968** NO: 13 G; Int 1-7; 1 Fum. **Total:** 75 G; KR 1-18 18.0; Int 1-7; 1 Fum.

OLIE CORDILL Cordill, Olie James Jr. 6'3", 185 **DB-P-OE**
Col: Memphis *HS:* Lafayette [LA] B: 6/20/1943, Houston, TX
Drafted: 1965 Round 11 Cle

		Punting		
Year Team	G	Punts	Yds	Avg
1967 SD	3	3	145	48.3
1968 Atl	1	0	0	—
1969 NO	12	42	1719	40.9
NFL Total	16	45	1864	41.4

OLIE CORDILL Cordill, Olie James Sr. 6'2", 190 **HB-P**
Col: Rice *HS:* Big Spring [TX] B: 4/28/1916, Big Spring, TX
D: 11/14/1988, Spicewood, TX *Drafted:* 1940 Round 1 Cle
1940 Cle: 10 G; Rush 24-73 3.0; Rec 14-158 11.3 2 TD; Int 1-2; Punt 5-224 44.8; 12 Pt.

SAM CORDOVANO Cordovano, Samuel S 5'11", 185 **G**
Col: Georgetown *HS:* Canisius Prep [Buffalo, NY] B: 12/10/1906, Adams, PA D: 7/13/1995, Hilton Head Island, SC
1930 Nwk: 9 G.

WALT COREY Corey, Walter Martin 6'2", 240 **LB**
Col: Miami (Fla.) *HS:* Derry Twp. [Cooperstown, PA] B: 5/9/1938, Latrobe, PA
1960 DalT: 14 G; Int 3-20. **1962** DalT: 14 G. **1963** KC: 12 G. **1964** KC: 13 G; Int 1-17. **1965** KC: 7 G. **1966** KC: 9 G. **Total:** 69 G; Int 4-37.

CHUCK CORGAN Corgan, Charles Howard 6'0", 183 **BB-OE-WB-TB**
Col: Arkansas *HS:* Wagoner [OK] B: 12/4/1902, Wagoner, OK
D: 6/13/1928, Wagoner, OK
1924 KC: 9 G; Rush 1 TD; Rec 2 TD; Scor 26, 2 XK; 1 Fum TD; Tot TD 4. **1925** KC: 2 G; Rec 1 TD; 6 Pt. **1926** Har-KC: 8 G. Har: 7 G. KC: 1 G. **1927** NYG: 11 G. **Total:** 30 G; Rush 1 TD; Rec 3 TD; 1 Fum TD; Tot TD 5.

MIKE CORGAN Corgan, Michael Henry 5'10", 188 **FB-LB**
Col: Notre Dame *HS:* Alma [MI] B: 10/26/1918, Olongopo, Philippines
D: 5/28/1989, Lincoln, NE
1943 Det: 4 G; Rush 5-14 2.8; Rec 1-9 9.0.

JOHN CORKER Corker, John B 6'5", 240 **LB**
Col: Oklahoma State *HS:* South Miami [Miami, FL] B: 12/29/1958, Miami, FL *Drafted:* 1980 Round 5 Hou
1980 Hou: 16 G; **1** Fum TD; 6 Pt. **1981** Hou: 11 G. **1982** Hou: 3 G; 1 Sac. **1988** GB: 2 G. **Total:** 32 G; 1 Fum TD; 6 Pt; 1 Sac.

ANTHONY CORLEY Corley, Anthony George 6'0", 210 **RB**
Col: Nevada-Reno *HS:* Hug [Reno, NV] B: 8/10/1960, Reno, NV
1984 Pit: 14 G; Rush 18-89 4.9; KR 1-15 15.0. **1985** SD: 4 G. **Total:** 18 G; Rush 18-89 4.9; KR 1-15 15.0.

CHRIS CORLEY Corley, Christopher Ramon 6'4", 285 **TE**
Col: South Carolina *HS:* Irmo [Columbia, SC] B: 10/24/1963, Columbia, SC
1987 Sea: 1 G.

BERT CORLEY Corley, Elbert Ellis 6'2", 210 **C-LB**
(Mule) *Col:* Mississippi State *HS:* Okolona [MS] B: 9/9/1920, Okolona, MS D: 9/22/1988, Tupelo, MS
AAFC **1947** BufA: 13 G; Int 1-41. **1948** BalA: 9 G. **Total:** 22 G; Int 1-41.

JOE CORMIER Cormier, Joseph Daily 6'6", 230 **LB**
Col: USC *HS:* Junipero Serra [Gardena, CA] B: 5/3/1963, Los Angeles, CA
1987 LARd: 2 G; 1 Sac.

JOE CORN Corn, Joseph Huey 5'6", 168 **HB-DB**
B: 10/5/1923
1948 LARm: 9 G; Rush 11-27 2.5; PR 4-49 12.3; KR 5-112 22.4; 2 Fum.

JERRY CORNELISON Cornelison, Jerry G 6'4", 250 **OT**
Col: Southern Methodist *HS:* Temple [TX] B: 9/13/1936, Dallas, TX
Drafted: 1958 Round 16 Cle
1960 DalT: 14 G. **1961** DalT: 14 G. **1962** DalT: 14 G. **1964** KC: 14 G. **1965** KC: 14 G. **Total:** 70 G.

CHARLES CORNELIUS Cornelius, Charles Edward 5'9", 176 **DB**
Col: Bethune-Cookman *HS:* Delray Beach [FL] B: 7/27/1952, Boynton Beach, FL
1977 Mia: 13 G. **1978** Mia: 16 G; PR 1-5 5.0; Int 1-21. **1979** SF: 16 G; Int 3-54. **1980** SF: 16 G. **Total:** 61 G; PR 1-5 5.0; Int 4-75.

BO CORNELL Cornell, Robert Paul 6'2", 220 **LB-RB**
Col: Washington *HS:* Roosevelt [Seattle, WA] B: 3/7/1949, Seattle, WA
Drafted: 1971 Round 2 Cle
1971 Cle: 14 G; Rush 11-12 1.1; Rec 1-18 18.0; KR 1-19 19.0; 1 Fum. **1972** Cle: 14 G; Rush 7-8 1.1; Rec 2-7 3.5. **1973** Buf: 14 G; Rush 4-13 3.3; KR 1-2 2.0. **1974** Buf: 14 G; KR 3-45 15.0; 1 Fum. **1975** Buf: 14 G; KR 3-38 12.7. **1976** Buf: 14 G; KR 2-32 16.0. **1977** Buf: 12 G; 1 Fum TD; 6 Pt. **Total:** 96 G; Rush 22-33 1.5; Rec 3-25 8.3; KR 10-136 13.6; 1 Fum TD; 6 Pt; 2 Fum.

MARTIN CORNELSON Cornelson, Martin Shaw 6'1", 230 **C**
Col: North Carolina State *HS:* Episcopal [Alexandria, VA] B: 6/4/1961, Clinton, SC
1987 NYJ: 3 G.

FRANK CORNISH Cornish, Frank Edgar 6'4", 292 **C-OG**
Col: UCLA *HS:* Mount Carmel [Chicago, IL] B: 9/24/1967, Chicago, IL
Drafted: 1990 Round 6 SD
1990 SD: 16 G. **1991** SD: 16 G. **1992** Dal: 11 G. **1993** Dal: 14 G. **1994** Min: 7 G. **1995** Jac-Phi: 5 G. Jac: 3 G. Phi: 2 G. **Total:** 69 G.

FRANK CORNISH Cornish, Frank Edgar III 6'4", 282 **DT**
Col: Grambling State *HS:* George Washington Carver [New Orleans, LA]
B: 6/20/1944, New Orleans, LA *Drafted:* 1965 Round 11 ChiB
1966 ChiB: 14 G. **1967** ChiB: 14 G; Int 2-10. **1968** ChiB: 13 G. **1969** ChiB: 14 G. **1970** Cin-Mia: 12 G. Cin: 1 G. Mia: 11 G. **1971** Mia: 10 G. **1972** Buf: 6 G. **Total:** 83 G; Int 2-10.

AL CORNSWEET Cornsweet, Albert Charles 5'7", 180 **FB**
Col: Brown *HS:* Shaker Heights [OH] B: 7/16/1906, Cleveland, OH
D: 10/16/1991, Falls Church, VA
1931 Cle: 4 G.

FRED CORNWELL Cornwell, Frederick Keith 6'6", 236 **TE**
Col: USC *HS:* Canyon [Canyon County, CA] B: 8/7/1961, Osborne, KS
Drafted: 1984 Round 3 Dal
1984 Dal: 14 G; Rec 2-23 11.5 1 TD; 6 Pt. **1985** Dal: 16 G; Rec 6-77 12.8 1 TD; 6 Pt. **Total:** 30 G; Rec 8-100 12.5 2 TD; 12 Pt.

BOB CORONADO Coronado, Robert H 6'2", 195 **WR**
Col: Vallejo JC CA; U. of Pacific *HS:* Vallejo [CA] B: 5/22/1936, Vallejo, CA *Drafted:* 1959 Round 10 ChiB
1961 Pit: 5 G; Rush 1-(-7) -7.0; Rec 3-32 10.7.

FRANK CORRAL Corral, John Frank 6'2", 224 **K**
Col: Riverside CC CA; UCLA *HS:* Norte Vista [Riverside, CA]
B: 6/16/1955, Chihuahua, Mexico *Drafted:* 1978 Round 3 LARm
1981 LARm: Pass 1-0. **Total:** Pass 1-0.

		Punting		
Year Team	G	Punts	Yds	Avg
1978 LARm	16	0	0	—
1979 LARm	16	0	0	—
1980 LARm	16	76	3002	39.5
1981 LARm	16	89	3735	42.0
NFL Total	64	165	6737	40.8

			Scoring					
Year Team	Pts	FG	FGA	FG%	XK	XKA	XK%	Fum
1978 LARm	**118**	**29**	**43**	67.4	31	33	93.9	0
1979 LARm	75	13	25	52.0	36	39	92.3	0
1980 LARm	99	16	30	53.3	51	52	98.1	1
1981 LARm	87	17	26	65.4	36	36	100.0	0
NFL Total	379	75	124	60.5	154	160	96.3	1

CHUCK CORREAL Correal, Charles Alan 6'3", 247 **C**
Col: Penn State *HS:* Laurel Highlands [Union Town, PA] B: 5/17/1956, Uniontown, PA *Drafted:* 1979 Round 8 Phi
1980 Atl: 16 G.

KIP CORRINGTON Corrington, Kip Alan 6'0", 175 **DB**
Col: Texas A&M *HS:* A & M Consolidated [College Station, TX] B: 4/12/1965, Ames, IA *Drafted:* 1988 Round 9 Det
1989 Den: 16 G; Int 1-8. **1990** Den: 16 G. **Total:** 32 G; Int 1-8.

RICO CORSETTI Corsetti, Enrico S 6'1", 225 **LB**
Col: Bates *HS:* Belmont Hill [Belmont, MA] B: 1/13/1963, Newton, MA
1987 NE: 2 G.

CHRIS CORTEMEGLIA Cortemeglia, Christopher 6'0", 210 **WB**
Col: Southern Methodist *HS:* Bryan [TX] B: 9/21/1903, Bryan, TX D: 3/14/1989, Houston, TX
1927 Fra: 2 G.

JULIO CORTES Cortes, Julio Ceasar 6'0", 226 **LB**
Col: Miami (Fla.) *HS:* Christopher Columbus [Miami, FL] B: 8/13/1962, New York, NY
1987 Sea: 3 G.

BRUCE CORTEZ Cortez, Bruce Ford 6'0", 175 **DB**
Col: Missouri Southern State; Parsons *HS:* Carthage [MO] B: 10/29/1945, Carthage, MO *Drafted:* 1967 Round 16 NO
1967 NO: 1 G.

ANTHONY CORVINO Corvino, Anthony 6'1", 262 **OG-OT**
Col: Southern Connecticut State B: 9/15/1965
1987 NYJ: 2 G.

QUENTIN CORYATT Coryatt, Quentin John 6'3", 250 **LB**
Col: Texas A&M *HS:* Robert E. Lee [Baytown, TX] B: 8/1/1970, St. Croix, Virgin Islands *Drafted:* 1992 Round 1 Ind
1992 Ind: 7 G; 2 Sac. **1993** Ind: 16 G; 1 Sac. **1994** Ind: 16 G; 1 Fum TD; 6 Pt; 1 Sac. **1995** Ind: 16 G; Int 1-6; 2.5 Sac. **1996** Ind: 8 G. **1997** Ind: 15 G; Int 2-3; 2 Sac. **Total:** 78 G; Int 3-9; 1 Fum TD; 6 Pt; 8.5 Sac.

RED CORZINE Corzine, Lester Howard 6'0", 213 **LB-BB-FB**
(Lefty) *Col:* Davis & Elkins *HS:* Anna [IL]; Monmouth HS [IL] B: 1/19/1909, Balcom, IL
1933 Cin: Pass 7-4 57.1%, 47 6.71 1 Int; Rec 2-38 19.0. **1934** Cin-StL: Pass 11-5 45.5%, 33 3.00 2 Int; Rec 2-22 11.0. Cin: Pass 11-5 45.5%, 33 3.00 2 Int; Rec 2-22 11.0. **1936** NYG: Rec 1-36 36.0 1 TD. **1937** NYG: Pass 1-0; Rec 9-75 8.3 1 TD. **Total:** Pass 19-9 47.4%, 80 4.21 3 Int; Rec 14-171 12.2 2 TD.

		Rushing				Tot
Year Team	G	Att	Yds	Avg	TD	TD
1933 Cin	9	100	239	2.4	1	1
1934 Cin-StL	10	62	167	2.7	1	1
1934 Cin	8	58	162	2.8	0	0
1934 StL	2	4	5	1.3	1	1
1935 NYG	11	32	105	3.3	0	1
1936 NYG	10	7	12	1.7	0	1
1937 NYG	11	8	23	2.9	0	1
NFL Total	51	209	546	2.6	2	5

DOUG COSBIE Cosbie, Douglas Durant 6'6", 236 **TE**
Col: De Anza Coll. CA (J.C.); Holy Cross; Santa Clara *HS:* St. Francis [Mountain View, CA] B: 3/27/1956, Palo Alto, CA *Drafted:* 1979 Round 3 Dal
1980 Dal: KR 1-13 13.0. **1981** Dal: Rush 4-33 8.3; KR 1-0. **1982** Dal: Rush 1-(-2) -2.0; KR 1-4 4.0. **1983** Dal: KR 2-17 8.5. **1986** Dal: Rush 1-9 9.0. **1987** Dal: Rush 1-(-5) -5.0. **Total:** Rush 7-35 5.0; KR 5-34 6.8.

		Receiving				
Year Team	G	Rec	Yds	Avg	TD	Fum
1979 Dal	16	5	36	7.2	0	1
1980 Dal	16	2	11	5.5	1	0
1981 Dal	16	17	225	13.2	5	1
1982 Dal	9	30	441	14.7	4	0
1983 Dal	16	46	588	12.8	6	0
1984 Dal	16	60	789	13.2	4	1
1985 Dal	16	64	793	12.4	6	2
1986 Dal	16	28	312	11.1	1	0
1987 Dal	12	36	421	11.7	3	0
1988 Dal	11	12	112	9.3	0	0
NFL Total	144	300	3728	12.4	30	5

THOMAS COSGROVE Cosgrove, Thomas 5'11", 175 **HB**
Col: No College
1935 Pit: 1 G; Rush 3-18 6.0.

BRUCE COSLET Coslet, Bruce Noel 6'4", 227 **TE**
Col: U. of Pacific *HS:* Oakdale [CA] B: 8/5/1946, Oakdale, CA
1973 Cin: KR 1-0. **1975** Cin: Rush 1-1 1.0. **Total:** Rush 1-1 1.0; KR 1-0.

		Receiving				
Year Team	G	Rec	Yds	Avg	TD	Fum
1969 Cin	8	1	39	39.0	1	0
1970 Cin	14	8	98	12.3	1	0
1971 Cin	14	21	356	17.0	4	3
1972 Cin	10	5	48	9.6	1	0
1973 Cin	13	9	123	13.7	0	0
1974 Cin	14	2	24	12.0	0	0
1975 Cin	14	10	117	11.7	0	0
1976 Cin	14	5	73	14.6	2	0
NFL Total	101	61	878	14.4	9	3

DON COSNER Cosner, Donald Stewart 6'2", 200 **WB-DB**
Col: Montana State *HS:* Malta [MT] B: 2/16/1917, Malta, MT
1939 ChiC: 1 G.

ERIC COSS Coss, Eric 6'3", 270 **C**
Col: Temple *HS:* Bethel Park [PA] B: 6/12/1963
1987 NYJ: 3 G.

DAVE COSTA Costa, David Joseph 6'2", 250 **DT-DE**
Col: Northeastern JC CO; Utah *HS:* Saunders Trade & Tech [Yonkers, NY] B: 10/27/1941, Yonkers, NY *Drafted:* 1963 Round 7 Oak
1963 Oak: 14 G. **1964** Oak: 14 G. **1965** Oak: 14 G. **1966** Buf: 14 G; KR 1-0. **1967** Den: 14 G. **1968** Den: 14 G. **1969** Den: 14 G. **1970** Den: 14 G. **1971** Den: 14 G. **1972** SD: 14 G; Scor **1** Saf; 2 Pt. **1973** SD: 14 G. **1974** Buf: 14 G. **Total:** 168 G; KR 1-0; Scor 1 Saf; 2 Pt.

PAUL COSTA Costa, Sebastian Paul 6'6", 268 **TE-OT**
Col: Northeastern JC CO; Notre Dame *HS:* Port Chester [NY] B: 12/7/1941, Yonkers, NY *Drafted:* 1964 Round 14 KC
1966 Buf: Rush 0-1. **1968** Buf: Rush 2-11 5.5 1 TD; KR 5-68 13.6. **1970** Buf: KR 1-0. **Total:** Rush 2-12 6.0 1 TD; KR 6-68 11.3.

		Receiving					Tot
Year Team	G	Rec	Yds	Avg	TD	Fum	TD
1965 Buf	10	21	401	19.1	0	1	0
1966 Buf	14	27	400	14.8	3	0	3
1967 Buf	14	39	726	18.6	2	2	2
1968 Buf	14	15	172	11.5	1	0	2
1969 Buf	14	0	0	—	0	0	0
1970 Buf	14	0	0	—	0	0	0
1971 Buf	11	0	0	—	0	0	0
1972 Buf	9	0	0	—	0	0	0
NFL Total	100	102	1699	16.7	6	3	7

BRAD COSTELLO Costello, Brad 6'0", 231 **OT**
Col: Michigan State; Boston U. *HS:* Fairfield Prep [CT]; Holy Cross [Delran, NJ] B: 12/12/1974, Moorestown, NJ
1998 Cin: 3 G; Rush 1-0; Punt 10-495 49.5.

JOE COSTELLO Costello, Joseph Patrick Jr. 6'3", 245 **DE**
Col: Central Connecticut State *HS:* Stratford [CT] B: 6/1/1960, New York, NY
1986 Atl: 14 G; 2 Sac. **1987** Atl: 9 G. **1988** Atl: 6 G. **1989** LARd: 2 G. **Total:** 31 G; 2 Sac.

TOM COSTELLO Costello, Thomas Francis 6'4", 220 **LB**
Col: Dayton; Miami (Fla.) *HS:* Holy Cross [Queens, NY] B: 5/23/1941, Queens, NY
1964 NYG: 2 G. **1965** NYG: 8 G. **Total:** 10 G.

VINCE COSTELLO Costello, Vincent 6'0", 230 **LB**
Col: Ohio U. *HS:* Magnolia [OH] B: 8/4/1932, Dellroy, OH
1961 Cle: 1 Fum TD. **1962** Cle: **1** Fum TD. **1966** Cle: Rec 1-(-7) -7.0. **Total:** Rec 1-(-7) -7.0; 2 Fum TD.

		Interceptions		
Year Team	G	Int	Yds	TD
1957 Cle	12	2	19	0
1958 Cle	12	0	0	0
1959 Cle	12	0	14	0
1960 Cle	12	0	0	0
1961 Cle	14	0	0	0
1962 Cle	13	3	40	0
1963 Cle	14	7	118	0
1964 Cle	14	2	21	0
1965 Cle	13	3	33	0
1966 Cle	14	1	0	0
1967 NYG	14	4	54	0
1968 NYG	2	0	0	0
NFL Total	146	22	299	0

JOE COSTER Coster, Howard Owen 5'10", 175 **T**
Col: Western Maryland; Maryland B: 11/24/1895 D: 8/20/1966
1921 Was: 1 G.

RAY COSTICT Costict, Ray Charles 6'0", 217 **LB**
Col: Mississippi State *HS:* Moss Point [MS] B: 3/19/1955, Moss Point, MS *Drafted:* 1977 Round 11 NE
1977 NE: 14 G. **1978** NE: 16 G. **1979** NE: 16 G; Int 1-22. **Total:** 46 G; Int 1-22.

ZED COSTON Coston, Fred Monroe 6′2″, 222 **C-LB**
Col: Texas A&M *HS:* Crozier Tech [Dallas, TX] B: 7/12/1915, Dallas, TX
Drafted: 1939 Round 5 Phi
1939 Phi: 1 G.

CHAD COTA Cota, Chad Garrett 6′1″, 198 **DB**
Col: Oregon *HS:* Ashland [OR] B: 8/13/1971, Ashland, OR
Drafted: 1995 Round 7 Car
1996 Car: 1 Sac. **1997** Car: 1 Sac. **1998** NO: 2 Sac. **Total:** 4 Sac.

		Interceptions			
Year Team	**G**	**Int**	**Yds**	**TD**	**Fum**
1995 Car	16	0	0	0	0
1996 Car	16	5	63	0	1
1997 Car	16	2	28	0	0
1998 NO	16	4	16	0	0
NFL Total	64	11	107	0	1

JEFF COTHRAN Cothran, Jeffrey Lance 6′1″, 249 **RB**
Col: Ohio State *HS:* Middletown [OH] B: 6/28/1971, Middletown, OH
Drafted: 1994 Round 3 Cin
1994 Cin: Rec 4-24 6.0 1 TD. **1995** Cin: Rec 8-44 5.5. **1996** Cin: Rec 7-49 7.0; KR 1-11 11.0. **Total:** Rec 19-117 6.2 1 TD; KR 1-11 11.0.

		Rushing					Tot
Year Team	**G**	**Att**	**Yds**	**Avg**	**TD**	**Fum**	**TD**
1994 Cin	14	26	85	3.3	0	0	1
1995 Cin	14	16	62	3.9	0	1	0
1996 Cin	11	15	44	2.9	1	0	1
NFL Total	39	57	191	3.4	1	1	2

PAIGE COTHREN Cothren, Jennings Paige 5′11″, 201 **K**
Col: Mississippi *HS:* Natchez [MS] B: 7/12/1935, Natchez, MS
Drafted: 1957 Round 22 LARm

		Scoring						
Year Team	**G**	**Pts**	**FG**	**FGA**	**FG%**	**XK**	**XKA**	**XK%**
1957 LARm	12	71	11	19	57.9	**38**	**38**	100.0
1958 LARm	12	84	**14**	25	**56.0**	42	42	**100.0**
1959 Phi	7	25	8	18	44.4	1	1	100.0
NFL Total	31	180	33	62	53.2	81	81	100.0

MARK COTNEY Cotney, John Mark 6′0″, 204 **DB**
Col: New Mexico Highlands; Cameron *HS:* Altus [OK] B: 6/26/1952, Altus, OK *Drafted:* 1975 Round 7 Hou
1975 Hou: PR 2-8 4.0; KR 10-189 18.9. **1976** TB: PR 3-26 8.7. **1978** TB: PR 5-38 7.6. **1983** TB: 1 Sac. **1984** TB: 2 Sac. **Total:** PR 10-72 7.2; KR 10-189 18.9; 3 Sac.

		Interceptions			
Year Team	**G**	**Int**	**Yds**	**TD**	**Fum**
1975 Hou	14	0	0	0	0
1976 TB	14	3	25	0	0
1977 TB	14	1	0	0	0
1978 TB	16	2	28	0	1
1979 TB	16	1	0	0	0
1980 TB	16	3	28	0	0
1982 TB	9	0	0	0	0
1983 TB	12	2	1	0	0
1984 TB	16	5	123	0	0
NFL Total	127	17	205	0	1

BARNEY COTTON Cotton, Barney T 6′5″, 264 **OG**
Col: Nebraska *HS:* Harry A. Burke [Omaha, NE] B: 9/30/1956, Omaha, NE *Drafted:* 1979 Round 3 Cin
1979 Cin: 13 G. **1980** StL: 16 G. **1981** StL: 16 G. **Total:** 45 G.

CRAIG COTTON Cotton, Craig Lee 6′5″, 216 **TE**
(Monk) *Col:* Youngstown State *HS:* Elizabeth [PA] B: 7/7/1947, Elizabeth, PA *Drafted:* 1969 Round 8 SD
1971 Det: KR 1-4 4.0. **1973** ChiB: KR 2-15 7.5. **Total:** KR 3-19 6.3.

		Receiving			
Year Team	**G**	**Rec**	**Yds**	**Avg**	**TD**
1969 Det	13	0	0	—	0
1970 Det	14	1	6	6.0	0
1971 Det	14	6	88	14.7	0
1972 Det	14	8	129	16.1	1
1973 ChiB	13	13	186	14.3	0
1975 SD	9	0	0	—	0
NFL Total	77	28	409	14.6	1

FEST COTTON Cotton, Fest James 6′2″, 255 **DT**
Col: Dayton *HS:* Paul L. Dunbar [Dayton, OH] B: 10/18/1949, Macon, MS
1972 Cle: 3 G.

FOD COTTON Cotton, Forrest George 6′1″, 195 **T**
Col: Notre Dame *HS:* Elgin [IL] B: 1/14/1901, Elgin, IL D: 3/6/1967, Kansas City, MO
1923 RI: 8 G. **1925** RI: 8 G. **Total:** 16 G.

RUSS COTTON Cotton, James Russell 6′2″, 196 **QB**
(King) *Col:* Texas-El Paso *HS:* Palestine [TX] B: 5/24/1915, Palestine, TX *Drafted:* 1941 Round 11 Pit
1942 Pit: 11 G; Rec 2-58 29.0; Int 1-0.

MARCUS COTTON Cotton, Marcus Glenn 6′3″, 225 **LB**
Col: USC *HS:* Castlemont [Oakland, CA] B: 8/11/1966, Los Angeles, CA *Drafted:* 1988 Round 2 Atl
1988 Atl: 11 G; 5 Sac. **1989** Atl: 16 G; 9 Sac. **1990** Atl-Cle: 14 G. Atl: 7 G. Cle: 7 G. **1991** Sea: 3 G. **Total:** 44 G; 14 Sac.

KENYON COTTON Cotton, Timothy 6′0″, 255 **RB**
Col: Southwestern Louisiana *HS:* Minden [LA] B: 2/23/1974, Bossier City, LA
1997 Bal: 15 G; Rush 2-2 1.0 1 TD; 6 Pt. **1998** Bal: 12 G; Rush 2-8 4.0; KR 2-33 16.5. **Total:** 27 G; Rush 4-10 2.5 1 TD; KR 2-33 16.5; 6 Pt.

DANA COTTRELL Cottrell, Dana Robert 6′3″, 234 **LB**
Col: Syracuse *HS:* Billerica [MA] B: 1/11/1974, Boston, MA
1998 NE: 2 G.

TED COTTRELL Cottrell, Theodore John 6′2″, 233 **LB**
Col: Delaware Valley *HS:* Chester [PA] B: 6/13/1947, Chester, PA
Drafted: 1969 Round 7 Atl
1969 Atl: 10 G. **1970** Atl: 14 G. **Total:** 24 G.

BILL COTTRELL Cottrell, William Henry 6′4″, 255 **OT-OG-C**
Col: Delaware Valley *HS:* Chester [PA] B: 9/18/1944, Chester, PA
1967 Det: 14 G. **1968** Det: 14 G. **1969** Det: 14 G. **1970** Det: 10 G. **1972** Den: 11 G. **Total:** 63 G.

DANNY COUGHLIN Coughlin, Daniel Martin 5′9″, 175 **WB**
Col: St. Thomas; Notre Dame B: 6/1897, Faribault, MN Deceased
1923 Min: 2 G.

FRANK COUGHLIN Coughlin, Francis Edward 6′3″, 220 **T**
Col: Notre Dame *HS:* Englewood [Chicago, IL] B: 2/28/1896, Chicago, IL D: 9/8/1951, Indianapolis, IN
1921 RI-Det-GB: 10 G. RI: 3 G. Det: 2 G. GB: 5 G. **Total:** 10 G.

TEX COULTER Coulter, DeWitt Echoles 6′4″, 250 **OT-DT-C-DE**
Col: Texas A&M; Cornell; Army *HS:* Masonic Home School [Fort Worth, TX] B: 10/26/1924, Ft.Worth, TX *Drafted:* 1947 Round 1 ChiC
1946 NYG: 9 G. **1947** NYG: 12 G; Rec 8-107 13.4 1 TD; KR 2-16 8.0; 6 Pt. **1948** NYG: 12 G. **1949** NYG: 12 G. **1951** NYG: 12 G; KR 1-12 12.0. **1952** NYG: 12 G; Rec 1-9 9.0. **Total:** 69 G; Rec 9-116 12.9 1 TD; KR 3-28 9.3; 6 Pt.

JOHNNY COUNTS Counts, John E Jr. 5′11″, 175 **HB**
Col: Illinois *HS:* New Rochelle [NY] B: 2/28/1939, Mount Pleasent, NY
Drafted: 1962 Round 24 NYT
1962 NYG: Rush 14-55 3.9; Rec 4-62 15.5; PR 8-33 4.1.
Total: Rush 14-55 3.9; Rec 4-62 15.5; PR 8-33 4.1.

		Kickoff Returns				
Year Team	**G**	**Ret**	**Yds**	**Avg**	**TD**	**Fum**
1962 NYG	14	26	784	30.2	**1**	4
1963 NYG	3	5	107	21.4	0	0
NFL Total	17	31	891	28.7	1	4

AL COUPPEE Couppee, Albert Wallace 6′0″, 225 **G-FB-BB-LB**
(Dictator; Coup) *Col:* Iowa *HS:* Thomas Jefferson [Council Bluffs, IA] B: 6/4/1920, Council Bluffs, IA D: 7/3/1998, Laguna Hills, CA
Drafted: 1942 Round 20 Was
1946 Was: 7 G; Rush 3-22 7.3.

STEVE COURSON Courson, Stephen Paul 6′1″, 274 **OG**
Col: South Carolina *HS:* Gettysburg [PA] B: 10/1/1955, Philadelphia, PA *Drafted:* 1977 Round 5 Pit
1978 Pit: 16 G. **1979** Pit: 16 G. **1980** Pit: 8 G. **1981** Pit: 16 G. **1982** Pit: 8 G. **1983** Pit: 9 G. **1984** TB: 14 G. **1985** TB: 16 G. **Total:** 103 G.

GERRY COURTNEY Courtney, Gerald L 6′0″, 195 **TB-DB**
Col: Syracuse *HS:* Ithaca [NY] B: 3/2/1918, Tulsa, OK D: 12/1963
1942 Bkn: 5 G; Pass 4-1 25.0%, 14 3.50 2 Int; Rush 8-12 1.5 1 TD; Rec 1-1 1.0; Int 1-32; 6 Pt.

MATT COURTNEY Courtney, Matthew Carter 5′11″, 194 **DB**
Col: Idaho State *HS:* Arapahoe [Littleton, CO] B: 12/21/1961, Greeley, CO
1987 SF: 3 G; Int 1-30; 1 Sac.

VINCE COURVILLE Courville, Vincent Eric 5′9″, 170 **WR**
Col: Ranger Coll. TX (J.C.); Texas Southern; Rice *HS:* Ball [Galveston, TX] B: 12/5/1959, Galveston, TX
1987 Dal: 2 G.

TERRY COUSIN Cousin, Terry Sean 5′9″, 182 **DB**
Col: South Carolina *HS:* Miami Beach Senior [FL] B: 4/11/1975
1997 ChiB: 6 G. **1998** ChiB: 16 G; Int 1-0. **Total:** 22 G; Int 1-0.

TOM COUSINEAU Cousineau, Thomas Michael 6'3", 225 LB
Col: Ohio State *HS:* St. Edwards [Lakewood, OH] B: 5/6/1957, Fairview Park, OH *Drafted:* 1979 Round 1 Buf
1982 Cle: 1 Sac. **1983** Cle: 4 Sac. **1985** Cle: 1.5 Sac. **Total:** 6.5 Sac.

		Interceptions		
Year Team	G	Int	Yds	TD
1982 Cle	9	1	6	0
1983 Cle	16	4	47	0
1984 Cle	16	2	9	0
1985 Cle	16	1	0	0
1986 SF	5	1	18	0
1987 SF	4	1	11	0
NFL Total	66	10	91	0

BRAD COUSINO Cousino, Bradley Gene 6'0", 218 LB
Col: Miami (Ohio) *HS:* Central Catholic [Toledo, OH] B: 4/5/1953, Toledo, OH
1975 Cin: 14 G; KR 1-0; 1 Fum. **1976** NYG: 6 G. **1977** Pit: 3 G.
Total: 23 G; KR 1-0; 1 Fum.

LARRY COUTRE Coutre, Lawrence Edward 5'10", 175 HB
Col: Notre Dame *HS:* St. George [Evanston, IL] B: 4/11/1928, Chicago, IL *Drafted:* 1950 Round 4 GB
1950 GB: Rec 17-206 12.1 2 TD. **1953** GB-Bal: Rec 1-(-4) -4.0; PR 5-43 8.6; KR 12-318 26.5. GB: Rec 1-(-4) -4.0; PR 1-5 5.0; KR 3-52 17.3. Bal: PR 4-38 9.5; KR 9-266 29.6. **Total:** Rec 18-202 11.2 2 TD; PR 5-43 8.6; KR 12-318 26.5.

		Rushing					Tot
Year Team	G	Att	Yds	Avg	TD	Fum	TD
1950 GB	12	41	283	6.9	1	1	3
1953 GB-Bal	10	22	39	1.8	0	0	0
1953 GB	7	22	39	1.8	0	0	0
1953 Bal	3	0	0	—	0	0	0
NFL Total	22	63	322	5.1	1	1	3

JIM COVERT Covert, James Paul 6'4", 277 OT
(Jimbo) *Col:* Pittsburgh *HS:* Freedom [PA] B: 3/22/1960, Conway, PA *Drafted:* 1983 Round 1 ChiB
1983 ChiB: 16 G. **1984** ChiB: 16 G. **1985** ChiB: 15 G. **1986** ChiB: 16 G. **1987** ChiB: 9 G. **1988** ChiB: 9 G. **1989** ChiB: 15 G. **1990** ChiB: 15 G. **Total:** 111 G.

TONY COVINGTON Covington, Anthony Lavonne 5'11", 192 DB
Col: Virginia *HS:* Parkland [Winston-Salem, NC] B: 12/26/1967, Winston-Salem, NC *Drafted:* 1991 Round 4 TB
1991 TB: 16 G; Int 3-21; 1 Sac. **1992** TB: 1 G. **1994** TB: 14 G; Int 1-38. **1995** Sea: 11 G. **Total:** 42 G; Int 4-59; 1 Sac.

DAMIEN COVINGTON Covington, Damien Emere 5'11", 236 LB
Col: North Carolina State *HS:* Overbrook Regional [Pine Hill, NJ] B: 12/4/1972, Berlin, NJ *Drafted:* 1995 Round 3 Buf
1995 Buf: 13 G. **1996** Buf: 9 G. **1997** Buf: 8 G; Int 1-6; 0.5 Sac. **Total:** 30 G; Int 1-6; 0.5 Sac.

JAIME COVINGTON Covington, Jaime A 6'1", 234 RB
Col: Syracuse *HS:* Bayside [Queens, NY] B: 12/12/1962
1987 NYG: 2 G; Rush 4-0; Rec 1-9 9.0.

JOHN COVINGTON Covington, John Shaft 6'0", 198 DB
Col: Notre Dame *HS:* Winter Haven [FL] B: 4/22/1972, Winter Haven, FL *Drafted:* 1994 Round 5 Ind
1994 Ind: 3 G.

CHARLEY COWAN Cowan, Charles Edward 6'5", 265 OT-OG
Col: New Mexico Highlands *HS:* Buffalo [WV] B: 6/19/1938, Braeholm, WV D: 4/29/1998, Whittier, CA *Drafted:* 1961 Round 4 LARm
1961 LARm: 14 G. **1962** LARm: 14 G. **1963** LARm: 14 G; KR 2-0. **1964** LARm: 14 G. **1965** LARm: 13 G. **1966** LARm: 14 G. **1967** LARm: 14 G. **1968** LARm: 13 G. **1969** LARm: 14 G. **1970** LARm: 14 G. **1971** LARm: 14 G. **1972** LARm: 13 G. **1973** LARm: 14 G. **1974** LARm: 14 G. **1975** LARm: 13 G; Rec 1-1 1.0. **Total:** 206 G; Rec 1-1 1.0; KR 2-0.

LARRY COWAN Cowan, Lawrence Donnell 5'11", 194 RB
Col: Jackson State *HS:* Mattie T. Blount [Prichard, AL] B: 7/11/1960, Mobile, AL *Drafted:* 1982 Round 7 Mia
1982 Mia-NE: 8 G; Rush 1-3 3.0. Mia: 2 G; Rush 1-3 3.0. NE: 6 G. **Total:** 8 G; Rush 1-3 3.0.

LES COWAN Cowan, Leslie Lowden 6'5", 235 DT-DE
Col: McMurry *HS:* Hamlin [TX] B: 12/24/1925, Stamford, TX D: 3/9/1979, Weatherford, TX *Drafted:* 1950 Round 9 LARm
1951 ChiB: 9 G.

BOB COWAN Cowan, Robert George 5'11", 185 HB-DB
Col: Michigan; Indiana *HS:* North Side [Fort Wayne, IN] B: 1/2/1923, Ft. Wayne, IN
AAFC **1947** CleA: Rec 5-60 12.0 1 TD; KR 3-55 18.3. **1948** CleA: Rec 15-265 17.7 4 TD; KR 3-53 17.7. **1949** BalA: Rec 1-26 26.0; Int 3-17. **Total:** Rec 21-351 16.7 5 TD; KR 6-108 18.0; Int 3-17.

		Rushing				Tot
Year Team	G	Att	Yds	Avg	TD	TD
1947 CleA	10	38	181	4.8	2	3
1948 CleA	14	33	99	3.0	1	5
1949 BalA	9	1	0	0.0	0	0
AAFC Total	33	72	280	3.9	3	8

SAM COWART Cowart, Samuel III 6'2", 239 LB
Col: Florida State *HS:* Mandarin [Jacksonville, FL] B: 2/26/1975, Jacksonville, FL *Drafted:* 1998 Round 2 Buf
1998 Buf: 16 G; Int 2-23.

BILL COWHER Cowher, William Laird 6'3", 225 LB
Col: North Carolina State *HS:* Carlynton [Carnegie, PA] B: 5/8/1957, Pittsburgh, PA
1980 Cle: 16 G. **1982** Cle: 9 G. **1983** Phi: 16 G. **1984** Phi: 4 G. **Total:** 45 G.

GERRY COWHIG Cowhig, Gerard Finbar 6'2", 215 LB-FB-DB
Col: Notre Dame *HS:* Mechanic Arts [Boston, MA]; Marianapolis Acad. [Thompson, CT] B: 7/5/1921, Boston, MA D: 12/6/1995, Van Nuys, CA *Drafted:* 1945 Round 6 Cle
1947 LARm: KR 2-29 14.5; Int 1-0. **1948** LARm: Rec 3-18 6.0; PR 1-3 3.0; KR 1-3 3.0; Int 1-9. **1949** LARm: KR 2-20 10.0; Int 4-62 1 TD. **1951** Phi: KR 1-12 12.0; 1 Fum TD. **Total:** Rec 3-18 6.0; PR 1-3 3.0; KR 6-64 10.7; Int 6-71 1 TD; 1 Fum TD.

		Rushing					Tot
Year Team	G	Att	Yds	Avg	TD	Fum	TD
1947 LARm	8	25	104	4.2	0	2	0
1948 LARm	12	46	206	4.5	2	0	2
1949 LARm	11	10	32	3.2	1	0	2
1950 ChiC	12	0	0	—	0	0	0
1951 Phi	11	0	0	—	0	0	1
NFL Total	54	81	342	4.2	3	2	5

AL COWLINGS Cowlings, Allen G 6'5", 255 DE-DT-LB
(A.C.) *Col:* USC *HS:* Galileo [San Francisco, CA] B: 6/16/1947, San Francisco, CA *Drafted:* 1970 Round 1 Buf
1970 Buf: 13 G. **1971** Buf: 14 G. **1972** Buf: 14 G. **1973** Hou: 14 G. **1974** Hou: 14 G. **1975** LARm: 5 G. **1976** Sea: 1 G. **1977** LARm: 14 G. **1979** SF: 12 G. **Total:** 101 G.

JOHN COWNE Cowne, John Kendall 6'2", 245 C
Col: Virginia Tech *HS:* Brentsville [Nokesville, VA] B: 5/23/1962, Fairfax, VA
1987 Was: 3 G.

AARON COX Cox, Aaron Dion 5'9", 174 WR
Col: Arizona State *HS:* Susan Miller Dorsey [Los Angeles, CA] B: 3/13/1965, Los Angeles, CA *Drafted:* 1988 Round 1 LARm

		Receiving				
Year Team	G	Rec	Yds	Avg	TD	Fum
1988 LARm	16	28	590	21.1	5	0
1989 LARm	16	20	340	17.0	3	1
1990 LARm	14	17	266	15.6	0	0
1991 LARm	15	15	216	14.4	0	1
1992 LARm	10	18	261	14.5	0	0
1993 Ind	11	4	59	14.8	0	0
NFL Total	82	102	1732	17.0	8	2

ARTHUR COX Cox, Arthur Dean 6'3", 262 TE
Col: Texas Southern *HS:* Plant City [FL] B: 2/5/1961, Plant City, FL
1987 Atl: KR 1-11 11.0. **Total:** KR 1-11 11.0.

		Receiving				
Year Team	G	Rec	Yds	Avg	TD	Fum
1983 Atl	16	9	83	9.2	1	1
1984 Atl	16	34	329	9.7	3	1
1985 Atl	16	33	454	13.8	2	0
1986 Atl	16	24	301	12.5	1	1
1987 Atl	12	11	101	9.2	0	2
1988 SD	16	18	144	8.0	0	0
1989 SD	16	22	200	9.1	2	0
1990 SD	16	14	93	6.6	1	2
1991 SD-Mia-Cle	13	5	53	10.6	0	0
1991 SD	8	5	53	10.6	0	0
1991 Mia	2	0	0	—	0	0
1991 Cle	3	0	0	—	0	0
NFL Total	137	170	1758	10.3	10	7

BRYAN COX Cox, Bryan Keith 6'4", 250 LB
Col: Western Illinois *HS:* East St. Louis [IL] B: 2/17/1968, St. Louis, MO *Drafted:* 1991 Round 5 Mia
1991 Mia: 13 G; 2 Sac. **1992** Mia: 16 G; Int 1-0; 14 Sac. **1993** Mia: 16 G; Int 1-26; 5 Sac. **1994** Mia: 16 G; 3 Sac. **1995** Mia: 16 G; Int 1-12; 7.5 Sac. **1996** ChiB: 9 G; **1** Fum TD; 6 Pt; 3 Sac. **1997** ChiB: 16 G; 5 Sac. **1998** NYJ: 16 G; Scor **1** Saf; 2 Pt; 6 Sac. **Total:** 118 G; Int 3-38; Scor 1 Saf; 1 Fum TD; 8 Pt; 45.5 Sac.

FRED COX Cox, Frederick William 5'11", 200 **K**
Col: Pittsburgh *HS:* Monongahela [PA] B: 12/11/1938, Monongahela, PA *Drafted:* 1961 Round 8 Cle
1970 Min: Pass 1-1 100.0%, -1 -1.00. **Total:** Pass 1-1 100.0%, -1 1.00.

Year Team	G	Punting Punts	Yds	Avg
1963 Min	14	70	2707	38.7
1964 Min	14	0	0	—
1965 Min	14	0	0	—
1966 Min	14	0	0	—
1967 Min	14	0	0	—
1968 Min	14	0	0	—
1969 Min	14	0	0	—
1970 Min	14	0	0	—
1971 Min	14	0	0	—
1972 Min	14	0	0	—
1973 Min	14	0	0	—
1974 Min	14	0	0	—
1975 Min	14	0	0	—
1976 Min	14	0	0	—
1977 Min	14	0	0	—
NFL Total	210	70	2707	38.7

Year Team	Scoring Pts	FG	FGA	FG%	XK	XKA	XK%
1963 Min	75	12	24	50.0	39	39	100.0
1964 Min	103	21	33	63.6	40	42	95.2
1965 Min	113	**23**	**35**	65.7	44	44	100.0
1966 Min	88	18	33	54.5	34	34	100.0
1967 Min	77	17	33	51.5	26	26	100.0
1968 Min	88	19	29	65.5	31	32	96.9
1969 Min	**121**	**26**	37	**70.3**	43	43	**100.0**
1970 Min	**125**	**30**	**46**	65.2	35	35	100.0
1971 Min	91	22	32	68.8	25	25	100.0
1972 Min	97	21	33	63.6	34	34	100.0
1973 Min	96	21	35	60.0	33	33	100.0
1974 Min	68	12	20	60.0	32	39	82.1
1975 Min	85	13	17	76.5	46	48	95.8
1976 Min	89	19	31	61.3	32	36	88.9
1977 Min	49	8	17	47.1	25	29	86.2
NFL Total	1365	282	455	62.0	519	539	96.3

GREG COX Cox, Gregory Mark 6'0", 223 **DB**
Col: Hartnell Coll. CA (J.C.); San Jose State *HS:* Walnut Ridge [Columbus, OH] B: 1/6/1965, Niagara Falls, NY
1988 SF: 15 G. **1989** NYG: 16 G; 1 Sac. **1990** SF: 13 G. **1991** SF: 11 G. **Total:** 55 G; 1 Sac.

JIM COX Cox, James Allen 6'3", 230 **TE**
Col: Miami (Fla.) *HS:* Christopher Columbus [Miami, FL] B: 12/21/1946, Baltimore, MD *Drafted:* 1968 Round 2 Mia
1968 Mia: 13 G; Rec 11-147 13.4; KR 0-41.

JIM COX Cox, James Ellingson 6'1", 208 **G-LB**
Col: California; Stanford *HS:* Christian Brothers [Sacramento, CA] B: 9/6/1920, St. Louis, MO
AAFC **1948** SF-A: 14 G.

BILLY COX Cox, John William 6'3", 189 **DB-HB-OE**
Col: Duke *HS:* Mount Airy [NC] B: 6/17/1929, Brandon, TX *Drafted:* 1951 Round 8 Was
1951 Was: 10 G; Rush 2-7 3.5; Int 2-0; Punt 28-1122 40.1. **1952** Was: 12 G; Rush 3-(-1) -0.3; Rec 2-19 9.5; Int 3-43; Punt 5-177 35.4; 1 Fum. **1955** Was: 4 G; Rec 5-71 14.2. **Total:** 26 G; Rush 5-6 1.2; Rec 7-90 12.9; Int 5-43; Punt 33-1299 39.4; 1 Fum.

LARRY COX Cox, Lawrence Donald 6'3", 255 **DT**
Col: Abilene Christian *HS:* Anson [TX] B: 11/12/1943, Anson, TX *Drafted:* 1966 Round 10 Den
1966 Den: 11 G. **1967** Den: 13 G. **1968** Den: 9 G. **Total:** 33 G.

NORM COX Cox, Norman Lawrence 6'2", 210 **QB-TB**
(Fuzzy) *Col:* Texas Christian *HS:* Grandfalls-Royalty [Grandfalls, TX] B: 9/22/1925, Stamford, TX
AAFC **1946** ChiA: 3 G; Rush 1-12 12.0. **1947** ChiA: 2 G; Pass 2-1 50.0%, 9 4.50; Rush 1-(-3) -3.0. **Total:** 5 G; Pass 2-1 50.0%, 9 4.50; Rush 2-9 4.5.

RON COX Cox, Ronald Eugene 6'2", 235 **LB**
Col: Fresno State *HS:* Washington [Fresno, CA] B: 2/27/1968, Fresno, CA *Drafted:* 1990 Round 2 ChiB
1990 ChiB: 13 G; 3 Sac. **1991** ChiB: 6 G; 1 Sac. **1992** ChiB: 16 G; 1 Sac. **1993** ChiB: 16 G; 2 Sac. **1994** ChiB: 15 G. **1995** ChiB: 16 G; Int 1-1. **1996** GB: 16 G. **1997** ChiB: 15 G; 1 Sac. **Total:** 113 G; Int 1-1; 8 Sac.

STEVE COX Cox, Stephen Everett 6'4", 195 **P-K**
Col: Tulsa; Arkansas *HS:* Charleston [AR] B: 5/11/1958, Shreveport, LA *Drafted:* 1981 Round 5 Cle
1981 Cle: Scor 0-1 FG. **1982** Cle: Rush 2-(-11) -5.5; Scor 0-1 FG. **1983** Cle: Scor 3, 1-1 100.0% FG. **1984** Cle: Pass 1-1 100.0%, 16 16.00; Scor 3, 1-3 33.3% FG. **1985** Was: Pass 1-1 100.0%, 11 11.00; Scor 0-1 FG. **1986** Was: Scor 9, 3-6 50.0% FG. **1987** Was: Scor 6, 1-2 50.0% FG, 3-3 100.0% XK. **Total:** Pass 2-2 100.0%, 27 13.50; Rush 2-(-11) -5.5; Scor 21, 6-15 40.0% FG, 3-3 100.0% XK.

Year Team	G	Punting Punts	Yds	Avg
1981 Cle	16	68	2884	42.4
1982 Cle	9	48	1877	39.1
1983 Cle	7	0	0	—
1984 Cle	16	74	3213	43.4
1985 Was	12	52	2175	41.8
1986 Was	16	75	3271	43.6
1987 Was	12	63	2571	40.8
1988 Was	1	6	221	36.8
NFL Total	89	386	16212	42.0

TOM COX Cox, Thomas Franklin 6'5", 260 **C**
Col: USC *HS:* Xenia [OH] B: 12/4/1962, Xenia, OH
1987 LARm: 3 G.

ROSS COYLE Coyle, Charles Ross 6'3", 195 **DB**
Col: Oklahoma *HS:* Marlow [OK] B: 3/23/1937, Marlow, OK
1961 LARm: 13 G.

ERIC COYLE Coyle, Eric Hudson 6'3", 260 **C**
Col: Colorado *HS:* Longmont [CO] B: 10/26/1963, Longmont, CO
1987 Was: 3 G.

CLAUDE CRABB Crabb, Claude Clarence 6'1", 192 **DB-WR**
Col: Monterey Peninsula Coll. CA (J.C.); Colorado *HS:* Monterey [CA] B: 3/8/1940, Monterey, CA *Drafted:* 1962 Round 19 Was
1964 Phi: Rec 1-14 14.0. **1965** Phi: Rec 2-41 20.5. **1966** LARm: Rec 1-47 47.0. **1967** LARm: PR 1-0. **Total:** Rec 4-102 25.5; PR 1-0.

Year Team	G	Interceptions Int	Yds	TD
1962 Was	13	6	30	0
1963 Was	13	3	82	1
1964 Phi	13	0	0	0
1965 Phi	10	0	0	0
1966 LARm	14	0	0	0
1967 LARm	14	1	23	0
1968 LARm	3	0	0	0
NFL Total	80	10	135	1

BOB CRABLE Crable, Robert Edward 6'3", 228 **LB**
Col: Notre Dame *HS:* Moeller [Cincinnati, OH] B: 9/22/1959, Cincinnati, OH *Drafted:* 1982 Round 1 NYJ
1982 NYJ: 9 G; 1 Sac. **1983** NYJ: 14 G; Int 1-0; 2 Sac. **1984** NYJ: 5 G. **1985** NYJ: 10 G; 1 Sac. **1986** NYJ: 16 G; Int 1-26; 3.5 Sac. **1987** NYJ: 12 G; Int 1-8; 2.5 Sac. **Total:** 66 G; Int 3-34; 10 Sac.

CLEM CRABTREE Crabtree, Clem Gurley 6'3", 225 **T-G**
Col: Wake Forest B: 11/11/1918, Durham, NC D: 1/1981
1940 Det: 9 G. **1941** Det: 9 G. **Total:** 18 G.

CLYDE CRABTREE Crabtree, Clyde 5'8", 160 **BB-WB-HB**
(Cannonball) *Col:* Northwestern; Florida *HS:* J. Sterling Morton [Cicero, IL] B: 11/3/1905, Altoona, IA D: 4/21/1994, South Miami, FL
1930 Fra-Min: 15 G. Fra: 14 G; Rush 1 TD; Rec 1 TD; Tot TD 2; 12 Pt. Min: 1 G. **Total:** 15 G; Rush 1 TD; Rec 1 TD; Tot TD 2; 12 Pt.

ERIC CRABTREE Crabtree, Eric Leslie 6'0", 185 **WR-DB**
(Tree) *Col:* Pittsburgh *HS:* Monessen [PA] B: 11/3/1944, Monessen, PA *Drafted:* 1966 Round 13 Den
1966 Den: KR 5-129 25.8. **1967** Den: Rush 2-2 1.0; PR 2-24 12.0; KR 1-26 26.0. **1968** Den: KR 1-30 30.0. **1970** Cin: Rush 3-23 7.7. **1971** Cin-NE: Rush 3-12 4.0. Cin: Rush 1-1 1.0. NE: Rush 2-11 5.5. **Total:** Rush 8-37 4.6; PR 2-24 12.0; KR 7-185 26.4.

Year Team	G	Receiving Rec	Yds	Avg	TD	Fum
1966 Den	14	1	38	38.0	0	1
1967 Den	14	46	716	15.6	5	0
1968 Den	14	35	601	17.2	5	0
1969 Cin	14	40	855	21.4	7	0
1970 Cin	14	19	231	12.2	2	1
1971 Cin-NE	13	23	222	9.7	3	0
1971 Cin	7	14	102	7.3	2	0
1971 NE	6	9	120	13.3	1	0
NFL Total	83	164	2663	16.2	22	2

NATE CRADDOCK Craddock, Nathaniel 6'1", 220 **FB**
Col: Parsons B: 12/3/1940, Des Moines, IA *Drafted:* 1963 Round 22 Bos
1963 Bal: 3 G; Rush 1-1 1.0; 1 Fum.

DONNIE CRAFT Craft, Donald Joseph 6'0", 206 **RB**
Col: Louisville *HS:* A. Crawford Mosley [Lynn Haven, FL] B: 11/19/1959, Panama City, FL *Drafted:* 1982 Round 12 Hou

Year Team	G	Rushing Att	Yds	Avg	TD	Receiving Rec	Yds	Avg	TD	Tot TD
1982 Hou	9	18	42	2.3	3	23	230	10.0	1	4
1983 Hou	15	55	147	2.7	0	12	99	8.3	0	0
1984 Hou	1	0	0	—	0	0	0	—	0	0
NFL Total	25	73	189	2.6	3	35	329	9.4	1	4

RUSS CRAFT Craft, William Russell 5′9″, 178 **DB-HB**
Col: Alabama *HS:* Wellsburg [WV] B: 10/15/1919, McEwan, TN
Drafted: 1943 Round 15 Phi
1946 Phi: Rec 4-48 12.0; KR 4-86 21.5. **1947** Phi: Rec 2-66 33.0 1 TD. **1948** Phi: Rec 4-138 34.5 2 TD. **1949** Phi: Rec 1-37 37.0; **1** Fum TD. **1950** Phi: Rec 1-14 14.0; KR 10-327 32.7 1 TD. **1951** Phi: KR 2-53 26.5. **1952** Phi: KR 1-18 18.0. **Total:** Rec 12-303 25.3 3 TD; KR 17-484 28.5 1 TD; 1 Fum TD.

Year Team	G	Rushing Att	Yds	Avg	TD	Punt Returns Ret	Yds	Avg	TD
1946 Phi	9	27	108	4.0	0	4	47	11.8	0
1947 Phi	10	5	-1	-0.2	0	1	5	5.0	0
1948 Phi	12	13	67	5.2	0	3	32	10.7	0
1949 Phi	10	11	5	0.5	0	3	50	16.7	0
1950 Phi	12	8	52	6.5	0	19	113	5.9	0
1951 Phi	12	0	0	—	0	2	0	0.0	0
1952 Phi	12	0	0	—	0	0	0	—	0
1953 Phi	12	0	0	—	0	0	0	—	0
1954 Pit	11	0	0	—	0	0	0	—	0
NFL Total	100	64	231	3.6	0	32	247	7.7	0

Year Team	Interceptions Int	Yds	TD	Fum	Tot TD
1946 Phi	3	105	0	4	0
1947 Phi	1	0	0	0	1
1948 Phi	0	0	0	2	2
1949 Phi	1	17	0	2	1
1950 Phi	7	70	0	1	1
1951 Phi	2	61	0	0	0
1952 Phi	1	32	1	0	1
1953 Phi	4	46	0	0	0
1954 Pit	3	120	1	0	1
NFL Total	22	451	2	9	7

JERRY CRAFTS Crafts, Jerry Wayne 6′5″, 343 **OT**
Col: Oklahoma; Louisville *HS:* Metro Christian Acad. [Tulsa, OK]
B: 1/6/1968, Tulsa, OK *Drafted:* 1991 Round 11 Ind
1992 Buf: 6 G. **1993** Buf: 16 G. **1994** Buf: 16 G. **1997** Phi: 15 G. **1998** Phi: 1 G. **Total:** 54 G.

CLARK CRAIG Craig, Clark Western 5′9″, 180 **E**
Col: Oklahoma Baptist; Pennsylvania *HS:* Shawnee [OK]
B: 6/19/1902, near Shawnee, OK D: 11/28/1977, Shawnee, OK
1925 Fra: 2 G.

NEAL CRAIG Craig, Cornelius Jr. 6′1″, 191 **DB**
Col: Fisk *HS:* Robert A. Taft [Cincinnati, OH] B: 4/21/1948, Cincinnati, OH *Drafted:* 1971 Round 7 Cin
1971 Cin: 12 G; Int 1-0. **1972** Cin: 14 G; Int 2-76 1 TD; 6 Pt. **1973** Cin: 14 G; Int 2-52. **1974** Buf: 14 G; KR 1-0; Int 1-55 1 TD; 6 Pt. **1975** Cle: 11 G; Rec 1-1 1.0; Int 1-0. **1976** Cle: 14 G; Int 1-8. **Total:** 79 G; Rec 1-1 1.0; KR 1-0; Int 8-191 2 TD; 12 Pt.

DOBIE CRAIG Craig, Dobie 6′5″, 200 **WR-HB**
Col: Baylor; Howard Payne *HS:* El Campo [TX] B: 2/14/1938, El Campo, TX
1962 Oak: Rush 1-8 8.0. **Total:** Rush 1-8 8.0.

Year Team	G	Receiving Rec	Yds	Avg	TD
1962 Oak	14	27	492	18.2	4
1963 Oak	12	7	196	28.0	2
1964 Hou	7	4	46	11.5	1
NFL Total	33	38	734	19.3	7

PACO CRAIG Craig, Francisco Luis 5′10″, 173 **WR**
Col: UCLA *HS:* Ramona [Riverside, CA] B: 2/2/1965, Santa Maria, CA
Drafted: 1988 Round 10 Det
1988 Det: 8 G; Rec 2-29 14.5.

LARRY CRAIG Craig, Lawrence Gantt 6′1″, 211 **BB-DE-LB-OE**
(Superman) *Col:* South Carolina *HS:* D.W. Daniel [Central, SC]
B: 6/27/1916, Six Mile, SC D: 5/31/1992, Ninety Six, SC *Drafted:* 1939 Round 4 GB
1939 GB: 11 G; Rush 2-6 3.0; Rec 3-44 14.7. **1940** GB: 11 G; Rush 3-9 3.0; Rec 6-67 11.2; Int 1-0. **1941** GB: 11 G; Rush 1-1 1.0; Rec 2-13 6.5. **1942** GB: 11 G; Rush 2-0; KR 2-24 12.0. **1943** GB: 10 G; Rush 1-3 3.0. **1944** GB: 10 G; Rec 2-17 8.5; KR 1-17 17.0; Int 1-20. **1945** GB: 10 G; KR 1-11 11.0; **1** Fum TD; 6 Pt. **1946** GB: 11 G; Rush 1-(-3) -3.0; KR 2-18 9.0. **1947** GB: 12 G; Rec 1-14 14.0. **1948** GB: 12 G. **1949** GB: 12 G. **Total:** 121 G; Rush 10-16 1.6; Rec 14-155 11.1; KR 6-70 11.7; Int 2-20; 1 Fum TD; 6 Pt.

REGGIE CRAIG Craig, Reginald Mark 6′1″, 187 **WR**
Col: Arkansas *HS:* Baytown [TX] B: 6/10/1953, Baytown, TX
1975 KC: 14 G; Rec 1-10 10.0; PR 4-19 4.8; KR 10-247 24.7; 1 Fum. **1976** KC: 1 G; KR 2-45 22.5. **1977** Cle-Buf: 9 G; Rec 1-5 5.0; PR 1-0; 1 Fum. Cle: 5 G; Rec 1-5 5.0; PR 1-0; 1 Fum. Buf: 4 G. **Total:** 24 G; Rec 2-15 7.5; PR 5-19 3.8; KR 12-292 24.3; 2 Fum.

ROGER CRAIG Craig, Roger Timothy 6′0″, 222 **RB**
Col: Nebraska *HS:* Central [Davenport, IA] B: 7/10/1960, Davenport, IA *Drafted:* 1983 Round 2 SF
1988 SF: KR 2-32 16.0. **1993** Min: KR 1-11 11.0. **Total:** KR 3-43 14.3.

Year Team	G	Rushing Att	Yds	Avg	TD	Receiving Rec	Yds	Avg	TD	Fum	Tot TD
1983 SF	16	176	725	4.1	8	48	427	8.9	4	6	12
1984 SF	16	155	649	4.2	7	71	675	9.5	3	3	10
1985 SF	16	214	1050	4.9	9	**92**	1016	11.0	6	5	15
1986 SF	16	204	830	4.1	7	81	624	7.7	0	4	7
1987 SF	14	215	815	3.8	3	66	492	7.5	1	5	4
1988 SF	16	310	1502	4.8	9	76	534	7.0	1	8	10
1989 SF	16	271	1054	3.9	6	49	473	9.7	1	4	7
1990 SF	11	141	439	3.1	1	25	201	8.0	0	2	1
1991 LARd	15	162	590	3.6	1	17	136	8.0	0	2	1
1992 Min	15	105	416	4.0	4	22	164	7.5	0	2	4
1993 Min	14	38	119	3.1	1	19	169	8.9	1	1	2
NFL Total	165	1991	8189	4.1	56	566	4911	8.7	17	42	73

STEVE CRAIG Craig, Steven Arthur 6′3″, 231 **TE**
Col: Northwestern *HS:* Garfield [Akron, OH] B: 3/13/1951, Akron, OH
Drafted: 1974 Round 3 Min
1974 Min: 14 G; Rec 4-26 6.5 1 TD; 6 Pt. **1975** Min: 14 G; Rec 6-68 11.3. **1976** Min: 14 G; Rec 3-33 11.0. **1977** Min: 14 G; Rec 1-14 14.0. **1978** Min: 16 G; Rec 4-31 7.8; KR 1-0. **Total:** 72 G; Rec 18-172 9.6 1 TD; KR 1-0; 6 Pt.

MILT CRAIN Crain, Thomas Milton 6′2″, 225 **FB-LB**
Col: Baylor *HS:* G. W. Brackenridge [San Antonio, TX] B: 12/25/1920, San Antonio, TX *Drafted:* 1943 Round 13 Pit
1944 Bos: Rec 1-16 16.0; PR 2-10 5.0; KR 2-33 16.5; Int 1-0; Punt 1-40 40.0.

Year Team	G	Rushing Att	Yds	Avg	TD
1944 Bos	10	26	78	3.0	0

JOE CRAKES Crakes, Joseph Henry 6′1″, 205 **OE-DE**
(Buster) *Col:* South Dakota B: 12/29/1907, Platte, SD D: 3/23/1976, Victorville, CA
1932 ChiC: 1 G. **1933** Cin: 9 G; Pass 1-0; Rec 4-40 10.0. **Total:** 10 G; Pass 1-0; Rec 4-40 10.0.

CARL CRAMER Cramer, Carl 5′11″, 184 **FB-WB-TB**
(Curly) *Col:* Hamline *HS:* Winnebago [MN] B: 12/20/1897, Winnebago, MN D: 2/1978, Canal Fulton, OH
1920 Cle: 7 G. **1921** Akr: 11 G; Rush 4 TD; Rec 1 TD; Scor 31, 1 XK; Tot TD 5. **1922** Akr: 10 G; Rush 6 TD; 36 Pt. **1923** Akr: 7 G. **1924** Akr: 8 G; Rush 1 TD; Scor 9, 1 FG. **1925** Akr: 5 G. **1926** Akr: 8 G. **Total:** 56 G; Rush 11 TD; Rec 1 TD; Scor 76, 1 FG, 1 XK; Tot TD 12.

DENNIS CRANE Crane, Dennis Walter 6′7″, 260 **DT-OT**
Col: USC; San Bernardino Valley Coll. CA (J.C.) *HS:* Colton [CA]
B: 2/23/1945, San Bernardino, CA *Drafted:* 1968 Round 4 Was
1968 Was: 14 G. **1969** Was: 10 G. **1970** NYG: 9 G. **Total:** 33 G.

GARY CRANE Crane, Gary Don 6′5″, 230 **LB**
Col: Arkansas State *HS:* Dexter [MO] B: 5/19/1946, Dexter, MO
Drafted: 1969 Round 14 Den
1969 Den: 6 G.

PAUL CRANE Crane, Paul Edward 6′3″, 212 **LB-C**
Col: Alabama *HS:* C.F. Vigor [Prichard, AL] B: 1/29/1944, Pascagoula, MS
1966 NYJ: 14 G; 1 Fum. **1967** NYJ: 11 G. **1968** NYJ: 13 G; Scor **1** Saf; 2 Pt; 1 Fum. **1969** NYJ: 14 G; Int 3-63 1 TD; Tot TD 2; 12 Pt. **1970** NYJ: 14 G. **1971** NYJ: 14 G; Int 1-23. **1972** NYJ: 8 G; Int 1-4. **Total:** 88 G; Int 5-90 1 TD; Scor 1 Saf; Tot TD 2; 14 Pt; 2 Fum.

MIKE CRANGLE Crangle, Michael 6′4″, 243 **DE**
Col: Cincinnati; Tennessee-Martin *HS:* Central [Akron, OH]
B: 2/3/1947, Chicago, IL *Drafted:* 1972 Round 4 NO
1972 NO: 13 G.

JACK CRANGLE Crangle, Walter Francis 6′1″, 200 **FB-WB**
Col: Illinois *HS:* Onarga [IL] B: 6/8/1899, Onarga, IL D: 9/1/1944, Independence, MO
1923 ChiC: 9 G; Rush 3 TD; 18 Pt.

BILL CRASS Crass, William Arthur 6′0″, 205 **FB-DB**
Col: Louisiana State *HS:* Electra [TX] B: 6/9/1911, Childress, TX
D: 5/27/1996, Pasadena, CA
1937 ChiC: 3 G; Pass 1-0; Rush 5-8 1.6.

BILL CRAVEN Craven, William Moten 5′11″, 190 **DB**
Col: Harvard *HS:* Frederick [MD] B: 12/18/1951, Ranson, WV
1976 Cle: 13 G.

AARON CRAVER Craver, Aaron LaRenze 6′0″, 218 **RB**
Col: El Camino Coll. CA (J.C.); Fresno State *HS:* Compton [CA]
B: 12/18/1968, Los Angeles, CA *Drafted:* 1991 Round 3 Mia
1994 Mia: Scor 1 2XP. **1996** Den: Pass 1-0. **1998** NO: Pass 1-0.
Total: Pass 2-0; Scor 1 2XP.

		Rushing				Receiving			
Year Team	G	Att	Yds	Avg	TD	Rec	Yds	Avg	TD
1991 Mia	14	20	58	2.9	1	8	67	8.4	0
1992 Mia	6	3	9	3.0	0	0	0	—	0
1994 Mia	8	6	43	7.2	0	24	237	9.9	0
1995 Den	16	73	333	4.6	5	43	369	8.6	1
1996 Den	15	59	232	3.9	2	39	297	7.6	1
1997 SD	15	20	71	3.6	0	4	26	6.5	0
1998 NO	16	45	180	4.0	2	33	214	6.5	2
NFL Total	90	226	926	4.1	10	151	1210	8.0	4

	Kickoff Returns					Tot
Year Team	Ret	Yds	Avg	TD	Fum	TD
1991 Mia	32	615	19.2	0	2	1
1992 Mia	8	174	21.8	0	0	0
1994 Mia	0	0	—	0	1	0
1995 Den	7	50	7.1	0	1	6
1996 Den	0	0	—	0	1	3
1997 SD	3	68	22.7	0	0	0
1998 NO	7	212	30.3	1	2	5
NFL Total	57	1119	19.6	1	7	15

CHARLES CRAWFORD Crawford, Charles D 6′2″, 235 **RB**
Col: Oklahoma State *HS:* Bristow [OK] B: 3/8/1964, Bristow, OK
Drafted: 1986 Supplemental Round 7 Phi

		Rushing				Kickoff Returns				
Year Team	G	Att	Yds	Avg	TD	Ret	Yds	Avg	TD	Fum
1986 Phi	16	28	88	3.1	1	27	497	18.4	0	1
1987 Phi	2	0	0	—	0	0	0	—	0	0
NFL Total	18	28	88	3.1	1	27	497	18.4	0	1

DENNY CRAWFORD Crawford, Denver Junior 6′0″, 190 **G-T**
Col: Tennessee *HS:* Kingsport [TN] B: 6/16/1921, Kingsport, TN
AAFC **1948** NY-A: 8 G.

DERRICK CRAWFORD Crawford, Derrick Lorenzo 5′10″, 185 **WR**
Col: Memphis *HS:* East [Memphis, TN] B: 9/3/1960, Memphis, TN
1986 SF: 10 G; Rec 5-70 14.0; PR 4-15 3.8; KR 15-280 18.7; 1 Fum.

EDDIE CRAWFORD Crawford, Edward Slater III 6′3″, 185 **DB-OE**
Col: Mississippi *HS:* Jackson Central [TN] B: 7/25/1934, Jackson, TN
Drafted: 1956 Round 13 NYG
1957 NYG: 12 G; Rec 2-40 20.0; KR 2-38 19.0; Int 1-3.

ELBERT CRAWFORD Crawford, Elbert 6′3″, 280 **C-OG**
Col: Arkansas *HS:* Hall [Little Rock, AR] B: 6/20/1966, Chicago, IL
Drafted: 1990 Round 8 LARm
1990 NE: 14 G. **1991** NE: 16 G. **Total:** 30 G.

FRED CRAWFORD Crawford, Frederick Eugene 6′2″, 200 **OE-DE-T**
Col: Duke *HS:* Tuscola [NC]; McCallie School [Chattanooga, TN]
B: 7/27/1910, Waynesville, NC D: 3/5/1974, Tallahassee, FL
1935 ChiB: 6 G; Rec 1-10 10.0.

HILTON CRAWFORD Crawford, Hilton 6′2″, 195 **DB**
(Crow) *Col:* Grambling State *HS:* DeSoto [Mansfield, LA]
B: 2/2/1945, Converse, LA *Drafted:* 1969 Round 9 SF
1969 Buf: 7 G; KR 3-74 24.7; 1 Fum.

JIM CRAWFORD Crawford, James Lee 6′1″, 205 **FB-HB**
Col: Wyoming *HS:* Greybull [WY] B: 8/26/1935, Greybull, WY
Drafted: 1957 Round 14 Pit
1960 Bos: Scor 14, 0-1 FG, 1 2XP. **1962** Bos: KR 2-24 12.0; Scor **1** 2XP.
1963 Bos: Pass 2-2 100.0%, 27 13.50. **Total:** Pass 2-2 100.0%, 27 13.50;
KR 2-24 12.0; Scor 46, 0-1 FG, 2 2XP.

		Rushing				Receiving					Tot
Year Team	G	Att	Yds	Avg	TD	Rec	Yds	Avg	TD	Fum	TD
1960 Bos	14	51	238	4.7	2	10	92	9.2	0	0	2
1961 Bos	10	41	148	3.6	0	9	85	9.4	0	1	0
1962 Bos	14	139	459	3.3	2	22	224	10.2	2	1	4
1963 Bos	14	71	233	3.3	1	10	89	8.9	0	1	1
1964 Bos	2	0	0	—	0	1	11	11.0	0	0	0
NFL Total	54	302	1078	3.6	5	52	501	9.6	2	3	7

KEITH CRAWFORD Crawford, Keith LaCharles 6′2″, 188 **WR-DB**
Col: Howard Payne *HS:* Westwood [Palestine, TX] B: 11/21/1970, Palestine, TX
1993 NYG: 7 G; Rec 1-6 6.0. **1995** GB: 13 G. **1996** StL: 16 G; KR 4-47 11.8. **1997** StL: 15 G; Rush 2-32 16.0; Rec 11-232 21.1. **1998** KC: 8 G.
Total: 59 G; Rush 2-32 16.0; Rec 12-238 19.8; KR 4-47 11.8.

KEN CRAWFORD Crawford, Kenneth James 5′11″, 185 **FB-BB-WB-C**
(Chief) *Col:* Miami (Ohio) *HS:* Urbana [OH]; Woodstock HS [OH]
B: 9/1898, Woodstock, OH D: 3/9/1957
1920 Akr: 7 G. **1921** Ham-Cin: 4 G. Ham: 1 G. Cin: 3 G. **1923** Day: 1 G.
1925 Ham: 1 G. **Total:** 13 G.

MIKE CRAWFORD Crawford, Michael Gerald 5′10″, 215 **RB**
Col: Moorpark Coll. CA (J.C.); Arizona State *HS:* Thousand Oaks [CA]
B: 1/3/1964, San Fernando, CA
1987 Cle: 3 G.

MIKE CRAWFORD Crawford, Michael Joseph 6′1″, 238 **LB**
Col: Nevada-Las Vegas *HS:* George Whittell [Zephyr Cove, NV]
B: 10/29/1974, Reno, NV *Drafted:* 1997 Round 6 Mia
1997 Mia: 7 G.

RUFUS CRAWFORD Crawford, Rufus 5′10″, 180 **RB**
Col: Virginia State *HS:* Hunter Juss [Gastonia, NC] B: 5/21/1955, Gastonia, NC
1978 Sea: Rush 8-19 2.4; Rec 4-25 6.3.

		Punt Returns				Kickoff Returns				
Year Team	G	Ret	Yds	Avg	TD	Ret	Yds	Avg	TD	Fum
1978 Sea	16	34	284	8.4	0	35	829	23.7	0	5

TIM CRAWFORD Crawford, Timothy Jr. 6′4″, 245 **LB**
Col: Texas Tech *HS:* Kashmere [Houston, TX] B: 12/17/1962, Houston, TX
1987 Cle: 3 G; 3 Sac.

VERNON CRAWFORD Crawford, Vernon Dean 6′4″, 245 **LB**
Col: San Francisco City Coll. CA (J.C.); Florida State *HS:* Texas City [TX]
B: 6/25/1974, Texas City, TX *Drafted:* 1997 Round 5 NE
1997 NE: 16 G. **1998** NE: 16 G. **Total:** 32 G.

MUSH CRAWFORD Crawford, Walter Charles 6′0″, 200 **G-T**
Col: Beloit; Lake Forest; Illinois *HS:* Newport [Waukegan, IL]
B: 12/23/1898, Waukegan, IL D: 10/27/1966, Roanoke, VA
1925 ChiB: 3 G. **1927** NYY: 9 G. **Total:** 12 G.

BILL CRAWFORD Crawford, William 6′2″, 235 **OG**
Col: British Columbia (Canada) B: 7/17/1937
1960 NYG: 4 G.

DICK CRAYNE Crayne, Richard Cherry 6′0″, 205 **FB-DB**
(Baldy) *Col:* Iowa *HS:* Fairfield [IA] B: 4/24/1913, West Chester, IA
D: 8/1985, Le Mars, IA *Drafted:* 1936 Round 1 Bkn
1936 Bkn: Pass 2-1 50.0%, 52 26.00; Rec 1-32 32.0; Scor 7, 1 XK.
1937 Bkn: Pass 4-2 50.0%, 20 5.00; Rec 1-4 4.0; Scor 3, 1 FG.
Total: Pass 6-3 50.0%, 72 12.00; Rec 2-36 18.0; Scor 10, 1 FG, 1 XK.

		Rushing			
Year Team	G	Att	Yds	Avg	TD
1936 Bkn	12	64	203	3.2	1
1937 Bkn	10	47	135	2.9	0
NFL Total	22	111	338	3.0	1

BOB CREECH Creech, Robert Edwin 6′3″, 236 **LB**
Col: Texas Christian *HS:* W.B. Ray [Corpus Christi, TX] B: 1/26/1949, Corpus Christi, TX *Drafted:* 1971 Round 14 Phi
1971 Phi: 3 G. **1972** Phi: 13 G. **1973** NO: 2 G. **Total:** 18 G.

LOU CREEKMUR Creekmur, Louis 6′4″, 246 **OT-OG-DT-DG**
Col: William & Mary *HS:* Woodbridge [NJ] B: 1/22/1927, Hopeland, NJ
Drafted: 1948 Round 24 Phi *HOF:* 1996
1950 Det: 12 G. **1951** Det: 12 G. **1952** Det: 12 G. **1953** Det: 12 G.
1954 Det: 12 G. **1955** Det: 12 G. **1956** Det: 12 G. **1957** Det: 12 G.
1958 Det: 12 G; KR 2-23 11.5. **1959** Det: 8 G. **Total:** 116 G; KR 2-23 11.5.

BILL CREGAR Cregar, William Osmund 5′11″, 195 **G-LB**
Col: Holy Cross *HS:* Frank H. Morrell [Irvington, NJ] B: 5/2/1925, Newark, NJ *Drafted:* 1947 Round 16 Pit
1947 Pit: 11 G. **1948** Pit: 12 G. **Total:** 23 G.

MILAN CREIGHTON Creighton, Milan Standish 6′0″, 190 **DE-OE**
(Crate) *Col:* Arkansas *HS:* Gothenburg [NE] B: 1/21/1908, Gothenburg, NE
1931 ChiC: 9 G; Rec 2 TD; 12 Pt. **1932** ChiC: 10 G; Rec 5-74 14.8.
1933 ChiC: 11 G; Rec 7-80 11.4. **1934** ChiC: 9 G; Rush 1-12 12.0;
Rec 6-84 14.0. **1935** ChiC: 8 G; Rec 1-8 8.0. **1936** ChiC: 6 G. **1937** ChiC: 2 G. **Total:** 55 G; Rush 1-12 12.0; Rec 19-246 12.9 2 TD; 12 Pt.

TED CREMER Cremer, Theodore Roosevelt 6′2″, 209 **DE-OE**
Col: Auburn *HS:* Phillips [Birmingham, AL] B: 3/16/1919, Corbin, KY
D: 11/20/1980, Birmingham, AL

		Receiving			
Year Team	G	Rec	Yds	Avg	TD
1946 Det	11	15	179	11.9	0
1947 Det	12	13	117	9.0	1
1948 Det-GB	7	0	0	—	0
1948 Det	4	0	0	—	0

1948 GB	3	0	0	—	0
NFL Total	30	28	296	10.6	1

CARL CRENNEL Crennel, Carl Lee 6′1″, 230 **LB**
Col: West Virginia *HS:* E.C. Glass [Lynchburg, VA] B: 9/14/1948, Lynchburg, VA *Drafted:* 1970 Round 9 Pit
1970 Pit: 3 G.

LEON CRENSHAW Crenshaw, Leon 6′7″, 280 **DT**
Col: Tuskegee *HS:* Hooper City [Sayreton, AL] B: 7/14/1943, Greenville, AL
1968 GB: 10 G.

WILLIS CRENSHAW Crenshaw, Willis Clarence 6′2″, 230 **RB**
(Rubbie) *Col:* Kansas State *HS:* Soldan [St. Louis, MO] B: 7/16/1941, St. Louis, MO *Drafted:* 1963 Round 9 StL

		Rushing				Receiving			
Year Team	**G**	**Att**	**Yds**	**Avg**	**TD**	**Rec**	**Yds**	**Avg**	**TD**
1964 StL	14	60	297	5.0	1	8	58	7.3	0
1965 StL	14	127	437	3.4	0	23	232	10.1	1
1966 StL	14	94	360	3.8	0	15	46	3.1	0
1967 StL	14	44	149	3.4	0	6	30	5.0	0
1968 StL	14	203	813	4.0	6	23	232	10.1	1
1969 StL	14	55	172	3.1	3	11	94	8.5	0
1970 Den	12	69	200	2.9	5	18	105	5.8	1
NFL Total	96	652	2428	3.7	15	104	797	7.7	3

	Kickoff Returns					Tot
Year Team	**Ret**	**Yds**	**Avg**	**TD**	**Fum**	**TD**
1964 StL	13	340	26.2	0	3	1
1965 StL	2	23	11.5	0	2	1
1966 StL	0	0	—	0	5	0
1967 StL	2	14	7.0	0	1	0
1968 StL	6	104	17.3	0	**8**	7
1969 StL	4	34	8.5	0	1	3
1970 Den	0	0	—	0	3	6
NFL Total	27	515	19.1	0	23	18

BOB CRESPINO Crespino, Robert 6′5″, 225 **TE**
Col: Mississippi *HS:* Greenville [MS] B: 1/11/1938, Duncan, MS
Drafted: 1961 Round 1 Cle
1967 NYG: KR 1-7 7.0. **Total:** KR 1-7 7.0.

		Receiving				
Year Team	**G**	**Rec**	**Yds**	**Avg**	**TD**	**Fum**
1961 Cle	13	2	62	31.0	1	1
1962 Cle	14	2	13	6.5	0	0
1963 Cle	14	2	22	11.0	1	0
1964 NYG	13	12	165	13.8	0	0
1965 NYG	14	7	57	8.1	4	0
1966 NYG	14	16	167	10.4	2	0
1967 NYG	14	10	125	12.5	1	0
1968 NYG	11	7	130	18.6	0	0
NFL Total	107	58	741	12.8	9	1

SMILEY CRESWELL Creswell, Smiley Lawrence III 6′4″, 251 **DE**
Col: Columbia Basin Coll. WA (J.C.); Michigan State *HS:* Monroe [WA] B: 12/11/1959, Everett, WA *Drafted:* 1983 Round 5 NE
1985 Phi: 3 G; 1 Sac.

RON CREWS Crews, Ronald Edward 6′4″, 256 **NT-DE**
Col: Notre Dame; Nevada-Las Vegas *HS:* Columbia [MO]
B: 10/9/1956, Springfield, IL *Drafted:* 1980 Round 4 Cle
1980 Cle: 16 G.

TERRY CREWS Crews, Terry Alan 6′2″, 245 **LB**
Col: Western Michigan *HS:* Flint Southwestern Acad. [MI]
B: 7/30/1968, Flint, MI *Drafted:* 1991 Round 11 LARm
1991 LARm: 6 G. **1993** SD: 10 G. **1995** Was: 16 G. **Total:** 32 G.

JAMES CRIBBS Cribbs, James Clark 6′3″, 269 **DE**
Col: Memphis *HS:* Hamilton [Memphis, TN] B: 7/10/1966, Memphis, TN *Drafted:* 1989 Round 12 Det
1989 Det: 7 G.

JOE CRIBBS Cribbs, Joe Stanier 5′11″, 190 **RB**
Col: Auburn *HS:* Sulligent [AL] B: 1/5/1958, Sulligent, AL
Drafted: 1980 Round 2 Buf
1980 Buf: Pass 1-1 100.0%, 13 13.00. **1981** Buf: Pass 1-1 100.0%, 9 9.00 1 TD. **1982** Buf: Pass 1-0, 1 Int. **1983** Buf: Pass 2-1 50.0%, 3 1.50. **Total:** Pass 5-3 60.0%, 25 5.00 1 TD 1 Int.

		Rushing				Receiving			
Year Team	**G**	**Att**	**Yds**	**Avg**	**TD**	**Rec**	**Yds**	**Avg**	**TD**
1980 Buf	16	306	1185	3.9	11	52	415	8.0	1
1981 Buf	15	257	1097	4.3	3	40	603	15.1	7
1982 Buf	7	134	633	4.7	3	13	99	7.6	0
1983 Buf	16	263	1131	4.3	3	57	524	9.2	7
1985 Buf	10	122	399	3.3	1	18	142	7.9	0
1986 SF	14	152	590	3.9	5	35	346	9.9	0
1987 SF	11	70	300	4.3	1	9	70	7.8	0
1988 Ind-Mia	13	5	21	4.2	0	0	0	—	0
1988 Ind	1	0	0	—	0	0	0	—	0
1988 Mia	12	5	21	4.2	0	0	0	—	0
NFL Total	102	1309	5356	4.1	27	224	2199	9.8	15

	Punt Returns				Kickoff Returns					Tot
Year Team	**Ret**	**Yds**	**Avg**	**TD**	**Ret**	**Yds**	**Avg**	**TD**	**Fum**	**TD**
1980 Buf	29	154	5.3	0	2	39	19.5	0	**16**	12
1981 Buf	0	0	—	0	0	0	—	0	12	10
1982 Buf	0	0	—	0	0	0	—	0	5	3
1983 Buf	0	0	—	0	0	0	—	0	6	10
1985 Buf	0	0	—	0	0	0	—	0	5	1
1986 SF	0	0	—	0	0	0	—	0	5	5
1987 SF	0	0	—	0	13	327	25.2	1	1	2
1988 Ind-Mia	0	0	—	0	**41**	863	21.0	0	1	0
1988 Mia	0	0	—	0	41	863	21.0	0	1	0
NFL Total	29	154	5.3	0	56	1229	21.9	1	51	43

BERNIE CRIMMINS Crimmins, Bernard Anthony 5′11″, 195 **G-LB-HB-FB**
Col: Notre Dame *HS:* St. Xavier [Louisville, KY] B: 4/19/1919, Louisville, KY D: 3/19/1993, West Lafayette, IN
1945 GB: 6 G; Int 1-12 1 TD; 6 Pt.

HAL CRISLER Crisler, Harold James 6′4″, 213 **OE-DE-DB**
Col: San Jose State; Iowa State *HS:* Richmond [CA] B: 12/31/1923, Richmond, CA Deceased
1946 Bos: Rush 4-6 1.5; KR 2-22 11.0. **1948** Was: PR 2-20 10.0; Int 2-52. **Total:** Rush 4-6 1.5; PR 2-20 10.0; KR 2-22 11.0; Int 2-52.

		Receiving				
Year Team	**G**	**Rec**	**Yds**	**Avg**	**TD**	**Fum**
1946 Bos	11	32	385	12.0	5	3
1947 Bos	10	25	363	14.5	2	0
1948 Was	11	33	599	18.2	6	2
1949 Was	11	26	388	14.9	4	1
1950 Bal	10	19	307	16.2	5	0
NFL Total	53	135	2042	15.1	22	6

JOEL CRISMAN Crisman, Joel Devere 6′5″, 300 **OG**
Col: USC *HS:* Grundy Center [IA] B: 2/3/1971, Cherokee, IA
1996 TB: 9 G.

CRIS CRISSY Crissy, William Robert 5′11″, 195 **DB**
Col: Princeton *HS:* Penn Yan Acad. [NY] B: 2/3/1959, Penn Yan, NY
Drafted: 1981 Round 12 NE
1981 Was: 1 G.

CHUCK CRIST Crist, Charles Thomas 6′2″, 205 **DB**
Col: Penn State *HS:* Salamanca [NY] B: 1/16/1951, Salamanca, NY
1972 NYG: KR 1-7 7.0. **1973** NYG: PR 1-7 7.0. **1976** NO: PR 1-8 8.0. **Total:** PR 2-15 7.5; KR 1-7 7.0.

		Interceptions			
Year Team	**G**	**Int**	**Yds**	**TD**	**Fum**
1972 NYG	14	1	14	0	0
1973 NYG	14	2	6	0	0
1974 NYG	13	3	20	0	0
1975 NO	8	3	69	0	0
1976 NO	14	1	20	0	0
1977 NO	14	4	6	0	1
1978 SF	15	6	159	0	1
NFL Total	92	20	294	0	2

JEFF CRISWELL Criswell, Jeffrey L 6′7″, 291 **OG-OT**
Col: Graceland *HS:* Lynnville-Sully [Sully, IA] B: 3/7/1964, Grinnell, IA
1987 Ind: 3 G. **1988** NYJ: 15 G. **1989** NYJ: 16 G. **1990** NYJ: 16 G. **1991** NYJ: 16 G. **1992** NYJ: 14 G. **1993** NYJ: 16 G. **1994** NYJ: 15 G. **1995** KC: 15 G. **1996** KC: 15 G. **1997** KC: 16 G. **1998** KC: 14 G. **Total:** 171 G.

KIRBY CRISWELL Criswell, Kirby Lynn 6′5″, 238 **LB-DE**
Col: Kansas *HS:* Grinnell [IA] B: 8/31/1957, Grinnell, IA *Drafted:* 1980 Round 2 Cin
1980 StL: 4 G. **1981** StL: 2 G. **Total:** 6 G.

RAY CRISWELL Criswell, Ray Alan 6′0″, 192 **P**
Col: Florida *HS:* Orange Park [FL] B: 8/16/1963, Lake City, FL
Drafted: 1986 Round 5 Phi
1987 TB: Rush 1-0. **1988** TB: Rush 2-0; Scor 1, 1-1 100.0% XK. **Total:** Rush 3-0; Scor 1, 1-1 100.0% XK.

		Punting			
Year Team	**G**	**Punts**	**Yds**	**Avg**	**Fum**
1987 TB	3	26	1046	40.2	1
1988 TB	16	68	2477	36.4	1
NFL Total	19	94	3523	37.5	2

HANK CRITCHFIELD Critchfield, Henry Brown 5′10″, 207 **C**
Col: Wooster *HS:* North [Columbus, OH] B: 6/14/1905, Columbus, OH D: 7/29/1980, Wooster, OH
1931 Cle: 9 G.

LARRY CRITCHFIELD Critchfield, Lawrence K 5′11″, 195 **G**
Col: Grove City *HS:* Confluence [PA] B: 1/6/1908, Ursina, PA D: 6/30/1965, Confluence, PA
1933 Pit: 11 G.

KEN CRITER Criter, Kenneth William 6′0″, 225 **LB**
Col: Wisconsin *HS:* New Holstein [WI] B: 2/17/1947, Fond du Lac, WI
1969 Den: 14 G; KR 3-31 10.3. **1970** Den: 14 G; KR 2-20 10.0. **1971** Den: 11 G; KR 5-81 16.2. **1972** Den: 8 G. **1973** Den: 14 G; PR 1-0; Scor 1 Saf; 2 Pt. **1974** Den: 14 G; KR 3-48 16.0. **Total:** 75 G; PR 1-0; KR 13-180 13.8; Scor 1 Saf; 2 Pt.

RAY CRITTENDEN Crittenden, Raymond C IV 6′1″, 192 **WR**
Col: Virginia Tech *HS:* Thomas Jefferson [Alexandria, VA]; Annandale HS [VA] B: 3/1/1970, Washington, DC
1993 NE: Rush 1-(-3) -3.0; PR 2-37 18.5. **1994** NE: PR 19-155 8.2.
Total: Rush 1-(-3) -3.0; PR 21-192 9.1.

		Receiving				Kickoff Returns				
Year Team	G	Rec	Yds	Avg	TD	Ret	Yds	Avg	TD	Fum
1993 NE	16	16	293	18.3	1	23	478	20.8	0	0
1994 NE	16	28	379	13.5	3	24	460	19.2	0	1
1997 SD	2	0	0	—	0	0	0	—	0	0
NFL Total	34	44	672	15.3	4	47	938	20.0	0	1

JACK CRITTENDON Crittendon, Jack 6′1″, 190 **OE**
Col: Wayne State (Mich.) *HS:* Ferndale [MI] B: 8/9/1930, Ferndale, MI D: 2/2/1993, Toronto, Canada
1954 ChiC: 10 G; Rec 5-48 9.6; Scor 0-1 FG.

JIM CROCICCHIA Crocicchia, James Francis 6′2″, 209 **QB**
Col: Pennsylvania *HS:* Holy Cross [Waterbury, CT] B: 2/19/1964, Waterbury, CT
1987 NYG: 1 G; Pass 15-6 40.0%, 89 5.93 1 TD; Rush 4-5 1.3; 2 Fum.

RAY CROCKETT Crockett, Donald Ray 5′10″, 185 **DB**
Col: Baylor *HS:* Duncanville [TX] B: 1/5/1967, Dallas, TX
Drafted: 1989 Round 4 Det
1989 Det: KR 1-8 8.0. **1990** Det: 1 Fum TD; 1 Sac. **1991** Det: 1 Sac. **1992** Det: 1 Sac. **1993** Det: 1 Sac. **1995** Den: PR 0-4; **1** Fum TD; 3 Sac. **1996** Den: 4 Sac. **1998** Den: 0.5 Sac. **Total:** PR 0-4; KR 1-8 8.0; 2 Fum TD; 11.5 Sac.

		Interceptions			Tot
Year Team	G	Int	Yds	TD	TD
1989 Det	16	1	5	0	0
1990 Det	16	3	17	0	1
1991 Det	16	6	141	1	1
1992 Det	15	4	50	0	0
1993 Det	16	2	31	0	0
1994 Den	14	2	6	0	0
1995 Den	16	0	0	0	1
1996 Den	15	2	34	0	0
1997 Den	16	4	18	0	0
1998 Den	16	3	105	1	1
NFL Total	156	27	407	2	4

HENRI CROCKETT Crockett, Henri Woodrau 6′2″, 251 **LB**
Col: Florida State *HS:* Ely [Pompano Beach, FL] B: 10/28/1974, Pompano Beach, FL *Drafted:* 1997 Round 4 Atl
1997 Atl: 16 G; 2 Sac. **1998** Atl: 10 G; 1 Sac. **Total:** 26 G; 3 Sac.

MONTE CROCKETT Crockett, Monte Julius 6′4″, 218 **TE**
Col: New Mexico Highlands *HS:* Lincoln [Hinton, WV] B: 7/14/1938, Talcott, WV
1960 Buf: PR 1-5 5.0. **1961** Buf: KR 1-0. **Total:** PR 1-5 5.0; KR 1-0.

		Receiving			
Year Team	G	Rec	Yds	Avg	TD
1960 Buf	14	14	173	12.4	1
1961 Buf	14	20	325	16.3	0
1962 Buf	12	1	14	14.0	0
NFL Total	40	35	512	14.6	1

BOBBY CROCKETT Crockett, Robert Paul 6′3″, 200 **WR**
Col: Arkansas *HS:* Dermott [AR] B: 4/3/1943, Briggsville, AR
Drafted: 1966 Round 10 Buf

		Receiving			
Year Team	G	Rec	Yds	Avg	TD
1966 Buf	14	31	533	17.2	3
1968 Buf	9	6	76	12.7	0
1969 Buf	5	4	50	12.5	0
NFL Total	28	41	659	16.1	3

WILLIS CROCKETT Crockett, Willis Robert 6′3″, 234 **LB**
Col: Georgia Tech *HS:* Coffee Co. [Douglas, GA] B: 8/25/1966, Douglas, GA *Drafted:* 1989 Round 5 Dal
1990 Dal: 13 G.

ZACK CROCKETT Crockett, Zachary Theopolis 6′2″, 246 **RB**
Col: Hinds CC MS; Florida State *HS:* Ely [Pompano Beach, FL]
B: 12/2/1972, Pompano Beach, FL *Drafted:* 1995 Round 3 Ind

		Rushing				Receiving					Tot
Year Team	G	Att	Yds	Avg	TD	Rec	Yds	Avg	TD	Fum	TD
1995 Ind	16	1	0	0.0	0	2	35	17.5	0	0	0
1996 Ind	5	31	164	5.3	0	11	96	8.7	1	2	1
1997 Ind	16	95	300	3.2	1	15	112	7.5	0	3	1
1998 Ind-Jac	12	2	5	2.5	0	2	5	2.5	0	1	0
1998 Ind	2	2	5	2.5	0	1	1	1.0	0	1	0
1998 Jac	10	0	0	—	0	1	4	4.0	0	0	0
NFL Total	49	129	469	3.6	1	30	248	8.3	1	6	2

MIKE CROEL Croel, Michael Stephen 6′3″, 238 **DE**
Col: Nebraska *HS:* Lincoln-Sudbury Regional [Sudbury, MA]
B: 6/6/1969, Detroit, MI *Drafted:* 1991 Round 1 Den
1991 Den: 13 G; 10 Sac. **1992** Den: 16 G; 5 Sac. **1993** Den: 16 G; Int 1-22 1 TD; 6 Pt; 5 Sac. **1994** Den: 13 G. **1995** NYG: 16 G; 1 Sac. **1996** Bal: 16 G; Int 1-16; 3 Sac. **1998** Sea: 12 G. **Total:** 102 G; Int 2-38 1 TD; 6 Pt; 24.0 Sac.

ABE CROFT Croft, Abe 6′0″, 183 **OE-DB**
Col: Southern Methodist B: 3/12/1920, Houston, TX D: 12/2/1972, Houston, TX *Drafted:* 1944 Round 3 ChiB
1944 ChiB: 10 G; Rec 9-140 15.6 2 TD; Int 1-19; 12 Pt. **1945** ChiB: 1 G; Rec 2-12 6.0. **Total:** 11 G; Rec 11-152 13.8 2 TD; Int 1-19; 12 Pt.

DON CROFT Croft, Donald Thomas 6′4″, 254 **DT**
Col: Texas-El Paso *HS:* Irving [TX] B: 1/7/1949, Temple, TX
Drafted: 1972 Round 5 Bal
1972 Buf: 14 G. **1974** Buf: 6 G. **1975** Buf: 13 G. **1976** Det: 1 G.
Total: 34 G.

LEE CROFT Croft, Leland Reynolds 6′1″, 190 **G-T**
Col: Wis.-Platteville *HS:* Mineral Point [WI] B: 11/5/1898, Mineral Point, WI D: 1/28/1984, Odessa, TX
1924 Rac: 1 G.

TINY CROFT Croft, Milburn Russell 6′3″, 287 **T**
Col: Alabama; Ripon *HS:* Steinmetz [Chicago, IL] B: 11/7/1920, Chicago, IL D: 1/22/1977, St.Germain, WI *Drafted:* 1942 Round 18 Was
1942 GB: 7 G. **1943** GB: 4 G. **1944** GB: 10 G. **1945** GB: 9 G. **1946** GB: 11 G. **1947** GB: 10 G. **Total:** 51 G.

WIN CROFT Croft, Winfield Scott 5′11″, 235 **G**
(Bill) *Col:* Utah *HS:* Lovell [WY] B: 2/28/1910, Cowley, WY D: 7/8/1993, Gallup, NM
1935 Bkn: 11 G. **1936** Pit: 9 G. **Total:** 20 G.

DON CROFTCHECK Croftcheck, Donald Anthony 6′2″, 230 **OG-LB**
Col: Indiana *HS:* Redstone [PA] B: 9/12/1942, Allison, PA
Drafted: 1965 Round 8 Was
1965 Was: 14 G. **1966** Was: 12 G; KR 2-36 18.0. **1967** ChiB: 9 G.
Total: 35 G; KR 2-36 18.0.

NOLAN CROMWELL Cromwell, Nolan Neil 6′1″, 200 **DB**
Col: Kansas *HS:* Ransom [KS] B: 1/30/1955, Smith Center, KS
Drafted: 1977 Round 2 LARm
1978 LARm: Rush 1-16 16.0 1 TD; PR 1-8 8.0. **1979** LARm: Rush 1-5 5.0 1 TD. **1980** LARm: Pass 1-0; Rush 2-0; Scor **1** 1XP. **1981** LARm: Rush 1-17 17.0. **1982** LARm: Rush 1-17 17.0 1 TD. **1983** LARm: Rush 1-0. **1985** LARm: KR 1-3 3.0; 1 Sac. **1987** LARm: 1 Sac.
Total: Pass 1-0; Rush 7-55 7.9 3 TD; PR 1-8 8.0; KR 1-3 3.0; Scor 1 1XP; 2 Sac.

		Interceptions				Tot
Year Team	G	Int	Yds	TD	Fum	TD
1977 LARm	14	0	0	0	0	0
1978 LARm	16	1	31	0	0	2
1979 LARm	16	5	109	0	0	1
1980 LARm	16	8	140	1	2	1
1981 LARm	16	5	94	0	0	0
1982 LARm	9	3	33	0	0	1
1983 LARm	16	3	76	1	0	1
1984 LARm	11	3	54	1	0	1
1985 LARm	16	2	5	0	0	0
1986 LARm	16	5	101	1	0	1
1987 LARm	15	2	28	0	0	0
NFL Total	161	37	671	4	2	8

PETE CRONAN Cronan, Peter Joseph 6′2″, 238 **LB**
Col: Boston College *HS:* Marian [Framingham, MA] B: 1/13/1955, Bourne, MA *Drafted:* 1977 Round 2 Sea
1977 Sea: 14 G. **1978** Sea: 15 G; Int 2-15. **1979** Sea: 16 G.
1981 Sea-Was: 15 G; KR 3-60 20.0. Sea: 5 G; KR 2-42 21.0. Was: 10 G;

KR 1-18 18.0. **1982** Was: 7 G. **1983** Was: 16 G; KR 1-17 17.0. **1984** Was: 3 G. **1985** Was: 4 G. **Total:** 90 G; KR 4-77 19.3; Int 2-15.

GENE CRONIN Cronin, Eugene Edward 6'2", 229 **DE-OG-LB**
(Geno; Bud) *Col:* U. of Pacific *HS:* C.K. McClatchy [Sacramento, CA] B: 11/20/1933, Spalding, NE *Drafted:* 1956 Round 7 Det
1956 Det: 12 G. **1957** Det: 12 G; KR 1-0. **1958** Det: 12 G. **1959** Det: 12 G. **1960** Dal: 11 G; Int 1-2. **1961** Was: 14 G. **1962** Was: 14 G. **Total:** 87 G; KR 1-0; Int 1-2.

FRITZ CRONIN Cronin, Francis B 5'11", 182 **E-G**
Col: St. Mary's (Minn.) *HS:* Kenosha [WI] B: 6/20/1905, Lake City, MN D: 3/1969, Manchester, NH
1927 Dul: 8 G.

JERRY CRONIN Cronin, Jeremiah George 6'0", 198 **E**
(The Bullet) *Col:* Rutgers *HS:* De La Salle Acad. [New York, NY] B: 12/12/1909, New York, NY D: 7/1984, Huntington, NY
1932 Bkn: 4 G.

JACK CRONIN Cronin, John Patrick 5'11", 178 **WB-TB-FB-BB**
Col: Boston College *HS:* Dean Acad. [Franklin, MA] B: 5/3/1903, Hingham, MA D: 1/18/1993, Jupiter, FL
1927 Prov: 12 G; PR **1** TD; 6 Pt. **1928** Prov: 8 G; Rush 3 TD; 18 Pt. **1929** Prov: 12 G; Rush 1 TD; 6 Pt. **1930** Prov: 10 G. **Total:** 42 G; Rush 4 TD; PR 1 TD; Tot TD 5; 30 Pt.

TOMMY CRONIN Cronin, Thomas V 5'9", 170 **HB**
(Paddy) *Col:* Loras; Marquette *HS:* Janesville [WI] B: 4/29/1896, Janesville, WI D: 4/24/1964, Janesville, WI
1922 GB: 5 G; Rush 1 TD; 6 Pt.

BILL CRONIN Cronin, William 5'10", 183 **FB-WB-TB-OE**
Col: Boston College *HS:* Hingham [MA] B: 4/18/1901 D: 4/1948
1927 Prov: 9 G; Rec 1 TD; 6 Pt. **1928** Prov: 9 G. **1929** Prov: 10 G. **Total:** 28 G; Rec 1 TD; 6 Pt.

BILL CRONIN Cronin, William F Jr. 6'5", 231 **TE**
Col: Boston College B: 11/20/1943, Lawrence, MA *Drafted:* 1965 Round 15 Oak
1965 Phi: 2 G. **1966** Mia: 14 G; Rec 7-83 11.9 1 TD; 6 Pt. **Total:** 16 G; Rec 7-83 11.9 1 TD; 6 Pt.

DOC CRONKHITE Cronkhite, Henry Oliver 6'5", 210 **OE-DE**
Col: Kansas State B: 3/10/1911 D: 12/26/1949, Wichita, KS
1934 Bkn: 6 G; Rec 1-3 3.0.

AL CROOK Crook, Alfred John 5'10", 190 **C-G-T**
Col: Washington & Jefferson *HS:* Central [Detroit, MI] B: 11/20/1897, Detroit, MI D: 2/17/1958
1925 Det: 8 G. **1926** Det: 8 G. **Total:** 16 G.

COREY CROOM Croom, Corey Vincent 5'11", 212 **RB**
Col: Ball State *HS:* Sandusky [OH] B: 5/22/1971, Sandusky, OH
1993 NE: Rec 8-92 11.5. **1994** NE: KR 10-172 17.2. **1995** NE: Rec 1-8 8.0. **Total:** Rec 9-100 11.1; KR 10-172 17.2.

		Rushing				
Year Team	**G**	**Att**	**Yds**	**Avg**	**TD**	**Fum**
1993 NE	14	60	198	3.3	1	1
1994 NE	16	0	0	—	0	1
1995 NE	13	13	54	4.2	0	0
NFL Total	43	73	252	3.5	1	2

SYLVESTER CROOM Croom, Sylvester Jr. 6'0", 235 **C**
Col: Alabama *HS:* Tuscaloosa [AL] B: 9/25/1954, Tuscaloosa, AL
1975 NO: 1 G.

CHRIS CROOMS Crooms, Christopher Dale 6'2", 211 **DB**
Col: Texas A&M *HS:* Robert E. Lee [Baytown, TX] B: 2/4/1969, Houston, TX *Drafted:* 1992 Round 5 LARm
1992 LARm: 16 G.

MARSHALL CROPPER Cropper, Marshall Joseph 6'4", 200 **WR**
Col: Maryland East. Shore *HS:* Mary Nottingham Smith [Accomack, VA] B: 4/1/1944, Wattsville, VA
1967 Pit: 7 G; Rec 1-11 11.0. **1968** Pit: 5 G; Rec 4-54 13.5; KR 3-53 17.7. **1969** Pit: 4 G; Rec 9-116 12.9. **Total:** 16 G; Rec 14-181 12.9; KR 3-53 17.7.

CLEVELAND CROSBY Crosby, Cleveland Pittsburgh 6'5", 250 **DE**
Col: Purdue; Arizona *HS:* East St. Louis [IL] B: 4/3/1956, West Point, MS *Drafted:* 1980 Round 2 Cle
1982 Bal: 9 G.

RON CROSBY Crosby, Ronald Cameron 6'3", 224 **LB**
Col: Penn State *HS:* South Allegheny [McKeesport, PA] B: 3/2/1955, McKeesport, PA *Drafted:* 1977 Round 5 Det
1978 NO: 14 G. **1979** NYJ: 12 G. **1980** NYJ: 16 G; Int 2-47. **1981** NYJ: 16 G. **1982** NYJ: 9 G. **1983** NYJ: 16 G; Rush 1-5 5.0. **Total:** 83 G; Rush 1-5 5.0; Int 2-47.

STEVE CROSBY Crosby, Steven Kent 5'11", 205 **RB**
Col: Kansas State; Fort Hays State *HS:* Pawnee Park [Great Bend, KS] B: 7/3/1950, Great Bend, KS *Drafted:* 1974 Round 17 NYG
1974 NYG: 9 G; Rush 14-55 3.9; Rec 2-44 22.0; KR 2-47 23.5; Punt 1-60 60.0; 1 Fum. **1975** NYG: 4 G; KR 1-14 14.0; Punt 1-28 28.0. **1976** NYG: 2 G; Rush 1-(-1) -1.0. **Total:** 15 G; Rush 15-54 3.6; Rec 2-44 22.0; KR 3-61 20.3; Punt 2-88 44.0; 1 Fum.

BILLIE CROSS Cross, Billie Jarrel 5'6", 151 **HB**
(Canadian Comet) *Col:* West Texas A&M *HS:* Canadian [TX] B: 5/3/1929, Fry, TX *Drafted:* 1951 Round 24 ChiC
1952 ChiC: KR 9-169 18.8. **1953** ChiC: KR 12-257 21.4. **Total:** KR 21-426 20.3.

		Rushing				Receiving			
Year Team	**G**	**Att**	**Yds**	**Avg**	**TD**	**Rec**	**Yds**	**Avg**	**TD**
1951 ChiC	12	53	283	5.3	3	18	322	17.9	3
1952 ChiC	12	71	347	4.9	2	17	234	13.8	2
1953 ChiC	12	51	196	3.8	1	17	285	16.8	1
NFL Total	36	175	826	4.7	6	52	841	16.2	6

	Punt Returns					
Year Team	**Ret**	**Yds**	**Avg**	**TD**	**Fum**	**Tot TD**
1951 ChiC	7	39	5.6	0	2	6
1952 ChiC	21	177	8.4	0	6	4
1953 ChiC	6	5	0.8	0	7	2
NFL Total	34	221	6.5	0	15	12

HOWARD CROSS Cross, Howard Edward Jr. 6'5", 260 **TE**
Col: Alabama *HS:* New Hope [AL] B: 8/8/1967, Huntsville, AL *Drafted:* 1989 Round 6 NYG
1990 NYG: KR 1-10 10.0. **1991** NYG: KR 1-11 11.0. **1993** NYG: KR 2-15 7.5. **Total:** KR 4-36 9.0.

		Receiving				
Year Team	**G**	**Rec**	**Yds**	**Avg**	**TD**	**Fum**
1989 NYG	16	6	107	17.8	1	1
1990 NYG	16	8	106	13.3	0	0
1991 NYG	16	20	283	14.2	2	1
1992 NYG	16	27	357	13.2	2	2
1993 NYG	16	21	272	13.0	5	0
1994 NYG	16	31	364	11.7	4	0
1995 NYG	15	18	197	10.9	0	0
1996 NYG	16	22	178	8.1	1	1
1997 NYG	16	21	150	7.1	2	1
1998 NYG	16	13	90	6.9	0	2
NFL Total	159	187	2104	11.3	17	8

IRV CROSS Cross, Irvin Acie 6'2", 195 **DB**
Col: Northwestern *HS:* Hammond [IN] B: 7/27/1939, Hammond, IN *Drafted:* 1961 Round 7 Phi

		Punt Returns				Kickoff Returns			
Year Team	**G**	**Ret**	**Yds**	**Avg**	**TD**	**Ret**	**Yds**	**Avg**	**TD**
1961 Phi	13	7	77	11.0	0	1	11	11.0	0
1962 Phi	14	1	2	2.0	0	2	72	36.0	0
1963 Phi	14	0	0	—	0	0	0	—	0
1964 Phi	14	0	0	—	0	0	0	—	0
1965 Phi	14	14	79	5.6	0	25	662	26.5	0
1966 LARm	14	12	82	6.8	0	12	348	29.0	0
1967 LARm	14	17	136	8.0	0	4	134	33.5	0
1968 LARm	14	0	0	—	0	0	0	—	0
1969 Phi	14	0	0	—	0	0	0	—	0
NFL Total	125	51	376	7.4	0	44	1227	27.9	0

	Interceptions			
Year Team	**Int**	**Yds**	**TD**	**Fum**
1961 Phi	2	36	0	0
1962 Phi	5	46	0	0
1963 Phi	2	6	0	0
1964 Phi	3	109	1	1
1965 Phi	3	1	0	2
1966 LARm	1	60	1	0
1967 LARm	2	0	0	5
1968 LARm	3	0	0	0
1969 Phi	1	0	0	0
NFL Total	22	258	2	8

JEFF CROSS Cross, Jeffrey Allen 6'4", 280 **DE**
Col: Missouri *HS:* Palo Verde [Blythe, CA] B: 3/25/1966, Riverside, CA *Drafted:* 1988 Round 9 Mia
1988 Mia: 16 G. **1989** Mia: 16 G; 10 Sac. **1990** Mia: 16 G; 11.5 Sac. **1991** Mia: 16 G; 7 Sac. **1992** Mia: 16 G; 5 Sac. **1993** Mia: 16 G; 10.5 Sac. **1994** Mia: 13 G; Int 1-0; 9.5 Sac. **1995** Mia: 16 G; 1 Fum; 6 Sac. **Total:** 125 G; Int 1-0; 1 Fum; 59.5 Sac.

JUSTIN CROSS Cross, Justin Allen 6'6", 263 **OT**
Col: Western State (Colo.) *HS:* Portsmouth [NH] B: 4/29/1959, Montreal, Canada *Drafted:* 1981 Round 10 Buf
1982 Buf: 9 G. **1983** Buf: 15 G. **1984** Buf: 7 G. **1985** Buf: 3 G. **1986** Buf: 10 G. **Total:** 44 G.

RANDY CROSS Cross, Randall Laureat 6'3", 259 **OG-C**
Col: UCLA *HS:* Crespi [Encino, CA] B: 4/25/1954, Brooklyn, NY
Drafted: 1976 Round 2 SF
1976 SF: 14 G. **1977** SF: 14 G; 1 Fum. **1978** SF: 9 G; 1 Fum. **1979** SF: 16 G. **1980** SF: 16 G. **1981** SF: 16 G. **1982** SF: 9 G. **1983** SF: 16 G. **1984** SF: 16 G. **1985** SF: 15 G. **1986** SF: 16 G. **1987** SF: 12 G. **1988** SF: 16 G. **Total:** 185 G; 2 Fum.

BOBBY CROSS Cross, Robert Joe 6'4", 240 **OT-DT**
Col: Kilgore Coll. TX (J.C.); Stephen F. Austin St. *HS:* Kilgore [TX]
B: 4/4/1931, Ranger, TX D: 6/18/1989, Kilgore, TX *Drafted:* 1952 Round 9 ChiB
1952 ChiB: 12 G. **1954** LARm: 12 G. **1955** LARm: 12 G. **1956** SF: 12 G. **1957** SF: 12 G. **1958** ChiC: 12 G. **1959** ChiC: 11 G; KR 1-0. **1960** Bos: 4 G. **Total:** 87 G; KR 1-0.

DAVE CROSSAN Crossan, David Harry 6'4", 245 **C**
Col: Maryland *HS:* Collingswood [NJ] B: 6/8/1940, Philadelphia, PA
Drafted: 1963 Round 3 Phi
1965 Was: 14 G. **1966** Was: 14 G; 1 Fum. **1967** Was: 11 G. **1968** Was: 14 G. **1969** Was: 6 G. **Total:** 59 G; 1 Fum.

LEON CROSSWHITE Crosswhite, Leon Mac 6'2", 215 **RB**
Col: Oklahoma *HS:* Hennessey [TX] B: 4/28/1951, Hennessey, TX
Drafted: 1973 Round 2 Det
1973 Det: 7 G; Rush 11-30 2.7 1 TD; Rec 1-4 4.0; 6 Pt. **1974** Det: 14 G; Rush 12-49 4.1 1 TD; Rec 3-31 10.3; KR 1-11 11.0; 6 Pt; 1 Fum. **Total:** 21 G; Rush 23-79 3.4 2 TD; Rec 4-35 8.8; KR 1-11 11.0; 12 Pt; 1 Fum.

DAVE CROSTON Croston, David Charles 6'5", 280 **OT**
Col: Iowa *HS:* East [Sioux City, IA] B: 11/10/1963, Sioux City, IA
Drafted: 1987 Round 3 GB
1988 GB: 16 G.

JIM CROTTY Crotty, James Richard 6'1", 190 **DB**
Col: Notre Dame *HS:* Falls [International Falls, MN] B: 3/31/1938, Storm Lake, IA *Drafted:* 1960 Round 12 Was
1960 Was: 9 G; Int 1-0; 1 Fum. **1961** Was-Buf: 10 G; Int 2-0. Was: 5 G. Buf: 5 G; Int 2-0. **1962** Buf: 3 G. **Total:** 22 G; Int 3-0; 1 Fum.

TERRY CROUCH Crouch, Terry Wayne 6'2", 278 **OG**
Col: Oklahoma *HS:* Skyline [Dallas, TX] B: 7/6/1959, Dallas, TX
Drafted: 1982 Round 5 Bal
1982 Bal: 9 G.

BILLY CROUCH Crouch, William Butler 6'1", 187 **C**
Col: Davidson *HS:* Cartersville [GA] B: 11/4/1898, Moorestown, TN
D: 2/23/1934, Washington, DC
1921 Was: 3 G.

DAVID CROUDIP Croudip, David Rodney 5'8", 183 **DB**
Col: Ventura Coll. CA (J.C.); San Diego State *HS:* Compton [CA]
B: 1/25/1958, Indianapolis, IN D: 10/10/1988, Duluth, GA
1984 LARm: 16 G. **1985** SD-Atl: 13 G. SD: 2 G. Atl: 11 G. **1986** Atl: 15 G; KR 1-20 20.0; Int 2-35. **1987** Atl: 12 G; KR 1-18 18.0; Int 2-40. **1988** Atl: 6 G. **Total:** 62 G; KR 2-38 19.0; Int 4-75.

RAY CROUSE Crouse, Marlon Ray 5'11", 214 **RB**
Col: Laney Coll. CA (J.C.); Nevada-Las Vegas *HS:* Encinal [Alameda, CA]; Berkeley HS [CA] B: 3/16/1959, Oakland, CA
1984 GB: Rec 9-93 10.3 1 TD.

		Rushing			
Year Team	**G**	**Att**	**Yds**	**Avg**	**TD**
1984 GB	16	53	169	3.2	0

JAKE CROUTHAMEL Crouthamel, John Jacob 6'0", 195 **HB**
Col: Dartmouth *HS:* Pennridge [Perkasie, PA] B: 6/27/1938, Perkasie, PA *Drafted:* 1960 Round 1 LAC
1960 Bos: 2 G; Rush 4-16 4.0; KR 2-27 13.5.

AL CROW Crow, Albert Lee 6'7", 260 **DT**
Col: William & Mary *HS:* Norfolk [VA]; Fork Union Mil. Acad. [VA]
B: 8/20/1932, Norfolk, VA *Drafted:* 1955 Round 28 NYG
1960 Bos: 3 G.

WAYNE CROW Crow, Charles Wayne 6'1", 205 **HB-DB**
Col: California *HS:* Corcoran [CA] B: 5/5/1938, Coolidge, AZ
Drafted: 1960 Round 8 StL
1960 Oak: Int 4-50. **1961** Oak: Pass 10-6 60.0%, 165 16.50; Scor 1 2XP. **1962** Buf: Pass 4-2 50.0%, 16 4.00 1 Int. **Total:** Pass 14-8 57.1%, 181 12.93 1 Int; Int 4-50; Scor 1 2XP.

		Rushing				Receiving			
Year Team	**G**	**Att**	**Yds**	**Avg**	**TD**	**Rec**	**Yds**	**Avg**	**TD**
1960 Oak	14	0	0	—	0	0	0	—	0
1961 Oak	14	119	490	4.1	2	17	105	6.2	0
1962 Buf	14	110	589	5.4	1	8	80	10.0	1
1963 Buf	5	6	6	1.0	0	5	69	13.8	0
NFL Total	47	235	1085	4.6	3	30	254	8.5	1

	Punting				Tot
Year Team	**Punts**	**Yds**	**Avg**	**Fum**	**TD**
1960 Oak	76	2958	38.9	0	0
1961 Oak	63	2613	41.5	1	2
1962 Buf	76	2946	38.8	1	2
1963 Buf	10	424	42.4	0	0
NFL Total	225	8941	39.7	2	4

JOHN DAVID CROW Crow, John David 6'2", 220 **HB-OE**
Col: Texas A&M *HS:* Springhill [LA] B: 7/8/1935, Marion, LA
Drafted: 1958 Round 1 ChiC
1958 ChiC: KR 6-145 24.2; **1** Fum TD. **1959** ChiC: KR 5-185 37.0. **1962** StL: PR 2-6 3.0. **Total:** PR 2-6 3.0; KR 11-330 30.0; 1 Fum TD.

		Passing							
Year Team	**G**	**Att**	**Comp**	**Comp%**	**Yds**	**YPA**	**TD**	**Int**	**Rating**
1958 ChiC	7	1	0	0.0	0	0.00	0	1	0.0
1959 ChiC	12	0	0	—	0	—	0	0	—
1960 StL	12	18	9	50.0	247	13.72	2	1	109.7
1961 StL	8	14	4	28.6	76	5.43	1	1	43.8
1962 StL	14	20	12	60.0	241	12.05	0	0	102.3
1963 StL	3	3	2	66.7	27	9.00	1	0	134.7
1964 StL	13	1	0	0.0	0	0.00	0	0	39.6
1965 SF	14	4	2	50.0	61	15.25	1	1	95.8
1966 SF	14	4	2	50.0	61	15.25	0	1	56.3
1967 SF	14	5	2	40.0	46	9.20	0	0	73.8
1968 SF	14	0	0	—	0	—	0	0	—
NFL Total	125	70	33	47.1	759	10.84	5	5	80.6

	Rushing				Receiving					Tot
Year Team	**Att**	**Yds**	**Avg**	**TD**	**Rec**	**Yds**	**Avg**	**TD**	**Fum**	**TD**
1958 ChiC	52	221	4.3	2	20	362	18.1	3	1	6
1959 ChiC	140	666	4.8	3	27	328	12.1	4	5	7
1960 StL	183	1071	**5.9**	6	25	462	18.5	3	**11**	9
1961 StL	48	192	4.0	1	20	306	15.3	3	1	4
1962 StL	192	751	3.9	14	23	246	10.7	3	**14**	17
1963 StL	9	34	3.8	0	0	0	—	0	0	0
1964 StL	163	554	3.4	7	23	257	11.2	1	5	8
1965 SF	132	514	3.9	2	28	493	17.6	7	5	9
1966 SF	121	477	3.9	1	30	341	11.4	3	1	4
1967 SF	113	479	4.2	2	31	373	12.0	3	1	5
1968 SF	4	4	1.0	0	31	531	17.1	5	0	5
NFL Total	1157	4963	4.3	38	258	3699	14.3	35	44	74

ORIEN CROW Crow, John Orien 6'2", 220 **C**
Col: Haskell Indian B: 9/7/1912, Salem, MO
1933 Bos: 11 G. **1934** Bos: 11 G; Rec 2-20 10.0. **Total:** 22 G; Rec 2-20 10.0.

LINDON CROW Crow, Lindon Oscar 6'1", 195 **DB**
Col: USC *HS:* Corcoran [CA] B: 4/4/1933, Denison, TX *Drafted:* 1955 Round 2 ChiC
1960 NYG: **1** Fum TD. **1963** LARm: Scor **1** Saf. **Total:** Scor 1 Saf; 1 Fum TD.

		Punt Returns				Interceptions				Tot
Year Team	**G**	**Ret**	**Yds**	**Avg**	**TD**	**Int**	**Yds**	**TD**	**Fum**	**TD**
1955 ChiC	12	0	0	—	0	3	11	0	0	0
1956 ChiC	12	1	21	21.0	0	**11**	170	0	0	0
1957 ChiC	12	0	0	—	0	1	0	0	0	0
1958 NYG	12	11	46	4.2	0	3	40	0	1	0
1959 NYG	12	11	66	6.0	0	5	54	**1**	1	1
1960 NYG	12	2	1	0.5	0	3	3	0	1	1
1961 LARm	14	0	0	—	0	6	117	0	0	0
1962 LARm	14	0	0	—	0	5	100	**1**	0	1
1963 LARm	14	0	0	—	0	0	0	0	0	0
1964 LARm	9	0	0	—	0	1	23	0	0	0
NFL Total	123	25	134	5.4	0	38	518	2	3	3

EARL CROWDER Crowder, Earl Franklin 6'0", 198 **BB-LB**
Col: Oklahoma *HS:* Cherokee [OK] B: 1/21/1915, Cherokee, OK
D: 2/6/1984, Cherokee, OK *Drafted:* 1939 Round 10 ChiC
1939 ChiC: 6 G; Pass 7-2 28.6%, 6 0.86; Rush 6-(-5) -0.8; Rec 2-59 29.5. **1940** Cle: 3 G; Rec 2-33 16.5. **Total:** 9 G; Pass 7-2 28.6%, 6 0.86; Rush 6-(-5) -0.8; Rec 4-92 23.0.

RANDY CROWDER Crowder, Randolph Channing 6'2", 242 **DT-NT-DE**
Col: Penn State *HS:* Farrell [PA] B: 7/30/1953, Sharon, PA
Drafted: 1974 Round 6 Mia
1974 Mia: 12 G. **1975** Mia: 13 G. **1976** Mia: 14 G. **1978** TB: 14 G. **1979** TB: 16 G. **1980** TB: 2 G. **Total:** 71 G.

LARRY CROWE Crowe, Larry Darnell 6'1", 198 **RB**
Col: Texas Southern *HS:* Valley View [TX] B: 1/8/1950, Diana, TX
Drafted: 1971 Round 8 Pit
1972 Phi: 1 G; Rush 1-2 2.0. **1975** Atl: 5 G. **Total:** 6 G; Rush 1-2 2.0.

PAUL CROWE Crowe, Paul James 6′1″, 195 **DB-HB-FB**
(Legs) *Col:* St. Mary's (Cal.) *HS:* Chino [CA] B: 10/23/1924, Chino, CA D: 12/13/1989
AAFC **1948** SF-A: 14 G; Rush 12-65 5.4; Rec 0-16 1 TD; PR 2-14 7.0; KR 2-18 9.0; Int 5-69 1 TD; Tot TD 2; 12 Pt. **1949** SF-A-LA-A: 9 G; Rush 3-2 0.7; PR 6-96 16.0; Int 1-25; 6 Pt. **Total:** 23 G; Rush 15-67 4.5; Rec 0-16 1 TD; PR 8-110 13.8; KR 2-18 9.0; Int 6-94 1 TD; Tot TD 3; 18 Pt.

NFL **1951** NYY: 9 G; Rec 3-20 6.7; Int 3-15.

GERMANE CROWELL Crowell, Germane L 6′3″, 213 **WR**
Col: Virginia *HS:* North Forsyth [Winston-Salem, NC] B: 9/13/1976, Winston-Salem, NC *Drafted:* 1998 Round 2 Det
1998 Det: Rush 1-35 35.0.

		Receiving				
Year Team	G	Rec	Yds	Avg	TD	Fum
1998 Det	14	25	464	18.6	3	1

ODIS CROWELL Crowell, Odis Leonard 6′2″, 220 **T**
Col: Amarillo Coll. TX (J.C.); Hardin-Simmons *HS:* Matador [TX] B: 10/7/1914, Matador, TX
AAFC **1947** SF-A: 2 G.

BERNIE CROWL Crowl, Richard Bernard 5′10″, 185 **G-C**
Col: Rutgers *HS:* Ridgefield Park [NJ] B: 3/25/1908, Brooklyn, NY
1930 Bkn: 2 G.

JIM CROWLEY Crowley, James Harold 5′9″, 165 **TB-HB**
(Sleepy Jim) *Col:* Notre Dame *HS:* Green Bay East [WI] B: 9/10/1902, Chicago, IL D: 1/15/1986, Scranton, PA
1925 GB-Prov: 3 G; Rec 1 TD; 6 Pt. GB: 2 G; Rec 1 TD; 6 Pt. Prov: 1 G. **Total:** 3 G; Rec 1 TD; 6 Pt.

JOE CROWLEY Crowley, Joseph A 6′0″, 194 **OE-DB**
Col: Dartmouth *HS:* Boston Latin [MA]; Kiski School [Saltsburg, PA] B: 4/6/1919, Brighton, MA
1944 Bos: 9 G; Rush 1-10 10.0; Rec 13-279 21.5 3 TD; Int 1-5; 18 Pt. **1945** Bos: 9 G; Rec 1-12 12.0; Int 1-45. **Total:** 18 G; Rush 1-10 10.0; Rec 14-291 20.8 3 TD; Int 2-50; 18 Pt.

RAE CROWTHER Crowther, Rae 5′11″, 175 **OE**
Col: Penn State; Colgate *HS:* Radnor [PA] B: 12/11/1902, Rosemont, PA D: 11/3/1980, Haddonfield, NJ
1925 Fra: 19 G; Rec 3 TD; 18 Pt. **1926** Fra: 14 G. **Total:** 33 G; Rec 3 TD; 18 Pt.

SAVILLE CROWTHER Crowther, Saville Evans 6′1″, 220 **G-T**
Col: Penn State; Colgate *HS:* Radnor [PA] B: 7/10/1901, Rosemont, PA D: 7/8/1962, Philadelphia, PA
1925 Fra: 2 G.

PHIL CROYLE Croyle, Philip Gordon 6′3″, 223 **LB**
Col: California *HS:* San Lorenzo [CA] B: 10/30/1947, Great Lakes, IL *Drafted:* 1971 Round 7 Hou
1971 Hou: 14 G. **1972** Hou: 12 G. **1973** Hou-Buf: 6 G. Hou: 1 G. Buf: 5 G. **Total:** 32 G.

DERRICK CRUDUP Crudup, Derrick 6′2″, 220 **DB-RB**
Col: Florida; Oklahoma *HS:* Boca Raton [FL] B: 2/15/1965, Delray Beach, FL *Drafted:* 1988 Round 7 LARd
1989 LARd: 4 G. **1991** LARd: 16 G. **Total:** 20 G.

BOB CRUM Crum, Robert Harvey 6′5″, 240 **DE**
Col: Arizona *HS:* Sunnyslope [Phoenix, AZ] B: 6/28/1951, Mesa, AZ *Drafted:* 1973 Round 3 Cle
1974 StL: 14 G; KR 1-1 1.0.

DWAYNE CRUMP Crump, Dwayne Anthony 5′11″, 180 **DB**
Col: Fresno City Coll. CA (J.C.); Pasadena City Coll. CA (J.C.); Fresno State *HS:* Madera [CA] B: 8/9/1950, Madera, CA *Drafted:* 1973 Round 6 StL
1973 StL: 14 G. **1974** StL: 14 G; Int 1-10. **1975** StL: 14 G; 6 Pt. **1976** StL: 13 G; KR 3-57 19.0. **Total:** 55 G; KR 3-57 19.0; Int 1-10; 6 Pt.

GEORGE CRUMP Crump, George Stanley 6′4″, 260 **DE**
Col: East Carolina *HS:* Indian River [Chesapeake, VA] B: 7/22/1959, Portsmouth, VA *Drafted:* 1982 Round 4 NE
1982 NE: 9 G; Scor **1** Saf; 2 Pt; 1 Sac.

HARRY CRUMP Crump, Harry M 6′1″, 205 **FB**
Col: Boston College *HS:* Westborough [MA] B: 6/18/1940, Framingham, MA
1963 Bos: Rec 6-46 7.7; KR 3-33 11.0.

		Rushing				
Year Team	G	Att	Yds	Avg	TD	Fum
1963 Bos	14	48	120	2.5	5	1

CARLESTER CRUMPLER Crumpler, Carlester Jr. 6′6″, 260 **TE**
Col: East Carolina *HS:* J.H. Rose [Greenville, NC] B: 9/5/1971, Greenville, NC *Drafted:* 1994 Round 7 Sea

		Receiving				
Year Team	G	Rec	Yds	Avg	TD	Fum
1994 Sea	9	2	19	9.5	0	0
1995 Sea	16	23	254	11.0	1	1
1996 Sea	16	26	258	9.9	0	1
1997 Sea	15	31	361	11.6	1	0
1998 Sea	11	6	52	8.7	1	0
NFL Total	67	88	944	10.7	3	2

DOUG CRUSAN Crusan, Douglas Gordon Jr. 6′5″, 250 **OT**
Col: Indiana *HS:* Monessen [PA] B: 7/26/1946, Monessen, PA *Drafted:* 1968 Round 1 Mia
1968 Mia: 14 G. **1969** Mia: 14 G. **1970** Mia: 14 G. **1971** Mia: 14 G. **1972** Mia: 11 G. **1973** Mia: 14 G. **1974** Mia: 1 G. **Total:** 82 G.

TOMMY CRUTCHER Crutcher, Tommy Joe 6′4″, 230 **LB**
Col: Texas Christian *HS:* McKinney [TX] B: 8/10/1941, McKinney, TX *Drafted:* 1964 Round 3 GB
1964 GB: 14 G; Rush 1-5 5.0; KR 2-54 27.0. **1965** GB: 14 G; KR 3-53 17.7; Int 1-4. **1966** GB: 14 G; Int 1-15. **1967** GB: 14 G; KR 3-48 16.0. **1968** NYG: 14 G. **1969** NYG: 14 G; Int 1-0. **1971** GB: 12 G. **1972** GB: 12 G. **Total:** 108 G; Rush 1-5 5.0; KR 8-155 19.4; Int 3-19.

BUDDY CRUTCHFIELD Crutchfield, Buddy 6′0″, 196 **DB**
Col: North Carolina Central *HS:* Athens Drive [Raleigh, NC] B: 3/7/1976, Raleigh, NC
1998 Was: 2 G.

DWAYNE CRUTCHFIELD Crutchfield, Dwayne A 6′0″, 235 **RB**
Col: Waldorf Coll. IA (J.C.); Garden City CC KS; Iowa State *HS:* North College Hill [Cincinnati, OH] B: 9/30/1959, Cincinnati, OH *Drafted:* 1982 Round 3 NYJ
1983 NYJ-Hou: Rec 19-133 7.0. NYJ: Rec 19-133 7.0. **1984** LARm: Rec 2-11 5.5 1 TD; KR 1-20 20.0. **Total:** Rec 21-144 6.9 1 TD; KR 1-20 20.0.

		Rushing					Tot
Year Team	G	Att	Yds	Avg	TD	Fum	TD
1982 NYJ	6	22	78	3.5	1	1	1
1983 NYJ-Hou	13	140	578	4.1	3	2	3
1983 NYJ	11	137	571	4.2	3	2	3
1983 Hou	2	3	7	2.3	0	0	0
1984 LARm	15	73	337	4.6	1	1	2
NFL Total	34	235	993	4.2	5	4	6

BOB CRYDER Cryder, Robert Joseph 6′4″, 275 **OG-OT**
Col: Alabama *HS:* O'Fallon [IL] B: 9/7/1956, East St. Louis, IL *Drafted:* 1978 Round 1 NE
1978 NE: 5 G. **1979** NE: 16 G. **1980** NE: 16 G. **1981** NE: 15 G. **1982** NE: 9 G. **1983** NE: 14 G. **1984** Sea: 16 G. **1985** Sea: 15 G. **1986** Sea: 1 G. **Total:** 107 G.

LARRY CSONKA Csonka, Lawrence Richard 6′3″, 237 **RB**
(Butch Cassidy; Zonk) *Col:* Syracuse *HS:* Stow [OH] B: 12/25/1946, Stow, OH *Drafted:* 1968 Round 1 Mia *HOF:* 1987

		Rushing				Receiving					Tot
Year Team	G	Att	Yds	Avg	TD	Rec	Yds	Avg	TD	Fum	TD
1968 Mia	11	138	540	3.9	6	11	118	10.7	1	3	7
1969 Mia	11	131	566	4.3	2	21	183	8.7	1	1	3
1970 Mia	14	193	874	4.5	6	11	94	8.5	0	3	6
1971 Mia	14	195	1051	**5.4**	7	13	113	8.7	1	0	8
1972 Mia	14	213	1117	5.2	6	5	48	9.6	0	2	6
1973 Mia	14	219	1003	4.6	5	7	22	3.1	0	3	5
1974 Mia	12	197	749	3.8	9	7	35	5.0	0	2	9
1976 NYG	12	160	569	3.6	4	6	39	6.5	0	2	4
1977 NYG	14	134	464	3.5	1	2	20	10.0	0	0	1
1978 NYG	14	91	311	3.4	6	7	73	10.4	0	1	6
1979 Mia	16	220	837	3.8	12	16	75	4.7	1	4	13
NFL Total	146	1891	8081	4.3	64	106	820	7.7	4	21	68

PAUL CUBA Cuba, Paul J 6′0″, 212 **T**
Col: Pittsburgh *HS:* New Castle [PA] B: 6/12/1908, New Castle, PA D: 8/12/1990, New Castle, PA
1933 Phi: 9 G. **1934** Phi: 10 G. **1935** Phi: 10 G. **Total:** 29 G.

WALT CUDZIK Cudzik, Walter Jacob 6′2″, 231 **C-LB**
(Mike) *Col:* Purdue *HS:* Harrison [Chicago, IL] B: 2/21/1932, Chicago, IL *Drafted:* 1954 Round 18 Was
1954 Was: 1 G. **1960** Bos: 14 G; Rec 1-11 11.0; Scor 0-1 FG. **1961** Bos: 14 G; KR 1-0. **1962** Bos: 14 G. **1963** Bos: 14 G. **1964** Buf: 14 G. **Total:** 71 G; Rec 1-11 11.0; KR 1-0; Scor 0-1 FG.

WARD CUFF Cuff, Ward Lloyd 6′1″, 192 **WB-DB-HB-FB**
Col: Marquette *HS:* Redwood Valley [Redwood Falls, MN] B: 8/12/1913, Redwood Falls, MN *Drafted:* 1937 Round 4 NYG
1941 NYG: KR 2-46 23.0. **1942** NYG: KR 3-78 26.0. **1943** NYG: Pass 1-0; KR 3-59 19.7. **1944** NYG: KR 2-63 31.5. **1945** NYG: KR 4-105 26.3. **Total:** Pass 1-0; KR 14-351 25.1.

Year Team	G	Rushing Att	Yds	Avg	TD	Receiving Rec	Yds	Avg	TD
1937 NYG	11	4	32	8.0	2	5	117	23.4	2
1938 NYG	11	18	38	2.1	0	8	114	14.3	1
1939 NYG	9	23	102	4.4	0	10	83	8.3	2
1940 NYG	8	15	86	5.7	1	13	220	16.9	1
1941 NYG	11	28	157	5.6	0	19	317	16.7	2
1942 NYG	11	38	189	5.0	0	16	267	16.7	2
1943 NYG	10	80	523	**6.5**	3	7	52	7.4	0
1944 NYG	10	76	425	5.6	0	11	135	12.3	2
1945 NYG	9	48	214	4.5	0	12	172	14.3	0
1946 ChiC	10	13	78	6.0	1	5	82	16.4	1
1947 GB	10	1	7	7.0	0	0	0	—	0
NFL Total	110	344	1851	5.4	7	106	1559	14.7	13

Year Team	Punt Returns Ret	Yds	Avg	TD	Interceptions Int	Yds	TD
1938 NYG	—	—	—	0	—	—	**1**
1940 NYG	—	—	—	0	2	16	0
1941 NYG	1	10	10.0	0	4	**152**	0
1942 NYG	4	54	13.5	0	1	43	0
1943 NYG	9	120	13.3	0	3	6	0
1944 NYG	11	115	10.5	0	2	31	0
1945 NYG	10	124	12.4	0	1	15	0
1946 ChiC	2	24	12.0	0	0	0	0
NFL Total	37	447	12.1	0	13	263	1

Year Team	Scoring Pts	FG	FGA	FG%	XK	XKA	XK%	Fum	Tot TD
1937 NYG	30	2	—	—	0	—	—	0	4
1938 NYG	45	**5**	9	55.6	**18**	**20**	90.0	0	2
1939 NYG	39	**7**	**16**	43.8	6	6	100.0	0	2
1940 NYG	36	5	8	62.5	9	9	100.0	0	2
1941 NYG	46	5	13	38.5	19	20	95.0	0	2
1942 NYG	39	3	11	27.3	18	18	100.0	0	2
1943 NYG	53	**3**	9	33.3	26	27	96.3	0	3
1944 NYG	17	1	4	25.0	2	2	100.0	0	2
1945 NYG	0	0	0	—	0	0	—	5	0
1946 ChiC	55	5	12	41.7	28	30	93.3	0	2
1947 GB	51	**7**	**16**	43.8	30	30	100.0	0	0
NFL Total	411	43	98	41.8	156	162	96.3	5	21

JIM CULBREATH Culbreath, James Clifford Jr. 6'0", 209 **RB**
Col: Oklahoma *HS:* Mitchell [Yeadon, PA] B: 10/21/1952, Yeadon, PA
Drafted: 1977 Round 10 GB
1977 GB: Rec 2-6 3.0; KR 5-82 16.4. **1978** GB: Rec 7-78 11.1; KR 4-58 14.5. **Total:** Rec 9-84 9.3; KR 9-140 15.6.

Year Team	G	Rushing Att	Yds	Avg	TD	Fum
1977 GB	13	12	53	4.4	0	1
1978 GB	12	30	92	3.1	0	1
1979 GB	4	5	8	1.6	0	0
1980 Phi-NYG	3	1	3	3.0	0	0
1980 Phi	2	1	3	3.0	0	0
1980 NYG	1	0	0	—	0	0
NFL Total	32	48	156	3.3	0	2

WILLIE CULLARS Cullars, Willie Edward 6'5", 250 **DE**
Col: Pratt CC KS; Kansas State *HS:* Central [Washington, GA]
B: 8/4/1951, Washington, GA *Drafted:* 1974 Round 7 Phi
1974 Phi: 13 G.

DAVID CULLEN Cullen, David Emerson 5'10", 230 **G**
Col: Geneva *HS:* Freedom [PA] B: 3/18/1905, Freedom, PA
D: 5/15/1982, Butler, PA
1931 Cle: 2 G.

DAVE CULLITY Cullity, David Richard 6'7", 275 **OT**
Col: Utah *HS:* La Serna [Whittier, CA] B: 6/15/1964, La Mirada, CA
1989 SF: 2 G.

JIM CULLOM Cullom, James Henry 5'11", 235 **OG**
(Truck) *Col:* California *HS:* Piedmont [CA] B: 11/5/1925, Healdsburg, CA D: 3/4/1998, Oakland, CA *Drafted:* 1950 Round 17 Was
1951 NYY: 2 G.

DERRICK CULLORS Cullors, Derrick Shane 6'0", 195 **RB**
Col: Texas Christian; Murray State *HS:* Lake Highlands [Dallas, TX]
B: 12/26/1972, Dallas, TX
1997 NE: Rec 2-8 4.0. **1998** NE: Rec 14-146 10.4 1 TD.
Total: Rec 16-154 9.6 1 TD.

Year Team	G	Rushing Ret	Yds	Avg	TD	Kickoff Returns Ret	Yds	Avg	TD	Fum	Tot TD
1997 NE	15	22	101	4.6	0	15	386	25.7	1	3	1
1998 NE	16	18	48	2.7	0	45	1085	24.1	0	1	1
NFL Total	31	40	149	3.7	0	60	1471	24.5	1	4	2

CURLEY CULP Culp, Curley 6'2", 265 **DT-OG**
Col: Arizona State *HS:* Yuma [AZ] B: 3/10/1946, Yuma, AZ
Drafted: 1968 Round 2 Den
1968 KC: 9 G. **1969** KC: 14 G. **1970** KC: 14 G. **1971** KC: 14 G. **1972** KC: 14 G. **1973** KC: 13 G. **1974** KC-Hou: 12 G. KC: 4 G. Hou: 8 G. **1975** Hou: 14 G; **1** Fum TD; 6 Pt. **1976** Hou: 14 G. **1977** Hou: 14 G; Int 1-25. **1978** Hou: 16 G. **1979** Hou: 16 G. **1980** Hou-Det: 13 G. Hou: 10 G. Det: 3 G. **1981** Det: 2 G. **Total:** 179 G; Int 1-25; 1 Fum TD; 6 Pt.

BRAD CULPEPPER Culpepper, John Broward 6'1", 275 **DT**
Col: Florida *HS:* Leon [Tallahassee, FL] B: 5/8/1969, Tallahassee, FL
Drafted: 1992 Round 10 Min
1992 Min: 11 G. **1993** Min: 15 G. **1994** TB: 16 G; KR 2-30 15.0; 4 Sac. **1995** TB: 16 G; 4 Sac. **1996** TB: 13 G; 1.5 Sac. **1997** TB: 16 G; 8.5 Sac. **1998** TB: 16 G; 9 Sac. **Total:** 103 G; KR 2-30 15.0; 27.0 Sac.

ED CULPEPPER Culpepper, Robert Edward 6'1", 255 **DT**
Col: Alabama *HS:* Manatee [Bradenton, FL] B: 1/21/1934, Bradenton, FL *Drafted:* 1955 Round 9 GB
1958 ChiC: 11 G. **1959** ChiC: 11 G. **1960** StL: 10 G. **1961** Min: 14 G. **1962** Hou: 14 G. **1963** Hou: 14 G. **Total:** 74 G.

WILLIE CULPEPPER Culpepper, Willie James 5'11", 155 **WR**
Col: Southwestern Louisiana *HS:* Jean Ribault [Jacksonville, FL]
B: 3/27/1967, Jacksonville, FL
1992 TB: 3 G.

AL CULVER Culver, Alvin Sager 6'2", 245 **T**
Col: Notre Dame *HS:* St.Thomas Acad. [St. Paul, MN] B: 6/11/1908, Wilmette, IL D: 2/7/1982, Plymouth, IN
1932 ChiB-GB: 4 G. ChiB: 3 G. GB: 1 G. **Total:** 4 G.

FRANK CULVER Culver, Franklin Z 5'11", 175 **C-OE**
Col: Syracuse *HS:* V. W. Scott [Toledo, OH] B: 4/24/1897, Toldeo, OH
D: 1/13/1969, Yonkers, NY
1923 Buf: 12 G. **1924** Roch-Buf: 9 G. Roch: 1 G. Buf: 8 G. **1925** Can: 8 G. **Total:** 29 G.

RODNEY CULVER Culver, Rodney Dwayne 5'9", 224 **RB**
Col: Notre Dame *HS:* St. Martin de Porres [Detroit, MI] B: 12/23/1969, Detroit, MI D: 5/11/1996, Miami, FL *Drafted:* 1992 Round 4 Ind
1993 Ind: KR 3-51 17.0; 1 Fum TD. **Total:** KR 3-51 17.0; 1 Fum TD.

Year Team	G	Rushing Att	Yds	Avg	TD	Receiving Rec	Yds	Avg	TD	Fum	Tot TD
1992 Ind	16	121	321	2.7	7	26	210	8.1	2	2	9
1993 Ind	16	65	150	2.3	3	11	112	10.2	1	3	5
1994 SD	3	8	63	7.9	0	0	0	—	0	0	0
1995 SD	8	47	155	3.3	3	5	21	4.2	0	0	3
NFL Total	43	241	689	2.9	13	42	343	8.2	3	5	17

GEORGE CUMBY Cumby, George Edward 6'0", 220 **LB**
Col: Oklahoma *HS:* Gorman [TX] B: 7/5/1956, Gorman, TX
Drafted: 1980 Round 1 GB
1980 GB: 9 G. **1981** GB: 16 G; Int 3-22. **1982** GB: 9 G; Int 1-4. **1983** GB: 15 G; 2 Sac. **1984** GB: 16 G; Int 1-7; 2.5 Sac. **1985** GB: 15 G. **1986** Buf: 11 G; 1 Sac. **1987** Phi: 1 G. **Total:** 92 G; Int 5-33; 5.5 Sac.

FRANK CUMISKEY Cumiskey, Frank Steven 6'2", 205 **OE-DE**
(Red) *Col:* Ohio State *HS:* Rayen [Youngstown, OH] B: 7/24/1911, Youngstown, OH D: 7/16/1982, Sun City, AZ
1937 Bkn: 9 G; Rec 5-50 10.0.

ED CUMMINGS Cummings, Edward Arthur 6'3", 232 **LB**
Col: Stanford *HS:* Anaconda [MT] B: 6/29/1941, Anaconda, MT
1964 NYJ: 11 G; Int 1-2. **1965** Den: 14 G. **Total:** 25 G; Int 1-2.

JOE CUMMINGS Cummings, Joe Edward 6'2", 242 **LB**
Col: Wyoming *HS:* Stevensville [MT] B: 6/8/1974, Missoula, MT
1996 SD: 3 G. **1998** Buf: 9 G; KR 1-21 21.0. **Total:** 12 G; KR 1-21 21.0.

MACK CUMMINGS Cummings, Mack 6'0", 195 **WR**
Col: East Tennessee State *HS:* Gainesville [FL] B: 3/3/1959, Gainesville, FL
1987 NYG: 1 G; KR 1-11 11.0.

ERNIE CUNEO Cuneo, Ernest L 5'9", 192 **G**
Col: Penn State; Columbia *HS:* Henry P. Becton [East Rutherford, NJ]
B: 5/27/1905, Carlstadt, NJ D: 3/2/1988, Arlington, VA
1929 Ora: 12 G. **1930** Bkn: 6 G. **Total:** 18 G.

T.J. CUNNINGHAM Cunningham, Anthony Jr. 6'0", 197 **DB**
Col: Colorado *HS:* Overland [Aurora, CO] B: 10/24/1972, Aurora, CO
Drafted: 1996 Round 6 Sea
1996 Sea: 9 G.

BENNIE CUNNINGHAM Cunningham, Bennie Lee Jr. 6'5", 254 **TE**
Col: Clemson *HS:* Seneca [SC] B: 12/23/1954, Laurens, SC
Drafted: 1976 Round 1 Pit

Year Team	G	Receiving Rec	Yds	Avg	TD	Fum
1976 Pit	12	5	49	9.8	1	0

1977 Pit	12	20	347	17.4	2	0
1978 Pit	6	16	321	20.1	2	1
1979 Pit	15	36	512	14.2	4	0
1980 Pit	15	18	232	12.9	2	0
1981 Pit	15	41	574	14.0	3	0
1982 Pit	9	21	277	13.2	2	0
1983 Pit	16	35	442	12.6	3	4
1984 Pit	7	4	64	16.0	1	0
1985 Pit	11	6	61	10.2	0	0
NFL Total	118	202	2879	14.3	20	5

CARL CUNNINGHAM Cunningham, Carl Madison 6'4", 230 **LB**
Col: Houston *HS:* Waltrip [Houston, TX] B: 7/23/1944, Houston, TX
Drafted: 1967 Round 4 Den
1967 Den: 13 G; Int 1-16. **1968** Den: 14 G; Int 1-3. **1969** Den: 14 G; Int 2-10. **1970** Den: 14 G. **1971** NO: 13 G. **Total:** 68 G; Int 4-29.

DOUGLAS CUNNINGHAM Cunningham, Douglas Scott 6'3", 195 **WR**
Col: Rice *HS:* Winston Churchill [San Antonio, TX] B: 11/14/1955, San Antonio, TX
1979 Min: 6 G; Rec 5-50 10.0.

ED CUNNINGHAM Cunningham, Edward Patrick 6'3", 288 **C-OG**
Col: Washington *HS:* Mount Vernon [Alexandria, VA] B: 8/17/1969, Washington, DC *Drafted:* 1992 Round 3 Pho
1992 Pho: 10 G. **1993** Pho: 15 G. **1994** Ariz: 16 G. **1995** Ariz: 9 G; 1 Fum. **1996** Sea: 11 G. **Total:** 61 G; 1 Fum.

ERIC CUNNINGHAM Cunningham, Eric Alan 6'3", 257 **OG**
Col: Penn State *HS:* South [Akron, OH] B: 3/16/1957, Akron, OH
Drafted: 1979 Round 4 NYJ
1979 NYJ: 11 G. **1980** NYJ: 6 G. **Total:** 17 G.

COOKIE CUNNINGHAM Cunningham, Harold Brewer 6'3", 210 **OE**
Col: Ohio State *HS:* Mount Vernon [OH] B: 2/4/1905, Mount Vernon, OH D: 11/3/1995, Leesburg, FL
1927 Cle: 5 G. **1929** ChiB: 11 G. **1931** SI: 10 G. **Total:** 26 G.

LEON CUNNINGHAM Cunningham, Horace Leon 6'3", 215 **LB-C**
Col: South Carolina *HS:* Smith [Atlanta, GA] B: 8/19/1931
D: 4/5/1987, Lono, AR *Drafted:* 1955 Round 8 Det
1955 Det: 8 G; KR 1-13 13.0.

JIM CUNNINGHAM Cunningham, James Walter 6'0", 224 **FB**
Col: Pittsburgh *HS:* Connellsville [PA] B: 3/11/1939, Connellsville, PA
Drafted: 1961 Round 3 Was
1961 Was: KR 4-80 20.0; Punt 1-46 46.0. **1962** Was: KR 2-54 27.0. **1963** Was: KR 6-96 16.0. **Total:** KR 12-230 19.2; Punt 1-46 46.0.

		Rushing				Receiving					Tot
Year Team	**G**	**Att**	**Yds**	**Avg**	**TD**	**Rec**	**Yds**	**Avg**	**TD**	**Fum**	**TD**
1961 Was	14	69	160	2.3	1	12	90	7.5	1	1	2
1962 Was	14	35	144	4.1	1	6	43	7.2	1	1	2
1963 Was	14	16	33	2.1	1	8	86	10.8	0	1	1
NFL Total	42	120	337	2.8	3	26	219	8.4	2	3	5

JAY CUNNINGHAM Cunningham, Jay 5'10", 185 **DB**
(Dart) *Col:* Bowling Green State *HS:* South [Youngstown, OH]
B: 10/9/1943, Youngstown, OH *Drafted:* 1965 Round 14 Bos
1965 Bos: PR 5-35 7.0; Int 2-16; Scor **1** Saf. **1967** Bos: PR 17-105 6.2; Int 1-54 1 TD. **Total:** PR 22-140 6.4; Int 3-70 1 TD; Scor 1 Saf.

		Kickoff Returns				
Year Team	**G**	**Ret**	**Yds**	**Avg**	**TD**	**Fum**
1965 Bos	14	17	374	22.0	0	2
1966 Bos	14	17	371	21.8	0	0
1967 Bos	12	30	627	20.9	0	2
NFL Total	40	64	1372	21.4	0	4

DOUG CUNNINGHAM Cunningham, Julian Douglas 6'0", 200 **RB**
Col: Mississippi *HS:* Louisville [MS] B: 9/14/1945, Louisville, MS
Drafted: 1967 Round 6 SF
1969 SF: Pass 3-3 100.0%, 48 16.00 1 TD. **Total:** Pass 3-3 100.0%, 48 16.00 1 TD.

		Rushing				Receiving			
Year Team	**G**	**Att**	**Yds**	**Avg**	**TD**	**Rec**	**Yds**	**Avg**	**TD**
1967 SF	14	43	212	4.9	2	13	121	9.3	0
1968 SF	10	6	7	1.2	0	2	25	12.5	0
1969 SF	14	147	541	3.7	3	51	484	9.5	0
1970 SF	12	128	443	3.5	3	35	209	6.0	0
1971 SF	14	25	98	3.9	1	19	188	9.9	0
1972 SF	4	8	32	4.0	0	0	0	—	0
1973 SF	14	44	165	3.8	1	15	118	7.9	0
1974 Was	2	5	17	3.4	0	2	26	13.0	0
NFL Total	84	406	1515	3.7	10	137	1171	8.5	0

	Punt Returns				Kickoff Returns				
Year Team	**Ret**	**Yds**	**Avg**	**TD**	**Ret**	**Yds**	**Avg**	**TD**	**Fum**
1967 SF	**27**	249	9.2	0	31	826	26.6	0	5
1968 SF	0	0	—	0	14	286	20.4	0	2
1969 SF	3	23	7.7	0	9	207	23.0	0	5
1970 SF	0	0	—	0	0	0	—	0	4
1971 SF	0	0	—	0	6	121	20.2	0	1
1973 SF	0	0	—	0	8	173	21.6	0	3
NFL Total	30	272	9.1	0	68	1613	23.7	0	20

RICK CUNNINGHAM Cunningham, Patrick Dante Ross 6'7", 311 **OT**
Col: Sacramento City Coll. CA (J.C.); Texas A&M *HS:* Beverly Hills [CA]
B: 1/4/1967, Los Angeles, CA *Drafted:* 1990 Round 4 Ind
1990 Ind: 2 G. **1992** Pho: 8 G. **1993** Pho: 16 G. **1994** Ariz: 11 G. **1995** Min: 11 G. **1996** Oak: 13 G; Rec 1-3 3.0 1 TD; 6 Pt. **1997** Oak: 7 G. **1998** Oak: 12 G. **Total:** 80 G; Rec 1-3 3.0 1 TD; 6 Pt.

RANDALL CUNNINGHAM Cunningham, Randall 6'4", 212 **QB**
Col: Nevada-Las Vegas *HS:* Santa Barbara [CA] B: 3/27/1963, Santa Barbara, CA *Drafted:* 1985 Round 2 Phi
1986 Phi: Punt 2-54 27.0. **1987** Phi: Rec 1-(-3) -3.0. **1988** Phi: Punt 3-167 55.7. **1989** Phi: Punt 6-319 53.2. **1994** Phi: Punt 1-80 80.0. **1997** Min: Punt 8-274 34.3. **1998** Min: Rec 1-(-3) -3.0; Scor 1 2XP. **Total:** Rec 2-(-6) -3.0; Punt 20-894 44.7; Scor 1 2XP.

		Passing							
Year Team	**G**	**Att**	**Comp**	**Comp%**	**Yds**	**YPA**	**TD**	**Int**	**Rating**
1985 Phi	6	81	34	42.0	548	6.77	1	8	29.8
1986 Phi	15	209	111	53.1	1391	6.66	8	7	72.9
1987 Phi	12	406	223	54.9	2786	6.86	23	12	83.0
1988 Phi	16	560	301	53.8	3808	6.80	24	16	77.6
1989 Phi	16	532	290	54.5	3400	6.39	21	15	75.5
1990 Phi	16	465	271	58.3	3466	7.45	30	13	91.6
1991 Phi	1	4	1	25.0	19	4.75	0	0	46.9
1992 Phi	15	384	233	60.7	2775	7.23	19	11	87.3
1993 Phi	4	110	76	69.1	850	7.73	5	5	88.1
1994 Phi	14	490	265	54.1	3229	6.59	16	13	74.4
1995 Phi	7	121	69	57.0	605	5.00	3	5	61.5
1997 Min	6	88	44	50.0	501	5.69	6	4	71.3
1998 Min	15	425	259	60.9	3704	8.72	34	10	**106.0**
NFL Total	143	3875	2177	56.2	27082	6.99	190	119	81.6

	Rushing				
Year Team	**Att**	**Yds**	**Avg**	**TD**	**Fum**
1985 Phi	29	205	7.1	0	3
1986 Phi	66	540	8.2	5	7
1987 Phi	76	505	6.6	3	**12**
1988 Phi	93	624	6.7	6	**12**
1989 Phi	104	621	**6.0**	4	17
1990 Phi	118	942	**8.0**	5	9
1992 Phi	87	549	6.3	5	**13**
1993 Phi	18	110	6.1	1	3
1994 Phi	65	288	4.4	3	10
1995 Phi	21	98	4.7	0	3
1997 Min	19	127	6.7	0	4
1998 Min	32	132	4.1	1	2
NFL Total	728	4741	6.5	33	95

RICHIE CUNNINGHAM Cunningham, Richard Anthony 5'10", 167 **K**
Col: Southwestern Louisiana *HS:* Terrebonne [Houma, LA]
B: 8/18/1970, Houma, LA *Drafted:* 1996

		Scoring						
Year Team	**G**	**Pts**	**FG**	**FGA**	**FG%**	**XK**	**XKA**	**XK%**
1997 Dal	16	126	**34**	37	91.9	24	24	100.0
1998 Dal	16	127	29	35	82.9	40	40	100.0
NFL Total	32	253	63	72	87.5	64	64	100.0

DICK CUNNINGHAM Cunningham, Richard Karekin 6'3", 245 **LB-OT**
Col: Arkansas *HS:* Thomas Jefferson [San Antonio, TX]
B: 10/12/1944, Boston, MA *Drafted:* 1966 Redshirt Round 4 Buf
1967 Buf: 14 G. **1968** Buf: 14 G. **1970** Buf: 14 G. **1971** Buf: 5 G. **1972** Buf: 9 G. **1973** Phi-Hou: 10 G. Phi: 9 G. Hou: 1 G. **Total:** 66 G.

SAM CUNNINGHAM Cunningham, Samuel Lewis Jr. 6'3", 226 **RB**
(Bam) *Col:* USC *HS:* Santa Barbara [CA] B: 8/15/1950, Santa Barbara, CA *Drafted:* 1973 Round 1 NE

		Rushing				Receiving					Tot
Year Team	**G**	**Att**	**Yds**	**Avg**	**TD**	**Rec**	**Yds**	**Avg**	**TD**	**Fum**	**TD**
1973 NE	14	155	516	3.3	4	15	144	9.6	1	10	5
1974 NE	10	166	811	4.9	9	22	214	9.7	2	2	11
1975 NE	13	169	666	3.9	6	32	253	7.9	2	**12**	8
1976 NE	11	172	824	4.8	3	27	299	11.1	0	5	3
1977 NE	14	270	1015	3.8	4	42	370	8.8	1	10	5
1978 NE	16	199	768	3.9	8	31	297	9.6	0	4	8
1979 NE	12	159	563	3.5	5	29	236	8.1	0	4	5
1981 NE	11	86	269	3.1	4	12	92	7.7	0	2	4
1982 NE	6	9	21	2.3	0	0	0	—	0	0	0
NFL Total	107	1385	5453	3.9	43	210	1905	9.1	6	49	49

GARY CUOZZO Cuozzo, Gary Samuel 6'0", 195 **QB**
Col: Virginia *HS:* Glen Ridge [NJ] B: 4/26/1941, Montclair, NJ

Year Team	G	Passing Att	Comp	Comp%	Yds	YPA	TD	Int	Rating
1963 Bal	5	17	10	58.8	104	6.12	0	0	76.6
1964 Bal	9	36	15	41.7	163	4.53	2	3	39.5
1965 Bal	7	105	54	51.4	700	6.67	7	4	79.1
1966 Bal	7	50	26	52.0	424	8.48	4	2	90.8
1967 NO	13	260	134	51.5	1562	6.01	7	12	59.8
1968 Min	4	33	24	72.7	297	9.00	1	0	110.3
1969 Min	9	98	49	50.0	693	7.07	4	5	65.6
1970 Min	12	257	128	49.8	1720	6.69	7	10	64.3
1971 Min	8	168	75	44.6	842	5.01	6	8	52.2
1972 StL	8	158	69	43.7	897	5.68	5	11	43.7
NFL Total	82	1182	584	49.4	7402	6.26	43	55	62.1

Year Team	Rushing Att	Yds	Avg	TD	Fum
1963 Bal	3	26	8.7	0	0
1964 Bal	7	-2	-0.3	0	1
1965 Bal	6	8	1.3	0	3
1966 Bal	1	9	9.0	0	0
1967 NO	19	43	2.3	1	2
1968 Min	1	4	4.0	0	1
1969 Min	3	-4	-1.3	0	2
1970 Min	17	61	3.6	0	3
1971 Min	15	24	1.6	0	2
1972 StL	4	7	1.8	0	3
NFL Total	76	176	2.3	1	17

KEITH CUPP Cupp, Keith Eric 6′6″, 301 **OT**
Col: Findlay *HS:* Leipsic [OH] B: 6/20/1964, Lima, OH
1987 Cin: 3 G.

BREE CUPPOLETTI Cuppoletti, Rudolph Bruno 5′10″, 200 **G-LB**
(Coop) *Col:* Mesabi CC (MN); Oregon *HS:* Roosevelt [Virginia, MN]
B: 6/19/1910, Virginia, MN D: 9/21/1960, Virginia, MN
1934 ChiC: 11 G. **1935** ChiC: 12 G; Rush 1-9 9.0. **1936** ChiC: 12 G. **1937** ChiC: 10 G. **1938** ChiC: 11 G. **1939** Phi: 10 G. **Total:** 66 G; Rush 1-9 9.0.

JEFF CURCHIN Curchin, Jeffery Mansfield 6′7″, 260 **OT-OG**
Col: Florida State *HS:* Ocala [FL] B: 12/17/1947, Binghamton, NY
Drafted: 1970 Round 6 ChiB
1970 ChiB: 14 G. **1971** ChiB: 12 G. **1972** Buf: 1 G. **Total:** 27 G.

TONY CURCILLO Curcillo, Anthony Jr. 6′1″, 200 **DB-HB**
Col: Ohio State *HS:* Elyria [OH] B: 5/27/1931, Long Branch, NJ
Drafted: 1953 Round 6 ChiC
1953 ChiC: 12 G; Rush 8-29 3.6; KR 1-17 17.0; Int 2-16; 2 Fum.

MIKE CURCIO Curcio, Michael A 6′1″, 237 **LB**
Col: Temple *HS:* Oakcrest [Mays Landing, NJ] B: 1/24/1957, Hudson, NY *Drafted:* 1980 Round 8 Phi
1981 Phi: 16 G. **1982** Phi: 5 G. **1983** GB: 13 G. **Total:** 34 G.

ARMAND CURE Cure, Armand Arthur 6′0″, 198 **HB-DB**
Col: Rhode Island *HS:* New Bedford [MA] B: 8/1/1919, New Bedford, MA
AAFC **1947** BalA: 1 G; Rush 2-(-1) -0.5.

WILL CURETON Cureton, William Joe 6′3″, 200 **QB**
Col: Texas A&M-Commerce *HS:* Whitewright [TX] B: 12/2/1950, Meridian, TX
1975 Cle: 1 G; Pass 32-10 31.3%, 95 2.97 1 TD 1 Int; Rush 1-1 1.0.

AUGUST CURLEY Curley, August Onorato 6′3″, 226 **LB**
Col: USC *HS:* Southwest [Atlanta, GA] B: 1/24/1960, Little Rock, AR
Drafted: 1983 Round 4 Det
1983 Det: 10 G; KR 1-7 7.0. **1984** Det: 8 G. **1985** Det: 16 G. **1986** Det: 4 G. **Total:** 38 G; KR 1-7 7.0.

HARRY CURRAN Curran, Harry Ambrose 5′10″, 180 **WB-DB**
(Duke) *Col:* Massachusetts *HS:* Marlboro [MA] B: 6/2/1894, Marlboro, MA D: 6/28/1976, South Pasadena, FL
1920 ChiC: 9 G. **1921** ChiC: 1 G. **Total:** 10 G.

PAT CURRAN Curran, Patrick Michael 6′4″, 238 **TE-RB**
Col: Iowa State; Lakeland *HS:* Solomon Juneau [Milwaukee, WI]
B: 9/21/1945, Milwaukee, WI *Drafted:* 1969 Round 6 LARm
1969 LARm: KR 2-28 14.0. **1970** LARm: Pass 2-0, 1 Int; KR 3-51 17.0. **1971** LARm: KR 3-35 11.7. **1972** LARm: KR 4-37 9.3. **1973** LARm: KR 1-24 24.0. **1974** LARm: KR 1-16 16.0. **1975** SD: KR 3-28 9.3; Scor **1** 1XP. **Total:** Pass 2-0, 1 Int; KR 17-219 12.9; Scor 1 1XP.

Year Team	G	Rushing Att	Yds	Avg	TD	Receiving Rec	Yds	Avg	TD	Fum	Tot TD
1969 LARm	1	0	0	—	0	0	0	—	0	0	0
1970 LARm	14	25	92	3.7	0	3	25	8.3	0	2	1
1971 LARm	14	0	0	—	0	1	2	2.0	1	0	1
1972 LARm	10	0	0	—	0	0	0	—	0	0	0
1973 LARm	14	0	0	—	0	5	56	11.2	1	0	1
1974 LARm	13	0	0	—	0	0	0	—	0	0	0
1975 SD	14	3	21	7.0	0	45	619	13.8	0	1	0
1976 SD	14	1	12	12.0	0	33	349	10.6	1	0	1
1977 SD	14	1	2	2.0	0	10	123	12.3	0	0	0
1978 SD	14	0	0	—	0	9	92	10.2	2	0	2
NFL Total	122	30	127	4.2	0	106	1266	11.9	5	3	6

WILLIE CURRAN Curran, William Martin 5′10″, 175 **WR**
Col: UCLA *HS:* Crespi [Encino, CA] B: 12/30/1959, Inglewood, CA
1982 Atl: 7 G. **1983** Atl: 16 G; Rec 1-15 15.0; KR 2-26 13.0; 1 Fum. **1984** Atl: 14 G; Rec 1-7 7.0; PR 9-21 2.3; KR 11-219 19.9; 2 Fum. **Total:** 37 G; Rec 2-22 11.0; PR 9-21 2.3; KR 13-245 18.8; 3 Fum.

MIKE CURRENT Current, Michael Wayne 6′5″, 274 **OT**
Col: Ohio State *HS:* Lima [OH] B: 9/17/1945, Lima, OH
Drafted: 1967 Round 3 Den
1967 Den-Mia: 4 G. Den: 3 G. Mia: 1 G. **1968** Den: 14 G. **1969** Den: 14 G. **1970** Den: 14 G. **1971** Den: 14 G. **1972** Den: 14 G. **1973** Den: 14 G. **1974** Den: 14 G. **1975** Den: 7 G. **1976** TB: 14 G. **1977** Mia: 14 G. **1978** Mia: 16 G. **1979** Mia: 16 G. **Total:** 169 G.

DAN CURRIE Currie, Daniel George 6′3″, 235 **LB**
(Dapper Dan) *Col:* Michigan State *HS:* St. Anthony's [Detroit, MI]
B: 6/27/1935, Detroit, MI *Drafted:* 1958 Round 1 GB
1958 GB: KR 2-14 7.0. **1966** LARm: KR 1-25 25.0. **Total:** KR 3-39 13.0.

Year Team	G	Interceptions Int	Yds	TD
1958 GB	12	0	0	0
1959 GB	12	1	25	0
1960 GB	12	4	75	0
1961 GB	14	3	59	1
1962 GB	12	0	0	0
1963 GB	14	1	23	0
1964 GB	14	2	11	0
1965 LARm	14	0	0	0
1966 LARm	14	0	0	0
NFL Total	118	11	193	1

HERSCHEL CURRIE Currie, Herschel Lamont 6′0″, 190 **DB**
Col: Chabot Coll. CA (J.C.); Oregon State *HS:* Yerba Buena [San Jose, CA] B: 9/8/1965, Chicago, IL
1994 Ariz: 1 G.

BILL CURRIER Currier, William Frank 6′0″, 196 **DB**
Col: South Carolina *HS:* Glen Burnie [MD] B: 1/5/1955, Glen Burnie, MD *Drafted:* 1977 Round 9 Hou
1980 NE: KR 6-98 16.3. **1982** NYG: 2 Sac. **1983** NYG: 1 Sac.
Total: KR 6-98 16.3; 3 Sac.

Year Team	G	Interceptions Int	Yds	TD
1977 Hou	14	2	0	0
1978 Hou	14	1	8	0
1979 Hou	16	0	0	0
1980 NE	16	0	0	0
1981 NYG	16	3	2	0
1982 NYG	9	1	0	0
1983 NYG	15	2	37	1
1984 NYG	9	1	7	0
1985 NYG	2	1	9	0
NFL Total	111	11	63	1

DON CURRIVAN Currivan, Donald F 6′0″, 193 **OE-DB-DE**
Col: Boston College *HS:* Mansfield [MA] B: 3/6/1920, Mansfield, MA
D: 5/16/1956, Hyannis, MA *Drafted:* 1943 Round 3 ChiC
1944 ChPt: KR 1-14 14.0. **1945** Bos: KR 1-3 3.0. **1946** Bos: PR 1-22 22.0; KR 1-14 14.0. **1947** Bos: Int 1-0. **1948** Bos-LARm: Rush 1-(-4) -4.0. LARm: Rush 1-(-4) -4.0. **1949** LARm: Int 5-31. **Total:** Rush 1-(-4) -4.0; PR 1-22 22.0; KR 3-31 10.3; Int 6-31.

Year Team	G	Receiving Rec	Yds	Avg	TD	Fum	Tot TD
1943 ChiC	7	5	78	15.6	1	0	2
1944 ChPt	10	7	163	23.3	2	0	2
1945 Bos	10	16	397	24.8	4	0	4
1946 Bos	11	11	262	23.8	4	1	4
1947 Bos	12	24	782	**32.6**	9	0	10
1948 Bos-LARm	13	12	218	18.2	3	0	4
1948 Bos	3	2	29	14.5	0	0	0
1948 LARm	10	10	189	18.9	3	0	4
1949 LARm	12	3	78	26.0	1	0	1
NFL Total	75	78	1978	25.4	24	1	27

CRAIG CURRY Curry, Craig Anthony 6′0″, 187 **DB**
Col: Texas *HS:* Kashmere [Houston, TX] B: 7/20/1961, Houston, TX
Drafted: 1984 Round 4 Ind
1984 TB: 5 G. **1985** TB: 16 G; 1 Sac. **1986** TB: 16 G; KR 1-6 6.0; Int 2-0. **1987** Ind: 3 G; Int 1-0. **Total:** 40 G; KR 1-6 6.0; Int 3-0; 1 Sac.

ERIC CURRY Curry, Eric Felece 6′5″, 270 **DE**
Col: Alabama *HS:* Thomasville [GA] B: 2/3/1970, Thomasville, GA
Drafted: 1993 Round 1 TB
1993 TB: 10 G; 5 Sac. **1994** TB: 15 G; 3 Sac. **1995** TB: 16 G; 2 Sac. **1996** TB: 12 G; 2 Sac. **1997** TB: 6 G. **1998** Jac: 11 G. **Total:** 70 G; 12 Sac.

BUDDY CURRY Curry, George Jessel 6′4″, 224 **LB**
Col: North Carolina *HS:* George Washington [Danville, VA]
B: 6/4/1958, Greenville, NC *Drafted:* 1980 Round 2 Atl
1980 Atl: 16 G; Int 3-13; **1** Fum TD; 6 Pt; 1 Fum. **1981** Atl: 16 G; Int 1-35 1 TD; 6 Pt. **1982** Atl: 9 G; Int 1-0; 1 Sac. **1983** Atl: 16 G; 4 Sac. **1984** Atl: 16 G; 0.5 Sac. **1985** Atl: 16 G; Int 1-0. **1986** Atl: 16 G; Int 1-32. **1987** Atl: 4 G. **Total:** 109 G; Int 7-80 1 TD; 1 Fum TD; Tot TD 2; 12 Pt; 1 Fum; 5.5 Sac.

IVORY CURRY Curry, Ivory 5′11″, 185 **DB**
Col: Florida *HS:* Miami Central [FL] B: 2/6/1961, Miami, FL
D: 8/22/1989, Brandon, FL
1987 TB: 3 G; PR 3-32 10.7; KR 3-53 17.7.

ROY CURRY Curry, Roy 6′1″, 185 **WR**
Col: Jackson State B: 11/9/1939 *Drafted:* 1963 Round 12 Pit
1963 Pit: 6 G; Rec 1-31 31.0 1 TD; KR 1-27 27.0; 6 Pt.

SHANE CURRY Curry, Shane Clifton 6′5″, 270 **DE**
Col: Georgia Tech; Miami (Fla.) *HS:* Princeton [Cincinatti, OH]
B: 4/7/1968, Cincinnati, OH D: 5/3/1992, Cincinnati, OH
Drafted: 1991 Round 2 Ind
1991 Ind: 9 G; 1 Sac.

BILL CURRY Curry, William Alexander 6′3″, 235 **LB-C**
Col: Georgia Tech *HS:* College Park [GA] B: 10/21/1942, College Park, GA *Drafted:* 1964 Round 20 GB
1965 GB: 14 G. **1966** GB: 14 G. **1967** Bal: 11 G. **1968** Bal: 14 G. **1969** Bal: 14 G. **1970** Bal: 14 G. **1971** Bal: 14 G. **1972** Bal: 14 G; 1 Fum. **1973** Hou: 4 G. **1974** LARm: 10 G. **Total:** 123 G; 1 Fum.

DON CURTIN Curtin, Don William 5′8″, 155 **BB**
(Red) *Col:* Marquette *HS:* West Division [Milwaukee, WI] B: 1902, Woodville, WI
1926 Mil-Rac: 4 G; Scor 7, 2 FG, 1 XK. Mil: 3 G; Scor 7, 2 FG, 1 XK. Rac: 1 G. **Total:** 4 G; Scor 7, 2 FG, 1 XK.

SCOTT CURTIS Curtis, Alston Scott 6′1″, 230 **LB**
Col: New Hampshire *HS:* Lynnfield [MA] B: 12/26/1964, Burlington, VT
1988 Phi: 16 G. **1989** Den: 16 G. **1990** Den: 9 G. **Total:** 41 G.

CANUTE CURTIS Curtis, Canute 6′2″, 250 **LB**
Col: West Virginia *HS:* Farmingdale [NY] B: 8/4/1974, Amityville, NY
Drafted: 1997 Round 6 Cin
1997 Cin: 3 G. **1998** Cin: 5 G. **Total:** 8 G.

ISAAC CURTIS Curtis, Isaac Fisher Jr. 6′1″, 192 **WR**
Col: California; San Diego State *HS:* Santa Ana [CA] B: 10/20/1950, Santa Ana, CA *Drafted:* 1973 Round 1 Cin

		Rushing				Receiving				
Year Team	**G**	**Att**	**Yds**	**Avg**	**TD**	**Rec**	**Yds**	**Avg**	**TD**	**Fum**
1973 Cin	14	2	-11	-5.5	0	45	843	18.7	9	0
1974 Cin	14	8	62	7.8	0	30	633	21.1	10	1
1975 Cin	14	6	-9	-1.5	0	44	934	**21.2**	7	1
1976 Cin	14	3	29	9.7	0	41	766	18.7	6	1
1977 Cin	8	0	0	—	0	20	338	16.9	2	0
1978 Cin	16	1	1	1.0	0	47	737	15.7	3	2
1979 Cin	16	2	-11	-5.5	0	32	605	18.9	8	1
1980 Cin	15	0	0	—	0	43	610	14.2	3	0
1981 Cin	15	0	0	—	0	37	609	16.5	2	1
1982 Cin	9	3	15	5.0	0	23	320	13.9	1	1
1983 Cin	16	0	0	—	0	42	571	13.6	2	1
1984 Cin	16	0	0	—	0	12	135	11.3	0	1
NFL Total	167	25	76	3.0	0	416	7101	17.1	53	10

MIKE CURTIS Curtis, James Michael 6′3″, 232 **LB-FB**
Col: Duke *HS:* Richard Montgomery [Rockville, MD] B: 3/27/1943, Washington, DC *Drafted:* 1965 Round 1 Bal
1965 Bal: Rush 6-1 0.2; Rec 1-5 5.0; KR 2-10 5.0. **1966** Bal: KR 3-64 21.3; **1** Fum TD. **Total:** Rush 6-1 0.2; Rec 1-5 5.0; KR 5-74 14.8; 1 Fum TD.

		Interceptions				Tot
Year Team	**G**	**Int**	**Yds**	**TD**	**Fum**	**TD**
1965 Bal	14	0	0	0	0	0
1966 Bal	12	0	0	0	0	1
1967 Bal	3	1	6	0	0	0
1968 Bal	14	2	38	1	0	1
1969 Bal	14	0	0	0	0	0
1970 Bal	14	5	50	0	0	0
1971 Bal	13	3	44	0	0	0
1972 Bal	14	4	74	1	0	1
1973 Bal	7	2	9	0	0	0
1974 Bal	14	3	24	0	0	0
1975 Bal	6	1	3	0	0	0
1976 Sea	14	2	40	0	1	0
1977 Was	14	1	1	0	0	0
1978 Was	13	1	0	0	0	0
NFL Total	166	25	289	2	1	3

BOBBY CURTIS Curtis, Robert Waymon 6′3″, 235 **LB**
Col: The Citadel; Jackson State; Savannah State *HS:* Jones Co. [Gray, GA] B: 10/23/1964, Macon, GA
1987 Was: 3 G; 1 Sac.

TOM CURTIS Curtis, Thomas Newton 6′1″, 196 **DB**
(T.C.) *Col:* Michigan *HS:* Aurora [OH] B: 11/1/1947, Cleveland, OH
Drafted: 1970 Round 14 Bal
1970 Bal: 10 G; PR 3-2 0.7; Int 1-0. **1971** Bal: 14 G; PR 7-15 2.1; KR 1-0; 1 Fum. **Total:** 24 G; PR 10-17 1.7; KR 1-0; Int 1-0; 1 Fum.

TRAVIS CURTIS Curtis, Travis Fennel 5′10″, 180 **DB**
Col: West Virginia *HS:* Winston Churchill [Potomac, MD] B: 9/27/1965, Washington, DC
1987 StL: 13 G; Int 5-65. **1988** Pho-Was: 13 G; Int 1-18; 1 Sac. Pho: 12 G; Int 1-18; 1 Sac. Was: 1 G. **1989** Min: 16 G; KR 1-18 18.0. **1990** NYJ: 14 G; Int 2-45. **1991** Was: 1 G. **Total:** 57 G; KR 1-18 18.0; Int 8-128; 1 Sac.

HARRY CURZON Curzon, Harry M 6′0″, 195 **OE-TB-BB-FB**
Col: No College B: 11/12/1894, Champaign, IL D: 4/25/1966, Coral Gables, FL
1925 Buf-Ham: 9 G; Pass 1 TD; Rec 1 TD; 6 Pt. Buf: 5 G; Rec 1 TD; 6 Pt. Ham: 4 G; Pass 1 TD. **1926** Lou-Ham: 5 G. Lou: 1 G. Ham: 4 G. **1928** ChiC: 1 G. **Total:** 15 G; Pass 1 TD; Rec 1 TD; 6 Pt.

PETE CUSICK Cusick, Peter Martin 6′1″, 255 **NT**
Col: Ohio State *HS:* Lakewood [OH] B: 10/27/1952, San Bernardino, CA *Drafted:* 1975 Round 3 NE
1975 NE: 13 G.

RANDY CUTHBERT Cuthbert, Randy Alan 6′2″, 225 **RB**
Col: Duke *HS:* Central Bucks West [Doylestown, PA] B: 1/16/1970, Landsdale, PA
1993 Pit: 10 G; Rush 1-7 7.0; Rec 1-3 3.0. **1994** Pit: 1 G. **Total:** 11 G; Rush 1-7 7.0; Rec 1-3 3.0.

HARRY CUTLER Cutler, Harry G Jr. 6′2″, 190 **T**
(King) *Col:* No College B: 9/13/1893 D: 4/24/1964, Dayton, OH
1920 Day: 7 G.

GARY CUTSINGER Cutsinger, Gary Leon 6′5″, 245 **DE**
Col: Oklahoma State *HS:* Elk City [OK] B: 2/4/1940, Perry, OK
Drafted: 1962 Round 4 Hou
1962 Hou: 14 G; Int 1-3. **1963** Hou: 14 G. **1964** Hou: 14 G. **1965** Hou: 14 G; Int 1-72. **1966** Hou: 14 G. **1968** Hou: 14 G. **Total:** 84 G; Int 2-75.

ANDY CVERCKO Cvercko, Andrew Bertram 6′1″, 243 **OG**
Col: Northwestern *HS:* Memorial [Campbell, OH] B: 11/6/1937, Campbell, OH *Drafted:* 1959 Round 5 GB
1960 GB: 12 G. **1961** Dal: 11 G. **1962** Dal: 14 G; KR 1-0. **1963** Cle-Was: 10 G. Cle: 2 G. Was: 8 G. **Total:** 47 G; KR 1-0.

HEC CYRE Cyre, Hector J 6′2″, 215 **T-G-E**
Col: Gonzaga B: 10/25/1901 D: 8/5/1971, Langley, WA
1926 GB: 10 G. **1928** NYY: 3 G. **Total:** 13 G.

ZIGGY CZAROBSKI Czarobski, Zygmont Peter 6′0″, 230 **T**
(AKA Sigismunt Peter Czarobski) *Col:* Notre Dame *HS:* Mount Carmel [Chicago, IL] B: 9/13/1922, Chicago, IL D: 7/1/1984, Chicago, IL
AAFC **1948** ChiA: 14 G. **1949** ChiA: 12 G. **Total:** 26 G.

JERRY DAANEN Daanen, Jerome Theodore 6′0″, 190 **WR**
(Fudge) *Col:* Miami (Fla.) *HS:* East [DePere, WI] B: 12/15/1944, Green Bay, WI *Drafted:* 1968 Round 8 StL
1968 StL: 14 G; Rec 4-35 8.8. **1969** StL: 9 G; Rec 2-12 6.0. **1970** StL: 14 G; Rec 2-31 15.5. **Total:** 37 G; Rec 8-78 9.8.

CARLTON DABNEY Dabney, Carlton Roland Jr. 6′5″, 259 **DT**
Col: Morgan State *HS:* Armstrong [Richmond, VA] B: 1/26/1947, Richmond, VA *Drafted:* 1968 Round 2 Atl
1968 Atl: 14 G; Int 1-3.

DAVE D'ADDIO D'Addio, David John 6′2″, 235 **RB**
Col: Maryland *HS:* Union [NJ] B: 7/13/1961, Newark, NJ
Drafted: 1984 Round 4 Det
1984 Det: 16 G; Rush 7-46 6.6; Rec 1-12 12.0; KR 1-0.

BILL DADDIO Daddio, Louis William 5′11″, 207 **DE-OE**
Col: Pittsburgh *HS:* Meadville [PA] B: 4/26/1916, Meadville, PA
D: 7/5/1989, Mount Lebanon, PA *Drafted:* 1939 Round 5 ChiC
AAFC **1946** BufA: 3 G; Scor 3, 3-3 100.0% XK.

NFL **1941** ChiC: 11 G; Rec 5-39 7.8; Scor 20, 4-8 50.0% FG, 8-9 88.9% XK. **1942** ChiC: 11 G; Rec 11-108 9.8 1 TD; Int 1-4; Scor 29, **5**-10 50.0% FG, 8-8 100.0% XK. **Total:** 22 G; Rec 16-147 9.2 1 TD; Int 1-4; Scor 49, 9-18 50.0% FG, 16-17 94.1% XK.

HARRIE DADMUN Dadmun, Harrie Holland 6'0", 235 G-T
(Hal) *Col:* Tufts; Harvard *HS:* Arlington [MA] B: 6/25/1894, Cambridge, MA D: 9/15/1980, Concord, MN
1920 Can: 5 G. **1921** NYG: 1 G. **Total:** 6 G.

TED DAFFER Daffer, Terrell Edwin 6'0", 198 DE
Col: Tennessee *HS:* Maury [Norfolk, VA] B: 9/24/1929, Norfolk, VA
Drafted: 1952 Round 21 ChiB
1954 ChiB: 12 G.

BERNARD DAFNEY Dafney, Bernard Eugene 6'5", 324 OG-OT
Col: Los Angeles Southwest Coll. CA (J.C.); Tennessee *HS:* John C. Fremont [Los Angeles, CA] B: 11/1/1968, Los Angeles, CA
Drafted: 1992 Round 9 Hou
1992 Min: 2 G. **1993** Min: 16 G. **1994** Min: 16 G. **1995** Ariz: 11 G. **1996** Pit: 14 G. **1997** Bal: 1 G. **Total:** 60 G.

FRED DAGATA DaGata, Frederick Albert 5'10", 187 FB
Col: Boston College; Providence *HS:* B.M.C. Durfee [Fall River, MA] B: 4/4/1908, Fall River, MA D: 5/1980, Fall River, MA
1931 Prov: 1 G.

FRANK D'AGOSTINO D'Agostino, Francis Joseph 6'1", 245 OG-OT
Col: Auburn *HS:* Northeast Catholic [Philadelphia, PA] B: 3/11/1934, Philadelphia, PA D: 9/29/1997, Tampa, FL *Drafted:* 1956 Round 2 Phi
1956 Phi: 12 G. **1960** NYT: 2 G. **Total:** 14 G.

LOU D'AGOSTINO D'Agostino, Louis 6'0", 235 RB
Col: Hofstra; Rhode Island *HS:* Lawrence [Cedarhurst, NY]
B: 12/12/1973, Brooklyn, NY
1996 NYJ: 9 G.

BOB DAHL Dahl, Robert Allen 6'5", 318 OG-OT
Col: Notre Dame *HS:* Chagrin Falls [OH] B: 1/15/1968, Chicago, IL
Drafted: 1991 Round 3 Cin
1992 Cle: 9 G. **1993** Cle: 16 G. **1994** Cle: 15 G. **1995** Cle: 16 G. **1996** Was: 15 G. **1997** Was: 11 G. **Total:** 82 G.

GEORGE DAHLGREN Dahlgren, George Arthur 5'10", 200 G-T
(Swede) *Col:* Wis.-La Crosse; Beloit B: 4/17/1887, La Crosse, WI D: 1/16/1940, Chicago, IL
1924 Ken: 4 G. **1925** Ham-RI: 4 G. Ham: 3 G. RI: 1 G. **1926** Ham: 2 G. **Total:** 10 G.

TOM DAHMS Dahms, Thomas G 6'5", 242 OT
Col: San Diego State *HS:* San Diego [CA] B: 4/19/1927, San Diego, CA D: 11/30/1988, Orange Co., CA
1951 LARm: 12 G. **1952** LARm: 12 G. **1953** LARm: 12 G. **1954** LARm: 12 G; KR 2-23 11.5. **1955** GB: 12 G. **1956** ChiC: 12 G. **1957** SF: 8 G. **Total:** 80 G; KR 2-23 11.5.

ANTHONY DAIGLE Daigle, Anthony John 5'10", 203 RB
Col: El Camino Coll. CA (J.C.); Arizona State; Fresno State *HS:* St. Patrick St. Vincent [Vallejo, CA] B: 4/5/1970, San Francisco, CA
Drafted: 1994 Round 6 KC
1994 Pit: 1 G.

TED DAILEY Dailey, Theodore E 5'9", 170 E
Col: Pittsburgh *HS:* Phillipsburg [NJ] B: 9/25/1908, Phillipsburg, NJ D: 10/3/1992, Syracuse, NY
1933 Pit: 10 G; Rush 1-1 1.0; Rec 7-66 9.4.

DAVE DALBY Dalby, David Merle 6'2", 248 C-OG
Col: UCLA *HS:* La Serna [Whittier, CA] B: 10/19/1950, Alexandria, MN
Drafted: 1972 Round 4 Oak
1972 Oak: 14 G. **1973** Oak: 14 G; 1 Fum. **1974** Oak: 14 G. **1975** Oak: 14 G. **1976** Oak: 14 G. **1977** Oak: 14 G. **1978** Oak: 16 G. **1979** Oak: 16 G; Rec 1-1 1.0. **1980** Oak: 16 G; 1 Fum. **1981** Oak: 16 G. **1982** LARd: 9 G. **1983** LARd: 16 G. **1984** LARd: 16 G. **1985** LARd: 16 G. **Total:** 205 G; Rec 1-1 1.0; 2 Fum.

CARROLL DALE Dale, Carroll Wayne 6'2", 200 WR
Col: Virginia Tech *HS:* J.J. Kelly [Wise, VA] B: 4/24/1938, Wise, VA
Drafted: 1960 Round 8 LARm
1963 LARm: Rush 1-12 12.0. **1967** GB: Rush 1-9 9.0. **1970** GB: Rush 2-9 4.5. **Total:** Rush 4-30 7.5.

		Receiving				
Year Team	**G**	**Rec**	**Yds**	**Avg**	**TD**	**Fum**
1960 LARm	12	19	336	17.7	3	0
1961 LARm	14	35	561	16.0	2	1
1962 LARm	14	29	584	20.1	3	0
1963 LARm	12	34	638	18.8	7	0
1964 LARm	13	32	544	17.0	2	1
1965 GB	13	20	382	19.1	2	1
1966 GB	14	37	876	**23.7**	7	0
1967 GB	14	35	738	21.1	5	0
1968 GB	14	42	818	19.5	8	1
1969 GB	14	45	879	19.5	6	0
1970 GB	14	49	814	16.6	2	2
1971 GB	14	31	598	19.3	4	0
1972 GB	14	16	317	19.8	1	0
1973 Min	13	14	192	13.7	0	0
NFL Total	189	438	8277	18.9	52	6

JEFFERY DALE Dale, Jeffery Dwayne 6'3", 211 DB
Col: Louisiana State *HS:* Winnfield [LA] B: 10/6/1962, Pineville, LA
Drafted: 1985 Round 2 SD
1985 SD: 16 G; Int 2-83 **1** TD; 6 Pt. **1986** SD: 16 G; Int 4-153. **1988** SD: 10 G. **Total:** 42 G; Int 6-236 1 TD; 6 Pt.

ROLAND DALE Dale, Roland Hall 6'3", 210 DE
Col: Mississippi *HS:* Magee [MS] B: 10/30/1927, Magee, MS
1950 Was: 11 G.

BILL DALEY Daley, William Edward 6'2", 210 FB-DB-LB
(Big Bill) *Col:* DePaul; Michigan; Minnesota; Columbia *HS:* Melrose [MN] B: 9/16/1919, Melrose, MN
AAFC **1946** BknA-MiaA: Rec 2-(-5) -2.5; KR 1-10 10.0. **1947** ChiA: Pass 6-3 50.0%, 70 11.67 1 TD 1 Int; Rec 12-116 9.7; PR 1-3 3.0; KR 7-145 20.7. **1948** NY-A: Rec 4-31 7.8; KR 4-88 22.0; Punt 1-41 41.0. **Total:** Pass 6-3 50.0%, 70 11.67 1 TD 1 Int; Rec 18-142 7.9; PR 1-3 3.0; KR 12-243 20.3; Punt 1-41 41.0.

		Rushing			
Year Team	**G**	**Att**	**Yds**	**Avg**	**TD**
1946 BknA-MiaA	3	14	63	4.5	0
1947 ChiA	14	121	447	3.7	4
1948 NY-A	7	40	102	2.6	1
AAFC Total	24	175	612	3.5	5

KEN DALLAFIOR Dallafior, Kenneth Ray 6'4", 276 OG-C-OT
Col: Minnesota *HS:* Madison [Madison Heights, MI] B: 8/26/1959, Royal Oak, MI *Drafted:* 1982 Round 5 Pit
1985 SD: 3 G. **1986** SD: 12 G. **1987** SD: 9 G. **1988** SD: 13 G. **1989** Det: 16 G; KR 2-13 6.5. **1990** Det: 16 G. **1991** Det: 6 G. **1992** Det: 12 G. **Total:** 87 G; KR 2-13 6.5.

DILLY DALLY Dally, ? 1 G
Col: No College *HS:* Pottsville [PA]
1926 Har: 6 G.

CHRIS DALMAN Dalman, Chris William 6'3", 287 OG-C
Col: Stanford *HS:* Palma [Salinas, CA] B: 3/15/1970, Salinas, CA
Drafted: 1993 Round 6 SF
1993 SF: 15 G. **1994** SF: 16 G; 1 Fum. **1995** SF: 15 G; Rec 1-(-1) -1.0; KR 3-29 9.7. **1996** SF: 16 G. **1997** SF: 13 G. **1998** SF: 15 G. **Total:** 90 G; Rec 1-(-1) -1.0; KR 3-29 9.7; 1 Fum.

PETE D'ALONZO D'Alonzo, Peter Joseph 5'10", 210 FB
Col: Villanova *HS:* Orange [NJ] B: 5/26/1929, Orange, NJ
Drafted: 1951 Round 4 Det
1951 Det: 12 G; Rush 2-11 5.5. **1952** Det: 4 G; Rush 5-7 1.4; Rec 2-4 2.0. **Total:** 16 G; Rush 7-18 2.6; Rec 2-4 2.0.

SLATS DALRYMPLE Dalrymple, Robert Hew 6'2", 210 C
Col: Indiana; Wabash *HS:* Wylie [Terre Haute, IN] B: 7/15/1896, Nelsonville, OH D: 5/23/1978, Dublin, GA
1922 Eva: 1 G.

LIONAL DALTON Dalton, Lional Deshawn 6'1", 320 DT
Col: Eastern Michigan *HS:* Cooley [Detroit, MI] B: 2/21/1975, Detroit, MI
1998 Bal: 2 G.

MOXIE DALTON Dalton, Maurice Jack 5'6", 165 BB-FB
(Leather) *Col:* Carroll (Wis.); Loras *HS:* Janesville [WI] B: 9/1894, Janesville, WI D: 2/9/1954
1922 Rac: 5 G.

OAKLEY DALTON Dalton, Oakley 6'6", 285 DT
Col: Jackson State *HS:* Gary [WV] B: 7/18/1952, Welch, WV
Drafted: 1977 Round 12 NO
1977 NO: 1 G.

BRAD DALUISO Daluiso, Bradley William 6'2", 215 K
Col: Grossmont Coll. CA (J.C.); San Diego State; UCLA *HS:* Valhalla [El Cajon, CA] B: 12/31/1967, San Diego, CA
1992 Den: Punt 10-467 46.7. **Total:** Punt 10-467 46.7.

		Scoring						
Year Team	**G**	**Pts**	**FG**	**FGA**	**FG%**	**XK**	**XKA**	**XK%**
1991 Atl-Buf	16	8	2	3	66.7	2	2	100.0
1991 Atl	2	8	2	3	66.7	2	2	100.0
1991 Buf	14	0	0	0	—	0	0	—
1992 Den	16	0	0	1	0.0	0	0	—
1993 NYG	15	3	1	3	33.3	0	0	—
1994 NYG	16	38	11	11	100.0	5	5	100.0
1995 NYG	16	88	20	28	71.4	28	28	100.0
1996 NYG	16	94	24	27	88.9	22	22	100.0
1997 NYG	16	93	22	32	68.8	27	29	93.1
1998 NYG	16	95	21	27	77.8	32	32	100.0
NFL Total	127	419	101	132	76.5	116	118	98.3

MIKE D'AMATO D'Amato, Michael Anthony 6'2", 205 DB
Col: Hofstra *HS:* Brooklyn Tech [NY] B: 3/3/1943, Brooklyn, NY
Drafted: 1968 Round 10 NYJ
1968 NYJ: 13 G; KR 1-32 32.0.

FRANK DAMIANI Damiani, Francis Anthony 6'1", 225 T
Col: Manhattan *HS:* Carnegie [PA] B: 7/27/1922, Carnegie, PA
1944 NYG: 4 G.

MAURY DAMKROGER Damkroger, Maurice Albert 6'2", 230 LB
Col: Nebraska *HS:* Lincoln Northwest [NE] B: 1/8/1952, Cambridge, NE *Drafted:* 1974 Round 7 NE
1974 NE: 11 G. **1975** NE: 2 G. **Total:** 13 G.

JOHN DAMORE Damore, John Lawrence 6'0", 228 C-OG
Col: Northwestern *HS:* Riverside [IL] B: 10/20/1933, Riverside, IL
Drafted: 1955 Round 13 NYG
1957 ChiB: 4 G; KR 1-7 7.0. **1959** ChiB: 8 G. **Total:** 12 G; KR 1-7 7.0.

BOLEY DANCEWICZ Dancewicz, Francis Joseph 5'10", 187 QB-DB
Col: Notre Dame *HS:* Classical [Lynn, MA] B: 10/3/1924, Lynn, MA
D: 6/26/1985, Boston, MA *Drafted:* 1946 Round 1 Bos
1946 Bos: Int 1-4. **1947** Bos: Punt 1-40 40.0. **Total:** Int 1-4; Punt 1-40 40.0.

		Passing							
Year Team	G	Att	Comp	Comp%	Yds	YPA	TD	Int	Rating
1946 Bos	8	34	13	38.2	162	4.76	1	6	24.0
1947 Bos	12	169	66	39.1	1203	7.12	11	18	46.4
1948 Bos	3	35	17	48.6	186	5.31	0	5	25.1
NFL Total	23	238	96	40.3	1551	6.52	12	29	40.1

	Rushing				
Year Team	Att	Yds	Avg	TD	Fum
1946 Bos	14	81	5.8	0	0
1947 Bos	47	145	3.1	1	3
1948 Bos	4	3	0.8	1	1
NFL Total	65	229	3.5	2	4

DICK DANEHE Danehe, Richard Michael 6'2", 235 T-C
Col: USC *HS:* Hickman [Columbia, MO] B: 9/10/1920, Memphis, TN
AAFC **1947** LA-A: 11 G. **1948** LA-A: 5 G. **Total:** 16 G.

NFL **1947** LA-A: 11 G. **1948** LA-A: 5 G. **Total:** 16 G.

JOE DANELO Danelo, Joseph Peter 5'9", 166 K
Col: Washington State *HS:* Gonzaga Prep [Spokane, WA] B: 9/2/1953, Spokane, WA *Drafted:* 1975 Round 10 Mia
1979 NYG: Rec 1-1 1.0. **Total:** Rec 1-1 1.0.

		Scoring						
Year Team	G	Pts	FG	FGA	FG%	XK	XKA	XK%
1975 GB	12	53	11	16	68.8	20	23	87.0
1976 NYG	14	44	8	21	38.1	20	21	95.2
1977 NYG	14	61	14	23	60.9	19	20	95.0
1978 NYG	16	90	21	29	72.4	27	29	93.1
1979 NYG	16	55	9	20	45.0	28	29	96.6
1980 NYG	16	75	16	24	66.7	27	28	96.4
1981 NYG	16	103	24	**38**	63.2	31	31	100.0
1982 NYG	9	54	12	21	57.1	18	18	100.0
1983 Buf	14	63	10	20	50.0	33	35	94.3
1984 Buf	9	41	8	16	50.0	17	17	100.0
NFL Total	136	639	133	228	58.3	240	251	95.6

ELDON DANENHAUER Danenhauer, Eldon Voss 6'5", 245 OT
(Big E) *Col:* Emporia State; Pittsburg State *HS:* Concordia [KS]
B: 10/4/1935, Clay Center, KS
1960 Den: 14 G. **1961** Den: 14 G. **1962** Den: 14 G; KR 1-11 11.0.
1963 Den: 9 G. **1964** Den: 14 G. **1965** Den: 14 G. **Total:** 79 G; KR 1-11 11.0.

BILL DANENHAUER Danenhauer, William Adolph 6'4", 245 DE
Col: Emporia State *HS:* Concordia [KS] B: 6/3/1934, Clay Center, KS
Drafted: 1956 Round 17 Bal
1960 Den-Bos: 7 G. Den: 4 G. Bos: 3 G. **Total:** 7 G.

GEORGE DANEY Daney, George Anthony 6'4", 240 OG
Col: Detroit Mercy; Texas-El Paso *HS:* Avella [PA] B: 2/2/1946, Washington, PA D: 2/15/1990, Raytown, MO *Drafted:* 1968 Round 1 KC
1968 KC: 14 G; KR 1-0. **1969** KC: 14 G; **1** Fum TD; 6 Pt. **1970** KC: 14 G.
1971 KC: 14 G. **1972** KC: 14 G. **1973** KC: 14 G. **1974** KC: 13 G.
Total: 97 G; KR 1-0; 1 Fum TD; 6 Pt.

EUGENE DANIEL Daniel, Eugene Jr. 5'11", 178 DB
Col: Louisiana State *HS:* Robert E. Lee [Baton Rouge, LA]
B: 5/4/1961, Baton Rouge, LA *Drafted:* 1984 Round 8 Ind
1985 Ind: PR 1-6 6.0. **1990** Ind: PR 1-0. **1992** Ind: 2 Sac. **Total:** PR 2-6 3.0; 2 Sac.

		Interceptions				Tot
Year Team	G	Int	Yds	TD	Fum	TD
1984 Ind	15	6	25	0	0	0
1985 Ind	16	8	53	0	1	0
1986 Ind	15	3	11	0	0	1
1987 Ind	12	2	34	0	0	0
1988 Ind	16	2	44	1	0	1
1989 Ind	15	1	34	0	0	0
1990 Ind	15	0	0	0	0	0
1991 Ind	16	3	22	0	0	0
1992 Ind	14	1	0	0	0	0
1993 Ind	16	1	17	0	0	0
1994 Ind	16	2	6	0	0	0
1995 Ind	16	3	142	1	0	1
1996 Ind	16	3	35	1	0	1
1997 Bal	9	3	60	0	0	0
NFL Total	207	38	483	3	1	4

KENNY DANIEL Daniel, Kenneth Ray 5'10", 180 DB
Col: Contra Costa Coll. CA (J.C.); San Jose State *HS:* John F. Kennedy [Richmond, CA] B: 6/1/1960, Martinez, CA
1984 NYG: 15 G; KR 1-52 52.0. **1986** Ind: 15 G; KR 5-109 21.8; Int 1-0.
1987 Ind: 2 G; KR 10-225 22.5; 2 Fum. **Total:** 32 G; KR 16-386 24.1; Int 1-0; 2 Fum.

WILLIE DANIEL Daniel, William Paul 5'11", 190 DB
Col: Mississippi State *HS:* Noxubee Co. [Macon, MS] B: 11/10/1937, New Albany, MS
1965 Pit: **1** Fum TD. **Total:** 1 Fum TD.

		Interceptions			Tot
Year Team	G	Int	Yds	TD	TD
1961 Pit	14	3	76	0	0
1962 Pit	13	5	85	**1**	1
1963 Pit	13	0	0	0	0
1964 Pit	14	2	4	0	0
1965 Pit	9	1	9	0	1
1966 Pit	12	0	0	0	0
1967 LARm	14	2	45	0	0
1968 LARm	14	0	0	0	0
1969 LARm	10	1	13	0	0
NFL Total	113	14	232	1	2

AVE DANIELL Daniell, Averell Edward 6'3", 215 T
(Li'l Abner) *Col:* Pittsburgh *HS:* Mount Lebanon [PA] B: 11/6/1914, Pittsburgh, PA D: 1/26/1999, Pittsburgh, PA *Drafted:* 1937 Round 2 GB
1937 GB-Bkn: 9 G. GB: 5 G. Bkn: 4 G. **Total:** 9 G.

JIM DANIELL Daniell, James Laughlin 6'2", 230 T
Col: Ohio State *HS:* Mount Lebanon [PA]; Kiski School [Saltsburg, PA]
B: 4/10/1918, Pittsburgh, PA D: 12/13/1983, Pittsburgh, PA
Drafted: 1942 Round 10 ChiB
AAFC **1946** CleA: 14 G.

NFL **1945** ChiB: 7 G; KR 1-14 14.0; 1 Fum.

CALVIN DANIELS Daniels, Calvin Richard 6'3", 236 LB
Col: North Carolina *HS:* Goldsboro [NC] B: 12/26/1958, Morehead City, NC *Drafted:* 1982 Round 2 KC
1982 KC: 9 G. **1983** KC: 16 G; KR 1-0; 2 Sac. **1984** KC: 16 G; Int 2-11; 4.5 Sac. **1985** KC: 16 G; 2.5 Sac. **1986** Was: 13 G; Int 1-4; 1 Sac.
Total: 70 G; KR 1-0; Int 3-15; 10 Sac.

CLEM DANIELS Daniels, Clemon C Jr. 6'1", 220 HB-DB
Col: Prairie View A&M *HS:* Edward Sewell Daly [McKinney, TX]
B: 7/9/1937, McKinney, TX
1960 DalT: PR 3-69 23.0; Int 3-10. **1961** Oak: PR 5-34 6.8. **1962** Oak: Pass 1-0. **1963** Oak: Pass 1-1 100.0%, 10 10.00. **1964** Oak: Pass 1-0.
1965 Oak: Pass 2-2 100.0%, 95 47.50. **1966** Oak: Pass 3-0, 1 Int.
1967 Oak: Pass 1-1 100.0%, 28 28.00. **Total:** Pass 9-4 44.4%, 133 14.78 1 Int; PR 8-103 12.9; Int 3-10.

		Rushing				Receiving			
Year Team	G	Att	Yds	Avg	TD	Rec	Yds	Avg	TD
1960 DalT	14	1	-2	-2.0	0	0	0	—	0
1961 Oak	8	31	154	5.0	2	13	150	11.5	0
1962 Oak	14	161	766	4.8	7	24	318	13.3	1
1963 Oak	14	215	**1099**	5.1	3	30	685	22.8	5
1964 Oak	14	173	824	4.8	2	42	696	16.6	6
1965 Oak	14	219	884	4.0	5	36	568	15.8	7
1966 Oak	14	204	801	3.9	7	40	652	16.3	3
1967 Oak	9	130	575	4.4	4	16	222	13.9	2
1968 SF	9	12	37	3.1	0	2	23	11.5	0
NFL Total	110	1146	5138	4.5	30	203	3314	16.3	24

	Kickoff Returns					Tot
Year Team	Ret	Yds	Avg	TD	Fum	TD
1960 DalT	9	162	18.0	0	1	0
1961 Oak	13	276	21.2	0	3	2

Year Team						
1962 Oak	24	530	22.1	0	8	8
1963 Oak	0	0	—	0	8	8
1964 Oak	1	32	32.0	0	9	8
1965 Oak	0	0	—	0	6	12
1966 Oak	0	0	—	0	7	10
1967 Oak	0	0	—	0	2	6
1968 SF	10	206	20.6	0	0	0
NFL Total	57	1206	21.2	0	44	54

DAVID DANIELS Daniels, David 6′1″, 190 **WR**
Col: Penn State *HS:* Sarasota [FL] B: 9/16/1969, Sarasota, FL
Drafted: 1991 Round 3 Sea
1991 Sea: 16 G; Rec 4-38 9.5; 1 Fum. **1992** Sea: 13 G; Rec 5-99 19.8. **Total:** 29 G; Rec 9-137 15.2; 1 Fum.

DAVE DANIELS Daniels, David Lee 6′3″, 245 **DT**
Col: Florida A&M *HS:* Central Acad. [East Palatka, FL] B: 4/5/1941, East Palatka, FL *Drafted:* 1965 Redshirt Round 6 Hou
1966 Oak: 14 G.

DEXTER DANIELS Daniels, Dexter Lavista 6′0″, 241 **LB**
Col: Florida *HS:* Valdosta [GA] B: 12/8/1973, Valdosta, GA
Drafted: 1996 Round 6 Bal
1996 Bal: 4 G.

JACK DANIELS Daniels, Jack 135 **TB**
Col: No College *HS:* Englewood [Chicago, IL] B: 1909, MI Deceased
1925 Mil: 1 G.

JEROME DANIELS Daniels, Jerome Alvonne 6′5″, 350 **OT**
Col: Northeastern *HS:* Bloomfield [CT] B: 9/13/1974, Hartford, CT
Drafted: 1997 Round 4 Mia
1998 Ariz: 8 G.

LESHUN DANIELS Daniels, LeShun 6′1″, 304 **OG**
Col: Ohio State *HS:* Warren G. Harding [Warren, OH] B: 5/30/1974, Warren, OH
1997 Min: 1 G.

PHILLIP DANIELS Daniels, Phillip Bernard 6′5″, 263 **DE**
Col: Georgia *HS:* Seminole Co. [Donalsonville, GA] B: 3/4/1973, Donalsonville, GA *Drafted:* 1996 Round 4 Sea
1996 Sea: 15 G; 2 Sac. **1997** Sea: 13 G; KR 1-(-2) -2.0; 1 Fum; 4 Sac. **1998** Sea: 16 G; 6.5 Sac. **Total:** 44 G; KR 1-(-2) -2.0; 1 Fum; 12.5 Sac.

DICK DANIELS Daniels, Richard Bernard 5′9″, 180 **DB**
Col: Pacific (Ore) *HS:* Jefferson [Portland, OR] B: 10/19/1944, Portland, OR
1966 Dal: 4 G. **1967** Dal: 14 G. **1968** Dal: 14 G; KR 9-193 21.4; Int 2-25. **1969** ChiB: 8 G; Int 3-37. **1970** ChiB: 13 G; Int 2-29. **Total:** 53 G; KR 9-193 21.4; Int 7-91.

GARY DANIELSON Danielson, Gary Dennis 6′2″, 195 **QB**
Col: Purdue *HS:* Divine Child [Dearborn, MI] B: 9/10/1951, Detroit, MI
1984 Det: Rec 1-22 22.0 1 TD. **Total:** Rec 1-22 22.0 1 TD.

		Passing							
Year Team	**G**	**Att**	**Comp**	**Comp%**	**Yds**	**YPA**	**TD**	**Int**	**Rating**
1976 Det	1	0	0	—	0	—	0	0	—
1977 Det	13	100	42	42.0	445	4.45	1	5	38.1
1978 Det	16	351	199	56.7	2294	6.54	18	17	73.5
1980 Det	16	417	244	58.5	3223	7.73	13	11	82.4
1981 Det	6	96	56	58.3	784	8.17	3	5	73.4
1982 Det	8	197	100	50.8	1343	6.82	10	14	60.1
1983 Det	10	113	59	52.2	720	6.37	7	4	78.0
1984 Det	15	410	252	61.5	3076	7.50	17	15	83.1
1985 Cle	8	163	97	59.5	1274	7.82	8	6	85.3
1987 Cle	6	33	25	75.8	281	8.52	4	0	140.3
1988 Cle	2	52	31	59.6	324	6.23	0	1	69.7
NFL Total	101	1932	1105	57.2	13764	7.12	81	78	76.6

	Rushing					Tot
Year Team	**Att**	**Yds**	**Avg**	**TD**	**Fum**	**TD**
1977 Det	7	62	8.9	0	0	0
1978 Det	22	93	4.2	0	5	0
1980 Det	48	232	4.8	2	11	2
1981 Det	9	23	2.6	2	2	2
1982 Det	23	92	4.0	0	6	0
1983 Det	6	8	1.3	0	2	0
1984 Det	41	218	5.3	3	7	4
1985 Cle	25	126	5.0	0	5	0
1987 Cle	1	0	0.0	0	2	0
1988 Cle	4	3	0.8	0	1	0
NFL Total	186	857	4.6	7	41	8

ERNIE DANJEAN Danjean, Ernest Joseph 6′0″, 230 **LB**
Col: Auburn *HS:* Behrman [New Orleans, LA] B: 3/5/1934, New Orleans, LA D: 6/22/1995, Belle Chasse, LA *Drafted:* 1957 Round 19 GB
1957 GB: 12 G.

RICK DANMEIER Danmeier, Richard Craig 6′0″, 194 **K**
Col: Lakewood CC MN; Sioux Falls *HS:* White Bear Lake [MN]
B: 4/8/1952, St. Paul, MN

		Scoring						
Year Team	**G**	**Pts**	**FG**	**FGA**	**FG%**	**XK**	**XKA**	**XK%**
1977 Min	1	0	0	0	—	0	0	—
1978 Min	16	72	12	19	63.2	36	37	97.3
1979 Min	16	67	13	22	59.1	28	31	90.3
1980 Min	16	81	16	26	61.5	33	38	86.8
1981 Min	16	97	21	25	84.0	34	37	91.9
1982 Min	9	47	8	14	57.1	23	23	100.0
NFL Total	74	364	70	106	66.0	154	166	92.8

ED DANOWSKI Danowski, Edward Frank 6′1″, 198 **QB-TB-DB-WB**
Col: Fordham *HS:* Riverhead [NY] B: 9/30/1911, Jamesport, NY
D: 2/1/1997, East Patchogue, NY
1939 NYG: Punt 29-1105 38.1. **1941** NYG: Rec 1-12 12.0; Punt 2-73 36.5. **Total:** Rec 1-12 12.0; Punt 31-1178 38.0.

		Passing							
Year Team	**G**	**Att**	**Comp**	**Comp%**	**Yds**	**YPA**	**TD**	**Int**	**Rating**
1934 NYG	8	32	15	**46.9**	230	7.19	2	3	52.9
1935 NYG	12	**113**	**57**	**50.4**	**794**	7.03	**10**	9	69.7
1936 NYG	12	104	47	45.2	515	4.95	5	10	36.8
1937 NYG	11	134	66	49.3	814	6.07	8	5	72.8
1938 NYG	11	129	**70**	54.3	848	6.57	7	8	66.9
1939 NYG	11	101	42	41.6	437	4.33	3	6	39.9
1941 NYG	6	24	12	50.0	179	7.46	2	3	63.0
NFL Total	71	637	309	48.5	3817	5.99	37	44	58.1

	Rushing			
Year Team	**Att**	**Yds**	**Avg**	**TD**
1934 NYG	75	248	3.3	0
1935 NYG	130	335	2.6	2
1936 NYG	91	259	2.8	0
1937 NYG	66	95	1.4	1
1938 NYG	48	215	4.5	1
1939 NYG	25	21	0.8	0
NFL Total	435	1173	2.7	4

FRED DANZIGER Danziger, Frederick W 5′11″, 175 **FB**
Col: Michigan State *HS:* Western [Detroit, MI] B: 1/12/1906, Detroit, MI D: 10/18/1948, Dearborn, MI
1931 Cle: 1 G.

JERRY DAPRATO DaPrato, Neno Joseph 5′10″, 185 **FB**
Col: Michigan State *HS:* Iron Mountain [MI] B: 1/14/1893, Iron Mountain, MI D: 4/29/1984, Parkesburg, PA
1921 Det: 6 G.

AL DARBY Darby, Alvis Russell 6′5″, 221 **TE**
Col: Florida *HS:* Miami Edison [FL] B: 9/14/1954, Miami, FL
Drafted: 1976 Round 6 Sea
1976 Sea-Hou: 3 G. Sea: 1 G. Hou: 2 G. **1978** TB: 6 G. **Total:** 9 G.

BYRON DARBY Darby, Byron Keith 6′4″, 260 **DE-NT-TE**
Col: USC *HS:* Inglewood [CA] B: 6/4/1960, Los Angeles, CA
Drafted: 1983 Round 5 Phi
1983 Phi: 16 G; KR 2-3 1.5; 1 Fum; 1 Sac. **1984** Phi: 16 G; 5 Sac. **1985** Phi: 10 G; 1.5 Sac. **1986** Phi: 16 G; Rec 2-16 8.0; 1 Sac. **1987** Ind: 12 G; 3 Sac. **1988** Ind: 16 G; 2 Sac. **1989** Det: 1 G. **Total:** 87 G; Rec 2-16 8.0; KR 2-3 1.5; 1 Fum; 13.5 Sac.

MATT DARBY Darby, Matthew Lamont 6′2″, 200 **DB**
Col: UCLA *HS:* Green Run [Virginia Beach, VA] B: 11/19/1968, Virginia Beach, VA *Drafted:* 1992 Round 5 Buf
1992 Buf: 16 G. **1993** Buf: 16 G; Int 2-32. **1994** Buf: 16 G; Int 4-20. **1995** Buf: 7 G; Int 2-37. **1996** Ariz: 15 G. **1997** Ariz: 11 G. **Total:** 81 G; Int 8-89.

PAUL DARBY Darby, Paul Willie 5′10″, 192 **WR**
Col: Southwest Texas State *HS:* Lyndon B. Johnson [Austin, TX]
B: 10/22/1956, Austin, TX *Drafted:* 1979 Round 12 NYJ
1979 NYJ: 15 G; PR 1-0. **1980** NYJ: 8 G; Rush 1-15 15.0; Rec 3-48 16.0 1 TD; KR 7-139 19.9; 6 Pt; 1 Fum. **Total:** 23 G; Rush 1-15 15.0; Rec 3-48 16.0 1 TD; PR 1-0; KR 7-139 19.9; 6 Pt; 1 Fum.

RAMSEY DARDAR Dardar, James Ramsey 6′2″, 264 **OG-OT**
Col: Louisiana State *HS:* Cecilia [LA] B: 10/3/1959, Cecilia, LA
Drafted: 1983 Round 3 StL
1984 StL: 16 G.

KIRBY DAR DAR Dar Dar, Kirby David 5′9″, 185 **WR**
Col: Syracuse *HS:* Thomas Jefferson [Tampa, FL] B: 3/27/1972, Morgan City, LA
1995 Mia: 1 G; KR 1-22 22.0. **1996** Mia: 11 G; KR 7-132 18.9. **1998** Mia: 2 G. **Total:** 14 G; KR 8-154 19.3.

THOM DARDEN Darden, Thomas Vincent 6'2", 195 DB
Col: Michigan *HS:* Sandusky [OH] B: 8/28/1950, Sandusky, OH
Drafted: 1972 Round 1 Cle
1974 Cle: 1 Fum TD. **1980** Cle: KR 1-(-1) -1.0. **Total:** KR 1-(-1) -1.0; 1 Fum TD.

		Punt Returns				Interceptions				Tot
Year Team	G	Ret	Yds	Avg	TD	Int	Yds	TD	Fum	TD
1972 Cle	14	15	61	4.1	0	3	64	0	0	0
1973 Cle	11	9	51	5.7	0	1	36	0	2	0
1974 Cle	14	21	173	8.2	0	8	105	0	1	1
1976 Cle	14	0	0	—	0	7	73	0	1	0
1977 Cle	14	0	0	—	0	6	107	**1**	1	1
1978 Cle	16	0	0	—	0	**10**	**200**	0	0	0
1979 Cle	16	0	0	—	0	5	125	1	0	1
1980 Cle	16	0	0	—	0	2	42	0	1	0
1981 Cle	13	0	0	—	0	3	68	0	0	0
NFL Total	128	45	285	6.3	0	45	820	2	6	3

DONOVIN DARIUS Darius, Donovin 6'1", 220 DB
(Double D) *Col:* Syracuse *HS:* Woodrow Wilson [Camden, NJ]
B: 8/12/1975, Camden, NJ *Drafted:* 1998 Round 1 Jac
1998 Jac: 14 G; 1 Fum TD; 6 Pt.

CHRIS DARKINS Darkins, Christopher Oji 6'0", 205 CB
(Darkside) *Col:* Minnesota *HS:* Starke Jesuit College Prep [Houston, TX] B: 4/30/1974, San Francisco, CA *Drafted:* 1996 Round 4 GB
1997 GB: 14 G; KR 4-68 17.0.

BOOB DARLING Darling, Bernard Edward 6'1", 206 C
Col: Wisconsin; Ripon; Beloit *HS:* Oshkosh [WI] B: 11/18/1903, Winnebago Co., WI D: 3/5/1968, Green Bay, WI
1927 GB: 1 G. **1928** GB: 7 G. **1929** GB: 11 G. **1930** GB: 13 G. **1931** GB: 4 G. **Total:** 36 G.

JAMES DARLING Darling, James Jackson 6'0", 250 LB
Col: Washington State *HS:* Kettle Falls [WA] B: 12/29/1974, Denver, CO *Drafted:* 1997 Round 2 Phi
1997 Phi: 16 G. **1998** Phi: 12 G; 2 Sac. **Total:** 28 G; 2 Sac.

BILL DARNALL Darnall, William Carlyle III 6'2", 197 WR
Col: North Carolina *HS:* Wakefield [Arlington, VA] B: 4/21/1944, Washington, DC *Drafted:* 1966 Redshirt Round 6 Mia
1968 Mia: 11 G; Rec 2-25 12.5. **1969** Mia: 2 G; Rec 1-13 13.0. **Total:** 13 G; Rec 3-38 12.7.

PHIL DARNS Darns, Phillip 6'3", 245 DE
Col: Mississippi Valley State *HS:* Tampa Bay Tech [Tampa, FL]
B: 7/27/1959, Tampa, FL
1984 TB: 2 G.

DAN DARRAGH Darragh, Daniel Meyer 6'3", 196 QB
Col: William & Mary *HS:* South Hills Catholic [Pittsburgh, PA]
B: 11/28/1946, Pittsburgh, PA *Drafted:* 1968 Round 13 Buf
1968 Buf: Rush 13-11 0.8. **1969** Buf: Rush 6-14 2.3. **1970** Buf: Rush 1-26 26.0. **Total:** Rush 20-51 2.6.

		Passing								
Year Team	G	Att	Comp	Comp%	Yds	YPA	TD	Int	Rating	Fum
1968 Buf	11	215	92	42.8	917	4.27	3	14	33.0	7
1969 Buf	3	52	24	46.2	365	7.02	1	6	36.6	2
1970 Buf	3	29	11	37.9	71	2.45	0	2	17.5	0
NFL Total	17	296	127	42.9	1353	4.57	4	22	30.4	9

BERNIE DARRE Darre, Bernard John 6'2", 230 OG
Col: Tulane *HS:* Alcee Fortier [New Orleans, LA] B: 11/8/1939, New Orleans, LA *Drafted:* 1960 Round 15 Was
1961 Was: 12 G.

CHRIS DARRINGTON Darrington, Christopher 5'10", 180 WR
Col: El Camino Coll. CA (J.C.); Weber State *HS:* Manual Arts [Los Angeles, CA] B: 7/13/1964
1987 Hou: 3 G; Rec 1-38 38.0.

BARRY DARROW Darrow, Barry Wayne 6'7", 260 OT
Col: Western Montana; Montana *HS:* C.M. Russell [Great Falls, MT]
B: 6/27/1950, Peoria, IL *Drafted:* 1973 Round 17 SD
1974 Cle: 13 G. **1975** Cle: 14 G. **1976** Cle: 14 G. **1977** Cle: 14 G. **1978** Cle: 16 G. **Total:** 71 G.

MATT DARWIN Darwin, Matthew Wayne 6'4", 268 OT-C
Col: Texas A&M *HS:* Cheyenne Mountain [Colorado Springs, CO]; Klein HS [Houston, TX] B: 3/11/1963, Houston, TX *Drafted:* 1986 Round 4 Phi
1986 Phi: 16 G. **1987** Phi: 12 G. **1988** Phi: 16 G. **1989** Phi: 15 G. **1990** Phi: 2 G. **Total:** 61 G.

DANE DASTILLUNG Dastillung, Harry 6'0", 190 G-T
Col: Marietta; Xavier (Ohio) *HS:* No High School B: 4/2/1897, Cincinnati, OH D: 11/30/1982, Cincinnati, OH
1921 Cin: 4 G.

RUSS DAUGHERITY Daugherity, Russell S 5'10", 175 WB
Col: Illinois *HS:* Streator [IL] B: 1/31/1902, Streator, IL D: 3/1971, Sierra Madre, CA
1927 Fra: 2 G.

DICK DAUGHERTY Daugherty, Richard Lee 6'1", 219 OG-LB-C
Col: Oregon *HS:* Thomas Jefferson [Richmond, OH] B: 3/31/1929, Moundsville, WV *Drafted:* 1951 Round 18 LARm
1951 LARm: 12 G. **1952** LARm: 12 G. **1953** LARm: 12 G. **1956** LARm: 12 G. **1957** LARm: 9 G; Int 1-32 1 TD; Scor **1** Saf; 8 Pt. **1958** LARm: 12 G; Int 1-12 1 TD; 6 Pt. **Total:** 69 G; Int 2-44 2 TD; Scor 1 Saf; 14 Pt.

BOB DAUGHERTY Daugherty, Robert J 6'1", 210 HB
Col: New Mexico Mil. Inst. (J.C.); Tulsa *HS:* Mountain View [CA]
B: 10/4/1942 *Drafted:* 1964 Round 8 SF
1966 SF: 4 G.

RON DAUGHERTY Daugherty, Ronald 6'3", 185 WR
Col: Northeastern Illinois B: 3/17/1958, Chicago, IL
1987 Min: 3 G; Rec 2-21 10.5.

LOU DAUKAS Daukas, Louis James 6'0", 203 LB-C
Col: Cornell *HS:* Cushing [Nashua, NH] B: 7/4/1921, Nashua, NH
AAFC **1947** BknA: 4 G; KR 1-1 1.0; Int 1-1.

NICK DAUKAS Daukas, Nicholas James 6'3", 220 T-G
Col: Dartmouth *HS:* Cushing [Nashua, NH] B: 12/11/1922, Nashua, NH
AAFC **1946** BknA: 8 G; Rec 2-19 9.5; Int 1-5. **1947** BknA: 7 G. **Total:** 15 G; Rec 2-19 9.5; Int 1-5.

RED DAUM Daum, Carl V 5'7", 166 E-BB-WB
Col: Akron *HS:* Central [Akron, OH] B: 9/18/1898, Akron, OH
D: 6/30/1959, Akron, OH
1922 Akr: 9 G; Pass 1 TD; Rec 1 TD; Int 1 TD; Tot TD 2; 12 Pt. **1923** Akr: 7 G. **1924** Akr: 8 G. **1925** Akr: 5 G; Rec 1 TD; 6 Pt. **1926** Akr: 8 G. **Total:** 37 G; Pass 1 TD; Rec 2 TD; Int 1 TD; Tot TD 3; 18 Pt.

MITCH DAUM Daum, Mitchell 6'5", 250 TE
Col: Wyoming *HS:* Kimball [NE] B: 11/13/1963, Kimball, NE
1987 Hou: 2 G.

CHARLES DAVENPORT Davenport, Charles Donald Jr. 6'3", 210 WR
Col: North Carolina State *HS:* Pine Forest [Fayetteville, NC]
B: 11/22/1968, Fayetteville, NC *Drafted:* 1992 Round 4 Pit
1992 Pit: 15 G; Rec 9-136 15.1; 1 Fum TD; 6 Pt. **1993** Pit: 16 G; Rec 4-51 12.8. **1994** Pit: 7 G. **Total:** 38 G; Rec 13-187 14.4; 1 Fum TD; 6 Pt.

WAYNE DAVENPORT Davenport, Raymond Wayne 6'4", 187 HB
(Mike) *Col:* Georgetown; Hardin-Simmons *HS:* San Saba [TX]
B: 12/16/1906, San Saba, TX
1931 GB: 2 G.

RON DAVENPORT Davenport, Ronald Donovan 6'2", 230 RB
Col: Louisville *HS:* Walter F. George [Atlanta, GA] B: 12/22/1962, Summerset, Bermuda *Drafted:* 1985 Round 6 Mia
1986 Mia: KR 16-285 17.8. **1988** Mia: KR 2-41 20.5. **1989** Mia: KR 1-19 19.0. **Total:** KR 19-345 18.2.

		Rushing				Receiving					Tot
Year Team	G	Att	Yds	Avg	TD	Rec	Yds	Avg	TD	Fum	TD
1985 Mia	16	98	370	3.8	11	13	74	5.7	2	2	13
1986 Mia	16	75	314	4.2	0	20	177	8.9	1	4	1
1987 Mia	10	32	114	3.6	1	27	249	9.2	1	0	2
1988 Mia	16	55	273	5.0	0	30	282	9.4	0	1	0
1989 Mia	9	14	56	4.0	1	3	19	6.3	0	0	1
NFL Total	67	274	1127	4.1	13	93	801	8.6	4	7	17

DON DAVEY Davey, Donald Vincent 6'4", 273 DE-DT
Col: Wisconsin *HS:* Lincoln [Manitowoc, WI] B: 4/8/1968, Scottsville, NY *Drafted:* 1991 Round 3 GB
1991 GB: 16 G; KR 1-8 8.0. **1992** GB: 9 G; KR 1-8 8.0. **1993** GB: 9 G. **1994** GB: 16 G; KR 1-6 6.0; 1.5 Sac. **1995** Jac: 16 G; 3 Sac. **1996** Jac: 16 G; 0.5 Sac. **1997** Jac: 10 G; 3 Sac. **Total:** 92 G; KR 3-22 7.3; 8 Sac.

JIM DAVID David, James Theodore 5'11", 178 DB
(Hatchet) *Col:* Colorado State *HS:* Chicora [Charleston, SC]
B: 12/2/1927, Florence, SC *Drafted:* 1952 Round 22 Det
1955 Det: PR 1-0. **Total:** PR 1-0.

		Interceptions			
Year Team	G	Int	Yds	TD	Fum
1952 Det	12	7	48	0	0
1953 Det	12	4	50	0	0
1954 Det	12	7	74	0	0
1955 Det	12	3	44	0	0
1956 Det	12	7	4	0	0
1957 Det	12	3	20	0	0
1958 Det	12	3	12	0	1
1959 Det	12	2	7	0	0
NFL Total	96	36	259	0	1

BOB DAVID David, Robert Joseph 6′0″, 219 **G-LB**
Col: Notre Dame; Villanova *HS:* Mount Carmel [Chicago, IL]
B: 1/15/1921, Blue Island, IL *Drafted:* 1947 Round 25 LARm
AAFC **1948** ChiA: 4 G.

NFL **1947** LARm: 8 G. **1948** LARm: 3 G. **Total:** 11 G.

STAN DAVID David, Stanley Chaunce 6′3″, 210 **LB**
Col: Texas Tech *HS:* Tucumcari [NM] B: 2/17/1962, North Platte, NE
Drafted: 1984 Round 7 Buf
1984 Buf: 16 G; KR 1-6 6.0; 6 Pt; 1 Sac.

NORBERTO DAVIDDS-GARRIDO Davidds-Garrido, Norberto Jr. 6′6″, 315 **OT**
Col: Mount San Antonio Coll. CA (J.C.); USC *HS:* William Workman [City of Industry, CA] B: 10/4/1972, La Puente, CA *Drafted:* 1996 Round 4 Car
1996 Car: 12 G. **1997** Car: 15 G. **1998** Car: 16 G. **Total:** 43 G.

BEN DAVIDSON Davidson, Benjamin Earl 6′8″, 275 **DE-DT**
Col: East Los Angeles Coll. CA (J.C.); Washington *HS:* Woodrow Wilson [Los Angeles, CA] B: 6/14/1940, Los Angeles, CA *Drafted:* 1961 Round 4 NYG
1961 GB: 14 G. **1962** Was: 14 G. **1963** Was: 14 G. **1964** Oak: 12 G. **1965** Oak: 14 G. **1966** Oak: 14 G. **1967** Oak: 14 G. **1968** Oak: 14 G. **1969** Oak: 14 G. **1970** Oak: 14 G. **1971** Oak: 14 G. **Total:** 152 G.

CHY DAVIDSON Davidson, Chy 5′11″, 175 **WR**
Col: Rhode Island *HS:* Bayside [Queens, NY] B: 5/9/1959, Queens, NY *Drafted:* 1981 Supplemental Round 1 NE
1984 NYJ: 3 G; KR 1-9 9.0. **1985** NYJ: 1 G. **Total:** 4 G; KR 1-9 9.0.

COTTON DAVIDSON Davidson, Francis Marion 6′1″, 182 **QB**
Col: Baylor *HS:* Gatesville [TX] B: 11/30/1931, Gatesville, TX
Drafted: 1954 Round 1 Bal
1957 Bal: KR 5-79 15.8. **1960** DalT: Rec 1-(-1) -1.0; Scor 16, 1-1 100.0% FG, 7-7 100.0% XK. **1961** DalT: Scor 26, 0-2 FG, 20-20 100.0% XK. **1962** DalT-Oak: Scor 25, 1-2 50.0% FG, 4-5 80.0% XK. Oak: Scor 25, 1-2 50.0% FG, 4-5 80.0% XK. **Total:** Rec 1-(-1) -1.0; KR 5-79 15.8; Scor 103, 2-5 40.0% FG, 31-32 96.9% XK.

		Passing							
Year Team	**G**	**Att**	**Comp**	**Comp%**	**Yds**	**YPA**	**TD**	**Int**	**Rating**
1954 Bal	12	64	28	43.8	309	4.83	0	5	26.1
1957 Bal	12	2	0	0.0	0	0.00	0	1	0.0
1960 DalT	14	379	179	47.2	2474	6.53	15	16	64.2
1961 DalT	14	330	151	45.8	2445	7.41	17	23	59.2
1962 DalT-Oak	14	321	119	37.1	1977	6.16	7	23	36.1
1962 DalT	1	0	0	—	0	—	0	0	—
1962 Oak	13	321	119	37.1	1977	6.16	7	23	36.1
1963 Oak	14	194	77	39.7	1276	6.58	11	**10**	60.0
1964 Oak	14	320	155	48.4	2497	7.80	21	19	72.1
1965 Oak	2	1	1	100.0	8	8.00	0	0	100.0
1966 Oak	14	139	59	42.4	770	5.54	2	11	32.4
1968 Oak	1	2	1	50.0	4	2.00	0	0	56.3
NFL Total	111	1752	770	43.9	11760	6.71	73	108	54.9

	Rushing				Punting			
Year Team	**Att**	**Yds**	**Avg**	**TD**	**Punts**	**Yds**	**Avg**	**Fum**
1954 Bal	11	31	2.8	0	72	2680	37.2	4
1957 Bal	0	0	—	0	47	1664	35.4	0
1960 DalT	14	36	2.6	1	58	2287	39.4	6
1961 DalT	21	123	5.9	1	62	2479	40.0	7
1962 DalT-Oak	25	54	2.2	3	41	1569	38.3	7
1962 DalT	0	0	—	0	3	117	39.0	0
1962 Oak	25	54	2.2	3	38	1452	38.2	7
1963 Oak	23	133	5.8	4	0	0	—	3
1964 Oak	29	167	5.8	2	0	0	—	6
1966 Oak	6	-11	-1.8	0	0	0	—	2
NFL Total	129	533	4.1	11	280	10679	38.1	35

GREG DAVIDSON Davidson, Gregory Merle 6′2″, 250 **C**
Col: North Texas *HS:* Dulles [Missouri City, TX] B: 4/24/1958, Independence, IA
1980 Hou: 14 G. **1981** Hou: 16 G. **1982** Hou: 9 G. **Total:** 39 G.

JEFF DAVIDSON Davidson, Jeffrey John 6′5″, 309 **OG-OT**
Col: Ohio State *HS:* Westerville-North [OH] B: 10/3/1967, Akron, OH
Drafted: 1990 Round 5 Den
1990 Den: 12 G. **1991** Den: 16 G. **1992** Den: 16 G. **Total:** 44 G.

JOE DAVIDSON Davidson, Joseph Burl 6′0″, 200 **G-C**
Col: Colgate; Oklahoma State *HS:* Ovid [MI] B: 1/24/1903, Durand, MI
D: 5/14/1982, Dallas, TX
1928 ChiC: 6 G. **1930** Nwk: 6 G. **Total:** 12 G.

KENNY DAVIDSON Davidson, Kenneth Darrell 6′5″, 280 **DE**
Col: Louisiana State *HS:* Huntington [Shreveport, LA] B: 8/17/1967, Shreveport, LA *Drafted:* 1990 Round 2 Pit
1990 Pit: 14 G; 3.5 Sac. **1991** Pit: 13 G. **1992** Pit: 16 G; 2 Sac. **1993** Pit: 16 G; Int 1-6; 1 Fum TD; 6 Pt; 2.5 Sac. **1994** Hou: 16 G; 6 Sac. **1995** Hou: 15 G; Int 1-3; 2 Sac. **1996** Cin: 3 G. **Total:** 93 G; Int 2-9; 1 Fum TD; 6 Pt; 16 Sac.

PETE DAVIDSON Davidson, Peter Stewart 6′5″, 255 **DT**
Col: The Citadel *HS:* Oakwood [Dayton, OH] B: 1/25/1937, Dayton, OH *Drafted:* 1960 Round 1 LAC
1960 Hou: 1 G.

BILL DAVIDSON Davidson, William A 6′0″, 182 **HB-DB-TB-OE**
Col: Temple *HS:* Mount Lebanon [PA] B: 6/15/1915, Pittsburgh, PA
D: 8/1970
1937 Pit: Pass 24-8 33.3%, 81 3.38 5 Int; Rec 4-169 42.3 2 TD; Int **1** TD. **1938** Pit: Pass 2-2 100.0%, 10 5.00; Rec 12-229 19.1. **1939** Pit: Pass 7-1 14.3%, 8 1.14; Rec 6-27 4.5. **Total:** Pass 33-11 33.3%, 99 3.00 5 Int; Rec 22-425 19.3 2 TD; Int 1 TD.

		Rushing				Tot
Year Team	**G**	**Att**	**Yds**	**Avg**	**TD**	**TD**
1937 Pit	11	101	293	2.9	1	4
1938 Pit	10	33	52	1.6	0	0
1939 Pit	7	21	27	1.3	0	0
NFL Total	28	155	372	2.4	1	4

DAVIS Davis 185 **G**
Col: Chicago Deceased
1920 Ham: 6 G.

SONNY DAVIS Davis, Albert Lee 5′11″, 215 **RB**
Col: Tennessee State *HS:* Alcoa [TN] B: 1/16/1948, Alcoa, TN
Drafted: 1971 Round 11 Phi
1971 Phi: Pass 1-0; Rec 11-46 4.2; KR 2-44 22.0.

		Rushing				
Year Team	**G**	**Att**	**Yds**	**Avg**	**TD**	**Fum**
1971 Phi	14	47	163	3.5	1	1

ANDRE DAVIS Davis, Andre 6′3″, 330 **DT**
Col: Southern University *HS:* Baker [LA] B: 10/7/1975, Baton Rouge, LA
1996 Jac: 2 G.

ANDY DAVIS Davis, Andrew Nathan Jr. 6′0″, 188 **DB**
Col: George Washington *HS:* McKinley [Washington, DC]
B: 7/28/1927, Indianapolis, IN *Drafted:* 1952 Round 2 Was
1952 Was: 8 G.

ANTHONY DAVIS Davis, Anthony 5′10″, 190 **RB**
Col: USC *HS:* San Fernando [CA] B: 9/8/1952, San Fernando, CA
Drafted: 1975 Round 2 NYJ
1977 TB: Rec 8-91 11.4; KR 15-277 18.5. **1978** Hou-LARm: KR 4-98 24.5. Hou: KR 4-98 24.5. **Total:** Rec 8-91 11.4; KR 19-375 19.7.

		Rushing				
Year Team	**G**	**Att**	**Yds**	**Avg**	**TD**	**Fum**
1977 TB	11	95	297	3.1	1	5
1978 Hou-LARm	4	3	7	2.3	0	0
1978 Hou	2	0	0	—	0	0
1978 LARm	2	3	7	2.3	0	0
NFL Total	15	98	304	3.1	1	5

ANTHONY DAVIS Davis, Anthony Darvise 6′0″, 235 **LB**
Col: Spokane CC WA; Utah *HS:* Pasco [WA] B: 3/7/1969, Pasco, WA
Drafted: 1992 Round 11 Hou
1993 Sea: 10 G. **1994** KC: 5 G. **1995** KC: 16 G; Int 1-11; 2 Sac. **1996** KC: 16 G; Int 2-37; 2.5 Sac. **1997** KC: 15 G; 3.5 Sac. **1998** KC: 16 G; Int 2-27; 4.5 Sac. **Total:** 78 G; Int 5-75; 12.5 Sac.

ANTONE DAVIS Davis, Antone Eugene 6′4″, 330 **OT**
Col: Tennessee *HS:* Peach Co. [Fort Valley, GA] B: 2/28/1967, Sweetwater, TX *Drafted:* 1991 Round 1 Phi
1991 Phi: 16 G. **1992** Phi: 15 G. **1993** Phi: 16 G. **1994** Phi: 16 G. **1995** Phi: 15 G. **1996** Atl: 16 G. **1997** Atl: 3 G. **Total:** 97 G.

SONNY DAVIS Davis, Arnold Allen 6′2″, 219 **LB**
Col: Baylor *HS:* W.B. Ray [Corpus Christi, TX] B: 9/25/1938, Corpus Christi, TX *Drafted:* 1961 Round 4 Dal
1961 Dal: 2 G.

BUDDY DAVIS Davis, Arthur E 6′2″, 235 **OT**
Col: Alabama State *HS:* Alabama State Lab. [Montgomery, AL]
B: 12/19/1929, Montgomery, AL D: 11/18/1987, Montgomery, AL
1953 ChiB: 2 G. **1954** ChiB: 1 G. **Total:** 3 G.

ART DAVIS Davis, Arthur Ganong 6′1″, 195 **HB**
Col: Mississippi State *HS:* Clarksdale [MS] B: 11/29/1934, Clarksdale, MS *Drafted:* 1956 Round 1 Pit
1956 Pit: 9 G; Rush 5-6 1.2; Rec 1-9 9.0; PR 3-5 1.7.

BEN DAVIS Davis, Benjamin Frank Jr. 5′11″, 180 **DB**
Col: Defiance *HS:* Fair Lawn [NJ]; Bridgton Acad. [North Bridgton, ME]
B: 10/30/1945, Birmingham, AL *Drafted:* 1967 Round 17 Cle

Year Team	G	Punt Returns Ret	Yds	Avg	TD	Kickoff Returns Ret	Yds	Avg	TD
1967 Cle	14	18	229	**12.7**	**1**	27	708	26.2	0
1968 Cle	14	9	11	1.2	0	8	152	19.0	0
1969 Cle	1	0	0	—	0	0	0	—	0
1970 Cle	7	0	0	—	0	0	0	—	0
1971 Cle	12	0	0	—	0	0	0	—	0
1972 Cle	14	0	0	—	0	0	0	—	0
1973 Cle	13	0	0	—	0	0	0	—	0
1974 Det	9	0	0	—	0	0	0	—	0
1975 Det	11	0	0	—	0	0	0	—	0
1976 Det	14	0	0	—	0	0	0	—	0
NFL Total	109	27	240	8.9	1	35	860	24.6	0

Year Team	Interceptions Int	Yds	TD	Fum	Tot TD
1967 Cle	1	9	0	2	1
1968 Cle	8	**162**	0	4	0
1970 Cle	1	0	0	0	0
1971 Cle	2	18	0	0	0
1972 Cle	3	10	0	0	0
1973 Cle	2	33	0	0	0
1974 Det	1	14	0	0	0
1975 Det	1	67	1	0	1
NFL Total	19	313	1	6	2

BRAD DAVIS Davis, Bradford Timothy 5′10″, 204 **RB**
Col: Louisiana State *HS:* Hammond [LA] B: 2/9/1953, Hammond, LA
Drafted: 1975 Round 9 Atl
1975 Atl: 3 G; KR 1-0. **1976** Atl: 1 G. **Total:** 4 G; KR 1-0.

BRIAN DAVIS Davis, Brian Wesely 6′2″, 190 **DB**
Col: Glendale CC AZ; Nebraska *HS:* Cortez [Phoenix, AZ]
B: 8/31/1963, Phoenix, AZ *Drafted:* 1987 Round 2 Was
1987 Was: 7 G. **1988** Was: 9 G; Int 1-11. **1989** Was: 15 G; PR 1-3 3.0; Int 4-40. **1990** Was: 7 G. **1991** Sea: 16 G; PR 1-1 1.0; Int 1-40 1 TD; 6 Pt. **1992** Sea: 13 G; Int 2-36. **1993** SD: 11 G; Int 1-0. **1994** Min: 9 G. **Total:** 87 G; PR 2-4 2.0; Int 9-127 1 TD; 6 Pt.

BRUCE DAVIS Davis, Bruce Edward 5′8″, 160 **WR**
Col: Baylor *HS:* Franklin D. Roosevelt [Dallas, TX] B: 2/25/1963, Dallas, TX *Drafted:* 1984 Round 2 Cle
1984 Cle: 14 G; Rush 1-6 6.0; Rec 7-119 17.0 2 TD; KR 18-369 20.5; 12 Pt; 2 Fum. **1987** SD: 1 G. **Total:** 15 G; Rush 1-6 6.0; Rec 7-119 17.0 2 TD; KR 18-369 20.5; 12 Pt; 2 Fum.

BRUCE DAVIS Davis, Bruce Edward 6′6″, 287 **OT-OG**
Col: UCLA *HS:* Lackey [Indian Head, MD] B: 6/21/1956, Rutherfordton, NC *Drafted:* 1979 Round 11 Oak
1979 Oak: 12 G. **1980** Oak: 16 G. **1981** Oak: 16 G. **1982** LARd: 9 G. **1983** LARd: 16 G. **1984** LARd: 16 G. **1985** LARd: 16 G. **1986** LARd: 16 G. **1987** LARd-Hou: 11 G. LARd: 4 G. Hou: 7 G. **1988** Hou: 16 G. **1989** Hou: 16 G. **Total:** 160 G.

CARL DAVIS Davis, Carl Lewis 6′0″, 194 **OE-T-C-G**
Col: Michigan; West Virginia *HS:* Charleston [WV] B: 5/19/1903, Charleston, WV D: 10/14/1959, Charleston, WV
1927 Fra: 8 G.

CHARLIE DAVIS Davis, Charles Douglas 5′11″, 200 **RB**
Col: Colorado *HS:* West Columbia [TX] B: 1/6/1952, West Columbia, TX *Drafted:* 1974 Round 2 Cin
1974 Cin: Rec 19-171 9.0; KR 12-243 20.3. **1976** TB: Rec 3-32 10.7; KR 4-73 18.3. **Total:** Rec 22-203 9.2; KR 16-316 19.8.

Year Team	G	Rushing Att	Yds	Avg	TD	Fum
1974 Cin	14	72	375	5.2	0	3
1976 TB	6	41	107	2.6	1	2
NFL Total	20	113	482	4.3	1	5

CHARLES DAVIS Davis, Charles Mack 6′1″, 269 **DT-NT**
Col: Texas Christian *HS:* Wortham [TX] B: 11/17/1951, Wortham, TX
Drafted: 1974 Round 9 Pit
1974 Pit: 14 G. **1975** StL: 14 G. **1976** StL: 14 G. **1977** StL: 14 G; 1 Fum TD; 6 Pt. **1978** StL: 1 G. **1979** StL: 16 G. **1980** Hou: 1 G. **Total:** 74 G; 1 Fum TD; 6 Pt.

WAYNE DAVIS Davis, Chris Wayne 6′1″, 213 **LB**
Col: Alabama *HS:* Gordo [AL] B: 3/10/1964, Tuscaloosa, AL
Drafted: 1987 Round 9 StL
1987 StL: 12 G. **1988** Pho: 16 G. **Total:** 28 G.

CHRIS DAVIS Davis, Christopher Weldon 6′1″, 225 **LB**
Col: Purdue; San Diego State *HS:* Springbrook [Silver Spring, MD]
B: 7/26/1963, Rahway, NJ
1987 NYG: 3 G.

CLARENCE DAVIS Davis, Clarence Eugene 5′10″, 195 **RB**
Col: East Los Angeles Coll. CA (J.C.); USC *HS:* George Washington [Los Angeles, CA] B: 6/28/1949, Birmingham, AL *Drafted:* 1971 Round 4 Oak

Year Team	G	Rushing Att	Yds	Avg	TD	Receiving Rec	Yds	Avg	TD
1971 Oak	14	54	321	5.9	2	15	97	6.5	0
1972 Oak	11	71	363	5.1	6	8	82	10.3	0
1973 Oak	13	116	609	5.3	4	7	76	10.9	0
1974 Oak	11	129	554	4.3	2	11	145	13.2	1
1975 Oak	11	112	486	4.3	4	11	126	11.5	1
1976 Oak	12	114	516	4.5	3	27	191	7.1	0
1977 Oak	14	194	787	4.1	5	16	124	7.8	0
1978 Oak	2	14	4	0.3	0	4	24	6.0	0
NFL Total	88	804	3640	4.5	26	99	865	8.7	2

Year Team	Kickoff Returns Ret	Yds	Avg	TD	Fum	Tot TD
1971 Oak	27	734	27.2	0	2	2
1972 Oak	18	464	25.8	0	4	6
1973 Oak	19	504	26.5	0	5	4
1974 Oak	3	107	35.7	0	0	3
1975 Oak	9	268	29.8	0	4	5
1976 Oak	0	0	—	0	6	3
1977 Oak	3	63	21.0	0	0	5
NFL Total	79	2140	27.1	0	21	28

DARRELL DAVIS Davis, Darrell Odell 6′2″, 258 **DE**
Col: Texas Christian *HS:* Midland [TX] B: 3/10/1966, Houston, TX
Drafted: 1990 Round 12 NYJ
1990 NYJ: 15 G; 1 Fum TD; 6 Pt; 5 Sac. **1991** NYJ: 13 G; 1 Sac. **Total:** 28 G; 1 Fum TD; 6 Pt; 6 Sac.

DAVE DAVIS Davis, David Glenn 6′0″, 175 **WR**
Col: Tennessee State *HS:* Alcoa [TN] B: 7/5/1948, Alcoa, TN
Drafted: 1971 Round 7 GB
1971 GB: 14 G; Rec 6-59 9.8; PR 6-36 6.0; KR 1-22 22.0; 1 Fum. **1972** GB: 10 G; Rush 2-0; Rec 4-119 29.8 1 TD; 6 Pt. **1973** Pit: 2 G; Rec 1-14 14.0. **1974** NO: 7 G; KR 1-14 14.0. **Total:** 33 G; Rush 2-0; Rec 11-192 17.5 1 TD; PR 6-36 6.0; KR 2-36 18.0; 6 Pt; 1 Fum.

DEXTER DAVIS Davis, Dexter Wendell Jackson 5′10″, 190 **DB**
Col: Clemson *HS:* Sumter [SC] B: 3/20/1970, Brooklyn, NY
Drafted: 1991 Round 4 Pho
1991 Pho: 11 G. **1992** Pho: 16 G; Int 2-27. **1993** Pho-LARm: 12 G. Pho: 6 G. LARm: 6 G. **1994** LARm: 4 G. **1995** StL: 16 G; 1 Sac. **Total:** 59 G; Int 2-27; 1 Sac.

DON DAVIS Davis, Donald Earl 6′1″, 240 **LB**
Col: Kansas *HS:* Olathe South [KS] B: 12/17/1972, Olathe, KS
1996 NO: 11 G. **1997** NO: 11 G. **1998** NO-TB: 9 G. NO: 4 G. TB: 5 G. **Total:** 31 G.

DON DAVIS Davis, Donald Earl 6′6″, 285 **DT**
Col: Rancho Santiago Coll. CA (J.C.); Los Angeles State *HS:* Santa Ana [CA] B: 12/16/1943, Santa Ana, CA *Drafted:* 1966 Round 2 NYG
1966 NYG: 14 G.

DONNIE DAVIS Davis, Donnie Ray 6′3″, 225 **WR-TE**
Col: Southern University *HS:* Phillis Wheatley [Houston, TX]
B: 9/18/1940, Opelousas, LA *Drafted:* 1962 Round 6 Dal
1962 Dal: 11 G; Rec 2-31 15.5; KR 4-66 16.5. **1970** Hou: 14 G; KR 2-0; 1 Fum. **Total:** 25 G; Rec 2-31 15.5; KR 6-66 11.0; 1 Fum.

DOUG DAVIS Davis, Douglas Sherone 6′4″, 255 **OT**
Col: Kentucky *HS:* Centerburg [OH] B: 7/22/1944, Elkton, MD
Drafted: 1966 Round 5 Min
1966 Min: 13 G. **1967** Min: 11 G. **1968** Min: 14 G. **1969** Min: 10 G. **1970** Min: 12 G. **1971** Min: 14 G. **1972** Min: 5 G. **Total:** 79 G.

DOC DAVIS Davis, Edward C 5′9″, 200 **G-T**
Col: Indiana B: 2/13/1889 D: 7/1963
1920 Mun-Day: 8 G. Mun: 1 G. Day: 7 G. **1922** Col: 1 G. **Total:** 9 G.

ELGIN DAVIS Davis, Elgin 5′10″, 192 **RB**
Col: Central Florida *HS:* Jean Ribault [Jacksonville, FL] B: 10/23/1965, Jacksonville, FL *Drafted:* 1987 Round 12 NE
1987 NE: 4 G; Rush 9-43 4.8; KR 5-134 26.8. **1988** NE: 5 G; KR 6-106 17.7; 1 Fum. **Total:** 9 G; Rush 9-43 4.8; KR 11-240 21.8; 1 Fum.

ERIC DAVIS Davis, Eric Wayne 5′11″, 185 **DB**
Col: Jacksonville State *HS:* Anniston [AL] B: 1/26/1968, Anniston, AL
Drafted: 1990 Round 2 SF
1990 SF: PR 5-38 7.6. **1993** SF: 1 Fum TD. **1995** SF: 1 Sac. **1998** Car: 1 Sac. **Total:** PR 5-38 7.6; 1 Fum TD; 2 Sac.

Year Team	G	Interceptions Int	Yds	TD	Fum	Tot TD
1990 SF	16	1	13	0	0	0
1991 SF	2	0	0	0	0	0
1992 SF	16	3	52	0	0	0
1993 SF	16	4	45	1	0	2
1994 SF	16	1	8	0	1	0
1995 SF	15	3	84	1	0	1
1996 Car	16	5	57	0	0	0
1997 Car	14	5	25	0	0	0

1998 Car	16	5	81	2	0	2
NFL Total	127	27	365	4	1	5

FRED DAVIS Davis, Frederick 5′10″, 182 **DB**
Col: Western Carolina *HS:* Decatur [GA] B: 7/18/1964
1987 Sea: 1 G.

FRED DAVIS Davis, Frederick Lee 6′3″, 244 **DT-OT**
Col: Alabama *HS:* Manual [Louisville, KY] B: 2/15/1918, Louisville, KY D: 3/10/1995, Selma, AL *Drafted:* 1941 Round 2 Was
1941 Was: 11 G. **1942** Was: 11 G. **1945** Was: 4 G. **1946** ChiB: 11 G. **1947** ChiB: 12 G; 1 Fum. **1948** ChiB: 12 G. **1949** ChiB: 12 G. **1950** ChiB: 12 G; KR 1-13 13.0. **1951** ChiB: 12 G; KR 3-26 8.7; 1 Fum. **Total:** 97 G; KR 4-39 9.8; 2 Fum.

GARY DAVIS Davis, Gary Curtis 5′10″, 202 **RB**
Col: Cal Poly-S.L.O. *HS:* Garey [Pomona, CA] B: 9/7/1954, Los Angeles, CA *Drafted:* 1976 Round 6 Mia
1977 Mia: PR 1-11 11.0. **1978** Mia: PR 2-36 18.0. **Total:** PR 3-47 15.7.

		Rushing				Receiving			
Year Team	**G**	**Att**	**Yds**	**Avg**	**TD**	**Rec**	**Yds**	**Avg**	**TD**
1976 Mia	14	31	160	5.2	1	2	8	4.0	0
1977 Mia	14	126	533	4.2	2	14	151	10.8	1
1978 Mia	14	62	313	5.0	3	24	218	9.1	0
1979 Mia	16	98	383	3.9	1	34	215	6.3	0
1980 TB	15	7	21	3.0	0	9	79	8.8	0
1981 TB	7	0	0	—	0	0	0	—	0
NFL Total	80	324	1410	4.4	7	83	671	8.1	1

	Kickoff Returns					Tot
Year Team	**Ret**	**Yds**	**Avg**	**TD**	**Fum**	**TD**
1976 Mia	26	617	23.7	0	1	1
1977 Mia	14	414	29.6	0	1	3
1978 Mia	13	251	19.3	0	3	3
1979 Mia	2	27	13.5	0	2	1
1980 TB	44	951	21.6	0	1	0
1981 TB	5	81	16.2	0	1	0
NFL Total	104	2341	22.5	0	9	8

GLENN DAVIS Davis, Glenn Ashby 6′0″, 180 **WR**
Col: Ohio State *HS:* Barberton [OH] B: 9/12/1934, Wellsburg, WV
1960 Det: 4 G; Rec 1-17 17.0. **1961** Det: 8 G; Rec 9-115 12.8; 1 Fum. **Total:** 12 G; Rec 10-132 13.2; 1 Fum.

GLENN DAVIS Davis, Glenn Woodward 5′9″, 172 **HB**
(Mr. Outside) *Col:* Cal Poly-Pomona; Army *HS:* Bonita [La Verne, CA] B: 12/26/1924, Burbank, CA *Drafted:* 1947 Round 1 Det
1950 LARm: Pass 5-3 60.0%, 97 19.40 2 TD; PR 3-24 8.0; KR 8-167 20.9. **1951** LARm: Pass 2-1 50.0%, 5 2.50; PR 15-85 5.7; KR 9-179 19.9. **Total:** Pass 7-4 57.1%, 102 14.57 2 TD; PR 18-109 6.1; KR 17-346 20.4.

		Rushing				Receiving					Tot
Year Team	**G**	**Att**	**Yds**	**Avg**	**TD**	**Rec**	**Yds**	**Avg**	**TD**	**Fum**	**TD**
1950 LARm	12	88	416	4.7	3	42	592	14.1	4	5	7
1951 LARm	11	64	200	3.1	1	8	90	11.3	1	3	2
NFL Total	23	152	616	4.1	4	50	682	13.6	5	8	9

GREG DAVIS Davis, Gregory Brian 6′0″, 202 **K**
Col: The Citadel *HS:* Lakeside [Atlanta, GA] B: 10/29/1965, Atlanta, GA *Drafted:* 1987 Round 9 TB
1987 Atl: Punt 6-191 31.8. **1992** Pho: Punt 4-167 41.8. **Total:** Punt 10-358 35.8.

		Scoring						
Year Team	**G**	**Pts**	**FG**	**FGA**	**FG%**	**XK**	**XKA**	**XK%**
1987 Atl	3	15	3	4	75.0	6	6	100.0
1988 Atl	16	82	19	30	63.3	25	27	92.6
1989 NE-Atl	15	94	23	34	67.6	25	28	89.3
1989 NE	9	61	16	23	69.6	13	16	81.3
1989 Atl	6	33	7	11	63.6	12	12	100.0
1990 Atl	16	106	22	33	66.7	40	40	100.0
1991 Pho	16	82	21	30	70.0	19	19	100.0
1992 Pho	16	67	13	26	50.0	28	28	100.0
1993 Pho	16	100	21	28	75.0	37	37	100.0
1994 Ariz	14	77	20	26	76.9	17	17	100.0
1995 Ariz	16	109	30	39	76.9	19	19	100.0
1996 Ariz	9	39	9	14	64.3	12	12	100.0
1997 Min-SD	16	109	26	34	76.5	31	32	96.9
1997 Min	4	31	7	10	70.0	10	10	100.0
1997 SD	12	78	19	24	79.2	21	22	95.5
1998 Oak	16	82	17	27	63.0	31	31	100.0
NFL Total	169	962	224	325	68.9	290	296	98.0

HARRISON DAVIS Davis, Harrison Paul III 6′4″, 219 **WR**
Col: Virginia *HS:* Bethel [Hampton, VA] B: 2/20/1952, Salisbury, NC *Drafted:* 1974 Round 4 SD
1974 SD: 12 G; Rush 2-(-7) -3.5; Rec 18-432 24.0 2 TD; PR 4-34 8.5; 12 Pt; 1 Fum.

HENRY DAVIS Davis, Henry Louis 6′3″, 235 **LB**
(Hatchet Man) *Col:* Grambling State *HS:* Clinton [LA] B: 11/8/1942, Slaughter, LA *Drafted:* 1968 Round 11 NYG
1968 NYG: 14 G. **1969** NYG: 13 G. **1970** Pit: 14 G. **1971** Pit: 14 G. **1972** Pit: 14 G; Int 2-32; 6 Pt. **1973** Pit: 14 G; Int 2-23. **Total:** 83 G; Int 4-55; 6 Pt.

HERB DAVIS Davis, Herbert A 5′11″, 173 **WB-E-BB**
Col: Xavier (Ohio) *HS:* Middletown [OH] B: 4/2/1899 D: 1/1/1986, San Lorenzo, CA
1925 Col: 4 G. **1926** Col: 6 G. **Total:** 10 G.

ERM DAVIS Davis, Hermit 5′11″, 205 **OE**
Col: Birmingham-Southern *HS:* Winston Co. [Double Springs, AL] B: 3/31/1911, Double Springs, AL
1936 ChiC: 2 G; Rec 1-36 36.0.

JACK DAVIS Davis, Jack Owen 6′2″, 235 **OG**
Col: Arizona *HS:* Heavener [OK] B: 2/19/1933, Heavener, OK
1960 Den: 2 G.

BOB DAVIS Davis, James Robert Jr. 6′1″, 180 **HB-P**
(Twenty Grand) *Col:* Kentucky B: 5/4/1914, Greenup, KY D: 7/1969, , FL
1938 Cle: Scor 0-1 XK. **1944** Bos: Punt 3-60 20.0. **1945** Bos: Punt 3-129 43.0. **Total:** Punt 6-189 31.5; Scor 30, 0-1 XK.

		Passing							
Year Team	**G**	**Att**	**Comp**	**Comp%**	**Yds**	**YPA**	**TD**	**Int**	**Rating**
1938 Cle	8	24	6	25.0	49	2.04	0	2	4.9
1942 Phi	10	0	0	—	0	—	0	0	—
1944 Bos	10	18	8	44.4	88	4.89	1	2	38.4
1945 Bos	10	10	5	50.0	73	7.30	3	0	113.8
1946 Bos	11	1	1	100.0	7	7.00	0	0	95.8
NFL Total	49	53	20	37.7	217	4.09	4	4	44.3

	Rushing				Receiving			
Year Team	**Att**	**Yds**	**Avg**	**TD**	**Rec**	**Yds**	**Avg**	**TD**
1938 Cle	22	100	4.5	0	3	31	10.3	0
1942 Phi	43	207	4.8	2	6	93	15.5	1
1944 Bos	95	363	3.8	1	19	97	5.1	0
1945 Bos	29	91	3.1	0	9	56	6.2	0
1946 Bos	41	143	3.5	0	10	150	15.0	1
NFL Total	230	904	3.9	3	47	427	9.1	2

	Punt Returns				Kickoff Returns			
Year Team	**Ret**	**Yds**	**Avg**	**TD**	**Ret**	**Yds**	**Avg**	**TD**
1942 Phi	10	84	8.4	0	9	140	15.6	0
1944 Bos	**22**	**271**	12.3	0	7	152	21.7	0
1945 Bos	11	94	8.5	0	6	131	21.8	0
1946 Bos	13	130	10.0	0	5	92	18.4	0
NFL Total	56	579	10.3	0	27	515	19.1	0

	Interceptions				Tot
Year Team	**Int**	**Yds**	**TD**	**Fum**	**TD**
1942 Phi	2	35	0	0	3
1944 Bos	4	48	0	0	1
1945 Bos	6	28	0	2	0
1946 Bos	7	129	0	3	1
NFL Total	19	240	0	5	5

JAMES DAVIS Davis, James Steven 6′0″, 193 **DB**
Col: Los Angeles Southwest Coll. CA (J.C.); Southern University *HS:* Crenshaw [Los Angeles, CA] B: 6/12/1957, Los Angeles, CA *Drafted:* 1981 Round 5 Oak
1982 LARd: 9 G; Int 2-**107 1** TD; 6 Pt; 1 Sac. **1983** LARd: 16 G; Int 1-10. **1984** LARd: 15 G; Int 1-8. **1985** LARd: 15 G. **1986** LARd: 16 G. **1987** LARd: 12 G; PR 1-0; 1 Fum. **Total:** 83 G; PR 1-0; Int 4-125 1 TD; 6 Pt; 1 Fum; 1 Sac.

JEFF DAVIS Davis, Jeffrey Eugene 6′0″, 230 **LB**
Col: Clemson *HS:* James B. Dudley [Greensboro, NC] B: 1/26/1960, Greensboro, NC *Drafted:* 1982 Round 5 TB
1982 TB: 9 G; KR 1-0; 1 Fum. **1983** TB: 15 G; 1.5 Sac. **1984** TB: 16 G; Int 1-0. **1985** TB: 16 G; Int 1-22; 2.5 Sac. **1986** TB: 16 G; Int 1-0. **1987** TB: 11 G. **Total:** 83 G; KR 1-0; Int 3-22; 1 Fum; 4 Sac.

JEROME DAVIS Davis, Jerome 6′1″, 260 **NT**
Col: Wabash Valley Coll. IL (J.C.); Ball State *HS:* Hughes [Cincinnati, OH] B: 2/27/1962, Cincinnati, OH
1987 Det: 3 G.

JERRY DAVIS Davis, Jerome W 5′10″, 178 **DB-HB**
(Weasel) *Col:* Southeastern Louisiana *HS:* Covington [LA] B: 1/5/1924, Savannah, GA *Drafted:* 1948 Round 17 ChiC
1948 ChiC: Rush 12-77 6.4; KR 15-437 29.1. **1949** ChiC: **1** Fum TD. **1950** ChiC: KR 2-53 26.5. **1951** ChiC: Rush 1-(-7) -7.0; Rec 4-24 6.0. **Total:** Rush 13-70 5.4; Rec 4-24 6.0; KR 17-490 28.8; 1 Fum TD.

Year Team	G	Punt Returns Ret	Yds	Avg	TD	Interceptions Int	Yds	TD	Fum	Tot TD
1948 ChiC	11	16	334	**20.9**	**2**	4	47	0	2	2
1949 ChiC	9	1	14	14.0	0	6	63	0	0	1
1950 ChiC	11	3	29	9.7	0	9	40	0	0	0
1951 ChiC	8	4	10	2.5	0	2	36	0	0	0
1952 Dal	7	1	11	11.0	0	3	118	1	0	1
NFL Total	46	25	398	15.9	2	24	304	1	2	4

JERRY DAVIS Davis, Jerry Wayne 5′11″, 182 **DB**
Col: Morris Brown *HS:* Ballard-Hudson [Macon, GA] B: 2/5/1951, Macon, GA
1975 NYJ: 6 G.

JOHN DAVIS Davis, John 155 **FB-WB-TB-BB**
Col: No College *HS:* Commerce [Columbus, OH] B: 1896 Deceased
1920 Col: 8 G.

BUTCH DAVIS Davis, John Charles 5′11″, 183 **DB**
Col: Missouri *HS:* Chillicothe [MO] B: 7/3/1948, La Jolla, CA
Drafted: 1970 Round 12 ChiB
1970 ChiB: 10 G; Int 1-0.

JOHN DAVIS Davis, John Henry 6′4″, 310 **OT-OG-C**
Col: Georgia Tech *HS:* Gilmer [Ellijay, GA] B: 8/22/1965, Ellijay, GA
Drafted: 1987 Round 11 Hou
1987 Hou: 6 G; KR 1-0; 1 Fum. **1988** Hou: 13 G. **1989** Buf: 16 G. **1990** Buf: 16 G. **1991** Buf: 12 G. **1992** Buf: 9 G. **1993** Buf: 16 G. **1994** Buf: 16 G. **Total:** 104 G; KR 1-0; 1 Fum.

ISAAC DAVIS Davis, John Isaac Eric Lamont 6′3″, 320 **OG**
Col: Arkansas *HS:* Malvern [AR] B: 4/8/1972, Malvern, AR
Drafted: 1994 Round 2 SD
1994 SD: 13 G. **1995** SD: 16 G. **1996** SD: 14 G. **1997** SD-NO: 15 G. SD: 12 G. NO: 3 G. **Total:** 58 G.

JACK DAVIS Davis, John James 6′0″, 225 **OG**
Col: Maryland *HS:* Gonzaga [Washington, DC]; Bladensburg HS [MD]
B: 3/12/1932, Braddock, PA *Drafted:* 1958 Round 15 Was
1960 Bos: 14 G.

JOHN DAVIS Davis, John Leonard 6′4″, 257 **TE**
Col: Cisco JC TX; Emporia State *HS:* Jasper [TX] B: 5/14/1973, Jasper, TX
1997 TB: 8 G; Rec 3-35 11.7. **1998** TB: 16 G; Rec 2-12 6.0 1 TD; 6 Pt. **Total:** 24 G; Rec 5-47 9.4 1 TD; 6 Pt.

JOHNNY DAVIS Davis, Johnny Lee 6′1″, 235 **RB**
Col: Alabama *HS:* Sidney Lanier [Montgomery, AL] B: 7/17/1956, Montgomery, AL *Drafted:* 1978 Round 2 TB
1978 TB: Rec 5-13 2.6. **1979** TB: Rec 5-57 11.4. **1980** TB: Rec 4-17 4.3. **1981** SF: Rec 3-(-1) -0.3; KR 1-0. **1983** Cle: Rec 5-20 4.0; KR 1-8 8.0. **Total:** Rec 22-106 4.8; KR 2-8 4.0.

Year Team	G	Rushing Att	Yds	Avg	TD	Fum
1978 TB	16	97	370	3.8	3	2
1979 TB	16	59	221	3.7	2	0
1980 TB	14	39	130	3.3	1	1
1981 SF	16	94	297	3.2	7	1
1982 Cle	2	4	3	0.8	1	0
1983 Cle	16	13	42	3.2	0	0
1984 Cle	16	3	15	5.0	1	0
1985 Cle	16	4	9	2.3	0	0
1986 Cle	6	0	0	—	0	0
1987 Cle	1	1	7	7.0	0	1
NFL Total	119	314	1094	3.5	15	5

JOE DAVIS Davis, Joseph Austin 6′2″, 195 **OE-DE**
Col: USC *HS:* Bountiful [UT] B: 11/20/1919, St. Anthony, ID
D: 5/26/1992, Bakersfield, CA
AAFC **1946** BknA: 14 G; Rec 22-337 15.3 1 TD; KR 2-32 16.0; Scor 7, 1-1 100.0% XK.

TYRONE DAVIS Davis, Joseph Tyrone 6′1″, 190 **DB**
Col: Clemson *HS:* Cedar Shoals [Athens, GA] B: 11/17/1961, Athens, GA *Drafted:* 1985 Round 3 NYG
1985 NYG: 7 G.

HARPER DAVIS Davis, Julius Harper Jr. 5′11″, 173 **DB**
(Hepo; Julie) *Col:* Mississippi State *HS:* Clarksdale [MS]
B: 12/11/1925, Clarksdale, MS *Drafted:* 1949 Round 2 Pit
AAFC **1949** LA-A: 11 G; Rush 13-33 2.5 1 TD; Rec 2-13 6.5; PR 2-37 18.5; KR 4-87 21.8; Int 2-5; 6 Pt.

NFL **1950** ChiB: 12 G; Rush 10-57 5.7 1 TD; Rec 2-15 7.5; PR 1-19 19.0; Int 5-59; 6 Pt. **1951** GB: 12 G; Rec 1-15 15.0; PR 2-21 10.5; Int 4-37. **Total:** 24 G; Rush 10-57 5.7 1 TD; Rec 3-30 10.0; PR 3-40 13.3; Int 9-96; 6 Pt.

KELVIN DAVIS Davis, Kelvin 6′2″, 260 **OG**
Col: Johnson C. Smith *HS:* East Orange [NJ] B: 2/7/1963
1987 NYG: 1 G.

KENNETH DAVIS Davis, Kenneth Earl 5′10″, 208 **RB**
Col: Texas Christian *HS:* Temple [TX] B: 4/16/1962, Williamson Co., TX
Drafted: 1986 Round 2 GB

Year Team	G	Rushing Att	Yds	Avg	TD	Receiving Rec	Yds	Avg	TD
1986 GB	16	114	519	4.6	0	21	142	6.8	1
1987 GB	10	109	413	3.8	3	14	110	7.9	0
1988 GB	9	39	121	3.1	1	11	81	7.4	0
1989 Buf	16	29	149	5.1	1	6	92	15.3	2
1990 Buf	16	64	302	4.7	4	9	78	8.7	1
1991 Buf	16	129	624	4.8	4	20	118	5.9	1
1992 Buf	16	139	613	4.4	6	15	80	5.3	0
1993 Buf	16	109	391	3.6	6	21	95	4.5	0
1994 Buf	16	91	381	4.2	2	18	82	4.6	0
NFL Total	131	823	3513	4.3	27	135	878	6.5	5

Year Team	Kickoff Returns Ret	Yds	Avg	TD	Fum	Tot TD
1986 GB	12	231	19.3	0	2	1
1987 GB	0	0	—	0	2	3
1988 GB	0	0	—	0	0	1
1989 Buf	3	52	17.3	0	2	3
1990 Buf	0	0	—	0	1	5
1991 Buf	4	73	18.3	0	0	5
1992 Buf	14	251	17.9	0	5	6
1993 Buf	8	100	12.5	0	3	6
1994 Buf	1	0	0.0	0	3	2
NFL Total	42	707	16.8	0	18	32

KYLE DAVIS Davis, Kyle Wayne 6′3″, 240 **C**
Col: Oklahoma *HS:* Altus [OK] B: 10/1/1952, Cordell, OK
Drafted: 1975 Round 5 Dal
1975 Dal: 14 G; 1 Fum. **1978** SF: 7 G. **Total:** 21 G; 1 Fum.

LEE DAVIS Davis, Lee Andrew 5′11″, 198 **DB**
Col: Mississippi *HS:* Amory [MS] B: 12/18/1962, Okolona, MS
Drafted: 1985 Round 5 Cin
1985 Cin: 7 G. **1987** Ind: 3 G; Int 1-7. **Total:** 10 G; Int 1-7.

LORENZO DAVIS Davis, Lorenzo Edward 5′11″, 185 **WR**
Col: Youngstown State *HS:* Dillard [Fort Lauderdale, FL] B: 2/12/1968, Fort Lauderdale, FL
1990 Pit: 4 G.

MARVIN DAVIS Davis, Marvin Daniel 6′4″, 252 **DE**
(Butch) *Col:* Wichita State *HS:* South Bay [FL] B: 6/6/1943, Jacksonville, FL *Drafted:* 1965 Redshirt Round 3 Den
1966 Den: 1 G.

MARVIN DAVIS Davis, Marvin Eugene 6′4″, 235 **LB**
Col: Southern University *HS:* Eden Gardens [Shreveport, LA]
B: 5/25/1952, Shreveport, LA
1974 Hou: 13 G.

MIKE DAVIS Davis, Michael Allen 6′1″, 192 **DB**
Col: Cincinnati *HS:* Springfield North [OH] B: 1/14/1972, Springfield, OH *Drafted:* 1994 Round 4 Hou
1994 Hou: 16 G. **1995** Cle: 3 G. **Total:** 19 G.

TONY DAVIS Davis, Michael Edward 5′11″, 212 **RB**
Col: Nebraska *HS:* Tecumseh [NE] B: 1/21/1953, Tecumseh, NE
Drafted: 1976 Round 4 Cin
1976 Cin: KR 4-21 5.3. **1977** Cin: KR 3-42 14.0. **1978** Cin: KR 3-51 17.0. **1979** TB: KR 4-33 8.3. **1980** TB: KR 4-58 14.5. **1981** TB: KR 3-51 17.0. **Total:** KR 21-256 12.2.

Year Team	G	Rushing Att	Yds	Avg	TD	Receiving Rec	Yds	Avg	TD
1976 Cin	14	36	178	4.9	1	4	29	7.3	0
1977 Cin	14	27	81	3.0	2	9	83	9.2	0
1978 Cin	14	21	57	2.7	2	2	23	11.5	0
1979 TB	16	0	0	—	0	0	0	—	0
1980 TB	15	5	24	4.8	0	12	115	9.6	1
1981 TB	16	2	5	2.5	0	0	0	—	0
NFL Total	89	91	345	3.8	5	27	250	9.3	1

Year Team	Punt Returns Ret	Yds	Avg	TD	Fum	Tot TD
1976 Cin	0	0	—	0	3	1
1977 Cin	19	220	11.6	0	3	2
1978 Cin	22	130	5.9	0	2	2
1979 TB	1	7	7.0	0	0	0
1980 TB	0	0	—	0	0	1
NFL Total	42	357	8.5	0	8	6

MIKE DAVIS Davis, Michael Leonar 6'3", 203 **DB**
Col: East Los Angeles Coll. CA (J.C.); Colorado *HS:* Alain Leroy Locke [Los Angeles, CA] B: 4/15/1956, Los Angeles, CA *Drafted:* 1977 Round 2 Oak
1979 Oak: PR 1-6 6.0. **1982** LARd: 2.5 Sac. **1983** LARd: 2 Sac. **1984** LARd: 5.5 Sac. **1985** LARd: 1 Sac. **Total:** PR 1-6 6.0; 11 Sac.

		Interceptions		
Year Team	G	Int	Yds	TD
1978 Oak	16	1	0	0
1979 Oak	16	2	22	0
1980 Oak	16	3	88	0
1981 Oak	7	1	0	0
1982 LARd	9	1	56	**1**
1983 LARd	16	1	3	0
1984 LARd	16	2	11	0
1985 LARd	11	0	0	0
1987 SD	8	0	0	0
NFL Total	115	11	180	1

MILT DAVIS Davis, Milton Eugene 6'1", 188 **DB**
Col: Los Angeles City Coll. CA (J.C.); UCLA *HS:* Thomas Jefferson [Los Angeles, CA] B: 5/31/1929, Muskogee, OK *Drafted:* 1954 Round 8 Det
1957 Bal: PR 1-0. **1959** Bal: KR 1-0. **Total:** PR 1-0; KR 1-0.

		Interceptions		
Year Team	G	Int	Yds	TD
1957 Bal	12	**10**	**219**	**2**
1958 Bal	10	4	40	0
1959 Bal	11	**7**	119	**1**
1960 Bal	12	6	32	0
NFL Total	45	27	410	3

NATHAN DAVIS Davis, Nathan Michael 6'5", 312 **DE**
Col: Indiana *HS:* Richmond [IN] B: 2/6/1974, Hartford, CT
Drafted: 1997 Round 2 Atl
1997 Atl: 2 G.

NORMAN DAVIS Davis, Norman 6'2", 245 **OG**
Col: Grambling State *HS:* Monroe [Cocoa, FL] B: 8/8/1945, Cocoa, FL
Drafted: 1967 Round 3 Bal
1967 Bal: 14 G; KR 1-8 8.0. **1969** NO: 12 G. **1970** Phi: 14 G. **Total:** 40 G; KR 1-8 8.0.

OLIVER DAVIS Davis, Oliver James 6'1", 203 **DB**
Col: Tennessee State *HS:* Mount Olive [Fort Mitchell, AR]
B: 8/29/1954, Columbus, GA *Drafted:* 1977 Round 4 Cle

		Interceptions		
Year Team	G	Int	Yds	TD
1977 Cle	14	3	71	0
1978 Cle	13	6	65	1
1979 Cle	16	1	33	0
1980 Cle	15	1	70	0
1981 Cin	10	0	0	0
1982 Cin	9	0	0	0
NFL Total	77	11	239	1

PAHL DAVIS Davis, Pahl George 5'10", 185 **G-OE-FB**
Col: Wis.-Oshkosh; Marquette *HS:* Oconto [WI] B: 3/26/1897, Oconto, WI D: 10/15/1971, Hemet, CA
1922 GB: 7 G.

PASCHALL DAVIS Davis, Paschall Tederall 6'2", 225 **LB**
Col: Trinity Valley CC TX; Texas A&M–Kingsville *HS:* Hearne [TX]
B: 6/5/1969, Bryan, TX
1995 StL: 3 G. **1996** StL: 10 G. **Total:** 13 G.

PAUL DAVIS Davis, Paul Calvin 6'2", 221 **LB**
Col: North Carolina *HS:* Appalachia [VA] B: 7/10/1958, Appalachia, VA
1981 Atl: 13 G. **1982** Atl: 9 G. **1983** NYG-StL: 9 G. NYG: 3 G. StL: 6 G. **Total:** 31 G.

PAUL DAVIS Davis, Paul James 6'1", 188 **FB-DB**
Col: Otterbein B: 3/21/1925, Ashland, KY D: 2/21/1989, Loxahatchee, FL *Drafted:* 1947 Round 22 Pit
1947 Pit: 5 G; Rush 4-5 1.3; 1 Fum. **1948** Pit: 6 G; Rush 2-(-1) -0.5; PR 4-34 8.5; KR 1-13 13.0; Int 1-7; 2 Fum. **Total:** 11 G; Rush 6-4 0.7; PR 4-34 8.5; KR 1-13 13.0; Int 1-7; 3 Fum.

PRESTON DAVIS Davis, Preston 5'11", 180 **DB**
Col: Baylor *HS:* Estacado [Lubbock, TX] B: 3/10/1962, Lubbock, TX
1984 Ind: 12 G; Int 1-3. **1985** Ind: 16 G; Int 2-14. **1986** Ind: 8 G. **Total:** 36 G; Int 3-17.

RALPH DAVIS Davis, Ralph Gordon 5'11", 205 **G**
Col: Wisconsin *HS:* Jefferson [WI] B: 5/30/1922, Seymour, WI
D: 9/26/1992, Northbrook, IL
1947 GB: 11 G. **1948** GB: 11 G. **Total:** 22 G.

RAY DAVIS Davis, Raymond Elswood 6'1", 198 **G-C-T-OE**
Col: Samford *HS:* Anniston [AL] B: 9/14/1907, Birmingham, AL
D: 8/26/1972, Fort Walton Beach, FL
1932 Port: 11 G. **1933** Port: 4 G. **Total:** 15 G.

LAMAR DAVIS Davis, Raymond Lamar 6'1", 185 **OE-DE**
(Racehorse) *Col:* Georgia *HS:* Glynn Acad. [Brunswick, GA]
B: 6/15/1921, Brunswick, GA
AAFC **1946** MiaA: Rush 14-64 4.6; PR 4-54 13.5; KR 5-235 47.0. **1947** BalA: Pass 1-0; Rush 3-14 4.7; PR 1-33 33.0; KR 2-44 22.0. **1948** BalA: PR 1-10 10.0. **1949** BalA: KR 1-13 13.0. **Total:** Pass 1-0; Rush 17-78 4.6; PR 6-97 16.2; KR 8-292 36.5.

		Receiving				Interceptions		
Year Team	G	Rec	Yds	Avg	TD	Int	Yds	TD
1946 MiaA	14	22	275	12.5	2	4	40	0
1947 BalA	13	46	515	11.2	2	1	12	0
1948 BalA	14	41	765	18.7	7	5	110	0
1949 BalA	12	38	548	14.4	1	1	35	0
AAFC Total	53	147	2103	14.3	12	11	197	0

REUBEN DAVIS Davis, Reuben Cordell 6'5", 302 **DE-DT**
Col: North Carolina *HS:* Grimsley [Greensboro, NC] B: 5/7/1965, Greensboro, NC *Drafted:* 1988 Round 9 TB
1988 TB: 16 G; 3 Sac. **1989** TB: 16 G; Int 1-13 1 TD; 6 Pt; 3 Sac. **1990** TB: 16 G; 1 Sac. **1991** TB: 12 G; 3.5 Sac. **1992** TB-Pho: 16 G; 2 Sac. TB: 5 G. Pho: 11 G; 2 Sac. **1993** Pho: 16 G; 1 Sac. **1994** SD: 16 G; 0.5 Sac. **1995** SD: 16 G; Scor **1** Saf; 2 Pt; 3.5 Sac. **1996** SD: 15 G; 3 Sac. **Total:** 139 G; Int 1-13 1 TD; Scor 1 Saf; 8 Pt; 20.5 Sac.

DICK DAVIS Davis, Richard C 5'11", 215 **RB**
Col: Nebraska *HS:* Omaha [NE] B: 11/28/1946, Omaha, NE
Drafted: 1969 Round 12 Cle
1970 Den-NO: Rec 4-29 7.3. NO: Rec 4-29 7.3. **Total:** Rec 4-29 7.3.

		Rushing			
Year Team	G	Att	Yds	Avg	TD
1970 Den-NO	6	27	94	3.5	0
1970 Den	2	0	0	—	0
1970 NO	4	27	94	3.5	0
NFL Total	6	27	94	3.5	0

CORBY DAVIS Davis, Richard Corbett 5'11", 212 **FB-K**
Col: Indiana *HS:* Lowell [IN] B: 12/18/1914, Lowell, IN D: 5/28/1968
Drafted: 1938 Round 1 Cle
1938 Cle: Pass 1-0; Rec 1-2 2.0; Scor 19, 1-1 100.0% XK. **1939** Cle: Rec 3-49 16.3; Punt 10-393 39.3; Scor 13, 1-2 50.0% FG, 4-4 100.0% XK. **1941** Cle: Rec 13-64 4.9; PR 1-6 6.0; Punt 2-75 37.5. **1942** Cle: Pass 2-1 50.0%, 22 11.00 1 Int; Rec 2-18 9.0; Int 1-3; Punt 7-275 39.3. **Total:** Pass 3-1 33.3%, 22 7.33 1 Int; Rec 19-133 7.0; PR 1-6 6.0; Int 1-3; Punt 19-743 39.1; Scor 32, 1-2 50.0% FG, 5-5 100.0% XK.

		Rushing			
Year Team	G	Att	Yds	Avg	TD
1938 Cle	11	71	202	2.8	3
1939 Cle	11	13	15	1.2	1
1941 Cle	8	31	110	3.5	0
1942 Cle	9	28	55	2.0	0
NFL Total	39	143	382	2.7	4

DICK DAVIS Davis, Richard Earl 6'2", 230 **DE**
Col: Vanderbilt; Kansas *HS:* Messick [Memphis, TN] B: 2/6/1938, Jackson, TN
1962 DalT: 12 G.

TED DAVIS Davis, Richard Kenneth 6'1", 232 **LB**
Col: Georgia Tech *HS:* Messick [Memphis, TN] B: 7/27/1942, Memphis, TN *Drafted:* 1964 Round 4 Bal
1964 Bal: 14 G; PR 1-0; KR 1-12 12.0. **1965** Bal: 14 G. **1966** Bal: 10 G; PR 2-7 3.5; Int 1-15. **1967** NO: 10 G. **1968** NO: 14 G. **1969** NO: 14 G. **1970** Mia: 14 G; Int 1-15. **Total:** 90 G; PR 3-7 2.3; KR 1-12 12.0; Int 2-30.

RICKY DAVIS Davis, Richard Terrell 6'1", 179 **DB**
Col: Alabama *HS:* Jess Lanier [Birmingham, AL] B: 5/18/1953, Birmingham, AL *Drafted:* 1975 Round 8 Cin
1975 Cin: 14 G; Int 1-26. **1976** TB: 11 G; Pass 1-1 100.0%, -7 -7.00. **1977** KC: 13 G. **Total:** 38 G; Pass 1-1 100.0%, -7 7.00; Int 1-26.

BOB DAVIS Davis, Robert Billingsley 5'11", 192 **DE-OE**
Col: Penn State *HS:* Monongahela [PA] B: 9/26/1921, Monongahela, PA D: 11/16/1998, Pleasant Hills, PA
1946 Pit: 11 G; Rec 1-13 13.0; **1** Fum TD; 6 Pt; 1 Fum. **1947** Pit: 11 G; Rec 5-145 29.0; KR 1-3 3.0. **1948** Pit: 12 G; Rec 2-14 7.0; KR 1-8 8.0; 1 Fum. **1949** Pit: 11 G. **1950** Pit: 10 G. **Total:** 55 G; Rec 8-172 21.5; KR 2-11 5.5; 1 Fum TD; 6 Pt; 2 Fum.

BOB DAVIS Davis, Robert Ellersie Jr. 6'2", 205 **QB**
Col: Virginia *HS:* Neptune [NJ] B: 9/15/1945, Neptune, NJ
Drafted: 1967 Round 2 Hou

Year Team	G	Passing Att	Comp	Comp%	Yds	YPA	TD	Int	Rating
1967 Hou	2	19	9	47.4	71	3.74	0	2	17.5
1968 Hou	6	86	33	38.4	441	5.13	0	6	26.4
1969 Hou	2	42	25	59.5	223	5.31	2	4	50.1
1970 NYJ	1	17	6	35.3	66	3.88	0	0	47.7
1971 NYJ	13	121	49	40.5	624	5.16	10	8	57.3
1972 NYJ	14	22	10	45.5	114	5.18	2	1	72.9
1973 NO	2	17	5	29.4	14	0.82	0	2	0.0
NFL Total	40	324	137	42.3	1553	4.79	14	23	42.1

Year Team	Rushing Att	Yds	Avg	TD	Fum
1967 Hou	5	32	6.4	0	2
1968 Hou	15	91	6.1	1	5
1969 Hou	3	2	0.7	0	3
1970 NYJ	2	11	5.5	0	0
1971 NYJ	18	154	8.6	1	3
1972 NYJ	6	32	5.3	0	0
1973 NO	3	10	3.3	0	2
NFL Total	52	332	6.4	2	15

ROB DAVIS Davis, Robert Emmett 6′3″, 290 **DT**
Col: Shippensburg *HS:* Eleanor Roosevelt [Greenbelt, MD]
B: 12/10/1968, Washington, DC
1996 ChiB: 16 G. **1997** GB: 7 G. **1998** GB: 16 G. **Total:** 39 G.

BOB DAVIS Davis, Robert Thomas Jr. 6′4″, 235 **T**
Col: Georgia Tech *HS:* Jordan Vocational [Columbus, GA] B: 5/3/1927, Columbus, GA *Drafted:* 1947 Round 4 NYG
1948 Bos: 12 G.

ROGER DAVIS Davis, Roger Wilfred 6′3″, 240 **OG-OT**
Col: Syracuse *HS:* Solon [OH] B: 6/23/1938, Cleveland, OH
Drafted: 1960 Round 1 ChiB
1960 ChiB: 12 G. **1961** ChiB: 14 G. **1962** ChiB: 9 G. **1963** ChiB: 13 G. **1964** LARm: 11 G. **1965** NYG: 3 G. **1966** NYG: 10 G; KR 1-0; 2 Fum. **Total:** 72 G; KR 1-0; 2 Fum.

RON DAVIS Davis, Ronald Rozelle 5′10″, 190 **DB**
Col: Tennessee *HS:* Bartlett [TN] B: 2/24/1972, Bartlett, TN
Drafted: 1995 Round 2 Atl
1995 Atl: 12 G.

RON DAVIS Davis, Ronald Willard 6′2″, 235 **OG**
Col: Virginia State *HS:* Deptford [NJ] B: 9/16/1950, Camden, NJ
Drafted: 1972 Round 16 SF
1973 StL: 2 G.

ROSEY DAVIS Davis, Roosevelt 6′5″, 260 **DE**
(Truck) *Col:* Tennessee State *HS:* Jim Hill [Jackson, MS]
B: 11/29/1941, Jackson, MS *Drafted:* 1965 Round 8 Bal
1965 NYG: 14 G. **1966** NYG: 7 G. **1967** NYG: 1 G. **Total:** 22 G.

RUSSELL DAVIS Davis, Russell W III 6′0″, 227 **RB**
Col: Michigan *HS:* Woodbridge [VA] B: 9/15/1956, Millen, GA
Drafted: 1979 Round 4 Pit
1980 Pit: KR 9-160 17.8. **1981** Pit: Rec 4-34 8.5; KR 1-8 8.0. **1982** Pit: Rec 1-11 11.0. **Total:** Rec 5-45 9.0; KR 10-168 16.8.

Year Team	G	Rushing Att	Yds	Avg	TD	Fum
1980 Pit	14	33	132	4.0	1	0
1981 Pit	16	47	270	5.7	1	3
1982 Pit	7	24	72	3.0	0	0
1983 Pit	5	0	0	—	0	0
NFL Total	42	104	474	4.6	2	3

SAM DAVIS Davis, Samuel Ruel 6′1″, 255 **OG**
Col: Allen *HS:* Northwestern [Jacksonville, FL] B: 7/5/1944, Jacksonville, FL
1967 Pit: 14 G. **1968** Pit: 14 G. **1969** Pit: 12 G; PR 1-0; KR 3-0; 2 Fum. **1970** Pit: 14 G. **1971** Pit: 12 G. **1972** Pit: 11 G. **1973** Pit: 12 G. **1974** Pit: 11 G. **1975** Pit: 14 G. **1976** Pit: 14 G. **1977** Pit: 11 G. **1978** Pit: 16 G. **1979** Pit: 13 G. **Total:** 168 G; PR 1-0; KR 3-0; 2 Fum.

SCOTT DAVIS Davis, Scott L 6′3″, 292 **OG**
Col: Iowa *HS:* Glenwood [IA] B: 1/29/1970, Glenwood, IA
Drafted: 1993 Round 6 NYG
1993 NYG: 4 G. **1994** NYG: 15 G. **1997** Atl: 2 G. **Total:** 21 G.

SCOTT DAVIS Davis, Scott Michael 6′7″, 280 **DE-LB-DT**
Col: Illinois *HS:* Plainfield [IL] B: 7/8/1965, Joliet, IL *Drafted:* 1988 Round 1 LARd
1988 LARd: 15 G; 5.5 Sac. **1989** LARd: 14 G; 5.5 Sac. **1990** LARd: 16 G; 10 Sac. **1991** LARd: 16 G; 6.5 Sac. **1994** LARd: 14 G. **Total:** 75 G; 27.5 Sac.

STAN DAVIS Davis, Stanley Wayne 5′10″, 180 **WR**
Col: Memphis *HS:* Manassas [Memphis, TN] B: 7/13/1950, Memphis, TN *Drafted:* 1973 Round 13 Phi
1973 Phi: 8 G; Rec 1-6 6.0; PR 2-0; KR 10-236 23.6; 1 Fum.

STEPHEN DAVIS Davis, Stephen Lamont 6′0″, 234 **RB**
Col: Auburn *HS:* Spartanburg [SC] B: 3/1/1974, Spartanburg, SC
Drafted: 1996 Round 4 Was
1997 Was: KR 3-62 20.7. **Total:** KR 3-62 20.7.

Year Team	G	Rushing Att	Yds	Avg	TD	Receiving Rec	Yds	Avg	TD	Fum	Tot TD
1996 Was	12	23	139	6.0	2	0	0	—	0	0	2
1997 Was	14	141	567	4.0	3	18	134	7.4	0	1	3
1998 Was	16	34	109	3.2	0	21	263	12.5	2	0	2
NFL Total	42	198	815	4.1	5	39	397	10.2	2	1	7

STEVE DAVIS Davis, Steven Timothy 6′1″, 218 **RB**
Col: Delaware State *HS:* Lylburn Downing [Lexington, VA]; Lexington HS [VA] B: 11/10/1948, Lexington, VA *Drafted:* 1971 Round 3 Pit

Year Team	G	Rushing Att	Yds	Avg	TD	Receiving Rec	Yds	Avg	TD
1972 Pit	11	20	85	4.3	1	1	5	5.0	0
1973 Pit	14	67	266	4.0	2	7	31	4.4	1
1974 Pit	14	71	246	3.5	2	11	152	13.8	1
1975 NYJ	14	70	290	4.1	1	6	56	9.3	0
1976 NYJ	12	94	418	4.4	3	8	57	7.1	0
NFL Total	65	322	1305	4.1	9	33	301	9.1	2

Year Team	Kickoff Returns Ret	Yds	Avg	TD	Fum	Tot TD
1972 Pit	7	207	29.6	0	3	1
1973 Pit	15	404	26.9	0	3	3
1974 Pit	12	269	22.4	0	3	3
1975 NYJ	20	483	24.2	0	1	1
1976 NYJ	0	0	—	0	6	3
NFL Total	54	1363	25.2	0	16	11

RED DAVIS Davis, Sylvester Edward 5′11″, 195 **TB**
Col: Geneva *HS:* Willard [OH] B: 11/14/1907, Franks, OH
D: 8/5/1988, Garden Grove, CA
1933 Port-Phi: 8 G; Pass 6-2 33.3%, 62 10.33 1 TD 3 Int; Rush 15-57 3.8 1 TD; Rec 4-50 12.5; Scor 9, 3 XK. Port: 1 G. Phi: 7 G; Pass 6-2 33.3%, 62 10.33 1 TD 3 Int; Rush 15-57 3.8 1 TD; Rec 4-50 12.5; Scor 9, 3 XK. **Total:** 8 G; Pass 6-2 33.3%, 62 10.33 1 TD 3 Int; Rush 15-57 3.8 1 TD; Rec 4-50 12.5.

TERRELL DAVIS Davis, Terrell 5′11″, 206 **RB**
Col: Long Beach State; Georgia *HS:* Abraham Lincoln [San Diego, CA]
B: 10/28/1972, San Diego, CA *Drafted:* 1995 Round 6 Den
1997 Den: Scor **3** 2XP. **Total:** Scor 3 2XP.

Year Team	G	Rushing Att	Yds	Avg	TD	Receiving Rec	Yds	Avg	TD	Fum	Tot TD
1995 Den	14	237	1117	4.7	7	49	367	7.5	1	5	8
1996 Den	16	345	1538	4.5	13	36	310	8.6	2	5	15
1997 Den	15	369	1750	4.7	**15**	42	287	6.8	0	4	15
1998 Den	16	392	**2008**	**5.1**	**21**	25	217	8.7	2	2	**23**
NFL Total	61	1343	6413	4.8	56	152	1181	7.8	5	16	61

TOMMY DAVIS Davis, Tommy Ray 6′0″, 215 **K**
Col: Louisiana State *HS:* Fair Park [Shreveport, LA] B: 10/13/1934, Shreveport, LA D: 4/2/1987, Millbrae, CA *Drafted:* 1957 Round 11 SF
1963 SF: Pass 1-0. **1965** SF: Rush 1-21 21.0. **1966** SF: Rush 3-43 14.3. **1969** SF: Rush 2-21 10.5. **Total:** Pass 1-0; Rush 6-85 14.2.

Year Team	G	Punting Punts	Yds	Avg
1959 SF	12	59	2694	45.7
1960 SF	12	62	2737	44.1
1961 SF	14	50	2269	45.4
1962 SF	14	48	2188	**45.6**
1963 SF	14	73	3311	45.4
1964 SF	14	79	3599	45.6
1965 SF	14	54	2471	45.8
1966 SF	14	63	2609	41.4
1967 SF	14	0	0	—
1968 SF	9	0	0	—
1969 SF	7	23	955	41.5
NFL Total	138	511	22833	44.7

Year Team	Scoring Pts	FG	FGA	FG%	XK	XKA	XK%
1959 SF	67	12	26	46.2	31	31	100.0
1960 SF	78	**19**	**32**	59.4	21	21	100.0
1961 SF	80	12	22	54.5	44	44	100.0
1962 SF	66	10	23	43.5	36	36	100.0
1963 SF	54	10	31	32.3	24	24	100.0
1964 SF	54	8	25	32.0	30	30	100.0
1965 SF	103	17	27	63.0	**52**	**53**	98.1
1966 SF	86	16	31	51.6	38	39	97.4
1967 SF	75	14	33	42.4	33	33	100.0
1968 SF	53	9	16	56.3	26	26	100.0

1969 SF	22	3	10	30.0	13	13	100.0
NFL Total	738	130	276	47.1	348	350	99.4

TRAVIS DAVIS Davis, Travis Horace 6′0″, 203 **DB**
Col: Notre Dame *HS:* Phineas Banning [Los Angeles, CA]
B: 1/10/1973, Wilmington, CA *Drafted:* 1995 Round 7 NO
1995 Jac: 9 G. **1996** Jac: 16 G; Int 2-0; 0.5 Sac. **1997** Jac: 16 G; KR 1-9 9.0; Int 1-23; 2 Sac. **1998** Jac: 16 G; Int 2-34; 0.5 Sac. **Total:** 57 G; KR 1-9 9.0; Int 5-57; 3 Sac.

TRAVIS DAVIS Davis, Travis Neil 6′2″, 279 **NT**
Col: Michigan State *HS:* Warren G. Harding [Warren, OH]
B: 5/10/1966, Warren, OH *Drafted:* 1990 Round 4 Pho
1990 NO: 2 G. **1991** Ind: 16 G. **Total:** 18 G.

GAINES DAVIS Davis, Trenton Gaines 5′11″, 230 **G**
Col: Texas Tech *HS:* St. Jo [TX] B: 10/20/1913 D: 12/1983, Waco, TX
1936 NYG: 6 G.

TROY DAVIS Davis, Troy 5′7″, 191 **RB**
Col: Iowa State *HS:* Miami Southridge [FL] B: 9/14/1975, Miami, FL
Drafted: 1997 Round 3 NO
1997 NO: KR 9-173 19.2. **1998** NO: KR 2-21 10.5. **Total:** KR 11-194 17.6.

		Rushing				Receiving				
Year Team	**G**	**Att**	**Yds**	**Avg**	**TD**	**Rec**	**Yds**	**Avg**	**TD**	**Fum**
1997 NO	16	75	271	3.6	0	13	85	6.5	0	3
1998 NO	14	55	143	2.6	1	16	99	6.2	0	1
NFL Total	30	130	414	3.2	1	29	184	6.3	0	4

TYREE DAVIS Davis, Tyree Bernard 5′9″, 175 **WR**
Col: Central Arkansas *HS:* Altheimer [AR] B: 9/23/1970, Altheimer, AR
Drafted: 1993 Round 7 TB
1995 TB: 1 G. **1997** Sea: 13 G; Rec 2-48 24.0; PR 16-104 6.5; KR 2-25 12.5; 1 Fum. **Total:** 14 G; Rec 2-48 24.0; PR 16-104 6.5; KR 2-25 12.5; 1 Fum.

TYRONE DAVIS Davis, Tyrone 6′4″, 240 **TE-WR**
Col: Virginia *HS:* Halifax Co. [South Boston, VA]; Fork Union Mil. Acad. [VA] B: 6/30/1972, Halifax, VA *Drafted:* 1995 Round 4 NYJ
1995 NYJ: 4 G; Rec 1-9 9.0. **1996** NYJ: 2 G; Rec 1-6 6.0. **1997** GB: 13 G; Rec 2-28 14.0 1 TD; 1 Fum TD; Tot TD 2; 12 Pt. **1998** GB: 13 G; Rec 18-250 13.9 7 TD; 42 Pt; 1 Fum. **Total:** 32 G; Rec 22-293 13.3 8 TD; 1 Fum TD; Tot TD 9; 54 Pt; 1 Fum.

VAN DAVIS Davis, Van Andrew Jr. 6′2″, 215 **DE-OE**
Col: Georgia *HS:* Philomath [GA] B: 10/5/1921, Philomath, GA
D: 7/11/1987, Carrollton, GA
AAFC **1947** NY-A: 13 G; Rec 8-179 22.4; KR 1-9 9.0. **1948** NY-A: 13 G; Rec 4-49 12.3 1 TD; Int 1-5; 6 Pt. **1949** NY-A: 11 G; Rec 2-26 13.0. **Total:** 37 G; Rec 14-254 18.1 1 TD; KR 1-9 9.0; Int 1-5; 6 Pt.

VERN DAVIS Davis, Vernon Charles 6′4″, 208 **DB**
Col: Western Michigan *HS:* Dowagiac [MI] B: 11/2/1949, Dowagiac, MI
1971 Phi: 3 G.

WAYNE DAVIS Davis, Wayne Elliott 5′11″, 175 **DB**
Col: Indiana State *HS:* Mount Healthy [Cincinnati, OH] B: 6/17/1963, Cincinnati, OH
1985 SD: 16 G; Int 2-29; 1 Sac. **1986** SD: 16 G. **1987** Buf: 10 G; Int 1-0. **1988** Buf: 16 G; Int 1-3. **1989** Buf-Was: 14 G; Int 1-11. Buf: 6 G. Was: 8 G; Int 1-11. **1990** Was: 1 G. **Total:** 73 G; Int 5-43; 1 Sac.

WENDELL DAVIS Davis, Wendell 6′2″, 246 **TE**
Col: Mississippi Gulf Coast CC; Temple *HS:* Moss Point [MS]
B: 10/24/1975, Escatawapa, MS
1998 SD: 11 G; Rec 4-23 5.8.

WENDELL DAVIS Davis, Wendell 5′10″, 201 **DB**
Col: Coffeyville CC KS; Oklahoma *HS:* North [Wichita, KS]
B: 6/27/1973, Wichita, KS *Drafted:* 1996 Round 6 Dal
1996 Dal: 13 G. **1997** Dal: 15 G. **Total:** 28 G.

WENDELL DAVIS Davis, Wendell Tyrone 5′11″, 188 **WR**
Col: Louisiana State *HS:* Fair Park [Shreveport, LA] B: 1/3/1966, Shreveport, LA *Drafted:* 1988 Round 1 ChiB
1988 ChiB: Rush 1-3 3.0; PR 3-17 5.7. **1992** ChiB: Rush 4-42 10.5. **Total:** Rush 5-45 9.0; PR 3-17 5.7.

		Receiving				
Year Team	**G**	**Rec**	**Yds**	**Avg**	**TD**	**Fum**
1988 ChiB	16	15	220	14.7	0	2
1989 ChiB	14	26	397	15.3	3	0
1990 ChiB	14	39	572	14.7	3	1
1991 ChiB	16	61	945	15.5	6	0
1992 ChiB	16	54	734	13.6	2	0
1993 ChiB	5	12	132	11.0	0	0
NFL Total	81	207	3000	14.5	14	3

BILLY DAVIS Davis, William Augusta III 6′1″, 205 **WR**
Col: Pittsburgh *HS:* Irvin [El Paso, TX] B: 7/6/1972, El Paso, TX
1998 Dal: Rush 4-15 3.8; KR 1-10 10.0. **Total:** Rush 4-15 3.8; KR 1-10 10.0.

		Receiving				
Year Team	**G**	**Rec**	**Yds**	**Avg**	**TD**	**Fum**
1995 Dal	16	0	0	—	0	0
1996 Dal	13	0	0	—	0	0
1997 Dal	16	3	33	11.0	0	0
1998 Dal	16	39	691	17.7	3	1
NFL Total	61	42	724	17.2	3	1

WILLIE DAVIS Davis, William Delford 6′3″, 243 **DE**
Col: Grambling State *HS:* Booker T. Washington [Texarkana, AR]
B: 7/24/1934, Lisbon, LA *Drafted:* 1956 Round 15 Cle *HOF:* 1981
1958 Cle: 12 G. **1959** Cle: 12 G. **1960** GB: 12 G; 6 Pt. **1961** GB: 14 G. **1962** GB: 14 G; **1** Fum TD; 6 Pt. **1963** GB: 14 G; Scor **1** Saf; 2 Pt. **1964** GB: 14 G. **1965** GB: 14 G; Int 1-21. **1966** GB: 14 G. **1967** GB: 14 G; Scor **1** Saf; 2 Pt. **1968** GB: 14 G. **1969** GB: 14 G; Int 1-0. **Total:** 162 G; Int 2-21; Scor 2 Saf; 1 Fum TD; Tot TD 2; 16 Pt.

BILL DAVIS Davis, William Dorris 6′1″, 234 **T**
(Big Bill) *Col:* Texas Tech *HS:* Grapevine [TX] B: 11/10/1916, Grapevine, TX D: 11/8/1994, Addison, TX *Drafted:* 1940 Round 11 ChiC
AAFC **1946** MiaA: 12 G.

NFL **1940** ChiC: 10 G. **1941** ChiC: 10 G; **1** Fum TD; 6 Pt. **1943** Bkn: 8 G. **Total:** 28 G; 1 Fum TD; 6 Pt.

BILLY DAVIS Davis, William Henry Jr. 6′4″, 210 **LB**
Col: Clemson *HS:* Mount Vernon [Alexandria, VA] B: 12/6/1961, Alexandria, VA
1984 StL: 1 G.

WILLIE DAVIS Davis, Willie Clark 6′0″, 180 **WR**
Col: Central Arkansas *HS:* Altheimer [AR] B: 10/10/1967, Little Rock, AR
1992 KC: Rush 1-(-11) -11.0. **1994** KC: Scor 1 2XP. **1996** Hou: Rush 1-15 15.0. **1997** Ten: Pass 1-1 100.0%, 22 22.00 1 TD. **Total:** Pass 1-1 100.0%, 22 22.00 1 TD; Rush 2-4 2.0; Scor 1 2XP.

		Receiving				
Year Team	**G**	**Rec**	**Yds**	**Avg**	**TD**	**Fum**
1991 KC	1	0	0	—	0	0
1992 KC	16	36	756	**21.0**	3	0
1993 KC	16	52	909	17.5	7	0
1994 KC	14	51	822	16.1	5	1
1995 KC	16	33	527	16.0	5	0
1996 Hou	16	39	464	11.9	6	1
1997 Ten	16	43	564	13.1	4	0
1998 Ten	13	32	461	14.4	3	0
NFL Total	108	286	4503	15.7	33	2

JERONE DAVISON Davison, Jerone Lamar 6′1″, 235 **RB**
Col: Solano C.C. CA; Arizona State *HS:* Picayune Memorial [MS]; Vallejo HS [CA] B: 9/16/1970, Picayune, MS
1996 Oak: 2 G; Rec 4-21 5.3. **1997** Oak: 8 G; Rush 2-4 2.0; Rec 2-34 17.0. **Total:** 10 G; Rush 2-4 2.0; Rec 6-55 9.2.

MIKE DAVLIN Davlin, Michael Francis 6′1″, 230 **OT**
Col: Notre Dame; San Francisco *HS:* Creighton Prep [Omaha, NE]
B: 11/2/1927, Omaha, NE D: 3/28/1996, Petaluma, CA
1955 Was: 9 G.

BRIAN DAWKINS Dawkins, Brian Patrick 5′11″, 200 **DB**
Col: Clemson *HS:* William M. Raines [Jacksonville, FL] B: 10/13/1973, Jacksonville, FL *Drafted:* 1996 Round 2 Phi
1996 Phi: 14 G; Int 3-41; 1 Sac. **1997** Phi: 15 G; Int 3-76 1 TD; 6 Pt. **1998** Phi: 14 G; Int 2-39; 1 Sac. **Total:** 43 G; Int 8-156 1 TD; 6 Pt; 2 Sac.

DALE DAWKINS Dawkins, Dale V 6′1″, 190 **WR**
Col: Miami (Fla.) *HS:* Vero Beach [FL] B: 10/30/1966, Vero Beach, FL
Drafted: 1990 Round 9 NYJ
1990 NYJ: 11 G; Rec 5-68 13.6. **1991** NYJ: 15 G; Rec 3-38 12.7; KR 2-22 11.0. **1992** NYJ: 6 G; KR 1-10 10.0. **1993** NYJ: 4 G. **Total:** 36 G; Rec 8-106 13.3; KR 3-32 10.7.

JOE DAWKINS Dawkins, Joseph III 6′0″, 223 **RB**
Col: Los Angeles City Coll. CA (J.C.); Wisconsin *HS:* John C. Fremont [Los Angeles, CA] B: 1/27/1948, Los Angeles, CA *Drafted:* 1970 Round 10 Hou
1970 Hou: PR 1-0. **Total:** PR 1-0.

		Rushing				Receiving			
Year Team	**G**	**Att**	**Yds**	**Avg**	**TD**	**Rec**	**Yds**	**Avg**	**TD**
1970 Hou	14	124	517	4.2	2	15	94	6.3	0
1971 Hou-Den	14	42	135	3.2	2	9	53	5.9	0
1971 Hou	6	42	135	3.2	2	9	53	5.9	0
1971 Den	8	0	0	—	0	0	0	—	0
1972 Den	14	56	243	4.3	2	18	242	13.4	0

Year Team	G								
1973 Den	14	160	706	4.4	2	30	329	11.0	0
1974 NYG	14	156	561	3.6	2	46	332	7.2	3
1975 NYG	14	129	438	3.4	2	24	245	10.2	0
1976 Hou	14	31	61	2.0	1	3	21	7.0	0
NFL Total	98	698	2661	3.8	13	145	1316	9.1	3

	Kickoff Returns					Tot
Year Team	Ret	Yds	Avg	TD	Fum	TD
1970 Hou	0	0	—	0	4	2
1971 Hou-Den	2	34	17.0	0	0	2
1971 Hou	0	0	—	0	0	2
1971 Den	2	34	17.0	0	0	0
1972 Den	15	357	23.8	0	3	2
1973 Den	10	222	22.2	0	4	2
1974 NYG	4	154	38.5	0	6	5
1975 NYG	1	32	32.0	0	5	2
1976 Hou	0	0	—	0	0	1
NFL Total	32	799	25.0	0	22	16

JULIUS DAWKINS Dawkins, Julius 6′1″, 196 **WR**
Col: Pittsburgh *HS:* Monessen [PA] B: 1/4/1961, Monessen, PA
Drafted: 1983 Round 12 Buf

		Receiving			
Year Team	G	Rec	Yds	Avg	TD
1983 Buf	11	11	123	11.2	1
1984 Buf	16	21	295	14.0	2
NFL Total	27	32	418	13.1	3

SEAN DAWKINS Dawkins, Sean Russell 6′4″, 215 **WR**
Col: California *HS:* Homestead [Cupertino, CA] B: 2/3/1971, Red Bank, NJ *Drafted:* 1993 Round 1 Ind

		Receiving				
Year Team	G	Rec	Yds	Avg	TD	Fum
1993 Ind	16	26	430	16.5	1	0
1994 Ind	16	51	742	14.5	5	1
1995 Ind	16	52	784	15.1	3	1
1996 Ind	15	54	751	13.9	1	1
1997 Ind	14	68	804	11.8	2	0
1998 NO	15	53	823	15.5	1	2
NFL Total	92	304	4334	14.3	13	5

TOMMY DAWKINS Dawkins, Tommy Earl 6′3″, 260 **DE**
Col: Lees-McRae JC NC; Appalachian State *HS:* Lexington [NC]
B: 5/8/1965, Lexington, NC
1987 Pit: 2 G; 1 Sac.

FRED DAWLEY Dawley, Frederick Martin 5′9″, 190 **FB-LB**
Col: Michigan B: 3/11/1921, Bay City, MI D: 4/13/1994, Palm City, FL
1944 Det: 2 G; Rush 2-16 8.0.

LAWRENCE DAWSEY Dawsey, Lawrence Leneir 6′0″, 195 **WR**
Col: Florida State *HS:* Northview [Dothan, AL] B: 11/16/1967, Dothan, AL *Drafted:* 1991 Round 3 TB
1991 TB: Rush 1-9 9.0 1 TD. **Total:** Rush 1-9 9.0 1 TD.

		Receiving					Tot
Year Team	G	Rec	Yds	Avg	TD	Fum	TD
1991 TB	16	55	818	14.9	3	0	4
1992 TB	15	60	776	12.9	1	1	1
1993 TB	4	15	203	13.5	0	0	0
1994 TB	10	46	673	14.6	1	0	1
1995 TB	12	30	372	12.4	0	0	0
1996 NYG	16	18	233	12.9	0	0	0
NFL Total	73	224	3075	13.7	5	1	6

STACEY DAWSEY Dawsey, Stacey L 5′9″, 154 **WR**
Col: Indiana *HS:* Manatee [Bradenton, FL] B: 10/24/1965, Bradenton, FL
1987 NO: 3 G; Rec 13-142 10.9; 2 Fum.

DALE DAWSON Dawson, Dale Anthony 6′0″, 213 **K**
Col: Eastern Kentucky *HS:* North Shore [West Palm Beach, FL]
B: 11/2/1964, West Palm Beach, FL
1987 Min: 3 G; Scor 7, 1-5 20.0% FG, 4-4 100.0% XK. **1988** Phi-GB: 5 G; Scor 13, 3-6 50.0% FG, 4-5 80.0% XK. Phi: 1 G; Scor 3, 0-1 FG, 3-3 100.0% XK. GB: 4 G; Scor 10, 3-5 60.0% FG, 1-2 50.0% XK. **Total:** 8 G; Scor 20, 4-11 36.4% FG, 8-9 88.9% XK.

DERMONTTI DAWSON Dawson, Dermontti Fara 6′2″, 288 **C-OG**
(Dirt) *Col:* Kentucky *HS:* Bryan Station [Lexington, KY] B: 6/17/1965, Lexington, KY *Drafted:* 1988 Round 2 Pit
1988 Pit: 8 G. **1989** Pit: 16 G. **1990** Pit: 16 G. **1991** Pit: 16 G; 2 Fum. **1992** Pit: 16 G. **1993** Pit: 16 G; 1 Fum. **1994** Pit: 16 G. **1995** Pit: 16 G. **1996** Pit: 16 G. **1997** Pit: 16 G. **1998** Pit: 16 G; 1 Fum. **Total:** 168 G; 4 Fum.

DOUG DAWSON Dawson, Douglas Arlin 6′3″, 288 **OG**
Col: Texas *HS:* Memorial [Houston, TX] B: 12/27/1961, Houston, TX
Drafted: 1984 Round 2 StL
1984 StL: 15 G. **1985** StL: 16 G. **1986** StL: 1 G. **1990** Hou: 16 G. **1991** Hou: 14 G. **1992** Hou: 16 G. **1993** Hou: 16 G. **1994** Cle: 12 G. **Total:** 106 G.

GIB DAWSON Dawson, Gilbert Henry 5′11″, 180 **HB**
Col: Texas *HS:* Douglas [AZ] B: 8/27/1930, Bisbee, AZ *Drafted:* 1953 Round 4 GB
1953 GB: 7 G; Rush 5-18 3.6; PR 7-72 10.3 **1** TD; KR 4-102 25.5; 6 Pt; 1 Fum.

LIN DAWSON Dawson, James Linwood 6′3″, 240 **TE**
Col: North Carolina State *HS:* Kinston [NC] B: 6/24/1959, Norfolk, VA
Drafted: 1981 Round 8 NE

		Receiving				
Year Team	G	Rec	Yds	Avg	TD	Fum
1981 NE	15	7	126	18.0	0	0
1982 NE	8	13	160	12.3	1	0
1983 NE	13	9	84	9.3	1	0
1984 NE	16	39	427	10.9	4	0
1985 NE	16	17	148	8.7	0	1
1987 NE	12	12	81	6.8	0	0
1988 NE	6	8	106	13.3	2	0
1989 NE	16	12	101	8.4	0	0
1990 NE	3	0	0	—	0	0
NFL Total	105	117	1233	10.5	8	1

LAKE DAWSON Dawson, Lake 6′1″, 204 **WR**
Col: Notre Dame *HS:* Federal Way [WA] B: 1/2/1972, Boston, MA
Drafted: 1994 Round 3 KC
1994 KC: Rush 3-24 8.0. **1995** KC: Rush 1-(-9) -9.0. **Total:** Rush 4-15 3.8.

		Receiving				
Year Team	G	Rec	Yds	Avg	TD	Fum
1994 KC	12	37	537	14.5	2	1
1995 KC	16	40	513	12.8	5	0
1996 KC	4	5	83	16.6	1	0
1997 KC	11	21	273	13.0	2	0
NFL Total	43	103	1406	13.7	10	1

LEN DAWSON Dawson, Leonard Ray 6′0″, 190 **QB**
Col: Purdue *HS:* Alliance [OH] B: 6/20/1935, Alliance, OH
Drafted: 1957 Round 1 Pit *HOF:* 1987
1957 Pit: Scor 0-1 FG, 0-2 XK. **Total:** Scor 54, 0-1 FG, 0-2 XK.

		Passing							
Year Team	G	Att	Comp	Comp%	Yds	YPA	TD	Int	Rating
1957 Pit	3	4	2	50.0	25	6.25	0	0	69.8
1958 Pit	4	6	1	16.7	11	1.83	0	2	0.0
1959 Pit	12	7	3	42.9	60	8.57	1	0	113.1
1960 Cle	2	13	8	61.5	23	1.77	0	0	65.9
1961 Cle	7	15	7	46.7	85	5.67	1	3	47.2
1962 DalT	14	310	189	**61.0**	2759	**8.90**	**29**	17	98.3
1963 KC	14	352	190	54.0	2389	6.79	**26**	19	77.5
1964 KC	14	354	199	**56.2**	2879	8.13	30	18	89.9
1965 KC	14	305	163	**53.4**	2262	7.42	**21**	14	81.3
1966 KC	14	284	159	**56.0**	2527	**8.90**	**26**	10	101.7
1967 KC	14	357	206	**57.7**	2651	7.43	24	17	83.7
1968 KC	14	224	131	**58.5**	2109	**9.42**	17	9	98.6
1969 KC	9	166	98	**59.0**	1323	7.97	9	13	69.9
1970 KC	14	262	141	53.8	1876	7.16	13	14	71.0
1971 KC	14	301	167	55.5	2504	8.32	15	13	81.6
1972 KC	14	305	175	57.4	1835	6.02	13	12	72.8
1973 KC	8	101	66	65.3	725	7.18	2	5	72.4
1974 KC	14	235	138	58.7	1573	6.69	7	13	65.8
1975 KC	12	140	93	**66.4**	1095	7.82	5	**4**	90.0
NFL Total	211	3741	2136	57.1	28711	7.67	239	183	82.6

	Rushing				
Year Team	Att	Yds	Avg	TD	Fum
1957 Pit	3	31	10.3	0	1
1958 Pit	2	-1	-0.5	0	0
1959 Pit	4	20	5.0	0	1
1960 Cle	1	0	0.0	0	1
1961 Cle	1	-10	-10.0	0	0
1962 DalT	38	252	6.6	3	**11**
1963 KC	37	272	7.4	2	4
1964 KC	40	89	2.2	2	16
1965 KC	43	142	3.3	2	7
1966 KC	24	167	7.0	0	5
1967 KC	20	68	3.4	0	6
1968 KC	20	40	2.0	0	4
1969 KC	1	3	3.0	0	0
1970 KC	11	46	4.2	0	5
1971 KC	12	24	2.0	0	8
1972 KC	15	75	5.0	0	2
1973 KC	6	40	6.7	0	4

1974 KC	11	28	2.5	0	6
1975 KC	5	7	1.4	0	4
NFL Total	294	1293	4.4	9	85

MIKE DAWSON Dawson, Michael Daniel 6′4″, 270 **DT-NT-DE**
Col: Arizona *HS:* Tucson [AZ] B: 10/16/1953, Dorking, England
Drafted: 1976 Round 1 StL
1976 StL: 13 G. **1977** StL: 14 G. **1978** StL: 16 G. **1979** StL: 16 G. **1980** StL: 4 G. **1981** StL: 16 G. **1982** StL: 9 G; Int 1-0; 3.5 Sac. **1983** Det: 16 G; 1 Sac. **1984** KC: 9 G; 1 Sac. **Total:** 113 G; Int 1-0; 5.5 Sac.

RHETT DAWSON Dawson, Rhett Motte 6′1″, 185 **WR**
Col: Florida State *HS:* Valdosta [GA] B: 12/22/1948, Valdosta, GA
Drafted: 1972 Round 10 Hou
1972 Hou: 14 G; Rec 6-78 13.0 1 TD; 6 Pt. **1973** Min: 2 G; Rec 2-24 12.0. **Total:** 16 G; Rec 8-102 12.8 1 TD; 6 Pt.

BILL DAWSON Dawson, William Alfred 6′3″, 240 **TE-DE**
(Red) *Col:* Florida State *HS:* Valdosta [GA] B: 12/4/1942
Drafted: 1964 Round 19 Bos
1965 Bos: 9 G.

AL DAY Day, Albert Edward 6′2″, 216 **LB**
Col: Eastern Michigan B: 3/18/1938
1960 Den: 14 G.

FRED DAY Day, Frederick Samuel 6′2″, 195 **T**
Col: Ohio Wesleyan B: 7/4/1896, Pandora, OH D: 5/18/1963, Fort Lauderdale, FL
1921 Cin: 1 G.

EAGLE DAY Day, Herman Sidney 6′0″, 183 **QB**
Col: Mississippi *HS:* Columbia [MS] B: 10/2/1932, Columbia, MS
Drafted: 1956 Round 17 Was
1959 Was: Pass 13-6 46.2%, 79 6.08 1 Int; Rush 3-27 9.0. **1960** Was: Pass 19-9 47.4%, 115 6.05 1 Int; Rush 3-1 0.3. **Total:** Pass 32-15 46.9%, 194 6.06 2 Int; Rush 6-28 4.7.

		Punting		
Year Team	**G**	**Punts**	**Yds**	**Avg**
1959 Was	4	0	0	—
1960 Was	12	59	2476	42.0
NFL Total	16	59	2476	42.0

TERRY DAY Day, Terry Lee 6′4″, 290 **DE**
Col: Holmes CC MS; Mississippi State *HS:* Williams-Sullivan [Durant, MS] B: 9/18/1974, Pickens, MS *Drafted:* 1997 Round 4 NYJ
1997 NYJ: 1 G.

TOM DAY Day, Thomas Frederick 6′2″, 262 **DE-OG-DT-OT**
(Tippy) *Col:* North Carolina A&T *HS:* Phelps Career [Washington, DC]
B: 8/20/1935, Washington, DC *Drafted:* 1960 Round 20 StL
1960 StL: 10 G. **1961** Buf: 12 G. **1962** Buf: 14 G. **1963** Buf: 14 G. **1964** Buf: 14 G. **1965** Buf: 14 G; Int 1-0. **1966** Buf: 14 G. **1967** SD: 11 G. **1968** Buf: 14 G. **Total:** 117 G; Int 1-0.

HARRY DAYHOFF Dayhoff, Harry Oscar 5′9″, 180 **WB-FB-TB-BB**
(Gump) *Col:* Bucknell *HS:* Steelton [PA] B: 5/25/1896, Gettysburg, PA D: 2/17/1963, Harrisburg, PA
1924 Fra: 11 G; Rush 2 TD; 12 Pt. **1925** Pott: 1 G. **Total:** 12 G; Rush 2 TD; 12 Pt.

TONY DAYKIN Daykin, Anthony Albert 6′1″, 215 **LB**
Col: Georgia Tech *HS:* Aquinas [Augusta, GA] B: 5/13/1955, Taipei, Taiwan *Drafted:* 1977 Round 11 Det
1977 Det: 14 G. **1978** Det: 16 G; Rush 1-8 8.0. **1979** Atl: 11 G. **1980** Atl: 16 G; KR 1-3 3.0. **1981** Atl: 16 G; Rush 1-2 2.0. **Total:** 73 G; Rush 2-10 5.0; KR 1-3 3.0.

RUFUS DEAL Deal, Rufus Copeland 6′0″, 220 **FB-BB-LB**
(Gus) *Col:* Auburn *HS:* Tuscaloosa Central [AL] B: 12/7/1917, Moundsville, AL *Drafted:* 1942 Round 2 Was
1942 Was: 6 G; Rush 5-12 2.4.

FRED DEAN Dean, Frederick Gregory 6′3″, 253 **OG**
Col: Texas Southern *HS:* Gainesville [FL] B: 3/30/1955, Gainesville, FL
1977 ChiB: Postseason only. **1978** Was: 8 G. **1979** Was: 15 G. **1980** Was: 12 G. **1982** Was: 5 G. **Total:** 40 G.

FRED DEAN Dean, Frederick Rudolph 6′3″, 230 **DE**
Col: Louisiana Tech *HS:* Ruston [LA] B: 2/24/1952, Arcadia, LA
Drafted: 1975 Round 2 SD
1975 SD: 14 G. **1976** SD: 14 G. **1977** SD: 11 G; Int 1-22 **1** TD; 1 Fum TD; Tot TD 2; 12 Pt. **1978** SD: 15 G. **1979** SD: 13 G. **1980** SD: 14 G. **1981** SD-SF: 14 G. SD: 3 G. SF: 11 G. **1982** SF: 9 G; 3.5 Sac. **1983** SF: 16 G; 17.5 Sac. **1984** SF: 5 G; 4 Sac. **1985** SF: 16 G; 3 Sac. **Total:** 141 G; Int 1-22 1 TD; 1 Fum TD; Tot TD 2; 12 Pt; 28.0 Sac.

HAL DEAN Dean, Hal Stone 6′0″, 205 **G-LB**
Col: Ohio State *HS:* Wooster [OH] B: 10/30/1922, Wooster, OH
1947 LARm: 12 G. **1948** LARm: 11 G; Int 1-0. **1949** LARm: 12 G; KR 1-0. **Total:** 35 G; KR 1-0; Int 1-0.

JIMMY DEAN Dean, James Daniel Jr. 6′4″, 252 **DE**
Col: Texas A&M *HS:* Brazoswood [Freeport, TX] B: 1/8/1955, Bryan, TX *Drafted:* 1977 Round 4 Buf
1978 Hou: 3 G.

KEVIN DEAN Dean, Kevin James 6′1″, 235 **LB**
Col: Texas Christian *HS:* Newton [TX] B: 2/5/1965, Newton, TX
1987 SF: 4 G.

RANDY DEAN Dean, Randolph Hume 6′3″, 195 **QB**
Col: Northwestern *HS:* Whitefish Bay [WI] B: 6/10/1955, Milwaukee, WI *Drafted:* 1977 Round 5 NYG
1978 NYG: Rush 14-94 6.7. **1979** NYG: Rush 8-56 7.0 1 TD. **Total:** Rush 22-150 6.8 1 TD.

		Passing							
Year Team	**G**	**Att**	**Comp**	**Comp%**	**Yds**	**YPA**	**TD**	**Int**	**Rating**
1977 NYG	1	0	0	—	0	—	0	0	—
1978 NYG	6	39	19	48.7	188	4.82	1	3	39.3
1979 NYG	16	26	11	42.3	91	3.50	0	2	19.9
NFL Total	23	65	30	46.2	279	4.29	1	5	31.5

TED DEAN Dean, Theodore Curtis 6′2″, 213 **HB-FB**
Col: Wichita State *HS:* Radnor [PA] B: 3/24/1938, Radnor, PA
Drafted: 1960 Round 4 Phi

		Rushing				Receiving			
Year Team	**G**	**Att**	**Yds**	**Avg**	**TD**	**Rec**	**Yds**	**Avg**	**TD**
1960 Phi	12	113	304	2.7	0	15	218	14.5	3
1961 Phi	14	66	321	4.9	2	21	335	16.0	1
1962 Phi	2	0	0	—	0	0	0	—	0
1963 Phi	14	79	268	3.4	0	14	108	7.7	0
1964 Min	2	5	30	6.0	0	1	23	23.0	0
NFL Total	44	263	923	3.5	2	51	684	13.4	4

	Punt Returns				Kickoff Returns					Tot
Year Team	**Ret**	**Yds**	**Avg**	**TD**	**Ret**	**Yds**	**Avg**	**TD**	**Fum**	**TD**
1960 Phi	16	65	4.1	0	**26**	**533**	20.5	0	4	3
1961 Phi	18	140	7.8	0	21	462	22.0	0	6	3
1962 Phi	0	0	—	0	4	83	20.8	0	0	0
1963 Phi	10	74	7.4	0	16	425	26.6	0	4	0
1964 Min	2	0	0.0	0	3	50	16.7	0	0	0
NFL Total	46	279	6.1	0	70	1553	22.2	0	14	6

TOM DEAN Dean, Thomas Edwards 6′2″, 248 **T**
Col: Arkansas State; Southern Methodist B: 5/27/1923, Fostoria, TX
Drafted: 1945 Round 2 Bos
1946 Bos: 9 G. **1947** Bos: 12 G. **Total:** 21 G.

FLOYD DEAN Dean, Thomas Floyd 6′4″, 236 **LB**
Col: Florida *HS:* Eagle Lake [FL] B: 8/19/1940 *Drafted:* 1962 Round 4 SF
1964 SF: 6 G. **1965** SF: 9 G. **Total:** 15 G.

VERNON DEAN Dean, Vernon 5′11″, 178 **DB**
Col: Los Angeles Valley Coll. CA (J.C.); U.S. International; San Diego State *HS:* Los Angeles [CA] B: 5/5/1959, Los Angeles, CA
Drafted: 1982 Round 2 Was
1983 Was: 1 Fum TD. **1985** Was: PR 1-0. **Total:** PR 1-0; 1 Fum TD.

		Interceptions			Tot
Year Team	**G**	**Int**	**Yds**	**TD**	**TD**
1982 Was	9	3	62	0	0
1983 Was	16	5	54	0	1
1984 Was	16	7	114	**2**	2
1985 Was	16	5	8	0	0
1986 Was	16	1	5	0	0
1987 Was	12	0	0	0	0
1988 Sea	16	1	31	0	1
NFL Total	101	22	274	2	4

WALTER DEAN Dean, Walter Kevin 5′10″, 216 **RB**
Col: Grambling State *HS:* Grambling State U. Lab [LA] B: 6/1/1968, Ruston, LA *Drafted:* 1991 Round 6 GB
1991 GB: 9 G; KR 1-0; 1 Fum.

KIKI DEAYALA DeAyala, Julian Luis 6′1″, 225 **LB**
Col: Texas *HS:* Memorial [Houston, TX] B: 10/23/1961, Miami, FL
Drafted: 1983 Round 6 Cin
1986 Cin: 16 G; 1 Sac. **1987** Cin: 12 G. **Total:** 28 G; 1 Sac.

STEVE DEBERG DeBerg, Steven Leroy 6′3″, 210 **QB**
Col: Fullerton Coll. CA (J.C.); San Jose State *HS:* Savanna [Anaheim, CA] B: 1/19/1954, Oakland, CA *Drafted:* 1977 Round 10 Dal

		Passing							
Year Team	**G**	**Att**	**Comp**	**Comp%**	**Yds**	**YPA**	**TD**	**Int**	**Rating**
1978 SF	12	302	137	45.4	1570	5.20	8	22	40.0
1979 SF	16	**578**	**347**	60.0	3652	6.32	17	21	73.1
1980 SF	11	321	186	57.9	1998	6.22	12	17	66.7
1981 Den	14	108	64	59.3	797	7.38	6	6	77.6

1982 Den	9	223	131	58.7	1405	6.30	7	11	67.2
1983 Den	10	215	119	55.3	1617	7.52	9	7	79.9
1984 TB	16	509	308	60.5	3554	6.98	19	18	79.3
1985 TB	11	370	197	53.2	2488	6.72	19	18	71.3
1986 TB	16	96	50	52.1	610	6.35	5	12	49.7
1987 TB	12	275	159	57.8	1891	6.88	14	7	85.3
1988 KC	13	414	224	54.1	2935	7.09	16	16	73.5
1989 KC	12	324	196	60.5	2529	7.81	11	16	75.8
1990 KC	16	444	258	58.1	3444	7.76	23	**4**	96.3
1991 KC	16	434	256	59.0	2965	6.83	17	14	79.3
1992 TB	6	125	76	60.8	710	5.68	3	4	71.1
1993 TB-Mia	8	227	136	59.9	1707	7.52	7	10	75.3
1993 TB	3	39	23	59.0	186	4.77	1	3	47.6
1993 Mia	5	188	113	60.1	1521	8.09	6	7	81.0
1998 Atl	8	59	30	50.8	369	6.25	3	1	80.4
NFL Total	206	5024	2874	57.2	34241	6.82	196	204	74.2

	Rushing				
Year Team	Att	Yds	Avg	TD	Fum
1978 SF	15	20	1.3	1	9
1979 SF	17	10	0.6	0	6
1980 SF	6	4	0.7	0	4
1981 Den	9	40	4.4	0	2
1982 Den	8	27	3.4	1	4
1983 Den	13	28	2.2	1	5
1984 TB	28	59	2.1	2	15
1985 TB	9	28	3.1	0	3
1986 TB	2	1	0.5	1	2
1987 TB	8	-8	-1.0	0	7
1988 KC	18	30	1.7	1	1
1989 KC	14	-8	-0.6	0	4
1990 KC	21	-5	-0.2	0	9
1991 KC	21	-15	-0.7	0	6
1992 TB	3	3	1.0	0	2
1993 TB-Mia	4	-4	-1.0	0	2
1993 TB	0	0	—	0	1
1993 Mia	4	-4	-1.0	0	1
1998 Atl	8	-10	-1.3	0	2
NFL Total	204	200	1.0	7	83

FRED DEBERNARDI DeBernardi, Frank Frederick 6′5″, 250 **DE**
Col: Texas-El Paso *HS:* William S. Hart [Newhall, CA] B: 3/2/1949, Santa Clarita, CA *Drafted:* 1972 Round 11 Bal
1974 KC: 7 G.

CASE DEBRUIJN deBruijn, Case 6′0″, 176 **P**
Col: Idaho State *HS:* Stonewall Jackson [Manassas, VA] B: 4/11/1960, Denhaague, Netherlands *Drafted:* 1982 Round 8 KC
1982 KC: 1 G; Punt 5-174 34.8.

NICK DECARBO DeCarbo, Nicholas Fred 5′9″, 185 **G**
Col: Duquesne *HS:* New Castle [PA] B: 3/21/1910, New Castle, PA D: 8/21/1991, Mayfield Heights, OH
1933 Pit: 11 G.

ART DECARLO DeCarlo, Arthur Anthony Jr. 6′2″, 196 **DB-OE**
Col: Georgia *HS:* East [Youngstown, OH] B: 3/23/1931, Youngstown, OH *Drafted:* 1953 Round 6 ChiB
1953 Pit: 12 G; PR 1-1 1.0; Int 5-83; 1 Fum. **1956** Was: 12 G; Int 1-11. **1957** Was-Bal: 8 G; Int 1-14. Was: 2 G. Bal: 6 G; Int 1-14. **1958** Bal: 12 G; Rec 1-10 10.0; KR 1-0. **1959** Bal: 8 G. **1960** Bal: 9 G; Rec 8-116 14.5. **Total:** 61 G; Rec 9-126 14.0; PR 1-1 1.0; KR 1-0; Int 7-108; 1 Fum.

FRANK DECLERK DeClerk, Francis P 5′9″, 191 **C**
Col: St. Ambrose B: 1899, NE Deceased
1923 RI: 6 G. **1924** RI: 8 G. **1925** RI: 6 G. **Total:** 20 G.

BILL DECORREVONT deCorrevont, William John 6′0″, 186 **DB-HB-TB-WB**
Col: Northwestern *HS:* Austin [Chicago, IL] B: 11/26/1918, Chicago, IL D: 9/6/1995, St. Petersburg, FL *Drafted:* 1942 Round 12 Was
1945 Was: Rec 4-36 9.0; PR 3-45 15.0. **1946** Det: Pass 19-8 42.1%, 155 8.16 2 TD 2 Int; Rec 10-278 27.8 2 TD; PR 6-81 13.5; Punt 5-293 58.6. **1947** ChiC: Rec 4-52 13.0; PR 8-61 7.6. **1948** ChiB: Rec 2-7 3.5; PR 4-61 15.3. **1949** ChiB: Rec 1-44 44.0. **Total:** Pass 19-8 42.1%, 155 8.16 2 TD 2 Int; Rec 21-417 19.9 2 TD; PR 21-248 11.8; Punt 5-293 58.6.

		Rushing				Kickoff Returns			
Year Team	G	Att	Yds	Avg	TD	Ret	Yds	Avg	TD
1945 Was	10	22	91	4.1	0	11	210	19.1	0
1946 Det	9	8	-32	-4.0	0	10	183	18.3	0
1947 ChiC	12	29	149	5.1	1	7	102	14.6	0
1948 ChiB	10	16	25	1.6	0	6	160	26.7	0
1949 ChiB	8	0	0	—	0	0	0	—	0
NFL Total	49	75	233	3.1	1	34	655	19.3	0

	Interceptions				Tot
Year Team	Int	Yds	TD	Fum	TD
1945 Was	0	0	0	2	0
1946 Det	0	0	0	4	2
1947 ChiC	1	0	0	2	1
1948 ChiB	5	37	0	0	0
1949 ChiB	4	53	0	0	0
NFL Total	10	90	0	8	3

DONNIE DEE Dee, Donald Francis Jr. 6′4″, 247 **TE**
Col: Tulsa *HS:* Oak Park [Kansas City, MO] B: 3/17/1965, Kansas City, MO *Drafted:* 1988 Round 11 Ind
1988 Ind: 13 G. **1989** Ind-Sea: 4 G. Ind: 1 G. Sea: 3 G. **Total:** 17 G.

BOB DEE Dee, Robert Henry 6′3″, 248 **DE-DT**
(Bubba) *Col:* Holy Cross *HS:* Braintree [MA] B: 5/18/1933, Quincy, MA D: 4/18/1979, Portsmouth, NH *Drafted:* 1955 Round 19 Was
1957 Was: 11 G. **1958** Was: 11 G. **1960** Bos: 14 G; Int 1-14; 1 Fum. **1961** Bos: 14 G. **1962** Bos: 14 G; KR 1-14 14.0. **1963** Bos: 14 G. **1964** Bos: 14 G. **1965** Bos: 14 G. **1966** Bos: 14 G. **1967** Bos: 14 G. **Total:** 134 G; KR 1-14 14.0; Int 1-14; 1 Fum.

DON DEEKS Deeks, Donald Phillips 6′4″, 238 **T-G**
Col: Washington *HS:* U.S. Grant [Portland, OR] B: 2/10/1923, Portland, OR D: 9/4/1995, Bend, OR *Drafted:* 1945 Round 4 Bos
1945 Bos: 7 G. **1946** Bos: 8 G. **1947** Bos-Was: 6 G. Bos: 3 G. Was: 3 G. **1948** GB: 8 G. **Total:** 29 G.

DICK DEER SLAYER Deer Slayer, Dick 190 **E**
Col: No College Deceased
1922 Oor: 2 G.

BOB DEES Dees, Robert Leslie 6′4″, 245 **OT-DT**
Col: Southwest Missouri State *HS:* Southwest [St. Louis, MO] B: 9/26/1929, St. Louis, MO *Drafted:* 1952 Round 18 LARm
1952 GB: 9 G; KR 1-20 20.0.

DERRICK DEESE Deese, Derrick 6′3″, 285 **OG-OT**
Col: El Camino Coll. CA (J.C.); USC *HS:* Culver City [CA] B: 5/17/1970, Culver City, CA
1994 SF: 16 G. **1995** SF: 2 G. **1996** SF: 16 G; KR 2-20 10.0. **1997** SF: 16 G. **1998** SF: 16 G. **Total:** 66 G; KR 2-20 10.0.

NICK DEFELICE DeFelice, Nicholas Francis 6′3″, 250 **OT**
Col: Southern Connecticut State *HS:* Derby [CT] B: 2/4/1940, Derby, CT
1965 NYJ: 14 G; KR 1-0.

LOU DEFILIPPO DeFilippo, Louis Phillip 6′2″, 225 **G**
Col: Purdue; Fordham *HS:* James Hillhouse [New Haven, CT] B: 8/28/1916, East Haven, CT *Drafted:* 1941 Round 4 NYG
1941 NYG: 11 G. **1945** NYG: 10 G; 1 Fum. **1946** NYG: 11 G. **1947** NYG: 4 G. **Total:** 36 G; 1 Fum.

JOE DEFOREST DeForest, Joseph John 6′1″, 240 **LB**
Col: Southwestern Louisiana *HS:* Titusville [FL] B: 4/17/1965, Teaneck, NJ
1987 NO: 3 G; 1 Sac.

CHRIS DEFRANCE DeFrance, Christopher Anthony 6′1″, 205 **WR**
Col: Bakersfield Coll. CA (J.C.); Arizona State *HS:* Corcoran [CA] B: 9/13/1956, Walco, AR *Drafted:* 1979 Round 6 Dal
1979 Was: 4 G.

BOB DEFRUITER DeFruiter, Robert Albert 6′0″, 190 **DB-HB**
(Fruits) *Col:* Nebraska *HS:* Lexington [NE] B: 6/3/1918, Smithfield, NE
1945 Was: 3 G; Rush 7-36 5.1; Rec 1-19 19.0; 1 Fum. **1946** Was: 7 G; Rush 2-(-2) -1.0; Rec 1-9 9.0. **1947** Was-Det: 9 G; Rush 1-(-2) -2.0; Int 3-8. Was: 1 G. Det: 8 G; Rush 1-(-2) -2.0; Int 3-8. **1948** LARm: 3 G; Rush 3-4 1.3. **Total:** 22 G; Rush 13-36 2.8; Rec 2-28 14.0; Int 3-8; 1 Fum.

DICK DEGEN Degen, Richard G 6′1″, 220 **LB**
Col: Cerritos Coll. CA (J.C.); Long Beach State *HS:* Bellflower [CA] B: 3/4/1942, Jamestown, ND
1965 SD: 12 G; Int 2-6. **1966** SD: 10 G; Int 1-7. **Total:** 22 G; Int 3-13.

ALLEN DEGRAFFENREID DeGraffenreid, Allen 6′4″, 293 **OT**
Col: Vanderbilt *HS:* Dunwoody [GA] B: 6/3/1974, Kansas City, MO
1998 Ariz: 5 G.

ALLEN DEGRAFFENREID DeGraffenreid, Allen Justice 6′3″, 200 **WR**
Col: Ohio State *HS:* Princeton [Cincinatti, OH] B: 5/1/1970, Cincinnati, OH
1993 Cin: 2 G.

TONY DEGRATE Degrate, Tony 6′4″, 280 **NT**
Col: Texas *HS:* Snyder [TX] B: 4/25/1962, Snyder, TX *Drafted:* 1985 Round 5 Cin
1985 GB: 1 G.

CY DEGREE DeGree, Walter George 6′1″, 210 **G-T**
Col: Notre Dame *HS:* St.Cloud [MN] B: 7/7/1898, St.Cloud, MN D: 11/1961, Detroit, MI
1921 Det: 7 G; Scor 3, 1 FG.

JACK DEGRENIER DeGrenier, Jack Thomas 6′1″, 225 **RB**
Col: Northern Arizona; Texas-Arlington *HS:* Holy Cross [River Grove, IL] B: 2/25/1951, Chicago, IL
1974 NO: Rec 4-13 3.3.

		Rushing			
Year Team	G	Att	Yds	Avg	TD
1974 NO	12	33	110	3.3	0

ART DEIBEL Deibel, Arthur Francis 6′3″, 220 **T-G**
Col: Lafayette *HS:* Clinton [OH] B: 4/3/1896, Clinton, OH D: 4/1984
1926 Can: 7 G.

CHARLES DEJURNETT DeJurnett, Charles Ray 6′4″, 263 **DT**
Col: West Los Angeles Coll. CA (J.C.); San Jose State *HS:* Crenshaw [Los Angeles, CA] B: 6/17/1952, Picayune, MS *Drafted:* 1974 Round 17 SD
1976 SD: 13 G. **1977** SD: 11 G. **1978** SD: 15 G. **1979** SD: 12 G. **1980** SD: 15 G. **1982** LARm: 4 G. **1983** LARm: 10 G. **1984** LARm: 16 G; 3 Sac. **1985** LARm: 15 G; 1 Sac. **1986** LARm: 7 G. **Total:** 118 G; 4 Sac.

AL DEKDEBRUN Dekdebrun, Allen Edward 5′11″, 185 **TB-QB-DB**
(Dek) *Col:* Cornell *HS:* Burgard [Buffalo, NY]; Wyoming Seminary [Kingston, PA] B: 5/11/1921, Buffalo, NY *Drafted:* 1946 Round 9 Bos
AAFC **1946** BufA: KR 6-116 19.3; Int 3-19. **1948** NY-A: PR 1-12 12.0; KR 1-15 15.0; Int 1-16. **Total:** PR 1-12 12.0; KR 7-131 18.7; Int 4-35.

		Passing							
Year Team	G	Att	Comp	Comp%	Yds	YPA	TD	Int	Rating
1946 BufA	14	66	28	42.4	517	7.83	8	8	70.1
1947 ChiA	12	75	45	60.0	556	7.41	5	7	66.3
1948 NY-A	4	20	10	50.0	149	7.45	0	2	35.2
AAFC Total	30	161	83	51.6	1222	7.59	13	17	64.0

	Rushing			
Year Team	Att	Yds	Avg	TD
1946 BufA	25	-55	-2.2	0
1947 ChiA	20	71	3.6	0
1948 NY-A	7	24	3.4	0
AAFC Total	52	40	0.8	0

NFL **1948** Bos: 2 G; Pass 3-1 33.3%, 2 0.67 1 Int; Rush 2-14 7.0.

PAUL DEKKER Dekker, Paul Nelson 6′5″, 220 **OE**
Col: Michigan State *HS:* Muskegon [MI] B: 2/24/1931, Muskegon, MI *Drafted:* 1953 Round 3 Was
1953 Was: 11 G; Rec 14-182 13.0 1 TD; 6 Pt.

JOE DELAMIELLEURE DeLamielleure, Joseph Michael 6′3″, 254 **OG**
Col: Michigan State *HS:* St. Clement [Center Line, MI] B: 3/16/1951, Detroit, MI *Drafted:* 1973 Round 1 Buf
1973 Buf: 14 G. **1974** Buf: 14 G. **1975** Buf: 14 G. **1976** Buf: 14 G. **1977** Buf: 14 G. **1978** Buf: 16 G. **1979** Buf: 16 G. **1980** Cle: 16 G. **1981** Cle: 16 G. **1982** Cle: 9 G. **1983** Cle: 16 G. **1984** Cle: 16 G. **1985** Buf: 10 G. **Total:** 185 G.

JEFF DELANEY Delaney, Jeffrey John 6′0″, 195 **DB**
Col: Pittsburgh *HS:* Upper St. Clair [Pittsburgh, PA] B: 10/25/1956, Pittsburgh, PA *Drafted:* 1979 Round 7 LARm
1980 LARm: 16 G; Int 2-42. **1981** Det-TB: 7 G. Det: 5 G. TB: 2 G. **1982** Bal: 8 G; 1 Sac. **1983** Bal: 11 G; Int 2-16. **Total:** 42 G; Int 4-58; 1 Sac.

JOE DELANEY Delaney, Joe Alton 5′10″, 184 **RB**
Col: Northwestern State-Louisiana *HS:* Haughton [LA] B: 10/30/1958, Henderson, TX D: 6/29/1983, Monroe, LA *Drafted:* 1981 Round 2 KC
1981 KC: KR 1-11 11.0. **Total:** KR 1-11 11.0.

		Rushing				Receiving				
Year Team	G	Att	Yds	Avg	TD	Rec	Yds	Avg	TD	Fum
1981 KC	15	234	1121	4.8	3	22	246	11.2	0	9
1982 KC	8	95	380	4.0	0	11	53	4.8	0	0
NFL Total	23	329	1501	4.6	3	33	299	9.1	0	9

DARROLL DELAPORTE DeLaPorte, Darroll Austin **BB**
Col: No College *HS:* South Division [Milwaukee, WI]; St. John's Mil. Acad. [Delafield, WI] B: 10/30/1903, Brown Co., WI D: 12/25/1980, Bartow, FL
1925 Mil: 1 G.

BOB DELAUER deLauer, Robert 6′1″, 218 **C-LB**
Col: USC *HS:* Herbert Hoover [San Diego, CA] B: 8/30/1920, San Francisco, CA *Drafted:* 1942 Round 10 Cle
1945 Cle: 2 G. **1946** LARm: 11 G; Scor 0-2 FG. **Total:** 13 G; Scor 0-2 FG.

JACK DEL BELLO Del Bello, Ameleto Vincent 6′1″, 190 **QB**
Col: Miami (Fla.) *HS:* South Philadelphia [Philadelphia, PA] B: 12/9/1927, Philadelphia, PA
1953 Bal: Rush 14-14 1.0.

		Passing								
Year Team	G	Att	Comp	Comp%	Yds	YPA	TD	Int	Rating	Fum
1953 Bal	5	61	27	44.3	229	3.75	1	5	25.9	2

TOM DELEONE DeLeone, Thomas Denning 6′2″, 248 **C**
Col: Ohio State *HS:* Theodore Roosevelt [Kent, OH] B: 8/13/1950, Ravenna, OH *Drafted:* 1972 Round 5 Cin
1972 Cin: 13 G. **1973** Cin: 14 G. **1974** Cle: 12 G. **1975** Cle: 14 G. **1976** Cle: 14 G. **1977** Cle: 14 G. **1978** Cle: 15 G. **1979** Cle: 16 G. **1980** Cle: 16 G. **1981** Cle: 8 G. **1982** Cle: 9 G. **1983** Cle: 16 G; 1 Fum. **1984** Cle: 15 G. **Total:** 176 G; 1 Fum.

BURT DELEVAN Delevan, Darrel Burton 6′2″, 236 **OT**
Col: Menlo Coll. CA (J.C.); U. of Pacific *HS:* Sacramento [CA] B: 12/2/1929, Westwood, CA *Drafted:* 1952 Round 7 LARm
1955 ChiC: 12 G; KR 2-0; 1 Fum. **1956** ChiC: 2 G. **Total:** 14 G; KR 2-0; 1 Fum.

JIM DEL GAIZO Del Gaizo, James Robert 6′1″, 198 **QB**
Col: Tampa; Syracuse *HS:* Revere [MA] B: 5/31/1947, Everett, MA
1972 Mia: Rush 1-0. **1973** GB: Rush 4-1 0.3. **1974** NYG: Rush 3-15 5.0. **Total:** Rush 8-16 2.0.

		Passing								
Year Team	G	Att	Comp	Comp%	Yds	YPA	TD	Int	Rating	Fum
1972 Mia	4	9	5	55.6	165	18.33	2	1	100.5	1
1973 GB	8	62	27	43.5	318	5.13	2	6	30.9	3
1974 NYG	4	32	12	37.5	165	5.16	0	3	15.8	0
NFL Total	16	103	44	42.7	648	6.29	4	10	37.3	4

AL DEL GRECO Del Greco, Albert Louis Jr. 5′10″, 196 **K**
Col: Auburn *HS:* Coral Gables [FL] B: 3/2/1962, Providence, RI
1988 Pho: Rush 1-8 8.0. **1995** Hou: Punt 1-15 15.0. **1997** Ten: Punt 1-32 32.0. **Total:** Rush 1-8 8.0; Punt 2-47 23.5.

		Scoring						
Year Team	G	Pts	FG	FGA	FG%	XK	XKA	XK%
1984 GB	9	61	9	12	75.0	34	34	100.0
1985 GB	16	95	19	26	73.1	38	40	95.0
1986 GB	16	80	17	27	63.0	29	29	100.0
1987 GB-StL	8	46	9	15	60.0	19	20	95.0
1987 GB	5	26	5	10	50.0	11	11	100.0
1987 StL	3	20	4	5	80.0	8	9	88.9
1988 Pho	16	78	12	21	57.1	42	44	95.5
1989 Pho	16	82	18	26	69.2	28	29	96.6
1990 Pho	16	82	17	27	63.0	31	31	100.0
1991 Hou	7	46	10	13	76.9	16	16	100.0
1992 Hou	16	104	21	27	77.8	41	41	100.0
1993 Hou	16	126	29	34	85.3	39	40	97.5
1994 Hou	16	66	16	20	80.0	18	18	100.0
1995 Hou	16	114	27	31	87.1	33	33	100.0
1996 Hou	16	131	32	38	84.2	35	35	100.0
1997 Ten	16	113	27	35	77.1	32	32	100.0
1998 Ten	16	136	**36**	39	92.3	28	28	100.0
NFL Total	216	1360	299	391	76.5	463	470	98.5

STEVE DELINE DeLine, Steven Braun 5′11″, 185 **K**
Col: Colorado State *HS:* Cherry Creek [Englewood, CO]; J.K. Mullen HS [Denver, CO] B: 8/19/1961, Denver, CO *Drafted:* 1987 Round 7 SF
1988 SD: 5 G; Scor 30, 6-8 75.0% FG, 12-12 100.0% XK. **1989** Phi: 3 G; Scor 12, 3-7 42.9% FG, 3-3 100.0% XK. **Total:** 8 G; Scor 42, 9-15 60.0% FG, 15-15 100.0% XK.

JIM DELISLE DeLisle, James Roger 6′4″, 255 **DT**
Col: Wisconsin *HS:* Newman [Wausau, WI] B: 1/20/1949, Wausau, WI
1971 GB: 9 G.

JEFF DELLENBACH Dellenbach, Jeffrey Alan 6′6″, 290 **OT-OG-C**
Col: Wisconsin *HS:* East [Wausau, WI] B: 2/14/1963, Wausau, WI *Drafted:* 1985 Round 4 Mia
1985 Mia: 11 G. **1986** Mia: 13 G. **1987** Mia: 11 G; 1 Fum. **1988** Mia: 16 G; 1 Fum. **1989** Mia: 16 G. **1990** Mia: 15 G. **1991** Mia: 15 G; KR 1-0. **1992** Mia: 16 G. **1993** Mia: 16 G; 1 Fum. **1994** Mia: 16 G; 1 Fum. **1995** NE: 15 G. **1996** NE-GB: 5 G. NE: 2 G. GB: 3 G. **1997** GB: 14 G. **1998** GB: 16 G. **Total:** 195 G; KR 1-0; 4 Fum.

SPIRO DELLERBA Dellerba, Spiro 5′11″, 200 **LB-FB**
Col: Ohio State *HS:* Ashtabula [OH] B: 1/25/1923, Ashtabula, OH D: 8/1968
AAFC **1947** CleA: Rec 1-14 14.0; KR 1-34 34.0. **1948** BalA: KR 1-12 12.0; Int 2-18. **Total:** Rec 1-14 14.0; KR 2-46 23.0; Int 2-18.

		Rushing			
Year Team	G	Att	Yds	Avg	TD
1947 CleA	8	29	176	6.1	0
1948 BalA	14	2	0	0.0	0
1949 BalA	9	0	0	—	0
AAFC Total	31	31	176	5.7	0

LARRY DELLINGER Dellinger, Lawrence 5′11″, 204 **G-T**
Col: No College *HS:* Osborn [OH]; U. of Dayton Prep [OH] B: 1893 Deceased
1920 Day: 6 G. **1921** Day: 7 G. **1922** Day: 3 G. **1923** Day: 7 G. **Total:** 23 G.

JOHNNY DELL ISOLA Dell Isola, John Joseph 5′11″, 201 **G-LB-C**
Col: Fordham *HS:* Everett [MA] B: 2/12/1912, Everett, MA
D: 10/21/1986, Arlington, MA
1934 NYG: 6 G. **1935** NYG: 9 G. **1936** NYG: 10 G. **1937** NYG: 9 G. **1938** NYG: 11 G. **1939** NYG: 11 G. **1940** NYG: 10 G; Int 1-16. **Total:** 66 G; Int 1-16.

RALPH DELOACH DeLoach, Ralph Alan 6′5″, 255 **DE**
Col: California *HS:* Sacramento [CA] B: 1/13/1957, Sacramento, CA
Drafted: 1979 Round 4 Dal
1981 NYJ: 1 G.

GREG DELONG DeLong, Gregory Andrew 6′4″, 250 **TE**
Col: North Carolina *HS:* Parkland [Orefield, PA] B: 4/3/1973, Orefield, PA
1996 Min: KR 1-3 3.0. **Total:** KR 1-3 3.0.

		Receiving				
Year Team	**G**	**Rec**	**Yds**	**Avg**	**TD**	**Fum**
1995 Min	2	6	38	6.3	0	0
1996 Min	16	8	34	4.3	0	0
1997 Min	16	8	75	9.4	0	1
1998 Min	15	8	58	7.3	0	0
NFL Total	49	30	205	6.8	0	1

KEITH DELONG DeLong, Keith Allen 6′2″, 245 **LB**
Col: Tennessee *HS:* Lawrence [KS] B: 8/14/1967, San Diego, CA
Drafted: 1989 Round 1 SF
1989 SF: 15 G; Int 1-1. **1990** SF: 16 G. **1991** SF: 15 G; 1 Sac. **1992** SF: 14 G; Int 1-2. **1993** SF: 4 G. **Total:** 64 G; Int 2-3; 1 Sac.

STEVE DELONG DeLong, Steven Cyril 6′2″, 252 **DE-DT**
Col: Tennessee *HS:* Oscar F. Smith [Chesapeake, VA] B: 7/3/1943, Norfolk, VA *Drafted:* 1965 Round 1 SD
1965 SD: 12 G. **1966** SD: 14 G. **1967** SD: 7 G. **1968** SD: 14 G. **1969** SD: 14 G. **1970** SD: 14 G; Int 1-5. **1971** SD: 14 G. **1972** ChiB: 14 G. **Total:** 103 G; Int 1-5.

JACK DELOPLAINE Deloplaine, Jack A 5′10″, 205 **RB**
Col: Salem *HS:* Pottstown [PA] B: 4/21/1954, Pottstown, PA
Drafted: 1976 Round 6 Pit
1976 Pit: Rec 1-3 3.0; PR 17-150 8.8; KR 17-385 22.6. **1977** Pit: PR 1-7 7.0; KR 1-18 18.0. **1978** Was-Pit: KR 1-19 19.0. Pit: KR 1-19 19.0. **1979** ChiB-Pit: Rec 2-13 6.5. ChiB: Rec 2-13 6.5. **Total:** Rec 3-16 5.3; PR 18-157 8.7; KR 19-422 22.2.

		Rushing				
Year Team	**G**	**Att**	**Yds**	**Avg**	**TD**	**Fum**
1976 Pit	14	17	91	5.4	2	3
1977 Pit	8	2	7	3.5	0	0
1978 Was-Pit	12	11	49	4.5	0	0
1978 Was	2	0	0	—	0	0
1978 Pit	10	11	49	4.5	0	0
1979 ChiB-Pit	6	7	18	2.6	0	0
1979 ChiB	5	7	18	2.6	0	0
1979 Pit	1	0	0	—	0	0
NFL Total	40	37	165	4.5	2	3

ROBERT DELPINO Delpino, Robert Lewis 6′0″, 205 **RB**
Col: Dodge City CC KS; Missouri *HS:* Dodge City [KS] B: 11/2/1965, Dodge City, KS *Drafted:* 1988 Round 5 LARm

		Rushing				Receiving			
Year Team	**G**	**Att**	**Yds**	**Avg**	**TD**	**Rec**	**Yds**	**Avg**	**TD**
1988 LARm	15	34	147	4.3	0	30	312	10.4	2
1989 LARm	16	78	368	4.7	1	34	334	9.8	1
1990 LARm	15	13	52	4.0	0	15	172	11.5	4
1991 LARm	16	214	688	3.2	9	55	617	11.2	1
1992 LARm	10	32	115	3.6	0	18	139	7.7	1
1993 Den	16	131	445	3.4	8	26	195	7.5	0
NFL Total	88	502	1815	3.6	18	178	1769	9.9	9

	Kickoff Returns					Tot
Year Team	**Ret**	**Yds**	**Avg**	**TD**	**Fum**	**TD**
1988 LARm	14	333	23.8	0	2	2
1989 LARm	17	334	19.6	0	1	2
1990 LARm	20	389	19.5	0	1	4
1991 LARm	4	54	13.5	0	3	10
1992 LARm	6	83	13.8	0	2	1
1993 Den	7	146	20.9	0	1	8
NFL Total	68	1339	19.7	0	10	27

JACK DEL RIO Del Rio, Jack L Jr. 6′4″, 246 **LB**
Col: USC *HS:* Hayward [CA] B: 4/4/1963, Castro Valley, CA
Drafted: 1985 Round 3 NO
1985 NO: **1** Fum TD. **1986** NO: Rush 1-16 16.0. **1987** KC: 3 Sac. **1988** KC: 1 Sac. **1989** Dal: 1 Fum TD. **1990** Dal: 1.5 Sac. **1992** Min: 2 Sac. **1993** Min: KR 1-4 4.0; 0.5 Sac. **1994** Min: 2 Sac. **1995** Min: 3 Sac. **Total:** Rush 1-16 16.0; KR 1-4 4.0; 2 Fum TD; 13 Sac.

		Interceptions			Tot
Year Team	**G**	**Int**	**Yds**	**TD**	**TD**
1985 NO	16	2	13	0	1
1986 NO	16	0	0	0	0
1987 KC	10	0	0	0	0
1988 KC	15	1	0	0	0
1989 Dal	14	0	0	0	1
1990 Dal	16	0	0	0	0
1991 Dal	16	0	0	0	0
1992 Min	16	2	92	1	1
1993 Min	16	4	3	0	0
1994 Min	16	3	5	0	0
1995 Min	9	1	15	0	0
NFL Total	160	13	128	1	3

TONY DELUCA DeLuca, Anthony Lawrence 6′4″, 250 **NT**
Col: Rhode Island *HS:* Greenwich [CT]; Milford Acad. [CT]
B: 11/16/1960, Greenwich, CT
1984 GB: 1 G.

SAM DELUCA DeLuca, Samuel Frank 6′2″, 250 **OG-OT**
Col: South Carolina *HS:* Lafayette [Brooklyn, NY] B: 5/2/1936, Brooklyn, NY *Drafted:* 1957 Round 2 NYG
1960 LAC: 14 G; KR 1-0. **1961** SD: 14 G. **1963** SD: 14 G. **1964** NYJ: 11 G. **1965** NYJ: 14 G. **1966** NYJ: 14 G. **Total:** 81 G; KR 1-0.

JERRY DELUCCA DeLucca, Gerald Joseph 6′2″, 247 **OT-DT**
Col: Tennessee; Middle Tennessee State *HS:* Peabody [MA]
B: 7/17/1936, Peabody, MA *Drafted:* 1957 Round 7 ChiB
1959 Phi: 12 G; KR 1-0. **1960** Bos: 12 G; KR 1-8 8.0. **1961** Bos: 14 G. **1962** Buf: 14 G; KR 1-0. **1963** Buf-Bos: 5 G. Buf: 2 G. Bos: 3 G. **1964** Bos: 2 G. **Total:** 59 G; KR 3-8 2.7.

AL DEMAO DeMao, Albert Marcellus 6′2″, 214 **C-LB**
Col: Duquesne *HS:* Arnold [PA] B: 2/29/1920, New Kensington, PA
Drafted: 1942 Round 9 Was
1945 Was: 5 G; Int 1-44. **1946** Was: 11 G; Int 2-18. **1947** Was: 12 G; Int 2-35. **1948** Was: 9 G; Int 1-22; 1 Fum. **1949** Was: 12 G; Int 1-3. **1950** Was: 12 G; Rec 1-4 4.0. **1951** Was: 12 G; Int 1-0. **1952** Was: 12 G. **1953** Was: 12 G. **Total:** 97 G; Rec 1-4 4.0; Int 8-122; 1 Fum.

BRIAN DEMARCO DeMarco, Brian Thomas 6′7″, 323 **OT-OG**
Col: Michigan State *HS:* Admiral King [Lorain, OH] B: 4/9/1972, Berea, OH *Drafted:* 1995 Round 2 Jac
1995 Jac: 16 G. **1996** Jac: 10 G. **1997** Jac: 14 G. **1998** Jac: 16 G. **Total:** 56 G.

MARIO DEMARCO DeMarco, Mario 5′11″, 200 **G-LB**
Col: Miami (Fla.) *HS:* Boonton [NJ] B: 7/24/1924, Boonton, NJ
D: 9/1967
1949 Det: 12 G.

BOB DEMARCO DeMarco, Robert Albert 6′2″, 248 **C-OG**
(Dee) *Col:* Indiana; Dayton *HS:* St. Mary's [Rutherford, NJ]
B: 9/16/1938, Jersey City, NJ *Drafted:* 1960 Round 14 StL
1961 StL: 4 G. **1962** StL: 14 G. **1963** StL: 14 G. **1964** StL: 12 G. **1965** StL: 14 G. **1966** StL: 9 G. **1967** StL: 14 G. **1968** StL: 14 G. **1969** StL: 12 G. **1970** Mia: 11 G. **1971** Mia: 14 G. **1972** Cle: 12 G. **1973** Cle: 13 G; 1 Fum. **1974** Cle: 14 G. **1975** LARm: 14 G; 2 Fum. **Total:** 185 G; 3 Fum.

JOHN DEMARIE Demarie, John E 6′3″, 246 **OG-OT-C**
Col: Louisiana State *HS:* La Grange [Lake Charles, LA] B: 8/28/1945, Lake Charles, LA *Drafted:* 1967 Round 6 Cle
1967 Cle: 14 G. **1968** Cle: 14 G. **1969** Cle: 14 G. **1970** Cle: 14 G. **1971** Cle: 14 G. **1972** Cle: 14 G. **1973** Cle: 14 G. **1974** Cle: 11 G. **1975** Cle: 14 G; 1 Fum. **1976** Sea: 9 G. **Total:** 132 G; 1 Fum.

GEORGE DEMAS Demas, George James 6′0″, 194 **G**
Col: Washington & Jefferson *HS:* Allegheny Prep [Pittsburgh, PA]; Kiski School [Saltsburg, PA] B: 1/7/1907, Johnstown, PA D: 11/1977, Miami, FL
1932 SI: 4 G. **1934** Bkn: 1 G. **Total:** 5 G.

CALVIN DEMERY Demery, Calvin Louis 6′1″, 190 **WR**
Col: Arizona State *HS:* South Mountain [Phoenix, AZ] B: 8/17/1950, Phoenix, AZ *Drafted:* 1972 Round 8 Min
1972 Min: 5 G.

GEORGE DEMKO Demko, George 6′3″, 240 **DE**
Col: Appalachian State B: 8/10/1935
1961 Pit: 1 G.

JOHN DEMMY Demmy, John 190 **T**
(AKA John Demyanovich) *Col:* No College *HS:* Bayonne [NJ]
B: 3/5/1904, Bayonne, NJ D: 3/1970, Bay Head, NJ
1930 SI: 6 G. **1931** SI: 3 G. **Total:** 9 G.

BILL DEMORY Demory, John William 6′2″, 195 **QB**
Col: Arizona *HS:* Cortez [Phoenix, AZ] B: 12/1/1950, Indianola, IA
1973 NYJ: 6 G; Pass 39-12 30.8%, 159 4.08 2 TD 8 Int; Rush 4-(-1) -0.3; 2 Fum. **1974** NYJ: 1 G. **Total:** 7 G; Pass 39-12 30.8%, 159 4.08 2 TD 8 Int; Rush 4-(-1) -0.3; 2 Fum.

BOB DEMOSS DeMoss, Robert Alonzo 6′2″, 175 **QB**
(De Mo) *Col:* Purdue *HS:* Dayton [KY] B: 1/27/1927, Dayton, KY
Drafted: 1949 Round 2 NYB
1949 NYB: 3 G; Pass 18-6 33.3%, 60 3.33 2 Int; Rush 5-1 0.2; 1 Fum.

FRANK DEMPSEY Dempsey, James Franklin 6′3″, 235 **OG-LB-OT**
Col: Florida *HS:* Miami Senior [FL] B: 5/27/1925, Dothan, AL
Drafted: 1950 Round 13 ChiB
1950 ChiB: 6 G. **1951** ChiB: 12 G. **1952** ChiB: 10 G; Int 1-13. **1953** ChiB: 11 G; PR 1-5 5.0. **Total:** 39 G; PR 1-5 5.0; Int 1-13.

JACK DEMPSEY Dempsey, John Bernard 6′2″, 225 **T**
Col: Bucknell *HS:* Ridley Park [PA] B: 3/12/1912, Scranton, PA
D: 8/26/1988, Saratoga, CA
1934 Phi-Pit: 2 G. Phi: 1 G. Pit: 1 G. **1937** Phi: 2 G. **Total:** 4 G.

TOM DEMPSEY Dempsey, Thomas John 6′2″, 255 **K**
Col: Palomar Coll. CA (J.C.) *HS:* San Dieguito [Encinitas, CA]
B: 1/12/1941, Milwaukee, WI

		Scoring						
Year Team	**G**	**Pts**	**FG**	**FGA**	**FG%**	**XK**	**XKA**	**XK%**
1969 NO	14	99	22	**41**	53.7	33	35	94.3
1970 NO	14	70	18	34	52.9	16	17	94.1
1971 Phi	5	49	12	17	**70.6**	13	14	**92.9**
1972 Phi	14	71	20	35	57.1	11	12	91.7
1973 Phi	14	106	24	40	60.0	34	34	100.0
1974 Phi	14	56	10	16	62.5	26	30	86.7
1975 LARm	14	94	21	26	80.8	31	36	86.1
1976 LARm	14	87	17	26	65.4	36	44	81.8
1977 Hou	5	20	4	6	66.7	8	11	72.7
1978 Buf	16	66	10	13	76.9	36	38	94.7
1979 Buf	3	11	1	4	25.0	8	11	72.7
NFL Total	127	729	159	258	61.6	252	282	89.4

FRED DENFELD Denfeld, Frederick 6′0″, 198 **G-T**
Col: Navy *HS:* Central [Duluth, MN] B: 10/26/1898, Duluth, MN
D: 1/18/1990, St. Paul, MN
1920 RI: 5 G. **1925** Dul: 3 G. **Total:** 8 G.

VERN DEN HERDER Den Herder, Vern Wayne 6′6″, 250 **DE-NT**
Col: Central Coll. (Iowa) *HS:* Sioux Center [IA] B: 11/28/1948, Le Mars, IA *Drafted:* 1971 Round 9 Mia
1971 Mia: 14 G. **1972** Mia: 14 G; Int 1-24. **1973** Mia: 14 G. **1974** Mia: 14 G. **1975** Mia: 14 G. **1976** Mia: 14 G. **1977** Mia: 11 G. **1978** Mia: 16 G; Rec 1-7 7.0 1 TD; 6 Pt. **1979** Mia: 16 G. **1980** Mia: 16 G. **1981** Mia: 16 G. **1982** Mia: 7 G. **Total:** 166 G; Rec 1-7 7.0 1 TD; Int 1-24; 6 Pt.

MARK DENNARD Dennard, Mark Wesley 6′1″, 253 **C**
Col: Texas A&M *HS:* Bay City [TX] B: 11/2/1955, Bay City, TX
Drafted: 1978 Round 10 Mia
1979 Mia: 16 G. **1980** Mia: 16 G. **1981** Mia: 11 G. **1982** Mia: 8 G. **1983** Mia: 8 G. **1984** Phi: 16 G. **1985** Phi: 16 G; 1 Fum. **Total:** 91 G; 1 Fum.

PRESTON DENNARD Dennard, Preston Jackson 6′1″, 185 **WR**
Col: New Mexico *HS:* South Mountain [Phoenix, AZ]; Marcos de Niza HS [Tempe, AZ] B: 11/28/1955, Cordele, GA
1979 LARm: Rush 4-32 8.0. **1980** LARm: Rush 2-20 10.0. **1981** LARm: Rush 6-29 4.8. **Total:** Rush 12-81 6.8.

		Receiving				
Year Team	**G**	**Rec**	**Yds**	**Avg**	**TD**	**Fum**
1978 LARm	11	3	35	11.7	0	0
1979 LARm	15	43	766	17.8	4	1
1980 LARm	16	36	596	16.6	6	0
1981 LARm	15	49	821	16.8	4	1
1982 LARm	9	25	383	15.3	2	0
1983 LARm	14	33	465	14.1	5	0
1984 Buf	16	30	417	13.9	7	1
1985 GB	16	13	182	14.0	2	1
NFL Total	112	232	3665	15.8	30	4

JERRY DENNERLEIN Dennerlein, Gerald 6′2″, 240 **T**
Col: St. Mary's (Cal.) *HS:* James A. Garfield [Los Angeles, CA]
B: 12/1/1915, Ambridge, PA *Drafted:* 1937 Round 3 NYG
1937 NYG: 11 G. **1940** NYG: 11 G. **Total:** 22 G.

MIKE DENNERY Dennery, Michael Kevin 6′0″, 222 **LB**
Col: Southern Mississippi *HS:* Cardinal Dougherty [Philadelphia, PA]
B: 6/26/1950, Philadelphia, PA *Drafted:* 1974 Round 13 Oak
1974 Oak: 14 G. **1975** Oak: 14 G; Scor **1** Saf; 2 Pt. **1976** Mia: 3 G. **Total:** 31 G; Scor 1 Saf; 2 Pt.

VINCE DENNERY Dennery, Vincent Paul 5′11″, 190 **OE-DE**
Col: Fordham *HS:* William L. Dickinson [Jersey City, NJ]
B: 11/17/1916, Jersey City, NJ D: 8/9/1989, Philadelphia, PA
1941 NYG: 9 G; Rec 1-65 65.0 1 TD; 6 Pt.

AUSTIN DENNEY Denney, Austin Cheek Jr. 6′2″, 230 **TE**
Col: Tennessee *HS:* Donelson Christian Acad. [Nashville, TN]
B: 1/2/1944, Nashville, TN *Drafted:* 1966 Round 11 Dal
1968 ChiB: Rush 1-(-1) -1.0. **1969** ChiB: Rush 1-4 4.0. **Total:** Rush 2-3 1.5.

		Receiving			
Year Team	**G**	**Rec**	**Yds**	**Avg**	**TD**
1967 ChiB	7	12	113	9.4	0
1968 ChiB	14	23	247	10.7	2
1969 ChiB	14	22	203	9.2	1
1970 Buf	14	14	201	14.4	0
1971 Buf	1	0	0	—	0
NFL Total	50	71	764	10.8	3

AL DENNIS Dennis, Albert Rudolph III 6′4″, 250 **OG**
Col: Grambling State *HS:* Greenville Park [Hammond, LA]
B: 6/24/1951, Independence, LA
1973 SD: 7 G. **1976** Cle: 10 G. **1977** Cle: 14 G. **Total:** 31 G.

GUY DENNIS Dennis, Guy Dorell 6′2″, 255 **OG-C**
Col: Florida *HS:* Ernest Ward [Walnut Hill, FL] B: 2/28/1947, Walnut Hill, FL *Drafted:* 1969 Round 5 Cin
1969 Cin: 14 G. **1970** Cin: 14 G. **1971** Cin: 14 G. **1972** Cin: 13 G; KR 1-11 11.0. **1973** Det: 10 G; KR 1-0; 1 Fum. **1974** Det: 12 G; KR 1-18 18.0. **1975** Det: 12 G; KR 1-0. **Total:** 89 G; KR 4-29 7.3; 1 Fum.

MARK DENNIS Dennis, Mark Francis 6′6″, 292 **OT**
Col: Illinois *HS:* Washington [IL] B: 4/15/1965, Junction City, KS
Drafted: 1987 Round 8 Mia
1987 Mia: 5 G. **1988** Mia: 13 G. **1989** Mia: 8 G. **1990** Mia: 16 G. **1991** Mia: 16 G. **1992** Mia: 16 G. **1993** Mia: 16 G. **1994** Cin: 7 G. **1995** Car: 12 G; Rec 1-3 3.0. **1996** Car: 16 G. **Total:** 125 G; Rec 1-3 3.0.

MIKE DENNIS Dennis, Michael Dwayne 5′10″, 190 **DB**
Col: Pasadena City Coll. CA (J.C.); Wyoming *HS:* John Muir [Pasadena, CA] B: 6/6/1958, Los Angeles, CA
1980 NYG: 13 G; Int 5-68. **1981** NYG: 16 G; KR 3-51 17.0; 6 Pt.
1982 NYG: 9 G; KR 3-68 22.7. **1983** NYG: 16 G; KR 1-54 54.0; Int 1-0.
1984 SD-NYJ: 6 G. SD: 2 G. NYJ: 4 G. **Total:** 60 G; KR 7-173 24.7; Int 6-68; 6 Pt.

MIKE DENNIS Dennis, Walter Michael 6′1″, 207 **RB**
Col: Mississippi *HS:* William B. Murrah [Jackson, MS] B: 7/22/1944, Philadelphia, MS *Drafted:* 1966 Round 3 Atl
1968 LARm: Pass 2-0; Rec 8-53 6.6; KR 2-2 1.0. **Total:** Pass 2-0; Rec 8-53 6.6; KR 2-2 1.0.

		Rushing			
Year Team	**G**	**Att**	**Yds**	**Avg**	**TD**
1968 LARm	14	29	136	4.7	0
1969 LARm	1	0	0	—	0
NFL Total	15	29	136	4.7	0

GLENN DENNISON Dennison, Glenn 6′3″, 225 **TE**
Col: Miami (Fla.) *HS:* Beaver Falls [PA] B: 11/17/1961, Beaver Falls, PA
Drafted: 1984 Round 2 NYJ
1984 NYJ: 16 G; Rush 1-4 4.0; Rec 16-141 8.8 1 TD; 6 Pt. **1987** Was: 2 G; Rec 2-8 4.0. **Total:** 18 G; Rush 1-4 4.0; Rec 18-149 8.3 1 TD; 6 Pt.

RICK DENNISON Dennison, Rick Steven 6′3″, 220 **LB**
Col: Colorado State *HS:* Rocky Mountain [Fort Collins, CO]
B: 6/22/1958, Kalispell, MT
1982 Den: 9 G. **1983** Den: 16 G. **1984** Den: 16 G; KR 2-27 13.5; 3 Sac.
1985 Den: 15 G. **1986** Den: 16 G; Int 1-5; 1 Sac. **1987** Den: 12 G; Int 1-10.
1988 Den: 16 G; Int 1-29; 0.5 Sac. **1989** Den: 15 G; Int 1-1; 1 Sac.
1990 Den: 13 G; 1 Sac. **Total:** 128 G; KR 2-27 13.5; Int 4-45; 6.5 Sac.

DOUG DENNISON Dennison, William Douglas 6′1″, 202 **RB**
Col: Kutztown *HS:* Lancaster [PA] B: 12/18/1951, Lancaster, PA
1974 Dal: Rec 2-23 11.5; KR 3-54 18.0. **1975** Dal: Rec 2-5 2.5; KR 13-262 20.2. **1976** Dal: Rec 8-67 8.4. **1977** Dal: Rec 1-9 9.0; KR 1-30 30.0. **1978** Dal: Rec 1-6 6.0; KR 3-63 21.0. **Total:** Rec 14-110 7.9; KR 20-409 20.5.

		Rushing				
Year Team	**G**	**Att**	**Yds**	**Avg**	**TD**	**Fum**
1974 Dal	12	16	52	3.3	4	1
1975 Dal	13	111	383	3.5	7	1
1976 Dal	14	153	542	3.5	6	3
1977 Dal	8	12	60	5.0	1	0
1978 Dal	5	14	75	5.4	1	0
NFL Total	52	306	1112	3.6	19	5

EARL DENNY Denny, Earl Livingston 6′1″, 205 **RB**
Col: Missouri *HS:* Golden City [MO] B: 7/21/1945, El Paso, TX
Drafted: 1967 Round 3 Min
1967 Min: 13 G; KR 1-18 18.0. **1968** Min: 14 G; Rush 2-9 4.5; KR 3-19 6.3; 1 Fum. **Total:** 27 G; Rush 2-9 4.5; KR 4-37 9.3; 1 Fum.

AL DENSON Denson, Alfred Freddie 6′2″, 208 **WR**
Col: Florida A&M *HS:* New Stanton [Jacksonville, FL] B: 1/2/1942, Jacksonville, FL *Drafted:* 1964 Round 6 Den
1964 Den: Scor 1 2XP. **1965** Den: Rush 1-(-4) -4.0. **1967** Den: Rush 1-(-2) -2.0. **1969** Den: Rush 1-9 9.0. **1971** Min: Rush 1-0. **Total:** Rush 4-3 0.8; Scor 1 2XP.

		Receiving				
Year Team	G	Rec	Yds	Avg	TD	Fum
1964 Den	14	25	383	15.3	1	2
1965 Den	14	9	102	11.3	0	0
1966 Den	14	36	725	20.1	3	0
1967 Den	14	46	899	19.5	**11**	0
1968 Den	8	34	586	17.2	5	0
1969 Den	13	53	809	15.3	10	0
1970 Den	14	47	646	13.7	2	0
1971 Min	7	10	125	12.5	0	0
NFL Total	98	260	4275	16.4	32	2

DAMON DENSON Denson, Damon Michael 6′4″, 305 **OG**
Col: Michigan *HS:* Baldwin [Pittsburgh, PA] B: 2/8/1975, Pittsburgh, PA *Drafted:* 1997 Round 4 NE
1997 NE: 1 G. **1998** NE: 11 G. **Total:** 12 G.

KEITH DENSON Denson, Keith Armando 5′8″, 165 **WR**
Col: Rancho Santiago Coll. CA (J.C.); San Diego State *HS:* Valley [Santa Ana, CA] B: 8/30/1952, Camp Lejeune, NC
1976 NYJ: 2 G; KR 6-129 21.5; 2 Fum.

MOSES DENSON Denson, Moses 6′1″, 215 **RB**
Col: Maryland East. Shore *HS:* South [Akron, OH] B: 7/6/1944, Vredenburgh, AL *Drafted:* 1972 Round 8 Was
1974 Was: KR 2-49 24.5. **Total:** KR 2-49 24.5.

		Rushing				Receiving				
Year Team	G	Att	Yds	Avg	TD	Rec	Yds	Avg	TD	Fum
1974 Was	13	103	391	3.8	0	26	174	6.7	2	1
1975 Was	13	56	195	3.5	0	13	81	6.2	0	1
NFL Total	26	159	586	3.7	0	39	255	6.5	2	2

BURNELL DENT Dent, Burnell Joseph 6′1″, 236 **LB**
Col: Tulane *HS:* Destrehan [LA] B: 3/16/1963, New Orleans, LA *Drafted:* 1986 Round 6 GB
1986 GB: 16 G. **1987** GB: 9 G. **1988** GB: 10 G; 1 Sac. **1989** GB: 16 G; Int 1-53. **1990** GB: 15 G; 1 Sac. **1991** GB: 14 G; 1.5 Sac. **1992** GB: 15 G; 1 Sac. **Total:** 95 G; Int 1-53; 4.5 Sac.

RICHARD DENT Dent, Richard Lamar 6′5″, 265 **DE**
Col: Tennessee State *HS:* J.C. Murphy [Atlanta, GA] B: 12/13/1960, Atlanta, GA *Drafted:* 1983 Round 8 ChiB
1983 ChiB: 16 G; 3 Sac. **1984** ChiB: 16 G; 17.5 Sac. **1985** ChiB: 16 G; Int 2-10 **1** TD; 6 Pt; **17** Sac. **1986** ChiB: 15 G; 11.5 Sac. **1987** ChiB: 12 G; 12.5 Sac. **1988** ChiB: 13 G; 10.5 Sac. **1989** ChiB: 15 G; Int 1-30; 9 Sac. **1990** ChiB: 16 G; Int 3-21; 1 Fum TD; 6 Pt; 12 Sac. **1991** ChiB: 16 G; Int 1-4; 10.5 Sac. **1992** ChiB: 16 G; 8.5 Sac. **1993** ChiB: 16 G; Int 1-24; 12.5 Sac. **1994** SF: 2 G; 2 Sac. **1995** ChiB: 3 G. **1996** Ind: 16 G; Scor 1 Saf; 2 Pt; 6.5 Sac. **1997** Phi: 15 G; 4.5 Sac. **Total:** 203 G; Int 8-89 1 TD; Scor 1 Saf; 1 Fum TD; Tot TD 2; 14 Pt; 137.5 Sac.

BOB DENTON Denton, Robert George 6′3″, 244 **DE-OT**
Col: San Joaquin Delta Coll. CA (J.C.); U. of Pacific *HS:* Stockton [CA] B: 7/24/1934, Fresno, CA *Drafted:* 1959 Round 6 Cle
1960 Cle: 12 G. **1961** Min: 14 G. **1962** Min: 14 G; KR 1-17 17.0. **1963** Min: 14 G. **1964** Min: 14 G. **Total:** 68 G; KR 1-17 17.0.

TIM DENTON Denton, Tim 5′11″, 182 **DB**
Col: Blinn Coll. TX (J.C.); Oklahoma; Sam Houston State *HS:* Ball [Galveston, TX] B: 2/2/1973, Galveston, TX
1998 Was: 16 G.

WINNIE DENTON Denton, Winfield Kirkpatrick 6′1″, 200 **G**
Col: DePauw *HS:* Central [Evansville, IN] B: 10/28/1896, Evansville, IN D: 11/2/1971, Evansville, IN
1922 Eva: 1 G.

JOHN DENVIR Denvir, John William 6′4″, 245 **OG**
Col: West Virginia; Colorado *HS:* Immaculate Conception [Connellsville, PA] B: 4/30/1938, Connellsville, PA *Drafted:* 1961 Round 12 GB
1962 Den: 11 G.

STEVE DEOSSIE DeOssie, Steven Leonard 6′2″, 248 **LB**
Col: Boston College *HS:* Don Bosco Technical [Boston, MA] B: 11/22/1962, Tacoma, WA *Drafted:* 1984 Round 4 Dal
1984 Dal: 16 G. **1985** Dal: 16 G. **1986** Dal: 16 G. **1987** Dal: 11 G. **1988** Dal: 16 G. **1989** NYG: 9 G; Int 1-10. **1990** NYG: 16 G. **1991** NYG: 16 G. **1992** NYG: 12 G. **1993** NYG-NYJ: 15 G. NYG: 8 G. NYJ: 7 G. **1994** NE: 16 G; KR 1-14 14.0. **1995** NE: 16 G. **Total:** 175 G; KR 1-14 14.0; Int 1-10.

CARMINE DEPASCAL DePascal, Carmine Ralph 6′0″, 188 **DB-E**
(Rip) *Col:* Wichita State *HS:* Swissvale [PA] B: 4/13/1918, Aliquippa, PA
1945 Pit: 1 G.

TOM DEPASO DePaso, Thomas James 6′2″, 222 **LB**
Col: Penn State *HS:* White Plains [NY] B: 2/22/1956, White Plains, NY *Drafted:* 1978 Round 10 Cin
1978 Cin: 12 G.

HENRY DEPAUL DePaul, Henry J 5′11″, 225 **G**
Col: Duquesne *HS:* Beaver Falls [PA] B: 4/12/1917, Beaver Falls, PA D: 10/28/1985, Beaver Falls, PA
1945 Pit: 4 G.

JACK DEPLER Depler, John Charles 5′10″, 220 **C-T**
(Fat) *Col:* Illinois *HS:* Lewistown [IL] B: 1/6/1899, Lewistown, IL D: 12/5/1970, Lewistown, IL
1921 Ham: 5 G. **1929** Ora: 2 G. **Total:** 7 G.

JOHN DEPNER Depner, John 5′9″, 180 **OE**
HS: Steele [Dayton, OH] B: 5/2/1907, PA D: 1/23/1978, Covington, KY
1929 Day: 1 G.

JERRY DEPOYSTER DePoyster, Jerry Dean 6′1″, 200 **K**
Col: Wyoming *HS:* Bellevue [NE] B: 7/6/1946, Omaha, NE *Drafted:* 1968 Round 2 Det
1968 Det: Rush 1-20 20.0; Scor 27, 3-15 20.0% FG, 18-20 90.0% XK. **1971** Oak: Rush 1-(-14) -14.0. **Total:** Rush 2-6 3.0; Scor 27, 3-15 20.0% FG, 18-20 90.0% XK.

		Punting		
Year Team	G	Punts	Yds	Avg
1968 Det	14	71	2868	40.4
1971 Oak	12	51	2013	39.5
1972 Oak	14	55	2031	36.9
NFL Total	40	177	6912	39.1

LEE DERAMUS DeRamus, Lee Collins 6′0″, 198 **WR**
Col: Wisconsin *HS:* Edgewood Regional [Atco, NJ] B: 8/24/1972, Stratford, NJ *Drafted:* 1995 Round 6 NO
1995 NO: 8 G; Rec 6-76 12.7. **1996** NO: 15 G; Rush 1-2 2.0; Rec 15-182 12.1 1 TD; 6 Pt. **Total:** 23 G; Rush 1-2 2.0; Rec 21-258 12.3 1 TD; 6 Pt.

JIM DERATT DeRatt, James Harold Jr. 6′0″, 203 **DB**
Col: North Carolina *HS:* Saratoga Central [NC] B: 1/19/1953, Wilson, NC
1975 NO: 6 G; PR 2-17 8.5.

DEAN DERBY Derby, Clarance Dean 6′0″, 185 **DB**
Col: Washington *HS:* Walla Walla [WA] B: 6/11/1935, Leavenworth, WA *Drafted:* 1957 Round 5 LARm
1957 Pit: Rush 18-49 2.7 1 TD; Rec 4-79 19.8; PR 9-32 3.6; KR 6-137 22.8; Scor 15, 2-4 50.0% FG, 3-3 100.0% XK. **1959** Pit: PR 9-16 1.8; KR 2-32 16.0. **Total:** Rush 18-49 2.7 1 TD; Rec 4-79 19.8; PR 18-48 2.7; KR 8-169 21.1; Scor 15, 2-4 50.0% FG, 3-3 100.0% XK.

		Interceptions			
Year Team	G	Int	Yds	TD	Fum
1957 Pit	8	0	0	0	3
1958 Pit	12	4	0	0	1
1959 Pit	12	**7**	127	0	0
1960 Pit	12	3	40	0	0
1961 Pit-Min	13	3	73	0	0
1961 Pit	5	0	0	0	0
1961 Min	8	3	73	0	0
1962 Min	11	4	0	0	0
NFL Total	68	21	240	0	4

GLENN DERBY Derby, Glenn Evans Jr. 6′6″, 290 **OT-OG**
Col: Wisconsin *HS:* Oconomowoc [WI] B: 6/27/1964, Oconomowoc, WI *Drafted:* 1988 Round 8 NO
1989 NO: 3 G. **1990** NO: 4 G. **Total:** 7 G.

JOHN DERBY Derby, John Leslie 6′0″, 232 **LB**
Col: Iowa *HS:* Oconomowoc [WI] B: 3/24/1968, Oconomowoc, WI
1992 Det: 1 G.

ART DEREMER Deremer, Arthur Martin 6′1″, 198 **C-LB**
Col: Niagara *HS:* Westinghouse [Pittsburgh, PA] B: 12/16/1917, Pittsburgh, PA *Drafted:* 1942 Round 11 Bkn
1942 Bkn: 5 G.

FRED DERIGGI DeRiggi, Fred John 6′2″, 268 **NT**
Col: Syracuse *HS:* West Scranton [Scranton, PA] B: 1/15/1967, Scranton, PA *Drafted:* 1990 Round 7 Buf
1990 NE: 2 G.

ROBERT DERLETH Derleth, Robert J 6′3″, 230 **T**
Col: Michigan *HS:* Barage [Marquette, MI] B: 1922, Marquette, MI *Drafted:* 1944 Round 29 Det
1947 Det: 1 G.

AL DEROGATIS DeRogatis, Albert John 6′4″, 238 **DT**
(De-Ro) *Col:* Duke *HS:* Central [Newark, NJ] B: 5/5/1927, Newark, NJ D: 12/26/1995, Neptune, NJ *Drafted:* 1949 Round 2 NYG
1949 NYG: 11 G; **1** Fum TD; 6 Pt. **1950** NYG: 12 G; **1** Fum TD; 6 Pt. **1951** NYG: 11 G. **1952** NYG: 12 G. **Total:** 46 G; 2 Fum TD; 12 Pt.

BRIAN DEROO DeRoo, Brian Charles 6′3″, 193 **WR**
Col: Redlands *HS:* Redlands [CA] B: 4/25/1956, Redlands, CA
Drafted: 1978 Round 5 NYG
1979 Bal: 16 G; Rec 4-82 20.5 1 TD; 6 Pt. **1980** Bal: 16 G; Rec 2-34 17.0. **1981** Bal: 16 G; Rec 1-38 38.0. **Total:** 48 G; Rec 7-154 22.0 1 TD; 6 Pt.

DAN DEROSE DeRose, Daniel Eugene 6′0″, 230 **LB**
Col: Colorado; Southern Colorado B: 1/25/1962
1987 NYG: 3 G; Int 1-10.

BEN DERR Derr, Benjamin Harrison 5′10″, 180 **WB-TB**
Col: Pennsylvania *HS:* Shattuck Mil. Acad. [Faribault, MN]
B: 6/25/1892, Turton, SD D: 7/3/1977, Mesa, AZ
1920 ChiT: 3 G. **1921** Ham: 4 G. **Total:** 7 G.

DAN DESANTIS DeSantis, Daniel Joseph 6′0″, 180 **HB-DB**
Col: Niagara *HS:* Niagara Falls [NY] B: 9/20/1918, Niagara Falls, NY
1941 Phi: Pass 7-3 42.9%, 78 11.14 1 TD 1 Int; Rec 4-53 13.3; PR 9-80 8.9; KR 6-144 24.0; Int 2-37; Punt 7-206 29.4; Scor 1, 1-1 100.0% XK.

		Rushing			
Year Team	G	Att	Yds	Avg	TD
1941 Phi	11	45	125	2.8	0

DICK DESCHAINE Deschaine, Richard 6′0″, 206 **K**
Col: No College *HS:* Menominee [MI] B: 4/28/1932, Menominee, MI

		Punting		
Year Team	G	Punts	Yds	Avg
1955 GB	12	56	2420	43.2
1956 GB	12	62	2649	42.7
1957 GB	12	63	2645	42.0
1958 Cle	12	50	2063	41.3
NFL Total	48	231	9777	42.3

CHUCK DESHANE DeShane, Charles Frederick 6′1″, 212 **G-LB-BB-DB**
Col: Alabama *HS:* Creston [Grand Rapids, MI] B: 12/10/1918, Waukesha, WI
1945 Det: 9 G; Rec 2-29 14.5; PR 5-107 21.4 1 TD; Int 3-75 1 TD; Scor 12, 0-2 FG; Tot TD 2; 12 Pt; 2 Fum. **1946** Det: 10 G; Pass 1-0; Rush 2-3 1.5; Rec 2-13 6.5; Int 1-3; Scor 10, 0-1 FG, 10-10 100.0% XK. **1947** Det: 11 G. **1948** Det: 10 G. **1949** Det: 8 G; Int 1-0. **Total:** 48 G; Pass 1-0; Rush 2-3 1.5; Rec 4-42 10.5; PR 5-107 21.4 1 TD; Int 5-78 1 TD; Scor 22, 0-3 FG, 10-10 100.0% XK; Tot TD 2; 2 Fum.

SHORTY DES JARDIEN Des Jardien, Paul Raymond 6′4″, 210 **C-OE**
Col: Chicago *HS:* Wendell Phillips [Chicago, IL] B: 8/24/1893, Coffeyville, KS D: 3/7/1956, Monrovia, CA
1920 ChiT: 8 G. **1922** Min: 1 G. **Total:** 9 G.

VERSIL DESKIN Deskin, Versil Eugene 6′0″, 200 **OE**
Col: Drake *HS:* East [Des Moines, IA] B: 2/14/1913, Avery, IA
D: 3/7/1992, Ankeny, IA
1935 ChiC: 1 G. **1936** ChiC: 9 G; Rec 3-60 20.0 1 TD; 6 Pt. **1937** ChiC: 11 G; Rec 3-48 16.0 1 TD; 6 Pt. **1938** ChiC: 11 G; Rec 6-57 9.5. **1939** ChiC: 10 G; Rec 4-84 21.0. **Total:** 42 G; Rec 16-249 15.6 2 TD; 12 Pt.

DON DESKINS Deskins, Donald Richard 6′3″, 240 **OG**
Col: Michigan *HS:* Westbury [NY] B: 5/10/1932, Brooklyn, NY
Drafted: 1960 Round 1 Oak
1960 Oak: 14 G; KR 1-15 15.0.

DARRELL DESS Dess, Darrell Charles 6′0″, 243 **OG-OT**
(D-D) *Col:* North Carolina State *HS:* Union [New Castle, PA]
B: 7/11/1935, New Castle, PA *Drafted:* 1958 Round 11 Was
1958 Pit: 12 G. **1959** NYG: 12 G. **1960** NYG: 9 G; Rec 1-3 3.0. **1961** NYG: 14 G. **1962** NYG: 14 G. **1963** NYG: 14 G. **1964** NYG: 14 G. **1965** Was: 13 G. **1966** Was-NYG: 11 G. Was: 1 G. NYG: 10 G. **1967** NYG: 14 G; Rush 0-1 1 TD; 6 Pt. **1968** NYG: 13 G. **1969** NYG: 6 G. **Total:** 146 G; Rush 0-1 1 TD; Rec 1-3 3.0; 6 Pt.

FRED DESTEFANO DeStefano, Frederick Walter 195 **FB-WB-BB**
Col: Princeton; Columbia; Northwestern *HS:* DeWitt Clinton [Bronx, NY]
B: 4/4/1900, Coal City, IL D: 6/27/1974, Houston, TX
1924 ChiC: 4 G; Rush 1 TD; 6 Pt. **1925** ChiC: 2 G. **Total:** 6 G; Rush 1 TD; 6 Pt.

WAYNE DESUTTER DeSutter, Wayne Edward 6′4″, 255 **OT**
Col: Illinois; Western Illinois *HS:* Atkinson [IL] B: 5/17/1944, Geneseo, IL *Drafted:* 1966 Round 12 Buf
1966 Buf: 14 G; KR 2-0.

HAROLD DETERS Deters, Harold Lee 6′0″, 200 **K**
Col: North Carolina State *HS:* Grainger [Kinston, NC] B: 1/16/1944, Du Bois, PA *Drafted:* 1967 Round 12 Dal
1967 Dal: 3 G; Scor 12, 1-4 25.0% FG, 9-10 90.0% XK.

KOY DETMER Detmer, Koy Dennis 6′0″, 180 **QB**
Col: Colorado *HS:* Mission [TX] B: 7/5/1973, San Antonio, TX
Drafted: 1997 Round 7 Phi
1998 Phi: Rush 7-20 2.9.

		Passing								
Year Team	G	Att	Comp	Comp%	Yds	YPA	TD	Int	Rating	Fum
1998 Phi	8	181	97	53.6	1011	5.59	5	5	67.7	1

TY DETMER Detmer, Ty Hubert 6′0″, 194 **QB**
Col: Brigham Young *HS:* Southwest [San Antonio, TX] B: 10/30/1967, San Marcos, TX *Drafted:* 1992 Round 9 GB

		Passing							
Year Team	G	Att	Comp	Comp%	Yds	YPA	TD	Int	Rating
1993 GB	3	5	3	60.0	26	5.20	0	0	73.8
1995 GB	4	16	8	50.0	81	5.06	1	1	59.6
1996 Phi	13	401	238	59.4	2911	7.26	15	13	80.8
1997 Phi	8	244	134	54.9	1567	6.42	7	6	73.9
1998 SF	16	38	24	63.2	312	8.21	4	3	91.1
NFL Total	44	704	407	57.8	4897	6.96	27	23	78.4

	Rushing				
Year Team	Att	Yds	Avg	TD	Fum
1993 GB	1	-2	-2.0	0	0
1995 GB	3	3	1.0	0	1
1996 Phi	31	59	1.9	1	7
1997 Phi	14	46	3.3	1	6
1998 SF	8	7	0.9	0	1
NFL Total	57	113	2.0	2	15

CHUCK DETWILER Detwiler, Charles Michael 6′0″, 185 **DB**
Col: Utah State *HS:* Glendora [CA] B: 3/6/1947, Rome, NY
1970 SD: 11 G; PR 1-(-5) -5.0; 1 Fum TD; 6 Pt; 1 Fum. **1971** SD: 1 G. **1972** SD: 13 G; KR 4-94 23.5. **1973** StL: 10 G; KR 3-55 18.3; Int 1-0; 1 Fum. **Total:** 35 G; PR 1-(-5) -5.0; KR 7-149 21.3; Int 1-0; 1 Fum TD; 6 Pt; 2 Fum.

JOHN DETWILLER Detwiller, John Ely 5′8″, 190 **FB-BB**
Col: Kansas *HS:* Smith Center [KS] B: 3/14/1892, Smith Center, KS
D: 2/6/1988, Smith Center, KS
1923 Ham: 3 G. **1924** Ham: 1 G. **Total:** 4 G.

DENNIS DEVAUGHN DeVaughn, Dennis Wayne 5′10″, 175 **DB**
Col: Bishop *HS:* Franklin D. Roosevelt [Dallas, TX] B: 10/28/1960, Los Angeles, CA *Drafted:* 1982 Round 5 Phi
1982 Phi: 4 G. **1983** Phi: 9 G. **Total:** 13 G.

KEVIN DEVINE Devine, Kevin L 5′9″, 179 **DB**
Col: California *HS:* Nogales [West Covina, CA] B: 12/11/1974, Jackson, MS
1997 Jac: 12 G. **1998** Jac: 5 G; Int 1-0. **Total:** 17 G; Int 1-0.

ROB DEVITA DeVita, Robert Gerard 6′2″, 222 **LB**
Col: Illinois Benedictine; Eastern Illinois *HS:* Central [Wheaton, IL]
B: 11/29/1965
1987 Sea: 1 G.

CHUCK DEVLIEGHER DeVliegher, Charles 6′4″, 265 **DT**
Col: Memphis *HS:* Stowe [PA] B: 1/2/1947, Paterson, NJ
Drafted: 1968 Round 14 Buf
1969 Buf: 4 G.

CHRIS DEVLIN Devlin, Christopher James 6′2″, 226 **LB**
Col: Penn State *HS:* North Allegheny [Wexford, PA] B: 11/22/1953, Wexford, PA *Drafted:* 1975 Round 7 Cin
1975 Cin: 14 G. **1976** Cin: 9 G; Int 1-2. **1978** Cin-ChiB: 7 G. Cin: 1 G. ChiB: 6 G. **Total:** 30 G; Int 1-2.

JOE DEVLIN Devlin, Joseph Gregory 6′5″, 261 **OT-OG**
Col: Iowa *HS:* Great Valley [Malvern, PA] B: 2/23/1954, Phoenixville, PA *Drafted:* 1976 Round 2 Buf
1976 Buf: 14 G. **1977** Buf: 14 G. **1978** Buf: 14 G. **1979** Buf: 16 G. **1980** Buf: 16 G. **1981** Buf: 16 G. **1982** Buf: 9 G. **1984** Buf: 16 G. **1985** Buf: 16 G. **1986** Buf: 16 G. **1987** Buf: 12 G. **1988** Buf: 16 G. **1989** Buf: 16 G. **Total:** 191 G.

MARK DEVLIN Devlin, Mark H Jr. 5′10″, 180 **BB**
(Spoke) *Col:* Holy Cross *HS:* St. John's Prep [Danvers, MA]
B: 12/5/1894, Lawrence, MA D: 12/11/1973, Lawrence, MA
1920 Cle-RI: 5 G. Cle: 4 G. RI: 1 G. **1921** NYG: 1 G. **Total:** 6 G.

MIKE DEVLIN Devlin, Michael Richard 6′2″, 305 **C-OG**
Col: Iowa *HS:* Cherokee [Marlton, NJ] B: 11/16/1969, Blacksburg, VA
Drafted: 1993 Round 5 Buf
1993 Buf: 12 G. **1994** Buf: 16 G. **1995** Buf: 16 G. **1996** Ariz: 11 G. **1997** Ariz: 15 G. **1998** Ariz: 15 G. **Total:** 85 G.

JED DEVRIES DeVries, Jed 6′6″, 282 **OT**
Col: Utah State *HS:* Weber [Ogden, UT] B: 1/6/1971, Ogden, UT
1995 Cle: 2 G.

JIM DEWAR Dewar, James Alexander Jr. 6′1″, 190 **DB-HB-WB**
Col: Indiana *HS:* Oak Park [IL] B: 6/17/1922, Oak Park, IL
D: 6/30/1989
AAFC **1947** CleA: 10 G; Rush 14-64 4.6 1 TD; PR 1-2 2.0; KR 1-25 25.0; Int 1-50; 6 Pt. **1948** BknA: 1 G. **Total:** 11 G; Rush 14-64 4.6 1 TD; PR 1-2 2.0; KR 1-25 25.0; Int 1-50; 6 Pt.

EBBY DEWEESE DeWeese, Everett 6′0″, 188 **G-BB**
Col: No College B: 1906, Miamisburg, OH Deceased
1927 Day: 6 G. **1928** Day: 1 G. **1930** Port: 11 G. **Total:** 18 G.

BILL DEWELL Dewell, William Austin 6′4″, 208 **OE-DE**
Col: Southern Methodist *HS:* Dodge City [KS] B: 1/2/1917, Concordia, KS *Drafted:* 1939 Round 4 Phi
1941 ChiC: Rush 1-(-1) -1.0. **Total:** Rush 1-(-1) -1.0.

		Receiving				
Year Team	**G**	**Rec**	**Yds**	**Avg**	**TD**	**Fum**
1940 ChiC	4	2	29	14.5	0	0
1941 ChiC	11	27	362	13.4	1	0
1945 ChiC	9	26	370	14.2	1	1
1946 ChiC	11	27	643	**23.8**	**7**	0
1947 ChiC	11	42	576	13.7	4	1
1948 ChiC	11	33	442	13.4	2	0
1949 ChiC	12	20	235	11.8	2	0
NFL Total	69	177	2657	15.0	17	2

HERB DEWITZ DeWitz, Herbert Arnold 5′9″, 175 **WB-BB**
Col: Nebraska *HS:* Stanton [NE] B: 8/14/1902, Stanton, NE Deceased
1927 Cle: 13 G; Rush 1 TD; Rec 1 TD; Tot TD 2; 12 Pt.

RUFE DEWITZ DeWitz, Rufus Elbeno 5′9″, 175 **WB-TB**
Col: Nebraska *HS:* Stanton [NE] B: 6/9/1900, Stanton, NE D: 3/1984, Roselle, IL
1924 KC: 8 G; Pass 1 TD; Scor 4, 1 FG, 1 XK. **1926** KC: 8 G; Rush 1 TD; 6 Pt. **Total:** 16 G; Pass 1 TD; Rush 1 TD; Scor 10, 1 FG, 1 XK.

WILLARD DEWVEALL Dewveall, Willard Charles 6′4″, 224 **OE**
(Duke) *Col:* Southern Methodist *HS:* Weatherford [TX] B: 4/29/1936, Springtown, TX *Drafted:* 1958 Round 2 ChiB

		Receiving				
Year Team	**G**	**Rec**	**Yds**	**Avg**	**TD**	**Fum**
1959 ChiB	11	20	420	21.0	3	0
1960 ChiB	12	43	804	18.7	5	0
1961 Hou	7	12	200	16.7	3	0
1962 Hou	14	33	576	17.5	5	0
1963 Hou	14	58	752	13.0	7	3
1964 Hou	14	38	552	14.5	4	1
NFL Total	72	204	3304	16.2	27	4

JAMES DEXTER Dexter, James Roland 6′7″, 319 **OT**
Col: South Carolina *HS:* West Springfield [Springfield, VA] B: 3/3/1973, Fort Ord, CA *Drafted:* 1996 Round 5 Ariz
1996 Ariz: 6 G. **1997** Ariz: 10 G. **1998** Ariz: 16 G. **Total:** 32 G.

ALAN DIAL Dial, Alan Roy 6′1″, 188 **DB**
Col: UCLA *HS:* Anniston [AL] B: 2/2/1965, Anniston, AL
1989 Phi: 1 G.

BENJY DIAL Dial, Benjamin Franklin 6′1″, 185 **QB**
Col: Eastern New Mexico *HS:* Farwell [TX] B: 5/21/1943, Memphis, TN *Drafted:* 1966 Round 13 Pit
1967 Phi: 1 G; Pass 3-1 33.3%, 5 1.67.

BUDDY DIAL Dial, Gilbert Leroy 6′1″, 194 **FL-OE**
Col: Rice *HS:* Magnolia [TX] B: 1/17/1937, Ponca City, OK *Drafted:* 1959 Round 2 NYG
1960 Pit: Rush 1-8 8.0. **1961** Pit: Rush 3-6 2.0. **Total:** Rush 4-14 3.5.

		Receiving				
Year Team	**G**	**Rec**	**Yds**	**Avg**	**TD**	**Fum**
1959 Pit	12	16	428	26.8	6	0
1960 Pit	12	40	972	**24.3**	9	0
1961 Pit	14	53	1047	19.8	12	3
1962 Pit	14	50	981	19.6	6	0
1963 Pit	14	60	1295	**21.6**	9	2
1964 Dal	10	11	178	16.2	0	0
1965 Dal	12	17	283	16.6	1	0
1966 Dal	10	14	252	18.0	1	0
NFL Total	98	261	5436	20.8	44	5

CHARLEY DIAMOND Diamond, Charles John 6′2″, 262 **OT**
(Chief) *Col:* Miami (Fla.) *HS:* Archbishop Curley [Miami, FL] B: 7/19/1936, Miami, FL
1960 DalT: 14 G. **1961** DalT: 14 G. **1962** DalT: 14 G. **1963** KC: 9 G. **Total:** 51 G.

BILL DIAMOND Diamond, William Michael 6′0″, 240 **OG**
Col: Miami (Fla.) *HS:* Archbishop Curley [Miami, FL] B: 8/14/1939, Miami, FL *Drafted:* 1962 Round 13 StL
1963 KC: 5 G.

RICH DIANA Diana, Richard 5′9″, 220 **RB**
Col: Yale *HS:* Hamden [CT] B: 9/6/1960, Hamden, CT *Drafted:* 1982 Round 5 Mia
1982 Mia: 9 G; Rush 8-31 3.9; Rec 2-21 10.5; KR 1-15 15.0; 1 Fum.

JORGE DIAZ Diaz, Jorge Armando 6′4″, 308 **OG**
Col: Kilgore Coll. TX (J.C.); Texas A&M–Kingsville *HS:* Katy [TX] B: 11/15/1973, New York, NY
1996 TB: 11 G. **1997** TB: 16 G. **1998** TB: 12 G. **Total:** 39 G.

DAVID DIAZ-INFANTE Diaz-Infante, Gustavo David Miguel 6′3″, 291 **OG-C**
Col: San Jose State *HS:* Bellarmine Prep [San Jose, CA] B: 3/31/1964, San Jose, CA
1987 SD: 3 G. **1996** Den: 9 G. **1997** Den: 16 G. **1998** Den: 10 G. **Total:** 38 G.

JACK DIBB Dibb, John 6′0″, 200 **T**
Col: Army *HS:* Jordan [Sandy, UT] B: 12/24/1903, England D: 6/30/1993, Pinehurst, NC
1930 Nwk: 3 G.

DORNE DIBBLE Dibble, Dorne Allen 6′2″, 195 **OE-DB**
Col: Michigan State *HS:* Adrian [MI] B: 4/26/1929, Adrian, MI *Drafted:* 1951 Round 3 Det
1951 Det: Int 1-26. **1956** Det: Rush 1-8 8.0. **1957** Det: Rush 1-5 5.0. **Total:** Rush 2-13 6.5; Int 1-26.

		Receiving			
Year Team	**G**	**Rec**	**Yds**	**Avg**	**TD**
1951 Det	12	30	613	20.4	6
1953 Det	12	16	274	17.1	3
1954 Det	12	46	768	16.7	6
1955 Det	8	14	179	12.8	2
1956 Det	12	32	597	18.7	2
1957 Det	12	8	121	15.1	0
NFL Total	68	146	2552	17.5	19

RICK DIBERNARDO DiBernardo, Richard Anthony 6′3″, 230 **LB**
Col: Notre Dame *HS:* Edison [Huntington Beach, CA] B: 6/12/1964, Redondo Beach, CA
1986 StL: 16 G. **1987** LARm: 3 G. **Total:** 19 G.

JIM DICK Dick, James Brian 6′1″, 230 **LB**
Col: North Dakota State B: 6/18/1964, IL
1987 Min: 3 G.

DAN DICKEL Dickel, Daniel Lee 6′3″, 225 **LB**
Col: Iowa *HS:* Mid-Prairie [Wellman, IA] B: 8/24/1952, Fort Riley, KS *Drafted:* 1974 Round 7 Bal
1974 Bal: 14 G; Int 1-5. **1975** Bal: 14 G. **1976** Bal: 14 G. **1977** Bal: 14 G. **1978** Det: 4 G. **Total:** 60 G; Int 1-5.

ANDY DICKERSON Dickerson, Andrew Charles 6′5″, 260 **OG**
Col: Miami (Fla.); California Lutheran *HS:* Cypress Lake [Fort Myers, FL] B: 3/10/1963, Philadelphia, PA
1987 LARd: 1 G.

ANTHONY DICKERSON Dickerson, Anthony Charles 6′2″, 220 **LB**
Col: Trinity Valley CC TX; Southern Methodist *HS:* Pearland [TX] B: 6/9/1957, Texas City, TX
1980 Dal: 16 G; Int 2-46. **1981** Dal: 16 G. **1982** Dal: 9 G; Int 1-4; 2.5 Sac. **1983** Dal: 16 G; Int 1-8; Scor 1 Saf; 2 Pt; 10.5 Sac. **1984** Dal: 16 G; Int 1-0; 2 Sac. **1985** Buf: 16 G. **Total:** 89 G; Int 5-58; Scor 1 Saf; 2 Pt; 15 Sac.

ERIC DICKERSON Dickerson, Eric Demetric 6′3″, 220 **RB**
Col: Southern Methodist *HS:* Sealy [TX] B: 9/2/1960, Sealy, TX *Drafted:* 1983 Round 1 LARm *HOF:* 1999
1984 LARm: Pass 1-0, 1 Int. **1986** LARm: Pass 1-1 100.0%, 15 15.00 1 TD. **Total:** Pass 2-1 50.0%, 15 7.50 1 TD 1 Int.

		Rushing				Receiving					Tot
Year Team	**G**	**Att**	**Yds**	**Avg**	**TD**	**Rec**	**Yds**	**Avg**	**TD**	**Fum**	**TD**
1983 LARm	16	**390**	**1808**	4.6	18	51	404	7.9	2	13	20
1984 LARm	16	379	**2105**	5.6	**14**	21	139	6.6	0	14	14
1985 LARm	14	292	1234	4.2	12	20	126	6.3	0	10	12
1986 LARm	16	**404**	**1821**	4.5	11	26	205	7.9	0	12	11
1987 LARm-Ind	12	283	1288	4.6	6	18	171	9.5	0	7	6
1987 LARm	3	60	277	4.6	1	5	38	7.6	0	2	1
1987 Ind	9	223	1011	4.5	5	13	133	10.2	0	5	5
1988 Ind	16	**388**	**1659**	4.3	14	36	377	10.5	1	5	15
1989 Ind	15	314	1311	4.2	7	30	211	7.0	1	10	8
1990 Ind	11	166	677	4.1	4	18	92	5.1	0	0	4
1991 Ind	10	167	536	3.2	2	41	269	6.6	1	6	3
1992 LARd	16	187	729	3.9	2	14	85	6.1	1	1	3
1993 Atl	4	26	91	3.5	0	6	58	9.7	0	0	0
NFL Total	146	2996	13259	4.4	90	281	2137	7.6	6	78	96

RON DICKERSON Dickerson, Ronald Lee Jr. 6′0″, 211 **RB-WR**
Col: Arkansas *HS:* State College [PA] B: 8/31/1971, Denver, CO
1994 KC: Rush 1-0; Rec 2-11 5.5. **Total:** Rush 1-0; Rec 2-11 5.5.

		Kickoff Returns				
Year Team	**G**	**Ret**	**Yds**	**Avg**	**TD**	**Fum**
1993 KC	6	11	237	21.5	0	0

1994 KC	9	21	472	22.5	0	1
NFL Total	15	32	709	22.2	0	1

CHARLIE DICKEY Dickey, Charles Joseph 6'3", 270 **OG**
Col: Scottsdale CC AZ; Arizona *HS:* Saguaro [Scottsdale, AZ]
B: 12/31/1962, Ottumwa, IA
1987 Pit: 1 G.

LYNN DICKEY Dickey, Clifford Lynn 6'3", 214 **QB**
Col: Kansas State *HS:* Osawatomie [KS] B: 10/19/1949, Paola, KS
Drafted: 1971 Round 3 Hou
1973 Hou: Scor **1** 1XP. **Total:** Scor 1 1XP.

		Passing							
Year Team	**G**	**Att**	**Comp**	**Comp%**	**Yds**	**YPA**	**TD**	**Int**	**Rating**
1971 Hou	7	57	19	33.3	315	5.53	0	9	13.3
1973 Hou	12	120	71	59.2	888	7.40	6	10	64.2
1974 Hou	14	113	63	55.8	704	6.23	2	8	50.9
1975 Hou	14	4	2	50.0	46	11.50	0	1	52.1
1976 GB	10	243	115	47.3	1465	6.03	7	14	52.2
1977 GB	9	220	113	51.4	1346	6.12	5	14	51.4
1979 GB	5	119	60	50.4	787	6.61	5	4	71.7
1980 GB	16	478	278	58.2	3529	7.38	15	25	70.0
1981 GB	13	354	204	57.6	2593	7.32	17	15	79.0
1982 GB	9	218	124	56.9	1790	8.21	12	14	75.3
1983 GB	16	484	289	59.7	**4458**	**9.21**	**32**	29	87.3
1984 GB	15	401	237	59.1	3195	7.97	25	19	85.6
1985 GB	12	314	172	54.8	2206	7.03	15	17	70.4
NFL Total	152	3125	1747	55.9	23322	7.46	141	179	70.9

	Rushing				
Year Team	**Att**	**Yds**	**Avg**	**TD**	**Fum**
1971 Hou	1	4	4.0	0	1
1973 Hou	6	9	1.5	0	5
1974 Hou	3	7	2.3	0	2
1975 Hou	1	3	3.0	0	0
1976 GB	11	19	1.7	1	7
1977 GB	5	24	4.8	0	1
1979 GB	5	13	2.6	0	2
1980 GB	19	11	0.6	1	13
1981 GB	19	6	0.3	0	8
1982 GB	13	19	1.5	0	5
1983 GB	21	12	0.6	3	9
1984 GB	18	6	0.3	3	3
1985 GB	18	-12	-0.7	1	8
NFL Total	140	121	0.9	9	64

CURTIS DICKEY Dickey, Curtis Raymond 6'1", 213 **RB**
Col: Texas A&M *HS:* Bryan [TX] B: 11/27/1956, Madisonville, TX
Drafted: 1980 Round 1 Bal
1980 Bal: KR 4-86 21.5. **1984** Ind: Pass 1-1 100.0%, 63 63.00 1 TD.
Total: Pass 1-1 100.0%, 63 63.00 1 TD; KR 4-86 21.5.

		Rushing				Receiving					Tot
Year Team	**G**	**Att**	**Yds**	**Avg**	**TD**	**Rec**	**Yds**	**Avg**	**TD**	**Fum**	**TD**
1980 Bal	15	176	800	4.5	11	25	204	8.2	2	3	13
1981 Bal	15	164	779	4.8	7	37	419	11.3	3	8	10
1982 Bal	8	66	232	3.5	1	21	228	10.9	0	3	1
1983 Bal	16	254	1122	4.4	4	24	483	20.1	3	9	7
1984 Ind	10	131	523	4.0	3	14	135	9.6	0	6	3
1985 Ind-Cle	7	11	40	3.6	0	3	30	10.0	0	0	0
1985 Ind	6	9	34	3.8	0	3	30	10.0	0	0	0
1985 Cle	1	2	6	3.0	0	0	0	—	0	0	0
1986 Cle	14	135	523	3.9	6	10	78	7.8	0	4	6
NFL Total	85	937	4019	4.3	32	134	1577	11.8	8	33	40

ELDRIDGE DICKEY Dickey, Eldridge Reno 6'2", 198 **WR**
Col: Tennessee State *HS:* Booker T. Washington [TX] B: 12/24/1945, Houston, TX *Drafted:* 1968 Round 1 Oak
1968 Oak: 11 G; Rec 1-34 34.0; PR 6-48 8.0; KR 1-17 17.0. **1971** Oak: 7 G; Rec 4-78 19.5 1 TD; 6 Pt. **Total:** 18 G; Rec 5-112 22.4 1 TD; PR 6-48 8.0; KR 1-17 17.0; 6 Pt.

WALLACE DICKEY Dickey, Wallace 6'3", 260 **OT**
Col: Victoria Coll. TX (J.C.); Southwest Texas State *HS:* Harlandale [San Antonio, TX] B: 2/15/1941, San Antonio, TX *Drafted:* 1965 Round 15 Det
1968 Den: 10 G; KR 1-13 13.0. **1969** Den: 12 G. **Total:** 22 G; KR 1-13 13.0.

PARNELL DICKINSON Dickinson, Parnell 6'2", 185 **QB**
Col: Mississippi Valley State *HS:* Brighton [AL] B: 3/14/1953, Brighton, AL *Drafted:* 1976 Round 7 TB
1976 TB: 8 G; Pass 39-15 38.5%, 210 5.38 1 TD 5 Int; Rush 13-103 7.9; 3 Fum.

BO DICKINSON Dickinson, Richard Lee 6'2", 220 **FB**
Col: Southern Mississippi *HS:* Hattiesburg [MS] B: 7/18/1935, Hattiesburg, MS *Drafted:* 1957 Round 6 ChiB
1960 DalT: KR 2-29 14.5. **1961** DalT: Scor 2 2XP. **1962** Den: KR 2-26 13.0. **1964** Oak: KR 1-0. **Total:** KR 5-55 11.0; Scor 2 2XP.

		Rushing				Receiving					Tot
Year Team	**G**	**Att**	**Yds**	**Avg**	**TD**	**Rec**	**Yds**	**Avg**	**TD**	**Fum**	**TD**
1960 DalT	14	35	143	4.1	1	3	38	12.7	0	2	1
1961 DalT	14	71	263	3.7	3	14	209	14.9	2	0	5
1962 Den	14	73	247	3.4	0	60	554	9.2	4	4	4
1963 Den-Hou	11	6	32	5.3	1	6	57	9.5	0	0	1
1963 Den	6	5	31	6.2	0	1	9	9.0	0	0	0
1963 Hou	5	1	1	1.0	1	5	48	9.6	0	0	1
1964 Oak	7	4	8	2.0	0	3	28	9.3	0	0	0
NFL Total	60	189	693	3.7	5	86	886	10.3	6	6	11

TOM DICKINSON Dickinson, Thomas Passmore 5'8", 175 **E**
Col: Detroit J.C.; Syracuse *HS:* Northwestern [Detroit, MI]
B: 7/20/1897, Detroit, MI Deceased
1920 Det: 3 G.

PAUL DICKSON Dickson, Paul Serafin 6'5", 252 **DT-OT**
Col: Baylor *HS:* Waco [TX] B: 2/26/1937, Waco, TX *Drafted:* 1959 Round 1 LARm
1959 LARm: 10 G; KR 1-0. **1960** Dal: 8 G. **1961** Min: 7 G. **1962** Min: 14 G. **1963** Min: 14 G. **1964** Min: 14 G. **1965** Min: 14 G. **1966** Min: 12 G. **1967** Min: 14 G. **1968** Min: 13 G. **1969** Min: 13 G. **1970** Min: 14 G; PR 1-1 1.0. **1971** StL: 5 G; PR 1-0. **Total:** 152 G; PR 2-1 0.5; KR 1-0.

CHUCK DICUS Dicus, Charles Wayne 6'0", 183 **WR**
Col: Arkansas *HS:* Garland [TX] B: 10/2/1948, Odessa, TX
Drafted: 1971 Round 7 SD
1971 SD: 14 G; Rush 1-(-2) -2.0; Rec 6-89 14.8 1 TD; 6 Pt. **1972** SD: 10 G; Rush 1-(-11) -11.0; Rec 18-227 12.6 2 TD; 12 Pt; 1 Fum.
Total: 24 G; Rush 2-(-13) -6.5; Rec 24-316 13.2 3 TD; 18 Pt; 1 Fum.

CLINT DIDIER Didier, Clint Bradley 6'5", 240 **TE**
Col: Columbia Basin Coll. WA (J.C.); Portland State *HS:* Connell [WA]
B: 4/4/1959, Connell, WA *Drafted:* 1981 Round 12 Was
1983 Was: 1 Fum TD. **1989** GB: KR 1-0. **Total:** KR 1-0; 1 Fum TD.

		Receiving					Tot
Year Team	**G**	**Rec**	**Yds**	**Avg**	**TD**	**Fum**	**TD**
1982 Was	8	2	10	5.0	1	0	1
1983 Was	16	9	153	17.0	4	1	5
1984 Was	11	30	350	11.7	5	0	5
1985 Was	16	41	433	10.6	4	0	4
1986 Was	14	34	691	20.3	4	0	4
1987 Was	9	13	178	13.7	1	0	1
1988 GB	15	5	37	7.4	1	1	1
1989 GB	16	7	71	10.1	1	0	1
NFL Total	105	141	1923	13.6	21	2	22

MARK DIDIO Didio, Mark Vincent 5'11", 181 **WR**
Col: Connecticut *HS:* Henninger [Syracuse, NY] B: 2/17/1969, Syracuse, NY
1992 Pit: 2 G; Rec 3-39 13.0.

JOHN DIDION Didion, John Lawrence 6'4", 245 **C-LB**
Col: Oregon State *HS:* Woodland [CA] B: 10/24/1947, Woodland, CA
Drafted: 1969 Round 7 Was
1969 Was: 14 G. **1970** Was: 10 G. **1971** NO: 14 G; 1 Fum. **1972** NO: 14 G; 1 Fum. **1973** NO: 14 G; 1 Fum. **1974** NO: 14 G. **Total:** 80 G; 3 Fum.

CHARLIE DIEHL Diehl, Charles Christian 6'0", 208 **G-T**
Col: Idaho *HS:* Filer [ID] B: 1/13/1905 D: 5/26/1981, Auburn Lake Trails, CA
1930 ChiC: 6 G. **1931** ChiC: 8 G. **1934** StL: 1 G. **Total:** 15 G.

DAVE DIEHL Diehl, David Douglas 6'0", 195 **OE-DE**
(Davey; The Danv) *Col:* Michigan State *HS:* Dansville [MI]
B: 9/30/1918, Dansville, MI D: 9/15/1994, Dansville, MI

		Receiving				Tot
Year Team	**G**	**Rec**	**Yds**	**Avg**	**TD**	**TD**
1939 Det	3	1	12	12.0	0	0
1940 Det	10	12	131	10.9	0	1
1944 Det	10	18	426	23.7	4	4
1945 Det	3	1	9	9.0	0	0
NFL Total	26	32	578	18.1	4	5

WALLY DIEHL Diehl, Glenn Walter 6'0", 204 **FB**
Col: Pennsylvania; Bucknell *HS:* Mount Carmel [PA] B: 1905, Mount Carmel, PA D: 5/29/1954, Philadelphia, PA
1928 Fra: 14 G; Pass 3 TD; Rush 3 TD; Rec 1 TD; Int **1** TD; Tot TD 5; 30 Pt. **1929** Fra: 18 G; Pass 1 TD; Rush 6 TD; 36 Pt. **1930** Fra: 6 G; Pass 1 TD. **Total:** 38 G; Pass 5 TD; Rush 9 TD; Rec 1 TD; Int 1 TD; Tot TD 11; 66 Pt.

JOHN DIEHL Diehl, John Albright 6'7", 265 **DT**
Col: Virginia *HS:* Frankford [Philadelphia, PA] B: 1/27/1936, Philadelphia, PA *Drafted:* 1958 Round 7 Bal
1961 Bal: 3 G. **1962** Bal: 14 G; KR 1-5 5.0; 1 Fum. **1963** Bal: 14 G. **1964** Bal: 14 G. **1965** Oak: 8 G. **Total:** 53 G; KR 1-5 5.0; 1 Fum.

DOUG DIEKEN Dieken, Douglas Heye 6'5", 254 **OT**
Col: Illinois *HS:* Streator [IL] B: 2/12/1949, Streator, IL *Drafted:* 1971 Round 6 Cle
1971 Cle: 14 G; KR 1-16 16.0; Scor 1 Saf; 2 Pt. **1972** Cle: 14 G. **1973** Cle: 14 G; KR 2-14 7.0. **1974** Cle: 14 G. **1975** Cle: 14 G. **1976** Cle: 14 G. **1977** Cle: 14 G. **1978** Cle: 16 G. **1979** Cle: 16 G. **1980** Cle: 16 G. **1981** Cle: 16 G. **1982** Cle: 9 G. **1983** Cle: 16 G; Rec 1-14 14.0 1 TD; 6 Pt. **1984** Cle: 16 G. **Total:** 203 G; Rec 1-14 14.0 1 TD; KR 3-30 10.0; Scor 1 Saf; 8 Pt.

DAN DIERDORF Dierdorf, Daniel Lee 6'3", 275 **OT-OG-C**
Col: Michigan *HS:* Glenwood [Canton, OH] B: 6/29/1949, Canton, OH *Drafted:* 1971 Round 2 StL *HOF:* 1996
1971 StL: 12 G; KR 1-0. **1972** StL: 14 G. **1973** StL: 14 G. **1974** StL: 14 G. **1975** StL: 14 G. **1976** StL: 14 G. **1977** StL: 12 G. **1978** StL: 16 G. **1979** StL: 2 G. **1980** StL: 16 G. **1981** StL: 16 G. **1982** StL: 9 G; 1 Fum. **1983** StL: 7 G. **Total:** 160 G; KR 1-0; 1 Fum.

SCOTT DIERKING Dierking, Scott Edward 5'10", 218 **RB**
Col: Purdue *HS:* West Chicago [IL] B: 5/24/1955, Great Lakes Naval Base, IL *Drafted:* 1977 Round 4 NYJ
1977 NYJ: KR 6-91 15.2. **1978** NYJ: Pass 1-0. **Total:** Pass 1-0; KR 6-91 15.2.

		Rushing				Receiving					Tot
Year Team	G	Att	Yds	Avg	TD	Rec	Yds	Avg	TD	Fum	TD
1977 NYJ	14	79	315	4.0	0	4	29	7.3	1	1	1
1978 NYJ	15	170	681	4.0	4	19	152	8.0	0	2	4
1979 NYJ	16	186	767	4.1	3	10	121	12.1	0	1	3
1980 NYJ	16	156	567	3.6	6	19	138	7.3	1	3	7
1981 NYJ	16	74	328	4.4	1	26	228	8.8	1	2	2
1982 NYJ	9	38	130	3.4	1	12	80	6.7	1	2	2
1983 NYJ	16	28	113	4.0	3	33	275	8.3	0	0	3
1984 TB	8	3	14	4.7	0	1	5	5.0	1	0	1
NFL Total	110	734	2915	4.0	18	124	1028	8.3	5	11	23

HERB DIETER Dieter, Herbert Erwin 6'1", 195 **G-T-OE**
Col: Pennsylvania *HS:* Masten Park [Buffalo, NY] B: 3/3/1896 Deceased
1922 Buf: 9 G.

CHRIS DIETERICH Dieterich, Christian Jeffrey 6'3", 262 **OT-OG**
Col: Suffolk Co. CC NY; North Carolina State *HS:* Ward Melville [Setaucket, NY] B: 7/27/1958, Freeport, NY *Drafted:* 1980 Round 6 Det
1980 Det: 8 G. **1981** Det: 7 G. **1982** Det: 5 G. **1983** Det: 16 G. **1984** Det: 16 G. **1985** Det: 9 G. **1986** Det: 3 G. **Total:** 64 G.

JOHN DIETTRICH Diettrich, John Michael 6'2", 190 **K**
Col: Ball State *HS:* Homestead [Fort Wayne, IN] B: 5/9/1963, Fort Wayne, IN
1987 Hou: 2 G; Scor 23, 6-6 100.0% FG, 5-5 100.0% XK.

DAVE DIFILIPPO diFilippo, David Edward 5'10", 210 **G**
Col: Villanova *HS:* West Catholic [Philadelphia, PA] B: 10/9/1916, Philadelphia, PA D: 8/29/1983, Ocean City, NJ
1941 Phi: 5 G.

SHELTON DIGGS Diggs, Shelton 6'1", 190 **WR**
Col: USC *HS:* San Bernardino [CA] B: 4/22/1955, San Bernardino, CA *Drafted:* 1977 Round 5 Atl
1977 NYJ: 7 G; Rush 1-16 16.0.

CURT DIGIACOMO DiGiacomo, Curt Joseph 6'4", 270 **OG-C**
Col: American River Coll. CA (J.C.); Arizona *HS:* Foothill [Sacramento, CA] B: 10/24/1963, San Diego, CA
1986 SD: 3 G. **1988** KC: 12 G. **Total:** 15 G.

BERNIE DIGRIS Digris, Bernard John 6'0", 212 **T-G**
Col: Holy Cross *HS:* Ansonia [CT]; St.John's Prep [Danvers, MA] B: 6/9/1919, Union City, CT D: 11/1/1978, Roanoke, VA
1943 ChiB: 2 G.

TRENT DILFER Dilfer, Trent Farris 6'4", 234 **QB**
Col: Fresno State *HS:* Aptos [CA] B: 3/13/1972, Santa Cruz, CA *Drafted:* 1994 Round 1 TB

		Passing							
Year Team	G	Att	Comp	Comp%	Yds	YPA	TD	Int	Rating
1994 TB	5	82	38	46.3	433	5.28	1	6	36.3
1995 TB	16	415	224	54.0	2774	6.68	4	18	60.1
1996 TB	16	482	267	55.4	2859	5.93	12	19	64.8
1997 TB	16	386	217	56.2	2555	6.62	21	11	82.8
1998 TB	16	429	225	52.4	2729	6.36	21	15	74.0
NFL Total	69	1794	971	54.1	11350	6.33	59	69	68.5

	Rushing				
Year Team	Att	Yds	Avg	TD	Fum
1994 TB	2	27	13.5	0	2
1995 TB	23	115	5.0	2	13
1996 TB	32	124	3.9	0	10
1997 TB	33	99	3.0	1	9
1998 TB	40	141	3.5	2	9
NFL Total	130	506	3.9	5	43

KEN DILGER Dilger, Kenneth Ray 6'5", 259 **TE**
Col: Illinois *HS:* Heritage Hills [Lincoln City, IN] B: 2/2/1971, Mariah Hill, IN *Drafted:* 1995 Round 2 Ind
1998 Ind: KR 1-14 14.0; Scor 1 2XP. **Total:** KR 1-14 14.0; Scor 1 2XP.

		Receiving				
Year Team	G	Rec	Yds	Avg	TD	Fum
1995 Ind	16	42	635	15.1	4	0
1996 Ind	16	42	503	12.0	4	1
1997 Ind	14	27	380	14.1	3	0
1998 Ind	16	31	303	9.8	1	0
NFL Total	62	142	1821	12.8	12	1

SCOTT DILL Dill, Gerald Scott 6'5", 294 **OG-OT-C**
Col: Memphis *HS:* W.A. Berry [Birmingham, AL] B: 4/5/1966, Birmingham, AL *Drafted:* 1988 Round 9 Pho
1988 Pho: 13 G. **1989** Pho: 16 G. **1990** TB: 3 G. **1991** TB: 8 G. **1992** TB: 4 G. **1993** TB: 16 G. **1994** TB: 16 G. **1995** TB: 12 G. **1996** Min: 9 G. **1997** Min: 13 G. **Total:** 110 G.

ELLIS DILLAHUNT Dillahunt, Ellis Arto Jr. 5'11", 198 **DB**
Col: East Carolina *HS:* Jacksonville [NC] B: 11/25/1964, New Bern, NC *Drafted:* 1988 Round 10 Cin
1988 Cin: 8 G.

STACEY DILLARD Dillard, Stacey Bertrand 6'5", 290 **DT-NT-DE**
Col: Oklahoma *HS:* Clarksville [TX] B: 9/17/1968, Clarksville, TX *Drafted:* 1992 Round 6 NYG
1992 NYG: 12 G. **1993** NYG: 16 G; 3 Sac. **1994** NYG: 16 G; 1.5 Sac. **1995** NYG: 15 G; 1 Sac. **Total:** 59 G; 5.5 Sac.

BOBBY DILLON Dillon, Bobby Dan 6'1", 180 **DB**
Col: Texas *HS:* Temple [TX] B: 2/23/1930, Temple, TX *Drafted:* 1952 Round 3 GB
1952 GB: PR 2-22 11.0. **1954** GB: PR 1-7 7.0. **1957** GB: PR 1-8 8.0. **Total:** PR 4-37 9.3.

		Interceptions			
Year Team	G	Int	Yds	TD	Fum
1952 GB	12	4	35	0	0
1953 GB	10	9	112	**1**	0
1954 GB	12	7	111	1	1
1955 GB	12	9	153	0	0
1956 GB	12	7	**244**	1	0
1957 GB	12	9	180	1	0
1958 GB	12	6	134	1	0
1959 GB	12	1	7	0	0
NFL Total	94	52	976	5	1

COREY DILLON Dillon, Corey James 6'1", 225 **RB**
Col: Garden City CC KS; Dixie Coll. UT (J.C.); Washington *HS:* Franklin [Seattle, WA] B: 10/24/1975, Seattle, WA *Drafted:* 1997 Round 2 Cin
1997 Cin: KR 6-182 30.3. **Total:** KR 6-182 30.3.

		Rushing				Receiving					Tot
Year Team	G	Att	Yds	Avg	TD	Rec	Yds	Avg	TD	Fum	TD
1997 Cin	16	233	1129	4.8	10	27	259	9.6	0	1	10
1998 Cin	15	262	1130	4.3	4	28	178	6.4	1	2	5
NFL Total	31	495	2259	4.6	14	55	437	7.9	1	3	15

TERRY DILLON Dillon, Terry Gilbert 6'0", 193 **DB**
Col: Montana *HS:* Hopkins [MN] B: 8/18/1941, Waukesha, WI D: 5/28/1964, Tarkio, MT *Drafted:* 1963 Round 18 Oak
1963 Min: 7 G.

STEVE DILS Dils, Stephen Whitfield 6'1", 190 **QB**
Col: Stanford *HS:* East Vancouver [Vancouver, WA] B: 12/8/1955, Seattle, WA *Drafted:* 1979 Round 4 Min

		Passing							
Year Team	G	Att	Comp	Comp%	Yds	YPA	TD	Int	Rating
1979 Min	1	0	0	—	0	—	0	0	—
1980 Min	16	51	32	62.7	352	6.90	3	0	102.7
1981 Min	2	102	54	52.9	607	5.95	1	2	66.1
1982 Min	9	26	11	42.3	68	2.62	0	0	49.8
1983 Min	16	444	239	53.8	2840	6.40	11	16	66.8
1984 Min-LARm	10	7	4	57.1	44	6.29	1	1	75.9
1984 Min	3	0	0	—	0	—	0	0	—
1984 LARm	7	7	4	57.1	44	6.29	1	1	75.9
1985 LARm	15	0	0	—	0	—	0	0	—
1986 LARm	15	129	59	45.7	693	5.37	4	4	60.0
1987 LARm	15	114	56	49.1	646	5.67	5	4	66.6
1988 Atl	7	99	49	49.5	566	5.72	2	5	52.8
NFL Total	106	972	504	51.9	5816	5.98	27	32	65.8

Year Team	Att	Yds	Avg	TD	Fum
	Rushing				
1980 Min	3	26	8.7	0	0
1981 Min	4	14	3.5	0	3
1982 Min	1	5	5.0	0	0
1983 Min	16	28	1.8	0	13
1985 LARm	2	-4	-2.0	0	0
1986 LARm	10	5	0.5	0	4
1987 LARm	7	-4	-0.6	0	2
1988 Atl	2	1	0.5	1	3
NFL Total	45	71	1.6	1	25

BUCKY DILTS Dilts, Douglas Riggs 5′9″, 185 **P**
Col: Georgia *HS:* W.F. Dykes [Atlanta, GA] B: 12/6/1953, Corpus Christi, TX
1977 Den: Rush 1-0. **1979** Bal: Rush 1-(-14) -14.0. **Total:** Rush 2-(-14) -7.0.

Year Team	G	Punts	Yds	Avg
		Punting		
1977 Den	14	90	3525	39.2
1978 Den	16	96	3494	36.4
1979 Bal	16	99	3657	36.9
NFL Total	46	285	10676	37.5

ANTHONY DILWEG Dilweg, Anthony Hume 6′3″, 215 **QB**
Col: Duke *HS:* Walt Whitman [Bethesda, MD] B: 3/28/1965, Wanshington, DC *Drafted:* 1989 Round 3 GB
1990 GB: Rush 21-114 5.4. **Total:** Rush 21-114 5.4.

Year Team	G	Att	Comp	Comp%	Yds	YPA	TD	Int	Rating	Fum
		Passing								
1989 GB	1	1	1	100.0	7	7.00	0	0	95.8	0
1990 GB	9	192	101	52.6	1267	6.60	8	7	72.1	10
NFL Total	10	193	102	52.8	1274	6.60	8	7	72.3	10

LAVVIE DILWEG Dilweg, LaVern Ralph 6′3″, 200 **OE-DE**
Col: Marquette *HS:* Washington [Milwaukee, WI] B: 1/11/1903, Milwaukee, WI D: 1/2/1968, St.Petersburg, FL
1926 Mil: 9 G. **1927** GB: 10 G; Rec 1 TD; Int 1 TD; Tot TD 2; 12 Pt. **1928** GB: 12 G. **1929** GB: 13 G; Rec 3 TD; 18 Pt. **1930** GB: 12 G; Rec 2 TD; Int 1 TD; Tot TD 3; 18 Pt. **1931** GB: 14 G; Rec 4 TD; Scor **1** 1XP; 25 Pt. **1932** GB: 14 G; Rec 5-83 16.6; Scor 1 1XP; 1 Pt. **1933** GB: 11 G; Rec 13-225 17.3. **1934** GB: 12 G; Rec 5-135 27.0 2 TD; 12 Pt. **Total:** 107 G; Rec 23-443 19.3 12 TD; Int 2 TD; Scor 2 1XP; Tot TD 14; 86 Pt.

BABE DIMANCHEFF Dimancheff, Boris Stephan 5′11″, 178 **HB-DB**
Col: Butler; Purdue *HS:* George Washington [Indianapolis, IN] B: 9/6/1922, Indianapolis, IN *Drafted:* 1944 Round 2 Bos
1945 Bos: PR 8-99 12.4; Int 1-0. **1946** Bos: PR 7-98 14.0; Int 1-7. **1952** ChiB: PR 1-0. **Total:** PR 16-197 12.3; Int 2-7.

Year Team	G	Att	Yds	Avg	TD	Rec	Yds	Avg	TD
		Rushing				Receiving			
1945 Bos	5	30	69	2.3	0	1	15	15.0	0
1946 Bos	8	57	238	4.2	0	5	121	24.2	1
1947 ChiC	12	30	116	3.9	0	22	438	19.9	4
1948 ChiC	12	27	117	4.3	1	13	260	20.0	3
1949 ChiC	10	38	151	4.0	3	10	130	13.0	1
1950 ChiC	7	8	5	0.6	0	5	53	10.6	0
1952 ChiB	9	17	106	6.2	1	5	69	13.8	1
NFL Total	63	207	802	3.9	5	61	1086	17.8	10

Year Team	Ret	Yds	Avg	TD	Fum	Tot TD
	Kickoff Returns					
1945 Bos	4	123	30.8	0	2	0
1946 Bos	5	86	17.2	0	4	1
1947 ChiC	10	180	18.0	0	1	4
1948 ChiC	6	118	19.7	0	0	4
1949 ChiC	2	43	21.5	0	0	4
1952 ChiB	4	110	27.5	0	1	2
NFL Total	31	660	21.3	0	8	15

TONY DIMIDIO DiMidio, Antonio James 6′3″, 250 **OT-C**
Col: West Chester *HS:* Upper Darby [PA] B: 8/20/1942, Bryn Mawr, PA *Drafted:* 1964 Round 9 KC
1966 KC: 14 G. **1967** KC: 12 G. **Total:** 26 G.

TOM DIMITROFF Dimitroff, Thomas George 5′11″, 200 **QB**
Col: Miami (Ohio) *HS:* Barberton [OH] B: 6/6/1935 D: 1/20/1996, Strongsville, OH *Drafted:* 1957 Round 25 Cle
1960 Bos: 3 G; Pass 2-0.

RICH DIMLER Dimler, Richard Alan 6′6″, 260 **NT-DT**
Col: USC *HS:* Bayonne [NJ] B: 7/18/1956, Bayonne, NJ *Drafted:* 1979 Round 5 Cle
1979 Cle: 12 G. **1980** GB: 3 G. **Total:** 15 G.

DON DIMMICK Dimmick, Donald 5′8″, 160 **WB**
Col: Hobart *HS:* Masten Park [Buffalo, NY] Deceased
1926 Buf: 1 G.

TOM DIMMICK Dimmick, Thomas Evans 6′6″, 253 **C-OT-LB**
Col: Houston *HS:* Lake Charles [LA] B: 5/1/1931, Opelousas, LA *Drafted:* 1956 Round 10 Phi
1956 Phi: 12 G. **1960** DalT: 13 G. **Total:** 25 G.

CHARLES DIMRY Dimry, Charles Louis III 6′0″, 176 **DB**
Col: Nevada-Las Vegas *HS:* Oceanside [NJ] B: 1/31/1966, San Diego, CA *Drafted:* 1988 Round 5 Atl
1989 Atl: 1 Sac. **1992** Den: PR 1-4 4.0. **Total:** PR 1-4 4.0; 1 Sac.

Year Team	G	Int	Yds	TD	Fum
		Interceptions			
1988 Atl	16	0	0	0	0
1989 Atl	16	2	72	0	0
1990 Atl	16	3	16	0	0
1991 Den	16	3	35	1	0
1992 Den	16	1	2	0	0
1993 Den	12	1	0	0	0
1994 TB	16	1	0	0	0
1995 TB	16	1	0	0	0
1996 TB	16	2	1	0	0
1997 Phi	15	2	25	0	1
1998 SD	16	3	38	0	0
NFL Total	171	19	189	1	1

MIKE DINGLE Dingle, Miquel Bryce 6′2″, 240 **RB**
Col: South Carolina *HS:* Berkeley [Moncks Corner, SC] B: 1/30/1969, Moncks Corner, SC *Drafted:* 1991 Round 8 Cin
1991 Cin: 8 G; Rush 21-91 4.3; Rec 5-23 4.6 1 TD; KR 7-176 25.1; 6 Pt.

NATE DINGLE Dingle, Nathan Hunter 6′2″, 252 **LB**
Col: Cincinnati *HS:* Wells [ME] B: 7/23/1971, East Machias, ME
1995 Phi: 6 G. **1996** Jac: 2 G. **1997** StL: 9 G. **Total:** 17 G.

TOM DINKEL Dinkel, Thomas 6′3″, 240 **LB**
Col: Kansas *HS:* Shawnee Heights [Tecumseh, KS] B: 7/25/1956, Topeka, KS *Drafted:* 1978 Round 5 Cin
1978 Cin: 16 G; Rush 1-20 20.0; Int 1-1. **1979** Cin: 16 G; Rush 2-14 7.0. **1980** Cin: 16 G. **1981** Cin: 16 G; KR 1-0. **1982** Cin: 9 G. **1983** Cin: 16 G; KR 1-1 1.0; 0.5 Sac. **1985** Cin: 13 G. **Total:** 102 G; Rush 3-34 11.3; KR 2-1 0.5; Int 1-1; 0.5 Sac.

HOWARD DINKINS Dinkins, Howard James Jr. 6′1″, 230 **LB**
Col: Florida State *HS:* Jean Ribault [Jacksonville, FL] B: 4/26/1969, Jacksonville, FL *Drafted:* 1992 Round 3 Atl
1993 Atl: 3 G.

TERRY DION Dion, Terry Mark 6′6″, 254 **DE**
Col: Oregon *HS:* Shelton [WA]; Auburn HS [WA] B: 11/22/1957, Shelton, WA *Drafted:* 1980 Round 4 Sea
1980 Sea: 9 G.

JERRY DIORIO Diorio, Gerald J 6′3″, 245 **TE**
Col: Michigan *HS:* Cardinal Mooney [Youngstown, OH] B: 1/11/1962, Youngstown, OH
1987 Det: 2 G.

RAYMOND DIPIERRO DiPierro, Ramon Frank 5′11″, 210 **OG**
Col: Ohio State *HS:* Edward D. Libbey [Toledo, OH] B: 8/22/1926, Toledo, OH
1950 GB: 12 G; KR 3-42 14.0. **1951** GB: 6 G. **Total:** 18 G; KR 3-42 14.0.

JOHNNIE DIRDEN Dirden, Johnnie B 6′0″, 190 **WR**
Col: Sam Houston State *HS:* Stephen F. Austin [Houston, TX] B: 3/14/1952, Houston, TX *Drafted:* 1978 Supplemental Round 1 Hou

Year Team	G	Ret	Yds	Avg	TD	Fum
		Kickoff Returns				
1978 Hou	16	32	780	24.4	0	1
1979 KC	4	7	154	22.0	0	1
1981 Pit	6	3	45	15.0	0	0
NFL Total	26	42	979	23.3	0	2

FRED DIRENZO DiRenzo, Frederick E 5′11″, 234 **RB**
Col: New Haven *HS:* Pope John [Sparta, NJ] B: 1/28/1961, Dover, NJ
1987 NYG: 1 G; Rush 1-5 5.0.

ROBERT DIRICO DiRico, Robert J 5′10″, 202 **RB**
Col: West Chester; Kutztown *HS:* Upper Merion [King of Prussia, PA] B: 11/22/1963, Norristown, PA
1987 NYG: Rec 2-22 11.0; KR 2-31 15.5.

Year Team	G	Att	Yds	Avg	TD	Fum
		Rushing				
1987 NYG	3	25	90	3.6	0	2

MIKE DIRKS Dirks, Marion Gearhart Jr. 6'2", 246 DT-OG
Col: Wyoming *HS:* Monticello [IA] B: 8/28/1946, Monticello, IA
Drafted: 1968 Round 5 Phi
1968 Phi: 14 G. **1969** Phi: 12 G. **1970** Phi: 12 G; 6 Pt. **1971** Phi: 5 G. **Total:** 43 G; 6 Pt.

TONY DISCENZO Discenzo, Anthony N 6'5", 240 OT
Col: Michigan State B: 1936
1960 Bos-Buf: 8 G. Bos: 5 G. Buf: 3 G. **Total:** 8 G.

LEO DISEND Disend, Leo 6'2", 224 T
(Moose; Iron Man) *Col:* Albright *HS:* Abraham Clark [Roselle, NJ] B: 11/7/1915, New York, NY D: 5/13/1985, Baldwin, NY
1938 Bkn: 11 G. **1939** Bkn: 11 G. **1940** GB: 5 G. **Total:** 27 G.

CHRIS DISHMAN Dishman, Chris 6'3", 320 OG
Col: Nebraska *HS:* Cozad [NE] B: 2/27/1974, Cozad, NE
Drafted: 1997 Round 4 Ariz
1997 Ariz: 8 G. **1998** Ariz: 12 G. **Total:** 20 G.

CRIS DISHMAN Dishman, Cris Edward 6'0", 187 DB
Col: Purdue *HS:* DeSales [Louisville, KY] B: 8/13/1965, Louisville, KY
Drafted: 1988 Round 5 Hou
1991 Hou: 1 Fum TD. **1993** Hou: 1 Fum TD. **1994** Hou: PR 1-0. **1997** Was: 1.5 Sac. **Total:** PR 1-0; 2 Fum TD; 1.5 Sac.

		Interceptions			Tot
Year Team	G	Int	Yds	TD	TD
1988 Hou	15	0	0	0	1
1989 Hou	16	4	31	0	1
1990 Hou	16	4	50	0	0
1991 Hou	15	6	61	0	1
1992 Hou	15	3	34	0	0
1993 Hou	16	6	74	0	1
1994 Hou	16	4	74	1	1
1995 Hou	15	3	17	0	0
1996 Hou	16	1	7	0	0
1997 Was	16	4	47	1	1
1998 Was	16	2	60	0	0
NFL Total	172	37	455	2	6

MIKE DITKA Ditka, Michael Keller 6'3", 228 TE
(Iron Mike) *Col:* Pittsburgh *HS:* Aliquippa [PA] B: 10/18/1939, Carnegie, PA *Drafted:* 1961 Round 1 ChiB *HOF:* 1988
1962 ChiB: **1** Fum TD. **1964** ChiB: 1 Fum TD. **1971** Dal: Rush 2-2 1.0; KR 3-30 10.0. **Total:** Rush 2-2 1.0; KR 3-30 10.0; 2 Fum TD.

		Receiving					Tot
Year Team	G	Rec	Yds	Avg	TD	Fum	TD
1961 ChiB	14	56	1076	19.2	12	2	12
1962 ChiB	14	58	904	15.6	5	4	6
1963 ChiB	14	59	794	13.5	8	0	8
1964 ChiB	14	75	897	12.0	5	2	6
1965 ChiB	14	36	454	12.6	2	1	2
1966 ChiB	14	32	378	11.8	2	0	2
1967 Phi	9	26	274	10.5	2	0	2
1968 Phi	11	13	111	8.5	2	0	2
1969 Dal	12	17	268	15.8	3	0	3
1970 Dal	14	8	98	12.3	0	0	0
1971 Dal	14	30	360	12.0	1	0	1
1972 Dal	14	17	198	11.6	1	0	1
NFL Total	158	427	5812	13.6	43	9	45

JOHN DITTRICH Dittrich, John Francis 6'1", 236 OG
Col: Wisconsin *HS:* Cudahy [WY] B: 5/7/1933, Sheboygan, WI D: 7/5/1995, Walnut Creek, CA
1956 ChiC: 12 G. **1959** GB: 12 G. **1960** Oak: 11 G. **1961** Buf: 12 G. **Total:** 47 G.

JOE DIVITO DiVito, Joseph Charles 6'2", 205 QB-P
Col: Boston College *HS:* St. Mary's [Lynn, MA] B: 9/2/1945
1968 Den: 3 G; Pass 6-1 16.7%, 16 2.67; Rush 1-(-1) -1.0; Punt 8-242 30.3; 1 Fum.

AL DIXON Dixon, Albert D 6'5", 230 TE
Col: Iowa State *HS:* East St. Louis [IL] B: 4/5/1954, Drew, MS
Drafted: 1977 Round 7 NYG
1980 KC: KR 1-0. **1981** KC: Rush 1-(-5) -5.0. **Total:** Rush 1-(-5) -5.0; KR 1-0.

		Receiving				
Year Team	G	Rec	Yds	Avg	TD	Fum
1977 NYG	8	6	78	13.0	0	0
1978 NYG	15	18	376	20.9	3	1
1979 NYG-KC	8	2	18	9.0	0	0
1979 NYG	5	2	18	9.0	0	0
1979 KC	3	0	0	—	0	0
1980 KC	12	7	115	16.4	1	1
1981 KC	16	29	356	12.3	2	0
1982 KC	8	18	251	13.9	2	0
1983 Phi	10	4	54	13.5	0	0
1984 SF	2	0	0	—	0	0
NFL Total	79	84	1248	14.9	8	2

CAL DIXON Dixon, Calvert Ray III 6'4", 287 C-OG
Col: Florida *HS:* Merritt Island [FL] B: 10/11/1969, Fort Lauderdale, FL
Drafted: 1992 Round 5 NYJ
1992 NYJ: 11 G; KR 1-6 6.0. **1993** NYJ: 16 G. **1994** NYJ: 15 G. **1995** NYJ: 13 G. **1996** Mia: 11 G. **Total:** 66 G; KR 1-6 6.0.

DAVID DIXON Dixon, David Tukatahi 6'5", 354 OG
Col: Ricks Coll. ID (J.C.); Arizona State *HS:* Pukekohe [Auckland, New Zealand] B: 1/5/1969, Papakura, New Zealand *Drafted:* 1992 Round 9 NE
1994 Min: 1 G. **1995** Min: 15 G. **1996** Min: 13 G. **1997** Min: 13 G. **1998** Min: 16 G. **Total:** 58 G.

DWAYNE DIXON Dixon, Dwayne Keith 6'1", 205 WR
Col: Florida *HS:* Santa Fe [Alachua, FL] B: 8/2/1962, Gainsville, FL
1984 TB: 10 G; Rec 5-69 13.8. **1987** TB: 2 G; Rec 1-18 18.0. **Total:** 12 G; Rec 6-87 14.5.

ERNEST DIXON Dixon, Ernest James 6'1", 243 LB
Col: South Carolina *HS:* Fort Mill [SC]; Fork Union Mil. Acad. [VA] B: 10/17/1971, York, SC
1994 NO: 15 G. **1995** NO: 16 G; Int 2-17; 1 Fum; 4 Sac. **1996** NO: 16 G. **1997** NO: 15 G; 0.5 Sac. **1998** Oak-KC: 4 G. Oak: 3 G. KC: 1 G. **Total:** 66 G; Int 2-17; 1 Fum; 4.5 Sac.

FLOYD DIXON Dixon, Floyd Eugene 5'9", 170 WR
Col: Stephen F. Austin St. *HS:* Hebert [Beaumont, TX] B: 4/9/1964, Beaumont, TX *Drafted:* 1986 Round 6 Atl
1986 Atl: Rush 11-67 6.1; KR 1-13 13.0. **1987** Atl: Rush 3-(-3) -1.0. **1988** Atl: Rush 7-69 9.9. **1989** Atl: Rush 2-(-23) -11.5. **1990** Atl: KR 1-0. **Total:** Rush 23-110 4.8; KR 2-13 6.5.

		Receiving				Punt Returns				
Year Team	G	Rec	Yds	Avg	TD	Ret	Yds	Avg	TD	Fum
1986 Atl	16	42	617	14.7	2	26	151	5.8	0	3
1987 Atl	12	36	600	16.7	5	0	0	—	0	0
1988 Atl	14	28	368	13.1	2	0	0	—	0	1
1989 Atl	16	25	357	14.3	2	0	0	—	0	0
1990 Atl	16	38	399	10.5	4	0	0	—	0	0
1991 Atl	10	12	146	12.2	1	0	0	—	0	0
1992 Phi	7	3	36	12.0	0	0	0	—	0	0
NFL Total	91	184	2523	13.7	16	26	151	5.8	0	4

GERALD DIXON Dixon, Gerald Scott 6'3", 250 LB
Col: South Carolina *HS:* Rock Hill [SC] B: 6/20/1969, Charlotte, NC
Drafted: 1992 Round 3 Cle
1993 Cle: 11 G. **1994** Cle: 16 G; 1 Sac. **1995** Cle: 16 G; KR 1-10 10.0; Int 2-48 1 TD; 6 Pt. **1996** Cin: 16 G; Int 1-10. **1997** Cin: 15 G; 8.5 Sac. **1998** SD: 16 G; 2.5 Sac. **Total:** 90 G; KR 1-10 10.0; Int 3-58 1 TD; 6 Pt; 12 Sac.

HANFORD DIXON Dixon, Hanford Lee 5'11", 186 DB
Col: Southern Mississippi *HS:* Theodore [AL] B: 12/25/1958, Mobile, AL *Drafted:* 1981 Round 1 Cle
1982 Cle: 1 Sac. **1983** Cle: 1 Sac. **Total:** 2 Sac.

		Interceptions			
Year Team	G	Int	Yds	TD	Fum
1981 Cle	16	0	0	0	0
1982 Cle	9	4	22	0	1
1983 Cle	16	3	41	0	0
1984 Cle	16	5	31	0	0
1985 Cle	16	3	65	0	0
1986 Cle	16	5	35	0	1
1987 Cle	12	3	5	0	0
1988 Cle	15	2	24	0	0
1989 Cle	15	1	2	0	0
NFL Total	131	26	225	0	2

HEWRITT DIXON Dixon, Hewritt Frederick Jr. 6'1", 230 RB-TE
Col: Florida A&M *HS:* A.L. Mebane [Alachua, FL] B: 1/8/1940, Alachua, FL D: 11/24/1992, Los Angeles, CA *Drafted:* 1963 Round 8 Den
1963 Den: PR 3-58 19.3; KR 9-195 21.7. **1964** Den: KR 6-89 14.8. **1965** Den: KR 1-8 8.0. **1968** Oak: Scor **1** 2XP. **Total:** PR 3-58 19.3; KR 16-292 18.3; Scor 1 2XP.

		Rushing				Receiving					Tot
Year Team	G	Att	Yds	Avg	TD	Rec	Yds	Avg	TD	Fum	TD
1963 Den	5	23	105	4.6	2	10	130	13.0	0	2	2
1964 Den	14	18	25	1.4	0	38	585	15.4	1	3	1
1965 Den	14	0	0	—	0	25	354	14.2	2	0	2
1966 Oak	14	68	277	4.1	5	29	345	11.9	4	2	9
1967 Oak	13	153	559	3.7	5	59	563	9.5	2	6	7
1968 Oak	14	206	865	4.2	2	38	360	9.5	2	5	4
1969 Oak	11	107	398	3.7	0	33	275	8.3	1	4	1
1970 Oak	14	197	861	4.4	1	31	207	6.7	1	6	2
NFL Total	99	772	3090	4.0	15	263	2819	10.7	13	28	28

JAMES DIXON Dixon, James Anthony 5′9″, 181 **WR-RB**
Col: Houston *HS:* Vernon [TX] B: 2/2/1967, Vernon, TX
1989 Dal: Rush 3-30 10.0. **1990** Dal: Rush 11-43 3.9. **Total:** Rush 14-73 5.2.

		Receiving				Kickoff Returns					Tot
Year Team	G	Rec	Yds	Avg	TD	Ret	Yds	Avg	TD	Fum	TD
1989 Dal	16	24	477	19.9	2	**47**	**1181**	25.1	**1**	4	3
1990 Dal	15	2	26	13.0	0	36	736	20.4	0	2	0
1991 Dal	7	0	0	—	0	18	398	22.1	0	1	0
NFL Total	38	26	503	19.3	2	101	2315	22.9	1	7	3

MARK DIXON Dixon, Mark Keller 6′4″, 300 **OG-OT**
Col: Virginia *HS:* Lucy Ragsdale [Jamestown, NC] B: 11/26/1970, Charlottesville, VA
1998 Mia: 11 G.

RANDY DIXON Dixon, Randall Charles 6′3″, 300 **OT-OG**
Col: Pittsburgh *HS:* Clewiston [FL] B: 3/12/1965, Clewiston, FL
Drafted: 1987 Round 4 Ind
1987 Ind: 3 G. **1988** Ind: 16 G. **1989** Ind: 16 G; 1 Fum TD; 6 Pt. **1990** Ind: 15 G. **1991** Ind: 12 G. **1992** Ind: 15 G. **1993** Ind: 15 G. **1994** Ind: 14 G. **1995** Ind: 12 G. **Total:** 118 G; 1 Fum TD; 6 Pt.

RICH DIXON Dixon, Richard Marvin 6′2″, 235 **LB**
Col: California *HS:* Mount Eden [Hayward, CA] B: 8/6/1959, Roswell, NM
1983 Atl: 14 G.

RICKEY DIXON Dixon, Rickey 5′11″, 183 **DB**
Col: Oklahoma *HS:* Wilmer-Hutchins [Hutchins, TX] B: 12/26/1966, Dallas, TX *Drafted:* 1988 Round 1 Cin
1988 Cin: 15 G; KR 1-18 18.0; Int 1-13. **1989** Cin: 16 G; Int 3-47. **1990** Cin: 13 G. **1991** Cin: 15 G; Int 2-62. **1992** Cin: 14 G. **1993** LARd: 9 G. **Total:** 82 G; KR 1-18 18.0; Int 6-122.

RONNIE DIXON Dixon, Ronnie Christopher 6′3″, 301 **DT-NT**
Col: Cincinnati *HS:* Clinton [NC] B: 5/10/1971, Clinton, NC
Drafted: 1993 Round 6 NO
1993 NO: 2 G. **1995** Phi: 16 G. **1996** Phi: 16 G. **1997** NYJ: 5 G. **1998** KC: 4 G. **Total:** 43 G.

TITUS DIXON Dixon, Titus L 5′6″, 152 **WR**
Col: Troy State *HS:* Clewiston [FL] B: 6/15/1966, Clewiston, FL
Drafted: 1989 Round 6 NYJ
1989 NYJ-Ind-Det: 4 G; KR 4-67 16.8; 1 Fum. NYJ: 3 G; KR 4-67 16.8; 1 Fum. Ind: 1 G. **Total:** 4 G; KR 4-67 16.8; 1 Fum.

JOE DIXON Dixon, Willie Joe Jr. 6′3″, 275 **NT**
Col: Tulsa *HS:* Pocola [OK] B: 1/8/1964, Fort Smith, AR
1987 Hou: 2 G.

ZACHARY DIXON Dixon, Zachary C 6′0″, 203 **RB**
Col: Dean Coll. MA (J.C.); Temple *HS:* Dorchester [Boston, MA]
B: 3/5/1956, Boston, MA *Drafted:* 1979 Round 11 Den
1984 Sea: PR 1-5 5.0. **Total:** PR 1-5 5.0.

		Rushing				Receiving			
Year Team	G	Att	Yds	Avg	TD	Rec	Yds	Avg	TD
1979 Den-NYG	8	3	9	3.0	0	0	0	—	0
1979 Den	5	3	9	3.0	0	0	0	—	0
1979 NYG	3	0	0	—	0	0	0	—	0
1980 Phi-Bal	6	2	8	4.0	0	1	5	5.0	0
1980 Phi	5	2	8	4.0	0	1	5	5.0	0
1980 Bal	1	0	0	—	0	0	0	—	0
1981 Bal	16	73	285	3.9	0	17	169	9.9	1
1982 Bal	9	58	249	4.3	1	20	185	9.3	0
1983 Bal-Sea	15	9	32	3.6	0	1	2	2.0	0
1983 Bal	2	5	14	2.8	0	1	2	2.0	0
1983 Sea	13	4	18	4.5	0	0	0	—	0
1984 Sea	13	52	149	2.9	2	2	6	3.0	0
NFL Total	67	197	732	3.7	3	41	367	9.0	1

	Kickoff Returns					Tot
Year Team	Ret	Yds	Avg	TD	Fum	TD
1979 Den-NYG	3	53	17.7	0	1	0
1979 Den	3	53	17.7	0	1	0
1980 Phi-Bal	2	30	15.0	0	0	0
1980 Phi	2	30	15.0	0	0	0
1981 Bal	36	737	20.5	0	1	1
1982 Bal	11	197	17.9	0	2	1
1983 Bal-Sea	**51**	**1171**	23.0	**1**	1	1
1983 Bal	2	23	11.5	0	0	0
1983 Sea	49	1148	23.4	1	1	1
1984 Sea	25	446	17.8	0	1	2
NFL Total	128	2634	20.6	1	6	5

DINGER DOANE Doane, Erling Joseph 5′10″, 190 **FB-WB-G-E**
Col: Tufts *HS:* Somerville [MA] B: 1895, Natick, MA D: 6/5/1949
1920 Cle: 4 G. **1921** NYG: 1 G. **1922** Mil: 9 G; Rush 1 TD; 6 Pt. **1923** Mil: 10 G; Rush 2 TD; 12 Pt. **1924** Mil: 11 G; Rush 4 TD; 24 Pt. **1925** Det: 11 G; Rush 5 TD; 30 Pt. **1926** Det: 12 G; Rush 2 TD; 1 Fum TD; Tot TD 3; 18 Pt. **1927** Pott: 2 G. Prov: 5 G. **Total:** 65 G; Rush 14 TD; 1 Fum TD; Tot TD 15; 90 Pt.

HERB DOBBINS Dobbins, Herbert 6′4″, 260 **OT**
Col: Mount San Antonio Coll. CA (J.C.); San Diego State *HS:* Pomona [CA] B: 6/22/1951, Statesville, NC
1974 Phi: 3 G.

OLLIE DOBBINS Dobbins, Oliver Wendel 6′0″, 182 **DB**
Col: Morgan State *HS:* West Philadelphia [Philadelphia, PA]
B: 11/30/1941, Philadelphia, PA *Drafted:* 1964 Round 18 Pit
1964 Buf: 14 G.

GLENN DOBBS Dobbs, Glenn Jr. 6′4″, 211 **TB-DB-QB**
Col: Tulsa *HS:* Frederick [OK] B: 7/12/1920, McKinney, TX
AAFC **1946** BknA: Rec 1-(-5) -5.0; KR 12-214 17.8; Int 2-44.
1947 BknA-LA-A: Rec 2-21 10.5; KR 5-119 23.8; Int 5-44. **1948** LA-A: Rec 2-11 5.5; KR 2-38 19.0; Int 1-32. **Total:** Rec 5-27 5.4; KR 19-371 19.5; Int 8-120.

		Passing							
Year Team	G	Att	Comp	Comp%	Yds	YPA	TD	Int	Rating
1946 BknA	12	269	135	50.2	1886	7.01	13	15	66.0
1947 BknA-LA-A	11	143	61	42.7	762	5.33	7	8	52.8
1948 LA-A	14	369	185	50.1	2403	6.51	21	20	67.4
1949 LA-A	12	153	65	42.5	825	5.39	4	9	44.2
AAFC Total	49	934	446	47.8	5876	6.29	45	52	61.0

	Rushing				Punt Returns			
Year Team	Att	Yds	Avg	TD	Ret	Yds	Avg	TD
1946 BknA	95	208	2.2	4	7	146	20.9	1
1947 BknA-LA-A	42	131	3.1	1	19	215	11.3	0
1948 LA-A	91	539	5.9	4	0	0	—	0
1949 LA-A	34	161	4.7	3	0	0	—	0
AAFC Total	262	1039	4.0	12	26	361	13.9	1

	Punting			Tot
Year Team	Punts	Yds	Avg	TD
1946 BknA	80	3826	47.8	6
1947 BknA-LA-A	44	1911	43.4	2
1948 LA-A	68	3336	49.1	4
1949 LA-A	39	1650	42.3	3
AAFC Total	231	10723	46.4	15

DICK DOBELEIT Dobeleit, Richard Frank 5′4″, 155 **WB-TB-BB-FB**
Col: Ohio State *HS:* Steele [Dayton, OH] B: 7/4/1903, Germany
D: 3/2/1978, Lake Wales, FL
1925 Day: 6 G. **1926** Day: 6 G. **Total:** 12 G.

BOB DOBELSTEIN Dobelstein, Robert Edward 5′11″, 214 **G-LB**
(Dobbie) *Col:* Tennessee *HS:* Central [Bridgeport, CT]
B: 10/27/1922, Bridgeport, CT *Drafted:* 1945 Round 4 ChiC
AAFC **1949** LA-A: 8 G.

NFL **1946** NYG: 10 G. **1947** NYG: 12 G. **1948** NYG: 11 G; Int 1-20 1 TD; 6 Pt. **Total:** 33 G; Int 1-20 1 TD; 6 Pt.

CONRAD DOBLER Dobler, Conrad Francis 6′3″, 254 **OG**
Col: Wyoming *HS:* 29 Palms [CA] B: 10/1/1950, Chicago, IL
Drafted: 1972 Round 5 StL
1972 StL: 12 G. **1973** StL: 12 G. **1974** StL: 14 G. **1975** StL: 14 G. **1976** StL: 14 G. **1977** StL: 14 G; 1 Fum TD; 6 Pt. **1978** NO: 3 G. **1979** NO: 16 G. **1980** Buf: 16 G. **1981** Buf: 14 G. **Total:** 129 G; 1 Fum TD; 6 Pt.

EMIL DOBRY Dobry, Emil A 5′11″, 175 **OE**
Col: No College B: 8/10/1895 D: 7/1972, Decatur, IL
1928 Fra: 1 G.

JOHN DOCKERY Dockery, John Patrick 6′0″, 185 **DB**
Col: Harvard *HS:* Brooklyn Prep [NY] B: 9/6/1944, Brooklyn, NY
1968 NYJ: 3 G. **1969** NYJ: 14 G; Rec 1-6 6.0; Int 5-98. **1970** NYJ: 14 G. **1971** NYJ: 14 G; Int 2-13. **1972** Pit: 6 G. **1973** Pit: 10 G; Int 1-0. **Total:** 61 G; Rec 1-6 6.0; Int 8-111.

AL DODD Dodd, Alvin Roy 6′0″, 185 **WR-DB**
Col: Northwestern State-Louisiana *HS:* West Jefferson [Harvey, LA]
B: 8/21/1945, New Orleans, LA D: 4/9/1987, Opelika, AL
Drafted: 1967 Round 4 ChiB
1969 NO: Rush 3-12 4.0. **1970** NO: Pass 1-0; Rush 5-31 6.2. **1971** NO: Rush 1-7 7.0. **Total:** Pass 1-0; Rush 9-50 5.6.

		Receiving				Punt Returns			
Year Team	G	Rec	Yds	Avg	TD	Ret	Yds	Avg	TD
1967 ChiB	6	0	0	—	0	3	8	2.7	0
1969 NO	14	37	600	16.2	1	15	106	7.1	0
1970 NO	14	28	484	17.3	1	14	129	9.2	0
1971 NO	10	15	298	19.9	0	13	88	6.8	0
1973 Atl	13	19	291	15.3	0	8	69	8.6	0

1974 Atl	14	12	130	10.8	1	27	344	12.7	0
NFL Total	71	111	1803	16.2	3	80	744	9.3	0

	Kickoff Returns					Tot
Year Team	Ret	Yds	Avg	TD	Fum	TD
1967 ChiB	3	34	11.3	0	0	0
1969 NO	8	171	21.4	0	0	1
1970 NO	15	319	21.3	0	1	2
1971 NO	12	252	21.0	0	2	0
1973 Atl	0	0	—	0	1	0
1974 Atl	0	0	—	0	1	1
NFL Total	38	776	20.4	0	5	4

DEDRICK DODGE Dodge, Dedrick Allen 6′2″, 184 **DB**
Col: Florida State *HS:* East Brunswick [NJ]; Mulberry HS [FL]
B: 6/14/1967, Neptune, NJ
1991 Sea: 11 G. **1992** Sea: 14 G; Int 1-13; 1 Sac. **1994** SF: 15 G. **1995** SF: 16 G; Int 1-13. **1996** SF: 16 G; Int 3-27. **1997** Den: 16 G. **1998** SD: 8 G. **Total:** 96 G; Int 5-53; 1 Sac.

KIRK DODGE Dodge, Kirk James 6′1″, 231 **LB**
Col: Fullerton Coll. CA (J.C.); Nevada-Las Vegas *HS:* Lowell [San Francisco, CA] B: 6/4/1962, Whittier, CA *Drafted:* 1984 Round 7 Atl
1984 Det: 11 G. **1986** Hou: 9 G. **1987** Den: 3 G. **Total:** 23 G.

DALE DODRILL Dodrill, Dale Fike 6′1″, 215 **DG-LB**
Col: Colorado State *HS:* Loveland [CO] B: 2/27/1926, Stockton, KS
Drafted: 1951 Round 6 Pit
1953 Pit: **1** Fum TD. **1958** Pit: PR 1-5 5.0. **Total:** PR 1-5 5.0; 1 Fum TD.

		Interceptions			Tot
Year Team	G	Int	Yds	TD	TD
1951 Pit	7	0	0	0	0
1952 Pit	12	0	0	0	1
1953 Pit	12	1	3	0	1
1954 Pit	12	3	28	0	0
1955 Pit	12	2	25	0	0
1956 Pit	12	1	1	0	0
1957 Pit	12	2	50	0	0
1958 Pit	12	1	13	0	0
1959 Pit	12	0	0	0	0
NFL Total	103	10	120	0	2

LES DODSON Dodson, James Leslie 6′1″, 180 **TB-DB**
Col: Mississippi *HS:* West Lowndes [Columbus, MS] B: 4/18/1916, Birmingham, AL *Drafted:* 1941 Round 12 Phi
1941 Pit: 2 G; Pass 8-1 12.5%, 7 0.88 3 Int; Rush 2-(-4) -2.0; Punt 1-34 34.0.

JOHN DOEHRING Doehring, John H 6′0″, 216 **HB-LB-TB-DB**
(Bull) *Col:* No College *HS:* West Division [Milwaukee, WI];Illinois Mil. School [IL]; Kentucky Mil. Inst. B: 11/6/1909, Milwaukee, WI
D: 11/18/1972, Milwaukee, WI
1933 ChiB: Rec 1-9 9.0. **1934** ChiB: Rec 1-14 14.0. **1936** ChiB: Rec 1-19 19.0. **Total:** Rec 3-42 14.0.

		Passing							
Year Team	G	Att	Comp	Comp%	Yds	YPA	TD	Int	Rating
1932 ChiB	7	26	10	38.5	203	7.81	2	1	76.3
1933 ChiB	8	26	5	19.2	123	4.73	1	8	20.0
1934 ChiB	2	11	3	27.3	48	4.36	1	0	75.6
1935 Pit	2	8	4	50.0	83	10.38	2	1	87.0
1936 ChiB	6	12	5	41.7	145	12.08	1	0	114.9
1937 ChiB	3	3	2	66.7	25	8.33	0	0	92.4
NFL Total	28	86	29	33.7	627	7.29	7	10	48.1

	Rushing			
Year Team	Att	Yds	Avg	TD
1932 ChiB	36	28	0.8	1
1933 ChiB	13	58	4.5	0
1934 ChiB	8	6	0.8	0
1935 Pit	3	-6	-2.0	0
1936 ChiB	18	101	5.6	0
1937 ChiB	9	33	3.7	0
NFL Total	87	220	2.5	1

SONNY DOELL Doell, Walter A 6′0″, 200 **T**
(Tex) *Col:* Texas *HS:* Mason [TX] B: 12/8/1906, Mason, TX
1933 Cin: 1 G.

FRED DOELLING Doelling, Fred Frank 5′10″, 190 **DB**
Col: Pennsylvania *HS:* Valparaiso [IN] B: 9/27/1938, Valparaiso, IN
1960 Dal: 2 G.

JERRY DOERGER Doerger, Jerome William 6′5″, 270 **C-OT**
Col: Wisconsin *HS:* La Salle [Cincinnati, OH] B: 7/18/1960, Cincinnati, OH *Drafted:* 1982 Round 8 ChiB
1982 ChiB: 2 G. **1985** SD: 8 G. **Total:** 10 G.

CHRIS DOERING Doering, Christopher Paul 6′4″, 195 **WR**
Col: Florida *HS:* P.K. Yonge Lab [Gainesville, FL] B: 5/19/1973, Gainesville, FL *Drafted:* 1996 Round 6 Jac
1996 Ind: 1 G; Rec 1-10 10.0. **1997** Ind: 2 G; Rec 2-12 6.0. **Total:** 3 G; Rec 3-22 7.3.

KEVIN DOGINS Dogins, Kevin Ray 6′1″, 295 **C**
Col: Texas A&M–Kingsville *HS:* Rice [Eagle Lake, TX] B: 12/7/1972, Eagle Lake, TX
1996 TB: 1 G. **1997** TB: Postseason only. **1998** TB: 6 G. **Total:** 7 G.

GEORGE DOHERTY Doherty, George Edward 6′1″, 218 **G-T**
Col: Louisiana Tech *HS:* Canton [MS] B: 9/5/1920, Camden, MS
D: 12/31/1987, Natchitoches, LA *Drafted:* 1944 Round 20 Bkn
AAFC **1946** NY-A-BufA: 13 G; KR 1-0. **1947** BufA: 11 G. **Total:** 24 G; KR 1-0.

NFL **1944** Bkn: 10 G. **1945** Bos: 9 G. **Total:** 19 G.

MEL DOHERTY Doherty, Melvin 5′11″, 190 **C**
Col: Marietta D: Cincinnati, OH
1921 Cin: 4 G.

TOM DOHRING Dohring, Tom Edward 6′6″, 290 **OT**
Col: Michigan *HS:* Divine Child [Dearborn, MI] B: 5/24/1968, Detroit, MI *Drafted:* 1991 Round 8 KC
1992 KC: 3 G.

STEVE DOIG Doig, Stephen Gugel 6′2″, 240 **LB**
Col: New Hampshire *HS:* North Reading [MA] B: 3/28/1960, Melrose, MA *Drafted:* 1982 Round 3 Det
1982 Det: 9 G. **1983** Det: 9 G. **1984** Det: 16 G. **1986** NE: 5 G. **1987** NE: 1 G. **Total:** 40 G.

PHIL DOKES Dokes, Philip Dennis 6′4″, 258 **DT-DE**
Col: Oklahoma State *HS:* Ole Main [Little Rock, AR] B: 9/7/1955, North Little Rock, AR D: 12/7/1990, Jacksonville, FL *Drafted:* 1977 Round 1 Buf
1977 Buf: 12 G. **1978** Buf: 10 G. **Total:** 22 G.

CLIFF DOLAWAY Dolaway, Clifford Theodore 6′0″, 215 **OE**
Col: Carnegie Mellon *HS:* Port Allegany [PA] B: 12/11/1913
D: 12/18/1968
1935 Pit: 4 G; Rec 2-42 21.0.

JACK DOLBIN Dolbin, John Tice 5′10″, 180 **WR**
Col: Wake Forest *HS:* Pottsville [PA] B: 10/12/1948, Pottsville, PA
1975 Den: Rush 5-72 14.4; **1** Fum TD. **1976** Den: Rush 2-5 2.5. **1977** Den: Rush 2-12 6.0; KR 0-14. **Total:** Rush 9-89 9.9; KR 0-14; 1 Fum TD.

		Receiving					Tot
Year Team	G	Rec	Yds	Avg	TD	Fum	TD
1975 Den	14	22	421	19.1	3	0	4
1976 Den	14	19	354	18.6	1	0	1
1977 Den	14	26	443	17.0	3	0	3
1978 Den	16	24	284	11.8	0	1	0
1979 Den	4	3	74	24.7	0	0	0
NFL Total	62	94	1576	16.8	7	1	8

CHRIS DOLEMAN Doleman, Christopher John 6′5″, 270 **DE-LB**
Col: Pittsburgh *HS:* Valley Forge Mil. Acad. [Wayne, PA]; William Penn [York, PA] B: 10/16/1961, Indianapolis, IN *Drafted:* 1985 Round 1 Min
1985 Min: 16 G; Int 1-5; 0.5 Sac. **1986** Min: 16 G; Int 1-59 1 TD; 6 Pt; 3 Sac. **1987** Min: 12 G; 11 Sac. **1988** Min: 16 G; 8 Sac. **1989** Min: 16 G; **21** Sac. **1990** Min: 16 G; Int 1-30; Scor 1 Saf; 2 Pt; 11 Sac. **1991** Min: 16 G; 7 Sac. **1992** Min: 16 G; Int 1-27 1 TD; Scor 1 Saf; 8 Pt; 14.5 Sac. **1993** Min: 16 G; Int 1-(-3); 12.5 Sac. **1994** Atl: 14 G; Int 1-2; 7 Sac. **1995** Atl: 16 G; 9 Sac. **1996** SF: 16 G; Int 2-1; **1** Fum TD; 6 Pt; 11 Sac. **1997** SF: 16 G; 12 Sac. **1998** SF: 16 G; 15 Sac. **Total:** 218 G; Int 8-121 2 TD; Scor 2 Saf; 1 Fum TD; Tot TD 3; 22 Pt; 142.5 Sac.

DON DOLL Doll, Donald LeRoy 5′10″, 185 **DB-HB**
Col: USC *HS:* Grant Union [Sacramento, CA] B: 8/29/1926, Los Angeles, CA *Drafted:* 1948 Round 9 Det
1949 Det: Rush 8-25 3.1 1 TD; Rec 1-(-5) -5.0; PR 5-52 10.4. **1950** Det: PR 5-71 14.2. **1951** Det: PR 5-39 7.8. **1953** Was: PR 1-2 2.0. **1954** LARm: PR 1-0. **Total:** Rush 8-25 3.1 1 TD; Rec 1-(-5) -5.0; PR 17-164 9.6.

		Kickoff Returns				Interceptions				Tot
Year Team	G	Ret	Yds	Avg	TD	Int	Yds	TD	Fum	TD
1949 Det	12	21	**536**	25.5	0	11	**301**	1	2	2
1950 Det	11	2	52	26.0	0	12	163	1	0	1
1951 Det	12	9	220	24.4	0	1	0	0	0	0
1952 Det	12	0	0	—	0	2	0	0	0	0
1953 Was	12	0	0	—	0	10	102	0	0	0
1954 LARm	12	0	0	—	0	5	51	0	0	0
NFL Total	71	32	808	25.3	0	41	617	2	2	3

TONY DOLLINGER Dollinger, Anthony Dennis 5′11″, 205 **RB**
Col: Evangel *HS:* Oconto [WI] B: 10/18/1962, Winter Park, FL
1987 Det: 2 G; Rush 8-22 2.8; Rec 3-25 8.3.

DICK DOLLY Dolly, John Richard 6′3″, 211 **OE-DE**
Col: West Virginia *HS:* Franklin [WV] B: 12/12/1917, Onego, WV
D: 5/30/1959, North Augusta, SC
1941 Pit: 9 G; Rush 1-2 2.0. **1945** Pit: 10 G; Rec 8-122 15.3. **Total:** 19 G; Rush 1-2 2.0; Rec 8-122 15.3.

PAUL DOMBROSKI Dombroski, Paul Matthew 6′0″, 185 **DB**
Col: Hawaii; Linfield *HS:* Leilehua [Wahiawa, HI] B: 8/8/1956, Sumter, SC
1980 KC: 16 G; Int 1-6. **1981** KC-NE: 11 G; KR 3-66 22.0. KC: 5 G; KR 1-21 21.0. NE: 6 G; KR 2-45 22.5. **1982** NE: 9 G; KR 1-19 19.0. **1983** NE: 7 G. **1984** NE: 14 G; Int 1-23. **1985** TB: 6 G. **Total:** 63 G; KR 4-85 21.3; Int 2-29.

JIM DOMBROWSKI Dombrowski, James Matthew 6′5″, 300 **OT-OG**
Col: Virginia; Hawaii *HS:* Williamsville South [NY] B: 10/19/1963, Williamsville, NY *Drafted:* 1986 Round 1 NO
1986 NO: 3 G. **1987** NO: 10 G. **1988** NO: 16 G. **1989** NO: 16 G. **1990** NO: 16 G. **1991** NO: 16 G. **1992** NO: 16 G. **1993** NO: 16 G. **1994** NO: 16 G. **1995** NO: 16 G. **1996** NO: 10 G. **Total:** 151 G.

LEON DOMBROWSKI Dombrowski, Leon Raymond 6′0″, 215 **LB**
Col: Delaware *HS:* Salesianum [Wilmington, DE] B: 4/9/1938, Wilmington, DE
1960 NYT: 1 G.

JOE DOMNANOVICH Domnanovich, Joseph John 6′1″, 213 **C-LB**
Col: Alabama *HS:* James Whitcomb Riley [South Bend, IN]
B: 3/18/1919, South Bend, IN
1946 Bos: 11 G. **1947** Bos: 8 G; Int 1-16. **1948** Bos: 12 G; PR 1-29 29.0; Int 1-6. **1949** NYB: 12 G; Int 1-28. **1950** NYY: 12 G. **1951** NYY: 12 G. **Total:** 67 G; PR 1-29 29.0; Int 3-50.

MARTY DOMRES Domres, Martin Francis 6′4″, 220 **QB**
Col: Columbia *HS:* Christian Brothers Acad. [Syracuse, NY]
B: 4/17/1947, Ithaca, NY *Drafted:* 1969 Round 1 SD

		Passing							
Year Team	**G**	**Att**	**Comp**	**Comp%**	**Yds**	**YPA**	**TD**	**Int**	**Rating**
1969 SD	10	112	47	42.0	631	5.63	2	10	29.3
1970 SD	8	55	28	50.9	491	8.93	2	4	63.5
1971 SD	4	12	7	58.3	97	8.08	1	3	72.6
1972 Bal	12	222	115	51.8	1392	6.27	11	**6**	76.6
1973 Bal	11	191	93	48.7	1153	6.04	9	13	55.2
1974 Bal	14	153	77	50.3	803	5.25	0	12	33.2
1975 Bal	14	10	8	80.0	123	12.30	1	0	151.3
1976 SF	5	14	7	50.0	101	7.21	0	1	44.0
1977 NYJ	12	40	17	42.5	113	2.83	1	1	47.9
NFL Total	90	809	399	49.3	4904	6.06	27	50	53.8

	Rushing				
Year Team	**Att**	**Yds**	**Avg**	**TD**	**Fum**
1969 SD	19	145	7.6	4	0
1970 SD	14	39	2.8	0	2
1971 SD	1	0	0.0	0	1
1972 Bal	30	137	4.6	1	4
1973 Bal	32	126	3.9	2	3
1974 Bal	22	145	6.6	2	2
1975 Bal	4	46	11.5	1	0
1976 SF	4	18	4.5	0	0
1977 NYJ	4	23	5.8	0	0
NFL Total	130	679	5.2	10	12

TOM DOMRES Domres, Thomas Bruce 6′3″, 260 **DT**
Col: Wisconsin *HS:* Gladstone [MI] B: 10/19/1946, Marshfiield, WI
Drafted: 1968 Round 10 Hou
1968 Hou: 14 G. **1969** Hou: 14 G; **1** Fum TD; 6 Pt. **1970** Hou: 14 G; Int 0-13. **1971** Hou-Den: 10 G. Hou: 5 G. Den: 5 G. **1972** Den: 11 G. **Total:** 63 G; Int 0-13; 1 Fum TD; 6 Pt.

JACK DONAHUE Donahue, John 6′2″, 230 **G-T**
Col: Boston College *HS:* Peabody [MA] B: 1905 Deceased
1926 Prov: 13 G.

MARK DONAHUE Donahue, Mark Joseph 6′3″, 256 **OG**
Col: Michigan *HS:* Brother Rice [Chicago, IL] B: 1/29/1956, Evergreen Park, IL *Drafted:* 1978 Round 11 Cin
1978 Cin: 15 G. **1979** Cin: 16 G. **Total:** 31 G.

MITCH DONAHUE Donahue, Mitchell Todd 6′2″, 254 **LB**
Col: Wyoming *HS:* Billings West [MT] B: 2/4/1968, Los Angeles, CA
Drafted: 1991 Round 4 SF
1991 SF: 13 G. **1992** SF: 2 G. **1993** Den: 13 G. **1994** Den: 3 G. **Total:** 31 G.

OSCAR DONAHUE Donahue, Oscar 6′3″, 195 **WR**
Col: San Francisco City Coll. CA (J.C.); San Jose State B: 6/7/1937
Drafted: 1962 Round 6 GB
1962 Min: 13 G; Rec 16-285 17.8 1 TD; 6 Pt.

GENE DONALDSON Donaldson, Eugene 5′9″, 215 **OG**
Col: Kentucky *HS:* Theodore Roosevelt [East Chicago, IL]
B: 9/29/1930 *Drafted:* 1953 Round 3 Cle
1953 Cle: 11 G; KR 1-7 7.0.

GENE DONALDSON Donaldson, Eugene Harold 6′2″, 230 **RB**
Col: Purdue *HS:* Irving [Birmingham, AL]; Clarksburg HS [WV]
B: 11/4/1942, Birmingham, AL *Drafted:* 1964 Round 11 Was
1967 Buf: 2 G; Rush 3-(-1) -0.3; Rec 1-20 20.0.

JEFF DONALDSON Donaldson, Jeffrey Michael 6′0″, 192 **DB**
Col: Colorado *HS:* Fort Collins [CO] B: 4/19/1962, Fort Collins, CO
Drafted: 1984 Round 9 Hou
1985 Hou: PR 6-35 5.8; KR 5-93 18.6; 1 Sac. **1986** Hou: **1** Fum TD; 1.5 Sac. **1987** Hou: 1 Sac. **1988** Hou: KR 1-5 5.0. **1991** Atl: 1 Sac. **1992** Atl: 1 Sac. **Total:** PR 6-35 5.8; KR 6-98 16.3; 1 Fum TD; 5.5 Sac.

		Interceptions			
Year Team	**G**	**Int**	**Yds**	**TD**	**Fum**
1984 Hou	16	0	0	0	0
1985 Hou	16	0	0	0	1
1986 Hou	16	1	0	0	0
1987 Hou	12	4	16	0	0
1988 Hou	16	4	29	0	0
1989 Hou	14	0	14	0	0
1990 KC	16	3	28	0	0
1991 Atl	16	0	0	0	0
1992 Atl	16	0	0	0	0
1993 Atl	13	0	0	0	0
NFL Total	151	12	87	0	1

JOHN DONALDSON Donaldson, John Colvin 5′10″, 180 **DB-TB**
Col: Georgia *HS:* Jesup [GA] B: 8/22/1925, Jesup, GA
AAFC **1949** LA-A-ChiA: 8 G; Pass 1-0; Rush 1-(-2) -2.0; PR 1-18 18.0; KR 1-27 27.0; Int 0-23.

RAY DONALDSON Donaldson, Raymond Canute 6′3″, 285 **C**
Col: Georgia *HS:* East [Rome, GA] B: 5/18/1958, Rome, GA
Drafted: 1980 Round 2 Bal
1980 Bal: 16 G. **1981** Bal: 16 G. **1982** Bal: 9 G. **1983** Bal: 16 G; 1 Fum. **1984** Ind: 16 G. **1985** Ind: 16 G. **1986** Ind: 16 G; 2 Fum. **1987** Ind: 12 G. **1988** Ind: 16 G; Rec 1-(-3) -3.0. **1989** Ind: 16 G; 1 Fum. **1990** Ind: 16 G. **1991** Ind: 3 G. **1992** Ind: 16 G; 1 Fum. **1993** Sea: 16 G; 1 Fum. **1994** Sea: 16 G; 2 Fum. **1995** Dal: 12 G. **1996** Dal: 16 G; 2 Fum. **Total:** 244 G; Rec 1-(-3) -3.0; 10 Fum.

WALDO DON CARLOS Don Carlos, Waldo Emerson 6′2″, 190 **C**
Col: Drake *HS:* Roosevelt [Des Moines, IA] B: 10/16/1909, Greenfield, IA
1931 GB: 12 G.

TOM DONCHEZ Donchez, Thomas Frederick 6′2″, 216 **RB**
Col: Penn State *HS:* Liberty [Bethlehem, PA] B: 3/10/1952, Bethlehem, PA *Drafted:* 1975 Round 4 Buf
1975 ChiB: 14 G.

BILLY DONCKERS Donckers, William Lewis 6′1″, 205 **QB**
Col: Columbia Basin Coll. WA (J.C.); San Diego State *HS:* Renton [WA]
B: 1/8/1951, Renton, WA
1976 StL: 1 G; Pass 1-1 100.0%, 16 16.00. **1977** StL: 5 G; Pass 5-5 100.0%, 38 7.60. **Total:** 6 G; Pass 6-6 100.0%, 54 9.00.

AL DONELLI Donelli, Allen A 5′7″, 165 **HB**
Col: Duquesne *HS:* South Fayette [McDonald, PA] B: 12/22/1917, Morgan, PA
1941 Pit: 7 G; Pass 8-2 25.0%, 13 1.63 1 TD 3 Int; Rush 15-20 1.3; Rec 2-25 12.5; PR 1-11 11.0; KR 4-83 20.8; Int 1-18; Punt 1-41 41.0. **1942** Pit: 4 G; Rush 2-(-4) -2.0. **Total:** 11 G; Pass 8-2 25.0%, 13 1.63 1 TD 3 Int; Rush 17-16 0.9; Rec 2-25 12.5; PR 1-11 11.0; KR 4-83 20.8; Int 1-18; Punt 1-41 41.0.

DOUG DONLEY Donley, Douglas Max 6′0″, 175 **WR**
Col: Ohio State *HS:* Cambridge [OH] B: 2/6/1959, Cambridge, OH
Drafted: 1981 Round 2 Dal
1981 Dal: PR 1-3 3.0. **1982** Dal: PR 1-14 14.0; KR 8-151 18.9. **1983** Dal: PR 1-1 1.0. **1984** Dal: Rush 2-5 2.5. **Total:** Rush 2-5 2.5; PR 3-18 6.0; KR 8-151 18.9.

		Receiving				
Year Team	**G**	**Rec**	**Yds**	**Avg**	**TD**	**Fum**
1981 Dal	11	3	32	10.7	0	0
1982 Dal	6	2	23	11.5	0	2
1983 Dal	11	18	370	20.6	2	0
1984 Dal	15	32	473	14.8	2	0
NFL Total	43	55	898	16.3	4	2

JIM DONLIN Donlin, James Mikeal 210 **G**
Col: No College B: 9/25/1900, Hartford, CT D: 11/26/1957, Manchester, CT
1926 Har: 2 G.

ROGER DONNAHOO Donnahoo, Roger J 6'0", 185 **DB**
Col: Michigan State *HS:* St. Mary's of Redford [Detroit, MI]
B: 8/5/1937, Greenville, SC
1960 NYT: 14 G; Int 5-89; **1** Fum TD; Tot TD 2; 12 Pt.

KEVIN DONNALLEY Donnalley, Kevin Dale 5'11", 177 **DB**
Col: North Dakota State *HS:* Central [Red Wing, MN] B: 1/17/1958, Warren, OH *Drafted:* 1981 Round 7 StL
1981 NE: 1 G.

KEVIN DONNALLEY Donnalley, Kevin Thomas 6'5", 305 **OG-OT**
Col: Davidson; North Carolina *HS:* Athens Drive [Raleigh, NC]
B: 6/10/1968, St. Louis, MO *Drafted:* 1991 Round 3 Hou
1991 Hou: 16 G. **1992** Hou: 16 G. **1993** Hou: 16 G. **1994** Hou: 13 G. **1995** Hou: 16 G. **1996** Hou: 16 G. **1997** Ten: 16 G. **1998** Mia: 14 G. **Total:** 123 G.

RICK DONNALLEY Donnalley, William Frederick 6'2", 261 **C-OG**
Col: North Carolina *HS:* Sanderson [Raleigh, NC] B: 12/11/1958, Wilmington, DE *Drafted:* 1981 Round 3 Pit
1982 Pit: 5 G; KR 1-8 8.0. **1983** Pit: 16 G; KR 0-2. **1984** Was: 15 G. **1985** Was: 13 G. **1986** KC: 16 G; 2 Fum. **1987** KC: 6 G. **Total:** 71 G; KR 1-10 10.0; 2 Fum.

BEN DONNELL Donnell, Ben Clay 6'5", 248 **DE**
Col: Vanderbilt *HS:* DuPont [Old Hickory, TN] B: 7/17/1936, Old Hickory, TN *Drafted:* 1959 Round 7 Det
1960 LAC: 3 G.

GEORGE DONNELLY Donnelly, George 6'3", 210 **DB**
Col: Illinois *HS:* De Kalb [IL] B: 9/4/1942, Chicago, IL *Drafted:* 1965 Round 1 SF
1965 SF: 14 G. **1966** SF: 7 G; PR 1-0; Int 2-16; 1 Fum. **1967** SF: 12 G. **Total:** 33 G; PR 1-0; Int 2-16; 1 Fum.

RICK DONNELLY Donnelly, Richard Patrick 6'0", 195 **P**
Col: Wyoming *HS:* Miller Place [NY] B: 5/17/1962, Miller Place, NY
1985 Atl: Rush 2-(-5) -2.5. **1986** Atl: Scor 1, 1-1 100.0% XK. **1987** Atl: Rush 3-(-6) -2.0. **Total:** Rush 5-(-11) -2.2; Scor 1, 1-1 100.0% XK.

		Punting			
Year Team	**G**	**Punts**	**Yds**	**Avg**	**Fum**
1985 Atl	11	59	2574	43.6	0
1986 Atl	16	78	3421	43.9	0
1987 Atl	12	61	2686	**44.0**	2
1988 Atl	16	**98**	3920	40.0	0
1990 Sea	16	67	2722	40.6	0
1991 Sea	3	13	505	38.8	0
NFL Total	74	376	15828	42.1	2

MARK D'ONOFRIO D'Onofrio, Mark Emil 6'2", 235 **LB**
Col: Penn State *HS:* North Bergen [NJ] B: 3/17/1969, Hoboken, NJ
Drafted: 1992 Round 2 GB
1992 GB: 2 G.

MIKE DONOHOE Donohoe, Michael Pierce 6'3", 225 **TE**
Col: San Francisco *HS:* Archbishop Riordan [San Francisco, CA]
B: 5/6/1945, San Francisco, CA *Drafted:* 1968 Round 9 Min
1968 Atl: 14 G; Rec 6-52 8.7 1 TD; KR 1-22 22.0; 6 Pt. **1970** Atl: 14 G; Rec 2-36 18.0 1 TD; 6 Pt. **1971** Atl: 9 G. **1973** GB: 13 G; Rec 1-10 10.0. **1974** GB: 14 G; Rec 1-8 8.0. **Total:** 64 G; Rec 10-106 10.6 2 TD; KR 1-22 22.0; 12 Pt.

BILL DONOHOE Donohoe, William Wilson 5'9", 165 **BB-WB-FB**
Col: Carnegie Mellon *HS:* Edgewood [Pittsburgh, PA] B: 1904
1927 Fra: 8 G; Rush 1 TD; Rec 1 TD; Tot TD 2; 12 Pt.

LEON DONOHUE Donohue, Leon 6'4", 245 **OG-OT**
Col: San Jose State *HS:* James Lick [San Jose, CA] B: 3/25/1939, Star City, AR *Drafted:* 1961 Round 9 SF
1962 SF: 14 G. **1963** SF: 14 G. **1964** SF: 14 G. **1965** Dal: 14 G. **1966** Dal: 14 G. **1967** Dal: 14 G. **Total:** 84 G.

ART DONOVAN Donovan, Arthur James Jr. 6'2", 263 **DT-OT**
Col: Boston College *HS:* Mount St. Michael's [Bronx, NY] B: 6/5/1925, Bronx, NY *Drafted:* 1947 Round 20 NYG *HOF:* 1968
1950 Bal: 12 G. **1951** NYY: 12 G. **1952** Dal: 6 G. **1953** Bal: 12 G; Scor **1** Saf; 2 Pt. **1954** Bal: 11 G. **1955** Bal: 12 G. **1956** Bal: 11 G. **1957** Bal: 12 G. **1958** Bal: 12 G. **1959** Bal: 12 G. **1960** Bal: 12 G. **1961** Bal: 14 G. **Total:** 138 G; Scor 1 Saf; 2 Pt.

PAT DONOVAN Donovan, Patrick Emery 6'5", 253 **OT**
Col: Stanford *HS:* Helena [MT] B: 7/1/1953, Helena, MT
Drafted: 1975 Round 4 Dal
1975 Dal: 13 G. **1976** Dal: 14 G. **1977** Dal: 14 G. **1978** Dal: 16 G. **1979** Dal: 16 G. **1980** Dal: 16 G. **1981** Dal: 16 G. **1982** Dal: 9 G. **1983** Dal: 15 G. **Total:** 129 G.

TOM DONOVAN Donovan, Thomas Edward 5'11", 179 **WR**
Col: Penn State *HS:* Holy Family [Huntington, NY] B: 1/13/1957, Queens, NY *Drafted:* 1980 Round 9 KC
1980 NO: 5 G.

JOHN DOOLAN Doolan, John James 6'1", 190 **DB-WB-OE-DE**
Col: Georgetown *HS:* St. Cecilia [Englewood NJ]; Seton Hall Prep [South Orange, NJ] B: 5/16/1919, Brooklyn, NY
1945 Was-NYG: 6 G; Rush 10-26 2.6; Rec 6-50 8.3; KR 3-87 29.0; 1 Fum. Was: 1 G. NYG: 5 G; Rush 10-26 2.6; Rec 6-50 8.3; KR 3-87 29.0; 1 Fum. **1946** NYG: 5 G; Rush 12-33 2.8; Rec 3-28 9.3; PR 3-49 16.3; 2 Fum. **1947** ChiC: 12 G; Rec 1-17 17.0. **1948** ChiC: 12 G. **Total:** 35 G; Rush 22-59 2.7; Rec 10-95 9.5; PR 3-49 16.3; KR 3-87 29.0; 3 Fum.

JIM DOOLEY Dooley, James William 6'4", 198 **OE-FL-HB-DB**
Col: Miami (Fla.) *HS:* Miami Senior [FL] B: 2/8/1930, Stoutsville, MO
Drafted: 1952 Round 1 ChiB
1952 ChiB: Rush 1-0; Int 5-30. **Total:** Rush 1-0; Int 5-30.

		Receiving				
Year Team	**G**	**Rec**	**Yds**	**Avg**	**TD**	**Fum**
1952 ChiB	12	0	0	—	0	0
1953 ChiB	12	53	841	15.9	4	1
1954 ChiB	12	34	658	19.4	7	0
1956 ChiB	3	4	47	11.8	0	0
1957 ChiB	12	37	530	14.3	1	0
1959 ChiB	12	41	580	14.1	3	0
1960 ChiB	12	36	426	11.8	1	1
1961 ChiB	6	6	90	15.0	0	0
NFL Total	81	211	3172	15.0	16	2

JOHN DOOLEY Dooley, John M 6'1", 224 **G-T**
Col: Syracuse; Bucknell *HS:* Solvay [NY] B: 9/29/1897, Fairmount, NY
D: 10/31/1991, Syracuse, NY
1922 Roch: 5 G. **1923** Mil: 1 G. **1924** Roch: 5 G. **1925** Roch: 6 G. **Total:** 17 G.

DAN DOORNINK Doornink, Daniel Glenn 6'3", 210 **RB**
Col: Washington State *HS:* Wapato [WA] B: 2/1/1956, Yakima, WA
Drafted: 1978 Round 7 NYG
1979 Sea: KR 1-13 13.0. **1982** Sea: Punt 1-54 54.0. **Total:** KR 1-13 13.0; Punt 1-54 54.0.

		Rushing				Receiving					Tot
Year Team	**G**	**Att**	**Yds**	**Avg**	**TD**	**Rec**	**Yds**	**Avg**	**TD**	**Fum**	**TD**
1978 NYG	12	60	306	5.1	1	12	66	5.5	0	2	1
1979 Sea	16	152	500	3.3	8	54	432	8.0	1	6	9
1980 Sea	15	100	344	3.4	3	31	237	7.6	2	2	5
1981 Sea	15	65	194	3.0	1	27	350	13.0	4	3	5
1982 Sea	8	45	178	4.0	0	22	176	8.0	0	2	0
1983 Sea	16	40	99	2.5	2	24	328	13.7	2	1	4
1984 Sea	16	57	215	3.8	0	31	365	11.8	2	0	2
1985 Sea	6	4	0	0.0	0	8	52	6.5	0	0	0
NFL Total	104	523	1836	3.5	15	209	2006	9.6	11	16	26

JIM DORAN Doran, James Robert 6'2", 201 **OE-DE**
Col: Buena Vista; Iowa State *HS:* Beaver [IA] B: 8/11/1927, Beaver, IA
D: 6/30/1994, Lake City, IA *Drafted:* 1951 Round 5 Det
1951 Det: Rush 2-23 11.5; Int 1-38. **1952** Det: Rush 1-36 36.0. **1959** Det: **1** Fum TD. **1961** Dal: KR 1-0. **Total:** Rush 3-59 19.7; KR 1-0; Int 1-38; 1 Fum TD.

		Receiving					Tot
Year Team	**G**	**Rec**	**Yds**	**Avg**	**TD**	**Fum**	**TD**
1951 Det	12	10	225	22.5	2	1	2
1952 Det	11	10	147	14.7	1	0	1
1953 Det	7	6	75	12.5	0	0	0
1954 Det	7	10	203	20.3	4	1	4
1955 Det	10	38	552	14.5	2	2	2
1956 Det	11	25	448	17.9	0	1	0
1957 Det	12	33	624	18.9	5	0	5
1958 Det	9	22	495	22.5	4	0	4
1959 Det	10	14	191	13.6	1	0	2
1960 Dal	12	31	554	17.9	3	0	3
1961 Dal	14	13	153	11.8	2	1	2
NFL Total	115	212	3667	17.3	24	6	25

JOE D'ORAZIO D'Orazio, Joseph 5'11", 220 **T**
Col: Ithaca B: 10/5/1914 D: 9/1972
1944 Det: 5 G.

ART DORFMAN Dorfman, Arthur 5'10", 210 **C**
Col: Boston U. B: 5/9/1908, Everett, MA
1929 Buf: 9 G.

TORIN DORN Dorn, Torin Damon 6'0", 190 **DB**
Col: North Carolina *HS:* Southfield [MI] B: 2/28/1968, Greenwood, SC
Drafted: 1990 Round 4 LARd
1990 LARd: 16 G. **1991** LARd: 16 G; Scor 1 Saf; 2 Pt. **1992** LARd: 15 G; Int 1-7. **1993** LARd: 15 G. **1995** StL: 12 G; Int 1-24 1 TD; **1** Fum TD; Tot TD 2; 12 Pt. **1996** StL: 9 G; Int 1-40. **Total:** 83 G; Int 3-71 1 TD; Scor 1 Saf; 1 Fum TD; Tot TD 2; 14 Pt.

THOM DORNBROOK Dornbrook, Thomas John 6′2″, 240 OG-C
Col: Kentucky *HS:* North Hills [Pittsburgh, PA] B: 12/1/1956, Pittsburgh, PA
1979 Pit: 16 G; PR 1-0; 1 Fum. **1980** Mia: 4 G. **Total:** 20 G; PR 1-0; 1 Fum.

KEITH DORNEY Dorney, Keith Robert 6′5″, 268 OT-OG
Col: Penn State *HS:* Emmaus [PA] B: 12/3/1957, Allentown, PA
Drafted: 1979 Round 1 Det
1979 Det: 16 G. **1980** Det: 9 G. **1981** Det: 16 G. **1982** Det: 9 G. **1983** Det: 13 G. **1984** Det: 16 G. **1985** Det: 16 G. **1986** Det: 12 G. **1987** Det: 5 G. **Total:** 112 G.

DALE DORNING Dorning, Dale Scott 6′5″, 260 DE
Col: Walla Walla CC WA; Oregon *HS:* Federal Way [WA] B: 2/7/1962, Burien, WA
1987 Sea: 3 G; 1.5 Sac.

AL DOROW Dorow, Albert Richard Jr. 6′0″, 193 QB
Col: Michigan State *HS:* Imlay City [MI] B: 11/15/1929, Imlay City, MI
Drafted: 1952 Round 3 Was
1960 NYT: Punt 6-264 44.0. **Total:** Punt 6-264 44.0.

		Passing							
Year Team	G	Att	Comp	Comp%	Yds	YPA	TD	Int	Rating
1954 Was	11	138	70	50.7	997	7.22	8	17	54.2
1955 Was	8	12	2	16.7	37	3.08	0	1	5.2
1956 Was	12	112	55	49.1	730	6.52	8	8	64.2
1957 Phi	6	36	17	47.2	212	5.89	1	4	35.6
1960 NYT	14	396	201	50.8	2748	6.94	**26**	26	67.8
1961 NYT	14	**438**	**197**	45.0	2651	6.05	19	30	50.7
1962 Buf	4	75	30	40.0	333	4.44	2	7	23.9
NFL Total	69	1207	572	47.4	7708	6.39	64	93	53.8

	Rushing				
Year Team	Att	Yds	Avg	TD	Fum
1954 Was	34	117	3.4	3	4
1955 Was	8	49	6.1	0	1
1956 Was	30	105	3.5	0	4
1957 Phi	17	52	3.1	2	1
1960 NYT	90	453	5.0	7	9
1961 NYT	54	317	5.9	4	10
1962 Buf	15	57	3.8	0	2
NFL Total	248	1150	4.6	16	31

ANDY DORRIS Dorris, Andrew Michael 6′4″, 238 DE
Col: New Mexico State *HS:* Bellaire [OH] B: 8/11/1951, Bellaire, OH
Drafted: 1973 Round 4 Cle
1973 StL-NO: 5 G. StL: 4 G. NO: 1 G. **1974** NO: 14 G. **1975** NO: 13 G. **1976** NO: 14 G. **1977** Sea-Hou: 9 G. Sea: 4 G. Hou: 5 G. **1978** Hou: 16 G. **1979** Hou: 16 G. **1980** Hou: 16 G. **1981** Hou: 15 G. **Total:** 118 G.

ANTHONY DORSETT Dorsett, Anthony Drew Jr. 5′11″, 200 DB
Col: Pittsburgh *HS:* Richland [Dallas, TX]; J.J. Pearce HS [Richardson, TX] B: 9/14/1973, Aliquippa, PA *Drafted:* 1996 Round 6 Hou
1996 Hou: 8 G. **1997** Ten: 16 G. **1998** Ten: 16 G. **Total:** 40 G.

TONY DORSETT Dorsett, Anthony Drew Sr. 5′11″, 192 RB
Col: Pittsburgh *HS:* Hopewell [Aliquippa, PA] B: 4/7/1954, Rochester, PA *Drafted:* 1977 Round 1 Dal *HOF:* 1994
1977 Dal: Pass 1-1 100.0%, 34 34.00. **1978** Dal: Pass 1-0; 1 Fum TD. **1980** Dal: Pass 1-0. **1982** Dal: Pass 1-0. **1983** Dal: Pass 1-0. **1984** Dal: Pass 1-0, 1 Int. **1988** Den: Pass 2-1 50.0%, 7 3.50 1 TD. **Total:** Pass 8-2 25.0%, 41 5.13 1 TD 1 Int; 1 Fum TD.

		Rushing				Receiving					Tot
Year Team	G	Att	Yds	Avg	TD	Rec	Yds	Avg	TD	Fum	TD
1977 Dal	14	208	1007	4.8	12	29	273	9.4	1	7	13
1978 Dal	16	290	1325	4.6	7	37	378	10.2	2	**12**	10
1979 Dal	14	250	1107	4.4	6	45	375	8.3	1	9	7
1980 Dal	15	278	1185	4.3	11	34	263	7.7	0	8	11
1981 Dal	16	342	1646	4.8	4	32	325	10.2	2	10	6
1982 Dal	9	**177**	745	4.2	5	24	179	7.5	0	6	5
1983 Dal	16	289	1321	4.6	8	40	287	7.2	1	5	9
1984 Dal	16	302	1189	3.9	6	51	459	9.0	1	12	7
1985 Dal	16	305	1307	4.3	7	46	449	9.8	3	7	10
1986 Dal	13	184	748	4.1	5	25	267	10.7	1	5	6
1987 Dal	12	130	456	3.5	1	19	177	9.3	1	3	2
1988 Den	16	181	703	3.9	5	16	122	7.6	0	6	5
NFL Total	173	2936	12739	4.3	77	398	3554	8.9	13	90	91

MATTHEW DORSETT Dorsett, Matthew Herbert 5′11″, 190 DB
Col: Southern University *HS:* McMain [New Orleans LA] B: 8/23/1973, New Orleans, LA
1995 GB: 10 G.

DEAN DORSEY Dorsey, Dean 5′11″, 190 K
Col: Toronto (Canada) B: 3/13/1957, Toronto, Canada
1988 Phi-GB: 6 G; Scor 27, 5-10 50.0% FG, 12-13 92.3% XK. Phi: 3 G; Scor 21, 4-7 57.1% FG, 9-9 100.0% XK. GB: 3 G; Scor 6, 1-3 33.3% FG, 3-4 75.0% XK. **Total:** 6 G; Scor 27, 5-10 50.0% FG, 12-13 92.3% XK.

ERIC DORSEY Dorsey, Eric Hall 6′5″, 280 DE
Col: Notre Dame *HS:* McLean [VA] B: 8/5/1964, Washington, DC
Drafted: 1986 Round 1 NYG
1986 NYG: 16 G. **1987** NYG: 12 G; KR 1-13 13.0; 1 Sac. **1988** NYG: 16 G; 3.5 Sac. **1989** NYG: 2 G. **1990** NYG: 16 G. **1991** NYG: 11 G; 0.5 Sac. **1992** NYG: 16 G; 2 Sac. **Total:** 89 G; KR 1-13 13.0; 7 Sac.

JOHN DORSEY Dorsey, John Michael 6′2″, 240 LB
Col: Connecticut *HS:* Fort Union [Leonardtown, MD] B: 8/31/1960, Leonardtown, MD *Drafted:* 1984 Round 4 GB
1984 GB: 16 G. **1985** GB: 16 G. **1986** GB: 16 G. **1987** GB: 12 G. **1988** GB: 16 G. **Total:** 76 G.

LARRY DORSEY Dorsey, Larry Darnell 6′1″, 195 WR
Col: Tennessee State *HS:* Corinth [MS] B: 8/15/1953, Corinth, MS
Drafted: 1976 Round 3 SD
1976 SD: Rush 1-(-12) -12.0. **1978** KC: PR 1-3 3.0. **Total:** Rush 1-(-12) -12.0; PR 1-3 3.0.

		Receiving				
Year Team	G	Rec	Yds	Avg	TD	Fum
1976 SD	13	8	108	13.5	0	1
1977 SD	13	10	198	19.8	2	0
1978 KC	16	9	169	18.8	2	0
NFL Total	42	27	475	17.6	4	1

NATE DORSEY Dorsey, Nathaniel Eugene 6′4″, 240 DE
Col: Mississippi Valley State *HS:* Middleton [Tampa, FL] B: 12/6/1950, Tampa, FL *Drafted:* 1973 Round 7 Pit
1973 NE: 2 G.

DICK DORSEY Dorsey, Richard LeRoy 6′3″, 200 WR
Col: Santa Monica Coll. CA (J.C.); USC; Oklahoma *HS:* Santa Monica [CA] B: 3/11/1936, Malvern, IA *Drafted:* 1958 Round 19 LARm
1962 Oak: 11 G; Rec 21-344 16.4 2 TD; 12 Pt.

NOBLE DOSS Doss, Noble Webster 6′0″, 186 HB-DB
Col: Texas *HS:* Temple [TX] B: 5/22/1920, Temple, TX *Drafted:* 1942 Round 11 Phi
AAFC **1949** NY-A: 4 G; Rush 5-15 3.0; KR 1-22 22.0.

NFL **1947** Phi: Rec 2-17 8.5; Int 2-31. **1948** Phi: Rec 8-96 12.0; PR 1-0; KR 1-26 26.0. **Total:** Rec 10-113 11.3; PR 1-0; KR 1-26 26.0; Int 2-31.

		Rushing				
Year Team	G	Att	Yds	Avg	TD	Fum
1947 Phi	9	11	45	4.1	0	0
1948 Phi	11	62	193	3.1	0	4
NFL Total	20	73	238	3.3	0	4

REGGIE DOSS Doss, Reginald Lee 6′4″, 265 DE-DT
Col: Hampton *HS:* Sam Houston [San Antonio, TX] B: 12/7/1956, Mobile, AL *Drafted:* 1978 Round 7 LARm
1978 LARm: 16 G. **1979** LARm: 16 G. **1980** LARm: 16 G. **1981** LARm: 16 G. **1982** LARm: 9 G; 4 Sac. **1983** LARm: 16 G; 5 Sac. **1984** LARm: 16 G; 8.5 Sac. **1985** LARm: 16 G; Scor 1 Saf; 2 Pt; 2.5 Sac. **1986** LARm: 16 G. **1987** LARm: 12 G. **Total:** 149 G; Scor 1 Saf; 2 Pt; 20 Sac.

AL DOTSON Dotson, Alphonse Alan 6′4″, 260 DT
Col: Grambling State *HS:* Jack Yates [Houston, TX] B: 2/25/1943, Houston, TX *Drafted:* 1965 Redshirt Round 1 KC
1965 KC: 1 G. **1966** Mia: 9 G. **1968** Oak: 13 G. **1969** Oak: 13 G; Scor 1 Saf; 2 Pt. **1970** Oak: 11 G. **Total:** 47 G; Scor 1 Saf; 2 Pt.

EARL DOTSON Dotson, Earl Christopher 6′4″, 315 OT
Col: Tyler JC TX; Texas A&M–Kingsville *HS:* West Brook [Beaumont, TX] B: 12/17/1970, Beaumont, TX *Drafted:* 1993 Round 3 GB
1993 GB: 13 G. **1994** GB: 4 G. **1995** GB: 16 G. **1996** GB: 15 G. **1997** GB: 13 G. **1998** GB: 16 G. **Total:** 77 G.

DEWAYNE DOTSON Dotson, Jack DeWayne 6′1″, 254 LB
Col: Mississippi *HS:* Hendersonville [TN] B: 6/10/1971, Nashville, TN
Drafted: 1994 Round 4 Dal
1994 Mia: Postseason only. **1995** Mia: 15 G. **1997** Mia: 10 G; Rec 1-4 4.0. **Total:** 25 G; Rec 1-4 4.0.

SANTANA DOTSON Dotson, Santana N 6′5″, 278 DT-DE
(S.D.) *Col:* Baylor *HS:* Jack Yates [Houston, TX] B: 12/19/1969, New Orleans, LA *Drafted:* 1992 Round 5 TB
1992 TB: 16 G; 1 Fum TD; 6 Pt; 10 Sac. **1993** TB: 16 G; 5 Sac. **1994** TB: 16 G; 3 Sac. **1995** TB: 16 G; 5 Sac. **1996** GB: 16 G; 5.5 Sac. **1997** GB: 16 G; 5.5 Sac. **1998** GB: 16 G; 3 Sac. **Total:** 112 G; 1 Fum TD; 6 Pt; 37 Sac.

JOHN DOTTLEY Dottley, John Albert 6′1″, 200 FB
(Kayo) *Col:* Mississippi *HS:* McGehee [AR] B: 8/25/1928, Birmingham, AL *Drafted:* 1950 Round 2 ChiB

		Rushing				Receiving					Tot
Year Team	G	Att	Yds	Avg	TD	Rec	Yds	Avg	TD	Fum	TD
1951 ChiB	12	127	670	5.3	3	14	225	16.1	1	3	4
1952 ChiB	5	65	302	4.6	3	9	113	12.6	1	0	4

1953 ChiB	10	58	150	2.6	1	5	21	4.2	0	4	1
NFL Total	27	250	1122	4.5	7	28	359	12.8	2	7	9

DAN DOUBIAGO Doubiago, Daniel Clarke 6'5", 283 **OT**
Col: Utah *HS:* Mendocino [CA] B: 9/25/1960, Escondido, CA
1987 KC: 3 G.

JAP DOUDS Douds, Forrest McCreery 5'10", 216 **T-G-C-LB**
Col: Washington & Jefferson *HS:* Rochester [PA]; Bellefonte Acad. [PA] B: 4/21/1905, Rochester, PA D: 8/16/1979, Sewickley, PA
1930 Prov-Port: 12 G. Prov: 9 G. Port: 3 G. **1931** Port: 13 G. **1932** ChiC: 10 G. **1933** Pit: 7 G; Rush 1-2 2.0. **1934** Pit: 11 G. **Total:** 53 G; Rush 1-2 2.0.

PHIL DOUGHERTY Dougherty, Philip Francis 5'11", 185 **C-LB**
Col: Santa Clara *HS:* Mission [San Francisco, CA] B: 9/20/1912, San Francisco, CA *Drafted:* 1938 Round 7 ChiC
1938 ChiC: 8 G; Int **1** TD; 6 Pt.

BOB DOUGHERTY Dougherty, Robert William 6'1", 240 **LB**
Col: Cincinnati; Kentucky *HS:* Bellevue [KY] B: 4/20/1932, Bellevue, KY *Drafted:* 1954 Round 20 LARm
1957 LARm: 10 G; Int 1-6. **1958** Pit: 12 G. **1960** Oak: 14 G. **1961** Oak: 14 G; Int 2-12. **1962** Oak: 14 G; KR 1-20 20.0. **1963** Oak: 5 G. **Total:** 69 G; KR 1-20 20.0; Int 3-18.

GLENN DOUGHTY Doughty, Glenn Martin 6'2", 204 **WR**
Col: Michigan *HS:* Pershing [Detroit, MI] B: 1/30/1947, Detroit, MI *Drafted:* 1972 Round 2 Bal
1977 Bal: KR 1-0. **Total:** KR 1-0.

		Rushing				Receiving				
Year Team	**G**	**Att**	**Yds**	**Avg**	**TD**	**Rec**	**Yds**	**Avg**	**TD**	**Fum**
1972 Bal	5	2	33	16.5	0	3	31	10.3	0	0
1973 Bal	14	10	96	9.6	0	25	587	23.5	4	0
1974 Bal	13	7	51	7.3	0	24	300	12.5	2	0
1975 Bal	14	1	5	5.0	0	39	666	17.1	4	0
1976 Bal	14	3	7	2.3	0	40	628	15.7	5	2
1977 Bal	13	2	11	5.5	0	28	435	15.5	4	0
1978 Bal	15	1	-1	-1.0	0	25	390	15.6	3	1
1979 Bal	15	0	0	—	0	35	510	14.6	2	0
NFL Total	103	26	202	7.8	0	219	3547	16.2	24	3

DAVID DOUGLAS Douglas, David Glenn 6'4", 280 **OT-OG-C**
Col: Tennessee *HS:* Rhea Co. [Evensville, TN] B: 3/20/1963, Spring City, TN *Drafted:* 1986 Round 8 Cin
1986 Cin: 14 G. **1987** Cin: 12 G. **1988** Cin: 14 G. **1989** NE: 5 G. **1990** NE: 11 G. **Total:** 56 G.

DERRICK DOUGLAS Douglas, Derrick DeWayne 5'10", 222 **RB**
Col: Louisiana Tech *HS:* Captain Shreve [Shreveport, LA] B: 8/10/1968, Shreveport, LA *Drafted:* 1990 Round 6 TB
1991 Cle: 2 G.

EVERETT DOUGLAS Douglas, Everett Dewayne 6'3", 240 **OT**
Col: Florida *HS:* Kissimmee [FL] B: 12/22/1931 *Drafted:* 1953 Round 4 NYG
1953 NYG: 10 G.

BEN DOUGLAS Douglas, Frank Benjamin 6'0", 185 **HB**
Col: Grinnell *HS:* Grant [Cedar Rapids, IA] B: 3/12/1909, Denver, CO D: 12/4/1985, Brandon, FL
1933 Bkn: 6 G; Rush 4-6 1.5; Rec 5-86 17.2 1 TD; 6 Pt.

FREDDIE DOUGLAS Douglas, Freddie Joe 5'9", 185 **WR**
Col: Arkansas *HS:* McGehee [AR] B: 3/28/1954, McGehee, AR
1976 TB: 7 G; Rec 3-58 19.3; PR 4-78 19.5; KR 7-167 23.9.

HUGH DOUGLAS Douglas, Hugh Lamont 6'2", 270 **DE**
Col: Central State (Ohio) *HS:* Mansfield [OH] B: 8/23/1971, Mansfield, OH *Drafted:* 1995 Round 1 NYJ
1995 NYJ: 15 G; 10 Sac. **1996** NYJ: 10 G; **1** Fum TD; 6 Pt; 8 Sac. **1997** NYJ: 15 G; 4 Sac. **1998** Phi: 15 G; 12.5 Sac. **Total:** 55 G; 1 Fum TD; 6 Pt; 34.5 Sac.

JAY DOUGLAS Douglas, Jay Rufus 6'6", 250 **C**
Col: Arkansas; Memphis *HS:* North Little Rock [AR] B: 9/1/1950, Palio, KS *Drafted:* 1973 Round 11 SD
1973 SD: 14 G; KR 1-0. **1974** SD: 14 G. **Total:** 28 G; KR 1-0.

JOHN DOUGLAS Douglas, John Henry 6'1", 195 **DB**
(Blue) *Col:* Texas Southern *HS:* Como [Fort Worth, TX] B: 1/12/1945, Fort Worth, TX *Drafted:* 1967 Round 5 NO
1967 NO: 14 G; PR 2-15 7.5; KR 1-17 17.0; Int 1-19. **1968** NO: 14 G; KR 1-10 10.0. **1969** Hou: 8 G. **Total:** 36 G; PR 2-15 7.5; KR 2-27 13.5; Int 1-19.

JOHN DOUGLAS Douglas, John Louis 6'2", 228 **LB**
Col: Missouri *HS:* Columbia [MO] B: 9/6/1945, Columbia, MD
1970 NYG: 14 G; KR 1-16 16.0. **1971** NYG: 14 G; KR 1-7 7.0. **1972** NYG: 14 G; KR 4-43 10.8; Int 1-0. **1973** NYG: 14 G; Int 1-0. **Total:** 56 G; KR 6-66 11.0; Int 2-0.

LELAND DOUGLAS Douglas, Leland Cleveland 6'0", 179 **WR**
Col: Baylor *HS:* Hebert [Beaumont, TX] B: 9/23/1963, Beaumont, TX
1987 Mia: 3 G; Rec 9-92 10.2 1 TD; 6 Pt.

MERRILL DOUGLAS Douglas, Merrill George 6'0", 204 **FB-HB**
Col: Utah *HS:* Olympus [Salt Lake City, UT] B: 3/15/1936, Salt Lake City, UT *Drafted:* 1958 Round 6 ChiB
1959 ChiB: Rec 1-17 17.0. **1960** ChiB: Rec 2-11 5.5. **1961** Dal: Rec 1-(-2) -2.0; KR 1-12 12.0. **1962** Phi: KR 6-136 22.7. **Total:** Rec 4-26 6.5; KR 7-148 21.1.

		Rushing				
Year Team	**G**	**Att**	**Yds**	**Avg**	**TD**	**Fum**
1958 ChiB	12	10	53	5.3	0	1
1959 ChiB	12	24	47	2.0	2	0
1960 ChiB	12	11	82	7.5	0	0
1961 Dal	6	5	24	4.8	0	0
1962 Phi	13	4	7	1.8	0	0
NFL Total	55	54	213	3.9	2	1

OMAR DOUGLAS Douglas, Omar Kareem 5'10", 170 **WR**
Col: Minnesota *HS:* Isidore Newman [New Orleans, LA] B: 6/3/1972, New Orleans, LA
1994 NYG: 6 G. **1995** NYG: 8 G; Rec 2-15 7.5; KR 1-13 13.0; **1** Fum TD; 6 Pt; 1 Fum. **1996** NYG: 4 G; Rec 1-8 8.0; KR 1-11 11.0. **Total:** 18 G; Rec 3-23 7.7; KR 2-24 12.0; 1 Fum TD; 6 Pt; 1 Fum.

OTIS DOUGLAS Douglas, Otis Whitfield Jr. 6'1", 224 **T**
Col: William & Mary *HS:* Reedville [VA] B: 7/25/1911, Reedville, VA D: 3/21/1989, Kilmarnock, VA
1946 Phi: 11 G. **1947** Phi: 12 G. **1948** Phi: 5 G. **1949** Phi: 2 G. **Total:** 30 G.

BOB DOUGLAS Douglas, Robert 6'0", 195 **FB-DB**
Col: Kansas State B: 1915
1938 Pit: 2 G; Rush 4-10 2.5.

STEVE DOUGLAS Douglas, Stephen 200 **G-T**
Col: No College *HS:* Marquette Acad. [Milwaukee, WI]
1926 Mil: 2 G.

LEO DOUGLASS Douglass, Leo Frederick 5'11", 190 **FB-TB**
Col: Lehigh; Vermont *HS:* Wakefield [MA] B: 2/13/1901, Wakefield, MA D: 4/3/1985, Wakefield, MA
1926 Bkn-Fra: 6 G. Bkn: 4 G. Fra: 2 G. **Total:** 6 G.

MAURICE DOUGLASS Douglass, Maurice Gerrard 5'11", 203 **DB**
Col: Kentucky *HS:* Madison [Trotwood, IL] B: 2/12/1964, Muncie, IN *Drafted:* 1986 Round 8 ChiB
1986 ChiB: 4 G. **1987** ChiB: 12 G; Int 2-0. **1988** ChiB: 15 G; Int 1-35; 1 Fum. **1989** ChiB: 10 G; Int 1-0. **1990** ChiB: 11 G. **1991** ChiB: 16 G. **1992** ChiB: 16 G. **1993** ChiB: 16 G. **1994** ChiB: 16 G; Int 1-18; 1.5 Sac. **1995** NYG: 8 G; 1 Sac. **1996** NYG: 15 G; Int 1-32 1 TD; 6 Pt. **Total:** 139 G; Int 6-85 1 TD; 6 Pt; 1 Fum; 2.5 Sac.

MIKE DOUGLASS Douglass, Michael Reese 6'0", 220 **LB**
Col: Los Angeles City Coll. CA (J.C.); Arizona State; San Diego State *HS:* David Starr Jordan [Los Angeles, CA] B: 3/15/1955, St. Louis, MO *Drafted:* 1978 Round 5 GB
1982 GB: 3 Sac. **1983** GB: **2** Fum TD; 5.5 Sac. **1984** GB: 9 Sac. **1985** GB: 1.5 Sac. **Total:** 2 Fum TD; 19 Sac.

		Interceptions				Tot
Year Team	**G**	**Int**	**Yds**	**TD**	**Fum**	**TD**
1978 GB	16	0	0	0	0	0
1979 GB	16	3	73	0	0	0
1980 GB	16	0	0	0	0	0
1981 GB	16	3	20	0	0	0
1982 GB	9	2	55	0	0	0
1983 GB	15	0	0	0	0	2
1984 GB	16	0	0	0	0	0
1985 GB	15	2	126	**1**	1	1
1986 SD	7	0	0	0	0	0
NFL Total	126	10	274	1	1	3

BOBBY DOUGLASS Douglass, Robert Gilchrist 6'4", 225 **QB**
Col: Kansas *HS:* El Dorado [KS] B: 6/22/1947, Manhattan, KS *Drafted:* 1969 Round 2 ChiB
1971 ChiB: Scor **1** 1XP. **1976** NO: Rec 1-(-2) -2.0. **Total:** Rec 1-(-2) -2.0; Scor 1 1XP.

		Passing							
Year Team	**G**	**Att**	**Comp**	**Comp%**	**Yds**	**YPA**	**TD**	**Int**	**Rating**
1969 ChiB	11	148	68	45.9	773	5.22	5	8	50.9
1970 ChiB	3	30	12	40.0	218	7.27	4	3	65.7
1971 ChiB	12	225	91	40.4	1164	5.17	5	15	37.0
1972 ChiB	14	198	75	37.9	1246	6.29	9	12	49.8
1973 ChiB	13	174	81	46.6	1057	6.07	5	7	59.0
1974 ChiB	7	100	41	41.0	387	3.87	2	4	42.4
1975 ChiB-SD	4	47	15	31.9	140	2.98	0	3	14.6
1975 ChiB	1	20	8	40.0	87	4.35	0	2	14.0
1975 SD	3	27	7	25.9	53	1.96	0	1	24.2
1976 NO	11	213	103	48.4	1288	6.05	4	8	58.2

1977 NO	4	31	16	51.6	130	4.19	1	3	33.7
1978 GB	12	12	5	41.7	90	7.50	1	1	61.1
NFL Total	91	1178	507	43.0	6493	5.51	36	64	48.5

	Rushing				
Year Team	Att	Yds	Avg	TD	Fum
1969 ChiB	51	408	8.0	2	7
1970 ChiB	7	22	3.1	0	1
1971 ChiB	39	284	7.3	3	4
1972 ChiB	141	968	**6.9**	8	9
1973 ChiB	94	525	5.6	5	7
1974 ChiB	36	229	6.4	1	0
1975 ChiB-SD	15	76	5.1	1	1
1975 ChiB	5	34	6.8	1	0
1975 SD	10	42	4.2	0	1
1976 NO	21	92	4.4	2	1
1977 NO	2	23	11.5	0	1
1978 GB	4	27	6.8	0	0
NFL Total	410	2654	6.5	22	31

TY DOUTHARD Douthard, Talib Yakee 6′1″, 215 **RB**
Col: Illinois *HS:* La Salle [Cincinnati, OH] B: 5/27/1973, Cincinnati, OH
1997 Cin: 1 G.

EARL DOUTHITT Douthitt, Earl Jr. 6′2″, 188 **DB**
Col: Iowa *HS:* John Hay [Cleveland, OH] B: 9/8/1952, Cleveland, OH
Drafted: 1975 Round 7 ChiB
1975 ChiB: 9 G; KR 13-333 25.6; 1 Fum.

EDDIE DOVE Dove, Edward Everest 6′2″, 181 **DB**
Col: Colorado *HS:* Loveland [CO] B: 4/4/1937, Hygiene, CO
Drafted: 1959 Round 3 SF
1963 SF-NYG: KR 3-56 18.7. NYG: KR 3-56 18.7. **Total:** KR 3-56 18.7.

		Punt Returns				Interceptions			
Year Team	G	Ret	Yds	Avg	TD	Int	Yds	TD	Fum
1959 SF	12	22	126	5.7	0	1	6	0	2
1960 SF	12	11	43	3.9	0	3	29	0	1
1961 SF	14	6	49	8.2	0	3	41	0	0
1962 SF	14	5	21	4.2	0	1	0	0	1
1963 SF-NYG	14	17	198	11.6	0	2	75	0	3
1963 SF	2	0	0	—	0	0	0	0	0
1963 NYG	12	17	198	11.6	0	2	75	0	3
NFL Total	66	61	437	7.2	0	10	151	0	7

JEROME DOVE Dove, Jerome 6′0″, 190 **DB**
Col: Hutchinson CC KS; Colorado State *HS:* Huntington [Newport News, VA]; Menchville HS [Newport News, VA] B: 10/3/1953, Newport News, VA *Drafted:* 1976 Round 8 Oak
1977 SD: 14 G; PR 1-3 3.0; Int 1-32; 1 Fum. **1978** SD: 14 G; Int 1-4. **1979** SD: 16 G. **1980** SD: 16 G. **Total:** 60 G; PR 1-3 3.0; Int 2-36; 1 Fum.

BOB DOVE Dove, Robert Leo Patrick 6′2″, 222 **DE-OE**
(Grandpappy) *Col:* Notre Dame *HS:* South [Youngstown, OH]
B: 2/21/1921, Youngstown, OH *Drafted:* 1943 Round 3 Was
AAFC **1946** ChiA: 14 G; Rec 7-67 9.6 1 TD; 6 Pt. **1947** ChiA: 13 G; Rec 6-61 10.2 1 TD; KR 1-16 16.0; 6 Pt. **Total:** 27 G; Rec 13-128 9.8 2 TD; KR 1-16 16.0; 12 Pt.

NFL **1948** ChiC: 12 G; Rush 1-(-2) -2.0. **1949** ChiC: 12 G. **1950** ChiC: 12 G; Int 1-0. **1951** ChiC: 12 G. **1952** ChiC: 11 G. **1953** ChiC-Det: 8 G. ChiC: 4 G. Det: 4 G. **1954** Det: 12 G. **Total:** 79 G; Rush 1-(-2) -2.0; Int 1-0.

WES DOVE Dove, Wesley Walker 6′7″, 270 **DE**
Col: Syracuse *HS:* Kenmore East [Tonawanda, NY] B: 2/9/1964, Buffalo, NY D: 3/24/1989, Gaithersburg, MD *Drafted:* 1987 Round 12 Sea
1987 Sea: 2 G.

HARLEY DOW Dow, Harley Duane 6′2″, 220 **OG-OT**
Col: San Jose State *HS:* Verdugo Hills [Tujunga, CA] B: 10/19/1925, Mt.Hope, KS *Drafted:* 1950 Round 11 SF
1950 SF: 12 G.

WOODY DOW Dow, Jess Lwood 6′0″, 195 **FB-DB-LB**
(Rowdy; Cub) *Col:* West Texas A&M *HS:* Littlefield [TX]
B: 12/16/1914, Littlefield, TX
1938 Phi: 10 G; Rush 4-20 5.0; Rec 5-88 17.6 1 TD; 6 Pt. **1939** Phi: 9 G; Rush 1-(-7) -7.0; Rec 5-58 11.6. **1940** Phi: 11 G. **Total:** 30 G; Rush 5-13 2.6; Rec 10-146 14.6 1 TD; 6 Pt.

KEN DOW Dow, Kenneth William 5′10″, 198 **FB-DB**
Col: Oregon State *HS:* Great Falls [MT] B: 11/18/1917, Euphrata, WA
D: 11/17/1988, Helena, MT *Drafted:* 1941 Round 14 Was
1941 Was: 2 G.

JERRY DOWD Dowd, Jerry 6′0″, 210 **C-LB**
Col: St. Mary's (Cal.) *HS:* Lowell [San Francisco, CA] B: 11/29/1916
D: 8/24/1995 *Drafted:* 1939 Round 7 Cle
1939 Cle: 9 G; Int **1** TD; 6 Pt.

HARRY DOWDA Dowda, Harry Clinton 6′2″, 195 **DB**
Col: Wake Forest *HS:* Hickory [NC]; West Fulton HS [Atlanta, GA]
B: 12/29/1922, Atlanta, GA D: 6/24/1996, Wintergreen, VA
Drafted: 1947 Round 17 Was
1949 Was: Rec 11-187 17.0 1 TD. **1950** Was: Rec 2-16 8.0. **1951** Was: Rec 2-54 27.0; KR 13-341 26.2. **1952** Was: Rec 3-20 6.7 1 TD.
Total: Rec 18-277 15.4 2 TD; KR 13-341 26.2.

		Rushing				Interceptions				Tot
Year Team	G	Att	Yds	Avg	TD	Int	Yds	TD	Fum	TD
1949 Was	12	65	239	3.7	2	3	36	0	3	3
1950 Was	12	23	47	2.0	0	4	28	1	1	1
1951 Was	12	29	111	3.8	0	0	0	0	2	0
1952 Was	12	6	5	0.8	0	2	34	0	1	1
1953 Was	12	1	3	3.0	0	5	67	**1**	1	1
1954 Phi	12	0	0	—	0	2	34	0	0	0
1955 Phi	12	0	0	—	0	0	0	0	0	0
NFL Total	84	124	405	3.3	2	16	199	2	8	6

MARCUS DOWDELL Dowdell, Marcus Llewellyn 6′0″, 188 **WR**
Col: Tennessee State *HS:* Banks [Birmingham, AL] B: 5/22/1970, Birmingham, AL *Drafted:* 1992 Round 10 NO
1993 NO: KR 0-52. **1995** Ariz: KR 18-344 19.1. **1996** Ariz: KR 5-122 24.4.
Total: KR 23-518 22.5.

		Receiving				Punt Returns				
Year Team	G	Rec	Yds	Avg	TD	Ret	Yds	Avg	TD	Fum
1992 NO	4	1	6	6.0	0	12	37	3.1	0	4
1993 NO	9	6	46	7.7	1	0	0	—	0	1
1995 Ariz	13	10	96	9.6	0	1	0	0.0	0	1
1996 Ariz	15	20	318	15.9	2	34	297	8.7	0	6
NFL Total	41	37	466	12.6	3	47	334	7.1	0	12

COREY DOWDEN Dowden, Corey 5′11″, 190 **DB**
Col: Tulane *HS:* McDonogh [New Orleans, LA] B: 10/18/1968, New Orleans, LA
1996 GB-Bal: 12 G; Int 1-5. GB: 9 G; Int 1-5. Bal: 3 G. **1997** ChiB: 2 G.
Total: 14 G; Int 1-5.

STEVE DOWDEN Dowden, Steve Henry 6′2″, 235 **OT**
Col: Baylor *HS:* Odessa [TX] B: 2/24/1929, Natchitoches, LA
Drafted: 1952 Round 10 Det
1952 GB: 12 G.

MIKE DOWDLE Dowdle, Donald Michael 6′3″, 235 **LB-FB**
Col: Texas *HS:* Graham [TX] B: 12/6/1937, Eliasville, TX
D: 12/5/1993, Houston, TX *Drafted:* 1960 Round 15 SF
1960 Dal: 2 G; KR 2-22 11.0. **1961** Dal: 14 G; KR 2-33 16.5; Int 1-14. **1962** Dal: 14 G; Int 1-7. **1963** SF: 13 G; Int 2-6. **1964** SF: 14 G; Int 1-14. **1965** SF: 10 G. **1966** SF: 14 G; Int 1-27 1 TD; 6 Pt. **Total:** 81 G; KR 4-55 13.8; Int 6-68 1 TD; 6 Pt.

MULE DOWELL Dowell, Gwyn Clark 6′2″, 206 **FB-DB-LB**
Col: Texas Tech *HS:* Royse City [TX] B: 6/27/1913, Ben Franklin, TX
D: 8/12/1992, Richardson, TX
1936 ChiC: Pass 2-1 50.0%, 6 3.00. **Total:** Pass 2-1 50.0%, 6 3.00.

		Rushing			
Year Team	G	Att	Yds	Avg	TD
1935 ChiC	5	6	4	0.7	0
1936 ChiC	10	54	151	2.8	0
NFL Total	15	60	155	2.6	0

BOYD DOWLER Dowler, Boyd Hamilton 6′5″, 224 **FL-DE-WR**
Col: Colorado *HS:* Cheyenne [WY] B: 10/18/1937, Rock Springs, WY
Drafted: 1959 Round 3 GB
1959 GB: Rush 1-20 20.0. **1960** GB: Rush 1-8 8.0. **Total:** Rush 2-28 14.0.

		Receiving				Punting			
Year Team	G	Rec	Yds	Avg	TD	Punts	Yds	Avg	Fum
1959 GB	12	32	549	17.2	4	0	0	—	0
1960 GB	12	30	505	16.8	2	18	729	40.5	0
1961 GB	14	36	633	17.6	3	38	1674	44.1	0
1962 GB	14	49	724	14.8	2	36	1550	43.1	1
1963 GB	14	53	901	17.0	6	0	0	—	4
1964 GB	14	45	623	13.8	5	0	0	—	1
1965 GB	14	44	610	13.9	4	0	0	—	1
1966 GB	14	29	392	13.5	0	0	0	—	1
1967 GB	14	54	836	15.5	4	0	0	—	0
1968 GB	14	45	668	14.8	6	0	0	—	0
1969 GB	14	31	477	15.4	4	1	34	34.0	0
1971 Was	12	26	352	13.5	0	0	0	—	1
NFL Total	162	474	7270	15.3	40	93	3987	42.9	9

TOMMY DOWLER Dowler, Thomas Moran 5′8″, 160 **WB**
(Flash) *Col:* Colgate *HS:* East [Erie, PA] B: 7/3/1908, Erie, PA
D: 12/6/1986, Atlanta, GA
1931 Bkn: 2 G.

BRIAN DOWLING Dowling, Brian John 6'2", 210 **QB**
Col: Yale *HS:* St. Ignatius [Cleveland, OH] B: 4/1/1947, Cleveland, OH
Drafted: 1969 Round 11 Min
1972 NE: Rush 7-35 5.0 3 TD. **Total:** Rush 7-35 5.0 3 TD.

		Passing							
Year Team	G	Att	Comp	Comp%	Yds	YPA	TD	Int	Rating
1972 NE	14	54	29	53.7	383	7.09	2	1	81.0
1973 NE	11	0	0	—	0	—	0	0	—
1977 GB	2	1	0	0.0	0	0.00	0	0	39.6
NFL Total	27	55	29	52.7	383	6.96	2	1	79.6

PAT DOWLING Dowling, Patrick Arthur 5'11", 185 **OE**
(Smoke Screen) *Col:* DePaul *HS:* St. Patrick [Chicago, IL]
B: 4/14/1901, Chicago, IL D: 7/1984, Chicago, IL
1929 ChiC: 13 G.

SEAN DOWLING Dowling, Sean 6'4", 280 **OG-OT**
Col: C.W. Post *HS:* Oyster Bay [NY] B: 2/19/1963, New York, NY
1987 Buf: 3 G.

WALT DOWNING Downing, Walter Tyson 6'3", 259 **OG-C**
Col: Michigan *HS:* Coatesville [PA] B: 6/11/1956, Coatesville, PA
Drafted: 1978 Round 2 SF
1978 SF: 16 G; KR 2-13 6.5; 1 Fum. **1979** SF: 16 G. **1980** SF: 14 G.
1981 SF: 16 G. **1982** SF: 9 G. **1983** SF: 12 G. **Total:** 83 G; KR 2-13 6.5;
1 Fum.

GARY DOWNS Downs, Gary McLinton Jr. 6'1", 212 **RB**
Col: North Carolina State *HS:* William H. Spencer [Columbus, GA]
B: 6/6/1972, Columbus, GA *Drafted:* 1994 Round 3 NYG
1994 NYG: Rec 2-15 7.5. **1996** NYG: Rec 3-20 6.7. **1998** Atl: Rec 4-31
7.8. **Total:** Rec 9-66 7.3.

		Rushing				
Year Team	G	Att	Yds	Avg	TD	Fum
1994 NYG	14	15	51	3.4	0	1
1995 Den	2	0	0	—	0	0
1996 NYG	6	29	94	3.2	0	1
1997 Atl	16	0	0	—	0	0
1998 Atl	16	1	4	4.0	0	0
NFL Total	54	45	149	3.3	0	2

MICHAEL DOWNS Downs, Michael Lynn 6'3", 205 **DB**
Col: Rice *HS:* South Oak Cliff [Dallas, TX] B: 6/9/1959, Dallas, TX
1982 Dal: 1 Fum TD; 1 Sac. **1983** Dal: 1 Fum TD; 1.5 Sac. **1984** Dal:
3.5 Sac. **1985** Dal: 0.5 Sac. **1986** Dal: 1 Sac. **1988** Dal: 0.5 Sac.
Total: 2 Fum TD; 8 Sac.

		Interceptions			Tot
Year Team	G	Int	Yds	TD	TD
1981 Dal	15	7	81	0	0
1982 Dal	9	1	22	0	1
1983 Dal	16	4	80	0	1
1984 Dal	16	7	126	1	1
1985 Dal	16	3	11	0	0
1986 Dal	16	6	54	0	0
1987 Dal	12	4	56	0	0
1988 Dal	16	2	3	0	0
1989 Pho	5	1	37	0	0
NFL Total	121	35	470	1	3

BOB DOWNS Downs, Robert LeRoy 5'10", 210 **OG**
Col: USC *HS:* Alhambra [CA] B: 1927, Los Angeles, CA
1951 SF: 1 G.

XAVIER DOWNWIND Downwind, Xavier 6'0", 200 **T-OE**
(Red Fang; Chief) *Col:* Carlisle B: 12/24/1893, Red Lake Indian
Reservation, MN D: 7/24/1968, Bemidji, MN
1922 Oor: 5 G. **1923** Oor: 2 G. **Total:** 7 G.

PERRY DOWRICK Dowrick, Pirre 172 **FB**
Col: No College *HS:* Business [Washington, DC] B: 7/1894,
Washington, DC Deceased
1921 Was: 2 G.

TODD DOXZON Doxzon, Todd Matthew 6'1", 186 **WR**
Col: Iowa State *HS:* Millard North [Omaha, NE] B: 3/28/1975, Sioux
City, IA
1998 Mia: 9 G; Rush 2-6 3.0.

EDDIE DOYLE Doyle, Edward James 5'9", 173 **E**
Col: Army *HS:* North [Syracuse, NY] B: 8/17/1898, New York, NY
D: 11/8/1942, Morocco
1924 Fra: 10 G; Rec 2 TD; 12 Pt. **1925** Pott: 9 G; Rec 1 TD; 6 Pt.
Total: 19 G; Rec 3 TD; 18 Pt.

ED DOYLE Doyle, Edward Joseph 5'10", 190 **G**
(E.J.) *Col:* Canisius *HS:* Hutchinson [Buffalo, NY]; Canisius Prep
[Buffalo, NY] B: 7/7/1906, Buffalo, NY Deceased
1927 Buf: 5 G.

DICK DOYLE Doyle, Richard Albert 6'0", 193 **DB**
(Skip) *Col:* Ohio State *HS:* Rochester [PA] B: 3/25/1930
Drafted: 1952 Round 27 Pit
1955 Pit: 12 G; Int 1-4. **1960** Den: 6 G; Int 1-24. **Total:** 18 G; Int 2-28.

TED DOYLE Doyle, Theodore Dennison 6'2", 224 **T-G**
Col: Northeast CC NE; Nebraska *HS:* Curtis [NE] B: 1/12/1914,
Maywood, NE *Drafted:* 1938 Round 6 NYG
1938 Pit: 9 G. **1939** Pit: 9 G. **1940** Pit: 6 G. **1941** Pit: 9 G. **1942** Pit: 11 G.
1943 PhPt: 10 G. **1944** ChPt: 10 G. **1945** Pit: 10 G; Int 1-50 1 TD; 6 Pt.
Total: 74 G; Int 1-50 1 TD; 6 Pt.

CORNELIUS DOZIER Dozier, Cornelius Leslie 6'2", 190 **DB**
Col: Southern Methodist *HS:* South Oak Cliff [Dallas, TX] B: 2/5/1964,
Ennis, TX
1987 KC: 2 G.

D.J. DOZIER Dozier, William Henry Jr. 6'0", 200 **RB**
Col: Penn State *HS:* Kempsville [Virginia Beach, VA] B: 9/21/1965,
Norfolk, VA *Drafted:* 1987 Round 1 Min
1987 Min: KR 2-23 11.5. **1988** Min: KR 5-105 21.0. **1989** Min: Pass 1-1
100.0%, 19 19.00 1 TD; KR 12-258 21.5. **1991** Det: KR 4-60 15.0.
Total: Pass 1-1 100.0%, 19 19.00 1 TD; KR 23-446 19.4.

		Rushing				Receiving					Tot
Year Team	G	Att	Yds	Avg	TD	Rec	Yds	Avg	TD	Fum	TD
1987 Min	9	69	257	3.7	5	12	89	7.4	2	2	7
1988 Min	8	42	167	4.0	2	5	49	9.8	0	0	2
1989 Min	14	46	207	4.5	0	14	148	10.6	0	2	0
1990 Min	6	6	12	2.0	0	1	12	12.0	0	0	0
1991 Det	6	9	48	5.3	0	1	3	3.0	0	0	0
NFL Total	43	172	691	4.0	7	33	301	9.1	2	4	9

CHRIS DRAFT Draft, Chris 5'11", 225 **LB**
Col: Stanford *HS:* Valencia [Placentia, CA] B: 2/26/1976, Anaheim, CA
Drafted: 1998 Round 6 ChiB
1998 ChiB: 1 G.

OSCAR DRAGON Dragon, Oscar Lee 6'0", 214 **RB**
Col: Arizona State *HS:* Chowchilla [CA] B: 3/2/1950, Madera, CA
Drafted: 1972 Round 17 SD
1972 SD: 13 G; Rush 9-30 3.3.

JERRY DRAKE Drake, Jerry 6'5", 298 **DE**
Col: Ulster County CC NY; Hastings *HS:* Kingston [NY] B: 7/9/1969,
Kingston, NY
1995 Ariz: 2 G. **1996** Ariz: 11 G. **1998** Ariz: 1 G. **Total:** 14 G.

JOE DRAKE Drake, Joe Lynn 6'2", 290 **NT**
Col: Arizona *HS:* Galileo [San Francisco, CA] B: 5/28/1963, San
Francisco, CA *Drafted:* 1985 Round 9 Phi
1985 Phi: 16 G. **1987** SF: 3 G. **Total:** 19 G.

JOHNNY DRAKE Drake, John William 6'1", 213 **FB-DB-LB-WB**
Col: Purdue *HS:* Bowen [Chicago, IL] B: 3/27/1916, Chicago, IL
D: 3/25/1973, Detroit, MI *Drafted:* 1937 Round 1 Cle
1937 Cle: Pass 1-0. **1938** Cle: Pass 3-1 33.3%, 8 2.67. **1940** Cle:
Pass 4-2 50.0%, 16 4.00 2 TD; Int 1-2; Scor 56, 0-1 FG, 2-5 40.0% XK.
1941 Cle: Pass 2-0; KR 4-64 16.0; Int 2-66. **Total:** Pass 10-3 30.0%, 24
2.40 2 TD; KR 4-64 16.0; Int 3-68; Scor 164, 0-1 FG, 2-5 40.0% XK.

		Rushing				Receiving				Tot
Year Team	G	Att	Yds	Avg	TD	Rec	Yds	Avg	TD	TD
1937 Cle	11	98	333	3.4	3	10	172	17.2	2	5
1938 Cle	11	74	188	2.5	1	2	13	6.5	0	1
1939 Cle	11	118	453	3.8	**9**	5	53	10.6	0	9
1940 Cle	11	134	480	3.6	**9**	8	81	10.1	0	**9**
1941 Cle	11	101	246	2.4	2	16	211	13.2	1	3
NFL Total	55	525	1700	3.2	24	41	530	12.9	3	27

TROY DRAKE Drake, Troy Adam 6'6", 294 **OT**
Col: Indiana *HS:* Byron [IL] B: 5/15/1972, Rockford, IL
1995 Phi: 1 G. **1996** Phi: 11 G. **1997** Phi: 9 G. **1998** Was: 11 G.
Total: 32 G.

BILL DRAKE Drake, William Donald 6'1", 195 **DB-WR**
Col: Oregon *HS:* Jefferson [Portland, OR] B: 5/22/1950, Portland, OR
1973 LARm: 4 G. **1974** LARm: 9 G. **Total:** 13 G.

TYRONNE DRAKEFORD Drakeford, Tyronne James 5'11", 185 **DB**
Col: Virginia Tech *HS:* North Central [Camden, SC]; Fork Union Mil.
Acad. [VA] B: 6/21/1971, Camden, SC *Drafted:* 1994 Round 2 SF
1995 SF: 1 Sac. **1996** SF: 2 Sac. **1997** SF: KR 1-24 24.0. **Total:** KR 1-24
24.0; 3 Sac.

		Interceptions			
Year Team	G	Int	Yds	TD	Fum
1994 SF	13	1	6	0	0
1995 SF	16	5	54	0	1
1996 SF	16	1	11	0	0
1997 SF	16	5	15	0	0

1998 NO	16	4	76	1	0
NFL Total	77	16	162	1	1

DWIGHT DRANE Drane, Dwight 6'2", 204 **DB**
Col: Oklahoma *HS:* Miami Central [FL] B: 5/6/1962, Miami, FL
Drafted: 1984 Supplemental Round 1 Buf
1986 Buf: 13 G; 1 Sac. **1987** Buf: 11 G; 1 Sac. **1988** Buf: 16 G. **1989** Buf: 16 G; Int 1-25. **1990** Buf: 12 G. **1991** Buf: 14 G. **Total:** 82 G; Int 1-25; 2 Sac.

LEO DRAVELING Draveling, Leo Frank 6'2", 210 **T**
(Firpo) *Col:* Michigan *HS:* Port Huron [MI] B: 6/23/1907, Port Huron, MI D: 7/2/1955, Port Huron, MI
1933 Cin: 9 G.

CLARENCE DRAYER Drayer, Clarence Tilghman 6'4", 225 **T**
(Shorty) *Col:* Illinois *HS:* Indianapolis Tech [IN] B: 8/29/1901, Columbus, OH D: 10/8/1977, Indianapolis, IN
1925 Day: 4 G.

TROY DRAYTON Drayton, Troy Anthony 6'3", 260 **TE**
Col: Penn State *HS:* Highspire [Steelton, PA] B: 6/29/1970, Harrisburg, PA *Drafted:* 1993 Round 2 LARm
1993 LARm: Rush 1-7 7.0; KR 1-(-15) -15.0. **1994** LARm: Rush 1-4 4.0. **1996** StL-Mia: Scor 1 2XP. Mia: Scor 1 2XP. **Total:** Rush 2-11 5.5; KR 1-(-15) -15.0; Scor 1 2XP.

		Receiving				
Year Team	**G**	**Rec**	**Yds**	**Avg**	**TD**	**Fum**
1993 LARm	16	27	319	11.8	4	1
1994 LARm	16	32	276	8.6	6	0
1995 StL	16	47	458	9.7	4	2
1996 StL-Mia	13	28	331	11.8	0	0
1996 StL	3	2	11	5.5	0	0
1996 Mia	10	26	320	12.3	0	0
1997 Mia	16	39	558	14.3	4	0
1998 Mia	15	30	334	11.1	3	0
NFL Total	92	203	2276	11.2	21	3

CHUCK DRAZENOVICH Drazenovich, Charles Mark 6'1", 225 **LB-FB**
Col: Penn State *HS:* Brownsville [PA] B: 8/7/1927, Jere, WV
D: 2/27/1992, Annandale, VA *Drafted:* 1949 Round 9 Det
1950 Was: Rec 3-38 12.7; KR 3-38 12.7. **1951** Was: Rec 1-27 27.0. **1952** Was: Rec 4-62 15.5. **1954** Was: Rec 1-15 15.0; KR 1-17 17.0. **1955** Was: Rec 1-(-3) -3.0. **Total:** Rec 10-139 13.9; KR 4-55 13.8.

		Rushing				Interceptions			
Year Team	**G**	**Att**	**Yds**	**Avg**	**TD**	**Int**	**Yds**	**TD**	**Fum**
1950 Was	12	35	155	4.4	1	2	43	0	3
1951 Was	9	34	76	2.2	3	2	27	0	1
1952 Was	12	29	66	2.3	3	3	58	0	1
1953 Was	8	11	27	2.5	1	0	0	0	0
1954 Was	12	8	6	0.8	0	1	5	0	2
1955 Was	12	0	0	—	0	2	10	0	0
1956 Was	12	0	0	—	0	0	0	0	0
1957 Was	12	0	0	—	0	2	6	0	0
1958 Was	12	0	0	—	0	2	16	0	0
1959 Was	12	0	0	—	0	1	0	0	0
NFL Total	113	117	330	2.8	8	15	165	0	7

DAVE DRECHSLER Drechsler, David Edwin 6'3", 264 **OG**
Col: North Carolina *HS:* West Rowan [Mount Ulla, NC] B: 7/18/1960, Bethesda, MD *Drafted:* 1983 Round 2 GB
1983 GB: 16 G; KR 1-1 1.0. **1984** GB: 16 G. **Total:** 32 G; KR 1-1 1.0.

FERD DREHER Dreher, Ferdinand Adolphus 6'3", 205 **E**
Col: Arkansas State; Denver *HS:* Jonesboro [AR] B: 2/23/1913, Jonesboro, AR *Drafted:* 1938 Round 10 ChiB
1938 ChiB: 3 G; Rec 3-69 23.0 1 TD; 6 Pt.

CHRIS DRESSEL Dressel, Christopher John 6'4", 238 **TE**
Col: Stanford *HS:* El Dorado [Placentia, CA] B: 2/7/1961, Placentia, CA *Drafted:* 1983 Round 3 Hou
1983 Hou: Rush 1-3 3.0; KR 4-40 10.0. **1990** NYJ: KR 1-7 7.0. **1991** NYJ: KR 1-0. **Total:** Rush 1-3 3.0; KR 6-47 7.8.

		Receiving				
Year Team	**G**	**Rec**	**Yds**	**Avg**	**TD**	**Fum**
1983 Hou	16	32	316	9.9	4	0
1984 Hou	16	40	378	9.5	2	1
1985 Hou	16	3	17	5.7	1	0
1986 Hou	16	0	0	—	0	0
1987 SF	1	1	8	8.0	0	0
1989 KC-NYJ	15	12	191	15.9	1	1
1989 KC	7	9	136	15.1	1	1
1989 NYJ	8	3	55	18.3	0	0
1990 NYJ	15	6	66	11.0	0	1
1991 NYJ	15	17	122	7.2	0	0
1992 SF	1	0	0	—	0	0
NFL Total	111	111	1098	9.9	8	3

CHUCK DRESSEN Dressen, Charles Walter 5'6", 147 **BB-QB**
Col: No College *HS:* Assumption [East St. Louis, IL] B: 9/20/1898, Decatur, IL D: 8/10/1966, Detroit, MI
1920 Sta: 4 G. **1922** Rac: 7 G; Pass 1 TD; Rush 2 TD; 12 Pt. **1923** Rac: 1 G. **Total:** 12 G; Pass 1 TD; Rush 2 TD; 12 Pt.

DOUG DRESSLER Dressler, Douglas J 6'3", 228 **RB**
Col: Coll. of Marin CA (J.C.); Cal State-Chico *HS:* Las Vegas [NV]
B: 8/19/1948, Beaver Falls, PA
1970 Cin: KR 4-48 12.0. **1971** Cin: KR 1-20 20.0; Punt 1-34 34.0. **1974** Cin: KR 3-32 10.7. **1975** NE-KC: KR 1-18 18.0; Punt 4-100 25.0. KC: KR 1-18 18.0; Punt 4-100 25.0. **Total:** KR 9-118 13.1; Punt 5-134 26.8.

		Rushing				Receiving					Tot
Year Team	**G**	**Att**	**Yds**	**Avg**	**TD**	**Rec**	**Yds**	**Avg**	**TD**	**Fum**	**TD**
1970 Cin	14	18	77	4.3	0	0	0	—	0	2	0
1971 Cin	14	54	204	3.8	1	19	145	7.6	0	1	1
1972 Cin	14	128	565	4.4	6	39	348	8.9	1	4	7
1974 Cin	13	72	255	3.5	2	29	196	6.8	0	5	2
1975 NE-KC	13	6	24	4.0	0	3	6	2.0	1	0	1
1975 NE	5	3	8	2.7	0	1	-1	-1.0	0	0	0
1975 KC	8	3	16	5.3	0	2	7	3.5	1	0	1
NFL Total	68	278	1125	4.0	9	90	695	7.7	2	12	11

WILLIE DREWREY Drewrey, Willie James 5'7", 164 **WR**
Col: West Virginia *HS:* Northern Burlington Co. [Columbus, NJ]
B: 4/28/1963, Columbus, NJ *Drafted:* 1985 Round 11 Hou
1985 Hou: Rush 2-(-4) -2.0. **Total:** Rush 2-(-4) -2.0.

		Receiving				Punt Returns			
Year Team	**G**	**Rec**	**Yds**	**Avg**	**TD**	**Ret**	**Yds**	**Avg**	**TD**
1985 Hou	14	2	28	14.0	0	24	215	9.0	0
1986 Hou	15	18	299	16.6	0	34	262	7.7	0
1987 Hou	12	11	148	13.5	0	3	11	3.7	0
1988 Hou	14	11	172	15.6	1	2	8	4.0	0
1989 TB	16	14	157	11.2	1	20	220	11.0	0
1990 TB	16	7	182	26.0	1	23	184	8.0	0
1991 TB	16	26	375	14.4	2	38	360	9.5	0
1992 TB	9	16	237	14.8	2	7	62	8.9	0
1993 Hou	16	1	3	3.0	0	41	275	6.7	0
NFL Total	128	106	1601	15.1	7	192	1597	8.3	0

	Kickoff Returns				
Year Team	**Ret**	**Yds**	**Avg**	**TD**	**Fum**
1985 Hou	26	642	24.7	0	2
1986 Hou	25	500	20.0	0	3
1987 Hou	8	136	17.0	0	0
1988 Hou	1	10	10.0	0	0
1989 TB	1	26	26.0	0	0
1990 TB	14	244	17.4	0	1
1991 TB	12	246	20.5	0	3
1993 Hou	15	293	19.5	0	2
NFL Total	102	2097	20.6	0	11

TED DREWS Drews, Theodore Williams 6'0", 185 **E**
Col: Princeton *HS:* St. Albans [Washington, DC] B: 12/15/1902, Chicago, IL D: 4/15/1982, Daytona Beach, FL
1926 Bkn: 3 G. **1928** ChiB: 7 G; Scor **1** 1XP; 1 Pt. **Total:** 10 G; Scor 1 1XP; 1 Pt.

WALLY DREYER Dreyer, Walter Otto 5'10", 165 **HB-DB**
(Kid) *Col:* Michigan; Wisconsin *HS:* Washington [Milwaukee, WI]; University HS [Milwaukee , WI] B: 2/25/1923, Milwaukee, WI
Drafted: 1947 Round 15 ChiB
1949 ChiB: Rec 7-94 13.4; PR 13-130 10.0; KR 13-338 26.0. **1950** GB: PR 3-48 16.0; Int 5-62 1 TD. **Total:** Rec 7-94 13.4; PR 16-178 11.1; KR 13-338 26.0; Int 5-62 1 TD.

		Rushing				
Year Team	**G**	**Att**	**Yds**	**Avg**	**TD**	**Fum**
1949 ChiB	12	45	172	3.8	0	3
1950 GB	12	1	0	0.0	0	0
NFL Total	24	46	172	3.7	0	3

PADDY DRISCOLL Driscoll, John Leo 5'11", 160 **TB-HB-BB-QB**
Col: Northwestern *HS:* Evanston Twp. [Evanston, IL] B: 1/11/1895, Evanston, IL D: 6/28/1968, Chicago, IL *HOF:* 1965
1921 ChiC: Pass 1 TD; Rush 2 TD; PR **1** TD. **1922** ChiC: Pass 1 TD; Rec **2** TD. **1923** ChiC: Pass 1 TD; Rush 6 TD; Rec 1 TD. **1924** ChiC: Pass 2 TD; Rush 1 TD. **1925** ChiC: Rush 4 TD. **1926** ChiB: Pass **6** TD; Rush 4 TD; Rec 1 TD; 1 Fum TD. **1927** ChiB: Pass 3 TD; Rush 5 TD. **1928** ChiB: Pass 2 TD; Rush 2 TD. **1929** ChiB: Rush 1 TD.
Total: Pass 16 TD; Rush 25 TD; Rec 4 TD; PR 1 TD; 1 Fum TD.

		Scoring							Tot
Year Team	**G**	**Pts**	**FG**	**FGA**	**FG%**	**XK**	**XKA**	**XK%**	**TD**
1920 ChiC-Sta	10	—	—	—	—	—	—	—	—
1920 ChiC	9	—	—	—	—	—	—	—	—
1920 Sta	1	—	—	—	—	—	—	—	—

1921 ChiC	8	25	1	—	—	4	—	—	3
1922 ChiC	11	40	**8**	—	—	4	—	—	2
1923 ChiC	10	**78**	**10**	—	—	6	—	—	**7**
1924 ChiC	10	34	7	—	—	7	—	—	1
1925 ChiC	13	67	**11**	—	—	10	—	—	4
1926 ChiB	16	**86**	**12**	—	—	14	—	—	6
1927 ChiB	14	43	2	—	—	7	—	—	5
1928 ChiB	12	20	0	—	—	8	—	—	2
1929 ChiB	14	9	0	—	—	3	—	—	1
NFL Total	118	402	51	—	—	63	—	—	31

JOE DRISKILL Driskill, Joseph Guyon 6'1", 195 **DB**
Col: Northeast Louisiana *HS:* Arcadia [LA] B: 8/10/1937, Arcadia, LA
1960 StL: 6 G; KR 1-0; 1 Fum. **1961** StL: 14 G; PR 1-8 8.0; KR 2-8 4.0.
Total: 20 G; PR 1-8 8.0; KR 3-8 2.7; 1 Fum.

STACEY DRIVER Driver, Stacey Staphon 5'7", 190 **RB**
Col: Clemson *HS:* Griffin [GA] B: 3/4/1964, Griffin, GA
1987 Cle: 2 G; Rush 9-31 3.4; KR 1-16 16.0; 1 Fum.

SHANE DRONETT Dronett, Carlton Shane 6'6", 281 **DT-DE**
Col: Texas *HS:* Bridge City [TX] B: 1/12/1971, Orange, TX
Drafted: 1992 Round 2 Den
1992 Den: 16 G; 6.5 Sac. **1993** Den: 16 G; Int 2-13; 7 Sac. **1994** Den: 16 G; 6 Sac. **1995** Den: 13 G; 2 Sac. **1996** Atl-Det: 12 G. Atl: 5 G. Det: 7 G. **1997** Atl: 16 G; 3 Sac. **1998** Atl: 16 G; 6.5 Sac. **Total:** 105 G; Int 2-13; 31.0 Sac.

JEFF DROST Drost, Jeffrey Wayne 6'5", 286 **DT**
Col: Iowa *HS:* Indianola [IA] B: 1/27/1964, San Angelo, TX
Drafted: 1987 Round 8 GB
1987 GB: 2 G; 2 Sac.

TOM DROUGAS Drougas, Thomas Christopher Jr. 6'4", 257 **OT-OG**
Col: Oregon *HS:* Sunset [Beaverton, OR] B: 12/25/1949, Portland, OR
Drafted: 1972 Round 1 Bal
1972 Bal: 14 G. **1973** Bal: 13 G. **1974** Den-KC: 10 G. Den: 3 G. KC: 7 G.
1975 Mia: 14 G. **1976** Mia: 14 G. **Total:** 65 G.

DARREN DROZDOV Drozdov, Darren 6'3", 281 **NT**
Col: Maryland *HS:* Fork Union Mil. Acad. [VA] B: 4/7/1969, Mays Landing, NJ
1993 Den: 6 G.

JIM DRUCKENMILLER Druckenmiller, James David Jr. 6'4", 241 **QB**
Col: Virginia Tech *HS:* Northhampton [PA]; Fork Union Mil. Acad. [VA]
B: 9/19/1972, Allentown, PA *Drafted:* 1997 Round 1 SF
1997 SF: Rush 10-(-6) -0.6. **1998** SF: Rush 3-(-4) -1.3.
Total: Rush 13-(-10) -0.8.

		Passing							
Year Team	**G**	**Att**	**Comp**	**Comp%**	**Yds**	**YPA**	**TD**	**Int**	**Rating**
1997 SF	4	52	21	40.4	239	4.60	1	4	29.2
1998 SF	2	0	0	—	0	—	0	0	—
NFL Total	6	52	21	40.4	239	4.60	1	4	29.2

AL DRULIS Drulis, Albert Anthony 5'10", 193 **LB-FB-BB-QB**
Col: Temple *HS:* Girardville [PA] B: 8/30/1921, Girardville, PA
Drafted: 1943 Round 27 ChiC
1945 ChiC: 9 G; Rush 12-49 4.1; Rec 6-49 8.2; KR 4-44 11.0; 1 Fum.
1946 ChiC: 5 G; Rush 1-0. **1947** Pit: 10 G. **Total:** 24 G; Rush 13-49 3.8; Rec 6-49 8.2; KR 4-44 11.0; 1 Fum.

CHUCK DRULIS Drulis, Charles John 5'10", 216 **LB-OG**
Col: Temple *HS:* Girardville [PA] B: 3/8/1918, Girardville, PA
D: 8/23/1972, Little Rock, AR
1942 ChiB: 11 G; Int 1-41. **1945** ChiB: 3 G. **1946** ChiB: 11 G; Int 1-8.
1947 ChiB: 12 G. **1948** ChiB: 12 G; Int 1-2. **1949** ChiB: 12 G; Int 1-0.
1950 GB: 11 G. **Total:** 72 G; Int 4-51.

ROBERT DRUMMOND Drummond, Robert C 6'1", 205 **RB**
Col: Syracuse *HS:* Jamesville-DeWitt [DeWitt, NY] B: 6/21/1967, Apopka, FL *Drafted:* 1989 Round 3 Phi
1989 Phi: Rec 17-180 10.6 1 TD. **1990** Phi: Rec 5-39 7.8.
Total: Rec 22-219 10.0 1 TD.

		Rushing					Tot
Year Team	**G**	**Att**	**Yds**	**Avg**	**TD**	**Fum**	**TD**
1989 Phi	16	32	127	4.0	0	0	1
1990 Phi	4	8	33	4.1	1	0	1
1991 Phi	16	12	27	2.3	2	1	2
NFL Total	36	52	187	3.6	3	1	4

WOP DRUMSTEAD Drumstead, Walter 185 **G**
(AKA Walter Dremstadt) *Col:* No College B: 9/1898, Hammond, IN
Deceased
1925 Ham: 1 G.

ELBERT DRUNGO Drungo, Elbert J Jr. 6'5", 265 **OT-OG**
Col: Tennessee State *HS:* R.E. Hunt [Columbus, MS] B: 4/30/1943, Columbus, MS *Drafted:* 1969 Round 3 Hou
1969 Hou: 14 G. **1970** Hou: 14 G; KR 1-25 25.0. **1971** Hou: 11 G.
1973 Hou: 14 G. **1974** Hou: 13 G. **1975** Hou: 13 G. **1976** Hou: 14 G.
1977 Hou: 14 G. **1978** Buf: 13 G. **Total:** 120 G; KR 1-25 25.0.

HOOT DRURY Drury, Lyle Thomas 6'4", 189 **E**
Col: St. Louis *HS:* Moscow [ID] B: 2/18/1906 D: 8/26/1989, Itasca, IL
1930 ChiB: 14 G. **1931** ChiB: 10 G; Rec 1 TD; 6 Pt. **Total:** 24 G; Rec 1 TD; 6 Pt.

RICH DRUSCHEL Druschel, Richard Dennis 6'2", 248 **OT-OG**
Col: North Carolina State *HS:* Hempfield Area [Greensburg, PA]
B: 1/15/1952, Ellwood City, PA *Drafted:* 1974 Round 6 Pit
1974 Pit: 11 G.

JOHNNY DRUZE Druze, John Francis 6'0", 195 **OE**
Col: Fordham *HS:* Frank H. Morrell [Irvington, NJ] B: 7/3/1914, Newark, NJ *Drafted:* 1938 Round 9 Bkn
1938 Bkn: 10 G; Rec 4-29 7.3.

FRED DRYER Dryer, John Frederick 6'6", 240 **DE**
Col: El Camino Coll. CA (J.C.); San Diego State *HS:* Lawndale [CA]
B: 7/6/1946, Hawthorne, CA *Drafted:* 1969 Round 1 NYG
1969 NYG: 14 G. **1970** NYG: 14 G. **1971** NYG: 14 G; KR 1-0. **1972** LARm: 14 G. **1973** LARm: 14 G; Scor **2** Saf; 4 Pt. **1974** LARm: 14 G. **1975** LARm: 14 G; Int 1-20 1 TD; 6 Pt. **1976** LARm: 14 G. **1977** LARm: 14 G.
1978 LARm: 16 G. **1979** LARm: 16 G. **1980** LARm: 16 G. **1981** LARm: 2 G. **Total:** 176 G; KR 1-0; Int 1-20 1 TD; Scor 2 Saf; 10 Pt.

RON DRZEWIECKI Drzewiecki, Ronald John 5'11", 185 **HB-DB**
Col: Marquette *HS:* Boys Tech [Milwaukee, WI] B: 1/25/1933, Milwaukee, WI *Drafted:* 1955 Round 1 ChiB
1955 ChiB: Rush 10-54 5.4 1 TD; Rec 1-1 1.0. **1957** ChiB: Rush 5-11 2.2; Rec 1-7 7.0. **Total:** Rush 15-65 4.3 1 TD; Rec 2-8 4.0.

		Punt Returns				Kickoff Returns				
Year Team	**G**	**Ret**	**Yds**	**Avg**	**TD**	**Ret**	**Yds**	**Avg**	**TD**	**Fum**
1955 ChiB	12	20	100	5.0	0	25	591	23.6	0	3
1957 ChiB	8	22	64	2.9	0	13	315	24.2	0	0
NFL Total	20	42	164	3.9	0	38	906	23.8	0	3

GEORGE DUARTE Duarte, George Luis 5'9", 178 **DB**
Col: Arizona State; Northern Arizona *HS:* Sunnydale [AZ] B: 2/9/1964, Tuscon, AZ
1987 ChiB: 3 G; PR 8-64 8.0; 1 Fum.

ELBERT DUBENION Dubenion, Elbert 5'11", 187 **WR-HB**
(Golden Wheels) *Col:* Bluffton *HS:* South [Columbus, OH]
B: 2/16/1933, Griffin, GA *Drafted:* 1959 Round 14 Cle
1960 Buf: PR 2-6 3.0. **1961** Buf: PR 1-3 3.0. **Total:** PR 3-9 3.0.

		Rushing				Receiving			
Year Team	**G**	**Att**	**Yds**	**Avg**	**TD**	**Rec**	**Yds**	**Avg**	**TD**
1960 Buf	14	16	94	5.9	1	42	752	17.9	7
1961 Buf	14	17	173	10.2	2	31	461	14.9	6
1962 Buf	14	7	40	5.7	0	33	571	17.3	5
1963 Buf	14	0	0	—	0	53	959	18.1	4
1964 Buf	14	1	20	20.0	0	42	1139	**27.1**	10
1965 Buf	3	0	0	—	0	18	281	15.6	1
1966 Buf	14	3	16	5.3	0	50	747	14.9	2
1967 Buf	12	2	-17	-8.5	0	25	384	15.4	0
1968 Buf	4	0	0	—	0	0	0	—	0
NFL Total	103	46	326	7.1	3	294	5294	18.0	35

	Kickoff Returns					Tot
Year Team	**Ret**	**Yds**	**Avg**	**TD**	**Fum**	**TD**
1960 Buf	4	68	17.0	0	3	8
1961 Buf	16	329	20.6	0	1	8
1962 Buf	7	231	33.0	**1**	1	6
1963 Buf	13	333	25.6	0	2	4
1964 Buf	0	0	—	0	0	10
1965 Buf	0	0	—	0	0	1
1966 Buf	0	0	—	0	0	2
NFL Total	40	961	24.0	1	7	39

GREG DUBINETZ Dubinetz, Gregory George 6'4", 260 **OG**
Col: Yale *HS:* Lake Forest [IL] B: 4/15/1954, Chicago, IL
Drafted: 1975 Round 9 Cin
1979 Was: 15 G.

TOM DUBLINSKI Dublinski, Thomas Eugene Jr. 6'2", 212 **QB**
(Dubber; T.D.) *Col:* Utah *HS:* Hinsdale Central [IL] B: 8/8/1930, Chicago, IL *Drafted:* 1952 Round 8 Det

		Passing							
Year Team	**G**	**Att**	**Comp**	**Comp%**	**Yds**	**YPA**	**TD**	**Int**	**Rating**
1952 Det	6	6	1	16.7	39	6.50	0	1	14.6
1953 Det	7	30	14	46.7	174	5.80	0	5	25.6
1954 Det	12	138	77	55.8	1073	7.78	8	**7**	79.2

1958 NYG	1	3	1	33.3	14	4.67	0	0	49.3
1960 Den	3	0	0	—	0	—	0	0	—
NFL Total	29	177	93	52.5	1300	7.34	8	13	60.9

	Rushing				
Year Team	Att	Yds	Avg	TD	Fum
1952 Det	1	3	3.0	0	0
1953 Det	6	39	6.5	0	2
1954 Det	21	76	3.6	1	5
NFL Total	28	118	4.2	1	7

MAURY DUBOFSKY Dubofsky, Maurice 5'10", 210 G
(Mush) *Col:* Georgetown *HS:* Weaver [Hartford, CT] B: 1909, Hartford, CT D: 1/25/1970, Bethesda, MD
1932 NYG: 5 G.

PHIL DUBOIS DuBois, Philip Donn 6'2", 220 TE
Col: San Diego State *HS:* Norwalk [CA] B: 11/16/1956, Rochester, MN
1979 Was: 15 G. **1980** Was: 2 G; Rec 1-16 16.0. **Total:** 17 G; Rec 1-16 16.0.

DEMETRIUS DUBOSE DuBose, Adolphus Demetrius 6'1", 240 LB
Col: Notre Dame *HS:* Bishop O'Dea [Seattle, WA] B: 3/23/1971, Seattle, WA *Drafted:* 1993 Round 2 TB
1993 TB: 15 G. **1994** TB: 16 G. **1995** TB: 15 G. **1996** TB: 14 G. **Total:** 60 G.

DOUG DUBOSE DuBose, Donald Douglas 5'11", 190 RB
Col: Nebraska *HS:* Montville [Oakdale, CT] B: 3/14/1964, New London, CT
1987 SF: Rec 4-37 9.3. **1988** SF: Rec 6-57 9.5. **Total:** Rec 10-94 9.4.

		Rushing				Kickoff Returns				
Year Team	G	Att	Yds	Avg	TD	Ret	Yds	Avg	TD	Fum
1987 SF	2	10	33	3.3	0	0	0	—	0	0
1988 SF	14	24	116	4.8	2	32	608	19.0	0	2
NFL Total	16	34	149	4.4	2	32	608	19.0	0	2

JIMMY DUBOSE DuBose, Jimmy DuWayne 5'11", 217 RB
Col: Florida *HS:* Sarasota [FL] B: 10/25/1954, Enterprise, AL *Drafted:* 1976 Round 2 TB
1976 TB: Rec 5-26 5.2; KR 1-34 34.0. **1977** TB: Rec 11-89 8.1. **1978** TB: Rec 1-3 3.0. **Total:** Rec 17-118 6.9; KR 1-34 34.0.

		Rushing				
Year Team	G	Att	Yds	Avg	TD	Fum
1976 TB	14	20	62	3.1	0	1
1977 TB	13	71	284	4.0	0	0
1978 TB	6	93	358	3.8	4	1
NFL Total	33	184	704	3.8	4	2

WALT DUBZINSKI Dubzinski, Walter John 5'10", 205 LB-C-G
Col: Boston College *HS:* Gardner [MA] B: 10/26/1919, Gardner, MA
1943 NYG: 5 G; Int 1-0. **1944** Bos: 3 G. **Total:** 8 G; Int 1-0.

MARK DUCKENS Duckens, Mark Anthony 6'4", 270 DE-DT
Col: Wichita State; Arizona State *HS:* North [Wichita, KS] B: 3/4/1965, Wichita, KS
1989 NYG: 15 G. **1990** Det: 15 G; 3 Sac. **1992** TB: 5 G. **Total:** 35 G; 3 Sac.

KENNY DUCKETT Duckett, Kenneth Wayne 6'0", 184 WR
Col: Wake Forest *HS:* R.J. Reynolds [Winston-Salem, NC] B: 10/1/1959, Winston-Salem, NC D: 4/5/1998, Winston-Salem, NC *Drafted:* 1982 Round 3 NO
1983 NO: Rush 2-(-16) -8.0. **1984** NO: Rush 1-(-3) -3.0. **Total:** Rush 3-(-19) -6.3.

		Receiving				Kickoff Returns				
Year Team	G	Rec	Yds	Avg	TD	Ret	Yds	Avg	TD	Fum
1982 NO	7	12	196	16.3	2	2	39	19.5	0	0
1983 NO	14	19	283	14.9	2	33	719	21.8	0	1
1984 NO	11	3	24	8.0	0	29	580	20.0	0	0
1985 NO-Dal	4	0	0	—	0	9	173	19.2	0	1
1985 NO	1	0	0	—	0	0	0	—	0	0
1985 Dal	3	0	0	—	0	9	173	19.2	0	1
NFL Total	36	34	503	14.8	4	73	1511	20.7	0	2

FOREY DUCKETT Duckett, William Forey 6'3", 195 DB
Col: Nevada-Reno *HS:* Pinole Valley [Pinole, CA] B: 2/5/1970, Oakland, CA *Drafted:* 1993 Round 5 Cin
1994 Cin-GB-Sea: 7 G. Cin: 2 G. GB: 3 G. Sea: 2 G. **Total:** 7 G.

ROBERT DUCKSWORTH Ducksworth, Robert Charles Jr. 5'11", 200 DB
Col: Southern Mississippi *HS:* Biloxi [MS] B: 1/5/1963, Biloxi, MS *Drafted:* 1986 Round 8 NYJ
1986 NYJ: 2 G.

BOBBY DUCKWORTH Duckworth, Bobby Ray 6'3", 198 WR
Col: Arkansas *HS:* Hamburg [AR] B: 11/27/1958, Crossett, AR *Drafted:* 1981 Round 6 SD

		Receiving				
Year Team	G	Rec	Yds	Avg	TD	Fum
1982 SD	5	2	77	38.5	0	0
1983 SD	16	20	422	21.1	5	0
1984 SD	16	25	715	28.6	4	1
1985 LARm	14	25	422	16.9	3	0
1986 LARm-Phi	11	10	148	14.8	1	0
1986 LARm	7	9	141	15.7	1	0
1986 Phi	4	1	7	7.0	0	0
NFL Total	62	82	1784	21.8	13	1

JOE DUCKWORTH Duckworth, Joseph Walter 6'2", 220 OE-DE
Col: Colgate *HS:* Bloomfield [NJ]; Bordertown Mil. Inst. [NJ] B: 7/3/1921, Orange, NJ
1947 Was: 12 G; Rec 14-250 17.9 3 TD; 18 Pt.

MOON DUCOTE Ducote, Richard Joseph 5'11", 190 WB-TB
Col: Auburn B: 8/28/1897 D: 9/1985, Plaucheville, LA
1920 Cle: 1 G.

MARK DUDA Duda, Mark David 6'3", 273 DT
Col: Maryland *HS:* Wyoming Valley West [Plymouth, PA] B: 2/4/1961, Wilkes-Barre, PA *Drafted:* 1983 Round 4 StL
1983 StL: 14 G; KR 1-12 12.0; 1 Sac. **1984** StL: 8 G; 3 Sac. **1985** StL: 16 G; 5.5 Sac. **1986** StL: 14 G. **1987** StL: 3 G. **Total:** 55 G; KR 1-12 12.0; 9.5 Sac.

JOE DUDEK Dudek, Joseph Anthony 6'0", 200 RB
Col: Plymouth State *HS:* North Quincy [Quincy, MA] B: 1/22/1964, Boston, MA
1987 Den: Rec 7-41 5.9.

		Rushing				
Year Team	G	Att	Yds	Avg	TD	Fum
1987 Den	2	35	154	4.4	2	4

MITCH DUDEK Dudek, Mitchell Richard 6'4", 245 OT
Col: Xavier (Ohio) *HS:* St. George [Evanston, IL] B: 11/9/1943, Evanston, IL *Drafted:* 1965 Round 19 NYJ
1966 NYJ: 14 G.

DICK DUDEN Duden, Henry Richard Jr. 6'3", 212 DE-OE
Col: Navy *HS:* Phillips Exeter Acad. [Exeter, NH]; Phillips Andover Acad. [Andover, MA] B: 11/29/1924, Pottstown, PA
1949 NYG: 12 G; Rec 2-15 7.5.

ANDY DUDISH Dudish, Andrew Charles 5'11", 182 HB-DB
Col: Georgia *HS:* Hanover [PA] B: 10/13/1921, Wilkes-Barre, PA
AAFC **1946** BufA: Rec 2-33 16.5; PR 5-73 14.6; KR 7-196 28.0.
1947 BalA: Rec 7-130 18.6 1 TD; PR 5-121 24.2; KR 8-184 23.0.
Total: Rec 9-163 18.1 1 TD; PR 10-194 19.4; KR 15-380 25.3.

		Rushing				Tot
Year Team	G	Att	Yds	Avg	TD	TD
1946 BufA	11	30	106	3.5	0	0
1947 BalA	14	28	30	1.1	1	2
AAFC Total	25	58	136	2.3	1	2

NFL **1948** Det: 4 G; Rush 1-5 5.0; PR 2-10 5.0; KR 2-38 19.0.

BRIAN DUDLEY Dudley, Brian Christopher 6'1", 180 DB
Col: Bethune-Cookman *HS:* Fairfax [Los Angeles, CA] B: 8/30/1960, Los Angeles, CA
1987 Cle: 3 G.

PAUL DUDLEY Dudley, Paul Eugene 6'0", 185 HB
Col: Arkansas *HS:* Sallisaw [OK] B: 1/16/1939, Fort Smith, AR *Drafted:* 1961 Round 4 GB
1962 NYG: Pass 1-0, 1 Int; Rec 9-112 12.4 1 TD; KR 8-229 28.6.
1963 Phi: Rec 1-8 8.0. **Total:** Pass 1-0, 1 Int; Rec 10-120 12.0 1 TD; KR 8-229 28.6.

		Rushing				
Year Team	G	Att	Yds	Avg	TD	Fum
1962 NYG	11	27	100	3.7	0	2
1963 Phi	10	11	21	1.9	0	0
NFL Total	21	38	121	3.2	0	2

RICKEY DUDLEY Dudley, Rickey 6'6", 250 TE
Col: Ohio State *HS:* Henderson [TX] B: 7/15/1972, Henderson, TX *Drafted:* 1996 Round 1 Oak
1998 Oak: Rush 1-(-2) -2.0; Scor 1 2XP. **Total:** Rush 1-(-2) -2.0; Scor 1 2XP.

		Receiving				
Year Team	G	Rec	Yds	Avg	TD	Fum
1996 Oak	16	34	386	11.4	4	1
1997 Oak	16	48	787	16.4	7	0
1998 Oak	16	36	549	15.3	5	1
NFL Total	48	118	1722	14.6	16	2

BILL DUDLEY Dudley, William McGarvey 5'10", 182 **HB-TB-DB**
(Bullet Bill) *Col:* Virginia *HS:* Graham [Bluefield, VA] B: 12/24/1919, Bluefield, VA *Drafted:* 1942 Round 1 Pit *HOF:* 1966
1948 Det: 1 Fum TD. **Total:** 1 Fum TD.

		Passing							
Year Team	G	Att	Comp	Comp%	Yds	YPA	TD	Int	Rating
1942 Pit	11	94	35	37.2	438	4.66	2	5	37.5
1945 Pit	4	32	10	31.3	58	1.81	0	**2**	14.6
1946 Pit	11	90	32	35.6	452	5.02	2	9	20.5
1947 Det	9	4	3	75.0	24	6.00	2	0	129.2
1948 Det	7	1	0	0.0	0	0.00	0	1	0.0
1949 Det	12	0	0	—	0	—	0	0	—
1950 Was	12	0	0	—	0	—	0	0	—
1951 Was	12	1	1	100.0	13	13.00	0	0	118.8
1953 Was	12	0	0	—	0	—	0	0	—
NFL Total	90	222	81	36.5	985	4.44	6	17	28.1

	Rushing				Receiving			
Year Team	Att	Yds	Avg	TD	Rec	Yds	Avg	TD
1942 Pit	**162**	**696**	4.3	5	1	24	24.0	0
1945 Pit	57	204	3.6	3	0	0	—	0
1946 Pit	**146**	**604**	4.1	2	4	109	27.3	1
1947 Det	80	302	3.8	2	27	375	13.9	7
1948 Det	33	97	2.9	0	20	210	10.5	6
1949 Det	125	402	3.2	3	27	190	7.0	2
1950 Was	66	339	5.1	1	22	172	7.8	1
1951 Was	91	398	4.4	2	22	303	13.8	1
1953 Was	5	15	3.0	0	0	0	—	0
NFL Total	765	3057	4.0	18	123	1383	11.2	18

	Punt Returns				Kickoff Returns			
Year Team	Ret	Yds	Avg	TD	Ret	Yds	Avg	TD
1942 Pit	20	**271**	13.6	0	11	298	**27.1**	**1**
1945 Pit	5	20	4.0	0	3	65	21.7	0
1946 Pit	**27**	**385**	14.3	0	14	280	20.0	0
1947 Det	11	182	16.5	**1**	15	359	23.9	0
1948 Det	8	67	8.4	0	10	204	20.4	0
1949 Det	11	199	18.1	1	13	246	18.9	0
1950 Was	12	185	15.4	1	1	43	43.0	0
1951 Was	22	172	7.8	0	11	248	22.5	0
1953 Was	8	34	4.3	0	0	0	—	0
NFL Total	124	1515	12.2	3	78	1743	22.3	1

	Interceptions			Punting		
Year Team	Int	Yds	TD	Punts	Yds	Avg
1942 Pit	3	60	0	18	572	31.8
1945 Pit	2	47	0	2	36	18.0
1946 Pit	**10**	**242**	**1**	60	2409	40.2
1947 Det	5	104	1	15	657	43.8
1948 Det	1	3	0	23	825	35.9
1949 Det	0	0	0	34	1278	37.6
1950 Was	2	3	0	14	585	41.8
1951 Was	0	0	0	27	942	34.9
NFL Total	23	459	2	193	7304	37.8

	Scoring								Tot
Year Team	Pts	FG	FGA	FG%	XK	XKA	XK%	Fum	TD
1942 Pit	0	0	0	—	0	0	—	0	6
1945 Pit	20	0	0	—	2	3	66.7	1	3
1946 Pit	48	2	7	28.6	12	14	85.7	8	5
1947 Det	0	0	0	—	0	0	—	4	11
1948 Det	0	0	0	—	0	0	—	6	7
1949 Det	81	5	14	35.7	30	32	93.8	8	6
1950 Was	64	5	10	50.0	31	31	100.0	5	3
1951 Was	69	10	13	**76.9**	21	22	**95.5**	4	3
1953 Was	58	11	22	50.0	25	25	100.0	0	0
NFL Total	484	33	66	50.0	121	127	95.3	36	44

DAVE DUERSON Duerson, David Russell 6'1", 207 **DB**
Col: Notre Dame *HS:* Muncie Northside [IN] B: 11/28/1960, Muncie, IN *Drafted:* 1983 Round 3 ChiB
1983 ChiB: KR 3-66 22.0. **1984** ChiB: PR 1-4 4.0; KR 4-95 23.8; 3 Sac. **1985** ChiB: PR 6-47 7.8; 2 Sac. **1986** ChiB: 7 Sac. **1987** ChiB: PR 1-10 10.0; 3 Sac. **1988** ChiB: 1 Sac. **1990** NYG: 1 Fum TD. **Total:** PR 8-61 7.6; KR 7-161 23.0; 1 Fum TD; 16 Sac.

		Interceptions			
Year Team	G	Int	Yds	TD	Fum
1983 ChiB	16	0	0	0	0
1984 ChiB	16	1	9	0	0
1985 ChiB	15	5	53	0	1
1986 ChiB	16	6	139	0	0
1987 ChiB	12	3	0	0	0
1988 ChiB	15	2	18	0	0
1989 ChiB	12	1	2	0	0
1990 NYG	16	1	0	0	0
1991 Pho	11	1	5	0	0
1992 Pho	15	0	0	0	0
1993 Pho	16	0	0	0	0
NFL Total	160	20	226	0	1

PAUL DUFAULT Dufault, Paul Henry 6'4", 255 **C**
Col: New Hampshire *HS:* Spaulding [Rochester, NH] B: 2/15/1964, Bridgeport, CT
1987 LARd: 1 G.

DON DUFEK Dufek, Donald Patrick 6'0", 195 **DB**
Col: Michigan *HS:* Pioneer [Grand Rapids, MI] B: 4/28/1954, Ann Arbor, MI *Drafted:* 1976 Round 5 Sea
1976 Sea: 14 G; KR 9-177 19.7. **1977** Sea: 13 G; KR 1-21 21.0; Int 2-26. **1979** Sea: 13 G. **1980** Sea: 8 G. **1981** Sea: 15 G; KR 3-45 15.0. **1982** Sea: 9 G; Int 1-16. **1983** Sea: 14 G; 2 Sac. **1984** Sea: 9 G. **Total:** 95 G; KR 13-243 18.7; Int 3-42; 2 Sac.

JOE DUFEK Dufek, Joseph Edward 6'4", 215 **QB**
Col: Yale *HS:* Theodore Roosevelt [Kent, OH] B: 8/23/1961, Ann Arbor, MI
1984 Buf: Rush 9-22 2.4 1 TD. **Total:** Rush 9-22 2.4 1 TD.

		Passing								
Year Team	G	Att	Comp	Comp%	Yds	YPA	TD	Int	Rating	Fum
1983 Buf	5	0	0	—	0	—	0	0	—	0
1984 Buf	5	150	74	49.3	829	5.53	4	8	52.9	1
NFL Total	10	150	74	49.3	829	5.53	4	8	52.9	1

JAMAL DUFF Duff, Jamal Edwin 6'7", 276 **DE-DT**
Col: San Diego State *HS:* Foothill [Santa Ana, CA] B: 3/11/1972, Columbus, OH *Drafted:* 1995 Round 6 NYG
1995 NYG: 15 G; 4 Sac. **1997** Was: 13 G; 2 Sac. **1998** Was: 13 G; 3 Sac. **Total:** 41 G; 9 Sac.

JOHN DUFF Duff, John Edward 6'7", 250 **TE**
Col: Saddleback Coll. CA (J.C.); New Mexico *HS:* Foothill [Santa Ana, CA] B: 7/31/1967, Columbus, OH
1993 LARd: 1 G. **1994** LARd: 4 G. **Total:** 5 G.

JIM DUFFT Dufft, James Henry 6'6", 250 **G-T**
Col: Rutgers; Fordham *HS:* Kelvin School [Mount Vernon, NY] B: 6/25/1896 Deceased
1921 Roch-NYG: 2 G. Roch: 1 G. NYG: 1 G. **1922** Mil: 8 G. **Total:** 10 G.

PAT DUFFY Duffy, Joseph Patrick 5'10", 185 **FB-TB-BB-WB**
Col: Dayton B: 12/6/1906, Dayton, OH D: 10/14/1965, Dayton, OH
1929 Day: 5 G; Scor 1, 1 XK.

ROGER DUFFY Duffy, Roger Thomas 6'3", 300 **OG**
Col: Penn State *HS:* Central Catholic [Canton, OH] B: 7/16/1967, Pittsburgh, PA *Drafted:* 1990 Round 8 NYJ
1990 NYJ: 16 G; KR 1-8 8.0. **1991** NYJ: 12 G. **1992** NYJ: 16 G; KR 1-7 7.0. **1993** NYJ: 16 G. **1994** NYJ: 16 G. **1995** NYJ: 16 G. **1996** NYJ: 16 G. **1997** NYJ: 15 G; 2 Fum. **1998** Pit: 16 G. **Total:** 139 G; KR 2-15 7.5; 2 Fum.

DUKES DUFORD Duford, Wilfred Joseph 5'10", 180 **E-BB-HB**
Col: Marquette *HS:* Niagara [WI] B: 6/11/1898, Menomonee, WI D: 5/8/1981, Davenport, IA
1924 GB: 3 G.

DAN DUFOUR Dufour, Daniel Arthur 6'5", 280 **OG**
Col: UCLA *HS:* Classical [Lynn, MA] B: 10/18/1960, Lynn, MA
1983 Atl: 16 G. **1984** Atl: 6 G. **Total:** 22 G.

FRED DUGAN Dugan, John Frederick 6'3", 205 **OE**
(Butch) *Col:* Dayton *HS:* Stamford [CT] B: 5/12/1933, Stamford, CT *Drafted:* 1957 Round 7 SF
1962 Was: Rush 1-(-9) -9.0. **Total:** Rush 1-(-9) -9.0.

		Receiving				
Year Team	G	Rec	Yds	Avg	TD	Fum
1958 SF	12	9	122	13.6	0	0
1959 SF	12	6	72	12.0	0	0
1960 Dal	12	29	461	15.9	1	1
1961 Was	13	53	817	15.4	4	1
1962 Was	12	36	466	12.9	5	0
1963 Was	14	20	288	14.4	3	0
NFL Total	75	153	2226	14.5	13	2

LEN DUGAN Dugan, Leonard Mark 6'0", 218 **C-LB**
Col: Wichita State *HS:* McCracken [KS] B: 2/19/1910 D: 6/22/1967
1936 NYG: 3 G. **1937** ChiC: 11 G. **1938** ChiC: 8 G. **1939** ChiC-Pit: 5 G. ChiC: 4 G. Pit: 1 G. **Total:** 27 G.

BILL DUGAN Dugan, William H 6'4", 275 **OG-OT**
Col: Penn State *HS:* Hornell [NY] B: 6/5/1959, Hornell, NY *Drafted:* 1981 Round 3 Sea
1981 Sea: 16 G. **1982** Sea: 9 G. **1983** Sea: 15 G. **1984** Min: 1 G. **1987** NYG: 3 G. **Total:** 44 G.

EDDIE DUGGAN Duggan, Edward Dean 6'0", 200 **FB**
Col: Notre Dame *HS:* Whiteland [IN]; Greenwood HS [IN]
B: 5/19/1891, Franklin, IN D: 10/16/1950, Houston, TX
1921 RI: 3 G.

GIL DUGGAN Duggan, Gilford Earl 6'3", 229 **T**
(Cactus Face) *Col:* Oklahoma *HS:* Benton [AR] B: 12/26/1914, Benton, AR D: 10/18/1974, Harrah, OK *Drafted:* 1939 Round 13 NYG
AAFC **1946** LA-A: 11 G. **1947** BufA: 12 G. **Total:** 23 G.

NFL **1940** NYG: 10 G. **1942** ChiC: 11 G; Int 1-0. **1943** ChiC: 10 G. **1944** ChPt: 10 G. **1945** ChiC: 8 G. **Total:** 49 G; Int 1-0.

JACK DUGGER Dugger, John Richard 6'3", 230 **T-DE**
Col: Ohio State *HS:* McKinley [Canton, OH] B: 1/13/1923, Pittsburgh, PA D: 2/23/1988, Charlotte, NC *Drafted:* 1945 Round 2 Pit
AAFC **1946** BufA: 7 G; Rec 1-15 15.0; 6 Pt.

NFL **1947** Det: 12 G; Int 1-6. **1948** Det: 12 G. **1949** ChiB: 6 G; Rec 1-11 11.0; KR 1-8 8.0. **Total:** 30 G; Rec 1-11 11.0; KR 1-8 8.0; Int 1-6.

HERB DUGGINS Duggins, George Herbert 6'3", 200 **OE-DE**
Col: Purdue *HS:* New Albany [IN] B: 3/25/1912, New Albany, IN D: 7/20/1988, Yelm, WA
1934 ChiC: 11 G; Rec 5-52 10.4.

PAUL DUHART Duhart, Paul Albert 6'0", 180 **HB-DB-QB**
Col: Florida B: 12/30/1920, Montreal, Canada *Drafted:* 1945 Round 1 Pit
1944 GB: Pass 13-4 30.8%, 42 3.23; Rec 9-176 19.6 2 TD; PR 3-32 10.7; KR 1-18 18.0; Int 4-23. **1945** Pit-Bos: Pass 9-3 33.3%, 27 3.00 2 Int; KR 4-81 20.3. Pit: Pass 3-1 33.3%, 1 0.33; KR 2-49 24.5. Bos: Pass 6-2 33.3%, 26 4.33 2 Int; KR 2-32 16.0. **Total:** Pass 22-7 31.8%, 69 3.14 2 Int; Rec 9-176 19.6 2 TD; PR 3-32 10.7; KR 5-99 19.8; Int 4-23.

		Rushing				Tot
Year Team	**G**	**Att**	**Yds**	**Avg**	**TD**	**TD**
1944 GB	8	51	183	3.6	2	4
1945 Pit-Bos	5	17	17	1.0	1	1
1945 Pit	2	11	7	0.6	1	1
1945 Bos	3	6	10	1.7	0	0
NFL Total	13	68	200	2.9	3	5

A.J. DUHE Duhe, Adam Joseph Jr. 6'4", 247 **LB-DE**
Col: Louisiana State *HS:* Leon Goudchaux [Reserve, LA]
B: 11/27/1955, New Orleans, LA *Drafted:* 1977 Round 1 Mia
1977 Mia: 14 G. **1978** Mia: 13 G; Scor **1** Saf; 2 Pt. **1979** Mia: 13 G. **1980** Mia: 16 G. **1981** Mia: 16 G; Int 1-11. **1982** Mia: 9 G; Int 1-0; 2 Sac. **1983** Mia: 15 G; 5.5 Sac. **1984** Mia: 12 G; KR 1-0; Int 1-7; 1 Sac. **Total:** 108 G; KR 1-0; Int 3-18; Scor 1 Saf; 2 Pt; 8.5 Sac.

BOBBY DUHON Duhon, Robert Joseph Jr. 6'0", 195 **RB**
Col: Tulane *HS:* Abbeville [LA] B: 9/24/1946, Abbeville, LA
Drafted: 1968 Round 3 NYG
1968 NYG: Pass 2-2 100.0%, 24 12.00. **1970** NYG: Pass 2-2 100.0%, 28 14.00. **1971** NYG: Pass 1-0, 1 Int. **Total:** Pass 5-4 80.0%, 52 10.40 1 Int.

		Rushing				Receiving			
Year Team	**G**	**Att**	**Yds**	**Avg**	**TD**	**Rec**	**Yds**	**Avg**	**TD**
1968 NYG	13	101	362	3.6	3	37	373	10.1	1
1970 NYG	14	18	111	6.2	0	4	58	14.5	0
1971 NYG	13	93	344	3.7	1	25	266	10.6	0
1972 NYG	4	9	23	2.6	0	2	20	10.0	0
NFL Total	44	221	840	3.8	4	68	717	10.5	1

	Punt Returns				Kickoff Returns					Tot
Year Team	**Ret**	**Yds**	**Avg**	**TD**	**Ret**	**Yds**	**Avg**	**TD**	**Fum**	**TD**
1968 NYG	7	34	4.9	0	13	214	16.5	0	5	4
1970 NYG	19	157	8.3	**1**	14	255	18.2	0	4	1
1971 NYG	12	77	6.4	0	11	200	18.2	0	6	1
1972 NYG	2	20	10.0	0	2	47	23.5	0	0	0
NFL Total	40	288	7.2	1	40	716	17.9	0	15	6

STEVE DUICH Duich, Steven John 6'3", 248 **OG**
Col: San Diego Mesa Coll. CA (J.C.); San Diego State *HS:* St. Augustine [San Diego, CA] B: 2/28/1946, Long Beach, CA *Drafted:* 1968 Round 5 GB
1968 Atl: 12 G. **1969** Was: 11 G. **Total:** 23 G.

PAUL DUKE Duke, Paul Anderson 6'1", 210 **C-LB**
Col: Georgia Tech *HS:* Druid Hills [Atlanta, GA]; Boys High [Atlanta, GA]
B: 9/24/1924, DeKalb Co., GA
AAFC **1947** NY-A: 10 G.

JAMIE DUKES Dukes, Jamie Donnell 6'1", 285 **OG-C**
Col: Florida State *HS:* Evans [Orlando, FL] B: 6/14/1964, Schenectedy, NY
1986 Atl: 14 G. **1987** Atl: 4 G. **1988** Atl: 12 G; KR 1-13 13.0. **1989** Atl: 16 G. **1990** Atl: 16 G; 1 Fum. **1991** Atl: 16 G. **1992** Atl: 16 G. **1993** Atl: 16 G. **1994** GB: 6 G. **1995** Ariz: 8 G. **Total:** 124 G; KR 1-13 13.0; 1 Fum.

MIKE DUKES Dukes, Michael Francis 6'3", 235 **LB**
Col: Clemson *HS:* Southwest De Kalb [Decatur, GA] B: 3/16/1936, Louisville, KY *Drafted:* 1959 Round 14 SF
1960 Hou: 11 G; KR 4-58 14.5; Int 2-34. **1961** Hou: 14 G; KR 4-57 14.3; Int 1-5. **1962** Hou: 14 G; Int 2-11. **1963** Hou: 14 G; Int 1-4. **1964** Bos: 14 G; KR 2-33 16.5; Int 1-6. **1965** Bos-NYJ: 14 G; KR 3-45 15.0; Int 1-10. Bos: 11 G; KR 3-45 15.0; Int 1-10. NYJ: 3 G. **Total:** 81 G; KR 13-193 14.8; Int 8-70.

BILL DULAC DuLac, William Frank 6'4", 260 **OG**
Col: Eastern Michigan *HS:* Bishop Gallagher [Harper Woods, MI]
B: 1/15/1951, Detroit, MI *Drafted:* 1973 Round 7 LARm
1974 NE: 13 G. **1975** NE: 13 G. **Total:** 26 G.

MIKE DULANEY Dulaney, Michael Wayne 6'0", 245 **RB**
(AKA Mike Faulkerson) *Col:* North Carolina *HS:* Dobyns-Bennett [Kinsport, TN] B: 9/9/1970, Kingsport, TN
1995 ChiB: 5 G; Rec 2-22 11.0. **1996** ChiB: 16 G; Rec 1-1 1.0 1 TD; KR 4-63 15.8; 6 Pt. **1997** ChiB: 7 G; PR 1-0; 1 Fum. **1998** Car: 8 G. **Total:** 36 G; Rec 3-23 7.7 1 TD; PR 1-0; KR 4-63 15.8; 6 Pt; 1 Fum.

CHRIS DULIBAN Duliban, Christopher E 6'2", 216 **LB**
Col: Texas *HS:* Spring Woods [Houston, TX] B: 1/9/1963, Champaign, IL *Drafted:* 1986 Round 12 Dal
1987 Dal: 3 G; 2 Sac.

GARY DULIN Dulin, Gary Wayne 6'4", 275 **DE-DT**
Col: Ohio State *HS:* North Hopkins [Madisonville, KY] B: 1/20/1957, Madisonville, KY
1986 StL: 3 G. **1987** StL: 3 G; 0.5 Sac. **Total:** 6 G; 0.5 Sac.

MIKE DUMAS Dumas, Michael Dion 6'0", 190 **DB**
Col: Indiana *HS:* Lowell [MI] B: 3/18/1969, Grand Rapids, MI
Drafted: 1991 Round 2 Hou
1991 Hou: 13 G; Int 1-19; 1 Fum TD; 6 Pt. **1992** Hou: 16 G; Int 1-0. **1994** Buf: 14 G. **1995** Jac: 14 G; Int 1-0. **1997** SD: 16 G; Int 1-0; 1 Sac. **1998** SD: 3 G; 1 Sac. **Total:** 76 G; Int 4-19; 1 Fum TD; 6 Pt; 2 Sac.

TROY DUMAS Dumas, Troy 6'3", 242 **LB**
Col: Nebraska *HS:* East [Cheyenne, WY] B: 9/30/1972, Riverside, CA
Drafted: 1995 Round 3 KC
1996 KC: 6 G. **1997** KC-StL: 10 G; 1 Sac. KC: 8 G; 1 Sac. StL: 2 G. **Total:** 16 G; 1 Sac.

JON DUMBAULD Dumbauld, Jonathan Jordan 6'4", 259 **DE**
Col: Kentucky *HS:* Troy [OH] B: 2/14/1963, Anaheim, CA
Drafted: 1986 Round 10 NO
1986 NO: 9 G. **1987** Phi: 6 G. **1988** Phi-NO: 2 G. Phi: 1 G. NO: 1 G. **Total:** 17 G.

DOUG DUMLER Dumler, Douglas Marvin 6'3", 243 **C**
Col: Nebraska *HS:* Walther Lutheran [Melrose Park, IL] B: 12/15/1950, Hoisington, KS *Drafted:* 1973 Round 5 NE
1973 NE: 14 G; 1 Fum. **1974** NE: 14 G. **1975** NE: 14 G. **1976** Min: 14 G. **1977** Min: 14 G. **Total:** 70 G; 1 Fum.

JOE DUMOE DuMoe, Joseph Thomas 5'9", 178 **E**
(Stub) *Col:* Syracuse; Fordham; Lafayette *HS:* Central [Duluth, MN]
B: 9/11/1894, Duluth, MN D: 2/23/1959
1920 Roch: 2 G. **1921** Roch: 2 G. **Total:** 4 G.

BILLY DUMOE DuMoe, William G 5'10", 175 **E**
Col: No College *HS:* Central [Duluth, MN] B: 3/14/1898, Canosia Twp., MN D: 5/1983, Minneapolis, MN
1921 GB: 6 G; Rec 1 TD; Int **1** TD; Tot TD 2; 12 Pt.

JIM DUMONT Dumont, James 6'1", 224 **LB**
Col: Rutgers *HS:* Neshaminy [Langhorne, PA] B: 7/16/1961, Bristol, PA *Drafted:* 1984 Round 7 Cle
1984 Cle: 12 G.

CRAIG DUNAWAY Dunaway, Craig Carter 6'2", 233 **TE**
Col: Michigan *HS:* Upper St. Clair [Pittsburgh, PA] B: 3/27/1961, Lake Charles, LA *Drafted:* 1983 Round 8 Pit
1983 Pit: 11 G.

DAVE DUNAWAY Dunaway, David Harry 6'2", 205 **WR-P**
Col: Duke *HS:* Jacksonville [NC] B: 1/19/1945, Philadelphia, PA
Drafted: 1967 Round 2 GB
1968 GB-Atl: 10 G. GB: 2 G. Atl: 8 G. **1969** NYG: 3 G; Rush 1-4 4.0; Rec 2-37 18.5; Punt 13-497 38.2. **Total:** 13 G; Rush 1-4 4.0; Rec 2-37 18.5; Punt 13-497 38.2.

JIM DUNAWAY Dunaway, James Kenneth 6'4", 277 **DT**
Col: Mississippi *HS:* Columbia [MS] B: 9/3/1941, Columbia, MS
Drafted: 1963 Round 2 Buf
1963 Buf: 14 G. **1964** Buf: 14 G. **1965** Buf: 14 G; KR 1-0. **1966** Buf: 14 G; 6 Pt. **1967** Buf: 14 G; Int 1-8. **1968** Buf: 14 G. **1969** Buf: 14 G. **1970** Buf: 14 G. **1971** Buf: 14 G. **1972** Mia: 6 G. **Total:** 132 G; KR 1-0; Int 1-8; 6 Pt.

JUBILEE DUNBAR Dunbar, Allen 6'0", 196 **WR**
Col: Southern University *HS:* Washington [Lake Charles, LA]
B: 5/17/1949, New Orleans, LA *Drafted:* 1972 Round 3 SF
1973 NO: Rush 3-3 1.0. **Total:** Rush 3-3 1.0.

Year Team	G	Receiving Rec	Yds	Avg	TD	Fum
1973 NO	14	23	447	19.4	4	1
1974 Cle	5	6	74	12.3	0	0
NFL Total	19	29	521	18.0	4	1

KARL DUNBAR Dunbar, Karmichael MacKenzie II 6′4″, 275 **DE**
Col: Louisiana State *HS:* Plaisance [Opelousas, LA] B: 5/18/1967, Opelousas, LA *Drafted:* 1990 Round 8 Pit
1993 NO: 13 G. **1994** Ariz: 4 G. **1995** Ariz: 4 G. **Total:** 21 G.

VAUGHN DUNBAR Dunbar, Vaughn Allen 5′10″, 204 **RB**
Col: Northeastern State (Okla.); Indiana *HS:* R. Nelson Snider [Fort Wayne, IN] B: 9/4/1968, Fort Wayne, IN *Drafted:* 1992 Round 1 NO
1992 NO: Rec 9-62 6.9; KR 10-187 18.7. **1994** NO: KR 1-28 28.0. **1995** NO-Jac: Rec 2-11 5.5; KR 2-32 16.0. Jac: Rec 2-11 5.5; KR 2-32 16.0. **Total:** Rec 11-73 6.6; KR 13-247 19.0.

Year Team	G	Rushing Att	Yds	Avg	TD	Fum
1992 NO	16	154	565	3.7	3	3
1994 NO	8	3	9	3.0	0	0
1995 NO-Jac	15	110	361	3.3	2	0
1995 NO	1	0	0	—	0	0
1995 Jac	14	110	361	3.3	2	0
NFL Total	39	267	935	3.5	5	3

CLYDE DUNCAN Duncan, Clyde Lewis 6′1″, 202 **WR**
Col: Tennessee *HS:* Oxon Hill [MD] B: 2/5/1961, Oxen Hill, MD *Drafted:* 1984 Round 1 StL
1985 StL: Rec 4-39 9.8 1 TD. **Total:** Rec 4-39 9.8 1 TD.

Year Team	G	Kickoff Returns Ret	Yds	Avg	TD	Fum
1984 StL	8	0	0	—	0	0
1985 StL	11	28	550	19.6	0	3
NFL Total	19	28	550	19.6	0	3

CURTIS DUNCAN Duncan, Curtis Everett 5′11″, 184 **WR**
Col: Northwestern *HS:* Redford [Detroit, MI] B: 1/26/1965, Detroit, MI *Drafted:* 1987 Round 10 Hou
1987 Hou: PR 8-23 2.9. **1988** Hou: PR 4-47 11.8. **1989** Hou: Rush 1-0. **1991** Hou: PR 1-(-1) -1.0. **Total:** Rush 1-0; PR 13-69 5.3.

		Receiving				Kickoff Returns				
Year Team	G	Rec	Yds	Avg	TD	Ret	Yds	Avg	TD	Fum
1987 Hou	10	13	237	18.2	5	28	546	19.5	0	0
1988 Hou	16	22	302	13.7	1	1	34	34.0	0	0
1989 Hou	16	43	613	14.3	5	0	0	—	0	1
1990 Hou	16	66	785	11.9	1	0	0	—	0	1
1991 Hou	16	55	588	10.7	4	0	0	—	0	1
1992 Hou	16	82	954	11.6	1	0	0	—	0	0
1993 Hou	12	41	456	11.1	3	0	0	—	0	0
NFL Total	102	322	3935	12.2	20	29	580	20.0	0	3

FRANK DUNCAN Duncan, Frank Milton 6′1″, 190 **DB**
Col: Coll. of San Mateo CA (J.C.); San Francisco State *HS:* Jefferson [Daly City, CA] B: 11/16/1956, San Francisco, CA *Drafted:* 1979 Round 12 SD
1979 SD: 4 G. **1980** SD: 15 G; KR 5-85 17.0. **1981** SD: 7 G; Int 1-0. **Total:** 26 G; KR 5-85 17.0; Int 1-0.

RANDY DUNCAN Duncan, Hearst Randolph Jr. 6′0″, 185 **QB**
Col: Iowa *HS:* Roosevelt [Des Moines, IA] B: 3/15/1937, Osage, IA *Drafted:* 1959 Round 1 GB
1961 DalT: Rush 5-42 8.4.

		Passing								
Year Team	G	Att	Comp	Comp%	Yds	YPA	TD	Int	Rating	Fum
1961 DalT	14	67	25	37.3	361	5.39	1	3	41.9	3

HOWARD DUNCAN Duncan, Howard D 6′3″, 225 **C**
Col: Ohio State *HS:* Lakewood [OH] B: 11/8/1924 D: 7/1986, Tuscon, AZ
1948 Det: 1 G.

JIM DUNCAN Duncan, James 6′2″, 200 **DB**
Col: Maryland East. Shore *HS:* Bar Street [Lancaster, SC] B: 8/3/1946, Lancaster, SC D: 10/20/1972, Lancaster, SC *Drafted:* 1968 Round 4 Bal
1970 Bal: Int 2-56. **Total:** Int 2-56.

Year Team	G	Kickoff Returns Ret	Yds	Avg	TD	Fum
1969 Bal	13	19	560	29.5	**1**	1
1970 Bal	14	20	707	**35.4**	1	2
1971 Bal	11	3	102	34.0	0	2
NFL Total	38	42	1369	32.6	2	5

BRIAN DUNCAN Duncan, James Brian 6′0″, 201 **RB**
Col: Southern Methodist *HS:* Graham [TX] B: 3/31/1952, Olney, TX
1976 Cle: 14 G; Rush 11-44 4.0; Rec 6-49 8.2 1 TD; KR 6-145 24.2; 6 Pt; 1 Fum. **1977** Cle: 14 G; Rush 5-16 3.2; Rec 1-5 5.0 1 TD; KR 15-298 19.9; 6 Pt. **1978** Hou: 5 G; Rush 1-0; Rec 2-0; KR 2-38 19.0. **Total:** 33 G; Rush 17-60 3.5; Rec 9-54 6.0 2 TD; KR 23-481 20.9; 12 Pt; 1 Fum.

JIM DUNCAN Duncan, James Hampton 6′2″, 205 **DE**
Col: Duke; Wake Forest *HS:* Reidsville [NC] B: 5/2/1925, Reidsville, NC *Drafted:* 1950 Round 9 Cle
1950 NYG: 8 G. **1951** NYG: 12 G; Int 2-19. **1952** NYG: 12 G; Int 2-24. **1953** NYG: 11 G; Int 3-39. **Total:** 43 G; Int 7-82.

JAMIE DUNCAN Duncan, Jamie 6′0″, 244 **LB**
Col: Vanderbilt *HS:* Christiana [Newark, DE] B: 7/20/1975, Wilmington, DE *Drafted:* 1998 Round 3 TB
1998 TB: 14 G.

KEN DUNCAN Duncan, Kenneth W 6′2″, 210 **P**
Col: Tulsa *HS:* Carpinteria [CA] B: 2/28/1946, Rock Island, IL *Drafted:* 1971 Round 17 Min
1971 GB: 2 G; Punt 6-216 36.0.

SPEEDY DUNCAN Duncan, Leslie Herbert 5′10″, 180 **DB**
Col: Jackson State *HS:* Druid [Tuscaloosa, AL] B: 8/10/1942, Tuscaloosa, AL
1967 SD: **1** Fum TD. **Total:** 1 Fum TD.

		Punt Returns				Kickoff Returns			
Year Team	G	Ret	Yds	Avg	TD	Ret	Yds	Avg	TD
1964 SD	5	4	19	4.8	0	9	318	35.3	0
1965 SD	14	30	**464**	**15.5**	**2**	26	612	23.5	0
1966 SD	14	18	238	**13.2**	**1**	25	642	25.7	0
1967 SD	14	36	434	12.1	0	9	231	25.7	0
1968 SD	10	18	206	11.4	1	25	586	23.4	0
1969 SD	14	27	280	10.4	0	21	587	28.0	0
1970 SD	6	5	10	2.0	0	19	410	21.6	0
1971 Was	14	22	233	**10.6**	0	27	724	26.8	0
1972 Was	8	11	70	6.4	0	15	364	24.3	0
1973 Was	14	28	228	8.1	0	4	65	16.3	0
1974 Was	2	3	19	6.3	0	0	0	—	0
NFL Total	115	202	2201	10.9	4	180	4539	25.2	0

	Interceptions				Tot
Year Team	Int	Yds	TD	Fum	TD
1964 SD	1	3	0	3	0
1965 SD	4	30	0	2	2
1966 SD	7	67	0	3	1
1967 SD	2	100	1	1	3
1968 SD	1	4	0	3	1
1969 SD	6	118	1	4	1
1970 SD	0	0	0	1	0
1971 Was	1	46	1	4	1
1972 Was	1	8	0	2	0
1973 Was	1	6	0	3	0
NFL Total	24	382	3	26	9

MAURY DUNCAN Duncan, Maurice Perry 6′1″, 185 **QB**
Col: San Francisco State *HS:* Berkeley [CA] B: 7/18/1931, Oakland, CA
1954 SF: 6 G; Pass 14-4 28.6%, 82 5.86 2 Int. **1955** SF: 11 G; Pass 12-4 33.3%, 40 3.33; Rush 1-(-5) -5.0; 1 Fum. **Total:** 17 G; Pass 26-8 30.8%, 122 4.69 2 Int; Rush 1-(-5) -5.0; 1 Fum.

RICK DUNCAN Duncan, Richard Joe 6′0″, 208 **P-K**
Col: Pierce Coll. CA (J.C.); Eastern Montana *HS:* Mattoon [IL] B: 8/14/1941, Mattoon, IL
1967 Den: 2 G; Scor 9, 2-5 40.0% FG, 3-3 100.0% XK. **1968** Phi: 1 G; Punt 5-228 45.6. **1969** Det: 1 G; Punt 3-77 25.7. **Total:** 4 G; Punt 8-305 38.1; Scor 9, 2-5 40.0% FG, 3-3 100.0% XK.

RON DUNCAN Duncan, Ronald Neely 6′6″, 255 **TE**
Col: Wittenberg *HS:* Glen Rock [NJ] B: 9/8/1943, Lakeland, FL
1967 Cle: 3 G.

BOB DUNCUM Duncum, Robert Eldon 6′3″, 255 **OT**
Col: West Texas A&M *HS:* William B. Travis [Austin, TX] B: 8/14/1944, Austin, TX *Drafted:* 1967 Round 13 StL
1968 StL: 4 G.

KEN DUNEK Dunek, Kenneth Robert 6′6″, 235 **TE**
Col: Paducah CC KY; Memphis *HS:* Marengo [IL] B: 6/20/1957, Chicago, IL
1980 Phi: 2 G.

TONY DUNGY Dungy, Anthony Kevin 6′0″, 188 **DB-QB**
Col: Minnesota *HS:* Parkside [Jackson, MI] B: 10/6/1955, Jackson, MI
1977 Pit: 14 G; Pass 8-3 37.5%, 43 5.38 2 Int; Rush 3-8 2.7; Int 3-37; 1 Fum. **1978** Pit: 16 G; Int 6-95. **1979** SF: 15 G; PR 8-52 6.5; 1 Fum. **Total:** 45 G; Pass 8-3 37.5%, 43 5.38 2 Int; Rush 3-8 2.7; PR 8-52 6.5; Int 9-132; 2 Fum.

TOM DUNIVEN Duniven, James Thomas 6'3", 210 **QB**
Col: Texas Tech *HS:* McLean [TX] B: 5/20/1954, Pampa, TX
Drafted: 1977 Round 6 Cin
1977 Hou: 1 G.

LENNY DUNLAP Dunlap, Leonard 6'1", 195 **DB**
Col: Kilgore Coll. TX (J.C.); North Texas *HS:* Carverdale [Houston, TX]
B: 6/25/1949, Monroe, LA *Drafted:* 1971 Round 1 Bal
1971 Bal: KR 1-28 28.0. **1972** SD: KR 12-271 22.6; Int 5-67. **1974** SD: KR 1-19 19.0. **1975** Det: KR 1-19 19.0. **Total:** KR 15-337 22.5; Int 5-67.

		Punt Returns				
Year Team	**G**	**Ret**	**Yds**	**Avg**	**TD**	**Fum**
1971 Bal	4	8	112	14.0	0	1
1972 SD	14	19	179	9.4	0	6
1973 SD	14	0	0	—	0	0
1974 SD	8	0	0	—	0	0
1975 Det	6	0	0	—	0	0
NFL Total	46	27	291	10.8	0	7

BOB DUNLAP Dunlap, Robert Louis 6'1", 191 **DB-QB**
Col: Oklahoma *HS:* Haskell [OK] B: 10/29/1912, Haskell, OK
D: 7/30/1966, Wilmette, IL
1935 ChiB: 12 G; Pass 37-11 29.7%, 121 3.27 1 TD 2 Int; Rush 7-(-16) -2.3; Rec 1-9 9.0. **1936** NYG: 5 G; Pass 1-0; Rush 8-20 2.5. **Total:** 17 G; Pass 38-11 28.9%, 121 3.18 1 TD 2 Int; Rush 15-4 0.3; Rec 1-9 9.0.

COYE DUNN Dunn, Coye Elvis 6'0", 198 **WB-DB**
Col: USC *HS:* San Diego [CA] B: 3/7/1916, Vilas, CO
1943 Was: 3 G.

DAVID DUNN Dunn, David Leon 6'3", 215 **WR**
Col: Bakersfield Coll. CA (J.C.); Fresno State *HS:* Samuel F.B. Morse [San Diego, CA] B: 6/10/1972, San Diego, CA *Drafted:* 1995 Round 5 Cin
1995 Cin: Pass 1-0; Rush 1-(-13) -13.0. **1996** Cin: PR 7-54 7.7.
Total: Pass 1-0; Rush 1-(-13) -13.0; PR 7-54 7.7.

		Receiving				Kickoff Returns					Tot
Year Team	**G**	**Rec**	**Yds**	**Avg**	**TD**	**Ret**	**Yds**	**Avg**	**TD**	**Fum**	**TD**
1995 Cin	16	17	209	12.3	1	50	1092	21.8	0	2	1
1996 Cin	16	32	509	15.9	1	35	782	22.3	1	1	2
1997 Cin	14	27	414	15.3	2	19	487	25.6	0	1	2
1998 Cin-Pit	11	9	87	9.7	0	21	525	25.0	0	1	0
1998 Cin	1	0	0	—	0	0	0	—	0	0	0
1998 Pit	10	9	87	9.7	0	21	525	25.0	0	1	0
NFL Total	57	85	1219	14.3	4	125	2886	23.1	1	5	5

GARY DUNN Dunn, Gary Edward 6'3", 258 **NT-DT-DE**
Col: Miami (Fla.) *HS:* Coral Gables [FL] B: 8/24/1953, Coral Gables, FL
Drafted: 1976 Round 6 Pit
1976 Pit: 5 G. **1978** Pit: 16 G. **1979** Pit: 16 G. **1980** Pit: 16 G. **1981** Pit: 16 G. **1982** Pit: 9 G; 6 Sac. **1983** Pit: 13 G; 6 Sac. **1984** Pit: 16 G; 1 Sac. **1985** Pit: 10 G; 2.5 Sac. **1986** Pit: 16 G; 2.5 Sac. **1987** Pit: 13 G.
Total: 146 G; 18 Sac.

JASON DUNN Dunn, Jason Adam 6'4", 259 **TE**
Col: Eastern Kentucky *HS:* Harrodsburg [KY] B: 11/15/1973, Harrodsburg, KY *Drafted:* 1996 Round 2 Phi
1997 Phi: KR 2-32 16.0. **1998** Phi: Rush 1-(-5) -5.0. **Total:** Rush 1-(-5) -5.0; KR 2-32 16.0.

		Receiving				
Year Team	**G**	**Rec**	**Yds**	**Avg**	**TD**	**Fum**
1996 Phi	16	15	332	22.1	2	0
1997 Phi	15	7	93	13.3	2	0
1998 Phi	10	18	132	7.3	0	1
NFL Total	41	40	557	13.9	4	1

RED DUNN Dunn, Joseph Aloysius 5'11", 177 **BB-TB**
Col: Marquette *HS:* Marquette Acad. [Milwaukee, WI] B: 6/21/1901, Milwaukee, WI D: 1/15/1957, Milwaukee, WI
1924 Mil: 13 G; Pass 6 TD; Rush 2 TD; Scor 47, 7 FG, 14 XK. **1925** ChiC: 10 G; Pass 9 TD; Rush 3 TD; Scor 28, 10 XK. **1926** ChiC: 11 G; Pass 2 TD; Scor 15, 4 FG, 3 XK. **1927** GB: 10 G; Pass 3 TD; Rec 1 TD; Scor 13, 7 XK. **1928** GB: 12 G; Pass 4 TD; Scor 1, 1 XK. **1929** GB: 11 G; Pass 5 TD; Scor 17, 2 FG, 11 XK. **1930** GB: 13 G; Pass 11 TD; Scor 14, **14** XK. **1931** GB: 12 G; Pass **8** TD; Scor 15, **15** XK. **Total:** 92 G; Pass 48 TD; Rush 5 TD; Rec 1 TD; Scor 150, 13 FG, 75 XK; Tot TD 6.

K.D. DUNN Dunn, Keldrick Arthur 6'3", 235 **TE**
Col: Clemson *HS:* Gordon [Decatur, GA] B: 4/28/1963, Fort Hood, TX
Drafted: 1985 Round 5 StL
1985 TB: 7 G. **1986** TB: 7 G; Rec 3-83 27.7; KR 1-0. **1987** Was: 3 G. **1988** NYJ: 15 G; Rec 6-67 11.2. **1989** NYJ: 1 G; Rec 2-13 6.5.
Total: 33 G; Rec 11-163 14.8; KR 1-0.

PAUL DUNN Dunn, Paul Jr. 6'0", 210 **RB**
Col: San Diego City Coll. CA (J.C.); San Francisco State; U.S. International *HS:* San Diego [CA] B: 7/14/1948, Little Rock, AR
Drafted: 1970 Round 13 Cin
1970 Cin: 5 G.

PERRY LEE DUNN Dunn, Perry Lee 6'2", 210 **RB**
Col: Mississippi *HS:* Natchez [MS] B: 1/20/1941, Natchez, MS
Drafted: 1964 Round 4 Dal
1964 Dal: Pass 2-0; KR 2-33 16.5. **1966** Atl: Pass 2-0, 2 Int; KR 2-36 18.0. **1967** Atl: Pass 2-1 50.0%, 32 16.00 1 TD; KR 7-128 18.3. **Total:** Pass 6-1 16.7%, 32 5.33 1 TD 2 Int; KR 11-197 17.9.

		Rushing				Receiving					Tot
Year Team	**G**	**Att**	**Yds**	**Avg**	**TD**	**Rec**	**Yds**	**Avg**	**TD**	**Fum**	**TD**
1964 Dal	14	26	103	4.0	1	2	30	15.0	0	1	1
1965 Dal	13	54	171	3.2	2	8	74	9.3	1	2	3
1966 Atl	14	22	52	2.4	0	5	45	9.0	0	2	0
1967 Atl	14	27	63	2.3	0	13	111	8.5	0	3	0
1968 Atl	14	72	219	3.0	3	9	118	13.1	0	3	3
1969 Bal	5	13	45	3.5	0	5	30	6.0	0	1	0
NFL Total	74	214	653	3.1	6	42	408	9.7	1	12	7

BOB DUNN Dunn, Robert E 6'1", 200 **C-T**
(Baron) *Col:* New York U. *HS:* Dean Acad. [Franklin, MA]
1929 SI: 6 G.

RODDY DUNN Dunn, Roderick 5'10", 200 **T**
Col: Syracuse *HS:* Central [Duluth, MN] B: 8/8/1895, Duluth, MN
D: 12/20/1961, Los Angeles, CA
1923 Dul: 2 G.

WARRICK DUNN Dunn, Warrick De'Mon 5'8", 178 **RB**
Col: Florida State *HS:* Baton Rouge Catholic [LA] B: 1/5/1975, Baton Rouge, LA *Drafted:* 1997 Round 1 TB
1997 TB: PR 5-48 9.6; KR 6-129 21.5. **1998** TB: KR 1-25 25.0.
Total: PR 5-48 9.6; KR 7-154 22.0.

		Rushing				Receiving					Tot
Year Team	**G**	**Att**	**Yds**	**Avg**	**TD**	**Rec**	**Yds**	**Avg**	**TD**	**Fum**	**TD**
1997 TB	16	224	978	4.4	4	39	462	11.8	3	4	7
1998 TB	16	245	1026	4.2	2	44	344	7.8	0	1	2
NFL Total	32	469	2004	4.3	6	83	806	9.7	3	5	9

PAT DUNNE Dunne, Patrick 182 **FB**
Col: No College B: 1888 Deceased
1920 Det: 8 G. **1921** Det: 2 G. **Total:** 10 G.

PAT DUNNIGAN Dunnigan, Merton 5'10", 210 **T-G-E**
Col: Minnesota *HS:* West [Minneapolis, MN] B: 1/24/1894, Bay City, MI Deceased
1922 GB: 2 G. **1924** Min: 5 G. **1925** Mil: 6 G. **1926** Mil: 8 G. **Total:** 21 G.

PAT DUNSMORE Dunsmore, Patrick Neil 6'3", 237 **TE**
Col: Drake *HS:* Ankeny [IA] B: 10/2/1957, Duluth, MN *Drafted:* 1983 Round 4 ChiB
1983 ChiB: 16 G; Rec 8-102 12.8. **1984** ChiB: 11 G; Rec 9-106 11.8 1 TD; 6 Pt. **Total:** 27 G; Rec 17-208 12.2 1 TD; 6 Pt.

BILL DUNSTAN Dunstan, William Elwyn 6'4", 250 **DT**
Col: Utah State *HS:* Skyline [Oakland, CA] B: 1/3/1949, Oakland, CA
Drafted: 1971 Round 14 SF
1973 Phi: 14 G. **1974** Phi: 14 G; 1 Fum TD; 6 Pt. **1975** Phi: 14 G. **1976** Phi: 14 G. **1977** Buf: 14 G; KR 1-9 9.0. **1979** LARm: 10 G. **Total:** 80 G; KR 1-9 9.0; 1 Fum TD; 6 Pt.

ELWYN DUNSTAN Dunstan, William Elywn Jr. 6'3", 238 **HB-T**
(Moose) *Col:* Portland *HS:* Castlemont [Oakland, CA] B: 2/4/1915, San Francisco, CA
1938 ChiC: 4 G. **1939** ChiC-Cle: 8 G; Rush 3-2 0.7. ChiC: 1 G; Rush 3-2 0.7. Cle: 7 G. **1940** Cle: 10 G; Rush 1-4 4.0. **1941** Cle: 11 G; PR 1-35 35.0 **1** TD; 6 Pt. **Total:** 33 G; Rush 4-6 1.5; PR 1-35 35.0 1 TD; 6 Pt.

REGGIE DUPARD Dupard, Jon Reginald 5'11", 206 **RB**
Col: Southern Methodist *HS:* John Curtis Christian [River Ridge, LA]
B: 10/30/1963, New Orleans, LA *Drafted:* 1986 Round 1 NE
1986 NE: KR 3-50 16.7. **1987** NE: KR 4-61 15.3. **1990** Was: KR 2-0.
Total: KR 9-111 12.3.

		Rushing				Receiving				
Year Team	**G**	**Att**	**Yds**	**Avg**	**TD**	**Rec**	**Yds**	**Avg**	**TD**	**Fum**
1986 NE	6	15	39	2.6	0	0	0	—	0	1
1987 NE	8	94	318	3.4	3	3	1	0.3	0	2
1988 NE	16	52	151	2.9	2	34	232	6.8	0	1
1989 NE-Was	14	37	111	3.0	1	6	70	11.7	0	1
1989 NE	7	25	63	2.5	1	6	70	11.7	0	1
1989 Was	7	12	48	4.0	0	0	0	—	0	0
1990 Was	7	19	85	4.5	0	0	0	—	0	0
NFL Total	51	217	704	3.2	6	43	303	7.0	0	5

MARK DUPER Duper, Mark Super 5'9", 185 **WR**
(AKA Mark Kirby Dupas) *Col:* Northwestern State-Louisiana
HS: Moreauville [LA] B: 1/25/1959, Pineville, LA *Drafted:* 1982 Round 2 Mia
1986 Mia: Rush 1-(-10) -10.0. **Total:** Rush 1-(-10) -10.0.

Year Team	G	Receiving Rec	Yds	Avg	TD	Fum
1982 Mia	2	0	0	—	0	0
1983 Mia	16	51	1003	19.7	10	0
1984 Mia	16	71	1306	18.4	8	0
1985 Mia	9	35	650	18.6	3	1
1986 Mia	16	67	1313	19.6	11	0
1987 Mia	11	33	597	18.1	8	0
1988 Mia	13	39	626	16.1	1	0
1989 Mia	15	49	717	14.6	1	0
1990 Mia	16	52	810	15.6	5	1
1991 Mia	16	70	1085	15.5	5	0
1992 Mia	16	44	762	17.3	7	2
NFL Total	146	511	8869	17.4	59	4

CHARLIE DUPRE Dupre, Charles Leroy 6′1″, 195 **DB**
Col: Baylor *HS:* Texas City [TX] B: 11/11/1933, Texas City, TX
Drafted: 1956 Round 6 ChiC
1960 NYT: 14 G.

L.G. DUPRE Dupre, Louis George 5′11″, 190 **HB**
(Long Gone) *Col:* Baylor *HS:* Texas City [TX] B: 9/10/1932, New Orleans, LA *Drafted:* 1955 Round 3 Bal
1956 Bal: KR 7-148 21.1; Punt 25-953 38.1. **1957** Bal: Punt 3-75 25.0. **1958** Bal: Punt 1-(-4) -4.0. **1959** Bal: Pass 1-0. **1960** Dal: KR 2-44 22.0. **1961** Dal: PR 2-4 2.0; KR 6-110 18.3. **Total:** Pass 1-0; PR 2-4 2.0; KR 15-302 20.1; Punt 29-1024 35.3.

Year Team	G	Rushing Att	Yds	Avg	TD	Receiving Rec	Yds	Avg	TD	Fum	Tot TD
1955 Bal	11	88	338	3.8	1	10	153	15.3	0	2	1
1956 Bal	11	49	182	3.7	2	16	216	13.5	2	4	4
1957 Bal	12	101	375	3.7	2	32	339	10.6	2	1	4
1958 Bal	10	95	390	4.1	3	13	111	8.5	0	2	3
1959 Bal	4	23	54	2.3	0	6	47	7.8	1	0	1
1960 Dal	11	104	362	3.5	3	21	216	10.3	2	5	5
1961 Dal	10	16	60	3.8	0	6	49	8.2	0	2	0
NFL Total	69	476	1761	3.7	11	104	1131	10.9	7	16	18

BILLY JOE DUPREE DuPree, Billy Joe 6′4″, 225 **TE**
Col: Michigan State *HS:* Richardson [West Monroe, LA] B: 3/7/1950, Monroe, LA *Drafted:* 1973 Round 1 Dal
1977 Dal: KR 0-24. **Total:** KR 0-24.

Year Team	G	Rushing Att	Yds	Avg	TD	Receiving Rec	Yds	Avg	TD	Fum	Tot TD
1973 Dal	14	2	2	1.0	0	29	392	13.5	5	0	5
1974 Dal	14	4	43	10.8	0	29	466	16.1	4	1	4
1975 Dal	14	1	3	3.0	0	9	138	15.3	1	0	1
1976 Dal	14	7	50	7.1	0	42	680	16.2	2	2	2
1977 Dal	14	3	9	3.0	0	28	347	12.4	3	1	3
1978 Dal	16	1	15	15.0	0	34	509	15.0	9	3	9
1979 Dal	16	2	19	9.5	0	29	324	11.2	5	1	5
1980 Dal	16	4	19	4.8	0	29	312	10.8	7	1	7
1981 Dal	16	1	12	12.0	0	19	214	11.3	2	0	2
1982 Dal	9	1	6	6.0	1	7	41	5.9	2	0	3
1983 Dal	16	0	0	—	0	12	142	11.8	1	0	1
NFL Total	159	26	178	6.8	1	267	3565	13.4	41	9	42

MARCUS DUPREE Dupree, Marcus L 6′2″, 225 **RB**
Col: Oklahoma *HS:* Philadelphia [MS] B: 5/22/1964, Philadelphia, MS
Drafted: 1986 Round 12 LARm
1991 LARm: Rec 6-46 7.7. **Total:** Rec 6-46 7.7.

Year Team	G	Rushing Att	Yds	Avg	TD	Fum
1990 LARm	7	19	72	3.8	0	0
1991 LARm	8	49	179	3.7	1	1
NFL Total	15	68	251	3.7	1	1

MYRON DUPREE Dupree, Myron Ray 5′11″, 180 **DB**
Col: North Carolina Central *HS:* Rocky Mount [NC] B: 10/15/1961, New York, NY *Drafted:* 1983 Round 7 Den
1983 Den: 16 G.

PETE DURANKO Duranko, Peter Nicholas 6′2″, 250 **DE-DT**
Col: Notre Dame *HS:* Bishop McCort [Johnstown, PA] B: 12/15/1943, Johnstown, PA *Drafted:* 1966 Redshirt Round 2 Den
1967 Den: 14 G. **1968** Den: 14 G. **1969** Den: 14 G. **1970** Den: 14 G. **1972** Den: 14 G. **1973** Den: 14 G. **1974** Den: 14 G. **Total:** 98 G.

DON DURDAN Durdan, Donald Edgar 5′9″, 175 **HB-DB**
Col: Oregon State *HS:* Eureka [CA]; Phillips Exeter Acad. [Exeter, NH]
B: 9/21/1920, Arcata, CA D: 6/28/1971, Corvallis, OR
AAFC **1946** SF-A: Rec 2-27 13.5 1 TD; PR 3-37 12.3; Int 2-38; Punt 6-239 39.8. **Total:** Rec 2-27 13.5 1 TD; PR 3-37 12.3; Int 2-38; Punt 6-239 39.8.

Year Team	G	Rushing Att	Yds	Avg	TD
1946 SF-A	12	32	132	4.1	0
1947 SF-A	1	1	2	2.0	0
AAFC Total	13	33	134	4.1	0

CLARENCE DUREN Duren, Clarence Edward 6′1″, 190 **DB**
(Jason) *Col:* Los Angeles City Coll. CA (J.C.); California *HS:* Gardena [CA] B: 12/9/1950, Compton, CA

Year Team	G	Interceptions Int	Yds	TD
1973 StL	11	2	13	0
1974 StL	14	2	29	0
1975 StL	13	1	23	0
1976 StL	13	1	8	0
1977 SD	14	4	45	0
NFL Total	65	10	118	0

STEVE DURHAM Durham, Steven Allen 6′5″, 256 **DE**
Col: Clemson *HS:* James F. Byrnes [Duncan, SC] B: 10/11/1958, Greer, SC *Drafted:* 1981 Round 6 Sea
1982 Bal: 8 G.

JACK DURISHAN Durishan, John Donald 6′2″, 230 **T-G**
Col: Pittsburgh *HS:* Hazleton [PA] B: 7/7/1922 D: 5/13/1977
AAFC **1947** NY-A: 6 G; KR 1-3 3.0.

CHARLIE DURKEE Durkee, Charles Michael 5′11″, 165 **K**
(Mickey) *Col:* Oklahoma State *HS:* L.D. Bell [Hurst, TX] B: 6/25/1944, Tulsa, OK

Year Team	G	Scoring Pts	FG	FGA	FG%	XK	XKA	XK%
1967 NO	14	69	14	32	43.8	27	27	100.0
1968 NO	14	84	19	**37**	51.4	27	27	100.0
1971 NO	12	72	16	23	69.6	24	25	96.0
1972 NO	6	18	3	9	33.3	9	9	100.0
NFL Total	46	243	52	101	51.5	87	88	98.9

JOHN DURKO Durko, John Joseph 6′4″, 235 **E**
Col: Albright *HS:* Mahanoy City [PA] B: 7/23/1914, Mahanoy City, PA
D: 1/1/1963
1944 Phi: 6 G; Rec 2-31 15.5 1 TD; 6 Pt. **1945** ChiC: 1 G. **Total:** 7 G; Rec 2-31 15.5 1 TD; 6 Pt.

SANDY DURKO Durko, Sandy Vincent 6′1″, 185 **DB**
Col: USC *HS:* West Covina [CA] B: 8/29/1948, Los Angeles, CA
Drafted: 1970 Round 6 Cin
1970 Cin: 1 G. **1971** Cin: 14 G; Rush 1-7 7.0; PR 6-14 2.3; Int 4-46; 1 Fum. **1973** NE: 14 G; PR 3-21 7.0; Int 3-26; 2 Fum. **1974** NE: 11 G; PR 1-1 1.0; KR 1-0. **Total:** 40 G; Rush 1-7 7.0; PR 10-36 3.6; KR 1-0; Int 7-72; 3 Fum.

JEFF DURKOTA Durkota, Jeffrey George 6′0″, 205 **FB-LB**
Col: Penn State *HS:* Edensburg-Cambria [PA] B: 12/20/1923, Pittsburgh, PA
AAFC **1948** LA-A: 12 G; Rush 14-66 4.7; Rec 2-12 6.0; KR 9-198 22.0; Int 1-18.

MICHAEL DURRETTE Durrette, Michael Ray 6′4″, 280 **OG**
Col: Ferrum; West Virginia *HS:* Miller Military School [Albemarle, VA]
B: 8/11/1957, Charlottesville, VA
1986 SF: 9 G. **1987** SF: 3 G. **Total:** 12 G.

MARK DUSBABEK Dusbabek, Mark Edward 6′3″, 232 **LB**
Col: Minnesota *HS:* Faribault [MN] B: 6/23/1964, Faribault, MN
Drafted: 1987 Round 4 Hou
1989 Min: 16 G; Int 1-2. **1990** Min: 14 G; Scor **1** Saf; 2 Pt. **1991** Min: 1 G. **Total:** 31 G; Int 1-2; Scor 1 Saf; 2 Pt.

BRAD DUSEK Dusek, John Bradley 6′2″, 220 **LB**
Col: Texas A&M *HS:* Temple [TX] B: 12/13/1950, Temple, TX
Drafted: 1973 Round 3 NE
1974 Was: 14 G; KR 1-0. **1975** Was: 14 G; **1** Fum TD; 6 Pt. **1976** Was: 14 G; Int 1-0; **1** Fum TD; 6 Pt. **1977** Was: 14 G; Int 1-0. **1978** Was: 16 G; Int 1-11; 1 Fum TD; 6 Pt. **1979** Was: 16 G; Int 1-0. **1980** Was: 16 G. **1981** Was: 10 G. **Total:** 114 G; KR 1-0; Int 4-11; 3 Fum TD; 18 Pt.

BILL DUSENBERY Dusenbery, William 6′2″, 198 **RB**
Col: Johnson C. Smith *HS:* Dunbar [Lexington, NC] B: 9/15/1948, Washington, DC *Drafted:* 1970 Round 2 Hou
1970 NO: 8 G; Rush 4-6 1.5; KR 10-183 18.3.

JOE DUSOSSOIT DuSossoit, Florimond Joseph 5′11″, 185 **E**
(AKA Florimund DuSossoit Duke) *Col:* Dartmouth *HS:* Brookline [MA]
B: 10/2/1895, Rochester, NY D: 4/4/1969, Phoenix, AZ
1921 NYG: 1 G.

JOHN DUTTON Dutton, John Owen 6′6″, 266 **DT-DE**
Col: Nebraska *HS:* Rapid City [SD] B: 2/6/1951, Rapid City, SD
Drafted: 1974 Round 1 Bal
1974 Bal: 14 G. **1975** Bal: 14 G. **1976** Bal: 14 G. **1977** Bal: 12 G. **1978** Bal: 14 G. **1979** Dal: 8 G. **1980** Dal: 16 G; Int 1-38 1 TD; 6 Pt. **1981** Dal: 16 G; Scor 1 Saf; 2 Pt. **1982** Dal: 9 G; 2 Sac. **1983** Dal: 16 G; 4.5 Sac. **1984** Dal: 16 G; Scor **1** Saf; 2 Pt; 2.5 Sac. **1985** Dal: 16 G; 4 Sac.

1986 Dal: 16 G; 5 Sac. **1987** Dal: 4 G. **Total:** 185 G; Int 1-38 1 TD; Scor 2 Saf; 10 Pt; 18 Sac.

BILL DUTTON Dutton, William Earl 5′10″, 180 **HB-DB**
Col: Pittsburgh B: 12/9/1918, Morgantown, WV D: 8/2/1951, Pittsburgh, PA *Drafted:* 1943 Round 2 Was
1946 Pit: Pass 6-4 66.7%, 31 5.17; Rec 2-68 34.0; PR 3-36 12.0; KR 1-22 22.0.

		Rushing			
Year Team	**G**	**Att**	**Yds**	**Avg**	**TD**
1946 Pit	11	53	169	3.2	2

EARL DUVALL Duvall, Earl S 6′0″, 220 **G-T-E**
(Mooney; Rowdy) *Col:* Ohio U. *HS:* Ashville [OH] B: 6/20/1899, Duvall, OH D: 8/6/1966, Marble Cliff, OH
1924 Col: 8 G. **1925** Col: 8 G. **1926** Col: 5 G. **Total:** 21 G.

BEN DVORAK Dvorak, Benjamin Anton 5′10″, 170 **TB**
Col: Minnesota *HS:* New Prague [MN] B: 1/20/1895 D: 5/7/1974, Minneapolis, MN
1921 Min: 4 G; Rush 2 TD; 12 Pt.

RICK DVORAK Dvorak, Richard Joseph 6′4″, 240 **DE**
Col: Wichita State *HS:* Spearville [KS] B: 4/21/1952, Spearville, KS
Drafted: 1974 Round 3 NYG
1974 NYG: 13 G. **1975** NYG: 14 G. **1976** NYG: 14 G. **1977** NYG-Mia: 6 G. NYG: 5 G. Mia: 1 G. **Total:** 47 G.

TIM DWIGHT Dwight, Timothy John Jr. 5′8″, 184 **WR**
(Mutt) *Col:* Iowa *HS:* Iowa City [IA] B: 7/13/1975, Iowa City, IA
Drafted: 1998 Round 4 Atl
1998 Atl: Pass 2-1 50.0%, 22 11.00; Rush 8-19 2.4; Rec 4-94 23.5 1 TD.

		Punt Returns				Kickoff Returns					Tot
Year Team	**G**	**Ret**	**Yds**	**Avg**	**TD**	**Ret**	**Yds**	**Avg**	**TD**	**Fum**	**TD**
1998 Atl	12	31	263	8.5	0	36	973	27.0	1	3	2

DAN DWORSKY Dworsky, Daniel Leonard 6′0″, 211 **LB-BB**
(Deacon; Bull) *Col:* Michigan *HS:* Washington [Sioux Falls, SD]
B: 10/4/1927, Minneapolis, MN
AAFC **1949** LA-A: 11 G; KR 1-14 14.0; Int 1-3.

MIKE DWYER Dwyer, Francis Michael II 6′3″, 280 **DT**
Col: Rhode Island; Massachusetts *HS:* Barnstable [Hyannis, MA]
B: 6/13/1963, Boston, MA
1987 Dal: 3 G; 1 Sac.

JACK DWYER Dwyer, John Joseph 5′11″, 175 **DB**
Col: Los Angeles City Coll. CA (J.C.); Loyola Marymount *HS:* Alexander Hamilton [Los Angeles, CA] B: 1/15/1927, Los Angeles, CA
Drafted: 1951 Round 5 Phi
1951 Was: PR 7-22 3.1; KR 1-19 19.0. **1952** LARm: **2** Fum TD.
1954 LARm: PR 6-18 3.0; KR 3-65 21.7. **Total:** PR 13-40 3.1; KR 4-84 21.0; 2 Fum TD.

		Interceptions				Tot
Year Team	**G**	**Int**	**Yds**	**TD**	**Fum**	**TD**
1951 Was	12	1	14	0	1	0
1952 LARm	9	4	48	0	0	2
1953 LARm	12	2	31	**1**	0	1
1954 LARm	11	4	90	1	1	1
1955 LARm	2	0	0	0	0	0
NFL Total	46	11	183	2	2	4

BOB DWYER Dwyer, Robert E 5′9″, 160 **WB**
Col: Georgetown B: 8/30/1905, Orange, NJ D: 3/27/1974, Washington, DC
1929 Ora: 1 G.

MIKE DYAL Dyal, Michael Eben 6′2″, 240 **TE**
Col: Texas A&M–Kingsville *HS:* Tivy [Kerrville, TX] B: 5/20/1966, San Antonio, TX

		Receiving				
Year Team	**G**	**Rec**	**Yds**	**Avg**	**TD**	**Fum**
1989 LARd	16	27	499	18.5	2	0
1990 LARd	3	3	51	17.0	0	0
1992 KC	3	1	7	7.0	0	0
1993 KC-SD	10	7	83	11.9	0	1
1993 KC	6	7	83	11.9	0	1
1993 SD	4	0	0	—	0	0
NFL Total	32	38	640	16.8	2	1

ERNEST DYE Dye, Ernest Thaddius 6′6″, 330 **OT-OG**
Col: Itawamba CC MS; South Carolina *HS:* Greenwood [SC]
B: 7/15/1971, Greenwood, SC *Drafted:* 1993 Round 1 Pho
1993 Pho: 7 G. **1994** Ariz: 16 G. **1995** Ariz: 6 G. **1996** Ariz: 8 G. **1997** StL: 13 G. **Total:** 50 G.

LES DYE Dye, Lester Henry 6′1″, 181 **E**
Col: Syracuse *HS:* Wellsville [NY]; Dickinson Sem. [Williamsport, PA]
B: 7/15/1916, Forestville, NY

		Receiving				
Year Team	**G**	**Rec**	**Yds**	**Avg**	**TD**	**Fum**
1944 Was	9	24	281	11.7	2	0
1945 Was	10	8	84	10.5	2	1
NFL Total	19	32	365	11.4	4	1

HENRY DYER Dyer, Henry Louis 6′2″, 230 **RB**
Col: Grambling State *HS:* Chaneyville [Zachary, LA] B: 1/28/1945, Baton Rouge, LA *Drafted:* 1966 Round 4 LARm
1966 LARm: KR 5-61 12.2. **1968** LARm: Rec 8-37 4.6. **1969** Was: Rec 2-86 43.0 1 TD; KR 11-207 18.8. **1970** Was: Rec 4-37 9.3; KR 5-78 15.6. **Total:** Rec 14-160 11.4 1 TD; KR 21-346 16.5.

		Rushing					Tot
Year Team	**G**	**Att**	**Yds**	**Avg**	**TD**	**Fum**	**TD**
1966 LARm	8	0	0	—	0	0	0
1968 LARm	8	55	136	2.5	1	1	1
1969 Was	13	6	18	3.0	0	1	1
1970 Was	12	21	102	4.9	0	2	0
NFL Total	41	82	256	3.1	1	4	2

KEN DYER Dyer, Kenneth James 6′3″, 190 **DB-WR**
(The Blade) *Col:* Arizona State *HS:* Ann Arbor [MI] B: 3/16/1946, Ann Arbor, MI *Drafted:* 1968 Round 4 SD
1968 SD: 14 G; Rec 1-22 22.0; **1** Fum TD; 6 Pt. **1970** Cin: 12 G; Int 3-45. **1971** Cin: 1 G. **Total:** 27 G; Rec 1-22 22.0; Int 3-45; 1 Fum TD; 6 Pt.

DONALD DYKES Dykes, Donald Ray 5′11″, 182 **DB**
Col: Southeastern Louisiana *HS:* Hammond [LA] B: 8/24/1955, Independence, MO *Drafted:* 1979 Round 3 NYJ
1979 NYJ: 16 G. **1980** NYJ: 16 G; Int 5-1. **1981** NYJ: 14 G. **1982** SD: 1 G. **Total:** 47 G; Int 5-1.

HART LEE DYKES Dykes, Hart Lee Jr. 6′4″, 218 **WR**
Col: Oklahoma State *HS:* Bay City [TX] B: 9/2/1966, Bay City, TX
Drafted: 1989 Round 1 NE

		Receiving				
Year Team	**G**	**Rec**	**Yds**	**Avg**	**TD**	**Fum**
1989 NE	16	49	795	16.2	5	3
1990 NE	10	34	549	16.1	2	0
NFL Total	26	83	1344	16.2	7	3

SEAN DYKES Dykes, Sean Rene 5′10″, 170 **DB**
Col: Eastern Arizona Coll. (J.C.); Bowling Green State *HS:* Joseph S. Clark [New Orleans, LA] B: 8/8/1964, New Orleans, LA
1987 NYJ: 6 G.

CHRIS DYKO Dyko, Christopher Edward 6′6″, 305 **OT**
Col: Washington State *HS:* University [Spokane, WA] B: 3/16/1966, Champaign, IL *Drafted:* 1989 Round 8 ChiB
1989 ChiB: 8 G.

KEVIN DYSON Dyson, Kevin 6′1″, 201 **WR**
Col: Utah *HS:* Clearfield [UT] B: 6/23/1975, Clinton, UT
Drafted: 1998 Round 1 Ten
1998 Ten: 13 G; Rush 1-4 4.0; Rec 21-263 12.5 2 TD; 12 Pt.

MATT DYSON Dyson, Matthew Allen Jr. 6′3″, 275 **LB**
Col: Michigan *HS:* La Plata [MD] B: 8/1/1972, La Plata, MD
Drafted: 1995 Round 5 Oak
1995 Oak: 4 G.

JAMES EADDY Eaddy, James 6′2″, 280 **NT**
Col: C.W. Post; New York Tech B: 5/31/1963, Queens, NY
1987 Cin: 2 G.

ALEX EAGLE Eagle, Alexander Franklin Jr. 6′2″, 220 **T**
(Web) *Col:* Oregon *HS:* Lowell [San Francisco, CA] B: 3/19/1913, San Francisco, CA
1935 Bkn: 10 G.

EAGLE FEATHER Eagle Feather **HB**
(AKA Pierce) *Col:* No College Deceased
1922 Oor: 7 G; Rush 1 TD; 6 Pt. **1923** Oor: 11 G. **Total:** 18 G; Rush 1 TD; 6 Pt.

LARRY EAGLIN Eaglin, Lawrence 6′3″, 195 **DB**
Col: Stephen F. Austin St. *HS:* Hull-Daisetta [Daisetta, TX]
B: 8/27/1948, Raywood, TX *Drafted:* 1973 Round 11 Hou
1973 Hou: 11 G; KR 3-76 25.3; 6 Pt; 1 Fum.

KAY EAKIN Eakin, Oliver Kay Jr. 6′0″, 180 **QB-DB-WB-HB**
Col: Arkansas *HS:* Robert E. Lee [Marianna, AR] B: 8/3/1917, Atkins, AR D: 2/15/1993, Fort Smith, AR *Drafted:* 1940 Round 1 Pit
AAFC **1946** MiaA: 13 G; Pass 45-19 42.2%, 331 7.36 2 TD 5 Int; Rush 15-(-41) -2.7; Rec 6-67 11.2; PR 3-30 10.0; KR 4-51 12.8; Int 2-31; Punt 37-1530 41.4.

NFL **1940** NYG: Punt 11-454 41.3. **1941** NYG: Rec 5-81 16.2 1 TD; Int 2-33; Punt 20-949 47.5; Scor 6, 0-1 FG. **Total:** Rec 5-81 16.2 1 TD; Int 2-33; Punt 31-1403 45.3; Scor 6, 0-1 FG.

		Passing							
Year Team	G	Att	Comp	Comp%	Yds	YPA	TD	Int	Rating
1940 NYG	7	43	17	39.5	199	4.63	0	3	25.2
1941 NYG	11	19	5	26.3	71	3.74	1	4	20.6
NFL Total	18	62	22	35.5	270	4.35	1	7	15.6

	Rushing			
Year Team	Att	Yds	Avg	TD
1940 NYG	14	20	1.4	0
1941 NYG	27	-5	-0.2	0
NFL Total	41	15	0.4	0

RALPH EARHART Earhart, Ralph Gloyd 5'10", 165 **HB-DB**
(Scooter) *Col:* Pittsburg State; Texas Tech *HS:* Lefors [TX]
B: 3/29/1924, Milburn, OK *Drafted:* 1948 Round 30 GB
1948 GB: Rec 17-194 11.4 2 TD; KR 2-51 25.5. **1949** GB: Rec 5-109 21.8; KR 11-187 17.0. **Total:** Rec 22-303 13.8 2 TD; KR 13-238 18.3.

		Rushing				Punt Returns					Tot
Year Team	G	Att	Yds	Avg	TD	Ret	Yds	Avg	TD	Fum	TD
1948 GB	12	30	140	4.7	1	11	137	12.5	0	0	3
1949 GB	12	20	54	2.7	0	14	161	11.5	1	5	1
NFL Total	24	50	194	3.9	1	25	298	11.9	1	5	4

ROBIN EARL Earl, Robin Daniel 6'5", 242 **RB-TE**
Col: Washington *HS:* Kent-Meridian [Kent, WA] B: 3/18/1955, Boise, ID *Drafted:* 1977 Round 3 ChiB
1977 ChiB: KR 2-38 19.0. **1978** ChiB: KR 3-48 16.0. **1980** ChiB: KR 1-11 11.0. **Total:** KR 6-97 16.2.

		Rushing				Receiving					Tot
Year Team	G	Att	Yds	Avg	TD	Rec	Yds	Avg	TD	Fum	TD
1977 ChiB	14	56	233	4.2	1	6	32	5.3	0	1	1
1978 ChiB	16	3	17	5.7	0	1	1	1.0	0	0	0
1979 ChiB	13	35	132	3.8	0	8	56	7.0	0	3	0
1980 ChiB	16	0	0	—	0	18	223	12.4	3	0	3
1981 ChiB	16	0	0	—	0	10	118	11.8	1	0	1
1982 ChiB	9	0	0	—	0	4	56	14.0	0	0	0
NFL Total	84	94	382	4.1	1	47	486	10.3	4	4	5

JIM EARLEY Earley, James H 6'1", 230 **RB**
Col: Michigan State *HS:* Paul L. Dunbar [Dayton, OH] B: 1/23/1956, Dayton, OH *Drafted:* 1978 Round 7 NYJ
1978 NYJ: 2 G.

GUY EARLY Early, Guy Burdette 6'3", 210 **G-FB**
Col: Miami (Ohio) *HS:* Jamestown [OH]; Swavely Prep [VA] B: 10/1892 Deceased
1920 Day: 4 G. **1921** Cin: 1 G. **Total:** 5 G.

QUINN EARLY Early, Quinn Remar 6'0", 190 **WR**
Col: Iowa *HS:* Great Neck [NY] B: 4/13/1965, West Hempstead, NY *Drafted:* 1988 Round 3 SD
1988 SD: Rush 7-63 9.0. **1989** SD: Rush 1-19 19.0. **1991** NO: Rush 3-13 4.3; KR 9-168 18.7. **1992** NO: Rush 3-(-1) -0.3. **1993** NO: Rush 2-32 16.0. **1994** NO: Rush 2-10 5.0. **1995** NO: Rush 2-(-3) -1.5. **1996** Buf: Rush 3-39 13.0; Scor 1 2XP. **Total:** Rush 23-172 7.5; KR 9-168 18.7; Scor 1 2XP.

		Receiving				
Year Team	G	Rec	Yds	Avg	TD	Fum
1988 SD	16	29	375	12.9	4	1
1989 SD	6	11	126	11.5	0	0
1990 SD	14	15	238	15.9	1	0
1991 NO	15	32	541	16.9	2	2
1992 NO	16	30	566	18.9	5	0
1993 NO	16	45	670	14.9	6	1
1994 NO	16	82	894	10.9	4	0
1995 NO	16	81	1087	13.4	8	1
1996 Buf	16	50	798	16.0	4	0
1997 Buf	16	60	853	14.2	5	0
1998 Buf	16	19	217	11.4	1	0
NFL Total	163	454	6365	14.0	40	5

BLAINE EARON Earon, Blaine Allen 6'1", 195 **DE**
Col: Duke *HS:* Altoona [PA] B: 1/15/1927, Altoona, PA *Drafted:* 1952 Round 19 Det
1952 Det: 12 G; KR 3-25 8.3. **1953** Det: 6 G. **Total:** 18 G; KR 3-25 8.3.

JUG EARP Earp, Francis Lewis 6'0", 236 **C-T-G**
(Jugger) *Col:* Monmouth (N.J.) *HS:* Monmouth [IL] B: 7/22/1897, Monmouth, IL D: 1/8/1969, Green Bay, WI
1921 RI: 6 G. **1922** RI-GB: 9 G. RI: 2 G. GB: 7 G. **1923** GB: 8 G. **1924** GB: 11 G. **1925** Fra-GB: 14 G. Fra: 1 G. GB: 13 G. **1926** GB: 12 G. **1927** GB-NYY: 13 G. GB: 10 G. NYY: 3 G. **1928** GB: 13 G. **1929** GB: 11 G. **1930** GB: 13 G. **1931** GB: 12 G. **1932** GB: 10 G. **Total:** 132 G.

KENNY EASLEY Easley, Kenneth Mason Jr. 6'3", 206 **DB**
Col: UCLA *HS:* Oscar F. Smith [Chesapeake, VA] B: 1/15/1959, Chesapeake, VA *Drafted:* 1981 Round 1 Sea
1982 Sea: 2 Sac. **1983** Sea: 3 Sac. **1985** Sea: 2 Sac. **1986** Sea: 1 Sac. **Total:** 8 Sac.

		Punt Returns				Interceptions			
Year Team	G	Ret	Yds	Avg	TD	Int	Yds	TD	Fum
1981 Sea	14	0	0	—	0	3	155	1	0
1982 Sea	8	1	15	15.0	0	4	48	0	0
1983 Sea	16	1	6	6.0	0	7	106	0	0
1984 Sea	16	16	194	12.1	0	**10**	126	**2**	0
1985 Sea	13	8	87	10.9	0	2	22	0	2
1986 Sea	10	0	0	—	0	2	34	0	0
1987 Sea	12	0	0	—	0	4	47	0	0
NFL Total	89	26	302	11.6	0	32	538	3	2

WALT EASLEY Easley, Walter Edward 6'2", 226 **RB**
Col: West Virginia *HS:* Stonewall Jackson [Charleston, WV]
B: 9/8/1957, Charleston, WV
1981 SF: Pass 1-1 100.0%, 5 5.00; Rec 9-62 6.9. **Total:** Pass 1-1 100.0%, 5 5.00; Rec 9-62 6.9.

		Rushing				
Year Team	G	Att	Yds	Avg	TD	Fum
1981 SF	12	76	224	2.9	1	2
1982 SF	1	5	11	2.2	0	0
NFL Total	13	81	235	2.9	1	2

RICKY EASMON Easmon, Charles Richard 5'10", 158 **DB**
Col: Florida *HS:* Dunnellon [FL] B: 7/3/1963, Inverness, FL
1985 Dal-TB: 14 G. Dal: 8 G. TB: 6 G. **1986** TB: 9 G; Int 1-0. **Total:** 23 G; Int 1-0.

JOHN EASON Eason, Areenouis John 6'2", 220 **WR**
Col: Florida A&M *HS:* Howard [Ocala, FL] B: 7/30/1945, Ocala, FL *Drafted:* 1968 Round 9 Oak
1968 Oak: 3 G.

TONY EASON Eason, Charles Carroll IV 6'4", 212 **QB**
Col: American River Coll. CA (J.C.); Illinois *HS:* Delta [Clarksburg, CA] B: 10/8/1959, Blythe, CA *Drafted:* 1983 Round 1 NE

		Passing							
Year Team	G	Att	Comp	Comp%	Yds	YPA	TD	Int	Rating
1983 NE	16	95	46	48.4	557	5.86	1	5	48.4
1984 NE	16	431	259	60.1	3228	7.49	23	8	93.4
1985 NE	16	299	168	56.2	2156	7.21	11	17	67.5
1986 NE	15	448	276	61.6	3328	7.43	19	10	89.2
1987 NE	4	79	42	53.2	453	5.73	3	2	72.4
1988 NE	2	43	28	65.1	249	5.79	0	2	61.1
1989 NE-NYJ	5	141	79	56.0	1016	7.21	4	6	70.5
1989 NE	3	105	57	54.3	761	7.25	3	4	71.2
1989 NYJ	2	36	22	61.1	255	7.08	1	2	68.6
1990 NYJ	16	28	13	46.4	155	5.54	0	1	49.0
NFL Total	90	1564	911	58.2	11142	7.12	61	51	79.7

	Rushing				
Year Team	Att	Yds	Avg	TD	Fum
1983 NE	19	39	2.1	0	5
1984 NE	40	154	3.9	5	7
1985 NE	22	70	3.2	1	4
1986 NE	35	170	4.9	0	4
1987 NE	3	25	8.3	0	1
1988 NE	5	18	3.6	0	0
1989 NE-NYJ	3	-2	-0.7	0	3
1989 NE	2	-2	-1.0	0	1
1989 NYJ	1	0	0.0	0	2
1990 NYJ	7	29	4.1	0	2
NFL Total	134	503	3.8	6	26

ROGER EASON Eason, Charles Roger 6'2", 227 **G**
Col: Oklahoma *HS:* Central [Oklahoma City, OK] B: 7/31/1918, Paul's Valley, OK D: 4/28/1998, Houston, TX *Drafted:* 1942 Round 3 Cle
1945 Cle: 2 G. **1946** LARm: 9 G. **1947** LARm: 11 G. **1948** LARm: 10 G. **1949** GB: 12 G. **Total:** 44 G.

BO EASON Eason, James Lawrence 6'2", 200 **DB**
Col: California-Davis *HS:* Delta [Clarksburg, CA] B: 3/10/1961, Walnut Grove, CA *Drafted:* 1984 Round 2 Hou
1984 Hou: 10 G; Int 1-20; 1 Sac. **1985** Hou: 16 G; Int 3-55; 1 Fum; 2.5 Sac. **1986** Hou: 9 G; Int 2-16; 1 Fum. **1987** Hou: 3 G. **Total:** 38 G; Int 6-91; 2 Fum; 3.5 Sac.

RON EAST East, Ronald Allan 6'4", 250 **DT-DE**
Col: Columbia Basin Coll. WA (J.C.); Montana State *HS:* Lincoln [Portland, OR] B: 8/26/1943, Portland, OR
1967 Dal: 14 G. **1968** Dal: 14 G. **1969** Dal: 14 G. **1970** Dal: 14 G. **1971** SD: 14 G. **1972** SD: 12 G. **1973** SD: 13 G; KR 1-8 8.0. **1975** Cle: 14 G; Scor 1 Saf; 2 Pt. **1976** Atl: 14 G. **1977** Sea: 14 G. **Total:** 137 G; KR 2-8 4.0; Scor 1 Saf; 2 Pt.

RAY EASTERLING Easterling, Charles Ray 6'0", 195 **DB**
Col: Richmond *HS:* Collegiate School [Richmond, VA] B: 9/3/1949, Richmond, VA *Drafted:* 1972 Round 9 Atl
1974 Atl: KR 2-34 17.0. **Total:** KR 2-34 17.0.

		Interceptions		
Year Team	**G**	**Int**	**Yds**	**TD**
1972 Atl	8	0	0	0
1973 Atl	1	0	0	0
1974 Atl	14	0	0	0
1975 Atl	14	3	32	0
1976 Atl	14	3	33	0
1977 Atl	14	4	46	0
1978 Atl	2	1	1	0
1979 Atl	16	2	5	0
NFL Total	83	13	117	0

IRV EATMAN Eatman, Irvin Humphrey 6'7", 298 **OT**
Col: UCLA *HS:* Meadowdale [Dayton, OH] B: 1/1/1961, Birmingham, AL *Drafted:* 1983 Round 8 KC
1986 KC: 16 G. **1987** KC: 12 G. **1988** KC: 16 G. **1989** KC: 13 G. **1990** KC: 12 G. **1991** NYJ: 16 G. **1992** NYJ: 12 G. **1993** LARm: 16 G. **1994** Atl: 4 G. **1995** Hou: 16 G. **1996** Hou: 16 G. **Total:** 149 G.

CHAD EATON Eaton, Chad Everett 6'5", 295 **DT**
Col: Washington State *HS:* Gov. John R. Rogers [Puyallup, WA] B: 4/6/1972, Exeter, NH *Drafted:* 1995 Round 7 Ariz
1996 NE: 4 G; 1 Sac. **1997** NE: 16 G; 1 Sac. **1998** NE: 15 G; KR 1-13 13.0; 6 Sac. **Total:** 35 G; KR 1-13 13.0; 8 Sac.

LOU EATON Eaton, Louis Standish 6'2", 215 **T**
Col: California B: 1915
1945 NYG: 2 G.

SCOTT EATON Eaton, Thomas Scott 6'3", 205 **DB**
Col: Oregon State *HS:* Medford [OR] B: 8/20/1944, Salem, OR *Drafted:* 1967 Round 8 NYG
1967 NYG: Rec 1-18 18.0. **1968** NYG: KR 1-2 2.0. **Total:** Rec 1-18 18.0; KR 1-2 2.0.

		Interceptions		
Year Team	**G**	**Int**	**Yds**	**TD**
1967 NYG	12	2	7	0
1968 NYG	14	4	20	0
1969 NYG	14	2	23	1
1970 NYG	8	2	8	0
1971 NYG	12	1	0	0
NFL Total	60	11	58	1

TRACEY EATON Eaton, Tracey Bruce 6'1", 195 **DB**
Col: Portland State *HS:* Medford [OR] B: 7/19/1965, Medford, OR *Drafted:* 1988 Round 7 Hou
1988 Hou: 1 G. **1989** Hou: 16 G; Int 3-33. **1990** Pho: 11 G. **1991** Atl: 16 G. **1993** Atl: 16 G; Int 1-0. **Total:** 60 G; Int 4-33.

VIC EATON Eaton, Victor Roe 6'2", 200 **QB-DB**
Col: Missouri *HS:* Lafayette [St. Joseph, MO] B: 1/3/1933, Savannah, MO *Drafted:* 1955 Round 11 Pit
1955 Pit: Pass 2-0; PR 23-73 3.2.

		Punting		
Year Team	**G**	**Punts**	**Yds**	**Avg**
1955 Pit	12	66	2522	38.2

HARRY EBDING Ebding, Harry Joseph 5'11", 199 **OE-DE**
(Irish) *Col:* St. Mary's (Cal.) *HS:* Walla Walla [WA] B: 9/12/1906, Walla Walla, WA D: 9/11/1980, Mecca, CA
1937 Det: **2** Fum TD. **Total:** 2 Fum TD.

		Receiving				Tot
Year Team	**G**	**Rec**	**Yds**	**Avg**	**TD**	**TD**
1931 Port	14	—	—	—	0	0
1932 Port	12	14	171	12.2	1	1
1933 Port	11	8	125	15.6	0	0
1934 Det	12	10	**264**	**26.4**	2	2
1935 Det	11	8	128	16.0	1	1
1936 Det	11	10	194	19.4	3	4
1937 Det	10	5	89	17.8	1	3
NFL Total	81	55	971	17.7	8	11

RICK EBER Eber, Richard Lee 6'0", 185 **WR**
Col: El Camino Coll. CA (J.C.); Tulsa *HS:* Redondo [Redondo Beach, CA] B: 4/17/1945, Torrance, CA *Drafted:* 1968 Round 6 Atl
1968 Atl: 1 G. **1969** SD: 5 G; Rec 9-141 15.7 1 TD; 6 Pt. **1970** SD: 6 G; Rec 2-43 21.5. **Total:** 12 G; Rec 11-184 16.7 1 TD; 6 Pt.

JESS EBERDT Eberdt, Jess Samuel 6'2", 215 **C**
Col: Alabama *HS:* Blytheville [AR]; Lakeside HS [Lake Village, AR] B: 4/17/1908, Blytheville, AR D: 1/29/1995, Williamsburg, VA
1932 Bkn: 4 G.

HAL EBERSOLE Ebersole, Harold Leon 6'3", 190 **G**
Col: Cornell *HS:* Montclair Acad. [Montclair, NJ] B: 9/24/1899, St. Louis, MO D: 9/25/1984, Atlanta, GA
1923 Cle: 2 G.

JOHN EBERSOLE Ebersole, John Joel 6'3", 234 **LB**
Col: Penn State *HS:* Altoona [PA] B: 11/5/1948, Altoona, PA *Drafted:* 1970 Round 4 NYJ
1970 NYJ: 14 G. **1971** NYJ: 14 G. **1972** NYJ: 14 G. **1973** NYJ: 13 G; Int 1-0. **1974** NYJ: 14 G; Int 3-48. **1975** NYJ: 13 G; Int 2-21. **1976** NYJ: 13 G; Int 1-0. **1977** NYJ: 13 G; Int 1-0. **Total:** 108 G; Int 8-69.

BEANIE EBERTS Eberts, Bernard L 5'11", 198 **G-T-BB**
(Dutch) *Col:* Catholic *HS:* Aquinas [Columbus, OH] B: 5/21/1901, Columbus, OH D: 4/20/1983, Chevy Chase, MD
1924 Min: 3 G.

RAY EBLI Ebli, Raymond Henry 6'3", 210 **DE-OE**
(Lil' Abner) *Col:* Notre Dame *HS:* St.Ambrose [Ironwood, MI] B: 10/6/1919, Ironwood, MI
AAFC **1946** BufA: 9 G; Rec 2-15 7.5 1 TD; 6 Pt. **1947** ChiA: 5 G; Rec 4-38 9.5 1 TD; 6 Pt. **Total:** 14 G; Rec 6-53 8.8 2 TD; 12 Pt.

NFL **1942** ChiC: 6 G; Rec 6-83 13.8.

BYRON EBY Eby, Byron 6'0", 185 **TB-WB**
Col: Ohio State *HS:* Chillicothe [OH] B: 12/11/1904 D: 9/11/1990
1930 Port: 3 G; Pass 1 TD; Rec 1 TD; 6 Pt.

SCOTT ECCLES Eccles, Scott Michael 6'5", 240 **TE**
Col: Cabrillo Coll. CA (J.C.); Eastern New Mexico *HS:* Leland [San Jose, CA] B: 6/28/1963, New Orleans, LA *Drafted:* 1987 Round 9 LARd
1987 Hou: 1 G.

DONNIE ECHOLS Echols, Donald Wayne 6'4", 240 **TE**
Col: Oklahoma State *HS:* Franklin D. Roosevelt [Dallas, TX] B: 12/16/1957, Dallas, TX
1987 Cle: 3 G.

FATE ECHOLS Echols, Fate Leonard 6'1", 260 **OT-DT**
Col: Northwestern *HS:* Michael Washington [South Bend, IN] B: 6/29/1939, Union Springs, AL *Drafted:* 1962 Round 1 StL
1962 StL: 5 G. **1963** StL: 3 G. **Total:** 8 G.

TERRY ECHOLS Echols, Terry Lee 6'0", 220 **LB**
Col: Marshall *HS:* Mullens [WV] B: 1/10/1962, Mullens, WV
1984 Pit: 4 G.

KEITH ECK Eck, Keith Curren 6'5", 255 **C-OG**
Col: UCLA *HS:* Crespi [Encino, CA] B: 11/28/1955, Newport Beach, CA
1979 NYG: 13 G.

GUS ECKBERG Eckberg, Gustavus Anthony 5'9", 180 **FB**
Col: Minnesota; West Virginia *HS:* North [Minneapolis, MN] B: 8/25/1898, Minneapolis, MN Deceased
1925 Cle: 1 G.

ED ECKER Ecker, Enrique Edward 6'7", 276 **OT-DT**
Col: John Carroll *HS:* St. Ignatius [Cleveland, OH] B: 1/21/1923, Cleveland, OH D: 1/4/1990, Los Angeles, CA
AAFC **1948** ChiA: 8 G.

NFL **1947** ChiB: 12 G. **1950** GB: 12 G. **1951** GB: 7 G. **1952** Was: 9 G. **Total:** 40 G.

OX ECKHARDT Eckhardt, Oscar George Jr. 6'1", 190 **FB-WB**
(Mr. Zero) *Col:* Texas *HS:* Stephen F. Austin [Austin, TX] B: 12/23/1901, Yorktown, TX D: 4/22/1951, Yorktown, TX
1928 NYG: 11 G; Rush 2 TD; Scor 13, 1 XK.

BOB ECKL Eckl, Robert Joseph 6'1", 233 **T**
Col: Wisconsin *HS:* Washington [Milwaukee, WI] B: 11/20/1917, Milwaukee, WI D: 9/1961
1945 ChiC: 6 G.

BRAD ECKLUND Ecklund, Bradford Sterling 6'3", 215 **C-LB**
(Whitey) *Col:* Oregon *HS:* Milwaukie [OR] B: 5/9/1922, Los Angeles, CA
AAFC **1949** NY-A: 12 G.

NFL **1950** NYY: 12 G. **1951** NYY: 12 G. **1952** Dal: 12 G. **1953** Bal: 12 G. **Total:** 48 G.

DOLPH ECKSTEIN Eckstein, Adolph William 5'10", 185 **C**
Col: Brown *HS:* Battin [Elizabeth, NJ] B: 5/7/1902, Elizabeth, NJ D: 6/28/1963, Providence, RI
1925 Prov: 12 G. **1926** Prov: 13 G. **Total:** 25 G.

JERRY ECKWOOD Eckwood, Jerry Louis 6'0", 198 **RB**
Col: Arkansas *HS:* Brinkley [AR] B: 12/26/1954, Brinkley, AR *Drafted:* 1979 Round 3 TB
1979 TB: Pass 1-0. **1980** TB: Pass 4-0. **Total:** Pass 5-0.

Year Team	G	Rushing Att	Yds	Avg	TD	Receiving Rec	Yds	Avg	TD	Fum	Tot TD
1979 TB	16	194	690	3.6	2	22	268	12.2	0	9	2
1980 TB	15	149	504	3.4	2	47	475	10.1	1	7	3
1981 TB	16	172	651	3.8	2	24	213	8.9	0	3	2
NFL Total	47	515	1845	3.6	6	93	956	10.3	1	19	7

FLOYD EDDINGS Eddings, Floyd Jr. 5′11″, 177 **WR**
Col: California *HS:* Phillips [Birmingham, AL]; Ganesna HS [Birmingham, AL] B: 12/15/1958, Birmingham, AL
1982 NYG: Rush 2-12 6.0. **1983** NYG: Rush 1-3 3.0. **Total:** Rush 3-15 5.0.

Year Team	G	Receiving Rec	Yds	Avg	TD
1982 NYG	4	14	275	19.6	0
1983 NYG	9	14	231	16.5	0
NFL Total	13	28	506	18.1	0

NICK EDDY Eddy, Nicholas Matthew 6′1″, 210 **RB**
Col: Notre Dame *HS:* Tracy [CA] B: 8/23/1944, Dunsmuir, CA
Drafted: 1966 Round 2 Det
1968 Det: Rec 8-91 11.4; PR 4-10 2.5. **1969** Det: Rec 10-78 7.8 1 TD; PR 1-5 5.0. **1970** Det: Rec 4-22 5.5; PR 4-25 6.3; KR 7-168 24.0. **1972** Det: Rec 2-46 23.0 1 TD. **Total:** Rec 24-237 9.9 2 TD; PR 9-40 4.4; KR 7-168 24.0.

Year Team	G	Rushing Att	Yds	Avg	TD	Fum	Tot TD
1968 Det	5	48	176	3.7	0	3	0
1969 Det	11	78	272	3.5	2	1	3
1970 Det	11	18	47	2.6	1	2	1
1972 Det	2	8	28	3.5	0	0	1
NFL Total	29	152	523	3.4	3	6	5

BRAD EDELMAN Edelman, Bradley Martin 6′6″, 265 **OG**
Col: Missouri *HS:* Parkway North [Creve Coeur, MO] B: 9/3/1960, Jacksonville, FL *Drafted:* 1982 Round 2 NO
1982 NO: 9 G. **1983** NO: 16 G. **1984** NO: 11 G. **1985** NO: 8 G. **1986** NO: 13 G. **1987** NO: 11 G. **1988** NO: 14 G. **1989** NO: 8 G. **Total:** 90 G.

BILL EDGAR Edgar, Alexander Willis 6′2″, 185 **G-FB-WB-TB**
Col: Washington & Jefferson; Pittsburgh; Bucknell *HS:* Wilkinsburg [PA]; Kiski School [Saltsburg, PA] B: 9/17/1898, Morning Sun, IA
D: 12/18/1970, Butler, PA
1923 Buf-Akr: 5 G. Buf: 2 G. Akr: 3 G. **Total:** 5 G.

SHAYNE EDGE Edge, Randall Shayne 5′11″, 180 **P**
Col: Florida *HS:* Columbia [Lake City, FL] B: 8/21/1971, Newton Co., GA
1996 Pit: 4 G; Rush 1-(-16) -16.0; Punt 17-675 39.7.

BOOKER EDGERSON Edgerson, Booker Tyrone 5′10″, 183 **DB**
Col: Western Illinois *HS:* Rock Island [IL] B: 7/5/1939, Baxter, AR
1962 Buf: PR 1-1 1.0. **1967** Buf: PR 1-2 2.0. **1969** Buf: **1** Fum TD.
Total: PR 2-3 1.5; 1 Fum TD.

Year Team	G	Interceptions Int	Yds	TD	Fum	Tot TD
1962 Buf	14	6	111	0	1	0
1963 Buf	14	1	0	0	0	0
1964 Buf	10	4	130	0	0	0
1965 Buf	14	5	55	0	0	0
1966 Buf	7	0	0	0	0	0
1967 Buf	14	2	25	0	0	0
1968 Buf	13	4	100	**2**	0	2
1969 Buf	14	1	0	0	0	1
1970 Den	6	0	0	0	0	0
NFL Total	106	23	421	2	1	3

DEKE EDLER Edler, Robert Karl 5′9″, 170 **WB**
Col: Ohio Wesleyan *HS:* Galion [OH] B: 8/29/1898 D: 6/1/1953, Peoria, IL
1923 Cle: 5 G; Rush 1 TD; 6 Pt.

BOBBY JOE EDMONDS Edmonds, Bobby Joe Jr. 5′11″, 190 **RB**
Col: Arkansas *HS:* Lutheran North [St. Louis, MO] B: 9/26/1964, Nashville, TN *Drafted:* 1986 Round 5 Sea
1986 Sea: Rush 1-(-11) -11.0. **1995** TB: Rush 5-28 5.6; Rec 1-8 8.0.
Total: Rush 6-17 2.8; Rec 1-8 8.0.

Year Team	G	Punt Returns Ret	Yds	Avg	TD	Kickoff Returns Ret	Yds	Avg	TD	Fum
1986 Sea	15	34	419	**12.3**	1	34	764	22.5	0	4
1987 Sea	11	20	251	12.6	0	27	564	20.9	0	1
1988 Sea	16	35	340	9.7	0	40	900	22.5	0	2
1989 LARd	7	16	168	10.5	0	14	271	19.4	0	0
1995 TB	16	29	293	10.1	0	58	1147	19.8	0	1
NFL Total	65	134	1471	11.0	1	173	3646	21.1	0	8

VAN EDMONDSON Edmondson, August Van 5′10″, 210 **C**
(Gus) *Col:* Oklahoma *HS:* Maysville [AR] B: 6/8/1899, Delaware Co., OK Deceased
1926 Buf: 5 G.

FERRELL EDMUNDS Edmunds, Ferrell Jr. 6′6″, 254 **TE**
Col: Maryland *HS:* George Washington [Danville, VA] B: 4/16/1965, South Boston, VA *Drafted:* 1988 Round 3 Mia
1988 Mia: Rush 1-(-8) -8.0; KR 1-20 20.0. **1990** Mia: Rush 1-(-7) -7.0.
Total: Rush 2-(-15) -7.5; KR 1-20 20.0.

Year Team	G	Receiving Rec	Yds	Avg	TD	Fum
1988 Mia	16	33	575	17.4	3	4
1989 Mia	16	32	382	11.9	3	1
1990 Mia	16	31	446	14.4	1	2
1991 Mia	8	11	118	10.7	2	0
1992 Mia	10	10	91	9.1	1	0
1993 Sea	16	24	239	10.0	2	1
1994 Sea	7	7	43	6.1	0	1
NFL Total	89	148	1894	12.8	12	9

RANDY EDMUNDS Edmunds, George Randall 6′2″, 220 **LB**
Col: Georgia Tech *HS:* Lincoln Co. [Lincolnton, GA] B: 6/24/1946, Washington, GA *Drafted:* 1968 Round 8 Mia
1968 Mia: 14 G; Int 1-1. **1969** Mia: 14 G. **1971** NE: 14 G. **1972** Bal: 3 G.
Total: 45 G; Int 1-1.

TURK EDWARDS Edwards, Albert Glen 6′2″, 255 **T**
Col: Washington State *HS:* Clarkston [WA] B: 9/28/1907, Mold, WA
D: 1/12/1973, Seattle, WA *HOF:* 1969
1932 Bos: 6 G; 6 Pt. **1933** Bos: 12 G. **1934** Bos: 12 G. **1935** Bos: 11 G. **1936** Bos: 12 G. **1937** Was: 11 G. **1938** Was: 9 G; 6 Pt. **1939** Was: 11 G; Scor 0-1 XK. **1940** Was: 2 G. **Total:** 86 G; Scor 12, 0-1 XK; 12 Pt.

AL EDWARDS Edwards, Albert Jr. 5′8″, 171 **WR**
Col: Northwestern State-Louisiana *HS:* Alfred Bonnabel [Metairie, LA]
B: 5/18/1967, New Orleans, LA *Drafted:* 1990 Round 11 Buf
1991 Buf: Rush 1-17 17.0. **1992** Buf: Rush 1-8 8.0. **Total:** Rush 2-25 12.5.

Year Team	G	Receiving Rec	Yds	Avg	TD	Punt Returns Ret	Yds	Avg	TD
1990 Buf	14	2	11	5.5	0	14	92	6.6	0
1991 Buf	16	22	228	10.4	1	13	69	5.3	0
1992 Buf	7	2	25	12.5	0	0	0	—	0
NFL Total	37	26	264	10.2	1	27	161	6.0	0

Year Team	Kickoff Returns Ret	Yds	Avg	TD	Fum	Tot TD
1990 Buf	11	256	23.3	0	0	0
1991 Buf	31	623	20.1	**1**	2	2
1992 Buf	12	274	22.8	0	1	0
NFL Total	54	1153	21.4	1	3	2

ANTHONY EDWARDS Edwards, Anthony Quinn 5′10″, 195 **WR**
Col: New Mexico Highlands *HS:* Casa Grande Union [AZ]
B: 5/26/1966, Casa Grande, AZ
1996 Ariz: Rush 1-(-8) -8.0. **Total:** Rush 1-(-8) -8.0.

Year Team	G	Receiving Rec	Yds	Avg	TD	Punt Returns Ret	Yds	Avg	TD
1989 Phi	9	2	74	37.0	0	7	64	9.1	0
1990 Phi	5	0	0	—	0	8	60	7.5	0
1991 Pho	13	0	0	—	0	1	7	7.0	0
1992 Pho	16	14	147	10.5	1	0	0	—	0
1993 Pho	16	13	326	25.1	1	3	12	4.0	0
1995 Ariz	15	29	417	14.4	2	18	131	7.3	0
1996 Ariz	16	29	311	10.7	1	5	46	9.2	0
1997 Ariz	16	20	203	10.2	0	1	-1	-1.0	0
NFL Total	106	107	1478	13.8	5	43	319	7.4	0

Year Team	Kickoff Returns Ret	Yds	Avg	TD	Fum
1989 Phi	3	23	7.7	0	2
1990 Phi	3	36	12.0	0	2
1991 Pho	13	261	20.1	0	0
1992 Pho	8	143	17.9	0	0
1993 Pho	3	51	17.0	0	0
1995 Ariz	3	50	16.7	0	0
1996 Ariz	0	0	—	0	1
NFL Total	33	564	17.1	0	5

ANTONIO EDWARDS Edwards, Antonio 6′3″, 271 **DE**
Col: Valdosta State *HS:* Colquitt Co. [Moultrie, GA] B: 3/10/1970, Moultrie, GA *Drafted:* 1993 Round 8 Sea
1993 Sea: 9 G; Scor 1 Saf; 2 Pt; 3 Sac. **1994** Sea: 15 G; 2.5 Sac. **1995** Sea: 13 G; 1 Fum TD; 6 Pt; 5.5 Sac. **1996** Sea: 12 G; 2 Sac. **1997** Sea-NYG: 4 G. Sea: 1 G. NYG: 3 G. **1998** Atl: 15 G; 1 Fum TD; 6 Pt; 1 Sac. **Total:** 68 G; Scor 1 Saf; 2 Fum TD; 14 Pt; 14 Sac.

BRAD EDWARDS Edwards, Bradford Wayne 6'2", 207 **DB**
Col: South Carolina *HS:* Douglas Byrd [Fayetteville, NC] B: 3/22/1966, Lumberton, NC *Drafted:* 1988 Round 2 Min

		Interceptions		
Year Team	G	Int	Yds	TD
1988 Min	16	2	47	1
1989 Min	9	1	18	0
1990 Was	16	2	33	0
1991 Was	16	4	52	0
1992 Was	16	6	157	1
1993 Was	16	1	17	0
1994 Atl	4	0	0	0
1995 Atl	13	0	0	0
1996 Atl	16	2	15	0
NFL Total	122	18	339	2

BUD EDWARDS Edwards, Charles Halleck 5'11", 190 **FB-WB-HB-TB**
Col: Brown *HS:* Moses Brown School [Providence, RI] B: 3/21/1908, Chicago, IL D: 8/11/1986, Scottsdale, AZ
1930 Prov: 9 G; Rec 1 TD; 6 Pt. **1931** ChiB-Prov: 10 G. ChiB: 1 G. Prov: 9 G. **Total:** 19 G; Rec 1 TD; 6 Pt.

CID EDWARDS Edwards, Cleophus J 6'3", 230 **RB**
Col: Tennessee State *HS:* Selma [AL] B: 10/10/1943, Selma, AL
1971 StL: KR 2-41 20.5. **Total:** KR 2-41 20.5.

		Rushing				Receiving					Tot
Year Team	G	Att	Yds	Avg	TD	Rec	Yds	Avg	TD	Fum	TD
1968 StL	14	31	214	6.9	1	1	2	2.0	0	0	1
1969 StL	14	107	504	4.7	3	23	309	13.4	0	3	3
1970 StL	11	70	350	5.0	1	19	150	7.9	1	2	2
1971 StL	12	108	316	2.9	4	12	122	10.2	0	8	4
1972 SD	12	157	679	4.3	5	40	557	13.9	2	4	7
1973 SD	13	133	609	4.6	1	25	164	6.6	0	3	1
1974 SD	10	65	261	4.0	0	13	102	7.8	0	2	0
1975 ChiB	8	27	73	2.7	0	11	86	7.8	1	1	1
NFL Total	94	698	3006	4.3	15	144	1492	10.4	4	23	19

DAN EDWARDS Edwards, Dan Moody 6'1", 197 **OE-DE**
Col: Georgia *HS:* Gatesville [TX] B: 7/18/1926, Osage, TX
AAFC **1948** BknA: KR 1-21 21.0. **1949** ChiA: KR 2-29 14.5 1 TD. **Total:** KR 3-50 16.7 1 TD.

		Receiving				Tot
Year Team	G	Rec	Yds	Avg	TD	TD
1948 BknA	11	23	176	7.7	0	0
1949 ChiA	12	42	573	13.6	3	4
AAFC Total	23	65	749	11.5	3	4

NFL Statistics

		Receiving				
Year Team	G	Rec	Yds	Avg	TD	Fum
1950 NYY	12	52	775	14.9	6	1
1951 NYY	10	39	509	13.1	3	0
1952 Dal	1	3	22	7.3	0	0
1953 Bal	12	35	312	8.9	3	0
1954 Bal	12	40	531	13.3	1	0
NFL Total	47	169	2149	12.7	13	1

DAVE EDWARDS Edwards, David Lee 6'0", 195 **DB**
Col: Illinois *HS:* Columbia [Decatur, GA] B: 3/31/1962, Senoia, GA
1985 Pit: 14 G. **1986** Pit: 16 G; Scor **1** Saf; 2 Pt. **1987** Pit: 3 G; Int 1-0. **Total:** 33 G; Int 1-0; Scor 1 Saf; 2 Pt.

DAVE EDWARDS Edwards, David Monroe 6'1", 225 **LB**
Col: Auburn *HS:* Abbeville [AL] B: 12/14/1939, Columbia, AL
Drafted: 1962 Round 25 Den

		Interceptions			
Year Team	G	Int	Yds	TD	Fum
1963 Dal	14	1	17	0	0
1964 Dal	14	1	1	0	1
1965 Dal	14	2	0	0	0
1966 Dal	14	1	12	0	0
1967 Dal	14	3	34	1	0
1968 Dal	14	0	0	0	0
1969 Dal	14	1	0	0	0
1970 Dal	13	2	2	0	0
1971 Dal	14	2	0	0	0
1972 Dal	14	0	0	0	0
1973 Dal	14	0	0	0	0
1974 Dal	14	0	0	0	0
1975 Dal	14	0	0	0	0
NFL Total	181	13	66	1	1

DENNIS EDWARDS Edwards, Dennis Ray 6'4", 253 **DE**
Col: USC *HS:* Edison [Stockton, CA] B: 10/6/1959, Stockton, CA
1987 LARm: 3 G; 1 Sac.

DIXON EDWARDS Edwards, Dixon Voldean III 6'1", 230 **LB**
Col: Michigan State *HS:* Aiken [Cincinnati, OH] B: 3/25/1968, Cincinnati, OH *Drafted:* 1991 Round 2 Dal
1991 Dal: 11 G; Int 1-36 1 TD; 6 Pt. **1992** Dal: 16 G; KR 1-0. **1993** Dal: 16 G; 1.5 Sac. **1994** Dal: 16 G; 1 Sac. **1995** Dal: 15 G. **1996** Min: 14 G; Int 1-18; 3.5 Sac. **1997** Min: 16 G; 1.5 Sac. **1998** Min: 15 G. **Total:** 119 G; KR 1-0; Int 2-54 1 TD; 6 Pt; 7.5 Sac.

DONNIE EDWARDS Edwards, Donald Lewis 6'2", 236 **LB**
Col: UCLA *HS:* Chula Vista [CA] B: 4/6/1973, San Diego, CA
Drafted: 1996 Round 4 KC
1996 KC: 15 G; Int 1-22. **1997** KC: 16 G; Int 2-15; 2.5 Sac. **1998** KC: 15 G; 6 Sac. **Total:** 46 G; Int 3-37; 8.5 Sac.

EARL EDWARDS Edwards, Earl 6'7", 260 **DT-DE**
Col: Wichita State *HS:* Howard W. Blake [Tampa, FL] B: 3/17/1946, Statesboro, GA *Drafted:* 1969 Round 5 SF
1969 SF: 14 G; Rec 1-1 1.0; KR 3-3 1.0; 1 Fum. **1970** SF: 14 G. **1971** SF: 14 G. **1972** SF: 13 G. **1973** Buf: 14 G. **1974** Buf: 14 G. **1975** Buf: 14 G. **1976** Cle: 14 G. **1977** Cle: 14 G. **1978** Cle: 16 G. **1979** GB: 9 G. **Total:** 150 G; Rec 1-1 1.0; KR 3-3 1.0; 1 Fum.

EDDIE EDWARDS Edwards, Eddie Lee 6'5", 256 **DE-DT**
Col: Arizona Western Coll. (J.C.); Miami (Fla.) *HS:* Fort Pierce Central [FL] B: 4/25/1954, Sumter, SC *Drafted:* 1977 Round 1 Cin
1977 Cin: 12 G. **1978** Cin: 16 G; Int 1-2. **1979** Cin: 14 G. **1980** Cin: 16 G. **1981** Cin: 14 G. **1982** Cin: 9 G; 6 Sac. **1983** Cin: 16 G; 13 Sac. **1984** Cin: 16 G; 9 Sac. **1985** Cin: 16 G; 8.5 Sac. **1986** Cin: 16 G; **1** Fum TD; 6 Pt; 6.5 Sac. **1987** Cin: 14 G; 4 Sac. **1988** Cin: 11 G; 0.5 Sac. **Total:** 170 G; Int 1-2; 1 Fum TD; 6 Pt; 47.5 Sac.

EMMETT EDWARDS Edwards, Emmett Lee 6'1", 187 **WR**
Col: Kansas *HS:* Central [Kansas City, MO] B: 6/6/1952, Tulsa, OK
Drafted: 1975 Round 2 Hou
1975 Hou: 11 G; Rush 1-(-4) -4.0; Rec 2-22 11.0. **1976** Hou-Buf: 9 G; Rush 1-0; Rec 2-53 26.5. Hou: 3 G. Buf: 6 G; Rush 1-0; Rec 2-53 26.5. **Total:** 20 G; Rush 2-(-4) -2.0; Rec 4-75 18.8.

GLEN EDWARDS Edwards, Glen 6'0", 185 **DB**
Col: Florida A&M *HS:* Gibbs [St. Petersburg, FL] B: 7/31/1947, St. Petersburg, FL
1971 Pit: KR 9-198 22.0. **1972** Pit: KR 1-18 18.0. **1973** Pit: KR 1-10 10.0. **1974** Pit: KR 2-31 15.5. **Total:** KR 13-257 19.8.

		Punt Returns				Interceptions			
Year Team	G	Ret	Yds	Avg	TD	Int	Yds	TD	Fum
1971 Pit	8	1	0	0.0	0	1	20	0	0
1972 Pit	12	22	202	9.2	0	1	14	0	4
1973 Pit	14	34	336	9.9	0	6	186	1	2
1974 Pit	14	16	128	8.0	0	5	153	1	1
1975 Pit	14	25	267	10.7	0	3	68	0	0
1976 Pit	14	1	8	8.0	0	6	95	0	0
1977 Pit	13	0	0	—	0	3	116	0	0
1978 SD	14	0	0	—	0	3	43	0	0
1979 SD	15	0	0	—	0	4	99	0	0
1980 SD	16	4	17	4.3	0	5	122	1	0
1981 SD	8	1	1	1.0	0	2	45	0	1
NFL Total	142	104	959	9.2	0	39	961	3	8

HERMAN EDWARDS Edwards, Herman Lee 6'0", 194 **DB**
Col: Monterey Peninsula Coll. CA (J.C.); California; San Diego State
HS: Monterey [CA] B: 4/27/1954, Fort Monmouth, NJ
1978 Phi: 1 Fum TD. **Total:** 1 Fum TD.

		Interceptions				Tot
Year Team	G	Int	Yds	TD	Fum	TD
1977 Phi	14	6	9	0	1	0
1978 Phi	16	7	59	0	1	1
1979 Phi	16	3	6	0	0	0
1980 Phi	16	3	12	0	0	0
1981 Phi	16	3	1	0	0	0
1982 Phi	9	5	3	0	0	0
1983 Phi	16	1	0	0	0	0
1984 Phi	16	2	0	0	0	0
1985 Phi	16	3	8	**1**	0	1
1986 LARm-Atl	7	0	0	0	0	0
1986 LARm	4	0	0	0	0	0
1986 Atl	3	0	0	0	0	0
NFL Total	142	33	98	1	2	2

CAP EDWARDS Edwards, Howard Eugene 6'0", 207 **G**
Col: Notre Dame *HS:* South Bend Central [IN] B: 5/1888, South Bend, IN D: 11/23/1944, South Bend, IN
1920 Can: 7 G. **1921** Can: 2 G. **1922** Tol: 9 G. **1923** Cle: 2 G. **1924** Cle: 7 G. **Total:** 27 G.

JIMMY EDWARDS Edwards, James Leroy 5'9", 185 **RB**
Col: Oklahoma; Northeast Louisiana *HS:* Classen [Oklahoma City, OK] B: 9/19/1952, Oklahoma City, OK
1979 Min: Rec 1-2 2.0.

Year Team	G	Punt Returns Ret	Yds	Avg	TD	Kickoff Returns Ret	Yds	Avg	TD	Fum
1979 Min	14	33	186	5.6	0	44	1103	25.1	0	10

KELVIN EDWARDS Edwards, Kelvin Mack 6′2″, 202 **WR**
Col: Liberty *HS:* Russell [East Point, GA] B: 7/19/1964, Birmingham, AL *Drafted:* 1986 Round 4 NO
1986 NO: Rush 1-6 6.0; PR 3-2 0.7. **1987** Dal: Rush 2-61 30.5 1 TD; PR 8-75 9.4; KR 7-155 22.1. **Total:** Rush 3-67 22.3 1 TD; PR 11-77 7.0; KR 7-155 22.1.

Year Team	G	Receiving Rec	Yds	Avg	TD	Fum	Tot TD
1986 NO	14	10	132	13.2	0	2	0
1987 Dal	13	34	521	15.3	3	1	4
1988 Dal	8	5	93	18.6	0	1	0
NFL Total	35	49	746	15.2	3	4	4

LLOYD EDWARDS Edwards, Lloyd B 6′3″, 248 **TE**
Col: Los Angeles Harbor Coll. CA (J.C.); San Diego State *HS:* Nathaniel Narbonne [Los Angeles, CA] B: 11/26/1946, Long Beach, CA
Drafted: 1969 Round 3 Oak
1969 Oak: 14 G.

MARC EDWARDS Edwards, Marc Alexander 6′0″, 229 **RB**
Col: Notre Dame *HS:* Norwood [OH] B: 11/17/1974, Cincinnati, OH
Drafted: 1997 Round 2 SF
1997 SF: KR 1-30 30.0. **Total:** KR 1-30 30.0.

Year Team	G	Rushing Att	Yds	Avg	TD	Receiving Rec	Yds	Avg	TD	Tot TD
1997 SF	15	5	17	3.4	0	6	48	8.0	0	0
1998 SF	16	22	94	4.3	1	22	218	9.9	2	3
NFL Total	31	27	111	4.1	1	28	266	9.5	2	3

MARSHALL EDWARDS Edwards, Marshall 6′1″, 190 **FB-LB**
Col: Wake Forest B: 4/1/1916
1943 Bkn: 1 G; Rush 1-5 5.0; Rec 1-(-4) -4.0.

RANDY EDWARDS Edwards, Richard Randolph 6′4″, 264 **DE-NT**
Col: Alabama *HS:* Joseph Wheeler [Marietta, GA] B: 3/9/1961, Marietta, GA
1984 Sea: 13 G; 1.5 Sac. **1985** Sea: 16 G; 10.5 Sac. **1986** Sea: 16 G; KR 1-13 13.0; 4 Sac. **1987** Sea: 7 G. **Total:** 52 G; KR 1-13 13.0; 16 Sac.

ROBERT EDWARDS Edwards, Robert Lee III 5′11″, 218 **RB**
Col: Georgia *HS:* Washington Co. [Sandersville, GA] B: 10/2/1974, Tennille, GA *Drafted:* 1998 Round 1 NE

Year Team	G	Rushing Att	Yds	Avg	TD	Receiving Rec	Yds	Avg	TD	Fum	Tot TD
1998 NE	16	291	1115	3.8	9	35	331	9.5	3	5	12

STAN EDWARDS Edwards, Stanley J 6′0″, 208 **RB**
Col: Michigan *HS:* Kettering [Detroit, MI] B: 5/20/1960, Detroit, MI
Drafted: 1982 Round 3 Hou

Year Team	G	Rushing Att	Yds	Avg	TD	Receiving Rec	Yds	Avg	TD	Fum	Tot TD
1982 Hou	7	15	58	3.9	0	9	53	5.9	0	0	0
1983 Hou	14	16	40	2.5	0	9	79	8.8	1	0	1
1984 Hou	14	60	267	4.5	1	20	151	7.6	0	2	1
1985 Hou	15	25	96	3.8	1	7	71	10.1	0	0	1
1986 Hou	3	1	3	3.0	0	0	0	—	0	0	0
1987 Det	3	32	69	2.2	0	7	82	11.7	0	3	0
NFL Total	56	149	533	3.6	2	52	436	8.4	1	5	3

TOM EDWARDS Edwards, Thomas Leighton 5′11″, 185 **T**
Col: Central Michigan; Michigan *HS:* Central Lake [MI] B: 12/12/1899, Traverse City, MI D: 1/28/1980, Central Lake, MI
1926 Det: 12 G.

TIM EDWARDS Edwards, Timothy 6′1″, 270 **DT**
Col: Delta State *HS:* Neshoba Central [Philadelphia, MS]
B: 8/29/1968, Philadelphia, MS *Drafted:* 1991 Round 12 NE
1992 NE: 14 G; 1 Sac.

VERNON EDWARDS Edwards, Vernon Lajvin 6′4″, 255 **DE**
Col: Southern Methodist *HS:* Kashmere [Houston, TX] B: 6/23/1972, Houston, TX
1996 SD: 5 G; KR 1-0; 1 Sac.

WELDON EDWARDS Edwards, Weldon Bertrand 6′0″, 225 **T**
(Scratch) *Col:* Texas-Arlington; Texas Christian *HS:* Comanche [TX]
B: 4/15/1924, Comanche, TX D: 5/6/1988, Tulsa, OK *Drafted:* 1947 Round 12 Was
1948 Was: 5 G.

MONK EDWARDS Edwards, William Bennett 6′3″, 213 **G-T-LB**
Col: Baylor *HS:* Beaumont [TX] B: 7/19/1920, Ireland, TX
Drafted: 1940 Round 16 NYG
1940 NYG: 9 G. **1941** NYG: 11 G. **1942** NYG: 11 G. **1946** NYG: 10 G.
Total: 41 G.

EGAN Egan 175 **E-WB-BB**
Col: DePaul *HS:* St. Ignatius [Chicago, IL] Deceased
1920 ChiC: 7 G. **1921** ChiC: 1 G. **1922** ChiC: 9 G. **1923** ChiC: 4 G.
1924 Ken: 2 G. **Total:** 23 G.

DICK EGAN Egan, Richard Francis **G**
Col: Wilmington *HS:* Wilmington [OH] B: 2/2/1904, Wilmington, OH
D: 5/15/1984, Middletown, OH
1924 Day: 3 G.

DOUG EGGERS Eggers, Douglas Boyd 6′0″, 213 **LB**
Col: South Dakota State *HS:* Wagner [SD] B: 9/21/1930, Wagner, SD
1954 Bal: 11 G; Int 3-18. **1955** Bal: 12 G. **1956** Bal: 12 G; Int 1-6.
1957 Bal: 11 G. **1958** ChiC: 8 G. **Total:** 54 G; Int 4-24.

RON EGLOFF Egloff, Ronald Barry 6′5″, 230 **TE**
Col: Wisconsin *HS:* Plymouth [MI] B: 10/3/1955, Garden City, MI
1979 Den: KR 1-0. **1981** Den: KR 1-7 7.0. **1984** SD: KR 2-20 10.0.
Total: KR 4-27 6.8.

Year Team	G	Receiving Rec	Yds	Avg	TD	Fum
1977 Den	13	2	27	13.5	0	0
1978 Den	8	4	33	8.3	1	0
1979 Den	15	5	70	14.0	0	0
1980 Den	16	6	85	14.2	0	0
1981 Den	16	17	231	13.6	1	2
1982 Den	9	10	96	9.6	0	0
1983 Den	16	20	205	10.3	2	0
1984 SD	12	11	92	8.4	0	0
NFL Total	105	75	839	11.2	4	2

PATRICK EGU Egu, Okechukwu Patrick 5′11″, 205 **RB**
Col: Nevada-Reno *HS:* John F. Kennedy [Richmond, CA]
B: 2/20/1967, Owerri, Nigeria *Drafted:* 1989 Round 9 TB
1989 NE: 7 G; Rush 3-20 6.7 1 TD; KR 2-26 13.0; 6 Pt; 1 Fum.

CHUCK EHIN Ehin, Charles Kalev 6′4″, 261 **NT-DE-LB**
Col: Brigham Young *HS:* Layton [UT] B: 7/1/1961, Marysville, CA
Drafted: 1983 Round 12 SD
1983 SD: 9 G. **1984** SD: 16 G; 2 Sac. **1985** SD: 16 G; 1.5 Sac. **1986** SD: 12 G; 2.5 Sac. **1987** SD: 12 G; 1 Fum; 3.5 Sac. **Total:** 65 G; 1 Fum; 9.5 Sac.

TOM EHLERS Ehlers, Thomas Slick 6′2″, 218 **LB**
Col: Kentucky *HS:* John Adams [South Bend, IN] B: 7/14/1952, South Bend, IN *Drafted:* 1975 Round 13 Phi
1975 Phi: 14 G. **1976** Phi: 14 G; KR 1-8 8.0; Int 1-27. **1977** Phi: 14 G.
1978 Buf: 8 G. **Total:** 50 G; KR 1-8 8.0; Int 1-27.

CLYDE EHRHARDT Ehrhardt, Clyde Walter 6′1″, 232 **C-LB**
(Egbert) *Col:* Georgia *HS:* Morgan Prep [Petersburg, TN]
B: 7/4/1921, Bardwell, KY D: 2/4/1963
1946 Was: 10 G; Int 1-38. **1948** Was: 12 G; Int 2-29. **1949** Was: 12 G.
Total: 34 G; Int 3-67.

JOE EHRMANN Ehrmann, Joseph Charles 6′5″, 260 **DT**
Col: Syracuse *HS:* Riverside [Buffalo, NY] B: 3/29/1949, Buffalo, NY
Drafted: 1973 Round 1 Bal
1973 Bal: 12 G. **1974** Bal: 14 G. **1975** Bal: 14 G. **1976** Bal: 14 G.
1977 Bal: 9 G. **1978** Bal: 14 G. **1979** Bal: 15 G. **1980** Bal: 16 G; Int 1-5.
1981 Det: 4 G. **1982** Det: 9 G; 3 Sac. **Total:** 121 G; Int 1-5; 3 Sac.

JOHN EIBNER Eibner, John R 6′2″, 228 **T**
Col: Kentucky *HS:* Jeannette [PA]; Mount Sterling HS [KY]
B: 3/13/1914, Elyria, OH D: 11/1973 *Drafted:* 1941 Round 13 Pit
1941 Phi: 11 G. **1942** Phi: 10 G. **1946** Phi: 9 G. **Total:** 30 G.

RAY EICHENLAUB Eichenlaub, Raymond Joseph 6′0″, 225 **FB**
Col: Notre Dame *HS:* East [Columbus, OH] B: 7/15/1892, Columbus, OH D: 11/9/1949, Chicago, IL
1925 Col: 4 G.

ED EIDEN Eiden, Edmund Joseph 6′0″, 205 **C-LB**
(Beef) *Col:* Scranton *HS:* St. Mary's [Scranton, PA] B: 11/16/1921, Scranton, PA
1944 Det: 1 G.

JIM EIDEN Eiden, Harold Charles 5′8″, 185 **T**
Col: No College *HS:* DePaul Acad. [Chicago, IL] B: 10/16/1901, Evanston, IL D: 4/17/1990, Stuart, FL
1926 Lou: 1 G.

JIM EIDSON Eidson, James Milton 6′3″, 264 **OG-C**
Col: Mississippi State *HS:* Morgan Co. [Hartselle, AL] B: 5/10/1954, Anderson, SC *Drafted:* 1976 Round 2 Dal
1976 Dal: 9 G.

JIM EIFRID Eifrid, James Eifrid 6'1", 240 **LB**
Col: Colorado State *HS:* Central Catholic [Fort Wayne, IN]
B: 10/22/1938, Fort Wayne, IN *Drafted:* 1960 Round 1 NYT
1961 Den: 1 G.

VIRGIL EIKENBERG Eikenberg, Charles Virgil 6'2", 205 **QB**
Col: Southwestern Louisiana; Rice *HS:* Boling [TX] B: 2/22/1924, Old Gulf, TX D: 1/30/1987, Houston, TX *Drafted:* 1945 Round 18 Bkn
1948 ChiC: 9 G; Pass 19-6 31.6%, 116 6.11 3 TD 2 Int; Rush 2-9 4.5; Punt 2-72 36.0.

PAT EILERS Eilers, Patrick Christopher 5'11", 195 **DB**
Col: Notre Dame *HS:* St. Thomas Acad. [St. Paul, MN] B: 9/3/1966, St. Paul, MN
1990 Min: 8 G. **1991** Min: 16 G; KR 5-99 19.8. **1992** Was: 1 G. **1993** Was: 11 G. **1994** Was: 16 G. **1995** ChiB: 9 G. **Total:** 61 G; KR 5-99 19.8.

MIKE EISCHEID Eischeid, Michael Duncan 6'0", 190 **K**
Col: Upper Iowa *HS:* Fayette [IA] B: 9/29/1940, Orange City, IA
1966 Oak: Scor 70, 11-26 42.3% FG, 37-37 100.0% XK. **1968** Oak: Rush 2-41 20.5. **1969** Oak: Rush 1-10 10.0. **1972** Min: Rush 1-(-13) -13.0. **1974** Min: Pass 1-1 100.0%, 6 6.00. **Total:** Pass 1-1 100.0%, 6 6.00; Rush 4-38 9.5; Scor 70, 11-26 42.3% FG, 37-37 100.0% XK.

		Punting			
Year Team	G	Punts	Yds	Avg	Fum
1966 Oak	12	65	2703	41.6	0
1967 Oak	14	76	3364	44.3	0
1968 Oak	14	64	2788	43.6	0
1969 Oak	14	69	2944	42.7	0
1970 Oak	14	79	3121	39.5	0
1971 Oak	2	11	461	41.9	0
1972 Min	14	62	2651	42.8	2
1973 Min	14	66	2628	39.8	0
1974 Min	14	73	2636	36.1	0
NFL Total	112	565	23296	41.2	2

LARRY EISENHAUER Eisenhauer, Lawrence Conway 6'5", 250 **DE**
Col: Boston College *HS:* Chaminade [Mineola, NY] B: 2/22/1940, Hicksville, NY *Drafted:* 1961 Round 6 Bos
1961 Bos: 14 G. **1962** Bos: 14 G. **1963** Bos: 14 G; Int 1-0. **1964** Bos: 14 G. **1965** Bos: 14 G. **1966** Bos: 14 G. **1967** Bos: 9 G. **1968** Bos: 8 G. **1969** Bos: 14 G. **Total:** 115 G; Int 1-0.

JOHN EISENHOOTH Eisenhooth, John Levere III 6'2", 265 **NT**
Col: Lock Haven *HS:* Bald Eagle Area [Wingate, MD] B: 3/3/1962, Harrisburg, PA
1987 Sea: 1 G.

STAN EISENHOOTH Eisenhooth, Stanley Emerson 6'5", 287 **C-OT**
Col: Arizona Western Coll. (J.C.); Towson State *HS:* Bald Eagle Area [Wingate, MD] B: 7/8/1963, Harrisburg, PA
1988 Sea: 13 G. **1989** Ind: 16 G. **Total:** 29 G.

ALFRED EISSLER Eissler, Alfred F **HB**
Col: No College *HS:* Oak Park [IL]; Lake Forest Acad. [IL] B: 11/1896, Cicero, IL D: 11/19/1954, Albion, MI
1920 ChiT: 2 G.

ANDY EKERN Ekern, Anderson Erik 6'6", 265 **OT**
Col: Missouri *HS:* Mexico [MO] B: 7/26/1961, Columbia, MO
Drafted: 1983 Round 12 NE
1984 Ind: 2 G.

CARL EKERN Ekern, Carl Frederick 6'3", 223 **LB**
Col: San Jose State *HS:* Fremont [Sunnyvale, CA] B: 5/27/1954, Richland, WA D: 8/1/1990, Ridgecrest, CA *Drafted:* 1976 Round 5 LARm
1976 LARm: 14 G. **1977** LARm: 14 G; KR 1-8 8.0. **1978** LARm: 16 G. **1980** LARm: 15 G. **1981** LARm: 16 G. **1982** LARm: 3 G; Int 1-9. **1983** LARm: 16 G; Int 1-1. **1984** LARm: 16 G; 1 Sac. **1985** LARm: 16 G; Int 2-55 **1** TD; 6 Pt. **1986** LARm: 13 G; 1 Sac. **1987** LARm: 11 G; Int 1-7. **1988** LARm: 16 G. **Total:** 166 G; KR 1-8 8.0; Int 5-72 1 TD; 6 Pt; 2 Sac.

CLEVELAND ELAM Elam, Cleveland 6'4", 252 **DT-DE**
Col: Tennessee State *HS:* Lester [Memphis, TN] B: 4/5/1952, Memphis, TN *Drafted:* 1975 Round 4 SF
1975 SF: 14 G. **1976** SF: 14 G; **1** Fum TD; 6 Pt; 1 Fum. **1977** SF: 14 G. **1978** SF: 12 G. **1979** Det: 8 G. **Total:** 62 G; 1 Fum TD; 6 Pt; 1 Fum.

JASON ELAM Elam, Jason Douglas 5'11", 197 **K**
Col: Hawaii *HS:* Brookwood [Snellville, GA] B: 3/8/1970, Fort Walton Beach, FL *Drafted:* 1993 Round 3 Den
1995 Den: Punt 1-17 17.0. **Total:** Punt 1-17 17.0.

		Scoring						
Year Team	G	Pts	FG	FGA	FG%	XK	XKA	XK%
1993 Den	16	119	26	35	74.3	41	42	97.6
1994 Den	16	119	30	37	81.1	29	29	100.0
1995 Den	16	132	31	38	81.6	39	39	100.0
1996 Den	16	109	21	28	75.0	46	46	100.0
1997 Den	15	124	26	36	72.2	46	46	100.0
1998 Den	16	127	23	27	85.2	58	58	100.0
NFL Total	95	730	157	201	78.1	259	260	99.6

ONZY ELAM Elam, Onzy Warren 6'2", 225 **LB**
Col: Tennessee State *HS:* Miami Northwestern [FL] B: 12/1/1964, Miami, FL *Drafted:* 1987 Round 3 NYJ
1987 NYJ: 5 G. **1988** NYJ: 4 G. **1989** Dal: 1 G. **Total:** 10 G.

DONNIE ELDER Elder, Donald Eugene 5'9", 175 **DB**
Col: Memphis *HS:* Brainerd [Chattanooga, TN] B: 12/13/1962, Chattanooga, TN *Drafted:* 1985 Round 3 NYJ
1988 TB: PR 1-0; Int 3-9. **1989** TB: Int 1-0. **1990** SD: Int 1-0; 0.5 Sac. **1991** SD: Int 1-0; 1 Sac. **Total:** PR 1-0; Int 6-9; 1.5 Sac.

		Kickoff Returns				
Year Team	G	Ret	Yds	Avg	TD	Fum
1985 NYJ	10	3	42	14.0	0	1
1986 Pit-Det	12	22	435	19.8	0	1
1986 Pit	9	21	425	20.2	0	1
1986 Det	3	1	10	10.0	0	0
1988 TB	16	34	772	22.7	0	1
1989 TB	16	40	685	17.1	0	2
1990 SD	12	24	571	23.8	0	2
1991 SD	16	27	535	19.8	0	1
NFL Total	82	150	3040	20.3	0	8

MOHAMMED ELEWONIBI Elewonibi, Mohammed Thomas David 6'4", 298 **OT**
(Mo) *Col:* Snow Coll. UT (J.C.); Brigham Young *HS:* Mount Douglas Sec. School [Victoria, Canada] B: 12/16/1965, Lagos, Nigeria
Drafted: 1990 Round 3 Was
1992 Was: 5 G. **1993** Was: 15 G. **1995** Phi: 6 G. **Total:** 26 G.

CLIFTON ELEY Eley, Clifton 6'5", 230 **TE**
Col: Mississippi State *HS:* Clarksdale [MS] B: 6/21/1961, Clarksdale, MS
1987 Min: 2 G.

MONROE ELEY Eley, Monroe 6'2", 210 **RB**
Col: Palo Verde Coll. CA (J.C.); Arizona State *HS:* Central [Nashville, NC] B: 4/17/1949, Rocky Mount, NC *Drafted:* 1974 Round 5 Atl
1975 Atl: PR 7-61 8.7; KR 8-131 16.4. **1977** Atl: Rec 9-60 6.7; KR 1-16 16.0. **Total:** Rec 9-60 6.7; PR 7-61 8.7; KR 9-147 16.3.

		Rushing				
Year Team	G	Att	Yds	Avg	TD	Fum
1975 Atl	6	1	3	3.0	0	3
1977 Atl	7	97	273	2.8	1	0
NFL Total	13	98	276	2.8	1	3

BRUCE ELIA Elia, Bruce Louis 6'1", 222 **LB**
Col: Ohio State *HS:* Cliffside Park [NJ] B: 1/10/1953, Hoboken, NJ
Drafted: 1975 Round 4 Mia
1975 Mia: 14 G. **1976** SF: 12 G. **1977** SF: 13 G; PR 1-1 1.0. **1978** SF: 16 G; Rush 1-0; 1 Fum. **Total:** 55 G; Rush 1-0; PR 1-1 1.0; 1 Fum.

HOMER ELIAS Elias, Homer Cary 6'3", 255 **OG-OT**
Col: Tennessee State *HS:* Mount Olive [Seale, AL] B: 5/1/1955, Fort Benning, GA *Drafted:* 1978 Round 4 Det
1978 Det: 16 G. **1979** Det: 15 G. **1980** Det: 14 G. **1981** Det: 16 G. **1982** Det: 9 G. **1983** Det: 14 G. **1984** Det: 12 G. **Total:** 96 G.

KEITH ELIAS Elias, Keith Hector 5'9", 198 **RB**
Col: Princeton *HS:* Lacey Twp. [Lanoka Harbor, NJ] B: 2/3/1972, Lacey Twp., NJ
1995 NYG: Rec 9-69 7.7. **1996** NYG: Rec 8-51 6.4. **1998** Ind: Rec 1-11 11.0; KR 14-317 22.6. **Total:** Rec 18-131 7.3; KR 14-317 22.6.

		Rushing			
Year Team	G	Att	Yds	Avg	TD
1994 NYG	2	2	4	2.0	0
1995 NYG	15	10	44	4.4	0
1996 NYG	9	9	24	2.7	0
1998 Ind	13	8	24	3.0	0
NFL Total	39	29	96	3.3	0

DON ELIASON Eliason, Donald Carlton 6'2", 215 **OE-DE**
Col: Hamline *HS:* Harding [St. Paul, MN] B: 7/24/1918, Owatonna, MN
1942 Bkn: 4 G; Rec 1-36 36.0. **1946** Bos: 3 G; Rec 1-9 9.0; Scor 0-1 XK. **Total:** 7 G; Rec 2-45 22.5; Scor 0-1 XK.

JIM ELIOPULOS Eliopulos, James A 6'2", 230 **LB**
Col: Westminster (Mo.); Wyoming *HS:* Central [Cheyenne, WY]
B: 4/18/1959, Dearborn, MI *Drafted:* 1982 Round 3 Dal
1983 StL-NYJ: 12 G. StL: 4 G. NYJ: 8 G. **1984** NYJ: 11 G. **1985** NYJ: 8 G. **Total:** 31 G.

EV ELKINS Elkins, Everett Lee 5'11", 190 **WB-DB**
(Boot) *Col:* Marshall *HS:* Hamlin [WV] B: 11/17/1917, Hamlin, WV
D: 6/8/1977, Hamlin, WV
1940 ChiC: 1 G.

CHIEF ELKINS Elkins, Fait Vernon 5'11", 190 **DB-WB-FB-LB**
(Pete) *Col:* Haskell Indian; Southwestern Oklahoma State; Nebraska *HS:* Haskell [OK] B: 8/16/1899, Utica, NY D: 8/1966, Philadelphia, PA
1928 Fra: 10 G; KR **1** TD; Int **1** TD; Scor 13, 1 XK; Tot TD 2.
1929 Fra-ChiC: 9 G; Scor 3, 1 FG. Fra: 7 G. ChiC: 2 G; Scor 3, 1 FG.
1933 Cin: 1 G. **Total:** 20 G; KR 1 TD; Int 1 TD; Scor 16, 1 FG, 1 XK; Tot TD 2.

LARRY ELKINS Elkins, Lawrence Clayton 6'1", 192 **WR**
Col: Baylor *HS:* Brownwood [TX] B: 7/28/1943, Brownwood, TX
Drafted: 1965 Round 1 Hou
1966 Hou: 14 G; Rec 21-283 13.5 3 TD; 18 Pt. **1967** Hou: 4 G; Rush 2-19 9.5; Rec 3-32 10.7. **Total:** 18 G; Rush 2-19 9.5; Rec 24-315 13.1 3 TD; 18 Pt.

MIKE ELKINS Elkins, Michael David 6'3", 221 **QB**
Col: Wake Forest *HS:* Grimsley [Greensboro, NC] B: 7/20/1966, Greensboro, NC *Drafted:* 1989 Round 2 KC
1989 KC: 1 G; Pass 2-1 50.0%, 5 2.50 1 Int.

BILL ELKO Elko, William 6'5", 278 **OG-NT**
Col: Arizona State; Louisiana State *HS:* Windber [PA] B: 12/28/1959, New York, NY *Drafted:* 1983 Round 7 SD
1983 SD: 11 G; 0.5 Sac. **1984** SD: 15 G; 1.5 Sac. **1987** Ind: 3 G; 1 Sac. **Total:** 29 G; 3 Sac.

HENRY ELLARD Ellard, Henry Austin 5'11", 180 **WR**
Col: Fresno State *HS:* Herbert Hoover [Fresno, CA] B: 7/21/1961, Fresno, CA *Drafted:* 1983 Round 2 LARm
1983 LARm: Rush 3-7 2.3; KR 15-314 20.9. **1984** LARm: Rush 3-(-5) -1.7; KR 2-24 12.0. **1985** LARm: Rush 3-8 2.7. **1986** LARm: Rush 1-(-15) -15.0; KR 1-18 18.0. **1987** LARm: Rush 1-4 4.0; KR 1-8 8.0. **1988** LARm: Rush 1-7 7.0. **1989** LARm: Rush 2-10 5.0. **1990** LARm: Rush 2-21 10.5. **1993** LARm: Rush 2-18 9.0. **1994** Was: Rush 1-(-5) -5.0.
Total: Rush 19-50 2.6; KR 19-364 19.2.

		Receiving				Punt Returns					Tot
Year Team	G	Rec	Yds	Avg	TD	Ret	Yds	Avg	TD	Fum	TD
1983 LARm	12	16	268	16.8	0	16	217	**13.6**	**1**	2	1
1984 LARm	16	34	622	18.3	6	30	403	13.4	**2**	4	8
1985 LARm	16	54	811	15.0	5	37	501	13.5	1	5	6
1986 LARm	9	34	447	13.1	4	14	127	9.1	0	3	4
1987 LARm	12	51	799	15.7	3	15	107	7.1	0	3	3
1988 LARm	16	86	**1414**	16.4	10	17	119	7.0	0	3	10
1989 LARm	14	70	1382	19.7	8	2	20	10.0	0	0	8
1990 LARm	15	76	1294	17.0	4	2	15	7.5	0	4	4
1991 LARm	16	64	1052	16.4	3	0	0	—	0	1	3
1992 LARm	16	47	727	15.5	3	0	0	—	0	0	3
1993 LARm	16	61	945	15.5	2	2	18	9.0	0	0	2
1994 Was	16	74	1397	18.9	6	0	0	—	0	1	6
1995 Was	15	56	1005	17.9	5	0	0	—	0	1	5
1996 Was	16	52	1014	**19.5**	2	0	0	—	0	0	2
1997 Was	16	32	485	15.2	4	0	0	—	0	0	4
1998 NE-Was	7	7	115	16.4	0	0	0	—	0	0	0
1998 NE	5	5	86	17.2	0	0	0	—	0	0	0
1998 Was	2	2	29	14.5	0	0	0	—	0	0	0
NFL Total	228	814	13777	16.9	65	135	1527	11.3	4	27	69

JACK ELLENA Ellena, Jack Duane 6'1", 225 **OG-LB**
Col: Lassen Coll. CA (J.C.); UCLA *HS:* Lassen [Susanville, CA] B: 10/27/1931, Susanville, CA *Drafted:* 1953 Round 19 LARm
1955 LARm: 12 G; PR 0-9. **1956** LARm: 9 G. **Total:** 21 G; PR 0-9.

BILL ELLENBOGEN Ellenbogen, William A 6'5", 258 **OG-OT**
Col: Buffalo; Virginia Tech *HS:* New Rochelle [NY] B: 12/8/1950, Glen Cove, NY
1976 NYG: 11 G. **1977** NYG: 12 G. **Total:** 23 G.

RICH ELLENDER Ellender, Richard 5'11", 171 **RB**
Col: McNeese State *HS:* Sulphur [LA] B: 6/9/1957, Sulphur, LA
Drafted: 1979 Round 9 Hou
1979 Hou: Rec 1-15 15.0; KR 24-514 21.4.

		Punt Returns				
Year Team	G	Ret	Yds	Avg	TD	Fum
1979 Hou	13	31	203	6.5	0	4

GENE ELLENSON Ellenson, Eugene 6'1", 210 **T**
Col: Georgia *HS:* Miami Senior [FL] B: 3/24/1921, Chippewa Falls, WI D: 3/17/1995, Gainsville, FL
AAFC **1946** MiaA: 13 G.

CARL ELLER Eller, Carl Lee 6'6", 247 **DE**
Col: Minnesota *HS:* Atkins [Winston-Salem, NC] B: 2/25/1942, Winston-Salem, NC *Drafted:* 1964 Round 1 Min
1964 Min: 14 G; 1 Fum TD; 6 Pt. **1965** Min: 14 G; Scor **1** Saf; 2 Pt.
1966 Min: 14 G. **1967** Min: 14 G. **1968** Min: 14 G. **1969** Min: 14 G.
1970 Min: 14 G. **1971** Min: 14 G. **1972** Min: 14 G. **1973** Min: 14 G.
1974 Min: 14 G. **1975** Min: 14 G; Int 1-1. **1976** Min: 13 G. **1977** Min: 14 G; Scor 1 Saf; 2 Pt. **1978** Min: 14 G. **1979** Sea: 16 G. **Total:** 225 G; Int 1-1; Scor 2 Saf; 1 Fum TD; 10 Pt.

DON ELLERSICK Ellersick, Donald K 6'1", 193 **DB**
Col: Washington State *HS:* Newport [Bellevue, WA] B: 5/7/1938, Ione, WA *Drafted:* 1960 Round 6 LARm
1960 LARm: 12 G; Int 2-12.

GARY ELLERSON Ellerson, Gary Tobius 5'11", 220 **RB**
Col: Wisconsin *HS:* Monroe [Albany, GA] B: 7/17/1963, Albany, GA
Drafted: 1985 Round 7 GB
1985 GB: Rec 2-15 7.5. **1986** GB: Rec 12-130 10.8. **1987** Det: Rec 5-48 9.6 1 TD. **Total:** Rec 19-193 10.2 1 TD.

		Rushing				Kickoff Returns					Tot
Year Team	G	Ret	Yds	Avg	TD	Ret	Yds	Avg	TD	Fum	TD
1985 GB	15	32	205	6.4	2	29	521	18.0	0	3	2
1986 GB	16	90	287	3.2	3	7	154	22.0	0	3	3
1987 Det	8	47	196	4.2	3	0	0	—	0	0	4
NFL Total	39	169	688	4.1	8	36	675	18.8	0	6	9

AL ELLIOTT Elliott, Alvah Charles 5'9", 175 **TB-WB**
(Rowdy) *Col:* Wisconsin *HS:* Muscoda [WI] B: 10/13/1894, Muscoda, WI D: 12/18/1975, Naperville, IL
1922 Rac: 11 G; Rush 2 TD; 12 Pt. **1923** Rac: 10 G; Rec 2 TD; 12 Pt.
1924 Rac: 7 G; Pass 1 TD; Rush 1 TD; Scor 9, 1 FG. **Total:** 28 G; Pass 1 TD; Rush 3 TD; Rec 2 TD; Scor 33, 1 FG; Tot TD 5.

TONY ELLIOTT Elliott, Anthony Fitzgerald 5'10", 195 **DB**
Col: Central Michigan *HS:* Finney [Detroit, MI] B: 1/10/1964, Detroit, MI
1987 GB: 1 G.

TONY ELLIOTT Elliott, Anthony Robert 6'2", 282 **NT**
Col: Wisconsin; North Texas *HS:* Warren G. Harding [Bridgeport, CT] B: 4/23/1959, New York, NY *Drafted:* 1982 Round 5 NO
1982 NO: 9 G. **1983** NO: 12 G; 5.5 Sac. **1984** NO: 4 G. **1985** NO: 16 G; 1 Sac. **1986** NO: 15 G; 3.5 Sac. **1987** NO: 14 G; 2 Sac. **1988** NO: 14 G; 1 Sac. **Total:** 84 G; 13 Sac.

CARL ELLIOTT Elliott, Carlton Batt Jr. 6'4", 230 **OE-DE**
(Stretch) *Col:* Virginia *HS:* Laurel [DE] B: 11/12/1927, Laurel, DE
Drafted: 1950 Round 13 GB
1951 GB: KR 1-14 14.0. **1953** GB: **1** Fum TD. **Total:** KR 1-14 14.0; 1 Fum TD.

		Receiving				Tot
Year Team	G	Rec	Yds	Avg	TD	TD
1951 GB	12	35	317	9.1	5	5
1952 GB	12	12	114	9.5	1	1
1953 GB	12	13	150	11.5	0	1
1954 GB	12	0	0	—	0	0
NFL Total	48	60	581	9.7	6	7

CHARLIE ELLIOTT Elliott, Charles Junior 6'2", 240 **T**
(Chuck) *Col:* Oregon *HS:* Eugene [OR] B: 12/30/1921, Corvallis, OR D: 9/15/1980, Oregon City, OR
AAFC **1947** NY-A: 10 G. **1948** ChiA-SF-A: 4 G. **Total:** 14 G.

JOHN ELLIOTT Elliott, Darrell John 6'4", 244 **DT-DE**
Col: Texas *HS:* Warren [TX] B: 10/26/1944, Beaumont, TX
Drafted: 1967 Round 7 NYJ
1967 NYJ: 13 G. **1968** NYJ: 14 G. **1969** NYJ: 14 G. **1970** NYJ: 14 G; Scor **1** Saf; 2 Pt. **1971** NYJ: 4 G. **1972** NYJ: 13 G. **1973** NYJ: 13 G. **Total:** 85 G; Scor 1 Saf; 2 Pt.

MATT ELLIOTT Elliott, Eric Matthew 6'3", 288 **OG-C**
Col: Michigan *HS:* Carmel [IN] B: 10/1/1968, Carmel, IN
Drafted: 1992 Round 12 Was
1992 Was: 16 G. **1995** Car: 15 G. **1996** Car: 16 G. **1997** Car: 16 G. **Total:** 63 G.

JIM ELLIOTT Elliott, James Lawrence 5'11", 184 **P**
Col: Presbyterian *HS:* Herschel V. Jenkins [Savannah, GA] B: 8/18/1944, Montgomery, AL

		Punting			
Year Team	G	Punts	Yds	Avg	Fum
1967 Pit	14	72	2744	38.1	1

JUMBO ELLIOTT Elliott, John Stuart 6'7", 308 **OT**
Col: Michigan *HS:* Sachem [Lake Ronkonkoma, NY] B: 4/1/1965, Lake Ronkonkoma, NY *Drafted:* 1988 Round 2 NYG
1988 NYG: 16 G. **1989** NYG: 13 G. **1990** NYG: 8 G. **1991** NYG: 16 G. **1992** NYG: 16 G. **1993** NYG: 11 G. **1994** NYG: 16 G. **1995** NYG: 16 G. **1996** NYJ: 14 G. **1997** NYJ: 13 G. **1998** NYJ: 16 G. **Total:** 155 G.

LENVIL ELLIOTT Elliott, Lenvil Olon 6'0", 205 **RB**
Col: Northeast Missouri State *HS:* Richmond [MO] B: 9/2/1951, Lexington, MO *Drafted:* 1973 Round 10 Cin
1974 Cin: Pass 1-1 100.0%, 17 17.00. **Total:** Pass 1-1 100.0%, 17 17.00.

		Rushing				Receiving			
Year Team	G	Att	Yds	Avg	TD	Rec	Yds	Avg	TD
1973 Cin	6	22	122	5.5	1	1	12	12.0	1

1974 Cin	10	68	345	5.1	1	18	187	10.4	1
1975 Cin	14	71	308	4.3	1	20	196	9.8	3
1976 Cin	12	69	276	4.0	0	22	188	8.5	3
1977 Cin	14	65	269	4.1	0	29	238	8.2	1
1978 Cin	10	29	75	2.6	0	12	100	8.3	0
1979 SF	16	33	135	4.1	3	23	197	8.6	0
1980 SF	15	76	341	4.5	2	27	285	10.6	1
1981 SF	4	7	29	4.1	0	7	81	11.6	0
NFL Total	101	440	1900	4.3	8	159	1484	9.3	10

	Kickoff Returns					Tot
Year Team	**Ret**	**Yds**	**Avg**	**TD**	**Fum**	**TD**
1973 Cin	0	0	—	0	0	2
1974 Cin	1	2	2.0	0	3	2
1975 Cin	13	272	20.9	0	2	4
1976 Cin	5	98	19.6	0	5	3
1977 Cin	1	23	23.0	0	1	1
1978 Cin	0	0	—	0	1	0
1979 SF	9	170	18.9	0	2	3
1980 SF	18	321	17.8	0	5	3
1981 SF	0	0	—	0	2	0
NFL Total	47	886	18.9	0	21	18

LIN ELLIOTT Elliott, Lindley Franklin Jr. 6'0", 182 **K**
Col: Texas Tech *HS:* Waco [TX]; Richfield HS [Waco, TX] B: 11/1/1968, Euless, TX

		Scoring						
Year Team	**G**	**Pts**	**FG**	**FGA**	**FG%**	**XK**	**XKA**	**XK%**
1992 Dal	16	119	24	35	68.6	47	48	97.9
1993 Dal	2	8	2	4	50.0	2	3	66.7
1994 KC	16	105	25	30	83.3	30	30	100.0
1995 KC	16	106	24	30	80.0	34	37	91.9
NFL Total	50	338	75	99	75.8	113	118	95.8

TED ELLIOTT Elliott, Theodore 6'6", 275 **NT**
Col: Mankato State *HS:* Simley [Inver Grove Heights, MN]
B: 11/16/1964, Inver Grove Heights, MN
1987 NO: 3 G.

DOC ELLIOTT Elliott, Wallace John 5'10", 209 **FB-TB-WB**
Col: Lafayette *HS:* Rayen [Youngstown, OH]; Kiski School [Saltsburg, PA] B: 4/6/1900, Youngstown, OH D: 1/11/1976, Fort Myers, FL
1922 Can: 7 G; Rush 2 TD; 12 Pt. **1923** Can: 9 G; Rush 6 TD; 36 Pt. **1924** Cle: 7 G; Rush 6 TD; Scor 40, 1 FG, 1 XK. **1925** Cle: 14 G; Pass 1 TD; Rush 2 TD; Scor 27, 3 FG, 6 XK. **1931** Cle: 2 G; Rush 1 TD; 6 Pt. **Total:** 39 G; Pass 1 TD; Rush 17 TD; Scor 121, 4 FG, 7 XK.

ALLAN ELLIS Ellis, Allan Delon 5'11", 185 **DB**
Col: UCLA *HS:* Centennial [Compton, CA] B: 8/19/1951, Los Angeles, CA *Drafted:* 1973 Round 5 ChiB

		Interceptions		
Year Team	**G**	**Int**	**Yds**	**TD**
1973 ChiB	14	1	12	0
1974 ChiB	14	3	32	0
1975 ChiB	14	2	4	0
1976 ChiB	14	6	47	1
1977 ChiB	14	6	23	0
1979 ChiB	8	3	67	0
1980 ChiB	16	1	0	0
1981 SD	11	0	0	0
NFL Total	105	22	185	1

DREW ELLIS Ellis, Benjamin Drew 6'1", 215 **T**
Col: Texas Christian *HS:* Perryton [TX] B: 12/27/1914, Ochiltree Co., TX D: 5/18/1988, Perryton, TX *Drafted:* 1937 Round 3 Phi
1938 Phi: 11 G. **1939** Phi: 11 G; Rush 1-6 6.0. **Total:** 22 G; Rush 1-6 6.0.

CLARENCE ELLIS Ellis, Clarence Joseph Jr. 5'11", 193 **DB**
Col: Notre Dame *HS:* Central [Grand Rapids, MI] B: 2/11/1950, Grand Rapids, MI *Drafted:* 1972 Round 1 Atl
1972 Atl: 13 G; PR 1-13 13.0; Int 3-13. **1973** Atl: 14 G; Int 2-90. **1974** Atl: 14 G; Int 3-11; 1 Fum. **Total:** 41 G; PR 1-13 13.0; Int 8-114; 1 Fum.

CRAIG ELLIS Ellis, Craig 5'11", 185 **RB**
Col: Santa Barbara City Coll. CA (J.C.); San Diego State *HS:* John H. Francis Polytechnic [Sun Valley, CA] B: 1/26/1961, Los Angeles, CA
1986 Mia: PR 24-149 6.2. **1987** LARd: Rec 5-39 7.8. **Total:** Rec 5-39 7.8; PR 24-149 6.2.

		Rushing				Kickoff Returns				
Year Team	**G**	**Att**	**Yds**	**Avg**	**TD**	**Ret**	**Yds**	**Avg**	**TD**	**Fum**
1986 Mia	9	3	6	2.0	0	25	541	21.6	0	1
1987 LARd	3	33	138	4.2	2	0	0	—	0	1
NFL Total	12	36	144	4.0	2	25	541	21.6	0	2

ED ELLIS Ellis, Edward 6'7", 340 **OT**
Col: Buffalo *HS:* Hamden [CT] B: 10/13/1975, Hamden, CT
Drafted: 1997 Round 4 NE
1997 NE: 1 G. **1998** NE: 7 G. **Total:** 8 G.

GERRY ELLIS Ellis, Gerry Lynn 5'11", 221 **RB**
Col: Fort Scott CC KS; Missouri *HS:* Hickman [Columbia, MO]
B: 11/12/1957, Columbia, MO *Drafted:* 1980 Round 7 LARm
1981 GB: Pass 2-1 50.0%, 23 11.50. **1983** GB: Pass 5-2 40.0%, 31 6.20 1 TD 1 Int. **1984** GB: Pass 4-1 25.0%, 17 4.25. **1985** GB: Pass 1-0; KR 13-247 19.0. **Total:** Pass 12-4 33.3%, 71 5.92 1 TD 1 Int; KR 13-247 19.0.

		Rushing				Receiving					Tot
Year Team	**G**	**Att**	**Yds**	**Avg**	**TD**	**Rec**	**Yds**	**Avg**	**TD**	**Fum**	**TD**
1980 GB	15	126	545	4.3	5	48	496	10.3	3	7	8
1981 GB	16	196	860	4.4	4	65	499	7.7	3	5	7
1982 GB	9	62	228	3.7	1	18	140	7.8	0	6	1
1983 GB	15	141	696	4.9	4	52	603	11.6	2	7	6
1984 GB	16	123	581	4.7	4	36	312	8.7	2	2	6
1985 GB	16	104	571	5.5	5	24	206	8.6	0	2	5
1986 GB	16	84	345	4.1	2	24	258	10.8	0	4	2
NFL Total	103	836	3826	4.6	25	267	2514	9.4	10	33	35

GREG ELLIS Ellis, Gregory Lemont 6'6", 286 **DE**
Col: North Carolina *HS:* East Wake [Wendell, NC] B: 8/14/1975, Wendell, NC *Drafted:* 1998 Round 1 Dal
1998 Dal: 16 G; 3 Sac.

HERB ELLIS Ellis, Herbert Wayne 6'2", 205 **C-LB**
Col: Texas A&M B: 12/18/1925, Vernon, TX Deceased
1949 NYB: 12 G.

JIM ELLIS Ellis, James Kevin 6'3", 240 **LB**
Col: Boise State *HS:* Redondo [Redondo Beach, CA] B: 3/25/1964, Pomona, CA *Drafted:* 1987 Round 10 LARd
1987 LARd: 3 G.

JOHN ELLIS Ellis, John Wharton 5'10", 212 **G**
Col: Vanderbilt *HS:* Sherman [TX] B: 12/21/1919, Sherman, TX
1944 Bkn: 6 G.

KEN ELLIS Ellis, Kenneth Alfonzo 5'10", 190 **DB**
Col: Southern University *HS:* Ralph J. Bunche [Woodbine, GA]
B: 9/27/1947, Woodbine, GA *Drafted:* 1970 Round 4 GB

		Punt Returns				Kickoff Returns			
Year Team	**G**	**Ret**	**Yds**	**Avg**	**TD**	**Ret**	**Yds**	**Avg**	**TD**
1970 GB	13	7	27	3.9	0	22	451	20.5	0
1971 GB	14	22	107	4.9	0	1	22	22.0	0
1972 GB	14	14	215	**15.4**	**1**	1	10	10.0	0
1973 GB	14	11	47	4.3	0	12	319	26.6	0
1974 GB	14	3	3	1.0	0	0	0	—	0
1975 GB	14	6	27	4.5	0	0	0	—	0
1976 Hou-Mia	13	0	0	—	0	0	0	—	0
1976 Hou	1	0	0	—	0	0	0	—	0
1976 Mia	12	0	0	—	0	0	0	—	0
1977 Cle	9	0	0	—	0	5	80	16.0	0
1979 Det-LARm	10	8	43	5.4	0	0	0	—	0
1979 Det	7	8	43	5.4	0	0	0	—	0
1979 LARm	3	0	0	—	0	0	0	—	0
NFL Total	115	71	469	6.6	1	41	882	21.5	0

	Interceptions				Tot
Year Team	**Int**	**Yds**	**TD**	**Fum**	**TD**
1970 GB	3	69	0	3	0
1971 GB	6	10	0	0	1
1972 GB	4	106	1	2	2
1973 GB	3	53	1	1	1
1974 GB	3	56	1	1	1
1975 GB	1	0	0	0	0
1976 Hou-Mia	2	40	0	0	0
1976 Mia	2	40	0	0	0
1977 Cle	0	0	0	1	0
1979 Det-LARm	0	0	0	1	0
1979 Det	0	0	0	1	0
NFL Total	22	334	3	9	5

RAY ELLIS Ellis, Kerwin Ray 6'1", 192 **DB**
Col: Ohio State *HS:* McKinley [Canton, OH] B: 4/27/1959, Canton, OH
Drafted: 1981 Round 12 Phi
1983 Phi: KR 7-119 17.0. **1984** Phi: KR 2-25 12.5. **1985** Phi: 2 Sac. **1986** Cle: 1 Sac. **1987** Cle: **1** Fum TD. **Total:** KR 9-144 16.0; 1 Fum TD; 3 Sac.

		Interceptions			
Year Team	**G**	**Int**	**Yds**	**TD**	**Fum**
1981 Phi	16	0	0	0	0
1982 Phi	9	0	0	0	0
1983 Phi	16	1	18	0	0
1984 Phi	16	7	119	0	1
1985 Phi	16	4	32	0	0
1986 Cle	15	2	12	0	0

1987 Cle	12	0	0	0	0
NFL Total	100	14	181	0	1

KWAME ELLIS Ellis, Kwame Delaney 5'10", 188 **DB**
Col: Stanford *HS:* Skyline [Oakland, CA] B: 2/27/1974, Berkeley, CA
1996 NYJ: 8 G.

LARRY ELLIS Ellis, Lawrence Richard Jr. 6'1", 204 **LB**
Col: Syracuse *HS:* York [ME]; Cheshire Acad. [CT] B: 5/27/1922, York, ME D: 8/24/1988, Auburn, NY
1948 Det: 4 G.

ROGER ELLIS Ellis, Roger Calvin 6'3", 233 **LB-C**
Col: Maine *HS:* Westwood [MA] B: 2/1/1938, Boston, MA
Drafted: 1959 Round 14 NYG
1960 NYT: 14 G; Int 1-0. **1961** NYT: 14 G; KR 3-25 8.3; 1 Fum. **1962** NYT: 14 G. **1963** NYJ: 1 G. **Total:** 43 G; KR 3-25 8.3; Int 1-0; 1 Fum.

WALT ELLIS Ellis, Walter Joseph 5'11", 224 **T**
(Speed) *Col:* Detroit Mercy *HS:* Suffield [CT] B: 11/1898, Groton, CT Deceased
1924 Col: 8 G. **1925** Col-Det: 10 G. Col: 9 G. Det: 1 G. **1926** ChiC: 10 G. **1927** ChiC: 8 G. **Total:** 36 G.

GLENN ELLISON Ellison, Glenn F 6'1", 215 **RB**
Col: Arkansas *HS:* Paxon [Jacksonville, FL] B: 3/9/1947, Jacksonville, FL
1971 Oak: 1 G.

JERRY ELLISON Ellison, Jerry Ernest 5'10", 204 **RB**
Col: Tennessee-Chattanooga *HS:* Glenn Hills [Augusta, GA]
B: 12/20/1971, Augusta, GA
1995 TB: KR 15-261 17.4. **1997** TB: KR 2-61 30.5. **1998** TB: KR 1-19 19.0. **Total:** KR 18-341 18.9.

		Rushing				Receiving				
Year Team	**G**	**Att**	**Yds**	**Avg**	**TD**	**Rec**	**Yds**	**Avg**	**TD**	**Fum**
1995 TB	16	26	218	8.4	5	7	44	6.3	0	0
1996 TB	16	35	106	3.0	0	18	208	11.6	0	2
1997 TB	16	2	10	5.0	0	1	8	8.0	0	0
1998 TB	16	9	24	2.7	0	0	0	—	0	0
NFL Total	64	72	358	5.0	5	26	260	10.0	0	2

MARK ELLISON Ellison, Marshall Mark 6'2", 250 **OG**
Col: Dayton *HS:* Westinghouse [Pittsburgh, PA] B: 4/15/1948, Pittsburgh, PA *Drafted:* 1971 Round 11 NYG
1972 NYG: 14 G. **1973** NYG: 14 G. **Total:** 28 G.

'OMAR ELLISON Ellison, 'Omar Ryan 6'1", 200 **WR**
Col: Florida State *HS:* Griffin [GA] B: 10/8/1971, Griffin, GA
Drafted: 1995 Round 5 SD
1995 SD: 2 G; Rec 1-6 6.0. **1996** SD: 10 G; Rec 3-15 5.0. **Total:** 12 G; Rec 4-21 5.3.

RIKI ELLISON Ellison, Riki Morgan 6'2", 225 **LB**
Col: USC *HS:* Amphitheater [Tucson, AZ] B: 8/15/1960, Christchurch, New Zealand *Drafted:* 1983 Round 5 SF
1983 SF: 16 G. **1984** SF: 16 G; 2 Sac. **1985** SF: 16 G; 1 Sac. **1986** SF: 16 G. **1987** SF: 3 G. **1988** SF: 13 G; 1 Sac. **1990** LARd: 16 G; Int 1-7. **1991** LARd: 16 G. **1992** LARd: 12 G; 1 Sac. **Total:** 124 G; Int 1-7; 5 Sac.

WILLIE ELLISON Ellison, William Henry 6'2", 210 **RB**
(Hank) *Col:* Texas Southern *HS:* George Washington Carver [Lockhart, TX] B: 11/1/1945, Lockhart, TX *Drafted:* 1967 Round 2 LARm
1968 LARm: Pass 1-0. **1969** LARm: Pass 2-0. **Total:** Pass 3-0.

		Rushing				Receiving			
Year Team	**G**	**Att**	**Yds**	**Avg**	**TD**	**Rec**	**Yds**	**Avg**	**TD**
1967 LARm	14	14	84	6.0	0	1	18	18.0	0
1968 LARm	14	151	616	4.1	5	20	248	12.4	2
1969 LARm	14	20	56	2.8	1	4	31	7.8	1
1970 LARm	14	90	381	4.2	5	10	84	8.4	2
1971 LARm	14	211	1000	4.7	4	32	238	7.4	0
1972 LARm	13	170	764	4.5	5	23	141	6.1	1
1973 KC	10	108	411	3.8	2	9	64	7.1	0
1974 KC	5	37	114	3.1	2	5	64	12.8	0
NFL Total	98	801	3426	4.3	24	104	888	8.5	6

	Kickoff Returns					Tot
Year Team	**Ret**	**Yds**	**Avg**	**TD**	**Fum**	**TD**
1967 LARm	13	340	26.2	0	1	0
1968 LARm	12	268	22.3	0	3	7
1969 LARm	2	38	19.0	0	0	2
1970 LARm	1	20	20.0	0	4	7
1971 LARm	0	0	—	0	8	4
1972 LARm	14	345	24.6	0	3	6
1973 KC	0	0	—	0	3	2
1974 KC	0	0	—	0	2	2
NFL Total	42	1011	24.1	0	24	30

LUTHER ELLISS Elliss, Luther John 6'5", 294 **DE-DT**
Col: Utah *HS:* Mancos [CO] B: 3/22/1973, Mancos, CO
Drafted: 1995 Round 1 Det
1995 Det: 16 G. **1996** Det: 14 G; 6.5 Sac. **1997** Det: 16 G; 8.5 Sac. **1998** Det: 16 G; 3 Sac. **Total:** 62 G; 18 Sac.

BUD ELLOR Ellor, Albert Wesley 6'2", 205 **G-OE**
(Hod; Bert) *Col:* Bucknell *HS:* Bloomfield [NJ] B: 1905, Bloomfield, NJ D: 2/11/1932, Jersey City, NJ
1930 Nwk: 12 G; 6 Pt.

SWEDE ELLSTROM Ellstrom, Marvin Lawrence 6'1", 203 **HB-LB**
Col: Northern Oklahoma Coll. (J.C.); Oklahoma *HS:* Moline [IL]; Waynesburg HS [PA] B: 5/15/1906, Moline, IL D: 4/25/1994, Tonkawa, OK
1934 Bos-Phi: Pass 16-3 18.8%, 40 2.50 1 TD 5 Int; Rec 1-18 18.0. Bos: Pass 2-0. Phi: Pass 14-3 21.4%, 40 2.86 1 TD 5 Int; Rec 1-18 18.0. **1935** Pit: Pass 7-6 85.7%, 68 9.71; Rec 1-12 12.0. **Total:** Pass 23-9 39.1%, 108 4.70 1 TD 5 Int; Rec 2-30 15.0.

		Rushing			
Year Team	**G**	**Att**	**Yds**	**Avg**	**TD**
1934 Bos-Phi	11	82	319	3.9	1
1934 Bos	3	10	32	3.2	0
1934 Phi	8	72	287	4.0	1
1935 Pit	3	10	14	1.4	0
1936 ChiC	1	4	12	3.0	0
NFL Total	15	96	345	3.6	1

PERCY ELLSWORTH Ellsworth, Percy Daniel III 6'2", 213 **DB**
Col: Virginia *HS:* Southampton [Courtland, VA] B: 10/19/1974, Drewryville, VA

		Interceptions		
Year Team	**G**	**Int**	**Yds**	**TD**
1996 NYG	14	3	62	0
1997 NYG	16	4	40	0
1998 NYG	16	5	92	2
NFL Total	46	12	194	2

CHARLEY ELLZEY Ellzey, Charles Melvin Jr. 6'3", 240 **C-LB**
Col: Southern Mississippi *HS:* Meridian [MS] B: 2/17/1938, Meridian, MS *Drafted:* 1960 Round 3 StL
1960 StL: 9 G. **1961** StL: 5 G. **Total:** 14 G.

HICHAM EL-MASHTOUB El-Mashtoub, Hicham 6'2", 288 **C-OG**
Col: Arizona *HS:* Polyvalente Georges-Vanier Sec. School [Montreal, Canada] B: 5/11/1972, Lebanon *Drafted:* 1995 Round 6 Hou
1995 Hou: 2 G. **1996** Hou: 1 G. **Total:** 3 G.

DAVE ELMENDORF Elmendorf, David Cole 6'1", 195 **DB**
Col: Texas A&M *HS:* Westbury [Houston, TX] B: 6/20/1949, San Antonio, TX *Drafted:* 1971 Round 3 LARm
1973 LARm: KR 2-23 11.5. **Total:** KR 2-23 11.5.

		Punt Returns				Interceptions			
Year Team	**G**	**Ret**	**Yds**	**Avg**	**TD**	**Int**	**Yds**	**TD**	**Fum**
1971 LARm	14	0	0	—	0	2	32	0	0
1972 LARm	14	3	56	18.7	0	3	29	0	0
1973 LARm	14	22	187	8.5	0	1	16	0	3
1974 LARm	14	17	134	7.9	0	7	186	**2**	1
1975 LARm	14	15	125	8.3	0	4	48	0	1
1976 LARm	14	0	0	—	0	2	0	0	0
1977 LARm	14	0	0	—	0	2	51	0	0
1978 LARm	16	0	0	—	0	3	20	0	0
1979 LARm	16	0	0	—	0	3	39	0	0
NFL Total	130	57	502	8.8	0	27	421	2	5

DOUG ELMORE Elmore, James Douglas 6'0", 188 **DB-P**
Col: Mississippi *HS:* Pickens Co. [Reform, AL] B: 12/15/1939, Reform, AL *Drafted:* 1961 Round 13 Was
1962 Was: Pass 1-0; Rush 1-(-14) -14.0; Int 2-28.

		Punting			
Year Team	**G**	**Punts**	**Yds**	**Avg**	**Fum**
1962 Was	14	54	1860	34.4	1

SHORTY ELNESS Elness, Leland 5'8", 166 **HB-QB**
Col: Bradley *HS:* Windom [MN] B: 5/10/1906 D: 11/3/1965
1929 ChiB: 4 G.

JOEY ELOMS Eloms, Joey 5'10", 181 **DB**
Col: Indiana *HS:* River Forest [Fort Wayne, IN] B: 4/4/1976, Fort Wayne, IN
1998 Sea: 1 G.

JIMBO ELROD Elrod, James Whittington 6'0", 220 **LB**
Col: Oklahoma *HS:* East Central [Tulsa, OK] B: 5/25/1954, Memphis, TN *Drafted:* 1976 Round 5 KC
1976 KC: 6 G; Int 1-3. **1977** KC: 14 G. **1978** KC: 16 G. **1979** Hou: 4 G. **Total:** 40 G; Int 1-3.

EARL ELSER Elser, Earl Howard 6'1", 229 **T**
Col: Butler *HS:* Emerson [Gary, IN] B: 3/21/1908 D: 8/1974, Gary, IN
1933 Port: 4 G. **1934** Cin-StL: 9 G. Cin: 8 G. StL: 1 G. **Total:** 13 G.

EARL ELSEY Elsey, Earl D 5'8", 175 **HB-DB**
Col: Santa Monica Coll. CA (J.C.); Loyola Marymount *HS:* Manual Arts [Los Angeles, CA] B: 1919 Deceased
AAFC **1946** LA-A: Rec 14-179 12.8; PR 9-147 16.3; KR 15-335 22.3; Int 2-2.

		Rushing			
Year Team	**G**	**Att**	**Yds**	**Avg**	**TD**
1946 LA-A	13	47	165	3.5	0

NEIL ELSHIRE Elshire, Neil James 6'6", 260 **DE**
Col: Oregon *HS:* South Albany [OR] B: 3/8/1958, Salem, OR
1981 Min: 4 G. **1982** Min: 5 G; KR 1-7 7.0; 1 Sac. **1983** Min: 16 G; 9.5 Sac. **1984** Min: 12 G; 3.5 Sac. **1985** Min: 16 G; Scor 1 Saf; 2 Pt; 5 Sac. **1986** Min: 10 G. **Total:** 63 G; KR 1-7 7.0; Scor 1 Saf; 2 Pt; 19 Sac.

DUTCH ELSTON Elston, Arthur Warren 5'11", 190 **C**
Col: Georgia Mil. Coll. (J.C.); South Carolina *HS:* Morrison R. Waite [Toledo, OH] B: 11/19/1918, Texhoma, TX D: 9/10/1989, Daly City, CA
AAFC **1946** SF-A: 13 G; Int 1-34. **1947** SF-A: 9 G; Int 2-13. **1948** SF-A: 12 G; Int 1-0. **Total:** 34 G; Int 4-47.

NFL **1942** Cle: 11 G; Rush 1-15 15.0; Rec 4-58 14.5; KR 2-46 23.0.

LEO ELTER Elter, Leo William 5'10", 201 **FB-HB**
(Ducky) *Col:* Duquesne; Villanova *HS:* Shaler [Pittsburgh, PA]
B: 10/21/1929, Pittsburgh, PA
1953 Pit: KR 1-23 23.0. **1954** Pit: KR 2-32 16.0. **1956** Was: KR 4-87 21.8. **Total:** KR 7-142 20.3.

		Rushing				Receiving					Tot
Year Team	**G**	**Att**	**Yds**	**Avg**	**TD**	**Rec**	**Yds**	**Avg**	**TD**	**Fum**	**TD**
1953 Pit	12	26	81	3.1	0	3	29	9.7	0	0	0
1954 Pit	11	13	54	4.2	0	4	16	4.0	0	1	0
1955 Was	11	97	361	3.7	3	13	219	16.8	1	4	4
1956 Was	12	145	544	3.8	2	11	99	9.0	0	7	2
1957 Was	12	45	211	4.7	2	6	94	15.7	1	2	3
1958 Pit	7	37	104	2.8	2	6	68	11.3	0	2	2
1959 Pit	8	8	25	3.1	0	3	31	10.3	0	1	0
NFL Total	73	371	1380	3.7	9	46	556	12.1	2	17	11

JOHN ELWAY Elway, John Albert 6'3", 215 **QB**
Col: Stanford *HS:* Granada Hills [Los Angeles, CA] B: 6/28/1960, Port Angeles, WA *Drafted:* 1983 Round 1 Bal
1986 Den: Rec 1-23 23.0 1 TD. **1987** Den: Punt 1-31 31.0. **1988** Den: Punt 3-117 39.0. **1989** Den: Punt 1-34 34.0. **1990** Den: Punt 1-37 37.0. **1991** Den: Rec 1-24 24.0; Punt 1-34 34.0. **1995** Den: Scor 1 2XP. **1998** Den: Rec 1-14 14.0. **Total:** Rec 3-61 20.3 1 TD; Punt 7-253 36.1; Scor 1 2XP.

		Passing							
Year Team	**G**	**Att**	**Comp**	**Comp%**	**Yds**	**YPA**	**TD**	**Int**	**Rating**
1983 Den	11	259	123	47.5	1663	6.42	7	14	54.9
1984 Den	15	380	214	56.3	2598	6.84	18	15	76.8
1985 Den	16	**605**	327	54.0	3891	6.43	22	23	70.2
1986 Den	16	504	280	55.6	3485	6.91	19	13	79.0
1987 Den	12	410	224	54.6	3198	7.80	19	12	83.4
1988 Den	15	496	274	55.2	3309	6.67	17	19	71.4
1989 Den	15	416	223	53.6	3051	7.33	18	18	73.7
1990 Den	16	502	294	58.6	3526	7.02	15	14	78.5
1991 Den	16	451	242	53.7	3253	7.21	13	12	75.4
1992 Den	12	316	174	55.1	2242	7.09	10	17	65.7
1993 Den	16	**551**	**348**	63.2	**4030**	7.31	25	10	92.8
1994 Den	14	494	307	62.1	3490	7.06	16	10	85.7
1995 Den	16	542	316	58.3	3970	7.32	26	14	86.4
1996 Den	15	466	287	61.6	3328	7.14	26	14	89.2
1997 Den	16	502	280	55.8	3635	7.24	27	11	87.5
1998 Den	13	356	210	59.0	2806	7.88	22	10	93.0
NFL Total	234	7250	4123	56.9	51475	7.10	300	226	79.9

	Rushing					Tot
Year Team	**Att**	**Yds**	**Avg**	**TD**	**Fum**	**TD**
1983 Den	28	146	5.2	1	6	1
1984 Den	56	237	4.2	1	14	1
1985 Den	51	253	5.0	0	7	0
1986 Den	52	257	4.9	1	8	2
1987 Den	66	304	4.6	4	2	4
1988 Den	54	234	4.3	1	7	1
1989 Den	48	244	5.1	3	9	3
1990 Den	50	258	5.2	3	8	3
1991 Den	55	255	4.6	6	**12**	6
1992 Den	34	94	2.8	2	12	2
1993 Den	44	153	3.5	0	8	0
1994 Den	58	235	4.1	4	11	4
1995 Den	41	176	4.3	1	9	1
1996 Den	50	249	5.0	4	6	4
1997 Den	50	218	4.4	1	11	1
1998 Den	37	94	2.5	1	7	1
NFL Total	774	3407	4.4	33	137	34

JACK ELWELL Elwell, John Matthew 6'3", 200 **WR**
Col: Purdue *HS:* Cathedral Latin [Cleveland, OH] B: 8/1/1940, Cleveland, OH *Drafted:* 1962 Round 6 StL
1962 StL: 13 G; Rec 1-11 11.0.

HAROLD ELY Ely, Harold E 6'2", 268 **T**
Col: Iowa *HS:* Roosevelt [Des Moines, IA] B: 12/26/1909, Des Moines, IA D: 7/12/1983, Jasper, AL
1932 ChiB-Bkn: 9 G. ChiB: 6 G. Bkn: 3 G. **1933** Bkn: 10 G. **1934** Bkn: 11 G. **Total:** 30 G.

LARRY ELY Ely, Lawrence Orlo Jr. 6'1", 230 **LB**
Col: Iowa *HS:* Roosevelt [Des Moines, IA] B: 12/19/1947, Iowa City, IA
Drafted: 1970 Round 16 Cin
1970 Cin: 11 G. **1971** Cin: 6 G. **1975** ChiB: 12 G; Int 1-2. **Total:** 29 G; Int 1-2.

PAUL ELZEY Elzey, Paul Vincent 6'3", 235 **LB**
Col: Toledo *HS:* St. Francis DeSales [Toledo, OH] B: 5/13/1946, Toledo, OH *Drafted:* 1968 Round 5 Bal
1968 Cin: 5 G.

BERT EMANUEL Emanuel, Bert Tyrone 5'10", 180 **WR**
Col: UCLA; Rice *HS:* Langham Creek [Houston, TX] B: 10/26/1970, Kansas City, MO *Drafted:* 1994 Round 2 Atl
1994 Atl: Pass 1-0, 1 Int; Rush 2-4 2.0. **1995** Atl: Rush 1-0. **1998** TB: Rush 1-11 11.0. **Total:** Pass 1-0, 1 Int; Rush 4-15 3.8.

		Receiving				
Year Team	**G**	**Rec**	**Yds**	**Avg**	**TD**	**Fum**
1994 Atl	16	46	649	14.1	4	0
1995 Atl	16	74	1039	14.0	5	2
1996 Atl	14	75	921	12.3	6	0
1997 Atl	16	65	991	15.2	9	2
1998 TB	11	41	636	15.5	2	0
NFL Total	73	301	4236	14.1	26	4

CHARLES EMANUEL Emanuel, Charles Edward 6'0", 196 **DB**
Col: West Virginia *HS:* South Fork [Stuart, FL] B: 6/3/1973, Stuart, FL
1997 Phi: 5 G.

FRANK EMANUEL Emanuel, Thomas Frank 6'3", 225 **LB**
Col: Tennessee *HS:* Newport News [VA] B: 12/4/1942, Clio, SC
Drafted: 1966 Round 2 Mia
1966 Mia: 14 G; Int 1-14. **1967** Mia: 14 G; Int 1-24. **1968** Mia: 14 G; Int 2-8; 6 Pt. **1969** Mia: 14 G. **1970** NO: 3 G. **Total:** 59 G; Int 4-46; 6 Pt.

JOHN EMBREE Embree, John William 6'4", 194 **WR**
Col: Compton CC CA *HS:* Centennial [Compton, CA] B: 7/13/1944, St. Louis, MO

		Receiving			
Year Team	**G**	**Rec**	**Yds**	**Avg**	**TD**
1969 Den	13	29	469	16.2	5
1970 Den	7	4	50	12.5	0
NFL Total	20	33	519	15.7	5

JON EMBREE Embree, Jon William 6'2", 234 **TE**
Col: Colorado *HS:* Cherry Creek [Englewood, CO] B: 10/15/1965, Los Angeles, CA *Drafted:* 1987 Round 6 LARm
1987 LARm: 1 G. **1988** LARm: 12 G. **Total:** 13 G.

MEL EMBREE Embree, Melvin Belton 6'3", 190 **OE**
Col: Pepperdine *HS:* Los Angeles Polytechnic [Los Angeles, CA]
B: 1/26/1927, Los Angeles, CA D: 8/30/1996, Los Angeles, CA

		Receiving			
Year Team	**G**	**Rec**	**Yds**	**Avg**	**TD**
1953 Bal	12	23	272	11.8	1
1954 ChiC	5	2	20	10.0	0
NFL Total	17	25	292	11.7	1

BOB EMERICK Emerick, Robert William 6'2", 225 **T-G**
Col: Miami (Ohio) *HS:* Hamilton [OH] B: 2/21/1913, Stockton, CA
1934 Det: 9 G. **1937** Cle: 11 G. **Total:** 20 G.

OX EMERSON Emerson, Gover Conner 5'11", 203 **G-LB-C**
Col: Texas *HS:* Orange [TX] B: 12/18/1907, Douglass, TX
D: 11/26/1998, Austin, TX
1931 Port: 12 G. **1932** Port: 12 G. **1933** Port: 11 G. **1934** Det: 13 G. **1935** Det: 7 G. **1936** Det: 10 G. **1937** Det: 10 G. **1938** Bkn: 11 G. **Total:** 86 G.

VERN EMERSON Emerson, Vernon Merlin 6'5", 260 **OT**
Col: Minnesota-Duluth *HS:* Isle [MN] B: 9/2/1945, Anoka, MN
Drafted: 1968 Round 12 StL
1969 StL: 5 G. **1970** StL: 14 G. **1971** StL: 4 G. **Total:** 23 G.

LARRY EMERY Emery, Larry George Jr. 5′9″, 195 **RB**
Col: Wisconsin *HS:* Northeast [Macon, GA] B: 7/13/1964, Macon, GA *Drafted:* 1987 Round 12 Atl
1987 Atl: 5 G; Rush 1-5 5.0; Rec 5-31 6.2; KR 21-440 21.0.

CARLOS EMMONS Emmons, Carlos Antoine 6′5″, 246 **LB**
Col: Arkansas State *HS:* Greenwood [MS] B: 9/3/1973, Greenwood, MS *Drafted:* 1996 Round 7 Pit
1996 Pit: 15 G; 2.5 Sac. **1997** Pit: 5 G. **1998** Pit: 15 G; Int 1-2; 3.5 Sac. **Total:** 35 G; Int 1-2; 6 Sac.

FRANK EMMONS Emmons, Frank Boone 6′1″, 213 **FB-HB-LB**
(Wild Horse) *Col:* Oregon *HS:* Beaverton [OR] B: 9/17/1918, Portland, OR *Drafted:* 1940 Round 5 Phi
1940 Phi: Rec 3-19 6.3 1 TD.

		Rushing				Tot
Year Team	G	Att	Yds	Avg	TD	TD
1940 Phi	11	29	77	2.7	1	2

RED EMSLIE Emslie, Percy Gordon **G**
Col: No College B: 4/29/1895, Buffalo, NY D: 8/3/1964, Buffalo, NY
1923 Roch: 1 G.

STEVE EMTMAN Emtman, Steven Charles 6′4″, 290 **DT-DE**
Col: Washington *HS:* Cheney [WA] B: 4/16/1970, Spokane, WA *Drafted:* 1992 Round 1 Ind
1992 Ind: 9 G; Int 1-90 1 TD; 6 Pt; 3 Sac. **1993** Ind: 5 G; 1 Sac. **1994** Ind: 4 G; 1 Sac. **1995** Mia: 16 G; 1 Sac. **1996** Mia: 13 G; 2 Sac. **1997** Was: 3 G. **Total:** 50 G; Int 1-90 1 TD; 6 Pt; 8 Sac.

DICK ENDERLE Enderle, Richard Allyn 6′2″, 250 **OG**
Col: Minnesota *HS:* Elbow Lake [MN] B: 11/6/1947, Breckenridge, MN *Drafted:* 1969 Round 7 Atl
1969 Atl: 14 G. **1970** Atl: 12 G. **1971** Atl: 14 G; KR 1-20 20.0. **1972** NYG: 14 G; KR 1-0. **1973** NYG: 14 G. **1974** NYG: 14 G. **1975** NYG: 9 G. **1976** SF-GB: 5 G. SF: 2 G. GB: 3 G. **Total:** 96 G; KR 2-20 10.0.

AL ENDRESS Endress, Albert James 6′2″, 200 **DE-OE**
(Sonny) *Col:* St. Mary's (Cal.); San Francisco State *HS:* St. Elizabeth [Oakland, CA] B: 2/18/1929, Oakland, CA
1952 SF: 2 G.

VIC ENDRESS Endress, Victor F **BB**
Col: No College *HS:* Central [Evansville, IN] B: 5/25/1903, Evansville, IN D: 8/29/1970, Moline, IL
1922 Eva: 1 G.

TINY ENGEBRETSEN Engebretsen, Paul J 6′1″, 238 **G-T**
Col: Northwestern *HS:* Chariton [IA] B: 7/27/1910, Chariton, IA D: 3/31/1979, Chariton, IA
1932 ChiB: 14 G; Scor 13, 1 FG, **10** XK. **1933** Pit-ChiC: 11 G; Scor 1, 1 XK. Pit: 9 G; Scor 1, 1 XK. ChiC: 2 G. **1934** Bkn-GB: 10 G. Bkn: 5 G. GB: 5 G. **1935** GB: 9 G; Scor 1, 1 XK. **1936** GB: 11 G; Scor 17, 5 FG, 2 XK. **1937** GB: 9 G; Scor 8, 1 FG, 5 XK. **1938** GB: 10 G; Scor 15, 2-4 50.0% FG, 9-9 100.0% XK. **1939** GB: 11 G; Scor 30, 4-8 50.0% FG, **18**-19 94.7% XK. **1940** GB: 8 G; Scor 11, 1-5 20.0% FG, 8-8 100.0% XK. **1941** GB: 1 G; Scor 3, 1-3 33.3% FG. **Total:** 94 G; Scor 99, 15-20 40.0% FG, 54-36 97.2% XK.

GREG ENGEL Engel, Gregory Allen 6′3″, 285 **C**
Col: Illinois *HS:* Bloomington [IL] B: 1/18/1971, Davenport, IA
1995 SD: 10 G; KR 0-1. **1996** SD: 12 G. **1997** SD: 9 G. **Total:** 31 G; KR 0-1.

STEVE ENGEL Engel, William Stephen 6′1″, 218 **RB**
Col: Colorado *HS:* Englewood [CO] B: 10/13/1947, Englewood, CO *Drafted:* 1970 Round 5 Cle
1970 Cle: 3 G.

JOE ENGELHARD Engelhard, Joseph Adolphus 5′11″, 185 **TB-WB**
Col: Rose Hulman Tech *HS:* Male [Louisville, KY] B: 10/15/1898, Owensboro, KY D: 7/4/1981, Louisville, KY
1921 Lou: 1 G. **1922** Lou: 1 G. **Total:** 2 G.

WUERT ENGELMANN Engelmann, Wuert 6′3″, 191 **DB-HB-TB-BB**
Col: South Dakota State *HS:* Miller [SD] B: 2/11/1908, Miller, SD D: 1/8/1979, Green Bay, WI
1930 GB: Rec 2 TD. **1931** GB: Rec 2 TD; KR **1** TD. **1932** GB: Rec 1-33 33.0; Int **1** TD. **1933** GB: Rec 4-54 13.5; Int **1** TD. **Total:** Rec 5-87 17.4 4 TD; KR 1 TD; Int 2 TD.

		Rushing				Tot
Year Team	G	Att	Yds	Avg	TD	TD
1930 GB	9	—	—	—	1	3
1931 GB	14	—	—	—	1	4
1932 GB	12	35	184	5.3	0	1
1933 GB	9	23	79	3.4	0	2
NFL Total	44	58	263	4.5	2	10

ERIC ENGLAND England, Eric Jevon 6′2″, 280 **DE**
Col: Texas A&M *HS:* Willowridge [Sugar Land, TX] B: 4/25/1971, Fort Wayne, IN *Drafted:* 1994 Round 3 Ariz
1994 Ariz: 11 G. **1995** Ariz: 15 G. **1996** Ariz: 11 G. **Total:** 37 G.

DEREK ENGLER Engler, Derek Michael 6′5″, 300 **C**
Col: Wisconsin *HS:* Cretin-Derham Hall [St. Paul, MN] B: 7/11/1974, St. Paul, MN
1997 NYG: 5 G; 1 Fum. **1998** NYG: 11 G. **Total:** 16 G; 1 Fum.

RICK ENGLES Engles, Richard B 5′11″, 177 **P**
Col: Tulsa *HS:* Central [Tulsa, OK] B: 8/18/1954, Tulsa, OK *Drafted:* 1976 Round 3 Sea
1976 Sea: Pass 1-1 100.0%, 8 8.00; Rush 3-37 12.3. **1978** Phi: Pass 1-1 100.0%, -2 -2.00; Rush 1-16 16.0. **Total:** Pass 2-2 100.0%, 6 3.00; Rush 4-53 13.3.

		Punting			
Year Team	G	Punts	Yds	Avg	Fum
1976 Sea	14	80	3067	38.3	0
1977 Sea-Pit	2	9	306	34.0	0
1977 Sea	1	4	137	34.3	0
1977 Pit	1	5	169	33.8	0
1978 Phi	6	33	1307	39.6	1
NFL Total	22	122	4680	38.4	1

KEITH ENGLISH English, Keith Alan 6′3″, 220 **P**
Col: Colorado *HS:* Greeley West [CO] B: 3/10/1966, Denver, CO
1990 LARm: Rush 2-(-19) -9.5.

		Punting		
Year Team	G	Punts	Yds	Avg
1990 LARm	16	68	2663	39.2

DOUG ENGLISH English, Lowell Douglas 6′5″, 255 **DT-NT**
Col: Texas *HS:* Bryan Adams [Dallas, TX] B: 8/25/1953, Dallas, TX *Drafted:* 1975 Round 2 Det
1975 Det: 14 G. **1976** Det: 7 G. **1977** Det: 14 G; Scor 1 Saf; 2 Pt. **1978** Det: 14 G. **1979** Det: 16 G; Scor **1** Saf; 2 Pt. **1981** Det: 16 G. **1982** Det: 9 G; 4.5 Sac. **1983** Det: 15 G; Scor **2** Saf; 4 Pt; 13 Sac. **1984** Det: 16 G; 5 Sac. **1985** Det: 10 G; 2.5 Sac. **Total:** 131 G; Scor **4** Saf; 8 Pt; 25.0 Sac.

HARRY ENGLUND Englund, Harry C 6′0″, 185 **E-HB**
(Skin) *Col:* No College *HS:* Rockford Central [IL] B: 8/13/1900, Rockford, IL D: 3/16/1989, Rockford, IL
1921 Sta: 5 G. **1922** ChiB: 11 G. **Total:** 16 G.

BOBBY ENGRAM Engram, Simon III 5′10″, 192 **WR**
Col: Penn State *HS:* Camden [SC] B: 1/7/1973, Camden, SC *Drafted:* 1996 Round 2 ChiB
1997 ChiB: Scor 1 2XP. **1998** ChiB: Rush 1-3 3.0. **Total:** Rush 1-3 3.0; Scor 1 2XP.

		Receiving				Punt Returns			
Year Team	G	Rec	Yds	Avg	TD	Ret	Yds	Avg	TD
1996 ChiB	16	33	389	11.8	6	31	282	9.1	0
1997 ChiB	11	45	399	8.9	2	1	4	4.0	0
1998 ChiB	16	64	987	15.4	5	0	0	—	0
NFL Total	43	142	1775	12.5	13	32	286	8.9	0

	Kickoff Returns				
Year Team	Ret	Yds	Avg	TD	Fum
1996 ChiB	25	580	23.2	0	2
1997 ChiB	2	27	13.5	0	1
1998 ChiB	0	0	—	0	1
NFL Total	27	607	22.5	0	4

ART ENGSTROM Engstrom, Arthur Edward 5′9″, 185 **G**
Col: Chicago *HS:* Valparaiso [IN] B: 8/23/1901, Knox, IN Deceased
1924 Dul: 1 G.

STEVE ENICH Enich, Steve 5′10″, 212 **G**
Col: Marquette *HS:* Hibbing [MN] B: 4/21/1923, Hibbing, MN *Drafted:* 1945 Round 4 Bkn
1945 ChiC: 5 G.

CURTIS ENIS Enis, Curtis T 6′0″, 242 **RB**
Col: Penn State *HS:* Mississinawa Valley [Union City, OH]; Kiski School [Saltsburg, PA] B: 6/15/1976, Union City, OH *Drafted:* 1998 Round 1 ChiB
1998 ChiB: Rec 6-20 3.3.

		Rushing				
Year Team	G	Att	Yds	Avg	TD	Fum
1998 ChiB	9	133	497	3.7	0	1

HUNTER ENIS Enis, George Hunter 6′2″, 195 **QB**
Col: Texas Christian *HS:* Fort Worth Polytechnic [TX] B: 12/10/1936, Fort Worth, TX

Year Team	G	Passing Att	Comp	Comp%	Yds	YPA	TD	Int	Rating
1960 DalT	14	54	30	55.6	357	6.61	1	2	66.7
1961 SD	13	55	23	41.8	365	6.64	2	3	54.0
1962 Den-Oak	11	51	27	52.9	225	4.41	1	1	62.9
1962 Den	4	2	1	50.0	8	4.00	0	0	60.4
1962 Oak	7	49	26	53.1	217	4.43	1	1	63.1
NFL Total	38	160	80	50.0	947	5.92	4	6	61.1

Year Team	Rushing Att	Yds	Avg	TD	Fum
1960 DalT	9	23	2.6	3	0
1961 SD	16	13	0.8	2	4
1962 Den-Oak	2	24	12.0	0	0
1962 Oak	2	24	12.0	0	0
NFL Total	27	60	2.2	5	4

FRED ENKE Enke, Frederick William Jr. 6′1″, 208 **QB-HB**
Col: Arizona *HS:* Tucson [AZ] B: 12/15/1924, Louisville, KY
1948 Det: Rec 1-6 6.0; KR 5-76 15.2. **1949** Det: Rec 1-14 14.0. **1950** Det: PR 1-3 3.0; KR 1-11 11.0. **1952** Phi: Rec 2-19 9.5. **Total:** Rec 4-39 9.8; PR 1-3 3.0; KR 6-87 14.5.

Year Team	G	Passing Att	Comp	Comp%	Yds	YPA	TD	Int	Rating
1948 Det	12	221	100	45.2	1328	6.01	11	17	49.4
1949 Det	12	142	63	44.4	793	5.58	6	5	61.7
1950 Det	12	53	22	41.5	424	8.00	5	7	61.9
1951 Det	12	9	2	22.2	22	2.44	0	1	0.0
1952 Phi	9	67	22	32.8	377	5.63	1	5	26.8
1953 Bal	8	169	71	42.0	1054	6.24	8	15	41.9
1954 Bal	3	28	17	60.7	171	6.11	0	3	38.5
NFL Total	68	689	297	43.1	4169	6.05	31	53	46.2

Year Team	Rushing Att	Yds	Avg	TD	Fum
1948 Det	74	365	4.9	0	8
1949 Det	36	134	3.7	1	6
1950 Det	9	16	1.8	0	3
1951 Det	4	6	1.5	0	0
1952 Phi	14	25	1.8	0	2
1953 Bal	28	91	3.3	0	5
1954 Bal	5	3	0.6	0	1
NFL Total	170	640	3.8	1	25

REX ENRIGHT Enright, Rex Edward 5′10″, 198 **FB**
Col: Notre Dame *HS:* Rockford Central [IL] B: 3/19/1901, Rockford, IL D: 4/6/1960, Columbia, SC
1926 GB: 10 G; Rush 1 TD; 6 Pt. **1927** GB: 9 G; Rush 2 TD; Rec 2 TD; Tot TD 4; 24 Pt. **Total:** 19 G; Rush 3 TD; Rec 2 TD; Tot TD 5; 30 Pt.

BILL ENYART Enyart, William Donald 6′4″, 235 **RB-LB**
(Earthquake) *Col:* Oregon State *HS:* Medford [OR] B: 4/28/1947, Pawhuska, OK *Drafted:* 1969 Round 2 Buf
1969 Buf: KR 1-12 12.0. **1970** Buf: KR 3-60 20.0. **Total:** KR 4-72 18.0.

Year Team	G	Rushing Att	Yds	Avg	TD	Receiving Rec	Yds	Avg	TD	Fum	Tot TD
1969 Buf	14	47	191	4.1	1	19	186	9.8	2	2	3
1970 Buf	14	58	196	3.4	0	35	235	6.7	1	2	1
1971 Oak	1	0	0	—	0	0	0	—	0	0	0
NFL Total	29	105	387	3.7	1	54	421	7.8	3	4	4

PAT EPPERSON Epperson, John Patrick 6′3″, 225 **OE**
Col: Los Angeles Valley Coll. CA (J.C.); Adams State *HS:* Verdugo Hills [Tujunga, CA] B: 11/3/1935, Los Angeles, CA
1960 Den: 9 G; Rec 11-99 9.0.

JACK EPPS Epps, John Michael 6′0″, 197 **DB**
Col: Northeastern Oklahoma A&M (J.C.); Kansas State *HS:* Shawnee Mission West [KS] B: 3/20/1963, Tulsa, OK
1987 KC: 3 G.

PHIL EPPS Epps, Phillip Earl 5′10″, 165 **WR**
Col: Texas Christian *HS:* Atlanta [TX] B: 11/11/1958, Atlanta, TX
Drafted: 1982 Round 12 GB
1985 GB: Rush 5-103 20.6 1 TD. **1986** GB: Rush 4-18 4.5. **1987** GB: Rush 1-0. **1989** NYJ: Rush 1-14 14.0. **Total:** Rush 11-135 12.3 1 TD.

Year Team	G	Receiving Rec	Yds	Avg	TD	Punt Returns Ret	Yds	Avg	TD
1982 GB	9	10	226	22.6	2	20	150	7.5	0
1983 GB	16	18	313	17.4	0	36	324	9.0	1
1984 GB	16	26	435	16.7	3	29	199	6.9	0
1985 GB	16	44	683	15.5	3	15	146	9.7	0
1986 GB	12	49	612	12.5	4	0	0	—	0
1987 GB	10	34	516	15.2	2	0	0	—	0
1988 GB	6	11	99	9.0	0	0	0	—	0
1989 NYJ	10	8	108	13.5	0	0	0	—	0
NFL Total	95	200	2992	15.0	14	100	819	8.2	1

Year Team	Kickoff Returns Ret	Yds	Avg	TD	Fum	Tot TD
1982 GB	0	0	—	0	1	2
1983 GB	0	0	—	0	2	1
1984 GB	12	232	19.3	0	1	3
1985 GB	12	279	23.3	0	1	4
1986 GB	1	21	21.0	0	0	4
1987 GB	0	0	—	0	1	2
1989 NYJ	9	154	17.1	0	0	0
NFL Total	34	686	20.2	0	6	16

BOBBY EPPS Epps, Robert Hezekiah 5′9″, 198 **FB**
Col: Pittsburgh *HS:* Swissvale [PA] B: 3/25/1932, Swissvale, PA
Drafted: 1954 Round 14 NYG
1954 NYG: Rec 5-20 4.0. **1955** NYG: Rec 5-8 1.6. **1957** NYG: Pass 1-0; Rec 8-81 10.1. **Total:** Pass 1-0; Rec 18-109 6.1.

Year Team	G	Rushing Att	Yds	Avg	TD	Fum
1954 NYG	10	30	110	3.7	0	1
1955 NYG	9	95	375	3.9	2	1
1957 NYG	12	63	286	4.5	0	1
NFL Total	31	188	771	4.1	2	3

TORY EPPS Epps, Torrean Douglas 6′0″, 280 **NT-DT**
Col: Memphis *HS:* Uniontown [PA] B: 5/28/1967, Uniontown, PA
Drafted: 1990 Round 8 Atl
1990 Atl: 16 G; 3 Sac. **1991** Atl: 16 G; 1.5 Sac. **1992** Atl: 16 G.
1993 Atl-ChiB: 5 G. Atl: 2 G. ChiB: 3 G. **1994** ChiB: 5 G; 1 Sac. **1995** NO: 12 G. **Total:** 70 G; 5.5 Sac.

DICK ERDLITZ Erdlitz, Richard Alfred 5′10″, 181 **HB-DB**
(Automatic) *Col:* Northwestern *HS:* Oshkosh [WI] B: 2/16/1920, Menominee, MI
AAFC **1946** MiaA: Pass 1-1 100.0%, 10 10.00; Rec 7-31 4.4; KR 6-104 17.3; Int 1-12; Scor 34, 2-7 28.6% FG, 22-22 100.0% XK.

Year Team	G	Rushing Att	Yds	Avg	TD
1946 MiaA	14	26	38	1.5	1

NFL **1942** Phi: Rec 5-78 15.6; KR 1-25 25.0; Int 1-0; Scor 14, 8-8 100.0% XK. **1945** Phi: Int 1-3. **Total:** Rec 5-78 15.6; KR 1-25 25.0; Int 2-3; Scor 14, 8-8 100.0% XK.

Year Team	G	Rushing Att	Yds	Avg	TD
1942 Phi	10	21	69	3.3	1
1945 Phi	7	6	24	4.0	0
NFL Total	17	27	93	3.4	1

ARCHIE EREHART Erehart, Archibald Dean 5′8″, 165 **WB**
Col: Indiana B: 3/27/1894 Deceased
1920 Mun: 1 G.

RICH ERENBERG Erenberg, Richard Mark 5′10″, 200 **RB**
Col: Colgate *HS:* Horace Greeley [Chappaqua, NY] B: 4/17/1962, Chappaqua, NY *Drafted:* 1984 Round 9 Pit

Year Team	G	Rushing Att	Yds	Avg	TD	Receiving Rec	Yds	Avg	TD
1984 Pit	16	115	405	3.5	2	38	358	9.4	1
1985 Pit	14	17	67	3.9	0	33	326	9.9	3
1986 Pit	16	42	170	4.0	1	27	217	8.0	3
NFL Total	46	174	642	3.7	3	98	901	9.2	7

Year Team	Kickoff Returns Ret	Yds	Avg	TD	Fum	Tot TD
1984 Pit	28	575	20.5	0	3	3
1985 Pit	21	441	21.0	0	1	3
1986 Pit	0	0	—	0	1	4
NFL Total	49	1016	20.7	0	5	10

SWEDE ERICKSON Erickson, ? 215 **E**
(Goats)
1924 Ken: 1 G.

BUD ERICKSON Erickson, Carlton Lyons 6′1″, 198 **C-LB**
Col: Washington *HS:* Bothell [WA] B: 4/10/1916, Bothell, WA
1938 Was: 2 G. **1939** Was: 1 G. **Total:** 3 G.

CRAIG ERICKSON Erickson, Craig Neil 6′2″, 209 **QB**
Col: Miami (Fla.) *HS:* Cardinal Newman [West Palm Beach, FL]
B: 5/17/1969, Boynton Beach, FL *Drafted:* 1992 Round 4 TB

		Passing							
Year Team	G	Att	Comp	Comp%	Yds	YPA	TD	Int	Rating
1992 TB	6	26	15	57.7	121	4.65	0	0	69.6
1993 TB	16	457	233	51.0	3054	6.68	18	21	66.4
1994 TB	15	399	225	56.4	2919	7.32	16	10	82.5
1995 Ind	6	83	50	60.2	586	7.06	3	4	73.7
1996 Mia	7	99	55	55.6	780	7.88	4	2	86.3
1997 Mia	2	28	13	46.4	165	5.89	0	1	50.4
NFL Total	52	1092	591	54.1	7625	6.98	41	38	74.3

	Rushing				
Year Team	Att	Yds	Avg	TD	Fum
1992 TB	1	-1	-1.0	0	0
1993 TB	26	96	3.7	0	9
1994 TB	26	68	2.6	1	6
1995 Ind	9	14	1.6	0	2
1996 Mia	11	16	1.5	0	4
1997 Mia	4	8	2.0	0	2
NFL Total	77	201	2.6	1	23

HAROLD ERICKSON Erickson, Harold 195 **T**
(Sox) *Col:* No College *HS:* Central [Minnepolis, MN] Deceased
1921 Min: 4 G. **1922** Min: 4 G. **Total:** 8 G.

HAL ERICKSON Erickson, Harold A 5'9", 193 **WB-TB-FB-BB**
(Swede; Bull) *Col:* St. Olaf; Washington & Jefferson B: 3/10/1899, Maynard, MN D: 1/28/1963
1923 Mil: 11 G; Rush 1 TD; 6 Pt. **1924** Mil: 4 G; Rec 3 TD; 18 Pt. **1925** ChiC: 14 G; Rush 2 TD; Rec **4** TD; Int 1 TD; Tot TD 7; 42 Pt. **1926** ChiC: 11 G; Rec 1 TD; 6 Pt. **1927** ChiC: 8 G. **1928** ChiC: 6 G; Int **1** TD; 6 Pt. **1929** Min: 10 G; Scor 4, 1 FG, 1 XK. **1930** Min: 4 G. **Total:** 68 G; Rush 3 TD; Rec 8 TD; Int 2 TD; Scor 82, 1 FG, 1 XK; Tot TD 13.

BERNIE ERICKSON Erickson, John Bernard 6'2", 240 **LB**
(Beast) *Col:* Abilene Christian *HS:* Clifton [TX] B: 10/16/1944, Clifton, TX *Drafted:* 1967 Round 5 SD
1967 SD: 13 G; KR 1-0; Int 1-17. **1968** SD-Cin: 13 G. SD: 8 G. Cin: 5 G. **Total:** 26 G; KR 1-0; Int 1-17.

MICKEY ERICKSON Erickson, Milton Leroy 6'2", 208 **C**
Col: Northwestern *HS:* Moline [IL] B: 5/16/1905, Cambridge, MN D: 1/26/1984, Phoenix, AZ
1930 ChiC: 12 G. **1931** ChiC: 8 G. **1932** ChiC-Bos: 10 G. ChiC: 1 G. Bos: 9 G. **Total:** 30 G.

WALDEN ERICKSON Erickson, Walden D 6'1", 205 **T**
Col: Washington B: 9/3/1902 D: 12/1968, Chicago, IL
1927 Pott: 12 G.

BILL ERICKSON Erickson, William Clarence 6'2", 210 **G-LB**
Col: North Carolina; Mississippi *HS:* Bayside [Queens, NY] B: 12/4/1921 D: Queens, NY *Drafted:* 1948 Round 6 NYG
AAFC **1949** NY-A: 6 G.

NFL **1948** NYG: 9 G.

TOM ERLANDSON Erlandson, Thomas Dean Jr. 6'1", 220 **LB**
Col: Washington *HS:* Smoky Hills [Aurora, CO] B: 6/19/1966, Denver, CO *Drafted:* 1988 Round 12 Buf
1988 Buf: 4 G.

TOM ERLANDSON Erlandson, Thomas Dean Sr. 6'3", 235 **LB**
Col: Washington State *HS:* Bellingham [WA] B: 3/24/1940, Seattle, WA
1962 Den: 4 G; Int 1-3. **1963** Den: 11 G. **1964** Den: 5 G. **1965** Den: 14 G; Int 1-3. **1966** Mia: 14 G; Int 3-31 1 TD; 6 Pt. **1967** Mia: 10 G; Int 1-37. **1968** SD: 10 G; Int 2-22. **Total:** 68 G; Int 8-96 1 TD; 6 Pt.

JACK ERNST Ernst, John Oliver 5'11", 180 **BB-TB-WB**
Col: Lafayette *HS:* South [Youngstown, OH] B: 12/4/1899, Llewellyn, PA D: 3/9/1968, South Williamsport, PA
1925 Pott: 12 G; Pass **8** TD; Rush 2 TD; PR **1** TD; Scor 19, 1 XK; Tot TD 3. **1926** Pott: 10 G; Pass 1 TD; Rec 1 TD; 6 Pt. **1927** Pott: 12 G; Pass 1 TD. **1928** Pott-NYY: 11 G; Pass 3 TD; Rec 2 TD; 12 Pt. Pott: 10 G; Pass 3 TD; Rec 2 TD; 12 Pt. NYY: 1 G. **1929** Bost: 7 G; Scor 1, 1 XK. **1930** Fra: 8 G; Pass 1 TD; Rec 1 TD; 6 Pt. **Total:** 60 G; Pass 14 TD; Rush 2 TD; Rec 4 TD; PR 1 TD; Tot TD 7.

MIKE ERNST Ernst, Michael Paul 6'1", 190 **QB**
Col: Cerritos Coll. CA (J.C.); Cal State-Fullerton *HS:* Pius X [Downey, CA] B: 10/12/1950, Lynwood, CA
1972 Den: 1 G; Pass 4-1 25.0%, 10 2.50; Rush 1-4 4.0. **1973** Cin: 1 G. **Total:** 2 G; Pass 4-1 25.0%, 10 2.50; Rush 1-4 4.0.

RICKY ERVINS Ervins, Ricky 5'7", 200 **RB**
Col: USC *HS:* John Muir [Pasadena, CA] B: 12/7/1968, Fort Wayne, IN *Drafted:* 1991 Round 3 Was
1991 Was: KR 11-232 21.1. **1993** Was: KR 2-29 14.5. **1994** Was: KR 1-17 17.0. **1995** SF: KR 5-32 6.4. **Total:** KR 19-310 16.3.

		Rushing				Receiving					Tot
Year Team	G	Att	Yds	Avg	TD	Rec	Yds	Avg	TD	Fum	TD
1991 Was	15	145	680	4.7	3	16	181	11.3	1	1	4
1992 Was	16	151	495	3.3	2	32	252	7.9	0	1	2
1993 Was	15	50	201	4.0	0	16	123	7.7	0	2	0
1994 Was	16	185	650	3.5	3	51	293	5.7	1	1	4
1995 SF	14	23	88	3.8	0	2	21	10.5	0	0	0
NFL Total	76	554	2114	3.8	8	117	870	7.4	2	5	10

TERRY ERWIN Erwin, Terrence Lester 6'0", 190 **RB**
Col: Boston College *HS:* Beverly [MA] B: 8/30/1946, Weymouth, MA
1968 Den: 9 G; Rush 24-76 3.2; Rec 2-21 10.5; KR 3-55 18.3; 1 Fum.

RUSSELL ERXLEBEN Erxleben, Russell Allen 6'4", 223 **P**
Col: Texas *HS:* Seguin [TX] B: 1/13/1957, Seguin, TX *Drafted:* 1979 Round 1 NO
1979 NO: Pass 1-0, 1 Int; Scor 10, 2-2 100.0% FG, 4-4 100.0% XK. **1980** NO: Pass 1-0; Scor 8, 2-5 40.0% FG, 2-2 100.0% XK. **1981** NO: Rush 2-10 5.0. **1982** NO: Pass 2-1 50.0%, 39 19.50 1 TD; Scor 1, 0-1 FG, 1-1 100.0% XK. **1983** NO: Pass 1-1 100.0%, 24 24.00; Rush 2-(-9) -4.5. **Total:** Pass 5-2 40.0%, 63 12.60 1 TD 1 Int; Rush 4-1 0.3; Scor 19, 4-8 50.0% FG, 7-7 100.0% XK.

		Punting			
Year Team	G	Punts	Yds	Avg	Fum
1979 NO	1	4	148	37.0	0
1980 NO	16	89	3499	39.3	0
1981 NO	16	66	2672	40.5	1
1982 NO	9	46	1976	43.0	0
1983 NO	16	74	3034	41.0	0
1987 Det	1	1	52	52.0	0
NFL Total	59	280	11381	40.6	1

HERB ESCHBACH Eschbach, Herbert Heins 6'0", 190 **C**
Col: Penn State *HS:* Franklin and Marshall Acad. [Lancaster, PA] B: 4/26/1907, Lancaster, PA Deceased
1930 Prov: 7 G. **1931** Prov: 4 G. **Total:** 11 G.

LEN ESHMONT Eshmont, Leonard Charles 5'11", 179 **HB-DB-FB**
Col: Fordham *HS:* Mount Carmel [PA] B: 8/26/1917, Mount Carmel, PA D: 5/12/1957, Charlottesville, VA *Drafted:* 1941 Round 3 NYG
AAFC **1946** SF-A: Pass 2-1 50.0%, 42 21.00 1 TD; PR 2-25 12.5; KR 10-264 26.4. **1947** SF-A: PR 1-3 3.0; KR 9-177 19.7. **1948** SF-A: KR 1-32 32.0. **1949** SF-A: KR 1-13 13.0. **Total:** Pass 2-1 50.0%, 42 21.00 1 TD; PR 3-28 9.3; KR 21-486 23.1.

		Rushing				Receiving			
Year Team	G	Att	Yds	Avg	TD	Rec	Yds	Avg	TD
1946 SF-A	10	73	340	4.7	6	17	287	16.9	2
1947 SF-A	13	84	381	4.5	0	19	303	15.9	2
1948 SF-A	13	50	296	5.9	1	14	214	15.3	0
1949 SF-A	12	25	164	6.6	0	3	107	35.7	2
AAFC Total	48	232	1181	5.1	7	53	911	17.2	6

	Interceptions			Tot
Year Team	Int	Yds	TD	TD
1946 SF-A	0	0	0	9
1947 SF-A	6	72	0	2
1948 SF-A	1	0	0	2
1949 SF-A	3	56	0	2
AAFC Total	10	128	0	15

NFL **1941** NYG: Pass 3-2 66.7%, 32 10.67 1 TD; Rec 1-4 4.0; PR 6-131 21.8; KR 2-54 27.0; Punt 11-433 39.4.

		Rushing			
Year Team	G	Att	Yds	Avg	TD
1941 NYG	9	50	164	3.3	0

BOOMER ESIASON Esiason, Norman Julius 6'5", 224 **QB**
Col: Maryland *HS:* East Islip [Islip Terrace, NY] B: 4/17/1961, West Islip, NY *Drafted:* 1984 Round 2 Cin
1986 Cin: Punt 1-31 31.0. **1987** Cin: Punt 2-68 34.0. **1988** Cin: Punt 1-21 21.0. **1993** NYJ: Rec 1-(-8) -8.0. **1996** Ariz: Scor 1 2XP. **Total:** Rec 1-(-8) -8.0; Punt 4-120 30.0; Scor 1 2XP.

		Passing							
Year Team	G	Att	Comp	Comp%	Yds	YPA	TD	Int	Rating
1984 Cin	10	102	51	50.0	530	5.20	3	3	62.9
1985 Cin	15	431	251	58.2	3443	7.99	27	12	93.2
1986 Cin	16	469	273	58.2	3959	**8.44**	24	17	87.7
1987 Cin	12	440	240	54.5	3321	7.55	16	19	73.1
1988 Cin	16	388	223	57.5	3572	**9.21**	28	14	**97.4**
1989 Cin	16	455	258	56.7	3525	7.75	28	11	92.1
1990 Cin	16	402	224	55.7	3031	7.54	24	22	77.0
1991 Cin	14	413	233	56.4	2883	6.98	13	16	72.5
1992 Cin	12	278	144	51.8	1407	5.06	11	15	57.0
1993 NYJ	16	473	288	60.9	3421	7.23	16	11	84.5
1994 NYJ	15	440	255	58.0	2782	6.32	17	13	77.3

1995 NYJ	12	389	221	56.8	2275	5.85	16	15	71.4
1996 Ariz	10	339	190	56.0	2293	6.76	11	14	70.6
1997 Cin	7	186	118	63.4	1478	7.95	13	2	106.9
NFL Total	187	5205	2969	57.0	37920	7.29	247	184	81.1

	Rushing				
Year Team	Att	Yds	Avg	TD	Fum
1984 Cin	19	63	3.3	2	4
1985 Cin	33	79	2.4	1	9
1986 Cin	44	146	3.3	1	12
1987 Cin	52	241	4.6	0	10
1988 Cin	43	248	5.8	1	5
1989 Cin	47	278	5.9	0	8
1990 Cin	49	157	3.2	0	11
1991 Cin	24	66	2.8	0	10
1992 Cin	21	66	3.1	0	12
1993 NYJ	45	118	2.6	1	13
1994 NYJ	28	59	2.1	0	11
1995 NYJ	19	14	0.7	0	12
1996 Ariz	15	52	3.5	1	5
1997 Cin	8	11	1.4	0	1
NFL Total	447	1598	3.6	7	123

AL ESPIE Espie, David Allen **T**
Col: No College *HS:* Male [Louisville, KY]; Greenbrier Mil. Acad. [Lewisburg, WV] B: 1900, Kuttawa, KY D: 3/25/1961, Louisville, KY
1923 Lou: 1 G.

ALEX ESPINOZA Espinoza, Alex A 6'1", 193 **QB**
Col: Cal State-Fullerton; Iowa State *HS:* St. Paul [East Los Angeles, CA] B: 5/31/1964, Los Angles, CA
1987 KC: 1 G; Pass 14-9 64.3%, 69 4.93 2 Int; Rush 1-5 5.0.

MIKE ESPOSITO Esposito, Michael John 6'0", 183 **RB**
Col: Boston College *HS:* Wilmington [MA] B: 4/24/1953, Everett, MA
Drafted: 1975 Round 7 Atl
1976 Atl: Pass 1-0; Rec 17-88 5.2; PR 1-6 6.0; KR 1-12 12.0. **1977** Atl: Pass 1-0; Rec 1-(-1) -1.0; Int 1-55. **1978** Atl: Rec 3-10 3.3.
Total: Pass 2-0; Rec 21-97 4.6; PR 1-6 6.0; KR 1-12 12.0; Int 1-55.

		Rushing				
Year Team	G	Att	Yds	Avg	TD	Fum
1976 Atl	10	60	317	5.3	2	4
1977 Atl	14	34	101	3.0	0	0
1978 Atl	16	7	21	3.0	0	0
NFL Total	40	101	439	4.3	2	4

CLARENCE ESSER Esser, Clarence Joseph 6'0", 190 **DE-T**
Col: Wisconsin *HS:* Central [Madison, WI] B: 3/27/1921, Madison, WI
Drafted: 1947 Round 18 ChiC
1947 ChiC: 7 G.

RON ESSINK Essink, Ronald Arden 6'6", 260 **OT-TE**
Col: Grand Valley State *HS:* Zeeland [MI] B: 7/30/1958, Zeeland, MI
Drafted: 1980 Round 10 Sea
1980 Sea: 16 G; Rec 1-2 2.0 1 TD; 6 Pt. **1981** Sea: 16 G. **1982** Sea: 7 G. **1983** Sea: 16 G. **1984** Sea: 16 G. **1985** Sea: 12 G. **Total:** 83 G; Rec 1-2 2.0 1 TD; 6 Pt.

CHARLIE ESSMAN Essman, Charles Peter 6'0", 220 **G**
Col: Christian Brothers (Mo.) B: 1/31/1881, Jackson, OH
D: 10/12/1965, Columbus, OH
1920 Col: 1 G.

RICHARD ESTELL Estell, Richard Wayne 6'2", 210 **WR**
Col: Kansas *HS:* J.C. Harmon [Kansas City, KS] B: 10/12/1963, Kansas City, KS
1987 KC: 2 G; Rec 3-24 8.0.

MIKE ESTEP Estep, Michael Lawrence 6'4", 270 **OG-OT**
Col: Bowling Green State *HS:* Newark [OH] B: 12/29/1963, Northampton, England
1987 GB-Buf: 3 G. GB: 1 G. Buf: 2 G. **Total:** 3 G.

DON ESTES Estes, Donald Olarey 6'3", 250 **OG**
Col: Louisiana State *HS:* Brookhaven [MS] B: 10/14/1938, Tomball, TX
Drafted: 1963 Round 2 Hou
1966 SD: 5 G.

LARRY ESTES Estes, Lawrence G 6'6", 255 **DE**
Col: Alcorn State *HS:* Louisville [MS] B: 12/9/1946, Lousville, MS
Drafted: 1970 Round 8 NO
1970 NO: 14 G. **1971** NO: 8 G. **1972** Phi: 7 G. **1975** KC: 4 G. **1976** KC: 14 G. **Total:** 47 G.

SAM ETCHEVERRY Etcheverry, Samuel 5'11", 190 **QB-P**
Col: Denver *HS:* Carlsbad [NM] B: 5/20/1930, Carlsbad, NM

		Passing							
Year Team	G	Att	Comp	Comp%	Yds	YPA	TD	Int	Rating
1961 StL	14	196	96	49.0	1275	6.51	14	11	70.4
1962 StL	14	106	58	54.7	707	6.67	2	10	42.5
NFL Total	28	302	154	51.0	1982	6.56	16	21	60.6

	Rushing				Punting			
Year Team	Att	Yds	Avg	TD	Punts	Yds	Avg	Fum
1961 StL	33	73	2.2	0	0	0	—	**15**
1962 StL	8	5	0.6	0	59	2259	38.3	6
NFL Total	41	78	1.9	0	59	2259	38.3	21

CARL ETELMAN Etelman, Carl Edward 5'8", 160 **BB-WB-TB**
(Midget) *Col:* Boston U.; Harvard; Tufts *HS:* Fairhaven [MA]
B: 4/2/1900, Fairhaven, MA Deceased
1926 Prov: 1 G.

CARLOS ETHEREDGE Etheredge, Carlos Sebastian 6'5", 236 **TE**
Col: Miami (Fla.) *HS:* Del Norte [Albuquerque, NM] B: 8/10/1970, Albuquerque, NM *Drafted:* 1993 Round 6 Ind
1994 Ind: 9 G; Rec 1-6 6.0; KR 2-23 11.5.

DAVE ETHERLY Etherly, David 6'1", 190 **DB**
Col: Oregon State; Portland State *HS:* Lakeridge [Lake Oswego, OR]
B: 12/22/1962, Alburgu, Mexico
1987 Was: 3 G.

JOE ETHRIDGE Ethridge, Joe Paul 6'0", 230 **T**
Col: Southern Methodist *HS:* Kermit [TX] B: 4/15/1928, Conway, TX
Drafted: 1949 Round 6 GB
1949 GB: 12 G; Scor 4, 1-2 50.0% FG, 1-1 100.0% XK.

RAY ETHRIDGE Ethridge, Raymond Arthur Jr. 5'10", 180 **WR**
Col: Pasadena City Coll. CA (J.C.) *HS:* Crawford [San Diego, CA]
B: 12/12/1968, San Diego, CA *Drafted:* 1992 Round 3 SD
1996 Bal: 14 G; Rec 2-24 12.0; PR 1-3 3.0; KR 8-171 21.4. **1997** Bal: 2 G; PR 5-21 4.2; KR 2-37 18.5; 2 Fum. **Total:** 16 G; Rec 2-24 12.0; PR 6-24 4.0; KR 10-208 20.8; 2 Fum.

LEROY ETIENNE Etienne, LeRoy Joseph 6'2", 245 **LB**
Col: Nebraska *HS:* New Iberia [LA] B: 7/21/1966, Lafayette, LA
1990 SF: 10 G.

EARL ETTENHAUS Ettenhaus, Earl **G**
Col: No College *HS:* Perry [NY] B: 1902, Perry, NY Deceased
1921 Roch: 1 G.

BOB ETTER Etter, Robert Glenn 5'11", 157 **K**
Col: Georgia *HS:* Chattanooga [TN] B: 8/8/1945, Chattanooga, TN

		Scoring						
Year Team	G	Pts	FG	FGA	FG%	XK	XKA	XK%
1968 Atl	14	50	11	21	52.4	17	19	89.5
1969 Atl	14	78	15	30	50.0	33	33	100.0
NFL Total	28	128	26	51	51.0	50	52	96.2

DON ETTINGER Ettinger, Donald Nesbitt 6'2", 213 **LB-OG**
(Red) *Col:* Kansas *HS:* William Chrisman [Independence, MO]
B: 11/20/1922, Independence, MO D: 2/13/1992, Cookeville, KS
Drafted: 1948 Round 19 NYG
1948 NYG: 10 G; Int 2-14. **1949** NYG: 11 G; Int 2-7. **1950** NYG: 12 G.
Total: 33 G; Int 4-21.

BYRON EVANS Evans, Byron Nelson 6'2", 235 **LB**
Col: Arizona *HS:* South Mountain [Phoenix, AZ] B: 2/23/1964, Pheonix, AZ *Drafted:* 1987 Round 4 Phi
1989 Phi: 2 Sac. **1990** Phi: 1 Sac. **1993** Phi: 1 Fum TD. **1994** Phi: 0.5 Sac.
Total: 1 Fum TD; 3.5 Sac.

		Interceptions				Tot
Year Team	G	Int	Yds	TD	Fum	TD
1987 Phi	12	1	12	0	0	0
1988 Phi	16	0	0	0	0	0
1989 Phi	16	3	23	0	0	0
1990 Phi	16	1	43	1	0	1
1991 Phi	16	2	46	0	1	0
1992 Phi	16	4	76	0	0	0
1993 Phi	11	1	8	0	0	1
1994 Phi	10	1	6	0	0	0
NFL Total	113	13	214	1	1	2

CHUCK EVANS Evans, Charles Allen III 6'3", 235 **LB**
Col: Stanford *HS:* West Covina [CA] B: 12/19/1956, West Covina, CA
Drafted: 1980 Round 8 NO
1980 NO: 10 G. **1981** NO: 16 G. **Total:** 26 G.

CHUCK EVANS Evans, Charles Jr. 6'1", 240 **RB**
Col: Clark Atlanta *HS:* Glenn Hills [Augusta, GA] B: 4/16/1967, Augusta, GA *Drafted:* 1992 Round 11 Min
1993 Min: KR 1-11 11.0. **1994** Min: KR 1-4 4.0. **1997** Min: Scor 1 2XP.
Total: KR 2-15 7.5; Scor 1 2XP.

		Rushing				Receiving				Tot
Year Team	G	Att	Yds	Avg	TD	Rec	Yds	Avg	TD	TD
1993 Min	3	14	32	2.3	0	4	39	9.8	0	0

1994 Min	14	6	20	3.3	0	1	2	2.0	0	0
1995 Min	16	19	59	3.1	1	18	119	6.6	1	2
1996 Min	16	13	29	2.2	0	22	135	6.1	0	0
1997 Min	16	43	157	3.7	2	21	152	7.2	0	2
1998 Min	16	23	67	2.9	1	12	84	7.0	0	1
NFL Total	81	118	364	3.1	4	78	531	6.8	1	5

DAVID EVANS Evans, David Wayne 6'0", 178 **DB**
Col: Central Arkansas *HS:* Paul H. Pewitt [Naples, TX] B: 5/1/1959, Naples, TX
1986 Min: 16 G. **1987** Min: 3 G. **Total:** 19 G.

DONALD EVANS Evans, Donald Lee 6'2", 282 **DE-DT**
Col: Winston-Salem State *HS:* Athens Drive [Raleigh, NC]
B: 3/14/1964, Raleigh, NC *Drafted:* 1987 Round 2 LARm
1987 LARm: 1 G; Rush 3-10 3.3. **1988** Phi: 5 G. **1990** Pit: 16 G; 3 Sac. **1991** Pit: 16 G; 2 Sac. **1992** Pit: 16 G; 3 Sac. **1993** Pit: 16 G; 6.5 Sac. **1994** NYJ: 16 G; 0.5 Sac. **1995** NYJ: 4 G; 2 Sac. **Total:** 90 G; Rush 3-10 3.3; 17 Sac.

DOUG EVANS Evans, Douglas Edwards 6'1", 190 **DB**
(Greyhound) *Col:* Louisiana Tech *HS:* Haynesville [LA] B: 5/13/1970, Shreveport, LA *Drafted:* 1993 Round 6 GB
1994 GB: 1 Sac. **1995** GB: PR 1-0; 1 Sac. **1996** GB: 3 Sac. **1997** GB: 1 Sac. **Total:** PR 1-0; 6 Sac.

		Interceptions			
Year Team	**G**	**Int**	**Yds**	**TD**	**Fum**
1993 GB	16	1	0	0	0
1994 GB	16	1	0	0	0
1995 GB	16	2	24	0	1
1996 GB	16	5	102	1	1
1997 GB	15	3	33	0	0
1998 Car	9	2	18	0	0
NFL Total	88	14	177	1	2

EARL EVANS Evans, Earl 5'11", 204 **T-G**
(Buck) *Col:* Marquette; Harvard *HS:* Albia [IA] B: 4/14/1900, Lucas, IA D: 3/18/1992, San Francisco, CA
1925 ChiC: 14 G; 1 Fum TD; 6 Pt. **1926** ChiB: 14 G. **1927** ChiB: 11 G. **1928** ChiB: 10 G. **1929** ChiB: 6 G. **Total:** 55 G; 1 Fum TD; 6 Pt.

FRED EVANS Evans, Frederick Owen Jr. 5'11", 185 **HB-DB**
(Dippy) *Col:* Notre Dame *HS:* James Whitcomb Riley [South Bend, IN]
B: 5/23/1921, Grand Rapids, MI *Drafted:* 1943 Round 2 ChiB
AAFC **1946** CleA: Rec 1-7 7.0; PR 1-0; Int 1-21; Punt 8-296 37.0.
1947 BufA-ChiA: Pass 2-0; Rec 5-84 16.8 1 TD; PR 5-30 6.0; KR 9-159 17.7; Punt 2-73 36.5. **Total:** Pass 2-0; Rec 6-91 15.2 1 TD; PR 6-30 5.0; KR 9-159 17.7; Int 1-21; Punt 10-369 36.9.

		Rushing				Tot
Year Team	**G**	**Att**	**Yds**	**Avg**	**TD**	**TD**
1946 CleA	6	8	27	3.4	0	0
1947 BufA-ChiA	13	31	124	4.0	1	2
AAFC Total	19	39	151	3.9	1	2

NFL **1948** ChiB: 3 G; Rush 10-15 1.5; Rec 1-(-2) -2.0; PR 1-15 15.0; 2 Fum TD; 12 Pt.

JERRY EVANS Evans, Gerald Kristen 6'4", 250 **TE**
Col: Toledo *HS:* Admiral King [Lorain, OH] B: 9/28/1968, Lorain, OH
1994 Den: KR 1-6 6.0. **Total:** KR 1-6 6.0.

		Receiving				
Year Team	**G**	**Rec**	**Yds**	**Avg**	**TD**	**Fum**
1993 Den	14	0	0	—	0	0
1994 Den	16	13	127	9.8	2	0
1995 Den	13	12	124	10.3	1	1
NFL Total	43	25	251	10.0	3	1

GREG EVANS Evans, Gregory G 6'1", 217 **DB**
Col: Texas Christian *HS:* Daingerfield [TX] B: 6/28/1971, Daingerfield, TX
1995 Buf: 16 G; Int 1-18. **1998** Was: 13 G. **Total:** 29 G; Int 1-18.

CHARLIE EVANS Evans, Jack Charles 6'1", 220 **RB**
Col: Utah; USC *HS:* Gardena [CA] B: 1/10/1948, Gardena, CA
Drafted: 1971 Round 14 NYG
1974 Was: KR 4-60 15.0. **Total:** KR 4-60 15.0.

		Rushing				Receiving					Tot
Year Team	**G**	**Att**	**Yds**	**Avg**	**TD**	**Rec**	**Yds**	**Avg**	**TD**	**Fum**	**TD**
1971 NYG	6	48	171	3.6	5	13	144	11.1	0	2	5
1972 NYG	8	91	317	3.5	4	26	182	7.0	1	6	5
1973 NYG	5	34	77	2.3	1	13	100	7.7	0	2	1
1974 Was	6	32	79	2.5	2	2	44	22.0	0	2	2
NFL Total	25	205	644	3.1	12	54	470	8.7	1	12	13

JIM EVANS Evans, James 6'1", 190 **WR**
Col: Howard Coll. TX (J.C.); Texas-El Paso *HS:* Big Spring [TX]
B: 10/24/1939 *Drafted:* 1964 Round 4 NYJ
1964 NYJ: 12 G; Rec 7-56 8.0; KR 13-259 19.9; 1 Fum. **1965** NYJ: 9 G; Rec 2-24 12.0. **Total:** 21 G; Rec 9-80 8.9; KR 13-259 19.9; 1 Fum.

JAMES EVANS Evans, James Marcus 6'0", 220 **RB**
Col: Southern University *HS:* Mattie T. Blount [Prichard, AL]
B: 8/17/1963, Prichard, AL *Drafted:* 1987 Round 10 KC
1987 KC: 2 G.

DALE EVANS Evans, Jay Dale 6'3", 210 **HB**
Col: Kansas State *HS:* Highland Park [Topeka, KS] B: 9/10/1939, St. Francis, KS *Drafted:* 1961 Round 6 Den
1961 Den: 5 G.

JOHNNY EVANS Evans, John Albert Jr. 6'1", 197 **P-QB**
Col: North Carolina State *HS:* T. Wingate Andrews [High Point, NC]
B: 2/18/1956, High Point, NC *Drafted:* 1978 Round 2 Cle
1978 Cle: Pass 1-1 100.0%, 19 19.00; Rush 2-12 6.0. **1979** Cle: Pass 2-1 50.0%, 14 7.00. **1980** Cle: Rush 3-(-6) -2.0. **Total:** Pass 3-2 66.7%, 33 11.00; Rush 5-6 1.2.

		Punting		
Year Team	**G**	**Punts**	**Yds**	**Avg**
1978 Cle	16	79	3089	39.1
1979 Cle	16	69	2844	41.2
1980 Cle	16	66	2530	38.3
NFL Total	48	214	8463	39.5

JACK EVANS Evans, John Alexander 5'9", 175 **BB**
Col: California *HS:* Long Beach Polytechnic [CA] B: 8/17/1906, Colorado Springs, CO D: 9/5/1988, Claremont, CA
1929 GB: 3 G.

JOHN EVANS Evans, John Stuart 6'2", 243 **TE**
Col: Stephen F. Austin St. *HS:* Cy-Fair [Cypress, TX] B: 6/13/1964, Houston, TX
1987 Atl: 1 G; Rec 1-8 8.0.

JON EVANS Evans, Jon Albert 6'4", 205 **OE**
Col: Oklahoma State *HS:* Bartlesville [OK] B: 1/31/1936, Tyler, TX
D: 8/19/1979, Raleigh, NC *Drafted:* 1958 Round 26 Pit
1958 Pit: 1 G.

LARRY EVANS Evans, Lawrence Eugene 6'2", 216 **LB**
Col: Mississippi College *HS:* Biloxi [MS] B: 7/11/1953, Biloxi, MS
Drafted: 1976 Round 14 Den
1976 Den: 14 G. **1977** Den: 14 G; Int 1-0. **1978** Den: 16 G. **1979** Den: 16 G. **1980** Den: 16 G; Int 1-13. **1981** Den: 16 G; Int 1-1. **1982** Den: 9 G. **1983** SD: 3 G. **Total:** 104 G; Int 3-14.

LEOMONT EVANS Evans, Leomont Dozier 6'1", 202 **DB**
Col: Clemson *HS:* Abbeville [SC] B: 7/12/1974, Abbeville, SC
Drafted: 1996 Round 5 Was
1996 Was: 12 G. **1997** Was: 16 G. **1998** Was: 16 G; Int 3-77; 1 Sac. **Total:** 44 G; Int 3-77; 1 Sac.

LEON EVANS Evans, Leon 6'5", 282 **DE**
Col: Miami (Fla.) *HS:* Montgomery Blair [Silver Spring, MD]
B: 10/12/1961, Silver Spring, MD
1985 Det: 8 G. **1986** Det: 16 G; KR 1-0. **Total:** 24 G; KR 1-0.

LON EVANS Evans, Lon Worth 6'2", 223 **G-T**
Col: Texas Christian *HS:* Forth Worth Polytechnic [TX] B: 12/25/1911, Fort Worth, TX D: 12/11/1992, Fort Worth, TX
1933 GB: 12 G. **1934** GB: 11 G. **1935** GB: 11 G. **1936** GB: 12 G. **1937** GB: 11 G. **Total:** 57 G.

MIKE EVANS Evans, Michael James 6'3", 269 **DT-DE**
Col: Michigan *HS:* Cushing Acad. [Ashburnham, MA] B: 6/2/1967, St. Croix, Virgin Islands *Drafted:* 1992 Round 4 KC
1992 KC: 12 G.

JOSH EVANS Evans, Mijoshki Antwon 6'2", 283 **DT-DE**
Col: Alabama-Birmingham *HS:* Lanett West [Valley, AL] B: 9/6/1972, Langdale, AL
1995 Hou: 7 G. **1996** Hou: 8 G. **1997** Ten: 15 G; 2 Sac. **1998** Ten: 14 G; 3.5 Sac. **Total:** 44 G; 5.5 Sac.

MURRAY EVANS Evans, Murray Charles 6'1", 210 **BB-DB-LB-QB**
Col: Hardin-Simmons *HS:* Burkburnett [TX] B: 6/23/1919, Goodlettsville, TN *Drafted:* 1942 Round 6 Det
1942 Det: 10 G; Pass 17-7 41.2%, 64 3.76 1 Int; Rush 1-(-1) -1.0; Rec 2-32 16.0. **1943** Det: 9 G; Pass 5-1 20.0%, 8 1.60 2 Int; Rush 2-3 1.5; Rec 3-31 10.3. **Total:** 19 G; Pass 22-8 36.4%, 72 3.27 3 Int; Rush 3-2 0.7; Rec 5-63 12.6.

NORM EVANS Evans, Norman Earl 6'5", 250 **OT**
Col: Texas Christian *HS:* Donna [TX] B: 9/28/1942, Santa FE, NM
Drafted: 1965 Round 14 Hou
1965 Hou: 14 G; 6 Pt. **1966** Mia: 14 G. **1967** Mia: 14 G. **1968** Mia: 13 G. **1969** Mia: 13 G. **1970** Mia: 14 G. **1971** Mia: 14 G. **1972** Mia: 14 G.

1973 Mia: 14 G. **1974** Mia: 14 G. **1975** Mia: 14 G. **1976** Sea: 10 G. **1977** Sea: 13 G. **1978** Sea: 13 G. **Total:** 188 G; 6 Pt.

RAY EVANS Evans, Raymond L 6'1", 225 **OG-OT-DT**
(Sugar) *Col:* Texas-El Paso *HS:* Odessa [TX] B: 1/10/1924, Electra, TX *Drafted:* 1945 Round 22 Cle
AAFC **1949** SF-A: 10 G.

NFL **1950** SF: 12 G; KR 1-2 2.0.

RAY EVANS Evans, Raymond Richard 6'1", 195 **TB-DB**
Col: Kansas *HS:* Wyandotte [Kansas City, KS] B: 9/22/1922, Kansas City, KS *Drafted:* 1944 Round 1 ChiB
1948 Pit: Rec 7-93 13.3; PR 10-133 13.3; KR 7-122 17.4.

		Passing							
Year Team	**G**	**Att**	**Comp**	**Comp%**	**Yds**	**YPA**	**TD**	**Int**	**Rating**
1948 Pit	9	137	64	46.7	924	6.74	5	17	41.7

	Rushing				
Year Team	**Att**	**Yds**	**Avg**	**TD**	**Fum**
1948 Pit	99	343	3.5	2	9

REGGIE EVANS Evans, Reginald Leon 5'11", 201 **RB**
Col: Richmond *HS:* York [Yorktown, VA] B: 1/5/1959, Newport News, VA
1983 Was: 15 G; Rush 16-11 0.7 4 TD; KR 10-141 14.1; 24 Pt.

DICK EVANS Evans, Richard Jacob 6'3", 205 **OE-DB-DE**
(Whitey) *Col:* Iowa *HS:* DePaul Acad. [Chicago, IL] B: 5/31/1917, Chicago, IL
1940 GB: 7 G; Rec 2-40 20.0. **1941** ChiC: 7 G; Rec 3-34 11.3. **1942** ChiC: 3 G. **1943** GB: 10 G; Rec 8-71 8.9. **Total:** 27 G; Rec 13-145 11.2.

BOB EVANS Evans, Robert Delbert 6'3", 250 **DE**
Col: Texas A&M *HS:* Thorndale [TX] B: 2/9/1942, Houston, TX
Drafted: 1965 Round 18 SD
1965 Hou: 4 G.

RUSSELL EVANS Evans, Russell Allen 5'8", 165 **WR**
Col: Northeast Missouri State *HS:* Rolla [MO] B: 2/3/1965
1987 Sea: 1 G.

SCOTT EVANS Evans, Scott Allen 6'3", 261 **DE**
Col: Oklahoma *HS:* Edmond Memorial [OK] B: 3/29/1968, Cincinnati, OH *Drafted:* 1991 Round 8 Pho
1991 Pho: 1 G.

VINCE EVANS Evans, Vincent Tobias 6'2", 211 **QB**
Col: Los Angeles City Coll. CA (J.C.); USC *HS:* Ben L. Smith [Greensboro, NC] B: 6/14/1955, Greensboro, NC *Drafted:* 1977 Round 6 ChiB
1977 ChiB: KR 13-253 19.5. **Total:** KR 13-253 19.5.

		Passing							
Year Team	**G**	**Att**	**Comp**	**Comp%**	**Yds**	**YPA**	**TD**	**Int**	**Rating**
1977 ChiB	7	0	0	—	0	—	0	0	—
1978 ChiB	3	3	1	33.3	38	12.67	0	1	42.4
1979 ChiB	4	63	32	50.8	508	8.06	4	5	66.1
1980 ChiB	13	278	148	53.2	2039	7.33	11	16	66.2
1981 ChiB	16	436	195	44.7	2354	5.40	11	20	51.1
1982 ChiB	4	28	12	42.9	125	4.46	0	4	16.8
1983 ChiB	9	145	76	52.4	1108	7.64	5	7	69.0
1987 LARd	3	83	39	47.0	630	7.59	5	4	72.9
1989 LARd	1	2	2	100.0	50	25.00	0	0	118.8
1990 LARd	5	1	1	100.0	36	36.00	0	0	118.8
1991 LARd	4	14	6	42.9	127	9.07	1	2	59.8
1992 LARd	5	53	29	54.7	372	7.02	4	3	78.5
1993 LARd	8	76	45	59.2	640	8.42	3	4	77.7
1994 LARd	9	33	18	54.5	222	6.73	2	0	95.8
1995 Oak	9	175	100	57.1	1236	7.06	6	8	71.5
NFL Total	100	1390	704	50.6	9485	6.82	52	74	63.0

	Rushing				
Year Team	**Att**	**Yds**	**Avg**	**TD**	**Fum**
1977 ChiB	1	0	0.0	0	3
1978 ChiB	6	23	3.8	0	0
1979 ChiB	12	72	6.0	1	1
1980 ChiB	60	306	5.1	8	4
1981 ChiB	43	218	5.1	3	13
1982 ChiB	2	0	0.0	0	1
1983 ChiB	22	142	6.5	1	4
1987 LARd	11	144	13.1	1	0
1989 LARd	1	16	16.0	0	1
1990 LARd	1	-2	-2.0	0	0
1991 LARd	8	20	2.5	0	0
1992 LARd	11	79	7.2	0	1
1993 LARd	14	51	3.6	0	4
1994 LARd	6	24	4.0	0	2
1995 Oak	14	36	2.6	0	5
NFL Total	212	1129	5.3	14	39

MIKE EVANS Evans, William Michael 6'5", 250 **C**
Col: Boston College *HS:* North Catholic [Philadelphia, PA]
B: 8/6/1946, Philadelphia, PA *Drafted:* 1968 Round 9 Phi
1968 Phi: 6 G. **1969** Phi: 13 G. **1970** Phi: 14 G; 1 Fum. **1971** Phi: 14 G. **1972** Phi: 12 G. **1973** Phi: 14 G. **Total:** 73 G; 1 Fum.

PAUL EVANSEN Evansen, Paul Arnold 6'3", 240 **G**
(Tiny) *Col:* Oregon State *HS:* Balboa [San Francisco, CA]
B: 5/10/1922, San Francisco, CA
AAFC **1948** SF-A: 1 G.

ERIC EVERETT Everett, Eric Eugene 5'10", 165 **DB**
Col: Texas Tech *HS:* Daingerfield [TX] B: 7/13/1966, Daingerfield, TX
Drafted: 1988 Round 5 Phi
1988 Phi: 16 G; Int 1-0. **1989** Phi: 16 G; Int 4-64 1 TD; 6 Pt. **1990** TB: 16 G; Int 3-28. **1991** KC: 11 G; 1 Sac. **1992** Min: 16 G. **Total:** 75 G; Int 8-92 1 TD; 6 Pt; 1 Sac.

JIM EVERETT Everett, James Samuel III 6'5", 212 **QB**
Col: Purdue *HS:* Eldorado [Albuquerque, NM] B: 1/3/1963, Emporia, KS *Drafted:* 1986 Round 1 Hou

		Passing							
Year Team	**G**	**Att**	**Comp**	**Comp%**	**Yds**	**YPA**	**TD**	**Int**	**Rating**
1986 LARm	6	147	73	49.7	1018	6.93	8	8	67.8
1987 LARm	11	302	162	53.6	2064	6.83	10	13	68.4
1988 LARm	16	517	308	59.6	3964	7.67	**31**	18	89.2
1989 LARm	16	518	304	58.7	4310	8.32	**29**	17	90.6
1990 LARm	16	554	307	55.4	3989	7.20	23	17	79.3
1991 LARm	16	490	277	56.5	3438	7.02	11	20	68.9
1992 LARm	16	475	281	59.2	3323	7.00	22	18	80.2
1993 LARm	10	274	135	49.3	1652	6.03	8	12	59.7
1994 NO	16	540	346	64.1	3855	7.14	22	18	84.9
1995 NO	16	567	345	60.8	3970	7.00	26	14	87.0
1996 NO	15	464	267	57.5	2797	6.03	12	16	69.4
1997 SD	4	75	36	48.0	457	6.09	1	4	49.7
NFL Total	158	4923	2841	57.7	34837	7.08	203	175	78.6

	Rushing				
Year Team	**Att**	**Yds**	**Avg**	**TD**	**Fum**
1986 LARm	16	46	2.9	1	2
1987 LARm	18	83	4.6	1	2
1988 LARm	34	104	3.1	0	7
1989 LARm	25	31	1.2	1	4
1990 LARm	20	31	1.6	1	4
1991 LARm	27	44	1.6	0	**12**
1992 LARm	32	133	4.2	0	5
1993 LARm	19	38	2.0	0	7
1994 NO	15	35	2.3	0	3
1995 NO	24	42	1.8	0	6
1996 NO	22	3	0.1	0	10
1997 SD	5	6	1.2	0	2
NFL Total	257	596	2.3	4	64

MAJOR EVERETT Everett, Major Donel 5'10", 215 **RB**
Col: Mississippi College *HS:* New Hebron [MS] B: 1/4/1960, New Hebron, MS
1983 Phi: Rec 2-18 9.0; KR 14-275 19.6. **1984** Phi: KR 3-40 13.3. **1985** Phi: Rec 4-25 6.3. **1987** Cle-Atl: Rec 8-41 5.1; KR 2-33 16.5. Cle: Rec 8-41 5.1. Atl: KR 2-33 16.5. **Total:** Rec 14-84 6.0; KR 19-348 18.3.

		Rushing				
Year Team	**G**	**Att**	**Yds**	**Avg**	**TD**	**Fum**
1983 Phi	16	5	7	1.4	0	0
1984 Phi	16	0	0	—	0	0
1985 Phi	15	4	13	3.3	0	2
1986 Cle	9	12	43	3.6	0	0
1987 Cle-Atl	11	34	95	2.8	0	0
1987 Cle	4	34	95	2.8	0	0
1987 Atl	7	0	0	—	0	0
NFL Total	67	55	158	2.9	0	2

THOMAS EVERETT Everett, Thomas Gregory 5'9", 185 **DB**
Col: Baylor *HS:* Daingerfield [TX] B: 11/21/1964, Daingerfield, TX
Drafted: 1987 Round 4 Pit
1987 Pit: PR 4-22 5.5. **1994** TB: PR 2-2 1.0. **1995** TB: 1 Sac.
Total: PR 6-24 4.0; 1 Sac.

		Interceptions			
Year Team	**G**	**Int**	**Yds**	**TD**	**Fum**
1987 Pit	12	3	22	0	1
1988 Pit	14	3	31	0	0
1989 Pit	16	3	68	0	1
1990 Pit	15	3	2	0	0
1991 Pit	16	4	53	0	0
1992 Dal	11	2	28	0	0
1993 Dal	16	2	25	0	0
1994 TB	15	1	26	0	0
1995 TB	13	0	0	0	0
NFL Total	128	21	255	0	2

STEVE EVERITT Everitt, Steven Michael 6'5", 295 **C-OG**
Col: Michigan *HS:* Miami Southridge [FL] B: 8/21/1970, Miami, FL
Drafted: 1993 Round 1 Cle
1993 Cle: 16 G. **1994** Cle: 15 G. **1995** Cle: 15 G. **1996** Bal: 8 G. **1997** Phi: 16 G. **1998** Phi: 13 G. **Total:** 83 G.

WILLIAM EVERS Evers, William 5'10", 175 **DB**
Col: Florida A&M *HS:* Cairo [GA] B: 9/24/1968, Cairo, GA
1990 Atl: 2 G. **1991** Atl: 2 G. **Total:** 4 G.

DICK EVEY Evey, Richard Theodore 6'4", 245 **DT-DE-OG**
Col: Tennessee *HS:* Springfield [OH] B: 2/12/1941, State College, PA
Drafted: 1964 Round 1 ChiB
1964 ChiB: 14 G. **1965** ChiB: 14 G; Int 1-15. **1966** ChiB: 14 G. **1967** ChiB: 12 G. **1968** ChiB: 14 G; Int 1-6. **1969** ChiB: 14 G. **1970** LARm: 9 G. **1971** Det: 11 G. **Total:** 102 G; Int 2-21.

NICK EYRE Eyre, Nicholas G 6'5", 276 **OT**
Col: Brigham Young *HS:* Las Vegas [NV] B: 6/16/1959, Las Vegas, NV
Drafted: 1981 Round 4 Hou
1981 Hou: 6 G.

VILNIS EZERINS Ezerins, Vilnis Raymond 6'2", 217 **RB**
(Ezz) *Col:* Wis.-Whitewater *HS:* Union Grove [WI] B: 4/22/1944, Latvia *Drafted:* 1966 Round 8 LARm
1968 LARm: 14 G; Rush 2-2 1.0; KR 1-0.

BLAKE EZOR Ezor, Blake 5'9", 181 **RB**
Col: Taft Coll. CA (J.C.); Michigan State *HS:* Bishop Gorman [Las Vegas, NV] B: 10/11/1966, Las Vegas, NV
1990 Den: 9 G; Rush 23-81 3.5; KR 13-214 16.5; 1 Fum.

NUU FAAOLA Faaola, Sinatausilinuu 5'11", 215 **RB**
Col: Hawaii *HS:* Farrington [Honolulu, HI] B: 1/15/1964, Honolulu, HI
Drafted: 1986 Round 9 NYJ
1986 NYJ: 12 G; Rush 3-5 1.7. **1987** NYJ: 12 G; Rush 14-43 3.1 2 TD; Rec 1-16 16.0; KR 1-4 4.0; 12 Pt. **1988** NYJ: 16 G; Rush 1-13 13.0; KR 2-9 4.5. **1989** NYJ-Mia: 12 G; Rush 2-10 5.0; Rec 1-8 8.0; KR 2-30 15.0. NYJ: 2 G. Mia: 10 G; Rush 2-10 5.0; Rec 1-8 8.0; KR 2-30 15.0. **Total:** 52 G; Rush 20-71 3.6 2 TD; Rec 2-24 12.0; KR 5-43 8.6; 12 Pt.

JASON FABINI Fabini, Jason T 6'7", 312 **OT**
Col: Cincinnati *HS:* Bishop Dwenger [Fort Wayne, IN] B: 8/25/1974, Fort Wayne, IN *Drafted:* 1998 Round 4 NYJ
1998 NYJ: 16 G.

ROB FADA Fada, Robert Alan 6'2", 265 **OG**
Col: Pittsburgh *HS:* Park Hills High School [Fairborn, OH] B: 5/7/1961, Fairborn, OH *Drafted:* 1983 Round 9 ChiB
1983 ChiB: 5 G. **1984** ChiB: 14 G. **1985** KC: 5 G. **Total:** 24 G.

JULIAN FAGAN Fagan, Julian Walter III 6'3", 205 **P**
Col: Mississippi *HS:* R.H. Watkins [Laurel, MS] B: 2/21/1948, Laurel, MS *Drafted:* 1970 Round 17 Hou
1970 NO: Rush 1-(-6) -6.0. **1971** NO: Rush 1-(-17) -17.0. **1973** NYJ: Rush 2-47 23.5. **Total:** Rush 4-24 6.0.

		Punting			
Year Team	**G**	**Punts**	**Yds**	**Avg**	**Fum**
1970 NO	14	77	3269	42.5	1
1971 NO	14	77	3188	41.4	0
1972 NO	14	71	2899	40.8	1
1973 NYJ	14	74	2744	37.1	0
NFL Total	56	299	12100	40.5	2

KEVIN FAGAN Fagan, Kevin Scott 6'3", 260 **DE**
Col: Miami (Fla.) *HS:* John I. Leonard [Lake Worth, FL] B: 4/25/1963, Lake Worth, FL *Drafted:* 1986 Round 4 SF
1987 SF: 7 G; 2 Sac. **1988** SF: 14 G; 3 Sac. **1989** SF: 16 G; 7 Sac. **1990** SF: 16 G; 9.5 Sac. **1991** SF: 8 G; 2 Sac. **1992** SF: 15 G; 1 Sac. **1993** SF: 7 G; 1 Sac. **Total:** 83 G; 25.5 Sac.

CARL FAGIOLO Fagiolo, Carl 6'0", 200 **G**
Col: No College B: 4/26/1917
1944 Phi: 2 G.

JOHN FAHAY Fahay, John Lloyd 6'0", 189 **OE-BB-G**
(Big Jawn) *Col:* St. Thomas; Marquette *HS:* Humboldt [St.Paul, MN] B: 6/16/1902, Mason City, IL D: 1/8/1980, Fort Lauderdale, FL
1925 Mil: 1 G. **1926** Rac: 2 G. **1929** Min: 5 G. **Total:** 8 G.

JIM FAHNHORST Fahnhorst, James John 6'4", 230 **LB**
Col: Minnesota *HS:* St. Cloud Technical [MN] B: 11/8/1958, St. Cloud, MN *Drafted:* 1982 Round 4 Min
1984 SF: 14 G; Int 2-9. **1985** SF: 15 G. **1986** SF: 16 G; Int 4-52; 1 Sac. **1987** SF: 11 G; Int 1-0. **1988** SF: 16 G. **1989** SF: 7 G. **1990** SF: 3 G. **Total:** 82 G; Int 7-61; 1 Sac.

KEITH FAHNHORST Fahnhorst, Keith Victor 6'6", 273 **OT**
Col: Minnesota *HS:* St. Cloud Technical [MN] B: 2/6/1952, St. Cloud, MN *Drafted:* 1974 Round 2 SF
1974 SF: 14 G. **1975** SF: 14 G; Rec 1-1 1.0; KR 1-13 13.0. **1976** SF: 13 G. **1977** SF: 14 G. **1978** SF: 15 G. **1979** SF: 16 G. **1980** SF: 16 G. **1981** SF: 16 G. **1982** SF: 9 G. **1983** SF: 16 G. **1984** SF: 15 G. **1985** SF: 16 G. **1986** SF: 16 G. **1987** SF: 3 G. **Total:** 193 G; Rec 1-1 1.0; KR 1-13 13.0.

FRED FAILING Failing, Fred C 5'11", 200 **G**
Col: Central Michigan B: 6/7/1904, Caro, MI D: 9/7/1972, Green Bay, WI
1930 ChiC: 1 G.

RICHARD FAIN Fain, Richard Alexander 5'10", 183 **DB**
Col: Florida *HS:* North Fort Myers [FL] B: 2/29/1968, North Fort Myers, FL *Drafted:* 1991 Round 6 Cin
1991 Cin-Pho: 8 G; Int 1-1. Cin: 6 G; Int 1-1. Pho: 2 G. **1992** ChiB: 16 G. **Total:** 24 G; Int 1-1.

TERRY FAIR Fair, Terrance Delon 5'9", 185 **DB**
Col: Tennessee *HS:* South Mountain [Phoenix, AZ] B: 7/20/1976, Phoenix, AZ *Drafted:* 1998 Round 1 Det
1998 Det: 1 Sac.

		Punt Returns				Kickoff Returns				
Year Team	**G**	**Ret**	**Yds**	**Avg**	**TD**	**Ret**	**Yds**	**Avg**	**TD**	**Fum**
1998 Det	14	30	189	6.3	0	51	1428	**28.0**	**2**	5

BILL FAIRBAND Fairband, William Robert 6'3", 228 **LB**
Col: Colorado *HS:* Los Gatos [CA] B: 6/11/1941, Los Gatos, CA
Drafted: 1967 Round 3 Oak
1967 Oak: 7 G. **1968** Oak: 2 G. **Total:** 9 G.

DON FAIRBANKS Fairbanks, Donald Lee 6'3", 253 **DE**
Col: Colorado *HS:* Alameda [Lakewood, CO] B: 2/13/1964, Lakewood, CO
1987 Sea: 3 G.

GREG FAIRCHILD Fairchild, Gregory Thompson 6'4", 258 **OG-OT-C**
Col: Tulsa *HS:* St. Mary's [St. Louis, MO] B: 3/10/1954, St. Louis, MO
Drafted: 1976 Round 4 Cin
1976 Cin: 12 G. **1977** Cin: 13 G; KR 1-6 6.0. **1978** Cle: 2 G. **Total:** 27 G; KR 1-6 6.0.

PAUL FAIRCHILD Fairchild, Paul Jay 6'4", 270 **OG-C**
Col: Ellsworth CC IA; Kansas *HS:* Gliden-Ralston [Glidden, IA]
B: 9/14/1961, Carroll, IA *Drafted:* 1984 Round 5 NE
1984 NE: 7 G. **1985** NE: 16 G. **1986** NE: 15 G. **1987** NE: 11 G. **1988** NE: 16 G. **1989** NE: 14 G. **1990** NE: 4 G. **Total:** 83 G.

ART FAIRCLOTH Faircloth, Arthur Terman 6'0", 190 **DB-QB-HB**
Col: North Carolina State; Guilford *HS:* Anacostia [Washington, DC]
B: 7/8/1921, Richmond, VA *Drafted:* 1944 Round 17 Bos
1947 NYG: 3 G; Pass 5-3 60.0%, 30 6.00 1 TD; Rush 10-9 0.9; KR 2-62 31.0; Punt 4-159 39.8; 1 Fum. **1948** NYG: 2 G; Rush 1-(-1) -1.0; Int 3-5. **Total:** 5 G; Pass 5-3 60.0%, 30 6.00 1 TD; Rush 11-8 0.7; KR 2-62 31.0; Int 3-5; Punt 4-159 39.8; 1 Fum.

LEONARD FAIRLEY Fairley, Leonard 5'11", 200 **DB**
Col: Alcorn State *HS:* M.F. Nichols [Biloxi, MS] B: 1/2/1951, Biloxi, MS
Drafted: 1974 Round 7 Hou
1974 Hou: 2 G.

ERIC FAIRS Fairs, Eric Jerome 6'3", 240 **LB**
Col: Memphis *HS:* Northside [Memphis, TN] B: 2/17/1964, Memphis, TN
1986 Hou: 12 G. **1987** Hou: 12 G. **1988** Hou: 16 G; Scor 1 Saf; 2 Pt. **1989** Hou: 16 G; KR 1-1 1.0; 2.5 Sac. **1990** Hou: 16 G. **1991** Hou: 16 G. **1992** Atl: 2 G. **Total:** 90 G; KR 1-1 1.0; Scor 1 Saf; 2 Pt; 2.5 Sac.

DERRICK FAISON Faison, Derrick 6'4", 200 **WR**
Col: Howard *HS:* Lake City [SC] B: 8/24/1967, Lake City, SC
1990 LARm: 15 G; Rec 3-27 9.0 1 TD; 6 Pt.

EARL FAISON Faison, William Earl 6'5", 270 **DE**
Col: Indiana *HS:* Huntington [Newport News, VA] B: 1/31/1939, Newport News, VA *Drafted:* 1961 Round 1 SD
1961 SD: 14 G; Int 2-14. **1962** SD: 8 G; Int 1-30. **1963** SD: 14 G; Scor **1** 2XP; 2 Pt. **1964** SD: 14 G; Int 1-42 **1** TD; 6 Pt. **1965** SD: 14 G; Int 1-24 1 TD; 6 Pt. **1966** SD-Mia: 9 G; Int 1-26; 1 Fum. SD: 3 G. Mia: 6 G; Int 1-26; 1 Fum. **Total:** 73 G; Int 6-136 2 TD; Scor 1 2XP; 14 Pt; 1 Fum.

NELLO FALASCHI Falaschi, Nello Donald 6'0", 195 **BB-LB**
(Flash) *Col:* Santa Clara *HS:* Bellarmine Prep [San Jose, CA]
B: 3/19/1913, Dos Palos, CA D: 7/29/1986, Oakland, CA
Drafted: 1937 Round 2 Was
1938 NYG: 9 G; Pass 1-0; Rush 1-6 6.0. **1939** NYG: 11 G; Rush 1-4 4.0; Rec 4-27 6.8. **1940** NYG: 11 G; Rec 2-9 4.5; Int 1-23. **1941** NYG: 11 G; Rec 1-3 3.0; KR 2-32 16.0; Int 1-10. **Total:** 42 G; Pass 1-0; Rush 2-10 5.0; Rec 7-39 5.6; KR 2-32 16.0; Int 2-33.

GUIL FALCON Falcon, Guilford W 5'10", 220 **FB**
(Hawk) *Col:* No College *HS:* Evanston Twp. [Evanston, IL]
B: 12/15/1892, Evanston, IL D: 7/28/1982, Hollywood, FL
1920 Ham-ChiT: 15 G. Ham: 8 G. ChiT: 7 G. **1921** Ham-Can: 8 G; Rush 2 TD; 12 Pt. Ham: 1 G. Can: 7 G; Rush 2 TD; 12 Pt. **1922** Tol: 9 G; Rush 1 TD; 6 Pt. **1923** Tol: 2 G. **1924** Ham: 5 G; Rush 2 TD; 12 Pt. **1925** Ham-Akr-Roch: 10 G. Ham: 1 G. Akr: 8 G. Roch: 1 G. **Total:** 49 G; Rush 5 TD; 30 Pt.

DICK FALCON Falcon, Ray C 5′9″, 175 **G**
Col: No College *HS:* Evanston Tech [IL]; Culver Mil. Acad. [IN] B: 1896, Evanston, IL Deceased
1920 ChiT: 2 G.

TERRY FALCON Falcon, Theodore Lee 6′3″, 260 **OG-OT**
Col: Minot State; Montana *HS:* Culbertson [MT] B: 8/30/1955, Culbertson, MT *Drafted:* 1978 Round 8 NE
1978 NE: 8 G. **1979** NE: 10 G. **1980** NYG: 13 G. **Total:** 31 G.

TONY FALKENSTEIN Falkenstein, Anthony Joseph 5′10″, 205 **FB-LB-BB**
(Hawk) *Col:* St. Mary's (Cal.) *HS:* Central [Pueblo, CO] B: 2/16/1915, Pueblo, CO D: 10/9/1994, Ceres, CA *Drafted:* 1938 Round 10 GB
1943 GB: Rec 3-39 13.0; KR 2-47 23.5. **1944** Bkn-Bos: Rec 1-21 21.0. Bos: Rec 1-21 21.0. **Total:** Rec 4-60 15.0; KR 2-47 23.5.

		Rushing			
Year Team	**G**	**Att**	**Yds**	**Avg**	**TD**
1943 GB	10	58	198	3.4	1
1944 Bkn-Bos	8	4	2	0.5	0
1944 Bkn	6	3	1	0.3	0
1944 Bos	2	1	1	1.0	0
NFL Total	18	62	200	3.2	1

MICKEY FALLON Fallon, Michael William 5′9″, 175 **G-E**
Col: Muhlenberg; Syracuse *HS:* Hartford Public [CT]; Williston Northampton School [Easthampton, MA] B: 4/15/1898, Hartford, CT D: 3/21/1972, New York, NY
1922 Mil: 8 G.

MIKE FALLS Falls, Michael Lee 6′2″, 240 **OG**
Col: Minnesota *HS:* Bemidji [MN] B: 3/3/1934, Bemidji, MN *Drafted:* 1956 Round 20 NYG
1960 Dal: 11 G. **1961** Dal: 14 G. **Total:** 25 G.

GARY FAMIGLIETTI Famiglietti, Gary J 6′0″, 225 **FB-LB-HB**
Col: Boston U. *HS:* Medford [MA] B: 11/28/1913, Boston, MA D: 7/13/1986, Chicago, IL *Drafted:* 1938 Round 2 ChiB
1939 ChiB: Rec 3-72 24.0; Scor 1, 1-1 100.0% XK. **1940** ChiB: Rec 1-11 11.0; Int 4-18. **1942** ChiB: Rec 1-12 12.0; KR 1-9 9.0; Int 1-10; Scor 48, 0-1 XK. **1943** ChiB: Rec 1-10 10.0. **1944** ChiB: Rec 1-23 23.0 1 TD. **1945** ChiB: Rec 4-42 10.5; KR 1-19 19.0. **1946** Bos: Pass 1-1 100.0%, 6 6.00; Rec 1-17 17.0; Scor 24, 0-1 FG. **Total:** Pass 1-1 100.0%, 6 6.00; Rec 12-187 15.6 1 TD; KR 2-28 14.0; Int 5-28; Scor 151, 0-1 FG, 1-2 50.0% XK.

		Rushing					Tot
Year Team	**G**	**Att**	**Yds**	**Avg**	**TD**	**Fum**	**TD**
1938 ChiB	9	33	129	3.9	0	0	0
1939 ChiB	10	33	128	3.9	0	0	0
1940 ChiB	11	93	320	3.4	4	0	4
1941 ChiB	7	36	101	2.8	1	0	1
1942 ChiB	10	118	503	4.3	**8**	0	8
1943 ChiB	10	64	229	3.6	2	0	2
1944 ChiB	10	63	282	4.5	2	0	3
1945 ChiB	10	65	235	3.6	3	2	3
1946 Bos	11	23	54	2.3	4	1	4
NFL Total	88	528	1981	3.8	24	3	25

ALAN FANECA Faneca, Alan Joseph Jr. 6′4″, 322 **OG**
Col: Louisiana State *HS:* Lamar [Houston, TX] B: 12/7/1976, New Orleans, LA *Drafted:* 1998 Round 1 Pit
1998 Pit: 16 G.

CHAD FANN Fann, Chad Fitzgerald 6′3″, 252 **TE**
Col: Mississippi; Florida A&M *HS:* Jean Ribault [Jacksonville, FL] B: 6/7/1970, Jacksonville, FL
1993 Pho: 1 G. **1994** Ariz: 16 G; Rec 12-96 8.0; 1 Fum. **1995** Ariz: 16 G; Rec 5-41 8.2; 1 Fum. **1997** SF: 11 G; Rec 5-78 15.6; KR 1-0. **1998** SF: 12 G. **Total:** 56 G; Rec 22-215 9.8; KR 1-0; 2 Fum.

MIKE FANNING Fanning, Michael LaVern 6′6″, 255 **DT-DE-NT**
Col: Notre Dame *HS:* Thomas Edison [Tulsa, OK] B: 2/2/1953, Mount Clemens, MI *Drafted:* 1975 Round 1 LARm
1975 LARm: 8 G. **1976** LARm: 14 G. **1977** LARm: 14 G. **1978** LARm: 16 G. **1979** LARm: 16 G. **1980** LARm: 15 G. **1981** LARm: 16 G. **1982** LARm: 8 G; 5 Sac. **1983** Det: 14 G; Scor 1 Saf; 2 Pt; 1 Sac. **1984** Sea: 16 G; 7 Sac. **Total:** 137 G; Scor 1 Saf; 2 Pt; 13 Sac.

STAN FANNING Fanning, Stanley Lynn 6′7″, 270 **OT-DE-DT**
Col: Idaho *HS:* Pullman [WA] B: 11/22/1937, Peoria, IL D: 11/21/1995 *Drafted:* 1960 Round 11 ChiB
1960 ChiB: 12 G. **1961** ChiB: 14 G. **1962** ChiB: 4 G. **1963** LARm: 10 G. **1964** Hou-Den: 12 G. Hou: 5 G. Den: 7 G. **Total:** 52 G.

KEN FANTETTI Fantetti, Kenneth Mark 6′2″, 230 **LB**
Col: Wyoming *HS:* Gresham [OR] B: 4/7/1957, Toledo, OR *Drafted:* 1979 Round 2 Det
1979 Det: 16 G; KR 2-18 9.0. **1980** Det: 16 G; Int 1-10. **1981** Det: 16 G; Int 2-18. **1982** Det: 9 G. **1983** Det: 16 G; Int 2-0; 1 Sac. **1984** Det: 14 G; Int 1-1; 1.5 Sac. **1985** Det: 8 G. **Total:** 95 G; KR 2-18 9.0; Int 6-29; 2.5 Sac.

LEDIO FANUCCHI Fanucchi, Ledio 6′2″, 225 **OT-DT**
Col: Fresno City Coll. CA (J.C.); Fresno State *HS:* Fresno [CA] B: 3/27/1931, Fresno, CA *Drafted:* 1954 Round 22 ChiC
1954 ChiC: 12 G.

MIKE FANUCCI Fanucci, Michael Joseph 6′4″, 235 **DE**
Col: Arizona State *HS:* Dunmore [PA] B: 9/25/1949, Scranton, PA *Drafted:* 1971 Round 9 Was
1972 Was: 14 G; KR 1-15 15.0. **1973** Hou: 13 G; KR 3-40 13.3. **1974** GB: 13 G. **Total:** 40 G; KR 4-55 13.8.

CHRIS FARASOPOULOS Farasopoulos, Chris Vitos 6′0″, 210 **DB**
Col: West Valley Coll. CA (J.C.); Brigham Young *HS:* Oak Grove [San Jose, CA]; North HS [Torrance, CA] B: 7/20/1949, Athens, Greece *Drafted:* 1971 Round 3 NYJ
1972 NYJ: Int 2-48. **1973** NYJ: Int 1-1. **1974** NO: Int 1-14. **Total:** Int 4-63.

		Punt Returns				Kickoff Returns				
Year Team	**G**	**Ret**	**Yds**	**Avg**	**TD**	**Ret**	**Yds**	**Avg**	**TD**	**Fum**
1971 NYJ	14	19	155	8.2	0	25	545	21.8	0	1
1972 NYJ	13	17	179	10.5	**1**	26	627	24.1	0	1
1973 NYJ	9	14	111	7.9	0	0	0	—	0	2
1974 NO	6	3	36	12.0	0	0	0	—	0	0
NFL Total	42	53	481	9.1	1	51	1172	23.0	0	4

HAP FARBER Farber, Louis Allen Jr. 6′1″, 220 **LB**
Col: Mississippi *HS:* William B. Murrah [Jackson, MS] B: 7/1/1948, Norfolk, VA *Drafted:* 1970 Round 7 Min
1970 Min-NO: 8 G. Min: 3 G. NO: 5 G. **Total:** 8 G.

NICK FARINA Farina, Ralph Robert 5′8″, 180 **C**
Col: Villanova *HS:* Steelton [PA] B: 2/21/1905, Steelton, PA D: 9/22/1984, Harrisburg, PA
1927 Pott: 1 G.

ANDY FARKAS Farkas, Andrew Geza 5′10″, 189 **FB-DB-HB-WB**
Col: Detroit Mercy *HS:* Catholic [Toledo, OH]; U. of Detroit HS [MI] B: 5/2/1916, Clay Center, OH *Drafted:* 1938 Round 1 Was
1938 Was: Scor **1** 1XP. **1939** Was: Scor **68**, 0-1 FG, 2-3 66.7% XK. **1942** Was: Scor 39, 3-3 100.0% XK. **Total:** Scor 228, 0-1 FG, 5-6 83.3% XK, 1 1XP.

		Rushing				Receiving			
Year Team	**G**	**Att**	**Yds**	**Avg**	**TD**	**Rec**	**Yds**	**Avg**	**TD**
1938 Was	9	75	315	4.2	**6**	9	66	7.3	0
1939 Was	11	**139**	547	3.9	5	16	437	27.3	5
1940 Was	1	1	0	0.0	0	0	0	—	0
1941 Was	11	85	224	2.6	2	12	77	6.4	0
1942 Was	10	125	468	3.7	3	11	143	13.0	2
1943 Was	10	110	327	3.0	5	19	202	10.6	4
1944 Was	10	21	85	4.0	0	4	29	7.3	0
1945 Det	8	31	137	4.4	0	9	132	14.7	2
NFL Total	70	587	2103	3.6	21	80	1086	13.6	13

	Punt Returns				Kickoff Returns			
Year Team	**Ret**	**Yds**	**Avg**	**TD**	**Ret**	**Yds**	**Avg**	**TD**
1939 Was	—	—	—	0	—	—	—	**1**
1941 Was	14	152	10.9	**1**	6	105	17.5	0
1942 Was	16	219	13.7	0	4	206	51.5	**1**
1943 Was	**15**	168	11.2	0	9	279	31.0	0
1944 Was	7	91	13.0	0	11	229	20.8	0
1945 Det	7	101	14.4	0	8	165	20.6	0
NFL Total	59	731	12.4	1	38	984	25.9	2

	Interceptions				Tot
Year Team	**Int**	**Yds**	**TD**	**Fum**	**TD**
1938 Was	—	—	0	0	6
1939 Was	—	—	0	0	**11**
1940 Was	1	0	0	0	0
1941 Was	4	27	0	0	3
1942 Was	3	26	0	0	6
1943 Was	0	0	0	0	9
1944 Was	3	31	0	0	0
1945 Det	0	0	0	1	2
NFL Total	11	84	0	1	37

DALE FARLEY Farley, Dale Rice 6′3″, 225 **LB**
Col: West Virginia *HS:* Sparta [TN] B: 9/27/1949, Sparta, TN *Drafted:* 1971 Round 3 Mia
1971 Mia: 4 G. **1972** Buf: 7 G; Int 1-42. **1973** Buf: 2 G. **Total:** 13 G; Int 1-42.

JOHN FARLEY Farley, John Howard 5′10″, 202 **RB**
Col: Sacramento State *HS:* Amos Alonzo Stagg [Stockton, CA] B: 8/11/1961, Stockton, CA *Drafted:* 1984 Round 4 Cin
1984 Cin: 13 G; Rush 7-11 1.6; Rec 2-11 5.5; KR 6-93 15.5; 1 Fum.

DICK FARLEY Farley, Richard Joseph 5'11", 185 **DB**
Col: Boston U. *HS:* St. John's Prep [Danvers, MA] B: 5/30/1946, Danvers, MA *Drafted:* 1968 Round 16 SD
1968 SD: 10 G. **1969** SD: 14 G. **Total:** 24 G.

DICK FARMAN Farman, Richard George 6'0", 219 **G-LB**
Col: Washington State *HS:* Kent [WA] B: 7/26/1916, Belmond, IA *Drafted:* 1939 Round 14 Was
1939 Was: 10 G. **1940** Was: 11 G. **1941** Was: 11 G. **1942** Was: 11 G. **1943** Was: 6 G. **Total:** 49 G.

TEDDY FARMER Farmer, Clanton Carter 5'11", 175 **RB**
Col: Mount San Antonio Coll. CA (J.C.); Oregon *HS:* Bassett [La Puente, CA] B: 9/8/1953, St. Louis, MO
1978 StL: 2 G; Rush 1-4 4.0.

DAVE FARMER Farmer, David W 6'0", 205 **RB**
Col: USC *HS:* William Workman [City of Industry, CA] B: 5/20/1954, Phoenix, AZ *Drafted:* 1977 Round 11 Atl
1978 TB: 3 G.

GEORGE FARMER Farmer, George III 5'10", 175 **WR**
Col: Santa Monica Coll. CA (J.C.); Southern University *HS:* Gardena [CA] B: 12/5/1958, Los Angeles, CA *Drafted:* 1980 Round 9 LARm
1983 LARm: Rush 1-(-9) -9.0. **1987** Mia: KR 3-56 18.7. **Total:** Rush 1-(-9) -9.0; KR 3-56 18.7.

		Receiving			
Year Team	**G**	**Rec**	**Yds**	**Avg**	**TD**
1982 LARm	8	17	344	20.2	2
1983 LARm	16	40	556	13.9	5
1984 LARm	14	7	75	10.7	0
1987 Mia	1	1	5	5.0	0
NFL Total	39	65	980	15.1	7

GEORGE FARMER Farmer, George Thaxton 6'4", 214 **WR**
Col: UCLA *HS:* La Puente [CA] B: 4/19/1948, Chattanooga, TN *Drafted:* 1970 Round 3 ChiB
1971 ChiB: Rush 1-11 11.0. **1972** ChiB: Rush 2-(-13) -6.5. **1973** ChiB: Rush 1-8 8.0. **Total:** Rush 4-6 1.5.

		Receiving				
Year Team	**G**	**Rec**	**Yds**	**Avg**	**TD**	**Fum**
1970 ChiB	11	31	496	16.0	2	0
1971 ChiB	14	46	737	16.0	5	1
1972 ChiB	14	14	380	27.1	2	0
1973 ChiB	14	15	219	14.6	1	1
1974 ChiB	9	5	45	9.0	0	0
1975 ChiB-Det	8	8	118	14.8	0	0
1975 ChiB	2	2	32	16.0	0	0
1975 Det	6	6	86	14.3	0	0
NFL Total	70	119	1995	16.8	10	2

RAY FARMER Farmer, Harvey Ray 6'3", 225 **LB**
Col: Duke *HS:* R.B. Glenn [Kernersville, NC] B: 7/1/1974, White Plains, NY *Drafted:* 1996 Round 4 Phi
1996 Phi: 16 G; Int 1-0; 1 Fum; 1 Sac. **1997** Phi: 14 G; 1 Sac. **1998** Phi: 2 G. **Total:** 32 G; Int 1-0; 1 Fum; 2 Sac.

KARL FARMER Farmer, Karl Anthony 5'11", 165 **WR**
Col: Los Angeles Southwest Coll. CA (J.C.); Pittsburgh *HS:* George Washington [Los Angeles, CA] B: 8/28/1954, Oklahoma City, OK *Drafted:* 1976 Round 7 Atl
1976 Atl: 1 G; PR 1-0. **1977** Atl: 14 G; Rush 1-4 4.0; Rec 2-39 19.5; KR 21-419 20.0; 2 Fum. **1978** TB: 2 G. **Total:** 17 G; Rush 1-4 4.0; Rec 2-39 19.5; PR 1-0; KR 21-419 20.0; 2 Fum.

LONNIE FARMER Farmer, Lonnie Wayne 6'0", 220 **LB**
Col: Tennessee-Chattanooga *HS:* Steubenville [OH] B: 3/28/1940, Steubenville, OH *Drafted:* 1964 Round 20 Bos
1964 Bos: 14 G. **1965** Bos: 3 G; Int 1-16. **1966** Bos: 14 G. **Total:** 31 G; Int 1-16.

ROGER FARMER Farmer, Roger Anderson 6'3", 195 **WR**
Col: Eastern Arizona Coll. (J.C.); Baker *HS:* Thomas Jefferson [Brooklyn, NY] B: 11/10/1955, Barbados
1979 NYJ: 4 G.

TOM FARMER Farmer, Thomas Manduis 5'11", 190 **HB-DB**
Col: Iowa *HS:* Wilson [Cedar Rapids, IA] B: 4/17/1921, Cedar Rapids, IA D: 7/1/1980, Iowa City, IA *Drafted:* 1943 Round 2 Cle
1946 LARm: Pass 2-0; PR 4-40 10.0; KR 4-129 32.3. **1947** Was: KR 4-118 29.5; Int 6-27. **1948** Was: PR 4-34 8.5; KR 8-192 24.0. **Total:** Pass 2-0; PR 8-74 9.3; KR 16-439 27.4; Int 6-27.

		Rushing				Receiving					Tot
Year Team	**G**	**Att**	**Yds**	**Avg**	**TD**	**Rec**	**Yds**	**Avg**	**TD**	**Fum**	**TD**
1946 LARm	8	28	90	3.2	1	6	17	2.8	0	1	1
1947 Was	10	15	29	1.9	1	8	137	17.1	0	0	1
1948 Was	9	52	188	3.6	1	12	148	12.3	2	2	3
NFL Total	27	95	307	3.2	3	26	302	11.6	2	3	5

JOHN FARQUHAR Farquhar, John Christian Mowat 6'6", 278 **TE**
Col: Duke *HS:* Menlo [CA] B: 3/22/1972, Stanford, CA
1996 TB-Pit: 5 G. TB: 1 G. Pit: 4 G. **1997** NO: 11 G; Rec 17-253 14.9 1 TD; 6 Pt. **1998** NO: 5 G; Rec 1-13 13.0. **Total:** 21 G; Rec 18-266 14.8 1 TD; 6 Pt.

D'MARCO FARR Farr, D'Marco Marcellus 6'1", 276 **DT**
Col: Washington *HS:* John F. Kennedy [Richmond, CA] B: 6/9/1971, San Pablo, CA
1994 LARm: 10 G; KR 1-16 16.0; 1 Sac. **1995** StL: 16 G; Int 1-5; 11.5 Sac. **1996** StL: 16 G; Int 1-5; 4.5 Sac. **1997** StL: 16 G; Int 1-22; 3 Sac. **1998** StL: 16 G; 7 Sac. **Total:** 74 G; KR 1-16 16.0; Int 3-32; 27.0 Sac.

MEL FARR Farr, Melvin Jr. 6'0", 222 **RB**
Col: UCLA *HS:* Brother Rice [Birmingham, MI] B: 8/12/1966, Santa Monica, CA *Drafted:* 1988 Round 9 Den
1989 LARm: 1 G.

MEL FARR Farr, Melvin Sr. 6'2", 210 **RB**
Col: UCLA *HS:* Hebert [Beaumont, TX] B: 11/3/1944, Beaumont, TX *Drafted:* 1967 Round 1 Det
1967 Det: Pass 2-0. **1969** Det: Pass 1-0. **Total:** Pass 3-0.

		Rushing				Receiving					Tot
Year Team	**G**	**Att**	**Yds**	**Avg**	**TD**	**Rec**	**Yds**	**Avg**	**TD**	**Fum**	**TD**
1967 Det	13	206	860	4.2	3	39	317	8.1	3	7	6
1968 Det	9	128	597	4.7	3	24	375	15.6	4	2	7
1969 Det	5	58	245	4.2	4	13	94	7.2	0	2	4
1970 Det	12	166	717	4.3	9	29	213	7.3	2	5	11
1971 Det	9	22	64	2.9	0	5	60	12.0	1	0	1
1972 Det	10	62	216	3.5	3	10	132	13.2	0	0	3
1973 Det	11	97	373	3.8	4	26	183	7.0	0	3	4
NFL Total	69	739	3072	4.2	26	146	1374	9.4	10	19	36

MIKE FARR Farr, Michael Anthony 5'10", 192 **WR**
Col: UCLA *HS:* Brother Rice [Birmingham, MI] B: 8/8/1967, Santa Monica, CA

		Receiving				
Year Team	**G**	**Rec**	**Yds**	**Avg**	**TD**	**Fum**
1990 Det	12	12	170	14.2	0	0
1991 Det	16	42	431	10.3	1	1
1992 Det	14	15	115	7.7	0	0
NFL Total	42	69	716	10.4	1	1

MILLER FARR Farr, Miller Jr. 6'1", 190 **DB**
Col: Wichita State *HS:* Hebert [Beaumont, TX] B: 4/8/1943, Beaumont, TX *Drafted:* 1965 Redshirt Round 1 Den
1965 Den-SD: KR 7-123 17.6. SD: KR 7-123 17.6. **1966** SD: KR 2-54 27.0. **1967** Hou: KR 1-17 17.0. **Total:** KR 10-194 19.4.

		Interceptions		
Year Team	**G**	**Int**	**Yds**	**TD**
1965 Den-SD	10	2	22	0
1965 Den	7	2	22	0
1965 SD	3	0	0	0
1966 SD	14	3	68	0
1967 Hou	14	**10**	**264**	**3**
1968 Hou	14	3	104	**2**
1969 Hou	14	6	48	0
1970 StL	14	5	38	1
1971 StL	14	2	13	0
1972 StL	13	3	21	0
1973 Det	6	1	0	0
NFL Total	113	35	578	6

KEN FARRAGUT Farragut, Kenneth David Jr. 6'4", 240 **C-LB**
Col: Mississippi *HS:* Moss Point [MS] B: 12/23/1928, Ponchatoula, LA *Drafted:* 1951 Round 6 Phi
1951 Phi: 11 G. **1952** Phi: 12 G. **1953** Phi: 12 G. **1954** Phi: 8 G. **Total:** 43 G.

VINNIE FARRAR Farrar, Venice 5'10", 200 **G-BB-LB**
Col: North Carolina State *HS:* Rayen [Youngstown, OH] B: 12/22/1910, Youngstown, OH D: 1/1/1973, Youngstown, OH
1938 Pit: 1 G. **1939** Pit: 6 G. **Total:** 7 G.

SCRAPPER FARRELL Farrell, Edward Francis Jr. 5'9", 204 **FB-DB**
Col: Muhlenberg *HS:* Catasauqua [PA] B: 7/12/1915, Catasauqua, PA D: 4/16/1986, Lebanon, PA
1938 Pit-Bkn: Pass 2-0, 1 Int. Bkn: Pass 2-0, 1 Int. **Total:** Pass 2-0, 1 Int.

		Rushing			
Year Team	**G**	**Att**	**Yds**	**Avg**	**TD**
1938 Pit-Bkn	12	109	425	3.9	3
1938 Pit	5	46	176	3.8	0
1938 Bkn	7	63	249	4.0	3
1939 Bkn	2	0	0	—	0
NFL Total	14	109	425	3.9	3

SEAN FARRELL Farrell, Sean Ward 6′3″, 260 **OG**
Col: Penn State *HS:* Westhampton Beach [NY] B: 5/25/1960, Southampton, NY *Drafted:* 1982 Round 1 TB
1982 TB: 9 G. **1983** TB: 10 G. **1984** TB: 15 G. **1985** TB: 14 G. **1986** TB: 16 G. **1987** NE: 14 G. **1988** NE: 15 G; Rec 1-4 4.0. **1989** NE: 14 G. **1990** Den: 5 G. **1991** Den: 5 G. **1992** Sea: 6 G. **Total:** 123 G; Rec 1-4 4.0.

PAUL FARREN Farren, Paul Vincent 6′5″, 272 **OT-OG**
Col: Boston U. *HS:* Cohasset [MA] B: 12/24/1960, Weymouth, MA *Drafted:* 1983 Round 12 Cle
1983 Cle: 16 G. **1984** Cle: 15 G. **1985** Cle: 13 G. **1986** Cle: 16 G. **1987** Cle: 12 G. **1988** Cle: 15 G. **1989** Cle: 16 G. **1990** Cle: 16 G. **1991** Cle: 13 G. **Total:** 132 G.

CURT FARRIER Farrier, Curtis James 6′6″, 264 **DT**
Col: Montana State *HS:* Everett [WA] B: 6/25/1941, Yakima, WA *Drafted:* 1963 Round 10 KC
1963 KC: 5 G. **1964** KC: 14 G. **1965** KC: 8 G. **Total:** 27 G.

BO FARRINGTON Farrington, John R 6′3″, 217 **WR**
Col: Prairie View A&M *HS:* Jack Yates [Houston, TX] B: 1/18/1936, DeWalt, TX D: 7/26/1964, Rensselaer, IN *Drafted:* 1960 Round 16 ChiB
1960 ChiB: Rush 1-(-2) -2.0. **Total:** Rush 1-(-2) -2.0.

		Receiving				
Year Team	**G**	**Rec**	**Yds**	**Avg**	**TD**	**Fum**
1960 ChiB	6	0	0	—	0	0
1961 ChiB	11	21	349	16.6	4	1
1962 ChiB	14	13	197	15.2	1	0
1963 ChiB	14	21	335	16.0	2	0
NFL Total	45	55	881	16.0	7	1

JAMES FARRIOR Farrior, James Alfred Jr. 6′2″, 242 **LB**
Col: Virginia *HS:* Matoaca [Ettrick, VA] B: 1/6/1975, Richmond, VA *Drafted:* 1997 Round 1 NYJ
1997 NYJ: 16 G; 1.5 Sac. **1998** NYJ: 12 G. **Total:** 28 G; 1.5 Sac.

JOHN FARRIS Farris, John Speed 6′4″, 245 **OG**
Col: Cerritos Coll. CA (J.C.); San Diego State B: 11/2/1943, Kansas City, MO *Drafted:* 1964 Round 17 SD
1965 SD: 14 G. **1966** SD: 14 G. **Total:** 28 G.

TOM FARRIS Farris, Thomas George 6′1″, 185 **QB-DB**
Col: Wisconsin *HS:* Englewood [Chicago, IL] B: 9/16/1920, Casper, WY *Drafted:* 1942 Round 9 GB
AAFC **1948** ChiA: 13 G; Pass 9-3 33.3%, 24 2.67 3 Int; Rush 4-5 1.3.

NFL **1946** ChiB: 11 G; Pass 21-8 38.1%, 108 5.14 1 TD 2 Int; Rush 12-(-11) -0.9; Rec 1-16 16.0; PR 2-4 2.0; KR 1-27 27.0; Int 4-43; 2 Fum. **1947** ChiB: 9 G; Pass 2-0; Rush 1-(-3) -3.0; Int 1-2. **Total:** 20 G; Pass 23-8 34.8%, 108 4.70 1 TD 2 Int; Rush 13-(-14) -1.1; Rec 1-16 16.0; PR 2-4 2.0; KR 1-27 27.0; Int 5-45; 2 Fum.

BRETT FARYNIARZ Faryniarz, Brett Allen 6′3″, 230 **LB**
Col: San Diego State *HS:* Cordova [Rancho Cordova, CA] B: 7/23/1965, Carmichael, CA
1988 LARm: 15 G; 1 Sac. **1989** LARm: 16 G; 3 Sac. **1990** LARm: 16 G; 2 Sac. **1991** LARm: 12 G. **1993** SF: 2 G. **1994** Hou: 16 G. **1995** Car: 15 G. **Total:** 92 G; 6 Sac.

CHUCK FAUCETTE Faucette, Charles Jr. 6′3″, 242 **LB**
Col: Maryland *HS:* Willingboro [NJ] B: 10/7/1963, Levittown, PA *Drafted:* 1987 Round 10 NYG
1987 SD: 2 G. **1988** SD: 8 G; Int 1-2. **Total:** 10 G; Int 1-2.

MARSHALL FAULK Faulk, Marshall William 5′10″, 208 **RB**
Col: San Diego State *HS:* George Washington Carver [New Orleans, LA] B: 2/26/1973, New Orleans, LA *Drafted:* 1994 Round 1 Ind

		Rushing				Receiving					Tot
Year Team	**G**	**Att**	**Yds**	**Avg**	**TD**	**Rec**	**Yds**	**Avg**	**TD**	**Fum**	**TD**
1994 Ind	16	314	1282	4.1	11	52	522	10.0	1	5	12
1995 Ind	16	289	1078	3.7	11	56	475	8.5	3	8	14
1996 Ind	13	198	587	3.0	7	56	428	7.6	0	2	7
1997 Ind	16	264	1054	4.0	7	47	471	10.0	1	5	8
1998 Ind	16	324	1319	4.1	6	86	908	10.6	4	3	10
NFL Total	77	1389	5320	3.8	42	297	2804	9.4	9	23	51

CHRIS FAULKNER Faulkner, Christopher Alan 6′4″, 255 **TE**
Col: Florida *HS:* Hamilton Heights [Arcadia, IN] B: 4/13/1960, Tipton, IN *Drafted:* 1983 Round 4 Dal
1984 LARm: 8 G; Rec 1-6 6.0. **1985** SD: 9 G; Rec 1-12 12.0. **Total:** 17 G; Rec 2-18 9.0.

JEFF FAULKNER Faulkner, Jeffrey E 6′4″, 295 **DE**
Col: Southern University *HS:* American Senior [Hialeah, FL] B: 4/4/1964, St. Thomas, Virgin Islands
1987 KC: 3 G. **1990** Ind: 7 G; 2 Sac. **1991** Pho: 16 G; 2 Sac. **1992** Pho: 16 G; 0.5 Sac. **1993** NO-Was: 6 G; 1 Sac. NO: 1 G. Was: 5 G; 1 Sac. **1996** NYJ: 4 G. **Total:** 52 G; 5.5 Sac.

STALEY FAULKNER Faulkner, Staley 6′3″, 245 **OT**
Col: Texas *HS:* Denton [TX] B: 4/2/1941, Pampa, TX *Drafted:* 1963 Round 21 Hou
1964 Hou: 1 G.

TA'ASE FAUMUI Faumui, Ta'ase 6′3″, 278 **DE**
Col: Hawaii *HS:* Farrington [Honolulu, HI] B: 3/19/1971, Western Samoa *Drafted:* 1994 Round 4 Pit
1994 Pit: 5 G. **1995** Pit: 3 G. **Total:** 8 G.

WILSON FAUMUINA Faumuina, Wilson 6′5″, 275 **DT-DE-NT**
Col: San Jose State *HS:* Balboa [San Francisco, CA] B: 8/11/1954, American Samoa D: 9/26/1986, San Francisco, CA *Drafted:* 1977 Round 1 Atl
1977 Atl: 14 G. **1978** Atl: 16 G; Int 1-7. **1979** Atl: 14 G. **1980** Atl: 14 G. **1981** Atl: 16 G. **Total:** 74 G; Int 1-7.

CHRISTIAN FAURIA Fauria, Christian Ashley 6′4″, 245 **TE**
(Rocky) *Col:* Colorado *HS:* Crespi [Encino, CA] B: 9/22/1971, Los Angeles, CA *Drafted:* 1995 Round 2 Sea
1996 Sea: KR 1-8 8.0. **1998** Sea: KR 1-0. **Total:** KR 2-8 4.0.

		Receiving				
Year Team	**G**	**Rec**	**Yds**	**Avg**	**TD**	**Fum**
1995 Sea	14	17	181	10.6	1	0
1996 Sea	10	18	214	11.9	1	0
1997 Sea	16	10	110	11.0	0	0
1998 Sea	16	37	377	10.2	2	1
NFL Total	56	82	882	10.8	4	1

RON FAUROT Faurot, Ronald Edward 6′7″, 262 **DE-DT**
Col: Arkansas *HS:* L.D. Bell [Hurst, TX] B: 1/27/1962, Wichita, KS *Drafted:* 1984 Round 1 NYJ
1984 NYJ: 15 G; 2 Sac. **1985** NYJ: 5 G. **Total:** 20 G; 2 Sac.

FRANK FAUSCH Fausch, Franklin Leo 6′3″, 250 **FB**
(Whitey; Fox) *Col:* Kalamazoo *HS:* Benton Harbor [MI] B: 6/13/1895, Goshen, IN D: Goshen, IN
1921 Eva: 4 G; Rush 3 TD; 18 Pt. **1922** Eva: 3 G; Pass 1 TD. **Total:** 7 G; Pass 1 TD; Rush 3 TD; 18 Pt.

GEORGE FAUST Faust, George John 6′1″, 205 **BB-LB**
Col: Minnesota *HS:* North [Minneapolis, MN] B: 9/28/1917, Parkston, SD D: 5/28/1993, Edina, MN *Drafted:* 1939 Round 6 ChiC
1939 ChiC: 9 G; Pass 5-0, 1 Int; Rush 22-71 3.2; Rec 4-85 21.3; Punt 25-1101 **44.0**; Scor 1, 0-1 FG, 1-1 100.0% XK.

PAUL FAUST Faust, Paul Timothy 6′1″, 225 **LB**
Col: Minnesota *HS:* Edina [MN] B: 7/23/1943, Minneapolis, MN
1967 Min: 1 G.

DICK FAUST Faust, Richard A 6′1″, 208 **T-G-E**
Col: Otterbein *HS:* Steele [Dayton, OH] B: 1903 D: 4/15/1955
1924 Day: 1 G. **1928** Day: 7 G. **1929** Day: 6 G. **Total:** 14 G.

HAL FAVERTY Faverty, Harold Edward 6′2″, 220 **LB-DE-C**
Col: Wisconsin *HS:* Evanston Twp. [Evanston, IL] B: 9/26/1927, Hammond, IN *Drafted:* 1949 Round 15 ChiB
1952 GB: 11 G.

GREG FAVORS Favors, Gregory Bernard 6′1″, 236 **LB**
Col: Mississippi State *HS:* Southside [Atlanta, GA] B: 9/30/1974, Atlanta, GA *Drafted:* 1998 Round 4 KC
1998 KC: 16 G; 2 Sac.

BRETT FAVRE Favre, Brett Lorenzo 6′2″, 225 **QB**
(Country) *Col:* Southern Mississippi *HS:* Hancock Central [Pass Christian, MS] B: 10/10/1969, Gulfport, MS *Drafted:* 1991 Round 2 Atl
1992 GB: Rec 1-(-7) -7.0. **Total:** Rec 1-(-7) -7.0.

		Passing							
Year Team	**G**	**Att**	**Comp**	**Comp%**	**Yds**	**YPA**	**TD**	**Int**	**Rating**
1991 Atl	2	5	0	0.0	0	0.00	0	2	0.0
1992 GB	15	471	302	64.1	3227	6.85	18	13	85.3
1993 GB	16	522	318	60.9	3303	6.33	19	24	72.2
1994 GB	16	582	363	62.4	3882	6.67	33	14	90.7
1995 GB	16	570	359	63.0	**4413**	7.74	**38**	13	99.5
1996 GB	16	543	325	59.9	3899	7.18	**39**	13	95.8
1997 GB	16	513	304	59.3	3867	7.54	**35**	16	92.6
1998 GB	16	551	**347**	**63.0**	**4212**	7.64	31	23	87.8
NFL Total	113	3757	2318	61.7	26803	7.13	213	118	89.0

	Rushing				
Year Team	**Att**	**Yds**	**Avg**	**TD**	**Fum**
1992 GB	47	198	4.2	1	12
1993 GB	58	216	3.7	1	14
1994 GB	42	202	4.8	2	7
1995 GB	39	181	4.6	3	8
1996 GB	49	136	2.8	2	11
1997 GB	58	187	3.2	1	7
1998 GB	40	133	3.3	1	8
NFL Total	333	1253	3.8	11	67

CALVIN FAVRON Favron, Calvin Joseph 6′1″, 225 **LB**
Col: Southeastern Louisiana *HS:* White Castle [LA] B: 7/3/1957, New Orleans, LA *Drafted:* 1979 Round 2 StL
1979 StL: 16 G; KR 1-10 10.0. **1980** StL: 16 G. **1981** StL: 14 G; Int 1-42. **1982** StL: 4 G. **Total:** 50 G; KR 1-10 10.0; Int 1-42.

JAKE FAWCETT Fawcett, Jacob Robert 5′11″, 223 **T**
Col: Southern Methodist *HS:* Hillsboro [TX] B: 5/29/1919, Hillsboro, TX D: 6/1979, San Antonio, TX
1942 Cle: 10 G. **1943** Bkn: 10 G. **1944** Cle: 10 G; Rec 1-9 9.0; KR 2-2 1.0. **1946** LARm: 4 G; Int 1-5. **Total:** 34 G; Rec 1-9 9.0; KR 2-2 1.0; Int 1-5.

JOHN FAYLOR Faylor, John Joseph 6′1″, 197 **DB**
Col: Santa Clara *HS:* Archbishop Mitty [San Jose, CA] B: 2/10/1963, South Bend, IN
1987 SF: 3 G.

RON FAZIO Fazio, Ronald Anthony 6′4″, 242 **TE**
Col: Maryland *HS:* Willingboro [NJ] B: 6/5/1962, Meadowbrook, PA
1987 Phi: 1 G.

RICKY FEACHER Feacher, Ivory Ricky 5′10″, 174 **WR**
Col: Mississippi Valley State *HS:* Hernando [Brooksville, FL] B: 2/11/1954, Crystal River, FL *Drafted:* 1976 Round 10 NE
1976 NE-Cle: PR 13-142 10.9. Cle: PR 13-142 10.9. **1977** Cle: PR 2-15 7.5. **1979** Cle: Rush 1-(-1) -1.0. **1981** Cle: Rush 1-(-1) -1.0. **Total:** Rush 2-(-2) -1.0; PR 15-157 10.5.

		Receiving				Kickoff Returns				
Year Team	**G**	**Rec**	**Yds**	**Avg**	**TD**	**Ret**	**Yds**	**Avg**	**TD**	**Fum**
1976 NE-Cle	13	2	38	19.0	0	24	551	23.0	0	3
1976 NE	3	2	38	19.0	0	10	240	24.0	0	0
1976 Cle	10	0	0	—	0	14	311	22.2	0	3
1977 Cle	14	0	0	—	0	11	219	19.9	0	2
1978 Cle	16	4	76	19.0	0	0	0	—	0	0
1979 Cle	16	7	103	14.7	1	2	51	25.5	0	1
1980 Cle	16	10	244	24.4	4	0	0	—	0	0
1981 Cle	16	29	654	22.6	3	0	0	—	0	0
1982 Cle	9	28	408	14.6	3	0	0	—	0	0
1983 Cle	9	13	217	16.7	3	0	0	—	0	1
1984 Cle	16	22	382	17.4	1	0	0	—	0	0
NFL Total	125	115	2122	18.5	15	37	821	22.2	0	7

WILEY FEAGIN Feagin, Thomas Wiley 6′2″, 235 **OG**
Col: Texas; Houston *HS:* Conroe [TX] B: 8/28/1937, Conroe, TX
1961 Bal: 14 G. **1962** Bal: 14 G. **1963** Was: 2 G. **Total:** 30 G.

JEFF FEAGLES Feagles, Jeffrey Allan 6′1″, 202 **P**
Col: Scottsdale CC AZ; Miami (Fla.) *HS:* Gerard Catholic [Phoenix, AZ] B: 3/7/1966, Anaheim, CA
1988 NE: Rush 1-0. **1989** NE: Pass 2-0. **1990** Phi: Pass 1-0; Rush 2-3 1.5. **1991** Phi: Rush 3-(-1) -0.3. **1993** Phi: Rush 2-6 3.0. **1994** Ariz: Rush 2-8 4.0. **1995** Ariz: Rush 2-4 2.0. **1996** Ariz: Rush 1-0. **Total:** Pass 3-0; Rush 13-20 1.5.

		Punting			
Year Team	**G**	**Punts**	**Yds**	**Avg**	**Fum**
1988 NE	16	91	3482	38.3	0
1989 NE	16	63	2392	38.0	1
1990 Phi	16	72	3026	42.0	0
1991 Phi	16	**87**	3640	41.8	1
1992 Phi	16	82	3459	42.2	0
1993 Phi	16	83	3323	40.0	0
1994 Ariz	16	**98**	3997	40.8	0
1995 Ariz	16	72	3150	43.8	1
1996 Ariz	16	76	3328	43.8	1
1997 Ariz	16	91	4028	44.3	1
1998 Sea	16	81	3568	44.0	0
NFL Total	176	896	37393	41.7	5

TOM FEAMSTER Feamster, Thomas Ofey 6′7″, 260 **OT-DE**
Col: William & Mary; Florida State *HS:* Warwick [Newport News, VA] B: 10/23/1930, Warwick, VA *Drafted:* 1955 Round 4 LARm
1956 Bal: 12 G; Scor 24, 0-3 FG, 24-26 92.3% XK.

TOM FEARS Fears, Thomas Jesse 6′2″, 216 **OE**
Col: Santa Clara; UCLA *HS:* Manual Arts [Los Angeles, CA] B: 12/3/1923, Los Angeles, CA *Drafted:* 1945 Round 11 Cle *HOF:* 1970
1948 LARm: Rush 2-8 4.0; Int 2-37 1 TD. **1949** LARm: Rush 1-(-3) -3.0. **1951** LARm: Scor 24, 6-7 85.7% XK. **1952** LARm: Rush 1-0. **1953** LARm: Scor 32, 1-1 100.0% FG, 5-6 83.3% XK. **1954** LARm: Rush 1-10 10.0; Scor 19, 1-1 100.0% XK. **1955** LARm: Scor 12, 0-3 FG. **Total:** Rush 5-15 3.0; Int 2-37 1 TD; Scor 249, 1-4 25.0% FG, 12-14 85.7% XK.

		Receiving					Tot
Year Team	**G**	**Rec**	**Yds**	**Avg**	**TD**	**Fum**	**TD**
1948 LARm	12	**51**	698	13.7	4	0	5
1949 LARm	12	**77**	1013	13.2	**9**	0	9
1950 LARm	12	**84**	**1116**	13.3	7	3	7
1951 LARm	7	32	528	16.5	3	0	3
1952 LARm	12	48	600	12.5	6	0	6
1953 LARm	8	23	278	12.1	4	1	4
1954 LARm	10	36	546	15.2	3	0	3
1955 LARm	12	44	569	12.9	2	0	2
1956 LARm	2	5	49	9.8	0	0	0
NFL Total	87	400	5397	13.5	38	4	39

WILLIE FEARS Fears, Willie Bert Jr. 6′3″, 278 **DE**
Col: Holmes CC MS; Northwestern State-Louisiana *HS:* Barton [AR] B: 6/4/1964, Chicago, IL
1987 Cin: 3 G. **1990** Min: 2 G. **Total:** 5 G.

GRANT FEASEL Feasel, Grant Earl 6′7″, 278 **C**
Col: Abilene Christian *HS:* Barstow [CA] B: 6/28/1960, Barstow, CA *Drafted:* 1983 Round 6 Bal
1983 Bal: 11 G. **1984** Ind-Min: 15 G. Ind: 6 G. Min: 9 G. **1987** Sea: 12 G; 1 Fum. **1988** Sea: 16 G; 1 Fum. **1989** Sea: 16 G; Rec 1-5 5.0. **1990** Sea: 16 G. **1991** Sea: 15 G. **1992** Sea: 16 G. **Total:** 117 G; Rec 1-5 5.0; 2 Fum.

GREG FEASEL Feasel, Gregory Duane 6′7″, 300 **OT**
Col: Barstow Coll. CA (J.C.); Abilene Christian *HS:* Barstow [CA] B: 11/7/1958, Barstow, CA
1986 GB: 15 G. **1987** SD: 3 G. **Total:** 18 G.

BILL FEASTER Feaster, William George Jr. 6′0″, 205 **T-C**
(Vin) *Col:* Fordham *HS:* North Plainfield [NJ]; St. Benedict's Prep [Newark, NJ] B: 1904 D: 12/11/1950, Plainfield, NJ
1929 Ora: 12 G. **1930** Nwk: 10 G. **Total:** 22 G.

TINY FEATHER Feather, Elwin Elton 6′0″, 197 **DB-FB-BB-WB**
Col: Kansas State B: 2/23/1902
1928 Det: Rec 1 TD. **1929** NYG: Rec 1 TD; Int **1** TD. **1931** SI-NYG: Pass 1 TD. NYG: Pass 1 TD. **1932** NYG: Pass 5-1 20.0%, 15 3.00 1 Int; Rec 2-15 7.5. **1933** NYG: Rec 2-38 19.0. **1934** Cin: Rec 3-26 8.7. **Total:** Pass 5-1 20.0%, 15 3.00 1 TD 1 Int; Rec 7-79 11.3 2 TD; Int 1 TD.

		Rushing				Tot
Year Team	**G**	**Att**	**Yds**	**Avg**	**TD**	**TD**
1927 Cle	11	—	—	—	0	0
1928 Det	10	—	—	—	**6**	7
1929 NYG	15	—	—	—	1	3
1930 NYG	15	—	—	—	1	1
1931 SI-NYG	12	—	—	—	0	0
1931 SI	10	—	—	—	0	0
1931 NYG	2	—	—	—	0	0
1932 NYG	9	28	47	1.7	0	0
1933 NYG	9	2	4	2.0	0	0
1934 Cin	5	0	0	—	0	0
NFL Total	86	30	51	1.7	8	11

BEATTIE FEATHERS Feathers, William Beattie 5′10″, 185 **HB-DB**
(Big Chief) *Col:* Tennessee *HS:* Bristol [VA] B: 8/4/1908, Bristol, VA D: 3/10/1979, Winston-Salem, NC
1934 ChiB: Pass 12-4 33.3%, 41 3.42 2 TD 2 Int; Rec 6-174 29.0 1 TD; Scor **1** 1XP. **1935** ChiB: Pass 14-5 35.7%, 53 3.79 1 TD 2 Int; Rec 3-18 6.0. **1936** ChiB: Pass 11-1 9.1%, 10 0.91 1 TD 2 Int; Rec 2-5 2.5. **1937** ChiB: Pass 6-2 33.3%, 12 2.00. **1938** Bkn: Rec 3-34 11.3. **1939** Bkn: Rec 1-12 12.0. **Total:** Pass 43-12 27.9%, 116 2.70 4 TD 6 Int; Rec 15-243 16.2 1 TD; Scor 1 1XP.

		Rushing				Tot
Year Team	**G**	**Att**	**Yds**	**Avg**	**TD**	**TD**
1934 ChiB	11	119	**1004**	**8.4**	**8**	**9**
1935 ChiB	8	56	281	5.0	3	3
1936 ChiB	12	97	350	3.6	2	2
1937 ChiB	11	66	211	3.2	1	1
1938 Bkn	7	28	94	3.4	2	2
1939 Bkn	4	8	21	2.6	0	0
1940 GB	1	4	19	4.8	0	0
NFL Total	54	378	1980	5.2	16	17

CREIG FEDERICO Federico, Creig Ronald 6′2″, 205 **DB**
Col: Central Coll. (Iowa); Illinois State *HS:* James B. Conant [Hoffman Estates, IL] B: 5/7/1963, Chicago, IL
1987 Det: 3 G; 1 Sac.

JOHN FEDEROVITCH Federovitch, John Lawrence 6′5″, 261 **T**
(Ace) *Col:* Davis & Elkins *HS:* Redstone [PA] B: 6/26/1917, Wyano, PA *Drafted:* 1941 Round 7 ChiB
1941 ChiB: 11 G; Int 1-8. **1946** ChiB: 3 G. **Total:** 14 G; Int 1-8.

JOE FEDERSPIEL Federspiel, Joseph Michael 6′1″, 230 **LB**
Col: Kentucky *HS:* DeSales [Louisville, KY] B: 5/6/1950, Louisville, KY *Drafted:* 1972 Round 4 NO
1972 NO: 14 G. **1973** NO: 13 G; Int 1-1. **1974** NO: 14 G; KR 2-20 10.0; Int 1-9. **1975** NO: 14 G. **1976** NO: 14 G. **1977** NO: 14 G. **1978** NO: 16 G; Int 2-12. **1979** NO: 16 G; Int 1-4. **1980** NO: 15 G. **1981** Bal: 11 G. **Total:** 141 G; KR 2-20 10.0; Int 5-26.

WALT FEDORA Fedora, Walter Jack 6′1″, 190 **FB-DB**
Col: George Washington *HS:* Stephen Decatur [Decatur, IL] B: 9/15/1918, Decatur, IL D: 9/1968 *Drafted:* 1942 Round 20 Bkn
1942 Bkn: 8 G; Rush 16-34 2.1; KR 4-75 18.8.

GERRY FEEHERY Feehery, Gerald 6'2", 268 C-OG
Col: Syracuse *HS:* Cardinal O'Hara [Springfield, PA] B: 3/9/1960, Philadelphia, PA
1983 Phi: 2 G. **1984** Phi: 6 G. **1985** Phi: 15 G. **1986** Phi: 6 G. **1987** Phi: 12 G. **1988** KC: 6 G. **Total:** 47 G.

AL FEENEY Feeney, Albert George 6'0", 210 C
Col: Notre Dame *HS:* Emmerich Manual Training [Indianapolis, IN] B: 11/12/1891, Indianapolis, IN D: 11/12/1950, Indianapolis, IN
1920 Can: 11 G. **1921** Can: 8 G; Scor 6, 6 XK. **Total:** 19 G.

HOWARD FEGGINS Feggins, Howard Anthony 5'10", 190 DB
Col: North Carolina *HS:* Park View [South Hill, VA] B: 5/6/1965, South Hill, VA
1989 NE: 11 G; Int 1-4.

NICK FEHER Feher, Nicholas John 6'0", 224 OG
Col: Georgia *HS:* North [Youngstown, OH] B: 7/13/1926, Youngstown, OH D: 12/28/1992, Kingman, AZ *Drafted:* 1951 Round 10 SF
1951 SF: 12 G. **1952** SF: 6 G. **1953** SF: 10 G. **1954** SF: 12 G. **1955** Pit: 2 G. **Total:** 42 G.

BERNIE FEIBISH Feibish, Bernard 6'2", 223 C-LB
Col: New York U. *HS:* New Utrecht [Brooklyn, NY] B: 1918 Deceased
1941 Phi: 3 G; Int 1-9.

ANDY FEICHTINGER Feichtinger, Andrew Joseph 5'10", 170 OE
Col: No College *HS:* None B: 11/16/1897, Salem, OR D: 12/1962, OR
1920 Sta: 4 G.

LOU FEIST Feist, Louis 6'1", 200 E-T-FB
Col: Columbia; Canisius *HS:* Lafayette [Buffalo, NY] B: 1903 D: 11/12/1926, Buffalo, NY
1924 Buf: 10 G. **1925** Buf: 7 G. **1926** Buf: 5 G. **Total:** 22 G.

GENE FEKETE Fekete, Eugene H 6'0", 195 FB-LB
Col: Ohio State *HS:* Findley [OH] B: 8/31/1922, Sugar Creek, OH
AAFC **1946** CleA: Rec 1-2 2.0; KR 1-21 21.0.

		Rushing			
Year Team	**G**	**Att**	**Yds**	**Avg**	**TD**
1946 CleA	6	26	106	4.1	1

JOHN FEKETE Fekete, John Michael 5'11", 200 HB-DB
Col: Ohio U. *HS:* Findley [OH] B: 10/28/1919, Morgantown, WV D: 7/26/1988, Cleveland, OH
AAFC **1946** BufA: 3 G; Rush 1-(-1) -1.0.

NIP FELBER Felber, Frederick Emmett 6'2", 190 OE-DE
Col: North Dakota *HS:* Fairmont [MN] B: 3/25/1909, Le Seuer, MN D: 5/1978, Minot, SD
1932 Bos: 10 G. **1933** Phi: 1 G; Rec 1-8 8.0. **Total:** 11 G; Rec 1-8 8.0.

BILL FELDHAUS Feldhaus, William Bernard 6'0", 226 G-LB-T
(Butch) *Col:* Cincinnati *HS:* Hughes [Cincinnati, OH] B: 12/8/1912, Cincinnati, OH D: 6/2/1974, Cincinnati, OH
1937 Det: 11 G. **1938** Det: 11 G. **1939** Det: 10 G. **1940** Det: 11 G; Int 1-10. **Total:** 43 G; Int 1-10.

PAUL FELDHAUSEN Feldhausen, Paul Elvie 6'6", 260 OT
Col: Northland CC MN *HS:* Iron Mountain [MI] B: 6/14/1946, Madison, WI *Drafted:* 1968 Round 11 Bos
1968 Bos: 2 G.

TODD FELDMAN Feldman, Todd Mitchell 5'10", 184 WR
Col: Kent State *HS:* Haverford [Havertown, PA] B: 8/7/1962, Philadelphia, PA
1987 Mia: 1 G.

GENE FELKER Felker, Eugene Marvin 6'1", 198 OE
Col: Wisconsin *HS:* North Division [Milwaukee, WI] B: 3/4/1929, Milwaukee, WI *Drafted:* 1952 Round 19 Dal
1952 Dal: 6 G; Rec 6-63 10.5 1 TD; 6 Pt.

HAPPY FELLER Feller, James Patrick 5'11", 185 K
Col: Texas *HS:* Fredericksburg [TX] B: 6/13/1949, Fredericksburg, TX *Drafted:* 1971 Round 4 Phi
1971 Phi: 9 G; Scor 28, 6-20 30.0% FG, 10-10 100.0% XK. **1972** NO: 6 G; Scor 28, 6-11 54.5% FG, 10-11 90.9% XK. **1973** NO: 6 G; Scor 19, 4-12 33.3% FG, 7-7 100.0% XK. **Total:** 21 G; Scor 75, 16-43 37.2% FG, 27-28 96.4% XK.

MARK FELLOWS Fellows, Charles Mark 6'1", 233 LB
Col: Montana State *HS:* Choteau [MT] B: 2/26/1963, Billings, MT *Drafted:* 1985 Round 7 SD
1985 SD: 2 G. **1986** SD: 1 G. **Total:** 3 G.

RON FELLOWS Fellows, Ronald Lee 6'0", 178 DB
Col: Butler County CC KS; Missouri *HS:* Michael Washington [South Bend, IN] B: 11/7/1958, South Bend, IN *Drafted:* 1981 Round 7 Dal

		Punt Returns				Kickoff Returns			
Year Team	**G**	**Ret**	**Yds**	**Avg**	**TD**	**Ret**	**Yds**	**Avg**	**TD**
1981 Dal	16	11	44	4.0	0	8	170	21.3	0
1982 Dal	9	25	189	7.6	0	16	359	22.4	0
1983 Dal	16	10	75	7.5	0	43	855	19.9	0
1984 Dal	16	0	0	—	0	6	94	15.7	0
1985 Dal	13	0	0	—	0	0	0	—	0
1986 Dal	16	0	0	—	0	0	0	—	0
1987 LARd	12	2	19	9.5	0	0	0	—	0
1988 LARd	14	0	0	—	0	0	0	—	0
NFL Total	112	48	327	6.8	0	73	1478	20.2	0

	Interceptions				Tot
Year Team	**Int**	**Yds**	**TD**	**Fum**	**TD**
1982 Dal	0	0	0	3	0
1983 Dal	5	139	1	4	2
1984 Dal	3	3	0	3	0
1985 Dal	4	52	0	0	0
1986 Dal	5	46	1	0	1
1988 LARd	2	14	0	0	0
NFL Total	19	254	2	10	3

DICK FELT Felt, Richard George 6'1", 185 DB
Col: Brigham Young *HS:* Lehi [UT] B: 3/4/1933, Lehi, UT

		Interceptions		
Year Team	**G**	**Int**	**Yds**	**TD**
1960 NYT	14	2	7	0
1961 NYT	14	4	88	1
1962 Bos	14	5	73	0
1963 Bos	14	3	81	0
1964 Bos	9	2	10	0
1965 Bos	1	0	0	0
1966 Bos	14	2	35	0
NFL Total	80	18	294	1

ERIC FELTON Felton, Eric Norman 6'0", 200 DB
Col: Texas Tech *HS:* Lubbock [TX] B: 10/8/1955, Austin, TX *Drafted:* 1978 Round 5 NO
1978 NO: 16 G; Int 1-0. **1979** NO: 13 G; Int 4-53. **1980** NYG: 6 G. **Total:** 35 G; Int 5-53.

JOE FELTON Felton, Joseph James 6'2", 266 OG
Col: Albion *HS:* Bridgeport [Saginaw, MI] B: 10/16/1964, Saginaw, MI
1987 Det: 2 G.

RALPH FELTON Felton, Ralph Dwain 5'11", 210 LB-FB
Col: Maryland *HS:* Midway [PA] B: 5/21/1932, Midway, PA *Drafted:* 1954 Round 4 Was
1954 Was: 12 G; Rush 3-8 2.7; PR 1-0; KR 2-18 9.0; Int 2-7; Scor 19, 1-2 50.0% FG, 16-17 94.1% XK. **1955** Was: 12 G; PR 1-5 5.0; KR 1-12 12.0; 1 Fum. **1956** Was: 7 G. **1957** Was: 12 G; Int 1-6. **1958** Was: 8 G. **1959** Was: 12 G; Int 2-6. **1960** Was: 12 G. **1961** Buf: 14 G; Int 2-15. **1962** Buf: 4 G; Int 0-1; Scor 0-1 XK. **Total:** 93 G; Rush 3-8 2.7; PR 2-5 2.5; KR 3-30 10.0; Int 7-35; Scor 19, 1-2 50.0% FG, 16-18 88.9% XK; 1 Fum.

BOBBY FELTS Felts, Bobby 6'2", 202 HB
Col: Florida A&M *HS:* Miami Northwestern [FL] B: 6/26/1942, Miami, FL *Drafted:* 1965 Round 6 Bal
1965 Bal-Det: Pass 1-0; Rec 3-28 9.3; PR 3-27 9.0. Det: Pass 1-0; Rec 3-28 9.3; PR 3-27 9.0. **1966** Det: Rec 2-1 0.5; PR 2-20 10.0. **1967** Det: PR 1-(-1) -1.0. **Total:** Pass 1-0; Rec 5-29 5.8; PR 6-46 7.7.

		Rushing				Kickoff Returns				
Year Team	**G**	**Att**	**Yds**	**Avg**	**TD**	**Ret**	**Yds**	**Avg**	**TD**	**Fum**
1965 Bal-Det	14	22	58	2.6	0	18	422	23.4	0	3
1965 Bal	7	2	0	0.0	0	10	193	19.3	0	2
1965 Det	7	20	58	2.9	0	8	229	28.6	0	1
1966 Det	10	34	83	2.4	2	20	392	19.6	0	2
1967 Det	14	10	66	6.6	0	0	0	—	0	1
NFL Total	38	66	207	3.1	2	38	814	21.4	0	6

TOM FENA Fena, Thomas Mitchell 5'11", 200 G
Col: Denver *HS:* St. Mary's Prep [Berkeley, CA] B: 12/27/1909, Cleveland, OH D: 9/7/1985, Burlingame, CA
1937 Det: 2 G.

GARY FENCIK Fencik, John Gary 6'1", 194 DB
Col: Yale *HS:* Barrington [IL] B: 6/11/1954, Chicago, IL *Drafted:* 1976 Round 10 Mia
1984 ChiB: 1 Sac. **1986** ChiB: 1 Sac. **Total:** 2 Sac.

		Interceptions			
Year Team	**G**	**Int**	**Yds**	**TD**	**Fum**
1976 ChiB	13	0	0	0	0
1977 ChiB	14	4	33	0	0
1978 ChiB	16	4	77	0	0
1979 ChiB	14	6	31	0	0
1980 ChiB	15	1	8	0	0

1981 ChiB	16	6	121	1	0
1982 ChiB	9	2	2	0	0
1983 ChiB	7	2	34	0	0
1984 ChiB	16	5	102	0	1
1985 ChiB	16	5	43	0	0
1986 ChiB	16	3	37	0	0
1987 ChiB	12	0	0	0	0
NFL Total	164	38	488	1	1

DICK FENCL Fencl, Richard John 5′11″, 160 **OE-DE**
Col: Northwestern *HS:* St. Philip [Chicago, IL] B: 2/24/1909, Chicago, IL D: 6/25/1972, Chicago, IL
1933 Phi: 5 G; Rec 1-20 20.0.

CHUCK FENENBOCK Fenenbock, Charles Bernard 5′9″, 174 **TB-HB-DB-WB**
Col: UCLA *HS:* Pittsburg [CA] B: 8/28/1917, Oakland, CA
AAFC **1946** LA-A: Pass 1-0. **1947** LA-A: Pass 7-1 14.3%, 7 1.00 2 Int. **1948** LA-A-ChiA: Pass 15-4 26.7%, 136 9.07 2 TD 1 Int. **Total:** Pass 23-5 21.7%, 143 6.22 2 TD 3 Int.

		Rushing				Receiving			
Year Team	G	Att	Yds	Avg	TD	Rec	Yds	Avg	TD
1946 LA-A	13	50	420	8.4	3	11	67	6.1	0
1947 LA-A	14	58	185	3.2	3	20	276	13.8	2
1948 LA-A-ChiA	14	43	174	4.0	0	8	111	13.9	1
AAFC Total	41	151	779	5.2	6	39	454	11.6	3

	Punt Returns				Kickoff Returns				Tot
Year Team	Ret	Yds	Avg	TD	Ret	Yds	Avg	TD	TD
1946 LA-A	16	299	18.7	0	17	479	28.2	1	4
1947 LA-A	17	210	12.4	0	18	452	25.1	0	6
1948 LA-A-ChiA	17	169	9.9	0	14	311	22.2	0	1
AAFC Total	50	678	13.6	0	49	1242	25.3	1	11

NFL **1943** Det: Rec 5-45 9.0 1 TD; PR 6-54 9.0; KR 11-224 20.4; Int 1-28; Punt 4-184 46.0. **1945** Det: Rec 1-24 24.0; PR 5-69 13.8; KR 7-192 27.4; Int 1-10; Punt 29-1081 37.3; **1** Fum TD. **Total:** Rec 6-69 11.5 1 TD; PR 11-123 11.2; KR 18-416 23.1; Int 2-38; Punt 33-1265 38.3; 1 Fum TD.

		Passing							
Year Team	G	Att	Comp	Comp%	Yds	YPA	TD	Int	Rating
1943 Det	10	58	20	34.5	338	5.83	3	9	32.8
1945 Det	10	110	45	40.9	754	6.85	7	11	46.4
NFL Total	20	168	65	38.7	1092	6.50	10	20	41.7

	Rushing					Tot
Year Team	Att	Yds	Avg	TD	Fum	TD
1943 Det	46	180	3.9	0	0	1
1945 Det	72	143	2.0	1	5	2
NFL Total	118	323	2.7	1	5	3

GILL FENERTY Fenerty, Lawrence Gill 6′0″, 205 **RB**
Col: Holy Cross *HS:* Jesuit [New Orleans, LA] B: 8/24/1963, New Orleans, LA *Drafted:* 1986 Round 7 NO
1991 NO: PR 12-55 4.6. **Total:** PR 12-55 4.6.

		Rushing				Receiving			
Year Team	G	Att	Yds	Avg	TD	Rec	Yds	Avg	TD
1990 NO	15	73	355	4.9	2	18	209	11.6	0
1991 NO	16	139	477	3.4	3	26	235	9.0	2
NFL Total	31	212	832	3.9	5	44	444	10.1	2

	Kickoff Returns					Tot
Year Team	Ret	Yds	Avg	TD	Fum	TD
1990 NO	28	572	20.4	0	4	2
1991 NO	2	28	14.0	0	1	5
NFL Total	30	600	20.0	0	5	7

BOB FENIMORE Fenimore, Robert Dale 6′1″, 195 **HB-DB**
(The Blond Blizz) *Col:* Oklahoma State *HS:* Woodward [OK] B: 10/6/1925, Woodward, OK *Drafted:* 1947 Round 1 ChiB
1947 ChiB: Pass 3-2 66.7%, 27 9.00; Rec 15-219 14.6 2 TD; PR 2-16 8.0; Int 2-83.

		Rushing					Tot
Year Team	G	Att	Yds	Avg	TD	Fum	TD
1947 ChiB	10	53	189	3.6	1	4	3

CARL FENNEMA Fennema, Carl H 6′2″, 210 **C-LB**
Col: Compton CC CA; Washington *HS:* Woodrow Wilson [Long Beach, CA] B: 10/17/1926, San Francisco, CA
1948 NYG: 8 G; 6 Pt. **1949** NYG: 3 G. **Total:** 11 G; 6 Pt.

DERRICK FENNER Fenner, Derrick Steven 5′11″, 240 **RB**
Col: Gardner-Webb; North Carolina *HS:* Oxon Hill [MD] B: 4/6/1967, Washington, DC *Drafted:* 1989 Round 10 Sea
1992 Cin: KR 2-38 19.0. **Total:** KR 2-38 19.0.

		Rushing				Receiving					Tot
Year Team	G	Att	Yds	Avg	TD	Rec	Yds	Avg	TD	Fum	TD
1989 Sea	5	11	41	3.7	1	3	23	7.7	0	0	1
1990 Sea	16	215	859	4.0	**14**	17	143	8.4	1	3	15
1991 Sea	11	91	267	2.9	4	11	72	6.5	0	2	4
1992 Cin	16	112	500	4.5	7	7	41	5.9	1	1	8
1993 Cin	15	121	482	4.0	1	48	427	8.9	0	1	1
1994 Cin	16	141	468	3.3	1	36	276	7.7	1	6	2
1995 Oak	16	39	110	2.8	0	35	252	7.2	3	2	3
1996 Oak	16	67	245	3.7	4	31	252	8.1	4	0	8
1997 Oak	9	7	24	3.4	0	14	92	6.6	0	1	0
NFL Total	120	804	2996	3.7	32	202	1578	7.8	10	16	42

LANE FENNER Fenner, Lane Bryce 6′5″, 210 **WR**
Col: Florida State *HS:* North [Evansville, IN] B: 12/7/1945, Evansville, IN *Drafted:* 1968 Round 7 SD
1968 SD: 11 G.

HAROLD FENNER Fenner, Leonard Harold 5′10″, 171 **OE**
Col: No College *HS:* Stivers [Dayton, OH] B: 11/10/1895, Hillsboro, OH D: 4/1/1963, Cicinnati, OH
1920 Day: 8 G. **1921** Day: 8 G. **1922** Day: 6 G; Scor 3, 1 FG. **1923** Day: 5 G. **1924** Day: 7 G; Rec 1 TD; 6 Pt. **1925** Day: 8 G. **1926** Day: 6 G. **1927** Day: 6 G. **1929** Day: 6 G. **1930** Port: 1 G. **Total:** 61 G; Rec 1 TD; Scor 9, 1 FG.

RICK FENNEY Fenney, Ricky Dale 6′1″, 235 **RB**
Col: Washington *HS:* Snohomish [WA] B: 12/7/1964, Everett, WA *Drafted:* 1987 Round 8 Min
1989 Min: KR 1-12 12.0. **Total:** KR 1-12 12.0.

		Rushing				Receiving					Tot
Year Team	G	Att	Yds	Avg	TD	Rec	Yds	Avg	TD	Fum	TD
1987 Min	11	42	174	4.1	2	7	27	3.9	0	0	2
1988 Min	13	55	271	4.9	3	15	224	14.9	0	0	3
1989 Min	16	151	588	3.9	4	30	254	8.5	2	4	6
1990 Min	12	87	376	4.3	2	17	112	6.6	0	3	2
1991 Min	11	23	99	4.3	0	2	11	5.5	0	0	0
NFL Total	63	358	1508	4.2	11	71	628	8.8	2	7	13

DUKE FERGERSON Fergerson, Duke 6′1″, 189 **WR**
Col: Merced Coll. CA (J.C.); Washington State; San Diego State *HS:* Merced [CA] B: 4/21/1954, Boise, ID *Drafted:* 1976 Round 3 Dal
1977 Sea: PR 8-54 6.8; KR 11-240 21.8. **1978** Sea: KR 10-236 23.6. **Total:** PR 8-54 6.8; KR 21-476 22.7.

		Receiving				
Year Team	G	Rec	Yds	Avg	TD	Fum
1977 Sea	13	19	374	19.7	2	1
1978 Sea	16	11	116	10.5	0	1
1979 Sea	4	2	12	6.0	0	0
1980 Buf	9	3	41	13.7	0	0
NFL Total	42	35	543	15.5	2	2

CHARLEY FERGUSON Ferguson, Charles Edward 6′5″, 217 **WR-TE**
(High Pockets; Hooks) *Col:* Tennessee State *HS:* Galveston Central [TX] B: 11/13/1939, Dallas, TX
1966 Buf: KR 2-0. **Total:** KR 2-0.

		Receiving				
Year Team	G	Rec	Yds	Avg	TD	Fum
1961 Cle	12	2	68	34.0	1	0
1962 Min	10	14	364	26.0	6	0
1963 Buf	12	9	181	20.1	3	0
1965 Buf	12	21	262	12.5	2	1
1966 Buf	14	16	293	18.3	1	0
1969 Buf	4	0	0	—	0	0
NFL Total	64	62	1168	18.8	13	1

GENE FERGUSON Ferguson, Eugene Bransford 6′8″, 300 **OT-DT**
(Monster) *Col:* Norfolk State *HS:* Dunbar [Lynchburg, VA] B: 6/5/1947, Lynchburg, VA *Drafted:* 1969 Round 3 SD
1969 SD: 12 G. **1970** SD: 14 G. **1971** Hou: 14 G. **1972** Hou: 1 G. **Total:** 41 G.

HOWIE FERGUSON Ferguson, Howard Jr. 6′2″, 218 **FB**
Col: No College *HS:* New Iberia [LA] B: 8/5/1930, New Iberia, LA
1953 GB: KR 7-123 17.6. **1954** GB: KR 2-31 15.5. **1955** GB: KR 1-20 20.0. **1956** GB: KR 5-83 16.6. **1957** GB: Pass 1-0. **1958** GB: Pass 1-0. **Total:** Pass 2-0; KR 15-257 17.1.

		Rushing				Receiving					Tot
Year Team	G	Att	Yds	Avg	TD	Rec	Yds	Avg	TD	Fum	TD
1953 GB	11	52	134	2.6	0	15	86	5.7	0	4	0
1954 GB	12	83	276	3.3	0	41	398	9.7	0	8	0

1955 GB	12	192	859	4.5	4	22	153	7.0	0	8	4
1956 GB	11	99	367	3.7	0	22	214	9.7	0	6	0
1957 GB	12	59	216	3.7	1	15	107	7.1	1	2	2
1958 GB	7	59	268	4.5	1	12	121	10.1	0	1	1
1960 LAC	14	126	438	3.5	4	21	168	8.0	2	6	6
NFL Total	79	670	2558	3.8	10	148	1247	8.4	3	35	13

JIM FERGUSON Ferguson, James Thomas 6′4″, 240 **C-LB**
Col: Cerritos Coll. CA (J.C.); USC *HS:* Excelsior [Norwalk, CA]
B: 10/15/1942, Oakland, CA *Drafted:* 1968 Round 17 NO
1968 NO: 4 G. **1969** Atl-ChiB: 6 G; 1 Fum. Atl: 2 G; 1 Fum. ChiB: 4 G. **Total:** 10 G; 1 Fum.

JASON FERGUSON Ferguson, Jason Orlando 6′3″, 305 **DT**
Col: Itawamba CC MS; Georgia *HS:* Nettleton [MS] B: 11/28/1974, Nettleton, MS *Drafted:* 1997 Round 7 NYJ
1997 NYJ: 13 G; KR 1-1 1.0; 3.5 Sac. **1998** NYJ: 16 G; 4 Sac. **Total:** 29 G; KR 1-1 1.0; 7.5 Sac.

JOE FERGUSON Ferguson, Joe Carlton Jr. 6′1″, 195 **QB**
Col: Arkansas *HS:* Woodlawn [Shreveport, LA] B: 4/23/1950, Alvin, TX
Drafted: 1973 Round 3 Buf
1973 Buf: Rec 1-(-3) -3.0. **1978** Buf: Rec 1-(-6) -6.0. **1982** Buf: 1 Fum TD. **Total:** Rec 2-(-9) -4.5; 1 Fum TD.

		Passing							
Year Team	**G**	**Att**	**Comp**	**Comp%**	**Yds**	**YPA**	**TD**	**Int**	**Rating**
1973 Buf	14	164	73	44.5	939	5.73	4	10	45.8
1974 Buf	14	232	119	51.3	1588	6.84	12	12	69.0
1975 Buf	14	321	169	52.6	2426	7.56	**25**	17	81.3
1976 Buf	7	151	74	49.0	1086	7.19	9	**1**	90.0
1977 Buf	14	**457**	221	48.4	**2803**	6.13	12	24	54.8
1978 Buf	16	330	175	53.0	2136	6.47	16	15	70.5
1979 Buf	16	458	238	52.0	3572	7.80	14	15	74.4
1980 Buf	16	439	251	57.2	2805	6.39	20	18	74.5
1981 Buf	16	498	252	50.6	3652	7.33	24	20	74.1
1982 Buf	9	264	144	54.5	1597	6.05	7	16	56.3
1983 Buf	16	508	281	55.3	2995	5.90	26	25	69.3
1984 Buf	12	344	191	55.5	1991	5.79	12	17	63.5
1985 Det	8	54	31	57.4	364	6.74	2	3	67.2
1986 Det	6	155	73	47.1	941	6.07	7	7	62.9
1988 TB	2	46	31	67.4	368	8.00	3	1	104.3
1989 TB	5	90	44	48.9	533	5.92	3	6	50.8
1990 Ind	1	8	2	25.0	21	2.63	0	2	0.0
NFL Total	186	4519	2369	52.4	29817	6.60	196	209	68.4

	Rushing					Tot
Year Team	**Att**	**Yds**	**Avg**	**TD**	**Fum**	**TD**
1973 Buf	48	147	3.1	2	7	2
1974 Buf	54	111	2.1	2	**14**	2
1975 Buf	23	82	3.6	1	4	1
1976 Buf	18	81	4.5	0	2	0
1977 Buf	41	279	6.8	2	**12**	2
1978 Buf	27	76	2.8	0	5	0
1979 Buf	22	68	3.1	1	5	1
1980 Buf	31	65	2.1	0	9	0
1981 Buf	20	29	1.5	1	2	1
1982 Buf	16	46	2.9	1	5	2
1983 Buf	20	88	4.4	0	3	0
1984 Buf	19	102	5.4	0	8	0
1985 Det	4	12	3.0	1	1	1
1986 Det	5	25	5.0	0	3	0
1988 TB	1	0	0.0	0	1	0
1989 TB	4	6	1.5	0	1	0
NFL Total	353	1217	3.4	11	82	12

KEITH FERGUSON Ferguson, Keith Tyrone 6′5″, 252 **DE**
Col: Ohio State *HS:* Miami Edison [FL] B: 4/3/1959, Miami, FL
Drafted: 1981 Round 5 SD
1981 SD: 16 G. **1982** SD: 9 G; 4.5 Sac. **1983** SD: 16 G; 5 Sac. **1984** SD: 16 G; 8 Sac. **1985** SD-Det: 15 G; 2.5 Sac. SD: 10 G; 1 Sac. Det: 5 G; 1.5 Sac. **1986** Det: 16 G; Int 1-7; 1 Fum; 9.5 Sac. **1987** Det: 12 G; 6 Sac. **1988** Det: 14 G; 8.5 Sac. **1989** Det: 4 G. **1990** Det: 16 G; 3 Sac. **Total:** 134 G; Int 1-7; 1 Fum; 47.0 Sac.

KEVIN FERGUSON Ferguson, Kevin Howard 6′2″, 223 **TE**
Col: Virginia *HS:* Appomattox Co. [Appomattox, VA] B: 12/4/1965, Lynchburg, VA
1987 SD: 3 G.

LARRY FERGUSON Ferguson, Lawrence Pearly 5′10″, 195 **HB**
Col: Iowa *HS:* Madison [IL] B: 3/19/1940, Madison, IL *Drafted:* 1962 Round 4 Det
1963 Det: 7 G; Rush 13-23 1.8; Rec 2-8 4.0; PR 11-108 9.8; KR 9-231 25.7; 2 Fum.

BOB FERGUSON Ferguson, Robert Eugene 5′11″, 220 **FB**
Col: Ohio State *HS:* Troy [OH] B: 8/29/1939, Columbus, OH
Drafted: 1962 Round 1 Pit
1962 Pit: Rec 1-6 6.0; KR 2-30 15.0. **1963** Pit-Min: Rec 3-7 2.3. Pit: Rec 3-7 2.3. **Total:** Rec 4-13 3.3; KR 2-30 15.0.

		Rushing				
Year Team	**G**	**Att**	**Yds**	**Avg**	**TD**	**Fum**
1962 Pit	13	20	37	1.9	0	3
1963 Pit-Min	7	46	172	3.7	1	0
1963 Pit	5	43	171	4.0	1	0
1963 Min	2	3	1	0.3	0	0
NFL Total	20	66	209	3.2	1	3

TOM FERGUSON Ferguson, Thomas B 1 **T**
Col: No College B: 9/24/1893, IN D: 12/8/1979, Plantation, FL
1921 Lou: 2 G.

VAGAS FERGUSON Ferguson, Vasquero Diaz 6′1″, 204 **RB**
Col: Notre Dame *HS:* Richmond [IN] B: 3/6/1957, Richmond, IN
Drafted: 1980 Round 1 NE
1983 Hou-Cle: KR 2-36 18.0. Cle: KR 2-36 18.0. **Total:** KR 2-36 18.0.

		Rushing				Receiving				
Year Team	**G**	**Att**	**Yds**	**Avg**	**TD**	**Rec**	**Yds**	**Avg**	**TD**	**Fum**
1980 NE	16	211	818	3.9	2	22	173	7.9	0	3
1981 NE	13	78	340	4.4	3	4	39	9.8	0	1
1982 NE	2	1	5	5.0	0	0	0	—	0	0
1983 Hou-Cle	2	0	0	—	0	0	0	—	0	0
1983 Hou	1	0	0	—	0	0	0	—	0	0
1983 Cle	1	0	0	—	0	0	0	—	0	0
NFL Total	33	290	1163	4.0	5	26	212	8.2	0	4

BILL FERGUSON Ferguson, William Michael 6′3″, 225 **LB**
Col: Grossmont Coll. CA (J.C.); Washington; San Diego State
HS: Grossmont [La Mesa, CA] B: 7/7/1951, San Diego, CA
Drafted: 1973 Round 4 NYJ
1973 NYJ: 11 G. **1974** NYJ: 13 G. **Total:** 24 G.

FRITZ FERKO Ferko, John Frederick 6′1″, 242 **T**
Col: West Chester; Mount St. Mary's *HS:* Mauch Chunk [PA]
B: 7/6/1912 D: 3/1984, Perth Amboy, NJ
1937 Phi: 10 G. **1938** Phi: 2 G. **Total:** 12 G.

RON FERNANDES Fernandes, Ronald Michael 6′4″, 251 **DE**
Col: Eastern Michigan *HS:* Rocky River [OH]; Ypsilanti HS [MI]
B: 9/11/1951, Ypsilanti, MI *Drafted:* 1973 Round 10 Mia
1976 Bal: 13 G; Scor **1** Saf; 2 Pt. **1977** Bal: 14 G. **1979** Bal: 13 G. **Total:** 40 G; Scor 1 Saf; 2 Pt.

MANNY FERNANDEZ Fernandez, Manuel Jose 6′2″, 250 **DT**
Col: Chabot Coll. CA (J.C.); Utah *HS:* San Lorenzo [CA] B: 7/3/1946, Oakland, CA
1968 Mia: 13 G. **1969** Mia: 14 G. **1970** Mia: 13 G. **1971** Mia: 14 G. **1972** Mia: 14 G. **1973** Mia: 13 G. **1974** Mia: 12 G. **1975** Mia: 10 G. **Total:** 103 G.

MERVYN FERNANDEZ Fernandez, Mervyn 6′3″, 205 **WR**
Col: San Jose City Coll. CA (J.C.); De Anza Coll. CA (J.C.); San Jose State
HS: Andrew Hill [San Jose, CA] B: 12/29/1959, Merced, CA
Drafted: 1983 Round 10 LARd
1988 LARd: Rush 1-9 9.0. **1989** LARd: Rush 2-16 8.0. **1990** LARd: Rush 3-10 3.3. **Total:** Rush 6-35 5.8.

		Receiving				
Year Team	**G**	**Rec**	**Yds**	**Avg**	**TD**	**Fum**
1987 LARd	7	14	236	16.9	0	1
1988 LARd	16	31	805	26.0	4	0
1989 LARd	16	57	1069	18.8	9	3
1990 LARd	16	52	839	16.1	5	0
1991 LARd	16	46	694	15.1	1	0
1992 LARd	15	9	121	13.4	0	0
NFL Total	86	209	3764	18.0	19	4

VINCE FERRAGAMO Ferragamo, Vincent Anthony 6′3″, 212 **QB**
Col: California; Nebraska *HS:* Phineas Banning [Los Angeles, CA]
B: 4/24/1954, Torrance, CA *Drafted:* 1977 Round 4 LARm

		Passing							
Year Team	**G**	**Att**	**Comp**	**Comp%**	**Yds**	**YPA**	**TD**	**Int**	**Rating**
1977 LARm	3	15	9	60.0	83	5.53	2	0	114.7
1978 LARm	9	20	7	35.0	114	5.70	0	2	15.4
1979 LARm	8	110	53	48.2	778	7.07	5	10	49.0
1980 LARm	16	404	240	59.4	3199	7.92	30	19	89.7
1982 LARm	7	209	118	56.5	1609	7.70	9	9	77.6
1983 LARm	16	464	274	59.1	3276	7.06	22	23	75.9
1984 LARm	3	66	29	43.9	317	4.80	2	8	29.2
1985 Buf	10	287	149	51.9	1677	5.84	5	17	50.8
1986 GB	3	40	23	57.5	283	7.08	1	3	56.6
NFL Total	75	1615	902	55.9	11336	7.02	76	91	70.1

	Rushing				
Year Team	**Att**	**Yds**	**Avg**	**TD**	**Fum**
1977 LARm	1	0	0.0	0	0
1978 LARm	2	10	5.0	0	0
1979 LARm	3	-2	-0.7	0	2

1980 LARm	15	34	2.3	1	4
1982 LARm	4	3	0.8	1	1
1983 LARm	22	17	0.8	0	8
1984 LARm	4	0	0.0	0	0
1985 Buf	8	15	1.9	1	1
1986 GB	1	0	0.0	0	3
NFL Total	60	77	1.3	3	19

JACK FERRANTE Ferrante, Jack Anthony 6′1″, 197 **OE-DE**
(Blackjack) *Col:* No College *HS:* No High School B: 3/9/1916, Camden, NJ
1945 Phi: Int 1-15. **1947** Phi: KR 7-99 14.1. **Total:** KR 7-99 14.1; Int 1-15.

		Receiving			
Year Team	**G**	**Rec**	**Yds**	**Avg**	**TD**
1941 Phi	3	2	22	11.0	0
1944 Phi	10	3	66	22.0	1
1945 Phi	10	21	464	22.1	7
1946 Phi	11	28	451	16.1	4
1947 Phi	11	18	341	18.9	4
1948 Phi	12	28	444	15.9	7
1949 Phi	12	34	508	14.9	5
1950 Phi	12	35	588	16.8	3
NFL Total	81	169	2884	17.1	31

ORLANDO FERRANTE Ferrante, Orlando C 6′0″, 230 **OG**
Col: USC *HS:* Mount Carmel [Los Angeles, CA] B: 9/24/1932, Los Angeles, CA
1960 LAC: 14 G. **1961** SD: 14 G; KR 1-0; 1 Fum. **Total:** 28 G; KR 1-0; 1 Fum.

RON FERRARI Ferrari, Ronald Lee 6′0″, 212 **LB**
Col: Lakeland; Illinois *HS:* Moweaqua [IL] B: 7/30/1959, Springfield, IL *Drafted:* 1982 Round 7 SF
1982 SF: 9 G; KR 2-19 9.5. **1983** SF: 16 G; 3 Sac. **1984** SF: 11 G; 1 Sac. **1985** SF: 16 G. **1986** SF: 16 G. **Total:** 68 G; KR 2-19 9.5; 4 Sac.

EARL FERRELL Ferrell, Earl Thomas 6′0″, 225 **RB**
Col: East Tennessee State *HS:* Halifax Co. [South Boston, VA] B: 3/27/1958, Halifax, VA *Drafted:* 1982 Round 5 StL
1982 StL: PR 1-6 6.0; KR 4-88 22.0. **1983** StL: PR 1-17 17.0; KR 13-257 19.8. **1984** StL: KR 1-0. **1986** StL: KR 3-41 13.7. **1987** StL: KR 1-10 10.0. **1988** Pho: KR 2-25 12.5. **Total:** PR 2-23 11.5; KR 24-421 17.5.

		Rushing				Receiving					Tot
Year Team	**G**	**Att**	**Yds**	**Avg**	**TD**	**Rec**	**Yds**	**Avg**	**TD**	**Fum**	**TD**
1982 StL	9	0	0	—	0	0	0	—	0	0	0
1983 StL	16	7	53	7.6	1	0	0	—	0	2	1
1984 StL	16	44	203	4.6	1	26	218	8.4	1	3	2
1985 StL	11	46	208	4.5	2	25	277	11.1	2	2	4
1986 StL	16	124	548	4.4	0	56	434	7.8	3	6	3
1987 StL	11	113	512	4.5	7	23	262	11.4	0	0	7
1988 Pho	16	202	924	4.6	7	38	315	8.3	2	7	9
1989 Pho	15	149	502	3.4	6	18	122	6.8	0	2	6
NFL Total	110	685	2950	4.3	24	186	1628	8.8	8	22	32

BOB FERRELL Ferrell, Robert Steven 6′0″, 216 **RB**
Col: UCLA *HS:* Ganesha [Pomona, CA] B: 11/13/1952, Los Angeles, CA
1976 SF: Rec 1-9 9.0; KR 1-12 12.0. **1977** SF: Rec 2-12 6.0; KR 3-35 11.7. **1978** SF: Rec 16-123 7.7; KR 1-24 24.0. **1979** SF: Rec 2-4 2.0; KR 6-78 13.0. **1980** SF: PR 1-1 1.0. **Total:** Rec 21-148 7.0; PR 1-1 1.0; KR 11-149 13.5.

		Rushing				
Year Team	**G**	**Att**	**Yds**	**Avg**	**TD**	**Fum**
1976 SF	10	9	28	3.1	1	2
1977 SF	14	41	160	3.9	1	3
1978 SF	16	125	471	3.8	1	5
1979 SF	16	8	33	4.1	0	0
1980 SF	12	0	0	—	0	0
NFL Total	68	183	692	3.8	3	10

NEIL FERRIS Ferris, Neil George 5′11″, 181 **DB-HB**
(Ferris Can Wheel) *Col:* Loyola Marymount *HS:* Bell [CA] B: 10/31/1927, Bell, CA D: 1/30/1996, Lake Havasu City, AZ
1951 Was: 12 G; PR 2-1 0.5. **1952** Was-Phi: 12 G; Rush 11-22 2.0 1 TD; Rec 1-8 8.0; PR 2-11 5.5; KR 3-76 25.3; Int 0-3; 6 Pt. Was: 4 G; Rush 11-22 2.0 1 TD; Rec 1-8 8.0; PR 2-11 5.5; KR 3-76 25.3; 6 Pt. Phi: 8 G; Int 0-3. **1953** LARm: 5 G. **Total:** 29 G; Rush 11-22 2.0 1 TD; Rec 1-8 8.0; PR 4-12 3.0; KR 3-76 25.3; Int 0-3; 6 Pt.

LOU FERRY Ferry, Louis Anthony Jr. 6′2″, 244 **DT-OT**
Col: Villanova *HS:* St. James [Chester, PA] B: 12/1/1927, Chester, PA *Drafted:* 1949 Round 3 GB
1949 GB: 12 G. **1951** ChiC: 12 G. **1952** Pit: 12 G; 1 Fum TD; 6 Pt. **1953** Pit: 12 G; Scor **1** Saf; 2 Pt. **1954** Pit: 11 G. **1955** Pit: 12 G. **Total:** 71 G; Scor 1 Saf; 1 Fum TD; 8 Pt.

PAUL FERSEN Fersen, Paul Clinton 6′5″, 260 **OT**
Col: Georgia *HS:* North Fulton [Atlanta, GA] B: 2/16/1950, Columbus, GA *Drafted:* 1973 Round 14 NO
1973 NO: 3 G. **1974** NO: 1 G. **Total:** 4 G.

HOWARD FEST Fest, Howard Arthur 6′6″, 262 **OT-OG**
Col: Texas *HS:* Thomas Edison [San Antonio, TX] B: 4/11/1946, San Antonio, TX *Drafted:* 1968 Round 6 Cin
1968 Cin: 14 G. **1969** Cin: 14 G. **1970** Cin: 14 G. **1971** Cin: 14 G. **1972** Cin: 14 G. **1973** Cin: 14 G. **1974** Cin: 14 G. **1975** Cin: 14 G. **1976** TB: 14 G. **1977** TB: 1 G. **Total:** 127 G.

JIM FETHERSTON Fetherston, James Steven 6′2″, 225 **LB**
Col: California *HS:* Turlock [CA] B: 6/1/1945, Modesto, CA
1968 SD: 13 G; Int 1-0. **1969** SD: 14 G; KR 3-0. **Total:** 27 G; KR 3-0; Int 1-0.

GUS FETZ Fetz, Gustave 158 **HB**
Col: No College B: 1900 Deceased
1923 ChiB: 9 G; Rush 1 TD; 6 Pt.

JOHN FIALA Fiala, John Charles 6′2″, 232 **LB**
Col: Washington *HS:* Lake Washington [Kirkland, WA] B: 11/25/1973, Fullerton, CA *Drafted:* 1997 Round 6 Mia
1998 Pit: 16 G.

DAN FICCA Ficca, Daniel Robert 6′1″, 245 **OG**
Col: USC *HS:* Mount Carmel [Los Angeles, CA] B: 2/7/1939, Atlas, PA *Drafted:* 1961 Round 29 SD
1962 Oak: 14 G. **1963** NYJ: 14 G. **1964** NYJ: 14 G. **1965** NYJ: 14 G. **1966** NYJ: 14 G. **Total:** 70 G.

LEON FICHMAN Fichman, Leon 6′1″, 215 **T**
Col: Alabama *HS:* Los Angeles [CA] B: 2/23/1921, Los Angeles, CA
1946 Det: 11 G. **1947** Det: 1 G. **Total:** 12 G.

BRAD FICHTEL Fichtel, Brad Alan 6′2″, 285 **C**
Col: Eastern Illinois *HS:* Oswego [IL] B: 3/10/1970, Aurora, IL *Drafted:* 1993 Round 7 LARm
1994 LARm: 1 G.

ROSS FICHTNER Fichtner, Ross William 6′0″, 185 **DB**
(Rocky) *Col:* Purdue *HS:* McKeesport Tech [PA] B: 10/26/1938, McKeesport, PA *Drafted:* 1960 Round 3 Cle
1960 Cle: KR 1-0. **1961** Cle: KR 1-11 11.0. **Total:** KR 2-11 5.5.

		Interceptions			
Year Team	**G**	**Int**	**Yds**	**TD**	**Fum**
1960 Cle	12	0	0	0	0
1961 Cle	13	0	0	0	0
1962 Cle	14	7	76	0	0
1963 Cle	13	2	75	1	0
1964 Cle	8	2	67	0	0
1965 Cle	14	4	98	1	0
1966 Cle	14	8	152	1	0
1967 Cle	14	4	113	0	1
1968 NO	4	0	0	0	0
NFL Total	106	27	581	3	1

JAY FIEDLER Fiedler, Jay Brian 6′1″, 214 **QB**
Col: Dartmouth *HS:* Oceanside [NY] B: 12/29/1971, Brooklyn, NY
1995 Phi: Postseason only. **1998** Min: 5 G; Pass 7-3 42.9%, 41 5.86 1 Int; Rush 4-(-6) -1.5.

BILL FIEDLER Fiedler, William Ferdinand 5′9″, 200 **G**
Col: Pennsylvania *HS:* Pennington [Philadelphia, PA] B: 11/9/1914 D: 2/1976
1938 Phi: 1 G.

AMOD FIELD Field, Amod Lloyd 5′11″, 186 **WR**
Col: Montclair State *HS:* Passaic [NJ] B: 10/11/1967
1991 Pho: 2 G.

HARRY FIELD Field, Harry Nuuanu 6′1″, 226 **T**
Col: Hawaii; Oregon State *HS:* Punahou School [Honolulu, HI] B: 8/18/1911, Iao Valley, HI D: 5/23/1964, Honolulu, HI
1934 ChiC: 11 G. **1935** ChiC: 10 G. **1936** ChiC: 12 G. **Total:** 33 G.

DOAK FIELD Field, Richard Doak Jr. 6′2″, 228 **LB**
Col: Baylor *HS:* Burnet [TX] B: 10/8/1958, Burnet, TX *Drafted:* 1981 Round 7 Phi
1981 StL: 7 G.

DON FIELDER Fielder, Donald Sinclair 6′3″, 260 **DE**
Col: Golden West Coll. CA (J.C.); Kentucky *HS:* Rancho Alamitos [Garden Grove, CA] B: 10/20/1959, Las Cruces, NM
1985 TB: 11 G; 1 Sac.

ANTHONY FIELDINGS Fieldings, Anthony 6′1″, 237 **LB**
Col: Morningside *HS:* Eustis [FL] B: 7/9/1971, Eustis, FL
1995 Dal: 4 G.

JITTER FIELDS Fields, Alfred Gene 5'8", 185 **DB**
Col: Texas *HS:* H. Grady Spruce [Dallas, TX] B: 8/16/1962, Dallas, TX
Drafted: 1984 Round 5 NO
1984 NO: KR 19-356 18.7. **1987** Ind-KC: KR 1-13 13.0. KC: KR 1-13 13.0. **Total:** KR 20-369 18.5.

Year Team	G	Punt Returns Ret	Yds	Avg	TD	Fum
1984 NO	13	27	236	8.7	0	2
1987 Ind-KC	6	8	161	20.1	1	0
1987 Ind	1	0	0	—	0	0
1987 KC	5	8	161	20.1	1	0
NFL Total	19	35	397	11.3	1	2

ANGELO FIELDS Fields, Angelo Bertell 6'6", 321 **OT**
Col: Michigan State *HS:* Woodrow Wilson [Washington, DC]
B: 9/15/1957, Washington, DC *Drafted:* 1980 Round 2 Hou
1980 Hou: 16 G. **1981** Hou: 14 G. **1982** GB: Postseason only. **Total:** 30 G.

ANTHONY FIELDS Fields, Anthony Bernard 6'1", 192 **DB**
Col: Eastern Michigan *HS:* Northwestern [Detroit, MI] B: 1/17/1964, Mobile, AL
1987 Det: 3 G.

EDGAR FIELDS Fields, Edgar Eugene 6'2", 255 **DE-DT**
Col: Navarro Coll. TX (J.C.); Texas A&M *HS:* Lyndon B. Johnson [Austin, TX] B: 3/10/1954, Austin, TX *Drafted:* 1977 Round 3 Atl
1977 Atl: 14 G. **1978** Atl: 16 G; KR 2-21 10.5. **1979** Atl: 16 G. **1980** Atl: 14 G; KR 1-11 11.0. **1981** Det: 2 G. **Total:** 62 G; KR 3-32 10.7.

FLOYD FIELDS Fields, Floyd Cornelius 6'0", 208 **DB**
Col: Arizona State *HS:* Thornwood [South Holland, IL] B: 1/7/1969, South Holland, IL *Drafted:* 1991 Round 5 SD
1991 SD: 1 G. **1992** SD: 16 G; Int 1-0. **1993** SD: 13 G. **Total:** 30 G; Int 1-0.

GEORGE FIELDS Fields, George 6'3", 245 **DE-DT**
Col: Bakersfield Coll. CA (J.C.) *HS:* Berkeley [CA] B: 1936
1960 Oak: 14 G; Int 2-7. **1961** Oak: 1 G. **Total:** 15 G; Int 2-7.

GREG FIELDS Fields, Gregory Keith 6'7", 260 **DE**
Col: Hartnell Coll. CA (J.C.); Grambling State *HS:* Mission [San Francisco, CA] B: 1/23/1955, San Francisco, CA
1979 Bal: 16 G. **1980** Bal: 16 G. **Total:** 32 G.

JAIME FIELDS Fields, Jaime Dablang 5'11", 233 **LB**
Col: Washington *HS:* Lynwood [CA] B: 8/28/1970, Compton, CA
Drafted: 1993 Round 4 KC
1993 KC: 6 G. **1994** KC: 11 G. **Total:** 17 G.

JEFF FIELDS Fields, Jeff 6'3", 320 **NT**
Col: Hinds CC MS; Arkansas State *HS:* Jim Hill [Jackson, MS]
B: 7/3/1967, Jackson, MS *Drafted:* 1991 Round 9 LARm
1995 Car: 2 G.

JERRY FIELDS Fields, Jerry Eugene 6'1", 222 **LB**
Col: Ohio State *HS:* Coal Grove [OH] B: 5/24/1938, Ironton, OH
Drafted: 1961 Round 13 NYG
1961 NYT: 5 G; KR 1-19 19.0. **1962** NYT: 14 G. **Total:** 19 G; KR 1-19 19.0.

JOE FIELDS Fields, Joseph Charles Jr. 6'2", 250 **C-OG**
Col: Rutgers-Camden; Widener *HS:* Gloucester City Catholic [NJ]
B: 11/14/1953, Woodbury, NJ *Drafted:* 1975 Round 14 NYJ
1975 NYJ: 14 G; 1 Fum. **1976** NYJ: 14 G; 1 Fum. **1977** NYJ: 14 G. **1978** NYJ: 16 G. **1979** NYJ: 15 G. **1980** NYJ: 13 G. **1981** NYJ: 16 G; 1 Fum. **1982** NYJ: 9 G. **1983** NYJ: 12 G. **1984** NYJ: 16 G. **1985** NYJ: 15 G. **1986** NYJ: 9 G. **1987** NYJ: 10 G. **1988** NYG: 13 G. **Total:** 186 G; 3 Fum.

MARK FIELDS Fields, Mark Lee 6'2", 244 **LB**
Col: Los Angeles Southwest Coll. CA (J.C.); Washington State
HS: George Washington [Los Angeles, CA] B: 11/9/1972, Los Angeles, CA *Drafted:* 1995 Round 1 NO
1995 NO: 16 G; 1 Sac. **1996** NO: 16 G; 2 Sac. **1997** NO: 16 G; 1 Fum TD; 6 Pt; 8 Sac. **1998** NO: 15 G; 1 Fum TD; 6 Pt; 6 Sac. **Total:** 63 G; 2 Fum TD; 12 Pt; 17 Sac.

SCOTT FIELDS Fields, Scott 6'2", 220 **LB**
Col: USC *HS:* Bishop Amat [La Puente, CA] B: 4/22/1973, Ontario, CA
1996 Atl: 6 G.

RALPH FIFE Fife, Ralph Donald 6'0", 207 **G-LB**
Col: Pittsburgh *HS:* McKinley [Canton, OH] B: 1/26/1920, Pittsburgh, PA
1942 ChiC: 4 G. **1945** ChiC: 1 G. **1946** Pit: 10 G; KR 2-31 15.5. **Total:** 15 G; KR 2-31 15.5.

BILL FIFER Fifer, William Charles 6'4", 250 **OT**
Col: West Texas A&M *HS:* Tivy [Kerrville, TX] B: 10/26/1955, Kerrville, TX *Drafted:* 1978 Round 4 Det
1978 Det-NO: 12 G. Det: 8 G. NO: 4 G. **Total:** 12 G.

CEDRIC FIGARO Figaro, Cedric Noah 6'3", 255 **LB**
Col: Notre Dame *HS:* Lafayette [LA] B: 8/17/1966, Lafayette, LA
Drafted: 1988 Round 6 SD
1988 SD: 6 G. **1989** SD: 16 G; PR 1-0; KR 1-21 21.0; Int 1-2. **1990** SD: 16 G. **1991** Ind-Cle: 13 G; Int 1-9. Ind: 1 G. Cle: 12 G; Int 1-9. **1992** Cle: 16 G. **1995** StL: 16 G; 1 Sac. **1996** StL: 15 G; PR 1-0; 1 Fum. **Total:** 98 G; PR 2-0; KR 1-21 21.0; Int 2-11; 1 Fum; 1 Sac.

GEORGE FIGNER Figner, George Kendall 6'0", 185 **DB**
Col: Colorado *HS:* Centennial [Pueblo, CO] B: 4/30/1931, Dayton, OH
1953 ChiB: 5 G; Int 1-4.

DEON FIGURES Figures, Deon Juniel 6'0", 200 **DB**
Col: Colorado *HS:* Serra [Compton, CA] B: 1/20/1970, Bellflower, CA
Drafted: 1993 Round 1 Pit
1993 Pit: 15 G; PR 5-15 3.0; Int 1-78; 2 Fum. **1994** Pit: 16 G; 1 Sac. **1995** Pit: 14 G. **1996** Pit: 16 G; Int 2-13. **1997** Jac: 16 G; Int 5-48. **1998** Jac: 16 G; Int 1-0. **Total:** 93 G; PR 5-15 3.0; Int 9-139; 2 Fum; 1 Sac.

DAN FIKE Fike, Dan Clement Jr. 6'7", 280 **OG-OT**
Col: Florida *HS:* Pine Forest [Pensacola, FL] B: 6/16/1961, Mobile, AL
Drafted: 1983 Round 10 NYJ
1985 Cle: 13 G. **1986** Cle: 16 G. **1987** Cle: 12 G. **1988** Cle: 16 G. **1989** Cle: 13 G. **1990** Cle: 10 G. **1991** Cle: 16 G. **1992** Cle: 16 G. **1993** Pit: 3 G. **Total:** 115 G.

JACK FILAK Filak, John 6'0", 190 **T-G**
Col: Penn State *HS:* East Side [Newark, NJ] B: 10/13/1903
1927 Fra: 11 G. **1928** Fra: 14 G. **1929** Fra: 14 G. **Total:** 39 G.

FRANK FILCHOCK Filchock, Frank Joseph 5'11", 193 **TB-QB-DB-HB**
Col: Indiana *HS:* Redstone [PA] B: 10/8/1916, Crucible, PA
D: 6/20/1994, Lake Oswego, OK *Drafted:* 1938 Round 1 Pit
1938 Pit-Was: Rec 2-4 2.0. Was: Rec 2-4 2.0. **1940** Was: Int 4-1. **1941** Was: PR 7-157 **22.4** **1** TD; KR 5-126 25.2; Punt 1-35 35.0. **1944** Was: Rec 3-51 17.0; PR 3-5 1.7; KR 3-42 14.0. **1945** Was: Rec 3-33 11.0; PR 1-17 17.0; Int 1-0. **1946** NYG: Rec 1-(-6) -6.0; PR 6-50 8.3; KR 4-109 27.3; Int 1-19. **Total:** Rec 9-82 9.1; PR 17-229 13.5 1 TD; KR 12-277 23.1; Int 6-20; Punt 1-35 35.0.

Year Team	G	Passing Att	Comp	Comp%	Yds	YPA	TD	Int	Rating
1938 Pit-Was	12	101	41	40.6	469	4.64	3	11	25.6
1938 Pit	6	74	30	40.5	392	5.30	3	7	32.0
1938 Was	6	27	11	40.7	77	2.85	0	4	9.0
1939 Was	11	89	55	**61.8**	1094	12.29	**11**	7	111.6
1940 Was	10	54	28	51.9	460	8.52	6	9	78.2
1941 Was	11	68	28	41.2	327	4.81	1	11	21.8
1944 Was	10	147	**84**	**57.1**	1139	7.75	**13**	9	86.0
1945 Was	10	46	18	39.1	169	3.67	1	7	17.7
1946 NYG	11	169	87	51.5	1262	7.47	12	25	60.2
1950 Bal	1	3	1	33.3	1	0.33	0	0	42.4
NFL Total	76	677	342	50.5	4921	7.27	47	79	58.0

Year Team	Rushing Att	Yds	Avg	TD	Fum	Tot TD
1938 Pit-Was	69	198	2.9	1	0	1
1938 Pit	17	20	1.2	0	0	0
1938 Was	52	178	3.4	1	0	1
1939 Was	103	413	4.0	1	0	1
1940 Was	50	126	2.5	2	0	2
1941 Was	115	383	3.3	1	0	2
1944 Was	33	-34	-1.0	0	0	0
1945 Was	9	21	2.3	0	0	0
1946 NYG	98	371	3.8	2	5	2
NFL Total	477	1478	3.1	7	5	8

JIM FILES Files, James Dale 6'4", 240 **LB**
Col: Oklahoma *HS:* Southside [Fort Smith, AR] B: 1/16/1948, Paris, AR *Drafted:* 1970 Round 1 NYG
1970 NYG: 14 G; Int 1-8; Scor **1** Saf; 2 Pt. **1971** NYG: 14 G; Int 1-29. **1972** NYG: 14 G; Int 2-46 1 TD; 6 Pt; 1 Fum. **1973** NYG: 14 G; Int 1-22. **Total:** 56 G; Int 5-105 1 TD; Scor 1 Saf; 8 Pt; 1 Fum.

STEVE FILIPOWICZ Filipowicz, Stephen Charles 5'8", 200 **LB-FB-DB**
Col: Fordham *HS:* Kulpmont [PA] B: 6/28/1921, Donora, PA
D: 2/21/1975, Wilkes-Barre, PA *Drafted:* 1943 Round 1 NYG
1945 NYG: Pass 2-0; Rec 4-49 12.3 1 TD; PR 1-18 18.0; KR 1-32 32.0. **1946** NYG: Rec 7-84 12.0 1 TD; KR 1-16 16.0; Int 4-52 **1** TD. **Total:** Pass 2-0; Rec 11-133 12.1 2 TD; PR 1-18 18.0; KR 2-48 24.0; Int 4-52 1 TD.

Year Team	G	Rushing Att	Yds	Avg	TD	Fum	Tot TD
1945 NYG	10	53	142	2.7	1	1	2
1946 NYG	11	2	3	1.5	1	1	3
NFL Total	21	55	145	2.6	2	2	5

GENE FILIPSKI Filipski, Eugene Charles 5′11″, 185 **HB**
Col: Army; Villanova *HS:* Grant Union [Sacramento, CA] B: 6/14/1931, Sacramento, CA *Drafted:* 1953 Round 7 Cle
1956 NYG: Rec 3-37 12.3; PR 1-25 25.0. **1957** NYG: Rec 1-7 7.0; PR 20-91 4.6. **Total:** Rec 4-44 11.0; PR 21-116 5.5.

		Rushing				Kickoff Returns				
Year Team	G	Att	Yds	Avg	TD	Ret	Yds	Avg	TD	Fum
1956 NYG	12	13	85	6.5	1	19	390	20.5	0	3
1957 NYG	12	22	89	4.0	0	26	613	23.6	0	2
NFL Total	24	35	174	5.0	1	45	1003	22.3	0	5

JOHN FINA Fina, John Joseph 6′4″, 287 **OT**
Col: Arizona *HS:* Salpointe [Tucson, AZ] B: 3/11/1969, Rochester, MN *Drafted:* 1992 Round 1 Buf
1992 Buf: 16 G; Rec 1-1 1.0 1 TD; 6 Pt. **1993** Buf: 16 G; Rush 1-(-2) -2.0. **1994** Buf: 12 G. **1995** Buf: 16 G. **1996** Buf: 15 G. **1997** Buf: 16 G. **1998** Buf: 14 G. **Total:** 105 G; Rush 1-(-2) -2.0; Rec 1-1 1.0 1 TD; 6 Pt.

KARL FINCH Finch, Karl Lee 6′3″, 195 **WR**
Col: Modesto JC CA; Iowa; Cal Poly-S.L.O. *HS:* Modesto [CA] B: 7/7/1939, Modesto, CA
1962 LARm: 7 G.

BULL FINCH Finch, Olin 5′8″, 180 **BB-FB**
Col: Whittier B: 1893 D: 1956
1926 LA: 7 G.

STEVE FINCH Finch, Stephen 6′0″, 200 **WR**
Col: Elmhurst B: 1/2/1961, Great Lakes, IL
1987 Min: 1 G; Rec 3-54 18.0.

MIKE FINK Fink, Paul Michael 5′11″, 181 **DB**
Col: Missouri *HS:* Park Hill [Kansas City, MO] B: 12/24/1950, Kansas City, MO *Drafted:* 1973 Round 9 NO
1973 NO: 13 G; KR 5-81 16.2.

MATT FINKES Finkes, Matthew Scott 6′3″, 272 **DE**
Col: Ohio State *HS:* Piqua [OH] B: 2/12/1975, Piqua, OH *Drafted:* 1997 Round 6 Car
1997 NYJ: 8 G.

JIM FINKS Finks, James Edward 5′11″, 180 **QB-TB-DB**
Col: Tulsa *HS:* Salem [IL] B: 8/31/1927, St. Louis, MO D: 5/8/1994, New Orleans, LA *Drafted:* 1949 Round 12 Pit *HOF:* 1995
1949 Pit: Rec 1-17 17.0 1 TD; Int 1-14. **1950** Pit: Int 3-24. **1951** Pit: PR 1-20 20.0; Int 3-46 1 TD. **1952** Pit: Punt 4-156 39.0. **Total:** Rec 1-17 17.0 1 TD; PR 1-20 20.0; Int 7-84 1 TD; Punt 4-156 39.0.

		Passing							
Year Team	G	Att	Comp	Comp%	Yds	YPA	TD	Int	Rating
1949 Pit	11	71	24	33.8	322	4.54	2	8	19.0
1950 Pit	9	9	5	55.6	35	3.89	0	1	25.0
1951 Pit	12	24	14	58.3	201	8.38	1	1	82.1
1952 Pit	12	336	158	47.0	2307	6.87	**20**	19	66.2
1953 Pit	11	292	131	44.9	1484	5.08	8	14	49.8
1954 Pit	12	306	164	53.6	2003	6.55	14	19	63.4
1955 Pit	12	**344**	**165**	48.0	**2270**	6.60	10	26	47.7
NFL Total	79	1382	661	47.8	8622	6.24	55	88	54.7

	Rushing					Tot
Year Team	Att	Yds	Avg	TD	Fum	TD
1949 Pit	35	135	3.9	1	0	2
1950 Pit	1	2	2.0	0	0	0
1951 Pit	3	27	9.0	0	1	1
1952 Pit	23	37	1.6	5	7	5
1953 Pit	12	0	0.0	2	3	2
1954 Pit	9	17	1.9	0	4	0
1955 Pit	35	76	2.2	4	5	4
NFL Total	118	294	2.5	12	20	14

JACK FINLAY Finlay, Jack Alexander 6′1″, 217 **OG-LB**
Col: UCLA *HS:* Fairfax [Los Angeles, CA] B: 9/8/1921, Los Angeles, CA
1947 LARm: 12 G. **1948** LARm: 12 G. **1949** LARm: 12 G. **1950** LARm: 10 G; KR 2-14 7.0. **1951** LARm: 9 G. **Total:** 55 G; KR 2-14 7.0.

BERNIE FINN Finn, Bernard Francis 5′10″, 180 **BB-WB-TB-HB**
(Barney) *Col:* Holy Cross *HS:* St. Peter's Prep [Jersey City, NJ] B: 6/4/1907 D: 9/26/1993, Toms River, NJ
1930 Nwk-SI: 14 G. Nwk: 10 G. SI: 4 G. **1932** SI-ChiC: 3 G; Pass 1-1 100.0%, 9 9.00; Rush 3-9 3.0; Rec 3-37 12.3. SI: 1 G; Pass 1-1 100.0%, 9 9.00; Rush 3-9 3.0. ChiC: 2 G; Rec 3-37 12.3. **Total:** 17 G; Pass 1-1 100.0%, 9 9.00; Rush 3-9 3.0; Rec 3-37 12.3.

JACK FINN Finn, John Thomas 5′7″, 172 **BB-WB-BB-FB**
Col: Villanova; Moravian B: 8/27/1895, Bethlehem, PA D: 12/25/1970, Hellertown, PA
1924 Fra: 9 G; Rush 2 TD; Scor 20, 2 FG, 2 XK.

JIM FINNEGAN Finnegan, James Patrick 5′8″, 160 **OE-QB**
Col: St. Louis B: 1/20/1901, St. Louis, MO D: 9/6/1967, Crestwood, MO
1923 StL: 2 G.

GARY FINNERAN Finneran, Gary Joseph 6′3″, 240 **DT**
Col: USC *HS:* Cathedral [Los Angeles, CA] B: 2/23/1934
1960 LAC: 13 G. **1961** Oak: 13 G; 1 Fum. **Total:** 26 G; 1 Fum.

ROGER FINNIE Finnie, Roger Lewis 6′3″, 245 **OT-OG-DT**
Col: Florida A&M *HS:* Miami Senior [FL] B: 11/6/1945, Miami, FL *Drafted:* 1969 Round 14 NYJ
1969 NYJ: 14 G. **1970** NYJ: 3 G. **1971** NYJ: 7 G. **1972** NYJ: 14 G. **1973** StL: 12 G. **1974** StL: 14 G; KR 1-8 8.0. **1975** StL: 14 G. **1976** StL: 14 G. **1977** StL: 14 G. **1978** StL: 7 G. **1979** NO: 8 G. **Total:** 121 G; KR 1-8 8.0.

TOM FINNIN Finnin, Thomas R 6′2″, 262 **DT**
Col: Detroit Mercy *HS:* St.Augustine [San Diego, CA]; St.Ignatius HS [Chicago, IL] B: 9/28/1927, Chicago, IL *Drafted:* 1950 Round 24 NYG
1953 Bal: 11 G; KR 1-18 18.0; 1 Fum. **1954** Bal: 12 G; Scor **1** Saf; 2 Pt. **1955** Bal: 11 G. **1956** Bal: 10 G. **1957** ChiC-GB: 11 G. ChiC: 8 G. GB: 3 G. **Total:** 55 G; KR 1-18 18.0; Scor 1 Saf; 2 Pt; 1 Fum.

RUSS FINSTERWALD Finsterwald, Russell Weihr 5′9″, 165 **WB**
(Jube; Wild Bill) *Col:* Ohio U.; Syracuse *HS:* Athens [OH] B: 8/1896, Athens, OH D: 6/13/1962, Athens, OH
1920 Det: 2 G.

DAVE FINZER Finzer, David Mangan 6′1″, 195 **P**
Col: Illinois; DePauw *HS:* Loyola Acad. [Wilmette, IL] B: 2/3/1959, Chicago, IL
1984 ChiB: Rush 2-0. **1985** Sea: Pass 1-0, 1 Int; Rush 1-(-2) -2.0. **Total:** Pass 1-0, 1 Int; Rush 3-(-2) -0.7.

		Punting		
Year Team	G	Punts	Yds	Avg
1984 ChiB	16	83	3328	40.1
1985 Sea	12	68	2766	40.7
NFL Total	28	151	6094	40.4

DAVE FIORE Fiore, David Allan 6′4″, 288 **OT**
Col: Hofstra *HS:* Waldwick [NJ] B: 8/10/1974, Hackensack, NJ
1998 SF: 9 G.

AL FIORENTINO Fiorentino, Albert M 5′7″, 201 **G-LB**
Col: Boston College *HS:* Watertown [NY] B: 2/28/1917, Watertown, NY
1943 Was: 10 G. **1944** Was: 10 G; KR 1-5 5.0; Int 1-0. **1945** Bos: 8 G. **Total:** 28 G; KR 1-5 5.0; Int 1-0.

ED FIORENTINO Fiorentino, Edward Angelo 6′1″, 210 **DE**
Col: Boston College; Brown *HS:* Boston College [MA] B: 9/21/1923, Everett, MA D: 8/2/1989, Boston, MA *Drafted:* 1944 Round 10 Bos
1947 Bos: 4 G.

CLARKE FISCHER Fischer, Clarke John 5′8″, 165 **HB**
Col: Marquette; Campion; Catholic *HS:* Marquette Acad. [Milwaukee, WI] B: 3/30/1900, Hermansville, MI D: 10/21/1979, Pana, IL
1926 Mil: 2 G.

CLETE FISCHER Fischer, Cletus Paul 5′9″, 170 **HB-DB**
Col: Nebraska *HS:* St. Edward [NE] B: 6/11/1925, St. Edward, NE *Drafted:* 1949 Round 23 NYG
1949 NYG: Rec 3-45 15.0 1 TD; PR 7-64 9.1; KR 8-188 23.5; Int 2-10.

		Rushing			
Year Team	G	Att	Yds	Avg	TD
1949 NYG	11	26	72	2.8	0

MARK FISCHER Fischer, Mark Raymond 6′3″, 293 **C**
Col: Purdue *HS:* La Salle [Cincinnati, OH] B: 7/29/1974, Cincinnati, OH *Drafted:* 1998 Round 5 Was
1998 Was: 6 G.

PAT FISCHER Fischer, Patrick 5′9″, 170 **DB**
(Mouse) *Col:* Nebraska *HS:* West Side [Omaha, NE] B: 1/2/1940, St. Edward, NE *Drafted:* 1961 Round 17 StL
1961 StL: Rec 1-22 22.0; PR 4-18 4.5. **1962** StL: PR 4-37 9.3. **1963** StL: PR 9-25 2.8. **1964** StL: 1 Fum TD. **Total:** Rec 1-22 22.0; PR 17-80 4.7; 1 Fum TD.

		Kickoff Returns				Interceptions				Tot
Year Team	G	Ret	Yds	Avg	TD	Int	Yds	TD	Fum	TD
1961 StL	12	17	426	25.1	0	0	0	0	1	0
1962 StL	12	7	187	26.7	0	3	41	0	0	0
1963 StL	14	0	0	—	0	8	169	0	1	0
1964 StL	14	0	0	—	0	10	164	**2**	1	3
1965 StL	14	0	0	—	0	3	30	0	0	0
1966 StL	7	0	0	—	0	1	40	0	0	0
1967 StL	14	1	0	0.0	0	4	85	1	0	1
1968 Was	14	0	0	—	0	2	14	0	0	0
1969 Was	14	0	0	—	0	2	28	0	0	0

1970 Was	14	0	0	—	0	2	13	0	0	0
1971 Was	14	0	0	—	0	3	103	1	0	1
1972 Was	14	0	0	—	0	4	61	0	0	0
1973 Was	14	0	0	—	0	3	99	0	0	0
1974 Was	14	0	0	—	0	3	52	0	0	0
1975 Was	11	0	0	—	0	3	4	0	0	0
1976 Was	14	0	0	—	0	5	38	0	0	0
1977 Was	3	0	0	—	0	0	0	0	0	0
NFL Total	213	25	613	24.5	0	56	941	4	3	5

BILL FISCHER Fischer, William Anton 6'2", 248 **OT-OG-DT**
(Moose) *Col:* Notre Dame *HS:* Albert G. Lane Tech [Chicago, IL] B: 3/10/1927, Chicago, IL *Drafted:* 1949 Round 1 ChiC
1949 ChiC: 12 G; Int 1-3. **1950** ChiC: 12 G. **1951** ChiC: 12 G; KR 1-0. **1952** ChiC: 12 G; KR 1-0. **1953** ChiC: 11 G. **Total:** 59 G; KR 2-0; Int 1-3.

JOE FISHBACK Fishback, Joe Edward Jr. 6'0", 205 **DB**
Col: Carson-Newman *HS:* Austin-East [Knoxville, TN] B: 11/29/1967, Knoxville, TN
1991 Atl: 14 G; KR 3-29 9.7; 1 Fum TD; 6 Pt. **1992** NYJ-Atl: 13 G. NYJ: 5 G. Atl: 8 G. **1993** Dal: 6 G. **1994** Dal: 12 G. **Total:** 45 G; KR 3-29 9.7; 1 Fum TD; 6 Pt.

DICK FISHEL Fishel, Richard Edward 5'9", 190 **BB-LB-DB-WB**
Col: Syracuse *HS:* Morris [Bronx, NY] B: 9/19/1909, Brooklyn, NY D: 8/12/1972
1933 Bkn: 8 G; Pass 7-3 42.9%, 50 7.14 1 Int; Rush 22-61 2.8 1 TD; 6 Pt.

DARRELL FISHER Fisher, Darrell Charles 5'11", 190 **TB-FB**
Col: Iowa *HS:* Mormon Trail [Garden Grove, IA] B: 5/10/1903, IL Deceased
1925 Buf: 5 G.

DOUG FISHER Fisher, Douglas Gene 6'1", 225 **LB**
Col: Kings River CC CA; San Diego State *HS:* Caruthers [CA] B: 3/8/1947, Fresno, CA *Drafted:* 1969 Round 12 Pit
1969 Pit: 6 G. **1970** Pit: 4 G. **Total:** 10 G.

EDDIE FISHER Fisher, Edward 5'11", 210 **G**
Col: Columbia *HS:* Masten Park [Buffalo, NY] B: 7/18/1901, Tonawanda, NY D: 2/1984, Buffalo, NY
1925 Buf: 2 G.

ED FISHER Fisher, Edwin Louis 6'3", 249 **OG-DE-C**
Col: Arizona State *HS:* Lincoln [Stockton, CA] B: 5/31/1949, Stockton, CA
1974 Hou: 11 G. **1975** Hou: 14 G. **1976** Hou: 14 G. **1977** Hou: 14 G. **1978** Hou: 16 G. **1979** Hou: 16 G. **1980** Hou: 16 G. **1981** Hou: 16 G. **1982** Hou: 9 G. **Total:** 126 G.

EV FISHER Fisher, Everett Earl 5'11", 205 **BB-LB-OE-DE**
(King) *Col:* Santa Clara *HS:* Santa Rosa [CA] B: 3/1/1914 Deceased
1938 ChiC: 11 G; Rec 3-48 16.0. **1939** ChiC: 11 G; Rush 18-63 3.5; Rec 6-62 10.3. **1940** Pit: 4 G; Rec 2-12 6.0. **Total:** 26 G; Rush 18-63 3.5; Rec 11-122 11.1.

GEORGE FISHER Fisher, George Louis 6'0", 210 **T**
Col: Indiana *HS:* Clear Spring [IN] B: 8/17/1901, Jackson Co., IN D: 10/30/1968, Lewisburg, IN
1926 Ham: 2 G.

MIKE FISHER Fisher, James Michael 5'11", 172 **WR**
Col: Baylor *HS:* Gatesville [TX] B: 4/22/1958, Gatesville, TX *Drafted:* 1981 Round 8 StL
1981 StL: 2 G.

JEFF FISHER Fisher, Jeffrey Michael 5'11", 188 **DB**
Col: USC *HS:* William Howard Taft [Woodland Hills, CA] B: 2/25/1958, Culver City, CA *Drafted:* 1981 Round 7 ChiB
1981 ChiB: KR 7-102 14.6; Int 2-3. **1982** ChiB: KR 7-102 14.6; Int 3-19. **Total:** KR 14-204 14.6; Int 5-22.

		Punt Returns				
Year Team	G	Ret	Yds	Avg	TD	Fum
1981 ChiB	16	43	509	11.8	1	3
1982 ChiB	9	7	53	7.6	0	2
1983 ChiB	8	13	71	5.5	0	0
1984 ChiB	16	**57**	492	8.6	0	4
NFL Total	49	120	1125	9.4	1	9

RAY FISHER Fisher, Raymond Edward 6'0", 230 **DT-OT-OG**
Col: Eastern Illinois *HS:* Charleston [IL] B: 2/12/1934, Charleston, IL
1959 Pit: 12 G.

BOB FISHER Fisher, Robert Arthur 6'2", 220 **T**
Col: USC *HS:* Los Angeles Polytechnic [CA] B: 8/27/1916, Los Angeles, CA D: 5/29/1983, Laguna Beach, CA
1940 Was: 7 G.

BOB FISHER Fisher, Robert Lee 6'3", 240 **TE**
Col: Southern Methodist *HS:* William Blair [Pasadena, CA] B: 3/17/1958, Pasadena, CA *Drafted:* 1980 Round 12 ChiB
1980 ChiB: 16 G; Rec 12-203 16.9 2 TD; KR 3-32 10.7; 12 Pt. **1981** ChiB: 6 G; KR 1-9 9.0. **Total:** 22 G; Rec 12-203 16.9 2 TD; KR 4-41 10.3; 12 Pt.

ALEC FISHMAN Fishman, Alexander 5'11", 218 **G-FB**
Col: No College *HS:* Central [Evansville, IN] B: IL Deceased
1921 Eva: 5 G; Rush 1 TD; 6 Pt.

JASON FISK Fisk, Jason Michael 6'3", 292 **DT**
Col: Stanford *HS:* Davis [CA] B: 9/4/1972, Davis, CA *Drafted:* 1995 Round 7 Min
1995 Min: 8 G. **1996** Min: 16 G; Int 1-0; 1 Sac. **1997** Min: 16 G; Int 1-1; 3 Sac. **1998** Min: 16 G; 1.5 Sac. **Total:** 56 G; Int 2-1; 5.5 Sac.

BILL FISK Fisk, William G 6'0", 199 **OE-DE**
Col: USC *HS:* Alhambra [CA] B: 11/5/1916, Los Angeles, CA
Drafted: 1940 Round 2 Det
AAFC.

		Receiving			
Year Team	G	Rec	Yds	Avg	TD
1946 SF-A	14	19	186	9.8	1
1947 SF-A	14	5	39	7.8	0
1948 LA-A	13	9	102	11.3	0
AAFC Total	41	33	327	9.9	1

NFL **1940** Det: Rush 2-0. **1942** Det: KR 1-10 10.0. **1943** Det: KR 1-5 5.0. **Total:** Rush 2-0; KR 2-15 7.5.

		Receiving			
Year Team	G	Rec	Yds	Avg	TD
1940 Det	10	1	10	10.0	0
1941 Det	11	9	140	15.6	2
1942 Det	11	15	177	11.8	0
1943 Det	10	11	137	12.5	0
NFL Total	42	36	464	12.9	2

MAX FISKE Fiske, Max Joseph 6'0", 199 **TB-DB-OE-HB**
(Baxie) *Col:* DePaul *HS:* Pullman Tech [Chicago, IL] B: 9/27/1913, Chicago, IL D: 3/15/1973, Chicago, IL
1936 Pit: Rec 7-96 13.7. **1937** Pit: Rec 1-0. **Total:** Rec 8-96 12.0.

		Passing							
Year Team	G	Att	Comp	Comp%	Yds	YPA	TD	Int	Rating
1936 Pit	11	15	6	40.0	64	4.27	0	3	13.6
1937 Pit	7	43	17	39.5	318	7.40	4	4	58.1
1938 Pit	10	37	11	29.7	121	3.27	0	4	1.1
1939 Pit	1	0	0	—	0	—	0	0	—
NFL Total	29	95	34	35.8	503	5.29	4	11	28.4

	Rushing			
Year Team	Att	Yds	Avg	TD
1936 Pit	58	92	1.6	0
1937 Pit	28	44	1.6	0
1938 Pit	29	83	2.9	0
NFL Total	115	219	1.9	0

GALEN FISS Fiss, Galen Royce 6'0", 227 **LB**
Col: Kansas *HS:* Johnson [KS] B: 7/10/1931, Johnson, KS
Drafted: 1953 Round 13 Cle

		Interceptions		
Year Team	G	Int	Yds	TD
1956 Cle	12	1	4	0
1957 Cle	12	1	15	0
1958 Cle	12	0	0	0
1959 Cle	12	1	9	0
1960 Cle	12	1	19	0
1961 Cle	13	1	13	0
1962 Cle	14	4	81	0
1963 Cle	13	2	8	0
1964 Cle	13	1	24	0
1965 Cle	12	1	5	0
1966 Cle	14	0	0	0
NFL Total	139	13	178	0

JAMIE FITZGERALD Fitzgerald, Edgar James 6'0", 180 **DB**
Col: Idaho State *HS:* Gonzaga Prep [Spokane, WA] B: 4/30/1965, Spokane, WA
1987 Min: 2 G.

FRANCE FITZGERALD Fitzgerald, Francis J 5'10", 185 **HB**
Col: Detroit Mercy *HS:* Holyoke [MA] B: 5/20/1896, County Kerry, Ireland D: 3/6/1976, Springfield, MA
1923 Tol: 7 G.

FREEMAN FITZGERALD Fitzgerald, Freeman Charles 6'0", 195 **C-G**
Col: Notre Dame *HS:* Columbia Prep [Portland, OR] B: 8/21/1891, Jervis, OR D: 5/6/1942, Milwaukee, WI
1920 RI: 9 G. **1921** RI: 2 G. **Total:** 11 G.

GREG FITZGERALD Fitzgerald, Gregory M 6'4", 265 **DE**
Col: Iowa *HS:* Hoffman Estates [IL] B: 7/3/1963, Chicago, IL
1987 ChiB: 3 G.

JIM FITZGERALD Fitzgerald, James Peter 5′11″, 215 **C**
Col: Holy Cross *HS:* Westbrook Seminary [ME] B: 3/7/1907, Waltham, MA D: 9/23/1978, Boston, MA
1930 SI: 11 G. **1931** SI: 10 G. **Total:** 21 G.

JOHN FITZGERALD Fitzgerald, John Robert 6′5″, 255 **C-OG**
Col: Boston College *HS:* Southbridge [MA] B: 4/16/1948, Southbridge, MA *Drafted:* 1970 Round 4 Dal
1971 Dal: 14 G. **1972** Dal: 14 G. **1973** Dal: 14 G. **1974** Dal: 12 G. **1975** Dal: 14 G. **1976** Dal: 14 G. **1977** Dal: 12 G. **1978** Dal: 14 G; 1 Fum. **1979** Dal: 15 G. **1980** Dal: 14 G. **Total:** 137 G; 1 Fum.

JOE FITZGERALD Fitzgerald, Joseph 150 **OE**
Col: No College *HS:* Western [Detroit, MI] Deceased
1920 Det: 8 G.

KEVIN FITZGERALD Fitzgerald, Kevin Lee 6′3″, 235 **TE**
Col: Wis.-Eau Claire B: 6/30/1964
1987 GB: 1 G.

MICKEY FITZGERALD Fitzgerald, Marion Maxwell 6′2″, 235 **RB**
Col: Virginia Tech *HS:* E.C. Glass [Lynchburg, VA] B: 4/10/1958, Lynchburg, VA
1981 Atl-Phi: 2 G. Atl: 1 G. Phi: 1 G. **Total:** 2 G.

MIKE FITZGERALD Fitzgerald, Michael 5′10″, 180 **DB**
(Mickey) *Col:* Iowa State *HS:* Highland Park [MI] B: 5/4/1941, Detroit, MI
1966 Min: Int 1-18. **1967** Min-NYG-Atl: PR 2-4 2.0. Min: PR 1-4 4.0. Atl: PR 1-0. **Total:** PR 2-4 2.0; Int 1-18.

		Kickoff Returns				
Year Team	**G**	**Ret**	**Yds**	**Avg**	**TD**	**Fum**
1966 Min	9	14	301	21.5	0	0
1967 Min-NYG-Atl	10	12	240	20.0	0	1
1967 Min	6	0	0	—	0	0
1967 NYG	2	6	119	19.8	0	1
1967 Atl	2	6	121	20.2	0	0
NFL Total	19	26	541	20.8	0	1

PAUL FITZGIBBON Fitzgibbon, Paul Joseph 5′8″, 176 **BB-WB-HB-TB**
Col: Creighton *HS:* Cathedral [Sioux Falls, SD] B: 3/21/1903 Deceased
1926 Dul: 14 G; Rush 1 TD; 6 Pt. **1927** Fra: 11 G. **1928** ChiC: 6 G. **1930** GB: 9 G; Rush 1 TD; Rec 2 TD; Tot TD 3; 18 Pt. **1931** GB: 11 G; Pass 3 TD; Scor 1, 1 XK. **1932** GB: 4 G; Pass 5-1 20.0%, 9 1.80; Rush 2-(-1) -0.5; Rec 1-25 25.0. **Total:** 55 G; Pass 5-1 20.0%, 9 1.80 3 TD; Rush 2-(-1) -0.5 2 TD; Rec 1-25 25.0 2 TD; Tot TD 4.

STEVE FITZHUGH Fitzhugh, Stephen Allen 5′11″, 188 **DB**
Col: Miami (Ohio) *HS:* Walsh Jesuit [Akron, OH] B: 1/28/1963, Akron, OH
1987 Den: 3 G.

BOB FITZKE Fitzke, Paul Frederick Herman 5′10″, 195 **WB**
Col: Wyoming; Idaho *HS:* La Crosse [WI] B: 7/30/1900, La Crosse, WI D: 6/30/1950, Sacramento, CA
1925 Fra: 16 G; Rush 1 TD; 6 Pt.

SCOTT FITZKEE Fitzkee, Scott Austin 6′0″, 187 **WR**
Col: Penn State *HS:* Red Lion [PA] B: 4/8/1957, York, PA
Drafted: 1979 Round 5 Phi
1979 Phi: 15 G; Rec 8-105 13.1 1 TD; 6 Pt. **1980** Phi: 7 G; Rush 1-15 15.0; Rec 6-169 28.2 2 TD; 12 Pt. **1981** SD: 5 G. **1982** SD: 9 G; Rec 3-47 15.7 1 TD; 6 Pt. **Total:** 36 G; Rush 1-15 15.0; Rec 17-321 18.9 4 TD; 24 Pt.

JAMES FITZPATRICK FitzPatrick, James Joseph III 6′8″, 305 **OT-OG**
Col: USC *HS:* Beaverton [OR] B: 2/1/1964, Heidelberg, Germany
Drafted: 1986 Round 1 SD
1986 SD: 4 G. **1987** SD: 10 G. **1988** SD: 11 G. **1989** SD: 13 G. **1990** LARd: 11 G. **1991** LARd: 16 G. **Total:** 65 G.

JACK FLAGERMAN Flagerman, Jack Michael 6′0″, 218 **C-LB**
Col: St. Mary's (Cal.) *HS:* Tamalpais [Mill Valley, CA] B: 2/27/1922, San Francisco, CA
AAFC **1948** LA-A: 14 G; Rec 0-6.

TERRENCE FLAGLER Flagler, Robert Terrence 6′0″, 200 **RB**
Col: Clemson *HS:* Fernandina Beach [FL] B: 9/24/1964, New York, NY
Drafted: 1987 Round 1 SF

		Rushing				Receiving			
Year Team	**G**	**Att**	**Yds**	**Avg**	**TD**	**Rec**	**Yds**	**Avg**	**TD**
1987 SF	3	6	11	1.8	0	2	28	14.0	0
1988 SF	3	3	5	1.7	0	4	72	18.0	0
1989 SF	15	33	129	3.9	1	6	51	8.5	0
1990 Pho	13	13	85	6.5	1	13	130	10.0	1
1991 Pho	7	1	7	7.0	0	8	85	10.6	0
NFL Total	41	56	237	4.2	2	33	366	11.1	1

	Kickoff Returns					Tot
Year Team	**Ret**	**Yds**	**Avg**	**TD**	**Fum**	**TD**
1987 SF	3	31	10.3	0	2	0
1989 SF	32	643	20.1	0	5	1
1990 Pho	10	167	16.7	0	0	2
1991 Pho	12	208	17.3	0	0	0
NFL Total	57	1049	18.4	0	7	3

HARRY FLAHERTY Flaherty, Harry Edward 6′1″, 232 **LB**
Col: Holy Cross *HS:* Red Bank Catholic [NJ] B: 12/25/1961
1987 Dal: 2 G.

JIM FLAHERTY Flaherty, James Wilson 198 **OE-HB**
Col: Georgetown *HS:* Eastern [Washington, DC] B: 12/26/1895, Washington, DC D: 1/30/1978, Winter Haven, FL
1923 ChiB: 12 G.

RAY FLAHERTY Flaherty, Raymond Paul 6′0″, 190 **OE-DE**
(Red) *Col:* Washington State; Gonzaga *HS:* Gonzaga Prep [Spokane, WA] B: 9/1/1903, Spokane, WA D: 7/19/1994, Coeur d'Alene, ID
HOF: 1976
1929 NYG: Scor **1** 1XP. **1932** NYG: Pass 4-3 75.0%, 33 8.25.
Total: Pass 4-3 75.0%, 33 8.25; Scor 1 1XP.

		Receiving				Tot
Year Team	**G**	**Rec**	**Yds**	**Avg**	**TD**	**TD**
1927 NYY	13	—	—	—	**4**	4
1928 NYY-NYG	12	—	—	—	1	1
1928 NYY	11	—	—	—	1	1
1928 NYG	1	—	—	—	0	0
1929 NYG	15	—	—	—	**8**	8
1931 NYG	14	—	—	—	1	2
1932 NYG	12	**21**	**350**	16.7	**5**	5
1933 NYG	11	11	177	16.1	0	0
1934 NYG	9	8	76	9.5	1	1
1935 NYG	2	1	23	23.0	0	0
NFL Total	88	41	626	15.3	20	21

DICK FLAHERTY Flaherty, Richard Thomas 5′10″, 200 **OE**
Col: Gonzaga; Marquette *HS:* Gonzaga Prep [Spokane, WA] B: 8/8/1900, Seattle, WA D: 2/4/1984, Spokane, WA
1926 GB: 12 G; Rec 2 TD; 12 Pt.

TOM FLAHERTY Flaherty, Thomas Francis 6′3″, 223 **LB**
Col: Northwestern *HS:* St. Rita [Chicago, IL] B: 9/24/1964, Chicago, IL
Drafted: 1986 Round 11 Cin
1987 Cin: 3 G.

ED FLANAGAN Flanagan, Edward Joseph 6′3″, 245 **C**
(Bull) *Col:* Purdue *HS:* Altoona [PA] B: 2/23/1944, San Bernardino, PA *Drafted:* 1965 Round 5 Det
1965 Det: 14 G. **1966** Det: 14 G. **1967** Det: 14 G; Rush 0-5. **1968** Det: 14 G. **1969** Det: 14 G. **1970** Det: 14 G. **1971** Det: 14 G. **1972** Det: 14 G. **1973** Det: 14 G. **1974** Det: 13 G. **1975** SD: 14 G. **1976** SD: 12 G; 1 Fum. **Total:** 165 G; Rush 0-5; 1 Fum.

LATHAM FLANAGAN Flanagan, Latham 6′2″, 185 **OE**
(Pete) *Col:* Carnegie Mellon *HS:* Buckhannon [WV]; Montclair Acad. [Buckhannon, WV] B: 1/17/1907, Buckhannon, WV D: 5/18/1981, Eugene, OR
1931 ChiB-ChiC: 4 G. ChiB: 2 G. ChiC: 2 G. **Total:** 4 G.

MIKE FLANAGAN Flanagan, Michael Christopher 6′5″, 290 **C**
Col: UCLA *HS:* Rio Americano [Sacramento, CA] B: 11/10/1973, Washington, DC *Drafted:* 1996 Round 3 GB
1998 GB: 2 G.

DICK FLANAGAN Flanagan, Richard Eugene 6′0″, 216 **LB-OG-C-HB**
Col: Ohio State *HS:* Findley [OH] B: 10/31/1926, Sidney, OH
Drafted: 1948 Round 8 ChiB
1948 ChiB: 11 G; Rush 5-14 2.8. **1949** ChiB: 12 G; KR 5-88 17.6. **1950** ChiB-Det: 8 G. ChiB: 1 G. Det: 7 G. **1951** Det: 12 G; Int 2-0. **1952** Det: 12 G; Int 1-14. **1953** Pit: 12 G; Int 2-23. **1954** Pit: 5 G; Int 3-0. **1955** Pit: 12 G. **Total:** 84 G; Rush 5-14 2.8; KR 5-88 17.6; Int 8-37.

HOOT FLANAGAN Flanagan, William Harold 6′0″, 169 **TB-WB**
Col: West Virginia Wesleyan; Pittsburgh *HS:* Buckhannon [WV] B: 4/28/1901, Buckhannon, WV D: 2/3/1975, Martinsburg, WV
1925 Pott: 10 G; Pass 1 TD; Rush 5 TD; Int **2** TD; Tot TD 7; 42 Pt. **1926** Pott: 8 G. **Total:** 18 G; Pass 1 TD; Rush 5 TD; Int 2 TD; Tot TD 7; 42 Pt.

JIM FLANIGAN Flanigan, James Michael 6′3″, 240 **LB**
Col: Pittsburgh *HS:* North [West Mifflin, PA] B: 4/15/1945, Pittsburgh, PA *Drafted:* 1967 Round 2 GB
1967 GB: 12 G. **1968** GB: 13 G. **1969** GB: 4 G. **1970** GB: 11 G. **1971** NO: 14 G; Int 1-10. **Total:** 54 G; Int 1-10.

JIM FLANIGAN Flanigan, James Michael 6′2″, 285 **DT**
Col: Notre Dame *HS:* Southern Door [Brussels, WI] B: 8/27/1971, Green Bay, WI *Drafted:* 1994 Round 3 ChiB
1994 ChiB: 14 G; KR 2-26 13.0. **1995** ChiB: 16 G; Rush 1-0; Rec 2-6 3.0 2 TD; 12 Pt; 11 Sac. **1996** ChiB: 14 G; Rec 1-1 1.0 1 TD; 6 Pt; 5 Sac.

1997 ChiB: 16 G; Scor 1 2XP; 2 Pt; 6 Sac. **1998** ChiB: 16 G; 8.5 Sac. **Total:** 76 G; Rush 1-0; Rec 3-7 2.3 3 TD; KR 2-26 13.0; Scor 1 2XP; 20 Pt; 30.5 Sac.

JOHN FLANNERY Flannery, John Joseph 6′4″, 303 **OG-C**
Col: Syracuse *HS:* Pottsville [PA] B: 1/13/1969, Pottsville, PA
Drafted: 1991 Round 2 Hou
1991 Hou: 16 G; KR 1-0. **1992** Hou: 15 G; KR 1-12 12.0. **1994** Hou: 16 G. **1996** Dal: 1 G. **1997** Dal: 16 G. **1998** StL: 16 G; Rec 1-2 2.0; 2 Fum. **Total:** 80 G; Rec 1-2 2.0; KR 2-12 6.0; 2 Fum.

BILL FLANNIGAN Flannigan, William 210 **T**
Col: No College *HS:* Beloit [WI] B: 1902 Deceased
1926 Lou: 2 G.

PAUL FLATLEY Flatley, Paul Richard 6′1″, 187 **WR**
Col: Northwestern *HS:* Richmond [IN] B: 1/30/1941, Richmond, IN
Drafted: 1963 Round 4 Min

		Receiving				
Year Team	**G**	**Rec**	**Yds**	**Avg**	**TD**	**Fum**
1963 Min	14	51	867	17.0	4	1
1964 Min	10	28	450	16.1	3	0
1965 Min	14	50	896	17.9	7	1
1966 Min	13	50	777	15.5	3	0
1967 Min	13	23	232	10.1	0	1
1968 Atl	14	20	305	15.3	0	0
1969 Atl	14	45	834	18.5	6	1
1970 Atl	14	39	544	13.9	1	0
NFL Total	106	306	4905	16.0	24	4

WILLIE FLATTERY Flattery, Wilson Immel 5′11″, 220 **G-E**
(Pud) *Col:* Wooster *HS:* Wooster [OH] B: 2/4/1904, Wooster, OH
D: 4/4/1957, Wooster, OH
1925 Can: 6 G. **1926** Can: 10 G. **Total:** 16 G.

JACK FLAVIN Flavin, John Henry 5′11″, 187 **FB**
Col: Georgetown *HS:* Portland [ME] B: 1/1900, Portland, ME
D: 7/8/1965, New York, NY
1923 Buf: 1 G; Rush 2 TD; 12 Pt. **1924** Buf: 2 G. **Total:** 3 G; Rush 2 TD; 12 Pt.

BILL FLECKENSTEIN Fleckenstein, William P 6′1″, 208 **G-E-C-T**
Col: Carleton; Iowa *HS:* Faribault [MN] B: 11/4/1903, Faribault, MN
D: 1/25/1967, Los Angeles, CA
1925 ChiB: 16 G. **1926** ChiB: 10 G. **1927** ChiB: 11 G. **1928** ChiB: 12 G; 6 Pt. **1929** ChiB: 15 G. **1930** ChiB-Port: 12 G. ChiB: 2 G. Port: 10 G. **1931** Fra-Bkn: 8 G. Fra: 6 G. Bkn: 2 G. **Total:** 84 G; 6 Pt.

JACK FLEISCHMANN Fleischmann, Godfrey Jacob 5′6″, 184 **G**
(Butter) *Col:* Purdue *HS:* East Detroit [Eastpointe, MI] B: 8/15/1901, Monroe, MI D: 4/27/1988, Monroe, LA
1925 Det: 9 G. **1926** Det: 11 G. **1927** Prov: 14 G. **1928** Prov: 11 G. **1929** Prov: 12 G. **Total:** 57 G.

CORY FLEMING Fleming, Cory Lamont 6′1″, 216 **WR**
Col: Tennessee *HS:* Stratford [Nashville, TN] B: 3/19/1971, Nashville, TN *Drafted:* 1994 Round 3 SF
1994 Dal: 2 G. **1995** Dal: 16 G; Rec 6-83 13.8. **Total:** 18 G; Rec 6-83 13.8.

DON FLEMING Fleming, Donald Denver 6′0″, 188 **DB**
Col: Florida *HS:* Shadyside [OH] B: 6/11/1937, Bellaire, OH
D: 6/4/1963, Winter Park, FL *Drafted:* 1959 Round 28 ChiC
1960 Cle: KR 1-8 8.0. **Total:** KR 1-8 8.0.

		Interceptions		
Year Team	**G**	**Int**	**Yds**	**TD**
1960 Cle	12	5	85	0
1961 Cle	14	3	62	0
1962 Cle	12	2	13	0
NFL Total	38	10	160	0

GEORGE FLEMING Fleming, George 5′11″, 188 **HB-K**
Col: East Los Angeles Coll. CA (J.C.); Washington *HS:* Booker T. Washington [Dallas, TX] B: 6/29/1938, TX *Drafted:* 1961 Round 2 Oak
1961 Oak: Pass 1-0, 1 Int; Rec 10-49 4.9; PR 3-24 8.0; Scor 63, 11-26 42.3% FG, 24-25 96.0% XK.

		Rushing				Kickoff Returns				
Year Team	**G**	**Att**	**Yds**	**Avg**	**TD**	**Ret**	**Yds**	**Avg**	**TD**	**Fum**
1961 Oak	14	31	112	3.6	1	**29**	588	20.3	0	2

MARV FLEMING Fleming, Marvin Xavier 6′4″, 232 **TE**
Col: Utah *HS:* Compton [CA] B: 1/2/1942, Longview, TX
Drafted: 1963 Round 11 GB
1963 GB: KR 1-0. **Total:** KR 1-0.

		Receiving			
Year Team	**G**	**Rec**	**Yds**	**Avg**	**TD**
1963 GB	14	7	132	18.9	2
1964 GB	14	4	36	9.0	0
1965 GB	13	14	141	10.1	2
1966 GB	14	31	361	11.6	2
1967 GB	14	10	126	12.6	1
1968 GB	14	25	278	11.1	3
1969 GB	12	18	226	12.6	2
1970 Mia	14	18	205	11.4	0
1971 Mia	14	13	137	10.5	2
1972 Mia	14	13	156	12.0	1
1973 Mia	11	3	22	7.3	0
1974 Mia	14	1	3	3.0	1
NFL Total	162	157	1823	11.6	16

WILMER FLEMING Fleming, Wilmer Clarence 5′11″, 165 **WB**
Col: Mount Union *HS:* Cambridge [OH] B: 9/30/1901, Colton, OH
D: 3/13/1969, Toledo, OH
1925 Can: 1 G.

MACK FLENNIKEN Flenniken, Mack 6′1″, 200 **FB-TB-WB-BB**
Col: Centenary; Geneva *HS:* North Side [Fort Worth, TX] B: 1905
D: 5/26/1956, Geneva, PA
1930 ChiC: 10 G; Rush 3 TD; 18 Pt. **1931** NYG: 4 G; Pass 1 TD; Rush 1 TD; 6 Pt. **Total:** 14 G; Pass 1 TD; Rush 4 TD; 24 Pt.

ANDY FLETCHER Fletcher, Andrew 5′6″, 165 **FB**
Col: Maryland Deceased
1920 Buf: 2 G.

ARTHUR FLETCHER Fletcher, Arthur A 6′3″, 215 **OE**
Col: Washburn *HS:* Junction City [KS] B: 12/22/1924, Phoenix, AZ
1950 Bal: 1 G; Rec 2-18 9.0.

BILLY FLETCHER Fletcher, Billy Ray 5′10″, 190 **DB**
Col: Memphis *HS:* South Side [Memphis, TN] B: 5/2/1943, Memphis, TN
1966 Den: 1 G.

CHRIS FLETCHER Fletcher, Christopher C Jr. 5′11″, 185 **DB**
Col: Temple *HS:* East Orange [NJ] B: 12/25/1948, Morristown, NJ
Drafted: 1970 Round 9 SD

		Punt Returns				Kickoff Returns			
Year Team	**G**	**Ret**	**Yds**	**Avg**	**TD**	**Ret**	**Yds**	**Avg**	**TD**
1970 SD	13	16	137	8.6	0	17	382	22.5	0
1971 SD	14	12	68	5.7	0	11	217	19.7	0
1972 SD	1	0	0	—	0	0	0	—	0
1973 SD	9	0	0	—	0	0	0	—	0
1974 SD	12	0	0	—	0	0	0	—	0
1975 SD	14	0	0	—	0	0	0	—	0
1976 SD	13	0	0	—	0	0	0	—	0
NFL Total	76	28	205	7.3	0	28	599	21.4	0

	Interceptions			
Year Team	**Int**	**Yds**	**TD**	**Fum**
1970 SD	0	0	0	1
1971 SD	3	63	1	2
1974 SD	4	74	0	0
1975 SD	6	100	0	1
NFL Total	13	237	1	4

JOHN FLETCHER Fletcher, John Williams 6′3″, 293 **OG**
Col: Texas A&M–Kingsville *HS:* Foy H. Moody [Corpus Christi, TX]
B: 8/22/1965, Uvalde, TX
1987 Cin: 3 G.

LONDON FLETCHER Fletcher, London Levi 6′0″, 241 **LB**
Col: John Carroll *HS:* Villa Angela–St. Joseph [Cleveland, OH]
B: 5/19/1975, Cleveland, OH
1998 StL: 16 G; KR 5-72 14.4; 1 Fum.

OLLIE FLETCHER Fletcher, Oliver 6′3″, 210 **G-LB-G**
Col: Rancho Santiago Coll. CA (J.C.); USC *HS:* San Diego [CA]
B: 2/5/1923 D: 5/10/1994, Bullhead City, AZ
AAFC **1949** LA-A: 3 G.

SIMON FLETCHER Fletcher, Simon Raynard 6′5″, 240 **LB-DE**
Col: Houston *HS:* Bay City [TX] B: 2/18/1962, Bay City, TX
Drafted: 1985 Round 2 Den
1985 Den: 16 G; 1 Sac. **1986** Den: 16 G; 5.5 Sac. **1987** Den: 12 G; 4 Sac. **1988** Den: 16 G; Int 1-4; 9 Sac. **1989** Den: 16 G; 12 Sac. **1990** Den: 16 G; Scor **1** Saf; 2 Pt; 11 Sac. **1991** Den: 16 G; 13.5 Sac. **1992** Den: 16 G; 16 Sac. **1993** Den: 16 G; 13.5 Sac. **1994** Den: 16 G; Int 1-4; 7 Sac. **1995** Den: 16 G; 5 Sac. **Total:** 172 G; Int 2-8; Scor 1 Saf; 2 Pt; 97.5 Sac.

TERRELL FLETCHER Fletcher, Terrell Antoine 5′8″, 196 **RB**
Col: Wisconsin *HS:* Hazelwood East [St. Louis, MO] B: 9/14/1973, St. Louis, MO *Drafted:* 1995 Round 2 SD
1995 SD: PR 3-12 4.0; KR 4-65 16.3. **1998** SD: Pass 1-1 100.0%, 23 23.00 1 TD; KR 3-71 23.7. **Total:** Pass 1-1 100.0%, 23 23.00 1 TD; PR 3-12 4.0; KR 7-136 19.4.

		Rushing				Receiving					Tot
Year Team	**G**	**Att**	**Yds**	**Avg**	**TD**	**Rec**	**Yds**	**Avg**	**TD**	**Fum**	**TD**
1995 SD	16	26	140	5.4	1	3	26	8.7	0	2	1

1996 SD	16	77	282	3.7	0	61	476	7.8	2	1	2
1997 SD	13	51	161	3.2	0	39	292	7.5	0	4	0
1998 SD	12	153	543	3.5	5	30	188	6.3	0	1	5
NFL Total	57	307	1126	3.7	6	133	982	7.4	2	8	8

TOM FLICK Flick, Thomas Lyle 6′2″, 190 **QB**
Col: Washington *HS:* Belleville [WA] B: 8/30/1958, Patuxent River, MD
Drafted: 1981 Round 4 Was
1986 SD: Rush 6-5 0.8 1 TD. **Total:** Rush 6-5 0.8 1 TD.

		Passing								
Year Team	**G**	**Att**	**Comp**	**Comp%**	**Yds**	**YPA**	**TD**	**Int**	**Rating**	**Fum**
1981 Was	6	27	13	48.1	143	5.30	0	2	33.4	2
1982 NE	3	5	0	0.0	0	0.00	0	0	39.6	0
1984 Cle	1	1	1	100.0	2	2.00	0	0	79.2	1
1986 SD	11	73	33	45.2	361	4.95	2	8	29.9	1
NFL Total	21	106	47	44.3	506	4.77	2	10	25.9	4

PAUL FLINN Flinn, Paul Augustine 6′0″, 180 **E**
Col: Minnesota *HS:* Central [Duluth, MN] B: 9/11/1895, St. Paul, MN
D: 12/1980, St. Paul, MN
1922 Min: 3 G. **1923** Min: 8 G. **Total:** 11 G.

GEORGE FLINT Flint, George Howard 6′4″, 240 **OG**
Col: Arizona State *HS:* North [Phoenix, AZ] B: 2/26/1939, Erie, PA
1962 Buf: 14 G; KR 1-4 4.0. **1963** Buf: 9 G. **1964** Buf: 14 G. **1965** Buf: 14 G. **1968** Buf: 14 G. **Total:** 65 G; KR 1-4 4.0.

JUDSON FLINT Flint, Judson Rochelle 6′0″, 201 **DB**
Col: Memphis; California (Pa.) *HS:* Farrell [PA] B: 1/26/1957, Farrell, PA *Drafted:* 1979 Round 7 NE
1980 Cle: 13 G; KR 1-0. **1981** Cle: 16 G; Int 2-33. **1982** Cle: 9 G; Int 1-0. **1983** Buf: 1 G. **Total:** 39 G; KR 1-0; Int 3-33.

BRIAN FLONES Flones, Brian Lee 6′1″, 228 **LB**
Col: Washington State *HS:* Burlington-Edison [Burlington, WA]
B: 9/1/1959, Mount Vernon, WA
1981 Sea: 4 G. **1982** Sea: 9 G. **Total:** 13 G.

ANTHONY FLORENCE Florence, Anthony Westly 6′0″, 185 **CB**
Col: Bethune-Cookman *HS:* Atlantic [Delray Beach, FL]
B: 12/11/1966, Delray Beach, FL *Drafted:* 1989 Round 4 TB
1991 Cle: 6 G; 0.5 Sac.

PAUL FLORENCE Florence, Paul Robert 6′1″, 180 **OE**
(Pep) *Col:* Loyola (Chicago); Georgetown *HS:* Campion Prep [Prarie du Chien, WI]; Loyola Acad. [Wilmette, IL] B: 4/22/1900, Chicago, IL
D: 5/28/1986, Gainesville, FL
1920 ChiC: 9 G.

MIKE FLORES Flores, Michael Andre 6′3″, 256 **DE**
Col: Louisville *HS:* East [Youngstown, OH] B: 12/1/1966, Youngstown, OH *Drafted:* 1991 Round 11 Phi
1991 Phi: 4 G. **1992** Phi: 15 G. **1993** Phi: 16 G; Scor 1 Saf; 2 Pt; 3 Sac. **1994** Phi: 15 G; 3 Sac. **1995** Was: 11 G; 1 Sac. **Total:** 61 G; Scor 1 Saf; 2 Pt; 7 Sac.

TOM FLORES Flores, Thomas Raymond 6′1″, 202 **QB**
Col: Fresno City Coll. CA (J.C.); U. of Pacific *HS:* Sanger [CA]
B: 3/21/1937, Fresno, CA

		Passing							
Year Team	**G**	**Att**	**Comp**	**Comp%**	**Yds**	**YPA**	**TD**	**Int**	**Rating**
1960 Oak	14	252	136	**54.0**	1738	6.90	12	12	71.8
1961 Oak	14	366	190	51.9	2176	5.95	15	19	62.1
1963 Oak	14	247	113	45.7	2101	8.51	20	13	80.7
1964 Oak	14	200	98	49.0	1389	6.95	7	14	54.4
1965 Oak	14	269	122	45.4	1593	5.92	14	11	64.9
1966 Oak	14	306	151	49.3	2638	8.62	24	14	86.2
1967 Buf	14	64	22	34.4	260	4.06	0	8	8.1
1968 Buf	1	5	3	60.0	15	3.00	0	1	25.0
1969 Buf-KC	7	6	3	50.0	49	8.17	1	0	117.4
1969 Buf	2	5	2	40.0	16	3.20	0	0	48.8
1969 KC	5	1	1	100.0	33	33.00	1	0	158.3
NFL Total	106	1715	838	48.9	11959	6.97	93	92	67.6

	Rushing				
Year Team	**Att**	**Yds**	**Avg**	**TD**	**Fum**
1960 Oak	19	123	6.5	3	3
1961 Oak	23	36	1.6	1	8
1963 Oak	12	2	0.2	0	2
1964 Oak	11	64	5.8	0	3
1965 Oak	11	32	2.9	0	0
1966 Oak	5	50	10.0	1	2
1969 Buf-KC	1	0	0.0	0	0
1969 KC	1	0	0.0	0	0
NFL Total	82	307	3.7	5	18

JIM FLOWER Flower, James Tod Jr. 6′1″, 193 **T-OE-C-G**
(AKA Reeves) *Col:* Ohio State *HS:* Central [Akron, OH]
B: 10/17/1895, Akron, OH D: 5/6/1965, Fremont, OH
1920 Col: 4 G. **1921** Akr: 9 G. **1922** Akr: 10 G. **1923** Akr: 7 G. **1924** Akr: 8 G. **1925** Akr: 1 G. **Total:** 39 G.

BERNIE FLOWERS Flowers, Benjamin Bernard 6′2″, 190 **OE**
Col: Purdue *HS:* Erie Tech [PA] B: 2/14/1930, Erie, PA *Drafted:* 1953 Round 2 Bal
1956 Bal: 1 G.

CHARLIE FLOWERS Flowers, Charles 6′1″, 220 **FB**
(Flavy) *Col:* Mississippi *HS:* Robert E. Lee [Marianna, AR]
B: 6/28/1937, Marianna, AR *Drafted:* 1960 Round 1 LAC

		Rushing				Receiving					Tot
Year Team	**G**	**Att**	**Yds**	**Avg**	**TD**	**Rec**	**Yds**	**Avg**	**TD**	**Fum**	**TD**
1960 LAC	10	39	161	4.1	1	12	153	12.8	1	2	2
1961 SD	14	51	177	3.5	3	16	175	10.9	0	2	3
1962 NYT	4	21	78	3.7	0	7	55	7.9	0	0	0
NFL Total	28	111	416	3.7	4	35	383	10.9	1	4	5

KEITH FLOWERS Flowers, Keith Duane 6′0″, 211 **C-LB**
Col: Texas Christian *HS:* Perryton [TX] B: 4/24/1930, Perryton, TX
D: 11/12/1993, Richardson, TX *Drafted:* 1952 Round 11 Det
1952 Det-Dal: 9 G; Int 1-16; Scor 3, 3-5 60.0% XK. Det: 3 G. Dal: 6 G; Int 1-16; Scor 3, 3-5 60.0% XK. **Total:** 9 G; Int 1-16; Scor 3, 3-5 60.0% XK.

KENNY FLOWERS Flowers, Kenneth Charles 6′0″, 210 **RB**
Col: Clemson *HS:* Spruce Creek [Port Orange, FL] B: 3/14/1964, Daytona Beach, FL *Drafted:* 1987 Round 2 Atl
1987 Atl: Rec 7-50 7.1; KR 4-72 18.0. **Total:** Rec 7-50 7.1; KR 4-72 18.0.

		Rushing				
Year Team	**G**	**Att**	**Yds**	**Avg**	**TD**	**Fum**
1987 Atl	8	14	61	4.4	0	1
1989 Atl	8	13	24	1.8	1	0
NFL Total	16	27	85	3.1	1	1

LARRY FLOWERS Flowers, Larry Darnell 6′1″, 190 **DB**
Col: Texas Tech *HS:* Temple [TX] B: 4/19/1958, Temple, TX
Drafted: 1980 Round 4 TB
1981 NYG: 16 G; Int 1-9. **1982** NYG: 6 G. **1983** NYG: 14 G; Int 1-19; 1 Sac. **1984** NYG: 16 G. **1985** NYG-NYJ: 15 G. NYG: 9 G. NYJ: 6 G. **Total:** 67 G; Int 2-28; 1 Sac.

LETHON FLOWERS Flowers, Lethon III 6′0″, 213 **DB**
Col: Georgia Tech *HS:* Spring Valley [Columbia, SC] B: 1/14/1973, Columbia, SC *Drafted:* 1995 Round 5 Pit
1995 Pit: 10 G. **1996** Pit: 16 G. **1997** Pit: 10 G. **1998** Pit: 16 G; Int 1-2; 1 Sac. **Total:** 52 G; Int 1-2; 1 Sac.

DICK FLOWERS Flowers, Richard R 6′0″, 190 **QB**
(Posey) *Col:* Northwestern *HS:* South Bend Central [IN]
B: 8/13/1927, South Bend, IN
1953 Bal: 1 G; Pass 4-2 50.0%, 18 4.50.

RICHMOND FLOWERS Flowers, Richmond McDavid Jr. 6′0″, 180 **DB-WR**
Col: Tennessee *HS:* Sidney Lanier [Montgomery, AL] B: 6/13/1947, Montgomery, AL *Drafted:* 1969 Round 2 Dal
1969 Dal: 6 G; KR 11-238 21.6. **1970** Dal: 14 G; KR 1-3 3.0. **1971** Dal-NYG: 13 G; KR 8-156 19.5; Int 1-0; 1 Fum. Dal: 5 G. NYG: 8 G; KR 8-156 19.5; Int 1-0; 1 Fum. **1972** NYG: 14 G; Int 4-30. **1973** NYG: 8 G; Int 1-0. **Total:** 55 G; KR 20-397 19.9; Int 6-30; 1 Fum.

BOB FLOWERS Flowers, Robert O.C. 6′1″, 210 **C-LB**
Col: Texas; Texas Tech *HS:* Big Spring [TX] B: 8/6/1917, Big Spring, TX D: 12/8/1962, Big Spring, TX
1942 GB: 3 G. **1943** GB: 8 G; Int 1-0. **1944** GB: 8 G. **1945** GB: 10 G. **1946** GB: 10 G. **1947** GB: 12 G; Int 1-12. **1948** GB: 11 G; Int 4-21. **1949** GB: 1 G. **Total:** 63 G; Int 6-33.

BOBBY JACK FLOYD Floyd, Bobby Jack 6′0″, 210 **FB**
Col: Texas Christian *HS:* Paris [TX] B: 12/8/1929, Paris, TX
Drafted: 1952 Round 15 GB
1952 GB: Rec 11-129 11.7; KR 5-75 15.0. **1953** ChiB: Rec 9-63 7.0. **Total:** Rec 20-192 9.6; KR 5-75 15.0.

		Rushing				
Year Team	**G**	**Att**	**Yds**	**Avg**	**TD**	**Fum**
1952 GB	12	61	236	3.9	1	5
1953 ChiB	8	16	70	4.4	0	1
NFL Total	20	77	306	4.0	1	6

CHRIS FLOYD Floyd, Christopher Michael 6′0″, 231 **RB**
Col: Michigan *HS:* Cooley [Detroit, MI] B: 6/23/1975, Detroit, MI
Drafted: 1998 Round 3 NE
1998 NE: 16 G; Rush 6-22 3.7; Rec 1-6 6.0.

DON FLOYD Floyd, Donald Wayne 6′3″, 245 **DE**
Col: Texas Christian *HS:* Midlothian [TX] B: 7/10/1938, Abilene, TX D: 3/9/1980, Arlington, TX *Drafted:* 1960 Round 1 NYT
1960 Hou: 14 G. **1961** Hou: 14 G. **1962** Hou: 14 G; Int 4-50 **1** TD; 6 Pt. **1963** Hou: 9 G. **1964** Hou: 14 G; Int 0-8; 6 Pt. **1965** Hou: 14 G. **1966** Hou: 6 G. **1967** Hou: 12 G. **Total:** 97 G; Int 4-58 1 TD; Tot TD 2; 12 Pt.

ERIC FLOYD Floyd, Eric Cunningham 6′5″, 305 **OT-OG**
Col: Auburn *HS:* West [Rome, GA] B: 10/28/1965, Rome, GA
1990 SD: 16 G. **1991** SD: 2 G. **1992** Phi: 16 G. **1993** Phi: 3 G. **1995** Ariz: 1 G. **Total:** 38 G.

GEORGE FLOYD Floyd, George Jr. 5′11″, 190 **DB**
Col: Eastern Kentucky *HS:* Hernando [Brooksville, FL] B: 12/21/1960, Tampa, FL *Drafted:* 1982 Round 4 NYJ
1982 NYJ: 7 G. **1984** NYJ: 8 G. **Total:** 15 G.

JOHN FLOYD Floyd, John Manuel 6′1″, 195 **WR**
Col: Northeast Louisiana *HS:* Gladewater [TX] B: 9/10/1956, Big Sandy, TX *Drafted:* 1979 Round 4 SD
1979 SD: 8 G; Rec 10-152 15.2 1 TD; 6 Pt. **1980** SD: 15 G; Rec 1-31 31.0 1 TD; PR 1-0; 6 Pt. **1981** StL: 4 G; Rec 3-32 10.7. **Total:** 27 G; Rec 14-215 15.4 2 TD; PR 1-0; 12 Pt.

MALCOLM FLOYD Floyd, Malcolm Gregory Ali 6′0″, 194 **WR**
(AKA Malcolm Gregory Ali Seabron) *Col:* Fresno State *HS:* C.K. McClatchy [Sacramento, CA] B: 12/19/1972, San Francisco, CA *Drafted:* 1994 Round 3 Hou
1996 Hou: PR 7-74 10.6. **1997** Ten-StL: PR 4-15 3.8. StL: PR 4-15 3.8. **Total:** PR 11-89 8.1.

		Receiving				
Year Team	**G**	**Rec**	**Yds**	**Avg**	**TD**	**Fum**
1994 Hou	13	0	0	—	0	0
1995 Hou	15	12	167	13.9	1	0
1996 Hou	16	10	145	14.5	1	1
1997 Ten-StL	5	4	39	9.8	0	0
1997 Ten	1	0	0	—	0	0
1997 StL	4	4	39	9.8	0	0
NFL Total	49	26	351	13.5	2	1

OWEN FLOYD Floyd, Owen Glen 6′0″, 195 **C**
(Silvers) *Col:* Rose Hulman Tech *HS:* Garfield [Terre Haute, IN] B: 12/7/1896, Marshall, IN D: 9/26/1960, Beaumont, TX
1920 Mun: 1 G. **1921** Mun: 2 G. **Total:** 3 G.

VICTOR FLOYD Floyd, Victor Leonard 6′1″, 201 **RB**
Col: Florida State *HS:* Pensacola [FL] B: 1/24/1966, Pensacola, FL *Drafted:* 1989 Round 11 SD
1989 SD: 6 G; Rush 8-15 1.9; Rec 1-6 6.0; KR 3-12 4.0; 1 Fum.

WILLIAM FLOYD Floyd, William Ali 6′1″, 242 **RB**
(Bar-None) *Col:* Florida State *HS:* Lakewood [St. Petersburg, FL] B: 2/17/1972, St. Petersburg, FL *Drafted:* 1994 Round 1 SF
1998 Car: Pass 1-0, 1 Int; KR 1-22 22.0. **Total:** Pass 1-0, 1 Int; KR 1-22 22.0.

		Rushing				Receiving					Tot
Year Team	**G**	**Att**	**Yds**	**Avg**	**TD**	**Rec**	**Yds**	**Avg**	**TD**	**Fum**	**TD**
1994 SF	16	87	305	3.5	6	19	145	7.6	0	0	6
1995 SF	8	64	237	3.7	2	47	348	7.4	1	1	3
1996 SF	9	47	186	4.0	2	26	197	7.6	1	4	3
1997 SF	15	78	231	3.0	3	37	321	8.7	1	2	4
1998 Car	16	28	71	2.5	3	24	123	5.1	1	1	4
NFL Total	64	304	1030	3.4	16	153	1134	7.4	4	8	20

DARREN FLUTIE Flutie, Darren Paul 5′10″, 184 **WR**
Col: Boston College *HS:* Natick [MA] B: 11/18/1966, Baltimore, MD
1988 SD: 16 G; Rec 18-208 11.6 2 TD; PR 7-36 5.1; KR 1-10 10.0; 12 Pt; 2 Fum.

DOUG FLUTIE Flutie, Douglas Richard 5′10″, 176 **QB**
(Magic) *Col:* Boston College *HS:* Natick [MA] B: 10/23/1962, Manchester, MD *Drafted:* 1985 Round 11 LARm

		Passing							
Year Team	**G**	**Att**	**Comp**	**Comp%**	**Yds**	**YPA**	**TD**	**Int**	**Rating**
1986 ChiB	4	46	23	50.0	361	7.85	3	2	80.1
1987 ChiB-NE	2	25	15	60.0	199	7.96	1	0	98.6
1987 ChiB	1	0	0	—	0	—	0	0	—
1987 NE	1	25	15	60.0	199	7.96	1	0	98.6
1988 NE	11	179	92	51.4	1150	6.42	8	10	63.3
1989 NE	5	91	36	39.6	493	5.42	2	4	46.6
1998 Buf	13	354	202	57.1	2711	7.66	20	11	87.4
NFL Total	35	695	368	52.9	4914	7.07	34	27	75.8

	Rushing				
Year Team	**Att**	**Yds**	**Avg**	**TD**	**Fum**
1986 ChiB	9	36	4.0	1	3
1987 ChiB-NE	6	43	7.2	0	1
1987 NE	6	43	7.2	0	1
1988 NE	38	179	4.7	1	3
1989 NE	16	87	5.4	0	1
1998 Buf	48	248	5.2	1	3
NFL Total	117	593	5.1	3	11

DON FLYNN Flynn, Don Max 6′0″, 205 **DB-K**
Col: Houston *HS:* John Tyler [Tyler, TX] B: 9/14/1934
1960 DalT: 14 G; Int 3-65 1 TD; Scor 6, 0-1 FG; 6 Pt. **1961** DalT-NYT: 13 G; Int 2-9. DalT: 6 G; Int 2-9. NYT: 7 G. **Total:** 27 G; Int 5-74 1 TD; Scor 6, 0-1 FG; 6 Pt.

FURLONG FLYNN Flynn, Furlonge Harold 6′0″, 210 **G-T**
Col: Cornell *HS:* St. Bernard's [Cohoes, NY] B: 12/27/1901, Waterford, NY D: 11/1/1977, Vernon, CT
1926 Har: 9 G.

MIKE FLYNN Flynn, Michael Patrick 6′3″, 295 **OG**
Col: Maine *HS:* Cathedral [Springfield, MA] B: 6/15/1974, Doylestown, PA
1998 Bal: 3 G.

TOM FLYNN Flynn, Thomas Jeffrey 6′0″, 195 **DB**
Col: Pittsburgh *HS:* Penn Hills [Pittsburgh, PA] B: 3/24/1962, Verona, PA *Drafted:* 1984 Round 5 GB
1984 GB: PR 15-128 8.5. **1985** GB: PR 7-41 5.9; KR 1-20 20.0. **1988** NYG: PR 1-4 4.0. **Total:** PR 23-173 7.5; KR 1-20 20.0.

		Interceptions			
Year Team	**G**	**Int**	**Yds**	**TD**	**Fum**
1984 GB	15	9	106	0	1
1985 GB	16	1	7	0	0
1986 GB-NYG	9	1	0	0	0
1986 GB	7	1	0	0	0
1986 NYG	2	0	0	0	0
1987 NYG	12	0	0	0	0
1988 NYG	16	0	0	0	1
NFL Total	68	11	113	0	2

MARK FLYTHE Flythe, Mark Lloyd 6′7″, 270 **DE**
Col: Penn State *HS:* West Windsor-Plainsboro [Princeton Junction, NJ] B: 10/4/1968, Philadelphia, PA
1993 NYG: 2 G.

FRED FOGGIE Foggie, Fred Jerome 6′0″, 200 **DB**
Col: Minnesota *HS:* District 55 [Laurens, SC] B: 6/10/1969, Waterloo, SC
1992 Cle: 2 G. **1994** Pit: 3 G. **Total:** 5 G.

DESHAWN FOGLE Fogle, DeShawn Casey 6′1″, 220 **LB**
Col: Kansas State *HS:* Chapman [KS] B: 4/1/1975, Brooklyn, NY
1997 Phi: 5 G.

SPENCER FOLAU Folau, Spencer Sione 6′5″, 300 **OT**
Col: Idaho *HS:* Sequoia [Redwood City, CA] B: 4/5/1973, Nuku'Alofa, Tonga
1997 Bal: 10 G. **1998** Bal: 3 G. **Total:** 13 G.

HANK FOLDBERG Foldberg, Henry Christian Jr. 6′1″, 203 **OE-DE**
Col: Texas A&M; Army *HS:* Sunset [Dallas, TX] B: 3/12/1923, Dallas, TX
AAFC.

		Receiving			
Year Team	**G**	**Rec**	**Yds**	**Avg**	**TD**
1948 BknA	13	16	129	8.1	0
1949 ChiA	12	15	202	13.5	0
AAFC Total	25	31	331	10.7	0

DAVE FOLEY Foley, David Edward 6′5″, 255 **OT-C**
Col: Ohio State *HS:* Roger Bacon [Cincinnati, OH] B: 10/28/1947, Cincinnati, OH *Drafted:* 1969 Round 1 NYJ
1969 NYJ: 1 G. **1970** NYJ: 14 G. **1971** NYJ: 14 G. **1972** Buf: 12 G. **1973** Buf: 14 G. **1974** Buf: 14 G. **1975** Buf: 14 G. **1976** Buf: 14 G. **1977** Buf: 13 G. **Total:** 110 G.

GLENN FOLEY Foley, Glenn Edward 6′2″, 210 **QB**
Col: Boston College *HS:* Cherry Hill-East [NJ] B: 10/10/1970, Cherry Hill, NJ *Drafted:* 1994 Round 7 NYJ
1995 NYJ: Rush 1-9 9.0; Rec 1-(-9) -9.0. **1996** NYJ: Rush 7-40 5.7. **1997** NYJ: Rush 3-(-5) -1.7. **1998** NYJ: Rush 5-(-11) -2.2. **Total:** Rush 16-33 2.1; Rec 1-(-9) -9.0.

		Passing								
Year Team	**G**	**Att**	**Comp**	**Comp%**	**Yds**	**YPA**	**TD**	**Int**	**Rating**	**Fum**
1994 NYJ	1	8	5	62.5	45	5.63	0	1	38.0	0
1995 NYJ	1	29	16	55.2	128	4.41	0	1	52.1	0
1996 NYJ	5	110	54	49.1	559	5.08	3	7	46.7	1
1997 NYJ	6	97	56	57.7	705	7.27	3	1	86.5	1
1998 NYJ	5	108	58	53.7	749	6.94	4	6	64.9	1
NFL Total	18	352	189	53.7	2186	6.21	10	16	63.2	3

JIM FOLEY Foley, James Edward 5′8″, 165 TB-WB-FB
(Shrimp) *Col:* Syracuse *HS:* Suffield [CT] Deceased
1926 Har: 9 G.

STEVE FOLEY Foley, Stephen James 6′2″, 189 DB
Col: Tulane *HS:* Jesuit [New Orleans, LA] B: 11/11/1953, New Orleans, LA *Drafted:* 1975 Round 8 Den
1976 Den: PR 5-42 8.4. **1978** Den: Rush 1-14 14.0. **1984** Den: **1** Fum TD.
Total: Rush 1-14 14.0; PR 5-42 8.4; 1 Fum TD.

		Interceptions				Tot
Year Team	G	Int	Yds	TD	Fum	TD
1976 Den	14	4	95	0	1	0
1977 Den	13	3	22	0	0	0
1978 Den	16	6	84	0	0	0
1979 Den	16	6	14	0	1	0
1980 Den	16	4	115	0	0	0
1981 Den	16	5	81	0	0	0
1982 Den	1	0	0	0	0	0
1983 Den	14	5	28	0	1	0
1984 Den	16	6	97	1	0	2
1985 Den	12	3	47	0	0	0
1986 Den	16	2	39	0	0	0
NFL Total	150	44	622	1	3	2

STEVE FOLEY Foley, Steve 6′3″, 260 LB
Col: Northeast Louisiana *HS:* Hall [Little Rock, AR] B: 9/9/1975, Little Rock, AR *Drafted:* 1998 Round 3 Cin
1998 Cin: 10 G; 2 Sac.

TIM FOLEY Foley, Thomas David 6′0″, 194 DB
Col: Purdue *HS:* Loyola Acad. [Wilmette, IL] B: 1/22/1948, Evanston, IL *Drafted:* 1970 Round 3 Mia
1970 Mia: KR 1-0. **1974** Mia: Scor **1** Saf. **Total:** KR 1-0; Scor 1 Saf.

		Interceptions		
Year Team	G	Int	Yds	TD
1970 Mia	14	0	0	0
1971 Mia	14	4	14	0
1972 Mia	14	3	25	0
1973 Mia	11	2	22	0
1974 Mia	13	2	-2	0
1975 Mia	14	0	0	0
1976 Mia	2	0	0	0
1977 Mia	14	3	17	0
1978 Mia	16	6	12	0
1979 Mia	15	2	8	0
1980 Mia	7	0	0	0
NFL Total	134	22	96	0

TIM FOLEY Foley, Timothy John 6′6″, 275 OT
Col: Notre Dame *HS:* Roger Bacon [Cincinnati, OH] B: 5/30/1958, Cincinnati, OH *Drafted:* 1980 Round 2 Bal
1981 Bal: 6 G.

DICK FOLK Folk, Richard Armand 6′0″, 200 FB-DB
Col: Arkansas State; Illinois Wesleyan *HS:* Polo [IL] B: 5/21/1915, Polo, IL
1939 Bkn: 3 G.

LEE FOLKINS Folkins, Lloyd Leroy 6′5″, 215 TE-DE
Col: Washington *HS:* Roosevelt [Seattle, WA] B: 7/4/1939, Wallace, ID *Drafted:* 1961 Round 6 GB
1964 Dal: Rush 1-9 9.0; KR 1-0; Punt 15-497 33.1. **1965** Pit: **1** Fum TD.
Total: Rush 1-9 9.0; KR 1-0; Punt 15-497 33.1; 1 Fum TD.

		Receiving					Tot
Year Team	G	Rec	Yds	Avg	TD	Fum	TD
1961 GB	14	0	0	—	0	0	0
1962 Dal	14	39	536	13.7	6	0	6
1963 Dal	13	31	407	13.1	4	2	4
1964 Dal	14	5	41	8.2	0	0	0
1965 Pit	8	5	58	11.6	0	0	1
NFL Total	63	80	1042	13.0	10	2	11

BERYL FOLLET Follet, Beryl Millard 5′9″, 165 HB-TB
Col: New York U. *HS:* Worcester Acad. [MA] B: 4/26/1908, Manlius, IL D: 5/1/1982, Stony Brook, NY
1930 SI: 10 G. **1931** SI: 2 G. **Total:** 12 G.

BRENDAN FOLMAR Folmar, Brendan Arthur 6′1″, 200 QB
Col: California (Pa.) *HS:* California [Coal Center, PA] B: 4/2/1964, Birmingham, AL
1987 Det: 1 G.

STEVE FOLSOM Folsom, Steven Mark 6′5″, 235 TE
Col: Long Beach State; Utah *HS:* Santa Fe [Santa Fe Springs, CA] B: 3/21/1958, Los Angeles, CA *Drafted:* 1981 Round 10 Mia

		Receiving			
Year Team	G	Rec	Yds	Avg	TD
1981 Phi	3	0	0	—	0
1987 Dal	9	0	0	—	0
1988 Dal	16	9	84	9.3	2
1989 Dal	16	28	265	9.5	2
1990 Dal	1	0	0	—	0
NFL Total	45	37	349	9.4	4

JAMES FOLSTON Folston, James Edward 6′3″, 236 LB
Col: Northeast Louisiana *HS:* Cocoa [FL] B: 8/14/1971, Cocoa, FL *Drafted:* 1994 Round 2 LARd
1994 LARd: 7 G. **1995** Oak: 14 G. **1996** Oak: 12 G. **1997** Oak: 16 G. **1998** Oak: 16 G; Rec 1-(-1) -1.0; 1 Sac. **Total:** 65 G; Rec 1-(-1) -1.0; 1 Sac.

VERN FOLTZ Foltz, Vernon Jay 6′1″, 205 C-LB
Col: St. Vincent *HS:* Greensburg [PA]; Staunton Mil. Acad. [VA] B: 8/27/1918, Clearfield, PA
1944 Was: 10 G. **1945** Pit: 4 G. **Total:** 14 G.

ART FOLZ Folz, Arthur 5′7″, 157 BB-TB-WB
Col: Chicago *HS:* Englewood [Chicago, IL] B: 1903 Deceased
1923 ChiC: 4 G; Rush 1 TD; Scor **1** 1XP; 7 Pt. **1924** ChiC: 9 G; Rush 1 TD; 6 Pt. **1925** ChiC: 5 G; Rush 2 TD; Rec 1 TD; Tot TD 4; 24 Pt. **Total:** 18 G; Rush 4 TD; Rec 1 TD; Scor 1 1XP; Tot TD 6; 37 Pt.

AL FONTENOT Fontenot, Albert Paul III 6′4″, 275 DE
Col: Navarro Coll. TX (J.C.); Baylor *HS:* Jack Yates [Houston, TX] B: 9/17/1970, Houston, TX *Drafted:* 1993 Round 4 ChiB
1993 ChiB: 16 G; KR 1-8 8.0; 1 Sac. **1994** ChiB: 16 G; 4 Sac. **1995** ChiB: 13 G; Scor **1** Saf; 2 Pt; 2.5 Sac. **1996** ChiB: 16 G; 4.5 Sac. **1997** Ind: 16 G; 1 Fum TD; 6 Pt; 4.5 Sac. **1998** Ind: 7 G; 1 Sac. **Total:** 84 G; KR 1-8 8.0; Scor 1 Saf; 1 Fum TD; 8 Pt; 17.5 Sac.

CHRIS FONTENOT Fontenot, Christopher Dwight 6′3″, 250 TE
Col: McNeese State *HS:* Iota [LA] B: 7/11/1974, Lafayette, LA
1998 Phi: 5 G; Rec 8-90 11.3.

HERMAN FONTENOT Fontenot, Herman Joseph 6′0″, 206 RB
Col: Louisiana State *HS:* Charlton-Pollard [Beaumont, TX] B: 9/12/1963, St. Elizabeth, TX
1985 Cle: Pass 1-0. **1986** Cle: Pass 1-1 100.0%, 46 46.00 1 TD.
1987 Cle: Pass 1-1 100.0%, 14 14.00. **1988** Cle: Pass 1-0.
Total: Pass 4-2 50.0%, 60 15.00 1 TD.

		Rushing				Receiving			
Year Team	G	Att	Yds	Avg	TD	Rec	Yds	Avg	TD
1985 Cle	9	0	0	—	0	2	19	9.5	0
1986 Cle	16	25	105	4.2	1	47	559	11.9	1
1987 Cle	12	15	33	2.2	0	4	40	10.0	0
1988 Cle	16	28	87	3.1	0	19	170	8.9	1
1989 GB	16	17	69	4.1	1	40	372	9.3	3
1990 GB	14	17	76	4.5	0	31	293	9.5	1
NFL Total	83	102	370	3.6	2	143	1453	10.2	6

	Kickoff Returns					Tot
Year Team	Ret	Yds	Avg	TD	Fum	TD
1985 Cle	8	215	26.9	0	1	0
1986 Cle	7	99	14.1	0	2	2
1987 Cle	9	130	14.4	0	0	0
1988 Cle	21	435	20.7	0	0	2
1989 GB	2	30	15.0	0	0	4
1990 GB	3	88	29.3	0	1	1
NFL Total	50	997	19.9	0	4	9

JERRY FONTENOT Fontenot, Jerry Paul 6′3″, 286 C-OG
Col: Texas A&M *HS:* Lafayette [LA] B: 11/21/1966, Lafayette, LA *Drafted:* 1989 Round 3 ChiB
1989 ChiB: 16 G. **1990** ChiB: 16 G; 1 Fum. **1991** ChiB: 16 G. **1992** ChiB: 16 G; 1 Fum. **1993** ChiB: 16 G. **1994** ChiB: 16 G. **1995** ChiB: 16 G. **1996** ChiB: 16 G. **1997** NO: 16 G; 3 Fum. **1998** NO: 4 G. **Total:** 148 G; 5 Fum.

WAYNE FONTES Fontes, Wayne Howard Joseph 6′0″, 190 DB
Col: Michigan State *HS:* Wareham [MA]; McKinley HS [Canton, OH] B: 2/17/1939, New Bedford, MA *Drafted:* 1961 Round 22 NYT
1962 NYT: 9 G; Int 4-145 **1** TD; 6 Pt.

CHRIS FOOTE Foote, Christopher D 6′3″, 256 C-OG
Col: USC *HS:* Fairview [Boulder, CO] B: 12/2/1956, Louisville, KY *Drafted:* 1980 Round 6 Bal
1980 Bal: 16 G; KR 1-9 9.0. **1981** Bal: 16 G; KR 1-0. **1982** NYG: 7 G. **1983** NYG: 11 G. **1987** Min: 6 G. **1988** Min: 16 G. **1989** Min: 16 G. **1990** Min: 16 G. **Total:** 104 G; KR 2-9 4.5.

DAN FOOTMAN Footman, Daniel Ellis Jr. 6′5″, 290 DE-DT
Col: Florida State *HS:* Hillsborough [Tampa, FL] B: 1/13/1969, Tampa, FL *Drafted:* 1993 Round 2 Cle
1993 Cle: 8 G; 1 Sac. **1994** Cle: 16 G; 2.5 Sac. **1995** Cle: 16 G; 5 Sac. **1996** Bal: 10 G; 0.5 Sac. **1997** Ind: 16 G; 10.5 Sac. **1998** Ind: 3 G. **Total:** 69 G; 19.5 Sac.

MARLON FORBES Forbes, Marlon Darryl 6′1″, 215 **DB**
Col: Penn State *HS:* Central Islip [NY] B: 12/25/1971, Brooklyn, NY
1996 ChiB: 15 G. **1997** ChiB: 16 G. **1998** ChiB: 16 G. **Total:** 47 G.

ADRIAN FORD Ford, Adrian Grainger 5′10″, 190 **WB-OE-BB-FB**
Col: Lafayette *HS:* Niles [OH] B: 1/1/1904, Youngstown, OH
D: 7/7/1977, Youngstown, OH
1927 Pott-Fra: 11 G; Rush 2 TD; 12 Pt. Pott: 2 G. Fra: 9 G; Rush 2 TD; 12 Pt. **Total:** 11 G; Rush 2 TD; 12 Pt.

BRAD FORD Ford, Brad Jamar 5′10″, 170 **DB**
Col: Fresno City Coll. CA (J.C.); Alabama *HS:* Dadeville [AL]
B: 1/11/1974, Alexander City, AL *Drafted:* 1996 Round 4 Det
1996 Det: 14 G.

CHARLIE FORD Ford, Charles Glenn 6′3″, 185 **DB**
Col: Houston *HS:* Beaumont [TX] B: 12/10/1948, Beaumont, TX
Drafted: 1971 Round 2 ChiB

		Interceptions			
Year Team	**G**	**Int**	**Yds**	**TD**	**Fum**
1971 ChiB	14	5	46	0	1
1972 ChiB	14	7	104	0	0
1973 ChiB	13	2	50	0	1
1974 Phi	6	0	0	0	0
1975 Buf-NYG	13	1	19	0	0
1975 Buf	5	1	19	0	0
1975 NYG	8	0	0	0	0
NFL Total	60	15	219	0	2

CHRIS FORD Ford, Christopher David 6′1″, 185 **WR**
Col: Lamar *HS:* St. Thomas [Houston, TX] B: 5/20/1967, Houston, TX
1990 TB: 1 G.

COLE FORD Ford, Cole 6′2″, 210 **K**
Col: USC *HS:* Sabino [Tucson, AZ] B: 12/31/1972, Tucson, AZ
Drafted: 1995 Round 7 Pit

		Scoring						
Year Team	**G**	**Pts**	**FG**	**FGA**	**FG%**	**XK**	**XKA**	**XK%**
1995 Oak	5	41	8	9	88.9	17	18	94.4
1996 Oak	16	108	24	31	77.4	36	36	100.0
1997 Oak	16	72	13	22	59.1	33	35	94.3
1998 Buf	1	0	0	0	—	0	0	—
NFL Total	38	221	45	62	72.6	86	89	96.6

DARRYL FORD Ford, Darryl Dewayne 6′1″, 225 **LB**
Col: New Mexico State *HS:* Franklin D. Roosevelt [Dallas, TX]
B: 6/22/1966, Dallas, TX
1992 Pit-Det: 9 G. Pit: 8 G. Det: 1 G. **1993** Det: 11 G. **1994** Atl: 15 G. **Total:** 35 G.

FRED FORD Ford, Frederick 5′8″, 180 **HB**
Col: Cal Poly-Pomona *HS:* Tulare [CA] B: 3/30/1938
1960 Buf-LAC: Pass 1-0; Rec 1-5 5.0; PR 2-6 3.0; KR 18-400 22.2. Buf: Rec 1-5 5.0; KR 5-106 21.2. LAC: Pass 1-0; PR 2-6 3.0; KR 13-294 22.6. **Total:** Pass 1-0; Rec 1-5 5.0; PR 2-6 3.0; KR 18-400 22.2.

		Rushing			
Year Team	**G**	**Att**	**Yds**	**Avg**	**TD**
1960 Buf-LAC	9	38	194	5.1	2
1960 Buf	3	18	40	2.2	0
1960 LAC	6	20	154	7.7	2
NFL Total	9	38	194	5.1	2

GARRETT FORD Ford, Garrett William 6′2″, 230 **RB**
Col: West Virginia *HS:* DeMatha [Hyattsville, MD] B: 5/4/1945, Washington, DC *Drafted:* 1968 Round 3 Den
1968 Den: Rec 6-40 6.7.

		Rushing				
Year Team	**G**	**Att**	**Yds**	**Avg**	**TD**	**Fum**
1968 Den	14	41	186	4.5	1	1

HENRY FORD Ford, Henry 6′3″, 288 **DE-DT**
Col: Arkansas *HS:* Trimble Tech [Fort Worth, TX] B: 10/30/1971, Ft. Worth, TX *Drafted:* 1994 Round 1 Hou
1994 Hou: 11 G. **1995** Hou: 16 G; 4.5 Sac. **1996** Hou: 15 G; 1 Sac. **1997** Ten: 16 G; 5 Sac. **1998** Ten: 13 G; 1.5 Sac. **Total:** 71 G; 12 Sac.

HENRY FORD Ford, Henry 6′0″, 180 **HB-DB**
Col: Pittsburgh *HS:* Schenley [Pittsburgh, PA] B: 11/1/1931, Homestead, PA *Drafted:* 1955 Round 9 Cle
1955 Cle: Rush 2-1 0.5. **1956** Pit: Rush 12-26 2.2 2 TD; Rec 3-7 2.3; KR 6-135 22.5; Int 1-17. **Total:** Rush 14-27 1.9 2 TD; Rec 3-7 2.3; KR 6-135 22.5; Int 1-17.

		Punt Returns				
Year Team	**G**	**Ret**	**Yds**	**Avg**	**TD**	**Fum**
1955 Cle	2	4	15	3.8	0	1
1956 Pit	12	25	145	5.8	0	1
NFL Total	14	29	160	5.5	0	2

JAMES FORD Ford, James Leon 6′0″, 200 **RB**
(Jamie) *Col:* Texas Southern *HS:* New Stanton [Jacksonville, FL]
B: 9/11/1949, Jacksonville, FL *Drafted:* 1971 Round 13 Dal
1971 NO: Rec 7-54 7.7. **1972** NO: Rec 1-9 9.0. **Total:** Rec 8-63 7.9.

		Rushing				
Year Team	**G**	**Att**	**Yds**	**Avg**	**TD**	**Fum**
1971 NO	9	93	379	4.1	2	2
1972 NO	5	11	28	2.5	0	0
NFL Total	14	104	407	3.9	2	2

JOHN FORD Ford, John Allen Jr. 6′2″, 204 **WR**
Col: Virginia *HS:* Glades Central [Belle Glade, FL] B: 7/31/1966, Belle Glade, FL *Drafted:* 1989 Round 2 Det
1989 Det: 7 G; Rec 5-56 11.2.

BERNARD FORD Ford, K. Bernard 5′9″, 168 **WR**
Col: Marion Mil. Inst. AL (J.C.); Central Florida *HS:* Crisp Co. [Cordele, GA] B: 2/27/1966, Cordele, GA *Drafted:* 1988 Round 3 Buf
1989 Dal: 10 G; Rec 7-78 11.1 1 TD; 6 Pt. **1990** Hou: 14 G; Rec 10-98 9.8 1 TD; KR 14-219 15.6; 6 Pt; 2 Fum. **Total:** 24 G; Rec 17-176 10.4 2 TD; KR 14-219 15.6; 12 Pt; 2 Fum.

LEN FORD Ford, Leonard Guy Jr. 6′4″, 245 **DE-OE**
Col: Morgan State; Michigan *HS:* Armstrong [Washington, DC]
B: 2/18/1926, Washington, DC D: 3/13/1972, Detroit, MI *HOF:* 1976
AAFC **1948** LA-A: KR 1-24 24.0; Int 1-0. **1949** LA-A: Int 1-45.
Total: KR 1-24 24.0; Int 2-45.

		Receiving			
Year Team	**G**	**Rec**	**Yds**	**Avg**	**TD**
1948 LA-A	14	31	598	19.3	7
1949 LA-A	12	36	577	16.0	1
AAFC Total	26	67	1175	17.5	8

NFL **1950** Cle: 5 G. **1951** Cle: 12 G. **1952** Cle: 12 G; 1 Fum TD; 6 Pt. **1953** Cle: 12 G; Int 1-0. **1954** Cle: 12 G; Scor **1** Saf; 2 Pt. **1955** Cle: 12 G. **1956** Cle: 12 G. **1957** Cle: 11 G. **1958** GB: 11 G. **Total:** 99 G; Int 1-0; Scor 1 Saf; 1 Fum TD; 8 Pt.

MOSES FORD Ford, Moses 6′2″, 220 **WR**
Col: Fayetteville State *HS:* Dillon [SC] B: 2/9/1964, Dillon, SC
1987 Pit: 1 G.

SALEM FORD Ford, Salem Holland 5′7″, 150 **WB-TB-BB**
(Hot Rock) *Col:* Louisville *HS:* Male [Louisville, KY] B: 2/14/1896, Louisville, KY D: 6/16/1976, Louisville, KY
1922 Lou: 3 G. **1923** Lou: 1 G. **Total:** 4 G.

BRIAN FORDE Forde, Brian Michael 6′2″, 230 **LB**
Col: Washington State *HS:* Champlain Prep [Montreal, Canada]
B: 11/1/1963, Montreal, Canada *Drafted:* 1988 Round 7 NO
1988 NO: 16 G. **1989** NO: 16 G; Scor **1** Saf; 2 Pt. **1990** NO: 16 G. **1991** NO: 16 G. **Total:** 64 G; Scor 1 Saf; 2 Pt.

JIM FORDHAM Fordham, James Abner 5′11″, 215 **FB-LB**
Col: Georgia *HS:* Swainsboro [GA] B: 12/6/1916, Graymont, GA
D: 4/1969 *Drafted:* 1940 Round 6 ChiB
1944 ChiB: Rec 1-13 13.0; KR 2-42 21.0. **1945** ChiB: Rec 4-34 8.5. **Total:** Rec 5-47 9.4; KR 2-42 21.0.

		Rushing			
Year Team	**G**	**Att**	**Yds**	**Avg**	**TD**
1944 ChiB	10	73	381	5.2	4
1945 ChiB	9	45	153	3.4	1
NFL Total	19	118	534	4.5	5

TODD FORDHAM Fordham, Lindsey Todd 6′5″, 308 **OT**
(Earl) *Col:* Florida State *HS:* Tift Co. [Tifton, GA] B: 10/9/1973, Atlanta, GA
1997 Jac: 1 G. **1998** Jac: 11 G; KR 1-0. **Total:** 12 G; KR 1-0.

CHUCK FOREMAN Foreman, Walter Eugene 6′2″, 210 **RB**
Col: Miami (Fla.) *HS:* Frederick [MD] B: 10/26/1950, Frederick, MD
Drafted: 1973 Round 1 Min
1974 Min: KR 1-30 30.0. **1975** Min: KR 1-4 4.0. **Total:** KR 2-34 17.0.

		Rushing				Receiving					
Year Team	**G**	**Att**	**Yds**	**Avg**	**TD**	**Rec**	**Yds**	**Avg**	**TD**	**Fum**	**Tot TD**
1973 Min	12	182	801	4.4	4	37	362	9.8	2	6	6
1974 Min	13	199	777	3.9	9	53	586	11.1	6	6	**15**
1975 Min	14	280	1070	3.8	13	**73**	691	9.5	9	**12**	22
1976 Min	14	278	1155	4.2	13	55	567	10.3	1	7	**14**
1977 Min	14	270	1112	4.1	6	38	308	8.1	3	9	9
1978 Min	14	237	749	3.2	5	61	396	6.5	2	8	7
1979 Min	12	87	223	2.6	2	19	147	7.7	0	4	2
1980 NE	16	23	63	2.7	1	14	99	7.1	0	0	1
NFL Total	109	1556	5950	3.8	53	350	3156	9.0	23	52	76

BILL FORESTER Forester, George William 6'3", 237 LB-DT
Col: Southern Methodist *HS:* Woodrow Wilson [Dallas, TX]
B: 8/9/1932, Dallas, TX *Drafted:* 1953 Round 3 GB
1953 GB: KR 1-12 12.0. **1954** GB: KR 1-18 18.0. **1955** GB: KR 3-52 17.3. **1956** GB: KR 4-36 9.0. **1957** GB: KR 4-57 14.3. **1958** GB: KR 1-6 6.0. **1959** GB: Scor **1** Saf. **1960** GB: PR 1-7 7.0. **1961** GB: KR 3-55 18.3.
Total: PR 1-7 7.0; KR 17-236 13.9; Scor 1 Saf.

		Interceptions			
Year Team	G	Int	Yds	TD	Fum
1953 GB	12	1	0	0	0
1954 GB	12	1	21	0	0
1955 GB	12	4	32	0	1
1956 GB	12	4	35	0	0
1957 GB	12	4	79	0	1
1958 GB	12	0	0	0	0
1959 GB	12	2	48	0	1
1960 GB	12	2	18	0	0
1961 GB	14	2	33	0	0
1962 GB	14	0	0	0	0
1963 GB	14	1	13	0	0
NFL Total	138	21	279	0	3

HERSCHEL FORESTER Forester, Herschel Vincent 6'0", 230 OG
Col: Southern Methodist *HS:* Woodrow Wilson [Dallas, TX]
B: 4/14/1931, Dallas, TX *Drafted:* 1952 Round 8 Cle
1954 Cle: 12 G. **1955** Cle: 12 G. **1956** Cle: 12 G. **1957** Cle: 12 G.
Total: 48 G.

NICK FORKOVITCH Forkovitch, Nicholas John 5'11", 195 FB-LB
Col: William & Mary *HS:* McKeesport [PA] B: 3/1/1920, McKeesport, PA
AAFC **1948** BknA: 9 G; Rush 1-4 4.0.

PHIL FORNEY Forney, Philip L 6'2", 230 LB
Col: East Tennessee State *HS:* Central [Rutherfordton, NC]
B: 9/18/1963, Rutherfordton, NC
1987 StL: 3 G.

EDDIE FORREST Forrest, Edwin George 5'11", 215 G-LB
(Sea Pig) *Col:* Santa Clara *HS:* St. Ignatius [San Francisco, CA]
B: 6/12/1921, San Francisco, CA
AAFC **1946** SF-A: 11 G. **1947** SF-A: 14 G. **Total:** 25 G.

TOM FORREST Forrest, Thomas Wesley 6'2", 255 OG
Col: Cincinnati *HS:* DeMatha [Hyattsville, MD] B: 4/11/1952, Washington, DC *Drafted:* 1974 Round 8 SD
1974 ChiB: 8 G.

FRED FORSBERG Forsberg, Frederick Carl 6'1", 235 LB
Col: Washington *HS:* Woodrow Wilson [Tacoma, WA] B: 7/4/1944, Tacoma, WA *Drafted:* 1966 Round 14 Den
1968 Den: 13 G; KR 2-16 8.0; Int 1-6. **1970** Den: 14 G. **1971** Den: 14 G; KR 1-19 19.0; Int 3-75 1 TD; 6 Pt. **1972** Den: 9 G. **1973** Den-Buf: 13 G; KR 1-12 12.0; Int 1-7; 1 Fum. Den: 3 G; KR 1-12 12.0; Int 1-7; 1 Fum. Buf: 10 G. **1974** SD: 6 G. **Total:** 69 G; KR 4-47 11.8; Int 5-88 1 TD; 6 Pt; 1 Fum.

DUTCH FORST Forst, Arthur Henry 5'8", 195 FB
Col: Villanova *HS:* Villanova Prep [PA] B: 2/17/1891, Derby, CT
D: 10/1963, CT
1926 Prov: 2 G.

BEN FORSYTH Forsyth, Charles Benjamin 190 C
Col: Rochester; Syracuse *HS:* West Side [Rochester, NY]; Phillips Andover Acad. [Andover, MA] B: 6/4/1890, Rochester, NY
D: 11/11/1968, Rochester, NY
1920 Roch: 2 G.

ALDO FORTE Forte, Aldo John 6'0", 213 G-T
Col: Montana *HS:* Fenger [Chicago, IL] B: 1/20/1918, Chicago, IL
Drafted: 1939 Round 19 ChiB
1939 ChiB: 10 G. **1940** ChiB: 10 G. **1941** ChiB: 10 G. **1946** Det-ChiB: 9 G. Det: 3 G. ChiB: 6 G. **1947** GB: 10 G. **Total:** 49 G.

IKE FORTE Forte, Donald Ray 6'0", 203 RB
Col: Tyler JC TX; Arkansas *HS:* Texas [Texarkana] B: 3/8/1954, Texarkana, AR *Drafted:* 1976 Round 2 NE
1977 NE: PR 2-9 4.5. **1978** Was: PR 1-(-5) -5.0. **Total:** PR 3-4 1.3.

		Rushing				Receiving			
Year Team	G	Att	Yds	Avg	TD	Rec	Yds	Avg	TD
1976 NE	10	25	100	4.0	1	3	9	3.0	1
1977 NE	13	62	157	2.5	2	8	88	11.0	0
1978 Was	13	4	4	1.0	0	0	0	—	0
1979 Was	11	25	125	5.0	1	10	105	10.5	0
1980 Was	12	30	51	1.7	1	15	174	11.6	1
1981 NYG	5	19	74	3.9	0	3	11	3.7	0
NFL Total	64	165	511	3.1	5	39	387	9.9	2

	Kickoff Returns					Tot
Year Team	Ret	Yds	Avg	TD	Fum	TD
1976 NE	3	62	20.7	0	1	2
1977 NE	0	0	—	0	2	2
1978 Was	11	243	22.1	0	0	0
1979 Was	8	211	26.4	0	3	1
1980 Was	4	114	28.5	0	1	2
1981 NYG	0	0	—	0	1	0
NFL Total	26	630	24.2	0	8	7

BOB FORTE Forte, Robert Dominic 6'0", 199 HB-DB-LB
(Chick) *Col:* Arkansas *HS:* Lakeside [Lake Village, AR] B: 7/15/1922, Lake Village, AR D: 3/12/1996, Dallas, TX *Drafted:* 1943 Round 9 GB
1946 GB: Pass 7-3 42.9%, 28 4.00 1 TD 1 Int; Rec 2-5 2.5. **1947** GB: Pass 2-1 50.0%, 8 4.00; Rec 7-80 11.4 2 TD; PR 1-15 15.0; KR 2-28 14.0. **1948** GB: Rec 6-63 10.5 1 TD; KR 2-30 15.0. **1949** GB: Pass 1-0; Rec 7-85 12.1; PR 1-13 13.0; KR 7-159 22.7. **1950** GB: Pass 2-2 100.0%, 24 12.00; Rec 2-9 4.5; KR 3-73 24.3; Punt 3-107 35.7. **1952** GB: Pass 2-2 100.0%, 4 2.00. **Total:** Pass 14-8 57.1%, 64 4.57 1 TD 1 Int; Rec 24-242 10.1 3 TD; PR 2-28 14.0; KR 14-290 20.7; Punt 3-107 35.7.

		Rushing				Interceptions				Tot
Year Team	G	Att	Yds	Avg	TD	Int	Yds	TD	Fum	TD
1946 GB	9	17	73	4.3	0	2	23	0	1	0
1947 GB	12	29	80	2.8	0	9	140	1	1	3
1948 GB	12	12	30	2.5	0	5	56	0	1	1
1949 GB	12	40	135	3.4	0	2	17	0	1	0
1950 GB	12	9	13	1.4	0	1	5	0	0	0
1952 GB	12	0	0	—	0	4	50	0	0	0
1953 GB	11	0	0	—	0	0	0	0	0	0
NFL Total	80	107	331	3.1	0	23	291	1	4	4

ROMAN FORTIN Fortin, Roman Brian 6'5", 297 OT-OG-C
Col: Oregon; San Diego State *HS:* Ventura [CA] B: 2/26/1967, Columbus, OH *Drafted:* 1990 Round 8 Det
1991 Det: 16 G; Rec 1-4 4.0. **1992** Atl: 16 G; KR 1-5 5.0. **1993** Atl: 16 G. **1994** Atl: 16 G. **1995** Atl: 16 G; 2 Fum. **1996** Atl: 16 G. **1997** Atl: 3 G. **1998** SD: 16 G. **Total:** 115 G; Rec 1-4 4.0; KR 1-5 5.0; 2 Fum.

DANNY FORTMANN Fortmann, Daniel John 6'0", 210 G-LB
Col: Colgate *HS:* Pearl River [NY] B: 4/11/1916, Pearl River, NY
D: 5/24/1995, Los Angeles Co., CA *Drafted:* 1936 Round 9 ChiB
HOF: 1965
1936 ChiB: 12 G. **1937** ChiB: 10 G. **1938** ChiB: 11 G. **1939** ChiB: 11 G. **1940** ChiB: 10 G; Int 1-7. **1941** ChiB: 11 G; Int 3-7. **1942** ChiB: 11 G; Int 4-40; **1** Fum TD; 6 Pt. **1943** ChiB: 10 G. **Total:** 86 G; Int 8-54; 1 Fum TD; 6 Pt.

JOE FORTUNATO Fortunato, Joseph Francis 6'1", 225 LB
Col: Virginia Military; Mississippi State *HS:* Mingo Junction [OH]
B: 3/28/1930, Mingo Junction, OH *Drafted:* 1952 Round 7 ChiB
1957 ChiB: Rush 2-(-9) -4.5 1 TD. **1966** ChiB: **1** Fum TD.
Total: Rush 2-(-9) -4.5 1 TD; 1 Fum TD.

		Interceptions				Tot
Year Team	G	Int	Yds	TD	Fum	TD
1955 ChiB	12	0	0	0	0	0
1956 ChiB	12	2	30	1	0	1
1957 ChiB	12	0	0	0	1	1
1958 ChiB	12	1	5	0	0	0
1959 ChiB	12	2	10	0	0	0
1960 ChiB	12	0	0	0	0	0
1961 ChiB	14	3	34	0	0	0
1962 ChiB	14	3	44	0	0	0
1963 ChiB	14	2	30	0	0	0
1964 ChiB	13	0	0	0	0	0
1965 ChiB	14	2	0	0	0	0
1966 ChiB	14	1	3	0	0	1
NFL Total	155	16	156	1	1	3

ELLIOTT FORTUNE Fortune, Elliott David 6'4", 275 DT-DE
Col: Georgia Tech *HS:* Roosevelt [NY] B: 5/28/1974, Roosevelt, NY
1996 Bal: 14 G; 1 Sac.

HOSEA FORTUNE Fortune, Hosea Gerard 6'0", 174 WR
Col: Rice *HS:* Beverly Hills [CA] B: 3/4/1959, New Orleans, LA
1983 SD: 4 G; PR 4-16 4.0; 1 Fum.

BILL FORTUNE Fortune, William Peter 5'11", 218 G
Col: Michigan B: 10/14/1897, Joliet, IL D: 3/12/1947, Chicago, IL
1920 ChiC: 1 G. **1924** Ham: 4 G. **1925** Ham: 5 G. **Total:** 10 G.

JOHN FORURIA Foruria, John George 6'2", 205 DB
(Rocky) *Col:* Idaho *HS:* Emmett [ID] B: 11/26/1944, Emmett, ID
Drafted: 1967 Round 8 Pit
1967 Pit: 3 G. **1968** Pit: 6 G. **Total:** 9 G.

BOB FOSDICK Fosdick, Robert Everett 5'10", 225 T
Col: Iowa *HS:* West [Des Moines, IA] B: 11/11/1894, Knoxville, IA
D: 1/30/1990, Tucson, AZ
1923 Min: 5 G.

BARRY FOSTER Foster, Barry 5'10", 223 **RB**
Col: Arkansas *HS:* Duncanville [TX] B: 12/8/1968, Hurst, TX
Drafted: 1990 Round 5 Pit
1990 Pit: KR 3-29 9.7. **1992** Pit: Pass 1-0. **Total:** Pass 1-0; KR 3-29 9.7.

		Rushing				Receiving					Tot
Year Team	**G**	**Att**	**Yds**	**Avg**	**TD**	**Rec**	**Yds**	**Avg**	**TD**	**Fum**	**TD**
1990 Pit	16	36	203	5.6	1	1	2	2.0	0	2	1
1991 Pit	10	96	488	5.1	1	9	117	13.0	1	5	2
1992 Pit	16	**390**	1690	4.3	11	36	344	9.6	0	9	11
1993 Pit	9	177	711	4.0	8	27	217	8.0	1	3	9
1994 Pit	11	216	851	3.9	5	20	124	6.2	0	0	5
NFL Total	62	915	3943	4.3	26	93	804	8.6	2	19	28

DERRICK FOSTER Foster, Derrick 5'11", 205 **RB**
Col: William Paterson B: 10/12/1963
1987 NYJ: 3 G; Rush 1-9 9.0; Rec 1-9 9.0; PR 2-8 4.0.

EDDIE FOSTER Foster, Edward Ervin 5'10", 185 **WR**
Col: Houston *HS:* Kashmere [Houston, TX] B: 6/5/1954, Houston, TX
Drafted: 1977 Round 8 Hou
1977 Hou: 14 G; Rec 15-208 13.9; KR 1-31 31.0; 1 Fum. **1979** Hou: 1 G.
Total: 15 G; Rec 15-208 13.9; KR 1-31 31.0; 1 Fum.

FRED FOSTER Foster, Frederick Frank 5'11", 185 **FB-BB**
(Fritz) *Col:* Syracuse *HS:* Niagara Falls [NY]; Bethlehem Prep [PA]
B: 4/25/1898, Niagara Falls, NY D: 12/19/1968, Tallahassee, FL
1923 Buf-Roch: 2 G. Buf: 1 G. Roch: 1 G. **1924** Roch: 5 G. **Total:** 7 G.

GENE FOSTER Foster, Irving Eugene 6'0", 220 **RB**
Col: Arizona State *HS:* Memorial [Pennsville, NJ] B: 3/20/1942, Salem, NJ *Drafted:* 1965 Round 10 SD
1965 SD: Pass 3-2 66.7%, 31 10.33; KR 5-108 21.6. **1967** SD: Pass 1-0.
1968 SD: Pass 7-6 85.7%, 169 24.14. **1969** SD: Pass 5-2 40.0%, 39 7.80 1 TD; KR 1-1 1.0. **1970** SD: Pass 3-1 33.3%, 9 3.00. **Total:** Pass 19-11 57.9%, 248 13.05 1 TD; KR 6-109 18.2.

		Rushing				Receiving					Tot
Year Team	**G**	**Att**	**Yds**	**Avg**	**TD**	**Rec**	**Yds**	**Avg**	**TD**	**Fum**	**TD**
1965 SD	14	121	469	3.9	2	17	199	11.7	0	2	2
1966 SD	14	81	352	4.3	1	26	260	10.0	2	2	3
1967 SD	10	38	78	2.1	0	9	46	5.1	0	1	0
1968 SD	10	109	394	3.6	1	23	224	9.7	0	2	1
1969 SD	13	64	236	3.7	0	14	83	5.9	1	3	1
1970 SD	7	32	84	2.6	0	10	92	9.2	0	1	0
NFL Total	68	445	1613	3.6	4	99	904	9.1	3	11	7

WALLY FOSTER Foster, James Wallace 5'10", 165 **BB**
(Jim) *Col:* Bucknell *HS:* Oakmont [PA] B: 10/29/1902, Pittsburgh, PA
D: 8/31/1978, Oakmont, PA
1925 Buf: 9 G; Pass 1 TD; Scor 1, 1 XK.

JEROME FOSTER Foster, Jerome 6'2", 268 **DE-DT**
Col: Ohio State *HS:* Kettering [Detroit, MI] B: 7/25/1960, Detroit, MI
Drafted: 1983 Round 5 Hou
1983 Hou: 16 G; 3.5 Sac. **1984** Hou: 9 G; 1 Sac. **1986** Mia-NYJ: 15 G; 3 Sac. Mia: 14 G; 3 Sac. NYJ: 1 G. **1987** NYJ: 4 G. **Total:** 44 G; 7.5 Sac.

RALPH FOSTER Foster, Ralph Ellsworth Jr. 6'1", 240 **T**
(Burley) *Col:* Idaho; Oklahoma State *HS:* Perry [OK] B: 6/12/1917, Perry, OK *Drafted:* 1940 Round 17 ChiC
1945 ChiC: 9 G. **1946** ChiC: 10 G. **Total:** 19 G.

BOB FOSTER Foster, Robins J 5'10", 192 **TB-G-T-BB**
Col: No College B: 10/1886 Deceased
1922 Rac: 10 G; Rush 3 TD; 18 Pt. **1923** Rac: 8 G. **1924** Mil: 2 G.
Total: 20 G; Rush 3 TD; 18 Pt.

RON FOSTER Foster, Ronald Calvin 6'0", 200 **DB**
Col: Cal State-Northridge *HS:* William Howard Taft [Woodland Hills, CA]
B: 11/25/1963, Los Angeles, CA
1987 LARd: 3 G; KR 1-12 12.0.

ROY FOSTER Foster, Roy Allen 6'4", 282 **OG-OT**
Col: USC *HS:* Taft [Woodland Hills, CA]; Shawnee Mission West HS [Overland Park, KS] B: 5/24/1960, Los Angeles, CA *Drafted:* 1982 Round 1 Mia
1982 Mia: 9 G. **1983** Mia: 16 G. **1984** Mia: 16 G. **1985** Mia: 16 G.
1986 Mia: 16 G. **1987** Mia: 12 G. **1988** Mia: 15 G. **1989** Mia: 16 G.
1990 Mia: 16 G. **1991** SF: 16 G. **1992** SF: 16 G. **1993** SF: 1 G.
Total: 165 G.

WILL FOSTER Foster, William Henry 6'2", 230 **LB**
Col: Eastern Michigan *HS:* Washington [Massillon, OH] B: 10/2/1948, Grady, AL *Drafted:* 1972 Round 7 Phi
1973 NE: 9 G; **1** Fum TD; 6 Pt. **1974** NE: 12 G. **Total:** 21 G; 1 Fum TD; 6 Pt.

ELBERT FOULES Foules, Elbert 5'11", 185 **DB**
Col: Alcorn State *HS:* Greenville [MS] B: 7/4/1961, Greenville, MS
1983 Phi: PR 1-7 7.0. **1985** Phi: KR 1-7 7.0. **Total:** PR 1-7 7.0; KR 1-7 7.0.

		Interceptions		
Year Team	**G**	**Int**	**Yds**	**TD**
1983 Phi	16	1	0	0
1984 Phi	16	4	27	0
1985 Phi	16	0	0	0
1986 Phi	16	1	14	0
1987 Phi	9	4	6	0
NFL Total	73	10	47	0

JAMAL FOUNTAINE Fountaine, Jamal David 6'3", 240 **DE**
Col: Washington *HS:* Abraham Lincoln [San Francisco, CA]
B: 1/29/1971, San Francisco, CA
1995 SF: 7 G; 1 Sac. **1997** Atl: 3 G. **Total:** 10 G; 1 Sac.

JOHN FOURCADE Fourcade, John Charles 6'1", 208 **QB**
Col: Mississippi *HS:* Archbishop Shaw [Marrero, LA] B: 10/11/1960, Gretna, LA

		Passing							
Year Team	**G**	**Att**	**Comp**	**Comp%**	**Yds**	**YPA**	**TD**	**Int**	**Rating**
1987 NO	3	89	48	53.9	597	6.71	4	3	75.9
1988 NO	1	1	0	0.0	0	0.00	0	0	39.6
1989 NO	13	107	61	57.0	930	8.69	7	4	92.0
1990 NO	7	116	50	43.1	785	6.77	3	8	46.1
NFL Total	24	313	159	50.8	2312	7.39	14	15	70.1

	Rushing				
Year Team	**Att**	**Yds**	**Avg**	**TD**	**Fum**
1987 NO	19	134	7.1	0	1
1989 NO	14	91	6.5	1	2
1990 NO	15	77	5.1	1	4
NFL Total	48	302	6.3	2	7

KEITH FOURCADE Fourcade, Keith Joseph 5'11", 225 **LB**
Col: Mississippi *HS:* Archbishop Shaw [Marrero, LA] B: 10/20/1961, Marrero, LA
1987 NO: 2 G.

SID FOURNET Fournet, Sidney Fredrick 6'0", 235 **OG-LB-DB**
Col: Louisiana State *HS:* Bogalusa [LA] B: 8/27/1932, Bogalusa, LA
Drafted: 1955 Round 2 LARm
1955 LARm: 12 G. **1956** LARm: 12 G; Int 1-29. **1957** Pit: 2 G. **1960** DalT: 14 G. **1961** DalT: 14 G. **1962** NYT: 14 G; KR 1-0. **1963** NYJ: 14 G.
Total: 82 G; KR 1-0; Int 1-29.

DAN FOUTS Fouts, Daniel Francis 6'3", 204 **QB**
Col: Oregon *HS:* St. Ignatius [San Francisco, CA] B: 6/10/1951, San Francisco, CA *Drafted:* 1973 Round 3 SD *HOF:* 1993
1984 SD: Rec 1-0. **Total:** Rec 1-0.

		Passing							
Year Team	**G**	**Att**	**Comp**	**Comp%**	**Yds**	**YPA**	**TD**	**Int**	**Rating**
1973 SD	10	194	87	44.8	1126	5.80	6	13	46.0
1974 SD	11	237	115	48.5	1732	7.31	8	13	61.4
1975 SD	10	195	106	54.4	1396	7.16	2	10	59.3
1976 SD	14	359	208	57.9	2535	7.06	14	15	75.4
1977 SD	4	109	69	63.3	869	7.97	4	6	77.4
1978 SD	15	381	224	58.8	2999	7.87	24	20	83.0
1979 SD	16	530	332	**62.6**	**4082**	7.70	24	24	82.6
1980 SD	16	**589**	**348**	59.1	**4715**	8.01	30	24	84.7
1981 SD	16	**609**	**360**	59.1	**4802**	7.89	**33**	17	90.6
1982 SD	9	330	204	61.8	**2883**	**8.74**	**17**	11	93.3
1983 SD	10	340	215	63.2	2975	8.75	20	15	92.5
1984 SD	13	507	317	62.5	3740	7.38	19	17	83.4
1985 SD	14	430	254	59.1	3638	**8.46**	27	20	88.1
1986 SD	12	430	252	58.6	3031	7.05	16	22	71.4
1987 SD	11	364	206	56.6	2517	6.91	10	15	70.0
NFL Total	181	5604	3297	58.8	43040	7.68	254	242	80.2

	Rushing				
Year Team	**Att**	**Yds**	**Avg**	**TD**	**Fum**
1973 SD	7	32	4.6	0	2
1974 SD	19	63	3.3	1	4
1975 SD	23	170	7.4	2	3
1976 SD	18	65	3.6	0	8
1977 SD	6	13	2.2	0	4
1978 SD	20	43	2.2	2	10
1979 SD	26	49	1.9	2	13
1980 SD	23	15	0.7	2	11
1981 SD	22	56	2.5	0	9
1982 SD	9	8	0.9	1	2
1983 SD	12	-5	-0.4	1	5
1984 SD	12	-29	-2.4	0	8
1985 SD	11	-1	-0.1	0	13
1986 SD	4	-3	-0.8	0	4
1987 SD	12	0	0.0	2	10
NFL Total	224	476	2.1	13	106

AMOS FOWLER Fowler, Amos Emanuel 6′3″, 250 **C-OG**
Col: Southern Mississippi *HS:* Fort Walton Beach [FL] B: 2/11/1956, Pensacola, FL *Drafted:* 1978 Round 5 Det
1978 Det: 16 G. **1979** Det: 12 G. **1980** Det: 13 G. **1981** Det: 16 G. **1982** Det: 9 G. **1983** Det: 16 G. **1984** Det: 15 G. **Total:** 97 G.

BOBBY FOWLER Fowler, Bobby Lane 6′2″, 230 **FB**
Col: Texas-El Paso; Louisiana Tech *HS:* Angleton [TX] B: 9/11/1960, Temple, TX
1985 NO: 10 G; Rush 2-4 2.0; Rec 5-43 8.6; KR 4-78 19.5.

WAYNE FOWLER Fowler, Byron Wayne 6′3″, 260 **C**
Col: Baltimore City CC MD; Richmond *HS:* Glen Burnie [MD] B: 1/23/1948, Baltimore, MD *Drafted:* 1970 Round 7 Buf
1970 Buf: 10 G.

CHARLIE FOWLER Fowler, Charles Clark III 6′2″, 265 **OG**
Col: Auburn; Houston *HS:* Battle Ground Acad. [Franklin, TN] B: 11/10/1944, Nashville, TN *Drafted:* 1967 Round 12 Cle
1967 Mia: 6 G. **1968** Mia: 14 G. **Total:** 20 G.

DAN FOWLER Fowler, Daniel Gabriel 6′4″, 260 **OG**
Col: Kentucky *HS:* Euclid [OH] B: 4/12/1956, Euclid, OH *Drafted:* 1979 Round 10 NYG
1979 NYG: 1 G.

JERRY FOWLER Fowler, Jerry Marston 6′3″, 255 **OT**
Col: Northwestern State-Louisiana *HS:* Coushatta [LA] B: 4/26/1940, Shreveport, LA
1964 Hou: 4 G.

BOBBY FOWLER Fowler, Robert 5′11″, 212 **FB**
Col: Tennessee-Martin B: 1936
1962 NYT: 1 G; Rush 5-27 5.4.

AUBREY FOWLER Fowler, Robert Aubrey 5′10″, 160 **DB-HB**
(The Arkansas Traveler) *Col:* Arkansas Tech; Arkansas *HS:* Dumas [AR] B: 6/12/1920, Hamburg, AR D: 2/29/1996, Dumas, AR
AAFC **1948** BalA: 13 G; Rush 6-30 5.0; PR 4-41 10.3; KR 2-16 8.0; Int 3-0.

TODD FOWLER Fowler, Steven Todd 6′3″, 222 **RB**
Col: Trinity Valley CC TX; Stephen F. Austin St. *HS:* Van [TX] B: 6/9/1962, Van, TX
1985 Dal: 8 G; Rush 7-25 3.6; Rec 5-24 4.8; KR 3-48 16.0. **1986** Dal: 16 G; Rush 6-5 0.8; Rec 1-19 19.0; 1 Fum. **1987** Dal: 12 G; Rec 1-6 6.0. **1988** Dal: 16 G; Rush 3-6 2.0; Rec 10-64 6.4. **Total:** 52 G; Rush 16-36 2.3; Rec 17-113 6.6; KR 3-48 16.0; 1 Fum.

WILLMER FOWLER Fowler, Willmer 5′10″, 185 **HB**
Col: Northwestern *HS:* Mansfield [OH] B: 6/3/1937, Andalusia, AL *Drafted:* 1959 Round 8 Phi
1960 Buf: Rec 10-99 9.9; KR 12-201 16.8. **Total:** Rec 10-99 9.9; KR 12-201 16.8.

		Rushing				
Year Team	**G**	**Att**	**Yds**	**Avg**	**TD**	**Fum**
1960 Buf	11	93	370	4.0	1	2
1961 Buf	2	1	2	2.0	0	0
NFL Total	13	94	372	4.0	1	2

DENNIS FOWLKES Fowlkes, Dennis James 6′2″, 238 **LB**
Col: West Virginia *HS:* East [Columbus, OH] B: 3/11/1961, Columbus, OH
1983 Min: 11 G. **1984** Min: 14 G. **1985** Min: 15 G; 2 Sac. **1987** Mia: 3 G. **Total:** 43 G; 2 Sac.

CHAS FOX Fox, Charles Eldon III 5′11″, 180 **WR**
Col: Furman *HS:* Stevens [Rapid City, SD] B: 10/3/1963, Lafayette, IN *Drafted:* 1986 Round 4 KC
1986 StL: 4 G; Rec 5-59 11.8 1 TD; KR 6-161 26.8; 6 Pt.

MIKE FOX Fox, Michael James 6′8″, 285 **DE-DT**
Col: West Virginia *HS:* North [Akron, OH] B: 8/5/1967, Akron, OH *Drafted:* 1990 Round 2 NYG
1990 NYG: 16 G; 1.5 Sac. **1991** NYG: 15 G. **1992** NYG: 16 G; 2.5 Sac. **1993** NYG: 16 G; 4.5 Sac. **1994** NYG: 16 G; 1 Sac. **1995** Car: 16 G; 4.5 Sac. **1996** Car: 11 G; 2 Sac. **1997** Car: 11 G. **1998** Car: 16 G; 1 Sac. **Total:** 133 G; 17 Sac.

SAM FOX Fox, Samuel S 6′2″, 215 **OE-DE**
Col: Ohio State B: 5/4/1924, Washington, DC
1945 NYG: 8 G; Rec 10-120 12.0 2 TD; KR 1-14 14.0; 12 Pt.

SCOTT FOX Fox, Scott 6′2″, 222 **LB**
Col: Austin Peay State *HS:* Clinton [TN] B: 12/28/1963
1987 Hou: 2 G; 1 Sac.

TERRY FOX Fox, Terrence Patrick 6′1″, 208 **FB-LB**
Col: Miami (Fla.) B: 7/6/1918, Newark, NJ D: 4/1/1981, Miami, FL *Drafted:* 1941 Round 15 Pit
AAFC **1946** MiaA: 8 G; Rush 12-26 2.2; Rec 3-27 9.0; KR 1-24 24.0; Punt 2-88 44.0.
NFL **1941** Phi: 11 G; Rush 21-97 4.6; Rec 6-71 11.8; KR 1-16 16.0. **1945** Phi: 2 G. **Total:** 13 G; Rush 21-97 4.6; Rec 6-71 11.8; KR 1-16 16.0.

TIM FOX Fox, Timothy Richard 5′11″, 186 **DB**
Col: Ohio State *HS:* Glenwood [Canton, OH] B: 11/1/1953, Canton, OH *Drafted:* 1976 Round 1 NE
1978 NE: Scor **1** Saf. **1984** SD: 1 Sac. **Total:** Scor 1 Saf; 1 Sac.

		Interceptions			
Year Team	**G**	**Int**	**Yds**	**TD**	**Fum**
1976 NE	13	3	67	0	0
1977 NE	14	3	39	0	0
1978 NE	16	2	10	0	0
1979 NE	16	2	38	0	0
1980 NE	16	4	41	0	0
1981 NE	16	3	20	0	0
1982 SD	7	4	103	0	1
1983 SD	12	2	14	0	0
1984 SD	11	1	36	0	0
1985 LARm	6	2	8	0	0
1986 LARm	14	0	0	0	0
NFL Total	141	26	376	0	1

DION FOXX Foxx, Dion Lamont 6′3″, 254 **LB**
Col: James Madison *HS:* Meadowbrook [Richmond, VA] B: 6/11/1971, Richmond, VA
1994 Mia: 16 G. **1995** Mia-Was: 3 G; 0.5 Sac. Mia: 1 G; 0.5 Sac. Was: 2 G. **Total:** 19 G; 0.5 Sac.

DICK FRAHM Frahm, Herald Samuel 5′10″, 195 **DB-WB-HB**
Col: Nebraska *HS:* Beatrice [NE] B: 4/11/1906, Liberty, NE
1932 SI: 9 G; Rush 1-8 8.0; Rec 2-10 5.0; Scor 2, 2 XK. **1935** Phi-Bos: 2 G; Pass 1-1 100.0%, 12 12.00. Phi: 1 G. Bos: 1 G; Pass 1-1 100.0%, 12 12.00. **Total:** 11 G; Pass 1-1 100.0%, 12 12.00; Rush 1-8 8.0; Rec 2-10 5.0.

TODD FRAIN Frain, Todd Leslie 6′2″, 240 **TE**
Col: Nebraska *HS:* Treynor [IA] B: 1/31/1962, Council Bluffs, IA
1986 Was: 1 G. **1987** NE: 3 G; Rec 2-22 11.0. **Total:** 4 G; Rec 2-22 11.0.

BILL FRALIC Fralic, William P Jr. 6′5″, 280 **OG-OT**
Col: Pittsburgh *HS:* Penn Hills [Pittsburgh, PA] B: 10/31/1962, Penn Hills, PA *Drafted:* 1985 Round 1 Atl
1985 Atl: 15 G. **1986** Atl: 16 G. **1987** Atl: 12 G. **1988** Atl: 14 G. **1989** Atl: 15 G. **1990** Atl: 16 G. **1991** Atl: 12 G. **1992** Atl: 16 G. **1993** Det: 16 G; Rec 1-(-4) -4.0. **Total:** 132 G; Rec 1-(-4) -4.0.

DOUG FRANCE France, Frederick Douglas Jr. 6′5″, 270 **OT**
Col: Ohio State *HS:* Colonel White [Dayton, OH] B: 4/26/1953, Dayton, OH *Drafted:* 1975 Round 1 LARm
1975 LARm: 14 G. **1976** LARm: 14 G. **1977** LARm: 13 G. **1978** LARm: 16 G. **1979** LARm: 16 G. **1980** LARm: 16 G. **1981** LARm: 8 G. **1983** Hou: 13 G. **Total:** 110 G.

PETE FRANCESCHI Franceschi, Peter Louis 5′9″, 170 **HB-DB**
Col: San Francisco *HS:* Mission [San Francisco, CA] B: 9/28/1919, San Francisco, CA D: 7/22/1989, San Francisco, CA
AAFC **1946** SF-A: 9 G; Rush 8-(-5) -0.6 1 TD; Rec 3-35 11.7 1 TD; PR 1-6 6.0; Tot TD 2; 12 Pt.

JASON FRANCI Franci, Jason Arthur 6′1″, 210 **WR**
Col: Santa Rosa JC CA; California-Santa Barbara *HS:* Point Arena [CA] B: 10/17/1943, Fort Bragg, CA
1966 Den: 10 G; Rec 1-8 8.0.

DAVE FRANCIS Francis, David Lee 6′1″, 210 **FB**
Col: Ohio State *HS:* West [Columbus, OH] B: 4/15/1941, Columbus, OH *Drafted:* 1963 Round 7 Was
1963 Was: 8 G.

GENE FRANCIS Francis, Eugene Arthur 5′10″, 190 **FB**
Col: Chicago *HS:* Lindblom [Chicago, IL] B: 7/1/1903, Chicago, IL D: 11/1968, Wickenburg, AZ
1926 ChiC: 11 G; Int **1** TD; 6 Pt.

SAM FRANCIS Francis, Harrison Samuel 6′0″, 207 **FB-DB-HB-LB**
Col: Nebraska *HS:* Decatur [Oberlin, KS] B: 10/26/1913, Dunbar, NE *Drafted:* 1937 Round 1 Phi
1937 ChiB: Pass 6-3 50.0%, 34 5.67 1 TD 2 Int; Rec 1-(-9) -9.0; Int **1** TD; Scor 7, 1 XK. **1938** ChiB: Pass 3-1 33.3%; Rec 1-8 8.0; Scor 18, 0-2 XK. **1939** Pit-Bkn: Rec 2-5 2.5; Punt 13-488 37.5. Pit: Rec 1-5 5.0; Punt 10-389 38.9. Bkn: Rec 1-0; Punt 3-99 33.0. **1940** Bkn: Int 1-7; Punt 16-719 44.9; Scor 6, 0-1 FG. **Total:** Pass 9-4 44.4%, 34 3.78 1 TD 2 Int; Rec 4-4 1.0; Int 1-7 1 TD; Punt 29-1207 41.6; Scor 37, 0-1 FG, 1-2 XK.

		Rushing				Tot
Year Team	**G**	**Att**	**Yds**	**Avg**	**TD**	**TD**
1937 ChiB	8	48	129	2.7	0	1
1938 ChiB	11	85	297	3.5	3	3
1939 Pit-Bkn	10	76	230	3.0	1	1
1939 Pit	5	55	171	3.1	1	1

1939 Bkn	5	21	59	2.8	0	0
1940 Bkn	11	44	217	4.9	1	1
NFL Total	40	253	873	3.5	5	6

JAMES FRANCIS Francis, James Henry 6′5″, 253 **LB**
Col: Baylor *HS:* La Marque [TX] B: 8/4/1968, Houston, TX
Drafted: 1990 Round 1 Cin
1990 Cin: Scor **1** Saf; 8 Sac. **1991** Cin: 3 Sac. **1992** Cin: 6 Sac. **1993** Cin: 2 Sac. **1994** Cin: 4.5 Sac. **1995** Cin: 3 Sac. **1996** Cin: 3 Sac. **1997** Cin: 3.5 Sac. **Total:** Scor 1 Saf; 33 Sac.

		Interceptions		
Year Team	**G**	**Int**	**Yds**	**TD**
1990 Cin	16	1	17	1
1991 Cin	16	1	0	0
1992 Cin	14	3	108	1
1993 Cin	14	2	12	0
1994 Cin	16	0	0	0
1995 Cin	11	0	0	0
1996 Cin	16	3	61	1
1997 Cin	16	1	7	0
1998 Cin	14	0	0	0
NFL Total	133	11	205	3

JEFF FRANCIS Francis, Jeffrey Lee 6′4″, 225 **QB**
Col: Tennessee *HS:* Prospect [Mount Prospect, IL] B: 7/7/1966, Park Ridge, IL *Drafted:* 1989 Round 6 LARd
1990 Cle: 1 G; Pass 2-2 100.0%, 26 13.00.

JON FRANCIS Francis, Jon Charles Naekauna 5′11″, 207 **RB**
Col: Taft Coll. CA (J.C.); Colorado State; Boise State *HS:* Corvallis [OR]
B: 6/21/1964, Corvallis, OR *Drafted:* 1986 Round 7 NYG
1987 LARm: Rec 8-38 4.8 2 TD.

		Rushing			
Year Team	**G**	**Att**	**Yds**	**Avg**	**TD**
1987 LARm	9	35	138	3.9	0

JOE FRANCIS Francis, Joseph Charles 6′1″, 195 **QB-HB**
Col: Oregon State *HS:* Kamehameha School [Honolulu, HI]
B: 4/21/1936, Honolulu, HI *Drafted:* 1958 Round 5 GB
1958 GB: Pass 31-15 48.4%, 175 5.65 2 TD 2 Int. **1959** GB: Pass 18-5 27.8%, 91 5.06 1 Int; KR 2-52 26.0. **Total:** Pass 49-20 40.8%, 266 5.43 2 TD 3 Int; KR 2-52 26.0.

		Rushing				
Year Team	**G**	**Att**	**Yds**	**Avg**	**TD**	**Fum**
1958 GB	12	24	153	6.4	1	3
1959 GB	12	2	5	2.5	0	0
NFL Total	24	26	158	6.1	1	3

PHIL FRANCIS Francis, Phillip Kevin 6′1″, 205 **RB**
Col: Stanford *HS:* Beaverton [IL] B: 1/10/1957, Kewanee, IL
Drafted: 1979 Round 7 SF
1979 SF: KR 7-103 14.7. **1980** SF: KR 5-60 12.0. **Total:** KR 12-163 13.6.

		Rushing				Receiving				
Year Team	**G**	**Att**	**Yds**	**Avg**	**TD**	**Rec**	**Yds**	**Avg**	**TD**	**Fum**
1979 SF	16	31	118	3.8	1	32	198	6.2	0	2
1980 SF	5	7	36	5.1	0	3	23	7.7	0	0
NFL Total	21	38	154	4.1	1	35	221	6.3	0	2

RON FRANCIS Francis, Ronald Bernard 5′9″, 201 **DB**
Col: Baylor *HS:* La Marque [TX] B: 4/7/1964, La Marque, TX
Drafted: 1987 Round 2 Dal
1987 Dal: 11 G; Int 2-18 1 TD; 6 Pt. **1988** Dal: 13 G; Int 1-29. **1989** Dal: 15 G; Int 1-2. **1990** Dal: 15 G. **Total:** 54 G; Int 4-49 1 TD; 6 Pt.

RUSS FRANCIS Francis, Russell Ross 6′6″, 240 **TE**
Col: Oregon *HS:* Kailua [HI]; Pleasant Hill HS [OR] B: 4/3/1953, Seattle, WA *Drafted:* 1975 Round 1 NE
1976 NE: Rush 2-12 6.0. **1982** SF: Pass 1-1 100.0%, 45 45.00.
Total: Pass 1-1 100.0%, 45 45.00; Rush 2-12 6.0.

		Receiving				
Year Team	**G**	**Rec**	**Yds**	**Avg**	**TD**	**Fum**
1975 NE	14	35	636	18.2	4	1
1976 NE	13	26	367	14.1	3	1
1977 NE	10	16	229	14.3	4	0
1978 NE	15	39	543	13.9	4	1
1979 NE	12	39	557	14.3	5	0
1980 NE	15	41	664	16.2	8	0
1982 SF	9	23	278	12.1	2	2
1983 SF	16	33	357	10.8	4	2
1984 SF	10	23	285	12.4	2	1
1985 SF	16	44	478	10.9	3	2
1986 SF	16	41	505	12.3	1	0
1987 SF-NE	9	22	202	9.2	0	0
1987 SF	8	22	202	9.2	0	0
1987 NE	1	0	0	—	0	0
1988 NE	12	11	161	14.6	0	0
NFL Total	167	393	5262	13.4	40	10

WALLY FRANCIS Francis, Wallace Diron 5′11″, 190 **WR**
Col: Arkansas-Pine Bluff *HS:* Park Avenue [Franklin, LA] B: 11/7/1951, Franklin, LA *Drafted:* 1973 Round 5 Buf
1975 Atl: Rush 2-12 6.0. **1977** Atl: Rush 4-6 1.5. **1978** Atl: Rush 2-(-11) -5.5. **1980** Atl: Rush 1-2 2.0. **1981** Atl: Rush 1-8 8.0 1 TD.
Total: Rush 10-17 1.7 1 TD.

		Receiving				Kickoff Returns					Tot
Year Team	**G**	**Rec**	**Yds**	**Avg**	**TD**	**Ret**	**Yds**	**Avg**	**TD**	**Fum**	**TD**
1973 Buf	12	0	0	—	0	23	687	29.9	**2**	1	2
1974 Buf	14	0	0	—	0	37	947	25.6	0	0	0
1975 Atl	14	13	270	20.8	4	14	265	18.9	0	2	4
1976 Atl	14	2	24	12.0	0	9	156	17.3	0	0	0
1977 Atl	14	26	390	15.0	1	1	22	22.0	0	0	1
1978 Atl	16	45	695	15.4	3	0	0	—	0	0	3
1979 Atl	16	74	1013	13.7	8	0	0	—	0	3	8
1980 Atl	16	54	862	16.0	7	0	0	—	0	0	7
1981 Atl	16	30	441	14.7	4	0	0	—	0	1	5
NFL Total	132	244	3695	15.1	27	84	2077	24.7	2	7	30

GEORGE FRANCK Franck, George Henning 6′0″, 176 **WB-DB-FB**
(Sonny) *Col:* Minnesota *HS:* Central [Davenport, IA] B: 9/23/1918, Davenport, IA *Drafted:* 1941 Round 1 NYG
1941 NYG: Pass 1-0; PR 13-194 14.9; KR 4-120 30.0; Int 4-94.
1945 NYG: Pass 1-1 100.0%, 4 4.00; PR 1-18 18.0; KR 3-58 19.3.
1946 NYG: PR 4-58 14.5; KR 6-162 27.0. **1947** NYG: PR 6-60 10.0; KR 7-121 17.3; Int 1-0. **Total:** Pass 2-1 50.0%, 4 2.00; PR 24-330 13.8; KR 20-461 23.1; Int 5-94.

		Rushing				Receiving			
Year Team	**G**	**Att**	**Yds**	**Avg**	**TD**	**Rec**	**Yds**	**Avg**	**TD**
1941 NYG	11	48	101	2.1	3	8	95	11.9	1
1945 NYG	5	29	42	1.4	0	3	39	13.0	0
1946 NYG	10	43	270	6.3	0	6	137	22.8	1
1947 NYG	7	24	93	3.9	0	10	265	26.5	3
NFL Total	33	144	506	3.5	3	27	536	19.9	5

	Punting				Tot
Year Team	**Punts**	**Yds**	**Avg**	**Fum**	**TD**
1941 NYG	18	717	39.8	0	4
1945 NYG	22	832	37.8	2	0
1946 NYG	16	624	39.0	5	1
1947 NYG	7	297	42.4	3	3
NFL Total	63	2470	39.2	10	8

TOM FRANCKHAUSER Franckhauser, Thomas Anthony 6′0″, 195 **DB**
Col: Purdue *HS:* Central Catholic [Steubenville, OH] B: 5/26/1937, Steubenville, OH D: 4/17/1997, Houston, TX *Drafted:* 1959 Round 3 LARm
1960 Dal: PR 2-7 3.5. **1962** Min: PR 1-12 12.0. **Total:** PR 3-19 6.3.

		Kickoff Returns				Interceptions			
Year Team	**G**	**Ret**	**Yds**	**Avg**	**TD**	**Int**	**Yds**	**TD**	**Fum**
1959 LARm	12	0	0	—	0	3	2	0	0
1960 Dal	12	**26**	526	20.2	0	3	11	0	4
1961 Dal	6	0	0	—	0	1	23	0	0
1962 Min	14	0	0	—	0	4	27	0	0
1963 Min	14	4	94	23.5	0	2	59	0	0
NFL Total	58	30	620	20.7	0	13	122	0	4

MIKE FRANCKOWIAK Franckowiak, Michael Jerome 6′3″, 220 **RB-TE**
Col: Central Michigan *HS:* Western Catholic [Grand Rapids, MI]
B: 3/25/1953, Grand Rapids, MI *Drafted:* 1975 Round 3 Den
1975 Den: 14 G; Rush 1-1 1.0. **1976** Den: 14 G; Rush 12-25 2.1; Rec 4-42 10.5; KR 2-22 11.0; 1 Fum. **1977** Buf: 13 G; Rush 1-0; KR 1-9 9.0; 1 Fum. **1978** Buf: 16 G; KR 5-60 12.0. **Total:** 57 G; Rush 14-26 1.9; Rec 4-42 10.5; KR 8-91 11.4; 2 Fum.

BRIAN FRANCO Franco, Brian David 5′8″, 165 **K**
Col: Penn State *HS:* Glen Burnie [MD]; Altoona HS [PA] B: 12/3/1959, Annapolis, MD
1987 Cle: 2 G; Scor 11, 3-4 75.0% FG, 2-2 100.0% XK.

ED FRANCO Franco, Edmund Joseph 5′8″, 205 **T**
(Devil Doll) *Col:* Fordham *HS:* William L. Dickinson [Jersey City, NJ]
B: 4/24/1915, New York, NY D: 11/18/1992, Bayonne, NJ
Drafted: 1938 Round 3 Cle
1944 Bos: 10 G.

MALCOLM FRANK Frank, Baldwin Malcolm 5′8″, 178 **DB**
Col: Baylor *HS:* Central [Beaumont, TX] B: 12/5/1968, Mamou, LA
1992 Sea: 15 G.

DONALD FRANK Frank, Donald Lee 6′0″, 194 **DB**
Col: Winston-Salem State *HS:* Tarboro [NC] B: 10/24/1965, Edgecombe Co., NC
1990 SD: KR 8-172 21.5. **Total:** KR 8-172 21.5.

Year Team	G	Interceptions Int	Yds	TD
1990 SD	16	2	8	0
1991 SD	16	1	71	1
1992 SD	16	4	37	0
1993 SD	16	3	119	1
1994 LARd	16	1	8	0
1995 Min	12	3	72	0
NFL Total	92	14	315	2

JOHN FRANK Frank, John E 6′3″, 225 **TE**
Col: Ohio State *HS:* Mount Lebanon [PA] B: 4/17/1962, Pittsburgh, PA
Drafted: 1984 Round 2 SF
1985 SF: KR 1-1 1.0. **1986** SF: Rush 1-(-3) -3.0; KR 2-24 12.0. **1987** SF: Rush 1-2 2.0. **Total:** Rush 2-(-1) -0.5; KR 3-25 8.3.

Year Team	G	Receiving Rec	Yds	Avg	TD	Fum
1984 SF	15	7	60	8.6	1	0
1985 SF	16	7	50	7.1	1	0
1986 SF	16	9	61	6.8	2	0
1987 SF	12	26	296	11.4	3	2
1988 SF	7	16	195	12.2	3	0
NFL Total	66	65	662	10.2	10	2

JOE FRANK Frank, Joseph C 6′1″, 217 **T**
Col: Georgetown *HS:* James Monroe [Bronx, NY] B: 7/14/1915, Bronx, NY D: 8/11/1981, Queens, NY
1941 Phi: 11 G. **1942** Phi: 1 G. **1943** PhPt: 2 G. **Total:** 14 G.

PAUL FRANK Frank, Paul 200 **BB**
(Hap) *Col:* Waynesburg *HS:* Kiski School [Saltsburg, PA] B: 5/8/1907 D: 11/1970, Bridgeville, PA
1930 Nwk: 3 G.

BILL FRANK Frank, William B Jr. 6′5″, 255 **OT**
Col: San Diego City Coll. CA (J.C.); Colorado *HS:* West [Denver, CO] B: 4/13/1938, Denver, CO *Drafted:* 1963 Round 18 Dal
1964 Dal: 4 G.

IKE FRANKIAN Frankian, Malcolm J 5′11″, 208 **OE-DE**
Col: St. Mary's (Cal.) *HS:* Dinuba [CA] B: 4/3/1907, Worcester, MA D: 3/14/1963
1933 Bos: 12 G; Rec 6-75 12.5 1 TD; 6 Pt. **1934** NYG: 13 G; Rec 1-5 5.0. **1935** NYG: 12 G; Rec 7-39 5.6 1 TD; 6 Pt. **Total:** 37 G; Rec 14-119 8.5 2 TD; 12 Pt.

ANDRA FRANKLIN Franklin, Andra Bernard 5′10″, 225 **RB**
Col: Nebraska *HS:* Anniston [AL] B: 8/22/1959, Anniston, AL
Drafted: 1981 Round 2 Mia
1981 Mia: Rec 3-6 2.0 1 TD. **1982** Mia: Rec 3-9 3.0. **Total:** Rec 6-15 2.5 1 TD.

Year Team	G	Rushing Att	Yds	Avg	TD	Fum	Tot TD
1981 Mia	16	201	711	3.5	7	5	8
1982 Mia	9	**177**	701	4.0	7	3	7
1983 Mia	15	224	746	3.3	8	6	8
1984 Mia	2	20	74	3.7	0	0	0
NFL Total	42	622	2232	3.6	22	14	23

TONY FRANKLIN Franklin, Anthony Ray 5′8″, 182 **K**
Col: Texas A&M *HS:* Arlington Heights [Fort Worth, TX] B: 11/18/1956, Big Spring, TX *Drafted:* 1979 Round 3 Phi
1979 Phi: Punt 1-32 32.0. **1981** Phi: Punt 1-13 13.0. **1985** NE: Rush 1-(-5) -5.0. **Total:** Rush 1-(-5) -5.0; Punt 2-45 22.5.

Year Team	G	Scoring Pts	FG	FGA	FG%	XK	XKA	XK%
1979 Phi	16	105	23	31	74.2	36	39	92.3
1980 Phi	16	96	16	31	51.6	48	48	100.0
1981 Phi	16	101	20	31	64.5	41	43	95.3
1982 Phi	9	41	6	9	66.7	23	25	92.0
1983 Phi	16	69	15	26	57.7	24	27	88.9
1984 NE	16	108	22	28	78.6	42	42	100.0
1985 NE	16	112	24	30	80.0	40	41	97.6
1986 NE	16	**140**	**32**	**41**	78.0	44	45	97.8
1987 NE	14	82	15	26	57.7	37	38	97.4
1988 Mia	5	18	4	11	36.4	6	7	85.7
NFL Total	140	872	177	264	67.0	341	355	96.1

ARNOLD FRANKLIN Franklin, Arnold Lee 6′3″, 246 **TE**
Col: North Carolina *HS:* Princeton [Cincinnati, OH] B: 12/16/1963, Cincinnati, OH
1987 NE: 3 G.

BOBBY FRANKLIN Franklin, Bobby Ray 5′11″, 182 **DB**
Col: Mississippi *HS:* Clarksdale [MS] B: 10/5/1936, Clarksdale, MS
Drafted: 1960 Round 11 Cle
1960 Cle: PR 1-2 2.0; KR 1-23 23.0. **1961** Cle: Rush 1-12 12.0 1 TD. **1963** Cle: Rush 1-(-10) -10.0; KR 2-33 16.5. **1964** Cle: KR 1-1 1.0; Punt 1-36 36.0. **1965** Cle: Rush 1-(-11) -11.0; KR 1-0; Punt 4-118 29.5. **Total:** Rush 3-(-9) -3.0 1 TD; PR 1-2 2.0; KR 5-57 11.4; Punt 5-154 30.8.

Year Team	G	Interceptions Int	Yds	TD	Fum	Tot TD
1960 Cle	12	8	131	**2**	1	2
1961 Cle	14	2	20	0	1	1
1962 Cle	9	1	10	0	0	0
1963 Cle	14	2	26	0	1	0
1964 Cle	14	0	0	0	1	0
1965 Cle	14	0	0	0	1	0
1966 Cle	9	0	0	0	0	0
NFL Total	86	13	187	2	5	3

BYRON FRANKLIN Franklin, Byron Paul 6′1″, 179 **WR**
Col: Auburn *HS:* Sheffield [AL] B: 9/4/1958, Florence, AL
Drafted: 1981 Round 2 Buf
1981 Buf: Rush 1-(-11) -11.0; PR 5-45 9.0; KR 21-436 20.8. **1983** Buf: Rush 1-3 3.0. **1984** Buf: Rush 1-(-7) -7.0. **1985** Sea: Rush 1-5 5.0. **1986** Sea: Rush 1-2 2.0. **Total:** Rush 5-(-8) -1.6; PR 5-45 9.0; KR 21-436 20.8.

Year Team	G	Receiving Rec	Yds	Avg	TD	Fum
1981 Buf	13	2	29	14.5	0	2
1983 Buf	15	30	452	15.1	4	0
1984 Buf	16	69	862	12.5	4	4
1985 Sea	13	10	119	11.9	0	0
1986 Sea	14	33	547	16.6	2	0
1987 Sea	6	1	7	7.0	0	0
NFL Total	77	145	2016	13.9	10	6

CLEVELAND FRANKLIN Franklin, Cleveland 6′2″, 216 **RB**
Col: Baylor *HS:* Brenham [TX] B: 4/24/1955, Brenham, TX
Drafted: 1977 Round 8 Phi
1982 Bal: KR 1-8 8.0. **Total:** KR 1-8 8.0.

Year Team	G	Rushing Att	Yds	Avg	TD	Receiving Rec	Yds	Avg	TD	Fum
1977 Phi	14	1	0	0.0	0	0	0	—	0	0
1978 Phi	16	60	167	2.8	0	7	46	6.6	0	7
1980 Bal	13	83	264	3.2	2	14	112	8.0	0	2
1981 Bal	9	21	52	2.5	1	6	39	6.5	0	2
1982 Bal	9	43	152	3.5	0	9	61	6.8	0	2
NFL Total	61	208	635	3.1	3	36	258	7.2	0	13

DENNIS FRANKLIN Franklin, Dennis E 6′1″, 185 **WR**
Col: Michigan *HS:* Washington [Massillon, OH] B: 8/24/1953, Massillon, OH *Drafted:* 1975 Round 6 Det
1975 Det: 4 G; Rec 5-109 21.8. **1976** Det: 5 G; Rec 1-16 16.0. **Total:** 9 G; Rec 6-125 20.8.

GEORGE FRANKLIN Franklin, George Eugene 6′3″, 225 **RB**
Col: Texas A&M–Kingsville *HS:* Sam Houston [San Antonio, TX] B: 7/5/1954, Seguin, TX *Drafted:* 1977 Round 2 StL
1978 Atl: 15 G; Rush 1-(-8) -8.0; Rec 1-19 19.0; KR 11-258 23.5; 1 Fum.

JERRELL FRANKLIN Franklin, Jerrell Lynn 6′3″, 287 **OG**
Col: Northeastern Oklahoma A&M (J.C.); Kansas State; Southern University *HS:* Jack Yates [Houston, TX] B: 5/4/1959, Houston, TX
1987 Hou: 3 G.

JETHRO FRANKLIN Franklin, Jethro Fitzgerald 6′1″, 258 **DE**
Col: San Jose City Coll. CA (J.C.); Fresno State *HS:* Yerba Buena [San Jose, CA] B: 10/25/1965, St. Lazaire, France *Drafted:* 1988 Round 11 Hou
1989 Sea: 7 G.

KEITH FRANKLIN Franklin, Keith Lamont 6′2″, 230 **LB**
Col: Glendale CC CA; South Carolina *HS:* La Sierra [Riverside, CA]; Dorsey HS [Los Angeles, CA] B: 3/4/1970, Los Angeles, CA
1995 Oak: 2 G.

LARRY FRANKLIN Franklin, Lawrence Darnell 6′1″, 185 **WR**
Col: Jackson State *HS:* Hamilton [Memphis, TN] B: 8/2/1955, Memphis, TN
1978 TB: 2 G.

RED FRANKLIN Franklin, Norman Clifford 5′10″, 163 **TB-DB**
Col: Oregon State *HS:* Long Beach Polytechnic [CA] B: 12/13/1911, Hope, RI D: 12/1984, Santa Ana, CA
1935 Bkn: Rec 1-12 12.0. **Total:** Rec 1-12 12.0.

Year Team	G	Passing Att	Comp	Comp%	Yds	YPA	TD	Int	Rating
1935 Bkn	12	57	12	21.1	175	3.07	2	7	12.0
1936 Bkn	2	7	1	14.3	17	2.43	0	0	39.6
1937 Bkn	1	4	0	0.0	0	0.00	0	0	39.6
NFL Total	15	68	13	19.1	192	2.82	2	7	9.8

Year Team	Att	Rushing Yds	Avg	TD
1935 Bkn	100	284	2.8	3
1936 Bkn	15	70	4.7	1
1937 Bkn	4	12	3.0	0
NFL Total	119	366	3.1	4

PAT FRANKLIN Franklin, Patrick Dijon 6′1″, 232 **RB**
Col: Southwest Texas State; Houston *HS:* Bay City [TX] B: 8/16/1963, Bay City, TX *Drafted:* 1986 Round 7 Cin
1986 TB: 8 G; Rush 7-7 1.0; Rec 7-29 4.1 1 TD; KR 3-23 7.7; **1** Fum TD; Tot TD 2; 12 Pt; 1 Fum. **1987** Cin: 2 G. **Total:** 10 G; Rush 7-7 1.0; Rec 7-29 4.1 1 TD; KR 3-23 7.7; 1 Fum TD; Tot TD 2; 12 Pt; 1 Fum.

PAUL FRANKLIN Franklin, Paul R 6′2″, 198 **FB-LB-OE-DE**
(Ben) *Col:* Franklin (Ind.) *HS:* Plainfield [IN] B: 2/10/1906, Plainfield, IN D: 8/26/1959, Mount Prospect, IL

		Rushing			
Year Team	G	Att	Yds	Avg	TD
1931 ChiB	12	—	—	—	1
1932 ChiB	8	26	14	0.5	0
1933 ChiB	3	2	5	2.5	0
NFL Total	23	28	19	0.7	1

WILLIE FRANKLIN Franklin, Willie 6′2″, 195 **WR**
Col: Mesa CC AZ; Oklahoma *HS:* Abraham Lincoln [San Diego, CA] B: 10/9/1949, San Diego, CA
1972 Bal: 4 G.

RAY FRANKOWSKI Frankowski, Ray William 5′11″, 223 **G**
Col: Washington *HS:* Hammond [IN] B: 9/14/1917, Chicago, IL
AAFC **1946** LA-A: 12 G; 6 Pt. **1947** LA-A: 14 G. **1948** LA-A: 14 G. **Total:** 40 G; 6 Pt.

NFL **1945** GB: 2 G.

DENNIS FRANKS Franks, Dennis John 6′1″, 241 **C**
Col: Michigan *HS:* Bethel Park [PA] B: 5/29/1953, McKeesport, PA
1976 Phi: 14 G. **1977** Phi: 14 G. **1978** Phi: 16 G. **1979** Det: 13 G; 1 Fum. **Total:** 57 G; 1 Fum.

ELVIS FRANKS Franks, Elvis Andrea 6′4″, 252 **DE**
Col: Morgan State *HS:* Kirby [Woodville, TX] B: 7/9/1957, Doucette, TX *Drafted:* 1980 Round 5 Cle
1980 Cle: 16 G. **1981** Cle: 16 G. **1982** Cle: 9 G; 2 Sac. **1983** Cle: 16 G; 5 Sac. **1984** Cle: 16 G; 1.5 Sac. **1985** LARd: 3 G. **1986** LARd-NYJ: 7 G; 1 Sac. LARd: 4 G. NYJ: 3 G; 1 Sac. **Total:** 83 G; 9.5 Sac.

CHIEF FRANTA Franta, Herbert J 6′1″, 220 **T-G**
Col: St. Thomas *HS:* New Ulm [MN] B: 3/10/1905, New Ulm, MN Deceased
1929 Min: 10 G. **1930** Min-GB: 8 G. Min: 6 G. GB: 2 G. **Total:** 18 G.

JACK FRANTZ Frantz, John Edward 6′3″, 230 **C**
Col: California *HS:* Nevada Union [Grass Valley, CA] B: 7/1/1945, Kokomo, IN *Drafted:* 1968 Round 16 Buf
1968 Buf: 2 G.

NOLAN FRANZ Franz, Nolan Clarence 6′2″, 185 **WR**
Col: Tulane *HS:* East Jefferson [Metairie, LA] B: 9/11/1959, New Orleans, LA
1986 GB: 1 G; Rec 1-7 7.0.

TRACY FRANZ Franz, Tracy Mark 6′5″, 270 **OG**
Col: San Jose State *HS:* Rio Americano [Sacramento, CA] B: 3/26/1960, Sacramento, CA
1987 SF: 3 G.

PAUL FRASE Frase, Paul Miles 6′5″, 272 **DE-NT-DT**
Col: Syracuse *HS:* Spaulding [Rochester, NH] B: 5/6/1965, Elmira, NY *Drafted:* 1988 Round 6 NYJ
1988 NYJ: 16 G; 1 Sac. **1989** NYJ: 16 G; 2 Sac. **1991** NYJ: 16 G; 1 Fum. **1992** NYJ: 16 G; 5 Sac. **1993** NYJ: 16 G; 1 Sac. **1994** NYJ: 16 G; 1 Sac. **1995** Jac: 9 G; 1 Sac. **1996** Jac: 14 G. **1997** GB: 9 G. **1998** Bal: 11 G. **Total:** 139 G; 1 Fum; 11 Sac.

JIM FRASER Fraser, James Gallagher 6′3″, 236 **LB-P**
Col: Wisconsin *HS:* Germantown [Philadelphia, PA] B: 5/29/1936, Philadelphia, PA *Drafted:* 1959 Round 21 Cle
1962 Den: Int 1-2; Scor 2, 2-2 100.0% XK. **1963** Den: KR 1-0. **1964** Den: Int 1-1. **1965** KC: KR 1-5 5.0. **1966** Bos: Int 1-3. **Total:** KR 2-5 2.5; Int 3-6; Scor 2, 2-2 100.0% XK.

		Punting		
Year Team	G	Punts	Yds	Avg
1962 Den	14	55	2400	43.6
1963 Den	14	**81**	**3596**	**44.4**
1964 Den	14	73	3225	**44.2**
1965 KC	14	3	81	27.0
1966 Bos	14	55	2044	37.2
1968 NO	2	11	391	35.5
NFL Total	72	278	11737	42.2

AL FRAZIER Frazier, Adolphus Cornelius 5′11″, 180 **HB-WR**
Col: Florida A&M *HS:* Stanton [Jacksonville, FL] B: 5/28/1935, Jacksonville, FL *Drafted:* 1957 Round 20 ChiB
1961 Den: Pass 1-0, 1 Int; Scor 1 2XP. **Total:** Pass 1-0, 1 Int; Scor 1 2XP.

		Rushing				Receiving			
Year Team	G	Att	Yds	Avg	TD	Rec	Yds	Avg	TD
1961 Den	14	23	110	4.8	0	47	799	17.0	6
1962 Den	14	39	168	4.3	2	11	211	19.2	1
1963 Den	3	0	0	—	0	0	0	—	0
NFL Total	31	62	278	4.5	2	58	1010	17.4	7

	Punt Returns				Kickoff Returns					Tot
Year Team	Ret	Yds	Avg	TD	Ret	Yds	Avg	TD	Fum	TD
1961 Den	18	231	12.8	1	18	504	28.0	**1**	9	8
1962 Den	5	32	6.4	0	19	388	20.4	0	4	3
1963 Den	3	42	14.0	0	7	185	26.4	0	1	0
NFL Total	26	305	11.7	1	44	1077	24.5	1	14	11

CHARLEY FRAZIER Frazier, Charles Douglas 6′0″, 190 **WR**
(Razor) *Col:* Texas Southern *HS:* Marshall [Angleton, TX] B: 8/12/1939, Houston, TX
1964 Hou: Rush 1-(-4) -4.0. **1965** Hou: Rush 1-10 10.0. **1969** Bos: Rush 2-(-1) -0.5. **Total:** Rush 4-5 1.3.

		Receiving				
Year Team	G	Rec	Yds	Avg	TD	Fum
1962 Hou	14	7	155	22.1	1	0
1963 Hou	10	16	279	17.4	1	0
1964 Hou	11	29	404	13.9	1	0
1965 Hou	12	38	717	18.9	6	1
1966 Hou	14	57	1129	19.8	12	0
1967 Hou	13	23	253	11.0	1	0
1968 Hou	13	9	123	13.7	0	0
1969 Bos	14	19	306	16.1	7	2
1970 Bos	9	9	86	9.6	0	0
NFL Total	110	207	3452	16.7	29	3

CLIFF FRAZIER Frazier, Clifford Henry 6′4″, 265 **DT**
Col: Fort Scott CC KS; UCLA *HS:* Ballwin [MO] B: 11/23/1952, St. Louis, MO *Drafted:* 1976 Round 2 KC
1977 KC: 14 G.

CURT FRAZIER Frazier, Curtis 5′11″, 193 **DB**
Col: Contra Costa Coll. CA (J.C.); Fresno State *HS:* Berkeley [CA] B: 3/11/1945, Berkeley, CA
1968 Cin: 14 G.

PAUL FRAZIER Frazier, Daniel Paul 5′8″, 188 **RB**
Col: Northwestern State-Louisiana *HS:* Coushatta [LA] B: 11/12/1967, Beaumont, TX
1989 NO: Rec 3-25 8.3; KR 8-157 19.6.

		Rushing				
Year Team	G	Att	Yds	Avg	TD	Fum
1989 NO	15	25	112	4.5	1	1

DERRICK FRAZIER Frazier, Derrick Lothair 5′10″, 178 **DB**
Col: Texas A&M *HS:* Clements [Sugar Land, TX] B: 4/29/1970, Sugar Land, TX *Drafted:* 1993 Round 3 Phi
1994 Phi: 12 G. **1995** Phi: 7 G; Int 1-3. **1996** Ind: 6 G. **Total:** 25 G; Int 1-3.

FRANK FRAZIER Frazier, Frank Lee 6′5″, 290 **OG**
Col: Miami (Fla.) *HS:* Tampa Bay Tech [Tampa, FL] B: 6/15/1960, Tampa, FL
1987 Was: 3 G.

GUY FRAZIER Frazier, Guy Shelton 6′2″, 215 **LB**
Col: Wyoming *HS:* Cass Tech [Detroit, MI] B: 7/20/1959, Detroit, MI *Drafted:* 1981 Round 4 Cin
1981 Cin: 16 G. **1982** Cin: 9 G. **1983** Cin: 10 G; 1 Sac. **1984** Cin: 16 G; 2 Sac. **1985** Buf: 16 G; Int 1-8; 1 Sac. **1986** Buf: 7 G; 1 Sac. **Total:** 74 G; Int 1-8; 5 Sac.

LESLIE FRAZIER Frazier, Leslie Antonio 6′0″, 189 **DB**
Col: Alcorn State *HS:* Stephen D. Lee [Columbus, MS] B: 4/3/1959, Columbus, MS
1981 ChiB: KR 6-77 12.8. **1982** ChiB: 1 Sac. **Total:** KR 6-77 12.8; 1 Sac.

		Interceptions		
Year Team	G	Int	Yds	TD
1981 ChiB	13	0	0	0
1982 ChiB	9	2	0	0
1983 ChiB	16	7	135	1
1984 ChiB	11	5	89	0
1985 ChiB	16	6	119	**1**
NFL Total	65	20	343	2

RANDY FRAZIER Frazier, Phillip Randy 6'3", 235 **LB**
Col: Morehead State *HS:* Whitesburg [KY] B: 6/18/1964, Letcher Co., KY
1987 KC: 3 G.

WAYNE FRAZIER Frazier, William Wayne 6'3", 245 **C-LB**
Col: Auburn *HS:* Hillcrest [Evergreen, AL] B: 3/5/1939, Evergreen, AL
Drafted: 1961 Round 16 ChiB
1962 SD: 7 G. **1965** Hou: 14 G. **1966** KC: 14 G. **1967** Buf-KC: 13 G. Buf: 6 G. KC: 7 G. **Total:** 48 G.

WILLIE FRAZIER Frazier, Willie C 6'4", 225 **TE**
Col: Arkansas-Pine Bluff *HS:* Booker T. Washington [EL Dorado, AR]
B: 6/19/1942, El Dorado, AR
1964 Hou: KR 1-0. **1970** SD: Rush 5-120 24.0 1 TD; 1 Fum TD.
1971 Hou-KC: Rush 1-(-2) -2.0. KC: Rush 1-(-2) -2.0. **Total:** Rush 6-118 19.7 1 TD; KR 1-0; 1 Fum TD.

		Receiving					Tot
Year Team	**G**	**Rec**	**Yds**	**Avg**	**TD**	**Fum**	**TD**
1964 Hou	14	11	227	20.6	2	0	2
1965 Hou	12	37	521	14.1	8	0	8
1966 SD	14	9	144	16.0	2	0	2
1967 SD	14	57	922	16.2	10	3	10
1968 SD	9	16	237	14.8	3	0	3
1969 SD	11	17	205	12.1	0	1	0
1970 SD	14	38	497	13.1	6	1	8
1971 Hou-KC	14	10	154	15.4	0	1	0
1971 Hou	6	8	113	14.1	0	1	0
1971 KC	8	2	41	20.5	0	0	0
1972 KC	14	13	172	13.2	5	0	5
1975 Hou	5	1	9	9.0	0	0	0
NFL Total	121	209	3088	14.8	36	6	38

ANDY FREDERICK Frederick, Andrew Brian 6'6", 257 **OT**
Col: New Mexico *HS:* St. Joseph [Westchester, IL] B: 7/25/1954, Oak Park, IL *Drafted:* 1977 Round 5 Dal
1977 Dal: 13 G. **1978** Dal: 16 G. **1979** Dal: 16 G. **1980** Dal: 16 G.
1981 Dal: 16 G. **1982** Cle: 7 G. **1983** ChiB: 16 G. **1984** ChiB: 16 G.
1985 ChiB: 16 G. **Total:** 132 G.

MIKE FREDERICK Frederick, Thomas Michael 6'5", 280 **DE**
Col: Virginia *HS:* Neshaminy [Langhorne, PA] B: 8/6/1972, Abington, PA *Drafted:* 1995 Round 3 Cle
1995 Cle: 16 G; KR 2-16 8.0; 1.5 Sac. **1996** Bal: 16 G. **1997** Bal: 16 G.
1998 Bal: 10 G. **Total:** 58 G; KR 2-15 7.5; 1.5 Sac.

TUCKER FREDERICKSON Frederickson, Ivan Charles 6'2", 220 **RB**
Col: Auburn *HS:* South Broward [Hollywood, FL] B: 1/12/1943, Fort Lauderdale, FL *Drafted:* 1965 Round 1 NYG
1965 NYG: Pass 1-0, 1 Int. **1967** NYG: KR 1-19 19.0. **1968** NYG: KR 2-13 6.5. **Total:** Pass 1-0, 1 Int; KR 3-32 10.7.

		Rushing				Receiving					Tot
Year Team	**G**	**Att**	**Yds**	**Avg**	**TD**	**Rec**	**Yds**	**Avg**	**TD**	**Fum**	**TD**
1965 NYG	13	195	659	3.4	5	24	177	7.4	1	9	6
1967 NYG	10	97	311	3.2	2	19	153	8.1	0	3	2
1968 NYG	14	142	486	3.4	1	10	64	6.4	2	2	3
1969 NYG	5	33	136	4.1	0	14	95	6.8	1	0	1
1970 NYG	14	120	375	3.1	1	40	408	10.2	3	8	4
1971 NYG	10	64	242	3.8	0	21	114	5.4	1	1	1
NFL Total	66	651	2209	3.4	9	128	1011	7.9	8	23	17

ROB FREDRICKSON Fredrickson, Robert J 6'4", 240 **LB**
Col: Michigan State *HS:* St. Joseph [Detroit, MI] B: 5/13/1971, St. Joseph, MI *Drafted:* 1994 Round 1 LARd
1994 LARd: 16 G; 3 Sac. **1995** Oak: 16 G; Int 1-14; **1** Fum TD; 6 Pt.
1996 Oak: 10 G. **1997** Oak: 16 G; 2 Sac. **1998** Det: 16 G; Int 1-0; 2.5 Sac.
Total: 74 G; Int 2-14; 1 Fum TD; 6 Pt; 7.5 Sac.

SOLOMON FREELON Freelon, Solomon Jr. 6'2", 250 **OG**
Col: Grambling State *HS:* Carroll [Monroe, LA] B: 2/19/1951, Monroe, LA *Drafted:* 1972 Round 3 Hou
1972 Hou: 14 G. **1973** Hou: 11 G. **1974** Hou: 14 G. **Total:** 39 G.

ANTONIO FREEMAN Freeman, Antonio Michael 6'1", 191 **WR**
(Free) *Col:* Virginia Tech *HS:* Baltimore Polytechnic Inst. [MD]
B: 5/27/1972, Baltimore, MD *Drafted:* 1995 Round 3 GB
1997 GB: Rush 1-14 14.0. **1998** GB: Rush 3-5 1.7; Scor 1 2XP.
Total: Rush 4-19 4.8; Scor 1 2XP.

		Receiving				Punt Returns			
Year Team	**G**	**Rec**	**Yds**	**Avg**	**TD**	**Ret**	**Yds**	**Avg**	**TD**
1995 GB	11	8	106	13.3	1	37	292	7.9	0
1996 GB	12	56	933	16.7	9	0	0	—	0
1997 GB	16	81	1243	15.3	12	0	0	—	0
1998 GB	15	84	**1424**	17.0	14	0	0	—	0
NFL Total	54	229	3706	16.2	36	37	292	7.9	0

	Kickoff Returns				
Year Team	**Ret**	**Yds**	**Avg**	**TD**	**Fum**
1995 GB	24	556	23.2	0	7
1996 GB	1	16	16.0	0	3
1997 GB	0	0	—	0	1
NFL Total	25	572	22.9	0	11

JACK FREEMAN Freeman, Jack Lenard 6'0", 198 **G**
Col: Texas B: 1/20/1922, Mexia, TX
AAFC **1946** BknA: 12 G.

LORENZO FREEMAN Freeman, Lorenzo Z 6'5", 300 **NT-DT**
Col: Pittsburgh *HS:* Woodrow Wilson [Camden, NJ] B: 5/23/1964, Camden, NJ *Drafted:* 1987 Round 4 GB
1987 Pit: 6 G. **1988** Pit: 13 G. **1989** Pit: 16 G. **1990** Pit: 11 G; 2 Sac.
1991 NYG: 16 G; KR 1-0; 0.5 Sac. **Total:** 62 G; KR 1-0; 2.5 Sac.

MIKE FREEMAN Freeman, Michael 5'11", 179 **DB**
Col: Fresno City Coll. CA (J.C.); Fresno State *HS:* Fresno [CA]
B: 7/13/1944, Los Angeles, CA *Drafted:* 1968 Round 4 Min
1968 Atl: 9 G. **1969** Atl: 14 G; PR 4-30 7.5. **1970** Atl: 14 G; PR 3-15 5.0; KR 1-0; Int 1-3. **Total:** 37 G; PR 7-45 6.4; KR 1-0; Int 1-3.

MIKE FREEMAN Freeman, Michael Joseph 6'3", 256 **OG-C**
Col: Arizona *HS:* Sahuaro [Tucson, AZ]; Fountain Valley HS [CA]
B: 10/13/1961, Mount Holly, NJ
1984 Den: 9 G. **1986** Den: 4 G. **1987** Den: 13 G. **1988** LARd: 2 G.
Total: 28 G.

PHIL FREEMAN Freeman, Phillip Emery 5'11", 185 **WR**
Col: Arizona *HS:* St. Monica's [Santa Monica, CA] B: 12/9/1962, St. Paul, MN *Drafted:* 1985 Round 8 TB
1986 TB: Rec 14-229 16.4 2 TD. **1987** TB: Rush 1-1 1.0; Rec 8-141 17.6 2 TD. **Total:** Rush 1-1 1.0; Rec 22-370 16.8 4 TD.

		Kickoff Returns				
Year Team	**G**	**Ret**	**Yds**	**Avg**	**TD**	**Fum**
1985 TB	14	48	1085	22.6	0	1
1986 TB	15	31	582	18.8	0	1
1987 TB	8	0	0	—	0	1
NFL Total	37	79	1667	21.1	0	3

REGGIE FREEMAN Freeman, Reginald Prince 6'1", 233 **LB**
Col: Florida State *HS:* Clewiston [FL] B: 5/8/1970, Clewiston, FL
Drafted: 1993 Round 2 NO
1993 NO: 10 G.

BOBBY FREEMAN Freeman, Robert Clayton 6'1", 202 **DB-HB**
(Goose) *Col:* Auburn *HS:* Decatur [AL] B: 10/19/1932, Birmingham, AL *Drafted:* 1956 Round 5 LARm
1957 Cle: KR 1-15 15.0. **1958** Cle: Rush 2-1 0.5. **Total:** Rush 2-1 0.5; KR 1-15 15.0.

		Interceptions			
Year Team	**G**	**Int**	**Yds**	**TD**	**Fum**
1957 Cle	9	3	46	0	0
1958 Cle	12	3	21	0	0
1959 GB	12	2	22	0	0
1960 Phi	12	4	67	0	0
1961 Phi	14	0	0	0	0
1962 Was	14	3	48	0	1
NFL Total	73	15	204	0	1

RUSS FREEMAN Freeman, Russell Williams 6'7", 290 **OT**
Col: Georgia Tech *HS:* Allderdice [Pittsburgh, PA] B: 9/2/1969, Homestead, PA
1992 Den: 16 G. **1993** Den: 14 G. **1994** Den: 13 G. **1995** Oak: 15 G.
Total: 58 G.

STEVE FREEMAN Freeman, Steven Jay 5'11", 185 **DB**
Col: Mississippi State *HS:* Whitehaven [Memphis, TN] B: 5/8/1953, Lamesa, TX *Drafted:* 1975 Round 5 NE
1981 Buf: KR 1-0. **1982** Buf: 1 Sac. **1984** Buf: 2 Sac. **Total:** KR 1-0; 3 Sac.

		Interceptions		
Year Team	**G**	**Int**	**Yds**	**TD**
1975 Buf	14	2	44	1
1976 Buf	14	0	0	0
1977 Buf	14	1	4	0
1978 Buf	16	0	0	0
1979 Buf	16	3	62	1
1980 Buf	16	7	107	1
1981 Buf	16	0	0	0
1982 Buf	9	3	27	0
1983 Buf	16	3	40	0
1984 Buf	15	3	45	0
1985 Buf	16	0	0	0
1986 Buf	16	1	0	0
1987 Min	12	0	0	0
NFL Total	190	23	329	3

JESSE FREITAS Freitas, Jesse 5′10″, 170 **QB-DB**
Col: Santa Clara *HS:* Red Bluff [CA] B: 2/7/1921, Red Bluff, CA
AAFC **1946** SF-A: PR 1-10 10.0; Int 2-40. **1947** SF-A: Int 1-11; Punt 8-336 42.0. **Total:** PR 1-10 10.0; Int 3-51; Punt 8-336 42.0.

Year Team	G	Passing Att	Comp	Comp%	Yds	YPA	TD	Int	Rating
1946 SF-A	10	44	22	50.0	234	5.32	3	7	49.1
1947 SF-A	10	33	13	39.4	215	6.52	4	2	76.4
1948 ChiA	10	167	84	50.3	1425	8.53	14	16	67.9
1949 BufA	1	9	4	44.4	10	1.11	0	2	12.0
AAFC Total	31	253	123	48.6	1884	7.45	21	27	61.7

Year Team	Rushing Att	Yds	Avg	TD
1946 SF-A	6	-21	-3.5	0
1947 SF-A	6	-9	-1.5	0
1948 ChiA	24	25	1.0	0
1949 BufA	3	13	4.3	0
AAFC Total	39	8	0.2	0

JESSE FREITAS Freitas, Jesse Lee 6′1″, 203 **QB**
Col: Stanford; San Diego State *HS:* Serra [San Mateo, CA]
B: 9/10/1951, San Mateo, CA *Drafted:* 1974 Round 6 SD
1974 SD: Rush 6-16 2.7. **1975** SD: Rush 11-56 5.1. **Total:** Rush 17-72 4.2.

Year Team	G	Passing Att	Comp	Comp%	Yds	YPA	TD	Int	Rating	Fum
1974 SD	5	109	49	45.0	719	6.60	3	8	45.6	0
1975 SD	8	110	49	44.5	525	4.77	5	5	55.3	3
NFL Total	13	219	98	44.7	1244	5.68	8	13	50.5	3

ROCKY FREITAS Freitas, Rockne Crowningburg 6′6″, 270 **OT**
Col: Oregon State *HS:* Kamehameha School [Honolulu, HI]
B: 9/7/1945, Kailua, HI *Drafted:* 1967 Round 3 Pit
1968 Det: 6 G. **1969** Det: 14 G. **1970** Det: 14 G; Rec 1-(-8) -8.0. **1971** Det: 14 G. **1972** Det: 14 G. **1973** Det: 14 G. **1974** Det: 14 G. **1975** Det: 14 G. **1976** Det: 14 G. **1977** Det: 3 G. **1978** TB: 13 G. **Total:** 134 G; Rec 1-(-8) -8.0.

BARRY FRENCH French, Barry Alden 6′0″, 225 **OG-DG-OT**
(Bear) *Col:* Purdue *HS:* Washington [Sioux Falls, SD] B: 2/12/1922, Chamberlain, SD D: 3/16/1990, Vero Beach, FL *Drafted:* 1944 Round 17 ChiB
AAFC **1947** BalA: 14 G; KR 1-8 8.0. **1949** BalA: 11 G. **Total:** 25 G; KR 1-8 8.0.

NFL **1950** Bal: 12 G. **1951** Det: 12 G; KR 1-3 3.0. **Total:** 24 G; KR 1-3 3.0.

ERNEST FRENCH French, Ernest Clauzell 5′11″, 195 **DB**
Col: Alabama A&M *HS:* Baldwin Co. [Bay Minette, AL] B: 9/5/1959, Tensaw, AL
1982 Pit: 3 G; KR 2-38 19.0.

WALT FRENCH French, Walter Edward 5′7″, 155 **WB-TB-BB**
(Fitz; Piggy) *Col:* Rutgers; Army *HS:* Moorestown [NJ]; Pennington Prep [NJ] B: 7/12/1899, Moorestown, NJ D: 5/13/1984, Mountain Home, AR
1922 Roch: 1 G. **1925** Pott: 9 G; Rush 3 TD; Rec 2 TD; Tot TD 5; 30 Pt. **Total:** 10 G; Rush 3 TD; Rec 2 TD; Tot TD 5; 30 Pt.

GUS FREROTTE Frerotte, Gustave Joseph 6′3″, 228 **QB**
Col: Tulsa *HS:* Ford City [PA] B: 8/3/1971, Kittanning, PA
Drafted: 1994 Round 7 Was

Year Team	G	Passing Att	Comp	Comp%	Yds	YPA	TD	Int	Rating
1994 Was	4	100	46	46.0	600	6.00	5	5	61.3
1995 Was	16	396	199	50.3	2751	6.95	13	13	70.2
1996 Was	16	470	270	57.4	3453	7.35	12	11	79.3
1997 Was	13	402	204	50.7	2682	6.67	17	12	73.8
1998 Was	3	54	25	46.3	283	5.24	1	3	45.5
NFL Total	52	1422	744	52.3	9769	6.87	48	44	72.7

Year Team	Rushing Att	Yds	Avg	TD	Fum
1994 Was	4	1	0.3	0	4
1995 Was	22	16	0.7	1	7
1996 Was	28	16	0.6	0	12
1997 Was	25	65	2.6	2	8
1998 Was	3	20	6.7	0	0
NFL Total	82	118	1.4	3	31

MITCH FREROTTE Frerotte, Paul Mitchell 6′3″, 281 **OG**
Col: Penn State *HS:* Kittanning [PA] B: 3/30/1965, Kittanning, PA
1987 Buf: 12 G. **1990** Buf: 16 G. **1991** Buf: 16 G. **1992** Buf: 14 G; Rec 2-4 2.0 2 TD; KR 1-0; 12 Pt. **Total:** 58 G; Rec 2-4 2.0 2 TD; KR 1-0; 12 Pt.

GLENN FREY Frey, Glenn Joseph 5′10″, 193 **BB-DB**
(Wackie) *Col:* Temple *HS:* Pitman [PA] B: 3/6/1912, Tunkhannock, PA D: 1/5/1980, New Port Richey, FL
1936 Phi: 12 G; Rush 7-8 1.1; Rec 3-65 21.7. **1937** Phi: 6 G; Pass 1-0; Rush 5-11 2.2; Rec 4-19 4.8. **Total:** 18 G; Pass 1-0; Rush 12-19 1.6; Rec 7-84 12.0.

DICK FREY Frey, Richard H 6′2″, 235 **DE**
Col: Pasadena City Coll. CA (J.C.); Texas A&M *HS:* Mark Keppel [Alhambra, CA] B: 12/17/1929
1960 DalT: 14 G. **1961** Hou: 7 G. **Total:** 21 G.

RAY FRICK Frick, Raymond Augustus 6′1″, 205 **C-LB**
Col: Pennsylvania *HS:* Bloomfield [NJ] B: 1/16/1919, Bloomfield, NJ
Drafted: 1941 Round 3 Bkn
1941 Bkn: 3 G.

WALT FRICKEY Frickey, Walter Henry 5′11″, 220 **OE**
Col: No College B: 8/8/1895, Rochester, NY D: 3/12/1972, Rochester, NY
1920 Roch: 1 G.

LARRY FRIDAY Friday, Lawrence 6′4″, 215 **DB**
Col: Alcorn State; Mississippi State *HS:* Callaway [Jackson, MS]
B: 1/23/1958, Jackson, MS *Drafted:* 1981 Round 11 Cle
1987 Buf: 1 G.

MIKE FRIEDE Friede, Michael Gordon 6′3″, 205 **WR**
Col: Garden City CC KS; Indiana *HS:* Goodland [KS] B: 9/22/1957, Havre, MT *Drafted:* 1980 Round 3 Det

Year Team	G	Receiving Rec	Yds	Avg	TD
1980 Det-NYG	11	22	371	16.9	0
1980 Det	4	1	21	21.0	0
1980 NYG	7	21	350	16.7	0
1981 NYG	16	18	250	13.9	1
NFL Total	27	40	621	15.5	1

BOB FRIEDLUND Friedlund, Robert Memler 6′3″, 210 **DE-OE**
Col: Michigan State *HS:* Schenectady [NY]; Peekskill Mil. Acad. [NY]
B: 1/6/1920, Galesburg, IL D: 8/24/1991
1946 Phi: 2 G.

BENNY FRIEDMAN Friedman, Benjamin 5′10″, 183 **TB-DB**
(Bennah) *Col:* Michigan *HS:* East Tech [Cleveland, OH]; Glenville HS [Cleveland, OH] B: 3/18/1905, Cleveland, OH D: 11/23/1982, New York, NY
1927 Cle: Scor 23, 11 XK. **1928** Det: Scor **55**, **19** XK. **1929** NYG: Scor 32, **20** XK. **1930** NYG: Scor 49, 1 FG, 10 XK. **1932** Bkn: Rec 5-67 13.4; Scor 8, 1 FG, 5 XK. **1933** Bkn: Scor 6, 6 XK. **Total:** Rec 5-67 13.4; Scor 185, 2 FG, 71 XK.

Year Team	G	Passing Att	Comp	Comp%	Yds	YPA	TD	Int	Rating
1927 Cle	13	—	—	—	—	—	**11**	—	—
1928 Det	10	—	—	—	—	—	**9**	—	—
1929 NYG	15	—	—	—	—	—	**20**	—	—
1930 NYG	15	—	—	—	—	—	**13**	—	—
1931 NYG	9	—	—	—	—	—	3	—	—
1932 Bkn	11	74	23	31.1	319	4.31	5	10	28.9
1933 Bkn	7	80	42	**52.5**	594	7.43	5	7	61.1
1934 Bkn	1	13	5	38.5	16	1.23	0	2	7.1
NFL Total	81	167	70	41.9	929	5.56	66	19	60.2

Year Team	Rushing Att	Yds	Avg	TD
1927 Cle	—	—	—	2
1928 Det	—	—	—	**6**
1929 NYG	—	—	—	2
1930 NYG	—	—	—	6
1931 NYG	—	—	—	2
1932 Bkn	88	250	2.8	0
1933 Bkn	55	177	3.2	0
1934 Bkn	9	31	3.4	0
NFL Total	152	458	3.0	18

JAKE FRIEDMAN Friedman, Jacob **OE**
Col: No College *HS:* Waterbury [CT] B: 3/23/1896, Bridgeport, CT D: 11/9/1988, Port Salerno, FL
1926 Har: 3 G.

BOB FRIEDMAN Friedman, Robert Allen 6′2″, 215 **T**
(Buck) *Col:* Washington *HS:* Allentown [PA] B: 9/11/1921, Allentown, PA D: 12/9/1989, Fort Lauderdale, FL *Drafted:* 1943 Round 18 Phi
1944 Phi: 10 G; Int 1-2.

BEN FRIEND Friend, Benjamin W 6′5″, 248 **T**
Col: Louisiana State *HS:* Gulfport [MS] B: 1/30/1912 *Drafted:* 1939 Round 15 Cle
1939 Cle: 10 G.

MIKE FRIER Frier, Michael 6′5″, 300 **DE**
Col: Appalachian State *HS:* Jacksonville [NC] B: 3/20/1969, Jacksonville, NC *Drafted:* 1992 Round 7 Sea
1992 Cin: 15 G. **1993** Cin: 16 G; 1 Sac. **1994** Cin-Sea: 4 G. Cin: 1 G. Sea: 3 G. **Total:** 35 G; 1 Sac.

SHERWOOD FRIES Fries, Sherwood Marshall 6′1″, 235 **G-LB**
Col: Colorado State *HS:* Fairfax [Los Angeles, CA] B: 11/24/1920, Los Angeles, CA D: 12/9/1986, San Juan Capistrano, CA
1943 GB: 5 G; Int 2-6.

JOHN FRIESZ Friesz, John Melvin 6′4″, 214 **QB**
Col: Idaho *HS:* Coeur d'Alene [ID] B: 5/19/1967, Missoula, MT
Drafted: 1990 Round 6 SD

		Passing							
Year Team	**G**	**Att**	**Comp**	**Comp%**	**Yds**	**YPA**	**TD**	**Int**	**Rating**
1990 SD	1	22	11	50.0	98	4.45	1	1	58.5
1991 SD	16	487	262	53.8	2896	5.95	12	15	67.1
1993 SD	12	238	128	53.8	1402	5.89	6	**4**	72.8
1994 Was	16	180	105	58.3	1266	7.03	10	9	77.7
1995 Sea	6	120	64	53.3	795	6.63	6	3	80.4
1996 Sea	8	211	120	56.9	1629	7.72	8	4	86.4
1997 Sea	2	36	15	41.7	138	3.83	0	3	18.1
1998 Sea	6	49	29	59.2	409	8.35	2	2	82.8
NFL Total	67	1343	734	54.7	8633	6.43	45	41	72.9

	Rushing				
Year Team	**Att**	**Yds**	**Avg**	**TD**	**Fum**
1990 SD	1	3	3.0	0	0
1991 SD	10	18	1.8	0	10
1993 SD	10	3	0.3	0	2
1994 Was	1	1	1.0	0	2
1995 Sea	11	0	0.0	0	2
1996 Sea	12	1	0.1	0	7
1997 Sea	1	0	0.0	0	1
1998 Sea	5	5	1.0	0	0
NFL Total	51	31	0.6	0	24

DAVID FRISCH Frisch, David Joseph 6′7″, 260 **TE**
Col: Central Coll. (Iowa); Missouri; Colorado State *HS:* Northwest [House Springs, MO] B: 6/22/1970, Kirkwood, MO
1993 Cin: 11 G; Rec 6-43 7.2. **1994** Cin: 16 G. **1995** NE: 2 G; KR 1-8 8.0. **1996** Min: 10 G; Rec 3-27 9.0 1 TD; 6 Pt. **1997** Was: 2 G. **Total:** 41 G; Rec 9-70 7.8 1 TD; KR 1-8 8.0; 6 Pt.

TONI FRITSCH Fritsch, Anton 5′7″, 190 **K**
Col: No College *HS:* No High School B: 7/10/1945, Petronell, Austria

		Scoring						
Year Team	**G**	**Pts**	**FG**	**FGA**	**FG%**	**XK**	**XKA**	**XK%**
1971 Dal	2	17	5	8	62.5	2	2	100.0
1972 Dal	14	99	21	36	58.3	36	36	100.0
1973 Dal	13	97	18	28	64.3	**43**	**43**	100.0
1975 Dal	14	104	**22**	**35**	62.9	38	40	95.0
1976 SD	5	29	6	12	50.0	11	14	78.6
1977 Hou	9	55	12	16	**75.0**	19	20	**95.0**
1978 Hou	16	73	14	18	77.8	31	32	96.9
1979 Hou	16	104	21	25	**84.0**	41	43	**95.3**
1980 Hou	15	83	19	24	**79.2**	26	27	**96.3**
1981 Hou	16	77	15	22	68.2	32	34	94.1
1982 NO	5	20	4	7	57.1	8	9	88.9
NFL Total	125	758	157	231	68.0	287	300	95.7

ERNIE FRITSCH Fritsch, Ernest A 6′0″, 230 **LB**
Col: Detroit Mercy *HS:* Central Catholic [Canton, OH] B: 1/14/1937, Masillon, OH
1960 StL: 1 G.

LOUIE FRITSCH Fritsch, Louis E 240 **G**
Col: Georgetown (Ky.) *HS:* Central [Evansville, IN] B: 10/9/1879, Evansville, IN D: 1/20/1958, Indianapolis, IN
1921 Eva: 1 G.

TED FRITSCH Fritsch, Theodore Edward 5′10″, 210 **FB-LB**
Col: Wis.-Stevens Point *HS:* Spencer [WI] B: 10/31/1920, Spencer, WI D: 10/5/1979, Green Bay, WI
1942 GB: PR 1-31 31.0; Punt 3-122 40.7. **1943** GB: Punt 5-151 30.2. **1944** GB: Punt 10-408 40.8. **1946** GB: Punt 1-52 52.0. **1948** GB: 1 Fum TD. **1949** GB: Pass 1-0. **Total:** Pass 1-0; PR 1-31 31.0; Punt 19-733 38.6; 1 Fum TD.

		Rushing				Receiving			
Year Team	**G**	**Att**	**Yds**	**Avg**	**TD**	**Rec**	**Yds**	**Avg**	**TD**
1942 GB	11	74	323	4.4	0	9	60	6.7	0
1943 GB	10	54	169	3.1	4	2	55	27.5	0
1944 GB	9	94	322	3.4	4	3	5	1.7	0
1945 GB	10	89	282	3.2	7	3	13	4.3	0
1946 GB	11	128	444	3.5	**9**	2	13	6.5	1
1947 GB	12	68	247	3.6	6	0	0	—	0
1948 GB	12	37	173	4.7	0	0	0	—	0
1949 GB	12	69	227	3.3	1	6	81	13.5	0
1950 GB	12	7	13	1.9	0	0	0	—	0
NFL Total	99	620	2200	3.5	31	25	227	9.1	1

	Kickoff Returns				Interceptions		
Year Team	**Ret**	**Yds**	**Avg**	**TD**	**Int**	**Yds**	**TD**
1942 GB	2	43	21.5	0	0	0	0
1943 GB	4	99	24.8	0	0	0	0
1944 GB	11	288	26.2	0	6	115	1
1945 GB	8	279	**34.9**	0	1	69	1
1946 GB	3	68	22.7	0	1	15	0
1947 GB	5	100	20.0	0	1	12	0
1948 GB	1	17	17.0	0	1	52	0
1949 GB	1	23	23.0	0	0	0	0
1950 GB	2	34	17.0	0	0	0	0
NFL Total	37	951	25.7	0	10	263	2

	Scoring								Tot
Year Team	**Pts**	**FG**	**FGA**	**FG%**	**XK**	**XKA**	**XK%**	**Fum**	**TD**
1942 GB	13	4	5	**80.0**	1	1	**100.0**	0	0
1943 GB	24	0	2	0.0	0	0	—	0	4
1944 GB	0	0	0	—	0	0	—	0	5
1945 GB	57	3	8	37.5	0	0	—	2	8
1946 GB	**100**	**9**	**17**	52.9	13	15	86.7	3	**10**
1947 GB	56	6	13	**46.2**	2	2	**100.0**	1	6
1948 GB	29	6	16	37.5	5	6	83.3	2	1
1949 GB	32	5	**20**	25.0	11	13	84.6	2	1
1950 GB	39	3	17	17.6	30	33	90.9	0	0
NFL Total	380	36	98	36.7	62	70	88.6	10	35

TED FRITSCH Fritsch, Theodore Edward Jr. 6′2″, 242 **C**
Col: St. Norbert *HS:* Premontre [Green Bay, WI] B: 8/26/1950, Green Bay, WI
1972 Atl: 14 G. **1973** Atl: 14 G. **1974** Atl: 14 G; PR 1-0; KR 1-0; 2 Fum. **1976** Was: 14 G. **1977** Was: 14 G. **1978** Was: 16 G. **1979** Was: 16 G. **Total:** 102 G; PR 1-0; KR 1-0; 2 Fum.

GEORGE FRITTS Fritts, George Henry Jr. 5′11″, 205 **T**
Col: Clemson *HS:* Lenoir City [TN] B: 12/30/1919, Lenoir City, TN D: 2/7/1987, Savannah, GA
1945 Phi: 10 G.

STAN FRITTS Fritts, Stanley Allan 6′1″, 215 **RB**
Col: Murray State; North Carolina State *HS:* Oak Ridge [TN]
B: 12/18/1952, Oak Ridge, TN *Drafted:* 1975 Round 4 Cin
1975 Cin: Pass 4-2 50.0%, 31 7.75; Rec 6-63 10.5 2 TD. **1976** Cin: Rec 9-75 8.3; KR 1-10 10.0. **Total:** Pass 4-2 50.0%, 31 7.75; Rec 15-138 9.2 2 TD; KR 1-10 10.0.

		Rushing					Tot
Year Team	**G**	**Att**	**Yds**	**Avg**	**TD**	**Fum**	**TD**
1975 Cin	13	94	375	4.0	8	1	10
1976 Cin	13	47	200	4.3	3	1	3
NFL Total	26	141	575	4.1	11	2	13

RALPH FRITZ Fritz, Ralph C 5′9″, 202 **G**
Col: Michigan *HS:* Valley [New Kensington, PA]; Kiski School [Saltsburg, PA] B: 11/23/1917, New Kensington, PA *Drafted:* 1941 Round 8 Pit
1941 Phi: 10 G.

JIM FRITZSCHE Fritzsche, James Brian 6′8″, 265 **OT-OG**
Col: Purdue *HS:* Valley Forge [Parma Heights, OH] B: 10/11/1960, Parma, OH *Drafted:* 1982 Round 8 Phi
1983 Phi: 15 G; KR 2-17 8.5.

WILLIAM FRIZZELL Frizzell, William Jasper 6′3″, 203 **DB**
Col: North Carolina Central *HS:* J.H. Rose [Greenville, NC]
B: 9/8/1962, Greenville, NC *Drafted:* 1984 Round 10 Det
1987 Phi: 1 Sac. **1989** Phi: 1.5 Sac. **1990** Phi: 1.5 Sac. **Total:** 4 Sac.

		Interceptions		
Year Team	**G**	**Int**	**Yds**	**TD**
1984 Det	16	0	0	0
1985 Det	8	1	3	0
1986 Phi	8	0	0	0
1987 Phi	12	0	0	0
1988 Phi	16	3	19	0
1989 Phi	16	4	58	0
1990 Phi	16	3	91	1
1991 TB	16	0	0	0
1992 Phi	10	0	0	0
1993 Phi	16	0	0	0
NFL Total	134	11	171	1

LEN FRKETICH Frketich, Leonard Lawrence 6′1″, 290 **T**
(Ferky) *Col:* Penn State *HS:* Monessen [PA] B: 11/18/1917, Monessen, PA
1945 Pit: 2 G.

BILL FROHBOSE Frohbose, William Joseph 6′0″, 185 **DB**
Col: Miami (Fla.) *HS:* Archbishop Curley [Miami, FL] B: 5/20/1952, Washington, DC
1974 Det: 2 G.

ANDY FRONCZEK Fronczek, Andrew Anthony 6′0″, 200 **T**
Col: Richmond *HS:* Thornton Twp. [Harvey, IL] B: 9/21/1916, Harvey, IL
1941 Bkn: 11 G.

JOHN FRONGILLO Frongillo, John Richard 6′3″, 255 **C-OG**
Col: Cerritos Coll. CA (J.C.); Baylor *HS:* Bellflower [CA] B: 10/12/1939, Mansfield, MA *Drafted:* 1961 Round 28 Hou
1962 Hou: 14 G. **1963** Hou: 3 G. **1964** Hou: 14 G. **1965** Hou: 9 G. **1966** Hou: 14 G. **Total:** 54 G.

KEN FROST Frost, Carroll Kenneth 6′4″, 242 **DT**
Col: Tennessee *HS:* Franklin [TN] B: 11/17/1938, Brentwood, TN
1961 Dal: 14 G; Int 1-0. **1962** Dal: 3 G. **Total:** 17 G; Int 1-0.

SCOTT FROST Frost, Scott Andrew 6′3″, 219 **DB**
Col: Stanford; Nebraska *HS:* Wood River [NE] B: 1/4/1975, Wood River, NE *Drafted:* 1998 Round 3 NYJ
1998 NYJ: 13 G; PR 1-0; 1 Fum.

JIM FRUGONE Frugone, James Gregory 5′10″, 165 **TB**
(Babe) *Col:* Syracuse *HS:* Commercial [Brooklyn, NY] B: 10/23/1897, Brooklyn, NY D: 6/7/1972, Brooklyn, NY
1925 NYG: 3 G.

BABE FRUMP Frump, Maurice Elwood 6′0″, 225 **G**
Col: Ohio Wesleyan *HS:* Hillsboro [IL]; Lake Forest Acad. [IL]
B: 7/15/1901, OH D: 8/14/1979, Boynton Beach, FL
1930 ChiB: 9 G.

ED FRUTIG Frutig, Edward C 6′1″, 190 **OE-DB-DE**
Col: Michigan *HS:* River Rouge [MI] B: 8/19/1918, River Rouge, MI
Drafted: 1941 Round 3 GB
1941 GB: 8 G; Rush 1-11 11.0; Rec 2-40 20.0. **1945** GB-Det: 9 G; Rec 2-5 2.5 1 TD; KR 1-12 12.0; 6 Pt; 1 Fum. GB: 1 G. Det: 8 G; Rec 2-5 2.5 1 TD; KR 1-12 12.0; 6 Pt; 1 Fum. **1946** Det: 7 G; Rec 8-72 9.0 2 TD; KR 1-17 17.0; 12 Pt. **Total:** 24 G; Rush 1-11 11.0; Rec 12-117 9.8 3 TD; KR 2-29 14.5; 18 Pt; 1 Fum.

HARRY FRY Fry, Harry Glen 6′3″, 210 **E**
Col: Bucknell *HS:* Picture Rooks [PA] B: 10/4/1909, Hughesville, PA
1932 SI: 5 G.

BOB FRY Fry, Robert Moellering 6′4″, 235 **OT-OG**
Col: Kentucky *HS:* Elder [Cincinnati, OH] B: 11/11/1930, Cincinnati, OH *Drafted:* 1953 Round 3 LARm
1953 LARm: 12 G. **1956** LARm: 12 G. **1957** LARm: 12 G. **1958** LARm: 12 G; KR 2-23 11.5; 1 Fum. **1959** LARm: 12 G. **1960** Dal: 12 G. **1961** Dal: 14 G. **1962** Dal: 14 G. **1963** Dal: 14 G. **1964** Dal: 12 G. **Total:** 126 G; KR 2-23 11.5; 1 Fum.

WES FRY Fry, Wesley Leonard 5′10″, 190 **FB-BB-WB-TB**
(Cowboy) *Col:* Iowa *HS:* Hartley [IA] B: 12/10/1902, Hartley, IA
D: 11/11/1970, La Mesa, CA
1927 NYY: 15 G; Pass 1 TD; Rush 3 TD; Int 1 TD; Scor 25, 1 XK; Tot TD 4.

IRVING FRYAR Fryar, Irving Dale 6′0″, 200 **WR**
Col: Nebraska *HS:* Rancocas Valley Regional [Mount Holly, NJ]
B: 9/28/1962, Mount Holly, NJ *Drafted:* 1984 Round 1 NE
1991 NE: Pass 1-0. **1994** Mia: Scor 2 2XP. **Total:** Pass 1-0; Scor 2 2XP.

		Rushing				Receiving			
Year Team	**G**	**Att**	**Yds**	**Avg**	**TD**	**Rec**	**Yds**	**Avg**	**TD**
1984 NE	14	2	-11	-5.5	0	11	164	14.9	1
1985 NE	16	7	27	3.9	1	39	670	17.2	7
1986 NE	14	4	80	20.0	0	43	737	17.1	6
1987 NE	12	9	52	5.8	0	31	467	15.1	5
1988 NE	15	6	12	2.0	0	33	490	14.8	5
1989 NE	11	2	15	7.5	0	29	537	18.5	3
1990 NE	16	2	-4	-2.0	0	54	856	15.9	4
1991 NE	16	2	11	5.5	0	68	1014	14.9	3
1992 NE	15	1	6	6.0	0	55	791	14.4	4
1993 Mia	16	3	-4	-1.3	0	64	1010	15.8	5
1994 Mia	16	0	0	—	0	73	1270	17.4	7
1995 Mia	16	0	0	—	0	62	910	14.7	8
1996 Phi	16	1	-4	-4.0	0	88	1195	13.6	11
1997 Phi	16	0	0	—	0	86	1316	15.3	6
1998 Phi	16	3	46	15.3	0	48	556	11.6	2
NFL Total	225	42	226	5.4	1	784	11983	15.3	77

	Punt Returns				Kickoff Returns					Tot
Year Team	**Ret**	**Yds**	**Avg**	**TD**	**Ret**	**Yds**	**Avg**	**TD**	**Fum**	**TD**
1984 NE	36	347	9.6	0	5	95	19.0	0	4	1
1985 NE	37	520	**14.1**	**2**	3	39	13.0	0	4	10
1986 NE	35	366	10.5	1	10	192	19.2	0	4	7
1987 NE	18	174	9.7	0	6	119	19.8	0	2	5
1988 NE	38	398	10.5	0	1	3	3.0	0	2	5
1989 NE	12	107	8.9	0	1	47	47.0	0	2	3
1990 NE	28	133	4.8	0	0	0	—	0	1	4
1991 NE	2	10	5.0	0	0	0	—	0	2	3
1992 NE	0	0	—	0	0	0	—	0	0	4
1993 Mia	0	0	—	0	1	10	10.0	0	0	5
1994 Mia	0	0	—	0	0	0	—	0	0	7
1995 Mia	0	0	—	0	0	0	—	0	0	8
1996 Phi	0	0	—	0	0	0	—	0	0	11
1997 Phi	0	0	—	0	0	0	—	0	1	6
1998 Phi	0	0	—	0	0	0	—	0	0	2
NFL Total	206	2055	10.0	3	27	505	18.7	0	22	81

DAVID FRYE Frye, David William 6′2″, 223 **LB**
Col: Rancho Santiago Coll. CA (J.C.); Purdue *HS:* Woodward [Cincinnati, OH] B: 6/21/1961, Cincinnati, OH
1983 Atl: 16 G; 1 Sac. **1984** Atl: 16 G; 2 Sac. **1985** Atl: 14 G; Int 1-20; 4 Sac. **1986** Mia: 9 G. **1987** Mia: 12 G; 1 Sac. **1988** Mia: 8 G. **1989** Mia: 11 G; 1 Sac. **Total:** 86 G; Int 1-20; 9 Sac.

PHIL FRYE Frye, Philip Todd 5′11″, 180 **RB**
Col: Utah State; California Lutheran *HS:* John Marshall [Rochester, MN]
B: 12/20/1958, Washington, DC
1987 Min: 1 G; Rush 4-4 1.0; Rec 3-25 8.3.

BRIAN FRYER Fryer, Brian 6′1″, 185 **WR**
Col: Edmonton (Canada) B: 7/16/1953, Edmonton, Canada
Drafted: 1976 Round 8 Was
1976 Was: 4 G; KR 9-166 18.4.

KENNY FRYER Fryer, Kenneth Wesley 6′0″, 200 **TB-DB**
Col: West Virginia *HS:* Wellsburg [WV] B: 11/17/1918, Wellsburg, WV
1944 Bkn: 3 G; Pass 24-9 37.5%, 91 3.79 2 Int; Rush 15-15 1.0; Punt 7-273 39.0.

CHRIS FUAMATU-MA'AFALA Fuamatu-Ma'afala, Chris 5′11″, 252 **RB**
Col: Utah *HS:* St. Louis [Honolulu, HI] B: 3/4/1977, Honolulu, HI
Drafted: 1998 Round 6 Pit
1998 Pit: 12 G; Rush 7-30 4.3 2 TD; Rec 9-84 9.3 1 TD; Tot TD 3; 18 Pt.

DOM FUCCI Fucci, Dominic A 5′11″, 190 **DB**
Col: Kentucky *HS:* Washington [New Village, NJ] B: 9/14/1928, New Village, NJ D: 6/22/1987, Lexington, KY *Drafted:* 1951 Round 18 Was
1955 Det: 12 G; Punt 2-72 36.0.

JEAN FUGETT Fugett, Jean Schloss Jr. 6′3″, 225 **TE-WR**
Col: Amherst *HS:* Cardinal Gibbons [Baltimore, MD] B: 12/16/1951, Baltimore, MD *Drafted:* 1972 Round 13 Dal
1972 Dal: Rush 3-2 0.7; KR 1-0. **1973** Dal: Rush 1-34 34.0. **1975** Dal: Rush 1-2 2.0. **1976** Was: Rush 2-0. **Total:** Rush 7-38 5.4; KR 1-0.

		Receiving				
Year Team	**G**	**Rec**	**Yds**	**Avg**	**TD**	**Fum**
1972 Dal	14	7	94	13.4	0	0
1973 Dal	12	9	168	18.7	3	0
1974 Dal	12	4	60	15.0	1	0
1975 Dal	14	38	488	12.8	3	0
1976 Was	12	27	334	12.4	6	2
1977 Was	14	36	631	17.5	5	1
1978 Was	14	25	367	14.7	7	0
1979 Was	11	10	128	12.8	3	1
NFL Total	103	156	2270	14.6	28	4

DICK FUGLER Fugler, Richard Guy 6′2″, 238 **OT-DT**
Col: Tulane *HS:* White Oak [TX] B: 7/19/1931, Dallas, TX
Drafted: 1952 Round 5 ChiC
1952 Pit: 12 G. **1954** ChiC: 12 G. **Total:** 24 G.

DAVID FULCHER Fulcher, David Dwaye 6′3″, 236 **DB**
Col: Arizona State *HS:* John C. Fremont [Los Angeles, CA]
B: 9/28/1964, Los Angeles, CA *Drafted:* 1986 Round 3 Cin
1986 Cin: 2 Sac. **1987** Cin: KR 1-0; 3 Sac. **1988** Cin: 1.5 Sac. **1990** Cin: Scor **1** Saf; 1 Sac. **1992** Cin: 1 Sac. **Total:** KR 1-0; Scor 1 Saf; 8.5 Sac.

		Interceptions			
Year Team	**G**	**Int**	**Yds**	**TD**	**Fum**
1986 Cin	16	4	20	0	0
1987 Cin	11	3	30	0	0
1988 Cin	16	5	38	1	1
1989 Cin	16	8	87	0	0
1990 Cin	13	4	20	0	0
1991 Cin	16	4	51	1	1
1992 Cin	12	3	0	0	0
1993 LARd	3	0	0	0	0
NFL Total	103	31	246	2	2

BILL FULCHER Fulcher, William Marcus Jr. 6′0″, 193 **LB-OG**
Col: Georgia Tech *HS:* Richmond Acad. [Atlanta, GA] B: 2/9/1934, Augusta, GA
1956 Was: 9 G; Int 1-0. **1957** Was: 2 G. **1958** Was: 12 G. **Total:** 23 G; Int 1-0.

SCOTT FULHAGE Fulhage, Scott Alan 5′11″, 191 P
Col: Kansas State *HS:* Beloit [KS] B: 1/17/1961, Beloit, KS
1989 Atl: Pass 1-1 100.0%, 12 12.00; Rush 1-0. **1992** Atl: Rush 1-0.
Total: Pass 1-1 100.0%, 12 12.00; Rush 2-0.

		Punting			
Year Team	G	Punts	Yds	Avg	Fum
1987 Cin	11	52	2168	41.7	0
1988 Cin	13	44	1672	38.0	0
1989 Atl	16	84	3472	41.3	1
1990 Atl	16	70	2913	41.6	0
1991 Atl	16	81	3470	42.8	0
1992 Atl	16	68	2818	41.4	0
NFL Total	88	399	16513	41.4	1

CHARLEY FULLER Fuller, Charles Earl 5′11″, 175 HB
(Tornado) *Col:* San Francisco State *HS:* Vallejo [CA] B: 1/22/1939, Vicksburg, MS *Drafted:* 1961 Round 19 Oak
1961 Oak: Pass 1-0; Rec 12-277 23.1 2 TD; PR 4-52 13.0; KR 8-155 19.4.
1962 Oak: Rec 5-67 13.4. **Total:** Pass 1-0; Rec 17-344 20.2 2 TD; PR 4-52 13.0; KR 8-155 19.4.

		Rushing				
Year Team	G	Att	Yds	Avg	TD	Fum
1961 Oak	14	38	134	3.5	0	5
1962 Oak	3	0	0	—	0	0
NFL Total	17	38	134	3.5	0	5

COREY FULLER Fuller, Corey Bushe 5′10″, 204 DB
Col: Florida State *HS:* James S. Rickards [Tallahassee, FL]
B: 5/1/1971, Tallahassee, FL *Drafted:* 1995 Round 2 Min
1995 Min: **1** Fum TD; 0.5 Sac. **1998** Min: 1 Sac. **Total:** 1 Fum TD; 1.5 Sac.

		Interceptions		
Year Team	G	Int	Yds	TD
1995 Min	16	1	0	0
1996 Min	16	3	3	0
1997 Min	16	2	24	0
1998 Min	16	4	36	0
NFL Total	64	10	63	0

EDDIE FULLER Fuller, Eddie Jerome 5′9″, 201 RB
Col: Louisiana State *HS:* Leesville [LA] B: 6/22/1968, Leesville, LA
Drafted: 1990 Round 4 Buf
1991 Buf: 5 G; KR 8-125 15.6. **1992** Buf: 8 G; Rush 6-39 6.5; Rec 2-17 8.5; KR 8-134 16.8. **1993** Buf: 7 G. **Total:** 20 G; Rush 6-39 6.5; Rec 2-17 8.5; KR 16-259 16.2.

FRANK FULLER Fuller, Frank Andrew 6′4″, 244 OT-OG-C-DE
Col: Kentucky *HS:* Du Bois [PA] B: 8/8/1929, Du Bois, PA
D: 12/10/1993, Los Angeles, CA *Drafted:* 1952 Round 26 LARm
1953 LARm: 9 G. **1955** LARm: 12 G. **1957** LARm: 10 G. **1958** LARm: 12 G. **1959** ChiC: 10 G. **1960** StL: 9 G; Scor **1** Saf; 2 Pt. **1961** StL: 14 G. **1962** StL: 14 G. **1963** Phi: 5 G. **Total:** 95 G; Scor 1 Saf; 2 Pt.

JAMES FULLER Fuller, James Ray 6′0″, 208 DB
Col: Walla Walla CC WA; Portland State *HS:* Stadium [Tacoma, WA]
B: 8/5/1969, Tacoma, WA *Drafted:* 1992 Round 8 SD
1992 SD: Postseason only. **1993** SD: 10 G. **1996** Phi: 13 G; Int 1-4.
Total: 23 G; Int 1-4.

JEFF FULLER Fuller, Jeffery Avery 6′2″, 216 DB-LB
Col: Texas A&M *HS:* Franklin D. Roosevelt [Dallas, TX] B: 8/8/1962, Dallas, TX *Drafted:* 1984 Round 5 SF
1984 SF: 1.5 Sac. **1985** SF: 2 Sac. **1986** SF: 2.5 Sac. **1987** SF: Scor **1** Saf; 2 Sac. **1988** SF: 1 Sac. **Total:** Scor 1 Saf; 9 Sac.

		Interceptions			
Year Team	G	Int	Yds	TD	Fum
1984 SF	13	1	38	0	0
1985 SF	16	1	4	0	0
1986 SF	6	4	44	0	2
1987 SF	14	0	0	0	0
1988 SF	16	4	18	0	0
1989 SF	6	0	0	0	0
NFL Total	71	10	104	0	2

JOE FULLER Fuller, Joe Robert 5′11″, 180 DB
Col: Northern Iowa *HS:* Central [Minneapolis, MN] B: 9/25/1964, Milligan, FL
1990 SD: 4 G; Int 1-5. **1991** GB: 16 G. **Total:** 20 G; Int 1-5.

JOHNNY FULLER Fuller, John Charles 6′0″, 186 DB
(Splinter) *Col:* Lamar *HS:* South Park [Beaumont, TX] B: 3/3/1946, Beaumont, TX *Drafted:* 1968 Round 4 SF
1968 SF: KR 1-23 23.0; Int 2-3. **1969** SF: KR 8-155 19.4; Int 1-31.
1970 SF: KR 1-8 8.0; Int 1-20. **1971** SF: Int 2-57. **1972** SF: Int 1-0.
1974 NO: Int 1-16. **Total:** KR 10-186 18.6; Int 8-127.

		Punt Returns				
Year Team	G	Ret	Yds	Avg	TD	Fum
1968 SF	14	12	33	2.8	0	2
1969 SF	7	5	12	2.4	0	1
1970 SF	14	4	29	7.3	0	2
1971 SF	14	3	31	10.3	0	0
1972 SF	14	1	9	9.0	0	0
1973 NO	13	0	0	—	0	0
1974 NO	12	0	0	—	0	0
1975 NO	11	0	0	—	0	0
NFL Total	99	25	114	4.6	0	5

LARRY FULLER Fuller, Lawrence 5′10″, 192 HB-DB-LB
Col: No College B: 1/28/1923, Faust, NY D: 2/18/1992, Tupper Lake, NY
1944 Was: 5 G; Rush 4-10 2.5; Rec 5-82 16.4 1 TD; 6 Pt. **1945** Was-ChiC: 2 G. Was: 1 G. ChiC: 1 G. **Total:** 7 G; Rush 4-10 2.5; Rec 5-82 16.4 1 TD; 6 Pt.

MIKE FULLER Fuller, Michael Darwin 5′10″, 188 DB
Col: Auburn *HS:* John S. Shaw [Mobile, AL] B: 4/7/1953, Jackson, MS
Drafted: 1975 Round 3 SD
1976 SD: Scor **1** 1XP. **1977** SD: Rush 1-7 7.0 1 TD. **1979** SD: Pass 1-0; Rush 1-0. **1980** SD: Rush 2-0. **Total:** Pass 1-0; Rush 4-7 1.8 1 TD; Scor 1 1XP.

		Punt Returns				Kickoff Returns			
Year Team	G	Ret	Yds	Avg	TD	Ret	Yds	Avg	TD
1975 SD	14	36	410	11.4	1	31	725	23.4	0
1976 SD	14	33	436	13.2	0	20	420	21.0	0
1977 SD	14	28	360	12.9	1	0	0	—	0
1978 SD	16	39	436	11.2	0	5	109	21.8	0
1979 SD	16	46	448	9.7	0	6	115	19.2	0
1980 SD	16	30	298	9.9	0	15	289	19.3	0
1981 Cin	15	23	177	7.7	0	1	34	34.0	0
1982 Cin	9	17	95	5.6	0	1	9	9.0	0
NFL Total	114	252	2660	10.6	2	79	1701	21.5	0

	Interceptions				Tot
Year Team	Int	Yds	TD	Fum	TD
1975 SD	1	1	0	5	1
1976 SD	1	0	0	3	0
1977 SD	5	61	0	2	2
1978 SD	4	44	1	1	1
1979 SD	4	39	0	4	0
1980 SD	0	0	0	3	0
1981 Cin	1	31	0	1	0
1982 Cin	1	0	0	2	0
NFL Total	17	176	1	21	4

RANDY FULLER Fuller, Randy Lamar 5′10″, 180 DB
Col: Tennessee State *HS:* William H. Spencer [Columbus, GA]
B: 6/2/1970, Griffin, GA *Drafted:* 1994 Round 4 Den
1994 Den: 10 G. **1995** Pit: 13 G. **1996** Pit: 14 G; Int 1-0. **1997** Pit: 12 G; 1 Sac. **1998** Atl: 13 G; 2 Sac. **Total:** 62 G; Int 1-0; 3 Sac.

STEVE FULLER Fuller, Stephen Ray 6′4″, 198 QB
Col: Clemson *HS:* Spartanburg [SC] B: 1/5/1957, Enid, OK
Drafted: 1979 Round 1 KC

		Passing							
Year Team	G	Att	Comp	Comp%	Yds	YPA	TD	Int	Rating
1979 KC	16	270	146	54.1	1484	5.50	6	14	55.8
1980 KC	14	320	193	60.3	2250	7.03	10	12	76.4
1981 KC	13	134	77	57.5	934	6.97	3	4	74.0
1982 KC	9	93	49	52.7	665	7.15	3	2	77.6
1984 ChiB	6	78	53	67.9	595	7.63	3	0	103.3
1985 ChiB	16	107	53	49.5	777	7.26	1	5	57.3
1986 ChiB	16	64	34	53.1	451	7.05	2	4	60.1
NFL Total	90	1066	605	56.8	7156	6.71	28	41	70.1

	Rushing				
Year Team	Att	Yds	Avg	TD	Fum
1979 KC	50	264	5.3	1	6
1980 KC	60	274	4.6	4	**16**
1981 KC	19	118	6.2	0	4
1982 KC	10	56	5.6	0	3
1984 ChiB	15	89	5.9	1	0
1985 ChiB	24	77	3.2	5	3
1986 ChiB	8	30	3.8	0	2
NFL Total	186	908	4.9	11	34

WILLIAM FULLER Fuller, William Henry Jr. 6′3″, 271 DE
Col: North Carolina *HS:* Indian River [Chesapeake, VA] B: 3/8/1962, Norfolk, VA *Drafted:* 1984 Supplemental Round 1 LARm
1986 Hou: 13 G; 1 Sac. **1987** Hou: 12 G; KR 1-0; 2 Sac. **1988** Hou: 16 G; Int 1-9; 8.5 Sac. **1989** Hou: 15 G; 6.5 Sac. **1990** Hou: 16 G; 8 Sac.
1991 Hou: 16 G; 15 Sac. **1992** Hou: 15 G; 1 Fum TD; 6 Pt; 8 Sac.
1993 Hou: 16 G; 10 Sac. **1994** Phi: 16 G; Scor **1** Saf; 2 Pt; 9.5 Sac.
1995 Phi: 14 G; 13 Sac. **1996** Phi: 16 G; 13 Sac. **1997** SD: 16 G; Int 1-0;

3 Sac. **1998** SD: 13 G; 3 Sac. **Total:** 194 G; KR 1-0; Int 2-9; Scor 1 Saf; 1 Fum TD; 8 Pt; 100.5 Sac.

ED FULLERTON Fullerton, Edward Reno 5′10″, 190 **DB**
Col: Maryland *HS:* West View [PA] B: 4/7/1931, Pittsburgh, PA
Drafted: 1953 Round 4 SF
1953 Pit: 1 G.

DARRELL FULLINGTON Fullington, Darrell 6′1″, 197 **DB**
Col: Miami (Fla.) *HS:* New Smyrna Beach [FL] B: 4/17/1964, New Smyrna Beach, FL *Drafted:* 1988 Round 5 Min
1990 Min: 1 Sac. **1992** TB: Rec 1-12 12.0. **Total:** Rec 1-12 12.0; 1 Sac.

		Interceptions		
Year Team	**G**	**Int**	**Yds**	**TD**
1988 Min	15	3	57	0
1989 Min	16	1	0	0
1990 Min	16	1	10	0
1991 NE-TB	16	2	13	0
1991 NE	5	0	0	0
1991 TB	11	2	13	0
1992 TB	16	3	25	0
NFL Total	79	10	105	0

BRENT FULLWOOD Fullwood, Brent Lanard 5′11″, 209 **RB**
Col: Auburn *HS:* St. Cloud [FL] B: 10/10/1963, Kissimmee, FL
Drafted: 1987 Round 1 GB

		Rushing				Receiving			
Year Team	**G**	**Att**	**Yds**	**Avg**	**TD**	**Rec**	**Yds**	**Avg**	**TD**
1987 GB	11	84	274	3.3	5	2	11	5.5	0
1988 GB	14	101	483	4.8	7	20	128	6.4	1
1989 GB	15	204	821	4.0	5	19	214	11.3	0
1990 GB-Cle	6	44	124	2.8	1	3	17	5.7	0
1990 GB	5	44	124	2.8	1	3	17	5.7	0
1990 Cle	1	0	0	—	0	0	0	—	0
NFL Total	46	433	1702	3.9	18	44	370	8.4	1

	Kickoff Returns					Tot
Year Team	**Ret**	**Yds**	**Avg**	**TD**	**Fum**	**TD**
1987 GB	24	510	21.3	0	2	5
1988 GB	21	421	20.0	0	6	8
1989 GB	11	243	22.1	0	6	5
1990 GB-Cle	6	119	19.8	0	1	1
1990 GB	0	0	—	0	1	1
1990 Cle	6	119	19.8	0	0	0
NFL Total	62	1293	20.9	0	15	19

DANNY FULTON Fulton, Daniel B 6′2″, 184 **WR**
Col: Nebraska; Nebraska-Omaha *HS:* Omaha Tech [NE] B: 9/2/1956, Memphis, TN *Drafted:* 1978 Round 3 Buf
1979 Buf: 6 G; Rec 2-34 17.0. **1981** Cle: 5 G; Rec 2-38 19.0. **1982** Cle: 9 G; Rec 1-9 9.0. **Total:** 20 G; Rec 5-81 16.2.

ED FULTON Fulton, Edward Ulmer 6′3″, 250 **OG**
Col: Maryland *HS:* Sparta [NJ] B: 1/27/1955, Abington, PA
Drafted: 1977 Round 3 LARm
1978 LARm: 4 G. **1979** Buf: 5 G. **Total:** 9 G.

KEN FULTON Fulton, Kenneth L **G**
Col: No College B: 6/5/1899, Muncie, IN D: 3/12/1948, Muncie, IN
1921 Mun: 1 G.

TED FULTON Fulton, Theodore Walton Jr. 6′0″, 196 **G-T**
(Curley) *Col:* Oglethorpe *HS:* Boys [Atlanta, GA] B: 11/5/1905, Memphis, TN D: 3/2/1991, Atlanta, GA
1931 Bkn: 12 G. **1932** Bkn: 1 G. **Total:** 13 G.

MIKE FULTZ Fultz, Michael Dwayne 6′5″, 278 **DT**
Col: Nebraska *HS:* Lincoln [NE] B: 1/28/1954, Lincoln, NE
Drafted: 1977 Round 2 NO
1977 NO: 12 G. **1978** NO: 12 G. **1979** NO: 13 G. **1980** NO: 12 G. **1981** Mia-Bal: 9 G. Mia: 4 G. Bal: 5 G. **Total:** 58 G.

TOM FUNCHESS Funchess, Thomas 6′5″, 265 **OT**
(Moose) *Col:* Jackson State *HS:* Crystal Springs [MS] B: 9/12/1944, Crystal Springs, MS *Drafted:* 1968 Round 2 Bos
1968 Bos: 14 G. **1969** Bos: 14 G. **1970** Bos: 11 G. **1971** Hou: 12 G. **1972** Hou: 14 G. **1973** Hou: 14 G. **1974** Mia: 8 G. **Total:** 87 G.

JOHN FUQUA Fuqua, John William 5′11″, 205 **RB**
(Frenchy) *Col:* Morgan State *HS:* East Detroit [Eastpointe, MI] B: 9/12/1946, Detroit, MI *Drafted:* 1969 Round 11 NYG
1971 Pit: PR 1-0. **1976** Pit: PR 11-77 7.0. **Total:** PR 12-77 6.4.

		Rushing				Receiving			
Year Team	**G**	**Att**	**Yds**	**Avg**	**TD**	**Rec**	**Yds**	**Avg**	**TD**
1969 NYG	13	20	89	4.5	0	3	11	3.7	0
1970 Pit	14	138	691	5.0	7	23	289	12.6	2
1971 Pit	12	155	625	4.0	4	49	427	8.7	1
1972 Pit	13	150	665	4.4	4	18	152	8.4	0
1973 Pit	11	117	457	3.9	2	17	150	8.8	0
1974 Pit	9	50	156	3.1	2	6	68	11.3	0
1975 Pit	14	74	285	3.9	1	18	146	8.1	0
1976 Pit	14	15	63	4.2	1	1	4	4.0	0
NFL Total	100	719	3031	4.2	21	135	1247	9.2	3

	Kickoff Returns					Tot
Year Team	**Ret**	**Yds**	**Avg**	**TD**	**Fum**	**TD**
1969 NYG	20	399	20.0	0	2	0
1970 Pit	0	0	—	0	7	9
1971 Pit	0	0	—	0	4	5
1972 Pit	0	0	—	0	1	4
1973 Pit	1	22	22.0	0	3	2
1974 Pit	0	0	—	0	0	2
1975 Pit	1	0	0.0	0	1	1
1976 Pit	4	75	18.8	0	2	1
NFL Total	26	496	19.1	0	20	24

RAY FUQUA Fuqua, Raymond Earl 6′0″, 190 **OE-DE**
Col: Southern Methodist B: 3/21/1912, Shreveport, LA D: 10/26/1983, Houston, TX
1935 Bkn: 10 G; Rec 8-82 10.3 1 TD; 6 Pt. **1936** Bkn: 12 G; Rec 1-2 2.0. **Total:** 22 G; Rec 9-84 9.3 1 TD; 6 Pt.

JIM FUREY Furey, James Andrew 6′0″, 228 **LB**
Col: Kansas State *HS:* Barringer [Newark, NJ] B: 9/22/1932, Newark, NJ *Drafted:* 1956 Round 13 Cle
1961 NYT: 9 G.

TONY FURJANIC Furjanic, Anthony Joseph 6′1″, 228 **LB**
Col: Notre Dame *HS:* Mount Carmel [Chicago, IL] B: 2/26/1964, Chicago, IL *Drafted:* 1986 Round 8 Buf
1986 Buf: 14 G. **1987** Buf: 8 G. **1988** Mia: 6 G. **Total:** 28 G.

STEVE FURNESS Furness, Stephen Robert 6′4″, 255 **DE-DT**
Col: Rhode Island *HS:* Bishop Hendricken [Warwick, RI] B: 12/5/1950, Providence, RI *Drafted:* 1972 Round 5 Pit
1972 Pit: 2 G. **1973** Pit: 6 G. **1974** Pit: 14 G. **1975** Pit: 14 G. **1976** Pit: 9 G; 1 Fum. **1977** Pit: 14 G. **1978** Pit: 10 G. **1979** Pit: 12 G. **1980** Pit: 16 G. **1981** Det: 9 G. **Total:** 106 G; 1 Fum.

WILL FURRER Furrer, William Mason 6′3″, 211 **QB**
Col: Virginia Tech *HS:* Pullman [WA]; Fork Union Mil. Acad. [VA]
B: 2/5/1968, Danville, PA *Drafted:* 1992 Round 4 ChiB
1995 Hou: Rush 8-20 2.5. **Total:** Rush 8-20 2.5.

		Passing								
Year Team	**G**	**Att**	**Comp**	**Comp%**	**Yds**	**YPA**	**TD**	**Int**	**Rating**	**Fum**
1992 ChiB	2	25	9	36.0	89	3.56	0	3	7.3	1
1995 Hou	7	99	48	48.5	483	4.88	2	7	40.1	3
NFL Total	9	124	57	46.0	572	4.61	2	10	31.4	4

TONY FURST Furst, Anthony Raymond 6′1″, 217 **T**
Col: Dayton *HS:* Chaminade [Dayton, OH] B: 4/26/1918, Dayton, OH
1940 Det: 9 G. **1941** Det: 10 G; Int 1-0. **1944** Det: 2 G. **Total:** 21 G; Int 1-0.

CHUCK FUSINA Fusina, Charles Anthony 6′1″, 197 **QB**
Col: Penn State *HS:* Sto-Rox [McKees Rocks, PA] B: 5/31/1957, Pittsburgh, PA *Drafted:* 1979 Round 5 TB
1979 TB: 1 G. **1980** TB: 2 G; Pass 4-2 50.0%, 18 4.50 1 Int; Rush 1-14 14.0. **1981** TB: 4 G; Pass 1-1 100.0%, 2 2.00 1 TD; Rush 3-3 1.0. **1986** GB: 7 G; Pass 32-19 59.4%, 178 5.56 1 Int; Rush 7-11 1.6; 4 Fum. **Total:** 14 G; Pass 37-22 59.5%, 198 5.35 1 TD 2 Int; Rush 11-28 2.5; 4 Fum.

TOM FUSSELL Fussell, Thomas Paul 6′3″, 250 **DE**
Col: Louisiana State *HS:* Istrouma [Baton Rouge, LA] B: 5/25/1945, Cleveland, OH *Drafted:* 1967 Round 8 Bos
1967 Bos: 12 G.

BOBBY FUTRELL Futrell, Bobby Lee 5′11″, 190 **DB**
Col: Elizabeth City State *HS:* Ahoskie [NC] B: 8/4/1962, Ahoskie, NC D: 5/31/1992, Tampa, FL
1987 TB: Int 2-46. **1988** TB: Int 1-26. **1989** TB: Int 1-1. **Total:** Int 4-73.

		Punt Returns				Kickoff Returns				
Year Team	**G**	**Ret**	**Yds**	**Avg**	**TD**	**Ret**	**Yds**	**Avg**	**TD**	**Fum**
1986 TB	16	14	67	4.8	0	5	115	23.0	0	1
1987 TB	12	24	213	8.9	0	31	609	19.6	0	2
1988 TB	16	27	283	10.5	0	2	38	19.0	0	4
1989 TB	16	12	76	6.3	0	4	58	14.5	0	1
1990 TB	1	0	0	—	0	0	0	—	0	0
NFL Total	61	77	639	8.3	0	42	820	19.5	0	8

STEVE GABBARD Gabbard, Stephen Edward 6′4″, 297 **DT**
Col: Florida State *HS:* Independence [Charlotte, NC] B: 7/19/1966, Lexington, KY
1991 GB: 4 G.

JOHN GABLER Gabler, John H **G**
Col: No College *HS:* Stivers [Dayton, OH] B: 4/16/1906, Dayton, OH D: 3/1975, Dayton, OH
1925 Day: 1 G.

ROMAN GABRIEL Gabriel, Roman Ildonzo Jr. 6'5", 220 **QB**
Col: North Carolina State *HS:* New Hanover [Wilmington, NC]
B: 8/5/1940, Wilmington, NC *Drafted:* 1962 Round 1 LARm
1968 LARm: Rec 1-(-5) -5.0. **Total:** Rec 1-(-5) -5.0.

		Passing							
Year Team	G	Att	Comp	Comp%	Yds	YPA	TD	Int	Rating
1962 LARm	6	101	57	56.4	670	6.63	3	2	78.4
1963 LARm	12	281	130	46.3	1947	6.93	8	11	62.7
1964 LARm	7	143	65	45.5	1236	8.64	9	5	82.4
1965 LARm	7	173	83	48.0	1321	7.64	11	**5**	83.0
1966 LARm	14	397	217	54.7	2540	6.40	10	16	65.9
1967 LARm	14	371	196	52.8	2779	7.49	25	13	85.2
1968 LARm	14	366	184	50.3	2364	6.46	19	16	70.0
1969 LARm	14	399	217	54.4	2549	6.39	**24**	7	86.8
1970 LARm	14	**407**	211	51.8	2552	6.27	16	12	72.2
1971 LARm	14	352	180	51.1	2238	6.36	17	10	75.4
1972 LARm	14	323	165	51.1	2027	6.28	12	15	63.8
1973 Phi	14	**460**	**270**	58.7	**3219**	7.00	**23**	12	86.0
1974 Phi	11	338	193	57.1	1867	5.52	9	12	66.8
1975 Phi	11	292	151	51.7	1644	5.63	13	11	67.8
1976 Phi	4	92	46	50.0	476	5.17	2	2	63.5
1977 Phi	13	3	1	33.3	15	5.00	0	0	50.7
NFL Total	183	4498	2366	52.6	29444	6.55	201	149	74.3

	Rushing				
Year Team	Att	Yds	Avg	TD	Fum
1962 LARm	18	93	5.2	0	2
1963 LARm	39	132	3.4	3	10
1964 LARm	11	5	0.5	1	9
1965 LARm	23	79	3.4	2	5
1966 LARm	52	176	3.4	3	10
1967 LARm	43	198	4.6	6	5
1968 LARm	34	139	4.1	4	6
1969 LARm	35	156	4.5	5	7
1970 LARm	28	104	3.7	1	6
1971 LARm	18	48	2.7	2	9
1972 LARm	14	16	1.1	1	6
1973 Phi	12	10	0.8	1	10
1974 Phi	14	76	5.4	0	6
1975 Phi	13	70	5.4	1	5
1976 Phi	4	2	0.5	0	9
NFL Total	358	1304	3.6	30	105

DENNIS GADBOIS Gadbois, Dennis Richard 6'1", 183 **WR**
Col: Boston U. *HS:* Biddleford [ME] B: 9/18/1963, Biddleford, ME
1987 NE: 3 G; Rec 3-51 17.0. **1988** NE: 2 G. **Total:** 5 G; Rec 3-51 17.0.

ROBERT GADDIS Gaddis, Robert 5'11", 178 **WR**
Col: Mississippi Valley State *HS:* W.H. Lanier [Jackson, MS]
B: 1/20/1952, Jackson, MS *Drafted:* 1975 Round 13 Pit
1976 Buf: 2 G; PR 1-6 6.0; KR 1-16 16.0; 1 Fum.

ORONDE GADSDEN Gadsden, Oronde Benjamin 6'2", 218 **WR**
Col: Winston-Salem State *HS:* Burks [Charleston, SC] B: 8/20/1971, Charleston, SC
1995 Dal: Postseason only.

		Receiving				
Year Team	G	Rec	Yds	Avg	TD	Fum
1998 Mia	16	48	713	14.9	7	2

MIKE GAECHTER Gaechter, Michael Theodore 6'0", 190 **DB**
Col: Oregon *HS:* Antelope Valley [Lancaster, CA] B: 1/9/1940, Santa Monica, CA
1962 Dal: PR 6-32 5.3; KR 1-16 16.0. **1963** Dal: PR 2-2 1.0. **1964** Dal: PR 5-24 4.8; KR 1-31 31.0. **Total:** PR 13-58 4.5; KR 2-47 23.5.

		Interceptions				Tot
Year Team	G	Int	Yds	TD	Fum	TD
1962 Dal	14	5	136	**1**	2	1
1963 Dal	14	3	140	0	2	0
1964 Dal	11	0	0	0	0	0
1965 Dal	14	2	21	0	0	1
1966 Dal	14	3	28	0	0	0
1967 Dal	14	2	0	0	0	0
1968 Dal	14	3	23	0	1	0
1969 Dal	13	3	72	0	0	0
NFL Total	108	21	420	1	5	2

DERRICK GAFFNEY Gaffney, Derrick Tyrone 6'1", 181 **WR**
Col: Florida *HS:* William M. Raines [Jacksonville, FL] B: 5/24/1955, Jacksonville, FL *Drafted:* 1978 Round 8 NYJ
1978 NYJ: Rush 2-(-2) -1.0. **1984** NYJ: KR 1-6 6.0. **Total:** Rush 2-(-2) -1.0; KR 1-6 6.0.

		Receiving			
Year Team	G	Rec	Yds	Avg	TD
1978 NYJ	16	38	691	18.2	3
1979 NYJ	16	32	534	16.7	1
1980 NYJ	13	24	397	16.5	2
1981 NYJ	16	14	246	17.6	0
1982 NYJ	9	11	207	18.8	1
1983 NYJ	16	17	243	14.3	0
1984 NYJ	12	19	285	15.0	0
1987 NYJ	2	1	10	10.0	0
NFL Total	100	156	2613	16.8	7

JIM GAFFNEY Gaffney, James Thomas 6'1", 204 **HB-DB**
Col: Tennessee *HS:* Allegany [Cumberland, MD] B: 4/21/1921, Cumberland, MD *Drafted:* 1944 Round 13 Was
1946 Was: Rec 7-85 12.1 1 TD; KR 1-24 24.0. **Total:** Rec 7-85 12.1 1 TD; KR 1-24 24.0.

		Rushing				
Year Team	G	Att	Yds	Avg	TD	Fum
1945 Was	2	1	-6	-6.0	0	0
1946 Was	10	25	96	3.8	0	4
NFL Total	12	26	90	3.5	0	4

JEFF GAFFNEY Gaffney, John Francis 6'2", 195 **K**
Col: Virginia *HS:* Walt Whitman [Bethesda, MD] B: 10/22/1964, Washington, DC
1987 SD: 3 G; Scor 13, 3-6 50.0% FG, 4-5 80.0% XK.

MONK GAFFORD Gafford, Roy Haynes Jr. 5'11", 195 **DB-HB-TB-WB**
Col: Auburn *HS:* Fort Deposit [AL] B: 10/1/1920, Fort Deposit, AL
D: 2/19/1987, Montgomery, AL
AAFC **1946** BknA-MiaA: Pass 5-1 20.0%, -3 -0.60 2 Int; Int 4-88; Punt 13-523 40.2. **1947** BknA: Int 3-16. **1948** BknA: Pass 39-17 43.6%, 268 6.87 4 TD 2 Int. **Total:** Pass 44-18 40.9%, 265 6.02 4 TD 4 Int; Int 7-104; Punt 13-523 40.2.

		Rushing				Receiving			
Year Team	G	Att	Yds	Avg	TD	Rec	Yds	Avg	TD
1946 BknA-MiaA	14	24	66	2.8	1	14	270	19.3	4
1947 BknA	14	46	232	5.0	1	8	113	14.1	0
1948 BknA	12	30	51	1.7	1	15	274	18.3	4
AAFC Total	40	100	349	3.5	3	37	657	17.8	8

	Punt Returns				Kickoff Returns				Tot
Year Team	Ret	Yds	Avg	TD	Ret	Yds	Avg	TD	TD
1946 BknA-MiaA	9	117	13.0	0	11	345	31.4	0	5
1947 BknA	11	186	16.9	0	21	565	26.9	0	1
1948 BknA	14	130	9.3	0	23	559	24.3	0	5
AAFC Total	34	433	12.7	0	55	1469	26.7	0	11

BOBBY GAGE Gage, Robert II 5'11", 175 **TB-DB**
Col: Clemson *HS:* Boys [Anderson, SC] B: 1/15/1927, Chester, SC
Drafted: 1949 Round 1 Pit
1949 Pit: Rec 1-8 8.0; KR 1-25 25.0; Int 5-58; Punt 4-163 40.8. **1950** Pit: Rec 6-127 21.2 2 TD; KR 9-196 21.8; Int 4-64; Punt 3-146 48.7.
Total: Rec 7-135 19.3 2 TD; KR 10-221 22.1; Int 9-122; Punt 7-309 44.1.

		Passing							
Year Team	G	Att	Comp	Comp%	Yds	YPA	TD	Int	Rating
1949 Pit	12	36	17	47.2	329	9.14	2	4	58.4
1950 Pit	10	58	21	36.2	294	5.07	1	5	23.2
NFL Total	22	94	38	40.4	623	6.63	3	9	34.4

	Rushing				Punt Returns					Tot
Year Team	Att	Yds	Avg	TD	Ret	Yds	Avg	TD	Fum	TD
1949 Pit	46	228	5.0	3	16	254	15.9	0	7	3
1950 Pit	39	106	2.7	3	14	192	13.7	0	5	5
NFL Total	85	334	3.9	6	30	446	14.9	0	12	8

STEVE GAGE Gage, Steven Glen 6'3", 210 **DB**
Col: Tulsa *HS:* Claremore [OK] B: 5/10/1964, Claremore, OK
Drafted: 1987 Round 6 Was
1987 Was: 4 G; Int 1-7. **1988** Was: 16 G; KR 5-60 12.0. **Total:** 20 G; KR 5-60 12.0; Int 1-7.

BOB GAGLIANO Gagliano, Robert Frank 6'3", 200 **QB**
Col: Glendale CC CA; U.S. International; Utah State *HS:* Herbert Hoover [Glendale, CA] B: 9/5/1958, Los Angeles, CA *Drafted:* 1981 Round 12 KC

		Passing							
Year Team	G	Att	Comp	Comp%	Yds	YPA	TD	Int	Rating
1982 KC	1	1	1	100.0	7	7.00	0	0	95.8
1983 KC	1	0	0	—	0	—	0	0	—
1987 SF	3	29	16	55.2	229	7.90	1	1	78.1
1989 Det	11	232	117	50.4	1671	7.20	6	12	61.2
1990 Det	9	159	87	54.7	1190	7.48	10	10	73.6
1991 SD	2	23	9	39.1	76	3.30	0	1	30.3
1992 SD	5	42	19	45.2	258	6.14	0	3	35.6
NFL Total	32	486	249	51.2	3431	7.06	17	27	62.7

	Rushing				
Year Team	Att	Yds	Avg	TD	Fum
1989 Det	41	192	4.7	4	3
1990 Det	46	145	3.2	0	5
1991 SD	3	19	6.3	0	2
1992 SD	3	-4	-1.3	0	1
NFL Total	93	352	3.8	4	11

LARRY GAGNER Gagner, Lawrence Joseph 6′3″, 240 **OG**
Col: Florida *HS:* Seabreeze [Daytona Beach, FL] B: 12/30/1943, Cleveland, OH *Drafted:* 1966 Round 2 Pit
1966 Pit: 14 G. **1967** Pit: 14 G. **1968** Pit: 12 G. **1969** Pit: 12 G. **1972** KC: 7 G. **Total:** 59 G.

DAVE GAGNON Gagnon, David John 5′10″, 210 **RB**
Col: Ferris State *HS:* St. Mary [Wayne, MI] B: 1/17/1951, Garden City, MI
1974 ChiB: 13 G; Rush 1-15 15.0; Rec 4-20 5.0; KR 2-32 16.0.

ROY GAGNON Gagnon, Roy Joseph Maurice 5′11″, 210 **G**
(Rosy) *Col:* Oregon *HS:* De La Salle [Minneapolis, MN] B: 1/6/1913, Minneapolis, MN
1935 Det: 4 G.

BOB GAIN Gain, Robert 6′3″, 256 **DT-DE-DG-OT**
Col: Kentucky *HS:* Weir [Weirton, WV] B: 6/21/1929, Akron, OH *Drafted:* 1951 Round 1 GB
1952 Cle: 6 G; KR 1-0; Scor 3, 3-3 100.0% XK. **1954** Cle: 2 G. **1955** Cle: 11 G. **1956** Cle: 12 G. **1957** Cle: 12 G. **1958** Cle: 12 G. **1959** Cle: 12 G. **1960** Cle: 12 G; Int 1-22 1 TD; 6 Pt. **1961** Cle: 14 G. **1962** Cle: 14 G. **1963** Cle: 14 G. **1964** Cle: 4 G. **Total:** 125 G; KR 1-0; Int 1-22 1 TD; Scor 9, 3-3 100.0% XK.

DERRICK GAINER Gainer, Derrick Luther 5′11″, 235 **RB**
Col: Florida A&M *HS:* Plant City [FL] B: 8/15/1966, Plant City, FL *Drafted:* 1989 Round 8 LARd
1990 Cle: Rec 7-85 12.1; KR 1-0. **1993** Dal: Rec 6-37 6.2. **Total:** Rec 13-122 9.4; KR 1-0.

		Rushing			
Year Team	G	Att	Yds	Avg	TD
1990 Cle	16	30	81	2.7	1
1992 LARd-Dal	7	2	10	5.0	0
1992 LARd	2	2	10	5.0	0
1992 Dal	5	0	0	—	0
1993 Dal	11	9	29	3.2	0
NFL Total	34	41	120	2.9	1

CHRIS GAINES Gaines, Christopher Randall 6′0″, 238 **LB**
Col: Vanderbilt *HS:* DuPont [Nashville, TN] B: 2/3/1965, Nashville, TN *Drafted:* 1988 Round 5 Pho
1988 Mia: 4 G.

CLARK GAINES Gaines, Clark Daniel 6′1″, 206 **RB**
Col: Lees-McRae JC NC; Wake Forest *HS:* Elbert Co. [Elberton, GA] B: 2/1/1954, Elberton, GA
1976 NYJ: KR 1-5 5.0. **1978** NYJ: KR 3-33 11.0. **1979** NYJ: KR 2-29 14.5. **Total:** KR 6-67 11.2.

		Rushing				Receiving					Tot
Year Team	G	Att	Yds	Avg	TD	Rec	Yds	Avg	TD	Fum	TD
1976 NYJ	14	157	724	4.6	3	41	400	9.8	2	4	5
1977 NYJ	14	158	595	3.8	3	55	469	8.5	1	3	4
1978 NYJ	16	44	154	3.5	2	3	23	7.7	0	1	2
1979 NYJ	16	186	905	4.9	0	29	219	7.6	0	1	0
1980 NYJ	5	36	174	4.8	0	36	310	8.6	3	2	3
1981 KC	1	0	0	—	0	0	0	—	0	0	0
1982 KC	9	1	0	0.0	0	2	17	8.5	0	0	0
NFL Total	75	582	2552	4.4	8	166	1438	8.7	6	11	14

GREG GAINES Gaines, Gregory Scott 6′3″, 220 **LB**
Col: Tennessee *HS:* DuPont [Old Hickory, TN] B: 10/16/1958, Martinsville, VA
1981 Sea: 8 G. **1983** Sea: 16 G; 1 Sac. **1984** Sea: 16 G; Int 1-18; 3.5 Sac. **1985** Sea: 16 G; 2 Sac. **1986** Sea: 16 G; Int 1-8; 5 Sac. **1987** Sea: 11 G. **1988** Sea: 6 G. **Total:** 89 G; Int 2-26; 11.5 Sac.

LAWRENCE GAINES Gaines, Lawrence Edward 6′1″, 237 **RB**
Col: Wyoming *HS:* Vernon [TX] B: 12/15/1953, Vernon, TX *Drafted:* 1976 Round 1 Det

		Rushing				Receiving					Tot
Year Team	G	Att	Yds	Avg	TD	Rec	Yds	Avg	TD	Fum	TD
1976 Det	14	155	659	4.3	4	23	130	5.7	1	7	5
1978 Det	13	54	178	3.3	1	2	16	8.0	0	1	1
1979 Det	16	23	55	2.4	0	0	0	—	0	1	0
NFL Total	43	232	892	3.8	5	25	146	5.8	1	9	6

SHELDON GAINES Gaines, Sheldon 5′9″, 155 **WR**
Col: Moorpark Coll. CA (J.C.); Long Beach State *HS:* Simi Valley [CA] B: 4/22/1964, Los Angeles, CA
1987 Buf: 3 G; Rec 9-115 12.8; 1 Fum.

WENDALL GAINES Gaines, Wendall Lewis 6′4″, 293 **DT**
Col: Oklahoma State *HS:* Frederick [OK] B: 1/17/1972, Vernon, TX
1995 Ariz: 16 G; Rec 14-117 8.4 2 TD; 12 Pt.

WENTFORD GAINES Gaines, Wentford Elijah 6′0″, 185 **DB**
Col: Ferrum; Tennessee Tech; Cincinnati *HS:* Westside [Anderson, SC] B: 2/4/1953, Anderson, SC *Drafted:* 1976 Round 9 Pit
1978 Pit-ChiB: 12 G; KR 10-240 24.0; Int 1-0; 2 Fum. Pit: 1 G. ChiB: 11 G; KR 10-240 24.0; Int 1-0; 2 Fum. **1979** ChiB: 16 G; Int 1-38. **1980** ChiB: 8 G. **Total:** 36 G; KR 10-240 24.0; Int 2-38; 2 Fum.

WILLIAM GAINES Gaines, William Albert 6′5″, 310 **DT**
Col: Florida *HS:* W.H. Lanier [Jackson, MS] B: 6/20/1971, Jackson, MS *Drafted:* 1994 Round 5 Mia
1994 Mia: 7 G. **1995** Was: 15 G; 2 Sac. **1996** Was: 16 G. **1997** Was: 13 G. **Total:** 51 G; 2 Sac.

CHARLIE GAINOR Gainor, Charles Edward 6′3″, 190 **DE**
Col: North Dakota *HS:* Milnor [ND] B: 11/22/1916, Sargeant, ND D: 9/10/1996, Fort Dodge, IA *Drafted:* 1939 Round 18 Phi
1939 ChiC: 1 G.

GEORGE GAISER Gaiser, George Nolan 6′4″, 255 **OT-OG**
Col: Southern Methodist *HS:* Thomas Jefferson [San Antonio, TX] B: 5/9/1945, San Antonio, TX *Drafted:* 1967 Round 7 Buf
1968 Den: 10 G.

BLANE GAISON Gaison, Blane Keith 6′0″, 185 **DB**
Col: Hawaii *HS:* Kamehameha School [Honolulu, HI] B: 5/13/1958, Kaneohe, HI
1981 Atl: 14 G; KR 3-43 14.3; Int 1-0. **1982** Atl: 9 G; KR 2-14 7.0; Int 1-0. **1983** Atl: 16 G; 1 Fum TD; 6 Pt. **1984** Atl: 15 G; KR 1-15 15.0. **Total:** 54 G; KR 6-72 12.0; Int 2-0; 1 Fum TD; 6 Pt.

TONY GAITER Gaiter, Tony Bernard Jr. 5′8″, 169 **WR**
Col: San Bernardino Valley Coll. CA (J.C.); Miami (Fla.) *HS:* Miami Killian [FL] B: 7/15/1974, Miami, FL *Drafted:* 1997 Round 6 NE
1997 NE: 1 G. **1998** SD: 5 G; PR 13-155 11.9; KR 16-295 18.4; 1 Fum. **Total:** 6 G; PR 13-155 11.9; KR 16-295 18.4; 1 Fum.

BOB GAITERS Gaiters, Robert James 5′11″, 210 **HB**
Col: Rancho Santiago Coll. CA (J.C.); New Mexico State *HS:* Zanesville [OH] B: 2/26/1938, Zanesville, OH *Drafted:* 1961 Round 2 NYG
1961 NYG: Pass 3-3 100.0%, 42 14.00 2 TD; Rec 11-54 4.9 1 TD. **1962** NYG-SF: Pass 2-0; Rec 5-47 9.4. NYG: Pass 2-0; Rec 3-34 11.3. SF: Rec 2-13 6.5. **1963** Den: Rec 1-74 74.0 1 TD. **Total:** Pass 5-3 60.0%, 42 8.40 2 TD; Rec 17-175 10.3 2 TD.

		Rushing				Kickoff Returns					Tot
Year Team	G	Ret	Yds	Avg	TD	Ret	Yds	Avg	TD	Fum	TD
1961 NYG	14	116	460	4.0	6	11	288	26.2	0	11	7
1962 NYG-SF	11	43	193	4.5	0	11	273	24.8	0	1	0
1962 NYG	2	7	35	5.0	0	0	0	—	0	0	0
1962 SF	9	36	158	4.4	0	11	273	24.8	0	1	0
1963 Den	6	9	20	2.2	0	11	225	20.5	0	1	1
NFL Total	31	168	673	4.0	6	33	786	23.8	0	13	8

HOKIE GAJAN Gajan, Howard Lee Jr. 5′11″, 220 **RB**
Col: Louisiana State *HS:* Baker [LA] B: 9/6/1959, Baton Rouge, LA *Drafted:* 1981 Round 10 NO
1982 NO: KR 1-18 18.0. **1983** NO: Pass 1-0. **1984** NO: Pass 1-1 100.0%, 34 34.00 1 TD. **Total:** Pass 2-1 50.0%, 34 17.00 1 TD; KR 1-18 18.0.

		Rushing				Receiving					Tot
Year Team	G	Att	Yds	Avg	TD	Rec	Yds	Avg	TD	Fum	TD
1982 NO	9	19	77	4.1	0	3	10	3.3	0	0	0
1983 NO	16	81	415	5.1	4	17	130	7.6	0	3	4
1984 NO	14	102	615	**6.0**	5	35	288	8.2	2	0	7
1985 NO	6	50	251	5.0	2	8	87	10.9	0	3	2
NFL Total	45	252	1358	5.4	11	63	515	8.2	2	6	13

STAN GALAZIN Galazin, Stanley Bernard 6′3″, 211 **C-LB**
Col: Villanova *HS:* Keystone Acad. [Wyoming, PA] B: 8/8/1915 D: 1/3/1989, Queens, NY
1937 NYG: 1 G. **1938** NYG: 5 G. **1939** NYG: 3 G. **Total:** 9 G.

SCOTT GALBRAITH Galbraith, Alan Scott 6′2″, 258 **TE**
Col: USC *HS:* Highlands [North Highlands, CA] B: 1/7/1967, Sacramento, CA *Drafted:* 1990 Round 7 Cle
1990 Cle: KR 3-16 5.3. **1991** Cle: KR 2-13 6.5. **1997** Dal: KR 2-24 12.0. **Total:** KR 7-53 7.6.

		Receiving			
Year Team	G	Rec	Yds	Avg	TD
1990 Cle	16	4	62	15.5	0
1991 Cle	16	27	328	12.1	0
1992 Cle	14	4	63	15.8	1

1993 Dal	7	1	1	1.0	1
1994 Dal	16	4	31	7.8	0
1995 Was	16	10	80	8.0	2
1996 Was	16	8	89	11.1	2
1997 Dal	16	2	16	8.0	0
1998 GB	1	0	0	—	0
NFL Total	118	60	670	11.2	6

TONY GALBREATH Galbreath, Anthony Dale 6'0", 228 **RB**
Col: Indian Hills CC IA; Missouri *HS:* Fulton [MO] B: 1/29/1954, Fulton, MO *Drafted:* 1976 Round 2 NO
1976 NO: PR 2-8 4.0. **1978** NO: Scor 42, 0-1 XK. **1979** NO: Pass 3-2 66.7%, 70 23.33 1 Int; Scor 67, 2-3 66.7% FG, 1-2 50.0% XK. **1980** NO: Pass 2-0. **1984** NYG: Pass 1-1 100.0%, 13 13.00. **1986** NYG: Pass 1-0; PR 3-1 0.3. **Total:** Pass 7-3 42.9%, 83 11.86 1 Int; PR 5-9 1.8; Scor 265, 2-3 66.7% FG, 1-3 33.3% XK.

		Rushing				Receiving			
Year Team	**G**	**Att**	**Yds**	**Avg**	**TD**	**Rec**	**Yds**	**Avg**	**TD**
1976 NO	14	136	570	4.2	7	54	420	7.8	1
1977 NO	14	168	644	3.8	3	41	265	6.5	0
1978 NO	16	186	635	3.4	5	74	582	7.9	2
1979 NO	15	189	708	3.7	9	58	484	8.3	1
1980 NO	16	81	308	3.8	3	57	470	8.2	2
1981 Min	14	42	198	4.7	2	18	144	8.0	0
1982 Min	8	39	116	3.0	1	17	153	9.0	0
1983 Min	13	113	474	4.2	4	45	348	7.7	2
1984 NYG	16	22	97	4.4	0	37	357	9.6	0
1985 NYG	16	29	187	6.4	0	30	327	10.9	1
1986 NYG	16	16	61	3.8	0	33	268	8.1	0
1987 NYG	12	10	74	7.4	0	26	248	9.5	0
NFL Total	170	1031	4072	3.9	34	490	4066	8.3	9

	Kickoff Returns					Tot
Year Team	**Ret**	**Yds**	**Avg**	**TD**	**Fum**	**TD**
1976 NO	20	399	20.0	0	7	8
1977 NO	0	0	—	0	3	3
1978 NO	0	0	—	0	6	7
1979 NO	0	0	—	0	5	10
1980 NO	6	86	14.3	0	3	5
1981 Min	1	16	16.0	0	2	2
1982 Min	0	0	—	0	1	1
1983 Min	0	0	—	0	4	6
1985 NYG	7	120	17.1	0	2	1
1986 NYG	0	0	—	0	3	0
1987 NYG	0	0	—	0	1	0
NFL Total	34	621	18.3	0	37	43

HARRY GALBREATH Galbreath, Harry Curtis 6'1", 280 **OG**
(Harry Love) *Col:* Tennessee *HS:* Clarksville [TN] B: 1/1/1965, Clarksville, TN *Drafted:* 1988 Round 8 Mia
1988 Mia: 16 G. **1989** Mia: 14 G. **1990** Mia: 16 G. **1991** Mia: 16 G. **1992** Mia: 16 G. **1993** GB: 16 G. **1994** GB: 16 G. **1995** GB: 16 G. **1996** NYJ: 15 G. **Total:** 141 G.

ARNIE GALIFFA Galiffa, Arnold Anthony 6'2", 193 **QB**
Col: Army *HS:* Donora [PA] B: 1/29/1927, Donora, PA D: 9/5/1978, Glenview, IL *Drafted:* 1950 Round 18 GB
1953 NYG: 3 G; Pass 13-4 30.8%, 129 9.92 1 TD 5 Int; Rush 5-1 0.2; 1 Fum. **1954** SF: 4 G; Pass 12-3 25.0%, 54 4.50; Rush 1-2 2.0. **Total:** 7 G; Pass 25-7 28.0%, 183 7.32 1 TD 5 Int; Rush 6-3 0.5; 1 Fum.

ED GALIGHER Galigher, Edward Albert 6'4", 255 **DE-DT**
Col: Chabot Coll. CA (J.C.); UCLA *HS:* Hayward [CA] B: 10/15/1950, Hayward, CA *Drafted:* 1972 Round 4 NYJ
1972 NYJ: 13 G. **1973** NYJ: 7 G. **1974** NYJ: 13 G. **1975** NYJ: 13 G. **1976** NYJ: 14 G. **1977** SF: 12 G. **1978** SF: 15 G. **Total:** 87 G.

WILLIE GALIMORE Galimore, Willie Lee 6'1", 187 **HB**
Col: Florida A&M *HS:* Excelsior [St. Augustine, FL] B: 3/30/1935, St. Augustine, FL D: 7/26/1964, Rensselaer, IN *Drafted:* 1956 Round 5 ChiB
1958 ChiB: Pass 1-0, 1 Int. **Total:** Pass 1-0, 1 Int.

		Rushing				Receiving			
Year Team	**G**	**Att**	**Yds**	**Avg**	**TD**	**Rec**	**Yds**	**Avg**	**TD**
1957 ChiB	12	127	538	4.2	5	15	201	13.4	2
1958 ChiB	12	130	619	4.8	8	8	151	18.9	3
1959 ChiB	12	58	199	3.4	1	10	125	12.5	2
1960 ChiB	12	74	368	5.0	1	3	35	11.7	0
1961 ChiB	14	153	707	4.6	4	33	502	15.2	3
1962 ChiB	7	43	233	5.4	2	5	56	11.2	0
1963 ChiB	13	85	321	3.8	5	13	131	10.1	0
NFL Total	82	670	2985	4.5	26	87	1201	13.8	10

	Kickoff Returns					Tot
Year Team	**Ret**	**Yds**	**Avg**	**TD**	**Fum**	**TD**
1957 ChiB	5	140	28.0	0	6	7
1958 ChiB	9	338	37.6	1	6	12
1959 ChiB	11	229	20.8	0	4	3
1960 ChiB	12	292	24.3	0	5	1
1961 ChiB	5	82	16.4	0	8	7
1962 ChiB	0	0	—	0	0	2
1963 ChiB	1	19	19.0	0	5	5
NFL Total	43	1100	25.6	1	34	37

BERNIE GALLAGHER Gallagher, Bernard John Jr. 6'0", 234 **G**
Col: Princeton; Pennsylvania *HS:* Southeast Catholic [Philadelphia, PA] B: 11/8/1921, Philadelphia, PA D: 11/17/1988, East Lansdowne, PA
AAFC **1947** LA-A: 8 G.

DAVE GALLAGHER Gallagher, David Dillon 6'4", 256 **DE**
Col: Michigan *HS:* Piqua [OH] B: 1/2/1952, Piqua, OH *Drafted:* 1974 Round 1 ChiB
1974 ChiB: 14 G; KR 1-16 16.0. **1975** NYG: 12 G. **1976** NYG: 14 G; Int 1-7; 1 Fum. **1978** Det: 1 G. **1979** Det: 10 G. **Total:** 51 G; KR 1-16 16.0; Int 1-7; 1 Fum.

ED GALLAGHER Gallagher, Edward Barto 6'1", 205 **T**
Col: Washington & Jefferson *HS:* Asbury Park [NJ] B: 2/3/1903, Philadelphia, PA D: 10/1963
1928 NYY: 11 G.

FRANK GALLAGHER Gallagher, Francis Joseph 6'2", 245 **OG**
Col: North Carolina *HS:* St. James [Chester, PA] B: 3/2/1943, Chester, PA
1967 Det: 13 G. **1968** Det: 14 G. **1969** Det: 14 G. **1970** Det: 14 G. **1971** Det: 14 G. **1972** Det: 14 G. **1973** Atl-Min: 7 G. Atl: 3 G. Min: 4 G. **Total:** 90 G.

ALLEN GALLAHER Gallaher, Allen Ross 6'3", 250 **OT**
Col: USC *HS:* Sylmar [CA] B: 11/13/1950, San Fernando, CA *Drafted:* 1973 Round 4 NE
1974 NE: 14 G.

HUGH GALLARNEAU Gallarneau, Hugh Harold 6'0", 190 **HB-DB**
(Duke) *Col:* Stanford *HS:* Morgan Park [Chicago, IL] B: 4/2/1917, Detroit, MI *Drafted:* 1941 Round 4 ChiB
1941 ChiB: PR 2-36 18.0; KR 2-35 17.5; Int 1-46 **1** TD. **1942** ChiB: PR 9-101 11.2; KR 5-151 30.2. **1945** ChiB: PR 3-7 2.3; KR 6-90 15.0; Int 2-6. **1946** ChiB: PR 10-99 9.9; KR 5-115 23.0. **1947** ChiB: KR 2-43 21.5; Int 1-9. **Total:** PR 24-243 10.1; KR 20-434 21.7; Int 4-61 1 TD.

		Rushing				Receiving					Tot
Year Team	**G**	**Att**	**Yds**	**Avg**	**TD**	**Rec**	**Yds**	**Avg**	**TD**	**Fum**	**TD**
1941 ChiB	11	49	304	6.2	**8**	11	204	18.5	2	0	11
1942 ChiB	10	68	292	4.3	4	14	291	20.8	3	0	7
1945 ChiB	8	75	260	3.5	2	7	58	8.3	1	3	3
1946 ChiB	11	112	476	4.3	6	12	185	15.4	1	7	8
1947 ChiB	12	39	89	2.3	6	7	56	8.0	0	4	6
NFL Total	52	343	1421	4.1	26	51	794	15.6	7	14	35

CHON GALLEGOS Gallegos, Chon Fernando 5'9", 175 **QB**
Col: San Jose City Coll. CA (J.C.); San Jose State *HS:* James Lick [San Jose, CA] B: 9/28/1939, Gallup, NM
1962 Oak: 6 G; Pass 35-18 51.4%, 298 8.51 2 TD 3 Int; Rush 3-25 8.3; 3 Fum.

JIM GALLERY Gallery, James Patrick 6'1", 190 **K**
Col: Minnesota *HS:* Morton [MN] B: 9/15/1961, Redwood Falls, MN *Drafted:* 1984 Round 10 TB
1987 StL: 13 G; Scor 57, 9-19 47.4% FG, 30-31 96.8% XK. **1989** Cin: 4 G; Scor 19, 2-6 33.3% FG, 13-13 100.0% XK. **1990** Min: 2 G. **Total:** 19 G; Scor 76, 11-25 44.0% FG, 43-44 97.7% XK.

NICK GALLERY Gallery, Nick Patrick 6'4", 245 **P**
Col: Iowa *HS:* East Buchanan [Winthrop, IA] B: 2/15/1975, Manchester, IA
1998 NYJ: 1 G; Punt 6-238 39.7.

TONY GALLOVICH Gallovich, Anthony Richard 5'9", 170 **WB-DB**
Col: Wake Forest B: 9/10/1917, Vandergrift, PA *Drafted:* 1941 Round 8 Cle
1941 Cle: 3 G; Rush 1-1 1.0.

DAVID GALLOWAY Galloway, David Lawrence 6'3", 277 **DT-DE**
Col: Florida *HS:* Brandon [FL] B: 2/16/1959, Tampa, FL *Drafted:* 1982 Round 2 StL
1982 StL: 5 G; 2 Sac. **1983** StL: 16 G; Int 1-17; Scor 1 Saf; 2 Pt; 12 Sac. **1984** StL: 14 G; 5.5 Sac. **1985** StL: 16 G; 3.5 Sac. **1986** StL: 14 G; 4.5 Sac. **1987** StL: 4 G; 1 Sac. **1988** Pho: 8 G; 2 Sac. **1989** Pho: 12 G; 5.5 Sac. **1990** Den: 10 G; 2 Sac. **Total:** 99 G; Int 1-17; Scor 1 Saf; 2 Pt; 38 Sac.

DUANE GALLOWAY Galloway, Duane Keith 5'8", 181 **DB**
Col: Santa Monica Coll. CA (J.C.); Arizona State *HS:* Crenshaw [Los Angeles, CA] B: 11/7/1961, Los Angeles, CA
1985 Det: 2 G. **1986** Det: 16 G; Int 4-58. **1987** Det: 10 G; Int 3-46. **Total:** 28 G; Int 7-104.

JOEY GALLOWAY Galloway, Joseph Scott 5'11", 188 **WR**
Col: Ohio State *HS:* Bellaire [OH] B: 11/20/1971, Bellaire, OH *Drafted:* 1995 Round 1 Sea
1995 Sea: KR 2-30 15.0. **Total:** KR 2-30 15.0.

Year Team	G	Rushing Att	Yds	Avg	TD	Receiving Rec	Yds	Avg	TD
1995 Sea	16	11	154	14.0	1	67	1039	15.5	7
1996 Sea	16	15	127	8.5	0	57	987	17.3	7
1997 Sea	15	9	72	8.0	0	72	1049	14.6	12
1998 Sea	16	9	26	2.9	0	65	1047	16.1	10
NFL Total	63	44	379	8.6	1	261	4122	15.8	36

Year Team	Punt Returns Ret	Yds	Avg	TD	Fum	Tot TD
1995 Sea	36	360	10.0	**1**	1	9
1996 Sea	15	158	10.5	1	2	8
1997 Sea	0	0	—	0	1	12
1998 Sea	25	251	10.0	**2**	1	12
NFL Total	76	769	10.1	4	5	41

MITCHELL GALLOWAY Galloway, Mitchell 5′8″, 178 **WR**
Col: East Carolina *HS:* Marlboro Co. [Bennettsville, SC] B: 10/8/1974, Chesterfield Co., SC
1997 Buf: 3 G; PR 2-15 7.5; KR 6-130 21.7; 1 Fum.

JOHN GALVIN Galvin, John Blake Jr. 6′3″, 226 **LB**
Col: Boston College *HS:* Lowell [MA] B: 7/9/1965, Lowell, MA
Drafted: 1988 Round 11 NYJ
1988 NYJ: 16 G. **1989** Min: 11 G. **1990** NYJ: 16 G. **1991** NYJ: 9 G.
Total: 52 G.

JOHN GALVIN Galvin, John E 5′10″, 170 **QB**
Col: Purdue *HS:* Leo [Chicago, IL] B: 12/7/1920, Chicago, IL
D: 12/23/1998, Oak Lawn, IL
AAFC **1947** BalA: Pass 6-3 50.0%, 34 5.67; Rush 1-(-4) -4.0; KR 2-38 19.0.

Year Team	G	Punting Punts	Yds	Avg
1947 BalA	13	66	2377	36.0

SCOTT GALYON Galyon, Gregory Scott 6′2″, 245 **LB**
Col: Tennessee *HS:* Seymour [TN] B: 3/23/1974, Seymour, TN
Drafted: 1996 Round 6 NYG
1996 NYG: 16 G. **1997** NYG: 16 G; 3 Sac. **1998** NYG: 10 G; 1 Sac.
Total: 42 G; 4 Sac.

VINCE GAMACHE Gamache, Vincent Lucky 5′11″, 174 **P**
(Lucky) *Col:* Cal State-Fullerton *HS:* Venice [Los Angeles, CA]
B: 11/18/1961, Los Angeles, CA

Year Team	G	Punting Punts	Yds	Avg
1986 Sea	16	79	3048	38.6
1987 LARd	3	13	519	39.9
NFL Total	19	92	3567	38.8

LU GAMBINO Gambino, Lucien Anthony 6′1″, 205 **FB-LB**
(Galloping Lou) *Col:* Indiana; Maryland *HS:* Crane Tech [Chicago, IL]; J. Sterling Morton HS [Cicero, IL] B: 9/21/1923, Berwyn, IL
AAFC **1948** BalA: Rec 6-28 4.7; KR 3-57 19.0. **1949** BalA: Rec 10-67 6.7 1 TD. **Total:** Rec 16-95 5.9 1 TD; KR 3-57 19.0.

Year Team	G	Rushing Att	Yds	Avg	TD	Tot TD
1948 BalA	9	54	194	3.6	1	1
1949 BalA	10	56	208	3.7	0	1
AAFC Total	19	110	402	3.7	1	2

DAVID GAMBLE Gamble, David Anthony 6′1″, 190 **WR**
Col: New Hampshire *HS:* Colonie Central [NY] B: 6/4/1971, Albany, NY
1997 Den: 2 G.

KENNY GAMBLE Gamble, Kenneth Patrick 5′10″, 197 **RB-DB**
Col: Colgate *HS:* Holyoke [MA]; Cushing Acad. [Ashburnham, MA]
B: 3/8/1965, Holyoke, MA *Drafted:* 1988 Round 10 KC
1988 KC: 16 G; Rec 1-(-7) -7.0; KR 15-291 19.4; Int 1-2; 1 Fum. **1989** KC: 2 G; Rush 6-24 4.0 1 TD; Rec 2-2 1.0; KR 3-55 18.3; 6 Pt. **1990** KC: 1 G.
Total: 19 G; Rush 6-24 4.0 1 TD; Rec 3-(-5) -1.7; KR 18-346 19.2; Int 1-2; 6 Pt; 1 Fum.

R.C. GAMBLE Gamble, R.C. Jr. 6′3″, 220 **RB**
Col: South Carolina State *HS:* Sterling [Greenville, SC] B: 9/27/1946, Greenville, SC *Drafted:* 1968 Round 4 Bos
1968 Bos: Rec 11-55 5.0 1 TD; KR 1-0. **1969** Bos: Rec 7-74 10.6; KR 1-23 23.0. **Total:** Rec 18-129 7.2 1 TD; KR 2-23 11.5.

Year Team	G	Rushing Att	Yds	Avg	TD	Fum	Tot TD
1968 Bos	14	78	311	4.0	1	3	2
1969 Bos	13	16	35	2.2	0	1	0
NFL Total	27	94	346	3.7	1	4	2

CHRIS GAMBOL Gambol, Christopher Hughes 6′6″, 303 **OT-OG**
Col: Iowa *HS:* Oxford [MI] B: 9/14/1964, Pittsburgh, PA
Drafted: 1987 Round 3 Ind
1988 Ind-SD: 12 G. Ind: 1 G. SD: 11 G. **1989** Det: 6 G. **1990** NE: 16 G.
Total: 34 G.

BOB GAMBOLD Gambold, Robert Lee 6′4″, 215 **QB**
Col: Washington State *HS:* Longview [WA] B: 2/5/1929, Longview, WA
Drafted: 1950 Round 24 ChiC
1953 Phi: 3 G; Pass 14-6 42.9%, 107 7.64 2 Int; Rush 2-(-2) -1.0; 1 Fum.

BILLY GAMBRELL Gambrell, William Edward 5′10″, 175 **WR**
Col: South Carolina *HS:* Athens [GA] B: 9/18/1941, Athens, GA
Drafted: 1963 Round 12 Bos
1964 StL: KR 4-92 23.0. **1965** StL: Rush 4-15 3.8; KR 9-216 24.0.
1966 StL: Rush 3-26 8.7; KR 1-16 16.0. **1968** Det: KR 1-12 12.0.
Total: Rush 7-41 5.9; KR 15-336 22.4.

Year Team	G	Receiving Rec	Yds	Avg	TD	Punt Returns Ret	Yds	Avg	TD	Fum
1963 StL	14	3	63	21.0	0	11	111	10.1	0	2
1964 StL	14	24	398	16.6	2	12	126	10.5	0	2
1965 StL	10	9	171	19.0	2	1	-1	-1.0	0	1
1966 StL	14	24	409	17.0	5	4	46	11.5	0	0
1967 StL	12	28	398	14.2	2	0	0	—	0	1
1968 Det	14	28	492	17.6	7	0	0	—	0	0
NFL Total	78	116	1931	16.6	18	28	282	10.1	0	6

KENDALL GAMMON Gammon, Kendall Robert 6′4″, 288 **C**
Col: Pittsburg State *HS:* Rose Hill [KS] B: 10/23/1968, Wichita, KS
Drafted: 1992 Round 11 Pit
1992 Pit: 16 G. **1993** Pit: 16 G. **1994** Pit: 16 G. **1995** Pit: 16 G. **1996** NO: 16 G. **1997** NO: 16 G. **1998** NO: 16 G. **Total:** 112 G.

RUSTY GANAS Ganas, Russell Lindberg 6′4″, 257 **DT**
Col: South Carolina *HS:* Ware Co. [Waycross, GA] B: 8/12/1949, Waycross, GA
1971 Bal: 1 G.

SONNY GANDEE Gandee, Sherwin Kenneth 6′1″, 216 **DE-LB**
Col: Ohio State *HS:* Garfield [Akron, OH]; Berea HS [OH]
B: 2/27/1929, Akron, OH *Drafted:* 1952 Round 9 Det
1952 Dal-Det: 10 G; Scor **1** Saf; 2 Pt. Dal: 2 G. Det: 8 G; Scor 1 Saf; 2 Pt.
1953 Det: 8 G; Int 1-0. **1954** Det: 11 G; Int 3-29. **1955** Det: 12 G; KR 1-7 7.0; **1** Fum TD; 6 Pt. **1956** Det: 12 G. **Total:** 53 G; KR 1-7 7.0; Int 4-29; Scor 1 Saf; 1 Fum TD; 8 Pt.

WAYNE GANDY Gandy, Wayne Lamar 6′4″, 300 **OT**
Col: Auburn *HS:* Haines City [FL] B: 2/10/1971, Haines City, FL
Drafted: 1994 Round 1 LARm
1994 LARm: 16 G. **1995** StL: 16 G. **1996** StL: 16 G. **1997** StL: 16 G.
1998 StL: 16 G. **Total:** 80 G.

MIKE GANN Gann, Michael Alan 6′5″, 271 **DE**
Col: Notre Dame *HS:* Lakewood [CO] B: 10/19/1963, Stillwater, OK
Drafted: 1985 Round 2 Atl
1985 Atl: 16 G; **1** Fum TD; 6 Pt; 4.5 Sac. **1986** Atl: 16 G; Scor **1** Saf; 2 Pt; 5.5 Sac. **1987** Atl: 12 G; 1 Sac. **1988** Atl: 16 G; **1** Fum TD; 6 Pt; 4 Sac.
1989 Atl: 16 G; 2 Sac. **1990** Atl: 16 G; 3.5 Sac. **1991** Atl: 5 G; Int 1-0.
1992 Atl: 13 G; 2 Sac. **1993** Atl: 8 G; 1 Sac. **Total:** 118 G; Int 1-0; Scor 1 Saf; 2 Fum TD; 14 Pt; 23.5 Sac.

CHRIS GANNON Gannon, Christopher Stephen 6′6″, 265 **DE-TE**
Col: Southwestern Louisiana *HS:* Orange Park [FL] B: 1/20/1966, Brandon, FL *Drafted:* 1989 Round 3 NE
1989 SD: 10 G. **1990** NE: 6 G; Rush 1-0; 1 Fum; 0.5 Sac. **1991** NE: 8 G.
1992 NE: 12 G; 1 Fum. **1993** NE: 4 G. **Total:** 40 G; Rush 1-0; 2 Fum; 0.5 Sac.

RICH GANNON Gannon, Richard Joseph 6′3″, 205 **QB**
Col: Delaware *HS:* St. Joseph's Prep [Philadelphia, PA] B: 12/20/1965, Philadelphia, PA *Drafted:* 1987 Round 4 NE
1989 Min: Postseason only. **1991** Min: Rec 1-0. **Total:** Rec 1-0.

Year Team	G	Passing Att	Comp	Comp%	Yds	YPA	TD	Int	Rating
1987 Min	4	6	2	33.3	18	3.00	0	1	2.8
1988 Min	3	15	7	46.7	90	6.00	0	0	66.0
1990 Min	14	349	182	52.1	2278	6.53	16	16	68.9
1991 Min	15	354	211	59.6	2166	6.12	12	6	81.5
1992 Min	12	279	159	57.0	1905	6.83	12	13	72.9
1993 Was	8	125	74	59.2	704	5.63	3	7	59.6
1995 KC	2	11	7	63.6	57	5.18	0	0	76.7
1996 KC	4	90	54	60.0	491	5.46	6	1	92.4
1997 KC	9	175	98	56.0	1144	6.54	7	4	79.8
1998 KC	12	354	206	58.2	2305	6.51	10	6	80.1
NFL Total	83	1758	1000	56.9	11158	6.35	66	54	75.6

Year Team	Rushing Att	Yds	Avg	TD	Fum
1988 Min	4	29	7.3	0	0
1990 Min	52	268	5.2	1	10

1991 Min	43	236	5.5	2	2
1992 Min	45	187	4.2	0	5
1993 Was	21	88	4.2	1	3
1995 KC	8	25	3.1	1	0
1996 KC	12	81	6.8	0	1
1997 KC	33	109	3.3	2	5
1998 KC	44	168	3.8	3	9
NFL Total	262	1191	4.5	10	35

AL GANSBERG Gansberg, Alfred Henry 5′11″, 187 **E-T**
Col: Miami (Ohio) *HS:* Highland Park [IL] B: 10/16/1901, Lake Forest, IL D: 8/24/1976, Evanston, IL
1926 Lou: 3 G.

BRIAN GANT Gant, Brian Keith 6′0″, 235 **LB**
Col: Illinois State *HS:* Theodore Roosevelt [Gary, IN] B: 9/6/1965, Gary, IN
1987 TB: 11 G; Int 1-5.

EARL GANT Gant, Earl Leon 6′0″, 207 **RB**
Col: Missouri *HS:* Manual [Peoria, IL] B: 7/6/1957, Chicago, IL
Drafted: 1979 Round 5 KC
1979 KC: Rec 15-101 6.7; KR 4-75 18.8. **1980** KC: Rec 9-68 7.6; KR 3-44 14.7. **Total:** Rec 24-169 7.0; KR 7-119 17.0.

		Rushing				
Year Team	**G**	**Att**	**Yds**	**Avg**	**TD**	**Fum**
1979 KC	16	56	196	3.5	1	2
1980 KC	4	9	32	3.6	0	3
NFL Total	20	65	228	3.5	1	5

KENNETH GANT Gant, Kenneth Dwayne 5′11″, 195 **DB**
Col: Albany State (Ga.) *HS:* Kathleen [Lakeland, FL] B: 4/18/1967, Bartow, FL *Drafted:* 1990 Round 9 Dal
1990 Dal: 12 G; Int 1-26. **1991** Dal: 16 G; KR 6-114 19.0; Int 1-0. **1992** Dal: 16 G; Int 3-19; 3 Sac. **1993** Dal: 12 G; KR 1-18 18.0; Int 1-0. **1994** Dal: 16 G; Int 1-0. **1995** TB: 16 G. **1996** TB: 16 G. **1997** TB: 9 G. **Total:** 113 G; KR 7-132 18.9; Int 7-45; 3 Sac.

REUBEN GANT Gant, Reuben Charles 6′4″, 230 **TE-WR**
Col: Oklahoma State *HS:* Washington [Tulsa, OK] B: 4/12/1952, Tulsa, OK *Drafted:* 1974 Round 1 Buf
1978 Buf: Rush 1-14 14.0. **Total:** Rush 1-14 14.0.

		Receiving				
Year Team	**G**	**Rec**	**Yds**	**Avg**	**TD**	**Fum**
1974 Buf	13	0	0	—	0	0
1975 Buf	14	9	107	11.9	2	0
1976 Buf	14	12	263	21.9	3	1
1977 Buf	14	41	646	15.8	2	0
1978 Buf	16	34	408	12.0	5	1
1979 Buf	14	19	245	12.9	2	1
1980 Buf	16	12	181	15.1	1	0
NFL Total	101	127	1850	14.6	15	3

MILT GANTENBEIN Gantenbein, Milton Edward 6′0″, 199 **OE-DE**
Col: Wisconsin *HS:* La Crosse [WI] B: 5/31/1909, New Albin, IA D: 12/18/1988, Carmichael, CA

		Receiving			
Year Team	**G**	**Rec**	**Yds**	**Avg**	**TD**
1931 GB	14	—	—	—	1
1932 GB	9	2	71	35.5	0
1933 GB	12	6	144	24.0	1
1934 GB	10	10	155	15.5	0
1935 GB	11	12	168	14.0	1
1936 GB	9	15	221	14.7	1
1937 GB	11	12	237	19.8	2
1938 GB	11	12	164	13.7	1
1939 GB	11	7	127	18.1	1
1940 GB	5	1	12	12.0	0
NFL Total	103	77	1299	16.9	8

JERRY GANTT Gantt, Jerome Floyd 6′4″, 266 **OT**
Col: North Carolina Central *HS:* James B. Dudley [Greensboro, NC] B: 8/20/1948, Greensboro, NC *Drafted:* 1970 Round 4 Buf
1970 Buf: 6 G.

GREG GANTT Gantt, Lewis Gregory 5′11″, 188 **P**
Col: Alabama *HS:* Woodlawn [Birmingham, AL] B: 10/30/1951, Birmingham, AL *Drafted:* 1974 Round 8 NYJ
1974 NYJ: Scor 1, 1-2 50.0% XK. **1975** NYJ: Pass 1-1 100.0%, 1 1.00. **Total:** Pass 1-1 100.0%, 1 1.00; Scor 1, 1-2 50.0% XK.

		Punting			
Year Team	**G**	**Punts**	**Yds**	**Avg**	**Fum**
1974 NYJ	14	75	2689	35.9	1
1975 NYJ	14	59	2156	36.5	1
NFL Total	28	134	4845	36.2	2

BOB GAONA Gaona, Robert John 6′3″, 243 **OT-DT**
Col: Wake Forest *HS:* Ambridge [PA] B: 1/3/1931 *Drafted:* 1953 Round 5 Pit
1953 Pit: 12 G; KR 1-0. **1954** Pit: 12 G; Rec 0-25. **1955** Pit: 12 G; KR 2-4 2.0. **1956** Pit: 12 G. **1957** Phi: 12 G; Rec 1-(-9) -9.0. **Total:** 60 G; Rec 1-16 16.0; KR 3-4 1.3.

MARK GARALCZYK Garalczyk, Mark Patrick 6′5″, 272 **DT-DE**
Col: Western Michigan *HS:* Fraser [MI] B: 8/12/1964, Roseville, MI
Drafted: 1987 Round 6 StL
1987 StL: 11 G; 2.5 Sac. **1988** Pho-NYJ: 13 G; 0.5 Sac. Pho: 6 G. NYJ: 7 G; 0.5 Sac. **Total:** 24 G; 3 Sac.

TONY GARBARCZYK Garbarczyk, Anthony Stephen 6′4″, 275 **DE**
Col: Nassau CC NY; Wake Forest *HS:* Hauppauge [NY] B: 1/20/1964, Queens, NY
1987 NYJ: 2 G.

TEDDY GARCIA Garcia, Alfonso Teddy 5′10″, 187 **K**
Col: Northeast Louisiana *HS:* Lewisville [TX] B: 6/4/1964, Caddo Parish, LA *Drafted:* 1988 Round 4 NE
1988 NE: 16 G; Scor 29, 6-13 46.2% FG, 11-16 68.8% XK. **1989** Min: 3 G; Scor 11, 1-5 20.0% FG, 8-8 100.0% XK. **1990** Hou: 9 G; Scor 68, 14-20 70.0% FG, 26-28 92.9% XK. **Total:** 28 G; Scor 108, 21-38 55.3% FG, 45-52 86.5% XK.

EDDIE GARCIA Garcia, Edgar Ivan 5′8″, 178 **K**
Col: Southern Methodist *HS:* Woodrow Wilson [Dallas, TX]
B: 4/15/1959, New Orleans, LA *Drafted:* 1982 Round 10 GB
1983 GB: 12 G. **1984** GB: 7 G; Scor 23, 3-9 33.3% FG, 14-15 93.3% XK. **Total:** 19 G; Scor 23, 3-9 33.3% FG, 14-15 93.3% XK.

FRANK GARCIA Garcia, Frank Benitez 6′0″, 205 **P**
Col: Arizona State; Nevada-Las Vegas; Arizona *HS:* Salpointe [Tucson, AZ] B: 6/5/1957, Tucson, AZ
1984 TB: Pass 1-0. **1986** TB: Rush 1-(-11) -11.0. **Total:** Pass 1-0; Rush 1-(-11) -11.0.

		Punting		
Year Team	**G**	**Punts**	**Yds**	**Avg**
1981 Sea	1	2	74	37.0
1983 TB	16	**95**	4008	42.2
1984 TB	16	68	2849	41.9
1985 TB	16	77	3233	42.0
1986 TB	16	77	3089	40.1
1987 TB	12	62	2409	38.9
NFL Total	77	381	15662	41.1

FRANK GARCIA Garcia, Frank Christopher 6′2″, 297 **OG-C**
Col: Washington *HS:* Maryvale [Phoenix, AZ] B: 1/28/1972, Phoenix, AZ *Drafted:* 1995 Round 4 Car
1995 Car: 15 G; 1 Fum. **1996** Car: 14 G. **1997** Car: 16 G; KR 1-11 11.0. **1998** Car: 14 G. **Total:** 59 G; KR 1-11 11.0; 1 Fum.

JIM GARCIA Garcia, James Ronald 6′4″, 250 **DE-DT**
Col: Purdue *HS:* Albert G. Lane Tech [Chicago, IL] B: 3/7/1944, Chicago, IL *Drafted:* 1965 Round 2 Cle
1965 Cle: 12 G. **1966** NYG: 10 G. **1967** NO: 12 G. **1968** Atl: 1 G. **Total:** 35 G.

BUBBA GARCIA Garcia, Jesse Clarence 5′11″, 185 **WR**
Col: Texas-El Paso *HS:* New Braunfels [TX] B: 10/18/1957, New Braunfels, TX *Drafted:* 1980 Round 6 KC
1980 KC: 5 G; Rec 3-27 9.0 1 TD; 6 Pt; 1 Fum. **1981** KC: 1 G. **Total:** 6 G; Rec 3-27 9.0 1 TD; 6 Pt; 1 Fum.

GUS GARDELLA Gardella, August Michael 190 **FB**
(Siki; Hope) *Col:* No College B: 7/22/1895, New York, NY
D: 6/4/1985, Bridgeport, CT
1922 GB: 7 G.

FRANK GARDEN Garden, Frank 5′11″, 188 **OE**
Col: No College Deceased
1920 RI: 2 G. **1923** Cle: 2 G. **1925** Cle: 1 G. **Total:** 5 G.

DARYL GARDENER Gardener, Daryl Ronald 6′6″, 315 **DE**
Col: Baylor *HS:* Lawton [OK] B: 2/25/1973, Baltimore, MD
Drafted: 1996 Round 1 Mia
1996 Mia: 16 G; 1 Sac. **1997** Mia: 16 G; 1.5 Sac. **1998** Mia: 16 G; Int 1-(-1); 1 Sac. **Total:** 48 G; Int 1-(-1); 3.5 Sac.

RON GARDIN Gardin, Ronald Lee 5′11″, 180 **DB-WR**
Col: Cameron; Arizona *HS:* Ansonia [CT] B: 9/25/1944, New Haven, CT *Drafted:* 1970 Round 6 Bal

		Punt Returns				Kickoff Returns				
Year Team	**G**	**Ret**	**Yds**	**Avg**	**TD**	**Ret**	**Yds**	**Avg**	**TD**	**Fum**
1970 Bal	13	28	330	11.8	**1**	11	265	24.1	0	5
1971 Bal-NE	9	6	89	14.8	0	14	321	22.9	0	2
1971 Bal	1	2	75	37.5	0	0	0	—	0	0
1971 NE	8	4	14	3.5	0	14	321	22.9	0	2
NFL Total	22	34	419	12.3	1	25	586	23.4	0	7

CARWELL GARDNER Gardner, Carwell Ernest 6′2″, 240 **FB**
Col: Kentucky; Louisville *HS:* Trinity [Louisville, KY] B: 11/27/1966, Baltimore, MD *Drafted:* 1990 Round 2 Buf
1991 Buf: KR 1-10 10.0. **1994** Buf: KR 1-6 6.0. **1995** Buf: Scor 1 2XP; 1 Fum TD. **1996** Bal: Scor 1 2XP. **Total:** KR 2-16 8.0; Scor 2 2XP; 1 Fum TD.

		Rushing				Receiving					Tot
Year Team	**G**	**Att**	**Yds**	**Avg**	**TD**	**Rec**	**Yds**	**Avg**	**TD**	**Fum**	**TD**
1990 Buf	7	15	41	2.7	0	0	0	—	0	0	0
1991 Buf	16	42	146	3.5	4	3	20	6.7	0	4	4
1992 Buf	16	40	166	4.2	2	7	67	9.6	0	0	2
1993 Buf	13	20	56	2.8	0	4	50	12.5	1	1	1
1994 Buf	16	41	135	3.3	4	11	89	8.1	0	1	4
1995 Buf	15	20	77	3.9	0	2	17	8.5	0	0	1
1996 Bal	13	26	108	4.2	0	7	28	4.0	0	0	0
1997 SD	5	7	20	2.9	0	2	10	5.0	0	0	0
NFL Total	101	211	749	3.5	10	36	281	7.8	1	6	12

ELLIS GARDNER Gardner, Ellis Peniston 6′5″, 257 **OT-OG**
Col: Georgia Tech *HS:* McCallie School [Chattanooga, TN] B: 9/16/1961, Chattanooga, TN *Drafted:* 1983 Round 6 KC
1983 KC: 8 G. **1984** Ind: 9 G. **Total:** 17 G.

MOOSE GARDNER Gardner, Milton LeRoy 6′1″, 220 **G**
Col: Wisconsin *HS:* Ashland [WI] B: 7/2/1894, Ashland, WI D: 12/23/1954, Rocky River, OH
1920 Det: 2 G. **1921** Det-Buf: 8 G. Det: 7 G. Buf: 1 G. **1922** GB: 9 G. **1923** GB: 9 G. **1924** GB: 11 G. **1925** GB: 13 G; 6 Pt. **1926** GB: 13 G. **Total:** 65 G; 6 Pt.

MOE GARDNER Gardner, Morris Jr. 6′2″, 265 **NT-DE-DT**
Col: Illinois *HS:* Cathedral [Indianapolis, IN] B: 8/10/1968, Indianapolis, IN *Drafted:* 1991 Round 4 Atl
1991 Atl: 16 G; 3 Sac. **1992** Atl: 16 G; 4.5 Sac. **1993** Atl: 16 G; 2 Sac. **1994** Atl: 16 G. **1995** Atl: 16 G; 0.5 Sac. **1996** Atl: 10 G. **Total:** 90 G; 10 Sac.

DONNIE GARDNER Gardner, Redondo Lee 6′3″, 260 **DE**
Col: Kentucky *HS:* Trinity [Louisville, KY] B: 2/17/1968, Lousville, KY *Drafted:* 1990 Round 7 TB
1991 Mia: 10 G; 1 Sac.

BIRDIE GARDNER Gardner, William 190 **T**
Col: Carlisle B: 1883 Deceased
1920 Can: 1 G.

CHRIS GARDOCKI Gardocki, Christopher Allen 6′1″, 200 **P-K**
Col: Clemson *HS:* Redan [Stone Mountain, GA] B: 2/7/1970, Stone Mountain, GA *Drafted:* 1991 Round 3 ChiB
1992 ChiB: Pass 3-1 33.3%, 43 14.33. **1993** ChiB: Pass 2-0. **1995** Ind: Pass 1-0. **Total:** Pass 6-1 16.7%, 43 7.17.

		Punting			
Year Team	**G**	**Punts**	**Yds**	**Avg**	**Fum**
1991 ChiB	4	0	0	—	0
1992 ChiB	16	79	3393	42.9	0
1993 ChiB	16	80	3080	38.5	1
1994 ChiB	16	76	2871	37.8	0
1995 Ind	16	63	2681	42.6	0
1996 Ind	16	68	3105	45.7	0
1997 Ind	16	67	3034	45.3	0
1998 Ind	16	79	3583	45.4	0
NFL Total	116	512	21747	42.5	1

CHRIS GARLICH Garlich, Christopher James 6′1″, 220 **LB**
Col: Missouri *HS:* Rockhurst [Kansas City, MO] B: 7/17/1957, St. Louis, MO
1979 StL: 9 G; KR 1-0.

DON GARLIN Garlin, Donald Arthur 5′11″, 188 **HB-DB**
Col: USC *HS:* Porterville [CA] B: 11/10/1926, Porterville, CA
AAFC **1949** SF-A: 11 G; Rush 21-113 5.4 1 TD; Rec 6-64 10.7; KR 1-21 21.0; Int 1-0; 6 Pt.

NFL **1950** SF: 8 G; Rush 3-3 1.0; KR 1-24 24.0.

JOHN GARLINGTON Garlington, John M 6′1″, 218 **LB**
Col: Louisiana State *HS:* Jonesboro-Hodge [Jonesboro, LA] B: 6/5/1946, Jonesboro, LA *Drafted:* 1968 Round 2 Cle
1968 Cle: 13 G; Int 1-0. **1969** Cle: 14 G; Int 2-4. **1970** Cle: 11 G; Int 1-6. **1971** Cle: 14 G; Int 1-0. **1972** Cle: 14 G; Int 1-10. **1973** Cle: 14 G; Int 1-10. **1974** Cle: 14 G; Int 2-33. **1975** Cle: 7 G. **1976** Cle: 14 G. **1977** Cle: 13 G. **Total:** 128 G; Int 9-63.

BILL GARNAAS Garnaas, Wilford Benjamin 5′11″, 187 **WB-BB-LB**
Col: Minnesota *HS:* Marshall [Minneapolis, MN] B: 10/8/1921, Oberon, ND *Drafted:* 1944 Round 6 ChiC
1946 Pit: 10 G; Rec 3-56 18.7 1 TD; KR 2-29 14.5; 6 Pt. **1947** Pit: 10 G; Rec 5-144 28.8 2 TD; KR 1-17 17.0; 12 Pt. **1948** Pit: 6 G; KR 1-18 18.0. **Total:** 26 G; Rec 8-200 25.0 3 TD; KR 4-64 16.0; 18 Pt.

CHARLIE GARNER Garner, Charles III 5′9″, 187 **RB**
Col: Tennessee *HS:* J.E.B. Stuart [Falls Church, VA] B: 2/13/1972, Fairfax, VA *Drafted:* 1994 Round 2 Phi

		Rushing				Receiving			
Year Team	**G**	**Att**	**Yds**	**Avg**	**TD**	**Rec**	**Yds**	**Avg**	**TD**
1994 Phi	10	109	399	3.7	3	8	74	9.3	0
1995 Phi	15	108	588	**5.4**	6	10	61	6.1	0
1996 Phi	15	66	346	5.2	1	14	92	6.6	0
1997 Phi	16	116	547	4.7	3	24	225	9.4	0
1998 Phi	10	96	381	4.0	4	19	110	5.8	0
NFL Total	66	495	2261	4.6	17	75	562	7.5	0

	Kickoff Returns				
Year Team	**Ret**	**Yds**	**Avg**	**TD**	**Fum**
1994 Phi	0	0	—	0	3
1995 Phi	29	590	20.3	0	2
1996 Phi	6	117	19.5	0	1
1997 Phi	0	0	—	0	1
1998 Phi	0	0	—	0	1
NFL Total	35	707	20.2	0	8

DWIGHT GARNER Garner, Dwight Eugene 5′8″, 183 **RB**
Col: California *HS:* Skyline [Oakland, CA] B: 10/25/1964, San Francisco, CA
1986 Was: 2 G; KR 7-142 20.3; 1 Fum.

HAL GARNER Garner, Hal E Jr. 6′4″, 228 **LB**
Col: Utah State *HS:* James Logan [Logan, UT] B: 1/18/1962, New Iberia, LA *Drafted:* 1985 Round 3 Buf
1985 Buf: 13 G. **1986** Buf: 16 G. **1988** Buf: 12 G; 1 Sac. **1990** Buf: 10 G; 0.5 Sac. **1991** Buf: 16 G. **Total:** 67 G; 1.5 Sac.

BOB GARNER Garner, Robert 5′10″, 189 **DB**
Col: Fresno State *HS:* Hanford [CA] B: 1935
1960 LAC: Int 2-2. **1961** Oak: Int 2-14. **1962** Oak: KR 1-8 8.0; Int 3-31. **Total:** KR 1-8 8.0; Int 7-47.

		Punt Returns				
Year Team	**G**	**Ret**	**Yds**	**Avg**	**TD**	**Fum**
1960 LAC	13	6	85	14.2	0	1
1961 Oak	13	2	5	2.5	0	2
1962 Oak	14	20	162	8.1	0	1
NFL Total	40	28	252	9.0	0	4

BOB GARNER Garner, Robert Edward 6′0″, 238 **G**
Col: No College *HS:* Hillsborough [Tampa, FL] B: 8/16/1923, North Adams, MA D: 12/1972
1945 NYG: 1 G.

SAM GARNES Garnes, Samuel Aaron 6′3″, 225 **DB**
Col: Cincinnati *HS:* DeWitt Clinton [Bronx, NY] B: 7/12/1974, Bronx, NY *Drafted:* 1997 Round 5 NYG
1997 NYG: 16 G; Int 1-95 1 TD; 6 Pt. **1998** NYG: 11 G; Int 1-13. **Total:** 27 G; Int 2-108 1 TD; 6 Pt.

DAVE GARNETT Garnett, David Eugene 6′2″, 216 **LB**
Col: Stanford *HS:* Naperville North [IL] B: 12/6/1970, Pittsburgh, PA
1993 Min: 16 G. **1994** Min: 9 G; KR 1-0. **1995** Den: 3 G. **1996** Min: 12 G. **Total:** 40 G; KR 1-0.

SCOTT GARNETT Garnett, Scott Aaron 6′2″, 271 **NT-DE**
Col: Washington *HS:* John Muir [Pasadena, CA] B: 12/3/1962, Harrisburg, PA *Drafted:* 1984 Round 8 Den
1984 Den: 16 G; 1 Sac. **1985** SF-SD: 8 G; 2 Sac. SF: 3 G; 1 Sac. SD: 5 G; 1 Sac. **1987** Buf: 3 G. **Total:** 27 G; 3 Sac.

BILL GARNJOST Garnjost, William Tecumseh Sherman 5′10″, 190 **G**
Col: Columbia *HS:* Yonkers [NY] B: 12/1892 D: 1958
1921 Eva: 5 G.

BUDGE GARRETT Garrett, Alfred Tennyson 5′9″, 200 **E-G-FB**
Col: Rutgers *HS:* Peddie School [Highstown, NJ] B: 4/17/1893, Muskogee, OK D: 6/11/1950, Verona, NJ
1920 Akr: 7 G. **1922** Mil: 6 G. **Total:** 13 G.

ALVIN GARRETT Garrett, Alvin Lynn 5′7″, 178 **WR-RB**
Col: Angelo State *HS:* Mineral Wells [TX] B: 10/1/1956, Mineral Wells, TX *Drafted:* 1979 Round 9 SD
1980 NYG: Rush 9-31 3.4. **1981** NYG-Was: Rush 1-2 2.0. NYG: Rush 1-2 2.0. **1983** Was: Rush 2-0. **Total:** Rush 12-33 2.8.

		Receiving				Punt Returns			
Year Team	**G**	**Rec**	**Yds**	**Avg**	**TD**	**Ret**	**Yds**	**Avg**	**TD**
1980 NYG	15	5	69	13.8	1	35	287	8.2	0
1981 NYG-Was	13	0	0	—	0	8	57	7.1	0
1981 NYG	9	0	0	—	0	8	57	7.1	0
1981 Was	4	0	0	—	0	0	0	—	0
1982 Was	9	1	6	6.0	0	0	0	—	0
1983 Was	15	25	332	13.3	1	0	0	—	0
1984 Was	3	1	5	5.0	0	0	0	—	0
NFL Total	55	32	412	12.9	2	43	344	8.0	0

Year Team	Kickoff Returns Ret	Yds	Avg	TD	Fum
1980 NYG	28	527	18.8	0	5
1981 NYG-Was	18	401	22.3	0	1
1981 NYG	16	361	22.6	0	1
1981 Was	2	40	20.0	0	0
1982 Was	2	35	17.5	0	0
1983 Was	2	50	25.0	0	0
NFL Total	50	1013	20.3	0	6

CARL GARRETT Garrett, Carl L 5′11″, 210 **RB**
Col: New Mexico Highlands *HS:* Fred Moore [Denton, TX]
B: 8/31/1947, Denton, TX *Drafted:* 1969 Round 3 Bos
1969 Bos: Pass 1-0. **1972** NE: Pass 1-0, 1 Int. **1973** ChiB: Pass 1-0.
Total: Pass 3-0, 1 Int.

		Rushing				Receiving			
Year Team	G	Att	Yds	Avg	TD	Rec	Yds	Avg	TD
1969 Bos	14	137	691	**5.0**	5	29	267	9.2	2
1970 Bos	13	88	272	3.1	4	26	216	8.3	0
1971 NE	14	181	784	4.3	1	22	265	12.0	1
1972 NE	10	131	488	3.7	5	30	410	13.7	0
1973 ChiB	13	175	655	3.7	5	23	292	12.7	0
1974 ChiB	7	96	346	3.6	1	16	132	8.3	1
1975 NYJ	13	122	566	4.6	5	19	180	9.5	1
1976 Oak	12	48	220	4.6	1	9	108	12.0	0
1977 Oak	14	53	175	3.3	1	8	61	7.6	2
NFL Total	110	1031	4197	4.1	28	182	1931	10.6	7

	Punt Returns				Kickoff Returns					Tot
Year Team	Ret	Yds	Avg	TD	Ret	Yds	Avg	TD	Fum	TD
1969 Bos	12	159	13.3	0	28	792	28.3	0	6	7
1970 Bos	17	168	9.9	0	24	511	21.3	0	1	4
1971 NE	8	124	15.5	0	24	538	22.4	0	8	2
1972 NE	6	36	6.0	0	16	410	25.6	0	5	5
1973 ChiB	0	0	—	0	16	486	**30.4**	0	13	5
1974 ChiB	0	0	—	0	0	0	—	0	2	2
1975 NYJ	0	0	—	0	7	159	22.7	0	4	6
1976 Oak	0	0	—	0	18	388	21.6	0	2	1
1977 Oak	0	0	—	0	21	420	20.0	0	2	3
NFL Total	43	487	11.3	0	154	3704	24.1	0	43	35

CURTIS GARRETT Garrett, Curtis L 6′5″, 302 **DE**
Col: Illinois; Illinois State *HS:* Thornton Twp. [Harvey, IL] B: 6/9/1962, Chicago Heights, IL
1987 NYG: 3 G.

DRAKE GARRETT Garrett, Drake F 5′9″, 183 **DB**
Col: Michigan State *HS:* Paul L. Dunbar [Dayton, OH] B: 3/19/1946, Dayton, OH *Drafted:* 1968 Round 4 Den
1968 Den: 14 G; KR 3-77 25.7; Int 2-6; 1 Fum. **1970** Den: 1 G.
Total: 15 G; KR 3-77 25.7; Int 2-6; 1 Fum.

JASON GARRETT Garrett, Jason Calvin 6′2″, 195 **QB**
Col: Columbia; Princeton *HS:* University School [Hunting Valley, OH]
B: 3/28/1966, Abington, PA
1993 Dal: Rush 8-(-8) -1.0. **1994** Dal: Rush 3-(-2) -0.7. **1995** Dal: Rush 1-(-1) -1.0. **1998** Dal: Rush 11-14 1.3. **Total:** Rush 23-3 0.1.

		Passing								
Year Team	G	Att	Comp	Comp%	Yds	YPA	TD	Int	Rating	Fum
1993 Dal	5	19	9	47.4	61	3.21	0	0	54.9	1
1994 Dal	2	31	16	51.6	315	10.16	2	1	95.5	0
1995 Dal	1	5	4	80.0	46	9.20	1	0	144.6	0
1996 Dal	1	3	3	100.0	44	14.67	0	0	118.8	0
1997 Dal	1	14	10	71.4	56	4.00	0	0	78.3	0
1998 Dal	8	158	91	57.6	1206	7.63	5	3	84.5	4
NFL Total	18	230	133	57.8	1728	7.51	8	4	85.9	5

J.D. GARRETT Garrett, John D 5′11″, 195 **HB**
Col: Grambling State *HS:* Natchitoches Central [LA] B: 11/28/1941, Natchitoches, LA *Drafted:* 1964 Round 8 Bos
1964 Bos: Rec 8-101 12.6; PR 2-28 14.0. **1965** Bos: Rec 7-49 7.0 2 TD; PR 1-19 19.0. **1966** Bos: Rec 1-7 7.0. **1967** Bos: Rec 1-12 12.0.
Total: Rec 17-169 9.9 2 TD; PR 3-47 15.7.

		Rushing				Kickoff Returns					Tot
Year Team	G	Ret	Yds	Avg	TD	Ret	Yds	Avg	TD	Fum	TD
1964 Bos	14	56	259	4.6	2	32	749	23.4	0	3	2
1965 Bos	12	42	147	3.5	1	12	232	19.3	0	1	3
1966 Bos	14	13	21	1.6	0	0	0	—	0	0	0
1967 Bos	10	5	7	1.4	0	4	73	18.3	0	1	1
NFL Total	50	116	434	3.7	3	48	1054	22.0	0	5	6

JOHN GARRETT Garrett, John Morgan 5′11″, 180 **WR**
Col: Columbia; Princeton *HS:* University School [Hunting Valley, OH]
B: 3/2/1965, Danville, PA
1989 Cin: 1 G; Rec 2-29 14.5.

LEN GARRETT Garrett, Leonard Neal 6′3″, 230 **TE**
Col: New Mexico Highlands *HS:* Waldo Mathew [Silsbee, TX]
B: 12/18/1947, Silsbee, TX *Drafted:* 1971 Round 15 GB
1971 GB: 14 G. **1972** GB: 14 G; Rec 4-66 16.5; KR 1-0. **1973** GB-NO: 14 G; Rec 2-30 15.0. GB: 2 G. NO: 12 G; Rec 2-30 15.0. **1974** NO: 10 G. **1975** NO-SF: 3 G. NO: 1 G. SF: 2 G. **Total:** 55 G; Rec 6-96 16.0; KR 1-0.

SHANE GARRETT Garrett, Marcus Shane 5′11″, 185 **WR**
Col: Texas A&M *HS:* Crowley [LA] B: 11/16/1967, Lafayette, LA
Drafted: 1991 Round 9 Cin
1991 Cin: 4 G; Rec 3-32 10.7; PR 1-7 7.0; KR 13-214 16.5; 1 Fum.

MIKE GARRETT Garrett, Michael Lockett 5′9″, 191 **RB**
Col: USC *HS:* Theodore Roosevelt [Los Angeles, CA] B: 4/12/1944, Los Angeles, CA *Drafted:* 1966 Round 20 KC
1966 KC: Pass 1-0; KR 14-323 23.1. **1967** KC: Pass 4-1 25.0%, 17 4.25 1 TD. **1968** KC: Pass 1-0, 1 Int. **1971** SD: Pass 1-1 100.0%, 53 53.00. **1972** SD: Pass 1-0. **1973** SD: Pass 1-0. **Total:** Pass 9-2 22.2%, 70 7.78 1 TD 1 Int; KR 14-323 23.1.

		Rushing				Receiving			
Year Team	G	Att	Yds	Avg	TD	Rec	Yds	Avg	TD
1966 KC	14	147	801	**5.4**	6	15	175	11.7	1
1967 KC	14	236	1087	4.6	9	46	261	5.7	1
1968 KC	13	164	564	3.4	3	33	359	10.9	3
1969 KC	14	168	732	4.4	6	43	432	10.0	2
1970 KC-SD	12	67	208	3.1	1	14	131	9.4	1
1970 KC	3	21	62	3.0	0	4	4	1.0	0
1970 SD	9	46	146	3.2	1	10	127	12.7	1
1971 SD	13	140	591	4.2	4	41	283	6.9	3
1972 SD	14	272	1031	3.8	6	31	245	7.9	1
1973 SD	10	114	467	4.1	0	15	124	8.3	1
NFL Total	104	1308	5481	4.2	35	238	2010	8.4	13

	Punt Returns					Tot
Year Team	Ret	Yds	Avg	TD	Fum	TD
1966 KC	17	139	8.2	**1**	5	8
1967 KC	4	22	5.5	0	6	10
1968 KC	2	4	2.0	0	6	6
1969 KC	8	28	3.5	0	4	8
1970 KC-SD	3	30	10.0	0	4	2
1970 KC	3	30	10.0	0	1	0
1970 SD	0	0	—	0	3	2
1971 SD	3	2	0.7	0	6	7
1972 SD	2	10	5.0	0	8	7
1973 SD	0	0	—	0	6	1
NFL Total	39	235	6.0	1	45	49

MIKE GARRETT Garrett, Michael Steven 6′1″, 184 **P**
Col: Georgia *HS:* Haralson Co. [Tallapoosa, GA] B: 6/13/1957, Atlanta, GA
1981 Bal: Rush 2-4 2.0.

		Punting		
Year Team	G	Punts	Yds	Avg
1981 Bal	16	78	3071	39.4

REGGIE GARRETT Garrett, Reginald Weldon 6′1″, 172 **WR**
Col: New Mexico Highlands; Eastern Michigan *HS:* Waldo Mathew [Silsbee, TX] B: 11/22/1951, Silsbee, TX
1974 Pit: 14 G. **1975** Pit: 14 G; Rec 13-178 13.7 1 TD; 6 Pt. **Total:** 28 G; Rec 13-178 13.7 1 TD; 6 Pt.

BOBBY GARRETT Garrett, Robert Driscoll 6′1″, 198 **QB**
Col: Stanford *HS:* South Pasadena [CA] B: 8/16/1932, Los Angeles, CA D: 12/5/1987, Westminster, CA *Drafted:* 1954 Round 1 Cle
1954 GB: 9 G; Pass 30-15 50.0%, 143 4.77 1 Int; Rush 1-(-3) -3.0; 2 Fum.

THURMAN GARRETT Garrett, Thurman Edward 6′3″, 268 **C-G**
(Goose) *Col:* Oklahoma State *HS:* Blackwell [OK] B: 2/17/1923, Blackwell, OK
1947 ChiB: 10 G; Int 1-2; Scor 0-1 FG. **1948** ChiB: 10 G. **Total:** 20 G; Int 1-2; Scor 0-1 FG.

DUB GARRETT Garrett, William Davis Jr. 6′1″, 235 **DG-OG-DT**
Col: Mississippi State *HS:* Dundee [MS] B: 1/29/1925, Dundee, MS
D: 7/1976 *Drafted:* 1948 Round 2 ChiB
AAFC **1948** BalA: 14 G; KR 1-6 6.0. **1949** BalA: 11 G. **Total:** 25 G; KR 1-6 6.0.

NFL **1950** ChiB: 3 G; **1** Fum TD; 6 Pt.

GARY GARRISON Garrison, Gary Lynn 6′2″, 193 **WR**
(The Ghost) *Col:* Long Beach City Coll. CA (J.C.); San Diego State
HS: R.A. Millikan [Long Beach, CA] B: 1/21/1944, Amarillo, TX
Drafted: 1965 Redshirt Round 1 SD
1966 SD: Rush 1-(-3) -3.0. **1967** SD: Rush 1-1 1.0. **1970** SD: Rush 4-7 1.8. **1971** SD: Rush 1-0. **1972** SD: Rush 2-(-6) -3.0. **1975** SD: Rush 3-30 10.0. **Total:** Rush 12-29 2.4.

Year Team	G	Receiving Rec	Yds	Avg	TD	Fum
1966 SD	14	46	642	14.0	4	0
1967 SD	14	44	772	17.5	2	0
1968 SD	14	52	1103	21.2	10	1
1969 SD	10	40	804	20.1	7	1
1970 SD	14	44	1006	**22.9**	12	0
1971 SD	14	42	889	21.2	6	0
1972 SD	14	52	744	14.3	7	0
1973 SD	7	14	292	20.9	2	0
1974 SD	14	41	785	19.1	5	1
1975 SD	14	27	438	16.2	2	0
1976 SD	2	2	58	29.0	1	0
1977 Hou	3	1	5	5.0	0	0
NFL Total	134	405	7538	18.6	58	3

WALT GARRISON Garrison, Walter Benton 6′0″, 205 **RB**
Col: Oklahoma State *HS:* Lewisville [TX] B: 7/23/1944, Denton, TX
Drafted: 1966 Round 5 Dal
1973 Dal: Pass 1-0. **Total:** Pass 1-0.

		Rushing				Receiving			
Year Team	G	Att	Yds	Avg	TD	Rec	Yds	Avg	TD
1966 Dal	14	16	62	3.9	1	2	18	9.0	0
1967 Dal	13	24	146	6.1	0	2	17	8.5	0
1968 Dal	14	45	271	6.0	5	7	111	15.9	0
1969 Dal	13	176	818	4.6	2	13	131	10.1	0
1970 Dal	11	126	507	4.0	3	21	205	9.8	2
1971 Dal	13	127	429	3.4	1	40	396	9.9	1
1972 Dal	14	167	784	4.7	7	37	390	10.5	3
1973 Dal	13	105	440	4.2	6	26	273	10.5	2
1974 Dal	14	113	429	3.8	5	34	253	7.4	1
NFL Total	119	899	3886	4.3	30	182	1794	9.9	9

	Kickoff Returns					Tot
Year Team	Ret	Yds	Avg	TD	Fum	TD
1966 Dal	20	445	22.3	0	0	1
1967 Dal	20	366	18.3	0	0	0
1968 Dal	0	0	—	0	0	5
1969 Dal	1	2	2.0	0	4	2
1970 Dal	0	0	—	0	2	5
1971 Dal	0	0	—	0	6	2
1972 Dal	0	0	—	0	6	10
1973 Dal	0	0	—	0	3	8
1974 Dal	0	0	—	0	5	6
NFL Total	41	813	19.8	0	26	39

GREGG GARRITY Garrity, Gregg David 5′10″, 171 **WR**
Col: Penn State *HS:* North Allegheny [Wexford, PA] B: 11/24/1960, Pittsburgh, PA *Drafted:* 1983 Round 5 Pit
1986 Phi: PR 17-187 11.0 1 TD. **1987** Phi: PR 4-16 4.0. **Total:** PR 21-203 9.7 1 TD.

		Receiving					Tot
Year Team	G	Rec	Yds	Avg	TD	Fum	TD
1983 Pit	15	19	279	14.7	1	1	1
1984 Pit-Phi	10	2	22	11.0	0	0	0
1984 Pit	6	2	22	11.0	0	0	0
1984 Phi	4	0	0	—	0	0	0
1985 Phi	12	7	142	20.3	0	0	0
1986 Phi	12	12	227	18.9	0	0	1
1987 Phi	12	12	242	20.2	2	2	2
1988 Phi	9	17	208	12.2	1	0	1
1989 Phi	9	13	209	16.1	2	0	2
NFL Total	79	82	1329	16.2	6	3	7

LARRY GARRON Garron, Lawrence Jr. 6′0″, 195 **HB**
Col: Western Illinois *HS:* Argo [Summit, IL] B: 5/23/1937, Mark, MS
1962 Bos: Pass 3-1 33.3%, 39 13.00. **1963** Bos: Pass 1-0; PR 1-23 23.0.
1964 Bos: Pass 2-0. **Total:** Pass 6-1 16.7%, 39 6.50; PR 1-23 23.0.

		Rushing				Receiving			
Year Team	G	Att	Yds	Avg	TD	Rec	Yds	Avg	TD
1960 Bos	4	8	27	3.4	0	1	8	8.0	0
1961 Bos	14	69	389	5.6	2	24	341	14.2	3
1962 Bos	11	67	392	5.9	2	18	236	13.1	3
1963 Bos	14	175	750	4.3	2	26	418	16.1	2
1964 Bos	14	183	585	3.2	2	40	350	8.8	7
1965 Bos	10	74	259	3.5	1	15	222	14.8	1
1966 Bos	14	101	319	3.2	4	30	416	13.9	5
1967 Bos	14	46	163	3.5	0	30	507	16.9	5
1968 Bos	4	36	97	2.7	1	1	4	4.0	0
NFL Total	99	759	2981	3.9	14	185	2502	13.5	26

	Kickoff Returns					Tot
Year Team	Ret	Yds	Avg	TD	Fum	TD
1960 Bos	1	21	21.0	0	0	0
1961 Bos	16	438	27.4	**1**	5	6
1962 Bos	24	686	28.6	**1**	7	6
1963 Bos	28	693	24.8	0	8	4
1964 Bos	10	198	19.8	0	9	9
1965 Bos	5	141	28.2	0	1	2
1966 Bos	2	49	24.5	0	3	9
1967 Bos	3	73	24.3	0	2	5
1968 Bos	0	0	—	0	2	1
NFL Total	89	2299	25.8	2	37	42

LEON GARROR Garror, Leon 6′0″, 180 **DB**
Col: Alcorn State *HS:* Lillie B. Williamson [Mobile, AL] B: 5/2/1948, Mobile, AL *Drafted:* 1972 Round 5 Buf
1972 Buf: 12 G. **1973** Buf: 4 G; Int 1-0. **Total:** 16 G; Int 1-0.

BEN GARRY Garry, Benjamin Earl 6′0″, 215 **RB**
Col: Southern Mississippi *HS:* Pascagoula [MS] B: 2/11/1956, Hazlehurst, MS *Drafted:* 1978 Round 6 Bal
1979 Bal: 11 G; Rush 13-41 3.2; Rec 3-9 3.0; KR 8-135 16.9; 1 Fum.
1980 Bal: 3 G; Rec 1-9 9.0; KR 3-55 18.3; 1 Fum. **Total:** 14 G; Rush 13-41 3.2; Rec 4-18 4.5; KR 11-190 17.3; 2 Fum.

CHRIS GARTNER Gartner, Sven Chris 6′0″, 170 **K**
Col: Indiana *HS:* Princeton [NJ] B: 7/12/1950, Gothenburg, Sweden
1974 Cle: 11 G.

HEC GARVEY Garvey, Arthur Aloysius 6′1″, 235 **G-T-E-C**
(Stretch) *Col:* Notre Dame *HS:* Holyoke [MA] B: 2/20/1900, Holyoke, MA D: 9/22/1973, Chicago, IL
1922 ChiB: 12 G. **1923** ChiB: 13 G. **1926** Har-Bkn: 5 G. Har: 4 G. Bkn: 1 G. **1927** NYG: 8 G. **1928** NYG: 11 G. **1929** Prov: 9 G. **1930** Bkn: 12 G. **1931** SI: 11 G. **Total:** 81 G.

FRANNY GARVEY Garvey, Francis Daniel 6′1″, 175 **E**
Col: Holy Cross B: 5/18/1901, Worcester, MA D: 11/18/1972, Chelsea, MA
1925 Prov: 9 G; 1 Fum TD; Tot TD 2; 12 Pt. **1926** Prov: 10 G; Scor **1** 1XP; 1 Pt. **Total:** 19 G; Scor 1 1XP; 1 Fum TD; Tot TD 2; 13 Pt.

CLEVELAND GARY Gary, Cleveland Everett 6′0″, 226 **RB**
Col: Georgia; Miami (Fla.) *HS:* South Fork [Stuart, FL] B: 5/4/1966, Stuart, FL *Drafted:* 1989 Round 1 LARm
1989 LARm: KR 1-4 4.0. **1993** LARm: Pass 1-1 100.0%, 8 8.00.
Total: Pass 1-1 100.0%, 8 8.00; KR 1-4 4.0.

		Rushing				Receiving					Tot
Year Team	G	Att	Yds	Avg	TD	Rec	Yds	Avg	TD	Fum	TD
1989 LARm	10	37	163	4.4	1	2	13	6.5	0	1	1
1990 LARm	15	204	808	4.0	**14**	30	150	5.0	1	12	15
1991 LARm	10	68	245	3.6	1	13	110	8.5	0	1	1
1992 LARm	16	279	1125	4.0	7	52	293	5.6	3	9	10
1993 LARm	15	79	293	3.7	1	36	289	8.0	1	1	2
1994 Mia	2	7	11	1.6	0	2	19	9.5	0	1	0
NFL Total	68	674	2645	3.9	24	135	874	6.5	5	25	29

KEITH GARY Gary, Keith Jerrold 6′3″, 263 **DE**
Col: Ferrum; Oklahoma *HS:* Chantilly [VA] B: 9/14/1959, Bethesda, MD *Drafted:* 1981 Round 1 Pit
1983 Pit: 16 G; 7.5 Sac. **1984** Pit: 16 G; 4 Sac. **1985** Pit: 12 G; 3 Sac.
1986 Pit: 16 G; 6.5 Sac. **1987** Pit: 11 G; 4 Sac. **1988** Pit: 15 G.
Total: 86 G; 25.0 Sac.

RUSSELL GARY Gary, Russell Craig 5′11″, 195 **DB**
Col: Nebraska *HS:* Central [Minneapolis, MN] B: 7/31/1959, Minneapolis, MN *Drafted:* 1981 Round 2 NO
1981 NO: 14 G; Int 1-0. **1982** NO: 9 G; Int 2-25; 3 Sac. **1983** NO: 14 G; Int 3-70; 1 Fum. **1984** NO: 16 G. **1985** NO: 2 G. **1986** NO-Phi: 13 G; Int 1-14. NO: 7 G; Int 1-14. Phi: 6 G. **1987** Phi: 12 G. **Total:** 80 G; Int 7-109; 1 Fum; 3 Sac.

DAN GARZA Garza, Daniel Robert 6′3″, 203 **OE**
Col: North Texas; Central Missouri State; Oregon *HS:* G. W. Brackenridge [San Antonio, TX] B: 2/21/1924, Anderson, SC
Drafted: 1948 Round 15 NYG
AAFC **1949** NY-A: 12 G; Rec 9-193 21.4; KR 1-21 21.0.

NFL Statistics

Year Team	G	Receiving Rec	Yds	Avg	TD	Fum
1951 NYY	11	31	470	15.2	4	1

SAMMY GARZA Garza, Samuel Mayorga Jr. 6′1″, 184 **QB**
Col: Texas-El Paso *HS:* Harlingen [TX] B: 7/10/1965, Corpus Christi, TX *Drafted:* 1987 Round 8 Sea
1987 StL: 2 G; Pass 20-11 55.0%, 183 9.15 1 TD 2 Int; Rush 8-31 3.9 1 TD; 6 Pt; 1 Fum.

MIKE GARZONI Garzoni, Michael John 5′11″, 218 **G**
Col: Santa Clara; Fresno State; USC *HS:* Santa Clara [Oxnard, CA]
B: 8/19/1923, Los Angeles, CA *Drafted:* 1947 Round 4 Was
AAFC **1948** NY-A: 2 G.

NFL **1947** Was: 10 G. **1948** NYG: 5 G; KR 1-0; 1 Fum. **Total:** 15 G; KR 1-0; 1 Fum.

SAM GASH Gash, Samuel Lee Jr. 6'0", 235 **RB**
Col: Penn State *HS:* Hendersonville [NC] B: 3/7/1969, Hendersonville, NC *Drafted:* 1992 Round 8 NE
1994 NE: KR 1-9 9.0. **1996** NE: Scor 1 2XP. **1998** Buf: KR 3-41 13.7.
Total: KR 4-50 12.5; Scor 1 2XP.

		Rushing				Receiving					Tot
Year Team	G	Att	Yds	Avg	TD	Rec	Yds	Avg	TD	Fum	TD
1992 NE	15	5	7	1.4	1	0	0	—	0	1	1
1993 NE	15	48	149	3.1	1	14	93	6.6	0	1	1
1994 NE	13	30	86	2.9	0	9	61	6.8	0	1	0
1995 NE	15	8	24	3.0	0	26	242	9.3	1	0	1
1996 NE	14	8	15	1.9	0	33	276	8.4	2	0	2
1997 NE	16	6	10	1.7	0	22	154	7.0	3	0	3
1998 Buf	16	11	32	2.9	0	19	165	8.7	3	0	3
NFL Total	104	116	323	2.8	2	123	991	8.1	9	3	11

THANE GASH Gash, Thane Alvin 6'0", 200 **DB**
Col: East Tennessee State *HS:* Hendersonville [NC] B: 9/1/1965, Hendersonville, NC *Drafted:* 1988 Round 7 Cle
1988 Cle: 16 G. **1989** Cle: 16 G; Int 3-65 **2** TD; 12 Pt; 2 Sac. **1990** Cle: 16 G; Int 1-16. **1992** SF: 16 G. **Total:** 64 G; Int 4-81 2 TD; 12 Pt; 2 Sac.

PERCELL GASKINS Gaskins, Percell McGahee 6'0", 230 **LB**
Col: Northwestern Okla. State; Kansas State *HS:* Seabreeze [Daytona Beach, FL] B: 4/25/1972, Daytona Beach, FL *Drafted:* 1996 Round 4 StL
1996 StL: 15 G. **1997** Car: 12 G. **Total:** 27 G.

JOE GASPARELLA Gasparella, Joseph Richard 6'4", 222 **QB-BB-DB**
Col: Notre Dame *HS:* Vandergrift [PA] B: 2/5/1927, Apollo, PA
Drafted: 1948 Round 4 Pit
1948 Pit: Rush 1-5 5.0. **1950** Pit: Rec 1-3 3.0. **Total:** Rush 1-5 5.0; Rec 1-3 3.0.

		Passing								
Year Team	G	Att	Comp	Comp%	Yds	YPA	TD	Int	Rating	Fum
1948 Pit	9	57	23	40.4	294	5.16	0	4	28.0	1
1950 Pit	11	54	23	42.6	383	7.09	3	5	47.1	0
1951 Pit-ChiC	6	2	0	0.0	0	0.00	0	1	0.0	0
1951 Pit	4	2	0	0.0	0	0.00	0	1	0.0	0
1951 ChiC	2	0	0	—	0	—	0	0	—	0
NFL Total	26	113	46	40.7	677	5.99	3	10	32.9	1

RON GASSERT Gassert, Ronald Earl 6'3", 260 **DT**
Col: Virginia *HS:* Bordentown Mil. Acad. [NJ] B: 7/22/1940, Campbelltown, PA *Drafted:* 1962 Round 4 GB
1962 GB: 10 G.

MARK GASTINEAU Gastineau, Marcus Dell 6'5", 266 **DE**
Col: Eastern Arizona Coll. (J.C.); Arizona State; East Central (OK)
HS: Round Valley [Springerville, AZ] B: 11/20/1956, Ardmore, OK
Drafted: 1979 Round 2 NYJ
1979 NYJ: 16 G. **1980** NYJ: 16 G. **1981** NYJ: 16 G. **1982** NYJ: 9 G; 6 Sac. **1983** NYJ: 16 G; 1 Fum TD; 6 Pt; **19** Sac. **1984** NYJ: 16 G; **1** Fum TD; 6 Pt; **22** Sac. **1985** NYJ: 16 G; 13.5 Sac. **1986** NYJ: 10 G; 2 Sac. **1987** NYJ: 15 G; 4.5 Sac. **1988** NYJ: 7 G; 7 Sac. **Total:** 137 G; 2 Fum TD; 12 Pt; 74 Sac.

GATES Gates **G**
Col: No College Deceased
1920 Det: 1 G.

LES GATEWOOD Gatewood, Lester Buddy 6'2", 198 **C-LB**
(Buddy) *Col:* Baylor; Tulane *HS:* Waco [TX] B: 5/30/1921, Dallas, TX
Drafted: 1943 Round 6 GB
1946 GB: 11 G. **1947** GB: 12 G. **Total:** 23 G.

TOM GATEWOOD Gatewood, Thomas Jr. 6'3", 215 **TE-WR**
Col: Notre Dame *HS:* Baltimore City College [MD] B: 3/7/1950, Baltimore, MD *Drafted:* 1972 Round 5 NYG
1972 NYG: 10 G. **1973** NYG: 7 G. **Total:** 17 G.

FRANK GATSKI Gatski, Frank 6'3", 233 **C-LB**
(Gunner) *Col:* Marshall; Auburn *HS:* Farmington [WV] B: 3/18/1922, Farmington, WV *HOF:* 1985
AAFC **1946** CleA: 10 G; Int 1-35 1 TD; 6 Pt. **1947** CleA: 12 G; KR 1-17 17.0; Int 2-0. **1948** CleA: 14 G. **1949** CleA: 12 G. **Total:** 48 G; KR 1-17 17.0; Int 3-35 1 TD; 6 Pt.

NFL **1950** Cle: 12 G. **1951** Cle: 12 G. **1952** Cle: 12 G. **1953** Cle: 12 G. **1954** Cle: 12 G. **1955** Cle: 12 G. **1956** Cle: 12 G. **1957** Det: 12 G.
Total: 96 G.

DENNIS GAUBATZ Gaubatz, Dennis Earl 6'2", 232 **LB**
Col: Louisiana State *HS:* West Columbia [TX] B: 2/11/1940, Needville, TX *Drafted:* 1963 Round 8 Det
1964 Det: Scor **1** Saf. **Total:** Scor 1 Saf.

		Interceptions		
Year Team	G	Int	Yds	TD
1963 Det	14	1	55	0
1964 Det	14	1	16	0
1965 Bal	14	1	5	0
1966 Bal	13	2	12	0
1967 Bal	14	2	10	0
1968 Bal	14	2	15	0
1969 Bal	12	1	11	0
NFL Total	95	10	124	0

BOB GAUDIO Gaudio, Angelo Robert 5'10", 219 **OG-LB-DG**
Col: Ohio State *HS:* Shaw [East Cleveland, OH] B: 7/13/1925, Ashtabula, OH
AAFC **1947** CleA: 14 G. **1948** CleA: 13 G; Rush 1-2 2.0. **1949** CleA: 12 G; Rush 1-(-2) -2.0. **Total:** 39 G; Rush 2-0.

NFL **1951** Cle: 12 G; KR 1-8 8.0; 1 Fum.

CHARLIE GAUER Gauer, Charles Edward Jr. 6'2", 213 **DE-FB-OE-LB**
Col: Colgate *HS:* Upper Darby [PA] B: 9/24/1921, Chicago, IL
D: 10/22/1973, Philadelphia, PA
1943 PhPt: 9 G; Rush 12-69 5.8; Rec 2-18 9.0; Int 1-0. **1944** Phi: 7 G; Rec 2-35 17.5; Int 1-2. **1945** Phi: 7 G. **Total:** 23 G; Rush 12-69 5.8; Rec 4-53 13.3; Int 2-2.

FRANK GAUL Gaul, Francis Edward 6'0", 200 **T**
(Speed) *Col:* Notre Dame *HS:* Cathedral Latin [Cleveland, OH]
B: 8/8/1926, Cleveland, OH *Drafted:* 1949 Round 20 NYB
1949 NYB: 12 G.

HAL GAULKE Gaulke, Harold M 5'8", 175 **BB-OE**
Col: No College *HS:* South [Columbus, OH] B: 8/1894, Columbus, OH Deceased
1920 Col: 10 G. **1921** Col: 4 G. **1922** Col: 7 G. **Total:** 21 G.

DON GAULT Gault, Donald J 6'2", 190 **QB**
Col: Hofstra *HS:* John Adams [Queens, NY] B: 8/30/1946, Lynbrook, NY
1970 Cle: 2 G; Pass 19-2 10.5%, 67 3.53 3 Int; 1 Fum.

BILLY GAULT Gault, William 6'1", 185 **HB**
Col: Texas Christian *HS:* North Side [Fort Worth, TX] B: 12/19/1936, Monroe, LA *Drafted:* 1961 Round 11 Cle
1961 Min: 4 G; KR 2-41 20.5.

WILLIE GAULT Gault, Willie James 6'0", 181 **WR**
Col: Tennessee *HS:* Griffin [GA] B: 9/5/1960, Griffin, GA
Drafted: 1983 Round 1 ChiB
1983 ChiB: Rush 4-31 7.8; PR 9-60 6.7. **1985** ChiB: Rush 5-18 3.6. **1986** ChiB: Rush 8-79 9.9. **1987** ChiB: Rush 2-16 8.0. **1988** LARd: Rush 1-4 4.0. **1992** LARd: Rush 1-6 6.0. **Total:** Rush 21-154 7.3; PR 9-60 6.7.

		Receiving				Kickoff Returns					Tot
Year Team	G	Rec	Yds	Avg	TD	Ret	Yds	Avg	TD	Fum	TD
1983 ChiB	16	40	836	20.9	8	13	276	21.2	0	1	8
1984 ChiB	16	34	587	17.3	6	1	12	12.0	0	1	6
1985 ChiB	16	33	704	21.3	1	22	577	26.2	1	0	2
1986 ChiB	16	42	818	19.5	5	1	20	20.0	0	1	5
1987 ChiB	12	35	705	20.1	7	0	0	—	0	0	7
1988 LARd	15	16	392	24.5	2	0	0	—	0	1	2
1989 LARd	16	28	690	24.6	4	1	16	16.0	0	0	4
1990 LARd	16	50	985	19.7	3	0	0	—	0	1	3
1991 LARd	16	20	346	17.3	4	0	0	—	0	0	4
1992 LARd	16	27	508	18.8	4	0	0	—	0	0	4
1993 LARd	15	8	64	8.0	0	7	187	26.7	0	0	0
NFL Total	170	333	6635	19.9	44	45	1088	24.2	1	5	45

STEVE GAUNTY Gaunty, Steven 5'10", 175 **WR**
Col: Northern Colorado *HS:* Thornton Twp. [Harvey, IL] B: 5/3/1957, Chicago, IL
1979 KC: 9 G; Rec 5-87 17.4 1 TD; KR 12-271 22.6; 6 Pt.

FRANK GAUSE Gause, Frank O 190 **C-G**
HS: North [Minneapolis, MN] B: 2/11/1905 D: 8/15/1972, Minneapolis, MN
1929 Min: 3 G.

DUTCH GAUSTAD Gaustad, Arthur M 212 **G**
(Heavy) *Col:* No College *HS:* None B: 6/1889, MN Deceased
1921 Min: 4 G. **1922** Min: 4 G. **1923** Min: 6 G. **Total:** 14 G.

PRENTICE GAUTT Gautt, Prentice 6'1", 210 **HB-FB**
Col: Oklahoma *HS:* Frederick Douglass [Oklahoma City, OK]
B: 2/8/1938, Oklahoma City, OK *Drafted:* 1960 Round 2 Cle
1960 Cle: KR 3-47 15.7. **1961** StL: Pass 11-6 54.5%, 100 9.09 1 TD 1 Int. **1962** StL: KR 6-124 20.7. **1963** StL: Pass 1-0. **1964** StL: KR 5-104 20.8. **1965** StL: Pass 1-0. **Total:** Pass 13-6 46.2%, 100 7.69 1 TD 1 Int; KR 14-275 19.6.

		Rushing				Receiving					Tot
Year Team	G	Att	Yds	Avg	TD	Rec	Yds	Avg	TD	Fum	TD
1960 Cle	12	28	159	5.7	1	1	10	10.0	0	0	1
1961 StL	14	129	523	4.1	3	12	132	11.0	3	3	6
1962 StL	13	114	470	4.1	2	16	240	15.0	0	1	2

1963 StL	1	3	5	1.7	0	1	3	3.0	0	0	0
1964 StL	13	59	191	3.2	1	9	72	8.0	1	1	2
1965 StL	7	44	175	4.0	2	9	128	14.2	0	2	2
1966 StL	14	110	370	3.4	1	16	114	7.1	1	0	2
1967 StL	14	142	573	4.0	1	15	202	13.5	1	0	2
NFL Total	88	629	2466	3.9	11	79	901	11.4	6	7	17

MIKE GAVAGAN Gavagan, Maurice Thomas 5′10″, 176 **BB**
Col: St. Bonaventure *HS:* Warsaw [NY] B: 4/10/1899, Warsaw, NY
Deceased
1923 Roch: 2 G.

CHUCK GAVIN Gavin, Charles E 6′1″, 250 **DE**
Col: Tennessee State *HS:* Oak Park [Laurel, MS] B: 12/26/1933, Lake, MS
1960 Den: 11 G. **1961** Den: 8 G; 6 Pt. **1962** Den: 14 G; Int 1-35.
1963 Den: 14 G. **Total:** 47 G; Int 1-35; 6 Pt.

BUCK GAVIN Gavin, Patrick M 5′10″, 179 **FB-TB-WB**
Col: No College B: 6/22/1895, NY D: 4/12/1981, Daytona Beach, FL
1920 Buf: 5 G. **1921** Det-RI: 6 G. Det: 3 G. RI: 3 G. **1922** RI-Buf: 10 G; Rush 6 TD; 36 Pt. RI: 7 G; Rush 5 TD; 30 Pt. Buf: 3 G; Rush 1 TD; 6 Pt.
1923 GB: 9 G. **1924** RI: 9 G; Rush 7 TD; 42 Pt. **1925** RI: 5 G. **1926** Ham: 3 G. **Total:** 47 G; Rush 13 TD; 78 Pt.

MOMCILO GAVRIC Gavric, Momcilo 5′10″, 167 **K**
(Gabbo) *Col:* Belgrade (Serbia) *HS:* Senj [Croatia] B: 8/4/1938, Senj, Croatia
1969 SF: 7 G; Scor 31, 3-11 27.3% FG, 22-24 91.7% XK.

BLENDA GAY Gay, Blenda Glen 6′5″, 254 **DE**
Col: Fayetteville State *HS:* H.B. Sugg [Farmville, NC] B: 11/22/1950, Greenville, NC D: 12/19/1976, Freeport, NY *Drafted:* 1973 Supplemental Round 1 Oak
1974 SD: 2 G; 1 Fum TD; 6 Pt. **1975** Phi: 14 G. **1976** Phi: 14 G.
Total: 30 G; 1 Fum TD; 6 Pt.

CHET GAY Gay, Chester Joseph 6′0″, 215 **T-G-C**
Col: Minnesota *HS:* Moose Lake [MN] B: 1/8/1900, Moose Lake, MN
D: 3/12/1978, Moose Lake, MN
1925 Buf: 8 G. **1926** Mil: 6 G. **Total:** 14 G.

EVERETT GAY Gay, Everett Carlton 6′2″, 209 **WR**
Col: Texas *HS:* Phillis Wheatley [Houston, TX] B: 10/23/1964, Houston, TX *Drafted:* 1987 Round 5 Dal
1988 Dal: 16 G; Rec 15-205 13.7 1 TD; 6 Pt; 1 Fum.

MATT GAY Gay, Matthew Gilbert 5′11″, 197 **DB**
Col: Kansas *HS:* Nicholas Senn [Chicago, IL] B: 4/3/1970, Chicago, IL
1994 KC: 2 G.

BILL GAY Gay, William Howard 6′5″, 250 **DE-DT-TE**
Col: San Diego City Coll. CA (J.C.); USC *HS:* Herbert Hoover [San Diego, CA] B: 5/28/1955, San Francisco, CA *Drafted:* 1978 Round 2 Den
1978 Det: 16 G. **1979** Det: 15 G; KR 1-0; **1** Fum TD; 6 Pt; 1 Fum.
1980 Det: 16 G. **1981** Det: 16 G. **1982** Det: 9 G; Int 1-7; 5 Sac. **1983** Det: 15 G; 13.5 Sac. **1984** Det: 16 G; 10 Sac. **1985** Det: 16 G; Int 1-7; 7.5 Sac.
1986 Det: 16 G; 6.5 Sac. **1987** Det: 11 G; 2 Sac. **1988** Min: 5 G.
Total: 151 G; KR 1-0; Int 2-14; 1 Fum TD; 6 Pt; 1 Fum; 44.5 Sac.

BILLY GAY Gay, William Theodore 5′11″, 180 **DB**
(Bib) *Col:* Notre Dame *HS:* Tilden [Chicago, IL] B: 11/12/1927, Chicago, IL *Drafted:* 1950 Round 7 ChiC
1951 ChiC: 3 G.

KENT GAYDOS Gaydos, Kent Bryan 6′6″, 225 **WR**
Col: Florida State *HS:* Winter Park [FL] B: 9/8/1949, South Bend, IN
Drafted: 1972 Round 12 Oak
1975 GB: 4 G.

CHUCK GAYER Gayer, Walter Edward 5′11″, 205 **T**
Col: St. Mary's (Minn.); Creighton *HS:* Janesville [MN]; St. Mary's HS [Winona, MN] B: 7/29/1901, Janesville, MN D: 1/1961
1926 Dul: 9 G.

RASHID GAYLE Gayle, Rashid Ali 5′8″, 175 **DB**
Col: Boise State *HS:* Roseville [CA] B: 4/16/1974, New York, NY
1996 Jac: 2 G.

SHAUN GAYLE Gayle, Shaun LaNard 5′11″, 198 **DB**
Col: Ohio State *HS:* Bethel [Hampton, VA] B: 3/8/1962, Newport News, VA *Drafted:* 1984 Round 10 ChiB
1990 ChiB: 1 Sac. **1993** ChiB: 1 Sac. **1995** SD: **1** Fum TD.
Total: 1 Fum TD; 2 Sac.

		Interceptions			Tot
Year Team	**G**	**Int**	**Yds**	**TD**	**TD**
1984 ChiB	15	1	-1	0	0
1985 ChiB	16	0	0	0	0
1986 ChiB	16	1	13	0	0
1987 ChiB	8	1	20	1	1
1988 ChiB	4	1	0	0	0
1989 ChiB	14	3	39	0	0
1990 ChiB	16	2	5	0	0
1991 ChiB	12	1	11	0	0
1992 ChiB	11	2	39	0	0
1993 ChiB	16	0	0	0	0
1994 ChiB	16	2	33	0	0
1995 SD	16	2	99	1	2
NFL Total	160	16	258	2	3

DOUG GAYNOR Gaynor, Douglas 6′2″, 205 **QB**
Col: Fresno City Coll. CA (J.C.); Long Beach State *HS:* Roosevelt [Fresno, CA] B: 7/5/1963, Fresno, CA *Drafted:* 1986 Round 4 Cin
1986 Cin: 1 G; Pass 3-3 100.0%, 30 10.00; Rush 1-4 4.0.

FRANK GAZIANO Gaziano, Francis Joseph 5′8″, 218 **G**
Col: Holy Cross *HS:* Waltham [MA] B: 5/2/1916, Realemonte, Italy
1944 Bos: 9 G.

RON GEATER Geater, Ronald Ray 6′6″, 272 **DE**
Col: Iowa *HS:* Marion [IA] B: 4/23/1969, Marion, IA *Drafted:* 1992 Round 7 Den
1992 Den: 3 G.

JUMPY GEATHERS Geathers, James Allen 6′7″, 283 **DE-NT-DT**
Col: Wichita State *HS:* Choppee [Georgetown, SC] B: 6/26/1960, Georgetown, SC *Drafted:* 1984 Round 2 NO
1984 NO: 16 G; 6 Sac. **1985** NO: 16 G; 6.5 Sac. **1986** NO: 16 G; 9 Sac.
1987 NO: 1 G. **1988** NO: 16 G; 3.5 Sac. **1989** NO: 15 G; 1 Sac. **1990** Was: 9 G; 3 Sac. **1991** Was: 16 G; 4.5 Sac. **1992** Was: 16 G; 5 Sac. **1993** Atl: 14 G; 3.5 Sac. **1994** Atl: 16 G; 8 Sac. **1995** Atl: 16 G; 7 Sac. **1996** Den: 16 G; 5 Sac. **Total:** 183 G; 62.0 Sac.

KEN GEDDES Geddes, Kenneth Lewis 6′3″, 235 **LB**
Col: Nebraska *HS:* Boys Town [NE] B: 9/27/1946, Jacksonville, FL
Drafted: 1970 Round 7 Det
1971 LARm: 14 G. **1972** LARm: 2 G. **1973** LARm: 14 G. **1974** LARm: 14 G; Int 2-15. **1975** LARm: 14 G; Int 1-4. **1976** Sea: 11 G. **1977** Sea: 14 G; Int 3-9. **1978** Sea: 12 G; PR 1-0; 1 Fum. **Total:** 95 G; PR 1-0; Int 6-28; 1 Fum.

BOB GEDDES Geddes, Robert Eric 6′2″, 240 **LB**
Col: Riverside CC CA; UCLA *HS:* Riverside Polytechnic [CA]
B: 4/22/1946, Seattle, WA *Drafted:* 1970 Round 14 LARm
1972 Den: 14 G. **1973** NE: 2 G. **1974** NE: 9 G; Int 2-32 1 TD; 6 Pt.
1975 NE: 13 G. **Total:** 38 G; Int 2-32 1 TD; 6 Pt.

GENE GEDMAN Gedman, Eugene William 5′11″, 195 **HB**
(The Baron) *Col:* Indiana *HS:* Duquesne [PA] B: 1/9/1932, Duquesne, PA D: 8/19/1974, Chicago, IL *Drafted:* 1953 Round 2 Det
1953 Det: PR 4-10 2.5; KR 2-47 23.5. **1957** Det: Pass 2-0; KR 6-158 26.3.
1958 Det: Pass 3-2 66.7%, 111 37.00 1 TD; KR 7-131 18.7.
Total: Pass 5-2 40.0%, 111 22.20 1 TD; PR 4-10 2.5; KR 15-336 22.4.

		Rushing				Receiving					Tot
Year Team	**G**	**Att**	**Yds**	**Avg**	**TD**	**Rec**	**Yds**	**Avg**	**TD**	**Fum**	**TD**
1953 Det	12	83	255	3.1	3	14	121	8.6	0	0	3
1956 Det	12	135	479	3.5	7	15	142	9.5	1	3	8
1957 Det	10	67	278	4.1	3	10	135	13.5	0	1	3
1958 Det	11	92	209	2.3	4	14	106	7.6	3	3	7
NFL Total	45	377	1221	3.2	17	53	504	9.5	4	7	21

CHRIS GEDNEY Gedney, Christopher Joseph 6′5″, 258 **TE**
Col: Syracuse *HS:* Liverpool [NY] B: 8/9/1970, Wilmington, DE
Drafted: 1993 Round 3 ChiB
1997 Ariz: Rush 1-15 15.0; KR 2-26 13.0. **1998** Ariz: KR 2-12 6.0.
Total: Rush 1-15 15.0; KR 4-38 9.5.

		Receiving				
Year Team	**G**	**Rec**	**Yds**	**Avg**	**TD**	**Fum**
1993 ChiB	7	10	98	9.8	0	1
1994 ChiB	7	13	157	12.1	3	1
1995 ChiB	14	5	52	10.4	0	0
1997 Ariz	16	23	261	11.3	4	1
1998 Ariz	16	22	271	12.3	1	1
NFL Total	60	73	839	11.5	8	4

MARK GEHRING Gehring, Mark 6′4″, 235 **TE**
Col: Olympic Coll. WA (J.C.); Eastern Washington *HS:* Mount Rainier [Des Moines, WA] B: 4/16/1964, Burien, WA
1987 Hou: 6 G; Rec 5-64 12.8 1 TD; 6 Pt.

BRUCE GEHRKE Gehrke, Bruce R 6′2″, 190 **OE-DE**
Col: Columbia *HS:* Sewanhaka [Floral Park, NY] B: 9/12/1924, Long Island, NY D: 4/6/1976, Mineola, NY *Drafted:* 1948 Round 4 NYG
1948 NYG: 8 G; Rec 9-109 12.1 1 TD; 6 Pt.

FRED GEHRKE Gehrke, Clarence Fred 5′11″, 189 **HB-DB-TB**
Col: Utah *HS:* South [Salt Lake City, UT] B: 4/24/1918, Salt Lake City, UT
1940 Cle: Pass 1-0. **1946** LARm: Pass 1-1 100.0%, 29 29.00.
1947 LARm: Scor 13, 1-1 100.0% FG, 4-4 100.0% XK. **1948** LARm: Pass 1-0; Scor 19, 1-1 100.0% XK. **1949** LARm: Scor 32, 0-1 FG, 2-3 66.7% XK. **Total:** Pass 3-1 33.3%, 29 9.67; Scor 154, 1-2 50.0% FG, 7-8 87.5% XK.

Year Team	G	Rushing Att	Yds	Avg	TD	Receiving Rec	Yds	Avg	TD
1940 Cle	3	0	0	—	0	1	-2	-2.0	0
1945 Cle	10	74	467	**6.3**	7	8	90	11.3	1
1946 LARm	10	71	371	**5.2**	3	11	83	7.5	2
1947 LARm	11	59	304	5.2	0	6	19	3.2	0
1948 LARm	12	56	246	4.4	1	16	173	10.8	1
1949 LARm	12	58	203	3.5	2	9	140	15.6	2
1950 ChiC-SF	11	25	73	2.9	1	5	26	5.2	1
1950 ChiC	7	3	4	1.3	0	2	-3	-1.5	0
1950 SF	4	22	69	3.1	1	3	29	9.7	1
NFL Total	69	343	1664	4.9	14	56	529	9.4	7

Year Team	Punt Returns Ret	Yds	Avg	TD	Kickoff Returns Ret	Yds	Avg	TD
1945 Cle	8	120	**15.0**	0	9	173	19.2	0
1946 LARm	8	59	7.4	0	8	186	23.3	0
1947 LARm	4	112	28.0	**1**	2	29	14.5	0
1948 LARm	19	217	11.4	0	17	464	27.3	**1**
1950 ChiC-SF	5	44	8.8	0	2	57	28.5	0
1950 SF	5	44	8.8	0	2	57	28.5	0
NFL Total	44	552	12.5	1	38	909	23.9	1

Year Team	Interceptions Int	Yds	TD	Fum	Tot TD
1945 Cle	4	16	0	3	8
1946 LARm	3	63	0	2	5
1947 LARm	1	0	0	3	1
1948 LARm	2	29	0	4	3
1949 LARm	0	0	0	0	5
1950 ChiC-SF	3	23	0	2	2
1950 ChiC	3	23	0	0	0
1950 SF	0	0	0	2	2
NFL Total	13	131	0	14	24

JACK GEHRKE Gehrke, John Fred 6′0″, 178 **WR**
Col: Utah *HS:* South [Salt Lake City, UT] B: 1/14/1946, Salt Lake City, UT *Drafted:* 1968 Round 10 KC
1968 KC: 2 G. **1969** Cin: 10 G; Pass 1-1 100.0%, 13 13.00. **1971** Den: 14 G; Pass 2-1 50.0%, 19 9.50; Rush 1-2 2.0; Rec 14-254 18.1. **Total:** 26 G; Pass 3-2 66.7%, 32 10.67; Rush 1-2 2.0; Rec 14-254 18.1.

CHRIS GEILE Geile, Christopher L 6′4″, 305 **OG**
Col: Chabot Coll. CA (J.C.); Eastern Illinois *HS:* Amador Valley [Pleasanton, CA] B: 4/14/1964, Anaheim, CA
1987 Det: 3 G.

CHUCK GELATKA Gelatka, Charles Thomas 6′1″, 185 **OE-DB-DE**
Col: Mississippi State *HS:* Francis W. Parker [Chicago, IL] B: 1/28/1914, Chicago, IL *Drafted:* 1937 Round 10 NYG
1937 NYG: 4 G; Rec 1-17 17.0. **1938** NYG: 10 G; Rec 7-106 15.1 1 TD; Int **1** TD; Tot TD 2; 12 Pt. **1939** NYG: 10 G; Rec 6-71 11.8. **1940** NYG: 10 G; Rec 6-56 9.3. **Total:** 34 G; Rec 20-250 12.5 1 TD; Int 1 TD; Tot TD 2; 12 Pt.

STAN GELBAUGH Gelbaugh, Stanley Morris 6′3″, 208 **QB**
Col: Maryland *HS:* Cumberland Valley [Mechanicsburg, PA] B: 12/4/1962, Carlisle, PA *Drafted:* 1986 Round 6 Dal

Year Team	G	Passing Att	Comp	Comp%	Yds	YPA	TD	Int	Rating
1989 Buf	1	0	0	—	0	—	0	0	—
1991 Pho	6	118	61	51.7	674	5.71	3	10	42.1
1992 Sea	10	255	121	47.5	1307	5.13	6	11	52.9
1993 Sea	1	5	3	60.0	39	7.80	0	1	45.0
1994 Sea	1	11	7	63.6	80	7.27	1	0	115.7
1996 Sea	1	2	0	0.0	0	0.00	0	0	39.6
NFL Total	20	391	192	49.1	2100	5.37	10	22	50.5

Year Team	Rushing Att	Yds	Avg	TD	Fum
1989 Buf	1	-3	-3.0	0	0
1991 Pho	9	23	2.6	0	4
1992 Sea	16	79	4.9	0	9
1993 Sea	1	-1	-1.0	0	1
1994 Sea	1	10	10.0	0	0
NFL Total	28	108	3.9	0	14

PETE GENT Gent, George Davis 6′4″, 205 **WR**
Col: Michigan State *HS:* Bangor [MI] B: 8/23/1942, Bangor, MI
1968 Dal: Rush 2-(-5) -2.5. **Total:** Rush 2-(-5) -2.5.

Year Team	G	Receiving Rec	Yds	Avg	TD	Fum
1964 Dal	7	0	0	—	0	0
1965 Dal	10	16	233	14.6	2	1
1966 Dal	14	27	474	17.6	1	0
1967 Dal	7	9	88	9.8	1	0
1968 Dal	10	16	194	12.1	0	0
NFL Total	48	68	989	14.5	4	1

BYRON GENTRY Gentry, Byron B 5′11″, 227 **G**
(Pills) *Col:* USC *HS:* Corcoran [CA] B: 10/20/1913 D: 2/10/1992, Templeton, CA
1937 Pit: 3 G. **1938** Pit: 11 G. **1939** Pit: 11 G. **Total:** 25 G.

CURT GENTRY Gentry, Curtis William 6′0″, 185 **DB**
Col: Maryland East. Shore *HS:* Portsmouth [OH] B: 8/8/1941, Waco, TX *Drafted:* 1966 Round 17 ChiB
1966 ChiB: 13 G; Int 1-0; 1 Fum. **1967** ChiB: 14 G; Int 4-25. **1968** ChiB: 11 G; Int 1-7. **Total:** 38 G; Int 6-32; 1 Fum.

DALE GENTRY Gentry, Dale LuAuverene 6′3″, 223 **OE-DE**
Col: St. Mary's (Cal.); Washington State *HS:* Walla Walla [WA] B: 7/2/1917, Umapine, OR D: 1/30/1966
AAFC **1946** LA-A: Rush 5-29 5.8 1 TD; PR 1-14 14.0. **Total:** Rush 5-29 5.8 1 TD; PR 1-14 14.0.

Year Team	G	Receiving Rec	Yds	Avg	TD	Tot TD
1946 LA-A	14	24	341	14.2	3	5
1947 LA-A	14	22	352	16.0	2	2
1948 LA-A	14	28	308	11.0	0	0
AAFC Total	42	74	1001	13.5	5	7

DENNIS GENTRY Gentry, Dennis Louis 5′8″, 181 **RB-WR**
Col: Baylor *HS:* Dunbar [Lubbock, TX] B: 2/10/1959, Lubbock, TX *Drafted:* 1982 Round 4 ChiB
1982 ChiB: PR 17-89 5.2. **1985** ChiB: PR 0-47. **Total:** PR 17-136 8.0.

Year Team	G	Rushing Att	Yds	Avg	TD	Receiving Rec	Yds	Avg	TD
1982 ChiB	9	4	21	5.3	0	1	9	9.0	0
1983 ChiB	15	16	65	4.1	0	2	8	4.0	0
1984 ChiB	16	21	79	3.8	1	4	29	7.3	0
1985 ChiB	16	30	160	5.3	2	5	77	15.4	0
1986 ChiB	15	11	103	9.4	1	19	238	12.5	0
1987 ChiB	12	6	41	6.8	0	17	183	10.8	1
1988 ChiB	16	7	86	12.3	1	33	486	14.7	3
1989 ChiB	16	17	106	6.2	0	39	463	11.9	1
1990 ChiB	14	11	43	3.9	0	23	320	13.9	2
1991 ChiB	15	9	58	6.4	0	16	149	9.3	0
1992 ChiB	15	5	2	0.4	0	12	114	9.5	0
NFL Total	159	137	764	5.6	5	171	2076	12.1	7

Year Team	Kickoff Returns Ret	Yds	Avg	TD	Fum	Tot TD
1982 ChiB	9	161	17.9	0	4	0
1983 ChiB	7	130	18.6	0	1	0
1984 ChiB	11	209	19.0	0	0	1
1985 ChiB	18	466	25.9	1	0	3
1986 ChiB	20	576	**28.8**	**1**	0	3
1987 ChiB	25	621	24.8	1	2	2
1988 ChiB	27	578	21.4	0	2	4
1989 ChiB	28	667	23.8	0	1	1
1990 ChiB	18	388	21.6	0	1	2
1991 ChiB	13	227	17.5	0	1	0
1992 ChiB	16	330	20.6	0	0	0
NFL Total	192	4353	22.7	3	12	16

LEE GENTRY Gentry, Elmer Lee 6′0″, 198 **HB**
Col: Tulsa B: 12/1/1918, Shawnee, OK D: 12/1992 *Drafted:* 1941 Round 20 Was
1941 Was: 5 G; Rush 5-13 2.6; Int 1-9.

WELDON GENTRY Gentry, Weldon Christopher 5′10″, 195 **G**
(Cash; Spot) *Col:* Arkansas; Oklahoma *HS:* Lawton [OK] B: 9/9/1906, Lawton, OK D: 3/19/1990, Oklahoma City, OK
1930 Prov: 4 G. **1931** Prov: 7 G. **Total:** 11 G.

CARL GEORGE George, Carl W 5′11″, 175 **G**
Col: Carroll (Wis.); Loras *HS:* Ashland [WI] B: 3/13/1892, NY D: 10/8/1965, Union County, OH
1922 Rac: 3 G.

ED GEORGE George, Edward Gary 6′4″, 270 **OT**
Col: Ferrum; Wake Forest *HS:* E.C. Glass [Lynchburg, VA] B: 8/10/1946, Norfolk, VA *Drafted:* 1970 Round 4 Pit
1975 Bal: 12 G. **1976** Phi: 14 G. **1977** Phi: 14 G. **1978** Phi: 16 G. **Total:** 56 G.

EDDIE GEORGE George, Edward Nathan 6′3″, 240 **RB**
Col: Ohio State *HS:* Abington [PA]; Fork Union Mil. Acad. [VA] B: 9/24/1973, Philadelphia, PA *Drafted:* 1996 Round 1 Hou
1997 Ten: Scor 1 2XP. **1998** Ten: Scor 1 2XP. **Total:** Scor 2 2XP.

Year Team	G	Rushing Att	Yds	Avg	TD	Receiving Rec	Yds	Avg	TD	Fum	Tot TD
1996 Hou	16	335	1368	4.1	8	23	182	7.9	0	3	8

1997 Ten	16	357	1399	3.9	6	7	44	6.3	1	4	7
1998 Ten	16	348	1294	3.7	5	37	310	8.4	1	7	6
NFL Total	48	1040	4061	3.9	19	67	536	8.0	2	14	21

JEFF GEORGE George, Jeffrey L 6′1″, 185 **DB**
Col: Highland CC KS; Illinois State *HS:* Atchison [KS] B: 12/24/1957, Atchison, KS
1987 TB: 2 G.

JEFF GEORGE George, Jeffrey Scott 6′4″, 218 **QB**
Col: Purdue; Illinois *HS:* Warren Central [Indianapolis, IN]
B: 12/8/1967, Indianapolis, IN *Drafted:* 1990 Round 1 Ind

		Passing							
Year Team	**G**	**Att**	**Comp**	**Comp%**	**Yds**	**YPA**	**TD**	**Int**	**Rating**
1990 Ind	13	334	181	54.2	2152	6.44	16	13	73.8
1991 Ind	16	485	292	60.2	2910	6.00	10	12	73.8
1992 Ind	10	306	167	54.6	1963	6.42	7	15	61.5
1993 Ind	13	407	234	57.5	2526	6.21	8	6	76.3
1994 Atl	16	524	322	61.5	3734	7.13	23	18	83.3
1995 Atl	16	557	336	60.3	4143	7.44	24	11	89.5
1996 Atl	3	99	56	56.6	698	7.05	3	3	76.1
1997 Oak	16	521	290	55.7	**3917**	7.52	29	9	91.2
1998 Oak	8	169	93	55.0	1186	7.02	4	5	72.7
NFL Total	111	3402	1971	57.9	23229	6.83	124	92	79.7

	Rushing				
Year Team	**Att**	**Yds**	**Avg**	**TD**	**Fum**
1990 Ind	11	2	0.2	1	4
1991 Ind	16	36	2.3	0	8
1992 Ind	14	26	1.9	1	6
1993 Ind	13	39	3.0	0	4
1994 Atl	30	66	2.2	0	**12**
1995 Atl	27	17	0.6	0	6
1996 Atl	5	10	2.0	0	3
1997 Oak	17	44	2.6	0	7
1998 Oak	8	2	0.3	0	7
NFL Total	141	242	1.7	2	57

MATT GEORGE George, Matthew Michael 5′11″, 190 **P-K**
Col: Chapman *HS:* Canyon [Canyon Country, CA] B: 1/13/1975, Santa Clarita, CA
1998 Pit: 1 G; Scor 2, 0-1 FG, 2-2 100.0% XK.

RAY GEORGE George, Raymond Edward 6′0″, 229 **T**
Col: USC *HS:* Loyola [Los Angeles, CA] B: 1/7/1918, St. Louis, MO
D: 1/12/1995, Costa Mesa, CA *Drafted:* 1939 Round 8 Det
1939 Det: 11 G. **1940** Phi: 2 G. **Total:** 13 G.

RON GEORGE George, Ronald Lawrence 6′2″, 233 **LB**
Col: Air Force; Stanford *HS:* American School [Heidelberg, Germany]
B: 3/20/1970, Heidelberg, Germany *Drafted:* 1993 Round 5 Atl
1993 Atl: 12 G; 1 Sac. **1994** Atl: 16 G. **1995** Atl: 16 G; KR 3-45 15.0. **1996** Atl: 16 G; 2 Sac. **1997** Min: 16 G; KR 1-10 10.0. **1998** KC: 16 G. **Total:** 92 G; KR 4-55 13.8; 3 Sac.

SPENCER GEORGE George, Spencer James 5′9″, 202 **RB**
Col: Rice *HS:* Hamshire-Fannett [Hamshire, TX] B: 10/28/1973, Beaumont, TX
1997 Ten: 5 G. **1998** Ten: 5 G. **Total:** 10 G.

STEVE GEORGE George, Stephen Elwood 6′5″, 265 **DT**
Col: Houston *HS:* Plano [TX] B: 4/11/1951, Sulphur Springs, TX
Drafted: 1974 Round 3 StL
1974 StL: 13 G. **1976** Atl: 1 G. **Total:** 14 G.

TIM GEORGE George, Timothy Anderson 6′5″, 225 **WR**
Col: Carson-Newman *HS:* Alcoa [TN] B: 10/4/1951, Alcoa, TN
Drafted: 1973 Round 3 Cin
1973 Cin: 12 G; Rec 2-28 14.0. **1974** Cle: 8 G. **Total:** 20 G; Rec 2-28 14.0.

BILL GEORGE George, William J 6′2″, 237 **LB-OG-DT**
Col: Wake Forest *HS:* Waynesburg [PA] B: 10/27/1929, Waynesburg, PA D: 9/30/1982, Davis Junction, IL *Drafted:* 1951 Round 2 ChiB
HOF: 1974
1953 ChiB: Scor 0-1 FG. **1954** ChiB: Scor 25, 4-6 66.7% FG, 13-14 92.9% XK. **1958** ChiB: Scor 1, 1-1 100.0% XK. **1961** ChiB: Scor 0-1 FG. **Total:** Scor 26, 4-8 50.0% FG, 14-15 93.3% XK.

		Interceptions		
Year Team	**G**	**Int**	**Yds**	**TD**
1952 ChiB	12	0	0	0
1953 ChiB	12	0	0	0
1954 ChiB	12	2	9	0
1955 ChiB	12	2	13	0
1956 ChiB	12	2	9	0
1957 ChiB	12	0	0	0
1958 ChiB	12	1	5	0
1959 ChiB	12	2	20	0
1960 ChiB	12	1	12	0
1961 ChiB	14	3	18	0
1962 ChiB	13	2	26	0
1963 ChiB	14	1	4	0
1964 ChiB	8	2	28	0
1965 ChiB	2	0	0	0
1966 LARm	14	0	0	0
NFL Total	173	18	144	0

SID GEPFORD Gepford, Sidney 5′6″, 152 **HB**
Col: Millikin; Bethany (W.V.) *HS:* Stephen Decatur [Decatur, IL]
B: 12/1896, Decatur, IL Deceased
1920 Sta: 2 G.

JOHN GERAK Gerak, John Matthew 6′3″, 290 **OG-C**
Col: Penn State *HS:* Struthers [OH] B: 1/6/1970, Youngstown, OH
Drafted: 1993 Round 3 Min
1993 Min: 4 G. **1994** Min: 13 G. **1995** Min: 16 G; Rec 1-3 3.0; KR 1-19 19.0. **1996** Min: 14 G; KR 1-13 13.0. **1997** StL: 16 G. **Total:** 63 G; Rec 1-3 3.0; KR 2-32 16.0.

PATSY GERARDI Gerardi, Pasqual 165 **OE**
Col: No College B: 2/27/1892, Washington, DC D: 6/13/1973, Kensington, MD
1921 Was: 1 G.

WOODY GERBER Gerber, Elwood George 6′0″, 223 **G**
Col: Alabama *HS:* Naperville Central [IL] B: 8/7/1920, Kankakee, IL
1941 Phi: 5 G. **1942** Phi: 11 G; Int 1-0. **Total:** 16 G; Int 1-0.

TOM GEREDINE Geredine, Thomas Allen 6′2″, 195 **WR**
Col: Northeast Missouri State *HS:* Central [Kansas City, MO]
B: 6/17/1950, St. Louis, MO *Drafted:* 1973 Round 4 Atl
1973 Atl: Rush 1-(-3) -3.0; Rec 12-231 19.3 1 TD. **1974** Atl: Rec 4-69 17.3. **1976** LARm: Rush 1-8 8.0; Rec 1-23 23.0 1 TD. **Total:** Rush 2-5 2.5; Rec 17-323 19.0 2 TD.

		Kickoff Returns				
Year Team	**G**	**Ret**	**Yds**	**Avg**	**TD**	**Fum**
1973 Atl	12	9	211	23.4	0	1
1974 Atl	12	9	219	24.3	0	0
1976 LARm	10	9	181	20.1	0	0
NFL Total	34	27	611	22.6	0	1

ROY GERELA Gerela, Carl Roy 5′10″, 185 **K**
Col: New Mexico State *HS:* Rockville [MD]; Kalani HS [Honolulu, HI]
B: 4/2/1948, Sarrail, Canada *Drafted:* 1969 Round 4 Hou

		Punting		
Year Team	**G**	**Punts**	**Yds**	**Avg**
1969 Hou	14	41	1656	40.4
1970 Hou	14	0	0	—
1971 Pit	14	0	0	—
1972 Pit	14	1	29	29.0
1973 Pit	14	0	0	—
1974 Pit	14	0	0	—
1975 Pit	14	0	0	—
1976 Pit	14	0	0	—
1977 Pit	14	0	0	—
1978 Pit	16	0	0	—
1979 SD	3	0	0	—
NFL Total	145	42	1685	40.1

	Scoring							
Year Team	**Pts**	**FG**	**FGA**	**FG%**	**XK**	**XKA**	**XK%**	**Fum**
1969 Hou	86	19	40	47.5	29	29	100.0	1
1970 Hou	77	18	32	56.3	23	23	100.0	0
1971 Pit	78	17	27	63.0	27	27	100.0	0
1972 Pit	119	28	41	68.3	35	36	97.2	0
1973 Pit	123	29	43	67.4	36	37	97.3	0
1974 Pit	93	20	29	69.0	33	35	94.3	0
1975 Pit	95	17	21	81.0	44	46	95.7	0
1976 Pit	82	14	26	53.8	40	43	93.0	0
1977 Pit	61	9	14	64.3	34	37	91.9	0
1978 Pit	80	12	26	46.2	44	45	97.8	0
1979 SD	9	1	7	14.3	6	7	85.7	0
NFL Total	903	184	306	60.1	351	365	96.2	1

CHRIS GERHARD Gerhard, Christopher Anthony 5′10″, 185 **DB**
Col: East Stroudsburg *HS:* Catasauqua [PA]; Fork Union Military Academy [VA] B: 7/6/1964, Allentown, PA
1987 Phi: 3 G.

TOM GERHART Gerhart, Thomas Edward 6′1″, 195 **SAF**
Col: Salem (NC); Ohio U. *HS:* Cedar Crest [Lebanon, PA] B: 6/4/1965, Lebanon, PA
1992 Phi: 1 G.

JOE GERI Geri, Joseph Steven 5′10″, 185 **TB-HB**
Col: Georgia *HS:* Phoenixville [PA] B: 10/20/1924, Phoenixville, PA
Drafted: 1949 Round 4 Pit
1949 Pit: PR 2-28 14.0; Scor 45, 1-1 100.0% FG, 12-13 92.3% XK. **1950** Pit: Rec 1-33 33.0 1 TD; Scor 64, 8-14 57.1% FG, 22-22 100.0% XK. **1951** Pit: Rec 3-59 19.7 1 TD; KR 2-108 54.0; Scor 67, 7-14 50.0% FG, 22-23 95.7% XK. **1952** ChiC: Scor 28, 2-18 11.1% FG, 22-24

91.7% XK. **Total:** Rec 4-92 23.0 2 TD; PR 2-28 14.0; KR 2-108 54.0; Scor 204, 18-47 38.3% FG, 78-82 95.1% XK.

		Passing							
Year Team	G	Att	Comp	Comp%	Yds	YPA	TD	Int	Rating
1949 Pit	12	77	31	40.3	554	7.19	5	5	60.2
1950 Pit	12	113	41	36.3	866	7.66	6	15	42.4
1951 Pit	12	90	29	32.2	506	5.62	2	7	27.4
1952 ChiC	12	0	0	—	0	—	0	0	—
NFL Total	48	280	101	36.1	1926	6.88	13	27	36.7

	Rushing				Punting				Tot
Year Team	Att	Yds	Avg	TD	Punts	Yds	Avg	Fum	TD
1949 Pit	133	543	4.1	5	43	1856	43.2	4	5
1950 Pit	**188**	705	3.8	2	55	2237	40.7	12	3
1951 Pit	90	252	2.8	3	73	2787	38.2	5	4
1952 ChiC	20	50	2.5	0	29	1094	37.7	0	0
NFL Total	431	1550	3.6	10	200	7974	39.9	21	12

JIMMY GERMAN German, James 6'0", 180 **TB-DB**
Col: Centre *HS:* Manual [Louisville, KY] B: 11/6/1917, Louisville, KY D: 8/8/1945, Burma *Drafted:* 1939 Round 9 Was
1939 Was: 8 G; Pass 12-6 50.0%, 97 8.08 1 TD 2 Int; Rush 17-58 3.4 2 TD; 12 Pt. **1940** ChiC: 1 G. **Total:** 9 G; Pass 12-6 50.0%, 97 8.08 1 TD 2 Int; Rush 17-58 3.4 2 TD; 12 Pt.

JAMMI GERMAN German, Jammi Darnell 6'0", 187 **WR**
Col: Miami (Fla.) *HS:* Fort Myers [FL] B: 7/4/1974, Fort Myers, FL *Drafted:* 1998 Round 3 Atl
1998 Atl: 6 G.

WILLIE GERMANY Germany, Willie James Jr. 6'0", 192 **DB**
Col: Morgan State *HS:* Howard [Ellicott City, MD] B: 5/9/1948, Columbus, GA *Drafted:* 1971 Round 7 Was
1972 Atl: 12 G; KR 2-5 2.5; 2 Fum. **1973** Det: 6 G; KR 1-0. **1975** Hou: 14 G; Int 2-15; **1** Fum TD; 6 Pt. **1976** NE: 10 G. **Total:** 42 G; KR 3-5 1.7; Int 2-15; 1 Fum TD; 6 Pt; 2 Fum.

CARL GERSBACH Gersbach, Carl Robert 6'1", 230 **LB**
Col: Duke; West Chester *HS:* Swarthmore [PA] B: 1/8/1947, Syracuse, NY
1970 Phi: 6 G. **1971** Min: 13 G. **1972** Min: 14 G. **1973** SD: 14 G; Int 1-9. **1974** SD: 12 G; Int 1-0. **1975** ChiB: 10 G; Int 1-4. **1976** StL: 7 G. **Total:** 76 G; Int 3-13.

RICK GERVAIS Gervais, Richard Paul 5'11", 190 **DB**
Col: Stanford *HS:* Bend [OR] B: 11/4/1959, Bend, OR
1981 SF: 8 G. **1982** SF: 8 G. **1983** SF: 5 G; 1 Sac. **Total:** 21 G; 1 Sac.

JOHN GESEK Gesek, John Christian Jr. 6'5", 282 **OG-C**
Col: Diablo Valley Coll. CA (J.C.); Sacramento State *HS:* San Ramon Valley [Danville, CA]; Bellflower HS [CA] B: 2/18/1963, San Francisco, CA *Drafted:* 1987 Round 10 LARd
1987 LARd: 3 G. **1988** LARd: 12 G; 1 Fum. **1989** LARd: 16 G. **1990** Dal: 15 G. **1991** Dal: 16 G. **1992** Dal: 16 G; Rec 1-4 4.0; 1 Fum. **1993** Dal: 14 G. **1994** Was: 15 G. **1995** Was: 16 G. **Total:** 123 G; Rec 1-4 4.0; 2 Fum.

GORHAM GETCHELL Getchell, Charles Gorham 6'4", 225 **OE-DE**
(Getch) *Col:* Temple *HS:* Jenkintown [PA] B: 8/14/1920, Abington, PA D: 7/7/1980, Manhattan Beach, CA
AAFC **1947** BalA: 8 G; Rec 2-17 8.5.

CHARLIE GETTY Getty, Charles Matthew 6'4", 265 **OT-OG**
Col: Penn State *HS:* Pompton Lakes [NJ] B: 7/24/1952, Pompton Lakes, NJ *Drafted:* 1974 Round 2 KC
1974 KC: 14 G. **1975** KC: 14 G. **1976** KC: 14 G; Rec 1-(-5) -5.0. **1977** KC: 14 G; KR 1-15 15.0. **1978** KC: 16 G. **1979** KC: 16 G. **1980** KC: 6 G. **1981** KC: 16 G. **1982** KC: 9 G. **1983** GB: 15 G. **Total:** 134 G; Rec 1-(-5) -5.0; KR 1-15 15.0.

LEE GETZ Getz, E. Lee 6'3", 250 **OG**
Col: Rutgers *HS:* Voorhees [Glen Gardener, NJ] B: 4/2/1964, Hunterton Co., NJ
1987 KC: 3 G.

FRED GETZ Getz, Frederick 6'1", 192 **OE**
Col: Tennessee-Chattanooga B: 1909, Memphis, TN Deceased
1930 Bkn: 1 G.

BILL GEYER Geyer, William Herbert Jr. 5'10", 173 **HB-DB**
Col: Colgate *HS:* Bloomfield [NJ] B: 10/3/1919, Bloomfield, NJ *Drafted:* 1942 Round 9 ChiB
1942 ChiB: Rec 1-22 22.0; PR 2-28 14.0. **1943** ChiB: Rec 5-123 24.6 2 TD; PR 1-8 8.0; KR 2-71 35.5; Int 2-0. **1946** ChiB: KR 1-14 14.0. **Total:** Rec 6-145 24.2 2 TD; PR 3-36 12.0; KR 3-85 28.3; Int 2-0.

		Rushing				Tot
Year Team	G	Att	Yds	Avg	TD	TD
1942 ChiB	5	9	18	2.0	0	0
1943 ChiB	3	16	36	2.3	1	4
1946 ChiB	1	0	0	—	0	0
NFL Total	9	25	54	2.2	1	4

LOU GHECAS Ghecas, Louis James 5'9", 175 **HB-DB**
Col: Georgetown B: 7/14/1918, Danbury, CT D: 5/13/1997, Wilmington, DE
1941 Phi: 8 G; Rush 2-0; PR 1-11 11.0; KR 1-17 17.0.

MILT GHEE Ghee, Milton Pomeroy Jr. 5'7", 167 **BB-TB**
Col: Dartmouth *HS:* Oak Park [IL] B: 11/17/1891, Wilmette, IL D: 3/16/1975, Corte Madera, CA
1920 ChiT: 8 G. **1921** Cle: 5 G; Pass 1 TD; Rush 2 TD; 12 Pt. **Total:** 13 G; Pass 1 TD; Rush 2 TD; 12 Pt.

VERN GHERSANICH Ghersanich, Vernon George 5'11", 219 **G-LB**
Col: Auburn *HS:* Warren Easton [New Orleans, LA] B: 12/22/1919, New Orleans, LA Deceased
1943 ChiC: 4 G; Int 1-19.

RALPH GIACOMARRO Giacomarro, Ralph J 6'1", 190 **P**
Col: Penn State *HS:* Saddle Brook [NJ] B: 1/17/1961, Passaic, NJ *Drafted:* 1983 Round 10 Atl
1983 Atl: Pass 1-1 100.0%, 23 23.00; Rush 2-13 6.5. **1984** Atl: Rush 1-0. **Total:** Pass 1-1 100.0%, 23 23.00; Rush 3-13 4.3.

		Punting			
Year Team	G	Punts	Yds	Avg	Fum
1983 Atl	16	70	2823	40.3	1
1984 Atl	16	68	2855	42.0	1
1985 Atl	5	29	1157	39.9	0
1987 Den	3	18	757	42.1	0
NFL Total	40	185	7592	41.0	2

LOUIE GIAMMONA Giammona, Louis Jean 5'9", 180 **RB**
Col: Utah State *HS:* Calistoga [CA] B: 3/3/1953, St. Helena, CA *Drafted:* 1976 Round 8 NYJ
1976 NYJ: PR 12-117 9.8. **1979** Phi: PR 5-42 8.4. **1980** Phi: Pass 3-3 100.0%, 55 18.33 1 TD; PR 1-8 8.0. **1982** Phi: Pass 1-0, 1 Int. **Total:** Pass 4-3 75.0%, 55 13.75 1 TD 1 Int; PR 18-167 9.3.

		Rushing				Receiving			
Year Team	G	Att	Yds	Avg	TD	Rec	Yds	Avg	TD
1976 NYJ	14	39	150	3.8	1	15	145	9.7	0
1978 Phi	7	4	6	1.5	0	0	0	—	0
1979 Phi	15	15	38	2.5	0	0	0	—	0
1980 Phi	16	97	361	3.7	4	17	178	10.5	1
1981 Phi	8	35	98	2.8	1	6	54	9.0	1
1982 Phi	9	11	29	2.6	1	8	67	8.4	0
NFL Total	69	201	682	3.4	7	46	444	9.7	2

	Kickoff Returns					Tot
Year Team	Ret	Yds	Avg	TD	Fum	TD
1976 NYJ	23	527	22.9	0	5	1
1978 Phi	12	245	20.4	0	0	0
1979 Phi	15	294	19.6	0	0	0
1980 Phi	7	82	11.7	0	5	5
1981 Phi	1	19	19.0	0	2	2
1982 Phi	0	0	—	0	1	1
NFL Total	58	1167	20.1	0	13	9

HAL GIANCANELLI Giancanelli, Harold Arthur 5'10", 182 **HB-FL**
(Skippy) *Col:* Loyola Marymount *HS:* Abraham Lincoln [Los Angeles, CA] B: 5/21/1929, Farr, CO
1953 Phi: PR 4-11 2.8. **1955** Phi: PR 5-30 6.0. **1956** Phi: PR 4-22 5.5. **Total:** PR 13-63 4.8.

		Rushing				Receiving			
Year Team	G	Att	Yds	Avg	TD	Rec	Yds	Avg	TD
1953 Phi	12	44	131	3.0	1	20	346	17.3	5
1954 Phi	10	33	47	1.4	0	14	195	13.9	4
1955 Phi	12	97	385	4.0	2	25	379	15.2	1
1956 Phi	7	42	148	3.5	1	10	104	10.4	0
NFL Total	41	216	711	3.3	4	69	1024	14.8	10

	Kickoff Returns					Tot
Year Team	Ret	Yds	Avg	TD	Fum	TD
1953 Phi	2	45	22.5	0	5	6
1954 Phi	17	387	22.8	0	1	4
1955 Phi	11	267	24.3	0	8	3
1956 Phi	8	187	23.4	0	2	1
NFL Total	38	886	23.3	0	16	14

MARIO GIANELLI Gianelli, Mario 6'0", 265 **DG-OG**
(Yo-Yo) *Col:* Boston College *HS:* Everett [MA] B: 12/24/1920, Everett, MA *Drafted:* 1945 Round 20 Bos
1948 Phi: 12 G. **1949** Phi: 10 G; Scor **1** Saf; 2 Pt. **1950** Phi: 12 G. **1951** Phi: 10 G. **Total:** 44 G; Scor 1 Saf; 2 Pt.

FRANK GIANNETTI Giannetti, Frank John 6'2", 267 **NT**
Col: Penn State *HS:* Toms River-East [NJ] B: 3/14/1968, Toms River, NJ *Drafted:* 1991 Round 10 Ind
1991 Ind: 3 G.

JACK GIANNONI Giannoni, John Michael 6'2", 225 **OE-DE**
Col: St. Mary's (Cal.) *HS:* Sacramento [CA] B: 8/27/1914, Sacramento, CA
1938 Cle: 3 G.

NICK GIAQUINTO Giaquinto, Nicholas Albert 5'11", 205 **RB**
Col: Bridgeport; Connecticut *HS:* Stratford [CT] B: 4/4/1955, Bridgeport, CT
1980 Mia: PR 7-35 5.0; KR 9-146 16.2; **1** Fum TD. **1981** Mia-Was: KR 1-22 22.0. Mia: KR 1-22 22.0. **1982** Was: PR 5-34 6.8; KR 1-21 21.0. **1983** Was: PR 2-12 6.0; KR 1-0. **Total:** PR 14-81 5.8; KR 12-189 15.8; 1 Fum TD.

		Rushing				Receiving				Tot
Year Team	G	Att	Yds	Avg	TD	Rec	Yds	Avg	TD	TD
1980 Mia	16	5	16	3.2	0	24	192	8.0	1	2
1981 Mia-Was	14	20	104	5.2	0	12	93	7.8	2	2
1981 Mia	8	3	31	10.3	0	7	38	5.4	1	1
1981 Was	6	17	73	4.3	0	5	55	11.0	1	1
1982 Was	7	1	5	5.0	0	2	65	32.5	0	0
1983 Was	16	14	53	3.8	1	27	372	13.8	0	1
NFL Total	53	40	178	4.5	1	65	722	11.1	3	5

BILL GIAVER Giaver, Einar William 5'9", 190 **WB-TB-FB-BB**
Col: Georgia Tech B: 5/29/1898, Chicago, IL Deceased
1922 Ham: 5 G. **1923** RI: 7 G; Rush 4 TD; 24 Pt. **1924** Rac: 10 G. **1925** Ham: 4 G. **1926** Lou: 2 G. **Total:** 28 G; Rush 4 TD; 24 Pt.

JIM GIBBONS Gibbons, James Edwin 6'2", 220 **OE-TE**
(Gib) *Col:* Iowa *HS:* Lindblom [Chicago, IL] B: 9/26/1936, Chicago, IL *Drafted:* 1958 Round 5 Cle
1958 Det: KR 1-4 4.0. **1961** Det: PR 1-14 14.0. **Total:** PR 1-14 14.0; KR 1-4 4.0.

		Receiving				
Year Team	G	Rec	Yds	Avg	TD	Fum
1958 Det	12	25	367	14.7	2	0
1959 Det	12	31	431	13.9	1	2
1960 Det	12	51	604	11.8	2	0
1961 Det	14	45	566	12.6	1	0
1962 Det	14	33	318	9.6	2	0
1963 Det	14	32	412	12.9	1	0
1964 Det	14	45	605	13.4	8	0
1965 Det	13	12	111	9.3	2	0
1966 Det	7	1	2	2.0	1	0
1967 Det	14	10	107	10.7	0	0
1968 Det	14	2	38	19.0	0	0
NFL Total	140	287	3561	12.4	20	2

MIKE GIBBONS Gibbons, Michael Leslie 6'4", 262 **OT**
Col: Southwestern Oklahoma State *HS:* Duncan [OK]; Colorado City HS [TX] B: 1/23/1951, Duncan, OK
1976 NYG: 11 G. **1977** NYG: 5 G. **Total:** 16 G.

DONNIE GIBBS Gibbs, Donald R 6'2", 205 **P**
Col: Texas Christian *HS:* Robert E. Lee [Tyler, TX] B: 12/31/1945, Tyler, TX
1974 NO: 1 G; Punt 3-99 33.0; 2 Fum.

SONNY GIBBS Gibbs, Guy Gilbert Jr. 6'7", 230 **QB**
Col: Texas Christian *HS:* Graham [TX] B: 10/25/1939, Graham, TX *Drafted:* 1962 Round 2 Dal
1964 Det: 2 G; Pass 3-1 33.3%, 3 1.00 1 Int.

PAT GIBBS Gibbs, Patrick Henry 5'10", 188 **DB**
Col: Lamar *HS:* Stark [Orange, TX] B: 4/5/1950, Marshall, TX *Drafted:* 1972 Round 9 Phi
1972 Phi: 2 G; PR 1-8 8.0; KR 3-61 20.3; 1 Fum.

ANDY GIBLER Gibler, James Andrew 6'4", 235 **TE**
Col: Missouri *HS:* Grandview [MO] B: 4/30/1961, Independence, MO
1983 Cin: 2 G.

ROBERT GIBLIN Giblin, Robert James 6'2", 205 **DB**
Col: Houston *HS:* Groves [Port Neches, TX] B: 11/18/1952, Omaha, NE *Drafted:* 1975 Round 4 NYG
1975 NYG: 12 G. **1977** StL: 11 G. **Total:** 23 G.

ABE GIBRON Gibron, Abraham 5'11", 243 **OG-DG**
Col: Valparaiso; Purdue *HS:* Isaac C. Elston [Michigan City, IN] B: 9/22/1925, Michigan City, IN D: 9/23/1997, Belleair, FL *Drafted:* 1949 Round 6 NYG
AAFC **1949** BufA: 10 G; Rec 0-3.

NFL **1950** Cle: 12 G. **1951** Cle: 12 G; KR 1-0. **1952** Cle: 12 G; KR 1-0. **1953** Cle: 10 G. **1954** Cle: 12 G. **1955** Cle: 12 G. **1956** Cle-Phi: 9 G. Cle: 7 G. Phi: 2 G. **1957** Phi: 12 G. **1958** ChiB: 12 G; KR 1-12 12.0. **1959** ChiB: 12 G. **Total:** 115 G; KR 3-12 4.0.

ALEC GIBSON Gibson, Alexander Raymond 6'4", 270 **DE**
Col: Ventura Coll. CA (J.C.); Illinois *HS:* Ventura [CA] B: 12/9/1963, Columbus, OH
1987 Was: 3 G.

ANTONIO GIBSON Gibson, Antonio Marice 6'3", 206 **DB**
Col: Hinds CC MS; Cincinnati *HS:* William B. Murrah [Jackson, MS] B: 7/5/1962, Jackson, MS
1986 NO: 16 G; Int 2-43; 3 Sac. **1987** NO: 10 G; Int 1-17. **1988** NO: 10 G; 2 Sac. **1989** NO: 16 G; 1 Fum. **1992** NO: 6 G. **Total:** 58 G; Int 3-60; 1 Fum; 5 Sac.

JOE GIBSON Gibson, Billy Joe 6'3", 213 **LB-DE-C-OE**
Col: Cameron; Tulsa *HS:* Electra [TX] B: 6/28/1919, Nocona, TX
AAFC **1946** BknA: 14 G. **1947** BknA: 14 G. **Total:** 28 G.

NFL **1942** Cle: 11 G; Rec 6-79 13.2. **1943** Was: 5 G. **1944** Cle: 10 G. **Total:** 26 G; Rec 6-79 13.2.

CLAUDE GIBSON Gibson, Claude Andrew 6'1", 190 **DB**
Col: North Carolina State *HS:* Lee H. Edwards [Asheville, NC] B: 5/26/1939, Spruce Pine, NC *Drafted:* 1961 Round 7 SD
1961 SD: KR 3-17 5.7; Scor 1 2XP. **1962** SD: KR 2-55 27.5. **1963** Oak: KR 2-10 5.0. **1965** Oak: KR 9-186 20.7. **Total:** KR 16-268 16.8; Scor 1 2XP.

		Punt Returns				Interceptions				Tot
Year Team	G	Ret	Yds	Avg	TD	Int	Yds	TD	Fum	TD
1961 SD	14	14	209	14.9	0	5	43	0	1	0
1962 SD	14	10	89	8.9	0	8	85	**1**	2	1
1963 Oak	14	**26**	**307**	**11.8**	**2**	3	18	0	1	2
1964 Oak	14	29	**419**	14.4	0	2	74	0	2	0
1965 Oak	14	**31**	357	11.5	1	4	53	0	1	1
NFL Total	70	110	1381	12.6	3	22	273	1	7	4

DAMON GIBSON Gibson, Damon O'Keith 5'8", 185 **WR**
Col: Iowa *HS:* Forest Brook [Houston, TX] B: 2/25/1975, Houston, TX
1998 Cin: Rush 1-9 9.0; Rec 19-258 13.6 3 TD; KR 17-372 21.9.

		Punt Returns					Tot
Year Team	G	Ret	Yds	Avg	TD	Fum	TD
1998 Cin	16	27	218	8.1	1	3	4

DENNIS GIBSON Gibson, Dennis Michael 6'2", 240 **LB**
Col: Iowa State *HS:* Ankeny [IA] B: 2/8/1964, Des Moines, IA *Drafted:* 1987 Round 8 Det
1987 Det: 12 G; Int 1-5; 1 Sac. **1988** Det: 16 G; 0.5 Sac. **1989** Det: 6 G; Int 1-10. **1990** Det: 11 G. **1991** Det: 16 G. **1992** Det: 16 G. **1993** Det: 15 G; Int 1-0; 1 Sac. **1994** SD: 16 G. **1995** SD: 13 G. **Total:** 121 G; Int 3-15; 2.5 Sac.

BUTCH GIBSON Gibson, Denver E 5'9", 204 **G-T**
Col: Grove City *HS:* Canton Central Catholic [OH]; McKinley HS [Canton, OH] B: 1904, Middlebranch, OH D: 5/1960
1930 NYG: 14 G. **1931** NYG: 14 G. **1932** NYG: 12 G. **1933** NYG: 14 G. **1934** NYG: 13 G. **Total:** 67 G.

ERNEST GIBSON Gibson, Ernest Gerard 5'10", 189 **DB**
Col: Furman *HS:* Bishop Kenney [Jacksonville, FL] B: 10/3/1961, Jacksonville, FL *Drafted:* 1984 Round 6 NE
1984 NE: 15 G; PR 1-3 3.0; Int 2-4. **1985** NE: 9 G. **1986** NE: 15 G. **1987** NE: 12 G; Int 2-17. **1988** NE: 16 G. **1989** Mia: 5 G; PR 1-(-1) -1.0. **Total:** 72 G; PR 2-2 1.0; Int 4-21.

GEORGE GIBSON Gibson, George Randall 6'0", 210 **G**
Col: Minnesota *HS:* Medford [OK] B: 10/2/1905, Kendaia, NY
1930 Fra-Min: 14 G. Fra: 5 G. Min: 9 G. **Total:** 14 G.

OLIVER GIBSON Gibson, Oliver Donnovan 6'2", 298 **DT**
Col: Notre Dame *HS:* Romeoville [IL] B: 3/15/1972, Chicago, IL *Drafted:* 1995 Round 4 Pit
1995 Pit: 12 G; KR 1-10 10.0. **1996** Pit: 16 G; 2.5 Sac. **1997** Pit: 16 G; 1 Sac. **1998** Pit: 16 G; KR 1-9 9.0; 2 Sac. **Total:** 60 G; KR 2-19 9.5; 5.5 Sac.

PAUL GIBSON Gibson, Paul Dean 6'2", 195 **WR**
Col: Texas-El Paso *HS:* Carlsbad [NM] B: 6/20/1948, Paris, AR D: 5/23/1975, El Paso, TX *Drafted:* 1972 Round 8 Buf
1972 GB: 1 G.

PAUL GIBSON Gibson, Paul Edward 6'2", 195 **OE-DB-DE**
Col: North Carolina State *HS:* Mineral Springs [NC] B: 10/28/1921, Winston Salem, NC D: 1975
AAFC **1947** BufA: 14 G; Rec 8-154 19.3. **1948** BufA: 7 G; Rec 11-216 19.6. **1949** BufA: 9 G; Rec 3-32 10.7; Int 1-9. **Total:** 30 G; Rec 22-402 18.3; Int 1-9.

DICK GIBSON Gibson, Richard M 6'0", 188 **T-G**
Col: Centre *HS:* Male [Louisville, KY] B: 12/5/1900 D: 11/23/1968, Greenville, IN
1922 Lou: 2 G. **1923** Lou: 3 G. **Total:** 5 G.

TOM GIBSON Gibson, Thomas Anthony 6'7", 257 **DE-DT**
Col: Northern Arizona *HS:* Saugus [CA] B: 12/20/1963, San Fernando, CA *Drafted:* 1987 Round 5 NE
1989 Cle: 16 G; 2 Sac. **1990** Cle: 12 G; 1 Sac. **1991** LARm: 5 G. **Total:** 33 G; 3 Sac.

FRANK GIDDENS Giddens, Frank David 6′7″, 300 **OT**
Col: New Mexico *HS:* Carlsbad [NM] B: 1/20/1959, Lubbock, TX
1981 Phi: 16 G. **1982** Phi: 9 G. **Total:** 25 G.

WIMPY GIDDENS Giddens, Herschel Orine 6′2″, 220 **T**
Col: Louisiana Tech *HS:* Ringgold [LA] B: 11/25/1914, Ringgold, LA
1938 Phi: 9 G. **1944** Bos: 7 G. **Total:** 16 G.

JON GIESLER Giesler, Jon William 6′5″, 262 **OT**
Col: Michigan *HS:* Woodmore [Elmore, OH] B: 12/23/1956, Toledo, OH *Drafted:* 1979 Round 1 Mia
1979 Mia: 16 G. **1980** Mia: 10 G. **1981** Mia: 16 G. **1982** Mia: 9 G. **1983** Mia: 16 G. **1984** Mia: 16 G. **1985** Mia: 13 G. **1986** Mia: 7 G. **1987** Mia: 10 G. **1988** Mia: 13 G. **Total:** 126 G.

FRANK GIFFORD Gifford, Frank Newton 6′1″, 197 **HB-WR-DB**
Col: Bakersfield Coll. CA (J.C.); USC *HS:* Bakersfield [CA]
B: 8/16/1930, Santa Monica, CA *Drafted:* 1952 Round 1 NYG
HOF: 1977
1952 NYG: PR 1-3 3.0; KR 4-124 31.0; Int 1-46. **1953** NYG: PR 16-106 6.6; KR 13-327 25.2; Int 1-66 **1** TD; Scor 47, 1-5 20.0% FG, 2-2 100.0% XK. **1954** NYG: PR 4-4 1.0; KR 1-29 29.0. **1955** NYG: KR 5-114 22.8. **1956** NYG: Scor 65, 1-2 50.0% FG, 8-9 88.9% XK.
Total: PR 21-113 5.4; KR 23-594 25.8; Int 2-112 1 TD; Scor 484, 2-7 28.6% FG, 10-11 90.9% XK.

		Passing							
Year Team	**G**	**Att**	**Comp**	**Comp%**	**Yds**	**YPA**	**TD**	**Int**	**Rating**
1952 NYG	10	2	1	50.0	18	9.00	1	0	120.8
1953 NYG	12	6	3	50.0	47	7.83	1	0	116.0
1954 NYG	9	8	4	50.0	155	19.38	3	1	95.8
1955 NYG	11	6	2	33.3	96	16.00	2	0	121.5
1956 NYG	12	5	2	40.0	35	7.00	2	1	64.6
1957 NYG	12	6	4	66.7	143	23.83	2	0	149.3
1958 NYG	10	10	3	30.0	109	10.90	1	1	66.3
1959 NYG	11	11	5	45.5	151	13.73	2	2	92.0
1960 NYG	8	6	3	50.0	24	4.00	0	1	20.8
1962 NYG	14	2	1	50.0	12	6.00	0	0	68.8
1963 NYG	14	0	0	—	0	—	0	0	—
1964 NYG	13	1	1	100.0	33	33.00	0	0	118.8
NFL Total	136	63	29	46.0	823	13.06	14	6	92.5

	Rushing				Receiving					Tot
Year Team	**Att**	**Yds**	**Avg**	**TD**	**Rec**	**Yds**	**Avg**	**TD**	**Fum**	**TD**
1952 NYG	38	116	3.1	0	5	36	7.2	0	3	0
1953 NYG	50	157	3.1	2	18	292	16.2	4	2	7
1954 NYG	66	368	5.6	2	14	154	11.0	1	7	3
1955 NYG	86	351	4.1	3	33	437	13.2	4	5	7
1956 NYG	159	819	5.2	5	51	603	11.8	4	5	9
1957 NYG	136	528	3.9	5	41	588	14.3	4	9	9
1958 NYG	115	468	4.1	8	29	330	11.4	2	3	10
1959 NYG	106	540	5.1	3	42	768	18.3	4	5	7
1960 NYG	77	232	3.0	4	24	344	14.3	3	6	7
1962 NYG	2	18	9.0	1	39	796	20.4	7	1	8
1963 NYG	4	10	2.5	0	42	657	15.6	7	2	7
1964 NYG	1	2	2.0	1	29	429	14.8	3	0	4
NFL Total	840	3609	4.3	34	367	5434	14.8	43	48	78

BOB GIFFORD Gifford, Robert F 6′0″, 200 **BB-LB**
Col: Denver *HS:* South [Denver, CO] B: 11/12/1918, Chicago, IL
D: 8/31/1994, Westminster, CO *Drafted:* 1942 Round 7 Bkn
1942 Bkn: 5 G.

WAYNE GIFT Gift, Leland Wayne 5′8″, 175 **BB-DB**
Col: Purdue *HS:* McKinley [Canton, OH] B: 10/21/1915, Medina, OH
1937 Cle: 10 G; Pass 3-0; Rush 3-7 2.3; Rec 3-20 6.7.

DAREN GILBERT Gilbert, Daren K 6′6″, 285 **OT**
Col: Cal State-Fullerton *HS:* Dominguez [Compton, CA] B: 10/3/1963, San Diego, CA *Drafted:* 1985 Round 2 NO
1985 NO: 16 G. **1986** NO: 9 G. **1987** NO: 6 G. **1988** NO: 11 G.
Total: 42 G.

FREDDIE GILBERT Gilbert, Freddie Gene 6′4″, 275 **DE**
Col: Georgia *HS:* Griffin [GA] B: 4/8/1962, Griffin, GA *Drafted:* 1984 Supplemental Round 1 Den
1986 Den: 15 G; 4 Sac. **1987** Den: 7 G. **1988** Den: 13 G; 1 Sac. **1989** Pho: 2 G. **Total:** 37 G; 5 Sac.

GALE GILBERT Gilbert, Gale Reed 6′3″, 209 **QB**
Col: California *HS:* Red Bluff [CA] B: 12/20/1961, Red Bluff, CA
1985 Sea: Rush 7-4 0.6. **1986** Sea: Rush 3-8 2.7. **1994** SD: Rush 8-(-3) -0.4. **1995** SD: Rush 6-11 1.8. **Total:** Rush 24-20 0.8.

		Passing								
Year Team	**G**	**Att**	**Comp**	**Comp%**	**Yds**	**YPA**	**TD**	**Int**	**Rating**	**Fum**
1985 Sea	9	40	19	47.5	218	5.45	1	2	51.9	1
1986 Sea	16	76	42	55.3	485	6.38	3	3	71.4	1
1990 Buf	1	15	8	53.3	106	7.07	2	2	76.0	0
1993 Buf	1	0	0	—	0	—	0	0	—	0
1994 SD	15	67	41	61.2	410	6.12	3	1	87.3	0
1995 SD	16	61	36	59.0	325	5.33	0	4	46.1	2
NFL Total	58	259	146	56.4	1544	5.96	9	12	66.2	4

KLINE GILBERT Gilbert, Kline 6′2″, 233 **OT-OG**
Col: Mississippi *HS:* Hollandale [MS] B: 11/22/1930, Hollandale, MS
D: 6/14/1987, Jackson, MS *Drafted:* 1953 Round 6 ChiB
1953 ChiB: 12 G. **1954** ChiB: 12 G. **1955** ChiB: 12 G. **1956** ChiB: 12 G. **1957** ChiB: 12 G. **Total:** 60 G.

LEWIS GILBERT Gilbert, Lewis Howe Jr. 6′4″, 225 **TE**
Col: Florida *HS:* Naples [FL] B: 5/24/1956, Naples, FL
1978 Atl: 4 G. **1980** Phi-SF: 9 G; Rec 1-7 7.0. Phi: 3 G; Rec 1-7 7.0. SF: 6 G. **1981** LARm: 6 G. **Total:** 19 G; Rec 1-7 7.0.

SEAN GILBERT Gilbert, Sean 6′5″, 318 **DT-DE**
Col: Pittsburgh *HS:* Aliquippa [PA] B: 4/10/1970, Aliquippa, PA
Drafted: 1992 Round 1 LARm
1992 LARm: 16 G; 5 Sac. **1993** LARm: 16 G; 10.5 Sac. **1994** LARm: 14 G; Scor **1** Saf; 2 Pt; 3 Sac. **1995** StL: 14 G; 5.5 Sac. **1996** Was: 16 G; 3 Sac. **1998** Car: 16 G; 6 Sac. **Total:** 92 G; Scor 1 Saf; 2 Pt; 33 Sac.

WALLY GILBERT Gilbert, Walter John 6′1″, 180 **TB-WB**
Col: Valparaiso *HS:* Denfeld [Duluth, MN] B: 12/19/1900, Oscoda, MI
D: 9/7/1958, Duluth, MN
1923 Dul: 7 G; Rush 1 TD; 6 Pt. **1924** Dul: 5 G; Pass 2 TD; Int **1** TD; Scor 18, 3 FG, 3 XK. **1925** Dul: 2 G; Pass 1 TD. **1926** Dul: 3 G.
Total: 17 G; Pass 3 TD; Rush 1 TD; Int 1 TD; Scor 24, 3 FG, 3 XK; Tot TD 2.

TOM GILBURG Gilburg, Thomas deMagnin 6′5″, 245 **OT-P**
Col: Syracuse *HS:* Horace Greeley [Chappaqua, NY] B: 11/27/1938, Bronxville, NY *Drafted:* 1961 Round 2 Bal
1963 Bal: KR 3-29 9.7. **1964** Bal: KR 1-19 19.0. **Total:** KR 4-48 12.0.

		Punting		
Year Team	**G**	**Punts**	**Yds**	**Avg**
1961 Bal	14	42	1804	43.0
1962 Bal	14	57	2384	41.8
1963 Bal	13	52	2173	41.8
1964 Bal	14	27	1106	41.0
1965 Bal	14	54	2139	39.6
NFL Total	69	232	9606	41.4

COOKIE GILCHRIST Gilchrist, Carlton Chester 6′3″, 251 **FB**
HS: Har-Brack Union [Brackenridge, PA] B: 5/25/1935, Brackenridge, PA
1962 Buf: KR 7-150 21.4; Scor 128, 8-20 40.0% FG, 14-17 82.4% XK.
1963 Buf: Pass 1-1 100.0%, 35 35.00. **Total:** Pass 1-1 100.0%, 35 35.00; KR 7-150 21.4; Scor 296, 8-20 40.0% FG, 14-17 82.4% XK.

		Rushing				Receiving					Tot
Year Team	**G**	**Att**	**Yds**	**Avg**	**TD**	**Rec**	**Yds**	**Avg**	**TD**	**Fum**	**TD**
1962 Buf	14	214	**1096**	5.1	**13**	24	319	13.3	2	7	15
1963 Buf	14	**232**	979	4.2	**12**	24	211	8.8	2	8	14
1964 Buf	14	**230**	**981**	4.3	**6**	30	345	11.5	0	6	6
1965 Den	14	**252**	954	3.8	**6**	18	154	8.6	1	8	7
1966 Mia	8	72	262	3.6	0	13	110	8.5	1	1	1
1967 Den	1	10	21	2.1	0	1	-4	-4.0	0	0	0
NFL Total	65	1010	4293	4.3	37	110	1135	10.3	6	30	43

GEORGE GILCHRIST Gilchrist, George Robert Jr. 6′0″, 260 **DT-DG**
Col: Tennessee State *HS:* Manassas [Memphis, TN] B: 1/9/1928, Memphis, TN D: 7/1980, Chicago, IL
1953 ChiC: 11 G.

DENNY GILDEA Gildea, Dennis Anthony 5′9″, 190 **C-T-G**
Col: Holy Cross *HS:* Boston College [MA] B: 10/9/1898, Boston, MA
D: 2/22/1976, Lynn, MA
1926 Har: 7 G.

JOHNNY GILDEA Gildea, John Thomas 6′2″, 205 **TB-BB-DB-LB**
Col: St. Bonaventure *HS:* Perkiomen School [Pennsburg, PA]
B: 3/9/1910, Boston Run, PA D: 11/20/1979, Tamaqua, PA
1935 Pit: Rec 4-61 15.3. **1936** Pit: Rec 5-70 14.0. **1937** Pit: Rec 3-47 15.7. **1938** NYG: Rec 1-3 3.0; Scor 0-2 FG, 0-1 XK. **Total:** Rec 13-181 13.9; Scor 6, 0-2 FG, 0-1 XK.

		Passing							
Year Team	**G**	**Att**	**Comp**	**Comp%**	**Yds**	**YPA**	**TD**	**Int**	**Rating**
1935 Pit	12	105	28	26.7	529	5.04	2	20	14.8
1936 Pit	12	29	9	31.0	147	5.07	1	5	21.0
1937 Pit	11	47	14	29.8	288	6.13	2	9	27.2
1938 NYG	9	0	0	—	0	—	0	0	—
NFL Total	44	181	51	28.2	964	5.33	5	34	18.9

	Rushing			
Year Team	**Att**	**Yds**	**Avg**	**TD**
1935 Pit	49	1	0.0	0
1936 Pit	35	31	0.9	0
1937 Pit	49	65	1.3	1

1938 NYG	1	2	2.0	0
NFL Total	134	99	0.7	1

JASON GILDON Gildon, Jason Larue 6'3", 245 **LB**
Col: Oklahoma State *HS:* Altus [OK] B: 7/31/1972, Altus, OK
Drafted: 1994 Round 3 Pit
1994 Pit: 16 G; 2 Sac. **1995** Pit: 16 G; 3 Sac. **1996** Pit: 14 G; 7 Sac. **1997** Pit: 16 G; 1 Fum TD; 6 Pt; 5 Sac. **1998** Pit: 16 G; 11 Sac. **Total:** 78 G; 1 Fum TD; 6 Pt; 28.0 Sac.

JIMMIE GILES Giles, Jimmie Jr. 6'3", 239 **TE**
Col: Alcorn State *HS:* Greenville [MS] B: 11/8/1954, Natchez, MS
Drafted: 1977 Round 3 Hou
1977 Hou: Rush 1-(-10) -10.0. **1978** TB: Rush 1-(-1) -1.0; KR 5-60 12.0. **1979** TB: Rush 2-7 3.5. **1982** TB: Rush 1-1 1.0. **Total:** Rush 5-(-3) -0.6; KR 5-60 12.0.

		Receiving				
Year Team	G	Rec	Yds	Avg	TD	Fum
1977 Hou	14	17	147	8.6	0	0
1978 TB	16	23	324	14.1	2	1
1979 TB	16	40	579	14.5	7	0
1980 TB	16	33	602	18.2	4	2
1981 TB	16	45	786	17.5	6	0
1982 TB	9	28	499	17.8	3	2
1983 TB	11	25	349	14.0	1	1
1984 TB	14	24	310	12.9	2	0
1985 TB	16	43	673	15.7	8	3
1986 TB-Det	16	37	376	10.2	4	0
1986 TB	7	18	178	9.9	1	0
1986 Det	9	19	198	10.4	3	0
1987 Det-Phi	12	13	157	12.1	1	0
1987 Det	4	6	62	10.3	0	0
1987 Phi	8	7	95	13.6	1	0
1988 Phi	16	6	57	9.5	1	0
1989 Phi	16	16	225	14.1	2	0
NFL Total	188	350	5084	14.5	41	9

OWEN GILL Gill, Owen 6'1", 230 **RB**
Col: Iowa *HS:* Samuel J. Tilden [Brooklyn, NY] B: 2/19/1962, London, England *Drafted:* 1985 Round 2 Sea
1985 Ind: Rec 5-52 10.4; KR 1-6 6.0. **1986** Ind: Rec 16-137 8.6; KR 5-73 14.6. **Total:** Rec 21-189 9.0; KR 6-79 13.2.

		Rushing				
Year Team	G	Att	Yds	Avg	TD	Fum
1985 Ind	15	45	262	5.8	2	1
1986 Ind	16	53	228	4.3	1	4
1987 LARm	1	0	0	—	0	0
NFL Total	32	98	490	5.0	3	5

RANDY GILL Gill, Randy 6'2", 230 **LB**
Col: Mount Hood CC OR; San Jose State *HS:* Hollywood [Los Angeles, CA] B: 8/1/1956, Los Angeles, CA *Drafted:* 1978 Round 10 StL
1978 StL-TB: 8 G. StL: 7 G. TB: 1 G. **Total:** 8 G.

ROGER GILL Gill, Roger Ewing 6'1", 200 **WR-HB**
Col: Texas Tech *HS:* Harlandale [San Antonio, TX] B: 10/14/1940, League City, TX *Drafted:* 1963 Round 12 Phi
1964 Phi: 12 G; Rec 4-58 14.5; PR 6-61 10.2; KR 7-167 23.9. **1965** Phi: 13 G; Rec 1-27 27.0; PR 2-28 14.0; KR 1-0. **Total:** 25 G; Rec 5-85 17.0; PR 8-89 11.1; KR 8-167 20.9.

SLOK GILL Gill, Sloko 5'7", 180 **C-LB-G**
Col: Youngstown State *HS:* Memorial [Campbell, OH] B: 3/8/1918, Campbell, OH D: 12/22/1995, Boardman, OH
1942 Det: 11 G; Int 1-9.

JOHN GILLEN Gillen, John Francis 6'3", 227 **LB**
Col: Illinois *HS:* St. Viator [Arlington Heights, IL] B: 11/5/1958, Arlington Heights, IL *Drafted:* 1981 Round 5 StL
1981 StL: 16 G. **1982** StL: 4 G. **1983** NE: 8 G. **Total:** 28 G.

FERNANDARS GILLESPIE Gillespie, Fernandars 5'10", 185 **RB**
(Scoop) *Col:* William Jewell *HS:* Southwest [St. Louis, MO]
B: 2/26/1962, St. Louis, MO *Drafted:* 1984 Round 12 Pit
1984 Pit: 14 G; Rush 7-18 2.6; Rec 1-12 12.0; KR 1-12 12.0; 1 Fum.

WILLIE GILLESPIE Gillespie, Willie E 5'9", 170 **WR**
Col: East Mississippi CC; Tennessee-Chattanooga *HS:* Starkville [MS]
B: 10/24/1961, Starkville, MS
1986 TB: 2 G; Rec 1-18 18.0. **1987** Min: 1 G; Rec 2-28 14.0. **Total:** 3 G; Rec 3-46 15.3.

FRED GILLETT Gillett, Frederick L 6'3", 225 **HB-OE**
Col: Los Angeles State *HS:* Hollywood [Los Angeles, CA]
B: 12/16/1936 *Drafted:* 1962 Round 19 Bal
1962 SD: 6 G; Rush 2-8 4.0. **1964** Oak: 3 G. **Total:** 9 G; Rush 2-8 4.0.

JIM GILLETTE Gillette, James Thomas Jr. 6'1", 185 **HB-DB-TB**
Col: Virginia *HS:* Courtland [Spotsylvania, VA] B: 12/19/1917, Courtland, VA D: 1/9/1990, Richmond, VA *Drafted:* 1940 Round 16 GB
1940 Cle: Pass 4-0, 2 Int. **1944** Cle: PR 1-16 16.0; KR 4-115 28.8. **1945** Cle: Rec 6-48 8.0; PR 7-53 7.6; KR 4-66 16.5. **1946** Bos: Rec 5-96 19.2 1 TD; PR 2-62 31.0; KR 3-43 14.3. **1947** GB: Rec 12-224 18.7 1 TD; PR 11-168 15.3; KR 3-66 22.0. **1948** Det: Rec 1-8 8.0; PR 2-10 5.0. **Total:** Pass 4-0, 2 Int; Rec 24-376 15.7 2 TD; PR 23-309 13.4; KR 14-290 20.7.

		Rushing				Interceptions				Tot
Year Team	G	Att	Yds	Avg	TD	Int	Yds	TD	Fum	TD
1940 Cle	4	1	1	1.0	0	0	0	0	0	0
1944 Cle	7	26	131	5.0	2	3	29	0	0	2
1945 Cle	10	63	390	6.2	1	4	8	0	2	1
1946 Bos	11	30	99	3.3	1	1	5	0	1	2
1947 GB	10	50	207	4.1	0	0	0	0	2	1
1948 Det	10	2	3	1.5	0	6	17	0	0	0
NFL Total	52	172	831	4.8	4	14	59	0	5	6

WALKER GILLETTE Gillette, Walker Adams 6'5", 200 **WR**
Col: Richmond *HS:* Southampton [Courtland, VA]; Courtland HS [VA]
B: 3/16/1947, Norfolk, VA *Drafted:* 1970 Round 1 SD
1976 NYG: Rush 1-(-4) -4.0. **Total:** Rush 1-(-4) -4.0.

		Receiving				
Year Team	G	Rec	Yds	Avg	TD	Fum
1970 SD	13	2	21	10.5	0	0
1971 SD	12	10	147	14.7	2	0
1972 StL	14	33	550	16.7	2	1
1973 StL	14	20	244	12.2	1	2
1974 NYG	11	29	466	16.1	3	0
1975 NYG	14	43	600	14.0	2	1
1976 NYG	13	16	263	16.4	2	0
NFL Total	91	153	2291	15.0	12	4

JOHN GILLIAM Gilliam, John Rally 6'1", 195 **WR-HB**
(Tally) *Col:* South Carolina State *HS:* Brewer [Greenwood, SC]
B: 8/7/1945, Greenwood, SC *Drafted:* 1967 Round 2 NO
1967 NO: PR 7-13 1.9. **1968** NO: PR 15-60 4.0. **1971** StL: PR 1-21 21.0. **Total:** PR 23-94 4.1.

		Rushing				Receiving			
Year Team	G	Att	Yds	Avg	TD	Rec	Yds	Avg	TD
1967 NO	13	7	41	5.9	0	22	264	12.0	1
1968 NO	14	2	36	18.0	0	24	284	11.8	0
1969 StL	14	1	-4	-4.0	0	52	997	19.2	9
1970 StL	14	5	68	13.6	1	45	952	21.2	5
1971 StL	14	2	16	8.0	0	42	837	19.9	3
1972 Min	14	8	14	1.8	0	47	1035	**22.0**	7
1973 Min	14	5	71	14.2	1	42	907	21.6	8
1974 Min	14	2	16	8.0	0	26	578	22.2	5
1975 Min	14	3	35	11.7	0	50	777	15.5	7
1976 Atl	14	0	0	—	0	21	292	13.9	2
1977 ChiB-NO	12	0	0	—	0	11	133	12.1	1
1977 ChiB	2	0	0	—	0	0	0	—	0
1977 NO	10	0	0	—	0	11	133	12.1	1
NFL Total	151	35	293	8.4	2	382	7056	18.5	48

	Kickoff Returns					Tot
Year Team	Ret	Yds	Avg	TD	Fum	TD
1967 NO	16	481	30.1	1	2	2
1968 NO	15	328	21.9	0	0	0
1969 StL	11	339	30.8	**1**	1	10
1970 StL	5	107	21.4	0	3	6
1971 StL	0	0	—	0	2	3
1972 Min	14	369	26.4	0	2	7
1973 Min	10	174	17.4	0	1	9
1974 Min	3	86	28.7	0	0	5
1975 Min	0	0	—	0	1	7
1976 Atl	0	0	—	0	0	2
1977 ChiB-NO	0	0	—	0	0	1
1977 NO	0	0	—	0	0	1
NFL Total	74	1884	25.5	2	12	52

JON GILLIAM Gilliam, Jon Ray 6'2", 240 **C**
Col: Oklahoma State; Texas A&M-Commerce *HS:* Hillcrest [Dallas, TX]
B: 10/22/1938, Oklahoma City, OK *Drafted:* 1960 Round 1 Buf
1961 DalT: 14 G; KR 1-23 23.0. **1962** DalT: 14 G. **1963** KC: 14 G. **1964** KC: 14 G. **1965** KC: 14 G. **1966** KC: 1 G. **1967** KC: 5 G. **Total:** 76 G; KR 1-23 23.0.

JOE GILLIAM Gilliam, Joseph Wiley Jr. 6'2", 187 **QB**
(Jefferson Street Joe) *Col:* Tennessee State *HS:* Pearl [Nashville, TN]
B: 12/29/1950, Charleston, WV *Drafted:* 1972 Round 11 Pit
1972 Pit: Rush 2-0. **1973** Pit: Rush 6-23 3.8. **1974** Pit: Rush 14-41 2.9 1 TD. **Total:** Rush 22-64 2.9 1 TD.

Year Team	G	Passing Att	Comp	Comp%	Yds	YPA	TD	Int	Rating	Fum
1972 Pit	2	11	7	63.6	48	4.36	0	0	73.3	0
1973 Pit	5	60	20	33.3	331	5.52	2	6	24.4	3
1974 Pit	9	212	96	45.3	1274	6.01	4	8	55.4	5
1975 Pit	4	48	24	50.0	450	9.38	3	3	77.6	0
NFL Total	20	331	147	44.4	2103	6.35	9	17	53.2	8

CORY GILLIARD Gilliard, Cory Rashad 6'0", 210 **DB**
Col: Ball State *HS:* Danbury [CT]; North Central HS [Indianapolis, NY] B: 10/10/1974, Bronx, NY *Drafted:* 1997 Round 4 Den
1997 Cin: 1 G.

FRED GILLIES Gillies, Frederick Montague 6'3", 218 **T**
(Boo) *Col:* Cornell *HS:* University [Chicago, IL] B: 12/9/1895, Chicago, IL D: 5/8/1974, Flossmoor, IL
1920 ChiC: 9 G. **1921** ChiC: 8 G. **1922** ChiC: 11 G. **1923** ChiC: 11 G. **1924** ChiC: 10 G. **1925** ChiC: 14 G. **1926** ChiC: 7 G. **1928** ChiC: 1 G. **Total:** 71 G.

GALE GILLINGHAM Gillingham, Gale Herbert 6'3", 255 **OG-DT**
Col: Minnesota *HS:* Little Falls [MN] B: 2/3/1944, Madison, WI *Drafted:* 1966 Round 1 GB
1966 GB: 14 G. **1967** GB: 14 G. **1968** GB: 14 G. **1969** GB: 14 G; KR 1-13 13.0. **1970** GB: 14 G. **1971** GB: 14 G. **1972** GB: 2 G. **1973** GB: 14 G. **1974** GB: 14 G. **1976** GB: 14 G. **Total:** 128 G; KR 1-13 13.0.

DON GILLIS Gillis, Donald 6'3", 245 **C**
Col: Del Mar Coll. TX (J.C.); Rice *HS:* West Oso [Corpus Christi, TX] B: 3/31/1935, Corpus Christi, TX *Drafted:* 1957 Round 8 Cle
1958 ChiC: 12 G. **1959** ChiC: 12 G. **1960** StL: 12 G. **1961** StL: 9 G. **Total:** 45 G.

JOE GILLIS Gillis, Joseph Augustus 5'8", 210 **G-T**
Col: Tufts; Detroit Mercy *HS:* Medford [MA] B: 4/24/1896, Medford, MA D: 12/19/1967, Detroit, MI
1923 Tol: 7 G.

HANK GILLO Gillo, Henry Charles 5'10", 195 **FB-WB-BB-TB**
Col: Colgate *HS:* South Division [Milwaukee, WI] B: 10/5/1894, Milwaukee, WI D: 9/6/1948, Manchester Twp., Green Lake Co, WI
1920 Ham: 7 G. **1921** Ham: 1 G. **1922** Rac: 11 G; Rush 5 TD; Scor **52**, 6 FG, 4 XK. **1923** Rac: 10 G; Rush 2 TD; Scor 44, 8 FG, 8 XK. **1924** Rac: 10 G; Rush 3 TD; Scor 48, 8 FG, 6 XK. **1925** Mil: 2 G. **1926** Rac: 4 G. **Total:** 45 G; Rush 10 TD; Scor 144, 22 FG, 18 XK.

HORACE GILLOM Gillom, Horace Albert 6'1", 221 **DE-OE**
Col: Ohio State; Nevada-Reno *HS:* Washington [Massillon, OH] B: 3/3/1921, Roanoke, AL
AAFC **1947** CleA: Int 1-29. **1948** CleA: KR 3-10 3.3. **1949** CleA: Rush 2-8 4.0. **Total:** Rush 2-8 4.0; KR 3-10 3.3; Int 1-29.

Year Team	G	Receiving Rec	Yds	Avg	TD	Punting Punts	Yds	Avg
1947 CleA	14	2	24	12.0	0	47	2096	44.6
1948 CleA	13	20	295	14.8	1	6	227	37.8
1949 CleA	12	23	359	15.6	0	54	2011	37.2
AAFC Total	39	45	678	15.1	1	107	4334	40.5

NFL **1950** Cle: Pass 1-1 100.0%, 3 3.00; KR 3-51 17.0. **1951** Cle: KR 2-25 12.5; 1 Fum TD. **1952** Cle: KR 1-2 2.0. **1955** Cle: Rush 1-(-15) -15.0. **Total:** Pass 1-1 100.0%, 3 3.00; Rush 1-(-15) -15.0; KR 6-78 13.0; 1 Fum TD.

Year Team	G	Receiving Rec	Yds	Avg	TD	Punting Punts	Yds	Avg	Fum	Tot TD
1950 Cle	12	2	54	27.0	1	66	2849	43.2	0	1
1951 Cle	12	11	164	14.9	0	73	**3321**	**45.5**	1	1
1952 Cle	12	4	45	11.3	1	61	2787	**45.7**	1	1
1953 Cle	12	7	80	11.4	0	63	2760	43.8	1	0
1954 Cle	12	5	62	12.4	0	52	2230	42.9	0	0
1955 Cle	12	0	0	—	0	58	2389	41.2	0	0
1956 Cle	5	0	0	—	0	12	536	44.7	0	0
NFL Total	77	29	405	14.0	2	385	16872	43.8	3	3

BOB GILLSON Gillson, Robert William 6'0", 208 **G**
Col: Colgate *HS:* Binghamton [NY] B: 5/4/1905, Binghamton, NY D: 11/16/1992, Phoenix, AZ
1930 Bkn: 12 G. **1931** Bkn: 11 G. **Total:** 23 G.

WILLIE GILLUS Gillus, Willie Harden 6'4", 215 **QB**
Col: Norfolk State *HS:* Greensville Co. [Emporia, VA] B: 9/1/1963, Emporia, VA
1987 GB: 1 G; Pass 5-2 40.0%, 28 5.60.

HARRY GILMER Gilmer, Harry Vincent Jr. 6'0", 169 **QB-DB-HB**
Col: Alabama *HS:* Woodlawn [Birmingham, AL] B: 4/14/1926, Birmingham, AL *Drafted:* 1948 Round 1 Was
1949 Was: Rec 5-37 7.4. **1951** Was: PR 6-132 22.0; Int 5-79. **1952** Was: Rec 15-143 9.5 1 TD; PR 3-28 9.3; KR 7-157 22.4. **Total:** Rec 20-180 9.0 1 TD; PR 9-160 17.8; KR 7-157 22.4; Int 5-79.

Year Team	G	Passing Att	Comp	Comp%	Yds	YPA	TD	Int	Rating
1948 Was	1	5	2	40.0	69	13.80	0	0	87.5
1949 Was	12	132	49	37.1	869	6.58	4	15	31.0
1950 Was	10	141	63	44.7	948	6.72	8	12	50.8
1951 Was	10	68	31	45.6	391	5.75	1	6	32.2
1952 Was	12	58	31	53.4	555	9.57	4	4	80.7
1954 Was	12	7	2	28.6	18	2.57	0	1	0.0
1955 Det	8	122	58	47.5	633	5.19	2	**4**	55.1
1956 Det	11	46	27	58.7	303	6.59	4	3	80.3
NFL Total	76	579	263	45.4	3786	6.54	23	45	48.0

Year Team	Rushing Att	Yds	Avg	TD	Fum	Tot TD
1949 Was	31	167	5.4	0	2	0
1950 Was	22	145	6.6	1	6	1
1951 Was	19	141	7.4	0	4	0
1952 Was	100	365	3.7	0	4	1
1954 Was	6	19	3.2	0	2	0
1955 Det	15	67	4.5	0	2	0
1956 Det	8	19	2.4	0	1	0
NFL Total	201	923	4.6	1	21	2

JIM GILMORE Gilmore, James Thomas 6'5", 269 **OT-OG**
Col: Villanova; Ohio State *HS:* Northwest Catholic [Philadelphia, PA] B: 12/19/1962, Philadelphia, PA
1986 Phi: 2 G. **1987** Mia: 3 G. **Total:** 5 G.

JOHNNY GILROY Gilroy, Roland John 5'11", 178 **BB-WB-TB**
Col: Georgetown *HS:* Haverhill [MA] B: 10/24/1895, Hudson, MA D: 6/1983, Smithtown, NY
1920 Can-Cle: 8 G. Can: 6 G. Cle: 2 G. **1921** Was: 1 G. **Total:** 9 G.

HUBERT GINN Ginn, Hubert A 5'10", 185 **RB**
(Wizard) *Col:* Florida A&M *HS:* Tompkins [Savannah, GA] B: 1/4/1947, Savannah, GA *Drafted:* 1970 Round 9 Mia
1972 Mia: Rec 1-23 23.0. **1973** Mia-Bal: Rec 3-2 0.7. Bal: Rec 3-2 0.7. **1974** Mia: Rec 2-3 1.5. **1975** Mia: Rec 3-21 7.0; PR 1-4 4.0. **Total:** Rec 9-49 5.4; PR 1-4 4.0.

Year Team	G	Rushing Att	Yds	Avg	TD	Kickoff Returns Ret	Yds	Avg	TD	Fum
1970 Mia	12	5	-1	-0.2	0	5	59	11.8	0	2
1971 Mia	14	22	97	4.4	0	10	252	25.2	0	2
1972 Mia	14	27	142	5.3	1	1	25	25.0	0	1
1973 Mia-Bal	12	16	47	2.9	0	9	198	22.0	0	0
1973 Mia	3	0	0	—	0	0	0	—	0	0
1973 Bal	9	16	47	2.9	0	9	198	22.0	0	0
1974 Mia	9	26	99	3.8	2	12	235	19.6	0	2
1975 Mia	11	21	78	3.7	0	9	235	26.1	0	1
1976 Oak	7	10	53	5.3	0	1	27	27.0	0	0
1977 Oak	10	5	6	1.2	0	3	74	24.7	0	1
1978 Oak	1	0	0	—	0	0	0	—	0	0
NFL Total	90	132	521	3.9	3	50	1105	22.1	0	9

TOMMIE GINN Ginn, Tommie Webster 6'3", 253 **OG-C**
Col: Arkansas *HS:* Berryville [AR] B: 1/25/1958, Scotia, CA *Drafted:* 1980 Round 5 Det
1980 Det: 14 G. **1981** Det: 13 G. **Total:** 27 G.

JERRY GINNEY Ginney, Jerald Warren 5'11", 217 **G**
Col: Santa Clara *HS:* Lowell [San Francisco, CA] B: 4/9/1916, Dayton, OH D: 10/22/1984, San Jose, CA *Drafted:* 1939 Round 4 NYG
1940 Phi: 1 G.

PAUL GIPSON Gipson, Paul Theodis 6'0", 210 **RB**
Col: Houston *HS:* Washington [Conroe, TX] B: 3/21/1946, Jacksonville, TX D: 1/16/1985, Houston, TX *Drafted:* 1969 Round 2 Atl
1969 Atl: Pass 1-0, 1 Int; Rec 4-33 8.3; KR 9-145 16.1. **1970** Atl: Rec 16-186 11.6 3 TD; KR 8-189 23.6. **1971** Det: Rec 1-21 21.0; KR 5-105 21.0. **Total:** Pass 1-0, 1 Int; Rec 21-240 11.4 3 TD; KR 22-439 20.0.

Year Team	G	Rushing Att	Yds	Avg	TD	Fum	Tot TD
1969 Atl	10	62	303	4.9	1	**8**	1
1970 Atl	13	52	177	3.4	0	2	3
1971 Det	5	4	12	3.0	0	0	0
1973 NE	5	5	-1	-0.2	0	1	0
NFL Total	33	123	491	4.0	1	11	4

TOM GIPSON Gipson, Thomas Allen 6'7", 280 **DT**
Col: North Texas *HS:* Fulton [Rockport, TX] B: 7/28/1948, Refugio, TX *Drafted:* 1971 Round 14 Oak
1971 Oak: 4 G.

JUG GIRARD Girard, Earl Francis 5'11", 176 **HB-OE-DB-QB**
Col: Wisconsin *HS:* Marinette [WI] B: 1/25/1927, Marinette, WI
D: 1/17/1997, Rochester Hills, MI *Drafted:* 1948 Round 1 GB
1948 GB: Int 1-34. **1949** GB: Int 1-41. **1950** GB: Int 1-6. **1951** GB: Int 5-25. **1957** Pit: Scor 29, 1-3 33.3% FG, 2-3 66.7% XK.
Total: Int 8-106; Scor 113, 1-3 33.3% FG, 2-3 66.7% XK.

		Passing							
Year Team	**G**	**Att**	**Comp**	**Comp%**	**Yds**	**YPA**	**TD**	**Int**	**Rating**
1948 GB	10	14	4	28.6	117	8.36	1	1	56.0
1949 GB	12	175	62	35.4	881	5.03	4	12	31.6
1950 GB	12	0	0	—	0	—	0	0	—
1951 GB	12	0	0	—	0	—	0	0	—
1952 Det	11	4	0	0.0	0	0.00	0	0	39.6
1953 Det	11	1	0	0.0	0	0.00	0	0	39.6
1954 Det	12	0	0	—	0	—	0	0	—
1955 Det	12	1	0	0.0	0	0.00	0	0	39.6
1956 Det	10	1	1	100.0	19	19.00	0	0	118.8
1957 Pit	12	1	0	0.0	0	0.00	0	0	39.6
NFL Total	114	197	67	34.0	1017	5.16	5	13	32.9

	Rushing				Receiving			
Year Team	**Att**	**Yds**	**Avg**	**TD**	**Rec**	**Yds**	**Avg**	**TD**
1948 GB	13	26	2.0	0	1	2	2.0	0
1949 GB	45	198	4.4	1	1	13	13.0	0
1950 GB	14	39	2.8	0	4	89	22.3	0
1951 GB	4	20	5.0	0	10	220	22.0	2
1952 Det	61	222	3.6	2	17	316	18.6	2
1953 Det	19	73	3.8	0	2	24	12.0	0
1954 Det	9	36	4.0	0	27	421	15.6	7
1955 Det	10	27	2.7	0	23	301	13.1	0
1956 Det	17	67	3.9	0	3	33	11.0	0
1957 Pit	2	-5	-2.5	0	21	419	20.0	4
NFL Total	194	703	3.6	3	109	1838	16.9	15

	Punt Returns				Kickoff Returns			
Year Team	**Ret**	**Yds**	**Avg**	**TD**	**Ret**	**Yds**	**Avg**	**TD**
1948 GB	0	0	—	0	1	20	20.0	0
1949 GB	11	70	6.4	0	2	45	22.5	0
1950 GB	0	0	—	0	1	25	25.0	0
1951 GB	1	9	9.0	0	0	0	—	0
1952 Det	0	0	—	0	2	31	15.5	0
1953 Det	9	86	9.6	0	9	252	28.0	0
1954 Det	9	22	2.4	0	12	248	20.7	0
1955 Det	9	25	2.8	0	7	117	16.7	0
1956 Det	2	7	3.5	0	0	0	—	0
NFL Total	41	219	5.3	0	34	738	21.7	0

	Punting				Tot
Year Team	**Punts**	**Yds**	**Avg**	**Fum**	**TD**
1948 GB	8	320	40.0	2	0
1949 GB	**69**	2694	39.0	4	1
1950 GB	71	2715	38.2	1	0
1951 GB	52	2101	40.4	1	2
1952 Det	0	0	—	3	4
1954 Det	63	2585	41.0	0	7
1955 Det	56	2310	41.3	2	0
1956 Det	10	448	44.8	0	0
1957 Pit	**68**	2754	40.5	1	4
NFL Total	397	15927	40.1	14	18

MIKE GISLER Gisler, Michael 6'4", 295 **OG-C**
Col: Houston *HS:* Runge [TX] B: 8/26/1969, Runge, TX *Drafted:* 1992 Round 11 NO
1993 NE: 12 G. **1994** NE: 15 G. **1995** NE: 16 G; KR 2-19 9.5; 1 Fum. **1996** NE: 14 G; KR 1-9 9.0. **1997** NE: 16 G. **1998** NYJ: 16 G. **Total:** 89 G; KR 3-28 9.3; 1 Fum.

ANDREW GISSINGER Gissinger, Andrew III 6'5", 280 **OT**
Col: Syracuse *HS:* Valley Forge [Parma Heights, OH] B: 7/4/1959, Barberton, OH *Drafted:* 1981 Round 6 SD
1982 SD: 9 G; KR 1-0. **1983** SD: 16 G. **1984** SD: 16 G; Rec 1-3 3.0.
Total: 41 G; Rec 1-3 3.0; KR 1-0.

PATSY GIUGLIANO Giugliano, Pasquale Raphael 5'4", 140 **BB**
(Jule) *Col:* No College *HS:* Maie [Louisville, KY]; Dupont Manual HS [Louisville, KY] B: 12/11/1900, Louisville, KY D: 3/1976, Louisville, KY
1923 Lou: 1 G.

REGGIE GIVENS Givens, Reggie 6'0", 234 **LB**
Col: Penn State *HS:* Sussex Central [VA] B: 10/3/1971, Emporia, VA
Drafted: 1993 Round 8 Dal
1998 SF: 16 G.

ERNEST GIVINS Givins, Ernest Pastell Jr. 5'9", 172 **WR**
Col: Northeastern Oklahoma A&M (J.C.); Louisville *HS:* Lakewood [St. Petersburg, FL] B: 9/3/1964, St. Petersburg, FL *Drafted:* 1986 Round 2 Hou
1986 Hou: Pass 2-0. **1994** Hou: KR 1-27 27.0. **Total:** Pass 2-0; KR 1-27 27.0.

		Rushing				Receiving			
Year Team	**G**	**Att**	**Yds**	**Avg**	**TD**	**Rec**	**Yds**	**Avg**	**TD**
1986 Hou	15	9	148	16.4	1	61	1062	17.4	3
1987 Hou	12	1	-13	-13.0	0	53	933	17.6	6
1988 Hou	16	4	26	6.5	0	60	976	16.3	5
1989 Hou	15	0	0	—	0	55	794	14.4	3
1990 Hou	16	3	65	21.7	0	72	979	13.6	9
1991 Hou	16	4	30	7.5	0	70	996	14.2	5
1992 Hou	16	7	75	10.7	0	67	787	11.7	10
1993 Hou	16	6	19	3.2	0	68	887	13.0	4
1994 Hou	16	1	-5	-5.0	0	36	521	14.5	1
1995 Jac	9	0	0	—	0	29	280	9.7	3
NFL Total	147	35	345	9.9	1	571	8215	14.4	49

	Punt Returns					Tot
Year Team	**Ret**	**Yds**	**Avg**	**TD**	**Fum**	**TD**
1986 Hou	8	80	10.0	0	0	4
1987 Hou	0	0	—	0	2	6
1988 Hou	0	0	—	0	1	5
1989 Hou	0	0	—	0	0	3
1990 Hou	0	0	—	0	1	9
1991 Hou	11	107	9.7	0	3	5
1992 Hou	0	0	—	0	3	10
1993 Hou	0	0	—	0	2	4
1994 Hou	37	210	5.7	1	3	2
1995 Jac	2	-7	-3.5	0	1	3
NFL Total	58	390	6.7	1	16	51

SCOTTY GLACKEN Glacken, Edward Scott 6'0", 190 **QB**
Col: Duke *HS:* St. John's [Washington, DC] B: 7/28/1944, Washington, DC *Drafted:* 1966 Round 7 Den
1966 Den: 8 G; Pass 11-6 54.5%, 84 7.64 1 TD; Rush 2-(-1) -0.5.
1967 Den: 2 G; Pass 4-0; Rush 1-10 10.0. **Total:** 10 G; Pass 15-6 40.0%, 84 5.60 1 TD; Rush 3-9 3.0.

CHET GLADCHUK Gladchuk, Chester Stephen 6'4", 248 **C-T-LB**
Col: Boston College *HS:* Warren G. Harding [Bridgeport, CT]
B: 4/4/1917, Bridgeport, CT D: 9/4/1967, Northampton, MA
Drafted: 1941 Round 1 Pit
1941 NYG: 7 G; Int 1-16. **1946** NYG: 11 G; 1 Fum. **1947** NYG: 10 G.
Total: 28 G; Int 1-16; 1 Fum.

MACK GLADDEN Gladden, James Mack 6'2", 195 **OE-DE**
Col: Missouri B: 5/22/1909, Turley, MO D: 3/1985, Rolla, MO
1934 StL: 3 G.

BOB GLADIEUX Gladieux, Robert Joseph 5'11", 195 **RB**
Col: Notre Dame *HS:* Louisville [OH] B: 1/2/1947, Louisville, OH
Drafted: 1969 Round 8 Bos
1969 Bos: KR 4-61 15.3. **1971** NE: Pass 2-1 50.0%, 48 24.00; PR 4-0; KR 6-85 14.2. **1972** NE: Pass 1-0, 1 Int; PR 2-(-6) -3.0. **Total:** Pass 3-1 33.3%, 48 16.00 1 Int; PR 6-(-6) -1.0; KR 10-146 14.6.

		Rushing				Receiving				
Year Team	**G**	**Att**	**Yds**	**Avg**	**TD**	**Rec**	**Yds**	**Avg**	**TD**	**Fum**
1969 Bos	10	0	0	—	0	0	0	—	0	0
1970 Bos-Buf	10	4	8	2.0	0	0	0	—	0	0
1970 Bos	8	4	8	2.0	0	0	0	—	0	0
1970 Buf	2	0	0	—	0	0	0	—	0	0
1971 NE	14	37	175	4.7	0	6	60	10.0	0	3
1972 NE	11	24	56	2.3	0	19	192	10.1	0	3
NFL Total	45	65	239	3.7	0	25	252	10.1	0	6

CHARLES GLADMAN Gladman, Charles R 5'11", 205 **RB**
Col: Pittsburgh *HS:* Garfield [Akron, OH] B: 9/2/1966, Akron, OH
1987 TB: 2 G; Rush 12-29 2.4; Rec 2-8 4.0; KR 1-16 16.0.

TONY GLADNEY Gladney, Anthony Lamont 6'3", 200 **WR**
Col: Nevada-Las Vegas *HS:* San Mateo [CA] B: 7/20/1964, San Mateo, CA
1987 SF: 2 G; Rec 4-60 15.0.

JOE GLAMP Glamp, Joseph J 5'11", 180 **HB-DB**
Col: Louisiana State *HS:* Mount Pleasant [PA] B: 5/13/1921
D: 1/13/1989, Greensburg, PA
1947 Pit: Scor 48, 6-14 42.9% FG, 30-31 96.8% XK. **1948** Pit: Pass 1-0; Rec 9-138 15.3 2 TD; PR 1-15 15.0; KR 7-158 22.6; Scor 56, 4-10 40.0% FG, 26-27 96.3% XK. **1949** Pit: Rec 1-14 14.0; Scor 21, 1-6 16.7% FG, 18-18 100.0% XK. **Total:** Pass 1-0; Rec 10-152 15.2 2 TD; PR 1-15 15.0; KR 7-158 22.6; Scor 125, 11-30 36.7% FG, 74-76 97.4% XK.

		Rushing					Tot
Year Team	**G**	**Att**	**Yds**	**Avg**	**TD**	**Fum**	**TD**
1947 Pit	12	1	2	2.0	0	0	0
1948 Pit	12	28	167	6.0	1	1	3
1949 Pit	8	3	-8	-2.7	0	0	0
NFL Total	32	32	161	5.0	1	1	3

BRIAN GLASGOW Glasgow, Brian Gene 6′2″, 230 **TE**
Col: Northern Illinois *HS:* Dwight D. Eisenhower [Blue Island, IL]
B: 6/9/1961, Burlington, IA
1987 ChiB: 3 G; Rec 2-16 8.0.

NESBY GLASGOW Glasgow, Nesby Lee 5′10″, 185 **DB**
Col: Washington *HS:* Gardena [CA] B: 4/15/1957, Los Angeles, CA
Drafted: 1979 Round 8 Bal
1983 Bal: 1 Sac. **1985** Ind: 2 Sac. **1987** Ind: 0.5 Sac. **1989** Sea: Rec 1-4 4.0; 1 Fum TD. **1990** Sea: 2 Sac. **1991** Sea: 2.5 Sac. **1992** Sea: 1 Sac.
Total: Rec 1-4 4.0; 1 Fum TD; 9 Sac.

		Punt Returns				Kickoff Returns			
Year Team	**G**	**Ret**	**Yds**	**Avg**	**TD**	**Ret**	**Yds**	**Avg**	**TD**
1979 Bal	16	44	352	8.0	1	50	1126	22.5	0
1980 Bal	16	23	187	8.1	0	33	743	22.5	0
1981 Bal	14	0	0	—	0	1	35	35.0	0
1982 Bal	9	4	24	6.0	0	0	0	—	0
1983 Bal	16	1	9	9.0	0	0	0	—	0
1984 Ind	16	7	79	11.3	0	0	0	—	0
1985 Ind	16	0	0	—	0	0	0	—	0
1986 Ind	14	0	0	—	0	0	0	—	0
1987 Ind	11	0	0	—	0	0	0	—	0
1988 Sea	16	1	0	0.0	0	0	0	—	0
1989 Sea	16	0	0	—	0	0	0	—	0
1990 Sea	16	0	0	—	0	1	2	2.0	0
1991 Sea	16	0	0	—	0	0	0	—	0
1992 Sea	13	0	0	—	0	0	0	—	0
NFL Total	205	80	651	8.1	1	85	1906	22.4	0

	Interceptions				Tot
Year Team	**Int**	**Yds**	**TD**	**Fum**	**TD**
1979 Bal	1	-1	0	8	1
1980 Bal	4	65	0	5	0
1981 Bal	2	35	0	0	0
1983 Bal	3	35	0	0	0
1984 Ind	1	8	0	1	0
1987 Ind	1	0	0	0	0
1988 Sea	2	19	0	1	0
1989 Sea	0	0	0	0	1
1990 Sea	0	0	0	1	0
1991 Sea	1	28	0	0	0
NFL Total	15	189	0	16	2

CHIP GLASS Glass, Charles Ferdinand 6′4″, 235 **TE**
Col: Florida State *HS:* Chamberlain [Tampa, FL] B: 6/25/1947, Homestead, FL *Drafted:* 1969 Round 3 Cle
1970 Cle: KR 1-0. **1971** Cle: KR 1-1 1.0. **Total:** KR 2-1 0.5.

		Receiving				
Year Team	**G**	**Rec**	**Yds**	**Avg**	**TD**	**Fum**
1969 Cle	14	4	91	22.8	2	0
1970 Cle	14	19	403	21.2	2	2
1971 Cle	14	1	4	4.0	1	0
1972 Cle	14	5	61	12.2	0	1
1973 Cle	12	2	60	30.0	0	0
1974 NYG	13	3	23	7.7	0	0
NFL Total	81	34	642	18.9	5	3

GLENN GLASS Glass, Glenn Murray 6′1″, 205 **DB-WR**
(Red) *Col:* Tennessee *HS:* Clewiston [FL] B: 2/16/1940, Holopaw, FL
Drafted: 1962 Round 17 ChiB
1962 Pit: 7 G; KR 16-396 24.8. **1963** Pit: 14 G; KR 2-46 23.0; Int 1-29. **1964** Phi: 13 G; PR 1-0; KR 1-12 12.0; Int 1-18. **1965** Phi: 12 G; Rec 15-201 13.4. **1966** Atl-Den: 9 G; KR 1-11 11.0. Atl: 3 G; KR 1-11 11.0. Den: 6 G. **Total:** 55 G; Rec 15-201 13.4; PR 1-0; KR 20-465 23.3; Int 2-47.

LELAND GLASS Glass, Leland Strother 6′0″, 185 **WR**
Col: Oregon *HS:* Sacramento [CA] B: 11/5/1950, Sacramento, CA
Drafted: 1972 Round 8 GB
1972 GB: Rush 2-13 6.5; PR 1-1 1.0. **Total:** Rush 2-13 6.5; PR 1-1 1.0.

		Receiving			
Year Team	**G**	**Rec**	**Yds**	**Avg**	**TD**
1972 GB	14	15	261	17.4	1
1973 GB	12	11	119	10.8	0
NFL Total	26	26	380	14.6	1

WILLIAM GLASS Glass, William Parker 6′4″, 261 **OG**
Col: Baylor *HS:* Duncanville [TX] B: 12/21/1957, Harlingten, TX
Drafted: 1980 Round 4 Cin
1980 Cin: 15 G.

BILL GLASS Glass, William Sheppeard 6′5″, 252 **DE-C-OT**
Col: Baylor *HS:* W.B. Ray [Corpus Christi, TX] B: 8/16/1935, Texarkana, TX *Drafted:* 1957 Round 1 Det
1958 Det: 12 G. **1959** Det: 12 G. **1960** Det: 12 G. **1961** Det: 14 G. **1962** Cle: 14 G. **1963** Cle: 14 G. **1964** Cle: 14 G. **1965** Cle: 14 G; Int 1-0. **1966** Cle: 14 G; **1** Fum TD; 6 Pt. **1967** Cle: 14 G; Int 1-0. **1968** Cle: 10 G; Int 2-21 1 TD; 6 Pt. **Total:** 144 G; Int 4-21 1 TD; 1 Fum TD; Tot TD 2; 12 Pt.

BILL GLASSGOW Glassgow, Willis Allen 5′10″, 190 **TB-WB**
Col: Nebraska; Iowa *HS:* Shenandoah [IA] B: 4/21/1907, Wheeling, MO D: 1959, Cedar Rapids, IA
1930 Port: 12 G; Pass 1 TD; Rush 3 TD; KR **1** TD; Scor 28, 4 XK; Tot TD 4. **1931** ChiC: 9 G. **Total:** 21 G; Pass 1 TD; Rush 3 TD; KR 1 TD; Tot TD 4.

TOM GLASSIC Glassic, Thomas Joseph 6′3″, 254 **OG**
Col: Virginia *HS:* Watchung [NJ] B: 4/17/1954, Elizabeth, NJ
Drafted: 1976 Round 1 Den
1976 Den: 14 G. **1977** Den: 14 G. **1978** Den: 11 G. **1979** Den: 16 G. **1980** Den: 13 G. **1981** Den: 16 G. **1982** Den: 9 G. **1983** Den: 12 G. **Total:** 105 G.

FRANK GLASSMAN Glassman, Frank 6′0″, 210 **G-T**
Col: Wilmington; Bliss College *HS:* Central [Columbus, OH]
B: 5/14/1908, Columbus, OH D: 8/1/1996, Columbus, OH
1929 Buf: 9 G.

MORRIS GLASSMAN Glassman, Morris 5′10″, 166 **OE**
Col: No College *HS:* Commerce [Columbus, OH] B: 2/19/1900, Russia D: 2/18/1980, Columbus, OH
1921 Col: 9 G. **1922** Col: 6 G. **Total:** 15 G.

FRED GLATZ Glatz, Fred Joseph 6′1″, 200 **OE**
Col: Pittsburgh *HS:* Central Catholic [Pittsburgh, PA] B: 7/31/1933, Pittsburgh, PA *Drafted:* 1956 Round 20 Pit
1956 Pit: 4 G; Punt 25-984 39.4.

CHARLES GLAZE Glaze, Charles Otis 5′11″, 200 **DB**
Col: South Carolina State *HS:* Lincoln Co. [Lincolnton, GA]
B: 9/12/1965, Lincolnton, GA
1987 Sea: 3 G; Int 2-53; 2 Sac.

BOB GLAZEBROOK Glazebrook, Robert 6′1″, 200 **DB**
Col: Fresno City Coll. CA (J.C.); Fresno State *HS:* Herbert Hoover [Fresno, CA] B: 3/7/1956, Fresno, CA *Drafted:* 1978 Round 11 Oak
1978 Atl: 8 G. **1979** Atl: 13 G; Rec 1-20 20.0; PR 1-(-1) -1.0. **1980** Atl: 16 G; Int 2-6. **1981** Atl: 16 G; Int 2-21. **1982** Atl: 9 G; Int 1-10; 1 Fum TD; 6 Pt. **1983** Atl: 16 G; KR 2-0; Int 3-30; 1 Fum. **Total:** 78 G; Rec 1-20 20.0; PR 1-(-1) -1.0; KR 2-0; Int 8-67; 1 Fum TD; 6 Pt; 1 Fum.

AARON GLENN Glenn, Aaron DeVon 5′9″, 185 **DB**
Col: Navarro Coll. TX (J.C.); Texas A&M *HS:* Chester W. Nimitz [Houston, TX] B: 7/16/1972, Humble, TX *Drafted:* 1994 Round 1 NYJ

		Kickoff Returns				Interceptions				Tot
Year Team	**G**	**Ret**	**Yds**	**Avg**	**TD**	**Int**	**Yds**	**TD**	**Fum**	**TD**
1994 NYJ	15	27	582	21.6	0	0	0	0	2	0
1995 NYJ	16	1	12	12.0	0	1	17	0	0	0
1996 NYJ	16	1	6	6.0	0	4	113	**2**	0	2
1997 NYJ	16	28	741	26.5	1	1	5	0	1	1
1998 NYJ	13	24	585	24.4	0	6	23	0	1	1
NFL Total	76	81	1926	23.8	1	12	158	2	4	4

HOWARD GLENN Glenn, Howard Earl 6′0″, 235 **OG**
Col: Linfield *HS:* Louisville Colored [MS] B: 9/26/1934, Vancouver, Canada D: 10/9/1960, Houston, TX
1960 NYT: 4 G.

KERRY GLENN Glenn, Kerry Raymond 5′9″, 175 **DB**
Col: Minnesota *HS:* East St. Louis [IL] B: 1/3/1962, East St. Louis, IL
Drafted: 1985 Round 10 NYJ
1985 NYJ: 16 G; KR 5-71 14.2; Int 4-15 **1** TD; 6 Pt. **1986** NYJ: 1 G. **1987** NYJ: 8 G; 0.5 Sac. **1989** NYJ: 14 G; Int 1-0; 0.5 Sac. **1990** Mia: 16 G; Int 2-31 1 TD; 6 Pt; 1 Sac. **1991** Mia: 3 G. **1992** Mia: 16 G. **Total:** 74 G; KR 5-71 14.2; Int 7-46 2 TD; 12 Pt; 2 Sac.

TARIK GLENN Glenn, Tarik 6′5″, 335 **OT**
(T-Bone) *Col:* California *HS:* Bishop O'Dowd [Oakland, CA]
B: 5/25/1976, Cleveland, OH *Drafted:* 1997 Round 1 Ind
1997 Ind: 16 G; Rec 1-3 3.0. **1998** Ind: 16 G. **Total:** 32 G; Rec 1-3 3.0.

TERRY GLENN Glenn, Terry Tyree 5′11″, 185 **WR**
Col: Ohio State *HS:* Brookhaven [Columbus, OH] B: 7/23/1974, Columbus, OH *Drafted:* 1996 Round 1 NE
1996 NE: Rush 5-42 8.4. **1998** NE: Rush 2-(-1) -0.5. **Total:** Rush 7-41 5.9.

		Receiving				
Year Team	**G**	**Rec**	**Yds**	**Avg**	**TD**	**Fum**
1996 NE	15	90	1132	12.6	6	1
1997 NE	9	27	431	16.0	2	1
1998 NE	10	50	792	15.8	3	0
NFL Total	34	167	2355	14.1	11	2

VENCIE GLENN Glenn, Vencie Lenard 6′0″, 191 **DB**
Col: Indiana State *HS:* John F. Kennedy [Silver Spring, MD]
B: 10/26/1964, Grambling, LA *Drafted:* 1986 Round 2 NE
1987 SD: 0.5 Sac. **1988** SD: 1 Sac. **1989** SD: 1 Fum TD; 1 Sac. **1991** NO: KR 1-10 10.0. **1994** Min: 1 Sac. **Total:** KR 1-10 10.0; 1 Fum TD; 3.5 Sac.

Year Team	G	Interceptions Int	Yds	TD	Tot TD
1986 NE-SD	16	2	31	0	0
1986 NE	4	0	0	0	0
1986 SD	12	2	31	0	0
1987 SD	12	4	**166**	1	1
1988 SD	16	1	0	0	0
1989 SD	16	4	52	0	1
1990 SD	14	1	0	0	0
1991 NO	16	4	35	0	0
1992 Min	16	5	65	0	0
1993 Min	16	5	49	0	0
1994 Min	16	4	55	0	0
1995 NYG	15	5	91	1	1
NFL Total	153	35	544	2	3

BILL GLENN Glenn, William Joseph 6'0", 157 **QB-DB**
Col: Eastern Illinois *HS:* Fairfield [IL] B: 3/15/1918, St. Louis, MO
Drafted: 1941 Round 19 ChiB
1944 ChiB: 2 G; Pass 4-1 25.0%, 22 5.50; Rush 1-1 1.0.

GEORGE GLENNIE Glennie, George William 6'2", 185 **G-E-T**
Col: Ripon B: 3/30/1902, North Andover, MA D: 6/8/1980, Andover, MA
1926 Rac: 5 G.

EDDIE GLICK Glick, Edward Isadore 5'8", 165 **TB-HB-BB**
Col: Lawrence; Marquette *HS:* Marinette [WI] B: 4/23/1900, Marinette, WI D: 8/13/1976, DePere, WI
1922 GB: 6 G.

FRED GLICK Glick, Frederick Couture 6'1", 195 **DB**
(Bear) *Col:* Colorado State *HS:* Poudre [Fort Collins, CO]
B: 2/25/1937, Aurora, CO *Drafted:* 1959 Round 23 ChiC

Year Team	G	Punt Returns Ret	Yds	Avg	TD	Kickoff Returns Ret	Yds	Avg	TD
1959 ChiC	1	0	0	—	0	0	0	—	0
1960 StL	4	0	0	—	0	0	0	—	0
1961 Hou	12	0	0	—	0	0	0	—	0
1962 Hou	14	12	79	6.6	0	1	22	22.0	0
1963 Hou	14	19	171	9.0	0	20	451	22.6	0
1964 Hou	14	6	32	5.3	0	1	27	27.0	0
1965 Hou	14	7	44	6.3	0	4	84	21.0	0
1966 Hou	10	0	0	—	0	0	0	—	0
NFL Total	83	44	326	7.4	0	26	584	22.5	0

Year Team	Interceptions Int	Yds	TD	Fum
1961 Hou	4	28	0	0
1962 Hou	3	53	0	0
1963 Hou	**12**	180	1	3
1964 Hou	5	54	0	0
1965 Hou	2	18	0	1
1966 Hou	4	57	0	1
NFL Total	30	390	1	5

GARY GLICK Glick, Gary Gaylen 6'2", 195 **DB-HB**
Col: Colorado State *HS:* LaPorte [CO] B: 5/14/1930, Grant, NE
Drafted: 1956 Round 1 Pit
1956 Pit: Scor 28, 4-7 57.1% FG, 16-17 94.1% XK. **1957** Pit: PR 1-0; Scor 25, 5-18 27.8% FG, 10-12 83.3% XK. **1958** Pit: PR 2-0; **1** Fum TD. **1959** Pit-Was: PR 1-9 9.0. Was: PR 1-9 9.0. **1960** Was: Rush 1-15 15.0; **1** Fum TD. **Total:** Rush 1-15 15.0; PR 4-9 2.3; Scor 65, 9-25 36.0% FG, 26-29 89.7% XK; 2 Fum TD.

Year Team	G	Interceptions Int	Yds	TD	Fum
1956 Pit	8	0	0	0	0
1957 Pit	12	2	0	0	0
1958 Pit	12	2	60	0	0
1959 Pit-Was	11	2	35	0	0
1959 Pit	2	0	0	0	0
1959 Was	9	2	35	0	0
1960 Was	11	3	4	0	1
1961 Bal	11	4	18	0	0
1963 SD	6	1	13	0	0
NFL Total	71	14	130	0	1

NORM GLOCKSON Glockson, Norman Stanley 6'2", 230 **G**
(Tango) *Col:* No College B: 6/15/1894, Blue Island, IL D: 8/5/1955, Maywood, IL
1922 Rac: 1 G.

FRED GLODEN Gloden, Frederick Jean Jr. 5'10", 187 **HB-DB**
Col: Tulane *HS:* Dubuque [IA] B: 12/21/1918, Dubuque, IA
AAFC **1946** MiaA: 7 G; Rush 13-24 1.8 1 TD; KR 1-20 20.0; 6 Pt.
NFL **1941** Phi: 6 G; Rush 22-55 2.5; Rec 2-13 6.5.

CLYDE GLOSSON Glosson, Clyde P 5'11", 175 **WR**
Col: Texas-El Paso *HS:* Phillis Wheatley [Houston, TX] B: 1/22/1947, San Antonio, TX *Drafted:* 1970 Round 7 KC
1970 Buf: 11 G; Rec 2-16 8.0; KR 4-61 15.3.

ANDREW GLOVER Glover, Andrew Lee 6'6", 250 **TE**
Col: Grambling State *HS:* East Ascension [Gonzales, LA]
B: 8/12/1967, New Orleans, LA *Drafted:* 1991 Round 10 LARd

Year Team	G	Receiving Rec	Yds	Avg	TD	Fum
1991 LARd	16	5	45	9.0	3	0
1992 LARd	16	15	178	11.9	1	1
1993 LARd	15	4	55	13.8	1	0
1994 LARd	16	33	371	11.2	2	0
1995 Oak	16	26	220	8.5	3	0
1996 Oak	14	9	101	11.2	1	0
1997 Min	13	32	378	11.8	3	0
1998 Min	16	35	522	14.9	5	0
NFL Total	122	159	1870	11.8	19	1

CLYDE GLOVER Glover, Clyde M 6'6", 280 **DT**
Col: Walla Walla CC WA; Fresno State *HS:* Sunset [Las Vegas, NV]
B: 7/16/1960, New Orleans, LA
1987 SF: 13 G; 2 Sac.

KEVIN GLOVER Glover, Kevin Bernard 6'2", 278 **C-OG**
Col: Maryland *HS:* Largo [Upper Marlboro, MD] B: 6/17/1963, Washington, DC *Drafted:* 1985 Round 2 Det
1985 Det: 10 G. **1986** Det: 4 G. **1987** Det: 12 G; KR 1-19 19.0. **1988** Det: 16 G. **1989** Det: 16 G. **1990** Det: 16 G. **1991** Det: 16 G. **1992** Det: 7 G. **1993** Det: 16 G. **1994** Det: 16 G. **1995** Det: 16 G; 2 Fum. **1996** Det: 16 G. **1997** Det: 16 G. **1998** Sea: 8 G. **Total:** 185 G; KR 1-19 19.0; 2 Fum.

LA'ROI GLOVER Glover, La'Roi Damon 6'2", 285 **DT**
Col: San Diego State *HS:* Point Loma [San Diego, CA] B: 7/4/1974, San Diego, CA *Drafted:* 1996 Round 5 Oak
1996 Oak: 2 G. **1997** NO: 15 G; 6.5 Sac. **1998** NO: 16 G; Int 1-0; 10 Sac. **Total:** 33 G; Int 1-0; 16.5 Sac.

RICH GLOVER Glover, Richard Edward 6'1", 240 **DT**
Col: Nebraska *HS:* Henry Snyder [Jersey City, NJ] B: 2/6/1950, Bayonne, NJ *Drafted:* 1973 Round 3 NYG
1973 NYG: 13 G. **1975** Phi: 14 G. **Total:** 27 G.

LARRY GLUECK Glueck, Lawrence David 6'0", 190 **DB**
Col: Villanova *HS:* Landsdale Catholic [PA] B: 10/5/1941, Norristown, PA *Drafted:* 1963 Round 3 ChiB
1963 ChiB: 14 G; Int 1-14. **1964** ChiB: 11 G. **1965** ChiB: 12 G. **Total:** 37 G; Int 1-14.

PAUL GOAD Goad, Paul Ellis 6'0", 195 **FB**
Col: Vanderbilt; Abilene Christian *HS:* Little Rock Central [AR]
B: 9/7/1934, Cincinnati, OH D: 11/29/1978, Little Rock, AR
Drafted: 1956 Round 25 SF
1956 SF: 4 G; KR 1-18 18.0.

TIM GOAD Goad, Timothy Ray 6'3", 280 **NT-DT**
Col: North Carolina *HS:* Patrick Co. [Stuart, VA] B: 2/28/1966, Claudville, VA *Drafted:* 1988 Round 4 NE
1988 NE: 16 G; 2 Sac. **1989** NE: 16 G; 1 Sac. **1990** NE: 16 G; 2.5 Sac. **1991** NE: 16 G. **1992** NE: 16 G; 1 Fum TD; 6 Pt; 2.5 Sac. **1993** NE: 16 G; 0.5 Sac. **1994** NE: 13 G; 3 Sac. **1995** Cle: 16 G. **1996** Bal: 16 G; 3 Sac. **Total:** 141 G; 1 Fum TD; 6 Pt; 14.5 Sac.

ART GOB Gob, Arthur Jerome 6'4", 230 **DE**
Col: Pittsburgh *HS:* Baldwin [Pittsburgh, PA] B: 1/7/1937, Pittsburgh, PA *Drafted:* 1959 Round 22 Was
1959 Was: 11 G; KR 1-0; Scor **1** Saf; 2 Pt. **1960** Was-LAC: 4 G. Was: 1 G. LAC: 3 G. **Total:** 15 G; KR 1-0; Scor 1 Saf; 2 Pt.

LES GOBLE Goble, Lester Bois 5'11", 158 **HB-DB**
Col: Alfred *HS:* Waverly [NY] B: 7/23/1932, Waverly, NY
Drafted: 1954 Round 13 ChiC
1954 ChiC: Rec 1-(-1) -1.0; PR 22-51 2.3; Int 1-3. **Total:** Rec 1-(-1) -1.0; PR 22-51 2.3; Int 1-3.

Year Team	G	Rushing Ret	Yds	Avg	TD	Kickoff Returns Ret	Yds	Avg	TD	Fum	Tot TD
1954 ChiC	12	30	42	1.4	1	27	749	27.7	**2**	5	3
1955 ChiC	9	7	11	1.6	0	8	160	20.0	0	0	0
NFL Total	21	37	53	1.4	1	35	909	26.0	2	5	3

ED GODDARD Goddard, Edwin Vinson 5'10", 183 **TB-DB-WB**
(Rip) *Col:* Washington State *HS:* Escondido [CA] B: 10/28/1914, San Diego, CA D: 7/20/1992, Lake San Marcos, CA *Drafted:* 1937 Round 1 Bkn
1937 Bkn-Cle: Rec 6-61 10.2; Scor 13, 1 XK. Bkn: Rec 3-18 6.0. Cle: Rec 3-43 14.3; Scor 7, 1 XK. **1938** Cle: Rec 6-128 21.3 1 TD; Scor 7, 1-1 100.0% XK. **Total:** Rec 12-189 15.8 1 TD; Scor 20, 2-1 100.0% XK.

		Passing							
Year Team	G	Att	Comp	Comp%	Yds	YPA	TD	Int	Rating
1937 Bkn-Cle	8	41	13	31.7	180	4.39	1	8	15.3
1937 Bkn	4	23	4	17.4	46	2.00	1	5	14.5
1937 Cle	4	18	9	50.0	134	7.44	0	3	35.2
1938 Cle	10	43	19	44.2	238	5.53	0	6	22.4
NFL Total	18	84	32	38.1	418	4.98	1	14	18.9

	Rushing				Tot
Year Team	Att	Yds	Avg	TD	TD
1937 Bkn-Cle	57	162	2.8	2	2
1937 Bkn	19	65	3.4	1	1
1937 Cle	38	97	2.6	1	1
1938 Cle	40	-16	-0.4	0	1
NFL Total	97	146	1.5	2	3

CHRIS GODFREY Godfrey, Christopher James 6′3″, 263 **OG-OT-DE-DT**
Col: Michigan *HS:* De La Salle [Detroit, MI]; Lake HS [Miami, FL]
B: 5/17/1958, Detroit, MI
1980 NYJ: 6 G. **1984** NYG: 10 G. **1985** NYG: 16 G. **1986** NYG: 16 G. **1987** NYG: 8 G. **1988** Sea: 9 G. **Total:** 65 G.

HERB GODFREY Godfrey, Herbert L 6′1″, 187 **OE-DE**
Col: Washington State *HS:* Lincoln [Tacoma, WA] B: 8/23/1919, Port Angeles, WA
1942 Cle: 3 G.

RANDALL GODFREY Godfrey, Randall Euralentris 6′2″, 245 **LB**
Col: Georgia *HS:* Lowndes [Valdosta, GA] B: 4/6/1973, Valdosta, GA
Drafted: 1996 Round 2 Dal
1996 Dal: 16 G. **1997** Dal: 16 G; 1 Sac. **1998** Dal: 16 G; Int 1-0; 3 Sac. **Total:** 48 G; Int 1-0; 4 Sac.

WALT GODWIN Godwin, Walter Hampton 5′7″, 205 **G**
Col: Georgia Tech *HS:* Lamar Co. [Barnesville, GA] B: 9/29/1899
D: 10/1954
1929 SI: 9 G.

BILL GODWIN Godwin, William Domont 6′3″, 241 **C-LB**
Col: Georgia *HS:* Blytheville [AR] B: 5/8/1919 *Drafted:* 1943 Round 8 ChiC
1947 Bos: 12 G; Int 2-27. **1948** Bos: 12 G. **Total:** 24 G; Int 2-27.

LEO GOEAS Goeas, Leo Douglas 6′4″, 300 **OT-OG**
Col: Hawaii *HS:* Kamehameha School [Honolulu, HI] B: 8/15/1966, Honolulu, HI *Drafted:* 1990 Round 3 SD
1990 SD: 15 G. **1991** SD: 9 G. **1992** SD: 16 G. **1993** LARm: 16 G. **1994** LARm: 13 G. **1995** StL: 15 G. **1996** StL: 16 G. **1997** Bal: 11 G. **Total:** 111 G.

BRAD GOEBEL Goebel, Bradley Arlen 6′3″, 202 **QB**
Col: Baylor *HS:* Cuero [TX] B: 10/13/1967, Cuero, TX
1991 Phi: Rush 1-2 2.0. **Total:** Rush 1-2 2.0.

		Passing								
Year Team	G	Att	Comp	Comp%	Yds	YPA	TD	Int	Rating	Fum
1991 Phi	5	56	30	53.6	267	4.77	0	6	27.0	2
1992 Cle	1	3	2	66.7	32	10.67	0	0	102.1	0
1994 Cle	1	0	0	—	0	—	0	0	—	0
NFL Total	7	59	32	54.2	299	5.07	0	6	28.8	2

HANK GOEBEL Goebel, Henry Walter 6′7″, 270 **OT**
Col: Cal State-Fullerton *HS:* Corona Del Mar [Newport Beach, CA]
B: 11/1/1964, Evergreen Park, IL *Drafted:* 1986 Round 8 LARm
1987 LARm: 3 G.

JOE GOEBEL Goebel, Joseph Robert 6′5″, 264 **C**
Col: UCLA *HS:* Midland [TX] B: 12/12/1963, Tulsa, OK *Drafted:* 1987 Round 11 SD
1987 SD: 2 G.

PAUL GOEBEL Goebel, Paul Gordon 6′3″, 199 **OE**
Col: Michigan *HS:* Grand Rapids Union [MS] B: 5/28/1901, Grand Rapids, MI D: 1/26/1988, Grand Rapids, MI
1923 Col: 10 G; Pass 1 TD; Rec 1 TD; Scor 8, 2 XK. **1924** Col: 8 G; Rec 2 TD; 1 Fum TD; Tot TD 3; 18 Pt. **1925** Col: 8 G. **Total:** 26 G; Pass 1 TD; Rec 3 TD; 1 Fum TD; Tot TD 4.

GEORGE GOEDDEKE Goeddeke, George Aloysius 6′3″, 253 **OG-OT-C**
Col: Notre Dame *HS:* St. David's [Detroit, MI] B: 7/29/1945, Detroit, MI
Drafted: 1967 Round 3 Den
1967 Den: 10 G. **1968** Den: 14 G. **1969** Den: 14 G. **1970** Den: 14 G. **1971** Den: 12 G. **1972** Den: 2 G. **Total:** 66 G.

ART GOERKE Goerke, Arthur C 5′6″, 165 **OE**
Col: No College *HS:* Tonawanda [NY] B: 9/14/1896, NY D: 2/5/1970, Rochester, NY
1921 Ton: 1 G.

GUS GOETZ Goetz, Angus Gerald 6′3″, 198 **T-OE**
Col: Michigan *HS:* Sault Ste. Marie [MI] B: 7/6/1897, De Tour, MI
D: 7/24/1977, Grosse Pointe, MI
1922 Buf: 7 G. **1923** Col: 2 G. **Total:** 9 G.

CLARK GOFF Goff, Clark William 6′3″, 235 **T**
Col: Florida *HS:* Scott Twp. [North Braddock, PA] B: 1918
D: 2/3/1998, Pittsburgh, PA *Drafted:* 1940 Round 5 Pit
1940 Pit: 11 G.

MIKE GOFF Goff, Michael J 6′5″, 316 **OG**
Col: Iowa *HS:* La Salle-Peru Twp. [La Salle, IL] B: 1/6/1976, Spring Valley, IL *Drafted:* 1998 Round 3 Cin
1998 Cin: 10 G.

ROBERT GOFF Goff, Robert Lamar 6′3″, 272 **DE-DT**
(Pig) *Col:* Butler County CC KS; Auburn *HS:* Bayshore [Bradenton, FL]
B: 10/2/1965, Rochester, NY *Drafted:* 1988 Round 4 TB
1988 TB: 16 G; 2 Sac. **1989** TB: 12 G; 4 Sac. **1990** NO: 15 G. **1991** NO: 15 G; 2 Sac. **1992** NO: 16 G; **2** Fum TD; 12 Pt. **1993** NO: 16 G; 2 Sac. **1994** NO: 16 G. **1995** NO: 11 G; 1.5 Sac. **1996** Min: 5 G. **Total:** 122 G; 2 Fum TD; 12 Pt; 11.5 Sac.

WILLARD GOFF Goff, Willard E Jr. 6′3″, 268 **DT**
Col: Dodge City CC KS; West Texas A&M; Illinois *HS:* Springfield [CO]
B: 10/17/1961, Lamar, CO
1985 Atl: 7 G. **1987** SD: 1 G. **Total:** 8 G.

DERREL GOFOURTH Gofourth, Derrel Glen 6′3″, 260 **OG-C**
Col: Oklahoma State *HS:* Parsons [KS] B: 3/20/1955, Parsons, KS
Drafted: 1977 Round 7 GB
1977 GB: 13 G; KR 1-13 13.0. **1978** GB: 16 G. **1979** GB: 16 G. **1980** GB: 16 G. **1981** GB: 15 G. **1982** GB: 9 G. **1983** SD: 15 G. **1984** SD: 16 G; KR 1-0. **Total:** 116 G; KR 2-13 6.5.

KEVIN GOGAN Gogan, Kevin Patrick 6′7″, 317 **OT-OG**
Col: Washington *HS:* Sacred Heart [San Francisco, CA] B: 11/2/1964, San Francisco, CA *Drafted:* 1987 Round 8 Dal
1987 Dal: 11 G. **1988** Dal: 15 G. **1989** Dal: 13 G. **1990** Dal: 16 G. **1991** Dal: 16 G. **1992** Dal: 16 G. **1993** Dal: 16 G. **1994** LARd: 16 G. **1995** Oak: 16 G. **1996** Oak: 16 G. **1997** SF: 16 G. **1998** SF: 16 G. **Total:** 183 G.

KEITH GOGANIOUS Goganious, Keith Lorenzo 6′2″, 237 **LB**
Col: Penn State *HS:* Green Run [Virginia Beach, VA] B: 12/7/1968, Virginia Beach, VA *Drafted:* 1992 Round 3 Buf
1992 Buf: 13 G. **1993** Buf: 16 G; 1 Sac. **1994** Buf: 16 G. **1995** Jac: 16 G; Int 2-11. **1996** Bal: 13 G. **Total:** 74 G; Int 2-11; 1 Sac.

CHARLIE GOGOLAK Gogolak, Charles Paul 5′10″, 165 **K**
Col: Princeton *HS:* Ogdensburg Free Acad. [NY] B: 12/29/1944, Rapahidveg, Hungary *Drafted:* 1966 Round 1 Was

		Scoring						
Year Team	G	Pts	FG	FGA	FG%	XK	XKA	XK%
1966 Was	14	105	22	34	64.7	39	41	95.1
1967 Was	1	6	1	4	25.0	3	3	100.0
1968 Was	14	57	9	19	47.4	30	31	96.8
1970 Bos	6	11	2	7	28.6	5	5	100.0
1971 NE	14	64	12	21	57.1	28	28	100.0
1972 NE	6	27	6	8	75.0	9	9	100.0
NFL Total	55	270	52	93	55.9	114	117	97.4

PETE GOGOLAK Gogolak, Peter Kornel 6′1″, 190 **K**
Col: Cornell *HS:* Ogdensburg Free Acad. [NY] B: 4/18/1942, Budapest, Hungary *Drafted:* 1964 Round 12 Buf
1969 NYG: Punt 12-491 40.9. **Total:** Punt 12-491 40.9.

		Scoring						
Year Team	G	Pts	FG	FGA	FG%	XK	XKA	XK%
1964 Buf	14	102	19	29	**65.5**	45	**46**	**97.8**
1965 Buf	14	115	**28**	**46**	60.9	31	31	100.0
1966 NYG	14	77	16	28	57.1	29	31	93.5
1967 NYG	9	46	6	10	60.0	28	29	96.6
1968 NYG	14	78	14	24	58.3	36	36	100.0
1969 NYG	14	66	11	21	52.4	33	33	100.0
1970 NYG	14	107	25	41	61.0	32	32	100.0
1971 NYG	14	48	6	17	35.3	30	30	100.0
1972 NYG	14	97	21	31	67.7	34	38	89.5
1973 NYG	14	76	17	28	60.7	25	25	100.0
1974 NYG	14	51	10	19	52.6	21	23	91.3
NFL Total	149	863	173	294	58.8	344	354	97.2

DAN GOICH Goich, Dandennis John 6′4″, 240 **DT**
Col: West Hills CC CA (J.C.); California *HS:* Mount Carmel [Chicago, IL]
B: 4/30/1944, Chicago, IL *Drafted:* 1966 Round 8 StL
1969 Det: 14 G. **1970** Det: 14 G. **1971** NO: 10 G. **1972** NYG: 4 G. **1973** NYG: 14 G. **Total:** 56 G.

MARSHALL GOLDBERG Goldberg, Marshall 5′11″, 190 **TB-DB-FB-HB**
(Biggie) *Col:* Pittsburgh *HS:* Elkins [WV] B: 10/25/1917, Elkins, WV
Drafted: 1939 Round 2 ChiC
1939 ChiC: Pass 7-1 14.3%, 4 0.57 1 Int. **1940** ChiC: Pass 2-0; Punt 1-47 47.0. **1941** ChiC: Pass 19-7 36.8%, 111 5.84 1 TD 2 Int; PR 12-152 12.7. **1942** ChiC: PR 6-60 10.0. **1943** ChiC: PR 1-15 15.0. **1946** ChiC: PR 1-11 11.0. **1947** ChiC: PR 1-21 21.0. **Total:** Pass 28-8 28.6%, 115 4.11 1 TD 3 Int; PR 21-259 12.3; Punt 1-47 47.0.

		Rushing				Receiving			
Year Team	G	Att	Yds	Avg	TD	Rec	Yds	Avg	TD
1939 ChiC	10	56	152	2.7	2	5	90	18.0	1
1940 ChiC	11	87	325	3.7	2	2	29	14.5	1
1941 ChiC	11	117	427	3.6	3	16	313	19.6	1
1942 ChiC	11	116	369	3.2	1	9	108	12.0	0
1943 ChiC	1	6	6	1.0	0	4	31	7.8	1
1946 ChiC	10	43	210	4.9	3	17	152	8.9	1
1947 ChiC	12	51	155	3.0	0	7	52	7.4	0
1948 ChiC	11	0	0	—	0	0	0	—	0
NFL Total	77	476	1644	3.5	11	60	775	12.9	5

	Kickoff Returns				Interceptions				Tot
Year Team	Ret	Yds	Avg	TD	Int	Yds	TD	Fum	TD
1939 ChiC	—	—	—	0	—	—	0	0	3
1940 ChiC	—	—	—	0	2	15	0	0	3
1941 ChiC	**12**	**290**	24.2	0	**7**	54	0	0	4
1942 ChiC	**15**	**393**	26.2	**1**	3	39	0	0	2
1943 ChiC	2	53	26.5	0	1	0	0	0	1
1946 ChiC	5	108	21.6	0	4	46	0	3	4
1947 ChiC	0	0	—	0	0	0	0	1	0
1948 ChiC	0	0	—	0	2	9	0	0	0
NFL Total	34	844	24.8	1	19	163	0	4	17

BILL GOLDBERG Goldberg, William Scott 6′2″, 272 **NT-DT**
Col: Georgia *HS:* Thomas Edison [Tulsa, OK] B: 12/27/1966, Tulsa, OK
Drafted: 1990 Round 11 LARm
1992 Atl: 4 G. **1993** Atl: 5 G. **1994** Atl: 5 G. **Total:** 14 G.

TIM GOLDEN Golden, Timothy George 6′1″, 220 **LB**
Col: Florida *HS:* Boyd H. Anderson [Lauderdale Lakes, FL]
B: 11/15/1959, Pahokee, FL
1982 NE: 9 G. **1983** NE: 16 G; KR 1-10 10.0. **1984** NE: 15 G. **1985** Phi: 2 G. **Total:** 42 G; KR 1-10 10.0.

BUCKETS GOLDENBERG Goldenberg, Charles Robert 5′10″, 220 **G-LB-BB-DB**
Col: Wisconsin *HS:* West Division [Milwaukee, WI] B: 3/10/1910, Odessa, Ukraine D: 4/16/1986, Glendale, WI
1933 GB: Rec 4-43 10.8 1 TD; Int **1** TD. **1934** GB: Rec 4-26 6.5. **1935** GB: Rec 3-42 14.0. **1937** GB: Int **1** TD. **1940** GB: Int 1-5. **1941** GB: Int 1-0. **1942** GB: Int 4-31. **1943** GB: Int 2-37. **Total:** Rec 11-111 10.1 1 TD; Int 8-73 2 TD.

		Rushing				Tot
Year Team	G	Att	Yds	Avg	TD	TD
1933 GB	11	52	213	4.1	4	**7**
1934 GB	10	30	73	2.4	2	2
1935 GB	11	16	52	3.3	0	0
1936 GB	7	6	9	1.5	0	0
1937 GB	8	4	18	4.5	0	1
1938 GB	11	0	0	—	0	0
1939 GB	9	0	0	—	0	0
1940 GB	11	0	0	—	0	0
1941 GB	8	0	0	—	0	0
1942 GB	11	0	0	—	0	0
1943 GB	10	0	0	—	0	0
1944 GB	9	0	0	—	0	0
1945 GB	4	0	0	—	0	0
NFL Total	120	108	365	3.4	6	10

JOE GOLDING Golding, Joseph Griffith 6′0″, 184 **DB-HB**
Col: Oklahoma *HS:* Eufaula [OK] B: 2/26/1921, Eufaula, OK
D: 12/26/1971, near Muskogee, OK
1947 Bos: PR 7-63 9.0. **1948** Bos: PR 10-129 12.9. **1949** NYB: PR 5-27 5.4. **1950** NYY: **1** Fum TD. **Total:** PR 22-219 10.0; 1 Fum TD.

		Rushing				Receiving			
Year Team	G	Att	Yds	Avg	TD	Rec	Yds	Avg	TD
1947 Bos	12	26	71	2.7	1	6	52	8.7	2
1948 Bos	12	24	36	1.5	0	9	159	17.7	4
1949 NYB	11	63	240	3.8	0	12	78	6.5	2
1950 NYY	12	1	2	2.0	0	0	0	—	0
1951 NYY	11	0	0	—	0	0	0	—	0
NFL Total	58	114	349	3.1	1	27	289	10.7	8

	Kickoff Returns				Interceptions				Tot
Year Team	Ret	Yds	Avg	TD	Int	Yds	TD	Fum	TD
1947 Bos	9	173	19.2	0	5	87	0	3	3
1948 Bos	7	192	27.4	0	4	205	**2**	3	6
1949 NYB	13	289	22.2	0	1	65	1	6	3
1950 NYY	0	0	—	0	7	145	1	0	2
1951 NYY	0	0	—	0	2	9	0	0	0
NFL Total	29	654	22.6	0	19	511	4	12	14

SAM GOLDMAN Goldman, Samuel 6′3″, 228 **OE-DE**
Col: Ohio State; Samford *HS:* John Adams [Cleveland, OH]
B: 11/10/1916, Cleveland, OH D: 11/8/1978, Pensacola, FL
1944 Bos: 4 G; Rec 2-21 10.5; KR 1-0. **1946** Bos: 11 G; Rush 2-(-3) -1.5; Rec 15-154 10.3; KR 2-41 20.5; 2 Fum. **1947** Bos: 12 G; Rec 1-9 9.0; KR 1-1 1.0. **1948** ChiC: 11 G. **1949** Det: 8 G. **Total:** 46 G; Rush 2-(-3) -1.5; Rec 18-184 10.2; KR 4-42 10.5; 2 Fum.

JOHN GOLDSBERRY Goldsberry, John Gerard 6′2″, 245 **DT-OT**
Col: Indiana *HS:* Roosevelt [Ypsilanti, MI]; John Adams HS [South Bend, IN] B: 11/22/1926, Indianapolis, IN D: 1/23/1972
Drafted: 1949 Round 4 ChiC
1949 ChiC: 10 G; Int 1-36. **1950** ChiC: 10 G. **Total:** 20 G; Int 1-36.

EARL GOLDSMITH Goldsmith, Arthur Earl 182 **OE-WB**
(Goney) *Col:* Indiana *HS:* Central [Evansville, IN] B: 4/14/1894, Evansville, IN D: 1/9/1971, Richmond, VA
1921 Eva: 5 G; 1 Fum TD; 6 Pt. **1922** Eva: 2 G. **Total:** 7 G; 1 Fum TD; 6 Pt.

WEN GOLDSMITH Goldsmith, Wendell Eugene 6′0″, 202 **C-LB**
Col: Emporia State *HS:* Malvern [KS] B: 12/15/1917, Malvern, KS
1940 NYG: 1 G.

AL GOLDSTEIN Goldstein, Alan 6′0″, 204 **OE**
Col: North Carolina *HS:* Lafayette [Brooklyn, NY] B: 1/8/1936, Brooklyn, NY D: 10/14/1991, West Bloomfield, MI *Drafted:* 1960 Round 1 Buf
1960 Oak: Rush 3-(-2) -0.7 1 TD.

		Receiving				Tot
Year Team	G	Rec	Yds	Avg	TD	TD
1960 Oak	14	27	354	13.1	1	2

RALPH GOLDSTON Goldston, Ralph Peter 5′11″, 195 **HB-DB**
(Goldie) *Col:* Indiana; Youngstown State *HS:* Memorial [Campbell, OH]
B: 2/25/1929, Campbell, OH *Drafted:* 1952 Round 11 Phi
1952 Phi: Rec 2-12 6.0. **1955** Phi: Rec 2-8 4.0. **Total:** Rec 4-20 5.0.

		Rushing				
Year Team	G	Att	Yds	Avg	TD	Fum
1952 Phi	9	65	210	3.2	3	2
1954 Phi	8	0	0	—	0	0
1955 Phi	10	14	-7	-0.5	0	2
NFL Total	27	79	203	2.6	3	4

ARCHIE GOLEMBESKI Golembeski, Anthony Edward 5′10″, 185 **E-G-C-LB**
Col: Holy Cross *HS:* Worcester Classical [MA] B: 5/25/1900, Lyon Mountain, KY D: 3/9/1976, Worcester, MA
1925 Prov: 11 G; 2 Fum TD; 12 Pt. **1926** Prov: 9 G; Rec 1 TD; Scor 7, 1 XK. **1929** Prov: 8 G. **Total:** 28 G; Rec 1 TD; 2 Fum TD; Tot TD 3.

JOHN GOLEMGESKE Golemgeske, John William 6′2″, 225 **T-G**
Col: Wisconsin *HS:* Waukesha [WI] B: 11/14/1915, Waukesha, WI
Drafted: 1937 Round 6 Bkn
1937 Bkn: 10 G. **1938** Bkn: 11 G. **1939** Bkn: 11 G. **1940** Bkn: 10 G. **Total:** 42 G.

MIKE GOLIC Golic, Michael Louis 6′5″, 274 **DT-NT-DE**
Col: Notre Dame *HS:* St. Joseph [Cleveland, OH] B: 12/12/1962, Willowick, OH *Drafted:* 1985 Round 10 Hou
1986 Hou: 16 G; 1 Sac. **1987** Hou-Phi: 8 G. Hou: 2 G. Phi: 6 G. **1988** Phi: 12 G; 1 Sac. **1989** Phi: 16 G; Int 1-23; 3 Sac. **1990** Phi: 16 G; Int 1-12; 2 Sac. **1991** Phi: 16 G; Int 1-13; 2.5 Sac. **1992** Phi: 16 G; 2 Sac. **1993** Mia: 15 G. **Total:** 115 G; Int 3-48; 11.5 Sac.

BOB GOLIC Golic, Robert Perry 6′2″, 264 **NT-LB-DE**
Col: Notre Dame *HS:* St. Joseph [Cleveland, OH] B: 10/26/1957, Cleveland, OH *Drafted:* 1979 Round 2 NE
1979 NE: 1 G. **1980** NE: 16 G. **1981** NE: 16 G. **1982** Cle: 6 G; 4 Sac. **1983** Cle: 16 G; Int 1-7 1 TD; 6 Pt; 3.5 Sac. **1984** Cle: 15 G; 2 Sac. **1985** Cle: 16 G; 3 Sac. **1986** Cle: 16 G. **1987** Cle: 12 G; 1.5 Sac. **1988** Cle: 16 G. **1989** LARd: 16 G; 3.5 Sac. **1990** LARd: 16 G; 4 Sac. **1991** LARd: 16 G; 1 Sac. **1992** LARd: 9 G. **Total:** 187 G; Int 1-7 1 TD; 6 Pt; 22.5 Sac.

RUDY GOLLOMB Gollomb, Rudolph Peter 5′11″, 205 **G**
Col: Wisconsin; Carroll (Wis.) B: 11/6/1910, Oshkosh, WI
D: 9/11/1991, Oshkosh, WI
1936 Phi: 4 G.

GENE GOLSEN Golsen, Eugene William 5′11″, 188 **FB-TB**
Col: Georgetown *HS:* Loyola Acad. [Wilmette, IL]; Georgetown Prep [Washington, DC] B: 7/6/1902 D: 11/19/1935, Bound Brook, NJ
1926 Lou: 3 G.

TOM GOLSEN Golsen, Thomas Joseph 5'11", 175 **G**
Col: Georgetown *HS:* Loyola Acad. [Wilmette, IL] B: 7/6/1902
D: 11/23/1986, Chicago, IL
1926 Lou: 1 G.

JERRY GOLSTEYN Golsteyn, Jerry Mark 6'4", 207 **QB**
Col: Northern Illinois *HS:* Central [West Allis, WI] B: 8/6/1954, West Allis, WI *Drafted:* 1976 Round 12 NYG
1977 NYG: Rush 3-(-4) -1.3. **1978** NYG: Rush 1-(-3) -3.0. **1979** Det-Bal: Rush 1-0. Det: Rush 1-0. **1983** TB: Rush 5-3 0.6. **Total:** Rush 10-(-4) -0.4.

		Passing									
Year Team	**G**	**Att**	**Comp**	**Comp%**	**Yds**	**YPA**	**TD**	**Int**	**Rating**	**Fum**
1977 NYG	6	70	31	44.3	416	5.94	2	8	33.7	1
1978 NYG	7	40	12	30.0	110	2.75	0	1	29.2	1
1979 Det-Bal	2	9	2	22.2	16	1.78	0	2	0.0	1
1979 Det	1	9	2	22.2	16	1.78	0	2	0.0	1
1979 Bal	1	0	0	—	0	—	0	0	—	0
1982 TB	1	1	0	0.0	0	0.00	0	0	39.6	0
1983 TB	5	97	47	48.5	535	5.52	0	2	56.9	3
NFL Total	21	217	92	42.4	1077	4.96	2	13	36.2	6

RICK GOLTZ Goltz, Ricardo Eugene 6'4", 255 **DE**
Col: Simon Fraser (Canada); British Columbia (Canada) *HS:* John Oliver Sec. School [Vancouver, Canada] B: 3/19/1955, Vancouver, Canada
1987 LARd: 1 G.

CHRIS GOLUB Golub, Christopher David 6'2", 196 **DB**
Col: Kansas *HS:* Shawnee Mission North [KS] B: 12/2/1954, Kansas City, MO *Drafted:* 1977 Round 7 KC
1977 KC: 1 G.

BILL GOMPERS Gompers, William George 6'1", 185 **HB-DB**
(Bushel Foot) *Col:* Notre Dame *HS:* Central Catholic [Wheeling, WV]
B: 3/20/1928, Wheeling, WV
AAFC **1948** BufA: PR 1-10 10.0; KR 4-62 15.5; Int 2-74.

		Rushing			
Year Team	**G**	**Att**	**Yds**	**Avg**	**TD**
1948 BufA	14	48	219	4.6	1

GEORGE GONDA Gonda, George John 5'10", 175 **HB-DB**
Col: Duquesne *HS:* Redstone [PA] B: 2/23/1919, Alverton, PA
1942 Pit: 5 G; Rush 17-147 8.6 2 TD; Rec 1-7 7.0; PR 2-17 8.5; Int 1-37; 12 Pt.

GOOSE GONSOULIN Gonsoulin, Austin William 6'3", 210 **DB**
Col: Baylor *HS:* Thomas Jefferson [Port Arthur, TX] B: 6/7/1938, Port Arthur, TX *Drafted:* 1960 Round 2 DalT
1961 Den: KR 1-34 34.0. **1963** Den: KR 0-4. **1965** Den: Scor 1 2XP.
1967 SF: PR 1-0. **Total:** PR 1-0; KR 1-38 38.0; Scor 1 2XP.

		Interceptions		
Year Team	**G**	**Int**	**Yds**	**TD**
1960 Den	14	**11**	98	0
1961 Den	14	6	76	0
1962 Den	14	7	88	**1**
1963 Den	14	6	64	1
1964 Den	14	7	125	0
1965 Den	14	6	91	0
1966 Den	10	0	0	0
1967 SF	14	3	9	0
NFL Total	108	46	551	2

BOB GONYA Gonya, Robert James 6'2", 215 **T-OE-DE**
Col: Northwestern *HS:* Mount Carmel [Chicago, IL] B: 6/15/1910, Chicago, IL
1933 Phi: 2 G. **1934** Phi: 9 G; Rec 1-4 4.0 1 TD; 6 Pt. **Total:** 11 G; Rec 1-4 4.0 1 TD; 6 Pt.

JOHN GONZAGA Gonzaga, John Louis 6'3", 247 **OT-OG-DT-DE**
Col: No College *HS:* Mount Diablo [Concord, CA] B: 3/6/1933, Martinez, CA
1956 SF: 9 G; KR 1-6 6.0. **1957** SF: 12 G. **1958** SF: 12 G. **1959** SF: 12 G. **1960** Dal: 11 G. **1961** Det: 13 G. **1962** Det: 14 G. **1963** Det: 14 G. **1964** Det: 14 G. **1965** Det: 10 G. **1966** Den: 11 G. **Total:** 132 G; KR 1-6 6.0.

TONY GONZALEZ Gonzalez, Anthony David 6'4", 250 **TE**
Col: California *HS:* Huntington Beach [CA] B: 2/27/1976, Torrance, CA
Drafted: 1997 Round 1 KC
1997 KC: Scor 1 2XP. **Total:** Scor 1 2XP.

		Receiving				
Year Team	**G**	**Rec**	**Yds**	**Avg**	**TD**	**Fum**
1997 KC	16	33	368	11.2	2	0
1998 KC	16	59	621	10.5	2	3
NFL Total	32	92	989	10.8	4	3

LEON GONZALEZ Gonzalez, Leon Eugene III 5'10", 162 **WR**
(Speedy) *Col:* Bethune-Cookman *HS:* Jean Ribault [Jacksonville, FL]
B: 9/21/1963, Jacksonville, FL *Drafted:* 1985 Round 8 Dal
1985 Dal: 11 G; Rec 3-28 9.3; PR 15-58 3.9; 1 Fum. **1987** Atl: 2 G; Rec 3-40 13.3. **Total:** 13 G; Rec 6-68 11.3; PR 15-58 3.9; 1 Fum.

NOE GONZALEZ Gonzalez, Noe Mio 6'1", 210 **RB**
Col: Southwest Texas State *HS:* San Diego [TX] B: 2/5/1951, Alice, TX
Drafted: 1974 Round 12 Oak
1974 NE: 2 G.

JEFF GOOCH Gooch, Jeffrey Lance 5'11", 224 **LB**
Col: Austin Peay State *HS:* Overton [Nashville, TN] B: 10/31/1974, Nashville, TN
1996 TB: 15 G. **1997** TB: 14 G. **1998** TB: 16 G; 1 Sac. **Total:** 45 G; 1 Sac.

TOM GOOD Good, Thomas Maynard 6'0", 230 **LB**
Col: Marshall *HS:* Clendenon [WV] B: 12/23/1944, South Charleston, WV *Drafted:* 1965 Redshirt Round 6 SD
1966 SD: 2 G.

ROYCE GOODBREAD Goodbread, Royce Ethelbert 5'11", 207 **WB-HB-TB**
Col: Florida *HS:* St.Petersburg [FL] B: 1908, Crystal River, FL
1930 Fra-Min: 14 G. Fra: 13 G; Rec 1 TD; 6 Pt. Min: 1 G. **1931** Prov: 4 G.
Total: 18 G; Rec 1 TD; 6 Pt.

KELLY GOODBURN Goodburn, Kelly Joe 6'2", 195 **P**
Col: Emporia State; Iowa State *HS:* Eastwood [Correctionville, IA]
B: 4/14/1962, Cherokee, IA
1987 KC: Rush 1-16 16.0. **1988** KC: Rush 1-15 15.0. **1990** KC-Was: Rush 1-5 5.0. KC: Rush 1-5 5.0. **1992** Was: Rush 2-1 0.5.
Total: Rush 5-37 7.4.

		Punting		
Year Team	**G**	**Punts**	**Yds**	**Avg**
1987 KC	13	59	2412	40.9
1988 KC	16	76	3059	40.3
1989 KC	16	67	2688	40.1
1990 KC-Was	7	28	1030	36.8
1990 KC	3	17	653	38.4
1990 Was	4	11	377	34.3
1991 Was	16	52	2070	39.8
1992 Was	16	64	2555	39.9
1993 Was	1	5	197	39.4
NFL Total	85	351	14011	39.9

CHRIS GOODE Goode, Christopher Kimberly 6'0", 195 **DB**
Col: North Alabama; Alabama *HS:* Hazelwood [Town Creek, AL]
B: 9/17/1963, Town Creek, AL *Drafted:* 1987 Round 10 Ind
1987 Ind: 8 G. **1988** Ind: 13 G; Int 2-53. **1989** Ind: 15 G. **1990** Ind: 16 G; Int 1-10; 1 Fum TD; 6 Pt. **1991** Ind: 15 G; Int 2-27; 2 Sac. **1992** Ind: 15 G; Int 2-93. **1993** Ind: 14 G. **Total:** 96 G; Int 7-183; 1 Fum TD; 6 Pt; 2 Sac.

CONRAD GOODE Goode, Conrad Lawrence 6'6", 285 **OT-OG-C**
Col: Missouri *HS:* Parkway Central [Chesterfield, MO] B: 1/19/1962, St. Louis, MO *Drafted:* 1984 Round 4 NYG
1984 NYG: 8 G. **1985** NYG: 16 G. **1987** TB: 11 G. **Total:** 35 G.

DON GOODE Goode, Donald Ray 6'2", 234 **LB**
Col: Kansas *HS:* Booker T. Washington [Houston, TX] B: 6/21/1951, Houston, TX *Drafted:* 1974 Round 1 SD
1978 SD: PR 1-0. **1979** SD: PR 1-0. **Total:** PR 2-0.

		Interceptions			
Year Team	**G**	**Int**	**Yds**	**TD**	**Fum**
1974 SD	14	0	0	0	0
1975 SD	13	1	37	0	0
1976 SD	14	6	82	0	1
1977 SD	14	0	0	0	0
1978 SD	14	1	0	0	0
1979 SD	12	1	0	0	0
1980 Cle	15	0	0	0	0
1981 Cle	16	1	1	0	0
NFL Total	112	10	120	0	1

IRV GOODE Goode, Irvin Lee 6'5", 255 **OG-OT-C**
Col: Kentucky *HS:* Holmes [Covington, KY]; Boone Co. HS [Florence, KY] B: 10/12/1940, Newport, KY *Drafted:* 1962 Round 1 StL
1962 StL: 14 G. **1963** StL: 13 G; KR 1-0. **1964** StL: 14 G. **1965** StL: 12 G. **1966** StL: 11 G. **1967** StL: 14 G. **1968** StL: 14 G. **1969** StL: 14 G. **1970** StL: 14 G. **1971** StL: 14 G; 1 Fum. **1973** Mia: 14 G. **1974** Mia: 14 G; 1 Fum. **Total:** 162 G; KR 1-0; 2 Fum.

JOHN GOODE Goode, John Timothy 6'2", 233 **TE**
Col: Youngstown State *HS:* Benedictine [Cleveland, OH]
B: 11/5/1962, Cleveland Heights, OH *Drafted:* 1984 Round 5 StL
1984 StL: 16 G; Rec 3-23 7.7. **1985** Phi: 14 G. **Total:** 30 G; Rec 3-23 7.7.

KERRY GOODE Goode, Kerry DeAnglo 5′11″, 200 **RB**
Col: Alabama *HS:* Hazelwood [Town Creek, AL] B: 7/28/1965, Town Creek, AL *Drafted:* 1988 Round 7 TB
1988 TB: Rec 7-68 9.7; Scor 1 Saf. **1989** Mia: KR 1-8 8.0. **Total:** Rec 7-68 9.7; KR 1-8 8.0; Scor 1 Saf.

		Rushing			
Year Team	**G**	**Att**	**Yds**	**Avg**	**TD**
1988 TB	14	63	231	3.7	0
1989 Mia	1	0	0	—	0
NFL Total	15	63	231	3.7	0

ROB GOODE Goode, Robert Leslie 6′4″, 222 **FB-HB-LB-DB**
Col: Texas A&M *HS:* Bastrop [TX] B: 6/5/1927, Roby, TX
Drafted: 1949 Round 1 Was
1949 Was: KR 3-50 16.7; Int 2-25. **1950** Was: Int 2-29. **1954** Was: KR 16-284 17.8; **1** Fum TD. **1955** Was-Phi: KR 2-36 18.0. Phi: KR 2-36 18.0. **Total:** KR 21-370 17.6; Int 4-54; 1 Fum TD.

		Rushing				Receiving					Tot
Year Team	**G**	**Att**	**Yds**	**Avg**	**TD**	**Rec**	**Yds**	**Avg**	**TD**	**Fum**	**TD**
1949 Was	12	61	261	4.3	2	16	279	17.4	0	0	2
1950 Was	12	136	560	4.1	5	19	160	8.4	1	8	6
1951 Was	12	208	951	4.6	**9**	3	45	15.0	0	**9**	9
1954 Was	12	108	462	4.3	0	4	4	1.0	0	10	1
1955 Was-Phi	11	83	297	3.6	0	11	152	13.8	0	4	0
1955 Was	3	7	23	3.3	0	1	15	15.0	0	0	0
1955 Phi	8	76	274	3.6	0	10	137	13.7	0	4	0
NFL Total	59	596	2531	4.2	16	53	640	12.1	1	31	18

TOM GOODE Goode, Thomas Guinn 6′3″, 245 **LB-C**
Col: Mississippi State *HS:* West Point [MS] B: 12/1/1938, West Point, MS *Drafted:* 1961 Round 2 Hou
1962 Hou: 14 G. **1963** Hou: 14 G. **1964** Hou: 14 G. **1965** Hou: 14 G. **1966** Mia: 14 G. **1967** Mia: 14 G; 1 Fum. **1968** Mia: 14 G. **1969** Mia: 14 G. **1970** Bal: 1 G. **Total:** 113 G; 1 Fum.

DARRYL GOODLOW Goodlow, Darryl 6′2″, 235 **LB**
Col: Oklahoma *HS:* Maplewood-Richmond Heights [Maplewood, MO] B: 11/2/1960, St. Louis, MO *Drafted:* 1984 Supplemental Round 2 Phi
1987 LARd: 2 G.

EUGENE GOODLOW Goodlow, Eugene 6′2″, 185 **WR**
Col: Kansas State *HS:* McQuaid [Rochester, NY] B: 12/19/1958, St. Louis, MO *Drafted:* 1982 Round 3 NO
1983 NO: Rush 1-3 3.0. **1984** NO: Rush 1-5 5.0. **1985** NO: Rush 1-3 3.0. **Total:** Rush 3-11 3.7.

		Receiving				
Year Team	**G**	**Rec**	**Yds**	**Avg**	**TD**	**Fum**
1983 NO	16	41	487	11.9	2	0
1984 NO	10	22	281	12.8	3	0
1985 NO	12	32	603	18.8	3	0
1986 NO	16	20	306	15.3	2	1
NFL Total	54	115	1677	14.6	10	1

AUBREY GOODMAN Goodman, Aubrey Louis 6′3″, 225 **T**
Col: Baylor; Chicago *HS:* Waco [TX] B: 2/18/1904, Lott, TX
D: 3/7/1972, Waco, TX
1927 ChiC: 1 G.

BRIAN GOODMAN Goodman, Brian Harbert 6′2″, 250 **OG**
Col: Los Angeles Valley Coll. CA (J.C.); UCLA *HS:* Hollywood [Los Angeles, CA] B: 12/7/1949, Los Angeles, CA
1973 Hou: 3 G. **1974** Hou: 14 G. **Total:** 17 G.

HARVEY GOODMAN Goodman, Harvey Franklin 6′4″, 260 **OG**
Col: Los Angeles City Coll. CA (J.C.); Colorado *HS:* Hollywood [Los Angeles, CA] B: 9/16/1952, Los Angeles, CA *Drafted:* 1975 Round 5 StL
1976 Den: 14 G; KR 1-8 8.0.

HANK GOODMAN Goodman, Henry Joseph 6′4″, 230 **T**
Col: St. Bonaventure; George Washington; West Virginia *HS:* Bradford [PA] B: 4/18/1917, Bradford, PA
1942 Det: 11 G.

JOHN GOODMAN Goodman, John Richard 6′6″, 253 **DE-DT-NT**
Col: Oklahoma *HS:* L.V. Berkner [Richardson, TX] B: 11/21/1958, Oklahoma City, OK *Drafted:* 1980 Round 2 Pit
1981 Pit: 15 G. **1982** Pit: 9 G; 1.5 Sac. **1983** Pit: 14 G; 1 Sac. **1984** Pit: 14 G; 2.5 Sac. **1985** Pit: 12 G; 2 Sac. **Total:** 64 G; 7 Sac.

LES GOODMAN Goodman, Leslie Edward Jr. 5′11″, 206 **RB**
Col: Yankton *HS:* Port Jefferson [NY] B: 9/1/1950, Port Jefferson, NY
Drafted: 1972 Round 3 Atl
1973 GB: Rec 2-19 9.5. **1974** GB: Rec 5-19 3.8; KR 4-49 12.3. **Total:** Rec 7-38 5.4; KR 4-49 12.3.

		Rushing				
Year Team	**G**	**Att**	**Yds**	**Avg**	**TD**	**Fum**
1973 GB	6	18	88	4.9	1	2
1974 GB	13	20	101	5.1	0	1
NFL Total	19	38	189	5.0	1	3

DON GOODMAN Goodman, Weldon Charles 5′11″, 214 **RB**
Col: Cincinnati *HS:* Crenshaw [Los Angeles, CA] B: 4/23/1959, Los Angeles, CA
1987 StL: 3 G.

CLYDE GOODNIGHT Goodnight, Clyde Davis 6′1″, 205 **OE-DB**
(Nip) *Col:* Tulsa *HS:* Holland [TX] B: 3/3/1924, Holland, TX
Drafted: 1945 Round 2 GB
1945 GB: Rush 8-26 3.3; KR 1-8 8.0. **1947** GB: Rush 1-(-1) -1.0; KR 1-7 7.0. **1948** GB: KR 1-12 12.0. **1950** Was: KR 1-12 12.0. **Total:** Rush 9-25 2.8; KR 4-39 9.8.

		Receiving				
Year Team	**G**	**Rec**	**Yds**	**Avg**	**TD**	**Fum**
1945 GB	10	7	283	40.4	3	1
1946 GB	8	16	308	19.3	1	0
1947 GB	11	38	593	15.6	6	0
1948 GB	8	28	448	16.0	3	2
1949 GB-Was	11	11	150	13.6	0	0
1949 GB	1	0	0	—	0	0
1949 Was	10	11	150	13.6	0	0
1950 Was	10	12	185	15.4	2	0
NFL Total	58	112	1967	17.6	15	3

OWEN GOODNIGHT Goodnight, Owen Letcher Jr. 6′0″, 200 **TB-DB**
Col: Hardin-Simmons *HS:* Holland [TX] B: 8/27/1917, Holland, TX
D: 5/13/1967, San Marcos, TX *Drafted:* 1940 Round 15 Cle
1941 Cle: 9 G; Pass 36-12 33.3%, 182 5.06 1 TD 5 Int; Rush 21-(-54) -2.6; PR 2-27 13.5; KR 5-103 20.6; Int 2-13; Punt 16-637 39.8.

BOB GOODRIDGE Goodridge, Robert Wayne 6′2″, 190 **WR**
Col: Vanderbilt *HS:* Wyoming [Cincinatti, OH] B: 5/11/1946, Boston, MA *Drafted:* 1968 Round 6 Min
1968 Min: 11 G; Rec 1-5 5.0.

CHARLIE GOODRUM Goodrum, Charles Leo 6′3″, 256 **OT-OG**
Col: Florida A&M *HS:* Dillard [Fort Lauderdale, FL] B: 1/11/1950, Miami, FL *Drafted:* 1972 Round 9 Min
1973 Min: 10 G. **1974** Min: 12 G. **1975** Min: 14 G. **1976** Min: 14 G. **1977** Min: 14 G. **1978** Min: 16 G. **1979** Min: 15 G. **Total:** 95 G.

JOHN GOODSON Goodson, John Warren 6′3″, 204 **P**
Col: Texas *HS:* Spring Woods [Houston, TX] B: 3/18/1960, Houston, TX *Drafted:* 1982 Round 8 Pit

		Punting		
Year Team	**G**	**Punts**	**Yds**	**Avg**
1982 Pit	9	49	1981	40.4

MARK GOODSPEED Goodspeed, Mark Judson 6′5″, 270 **OT**
Col: Nebraska *HS:* Rockhurst [Kansas City, MO] B: 12/1/1956, Kansas City, KS D: 1/10/1998, Kansas City, MO *Drafted:* 1980 Round 9 Mia
1980 StL: 3 G.

TOD GOODWIN Goodwin, Charles Tod 6′0″, 184 **OE-DE**
Col: West Virginia *HS:* Bellaire [OH] B: 12/5/1911, Wheeling, WV
1936 NYG: Rush 3-(-1) -0.3. **Total:** Rush 3-(-1) -0.3.

		Receiving			
Year Team	**G**	**Rec**	**Yds**	**Avg**	**TD**
1935 NYG	12	**26**	432	16.6	4
1936 NYG	8	7	79	11.3	2
NFL Total	20	33	511	15.5	6

DOUG GOODWIN Goodwin, Douglas McArthur 6′2″, 228 **RB**
Col: Maryland East. Shore *HS:* Burke [Charleston, SC] B: 3/11/1942, Charleston, SC *Drafted:* 1965 Round 11 Buf
1966 Buf: 3 G. **1968** Atl: 2 G. **Total:** 5 G.

EARL GOODWIN Goodwin, Earl 6′1″, 195 **OE**
Col: West Texas A&M; Bucknell *HS:* Joy Coy [CO] B: 1/21/1901, Paducah, TX D: 7/1/1976, Durango, CO
1928 Pott: 8 G.

MYRL GOODWIN Goodwin, Myrl 6′1″, 195 **WB-BB-OE**
Col: West Texas A&M; Bucknell *HS:* Joy Coy [CO] B: 1/21/1901, Paducah, TX D: 2/14/1979, Reno, NV
1928 Pott: 4 G.

HUNTER GOODWIN Goodwin, Robert Hunter 6′5″, 271 **TE**
Col: Texas A&M–Kingsville; Texas A&M *HS:* Bellville [TX]
B: 10/10/1972, Bellville, TX *Drafted:* 1996 Round 4 Min
1996 Min: 9 G; Rec 1-24 24.0. **1997** Min: 16 G; Rec 7-61 8.7. **1998** Min: 15 G; Rec 3-16 5.3. **Total:** 40 G; Rec 11-101 9.2.

RON GOODWIN Goodwin, Ronald Ray 5'11", 180 **WR**
Col: Baylor *HS:* Odessa [TX] B: 1/9/1941, Phillips, TX *Drafted:* 1963 Round 16 Phi
1964 Phi: Rush 1-(-23) -23.0. **1967** Phi: Rush 1-1 1.0. **Total:** Rush 2-(-22) -11.0.

		Receiving			
Year Team	**G**	**Rec**	**Yds**	**Avg**	**TD**
1963 Phi	10	15	215	14.3	4
1964 Phi	14	23	335	14.6	3
1965 Phi	11	18	252	14.0	1
1966 Phi	12	16	212	13.3	1
1967 Phi	7	6	65	10.8	0
1968 Phi	2	0	0	—	0
NFL Total	56	78	1079	13.8	9

JOHN GOODYEAR Goodyear, John Martin 6'0", 190 **WB-DB**
Col: Marquette *HS:* Lyons Twp. [La Grange, IL] B: 6/10/1920, La Grange, IL *Drafted:* 1942 Round 8 Was
1942 Was: 3 G; Rush 2-1 0.5.

SHAG GOOLSBY Goolsby, James Earl 6'2", 185 **C-LB**
Col: Mississippi State *HS:* Steven D. Lee [Columbus, MS]
B: 7/24/1917, Columbus, MS D: 5/7/1975, Columbus, MS
Drafted: 1940 Round 12 Cle
1940 Cle: 8 G.

TOM GOOSBY Goosby, Thomas Aaron 6'0", 235 **OG-LB**
Col: Baldwin-Wallace *HS:* Alliance [OH] B: 5/24/1939, Alliance, OH
Drafted: 1962 Round 15 Cle
1963 Cle: 1 G. **1966** Was: 14 G; KR 1-0. **Total:** 15 G; KR 1-0.

RON GOOVERT Goovert, Ronald Edward 5'11", 225 **LB**
Col: Michigan State *HS:* Hazel Park [MI] B: 2/15/1944, Detroit, MI
1967 Det: 14 G; KR 2-40 20.0.

ALEX GORDON Gordon, Alex Groncier 6'5", 246 **LB**
Col: Cincinnati *HS:* Englewood [Jacksonville, FL] B: 9/14/1964, Jacksonville, FL *Drafted:* 1987 Round 2 NYJ
1987 NYJ: 12 G; 5 Sac. **1988** NYJ: 13 G; 3 Sac. **1989** NYJ: 16 G; Int 1-2; 1 Sac. **1990** LARd: 10 G. **1991** Cin: 14 G; Scor 1 Saf; 2 Pt; 2 Sac. **1992** Cin: 15 G; 1 Sac. **1993** Cin: 16 G. **Total:** 96 G; Int 1-2; Scor 1 Saf; 2 Pt; 12 Sac.

BOBBY GORDON Gordon, Bobby Lee 6'0", 195 **DB**
Col: Tennessee *HS:* Giles Co. [Pulaski, TN] B: 12/7/1935, Pulaski, TN D: 8/16/1990, Strawberry Plains, TN
1958 ChiC: Rush 2-10 5.0; PR 1-12 12.0; Int 2-27. **1960** Hou: Int 3-45. **Total:** Rush 2-10 5.0; PR 1-12 12.0; Int 5-72.

		Punting		
Year Team	**G**	**Punts**	**Yds**	**Avg**
1958 ChiC	12	55	2089	38.0
1960 Hou	13	0	0	—
NFL Total	25	55	2089	38.0

CORNELL GORDON Gordon, Cornell Kermit 6'0", 187 **DB**
Col: North Carolina A&T *HS:* Booker T. Washington [Norfolk, VA]
B: 1/6/1941, Norfolk, VA *Drafted:* 1964 Round 23 NYJ

		Interceptions			
Year Team	**G**	**Int**	**Yds**	**TD**	**Fum**
1965 NYJ	14	2	7	0	0
1966 NYJ	10	0	0	0	0
1967 NYJ	2	1	14	0	0
1968 NYJ	14	2	0	0	0
1969 NYJ	14	4	23	0	1
1970 Den	14	3	26	0	0
1971 Den	14	2	21	0	0
1972 Den	1	0	0	0	0
NFL Total	83	14	91	0	1

DARRIEN GORDON Gordon, Darrien X Jamal 5'11", 184 **DB**
Col: Stanford *HS:* Shawnee [OK] B: 11/14/1970, Shawnee, OK
Drafted: 1993 Round 1 SD
1996 SD: 2 Sac. **1997** Den: 2 Sac. **Total:** 4 Sac.

		Punt Returns				Interceptions				Tot
Year Team	**G**	**Ret**	**Yds**	**Avg**	**TD**	**Int**	**Yds**	**TD**	**Fum**	**TD**
1993 SD	16	31	395	12.7	0	1	3	0	4	0
1994 SD	16	36	475	13.2	**2**	4	32	0	2	2
1996 SD	16	36	537	14.9	1	2	55	0	3	1
1997 Den	16	40	543	13.6	**3**	4	64	1	3	4
1998 Den	16	34	379	11.1	0	4	125	1	1	1
NFL Total	80	177	2329	**13.2**	6	15	279	2	13	8

SONNY GORDON Gordon, Denman Preston 5'11", 192 **DB**
Col: Ohio State *HS:* Middletown [OH] B: 7/30/1965, Lynn, MA
Drafted: 1987 Round 6 Cin
1987 TB: 7 G.

DWAYNE GORDON Gordon, Dwayne Kirk 6'1", 240 **LB**
Col: New Hampshire *HS:* Arlington [Lagrangeville, NY] B: 11/2/1969, White Plains, NY *Drafted:* 1993 Round 8 Mia
1993 Atl: 5 G; 1 Fum. **1994** Atl: 16 G. **1995** SD: 16 G; 1 Sac. **1996** SD: 13 G. **1997** NYJ: 16 G; 1 Sac. **1998** NYJ: 16 G; Int 1-31 1 TD; 6 Pt. **Total:** 82 G; Int 1-31 1 TD; 6 Pt; 1 Fum; 2 Sac.

IRA GORDON Gordon, Ira Laverne 6'3", 275 **OG-OT**
Col: Phoenix Coll. AZ (J.C.); Kansas State *HS:* Combs-McIntyre [Oak Grove, LA] B: 5/5/1947, Kilbourne, LA *Drafted:* 1970 Round 8 Phi
1970 SD: 8 G. **1971** SD: 14 G. **1972** SD: 6 G. **1973** SD: 6 G. **1974** SD: 14 G. **1975** SD: 14 G. **Total:** 62 G.

JOHN GORDON Gordon, John David 6'6", 260 **DT**
Col: Hawaii *HS:* East Detroit [Eastpointe, MI] B: 8/29/1948, Detroit, MI
1972 Det: 2 G.

LARRY GORDON Gordon, Larry Wayne 6'4", 230 **LB**
Col: Arizona State *HS:* Combs-McIntyre [Oak Grove, LA]; Phoenix Union HS [AZ] B: 7/8/1953, Monroe, LA D: 6/25/1983, Phoenix, AZ
Drafted: 1976 Round 1 Mia
1976 Mia: 14 G. **1977** Mia: 14 G; Int 1-27. **1978** Mia: 16 G; Int 3-35. **1979** Mia: 16 G; Int 2-33. **1980** Mia: 15 G; Int 1-11. **1981** Mia: 16 G; Scor **1** Saf; 2 Pt. **1982** Mia: 9 G; Int 1-15; 3 Sac. **Total:** 100 G; Int 8-121; Scor 1 Saf; 2 Pt; 3 Sac.

LOU GORDON Gordon, Louis James 6'5", 224 **T-G-OE-DE**
Col: Illinois *HS:* Albert G. Lane Tech [Chicago, IL] B: 7/15/1908, Chicago, IL D: 4/4/1976, Chicago, IL
1930 ChiC: 10 G. **1931** ChiC-Bkn: 7 G. ChiC: 1 G. Bkn: 6 G. **1932** ChiC: 8 G. **1933** ChiC: 11 G; Rec 1-8 8.0. **1934** ChiC: 11 G. **1935** ChiC: 12 G. **1936** GB: 12 G. **1937** GB: 10 G. **1938** ChiB: 2 G. **Total:** 83 G; Rec 1-8 8.0.

DICK GORDON Gordon, Richard Frederick 5'11", 190 **WR**
Col: Michigan State *HS:* Walnut Hills [Cincinnati, OH] B: 1/1/1944, Cincinnati, OH *Drafted:* 1965 Round 7 ChiB
1965 ChiB: Rush 2-10 5.0. **1966** ChiB: Rush 1-2 2.0. **1967** ChiB: Rush 3-(-7) -2.3. **1969** ChiB: Rush 2-28 14.0. **1970** ChiB: Rush 4-17 4.3. **1973** LARm-GB: Rush 2-15 7.5. LARm: Rush 1-19 19.0. GB: Rush 1-(-4) -4.0. **1974** SD: Rush 1-25 25.0. **Total:** Rush 15-90 6.0.

		Receiving				Punt Returns			
Year Team	**G**	**Rec**	**Yds**	**Avg**	**TD**	**Ret**	**Yds**	**Avg**	**TD**
1965 ChiB	14	13	279	21.5	3	1	-3	-3.0	0
1966 ChiB	14	15	210	14.0	1	4	-5	-1.3	0
1967 ChiB	14	31	534	17.2	5	12	82	6.8	0
1968 ChiB	14	29	477	16.4	4	1	5	5.0	0
1969 ChiB	14	36	414	11.5	4	1	11	11.0	0
1970 ChiB	14	**71**	1026	14.5	**13**	0	0	—	0
1971 ChiB	13	43	610	14.2	5	0	0	—	0
1972 LARm	4	3	29	9.7	1	4	20	5.0	0
1973 LARm-GB	7	0	0	—	0	0	0	—	0
1973 LARm	5	0	0	—	0	0	0	—	0
1973 GB	2	0	0	—	0	0	0	—	0
1974 SD	7	2	15	7.5	0	8	39	4.9	0
NFL Total	115	243	3594	14.8	36	31	149	4.8	0

	Kickoff Returns					Tot
Year Team	**Ret**	**Yds**	**Avg**	**TD**	**Fum**	**TD**
1965 ChiB	14	242	17.3	0	1	3
1966 ChiB	19	521	27.4	0	4	1
1967 ChiB	16	397	24.8	0	2	5
1968 ChiB	3	97	32.3	0	1	4
1969 ChiB	6	105	17.5	0	0	4
1970 ChiB	0	0	—	0	2	**13**
1971 ChiB	0	0	—	0	0	5
1972 LARm	4	141	35.3	0	1	1
1973 LARm-GB	3	68	22.7	0	0	0
1973 LARm	3	68	22.7	0	0	0
1974 SD	14	354	25.3	0	4	0
NFL Total	79	1925	24.4	0	15	36

STEVE GORDON Gordon, Steve Duane 6'3", 288 **C**
Col: California *HS:* Nevada Union [Grass Valley, CA] B: 4/15/1969, Fort Ord, CA *Drafted:* 1992 Round 10 NE
1998 SF: 13 G.

TIM GORDON Gordon, Timothy Carvelle 6'0", 188 **DB**
Col: Tulsa *HS:* Ardmore [OK] B: 5/7/1965, Ardmore, OK
1987 Atl: 11 G; Int 2-28. **1988** Atl: 16 G; KR 14-209 14.9; Int 2-10; 1 Fum; 1 Sac. **1989** Atl: 14 G; Int 4-60. **1990** Atl: 5 G; KR 1-43 43.0. **1991** NE: 11 G. **1992** NE: 10 G. **Total:** 67 G; KR 15-252 16.8; Int 8-98; 1 Fum; 1 Sac.

JOHN GORDY Gordy, John Thomas 6'3", 248 **OG**
Col: Tennessee *HS:* Isaac Litton [Nashville, TN] B: 6/17/1935, Nashville, TN *Drafted:* 1957 Round 2 Det
1957 Det: 12 G. **1959** Det: 12 G. **1960** Det: 12 G. **1961** Det: 14 G. **1962** Det: 14 G. **1963** Det: 14 G. **1964** Det: 14 G. **1965** Det: 14 G. **1966** Det: 14 G. **1967** Det: 14 G. **Total:** 134 G.

GORDON GORE Gore, Wilfred Gordon 6′0″, 215 **HB**
(Cake) *Col:* Southwestern Oklahoma State *HS:* Hominy [OK]
B: 6/28/1913, Clinton, OK
1939 Det: 7 G; Pass 1-0; Rush 8-7 0.9; Rec 1-20 20.0.

CHUCK GORECKI Gorecki, Charles Michael 6′4″, 237 **LB**
Col: Boston College *HS:* Conestoga [Berwyn, PA] B: 4/7/1964, Bryn Mawr, PA
1987 Phi: 3 G.

ALEX GORGAL Gorgal, Alex 5′9″, 180 **FB-WB**
Col: No College *HS:* No High School B: 1/16/1900, Czechoslovakia
D: 6/1/1986, Peru, IL
1923 RI: 5 G.

KEN GORGAL Gorgal, Kenneth Robert 6′2″, 200 **DB**
Col: Purdue *HS:* St.Bede [Peru, IL] B: 2/13/1929, La Salle, IL
Drafted: 1950 Round 6 Cle
1950 Cle: PR 4-83 20.8. **1954** Cle: PR 1-0; KR 1-11 11.0. **Total:** PR 5-83 16.6; KR 1-11 11.0.

		Interceptions			
Year Team	**G**	**Int**	**Yds**	**TD**	**Fum**
1950 Cle	12	6	23	0	1
1953 Cle	12	4	25	0	0
1954 Cle	11	1	53	1	0
1955 ChiB	12	6	107	0	0
1956 ChiB-GB	11	2	2	0	0
1956 ChiB	6	0	0	0	0
1956 GB	5	2	2	0	0
NFL Total	58	19	210	1	1

PETE GORGONE Gorgone, Pietro Orris 6′0″, 220 **HB**
Col: Muhlenberg *HS:* Windber [PA] B: 5/8/1920, Bruca, Sicily, Italy
D: 12/1/1992, Salisbury Twp., PA
1946 NYG: 9 G.

WALT GORINSKI Gorinski, Walter A 6′1″, 207 **FB**
Col: Louisiana State *HS:* Mutual [PA] B: 12/20/1919, Mutual, PA
D: 7/3/1977, Bossier City, LA *Drafted:* 1943 Round 17 Phi
1946 Pit: 6 G; Rush 1-3 3.0.

STACY GORE Gore, Stacy Lynn 6′0″, 200 **P**
Col: Arkansas State *HS:* Palestine [AR] B: 5/20/1963, Jonesboro, AR
1987 Mia: 3 G; Punt 14-502 35.9.

BUD GORMAN Gorman, Earl Patrick 210 **G-T**
(Pat) *Col:* No College B: 6/27/1896, Halder, WI D: 11/6/1962, Milwaukee, WI
1922 Rac: 11 G. **1923** Rac: 10 G. **1924** Ken: 3 G. **Total:** 24 G.

DOC GORMAN Gorman, Otho Addison **OE**
Col: St. Louis *HS:* Springfield [IL] B: 7/23/1893, Pawnee, IL
D: 9/22/1938, Evansville, IN
1921 Eva: 1 G.

TOM GORMLEY Gormley, Thomas Francis 5′11″, 225 **G-T**
Col: Villanova; Ursinus; Catholic; Georgetown *HS:* Naugatuck [CT]
B: 8/9/1891, Bridgeport, CT D: 7/24/1951, Washington, DC
1920 Cle-Can: 9 G. Cle: 8 G. Can: 1 G. **1921** NYG-Was: 3 G. NYG: 1 G. Was: 2 G. **Total:** 12 G.

FLOP GORRILL Gorrill, Charles Virgil 5′11″, 178 **E**
Col: Ohio State *HS:* Fostoria [OH] B: 1903 Deceased
1926 Col: 7 G; Rec 1 TD; 6 Pt.

ANTONIO GOSS Goss, Antonio Derrell 6′4″, 228 **LB**
Col: North Carolina *HS:* Randleman [NC] B: 8/11/1966, Randleman, NC *Drafted:* 1989 Round 12 SF
1989 SF: 8 G. **1991** SF: 14 G. **1992** SF: 16 G. **1993** SF: 14 G. **1994** SF: 16 G. **1995** SF: 16 G. **1996** StL: 8 G; 1 Sac. **Total:** 92 G; 1 Sac.

DON GOSS Goss, Robert Donald 6′5″, 260 **OT-DT**
Col: Southern Methodist *HS:* Sunset [Dallas, TX] B: 5/19/1933, Dallas, TX *Drafted:* 1954 Round 10 Cle
1956 Cle: 6 G.

GENE GOSSAGE Gossage, Ezra Gene 6′3″, 240 **DE-DT-OG**
Col: Northwestern *HS:* Wadsworth [OH] B: 2/17/1935, Columbia, TN
Drafted: 1960 Round 1 DalT
1960 Phi: 12 G. **1961** Phi: 14 G. **1962** Phi: 14 G. **Total:** 40 G.

BRUCE GOSSETT Gossett, Daniel Bruce 6′1″, 204 **K**
Col: Ferrum; Clarion; Duquesne; Richmond *HS:* Cecil Twp. [Venice, PA]
B: 11/9/1941, Canonsburg, PA
1974 SF: Punt 2-56 28.0. **Total:** Punt 2-56 28.0.

		Scoring						
Year Team	**G**	**Pts**	**FG**	**FGA**	**FG%**	**XK**	**XKA**	**XK%**
1964 LARm	14	85	18	24	**75.0**	31	33	**93.9**
1965 LARm	14	75	15	26	57.7	30	32	93.8
1966 LARm	14	**113**	**28**	**49**	57.1	29	29	100.0
1967 LARm	14	108	20	**43**	46.5	**48**	**48**	100.0
1968 LARm	14	88	17	31	54.8	37	37	100.0
1969 LARm	14	102	22	34	64.7	36	36	100.0
1970 SF	14	102	21	31	67.7	39	**41**	95.1
1971 SF	14	101	23	36	63.9	32	32	100.0
1972 SF	14	95	18	29	62.1	41	42	97.6
1973 SF	14	104	26	33	**78.8**	26	26	**100.0**
1974 SF	14	58	11	24	45.8	25	27	92.6
NFL Total	154	1031	219	360	60.8	374	383	97.7

JEFF GOSSETT Gossett, Jeffery Alan 6′2″, 195 **P**
Col: Eastern Illinois *HS:* Charleston [IL] B: 1/25/1957, Charleston, IL
1985 Cle: Pass 1-0. **1986** Cle: Pass 2-1 50.0%, 30 15.00 1 Int.
1989 LARd: Pass 1-0. **1991** LARd: Pass 1-1 100.0%, 34 34.00.
1992 LARd: Rush 1-(-12) -12.0. **1993** LARd: Rush 1-(-10) -10.0.
1996 Oak: Rush 3-28 9.3; KR 1-0. **Total:** Pass 5-2 40.0%, 64 12.80 1 Int; Rush 5-6 1.2; KR 1-0.

		Punting			
Year Team	**G**	**Punts**	**Yds**	**Avg**	**Fum**
1981 KC	7	29	1141	39.3	0
1982 KC	8	33	1366	41.4	0
1983 Cle	16	70	2854	40.8	0
1985 Cle	16	81	3261	40.3	0
1986 Cle	16	83	3423	41.2	0
1987 Cle-Hou	9	44	1777	40.4	0
1987 Cle	5	19	769	40.5	0
1987 Hou	4	25	1008	40.3	0
1988 LARd	16	91	3804	41.8	0
1989 LARd	16	67	2711	40.5	0
1990 LARd	16	60	2315	38.6	0
1991 LARd	16	67	2961	44.2	0
1992 LARd	16	77	3255	42.3	1
1993 LARd	16	71	2971	41.8	0
1994 LARd	16	77	3377	43.9	0
1995 Oak	16	75	3089	41.2	0
1996 Oak	12	57	2264	39.7	1
NFL Total	212	982	40569	41.3	2

PRESTON GOTHARD Gothard, Sherrill Preston 6′4″, 239 **TE**
Col: Alabama *HS:* Lowndes Acad. [Montgomery, AL] B: 2/23/1962, Montgomery, AL

		Receiving			
Year Team	**G**	**Rec**	**Yds**	**Avg**	**TD**
1985 Pit	16	6	83	13.8	0
1986 Pit	16	21	246	11.7	1
1987 Pit	2	2	9	4.5	1
1988 Pit	16	12	121	10.1	1
NFL Total	50	41	459	11.2	3

LEN GOTSHALK Gotshalk, Leonard William 6′4″, 259 **OT-OG**
Col: Santa Rosa JC CA; Humboldt State *HS:* Lakeport [CA]
B: 10/21/1949, Lakeport, CA *Drafted:* 1971 Round 8 Phi
1972 Atl: 14 G. **1973** Atl: 14 G. **1974** Atl: 10 G. **1975** Atl: 14 G. **1976** Atl: 14 G. **Total:** 66 G.

DARREN GOTTSCHALK Gottschalk, Darren K 6′4″, 225 **TE**
Col: California Lutheran *HS:* South Tahoe [South Lake Tahoe, CA]
B: 12/1/1964, Merced, CA
1987 NO: 1 G.

KURT GOUVEIA Gouveia, Kurt Keola 6′1″, 233 **LB**
Col: Brigham Young *HS:* Waianae [HI] B: 9/14/1964, Honolulu, HI
Drafted: 1986 Round 8 Was
1989 Was: KR 1-0. **1990** Was: KR 2-23 11.5; 1 Fum TD; 1 Sac. **1991** Was: KR 3-12 4.0. **1992** Was: KR 1-7 7.0; 1 Sac. **1993** Was: 1.5 Sac. **1996** SD: 1 Sac. **1998** SD: 0.5 Sac. **Total:** KR 7-42 6.0; 1 Fum TD; 5 Sac.

		Interceptions			Tot
Year Team	**G**	**Int**	**Yds**	**TD**	**TD**
1987 Was	11	0	0	0	0
1988 Was	16	0	0	0	0
1989 Was	15	1	1	0	0
1990 Was	16	0	0	0	1
1991 Was	14	1	22	0	0
1992 Was	16	3	43	0	0
1993 Was	16	1	59	1	1
1994 Was	14	1	7	0	0
1995 Phi	16	1	20	0	0
1996 SD	16	3	41	0	0
1997 SD	7	1	0	0	0
1998 SD	14	0	0	0	0
NFL Total	171	12	193	1	2

PAUL GOVERNALI Governali, Paul Vincent 5′11″, 193 **QB**
(Pitchin' Paul) *Col:* Columbia *HS:* Evander Childs [Bronx, NY]
B: 1/5/1921, Bronx, NY D: 2/14/1978, San Diego, CA *Drafted:* 1943 Round 1 Bkn
1946 Bos: Punt 11-481 43.7. **1947** Bos-NYG: Punt 4-142 35.5. NYG: Punt 4-142 35.5. **Total:** Punt 15-623 41.5.

Year Team	G	Passing Att	Comp	Comp%	Yds	YPA	TD	Int	Rating
1946 Bos	11	192	83	43.2	1293	6.73	13	10	67.0
1947 Bos-NYG	12	252	108	42.9	1775	7.04	17	22	53.3
1947 Bos	4	55	23	41.8	314	5.71	3	6	39.3
1947 NYG	8	197	85	43.1	1461	7.42	14	16	58.8
1948 NYG	9	56	27	48.2	280	5.00	1	**1**	61.6
NFL Total	32	500	218	43.6	3348	6.70	31	33	59.5

Year Team	Rushing Att	Yds	Avg	TD	Fum
1946 Bos	33	-186	-5.6	2	2
1947 Bos-NYG	40	151	3.8	2	6
1947 Bos	4	19	4.8	0	3
1947 NYG	36	132	3.7	2	3
1948 NYG	6	-48	-8.0	0	1
NFL Total	79	-83	-1.1	4	9

CORNELL GOWDY Gowdy, Cornell Anthony 6′1″, 196 **DB**
Col: Morgan State *HS:* Central [Capitol Heights, MD] B: 10/2/1963, Washington, DC
1986 Dal: 3 G. **1987** Pit: 13 G; KR 1-0; Int 2-50 1 TD; 6 Pt. **1988** Pit: 16 G; Int 1-24. **Total:** 32 G; KR 1-0; Int 3-74 1 TD; 6 Pt.

TOBY GOWIN Gowin, Toby Lee 5′10″, 167 **P**
Col: North Texas *HS:* Jacksonville [TX] B: 3/30/1975, Jacksonville, TX
1997 Dal: Scor 0-1 FG. **1998** Dal: Rush 1-33 33.0. **Total:** Rush 1-33 33.0; Scor 0-1 FG.

Year Team	G	Punting Punts	Yds	Avg
1997 Dal	16	86	3592	41.8
1998 Dal	16	77	3342	43.4
NFL Total	32	163	6934	42.5

HIPPO GOZDOWSKI Gozdowski, Casimir 1 **FB-G-C**
(Kazmiera Gozdowski) *Col:* No College B: 3/4/1897 D: 7/1976, Spring Lake, NJ
1922 Tol: 3 G; Rush 2 TD; 12 Pt.

TED GRABINSKI Grabinski, Thaddeus 6′2″, 207 **LB-C-G**
Col: Duquesne *HS:* Ambridge [PA] B: 2/6/1916
1939 Pit: 10 G. **1940** Pit: 11 G. **Total:** 21 G.

GENE GRABOSKY Grabosky, Harry Eugene 6′5″, 275 **DT**
Col: Syracuse *HS:* Liverpool [NY] B: 9/1/1936, Syracuse, NY
Drafted: 1959 Round 26 Was
1960 Buf: 3 G.

JIM GRABOWSKI Grabowski, James Steven 6′2″, 220 **RB**
Col: Illinois *HS:* Taft [Chicago, IL] B: 9/9/1944, Chicago, IL
Drafted: 1966 Round 1 GB

Year Team	G	Rushing Att	Yds	Avg	TD	Receiving Rec	Yds	Avg	TD	Fum	Tot TD
1966 GB	14	29	127	4.4	1	4	13	3.3	0	2	1
1967 GB	9	120	466	3.9	2	12	171	14.3	1	3	3
1968 GB	14	135	518	3.8	3	18	210	11.7	1	6	4
1969 GB	14	73	261	3.6	1	12	98	8.2	1	2	2
1970 GB	12	67	210	3.1	1	19	83	4.4	0	0	1
1971 ChiB	12	51	149	2.9	0	17	100	5.9	0	3	0
NFL Total	75	475	1731	3.6	8	82	675	8.2	3	16	11

LES GRACE Grace, Leslie 5′11″, 200 **E**
(Red) *Col:* Temple *HS:* Willmar [NJ] D: 8/19/1968
1930 Nwk: 2 G.

SAM GRADDY Graddy, Samuel Louis 5′10″, 165 **WR**
Col: Tennessee *HS:* Northside [Atlanta, GA] B: 2/10/1964, Gaffney, SC
1988 Den: Rec 1-30 30.0. **1990** LARd: Rec 1-47 47.0 1 TD. **1991** LARd: Rec 6-195 32.5 1 TD. **1992** LARd: Rec 10-205 20.5 1 TD.
Total: Rec 18-477 26.5 3 TD.

Year Team	G	Kickoff Returns Ret	Yds	Avg	TD	Fum
1987 Den	1	0	0	—	0	0
1988 Den	7	0	0	—	0	0
1990 LARd	16	0	0	—	0	0
1991 LARd	12	22	373	17.0	0	1
1992 LARd	7	5	85	17.0	0	0
NFL Total	43	27	458	17.0	0	1

RANDY GRADISHAR Gradishar, Randolph Charles 6′3″, 233 **LB**
Col: Ohio State *HS:* Champion [OH] B: 3/3/1952, Warren, OH
Drafted: 1974 Round 1 Den
1978 Den: 1 Fum TD. **1982** Den: 2 Sac. **1983** Den: 2.5 Sac.
Total: 1 Fum TD; 4.5 Sac.

Year Team	G	Interceptions Int	Yds	TD	Fum	Tot TD
1974 Den	14	0	0	0	0	0
1975 Den	14	3	77	1	0	1
1976 Den	14	3	44	1	0	1
1977 Den	14	3	56	0	1	0
1978 Den	16	4	19	0	1	1
1979 Den	16	0	0	0	0	0
1980 Den	16	2	96	1	0	1
1981 Den	16	4	38	0	0	0
1982 Den	9	0	0	0	0	0
1983 Den	16	1	5	0	0	0
NFL Total	145	20	335	3	2	4

GARRY GRADY Grady, Garry L 5′10″, 185 **DB**
Col: Eastern Michigan *HS:* Plymouth [MI] B: 10/11/1946, Northville, MI
1969 Mia: 2 G.

DAVE GRAF Graf, David Francis 6′2″, 215 **LB**
Col: Penn State *HS:* Dunkirk [NY] B: 8/5/1953, Dunkirk, NY
Drafted: 1975 Round 17 Cle
1975 Cle: 14 G; Int 1-19; 1 Fum. **1976** Cle: 14 G; KR 1-15 15.0. **1977** Cle: 14 G. **1978** Cle: 7 G. **1979** Cle: 16 G. **1981** Was: 6 G. **Total:** 71 G; KR 1-15 15.0; Int 1-19; 1 Fum.

RICK GRAF Graf, Richard Glenn 6′5″, 244 **LB**
Col: Wisconsin *HS:* James Madison Memorial [Madison, WI]
B: 8/29/1964, Iowa City, IA *Drafted:* 1987 Round 2 Mia
1987 Mia: 12 G; 1 Sac. **1988** Mia: 16 G; Int 1-14; 1 Sac. **1989** Mia: 4 G; 1 Sac. **1990** Mia: 8 G; KR 1-6 6.0. **1991** Hou: 12 G. **1992** Hou: 16 G; Int 1-0; 1 Sac. **1993** Was: 5 G. **Total:** 73 G; KR 1-6 6.0; Int 2-14; 4 Sac.

NEIL GRAFF Graff, Neil Howard 6′3″, 205 **QB**
Col: Wisconsin *HS:* Lincoln [Sioux Falls, SD] B: 1/12/1950, Sioux Falls, SD *Drafted:* 1972 Round 16 Min
1974 NE: 14 G; Pass 1-1 100.0%, 20 20.00. **1975** NE: 11 G; Pass 35-18 51.4%, 221 6.31 2 TD 3 Int; Rush 2-2 1.0; 1 Fum. **1977** Pit: 4 G; Pass 12-6 50.0%, 47 3.92; Rush 5-3 0.6. **Total:** 29 G; Pass 48-25 52.1%, 288 6.00 2 TD 3 Int; Rush 7-5 0.7; 1 Fum.

SCOTT GRAGG Gragg, Christopher Scott 6′8″, 325 **OT**
(Lurch) *Col:* Montana *HS:* Silverton [OR] B: 2/28/1972, Altus, OK
Drafted: 1995 Round 2 NYG
1995 NYG: 13 G. **1996** NYG: 16 G. **1997** NYG: 16 G. **1998** NYG: 16 G. **Total:** 61 G.

AARON GRAHAM Graham, Aaron Geddes 6′4″, 293 **C**
Col: Nebraska *HS:* Denton [TX] B: 5/22/1973, Las Vegas, NM
Drafted: 1996 Round 4 Ariz
1996 Ariz: 16 G. **1997** Ariz: 16 G. **1998** Ariz: 14 G. **Total:** 46 G.

AL GRAHAM Graham, Alfred 6′0″, 215 **G**
(Pup) *Col:* No College B: 9/27/1905 D: 10/18/1969, Knoxville, TN
1925 Day: 8 G. **1926** Day: 6 G. **1927** Day: 8 G; 1 Fum TD; 6 Pt. **1928** Day: 7 G. **1929** Day: 5 G; 1 Fum TD; 6 Pt. **1930** Port-Prov: 12 G. Port: 3 G. Prov: 9 G. **1931** Prov: 11 G. **1932** ChiC: 8 G. **1933** ChiC: 8 G. **Total:** 73 G; 2 Fum TD; 12 Pt.

ART GRAHAM Graham, Arthur William III 6′1″, 205 **WR**
Col: Boston College *HS:* Matignon [Cambridge, MA] B: 7/31/1941, Somerville, MA *Drafted:* 1963 Round 1 Bos
1967 Bos: Rush 1-(-5) -5.0. **1968** Bos: PR 2-11 5.5; KR 1-9 9.0.
Total: Rush 1-(-5) -5.0; PR 2-11 5.5; KR 1-9 9.0.

Year Team	G	Receiving Rec	Yds	Avg	TD	Fum
1963 Bos	14	21	550	26.2	5	1
1964 Bos	14	45	720	16.0	6	0
1965 Bos	10	25	316	12.6	0	0
1966 Bos	14	51	673	13.2	4	0
1967 Bos	12	41	606	14.8	4	1
1968 Bos	11	16	242	15.1	1	0
NFL Total	75	199	3107	15.6	20	2

CLARENCE GRAHAM Graham, Clarence 1 **WB-BB**
Col: No College
1928 Day: 2 G.

DAVE GRAHAM Graham, David Elliott 6′3″, 250 **OT**
Col: Virginia *HS:* Roger Ludlowe [Fairfield, CT] B: 2/1/1939, Bridgeport, CT *Drafted:* 1960 Round 13 Phi
1963 Phi: 14 G. **1964** Phi: 13 G. **1965** Phi: 14 G. **1966** Phi: 14 G. **1968** Phi: 14 G; KR 1-8 8.0. **1969** Phi: 14 G; KR 2-5 2.5. **Total:** 83 G; KR 3-13 4.3.

DAVID GRAHAM Graham, David Jerome 6′6″, 250 **DE-NT**
Col: Morehouse *HS:* Florida A & M University [Tallahassee, FL]
B: 4/6/1959, Chicago, IL
1982 Sea: 3 G. **1987** Sea: 3 G. **Total:** 6 G.

DERRICK GRAHAM Graham, Dettrice Andrew 6′4″, 310 **OT-OG**
Col: Appalachian State *HS:* Groveland [FL] B: 3/18/1967, Groveland, FL *Drafted:* 1990 Round 5 KC
1990 KC: 6 G. **1991** KC: 16 G. **1992** KC: 2 G. **1993** KC: 11 G. **1994** KC: 16 G. **1995** Car: 11 G. **1996** Sea: 16 G. **1997** Sea: 9 G. **1998** Oak: 12 G. **Total:** 99 G.

DON GRAHAM Graham, Donald John 6′2″, 244 **LB**
Col: Penn State *HS:* Brentwood [Pittsburgh, PA] B: 1/31/1964, Pittsburgh, PA *Drafted:* 1987 Round 4 TB
1987 TB: 2 G. **1988** Buf: 10 G. **1989** Was: 1 G. **Total:** 13 G.

FRED GRAHAM Graham, Frederick Hartley 6′0″, 175 **OE**
Col: Indiana State; West Virginia *HS:* Morgantown [WV] B: 12/11/1900, Masontown, WV D: 8/29/1952, Fairmont, WV
1926 Fra-Prov: 2 G. Fra: 1 G. Prov: 1 G. **Total:** 2 G.

HASON GRAHAM Graham, Hason Aaron 5′10″, 176 **WR**
Col: Hinds CC MS; Georgia *HS:* S.W. DeKalb [Decatur, GA]
B: 3/21/1971, Decatur, GA
1995 NE: 10 G; Rec 10-156 15.6 2 TD; 12 Pt. **1996** NE: 9 G; Rec 5-64 12.8. **Total:** 19 G; Rec 15-220 14.7 2 TD; 12 Pt.

JAY GRAHAM Graham, Herman Jason 5′11″, 220 **RB**
Col: Tennessee *HS:* Concord [NC] B: 7/14/1975, Concord, NC
Drafted: 1997 Round 3 Bal
1997 Bal: Rec 12-51 4.3; KR 6-115 19.2. **1998** Bal: Rec 5-41 8.2; KR 3-52 17.3. **Total:** Rec 17-92 5.4; KR 9-167 18.6.

		Rushing				
Year Team	G	Att	Yds	Avg	TD	Fum
1997 Bal	13	81	299	3.7	2	2
1998 Bal	5	35	109	3.1	0	0
NFL Total	18	116	408	3.5	2	2

KENNY GRAHAM Graham, James Kenneth 6′0″, 210 **DB**
(Pony) *Col:* Washington State *HS:* Santa Monica [CA] B: 11/25/1941, Texarkana, TX *Drafted:* 1964 Round 13 SD
1964 SD: KR 7-172 24.6. **Total:** KR 7-172 24.6.

		Punt Returns				Interceptions			
Year Team	G	Ret	Yds	Avg	TD	Int	Yds	TD	Fum
1964 SD	14	2	24	12.0	0	4	24	0	0
1965 SD	14	5	36	7.2	0	5	108	1	0
1966 SD	13	2	15	7.5	0	5	70	1	0
1967 SD	13	3	46	15.3	0	2	76	1	0
1968 SD	14	13	61	4.7	0	5	87	0	3
1969 SD	14	3	15	5.0	0	4	112	**2**	4
1970 Cin-Pit	8	1	41	41.0	0	3	31	0	0
1970 Cin	5	1	41	41.0	0	3	31	0	0
1970 Pit	3	0	0	—	0	0	0	0	0
NFL Total	90	29	238	8.2	0	28	508	5	7

SCOTTIE GRAHAM Graham, James Otis 5′9″, 217 **RB**
Col: Ohio State *HS:* Long Beach [NY] B: 3/28/1969, Long Beach, NY
Drafted: 1992 Round 7 Pit
1993 Min: Rec 7-46 6.6; KR 1-16 16.0. **1994** Min: Rec 1-1 1.0. **1995** Min: Rec 4-30 7.5. **1996** Min: Rec 7-48 6.9. **1997** Cin: Rec 1-1 1.0.
Total: Rec 20-126 6.3; KR 1-16 16.0.

		Rushing			
Year Team	G	Att	Yds	Avg	TD
1992 NYJ	2	14	29	2.1	0
1993 Min	7	118	488	4.1	3
1994 Min	16	64	207	3.2	2
1995 Min	16	110	406	3.7	2
1996 Min	11	57	138	2.4	0
1997 Cin	5	1	-1	-1.0	0
NFL Total	57	364	1267	3.5	7

JEFF GRAHAM Graham, Jeffrey Todd 6′2″, 200 **WR**
Col: Ohio State *HS:* Alter [Kettering, OH] B: 2/14/1969, Dayton, OH
Drafted: 1991 Round 2 Pit
1991 Pit: KR 3-48 16.0. **1994** ChiB: Scor 1 2XP. **1995** ChiB: KR 1-12 12.0. **Total:** KR 4-60 15.0; Scor 1 2XP.

		Receiving				Punt Returns					Tot
Year Team	G	Rec	Yds	Avg	TD	Ret	Yds	Avg	TD	Fum	TD
1991 Pit	13	2	21	10.5	0	8	46	5.8	0	0	0
1992 Pit	14	49	711	14.5	1	0	0	—	0	0	1
1993 Pit	15	38	579	15.2	0	0	0	—	0	0	0
1994 ChiB	16	68	944	13.9	4	15	140	9.3	1	1	5
1995 ChiB	16	82	1301	15.9	4	23	183	8.0	0	3	4
1996 NYJ	11	50	788	15.8	6	0	0	—	0	0	6
1997 NYJ	16	42	542	12.9	2	0	0	—	0	0	2
1998 Phi	15	47	600	12.8	2	0	0	—	0	0	2
NFL Total	116	378	5486	14.5	19	46	369	8.0	1	4	20

KENT GRAHAM Graham, Kent Douglas 6′5″, 231 **QB**
Col: Notre Dame; Ohio State *HS:* North [Wheaton, IL] B: 11/1/1968, Winfield, LA *Drafted:* 1992 Round 8 NYG
1998 NYG: Rec 1-16 16.0. **Total:** Rec 1-16 16.0.

		Passing							
Year Team	G	Att	Comp	Comp%	Yds	YPA	TD	Int	Rating
1992 NYG	6	97	42	43.3	470	4.85	1	4	44.6
1993 NYG	9	22	8	36.4	79	3.59	0	0	47.3
1994 NYG	13	53	24	45.3	295	5.57	3	2	66.2
1996 Ariz	10	274	146	53.3	1624	5.93	12	7	75.1
1997 Ariz	8	250	130	52.0	1408	5.63	4	5	65.9
1998 NYG	11	205	105	51.2	1219	5.95	7	5	70.8
NFL Total	57	901	455	50.5	5095	5.65	27	23	67.1

	Rushing				
Year Team	Att	Yds	Avg	TD	Fum
1992 NYG	6	36	6.0	0	1
1993 NYG	2	-3	-1.5	0	0
1994 NYG	2	11	5.5	0	2
1996 Ariz	21	87	4.1	0	5
1997 Ariz	13	23	1.8	2	5
1998 NYG	27	138	5.1	2	2
NFL Total	71	292	4.1	4	15

LES GRAHAM Graham, Lester James 6′0″, 215 **G**
Col: Tulsa *HS:* Hominy [OK] B: 7/1/1916, Hominy, OK Deceased
1938 Det: 11 G.

MIKE GRAHAM Graham, Michael N 6′0″, 200 **FB-LB**
(The Greek Ground Gripper) *Col:* Cincinnati *HS:* Warren G. Harding [Warren, OH] B: 4/3/1925, Warren, OH
AAFC **1948** LA-A: 14 G; Rush 19-69 3.6 1 TD; Rec 0-2; KR 6-145 24.2; Int 1-20; 6 Pt.

MILT GRAHAM Graham, Milton Russell 6′6″, 235 **OT-DT**
Col: Colgate *HS:* Columbia [Rensselaer, NY] B: 7/28/1934
1961 Bos: 3 G. **1962** Bos: 14 G. **1963** Bos: 11 G. **Total:** 28 G.

OTTO GRAHAM Graham, Otto Everett Jr. 6′1″, 196 **QB-DB**
Col: Northwestern *HS:* Waukegan [IL] B: 12/6/1921, Waukegan, IL
Drafted: 1944 Round 1 Det *HOF:* 1965
AAFC **1946** CleA: PR 12-129 10.8; Int 5-102 1 TD. **1947** CleA: PR 10-121 12.1; Int 1-0. **1948** CleA: PR 1-12 12.0; Int 1-0. **Total:** PR 23-262 11.4; Int 7-102 1 TD.

		Passing							
Year Team	G	Att	Comp	Comp%	Yds	YPA	TD	Int	Rating
1946 CleA	14	174	95	54.6	1834	10.54	17	5	112.1
1947 CleA	14	269	163	60.6	2753	10.23	25	11	109.2
1948 CleA	14	333	173	52.0	2713	8.15	25	15	85.6
1949 CleA	12	285	161	56.5	2785	9.77	19	10	97.5
AAFC Total	54	1061	592	55.8	10085	9.51	86	41	99.1

	Rushing				Tot
Year Team	Att	Yds	Avg	TD	TD
1946 CleA	30	-125	-4.2	1	2
1947 CleA	19	72	3.8	1	1
1948 CleA	23	146	6.3	6	6
1949 CleA	27	107	4.0	3	3
AAFC Total	99	200	2.0	11	12

NFL **1951** Cle: 1 Fum TD. **Total:** 1 Fum TD.

		Passing							
Year Team	G	Att	Comp	Comp%	Yds	YPA	TD	Int	Rating
1950 Cle	12	253	137	54.2	1943	7.68	14	20	64.7
1951 Cle	12	265	147	55.5	2205	8.32	17	16	79.2
1952 Cle	12	**364**	**181**	49.7	**2816**	7.74	**20**	24	66.6
1953 Cle	12	258	167	**64.7**	**2722**	**10.55**	11	9	99.7
1954 Cle	12	240	142	**59.2**	2092	8.72	11	17	73.5
1955 Cle	12	185	98	**53.0**	1721	**9.30**	15	8	94.0
NFL Total	72	1565	872	55.7	13499	**8.63**	88	94	78.2

	Rushing					Tot
Year Team	Att	Yds	Avg	TD	Fum	TD
1950 Cle	55	145	2.6	6	6	6
1951 Cle	35	29	0.8	3	7	4
1952 Cle	42	130	3.1	4	4	4
1953 Cle	43	143	3.3	6	8	6
1954 Cle	63	114	1.8	8	3	8
1955 Cle	68	121	1.8	6	7	6
NFL Total	306	682	2.2	33	35	34

ROGER GRAHAM Graham, Roger Alton 5′10″, 217 **RB**
Col: New Haven *HS:* Spring Valley [NY] B: 11/8/1972, Bronx, NY
1996 Jac: 1 G.

LYLE GRAHAM Graham, Samuel Lyle 6'3", 210 **C-LB**
Col: Richmond *HS:* Farmville [VA] B: 10/28/1915, Kenbridge, VA
1941 Phi: 11 G; Int 2-39.

TOM GRAHAM Graham, Thomas 6'3", 210 **G**
Col: Temple *HS:* Alhambra [CA] B: 8/14/1909 D: 8/1961
1935 Phi: 2 G.

TOM GRAHAM Graham, Thomas Lawrence 6'2", 235 **LB**
Col: Oregon *HS:* Nathaniel Narbonne [Los Angeles, CA] B: 4/15/1950, Los Angeles, CA *Drafted:* 1972 Round 4 Den
1972 Den: 14 G; Int 2-10. **1973** Den: 14 G. **1974** Den-KC: 13 G. Den: 5 G. KC: 8 G. **1975** SD: 14 G; Int 2-5; 1 Fum. **1976** SD: 10 G; Int 3-55. **1977** SD: 12 G. **1978** Buf: 11 G. **Total:** 88 G; Int 7-70; 1 Fum.

WILLIAM GRAHAM Graham, William Roger 5'11", 191 **DB**
Col: Texas *HS:* Silsbee [TX] B: 9/27/1959, Silsbee, TX *Drafted:* 1982 Round 5 Det
1982 Det: 7 G. **1983** Det: 14 G. **1984** Det: 14 G; Int 3-22. **1985** Det: 16 G; Int 3-22; 1 Sac. **1986** Det: 16 G; KR 3-72 24.0. **1987** Det: 2 G. **Total:** 69 G; KR 3-72 24.0; Int 6-44; 1 Sac.

ED GRAIN Grain, Edwin Elswin III 6'0", 230 **G**
Col: Pennsylvania *HS:* Baltimore Polytechnic Inst. [MD] B: 2/25/1922, Baltimore, MD D: 10/6/1984, Evanston, IL
AAFC **1947** NY-A-BalA: 12 G. **1948** BalA: 11 G. **Total:** 23 G.

JOHN GRANBY Granby, John Edward Jr. 6'1", 200 **WR**
Col: Virginia Tech *HS:* Floyd E. Kellam [Virginia Beach, VA]
B: 11/11/1968, Virginia Beach, VA *Drafted:* 1992 Round 12 Den
1992 Den: 4 G.

KEN GRANDBERRY Grandberry, Kenneth James 6'0", 195 **RB**
Col: Washington State *HS:* Laughbon [Dupont, WA] B: 1/25/1952, Waco, TX *Drafted:* 1974 Round 8 ChiB
1974 ChiB: KR 22-568 25.8.

		Rushing				Receiving				
Year Team	G	Att	Yds	Avg	TD	Rec	Yds	Avg	TD	Fum
1974 ChiB	14	144	475	3.3	2	30	212	7.1	0	8

SONNY GRANDELIUS Grandelius, Everett John 6'0", 195 **HB**
Col: Michigan State *HS:* Muskegon Heights [MI] B: 4/16/1929, Muskegon, MI *Drafted:* 1951 Round 3 NYG
1953 NYG: Rec 15-80 5.3.

		Rushing				
Year Team	G	Att	Yds	Avg	TD	Fum
1953 NYG	12	108	278	2.6	1	3

RUFUS GRANDERSON Granderson, Rufus Will 6'5", 277 **DT**
HS: Temple [TX] B: 8/13/1936, Waco, TX *Drafted:* 1959 Round 19 Det
1960 DalT: 6 G.

GEORGE GRANDINETTE Grandinette, George J 5'9", 215 **G**
Col: Fordham *HS:* James Hillhouse [New Haven, CT]; Bridgton Acad. [North Bridgton, ME] B: 4/13/1917, New Haven, CT D: 4/16/1984, Lauderdale Lakes, FL
1943 Bkn: 10 G.

GARDIE GRANGE Grange, Garland Arthur 6'0", 173 **OE**
Col: Illinois *HS:* Wheaton [IL] B: 12/2/1906, Forksville, PA
D: 5/28/1981, Miami, FL
1929 ChiB: 14 G; Rec 2 TD; 12 Pt. **1930** ChiB: 12 G; Scor 1, 1 XK. **1931** ChiB: 12 G; Rec 1 TD; Scor 7, 1 XK. **Total:** 38 G; Rec 3 TD.

RED GRANGE Grange, Harold Edward 6'0", 180 **HB-DB-TB-BB**
(The Galloping Ghost) *Col:* Illinois *HS:* Wheaton [IL] B: 6/13/1903, Forksville, PA D: 1/28/1991, Lake Wales, FL *HOF:* 1963
1925 ChiB: Int 1 TD. **1929** ChiB: Scor **1** 1XP. **1930** ChiB: Rec 2 TD; Scor **1** 1XP. **1931** ChiB: Rec 2 TD. **1932** ChiB: Rec 11-168 15.3 4 TD. **1933** ChiB: Rec 3-74 24.7. **1934** ChiB: Rec 2-46 23.0 2 TD. **Total:** Rec 16-288 18.0 10 TD; Int 1 TD; Scor 2 1XP.

		Passing							
Year Team	G	Att	Comp	Comp%	Yds	YPA	TD	Int	Rating
1925 ChiB	5	—	—	—	—	—	1	—	—
1927 NYY	13	—	—	—	—	—	0	—	—
1929 ChiB	14	—	—	—	—	—	2	—	—
1930 ChiB	14	—	—	—	—	—	3	—	—
1931 ChiB	13	—	—	—	—	—	1	—	—
1932 ChiB	12	13	5	38.5	96	7.38	0	0	64.9
1933 ChiB	13	33	13	39.4	169	5.12	2	**3**	38.6
1934 ChiB	12	25	6	24.0	81	3.24	1	7	14.3
NFL Total	96	71	24	33.8	346	4.87	10	10	50.6

	Rushing				Tot
Year Team	Att	Yds	Avg	TD	TD
1925 ChiB	—	—	—	2	3
1927 NYY	—	—	—	1	1
1929 ChiB	—	—	—	2	2
1930 ChiB	—	—	—	6	8
1931 ChiB	—	—	—	5	7
1932 ChiB	57	136	2.4	3	**7**
1933 ChiB	81	277	3.4	1	1
1934 ChiB	32	156	4.9	1	3
NFL Total	170	569	3.3	21	32

CHARLEY GRANGER Granger, Charles 6'2", 240 **OT**
Col: Southern University *HS:* Booker T. Washington [Lake Charles, LA]
B: 8/9/1938, Lake Charles, LA *Drafted:* 1961 Round 26 Bos
1961 Dal-StL: 14 G. Dal: 8 G. StL: 6 G. **Total:** 14 G.

HOYLE GRANGER Granger, Hoyle John 6'1", 225 **RB**
Col: Mississippi State *HS:* Oberlin [LA] B: 3/7/1944, Oberlin, LA
Drafted: 1966 Round 5 Hou
1970 Hou: KR 1-0. **1972** Hou: KR 1-5 5.0. **Total:** KR 2-5 2.5.

		Rushing				Receiving					Tot
Year Team	G	Att	Yds	Avg	TD	Rec	Yds	Avg	TD	Fum	TD
1966 Hou	11	56	388	6.9	1	12	104	8.7	1	0	2
1967 Hou	14	236	1194	5.1	6	31	300	9.7	3	1	9
1968 Hou	13	202	848	4.2	7	26	361	13.9	0	3	7
1969 Hou	13	186	740	4.0	3	27	330	12.2	1	1	4
1970 Hou	5	51	169	3.3	1	11	118	10.7	0	2	1
1971 NO	14	32	139	4.3	1	12	52	4.3	0	1	1
1972 Hou	13	42	175	4.2	0	15	74	4.9	0	2	0
NFL Total	83	805	3653	4.5	19	134	1339	10.0	5	10	24

NORM GRANGER Granger, Norman Lance 5'9", 225 **RB**
Col: Iowa *HS:* Barringer [Newark, NJ] B: 9/14/1961, Newark, NJ
Drafted: 1984 Round 5 Dal
1984 Dal: 15 G; KR 2-6 3.0. **1987** Atl: 3 G; Rush 6-12 2.0; Rec 2-34 17.0; 1 Fum. **Total:** 18 G; Rush 6-12 2.0; Rec 2-34 17.0; KR 2-6 3.0; 1 Fum.

DAVE GRANNELL Grannell, David Matthew 6'4", 230 **TE**
Col: Arizona State *HS:* Thomas Jefferson [Denver, CO] B: 10/4/1952, Denver, CO *Drafted:* 1974 Round 11 SD
1974 SD: 9 G; Rec 3-51 17.0.

AARON GRANT Grant, Aaron T Jr. 6'2", 285 **C**
(Heavy) *Col:* Tennessee Wesleyan; Tennessee-Chattanooga
HS: Maryville [TN] B: 7/3/1908, Roane Co., TN D: 9/1966
1930 Port: 1 G.

AFRICAN GRANT Grant, African Nigeria 6'0", 200 **DB**
Col: Illinois *HS:* Dwight Morrow [Englewood, NJ] B: 8/2/1965, New York, NY
1990 Mia: 4 G.

ALAN GRANT Grant, Alan Hays 5'10", 187 **DB**
Col: Stanford *HS:* St. Francis [La Canada, CA] B: 10/1/1966, Pasadena, CA *Drafted:* 1990 Round 4 Ind
1990 Ind: KR 15-280 18.7; Int 1-25 1 TD. **1991** Ind: KR 3-20 6.7. **1992** SF: KR 3-70 23.3. **1993** SF-Cin: Int 1-17. Cin: Int 1-17. **1994** Was: Int 1-0. **Total:** KR 21-370 17.6; Int 3-42 1 TD.

		Punt Returns				
Year Team	G	Ret	Yds	Avg	TD	Fum
1990 Ind	16	2	6	3.0	0	1
1991 Ind	16	2	6	3.0	0	0
1992 SF	15	29	249	8.6	0	1
1993 SF-Cin	12	0	0	—	0	0
1993 SF	3	0	0	—	0	0
1993 Cin	9	0	0	—	0	0
1994 Was	13	0	0	—	0	0
NFL Total	72	33	261	7.9	0	2

DARRYL GRANT Grant, Darryl Baris 6'1", 269 **DT-OG-C-OT**
Col: Rice *HS:* Highlands [San Antonio, TX] B: 11/22/1959, San Antonio, TX *Drafted:* 1981 Round 9 Was
1981 Was: 15 G; KR 1-20 20.0. **1982** Was: 9 G; 2.5 Sac. **1983** Was: 16 G; 2.5 Sac. **1984** Was: 15 G; **1** Fum TD; 6 Pt; 8 Sac. **1985** Was: 8 G; 1.5 Sac. **1986** Was: 16 G; 2 Sac. **1987** Was: 12 G; 2 Sac. **1988** Was: 16 G; 4 Sac. **1989** Was: 16 G; Int 2-0; 3.5 Sac. **1990** Was: 16 G; 1 Sac. **1991** TB: 2 G. **Total:** 141 G; KR 1-20 20.0; Int 2-0; 1 Fum TD; 6 Pt; 27.0 Sac.

DAVID GRANT Grant, David John 6'4", 277 **NT**
Col: West Virginia *HS:* Belleville [NJ] B: 9/17/1965, Belleville, NJ
Drafted: 1988 Round 4 Cin
1988 Cin: 16 G; 5 Sac. **1989** Cin: 16 G; 0.5 Sac. **1990** Cin: 16 G; 1 Sac. **1991** Cin: 13 G; Int 1-0; 2 Sac. **1992** TB: 2 G. **1993** GB: 7 G. **Total:** 70 G; Int 1-0; 8.5 Sac.

FRANK GRANT Grant, Frank 5'11", 181 **WR**
Col: Southern Colorado *HS:* East Side [Newark, NJ] B: 2/15/1950, Brooklyn, NY *Drafted:* 1972 Round 13 Was
1974 Was: Rush 1-(-10) -10.0. **1975** Was: Rush 3-46 15.3; KR 0-16. **1976** Was: Rush 1-(-9) -9.0. **Total:** Rush 5-27 5.4; KR 0-16.

		Receiving				
Year Team	G	Rec	Yds	Avg	TD	Fum
1973 Was	13	1	12	12.0	1	0
1974 Was	14	9	196	21.8	1	0

1975 Was	14	41	776	18.9	8	2
1976 Was	14	50	818	16.4	5	0
1977 Was	14	34	480	14.1	3	0
1978 Was-TB	16	14	204	14.6	0	0
1978 Was	6	6	92	15.3	0	0
1978 TB	10	8	112	14.0	0	0
NFL Total	85	149	2486	16.7	18	2

BUD GRANT Grant, Harold Peter Jr. 6′3″, 199 **OE-DE**
Col: Minnesota *HS:* Central [Superior, WI] B: 5/20/1927, Superior, WI
Drafted: 1950 Round 1 Phi
1951 Phi: PR 1-9 9.0. **Total:** PR 1-9 9.0.

		Receiving				
Year Team	**G**	**Rec**	**Yds**	**Avg**	**TD**	**Fum**
1951 Phi	12	0	0	—	0	0
1952 Phi	12	56	997	17.8	7	4
NFL Total	24	56	997	17.8	7	4

DUCKY GRANT Grant, Hugh E 5′11″, 175 **BB**
Col: St. Mary's (Cal.) *HS:* St.Mary's [Moraga, CA] B: 12/24/1902
D: 9/1985, Fountain Valley, CA
1928 ChiC: 6 G; Scor 1, 1 XK.

JOHN GRANT Grant, John David 6′3″, 241 **DE-NT-DT**
Col: USC *HS:* Capital [Boise, ID] B: 6/28/1950, Boise, ID
Drafted: 1973 Round 7 Den
1973 Den: 13 G. **1974** Den: 13 G. **1975** Den: 14 G. **1976** Den: 13 G. **1977** Den: 14 G; KR 1-8 8.0. **1978** Den: 16 G. **1979** Den: 16 G; KR 1-25 25.0. **Total:** 99 G; KR 2-33 16.5.

LEN GRANT Grant, Leonard W 6′3″, 235 **T**
(Galahad; Fish) *Col:* New York U. *HS:* Dedham [MA]; Dean Acad. [Franklin, MA] B: 1/17/1906, Boston, MA D: 8/6/1938, Dedham, MA
1930 NYG: 12 G. **1931** NYG: 11 G. **1932** NYG: 12 G. **1933** NYG: 14 G. **1934** NYG: 12 G. **1935** NYG: 12 G. **1936** NYG: 10 G. **1937** NYG: 9 G. **Total:** 92 G.

OTIS GRANT Grant, Otis 6′3″, 197 **WR**
Col: Michigan State *HS:* George Washington Carver [Atlanta, GA]
B: 8/13/1961, Atlanta, GA *Drafted:* 1983 Round 5 LARm
1983 LARm: Rush 2-(-10) -5.0. **1987** Phi: Pass 1-0; Rush 1-20 20.0. **Total:** Pass 1-0; Rush 3-10 3.3.

		Receiving				
Year Team	**G**	**Rec**	**Yds**	**Avg**	**TD**	**Fum**
1983 LARm	16	12	221	18.4	1	1
1984 LARm	14	9	64	7.1	0	0
1987 Phi	3	16	280	17.5	0	0
NFL Total	33	37	565	15.3	1	1

REGGIE GRANT Grant, Reginald Leon 5′9″, 185 **DB**
Col: Oregon *HS:* Sealth [Seattle, WA] B: 9/2/1955, Atlanta, GA
Drafted: 1978 Round 9 NYJ
1978 NYJ: 14 G.

BOB GRANT Grant, Robert Bernard 6′2″, 225 **LB**
Col: Wake Forest *HS:* Georgetown [NC] B: 10/14/1946, Jacksonville, NC *Drafted:* 1968 Round 2 Bal
1968 Bal: 7 G. **1969** Bal: 14 G; Int 3-0. **1970** Bal: 14 G; KR 1-21 21.0; Int 2-39 1 TD; 6 Pt. **1971** Was: 6 G. **Total:** 41 G; KR 1-21 21.0; Int 5-39 1 TD; 6 Pt.

ROSIE GRANT Grant, Ross Stewart 5′10″, 198 **G-C-LB**
Col: New York U. *HS:* Marblehead [MA] B: 4/16/1908, Chicago, IL
D: 4/26/1974, Cedar Lake, IN
1932 SI: 12 G. **1933** Cin: 8 G. **1934** Cin: 2 G. **Total:** 22 G.

RUPERT GRANT Grant, Rupert Jr. 6′1″, 233 **RB**
Col: Howard *HS:* Calvin Coolidge [Washington, DC] B: 11/5/1973, Washington, DC
1995 NE: 7 G; Rec 1-4 4.0; KR 1-7 7.0.

STEVE GRANT Grant, Stephen Mitchell 6′0″, 240 **LB**
Col: West Virginia *HS:* Miami Southridge [FL] B: 12/23/1969, Miami, FL *Drafted:* 1992 Round 10 Ind
1992 Ind: 16 G. **1993** Ind: 16 G. **1994** Ind: 16 G. **1995** Ind: 15 G; Int 1-9; 2 Sac. **1996** Ind: 11 G; 1 Sac. **1997** Ind: 9 G. **Total:** 83 G; Int 1-9; 3 Sac.

WES GRANT Grant, Wesley Louis 6′3″, 245 **DE-DT**
(Butch) *Col:* Santa Monica Coll. CA (J.C.); UCLA *HS:* Los Angeles [CA]
B: 9/24/1946, Los Angeles, CA *Drafted:* 1970 Round 4 NYG
1971 Buf-SD: 5 G. Buf: 3 G. SD: 2 G. **1972** Cle: 3 G. **1973** Hou: 3 G. **Total:** 11 G.

WILL GRANT Grant, Wilfred L 6′3″, 254 **C**
Col: Idaho State; Kentucky *HS:* Thayer Acad. [Braintree, MA]; Milford Acad. [CT] B: 3/7/1954, Milton, MA *Drafted:* 1978 Round 10 Buf
1978 Buf: 16 G. **1979** Buf: 16 G. **1980** Buf: 16 G. **1981** Buf: 16 G. **1982** Buf: 9 G. **1983** Buf: 16 G. **1984** Buf: 16 G. **1985** Buf: 16 G. **1986** Sea: 7 G. **1987** Buf: 1 G. **Total:** 129 G.

LARRY GRANTHAM Grantham, James Larry 6′0″, 210 **LB**
Col: Mississippi *HS:* Crystal Springs [MS] B: 9/16/1938, Crystal Springs, MS *Drafted:* 1960 Round 1 NYT
1962 NYT: **1** Fum TD. **Total:** 1 Fum TD.

		Interceptions				Tot
Year Team	**G**	**Int**	**Yds**	**TD**	**Fum**	**TD**
1960 NYT	14	5	13	0	1	0
1961 NYT	11	1	30	0	0	0
1962 NYT	14	2	2	0	0	1
1963 NYJ	14	3	89	0	0	1
1964 NYJ	14	2	32	0	0	0
1965 NYJ	14	1	0	0	0	0
1966 NYJ	14	1	14	0	1	0
1967 NYJ	14	5	77	0	0	0
1968 NYJ	13	0	0	0	0	0
1969 NYJ	14	0	0	0	0	0
1970 NYJ	14	3	51	1	0	1
1971 NYJ	14	1	0	0	0	0
1972 NYJ	11	0	0	0	0	0
NFL Total	175	24	308	1	2	3

BILLY GRANVILLE Granville, William Lamont 6′3″, 252 **LB**
Col: Duke *HS:* Lawrenceville School [NJ] B: 3/11/1974, Trenton, NJ
1997 Cin: 12 G. **1998** Cin: 16 G. **Total:** 28 G.

PAUL GRASMANIS Grasmanis, Paul Ryan 6′2″, 298 **DT**
Col: Notre Dame *HS:* Jenison [MI] B: 8/2/1974, Grand Rapids, MI
Drafted: 1996 Round 4 ChiB
1996 ChiB: 14 G. **1997** ChiB: 16 G; 0.5 Sac. **1998** ChiB: 15 G; 1 Sac. **Total:** 45 G; 1.5 Sac.

CARL GRATE Grate, Carl F 6′0″, 215 **G-LB**
Col: Georgia *HS:* McClain [Greenfield, OH] B: 1920 *Drafted:* 1944 Round 11 NYG
1945 NYG: 6 G.

WILLIE GRATE Grate, Willie 6′4″, 225 **TE**
Col: South Carolina State *HS:* Whittermore [Conway, SC]
B: 5/25/1946, Georgetown, SC *Drafted:* 1969 Round 6 Hou
1969 Buf: 11 G; Rec 1-19 19.0 1 TD; 6 Pt. **1970** Buf: 14 G; Rec 7-147 21.0 2 TD; 12 Pt; 1 Fum. **Total:** 25 G; Rec 8-166 20.8 3 TD; 18 Pt; 1 Fum.

GORDON GRAVELLE Gravelle, Gordon Carr 6′5″, 250 **OT**
Col: Brigham Young *HS:* Ygnacio Valley [Concord, CA] B: 6/12/1949, Oakland, CA *Drafted:* 1972 Round 2 Pit
1972 Pit: 14 G. **1973** Pit: 6 G. **1974** Pit: 14 G. **1975** Pit: 14 G. **1976** Pit: 6 G. **1977** NYG: 14 G. **1978** NYG: 16 G. **1979** NYG-LARm: 12 G. NYG: 4 G. LARm: 8 G. **Total:** 96 G.

MARSHARNE GRAVES Graves, Marsharne DeWayne 6′3″, 268 **OT**
Col: Arizona *HS:* Abraham Lincoln [San Francisco, CA] B: 7/8/1962, Memphis, TN
1984 Den: 1 G. **1987** Ind: 3 G. **Total:** 4 G.

RORY GRAVES Graves, Rory Anthony 6′6″, 288 **OT**
Col: Ohio State *HS:* Columbia [Decatur, GA] B: 7/21/1963, Atlanta, GA
1988 LARd: 16 G. **1989** LARd: 15 G. **1990** LARd: 15 G. **1991** LARd: 3 G. **Total:** 49 G.

RAY GRAVES Graves, Samuel Ray 6′1″, 205 **C**
(Parson) *Col:* Tennessee Wesleyan; Tennessee *HS:* Rockwood [TN]; Central HS [Knoxville, TN] B: 12/31/1918, Rockwood, TN
Drafted: 1942 Round 9 Phi
1942 Phi: 11 G; Int 1-0; Scor 1, 1-1 100.0% XK. **1943** PhPt: 10 G; Int 1-15. **1946** Phi: 7 G. **Total:** 28 G; Int 2-15; Scor 1, 1-1 100.0% XK.

TOM GRAVES Graves, Thomas Edward Jr. 6′3″, 228 **LB**
Col: Michigan State *HS:* Lake Taylor [Norfolk, VA] B: 12/18/1955, Norfolk, VA *Drafted:* 1979 Round 8 Pit
1979 Pit: 11 G.

WHITE GRAVES Graves, White Solomon III 6′0″, 190 **DB**
Col: Louisiana State *HS:* Crystal Springs [MS] B: 3/20/1942, Jackson, MS *Drafted:* 1965 Round 17 Bos
1965 Bos: 14 G; Int 2-0. **1966** Bos: 14 G; PR 1-5 5.0; Int 1-0. **1967** Bos: 12 G. **1968** Cin: 2 G. **Total:** 42 G; PR 1-5 5.0; Int 3-0.

CARLTON GRAY Gray, Carlton Patrick 6′0″, 195 **DB**
Col: UCLA *HS:* Forest Park [OH] B: 6/26/1971, Cincinnati, OH
Drafted: 1993 Round 2 Sea
1993 Sea: 1 Sac. **1998** NYG: 1 Sac. **Total:** 2 Sac.

		Interceptions			
Year Team	**G**	**Int**	**Yds**	**TD**	**Fum**
1993 Sea	10	3	33	0	0
1994 Sea	11	2	0	0	0
1995 Sea	16	4	45	0	1
1996 Sea	16	0	3	0	0
1997 Ind	15	2	0	0	0
1998 NYG	14	1	36	0	0
NFL Total	82	12	117	0	1

CECIL GRAY Gray, Cecil Talik 6'4", 288 **OT-OG-DT**
Col: North Carolina *HS:* Archbishop Molloy [Queens, NY]; Norfolk Catholic HS [VA] B: 2/16/1968, New York, NY *Drafted:* 1990 Round 9 Phi
1990 Phi: 12 G. **1991** Phi: 2 G. **1992** GB: 2 G. **1993** Ind: 6 G. **1994** Ind: 16 G. **1995** Ariz: 7 G. **Total:** 45 G.

CHRIS GRAY Gray, Christopher William 6'3", 296 **OG-OT**
Col: Auburn *HS:* Homewood [AL] B: 6/19/1970, Birmingham, AL
Drafted: 1993 Round 5 Mia
1993 Mia: 5 G. **1994** Mia: 16 G. **1995** Mia: 10 G. **1996** Mia: 11 G. **1997** ChiB: 8 G. **1998** Sea: 15 G. **Total:** 65 G.

DAN GRAY Gray, Daniel Thomas 6'6", 240 **DT**
Col: Rutgers *HS:* Belvidere [NJ] B: 1/29/1956, Phillipsburg, NJ
Drafted: 1978 Round 5 Det
1978 Det: 14 G.

DAVID GRAY Gray, David Allen 6'0", 187 **DB**
Col: East Los Angeles Coll. CA (J.C.); Oregon State; San Diego State
HS: Manual Arts [Los Angeles, CA] B: 3/28/1955, San Diego, CA
1979 NO: 16 G; Int 1-32.

DERWIN GRAY Gray, Derwin Lamont 5'11", 198 **DB**
Col: Brigham Young *HS:* Judson [Converse, TX] B: 4/9/1971, San Antonio, TX *Drafted:* 1993 Round 4 Ind
1993 Ind: 11 G. **1994** Ind: 16 G; KR 0-4. **1995** Ind: 16 G; Int 1-10. **1996** Ind: 10 G. **1997** Ind: 11 G. **1998** Car: 3 G. **Total:** 67 G; KR 0-4; Int 1-10.

EARNEST GRAY Gray, Earnest L 6'3", 195 **WR**
Col: Memphis *HS:* Greenwood [MS] B: 3/2/1957, Greenwood, MS
Drafted: 1979 Round 2 NYG
1979 NYG: Rush 2-2 1.0; KR 1-0. **Total:** Rush 2-2 1.0; KR 1-0.

		Receiving				
Year Team	**G**	**Rec**	**Yds**	**Avg**	**TD**	**Fum**
1979 NYG	16	28	537	19.2	4	1
1980 NYG	16	52	777	14.9	10	1
1981 NYG	16	22	360	16.4	2	1
1982 NYG	9	25	426	17.0	4	0
1983 NYG	16	78	1139	14.6	5	0
1984 NYG	12	38	529	13.9	2	0
1985 StL	5	3	22	7.3	0	0
NFL Total	90	246	3790	15.4	27	3

HECTOR GRAY Gray, Hector Bernard 6'1", 192 **DB**
Col: Florida State *HS:* Miami Springs [FL] B: 1/2/1957, Miami, FL
1981 Det: 16 G; Int 1-0. **1982** Det: 8 G; Int 1-5. **1983** Det: 1 G. **Total:** 25 G; Int 2-5.

JACK GRAY Gray, Jack 175 **E**
Deceased
1923 StL-GB: 5 G. StL: 4 G. GB: 1 G. **Total:** 5 G.

JIM GRAY Gray, James H 6'0", 180 **DB**
Col: Toledo *HS:* White Plains [NY] B: 8/23/1941 *Drafted:* 1965 Round 11 NYJ
1966 NYJ: 6 G; KR 5-77 15.4. **1967** Phi: 3 G; KR 1-30 30.0. **Total:** 9 G; KR 6-107 17.8.

JERRY GRAY Gray, Jerry Don 6'0", 183 **DB**
Col: Texas *HS:* Estacado [Lubbock, TX] B: 12/16/1962, Lubbock, TX
Drafted: 1985 Round 1 LARm
1988 LARm: PR 1-1 1.0. **1991** LARm: PR 1-9 9.0. **Total:** PR 2-10 5.0.

		Interceptions			Tot
Year Team	**G**	**Int**	**Yds**	**TD**	**TD**
1985 LARm	16	0	0	0	0
1986 LARm	16	8	101	0	0
1987 LARm	12	2	35	0	1
1988 LARm	16	3	83	1	1
1989 LARm	16	6	48	1	1
1990 LARm	12	0	0	0	0
1991 LARm	16	3	83	1	1
1992 Hou	16	6	24	0	0
1993 TB	14	0	0	0	0
NFL Total	134	28	374	3	4

JOHNNIE GRAY Gray, Johnnie Lee 5'11", 185 **DB**
Col: Allan Hancock Coll. CA (J.C.); Cal State-Fullerton *HS:* Lompoc [CA]
B: 12/18/1953, Lake Charles, LA
1976 GB: KR 1-23 23.0. **1980** GB: KR 5-63 12.6. **1981** GB: KR 2-24 12.0. **1982** GB: KR 2-29 14.5. **1983** GB: KR 11-178 16.2. **Total:** KR 21-317 15.1.

		Punt Returns				Interceptions			
Year Team	**G**	**Ret**	**Yds**	**Avg**	**TD**	**Int**	**Yds**	**TD**	**Fum**
1975 GB	14	1	27	27.0	0	1	7	0	0
1976 GB	14	37	307	8.3	0	4	101	1	0
1977 GB	14	10	68	6.8	0	1	12	0	0
1978 GB	16	11	95	8.6	0	3	66	0	1
1979 GB	16	13	61	4.7	0	5	66	0	3
1980 GB	16	4	41	10.3	0	5	54	0	0
1981 GB	9	1	0	0.0	0	0	0	0	0
1982 GB	9	6	48	8.0	0	1	21	0	0
1983 GB	16	2	9	4.5	0	2	5	0	2
NFL Total	124	85	656	7.7	0	22	332	1	6

KEN GRAY Gray, Kenneth Don 6'2", 245 **OG-LB**
Col: Howard Payne *HS:* Llano [TX] B: 3/10/1936, San Saba, TX
Drafted: 1958 Round 6 GB
1958 ChiC: 10 G. **1959** ChiC: 12 G; KR 1-11 11.0. **1960** StL: 10 G. **1961** StL: 13 G. **1962** StL: 14 G. **1963** StL: 14 G; KR 1-0. **1964** StL: 14 G; KR 2-0. **1965** StL: 14 G. **1966** StL: 11 G. **1967** StL: 13 G. **1968** StL: 14 G. **1969** StL: 12 G. **1970** Hou: 11 G. **Total:** 162 G; KR 4-11 2.8.

KEVIN GRAY Gray, Kevin 5'11", 179 **CB**
Col: Kennedy King Coll. IL (J.C.); Eastern Illinois *HS:* Hyde Park [Chicago, IL] B: 9/11/1957, Chicago, IL
1982 NO: 8 G.

LEON GRAY Gray, Leon 6'3", 256 **OT**
Col: Jackson State *HS:* East Side [Olive Branch, MS] B: 11/15/1951, Olive Branch, MS *Drafted:* 1973 Round 3 Mia
1973 NE: 9 G. **1974** NE: 14 G. **1975** NE: 14 G. **1976** NE: 14 G. **1977** NE: 11 G. **1978** NE: 16 G. **1979** Hou: 16 G. **1980** Hou: 14 G. **1981** Hou: 16 G. **1982** NO: 7 G. **1983** NO: 11 G. **Total:** 142 G.

MEL GRAY Gray, Melvin Dean 5'9", 175 **WR**
Col: Fort Scott CC KS; Missouri *HS:* Montgomery [Santa Rosa, CA]
B: 9/28/1948, Fresno, CA *Drafted:* 1971 Round 6 StL
1971 StL: Rush 2-56 28.0. **1972** StL: PR 2-(-4) -2.0. **1975** StL: Rush 1-6 6.0; PR 7-53 7.6. **1977** StL: Rush 1-(-1) -1.0. **1978** StL: Rush 5-51 10.2 1 TD. **1979** StL: Rush 4-41 10.3. **1980** StL: Rush 1-(-3) -3.0. **1981** StL: Rush 1-4 4.0. **Total:** Rush 15-154 10.3 1 TD; PR 9-49 5.4.

		Receiving				Kickoff Returns					Tot
Year Team	**G**	**Rec**	**Yds**	**Avg**	**TD**	**Ret**	**Yds**	**Avg**	**TD**	**Fum**	**TD**
1971 StL	14	18	534	29.7	4	30	740	24.7	0	1	4
1972 StL	7	3	62	20.7	0	17	378	22.2	0	1	0
1973 StL	12	29	513	17.7	7	4	73	18.3	0	0	7
1974 StL	14	39	770	19.7	6	0	0	—	0	0	6
1975 StL	14	48	926	19.3	**11**	0	0	—	0	1	11
1976 StL	11	36	686	19.1	5	0	0	—	0	0	5
1977 StL	14	38	782	20.6	5	0	0	—	0	0	5
1978 StL	13	44	871	19.8	1	0	0	—	0	0	2
1979 StL	13	25	447	17.9	1	0	0	—	0	1	1
1980 StL	16	40	709	17.7	3	0	0	—	0	0	3
1981 StL	12	27	310	11.5	2	0	0	—	0	0	2
1982 StL	5	4	34	8.5	0	0	0	—	0	0	0
NFL Total	145	351	6644	18.9	45	51	1191	23.4	0	4	46

MEL GRAY Gray, Melvin Junius 5'9", 167 **RB-WR**
Col: Coffeyville CC KS; Purdue *HS:* Lafayette [Williamsburg, VA]
B: 3/16/1961, Williamsburg, VA *Drafted:* 1984 Supplemental Round 2 NO
1986 NO: Rush 6-29 4.8; Rec 2-45 22.5. **1987** NO: Rush 8-37 4.6 1 TD; Rec 6-30 5.0. **1989** Det: Rush 3-22 7.3; Rec 2-47 23.5. **1991** Det: Rush 2-11 5.5; Rec 3-42 14.0. **Total:** Rush 19-99 5.2 1 TD; Rec 13-164 12.6.

		Punt Returns				Kickoff Returns					Tot
Year Team	**G**	**Ret**	**Yds**	**Avg**	**TD**	**Ret**	**Yds**	**Avg**	**TD**	**Fum**	**TD**
1986 NO	16	0	0	—	0	31	866	27.9	**1**	0	1
1987 NO	12	24	352	**14.7**	0	30	636	21.2	0	3	1
1988 NO	14	25	305	12.2	1	32	670	20.9	0	5	1
1989 Det	10	11	76	6.9	0	24	640	26.7	0	0	0
1990 Det	16	34	361	10.6	0	41	939	22.9	0	4	0
1991 Det	16	25	385	**15.4**	1	36	**929**	**25.8**	0	3	1
1992 Det	15	18	175	9.7	1	**42**	1006	24.0	1	0	2
1993 Det	11	23	197	8.6	0	28	688	24.6	**1**	3	1
1994 Det	16	21	233	11.1	0	45	1276	**28.4**	**3**	3	3
1995 Hou	15	30	303	10.1	0	53	1183	22.3	0	5	0
1996 Hou	14	22	205	9.3	0	50	1224	24.5	0	4	0
1997 Ten-Phi	14	19	161	8.5	0	9	193	21.4	0	1	0
1997 Ten	11	17	144	8.5	0	8	185	23.1	0	1	0
1997 Phi	3	2	17	8.5	0	1	8	8.0	0	0	0
NFL Total	169	252	2753	10.9	3	**421**	**10250**	24.3	**6**	31	10

MOSES GRAY Gray, Moses William 6'3", 260 **OT-DT**
Col: Indiana *HS:* Conemaugh Twp. [Davidsville, PA] B: 4/12/1937, Conemaugh, PA *Drafted:* 1961 Round 27 NYT
1961 NYT: 3 G. **1962** NYT: 2 G. **Total:** 5 G.

OSCAR GRAY Gray, Oscar Ray 6'1", 255 **FB**
Col: Arkansas *HS:* M.B. Smiley [Houston, TX] B: 9/25/1972, Houston, TX
1996 Sea: 9 G; Rush 2-4 2.0; Rec 1-5 5.0.

PAUL GRAY Gray, Paul David 6'2", 231 **LB**
Col: Western Kentucky *HS:* Daviess Co. [Owensboro, KY]
B: 6/20/1962, Tulsa, OK *Drafted:* 1984 Round 10 NO
1987 Atl: 2 G.

SAM GRAY Gray, Samuel Wilbur 6′0″, 195 DE-OE
Col: Tulsa B: 1/1/1919, Independence, KS D: 6/12/1979, Houston, TX
Drafted: 1944 Round 12 Pit
1946 Pit: 6 G; Rec 1-20 20.0. **1947** Pit: 10 G. **Total:** 16 G; Rec 1-20 20.0.

TIM GRAY Gray, Timothy 6′1″, 200 DB
Col: Navarro Coll. TX (J.C.); Texas A&M *HS:* Kashmere [Houston, TX]
B: 11/11/1952, Houston, TX *Drafted:* 1975 Round 1 StL
1975 StL: KR 1-20 20.0. **1977** KC: **2** Fum TD. **Total:** KR 1-20 20.0; 2 Fum TD.

		Interceptions			
Year Team	**G**	**Int**	**Yds**	**TD**	**Fum**
1975 StL	14	0	0	0	0
1976 KC	12	4	19	0	0
1977 KC	10	2	16	0	0
1978 KC	14	6	118	0	0
1979 SF	16	1	20	0	1
NFL Total	66	13	173	0	1

TORRIAN GRAY Gray, Torrian Deshon 6′0″, 200 DB
Col: Virginia Tech *HS:* Kathleen [Lakeland, FL] B: 3/18/1974, Bartow, FL *Drafted:* 1997 Round 2 Min
1997 Min: 16 G. **1998** Min: 9 G; Int 1-11; 1 Sac. **Total:** 25 G; Int 1-11; 1 Sac.

BILL GRAY Gray, William Robertson Jr. 5′11″, 210 G-C-BB
Col: USC; Oregon State *HS:* Benson Polytechnic [Portland, OR]
B: 12/27/1922, Portland, OR D: 7/1978, Manassas, VA *Drafted:* 1947 Round 5 Was
1947 Was: 12 G. **1948** Was: 12 G. **Total:** 24 G.

MIKE GRAYBILL Graybill, Michael Alton 6′7″, 275 OT
Col: Boston U. *HS:* DeMatha [Hyattsville, MD] B: 10/14/1966, Washington, DC *Drafted:* 1989 Round 7 Cle
1989 Cle: 6 G.

GRAY HORSE Gray Horse 5′8″, 190 HB
Col: No College Deceased
1923 Oor: 2 G.

DAVID GRAYSON Grayson, David Lee Jr. 6′2″, 230 LB
Col: Cal Poly-Pomona; Fresno State *HS:* Abraham Lincoln [San Diego, CA] B: 2/27/1964, San Diego, CA *Drafted:* 1987 Round 8 SF
1987 Cle: 11 G; KR 1-6 6.0; **1** Fum TD; 6 Pt; 1 Sac. **1988** Cle: 16 G; 5 Sac.
1989 Cle: 10 G; Int 2-25 1 TD; 1 Fum TD; Tot TD 2; 12 Pt; 1 Sac.
1990 Cle: 16 G; Int 1-3; 1 Sac. **1991** SD: 1 G. **Total:** 54 G; KR 1-6 6.0; Int 3-28 1 TD; 2 Fum TD; Tot TD 3; 18 Pt; 8 Sac.

DAVE GRAYSON Grayson, David Lee Sr. 5′10″, 187 DB
Col: San Diego City Coll. CA (J.C.); Oregon *HS:* Abraham Lincoln [San Diego, CA] B: 6/6/1939, San Diego, CA
1962 DalT: PR 1-0. **1963** KC: PR 1-2 2.0. **1967** Oak: PR 3-11 3.7.
1969 Oak: PR 4-28 7.0. **Total:** PR 9-41 4.6.

		Kickoff Returns				Interceptions				Tot
Year Team	**G**	**Ret**	**Yds**	**Avg**	**TD**	**Int**	**Yds**	**TD**	**Fum**	**TD**
1961 DalT	13	16	453	**28.3**	0	3	99	1	0	1
1962 DalT	14	18	535	29.7	0	4	6	0	1	0
1963 KC	14	20	564	28.2	**1**	5	17	0	2	1
1964 KC	14	30	679	22.6	0	7	**187**	0	2	0
1965 Oak	14	1	34	34.0	0	3	145	**2**	0	2
1966 Oak	14	6	128	21.3	0	3	64	0	0	0
1967 Oak	14	19	405	21.3	0	4	63	0	2	0
1968 Oak	14	0	0	—	0	**10**	195	1	0	1
1969 Oak	14	0	0	—	0	8	132	1	0	1
1970 Oak	14	0	0	—	0	1	25	0	0	0
NFL Total	139	110	2798	25.4	1	48	933	5	7	6

TONY GRAZIANI Graziani, Anthony Robert 6′2″, 210 QB
Col: Oregon *HS:* Thomas Downey [Modesto, CA] B: 12/23/1973, Las Vegas, NV *Drafted:* 1997 Round 7 Atl
1997 Atl: Rush 3-19 6.3. **1998** Atl: Rush 4-21 5.3. **Total:** Rush 7-40 5.7.

		Passing							
Year Team	**G**	**Att**	**Comp**	**Comp%**	**Yds**	**YPA**	**TD**	**Int**	**Rating**
1997 Atl	3	23	7	30.4	41	1.78	0	2	3.7
1998 Atl	3	33	16	48.5	199	6.03	0	2	42.4
NFL Total	6	56	23	41.1	240	4.29	0	4	24.4

ELVIS GRBAC Grbac, Elvis 6′5″, 232 QB
Col: Michigan *HS:* St. Joseph [Cleveland, OH] B: 8/13/1970, Cleveland, OH *Drafted:* 1993 Round 8 SF

		Passing							
Year Team	**G**	**Att**	**Comp**	**Comp%**	**Yds**	**YPA**	**TD**	**Int**	**Rating**
1994 SF	11	50	35	70.0	393	7.86	2	1	98.2
1995 SF	16	183	127	69.4	1469	8.03	8	5	96.6
1996 SF	15	197	122	61.9	1236	6.27	8	10	72.2
1997 KC	10	314	179	57.0	1943	6.19	11	6	79.1
1998 KC	8	188	98	52.1	1142	6.07	5	12	53.1
NFL Total	60	932	561	60.2	6183	6.63	34	34	76.8

	Rushing				
Year Team	**Att**	**Yds**	**Avg**	**TD**	**Fum**
1994 SF	13	1	0.1	0	5
1995 SF	20	33	1.7	2	2
1996 SF	23	21	0.9	2	0
1997 KC	30	168	5.6	1	1
1998 KC	7	27	3.9	0	1
NFL Total	93	250	2.7	5	9

GARY GREAVES Greaves, Gary 6′3″, 235 OT
Col: Miami (Fla.) *HS:* Baldwin [Pittsburgh, PA] B: 10/28/1935
1960 Hou: 7 G.

DICK GRECNI Grecni, Richard 6′1″, 230 LB
Col: Ohio U. *HS:* Garfield [Akron, OH] B: 3/27/1938, Akron, OH
Drafted: 1960 Round 13 Cle
1961 Min: 12 G; Int 1-16.

DON GRECO Greco, Donald 6′3″, 260 OG
Col: Western Illinois *HS:* Riverview Gardens [St. Louis, MO]
B: 4/1/1959, St. Louis, MO *Drafted:* 1981 Round 3 Det
1982 Det: 9 G. **1983** Det: 12 G. **1984** Det: 16 G. **1985** Det: 8 G.
Total: 45 G.

BUCKY GREELEY Greeley, Paul Domero 6′2″, 285 C
Col: Penn State *HS:* James M. Coughlin [Wilkes-Barre, PA]
B: 7/30/1972, Wilkes-Barre, PA
1997 Car: 6 G.

AHMAN GREEN Green, Ahman 6′0″, 213 RB
Col: Nebraska *HS:* Central [Omaha, NE] B: 2/16/1977, Omaha, NE
Drafted: 1998 Round 3 Sea
1998 Sea: Rec 3-2 0.7.

		Rushing				Kickoff Returns				
Year Team	**G**	**Att**	**Yds**	**Avg**	**TD**	**Ret**	**Yds**	**Avg**	**TD**	**Fum**
1998 Sea	16	35	209	6.0	1	27	620	23.0	0	1

ALLEN GREEN Green, Allen Leldon 6′2″, 216 K
Col: Mississippi *HS:* Hanceville [AL] B: 2/15/1938, Hanceville, AL
Drafted: 1961 Round 8 NYG
1961 Dal: Scor 34, 5-15 33.3% FG, 19-19 100.0% XK.

		Punting		
Year Team	**G**	**Punts**	**Yds**	**Avg**
1961 Dal	14	61	2236	36.7

TONY GREEN Green, Anthony Edward 5′9″, 185 RB
Col: Florida *HS:* Riverview [Sarasota, FL] B: 9/26/1956, Rochester, NY
Drafted: 1978 Round 6 Was
1978 Was: Rush 22-82 3.7 1 TD; Rec 4-89 22.3. **Total:** Rush 22-82 3.7 1 TD; Rec 4-89 22.3.

		Punt Returns				Kickoff Returns					Tot
Year Team	**G**	**Ret**	**Yds**	**Avg**	**TD**	**Ret**	**Yds**	**Avg**	**TD**	**Fum**	**TD**
1978 Was	16	42	443	10.5	**1**	34	870	25.6	**1**	7	3
1979 NYG-Sea	15	19	138	7.3	0	32	651	20.3	0	5	0
1979 NYG	4	3	17	5.7	0	12	214	17.8	0	0	0
1979 Sea	11	16	121	7.6	0	20	437	21.9	0	5	0
NFL Total	31	61	581	9.5	1	66	1521	23.0	1	12	3

BUBBA GREEN Green, Anthony Wayne 6′4″, 278 DT
Col: North Carolina State *HS:* Millville [NJ] B: 9/30/1957, Cape May, NJ *Drafted:* 1981 Round 6 Bal
1981 Bal: 15 G; Int 1-3.

ARTHUR GREEN Green, Arthur 5′11″, 198 RB
(Artie) *Col:* Albany State (Ga.) *HS:* Howard [Atlanta, GA]
B: 9/18/1947, Atlanta, GA
1972 NO: 7 G; Rush 14-51 3.6; Rec 7-49 7.0; KR 8-187 23.4.

ERIC GREEN Green, Bernard Eric 6′5″, 280 TE
Col: Liberty *HS:* Alfred E. Beach [Savannah, GA] B: 6/22/1967, Savannah, GA *Drafted:* 1990 Round 1 Pit
1990 Pit: KR 1-16 16.0. **1995** Mia: Scor 1 2XP. **Total:** KR 1-16 16.0; Scor 1 2XP.

		Receiving				
Year Team	**G**	**Rec**	**Yds**	**Avg**	**TD**	**Fum**
1990 Pit	13	34	387	11.4	7	1
1991 Pit	11	41	582	14.2	6	2
1992 Pit	7	14	152	10.9	2	0
1993 Pit	16	63	942	15.0	5	3
1994 Pit	15	46	618	13.4	4	2
1995 Mia	14	43	499	11.6	3	0
1996 Bal	6	15	150	10.0	1	0
1997 Bal	16	65	601	9.2	5	1

1998 Bal	12	34	422	12.4	1	4
NFL Total	110	355	4353	12.3	34	13

BOBBY JOE GREEN Green, Bobby Joe 5′11″, 175 **P**
Col: Florida *HS:* College [Bartlesville, OK] B: 5/7/1936, Vernon, TX D: 5/28/1993, Gainesville, FL *Drafted:* 1960 Round 2 Den
1961 Pit: Pass 1-0; Rush 2-37 18.5; Scor 0-1 FG. **1963** ChiB: Pass 1-0; Rush 2-(-10) -5.0. **1964** ChiB: Rush 2-(-2) -1.0. **1968** ChiB: Rush 1-4 4.0. **1969** ChiB: Pass 2-2 100.0%, 30 15.00; Rush 1-17 17.0. **1970** ChiB: Pass 2-2 100.0%, 37 18.50; Rush 1-7 7.0. **1971** ChiB: Pass 2-1 50.0%, 13 6.50. **1972** ChiB: Pass 2-1 50.0%, 23 11.50 1 Int. **Total:** Pass 10-6 60.0%, 103 10.30 1 Int; Rush 9-53 5.9; Scor 0-1 FG.

		Punting			
Year Team	**G**	**Punts**	**Yds**	**Avg**	**Fum**
1960 Pit	12	**64**	**2829**	44.2	0
1961 Pit	14	73	3431	47.0	0
1962 ChiB	14	69	3018	43.7	1
1963 ChiB	14	64	2974	46.5	0
1964 ChiB	14	71	3161	44.5	0
1965 ChiB	14	58	2479	42.7	0
1966 ChiB	14	**80**	**3358**	42.0	0
1967 ChiB	14	79	3392	42.9	0
1968 ChiB	7	27	1142	42.3	0
1969 ChiB	14	76	2964	39.0	0
1970 ChiB	14	83	3395	40.9	0
1971 ChiB	14	77	3095	40.2	0
1972 ChiB	14	67	2758	41.2	1
1973 ChiB	14	**82**	3321	40.5	0
NFL Total	187	970	41317	42.6	2

BOYCE GREEN Green, Boyce Keith 5′11″, 215 **RB**
Col: Carson-Newman *HS:* Beaufort [SC] B: 6/24/1960, Beaufort, SC *Drafted:* 1983 Round 11 Cle
1986 KC: Pass 1-0, 1 Int. **Total:** Pass 1-0, 1 Int.

		Rushing				Receiving			
Year Team	**G**	**Att**	**Yds**	**Avg**	**TD**	**Rec**	**Yds**	**Avg**	**TD**
1983 Cle	13	104	497	4.8	3	25	167	6.7	1
1984 Cle	16	202	673	3.3	0	12	124	10.3	1
1985 Cle	13	0	0	—	0	0	0	—	0
1986 KC	16	90	314	3.5	3	19	137	7.2	0
1987 Sea	2	21	77	3.7	0	0	0	—	0
NFL Total	60	417	1561	3.7	6	56	428	7.6	2

	Kickoff Returns					Tot
Year Team	**Ret**	**Yds**	**Avg**	**TD**	**Fum**	**TD**
1983 Cle	17	350	20.6	0	4	4
1984 Cle	0	0	—	0	3	1
1985 Cle	2	20	10.0	0	0	0
1986 KC	10	254	25.4	**1**	3	4
1987 Sea	1	20	20.0	0	0	0
NFL Total	30	644	21.5	1	10	9

CHARLIE GREEN Green, Charles Harold 6′0″, 190 **QB**
Col: Wittenberg *HS:* Milton Union [West Milton, OH] B: 3/14/1943, Dayton, OH *Drafted:* 1965 Round 13 Bos
1966 Oak: 14 G; Pass 2-2 100.0%, 17 8.50.

CHRIS GREEN Green, Christopher Allen 5′11″, 192 **DB**
Col: Illinois *HS:* Lawrenceburg [IN] B: 2/26/1968, Lawrenceburg, IN *Drafted:* 1991 Round 7 Mia
1991 Mia: 16 G. **1992** Mia: 4 G. **1993** Mia: 14 G; Int 2-0. **1994** Mia: 16 G. **1995** Buf: 16 G; KR 2-37 18.5. **Total:** 66 G; KR 2-37 18.5; Int 2-0.

CLEVELAND GREEN Green, Cleveland Carl 6′3″, 265 **OT**
Col: Southern University *HS:* Hinds Co. [Utica, MS] B: 9/11/1957, Bolton, MS
1979 Mia: 16 G. **1980** Mia: 12 G. **1981** Mia: 6 G. **1982** Mia: 3 G. **1983** Mia: 16 G. **1984** Mia: 16 G. **1985** Mia: 12 G. **1986** Mia: 11 G. **Total:** 92 G.

CORNELL GREEN Green, Cornell 6′3″, 208 **DB**
Col: Utah State *HS:* Richmond [CA] B: 2/10/1940, Oklahoma City, OK
1963 Dal: **1** Fum TD. **1965** Dal: **1** Fum TD. **1969** Dal: KR 2-0. **1971** Dal: KR 1-0. **Total:** KR 3-0; 2 Fum TD.

		Interceptions				Tot
Year Team	**G**	**Int**	**Yds**	**TD**	**Fum**	**TD**
1962 Dal	14	0	0	0	0	0
1963 Dal	14	7	211	0	0	1
1964 Dal	14	0	0	0	0	0
1965 Dal	14	3	49	0	0	1
1966 Dal	14	4	88	1	0	1
1967 Dal	14	7	52	0	1	0
1968 Dal	14	4	74	1	0	1
1969 Dal	14	2	0	0	0	0
1970 Dal	14	1	59	0	0	0
1971 Dal	14	2	16	0	1	0
1972 Dal	14	2	1	0	0	0
1973 Dal	14	0	0	0	0	0
1974 Dal	14	2	2	0	0	0
NFL Total	182	34	552	2	2	4

CURTIS GREEN Green, Curtis 6′3″, 256 **DE-NT-DT**
Col: Alabama State *HS:* James A. Shanks [Quincy, FL] B: 6/3/1957, Quincy, FL *Drafted:* 1981 Round 2 Det
1981 Det: 14 G. **1982** Det: 7 G; 1 Sac. **1983** Det: 16 G; 4.5 Sac. **1984** Det: 16 G; 8.5 Sac. **1985** Det: 15 G; 7 Sac. **1986** Det: 16 G; 3.5 Sac. **1987** Det: 12 G; KR 1-0; 1 Fum; 2.5 Sac. **1988** Det: 11 G; 2 Sac. **1989** Det: 16 G. **Total:** 123 G; KR 1-0; 1 Fum; 29.0 Sac.

DARRELL GREEN Green, Darrell Ray 5′8″, 176 **DB**
Col: Texas A&M–Kingsville *HS:* Jesse H. Jones [Houston, TX] B: 2/15/1960, Houston, TX *Drafted:* 1983 Round 1 Was
1985 Was: Rush 1-6 6.0. **1987** Was: **1** Fum TD. **1988** Was: 1 Sac. **1993** Was: 1 Fum TD. **1997** Was: KR 1-9 9.0. **Total:** Rush 1-6 6.0; KR 1-9 9.0; 2 Fum TD; 1 Sac.

		Punt Returns				Interceptions				Tot
Year Team	**G**	**Ret**	**Yds**	**Avg**	**TD**	**Int**	**Yds**	**TD**	**Fum**	**TD**
1983 Was	16	4	29	7.3	0	2	7	0	1	0
1984 Was	16	2	13	6.5	0	5	91	1	0	1
1985 Was	16	16	214	13.4	0	2	0	0	2	0
1986 Was	16	12	120	10.0	0	5	9	0	1	0
1987 Was	12	5	53	10.6	0	3	65	0	0	1
1988 Was	15	9	103	11.4	0	1	12	0	1	0
1989 Was	7	1	11	11.0	0	2	0	0	1	0
1990 Was	16	1	6	6.0	0	4	20	1	0	1
1991 Was	16	0	0	—	0	5	47	0	0	0
1992 Was	8	0	0	—	0	1	15	0	0	0
1993 Was	16	1	27	27.0	0	4	10	0	0	1
1994 Was	16	0	0	—	0	3	32	1	0	1
1995 Was	16	0	0	—	0	3	42	1	0	1
1996 Was	16	0	0	—	0	3	84	1	0	1
1997 Was	16	0	0	—	0	1	83	1	0	1
1998 Was	16	0	0	—	0	3	36	0	0	0
NFL Total	234	51	576	11.3	0	47	553	6	6	8

DAVE GREEN Green, David Elliott 5′11″, 206 **P**
Col: Ohio U. *HS:* Athens [OH] B: 9/21/1949, Mason City, IA *Drafted:* 1972 Round 17 Cin
1974 Cin: Pass 2-1 50.0%, 22 11.00. **1975** Cin: Pass 1-0; Scor 70, 10-21 47.6% FG, 40-45 88.9% XK. **1976** TB: Rush 1-0; Rec 1-9 9.0; Scor 35, 8-14 57.1% FG, 11-14 78.6% XK. **1977** TB: Pass 2-2 100.0%, 59 29.50; Rush 1-0; Scor 17, 4-7 57.1% FG, 5-6 83.3% XK. **1978** TB: Pass 3-2 66.7%, 25 8.33; Rush 1-0; Scor 3, 1-1 100.0% FG. **Total:** Pass 8-5 62.5%, 106 13.25; Rush 3-0; Rec 1-9 9.0; Scor 125, 23-43 53.5% FG, 56-65 86.2% XK.

		Punting			
Year Team	**G**	**Punts**	**Yds**	**Avg**	**Fum**
1973 Hou	4	22	868	39.5	0
1974 Cin	14	66	2701	40.9	0
1975 Cin	14	68	2655	39.0	0
1976 TB	14	92	3619	39.3	1
1977 TB	14	98	3948	40.3	0
1978 TB	16	100	4092	40.9	0
NFL Total	76	446	17883	40.1	1

DAVID GREEN Green, David Fendell 5′10″, 200 **RB**
Col: Chowan Coll. NC; Edinboro *HS:* Richlands [NC] B: 9/7/1953, Jacksonville, NC
1982 Cle: 9 G; KR 1-13 13.0.

DAVID GREEN Green, David G 5′11″, 193 **RB**
Col: Boston College *HS:* Fox Lane [Mount Kisco, NY] B: 4/18/1972, Mount Kisco, NY
1995 NE: 2 G.

DONNIE GREEN Green, Donald Gerald 6′7″, 272 **OT**
(Clyde) *Col:* Purdue *HS:* Crestwood [Chesapeake, VA] B: 7/12/1948, Washington, DC *Drafted:* 1971 Round 5 Buf
1971 Buf: 10 G. **1972** Buf: 14 G. **1973** Buf: 14 G. **1974** Buf: 10 G; Rec 1-0. **1975** Buf: 14 G. **1976** Buf: 13 G. **1977** Phi: 10 G. **1978** Det: 7 G. **Total:** 92 G; Rec 1-0.

JACQUEZ GREEN Green, D'Tanyian Jacquez 5′9″, 172 **WR**
Col: Florida *HS:* Peach Co. [Fort Valley, GA] B: 1/15/1976, Fort Valley, GA *Drafted:* 1998 Round 2 TB
1998 TB: Rush 3-12 4.0; Rec 14-251 17.9 2 TD; KR 10-229 22.9.

		Punt Returns					Tot
Year Team	**G**	**Ret**	**Yds**	**Avg**	**TD**	**Fum**	**TD**
1998 TB	12	30	453	15.1	1	5	3

ERNIE GREEN Green, Ernest E 6′2″, 205 **HB-FB**
Col: Louisville *HS:* William H. Spencer [Columbus, GA] B: 10/15/1938, Columbus, GA *Drafted:* 1962 Round 14 GB
1962 Cle: PR 5-31 6.2. **1963** Cle: PR 6-79 13.2. **Total:** PR 11-110 10.0.

Year Team	G	Rushing Att	Yds	Avg	TD	Receiving Rec	Yds	Avg	TD
1962 Cle	13	31	139	4.5	0	17	194	11.4	1
1963 Cle	14	87	526	6.0	0	28	305	10.9	3
1964 Cle	14	109	491	4.5	6	25	283	11.3	4
1965 Cle	13	111	436	3.9	2	25	298	11.9	2
1966 Cle	14	144	750	5.2	3	45	445	9.9	6
1967 Cle	13	145	710	4.9	4	39	369	9.5	2
1968 Cle	8	41	152	3.7	0	16	142	8.9	2
NFL Total	89	668	3204	4.8	15	195	2036	10.4	20

Year Team	Kickoff Returns Ret	Yds	Avg	TD	Fum	Tot TD
1962 Cle	13	250	19.2	0	2	1
1963 Cle	18	394	21.9	0	2	3
1964 Cle	0	0	—	0	1	10
1965 Cle	1	4	4.0	0	3	4
1966 Cle	0	0	—	0	2	9
1967 Cle	0	0	—	0	1	6
1968 Cle	0	0	—	0	0	2
NFL Total	32	648	20.3	0	11	35

E.G. GREEN Green, Ernest III 5′11″, 188 **WR**
Col: Florida State *HS:* Fort Walton Beach [FL] B: 6/28/1975, Fort Walton Beach, FL *Drafted:* 1998 Round 3 Ind
1998 Ind: 11 G; Rec 15-177 11.8 1 TD; 6 Pt.

GARY GREEN Green, Gary Francis 5′11″, 187 **DB**
Col: Baylor *HS:* Sam Houston [San Antonio, TX] B: 10/22/1955, San Antonio, TX *Drafted:* 1977 Round 1 KC
1977 KC: PR 14-115 8.2. **1978** KC: PR 1-6 6.0; KR 1-27 27.0. **1984** LARm: 2 Sac. **1985** LARm: 1 Sac. **Total:** PR 15-121 8.1; KR 1-27 27.0; 3 Sac.

Year Team	G	Interceptions Int	Yds	TD	Fum
1977 KC	11	3	19	0	3
1978 KC	16	1	0	0	0
1979 KC	16	5	148	0	0
1980 KC	16	2	25	0	1
1981 KC	16	5	37	0	0
1982 KC	9	2	42	**1**	0
1983 KC	16	6	59	0	0
1984 LARm	16	3	88	0	0
1985 LARm	16	6	84	**1**	0
NFL Total	132	33	502	2	4

GASTON GREEN Green, Gaston Alfred III 5′10″, 189 **RB**
Col: UCLA *HS:* Gardena [CA] B: 8/1/1966, Los Angeles, CA
Drafted: 1988 Round 1 LARm

Year Team	G	Rushing Att	Yds	Avg	TD	Receiving Rec	Yds	Avg	TD
1988 LARm	10	35	117	3.3	0	6	57	9.5	0
1989 LARm	6	26	73	2.8	0	1	-5	-5.0	0
1990 LARm	15	68	261	3.8	0	2	23	11.5	1
1991 Den	13	261	1037	4.0	4	13	78	6.0	0
1992 Den	14	161	648	4.0	2	10	79	7.9	0
NFL Total	58	551	2136	3.9	6	32	232	7.3	1

Year Team	Kickoff Returns Ret	Yds	Avg	TD	Fum	Tot TD
1988 LARm	17	345	20.3	0	1	0
1989 LARm	0	0	—	0	1	0
1990 LARm	25	560	22.4	1	1	2
1991 Den	0	0	—	0	4	4
1992 Den	5	76	15.2	0	0	2
NFL Total	47	981	20.9	1	7	8

HAROLD GREEN Green, Harold Jr. 6′2″, 222 **RB**
Col: South Carolina *HS:* Stratford [Goose Creek, SC] B: 1/29/1968, Ladson, SC *Drafted:* 1990 Round 2 Cin
1991 Cin: KR 4-66 16.5. **1994** Cin: KR 5-113 22.6. **1996** StL: Scor 1 2XP. **1997** Atl: KR 1-23 23.0. **1998** Atl: KR 1-24 24.0. **Total:** KR 11-226 20.5; Scor 1 2XP.

Year Team	G	Rushing Att	Yds	Avg	TD	Receiving Rec	Yds	Avg	TD	Fum	Tot TD
1990 Cin	12	83	353	4.3	1	12	90	7.5	1	2	2
1991 Cin	14	158	731	4.6	2	16	136	8.5	0	2	2
1992 Cin	16	265	1170	4.4	2	41	214	5.2	0	1	2
1993 Cin	15	215	589	2.7	0	22	115	5.2	0	3	0
1994 Cin	14	76	223	2.9	1	27	267	9.9	1	1	2
1995 Cin	15	171	661	3.9	2	27	182	6.7	1	2	3
1996 StL	16	127	523	4.1	4	37	246	6.6	1	2	5
1997 Atl	16	36	78	2.2	1	29	360	12.4	0	0	1
1998 Atl	6	20	37	1.9	0	2	34	17.0	0	1	0
NFL Total	124	1151	4365	3.8	13	213	1644	7.7	4	14	17

HUGH GREEN Green, Hugh Donell 6′2″, 225 **LB**
Col: Pittsburgh *HS:* North [Natchez, MS] B: 7/27/1959, Natchez, MS
Drafted: 1981 Round 1 TB
1981 TB: 16 G; Int 2-56. **1982** TB: 9 G; Int 1-31; 2.3 Sac. **1983** TB: 16 G; Int 2-54 **2** TD; 12 Pt; 1 Fum; 3.5 Sac. **1984** TB: 8 G; 4 Sac. **1985** TB-Mia: 16 G; Int 1-28; 7.5 Sac. TB: 5 G; 2.5 Sac. Mia: 11 G; Int 1-28; 5 Sac. **1986** Mia: 3 G; 4 Sac. **1987** Mia: 9 G. **1988** Mia: 16 G; 2.5 Sac. **1989** Mia: 16 G; 7.5 Sac. **1990** Mia: 16 G; 2 Sac. **1991** Mia: 11 G; 1 Sac. **Total:** 136 G; Int 6-169 2 TD; 12 Pt; 1 Fum; 34.3 Sac.

JACOB GREEN Green, Jacob Carl 6′3″, 255 **DE**
Col: Texas A&M *HS:* Kashmere [Houston, TX] B: 1/21/1957, Pasadena, TX *Drafted:* 1980 Round 1 Sea
1980 Sea: 14 G. **1981** Sea: 16 G. **1982** Sea: 9 G; 3 Sac. **1983** Sea: 16 G; Int 1-73 1 TD; 6 Pt; 16 Sac. **1984** Sea: 16 G; 13 Sac. **1985** Sea: 16 G; Int 1-19 **1** TD; **1** Fum TD; Tot TD 2; 12 Pt; 13.5 Sac. **1986** Sea: 16 G; 12 Sac. **1987** Sea: 12 G; 9.5 Sac. **1988** Sea: 16 G; **1** Fum TD; 6 Pt; 9 Sac. **1989** Sea: 15 G; 3 Sac. **1990** Sea: 16 G; 12.5 Sac. **1991** Sea: 16 G; Int 1-(-2); 6 Sac. **1992** SF: 2 G. **Total:** 180 G; Int 3-90 2 TD; 2 Fum TD; Tot TD 4; 24 Pt; 97.5 Sac.

JERRY GREEN Green, Jerome Albert 6′0″, 190 **OE**
Col: Georgia Tech *HS:* Henry Grady [Atlanta, GA] B: 4/16/1936, Atlanta, GA D: 12/12/1994
1960 Bos: 2 G; Rec 3-52 17.3.

JESSIE GREEN Green, Jessie Ray 6′3″, 191 **WR**
Col: Trinity Valley CC TX; Tulsa *HS:* Malakoff [TX] B: 2/21/1954, Malakoff, TX *Drafted:* 1976 Round 10 GB
1976 GB: 1 G. **1979** Sea: 12 G; Rec 1-9 9.0. **1980** Sea: 11 G; Rec 4-47 11.8; KR 15-274 18.3; 6 Pt; 1 Fum. **Total:** 24 G; Rec 5-56 11.2; KR 15-274 18.3; 6 Pt; 1 Fum.

JOHNNY GREEN Green, John Edward 6′3″, 198 **QB**
Col: Tennessee-Chattanooga B: 10/12/1937, West Point, MS
Drafted: 1959 Round 21 Pit
1960 Buf: Rec 1-0. **1962** NYT: Punt 3-121 40.3. **Total:** Rec 1-0; Punt 3-121 40.3.

Year Team	G	Passing Att	Comp	Comp%	Yds	YPA	TD	Int	Rating
1960 Buf	10	228	89	39.0	1267	5.56	10	**10**	54.1
1961 Buf	8	126	56	44.4	903	7.17	6	5	68.3
1962 NYT	11	258	128	49.6	1741	6.75	10	18	55.4
1963 NYJ	1	6	2	33.3	10	1.67	0	1	2.8
NFL Total	30	618	275	44.5	3921	6.34	26	34	56.7

Year Team	Rushing Att	Yds	Avg	TD	Fum
1960 Buf	21	29	1.4	2	9
1961 Buf	14	15	1.1	1	4
1962 NYT	17	35	2.1	3	6
NFL Total	52	79	1.5	6	19

JOHN GREEN Green, John Lincoln 6′1″, 192 **DE-OE**
Col: Tulsa *HS:* Arp [TX] B: 10/14/1921, Hastings, OK D: 3/6/1989, Bergland, MI *Drafted:* 1944 Round 14 Phi
1947 Phi: 12 G. **1948** Phi: 12 G; KR 2-24 12.0; 1 Fum. **1949** Phi: 7 G; KR 2-33 16.5. **1950** Phi: 12 G; KR 1-14 14.0; **1** Fum TD; 6 Pt. **1951** Phi: 1 G. **Total:** 44 G; KR 5-71 14.2; 1 Fum TD; 6 Pt; 1 Fum.

JOE GREEN Green, Joseph David 5′11″, 195 **DB**
(Little Joe) *Col:* Bowling Green State *HS:* V. W. Scott [Toledo, OH] B: 3/6/1947, Aberdeen, MS
1970 NYG: 14 G; KR 2-26 13.0. **1971** NYG: 14 G; KR 5-106 21.2; **1** Fum TD; 6 Pt; 1 Fum. **Total:** 28 G; KR 7-132 18.9; 1 Fum TD; 6 Pt; 1 Fum.

LARRY GREEN Green, Lawrence Edward 6′0″, 180 **OE**
Col: Georgetown *HS:* Haverhill [MA] B: 6/3/1894, Yorkshire, England D: 11/29/1976, St. Petersburg, FL
1920 Can: 4 G.

MARK GREEN Green, Mark Anthony 5′11″, 184 **RB**
Col: Notre Dame *HS:* Riverside Polytechnic [CA] B: 3/22/1967, Riverside, CA *Drafted:* 1989 Round 5 ChiB
1989 ChiB: Rec 5-48 9.6; PR 16-141 8.8. **1990** ChiB: Rec 4-26 6.5 1 TD. **1991** ChiB: Rec 6-54 9.0; PR 3-9 3.0. **1992** ChiB: Rec 7-85 12.1. **Total:** Rec 22-213 9.7 1 TD; PR 19-150 7.9.

Year Team	G	Rushing Ret	Yds	Avg	TD	Kickoff Returns Ret	Yds	Avg	TD	Fum	Tot TD
1989 ChiB	10	5	46	9.2	1	11	239	21.7	0	0	1
1990 ChiB	12	27	126	4.7	0	7	112	16.0	0	0	1
1991 ChiB	16	61	217	3.6	3	4	69	17.3	0	4	3
1992 ChiB	15	23	107	4.7	2	11	224	20.4	0	0	2
NFL Total	53	116	496	4.3	6	33	644	19.5	0	4	7

MIKE GREEN Green, Michael James 6′0″, 235 **LB**
Col: Oklahoma State *HS:* Lincoln [Port Arthur, TX] B: 6/29/1961, Port Arthur, TX *Drafted:* 1983 Round 9 SD
1983 SD: 16 G; Int 1-3; 1 Sac. **1984** SD: 16 G; 1 Sac. **1985** SD: 15 G; Int 2-17; 1 Sac. **Total:** 47 G; Int 3-20; 3 Sac.

PAUL GREEN Green, Paul Earl 6′3″, 236 **TE**
Col: USC *HS:* West [Clovis, CA] B: 10/8/1966, Coalinga, CA
Drafted: 1989 Round 8 Den
1989 Den: Postseason only.

		Receiving				
Year Team	**G**	**Rec**	**Yds**	**Avg**	**TD**	**Fum**
1992 Sea	4	9	67	7.4	1	0
1993 Sea	15	23	178	7.7	1	0
1994 Sea	16	30	208	6.9	1	1
1996 NO	14	7	91	13.0	0	0
NFL Total	49	69	544	7.9	3	1

ROBERT GREEN Green, Robert David 5′8″, 212 **RB**
Col: William & Mary *HS:* Friendly [Fort Washington, MD] B: 9/10/1970, Washington, DC
1992 Was: KR 1-9 9.0. **1993** ChiB: KR 9-141 15.7. **1994** ChiB: KR 6-77 12.8. **1995** ChiB: KR 3-29 9.7. **Total:** KR 19-256 13.5.

		Rushing				Receiving					Tot
Year Team	**G**	**Att**	**Yds**	**Avg**	**TD**	**Rec**	**Yds**	**Avg**	**TD**	**Fum**	**TD**
1992 Was	15	8	46	5.8	0	1	5	5.0	0	0	0
1993 ChiB	16	15	29	1.9	0	13	63	4.8	0	0	0
1994 ChiB	15	25	122	4.9	0	24	199	8.3	2	1	2
1995 ChiB	12	107	570	5.3	3	28	246	8.8	0	2	3
1996 ChiB	10	60	249	4.2	0	13	78	6.0	0	3	0
1997 Min	3	6	22	3.7	0	1	5	5.0	0	0	0
NFL Total	71	221	1038	4.7	3	80	596	7.5	2	6	5

ROGERICK GREEN Green, Rogerick 6′0″, 182 **DB**
Col: Kansas State *HS:* West Campus [San Antonio, TX] B: 12/15/1969, San Antonio, TX *Drafted:* 1992 Round 5 TB
1992 TB: 1 G. **1994** TB: 11 G; KR 2-33 16.5. **1995** Jac: 14 G. **Total:** 26 G; KR 2-33 16.5.

RON GREEN Green, Ronald Morris 6′1″, 200 **WR**
Col: North Dakota *HS:* Central [ND] B: 11/27/1943, Fargo, ND
Drafted: 1966 Round 9 Min
1967 Cle: 4 G. **1968** Cle: 1 G. **Total:** 5 G.

ROY GREEN Green, Roy Calvin 6′0″, 195 **WR-DB**
Col: Henderson State *HS:* Magnolia [AR] B: 6/30/1957, Magnolia, AR
Drafted: 1979 Round 4 StL
1980 StL: Int 1-10. **1981** StL: Rush 3-60 20.0 1 TD; Int 3-44. **1982** StL: Pass 1-0; Rush 6-8 1.3. **1983** StL: Rush 4-49 12.3. **1984** StL: Rush 1-(-10) -10.0. **1985** StL: Rush 1-2 2.0. **1986** StL: Rush 2-(-4) -2.0. **1987** StL: Rush 2-34 17.0. **1988** Pho: Rush 4-1 0.3. **1990** Pho: Pass 1-1 100.0%, 20 20.00. **Total:** Pass 2-1 50.0%, 20 10.00; Rush 23-140 6.1 1 TD; Int 4-54.

		Receiving				Punt Returns			
Year Team	**G**	**Rec**	**Yds**	**Avg**	**TD**	**Ret**	**Yds**	**Avg**	**TD**
1979 StL	16	1	15	15.0	0	8	42	5.3	0
1980 StL	15	0	0	—	0	16	168	10.5	1
1981 StL	16	33	708	21.5	4	0	0	—	0
1982 StL	9	32	453	14.2	3	3	20	6.7	0
1983 StL	16	78	1227	15.7	**14**	0	0	—	0
1984 StL	16	78	**1555**	19.9	12	0	0	—	0
1985 StL	13	50	693	13.9	5	0	0	—	0
1986 StL	11	42	517	12.3	6	0	0	—	0
1987 StL	12	43	731	17.0	4	0	0	—	0
1988 Pho	16	68	1097	16.1	7	0	0	—	0
1989 Pho	12	44	703	16.0	7	0	0	—	0
1990 Pho	16	53	797	15.0	4	0	0	—	0
1991 Phi	13	29	364	12.6	0	0	0	—	0
1992 Phi	9	8	105	13.1	0	0	0	—	0
NFL Total	190	559	8965	16.0	66	27	230	8.5	1

	Kickoff Returns					Tot
Year Team	**Ret**	**Yds**	**Avg**	**TD**	**Fum**	**TD**
1979 StL	41	1005	24.5	**1**	4	1
1980 StL	32	745	23.3	0	2	1
1981 StL	8	135	16.9	0	2	5
1982 StL	0	0	—	0	1	3
1983 StL	1	14	14.0	0	3	14
1984 StL	1	18	18.0	0	1	12
1985 StL	0	0	—	0	2	5
1986 StL	0	0	—	0	1	6
1987 StL	0	0	—	0	1	4
1988 Pho	0	0	—	0	0	7
1989 Pho	0	0	—	0	2	7
1990 Pho	1	15	15.0	0	1	4
1991 Phi	5	70	14.0	0	0	0
NFL Total	89	2002	22.5	1	20	69

SAMMY GREEN Green, Samuel Lee 6′2″, 228 **LB**
Col: Florida *HS:* Fort Meade [FL] B: 10/12/1954, Bradenton, FL
Drafted: 1976 Round 2 Sea
1976 Sea: 14 G. **1977** Sea: 14 G; Int 1-9. **1978** Sea: 16 G; Int 1-0. **1979** Sea: 16 G; Int 1-91 1 TD; 6 Pt. **1980** Hou: 2 G. **Total:** 62 G; Int 3-100 1 TD; 6 Pt.

TIM GREEN Green, Timothy John 6′2″, 249 **LB-DE**
Col: Syracuse *HS:* Liverpool [NY] B: 12/16/1963, Liverpool, NY
Drafted: 1986 Round 1 Atl
1986 Atl: 11 G. **1987** Atl: 9 G; 1 Sac. **1988** Atl: 10 G; 4 Sac. **1989** Atl: 16 G; 1 Fum; 5 Sac. **1990** Atl: 16 G; Scor **1** Saf; 2 Pt; 6 Sac. **1991** Atl: 16 G; 5 Sac. **1992** Atl: 12 G; 3 Sac. **1993** Atl: 9 G. **Total:** 99 G; Scor 1 Saf; 2 Pt; 1 Fum; 24.0 Sac.

TRENT GREEN Green, Trent Jason 6′3″, 215 **QB**
Col: Indiana *HS:* Vianny [St. Louis, MO] B: 7/9/1970, St. Louis, MO
Drafted: 1993 Round 8 SD
1998 Was: Rec 2-(-8) -4.0. **Total:** Rec 2-(-8) -4.0.

		Passing							
Year Team	**G**	**Att**	**Comp**	**Comp%**	**Yds**	**YPA**	**TD**	**Int**	**Rating**
1997 Was	1	1	0	0.0	0	0.00	0	0	39.6
1998 Was	15	509	278	54.6	3441	6.76	23	11	81.8
NFL Total	16	510	278	54.5	3441	6.75	23	11	81.7

	Rushing				
Year Team	**Att**	**Yds**	**Avg**	**TD**	**Fum**
1998 Was	42	117	2.8	2	**14**
NFL Total	42	117	2.8	2	14

VAN GREEN Green, Van Harold 6′1″, 192 **DB**
Col: Shaw *HS:* Auburndale [FL] B: 4/21/1951, Auburndale, FL
Drafted: 1973 Round 6 Cle
1973 Cle: 14 G; **1** Fum TD; 6 Pt. **1974** Cle: 14 G; Rec 1-27 27.0; Int 2-56 1 TD; 6 Pt. **1975** Cle: 14 G; Rec 1-(-1) -1.0; PR 1-0; Int 1-0; 1 Fum. **1976** Cle-Buf: 6 G. Cle: 1 G. Buf: 5 G. **Total:** 48 G; Rec 2-26 13.0; PR 1-0; Int 3-56 1 TD; 1 Fum TD; Tot TD 2; 12 Pt; 1 Fum.

VICTOR GREEN Green, Victor Bernard 5′11″, 200 **DB**
Col: Copiah-Lincoln CC MS; Akron *HS:* Americus [GA] B: 12/8/1969, Americus, GA
1994 NYJ: 1 Sac. **1995** NYJ: 2 Sac. **1996** NYJ: 2 Sac. **1997** NYJ: 1 Sac. **1998** NYJ: 1 Sac. **Total:** 7 Sac.

		Interceptions		
Year Team	**G**	**Int**	**Yds**	**TD**
1993 NYJ	11	0	0	0
1994 NYJ	16	0	0	0
1995 NYJ	16	1	2	0
1996 NYJ	16	2	27	0
1997 NYJ	16	3	89	0
1998 NYJ	16	4	99	0
NFL Total	91	10	217	0

VEE GREEN Green, Vivian Julius 6′0″, 195 **T**
Col: Illinois *HS:* Urbana [IL] B: 10/9/1900, Oakwood, IL
D: 5/13/1967, Urbana, IL
1926 Lou: 2 G.

ALEX GREEN Green, William Alexander 6′1″, 194 **DB**
Col: Indiana *HS:* Glenbard West [Glen Ellyn, IL] B: 11/3/1965
1987 Dal: 3 G; Int 1-0.

WILLIE GREEN Green, Willie Aaron 6′4″, 185 **WR**
Col: Tennessee Mil. Acad. (J.C.); Mississippi *HS:* Clarke Central [Athens, GA] B: 4/2/1966, Athens, GA *Drafted:* 1990 Round 8 Det
1996 Car: Rush 1-1 1.0. **Total:** Rush 1-1 1.0.

		Receiving				
Year Team	**G**	**Rec**	**Yds**	**Avg**	**TD**	**Fum**
1991 Det	16	39	592	15.2	7	0
1992 Det	15	33	586	17.8	5	1
1993 Det	16	28	462	16.5	2	0
1994 TB	5	9	150	16.7	0	0
1995 Car	16	47	882	18.8	6	1
1996 Car	15	46	614	13.3	3	0
1997 Den	16	19	240	12.6	2	0
1998 Den	15	16	194	12.1	1	0
NFL Total	114	237	3720	15.7	26	2

WOODY GREEN Green, Woodrow Jr. 6′0″, 205 **RB**
Col: Arizona State *HS:* Jefferson [Portland, OR] B: 6/20/1951, Warren, OR *Drafted:* 1974 Round 1 KC
1974 KC: PR 5-21 4.2; KR 1-16 16.0. **1975** KC: KR 16-343 21.4. **1976** KC: KR 3-82 27.3. **Total:** PR 5-21 4.2; KR 20-441 22.1.

		Rushing				Receiving					Tot
Year Team	**G**	**Att**	**Yds**	**Avg**	**TD**	**Rec**	**Yds**	**Avg**	**TD**	**Fum**	**TD**
1974 KC	10	135	509	3.8	3	26	247	9.5	1	5	4
1975 KC	12	167	611	3.7	5	23	215	9.3	1	6	6

1976 KC	6	73	322	4.4	1	9	100	11.1	0	2	1
NFL Total	28	375	1442	3.8	9	58	562	9.7	2	13	11

BEN GREENBERG Greenberg, Benjamin Norman 5'9", 170 **FB-TB**
Col: Rutgers *HS:* Leonia [NJ] B: 1907
1930 Bkn: 2 G.

AL GREENE Greene, Albert 5'8", 165 **WB**
(AKA Albert Greenstein) *Col:* No College *HS:* Haverhill [MA]
B: 3/1/1901, Russia D: 1/19/1977, North Miami, FL
1922 Mil: 2 G.

ANDREW GREENE Greene, Andrew Kirkpatrick 6'3", 304 **OG**
Col: Indiana *HS:* Pickering Sec. School [Ajax, Canada] B: 9/24/1969, Kingston, Jamaica *Drafted:* 1995 Round 2 Mia
1995 Mia: 6 G. **1998** Sea: 4 G. **Total:** 10 G.

TONY GREENE Greene, Anthony 5'10", 170 **DB**
Col: Maryland *HS:* Gaithersburg [MD] B: 8/29/1949, Clocksburg, MD
1972 Buf: PR 2-18 9.0; KR 15-378 25.2. **1973** Buf: KR 1-7 7.0. **1977** Buf: Scor 1 Saf. **Total:** PR 2-18 9.0; KR 16-385 24.1; Scor 1 Saf.

		Interceptions			
Year Team	**G**	**Int**	**Yds**	**TD**	**Fum**
1971 Buf	14	0	0	0	0
1972 Buf	14	3	45	1	2
1973 Buf	14	1	0	0	0
1974 Buf	12	9	157	0	0
1975 Buf	14	6	81	0	0
1976 Buf	14	5	135	1	0
1977 Buf	14	9	144	0	0
1978 Buf	16	3	56	0	0
1979 Buf	16	1	10	0	0
NFL Total	128	37	628	2	2

A.J. GREENE Greene, Anthony Jerome 5'8", 167 **DB**
Col: Wake Forest *HS:* East Henderson [East Flat Rock, NC]
B: 6/24/1966, Hendersonville, NC *Drafted:* 1989 Round 9 NYG
1991 NYG: 2 G.

JOE GREENE Greene, Charles Edward 6'4", 275 **DT**
(Mean Joe) *Col:* North Texas *HS:* Dunbar [Temple, TX] B: 9/24/1946, Temple, TX *Drafted:* 1969 Round 1 Pit *HOF:* 1987
1969 Pit: 14 G. **1970** Pit: 14 G. **1971** Pit: 14 G. **1972** Pit: 14 G. **1973** Pit: 14 G. **1974** Pit: 14 G; Int 1-26; 1 Fum. **1975** Pit: 10 G. **1976** Pit: 14 G. **1977** Pit: 13 G. **1978** Pit: 16 G. **1979** Pit: 15 G. **1980** Pit: 15 G. **1981** Pit: 14 G. **Total:** 181 G; Int 1-26; 1 Fum.

DOUG GREENE Greene, Douglas Parks 6'2", 205 **DB**
Col: Lakewood CC MN; Texas A&M–Kingsville *HS:* Jack Yates [Houston, TX] B: 2/10/1956, Los Angeles, CA *Drafted:* 1978 Round 3 StL
1978 StL: 15 G. **1979** Buf: 15 G; Int 1-21. **1980** Buf: 8 G. **Total:** 38 G; Int 1-21.

ED GREENE Greene, Edward 5'11", 185 **G-E**
(Babe) *Col:* Loyola (Chicago) B: 9/28/1900 D: 9/1960
1926 ChiC: 9 G.

FRANK GREENE Greene, Frank Stokes 5'11", 190 **BB-DB**
Col: Tulsa *HS:* Coronado [CA] B: 3/29/1910, San Diego, CA Deceased
1934 ChiC: Pass 41-7 17.1%, 71 1.73 **2** Int; Rec 4-32 8.0.

		Rushing			
Year Team	**G**	**Att**	**Yds**	**Avg**	**TD**
1934 ChiC	11	31	82	2.6	0

GEORGE GREENE Greene, George Everett 6'0", 194 **DB**
(Tiger) *Col:* Western Carolina *HS:* East Henderson [East Flat Rock, NC] B: 2/15/1962, Hendersonville, NC
1985 Atl: 10 G; Int 2-27. **1986** GB: 13 G; Int 2-0; 1 Sac. **1987** GB: 11 G; Int 1-11. **1988** GB: 16 G; 1 Sac. **1989** GB: 16 G; Int 1-0; 1 Fum; 2 Sac. **1990** GB: 16 G; 6 Pt. **Total:** 82 G; Int 6-38; 6 Pt; 1 Fum; 4 Sac.

JOHN GREENE Greene, John Joseph 6'0", 210 **OE-DE-DB-BB**
Col: Michigan *HS:* Westinghouse [Pittsburgh, PA]; Kiski School [Saltsburg, PA] B: 4/21/1920, Pittsburgh, PA *Drafted:* 1944 Round 5 Det
1944 Det: Int 2-22. **1945** Det: Int 3-65. **1946** Det: KR 2-29 14.5; Scor **1** Saf. **1947** Det: KR 2-19 9.5. **1948** Det: KR 1-11 11.0. **1950** Det: **1** Fum TD. **Total:** KR 5-59 11.8; Int 5-87; Scor 1 Saf; 1 Fum TD.

		Receiving					Tot
Year Team	**G**	**Rec**	**Yds**	**Avg**	**TD**	**Fum**	**TD**
1944 Det	9	0	0	—	0	0	0
1945 Det	10	26	550	21.2	5	0	5
1946 Det	11	20	289	14.5	2	0	2
1947 Det	12	38	621	16.3	5	1	5
1948 Det	12	25	595	**23.8**	5	0	5
1949 Det	12	42	542	12.9	7	1	7
1950 Det	12	22	368	16.7	2	0	3
NFL Total	78	173	2965	17.1	26	2	27

KEN GREENE Greene, Kenneth Edward 6'3", 203 **DB**
Col: Washington State *HS:* Omak [WA] B: 5/8/1956, Lewiston, ID
Drafted: 1978 Round 1 StL
1984 SD: 1 Sac. **Total:** 1 Sac.

		Interceptions		
Year Team	**G**	**Int**	**Yds**	**TD**
1978 StL	16	0	0	0
1979 StL	16	3	37	0
1980 StL	12	4	41	0
1981 StL	15	7	111	0
1982 StL	8	1	2	0
1983 SD	16	0	0	0
1984 SD	15	0	0	0
NFL Total	98	15	191	0

KEVIN GREENE Greene, Kevin Darwin 6'3", 247 **LB-DE**
Col: Auburn *HS:* South [Granite City, IL] B: 7/31/1962, New York, NY
Drafted: 1985 Round 5 LARm
1985 LARm: 15 G. **1986** LARm: 16 G; 7 Sac. **1987** LARm: 9 G; Int 1-25 1 TD; 6 Pt; 6.5 Sac. **1988** LARm: 16 G; Int 1-10; Scor 1 Saf; 2 Pt; 16.5 Sac. **1989** LARm: 16 G; 16.5 Sac. **1990** LARm: 15 G; 13 Sac. **1991** LARm: 16 G; Scor 1 Saf; 2 Pt; 3 Sac. **1992** LARm: 16 G; Scor 1 Saf; 2 Pt; 10 Sac. **1993** Pit: 16 G; 12.5 Sac. **1994** Pit: 16 G; **14** Sac. **1995** Pit: 16 G; Int 1-0; 9 Sac. **1996** Car: 16 G; **1** Fum TD; 6 Pt; **14.5** Sac. **1997** SF: 14 G; 1 Fum TD; 6 Pt; 10.5 Sac. **1998** Car: 15 G; Int 2-18; 15 Sac. **Total:** 212 G; Int 5-53 1 TD; Scor 3 Saf; 2 Fum TD; Tot TD 3; 24 Pt; 148 Sac.

MARCELLUS GREENE Greene, Marcellus Lamont 6'0", 185 **DB**
Col: Arizona *HS:* Shortridge [Indianapolis, IN] B: 12/12/1957, Indianapolis, IN *Drafted:* 1981 Round 11 LARm
1984 Min: 14 G.

NELSON GREENE Greene, Nelson 6'2", 235 **T**
Col: Tulsa *HS:* Shawnee [OK] B: 3/21/1924, Houston, TX
D: 5/3/1983, Houston, TX
AAFC **1948** NY-A: 14 G.

SCOTT GREENE Greene, Scott 5'11", **RB**
Col: Michigan State *HS:* Canandaigua Acad. [NY] B: 6/1/1972, Honeoye, NY *Drafted:* 1996 Round 6 Car
1996 Car: KR 2-10 5.0. **1997** Car: KR 3-18 6.0. **Total:** KR 5-28 5.6.

		Rushing				Receiving					Tot
Year Team	**G**	**Att**	**Yds**	**Avg**	**TD**	**Rec**	**Yds**	**Avg**	**TD**	**Fum**	**TD**
1996 Car	8	0	0	—	0	2	7	3.5	1	0	1
1997 Car	16	45	157	3.5	1	40	277	6.9	1	1	2
1998 Ind	5	0	0	—	0	1	2	2.0	0	0	0
NFL Total	29	45	157	3.5	1	43	286	6.7	2	1	3

DANNY GREENE Greene, Theodore Daniel II 5'11", 190 **WR**
Col: Washington *HS:* Compton [CA] B: 12/26/1961, Compton, CA
Drafted: 1985 Round 3 Sea
1985 Sea: 4 G; Rec 2-10 5.0 1 TD; PR 11-60 5.5; KR 5-144 28.8; 6 Pt; 1 Fum.

TED GREENE Greene, Theodore William 6'1", 230 **LB**
Col: Tampa B: 1/25/1932
1960 DalT: 14 G; Int 3-26. **1961** DalT: 14 G; Int 1-30. **1962** DalT: 4 G. **Total:** 32 G; Int 4-56.

TOM GREENE Greene, Thomas W 6'1", 190 **QB-P**
Col: Holy Cross *HS:* Loyola [Baltimore, MD] B: 1938
1960 Bos: Rush 7-44 6.3; KR 1-3 3.0. **Total:** Rush 7-44 6.3; KR 1-3 3.0.

		Passing							
Year Team	**G**	**Att**	**Comp**	**Comp%**	**Yds**	**YPA**	**TD**	**Int**	**Rating**
1960 Bos	10	63	27	42.9	251	3.98	1	6	20.1
1961 DalT	1	0	0	—	0	—	0	0	—
NFL Total	11	63	27	42.9	251	3.98	1	6	20.1

	Punting			
Year Team	**Punts**	**Yds**	**Avg**	**Fum**
1960 Bos	61	2253	36.9	2
NFL Total	61	2253	36.9	2

TRACY GREENE Greene, Tracy Lamar 6'5", 282 **TE**
Col: Grambling State *HS:* Grambling State U. Lab [LA] B: 11/5/1972, Monroe, LA *Drafted:* 1994 Round 7 KC
1994 KC: 7 G; Rec 6-69 11.5 1 TD; 6 Pt. **1995** Pit: 16 G; KR 1-7 7.0. **Total:** 23 G; Rec 6-69 11.5 1 TD; KR 1-7 7.0; 6 Pt.

NORM GREENEY Greeney, Norman Junior 5'11", 212 **G-T**
Col: Notre Dame *HS:* John Marshall [Cleveland, OH] B: 5/7/1910, Cleveland, OH D: 10/20/1985, Kelleys Island, OH
1933 GB: 7 G. **1934** Pit: 11 G. **1935** Pit: 1 G. **Total:** 19 G.

TOM GREENFIELD Greenfield, Thomas Guy 6'4", 213 **C-LB**
Col: Arizona *HS:* Peoria [AZ] B: 11/10/1917, Glendale, AZ
Drafted: 1939 Round 13 GB
1939 GB: 8 G; **1** Fum TD; 6 Pt. **1940** GB: 9 G; Int 1-5. **1941** GB: 5 G.
Total: 22 G; Int 1-5; 1 Fum TD; 6 Pt.

BOB GREENHALGH Greenhalgh, Robert Clyde 6'1", 200 **FB**
Col: Notre Dame; San Francisco *HS:* Central [Fargo, ND] B: 5/23/1924
Drafted: 1948 Round 29 NYG
1949 NYG: Rec 3-23 7.7.

		Rushing				
Year Team	**G**	**Att**	**Yds**	**Avg**	**TD**	**Fum**
1949 NYG	10	62	188	3.0	0	1

DUKE GREENICH Greenich, Harley Max 5'11", 185 **HB-DB**
Col: Mississippi *HS:* Coldwater [MI] B: 10/16/1921, Coldwater, MI
D: 3/4/1989, Huntington, NY
1944 ChiB: 1 G.

FRITZ GREENLEE Greenlee, William Frederick 6'2", 230 **LB**
Col: Northern Arizona *HS:* Franklin [Seattle, WA] B: 11/5/1943, Des Moines, IA
1969 SF: 4 G.

DONN GREENSHIELDS Greenshields, Donn 6'1", 190 **T**
Col: Penn State *HS:* Glenville [Cleveland, OH] B: 5/1/1904 Deceased
1932 Bkn: 11 G. **1933** Bkn: 2 G. **Total:** 13 G.

CARL GREENWOOD Greenwood, Carlanditt Keith 5'11", 186 **DB**
Col: UCLA *HS:* Carroll [Corpus Christi, TX] B: 3/11/1972, Fort Ord, CA
Drafted: 1995 Round 5 NYJ
1995 NYJ: 10 G. **1996** NYJ: 14 G. **Total:** 24 G.

DAVID GREENWOOD Greenwood, David Mark 6'3", 210 **DB**
Col: Wisconsin *HS:* Park Falls [WI] B: 3/25/1960, Park Falls, WI
Drafted: 1983 Round 8 NO
1985 TB: 16 G; Int 5-15; 2 Fum; 3 Sac. **1986** GB: 9 G; 3 Sac. **1988** LARd: 2 G. **Total:** 27 G; Int 5-15; 2 Fum; 6 Sac.

DON GREENWOOD Greenwood, Donald Adams 6'0", 190 **DB-HB-FB-LB**
Col: Missouri; Illinois *HS:* Southwest [Kansas City, MO] B: 2/18/1921, Detroit, MI D: 3/21/1983, Princeville, IL
AAFC **1946** CleA: Pass 1-1 100.0%, 27 27.00; Rec 4-0; KR 5-105 21.0; Int 2-56. **1947** CleA: Rec 5-49 9.8; Int 4-19. **Total:** Pass 1-1 100.0%, 27 27.00; Rec 9-49 5.4; KR 5-105 21.0; Int 6-75.

		Rushing			
Year Team	**G**	**Att**	**Yds**	**Avg**	**TD**
1946 CleA	13	77	274	3.6	6
1947 CleA	11	18	94	5.2	0
AAFC Total	24	95	368	3.9	6

NFL **1945** Cle: Rec 3-72 24.0; KR 5-106 21.2.

		Rushing				
Year Team	**G**	**Att**	**Yds**	**Avg**	**TD**	**Fum**
1945 Cle	9	101	376	3.7	4	6

GLENN GREENWOOD Greenwood, Glenn Jackson 5'10", 185 **FB**
Col: Iowa *HS:* Webster City [IA] B: 2/5/1896, IA D: 7/1/1970, Los Angeles, CA
1926 Lou: 1 G.

L.C. GREENWOOD Greenwood, L.C. Henderson 6'6", 245 **DE**
Col: Arkansas-Pine Bluff *HS:* Roger [Canton, MS] B: 9/8/1946, Canton, MS *Drafted:* 1969 Round 10 Pit
1969 Pit: 12 G. **1970** Pit: 12 G. **1971** Pit: 14 G. **1972** Pit: 13 G. **1973** Pit: 14 G. **1974** Pit: 14 G; Scor **1** Saf; 2 Pt. **1975** Pit: 14 G. **1976** Pit: 13 G. **1977** Pit: 9 G. **1978** Pit: 14 G. **1979** Pit: 12 G. **1980** Pit: 15 G. **1981** Pit: 14 G. **Total:** 170 G; Scor 1 Saf; 2 Pt.

AL GREER Greer, Albert 6'4", 190 **OE**
(Jake) *Col:* Jackson State B: 4/15/1940, Anniston, AL *Drafted:* 1963 Round 18 Det
1963 Det: 1 G.

CHARLIE GREER Greer, Charles Anthony 6'0", 205 **DB**
Col: Colorado *HS:* South Fulton [East Point, GA] B: 4/4/1946, Atlanta, GA *Drafted:* 1968 Round 13 Den
1968 Den: KR 2-41 20.5. **Total:** KR 2-41 20.5.

		Punt Returns				Interceptions			
Year Team	**G**	**Ret**	**Yds**	**Avg**	**TD**	**Int**	**Yds**	**TD**	**Fum**
1968 Den	14	9	53	5.9	0	4	18	0	1
1969 Den	12	1	36	36.0	0	2	13	0	0
1970 Den	14	14	123	8.8	0	4	20	0	2
1971 Den	13	11	46	4.2	0	3	32	0	0
1972 Den	14	4	67	16.8	**1**	2	18	0	0
1973 Den	10	3	11	3.7	0	1	1	0	1
1974 Den	11	13	90	6.9	0	1	23	0	2
NFL Total	88	55	426	7.7	1	17	125	0	6

CURTIS GREER Greer, Curtis William 6'4", 255 **DE**
Col: Michigan *HS:* Cass Tech [Detroit, MI] B: 11/10/1957, Detroit, MI
Drafted: 1980 Round 1 StL
1980 StL: 11 G. **1981** StL: 16 G. **1982** StL: 9 G; 7.5 Sac. **1983** StL: 16 G; 16 Sac. **1984** StL: 16 G; 14 Sac. **1985** StL: 16 G; 7 Sac. **1987** StL: 10 G; 6 Sac. **Total:** 94 G; 50.5 Sac.

DONOVAN GREER Greer, Donovan Orlando 5'9", 178 **CB**
Col: Texas A&M *HS:* Elsik [Alief, TX] B: 9/11/1974, Houston, TX
1997 Atl-NO: 7 G. Atl: 1 G. NO: 6 G. **1998** Buf: 11 G. **Total:** 18 G.

JIM GREER Greer, James Daniel 6'3", 215 **OE**
Col: Elizabeth City State *HS:* Douglass [Huntington, WV] B: 7/7/1931, Huntington, WV *Drafted:* 1955 Round 23 Cle
1960 Den: 14 G; Rec 22-284 12.9 1 TD; KR 1-11 11.0; 6 Pt.

TERRY GREER Greer, Terry Lee 6'1", 192 **WR**
Col: Alabama State *HS:* Messick [Memphis, TN] B: 9/27/1957, Memphis, TN *Drafted:* 1980 Round 11 LARm
1989 SF: PR 1-3 3.0; KR 1-17 17.0. **Total:** PR 1-3 3.0; KR 1-17 17.0.

		Receiving				
Year Team	**G**	**Rec**	**Yds**	**Avg**	**TD**	**Fum**
1986 Cle	11	3	51	17.0	0	0
1987 SF	3	6	111	18.5	1	0
1988 SF	10	8	120	15.0	0	0
1989 SF	11	1	26	26.0	0	1
1990 Det	15	20	332	16.6	3	0
NFL Total	50	38	640	16.8	4	1

TED GREFE Grefe, Theodore Fred 6'0", 205 **OE-DE**
Col: Northwestern *HS:* Roosevelt [Des Moines, IA] B: 10/26/1917, Des Moines, IA D: 10/27/1989, Fairfax, VA
1945 Det: 2 G.

FORREST GREGG Gregg, Alvis Forrest 6'4", 249 **OT-OG-DT**
Col: Southern Methodist *HS:* Sulphur Springs [TX] B: 10/18/1933, Birthright, TX *Drafted:* 1956 Round 2 GB *HOF:* 1977
1956 GB: 11 G. **1958** GB: 12 G. **1959** GB: 12 G. **1960** GB: 12 G. **1961** GB: 14 G. **1962** GB: 14 G. **1963** GB: 14 G. **1964** GB: 14 G. **1965** GB: 14 G. **1966** GB: 14 G. **1967** GB: 14 G. **1968** GB: 14 G. **1969** GB: 14 G. **1970** GB: 14 G; KR 2-21 10.5. **1971** Dal: 6 G.
Total: 193 G; KR 2-21 10.5.

EDD GREGG Gregg, Edd R 5'6", 135 **OE**
Col: Kentucky *HS:* Manual [Louisville, KY] B: 8/4/1897, Louisville, KY
D: 11/9/1961, Louisville, KY
1922 Lou: 2 G.

BOB GREGOR Gregor, Robert Lee 6'2", 192 **DB**
Col: Washington State *HS:* Monte Vista [Danville, CA] B: 2/10/1957, Riverside, CA *Drafted:* 1980 Round 4 SD
1981 SD: 14 G; KR 3-47 15.7; Int 2-11. **1982** SD: 4 G; Int 1-6. **1983** SD: 5 G. **1984** SD: 7 G; Int 1-12. **Total:** 30 G; KR 3-47 15.7; Int 4-29.

BEN GREGORY Gregory, Bennett Maurice 6'0", 220 **RB**
Col: Nebraska *HS:* Uniontown [PA] B: 10/31/1946, Uniontown, PA
D: 4/10/1997, Boulder, CO *Drafted:* 1968 Round 5 Buf
1968 Buf: Rec 5-21 4.2.

		Rushing				
Year Team	**G**	**Att**	**Yds**	**Avg**	**TD**	**Fum**
1968 Buf	6	52	283	5.4	1	2

BRUCE GREGORY Gregory, Bruce Robert 5'10", 170 **WB**
Col: Michigan *HS:* Ann Arbor [MI] B: 5/13/1903, Battle Creek, MI
D: 12/26/1960, Frederick, MD
1926 Det: 12 G; Rec 2 TD; 12 Pt.

JACK GREGORY Gregory, Earl Jackson 6'2", 210 **G**
Col: Tennessee-Chattanooga *HS:* Okolona [MS] B: 2/14/1916, Okolona, MS *Drafted:* 1940 Round 13 Cle
1941 Cle: 7 G.

JACK GREGORY Gregory, Earl Jackson Jr. 6'5", 250 **DE**
Col: Tennessee-Chattanooga; Delta State *HS:* Okolona [MS]
B: 10/3/1944, Okolona, MS *Drafted:* 1966 Round 9 Cle
1967 Cle: 14 G. **1968** Cle: 14 G. **1969** Cle: 14 G; Int 1-12. **1970** Cle: 14 G. **1971** Cle: 14 G. **1972** NYG: 14 G. **1973** NYG: 13 G. **1974** NYG: 14 G. **1975** NYG: 14 G. **1976** NYG: 11 G. **1977** NYG: 14 G. **1978** NYG: 16 G. **1979** Cle: 16 G. **Total:** 182 G; Int 1-12.

GIL GREGORY Gregory, Frank Gilbert 5'11", 165 **FB-WB**
Col: Williams B: 1/18/1898, Newark, NJ D: 11/11/1980, Hamburg, NY
1923 Buf: 1 G. **1924** Buf: 3 G. **Total:** 4 G.

GARLAND GREGORY Gregory, Garland D 5'11", 185 **G-LB**
(Greg) *Col:* Louisiana Tech *HS:* Columbia [LA] B: 3/8/1919, Columbia, LA
AAFC **1946** SF-A: 13 G; KR 1-0. **1947** SF-A: 14 G; PR 1-31 31.0.
Total: 27 G; PR 1-31 31.0; KR 1-0.

GLYNN GREGORY Gregory, Glynn Stephens 6'2", 195 **OE-DB**
Col: Southern Methodist *HS:* Abilene [TX] B: 7/6/1939, Paris, TX
Drafted: 1961 Round 9 Dal
1961 Dal: 14 G; Rec 3-30 10.0; Int 1-21. **1962** Dal: 6 G; Rec 3-70 23.3.
Total: 20 G; Rec 6-100 16.7; Int 1-21.

KEN GREGORY Gregory, Kenneth 6'1", 190 **OE**
Col: Whittier *HS:* Whittier [CA] B: 2/1/1937 *Drafted:* 1961 Round 4 Bal
1961 Bal: 14 G; KR 1-3 3.0. **1962** Phi: 2 G. **1963** NYJ: 14 G; Rec 9-90 10.0. **Total:** 30 G; Rec 9-90 10.0; KR 1-3 3.0.

MIKE GREGORY Gregory, Mitchell Oscar 5'11", 215 **C**
Col: Denison *HS:* Doane Acad. [Granville, OH] B: 7/30/1905, Pittsburgh, PA D: 7/30/1957, Granville, OH
1931 Cle: 7 G.

TED GREGORY Gregory, Theodore Anthony 6'1", 260 **NT**
Col: Syracuse *HS:* East Islip [Islip Terrace, NY] B: 2/11/1965, Queens, NY *Drafted:* 1988 Round 1 Den
1988 NO: 3 G; 1 Sac.

BILL GREGORY Gregory, William Penn Jr. 6'5", 255 **DT-DE**
Col: Wisconsin *HS:* Lincoln [La Marque, TX] B: 12/14/1949, Galveston, TX *Drafted:* 1971 Round 3 Dal
1971 Dal: 14 G. **1972** Dal: 13 G. **1973** Dal: 14 G. **1974** Dal: 14 G. **1975** Dal: 14 G; Int 1-3. **1976** Dal: 14 G. **1977** Dal: 13 G. **1978** Sea: 16 G; Int 1-3. **1979** Sea: 16 G. **1980** Sea: 14 G. **Total:** 142 G; Int 2-6.

HANK GREMMINGER Gremminger, Charles Henry 6'1", 201 **DB**
Col: Baylor *HS:* Weatherford [TX] B: 9/1/1933, Windthorst, TX
Drafted: 1956 Round 7 GB
1956 GB: KR 1-6 6.0. **Total:** KR 1-6 6.0.

		Interceptions			
Year Team	**G**	**Int**	**Yds**	**TD**	**Fum**
1956 GB	12	2	36	0	0
1957 GB	12	5	93	0	1
1958 GB	12	3	15	0	0
1959 GB	12	1	45	0	0
1960 GB	12	3	52	0	0
1961 GB	14	5	54	0	0
1962 GB	14	5	88	0	0
1963 GB	14	3	25	0	0
1964 GB	13	1	13	0	0
1965 GB	8	0	0	0	0
1966 LARm	8	1	0	0	0
NFL Total	131	29	421	0	1

BOB GRESHAM Gresham, Robert Clark 5'11", 195 **RB**
Col: West Virginia *HS:* Big Creek [War, WV] B: 7/9/1948, Porter, AL
Drafted: 1971 Round 8 NO
1972 NO: Pass 1-0. **1976** NYJ: Pass 1-1 100.0%, 29 29.00.
Total: Pass 2-1 50.0%, 29 14.50.

		Rushing				Receiving			
Year Team	**G**	**Att**	**Yds**	**Avg**	**TD**	**Rec**	**Yds**	**Avg**	**TD**
1971 NO	13	127	383	3.0	6	17	203	11.9	0
1972 NO	14	121	381	3.1	3	29	192	6.6	0
1973 Hou	13	104	400	3.8	2	28	244	8.7	1
1974 Hou	14	3	6	2.0	0	3	19	6.3	0
1975 NYJ	10	25	98	3.9	1	2	4	2.0	0
1976 NYJ	11	30	92	3.1	0	11	66	6.0	0
NFL Total	75	410	1360	3.3	12	90	728	8.1	1

	Kickoff Returns					Tot
Year Team	**Ret**	**Yds**	**Avg**	**TD**	**Fum**	**TD**
1971 NO	3	60	20.0	0	3	6
1972 NO	0	0	—	0	5	3
1973 Hou	27	723	26.8	1	5	4
1974 Hou	9	180	20.0	0	2	0
1975 NYJ	7	153	21.9	0	2	1
1976 NYJ	0	0	—	0	1	0
NFL Total	46	1116	24.3	1	18	14

VISCO GRGICH Grgich, Visco Gerald 5'11", 217 **OG-LB-DG-OT**
(Bosco; Garbag) *Col:* Santa Clara *HS:* West Seattle [Seattle, WA]
B: 1/19/1923, Zlarin, Yugoslavia *Drafted:* 1946 Round 24 ChiB
AAFC **1946** SF-A: 12 G. **1947** SF-A: 14 G; KR 1-21 21.0. **1948** SF-A: 14 G. **1949** SF-A: 12 G. **Total:** 52 G; KR 1-21 21.0.

NFL **1950** SF: 12 G; Int 1-37. **1951** SF: 12 G. **1952** SF: 2 G. **Total:** 26 G; Int 1-37.

MARRIO GRIER Grier, Marrio Darnell 5'10", 229 **RB**
Col: Clemson; Tennessee-Chattanooga *HS:* Independence [Charlotte, NC] B: 12/5/1971, Charlotte, NC *Drafted:* 1996 Round 6 NE
1996 NE: Pass 1-0; Rec 1-8 8.0. **Total:** Pass 1-0; Rec 1-8 8.0.

		Rushing			
Year Team	**G**	**Att**	**Yds**	**Avg**	**TD**
1996 NE	16	27	105	3.9	1
1997 NE	16	33	75	2.3	1
NFL Total	32	60	180	3.0	2

ROSEY GRIER Grier, Roosevelt 6'5", 284 **DT-DE**
Col: Penn State *HS:* Abraham Clark [Roselle, NJ] B: 7/14/1932, Cuthbert, GA *Drafted:* 1955 Round 3 NYG
1955 NYG: 12 G. **1956** NYG: 12 G. **1958** NYG: 10 G. **1959** NYG: 12 G. **1960** NYG: 12 G; Scor **1** Saf; 2 Pt. **1961** NYG: 14 G. **1962** NYG: 13 G. **1963** LARm: 14 G. **1964** LARm: 14 G. **1965** LARm: 14 G. **1966** LARm: 14 G; Scor **1** Saf; 2 Pt. **Total:** 141 G; Scor 2 Saf; 4 Pt.

BRIAN GRIESE Griese, Brian David 6'3", 215 **QB**
Col: Michigan *HS:* Christopher Columbus [Miami, FL] B: 3/18/1975, Miami, FL *Drafted:* 1998 Round 3 Den
1998 Den: 1 G; Pass 3-1 33.3%, 2 0.67 1 Int; Rush 4-(-4) -1.0; 1 Fum.

BOB GRIESE Griese, Robert Allen 6'1", 190 **QB**
Col: Purdue *HS:* Rex Mundi [Evansville, IN] B: 2/3/1945, Evansville, IN
Drafted: 1967 Round 1 Mia *HOF:* 1990

		Passing							
Year Team	**G**	**Att**	**Comp**	**Comp%**	**Yds**	**YPA**	**TD**	**Int**	**Rating**
1967 Mia	12	331	166	50.2	2005	6.06	15	18	61.6
1968 Mia	13	355	186	52.4	2473	6.97	21	16	75.7
1969 Mia	9	252	121	48.0	1695	6.73	10	16	56.9
1970 Mia	14	245	142	58.0	2019	8.24	12	17	72.1
1971 Mia	14	263	145	55.1	2089	7.94	19	9	90.9
1972 Mia	6	97	53	54.6	638	6.58	4	4	71.6
1973 Mia	13	218	116	53.2	1422	6.52	17	8	84.3
1974 Mia	13	253	152	60.1	1968	7.78	16	15	80.9
1975 Mia	10	191	118	61.8	1693	**8.86**	14	13	86.6
1976 Mia	13	272	162	59.6	2097	7.71	11	12	78.9
1977 Mia	14	307	180	58.6	2252	7.34	**22**	13	**87.8**
1978 Mia	11	235	148	**63.0**	1791	7.62	11	11	82.4
1979 Mia	14	310	176	56.8	2160	6.97	14	16	72.0
1980 Mia	5	100	61	61.0	790	7.90	6	4	89.2
NFL Total	161	3429	1926	56.2	25092	7.32	192	172	77.1

	Rushing				
Year Team	**Att**	**Yds**	**Avg**	**TD**	**Fum**
1967 Mia	37	157	4.2	1	3
1968 Mia	42	230	5.5	1	1
1969 Mia	21	102	4.9	0	5
1970 Mia	26	89	3.4	2	5
1971 Mia	26	82	3.2	0	9
1972 Mia	3	11	3.7	1	0
1973 Mia	13	20	1.5	0	5
1974 Mia	16	66	4.1	1	5
1975 Mia	17	59	3.5	1	2
1976 Mia	23	108	4.7	0	3
1977 Mia	16	30	1.9	0	6
1978 Mia	9	10	1.1	0	3
1979 Mia	11	30	2.7	0	4
1980 Mia	1	0	0.0	0	1
NFL Total	261	994	3.8	7	52

HAL GRIFFEN Griffen, Harold Winslow 6'1", 247 **C-T**
(Tubby) *Col:* Iowa *HS:* Sioux City [IA] B: 3/1/1902, Sioux City, IA Deceased
1928 GB: 5 G. **1930** Port: 2 G. **1932** Port: 2 G. **Total:** 9 G.

ARCHIE GRIFFIN Griffin, Archie Mason 5'9", 189 **RB**
Col: Ohio State *HS:* Eastmoor [Columbus, OH] B: 8/24/1954, Columbus, OH *Drafted:* 1976 Round 1 Cin
1976 Cin: KR 3-56 18.7. **1977** Cin: Pass 1-1 100.0%, 18 18.00 1 TD; KR 9-192 21.3. **1978** Cin: Pass 3-2 66.7%, 21 7.00 1 TD; KR 4-94 23.5. **1981** Cin: KR 6-119 19.8. **Total:** Pass 4-3 75.0%, 39 9.75 2 TD; KR 22-461 21.0.

		Rushing				Receiving					Tot
Year Team	**G**	**Att**	**Yds**	**Avg**	**TD**	**Rec**	**Yds**	**Avg**	**TD**	**Fum**	**TD**
1976 Cin	14	138	625	4.5	3	16	138	8.6	0	2	3
1977 Cin	12	137	549	4.0	0	28	240	8.6	0	3	0
1978 Cin	16	132	484	3.7	0	35	284	8.1	3	6	3
1979 Cin	16	140	688	4.9	0	43	417	9.7	2	3	2
1980 Cin	15	85	260	3.1	0	28	196	7.0	0	1	0
1981 Cin	16	47	163	3.5	3	20	160	8.0	1	0	4
1982 Cin	9	12	39	3.3	1	22	172	7.8	0	0	1
NFL Total	98	691	2808	4.1	7	192	1607	8.4	6	15	13

BOBBIE GRIFFIN Griffin, Bobbie Joel 6'0", 180 **DB**
Col: Baylor *HS:* Milby [Houston, TX] B: 5/27/1928, Fort Worth, TX
Drafted: 1950 Round 19 NYY
1951 NYY: 12 G; PR 4-46 11.5; Int 4-27.

COURTNEY GRIFFIN Griffin, Courtney 5′10″, 180 **DB**
Col: Fresno State *HS:* Central Unified [Fresno, CA] B: 12/19/1966, Madera, CA
1993 LARm: 7 G.

DON GRIFFIN Griffin, Donald Dean 5′11″, 190 **HB-DB**
Col: Illinois *HS:* Fenger [Chicago, IL] B: 10/15/1922, Benton Harbor, MI
AAFC **1946** ChiA: Pass 1-0, 1 Int; Rec 5-28 5.6; KR 2-31 15.5; Int 1-19.

		Rushing			
Year Team	**G**	**Att**	**Yds**	**Avg**	**TD**
1946 ChiA	13	28	13	0.5	0

DON GRIFFIN Griffin, Donald Frederick 6′0″, 176 **DB**
Col: Middle Tennessee State *HS:* Mitchell Baker [Camilla, GA]
B: 3/17/1964, Pelham, GA *Drafted:* 1986 Round 6 SF
1986 SF: KR 5-97 19.4; 1 Sac. **1988** SF: 1 Sac. **1990** SF: KR 1-15 15.0. **1991** SF: 1 Fum TD. **1994** Cle: 4 Sac. **1996** Phi: 0.5 Sac. **Total:** KR 6-112 18.7; 1 Fum TD; 6.5 Sac.

		Punt Returns				Interceptions				Tot
Year Team	**G**	**Ret**	**Yds**	**Avg**	**TD**	**Int**	**Yds**	**TD**	**Fum**	**TD**
1986 SF	16	38	377	9.9	1	3	0	0	3	1
1987 SF	12	9	79	8.8	0	5	1	0	0	0
1988 SF	10	4	28	7.0	0	0	0	0	0	0
1989 SF	16	1	9	9.0	0	2	6	0	0	0
1990 SF	16	16	105	6.6	0	3	32	0	1	0
1991 SF	16	0	0	—	0	1	0	0	0	1
1992 SF	16	6	69	11.5	0	5	4	0	1	0
1993 SF	12	0	0	—	0	3	6	0	0	0
1994 Cle	15	0	0	—	0	2	2	0	1	0
1995 Cle	16	0	0	—	0	1	0	0	0	0
1996 Phi	16	0	0	—	0	0	0	0	0	0
NFL Total	161	74	667	9.0	1	25	51	0	6	2

JIM GRIFFIN Griffin, James Bauman 6′3″, 265 **DE**
Col: Grambling State *HS:* William Oscar Boston [Lake Charles, LA]
B: 2/8/1942, Lake Charles, LA *Drafted:* 1964 Round 15 SF
1966 SD: 14 G. **1967** SD: 14 G. **1968** Cin: 14 G; **1** Fum TD; 6 Pt. **Total:** 42 G; 1 Fum TD; 6 Pt.

JAMES GRIFFIN Griffin, James Victor 6′2″, 197 **DB**
Col: Middle Tennessee State *HS:* Mitchell Baker [Camilla, GA]
B: 9/7/1961, Camilla, GA *Drafted:* 1983 Round 7 Cin
1985 Cin: KR 1-0; 1 Sac. **1986** Det: 2 Sac. **1987** Det: 1 Sac. **1988** Det: 1 Sac. **1989** Det: KR 1-1 1.0; 0.5 Sac. **Total:** KR 2-1 0.5; 5.5 Sac.

		Interceptions		
Year Team	**G**	**Int**	**Yds**	**TD**
1983 Cin	16	1	41	1
1984 Cin	16	1	57	1
1985 Cin	16	7	116	**1**
1986 Det	16	2	34	0
1987 Det	12	6	130	0
1988 Det	16	2	31	0
1989 Det	16	0	0	0
NFL Total	108	19	409	3

JEFF GRIFFIN Griffin, Jeffrey Earl 6′0″, 185 **DB**
Col: Utah *HS:* Phineas Banning [Los Angeles, CA] B: 7/19/1958, Carson, CA *Drafted:* 1981 Round 3 StL
1981 StL: 16 G; KR 2-34 17.0; Int 1-4. **1982** StL: 9 G; KR 1-12 12.0; Int 1-8. **1983** StL: 3 G. **1984** StL: 8 G; Int 2-0. **1985** StL: 12 G. **1987** Phi: 2 G; 1 Sac. **Total:** 50 G; KR 3-46 15.3; Int 4-12; 1 Sac.

JOHN GRIFFIN Griffin, John Watson 6′1″, 190 **DB**
Col: Memphis *HS:* East [Nashville, TN] B: 11/2/1939, Nashville, TN
Drafted: 1963 Round 4 LARm
1963 LARm: 10 G. **1964** Den: 7 G. **1965** Den: 14 G; Int 4-109 1 TD; Tot TD 2; 12 Pt. **1966** Den: 5 G. **Total:** 36 G; Int 4-109 1 TD; Tot TD 2; 12 Pt.

KEITH GRIFFIN Griffin, Keith B 5′8″, 185 **RB**
Col: Miami (Fla.) *HS:* Eastmoor [Columbus, OH] B: 10/26/1961, Columbus, OH *Drafted:* 1984 Round 10 Was

		Rushing				Receiving			
Year Team	**G**	**Att**	**Yds**	**Avg**	**TD**	**Rec**	**Yds**	**Avg**	**TD**
1984 Was	16	97	408	4.2	0	8	43	5.4	0
1985 Was	16	102	473	4.6	3	37	285	7.7	0
1986 Was	16	62	197	3.2	0	11	110	10.0	0
1987 Was	9	62	242	3.9	0	3	13	4.3	1
1988 Was	8	6	23	3.8	0	2	9	4.5	1
NFL Total	65	329	1343	4.1	3	61	460	7.5	2

	Kickoff Returns					Tot
Year Team	**Ret**	**Yds**	**Avg**	**TD**	**Fum**	**TD**
1984 Was	9	164	18.2	0	7	0
1985 Was	7	142	20.3	0	1	3
1986 Was	8	156	19.5	0	0	0
1987 Was	25	478	19.1	0	3	1
1988 Was	3	45	15.0	0	0	1
NFL Total	52	985	18.9	0	11	5

LARRY GRIFFIN Griffin, Larry Anthony 6′0″, 197 **DB**
Col: North Carolina *HS:* Great Bridge [Chesapeake, VA] B: 1/11/1963, Chesapeake, VA *Drafted:* 1986 Round 8 Hou
1989 Pit: KR 1-21 21.0. **1990** Pit: KR 2-16 8.0. **Total:** KR 3-37 12.3.

		Interceptions			
Year Team	**G**	**Int**	**Yds**	**TD**	**Fum**
1986 Hou	3	0	0	0	0
1987 Pit	7	2	2	0	0
1988 Pit	15	2	63	0	1
1989 Pit	16	1	15	0	0
1990 Pit	16	4	75	0	1
1991 Pit	6	1	22	0	0
1992 Pit	14	3	98	1	0
1993 Pit	12	0	0	0	0
NFL Total	89	13	275	1	2

LEONARD GRIFFIN Griffin, Leonard James Jr. 6′4″, 268 **DE-NT**
Col: Grambling State *HS:* Lake Providence [LA] B: 9/22/1962, Lake Providence, LA *Drafted:* 1986 Round 3 KC
1986 KC: 9 G; 2 Sac. **1987** KC: 12 G. **1988** KC: 15 G; 2 Sac. **1989** KC: 16 G; 6.5 Sac. **1990** KC: 16 G; 3.5 Sac. **1991** KC: 16 G. **1992** KC: 15 G; 2.5 Sac. **1993** KC: 4 G. **Total:** 103 G; 16.5 Sac.

RAY GRIFFIN Griffin, Raymond Eric 5′10″, 186 **DB**
Col: Ohio State *HS:* Eastmoor [Columbus, OH] B: 6/29/1956, Columbus, OH *Drafted:* 1978 Round 2 Cin
1983 Cin: 1 Sac. **Total:** 1 Sac.

		Kickoff Returns				Interceptions		
Year Team	**G**	**Ret**	**Yds**	**Avg**	**TD**	**Int**	**Yds**	**TD**
1978 Cin	15	37	787	21.3	0	0	0	0
1979 Cin	12	1	15	15.0	0	4	167	1
1980 Cin	16	0	0	—	0	2	80	**2**
1981 Cin	8	2	31	15.5	0	0	0	0
1982 Cin	9	0	0	—	0	1	21	0
1983 Cin	16	0	0	—	0	2	24	0
1984 Cin	12	0	0	—	0	2	13	0
NFL Total	88	40	833	20.8	0	11	305	3

BOB GRIFFIN Griffin, Robert Lloyd 6′3″, 235 **LB**
Col: Arkansas *HS:* Frederick [OK] B: 2/12/1929, Fort Worth, TX
Drafted: 1952 Round 2 LARm
1953 LARm: 2 G. **1954** LARm: 12 G. **1955** LARm: 12 G; Int 1-20; Scor **1** Saf; 2 Pt. **1956** LARm: 6 G. **1957** LARm: 12 G. **1961** StL: 5 G. **Total:** 49 G; Int 1-20; Scor 1 Saf; 2 Pt.

STEVE GRIFFIN Griffin, Stephen Giovanni 5′10″, 205 **RB**
Col: Tennessee State *HS:* C. Leon King [Tampa, FL] B: 8/14/1964
1987 KC: 1 G; KR 1-16 16.0.

STEVE GRIFFIN Griffin, Steven Broadus 5′10″, 185 **RB**
Col: Clemson *HS:* South Mecklenburg [Charlotte, NC] B: 12/17/1963, Charlotte, NC
1987 Atl: 4 G; Rush 1-(-2) -2.0; KR 1-21 21.0.

STEVE GRIFFIN Griffin, Steven Leroy 5′11″, 198 **WR**
Col: Purdue *HS:* Miami Norland [FL] B: 12/24/1964, Miami, FL
Drafted: 1986 Round 12 Atl
1987 Atl: 2 G.

WADE GRIFFIN Griffin, Wade Hampton Jr. 6′5″, 260 **OT**
Col: Mississippi *HS:* Winona [MS] B: 8/7/1954, Winona, MS
1977 Bal: 14 G; KR 1-6 6.0. **1978** Bal: 16 G. **1979** Bal: 16 G; KR 1-8 8.0. **1980** Bal: 16 G. **1981** Bal: 15 G. **Total:** 77 G; KR 2-14 7.0.

GLYNN GRIFFING Griffing, Wilburn Glynn 6′1″, 200 **QB**
Col: Mississippi *HS:* Culkin Acad. [Vicksburg, MS] B: 12/1/1940, Bentonia, MS *Drafted:* 1962 Round 4 NYG
1963 NYG: 13 G; Pass 40-16 40.0%, 306 7.65 3 TD 4 Int; Rush 5-20 4.0; 1 Fum.

FORREST GRIFFITH Griffith, Forrest Martin 5′11″, 190 **HB**
Col: Kansas *HS:* Lee's Summit [MO] B: 2/15/1928, Lee's Summit, MO
Drafted: 1950 Round 5 NYG
1950 NYG: Rec 1-26 26.0. **1951** NYG: Rec 2-19 9.5; KR 2-28 14.0. **Total:** Rec 3-45 15.0; KR 2-28 14.0.

		Rushing				
Year Team	**G**	**Att**	**Yds**	**Avg**	**TD**	**Fum**
1950 NYG	6	45	162	3.6	2	3
1951 NYG	10	54	115	2.1	0	7
NFL Total	16	99	277	2.8	2	10

HOMER GRIFFITH Griffith, Homer Oliver Jr. 5′11″, 165 **TB-DB**
Col: USC *HS:* Fairfax [Los Angeles, CA] B: 7/24/1912, Los Angeles, CA D: 1/31/1990, Tarzana, CA
1934 ChiC: Pass 29-8 27.6%, 51 1.76 3 Int; PR **1** TD; KR **1** TD.

Year Team	G	Rushing Att	Yds	Avg	TD	Tot TD
1934 ChiC	9	57	66	1.2	0	2

HOWARD GRIFFITH Griffith, Howard Thomas 6′0″, 230 **RB**
Col: Illinois *HS:* Percy L. Julian [Chicago, IL] B: 11/17/1967, Chicago, IL *Drafted:* 1991 Round 9 Ind
1993 LARm: KR 8-169 21.1. **1994** LARm: KR 2-35 17.5. **Total:** KR 10-204 20.4.

Year Team	G	Rushing Att	Yds	Avg	TD	Receiving Rec	Yds	Avg	TD	Fum	Tot TD
1993 LARm	15	0	0	—	0	0	0	—	0	0	0
1994 LARm	16	9	30	3.3	0	16	113	7.1	1	0	1
1995 Car	15	65	197	3.0	1	11	63	5.7	1	1	2
1996 Car	16	12	7	0.6	1	27	223	8.3	1	1	2
1997 Den	15	9	34	3.8	0	11	55	5.0	0	0	0
1998 Den	14	4	13	3.3	0	15	97	6.5	3	0	3
NFL Total	91	99	281	2.8	2	80	551	6.9	6	2	8

RICH GRIFFITH Griffith, Richard Pope 6′5″, 262 **TE**
Col: Arizona *HS:* Catalina [Tucson, AZ] B: 7/31/1969, Batesville, AR *Drafted:* 1993 Round 5 NE
1993 NE: 3 G. **1995** Jac: 16 G; Rec 16-243 15.2; KR 1-9 9.0. **1996** Jac: 16 G; Rec 5-53 10.6; KR 2-24 12.0. **1997** Jac: 16 G. **1998** Jac: 7 G. **Total:** 58 G; Rec 21-296 14.1; KR 3-33 11.0.

ROBERT GRIFFITH Griffith, Robert Otis 5′11″, 194 **DB**
Col: San Diego State *HS:* Mount Miguel [Spring Valley, CA] B: 11/30/1970, Lanham, MD
1995 Min: 0.5 Sac. **1996** Min: 2 Sac. **Total:** 2.5 Sac.

Year Team	G	Interceptions Int	Yds	TD	Fum
1994 Min	15	0	0	0	0
1995 Min	16	0	0	0	0
1996 Min	14	4	67	0	1
1997 Min	16	2	26	0	0
1998 Min	16	5	25	0	0
NFL Total	77	11	118	0	1

RUSS GRIFFITH Griffith, Russell M 5′11″, 175 **P**
Col: Utah State; Weber State *HS:* Judge Memorial [Salt Lake City, UT] B: 2/5/1964
1987 Sea: 2 G; Rush 1-0; Punt 11-386 35.1.

RED GRIFFITHS Griffiths, Percy Wilfrid 5′8″, 190 **G**
Col: Bloomsburg; Penn State *HS:* Taylor [PA] B: 3/30/1893, Taylor, PA D: 6/12/1983, Clearwater, FL
1921 Can: 1 G.

JOHN GRIGAS Grigas, John Joseph 6′0″, 204 **FB-LB-DB**
Col: Holy Cross *HS:* Chelsea [MA] B: 8/19/1920, Chelsea, MA *Drafted:* 1943 Round 2 ChiC
1943 ChiC: PR 2-(-2) -1.0; Int 5-42. **1944** ChPt: PR 5-40 8.0; Int 1-2; Punt 12-424 35.3. **1945** Bos: Int 1-3. **1946** Bos: Int 1-0; Punt 1-45 45.0. **Total:** PR 7-38 5.4; Int 8-47; Punt 13-469 36.1.

Year Team	G	Passing Att	Comp	Comp%	Yds	YPA	TD	Int	Rating
1943 ChiC	10	19	4	21.1	98	5.16	0	4	9.0
1944 ChPt	9	131	50	38.2	690	5.27	6	21	31.5
1945 Bos	10	14	5	35.7	85	6.07	0	1	27.4
1946 Bos	11	2	1	50.0	16	8.00	0	1	37.5
1947 Bos	9	0	0	—	0	—	0	0	—
NFL Total	49	166	60	36.1	889	5.36	6	27	27.0

Year Team	Rushing Att	Yds	Avg	TD	Receiving Rec	Yds	Avg	TD
1943 ChiC	105	333	3.2	3	19	225	11.8	0
1944 ChPt	185	610	3.3	3	2	33	16.5	0
1945 Bos	64	160	2.5	2	5	59	11.8	0
1946 Bos	84	426	5.1	2	3	61	20.3	1
1947 Bos	27	52	1.9	0	1	1	1.0	0
NFL Total	465	1581	3.4	10	30	379	12.6	1

Year Team	Kickoff Returns Ret	Yds	Avg	TD	Fum	Tot TD
1943 ChiC	3	72	24.0	0	0	3
1944 ChPt	**23**	**471**	20.5	0	0	3
1945 Bos	4	65	16.3	0	4	2
1946 Bos	1	8	8.0	0	3	3
1947 Bos	1	19	19.0	0	1	0
NFL Total	32	635	19.8	0	8	11

TEX GRIGG Grigg, Cecil Burkett 5′11″, 191 **BB-TB-WB**
(Ranger) *Col:* Austin; Texas *HS:* Sherman [TX] B: 2/15/1891, Nashville, TN D: 9/5/1968, Houston, TX
1920 Can: 12 G. **1921** Can: 7 G; Pass 2 TD; Int **1** TD; 6 Pt. **1922** Can: 4 G. **1923** Can: 12 G; Pass 1 TD; Rush 3 TD; Rec 1 TD; Tot TD 4; 24 Pt. **1924** Roch: 1 G. **1925** Roch: 7 G; Scor 2, 2 XK. **1926** NYG: 12 G. **1927** Fra: 1 G. **Total:** 56 G; Pass 3 TD; Rush 3 TD; Rec 1 TD; Int 1 TD; Tot TD 5.

CHUBBY GRIGG Grigg, Forrest Porter Jr. 6′2″, 294 **OT-DT**
Col: Tulsa *HS:* Longview [TX] B: 1/10/1926, El Dorado, AR D: 10/10/1983, Ore City, TX
AAFC **1946** BufA: 8 G. **1947** ChiA: 13 G. **1948** CleA: 14 G. **1949** CleA: 12 G; Rec 0-2. **Total:** 47 G; Rec 0-2.

NFL **1950** Cle: 11 G; Scor 12, 1-2 50.0% FG, 9-9 100.0% XK. **1951** Cle: 11 G. **1952** Dal: 10 G; Scor 9, 0-3 FG, 9-12 75.0% XK. **Total:** 32 G; Scor 21, 1-5 20.0% FG, 18-21 85.7% XK.

ANTHONY GRIGGS Griggs, Anthony G 6′3″, 227 **LB**
Col: Villanova; Ohio State *HS:* John F. Kennedy [Willingboro, NJ] B: 2/12/1960, Lawton, OK *Drafted:* 1982 Round 4 Phi
1982 Phi: 9 G. **1983** Phi: 16 G; Int 3-61; 1 Sac. **1984** Phi: 16 G; 3 Sac. **1985** Phi: 16 G. **1986** Cle: 16 G. **1987** Cle: 12 G. **1988** Cle: 5 G. **Total:** 90 G; Int 3-61; 4 Sac.

DAVID GRIGGS Griggs, David Wesley 6′3″, 250 **LB-DE**
Col: Virginia *HS:* Pennsauken [NJ] B: 2/5/1967, Camden, NJ D: 6/19/1995, Davie, FL *Drafted:* 1989 Round 7 NO
1989 Mia: 5 G. **1990** Mia: 16 G; 5.5 Sac. **1991** Mia: 16 G; 5.5 Sac. **1992** Mia: 16 G; 3 Sac. **1993** Mia: 9 G; 0.5 Sac. **1994** SD: 16 G; Int 1-11. **Total:** 78 G; Int 1-11; 14.5 Sac.

HAL GRIGGS Griggs, Haldane Alfred 5′10″, 170 **BB-TB**
Col: Butler *HS:* Indianapolis Tech [IN] B: 11/27/1900, Toronto, Canada Deceased
1926 Akr: 5 G; Rush 2 TD; 12 Pt.

PERRY GRIGGS Griggs, Perry 5′10″, 183 **WR**
Col: Troy State *HS:* Lanett [AL] B: 9/17/1954, Lafayette, AL *Drafted:* 1977 Round 5 NYJ
1977 Bal: 1 G; KR 1-12 12.0; 1 Fum.

BILLY GRIGGS Griggs, William Edward III 6′3″, 230 **TE**
Col: Virginia *HS:* Pennsauken [NJ] B: 8/4/1962, Camden, NJ *Drafted:* 1984 Round 8 NYJ
1987 NYJ: KR 1-13 13.0. **Total:** KR 1-13 13.0.

Year Team	G	Receiving Rec	Yds	Avg	TD	Fum
1985 NYJ	16	0	0	—	0	0
1986 NYJ	16	0	0	—	0	0
1987 NYJ	12	2	17	8.5	1	0
1988 NYJ	15	14	133	9.5	0	1
1989 NYJ	5	9	112	12.4	0	0
NFL Total	64	25	262	10.5	1	1

FRANK GRIGONIS Grigonis, Frank John 5′10″, 182 **FB-LB**
Col: Tennessee-Chattanooga *HS:* Thornton Fractional North [Calumet City, IL] B: 10/10/1916, Calumet City, IL
1942 Det: Rec 1-17 17.0; Int 1-26.

Year Team	G	Rushing Att	Yds	Avg	TD
1942 Det	10	37	131	3.5	1

BOB GRIM Grim, Robert Lee 6′0″, 200 **WR**
Col: Oregon State *HS:* Red Bluff [CA] B: 5/8/1945, Oakland, CA *Drafted:* 1967 Round 2 Min
1967 Min: Rush 1-20 20.0. **1971** Min: Pass 1-0; Rush 6-127 21.2. **1973** NYG: Rush 1-(-10) -10.0. **1975** ChiB: Pass 1-0. **Total:** Pass 2-0; Rush 8-137 17.1.

Year Team	G	Receiving Rec	Yds	Avg	TD	Punt Returns Ret	Yds	Avg	TD
1967 Min	13	6	108	18.0	1	25	101	4.0	0
1968 Min	2	0	0	—	0	0	0	—	0
1969 Min	14	10	155	15.5	1	4	12	3.0	0
1970 Min	14	23	287	12.5	0	5	46	9.2	0
1971 Min	14	45	691	15.4	7	7	44	6.3	0
1972 NYG	13	5	67	13.4	1	7	10	1.4	0
1973 NYG	14	37	593	16.0	2	0	0	—	0
1974 NYG	14	28	466	16.6	2	0	0	—	0
1975 ChiB	14	28	374	13.4	2	0	0	—	0
1976 Min	8	9	108	12.0	0	0	0	—	0
1977 Min	14	3	65	21.7	0	11	69	6.3	0
NFL Total	134	194	2914	15.0	16	59	282	4.8	0

Year Team	Kickoff Returns Ret	Yds	Avg	TD	Fum
1967 Min	22	493	22.4	0	3

1969 Min	0	0	—	0	1
1970 Min	0	0	—	0	1
1971 Min	3	52	17.3	0	0
1972 NYG	0	0	—	0	3
1973 NYG	0	0	—	0	1
1974 NYG	0	0	—	0	1
1977 Min	1	4	4.0	0	3
NFL Total	26	549	21.1	0	13

BILLY GRIMES Grimes, Billy Joe 6′1″, 195 **HB**
(Comanche Kid) *Col:* Oklahoma State *HS:* Comanche [OK]
B: 7/27/1927, County Line, OK *Drafted:* 1949 Round 2 ChiB
AAFC **1949** LA-A: Pass 3-3 100.0%, 105 35.00 1 TD; Rec 13-189 14.5 2 TD; PR 5-67 13.4; KR 16-411 25.7.

		Rushing				Tot
Year Team	G	Att	Yds	Avg	TD	TD
1949 LA-A	12	83	429	5.2	4	6

NFL Statistics

		Rushing				Receiving			
Year Team	G	Att	Yds	Avg	TD	Rec	Yds	Avg	TD
1950 GB	12	84	480	5.7	5	17	261	15.4	1
1951 GB	12	44	123	2.8	1	15	170	11.3	1
1952 GB	12	17	59	3.5	0	0	0	—	0
NFL Total	36	145	662	4.6	6	32	431	13.5	2

	Punt Returns				Kickoff Returns					Tot
Year Team	Ret	Yds	Avg	TD	Ret	Yds	Avg	TD	Fum	TD
1950 GB	29	**555**	19.1	**2**	26	600	23.1	0	8	8
1951 GB	16	100	6.3	0	23	582	25.3	0	5	2
1952 GB	18	179	9.9	0	18	422	23.4	0	5	0
NFL Total	63	834	13.2	2	67	1604	23.9	0	18	10

GEORGE GRIMES Grimes, George Stanley 5′11″, 190 **DB-WB**
Col: North Carolina; Virginia *HS:* Tazewell [VA] B: 7/3/1922, Jewell Ridge, VA D: 4/1971 *Drafted:* 1948 Round 4 LARm
1948 Det: 9 G; Rush 1-8 8.0; Rec 1-17 17.0 1 TD; PR 1-4 4.0; Int 1-26; Punt 28-1006 35.9; Scor 6, 0-1 XK; 6 Pt; 1 Fum.

PHIL GRIMES Grimes, Philip 6′4″, 230 **DE**
Col: Central Missouri State *HS:* Fort Zumwalt [St. Peters, MO]
B: 2/26/1965, Montgomery, AL
1987 LARd: 2 G.

RANDY GRIMES Grimes, Randall Collins 6′4″, 270 **C-OG**
Col: Baylor *HS:* Robert E. Lee [Tyler, TX] B: 7/20/1960, Tyler, TX
Drafted: 1983 Round 2 TB
1983 TB: 15 G. **1984** TB: 10 G. **1985** TB: 16 G. **1986** TB: 16 G. **1987** TB: 12 G. **1988** TB: 16 G. **1989** TB: 16 G. **1990** TB: 15 G; 1 Fum. **1992** TB: 2 G. **Total:** 118 G; 1 Fum.

DAN GRIMM Grimm, Daniel Jay 6′3″, 245 **OG**
Col: Colorado *HS:* Roosevelt [Des Moines, IA] B: 2/7/1941, Perry, IA
Drafted: 1963 Round 5 GB
1963 GB: 14 G. **1964** GB: 14 G. **1965** GB: 14 G; KR 1-0. **1966** Atl: 14 G. **1967** Atl: 2 G. **1968** Atl: 14 G; KR 1-4 4.0. **1969** Bal-Was: 8 G. Bal: 2 G. Was: 6 G. **Total:** 80 G; KR 2-4 2.0.

RUSS GRIMM Grimm, Russell Scott 6′3″, 273 **OG-C**
Col: Pittsburgh *HS:* Southmoreland [Alverton, PA] B: 5/2/1959, Scottsdale, PA *Drafted:* 1981 Round 3 Was
1981 Was: 14 G. **1982** Was: 9 G. **1983** Was: 16 G. **1984** Was: 16 G. **1985** Was: 16 G. **1986** Was: 15 G. **1987** Was: 6 G. **1988** Was: 5 G. **1989** Was: 12 G. **1990** Was: 15 G. **1991** Was: 16 G. **Total:** 140 G.

ED GRIMSLEY Grimsley, Edward Paul 6′0″, 235 **LB**
Col: Akron *HS:* McKinley [Canton, OH] B: 3/22/1963, Canton, OH
1987 Ind: 5 G; 1 Sac.

JOHN GRIMSLEY Grimsley, John Glenn 6′2″, 235 **LB**
Col: Kentucky *HS:* McKinley [Canton, OH] B: 2/25/1962, Canton, OH
Drafted: 1984 Round 6 Hou
1984 Hou: 16 G. **1985** Hou: 15 G. **1986** Hou: 16 G; 1 Sac. **1987** Hou: 12 G. **1988** Hou: 16 G; Int 1-9; 1 Sac. **1989** Hou: 16 G. **1990** Hou: 15 G. **1992** Mia: 14 G. **1993** Mia: 13 G. **Total:** 133 G; Int 1-9; 2 Sac.

CLIF GROCE Groce, Clifton Allen 5′11″, 245 **RB**
Col: Texas A&M *HS:* Texas A&M [College Station, TX] B: 7/30/1972, College Station, TX
1996 Ind: Rec 13-106 8.2; KR 1-18 18.0. **1997** Ind: KR 1-15 15.0.
Total: Rec 13-106 8.2; KR 2-33 16.5.

		Rushing				
Year Team	G	Att	Yds	Avg	TD	Fum
1995 Ind	1	0	0	—	0	0
1996 Ind	15	46	184	4.0	0	2
1997 Ind	7	10	66	6.6	0	0
NFL Total	23	56	250	4.5	0	2

RON GROCE Groce, Ronald 6′2″, 211 **RB**
Col: Macalester *HS:* Central [Minneapolis, MN] B: 7/1/1954, Minneapolis, MN *Drafted:* 1976 Round 15 Min
1976 Min: 4 G; Rush 3-18 6.0; 1 Fum.

STEVE GROGAN Grogan, Steven James 6′4″, 210 **QB**
Col: Kansas State *HS:* Ottawa [KS] B: 7/24/1953, San Antonio, TX
Drafted: 1975 Round 5 NE
1976 NE: **1** Fum TD. **1981** NE: Rec 2-27 13.5. **1983** NE: Rec 1-(-8) -8.0.
Total: Rec 3-19 6.3; 1 Fum TD.

		Passing							
Year Team	G	Att	Comp	Comp%	Yds	YPA	TD	Int	Rating
1975 NE	13	274	139	50.7	1976	7.21	11	18	60.4
1976 NE	14	302	145	48.0	1903	6.30	18	20	60.6
1977 NE	14	305	160	52.5	2162	7.09	17	21	65.2
1978 NE	16	362	181	50.0	2824	7.80	15	23	63.6
1979 NE	16	423	206	48.7	3286	7.77	**28**	20	77.4
1980 NE	12	306	175	57.2	2475	**8.09**	18	22	73.1
1981 NE	8	216	117	54.2	1859	**8.61**	7	16	63.0
1982 NE	6	122	66	54.1	930	7.62	7	**4**	84.4
1983 NE	12	303	168	55.4	2411	7.96	15	12	81.4
1984 NE	3	68	32	47.1	444	6.53	3	6	46.4
1985 NE	7	156	85	54.5	1311	8.40	7	5	84.1
1986 NE	4	102	62	60.8	976	9.57	9	2	113.8
1987 NE	7	161	93	57.8	1183	7.35	10	9	78.2
1988 NE	6	140	67	47.9	834	5.96	4	13	37.6
1989 NE	7	261	133	51.0	1697	6.50	9	14	60.8
1990 NE	4	92	50	54.3	615	6.68	4	3	76.1
NFL Total	149	3593	1879	52.3	26886	7.48	182	208	69.6

	Rushing					Tot
Year Team	Att	Yds	Avg	TD	Fum	TD
1975 NE	30	110	3.7	3	6	3
1976 NE	60	397	6.6	12	6	13
1977 NE	61	324	5.3	1	7	1
1978 NE	81	539	6.7	5	9	5
1979 NE	64	368	5.8	2	12	2
1980 NE	30	112	3.7	1	4	1
1981 NE	12	49	4.1	2	5	2
1982 NE	9	42	4.7	1	2	1
1983 NE	23	108	4.7	2	4	2
1984 NE	7	12	1.7	0	4	0
1985 NE	20	29	1.5	2	6	2
1986 NE	9	23	2.6	1	2	1
1987 NE	20	37	1.9	2	8	2
1988 NE	6	12	2.0	1	2	1
1989 NE	9	19	2.1	0	3	0
1990 NE	4	-5	-1.3	0	1	0
NFL Total	445	2176	4.9	35	81	36

BILL GROMAN Groman, William Frederick 6′0″, 194 **WR**
Col: Heidelberg *HS:* Columbian [Tiffin, OH] B: 7/17/1936, Triffin, OH
1960 Hou: Pass 1-1 100.0%, 3 3.00 1 TD. **1961** Hou: Pass 1-0; Rush 1-2 2.0 1 TD. **1963** Den: KR 0-9. **Total:** Pass 2-1 50.0%, 3 1.50 1 TD; Rush 1-2 2.0 1 TD; KR 0-9.

		Receiving					Tot
Year Team	G	Rec	Yds	Avg	TD	Fum	TD
1960 Hou	14	72	**1473**	**20.5**	12	2	12
1961 Hou	14	50	1175	**23.5**	**17**	0	**18**
1962 Hou	14	21	328	15.6	3	0	3
1963 Den	14	27	437	16.2	3	1	3
1964 Buf	5	4	68	17.0	1	0	1
1965 Buf	5	0	0	—	0	0	0
NFL Total	66	174	3481	20.0	36	3	37

JERRY GROOM Groom, Jerome Paul 6′3″, 236 **DT-C-LB**
(Boomer) *Col:* Notre Dame *HS:* Dowling [West Des Moines, IA]
B: 8/15/1929, Des Moines, IA *Drafted:* 1951 Round 1 ChiC
1951 ChiC: 12 G. **1952** ChiC: 12 G. **1953** ChiC: 12 G. **1954** ChiC: 11 G. **1955** ChiC: 11 G. **Total:** 58 G.

MEL GROOMES Groomes, Melvin Harold 6′0″, 178 **DB-WB-HB**
Col: Indiana *HS:* Trenton Central [NJ] B: 3/6/1927, Trenton, NJ
1948 Det: 6 G; Rush 2-1 0.5; Rec 2-18 9.0; 1 Fum. **1949** Det: 3 G; Rush 1-1 1.0; Rec 3-33 11.0 1 TD; Int 1-25; 6 Pt. **Total:** 9 G; Rush 3-2 0.7; Rec 5-51 10.2 1 TD; Int 1-25; 6 Pt; 1 Fum.

ELOIS GROOMS Grooms, Elois 6′4″, 249 **DE-DT**
Col: Tennessee Tech *HS:* Tompkinsville [KY] B: 5/20/1953, Tompkinsville, KY *Drafted:* 1975 Round 3 NO
1975 NO: 10 G. **1976** NO: 11 G. **1977** NO: 14 G; Rec 1-3 3.0 1 TD; 6 Pt. **1978** NO: 16 G. **1979** NO: 16 G; Int 1-(-2); Scor **1** Saf; 2 Pt. **1980** NO: 16 G; Int 1-37. **1981** NO: 16 G. **1982** StL: 9 G; 4.5 Sac. **1983** StL: 11 G; Int 1-10; 1 Fum TD; 6 Pt; 1 Sac. **1984** StL: 11 G; 2 Sac. **1985** StL: 5 G; 1 Sac. **1987** Phi: 3 G; 2 Sac. **Total:** 138 G; Rec 1-3 3.0 1 TD; Int 3-45; Scor 1 Saf; 1 Fum TD; Tot TD 2; 14 Pt; 10.5 Sac.

EARL GROS Gros, Earl Roy 6'3", 220 **RB**
Col: Louisiana State *HS:* Terrebonne [Houma, LA] B: 8/29/1940, Lafourche Parish, LA *Drafted:* 1962 Round 1 GB
1962 GB: KR 1-7 7.0. **1963** GB: KR 17-430 25.3. **1964** Phi: Pass 1-0; KR 2-38 19.0. **1965** Phi: Pass 2-1 50.0%, 63 31.50 1 TD. **1966** Phi: Pass 1-0. **Total:** Pass 4-1 25.0%, 63 15.75 1 TD; KR 20-475 23.8.

		Rushing				Receiving					Tot
Year Team	**G**	**Att**	**Yds**	**Avg**	**TD**	**Rec**	**Yds**	**Avg**	**TD**	**Fum**	**TD**
1962 GB	14	29	155	5.3	2	0	0	—	0	1	2
1963 GB	14	48	203	4.2	2	1	19	19.0	0	6	2
1964 Phi	13	154	748	4.9	2	29	234	8.1	0	2	2
1965 Phi	14	145	479	3.3	7	29	271	9.3	2	5	9
1966 Phi	14	102	396	3.9	7	18	214	11.9	2	3	9
1967 Pit	12	72	252	3.5	1	19	175	9.2	0	1	1
1968 Pit	13	151	579	3.8	3	27	211	7.8	3	3	6
1969 Pit	13	116	343	3.0	4	17	131	7.7	3	4	7
1970 NO	1	4	2	0.5	0	2	0	0.0	0	0	0
NFL Total	108	821	3157	3.8	28	142	1255	8.8	10	25	38

AL GROSS Gross, Alfred Ellis Jr. 6'3", 191 **DB**
Col: Arizona *HS:* Franklin [Stockton, CA] B: 1/4/1961, Stockton, CA *Drafted:* 1983 Round 9 Dal
1986 Cle: **1** Fum TD. **Total:** 1 Fum TD.

		Interceptions			Tot
Year Team	**G**	**Int**	**Yds**	**TD**	**TD**
1983 Cle	16	1	18	0	0
1984 Cle	16	5	103	0	0
1985 Cle	16	5	109	**1**	1
1986 Cle	4	0	0	0	1
1987 Cle	6	0	0	0	0
NFL Total	58	11	230	1	2

ANDY GROSS Gross, Andrew 6'0", 230 **OG**
(BoBo) *Col:* Auburn *HS:* Thomas Jefferson [Elizabeth, NJ] B: 10/13/1945, Burkam, Austria
1967 NYG: 14 G. **1968** NYG: 14 G. **Total:** 28 G.

GEORGE GROSS Gross, George 6'3", 270 **DT**
(Mr. Muscles) *Col:* Auburn *HS:* Thomas Jefferson [Elizabeth, NJ] B: 1/26/1941, Weilau, Romania *Drafted:* 1962 Round 16 SD
1963 SD: 14 G. **1964** SD: 14 G. **1965** SD: 14 G. **1966** SD: 14 G. **1967** SD: 14 G. **Total:** 70 G.

LEE GROSS Gross, Lee Monroe III 6'3", 237 **C**
Col: Auburn *HS:* Robert E. Lee [Montgomery, AL] B: 7/29/1953, Montgomery, AL *Drafted:* 1975 Round 2 NO
1975 NO: 9 G. **1976** NO: 14 G. **1977** NO: 9 G. **1979** Bal: 16 G. **Total:** 48 G.

LEE GROSSCUP Grosscup, Clyde Lee 6'1", 187 **QB**
Col: Santa Monica Coll. CA (J.C.); Washington; Utah *HS:* Santa Monica [CA] B: 12/27/1936, Santa Monica, CA *Drafted:* 1959 Round 1 NYG
1960 NYG: Rush 3-1 0.3. **1961** NYG: Rush 2-10 5.0. **1962** NYT: Rush 8-62 7.8. **Total:** Rush 13-73 5.6.

		Passing								
Year Team	**G**	**Att**	**Comp**	**Comp%**	**Yds**	**YPA**	**TD**	**Int**	**Rating**	**Fum**
1960 NYG	4	25	11	44.0	144	5.76	1	1	59.4	2
1961 NYG	4	22	5	22.7	87	3.95	1	3	19.1	0
1962 NYT	8	126	57	45.2	855	6.79	8	8	62.8	5
NFL Total	16	173	73	42.2	1086	6.28	10	12	53.8	7

BURT GROSSMAN Grossman, Burton L 6'4", 270 **DE**
Col: Pittsburgh *HS:* Archbishop Carroll [Radnor, PA] B: 4/10/1967, Philadelphia, PA *Drafted:* 1989 Round 1 SD
1989 SD: 16 G; 10 Sac. **1990** SD: 15 G; Scor **1** Saf; 2 Pt; 10 Sac. **1991** SD: 16 G; 5.5 Sac. **1992** SD: 15 G; Scor **2** Saf; 4 Pt; 8 Sac. **1993** SD: 10 G; 4.5 Sac. **1994** Phi: 14 G; 5.5 Sac. **Total:** 86 G; Scor 3 Saf; 6 Pt; 43.5 Sac.

RANDY GROSSMAN Grossman, Curt Randy 6'1", 218 **TE**
Col: Temple *HS:* Haverford [Havertown, PA] B: 9/20/1952, Philadelphia, PA

		Receiving				
Year Team	**G**	**Rec**	**Yds**	**Avg**	**TD**	**Fum**
1974 Pit	14	13	164	12.6	0	0
1975 Pit	14	11	135	12.3	1	0
1976 Pit	14	15	181	12.1	1	0
1977 Pit	13	5	57	11.4	0	0
1978 Pit	16	37	448	12.1	1	1
1979 Pit	16	12	217	18.1	1	0
1980 Pit	15	23	293	12.7	0	0
1981 Pit	16	3	19	6.3	1	0
NFL Total	118	119	1514	12.7	5	1

JACK GROSSMAN Grossman, Jack 6'1", 193 **DB-TB-FB-WB**
Col: Rutgers *HS:* James Madison [Brooklyn, NY] B: 11/1/1910, Poland D: 2/6/1983, Hollywood, FL
1932 Bkn: Rec 8-129 16.1 3 TD. **1934** Bkn: Rec 11-161 14.6 1 TD; PR **1** TD. **1935** Bkn: Rec 4-66 16.5; Scor 13, 1 XK. **Total:** Rec 23-356 15.5 4 TD; PR 1 TD.

		Passing							
Year Team	**G**	**Att**	**Comp**	**Comp%**	**Yds**	**YPA**	**TD**	**Int**	**Rating**
1932 Bkn	12	32	11	34.4	178	5.56	0	3	14.8
1934 Bkn	11	8	1	12.5	47	5.88	1	3	51.6
1935 Bkn	11	35	9	25.7	149	4.26	0	7	5.2
NFL Total	34	75	21	28.0	374	4.99	1	13	12.7

	Rushing				Tot
Year Team	**Att**	**Yds**	**Avg**	**TD**	**TD**
1932 Bkn	129	323	2.5	2	5
1934 Bkn	35	115	3.3	0	2
1935 Bkn	67	208	3.1	2	2
NFL Total	231	646	2.8	4	9

REX GROSSMAN Grossman, Rex Daniel 6'1", 215 **LB-FB-K**
Col: Indiana *HS:* Huntington [IN] B: 2/5/1924, Huntington, IN D: 6/13/1980, Bloomington, IN *Drafted:* 1948 Round 27 Phi
AAFC **1948** BalA: 14 G; Rush 8-(-3) -0.4; Int 2-13; Scor 73, 10-18 55.6% FG, 43-43 100.0% XK. **1949** BalA: 11 G; Pass 1-0, 1 Int; Punt 28-1087 38.8; Scor 37, 6-11 54.5% FG, 19-19 100.0% XK. **Total:** 25 G; Pass 1-0, 1 Int; Rush 8-(-3) -0.4; Int 2-13; Punt 28-1087 38.8; Scor 110, 16-29 55.2% FG, 62-62 100.0% XK.

NFL **1950** Bal-Det: 12 G; Rec 1-4 4.0; KR 1-15 15.0; Scor 16, 0-3 FG, 16-19 84.2% XK. Bal: 8 G; Rec 1-4 4.0; Scor 16, 0-3 FG, 16-19 84.2% XK. Det: 4 G; KR 1-15 15.0. **Total:** 12 G; Rec 1-4 4.0; KR 1-15 15.0; Scor 16, 0-3 FG, 16-19 84.2% XK.

GEORGE GROSVENOR Grosvenor, George Alfred 6'0", 174 **TB-DB-HB**
(Tarzan) *Col:* Colorado *HS:* Boulder [CO] B: 8/4/1911, Jefferson, OK
1936 ChiB-ChiC: Rec 1-6 6.0; PR **1** TD. ChiC: Rec 1-6 6.0; PR 1 TD. **Total:** Rec 1-6 6.0; PR 1 TD.

		Passing							
Year Team	**G**	**Att**	**Comp**	**Comp%**	**Yds**	**YPA**	**TD**	**Int**	**Rating**
1935 ChiB	11	15	6	40.0	69	4.60	0	1	26.8
1936 ChiB-ChiC	10	34	12	35.3	173	5.09	0	6	13.1
1936 ChiB	1	0	0	—	0	—	0	0	—
1936 ChiC	9	34	12	35.3	173	5.09	0	6	13.1
1937 ChiC	11	50	21	42.0	325	6.50	3	7	44.6
NFL Total	32	99	39	39.4	567	5.73	3	14	29.3

	Rushing				Tot
Year Team	**Att**	**Yds**	**Avg**	**TD**	**TD**
1935 ChiB	55	234	4.3	0	0
1936 ChiB-ChiC	170	612	3.6	4	5
1936 ChiB	1	3	3.0	0	0
1936 ChiC	169	609	3.6	4	5
1937 ChiC	143	461	3.2	2	2
NFL Total	368	1307	3.6	6	7

JEFF GROTH Groth, Jeffrey Eugene 5'10", 176 **WR**
Col: Bowling Green State *HS:* Chagrin Falls [OH] B: 7/2/1957, Mankato, MN *Drafted:* 1979 Round 8 Mia
1979 Mia-Hou: KR 1-21 21.0. Hou: KR 1-21 21.0. **1980** Hou: KR 12-216 18.0. **1981** NO: Rush 2-27 13.5; KR 3-50 16.7. **1982** NO: Rush 1-1 1.0. **1983** NO: Rush 1-15 15.0. **Total:** Rush 4-43 10.8; KR 16-287 17.9.

		Receiving				Punt Returns				
Year Team	**G**	**Rec**	**Yds**	**Avg**	**TD**	**Ret**	**Yds**	**Avg**	**TD**	**Fum**
1979 Mia-Hou	10	1	6	6.0	0	0	0	—	0	0
1979 Mia	4	0	0	—	0	0	0	—	0	0
1979 Hou	6	1	6	6.0	0	0	0	—	0	0
1980 Hou	16	4	47	11.8	0	1	0	0.0	0	2
1981 NO	15	20	380	19.0	1	37	436	11.8	0	0
1982 NO	9	30	383	12.8	1	21	144	6.9	0	1
1983 NO	16	49	585	11.9	1	39	275	7.1	0	3
1984 NO	16	33	487	14.8	0	6	32	5.3	0	0
1985 NO	12	15	238	15.9	2	1	0	0.0	0	0
NFL Total	94	152	2126	14.0	5	105	887	8.4	0	6

BOB GROTTKAU Grottkau, Robert Fred 6'4", 228 **OG**
Col: Oregon *HS:* Oakland [CA] B: 3/22/1937, San Rafael, CA *Drafted:* 1959 Round 4 Det
1959 Det: 12 G. **1960** Det: 5 G. **1961** Dal: 13 G. **Total:** 30 G.

ROGER GROVE Grove, Roger Robert 6'0", 182 **DB-BB-HB**
(Roy) *Col:* Michigan State *HS:* Sturgis [MI] B: 6/19/1908, Greenville, OH D: 12/19/1986, Torrance, CA
1931 GB: Pass 2 TD; Scor 2, 2 XK. **1932** GB: Scor 23, 5 XK. **1933** GB: Pass 3-1 33.3%, 44 14.67; Scor 8, 8 XK. **1934** GB: Pass 10-5 50.0%, 34 3.40; Scor 25, 1 XK. **Total:** Pass 13-6 46.2%, 78 6.00 2 TD.

Year Team	G	Rushing Att	Yds	Avg	TD	Receiving Rec	Yds	Avg	TD	Tot TD
1931 GB	14	—	—	—	0	—	—	—	0	0
1932 GB	11	12	21	1.8	0	9	149	16.6	3	3
1933 GB	13	1	4	4.0	0	17	215	12.6	0	0
1934 GB	10	62	262	4.2	1	6	125	20.8	3	4
1935 GB	3	7	21	3.0	0	0	0	—	0	0
NFL Total	51	82	308	3.8	1	32	489	15.3	6	7

GEORGE GROVES Groves, George Noah 5′11″, 195 **G-LB**
Col: Marquette *HS:* Rossville [IL] B: 6/10/1921, Hammond, IN
AAFC **1947** BufA: 7 G. **1948** BalA: 2 G. **Total:** 9 G.

MONTY GROW Grow, Monty Ray 6′3″, 214 **DB**
Col: Florida *HS:* Citrus [Inverness, FL] B: 9/4/1971, Inverness, FL
1994 KC: 15 G; Int 1-21; 1 Fum. **1995** Jac: 4 G; Int 1-2. **Total:** 19 G; Int 2-23; 1 Fum.

LOU GROZA Groza, Louis Roy 6′3″, 240 **OT-DT-K**
(The Toe) *Col:* Ohio State *HS:* Martins Ferry [OH] B: 1/25/1924, Martins Ferry, OH *HOF:* 1974
AAFC **1949** CleA: KR 1-2 2.0. **Total:** KR 1-2 2.0.

Year Team	G	Scoring Pts	FG	FGA	FG%	XK	XKA	XK%
1946 CleA	14	84	13	29	44.8	45	47	95.7
1947 CleA	12	60	7	19	36.8	39	42	92.9
1948 CleA	14	75	8	19	42.1	51	52	98.1
1949 CleA	12	40	2	9	22.2	34	35	97.1
AAFC Total	52	259	30	76	39.5	169	176	96.0

NFL **1950** Cle: Pass 1-0; Rec 1-23 23.0 1 TD. **1963** Cle: Pass 1-0, 1 Int. **1965** Cle: Pass 1-0. **1966** Cle: Pass 1-1 100.0%, -7 -7.00. **Total:** Pass 4-1 25.0%, -7 1.75 1 Int; Rec 1-23 23.0 1 TD.

Year Team	G	Scoring Pts	FG	FGA	FG%	XK	XKA	XK%
1950 Cle	10	74	**13**	**19**	**68.4**	29	29	**100.0**
1951 Cle	12	73	10	**23**	43.5	**43**	43	100.0
1952 Cle	12	89	**19**	**33**	57.6	32	32	100.0
1953 Cle	12	108	**23**	**26**	**88.5**	39	40	**97.5**
1954 Cle	12	85	**16**	24	**66.7**	37	38	**97.4**
1955 Cle	12	77	11	22	50.0	**44**	**45**	97.8
1956 Cle	12	51	11	20	55.0	18	18	100.0
1957 Cle	12	**77**	**15**	22	68.2	32	32	100.0
1958 Cle	12	60	8	19	42.1	36	38	94.7
1959 Cle	12	48	5	16	31.3	33	37	89.2
1961 Cle	14	85	16	23	**69.6**	37	38	**97.4**
1962 Cle	14	75	14	31	45.2	33	35	94.3
1963 Cle	14	85	15	23	**65.2**	40	43	**93.0**
1964 Cle	14	115	22	33	66.7	49	49	100.0
1965 Cle	14	93	16	25	64.0	45	45	100.0
1966 Cle	14	78	9	23	39.1	51	52	98.1
1967 Cle	14	76	11	23	47.8	43	43	100.0
NFL Total	216	1349	234	405	57.8	641	657	97.6

CHARLIE GRUBE Grube, Charles William 5′10″, 175 **OE**
Col: Michigan *HS:* Arthur Hill [Saginaw, MI] B: 6/11/1904, Saginaw, MI D: 1/21/1976, Hollywood, FL
1926 Det: 2 G.

FRANK GRUBE Grube, Franklin Thomas 5′9″, 180 **OE**
(Hans) *Col:* Lafayette *HS:* Easton [PA] B: 1/7/1905, Easton, PA D: 7/2/1945, New York, NY
1928 NYY: 11 G; Scor 1, 1 XK.

HERB GRUBER Gruber, Herbert C 5′9″, 155 **OE**
Col: Kentucky *HS:* Male [Louisville, KY] B: 12/22/1901, Shelbyville, KY D: 2/1/1979, St. Matthews, KY
1921 Lou: 2 G. **1922** Lou: 3 G. **1923** Lou: 3 G. **Total:** 8 G.

PAUL GRUBER Gruber, Paul Blake 6′5″, 292 **OT**
Col: Wisconsin *HS:* Sauk Prairie [Prairie du Sac, WI] B: 2/24/1965, Madison, WI *Drafted:* 1988 Round 1 TB
1988 TB: 16 G. **1989** TB: 16 G. **1990** TB: 16 G. **1991** TB: 16 G. **1992** TB: 16 G. **1993** TB: 10 G. **1994** TB: 16 G. **1995** TB: 16 G. **1996** TB: 13 G. **1997** TB: 16 G. **1998** TB: 16 G. **Total:** 167 G.

BOB GRUBER Gruber, Robert Leon Jr. 6′5″, 275 **OT**
Col: Pittsburgh *HS:* Greenville [TX] B: 6/7/1958, Del Rio, TX *Drafted:* 1980 Round 10 LARm
1987 GB: 1 G.

SAM GRUNEISEN Gruneisen, Samuel Kenneth 6′1″, 242 **C-OG-LB**
Col: Villanova *HS:* St. Xavier [Louisville, KY] B: 1/16/1941, Louisville, KY *Drafted:* 1962 Round 25 SD
1962 SD: 9 G. **1963** SD: 7 G. **1964** SD: 11 G; 2 Fum. **1965** SD: 14 G; 1 Fum. **1966** SD: 14 G; KR 1-0. **1967** SD: 14 G. **1968** SD: 14 G. **1969** SD: 14 G. **1970** SD: 14 G. **1971** SD: 2 G. **1972** SD: 7 G. **1973** Hou: 10 G. **Total:** 130 G; KR 1-0; 3 Fum.

TIM GRUNHARD Grunhard, Timothy Gerard 6′2″, 304 **C**
Col: Notre Dame *HS:* St. Laurence [Burbank, IL] B: 5/17/1968, Chicago, IL *Drafted:* 1990 Round 2 KC
1990 KC: 14 G. **1991** KC: 16 G. **1992** KC: 12 G. **1993** KC: 16 G; 1 Fum. **1994** KC: 16 G. **1995** KC: 16 G. **1996** KC: 16 G. **1997** KC: 16 G. **1998** KC: 16 G. **Total:** 138 G; 1 Fum.

BOB GRUPP Grupp, Robert William 5′11″, 193 **P**
Col: Duke *HS:* Neshaminy [Langhorne, PA] B: 5/8/1955, Philadelphia, PA *Drafted:* 1977 Round 7 NYJ
1979 KC: Pass 1-0. **1980** KC: Rush 3-(-14) -4.7. **1981** KC: Rush 1-(-19) -19.0. **Total:** Pass 1-0; Rush 4-(-33) -8.3.

Year Team	G	Punting Punts	Yds	Avg	Fum
1979 KC	16	89	3883	**43.6**	0
1980 KC	16	84	3317	39.5	2
1981 KC	9	41	1556	38.0	0
NFL Total	41	214	8756	40.9	2

MIKE GRUTTADAURIA Gruttadauria, Michael Jason 6′3″, 297 **C**
Col: Central Florida *HS:* Tarpon Springs [FL] B: 12/6/1972, Fort Lauderdale, FL
1996 StL: 9 G. **1997** StL: 14 G; Rec 1-0. **1998** StL: 11 G. **Total:** 34 G; Rec 1-0.

AL GRYGO Grygo, Aloysius Joseph 5′10″, 173 **HB-DB**
(Twinkletoes) *Col:* South Carolina B: 8/14/1918, Erie, PA D: 9/27/1971, Columbia, SC
1944 ChiB: Rec 5-42 8.4; PR 11-100 9.1; KR 7-162 23.1; Int 4-79; Punt 4-123 30.8. **1945** ChiB: Pass 1-1 100.0%, 11 11.00; Rec 5-68 13.6 1 TD; PR 6-44 7.3; KR 4-80 20.0; Int 3-9; Punt 2-86 43.0. **Total:** Pass 1-1 100.0%, 11 11.00; Rec 10-110 11.0 1 TD; PR 17-144 8.5; KR 11-242 22.0; Int 7-88; Punt 6-209 34.8.

Year Team	G	Rushing Att	Yds	Avg	TD	Fum	Tot TD
1944 ChiB	9	53	322	**6.1**	2	0	2
1945 ChiB	10	23	98	4.3	0	1	1
NFL Total	19	76	420	5.5	2	1	3

DARRELL GRYMES Grymes, Darrell Anthony 6′2″, 182 **WR**
Col: Central State (Ohio) *HS:* Spingarn [Washington, DC] B: 12/4/1961, Washington, DC
1987 Det: 2 G; Rec 9-140 15.6 2 TD; 12 Pt.

CHICK GUARNIERI Guarnieri, George Albert 5′10″, 175 **E**
Col: Niagara; Canisius *HS:* Ashtabula [OH] B: 7/1/1899, Ashtabula, OH D: 4/1980, Ashtabula, OH
1924 Buf: 11 G; Rec 2 TD; 12 Pt. **1925** Can: 1 G. **Total:** 12 G; Rec 2 TD; 12 Pt.

PAT GUCCIARDO Gucciardo, Pasquale John 5′11″, 185 **DB**
Col: Kent State *HS:* Wickliffe [OH] B: 4/21/1944
1966 NYJ: 1 G.

PETE GUDAUSKAS Gudauskas, Peter 6′2″, 219 **G-LB**
(Toe) *Col:* Murray State *HS:* Georgetown Twp. [KY] B: 10/19/1916, Georgetown, IL
1940 Cle: 1 G; Scor 1, 1-2 50.0% XK. **1943** ChiB: 6 G. **1944** ChiB: 10 G; Int 1-26; Scor 36, **36-37** 97.3% XK. **1945** ChiB: 8 G; Int 1-0; Scor 30, 1-2 50.0% FG, 27-27 100.0% XK. **Total:** 25 G; Int 2-26; Scor 67, 1-2 50.0% FG, 64-66 97.0% XK.

LEN GUDD Gudd, Leonard William 6′3″, 212 **OE-DE**
Col: Temple *HS:* Mahanoy City [PA] B: 9/25/1910, Taylor Springs, IL D: 6/5/1992
1934 Phi: 1 G.

HENRY GUDE Gude, Henry Paul 6′1″, 225 **C-G**
Col: Vanderbilt B: 2/25/1919, Memphis, TN *Drafted:* 1942 Round 12 ChiB
1946 Phi: 2 G; KR 1-0.

SCOTT GUDMUNDSON Gudmundson, Wayne Scott 5′10″, 178 **QB-DB**
(Slick; Scotty) *Col:* George Washington B: 4/3/1921, Ogden, UT
1944 Bos: PR 1-27 27.0; KR 3-55 18.3; Punt 12-402 33.5. **1945** Bos: Rec 1-(-8) -8.0; PR 4-36 9.0; Int 2-23; Punt 17-612 36.0. **Total:** Rec 1-(-8) -8.0; PR 5-63 12.6; KR 3-55 18.3; Int 2-23; Punt 29-1014 35.0.

Year Team	G	Passing Att	Comp	Comp%	Yds	YPA	TD	Int	Rating
1944 Bos	7	38	16	42.1	226	5.95	1	4	31.1
1945 Bos	10	43	17	39.5	299	6.95	1	5	32.2
NFL Total	17	81	33	40.7	525	6.48	2	9	31.7

Year Team	Rushing Att	Yds	Avg	TD	Fum
1944 Bos	14	-21	-1.5	0	0
1945 Bos	23	4	0.2	0	3
NFL Total	37	-17	-0.5	0	3

MIKE GUENDLING Guendling, Michael Anthony 6'3", 238 **LB**
Col: Northwestern *HS:* St. Viator [Arlington Heights, IL] B: 6/18/1962, Chicago, IL *Drafted:* 1984 Round 2 SD
1985 SD: 9 G.

JIM GUENO Gueno, James Andre 6'2", 220 **LB**
Col: Tulane *HS:* Crowley [LA] B: 1/15/1954, Crowley, LA
Drafted: 1976 Round 9 GB
1976 GB: 14 G. **1977** GB: 14 G; KR 1-0. **1978** GB: 15 G; KR 1-9 9.0. **1979** GB: 16 G; Rec 1-23 23.0. **1980** GB: 16 G. **Total:** 75 G; Rec 1-23 23.0; KR 2-9 4.5.

DICK GUESMAN Guesman, Richard Eugene 6'4", 255 **DT-K**
Col: West Virginia *HS:* Brownsville [PA] B: 1/22/1938, Brownsville, PA
Drafted: 1959 Round 6 Det
1960 NYT: 10 G. **1961** NYT: 14 G; Scor 39, 5-15 33.3% FG, 24-26 92.3% XK. **1962** NYT: 7 G; Scor 2, 0-1 FG, 2-2 100.0% XK. **1963** NYJ: 14 G; Scor 57, 9-24 37.5% FG, 30-30 100.0% XK. **1964** Den: 14 G; Scor 31, 6-22 27.3% FG, 13-15 86.7% XK. **Total:** 59 G; Scor 129, 20-62 32.3% FG, 69-73 94.5% XK.

TERRY GUESS Guess, Terry 6'0", 200 **WR**
Col: Georgia Mil. Coll. (J.C.); Gardner-Webb *HS:* Edisto [Cordova, SC]
B: 9/22/1974, Orangeburg, SC *Drafted:* 1996 Round 5 NO
1996 NO: 3 G; Rush 2-(-4) -2.0; Rec 2-69 34.5 1 TD; PR 1-7 7.0; 6 Pt.

ROY GUFFEY Guffey, Roy Cornelius 6'0", 194 **OE-T**
Col: Oklahoma *HS:* Shawnee [OK] B: 9/18/1902, Columbus Grove, OH D: 3/25/1994, Dallas, TX
1926 Buf: 9 G; Rec 1 TD; 6 Pt.

NEAL GUGGEMOS Guggemos, Neal Evan 6'0", 187 **DB**
Col: St. Thomas *HS:* Holy Trinity [Winsted, MN] B: 6/14/1964, Winsted, MN
1987 Min: Int 1-26. **Total:** Int 1-26.

		Kickoff Returns				
Year Team	**G**	**Ret**	**Yds**	**Avg**	**TD**	**Fum**
1986 Min	4	0	0	—	0	0
1987 Min	12	36	808	22.4	0	4
1988 NYG	11	17	344	20.2	0	2
NFL Total	27	53	1152	21.7	0	6

RALPH GUGLIELMI Guglielmi, Ralph Vincent 6'1", 196 **QB**
(Goog) *Col:* Notre Dame *HS:* Grandview Heights [OH] B: 6/26/1933, Columbus, OH *Drafted:* 1955 Round 1 Was

		Passing							
Year Team	**G**	**Att**	**Comp**	**Comp%**	**Yds**	**YPA**	**TD**	**Int**	**Rating**
1955 Was	9	62	20	32.3	242	3.90	2	4	29.1
1958 Was	8	81	34	42.0	458	5.65	2	6	38.0
1959 Was	9	89	36	40.4	617	6.93	4	11	40.1
1960 Was	11	223	125	56.1	1547	6.94	9	19	55.7
1961 StL	9	116	56	48.3	927	7.99	5	8	61.2
1962 NYG	14	31	14	45.2	210	6.77	2	1	76.0
1963 NYG-Phi	6	24	7	29.2	118	4.92	0	3	8.0
1963 NYG	2	17	5	29.4	89	5.24	0	3	9.3
1963 Phi	4	7	2	28.6	29	4.14	0	0	44.3
NFL Total	66	626	292	46.6	4119	6.58	24	52	46.5

	Rushing				
Year Team	**Att**	**Yds**	**Avg**	**TD**	**Fum**
1955 Was	18	51	2.8	1	0
1958 Was	17	74	4.4	0	2
1959 Was	26	97	3.7	0	2
1960 Was	79	247	3.1	0	6
1961 StL	22	101	4.6	1	7
1962 NYG	11	40	3.6	0	1
1963 NYG-Phi	4	23	5.8	0	2
1963 NYG	3	3	1.0	0	1
1963 Phi	1	20	20.0	0	1
NFL Total	177	633	3.6	2	20

KEVIN GUIDRY Guidry, Kevin Dale 6'0", 176 **DB**
Col: Louisiana State *HS:* Lake Charles [LA] B: 5/16/1964, Lake Charles, LA *Drafted:* 1988 Round 3 Den
1988 Den: 14 G. **1989** Pho: 3 G. **Total:** 17 G.

PAUL GUIDRY Guidry, Paul Michael 6'3", 227 **LB**
Col: Louisiana State; McNeese State *HS:* Breaux Bridge [LA]
B: 1/14/1944, Breaux Bridge, LA *Drafted:* 1966 Round 8 Buf
1966 Buf: 14 G. **1967** Buf: 14 G; KR 1-0; 1 Fum. **1968** Buf: 14 G; Int 1-21. **1969** Buf: 8 G; Int 2-39. **1970** Buf: 14 G. **1971** Buf: 14 G; Int 1-13. **1972** Buf: 14 G; Int 1-0. **1973** Hou: 14 G. **Total:** 106 G; KR 1-0; Int 5-73; 1 Fum.

RUSTY GUILBEAU Guilbeau, David Ruston 6'4", 242 **LB-DE**
Col: McNeese State *HS:* Sunset [LA] B: 11/20/1958, Opalousas, LA
Drafted: 1982 Round 3 StL
1982 NYJ: 4 G. **1983** NYJ: 16 G; 1 Sac. **1984** NYJ: 16 G. **1985** NYJ: 14 G; 2 Sac. **1986** NYJ: 6 G. **1987** Cle: 1 G. **Total:** 57 G; 3 Sac.

TONY GUILLORY Guillory, Anthony R 6'4", 236 **LB**
Col: Nebraska; Lamar *HS:* Hebert [Beaumont, TX] B: 11/10/1942, Opelousas, LA *Drafted:* 1965 Round 7 LARm
1965 LARm: 14 G. **1967** LARm: 14 G. **1968** LARm: 13 G. **1969** Phi: 12 G. **Total:** 53 G.

JOHN GUILLORY Guillory, John Lee 5'10", 190 **DB**
Col: Merritt Coll. CA (J.C.); Stanford *HS:* St. Mary's Prep [Berkeley, CA]
B: 7/28/1945, Berkeley, CA
1969 Cin: 11 G; PR 1-0; KR 8-170 21.3; Int 1-0; 2 Fum. **1970** Cin: 7 G. **Total:** 18 G; PR 1-0; KR 8-170 21.3; Int 1-0; 2 Fum.

MIKE GULIAN Gulian, Mianese J 6'0", 205 **T**
(Doggie) *Col:* Brown *HS:* Newton [MA] B: 7/29/1900, Marash, Armenia D: 1/10/1970, Boston, MA
1923 Buf: 11 G. **1924** Fra: 14 G. **1925** Prov: 8 G. **1926** Prov: 13 G. **1927** Prov: 2 G. **Total:** 48 G.

ERIC GULIFORD Guliford, Eric Andre 5'8", 170 **WR**
Col: Arizona State *HS:* Peoria [AZ] B: 10/25/1969, Kansas City, KS
1995 Car: Pass 2-1 50.0%, 46 23.00 1 Int; Rush 2-2 1.0. **1997** NO: Rush 1-(-2) -2.0. **Total:** Pass 2-1 50.0%, 46 23.00 1 Int; Rush 3-0.

		Receiving				Punt Returns			
Year Team	**G**	**Rec**	**Yds**	**Avg**	**TD**	**Ret**	**Yds**	**Avg**	**TD**
1993 Min	10	1	45	45.0	0	29	212	7.3	0
1994 Min	7	0	0	—	0	5	14	2.8	0
1995 Car	14	29	444	15.3	1	43	475	11.0	**1**
1997 NO	16	27	362	13.4	1	47	498	10.6	0
1998 NO	5	10	124	12.4	0	10	101	10.1	0
NFL Total	52	67	975	14.6	2	134	1300	9.7	1

	Kickoff Returns					Tot
Year Team	**Ret**	**Yds**	**Avg**	**TD**	**Fum**	**TD**
1993 Min	5	101	20.2	0	1	0
1994 Min	0	0	—	0	1	0
1995 Car	0	0	—	0	1	2
1997 NO	43	1128	26.2	1	2	2
1998 NO	18	431	23.9	0	1	0
NFL Total	66	1660	25.2	1	6	4

DAVID GULLEDGE Gulledge, David 6'1", 203 **DB**
Col: Jacksonville State *HS:* Pell City [AL] B: 10/26/1967, Pell City, AL
Drafted: 1991 Round 11 Was
1992 Was: 4 G.

DON GULSETH Gulseth, Donald Maurice 6'1", 240 **LB**
Col: North Dakota *HS:* Jefferson [Alexandria, MN] B: 9/11/1942, Tracy, MN
1966 Den: 5 G.

GEORGE GULYANICS Gulyanics, George 6'0", 198 **HB-DB**
Col: Jones Co. JC MS; Alabama *HS:* Mishawaka [IN] B: 6/11/1921, Mishawaka, IN D: 1/19/1990, Mishawaka, IN
1947 ChiB: Pass 2-1 50.0%, 55 27.50 1 Int; PR 1-7 7.0; KR 5-124 24.8; Int 2-36. **1949** ChiB: Pass 1-0. **1950** ChiB: Pass 1-1 100.0%, 16 16.00. **Total:** Pass 4-2 50.0%, 71 17.75 1 Int; PR 1-7 7.0; KR 5-124 24.8; Int 2-36.

		Rushing				Receiving			
Year Team	**G**	**Att**	**Yds**	**Avg**	**TD**	**Rec**	**Yds**	**Avg**	**TD**
1947 ChiB	12	35	212	6.1	4	3	22	7.3	0
1948 ChiB	12	119	439	3.7	4	8	130	16.3	1
1949 ChiB	11	102	452	4.4	5	16	165	10.3	1
1950 ChiB	12	146	571	3.9	2	12	137	11.4	0
1951 ChiB	12	105	403	3.8	4	13	146	11.2	0
1952 ChiB	2	2	4	2.0	0	0	0	—	0
NFL Total	61	509	2081	4.1	19	52	600	11.5	2

	Punting				Tot
Year Team	**Punts**	**Yds**	**Avg**	**Fum**	**TD**
1947 ChiB	23	1031	**44.8**	1	4
1948 ChiB	55	2432	44.2	3	5
1949 ChiB	29	1368	47.2	1	6
1950 ChiB	6	201	33.5	6	2
1951 ChiB	0	0	—	4	4
NFL Total	113	5032	44.5	15	21

MIKE GUMAN Guman, Michael Donald 6'2", 216 **RB**
Col: Penn State *HS:* Bethlehem Catholic [Fredericktown, PA]
B: 4/21/1958, Allentown, PA *Drafted:* 1980 Round 6 LARm
1980 LARm: Pass 1-1 100.0%, 31 31.00 1 TD; PR 2-6 3.0; KR 2-25 12.5. **1981** LARm: Pass 1-1 100.0%, 7 7.00 1 TD; KR 1-10 10.0. **1982** LARm: Pass 1-0, 1 Int; KR 8-102 12.8. **1983** LARm: KR 2-30 15.0. **1984** LARm: KR 1-43 43.0 **1** TD. **1985** LARm: KR 2-30 15.0. **1986** LARm: KR 2-28 14.0. **1987** LARm: KR 2-18 9.0. **Total:** Pass 3-2 66.7%, 38 12.67 2 TD 1 Int; PR 2-6 3.0; KR 20-286 14.3 1 TD.

Year Team	G	Rushing Att	Yds	Avg	TD	Receiving Rec	Yds	Avg	TD	Fum	Tot TD
1980 LARm	16	100	410	4.1	4	14	131	9.4	0	4	4
1981 LARm	16	115	433	3.8	4	18	130	7.2	0	2	4
1982 LARm	9	69	266	3.9	2	31	310	10.0	0	3	2
1983 LARm	16	7	42	6.0	0	34	347	10.2	4	0	4
1984 LARm	16	1	2	2.0	0	19	161	8.5	0	0	1
1985 LARm	8	11	32	2.9	0	3	23	7.7	0	0	0
1986 LARm	12	2	2	1.0	0	9	68	7.6	0	1	0
1987 LARm	12	36	98	2.7	1	22	263	12.0	0	0	1
1988 LARm	1	1	1	1.0	0	0	0	—	0	0	0
NFL Total	106	342	1286	3.8	11	150	1433	9.6	4	10	16

ANDY GUMP Gump, Andrew 210 **G-T**
Col: No College Deceased
1922 Col: 3 G.

BOB GUNDERMAN Gunderman, Robert Edward 6′3″, 220 **OE**
Col: Virginia *HS:* Franklin [Somerset, NJ] B: 10/8/1934, Sparta, NJ
Drafted: 1957 Round 19 Det
1957 Pit: 1 G.

HARRY GUNDERSON Gunderson, Arthur Henry 6′2″, 203 **C-G**
(King) *Col:* Iowa *HS:* Rolfe [IA] B: 11/9/1887, Rolfe, IA
D: 11/24/1975, Everett, WA
1920 RI: 4 G. **1921** Min: 4 G. **1922** Min: 2 G. **Total:** 10 G.

HERMAN GUNDLACH Gundlach, Herman Jr. 6′0″, 205 **G**
Col: Harvard *HS:* Houghton [MI]; Worcester Acad. [MA] B: 7/16/1913, Houghton, MI
1935 Bos: 2 G.

JIMMY GUNN Gunn, James 6′1″, 220 **LB**
Col: USC *HS:* Abraham Lincoln [San Diego, CA] B: 11/27/1948, Augusta, AR *Drafted:* 1970 Round 13 ChiB
1970 ChiB: 14 G. **1971** ChiB: 14 G; Int 1-5. **1972** ChiB: 14 G. **1973** ChiB: 3 G. **1974** ChiB: 14 G. **1975** ChiB-NYG: 14 G; Int 1-5. ChiB: 4 G; Int 1-5. NYG: 10 G. **1976** TB: 13 G. **Total:** 86 G; Int 2-10.

LANCE GUNN Gunn, Lance Cameron 6′3″, 222 **DB**
Col: Texas *HS:* North Shore [Houston, TX] B: 1/9/1970, Whiteman AFB, MO *Drafted:* 1993 Round 7 Cin
1993 Cin: 8 G.

MARK GUNN Gunn, Mark Pierre 6′5″, 288 **DE-DT**
Col: Merced Coll. CA (J.C.); Pittsburgh *HS:* Glenville [Cleveland, OH]
B: 7/24/1968, Cleveland, OH *Drafted:* 1991 Round 4 NYJ
1991 NYJ: 15 G. **1992** NYJ: 16 G; 2 Sac. **1993** NYJ: 12 G. **1994** NYJ: 3 G. **1995** Phi: 12 G; 0.5 Sac. **1996** Phi-NYJ: 12 G; 2 Sac. Phi: 3 G. NYJ: 9 G; 2 Sac. **Total:** 70 G; 4.5 Sac.

RILEY GUNNELS Gunnels, John Riley Jr. 6′3″, 253 **DT-DE**
Col: Georgia *HS:* Calhoun [GA] B: 9/24/1937, Atlanta, GA
Drafted: 1959 Round 10 Pit
1960 Phi: 12 G. **1961** Phi: 14 G. **1962** Phi: 14 G. **1963** Phi: 9 G. **1964** Phi: 14 G. **1965** Pit: 14 G. **1966** Pit: 14 G; Int 1-2. **Total:** 91 G; Int 1-2.

HARRY GUNNER Gunner, Harry James 6′6″, 250 **DE**
(The Cisco Kid) *Col:* Cisco JC TX; Oregon State *HS:* Lincoln [Port Arthur, TX] B: 11/25/1944, Port Arthur, TX *Drafted:* 1968 Round 8 Cin
1968 Cin: 14 G; Int 1-20; Scor 1 Saf; 2 Pt. **1969** Cin: 14 G; KR 1-0; Int 1-70 1 TD; 6 Pt; 1 Fum. **1970** ChiB: 14 G. **Total:** 42 G; KR 1-0; Int 2-90 1 TD; Scor 1 Saf; 8 Pt; 1 Fum.

MIKE GUNTER Gunter, Micheal Wayne 5′11″, 205 **RB**
Col: Tulsa *HS:* Gladewater [TX] B: 2/18/1961, Gladewater, TX
Drafted: 1984 Round 4 TB
1984 KC: 4 G; Rush 15-12 0.8.

AL GURSKY Gursky, Albert Lenart 6′1″, 215 **LB**
Col: Penn State *HS:* Governor Mifflin [Shillington, PA] B: 11/23/1940, West Reading, PA *Drafted:* 1962 Round 12 NYG
1963 NYG: 2 G.

MIKE GUSSIE Gussie, Michael 6′0″, 204 **G-LB**
Col: West Virginia B: 9/16/1917, Everettstown, PA D: 2/24/1977, Alexandria, VA *Drafted:* 1940 Round 13 Bkn
1940 Bkn: 8 G; Rec 1-9 9.0 1 TD; 6 Pt.

ED GUSTAFSON Gustafson, Edsel Warren 6′3″, 205 **C-LB**
Col: Dartmouth; George Washington *HS:* Moline [IL] B: 4/4/1922, Moline, IL
AAFC **1947** BknA: 13 G. **1948** BknA: 14 G; Rush 1-7 7.0. **Total:** 27 G; Rush 1-7 7.0.

JIM GUSTAFSON Gustafson, James Joel 6′1″, 177 **WR**
Col: St. Thomas *HS:* Lincoln [Bloomington, MN] B: 3/16/1961, Minneapolis, MN
1987 Min: Rush 1-(-2) -2.0. **Total:** Rush 1-(-2) -2.0.

Year Team	G	Receiving Rec	Yds	Avg	TD
1986 Min	14	5	61	12.2	2
1987 Min	12	4	55	13.8	0
1988 Min	16	15	231	15.4	1
1989 Min	16	14	144	10.3	2
NFL Total	58	38	491	12.9	5

GRANT GUTHRIE Guthrie, Grant Morrow Jr. 6′0″, 210 **K**
Col: Florida State *HS:* Claymont [DE] B: 2/9/1948, Waynesboro, PA
Drafted: 1970 Round 6 Buf
1970 Buf: 14 G; Scor 54, 10-19 52.6% FG, 24-25 96.0% XK. **1971** Buf: 6 G; Scor 17, 3-10 30.0% FG, 8-9 88.9% XK. **Total:** 20 G; Scor 71, 13-29 44.8% FG, 32-34 94.1% XK.

KEITH GUTHRIE Guthrie, Keith Edwin 6′4″, 264 **NT**
Col: Texas A&M *HS:* John Tyler [Tyler, TX] B: 8/17/1961, Tyler, TX
Drafted: 1984 Round 6 SD
1984 SD: 11 G.

BROCK GUTIERREZ Gutierrez, James Brock 6′3″, 300 **C**
Col: Central Michigan *HS:* Charlotte [MI] B: 9/25/1973, Charlotte, MI
1997 Cin: 5 G. **1998** Cin: 1 G. **Total:** 6 G.

AL GUTKNECHT Gutknecht, Albert Rudolph 6′0″, 205 **G-LB**
(Goose; Dutch) *Col:* Niagara *HS:* Arnold [PA] B: 6/11/1917, Arnold, PA D: 3/25/1996, Springdale, PA
1943 Bkn: 2 G. **1944** Cle: 1 G. **Total:** 3 G.

ACE GUTOWSKY Gutowsky, Leroy Erwin 5′11″, 201 **FB-LB-DB-TB**
Col: Oklahoma City *HS:* Kingfisher [OK] B: 8/2/1909, Komolty, Russia
D: 12/4/1976, Oklahoma City, OK
1935 Det: Rec 1-9 9.0. **1936** Det: Rec 1-30 30.0. **1938** Det: Rec 1-25 25.0. **Total:** Rec 3-64 21.3.

Year Team	G	Passing Att	Comp	Comp%	Yds	YPA	TD	Int	Rating
1932 Port	8	3	1	33.3	26	8.67	0	0	66.0
1933 Port	10	11	4	36.4	24	2.18	1	1	37.3
1934 Det	13	12	2	16.7	12	1.00	0	3	0.0
1935 Det	12	9	5	55.6	95	10.56	2	1	92.4
1936 Det	12	13	2	15.4	21	1.62	0	4	0.0
1937 Det	11	8	1	12.5	30	3.75	0	2	3.1
1938 Det	11	7	3	42.9	41	5.86	0	0	62.2
1939 Bkn	9	1	1	100.0	5	5.00	0	0	87.5
NFL Total	86	64	19	29.7	254	3.97	3	11	19.7

Year Team	Rushing Att	Yds	Avg	TD
1932 Port	63	247	3.9	3
1933 Port	103	385	3.7	1
1934 Det	**146**	517	3.5	5
1935 Det	102	296	2.9	2
1936 Det	191	827	4.3	6
1937 Det	128	361	2.8	1
1938 Det	131	444	3.4	2
1939 Bkn	58	202	3.5	0
NFL Total	922	3279	3.6	20

BILL GUTTERON Gutteron, William Alexander 5′5″, 155 **BB**
(Little Giant) *Col:* Nevada-Reno *HS:* San Diego [CA] B: 11/26/1899, Belize D: 5/30/1987, Middleton, WI
1926 LA: 2 G.

CHARLIE GUY Guy, Charles Howgate 6′0″, 170 **C-G-BB**
(Boots) *Col:* Dartmouth; Washington & Jefferson B: 12/5/1896, Schenectady, NY D: 4/9/1974, Tampa, FL
1920 Det: 7 G. **1921** Det-Buf: 12 G. Det: 7 G. Buf: 5 G. **1922** Buf: 10 G. **1923** Cle: 7 G. **1925** Day: 5 G. **Total:** 41 G.

LOUIS GUY Guy, Louis Burton Jr. 6′0″, 190 **DB**
Col: Mississippi *HS:* McComb [MS] B: 5/26/1941, McComb, MS
Drafted: 1963 Round 3 Phi
1963 NYG: 5 G; KR 3-44 14.7; 1 Fum. **1964** Oak: 6 G. **Total:** 11 G; KR 3-44 14.7; 1 Fum.

BUZZ GUY Guy, Melwood Norman 6′3″, 248 **OG-DT-OT**
Col: Duke *HS:* Lincoln [Ellwood City, PA] B: 3/20/1936, New Castle, PA *Drafted:* 1958 Round 3 Cle
1958 NYG: 10 G. **1959** NYG: 12 G. **1960** Dal: 12 G. **1961** Hou-Den: 10 G. Hou: 1 G. Den: 9 G. **Total:** 44 G.

RAY GUY Guy, William Ray 6′3″, 195 **P**
Col: Southern Mississippi *HS:* Thomson [GA] B: 12/22/1949, Swainsboro, GA *Drafted:* 1973 Round 1 Oak
1973 Oak: Rush 1-21 21.0. **1974** Oak: Pass 1-0, 1 Int. **1975** Oak: Pass 1-1 100.0%, 22 22.00. **1976** Oak: Rush 1-0; Scor 0-1 XK. **1980** Oak: Pass 1-1 100.0%, 32 32.00; Rush 3-38 12.7. **1982** LARd: Rush 2-(-3) -1.5. **1983** LARd: Rush 2-(-13) -6.5. **1985** LARd: Rush 1-0. **1986** LARd: Rush 1-0. **Total:** Pass 3-2 66.7%, 54 18.00 1 Int; Rush 11-43 3.9; Scor 0-1 XK.

Year Team	G	Punting Punts	Yds	Avg	Fum
1973 Oak	14	69	3127	45.3	0

1974 Oak	14	74	3124	**42.2**	1
1975 Oak	14	68	2979	**43.8**	0
1976 Oak	14	67	2785	41.6	1
1977 Oak	14	59	2552	**43.3**	0
1978 Oak	16	81	3462	42.7	0
1979 Oak	16	69	2939	42.6	0
1980 Oak	16	71	3099	43.6	0
1981 Oak	16	96	4195	43.7	1
1982 LARd	9	47	1839	39.1	0
1983 LARd	16	78	3336	42.8	0
1984 LARd	16	91	3809	41.9	0
1985 LARd	16	89	3627	40.8	1
1986 LARd	16	90	3620	40.2	1
NFL Total	207	1049	44493	42.4	5

THOMAS GUYNES Guynes, Thomas 6′5″, 300 **OT**
(Hez) *Col:* Michigan *HS:* McNamara [Kankakee, IL] B: 9/9/1974, Marion, IN
1997 Ariz: 4 G.

JOE GUYON Guyon, Joseph Napoleon 5′10″, 195 **TB-WB-BB-FB**
(Brave Man) *Col:* Carlisle; Georgia Tech *HS:* Keewatin Acad. [Prairie Du Chien, WI] B: 11/26/1892, White Earth, MN D: 11/27/1971, Louisville, KY *HOF:* 1966
1920 Can: 13 G. **1921** Was-Cle: 9 G; Pass 1 TD; Rush 2 TD; Int **1** TD; Scor 28, 10 XK; Tot TD 3. Was: 1 G. Cle: 8 G; Pass 1 TD; Rush 2 TD; Int 1 TD; Scor 28, 10 XK; Tot TD 3. **1922** Oor: 9 G; Rush 4 TD; Rec 1 TD; Scor 33, 2 XK, **1** 1XP; Tot TD 5. **1923** Oor: 4 G; Pass 1 TD; Rush 1 TD; Int **1** TD; Tot TD 2; 12 Pt. **1924** RI: 3 G. **1925** KC: 1 G. **1927** NYG: 7 G. **Total:** 46 G; Pass 2 TD; Rush 7 TD; Rec 1 TD; Int 2 TD; Scor 1 1XP; Tot TD 10.

MYRON GUYTON Guyton, Myron Mynard 6′1″, 205 **DB**
Col: Eastern Kentucky *HS:* Central [Thomasville, GA] B: 8/26/1967, Metcalf, GA *Drafted:* 1989 Round 8 NYG
1994 NE: KR 1-(-1) -1.0. **Total:** KR 1-(-1) -1.0.

		Interceptions			
Year Team	**G**	**Int**	**Yds**	**TD**	**Fum**
1989 NYG	16	2	27	0	0
1990 NYG	16	1	0	0	0
1991 NYG	16	0	0	0	0
1992 NYG	4	0	0	0	0
1993 NYG	16	2	34	0	0
1994 NE	16	2	18	0	0
1995 NE	14	3	68	0	1
NFL Total	98	10	147	0	1

JOHN GUZIK Guzik, John Joseph 6′4″, 270 **NT-DE**
Col: Ohio U. *HS:* Midpark [Middleburg Heights, OH] B: 9/25/1962, Cleveland, OH
1987 NE: 3 G.

JOHN GUZIK Guzik, John Paul III 6′3″, 231 **LB**
Col: Pittsburgh *HS:* Cecil Twp. [Venice, PA] B: 7/12/1936, Lawrence, PA *Drafted:* 1958 Round 4 LARm
1959 LARm: 12 G. **1960** LARm: 12 G. **1961** Hou: 3 G. **Total:** 27 G.

ROSS GWINN Gwinn, Charles Ross 6′3″, 273 **OG**
Col: Northwestern State-Louisiana *HS:* Natchitoches Central [LA] B: 7/25/1944, Deport, TX
1968 NO: 2 G.

MILO GWOSDEN Gwosden, Milo Jr. 6′0″, 185 **E**
Col: Indiana (Pa.); Pittsburgh *HS:* Woodlawn [PA] B: 10/20/1898, Angram, Austria D: 10/25/1959, Pittsburgh, PA
1925 Buf: 6 G.

BOB HAAK Haak, Robert Ally 6′1″, 245 **T-G**
(Spanky) *Col:* Indiana *HS:* Hammond [IN] B: 3/26/1916, Hammond, IN D: 11/1/1992, Bloomington, IN *Drafted:* 1939 Round 2 Bkn
1939 Bkn: 10 G.

BRUNO HAAS Haas, Bruno Philip 5′10″, 180 **WB-BB**
(Boon) *Col:* No College *HS:* Worcester Tech [MA] B: 5/5/1891, Worcester, MA D: 6/5/1952, Sarasota, FL
1921 Akr-Cle: 8 G. Akr: 1 G. Cle: 9 G; Rec 1 TD; 6 Pt. **1922** Day: 1 G. **Total:** 11 G; Rec 1 TD; 6 Pt.

BOB HAAS Haas, Robert J **BB-WB**
Col: No College *HS:* Fairmont [Kettering, OH] B: 5/25/1906, Springfield, OH D: 9/1979, Huntsville, OH
1929 Day: 5 G.

ANDY HAASE Haase, Andrew Scott 6′4″, 260 **TE**
Col: Northern Colorado *HS:* Rampart [Colorado Springs, CO] B: 7/10/1974, Odessa, WA
1998 NYG: 7 G; Rec 2-33 16.5.

IRA HAAVEN Haaven, Ira Laen 6′2″, 192 **OE**
(Ike) *Col:* Minnesota-Crookston; Hamline *HS:* McIntosh [MN] B: 6/6/1894, McIntosh, MN D: 6/28/1971, Minneapolis, MN
1923 Dul: 3 G.

BRIAN HABIB Habib, Brian Richard 6′7″, 299 **OT-OG**
Col: Washington *HS:* Ellensburg [WA] B: 12/2/1964, Ellensburg, WA *Drafted:* 1988 Round 10 Min
1989 Min: 16 G. **1990** Min: 16 G. **1991** Min: 16 G. **1992** Min: 16 G. **1993** Den: 16 G. **1994** Den: 16 G. **1995** Den: 16 G. **1996** Den: 16 G. **1997** Den: 14 G. **1998** Sea: 16 G. **Total:** 158 G.

BILL HACHTEN Hachten, William Andrews 6′0″, 210 **G-LB**
(Red Dog) *Col:* California; Stanford *HS:* Huntington Park [CA] B: 11/30/1924, Wichita, KS
1947 NYG: 8 G.

DALE HACKBART Hackbart, Dale Leonard 6′3″, 210 **DB**
Col: Wisconsin *HS:* East [Madison, WI] B: 7/21/1938, Madison, WI *Drafted:* 1960 Round 5 GB
1962 Was: Punt 2-78 39.0. **Total:** Punt 2-78 39.0.

		Interceptions			
Year Team	**G**	**Int**	**Yds**	**TD**	**Fum**
1960 GB	12	0	0	0	0
1961 GB-Was	14	6	128	**2**	0
1961 GB	2	0	0	0	0
1961 Was	12	6	128	2	0
1962 Was	14	3	49	0	0
1963 Was	14	1	7	0	0
1966 Min	14	5	73	1	0
1967 Min	13	2	45	1	0
1968 Min	14	0	0	0	0
1969 Min	12	0	0	0	0
1970 Min	14	0	0	0	0
1971 StL	14	1	11	0	0
1972 StL	14	1	22	0	1
1973 Den	3	0	0	0	0
NFL Total	152	19	335	4	1

JOHNNY HACKENBRUCK Hackenbruck, John Anthony 6′2″, 215 **T**
Col: Oregon State *HS:* The Dalles [OR] B: 10/20/1915, The Dalles, OR D: 10/26/1988, Corvallis, OR *Drafted:* 1940 Round 15 Det
1940 Det: 7 G.

DINO HACKETT Hackett, Barry Dean 6′3″, 228 **LB**
Col: Appalachian State *HS:* Southern Guilford [Greensboro, NC] B: 6/28/1964, Greensboro, NC *Drafted:* 1986 Round 2 KC
1986 KC: 16 G; Int 1-0. **1987** KC: 11 G; 2 Sac. **1988** KC: 13 G; Scor 1 Saf; 2 Pt; 3 Sac. **1989** KC: 13 G. **1990** KC: 16 G; 3 Sac. **1991** KC: 16 G; 1 Sac. **1993** Sea: 3 G. **Total:** 88 G; Int 1-0; Scor 1 Saf; 2 Pt; 9 Sac.

JOEY HACKETT Hackett, Joseph Glenn 6′5″, 267 **TE**
Col: Elon *HS:* Southern Guilford [Greensboro, NC] B: 9/29/1958, Greensboro, NC
1986 Den: 16 G; Rec 3-48 16.0. **1987** GB: 11 G. **1988** GB: 9 G; Rec 1-2 2.0 1 TD; KR 1-9 9.0; 6 Pt. **Total:** 36 G; Rec 4-50 12.5 1 TD; KR 1-9 9.0; 6 Pt.

ELMER HACKNEY Hackney, Elmer Loyd 6′2″, 205 **FB-LB-DB**
(One-Man Gang) *Col:* Kansas State *HS:* Decatur [Oberlin, KS] B: 7/8/1916, Oberlin, KS D: 5/30/1969, Manhattan, KS *Drafted:* 1940 Round 11 Phi
1940 Phi: Rec 2-4 2.0. **1941** Pit: Pass 1-0; Rec 1-10 10.0; PR 1-3 3.0. **1942** Det: Rec 3-22 7.3; KR 1-4 4.0. **1943** Det: Pass 3-1 33.3%, -1 -0.33; Rec 5-51 10.2; PR 1-40 40.0 **1** TD; KR 2-36 18.0; Int 2-94. **1944** Det: Pass 1-1 100.0%, 19 19.00; Rec 8-48 6.0 1 TD; Int 3-41. **Total:** Pass 5-2 40.0%, 18 3.60; Rec 19-135 7.1 1 TD; PR 2-43 21.5 1 TD; KR 3-40 13.3; Int 5-135.

		Rushing					Tot
Year Team	**G**	**Att**	**Yds**	**Avg**	**TD**	**Fum**	**TD**
1940 Phi	8	32	101	3.2	1	0	1
1941 Pit	11	63	253	4.0	1	0	1
1942 Det	8	34	208	6.1	2	0	2
1943 Det	10	27	87	3.2	2	0	3
1944 Det	10	58	184	3.2	4	0	5
1945 Det	8	6	13	2.2	0	1	0
1946 Det	6	0	0	—	0	0	0
NFL Total	61	220	846	3.8	10	1	12

GARY HADD Hadd, Gary Alan 6′4″, 274 **DT-NT**
Col: Minnesota *HS:* Burnsville [MN] B: 10/19/1965, St. Paul, MN *Drafted:* 1988 Round 8 Det
1988 Det: 5 G. **1989** Pho: 10 G. **Total:** 15 G.

AL HADDEN Hadden, Aldous Bernard 5′9″, 186 **WB-FB-TB-HB**
Col: Ohio State; Washington & Jefferson *HS:* V. W. Scott [Toledo, OH] B: 11/8/1899, Toledo, OH D: 2/26/1969, Toledo, OH
1925 Det: 12 G; Rush 1 TD; Rec 3 TD; Tot TD 4; 24 Pt. **1926** Det: 12 G; Rec 1 TD; 6 Pt. **1927** Prov: 10 G. **1928** ChiB-Prov: 10 G. ChiB: 1 G. Prov: 9 G. **1929** Prov: 9 G. **1930** Prov: 9 G. **Total:** 62 G; Rush 1 TD; Rec 4 TD; Tot TD 5; 30 Pt.

MICHAEL HADDIX Haddix, Michael Mcglamery 6'2", 225 **RB**
Col: Mississippi State *HS:* Walnut [MS] B: 12/27/1961, Tippah Co., MS *Drafted:* 1983 Round 1 Phi
1983 Phi: KR 3-51 17.0. **1987** Phi: KR 2-16 8.0. **Total:** KR 5-67 13.4.

		Rushing				Receiving					Tot
Year Team	G	Att	Yds	Avg	TD	Rec	Yds	Avg	TD	Fum	TD
1983 Phi	14	91	220	2.4	2	23	254	11.0	0	4	2
1984 Phi	14	48	130	2.7	1	33	231	7.0	0	2	1
1985 Phi	16	67	213	3.2	0	43	330	7.7	0	2	0
1986 Phi	16	79	276	3.5	0	26	150	5.8	0	1	0
1987 Phi	12	59	165	2.8	0	7	58	8.3	0	1	0
1988 Phi	16	57	185	3.2	0	12	82	6.8	0	1	0
1989 GB	16	44	135	3.1	0	15	111	7.4	1	2	1
1990 GB	16	98	311	3.2	0	13	94	7.2	2	3	2
NFL Total	120	543	1635	3.0	3	172	1310	7.6	3	16	6

WAYNE HADDIX Haddix, Samuel LaWayne 6'1", 203 **DB**
Col: Liberty *HS:* Middleton [TN] B: 7/23/1965, Bolivar, TN
1987 NYG: 5 G. **1988** NYG: 7 G; KR 6-123 20.5; 1 Fum. **1990** TB: 16 G; Int 7-**231 3** TD; 18 Pt; 1 Fum. **1991** TB-Cin: 13 G. TB: 6 G. Cin: 7 G. **Total:** 41 G; KR 6-123 20.5; Int 7-231 3 TD; 18 Pt; 2 Fum.

JACK HADEN Haden, Jack Craydon 6'4", 233 **T**
Col: Arkansas *HS:* Central [Fort Worth, TX] B: 10/2/1914, Fort Worth, TX D: 1/25/1996, Odessa, TX
1936 NYG: 9 G. **1937** NYG: 10 G. **1938** NYG: 11 G. **Total:** 30 G.

NICK HADEN Haden, Nicholas Scott 6'2", 270 **OG-C**
Col: Penn State *HS:* Montour [McKees Rocks, PA] B: 11/7/1962, Pittsburgh, PA *Drafted:* 1985 Round 7 LARd
1986 Phi: 8 G.

PAT HADEN Haden, Patrick Capper 5'11", 182 **QB**
Col: USC *HS:* Bishop Amat [La Puente, CA] B: 1/23/1953, Westbury, NY *Drafted:* 1975 Round 7 LARm

		Passing							
Year Team	G	Att	Comp	Comp%	Yds	YPA	TD	Int	Rating
1976 LARm	10	105	60	57.1	896	8.53	8	4	94.8
1977 LARm	12	216	122	56.5	1551	7.18	11	**6**	84.5
1978 LARm	16	444	229	51.6	2995	6.75	13	19	65.1
1979 LARm	10	290	163	56.2	1854	6.39	11	14	68.1
1980 LARm	4	41	19	46.3	185	4.51	0	4	19.9
1981 LARm	13	267	138	51.7	1815	6.80	9	13	64.4
NFL Total	65	1363	731	53.6	9296	6.82	52	60	69.6

	Rushing				
Year Team	Att	Yds	Avg	TD	Fum
1976 LARm	25	84	3.4	4	0
1977 LARm	29	106	3.7	2	4
1978 LARm	33	206	6.2	0	7
1979 LARm	16	97	6.1	0	4
1980 LARm	3	12	4.0	0	1
1981 LARm	18	104	5.8	0	5
NFL Total	124	609	4.9	6	21

JOHN HADL Hadl, John Willard 6'1", 214 **QB**
Col: Kansas *HS:* Lawrence [KS] B: 2/15/1940, Lawrence, KS
Drafted: 1962 Round 3 SD
1966 SD: Rec 2-(-13) -6.5. **1972** SD: Rec 1-4 4.0. **Total:** Rec 3-(-9) -3.0.

		Passing							
Year Team	G	Att	Comp	Comp%	Yds	YPA	TD	Int	Rating
1962 SD	14	260	107	41.2	1632	6.28	15	24	43.3
1963 SD	14	64	28	43.8	502	7.84	6	6	63.4
1964 SD	14	274	147	53.6	2157	7.87	18	15	78.7
1965 SD	14	348	174	50.0	**2798**	**8.04**	20	21	71.3
1966 SD	14	375	200	53.3	2846	7.59	23	14	83.0
1967 SD	14	427	217	50.8	3365	7.88	24	22	74.5
1968 SD	14	**440**	**208**	47.3	**3473**	7.89	**27**	32	64.5
1969 SD	14	324	158	48.8	2253	6.95	10	11	67.8
1970 SD	14	327	162	49.5	2388	7.30	22	15	77.1
1971 SD	14	**431**	**233**	54.1	**3075**	7.13	**21**	25	68.9
1972 SD	14	370	190	51.4	2449	6.62	15	26	56.7
1973 LARm	14	258	135	52.3	2008	7.78	22	11	88.8
1974 LARm-GB	14	299	142	47.5	1752	5.86	8	14	55.5
1974 LARm	6	115	53	46.1	680	5.91	5	6	57.9
1974 GB	8	184	89	48.4	1072	5.83	3	8	54.0
1975 GB	14	353	191	54.1	2095	5.93	6	21	52.8
1976 Hou	14	113	60	53.1	634	5.61	7	8	60.9
1977 Hou	14	24	11	45.8	76	3.17	0	3	13.9
NFL Total	224	4687	2363	50.4	33503	7.15	244	268	67.4

	Rushing				Punting			
Year Team	Att	Yds	Avg	TD	Punts	Yds	Avg	Fum
1962 SD	40	139	3.5	1	0	0	—	8
1963 SD	8	26	3.3	0	2	75	37.5	0
1964 SD	20	70	3.5	1	62	2447	39.5	6
1965 SD	28	91	3.3	1	38	1544	40.6	**9**
1966 SD	38	95	2.5	2	0	0	—	4
1967 SD	37	107	2.9	3	2	70	35.0	6
1968 SD	23	14	0.6	2	0	0	—	6
1969 SD	26	109	4.2	2	0	0	—	3
1970 SD	28	188	6.7	1	1	30	30.0	3
1971 SD	18	75	4.2	1	0	0	—	4
1972 SD	22	99	4.5	1	0	0	—	7
1973 LARm	14	5	0.4	0	0	0	—	1
1974 LARm-GB	19	25	1.3	0	0	0	—	6
1974 LARm	11	28	2.5	0	0	0	—	2
1974 GB	8	-3	-0.4	0	0	0	—	4
1975 GB	20	47	2.4	0	0	0	—	7
1976 Hou	7	11	1.6	0	0	0	—	2
1977 Hou	3	11	3.7	1	0	0	—	1
NFL Total	351	1112	3.2	16	105	4166	39.7	73

DAVID HADLEY Hadley, David 5'9", 186 **DB**
Col: Alcorn State *HS:* West Amory [Amory, MS] B: 10/8/1948, Amory, MS *Drafted:* 1970 Round 3 KC
1970 KC: 14 G. **1971** KC: 14 G; Int 1-0. **Total:** 28 G; Int 1-0.

RON HADLEY Hadley, Ronald Arthur 6'2", 240 **LB**
Col: Washington *HS:* Boise [ID] B: 11/9/1963, Caldwell, ID
Drafted: 1986 Round 5 NYJ
1987 SF: 3 G. **1988** SF: 3 G. **Total:** 6 G.

JIM HADNOT Hadnot, James Weldon 6'2", 244 **RB**
Col: Texas Tech *HS:* Jasper [TX] B: 7/11/1957, Jasper, TX
Drafted: 1980 Round 3 KC
1981 KC: Pass 1-0, 1 Int. **Total:** Pass 1-0, 1 Int.

		Rushing				Receiving				
Year Team	G	Att	Yds	Avg	TD	Rec	Yds	Avg	TD	Fum
1980 KC	13	76	244	3.2	2	15	97	6.5	0	4
1981 KC	16	140	603	4.3	3	23	215	9.3	0	4
1982 KC	9	46	172	3.7	0	14	96	6.9	0	1
1983 KC	5	4	10	2.5	0	2	18	9.0	0	0
NFL Total	43	266	1029	3.9	5	54	426	7.9	0	9

BARNEY HAFEN Hafen, Banard Ervin 6'2", 195 **OE-DE**
Col: Utah *HS:* Dixie [St. George, UT] B: 11/20/1921, Santa Clara, UT
Drafted: 1948 Round 19 Det
1949 Det: 12 G; Rec 1-10 10.0. **1950** Det: 12 G. **Total:** 24 G; Rec 1-10 10.0.

MIKE HAFFNER Haffner, Michael Arthur 6'2", 200 **WR**
Col: UCLA *HS:* Baldwin Park [CA] B: 7/7/1942, Waterloo, IA
1968 Den: Pass 1-1 100.0%, 18 18.00; Rush 2-2 1.0. **1970** Den: Rush 1-1 1.0. **Total:** Pass 1-1 100.0%, 18 18.00; Rush 3-3 1.0.

		Receiving				
Year Team	G	Rec	Yds	Avg	TD	Fum
1968 Den	14	12	232	19.3	1	0
1969 Den	9	35	563	16.1	5	0
1970 Den	11	12	196	16.3	1	1
1971 Cin	3	0	0	—	0	0
NFL Total	37	59	991	16.8	7	1

ROGER HAGBERG Hagberg, Roger Wheeler 6'1", 215 **RB-TE**
Col: Minnesota *HS:* Rochester [MN] B: 2/28/1939, Winnebago, MN
D: 4/15/1970, Walnut Creek, CA *Drafted:* 1961 Round 10 GB
1965 Oak: PR 1-3 3.0; KR 3-50 16.7. **1966** Oak: KR 1-13 13.0. **1967** Oak: KR 2-12 6.0. **1968** Oak: KR 1-21 21.0. **Total:** PR 1-3 3.0; KR 7-96 13.7.

		Rushing				Receiving					Tot
Year Team	G	Att	Yds	Avg	TD	Rec	Yds	Avg	TD	Fum	TD
1965 Oak	14	48	171	3.6	1	12	121	10.1	0	1	1
1966 Oak	14	62	282	4.5	0	21	248	11.8	1	3	1
1967 Oak	12	44	146	3.3	2	11	114	10.4	1	1	3
1968 Oak	14	39	164	4.2	1	8	78	9.8	1	0	2
1969 Oak	14	1	3	3.0	0	6	84	14.0	1	0	1
NFL Total	68	194	766	3.9	4	58	645	11.1	4	5	8

SWEDE HAGBERG Hagberg, Rudolph E 6'4", 219 **C-WB-FB-T**
Col: West Virginia *HS:* Follansbee [WV] B: 6/18/1907, Charleroi, PA
D: 11/25/1960, Steubenville, OH
1929 Buf: 9 G; Rec 3 TD; 18 Pt. **1930** Bkn: 12 G; Int 1 TD; 6 Pt.
Total: 21 G; Rec 3 TD; Int 1 TD; Tot TD 4; 24 Pt.

FRED HAGEMAN Hageman, Fred John 6'5", 242 **LB-C**
Col: Kansas *HS:* Batesville [AR] B: 6/30/1937, Bunkie, LA
Drafted: 1960 Round 8 NYG
1961 Was: 13 G. **1962** Was: 14 G. **1963** Was: 14 G. **1964** Was: 14 G.
Total: 55 G.

HALVOR HAGEN Hagen, Halvor Reini 6'5", 245 **OG-DE-OT-C**
Col: Shoreline CC WA; Weber State *HS:* Ballard [Seattle, WA]
B: 2/4/1947, Oslo, Norway *Drafted:* 1969 Round 3 Dal
1969 Dal: 12 G. **1970** Dal: 6 G. **1971** NE: 14 G; KR 1-7 7.0. **1972** NE: 12 G. **1973** Buf: 5 G. **1974** Buf: 8 G. **1975** Buf: 13 G. **Total:** 70 G; KR 1-7 7.0.

MIKE HAGEN Hagen, Michael Christopher 6′0″, 240 **RB**
Col: Walla Walla CC WA; Montana *HS:* Auburn [WA] B: 6/30/1959, Auburn, WA
1987 Sea: 2 G; Rush 2-3 1.5.

VERN HAGENBUCKLE Hagenbuckle, Vernon Bertram 5′8″, 185 **OE-G**
(Hookey) *Col:* Dartmouth *HS:* Mount Vernon [NY] B: 12/6/1901, Mount Vernon, NY Deceased
1926 Prov: 2 G.

BRITT HAGER Hager, Britt Harley 6′1″, 231 **LB**
Col: Texas *HS:* Permian [Odessa, TX] B: 2/20/1966, Odessa, TX
Drafted: 1989 Round 3 Phi
1989 Phi: 16 G. **1990** Phi: 16 G; KR 1-0. **1991** Phi: 16 G. **1992** Phi: 10 G. **1993** Phi: 16 G; Int 1-19; 1 Sac. **1994** Phi: 16 G; Int 1-0; 1 Sac. **1995** Den: 16 G; Int 1-19. **1996** Den: 2 G. **1997** StL: 13 G. **Total:** 121 G; KR 1-0; Int 3-38; 2 Sac.

JACK HAGERTY Hagerty, John Leo 5′9″, 164 **TB-WB-BB-FB**
(Black Jack) *Col:* Georgetown *HS:* Dorchester [Boston, MA]
B: 7/3/1903, Boston, MA D: 3/23/1982, Washington, DC
1926 NYG: 10 G; Rush 1 TD; Rec 1 TD; Tot TD 2; 12 Pt. **1927** NYG: 12 G; Rush 1 TD; Rec 1 TD; PR **1** TD; Tot TD 3; 18 Pt. **1928** NYG: 11 G. **1929** NYG: 14 G; Pass 1 TD; Rec 2 TD; KR **1** TD; Tot TD 3; 18 Pt. **1930** NYG: 12 G; Rush 2 TD; Rec 3 TD; Tot TD 5; 30 Pt. **1932** NYG: 4 G; Pass 32-17 **53.1**%, 158 4.94 2 TD 2 Int; Rush 10-22 2.2; Scor 2, 2 XK. **Total:** 63 G; Pass 32-17 53.1%, 158 4.94 3 TD 2 Int; Rush 10-22 2.2 4 TD; Rec 7 TD; PR 1 TD; KR 1 TD; Tot TD 13.

HORSE HAGERTY Hagerty, Loris James 5′10″, 185 **FB-TB**
Col: Iowa *HS:* Greeley [CO] B: 4/16/1905, Blanchard, IA
D: 3/26/1991
1930 Bkn: 9 G.

DOC HAGGERTY Haggerty, John F 6′0″, 205 **G**
Col: Tufts B: 5/9/1895, OH D: 7/1964, NY
1920 Cle-Can: 6 G. Cle: 5 G. Can: 1 G. **1921** NYG: 1 G. **Total:** 7 G.

MIKE HAGGERTY Haggerty, Michael K 6′4″, 245 **OT**
Col: Miami (Fla.) *HS:* Shrine [Royal Oak, MI] B: 10/14/1945, Royal Oak, MI *Drafted:* 1967 Round 6 Pit
1967 Pit: 14 G. **1968** Pit: 1 G. **1969** Pit: 14 G. **1970** Pit: 14 G. **1971** NE: 13 G. **1973** Det: 4 G. **Total:** 60 G.

STEVE HAGGERTY Haggerty, Steven Thomas 5′10″, 175 **WR**
Col: Colorado; Nevada-Las Vegas *HS:* Arapahoe [Littleton, CO]
B: 5/17/1953, Denver, CO *Drafted:* 1975 Round 10 Den
1975 Den: 1 G.

ODELL HAGGINS Haggins, Odell Jr. 6′2″, 278 **NT**
Col: Florida State *HS:* Bartow [FL] B: 2/27/1967, Lakeland, FL
Drafted: 1990 Round 9 SF
1991 Buf: 5 G.

ISAAC HAGINS Hagins, Isaac Ben 5′9″, 179 **WR**
Col: Southern University *HS:* C.E. Byrd [Shreveport, LA] B: 3/2/1954, Shreveport, LA *Drafted:* 1976 Round 9 Min
1976 TB: PR 1-2 2.0. **1977** TB: Rush 1-2 2.0; PR 17-85 5.0. **1978** TB: PR 4-23 5.8. **1980** TB: Rush 3-24 8.0. **Total:** Rush 4-26 6.5; PR 22-110 5.0.

		Receiving				Kickoff Returns				
Year Team	**G**	**Rec**	**Yds**	**Avg**	**TD**	**Ret**	**Yds**	**Avg**	**TD**	**Fum**
1976 TB	1	0	0	—	0	2	35	17.5	0	0
1977 TB	13	15	196	13.1	0	21	493	23.5	0	3
1978 TB	4	6	65	10.8	0	4	69	17.3	0	1
1979 TB	16	39	692	17.7	3	9	196	21.8	0	1
1980 TB	16	23	364	15.8	2	4	82	20.5	0	0
NFL Total	50	83	1317	15.9	5	40	875	21.9	0	5

SCOTT HAGLER Hagler, William Scott 5′8″, 160 **K**
Col: South Carolina *HS:* Dublin [GA] B: 7/19/1964
1987 Sea: 2 G; Scor 10, 2-2 100.0% FG, 4-4 100.0% XK.

JAY HAGOOD Hagood, Jay Dwight 6′4″, 306 **OT**
Col: Virginia Tech *HS:* Easley [SC]; Fork Union Mil. Acad. [VA]
B: 8/9/1973, Easley, SC
1997 NYJ: 2 G.

RICKEY HAGOOD Hagood, Rickey Gabriel 6′2″, 286 **NT**
Col: South Carolina *HS:* Wren [Piedmont, SC] B: 4/24/1961, Easley, SC *Drafted:* 1984 Round 4 Sea
1984 SD: 2 G.

JOHN HAGY Hagy, John Kevin 5′11″, 190 **DB**
Col: Texas *HS:* John Marshall [San Antonio, TX] B: 12/9/1965, Okinawa *Drafted:* 1988 Round 8 Buf
1988 Buf: 3 G. **1989** Buf: 9 G. **1990** Buf: 16 G; Int 2-23. **Total:** 28 G; Int 2-23.

RAY HAHN Hahn, Raymond Dryer 5′10″, 190 **OE**
Col: Kansas State *HS:* Clay Center [KS] B: 11/19/1897, Clay Center, KS D: 11/8/1989, McPherson, KS
1926 Ham: 3 G.

MIKE HAIGHT Haight, Michael James 6′4″, 281 **OG-OT**
Col: Iowa *HS:* Beckman [Dyersville, IA] B: 10/6/1962, Manchester, IA
Drafted: 1986 Round 1 NYJ
1986 NYJ: 2 G. **1987** NYJ: 6 G. **1988** NYJ: 14 G. **1989** NYJ: 13 G. **1990** NYJ: 14 G. **1991** NYJ: 7 G. **1992** Was: 7 G. **Total:** 63 G.

MAC HAIK Haik, Joseph Michael 6′1″, 195 **WR**
Col: Mississippi *HS:* Meridian [MS] B: 1/19/1946, Meridian, MS
Drafted: 1968 Round 2 Hou
1968 Hou: Rush 2-7 3.5. **1969** Hou: Rush 2-21 10.5. **Total:** Rush 4-28 7.0.

		Receiving				
Year Team	**G**	**Rec**	**Yds**	**Avg**	**TD**	**Fum**
1968 Hou	14	32	584	18.3	8	0
1969 Hou	13	27	375	13.9	1	1
1970 Hou	13	17	190	11.2	0	3
1971 Hou	4	0	0	—	0	0
NFL Total	44	76	1149	15.1	9	4

BY HAINES Haines, Byron Dalton 5′11″, 185 **HB-DB**
Col: Washington *HS:* Bend [OR] B: 11/30/1914, Bend, OR
Drafted: 1937 Round 7 Pit
1937 Pit: 5 G; Pass 6-1 16.7%, 14 2.33 1 Int; Rush 24-29 1.2; Rec 2-17 8.5.

KRIS HAINES Haines, David Kris 5′11″, 183 **WR**
Col: Notre Dame *HS:* Sidney [OH] B: 7/23/1957, Akron, OH
Drafted: 1979 Round 9 Was
1979 Was-ChiB: 3 G. Was: 1 G. ChiB: 2 G. **1980** ChiB: 16 G; Rec 4-83 20.8; KR 1-0. **1981** ChiB: 1 G. **1987** Buf: 1 G. **Total:** 21 G; Rec 4-83 20.8; KR 1-0.

HOOT HAINES Haines, Harry Jepson 6′0″, 205 **T-G-OE**
(Red) *Col:* Colgate *HS:* Germantown [Philadelphia, PA] B: 2/25/1907, Philadelphia, PA D: 8/17/1965, Brighton, NY
1930 Bkn: 8 G. **1931** Bkn-SI: 9 G. Bkn: 7 G. SI: 2 G. **Total:** 17 G.

HINKEY HAINES Haines, Henry Luther 5′10″, 170 **TB-BB-FB-WB**
Col: Lebanon Valley; Penn State *HS:* Red Lion [PA] B: 12/23/1898, Red Lion, PA D: 1/9/1979, Sharon Hill, PA
1925 NYG: 11 G; Rush 2 TD; Rec 1 TD; Tot TD 3; 18 Pt. **1926** NYG: 12 G; Rush 5 TD; Rec 1 TD; Tot TD 6; 36 Pt. **1927** NYG: 13 G; Rush 1 TD; Rec **4** TD; PR **1** TD; Tot TD **6**; 36 Pt. **1928** NYG: 9 G; Rush 4 TD; PR **1** TD; Tot TD 5; 30 Pt. **1929** SI: 4 G; Pass 1 TD; Rush 2 TD; 12 Pt. **1931** SI: 4 G. **Total:** 53 G; Pass 1 TD; Rush 14 TD; Rec 6 TD; PR 2 TD; Tot TD 22; 132 Pt.

JOHN HAINES Haines, John Yancy 6′6″, 266 **NT-DE-DT**
Col: Texas *HS:* Arlington Heights [Fort Worth, TX] B: 12/16/1961, Fort Worth, TX *Drafted:* 1984 Round 7 Min
1984 Min: 8 G; 2 Sac. **1986** Ind: 11 G. **Total:** 19 G; 2 Sac.

CARL HAIRSTON Hairston, Carl Blake 6′3″, 260 **DE-DT-LB**
Col: Maryland East. Shore *HS:* Martinsville [VA] B: 12/15/1952, Martinsville, VA *Drafted:* 1976 Round 7 Phi
1976 Phi: 14 G. **1977** Phi: 14 G. **1978** Phi: 16 G. **1979** Phi: 15 G. **1980** Phi: 16 G; Int 1-0. **1981** Phi: 16 G. **1982** Phi: 9 G; 4 Sac. **1983** Phi: 16 G; 5 Sac. **1984** Cle: 16 G; 4 Sac. **1985** Cle: 16 G; 7 Sac. **1986** Cle: 16 G; 9 Sac. **1987** Cle: 14 G; Int 0-40; 8 Sac. **1988** Cle: 14 G; 3 Sac. **1989** Cle: 16 G; 6.5 Sac. **1990** Pho: 16 G; 1 Sac. **Total:** 224 G; Int 1-40; 47.5 Sac.

RUSSELL HAIRSTON Hairston, Russell Jonathan 6′3″, 208 **DB**
Col: Kentucky *HS:* Eleanor Roosevelt [Greenbelt, MD] B: 2/10/1964
1987 Pit: 3 G; Rec 2-16 8.0 1 TD; 6 Pt; 1 Fum.

STACEY HAIRSTON Hairston, Stacey 5′9″, 185 **DB**
Col: Ohio Northern *HS:* South [Columbus, OH] B: 8/16/1967, Columbus, OH
1993 Cle: 16 G. **1994** Cle: 15 G. **Total:** 31 G.

CHUCK HAJEK Hajek, Charles Joseph 6′1″, 210 **C-LB**
Col: South Carolina; Northwestern *HS:* J. Sterling Morton [Cicero, IL]
B: 11/11/1910, Chicago, IL D: 2/21/1979, Centerport, NY
1934 Phi: 11 G.

ALI HAJI-SHEIKH Haji-Sheikh, Ali 6′0″, 172 **K**
Col: Michigan *HS:* Arlington [TX] B: 1/11/1961, Ann Arbor, MI
Drafted: 1983 Round 9 NYG

		Scoring						
Year Team	**G**	**Pts**	**FG**	**FGA**	**FG%**	**XK**	**XKA**	**XK%**
1983 NYG	16	127	**35**	42	83.3	22	23	95.7
1984 NYG	16	83	17	33	51.5	32	35	91.4
1985 NYG	2	11	2	5	40.0	5	5	100.0
1986 Atl	6	34	9	12	75.0	7	8	87.5
1987 Was	11	68	13	19	68.4	29	32	90.6
NFL Total	51	323	76	111	68.5	95	103	92.2

AZ-ZAHIR HAKIM Hakim, Az-zahir Ali 5'10", 179 **WR**
Col: San Diego State *HS:* Fairfax [Los Angeles, CA] B: 6/3/1977, Los Angeles, CA *Drafted:* 1998 Round 4 StL
1998 StL: 9 G; Rush 2-30 15.0 1 TD; Rec 20-247 12.4 1 TD; Tot TD 2; 12 Pt; 1 Fum.

MIKE HALAPIN Halapin, Richard Michael 6'4", 294 **DT**
Col: Pittsburgh *HS:* Kiski Area [Vandergrift, PA] B: 7/1/1973, New Kensington, PA
1996 Hou: 9 G. **1997** Ten: 3 G. **Total:** 12 G.

GEORGE HALAS Halas, George Stanley 6'0", 182 **OE**
(Papa Bear) *Col:* Illinois *HS:* Crane [Chicago, IL] B: 2/2/1895, Chicago, IL D: 10/31/1983, Chicago, IL *HOF:* 1963
1920 Sta: 12 G. **1921** Sta: 11 G; Rec **3** TD; 18 Pt. **1922** ChiB: 12 G; Rush 1 TD; Rec 1 TD; Scor 2 1XP; Tot TD 2; 14 Pt. **1923** ChiB: 13 G; 1 Fum TD; 6 Pt. **1924** ChiB: 11 G. **1925** ChiB: 17 G. **1926** ChiB: 15 G. **1927** ChiB: 10 G; Rec 1 TD; Int 1 TD; 1 Fum TD; Tot TD 3; 18 Pt. **1928** ChiB: 4 G; Rec 1 TD; 6 Pt. **Total:** 105 G; Rush 1 TD; Rec 6 TD; Int 1 TD; Scor 2 1XP; 2 Fum TD; Tot TD 10; 62 Pt.

CHRIS HALE Hale, Christopher 5'7", 164 **DB**
Col: Glendale CC AZ; Nebraska; USC *HS:* Monrovia [CA] B: 1/4/1966, Monrovia, CA *Drafted:* 1989 Round 7 Buf
1989 Buf: 16 G. **1990** Buf: 8 G; PR 10-76 7.6. **1991** Buf: 5 G; Int 1-0. **1992** Buf: 14 G; PR 14-175 12.5; Scor 1 Saf; 2 Pt. **Total:** 43 G; PR 24-251 10.5; Int 1-0; Scor 1 Saf; 2 Pt.

DAVE HALE Hale, David Robert 6'8", 255 **DT-DE**
(Hondo) *Col:* Ottawa (Ks) *HS:* Benson [Omaha, NE] B: 6/21/1947, McCook, NE *Drafted:* 1969 Round 12 ChiB
1969 ChiB: 3 G. **1970** ChiB: 14 G. **1971** ChiB: 12 G. **1973** ChiB: 1 G. **Total:** 30 G.

ART HALEY Haley, Arthur Reed 5'10", 175 **TB-WB**
Col: Akron *HS:* Cuyahoga Falls [OH] B: 1895, Beaver Falls, PA D: 2/14/1946, Zanesville, OH
1920 Can: 1 G. **1921** Day: 2 G. **1923** Akr: 3 G. **Total:** 6 G.

CHARLES HALEY Haley, Charles Lewis 6'5", 242 **DE-LB**
Col: James Madison *HS:* William Campbell [Naruna, VA] B: 1/6/1964, Gladys, VA *Drafted:* 1986 Round 4 SF
1986 SF: 16 G; Int 1-8; 1 Fum; 12 Sac. **1987** SF: 12 G; 6.5 Sac. **1988** SF: 16 G; Scor 1 Saf; 2 Pt; 11.5 Sac. **1989** SF: 16 G; 1 Fum TD; 6 Pt; 10.5 Sac. **1990** SF: 16 G; 16 Sac. **1991** SF: 14 G; 7 Sac. **1992** Dal: 15 G; 6 Sac. **1993** Dal: 14 G; 4 Sac. **1994** Dal: 16 G; Int 1-1; 12.5 Sac. **1995** Dal: 13 G; 10.5 Sac. **1996** Dal: 5 G; 1 Sac. **1998** SF: Postseason only. **Total:** 153 G; Int 2-9; Scor 1 Saf; 1 Fum TD; 8 Pt; 1 Fum; 97.5 Sac.

DARRYL HALEY Haley, Darryl 6'4", 269 **OT-OG**
Col: Utah *HS:* Alain Leroy Locke [Los Angeles, CA] B: 2/16/1961, Los Angeles, CA *Drafted:* 1982 Round 2 NE
1982 NE: 9 G. **1983** NE: 16 G. **1984** NE: 16 G. **1986** NE: 16 G. **1987** Cle: 9 G. **1988** GB: 13 G. **Total:** 79 G.

DICK HALEY Haley, George Richard Jr. 5'10", 193 **DB-HB-FL-OE**
Col: Pittsburgh *HS:* Midway [PA] B: 10/2/1937, Midway, PA *Drafted:* 1959 Round 9 Was
1959 Was: Rush 14-51 3.6 1 TD; Rec 2-14 7.0; PR 7-15 2.1. **1960** Was: Rec 3-21 7.0. **1961** Min-Pit: Rec 3-43 14.3. Min: Rec 3-43 14.3. **1962** Pit: PR 1-13 13.0. **1963** Pit: PR 12-59 4.9. **Total:** Rush 14-51 3.6 1 TD; Rec 8-78 9.8; PR 20-87 4.4.

		Kickoff Returns				Interceptions				Tot
Year Team	**G**	**Ret**	**Yds**	**Avg**	**TD**	**Int**	**Yds**	**TD**	**Fum**	**TD**
1959 Was	12	17	346	20.4	0	1	15	0	2	1
1960 Was	10	0	0	—	0	0	0	0	0	0
1961 Min-Pit	12	13	278	21.4	0	1	0	0	1	0
1961 Min	4	0	0	—	0	0	0	0	1	0
1961 Pit	8	13	278	21.4	0	1	0	0	0	0
1962 Pit	14	7	105	15.0	0	4	26	0	0	0
1963 Pit	14	0	0	—	0	6	65	1	1	1
1964 Pit	13	0	0	—	0	2	11	0	0	0
NFL Total	75	37	729	19.7	0	14	117	1	4	2

RONNIE HALIBURTON Haliburton, Ronnie Maurice 6'4", 230 **TE**
Col: Louisiana State *HS:* Lincoln [Port Arthur, TX] B: 4/14/1968, New Orleans, LA *Drafted:* 1990 Round 6 Den
1990 Den: 9 G. **1991** Den: 8 G. **Total:** 17 G.

EDDIE HALICKI Halicki, Edward Henry 5'9", 185 **TB-FB-WB-HB**
Col: Bucknell *HS:* Hanover Area [Wilkes-Barre, PA] B: 12/23/1905, Kingston, PA D: 4/27/1986, Ashley, PA
1929 Fra: 17 G; Rush 3 TD; Rec 3 TD; Scor 45, 1 FG, 6 XK; Tot TD 6. **1930** Fra-Min: 14 G; Pass 1 TD; Rush 3 TD; Rec 1 TD; Scor 30, 5 XK, **1** 1XP; Tot TD 4. Fra: 13 G; Pass 1 TD; Rush 3 TD; Rec 1 TD; Scor 29, 5 XK; Tot TD 4. Min: 1 G. **Total:** 31 G; Pass 1 TD; Rush 6 TD; Rec 4 TD; Scor 74, 1 FG, 11 XK; Tot TD 10.

ALVIN HALL Hall, Alvin 6'0", 198 **DB**
HS: Wendell Phillips [Chicago, IL] B: 8/12/1934, Fayette, MS
1961 LARm: 9 G; Int 0-10. **1962** LARm: 14 G; PR 4-21 5.3; KR 8-178 22.3; Int 1-0; 1 Fum. **1963** LARm: 3 G; KR 1-0. **Total:** 26 G; PR 4-21 5.3; KR 9-178 19.8; Int 1-10; 1 Fum.

ALVIN HALL Hall, Alvin Eugene 5'10", 193 **DB**
Col: Miami (Ohio) *HS:* Fairview [Dayton, OH] B: 8/12/1958, Dayton, OH
1981 Det: Int 1-60 1 TD. **1982** Det: Int 1-2. **1983** Det: PR 8-109 13.6; Int 2-18. **1984** Det: PR 7-30 4.3; Int 2-64. **1985** Det: 1 Sac. **1987** Det: Int 1-0. **Total:** PR 15-139 9.3; Int 7-144 1 TD; 1 Sac.

		Kickoff Returns					Tot
Year Team	**G**	**Ret**	**Yds**	**Avg**	**TD**	**Fum**	**TD**
1981 Det	16	25	525	21.0	0	1	1
1982 Det	9	16	426	26.6	**1**	1	1
1983 Det	16	23	492	21.4	0	1	0
1984 Det	16	19	385	20.3	0	3	0
1985 Det	16	39	886	22.7	0	2	0
1987 Det	3	6	105	17.5	0	1	0
NFL Total	76	128	2819	22.0	1	9	2

CHRIS HALL Hall, Charles Christopher 6'2", 184 **SAF**
Col: East Carolina *HS:* Pemberton Twp. [Pemberton, NJ] B: 4/25/1970, Fort Dix, NJ *Drafted:* 1992 Round 9 Dal
1993 Dal: 1 G.

KEN HALL Hall, Charles Kenneth 6'1", 205 **HB-P**
(The Sugarland E) *Col:* Texas A&M *HS:* Sugar Land [TX] B: 12/13/1935, Sugar Land, TX *Drafted:* 1958 Round 14 Bal
1959 ChiC: Rec 4-60 15.0 1 TD; PR 3-91 30.3 1 TD. **1960** Hou: PR 6-72 12.0; Punt 6-210 35.0. **1961** Hou-StL: Rec 4-58 14.5 1 TD; PR 2-1 0.5; Punt 8-238 29.8. Hou: Rec 1-20 20.0 1 TD; PR 2-1 0.5; Punt 8-238 29.8. StL: Rec 3-38 12.7. **Total:** Rec 8-118 14.8 2 TD; PR 11-164 14.9 1 TD; Punt 14-448 32.0.

		Rushing				Kickoff Returns					Tot
Year Team	**G**	**Ret**	**Yds**	**Avg**	**TD**	**Ret**	**Yds**	**Avg**	**TD**	**Fum**	**TD**
1959 ChiC	12	14	81	5.8	0	6	99	16.5	0	3	2
1960 Hou	11	30	118	3.9	0	19	594	**31.3**	1	3	1
1961 Hou-StL	11	7	13	1.9	0	6	140	23.3	0	0	1
1961 Hou	3	7	13	1.9	0	6	140	23.3	0	0	1
1961 StL	8	0	0	—	0	0	0	—	0	0	0
NFL Total	34	51	212	4.2	0	31	833	26.9	1	6	4

CHARLIE HALL Hall, Charles Leslie 6'3", 220 **LB**
Col: Houston *HS:* Yoakum [TX] B: 12/2/1948, Yoakum, TX *Drafted:* 1971 Round 3 Cle
1973 Cle: PR 1-0. **1975** Cle: **1** Fum TD. **Total:** PR 1-0; 1 Fum TD.

		Interceptions			Tot
Year Team	**G**	**Int**	**Yds**	**TD**	**TD**
1971 Cle	14	0	0	0	0
1972 Cle	14	1	12	0	0
1973 Cle	14	0	0	0	0
1974 Cle	14	3	54	1	1
1975 Cle	14	2	28	0	1
1976 Cle	14	1	12	0	0
1977 Cle	14	1	2	0	0
1978 Cle	16	1	6	0	0
1979 Cle	16	2	14	0	0
1980 Cle	16	2	3	0	0
NFL Total	146	13	131	1	2

CHARLIE HALL Hall, Charles Val Jr. 6'1", 195 **DB**
Col: Pittsburgh *HS:* Lower Merion [Ardmore, PA] B: 3/31/1948, Philadelphia, PA D: 5/14/1998, Orangeburg County, SC *Drafted:* 1971 Round 3 GB
1971 GB: 14 G. **1972** GB: 14 G. **1973** GB: 13 G. **1974** GB: 14 G; Int 2-22. **1975** GB: 14 G; PR 1-0; 1 Fum. **1976** GB: 14 G; Rec 1-18 18.0. **Total:** 83 G; Rec 1-18 18.0; PR 1-0; Int 2-22; 1 Fum.

COURTNEY HALL Hall, Courtney Caesar 6'1", 281 **C-OG**
Col: Rice *HS:* Phineas Banning [Los Angeles, CA] B: 8/26/1968, Los Angeles, CA *Drafted:* 1989 Round 2 SD
1989 SD: 16 G; 1 Fum. **1990** SD: 16 G. **1991** SD: 16 G. **1992** SD: 16 G. **1993** SD: 16 G. **1994** SD: 15 G. **1995** SD: 16 G. **1996** SD: 7 G. **Total:** 118 G; 1 Fum.

DANA HALL Hall, Dana Eric 6'3", 208 **DB**
Col: Washington *HS:* Ganesha [Pomona, CA] B: 7/8/1969, Bellflower, CA *Drafted:* 1992 Round 1 SF
1992 SF: 15 G; Int 2-34; 1 Sac. **1993** SF: 13 G. **1994** SF: 16 G; Int 2-0. **1995** Cle: 15 G; Int 2-41; 1 Sac. **1996** Jac: 16 G; Int 1-20. **1997** Jac: 16 G; Rec 1-22 22.0. **Total:** 91 G; Rec 1-22 22.0; Int 7-95; 2 Sac.

DARRYL HALL Hall, Darryl Cavada 5'10", 185 **DB**
Col: Long Beach City Coll. CA (J.C.); San Diego State *HS:* R.A. Millikan [Long Beach, CA] B: 10/23/1959, Greensboro, NC
1987 LARm: 1 G.

DARRYL HALL Hall, Darryl Edgar 6′2″, 210 **DB**
Col: Washington *HS:* Lompoc [CA] B: 8/1/1966, Oscoda, MI
1993 Den: 16 G; Int 1-0. **1994** Den: 16 G. **1995** SF: 12 G. **Total:** 44 G; Int 1-0.

DELTON HALL Hall, Delton Dwayne 6′1″, 202 **DB**
Col: Clemson *HS:* Grimsley [Greensboro, NC] B: 1/16/1965, Greensboro, NC *Drafted:* 1987 Round 2 Pit
1987 Pit: 12 G; Int 3-29 1 TD; **1** Fum TD; Tot TD 2; 12 Pt; 1 Fum. **1988** Pit: 14 G. **1989** Pit: 16 G; Int 1-6. **1990** Pit: 12 G; Int 1-0. **1991** Pit: 6 G. **1992** SD: 16 G; 1 Sac. **Total:** 76 G; Int 5-35 1 TD; 1 Fum TD; Tot TD 2; 12 Pt; 1 Fum; 1 Sac.

DINO HALL Hall, Donald Richard 5′7″, 165 **RB**
Col: Rowan *HS:* Pleasantville [NJ] B: 12/6/1955, Atlantic City, NJ
1979 Cle: Rec 2-14 7.0. **1982** Cle: Rec 5-78 15.6 1 TD. **1983** Cle: Rec 4-33 8.3. **Total:** Rec 11-125 11.4 1 TD.

		Rushing				Punt Returns			
Year Team	**G**	**Att**	**Yds**	**Avg**	**TD**	**Ret**	**Yds**	**Avg**	**TD**
1979 Cle	11	22	152	6.9	1	29	295	10.2	0
1980 Cle	16	2	26	13.0	0	6	41	6.8	0
1981 Cle	12	0	0	—	0	33	248	7.5	0
1982 Cle	9	2	14	7.0	0	4	33	8.3	0
1983 Cle	16	1	2	2.0	0	39	284	7.3	0
NFL Total	64	27	194	7.2	1	111	901	8.1	0

	Kickoff Returns					Tot
Year Team	**Ret**	**Yds**	**Avg**	**TD**	**Fum**	**TD**
1979 Cle	50	1014	20.3	0	5	1
1980 Cle	32	691	21.6	0	0	0
1981 Cle	36	813	22.6	0	5	0
1982 Cle	22	430	19.5	0	0	1
1983 Cle	11	237	21.5	0	0	0
NFL Total	151	3185	21.1	0	10	2

FORREST HALL Hall, Forrest John 5′8″, 158 **RB**
(Scooter) *Col:* Duquesne; San Francisco *HS:* St. Joseph's Prep [Philadelphia, PA] B: 10/29/1921, Oil City, PA
AAFC **1948** SF-A: Rec 4-87 21.8; PR 3-97 32.3; KR 13-369 28.4.

		Rushing			
Year Team	**G**	**Att**	**Yds**	**Avg**	**TD**
1948 SF-A	14	66	413	6.3	2

GALEN HALL Hall, Galen Samuel 5′10″, 216 **QB**
Col: Penn State *HS:* Williamsburg [PA] B: 8/14/1940, Altoona, PA
1962 Was: Rush 2-2 1.0 1 TD. **1963** NYJ: Rush 9-24 2.7 1 TD. **Total:** Rush 11-26 2.4 2 TD.

		Passing								
Year Team	**G**	**Att**	**Comp**	**Comp%**	**Yds**	**YPA**	**TD**	**Int**	**Rating**	**Fum**
1962 Was	3	32	19	59.4	274	8.56	2	1	95.1	0
1963 NYJ	13	118	45	38.1	611	5.18	3	9	32.1	4
NFL Total	16	150	64	42.7	885	5.90	5	10	45.6	4

HAROLD HALL Hall, Harold Benjamin 6′2″, 210 **C-LB**
Col: Springfield *HS:* Erasmus Hall [Brooklyn, NY] B: 4/29/1914, Brooklyn, NY D: 8/4/1992, Longwood, FL
1942 NYG: 1 G.

HARRY HALL Hall, Harry Archibald 5′11″, 165 **BB-TB**
(Swede) *Col:* Chicago; Illinois *HS:* Waukegan [IL] B: 10/5/1902, Waukegan, IL D: 2/25/1951, Minneapolis, MN
1925 RI: 1 G.

RAY HALL Hall, Hayward Ray 6′4″, 294 **DT**
Col: Washington State *HS:* Bishop O'Dea [Seattle, WA] B: 3/2/1971, Seattle, WA
1995 Jac: 12 G.

IRV HALL Hall, Irving Alger Jr. 6′0″, 210 **FB-LB**
(Shine) *Col:* Brown *HS:* Tilton [Melrose, MA]; Dean Acad. [Franklin, MA] B: 11/23/1913, Raynham, MA D: 1/24/1964, Orlando, FL
Drafted: 1939 Round 16 Phi
1942 Phi: 8 G; Rush 8-14 1.8; Rec 2-18 9.0; KR 1-22 22.0; Punt 1-36 36.0.

JAMES HALL Hall, James 6′1″, 252 **LB**
Col: Northwestern State-Louisiana *HS:* North [Natchez, MS]
B: 1/27/1963, Natchez, MS
1987 Atl: 3 G.

JOHN HALL Hall, John 6′3″, 222 **K**
Col: Wisconsin *HS:* Port Charlotte [FL] B: 3/17/1974, Port Charlotte, FL
1997 NYJ: Punt 3-144 48.0. **Total:** Punt 3-144 48.0.

		Scoring						
Year Team	**G**	**Pts**	**FG**	**FGA**	**FG%**	**XK**	**XKA**	**XK%**
1997 NYJ	16	120	28	**41**	68.3	36	36	100.0
1998 NYJ	16	120	25	35	71.4	45	46	97.8
NFL Total	32	240	53	76	69.7	81	82	98.8

JOHNNY HALL Hall, John Robert 6′0″, 196 **WB-DB**
Col: Texas Christian *HS:* Kaufman [TX] B: 12/14/1916, Kaufman, TX
Drafted: 1939 Round 7 GB
1940 ChiC: Pass 3-0, 2 Int; KR **1** TD; Int 1-50 **1** TD. **1941** ChiC: Pass 1-0; KR 6-140 23.3. **1942** Det: Pass 1-0; PR 4-38 9.5; KR 4-86 21.5; Int 1-9. **1943** ChiC: Pass 4-2 50.0%, 24 6.00 2 Int; PR 1-17 17.0; KR 2-35 17.5; Int 2-49. **Total:** Pass 9-2 22.2%, 24 2.67 4 Int; PR 5-55 11.0; KR 12-261 21.8 1 TD; Int 4-108 1 TD.

		Rushing				Receiving				Tot
Year Team	**G**	**Att**	**Yds**	**Avg**	**TD**	**Rec**	**Yds**	**Avg**	**TD**	**TD**
1940 ChiC	11	41	88	2.1	1	4	111	27.8	2	5
1941 ChiC	11	53	165	3.1	2	16	302	18.9	2	4
1942 Det	7	2	-8	-4.0	0	1	42	42.0	0	0
1943 ChiC	8	22	51	2.3	0	7	82	11.7	1	1
NFL Total	37	118	296	2.5	3	28	537	19.2	5	10

JOHN HALL Hall, John Wesley Jr. 6′1″, 220 **DE**
Col: Iowa *HS:* Crane [Chicago, IL] B: 6/30/1933, Chicago, IL
Drafted: 1955 Round 3 Cle
1955 NYG: 2 G.

LEMANSKI HALL Hall, Lemanski 6′0″, 231 **LB**
Col: Alabama *HS:* Valley [AL] B: 11/24/1970, Valley, AL
Drafted: 1994 Round 7 Hou
1995 Hou: 12 G. **1996** Hou: 3 G. **1997** Ten: 16 G; 2 Sac. **1998** ChiB: 15 G. **Total:** 46 G; 2 Sac.

PARKER HALL Hall, Linus Parker 6′0″, 198 **QB-HB**
(Bullet) *Col:* Mississippi *HS:* Tunica [MS] B: 12/10/1916, Tunica, MS
Drafted: 1939 Round 1 Cle
AAFC **1946** SF-A: 11 G; Pass 8-2 25.0%, 15 1.88; Rush 17-31 1.8; Rec 2-25 12.5; KR 1-22 22.0.

NFL **1939** Cle: Rec 1-(-16) -16.0. **1940** Cle: Int 2-0. **1941** Cle: KR 7-131 18.7; Int 2-0. **1942** Cle: KR 10-155 15.5; Int 3-60. **Total:** Rec 1-(-16) -16.0; KR 17-286 16.8; Int 7-60.

		Passing							
Year Team	**G**	**Att**	**Comp**	**Comp%**	**Yds**	**YPA**	**TD**	**Int**	**Rating**
1939 Cle	11	**208**	**106**	51.0	1227	5.90	9	13	57.5
1940 Cle	11	183	77	42.1	1108	6.05	7	16	38.7
1941 Cle	10	190	84	44.2	863	4.54	7	19	30.5
1942 Cle	10	140	62	44.3	815	5.82	7	19	40.3
NFL Total	42	721	329	45.6	4013	5.57	30	67	38.5

	Rushing				Punt Returns			
Year Team	**Att**	**Yds**	**Avg**	**TD**	**Ret**	**Yds**	**Avg**	**TD**
1939 Cle	120	458	3.8	2	—	—	—	0
1940 Cle	94	365	3.9	1	—	—	—	0
1941 Cle	57	232	4.1	2	13	125	9.6	0
1942 Cle	41	-3	-0.1	1	12	148	12.3	0
NFL Total	312	1052	3.4	6	25	273	10.9	0

	Punting		
Year Team	**Punts**	**Yds**	**Avg**
1939 Cle	**58**	**2369**	40.8
1940 Cle	**57**	**2489**	43.7
1941 Cle	**49**	1967	40.1
1942 Cle	36	1397	38.8
NFL Total	200	8222	41.1

MARK HALL Hall, Mark James 6′4″, 285 **DE**
Col: Mississippi Gulf Coast CC; Southwestern Louisiana *HS:* Patterson [LA] B: 8/21/1965, Morgan City, LA *Drafted:* 1989 Round 7 GB
1989 GB: 7 G; 1 Sac. **1990** GB: 3 G. **Total:** 10 G; 1 Sac.

PETE HALL Hall, Peter William 6′2″, 200 **OE**
Col: Marquette *HS:* Farrell [PA] B: 2/28/1939, Sharon, PA
Drafted: 1960 Round 12 NYG
1961 NYG: 12 G; Rec 2-22 11.0.

RANDY HALL Hall, Randy Lee 6′3″, 190 **DB**
Col: Idaho *HS:* East Wenatchee [WA] B: 2/8/1952, East Wenatchee, WA *Drafted:* 1974 Round 13 Bal
1974 Bal: 14 G. **1976** Bal: 13 G. **Total:** 27 G.

RHETT HALL Hall, Rhett Floyd 6′2″, 270 **DT**
Col: Gavilan Coll. CA (J.C.); California *HS:* Live Oak [Morgan Hill, CA]
B: 12/5/1968, San Jose, CA *Drafted:* 1991 Round 6 TB
1991 TB: 16 G; 1 Sac. **1992** TB: 4 G. **1993** TB: 1 G. **1994** SF: 12 G; 4 Sac. **1995** Phi: 2 G; 1 Sac. **1996** Phi: 16 G; **1** Fum TD; 6 Pt; 4.5 Sac. **1997** Phi: 15 G; Int 1-39; 8 Sac. **1998** Phi: 2 G. **Total:** 68 G; Int 1-39; 1 Fum TD; 6 Pt; 18.5 Sac.

DICK HALL Hall, Richard Lewis 6′2″, 220 T
Col: Butler; Illinois *HS:* Logansport [IN] B: 6/6/1903, Logansport, IN D: 9/6/1971, Homewood, IL
1927 NYY: 15 G.

RON HALL Hall, Ronald Edwin 6′4″, 245 TE
Col: Cal Poly-Pomona; Hawaii *HS:* San Pasqual [Escondido, CA] B: 3/15/1964, Fort Huachuca, AZ *Drafted:* 1987 Round 4 TB
1990 TB: KR 1-0. **1991** TB: KR 1-1 1.0. **Total:** KR 2-1 0.5.

		Receiving				
Year Team	G	Rec	Yds	Avg	TD	Fum
1987 TB	10	16	169	10.6	1	0
1988 TB	15	39	555	14.2	0	0
1989 TB	16	30	331	11.0	2	0
1990 TB	16	31	464	15.0	2	0
1991 TB	15	31	284	9.2	0	1
1992 TB	12	39	351	9.0	4	0
1993 TB	16	23	268	11.7	1	0
1994 Det	13	10	106	10.6	0	1
1995 Det	6	11	81	7.4	0	0
NFL Total	119	230	2609	11.3	10	2

RON HALL Hall, Ronald Gene 6′0″, 190 DB
(Haystacks) *Col:* Missouri Valley *HS:* Granite City [IL] B: 4/30/1937, Goreville, IL *Drafted:* 1959 Round 28 Pit
1959 Pit: PR 5-23 4.6; KR 1-22 22.0. **1962** Bos: PR 1-0. **Total:** PR 6-23 3.8; KR 1-22 22.0.

		Interceptions		
Year Team	G	Int	Yds	TD
1959 Pit	2	1	0	0
1961 Bos	9	2	12	0
1962 Bos	14	3	94	**1**
1963 Bos	14	3	24	0
1964 Bos	14	11	148	0
1965 Bos	14	3	35	0
1966 Bos	14	6	159	0
1967 Bos	9	1	4	0
NFL Total	90	30	476	1

STEVE HALL Hall, Steven Lamont 6′0″, 205 DB
Col: Kentucky *HS:* New Haven [IN] B: 4/15/1973, Fort Wayne, IN
1996 Min-Ind: 3 G. Min: 1 G. Ind: 2 G. **Total:** 3 G.

TOM HALL Hall, Thomas Francis 6′1″, 195 WR-DB
Col: Minnesota *HS:* Salesianum [Wilmington, DE] B: 4/3/1940, Wilmington, DE *Drafted:* 1962 Round 7 Det
1962 Det: KR 1-16 16.0. **1963** Det: PR 10-107 10.7; KR 6-143 23.8; Int 3-45. **1964** Min: Rush 4-(-4) -1.0. **1965** Min: PR 3-21 7.0; KR 4-93 23.3. **1966** Min: KR 7-141 20.1. **Total:** Rush 4-(-4) -1.0; PR 13-128 9.8; KR 18-393 21.8; Int 3-45.

		Receiving				
Year Team	G	Rec	Yds	Avg	TD	Fum
1962 Det	13	0	0	—	0	0
1963 Det	14	3	29	9.7	1	2
1964 Min	14	23	325	14.1	2	0
1965 Min	14	15	287	19.1	2	3
1966 Min	14	23	271	11.8	2	1
1967 NO	11	19	249	13.1	0	1
1968 Min	13	19	268	14.1	1	0
1969 Min	3	1	12	12.0	0	0
NFL Total	96	103	1441	14.0	8	7

TIM HALL Hall, Timothy 5′11″, 218 RB
Col: Kemper Mil. School MO (J.C.); Robert Morris *HS:* Northeast [Kansas City, MO] B: 2/15/1974, Kansas City, MO D: 9/30/1998, Kansas City, MO *Drafted:* 1996 Round 6 Oak
1997 Oak: Rec 1-9 9.0; KR 9-182 20.2. **Total:** Rec 1-9 9.0; KR 9-182 20.2.

		Rushing			
Year Team	G	Att	Yds	Avg	TD
1996 Oak	2	3	7	2.3	0
1997 Oak	16	23	120	5.2	0
NFL Total	18	26	127	4.9	0

TRAVIS HALL Hall, Travis Todd 6′5″, 285 DE
Col: Brigham Young *HS:* West Jordan [UT] B: 8/3/1972, Kenai, AK *Drafted:* 1995 Round 6 Atl
1995 Atl: 1 G. **1996** Atl: 14 G; 6 Sac. **1997** Atl: 16 G; 10.5 Sac. **1998** Atl: 14 G; 4.5 Sac. **Total:** 45 G; 21 Sac.

WILLIE HALL Hall, William Charles 6′2″, 223 LB
Col: USC *HS:* Pulaski [New Britain, CT] B: 9/30/1949, Montrose, GA *Drafted:* 1972 Round 2 NO
1972 NO: 14 G. **1973** NO: 7 G. **1975** Oak: 7 G. **1976** Oak: 14 G; Int 2-17. **1977** Oak: 14 G; Int 1-0; 1 Fum TD; 6 Pt. **1978** Oak: 11 G; Int 2-18. **Total:** 67 G; Int 5-35; 1 Fum TD; 6 Pt.

WINDLAN HALL Hall, Windlan Edsel 5′11″, 178 DB
Col: Arizona State *HS:* Gardena [CA] B: 3/11/1950, Los Angeles, CA *Drafted:* 1972 Round 4 SF
1972 SF: 14 G; Int 1-0. **1973** SF: 14 G; KR 1-14 14.0; Int 1-0; **1** Fum TD; Tot TD 2; 12 Pt. **1974** SF: 13 G. **1975** SF: 13 G; KR 1-18 18.0. **1976** Min: 14 G. **1977** Min-Was: 13 G. Min: 5 G. Was: 8 G. **Total:** 81 G; KR 2-32 16.0; Int 2-0; 1 Fum TD; Tot TD 2; 12 Pt.

DICK HALLADAY Halladay, Robert Thayer 6′0″, 175 OE-WB
(Death) *Col:* Chicago *HS:* Hyde Park [Chicago, IL] B: 10/29/1900, Chicago, IL D: 11/12/1988, Hinsdale, IL
1923 Rac: 7 G; Rec 1 TD; 6 Pt. **1924** Rac: 10 G; Rec 1 TD; 6 Pt. **Total:** 17 G; Rec 2 TD; 12 Pt.

NEIL HALLECK Halleck, Neil 190 BB-WB
Col: No College *HS:* South [Youngstown, OH] B: 1902
1924 Col: 6 G.

PAUL HALLECK Halleck, Paul Charles 6′0″, 195 OE-DE
Col: Ohio U. *HS:* Wayne Twp. [Williamsfield, OH] B: 7/11/1912, Youngstown, OH D: 3/1974
1937 Cle: 11 G; Rec 3-57 19.0.

BOB HALLEN Hallen, Robert Joseph 6′4″, 292 C
Col: Kent State *HS:* Mentor [OH] B: 3/9/1975, Cleveland, OH *Drafted:* 1998 Round 2 Atl
1998 Atl: 12 G.

ALAN HALLER Haller, Alan Glenn 5′11″, 185 DB
Col: Michigan State *HS:* J.W. Sexton [Lansing, MI] B: 8/9/1970, Lansing, MI *Drafted:* 1992 Round 5 Pit
1992 Pit-Cle: 6 G. Pit: 3 G. Cle: 3 G. **1993** Pit: 4 G. **1995** Car: 2 G. **Total:** 12 G.

JACK HALLIDAY Halliday, Jack P 6′3″, 238 OT-DT
Col: Southern Methodist *HS:* Woodrow Wilson [Dallas, TX] B: 6/2/1928 *Drafted:* 1950 Round 5 Bal
1951 LARm: 11 G.

TY HALLOCK Hallock, Ty Edward 6′2″, 252 TE-RB-LB
Col: Michigan State *HS:* Greenville [MI] B: 4/30/1971, Grand Rapids, MI *Drafted:* 1993 Round 7 Det
1993 Det: KR 1-11 11.0. **1997** Jac: Rush 4-21 5.3; KR 1-6 6.0. **1998** ChiB: Rush 13-41 3.2 1 TD. **Total:** Rush 17-62 3.6 1 TD; KR 2-17 8.5.

		Receiving					Tot
Year Team	G	Rec	Yds	Avg	TD	Fum	TD
1993 Det	16	8	88	11.0	2	0	2
1994 Det	15	7	75	10.7	0	0	0
1996 Jac	7	1	5	5.0	0	0	0
1997 Jac	15	18	131	7.3	1	0	1
1998 ChiB	16	25	166	6.6	0	3	1
NFL Total	69	59	465	7.9	3	3	4

DIMP HALLORAN Halloran, Clarence R 5′8″, 175 TB
Col: Boston College; Fordham *HS:* Framingham [MA] B: 5/27/1896, Framingham, MA D: 11/17/1970, Framingham, MA
1926 Har: 3 G.

SHAWN HALLORAN Halloran, Shawn Michael 6′4″, 217 QB
Col: Boston College *HS:* Oakmont [Ashburnham, MA] B: 4/23/1964, Gardner, MA
1987 StL: 3 G; Pass 42-18 42.9%, 263 6.26 1 Int; Rush 3-(-9) -3.0; 1 Fum.

STONE HALLQUIST Hallquist, Stone Conrad 5′9″, 168 HB-TB
Col: Middlebury *HS:* South Division [Milwaukee, WI] B: 4/8/1902, Soderholm, Sweden D: 6/1/1981, Sun City, AZ
1926 Mil: 9 G.

RON HALLSTROM Hallstrom, Ronald David 6′6″, 300 OT-OG
Col: Central Coll. (Iowa); Iowa *HS:* Moline [IL] B: 6/11/1959, Holden, MA *Drafted:* 1982 Round 1 GB
1982 GB: 6 G. **1983** GB: 16 G. **1984** GB: 16 G. **1985** GB: 16 G. **1986** GB: 16 G. **1987** GB: 12 G. **1988** GB: 16 G. **1989** GB: 16 G. **1990** GB: 16 G. **1991** GB: 16 G. **1992** GB: 16 G. **1993** Phi: 12 G. **Total:** 174 G.

BUCK HALPERIN Halperin, Robert Sherman 5′11″, 200 TB
Col: No College B: 1/26/1908, Chicago, IL D: 3/8/1985, Palm Springs, CA
1932 Bkn: 2 G; Pass 2-1 50.0%, 23 11.50; Rush 9-(-4) -0.4.

WILLIE HALPERN Halpern, William 5′11″, 220 G-T
Col: CCNY B: 7/10/1908, Brooklyn, NY D: 11/24/1990, Hollywood, FL
1930 SI: 3 G.

BERNIE HALSTROM Halstrom, Bernhard Christian 5′9″, 160 BB-WB-FB
Col: Illinois *HS:* Hyde Park [Chicago, IL] B: 4/18/1895, Chicago, IL Deceased
1920 ChiC: 8 G. **1921** ChiC: 5 G. **Total:** 13 G.

JIM HALUSKA Haluska, James David 6′0″, 190 **QB**
(Bombo) *Col:* Wisconsin *HS:* St. Catherine's [Racine, WI]
B: 10/9/1932, Racine, WI *Drafted:* 1954 Round 30 ChiB
1956 ChiB: 5 G; Pass 4-1 25.0%, 8 2.00.

DEAN HALVERSON Halverson, Robert Dean 6′2″, 230 **LB**
Col: Washington *HS:* Olympia [WA] B: 8/24/1946, Olympia, WA
Drafted: 1968 Round 13 LARm
1968 LARm: 1 G. **1970** Atl: 7 G. **1971** LARm: 12 G. **1972** LARm: 14 G. **1973** Phi: 5 G. **1974** Phi: 13 G; Int 1-0; 1 Fum. **1975** Phi: 14 G.
Total: 66 G; Int 1-0; 1 Fum.

BILL HALVERSON Halverson, William Meral 6′3″, 242 **T**
Col: Oregon State *HS:* Benson Polytechnic [Portland, OR]
B: 5/4/1919, Davenport, IA *Drafted:* 1942 Round 8 Phi
1942 Phi: 8 G.

JACK HAM Ham, Jack Raphael Jr. 6′1″, 225 **LB**
Col: Penn State *HS:* Bishop McCourt [Johnstown PA]; Massanutten Prep [Woodstock, VA] B: 12/23/1948, Johnstown, PA *Drafted:* 1971 Round 2 Pit *HOF:* 1988
1973 Pit: **1** Fum TD. **1982** Pit: 3 Sac. **Total:** 1 Fum TD; 3 Sac.

		Interceptions				Tot
Year Team	G	Int	Yds	TD	Fum	TD
1971 Pit	14	2	4	0	0	0
1972 Pit	14	7	83	1	1	1
1973 Pit	13	2	30	0	0	1
1974 Pit	14	5	13	0	0	0
1975 Pit	14	1	2	0	0	0
1976 Pit	14	2	13	0	0	0
1977 Pit	14	4	17	0	1	0
1978 Pit	14	3	7	0	0	0
1979 Pit	15	2	8	0	0	0
1980 Pit	16	2	16	0	0	0
1981 Pit	12	1	23	0	0	0
1982 Pit	8	1	2	0	0	0
NFL Total	162	32	218	1	2	2

JACK HAMAN Haman, John Adam 6′2″, 215 **C-LB**
Col: Northwestern *HS:* Naperville Central [IL] B: 8/18/1918, Naperville, IL D: 9/1972 *Drafted:* 1940 Round 3 Cle
1940 Cle: 11 G; Rec 1-5 5.0; Int 5-80 **1** TD; 6 Pt. **1941** Cle: 10 G; Int 1-6.
Total: 21 G; Rec 1-5 5.0; Int 6-86 1 TD; 6 Pt.

STEVE HAMAS Hamas, Steven V 6′0″, 195 **FB-WB**
Col: Penn State *HS:* Henry P. Becton [East Rutherford, NJ]
B: 1/9/1907, Passaic, NJ D: 10/11/1974, Northport, NY
1929 Ora: 12 G.

ERNIE HAMBACHER Hambacher, Ernest Adam 5′8″, 170 **FB-TB**
Col: Bucknell *HS:* Bloomfield [NJ] B: 12/12/1906, Bloomfield, NJ
D: 9/3/1990
1929 Ora: 3 G.

DARREN HAMBRICK Hambrick, Darren 6′1″, 227 **LB**
Col: Florida; South Carolina *HS:* Pasco [Dade City, FL] B: 8/30/1975, Lacoochee, FL *Drafted:* 1998 Round 5 Dal
1998 Dal: 14 G.

MIKE HAMBY Hamby, Michael Bradley 6′4″, 270 **DE**
Col: Utah State *HS:* Lehi [UT] B: 11/12/1962, Salt Lake City, UT
Drafted: 1985 Round 6 Buf
1986 Buf: 16 G; 1 Sac.

DEAN HAMEL Hamel, Dean Edward 6′3″, 279 **DT**
Col: Coffeyville CC KS; Tulsa *HS:* Warren Mott [Warren, MI]
B: 7/7/1961, Detroit, MI *Drafted:* 1985 Round 12 Was
1985 Was: 16 G; KR 1-14 14.0; 6 Sac. **1986** Was: 16 G. **1987** Was: 12 G. **1988** Was: 16 G; 2 Sac. **1989** Dal: 16 G; 3.5 Sac. **1990** Dal: 12 G; 1 Sac.
Total: 88 G; KR 1-14 14.0; 12.5 Sac.

TEX HAMER Hamer, Ernest Alexander 6′1″, 191 **FB-WB-TB**
Col: Pennsylvania *HS:* San Antonio Mil. Acad. [San Antonio, TX]
B: 10/4/1901, Junction, TX D: 5/9/1981, Dallas, TX
1924 Fra: 14 G; Pass 4 TD; Rush **12** TD; Tot TD **12**; 72 Pt. **1925** Fra: 19 G; Pass 1 TD; Rush 5 TD; Int **2** TD; Scor 45, 3 XK; Tot TD 7. **1926** Fra: 17 G; Rush 2 TD; Scor 15, 3 XK. **1927** Fra: 5 G. **Total:** 55 G; Pass 5 TD; Rush 19 TD; Int 2 TD; Tot TD 21.

BOBBY HAMILTON Hamilton, Bobby Jerome 6′5″, 280 **DE**
Col: Southern Mississippi *HS:* East Marion [Columbia, MS]
B: 1/7/1971, Denver, CO
1996 NYJ: 15 G; 4.5 Sac. **1997** NYJ: 16 G; KR 1-0; 1 Sac. **1998** NYJ: 16 G. **Total:** 47 G; KR 1-0; 5.5 Sac.

CONRAD HAMILTON Hamilton, Conrad 5′10″, 195 **DB**
Col: New Mexico Mil. Inst. (J.C.); Eastern New Mexico *HS:* Alamogordo [NM] B: 11/5/1974, Alamogordo, NM *Drafted:* 1996 Round 7 NYG
1996 NYG: 15 G; KR 19-382 20.1; Int 1-29. **1997** NYG: 14 G; Int 1-18. **1998** NYG: 16 G; Int 1-17; 1 Sac. **Total:** 45 G; KR 19-382 20.1; Int 3-64; 1 Sac.

DARRELL HAMILTON Hamilton, Darrell Franklin 6′5″, 298 **OT**
Col: North Carolina *HS:* Anacostia [Washington, DC] B: 5/11/1965, Washington, DC *Drafted:* 1989 Round 3 Den
1990 Den: 15 G. **1991** Den: 6 G. **Total:** 21 G.

HARRY HAMILTON Hamilton, Harry Edwin 6′0″, 194 **DB**
Col: Penn State *HS:* John S. Fine [Nanticoke, PA] B: 11/29/1962, Queens, NY *Drafted:* 1984 Round 7 NYJ
1985 NYJ: 1 Sac. **Total:** 1 Sac.

		Interceptions			
Year Team	G	Int	Yds	TD	Fum
1984 NYJ	8	0	0	0	0
1985 NYJ	11	2	14	0	0
1986 NYJ	15	1	29	0	0
1987 NYJ	12	3	25	0	0
1988 TB	16	6	123	0	1
1989 TB	13	6	70	0	0
1990 TB	16	5	39	0	1
1991 TB	7	0	0	0	0
NFL Total	98	23	300	0	2

JAMES HAMILTON Hamilton, James Samuel Jr. 6′5″, 243 **LB**
Col: North Carolina *HS:* Richmond Co. [Hamlet, NC] B: 4/17/1974, Hartford, CT *Drafted:* 1997 Round 3 Jac
1997 Jac: 9 G; 1 Sac. **1998** Jac: 7 G. **Total:** 16 G; 1 Sac.

KEITH HAMILTON Hamilton, Keith Lamarr 6′6″, 288 **DT-DE**
(Hammer) *Col:* Pittsburgh *HS:* Heritage [Lynchburg, VA]
B: 5/25/1971, Paterson, NJ *Drafted:* 1992 Round 4 NYG
1992 NYG: 16 G; 3.5 Sac. **1993** NYG: 16 G; Scor 1 Saf; 2 Pt; 11.5 Sac. **1994** NYG: 15 G; 6.5 Sac. **1995** NYG: 14 G; 1 Fum; 2 Sac. **1996** NYG: 14 G; 3 Sac. **1997** NYG: 16 G; 8 Sac. **1998** NYG: 16 G; 7 Sac.
Total: 107 G; Scor 1 Saf; 2 Pt; 1 Fum; 41.5 Sac.

ANDY HAMILTON Hamilton, Ladell Andrews Jr. 6′3″, 190 **WR**
Col: Louisiana State *HS:* Ruston [LA] B: 11/8/1950, Ruston, LA
Drafted: 1972 Round 4 KC
1973 KC: 5 G; Rec 2-35 17.5. **1974** KC: 10 G; Rec 2-25 12.5. **1975** NO: 9 G; Rec 12-210 17.5. **Total:** 24 G; Rec 16-270 16.9.

SKIP HAMILTON Hamilton, Lenwood 6′2″, 265 **DT**
Col: North Carolina State; Southern University *HS:* Wilson [Easton, PA]
B: 5/14/1959, Philadelphia, PA
1987 Phi: 1 G.

MALCOLM HAMILTON Hamilton, Malcolm Xavier 6′1″, 238 **LB**
Col: Baylor *HS:* Permian [Odessa, TX] B: 12/31/1972, Dallas, TX
1998 Was: 2 G.

MICHAEL HAMILTON Hamilton, Michael Antonio 6′2″, 245 **LB**
Col: North Carolina A&T *HS:* Southside [Greenville, SC] B: 12/3/1973, Greenville, SC *Drafted:* 1997 Round 3 SD
1997 SD: 6 G. **1998** SD: 13 G. **Total:** 19 G.

RAY HAMILTON Hamilton, Raymond 6′4″, 212 **OE-DE**
(Bones) *Col:* Arkansas *HS:* Sheridan [AR] B: 1/21/1916, Sheridan, AR *Drafted:* 1938 Round 4 Cle
1947 LARm: KR 1-10 10.0. **Total:** KR 1-10 10.0.

		Receiving			
Year Team	G	Rec	Yds	Avg	TD
1938 Cle	9	10	187	18.7	0
1939 Det	8	3	53	17.7	0
1944 Cle	9	3	113	37.7	1
1945 Cle	9	4	50	12.5	0
1946 LARm	11	8	92	11.5	0
1947 LARm	12	12	193	16.1	1
NFL Total	58	40	688	17.2	2

RAY HAMILTON Hamilton, Raymond Lee 6′1″, 244 **NT-DE**
(Sugar Bear) *Col:* Oklahoma *HS:* Frederick Douglass [Oklahoma City, OK] B: 1/20/1951, Omaha, NE *Drafted:* 1973 Round 14 NE
1973 NE: 14 G. **1974** NE: 14 G. **1975** NE: 14 G; **1** Fum TD; 6 Pt. **1976** NE: 14 G. **1977** NE: 14 G. **1978** NE: 16 G. **1979** NE: 16 G. **1980** NE: 15 G. **1981** NE: 15 G; KR 1-0; 1 Fum. **Total:** 132 G; KR 1-0; 1 Fum TD; 6 Pt; 1 Fum.

RICK HAMILTON Hamilton, Richard 6′2″, 241 **LB**
Col: Central Florida *HS:* Citrus [Inverness, FL] B: 4/19/1970, Inverness, FL *Drafted:* 1993 Round 3 Was
1993 Was: 16 G. **1994** Was-KC: 3 G. Was: 1 G. KC: 2 G. **1996** NYJ: 15 G; 1.5 Sac. **Total:** 34 G; 1.5 Sac.

RUFFIN HAMILTON Hamilton, Ruffin III 6′1″, 235 **LB**
(Ruff) *Col:* Tulane *HS:* Northeast [Zachary, LA] B: 3/2/1971, Detroit, MI *Drafted:* 1994 Round 6 GB
1994 GB: 5 G. **1997** Atl: 12 G. **1998** Atl: 16 G. **Total:** 33 G.

STEVE HAMILTON Hamilton, Steven 6'4", 263 **DE-DT**
Col: East Carolina *HS:* East [Williamsville, NY]; Fork Union Mil. Acad. [VA] B: 9/28/1961, Niagara Falls, NY *Drafted:* 1984 Round 2 Was
1985 Was: 7 G; 1 Sac. **1986** Was: 12 G; 4.5 Sac. **1987** Was: 12 G; 1 Sac. **1988** Was: 15 G; KR 1-7 7.0. **Total:** 46 G; KR 1-7 7.0; 6.5 Sac.

WES HAMILTON Hamilton, Wesley Dean 6'3", 261 **OG**
Col: Tulsa *HS:* Homewood-Flossmoor [Flossmoor, IL] B: 4/24/1953, Texas City, TX *Drafted:* 1976 Round 3 Min
1976 Min: 13 G. **1977** Min: 14 G. **1978** Min: 16 G. **1979** Min: 16 G. **1980** Min: 13 G. **1981** Min: 16 G. **1982** Min: 9 G. **1983** Min: 15 G. **1984** Min: 4 G. **Total:** 116 G.

GENE HAMLIN Hamlin, Eugene Robert 6'3", 245 **C**
Col: Western Michigan *HS:* Redford [Detroit, MI] B: 7/26/1946, Detroit, MI
1970 Was: 4 G. **1971** ChiB: 7 G. **1972** Det: 5 G. **Total:** 16 G.

BOB HAMM Hamm, Robert 6'4", 260 **DE**
Col: Nevada-Reno *HS:* St. Francis [Mountain View, CA] B: 4/24/1959, Kansas City, MO
1983 Hou: 16 G; 3 Sac. **1984** Hou: 12 G; 2 Sac. **1985** KC: 14 G; 1 Sac. **1987** Ind: 3 G. **Total:** 45 G; 6 Sac.

MAL HAMMACK Hammack, alcolm Eugene 6'2", 205 **FB-OE-TE-LB**
Col: Texas-Arlington; Florida *HS:* Roscoe [TX] B: 6/19/1933, Roscoe, TX *Drafted:* 1955 Round 3 ChiC
1955 ChiC: KR 2-32 16.0. **1957** ChiC: KR 2-33 16.5. **1959** ChiC: PR 0-17 1 TD; KR 1-0. **1960** StL: KR 2-23 11.5. **1961** StL: KR 1-8 8.0. **1962** StL: KR 2-36 18.0. **1963** StL: KR 4-60 15.0. **1964** StL: KR 2-61 30.5. **1965** StL: KR 3-34 11.3. **Total:** PR 0-17 1 TD; KR 19-287 15.1.

		Rushing				Receiving					Tot
Year Team	G	Att	Yds	Avg	TD	Rec	Yds	Avg	TD	Fum	TD
1955 ChiC	9	51	160	3.1	2	5	13	2.6	0	5	2
1957 ChiC	12	30	158	5.3	0	1	14	14.0	0	1	0
1958 ChiC	10	35	121	3.5	1	3	11	3.7	0	3	1
1959 ChiC	12	49	237	4.8	0	4	69	17.3	0	6	1
1960 StL	9	96	347	3.6	2	4	36	9.0	0	7	2
1961 StL	7	18	79	4.4	1	5	70	14.0	0	0	1
1962 StL	14	38	160	4.2	1	4	27	6.8	0	2	1
1963 StL	13	3	16	5.3	0	1	15	15.0	0	2	0
1964 StL	14	0	0	—	0	0	0	—	0	0	0
1965 StL	14	0	0	—	0	0	0	—	0	0	0
1966 StL	14	0	0	—	0	0	0	—	0	0	0
NFL Total	128	320	1278	4.0	7	27	255	9.4	0	26	8

MIKE HAMMERSTEIN Hammerstein, Michael Scott 6'4", 270 **DE-NT**
Col: Michigan *HS:* Wapakoneta [OH] B: 3/29/1963, Kokomo, IN *Drafted:* 1986 Round 3 Cin
1986 Cin: 15 G; 1 Sac. **1987** Cin: 11 G; 1 Sac. **1989** Cin: 15 G; 1.5 Sac. **1990** Cin: 15 G; 2 Sac. **Total:** 56 G; 5.5 Sac.

CHING HAMMILL Hammill, James E III 5'7", 158 **BB**
Col: Connecticut; Villanova; Georgetown *HS:* Bridgeport [CT] D: 11/25/1926, Bridgeport, CT
1925 Prov: 1 G.

GARY HAMMOND Hammond, Gary Allen 5'11", 184 **WR-RB**
Col: Southern Methodist *HS:* Thomas Jefferson [Port Arthur, TX] B: 7/31/1949, Port Arthur, TX *Drafted:* 1972 Round 3 NYJ
1973 StL: Pass 1-0; Rush 4-11 2.8; Rec 4-39 9.8. **1974** StL: Pass 1-1 100.0%, 81 81.00; Rec 2-14 7.0. **1975** StL: Rush 3-13 4.3; Rec 2-6 3.0. **1976** StL: Rec 1-5 5.0. **Total:** Pass 2-1 50.0%, 81 40.50; Rush 7-24 3.4; Rec 9-64 7.1.

		Punt Returns				Kickoff Returns				
Year Team	G	Ret	Yds	Avg	TD	Ret	Yds	Avg	TD	Fum
1973 StL	9	11	80	7.3	0	12	314	26.2	0	3
1974 StL	12	17	125	7.4	0	11	268	24.4	0	0
1975 StL	14	9	70	7.8	0	13	254	19.5	0	0
1976 StL	14	3	16	5.3	0	2	36	18.0	0	1
NFL Total	49	40	291	7.3	0	38	872	22.9	0	4

HENRY HAMMOND Hammond, Henry Thomas 5'11", 190 **OE-DE**
Col: Rhodes *HS:* Central [Memphis, TN] B: 2/23/1913, Memphis, TN *Drafted:* 1937 Round 4 ChiB
1937 ChiB: 6 G.

KIM HAMMOND Hammond, Kim Crane 6'1", 190 **QB**
Col: Florida State *HS:* Melbourne [FL] B: 10/12/1944, Miami, FL *Drafted:* 1968 Round 6 Mia
1968 Mia: 3 G; Pass 26-13 50.0%, 116 4.46 2 Int; Rush 1-0. **1969** Bos: 3 G; Pass 6-2 33.3%, 31 5.17; Scor **1** 2XP; 2 Pt. **Total:** 6 G; Pass 32-15 46.9%, 147 4.59 2 Int; Rush 1-0; Scor 1 2XP; 2 Pt.

BOBBY HAMMOND Hammond, Robert Lee 5'10", 171 **RB**
Col: Morgan State *HS:* Bayside [Queens, NY] B: 2/20/1952, Orangeburg, SC

		Rushing				Receiving			
Year Team	G	Att	Yds	Avg	TD	Rec	Yds	Avg	TD
1976 NYG	2	0	0	—	0	0	0	—	0
1977 NYG	14	154	577	3.7	3	19	136	7.2	0
1978 NYG	14	131	554	4.2	1	20	173	8.7	2
1979 NYG-Was	9	2	5	2.5	0	2	16	8.0	0
1979 NYG	4	0	0	—	0	0	0	—	0
1979 Was	5	2	5	2.5	0	2	16	8.0	0
1980 Was	15	45	265	5.9	0	24	203	8.5	1
NFL Total	54	332	1401	4.2	4	65	528	8.1	3

	Punt Returns				Kickoff Returns					Tot
Year Team	Ret	Yds	Avg	TD	Ret	Yds	Avg	TD	Fum	TD
1976 NYG	0	0	—	0	2	44	22.0	0	0	0
1977 NYG	32	334	10.4	1	19	419	22.1	0	3	4
1978 NYG	22	157	7.1	0	15	290	19.3	0	4	3
1979 NYG-Was	13	75	5.8	0	25	544	21.8	0	2	0
1979 NYG	6	21	3.5	0	11	230	20.9	0	2	0
1979 Was	7	54	7.7	0	14	314	22.4	0	0	0
1980 Was	0	0	—	0	0	0	—	0	0	1
NFL Total	67	566	8.4	1	61	1297	21.3	0	9	8

STEVE HAMMOND Hammond, Steven Reed 6'4", 225 **LB**
Col: Wake Forest *HS:* Sanford H. Calhoun [Merrick, NY] B: 2/25/1960, Hartford, CT
1988 NYJ: 2 G.

WAYNE HAMMOND Hammond, Wayne Roger 6'5", 257 **DT**
Col: Montana State *HS:* Anoka [MN] B: 1/30/1953, Minneapolis, MN *Drafted:* 1975 Round 5 LARm
1976 Den: 5 G.

SHELLY HAMMONDS Hammonds, Shelton Cornelius 5'10", 189 **DB**
Col: Penn State *HS:* Barnwell [SC] B: 2/13/1971, Barnwell, SC *Drafted:* 1994 Round 5 Min
1995 Min: 1 G.

ALONZO HAMPTON Hampton, Alonzo 5'10", 191 **DB**
Col: Riverside CC CA; Pittsburgh *HS:* Jefferson [Edgewater, CA] B: 1/19/1967, Butler, AL *Drafted:* 1990 Round 4 Min
1990 Min: 10 G. **1991** TB: 15 G; Int 1-12. **Total:** 25 G; Int 1-12.

DAN HAMPTON Hampton, Daniel Oliver 6'5", 264 **DT-DE**
(Danimal) *Col:* Arkansas *HS:* Jacksonville [AR] B: 9/19/1957, Oklahoma City, OK *Drafted:* 1979 Round 1 ChiB
1979 ChiB: 16 G. **1980** ChiB: 16 G. **1981** ChiB: 16 G. **1982** ChiB: 9 G; 9 Sac. **1983** ChiB: 11 G; 5 Sac. **1984** ChiB: 15 G; 11.5 Sac. **1985** ChiB: 16 G; 6.5 Sac. **1986** ChiB: 16 G; Scor **1** Saf; 2 Pt; 10 Sac. **1987** ChiB: 8 G; 3.5 Sac. **1988** ChiB: 16 G; 9.5 Sac. **1989** ChiB: 4 G; 2 Sac. **1990** ChiB: 14 G. **Total:** 157 G; Scor 1 Saf; 2 Pt; 57.0 Sac.

DAVE HAMPTON Hampton, David 6'0", 210 **RB**
(Scooter) *Col:* Wyoming *HS:* Ann Arbor [MI] B: 5/7/1947, Akron, OH *Drafted:* 1969 Round 9 GB

		Rushing				Receiving			
Year Team	G	Att	Yds	Avg	TD	Rec	Yds	Avg	TD
1969 GB	14	80	365	4.6	4	15	216	14.4	2
1970 GB	6	48	115	2.4	0	7	23	3.3	0
1971 GB	13	67	307	4.6	3	3	37	12.3	1
1972 Atl	13	230	995	4.3	6	23	244	10.6	1
1973 Atl	14	263	997	3.8	4	25	273	10.9	1
1974 Atl	9	127	464	3.7	2	13	111	8.5	0
1975 Atl	14	250	1002	4.0	5	21	195	9.3	1
1976 Atl-Phi	10	83	291	3.5	1	12	57	4.8	0
1976 Atl	2	12	24	2.0	0	0	0	—	0
1976 Phi	8	71	267	3.8	1	12	57	4.8	0
NFL Total	93	1148	4536	4.0	25	119	1156	9.7	6

	Kickoff Returns					Tot
Year Team	Ret	Yds	Avg	TD	Fum	TD
1969 GB	22	582	26.5	**1**	7	7
1970 GB	6	188	31.3	1	3	1
1971 GB	**46**	**1314**	28.6	1	7	5
1972 Atl	25	535	21.4	0	9	7
1973 Atl	11	258	23.5	0	7	5
1974 Atl	0	0	—	0	5	2
1975 Atl	0	0	—	0	8	6
1976 Atl-Phi	3	46	15.3	0	5	1
1976 Atl	0	0	—	0	1	0
1976 Phi	3	46	15.3	0	4	1
NFL Total	113	2923	25.9	3	51	34

KWANTE HAMPTON Hampton, Kwante Lavon 6'1", 182 **WR**
Col: Oregon; Long Beach State *HS:* Van Nuys [CA] B: 12/11/1963, Los Angeles, CA
1987 Atl: 1 G.

LORENZO HAMPTON Hampton, Lorenzo Timothy 5'11", 205 **RB**
Col: Florida *HS:* Lake Wales [FL] B: 3/12/1962, Lake Wales, FL *Drafted:* 1985 Round 1 Mia

Year Team	G	Rushing Att	Yds	Avg	TD	Receiving Rec	Yds	Avg	TD
1985 Mia	16	105	369	3.5	3	8	56	7.0	0
1986 Mia	16	186	830	4.5	9	61	446	7.3	3
1987 Mia	12	75	289	3.9	1	23	223	9.7	0
1988 Mia	16	117	414	3.5	9	23	204	8.9	3
1989 Mia	10	17	47	2.8	0	8	25	3.1	0
NFL Total	70	500	1949	3.9	22	123	954	7.8	6

Year Team	Kickoff Returns Ret	Yds	Avg	TD	Fum	Tot TD
1985 Mia	45	1020	22.7	0	3	3
1986 Mia	9	182	20.2	0	4	12
1987 Mia	16	304	19.0	0	4	1
1988 Mia	9	216	24.0	0	2	12
1989 Mia	17	303	17.8	0	1	0
NFL Total	96	2025	21.1	0	14	28

RODNEY HAMPTON Hampton, Rodney Craig 5′11″, 221 **RB**
Col: Georgia *HS:* Kashmere [Houston, TX] B: 4/3/1969, Houston, TX
Drafted: 1990 Round 1 NYG
1994 NYG: Scor 1 2XP. **1995** NYG: Scor 1 2XP. **Total:** Scor 2 2XP.

Year Team	G	Rushing Att	Yds	Avg	TD	Receiving Rec	Yds	Avg	TD
1990 NYG	15	109	455	4.2	2	32	274	8.6	2
1991 NYG	14	256	1059	4.1	10	43	283	6.6	0
1992 NYG	16	257	1141	4.4	14	28	215	7.7	0
1993 NYG	12	292	1077	3.7	5	18	210	11.7	0
1994 NYG	14	327	1075	3.3	6	14	103	7.4	0
1995 NYG	16	306	1182	3.9	10	24	142	5.9	0
1996 NYG	15	254	827	3.3	1	15	82	5.5	0
1997 NYG	2	23	81	3.5	1	0	0	—	0
NFL Total	104	1824	6897	3.8	49	174	1309	7.5	2

Year Team	Kickoff Returns Ret	Yds	Avg	TD	Fum	Tot TD
1990 NYG	20	340	17.0	0	2	4
1991 NYG	10	204	20.4	0	5	10
1992 NYG	0	0	—	0	1	14
1993 NYG	0	0	—	0	2	5
1994 NYG	0	0	—	0	0	6
1995 NYG	0	0	—	0	5	10
1996 NYG	0	0	—	0	3	1
1997 NYG	0	0	—	0	0	1
NFL Total	30	544	18.1	0	18	51

JAMES HAMRICK Hamrick, James McNeil 5′11″, 177 **K**
Col: Rice *HS:* Annandale [VA]; Angleton HS [TX] B: 8/31/1963, Jacksonville, FL
1987 KC: 3 G; Scor 10, 2-2 100.0% FG, 4-4 100.0% XK.

CHRIS HANBURGER Hanburger, Christian Jr. 6′2″, 218 **LB**
Col: North Carolina *HS:* Hampton [VA] B: 8/13/1941, Fort Bragg, NC
Drafted: 1965 Round 18 Was
1965 Was: KR 1-0. **1967** Was: Rec 1-1 1.0. **1969** Was: **1** Fum TD.
1970 Was: KR 2-33 16.5. **1971** Was: **1** Fum TD. **1974** Was: 1 Fum TD.
Total: Rec 1-1 1.0; KR 3-33 11.0; 3 Fum TD.

Year Team	G	Interceptions Int	Yds	TD	Tot TD
1965 Was	14	1	14	0	0
1966 Was	13	1	1	0	0
1967 Was	13	0	0	0	0
1968 Was	14	2	53	1	1
1969 Was	14	0	0	0	1
1970 Was	14	1	12	0	0
1971 Was	14	1	17	0	1
1972 Was	14	4	98	1	1
1973 Was	14	1	45	0	0
1974 Was	14	4	6	0	1
1975 Was	14	3	81	0	0
1976 Was	14	1	20	0	0
1977 Was	5	0	0	0	0
1978 Was	16	0	0	0	0
NFL Total	187	19	347	2	5

ANTHONY HANCOCK Hancock, Anthony Duane 6′0″, 200 **WR**
Col: Tennessee *HS:* John Hay [Cleveland, OH] B: 6/10/1960, Cleveland, OH *Drafted:* 1982 Round 1 KC

Year Team	G	Receiving Rec	Yds	Avg	TD	Punt Returns Ret	Yds	Avg	TD
1982 KC	9	7	116	16.6	1	12	103	8.6	0
1983 KC	16	37	584	15.8	1	14	81	5.8	0
1984 KC	14	10	217	21.7	1	3	14	4.7	0
1985 KC	16	15	286	19.1	2	0	0	—	0
1986 KC	4	4	63	15.8	0	0	0	—	0
NFL Total	59	73	1266	17.3	5	29	198	6.8	0

Year Team	Kickoff Returns Ret	Yds	Avg	TD	Fum
1982 KC	27	609	22.6	0	1
1983 KC	29	515	17.8	0	2
1984 KC	2	32	16.0	0	1
1985 KC	6	125	20.8	0	1
NFL Total	64	1281	20.0	0	5

MIKE HANCOCK Hancock, Carl Michael 6′4″, 220 **TE**
Col: Yuba Coll. CA (J.C.); Idaho State *HS:* Williams [CA] B: 2/25/1950, Woodlake, CA *Drafted:* 1973 Round 8 Was
1973 Was: 10 G; Rec 2-3 1.5 2 TD; 12 Pt. **1974** Was: 11 G. **Total:** 21 G; Rec 2-3 1.5 2 TD; 12 Pt.

KEVIN HANCOCK Hancock, Kevin Drew 6′2″, 224 **LB**
Col: Baylor *HS:* Texas City [TX] B: 1/6/1962, Longview, TX
Drafted: 1985 Round 4 Det
1987 Ind: 1 G.

JON HAND Hand, Jon Thomas 6′7″, 300 **DE**
Col: Alabama *HS:* Sylacauga [AL] B: 11/13/1963, Sylacauga, AL
Drafted: 1986 Round 1 Ind
1986 Ind: 15 G; Int 1-8; 5 Sac. **1987** Ind: 12 G; 1 Sac. **1988** Ind: 15 G; 5 Sac. **1989** Ind: 16 G; 10 Sac. **1990** Ind: 12 G; 3 Sac. **1991** Ind: 16 G; 5 Sac. **1992** Ind: 15 G; 1 Sac. **1993** Ind: 15 G; 5.5 Sac. **1994** Ind: 5 G. **Total:** 121 G; Int 1-8; 35.5 Sac.

LARRY HAND Hand, Lawrence Thomas 6′4″, 250 **DE-DT**
Col: Appalachian State *HS:* Butler [NJ] B: 7/10/1940, Paterson, NJ
Drafted: 1964 Round 10 Det
1965 Det: 14 G. **1966** Det: 14 G. **1967** Det: 14 G; Int 2-6 2 TD; 12 Pt. **1968** Det: 1 G. **1969** Det: 14 G. **1970** Det: 14 G; Int 1-62 1 TD; 6 Pt. **1971** Det: 14 G. **1972** Det: 14 G. **1973** Det: 14 G. **1974** Det: 13 G. **1975** Det: 14 G; Int 1-38. **1976** Det: 10 G; Int 1-4. **1977** Det: 14 G. **Total:** 164 G; Int 5-110 3 TD; 18 Pt.

NORMAN HAND Hand, Norman L 6′3″, 330 **DT**
Col: Itawamba CC MS; Mississippi *HS:* Walterboro [SC] B: 9/4/1972, Queens, NY *Drafted:* 1995 Round 5 Mia
1996 Mia: 9 G; 0.5 Sac. **1997** SD: 15 G; 1 Sac. **1998** SD: 16 G; Int 2-47; 6 Sac. **Total:** 40 G; Int 2-47; 7.5 Sac.

PHIL HANDLER Handler, Philip Jacob 6′0″, 212 **G**
(Motsy) *Col:* Texas Christian *HS:* Central [Fort Worth, TX]
B: 7/21/1908, Fort Worth, TX D: 12/8/1968, Skokie, IL
1930 ChiC: 9 G. **1931** ChiC: 7 G. **1932** ChiC: 9 G. **1933** ChiC: 8 G. **1934** ChiC: 8 G. **1935** ChiC: 10 G. **1936** ChiC: 2 G. **Total:** 53 G.

DICK HANDLEY Handley, Richard H 6′1″, 215 **C-LB**
Col: Coll. of the Sequoias CA (J.C.); USC; Fresno State *HS:* Corcoran [CA] B: 5/22/1922, Tulane, CA
AAFC **1947** BalA: 14 G.

CARL HANKE Hanke, Carl Christopher 6′0″, 190 **E**
Col: Minnesota B: 12/31/1897 D: 5/1964, Chicago, IL
1921 Ham: 5 G; 1 Fum TD; 6 Pt. **1922** ChiB-Ham: 3 G. ChiB: 2 G. Ham: 1 G. **1923** Ham: 7 G. **1924** ChiC: 8 G; Rec 1 TD; 1 Fum TD; Tot TD 2; 12 Pt. **Total:** 23 G; Rec 1 TD; 2 Fum TD; Tot TD 3; 18 Pt.

RAY HANKEN Hanken, Raymond George 5′11″, 190 **OE-DE**
Col: George Washington *HS:* Sacred Heart [Oelwein, IA] B: 12/3/1911 D: 11/1980, Vienna, VA
1937 NYG: 11 G; Rec 4-51 12.8. **1938** NYG: 10 G; Rec 5-73 14.6 2 TD; 12 Pt. **Total:** 21 G; Rec 9-124 13.8 2 TD; 12 Pt.

BEN HANKS Hanks, Benjamin Ujean 6′2″, 223 **LB**
Col: Florida *HS:* Miami Senior [FL] B: 7/31/1971, Miami, FL
1996 Min: 12 G. **1997** Det: 2 G. **Total:** 14 G.

MERTON HANKS Hanks, Merton Edward 6′2″, 185 **DB**
Col: Iowa *HS:* Lake Highlands [Dallas, TX] B: 3/12/1968, Dallas, TX
Drafted: 1991 Round 5 SF
1992 SF: PR 1-48 48.0 1 TD. **1994** SF: 0.5 Sac. **1995** SF: PR 1-0; **1** Fum TD. **1997** SF: 1 Fum TD. **1998** SF: 0.5 Sac. **Total:** PR 2-48 24.0 1 TD; 2 Fum TD; 1 Sac.

Year Team	G	Interceptions Int	Yds	TD	Fum	Tot TD
1991 SF	13	0	0	0	0	0
1992 SF	16	2	5	0	0	1
1993 SF	16	3	104	1	0	1
1994 SF	16	7	93	0	1	0
1995 SF	16	5	31	0	0	1
1996 SF	16	4	7	0	0	0
1997 SF	16	6	103	1	0	2
1998 SF	16	4	37	0	0	0
NFL Total	125	31	380	2	1	5

KARL HANKTON Hankton, Karl Christopher 6′3″, 200 **WR**
Col: Valley Forge J.C. PA; Louisiana State; Trinity (Ill.) *HS:* Valley Forge Mil. Acad. [Wayne, PA] B: 7/24/1970, New Orleans, LA
1998 Phi: 10 G; Rush 1-(-4) -4.0; KR 1-18 18.0.

BO HANLEY Hanley, Edward Louis 5′7″, 150 **WB**
Col: Marquette B: 12/14/1887, Milwaukee, WI D: 9/21/1980, Milwaukee, WI
1920 Det: 3 G.

DICK HANLEY Hanley, Richard Edgar 5′10″, 175 **WB**
Col: Washington; Washington State *HS:* Burlington [WA]; Bellingham HS [WA]; North Central HS [Spokane, WA] B: 11/19/1894, Cloquet, MN D: 12/16/1970, Palo Alto, CA
1924 Rac: 1 G.

BOB HANLON Hanlon, Robert Seldon 6′1″, 195 **DB-HB**
Col: Notre Dame; Loras *HS:* Leo [Chicago, IL] B: 8/24/1924, Springfield, OH D: 7/20/1995, Chicago, IL *Drafted:* 1948 Round 12 ChiC
1948 ChiC: 10 G; Rush 6-11 1.8; Int 1-25. **1949** Pit: 12 G; Rush 6-13 2.2; Rec 1-4 4.0; KR 11-213 19.4; Int 3-29; 1 Fum. **Total:** 22 G; Rush 12-24 2.0; Rec 1-4 4.0; KR 11-213 19.4; Int 4-54; 1 Fum.

ZIP HANNA Hanna, Elzaphan McConnell 5′10″, 218 **G**
Col: South Carolina B: 12/1/1916, Chester, SC
1945 Was: 9 G.

JIM HANNA Hanna, Jimmy Glenn 6′4″, 255 **NT**
Col: Louisville *HS:* Forest Hill [West Palm Beach, FL] B: 8/10/1971, West Palm Beach, FL
1994 NO: 7 G.

CHARLEY HANNAH Hannah, Charles Alvin 6′5″, 260 **OG-OT-DE**
Col: Alabama *HS:* Baylor Prep [Chattanooga, TN] B: 7/26/1955, Albertville, AL *Drafted:* 1977 Round 3 TB
1977 TB: 9 G. **1978** TB: 16 G; 1 Fum. **1979** TB: 14 G. **1980** TB: 16 G; Pass 1-0. **1981** TB: 15 G. **1982** TB: 7 G. **1983** LARd: 16 G. **1984** LARd: 15 G. **1985** LARd: 15 G. **1986** LARd: 12 G. **1987** LARd: 5 G. **1988** LARd: 8 G. **Total:** 148 G; Pass 1-0; 1 Fum.

HERB HANNAH Hannah, Herbert 6′3″, 220 **OT**
Col: Alabama *HS:* West Limestone [Lester, AL] B: 7/21/1921, Laoma, TN *Drafted:* 1951 Round 6 NYG
1951 NYG: 12 G; Rec 0-8.

JOHN HANNAH Hannah, John Allen 6′2″, 265 **OG**
Col: Alabama *HS:* Albertville [AL]; Baylor Prep [Chattanooga, TN] B: 4/4/1951, Canton, GA *Drafted:* 1973 Round 1 NE *HOF:* 1991
1973 NE: 13 G; KR 1-0. **1974** NE: 14 G; 1 Fum TD; 6 Pt. **1975** NE: 14 G. **1976** NE: 14 G. **1977** NE: 11 G. **1978** NE: 16 G. **1979** NE: 16 G. **1980** NE: 16 G. **1981** NE: 16 G. **1982** NE: 8 G. **1983** NE: 16 G. **1984** NE: 15 G. **1985** NE: 14 G. **Total:** 183 G; KR 1-0; 1 Fum TD; 6 Pt.

TRAVIS HANNAH Hannah, Travis Lamont 5′7″, 161 **WR**
Col: USC *HS:* Hawthorne [CA] B: 1/31/1970, Los Angeles, CA *Drafted:* 1993 Round 4 Hou
1993 Hou: 12 G. **1994** Hou: 9 G; Rec 3-24 8.0; PR 9-58 6.4; KR 5-116 23.2; 1 Fum. **1995** Hou: 16 G; Rush 1-5 5.0; Rec 10-142 14.2; PR 5-36 7.2. **Total:** 37 G; Rush 1-5 5.0; Rec 13-166 12.8; PR 14-94 6.7; KR 5-116 23.2; 1 Fum.

CHUCK HANNEMAN Hanneman, Charles Bennett 6′0″, 220 **OE-DE**
Col: Eastern Michigan *HS:* Grosse Pointe [MI] B: 9/26/1914, Flint, MI
1937 Det: Rush 2-53 26.5 1 TD. **1938** Det: Rush 1-6 6.0. **1939** Det: Punt 1-31 31.0; Scor 29, 4-5 **80.0%** FG, 5-5 **100.0%** XK. **1940** Det: Int 2-34; Scor 16, 2-4 50.0% FG, 10-10 100.0% XK. **1941** Det-Cle: Scor 13, 1-4 25.0% FG, 4-4 100.0% XK. Det: Scor 13, 1-4 25.0% FG, 4-4 100.0% XK. **Total:** Rush 3-59 19.7 1 TD; Int 2-34; Punt 1-31 31.0; Scor 70, 7-13 53.8% FG, 19-19 100.0% XK.

		Receiving				Tot
Year Team	**G**	**Rec**	**Yds**	**Avg**	**TD**	**TD**
1937 Det	10	1	9	9.0	0	1
1938 Det	10	4	80	20.0	1	1
1939 Det	10	12	257	21.4	2	2
1940 Det	9	14	224	16.0	0	0
1941 Det-Cle	7	4	48	12.0	1	1
1941 Det	6	4	48	12.0	1	1
1941 Cle	1	0	0	—	0	0
NFL Total	46	35	618	17.7	4	5

CRAIG HANNEMAN Hanneman, Craig Lewis 6′3″, 240 **DE-DT**
Col: Oregon State *HS:* South Salem [Salem, OR] B: 7/1/1949, Salem, OR *Drafted:* 1971 Round 6 Pit
1972 Pit: 13 G. **1973** Pit: 14 G; KR 1-20 20.0. **1974** NE: 9 G. **1975** NE: 11 G. **Total:** 47 G; KR 1-20 20.0.

CLIFF HANNEMANN Hannemann, Clifford Paul 6′2″, 235 **LB**
Col: Fresno State *HS:* Clovis West [Fresno, CA] B: 10/21/1964, Duarte, CA
1987 Cle: 3 G.

DAVE HANNER Hanner, Joel David 6′2″, 257 **DT**
(Hawg) *Col:* Arkansas *HS:* Parkin [AR] B: 5/22/1930, Parkin, AR *Drafted:* 1952 Round 5 GB
1952 GB: 12 G. **1953** GB: 12 G; Int 1-2. **1954** GB: 12 G. **1955** GB: 12 G. **1956** GB: 12 G. **1957** GB: 12 G. **1958** GB: 12 G. **1959** GB: 12 G; Scor **1** Saf; 2 Pt. **1960** GB: 12 G. **1961** GB: 13 G; Int 1-1. **1962** GB: 14 G; Int 1-0. **1963** GB: 14 G; Int 1-0. **1964** GB: 11 G. **Total:** 160 G; Int 4-3; Scor 1 Saf; 2 Pt.

TOM HANNON Hannon, Thomas Edward 5′11″, 193 **DB**
Col: Michigan State *HS:* Washington [Massillon, OH] B: 3/5/1955, Massillon, OH *Drafted:* 1977 Round 3 Min
1981 Min: Scor **1** Saf. **1983** Min: 0.5 Sac. **Total:** Scor 1 Saf; 0.5 Sac.

		Interceptions			
Year Team	**G**	**Int**	**Yds**	**TD**	**Fum**
1977 Min	12	0	0	0	0
1978 Min	16	2	0	0	0
1979 Min	16	4	85	0	0
1980 Min	16	4	89	1	1
1981 Min	16	4	28	0	0
1982 Min	9	0	0	0	0
1983 Min	16	0	0	0	0
1984 Min	16	1	0	0	0
NFL Total	117	15	202	1	1

JIM HANNULA Hannula, James Frank 6′6″, 264 **OT**
Col: Northern Illinois *HS:* St. Edward [Elgin, IL] B: 7/2/1959, Elgin, IL *Drafted:* 1981 Round 9 Cin
1983 Cin: 15 G.

DUKE HANNY Hanny, Frank Mathew 6′0″, 199 **OE-T-G-FB**
Col: Indiana *HS:* Aurora East [IL] B: 12/10/1897, Aurora, IL Deceased
1923 ChiB: 12 G; Rec 1 TD; 6 Pt. **1924** ChiB: 11 G; Int **1** TD; 6 Pt. **1925** ChiB: 17 G; Int 1 TD; 6 Pt. **1926** ChiB: 16 G; Rec **4** TD; 24 Pt. **1927** ChiB: 14 G. **1928** Prov: 11 G; Int **1** TD; 6 Pt. **1929** Prov: 11 G; Scor 1, 1 XK. **1930** GB-Port: 6 G. GB: 2 G. Port: 4 G. **Total:** 98 G; Rec 5 TD; Int 3 TD; Tot TD 8.

MATT HANOUSEK Hanousek, Matthew Joseph 6′4″, 265 **OG-OT**
Col: Drake; Utah State *HS:* St. Thomas Acad. [St. Paul, MN] B: 8/16/1963, St. Paul, MN
1987 Sea: 3 G.

TERRY HANRATTY Hanratty, Terrence Hugh 6′1″, 210 **QB**
Col: Notre Dame *HS:* Butler [PA] B: 1/19/1948, Butler, PA *Drafted:* 1969 Round 2 Pit
1969 Pit: Rush 10-106 10.6. **1970** Pit: Rush 4-(-5) -1.3. **1971** Pit: Rush 1-3 3.0 1 TD. **1973** Pit: Rush 3-0. **1974** Pit: Rush 1-(-6) -6.0. **1975** Pit: Rush 1-0. **1976** TB: Rush 1-1 1.0. **Total:** Rush 21-99 4.7 1 TD.

		Passing								
Year Team	**G**	**Att**	**Comp**	**Comp%**	**Yds**	**YPA**	**TD**	**Int**	**Rating**	**Fum**
1969 Pit	8	126	52	41.3	716	5.68	8	13	41.7	3
1970 Pit	13	163	64	39.3	842	5.17	5	8	46.1	1
1971 Pit	6	29	7	24.1	159	5.48	2	3	33.3	0
1972 Pit	7	4	2	50.0	23	5.75	0	0	67.7	1
1973 Pit	9	69	31	44.9	643	9.32	8	5	86.8	4
1974 Pit	3	26	3	11.5	95	3.65	1	5	15.5	1
1975 Pit	1	0	0	—	0	—	0	0	—	0
1976 TB	3	14	6	42.9	32	2.29	0	1	20.5	1
NFL Total	50	431	165	38.3	2510	5.82	24	35	43.0	11

BRIAN HANSEN Hansen, Brian Dean 6′4″, 215 **P**
Col: Sioux Falls *HS:* West Sioux [Hawarden, IA] B: 10/26/1960, Hawarden, IA *Drafted:* 1984 Round 9 NO
1984 NO: Rush 2-(-27) -13.5. **1985** NO: Pass 1-1 100.0%, 8 8.00. **1986** NO: Rush 1-0. **1987** NO: Rush 2-(-6) -3.0. **1988** NO: Rush 1-10 10.0. **1990** NE: Rush 1-0. **1991** Cle: Pass 1-1 100.0%, 11 11.00 1 TD; Rush 2-(-3) -1.5. **1996** NYJ: Rush 1-1 1.0. **1997** NYJ: Pass 1-1 100.0%, 26 26.00. **Total:** Pass 3-3 100.0%, 45 15.00 1 TD; Rush 10-(-25) -2.5.

		Punting			
Year Team	**G**	**Punts**	**Yds**	**Avg**	**Fum**
1984 NO	16	69	3020	43.8	0
1985 NO	16	89	3763	42.3	0
1986 NO	16	81	3456	42.7	1
1987 NO	12	52	2104	40.5	0
1988 NO	16	72	2913	40.5	0
1990 NE	16	**90**	**3752**	41.7	1
1991 Cle	16	80	3397	42.5	0
1992 Cle	16	74	3083	41.7	1
1993 Cle	16	82	3632	44.3	0
1994 NYJ	16	84	3534	42.1	0
1995 NYJ	16	**99**	**4090**	41.3	0
1996 NYJ	16	74	3293	44.5	0
1997 NYJ	15	71	3068	43.2	0
1998 NYJ	7	31	1233	39.8	0
NFL Total	210	1048	44338	42.3	3

BRUCE HANSEN Hansen, Bruce B 6′1″, 225 **RB**
Col: Brigham Young *HS:* American Fork [UT] B: 9/18/1961, American Fork, UT
1987 NE: 6 G; Rush 16-44 2.8; Rec 1-22 22.0; KR 1-14 14.0.

CLIFF HANSEN Hansen, Clifford Harold 6′1″, 190 **HB**
Col: Luther *HS:* Minnewaska [Glenwood, MN] B: 6/29/1910, Thief River Falls, MN
1933 ChiC: 5 G; Pass 10-1 10.0%, 8 0.80 3 Int; Rush 9-55 6.1.

CARL HANSEN Hansen, David Carl 6′5″, 282 **DE**
Col: Stanford *HS:* Stratford [TX] B: 1/25/1976, Houston, TX
Drafted: 1998 Round 6 Sea
1998 NYJ: 5 G.

DON HANSEN Hansen, Donald Ray 6′2″, 235 **LB**
Col: Illinois *HS:* Francis Joseph Reitz [Evansville, IN] B: 8/20/1944, Warrick Co., IN *Drafted:* 1966 Round 3 Min

		Interceptions			
Year Team	**G**	**Int**	**Yds**	**TD**	**Fum**
1966 Min	13	0	0	0	0
1967 Min	12	0	0	0	0
1969 Atl	11	2	51	0	0
1970 Atl	14	1	15	0	0
1971 Atl	14	3	56	1	0
1972 Atl	14	1	0	0	0
1973 Atl	14	1	0	0	1
1974 Atl	14	1	0	0	0
1975 Atl	14	1	1	0	0
1976 Sea-GB	14	0	0	0	0
1976 Sea	2	0	0	0	0
1976 GB	12	0	0	0	0
1977 GB	8	0	0	0	0
NFL Total	142	10	123	1	1

WAYNE HANSEN Hansen, George Wayne 6′2″, 231 **LB-C-OG-OT**
Col: Texas-El Paso *HS:* Monahans [TX] B: 10/6/1928, McCamey, TX D: 8/24/1987, El Paso, TX *Drafted:* 1950 Round 6 ChiB
1950 ChiB: 12 G. **1951** ChiB: 12 G; KR 1-23 23.0; 1 Fum. **1952** ChiB: 10 G. **1953** ChiB: 12 G. **1954** ChiB: 12 G; Int 1-57; **1** Fum TD; 6 Pt; 1 Fum. **1955** ChiB: 12 G. **1956** ChiB: 12 G; Int 1-11. **1957** ChiB: 12 G; Int 1-34. **1958** ChiB: 5 G; Int 1-12. **1960** Dal: 12 G; Int 2-14. **Total:** 111 G; KR 1-23 23.0; Int 6-128; 1 Fum TD; 6 Pt; 2 Fum.

HAL HANSEN Hansen, Harlan C 5′10″, 200 **FB-OE**
(King Hal) *Col:* Minnesota *HS:* West [Minneapolis, MN] B: 9/3/1892, Anita, IA D: 9/18/1977, Des Moines, IA
1923 GB: 1 G.

PHIL HANSEN Hansen, Philip Allen 6′5″, 278 **DE**
Col: North Dakota State *HS:* Oakes [ND] B: 5/20/1968, Ellendale, ND
Drafted: 1991 Round 2 Buf
1991 Buf: 14 G; 2 Sac. **1992** Buf: 16 G; 8 Sac. **1993** Buf: 11 G; 3.5 Sac. **1994** Buf: 16 G; 5.5 Sac. **1995** Buf: 16 G; 10 Sac. **1996** Buf: 16 G; 8 Sac. **1997** Buf: 16 G; Scor **1** Saf; 2 Pt; 6 Sac. **1998** Buf: 15 G; 1 Fum TD; 6 Pt; 7.5 Sac. **Total:** 120 G; Scor 1 Saf; 1 Fum TD; 8 Pt; 50.5 Sac.

RON HANSEN Hansen, Ronald Melrich 6′0″, 220 **OG-LB**
Col: Minnesota *HS:* Northfield [MN] B: 2/10/1932, Northfield, MN
Drafted: 1954 Round 28 Was
1954 Was: 12 G.

ROSCOE HANSEN Hansen, Roscoe Harold Jr. 6′3″, 215 **OT-DT**
(Rock) *Col:* North Carolina B: 9/24/1929, New York, NY
Drafted: 1951 Round 29 Phi
1951 Phi: 9 G.

DALE HANSEN Hansen, Warren Dale 6′3″, 223 **T-DE**
Col: Michigan State *HS:* Southwestern [Detroit, MI] B: 1/27/1921, Detroit, MI D: 5/6/1978, Birmingham, MI
1944 Det: 2 G. **1948** Det: 12 G. **Total:** 14 G.

TIM HANSHAW Hanshaw, Timothy Eugene 6′5″, 300 **OG**
Col: Brigham Young *HS:* West Valley [Spokane, WA] B: 4/27/1970, Spokane, WA *Drafted:* 1995 Round 4 SF
1996 SF: 1 G. **1997** SF: 13 G. **1998** SF: 16 G. **Total:** 30 G.

HAL HANSON Hanson, Harold Walter **G**
Col: Minnesota *HS:* Stewart [MN] B: 8/10/1905, Stewart, MN D: 9/29/1977, Mora, MN
1928 Fra: 16 G. **1929** Fra: 18 G. **1930** Fra-Min: 17 G. Fra: 16 G. Min: 1 G. **Total:** 51 G.

HAL HANSON Hanson, Harold William 6′1″, 190 **C-G-T**
Col: South Dakota B: 11/18/1895, La Crosse, WI D: 10/10/1973, Sarasota, FL
1921 RI: 6 G. **1923** Min: 1 G. **Total:** 7 G.

HOMER HANSON Hanson, Homer Peter 6′0″, 217 **G-C-LB**
Col: Kansas State *HS:* Riley [KS] B: 7/25/1910, Riley, KS D: 10/5/1989, Marysville, KS
1934 Cin: 2 G. **1935** ChiC-Phi: 2 G. ChiC: 1 G. Phi: 1 G. **1936** ChiC: 1 G. **Total:** 5 G.

JASON HANSON Hanson, Jason Douglas 5′11″, 183 **K**
Col: Washington State *HS:* Mead [Spokane, WA] B: 6/17/1970, Spokane, WA *Drafted:* 1992 Round 2 Det
1995 Det: Punt 1-34 34.0. **1996** Det: Punt 1-24 24.0. **1998** Det: Punt 3-94 31.3. **Total:** Punt 5-152 30.4.

		Scoring						
Year Team	**G**	**Pts**	**FG**	**FGA**	**FG%**	**XK**	**XKA**	**XK%**
1992 Det	16	93	21	26	80.8	30	30	100.0
1993 Det	16	130	34	43	79.1	28	28	100.0
1994 Det	16	93	18	27	66.7	39	40	97.5
1995 Det	16	132	28	34	82.4	**48**	**48**	100.0
1996 Det	16	72	12	17	70.6	36	36	100.0
1997 Det	16	117	26	29	89.7	39	40	97.5
1998 Det	16	114	29	33	87.9	27	29	93.1
NFL Total	112	751	168	209	80.4	247	251	98.4

MARK HANSON Hanson, Mark 6′2″, 260 **OG**
Col: Mankato State B: 2/3/1965, Faribault, MN
1987 Min: 1 G.

RAY HANSON Hanson, Raymond W 5′11″, 190 **G-C-T**
Col: Ohio State; Ohio Wesleyan *HS:* London [OH] B: 7/16/1893, London, OH D: 9/1968, Minerva, OH
1923 Col: 2 G.

DICK HANSON Hanson, Richard Alan 6′6″, 280 **OT**
Col: North Dakota State *HS:* Central [Fargo, ND] B: 12/25/1949, Hillsboro, ND
1971 NYG: 3 G.

STEVE HANSON Hanson, Steven Harold 6′2″, 192 **E**
Col: Carthage *HS:* Racine [WI] B: 4/27/1902, Racine Co., WI D: 8/1/1981, Racine, WI
1926 Lou: 1 G.

SWEDE HANSON Hanson, Thomas Tucker 6′1″, 192 **FB-DB-LB-TB**
Col: Temple *HS:* Leonardo [NJ] B: 11/10/1907, Navesink, NJ D: 8/5/1970, Philadelphia, PA
1933 Phi: Rec 10-186 18.6 1 TD. **1934** Phi: Rec 5-22 4.4; Int **1** TD; Scor 50, 2 XK. **1935** Phi: Rec 4-82 20.5. **1936** Phi: Rec 3-33 11.0. **1938** Pit: Rec 1-2 2.0. **Total:** Rec 23-325 14.1 1 TD; Int 1 TD.

		Passing							
Year Team	**G**	**Att**	**Comp**	**Comp%**	**Yds**	**YPA**	**TD**	**Int**	**Rating**
1931 Bkn	11	—	—	—	—	—	0	—	—
1932 SI	3	10	2	20.0	31	3.10	0	3	0.4
1933 Phi	9	28	7	25.0	50	1.79	0	4	0.0
1934 Phi	11	12	4	33.3	28	2.33	0	2	2.8
1935 Phi	11	1	1	100.0	23	23.00	0	0	118.8
1936 Phi	12	15	0	0.0	0	0.00	0	4	0.0
1937 Phi	2	2	0	0.0	0	0.00	0	0	39.6
1938 Pit	5	0	0	—	0	—	0	0	—
NFL Total	64	68	14	20.6	132	1.94	0	13	0.0

	Rushing				Tot
Year Team	**Att**	**Yds**	**Avg**	**TD**	**TD**
1932 SI	46	165	3.6	1	1
1933 Phi	133	475	3.6	3	4
1934 Phi	**146**	805	5.5	7	8
1935 Phi	77	209	2.7	0	0
1936 Phi	119	359	3.0	1	1
1937 Phi	18	59	3.3	1	1
1938 Pit	15	50	3.3	0	0
NFL Total	554	2122	3.8	13	15

BYRON HANSPARD Hanspard, Byron Courtenay 5′10″, 198 **RB**
Col: Texas Tech *HS:* De Soto [TX] B: 1/23/1976, Dallas, TX
Drafted: 1997 Round 2 Atl
1997 Atl: Rec 6-53 8.8 1 TD.

		Rushing				Kickoff Returns					Tot
Year Team	**G**	**Ret**	**Yds**	**Avg**	**TD**	**Ret**	**Yds**	**Avg**	**TD**	**Fum**	**TD**
1997 Atl	16	53	335	6.3	0	40	987	24.7	**2**	3	3

BOB HANTLA Hantla, Robert Dean 6′1″, 230 **OG-LB-DE**
Col: Kansas *HS:* Meade [KS] B: 10/3/1931, St.John, KS
Drafted: 1954 Round 5 SF
1954 SF: 12 G. **1955** SF: 12 G. **Total:** 24 G.

CHET HANULAK Hanulak, Chester Edward 5′10″, 185 **HB**
(Chet the Jet) *Col:* Maryland *HS:* Hackensack [NJ] B: 3/28/1933, Hackensack, NJ *Drafted:* 1954 Round 2 Cle
1954 Cle: Rec 6-80 13.3; KR 9-213 23.7. **1957** Cle: Pass 2-1 50.0%, 32 16.00 1 TD; Rec 3-38 12.7. **Total:** Pass 2-1 50.0%, 32 16.00 1 TD; Rec 9-118 13.1; KR 9-213 23.7.

		Rushing				Punt Returns				
Year Team	**G**	**Att**	**Yds**	**Avg**	**TD**	**Ret**	**Yds**	**Avg**	**TD**	**Fum**
1954 Cle	12	59	296	5.0	4	**27**	92	3.4	0	3

Year Team										
1957 Cle	12	125	375	3.0	3	11	29	2.6	0	1
NFL Total	24	184	671	3.6	7	38	121	3.2	0	4

PATRICK HAPE Hape, Patrick Stephen 6′4″, 256 **TE**
Col: Alabama *HS:* Brooks [Killen, AL] B: 6/6/1974, Killen, AL
Drafted: 1997 Round 5 TB
1997 TB: 14 G; Rush 1-1 1.0; Rec 4-22 5.5 1 TD; 6 Pt; 1 Fum. **1998** TB: 16 G; Rec 4-27 6.8; Scor 1 2XP; 2 Pt; 1 Fum. **Total:** 30 G; Rush 1-1 1.0; Rec 8-49 6.1 1 TD; Scor 1 2XP; 8 Pt; 2 Fum.

MERLE HAPES Hapes, Merle Alison 5′10″, 190 **FB-DB**
Col: Rancho Santiago Coll. CA (J.C.); Mississippi *HS:* Garden Grove [CA] B: 5/9/1919, Garden Grove, CA D: 7/18/1994, Biloxi, MS
Drafted: 1942 Round 1 NYG
1942 NYG: Pass 2-2 100.0%, -12 -6.00; Rec 10-79 7.9 2 TD; PR 11-170 15.5; KR 9-215 23.9; Int 3-49; Punt 15-557 37.1. **1946** NYG: Rec 3-40 13.3; PR 2-5 2.5; KR 2-43 21.5; Punt 12-479 39.9. **Total:** Pass 2-2 100.0%, -12 6.00; Rec 13-119 9.2 2 TD; PR 13-175 13.5; KR 11-258 23.5; Int 3-49; Punt 27-1036 38.4.

		Rushing					Tot
Year Team	**G**	**Att**	**Yds**	**Avg**	**TD**	**Fum**	**TD**
1942 NYG	11	95	363	3.8	3	0	5
1946 NYG	10	56	161	2.9	5	3	5
NFL Total	21	151	524	3.5	8	3	10

JIM HARBAUGH Harbaugh, James Joseph 6′3″, 215 **QB**
Col: Michigan *HS:* Pioneer [Ann Arbor, MI]; Palo Alto HS [CA]
B: 12/23/1963, Toledo, OH *Drafted:* 1987 Round 1 ChiB
1993 ChiB: Rec 1-1 1.0. **1995** Ind: Rec 1-(-9) -9.0. **Total:** Rec 2-(-8) -4.0.

		Passing							
Year Team	**G**	**Att**	**Comp**	**Comp%**	**Yds**	**YPA**	**TD**	**Int**	**Rating**
1987 ChiB	6	11	8	72.7	62	5.64	0	0	86.2
1988 ChiB	10	97	47	48.5	514	5.30	0	2	55.9
1989 ChiB	12	178	111	62.4	1204	6.76	5	9	70.5
1990 ChiB	14	312	180	57.7	2178	6.98	10	6	81.9
1991 ChiB	16	478	275	57.5	3121	6.53	15	16	73.7
1992 ChiB	16	358	202	56.4	2486	6.94	13	12	76.2
1993 ChiB	15	325	200	61.5	2002	6.16	7	11	72.1
1994 Ind	12	202	125	61.9	1440	7.13	9	6	85.8
1995 Ind	15	314	200	63.7	2575	**8.20**	17	**5**	**100.7**
1996 Ind	14	405	232	57.3	2630	6.49	13	11	76.3
1997 Ind	12	309	189	61.2	2060	6.67	10	4	86.2
1998 Bal	14	293	164	56.0	1839	6.28	12	11	72.9
NFL Total	156	3282	1933	58.9	22111	6.74	111	93	78.7

	Rushing				
Year Team	**Att**	**Yds**	**Avg**	**TD**	**Fum**
1987 ChiB	4	15	3.8	0	0
1988 ChiB	19	110	5.8	1	1
1989 ChiB	45	276	6.1	3	2
1990 ChiB	51	321	6.3	4	8
1991 ChiB	70	338	4.8	2	6
1992 ChiB	47	272	5.8	1	6
1993 ChiB	60	277	4.6	4	**15**
1994 Ind	39	223	5.7	0	1
1995 Ind	52	235	4.5	2	4
1996 Ind	48	192	4.0	1	8
1997 Ind	36	206	5.7	0	4
1998 Bal	40	172	4.3	0	7
NFL Total	511	2637	5.2	18	62

DAVE HARBOUR Harbour, David Lynn 6′4″, 265 **C**
Col: Illinois *HS:* St. Charles [IL] B: 10/23/1965, Boston, MA
1988 Was: 15 G; KR 1-6 6.0. **1989** Was: 16 G. **Total:** 31 G; KR 1-6 6.0.

JAMES HARBOUR Harbour, James Edward 6′1″, 192 **WR**
Col: Mississippi *HS:* Meridian [MS] B: 11/10/1962, Meridian, MS
Drafted: 1985 Round 7 Ind
1986 Ind: 9 G; Rec 4-46 11.5.

BUDDY HARDAWAY Hardaway, Milton Buddy Jr. 6′9″, 309 **OT**
Col: Blinn Coll. TX (J.C.); Oklahoma State *HS:* Seguin [TX]
B: 12/12/1954, Seguin, TX *Drafted:* 1978 Round 2 SD
1978 SD: 12 G.

BILLY HARDEE Hardee, Abraham Bill 6′0″, 184 **DB**
Col: Virginia Tech *HS:* Mulberry [FL] B: 8/12/1954, Lakeland, FL
1976 Den: 2 G. **1977** NYJ: 14 G; PR 1-17 17.0; KR 7-148 21.1; Int 1-0. **Total:** 16 G; PR 1-17 17.0; KR 7-148 21.1; Int 1-0.

DON HARDEMAN Hardeman, Donald Ray 6′2″, 235 **RB**
(Jaws) *Col:* Texas A&M–Kingsville *HS:* Killeen [TX] B: 8/13/1952, Killeen, TX *Drafted:* 1975 Round 1 Hou
1976 Hou: KR 7-171 24.4. **1978** Bal: KR 3-36 12.0. **Total:** KR 10-207 20.7.

		Rushing				Receiving					Tot
Year Team	**G**	**Att**	**Yds**	**Avg**	**TD**	**Rec**	**Yds**	**Avg**	**TD**	**Fum**	**TD**
1975 Hou	13	166	648	3.9	5	5	10	2.0	0	3	5
1976 Hou	13	32	114	3.6	1	7	25	3.6	0	0	1
1977 Hou	12	42	162	3.9	2	11	47	4.3	1	0	3
1978 Bal	13	48	244	5.1	0	10	88	8.8	0	1	0
1979 Bal	13	109	292	2.7	3	25	115	4.6	1	4	4
NFL Total	64	397	1460	3.7	11	58	285	4.9	2	8	13

BUDDY HARDEMAN Hardeman, Willie Riley Jr. 6′0″, 196 **RB**
Col: Iowa State *HS:* Auburn [NY] B: 10/21/1954, Auburn, NY
1979 Was: Pass 2-1 50.0%, 30 15.00 1 Int; PR 24-207 8.6; KR 19-404 21.3. **1980** Was: Pass 1-0. **Total:** Pass 3-1 33.3%, 30 10.00 1 Int; PR 24-207 8.6; KR 19-404 21.3.

		Rushing				Receiving				
Year Team	**G**	**Att**	**Yds**	**Avg**	**TD**	**Rec**	**Yds**	**Avg**	**TD**	**Fum**
1979 Was	10	31	124	4.0	0	21	197	9.4	1	4
1980 Was	15	40	132	3.3	0	16	178	11.1	0	2
NFL Total	25	71	256	3.6	0	37	375	10.1	1	6

BOBBY HARDEN Harden, Bobby Lee 6′0″, 192 **DB**
Col: Miami (Fla.) *HS:* Piper [Sunrise, FL] B: 2/8/1967, Pahokee, FL
Drafted: 1990 Round 12 Mia
1990 Mia: 1 G. **1991** Mia: 16 G; Int 2-39; 1 Sac. **1992** Mia: 4 G. **1993** Mia: 8 G. **Total:** 29 G; Int 2-39; 1 Sac.

DERRICK HARDEN Harden, Derrick 6′1″, 175 **WR**
Col: Ellsworth CC IA; Eastern New Mexico *HS:* South Division [Milwaukee, WI] B: 4/21/1964, Milwaukee, WI
1987 GB: 3 G; Rec 2-29 14.5; KR 4-72 18.0; 1 Fum.

LEE HARDEN Harden, Leon Maurice Jr. 5′11″, 195 **DB**
Col: Pratt CC KS; Texas-El Paso *HS:* Southeast [Kansas City, MO]
B: 8/17/1947, Kansas City, MO *Drafted:* 1969 Round 11 GB
1970 GB: 8 G; PR 2-(-7) -3.5; 1 Fum.

MIKE HARDEN Harden, Michael 6′1″, 192 **DB**
Col: Michigan *HS:* Central [Detroit, MI] B: 2/16/1958, Memphis, TN
Drafted: 1980 Round 5 Den
1980 Den: PR 2-36 18.0. **1985** Den: 1 Sac. **1986** Den: PR 1-41 41.0 1 TD. **1987** Den: PR 2-11 5.5. **1988** Den: PR 2-14 7.0. **1989** LARd: PR 1-11 11.0. **Total:** PR 8-113 14.1 1 TD; 1 Sac.

		Kickoff Returns				Interceptions				Tot
Year Team	**G**	**Ret**	**Yds**	**Avg**	**TD**	**Int**	**Yds**	**TD**	**Fum**	**TD**
1980 Den	16	12	214	17.8	0	0	0	0	1	0
1981 Den	16	11	178	16.2	0	2	34	0	0	0
1982 Den	5	0	0	—	0	2	3	0	0	0
1983 Den	15	1	9	9.0	0	4	127	0	0	0
1984 Den	16	1	4	4.0	0	6	79	1	1	1
1985 Den	16	0	0	—	0	5	100	**1**	0	1
1986 Den	16	0	0	—	0	6	179	2	0	3
1987 Den	12	0	0	—	0	4	85	0	0	0
1988 Den	16	1	9	9.0	0	4	36	0	1	0
1989 LARd	15	0	0	—	0	2	1	0	0	0
1990 LARd	15	0	0	—	0	3	19	0	0	0
NFL Total	158	26	414	15.9	0	38	663	4	3	5

PAT HARDER Harder, Marlin Martin 5′11″, 203 **FB-LB**
Col: Wisconsin *HS:* Washington [Milwaukee, WI] B: 5/6/1922, Milwaukee, WI D: 9/6/1992, Waukesha, WI *Drafted:* 1944 Round 1 ChiC
1946 ChiC: PR 1-10 10.0; KR 5-92 18.4. **1950** ChiC: KR 6-112 18.7. **1951** Det: Pass 1-0; KR 1-14 14.0. **Total:** Pass 1-0; PR 1-10 10.0; KR 12-218 18.2.

		Rushing				Receiving			
Year Team	**G**	**Att**	**Yds**	**Avg**	**TD**	**Rec**	**Yds**	**Avg**	**TD**
1946 ChiC	11	106	545	5.1	4	11	128	11.6	1
1947 ChiC	12	113	371	3.3	7	9	78	8.7	0
1948 ChiC	12	126	554	4.4	6	13	93	7.2	0
1949 ChiC	11	106	447	4.2	7	12	100	8.3	1
1950 ChiC	12	99	454	4.6	1	15	111	7.4	0
1951 Det	12	101	380	3.8	6	17	193	11.4	2
1952 Det	11	81	244	3.0	2	14	142	10.1	1
1953 Det	5	8	21	2.6	0	1	19	19.0	0
NFL Total	86	740	3016	4.1	33	92	864	9.4	5

	Scoring								Tot
Year Team	**Pts**	**FG**	**FGA**	**FG%**	**XK**	**XKA**	**XK%**	**Fum**	**TD**
1946 ChiC	35	0	0	—	5	5	100.0	4	5
1947 ChiC	**102**	**7**	10	70.0	39	40	97.5	7	7
1948 ChiC	**110**	7	**17**	41.2	**53**	**53**	100.0	3	6
1949 ChiC	**102**	3	5	60.0	**45**	**47**	95.7	3	8
1950 ChiC	40	4	9	44.4	22	24	91.7	0	1
1951 Det	57	3	5	60.0	0	0	—	4	8
1952 Det	85	11	23	47.8	34	35	97.1	0	3
1953 Det	0	0	0	—	0	0	—	1	0
NFL Total	531	35	69	50.7	198	204	97.1	22	38

STEVE HARDIN Hardin, Steven John 6′7″, 338 **OG**
Col: Oregon *HS:* Snohomish [WA] B: 12/30/1971, Bellevue, WA
1996 Ind: 1 G.

GREG HARDING Harding, Gregory 6′2″, 197 **DB**
Col: Nicholls State *HS:* Terrebonne [Houma, LA] B: 7/31/1960, New Orleans, LA
1984 NO: 3 G. **1987** Phi: 1 G. **Total:** 4 G.

ROGER HARDING Harding, Roger Paul 6′2″, 217 **C-LB**
Col: California *HS:* Acalanes [Lafayette, CA] B: 6/11/1923, Oakland, CA *Drafted:* 1945 Round 5 Cle
1945 Cle: 6 G; Int 1-16. **1946** LARm: 10 G; Int 1-14; 1 Fum. **1947** Phi: 6 G. **1948** Det: 11 G. **1949** NYB-GB: 9 G; Int 1-5. NYB: 3 G. GB: 6 G; Int 1-5. **Total:** 42 G; Int 3-35; 1 Fum.

DEE HARDISON Hardison, William David 6′4″, 274 **DE-NT-DT-DE**
Col: North Carolina *HS:* Hobbton [Newton Grove, NC] B: 5/2/1956, Jacksonville, NC *Drafted:* 1978 Round 2 Buf
1978 Buf: 16 G. **1979** Buf: 16 G. **1980** Buf: 16 G. **1981** NYG: Postseason only. **1982** NYG: 5 G. **1983** NYG: 16 G; 2.5 Sac. **1984** NYG: 15 G. **1985** NYG: 13 G. **1986** SD: 15 G; 6.5 Sac. **1987** SD: 3 G. **1988** KC: 7 G. **Total:** 122 G; 9 Sac.

CEDRICK HARDMAN Hardman, Cedrick Ward 6′3″, 255 **DE**
Col: North Texas *HS:* George Washington Carver [Houston, TX] B: 10/4/1948, Houston, TX *Drafted:* 1970 Round 1 SF
1970 SF: 14 G. **1971** SF: 14 G. **1972** SF: 14 G. **1973** SF: 14 G; Scor 1 Saf; 2 Pt. **1974** SF: 14 G. **1975** SF: 14 G. **1976** SF: 11 G. **1977** SF: 14 G. **1978** SF: 16 G. **1979** SF: 14 G. **1980** Oak: 16 G. **1981** Oak: 16 G; 1 Fum TD; 6 Pt. **Total:** 171 G; Scor 1 Saf; 1 Fum TD; 8 Pt.

ADRIAN HARDY Hardy, Adrian Paul 5′11″, 194 **DB**
Col: Northwestern State-Louisiana *HS:* Redeemer [New Orleans, LA] B: 8/16/1970, New Orleans, LA *Drafted:* 1993 Round 2 SF
1993 SF: 10 G. **1994** SF-Cin: 16 G; KR 8-185 23.1. SF: 2 G. Cin: 14 G; KR 8-185 23.1. **1995** Cin: 10 G. **Total:** 36 G; KR 8-185 23.1.

ANDRE HARDY Hardy, Andre Elton 6′1″, 233 **RB**
Col: San Diego City Coll. CA (J.C.); Weber State; St. Mary's (Cal.) *HS:* Herbert Hoover [San Diego, CA] B: 11/28/1961, San Diego, CA *Drafted:* 1984 Round 5 Phi
1984 Phi: Rec 2-22 11.0; KR 1-20 20.0. **1985** Sea: Rec 3-7 2.3. **1987** SF: Rec 1-7 7.0. **Total:** Rec 6-36 6.0; KR 1-20 20.0.

		Rushing				
Year Team	**G**	**Att**	**Yds**	**Avg**	**TD**	**Fum**
1984 Phi	6	14	41	2.9	0	0
1985 Sea	3	5	5	1.0	0	1
1987 SF	1	7	48	6.9	0	0
NFL Total	10	26	94	3.6	0	1

BRUCE HARDY Hardy, Bruce Alan 6′5″, 235 **TE-QB**
Col: Arizona State *HS:* Bingham [South Jordan, UT] B: 6/1/1956, Murray, UT *Drafted:* 1978 Round 9 Mia
1978 Mia: KR 2-27 13.5. **1979** Mia: Pass 1-0. **1983** Mia: Rush 1-2 2.0. **1985** Mia: KR 1-11 11.0. **1986** Mia: KR 3-39 13.0. **1987** Mia: KR 5-62 12.4. **1988** Mia: KR 1-17 17.0. **Total:** Pass 1-0; Rush 1-2 2.0; KR 12-156 13.0.

		Receiving				
Year Team	**G**	**Rec**	**Yds**	**Avg**	**TD**	**Fum**
1978 Mia	16	4	32	8.0	2	0
1979 Mia	16	30	386	12.9	3	0
1980 Mia	16	19	159	8.4	2	1
1981 Mia	16	15	174	11.6	0	1
1982 Mia	9	12	66	5.5	2	0
1983 Mia	15	22	202	9.2	0	0
1984 Mia	16	28	257	9.2	5	0
1985 Mia	16	39	409	10.5	4	1
1986 Mia	16	54	430	8.0	5	2
1987 Mia	12	28	292	10.4	2	1
1988 Mia	2	4	46	11.5	0	0
1989 Mia	1	1	2	2.0	0	0
NFL Total	151	256	2455	9.6	25	6

CARROLL HARDY Hardy, Carroll William 6′0″, 185 **HB**
Col: Colorado *HS:* Sturgis [SD] B: 5/18/1933, Sturgis, SD *Drafted:* 1955 Round 3 SF
1955 SF: 10 G; Rush 15-37 2.5; Rec 12-338 28.2 4 TD; KR 3-65 21.7; 24 Pt; 2 Fum.

CHARLIE HARDY Hardy, Charles 6′0″, 183 **WR**
Col: San Jose State *HS:* Oakland Technical [CA] B: 11/7/1933, Monroe, LA

		Receiving				
Year Team	**G**	**Rec**	**Yds**	**Avg**	**TD**	**Fum**
1960 Oak	14	24	423	17.6	3	1
1961 Oak	14	24	337	14.0	4	0
1962 Oak	5	6	80	13.3	0	0
NFL Total	33	54	840	15.6	7	1

CLIFF HARDY Hardy, Clifton 6′0″, 188 **DB**
Col: Michigan State *HS:* Roosevelt [Indianapolis, IN] B: 1/28/1947, Fairfield, AL *Drafted:* 1971 Round 11 ChiB
1971 ChiB: 1 G.

DARRYL HARDY Hardy, Darryl Gerrod 6′2″, 230 **LB**
Col: Tennessee *HS:* Princeton [Cincinatti, OH] B: 11/22/1968, Cincinnati, OH *Drafted:* 1992 Round 10 Atl
1995 Ariz-Dal: 9 G. Ariz: 4 G. Dal: 5 G. **1997** Dal-Sea: 14 G. Dal: 12 G. Sea: 2 G. **Total:** 23 G.

DAVID HARDY Hardy, David Robert 5′7″, 180 **K**
Col: Texas A&M *HS:* Huntsville [TX] B: 7/7/1959, Fort Worth, TX
1987 LARd: 2 G; Scor 7, 0-1 FG, 7-7 100.0% XK.

ED HARDY Hardy, Edgar Charles 6′4″, 242 **OG**
Col: Jackson State *HS:* Harper [Mendenhall, MS] B: 3/11/1951, Magee, MS *Drafted:* 1972 Round 7 SF
1973 SF: 3 G.

ISHAM HARDY Hardy, Isham Trotter 5′9″, 185 **G**
Col: William & Mary B: 3/28/1899, Blackstone, VA D: 1/23/1983, Richmond, VA
1923 Akr: 1 G. **1926** Akr: 2 G. **Total:** 3 G.

JIM HARDY Hardy, James Fred 6′0″, 180 **QB-DB**
Col: USC *HS:* Fairfax [Los Angeles, CA] B: 4/24/1923, San Pedro, CA *Drafted:* 1945 Round 1 Was
1946 LARm: Int 1-8. **1952** Det: Scor 1, 1-1 100.0% XK. **Total:** Int 1-8; Scor 13, 1-1 100.0% XK.

		Passing							
Year Team	**G**	**Att**	**Comp**	**Comp%**	**Yds**	**YPA**	**TD**	**Int**	**Rating**
1946 LARm	9	64	24	37.5	285	4.45	2	7	22.7
1947 LARm	9	57	23	40.4	388	6.81	5	7	53.7
1948 LARm	12	211	112	53.1	1390	6.59	14	7	82.1
1949 ChiC	12	150	63	42.0	748	4.99	10	13	44.0
1950 ChiC	11	257	117	45.5	1636	6.37	17	24	49.7
1951 ChiC	7	114	56	49.1	809	7.10	3	10	44.8
1952 Det	9	59	28	47.5	434	7.36	3	5	53.9
NFL Total	69	912	423	46.4	5690	6.24	54	73	53.1

	Rushing				Punting			
Year Team	**Att**	**Yds**	**Avg**	**TD**	**Punts**	**Yds**	**Avg**	**Fum**
1946 LARm	10	-10	-1.0	0	5	209	41.8	2
1947 LARm	3	-6	-2.0	0	10	263	26.3	2
1948 LARm	5	14	2.8	0	3	151	50.3	2
1949 ChiC	7	6	0.9	1	5	180	36.0	3
1950 ChiC	10	14	1.4	1	56	2208	39.4	9
1951 ChiC	12	38	3.2	0	0	0	—	2
1952 Det	5	16	3.2	0	0	0	—	0
NFL Total	52	72	1.4	2	79	3011	38.1	20

JOHN HARDY Hardy, John Louis 5′10″, 166 **DB**
Col: California *HS:* John Muir [Pasadena, CA] B: 6/11/1968, Pasadena, CA
1991 ChiB: 4 G.

KEVIN HARDY Hardy, Kevin Lamont 6′4″, 249 **LB**
Col: Illinois *HS:* William Henry Harrison [Evansville, IN] B: 7/24/1973, Evansville, IN *Drafted:* 1996 Round 1 Jac
1996 Jac: 16 G; Int 2-19; 5.5 Sac. **1997** Jac: 13 G; 2.5 Sac. **1998** Jac: 16 G; Int 2-40; 1.5 Sac. **Total:** 45 G; Int 4-59; 9.5 Sac.

KEVIN HARDY Hardy, Kevin Thomas 6′5″, 276 **DT**
Col: Notre Dame *HS:* St. Elizabeth [Oakland, CA] B: 7/28/1945, Oakland, CA *Drafted:* 1968 Round 1 NO
1968 SF: 12 G. **1970** GB: 14 G. **1971** SD: 13 G. **1972** SD: 6 G. **Total:** 45 G.

LARRY HARDY Hardy, Lawrence 6′3″, 234 **TE**
Col: Jackson State *HS:* Harper [Mendenhall, MS] B: 7/9/1956, Mendenhall, MS *Drafted:* 1978 Round 12 NO
1978 NO: KR 2-3 1.5. **Total:** KR 2-3 1.5.

		Receiving				
Year Team	**G**	**Rec**	**Yds**	**Avg**	**TD**	**Fum**
1978 NO	16	5	131	26.2	1	0
1979 NO	16	1	3	3.0	1	0
1980 NO	16	13	197	15.2	0	0
1981 NO	16	23	275	12.0	1	2
1982 NO	9	8	67	8.4	1	1
1983 NO	6	2	29	14.5	0	0
1984 NO	6	4	50	12.5	1	0
1985 NO	16	15	208	13.9	2	0
NFL Total	101	71	960	13.5	7	3

DICK HARDY Hardy, Richard Earle 5′10″, 210 **T**
Col: Boston College B: 9/1/1904, MA D: 2/27/1970, Togus, ME
1926 Rac: 5 G.

ROBERT HARDY Hardy, Robert Emmitt 6'2", 250 **DT**
Col: Jackson State *HS:* Booker T. Washington [Tulsa, OK]
B: 7/3/1956, Tulsa, OK *Drafted:* 1979 Round 10 Sea
1979 Sea: 16 G. **1980** Sea: 16 G. **1981** Sea: 14 G. **1982** Sea: 8 G; 2 Sac.
Total: 54 G; 2 Sac.

ROBERT HARDY Hardy, Robert Kenneth 5'10", 210 **RB**
Col: Lees-McRae JC NC; Carson-Newman *HS:* Gaffney [SC]
B: 9/1/1967, Gaffney, SC
1991 TB: 16 G; KR 8-119 14.9; 1 Fum.

TERRY HARDY Hardy, Terry 6'4", 266 **TE**
Col: Southern Mississippi *HS:* George Washington Carver [Montgomery, AL] B: 5/31/1976, Montgomery, AL *Drafted:* 1998 Round 5 Ariz
1998 Ariz: 9 G.

CECE HARE Hare, Cecil J 5'11", 195 **BB-LB-DB-HB**
Col: Gonzaga *HS:* Sheridan [OR] B: 3/2/1919, Glenbush, Canada
D: 4/14/1963
1941 Was: 11 G; Rush 5-19 3.8; Rec 1-25 25.0; Int 1-4. **1942** Was: 11 G; Rush 14-57 4.1; Rec 3-35 11.7 1 TD; PR 1-4 4.0; KR 1-11 11.0; **1** Fum TD; Tot TD 2; 12 Pt. **1945** Was: 9 G; Rush 3-0; Rec 3-83 27.7; KR 2-30 15.0; 1 Fum. **1946** NYG: 8 G; Rec 2-30 15.0; KR 1-19 19.0.
Total: 39 G; Rush 22-76 3.5; Rec 9-173 19.2 1 TD; PR 1-4 4.0; KR 4-60 15.0; Int 1-4; 1 Fum TD; Tot TD 2; 12 Pt; 1 Fum.

EDDIE HARE Hare, Edward Everett 6'4", 209 **P**
Col: Tulsa *HS:* Kilgore [TX] B: 5/30/1957, Ulysses, KS *Drafted:* 1979 Round 4 NE
1979 NE: Pass 1-1 100.0%, 4 4.00; Rush 1-0.

		Punting		
Year Team	**G**	**Punts**	**Yds**	**Avg**
1979 NE	16	83	3038	36.6

RAY HARE Hare, Raymond Lewis 6'1", 204 **BB-LB-DB-WB**
Col: Gonzaga *HS:* Sheridan [OR] B: 11/21/1917, North Battleford, Canada D: 6/2/1975, Chewelah, WA
AAFC **1946** NY-A: 4 G.

NFL **1941** Was: KR 3-57 19.0. **1942** Was: PR 1-0; KR 1-95 95.0 **1** TD; Int 1-0. **1943** Was: PR 1-5 5.0; KR 2-36 18.0; Int 3-13. **1944** Bkn: Pass 1-0; PR 2-5 2.5; KR 4-120 30.0; Int 1-12. **Total:** Pass 1-0; PR 4-10 2.5; KR 10-308 30.8 1 TD; Int 5-25.

		Rushing				Receiving				Tot
Year Team	**G**	**Att**	**Yds**	**Avg**	**TD**	**Rec**	**Yds**	**Avg**	**TD**	**TD**
1940 Was	5	1	2	2.0	0	0	0	—	0	0
1941 Was	11	12	51	4.3	1	12	87	7.3	0	1
1942 Was	11	27	197	7.3	1	5	57	11.4	0	2
1943 Was	10	21	96	4.6	0	2	9	4.5	0	0
1944 Bkn	10	72	196	2.7	0	9	206	22.9	1	1
NFL Total	47	133	542	4.1	2	28	359	12.8	1	4

TONY HARGAIN Hargain, Anthony Michael 6'0", 194 **WR**
Col: Oregon *HS:* Center [Elverta, CA] B: 12/26/1967, Palo Alto, CA
Drafted: 1991 Round 8 SF
1992 KC: 12 G; Rec 17-205 12.1.

EDD HARGETT Hargett, Edward Eugene 5'11", 185 **QB**
Col: Texas A&M *HS:* Linden-Kildare [Linden, TX] B: 6/26/1947, Marietta, TX *Drafted:* 1969 Round 16 NO
1969 NO: Rush 5-15 3.0. **1970** NO: Rush 4-7 1.8. **1971** NO: Rush 9-24 2.7 1 TD. **Total:** Rush 18-46 2.6 1 TD.

		Passing								
Year Team	**G**	**Att**	**Comp**	**Comp%**	**Yds**	**YPA**	**TD**	**Int**	**Rating**	**Fum**
1969 NO	6	52	31	59.6	403	7.75	0	0	84.1	0
1970 NO	10	175	78	44.6	1133	6.47	5	**5**	63.8	2
1971 NO	14	210	96	45.7	1191	5.67	6	5	63.4	1
1972 NO	14	0	0	—	0	—	0	0	—	0
1973 Hou	5	0	0	—	0	—	0	0	—	0
NFL Total	49	437	205	46.9	2727	6.24	11	10	66.0	3

JIM HARGROVE Hargrove, James Lawrence 6'2", 233 **LB**
(Red) *Col:* Howard Payne *HS:* Temple [TX] B: 2/21/1945, Temple, TX
Drafted: 1967 Round 14 Min
1967 Min: 14 G; Int 1-3; 6 Pt. **1969** Min: 6 G. **1970** Min: 12 G. **1971** StL: 14 G. **1972** StL: 10 G. **Total:** 56 G; Int 1-3; 6 Pt.

JIM HARGROVE Hargrove, Jimmy Rogers 6'2", 228 **RB**
Col: Wake Forest *HS:* Smithfield-Selma [Smithfield, NC]
B: 11/13/1957, Newton Grove, NC
1981 Cin: Rec 1-0. **1987** GB: Rec 1-6 6.0. **Total:** Rec 2-6 3.0.

		Rushing				
Year Team	**G**	**Att**	**Yds**	**Avg**	**TD**	**Fum**
1981 Cin	15	16	66	4.1	1	1
1987 GB	2	11	38	3.5	1	0
NFL Total	17	27	104	3.9	2	1

MARVIN HARGROVE Hargrove, Marvin Andre 5'10", 178 **WR**
Col: Richmond *HS:* Willingboro [NJ] B: 4/23/1968, Philadlphia, PA
1990 Phi: 7 G; Rec 1-34 34.0 1 TD; PR 12-83 6.9; KR 19-341 17.9; 6 Pt; 2 Fum.

LANCE HARKEY Harkey, Lance Marcel 5'10", 180 **DB**
Col: San Bernardino Valley Coll. CA (J.C.); Illinois *HS:* Alta Loma [CA]
B: 10/30/1965, Selma, AL
1987 LARd: 2 G; PR 2-17 8.5; KR 1-20 20.0.

LEM HARKEY Harkey, Lemuel Jr. 6'1", 205 **FB**
Col: Coll. of Emporia *HS:* Douglass [Lawton, OK] B: 1/7/1934, Oklahoma City, OK *Drafted:* 1955 Round 6 Pit
1955 SF: 4 G; Rush 6-27 4.5.

STEVE HARKEY Harkey, Stephen Douglas 6'0", 215 **RB**
Col: Georgia Tech *HS:* Westminster Boys School [Atlanta, GA]
B: 8/3/1949, Atlanta, GA *Drafted:* 1971 Round 16 NYJ
1971 NYJ: Rec 5-28 5.6; KR 1-2 2.0. **1972** NYJ: Rec 9-114 12.7.
Total: Rec 14-142 10.1; KR 1-2 2.0.

		Rushing				
Year Team	**G**	**Att**	**Yds**	**Avg**	**TD**	**Fum**
1971 NYJ	14	20	62	3.1	0	1
1972 NYJ	11	45	129	2.9	0	1
NFL Total	25	65	191	2.9	0	2

JIM HARLAN Harlan, James Thomas 6'4", 250 **OT**
Col: Howard Payne *HS:* C.E. Byrd [Shreveport, LA] B: 6/14/1954, Shreveport, LA *Drafted:* 1977 Round 6 SF
1978 Was: 14 G.

CHIC HARLEY Harley, Charles Wesley 5'8", 165 **HB**
Col: Ohio State *HS:* East [Columbus, OH] B: 9/15/1895, Columbus, OH D: 4/21/1974, Danville, OH
1921 Sta: 9 G; Pass 3 TD.

PAT HARLOW Harlow, Patrick Christopher 6'6", 295 **OT**
Col: USC *HS:* Norco [CA] B: 3/16/1969, Norco, CA *Drafted:* 1991 Round 1 NE
1991 NE: 16 G. **1992** NE: 16 G. **1993** NE: 16 G. **1994** NE: 16 G. **1995** NE: 10 G. **1996** Oak: 10 G. **1997** Oak: 16 G. **1998** Oak: 5 G. **Total:** 105 G.

ANDY HARMON Harmon, Andrew Phillip 6'4", 272 **DT-DE**
Col: Kent State *HS:* Centerville [OH] B: 4/6/1969, Dayton, OH
Drafted: 1991 Round 6 Phi
1991 Phi: 16 G. **1992** Phi: 16 G; 7 Sac. **1993** Phi: 16 G; 11.5 Sac.
1994 Phi: 16 G; Int 1-0; 9 Sac. **1995** Phi: 15 G; 11 Sac. **1996** Phi: 2 G; 1 Sac. **1997** Phi: 5 G. **Total:** 86 G; Int 1-0; 39.5 Sac.

CLARENCE HARMON Harmon, Clarence Junior 5'11", 204 **RB**
Col: Holmes CC MS; Mississippi State *HS:* Kosciusko [MS]
B: 11/30/1955, Kosciusko, MS
1977 Was: KR 1-18 18.0. **1978** Was: PR 1-5 5.0; KR 3-52 17.3. **1979** Was: PR 1-10 10.0; KR 5-63 12.6. **1982** Was: KR 1-13 13.0. **Total:** PR 2-15 7.5; KR 10-146 14.6.

		Rushing				Receiving					Tot
Year Team	**G**	**Att**	**Yds**	**Avg**	**TD**	**Rec**	**Yds**	**Avg**	**TD**	**Fum**	**TD**
1977 Was	12	94	310	3.3	0	14	119	8.5	1	1	1
1978 Was	16	34	141	4.1	0	11	112	10.2	1	0	1
1979 Was	16	65	267	4.1	0	32	434	13.6	5	3	5
1980 Was	16	128	484	3.8	4	54	534	9.9	4	4	8
1981 Was	5	1	4	4.0	0	11	98	8.9	0	0	0
1982 Was	9	38	168	4.4	1	11	86	7.8	0	0	1
NFL Total	74	360	1374	3.8	5	133	1383	10.4	11	8	16

DERRICK HARMON Harmon, Derrick Todd 5'10", 202 **RB**
Col: Cornell *HS:* Bayside [Queens, NY] B: 4/26/1963, New York, NY
Drafted: 1984 Round 9 SF
1984 SF: Pass 2-0; Rec 1-2 2.0. **1985** SF: Pass 1-0; Rec 14-123 8.8.
1986 SF: Rec 8-78 9.8. **Total:** Pass 3-0; Rec 23-203 8.8.

		Rushing				Kickoff Returns				
Year Team	**G**	**Att**	**Yds**	**Avg**	**TD**	**Ret**	**Yds**	**Avg**	**TD**	**Fum**
1984 SF	16	39	192	4.9	1	13	357	27.5	0	1
1985 SF	15	28	92	3.3	0	23	467	20.3	0	2
1986 SF	8	27	77	2.9	1	4	82	20.5	0	1
NFL Total	39	94	361	3.8	2	40	906	22.7	0	4

ED HARMON Harmon, Edward Charles 6'4", 235 **LB**
Col: Louisville *HS:* Bishop Gibbons [North Tonawanda, NY]
B: 12/16/1946, North Tonawanda, NY *Drafted:* 1968 Round 3 Dal
1969 Cin: 11 G.

HAM HARMON Harmon, Hamilton S 6'0", 220 **C-LB**
Col: Tulsa *HS:* Denton [TX] B: 4/2/1913 *Drafted:* 1937 Round 5 ChiC
1937 ChiC: 6 G.

KEVIN HARMON Harmon, Kevin Anthony 6'0", 190 **RB**
Col: Iowa *HS:* Bayside [Queens, NY] B: 10/26/1965, Queens, NY
Drafted: 1988 Round 4 Sea
1988 Sea: 5 G; Rush 2-13 6.5; KR 3-62 20.7. **1989** Sea: 4 G; Rush 1-24 24.0; KR 6-84 14.0. **Total:** 9 G; Rush 3-37 12.3; KR 9-146 16.2.

MIKE HARMON Harmon, Michael 6'0", 185 **WR**
Col: Mississippi *HS:* Kosciusko [MS] B: 7/24/1961, Kosciusko, MS
Drafted: 1983 Round 11 NYJ
1983 NYJ: 9 G; Rec 1-4 4.0; PR 12-109 9.1; 3 Fum.

RONNIE HARMON Harmon, Ronnie Keith 5'11", 200 **RB**
Col: Iowa *HS:* Bayside [Queens, NY] B: 5/7/1964, Queens, NY
Drafted: 1986 Round 1 Buf
1994 SD: Scor **3** 2XP. **Total:** Scor 3 2XP.

		Rushing				Receiving			
Year Team	G	Att	Yds	Avg	TD	Rec	Yds	Avg	TD
1986 Buf	14	54	172	3.2	0	22	185	8.4	1
1987 Buf	12	116	485	4.2	2	56	477	8.5	2
1988 Buf	16	57	212	3.7	1	37	427	11.5	3
1989 Buf	15	17	99	5.8	0	29	363	12.5	4
1990 SD	16	66	363	5.5	0	46	511	11.1	2
1991 SD	16	89	544	6.1	1	59	555	9.4	1
1992 SD	16	55	235	4.3	3	79	914	11.6	1
1993 SD	16	46	216	4.7	0	73	671	9.2	2
1994 SD	16	25	94	3.8	1	58	615	10.6	1
1995 SD	16	51	187	3.7	1	63	673	10.7	5
1996 Hou	16	29	131	4.5	1	42	488	11.6	2
1997 Ten-ChiB	12	10	36	3.6	0	18	197	10.9	0
1997 Ten	11	8	30	3.8	0	16	189	11.8	0
1997 ChiB	1	2	6	3.0	0	2	8	4.0	0
NFL Total	181	615	2774	4.5	10	582	6076	10.4	24

	Kickoff Returns					Tot
Year Team	Ret	Yds	Avg	TD	Fum	TD
1986 Buf	18	321	17.8	0	2	1
1987 Buf	1	30	30.0	0	2	4
1988 Buf	11	249	22.6	0	2	4
1989 Buf	18	409	22.7	0	2	4
1990 SD	0	0	—	0	1	2
1991 SD	2	25	12.5	0	2	2
1992 SD	7	96	13.7	0	4	4
1993 SD	1	18	18.0	0	0	2
1994 SD	9	157	17.4	0	0	2
1995 SD	4	25	6.3	0	1	6
1996 Hou	4	69	17.3	0	0	3
1997 Ten-ChiB	1	16	16.0	0	0	0
1997 Ten	1	16	16.0	0	0	0
NFL Total	76	1415	18.6	0	16	34

TOMMY HARMON Harmon, Thomas Dudley 6'1", 199 **HB-DB**
(Old 98) *Col:* Michigan *HS:* Horace Mann School [Gary, IN]
B: 9/28/1919, Rensselaer, IN D: 3/15/1990, Los Angeles, CA
Drafted: 1941 Round 1 ChiB
1946 LARm: Rec 10-199 19.9 2 TD; KR 6-134 22.3. **1947** LARm: Pass 3-1 33.3%, 31 10.33; Rec 5-89 17.8 1 TD; KR 9-208 23.1.
Total: Pass 3-1 33.3%, 31 10.33; Rec 15-288 19.2 3 TD; KR 15-342 22.8.

		Rushing				Punt Returns			
Year Team	G	Att	Yds	Avg	TD	Ret	Yds	Avg	TD
1946 LARm	10	47	236	5.0	2	5	57	11.4	0
1947 LARm	12	60	306	5.1	1	27	392	14.5	**1**
NFL Total	22	107	542	5.1	3	32	449	14.0	1

	Interceptions				Tot
Year Team	Int	Yds	TD	Fum	TD
1946 LARm	3	97	**1**	2	5
1947 LARm	8	136	1	3	4
NFL Total	11	233	2	5	9

TOM HARMON Harmon, Thomas Rockwell 6'4", 238 **OG**
Col: Gustavus Adolphus *HS:* Morningside [Edina, MN] B: 7/1/1945, Omaha, NE
1967 Atl: 10 G.

ART HARMS Harms, Arthur Gustav 6'1", 200 **T**
Col: Vermont *HS:* Flushing [Queens, NY] B: 6/25/1902, New York, NY
D: 7/24/1986, New Providence, NJ
1925 Fra: 9 G. **1926** NYG: 5 G. **Total:** 14 G.

JIM HARNESS Harness, James 5'11", 180 **DB**
Col: Mississippi State *HS:* Central [West Helena, AR] B: 4/6/1934, Dyersburg, TN *Drafted:* 1956 Round 21 Bal
1956 Bal: 1 G.

GEORGE HAROLD Harold, George Alton 6'3", 194 **DB**
Col: Allen *HS:* Lucy Craft Laney [Augusta, GA] B: 4/13/1942, Augusta, GA *Drafted:* 1965 Round 10 Bal
1966 Bal: 12 G. **1967** Bal: 2 G. **1968** Was: 8 G. **Total:** 22 G.

SHAWN HARPER Harper, Aaron Shawn 6'3", 290 **OT**
Col: North Iowa Area CC; Indiana *HS:* Independence [Columbus, OH]
B: 7/9/1968, Columbus, OH *Drafted:* 1992 Round 4 LARm
1995 Ind: 8 G.

ALVIN HARPER Harper, Alvin Craig 6'3", 210 **WR**
Col: Tennessee *HS:* Frostproof [FL] B: 7/6/1968, Lake Wells, FL
Drafted: 1991 Round 1 Dal
1992 Dal: Rush 1-15 15.0; Int 1-1. **1993** Dal: Pass 1-1 100.0%, 46 46.00.
Total: Pass 1-1 100.0%, 46 46.00; Rush 1-15 15.0; Int 1-1.

		Receiving				
Year Team	G	Rec	Yds	Avg	TD	Fum
1991 Dal	15	20	326	16.3	1	0
1992 Dal	16	35	562	16.1	4	1
1993 Dal	16	36	777	21.6	5	1
1994 Dal	16	33	821	**24.9**	8	2
1995 TB	13	46	633	13.8	2	0
1996 TB	12	19	289	15.2	1	1
1997 Was	12	2	65	32.5	0	0
NFL Total	100	191	3473	18.2	21	5

BRUCE HARPER Harper, Bruce S 5'8", 174 **RB-WR**
Col: Bergen CC NJ; Kutztown *HS:* Dwight Morrow [Englewood, NJ]
B: 6/20/1955, Englewood, NJ
1977 NYJ: Pass 1-0. **Total:** Pass 1-0.

		Rushing				Receiving			
Year Team	G	Att	Yds	Avg	TD	Rec	Yds	Avg	TD
1977 NYJ	14	44	198	4.5	0	21	209	10.0	1
1978 NYJ	16	58	303	5.2	2	13	196	15.1	2
1979 NYJ	16	65	282	4.3	0	17	250	14.7	2
1980 NYJ	15	45	126	2.8	0	50	634	12.7	3
1981 NYJ	16	81	393	4.9	4	52	459	8.8	1
1982 NYJ	9	20	125	6.3	0	14	177	12.6	1
1983 NYJ	9	51	354	6.9	1	48	413	8.6	2
1984 NYJ	4	10	48	4.8	1	5	71	14.2	0
NFL Total	99	374	1829	4.9	8	220	2409	11.0	12

	Punt Returns				Kickoff Returns					Tot
Year Team	Ret	Yds	Avg	TD	Ret	Yds	Avg	TD	Fum	TD
1977 NYJ	34	425	12.5	0	**42**	**1035**	24.6	0	7	1
1978 NYJ	30	378	12.6	**1**	**55**	**1280**	23.3	0	3	5
1979 NYJ	33	290	8.8	0	**55**	**1158**	21.1	0	6	2
1980 NYJ	28	242	8.6	0	49	1070	21.8	0	2	3
1981 NYJ	35	265	7.6	0	23	480	20.9	0	7	5
1982 NYJ	23	184	8.0	0	18	368	20.4	0	1	1
1983 NYJ	0	0	—	0	1	16	16.0	0	1	3
1984 NYJ	0	0	—	0	0	0	—	0	0	1
NFL Total	183	1784	9.7	1	243	5407	22.3	0	27	21

CHARLIE HARPER Harper, Charles Lynwood 6'0", 250 **OT-OG-DT**
Col: Oklahoma State *HS:* Broken Arrow [OK] B: 8/14/1944, Haskell, OK *Drafted:* 1966 Round 8 NYG
1966 NYG: 14 G. **1967** NYG: 14 G. **1968** NYG: 14 G. **1969** NYG: 14 G. **1970** NYG: 14 G. **1971** NYG: 14 G. **1972** NYG: 1 G. **Total:** 85 G.

DARRELL HARPER Harper, Darrell L 6'1", 195 **HB-K**
Col: Michigan *HS:* Royal Oak [MN] B: 6/18/1938 *Drafted:* 1960 Round 2 Buf
1960 Buf: 4 G; Rush 1-3 3.0; Scor 7, 2-3 66.7% FG, 1-2 50.0% XK.

DAVE HARPER Harper, David Douglas 6'1", 220 **LB**
Col: Humboldt State *HS:* Eureka [CA] B: 5/5/1966, Eureka, CA
Drafted: 1990 Round 11 Dal
1990 Dal: 6 G.

DWAYNE HARPER Harper, Dwayne Anthony 5'11", 175 **DB**
Col: South Carolina State *HS:* Orangeburg-Wilkinson [Orangeburg, SC]
B: 3/29/1966, Orangeburg, SC *Drafted:* 1988 Round 11 Sea
1988 Sea: 1 Sac. **1991** Sea: PR 1-5 5.0. **1992** Sea: 1 Fum TD.
Total: PR 1-5 5.0; 1 Fum TD; 1 Sac.

		Interceptions			
Year Team	G	Int	Yds	TD	Fum
1988 Sea	16	0	0	0	0
1989 Sea	16	2	15	0	0
1990 Sea	16	3	69	0	0
1991 Sea	16	4	84	0	0
1992 Sea	16	3	74	0	1
1993 Sea	14	1	0	0	0
1994 SD	16	3	28	0	0
1995 SD	16	4	12	0	0
1996 SD	6	1	0	0	0
1997 SD	12	2	43	0	0
1998 SD	1	1	12	0	0
NFL Total	145	24	337	0	1

JACK HARPER Harper, Jack Ridley 5′11″, 190 **RB**
Col: Florida *HS:* Lakeland [FL] B: 10/8/1944, Lakeland, FL
1967 Mia: Rec 11-212 19.3 3 TD; PR 4-15 3.8. **1968** Mia: PR 1-7 7.0; KR 1-18 18.0. **Total:** Rec 11-212 19.3 3 TD; PR 5-22 4.4; KR 1-18 18.0.

		Rushing					Tot
Year Team	G	Att	Yds	Avg	TD	Fum	TD
1967 Mia	9	41	197	4.8	1	3	4
1968 Mia	5	0	0	—	0	1	0
NFL Total	14	41	197	4.8	1	4	4

JOHN HARPER Harper, John III 6′3″, 230 **LB**
Col: Southern Illinois *HS:* Kingsbury [Memphis, TN] B: 6/12/1960, Memphis, TN *Drafted:* 1983 Round 4 Atl
1983 Atl: 13 G.

LASALLE HARPER Harper, LaSalle 6′1″, 235 **LB**
Col: Tyler JC TX; Arkansas *HS:* La Porte [TX] B: 5/16/1967, Galveston, TX *Drafted:* 1989 Round 9 ChiB
1989 NYG-ChiB: 4 G. NYG: 1 G. ChiB: 3 G. **Total:** 4 G.

MARK HARPER Harper, Mark 5′9″, 174 **DB**
Col: Alcorn State *HS:* Northside [Memphis, TN] B: 11/5/1961, Memphis, TN
1986 Cle: 16 G; Int 1-31. **1987** Cle: 12 G; Int 2-16; 1 Sac. **1988** Cle: 13 G; Int 2-13; 1 Sac. **1989** Cle: 16 G; Int 3-8; 1 Sac. **1990** Cle: 5 G. **Total:** 62 G; Int 8-68; 3 Sac.

MAURICE HARPER Harper, Maurice 6′4″, 227 **C-LB**
(Moose) *Col:* Austin *HS:* Sherman [TX] B: 5/14/1910, Bandera, TX D: 12/23/1991, Los Angeles, CA
1937 Phi: 9 G; Int **1** TD; 6 Pt. **1938** Phi: 11 G. **1939** Phi: 11 G. **1940** Phi: 9 G. **Total:** 40 G; Int 1 TD; 6 Pt.

MICHAEL HARPER Harper, Michael 5′10″, 180 **WR**
Col: USC *HS:* Hickman Mills [Kansas City, MO] B: 5/11/1961, Kansas City, MO *Drafted:* 1984 Round 11 LARm
1986 NYJ: KR 7-71 10.1. **1987** NYJ: PR 4-93 23.3 1 TD; KR 4-75 18.8. **1988** NYJ: KR 7-114 16.3. **1989** NYJ: Rush 1-3 3.0. **Total:** Rush 1-3 3.0; PR 4-93 23.3 1 TD; KR 18-260 14.4.

		Receiving				Tot
Year Team	G	Rec	Yds	Avg	TD	TD
1986 NYJ	16	0	0	—	0	0
1987 NYJ	3	18	225	12.5	1	2
1988 NYJ	10	0	0	—	0	0
1989 NYJ	6	7	127	18.1	0	0
NFL Total	35	25	352	14.1	1	2

ROGER HARPER Harper, Roger Michael 6′2″, 225 **DB**
Col: Ohio State *HS:* Independence [Columbus, OH] B: 10/26/1970, Columbus, OH *Drafted:* 1993 Round 2 Atl
1993 Atl: 16 G; 1 Fum. **1994** Atl: 10 G; Int 1-22; 1 Sac. **1995** Atl: 16 G; Int 1-0. **1996** Dal: 14 G; Int 2-30. **Total:** 56 G; Int 4-52; 1 Fum; 1 Sac.

ROLAND HARPER Harper, Roland 5′11″, 208 **RB**
(Bull) *Col:* Louisiana Tech *HS:* Eden Gardens [Shreveport, LA]; Captain Shreve HS [Shreveport,LA] B: 2/28/1953, Seguin, TX *Drafted:* 1975 Round 17 ChiB
1975 ChiB: KR 4-67 16.8. **1976** ChiB: KR 6-119 19.8. **1977** ChiB: Pass 2-0; KR 3-44 14.7. **1978** ChiB: Pass 1-0, 1 Int. **1982** ChiB: KR 2-10 5.0. **Total:** Pass 3-0, 1 Int; KR 15-240 16.0.

		Rushing				Receiving					Tot
Year Team	G	Att	Yds	Avg	TD	Rec	Yds	Avg	TD	Fum	TD
1975 ChiB	13	100	453	4.5	1	27	191	7.1	0	3	1
1976 ChiB	14	147	625	4.3	2	29	291	10.0	1	2	3
1977 ChiB	11	120	457	3.8	0	19	142	7.5	0	1	0
1978 ChiB	16	240	992	4.1	6	43	340	7.9	2	2	8
1980 ChiB	12	113	404	3.6	5	7	31	4.4	0	0	5
1981 ChiB	15	34	106	3.1	1	2	10	5.0	0	1	1
1982 ChiB	8	3	7	2.3	0	1	8	8.0	0	0	0
NFL Total	89	757	3044	4.0	15	128	1013	7.9	3	9	18

WILLIE HARPER Harper, Willie Miles 6′2″, 215 **LB**
Col: Nebraska *HS:* Jesup W. Scott [Toledo, OH] B: 7/30/1950, Toledo, OH *Drafted:* 1973 Round 2 SF
1973 SF: 14 G. **1974** SF: 14 G. **1975** SF: 13 G. **1976** SF: 14 G. **1977** SF: 12 G; Int 1-6. **1979** SF: 16 G. **1980** SF: 14 G. **1981** SF: 16 G. **1982** SF: 5 G; Int 1-0. **1983** SF: 16 G; Int 1-37; 3 Sac. **Total:** 134 G; Int 3-43; 3 Sac.

DENNIS HARRAH Harrah, Dennis Wayne 6′5″, 260 **OG-C**
Col: Miami (Fla.) *HS:* Stonewall Jackson [Charleston, WV] B: 3/9/1953, Charleston, WV *Drafted:* 1975 Round 1 LARm
1975 LARm: 14 G. **1976** LARm: 14 G; Rec 0-3. **1977** LARm: 8 G. **1978** LARm: 15 G. **1979** LARm: 13 G. **1980** LARm: 15 G. **1981** LARm: 15 G. **1982** LARm: 9 G. **1983** LARm: 15 G. **1984** LARm: 16 G. **1985** LARm: 10 G. **1986** LARm: 16 G. **1987** LARm: 8 G. **Total:** 168 G; Rec 0-3.

CHARLIE HARRAWAY Harraway, Charles Edward Jr. 6′2″, 215 **RB**
Col: San Jose State *HS:* American [Baumholder, Germany]; Monterey HS [CA] B: 9/21/1944, Oklahoma City, OK *Drafted:* 1966 Round 18 Cle
1966 Cle: KR 9-193 21.4. **1967** Cle: PR 1-7 7.0. **Total:** PR 1-7 7.0; KR 9-193 21.4.

		Rushing				Receiving					Tot
Year Team	G	Att	Yds	Avg	TD	Rec	Yds	Avg	TD	Fum	TD
1966 Cle	14	7	40	5.7	0	0	0	—	0	0	0
1967 Cle	14	5	-14	-2.8	0	0	0	—	0	0	0
1968 Cle	13	91	334	3.7	0	12	162	13.5	1	2	1
1969 Was	14	141	428	3.0	6	55	489	8.9	3	7	9
1970 Was	13	146	577	4.0	5	24	136	5.7	0	1	5
1971 Was	14	156	635	4.1	2	20	121	6.1	0	3	2
1972 Was	14	148	567	3.8	6	15	105	7.0	0	2	6
1973 Was	14	128	452	3.5	1	32	291	9.1	3	6	4
NFL Total	110	822	3019	3.7	20	158	1304	8.3	7	21	27

GARY HARRELL Harrell, Gary Lamar 5′7″, 170 **WR**
Col: Howard *HS:* Northwest Christian [Miami, FL] B: 1/23/1972, Miami, FL
1995 NYG: 4 G; PR 12-76 6.3; KR 1-23 23.0.

JAMES HARRELL Harrell, James Clearance Jr. 6′1″, 224 **LB**
Col: Florida *HS:* Chamberlain [Tampa, FL] B: 7/19/1957, Tampa, FL
1979 Det: 9 G. **1980** Det: 5 G. **1981** Det: 16 G; KR 1-0. **1982** Det: 9 G. **1983** Det: 16 G; 1 Sac. **1985** Det: 7 G; Int 1-20. **1986** Det: 16 G; 0.5 Sac. **1987** KC: 11 G. **Total:** 89 G; KR 1-0; Int 1-20; 1.5 Sac.

RICK HARRELL Harrell, Richard Lee 6′3″, 238 **C**
Col: Clemson *HS:* Morristown East [Morristown, TN] B: 8/8/1951, Morristown, TN *Drafted:* 1973 Round 6 NYJ
1973 NYJ: 4 G.

SAM HARRELL Harrell, Samuel Delmar Jr. 6′2″, 217 **RB**
Col: East Carolina *HS:* Ahoskie [NC] B: 2/7/1957, Ahoskie, NC *Drafted:* 1980 Round 11 Min
1981 Min: 4 G; Rush 1-7 7.0; Rec 2-23 11.5. **1982** Min: 1 G; KR 2-21 10.5; 1 Fum. **1987** Min: 1 G; Rush 5-8 1.6; Rec 3-20 6.7; KR 1-4 4.0; 1 Fum. **Total:** 6 G; Rush 6-15 2.5; Rec 5-43 8.6; KR 3-25 8.3; 2 Fum.

WILLARD HARRELL Harrell, Willard Race 5′8″, 182 **RB**
Col: U. of Pacific *HS:* Edison [Stockton, CA] B: 9/16/1952, Stockton, CA *Drafted:* 1975 Round 3 GB
1975 GB: Pass 5-3 60.0%, 61 12.20 3 TD. **1976** GB: Pass 4-1 25.0%, 40 10.00 1 TD 1 Int. **1977** GB: Pass 1-1 100.0%, 33 33.00. **1979** StL: Pass 1-0. **1982** StL: Pass 1-1 100.0%, 10 10.00. **Total:** Pass 12-6 50.0%, 144 12.00 4 TD 1 Int.

		Rushing				Receiving			
Year Team	G	Att	Yds	Avg	TD	Rec	Yds	Avg	TD
1975 GB	14	121	359	3.0	1	34	261	7.7	2
1976 GB	13	130	435	3.3	3	17	201	11.8	1
1977 GB	13	60	140	2.3	1	19	194	10.2	0
1978 StL	13	35	134	3.8	0	3	5	1.7	0
1979 StL	14	19	100	5.3	0	3	33	11.0	0
1980 StL	16	42	170	4.0	3	9	52	5.8	0
1981 StL	16	5	6	1.2	1	14	131	9.4	1
1982 StL	7	4	14	3.5	0	11	127	11.5	0
1983 StL	14	4	13	3.3	0	3	25	8.3	0
1984 StL	16	6	7	1.2	1	14	106	7.6	0
NFL Total	136	426	1378	3.2	10	127	1135	8.9	4

	Punt Returns				Kickoff Returns					Tot
Year Team	Ret	Yds	Avg	TD	Ret	Yds	Avg	TD	Fum	TD
1975 GB	21	136	6.5	0	3	78	26.0	0	11	3
1976 GB	3	-7	-2.3	0	0	0	—	0	9	4
1977 GB	28	253	9.0	1	3	48	16.0	0	3	2
1978 StL	21	196	9.3	**1**	19	389	20.5	0	4	1
1979 StL	32	205	6.4	0	22	497	22.6	0	5	0
1980 StL	11	31	2.8	0	19	348	18.3	0	3	3
1981 StL	1	8	8.0	0	7	118	16.9	0	0	2
1982 StL	1	1	1.0	0	8	150	18.8	0	0	0
1983 StL	5	31	6.2	0	3	62	20.7	0	1	0
1984 StL	0	0	—	0	13	231	17.8	0	0	1
NFL Total	123	854	6.9	2	97	1921	19.8	0	36	16

JOHN HARRINGTON Harrington, John Patrick 6′3″, 198 **OE-DE**
(Pinky) *Col:* Marquette *HS:* Reedsburg [WI] B: 4/15/1921, Reedsburg, WI D: 1/8/1992, Green Bay, WI
AAFC **1946** CleA: KR 2-16 8.0. **Total:** KR 2-16 8.0.

		Receiving			
Year Team	G	Rec	Yds	Avg	TD
1946 CleA	12	8	136	17.0	0
1947 ChiA	13	17	233	13.7	3
AAFC Total	25	25	369	14.8	3

LARUE HARRINGTON Harrington, LaRue Henry 6'0", 210 **RB**
Col: Norfolk State *HS:* I.C. Norcom [Portsmouth, VA] B: 6/28/1957, Norfolk, VA *Drafted:* 1980 Round 6 SD
1980 SD: 4 G; Rush 4-(-7) -1.8.

PERRY HARRINGTON Harrington, Perry Donell 5'11", 210 **RB**
Col: Jackson State *HS:* W.H. Lanier [Jackson, MS] B: 3/13/1958, Bentonia, MS *Drafted:* 1980 Round 2 Phi
1980 Phi: KR 6-104 17.3. **1983** Phi: KR 4-79 19.8. **1985** StL: KR 4-77 19.3. **Total:** KR 14-260 18.6.

		Rushing				Receiving				
Year Team	**G**	**Att**	**Yds**	**Avg**	**TD**	**Rec**	**Yds**	**Avg**	**TD**	**Fum**
1980 Phi	14	32	166	5.2	1	3	24	8.0	0	1
1981 Phi	4	34	140	4.1	2	9	27	3.0	0	1
1982 Phi	9	56	231	4.1	1	13	74	5.7	0	2
1983 Phi	15	23	98	4.3	1	1	19	19.0	0	1
1984 StL	6	3	6	2.0	0	0	0	—	0	0
1985 StL	11	7	42	6.0	1	0	0	—	0	1
NFL Total	59	155	683	4.4	6	26	144	5.5	0	6

AL HARRIS Harris, Alfred Carl 6'5", 250 **LB-DE**
Col: Arizona State *HS:* Leilehua [Wahiawa, HI] B: 12/31/1956, Bangor, ME *Drafted:* 1979 Round 1 ChiB
1979 ChiB: 4 G. **1980** ChiB: 16 G. **1981** ChiB: 16 G; Rec 1-18 18.0; Int 1-44 1 TD; 6 Pt. **1982** ChiB: 8 G; 3.5 Sac. **1983** ChiB: 13 G; 6 Sac. **1984** ChiB: 16 G; Int 1-34; 2 Sac. **1986** ChiB: 16 G; 2 Sac. **1987** ChiB: 12 G; 1.5 Sac. **1988** ChiB: 16 G; 3.5 Sac. **1989** Phi: 16 G; Int 2-18; Scor **1** Saf; 2 Pt; 2 Sac. **1990** Phi: 16 G. **Total:** 149 G; Rec 1-18 18.0; Int 4-96 1 TD; Scor 1 Saf; 8 Pt; 20.5 Sac.

AL HARRIS Harris, Alshinard 6'0", 185 **DB**
Col: Trinity Valley CC TX; Texas A&M–Kingsville *HS:* Ely [Pompano Beach, FL] B: 12/7/1974, Coconut Creek, FL *Drafted:* 1997 Round 6 TB
1998 Phi: 16 G; PR 1-(-2) -2.0; 1 Fum.

TONY HARRIS Harris, Anthony 6'2", 190 **DB**
Col: Toledo *HS:* John F. Kennedy [Cleveland, OH] B: 4/20/1949, Cleveland, OH *Drafted:* 1971 Round 4 SF
1971 SF: 4 G.

ANTHONY HARRIS Harris, Anthony Jerrod 6'1", 231 **LB**
Col: Auburn *HS:* Fort Pierce Westwood [FL] B: 1/25/1973, Fort Pierce, FL
1996 Mia: 7 G. **1997** Mia: 16 G; KR 1-0; 1 Sac. **1998** Mia: 5 G. **Total:** 28 G; KR 1-0; 1 Sac.

MICHAEL HARRIS Harris, Anthony Michael 6'4", 306 **C-OG**
Col: Grambling State *HS:* Booker T. Washington [Shreveport, LA] B: 8/30/1966, Shreveport, LA
1989 KC: 3 G.

ARCHIE HARRIS Harris, Archie Lee 6'6", 270 **OT**
Col: William & Mary *HS:* J.H.W. [Richmond, VA] B: 11/17/1964, Richmond, VA *Drafted:* 1987 Round 7 ChiB
1987 Den: 3 G.

BERNARDO HARRIS Harris, Bernardo Jamaine 6'2", 247 **LB**
Col: North Carolina *HS:* Chapel Hill [NC] B: 10/15/1971, Chapel Hill, NC
1995 GB: 11 G. **1996** GB: 16 G. **1997** GB: 16 G; Int 1-0; 1 Sac. **1998** GB: 16 G; 2 Sac. **Total:** 59 G; Int 1-0; 3 Sac.

CHUCK HARRIS Harris, Charles William 6'3", 255 **OT**
Col: North Iowa Area CC; West Virginia *HS:* Galena [IL] B: 10/7/1961, Columbus, OH
1987 ChiB: 3 G.

CLIFF HARRIS Harris, Clifford Allen 6'0", 188 **DB**
Col: Ouachita Baptist *HS:* Fayetteville [AR] B: 11/12/1948, Faytteville, AR

		Punt Returns				Kickoff Returns			
Year Team	**G**	**Ret**	**Yds**	**Avg**	**TD**	**Ret**	**Yds**	**Avg**	**TD**
1970 Dal	11	0	0	—	0	1	22	22.0	0
1971 Dal	14	17	129	7.6	0	29	823	28.4	0
1972 Dal	14	19	78	4.1	0	26	615	23.7	0
1973 Dal	14	3	20	6.7	0	6	148	24.7	0
1974 Dal	14	26	193	7.4	0	1	14	14.0	0
1975 Dal	14	0	0	—	0	0	0	—	0
1976 Dal	14	0	0	—	0	0	0	—	0
1977 Dal	14	1	-2	-2.0	0	0	0	—	0
1978 Dal	16	0	0	—	0	0	0	—	0
1979 Dal	16	0	0	—	0	0	0	—	0
NFL Total	141	66	418	6.3	0	63	1622	25.7	0

	Interceptions			
Year Team	**Int**	**Yds**	**TD**	**Fum**
1970 Dal	2	66	0	0
1971 Dal	2	0	0	4
1972 Dal	3	40	0	4
1973 Dal	2	9	0	0
1974 Dal	3	8	0	2
1975 Dal	3	58	1	0
1976 Dal	3	32	0	0
1977 Dal	5	7	0	0
1978 Dal	4	26	0	0
1979 Dal	2	35	0	0
NFL Total	29	281	1	10

BO HARRIS Harris, Clinton Lee Jr. 6'3", 225 **LB**
Col: Louisiana State *HS:* Captain Shreve [Shreveport, LA] B: 1/16/1953, Leesville, LA *Drafted:* 1975 Round 3 Cin
1975 Cin: 12 G. **1976** Cin: 14 G; Int 2-(-3); 1 Fum. **1977** Cin: 14 G; Int 2-17. **1978** Cin: 8 G. **1979** Cin: 15 G. **1980** Cin: 15 G. **1981** Cin: 16 G; Int 2-92. **1982** Cin: 9 G; Int 1-62 **1** TD; 6 Pt; 2 Sac. **Total:** 103 G; Int 7-168 1 TD; 6 Pt; 1 Fum; 2 Sac.

COREY HARRIS Harris, Corey Lamont 5'11", 200 **DB-WR**
Col: Vanderbilt *HS:* Ben Davis [Indianapolis, IN] B: 10/25/1969, Indianapolis, IN *Drafted:* 1992 Round 3 Hou
1992 Hou-GB: Rush 2-10 5.0; PR 6-17 2.8. Hou: PR 6-17 2.8. GB: Rush 2-10 5.0. **1993** GB: Rec 2-11 5.5. **1995** Sea: Int 3-(-5); **1** Fum TD. **1996** Sea: Int 1-25; 1 Sac. **1998** Bal: 1 Sac. **Total:** Rush 2-10 5.0; Rec 2-11 5.5; PR 6-17 2.8; Int 4-20; 1 Fum TD; 2 Sac.

		Kickoff Returns					Tot
Year Team	**G**	**Ret**	**Yds**	**Avg**	**TD**	**Fum**	**TD**
1992 Hou-GB	15	33	691	20.9	0	0	0
1992 Hou	5	10	206	20.6	0	0	0
1992 GB	10	23	485	21.1	0	0	0
1993 GB	11	16	482	30.1	0	0	0
1994 GB	16	29	618	21.3	0	1	0
1995 Sea	16	19	397	20.9	0	0	1
1996 Sea	16	7	166	23.7	0	0	0
1997 Mia	16	11	224	20.4	0	0	0
1998 Bal	16	35	965	27.6	1	2	1
NFL Total	106	150	3543	23.6	1	3	2

DARRYL HARRIS Harris, Darryl Lynn 5'10", 178 **RB**
Col: Arizona State *HS:* Garey [Pomona, CA] B: 2/20/1966, Jackson, MS
1988 Min: Rec 6-30 5.0.

		Rushing				Kickoff Returns				
Year Team	**G**	**Att**	**Yds**	**Avg**	**TD**	**Ret**	**Yds**	**Avg**	**TD**	**Fum**
1988 Min	14	34	151	4.4	1	39	833	21.4	0	1

DON HARRIS Harris, Donald Lesley 6'2", 185 **DB**
Col: Northland CC MN; Rutgers *HS:* Thomas Jefferson [Elizabeth, NJ] B: 2/8/1954, Elizabeth, NJ *Drafted:* 1977 Round 11 Was
1978 Was: 16 G; KR 6-99 16.5. **1979** Was: 16 G; KR 6-80 13.3. **1980** NYG: 11 G. **Total:** 43 G; KR 12-179 14.9.

DURIEL HARRIS Harris, Duriel LaDon Jr. 5'11", 179 **WR**
Col: New Mexico State *HS:* Austin [Port Arthur, TX] B: 11/27/1954, Port Arthur, TX *Drafted:* 1976 Round 3 Mia
1976 Mia: PR 9-79 8.8. **1979** Mia: Rush 1-20 20.0. **1982** Mia: Rush 1-13 13.0. **1983** Mia: Rush 1-0. **1984** Cle-Dal: PR 9-73 8.1. Cle: PR 9-73 8.1. **Total:** Rush 3-33 11.0; PR 18-152 8.4.

		Receiving				Kickoff Returns				
Year Team	**G**	**Rec**	**Yds**	**Avg**	**TD**	**Ret**	**Yds**	**Avg**	**TD**	**Fum**
1976 Mia	12	22	372	16.9	1	17	559	**32.9**	0	1
1977 Mia	14	34	601	17.7	5	4	91	22.8	0	0
1978 Mia	16	45	654	14.5	3	29	657	22.7	0	0
1979 Mia	15	42	798	19.0	3	0	0	—	0	0
1980 Mia	12	33	583	17.7	2	5	89	17.8	0	1
1981 Mia	15	53	911	17.2	2	1	20	20.0	0	0
1982 Mia	9	22	331	15.0	1	0	0	—	0	0
1983 Mia	12	15	260	17.3	1	0	0	—	0	0
1984 Cle-Dal	16	33	521	15.8	2	0	0	—	0	0
1984 Cle	11	32	512	16.0	2	0	0	—	0	0
1984 Dal	5	1	9	9.0	0	0	0	—	0	0
1985 Mia	6	3	24	8.0	0	0	0	—	0	1
NFL Total	127	302	5055	16.7	20	56	1416	25.3	0	3

DUD HARRIS Harris, Edmund Dudley 6'2", 240 **T**
Col: Ohio State; Marietta *HS:* East [Columbus, OH] B: 10/24/1903, Quitsna, NC D: 2/13/1989, Palm Springs, CA
1930 Port: 13 G.

AMOS HARRIS Harris, Edwin Amos 5'11", 175 **G**
Col: Mississippi State *HS:* Gulf Coast Mil. Acad. [MS] B: 1921
AAFC **1947** BknA: 14 G. **1948** BknA: 14 G; KR 1-10 10.0. **Total:** 28 G; KR 1-10 10.0.

ELMORE HARRIS Harris, Elmore Thomas 5'11", 175 **HB**
(Pepper) *Col:* Morgan State *HS:* Dover State [Normal, AL] B: 6/3/1922, Huntsville, AL D: 12/8/1968, Queens, NY
AAFC **1947** BknA: 10 G; Rush 3-(-2) -0.7; KR 14-329 23.5.

ELROY HARRIS Harris, Elroy Jr. 5'9", 218 **RB**
Col: Eastern Kentucky *HS:* Winter Park [FL] B: 8/18/1966, Orlando, FL
Drafted: 1989 Round 3 Sea
1989 Sea: 14 G; Rush 8-23 2.9; Rec 3-26 8.7; KR 18-334 18.6; 1 Fum.

ERIC HARRIS Harris, Eric Wayne 6'3", 198 **DB**
Col: Memphis *HS:* Hamilton [Memphis, TN] B: 8/11/1955, Memphis, TN *Drafted:* 1977 Round 4 KC
1984 LARm: 0.5 Sac. **Total:** 0.5 Sac.

		Interceptions		
Year Team	G	Int	Yds	TD
1980 KC	15	7	54	0
1981 KC	16	7	109	0
1982 KC	8	3	66	**1**
1983 LARm	16	4	100	0
1984 LARm	7	0	0	0
1985 LARm	9	0	0	0
NFL Total	71	21	329	1

FRANCO HARRIS Harris, Franco 6'2", 230 **RB**
Col: Penn State *HS:* Rancocas Valley Regional [Mount Holly, NJ]
B: 3/7/1950, Fort Dix, NJ *Drafted:* 1972 Round 1 Pit *HOF:* 1990
1972 Pit: KR 8-183 22.9. **1973** Pit: KR 1-23 23.0. **1975** Pit: KR 1-27 27.0.
1978 Pit: Pass 1-0. **Total:** Pass 1-0; KR 10-233 23.3.

		Rushing				Receiving					Tot
Year Team	G	Att	Yds	Avg	TD	Rec	Yds	Avg	TD	Fum	TD
1972 Pit	14	188	1055	5.6	10	21	180	8.6	1	7	11
1973 Pit	12	188	698	3.7	3	10	69	6.9	0	8	3
1974 Pit	12	208	1006	4.8	5	23	200	8.7	1	9	6
1975 Pit	14	262	1246	4.8	10	28	214	7.6	1	9	11
1976 Pit	14	289	1128	3.9	**14**	23	151	6.6	0	8	**14**
1977 Pit	14	300	1162	3.9	11	11	62	5.6	0	10	11
1978 Pit	16	310	1082	3.5	8	22	144	6.5	0	4	8
1979 Pit	15	267	1186	4.4	11	36	291	8.1	1	11	12
1980 Pit	13	208	789	3.8	4	30	196	6.5	2	7	6
1981 Pit	16	242	987	4.1	8	37	250	6.8	1	6	9
1982 Pit	9	140	604	4.3	2	31	249	8.0	0	1	2
1983 Pit	16	279	1007	3.6	5	34	278	8.2	2	10	7
1984 Sea	8	68	170	2.5	0	1	3	3.0	0	0	0
NFL Total	173	2949	12120	4.1	91	307	2287	7.4	9	90	100

FRANK HARRIS Harris, Frank Harmon 6'1", 196 **RB**
Col: Snow Coll. UT (J.C.); North Carolina State *HS:* Hampton [VA]
B: 7/1/1964, Waukesha, WI
1987 ChiB: 3 G; Rush 6-23 3.8.

FATTY HARRIS Harris, George Arthur **T**
Col: No College *HS:* Manual [Louisville, KY] B: 3/8/1884, Flemingsburg, KY D: 10/2/1963, Ashland, KY
1921 Lou: 1 G.

HARRY HARRIS Harris, Harry Frank 5'9", 175 **BB**
Col: West Virginia Wesleyan; West Virginia B: 9/10/1895 D: 3/1969, Martins Ferry, OH
1920 Akr: 11 G.

HANK HARRIS Harris, Henry Franklin 6'0", 265 **G-T**
(Demp) *Col:* Texas *HS:* Wilcox Co. [Camden, AL] B: 2/26/1923, Camden, AL *Drafted:* 1947 Round 6 Was
1947 Was: 10 G. **1948** Was: 2 G. **Total:** 12 G.

HERBERT HARRIS Harris, Herbert H Jr. 6'1", 206 **WR**
Col: Lamar *HS:* Kashmere [Houston, TX] B: 5/4/1961, Houston, TX
1986 NO: 7 G; Rec 11-148 13.5; KR 7-122 17.4; 1 Fum. **1987** NO: 2 G.
Total: 9 G; Rec 11-148 13.5; KR 7-122 17.4; 1 Fum.

IKE HARRIS Harris, Isiah Jr. 6'3", 210 **WR**
Col: Iowa State *HS:* West Memphis [AR] B: 11/27/1952, West Memphis, AR *Drafted:* 1974 Round 4 StL
1978 NO: Pass 1-0; Rush 2-22 11.0. **1979** NO: Rush 2-9 4.5.
Total: Pass 1-0; Rush 4-31 7.8.

		Receiving				
Year Team	G	Rec	Yds	Avg	TD	Fum
1975 StL	14	15	266	17.7	0	0
1976 StL	12	52	782	15.0	1	0
1977 StL	14	40	547	13.7	3	0
1978 NO	15	40	590	14.8	4	1
1979 NO	14	25	395	15.8	2	0
1980 NO	16	37	692	18.7	6	0
1981 NO	3	2	33	16.5	0	0
NFL Total	88	211	3305	15.7	16	1

JACKIE HARRIS Harris, Jackie Bernard 6'4", 244 **TE**
Col: Northeast Louisiana *HS:* Pine Bluff [AR] B: 1/4/1968, Pine Bluff, AR *Drafted:* 1990 Round 4 GB
1991 GB: Rush 1-1 1.0. **1994** TB: Scor 1 2XP. **1996** TB: Scor 1 2XP.
1998 Ten: KR 1-3 3.0. **Total:** Rush 1-1 1.0; KR 1-3 3.0; Scor 2 2XP.

		Receiving				
Year Team	G	Rec	Yds	Avg	TD	Fum
1990 GB	16	12	157	13.1	0	0
1991 GB	16	24	264	11.0	3	1
1992 GB	16	55	595	10.8	2	1
1993 GB	12	42	604	14.4	4	0
1994 TB	9	26	337	13.0	3	0
1995 TB	16	62	751	12.1	1	2
1996 TB	13	30	349	11.6	1	1
1997 TB	12	19	197	10.4	1	0
1998 Ten	16	43	412	9.6	2	0
NFL Total	126	313	3666	11.7	17	5

JIMMY HARRIS Harris, James Bedford 6'1", 178 **DB**
Col: Oklahoma *HS:* Terrell [TX] B: 11/12/1934, Terrell, TX
Drafted: 1957 Round 5 Phi
1957 Phi: PR 1-0. **1960** DalT: PR 1-5 5.0; KR 5-117 23.4. **Total:** PR 2-5 2.5; KR 5-117 23.4.

		Interceptions		
Year Team	G	Int	Yds	TD
1957 Phi	12	3	99	1
1958 LARm	12	4	51	0
1960 DalT	14	2	29	0
1961 Dal	11	2	13	0
NFL Total	49	11	192	1

JIM HARRIS Harris, James C 6'0", 173 **DB**
Col: Houston; Howard Payne *HS:* Brownwood [TX] B: 9/18/1946, Brownwood, TX *Drafted:* 1970 Round 7 Was
1970 Was: 3 G; KR 9-172 19.1; 1 Fum. **1971** Cin: 2 G. **Total:** 5 G; KR 9-172 19.1; 1 Fum.

JAMES HARRIS Harris, James Edward 6'6", 266 **DE**
Col: Temple *HS:* East St. Louis [IL] B: 5/13/1968, East St. Louis, IL
1993 Min: 6 G. **1994** Min: 16 G; Int 1-21; 1 Fum TD; 6 Pt; 2 Fum; 3 Sac.
1995 Min: 12 G; 1 Sac. **1996** StL: 16 G; 2 Sac. **1998** Oak: 16 G; 1 Sac.
Total: 66 G; Int 1-21; 1 Fum TD; 6 Pt; 2 Fum; 7 Sac.

JIM HARRIS Harris, James Jr. 6'4", 280 **DT**
(Diamond Jim) *Col:* Contra Costa Coll. CA (J.C.); Utah State
HS: Berkeley [CA] B: 2/24/1943, Lake Charles, LA *Drafted:* 1965 Round 7 NYJ
1965 NYJ: 14 G. **1966** NYJ: 14 G. **1967** NYJ: 14 G. **Total:** 42 G.

JAMES HARRIS Harris, James Larnell 6'4", 210 **QB**
Col: Grambling State *HS:* Carroll [Monroe, LA] B: 7/20/1947, Monroe, LA *Drafted:* 1969 Round 8 Buf

		Passing							
Year Team	G	Att	Comp	Comp%	Yds	YPA	TD	Int	Rating
1969 Buf	4	36	15	41.7	270	7.50	1	1	65.7
1970 Buf	7	50	24	48.0	338	6.76	3	4	56.9
1971 Buf	7	103	51	49.5	512	4.97	1	6	43.0
1973 LARm	8	11	7	63.6	68	6.18	0	0	80.9
1974 LARm	11	198	106	53.5	1544	7.80	11	6	85.1
1975 LARm	13	285	157	55.1	2148	7.54	14	15	73.8
1976 LARm	7	158	91	57.6	1460	9.24	8	6	89.6
1977 SD	9	211	109	51.7	1240	5.88	5	11	55.8
1978 SD	9	88	42	47.7	518	5.89	2	9	34.4
1979 SD	8	9	5	55.6	38	4.22	0	1	26.4
NFL Total	83	1149	607	52.8	8136	7.08	45	59	67.3

	Rushing				
Year Team	Att	Yds	Avg	TD	Fum
1969 Buf	10	25	2.5	0	3
1970 Buf	3	-8	-2.7	0	2
1971 Buf	6	42	7.0	0	3
1973 LARm	4	29	7.3	0	0
1974 LARm	42	112	2.7	5	7
1975 LARm	18	45	2.5	1	6
1976 LARm	12	76	6.3	2	5
1977 SD	10	13	1.3	2	4
1978 SD	10	7	0.7	0	5
1979 SD	6	26	4.3	0	1
NFL Total	121	367	3.0	10	36

JOHN HARRIS Harris, John Edward 6'2", 200 **DB**
Col: Arizona State *HS:* Miami Jackson [FL] B: 6/13/1956, Fort Benning, GA *Drafted:* 1978 Round 7 Sea
1978 Sea: PR 5-58 11.6. **1979** Sea: PR 8-70 8.8; KR 1-21 21.0. **1983** Sea: PR 2-27 13.5. **1984** Sea: KR 1-7 7.0; 1 Sac. **1985** Sea: PR 3-24 8.0.
Total: PR 18-179 9.9; KR 2-28 14.0; 1 Sac.

		Interceptions			
Year Team	G	Int	Yds	TD	Fum
1978 Sea	16	4	65	0	1
1979 Sea	14	2	30	0	1
1980 Sea	16	6	28	0	0
1981 Sea	16	10	155	2	1

Year Team					
1982 Sea	9	4	33	0	0
1983 Sea	16	2	15	0	0
1984 Sea	16	6	79	0	0
1985 Sea	16	7	20	0	0
1986 Min	16	3	69	0	0
1987 Min	12	3	20	0	0
1988 Min	13	3	46	0	0
NFL Total	160	50	560	2	3

JOHN HARRIS Harris, John Hiram 6′1″, 195 **DB-HB**
Col: Santa Monica Coll. CA (J.C.) *HS:* St. Peter Claver [San Antonio, TX] B: 5/7/1933, San Antonio, TX
1960 Oak: 14 G; KR 3-38 12.7. **1961** Oak: 14 G; Int 2-55. **Total:** 28 G; KR 3-38 12.7; Int 2-55.

JOHN HARRIS Harris, John T 196 **HB**
(Soldier) *Col:* No College B: 1898, CT Deceased
1926 Har: 2 G.

JON HARRIS Harris, Jonathan Cecil 6′7″, 300 **DE**
Col: Virginia *HS:* Kellenberg [Inwood, NY] B: 6/9/1974, Inwood, NY *Drafted:* 1997 Round 1 Phi
1997 Phi: 8 G; 1 Sac. **1998** Phi: 16 G; 1 Sac. **Total:** 24 G; 2 Sac.

JOE HARRIS Harris, Joseph Alexander 6′1″, 225 **LB**
Col: Georgia Tech *HS:* E.E. Smith [Fayetteville, NC] B: 12/6/1952, Fayetville, NC *Drafted:* 1975 Round 8 ChiB
1977 Was: 11 G. **1978** SF: 16 G. **1979** Min-LARm: 15 G; 6 Pt. Min: 2 G. LARm: 13 G; 6 Pt. **1980** LARm: 16 G. **1981** LARm: 16 G; Int 1-7; 1 Fum TD; 6 Pt. **1982** Bal: 9 G. **Total:** 83 G; Int 1-7; 1 Fum TD; Tot TD 2; 12 Pt.

KEN HARRIS Harris, Kenneth M 6′0″, 190 **FB**
(Bunk) *Col:* Syracuse; Columbia *HS:* Central [Duluth, MN] B: 6/1894, Duluth, MN Deceased
1923 Dul: 6 G; Pass 2 TD.

KENNY HARRIS Harris, Kenneth Lamont 6′1″, 198 **DB**
Col: North Carolina State *HS:* Northern [Durham, NC] B: 4/25/1975, Durham, NC
1997 Ariz: 11 G.

LEONARD HARRIS Harris, Leonard Milton Jr. 5′8″, 162 **WR**
Col: Austin; Texas Tech *HS:* McKinney [TX] B: 11/27/1960, McKinney, TX
1986 TB: PR 3-16 5.3. **1987** Hou: Rush 1-17 17.0. **1992** Hou: Rush 1-8 8.0. **Total:** Rush 2-25 12.5; PR 3-16 5.3.

		Receiving				Kickoff Returns				
Year Team	**G**	**Rec**	**Yds**	**Avg**	**TD**	**Ret**	**Yds**	**Avg**	**TD**	**Fum**
1986 TB	6	3	52	17.3	0	4	63	15.8	0	1
1987 Hou	3	10	164	16.4	0	3	87	29.0	0	0
1988 Hou	16	10	136	13.6	0	34	678	19.9	0	1
1989 Hou	11	13	202	15.5	2	14	331	23.6	0	1
1990 Hou	14	13	172	13.2	3	0	0	—	0	0
1991 Hou	9	8	101	12.6	0	2	34	17.0	0	0
1992 Hou	14	35	435	12.4	2	0	0	—	0	0
1993 Hou	4	4	53	13.3	1	0	0	—	0	0
1994 Atl	8	9	113	12.6	0	2	47	23.5	0	0
NFL Total	85	105	1428	13.6	8	59	1240	21.0	0	3

LEOTIS HARRIS Harris, Leotis 6′1″, 267 **OG**
Col: Arkansas *HS:* Hall [Little Rock, AR] B: 6/28/1955, Little Rock, AR *Drafted:* 1978 Round 6 GB
1978 GB: 13 G. **1979** GB: 15 G. **1980** GB: 16 G. **1981** GB: 16 G. **1982** GB: 9 G. **1983** GB: 5 G. **Total:** 74 G.

LEROY HARRIS Harris, Leroy 5′9″, 226 **RB**
Col: Fort Scott CC KS; Arkansas State *HS:* Savannah [GA] B: 7/3/1954, Savannah, GA *Drafted:* 1977 Round 5 Mia

		Rushing				Receiving					Tot
Year Team	**G**	**Att**	**Yds**	**Avg**	**TD**	**Rec**	**Yds**	**Avg**	**TD**	**Fum**	**TD**
1977 Mia	11	91	417	4.6	4	7	29	4.1	0	3	4
1978 Mia	15	123	512	4.2	2	25	211	8.4	0	5	2
1979 Phi	15	107	504	4.7	2	22	107	4.9	0	3	2
1980 Phi	15	104	341	3.3	3	15	207	13.8	1	2	4
1982 Phi	7	17	39	2.3	2	3	17	5.7	0	2	2
NFL Total	63	442	1813	4.1	13	72	571	7.9	1	15	14

LOU HARRIS Harris, Louis Richard 6′0″, 180 **DB**
Col: Kent State *HS:* Parker-Gray [Alexandria, VA] B: 3/25/1946, Washington, DC *Drafted:* 1968 Round 14 Pit
1968 Pit: 14 G; PR 6-21 3.5; KR 1-19 19.0.

MARK HARRIS Harris, Mark Edward 6′4″, 201 **WR**
Col: Ricks Coll. ID (J.C.); Southern Utah; Stanford *HS:* Box Elder [Brigham City, UT] B: 4/28/1970, Clovis, NM
1996 SF: 1 G. **1997** SF: 10 G; Rec 5-53 10.6. **1998** SF: 10 G; Rec 2-67 33.5. **Total:** 21 G; Rec 7-120 17.1.

MARSHALL HARRIS Harris, Marshall Kurt 6′6″, 261 **DE-NT**
Col: Texas Christian *HS:* Southwest [Fort Worth, TX] B: 12/6/1955, San Antonio, TX *Drafted:* 1979 Round 8 NYJ
1980 Cle: 16 G. **1981** Cle: 15 G. **1982** Cle: 9 G; 1.5 Sac. **1983** NE: 6 G; 0.5 Sac. **Total:** 46 G; 2 Sac.

MARV HARRIS Harris, Marvin Keith 6′1″, 237 **LB**
Col: Stanford *HS:* Coos Bay [OR] B: 7/8/1942, Coos Bay, OR *Drafted:* 1964 Round 13 LARm
1964 LARm: 14 G; KR 1-0.

M.L. HARRIS Harris, Michael Lee 6′5″, 238 **TE**
Col: Tampa; Kansas State *HS:* North [Columbus, OH] B: 1/16/1954, Columbus, OH
1980 Cin: Rush 1-0. **1982** Cin: Rush 2-(-3) -1.5. **1984** Cin: Rush 1-(-2) -2.0; KR 1-12 12.0. **Total:** Rush 4-(-5) -1.3; KR 1-12 12.0.

		Receiving				
Year Team	**G**	**Rec**	**Yds**	**Avg**	**TD**	**Fum**
1980 Cin	12	10	137	13.7	0	0
1981 Cin	15	13	181	13.9	2	1
1982 Cin	9	10	103	10.3	3	0
1983 Cin	12	8	66	8.3	2	0
1984 Cin	16	48	759	15.8	2	2
1985 Cin	10	10	123	12.3	1	0
NFL Total	74	99	1369	13.8	10	3

ODIE HARRIS Harris, Odie Lazar Jr. 6′0″, 190 **DB**
Col: Sam Houston State *HS:* Bryan [TX] B: 4/1/1966, Bryan, TX
1988 TB: 16 G; Int 2-26. **1989** TB: 16 G; Int 1-19. **1990** TB: 16 G. **1991** Cle: 16 G. **1992** Cle-Pho: 12 G. Cle: 4 G. Pho: 8 G. **1993** Pho: 16 G. **1994** Ariz: 13 G. **1995** Hou: 16 G; Int 2-0. **Total:** 121 G; Int 5-45.

RUDY HARRIS Harris, Onzell Andre 6′1″, 255 **RB**
Col: Clemson *HS:* Brockton [MA] B: 9/18/1971, Brockton, MA *Drafted:* 1993 Round 4 TB
1993 TB: 10 G; Rush 7-29 4.1; Rec 4-48 12.0. **1994** TB: 8 G; Rush 2-0; Rec 2-11 5.5; KR 1-12 12.0; 1 Fum. **Total:** 18 G; Rush 9-29 3.2; Rec 6-59 9.8; KR 1-12 12.0; 1 Fum.

PAUL HARRIS Harris, Paul Christopher 6′3″, 220 **LB**
Col: Alabama *HS:* Toulminville [Mobile, AL] B: 12/19/1954, Mobile, AL *Drafted:* 1977 Round 6 Pit
1977 TB: 14 G. **1978** Min-TB: 6 G. Min: 1 G. TB: 5 G. **Total:** 20 G.

PHIL HARRIS Harris, Philip Leon 6′0″, 195 **DB**
Col: Texas *HS:* Thomas Jefferson [San Antonio, TX] B: 9/13/1944, Jackson Hole, WY *Drafted:* 1966 Round 7 NYG
1966 NYG: 14 G; PR 5-7 1.4; KR 22-480 21.8; 1 Fum.

RAYMONT HARRIS Harris, Raymont LeShawn 6′0″, 226 **RB**
(Quiet Storm) *Col:* Ohio State *HS:* Admiral King [Lorain, OH] B: 12/23/1970, Lorain, OH *Drafted:* 1994 Round 4 ChiB
1994 ChiB: KR 1-18 18.0. **Total:** KR 1-18 18.0.

		Rushing				Receiving					Tot
Year Team	**G**	**Att**	**Yds**	**Avg**	**TD**	**Rec**	**Yds**	**Avg**	**TD**	**Fum**	**TD**
1994 ChiB	16	123	464	3.8	1	39	236	6.1	0	1	1
1995 ChiB	1	0	0	—	0	1	4	4.0	0	0	0
1996 ChiB	12	194	748	3.9	4	32	296	9.3	1	3	5
1997 ChiB	13	275	1033	3.8	10	28	115	4.1	0	1	10
1998 GB	8	79	228	2.9	1	10	68	6.8	0	3	1
NFL Total	50	671	2473	3.7	16	110	719	6.5	1	8	17

RICHARD HARRIS Harris, Richard Drew 6′5″, 260 **DE-DT**
(Panther) *Col:* Grambling State *HS:* Bethune [Shreveport, LA] B: 1/21/1948, Shreveport, LA *Drafted:* 1971 Round 1 Phi
1971 Phi: 14 G; KR 2-28 14.0. **1972** Phi: 14 G. **1973** Phi: 11 G. **1974** ChiB: 14 G. **1975** ChiB: 12 G. **1976** Sea: 14 G. **1977** Sea: 14 G. **Total:** 93 G; KR 2-28 14.0.

DICK HARRIS Harris, Richard May 5′11″, 187 **DB**
(Chucko) *Col:* McNeese State *HS:* San Pedro [CA] B: 7/24/1937, Denver, CO
1963 SD: KR 2-34 17.0. **1965** SD: KR 1-15 15.0. **Total:** KR 3-49 16.3.

		Punt Returns				Interceptions			
Year Team	**G**	**Ret**	**Yds**	**Avg**	**TD**	**Int**	**Yds**	**TD**	**Fum**
1960 LAC	14	13	105	8.1	0	5	56	1	1
1961 SD	14	0	0	—	0	7	140	**3**	0
1962 SD	14	7	95	13.6	0	5	52	0	1
1963 SD	14	4	43	10.8	0	8	83	1	0
1964 SD	6	0	0	—	0	3	82	0	0
1965 SD	14	3	8	2.7	0	1	0	0	0
NFL Total	76	27	251	9.3	0	29	413	5	2

RICKIE HARRIS Harris, Rickie Calvin 5′11″, 182 **DB**
Col: Arizona *HS:* John C. Fremont [Los Angeles, CA] B: 5/15/1943, St. Louis, MO

		Punt Returns				Kickoff Returns			
Year Team	G	Ret	Yds	Avg	TD	Ret	Yds	Avg	TD
1965 Was	14	31	377	12.2	1	5	96	19.2	0
1966 Was	13	18	108	6.0	**1**	20	405	20.3	0
1967 Was	14	23	208	9.0	0	25	580	23.2	0
1968 Was	14	19	144	7.6	0	23	579	25.2	0
1969 Was	14	14	158	11.3	**1**	19	458	24.1	0
1970 Was	14	14	10	0.7	0	10	208	20.8	0
1971 NE	14	5	19	3.8	0	0	0	—	0
1972 NE	14	4	5	1.3	0	0	0	—	0
NFL Total	111	128	1029	8.0	3	102	2326	22.8	0

	Interceptions				Tot
Year Team	Int	Yds	TD	Fum	TD
1965 Was	1	34	1	5	2
1966 Was	1	0	0	5	1
1967 Was	1	0	0	2	0
1968 Was	2	3	0	4	0
1969 Was	4	81	0	0	1
1970 Was	3	67	0	4	0
1971 NE	0	0	0	1	0
1972 NE	3	45	0	1	0
NFL Total	15	230	1	22	4

BOB HARRIS Harris, Robert Huel 6′2″, 219 **DB**
Col: Auburn *HS:* Cedar Grove [Decatur, GA] B: 11/11/1960, Everett, WA *Drafted:* 1983 Round 8 StL
1983 StL: 8 G; Int 3-10; 1 Sac. **1984** StL: 16 G; 2 Sac. **1985** StL: 10 G. **1987** KC: 3 G; 6 Pt. **Total:** 37 G; Int 3-10; 6 Pt; 3 Sac.

ROBERT HARRIS Harris, Robert Lee 6′4″, 295 **DE-DT**
Col: Southern University *HS:* Sun Coast [Riviera Beach, FL] B: 6/13/1969, Riviera Beach, FL *Drafted:* 1992 Round 2 Min
1992 Min: 7 G. **1993** Min: 16 G; 1 Sac. **1994** Min: 11 G; 2 Sac. **1995** NYG: 15 G; 5 Sac. **1996** NYG: 16 G; 4.5 Sac. **1997** NYG: 16 G; 10 Sac. **1998** NYG: 10 G; 3.5 Sac. **Total:** 91 G; 26.0 Sac.

ROD HARRIS Harris, Roderick World 5′10″, 183 **WR**
Col: Texas A&M *HS:* David W. Carter [Dallas, TX] B: 11/14/1966, Dallas, TX *Drafted:* 1989 Round 4 Hou
1991 Phi: Rec 2-28 14.0. **Total:** Rec 2-28 14.0.

		Punt Returns				Kickoff Returns				
Year Team	G	Ret	Yds	Avg	TD	Ret	Yds	Avg	TD	Fum
1989 NO	11	27	196	7.3	0	19	378	19.9	0	4
1990 Dal-Phi	11	28	214	7.6	0	2	44	22.0	0	3
1990 Dal	7	12	63	5.3	0	1	0	0.0	0	2
1990 Phi	4	16	151	9.4	0	1	44	44.0	0	1
1991 Phi	16	**53**	416	7.8	0	28	473	16.9	0	6
NFL Total	38	108	826	7.6	0	49	895	18.3	0	13

RONNIE HARRIS Harris, Ronnie James 5′11″, 179 **WR**
Col: Oregon *HS:* Valley Christian [San Jose, CA] B: 6/4/1970, Granada Hills, CA
1994 NE-Sea: Rec 1-11 11.0. NE: Rec 1-11 11.0. **1996** Sea: Rec 2-26 13.0. **1997** Sea: Rec 4-81 20.3. **1998** Sea-Atl: Rec 1-14 14.0. Atl: Rec 1-14 14.0. **Total:** Rec 8-132 16.5.

		Punt Returns				Kickoff Returns				
Year Team	G	Ret	Yds	Avg	TD	Ret	Yds	Avg	TD	Fum
1993 NE	5	23	201	8.7	0	6	90	15.0	0	2
1994 NE-Sea	2	3	26	8.7	0	0	0	—	0	1
1994 NE	1	3	26	8.7	0	0	0	—	0	1
1994 Sea	1	0	0	—	0	0	0	—	0	0
1995 Sea	13	3	23	7.7	0	1	29	29.0	0	0
1996 Sea	15	19	194	10.2	0	12	240	20.0	0	0
1997 Sea	13	21	144	6.9	0	14	318	22.7	0	4
1998 Sea-Atl	8	2	-6	-3.0	0	1	16	16.0	0	2
1998 Sea	2	1	-5	-5.0	0	0	0	—	0	1
1998 Atl	6	1	-1	-1.0	0	1	16	16.0	0	1
NFL Total	56	71	582	8.2	0	34	693	20.4	0	9

ROY HARRIS Harris, Roy Elliott 6′2″, 264 **DE-DT**
Col: Florida *HS:* West Orange [Winter Garden, FL] B: 3/26/1961, Winter Garden, FL
1984 Atl: 15 G; 1 Sac. **1985** Atl: 5 G. **1987** TB: 3 G; 1 Sac. **Total:** 23 G; 2 Sac.

SEAN HARRIS Harris, Sean Eugene 6′3″, 245 **LB**
Col: Arizona *HS:* Tuscon Magnet [AZ] B: 2/25/1972, Tuscon, AZ *Drafted:* 1995 Round 3 ChiB
1995 ChiB: 11 G. **1996** ChiB: 15 G. **1997** ChiB: 11 G. **1998** ChiB: 16 G; Int 1-0; 1 Sac. **Total:** 53 G; Int 1-0; 1 Sac.

DERRICK HARRIS Harris, Sidney Derrick 6′0″, 253 **RB**
Col: Miami (Fla.) *HS:* Willowridge [Sugar Land, TX] B: 9/18/1972, Angleton, TX *Drafted:* 1996 Round 6 StL
1996 StL: 11 G; Rush 3-5 1.7; Rec 4-17 4.3. **1998** StL: 16 G; Rush 14-38 2.7; Rec 12-57 4.8 2 TD; 12 Pt; 1 Fum. **Total:** 27 G; Rush 17-43 2.5; Rec 16-74 4.6 2 TD; 12 Pt; 1 Fum.

STEVE HARRIS Harris, Steven 5′11″, 194 **RB**
Col: Northern Iowa B: 12/12/1962, Chicago, IL
1987 Min: 2 G; Rush 4-3 0.8; Rec 2-17 8.5.

TIM HARRIS Harris, Timothy Allen 5′9″, 206 **RB**
Col: Washington State *HS:* Compton [CA] B: 6/15/1961, Compton, CA
1983 Pit: 14 G; Rush 2-15 7.5; PR 3-12 4.0; KR 18-289 16.1; 2 Fum.

TIM HARRIS Harris, Timothy David 6′6″, 260 **LB-DE**
Col: Memphis *HS:* Woodlawn [Birmingham, AL]; Memphis Catholic HS [TN] B: 9/10/1964, Birmingham, AL *Drafted:* 1986 Round 4 GB
1986 GB: 16 G; 8 Sac. **1987** GB: 12 G; 7 Sac. **1988** GB: 16 G; Scor **2** Saf; 10 Pt; 13.5 Sac. **1989** GB: 16 G; 19.5 Sac. **1990** GB: 16 G; 7 Sac. **1991** SF: 11 G; 3 Sac. **1992** SF: 16 G; 17 Sac. **1993** Phi: 4 G. **1994** SF: 5 G; 2 Sac. **1995** SF: 10 G; 4 Sac. **Total:** 122 G; Scor 2 Saf; 10 Pt; 81 Sac.

WALT HARRIS Harris, Walter Lee 5′11″, 194 **DB**
Col: Mississippi State *HS:* La Grange [GA] B: 8/10/1974, La Grange, GA *Drafted:* 1996 Round 1 ChiB

		Interceptions			
Year Team	G	Int	Yds	TD	Fum
1996 ChiB	15	2	0	0	0
1997 ChiB	16	5	30	0	1
1998 ChiB	14	4	41	1	0
NFL Total	45	11	71	1	1

WALTER HARRIS Harris, Walter Lee 6′1″, 195 **DB**
Col: Stanford *HS:* Lodi [CA] B: 4/1/1964, Stockton, CA
1987 SD: 3 G.

JACK HARRIS Harris, Welton John 5′11″, 190 **FB-OE-HB**
Col: Wisconsin *HS:* Racine [WI] B: 9/29/1902, Jackson, MI D: 12/28/1973, Indianapolis, IN
1925 GB: 11 G; Rush 1 TD; 6 Pt. **1926** GB: 10 G; Rush 2 TD; 12 Pt. **Total:** 21 G; Rush 3 TD; 18 Pt.

WENDELL HARRIS Harris, Wendell Preston 5′11″, 185 **DB-K**
Col: Louisiana State *HS:* Baton Rouge [LA] B: 10/2/1940, Baton Rouge, LA *Drafted:* 1962 Round 1 Bal
1962 Bal: KR 3-86 28.7; Int 2-52; Scor 9, 1-3 33.3% FG, 6-9 66.7% XK. **1963** Bal: KR 8-198 24.8. **1964** Bal: Int 1-20. **1965** Bal: Int 3-77. **1966** NYG: KR 1-9 9.0; Int 1-20; **1** Fum TD. **1967** NYG: Int 1-0; Scor 2, 0-1 FG, 2-2 100.0% XK. **Total:** KR 12-293 24.4; Int 8-169; Scor 17, 1-4 25.0% FG, 8-11 72.7% XK; 1 Fum TD.

		Punt Returns				
Year Team	G	Ret	Yds	Avg	TD	Fum
1962 Bal	14	8	61	7.6	0	4
1963 Bal	14	0	0	—	0	1
1964 Bal	14	17	214	12.6	0	2
1965 Bal	14	0	0	—	0	1
1966 NYG	13	0	0	—	0	1
1967 NYG	14	2	0	0.0	0	0
NFL Total	83	27	275	10.2	0	9

BILLY HARRIS Harris, William Andrews Jr. 6′2″, 204 **RB**
Col: Colorado *HS:* Galveston Central [TX] B: 1/17/1946, Galveston, TX *Drafted:* 1968 Round 13 Atl
1968 Atl: Rec 3-118 39.3 1 TD; KR 1-16 16.0. **1969** Min: Rec 2-13 6.5; KR 1-23 23.0. **Total:** Rec 5-131 26.2 1 TD; KR 2-39 19.5.

		Rushing				
Year Team	G	Att	Yds	Avg	TD	Fum
1968 Atl	6	53	144	2.7	0	1
1969 Min	13	6	13	2.2	0	0
1971 NO	1	1	1	1.0	0	0
NFL Total	20	60	158	2.6	0	1

WILLIAM HARRIS Harris, William Milton 6′4″, 239 **TE**
Col: Texas; Bishop *HS:* M.B. Smiley [Houston, TX] B: 2/10/1965, Houston, TX *Drafted:* 1987 Round 7 StL
1987 StL: 10 G; Rec 1-8 8.0. **1989** TB: 16 G; Rec 11-102 9.3 1 TD; 6 Pt. **1990** GB: 4 G. **Total:** 30 G; Rec 12-110 9.2 1 TD; 6 Pt.

BILLY HARRIS Harris, William Walter 6′2″, 196 **OE-DE**
Col: Hardin-Simmons B: 9/1/1914, Waco, TX D: 6/1979, San Benito, TX
1937 Pit: 1 G.

CHRIS HARRISON Harrison, Christopher Allen 6′3″, 290 **OG**
Col: Virginia *HS:* St. John's [Washington, DC] B: 2/25/1972, Washington, DC
1996 Det: 2 G.

DENNIS HARRISON Harrison, Dennis 6′8″, 275 **DE**
Col: Vanderbilt *HS:* Riverdale [Mufreesboro, TN] B: 7/31/1956, Cleveland, OH *Drafted:* 1978 Round 4 Phi
1978 Phi: 16 G; Int 1-12. **1979** Phi: 12 G. **1980** Phi: 15 G. **1981** Phi: 13 G. **1982** Phi: 9 G; 10.5 Sac. **1983** Phi: 16 G; 11.5 Sac. **1984** Phi: 16 G; 12 Sac. **1985** LARm: 12 G; 3 Sac. **1986** SF-Atl: 16 G; 1 Sac. SF: 5 G. Atl: 11 G; 1 Sac. **1987** Atl: 11 G; 1.5 Sac. **Total:** 136 G; Int 1-12; 39.5 Sac.

DWIGHT HARRISON Harrison, Dwight Webster 6′1″, 187 **WR-DB**
Col: Texas A&M–Kingsville *HS:* Beaumont [TX] B: 10/12/1948, Beaumont, TX *Drafted:* 1971 Round 2 Den
1971 Den: Rush 5-36 7.2; Rec 19-265 13.9 2 TD. **1972** Den-Buf: Rush 1-9 9.0; Rec 1-16 16.0; PR 1-2 2.0. Den: Rush 1-9 9.0. Buf: Rec 1-16 16.0; PR 1-2 2.0. **Total:** Rush 6-45 7.5; Rec 20-281 14.1 2 TD; PR 1-2 2.0.

		Interceptions				Tot
Year Team	G	Int	Yds	TD	Fum	TD
1971 Den	10	0	0	0	1	2
1972 Den-Buf	9	0	0	0	0	0
1972 Den	2	0	0	0	0	0
1972 Buf	7	0	0	0	0	0
1973 Buf	14	5	117	1	0	1
1974 Buf	13	1	24	0	0	0
1975 Buf	13	8	99	0	1	0
1976 Buf	12	1	18	0	0	0
1977 Buf	12	2	0	0	0	0
1978 Bal	15	0	0	0	0	0
1979 Bal	7	2	6	0	0	0
1980 Oak	3	0	0	0	0	0
NFL Total	108	19	264	1	2	3

ED HARRISON Harrison, Edward A 6′0″, 178 **E**
Col: Boston College *HS:* Brooklyn Prep [NY] B: 12/3/1902, New York, NY D: 5/1981, Bronxville, NY
1926 Bkn: 3 G.

PAT HARRISON Harrison, F.M. 6′2″, 215 **T**
Col: Samford *HS:* Thomasville [AL] B: 11/21/1911, Tallat Springs, AL
1937 Bkn: 3 G.

GLYNN HARRISON Harrison, Glynn Alan 5′11″, 191 **RB**
Col: Georgia *HS:* Columbia [Decatur, GA] B: 5/25/1954, Atlanta, GA *Drafted:* 1976 Round 9 SD
1976 KC: 8 G; Rush 16-41 2.6; Rec 1-12 12.0; KR 13-278 21.4; 1 Fum.

GRAN HARRISON Harrison, Granville Pearl 6′4″, 211 **DE-OE**
(Rock) *Col:* Mississippi State *HS:* Ashland [MS] B: 7/1/1917, Ashland, MS
1941 Phi: 1 G. **1942** Det: 4 G; Rec 3-21 7.0. **Total:** 5 G; Rec 3-21 7.0.

JIM HARRISON Harrison, Hulet James Jr. 6′4″, 235 **RB**
Col: Missouri *HS:* G. W. Brackenridge [San Antonio, TX] B: 9/10/1948, San Antonio, TX *Drafted:* 1971 Round 2 ChiB

		Rushing				Receiving					Tot
Year Team	G	Att	Yds	Avg	TD	Rec	Yds	Avg	TD	Fum	TD
1971 ChiB	2	5	13	2.6	0	2	18	9.0	0	0	0
1972 ChiB	14	167	622	3.7	2	8	30	3.8	1	7	3
1973 ChiB	13	100	370	3.7	1	21	200	9.5	2	2	3
1974 ChiB	9	36	94	2.6	1	5	38	7.6	0	0	1
NFL Total	38	308	1099	3.6	4	36	286	7.9	3	9	7

KENNY HARRISON Harrison, Kenneth Wayne 6′0″, 176 **WR**
Col: Southern Methodist *HS:* South Park [Beaumont, TX] B: 12/12/1953, Beaumont, TX *Drafted:* 1976 Round 9 SF
1977 SF: Pass 1-0; Rush 6-15 2.5. **1980** Was: Rush 2-(-11) -5.5. **Total:** Pass 1-0; Rush 8-4 0.5.

		Receiving				
Year Team	G	Rec	Yds	Avg	TD	Fum
1976 SF	11	3	65	21.7	0	0
1977 SF	14	15	217	14.5	1	4
1978 SF	8	16	320	20.0	0	0
1980 Was	9	8	66	8.3	0	0
NFL Total	42	42	668	15.9	1	4

MARTIN HARRISON Harrison, Martin Allen 6′5″, 252 **LB-DE**
Col: Washington *HS:* Newport [Bellevue, WA] B: 9/20/1967, Livermore, CA *Drafted:* 1990 Round 10 SF
1990 SF: 2 G. **1992** SF: 16 G; 3.5 Sac. **1993** SF: 11 G; 6 Sac. **1994** Min: 13 G. **1995** Min: 11 G; Int 1-15; 4.5 Sac. **1996** Min: 16 G; 7 Sac. **1997** Sea: 8 G. **Total:** 77 G; Int 1-15; 21 Sac.

MARVIN HARRISON Harrison, Marvin Daniel 6′0″, 181 **WR**
Col: Syracuse *HS:* Roman Catholic [Philadelphia, PA] B: 8/25/1972, Philadelphia, PA *Drafted:* 1996 Round 1 Ind
1996 Ind: Rush 3-15 5.0; PR 18-177 9.8. **1997** Ind: Rush 2-(-7) -3.5; Scor 2 2XP. **1998** Ind: Scor 1 2XP. **Total:** Rush 5-8 1.6; PR 18-177 9.8; Scor 3 2XP.

		Receiving				
Year Team	G	Rec	Yds	Avg	TD	Fum
1996 Ind	16	64	836	13.1	8	1
1997 Ind	16	73	866	11.9	6	2
1998 Ind	12	59	776	13.2	7	0
NFL Total	44	196	2478	12.6	21	3

MAX HARRISON Harrison, Maxwell Lamar 6′1″, 208 **OE-DE**
Col: Auburn *HS:* Escambia Co. [Altmore, AL] B: 1/29/1921, Cottonwood, AL
1940 NYG: 8 G; Rec 4-96 24.0.

NOLAN HARRISON Harrison, Nolan III 6′5″, 280 **DT-DE**
Col: Indiana *HS:* Homewood-Flossmoor [Flossmoor, IL] B: 1/25/1969, Chicago, IL *Drafted:* 1991 Round 6 LARd
1991 LARd: 14 G; 1 Sac. **1992** LARd: 14 G; Scor 1 Saf; 2 Pt; 2.5 Sac. **1993** LARd: 16 G; 3 Sac. **1994** LARd: 16 G; 5 Sac. **1995** Oak: 7 G. **1996** Oak: 15 G; 2 Sac. **1997** Pit: 16 G; 4 Sac. **1998** Pit: 9 G; 3.5 Sac. **Total:** 107 G; Scor 1 Saf; 2 Pt; 21 Sac.

REGGIE HARRISON Harrison, Reginald 5′11″, 218 **RB**
Col: Northeastern Oklahoma A&M (J.C.); Cincinnati *HS:* Washington Lee [Arlington, VA] B: 1/9/1951, Somerville, NJ *Drafted:* 1974 Round 9 StL
1974 StL-Pit: Rec 1-2 2.0; KR 4-72 18.0. Pit: Rec 1-2 2.0; KR 4-72 18.0. **1975** Pit: Rec 1-4 4.0. **1976** Pit: Rec 2-19 9.5; KR 1-26 26.0. **1977** Pit: Rec 3-11 3.7. **Total:** Rec 7-36 5.1; KR 5-98 19.6.

		Rushing				
Year Team	G	Att	Yds	Avg	TD	Fum
1974 StL-Pit	5	6	30	5.0	1	0
1974 StL	1	0	0	—	0	0
1974 Pit	4	6	30	5.0	1	0
1975 Pit	14	43	191	4.4	3	0
1976 Pit	12	54	235	4.4	4	1
1977 Pit	14	36	175	4.9	0	0
NFL Total	45	139	631	4.5	8	1

DICK HARRISON Harrison, Richard Proctor 6′0″, 195 **OE-DB**
Col: Boston College *HS:* Moses Brown School [Providence, RI] B: 4/13/1916, Buffalo, NY D: 5/30/1981, Boston, MA
1944 Bos: 4 G; Rec 1-9 9.0.

BOB HARRISON Harrison, Robert 5′11″, 185 **DB**
Col: Ohio U. *HS:* Vashon [St. Louis, MO] B: 11/15/1938, St. Louis, MO
1961 Bal: 13 G; PR 1-16 16.0; KR 11-250 22.7; Int 3-43.

ROB HARRISON Harrison, Robert 6′2″, 220 **DB**
Col: Coll of the Redwoods CA (J.C.); San Diego State; Sacramento State *HS:* Eureka [CA] B: 8/31/1963, Fortuna, CA *Drafted:* 1987 Round 10 LARd
1987 LARd: 2 G; Rush 9-49 5.4; Rec 2-18 9.0; 2 Fum.

BOB HARRISON Harrison, Robert Lucius Jr. 6′2″, 225 **LB**
Col: Oklahoma *HS:* Stamford [TX] B: 8/8/1937, Stamford, TX *Drafted:* 1959 Round 2 SF
1959 SF: 12 G. **1960** SF: 12 G; Int 1-6. **1961** SF: 14 G; Int 2-14. **1962** Phi: 13 G; Int 2-14. **1963** Phi: 9 G. **1964** Pit: 11 G. **1965** SF: 7 G. **1966** SF: 14 G. **1967** SF: 14 G. **Total:** 106 G; Int 5-34.

RODNEY HARRISON Harrison, Rodney Scott 6′1″, 203 **DB**
Col: Western Illinois *HS:* Marian Catholic [Chicago Heights, IL] B: 12/15/1972, Markham, IL *Drafted:* 1994 Round 5 SD
1996 SD: KR 1-10 10.0; 1 Sac. **1997** SD: PR 1-0; KR 1-40 40.0 1 TD; 1 Fum TD; 4 Sac. **1998** SD: 4 Sac. **Total:** PR 1-0; KR 2-50 25.0 1 TD; 1 Fum TD; 9 Sac.

		Interceptions				Tot
Year Team	G	Int	Yds	TD	Fum	TD
1994 SD	15	0	0	0	0	0
1995 SD	11	5	22	0	0	0
1996 SD	16	5	56	0	1	0
1997 SD	16	2	75	1	0	3
1998 SD	16	3	42	0	0	0
NFL Total	74	15	195	1	1	3

TODD HARRISON Harrison, Todd Lewis 6′4″, 260 **TE**
Col: North Carolina State *HS:* F.W. Buchholz [Gainesville, FL] B: 3/20/1969, Gainesville, FL *Drafted:* 1992 Round 5 ChiB
1992 TB: 1 G.

VIC HARRISON Harrison, Victor Mack 5′9″, 184 **WR**
Col: North Carolina *HS:* Warren Co. [Warrenton, NC] B: 2/9/1961, Vance Co., NC
1987 NO: 3 G.

ANTHONY HARRISON Harrison, Willie Anthony 6′1″, 195 **DB**
Col: Georgia Tech *HS:* Stephens Co. [Toccoa, GA] B: 9/26/1965, Toccoa, GA
1987 GB: 3 G; Int 1-0.

CARL HARRY Harry, Carl David 5′9″, 168 **WR**
Col: Utah *HS:* Fountain Valley [CA] B: 10/26/1967, Fountain Valley, CA
1989 Was: 1 G. **1992** Was: 1 G. **Total:** 2 G.

EMILE HARRY Harry, Emile Michael 5′11″, 175 **WR**
Col: Stanford *HS:* Fountain Valley [CA] B: 4/5/1963, Los Angeles, CA *Drafted:* 1985 Round 4 Atl
1986 KC: PR 6-20 3.3; KR 6-115 19.2. **1989** KC: Rush 1-9 9.0; PR 2-6 3.0. **1990** KC: PR 1-2 2.0. **1992** KC-LARm: Rush 1-27 27.0; PR 6-34 5.7.

KC: Rush 1-27 27.0. LARm: PR 6-34 5.7. **Total:** Rush 2-36 18.0; PR 15-62 4.1; KR 6-115 19.2.

Year Team	G	Receiving Rec	Yds	Avg	TD	Fum
1986 KC	12	9	211	23.4	1	1
1988 KC	16	26	362	13.9	1	0
1989 KC	16	33	430	13.0	2	1
1990 KC	16	41	519	12.7	2	0
1991 KC	12	35	431	12.3	3	0
1992 KC-LARm	11	6	58	9.7	0	0
1992 KC	7	5	46	9.2	0	0
1992 LARm	4	1	12	12.0	0	0
NFL Total	83	150	2011	13.4	9	2

BEN HART Hart, Benjamin Franklin 6′2″, 205 **DB**
Col: Oklahoma *HS:* Frederick Douglass [Oklahoma City, OK]
B: 8/19/1945, Oklahoma City, OK *Drafted:* 1967 Round 3 NO
1967 NO: 1 G; Int 1-21.

PETE HART Hart, Dee Whitfield 5′9″, 190 **FB**
Col: Hardin-Simmons *HS:* Aspermont [TX] B: 4/19/1933, Aspermont, TX
1960 NYT: Rec 3-19 6.3.

Year Team	G	Rushing Att	Yds	Avg	TD	Fum
1960 NYT	14	25	113	4.5	0	1

DOUG HART Hart, Douglas Wayne 6′0″, 190 **DB**
Col: Texas-Arlington *HS:* Handley [Fort Worth, TX] B: 6/3/1939, Fort Worth, TX
1965 GB: **1** Fum TD. **1967** GB: KR 1-8 8.0. **1971** GB: Scor 1 Saf.
Total: KR 1-8 8.0; Scor 1 Saf; 1 Fum TD.

Year Team	G	Interceptions Int	Yds	TD	Tot TD
1964 GB	14	1	0	0	0
1965 GB	14	4	29	0	1
1966 GB	14	1	40	1	1
1967 GB	14	0	0	0	0
1968 GB	14	1	24	0	0
1969 GB	14	3	156	1	1
1970 GB	14	3	114	1	1
1971 GB	14	2	73	0	1
NFL Total	112	15	436	3	5

HAROLD HART Hart, Harold Jerome 6′0″, 206 **RB**
Col: Texas Southern *HS:* New Stanton [Jacksonville, FL] B: 7/13/1952, Lake City, FL
1974 Oak: Rec 1-4 4.0; 1 Fum TD. **1975** Oak: Rec 6-27 4.5. **1978** Oak: Rec 1-1 1.0. **Total:** Rec 8-32 4.0; 1 Fum TD.

Year Team	G	Rushing Ret	Yds	Avg	TD	Kickoff Returns Ret	Yds	Avg	TD	Fum	Tot TD
1974 Oak	13	51	268	5.3	2	18	466	25.9	0	4	3
1975 Oak	9	56	173	3.1	3	17	518	30.5	**1**	2	4
1977 NYG	1	0	0	—	0	0	0	—	0	0	0
1978 Oak	7	7	44	6.3	0	11	252	22.9	0	1	0
NFL Total	30	114	485	4.3	5	46	1236	26.9	1	7	7

JIM HART Hart, James Warren 6′1″, 215 **QB**
Col: Southern Illinois *HS:* Niles West [Skokie, IL] B: 4/29/1944, Evanston, IL
1979 StL: Rec 1-(-4) -4.0. **Total:** Rec 1-(-4) -4.0.

Year Team	G	Passing Att	Comp	Comp%	Yds	YPA	TD	Int	Rating
1966 StL	1	11	4	36.4	29	2.64	0	0	44.9
1967 StL	14	397	192	48.4	3008	7.58	19	30	58.4
1968 StL	13	316	140	44.3	2059	6.52	15	18	58.2
1969 StL	9	169	84	49.7	1086	6.43	6	12	52.5
1970 StL	14	373	171	45.8	2575	6.90	14	18	61.5
1971 StL	11	243	110	45.3	1626	6.69	8	14	54.7
1972 StL	6	119	60	50.4	857	7.20	5	5	70.6
1973 StL	12	320	178	55.6	2223	6.95	15	10	80.0
1974 StL	14	**388**	200	51.5	2411	6.21	20	8	79.5
1975 StL	14	345	182	52.8	2507	7.27	19	19	71.7
1976 StL	14	388	218	56.2	2946	7.59	18	13	82.0
1977 StL	14	355	186	52.4	2542	7.16	13	20	64.3
1978 StL	15	477	240	50.3	3121	6.54	16	18	66.7
1979 StL	14	378	194	51.3	2218	5.87	9	20	55.2
1980 StL	15	425	228	53.6	2946	6.93	16	20	68.6
1981 StL	10	241	134	55.6	1694	7.03	11	14	68.7
1982 StL	4	33	19	57.6	199	6.03	1	0	85.3
1983 StL	5	91	50	54.9	592	6.51	4	8	53.0
1984 Was	2	7	3	42.9	26	3.71	0	0	53.3
NFL Total	201	5076	2593	51.1	34665	6.83	209	247	66.6

Year Team	Rushing Att	Yds	Avg	TD	Fum
1967 StL	13	36	2.8	3	4
1968 StL	19	20	1.1	6	3
1969 StL	7	16	2.3	2	1
1970 StL	18	18	1.0	0	6
1971 StL	13	9	0.7	0	2
1972 StL	9	17	1.9	0	3
1973 StL	3	-3	-1.0	0	2
1974 StL	10	21	2.1	2	5
1975 StL	11	7	0.6	1	7
1976 StL	8	7	0.9	0	4
1977 StL	11	18	1.6	0	5
1978 StL	11	11	1.0	2	5
1979 StL	6	11	1.8	0	5
1980 StL	9	11	1.2	0	4
1981 StL	3	2	0.7	0	4
1983 StL	5	12	2.4	0	5
1984 Was	3	-6	-2.0	0	0
NFL Total	159	207	1.3	16	65

JEFF HART Hart, Jeffery Allen 6′5″, 266 **OT**
Col: Oregon State *HS:* South Salem [Salem, OR] B: 9/10/1953, Portland, OR *Drafted:* 1975 Round 3 SF
1975 SF: 14 G; KR 2-28 14.0. **1976** NO: 14 G; KR 1-12 12.0. **1979** Bal: 16 G; KR 1-16 16.0. **1980** Bal: 16 G; KR 1-17 17.0. **1981** Bal: 16 G. **1982** Bal: 9 G. **1983** Bal: 14 G. **Total:** 99 G; KR 5-73 14.6.

LES HART Hart, Joseph Leslie 5′11″, 180 **BB**
Col: Colgate *HS:* Gorton [Yonkers, NY] B: 3/7/1908, Yonkers, NY
1931 SI: 5 G.

LEON HART Hart, Leon Joseph 6′5″, 257 **OE-DE-FB**
Col: Notre Dame *HS:* Turtle Creek [PA] B: 11/2/1928, Pittsburgh, PA
Drafted: 1950 Round 1 Det
1951 Det: Int 2-22. **1954** Det: **1** Fum TD. **1955** Det: KR 4-86 21.5.
Total: KR 4-86 21.5; Int 2-22; 1 Fum TD.

Year Team	G	Rushing Att	Yds	Avg	TD	Receiving Rec	Yds	Avg	TD	Fum	Tot TD
1950 Det	12	0	0	—	0	31	505	16.3	1	1	1
1951 Det	12	4	-6	-1.5	0	35	544	15.5	12	0	12
1952 Det	11	3	10	3.3	0	32	376	11.8	4	0	4
1953 Det	12	1	2	2.0	0	25	472	18.9	7	1	7
1954 Det	12	0	0	—	0	24	377	15.7	0	0	1
1955 Det	11	35	159	4.5	0	9	54	6.0	1	2	1
1956 Det	11	76	348	4.6	5	14	116	8.3	1	3	6
1957 Det	11	24	99	4.1	0	4	55	13.8	0	1	0
NFL Total	92	143	612	4.3	5	174	2499	14.4	26	8	32

LEO HART Hart, Marion Leo 6′3″, 203 **QB**
Col: Duke *HS:* Grainger [Kinston, NC] B: 3/3/1949, Kingston, NC
Drafted: 1971 Round 3 Atl
1971 Atl: 1 G; Pass 1-0. **1972** Buf: 2 G; Pass 15-6 40.0%, 53 3.53 3 Int; Rush 5-19 3.8; 2 Fum. **Total:** 3 G; Pass 16-6 37.5%, 53 3.31 3 Int; Rush 5-19 3.8; 2 Fum.

DICK HART Hart, Richard Kay 6′2″, 253 **OG**
Col: No College *HS:* Morrisville [PA] B: 3/4/1943, Morrisville, PA
1967 Phi: 14 G. **1968** Phi: 14 G. **1969** Phi: 14 G. **1970** Phi: 14 G.
1972 Buf: 5 G. **Total:** 61 G.

ROY HART Hart, Roy Jr. 6′1″, 280 **NT-DT**
Col: Northwest Mississippi CC; South Carolina *HS:* Tift Co. [Tifton, GA]
B: 7/10/1965, Tifton, GA *Drafted:* 1988 Round 6 Sea
1989 Sea: 16 G; 2 Sac. **1991** LARd: 1 G. **Total:** 17 G; 2 Sac.

TOMMY HART Hart, Tommy Lee 6′4″, 245 **DE-LB**
Col: Morris Brown *HS:* Ballard- Hudson [Macon, GA] B: 11/7/1944, Macon, GA *Drafted:* 1968 Round 10 SF
1968 SF: 5 G; KR 1-3 3.0. **1969** SF: 14 G. **1970** SF: 14 G; Int 1-0.
1971 SF: 14 G; **1** Fum TD; 6 Pt. **1972** SF: 14 G; Int 1-0. **1973** SF: 14 G.
1974 SF: 14 G. **1975** SF: 14 G; **1** Fum TD; 6 Pt. **1976** SF: 14 G; Scor **1** Saf; 2 Pt. **1977** SF: 14 G. **1978** ChiB: 16 G; Scor **1** Saf; 2 Pt.
1979 ChiB: 15 G. **1980** NO: 15 G. **Total:** 177 G; KR 1-3 3.0; Int 2-0; Scor 2 Saf; 2 Fum TD; 16 Pt.

MIKE HARTENSTINE Hartenstine, Michael Albert 6′3″, 251 **DE**
Col: Penn State *HS:* Liberty [Bethlehem, PA] B: 7/27/1953, Bethlehem, PA *Drafted:* 1975 Round 2 ChiB
1975 ChiB: 14 G; Scor **1** Saf; 2 Pt. **1976** ChiB: 14 G; Int 0-12 1 TD; 6 Pt.
1977 ChiB: 14 G. **1978** ChiB: 16 G. **1979** ChiB: 16 G. **1980** ChiB: 16 G.
1981 ChiB: 16 G. **1982** ChiB: 9 G; 3 Sac. **1983** ChiB: 16 G; 1 Fum TD; 6 Pt; 12 Sac. **1984** ChiB: 16 G; 7 Sac. **1985** ChiB: 16 G; 1 Sac.
1986 ChiB: 16 G; 1 Sac. **1987** Min: 5 G. **Total:** 184 G; Int 0-12 1 TD; Scor 1 Saf; 1 Fum TD; Tot TD 2; 14 Pt; 24.0 Sac.

JEFF HARTINGS Hartings, Jeffrey Allen 6′3″, 283 **OG**
Col: Penn State *HS:* St. Henry [OH] B: 9/7/1972, St. Henry, OH
Drafted: 1996 Round 1 Det
1996 Det: 11 G. **1997** Det: 16 G. **1998** Det: 13 G. **Total:** 40 G.

GREG HARTLE Hartle, Gregory Alan 6′2″, 225 **LB**
Col: Newberry *HS:* Newberry [SC] B: 2/14/1951, Savannah, GA
Drafted: 1974 Round 10 StL
1974 StL: 14 G. **1975** StL: 13 G; KR 1-20 20.0. **1976** StL: 1 G. **Total:** 28 G; KR 1-20 20.0.

FRANK HARTLEY Hartley, Frank 6′2″, 268 **TE**
Col: Illinois *HS:* Bogan [Chicago, IL] B: 12/15/1967, Chicago, IL
1998 SD: KR 1-11 11.0. **Total:** KR 1-11 11.0.

		Receiving				
Year Team	**G**	**Rec**	**Yds**	**Avg**	**TD**	**Fum**
1994 Cle	10	3	13	4.3	1	0
1995 Cle	15	11	137	12.5	1	1
1996 Bal	8	0	0	—	0	0
1997 SD	16	19	246	12.9	1	0
1998 SD	16	2	28	14.0	0	0
NFL Total	65	35	424	12.1	3	1

HOWARD HARTLEY Hartley, Howard Paul 6′0″, 185 **DB-HB-WB**
(Rabbit) *Col:* Duke *HS:* Ravenswood [WV] B: 9/26/1924, Ravenswood, WV
1948 Was: Rush 5-40 8.0 1 TD; Rec 1-10 10.0; KR 4-64 16.0. **1950** Pit: Rec 2-27 13.5; KR 1-44 44.0. **1951** Pit: KR 1-14 14.0. **Total:** Rush 5-40 8.0 1 TD; Rec 3-37 12.3; KR 6-122 20.3.

		Punt Returns				Interceptions			
Year Team	**G**	**Ret**	**Yds**	**Avg**	**TD**	**Int**	**Yds**	**TD**	**Fum**
1948 Was	12	2	41	20.5	0	3	76	0	3
1949 Pit	12	9	87	9.7	0	6	63	0	0
1950 Pit	12	5	23	4.6	0	5	84	0	3
1951 Pit	12	18	156	8.7	0	10	69	0	1
1952 Pit	9	1	34	34.0	0	4	51	0	1
NFL Total	57	35	341	9.7	0	28	343	0	8

KEN HARTLEY Hartley, Kenneth P 6′2″, 200 **P**
Col: Dean Coll. MA (J.C.); Catawba *HS:* King Philip [Wrentham, MA]
B: 4/28/1957, Bermuda, CO
1981 NE: 2 G; Punt 9-266 29.6.

FRED HARTMAN Hartman, Fred Lilburn 6′1″, 229 **T**
Col: Schreiner Coll.; Rice *HS:* Pampa [TX] B: 5/21/1917, Dallas, TX
D: 4/30/1984, Houston, TX *Drafted:* 1941 Round 8 ChiB
1947 ChiB: 11 G; Int 1-16 1 TD; 6 Pt. **1948** Phi: 12 G. **Total:** 23 G; Int 1-16 1 TD; 6 Pt.

JIM HARTMAN Hartman, James 6′2″, 205 **OE-DE**
Col: Colorado State B: 1913
1936 Bkn: 3 G.

BILL HARTMAN Hartman, William Coleman Jr. 6′0″, 188 **TB-DB-FB**
Col: Georgia Mil. Coll. (J.C.); Georgia *HS:* Upson [Thomaston, GA]
B: 3/17/1915, Thomaston, GA *Drafted:* 1938 Round 6 Was
1938 Was: Rec 1-6 6.0.

		Passing							
Year Team	**G**	**Att**	**Comp**	**Comp%**	**Yds**	**YPA**	**TD**	**Int**	**Rating**
1938 Was	10	77	38	49.4	558	7.25	4	10	51.1

	Rushing			
Year Team	**Att**	**Yds**	**Avg**	**TD**
1938 Was	71	195	2.7	0

PERRY HARTNETT Hartnett, Perry Edmund 6′5″, 278 **OG**
Col: Southern Methodist *HS:* Adidas [Galveston, TX] B: 4/28/1960, Galveston, TX *Drafted:* 1982 Round 5 ChiB
1982 ChiB: 9 G. **1983** ChiB: 2 G. **1987** GB: 1 G. **Total:** 12 G.

GEORGE HARTONG Hartong, George Howard 6′0″, 210 **G-T-C**
Col: Chicago *HS:* Joliet Twp. [Joliet, IL] B: 7/18/1896, Joliet, IL
D: 8/1973, Hinsdale, IL
1921 Ham: 3 G. **1923** Rac: 8 G. **1924** ChiC: 10 G. **Total:** 21 G.

LARRY HARTSHORN Hartshorn, Lawrence L 6′0″, 225 **OG**
Col: Kansas State *HS:* El Dorado [KS] B: 5/19/1933
1955 ChiC: 2 G.

CARTER HARTWIG Hartwig, Carter 6′0″, 205 **DB**
Col: USC *HS:* Central [Fresno, CA] B: 2/27/1956, Culver City, CA
Drafted: 1979 Round 8 Hou
1979 Hou: 16 G; KR 13-238 18.3; Int 2-24. **1980** Hou: 15 G; Int 1-0. **1981** Hou: 16 G; Int 3-78. **1982** Hou: 9 G. **1983** Hou: 16 G; 1 Sac. **1984** Hou: 14 G; Int 3-23. **Total:** 86 G; KR 13-238 18.3; Int 9-125; 1 Sac.

KEITH HARTWIG Hartwig, Malcolm Keith 6′0″, 186 **WR**
Col: Arizona *HS:* Central [Fresno, CA] B: 12/10/1953, Corona Del Mar, CA *Drafted:* 1977 Round 11 Min
1977 GB: 4 G.

JOHN HARTY Harty, John Daniel 6′4″, 260 **NT-DE**
Col: Iowa *HS:* Heelan [Sioux City, IA] B: 12/17/1958, Sioux City, IA
Drafted: 1981 Round 2 SF
1981 SF: 14 G. **1982** SF: 9 G; 2.5 Sac. **1983** SF: 5 G. **1985** SF: 7 G; Scor 1 Saf; 2 Pt. **1986** SF: 7 G. **Total:** 42 G; Scor 1 Saf; 2 Pt; 2.5 Sac.

BUG HARTZOG Hartzog, Howard Gallamore 5′11″, 195 **G-T-C**
Col: Baylor *HS:* San Marcos [TX] B: 4/11/1901, Terrell, TX
D: 5/18/1968, Marlin, TX
1928 NYG: 13 G.

CLAUDE HARVEY Harvey, Claude E 6′4″, 225 **LB**
Col: Prairie View A&M B: 3/27/1948, Willis, TX
1970 Hou: 5 G.

GEORGE HARVEY Harvey, George Everett 6′4″, 245 **OT**
Col: Kansas *HS:* Parsons [KS] B: 8/18/1945, Topeka, KS
Drafted: 1967 Round 6 NO
1967 NO: 6 G.

JIM HARVEY Harvey, James Britton Jr. 6′5″, 255 **OG-OT**
Col: Mississippi *HS:* Forest [MS] B: 8/20/1943, Jackson, MS
Drafted: 1965 Redshirt Round 2 Oak
1966 Oak: 14 G. **1967** Oak: 10 G. **1968** Oak: 14 G. **1969** Oak: 14 G. **1970** Oak: 14 G. **1971** Oak: 12 G. **Total:** 78 G.

JAMES HARVEY Harvey, James M 6′3″, 265 **OG-OT**
Col: Jackson State *HS:* Columbia [MS] B: 11/27/1965, New Orleans, LA
1987 KC: 3 G. **1988** KC: 1 G. **Total:** 4 G.

WADDEY HARVEY Harvey, James Wallace 6′4″, 282 **DT**
Col: Virginia Tech *HS:* Highland Springs [VA] B: 3/26/1947, Richmond, VA *Drafted:* 1969 Round 8 Buf
1969 Buf: 14 G; KR 1-11 11.0. **1970** Buf: 14 G. **Total:** 28 G; KR 1-11 11.0.

JOHN HARVEY Harvey, John Lewis 5′11″, 185 **RB**
Col: Texas-El Paso *HS:* Spring Valley [NY] B: 12/28/1966, New York, NY
1990 TB: Rec 11-86 7.8 1 TD; KR 12-207 17.3.

		Rushing				
Year Team	**G**	**Att**	**Yds**	**Avg**	**TD**	**Fum**
1990 TB	16	27	113	4.2	0	2

KEN HARVEY Harvey, Kenneth Ray 6′2″, 237 **LB**
Col: Laney Coll. CA (J.C.); California *HS:* Lanier [Austin, TX]
B: 5/6/1965, Austin, TX *Drafted:* 1988 Round 1 Pho
1988 Pho: 16 G; Scor 1 Saf; 2 Pt; 6 Sac. **1989** Pho: 16 G; 7 Sac. **1990** Pho: 16 G; 10 Sac. **1991** Pho: 16 G; 9 Sac. **1992** Pho: 10 G; 6 Sac. **1993** Pho: 16 G; 9.5 Sac. **1994** Was: 16 G; 13.5 Sac. **1995** Was: 16 G; 7.5 Sac. **1996** Was: 16 G; Int 1-2; 1 Fum; 9 Sac. **1997** Was: 15 G; 9.5 Sac. **1998** Was: 11 G; 2 Sac. **Total:** 164 G; Int 1-2; Scor 1 Saf; 2 Pt; 1 Fum; 89 Sac.

MARVIN HARVEY Harvey, Marvin Dwight 6′3″, 220 **TE-WR**
(Rock) *Col:* Southern Mississippi *HS:* Marianna [FL] B: 10/17/1959, Donalsonville, GA *Drafted:* 1981 Round 3 KC
1981 KC: 7 G.

MAURICE HARVEY Harvey, Maurice 5′10″, 190 **DB**
Col: Ball State *HS:* Princeton [Cincinatti, OH] B: 1/14/1956, Cincinatti, OH *Drafted:* 1978 Round 4 Oak
1978 Den: 16 G. **1980** Den: 15 G; Int 1-18. **1981** GB: 16 G; Int 6-217; 1 Fum. **1982** GB: 9 G; Int 2-32; 1 Fum TD; 6 Pt; 1 Sac. **1983** GB-Det: 13 G. GB: 4 G. Det: 9 G. **1984** TB: 15 G. **1987** Det: 2 G. **Total:** 86 G; Int 9-267; 1 Fum TD; 6 Pt; 1 Fum; 1 Sac.

NORM HARVEY Harvey, Norman C 6′0″, 196 **T-OE-C-G**
Col: Detroit Mercy *HS:* Calumet [MI] B: 8/27/1896, Calumet, MI
D: 2/1963, MI
1925 Buf: 5 G. **1926** Det: 8 G. **1927** Buf-NYY: 14 G. Buf: 5 G. NYY: 9 G. **1928** Prov: 9 G. **1929** Prov: 8 G. **Total:** 44 G.

RICHARD HARVEY Harvey, Richard Clemont Jr. 6′1″, 235 **LB**
Col: Tulane *HS:* Pascagoula [MS] B: 9/11/1966, Pascagoula, MS
Drafted: 1989 Round 11 Buf
1990 NE: 16 G. **1991** NE: 1 G. **1992** Buf: 12 G. **1993** Buf: 15 G. **1994** Den: 16 G. **1995** NO: 16 G; 2 Sac. **1996** NO: 14 G; 2 Sac. **1997** NO: 14 G; Int 1-7; 3 Sac. **1998** Oak: 16 G; Int 1-2; 4 Sac. **Total:** 120 G; Int 2-9; 11 Sac.

RICHARD HARVEY Harvey, Richard Clemont Sr. 6′2″, 190 **DB**
Col: Jackson State *HS:* 33rd Avenue [Gulfport, MS] B: 10/22/1945, Gulfport, MS *Drafted:* 1969 Round 8 LARm
1970 Phi: 4 G. **1971** NO: 3 G. **Total:** 7 G.

STACY HARVEY Harvey, Stacy Lamonte 6′4″, 245 **LB**
Col: Arizona State *HS:* Pasadena [CA] B: 3/8/1965, Pasadena, CA
1989 KC: 9 G.

FRANK HARVEY Harvey, Willie Frank 6'0", 245 RB
Col: Georgia *HS:* Terrell [Dawson, GA] B: 1/19/1971, Dawson, GA
Drafted: 1994 Round 7 Ariz
1994 Ariz: 2 G.

ALLEN HARVIN Harvin, Allen Nathaniel 5'9", 200 RB
Col: Cincinnati *HS:* Willingboro [NJ] B: 3/18/1959, Philadelphia, PA
1987 Was: 1 G.

JOHN HASBROUCK Hasbrouck, John Hutton 6'0", 190 WB-FB-E
(Ziggy) *Col:* Rutgers *HS:* Peekskill [NY] B: 1/20/1895, Port Ewen, NY
D: 10/19/1944, Port Ewen, NY
1921 Roch-RI: 5 G. Roch: 2 G. RI: 3 G. **Total:** 5 G.

CARLTON HASELRIG Haselrig, Carlton Lee 6'1", 293 DE
Col: Pittsburgh-Johnstown *HS:* Johnstown [PA] B: 1/22/1966, Johnstown, PA *Drafted:* 1989 Round 12 Pit
1990 Pit: 16 G. **1991** Pit: 16 G. **1992** Pit: 16 G. **1993** Pit: 9 G. **1995** NYJ: 11 G. **Total:** 68 G.

GEORGE HASENOHRL Hasenohrl, George Joseph 6'1", 260 DT
Col: Ohio State *HS:* Garfield Heights [OH] B: 3/10/1951, Cleveland, OH *Drafted:* 1973 Round 8 NYG
1974 NYG: 5 G.

JON HASKINS Haskins, Jon Radcliffe 6'2", 240 LB
Col: Stanford *HS:* Riverview [Sarasota, FL] B: 10/6/1975, Des Moines, IA *Drafted:* 1998 Round 7 SD
1998 SD: 2 G.

CLINT HASLERIG Haslerig, Clinton Edward 6'0", 189 WR-HB
Col: Michigan *HS:* Xavier [Cincinnati, OH] B: 4/9/1952, Cincinnati, OH
Drafted: 1974 Round 4 SF
1974 ChiB-Buf: 11 G. ChiB: 3 G. Buf: 8 G. **1975** Buf-Min: 10 G; Rush 2-9 4.5; Rec 2-28 14.0. Buf: 3 G; Rush 2-9 4.5. Min: 7 G; Rec 2-28 14.0.
1976 NYJ: 5 G. **Total:** 26 G; Rush 2-9 4.5; Rec 2-28 14.0.

JIM HASLETT Haslett, James Donald 6'3", 232 LB
Col: Indiana (Pa.) *HS:* Avalon [Pittsburgh, PA] B: 12/9/1955, Pittsburgh, PA *Drafted:* 1979 Round 2 Buf
1979 Buf: 16 G; Int 2-15. **1980** Buf: 16 G; Int 2-30. **1981** Buf: 16 G.
1982 Buf: 7 G; Rec 1-4 4.0. **1983** Buf: 5 G. **1984** Buf: 15 G; 3.5 Sac.
1985 Buf: 16 G; Int 1-40; 1 Fum; 1 Sac. **1987** NYJ: 3 G; Int 1-9.
Total: 94 G; Rec 1-4 4.0; Int 6-94; 1 Fum; 4.5 Sac.

WILBERT HASLIP Haslip, Wilbert 5'11", 212 RB
Col: Hawaii *HS:* Valley [Santa Ana, CA] B: 12/8/1956, El Centro, CA
Drafted: 1979 Round 8 SD
1979 KC: 5 G; Rush 2-1 0.5; KR 1-7 7.0.

HARALD HASSELBACH Hasselbach, Harald 6'6", 281 DE
Col: Washington *HS:* South Delta [Tsawassen, Canada] B: 9/22/1967, Amsterdam, Netherlands
1994 Den: 16 G; 2 Sac. **1995** Den: 16 G; 4 Sac. **1996** Den: 16 G; 2 Sac.
1997 Den: 16 G; 1.5 Sac. **1998** Den: 16 G; 3 Sac. **Total:** 80 G; 12.5 Sac.

DON HASSELBECK Hasselbeck, Donald William 6'7", 245 TE
Col: Colorado *HS:* La Salle [Cincinnati, OH] B: 4/1/1955, Cincinnati, OH *Drafted:* 1977 Round 2 NE
1981 NE: KR 1-7 7.0. **1985** NYG: KR 1-21 21.0. **Total:** KR 2-28 14.0.

		Receiving				
Year Team	G	Rec	Yds	Avg	TD	Fum
1977 NE	14	9	76	8.4	4	0
1978 NE	16	7	107	15.3	0	0
1979 NE	16	13	158	12.2	0	1
1980 NE	16	8	130	16.3	4	0
1981 NE	14	46	808	17.6	6	2
1982 NE	9	15	158	10.5	1	0
1983 NE-LARd	15	3	24	8.0	2	0
1983 NE	1	1	7	7.0	0	0
1983 LARd	14	2	17	8.5	2	0
1984 Min	16	1	10	10.0	0	0
1985 NYG	7	5	71	14.2	1	0
NFL Total	123	107	1542	14.4	18	3

ANDRE HASTINGS Hastings, Andre Orlando 6'1", 190 WR
Col: Georgia *HS:* Morrow [GA] B: 11/7/1971, Macon, GA
Drafted: 1993 Round 3 Pit
1993 Pit: KR 12-177 14.8. **1995** Pit: Rush 1-14 14.0. **1996** Pit: Rush 4-71 17.8; KR 1-42 42.0. **1997** NO: Rush 4-35 8.8; Scor 1 2XP. **1998** NO: Rush 3-32 10.7; KR 1-16 16.0. **Total:** Rush 12-152 12.7; KR 14-235 16.8; Scor 1 2XP.

		Receiving				Punt Returns					Tot
Year Team	G	Rec	Yds	Avg	TD	Ret	Yds	Avg	TD	Fum	TD
1993 Pit	6	3	44	14.7	0	0	0	—	0	0	0
1994 Pit	16	20	281	14.1	2	2	15	7.5	0	0	2
1995 Pit	16	48	502	10.5	1	48	474	9.9	**1**	1	2
1996 Pit	16	72	739	10.3	6	37	242	6.5	0	3	6
1997 NO	16	48	722	15.0	5	1	-2	-2.0	0	1	5
1998 NO	16	35	455	13.0	3	22	307	14.0	0	0	3
NFL Total	86	226	2743	12.1	17	110	1036	9.4	1	5	18

SANDY HASTINGS Hastings, Charles Elliot 5'8", 178 WB-BB-TB
Col: Pittsburgh *HS:* Brookville [PA]; Kiski School [Saltsburg, PA]
B: 1/24/1893, Brookville, PA Deceased
1920 Cle: 3 G.

GEORGE HASTINGS Hastings, George William 6'2", 190 T
Col: Ohio U. *HS:* Malden [MA] B: 9/21/1905, Malden, MA
D: 8/9/1981, Boston, MA
1930 Port: 1 G. **1931** Port: 1 G. **Total:** 2 G.

JAMES HASTY Hasty, James Edward 6'0", 203 DB
Col: Central Washington; Washington State *HS:* Franklin [Seattle, WA]
B: 5/23/1965, Seattle, WA *Drafted:* 1988 Round 3 NYJ
1988 NYJ: 1 Sac. **1990** NYJ: PR 1-0. **1994** NYJ: 3 Sac. **1996** KC:
1 Fum TD; 1 Sac. **1997** KC: 2 Sac. **1998** KC: 1 Sac. **Total:** PR 1-0; 1 Fum TD; 8 Sac.

		Interceptions				Tot
Year Team	G	Int	Yds	TD	Fum	TD
1988 NYJ	15	5	20	0	0	0
1989 NYJ	16	5	62	1	1	1
1990 NYJ	16	2	0	0	1	0
1991 NYJ	16	3	39	0	0	0
1992 NYJ	16	2	18	0	0	0
1993 NYJ	16	2	22	0	0	0
1994 NYJ	16	5	90	0	0	0
1995 KC	16	3	89	1	0	1
1996 KC	15	0	0	0	0	1
1997 KC	16	3	22	0	0	0
1998 KC	16	4	42	0	0	0
NFL Total	174	34	404	2	2	3

DALE HATCHER Hatcher, Roger Dale 6'2", 209 P
Col: Clemson *HS:* Cheraw [SC] B: 4/5/1963, Cheraw, SC
Drafted: 1985 Round 3 LARm
1989 LARm: Rush 1-0. **Total:** Rush 1-0.

		Punting		
Year Team	G	Punts	Yds	Avg
1985 LARm	16	87	3761	43.2
1986 LARm	16	97	3740	38.6
1987 LARm	15	76	**3140**	41.3
1988 LARm	7	36	1424	39.6
1989 LARm	16	73	2834	38.8
1991 LARm	13	63	2403	38.1
1993 Mia	16	58	2304	39.7
NFL Total	99	490	19606	40.0

RON HATCHER Hatcher, Ronald Allan 5'11", 215 FB
Col: Michigan State *HS:* Carnegie [PA] B: 7/3/1939, Pittsburgh, PA
Drafted: 1962 Round 8 Was
1962 Was: 3 G.

DERRICK HATCHETT Hatchett, Derrick Kingston 5'11", 182 DB
Col: Texas *HS:* John Jay [San Antonio, TX] B: 8/14/1958, Bryan, TX
Drafted: 1980 Round 1 Bal
1980 Bal: 16 G. **1981** Bal: 16 G; Int 2-8. **1982** Bal: 9 G; Int 1-0.
1983 Bal-Hou: 8 G; Int 4-36. Bal: 7 G; Int 4-36. Hou: 1 G. **Total:** 49 G; Int 7-44.

MATT HATCHETTE Hatchette, Matthew Isaac 6'2", 200 WR
(Rook) *Col:* Mercyhurst; Langston *HS:* Jefferson [Cleveland, OH]
B: 5/1/1974, Cleveland, OH *Drafted:* 1997 Round 7 Min
1997 Min: 16 G; Rec 3-54 18.0. **1998** Min: 5 G; Rec 15-216 14.4.
Total: 21 G; Rec 18-270 15.0.

RUSS HATHAWAY Hathaway, Russell Grant 5'11", 238 T-G
Col: Indiana *HS:* Dugger [IN]; Linton HS [IN] B: 1/14/1896, Terre Haute, IN D: 8/19/1988, Clay City, IN
1920 Mun-Day: 3 G. Mun: 1 G. Day: 2 G. **1921** Day: 9 G; Scor 24, 4 FG, 12 XK. **1922** Can-Day: 10 G; Scor 15, 2 FG, **8** XK, **1** 1XP. Can: 2 G. Day: 8 G; Scor 15, 2 FG, 8 XK, 1 1XP. **1923** Day: 8 G; Scor 10, 3 FG, 1 XK.
1924 Day: 8 G; Scor 6, 1 FG, 3 XK. **1925** Pott: 12 G. **1926** Pott: 10 G; Scor 3, 3 XK. **1927** Buf: 4 G. **Total:** 64 G; Scor 58, 10 FG, 27 XK, 1 1XP.

STEVE HATHAWAY Hathaway, Steven Francis 6'4", 238 LB
Col: West Virginia *HS:* Beaver [PA] B: 4/26/1962, Beaver, PA
Drafted: 1984 Round 12 Ind
1984 Ind: 6 G; KR 1-2 2.0.

DAVE HATHCOCK Hathcock, David Gary 6'0", 195 DB
(Buster) *Col:* Memphis *HS:* Kingsbury [Memphis, TN] B: 7/20/1943, Memphis, TN *Drafted:* 1966 Round 17 GB
1966 GB: 14 G. **1967** NYG: 6 G; PR 3-7 2.3; KR 14-315 22.5; 3 Fum.
Total: 20 G; PR 3-7 2.3; KR 14-315 22.5; 3 Fum.

JOHNNY HATLEY Hatley, Johnny Ray 6'3", 249 OG-DT
Col: Baylor; Sul Ross State *HS:* Uvalde [TX] B: 3/16/1930, Lometa, TX
Drafted: 1953 Round 16 ChiB
1953 ChiB: 10 G. **1954** ChiC: 12 G; KR 1-11 11.0. **1955** ChiC: 12 G; KR 2-13 6.5; 1 Fum. **1960** Den: 14 G. **Total:** 48 G; KR 3-24 8.0; 1 Fum.

TIM HAUCK Hauck, Timothy Christian 5′10″, 187 **DB**
Col: Pacific (Ore); Montana *HS:* Sweet Grass Co. [Big Timber, MT]
B: 12/20/1966, Butte, MT
1990 NE: 10 G. **1991** GB: 16 G. **1992** GB: 16 G; PR 1-2 2.0. **1993** GB: 13 G. **1994** GB: 13 G. **1995** Den: 16 G. **1996** Den: 16 G. **1997** Sea: 16 G. **1998** Ind: 16 G. **Total:** 132 G; PR 1-2 2.0.

ART HAUSER Hauser, Arthur A 6′0″, 237 **OT-OG**
Col: Xavier (Ohio) *HS:* Hartford [WI] B: 6/19/1929, Rubican, WI
Drafted: 1954 Round 5 LARm
1954 LARm: 12 G. **1955** LARm: 12 G; KR 2-17 8.5. **1956** LARm: 12 G. **1957** LARm: 12 G; 1 Fum TD; 6 Pt. **1959** ChiC-NYG: 6 G. ChiC: 2 G. NYG: 4 G. **1960** Bos: 8 G. **1961** Den: 14 G. **Total:** 76 G; KR 2-17 8.5; 1 Fum TD; 6 Pt.

KEN HAUSER Hauser, Kenneth 6′1″, 224 **FB-BB**
(One Round; Truck) *Col:* No College *HS:* South [Cleveland, OH]
B: 1899 Deceased
1927 Buf: 2 G. **1930** Nwk: 5 G. **Total:** 7 G.

EARL HAUSER Hauser, William Earl 6′1″, 190 **E-T**
Col: Miami (Ohio) *HS:* Covington [KY] B: 2/22/1897 D: 11/1974, Akron, OH
1920 Day: 6 G. **1921** Cin: 4 G; Rec 1 TD; 6 Pt. **Total:** 10 G; Rec 1 TD; 6 Pt.

LEN HAUSS Hauss, Leonard Moore 6′2″, 235 **C**
Col: Georgia *HS:* Jesup [GA] B: 7/11/1942, Jesup, GA *Drafted:* 1964 Round 9 Was
1964 Was: 14 G. **1965** Was: 14 G; 1 Fum. **1966** Was: 14 G. **1967** Was: 14 G. **1968** Was: 14 G. **1969** Was: 14 G. **1970** Was: 14 G. **1971** Was: 14 G. **1972** Was: 14 G. **1973** Was: 14 G. **1974** Was: 14 G. **1975** Was: 14 G. **1976** Was: 14 G. **1977** Was: 14 G; 1 Fum. **Total:** 196 G; 2 Fum.

CHARLIE HAVENS Havens, Charles William 5′10″, 205 **C**
Col: Colgate; Western Maryland *HS:* Rome Free Acad. [NY]
B: 7/12/1903, Rome, NY D: 5/12/1996, Gaithersburg, MD
1930 Fra: 13 G.

DAVE HAVERDICK Haverdick, David George 6′4″, 245 **DT**
Col: Morehead State *HS:* Glenwood [Canton, OH] B: 1/19/1948, Canton, OH *Drafted:* 1970 Round 13 Det
1970 Det: 8 G.

KEVIN HAVERDINK Haverdink, Kevin Dean 6′5″, 285 **OT**
Col: Western Michigan *HS:* Hamilton [MI] B: 10/20/1965, Holland, MI
Drafted: 1989 Round 5 NO
1989 NO: 16 G. **1990** NO: 15 G. **1991** NO: 10 G. **Total:** 41 G.

DENNIS HAVIG Havig, Dennis Eugene 6′2″, 253 **OG**
Col: Colorado *HS:* Powell [WY] B: 5/6/1949, Powell, WY
Drafted: 1971 Round 8 Atl
1972 Atl: 14 G. **1973** Atl: 14 G. **1974** Atl: 14 G. **1975** Atl: 13 G. **1976** Hou: 14 G. **1977** GB: 7 G. **Total:** 76 G.

SAM HAVRILAK Havrilak, Samuel Charles 6′2″, 195 **WR-RB**
Col: Bucknell *HS:* Monessen [PA] B: 12/13/1947, Charleroi, PA
Drafted: 1969 Round 8 Bal
1969 Bal: PR 13-56 4.3. **1970** Bal: Pass 2-2 100.0%, 82 41.00; KR 2-36 18.0. **1972** Bal: Pass 1-0. **Total:** Pass 3-2 66.7%, 82 27.33; PR 13-56 4.3; KR 2-36 18.0.

		Rushing				Receiving					Tot
Year Team	**G**	**Att**	**Yds**	**Avg**	**TD**	**Rec**	**Yds**	**Avg**	**TD**	**Fum**	**TD**
1969 Bal	14	5	49	9.8	1	1	5	5.0	0	4	1
1970 Bal	13	54	159	2.9	0	14	141	10.1	0	0	0
1971 Bal	14	0	0	—	0	1	12	12.0	0	0	0
1972 Bal	14	12	72	6.0	2	33	571	17.3	4	0	6
1973 Bal	14	2	9	4.5	0	1	9	9.0	0	0	0
1974 NO	6	0	0	—	0	1	23	23.0	0	0	0
NFL Total	75	73	289	4.0	3	51	761	14.9	4	4	7

ANDY HAWKINS Hawkins, Anthony James 6′2″, 225 **LB**
Col: Texas A&M–Kingsville *HS:* Van Vleck [TX] B: 3/31/1958, Bay City, TX *Drafted:* 1980 Round 10 TB
1980 TB: 16 G. **1981** TB: 16 G. **1982** TB: 9 G; 2.3 Sac. **1983** TB: 6 G; 3 Sac. **1986** SD: 10 G. **1987** SD: 2 G. **1988** KC: 7 G. **Total:** 66 G; 5.3 Sac.

ARTRELL HAWKINS Hawkins, Artrell 5′10″, 190 **DB**
Col: Cincinnati *HS:* Bishop McCort [Johnstown, PA] B: 11/24/1975, Johnstown, PA *Drafted:* 1998 Round 2 Cin
1998 Cin: 16 G; Int 3-21; 1 Sac.

BEN HAWKINS Hawkins, Benjamin Charles 6′1″, 180 **WR**
Col: Arizona State *HS:* Weequahic [Newark, NJ]; Nutley HS [NJ]
B: 3/22/1944, Newark, NJ *Drafted:* 1966 Round 3 Phi
1966 Phi: PR 9-47 5.2; KR 1-0. **1967** Phi: KR 10-250 25.0. **1968** Phi: KR 12-254 21.2. **1969** Phi: Rush 1-(-3) -3.0; PR 1-6 6.0. **1970** Phi: Rush 2-3 1.5; PR 10-16 1.6; KR 1-0. **1971** Phi: Rush 4-8 2.0; PR 1-6 6.0; 1 Fum TD. **1972** Phi: Rush 3-0. **Total:** Rush 10-8 0.8; PR 21-75 3.6; KR 24-504 21.0; 1 Fum TD.

		Receiving					Tot
Year Team	**G**	**Rec**	**Yds**	**Avg**	**TD**	**Fum**	**TD**
1966 Phi	14	14	143	10.2	0	3	0
1967 Phi	14	59	**1265**	21.4	10	1	10
1968 Phi	14	42	707	16.8	5	0	5
1969 Phi	14	43	761	17.7	8	1	8
1970 Phi	14	30	612	20.4	4	2	4
1971 Phi	14	37	650	17.6	4	1	5
1972 Phi	14	30	512	17.1	1	0	1
1973 Phi	4	6	114	19.0	0	0	0
1974 Cle	2	0	0	—	0	0	0
NFL Total	104	261	4764	18.3	32	8	33

ALEX HAWKINS Hawkins, Chilton Alexander 6′0″, 190 **RB-WR**
Col: South Carolina *HS:* South Charleston [WV] B: 7/2/1937, Welch, WV *Drafted:* 1959 Round 2 GB
1959 Bal: KR 1-21 21.0. **1962** Bal: Pass 1-0; KR 2-35 17.5. **1965** Bal: KR 2-0. **1966** Atl: KR 1-30 30.0. **Total:** Pass 1-0; KR 6-86 14.3.

		Rushing				Receiving			
Year Team	**G**	**Att**	**Yds**	**Avg**	**TD**	**Rec**	**Yds**	**Avg**	**TD**
1959 Bal	11	12	44	3.7	0	0	0	—	0
1960 Bal	12	76	267	3.5	2	25	280	11.2	3
1961 Bal	11	86	379	4.4	4	20	158	7.9	1
1962 Bal	13	29	87	3.0	4	4	37	9.3	0
1963 Bal	14	3	-2	-0.7	0	3	41	13.7	0
1964 Bal	14	0	0	—	0	2	42	21.0	1
1965 Bal	14	0	0	—	0	2	32	16.0	1
1966 Atl	12	0	0	—	0	44	661	15.0	2
1967 Atl-Bal	14	2	12	6.0	0	27	469	17.4	4
1967 Atl	3	0	0	—	0	0	0	—	0
1967 Bal	11	2	12	6.0	0	27	469	17.4	4
1968 Bal	10	0	0	—	0	2	31	15.5	0
NFL Total	125	208	787	3.8	10	129	1751	13.6	12

	Punt Returns					Tot
Year Team	**Ret**	**Yds**	**Avg**	**TD**	**Fum**	**TD**
1960 Bal	0	0	—	0	4	5
1961 Bal	4	20	5.0	0	3	5
1962 Bal	11	42	3.8	0	3	4
1963 Bal	17	156	9.2	0	0	0
1964 Bal	16	122	7.6	0	1	1
1965 Bal	4	18	4.5	0	0	1
1966 Atl	0	0	—	0	1	2
1967 Atl-Bal	0	0	—	0	0	4
1967 Bal	0	0	—	0	0	4
NFL Total	52	358	6.9	0	12	22

CLARENCE HAWKINS Hawkins, Clarence L 6′0″, 205 **RB**
Col: Florida A&M *HS:* Warwick [Tallahassee, FL] B: 7/15/1956, Tallahassee, FL
1979 Oak: 7 G; Rush 21-72 3.4; Rec 2-24 12.0 1 TD; KR 1-25 25.0; 6 Pt; 1 Fum.

COURTNEY HAWKINS Hawkins, Courtney Tyrone Jr. 5′9″, 183 **WR**
Col: Michigan State *HS:* Beecher [Flint, MI] B: 12/12/1969, Flint, MI
Drafted: 1992 Round 2 TB
1992 TB: KR 9-118 13.1. **1995** TB: Rush 4-5 1.3. **1996** TB: Rush 1-(-13) -13.0. **1997** Pit: Rush 5-17 3.4. **1998** Pit: Rush 10-41 4.1.
Total: Rush 20-50 2.5; KR 9-118 13.1.

		Receiving				Punt Returns				
Year Team	**G**	**Rec**	**Yds**	**Avg**	**TD**	**Ret**	**Yds**	**Avg**	**TD**	**Fum**
1992 TB	16	20	336	16.8	2	13	53	4.1	0	2
1993 TB	16	62	933	15.0	5	15	166	11.1	0	2
1994 TB	13	37	438	11.8	5	5	28	5.6	0	0
1995 TB	16	41	493	12.0	0	0	0	—	0	1
1996 TB	16	46	544	11.8	1	1	-1	-1.0	0	1
1997 Pit	15	45	555	12.3	3	4	68	17.0	0	1
1998 Pit	15	66	751	11.4	1	15	175	11.7	0	1
NFL Total	107	317	4050	12.8	17	53	489	9.2	0	8

FRANK HAWKINS Hawkins, Frank 5′9″, 210 **RB**
Col: Nevada-Reno *HS:* Western [Las Vegas, NV] B: 7/3/1959, Las Vegas, NV *Drafted:* 1981 Round 10 Oak
1981 Oak: KR 1-7 7.0. **1985** LARd: KR 1-14 14.0. **1986** LARd: KR 1-15 15.0. **Total:** KR 3-36 12.0.

		Rushing				Receiving					Tot
Year Team	**G**	**Att**	**Yds**	**Avg**	**TD**	**Rec**	**Yds**	**Avg**	**TD**	**Fum**	**TD**
1981 Oak	13	40	165	4.1	0	10	109	10.9	0	1	0
1982 LARd	9	27	54	2.0	2	7	35	5.0	1	1	3
1983 LARd	16	110	526	4.8	6	20	150	7.5	2	2	8
1984 LARd	16	108	376	3.5	3	7	51	7.3	0	3	3
1985 LARd	16	84	269	3.2	4	27	174	6.4	0	0	4
1986 LARd	16	58	245	4.2	0	25	166	6.6	0	0	0
1987 LARd	2	4	24	6.0	0	1	6	6.0	0	0	0
NFL Total	88	431	1659	3.8	15	97	691	7.1	3	7	18

GARLAND HAWKINS Hawkins, Garland Anthony 6'3", 253 **DE**
Col: Syracuse *HS:* DeMatha [Hyattsville, MD] B: 2/19/1970, Washington, DC
1995 ChiB: 1 G.

MIKE HAWKINS Hawkins, Michael Douglas 6'2", 235 **LB**
Col: Texas A&M–Kingsville *HS:* Van Vleck [TX] B: 10/29/1955, Bay City, TX *Drafted:* 1978 Round 7 NE
1978 NE: 12 G. **1979** NE: 16 G; Int 2-35 1 TD; 6 Pt. **1980** NE: 16 G; Int 2-5. **1981** NE: 15 G; Int 1-16. **1982** LARd: 3 G. **Total:** 62 G; Int 5-56 1 TD; 6 Pt.

NATE HAWKINS Hawkins, Nathaniel Alfred 6'1", 190 **WR**
Col: Nevada-Las Vegas *HS:* Booker T. Washington [Houston, TX] B: 2/8/1950, Houston, TX *Drafted:* 1972 Round 16 Pit
1975 Hou: 11 G; Rec 1-32 32.0.

RIP HAWKINS Hawkins, Ross Cooper 6'3", 235 **LB**
Col: North Carolina *HS:* Sewanee Mil. Acad. [TN] B: 4/21/1939, Winchester, TN *Drafted:* 1961 Round 2 Min
1962 Min: Scor 1 Saf. **Total:** Scor 1 Saf.

		Interceptions			
Year Team	**G**	**Int**	**Yds**	**TD**	**Fum**
1961 Min	14	5	70	0	0
1962 Min	14	1	3	0	1
1963 Min	14	1	6	0	1
1964 Min	14	2	85	**2**	0
1965 Min	14	3	68	1	0
NFL Total	70	12	232	3	2

STEVE HAWKINS Hawkins, Steven 6'5", 210 **WR**
Col: Tennessee State; Western Michigan *HS:* Central [Detroit, MI] B: 3/16/1971, Detroit, MI *Drafted:* 1994 Round 6 NE
1994 NE: 7 G; Rec 2-22 11.0.

WAYNE HAWKINS Hawkins, Wayne Allen 6'0", 240 **OG**
Col: U. of Pacific *HS:* Shasta Union [Redding, CA] B: 6/17/1938, Fort Peck, MT *Drafted:* 1960 Round 1 Den
1960 Oak: 14 G. **1961** Oak: 14 G. **1962** Oak: 14 G. **1963** Oak: 14 G. **1964** Oak: 14 G. **1965** Oak: 14 G. **1966** Oak: 14 G. **1967** Oak: 14 G. **1968** Oak: 10 G. **1969** Oak: 14 G. **Total:** 136 G.

BILL HAWKINS Hawkins, William E 6'6", 269 **DT-DE**
Col: Miami (Fla.) *HS:* South Broward [Hollywood, FL] B: 5/9/1966, Miami, FL *Drafted:* 1989 Round 1 LARm
1989 LARm: 13 G. **1990** LARm: 15 G; 3 Sac. **1991** LARm: 6 G. **1992** LARm: 8 G; 2 Sac. **Total:** 42 G; 5 Sac.

STEVE HAWORTH Haworth, Steven 5'11", 189 **DB**
Col: Oklahoma *HS:* Durant [OK] B: 9/16/1961, Manila, Philippines *Drafted:* 1983 Round 6 Hou
1983 Atl: 11 G. **1984** Atl: 5 G. **Total:** 16 G.

LES HAWS Haws, Harvey Lester 5'8", 165 **BB-TB**
Col: Dartmouth *HS:* Lower Merion [Ardmore, PA] B: 11/28/1899, Ardmore, PA D: 1/20/1966, Norristown, PA
1924 Fra: 13 G; Rush 3 TD; Rec 1 TD; Tot TD 4; 24 Pt. **1925** Fra: 13 G; Rush 1 TD; 6 Pt. **Total:** 26 G; Rush 4 TD; Rec 1 TD; Tot TD 5; 30 Pt.

KURT HAWS Haws, Kurt Leroy 6'5", 248 **TE**
Col: Mesa CC AZ; Utah *HS:* Mountain View [Mesa, AZ] B: 9/25/1969, Mesa, AZ *Drafted:* 1994 Round 4 Was
1994 Was: 6 G; KR 1-10 10.0.

ED HAWTHORNE Hawthorne, Edward William 6'1", 305 **NT**
Col: Minnesota *HS:* Parkway West [Ballwin, MO] B: 7/30/1970, St. Louis, MO
1995 Mia: 1 G.

GREG HAWTHORNE Hawthorne, Gregory Dale 6'2", 228 **RB-TE-WR**
Col: Baylor *HS:* Fort Worth Polytechnic [TX] B: 9/5/1956, Fort Worth, TX *Drafted:* 1979 Round 1 Pit
1979 Pit: KR 2-46 23.0. **1980** Pit: KR 9-169 18.8. **1981** Pit: KR 7-138 19.7. **1984** NE: KR 1-14 14.0. **1985** NE: KR 1-13 13.0. **1986** NE: KR 2-13 6.5. **Total:** KR 22-393 17.9.

		Rushing				Receiving					Tot
Year Team	**G**	**Att**	**Yds**	**Avg**	**TD**	**Rec**	**Yds**	**Avg**	**TD**	**Fum**	**TD**
1979 Pit	15	28	123	4.4	1	8	47	5.9	0	2	1
1980 Pit	15	63	226	3.6	4	12	158	13.2	0	6	4
1981 Pit	10	25	58	2.3	2	4	23	5.8	0	1	2
1982 Pit	9	15	68	4.5	0	12	182	15.2	3	0	3
1983 Pit	10	5	47	9.4	0	19	300	15.8	0	0	0
1984 NE	14	0	0	—	0	7	127	18.1	0	0	0
1985 NE	15	0	0	—	0	3	42	14.0	1	0	1
1986 NE	14	1	5	5.0	0	24	192	8.0	0	0	0
1987 Ind	3	0	0	—	0	3	41	13.7	0	0	0
NFL Total	105	137	527	3.8	7	92	1112	12.1	4	9	11

KEN HAYCRAFT Haycraft, Kenneth Clair 6'0", 178 **OE**
Col: Minnesota *HS:* East [Minneapolis, MN]; Central HS [Washington, DC] B: 2/16/1907, Bemidji, MN D: 6/29/1995, Kailua, HI
1929 Min: 10 G; Rec 2 TD; 12 Pt. **1930** Min-GB: 6 G. Min: 5 G. GB: 1 G. **Total:** 16 G; Rec 2 TD; 12 Pt.

AARON HAYDEN Hayden, Aaron Chautezz 6'0", 216 **RB**
Col: Tennessee *HS:* Mumford [Detroit, MI] B: 4/13/1973, Detroit, MI *Drafted:* 1995 Round 4 SD
1995 SD: Rec 5-53 10.6. **1996** SD: Rec 1-10 10.0. **1997** GB: Rec 2-11 5.5; KR 6-141 23.5. **1998** Phi: KR 1-22 22.0. **Total:** Rec 8-74 9.3; KR 7-163 23.3.

		Rushing				
Year Team	**G**	**Att**	**Yds**	**Avg**	**TD**	**Fum**
1995 SD	6	128	470	3.7	3	0
1996 SD	11	55	166	3.0	0	1
1997 GB	14	32	148	4.6	1	0
1998 Phi	1	0	0	—	0	0
NFL Total	32	215	784	3.6	4	1

KEN HAYDEN Hayden, Kenneth Mack 6'0", 205 **C-LB**
Col: Arkansas *HS:* Smackover [AR] B: 10/21/1917, Hamburg, AR D: 8/1968, Smackover, AR
1942 Phi: 9 G; Int 1-5. **1943** Was: 8 G. **Total:** 17 G; Int 1-5.

LEO HAYDEN Hayden, Leophus Jr. 6'0", 210 **RB**
Col: Ohio State *HS:* Roosevelt [Dayton, OH] B: 6/2/1948, Louisville, KY *Drafted:* 1971 Round 1 Min
1971 Min: 7 G. **1972** StL: 4 G; Rush 8-11 1.4 1 TD; Rec 1-17 17.0; 6 Pt; 2 Fum. **1973** StL: 2 G; KR 5-98 19.6. **Total:** 13 G; Rush 8-11 1.4 1 TD; Rec 1-17 17.0; KR 5-98 19.6; 6 Pt; 2 Fum.

HENRY HAYDUK Hayduk, Henry Harold 6'0", 200 **G**
Col: Washington State *HS:* Albert G. Lane Tech [Chicago, IL] B: 9/26/1913 D: 8/1969
1935 Bkn-Pit: 9 G; Rush 1-3 3.0. Bkn: 1 G. Pit: 8 G; Rush 1-3 3.0. **Total:** 9 G; Rush 1-3 3.0.

CHRIS HAYES Hayes, Christopher Kareem 6'0", 206 **DB**
Col: Washington State *HS:* San Gorgonio [San Bernardino, CA] B: 5/7/1972, San Bernardino, CA *Drafted:* 1996 Round 7 NYJ
1996 GB: 2 G. **1997** NYJ: 16 G. **1998** NYJ: 15 G. **Total:** 33 G.

DAVE HAYES Hayes, David Vincent 5'7", 165 **OE**
Col: Notre Dame *HS:* S. Manchester [CT]; Peddie Sch. [Hightstown, NJ]; PhillipsEx.Acad.[Exeter,NH] B: 3/1894, Hartford, CT Deceased
1921 RI-GB: 9 G; Rec 1 TD; 6 Pt. RI: 3 G; Rec 1 TD; 6 Pt. GB: 6 G. **1922** GB: 7 G. **Total:** 16 G; Rec 1 TD; 6 Pt.

DONALD HAYES Hayes, Donald Ross Jr. 6'4", 208 **WR**
Col: Wisconsin *HS:* East [Madison, WI] B: 7/13/1975, Madison, WI *Drafted:* 1998 Round 4 Car
1998 Car: 7 G; Rec 3-62 20.7.

ED HAYES Hayes, Edward Rogers 6'1", 185 **DB**
Col: Morgan State *HS:* Anderson [Jacksonville, FL] B: 8/14/1946, Jacksonville, FL *Drafted:* 1969 Round 4 Den
1970 Phi: 4 G; PR 2-6 3.0; KR 6-107 17.8; Int 1-2; 1 Fum.

ERIC HAYES Hayes, Eric Gerard 6'3", 292 **DT-DE-NT**
Col: Florida State *HS:* C. Leon King [Tampa, FL] B: 11/12/1967, Tampa, FL *Drafted:* 1990 Round 5 Sea
1990 Sea: 16 G. **1991** Sea: 5 G. **1992** LARm: 1 G. **1993** TB: 2 G. **Total:** 24 G.

GARY HAYES Hayes, Gary L 5'10", 180 **DB**
Col: Fresno State *HS:* El Cerrito [CA] B: 8/19/1957, Tuscon, AZ
1984 GB: 16 G; PR 4-24 6.0. **1985** GB: 16 G; PR 1-0; 1 Fum. **1986** GB: 10 G. **Total:** 42 G; PR 5-24 4.8; 1 Fum.

JIM HAYES Hayes, James William 6'4", 265 **DT-DE**
(Papa) *Col:* Jackson State *HS:* Harris [Meridian, MS] B: 11/26/1940, Meridian, MS
1965 Hou: 14 G. **1966** Hou: 14 G; KR 2-31 15.5. **Total:** 28 G; KR 2-31 15.5.

JARIUS HAYES Hayes, Jarius 6'3", 266 **TE**
Col: North Alabama *HS:* Muscle Shoals [AL] B: 3/27/1973, Sheffield, AL *Drafted:* 1996 Round 7 Ariz
1996 Ariz: 4 G. **1998** Ariz: 16 G. **Total:** 20 G.

JEFF HAYES Hayes, Jeffrey Clyde 5'11", 175 **P**
Col: North Carolina *HS:* Elkin [NC] B: 8/19/1959, Elkin, NC
1983 Was: Rush 2-63 31.5. **1984** Was: Rush 2-13 6.5. **1986** Cin: Rush 3-92 30.7 1 TD. **Total:** Rush 7-168 24.0 1 TD.

		Punting			
Year Team	**G**	**Punts**	**Yds**	**Avg**	**Fum**
1982 Was	9	51	1937	38.0	0
1983 Was	16	72	2796	38.8	0
1984 Was	16	72	2834	39.4	2
1985 Was	4	16	665	41.6	0

1986 Cin	16	56	1965	35.1	0
1987 Mia	2	7	274	39.1	0
NFL Total	63	274	10471	38.2	2

JOE HAYES Hayes, Joe Herman 5′9″, 185 **RB-WR**
Col: Texas A&M–Kingsville; Central Oklahoma *HS:* South Oak Cliff [Dallas, TX] B: 9/15/1960, Dallas, TX *Drafted:* 1984 Round 7 Phi
1984 Phi: 12 G; KR 22-441 20.0; 2 Fum.

JONATHAN HAYES Hayes, Jonathan Michael 6′5″, 242 **TE**
Col: Iowa *HS:* South Fayette [McDonald, PA] B: 8/11/1962, South Fayette Twp., PA *Drafted:* 1985 Round 2 KC
1985 KC: KR 1-0. **Total:** KR 1-0.

		Receiving				
Year Team	**G**	**Rec**	**Yds**	**Avg**	**TD**	**Fum**
1985 KC	16	5	39	7.8	1	0
1986 KC	16	8	69	8.6	0	0
1987 KC	12	21	272	13.0	2	0
1988 KC	16	22	233	10.6	1	0
1989 KC	16	18	229	12.7	2	1
1990 KC	12	9	83	9.2	1	0
1991 KC	16	19	208	10.9	2	1
1992 KC	16	9	77	8.6	2	0
1993 KC	16	24	331	13.8	1	1
1994 Pit	16	5	50	10.0	1	1
1995 Pit	16	11	113	10.3	0	0
1996 Pit	16	2	14	7.0	0	0
NFL Total	184	153	1718	11.2	13	4

LARRY HAYES Hayes, Larry Gene 6′3″, 230 **LB-C**
Col: Vanderbilt *HS:* Montgomery Bell Acad. [Nashville, TN] B: 7/21/1935, Nashville, TN
1961 NYG: 14 G; 6 Pt. **1962** LARm: 9 G. **1963** LARm: 9 G. **Total:** 32 G; 6 Pt.

LESTER HAYES Hayes, Lester 6′0″, 200 **DB**
(The Judge) *Col:* Texas A&M *HS:* Phillis Wheatley [Houston, TX] B: 1/22/1955, Houston, TX *Drafted:* 1977 Round 5 Oak
1977 Oak: KR 3-57 19.0. **1980** Oak: KR 1-0. **1985** LARd: KR 1-0. **1986** LARd: **1** Fum TD. **Total:** KR 5-57 11.4; 1 Fum TD.

		Interceptions				Tot
Year Team	**G**	**Int**	**Yds**	**TD**	**Fum**	**TD**
1977 Oak	14	1	27	0	1	0
1978 Oak	16	4	86	0	0	0
1979 Oak	16	7	100	**2**	0	2
1980 Oak	16	**13**	**273**	1	0	1
1981 Oak	16	3	0	0	0	0
1982 LARd	9	2	0	0	0	0
1983 LARd	16	2	49	0	0	0
1984 LARd	16	1	3	0	0	0
1985 LARd	16	4	27	**1**	0	1
1986 LARd	14	2	7	0	0	1
NFL Total	149	39	572	4	1	5

LUTHER HAYES Hayes, Luther E 6′4″, 202 **OE**
Col: USC *HS:* Abraham Lincoln [San Diego, CA] B: 1/1/1939, San Diego, CA *Drafted:* 1961 Round 27 SD
1961 SD: 14 G; Rec 14-280 20.0 3 TD; 18 Pt; 1 Fum.

MELVIN HAYES Hayes, Melvin Anthony 6′6″, 328 **OG-OT**
Col: Mississippi State *HS:* John Curtis Christian [River Ridge, LA] B: 4/28/1973, New Orleans, LA *Drafted:* 1995 Round 4 NYJ
1995 NYJ: 3 G. **1996** NYJ: 1 G. **Total:** 4 G.

MERCURY HAYES Hayes, Mercury Wayne 5′11″, 195 **WR**
Col: Michigan *HS:* Washington [Houston, TX] B: 1/1/1973, Houston, TX *Drafted:* 1996 Round 5 NO
1996 NO: 7 G; Rush 2-7 3.5; Rec 4-101 25.3; KR 2-30 15.0; 1 Fum. **1997** NO-Atl: 6 G. NO: 4 G. Atl: 2 G. **Total:** 13 G; Rush 2-7 3.5; Rec 4-101 25.3; KR 2-30 15.0; 1 Fum.

NORB HAYES Hayes, Norbert P 5′11″, 175 **OE-FB**
(Butts) *Col:* Marquette *HS:* Green Bay West [WI] B: 11/21/1896, Kaukauna, WI D: 7/1945
1922 Rac: 11 G. **1923** GB: 6 G. **Total:** 17 G.

RAY HAYES Hayes, Raymond 6′3″, 235 **FB**
Col: Maryland East. Shore; Central Oklahoma *HS:* Frederick Douglass [Oklahoma City, OK] B: 5/25/1935, Pawhuska, OK *Drafted:* 1961 Round 13 Min
1961 Min: Rec 16-121 7.6; KR 1-0.

		Rushing				
Year Team	**G**	**Att**	**Yds**	**Avg**	**TD**	**Fum**
1961 Min	13	73	319	4.4	2	5

RAY HAYES Hayes, Raymond Roy 6′5″, 248 **DT**
Col: Toledo *HS:* Clawson [MI] B: 9/5/1946, Hazel Park, MI *Drafted:* 1968 Round 12 NYJ
1968 NYJ: 6 G.

RUDY HAYES Hayes, Richard Rudolph 6′0″, 217 **LB**
Col: Clemson *HS:* Pickens [SC] B: 1/12/1935, Pickens, SC *Drafted:* 1959 Round 20 Pit
1959 Pit: 12 G; KR 1-19 19.0. **1960** Pit: 12 G; KR 1-11 11.0. **1962** Pit: 4 G. **Total:** 28 G; KR 2-30 15.0.

BOB HAYES Hayes, Robert Lee 5′11″, 185 **WR**
(Bullet Bob) *Col:* Florida A&M *HS:* Matthew W. Gilbert [Jacksonville, FL] B: 12/20/1942, Jacksonville, FL *Drafted:* 1964 Round 7 Dal
1965 Dal: Rush 4-(-8) -2.0 1 TD; KR 17-450 26.5. **1966** Dal: Rush 1-(-1) -1.0. **1967** Dal: KR 1-17 17.0. **1968** Dal: Rush 4-2 0.5; KR 1-20 20.0. **1969** Dal: Rush 4-17 4.3; KR 3-80 26.7. **1970** Dal: Rush 4-34 8.5 1 TD. **1971** Dal: Rush 3-18 6.0; KR 1-14 14.0. **1972** Dal: Rush 2-8 4.0. **1975** SF: Rush 2-(-2) -1.0. **Total:** Rush 24-68 2.8 2 TD; KR 23-581 25.3.

		Receiving				Punt Returns					Tot
Year Team	**G**	**Rec**	**Yds**	**Avg**	**TD**	**Ret**	**Yds**	**Avg**	**TD**	**Fum**	**TD**
1965 Dal	13	46	1003	**21.8**	**12**	12	153	12.8	0	3	13
1966 Dal	14	64	1232	19.3	**13**	17	106	6.2	0	3	13
1967 Dal	13	49	998	20.4	10	24	**276**	11.5	**1**	1	11
1968 Dal	14	53	909	17.2	10	15	312	**20.8**	**2**	2	12
1969 Dal	10	40	746	18.7	4	18	179	9.9	0	2	4
1970 Dal	13	34	889	26.1	10	15	116	7.7	0	5	11
1971 Dal	14	35	840	**24.0**	8	1	5	5.0	0	0	8
1972 Dal	12	15	200	13.3	0	0	0	—	0	1	0
1973 Dal	13	22	360	16.4	3	0	0	—	0	0	3
1974 Dal	12	7	118	16.9	1	2	11	5.5	0	0	1
1975 SF	4	6	119	19.8	0	0	0	—	0	0	0
NFL Total	132	371	7414	20.0	71	104	1158	11.1	3	17	76

TOM HAYES Hayes, Thomas J Jr. 6′1″, 199 **DB**
Col: Riverside CC CA; San Diego State *HS:* Rubidoux [Riverside, CA] B: 4/18/1946, Riverside, CA *Drafted:* 1971 Round 6 Atl
1971 Atl: **1** Fum TD. **Total:** 1 Fum TD.

		Interceptions			Tot
Year Team	**G**	**Int**	**Yds**	**TD**	**TD**
1971 Atl	14	3	27	0	3
1972 Atl	14	5	10	0	0
1973 Atl	14	4	142	**2**	2
1974 Atl	13	1	2	0	0
1975 Atl	14	4	16	0	0
1976 SD	9	2	37	1	1
NFL Total	78	19	234	3	6

WENDELL HAYES Hayes, Wendell 6′1″, 220 **RB**
Col: Humboldt State *HS:* McClymonds [Oakland, CA] B: 8/5/1940, Dallas, TX
1963 Dal: KR 2-48 24.0. **1965** Den: Pass 1-0, 1 Int; KR 4-93 23.3; Scor 1 2XP. **1967** Den: KR 3-104 34.7; Scor 1 2XP. **1969** KC: KR 2-81 40.5. **1971** KC: KR 4-75 18.8. **Total:** Pass 1-0, 1 Int; KR 15-401 26.7; Scor 2 2XP.

		Rushing				Receiving					Tot
Year Team	**G**	**Att**	**Yds**	**Avg**	**TD**	**Rec**	**Yds**	**Avg**	**TD**	**Fum**	**TD**
1963 Dal	1	0	0	—	0	0	0	—	0	0	0
1965 Den	14	130	526	4.0	5	24	294	12.3	2	5	7
1966 Den	11	105	417	4.0	1	8	49	6.1	0	0	1
1967 Den	14	85	255	3.0	4	13	125	9.6	0	4	4
1968 KC	11	85	340	4.0	4	12	108	9.0	1	1	5
1969 KC	14	62	208	3.4	4	9	64	7.1	0	2	4
1970 KC	14	109	381	3.5	5	26	219	8.4	0	3	5
1971 KC	14	132	537	4.1	1	16	150	9.4	1	1	2
1972 KC	13	128	536	4.2	0	31	295	9.5	3	0	3
1973 KC	13	95	352	3.7	2	18	134	7.4	0	2	2
1974 KC	14	57	206	3.6	2	4	23	5.8	0	0	2
NFL Total	133	988	3758	3.8	28	161	1461	9.1	7	18	35

BILLIE HAYES Hayes, William 6′1″, 175 **DB**
Col: Riverside CC CA; San Diego State *HS:* Rubidoux [Riverside, CA] B: 6/22/1947, Riverside, CA *Drafted:* 1970 Round 4 Cin
1972 NO: 14 G.

BRANDON HAYES Hayes, William Brandon 6′4″, 305 **OT**
Col: Central State (Ohio) *HS:* Muncie Southside [IN] B: 3/11/1973, Muncie, IN
1996 Car: 7 G.

BILL HAYHOE Hayhoe, William II 6′8″, 258 **OT**
Col: USC *HS:* Birmingham [Van Nuys, CA] B: 9/6/1946, Los Angeles, CA *Drafted:* 1969 Round 5 GB
1969 GB: 14 G. **1970** GB: 13 G. **1971** GB: 14 G. **1972** GB: 14 G. **1973** GB: 6 G. **Total:** 61 G.

CONWAY HAYMAN Hayman, Conway 6′3″, 264 **OG-OT**
Col: Delaware *HS:* Newark [DE] B: 1/9/1949, Wilmington, DE *Drafted:* 1971 Round 6 Was
1975 Hou: 14 G. **1976** Hou: 14 G. **1977** Hou: 12 G. **1978** Hou: 16 G. **1979** Hou: 16 G. **1980** Hou: 5 G. **Total:** 77 G.

GARY HAYMAN Hayman, Gary Wesley 6′1″, 198 **RB**
Col: Penn State *HS:* Newark [DE] B: 9/8/1951, Newark, DE
Drafted: 1974 Round 5 Buf
1974 Buf: Rush 7-31 4.4. **1975** Buf: Rush 10-30 3.0; KR 8-179 22.4.
Total: Rush 17-61 3.6; KR 8-179 22.4.

		Punt Returns				
Year Team	G	Ret	Yds	Avg	TD	Fum
1974 Buf	1	2	13	6.5	0	0
1975 Buf	14	25	216	8.6	0	3
NFL Total	15	27	229	8.5	0	3

ALVIN HAYMOND Haymond, Alvin Henry 6′0″, 194 **DB**
Col: Southern University *HS:* L.B. Landry [New Orleans, LA]
B: 8/31/1942, New Orleans, LA *Drafted:* 1964 Round 18 Bal

		Punt Returns				Kickoff Returns			
Year Team	G	Ret	Yds	Avg	TD	Ret	Yds	Avg	TD
1964 Bal	9	1	6	6.0	0	1	0	0.0	0
1965 Bal	14	**41**	**403**	9.8	0	20	614	30.7	0
1966 Bal	14	**40**	**347**	8.7	0	10	223	22.3	0
1967 Bal	8	26	155	6.0	0	13	326	25.1	0
1968 Phi	11	15	201	13.4	1	28	677	24.2	1
1969 LARm	14	33	**435**	**13.2**	0	16	375	23.4	0
1970 LARm	14	**53**	376	7.1	0	35	**1022**	29.2	1
1971 LARm	10	24	123	5.1	0	9	207	23.0	0
1972 Was	4	6	1	0.2	0	10	291	29.1	0
1973 Hou	6	14	101	7.2	0	28	703	25.1	0
NFL Total	104	253	2148	8.5	1	170	4438	26.1	2

	Interceptions				Tot
Year Team	Int	Yds	TD	Fum	TD
1965 Bal	3	47	1	1	1
1966 Bal	4	88	1	5	1
1967 Bal	2	33	0	0	0
1968 Phi	1	10	0	3	2
1969 LARm	0	0	0	3	0
1970 LARm	0	0	0	5	1
1971 LARm	0	0	0	4	0
1973 Hou	0	0	0	2	0
NFL Total	10	178	2	23	5

ABNER HAYNES Haynes, Abner 6′0″, 190 **HB**
Col: North Texas *HS:* Lincoln [Dallas, TX] B: 9/19/1937, Denton, TX
Drafted: 1960 Round 1 Oak
1960 DalT: Pass 1-0. **1962** DalT: Pass 1-0. **1963** KC: Pass 1-1 100.0%, 24 24.00. **1964** KC: Pass 1-0; **1** Fum TD. **1965** Den: Pass 1-0. **1966** Den: Pass 2-0, 2 Int. **Total:** Pass 7-1 14.3%, 24 3.43 2 Int; 1 Fum TD.

		Rushing				Receiving			
Year Team	G	Att	Yds	Avg	TD	Rec	Yds	Avg	TD
1960 DalT	14	**156**	**875**	5.6	**9**	55	576	10.5	3
1961 DalT	14	179	841	4.7	**9**	34	558	16.4	3
1962 DalT	14	221	1049	4.7	**13**	39	573	14.7	6
1963 KC	14	99	352	3.6	4	33	470	14.2	2
1964 KC	14	139	697	5.0	4	38	562	14.8	3
1965 Den	14	41	166	4.0	3	26	216	8.3	2
1966 Den	14	129	304	2.4	2	46	480	10.4	1
1967 Mia-NYJ	14	72	346	4.8	2	16	100	6.3	0
1967 Mia	11	56	274	4.9	2	16	100	6.3	0
1967 NYJ	3	16	72	4.5	0	0	0	—	0
NFL Total	112	1036	4630	4.5	46	287	3535	12.3	20

	Punt Returns				Kickoff Returns					Tot
Year Team	Ret	Yds	Avg	TD	Ret	Yds	Avg	TD	Fum	TD
1960 DalT	14	**215**	**15.4**	0	19	434	22.8	0	9	12
1961 DalT	19	196	10.3	0	8	270	33.8	**1**	**11**	13
1962 DalT	15	119	7.9	0	1	27	27.0	0	4	**19**
1963 KC	6	57	9.5	0	12	317	26.4	0	6	6
1964 KC	1	11	11.0	0	12	278	23.2	0	0	8
1965 Den	14	121	8.6	1	**34**	**901**	**26.5**	0	5	6
1966 Den	10	119	11.9	0	9	229	25.4	0	**11**	3
1967 Mia-NYJ	6	37	6.2	0	26	569	21.9	0	6	2
1967 Mia	6	37	6.2	0	22	444	20.2	0	6	2
1967 NYJ	0	0	—	0	4	125	31.3	0	0	0
NFL Total	85	875	10.3	1	121	3025	25.0	1	52	69

HALL HAYNES Haynes, Hall Gibson 6′0″, 187 **DB-HB**
Col: Santa Clara *HS:* Pasadena [CA] B: 10/3/1928, Duncan, OK
D: 6/13/1988, Santa Clara Co., CA *Drafted:* 1950 Round 2 Was
1950 Was: 12 G; Rush 2-20 10.0; PR 3-22 7.3; KR 5-214 42.8; Int 4-77 1 TD; Punt 19-756 39.8; 6 Pt. **1953** Was: 8 G; Rush 2-0; PR 5-92 18.4; KR 7-123 17.6; 1 Fum. **1954** LARm: 11 G; Int 1-0. **1955** LARm: 9 G.
Total: 40 G; Rush 4-20 5.0; PR 8-114 14.3; KR 12-337 28.1; Int 5-77 1 TD; Punt 19-756 39.8; 6 Pt; 1 Fum.

JAMES HAYNES Haynes, James 6′2″, 230 **LB**
Col: Coahoma CC MS; Mississippi Valley State *HS:* Tallulah [LA]
B: 8/9/1960, Tallulah, LA
1984 NO: 10 G. **1985** NO: 16 G; Rec 1-8 8.0; 2 Sac. **1986** NO: 16 G; Int 1-17 1 TD; 6 Pt; 2 Sac. **1987** NO: 12 G. **1988** NO: 4 G. **1989** NO: 3 G.
Total: 61 G; Rec 1-8 8.0; Int 1-17 1 TD; 6 Pt; 4 Sac.

JOE HAYNES Haynes, Joseph H 6′3″, 225 **C-G**
Col: Tulsa B: 3/26/1921, Barnsdall, OK
AAFC **1947** BufA: 9 G.

LOUIS HAYNES Haynes, Louis Jules 6′0″, 227 **LB**
Col: Bishop; North Texas *HS:* O. Perry Walker [New Orleans, LA]
B: 1/17/1960, New Orleans, LA *Drafted:* 1982 Round 4 KC
1982 KC: 6 G. **1983** KC: 5 G. **Total:** 11 G.

MARK HAYNES Haynes, Mark 5′11″, 194 **DB**
Col: Colorado *HS:* J.C. Harmon [Kansas City, KS] B: 11/6/1958, Kansas City, KS *Drafted:* 1980 Round 1 NYG
1980 NYG: KR 2-40 20.0. **1988** Den: 1 Sac. **Total:** KR 2-40 20.0; 1 Sac.

		Interceptions		
Year Team	G	Int	Yds	TD
1980 NYG	15	1	6	0
1981 NYG	16	1	9	0
1982 NYG	9	1	0	0
1983 NYG	15	3	18	0
1984 NYG	15	7	90	0
1985 NYG	5	0	0	0
1986 Den	11	0	0	0
1987 Den	12	3	39	1
1988 Den	15	1	0	0
1989 Den	14	0	0	0
NFL Total	127	17	162	1

MICHAEL HAYNES Haynes, Michael David 6′0″, 184 **WR**
Col: Eastern Arizona Coll. (J.C.); Northern Arizona *HS:* Joseph S. Clark [New Orleans, LA] B: 12/24/1965, New Orleans, LA *Drafted:* 1988 Round 7 Atl
1988 Atl: KR 6-113 18.8. **1989** Atl: Rush 4-35 8.8. **1994** NO: Rush 4-43 10.8. **1996** NO: Scor 1 2XP. **Total:** Rush 8-78 9.8; KR 6-113 18.8; Scor 1 2XP.

		Receiving				
Year Team	G	Rec	Yds	Avg	TD	Fum
1988 Atl	15	13	232	17.8	4	0
1989 Atl	13	40	681	17.0	4	0
1990 Atl	13	31	445	14.4	0	0
1991 Atl	16	50	1122	**22.4**	11	0
1992 Atl	14	48	808	16.8	10	0
1993 Atl	16	72	778	10.8	4	1
1994 NO	16	77	985	12.8	5	1
1995 NO	16	41	597	14.6	4	0
1996 NO	16	44	786	17.9	4	1
1997 Atl	12	12	154	12.8	1	0
NFL Total	147	428	6588	15.4	47	3

MIKE HAYNES Haynes, Michael James 6′2″, 192 **DB**
Col: Arizona State *HS:* John Marshall [Los Angeles, CA] B: 7/1/1953, Denison, TX *Drafted:* 1976 Round 1 NE *HOF:* 1997
1985 LARd: 1 Sac. **Total:** 1 Sac.

		Punt Returns				Interceptions				Tot
Year Team	G	Ret	Yds	Avg	TD	Int	Yds	TD	Fum	TD
1976 NE	14	45	608	13.5	2	8	90	0	3	2
1977 NE	14	24	200	8.3	0	5	54	0	4	0
1978 NE	16	14	183	13.1	0	6	123	1	1	1
1979 NE	16	5	16	3.2	0	3	66	0	1	0
1980 NE	13	17	140	8.2	0	1	31	0	2	1
1981 NE	8	6	12	2.0	0	1	3	0	0	0
1982 NE	9	0	0	—	0	4	26	0	0	0
1983 LARd	5	0	0	—	0	1	0	0	0	0
1984 LARd	16	0	0	—	0	6	**220**	1	0	1
1985 LARd	16	1	9	9.0	0	4	8	0	0	0
1986 LARd	13	0	0	—	0	2	28	0	0	0
1987 LARd	8	0	0	—	0	2	9	0	0	0
1988 LARd	16	0	0	—	0	3	30	0	0	0
1989 LARd	13	0	0	—	0	0	0	0	0	0
NFL Total	177	112	1168	10.4	2	46	688	2	11	5

REGGIE HAYNES Haynes, Reginold Eugene 6′2″, 229 **TE**
Col: Los Angeles City Coll. CA (J.C.); Nevada-Las Vegas *HS:* John Marshall [Los Angeles, CA] B: 9/15/1954, Denison, TX *Drafted:* 1977 Round 7 Was
1978 Was: 14 G; Rush 1-13 13.0; Rec 2-32 16.0.

TOMMY HAYNES Haynes, Thomas Walton 6′0″, 190 **DB**
Col: Mount San Antonio Coll. CA (J.C.); USC *HS:* Covina [CA]
B: 2/6/1963, Chicago, IL
1987 Dal: 3 G; Int 3-7; 3 Sac.

GEORGE HAYS Hays, George William 6'2", 211 **DE-DT**
Col: St. Bonaventure *HS:* Glassport [PA] B: 8/29/1924, Glassport, PA D: 1988
1950 Pit: 12 G. **1951** Pit: 12 G. **1952** Pit: 11 G; PR 1-3 3.0 1 TD; Int 1-1 1 TD; Tot TD 2; 12 Pt. **1953** GB: 9 G. **Total:** 44 G; PR 1-3 3.0 1 TD; Int 1-1 1 TD; Tot TD 2; 12 Pt.

HAROLD HAYS Hays, Leo Harold 6'2", 225 **LB**
Col: Southern Mississippi *HS:* Hattiesburg [MS] B: 9/24/1939, Gulfport, MS *Drafted:* 1962 Round 14 Dal
1963 Dal: 14 G. **1964** Dal: 14 G. **1965** Dal: 14 G. **1966** Dal: 14 G. **1967** Dal: 14 G. **1968** SF: 14 G; KR 2-21 10.5. **1969** SF: 12 G. **Total:** 96 G; KR 2-21 10.5.

AL HAYWOOD Haywood, Alfred 5'11", 215 **RB**
Col: Bethune-Cookman *HS:* Matthew W. Gilbert [Jacksonville, FL] B: 8/6/1948, Jacksonville, FL
1975 Den: 2 G.

TRACY HAYWORTH Hayworth, Tracy Keith 6'3", 260 **LB**
Col: Tennessee *HS:* Franklin Co. [Winchester, TN] B: 12/18/1967, Winchester, TN *Drafted:* 1990 Round 7 Det
1990 Det: 16 G; 4 Sac. **1991** Det: 16 G; Int 1-0; 1 Fum TD; 6 Pt; 2 Sac. **1992** Det: 4 G. **1993** Det: 11 G; 2 Sac. **1994** Det: 9 G; 1 Sac. **1995** Det: 16 G; 1 Sac. **Total:** 72 G; Int 1-0; 1 Fum TD; 6 Pt; 10 Sac.

ROBERT HAZELHURST Hazelhurst, Robert Gerald 6'0", 188 **HB-DB**
Col: Denver *HS:* South [Denver, CO] B: 7/21/1924, Denver, CO D: 11/11/1988, Denver, CO *Drafted:* 1947 Round 10 Bos
1948 Bos: 12 G; Rush 11-15 1.4; KR 2-31 15.5; Punt 2-102 51.0; 2 Fum.

MATT HAZELTINE Hazeltine, Matthew Emory Jr. 6'1", 220 **LB**
Col: California *HS:* Tamalpais [Mill Valley, CA] B: 8/2/1933, Ross, CA D: 1/13/1987, San Francisco, CA *Drafted:* 1955 Round 4 SF
1955 SF: KR 1-9 9.0. **1957** SF: PR 1-1 1.0; KR 1-23 23.0. **1959** SF: KR 2-26 13.0; **1** Fum TD. **1966** SF: **1** Fum TD. **Total:** PR 1-1 1.0; KR 4-58 14.5; 2 Fum TD.

		Interceptions			Tot
Year Team	**G**	**Int**	**Yds**	**TD**	**TD**
1955 SF	12	0	0	0	0
1956 SF	12	1	7	0	0
1957 SF	12	2	22	0	0
1958 SF	12	3	30	1	1
1959 SF	12	0	0	0	1
1960 SF	12	0	0	0	0
1961 SF	14	1	26	0	0
1962 SF	14	2	24	0	0
1963 SF	13	0	0	0	0
1964 SF	14	1	1	0	0
1965 SF	8	1	6	0	0
1966 SF	14	1	8	0	1
1967 SF	13	0	0	0	0
1968 SF	14	0	0	0	0
1970 NYG	14	1	6	0	0
NFL Total	190	13	130	1	3

MAJOR HAZELTON Hazelton, Major F 6'1", 185 **DB**
Col: Florida A&M *HS:* Bartow [FL] B: 9/9/1944, Bartow, FL *Drafted:* 1968 Round 3 ChiB
1968 ChiB: 14 G; PR 1-1 1.0; 1 Fum. **1969** ChiB: 9 G. **1970** NO: 3 G. **Total:** 26 G; PR 1-1 1.0; 1 Fum.

TED HAZELWOOD Hazelwood, Theodore Eugene 6'1", 235 **OT-DT**
Col: Purdue; North Carolina *HS:* Frankfort [IN] B: 4/25/1924, Silverwood, IN *Drafted:* 1946 Round 16 ChiB
AAFC **1949** ChiA: 9 G.

NFL **1953** Was: 6 G.

ANDY HEADEN Headen, Andrew Roosevelt 6'5", 240 **LB**
Col: Clemson *HS:* Eastern Randolph [Ramseur, NC] B: 7/8/1960, Asheboro, NC *Drafted:* 1983 Round 8 NYG
1983 NYG: 16 G; 5 Sac. **1984** NYG: 11 G; Int 1-4; **1** Fum TD; 6 Pt; 1 Sac. **1985** NYG: 16 G; Int 2-7; 5.5 Sac. **1986** NYG: 15 G; Int 1-1; 2.5 Sac. **1987** NYG: 12 G; Int 2-25; 2.5 Sac. **1988** NYG: 4 G; 3 Sac. **Total:** 74 G; Int 6-37; 1 Fum TD; 6 Pt; 19.5 Sac.

SHERRILL HEADRICK Headrick, Sherrill Darlon 6'2", 240 **LB**
Col: Texas Christian *HS:* North Side [Fort Worth, TX] B: 3/13/1937, Waco, TX
1961 DalT: PR 2-5 2.5. **Total:** PR 2-5 2.5.

		Interceptions		
Year Team	**G**	**Int**	**Yds**	**TD**
1960 DalT	12	2	9	0
1961 DalT	14	2	89	2
1962 DalT	14	3	30	0
1963 KC	14	2	49	1
1964 KC	14	1	0	0
1965 KC	14	1	1	0
1966 KC	14	2	22	0
1967 KC	12	1	7	0
1968 Cin	8	1	0	0
NFL Total	116	15	207	3

ED HEALEY Healey, Edward Francis Jr. 6'1", 207 **T-G-E**
Col: Dartmouth *HS:* Springfield Classical [MA] B: 12/28/1894, Indian Orchard, MA D: 12/10/1978, South Bend, IN *HOF:* 1964
1920 RI: 7 G. **1921** RI: 7 G; 1 Fum TD; 6 Pt. **1922** RI-ChiB: 10 G. RI: 7 G. ChiB: 3 G. **1923** ChiB: 12 G. **1924** ChiB: 11 G. **1925** ChiB: 17 G. **1926** ChiB: 14 G. **1927** ChiB: 11 G. **Total:** 89 G; 1 Fum TD; 6 Pt.

DON HEALY Healy, Michael Donald 6'3", 259 **DT-OG**
Col: Maryland *HS:* Rome Free Acad. [NY] B: 8/28/1936, Rome, NY *Drafted:* 1958 Round 3 ChiB
1958 ChiB: 12 G. **1959** ChiB: 12 G. **1960** Dal: 12 G. **1961** Dal: 14 G; Int 1-11. **1962** Buf: 1 G. **Total:** 51 G; Int 1-11.

CHIP HEALY Healy, William Raymond Jr. 6'2", 235 **LB**
Col: Vanderbilt *HS:* Baylor Prep [Chattanooga, TN] B: 8/16/1947, Atlanta, GA *Drafted:* 1969 Round 3 StL
1969 StL: 14 G. **1970** StL: 14 G. **Total:** 28 G.

JOE HEAP Heap, Joseph Lawrence 5'11", 185 **HB**
Col: Notre Dame *HS:* Holy Cross [New Orleans, LA] B: 10/26/1931, Abita Springs, LA *Drafted:* 1955 Round 1 NYG
1955 NYG: 12 G; Rush 8-29 3.6; PR 8-63 7.9; KR 12-230 19.2; 1 Fum.

WALT HEAP Heap, Walter Richmond Jr. 6'1", 210 **DB-BB-HB**
Col: Texas *HS:* Taylor [TX] B: 9/18/1921, Taylor, TX D: 5/20/1989, Dallas, TX
AAFC **1947** LA-A: Rush 5-3 0.6; Rec 2-0 1 TD. **1948** LA-A: Rush 3-12 4.0; Rec 2-9 4.5. **Total:** Rush 8-15 1.9; Rec 4-9 2.3 1 TD.

		Interceptions			Tot
Year Team	**G**	**Int**	**Yds**	**TD**	**TD**
1947 LA-A	13	5	107	1	2
1948 LA-A	14	5	94	1	1
AAFC Total	27	10	201	2	3

HERMAN HEARD Heard, Herman Willie Jr. 5'10", 184 **RB**
Col: Fort Lewis; Southern Colorado *HS:* South [Denver, CO] B: 11/24/1961, Denver, CO *Drafted:* 1984 Round 3 KC

		Rushing				Receiving					Tot
Year Team	**G**	**Att**	**Yds**	**Avg**	**TD**	**Rec**	**Yds**	**Avg**	**TD**	**Fum**	**TD**
1984 KC	16	165	684	4.1	4	25	223	8.9	0	5	4
1985 KC	16	164	595	3.6	4	31	257	8.3	2	4	6
1986 KC	15	71	295	4.2	2	17	83	4.9	0	4	2
1987 KC	12	82	466	5.7	3	14	118	8.4	0	5	3
1988 KC	12	106	438	4.1	0	20	198	9.9	0	2	0
1989 KC	16	63	216	3.4	0	25	246	9.8	1	2	1
NFL Total	87	651	2694	4.1	13	132	1125	8.5	3	22	16

LES HEARDEN Hearden, Lester Christopher 5'8", 165 **HB**
Col: Marquette; St. Ambrose *HS:* Green Bay East [WI] B: 4/24/1902, Lawrence, WI D: 12/25/1978, Green Bay, WI
1924 GB: 2 G; Rec 1 TD; 6 Pt.

TOM HEARDEN Hearden, Thomas Francis 5'9", 178 **HB-TB-BB**
(Red) *Col:* Notre Dame *HS:* Green Bay East [WI] B: 9/8/1904, Appleton, WI D: 12/27/1964, Green Bay, WI
1927 GB: 4 G. **1928** GB: 1 G. **1929** ChiB: 1 G. **Total:** 6 G.

GARRISON HEARST Hearst, Gerald Garrison 5'11", 219 **RB**
Col: Georgia *HS:* Lincoln Co. [Lincolnton, GA] B: 1/4/1971, Lincolnton, GA *Drafted:* 1993 Round 1 Pho
1993 Pho: Pass 1-0, 1 Int. **1994** Ariz: Pass 1-1 100.0%, 10 10.00 1 TD. **1995** Ariz: Pass 2-1 50.0%, 16 8.00. **1996** Cin: Scor 1 2XP. **1998** SF: Scor 1 2XP. **Total:** Pass 4-2 50.0%, 26 6.50 1 TD 1 Int; Scor 2 2XP.

		Rushing				Receiving					Tot
Year Team	**G**	**Att**	**Yds**	**Avg**	**TD**	**Rec**	**Yds**	**Avg**	**TD**	**Fum**	**TD**
1993 Pho	6	76	264	3.5	1	6	18	3.0	0	2	1
1994 Ariz	8	37	169	4.6	1	6	49	8.2	0	0	1
1995 Ariz	16	284	1070	3.8	1	29	243	8.4	1	12	2
1996 Cin	16	225	847	3.8	0	12	131	10.9	1	1	1
1997 SF	13	234	1019	4.4	4	21	194	9.2	2	2	6
1998 SF	16	310	1570	5.1	7	39	535	13.7	2	4	9
NFL Total	75	1166	4939	4.2	14	113	1170	10.4	6	21	20

DON HEATER Heater, Donald Perry 6'2", 205 **RB**
Col: Montana Tech *HS:* Thompson Falls [MT] B: 6/22/1950, Helena, MT *Drafted:* 1972 Round 6 StL
1972 StL: 2 G.

LARRY HEATER Heater, Larry 5'11", 205 **RB**
Col: Dixie Coll. UT (J.C.); Arizona *HS:* Rancho [North Las Vegas, NV] B: 1/9/1958, Cincinnati, OH *Drafted:* 1980 Round 6 KC
1980 NYG: Rec 10-139 13.9; KR 5-103 20.6. **1982** NYG: Rec 2-15 7.5; KR 5-84 16.8. **1983** NYG: KR 5-71 14.2. **Total:** Rec 12-154 12.8; KR 15-258 17.2.

Year Team	G	Rushing Att	Yds	Avg	TD	Fum
1980 NYG	14	111	360	3.2	3	1
1982 NYG	9	3	13	4.3	0	1
1983 NYG	6	0	0	—	0	0
NFL Total	29	114	373	3.3	3	2

RED HEATER Heater, William Alfred 6′2″, 220 **T**
Col: Syracuse *HS:* Reading [PA] B: 9/22/1918, Reading, PA
1940 Bkn: 8 G.

CLAYTON HEATH Heath, Clayton Donnie 5′11″, 195 **RB**
Col: Nassau CC NY; Wake Forest *HS:* Roosevelt [NY] B: 2/15/1951, Chester Co., SC *Drafted:* 1974 Round 13 Mia
1976 Buf-Mia: 8 G; Rush 1-0. Buf: 2 G. Mia: 6 G; Rush 1-0. **Total:** 8 G; Rush 1-0.

LEON HEATH Heath, Herman Leon 6′1″, 203 **FB**
(Mule Train) *Col:* Oklahoma *HS:* Hollis [OK] B: 10/27/1928, Hollis, OK
Drafted: 1951 Round 1 Was

Year Team	G	Rushing Att	Yds	Avg	TD	Receiving Rec	Yds	Avg	TD	Fum	Tot TD
1951 Was	11	64	159	2.5	0	1	3	3.0	0	3	0
1952 Was	11	90	388	4.3	2	23	146	6.3	1	5	3
1953 Was	9	76	266	3.5	4	5	45	9.0	0	4	4
NFL Total	31	230	813	3.5	6	29	194	6.7	1	12	7

JO JO HEATH Heath, Joseph Leroy 5′10″, 182 **DB**
Col: Pittsburgh *HS:* Monessen [PA] B: 3/9/1957, Monessen, PA
Drafted: 1980 Round 6 Cin
1980 Cin: 10 G; PR 6-29 4.8; KR 3-51 17.0. **1981** Phi: 15 G. **1987** NYJ: 2 G; Int 1-35. **Total:** 27 G; PR 6-29 4.8; KR 3-51 17.0; Int 1-35.

STAN HEATH Heath, Stanley R 6′1″, 190 **QB**
Col: Wisconsin; Nevada-Reno *HS:* Shorewood [WI] B: 3/5/1927, Toledo, OH *Drafted:* 1949 Round 1 GB
1949 GB: Rush 10-25 2.5 1 TD.

Year Team	G	Passing Att	Comp	Comp%	Yds	YPA	TD	Int	Rating	Fum
1949 GB	12	106	26	24.5	355	3.35	1	14	4.6	2

BOBBY HEBERT Hebert, Bobby Joseph Jr. 6′4″, 215 **QB**
Col: Northwestern State-Louisiana *HS:* South Lafourche [Galliano, LA]
B: 8/19/1960, Baton Rouge, LA
1985 NO: Rec 1-7 7.0 1 TD. **1986** NO: Rec 1-1 1.0. **1988** NO: Rec 2-0.
Total: Rec 4-8 2.0 1 TD.

Year Team	G	Passing Att	Comp	Comp%	Yds	YPA	TD	Int	Rating
1985 NO	6	181	97	53.6	1208	6.67	5	4	74.6
1986 NO	5	79	41	51.9	498	6.30	2	8	40.5
1987 NO	12	294	164	55.8	2119	7.21	15	9	82.9
1988 NO	16	478	280	58.6	3156	6.60	20	15	79.3
1989 NO	14	353	222	62.9	2686	7.61	15	15	82.7
1991 NO	9	248	149	60.1	1676	6.76	9	8	79.0
1992 NO	16	422	249	59.0	3287	7.79	19	16	82.9
1993 Atl	14	430	263	61.2	2978	6.93	24	17	84.0
1994 Atl	8	103	52	50.5	610	5.92	2	6	51.0
1995 Atl	4	45	28	62.2	313	6.96	2	1	88.5
1996 Atl	14	488	294	60.2	3152	6.46	22	25	72.9
NFL Total	118	3121	1839	58.9	21683	6.95	135	124	78.0

Year Team	Rushing Att	Yds	Avg	TD	Fum	Tot TD
1985 NO	12	26	2.2	0	1	1
1986 NO	5	14	2.8	0	3	0
1987 NO	13	95	7.3	0	4	0
1988 NO	37	79	2.1	0	9	0
1989 NO	25	87	3.5	0	2	0
1991 NO	18	56	3.1	0	5	0
1992 NO	32	95	3.0	0	3	0
1993 Atl	24	49	2.0	0	11	0
1994 Atl	9	43	4.8	0	2	0
1995 Atl	5	-1	-0.2	0	0	0
1996 Atl	15	59	3.9	1	10	1
NFL Total	195	602	3.1	1	50	2

BUD HEBERT Hebert, Darryl Ray 6′0″, 190 **DB**
Col: Oklahoma *HS:* South Park [Beaumont, TX] B: 10/12/1956, Beaumont, TX *Drafted:* 1980 Round 7 NYG
1980 NYG: 10 G; Int 1-0.

KEN HEBERT Hebert, Kenneth Daniel 6′0″, 200 **WR**
Col: Houston *HS:* Pampa [TX] B: 9/9/1944, San Bernardino, CA
Drafted: 1968 Round 3 Pit
1968 Pit: 3 G.

VAUGHN HEBRON Hebron, Vaughn Harlen 5′8″, 195 **RB**
Col: Virginia Tech *HS:* Cardinal Gibbons [Baltimore, MD] B: 10/7/1970, Baltimore, MD

Year Team	G	Rushing Att	Yds	Avg	TD	Receiving Rec	Yds	Avg	TD
1993 Phi	16	84	297	3.5	3	11	82	7.5	0
1994 Phi	16	82	325	4.0	2	18	137	7.6	0
1996 Den	16	49	262	5.3	0	7	43	6.1	0
1997 Den	16	49	222	4.5	1	3	36	12.0	0
1998 Den	15	9	31	3.4	1	2	5	2.5	0
NFL Total	79	273	1137	4.2	7	41	303	7.4	0

Year Team	Kickoff Returns Ret	Yds	Avg	TD	Fum	Tot TD
1993 Phi	3	35	11.7	0	5	3
1994 Phi	21	443	21.1	0	0	2
1996 Den	45	1099	24.4	0	3	0
1997 Den	43	1009	23.5	0	1	1
1998 Den	46	1216	26.4	1	0	2
NFL Total	158	3802	24.1	1	9	8

GEORGE HECHT Hecht, Alfred George 6′0″, 235 **G**
Col: Alabama *HS:* Bloom [Chicago Heights, IL] B: 9/17/1920, Chicago Heights, IL D: 10/24/1994, Collinsville, AL
AAFC **1947** ChiA: 10 G.

ANDY HECK Heck, Andrew Robert 6′6″, 298 **OT-OG**
Col: Notre Dame *HS:* W.T. Woodson [Fairfax, VA] B: 1/1/1967, Fargo, ND *Drafted:* 1989 Round 1 Sea
1989 Sea: 16 G. **1990** Sea: 16 G. **1991** Sea: 16 G. **1992** Sea: 13 G. **1993** Sea: 16 G. **1994** ChiB: 14 G. **1995** ChiB: 16 G. **1996** ChiB: 16 G. **1997** ChiB: 16 G. **1998** ChiB: 14 G. **Total:** 153 G.

RALPH HECK Heck, Ralph Adam 6′1″, 230 **LB**
Col: Colorado *HS:* Penn Hills [Pittsburgh, PA] B: 11/6/1941, Pittsburgh, PA *Drafted:* 1963 Round 11 Phi
1963 Phi: 14 G. **1964** Phi: 14 G. **1965** Phi: 12 G. **1966** Atl: 14 G; KR 1-0. **1967** Atl: 14 G. **1968** Atl: 13 G; Int 1-9. **1969** NYG: 14 G; Int 2-31. **1970** NYG: 14 G; Int 1-3. **1971** NYG: 11 G; Int 1-17; **1** Fum TD; 6 Pt. **Total:** 120 G; KR 1-0; Int 5-60; 1 Fum TD; 6 Pt.

BOB HECK Heck, Robert Elgin 6′4″, 210 **DE-OE**
Col: Purdue *HS:* Michael Washington [South Bend, IN] B: 6/17/1925, South Bend, IN
AAFC **1949** ChiA: 4 G.

STEVE HECKARD Heckard, Robert Stephen 6′1″, 195 **WR**
Col: USC; Davidson *HS:* R.J. Reynolds [Winston-Salem, NC]
B: 4/12/1943, Winston-Salem, NC
1965 LARm: 13 G; Rec 1-4 4.0. **1966** LARm: 12 G; Rec 5-102 20.4. **Total:** 25 G; Rec 6-106 17.7.

NORB HECKER Hecker, Norbert Earl 6′2″, 193 **DB-OE**
Col: Baldwin-Wallace *HS:* Olmsted Falls [OH] B: 5/26/1927, Berea, OH *Drafted:* 1951 Round 6 LARm
1951 LARm: Rec 4-35 8.8 1 TD; Scor 6, 0-1 FG. **1953** LARm: Rec 2-25 12.5. **1955** Was: Rec 3-31 10.3 1 TD; Scor 8, 0-1 FG, 2-2 100.0% XK. **1956** Was: **1** Fum TD. **Total:** Rec 9-91 10.1 2 TD; Scor 20, 0-2 FG, 2-2 100.0% XK; 1 Fum TD.

Year Team	G	Interceptions Int	Yds	TD	Tot TD
1951 LARm	10	3	74	0	1
1952 LARm	10	1	50	0	0
1953 LARm	12	7	91	0	0
1955 Was	12	6	52	0	1
1956 Was	12	8	26	0	1
1957 Was	8	3	39	0	0
NFL Total	64	28	332	0	3

ROBERT HECKER Hecker, Robert 6′1″, 185 **DB**
Col: Baldwin-Wallace B: 7/29/1925
1952 LARm-ChiC: 3 G. LARm: 2 G. ChiC: 1 G. **Total:** 3 G.

JOHNNY HECTOR Hector, Johnny Lindell 5′11″, 204 **RB**
Col: Texas A&M *HS:* New Iberia [LA] B: 11/26/1960, Lafayette, LA
Drafted: 1983 Round 2 NYJ
1988 NYJ: Pass 1-0. **Total:** Pass 1-0.

Year Team	G	Rushing Att	Yds	Avg	TD	Receiving Rec	Yds	Avg	TD
1983 NYJ	10	16	85	5.3	0	5	61	12.2	1
1984 NYJ	13	124	531	4.3	1	20	182	9.1	0
1985 NYJ	14	145	572	3.9	6	17	164	9.6	0
1986 NYJ	13	164	605	3.7	8	33	302	9.2	0
1987 NYJ	11	111	435	3.9	**11**	32	249	7.8	0
1988 NYJ	16	137	561	4.1	10	26	237	9.1	0
1989 NYJ	15	177	702	4.0	3	38	330	8.7	2
1990 NYJ	15	91	377	4.1	2	8	72	9.0	0
1991 NYJ	14	62	345	5.6	0	7	51	7.3	0

1992 NYJ	5	24	67	2.8	0	2	13	6.5	0
NFL Total	126	1051	4280	4.1	41	188	1661	8.8	3

	Kickoff Returns					Tot
Year Team	Ret	Yds	Avg	TD	Fum	TD
1983 NYJ	14	274	19.6	0	2	1
1984 NYJ	0	0	—	0	2	1
1985 NYJ	11	274	24.9	0	2	6
1986 NYJ	0	0	—	0	2	8
1987 NYJ	0	0	—	0	2	11
1988 NYJ	0	0	—	0	3	10
1989 NYJ	0	0	—	0	1	5
1990 NYJ	0	0	—	0	2	2
1991 NYJ	8	172	21.5	0	0	0
1992 NYJ	1	15	15.0	0	1	0
NFL Total	34	735	21.6	0	17	44

WILLIE HECTOR Hector, Willie Jr. 6′2″, 220 **OT**
Col: U. of Pacific *HS:* Tamalpais [Mill Valley, CA] B: 12/23/1939, New Iberia, LA *Drafted:* 1961 Round 5 LARm
1961 LARm: 12 G.

RANDY HEDBERG Hedberg, Randolph R 6′3″, 200 **QB**
Col: Minot State *HS:* Parshall [ND] B: 12/27/1954, Parshall, ND *Drafted:* 1977 Round 8 TB
1977 TB: Rush 9-35 3.9.

		Passing								
Year Team	G	Att	Comp	Comp%	Yds	YPA	TD	Int	Rating	Fum
1977 TB	7	90	25	27.8	244	2.71	0	10	0.0	2

PAT HEENAN Heenan, Patrick Dennis 6′2″, 191 **DB-OE**
Col: Notre Dame *HS:* University of Detroit [MI] B: 3/1/1938, Detroit, MI
1960 Was: 11 G; Int 1-25. **1961** Was: 1 G. **Total:** 12 G; Int 1-25.

GENE HEETER Heeter, Eugene Elwood 6′4″, 230 **TE**
Col: West Virginia *HS:* Windber [PA] B: 4/19/1941, Windber, PA *Drafted:* 1963 Round 8 SD
1963 NYJ: 9 G; Rec 8-160 20.0 1 TD; 6 Pt. **1964** NYJ: 14 G; Rec 13-153 11.8 1 TD; KR 1-0; 6 Pt. **1965** NYJ: 2 G; Rec 1-14 14.0. **Total:** 25 G; Rec 22-327 14.9 2 TD; KR 1-0; 12 Pt.

SHAWN HEFFERN Heffern, Shawn Patrick 6′5″, 270 **OT**
Col: Notre Dame *HS:* Carmel [IN] B: 3/15/1964, Toledo, OH
1987 Ind: 1 G.

DAVE HEFFERNAN Heffernan, David Roy 6′4″, 255 **OG**
Col: Miami (Fla.) *HS:* Christopher Columbus [Miami, FL] B: 10/28/1962, Boston, MA
1987 TB: 2 G.

VICTOR HEFLIN Heflin, Victor 6′0″, 184 **DB**
Col: Delaware State *HS:* Wayne [Huber Heights, OH] B: 7/7/1960, Springfield, MA *Drafted:* 1983 Round 6 Den
1983 StL: 8 G. **1984** StL: 16 G; Int 1-19. **Total:** 24 G; Int 1-19.

VINCE HEFLIN Heflin, Vincent George 6′0″, 185 **WR**
Col: Central State (Ohio) *HS:* Wayne [Huber Heights, OH] B: 7/7/1959, Dayton, OH
1982 Mia: 6 G; KR 2-49 24.5. **1983** Mia: 14 G; PR 1-19 19.0; KR 1-27 27.0. **1984** Mia: 16 G; PR 6-76 12.7; KR 9-130 14.4; 1 Fum. **1985** Mia: 5 G; Rec 6-98 16.3 1 TD; 6 Pt. **1986** TB: 6 G; Rec 3-42 14.0; KR 1-15 15.0; **1** Fum TD; 6 Pt. **Total:** 47 G; Rec 9-140 15.6 1 TD; PR 7-95 13.6; KR 13-221 17.0; 1 Fum TD; Tot TD 2; 12 Pt; 1 Fum.

LARRY HEFNER Hefner, Larry Douglas 6′2″, 230 **LB**
Col: Clemson *HS:* North Mecklenburg [Huntersville, NC] B: 8/2/1949, Charlotte, NC *Drafted:* 1972 Round 14 GB
1972 GB: 2 G. **1973** GB: 14 G; Int 1-3. **1974** GB: 14 G; PR 1-0. **1975** GB: 4 G. **Total:** 34 G; PR 1-0; Int 1-3.

GEORGE HEGAMIN Hegamin, George Russell 6′7″, 331 **OT**
Col: North Carolina State *HS:* Camden [NJ] B: 2/14/1973, Camden, NJ *Drafted:* 1994 Round 3 Dal
1994 Dal: 2 G. **1995** Dal: Postseason only. **1996** Dal: 16 G. **1997** Dal: 13 G. **1998** Phi: 16 G. **Total:** 47 G.

BILL HEGARTY Hegarty, William Michael 6′4″, 240 **DE-OT**
Col: Georgia; Villanova *HS:* Medford [MA]; St. Thomas Aquinas HS [Rochester, NY] B: 6/30/1931, Medford, MA
1953 Pit-Was: 3 G. Pit: 1 G. Was: 2 G. **Total:** 3 G.

MIKE HEGMAN Hegman, Michael William 6′1″, 227 **LB**
Col: Alabama A&M; Tennessee State *HS:* Northside [Memphis, TN] B: 1/17/1953, Memphis, TN *Drafted:* 1975 Round 7 Dal
1976 Dal: 14 G. **1977** Dal: 14 G; Int 1-0. **1978** Dal: 16 G. **1979** Dal: 16 G. **1980** Dal: 16 G; Int 2-2; **1** Fum TD; 6 Pt. **1981** Dal: 11 G. **1982** Dal: 9 G; 1.5 Sac. **1983** Dal: 16 G; 1 Fum TD; 6 Pt; 1 Sac. **1984** Dal: 16 G; Int 3-3; 3.5 Sac. **1985** Dal: 16 G; Int 1-7; 5.5 Sac. **1986** Dal: 16 G; 1 Sac. **1987** Dal: 10 G; 3 Sac. **Total:** 170 G; Int 7-12; 2 Fum TD; 12 Pt; 15.5 Sac.

JIMMY HEIDEL Heidel, James Byrnes 6′1″, 185 **DB**
Col: Mississippi *HS:* Yazoo City [MS] B: 12/1/1943, Yazoo City, MS *Drafted:* 1965 Round 9 StL
1966 StL: 14 G. **1967** NO: 14 G; Int 1-2. **Total:** 28 G; Int 1-2.

RALPH HEIKKINEN Heikkinen, Ralph I 5′10″, 180 **G**
Col: Michigan *HS:* Bessemer Twp. [Ramsay, MI] B: 5/14/1917, Hancock, MI D: 1/11/1990, Pontiac, MI *Drafted:* 1939 Round 12 Bkn
1939 Bkn: 3 G.

CHARLES HEILEMAN Heileman, Charles Donald 6′2″, 197 **OE-DE**
Col: Iowa State *HS:* Fort Dodge [IA] B: 1/25/1915, Fort Dodge, IA D: 2/23/1966, Clinton, IA *Drafted:* 1939 Round 5 ChiB
1939 ChiB: 2 G.

STEVE HEIMKREITER Heimkreiter, Steven 6′2″, 228 **LB**
Col: Notre Dame *HS:* Roger Bacon [Cincinnati, OH] B: 6/9/1957, Cincinnati, OH *Drafted:* 1979 Round 8 Bal
1980 Bal: 15 G.

JOHNNY HEIMSCH Heimsch, John Cyrus 5′10″, 175 **TB-HB**
Col: Marquette *HS:* Washington [Milwaukee, WI] B: 9/18/1902, Rosebush, MI D: 5/27/1991, Boulder Junction, WI
1926 Mil: 9 G; Rush 3 TD; 18 Pt.

LAKEI HEIMULI Heimuli, Lakei 5′11″, 219 **RB**
Col: Brigham Young *HS:* Kahuku [HI] B: 6/24/1965, Tonga *Drafted:* 1987 Round 9 ChiB
1987 ChiB: Rec 5-51 10.2 1 TD.

		Rushing				
Year Team	G	Att	Yds	Avg	TD	Fum
1987 ChiB	3	34	128	3.8	0	1

MEL HEIN Hein, Melvin Jack 6′2″, 225 **C-LB**
Col: Washington State *HS:* Burlington [WA]; Fairhaven HS [Bellingham, WA] B: 8/22/1909, Redding, CA D: 1/31/1992, San Clemente, CA *HOF:* 1963
1934 NYG: Rush 1-1 1.0; Rec 1-13 13.0. **1937** NYG: Rec 1-7 7.0. **1943** NYG: Pass 1-0. **Total:** Pass 1-0; Rush 1-1 1.0; Rec 2-20 10.0.

		Interceptions		
Year Team	G	Int	Yds	TD
1931 NYG	14	—	—	0
1932 NYG	12	—	—	0
1933 NYG	12	—	—	0
1934 NYG	13	—	—	0
1935 NYG	12	—	—	0
1936 NYG	11	—	—	0
1937 NYG	11	—	—	0
1938 NYG	11	—	—	**1**
1939 NYG	11	—	—	0
1940 NYG	11	2	15	0
1941 NYG	11	1	9	0
1942 NYG	11	1	2	0
1943 NYG	10	1	31	0
1944 NYG	10	3	14	0
1945 NYG	10	2	7	0
NFL Total	170	10	78	1

BOB HEIN Hein, Robert William 6′3″, 220 **DE-OE**
(AKA Bob Buck) *Col:* Kent State *HS:* John Adams [Cleveland, OH] B: 2/6/1921
AAFC **1947** BknA: 5 G; Rec 1-7 7.0.

KEN HEINEMAN Heineman, Kenneth Roy 5′9″, 168 **TB-DB**
Col: Texas-El Paso *HS:* El Paso [TX] B: 1/13/1918, Yorktown, TX *Drafted:* 1940 Round 6 Cle
1940 Cle: Int 1-5; Punt 2-63 31.5; Scor 1, 1-1 100.0% XK. **1943** Bkn: PR 10-78 7.8; KR **16-444** 27.8; Int 2-3; Punt 14-485 34.6. **Total:** PR 10-78 7.8; KR 16-444 27.8; Int 3-8; Punt 16-548 34.3; Scor 1, 1-1 100.0% XK.

		Passing							
Year Team	G	Att	Comp	Comp%	Yds	YPA	TD	Int	Rating
1940 Cle	3	8	3	37.5	74	9.25	1	1	71.9
1943 Bkn	8	57	18	31.6	285	5.00	3	8	27.2
NFL Total	11	65	21	32.3	359	5.52	4	9	32.9

	Rushing			
Year Team	Att	Yds	Avg	TD
1940 Cle	6	-5	-0.8	0
1943 Bkn	49	126	2.6	0
NFL Total	55	121	2.2	0

FRITZ HEINISCH Heinisch, Godfred F 5′10″, 173 **OE-WB-BB**
Col: No College B: 6/22/1900, Racine, WI D: 12/22/1983, Mount Pleasant, WI
1922 Rac: 5 G. **1923** Rac: 6 G. **1924** Ken: 3 G. **1926** Rac-Dul: 4 G. Rac: 3 G. Dul: 1 G. **Total:** 18 G.

PETE HEINLEIN Heinlein, George L 5′10″, 230 **G-T**
Col: No College B: 5/2/1893 D: Watertown, NY
1920 Roch: 3 G.

DON HEINRICH Heinrich, Donald Alan 6′0″, 182 **QB**
Col: Washington *HS:* Bremerton [WA] B: 9/19/1930, Bremerton, WA D: 2/29/1992, Saratoga, CA *Drafted:* 1952 Round 3 NYG

		Passing							
Year Team	G	Att	Comp	Comp%	Yds	YPA	TD	Int	Rating
1954 NYG	2	9	4	44.4	56	6.22	0	2	25.5
1955 NYG	10	67	31	46.3	413	6.16	2	2	63.8
1956 NYG	12	88	37	42.0	369	4.19	5	5	49.9
1957 NYG	4	26	11	42.3	224	8.62	1	1	70.0
1958 NYG	7	68	26	38.2	369	5.43	4	2	63.9
1959 NYG	8	58	22	37.9	329	5.67	1	6	23.5
1960 Dal	12	61	23	37.7	371	6.08	3	3	54.7
1962 Oak	1	29	10	34.5	156	5.38	1	2	36.0
NFL Total	56	406	164	40.4	2287	5.63	17	23	49.6

	Rushing				
Year Team	Att	Yds	Avg	TD	Fum
1954 NYG	1	0	0.0	0	1
1955 NYG	7	4	0.6	2	1
1956 NYG	5	-4	-0.8	0	2
1957 NYG	4	10	2.5	2	2
1958 NYG	5	4	0.8	1	1
1959 NYG	2	3	1.5	0	1
1960 Dal	2	3	1.5	0	0
1962 Oak	1	4	4.0	0	0
NFL Total	27	24	0.9	5	8

BOB HEINZ Heinz, Robert Kenneth 6′6″, 265 **DT-DE**
(Tree) *Col:* San Joaquin Delta Coll. CA (J.C.); U. of Pacific *HS:* Messemer [Milwaukee, WI]; Lincoln HS [Stockton, CA] B: 7/25/1947, Milwaukee, WI *Drafted:* 1969 Round 2 Mia
1969 Mia: 14 G. **1970** Mia: 14 G. **1971** Mia: 14 G. **1972** Mia: 11 G. **1973** Mia: 14 G. **1974** Mia: 14 G. **1976** Mia: 14 G. **1977** Mia: 14 G. **1978** Was: 2 G. **Total:** 111 G.

GEORGE HEKKERS Hekkers, George James 6′4″, 241 **T**
(Duke) *Col:* Wisconsin *HS:* Washington [Milwaukee, WI] B: 2/18/1923, Milwaukee, WI
AAFC **1946** MiaA: 8 G. **1947** BalA: 3 G. **Total:** 11 G.

NFL **1947** Det: 6 G. **1948** Det: 12 G. **1949** Det: 12 G; 1 Fum. **Total:** 30 G; 1 Fum.

PAUL HELD Held, Paul E 6′2″, 195 **QB**
(Pelican) *Col:* El Camino Coll. CA (J.C.); San Jose State *HS:* Redondo [Redondo Beach, CA] B: 10/20/1928, El Segundo, CA *Drafted:* 1953 Round 19 Det
1954 Pit: Rush 3-3 1.0; Scor 23, 3-5 60.0% FG, 14-16 87.5% XK. **1955** GB: Rush 1-8 8.0. **Total:** Rush 4-11 2.8; Scor 23, 3-5 60.0% FG, 14-16 87.5% XK.

		Passing								
Year Team	G	Att	Comp	Comp%	Yds	YPA	TD	Int	Rating	Fum
1954 Pit	8	73	24	32.9	305	4.18	1	6	17.2	1
1955 GB	2	4	2	50.0	27	6.75	0	0	71.9	0
NFL Total	10	77	26	33.8	332	4.31	1	6	20.0	1

CARL HELDT Heldt, Carl Diederich 6′2″, 206 **T**
Col: Purdue *HS:* Central [Evansville, IN] B: 3/20/1913, Evansville, IN D: 7/20/1983, Kerrville, TX
1935 Bkn: 6 G. **1936** Bkn: 12 G; Rec 2-39 19.5. **Total:** 18 G; Rec 2-39 19.5.

JACK HELDT Heldt, John Claussen 5′9″, 208 **C-G**
Col: Iowa *HS:* East Detroit [Eastpointe, MI] B: 12/2/1899, Calumet, MI D: 10/25/1975, Emmetsburg, IA
1923 Col: 1 G. **1926** Col: 6 G. **Total:** 7 G.

RON HELLER Heller, Ronald Jeffery 6′3″, 236 **TE**
Col: Oregon State *HS:* Clark Fork [ID] B: 9/18/1963, Gross Valley, CA

		Receiving				
Year Team	G	Rec	Yds	Avg	TD	Fum
1987 SF	13	12	165	13.8	3	1
1988 SF	16	14	140	10.0	0	0
1989 Atl	15	33	324	9.8	1	1
1990 Sea	16	13	157	12.1	1	0
1992 Sea	16	12	85	7.1	0	0
NFL Total	76	84	871	10.4	5	2

RON HELLER Heller, Ronald Ramon 6′6″, 290 **OT**
Col: Penn State *HS:* Farmingdale [NY] B: 8/25/1962, East Meadow, NY *Drafted:* 1984 Round 4 TB
1984 TB: 14 G. **1985** TB: 16 G. **1986** TB: 16 G; Rec 1-1 1.0 1 TD; 6 Pt. **1987** TB: 12 G. **1988** Phi: 15 G. **1989** Phi: 16 G. **1990** Phi: 16 G. **1991** Phi: 16 G. **1992** Phi: 12 G. **1993** Mia: 16 G. **1994** Mia: 16 G. **1995** Mia: 7 G. **Total:** 172 G; Rec 1-1 1.0 1 TD; 6 Pt.

WARREN HELLER Heller, Warren Willis 5′11″, 195 **TB-DB-HB**
(Fats) *Col:* Pittsburgh *HS:* Steelton [PA] B: 11/24/1910, Pittsburgh, PA D: 10/29/1982, Oakmont, PA
1934 Pit: Rec 6-96 16.0. **1935** Pit: Rec 2-16 8.0. **1936** Pit: Rec 12-160 13.3 3 TD. **Total:** Rec 20-272 13.6 3 TD.

		Passing							
Year Team	G	Att	Comp	Comp%	Yds	YPA	TD	Int	Rating
1934 Pit	12	112	31	27.7	511	4.56	2	15	12.5
1935 Pit	12	41	9	22.0	88	2.15	0	8	0.0
1936 Pit	12	5	0	0.0	0	0.00	0	1	0.0
NFL Total	36	158	40	25.3	599	3.79	2	24	7.5

	Rushing				Tot
Year Team	Att	Yds	Avg	TD	TD
1934 Pit	132	528	4.0	1	1
1935 Pit	37	112	3.0	0	0
1936 Pit	106	332	3.1	0	3
NFL Total	275	972	3.5	1	4

DALE HELLESTRAE Hellestrae, Dale Robert 6′5″, 282 **OT-OG-C**
Col: Southern Methodist *HS:* Saguaro [Scottsdale, AZ] B: 7/11/1962, Phoenix, AZ *Drafted:* 1985 Round 4 Buf
1985 Buf: 4 G. **1986** Buf: 8 G; 1 Fum. **1988** Buf: 16 G. **1990** Dal: 16 G. **1991** Dal: 16 G. **1992** Dal: 16 G. **1993** Dal: 16 G. **1994** Dal: 16 G. **1995** Dal: 16 G. **1996** Dal: 16 G. **1997** Dal: 16 G. **1998** Dal: 16 G. **Total:** 172 G; 1 Fum.

JERRY HELLUIN Helluin, Francis Jerome 6′2″, 272 **DT**
Col: Tulane *HS:* Catholic [Donaldsonville, LA] B: 8/8/1929, Houma, LA *Drafted:* 1951 Round 3 Cle
1952 Cle: 12 G. **1953** Cle: 6 G; **1** Fum TD; 6 Pt. **1954** GB: 12 G. **1955** GB: 12 G. **1956** GB: 12 G. **1957** GB: 12 G; Int 1-0. **1960** Hou: 14 G. **Total:** 80 G; Int 1-0; 1 Fum TD; 6 Pt.

JACK HELMS Helms, John Ancel 6′4″, 215 **DE**
Col: Georgia Tech *HS:* Charlotte [NC] B: 1921 *Drafted:* 1944 Round 17 Det
1946 Det: 7 G; Scor 13, 3-4 75.0% FG, 4-6 66.7% XK.

BARRY HELTON Helton, Barry Bret 6′3″, 205 **P**
Col: Colorado *HS:* Simla [CO] B: 1/2/1965, Colorado Springs, CO *Drafted:* 1988 Round 4 SF
1988 SF: Rush 1-0. **1989** SF: Rush 1-0. **1990** SF: Pass 1-1 100.0%. **1991** LARm: Pass 1-1 100.0%, 22 22.00. **Total:** Pass 2-2 100.0%, 22 11.00; Rush 2-0.

		Punting			
Year Team	G	Punts	Yds	Avg	Fum
1988 SF	15	78	3069	39.3	0
1989 SF	16	55	2226	40.5	1
1990 SF	16	69	2537	36.8	0
1991 LARm	3	11	453	41.2	0
NFL Total	50	213	8285	38.9	1

DARIUS HELTON Helton, Darius 6′2″, 260 **OG**
Col: North Carolina Central B: 10/2/1954, Charlotte, NC *Drafted:* 1977 Round 4 KC
1977 KC: 6 G.

CHUCK HELVIE Helvie, Charles L 5′8″, 185 **OE**
(Stump) *Col:* No College B: 10/8/1891, IN D: 5/17/1964, Columbus, OH
1920 Mun-Day: 5 G. Mun: 1 G. Day: 4 G. **1921** Mun: 2 G. **Total:** 7 G.

JOHN HELWIG Helwig, John Frank 6′2″, 208 **LB-DE**
Col: Notre Dame *HS:* Mount Carmel [Los Angeles, CA] B: 12/5/1927, Los Angeles, CA D: 12/2/1994, Pontiac, MI *Drafted:* 1950 Round 11 ChiB
1953 ChiB: 12 G; KR 1-12 12.0. **1954** ChiB: 12 G; Int 3-22. **1955** ChiB: 12 G. **1956** ChiB: 6 G. **Total:** 42 G; KR 1-12 12.0; Int 3-22.

BILL HEMPEL Hempel, William 6′0″, 235 **T**
(Butch) *Col:* Carroll (Wis.) *HS:* York [Elmhurst, IL] B: 2/10/1920, Lincoln, NE
1942 ChiB: 8 G.

DARRYL HEMPHILL Hemphill, Darryl Anthony 6′0″, 195 **DB**
Col: West Texas A&M *HS:* Thomas Jefferson [San Antonio, TX] B: 3/29/1960, San Antonio, TX *Drafted:* 1982 Round 10 NYJ
1982 Bal: 3 G.

HESSLEY HEMPSTEAD Hempstead, Hessley James II 6′1″, 295 **OG**
Col: Kansas *HS:* Upland [CA] B: 1/29/1972, Upland, CA *Drafted:* 1995 Round 7 Det
1995 Det: 2 G. **1996** Det: 13 G. **1997** Det: 16 G. **Total:** 31 G.

NATE HEMSLEY Hemsley, Nathaniel Richard 6′0″, 228 **LB**
Col: Syracuse *HS:* Delran [NJ] B: 5/15/1974, Willingboro, NJ
1997 Dal: 2 G. **1998** Dal: 3 G. **Total:** 5 G.

ANDY HENDEL Hendel, Andrew Carey 6'1", 230 LB
Col: North Carolina State *HS:* Irondequoit [NY] B: 3/4/1961, Rochester, NY
1986 Mia: 16 G.

LARRY HENDERSHOT Hendershot, Lawrence Leland 6'3", 240 LB
Col: Arizona State *HS:* Washington [Phoenix, AZ] B: 1/15/1944, Indianapolis, IN *Drafted:* 1967 Round 8 Was
1967 Was: 4 G.

HERB HENDERSON Henderson, Herbert Raymond 5'11", 170 TB
Col: Oberlin; Ohio State *HS:* Oberlin [OH] B: 6/21/1899, Oberlin, OH D: 1/14/1991, Odon, IN
1921 Eva: 4 G; Rush 4 TD; Scor 29, 5 XK.

JEROME HENDERSON Henderson, Jerome Virgil 5'10", 193 DB
Col: Clemson *HS:* West Iredell [Statesville, NC] B: 8/8/1969, Statesville, NC *Drafted:* 1991 Round 2 NE
1991 NE: Int 2-2. **1992** NE: Int 3-43. **1995** Phi: **1** Fum TD. **1996** NE: Int 2-7. **1997** NYJ: Int 1-45. **1998** NYJ: Int 1-21; 1 Fum TD; 1 Sac. **Total:** Int 9-118; 2 Fum TD; 1 Sac.

		Punt Returns				
Year Team	G	Ret	Yds	Avg	TD	Fum
1991 NE	16	27	201	7.4	0	2
1992 NE	16	0	0	—	0	0
1993 NE-Buf	3	0	0	—	0	0
1993 NE	1	0	0	—	0	0
1993 Buf	2	0	0	—	0	0
1994 Buf	12	0	0	—	0	0
1995 Phi	15	0	0	—	0	0
1996 NE	7	0	0	—	0	0
1997 NYJ	16	0	0	—	0	0
1998 NYJ	13	0	0	—	0	1
NFL Total	98	27	201	7.4	0	3

JOHN HENDERSON Henderson, John William 6'3", 195 WR
Col: Michigan *HS:* Roosevelt [Dayton, OH] B: 3/21/1943, Dayton, OH *Drafted:* 1965 Round 5 Phi

		Receiving				
Year Team	G	Rec	Yds	Avg	TD	Fum
1965 Det	12	8	140	17.5	1	0
1966 Det	13	6	121	20.2	0	0
1967 Det	14	13	144	11.1	0	0
1968 Min	7	4	42	10.5	0	0
1969 Min	14	34	553	16.3	5	0
1970 Min	14	31	527	17.0	2	0
1971 Min	7	2	18	9.0	0	0
1972 Min	12	10	190	19.0	2	1
NFL Total	93	108	1735	16.1	10	1

JON HENDERSON Henderson, Jon Elliott 6'0", 200 WR-DB
Col: Colorado State *HS:* Westinghouse [Pittsburgh, PA] B: 12/17/1944, Pittsburgh, PA *Drafted:* 1968 Round 3 Pit

		Receiving				Kickoff Returns				
Year Team	G	Rec	Yds	Avg	TD	Ret	Yds	Avg	TD	Fum
1968 Pit	14	3	26	8.7	0	29	589	20.3	0	2
1969 Pit	9	12	188	15.7	3	0	0	—	0	0
1970 Was	14	13	176	13.5	3	1	0	0.0	0	0
NFL Total	37	28	390	13.9	6	30	589	19.6	0	2

KEITH HENDERSON Henderson, Keith Pernell 6'1", 220 RB
Col: Georgia *HS:* Cartersville [GA] B: 8/4/1966, Cartersville, GA *Drafted:* 1989 Round 3 SF
1989 SF: KR 2-21 10.5. **1992** SF-Min: Pass 1-1 100.0%, 36 36.00 1 TD; KR 5-111 22.2. Min: Pass 1-1 100.0%, 36 36.00 1 TD; KR 5-111 22.2. **Total:** Pass 1-1 100.0%, 36 36.00 1 TD; KR 7-132 18.9.

		Rushing				Receiving				
Year Team	G	Att	Yds	Avg	TD	Rec	Yds	Avg	TD	Fum
1989 SF	6	7	30	4.3	1	3	130	43.3	0	1
1990 SF	2	6	14	2.3	0	4	35	8.8	0	0
1991 SF	14	137	561	4.1	2	30	303	10.1	0	4
1992 SF-Min	15	44	150	3.4	1	5	64	12.8	0	4
1992 SF	2	10	37	3.7	0	1	4	4.0	0	3
1992 Min	13	34	113	3.3	1	4	60	15.0	0	1
NFL Total	37	194	755	3.9	4	42	532	12.7	0	9

OTHELLO HENDERSON Henderson, Othello M 6'0", 204 DB
Col: UCLA *HS:* C.E. Ellison [Killeen, TX] B: 8/23/1972, Oakland, CA *Drafted:* 1993 Round 7 NO
1993 NO: 5 G. **1994** NO: 16 G. **Total:** 21 G.

REUBEN HENDERSON Henderson, Reuben Stanley 6'1", 196 DB
Col: Oklahoma State; San Diego State *HS:* Fontana [CA] B: 10/3/1958, Santa Monica, CA *Drafted:* 1981 Round 6 ChiB
1981 ChiB: 16 G; Int 4-84. **1982** ChiB: 4 G. **1983** SD: 14 G; 1 Sac. **1984** SD: 12 G; PR 1-0; 1 Fum. **Total:** 46 G; PR 1-0; Int 4-84; 1 Fum; 1 Sac.

TOM HENDERSON Henderson, Thomas Edward 6'2", 221 LB
(Hollywood) *Col:* Langston *HS:* Anderson [Austin, TX]; Douglass HS [Oklahoma City, OK] B: 3/1/1953, Austin, TX *Drafted:* 1975 Round 1 Dal
1975 Dal: 13 G; KR 4-130 32.5 **1** TD; 6 Pt; 1 Fum. **1976** Dal: 14 G; KR 0-12; Scor **1** Saf; 2 Pt. **1977** Dal: 14 G; KR 1-8 8.0; Int 3-79 **1** TD; 6 Pt. **1978** Dal: 15 G. **1979** Dal: 11 G. **1980** SF-Hou: 8 G; Int 1-3. SF: 1 G. Hou: 7 G; Int 1-3. **Total:** 75 G; KR 5-150 30.0 1 TD; Int 4-82 1 TD; Scor 1 Saf; Tot TD 2; 14 Pt; 1 Fum.

WILBUR HENDERSON Henderson, Wilbur W 195 HB
Col: No College B: 1898, IL Deceased
1920 Ham: 1 G.

WILLIAM HENDERSON Henderson, William Terrelle 6'1", 245 RB
(Boogey) *Col:* North Carolina *HS:* Thomas Dale [Chester, VA] B: 2/19/1971, Richmond, VA *Drafted:* 1995 Round 3 GB
1996 GB: KR 2-38 19.0. **Total:** KR 2-38 19.0.

		Rushing				Receiving					Tot
Year Team	G	Att	Yds	Avg	TD	Rec	Yds	Avg	TD	Fum	TD
1995 GB	15	7	35	5.0	0	3	21	7.0	0	0	0
1996 GB	16	39	130	3.3	0	27	203	7.5	1	1	1
1997 GB	16	31	113	3.6	0	41	367	9.0	1	1	1
1998 GB	16	23	70	3.0	2	37	241	6.5	1	1	3
NFL Total	63	100	348	3.5	2	108	832	7.7	3	3	5

WYATT HENDERSON Henderson, Wyatt Monroe 5'10", 180 DB
Col: Los Angeles Valley Coll. CA (J.C.); Fresno State *HS:* Fairfax [Los Angeles, CA] B: 11/10/1956, Bakersfield, CA
1981 SD: 15 G; KR 1-26 26.0.

WYMON HENDERSON Henderson, Wymon 5'10", 190 DB
Col: Allan Hancock Coll. CA (J.C.); Nevada-Las Vegas *HS:* North Miami Beach [FL] B: 12/15/1961, North Miami Beach, FL
1993 LARm: 1 Sac. **Total:** 1 Sac.

		Interceptions			
Year Team	G	Int	Yds	TD	Fum
1987 Min	12	4	33	0	0
1988 Min	16	1	13	0	0
1989 Den	16	3	58	0	1
1990 Den	15	2	71	1	0
1991 Den	16	2	53	0	0
1992 Den	15	4	79	1	0
1993 LARm	9	0	0	0	0
1994 LARm	15	0	0	0	0
NFL Total	114	16	307	2	1

ZAC HENDERSON Henderson, Zachary Ryall 6'1", 190 DB
Col: Oklahoma *HS:* Burkburnett [TX] B: 10/14/1955, Jena, LA
1980 Phi: 12 G.

DAVID HENDLEY Hendley, David 6'0", 188 DB
Col: Southern Connecticut State B: 6/29/1964
1987 NE: 2 G.

DICK HENDLEY Hendley, Dickson L 6'0", 198 BB
Col: Clemson *HS:* Greenville [SC] B: 8/6/1926 *Drafted:* 1951 Round 22 Pit
1951 Pit: 7 G.

JIM HENDLEY Hendley, James Willis Jr. 6'3", 257 C
Col: Florida State *HS:* Berrien [Nashville, GA] B: 10/25/1964, Valdosta, GA
1987 Atl: 3 G.

JERRY HENDREN Hendren, Jerry Wayne 6'2", 187 WR
Col: Idaho *HS:* Shadle Park [Spokane, WA] B: 11/4/1947, Spokane, WA *Drafted:* 1970 Round 4 Den
1970 Den: 10 G; KR 8-197 24.6.

JOHNNY HENDREN Hendren, John Crowther 5'10", 175 FB-TB-WB
Col: Bucknell *HS:* Northeast [Philadelphia, PA] B: 4/25/1897, Philadelphia, PA D: 6/3/1964, Media, PA
1920 Can: 3 G. **1921** Cle: 5 G; Rush 1 TD; 6 Pt. **Total:** 8 G; Rush 1 TD; 6 Pt.

BOB HENDREN Hendren, Robert Gerald 6'8", 244 OT-DT-DE
Col: Culver-Stockton; USC *HS:* Clarinda [IA] B: 8/10/1923, Burlington Junc., MO
1949 Was: 12 G. **1950** Was: 12 G. **1951** Was: 12 G; KR 2-21 10.5. **Total:** 36 G; KR 2-21 10.5.

DUTCH HENDRIAN Hendrian, Oscar George 5'9", 182 WB-FB-BB-TB
Col: DePauw; Detroit Mercy; Pittsburgh; Princeton *HS:* Central [Detroit, MI] B: 1/19/1896, Detroit, MI D: 12/13/1953, Los Angeles, CA
1923 Akr-Can: 9 G; Rush 1 TD; Scor 7, 1 XK. Akr: 5 G; Scor 1, 1 XK. Can: 4 G; Rush 1 TD; 6 Pt. **1924** GB: 11 G; Rush 3 TD; Scor 21, 1 FG. **1925** RI-NYG: 12 G; Rec 2 TD; Scor 22, 3 FG, 1 XK. RI: 1 G. NYG: 11 G; Rec 2 TD; Scor 22, 3 FG, 1 XK. **Total:** 32 G; Rush 4 TD; Rec 2 TD; Scor 50, 4 FG, 2 XK; Tot TD 6.

TED HENDRICKS Hendricks, Theodore Paul 6′7″, 220 LB
(The Mad Stork) *Col:* Miami (Fla.) *HS:* Hialeah [FL] B: 11/1/1947, Guatemala City, Guatemala *Drafted:* 1969 Round 2 Bal *HOF:* 1990
1971 Bal: **1** Fum TD. **1972** Bal: KR 1-0. **1974** GB: Scor **1** Saf. **1975** Oak: Scor **1** Saf. **1976** Oak: Scor **1** Saf. **1980** Oak: Scor **1** Saf. **1982** LARd: 7 Sac. **1983** LARd: 2 Sac. **Total:** KR 1-0; Scor **4** Saf; 1 Fum TD; 9 Sac.

		Interceptions				Tot
Year Team	G	Int	Yds	TD	Fum	TD
1969 Bal	14	0	0	0	0	0
1970 Bal	14	1	31	0	0	1
1971 Bal	14	5	70	0	0	1
1972 Bal	14	2	13	0	1	0
1973 Bal	14	3	33	0	0	1
1974 GB	14	5	74	0	0	0
1975 Oak	14	2	40	0	0	0
1976 Oak	14	1	9	0	0	0
1977 Oak	14	0	0	0	0	0
1978 Oak	16	3	29	0	0	0
1979 Oak	16	1	23	1	0	1
1980 Oak	16	3	10	0	0	0
1981 Oak	16	0	0	0	0	0
1982 LARd	9	0	0	0	0	0
1983 LARd	16	0	0	0	0	0
NFL Total	215	26	332	1	1	4

STEVE HENDRICKSON Hendrickson, Steven Daniel 6′0″, 250 LB-TE
Col: California *HS:* Napa [CA] B: 8/30/1966, Richmond, CA
Drafted: 1989 Round 6 SF
1989 Dal-SF: 15 G. Dal: 4 G. SF: 11 G. **1990** SD: 14 G; Rec 1-12 12.0. **1991** SD: 15 G; Rush 1-3 3.0 1 TD; Rec 4-36 9.0 1 TD; Tot TD 2; 12 Pt. **1992** SD: 16 G; KR 2-14 7.0. **1993** SD: 16 G; Rush 1-0; KR 2-25 12.5; Int 1-16. **1994** SD: 16 G; Rush 1-3 3.0. **1995** Phi-Hou: 8 G. Phi: 3 G. Hou: 5 G. **Total:** 100 G; Rush 3-6 2.0 1 TD; Rec 5-48 9.6 1 TD; KR 4-39 9.8; Int 1-16; Tot TD 2; 12 Pt.

DAVID HENDRIX Hendrix, David Tyrone 6′1″, 213 DB
Col: Georgia Tech *HS:* Meadowcreek [Norcross, GA] B: 5/29/1972, Jesup, GA
1995 SD: 5 G. **1996** SD: 14 G. **1997** SD: 4 G. **Total:** 23 G.

MANNY HENDRIX Hendrix, Manuel 5′10″, 180 DB
Col: Utah *HS:* South Mountain [Phoenix, AZ] B: 10/20/1964, Phoenix, AZ
1986 Dal: 13 G. **1987** Dal: 12 G. **1988** Dal: 16 G; Int 1-0. **1989** Dal: 16 G; 0.5 Sac. **1990** Dal: 16 G; Int 1-0. **1991** Dal: 16 G; Scor 1 Saf; 2 Pt. **Total:** 89 G; Int 2-0; Scor 1 Saf; 2 Pt; 0.5 Sac.

TIM HENDRIX Hendrix, Timothy John 6′5″, 241 TE
Col: Tennessee *HS:* De Soto [TX] B: 2/24/1965, De Soto, TX
1987 Dal: 3 G.

JOHN HENDY Hendy, John Herald 5′11″, 196 DB
Col: Long Beach State *HS:* Adrian Wilcox [Santa Clara, CA]
B: 10/9/1962, Guatemala City, Guatemala *Drafted:* 1985 Round 3 SD
1985 SD: 16 G; Int 4-139 **1** TD; 6 Pt.

BRIAN HENESEY Henesey, Brian P 5′10″, 215 RB
Col: Bucknell *HS:* Radnor [PA] B: 12/10/1969, Villanova, PA
1994 Ariz: 3 G; KR 6-108 18.0.

BRAD HENKE Henke, Brad William 6′3″, 275 DE-NT
Col: Palomar Coll. CA (J.C.); Iowa State; Arizona *HS:* Heritage [Littleton, CO] B: 4/10/1966, Columbus, NE *Drafted:* 1989 Round 4 NYG
1989 Den: 2 G.

ED HENKE Henke, Edgar Edwin 6′3″, 227 DE-LB-OG-DG
Col: Ventura Coll. CA (J.C.); USC *HS:* Ventura [CA] B: 12/13/1927, Ontario, CA *Drafted:* 1949 Round 13 Was
AAFC **1949** LA-A: 11 G; Rec 1-15 15.0.

NFL **1951** SF: 12 G. **1952** SF: 12 G; Rec 1-13 13.0. **1956** SF: 12 G. **1957** SF: 12 G. **1958** SF: 12 G. **1959** SF: 12 G. **1960** SF: 8 G. **1961** StL: 14 G. **1962** StL: 8 G. **1963** StL: 10 G. **Total:** 112 G; Rec 1-13 13.0.

KARL HENKE Henke, Karl Alfred 6′4″, 245 DT-DE
Col: Ventura Coll. CA (J.C.); Tulsa *HS:* Ventura [CA] B: 3/8/1945, Ventura, CA *Drafted:* 1968 Round 8 NYJ
1968 NYJ: 6 G. **1969** Bos: 10 G. **Total:** 16 G.

CAREY HENLEY Henley, Carey Ernest 5′10″, 201 HB
Col: Tennessee-Chattanooga *HS:* West Point [MS] B: 9/24/1936, West Point, MS *Drafted:* 1962 Round 21 Buf
1962 Buf: 1 G; Rush 3-2 0.7; KR 5-90 18.0.

JUNE HENLEY Henley, Charles Lee Jr. 5′10″, 226 RB
Col: Kansas *HS:* Brookhaven [Columbus, OH] B: 9/4/1975, Columbus, OH *Drafted:* 1997 Round 6 KC
1998 StL: KR 1-13 13.0.

		Rushing				Receiving				
Year Team	G	Att	Yds	Avg	TD	Rec	Yds	Avg	TD	Fum
1998 StL	11	88	313	3.6	3	35	252	7.2	0	1

DARRYL HENLEY Henley, Darryl Keith 5′9″, 172 DB
Col: UCLA *HS:* Damien [La Verne, CA] B: 10/30/1966, Los Angeles, CA *Drafted:* 1989 Round 2 LARm

		Punt Returns				Interceptions			
Year Team	G	Ret	Yds	Avg	TD	Int	Yds	TD	Fum
1989 LARm	15	28	266	9.5	0	1	10	0	1
1990 LARm	9	19	195	10.3	0	1	0	0	0
1991 LARm	16	13	110	8.5	0	3	22	0	1
1992 LARm	16	0	0	—	0	4	41	0	0
1993 LARm	5	1	8	8.0	0	0	0	0	0
1994 LARm	15	0	0	—	0	3	46	0	0
NFL Total	76	61	579	9.5	0	12	119	0	2

THOMAS HENLEY Henley, Thomas Henry III 5′11″, 185 WR
Col: Stanford *HS:* Damien [La Verne, CA] B: 7/28/1965, Hillsboro, TX
Drafted: 1987 Round 6 NO
1987 SF: 1 G; KR 1-21 21.0.

TOM HENNESSEY Hennessey, Thomas Edward 6′0″, 180 DB
Col: Holy Cross *HS:* Brookline [MA] B: 2/15/1942, Boston, MA
1965 Bos: 14 G; PR 5-21 4.2; Int 2-14; 1 Fum. **1966** Bos: 14 G; PR 7-39 5.6; Int 6-99; 2 Fum. **Total:** 28 G; PR 12-60 5.0; Int 8-113; 3 Fum.

JERRY HENNESSY Hennessy, Jerome Joseph 6′2″, 219 DE
(Three Star) *Col:* Santa Clara *HS:* Mount Carmel [Los Angeles, CA]
B: 2/22/1926, Los Angeles, CA *Drafted:* 1950 Round 13 ChiC
1950 ChiC: 7 G; KR 1-5 5.0. **1951** ChiC: 12 G; KR 1-11 11.0. **1952** Was: 12 G; Scor **1** Saf; 2 Pt. **1953** Was: 8 G. **Total:** 39 G; KR 2-16 8.0; Scor 1 Saf; 2 Pt.

JOHN HENNESSY Hennessy, John William 6′3″, 243 LB-DE
Col: Michigan *HS:* Gordon Tech [Chicago, IL] B: 3/12/1955, Chicago, IL *Drafted:* 1977 Round 10 NYJ
1977 NYJ: 14 G. **1978** NYJ: 16 G. **1979** NYJ: 16 G; KR 2-15 7.5.
Total: 46 G; KR 2-15 7.5.

CHARLEY HENNIGAN Hennigan, Charles Taylor 6′1″, 187 WR
Col: Louisiana State; Northwestern State-Louisiana *HS:* Minden [LA]
B: 3/19/1935, Bienville, LA

		Receiving				
Year Team	G	Rec	Yds	Avg	TD	Fum
1960 Hou	11	44	722	16.4	6	1
1961 Hou	14	82	**1746**	21.3	12	0
1962 Hou	14	54	867	16.1	8	0
1963 Hou	14	61	1051	17.2	10	0
1964 Hou	14	**101**	**1546**	15.3	8	1
1965 Hou	14	41	578	14.1	4	1
1966 Hou	14	27	313	11.6	3	0
NFL Total	95	410	6823	16.6	51	3

MIKE HENNIGAN Hennigan, Thomas Michael 6′2″, 217 LB
Col: Parsons; Tennessee Tech *HS:* Washington [IA] B: 10/24/1951, Washington, IA *Drafted:* 1973 Round 4 Det
1973 Det: 8 G. **1974** Det: 14 G. **1975** Det: 4 G; KR 1-13 13.0. **1976** NYJ: 12 G; KR 1-22 22.0. **1977** NYJ: 14 G. **1978** NYJ: 12 G; Int 3-76.
Total: 64 G; KR 2-35 17.5; Int 3-76.

DAN HENNING Henning, Daniel Ernest Jr. 6′0″, 195 QB
Col: William & Mary *HS:* St. Francis Prep [Brooklyn, NY] B: 6/21/1942, Bronx, NY
1966 SD: 1 G.

CHAD HENNINGS Hennings, Chad William 6′6″, 287 DE
Col: Air Force *HS:* Benton [Van Horne, IA] B: 10/20/1965, Elberton, IA
Drafted: 1988 Round 11 Dal
1992 Dal: 8 G. **1993** Dal: 13 G; KR 1-7 7.0. **1994** Dal: 16 G; 7 Sac. **1995** Dal: 16 G; 5.5 Sac. **1996** Dal: 15 G; 4.5 Sac. **1997** Dal: 11 G; 1 Fum TD; 6 Pt; 4.5 Sac. **1998** Dal: 16 G; 1 Sac. **Total:** 95 G; KR 1-7 7.0; 1 Fum TD; 6 Pt; 22.5 Sac.

RALPH HENRICUS Henricus, Ralph 6′0″, 175 TB
Col: No College *HS:* Cathedral [Rochester, NY] B: 6/1896, Rochester, NY Deceased
1922 Roch: 2 G.

BERNARD HENRY Henry, Bernard 6′1″, 180 WR
Col: Arizona State *HS:* John C. Fremont [Los Angeles, CA]
B: 4/9/1960, Los Angeles, CA

		Receiving			
Year Team	G	Rec	Yds	Avg	TD
1982 Bal	6	7	110	15.7	0
1983 Bal	15	30	416	13.9	4
1984 Ind	14	11	139	12.6	2
1985 Ind	1	2	31	15.5	0
1987 LARm	3	1	13	13.0	0
NFL Total	39	51	709	13.9	6

CHARLES HENRY Henry, Charles W 6′4″, 230 **TE**
Col: Miami (Fla.) *HS:* Northeast [St. Petersburg, FL] B: 4/18/1964, St. Petersburg, FL
1991 Mia: 6 G; Rec 2-17 8.5; KR 1-13 13.0.

FRITZ HENRY Henry, Fred Earl 190 **G**
Col: No College B: 11/30/1895, Columbus, OH D: 1/23/1974, Columbus, OH
1925 Akr: 1 G.

KEVIN HENRY Henry, Kevin Lerell 6′4″, 282 **DE**
Col: Mississippi State *HS:* John F. Kennedy [Mound Bayou, MS] B: 10/23/1968, Mound Bayou, MS *Drafted:* 1993 Round 4 Pit
1993 Pit: 12 G; Int 1-10; 1 Sac. **1994** Pit: 16 G. **1995** Pit: 14 G; 2 Sac. **1996** Pit: 12 G; 1.5 Sac. **1997** Pit: 16 G; Int 1-36; 4.5 Sac. **1998** Pit: 16 G; 4 Sac. **Total:** 86 G; Int 2-46; 13 Sac.

MAURICE HENRY Henry, Maurice Eugene 5′11″, 220 **LB**
Col: Kansas State *HS:* Salina Central [KS] B: 3/12/1967, Starkville, MS *Drafted:* 1990 Round 6 Det
1990 Phi: 7 G.

MIKE HENRY Henry, Michael Dennis 6′2″, 220 **LB**
Col: USC *HS:* Bell [CA] B: 8/15/1936, Los Angeles, CA *Drafted:* 1958 Round 9 Pit
1959 Pit: 12 G; Int 2-42. **1960** Pit: 12 G. **1961** Pit: 10 G; Int 1-8. **1962** LARm: 14 G; Int 1-10. **1963** LARm: 14 G; Int 5-43. **1964** LARm: 14 G. **Total:** 76 G; Int 9-103.

STEVE HENRY Henry, Steven Arlen 6′2″, 190 **DB**
Col: Emporia State *HS:* Nemaha Valley [Seneca, KS]; St. Peter & Paul HS [Seneca, KS] B: 3/5/1957, Kansas City, KS *Drafted:* 1979 Round 5 StL
1979 StL: 8 G. **1980** NYG: 5 G; Int 1-0. **1981** Bal: 2 G. **Total:** 15 G; Int 1-0.

TOM HENRY Henry, Thomas E 5′10″, 185 **WB**
Col: Louisiana State B: 4/1895, Alton, IL Deceased
1920 RI: 1 G.

URBAN HENRY Henry, Urban 6′4″, 265 **DT-DE**
Col: Georgia Tech *HS:* Berwick [LA] B: 6/7/1935, Berwick, LA
1961 LARm: 14 G. **1963** GB: 14 G. **1964** Pit: 10 G. **Total:** 38 G.

WALLY HENRY Henry, Wallace 5′8″, 175 **WR**
Col: San Diego City Coll. CA (J.C.); UCLA *HS:* Abraham Lincoln [San Diego, CA] B: 10/30/1954, San Diego, CA
1977 Phi: Rush 1-(-2) -2.0; Rec 2-16 8.0. **1980** Phi: Rec 4-68 17.0. **1981** Phi: Rush 1-(-2) -2.0; Rec 9-145 16.1 2 TD. **Total:** Rush 2-(-4) -2.0; Rec 15-229 15.3 2 TD.

		Punt Returns				Kickoff Returns					Tot
Year Team	G	Ret	Yds	Avg	TD	Ret	Yds	Avg	TD	Fum	TD
1977 Phi	10	2	25	12.5	0	0	0	—	0	0	0
1978 Phi	3	11	165	15.0	**1**	3	54	18.0	0	0	1
1979 Phi	12	35	320	9.1	0	28	668	23.9	0	2	0
1980 Phi	7	26	222	8.5	0	7	154	22.0	0	1	0
1981 Phi	16	**54**	396	7.3	0	25	533	21.3	0	4	2
1982 Phi	8	20	103	5.2	0	24	541	22.5	0	4	0
NFL Total	56	148	1231	8.3	1	87	1950	22.4	0	11	3

WILBUR HENRY Henry, Wilbur Amos 5′10″, 185 **G-C**
Col: Stanford B: 12/4/1891, Los Angeles, CA D: 11/9/1947, Los Angeles, CA
1930 SI: 2 G.

PETE HENRY Henry, Wilbur Francis 5′11″, 245 **T**
Col: Washington & Jefferson *HS:* Mansfield [OH] B: 10/31/1897, Mansfield, OH D: 2/7/1952, Washington, PA *HOF:* 1963
1920 Can: 13 G. **1921** Can: 10 G. **1922** Can: 12 G; Scor 10, 2 FG, 4 XK. **1923** Can: 12 G; Rec 1 TD; Scor 58, 9 FG, **25** XK. **1925** Can: 6 G; Pass 1 TD; Scor 8, 1 FG, 5 XK. **1926** Can: 13 G; Scor 3, 3 XK. **1927** NYG-Pott: 13 G; Scor 7, 2 FG, 1 XK. NYG: 4 G. Pott: 9 G; Scor 7, 2 FG, 1 XK. **1928** Pott: 7 G; Scor 2, 2 XK. **Total:** 86 G; Pass 1 TD; Rec 1 TD; Scor 88, 14 FG, 40 XK.

DICK HENSLEY Hensley, Richard Earl 6′4″, 213 **OE-DE**
Col: Kentucky *HS:* Williamson [WV] B: 9/8/1927, Williamson, WV *Drafted:* 1949 Round 11 NYG
1949 NYG: 11 G; Rec 3-24 8.0. **1952** Pit: 11 G; Rec 12-217 18.1 2 TD; 12 Pt. **1953** ChiB: 11 G; Rec 4-117 29.3; Scor **1** Saf; 2 Pt. **Total:** 33 G; Rec 19-358 18.8 2 TD; Scor 1 Saf; 14 Pt.

GARY HENSON Henson, Gary Owen 6′3″, 200 **OE**
Col: Colorado *HS:* East [Denver, CO] B: 9/8/1940, Oklahoma City, OK *Drafted:* 1962 Round 14 LARm
1963 Phi: 11 G; KR 3-21 7.0. **1964** Den: 1 G. **Total:** 12 G; KR 3-21 7.0.

CHAMP HENSON Henson, Harold R III 6′3″, 240 **RB**
Col: Ohio State *HS:* Teays Valley [Ashville, OH] B: 6/1/1953, Columbus, OH *Drafted:* 1975 Round 4 Min
1975 Cin: 6 G; Rush 11-38 3.5; Rec 1-(-2) -2.0; 1 Fum.

KEN HENSON Henson, Kenneth Wayne 6′6″, 260 **C**
Col: Texas Christian *HS:* San Angelo [TX] B: 4/11/1943, San Angelo, TX *Drafted:* 1964 Round 5 LARm
1965 Pit: 4 G.

LUTHER HENSON Henson, Luther Martin 6′0″, 275 **NT**
Col: Ohio State *HS:* Sandusky [OH] B: 3/25/1959, Sandusky, OH
1982 NE: 8 G; 1 Sac. **1983** NE: 4 G. **1984** NE: 9 G; 2 Sac. **Total:** 21 G; 3 Sac.

ANTHONY HENTON Henton, Oscar Anthony 6′1″, 224 **LB**
Col: Troy State *HS:* Jess Lanier [Bessemer, AL] B: 7/27/1963, Bessemer, AL *Drafted:* 1986 Round 9 Pit
1986 Pit: 16 G. **1988** Pit: 16 G. **Total:** 32 G.

CRAIG HENTRICH Hentrich, Craig Anthony 6′3″, 201 **P**
Col: Notre Dame *HS:* Marquette [Alton, IL] B: 5/18/1971, Alton, IL *Drafted:* 1993 Round 8 NYJ
1995 GB: Scor 14, 3-5 60.0% FG, 5-5 100.0% XK. **1996** GB: Pass 1-0. **1998** Ten: Pass 1-1 100.0%, 13 13.00; Rush 1-(-1) -1.0; Scor 0-1 FG. **Total:** Pass 2-1 50.0%, 13 6.50; Rush 1-(-1) -1.0; Scor 14, 3-6 50.0% FG, 5-5 100.0% XK.

		Punting		
Year Team	G	Punts	Yds	Avg
1994 GB	16	81	3351	41.4
1995 GB	16	65	2740	42.2
1996 GB	16	68	2886	42.4
1997 GB	16	75	3378	45.0
1998 Ten	16	69	3258	**47.2**
NFL Total	80	358	15613	43.6

LONNIE HEPBURN Hepburn, Lionel Lorenzo 5′11″, 180 **DB**
Col: Texas Southern *HS:* Miami Northwestern [FL] B: 5/12/1949, Miami, FL *Drafted:* 1971 Round 13 Mia
1971 Bal: 3 G. **1972** Bal: 14 G; Int 1-14. **1974** Den: 14 G; Int 0-22. **Total:** 31 G; Int 1-36.

ARNIE HERBER Herber, Arnold Charles 5′11″, 203 **TB-DB-QB-BB**
(Herbie) *Col:* Wisconsin; Regis *HS:* Green Bay West [WI] B: 4/2/1910, Green Bay, WI D: 10/14/1969, Green Bay, WI *HOF:* 1966
1930 GB: Rec 1 TD. **1932** GB: Int **1** TD. **1933** GB: Rec 3-27 9.0; Scor 1, 1 XK. **1935** GB: Rec 2-26 13.0; Scor 1, 1 XK. **1938** GB: Rec 5-84 16.8 2 TD; Scor 12, 0-1 FG. **1939** GB: Rec 1-18 18.0; Punt 24-957 39.9. **1940** GB: Int 2-0; Punt 13-504 38.8. **1944** NYG: Punt 1-39 39.0. **1945** NYG: Punt 1-51 51.0. **Total:** Rec 11-155 14.1 3 TD; Int 2-0 1 TD; Punt 39-1551 39.8; Scor 44, 0-1 FG, 2 XK.

		Passing							
Year Team	G	Att	Comp	Comp%	Yds	YPA	TD	Int	Rating
1930 GB	10	—	—	—	—	—	3	—	—
1931 GB	3	—	—	—	—	—	0	—	—
1932 GB	14	**101**	**37**	36.6	**639**	**6.33**	**9**	9	51.5
1933 GB	11	124	50	40.3	656	5.29	3	12	26.2
1934 GB	11	**115**	**42**	36.5	**799**	6.95	**8**	12	45.1
1935 GB	11	109	40	36.7	729	6.69	8	14	45.4
1936 GB	12	**173**	**77**	44.5	**1239**	7.16	**11**	13	58.9
1937 GB	9	104	47	45.2	684	6.58	7	10	50.0
1938 GB	8	55	22	40.0	336	6.11	3	4	48.8
1939 GB	10	139	57	41.0	1107	7.96	8	9	61.6
1940 GB	10	89	38	42.7	560	6.29	6	7	53.6
1944 NYG	10	86	36	41.9	651	7.57	6	8	53.0
1945 NYG	10	80	35	43.8	641	8.01	9	8	69.8
NFL Total	129	1175	481	40.9	8041	6.84	81	106	50.1

	Rushing					Tot
Year Team	Att	Yds	Avg	TD	Fum	TD
1930 GB	—	—	—	0	0	1
1931 GB	—	—	—	1	0	1
1932 GB	64	149	2.3	1	0	2
1933 GB	62	77	1.2	0	0	0
1934 GB	37	33	0.9	0	0	0
1935 GB	19	0	0.0	0	0	0
1936 GB	20	-32	-1.6	0	0	0
1937 GB	5	9	1.8	0	0	0
1938 GB	6	-1	-0.2	0	0	2
1939 GB	18	-11	-0.6	1	0	1
1940 GB	6	-23	-3.8	0	0	0
1944 NYG	7	-58	-8.3	0	0	0
1945 NYG	6	-27	-4.5	0	3	0
NFL Total	250	116	0.5	3	3	7

BILL HERCHMAN Herchman, William 6′2″, 246 **DT**
Col: Tyler JC TX; Texas Tech *HS:* Vernon [TX]; Lubbock HS [TX] B: 3/10/1933, Vernon, TX *Drafted:* 1956 Round 3 SF
1956 SF: 12 G; KR 1-6 6.0. **1957** SF: 12 G; Int 1-54 1 TD; 6 Pt. **1958** SF: 12 G. **1959** SF: 12 G; KR 1-7 7.0. **1960** Dal: 11 G. **1961** Dal: 14 G. **1962** Hou: 12 G. **Total:** 85 G; KR 2-13 6.5; Int 1-54 1 TD; 6 Pt.

JOE HERGERT Hergert, Joseph Martin 6′1″, 216 LB-K
Col: Florida *HS:* Daytona Beach [FL] B: 6/7/1936, Wilkes-Barre, PA
Drafted: 1959 Round 24 GB
1960 Buf: 10 G; Int 1-29 1 TD; Scor 12, 2-4 50.0% FG. **1961** Buf: 9 G; Int 1-0; Scor 18, 6-14 42.9% FG. **Total:** 19 G; Int 2-29 1 TD; Scor 30, 8-18 44.4% FG.

MATT HERKENHOFF Herkenhoff, Matthew Bernard 6′4″, 267 OT
Col: Minnesota *HS:* Melrose [MN] B: 4/2/1951, Melrose, MN
Drafted: 1974 Round 4 KC
1976 KC: 14 G. **1977** KC: 14 G. **1978** KC: 16 G. **1979** KC: 5 G. **1980** KC: 14 G. **1981** KC: 16 G. **1982** KC: 9 G. **1983** KC: 12 G. **1984** KC: 15 G. **1985** KC: 10 G. **Total:** 125 G.

ALAN HERLINE Herline, Alan Joseph 6′0″, 168 K-P
Col: Vanderbilt *HS:* Marist [Atlanta, GA] B: 9/16/1964, Monroe, LA
1987 NE: 3 G; Punt 25-861 34.4.

CHUCK HERMAN Herman, Charles Martin 6′3″, 250 OG
Col: Arkansas *HS:* North Little Rock, East [AR] B: 10/7/1958, North Little Rock, AR
1980 Atl: 2 G.

DAVE HERMAN Herman, David Jon 6′1″, 255 OG-OT
Col: Michigan State *HS:* Edon [OH] B: 9/3/1941, Bryan, OH
Drafted: 1963 Round 27 NYJ
1964 NYJ: 5 G. **1965** NYJ: 14 G. **1966** NYJ: 14 G. **1967** NYJ: 14 G. **1968** NYJ: 14 G. **1969** NYJ: 12 G. **1970** NYJ: 14 G. **1971** NYJ: 14 G. **1972** NYJ: 13 G. **1973** NYJ: 14 G. **Total:** 128 G.

ED HERMAN Herman, Edward Martin 5′10″, 175 OE
(Red) *Col:* Northwestern *HS:* Crane [Chicago, IL] B: 1/22/1902, Philadelphia, PA D: 5/31/1979, Evanston, IL
1925 RI: 1 G.

JOHNNY HERMANN Hermann, John Williams 6′1″, 180 DB
Col: UCLA *HS:* San Fernando [CA] B: 10/17/1933, San Fernando, CA
Drafted: 1956 Round 10 NYG
1956 NYG-Bal: 10 G; PR 1-0; KR 1-17 17.0. NYG: 2 G; PR 1-0; KR 1-17 17.0. Bal: 8 G. **Total:** 10 G; PR 1-0; KR 1-17 17.0.

DICK HERMANN Hermann, Richard Wallace 6′2″, 215 LB
Col: Florida State *HS:* Marianna [FL] B: 7/11/1942, Marianna, FL
1965 Oak: 14 G; KR 1-0.

TERRY HERMELING Hermeling, Terry Allen 6′5″, 255 OT-OG-DE
Col: Nevada-Reno *HS:* Santa Maria [CA] B: 4/25/1946, Santa Maria, CA
1970 Was: 5 G. **1971** Was: 8 G. **1972** Was: 14 G. **1973** Was: 13 G. **1975** Was: 9 G. **1976** Was: 12 G. **1977** Was: 13 G. **1978** Was: 16 G. **1979** Was: 16 G. **1980** Was: 14 G. **Total:** 120 G.

JOE HERNANDEZ Hernandez, Jose M 6′2″, 180 WR
Col: New Mexico Mil. Inst. (J.C.); Bakersfield Coll. CA (J.C.); Arizona *HS:* Garces Memorial [Bakersfield, CA] B: 2/9/1940, Bakersfield, CA
Drafted: 1962 Round 2 Was
1964 Was: 14 G; Rec 1-18 18.0; PR 5-49 9.8; KR 1-19 19.0; 2 Fum.

MATT HERNANDEZ Hernandez, Matthew J 6′6″, 260 OT
Col: Purdue *HS:* East Detroit [Eastpointe, MI] B: 10/16/1961, Detroit, MI *Drafted:* 1983 Round 8 Sea
1983 Sea: 8 G. **1984** Min: 13 G. **Total:** 21 G.

SCOTT HERNANDEZ Hernandez, Scott M 6′0″, 250 NT
Col: Kent State *HS:* Kenmore West [NY] B: 10/17/1959, Kenmore, NY
1987 Buf: 2 G.

DON HERNDON Herndon, Donald Eugene 6′0″, 195 HB
Col: Tampa *HS:* Hardee [Wauchula, FL] B: 6/4/1936 *Drafted:* 1958 Round 13 NYG
1960 NYT: 8 G; Rec 5-57 11.4 1 TD; KR 5-114 22.8; 6 Pt; 1 Fum.

JIMMY HERNDON Herndon, James Scott 6′8″, 318 OT
Col: Houston *HS:* Robert E. Lee [Baytown, TX] B: 8/30/1973, Baytown, TX *Drafted:* 1996 Round 5 Jac
1997 ChiB: 7 G. **1998** ChiB: 9 G. **Total:** 16 G.

KEN HEROCK Herock, Kenneth Barry 6′2″, 230 TE-LB
Col: West Virginia *HS:* Munhall [PA] B: 7/16/1941, Munhall, PA
1963 Oak: KR 1-3 3.0; **1** Fum TD. **Total:** KR 1-3 3.0; 1 Fum TD.

		Receiving					Tot
Year Team	G	Rec	Yds	Avg	TD	Fum	TD
1963 Oak	14	16	269	16.8	2	0	3
1964 Oak	14	23	360	15.7	2	2	2
1965 Oak	14	18	221	12.3	0	0	0
1967 Oak	12	1	-1	-1.0	0	0	0
1968 Cin	13	6	75	12.5	0	0	0
1969 Bos	6	0	0	—	0	0	0
NFL Total	73	64	924	14.4	4	2	5

FRED HERON Heron, Frederick Roger 6′4″, 260 DT-DE
(Rock) *Col:* San Jose State *HS:* Edison [Stockton, CA] B: 10/6/1944, Stockton, CA *Drafted:* 1966 Round 3 GB
1966 StL: 11 G. **1967** StL: 12 G. **1968** StL: 14 G. **1969** StL: 13 G. **1970** StL: 14 G. **1971** StL: 9 G. **1972** StL: 6 G. **Total:** 79 G.

BRIAN HEROSIAN Herosian, Brian Berge 6′3″, 200 DB
Col: Connecticut *HS:* Worcester Acad. [MA] B: 9/14/1950, Worcester, MA
1973 Bal: 12 G.

EFREN HERRERA Herrera, Efren 5′9″, 185 K
Col: UCLA *HS:* La Puente [CA] B: 7/30/1951, Guadalajara, Mexico
Drafted: 1974 Round 7 Det
1976 Dal: Punt 2-49 24.5. **1977** Dal: Punt 2-44 22.0. **1978** Sea: Punt 3-73 24.3. **1979** Sea: Rec 1-20 20.0; Punt 1-36 36.0. **1980** Sea: Rec 1-9 9.0; Punt 1-29 29.0. **Total:** Rec 2-29 14.5; Punt 9-231 25.7.

		Scoring						
Year Team	G	Pts	FG	FGA	FG%	XK	XKA	XK%
1974 Dal	11	57	8	13	61.5	33	33	100.0
1976 Dal	14	88	18	23	**78.3**	34	34	**100.0**
1977 Dal	14	93	18	29	62.1	**39**	41	95.1
1978 Sea	16	79	13	21	61.9	40	44	90.9
1979 Sea	16	100	19	23	82.6	43	46	93.5
1980 Sea	16	93	20	31	64.5	33	33	100.0
1981 Sea	12	59	12	17	70.6	23	25	92.0
1982 Buf	7	35	8	14	57.1	11	12	91.7
NFL Total	106	604	116	171	67.8	256	268	95.5

HOOT HERRIN Herrin, Houston R 5′10″, 208 C-G
Col: St. Mary's (Cal.) *HS:* Visalia [CA] B: 11/24/1904, OK
D: 4/6/1984, Visalia, CA
1931 Cle: 1 G.

GEORGE HERRING Herring, George W 6′2″, 200 QB-P
Col: Jones Co. JC MS; Southern Mississippi *HS:* Hokes Bluff [AL]
B: 6/18/1934, Gadsden, AL *Drafted:* 1960 Round 1 Hou
1961 Den: Rush 15-74 4.9 2 TD. **Total:** Rush 15-74 4.9 2 TD.

		Passing							
Year Team	G	Att	Comp	Comp%	Yds	YPA	TD	Int	Rating
1960 Den	14	22	9	40.9	137	6.23	0	1	43.2
1961 Den	14	211	93	44.1	1160	5.50	5	22	30.0
NFL Total	28	233	102	43.8	1297	5.57	5	23	29.3

	Punting			
Year Team	Punts	Yds	Avg	Fum
1960 Den	70	2610	37.3	1
1961 Den	80	3149	39.4	4
NFL Total	150	5759	38.4	5

HAL HERRING Herring, Harold Moreland 6′1″, 211 LB-C
Col: Auburn *HS:* Lanett [AL]; West Point HS [Cullman, AL]
B: 2/24/1924, Lanett, AL *Drafted:* 1949 Round 9 ChiC
AAFC **1949** BufA: 12 G; Int 1-1.

NFL **1950** Cle: 12 G; Int 2-12. **1951** Cle: 10 G; Int 1-28. **1952** Cle: 12 G. **Total:** 34 G; Int 3-40.

KIM HERRING Herring, Kimani Masai 5′11″, 210 DB
Col: Penn State *HS:* Solon [OH] B: 9/10/1975, Detroit, MI
Drafted: 1997 Round 2 Bal
1997 Bal: 15 G; 1 Sac. **1998** Bal: 7 G. **Total:** 22 G; 1 Sac.

DON HERRMANN Herrmann, Donald Bruce 6′2″, 205 WR
Col: Waynesburg *HS:* Chatham [NJ] B: 6/5/1947, Newark, NJ
Drafted: 1969 Round 15 NYG
1972 NYG: Rush 3-9 3.0. **1977** NO: Rush 1-(-17) -17.0. **Total:** Rush 4-(-8) -2.0.

		Receiving				
Year Team	G	Rec	Yds	Avg	TD	Fum
1969 NYG	12	33	423	12.8	5	1
1970 NYG	13	24	290	12.1	2	0
1971 NYG	9	27	297	11.0	1	0
1972 NYG	14	28	422	15.1	5	0
1973 NYG	14	43	520	12.1	2	1
1974 NYG	8	10	97	9.7	0	0
1975 NO	3	3	47	15.7	1	0
1976 NO	14	34	535	15.7	0	0
1977 NO	13	32	408	12.8	0	1
NFL Total	100	234	3039	13.0	16	3

MARK HERRMANN Herrmann, Mark Donald 6′4″, 200 QB
Col: Purdue *HS:* Carmel [IN] B: 1/8/1959, Cincinnati, OH
Drafted: 1981 Round 4 Den

		Passing							
Year Team	G	Att	Comp	Comp%	Yds	YPA	TD	Int	Rating
1982 Den	2	60	32	53.3	421	7.02	1	4	53.5

1983 Bal	2	36	18	50.0	256	7.11	0	3	38.7
1984 Ind	3	56	29	51.8	352	6.29	1	6	37.8
1985 SD	9	201	132	65.7	1537	7.65	10	10	84.5
1986 SD	6	97	51	52.6	627	6.46	2	3	66.8
1987 SD	3	57	37	64.9	405	7.11	1	5	55.1
1988 LARm	6	5	4	80.0	38	7.60	0	0	98.3
1989 LARm	3	5	4	80.0	59	11.80	0	1	76.3
1990 Ind	3	1	1	100.0	6	6.00	0	0	91.7
1991 Ind	2	19	11	57.9	137	7.21	0	3	40.8
1992 Ind	1	24	15	62.5	177	7.38	1	1	81.4
NFL Total	40	561	334	59.5	4015	7.16	16	36	64.3

	Rushing				
Year Team	**Att**	**Yds**	**Avg**	**TD**	**Fum**
1982 Den	3	7	2.3	1	1
1983 Bal	1	0	0.0	0	2
1985 SD	18	-8	-0.4	0	8
1986 SD	2	6	3.0	0	2
1987 SD	4	-1	-0.3	0	1
1988 LARm	1	-1	-1.0	0	0
1989 LARm	2	-1	-0.5	0	2
1991 Ind	1	-1	-1.0	0	0
1992 Ind	3	-2	-0.7	0	0
NFL Total	35	-1	0.0	1	16

JEFF HERROD Herrod, Jeff Sylvester 6′0″, 249 **LB**
Col: Mississippi *HS:* Banks [Birmingham, AL] B: 7/29/1966, Birmingham, AL *Drafted:* 1988 Round 9 Ind
1988 Ind: 16 G; 1 Sac. **1989** Ind: 15 G; 2 Sac. **1990** Ind: 13 G; Int 1-12; 4 Sac. **1991** Ind: 14 G; Int 1-25; 2.5 Sac. **1992** Ind: 16 G; Int 1-4; 2 Sac. **1993** Ind: 14 G; Int 1-29; 1 Fum TD; 6 Pt; 2 Sac. **1994** Ind: 15 G; 1 Sac. **1995** Ind: 16 G. **1996** Ind: 14 G; Int 1-68 1 TD; 6 Pt. **1997** Phi: 10 G. **1998** Ind: 10 G. **Total:** 153 G; Int 5-138 1 TD; 1 Fum TD; Tot TD 2; 12 Pt; 14.5 Sac.

BRUCE HERRON Herron, Bruce Wayne 6′2″, 220 **LB**
Col: New Mexico *HS:* Bloomington [TX] B: 4/14/1954, Victoria, TX *Drafted:* 1977 Round 7 Mia
1978 ChiB: 15 G. **1979** ChiB: 16 G; KR 1-0; 1 Fum. **1980** ChiB: 15 G; KR 1-5 5.0. **1981** ChiB: 16 G. **1982** ChiB: 9 G; 1 Sac. **Total:** 71 G; KR 2-5 2.5; 1 Fum; 1 Sac.

PAT HERRON Herron, James Patrick 5′10″, 170 **E**
Col: Pittsburgh *HS:* Monessen [PA] B: 8/12/1894, New Kensington, PA D: 12/21/1967, Monongahela, PA
1920 Cle: 1 G.

MACK HERRON Herron, Mack Willie 5′5″, 170 **RB**
Col: Hutchinson CC KS; Kansas State *HS:* David Farragut [Chicago, IL] B: 7/24/1948, Biloxi, MS *Drafted:* 1970 Round 6 Atl

		Rushing				Receiving			
Year Team	**G**	**Att**	**Yds**	**Avg**	**TD**	**Rec**	**Yds**	**Avg**	**TD**
1973 NE	14	61	200	3.3	2	18	265	14.7	1
1974 NE	14	231	824	3.6	7	38	474	12.5	5
1975 NE-Atl	11	62	274	4.4	0	5	50	10.0	0
1975 NE	7	61	274	4.5	0	5	50	10.0	0
1975 Atl	4	1	0	0.0	0	0	0	—	0
NFL Total	39	354	1298	3.7	9	61	789	12.9	6

	Punt Returns				Kickoff Returns					Tot
Year Team	**Ret**	**Yds**	**Avg**	**TD**	**Ret**	**Yds**	**Avg**	**TD**	**Fum**	**TD**
1973 NE	27	282	10.4	0	**41**	**1092**	26.6	1	7	4
1974 NE	35	517	14.8	0	28	629	22.5	0	12	12
1975 NE-Atl	22	183	8.3	0	13	264	20.3	0	8	0
1975 NE	12	89	7.4	0	2	75	37.5	0	7	0
1975 Atl	10	94	9.4	0	11	189	17.2	0	1	0
NFL Total	84	982	11.7	0	82	1985	24.2	1	27	16

KIRK HERSHEY Hershey, Kirk 6′2″, 215 **OE-DE**
Col: Carroll (Wis.); Cornell *HS:* William Penn Charter School [Philadelphia, PA] B: 7/7/1918, Philadelphia, PA D: 1/23/1979, North Palm Beach, FL *Drafted:* 1941 Round 17 Cle
1941 Cle-Phi: 8 G; Rec 1-11 11.0. Cle: 2 G. Phi: 6 G; Rec 1-11 11.0. **Total:** 8 G; Rec 1-11 11.0.

ROB HERTEL Hertel, Robert Alden 6′2″, 195 **QB**
Col: USC *HS:* Los Altos [Hacienda Heights, CA] B: 2/21/1955, Montebello, CA *Drafted:* 1978 Round 5 Cin
1978 Cin: 3 G; Pass 4-1 25.0%, 9 2.25; Rush 1-0; 1 Fum.

CRAIG HERTWIG Hertwig, John Craig 6′8″, 270 **OT**
Col: Georgia *HS:* Mark Smith [Macon, GA] B: 1/15/1952, Columbus, GA *Drafted:* 1975 Round 4 Det
1975 Det: 9 G. **1976** Det: 14 G. **1977** Det: 14 G. **Total:** 37 G.

FRANK HERTZ Hertz, Frank W 5′10″, 185 **E**
Col: Carroll (Wis.) *HS:* Waukesha [WI] B: 11/6/1902 D: 7/20/1963
1926 Mil: 8 G.

WALLY HESS Hess, Walter Bernard 5′9″, 174 **TB-BB-FB**
Col: Indiana *HS:* Hammond [IN] B: 10/28/1894 D: 8/1963, IN
1920 Ham: 2 G. **1921** Ham: 4 G. **1922** Ham: 6 G. **1923** Ham: 7 G. **1924** Ham: 4 G. **1925** Ham: 5 G; Pass 1 TD; Rec 1 TD; 6 Pt. **Total:** 28 G; Pass 1 TD; Rec 1 TD; 6 Pt.

JON HESSE Hesse, Jonathan Andrew 6′4″, 250 **LB**
Col: Nebraska *HS:* Southeast [Lincoln, NE] B: 6/6/1973, Lincoln, NE *Drafted:* 1997 Round 7 Jac
1998 StL: 5 G.

JIMMY HESTER Hester, James Conway 6′4″, 250 **TE**
(Boogie) *Col:* North Dakota *HS:* Central [Davenport, IA] B: 12/13/1944, Rock Island, IL *Drafted:* 1967 Round 14 NO
1969 NO: KR 1-4 4.0. **Total:** KR 1-4 4.0.

		Receiving				
Year Team	**G**	**Rec**	**Yds**	**Avg**	**TD**	**Fum**
1967 NO	5	2	10	5.0	0	0
1968 NO	14	17	300	17.6	2	0
1969 NO	10	3	44	14.7	1	0
1970 ChiB	5	7	54	7.7	0	1
NFL Total	34	29	408	14.1	3	1

JESSIE HESTER Hester, Jessie Lee 5′11″, 175 **WR**
Col: Florida State *HS:* Glades Central [Belle Glade, FL] B: 1/21/1963, Belle Glade, FL *Drafted:* 1985 Round 1 LARd
1985 LARd: Rush 1-13 13.0 1 TD. **1988** Atl: Rush 1-3 3.0. **1990** Ind: Rush 4-9 2.3. **1994** LARm: Rush 2-28 14.0. **Total:** Rush 8-53 6.6 1 TD.

		Receiving					Tot
Year Team	**G**	**Rec**	**Yds**	**Avg**	**TD**	**Fum**	**TD**
1985 LARd	16	32	665	20.8	4	0	5
1986 LARd	13	23	632	27.5	6	0	6
1987 LARd	10	1	30	30.0	0	0	0
1988 Atl	16	12	176	14.7	0	1	0
1990 Ind	16	54	924	17.1	6	0	6
1991 Ind	16	60	753	12.6	5	3	5
1992 Ind	16	52	792	15.2	1	0	1
1993 Ind	16	64	835	13.0	1	1	1
1994 LARm	16	45	644	14.3	3	1	3
1995 StL	12	30	399	13.3	3	0	3
NFL Total	147	373	5850	15.7	29	6	30

RAY HESTER Hester, Raymond William 6′2″, 215 **LB**
Col: Tulane *HS:* Holy Cross [New Orleans, LA] B: 3/31/1949, New Orleans, LA D: 5/16/1977, Metarie, LA
1971 NO: 14 G. **1972** NO: 7 G. **1973** NO: 6 G. **Total:** 27 G.

RON HESTER Hester, Ronald 6′2″, 222 **LB**
Col: Florida State *HS:* Umatilla [FL] B: 5/26/1959, Atlanta, GA *Drafted:* 1982 Round 6 Mia
1982 Mia: 9 G; 1 Sac.

CHRIS HETHERINGTON Hetherington, Christopher Raymond 6′3″, 249 **RB**
Col: Yale *HS:* Old Farms [Avon, CT] B: 11/27/1972, North Branford, CT
1996 Ind: 6 G; KR 1-16 16.0. **1997** Ind: 16 G; KR 2-23 11.5. **1998** Ind: 14 G; KR 5-71 14.2; 1 Fum. **Total:** 36 G; KR 8-110 13.8; 1 Fum.

DAVE HETTEMA Hettema, David Gary 6′5″, 250 **OT**
Col: Pasadena City Coll. CA (J.C.); New Mexico *HS:* Pasadena [CA] B: 11/7/1942, Pasadena, CA *Drafted:* 1965 Round 16 SF
1967 SF: 7 G. **1970** Atl: 6 G. **Total:** 13 G.

CHRIS HEWITT Hewitt, Christopher Horace 6′0″, 210 **DB**
Col: Cincinnati *HS:* Dwight Morrow [Englewood, NJ] B: 7/22/1974, Kingston, Jamaica
1997 NO: 11 G. **1998** NO: 16 G; 2 Sac. **Total:** 27 G; 2 Sac.

BILL HEWITT Hewitt, William Ernest 5′9″, 190 **OE-DE**
Col: Michigan *HS:* Central [Bay City, MI] B: 10/8/1909, Bay City, MI D: 1/14/1947, Sellersville, PA *HOF:* 1971
1932 ChiB: Rush 1-29 29.0 1 TD. **1933** ChiB: Pass 7-4 57.1%, 59 8.43 3 TD; Rush 2-1 0.5. **1934** ChiB: Pass 2-1 50.0%, 4 2.00; Rush 1-14 14.0. **1935** ChiB: Pass 1-0; Rush 1-0. **1936** ChiB: Rush 2-(-9) -4.5; **1** Fum TD. **1939** Phi: Rush 1-1 1.0. **Total:** Pass 10-5 50.0%, 63 6.30 3 TD; Rush 8-36 4.5 1 TD; 1 Fum TD.

		Receiving				Tot
Year Team	**G**	**Rec**	**Yds**	**Avg**	**TD**	**TD**
1932 ChiB	13	7	77	11.0	0	1
1933 ChiB	13	14	273	19.5	2	3
1934 ChiB	13	11	151	13.7	**5**	5
1935 ChiB	12	5	80	16.0	0	0
1936 ChiB	12	15	358	**23.9**	6	7
1937 Phi	11	16	197	12.3	5	5
1938 Phi	11	18	237	13.2	4	4
1939 Phi	10	15	243	16.2	1	1
1943 PhPt	6	2	22	11.0	0	0
NFL Total	101	103	1638	15.9	23	26

BOB HEWKO Hewko, Robert Todd 6′3″, 195 **QB**
Col: Florida *HS:* Upper Moreland [Williams Grove, PA] B: 6/8/1960, Abington, PA
1983 TB: 2 G.

BOB HEWS Hews, Robert Ellsworth 6′5″, 240 **OT-DE**
Col: Princeton *HS:* South Portland [ME] B: 12/30/1947, Portland, ME
Drafted: 1970 Round 6 KC
1971 Buf: 2 G.

CRAIG HEYWARD Heyward, Craig William 5′11″, 260 **RB**
(Ironhead) *Col:* Pittsburgh *HS:* Passaic [NJ] B: 9/26/1966, Passaic, NJ *Drafted:* 1988 Round 1 NO
1990 NO: Pass 1-0, 1 Int; KR 1-12 12.0. **1991** NO: Pass 1-1 100.0%, 44 44.00. **1992** NO: KR 1-14 14.0. **1993** ChiB: KR 1-12 12.0. **1994** Atl: KR 1-7 7.0. **1996** Atl: PR 1-0; KR 1-18 18.0. **Total:** Pass 2-1 50.0%, 44 22.00 1 Int; PR 1-0; KR 5-63 12.6.

		Rushing				Receiving					Tot
Year Team	**G**	**Att**	**Yds**	**Avg**	**TD**	**Rec**	**Yds**	**Avg**	**TD**	**Fum**	**TD**
1988 NO	11	74	355	4.8	1	13	105	8.1	0	0	1
1989 NO	16	49	183	3.7	1	13	69	5.3	0	2	1
1990 NO	16	129	599	4.6	4	18	121	6.7	0	3	4
1991 NO	7	76	260	3.4	4	4	34	8.5	1	0	5
1992 NO	16	104	416	4.0	3	19	159	8.4	0	1	3
1993 ChiB	16	68	206	3.0	0	16	132	8.3	0	1	0
1994 Atl	16	183	779	4.3	7	32	335	10.5	1	5	8
1995 Atl	16	236	1083	4.6	6	37	350	9.5	2	3	8
1996 Atl	15	72	321	4.5	3	16	168	10.5	0	0	3
1997 StL	16	34	84	2.5	1	8	77	9.6	0	1	1
1998 Ind	4	6	15	2.5	0	1	9	9.0	0	0	0
NFL Total	149	1031	4301	4.2	30	177	1559	8.8	4	16	34

RALPH HEYWOOD Heywood, Ralph Alvin 6′2″, 203 **OE-DE**
Col: USC *HS:* Huntington Park [CA] B: 9/11/1921, Los Angeles, CA
Drafted: 1944 Round 3 Det
AAFC **1946** ChiA: 14 G; Rec 20-287 14.4 4 TD; Punt 2-57 28.5; 24 Pt.

NFL **1948** Det-Bos: Rush 1-11 11.0; KR 1-8 8.0; **2** Fum TD. Bos: Rush 1-11 11.0; KR 1-8 8.0; 2 Fum TD. **1949** NYB: Rush 3-(-6) -2.0; **1** Fum TD. **Total:** Rush 4-5 1.3; KR 1-8 8.0; 3 Fum TD.

		Receiving				Punting				Tot
Year Team	**G**	**Rec**	**Yds**	**Avg**	**TD**	**Punts**	**Yds**	**Avg**	**Fum**	**TD**
1947 Det	12	13	198	15.2	2	0	0	—	2	2
1948 Det-Bos	10	14	208	14.9	1	46	1768	38.4	2	3
1948 Det	2	3	31	10.3	0	11	372	33.8	0	0
1948 Bos	8	11	177	16.1	1	35	1396	39.9	2	3
1949 NYB	12	37	499	13.5	3	20	697	34.9	1	4
NFL Total	34	64	905	14.1	6	66	2465	37.3	5	9

JESSE HIBBS Hibbs, Jesse John 6′0″, 195 **T**
Col: USC *HS:* Glendale [CA]; Lake Forest Acad. [IL] B: 1/11/1906, Normal, IL D: 2/4/1985, Los Angeles, CA
1931 ChiB: 9 G.

MIKE HIBLER Hibler, Michael Keith 6′1″, 235 **LB**
Col: Stanford *HS:* St. Francis [Mountain View, CA] B: 1/29/1946, Mountain View, CA *Drafted:* 1967 Round 5 Oak
1968 Cin: 11 G.

GENE HICKERSON Hickerson, Robert Eugene 6′3″, 248 **OG**
Col: Mississippi *HS:* Trezevant [Memphis, TN] B: 2/15/1935, Trenton, TN *Drafted:* 1957 Round 7 Cle
1958 Cle: 12 G. **1959** Cle: 12 G. **1960** Cle: 12 G. **1962** Cle: 12 G. **1963** Cle: 14 G. **1964** Cle: 14 G. **1965** Cle: 14 G. **1966** Cle: 14 G. **1967** Cle: 14 G. **1968** Cle: 14 G. **1969** Cle: 14 G. **1970** Cle: 14 G. **1971** Cle: 14 G. **1972** Cle: 14 G. **1973** Cle: 14 G. **Total:** 202 G.

RED HICKEY Hickey, Howard Wayne 6′2″, 204 **OE-DE**
Col: Arkansas *HS:* Clarksville [AR] B: 2/14/1917, Clarksville, AR
Drafted: 1941 Round 5 Phi
1941 Pit-Cle: Rush 7-7 1.0. Cle: Rush 7-7 1.0. **1946** LARm: KR 1-14 14.0. **Total:** Rush 7-7 1.0; KR 1-14 14.0.

		Receiving				
Year Team	**G**	**Rec**	**Yds**	**Avg**	**TD**	**Fum**
1941 Pit-Cle	10	21	294	14.0	4	0
1941 Pit	1	0	0	—	0	0
1941 Cle	9	21	294	14.0	4	0
1945 Cle	8	4	76	19.0	0	0
1946 LARm	8	8	213	26.6	3	0
1947 LARm	11	12	196	16.3	2	1
1948 LARm	12	30	509	17.0	7	0
NFL Total	49	75	1288	17.2	16	1

BO HICKEY Hickey, Thomas Henry 5′11″, 230 **RB**
Col: Maryland *HS:* Stamford Catholic [CT] B: 10/7/1945, Stamford, CT
Drafted: 1967 Round 14 StL
1967 Den: Rec 7-36 5.1 1 TD.

		Rushing					Tot
Year Team	**G**	**Att**	**Yds**	**Avg**	**TD**	**Fum**	**TD**
1967 Den	12	73	263	3.6	4	2	5

RAY HICKL Hickl, Raymond William 6′2″, 220 **LB**
Col: Blinn Coll. TX (J.C.); Texas A&M–Kingsville *HS:* Tidehaven [El Maton, TX] B: 12/24/1946, El Maton, TX *Drafted:* 1969 Round 9 NYG
1969 NYG: 9 G. **1970** NYG: 1 G. **Total:** 10 G.

DALLAS HICKMAN Hickman, Dallas Mark 6′6″, 238 **DE-LB**
Col: Kings River CC CA; California *HS:* Sierra [Tollhouse, CA]
B: 2/16/1952, Martinez, CA *Drafted:* 1975 Round 9 Was
1976 Was: 14 G. **1977** Was: 14 G. **1978** Was: 16 G. **1979** Was: 16 G. **1980** Was: 16 G. **1981** Bal-Was: 15 G. Bal: 5 G. Was: 10 G. **Total:** 91 G.

DONNIE HICKMAN Hickman, Donald J 6′2″, 261 **OG**
Col: USC *HS:* Flagstaff [AZ] B: 6/11/1955, Flagstaff, AZ
Drafted: 1977 Round 5 LARm
1978 Was-Det: 10 G. Was: 3 G. Det: 7 G. **Total:** 10 G.

HERMAN HICKMAN Hickman, Herman Michael Jr. 5′10″, 246 **G**
Col: Tennessee *HS:* Johnson City [TN]; Baylor Prep [Chattanooga, TN]
B: 10/1/1911, Johnson City, TN D: 4/25/1958, Washington, DC
1932 Bkn: 3 G. **1933** Bkn: 10 G; Scor 8, 2 FG, 2 XK. **1934** Bkn: 11 G. **Total:** 24 G; Scor 8, 2 FG, 2 XK.

KEVIN HICKMAN Hickman, Kevin Joseph 6′4″, 258 **TE**
Col: Navy *HS:* Holy Cross [Delran, NJ]; Marine Mil. Acad. [Harlington, TX] B: 8/20/1971, Cherry Hill, NJ *Drafted:* 1995 Round 6 Det
1995 Det: 6 G. **1997** Det: 4 G. **1998** Det: 3 G. **Total:** 13 G.

LARRY HICKMAN Hickman, Lawrence Dean 6′2″, 227 **FB**
Col: Baylor *HS:* Kilgore [TX] B: 10/9/1935, Spring Hill, TX
Drafted: 1959 Round 3 LARm
1959 ChiC: 12 G; Rush 5-18 3.6; Rec 1-11 11.0. **1960** GB: 12 G; Rush 7-22 3.1; KR 3-54 18.0. **Total:** 24 G; Rush 12-40 3.3; Rec 1-11 11.0; KR 3-54 18.0.

SKIP HICKS Hicks, Brian LaVell 6′0″, 230 **RB**
Col: UCLA *HS:* Burkburnett [TX] B: 10/13/1974, Corsicana, TX
Drafted: 1998 Round 3 Was
1998 Was: Rec 4-23 5.8.

		Rushing			
Year Team	**G**	**Att**	**Yds**	**Avg**	**TD**
1998 Was	9	122	433	3.5	8

CLIFF HICKS Hicks, Clifford Wendell Jr. 5′10″, 188 **DB**
Col: San Diego Mesa Coll. CA (J.C.); Oregon *HS:* Kearny [San Diego, CA] B: 8/18/1964, San Diego, CA *Drafted:* 1987 Round 3 LARm
1987 LARm: KR 4-119 29.8; Int 1-9. **1989** LARm: Int 2-27.
1990 LARm-Buf: Int 1-0; 1 Sac. Buf: Int 1-0; 1 Sac. **1991** Buf: Int 1-0.
1992 Buf: KR 1-5 5.0; 1 Sac. **1994** NYJ: KR 2-30 15.0. **Total:** KR 7-154 22.0; Int 5-36; 2 Sac.

		Punt Returns				
Year Team	**G**	**Ret**	**Yds**	**Avg**	**TD**	**Fum**
1987 LARm	11	13	110	8.5	0	1
1988 LARm	7	25	144	5.8	0	1
1989 LARm	15	4	39	9.8	0	0
1990 LARm-Buf	5	0	0	—	0	0
1990 LARm	1	0	0	—	0	0
1990 Buf	4	0	0	—	0	0
1991 Buf	16	12	203	16.9	0	1
1992 Buf	12	29	289	10.0	0	2
1993 NYJ	10	17	157	9.2	0	2
1994 NYJ	16	38	342	9.0	0	5
1995 Den	6	0	0	—	0	0
NFL Total	98	138	1284	9.3	0	12

DWIGHT HICKS Hicks, Dwight 6′1″, 190 **DB**
Col: Michigan *HS:* Pennsauken [NJ] B: 4/5/1956, Mount Holly, NJ
Drafted: 1978 Round 6 Det
1979 SF: KR 2-36 18.0. **1981** SF: KR 1-22 22.0; 1 Fum TD. **1985** SF: 1 Sac. **Total:** KR 3-58 19.3; 1 Fum TD; 1 Sac.

		Punt Returns				Interceptions				Tot
Year Team	**G**	**Ret**	**Yds**	**Avg**	**TD**	**Int**	**Yds**	**TD**	**Fum**	**TD**
1979 SF	8	13	120	9.2	0	5	57	0	0	0
1980 SF	16	12	58	4.8	0	4	73	0	0	0
1981 SF	16	19	171	9.0	0	9	**239**	1	1	2
1982 SF	9	10	54	5.4	0	3	5	0	0	0
1983 SF	15	0	0	—	0	2	102	**2**	0	2
1984 SF	16	0	0	—	0	3	42	0	1	0
1985 SF	16	0	0	—	0	4	68	0	1	0
1986 Ind	9	0	0	—	0	2	16	0	0	0
NFL Total	105	54	403	7.5	0	32	602	3	3	4

EDDIE HICKS Hicks, Edward James 6′2″, 210 **RB**
Col: East Carolina *HS:* Vance [Henderson, NC] B: 7/26/1955, Henderson, NC *Drafted:* 1979 Round 6 NYG
1979 NYG: 14 G; KR 3-51 17.0. **1980** NYG: 3 G; Rush 19-50 2.6; Rec 1-4 4.0; 2 Fum. **Total:** 17 G; Rush 19-50 2.6; Rec 1-4 4.0; KR 3-51 17.0; 2 Fum.

ERIC HICKS Hicks, Eric David 6′6″, 261 **DE**
Col: Maryland *HS:* Mercyhurst [Erie, PA] B: 6/17/1976, Erie, PA
1998 KC: 3 G.

IVAN HICKS Hicks, Ivan Lemuel 6′2″, 185 **DB**
Col: Michigan *HS:* Pennsauken [NJ] B: 6/30/1963, Camden, NJ
1987 Det: 1 G.

JOHN HICKS Hicks, John Charles Jr. 6′2″, 258 **OG**
Col: Ohio State *HS:* John Hay [Cleveland, OH] B: 3/21/1951, Cleveland, OH *Drafted:* 1974 Round 1 NYG
1974 NYG: 14 G. **1975** NYG: 14 G; Rec 1-5 5.0. **1976** NYG: 14 G. **1977** NYG: 10 G. **Total:** 52 G; Rec 1-5 5.0.

KERRY HICKS Hicks, Kerry Dale 6′6″, 283 **DE**
Col: Colorado *HS:* Highland [Salt Lake City, UT] B: 12/29/1972, Bountiful, UT *Drafted:* 1996 Round 7 Car
1997 KC: 2 G.

MARK HICKS Hicks, Mark Anthony 6′2″, 225 **LB**
Col: Arizona State *HS:* George Washington [Los Angeles, CA] B: 11/7/1960, Los Angeles, CA
1983 Sea: 10 G; 2.5 Sac. **1987** Det: 1 G. **Total:** 11 G; 2.5 Sac.

BRYAN HICKS Hicks, Mark Bryan 6′0″, 192 **DB**
Col: McNeese State *HS:* St. Louis [Lake Charles, LA] B: 1/24/1957, Lake Charles, LA *Drafted:* 1980 Round 5 Cin
1980 Cin: 16 G; KR 5-87 17.4; Int 1-8. **1981** Cin: 16 G; PR 1-4 4.0. **1982** Cin: 7 G. **Total:** 39 G; PR 1-4 4.0; KR 5-87 17.4; Int 1-8.

MAX HICKS Hicks, Max 175 **E**
Col: Geneva B: 7/1/1894 Deceased
1920 Ham: 1 G. **1921** Ham: 1 G. **Total:** 2 G.

MICHAEL HICKS Hicks, Michael 6′0″, 194 **RB**
Col: South Carolina State *HS:* Lamar [Barnsville, GA]; Robert E. Lee Inst. [Thomaston, GA] B: 2/1/1973, Barnsville, GA *Drafted:* 1996 Round 7 ChiB
1996 ChiB: Rec 1-(-1) -1.0. **Total:** Rec 1-(-1) -1.0.

		Rushing				
Year Team	**G**	**Att**	**Yds**	**Avg**	**TD**	**Fum**
1996 ChiB	4	27	92	3.4	0	1
1997 ChiB	3	4	14	3.5	0	0
NFL Total	7	31	106	3.4	0	1

R.W. HICKS Hicks, Richard Winslow 6′4″, 250 **C**
Col: West Los Angeles Coll. CA (J.C.); Southwestern (Tex.); Humboldt State *HS:* George Washington [Los Angeles, CA] B: 1/4/1951, Cleveland, OH
1975 Det: 14 G; 2 Fum.

ROBERT HICKS Hicks, Robert Otis Jr. 6′7″, 338 **OT**
Col: Mississippi State *HS:* Frederick Douglass [Atlanta, GA] B: 11/17/1974, Atlanta, GA *Drafted:* 1998 Round 3 Buf
1998 Buf: 9 G.

SYLVESTER HICKS Hicks, Sylvester 6′4″, 251 **DE**
Col: Tennessee State *HS:* North Side [Jackson, TN] B: 4/2/1955, Jackson, TN *Drafted:* 1978 Round 2 KC
1978 KC: 16 G. **1979** KC: 16 G. **1980** KC: 10 G. **1981** KC: 1 G. **Total:** 43 G.

TOM HICKS Hicks, Thomas Logan 6′4″, 235 **LB**
Col: Illinois *HS:* Willowbrook [Villa Park, IL] B: 12/18/1952, Chicago, IL *Drafted:* 1975 Round 6 ChiB
1976 ChiB: 14 G. **1977** ChiB: 12 G; Int 1-9. **1978** ChiB: 9 G. **1979** ChiB: 15 G; Int 3-85 1 TD; 6 Pt. **1980** ChiB: 14 G; Int 1-8. **Total:** 64 G; Int 5-102 1 TD; 6 Pt.

VICTOR HICKS Hicks, Victor Lonell 6′3″, 250 **TE**
Col: Oklahoma *HS:* Estacado [Lubbock, TX] B: 1/19/1957, Lubbock, TX *Drafted:* 1979 Round 5 LARm
1980 LARm: 16 G; Rush 1-19 19.0; Rec 23-318 13.8 3 TD; 18 Pt.

W.K. HICKS Hicks, Wilmer Kenzie 6′1″, 195 **DB**
(Contact) *Col:* Texas Southern *HS:* Dunbar [Texarkana, TX] B: 7/14/1942, Texarkana, AR
1965 Hou: PR 1-4 4.0; KR 7-181 25.9. **1971** NYJ: PR 1-0. **1972** NYJ: PR 3-25 8.3; KR 4-73 18.3. **Total:** PR 5-29 5.8; KR 11-254 23.1.

		Interceptions			
Year Team	**G**	**Int**	**Yds**	**TD**	**Fum**
1964 Hou	14	5	89	0	0
1965 Hou	14	**9**	**156**	0	0
1966 Hou	14	3	12	0	0
1967 Hou	14	3	122	0	0
1968 Hou	14	3	42	0	0
1969 Hou	14	4	36	0	0
1970 NYJ	14	8	99	0	0
1971 NYJ	13	4	46	0	1
1972 NYJ	14	1	43	0	0
NFL Total	125	40	645	0	1

ED HIEMSTRA Hiemstra, Edward Paul 6′0″, 200 **G**
Col: Sterling *HS:* Nampa [ID] B: 3/8/1920, Columbus, MT
1942 NYG: 11 G; Int 1-9.

ALEX HIGDON Higdon, Alexander 6′5″, 247 **TE**
Col: Ohio State *HS:* Princeton [Cincinatti, OH] B: 9/9/1966, Cincinatti, OH *Drafted:* 1988 Round 3 Atl
1988 Atl: 3 G; Rec 3-60 20.0 2 TD; 12 Pt.

AUSTIN HIGGINS Higgins, Austin George 5′9″, 168 **C-OE**
Col: No College *HS:* None B: 11/29/1897, Louisville, KY D: 3/3/1976, Louisville, KY
1921 Lou: 2 G. **1922** Lou: 4 G. **1923** Lou: 1 G. **Total:** 7 G.

JIM HIGGINS Higgins, James Benton Jr. 6′1″, 250 **OT-OG**
Col: Xavier (Ohio) *HS:* Purcell [Cincinnati, OH] B: 1/20/1942, Cincinnati, OH Deceased *Drafted:* 1964 Round 19 Cle
1966 Mia: 7 G.

JIM HIGGINS Higgins, James Benton Jr. 6′1″, 210 **G-LB**
Col: Trinity (Tex.) *HS:* Maypearl [TX] B: 1/10/1920, Maypearl, TX D: 6/6/1991, Beaumont, TX
1941 ChiC: 4 G.

LUKE HIGGINS Higgins, Luke Martin 6′0″, 210 **G**
Col: Notre Dame *HS:* Cliffside Park [NJ]; Marainapolis Acad. [Thompson, CT] B: 5/3/1920, Edgewater, NJ D: 10/11/1991
AAFC **1947** BalA: 11 G.

BOB HIGGINS Higgins, Robert Arlington 5′10″, 195 **E**
Col: Penn State *HS:* Peddie School [Highstown, NJ] B: 12/24/1893, Corning, NY D: 6/6/1969, State College, PA
1920 Can: 3 G. **1921** Can: 9 G; Rec 1 TD; Scor 14, 2 XK; 1 Fum TD; Tot TD 2. **Total:** 12 G; Rec 1 TD; 1 Fum TD; Tot TD 2.

TOM HIGGINS Higgins, Thomas Joseph John Jr. 6′2″, 235 **LB**
Col: North Carolina State *HS:* Colonia [NJ] B: 7/13/1954, Newark, NJ
1979 Buf: 16 G.

TOM HIGGINS Higgins, Thomas Joseph John Sr. 6′2″, 230 **OT-OG-DT**
Col: North Carolina *HS:* West Side [Newark, NJ] B: 2/26/1930, Newark, NJ *Drafted:* 1953 Round 6 ChiC
1953 ChiC: 12 G. **1954** Phi: 5 G. **1955** Phi: 12 G. **Total:** 29 G.

MARK HIGGS Higgs, Mark Deyon 5′7″, 199 **RB**
Col: Kentucky *HS:* Owensboro [KY] B: 4/11/1966, Chicago, IL *Drafted:* 1988 Round 8 Dal

		Rushing				Receiving			
Year Team	**G**	**Att**	**Yds**	**Avg**	**TD**	**Rec**	**Yds**	**Avg**	**TD**
1988 Dal	5	0	0	—	0	0	0	—	0
1989 Phi	15	49	184	3.8	0	3	9	3.0	0
1990 Mia	12	10	67	6.7	0	0	0	—	0
1991 Mia	14	231	905	3.9	4	11	80	7.3	0
1992 Mia	16	256	915	3.6	7	16	142	8.9	0
1993 Mia	16	186	693	3.7	3	10	72	7.2	0
1994 Mia-Ariz	11	62	195	3.1	0	0	0	—	0
1994 Mia	5	19	68	3.6	0	0	0	—	0
1994 Ariz	6	43	127	3.0	0	0	0	—	0
1995 Ariz	1	0	0	—	0	0	0	—	0
NFL Total	90	794	2959	3.7	14	40	303	7.6	0

	Kickoff Returns					Tot
Year Team	**Ret**	**Yds**	**Avg**	**TD**	**Fum**	**TD**
1988 Dal	2	31	15.5	0	0	0
1989 Phi	16	293	18.3	0	3	0
1990 Mia	10	210	21.0	0	1	1
1991 Mia	0	0	—	0	3	4
1992 Mia	0	0	—	0	5	7
1993 Mia	0	0	—	0	1	3
1994 Mia-Ariz	2	25	12.5	0	1	0
1994 Mia	0	0	—	0	1	0
1994 Ariz	2	25	12.5	0	0	0
1995 Ariz	2	26	13.0	0	0	0
NFL Total	32	585	18.3	0	14	15

LENNIE HIGH High, Lennie 5′11″, 195 **OE**
Col: Eastern Illinois B: 2/17/1895 D: 11/16/1975, LaHabra, CA
1920 Sta: 1 G.

ALONZO HIGHSMITH Highsmith, Alonzo Walter 6′1″, 234 **RB**
Col: Miami (Fla.) *HS:* Christopher Columbus [Miami, FL] B: 2/26/1965, Bartow, FL *Drafted:* 1987 Round 1 Hou

Year Team	G	Rushing Att	Yds	Avg	TD	Receiving Rec	Yds	Avg	TD	Fum	Tot TD
1987 Hou	8	29	106	3.7	1	4	55	13.8	1	2	2
1988 Hou	16	94	466	5.0	2	12	131	10.9	0	7	2
1989 Hou	16	128	531	4.1	4	18	201	11.2	2	6	6
1990 Dal	7	19	48	2.5	0	3	13	4.3	0	1	0
1991 Dal-TB	13	5	21	4.2	0	0	0	—	0	0	0
1991 Dal	2	0	0	—	0	0	0	—	0	0	0
1991 TB	11	5	21	4.2	0	0	0	—	0	0	0
1992 TB	5	8	23	2.9	0	5	28	5.6	0	0	0
NFL Total	65	283	1195	4.2	7	42	428	10.2	3	16	10

DON HIGHSMITH Highsmith, Donald Cornelius 6′0″, 210 **RB**
Col: Michigan State *HS:* New Brunswick [NJ] B: 3/12/1948, New Brunswick, NJ *Drafted:* 1970 Round 13 Oak
1971 Oak: Rec 10-109 10.9; PR 1-0; KR 21-454 21.6. **1972** Oak: Rec 2-34 17.0. **1973** GB: KR 1-18 18.0. **Total:** Rec 12-143 11.9; PR 1-0; KR 22-472 21.5.

Year Team	G	Rushing Att	Yds	Avg	TD	Fum
1970 Oak	8	2	2	1.0	0	0
1971 Oak	14	76	307	4.0	1	4
1972 Oak	8	9	11	1.2	1	2
1973 GB	7	7	7	1.0	0	1
NFL Total	37	94	327	3.5	2	7

BUZZ HIGHSMITH Highsmith, Walter 6′3″, 247 **OG-OT-C**
Col: Florida A&M *HS:* Roosevelt [Lake Wales, FL] B: 8/27/1943, Tampa, FL
1968 Den: 14 G. **1969** Den: 9 G. **1972** Hou: 9 G. **Total:** 32 G.

BEN HIGHTOWER Hightower, John Benjamin 6′2″, 184 **OE-DB**
Col: Sam Houston State *HS:* Beaumont [TX] B: 12/5/1918, Beaumont, TX *Drafted:* 1942 Round 11 Cle
1943 Det: Rush 1-(-5) -5.0; Int 1-9. **Total:** Rush 1-(-5) -5.0; Int 1-9.

Year Team	G	Receiving Rec	Yds	Avg	TD
1942 Cle	10	19	317	16.7	3
1943 Det	8	10	172	17.2	1
NFL Total	18	29	489	16.9	4

VAN HILES Hiles, Lavanda 6′0″, 195 **DB**
Col: Kentucky *HS:* Baton Rouge Episcopal [LA] B: 11/1/1975, Baton Rouge, LA *Drafted:* 1997 Round 5 ChiB
1997 ChiB: 16 G.

JAY HILGENBERG Hilgenberg, Jay Walter 6′3″, 259 **C-OG**
Col: Iowa *HS:* City [Iowa City, IA] B: 3/21/1959, Iowa City, IA
1981 ChiB: 16 G. **1982** ChiB: 9 G. **1983** ChiB: 16 G. **1984** ChiB: 16 G. **1985** ChiB: 16 G. **1986** ChiB: 16 G; 1 Fum. **1987** ChiB: 12 G. **1988** ChiB: 16 G; 1 Fum. **1989** ChiB: 16 G. **1990** ChiB: 14 G. **1991** ChiB: 16 G. **1992** Cle: 16 G. **1993** NO: 9 G; 1 Fum. **Total:** 188 G; 3 Fum.

JOEL HILGENBERG Hilgenberg, Joel C 6′3″, 250 **C-OG**
Col: Iowa *HS:* City [Iowa City, IA] B: 7/10/1962, Iowa City, IA *Drafted:* 1984 Round 4 NO
1984 NO: 10 G. **1985** NO: 15 G. **1986** NO: 16 G. **1987** NO: 12 G. **1988** NO: 16 G. **1989** NO: 16 G; 1 Fum. **1990** NO: 16 G; Rec 1-9 9.0. **1991** NO: 16 G; 1 Fum. **1992** NO: 16 G. **1993** NO: 9 G; 1 Fum. **Total:** 142 G; Rec 1-9 9.0; 3 Fum.

WALLY HILGENBERG Hilgenberg, Walter William 6′3″, 229 **LB-OG**
Col: Iowa *HS:* Wilton [IA] B: 9/19/1942, Marashalltown, IA *Drafted:* 1964 Round 4 Det
1964 Det: 14 G; KR 1-2 2.0. **1965** Det: 13 G. **1966** Det: 14 G. **1968** Min: 14 G. **1969** Min: 14 G. **1970** Min: 14 G; Int 2-33. **1971** Min: 14 G; Int 2-6. **1972** Min: 14 G; Int 1-17 1 TD; 6 Pt; 1 Fum. **1973** Min: 13 G; Int 1-6; **1** Fum TD; 6 Pt. **1974** Min: 13 G; PR 1-(-2) -2.0; Int 1-0; Scor **1** Saf; 2 Pt. **1975** Min: 14 G; Int 1-0. **1976** Min: 14 G. **1977** Min: 11 G. **1978** Min: 15 G. **1979** Min: 8 G. **Total:** 199 G; PR 1-(-2) -2.0; KR 1-2 2.0; Int 8-62 1 TD; Scor 1 Saf; 1 Fum TD; Tot TD 2; 14 Pt; 1 Fum.

RUSTY HILGER Hilger, Russell Todd 6′4″, 205 **QB**
Col: Oklahoma State *HS:* Southeast [Oklahoma City, OK] B: 5/9/1962, Oklahoma City, OK *Drafted:* 1985 Round 6 LARd

Year Team	G	Passing Att	Comp	Comp%	Yds	YPA	TD	Int	Rating
1985 LARd	4	13	4	30.8	54	4.15	1	0	70.7
1986 LARd	2	38	19	50.0	266	7.00	1	1	70.7
1987 LARd	5	106	55	51.9	706	6.66	2	6	55.8
1988 Det	11	306	126	41.2	1558	5.09	7	12	48.9
1991 Ind	1	1	0	0.0	0	0.00	0	0	39.6
NFL Total	23	464	204	44.0	2584	5.57	11	19	52.8

Year Team	Rushing Att	Yds	Avg	TD	Fum
1985 LARd	3	8	2.7	0	1
1986 LARd	6	48	8.0	0	3
1987 LARd	8	8	1.0	0	3
1988 Det	18	27	1.5	0	7
NFL Total	35	91	2.6	0	14

DREW HILL Hill, Andrew 5′9″, 170 **WR**
Col: Georgia Tech *HS:* Newnan [GA] B: 10/5/1956, Newnan, GA *Drafted:* 1979 Round 12 LARm
1979 LARm: PR 1-0. **1980** LARm: Rush 1-4 4.0. **1981** LARm: Rush 1-14 14.0; PR 2-22 11.0. **1987** Hou: Pass 1-0. **1991** Hou: Rush 1-1 1.0. **Total:** Pass 1-0; Rush 3-19 6.3; PR 3-22 7.3.

Year Team	G	Receiving Rec	Yds	Avg	TD	Kickoff Returns Ret	Yds	Avg	TD	Fum	Tot TD
1979 LARm	16	4	94	23.5	1	40	803	20.1	0	2	1
1980 LARm	16	19	416	21.9	2	43	880	20.5	**1**	2	3
1981 LARm	16	16	355	22.2	3	**60**	1170	19.5	0	1	3
1982 LARm	9	7	92	13.1	0	2	42	21.0	0	0	0
1984 LARm	16	14	390	27.9	4	26	543	20.9	0	0	4
1985 Hou	16	64	1169	18.3	9	1	22	22.0	0	0	9
1986 Hou	16	65	1112	17.1	5	0	0	—	0	0	5
1987 Hou	12	49	989	20.2	6	0	0	—	0	1	6
1988 Hou	16	72	1141	15.8	10	0	0	—	0	0	10
1989 Hou	14	66	938	14.2	8	0	0	—	0	1	8
1990 Hou	16	74	1019	13.8	5	0	0	—	0	0	5
1991 Hou	16	90	1109	12.3	4	0	0	—	0	2	4
1992 Atl	16	60	623	10.4	3	0	0	—	0	1	3
1993 Atl	16	34	384	11.3	0	0	0	—	0	0	0
NFL Total	211	634	9831	15.5	60	172	3460	20.1	1	10	61

TONY HILL Hill, Antonio LaVosia 6′6″, 250 **DE**
Col: Tennessee-Chattanooga *HS:* Warren Co. [Warrenton, GA] B: 10/23/1968, Augusta, GA *Drafted:* 1991 Round 4 Dal
1991 Dal: 8 G. **1992** Dal: 5 G. **Total:** 13 G.

BARRY HILL Hill, Barry Stephen 6′3″, 185 **DB**
Col: Iowa State *HS:* Carver [Delray Beach, FL] B: 1/26/1953, Eglin AFB, FL *Drafted:* 1975 Round 5 Mia
1975 Mia: 14 G. **1976** Mia: 6 G. **Total:** 20 G.

BRUCE HILL Hill, Bruce Edward 6′0″, 178 **WR**
Col: Arizona State *HS:* Antelope Valley [Lancaster, CA] B: 2/29/1964, Fort Dix, NJ *Drafted:* 1987 Round 4 TB
1987 TB: Rush 3-3 1.0; KR 1-8 8.0. **1988** TB: Rush 2-(-11) -5.5. **1990** TB: Rush 1-0. **Total:** Rush 6-(-8) -1.3; KR 1-8 8.0.

Year Team	G	Receiving Rec	Yds	Avg	TD	Fum
1987 TB	8	23	403	17.5	2	1
1988 TB	14	58	1040	17.9	9	2
1989 TB	16	50	673	13.5	5	2
1990 TB	13	42	641	15.3	5	0
1991 TB	6	17	185	10.9	2	0
NFL Total	57	190	2942	15.5	23	5

CALVIN HILL Hill, Calvin 6′4″, 227 **RB**
Col: Yale *HS:* Riverdale Country Day School [NY] B: 1/2/1947, Baltimore, MD *Drafted:* 1969 Round 1 Dal
1969 Dal: Pass 3-3 100.0%, 137 45.67 2 TD; KR 4-125 31.3. **1970** Dal: Pass 4-1 25.0%, 12 3.00. **1971** Dal: Pass 1-0, 1 Int. **1972** Dal: Pass 3-1 33.3%, 55 18.33 1 TD. **1973** Dal: Pass 1-0. **1976** Was: Pass 1-0. **Total:** Pass 13-5 38.5%, 204 15.69 3 TD 1 Int; KR 4-125 31.3.

Year Team	G	Rushing Att	Yds	Avg	TD	Receiving Rec	Yds	Avg	TD	Fum	Tot TD
1969 Dal	13	204	942	4.6	8	20	232	11.6	0	7	8
1970 Dal	12	153	577	3.8	4	13	95	7.3	0	4	4
1971 Dal	8	106	468	4.4	8	19	244	12.8	3	2	11
1972 Dal	14	245	1036	4.2	6	43	364	8.5	3	7	9
1973 Dal	14	273	1142	4.2	6	32	290	9.1	0	7	6
1974 Dal	12	185	844	4.6	7	12	134	11.2	0	5	7
1976 Was	14	79	301	3.8	1	7	100	14.3	0	4	1
1977 Was	14	69	257	3.7	0	18	154	8.6	1	3	1
1978 Cle	12	80	289	3.6	1	25	334	13.4	6	2	7
1979 Cle	14	53	193	3.6	1	38	381	10.0	2	1	3
1980 Cle	15	1	11	11.0	0	27	383	14.2	6	0	6
1981 Cle	14	4	23	5.8	0	17	150	8.8	2	1	2
NFL Total	156	1452	6083	4.2	42	271	2861	10.6	23	43	65

CHUCK HILL Hill, Charles Kelley 5′8″, 190 **FB-WB-OE**
Col: Iowa State *HS:* Corydon [IA] B: 5/26/1904 D: 1/19/1986, Saratoga, CA
1925 RI: 1 G.

CHARLEY HILL Hill, Charles Leland 6′0″, 183 **WB-FB-BB-TB**
(Chub) *Col:* Baker B: 1900, Paola, KS Deceased
1924 KC: 7 G; Rush 1 TD; 6 Pt. **1925** KC: 8 G; Rush 2 TD; Rec 2 TD; Scor 25, 1 XK; Tot TD 4. **1926** KC: 10 G; Pass 1 TD; Rush 1 TD; 6 Pt. **Total:** 25 G; Pass 1 TD; Rush 4 TD; Rec 2 TD; Tot TD 6.

DAVID HILL Hill, David Earl 6'2", 229 **TE**
Col: Texas A&M–Kingsville *HS:* Highlands [San Antonio, TX]
B: 1/1/1954, San Antonio, TX *Drafted:* 1976 Round 2 Det
1976 Det: Pass 1-0, 1 Int. **1977** Det: Pass 1-0; Rush 4-10 2.5. **1978** Det: Rush 3-12 4.0. **1979** Det: Rush 1-15 15.0. **Total:** Pass 2-0, 1 Int; Rush 8-37 4.6.

		Receiving				
Year Team	**G**	**Rec**	**Yds**	**Avg**	**TD**	**Fum**
1976 Det	14	19	249	13.1	5	2
1977 Det	14	32	465	14.5	2	1
1978 Det	16	53	633	11.9	4	1
1979 Det	16	47	569	12.1	3	1
1980 Det	16	39	424	10.9	1	1
1981 Det	15	33	462	14.0	4	1
1982 Det	9	22	252	11.5	4	0
1983 LARm	16	28	280	10.0	2	1
1984 LARm	16	31	300	9.7	1	2
1985 LARm	16	29	271	9.3	1	2
1986 LARm	16	14	202	14.4	1	1
1987 LARm	12	11	105	9.5	0	0
NFL Total	176	358	4212	11.8	28	13

DAVE HILL Hill, David Harris 6'5", 260 **OT**
Col: Auburn *HS:* Lanett [AL] B: 2/1/1941, Lanett, AL *Drafted:* 1963 Round 24 KC
1963 KC: 11 G. **1964** KC: 14 G. **1965** KC: 14 G. **1966** KC: 14 G. **1967** KC: 14 G; KR 1-0; 1 Fum. **1968** KC: 14 G. **1969** KC: 14 G. **1970** KC: 14 G. **1971** KC: 14 G. **1972** KC: 14 G. **1973** KC: 8 G. **1974** KC: 5 G. **Total:** 150 G; KR 1-0; 1 Fum.

DEREK HILL Hill, Derek Keith 6'1", 193 **WR**
Col: Arizona *HS:* Carson [CA] B: 11/4/1967, Detroit, MI
Drafted: 1989 Round 3 Pit
1989 Pit: PR 5-22 4.4. **1990** Pit: PR 1-0. **Total:** PR 6-22 3.7.

		Receiving				
Year Team	**G**	**Rec**	**Yds**	**Avg**	**TD**	**Fum**
1989 Pit	16	28	455	16.3	1	2
1990 Pit	16	25	391	15.6	0	1
NFL Total	32	53	846	16.0	1	3

DON HILL Hill, Donald Kinman 5'10", 175 **WB-HB-C**
Col: Stanford *HS:* Long Beach Polytechnic [CA] B: 9/18/1904, Hiawatha, KS D: 2/9/1967, Glendale, CA
1929 GB-ChiC: 16 G; Rec 1 TD; 6 Pt. GB: 3 G. ChiC: 13 G; Rec 1 TD; 6 Pt. **Total:** 16 G; Rec 1 TD; 6 Pt.

EDDIE HILL Hill, Eddie Wayne 6'2", 205 **RB**
Col: Memphis *HS:* Hillsboro [Nashville, TN] B: 5/13/1957, Nashville, TN *Drafted:* 1979 Round 2 LARm
1979 LARm: KR 15-305 20.3. **1981** Mia: Pass 1-1 100.0%, 14 14.00; KR 1-11 11.0. **1982** Mia: Pass 1-0. **1984** Mia: KR 1-14 14.0. **Total:** Pass 2-1 50.0%, 14 7.00; KR 17-330 19.4.

		Rushing				Receiving					Tot
Year Team	**G**	**Att**	**Yds**	**Avg**	**TD**	**Rec**	**Yds**	**Avg**	**TD**	**Fum**	**TD**
1979 LARm	16	29	114	3.9	1	4	36	9.0	1	4	2
1980 LARm	7	39	120	3.1	0	4	29	7.3	0	2	0
1981 Mia	11	37	146	3.9	1	12	73	6.1	1	2	2
1982 Mia	9	13	51	3.9	0	6	33	5.5	0	2	0
1983 Mia	16	2	12	6.0	0	0	0	—	0	0	0
1984 Mia	16	0	0	—	0	0	0	—	0	0	0
NFL Total	75	120	443	3.7	2	26	171	6.6	2	10	4

ERIC HILL Hill, Eric Dwayne 6'2", 258 **LB**
Col: Louisiana State *HS:* Ball [Galveston, TX] B: 11/14/1966, Blytheville, AR *Drafted:* 1989 Round 1 Pho
1989 Pho: 15 G; 1 Sac. **1990** Pho: 16 G; 1.5 Sac. **1991** Pho: 16 G; 1 Fum TD; 6 Pt; 1 Sac. **1992** Pho: 16 G; 1 Fum. **1993** Pho: 13 G; 1 Sac. **1994** Ariz: 16 G; 1.5 Sac. **1995** Ariz: 14 G; 2 Sac. **1996** Ariz: 16 G. **1997** Ariz: 11 G. **1998** StL: 15 G; Int 1-0; 1 Sac. **Total:** 148 G; Int 1-0; 1 Fum TD; 6 Pt; 1 Fum; 9 Sac.

FRED HILL Hill, Frederick Gordon 6'2", 215 **TE-WR**
Col: USC *HS:* Paramount [CA] B: 8/13/1943, Los Angeles, CA
Drafted: 1965 Round 4 Phi
1966 Phi: Rush 1-5 5.0. **Total:** Rush 1-5 5.0.

		Receiving			
Year Team	**G**	**Rec**	**Yds**	**Avg**	**TD**
1965 Phi	12	1	21	21.0	0
1966 Phi	14	29	304	10.5	0
1967 Phi	14	9	144	16.0	0
1968 Phi	14	30	370	12.3	3
1969 Phi	8	6	64	10.7	1
1970 Phi	14	3	10	3.3	1
1971 Phi	7	7	92	13.1	0
NFL Total	83	85	1005	11.8	5

GARY HILL Hill, Gary H 6'0", 200 **DB**
Col: USC *HS:* Rancho Alamitos [Garden Grove, CA] B: 6/29/1943
1965 Min: 8 G.

JERRY HILL Hill, Gerald Allen 5'11", 210 **RB**
Col: Wyoming *HS:* Lingle [WY] B: 10/12/1939, Torrington, WY
Drafted: 1961 Round 3 Bal
1963 Bal: PR 1-0; KR 2-32 16.0. **1964** Bal: KR 4-85 21.3. **1965** Bal: KR 1-3 3.0. **Total:** PR 1-0; KR 7-120 17.1.

		Rushing				Receiving					Tot
Year Team	**G**	**Att**	**Yds**	**Avg**	**TD**	**Rec**	**Yds**	**Avg**	**TD**	**Fum**	**TD**
1961 Bal	1	1	4	4.0	0	0	0	—	0	0	0
1963 Bal	14	100	440	4.4	5	22	304	13.8	1	8	6
1964 Bal	13	88	384	4.4	5	14	113	8.1	1	3	6
1965 Bal	14	147	516	3.5	5	20	112	5.6	0	4	5
1966 Bal	11	104	395	3.8	0	5	18	3.6	0	2	0
1967 Bal	14	90	311	3.5	2	19	156	8.2	0	1	2
1968 Bal	9	91	360	4.0	1	18	161	8.9	1	1	2
1969 Bal	14	49	143	2.9	2	11	44	4.0	0	3	2
1970 Bal	12	36	115	3.2	2	8	62	7.8	0	0	2
NFL Total	102	706	2668	3.8	22	117	970	8.3	3	22	25

GREG HILL Hill, Gregory LaMonte 5'11", 207 **RB**
Col: Texas A&M *HS:* David W. Carter [Dallas, TX] B: 2/23/1972, Dallas, TX *Drafted:* 1994 Round 1 KC

		Rushing				Receiving					Tot
Year Team	**G**	**Att**	**Yds**	**Avg**	**TD**	**Rec**	**Yds**	**Avg**	**TD**	**Fum**	**TD**
1994 KC	16	141	574	4.1	1	16	92	5.8	0	1	1
1995 KC	16	155	667	4.3	1	7	45	6.4	0	2	1
1996 KC	15	135	645	4.8	4	3	60	20.0	1	1	5
1997 KC	16	157	550	3.5	0	12	126	10.5	0	1	0
1998 StL	2	40	240	6.0	4	1	6	6.0	0	0	4
NFL Total	65	628	2676	4.3	10	39	329	8.4	1	5	11

GREG HILL Hill, Gregory Michael 6'1", 194 **DB**
Col: Oklahoma State *HS:* Stark [West Orange, TX] B: 2/12/1961, Orange, TX *Drafted:* 1983 Round 4 Hou
1983 Hou: 14 G. **1984** KC: 15 G; Int 2-(-1); 1 Fum. **1985** KC: 16 G; Int 3-37. **1986** KC: 13 G; Int 3-64 1 TD; 6 Pt. **1987** LARd-KC: 6 G. LARd: 2 G. KC: 4 G. **1988** KC: 15 G; Int 1-24. **Total:** 79 G; Int 9-124 1 TD; 6 Pt; 1 Fum.

HARLON HILL Hill, Harlon Junious 6'3", 199 **OE-DB**
Col: North Alabama *HS:* Lauderdale Co. [Rogersville, AL] B: 5/4/1932, Florence, AL *Drafted:* 1954 Round 15 ChiB
1956 ChiB: Pass 1-0; Rush 2-24 12.0. **1957** ChiB: Rush 2-7 3.5. **1959** ChiB: Rush 1-0. **1961** ChiB: Int 3-52. **1962** Pit-Det: Rush 7-72 10.3. Pit: Rush 7-72 10.3. **Total:** Pass 1-0; Rush 12-103 8.6; Int 3-52.

		Receiving					Tot
Year Team	**G**	**Rec**	**Yds**	**Avg**	**TD**	**Fum**	**TD**
1954 ChiB	12	45	1124	**25.0**	**12**	0	**12**
1955 ChiB	12	42	789	18.8	**9**	0	**9**
1956 ChiB	12	47	1128	**24.0**	11	0	11
1957 ChiB	8	21	483	23.0	2	1	2
1958 ChiB	8	27	365	13.5	3	0	3
1959 ChiB	11	36	578	16.1	3	1	3
1960 ChiB	12	5	98	19.6	0	0	0
1961 ChiB	14	3	51	17.0	0	0	0
1962 Pit-Det	14	7	101	14.4	0	0	0
1962 Pit	7	7	101	14.4	0	0	0
1962 Det	7	0	0	—	0	0	0
NFL Total	103	233	4717	20.2	40	2	40

COWBOY HILL Hill, Harry Franklin 5'8", 176 **TB-WB-BB**
(Dutch) *Col:* Oklahoma *HS:* Chickasha [OK] B: 3/30/1899, Pittsburg, OK D: 2/3/1966, Norman, OK
1923 Tol: 8 G; Rush 3 TD; 18 Pt. **1924** KC: 5 G. **1925** KC-NYG: 10 G; Rush 1 TD; 6 Pt. KC: 8 G; Rush 1 TD; 6 Pt. NYG: 2 G. **1926** NYG: 10 G; Rush 2 TD; 12 Pt. **Total:** 33 G; Rush 6 TD; 36 Pt.

BOB HILL Hill, Haskell 5'10", 190 **G**
(War Horse) *Col:* Carlisle B: 1890, NY Deceased
1922 Oor: 6 G.

IRV HILL Hill, Irvin Pate 6'1", 207 **FB-LB-BB-DB**
(Rusty) *Col:* Trinity (Tex.) *HS:* Arlington [TX] B: 12/8/1908, Fort Worth, TX D: 11/7/1978, Dallas, TX
1932 ChiC: Rec 3-28 9.3; Scor 22, 4 XK. **Total:** Rec 3-28 9.3.

		Rushing			
Year Team	**G**	**Att**	**Yds**	**Avg**	**TD**
1931 ChiC	9	—	—	—	0
1932 ChiC	7	45	162	3.6	3
1933 Bos	1	1	1	1.0	0
NFL Total	17	46	163	3.5	3

JACK HILL Hill, Jack Flint 6′1″, 185 **WR-K**
Col: Utah State *HS:* Davis [Kaysville, UT] B: 10/17/1932, Ogden, UT
1961 Den: 14 G; Rec 4-33 8.3; KR 1-23 23.0; Scor 31, 5-15 33.3% FG, 16-16 100.0% XK.

JIM HILL Hill, James Clifford 6′0″, 188 **DB**
Col: Tennessee *HS:* Maryville [TN] B: 7/21/1929, Knoxville, TN
D: 7/1970, Groveland, FL *Drafted:* 1951 Round 15 Det
1951 Det: 12 G. **1952** Det: 9 G; PR 1-2 2.0; Int 1-15. **1955** Pit: 10 G; Int 1-9. **Total:** 31 G; PR 1-2 2.0; Int 2-24.

J.D. HILL Hill, James D 6′1″, 202 **WR**
Col: Arizona State *HS:* Edison [Stockton, CA] B: 10/30/1948, Stockton, CA *Drafted:* 1971 Round 1 Buf
1971 Buf: Rush 1-2 2.0. **1972** Buf: Rush 1-11 11.0; PR 4-24 6.0; KR 2-32 16.0. **1973** Buf: PR 1-(-9) -9.0. **1975** Buf: Rush 1-1 1.0. **Total:** Rush 3-14 4.7; PR 5-15 3.0; KR 2-32 16.0.

		Receiving				
Year Team	**G**	**Rec**	**Yds**	**Avg**	**TD**	**Fum**
1971 Buf	5	11	216	19.6	2	0
1972 Buf	14	52	754	14.5	5	1
1973 Buf	14	29	422	14.6	0	2
1974 Buf	14	32	572	17.9	6	0
1975 Buf	14	36	667	18.5	7	0
1976 Det	1	1	2	2.0	0	0
1977 Det	11	24	247	10.3	1	0
NFL Total	73	185	2880	15.6	21	3

HAROLD HILL Hill, James Harold 6′0″, 200 **E**
(Bunker) *Col:* Samford *HS:* Etowah [Attalla, AL] B: 12/8/1914, Gadsden, AL
1938 Bkn: 8 G; Rec 3-61 20.3. **1939** Bkn: 9 G; Rec 7-150 21.4. **1940** Bkn: 9 G; Rec 1-9 9.0. **Total:** 26 G; Rec 11-220 20.0.

JIMMY HILL Hill, James Jr. 6′2″, 192 **DB**
Col: Sam Houston State *HS:* Booker T. Washington [Dallas, TX]
B: 6/27/1928, Dallas, TX
1955 ChiC: PR 1-0. **1957** ChiC: PR 1-9 9.0. **1959** ChiC: PR 1-0. **Total:** PR 3-9 3.0.

		Interceptions			Tot
Year Team	**G**	**Int**	**Yds**	**TD**	**TD**
1955 ChiC	9	0	0	0	0
1956 ChiC	12	5	21	0	0
1957 ChiC	10	3	53	0	0
1959 ChiC	12	2	4	0	1
1960 StL	12	0	0	0	0
1961 StL	13	4	92	1	1
1962 StL	14	2	15	0	0
1963 StL	12	3	126	1	1
1964 StL	10	0	0	0	0
1965 Det	4	1	9	0	0
1966 KC	3	0	0	0	0
NFL Total	111	20	320	2	3

JIM HILL Hill, James Webster 6′2″, 190 **DB**
Col: Texas A&M–Kingsville *HS:* Highlands [San Antonio, TX]
B: 10/21/1946, San Antonio, TX *Drafted:* 1968 Round 1 SD
1970 SD: KR 1-0. **Total:** KR 1-0.

		Interceptions		
Year Team	**G**	**Int**	**Yds**	**TD**
1969 SD	14	7	92	0
1970 SD	14	0	0	0
1971 SD	14	2	7	0
1972 GB	14	4	37	0
1973 GB	13	3	53	0
1974 GB	14	2	47	0
1975 Cle	11	1	56	1
NFL Total	94	19	292	1

JEFF HILL Hill, Jefferey Martin 5′11″, 178 **WR**
Col: Purdue *HS:* Mount Healthy [Cincinnati, OH] B: 9/24/1972, Mount Healthy, OH
1995 Cin: Rush 1-(-3) -3.0; Rec 4-44 11.0. **Total:** Rush 1-(-3) -3.0; Rec 4-44 11.0.

		Kickoff Returns				
Year Team	**G**	**Ret**	**Yds**	**Avg**	**TD**	**Fum**
1994 Cin	1	4	97	24.3	0	0
1995 Cin	16	17	454	26.7	0	0
1996 Cin	10	9	173	19.2	0	1
NFL Total	27	30	724	24.1	0	1

KID HILL Hill, John Anthony 5′11″, 185 **T**
(Bozo) *Col:* Amherst *HS:* Brighton [MA]; Portland Prep [ME]
B: 5/6/1904, Washington, DC D: 12/3/1973, Puerto Vallarta, Mexico
1926 NYG: 2 G.

JOHN HILL Hill, John Stark 6′2″, 249 **C-OT**
Col: Lehigh *HS:* Franklin [Somerset, NJ] B: 4/16/1950, East Orange, NJ *Drafted:* 1972 Round 6 NYG
1972 NYG: 14 G. **1973** NYG: 12 G; 1 Fum. **1974** NYG: 12 G. **1975** NO: 14 G. **1976** NO: 14 G. **1977** NO: 14 G. **1978** NO: 16 G. **1979** NO: 16 G. **1980** NO: 15 G. **1981** NO: 13 G. **1982** NO: 9 G. **1983** NO: 16 G. **1984** NO: 11 G. **1985** SF: 1 G. **Total:** 177 G; 1 Fum.

KENNY HILL Hill, Kenneth W 6′0″, 194 **DB**
Col: Yale *HS:* Oak Grove [LA] B: 7/25/1958, Oak Grove, LA
Drafted: 1980 Round 8 Oak
1984 NYG: 1 Sac. **1985** NYG: Int 2-30. **1986** NYG: Int 3-25; 1 Sac. **1987** NYG: Int 1-1; 1 Sac. **1989** KC: Int 1-3. **Total:** Int 7-59; 3 Sac.

		Kickoff Returns				
Year Team	**G**	**Ret**	**Yds**	**Avg**	**TD**	**Fum**
1981 Oak	9	1	21	21.0	0	0
1982 LARd	9	2	20	10.0	0	1
1983 LARd	16	0	0	—	0	0
1984 NYG	12	1	27	27.0	0	0
1985 NYG	12	11	186	16.9	0	1
1986 NYG	16	5	61	12.2	0	1
1987 NYG	12	0	0	—	0	0
1988 NYG	16	13	262	20.2	0	2
1989 KC	8	0	0	—	0	0
NFL Total	110	33	577	17.5	0	5

KENT HILL Hill, Kent Angelo 6′5″, 260 **OG-OT**
Col: Georgia Tech *HS:* Americus [GA] B: 3/7/1957, Americus, GA
Drafted: 1979 Round 1 LARm
1979 LARm: 16 G. **1980** LARm: 16 G. **1981** LARm: 16 G. **1982** LARm: 9 G. **1983** LARm: 16 G. **1984** LARm: 16 G. **1985** LARm: 16 G. **1986** LARm-Hou: 15 G. LARm: 2 G. Hou: 13 G. **1987** Hou: 12 G. **Total:** 132 G.

TONY HILL Hill, Leroy Anthony Jr. 6′2″, 199 **WR**
Col: Stanford *HS:* Long Beach Polytechnic [CA] B: 6/23/1956, San Diego, CA *Drafted:* 1977 Round 3 Dal
1977 Dal: KR 3-64 21.3. **1978** Dal: Pass 1-0; Rush 3-17 5.7. **1979** Dal: Rush 2-18 9.0; KR 1-32 32.0. **1980** Dal: Rush 4-27 6.8. **1981** Dal: Rush 1-(-3) -3.0. **1982** Dal: Rush 1-22 22.0. **1983** Dal: Rush 1-2 2.0. **1984** Dal: Rush 1-7 7.0. **1985** Dal: Pass 1-1 100.0%, 42 42.00; Rush 1-(-6) -6.0. **Total:** Pass 2-1 50.0%, 42 21.00; Rush 14-84 6.0; KR 4-96 24.0.

		Receiving				Punt Returns				
Year Team	**G**	**Rec**	**Yds**	**Avg**	**TD**	**Ret**	**Yds**	**Avg**	**TD**	**Fum**
1977 Dal	14	2	21	10.5	0	10	124	12.4	0	0
1978 Dal	16	46	823	17.9	6	11	101	9.2	0	1
1979 Dal	16	60	1062	17.7	10	6	43	7.2	0	1
1980 Dal	16	60	1055	17.6	8	0	0	—	0	0
1981 Dal	16	46	953	20.7	4	0	0	—	0	1
1982 Dal	9	35	526	15.0	1	0	0	—	0	0
1983 Dal	12	49	801	16.3	7	0	0	—	0	1
1984 Dal	11	58	864	14.9	5	0	0	—	0	0
1985 Dal	15	74	1113	15.0	7	0	0	—	0	2
1986 Dal	16	49	770	15.7	3	0	0	—	0	1
NFL Total	141	479	7988	16.7	51	27	268	9.9	0	7

LONZELL HILL Hill, Lonzell Ramon 5′11″, 189 **WR**
(Mo) *Col:* Washington *HS:* Amos Alonzo Stagg [Stockton, CA]
B: 9/25/1965, Stockton, CA *Drafted:* 1987 Round 2 NO
1987 NO: Rush 1-(-9) -9.0. **1988** NO: Pass 1-0; Rush 2-7 3.5; PR 10-108 10.8. **1989** NO: Rush 1-(-7) -7.0; PR 7-41 5.9; KR 1-13 13.0. **Total:** Pass 1-0; Rush 4-(-9) -2.3; PR 17-149 8.8; KR 1-13 13.0.

		Receiving				
Year Team	**G**	**Rec**	**Yds**	**Avg**	**TD**	**Fum**
1987 NO	10	19	322	16.9	2	0
1988 NO	16	66	703	10.7	7	3
1989 NO	16	48	636	13.3	4	1
1990 NO	13	3	35	11.7	0	0
NFL Total	55	136	1696	12.5	13	4

MACK LEE HILL Hill, Mack Lee 5′11″, 225 **FB-HB**
Col: Southern University *HS:* Carter-Parramore [Quincy, FL]
B: 8/17/1940, Quincy, FL D: 12/14/1965, Kansas City, MO

		Rushing				Receiving					Tot
Year Team	**G**	**Att**	**Yds**	**Avg**	**TD**	**Rec**	**Yds**	**Avg**	**TD**	**Fum**	**TD**
1964 KC	14	105	576	**5.5**	4	19	144	7.6	2	3	6
1965 KC	13	125	627	5.0	2	21	264	12.6	1	1	3
NFL Total	27	230	1203	5.2	6	40	408	10.2	3	4	9

NATE HILL Hill, Nathaniel 6′4″, 273 **DE**
Col: Auburn *HS:* La Grange [GA] B: 2/21/1966, La Grange, GA
Drafted: 1988 Round 6 GB
1988 GB-Mia: 4 G; KR 1-1 1.0. GB: 3 G; KR 1-1 1.0. Mia: 1 G. **Total:** 4 G; KR 1-1 1.0.

RALPH HILL Hill, Ralph Edward 6′1″, 245 **C**
Col: Florida A&M *HS:* Forrestville [Chicago, IL] B: 11/10/1949, Chicago, IL
1976 NYG: 14 G. **1977** NYG: 12 G; KR 1-11 11.0; 1 Fum. **Total:** 26 G; KR 1-11 11.0; 1 Fum.

RANDAL HILL Hill, Randal Thrill 5′10″, 180 **WR**
Col: Miami (Fla.) *HS:* Miami Killian [FL] B: 9/21/1969, Miami, FL
Drafted: 1991 Round 1 Mia
1991 Mia-Pho: KR 9-146 16.2. Mia: KR 1-33 33.0. Pho: KR 8-113 14.1. **1992** Pho: Rush 1-4 4.0. **1995** Mia: KR 12-287 23.9. **1996** Mia: KR 2-4 2.0. **1997** NO: Rush 1-11 11.0. **Total:** Rush 2-15 7.5; KR 23-437 19.0.

		Receiving				
Year Team	**G**	**Rec**	**Yds**	**Avg**	**TD**	**Fum**
1991 Mia-Pho	16	43	495	11.5	1	0
1991 Mia	1	0	0	—	0	0
1991 Pho	15	43	495	11.5	1	0
1992 Pho	16	58	861	14.8	3	2
1993 Pho	16	35	519	14.8	4	0
1994 Ariz	14	38	544	14.3	0	0
1995 Mia	12	12	260	21.7	0	0
1996 Mia	14	21	409	19.5	4	1
1997 NO	15	55	761	13.8	2	0
NFL Total	103	262	3849	14.7	14	3

RAY HILL Hill, Raymond Millous 6′0″, 182 **DB**
Col: Michigan State *HS:* Chadsey [Detroit, MI] B: 8/7/1975, Detroit, MI
1998 Buf-Mia: 6 G. Buf: 4 G. Mia: 2 G. **Total:** 6 G.

ROD HILL Hill, Rodrick 6′0″, 185 **DB**
Col: Kentucky State *HS:* Martin Luther King [Detroit, MI] B: 3/14/1959, Detroit, MI *Drafted:* 1982 Round 1 Dal
1983 Dal: KR 14-243 17.4; Int 2-12. **1985** Buf: Int 2-17. **Total:** KR 14-243 17.4; Int 4-29.

		Punt Returns				
Year Team	**G**	**Ret**	**Yds**	**Avg**	**TD**	**Fum**
1982 Dal	9	4	39	9.8	0	1
1983 Dal	14	30	232	7.7	0	2
1984 Buf	2	0	0	—	0	0
1985 Buf	10	16	120	7.5	0	1
1986 Buf-Det	9	1	0	0.0	0	1
1986 Buf	6	1	0	0.0	0	1
1986 Det	3	0	0	—	0	0
1987 LARd	4	0	0	—	0	0
NFL Total	48	51	391	7.7	0	5

SEAN HILL Hill, Sean Terrell 5′10″, 179 **DB**
Col: Montana State *HS:* Widefield [Colorado Springs, CO]
B: 8/14/1971, Dowagiac, MI *Drafted:* 1994 Round 7 Mia
1994 Mia: 16 G. **1995** Mia: 16 G; KR 1-38 38.0. **1996** Mia: 12 G; Int 1-0; **1** Fum TD; 6 Pt; 1 Sac. **Total:** 44 G; KR 1-38 38.0; Int 1-0; 1 Fum TD; 6 Pt; 1 Sac.

KING HILL Hill, Stuart King 6′3″, 212 **QB**
Col: Rice *HS:* Brazosport [Freeport, TX] B: 11/8/1936, Hamilton, TX
Drafted: 1958 Round 1 ChiC

		Passing							
Year Team	**G**	**Att**	**Comp**	**Comp%**	**Yds**	**YPA**	**TD**	**Int**	**Rating**
1958 ChiC	7	9	1	11.1	18	2.00	0	2	0.0
1959 ChiC	11	181	82	45.3	1015	5.61	7	13	46.2
1960 StL	12	55	20	36.4	205	3.73	1	5	16.1
1961 Phi	14	12	6	50.0	101	8.42	2	2	78.8
1962 Phi	14	61	31	50.8	361	5.92	0	5	34.9
1963 Phi	14	186	91	48.9	1213	6.52	10	17	49.9
1964 Phi	8	88	49	55.7	641	7.28	3	4	71.3
1965 Phi	7	113	60	53.1	857	7.58	5	10	55.8
1966 Phi	10	97	53	54.6	571	5.89	5	7	59.3
1967 Phi	1	7	2	28.6	33	4.71	1	0	86.3
1968 Phi-Min	11	71	33	46.5	531	7.48	3	6	50.9
1968 Phi	3	71	33	46.5	531	7.48	3	6	50.9
1968 Min	8	0	0	—	0	—	0	0	—
1969 StL	14	1	1	100.0	7	7.00	0	0	95.8
NFL Total	123	881	429	48.7	5553	6.30	37	71	49.3

	Rushing				Punting			
Year Team	**Att**	**Yds**	**Avg**	**TD**	**Punts**	**Yds**	**Avg**	**Fum**
1958 ChiC	1	0	0.0	0	0	0	—	1
1959 ChiC	39	167	4.3	5	3	118	39.3	**13**
1960 StL	16	47	2.9	1	5	198	39.6	3
1961 Phi	2	9	4.5	0	55	2403	43.7	0
1962 Phi	4	40	10.0	1	64	2747	42.9	1
1963 Phi	3	-1	-0.3	0	69	2972	43.1	3
1964 Phi	8	27	3.4	0	24	968	40.3	3
1965 Phi	7	20	2.9	2	19	813	42.8	0
1966 Phi	7	-2	-0.3	0	23	862	37.5	2
1968 Phi-Min	1	1	1.0	0	33	1354	41.0	1
1968 Phi	1	1	1.0	0	0	0	—	1
1968 Min	0	0	—	0	33	1354	41.0	0
1969 StL	0	0	—	0	73	2746	37.6	0
NFL Total	88	308	3.5	9	368	15181	41.3	27

IKE HILL Hill, Talmadge L 5′10″, 180 **WR-DB**
Col: Catawba *HS:* Atkins [Winston-Salem, NC] B: 4/15/1947, Winston-Salem, NC *Drafted:* 1970 Round 9 Oak
1971 Buf: Rec 5-55 11.0 1 TD. **1973** ChiB: Pass 1-1 100.0%, 35 35.00; Rush 3-(-14) -4.7; Rec 10-119 11.9. **1974** ChiB: Pass 1-0; Rec 7-109 15.6 1 TD. **Total:** Pass 2-1 50.0%, 35 17.50; Rush 3-(-14) -4.7; Rec 22-283 12.9 2 TD.

		Punt Returns				Kickoff Returns					Tot
Year Team	**G**	**Ret**	**Yds**	**Avg**	**TD**	**Ret**	**Yds**	**Avg**	**TD**	**Fum**	**TD**
1970 Buf	6	19	102	5.4	0	9	165	18.3	0	1	0
1971 Buf	14	14	133	9.5	**1**	12	280	23.3	0	2	2
1973 ChiB	14	36	204	5.7	1	27	637	23.6	1	6	2
1974 ChiB	13	33	183	5.5	0	0	0	—	0	1	1
1976 Mia	2	0	0	—	0	0	0	—	0	0	0
NFL Total	49	102	622	6.1	2	48	1082	22.5	1	10	5

TRAVIS HILL Hill, Travis LaVell 6′2″, 240 **LB**
Col: Nebraska *HS:* Pearland [TX] B: 10/3/1969, Texas City, TX
Drafted: 1993 Round 7 Cle
1994 Cle: 14 G; 6 Pt. **1995** Car-Cle: 7 G. Car: 3 G. Cle: 4 G. **Total:** 21 G; 6 Pt.

BILL HILL Hill, William 5′9″, 172 **DB**
Col: Rutgers *HS:* Howell [Farmingdale, NJ] B: 4/21/1959, Neptune, NJ
1987 Dal: 3 G.

WILL HILL Hill, Willie Jay 6′0″, 200 **DB**
Col: Ranger Coll. TX (J.C.); Bishop *HS:* Vero Beach [FL] B: 3/5/1963, Vero Beach, FL
1988 Cle: 16 G; 1 Sac.

WINSTON HILL Hill, Winston Cordell 6′4″, 270 **OT**
Col: Texas Southern *HS:* Weldon [Gladewater, TX] B: 10/23/1941, Seguin, TX *Drafted:* 1963 Round 11 Bal
1963 NYJ: 13 G. **1964** NYJ: 14 G. **1965** NYJ: 14 G. **1966** NYJ: 14 G. **1967** NYJ: 14 G. **1968** NYJ: 14 G. **1969** NYJ: 14 G. **1970** NYJ: 14 G. **1971** NYJ: 14 G. **1972** NYJ: 14 G. **1973** NYJ: 14 G. **1974** NYJ: 14 G. **1975** NYJ: 14 G. **1976** NYJ: 14 G. **1977** LARm: 3 G. **Total:** 198 G.

IRA HILLARY Hillary, Ira McDonald 5′10″, 190 **WR**
Col: South Carolina *HS:* Strom Thurmond [Edgefield, SC]
B: 11/13/1962, Edgefield, SC *Drafted:* 1985 Round 8 KC
1989 Cin: Rush 1-(-2) -2.0. **Total:** Rush 1-(-2) -2.0.

		Receiving				Punt Returns			
Year Team	**G**	**Rec**	**Yds**	**Avg**	**TD**	**Ret**	**Yds**	**Avg**	**TD**
1987 Cin	11	5	65	13.0	0	0	0	—	0
1988 Cin	16	5	76	15.2	1	17	166	9.8	0
1989 Cin	16	17	162	9.5	1	6	19	3.2	0
1990 Min	3	0	0	—	0	8	45	5.6	0
NFL Total	46	27	303	11.2	2	31	230	7.4	0

	Kickoff Returns				
Year Team	**Ret**	**Yds**	**Avg**	**TD**	**Fum**
1987 Cin	1	15	15.0	0	0
1988 Cin	12	195	16.3	0	0
1989 Cin	14	223	15.9	0	1
1990 Min	1	6	6.0	0	0
NFL Total	28	439	15.7	0	1

JERRY HILLEBRAND Hillebrand, Gerald John 6′3″, 240 **LB**
Col: Colorado *HS:* Central [Davenport, IA] B: 3/28/1940, Davenport, IA
Drafted: 1962 Round 1 NYG
1965 NYG: Scor 6, 0-1 FG. **1968** Pit: Rec 1-27 27.0. **Total:** Rec 1-27 27.0; Scor 18, 0-1 FG.

		Interceptions			
Year Team	**G**	**Int**	**Yds**	**TD**	**Fum**
1963 NYG	14	5	54	1	0
1964 NYG	11	1	9	0	0
1965 NYG	13	2	25	1	1
1966 NYG	11	1	31	1	0
1967 StL	14	0	0	0	0
1968 Pit	14	2	32	0	0
1969 Pit	10	1	14	0	0
1970 Pit	12	2	14	0	1
NFL Total	99	14	179	3	2

BILLY HILLENBRAND Hillenbrand, William Frank 6′0″, 188 **HB-DB-QB**
Col: Indiana *HS:* Memorial [Evansville, IN] B: 3/29/1922, Armstrong, IN
D: 7/14/1994, Indianapolis, IN
AAFC **1946** ChiA: Pass 3-0, 2 Int; Int 3-37. **1947** BalA: Pass 1-0, 1 Int; Int 1-48. **Total:** Pass 4-0, 3 Int; Int 4-85.

Year Team	G	Rushing Att	Yds	Avg	TD	Receiving Rec	Yds	Avg	TD
1946 ChiA	14	50	175	3.5	2	21	315	15.0	4
1947 BalA	13	66	204	3.1	2	39	702	18.0	7
1948 BalA	14	100	510	5.1	7	50	970	19.4	6
AAFC Total	41	216	889	4.1	11	110	1987	18.1	17

Year Team	Punt Returns Ret	Yds	Avg	TD	Kickoff Returns Ret	Yds	Avg	TD	Tot TD
1946 ChiA	13	180	13.8	1	8	220	27.5	1	8
1947 BalA	13	201	15.5	0	18	466	25.9	1	10
1948 BalA	18	231	12.8	0	16	356	22.3	0	13
AAFC Total	44	612	13.9	1	42	1042	24.8	2	31

ANDY HILLHOUSE Hillhouse, Andrew Fitch 6′2″, 190 **WB**
Col: Brown *HS:* Rutherford [NJ] B: 9/15/1896, Willimantic, CT
D: 3/6/1979, Boynton Beach, FL
1921 Buf: 1 G.

DALTON HILLIARD Hilliard, Dalton Andrea 5′8″, 204 **RB**
Col: Louisiana State *HS:* Patterson [LA] B: 1/21/1964, Patterson, LA
Drafted: 1986 Round 2 NO
1986 NO: Pass 3-1 33.3%, 29 9.67 1 TD. **1987** NO: Pass 1-1 100.0%, 23 23.00 1 TD. **1988** NO: Pass 2-1 50.0%, 27 13.50 1 TD. **1989** NO: Pass 1-1 100.0%, 35 35.00 1 TD. **Total:** Pass 7-4 57.1%, 114 16.29 4 TD.

Year Team	G	Rushing Att	Yds	Avg	TD	Receiving Rec	Yds	Avg	TD
1986 NO	16	121	425	3.5	5	17	107	6.3	0
1987 NO	12	123	508	4.1	7	23	264	11.5	1
1988 NO	16	204	823	4.0	5	34	335	9.9	1
1989 NO	16	344	1262	3.7	13	52	514	9.9	5
1990 NO	6	90	284	3.2	0	14	125	8.9	1
1991 NO	10	79	252	3.2	4	21	127	6.0	1
1992 NO	16	115	445	3.9	3	48	465	9.7	4
1993 NO	16	50	165	3.3	2	40	296	7.4	1
NFL Total	108	1126	4164	3.7	39	249	2233	9.0	14

Year Team	Kickoff Returns Ret	Yds	Avg	TD	Fum	Tot TD
1986 NO	0	0	—	0	3	5
1987 NO	10	248	24.8	0	4	8
1988 NO	6	111	18.5	0	3	6
1989 NO	1	20	20.0	0	7	**18**
1990 NO	0	0	—	0	2	1
1991 NO	0	0	—	0	3	5
1992 NO	7	130	18.6	0	6	7
1993 NO	1	17	17.0	0	2	3
NFL Total	25	526	21.0	0	30	53

IKE HILLIARD Hilliard, Isaac Jason 5′11″, 195 **WR**
Col: Florida *HS:* Patterson [LA] B: 4/5/1976, Patterson, LA
Drafted: 1997 Round 1 NYG
1998 NYG: Rush 1-4 4.0. **Total:** Rush 1-4 4.0.

Year Team	G	Receiving Rec	Yds	Avg	TD	Fum
1997 NYG	2	2	42	21.0	0	0
1998 NYG	16	51	715	14.0	2	2
NFL Total	18	53	757	14.3	2	2

RANDY HILLIARD Hilliard, Randy 5′11″, 165 **DB**
Col: Northwestern State-Louisiana *HS:* East Jefferson [Metairie, LA]
B: 2/6/1967, New Orleans, LA *Drafted:* 1990 Round 6 Cle
1990 Cle: 15 G. **1991** Cle: 14 G; Int 1-19; 2 Sac. **1992** Cle: 16 G; 1 Sac. **1993** Cle: 12 G; Int 1-54. **1994** Den: 15 G; Int 2-8. **1995** Den: 12 G. **1996** Den: 13 G; Int 1-27. **1997** Den: 14 G. **1998** ChiB: 9 G. **Total:** 120 G; Int 5-108; 3 Sac.

BILL HILLMAN Hillman, William Joseph 5′11″, 200 **FB-LB**
Col: Tennessee *HS:* Kane [PA] B: 11/11/1921, Erie, PA D: 1952
Drafted: 1947 Round 27 Det
1947 Det: 2 G; Rush 2-0; Rec 1-25 25.0; KR 1-15 15.0.

KENO HILLS Hills, Keno J 6′6″, 305 **OT-OG**
Col: Kent State; Southwestern Louisiana *HS:* Tampa Bay Tech [FL]
B: 6/13/1973, Tampa, FL *Drafted:* 1996 Round 6 NO
1996 NO: 1 G. **1997** NO: 9 G. **1998** NO: 12 G. **Total:** 22 G.

HAL HILPERT Hilpert, Harold 5′9″, 188 **OE-DE-WB-DB**
Col: Oklahoma City *HS:* Central [Oklahoma City, OK] B: 1908
1930 NYG: 10 G. **1933** Cin: 1 G. **Total:** 11 G.

CARL HILTON Hilton, Carl Patrick 6′3″, 232 **TE**
Col: Houston *HS:* Ball [Galveston, TX] B: 2/28/1964, Galveston, TX
Drafted: 1986 Round 7 Min
1986 Min: 16 G. **1987** Min: 11 G; Rec 2-16 8.0 2 TD; KR 1-13 13.0; 12 Pt. **1988** Min: 8 G; Rec 1-1 1.0 1 TD; 6 Pt. **1989** Min: 1 G. **Total:** 36 G; Rec 3-17 5.7 3 TD; KR 1-13 13.0; 18 Pt.

JOHN HILTON Hilton, John Justin 6′5″, 225 **TE**
Col: Richmond *HS:* Hermitage [Richmond, VA] B: 3/12/1942, Albany, NY *Drafted:* 1964 Round 6 Det
1966 Pit: KR 1-0. **1967** Pit: Rush 1-15 15.0; KR 1-0. **1968** Pit: KR 1-9 9.0. **Total:** Rush 1-15 15.0; KR 3-9 3.0.

Year Team	G	Receiving Rec	Yds	Avg	TD	Fum
1965 Pit	14	4	32	8.0	0	0
1966 Pit	14	46	603	13.1	4	1
1967 Pit	13	26	343	13.2	5	0
1968 Pit	14	20	285	14.3	1	0
1969 Pit	11	12	231	19.3	0	0
1970 GB	14	25	350	14.0	4	1
1971 Min	7	0	0	—	0	0
1972 Det	5	5	133	26.6	1	0
1973 Det	14	6	70	11.7	1	0
NFL Total	106	144	2047	14.2	16	2

ROY HILTON Hilton, Roy Lee 6′6″, 240 **DE**
(Bullet) *Col:* Jackson State *HS:* Parrish [Hazelhurst, MS]
B: 3/23/1943, Georgetown, MS *Drafted:* 1965 Round 15 Bal
1965 Bal: 14 G. **1966** Bal: 14 G. **1967** Bal: 14 G. **1968** Bal: 14 G; Int 1-13 1 TD; 6 Pt. **1969** Bal: 14 G. **1970** Bal: 14 G. **1971** Bal: 14 G. **1972** Bal: 14 G. **1973** Bal: 13 G. **1974** NYG: 14 G; 1 Fum TD; 6 Pt. **1975** Atl: 12 G. **Total:** 151 G; Int 1-13 1 TD; 1 Fum TD; Tot TD 2; 12 Pt.

SCOTT HILTON Hilton, Scott 6′4″, 230 **LB**
Col: Salem (NC) *HS:* Upper Moreland [Willow Grove, PA]
B: 5/28/1954, Harrisburg, PA
1979 SF: 7 G. **1980** SF: 13 G. **Total:** 20 G.

DICK HIMES Himes, Richard Dean 6′4″, 244 **OT**
Col: Ohio State *HS:* Canton South [OH] B: 5/25/1946, Canton, OH
Drafted: 1968 Round 3 GB
1968 GB: 14 G. **1969** GB: 14 G. **1970** GB: 11 G; KR 1-4 4.0. **1971** GB: 14 G. **1972** GB: 14 G. **1973** GB: 14 G. **1974** GB: 13 G. **1975** GB: 14 G. **1976** GB: 14 G. **1977** GB: 13 G. **Total:** 135 G; KR 1-4 4.0.

CURLY HINCHMAN Hinchman, Hubert Edward 5′10″, 190 **FB-TB-LB-BB**
Col: Butler *HS:* Greenfield [IN] B: 11/12/1907 D: 1/9/1968, Anderson, IN
1933 ChiC: Pass 4-2 50.0%, 33 8.25; Rec 1-9 9.0. **1934** ChiC-Det: Rec 1-18 18.0. Det: Rec 1-18 18.0. **Total:** Pass 4-2 50.0%, 33 8.25; Rec 2-27 13.5.

Year Team	G	Rushing Att	Yds	Avg	TD
1933 ChiC	10	49	156	3.2	0
1934 ChiC-Det	12	10	15	1.5	0
1934 ChiC	9	10	15	1.5	0
1934 Det	3	0	0	—	0
NFL Total	22	59	171	2.9	0

STAN HINDMAN Hindman, Stanley Chatham 6′3″, 235 **DE-DT**
Col: Mississippi *HS:* Newton [MS] B: 3/1/1944, Houlton, ME
Drafted: 1966 Round 1 SF
1966 SF: 14 G; KR 1-2 2.0. **1967** SF: 13 G. **1968** SF: 14 G; Int 1-25 1 TD; 6 Pt. **1969** SF: 10 G. **1970** SF: 8 G. **1971** SF: 9 G. **1974** SF: 8 G. **Total:** 76 G; KR 1-2 2.0; Int 1-25 1 TD; 6 Pt.

ANDRE HINES Hines, Andre Pierre 6′6″, 275 **OT**
Col: Stanford *HS:* St. Mary's Prep [Berkeley, CA] B: 2/28/1958, Oakland, CA *Drafted:* 1980 Round 2 Sea
1980 Sea: 9 G.

GLEN RAY HINES Hines, Glen Ray 6′5″, 265 **OT**
Col: Arkansas *HS:* El Dorado [AR] B: 10/26/1943, El Dorado, AR
Drafted: 1965 Redshirt Round 2 Hou
1966 Hou: 14 G. **1967** Hou: 14 G. **1968** Hou: 14 G. **1969** Hou: 14 G. **1970** Hou: 14 G. **1971** NO: 14 G. **1972** NO: 14 G. **1973** Pit: 14 G. **Total:** 112 G.

JIMMY HINES Hines, James 6′0″, 175 **WR**
Col: Texas Southern *HS:* McClymonds [Oakland, CA] B: 9/10/1946, Dumas, AR *Drafted:* 1968 Round 6 Mia
1969 Mia: 9 G; Rush 1-7 7.0; Rec 2-23 11.5; KR 1-22 22.0; 1 Fum. **1970** KC: 1 G. **Total:** 10 G; Rush 1-7 7.0; Rec 2-23 11.5; KR 1-22 22.0; 1 Fum.

BRYAN HINKLE Hinkle, Bryan Eric 6′1″, 222 **LB**
Col: Oregon *HS:* Central Kitsap [Silverdale, WA] B: 6/4/1959, Long Beach, CA *Drafted:* 1981 Round 6 Pit
1982 Pit: 1 Sac. **1984** Pit: 1 Fum TD; 5.5 Sac. **1985** Pit: 5 Sac. **1986** Pit: 4.5 Sac. **1987** Pit: 2 Sac. **1988** Pit: 0.5 Sac. **1990** Pit: 2 Sac. **1991** Pit: 2 Sac. **Total:** 1 Fum TD; 22.5 Sac.

Year Team	G	Interceptions Int	Yds	TD	Fum	Tot TD
1982 Pit	9	0	0	0	0	0
1983 Pit	16	1	14	1	0	1

1984 Pit	15	3	77	0	0	1
1985 Pit	14	0	0	0	0	0
1986 Pit	16	3	7	0	0	0
1987 Pit	12	3	15	0	1	0
1988 Pit	13	1	1	0	0	0
1989 Pit	13	1	4	0	0	0
1990 Pit	16	1	19	0	0	0
1991 Pit	14	2	68	1	0	1
1992 Pit	13	0	0	0	0	0
1993 Pit	12	0	0	0	0	0
NFL Total	163	15	205	2	1	3

GEORGE HINKLE Hinkle, George Allen Jr. 6′4″, 273 **DE-NT-DT**
Col: Arizona *HS:* Pacific [MO] B: 3/17/1965, St. Louis, MO
Drafted: 1988 Round 11 SD
1988 SD: 3 G; 3 Sac. **1989** SD: 14 G; 2.5 Sac. **1990** SD: 16 G; 0.5 Sac. **1991** SD: 13 G; 0.5 Sac. **1992** Min: 9 G. **1993** Cin: 13 G; 1 Sac. **Total:** 68 G; 7.5 Sac.

JACK HINKLE Hinkle, John M 6′0″, 195 **HB-DB-BB-LB**
Col: Syracuse *HS:* Milton [PA] B: 10/31/1917, Milton, PA
1940 NYG: Rec 3-23 7.7. **1941** Phi: KR 1-5 5.0. **1943** PhPt: Rec 1-3 3.0; PR 4-45 11.3; KR 11-217 19.7; Int 4-98; Punt 4-78 19.5; **1** Fum TD. **1944** Phi: Rec 2-34 17.0; PR 4-32 8.0; KR 6-134 22.3; Int 2-62 1 TD. **1945** Phi: Rec 1-8 8.0; PR 3-28 9.3; KR 1-17 17.0; Int 1-17. **1946** Phi: PR 1-4 4.0; KR 1-25 25.0; Int 2-37. **Total:** Rec 7-68 9.7; PR 12-109 9.1; KR 20-398 19.9; Int 9-214 1 TD; Punt 4-78 19.5; 1 Fum TD.

		Rushing					Tot
Year Team	**G**	**Att**	**Yds**	**Avg**	**TD**	**Fum**	**TD**
1940 NYG	3	0	0	—	0	0	0
1941 Phi	1	0	0	—	0	0	0
1943 PhPt	10	116	571	4.9	3	0	4
1944 Phi	10	92	421	4.6	2	0	3
1945 Phi	3	11	40	3.6	0	1	0
1946 Phi	10	18	33	1.8	0	0	0
1947 Phi	3	1	2	2.0	0	0	0
NFL Total	40	238	1067	4.5	5	1	7

CLARKE HINKLE Hinkle, William Clarke 5′11″, 202 **FB-LB-HB-DB**
Col: Bucknell *HS:* Toronto [OH] B: 4/10/1909, Toronto, OH
D: 11/9/1988, Steubenville, OH *HOF:* 1964
1940 GB: Int 2-11. **1941** GB: PR 2-61 30.5; KR 3-38 12.7; Int 1-2. **Total:** PR 2-61 30.5; KR 3-38 12.7; Int 3-13.

		Passing							
Year Team	**G**	**Att**	**Comp**	**Comp%**	**Yds**	**YPA**	**TD**	**Int**	**Rating**
1932 GB	13	1	1	100.0	23	23.00	0	0	118.8
1933 GB	13	27	12	44.4	147	5.44	0	3	22.2
1934 GB	12	19	9	47.4	87	4.58	0	2	21.1
1935 GB	9	0	0	—	0	—	0	0	—
1936 GB	12	2	1	50.0	10	5.00	0	0	64.6
1937 GB	11	3	2	66.7	43	14.33	0	0	109.7
1938 GB	11	2	1	50.0	6	3.00	0	0	56.3
1939 GB	11	0	0	—	0	—	0	0	—
1940 GB	10	0	0	—	0	—	0	0	—
1941 GB	11	0	0	—	0	—	0	0	—
NFL Total	113	54	26	48.1	316	5.85	0	5	28.0

	Rushing				Receiving			
Year Team	**Att**	**Yds**	**Avg**	**TD**	**Rec**	**Yds**	**Avg**	**TD**
1932 GB	95	331	3.5	3	0	0	—	0
1933 GB	139	413	3.0	4	6	38	6.3	0
1934 GB	144	359	2.5	1	11	113	10.3	1
1935 GB	77	273	3.5	2	1	-4	-4.0	0
1936 GB	100	476	4.8	5	0	0	—	0
1937 GB	129	552	4.3	**5**	8	116	14.5	2
1938 GB	114	299	2.6	3	7	98	14.0	4
1939 GB	135	381	2.8	5	4	70	17.5	0
1940 GB	109	383	3.5	2	4	28	7.0	1
1941 GB	**129**	393	3.0	5	8	78	9.8	1
NFL Total	1171	3860	3.3	35	49	537	11.0	9

	Punting		
Year Team	**Punts**	**Yds**	**Avg**
1939 GB	43	1751	40.7
1940 GB	22	819	37.2
1941 GB	22	980	44.5
NFL Total	87	3550	40.8

	Scoring							Tot
Year Team	**Pts**	**FG**	**FGA**	**FG%**	**XK**	**XKA**	**XK%**	**TD**
1932 GB	19	0	—	—	1	—	—	3
1933 GB	30	2	—	—	0	—	—	4
1934 GB	27	3	—	—	6	—	—	2
1935 GB	18	2	—	—	0	—	—	2
1936 GB	31	0	—	—	1	—	—	5
1937 GB	57	2	—	—	9	—	—	**7**
1938 GB	**58**	3	9	33.3	7	8	87.5	7
1939 GB	35	1	10	10.0	2	3	66.7	5
1940 GB	48	**9**	**14**	**64.3**	3	3	**100.0**	3
1941 GB	56	**6**	**14**	42.9	2	2	100.0	6
NFL Total	379	28	47	40.4	31	16	87.5	44

MIKE HINNANT Hinnant, Michael Wesley 6′3″, 268 **TE**
Col: Temple *HS:* Spingarn [Washington, DC] B: 9/8/1966, Washington, DC *Drafted:* 1988 Round 8 Pit
1988 Pit: 16 G; Rec 1-23 23.0. **1989** Pit: 5 G; KR 1-13 13.0. **1992** Det: 15 G; Rec 3-28 9.3. **Total:** 36 G; Rec 4-51 12.8; KR 1-13 13.0.

HAL HINTE Hinte, Harold Hale 6′1″, 195 **DE**
Col: Pittsburgh *HS:* Mount Hope [WV] B: 1/25/1920, Pittsburgh, PA
D: 2/3/1996, Jacksonville, FL
1942 GB-Pit: 4 G. GB: 1 G. Pit: 3 G. **Total:** 4 G.

CHUCK HINTON Hinton, Charles Dudley 6′5″, 260 **DT**
Col: North Carolina Central *HS:* Ligon [Raleigh, NC] B: 8/11/1939, Raleigh, NC D: 1/30/1999, Raleigh, NC *Drafted:* 1962 Round 2 Cle
1964 Pit: 14 G; Int 1-8 1 TD; 6 Pt. **1965** Pit: 14 G. **1966** Pit: 14 G. **1967** Pit: 14 G; **1** Fum TD; 6 Pt. **1968** Pit: 14 G. **1969** Pit: 14 G; Int 1-7; 1 Fum. **1970** Pit: 14 G. **1971** NYJ: 12 G. **1972** Bal: 13 G. **Total:** 123 G; Int 2-15 1 TD; 1 Fum TD; Tot TD 2; 12 Pt; 1 Fum.

CHUCK HINTON Hinton, Charles Richard 6′2″, 235 **C**
Col: Mississippi *HS:* Crosby [MS] B: 12/6/1942, Wilkinson, MS
Drafted: 1964 Round 15 NYG
1967 NYG: 10 G. **1968** NYG: 14 G; KR 1-12 12.0. **1969** NYG: 8 G; 1 Fum. **Total:** 32 G; KR 1-12 12.0; 1 Fum.

CHRIS HINTON Hinton, Christopher Jerrod 6′4″, 300 **OG-OT**
Col: Northwestern *HS:* Wendell Phillips [Chicago, IL] B: 7/31/1961, Chicago, IL *Drafted:* 1983 Round 1 Den
1983 Bal: 16 G. **1984** Ind: 6 G. **1985** Ind: 16 G. **1986** Ind: 16 G. **1987** Ind: 12 G. **1988** Ind: 14 G; Rec 1-1 1.0. **1989** Ind: 14 G. **1990** Atl: 15 G. **1991** Atl: 16 G. **1992** Atl: 16 G; Rec 1-(-2) -2.0. **1993** Atl: 16 G; Rec 1-(-8) -8.0. **1994** Min: 16 G. **1995** Min: 4 G. **Total:** 177 G; Rec 3-(-9) -3.0.

EDDIE HINTON Hinton, Edward Gerald 6′0″, 200 **WR**
Col: Oklahoma *HS:* Lawton [OK] B: 6/26/1947, Lawton, OK
Drafted: 1969 Round 1 Bal
1969 Bal: Rush 1-(-3) -3.0; KR 1-24 24.0. **1970** Bal: Rush 5-58 11.6 2 TD. **1971** Bal: Rush 4-56 14.0. **1973** Hou: Rush 1-(-2) -2.0; KR 8-141 17.6. **1974** NE: Rush 1-1 1.0; PR 1-0; KR 3-83 27.7. **Total:** Rush 12-110 9.2 2 TD; PR 1-0; KR 12-248 20.7.

		Receiving					Tot
Year Team	**G**	**Rec**	**Yds**	**Avg**	**TD**	**Fum**	**TD**
1969 Bal	12	13	269	20.7	1	0	1
1970 Bal	13	47	733	15.6	5	0	7
1971 Bal	14	25	436	17.4	2	0	2
1972 Bal	8	11	146	13.3	1	1	1
1973 Hou	11	13	202	15.5	1	1	1
1974 NE	9	2	36	18.0	0	1	0
NFL Total	67	111	1822	16.4	10	3	12

GRASSY HINTON Hinton, H.W. 6′0″, 185 **BB-TB**
Col: Texas Christian *HS:* Cleburne [TX] B: 6/30/1907 D: 12/10/1944, East Indies
1932 SI: 12 G; Pass 19-5 26.3%, 46 2.42 2 Int; Rush 19-64 3.4 1 TD; Rec 4-69 17.3; 6 Pt.

MARCUS HINTON Hinton, Marcus 6′4″, 260 **TE**
Col: Alcorn State *HS:* Stone [Wiggins, MS] B: 12/27/1971, Wiggins, MS
1996 Oak: 2 G.

MIKE HINTZ Hintz, Michael Kerry 6′1″, 190 **DB**
Col: Wis.-Platteville *HS:* South [Waukesha, WI] B: 8/8/1965, Eau Claire, WI
1987 ChiB: 3 G.

SAM HIPA Hipa, Samuel Vincent Kilaukea 5′11″, 165 **OE**
Col: Dayton *HS:* St. Louis [Honolulu, HI] B: 10/12/1900, Mapulhu, HI
D: 10/17/1961
1927 Day: 1 G. **1928** Day: 4 G. **Total:** 5 G.

I.M. HIPP Hipp, Isiah Moses Walter 5′11″, 201 **RB**
Col: Nebraska *HS:* Chapin [SC] B: 2/15/1956, Chapin, SC
Drafted: 1980 Round 4 Atl
1980 Oak: 1 G.

ERIC HIPPLE Hipple, Eric Ellsworth 6′2″, 196 **QB**
Col: Utah State *HS:* Earl Warren [Downey, CA] B: 9/16/1957, Lubbock, TX *Drafted:* 1980 Round 4 Det

		Passing							
Year Team	**G**	**Att**	**Comp**	**Comp%**	**Yds**	**YPA**	**TD**	**Int**	**Rating**
1980 Det	15	0	0	—	0	—	0	0	—
1981 Det	16	279	140	50.2	2358	8.45	14	15	73.4
1982 Det	9	86	36	41.9	411	4.78	2	4	45.3
1983 Det	16	387	204	52.7	2577	6.66	12	18	64.7
1984 Det	8	38	16	42.1	246	6.47	1	1	62.0

1985 Det	16	406	223	54.9	2952	7.27	17	18	73.6
1986 Det	16	305	192	**63.0**	1919	6.29	9	11	75.6
1988 Det	5	27	12	44.4	158	5.85	0	0	63.5
1989 Det	1	18	7	38.9	90	5.00	0	3	15.7
NFL Total	102	1546	830	53.7	10711	6.93	55	70	68.7

	Rushing				
Year Team	Att	Yds	Avg	TD	Fum
1981 Det	41	168	4.1	7	**14**
1982 Det	10	57	5.7	0	1
1983 Det	41	171	4.2	3	12
1984 Det	2	3	1.5	0	0
1985 Det	32	89	2.8	2	13
1986 Det	16	46	2.9	0	7
1988 Det	1	5	5.0	0	0
1989 Det	2	11	5.5	1	0
NFL Total	145	550	3.8	13	47

CLAUDE HIPPS Hipps, Claude Marion 6′1″, 189 **DB**
Col: Georgia *HS:* Waycross [GA] B: 4/21/1927, Hazlehurst, GA
Drafted: 1952 Round 7 Pit
1952 Pit: 12 G; Int 3-48. **1953** Pit: 5 G; Int 2-0. **Total:** 17 G; Int 5-48.

DOUG HIRE Hire, Douglas 6′2″, 245 **C**
Col: Linfield *HS:* Pearl City [HI] B: 4/22/1965
1987 Sea: 3 G.

BUCKETS HIRSCH Hirsch, Edward Norman 5′10″, 207 **LB-FB**
Col: Northwestern *HS:* Williamsville [NY] B: 3/26/1921, Clarence, NY
AAFC **1947** BufA: 14 G; Rush 4-7 1.8; Int 3-73 1 TD; 6 Pt. **1948** BufA: 13 G. **1949** BufA: 7 G. **Total:** 34 G; Rush 4-7 1.8; Int 3-73 1 TD; 6 Pt.

CRAZY LEGS HIRSCH Hirsch, Elroy Leon 6′2″, 190 **OE-HB-DE**
Col: Wisconsin; Michigan *HS:* Wausau [WI] B: 6/17/1923, Wausau, WI
Drafted: 1945 Round 1 Cle *HOF:* 1968
AAFC **1946** ChiA: Pass 20-12 60.0%, 156 7.80 1 TD 2 Int; PR 17-235 13.8 1 TD; KR 14-384 27.4 1 TD; Int 6-97; Scor 36, 0-1 XK. **1947** ChiA: Pass 1-0; PR 2-24 12.0; KR 6-172 28.7. **1948** ChiA: PR 2-27 13.5; KR 1-10 10.0; Int 2-59. **Total:** Pass 21-12 57.1%, 156 7.43 1 TD 2 Int; PR 21-286 13.6 1 TD; KR 21-566 27.0 1 TD; Int 8-156; Scor 66, 0-1 XK.

		Rushing				Receiving				Tot
Year Team	G	Att	Yds	Avg	TD	Rec	Yds	Avg	TD	TD
1946 ChiA	14	87	226	2.6	1	27	347	12.9	3	6
1947 ChiA	5	23	51	2.2	1	10	282	28.2	3	4
1948 ChiA	5	23	93	4.0	0	7	101	14.4	1	1
AAFC Total	24	133	370	2.8	2	44	730	16.6	7	11

NFL **1949** LARm: Int 2-55. **1950** LARm: Pass 1-0; Int 4-28; Scor 47, 5-5 100.0% XK. **1951** LARm: Scor **102**, 0-1 XK. **1953** LARm: Scor 28, 4-5 80.0% XK. **1954** LARm: Int 1-12. **Total:** Pass 1-0; Int 7-95; Scor 339, 9-11 81.8% XK.

		Rushing				Receiving					Tot
Year Team	G	Att	Yds	Avg	TD	Rec	Yds	Avg	TD	Fum	TD
1949 LARm	12	68	287	4.2	1	22	326	14.8	4	4	6
1950 LARm	12	2	19	9.5	0	42	687	16.4	7	0	7
1951 LARm	12	1	3	3.0	0	**66**	**1495**	**22.7**	**17**	0	**17**
1952 LARm	10	0	0	—	0	25	590	**23.6**	4	0	4
1953 LARm	12	1	-6	-6.0	0	61	941	15.4	4	2	4
1954 LARm	12	1	6	6.0	0	35	720	20.6	3	1	3
1955 LARm	9	0	0	—	0	25	460	18.4	2	0	2
1956 LARm	12	0	0	—	0	35	603	17.2	6	0	6
1957 LARm	12	1	8	8.0	0	32	477	14.9	6	0	6
NFL Total	103	74	317	4.3	1	343	6299	18.4	53	7	55

STEVE HIRSCH Hirsch, Steven Wendell 6′0″, 195 **DB**
Col: Northern Illinois *HS:* Lahser [Bloomfield Hills, MI] B: 5/18/1962, Pontiac, MI
1987 Det: 3 G.

JIMMY HITCHCOCK Hitchcock, Jimmy Davis Jr. 5′10″, 190 **DB**
Col: North Carolina *HS:* Concord [NC] B: 11/9/1970, Concord, NC
Drafted: 1995 Round 3 NE

		Interceptions		
Year Team	G	Int	Yds	TD
1995 NE	8	0	0	0
1996 NE	13	2	14	0
1997 NE	15	2	104	1
1998 Min	16	7	**242**	**3**
NFL Total	52	11	360	4

RAY HITCHCOCK Hitchcock, Raebern Brooks 6′2″, 289 **C**
Col: Minnesota *HS:* Johnson [St. Paul, MN] B: 6/20/1965, St. Paul, MN *Drafted:* 1987 Round 12 Was
1987 Was: 5 G.

BILL HITCHCOCK Hitchcock, William Frederick 6′6″, 296 **OT-OG**
Col: Purdue *HS:* Lindsay Place [Montreal, Canada] B: 8/26/1965, Kirkland, Canada *Drafted:* 1990 Round 8 Sea
1991 Sea: 16 G. **1992** Sea: 16 G. **1993** Sea: 14 G. **1994** Sea: 5 G. **Total:** 51 G.

JOEL HITT Hitt, Joel Reuben Jr. 6′1″, 180 **OE-DE**
Col: Mississippi College *HS:* Clinton [MS] B: 12/30/1912, Clinton, MS
Drafted: 1939 Round 13 Cle
1939 Cle: 3 G; Rush 1-3 3.0; Rec 4-51 12.8.

BILLY HIX Hix, Stewart William 6′2″, 215 **OE**
Col: Arkansas *HS:* Batesville [AR] B: 1/18/1929, Batesville, AR
Drafted: 1950 Round 14 Phi
1950 Phi: 11 G; Rec 2-25 12.5.

TERRY HOAGE Hoage, Terrell Lee 6′3″, 199 **DB**
Col: Georgia *HS:* Huntsville [TX] B: 4/11/1962, Ames, IA
Drafted: 1984 Round 3 NO
1985 NO: 1 Sac. **1987** Phi: 1 Sac. **1988** Phi: Rush 1-38 38.0 1 TD; 2 Sac. **1990** Phi: 1 Sac. **1994** Ariz: 1 Sac. **1995** Ariz: 1 Sac. **Total:** Rush 1-38 38.0 1 TD; 7 Sac.

		Interceptions			Tot
Year Team	G	Int	Yds	TD	TD
1984 NO	14	0	0	0	0
1985 NO	16	4	79	**1**	1
1986 Phi	16	1	18	0	0
1987 Phi	11	2	3	0	0
1988 Phi	16	8	116	0	1
1989 Phi	6	0	0	0	0
1990 Phi	16	1	0	0	0
1991 Was	6	0	0	0	0
1993 SF-Hou	7	0	0	0	0
1993 SF	4	0	0	0	0
1993 Hou	3	0	0	0	0
1994 Ariz	16	3	64	0	0
1995 Ariz	12	2	0	0	0
1996 Ariz	5	0	0	0	0
NFL Total	141	21	280	1	2

FRED HOAGLIN Hoaglin, George Frederick Jr. 6′4″, 250 **C**
Col: Pittsburgh *HS:* East Palestine [OH] B: 1/28/1944, Alliance, OH
Drafted: 1966 Round 6 Cle
1966 Cle: 6 G. **1967** Cle: 14 G; 1 Fum. **1968** Cle: 14 G. **1969** Cle: 14 G; 1 Fum. **1970** Cle: 14 G. **1971** Cle: 11 G. **1972** Cle: 14 G. **1973** Bal: 14 G; 1 Fum. **1974** Hou: 14 G. **1975** Hou: 14 G; 1 Fum. **1976** Sea: 13 G; 1 Fum. **Total:** 142 G; 5 Fum.

JOE HOAGUE Hoague, Joseph Daniell 6′2″, 203 **FB-DB-LB**
Col: Colgate *HS:* Gov. Plumer [Deerfield, NH] B: 2/8/1918, Brookline, MA D: 1/4/1991, Lakeville, MA *Drafted:* 1941 Round 11 Phi
1941 Pit: Pass 1-0; Rec 2-21 10.5 1 TD; KR 1-17 17.0; Punt 17-631 37.1. **1942** Pit: Pass 1-0; Int 1-15; Punt 2-88 44.0. **1946** Bos: Rec 1-4 4.0; Int 1-8. **Total:** Pass 2-0; Rec 3-25 8.3 1 TD; KR 1-17 17.0; Int 2-23; Punt 19-719 37.8.

		Rushing				Tot
Year Team	G	Att	Yds	Avg	TD	TD
1941 Pit	10	33	112	3.4	1	2
1942 Pit	11	65	168	2.6	1	1
1946 Bos	7	1	2	2.0	0	0
NFL Total	28	99	282	2.8	2	3

DICK HOAK Hoak, Richard John 5′11″, 195 **RB**
Col: Penn State *HS:* Jeannette [PA] B: 12/8/1939, Jeannette, PA
Drafted: 1961 Round 7 Pit
1961 Pit: Pass 3-1 33.3%, 13 4.33 1 TD 1 Int. **1962** Pit: Pass 1-0; KR 2-40 20.0. **1964** Pit: Pass 1-0. **1966** Pit: Pass 6-4 66.7%, 87 14.50 1 TD. **1967** Pit: Pass 8-4 50.0%, 69 8.63 1 TD 1 Int. **1968** Pit: Pass 16-7 43.8%, 188 11.75 1 Int. **1969** Pit: Pass 3-2 66.7%, 30 10.00; PR 1-9 9.0. **1970** Pit: Pass 2-2 100.0%, 40 20.00 1 TD. **Total:** Pass 40-20 50.0%, 427 10.68 4 TD 3 Int; PR 1-9 9.0; KR 2-40 20.0.

		Rushing				Receiving					Tot
Year Team	G	Att	Yds	Avg	TD	Rec	Yds	Avg	TD	Fum	TD
1961 Pit	14	85	302	3.6	0	3	18	6.0	0	1	0
1962 Pit	14	117	442	3.8	4	9	133	14.8	0	3	4
1963 Pit	12	216	679	3.1	6	11	118	10.7	1	4	7
1964 Pit	14	84	258	3.1	2	12	137	11.4	3	2	5
1965 Pit	14	131	426	3.3	5	19	228	12.0	1	6	6
1966 Pit	13	81	212	2.6	1	23	239	10.4	0	3	1
1967 Pit	14	52	142	2.7	1	17	111	6.5	1	2	2
1968 Pit	14	175	858	4.9	3	28	253	9.0	1	5	4
1969 Pit	14	151	531	3.5	2	20	190	9.5	1	4	3
1970 Pit	12	40	115	2.9	1	4	25	6.3	0	1	1
NFL Total	135	1132	3965	3.5	25	146	1452	9.9	8	31	33

LEROY HOARD Hoard, Leroy 5′11″, 225 **RB**
Col: Michigan *HS:* St. Augustine [New Orleans, LA] B: 5/15/1968, New Orleans, LA *Drafted:* 1990 Round 2 Cle
1990 Cle: KR 2-18 9.0. **1992** Cle: KR 2-34 17.0. **1993** Cle: Pass 1-0; KR 13-286 22.0. **1994** Cle: KR 2-30 15.0. **1995** Cle: KR 1-13 13.0. **1996** Bal-Car-Min: KR 1-19 19.0. Car: KR 1-19 19.0. **Total:** Pass 1-0; KR 21-400 19.0.

		Rushing				Receiving					Tot
Year Team	**G**	**Att**	**Yds**	**Avg**	**TD**	**Rec**	**Yds**	**Avg**	**TD**	**Fum**	**TD**
1990 Cle	14	58	149	2.6	3	10	73	7.3	0	6	3
1991 Cle	16	37	154	4.2	2	48	567	11.8	9	1	11
1992 Cle	16	54	236	4.4	0	26	310	11.9	1	3	1
1993 Cle	16	56	227	4.1	0	35	351	10.0	0	4	0
1994 Cle	16	209	890	4.3	5	45	445	9.9	4	8	9
1995 Cle	12	136	547	4.0	0	13	103	7.9	0	5	0
1996 Bal-Car-Min	11	125	492	3.9	3	11	133	12.1	0	3	3
1996 Bal	2	15	61	4.1	0	1	4	4.0	0	0	0
1996 Car	3	5	11	2.2	0	0	0	—	0	0	0
1996 Min	6	105	420	4.0	3	10	129	12.9	0	3	3
1997 Min	12	80	235	2.9	4	11	84	7.6	0	0	4
1998 Min	16	115	479	4.2	9	22	198	9.0	1	1	10
NFL Total	129	870	3409	3.9	26	221	2264	10.2	15	31	41

MIKE HOBAN Hoban, Michael Angel 6′2″, 235 **OG**
Col: Michigan *HS:* Gordon Tech [Chicago, IL] B: 1/19/1952, Chicago, IL
1974 ChiB: 1 G.

JIM HOBBINS Hobbins, James Patrick 6′6″, 275 **OG**
Col: Minnesota *HS:* Preble [Green Bay, WI] B: 6/4/1964, Green Bay, WI
1987 GB: 3 G.

BILL HOBBS Hobbs, Billie Glenn 6′0″, 221 **LB**
Col: Texas A&M *HS:* Tascosa [Amarillo, TX] B: 9/18/1946, Mount Pleasant, TX *Drafted:* 1969 Round 8 Phi
1969 Phi: 14 G. **1970** Phi: 12 G. **1971** Phi: 11 G; 6 Pt. **1972** NO: 6 G. **Total:** 43 G; 6 Pt.

DARYL HOBBS Hobbs, Daryl Ray 6′2″, 175 **WR**
Col: Santa Monica Coll. CA (J.C.); U. of Pacific *HS:* University [Los Angeles, CA] B: 5/23/1968, Victoria, TX
1995 Oak: Pass 1-0; PR 1-10 10.0; KR 1-20 20.0. **1996** Oak: Pass 1-1 100.0%, 7 7.00; PR 10-84 8.4; KR 1-14 14.0. **Total:** Pass 2-1 50.0%, 7 3.50; PR 11-94 8.5; KR 2-34 17.0.

		Receiving				
Year Team	**G**	**Rec**	**Yds**	**Avg**	**TD**	**Fum**
1993 LARd	3	0	0	—	0	0
1994 LARd	10	5	52	10.4	0	0
1995 Oak	16	38	612	16.1	3	0
1996 Oak	16	44	423	9.6	3	4
1997 NO-Sea	14	7	85	12.1	1	1
1997 NO	4	2	41	20.5	1	0
1997 Sea	10	5	44	8.8	0	1
NFL Total	59	94	1172	12.5	7	5

HOMER HOBBS Hobbs, Homer Brown 5′11″, 190 **OG-DG**
Col: Georgia *HS:* Lexington [SC] B: 2/13/1923, Lexington, SC
Drafted: 1949 Round 11 Was
AAFC **1949** SF-A: 12 G.

NFL **1950** SF: 10 G.

STEPHEN HOBBS Hobbs, Stephen 5′11″, 200 **WR**
Col: Copiah-Lincoln CC MS; North Alabama *HS:* Mendenhall [MS]
B: 11/14/1965, Mendenhall, MS
1990 Was: 7 G; Rec 1-18 18.0 1 TD; KR 6-92 15.3; 6 Pt. **1991** Was: 16 G; Rec 3-24 8.0; PR 1-10 10.0; KR 1-16 16.0. **1992** Was: 2 G. **Total:** 25 G; Rec 4-42 10.5 1 TD; PR 1-10 10.0; KR 7-108 15.4; 6 Pt.

MARION HOBBY Hobby, Marion Eugene Jr. 6′4″, 277 **DE**
Col: Tennessee *HS:* Shades Valley [Birmingham, AL] B: 11/7/1966, Birmingham, AL *Drafted:* 1990 Round 3 Min
1990 NE: 16 G; 3 Sac. **1991** NE: 15 G; KR 2-0; 2 Sac. **1992** NE: 11 G; KR 1-11 11.0. **Total:** 42 G; KR 3-11 3.7; 5 Sac.

BILLY JOE HOBERT Hobert, Billy Joe 6′3″, 230 **QB**
Col: Washington *HS:* Puyallup [WA] B: 1/8/1971, Puyallup, WA
Drafted: 1993 Round 3 LARd
1995 Oak: Rush 3-5 1.7. **1996** Oak: Rush 2-13 6.5; Punt 9-371 41.2. **1997** Buf-NO: Rush 14-43 3.1. Buf: Rush 2-7 3.5. NO: Rush 12-36 3.0. **1998** NO: Rush 2-13 6.5. **Total:** Rush 21-74 3.5; Punt 9-371 41.2.

		Passing								
Year Team	**G**	**Att**	**Comp**	**Comp%**	**Yds**	**YPA**	**TD**	**Int**	**Rating**	**Fum**
1995 Oak	4	80	44	55.0	540	6.75	6	4	80.2	0
1996 Oak	8	104	57	54.8	667	6.41	4	5	67.3	6
1997 Buf-NO	7	161	78	48.4	1024	6.36	6	10	55.5	3
1997 Buf	2	30	17	56.7	133	4.43	0	2	40.0	1
1997 NO	5	131	61	46.6	891	6.80	6	8	59.0	2
1998 NO	1	23	11	47.8	170	7.39	1	0	87.2	0
NFL Total	20	368	190	51.6	2401	6.52	17	19	66.2	9

LIFFORT HOBLEY Hobley, Liffort Wayne 6′0″, 207 **DB**
Col: Louisiana State *HS:* C.E. Byrd [Shreveport, LA] B: 5/12/1962, Shreveport, LA *Drafted:* 1985 Round 3 Pit
1985 StL: 5 G. **1987** Mia: 14 G; Int 2-7; **1** Fum TD; 6 Pt. **1988** Mia: 16 G; **1** Fum TD; 6 Pt. **1989** Mia: 16 G; Int 1-22; 1 Sac. **1990** Mia: 14 G; Int 1-15; 1 Fum; 3 Sac. **1992** Mia: 15 G; 2 Sac. **1993** Mia: 4 G; Int 1-17. **Total:** 84 G; Int 5-61; 2 Fum TD; 12 Pt; 1 Fum; 6 Sac.

FRED HOBSCHEID Hobscheid, Fred John 5′11″, 215 **T-G**
Col: Chicago *HS:* Hyde Park [Chicago, IL] B: 4/20/1904, Chicago, IL D: 4/1967
1926 Rac: 5 G.

BEN HOBSON Hobson, Benjamin Archie 5′10″, 190 **FB-BB-WB**
Col: No College *HS:* McKinley [St. Louis, MO] B: 7/25/1902, Kansas City, KS D: 7/5/1975, Leawood, KS
1926 Buf: 9 G; Rush 1 TD; 6 Pt. **1927** Buf: 5 G. **Total:** 14 G; Rush 1 TD; 6 Pt.

JOHN HOCK Hock, John Joseph 6′2″, 230 **OG-OT**
Col: Santa Clara *HS:* Mount Carmel [Los Angeles, CA] B: 3/7/1927, Pittsburgh, PA *Drafted:* 1950 Round 8 ChiC
1950 ChiC: 12 G; KR 1-5 5.0. **1953** LARm: 9 G. **1955** LARm: 12 G. **1956** LARm: 12 G. **1957** LARm: 12 G. **Total:** 57 G; KR 1-5 5.0.

MERWIN HODEL Hodel, Merwin Luther 6′2″, 205 **FB**
Col: Colorado *HS:* Rockford East [IL] B: 5/27/1931, Rockford, IL
Drafted: 1952 Round 4 NYG
1953 NYG: 2 G; Rush 5-11 2.2; Rec 2-(-15) -7.5; 1 Fum.

FLOYD HODGE Hodge, Floyd 6′0″, 195 **WR**
Col: Los Angeles Valley Coll. CA (J.C.); Utah *HS:* Centennial [Compton, CA] B: 7/18/1959, Compton, CA
1982 Atl: Rush 2-11 5.5; KR 1-23 23.0. **1983** Atl: Pass 2-1 50.0%, 28 14.00 1 Int. **1984** Atl: Rush 2-17 8.5. **Total:** Pass 2-1 50.0%, 28 14.00 1 Int; Rush 4-28 7.0; KR 1-23 23.0.

		Receiving				
Year Team	**G**	**Rec**	**Yds**	**Avg**	**TD**	**Fum**
1982 Atl	9	14	160	11.4	0	0
1983 Atl	12	25	280	11.2	4	0
1984 Atl	12	24	234	9.8	0	1
NFL Total	33	63	674	10.7	4	1

MILFORD HODGE Hodge, Milford 6′3″, 278 **DE-NT**
Col: Washington State *HS:* South San Francisco [CA] B: 3/11/1961, Los Angeles, CA *Drafted:* 1985 Round 8 NE
1986 NO-NE: 7 G; 1 Sac. NO: 1 G. NE: 6 G; 1 Sac. **1987** NE: 12 G; 1 Sac. **1988** NE: 15 G; 1 Sac. **1989** NE: 16 G; KR 2-19 9.5. **Total:** 50 G; KR 2-19 9.5; 3 Sac.

ERIC HODGES Hodges, Eric Neal 6′0″, 190 **WR**
Col: Florida *HS:* Central Philadelphia [Philadelphia, PA] B: 6/3/1964, Philadelphia, PA
1987 KC: 1 G.

HERMAN HODGES Hodges, J. Herman 6′1″, 198 **OE-DE**
(Country) *Col:* Samford *HS:* Geneva Co. [Hartford, AL]
B: 11/22/1914, Ozark, AL
1939 Bkn: 10 G; Rec 4-45 11.3; Int **1** TD; 6 Pt. **1940** Bkn: 9 G; Rec 3-38 12.7. **1941** Bkn: 11 G; Rec 12-128 10.7. **1942** Bkn: 10 G; Rec 4-74 18.5. **Total:** 40 G; Rec 23-285 12.4; Int 1 TD; 6 Pt.

NORM HODGINS Hodgins, Norman Francis Jr. 6′1″, 190 **DB**
Col: Louisiana State *HS:* Rummel [Metairie, LA] B: 3/1/1952, New Orleans, LA *Drafted:* 1974 Round 11 ChiB
1974 ChiB: 14 G; Pass 1-0; Rush 1-3 3.0; PR 2-8 4.0; 3 Fum.

PAT HODGSON Hodgson, Patrick Shannon 6′2″, 190 **WR**
Col: Georgia *HS:* Westminster [SC] B: 1/30/1944, Columbus, GA
1966 Was: 10 G.

TOM HODSON Hodson, Thomas Paul 6′3″, 195 **QB**
Col: Louisiana State *HS:* Central Lafourche [Mathews, LA]
B: 1/28/1967, Mathews, LA *Drafted:* 1990 Round 3 NE
1990 NE: Rush 12-79 6.6. **1991** NE: Rush 4-0. **1992** NE: Rush 5-11 2.2; Rec 1-(-6) -6.0. **Total:** Rush 21-90 4.3; Rec 1-(-6) -6.0.

		Passing								
Year Team	**G**	**Att**	**Comp**	**Comp%**	**Yds**	**YPA**	**TD**	**Int**	**Rating**	**Fum**
1990 NE	7	156	85	54.5	968	6.21	4	5	68.5	5
1991 NE	16	68	36	52.9	345	5.07	1	4	47.7	2
1992 NE	9	91	50	54.9	496	5.45	2	2	68.8	2
1995 NO	4	5	3	60.0	14	2.80	0	0	64.6	0
NFL Total	36	320	174	54.4	1823	5.70	7	11	64.1	9

BOB HOEL Hoel, Robert Malcolm 6′0″, 208 **G-T**
(Hub) *Col:* Pittsburgh *HS:* Evanston Twp. [Evanston, IL] B: 6/5/1913, Alden, MN
1935 Pit: 12 G. **1937** ChiC: 1 G. **1938** ChiC: 4 G. **Total:** 17 G.

DAVID HOELSCHER Hoelscher, David Henry 6′6″, 261 **DE**
Col: Eastern Kentucky *HS:* Versailles [OH] B: 11/27/1975, Coldwater, OH
1998 Was: 1 G.

DICK HOERNER Hoerner, Lester Junior 6′4″, 220 **FB**
Col: Iowa *HS:* Dubuque [IA] B: 7/25/1922, Dubuque, IA
Drafted: 1945 Round 17 Cle
1948 LARm: PR 1-6 6.0; KR 2-35 17.5; Int 1-6. **1949** LARm: Punt 1-43 43.0. **1951** LARm: KR 1-22 22.0. **1952** Dal: KR 1-33 33.0. **Total:** PR 1-6 6.0; KR 4-90 22.5; Int 1-6; Punt 1-43 43.0.

		Rushing				Receiving					Tot
Year Team	G	Att	Yds	Avg	TD	Rec	Yds	Avg	TD	Fum	TD
1947 LARm	4	30	124	4.1	2	1	20	20.0	0	2	2
1948 LARm	12	76	354	4.7	4	18	227	12.6	2	3	6
1949 LARm	12	155	582	3.8	6	17	213	12.5	0	7	6
1950 LARm	12	95	381	4.0	10	26	446	17.2	1	3	11
1951 LARm	12	94	569	6.1	6	8	102	12.8	1	5	7
1952 Dal	11	56	162	2.9	2	10	172	17.2	0	3	2
NFL Total	63	506	2172	4.3	30	80	1180	14.8	4	23	34

BOB HOERNSCHEMEYER Hoernschemeyer, Robert James 5′11″, 194 **HB-TB-DB-WB**
(Hunchy) *Col:* Indiana; Navy *HS:* Elder [Cincinnati, OH] B: 9/24/1925, Cincinnati, OH D: 6/17/1980, Detroit, MI *Drafted:* 1947 Round 9 NYG
AAFC **1946** ChiA: Rec 1-11 11.0; PR 6-91 15.2; Int 1-10; Punt 11-484 44.0. **1947** ChiA-BknA: Rec 1-4 4.0 1 TD; PR 1-19 19.0; Int 1-8; Punt 2-56 28.0. **1948** BknA: Rec 11-173 15.7 3 TD; PR 1-3 3.0; Punt 1-40 40.0. **1949** ChiA: PR 1-4 4.0; Punt 4-195 48.8. **Total:** Rec 13-188 14.5 4 TD; PR 9-117 13.0; Int 2-18; Punt 18-775 43.1.

		Passing							
Year Team	G	Att	Comp	Comp%	Yds	YPA	TD	Int	Rating
1946 ChiA	14	193	95	49.2	1266	6.56	14	14	64.4
1947 ChiA-BknA	14	173	73	42.2	926	5.35	4	11	40.8
1948 BknA	14	155	71	45.8	854	5.51	8	15	40.8
1949 ChiA	12	167	69	41.3	1063	6.37	6	11	47.6
AAFC Total	54	688	308	44.8	4109	5.97	32	51	48.9

	Rushing				Kickoff Returns				Tot
Year Team	Att	Yds	Avg	TD	Ret	Yds	Avg	TD	TD
1946 ChiA	111	375	3.4	0	9	275	30.6	0	0
1947 ChiA-BknA	152	704	4.6	5	1	11	11.0	0	6
1948 BknA	110	574	5.2	3	6	138	23.0	0	7
1949 ChiA	133	456	3.4	2	14	373	26.6	0	2
AAFC Total	506	2109	4.2	10	30	797	26.6	0	15

NFL **1950** Det: Pass 4-1 25.0%, 19 4.75 1 TD 1 Int; Punt 4-147 36.8. **1951** Det: Pass 4-2 50.0%, 46 11.50 2 TD; PR 2-16 8.0; KR 3-78 26.0. **1952** Det: Pass 4-2 50.0%, 14 3.50 2 TD 1 Int; KR 1-23 23.0. **1953** Det: Pass 5-2 40.0%, 16 3.20 1 TD 1 Int; KR 1-10 10.0. **1954** Det: Pass 7-3 42.9%, 81 11.57 3 TD 1 Int; KR 4-73 18.3. **1955** Det: Pass 2-1 50.0%, 17 8.50 1 TD 1 Int. **Total:** Pass 26-11 42.3%, 193 7.42 10 TD 5 Int; PR 2-16 8.0; KR 9-184 20.4; Punt 4-147 36.8.

		Rushing				Receiving					Tot
Year Team	G	Att	Yds	Avg	TD	Rec	Yds	Avg	TD	Fum	TD
1950 Det	10	84	471	5.6	1	8	78	9.8	1	1	2
1951 Det	11	132	678	5.1	2	23	263	11.4	3	3	5
1952 Det	10	106	457	4.3	4	17	139	8.2	0	3	4
1953 Det	12	101	482	4.8	7	23	282	12.3	2	3	9
1954 Det	11	94	242	2.6	2	20	153	7.7	1	3	3
1955 Det	5	36	109	3.0	1	5	36	7.2	0	1	1
NFL Total	59	553	2439	4.4	17	96	951	9.9	7	14	24

GEORGE HOEY Hoey, George William 5′10″, 174 **DB**
Col: Michigan *HS:* Central [Flint, MI] B: 11/14/1946, Gaffney, SC
Drafted: 1969 Round 14 Det
1971 StL: 6 G; KR 9-251 27.9 1 TD; 6 Pt. **1972** NE: 12 G; KR 9-210 23.3; Int 1-25; 1 Fum. **1973** NE: 13 G. **1974** SD: 13 G; PR 4-38 9.5; KR 3-73 24.3; Int 1-20; 1 Fum. **1975** Den-NYJ: 6 G. Den: 1 G. NYJ: 5 G. **Total:** 50 G; PR 4-38 9.5; KR 21-534 25.4 1 TD; Int 2-45; 6 Pt; 2 Fum.

PAUL HOFER Hofer, Paul David 6′0″, 195 **RB**
Col: Mississippi *HS:* Christian Brothers [Memphis, TN] B: 5/13/1952, Memphis, TN *Drafted:* 1976 Round 11 SF

		Rushing				Receiving			
Year Team	G	Att	Yds	Avg	TD	Rec	Yds	Avg	TD
1976 SF	14	18	74	4.1	0	4	45	11.3	1
1977 SF	14	34	106	3.1	0	5	46	9.2	0
1978 SF	16	121	465	3.8	7	12	170	14.2	0
1979 SF	15	123	615	5.0	7	58	662	11.4	2
1980 SF	6	60	293	4.9	1	41	467	11.4	2
1981 SF	12	60	193	3.2	1	27	244	9.0	0
NFL Total	77	416	1746	4.2	16	147	1634	11.1	5

	Kickoff Returns					Tot
Year Team	Ret	Yds	Avg	TD	Fum	TD
1976 SF	5	91	18.2	0	1	1
1977 SF	36	871	24.2	0	6	0
1978 SF	18	386	21.4	0	4	7
1979 SF	8	124	15.5	0	3	9
1980 SF	1	2	2.0	0	0	3
1981 SF	0	0	—	0	1	1
NFL Total	68	1474	21.7	0	15	21

GARY HOFFMAN Hoffman, Gary Edward 6′7″, 285 **OT**
Col: Santa Clara *HS:* Christian Brothers [Sacramento, CA]
B: 9/28/1961, Sacramento, CA *Drafted:* 1984 Round 10 GB
1984 GB: 1 G. **1987** SF: 3 G. **Total:** 4 G.

JACK HOFFMAN Hoffman, Jack Howard 6′5″, 234 **DE**
Col: Xavier (Ohio) *HS:* Purcell [Cincinnati, OH] B: 3/11/1930, Cincinnati, OH *Drafted:* 1952 Round 5 ChiB
1952 ChiB: 12 G; Int 1-7. **1955** ChiB: 12 G; Rec 6-86 14.3. **1956** ChiB: 12 G. **1957** ChiB: 12 G. **1958** ChiB: 7 G; Int 1-4. **Total:** 55 G; Rec 6-86 14.3; Int 2-11.

JAKE HOFFMAN Hoffman, Jacob H 5′8″, 188 **FB**
Col: No College *HS:* East Syracuse [NY] B: 7/21/1895, Syracuse, NY
D: 2/11/1977, Jordan, NY
1925 Roch: 4 G.

BILL HOFFMAN Hoffman, Jacob William 5′10″, 227 **G**
Col: Lehigh *HS:* Easton [PA] B: 8/6/1901, Raubsville, PA
D: 6/4/1994, Allentown, PA
1924 Fra: 1 G. **1925** Fra: 19 G. **1926** Fra: 16 G. **Total:** 36 G.

JOHN HOFFMAN Hoffman, John Frederick 6′7″, 260 **DE**
Col: USC; Hawaii *HS:* Western [Anaheim, CA] B: 8/2/1943, Santa Monica, CA
1969 Was: 13 G; **1** Fum TD; 6 Pt. **1970** Was: 13 G. **1971** ChiB: 1 G. **1972** StL-Den: 4 G. StL: 2 G. Den: 2 G. **Total:** 31 G; 1 Fum TD; 6 Pt.

JOHN HOFFMAN Hoffman, John Wilks 6′2″, 215 **FB-LB-DE-OE**
Col: Arkansas *HS:* Little Rock Central [AR] B: 12/8/1925, Little Rock, AR D: 4/15/1987, Little Rock, AR *Drafted:* 1949 Round 5 ChiB
1949 ChiB: KR 10-249 24.9. **1950** ChiB: PR 7-75 10.7; KR 2-52 26.0; Int 1-39 1 TD. **1952** ChiB: KR 2-34 17.0; Int 2-54. **1953** ChiB: KR 2-32 16.0; Int 1-27. **1954** ChiB: PR 1-5 5.0; KR 1-23 23.0. **1955** ChiB: Scor **1** Saf. **Total:** PR 8-80 10.0; KR 17-390 22.9; Int 4-120 1 TD; Scor 1 Saf.

		Rushing				Receiving					Tot
Year Team	G	Att	Yds	Avg	TD	Rec	Yds	Avg	TD	Fum	TD
1949 ChiB	12	53	216	4.1	1	25	373	14.9	2	1	3
1950 ChiB	12	42	154	3.7	0	8	161	20.1	2	1	3
1951 ChiB	12	1	-3	-3.0	0	28	394	14.1	2	0	2
1952 ChiB	4	0	0	—	0	1	9	9.0	0	0	0
1953 ChiB	12	32	95	3.0	3	28	341	12.2	1	2	4
1954 ChiB	12	39	178	4.6	1	28	354	12.6	1	4	2
1955 ChiB	12	94	454	4.8	0	11	153	13.9	1	3	1
1956 ChiB	12	56	272	4.9	2	7	85	12.1	0	2	2
NFL Total	88	317	1366	4.3	7	136	1870	13.8	9	13	17

DALTON HOFFMAN Hoffman, Johnie Dalton 6′0″, 207 **FB**
Col: Baylor *HS:* Ballinger [TX] B: 12/23/1941, Ballinger, TX
1964 Hou: 5 G; Rush 2-3 1.5 1 TD; Rec 1-1 1.0; KR 2-52 26.0; 6 Pt. **1965** Hou: 4 G; Rush 1-11 11.0. **Total:** 9 G; Rush 3-14 4.7 1 TD; Rec 1-1 1.0; KR 2-52 26.0; 6 Pt.

BOB HOFFMAN Hoffman, Wayne Robert 6′1″, 208 **LB-FB-BB**
Col: USC *HS:* Montebello [CA] B: 12/13/1917, Star City, WV
Drafted: 1940 Round 7 Was
AAFC **1949** LA-A: 12 G; Rec 2-21 10.5; KR 1-14 14.0; Int 1-7.

NFL **1940** Was: Int 1-6. **1947** LARm: Rec 2-22 11.0; KR 1-12 12.0; Int 1-14. **1948** LARm: Rec 3-28 9.3 1 TD; KR 2-19 9.5. **Total:** Rec 5-50 10.0 1 TD; KR 3-31 10.3; Int 2-20.

		Rushing					Tot
Year Team	G	Att	Yds	Avg	TD	Fum	TD
1940 Was	8	3	7	2.3	0	0	0
1941 Was	3	1	2	2.0	0	0	0
1946 LARm	10	43	162	3.8	3	0	3
1947 LARm	10	42	159	3.8	3	1	3
1948 LARm	11	22	68	3.1	4	1	5
NFL Total	42	111	398	3.6	10	2	11

DAVE HOFFMANN Hoffmann, David Paul 6′2″, 233 **LB**
Col: Washington *HS:* Pioneer [San Jose, CA] B: 7/24/1970, San Luis Obispo, CA *Drafted:* 1993 Round 6 ChiB
1993 Pit: 1 G.

MARC HOGAN Hogan, Marc Christian 6'0", 180 **DB**
Col: Tennessee *HS:* Brashear [Pittsburgh, PA] B: 4/21/1962, Pittsburgh, PA
1987 NYJ: 3 G; Int 1-5.

MIKE HOGAN Hogan, Michael L 6'2", 213 **RB**
Col: Tennessee-Chattanooga *HS:* East [Rome, GA] B: 11/1/1954, Floyd Co., GA *Drafted:* 1976 Round 9 Phi

		Rushing				Receiving					Tot
Year Team	G	Att	Yds	Avg	TD	Rec	Yds	Avg	TD	Fum	TD
1976 Phi	8	123	561	4.6	0	15	89	5.9	0	4	0
1977 Phi	12	155	546	3.5	0	19	118	6.2	1	6	1
1978 Phi	14	145	607	4.2	4	31	164	5.3	1	5	5
1979 SF	2	9	31	3.4	0	9	65	7.2	0	0	0
1980 Phi-NYG	13	34	90	2.6	2	5	46	9.2	0	0	2
1980 Phi	7	12	44	3.7	1	0	0	—	0	0	1
1980 NYG	6	22	46	2.1	1	5	46	9.2	0	0	1
NFL Total	49	466	1835	3.9	6	79	482	6.1	2	15	8

DARRELL HOGAN Hogan, Darrell 5'10", 210 **LB-OG**
Col: Baylor; Trinity (Tex.) *HS:* Hot Wells [TX] B: 7/2/1926, San Antonio, TX
1949 Pit: 12 G; Int 1-5. **1950** Pit: 12 G; Int 1-3. **1951** Pit: 12 G; Int 1-3. **1952** Pit: 12 G; Int 4-50 1 TD; 6 Pt; 1 Fum. **1953** Pit: 12 G. **Total:** 60 G; Int 7-61 1 TD; 6 Pt; 1 Fum.

PAUL HOGAN Hogan, Paul Timothy 5'8", 170 **WB-TB-BB-FB**
(Midge) *Col:* Notre Dame; Niagara; Washington & Jefferson; Detroit Mercy *HS:* Ashtabula [OH] B: 9/5/1898, Ashtabula, OH
D: 8/13/1976, Las Vegas, NV
1924 Akr: 6 G; Scor 5, 1 FG, 2 XK. **1925** Can: 6 G; Pass 3 TD. **1926** NYG-Fra: 13 G; Scor 5, 5 XK. NYG: 10 G; Scor 3, 3 XK. Fra: 3 G; Scor 2, 2 XK. **1927** ChiC: 1 G; Rush 1 TD; 6 Pt. **Total:** 26 G; Pass 3 TD; Rush 1 TD; Scor 16, 1 FG, 7 XK.

TOM HOGAN Hogan, Thomas Francis 6'2", 200 **T-C-G-E**
Col: Detroit Mercy; Fordham *HS:* Holyoke [MA] B: 4/26/1898, Boston, MA D: 1/27/1975, Boston, MA
1924 Min: 5 G. **1925** Det: 11 G. **1926** ChiC: 1 G. **Total:** 17 G.

MERRIL HOGE Hoge, Merril DuAine 6'2", 225 **RB**
Col: Idaho State *HS:* Highland [Pocatello, ID] B: 1/26/1965, Pocatello, ID *Drafted:* 1987 Round 10 Pit
1987 Pit: KR 1-13 13.0. **1992** Pit: KR 2-28 14.0. **1993** Pit: KR 3-33 11.0. **Total:** KR 6-74 12.3.

		Rushing				Receiving					Tot
Year Team	G	Att	Yds	Avg	TD	Rec	Yds	Avg	TD	Fum	TD
1987 Pit	13	3	8	2.7	0	7	97	13.9	1	0	1
1988 Pit	16	170	705	4.1	3	50	487	9.7	3	8	6
1989 Pit	16	186	621	3.3	8	34	271	8.0	0	2	8
1990 Pit	16	203	772	3.8	7	40	342	8.6	3	6	10
1991 Pit	16	165	610	3.7	2	49	379	7.7	1	3	3
1992 Pit	16	41	150	3.7	0	28	231	8.3	1	3	1
1993 Pit	16	51	249	4.9	1	33	247	7.5	4	0	5
1994 ChiB	5	6	24	4.0	0	13	79	6.1	0	0	0
NFL Total	114	825	3139	3.8	21	254	2133	8.4	13	22	34

GARY HOGEBOOM Hogeboom, Gary Keith 6'4", 205 **QB**
Col: Central Michigan *HS:* Northview [Grand Rapids, MI]
B: 8/21/1958, Grand Rapids, MI *Drafted:* 1980 Round 5 Dal

		Passing							
Year Team	G	Att	Comp	Comp%	Yds	YPA	TD	Int	Rating
1980 Dal	2	0	0	—	0	—	0	0	—
1981 Dal	1	0	0	—	0	—	0	0	—
1982 Dal	4	8	3	37.5	45	5.63	0	1	17.2
1983 Dal	6	17	11	64.7	161	9.47	1	1	90.6
1984 Dal	16	367	195	53.1	2366	6.45	7	14	63.7
1985 Dal	16	126	70	55.6	978	7.76	5	7	70.8
1986 Ind	5	144	85	59.0	1154	8.01	6	6	81.2
1987 Ind	6	168	99	58.9	1145	6.82	9	5	85.0
1988 Ind	9	131	76	58.0	996	7.60	7	7	77.7
1989 Pho	14	364	204	56.0	2591	7.12	14	19	69.5
NFL Total	79	1325	743	56.1	9436	7.12	49	60	71.9

	Rushing				
Year Team	Att	Yds	Avg	TD	Fum
1982 Dal	3	0	0.0	0	2
1983 Dal	6	-10	-1.7	0	0
1984 Dal	15	19	1.3	0	8
1985 Dal	8	48	6.0	1	0
1986 Ind	10	20	2.0	1	3
1987 Ind	3	3	1.0	0	1
1988 Ind	11	-8	-0.7	1	2
1989 Pho	27	89	3.3	1	5
NFL Total	83	161	1.9	4	21

D.D. HOGGARD Hoggard, William Benjamin 6'0", 188 **DB**
Col: North Carolina State *HS:* Bertie County [Windsor, NC]
B: 5/20/1961, Ahoskie, NC
1985 Cle: 2 G. **1986** Cle: 16 G. **1987** Cle: 1 G. **Total:** 19 G.

DOUG HOGLAND Hogland, M. Douglas 6'3", 245 **OG-OT**
(Hogs) *Col:* Oregon State *HS:* Bend [OR] B: 5/8/1931, Farmington, NM *Drafted:* 1953 Round 8 SF
1953 SF: 12 G; Rec 1-(-2) -2.0. **1954** SF: 12 G; KR 1-2 2.0. **1955** SF: 12 G. **1956** ChiC: 12 G. **1957** ChiC: 12 G. **1958** ChiC-Det: 12 G. ChiC: 2 G. Det: 10 G. **Total:** 72 G; Rec 1-(-2) -2.0; KR 1-2 2.0.

FRANK HOGUE Hogue, Francis E **BB-WB**
Col: No College B: 1/19/1899, Cleveland, OH D: 1/10/1967, Holmes Co., OH
1924 Akr: 3 G.

MURRELL HOGUE Hogue, Murrell E 6'1", 208 **T-G**
Col: Centenary *HS:* Powell Training [Shreveport, LA] B: 8/13/1904, Amarillo, TX D: 11/27/1990, Shreveport, LA
1928 NYY: 10 G. **1929** ChiC: 11 G. **1930** Min: 1 G. **Total:** 22 G.

MIKE HOHENSEE Hohensee, Michael Louis 6'0", 205 **QB**
Col: Mount San Antonio Coll. CA (J.C.); Minnesota *HS:* John A. Rowland [Rowland Heights, CA] B: 2/22/1961, Rowland Heights, CA
1987 ChiB: Rush 9-56 6.2.

		Passing								
Year Team	G	Att	Comp	Comp%	Yds	YPA	TD	Int	Rating	Fum
1987 ChiB	2	52	28	53.8	343	6.60	4	1	92.1	2

JOHN HOHMAN Hohman, John Carl 6'1", 245 **OG**
Col: Wisconsin *HS:* Proviso East [Maywood, IL] B: 10/23/1942, Antigo, WI *Drafted:* 1965 Round 8 Den
1965 Den: 10 G. **1966** Den: 14 G. **Total:** 24 G.

BOB HOHN Hohn, Robert Huber 6'0", 185 **DB**
Col: Nebraska *HS:* Beatrice [NE] B: 6/4/1941, Beatrice, NE
Drafted: 1964 Round 20 LARm
1965 Pit: 10 G. **1966** Pit: 4 G. **1967** Pit: 13 G; Int 2-0. **1968** Pit: 8 G. **1969** Pit: 11 G; Int 5-64. **Total:** 46 G; Int 7-64.

AL HOISINGTON Hoisington, Allan G 6'3", 200 **OE**
(Roadrunner) *Col:* Pasadena City Coll. CA (J.C.) *HS:* Van Nuys [CA]
B: 11/18/1933, Chicago, IL
1960 Oak-Buf: 14 G; Rec 8-141 17.6 2 TD; KR 2-25 12.5; 12 Pt. Oak: 9 G; Rec 4-96 24.0 2 TD; KR 2-25 12.5; 12 Pt. Buf: 5 G; Rec 4-45 11.3. **Total:** 14 G; Rec 8-141 17.6 2 TD; KR 2-25 12.5; 12 Pt.

JONATHAN HOKE Hoke, Jonathan David 5'11", 175 **DB**
Col: Ball State *HS:* Fairmont East [Kettering, OH] B: 1/24/1957, Hamilton, OH
1980 ChiB: 11 G.

STEVE HOKUF Hokuf, Stephen Melvin 6'0", 199 **BB-LB-OE-DE**
Col: Nebraska *HS:* Crete [NE] B: 9/26/1910, Wilber, NE
1933 Bos: Rec 2-19 9.5. **1934** Bos: Rec 6-34 5.7; Scor 4, 1 FG, 1 XK. **1935** Bos: Rec 1-1 1.0. **Total:** Rec 9-54 6.0; Scor 4, 1 FG, 1 XK.

		Passing							
Year Team	G	Att	Comp	Comp%	Yds	YPA	TD	Int	Rating
1933 Bos	12	18	8	44.4	105	5.83	0	0	63.4
1934 Bos	10	51	13	25.5	203	3.98	3	10	23.7
1935 Bos	7	1	0	0.0	0	0.00	0	0	39.6
NFL Total	29	70	21	30.0	308	4.40	3	10	20.1

	Rushing			
Year Team	Att	Yds	Avg	TD
1933 Bos	16	56	3.5	0
1934 Bos	25	98	3.9	0
1935 Bos	12	25	2.1	0
NFL Total	53	179	3.4	0

KELLY HOLCOMB Holcomb, Brian Kelly 6'2", 212 **QB**
Col: Middle Tennessee State *HS:* Lincoln Co. [Fayetteville, TN]
B: 7/9/1973, Fayetteville, TN
1997 Ind: Rush 5-5 1.0.

		Passing								
Year Team	G	Att	Comp	Comp%	Yds	YPA	TD	Int	Rating	Fum
1997 Ind	5	73	45	61.6	454	6.22	1	8	44.3	4

TEX HOLCOMB Holcomb, William L 6'2", 235 **T**
Col: Texas Tech *HS:* Sulphur Springs [TX] B: 6/21/1913, Amarillo, TX
D: 5/20/1974, Dallas, TX
1937 Pit-Phi: 8 G. Pit: 7 G. Phi: 1 G. **Total:** 8 G.

ROBERT HOLCOMBE Holcombe, Robert Wayne 5'11", 220 **RB**
Col: Illinois *HS:* Jeff Davis [Houston, TX]; Mesa HS [AZ]
B: 12/11/1975, Houston, TX *Drafted:* 1998 Round 2 StL
1998 StL: Rec 6-34 5.7.

Year Team	G	Rushing Att	Yds	Avg	TD
1998 StL	13	98	230	2.3	2

MIKE HOLD Hold, James Michel Jr. 6'0", 190 **QB**
Col: Mesa CC AZ; South Carolina *HS:* Corona del Sol [Tempe, AZ] B: 3/16/1963, Phoenix, AZ
1987 TB: 2 G; Pass 24-8 33.3%, 123 5.13 2 TD 1 Int; Rush 7-69 9.9.

SAM HOLDEN Holden, Samuel Lee Jr. 6'3", 258 **OT**
Col: Grambling State *HS:* Xavier Prep [New Orleans, LA]; St. Augustine [New Orleans, LA] B: 2/24/1947, Magnolia, MS *Drafted:* 1971 Round 2 NO
1971 NO: 9 G.

STEVE HOLDEN Holden, Steven Anthony 6'0", 195 **WR**
Col: Arizona State *HS:* Gardena [CA] B: 8/2/1951, Los Angeles, CA *Drafted:* 1973 Round 1 Cle
1974 Cle: Rush 1-6 6.0. **1975** Cle: Rush 2-(-4) -2.0. **Total:** Rush 3-2 0.7.

		Receiving				Punt Returns			
Year Team	G	Rec	Yds	Avg	TD	Ret	Yds	Avg	TD
1973 Cle	11	3	27	9.0	0	2	19	9.5	0
1974 Cle	10	30	452	15.1	3	0	0	—	0
1975 Cle	13	21	320	15.2	0	0	0	—	0
1976 Cle	14	8	128	16.0	1	31	205	6.6	0
1977 Cin	6	0	0	—	0	3	14	4.7	0
NFL Total	54	62	927	15.0	4	36	238	6.6	0

	Kickoff Returns				
Year Team	Ret	Yds	Avg	TD	Fum
1973 Cle	8	172	21.5	0	2
1974 Cle	0	0	—	0	1
1975 Cle	0	0	—	0	1
1976 Cle	19	461	24.3	0	3
1977 Cin	2	42	21.0	0	2
NFL Total	29	675	23.3	0	9

LEW HOLDER Holder, Lewis C 6'0", 191 **E**
Col: Texas *HS:* Woodrow Wilson [Dallas, TX] B: 10/10/1923, Dallas, TX
AAFC **1949** LA-A: 12 G; Rush 1-(-1) -1.0; Rec 5-71 14.2.

ERNIE HOLE Hole, Ernest **G**
(Sarp) *Col:* No College B: 1901 Deceased
1920 Mun: 1 G. **1921** Mun: 2 G. **Total:** 3 G.

MICKEY HOLE Hole, Michael 5'9", 180 **TB-FB-WB**
Col: No College B: 2/1892 Deceased
1920 Mun: 1 G. **1921** Mun: 2 G. **Total:** 3 G.

JOHN HOLECEK Holecek, John Francis 6'2", 240 **LB**
Col: Illinois *HS:* Marian Catholic [Steger, IL] B: 5/7/1972, Steger, IL *Drafted:* 1995 Round 5 Buf
1995 Buf: 1 G. **1997** Buf: 14 G; 1.5 Sac. **1998** Buf: 13 G. **Total:** 28 G; 1.5 Sac.

JIM HOLIFIELD Holifield, James Lee 6'3", 195 **DB**
(Rock) *Col:* Jackson State *HS:* Abrams [Bessemer, AL] B: 1/18/1946, Bessemer, AL *Drafted:* 1968 Round 12 NYG
1968 NYG: 14 G; KR 7-111 15.9. **1969** NYG: 14 G; KR 8-156 19.5; Int 1-5; 1 Fum. **Total:** 28 G; KR 15-267 17.8; Int 1-5; 1 Fum.

JOHN HOLIFIELD Holifield, Johnathan Mark 6'0", 202 **RB**
Col: West Virginia *HS:* Romulus [MI] B: 7/14/1964, Wayne, MI *Drafted:* 1987 Round 12 Cin
1989 Cin: 3 G; Rush 11-20 1.8; Rec 2-18 9.0; KR 1-0; 1 Fum.

BOB HOLLADAY Holladay, Robert B 5'11", 175 **DB**
Col: Tulsa *HS:* Columbia [LA] B: 3/13/1932, Shreveport, LA
1956 LARm-SF: 11 G; Int 1-0. LARm: 4 G. SF: 7 G; Int 1-0. **1957** SF: 7 G. **Total:** 18 G; Int 1-0.

DARIUS HOLLAND Holland, Darius Jerome 6'5", 313 **DT-DE**
(D.) *Col:* Colorado *HS:* Mayfield [Las Cruces, NM] B: 11/10/1973, Petersburg, VA *Drafted:* 1995 Round 3 GB
1995 GB: 14 G; 1.5 Sac. **1996** GB: 16 G. **1997** GB: 12 G. **1998** KC-Det: 16 G. KC: 6 G. Det: 10 G. **Total:** 58 G; 1.5 Sac.

JAMIE HOLLAND Holland, Jamie Lorenza 6'1", 192 **WR-RB**
Col: Butler County CC KS; Ohio State *HS:* Rolesville [Wake Forest, NC] B: 2/1/1964, Raleigh, NC *Drafted:* 1987 Round 7 SD
1987 SD: Rush 1-17 17.0. **1988** SD: Rush 3-19 6.3. **1989** SD: Rush 6-46 7.7. **Total:** Rush 10-82 8.2.

		Receiving				Kickoff Returns					Tot
Year Team	G	Rec	Yds	Avg	TD	Ret	Yds	Avg	TD	Fum	TD
1987 SD	12	6	138	23.0	0	19	410	21.6	0	0	0
1988 SD	16	39	536	13.7	1	31	810	26.1	**1**	1	2
1989 SD	16	26	336	12.9	0	29	510	17.6	0	0	0
1990 LARd	16	0	0	—	0	32	655	20.5	0	0	0
1991 LARd	16	0	0	—	0	22	421	19.1	0	0	0
1992 Cle	4	2	27	13.5	0	0	0	—	0	0	0
NFL Total	80	73	1037	14.2	1	133	2806	21.1	1	1	2

JOHN HOLLAND Holland, John Calvin 6'0", 190 **WR**
Col: Tennessee State *HS:* Middletown [OH] B: 2/28/1952, Beckley, WV *Drafted:* 1974 Round 2 Min
1975 Buf: PR 7-53 7.6; KR 4-67 16.8. **1976** Buf: PR 4-11 2.8; KR 4-62 15.5; **1** Fum TD. **Total:** PR 11-64 5.8; KR 8-129 16.1; 1 Fum TD.

		Receiving					Tot
Year Team	G	Rec	Yds	Avg	TD	Fum	TD
1974 Min	10	5	84	16.8	0	0	0
1975 Buf	12	7	144	20.6	1	0	1
1976 Buf	13	15	299	19.9	2	1	3
1977 Buf	3	8	107	13.4	0	1	0
NFL Total	38	35	634	18.1	3	2	4

JOHNNY HOLLAND Holland, Johnny Ray 6'2", 231 **LB**
Col: Texas A&M *HS:* Hempstead [TX] B: 3/11/1965, Bellville, TX *Drafted:* 1987 Round 2 GB
1987 GB: 12 G; Int 2-4; 1 Sac. **1988** GB: 13 G. **1989** GB: 16 G; Int 1-26. **1990** GB: 16 G; Int 1-32. **1991** GB: 16 G. **1992** GB: 14 G; Int 3-27; 2 Fum; 0.5 Sac. **1993** GB: 16 G; Int 2-41; 2 Fum; 2 Sac. **Total:** 103 G; Int 9-130; 4 Fum; 3.5 Sac.

VERN HOLLAND Holland, Vernon Edward 6'5", 268 **OT**
(Suki) *Col:* Tennessee State *HS:* Frederick Douglass [Sherman, TX] B: 6/27/1948, San Antonio, TX D: 4/20/1998, Nashville, TN *Drafted:* 1971 Round 1 Cin
1971 Cin: 14 G. **1972** Cin: 14 G. **1973** Cin: 14 G. **1974** Cin: 3 G. **1975** Cin: 14 G. **1976** Cin: 14 G. **1977** Cin: 14 G. **1978** Cin: 16 G. **1979** Cin: 16 G. **1980** Det-NYG: 12 G. Det: 2 G. NYG: 10 G. **Total:** 131 G.

JOHN HOLLAR Hollar, John Henry 6'0", 223 **FB-LB**
Col: Appalachian State *HS:* Appalachian [Boone, NC] B: 8/7/1922, Boone, NC *Drafted:* 1948 Round 11 ChiC
1948 Was: 9 G; Rush 4-7 1.8. **1949** Det-Was: 8 G; Rush 13-35 2.7 1 TD; Rec 4-38 9.5 1 TD; Tot TD 2; 12 Pt. Det: 6 G; Rush 8-21 2.6. Was: 2 G; Rush 5-14 2.8 1 TD; Rec 4-38 9.5 1 TD; Tot TD 2; 12 Pt. **Total:** 17 G; Rush 17-42 2.5 1 TD; Rec 4-38 9.5 1 TD; Tot TD 2; 12 Pt.

DONALD HOLLAS Hollas, Donald Wayne 6'3", 215 **QB**
Col: Rice *HS:* Lamar [Rosenberg, TX] B: 11/22/1967, Kingsville, TX *Drafted:* 1991 Round 4 Cin

		Passing							
Year Team	G	Att	Comp	Comp%	Yds	YPA	TD	Int	Rating
1991 Cin	8	55	32	58.2	310	5.64	1	4	49.8
1992 Cin	10	58	35	60.3	335	5.78	2	0	87.9
1994 Cin	2	2	0	0.0	0	0.00	0	1	0.0
1998 Oak	12	260	135	51.9	1754	6.75	10	16	60.6
NFL Total	32	375	202	53.9	2399	6.40	13	21	61.8

	Rushing				
Year Team	Att	Yds	Avg	TD	Fum
1991 Cin	12	66	5.5	0	3
1992 Cin	20	109	5.5	0	6
1998 Oak	29	120	4.1	1	10
NFL Total	61	295	4.8	1	19

HUGO HOLLAS Hollas, Hugo Andrew 6'1", 190 **DB**
Col: Rice *HS:* Bishop Forest [Schulenburg, TX] B: 11/30/1945, High Hill, TX D: 9/6/1995, Schulenburg, TX
1970 NO: PR 4-22 5.5. **1972** NO: KR 2-9 4.5. **Total:** PR 4-22 5.5; KR 2-9 4.5.

		Interceptions			
Year Team	G	Int	Yds	TD	Fum
1970 NO	11	5	79	0	0
1971 NO	14	5	56	0	0
1972 NO	14	1	14	0	1
1974 SF	7	0	0	0	0
NFL Total	46	11	149	0	1

ERIC HOLLE Holle, Eric Warner 6'5", 260 **DE-NT**
Col: Texas *HS:* Lyndon B. Johnson [Austin, TX] B: 9/5/1960, Houston, TX *Drafted:* 1984 Round 5 KC
1984 KC: 16 G; 0.5 Sac. **1985** KC: 16 G; 0.5 Sac. **1986** KC: 16 G; 1 Sac. **1987** KC: 8 G; 0.5 Sac. **Total:** 56 G; 2.5 Sac.

ED HOLLER Holler, James Edward 6'2", 235 **LB**
Col: South Carolina *HS:* Dreher [Columbia, SC] B: 1/23/1940, Bluefield, WV *Drafted:* 1963 Round 14 GB
1963 GB: 2 G. **1964** Pit: 13 G; Rush 1-8 8.0; Int 1-2; Punt 31-1334 43.0; 1 Fum. **Total:** 15 G; Rush 1-8 8.0; Int 1-2; Punt 31-1334 43.0; 1 Fum.

TOMMY HOLLERAN Holleran, Thomas **BB**
Col: No College *HS:* South [Akron, OH] B: 3/6/1892 D: 1/1976, Reynoldsburg, OH
1920 Akr: 1 G. **1922** Tol: 1 G; Pass 1 TD. **Total:** 2 G; Pass 1 TD.

TOM HOLLERAN Holleran, Thomas Vincent 5′7″, 165 **HB**
(Speed) *Col:* Pittsburgh *HS:* Kiski School [Saltsburg, PA]
B: 12/18/1896, Pittsburgh, PA D: 7/27/1972, Pittsburgh, PA
1923 Buf: 5 G; Rush 2 TD; 12 Pt.

KEN HOLLEY Holley, Kenneth Joseph 5′10″, 185 **QB**
Col: Holy Cross *HS:* St. John's Prep [Danvers, MA] B: 10/9/1919, Hartford, CT D: 3/1/1986, Livingston, NJ
AAFC **1946** MiaA: 5 G; Pass 11-3 27.3%, 36 3.27 4 Int; Rush 2-(-22) -11.0.

COREY HOLLIDAY Holliday, Corey Lamont 6′2″, 208 **WR**
Col: North Carolina *HS:* Huguenot [Richmond, VA] B: 1/31/1971, Richmond, VA
1995 Pit: 3 G. **1996** Pit: 11 G; Rec 1-7 7.0. **1997** Pit: 2 G. **Total:** 16 G; Rec 1-7 7.0.

VONNIE HOLLIDAY Holliday, Dimetry Giovonni 6′4″, 296 **DT**
Col: North Carolina *HS:* Camden [SC] B: 12/11/1975, Camden, SC
Drafted: 1998 Round 1 GB
1998 GB: 12 G; 8 Sac.

MARCUS HOLLIDAY Holliday, Marcus Edward 5′11″, 222 **RB**
Col: Memphis *HS:* Fairley [Memphis, TN] B: 7/16/1973, Memphis, TN
1996 StL: 1 G.

RON HOLLIDAY Holliday, Ronald C 5′9″, 168 **WR**
Col: Pittsburgh *HS:* Paoli Area [Berwyn, PA] B: 2/12/1948, West Chester, PA
1973 SD: 11 G; Pass 2-0, 1 Int; Rush 6-70 11.7; Rec 14-182 13.0; Scor **1** 1XP; 1 Pt; 1 Fum.

DOUG HOLLIE Hollie, James Douglas 6′4″, 265 **DE**
Col: San Francisco City Coll. CA (J.C.); Southern Methodist
HS: Highland Park [MI] B: 12/15/1960, Detroit, MI *Drafted:* 1984 Supplemental Round 3 Det
1987 Sea: 2 G. **1988** Sea: 3 G. **Total:** 5 G.

DWIGHT HOLLIER Hollier, Dwight Leon Jr. 6′2″, 246 **LB**
Col: North Carolina *HS:* Kecoughtan [Hampton, VA] B: 4/21/1969, Hampton, VA *Drafted:* 1992 Round 4 Mia
1992 Mia: 16 G; 1 Sac. **1993** Mia: 16 G. **1994** Mia: 11 G; Int 1-36. **1995** Mia: 16 G. **1996** Mia: 16 G; Int 1-11; 1 Sac. **1997** Mia: 16 G; KR 1-0. **1998** Mia: 16 G. **Total:** 107 G; KR 1-0; Int 2-47; 2 Sac.

JOE HOLLINGSWORTH Hollingsworth, Joseph DeWitt 6′0″, 200 **FB**
Col: Georgia; Eastern Kentucky *HS:* Lynch [KY] B: 6/20/1925, Durham, GA D: 8/18/1975, Lynch, KY
1949 Pit: 11 G; Pass 1-0; Rush 6-13 2.2; 1 Fum. **1950** Pit: 10 G; Rush 1-2 2.0; KR 1-22 22.0. **1951** Pit: 10 G; Rush 7-11 1.6; 1 Fum. **Total:** 31 G; Pass 1-0; Rush 14-26 1.9; KR 1-22 22.0; 2 Fum.

SHAWN HOLLINGSWORTH Hollingsworth, Shawn Lenor 6′2″, 260 **OT**
Col: New Mexico; Angelo State *HS:* Brownwood [TX] B: 12/4/1961, Brownwood, TX
1983 Den: 5 G.

LAMONT HOLLINQUEST Hollinquest, Bertrell Lamont 6′3″, 250 **LB**
Col: USC *HS:* Pius X [Downey, CA] B: 10/24/1970, Los Angeles, CA
Drafted: 1993 Round 8 Was
1993 Was: 16 G. **1994** Was: 14 G; Int 1-39; 0.5 Sac. **1996** GB: 16 G; Int 1-2. **1997** GB: 16 G. **1998** GB: 14 G. **Total:** 76 G; Int 2-41; 0.5 Sac.

DAVE HOLLIS Hollis, David Lanier 5′11″, 175 **DB**
Col: Nevada-Las Vegas *HS:* Gardena [CA] B: 4/4/1965, Los Angeles, CA
1988 KC-Sea: Int 2-32. Sea: Int 2-32. **Total:** Int 2-32.

		Punt Returns				Kickoff Returns				
Year Team	**G**	**Ret**	**Yds**	**Avg**	**TD**	**Ret**	**Yds**	**Avg**	**TD**	**Fum**
1987 Sea	11	6	33	5.5	0	10	263	26.3	0	0
1988 KC-Sea	8	3	28	9.3	0	13	261	20.1	0	1
1988 KC	2	3	28	9.3	0	6	106	17.7	0	1
1988 Sea	6	0	0	—	0	7	155	22.1	0	0
1989 Sea	10	18	164	9.1	0	15	247	16.5	0	1
NFL Total	29	27	225	8.3	0	38	771	20.3	0	2

MIKE HOLLIS Hollis, Michael Shane 5′7″, 179 **K**
Col: Idaho *HS:* Central Valley [Veradale, WA] B: 5/5/1972, Kellogg, ID

		Scoring						
Year Team	**G**	**Pts**	**FG**	**FGA**	**FG%**	**XK**	**XKA**	**XK%**
1995 Jac	16	87	20	27	74.1	27	28	96.4
1996 Jac	16	117	30	36	83.3	27	27	100.0
1997 Jac	16	**134**	31	36	86.1	41	41	100.0
1998 Jac	16	108	21	26	80.8	45	45	100.0
NFL Total	64	446	102	125	81.6	140	141	99.3

GUS HOLLOMON Hollomon, Gus Martin 6′3″, 195 **DB-P**
(Chopper) *Col:* Houston *HS:* French [Beaumont, TX] B: 10/23/1945, Beaumont, TX *Drafted:* 1968 Round 4 Den
1968 Den: KR 7-194 27.7; Int 1-16. **1969** Den: KR 1-0; Int 1-0. **1970** NYJ: Int 3-11. **1971** NYJ: Int 2-2. **1972** NYJ: Int 1-25. **Total:** KR 8-194 24.3; Int 8-54.

		Punting			
Year Team	**G**	**Punts**	**Yds**	**Avg**	**Fum**
1968 Den	13	0	0	—	2
1969 Den	14	47	1868	39.7	2
1970 NYJ	14	0	0	—	0
1971 NYJ	11	0	0	—	0
1972 NYJ	14	0	0	—	0
NFL Total	66	47	1868	39.7	4

TONY HOLLOWAY Holloway, Anthony Lambert 6′2″, 222 **DE-LB**
Col: Nebraska *HS:* West [Bellevue, NE] B: 4/21/1964, Puerto Rico
1987 KC: 1 G.

BRIAN HOLLOWAY Holloway, Brian Douglass 6′7″, 284 **OT-OG**
Col: Stanford *HS:* Winston Churchill [Potomac, MD] B: 7/25/1959, Omaha, NE *Drafted:* 1981 Round 1 NE
1981 NE: 16 G. **1982** NE: 9 G. **1983** NE: 16 G. **1984** NE: 16 G. **1985** NE: 16 G. **1986** NE: 15 G; Rec 1-5 5.0. **1987** LARd: 12 G. **1988** LARd: 2 G. **Total:** 102 G; Rec 1-5 5.0.

CORNELL HOLLOWAY Holloway, Cornell Duane 5′11″, 185 **DB**
Col: Pittsburgh *HS:* Alliance [OH] B: 1/30/1966, Alliance, OH
Drafted: 1989 Round 10 Cin
1990 Ind: 15 G. **1991** Ind: 10 G; Int 1-4; 1 Sac. **1992** Ind: 7 G. **Total:** 32 G; Int 1-4; 1 Sac.

DEREK HOLLOWAY Holloway, Derek Lance 5′7″, 166 **WR**
Col: Arkansas *HS:* Palmyra [NJ] B: 1/17/1961, Riverside, NJ
1986 Was: 9 G; Rec 1-7 7.0; KR 3-44 14.7. **1987** TB: 1 G. **Total:** 10 G; Rec 1-7 7.0; KR 3-44 14.7.

GLEN HOLLOWAY Holloway, Glen Leroy 6′3″, 250 **OG**
Col: North Texas *HS:* Roy Miller [Corpus Christi, TX] B: 9/16/1948, Corpus Christi, TX *Drafted:* 1970 Round 10 ChiB
1970 ChiB: 14 G. **1971** ChiB: 14 G. **1972** ChiB: 14 G; KR 1-28 28.0. **1973** ChiB: 14 G; KR 1-8 8.0. **1974** Cle: 14 G. **Total:** 70 G; KR 2-36 18.0.

JOHNNY HOLLOWAY Holloway, John Owen 5′11″, 181 **DB**
Col: Butler County CC KS; Northwestern; Kansas *HS:* Mirabeau B. Lamar [Houston, TX] B: 11/8/1963, Galveston, TX *Drafted:* 1986 Round 7 Dal
1986 Dal: 16 G; PR 1-0; Int 1-1; 1 Fum. **1987** StL: 3 G. **Total:** 19 G; PR 1-0; Int 1-1; 1 Fum.

RANDY HOLLOWAY Holloway, Randy 6′5″, 250 **DE**
Col: Pittsburgh *HS:* Sharon [PA] B: 8/26/1955, Sharon, PA
Drafted: 1978 Round 1 Min
1978 Min: 16 G. **1979** Min: 16 G. **1980** Min: 16 G; Scor **1** Saf; 2 Pt. **1981** Min: 16 G; 1 Fum TD; 6 Pt. **1982** Min: 9 G; Int 1-6; 2.5 Sac. **1983** Min: 16 G; 7.5 Sac. **1984** Min-StL: 14 G; 6.5 Sac. Min: 8 G; 5 Sac. StL: 6 G; 1.5 Sac. **Total:** 103 G; Int 1-6; Scor 1 Saf; 1 Fum TD; 8 Pt; 16.5 Sac.

STAN HOLLOWAY Holloway, Stanley O'Neil 6′2″, 218 **LB**
Col: California *HS:* Lowell [San Francisco, CA] B: 9/28/1957, San Francisco, CA
1980 NO: 11 G; KR 1-0; 1 Fum.

STEVE HOLLOWAY Holloway, Steven Weymon 6′3″, 235 **TE**
Col: Tennessee State *HS:* Jefferson Davis [Montgomery, AL]
B: 8/23/1964, Montgomery, AL
1987 TB: 6 G; Rec 10-127 12.7.

BOB HOLLY Holly, Robert Charles Jr. 6′2″, 197 **QB**
Col: Princeton *HS:* Clifton [NJ] B: 6/1/1960, Clifton, NJ
Drafted: 1982 Round 11 Was
1982 Was: Postseason only. **1983** Was: 5 G; Pass 1-1 100.0%, 5 5.00; Rush 4-13 3.3; 2 Fum. **1985** Atl: 4 G; Pass 39-24 61.5%, 295 7.56 1 TD 2 Int; Rush 3-36 12.0 1 TD; 6 Pt; 1 Fum. **Total:** 9 G; Pass 40-25 62.5%, 300 7.50 1 TD 2 Int; Rush 7-49 7.0 1 TD; 6 Pt; 3 Fum.

TONY HOLM Holm, Bernard Patrick 6′1″, 214 **FB-LB-TB-DB**
Col: Alabama *HS:* Fairfield [AL] B: 5/22/1908, Birmingham, AL
D: 7/15/1978, Waukegan, IL
1931 Port: Rec 1 TD. **1932** ChiC: Rec 1-9 9.0. **1933** Pit: Rec 2-13 6.5. **Total:** Rec 3-22 7.3 1 TD.

		Passing							
Year Team	**G**	**Att**	**Comp**	**Comp%**	**Yds**	**YPA**	**TD**	**Int**	**Rating**
1930 Prov	3	—	—	—	—	—	0	—	—
1931 Port	14	—	—	—	—	—	0	—	—
1932 ChiC	8	0	0	—	0	—	0	0	—
1933 Pit	9	52	17	32.7	406	7.81	2	13	35.1
NFL Total	34	52	17	32.7	406	7.81	2	13	35.1

Year Team	Rushing Att	Yds	Avg	TD	Tot TD
1931 Port	—	—	—	1	2
1932 ChiC	34	73	2.1	0	0
1933 Pit	58	160	2.8	0	0
NFL Total	92	233	2.5	1	2

JOHN HOLMAN Holman, John **T**
B: 1902, New Orleans, LA
1928 NYG: 1 G.

RODNEY HOLMAN Holman, Rodney Alan 6′3″, 238 **TE**
Col: Tulane *HS:* Ypsilanti [MI] B: 4/20/1960, Ypsilanti, MI
Drafted: 1982 Round 3 Cin
1986 Cin: KR 1-18 18.0. **1991** Cin: KR 1-15 15.0. **Total:** KR 2-33 16.5.

Year Team	G	Receiving Rec	Yds	Avg	TD	Fum
1982 Cin	9	3	18	6.0	1	0
1983 Cin	16	2	15	7.5	0	0
1984 Cin	16	21	239	11.4	1	1
1985 Cin	16	38	479	12.6	7	1
1986 Cin	16	40	570	14.3	2	1
1987 Cin	12	28	438	15.6	2	0
1988 Cin	16	39	527	13.5	3	2
1989 Cin	16	50	736	14.7	9	0
1990 Cin	16	40	596	14.9	5	1
1991 Cin	16	31	445	14.4	2	1
1992 Cin	16	26	266	10.2	2	0
1993 Det	16	25	244	9.8	2	1
1994 Det	15	17	163	9.6	0	1
1995 Det	16	5	35	7.0	0	0
NFL Total	212	365	4771	13.1	36	9

SCOTT HOLMAN Holman, Scott Huntington 6′2″, 195 **WR**
Col: Oregon *HS:* Beaverton [OR] B: 9/27/1962, Portland, OR
1986 StL: 3 G; Rec 3-41 13.7. **1987** NYJ: 3 G; Rec 15-155 10.3; 1 Fum.
Total: 6 G; Rec 18-196 10.9; 1 Fum.

WALTER HOLMAN Holman, Walter Ree 5′10″, 208 **RB**
Col: West Virginia State *HS:* Vaiden [MS] B: 4/6/1959, Vaiden, MS
1987 Was: 3 G; Rush 2-7 3.5.

WILLIE HOLMAN Holman, Willie Joseph 6′4″, 250 **DE-DT**
Col: South Carolina State *HS:* St. Mathews [TX] B: 2/27/1945, St. Mathews, TX *Drafted:* 1968 Round 7 ChiB
1968 ChiB: 14 G. **1969** ChiB: 14 G; KR 1-0. **1970** ChiB: 14 G. **1971** ChiB: 14 G. **1972** ChiB: 4 G. **1973** ChiB-Was: 11 G. ChiB: 6 G. Was: 5 G.
Total: 71 G; KR 1-0.

ROB HOLMBERG Holmberg, Robert Anthony 6′3″, 230 **LB**
Col: Navy; Penn State *HS:* Mount Pleasant [PA] B: 5/6/1971, McKeesport, PA *Drafted:* 1994 Round 7 LARd
1994 LARd: 16 G. **1995** Oak: 16 G; 1 Sac. **1996** Oak: 13 G; 1 Sac.
1997 Oak: 16 G; KR 1-15 15.0. **1998** Ind-NYJ: 12 G. Ind: 3 G. NYJ: 9 G.
Total: 73 G; KR 1-15 15.0; 2 Sac.

WALT HOLMER Holmer, Walter R 6′1″, 188 **TB-DB-FB-HB**
Col: Northwestern *HS:* Moline [IL] B: 12/5/1902, Moline, IL
D: 8/27/1976, Cashmere, WA
1929 ChiB: Scor 3, 1 FG. **1930** ChiB: Int 1 TD. **1932** ChiC: Scor 8, 2 XK.
Total: Int 1 TD; Scor 35, 1 FG, 2 XK.

Year Team	G	Passing Att	Comp	Comp%	Yds	YPA	TD	Int	Rating
1929 ChiB	15	—	—	—	—	—	5	—	—
1930 ChiB	12	—	—	—	—	—	0	—	—
1931 ChiC	9	—	—	—	—	—	0	—	—
1932 ChiC	10	78	25	32.1	449	5.76	2	**1**	56.0
1933 Bos-Pit	10	32	11	34.4	193	6.03	0	6	16.3
1933 Bos	6	5	2	40.0	35	7.00	0	2	25.0
1933 Pit	4	27	9	33.3	158	5.85	0	4	14.7
NFL Total	56	110	36	32.7	642	5.84	7	7	48.4

Year Team	Rushing Att	Yds	Avg	TD	Tot TD
1930 ChiB	—	—	—	2	3
1932 ChiC	65	230	3.5	1	1
1933 Bos-Pit	13	36	2.8	1	1
1933 Bos	9	28	3.1	1	1
1933 Pit	4	8	2.0	0	0
NFL Total	78	266	3.4	4	5

BRUCE HOLMES Holmes, Bruce Barton 6′2″, 235 **LB**
Col: Minnesota *HS:* Henry Ford [Detroit, MI] B: 10/24/1964, El Paso, TX *Drafted:* 1987 Round 12 KC
1987 KC: 3 G. **1993** Min: 1 G. **Total:** 4 G.

CLAYTON HOLMES Holmes, Clayton Antwan 5′10″, 185 **DB**
Col: Carson-Newman *HS:* Wilson [Florence, SC] B: 8/23/1969, Florence, SC *Drafted:* 1992 Round 3 Dal
1992 Dal: 15 G; KR 3-70 23.3. **1994** Dal: 16 G; PR 5-55 11.0; KR 4-89 22.3; Int 0-3; 1 Fum. **1995** Dal: 8 G; PR 4-35 8.8; KR 5-134 26.8; Int 1-0; 1 Fum. **Total:** 39 G; PR 9-90 10.0; KR 12-293 24.4; Int 1-3; 2 Fum.

DARICK HOLMES Holmes, Darick Lamon 6′0″, 226 **RB**
Col: Pasadena City Coll. CA (J.C.); Portland State *HS:* John Muir [Pasadena, CA] B: 7/1/1971, Pasadena, CA *Drafted:* 1995 Round 7 Buf
1996 Buf: Scor 1 2XP. **Total:** Scor 1 2XP.

Year Team	G	Rushing Att	Yds	Avg	TD	Receiving Rec	Yds	Avg	TD
1995 Buf	16	172	698	4.1	4	24	214	8.9	0
1996 Buf	16	189	571	3.0	4	16	102	6.4	1
1997 Buf	13	22	106	4.8	2	13	106	8.2	0
1998 Buf-GB	14	95	394	4.1	1	20	188	9.4	0
1998 Buf	3	2	8	4.0	0	1	9	9.0	0
1998 GB	11	93	386	4.2	1	19	179	9.4	0
NFL Total	59	478	1769	3.7	11	73	610	8.4	1

Year Team	Kickoff Returns Ret	Yds	Avg	TD	Fum	Tot TD
1995 Buf	39	799	20.5	0	4	4
1996 Buf	0	0	—	0	2	5
1997 Buf	23	430	18.7	0	1	2
1998 Buf-GB	1	20	20.0	0	1	1
1998 Buf	1	20	20.0	0	0	0
1998 GB	0	0	—	0	1	1
NFL Total	63	1249	19.8	0	8	12

DARRYL HOLMES Holmes, Darryl DeWayne 6′2″, 190 **DB**
Col: Fort Valley State *HS:* Northside [Warner Robins, GA] B: 9/6/1964, Birmingham, AL
1987 NE: 15 G; Int 1-4. **1988** NE: 16 G. **1989** NE: 13 G. **Total:** 44 G; Int 1-4.

DON HOLMES Holmes, Donald Ira 5′10″, 180 **WR**
Col: Gavilan Coll. CA (J.C.); Colorado; Mesa *HS:* Miami Northwestern [FL] B: 4/1/1961, Miami, FL *Drafted:* 1984 Round 12 Atl
1986 StL: KR 1-2 2.0. **1987** StL: KR 1-25 25.0. **Total:** KR 2-27 13.5.

Year Team	G	Receiving Rec	Yds	Avg	TD
1986 StL	12	0	0	—	0
1987 StL	11	11	132	12.0	0
1988 Pho	16	1	10	10.0	0
1989 Pho	15	13	271	20.8	1
1990 Pho	6	0	0	—	0
NFL Total	60	25	413	16.5	1

EARL HOLMES Holmes, Earl L 6′2″, 245 **LB**
Col: Florida A&M *HS:* Florida A&M University [Tallahassee, FL]
B: 4/28/1973, Tallahassee, FL *Drafted:* 1996 Round 4 Pit
1996 Pit: 3 G; 1 Sac. **1997** Pit: 16 G; 4 Sac. **1998** Pit: 14 G; Int 1-36; 1.5 Sac. **Total:** 33 G; Int 1-36; 6.5 Sac.

ERNIE HOLMES Holmes, Earnest Lee 6′3″, 260 **DT-NT**
Col: Texas Southern *HS:* Wiergate [TX] B: 7/11/1948, Jamestown, TX
Drafted: 1971 Round 8 Pit
1972 Pit: 14 G. **1973** Pit: 14 G. **1974** Pit: 13 G. **1975** Pit: 13 G. **1976** Pit: 14 G. **1977** Pit: 13 G. **1978** NE: 3 G. **Total:** 84 G.

PAT HOLMES Holmes, James Patrick 6′5″, 255 **DE-DT**
Col: Texas Tech *HS:* Del Rio [TX] B: 8/3/1940, Durant, OK
1966 Hou: 14 G. **1967** Hou: 14 G. **1968** Hou: 14 G. **1969** Hou: 14 G.
1970 Hou: 14 G. **1971** Hou: 14 G. **1972** Hou: 14 G. **1973** KC: 10 G; Int 1-17. **Total:** 108 G; Int 1-17.

JERRY HOLMES Holmes, Jerry Lee 6′2″, 175 **DB**
Col: Chowan Coll. NC; West Virginia *HS:* Bethel [Hampton, VA]
B: 12/22/1957, Newport News, VA
1987 NYJ: 1 Sac. **1990** GB: 1 Sac. **Total:** 2 Sac.

Year Team	G	Interceptions Int	Yds	TD	Tot TD
1980 NYJ	12	0	0	0	0
1981 NYJ	16	1	0	0	0
1982 NYJ	9	3	2	0	0
1983 NYJ	16	3	107	1	2
1986 NYJ	15	6	29	0	0
1987 NYJ	8	1	20	0	0
1988 Det	16	1	32	0	0
1989 Det	16	6	77	1	1
1990 GB	16	3	39	0	0
1991 GB	13	1	0	0	0
NFL Total	137	25	306	2	3

JACK HOLMES Holmes, John 5′11″, 210 **RB**
Col: Texas Southern *HS:* Rolling Fork [MS] B: 6/20/1953, Rolling Fork, MS *Drafted:* 1975 Round 15 Hou
1978 NO: KR 1-18 18.0. **1979** NO: KR 8-120 15.0. **1980** NO: Pass 3-1 33.3%, 23 7.67 1 TD. **1982** NO: Pass 1-0. **Total:** Pass 4-1 25.0%, 23 5.75 1 TD; KR 9-138 15.3.

		Rushing				Receiving					Tot
Year Team	**G**	**Att**	**Yds**	**Avg**	**TD**	**Rec**	**Yds**	**Avg**	**TD**	**Fum**	**TD**
1978 NO	11	2	4	2.0	0	0	0	—	0	0	0
1979 NO	16	17	68	4.0	0	3	19	6.3	0	1	0
1980 NO	16	38	119	3.1	2	29	226	7.8	1	0	3
1981 NO	16	58	194	3.3	2	38	206	5.4	0	0	2
1982 NO	5	2	8	4.0	0	1	2	2.0	0	0	0
NFL Total	64	117	393	3.4	4	71	453	6.4	1	1	5

JOHNNY HOLMES Holmes, John L 6′2″, 248 **DE**
Col: Florida A&M B: 11/3/1943
1966 Mia: 3 G.

KENNY HOLMES Holmes, Kenneth Jerome 6′4″, 270 **DE**
Col: Miami (Fla.) *HS:* Vero Beach [FL] B: 10/24/1973, Vero Beach, FL *Drafted:* 1997 Round 1 Ten
1997 Ten: 16 G; 7 Sac. **1998** Ten: 14 G; 2.5 Sac. **Total:** 30 G; 9.5 Sac.

LESTER HOLMES Holmes, Lester 6′4″, 304 **OG**
Col: Jackson State *HS:* Tylertown [MS] B: 9/27/1969, Tylertown, MS *Drafted:* 1993 Round 1 Phi
1993 Phi: 12 G. **1994** Phi: 16 G. **1995** Phi: 2 G. **1996** Phi: 16 G. **1997** Oak: 15 G. **1998** Ariz: 16 G. **Total:** 77 G.

MEL HOLMES Holmes, Melvin 6′3″, 251 **OG-OT**
Col: North Carolina A&T *HS:* Mays [Miami, FL] B: 1/22/1950, Miami, FL *Drafted:* 1971 Round 5 Pit
1971 Pit: 14 G. **1972** Pit: 14 G. **1973** Pit: 1 G. **Total:** 29 G.

MIKE HOLMES Holmes, Michael Raphael 6′2″, 193 **DB-WR**
Col: Texas Southern *HS:* Ball [Galveston, TX] B: 11/18/1950, Galveston, TX *Drafted:* 1973 Round 1 SF
1974 SF: PR 9-45 5.0; Int 3-26. **1975** SF: Rush 1-(-4) -4.0; Rec 16-220 13.8 1 TD. **1976** Buf-Mia: Rec 1-11 11.0. Mia: Rec 1-11 11.0. **Total:** Rush 1-(-4) -4.0; Rec 17-231 13.6 1 TD; PR 9-45 5.0; Int 3-26.

		Kickoff Returns				
Year Team	**G**	**Ret**	**Yds**	**Avg**	**TD**	**Fum**
1974 SF	13	25	612	24.5	0	6
1975 SF	14	2	59	29.5	0	1
1976 Buf-Mia	4	4	90	22.5	0	1
1976 Buf	1	4	90	22.5	0	0
1976 Mia	3	0	0	—	0	1
NFL Total	31	31	761	24.5	0	8

PRIEST HOLMES Holmes, Priest Anthony 5′9″, 205 **RB**
Col: Texas *HS:* John Marshall [San Antonio, TX] B: 10/7/1973, Fort Smith, AR
1997 Bal: KR 1-14 14.0. **1998** Bal: Pass 1-0, 1 Int; KR 2-30 15.0. **Total:** Pass 1-0, 1 Int; KR 3-44 14.7.

		Rushing				Receiving				
Year Team	**G**	**Att**	**Yds**	**Avg**	**TD**	**Rec**	**Yds**	**Avg**	**TD**	**Fum**
1997 Bal	7	0	0	—	0	0	0	—	0	0
1998 Bal	16	233	1008	4.3	7	43	260	6.0	0	3
NFL Total	23	233	1008	4.3	7	43	260	6.0	0	3

ROBERT HOLMES Holmes, Robert 5′9″, 221 **RB**
Col: Southern University *HS:* Sam Houston [Huntsville, TX] B: 10/5/1945, Huntsville, TX *Drafted:* 1968 Round 14 KC

		Rushing				Receiving			
Year Team	**G**	**Att**	**Yds**	**Avg**	**TD**	**Rec**	**Yds**	**Avg**	**TD**
1968 KC	14	174	866	5.0	7	19	201	10.6	0
1969 KC	14	150	612	4.1	2	26	266	10.2	3
1970 KC	14	63	206	3.3	3	23	173	7.5	1
1971 KC-Hou	14	112	323	2.9	4	19	154	8.1	0
1971 KC	6	21	35	1.7	0	2	16	8.0	0
1971 Hou	8	91	288	3.2	4	17	138	8.1	0
1972 Hou	6	43	172	4.0	0	6	32	5.3	0
1973 SD	13	78	289	3.7	7	19	151	7.9	0
1975 Hou	14	19	42	2.2	0	1	5	5.0	0
NFL Total	89	639	2510	3.9	23	113	982	8.7	4

	Kickoff Returns					Tot
Year Team	**Ret**	**Yds**	**Avg**	**TD**	**Fum**	**TD**
1968 KC	0	0	—	0	5	7
1969 KC	2	54	27.0	0	9	5
1970 KC	19	535	28.2	0	4	4
1971 KC-Hou	12	300	25.0	0	8	4
1971 KC	7	171	24.4	0	1	0
1971 Hou	5	129	25.8	0	7	4
1972 Hou	2	39	19.5	0	0	0
1973 SD	0	0	—	0	5	7
NFL Total	35	928	26.5	0	31	27

RON HOLMES Holmes, Ronald 6′4″, 261 **DE**
Col: Washington *HS:* Timberline [Lacey, WA] B: 8/26/1963, Fort Benning, GA *Drafted:* 1985 Round 1 TB
1985 TB: 16 G; 4.5 Sac. **1986** TB: 14 G; 2.5 Sac. **1987** TB: 10 G; 8 Sac. **1988** TB: 10 G; 4 Sac. **1989** Den: 15 G; 9 Sac. **1990** Den: 14 G; 3 Sac. **1991** Den: 15 G; 5 Sac. **1992** Den: 8 G; 0.5 Sac. **Total:** 102 G; 36.5 Sac.

RUDY HOLMES Holmes, Rudell Leron 5′10″, 178 **DB**
Col: Saddleback Coll. CA (J.C.); Drake *HS:* Mission Viejo [CA] B: 7/19/1952, Oakland, CA
1974 Atl: 8 G.

TOM HOLMOE Holmoe, Thomas Allen 6′2″, 190 **DB**
Col: Brigham Young *HS:* Valley [La Crescenta, CA] B: 3/7/1960, Los Angeles, CA *Drafted:* 1983 Round 4 SF
1983 SF: 16 G. **1984** SF: 16 G. **1986** SF: 16 G; Int 3-149 2 TD; 12 Pt. **1987** SF: 11 G; Int 1-0. **1988** SF: 16 G; Int 2-0. **1989** SF: 7 G; Int 1-23. **Total:** 82 G; Int 7-172 2 TD; 12 Pt.

PETE HOLOHAN Holohan, Peter Joseph 6′4″, 237 **TE**
Col: Notre Dame *HS:* Liverpool [NY] B: 7/25/1959, Albany, NY *Drafted:* 1981 Round 7 SD
1983 SD: Pass 1-0. **1984** SD: Pass 2-1 50.0%, 25 12.50 1 TD. **1985** SD: Pass 1-0; KR 1-0. **1986** SD: Pass 2-1 50.0%, 21 10.50. **1989** LARm: Rush 1-3 3.0. **Total:** Pass 6-2 33.3%, 46 7.67 1 TD; Rush 1-3 3.0; KR 1-0.

		Receiving				
Year Team	**G**	**Rec**	**Yds**	**Avg**	**TD**	**Fum**
1981 SD	7	1	14	14.0	0	0
1982 SD	9	0	0	—	0	0
1983 SD	16	23	272	11.8	2	0
1984 SD	15	56	734	13.1	1	0
1985 SD	15	42	458	10.9	3	1
1986 SD	16	29	356	12.3	1	0
1987 SD	12	20	239	12.0	0	0
1988 LARm	16	59	640	10.8	3	1
1989 LARm	16	51	510	10.0	2	1
1990 LARm	16	49	475	9.7	2	2
1991 KC	16	13	113	8.7	2	0
1992 Cle	9	20	170	8.5	0	0
NFL Total	163	363	3981	11.0	16	5

MIKE HOLOVAK Holovak, Michael Joseph 6′1″, 213 **FB-LB**
Col: Boston College *HS:* Seton Hall [Lansford, PA] B: 9/19/1919, Lansford, PA *Drafted:* 1943 Round 1 Cle
1946 LARm: Rec 2-6 3.0; KR 1-18 18.0. **1947** ChiB: Rec 7-119 17.0; KR 2-47 23.5. **1948** ChiB: Rec 4-30 7.5; Int 1-18. **Total:** Rec 13-155 11.9; KR 3-65 21.7; Int 1-18.

		Rushing				
Year Team	**G**	**Att**	**Yds**	**Avg**	**TD**	**Fum**
1946 LARm	11	55	211	3.8	3	2
1947 ChiB	12	51	281	5.5	1	0
1948 ChiB	11	30	228	7.6	2	0
NFL Total	34	136	720	5.3	6	2

BERNARD HOLSEY Holsey, Leonard Bernard 6′2″, 291 **DT-DE**
Col: Duke *HS:* Coosa [Rome, GA] B: 12/10/1973, Cave Spring, GA
1996 NYG: 16 G. **1997** NYG: 16 G; 3.5 Sac. **1998** NYG: 16 G. **Total:** 48 G; 3.5 Sac.

MIKE HOLSTON Holston, Michael Anthony 6′3″, 189 **WR**
Col: Hagerstown JC MD; Morgan State *HS:* Bladensburg [MD] B: 1/8/1958, Seat Pleasant, MD *Drafted:* 1981 Round 3 Hou

		Receiving			
Year Team	**G**	**Rec**	**Yds**	**Avg**	**TD**
1981 Hou	16	27	427	15.8	2
1982 Hou	9	5	116	23.2	1
1983 Hou	16	14	205	14.6	0
1984 Hou	16	22	287	13.0	1
1985 Hou-KC	7	6	76	12.7	0
1985 Hou	3	1	25	25.0	0
1985 KC	4	5	51	10.2	0
NFL Total	64	74	1111	15.0	4

HARRY HOLT Holt, Harry Thompson III 6′4″, 236 **TE**
Col: Arizona *HS:* Harlingen [TX]; Sunnyside HS [Tucson, AZ] B: 12/29/1957, Harlingen, TX
1983 Cle: Rush 3-8 2.7. **1984** Cle: Rush 1-12 12.0; KR 1-1 1.0. **1986** Cle: Rush 1-16 16.0 1 TD. **Total:** Rush 5-36 7.2 1 TD; KR 1-1 1.0.

		Receiving					Tot
Year Team	**G**	**Rec**	**Yds**	**Avg**	**TD**	**Fum**	**TD**
1983 Cle	15	29	420	14.5	3	1	3
1984 Cle	12	20	261	13.1	0	0	0
1985 Cle	11	10	95	9.5	1	1	1
1986 Cle	14	4	61	15.3	1	0	2

1987 SD	3	7	56	8.0	0	1	0
NFL Total	55	70	893	12.8	5	3	6

ISSIAC HOLT Holt, Issiac III 6'2", 200 **DB**
Col: Alcorn State *HS:* Carver [Birmingham, AL] B: 10/4/1962, Birmingham, AL *Drafted:* 1985 Round 2 Min
1988 Min: Scor 1 Saf. **1992** Dal: Scor 1 Saf. **Total:** Scor 2 Saf.

		Interceptions				Tot
Year Team	**G**	**Int**	**Yds**	**TD**	**Fum**	**TD**
1985 Min	15	1	0	0	0	0
1986 Min	16	8	54	0	1	1
1987 Min	9	2	7	0	0	0
1988 Min	13	2	15	0	0	0
1989 Min-Dal	14	1	90	1	0	1
1989 Min	5	1	90	1	0	1
1989 Dal	9	0	0	0	0	0
1990 Dal	15	3	72	1	0	1
1991 Dal	15	4	2	0	0	0
1992 Dal	16	2	11	0	0	0
NFL Total	113	23	251	2	1	3

JOHN HOLT Holt, John Stephanie 5'11", 180 **DB**
Col: West Texas A&M *HS:* Enid [OK] B: 5/14/1959, Lawton, OK
Drafted: 1981 Round 4 TB
1981 TB: KR 11-274 24.9; Int 1-13. **1983** TB: Int 3-43; 1 Sac. **1984** TB: Int 1-25. **1985** TB: Int 1-3. **1986** Ind: Int 1-80; 0.5 Sac. **Total:** KR 11-274 24.9; Int 7-164; 1.5 Sac.

		Punt Returns				
Year Team	**G**	**Ret**	**Yds**	**Avg**	**TD**	**Fum**
1981 TB	16	9	100	11.1	0	1
1982 TB	9	16	81	5.1	0	2
1983 TB	16	5	43	8.6	0	1
1984 TB	15	6	17	2.8	0	0
1985 TB	16	0	0	—	0	0
1986 Ind	16	0	0	—	0	0
1987 Ind	12	0	0	—	0	0
1988 Ind	9	0	0	—	0	0
NFL Total	109	36	241	6.7	0	4

PIERCE HOLT Holt, Leslie Pierce 6'4", 280 **DE-DT**
Col: Angelo State *HS:* Lamar [Rosenberg, TX] B: 1/1/1962, Marlin, TX
Drafted: 1988 Round 2 SF
1988 SF: 9 G; 5 Sac. **1989** SF: 16 G; 10.5 Sac. **1990** SF: 16 G; 5.5 Sac. **1991** SF: 13 G; 3 Sac. **1992** SF: 16 G; 5.5 Sac. **1993** Atl: 16 G; 6.5 Sac. **1994** Atl: 12 G. **1995** Atl: 11 G; 1 Sac. **Total:** 109 G; 37 Sac.

ROBERT HOLT Holt, Robert James 6'1", 182 **WR**
Col: Baylor *HS:* Grand Prairie [TX] B: 10/4/1959, Denison, TX
Drafted: 1981 Round 6 Buf
1982 Buf: 7 G; Rush 1-3 3.0; Rec 4-45 11.3; PR 10-45 4.5; KR 7-156 22.3; 2 Fum.

GLENN HOLTZMAN Holtzman, Glenn 6'3", 250 **OT-DT**
Col: Kilgore Coll. TX (J.C.); North Texas *HS:* Denton [TX]; Kilgore HS [TX] B: 10/9/1930, Shreveport, TX D: 5/6/1980, Reno, NV *Drafted:* 1954 Round 26 LARm
1955 LARm: 12 G. **1956** LARm: 12 G. **1957** LARm: 12 G. **1958** LARm: 12 G; Scor **1** Saf; 2 Pt. **Total:** 48 G; Scor 1 Saf; 2 Pt.

E.J. HOLUB Holub, Emil Joseph Jr. 6'4", 236 **LB-C**
Col: Texas Tech *HS:* Lubbock [TX] B: 1/5/1938, Schulenburg, TX
Drafted: 1961 Round 1 DalT
1961 DalT: 14 G; Int 1-0. **1962** DalT: 14 G; Int 2-8. **1963** KC: 14 G; Int 5-60. **1964** KC: 9 G. **1965** KC: 14 G; Int 1-8; 1 Fum. **1966** KC: 14 G. **1967** KC: 6 G. **1968** KC: 14 G. **1969** KC: 14 G. **1970** KC: 14 G. **Total:** 127 G; Int 9-76; 1 Fum.

GORDY HOLZ Holz, Gordon Francis 6'4", 260 **DT-OT**
Col: Minnesota *HS:* Rosemount [MN] B: 5/24/1933, St. Paul, MN
Drafted: 1955 Round 23 Pit
1960 Den: 14 G. **1961** Den: 14 G. **1962** Den: 14 G. **1963** Den: 14 G; Int 1-0. **1964** NYJ: 14 G. **Total:** 70 G; Int 1-0.

TOM HOLZER Holzer, Thomas Robert 6'4", 248 **DE**
Col: Louisville *HS:* Sacred Heart [Indianapolis, IN] B: 8/2/1945, Indianapolis, IN *Drafted:* 1967 Round 2 SF
1967 SF: 14 G.

DENNIS HOMAN Homan, Dennis Frank 6'1", 181 **WR**
Col: Alabama *HS:* Muscle Shoals [AL] B: 1/9/1946, Muscle Shoals, AL
Drafted: 1968 Round 1 Dal
1968 Dal: PR 1-0; KR 2-21 10.5. **1970** Dal: Rush 2-(-3) -1.5. **1971** KC: PR 10-61 6.1. **1972** KC: PR 2-9 4.5. **Total:** Rush 2-(-3) -1.5; PR 13-70 5.4; KR 2-21 10.5.

		Receiving				
Year Team	**G**	**Rec**	**Yds**	**Avg**	**TD**	**Fum**
1968 Dal	10	4	92	23.0	1	0
1969 Dal	11	12	240	20.0	0	0
1970 Dal	10	7	105	15.0	0	0
1971 KC	8	2	47	23.5	0	1
1972 KC	7	12	135	11.3	1	0
NFL Total	46	37	619	16.7	2	1

TWO-BITS HOMAN Homan, Ralph Henry 5'5", 145 **BB**
Col: Lebanon Valley *HS:* Lebanon [PA] B: 6/7/1898, Reading, PA
D: 2/1966, NY
1925 Fra: 16 G; Rec 1 TD; PR **1** TD; Tot TD 2; 12 Pt. **1926** Fra: 7 G; Rush 1 TD; Rec 2 TD; Tot TD 3; 18 Pt. **1927** Fra: 16 G; Rush 1 TD; Rec 1 TD; Tot TD 2; 12 Pt. **1928** Fra: 11 G; Rec 1 TD; 6 Pt. **1929** Fra: 17 G; Rec 2 TD; 12 Pt. **1930** Fra: 14 G. **Total:** 81 G; Rush 2 TD; Rec 7 TD; PR 1 TD; Tot TD 10; 60 Pt.

THOMAS HOMCO Homco, Thomas Ross 6'0", 245 **LB**
Col: Northwestern *HS:* Highland [IN] B: 1/8/1970, Hammond, IN
1993 LARm: 16 G; Int 1-6. **1994** LARm: 15 G. **1995** StL: 11 G. **1996** StL: 3 G. **Total:** 45 G; Int 1-6.

CHARLIE HONAKER Honaker, Charles Frank 5'11", 185 **OE**
Col: Ohio State *HS:* Huntington [WV] B: 10/11/1899, Russell, KY
D: 4/21/1974, Huntington, WV
1924 Cle: 6 G.

TODD HONS Hons, Todd Hank 6'1", 195 **QB**
Col: El Camino Coll. CA (J.C.); Arizona State *HS:* West [Torrance, CA]
B: 9/5/1961, Torrance, CA
1987 Det: Rush 5-49 9.8.

		Passing								
Year Team	**G**	**Att**	**Comp**	**Comp%**	**Yds**	**YPA**	**TD**	**Int**	**Rating**	**Fum**
1987 Det	3	92	43	46.7	552	6.00	5	5	61.5	2

ESTUS HOOD Hood, Estus III 5'11", 183 **DB**
Col: Illinois State *HS:* Eastridge [Kankakee, IL] B: 11/14/1955, Hattiesburg, MS *Drafted:* 1978 Round 3 GB
1978 GB: KR 3-74 24.7. **1983** GB: PR 1-0. **Total:** PR 1-0; KR 3-74 24.7.

		Interceptions		
Year Team	**G**	**Int**	**Yds**	**TD**
1978 GB	16	3	18	0
1979 GB	16	2	8	0
1980 GB	15	1	0	0
1981 GB	16	3	59	1
1982 GB	9	1	0	0
1983 GB	16	0	0	0
1984 GB	16	1	8	0
NFL Total	104	11	93	1

FRANK HOOD Hood, Franklin 6'0", 235 **HB-DB-BB**
Col: Pittsburgh *HS:* Bellefonte Acad. [PA] B: 1908 Deceased
1933 Pit: 3 G; Pass 18-6 33.3%, 45 2.50 4 Int; Rush 1-1 1.0.

WINFORD HOOD Hood, Winford DeWayne 6'3", 262 **OG-OT**
Col: Georgia *HS:* D.M. Therrell [Atlanta, GA] B: 3/29/1962, Atlanta, GA
Drafted: 1984 Round 8 Den
1984 Den: 16 G. **1985** Den: 16 G. **1986** Den: 9 G. **1987** Den: 3 G. **1988** Den: 3 G. **Total:** 47 G.

FAIR HOOKER Hooker, Fair Jr. 6'1", 190 **WR**
Col: Arizona State *HS:* Monrovia [CA] B: 5/22/1947, Los Angeles, CA
Drafted: 1969 Round 5 Cle

		Receiving			
Year Team	**G**	**Rec**	**Yds**	**Avg**	**TD**
1969 Cle	13	2	21	10.5	0
1970 Cle	13	28	490	17.5	2
1971 Cle	14	45	649	14.4	1
1972 Cle	14	32	441	13.8	2
1973 Cle	13	18	196	10.9	2
1974 Cle	7	4	48	12.0	1
NFL Total	74	129	1845	14.3	8

ALVIN HOOKS Hooks, Alvin Lee 5'11", 170 **WR**
Col: Cal State-Northridge *HS:* Grover Cleveland [Los Angeles, CA]
B: 5/7/1957, Los Angeles, CA
1981 Phi: 3 G.

JIM HOOKS Hooks, James Earl 5'11", 225 **RB**
Col: Central Oklahoma *HS:* James [Oklahoma City, OK]
B: 10/23/1950, Oklahoma City, OK *Drafted:* 1973 Round 4 Det
1973 Det: Rec 1-6 6.0; KR 2-52 26.0. **1974** Det: Rec 9-53 5.9. **1975** Det: Rec 1-5 5.0; KR 2-8 4.0. **Total:** Rec 11-64 5.8; KR 4-60 15.0.

		Rushing				
Year Team	**G**	**Att**	**Yds**	**Avg**	**TD**	**Fum**
1973 Det	11	19	110	5.8	0	1
1974 Det	8	44	143	3.3	0	1
1975 Det	12	4	-8	-2.0	0	0
1976 Det	1	0	0	—	0	0
NFL Total	32	67	245	3.7	0	2

ROLAND HOOKS Hooks, Roland 6'0", 197 **RB**
Col: North Carolina State *HS:* West Craven [Vanceboro, NC]
B: 1/2/1953, Brooklyn, NY *Drafted:* 1975 Round 10 Buf

		Rushing				Receiving			
Year Team	G	Att	Yds	Avg	TD	Rec	Yds	Avg	TD
1976 Buf	14	25	116	4.6	0	6	72	12.0	0
1977 Buf	14	128	497	3.9	0	16	195	12.2	0
1978 Buf	16	76	358	4.7	2	15	110	7.3	1
1979 Buf	16	89	320	3.6	6	26	254	9.8	0
1980 Buf	16	25	118	4.7	1	23	179	7.8	0
1981 Buf	16	51	250	4.9	3	10	140	14.0	2
1982 Buf	6	5	23	4.6	0	0	0	—	0
NFL Total	98	399	1682	4.2	12	96	950	9.9	3

	Punt Returns				Kickoff Returns					Tot
Year Team	Ret	Yds	Avg	TD	Ret	Yds	Avg	TD	Fum	TD
1976 Buf	11	45	4.1	0	23	521	22.7	0	4	0
1977 Buf	0	0	—	0	0	0	—	0	8	0
1978 Buf	3	12	4.0	0	7	124	17.7	0	2	3
1979 Buf	0	0	—	0	0	0	—	0	4	6
1980 Buf	8	90	11.3	0	7	109	15.6	0	3	1
1981 Buf	17	142	8.4	0	11	215	19.5	0	1	5
1982 Buf	4	13	3.3	0	0	0	—	0	0	0
NFL Total	43	302	7.0	0	48	969	20.2	0	22	15

HARRY HOOLIGAN Hooligan, Henry 6'2", 225 **FB**
Col: Bishop B: 9/13/1938
1965 Hou: 1 G.

TRELL HOOPER Hooper, John Lutrell 5'11", 182 **DB**
Col: Memphis *HS:* Jackson Central-Merry [Jackson, TN]
B: 12/22/1961, Brownsville, TN
1987 Mia: 3 G; PR 1-0; Int 2-11; **1** Fum TD; 6 Pt; 1 Fum.

MITCH HOOPES Hoopes, Mitchell Kent 6'1", 207 **P**
Col: Arizona *HS:* Bisbee [AZ] B: 7/8/1953, Bisbee, AZ *Drafted:* 1975 Round 8 Dal
1975 Dal: Pass 3-1 33.3%, 21 7.00; Rush 1-13 13.0. **1976** SD-Hou: Rush 2-10 5.0. SD: Rush 2-10 5.0. **Total:** Pass 3-1 33.3%, 21 7.00; Rush 3-23 7.7.

		Punting			
Year Team	G	Punts	Yds	Avg	Fum
1975 Dal	14	68	2676	39.4	0
1976 SD-Hou	10	49	1849	37.7	1
1976 SD	9	42	1628	38.8	1
1976 Hou	1	7	221	31.6	0
1977 Det	1	6	235	39.2	0
NFL Total	25	123	4760	38.7	1

HOUSTON HOOVER Hoover, Houston Roosevelt 6'2", 295 **OG-OT**
Col: Jackson State *HS:* Yazoo City [MS] B: 2/6/1965, Yazoo City, MS
Drafted: 1988 Round 6 Atl
1988 Atl: 15 G. **1989** Atl: 16 G. **1990** Atl: 16 G. **1991** Atl: 16 G. **1992** Atl: 16 G. **1993** Cle: 16 G. **1994** Mia: 3 G. **Total:** 98 G.

MELVIN HOOVER Hoover, Melvin Charles 6'0", 185 **WR**
Col: Arizona State *HS:* North Mecklenburg [Huntersville, NC]
B: 9/21/1959, Charlotte, NC *Drafted:* 1981 Round 6 NYG
1982 Phi: 7 G; Rush 1-5 5.0; KR 7-113 16.1. **1983** Phi: 11 G; Rec 10-221 22.1; PR 7-44 6.3; 3 Fum. **1984** Phi: 12 G; Rec 6-143 23.8 2 TD; 12 Pt. **1987** Det: 2 G. **Total:** 32 G; Rush 1-5 5.0; Rec 16-364 22.8 2 TD; PR 7-44 6.3; KR 7-113 16.1; 12 Pt; 3 Fum.

CHARLES HOPE Hope, Charles Edward 6'3", 303 **OG-C**
Col: Central State (Ohio) *HS:* William Penn [New Castle, DE]
B: 3/12/1970, Wilmington, DE
1994 GB: 6 G.

NEIL HOPE Hope, Neil Keith 6'2", 235 **LB**
Col: USC *HS:* Fairfax [Los Angeles, CA] B: 3/22/1963, Memphis, TN
1987 LARm: 3 G.

ANDY HOPKINS Hopkins, Andrew Pochae 5'10", 186 **RB**
Col: Stephen F. Austin St. *HS:* Ralph J. Bunche [Crockett, TX]
B: 10/19/1949, Crockett, TX *Drafted:* 1971 Round 15 Hou
1971 Hou: 2 G; Rush 2-2 1.0.

BRAD HOPKINS Hopkins, Bradley Donnell 6'3", 306 **OT**
Col: Illinois *HS:* Moline [IL] B: 9/5/1970, Columbia, SC *Drafted:* 1993 Round 1 Hou
1993 Hou: 16 G. **1994** Hou: 16 G. **1995** Hou: 16 G. **1996** Hou: 16 G. **1997** Ten: 16 G. **1998** Ten: 13 G. **Total:** 93 G.

TED HOPKINS Hopkins, Edward J 5'9", 180 **E**
Col: No College *HS:* McKinley [Canton, OH] B: 12/5/1890, Canton, OH D: 3/8/1973, Kettering, OH
1921 Col: 3 G. **1922** Col: 5 G. **Total:** 8 G.

JERRY HOPKINS Hopkins, Jerrell Wayne 6'2", 235 **LB**
Col: Texas A&M *HS:* Mart [TX] B: 1/24/1941, Chalk Bluff, TX
Drafted: 1963 Round 4 Hou
1963 Den: 7 G; Int 1-21. **1964** Den: 14 G; Int 2-11. **1965** Den: 14 G; Int 1-7. **1966** Den: 14 G; Int 2-9. **1967** Mia: 13 G. **1968** Oak: 5 G; KR 1-0. **Total:** 67 G; KR 1-0; Int 6-48.

ROY HOPKINS Hopkins, Roy Lee 6'1", 235 **RB**
Col: Texas Southern *HS:* Bruce [Gilmer, TX] B: 2/18/1945, Gilmer, TX
Drafted: 1967 Round 2 Hou
1967 Hou: KR 1-26 26.0. **1968** Hou: KR 1-21 21.0. **1970** Hou: KR 1-20 20.0. **Total:** KR 3-67 22.3.

		Rushing				Receiving					Tot
Year Team	G	Att	Yds	Avg	TD	Rec	Yds	Avg	TD	Fum	TD
1967 Hou	14	13	42	3.2	0	3	9	3.0	0	1	0
1968 Hou	13	31	104	3.4	0	4	40	10.0	0	0	0
1969 Hou	14	131	473	3.6	4	29	338	11.7	1	2	5
1970 Hou	12	57	207	3.6	3	14	142	10.1	0	0	3
NFL Total	53	232	826	3.6	7	50	529	10.6	1	3	8

THOMAS HOPKINS Hopkins, Thomas 6'6", 260 **OT**
Col: Alabama A&M *HS:* Choctaw Co. [Butler, AL] B: 1/13/1960, Butler, AL *Drafted:* 1983 Round 10 Cle
1983 Cle: 2 G.

WES HOPKINS Hopkins, Wesley Carl 6'1", 213 **DB**
Col: Southern Methodist *HS:* John Carroll [Birmingham, AL]
B: 9/26/1961, Birmingham, AL *Drafted:* 1983 Round 2 Phi
1983 Phi: 1 Sac. **1984** Phi: 1.5 Sac. **1985** Phi: 2 Sac. **1989** Phi: 3.5 Sac. **1990** Phi: 2 Sac. **1991** Phi: 2 Sac. **Total:** 12 Sac.

		Interceptions			
Year Team	G	Int	Yds	TD	Fum
1983 Phi	14	0	0	0	0
1984 Phi	16	5	107	0	0
1985 Phi	15	6	36	**1**	1
1986 Phi	4	0	0	0	0
1988 Phi	16	5	21	0	0
1989 Phi	16	0	0	0	0
1990 Phi	15	5	45	0	0
1991 Phi	16	5	26	0	0
1992 Phi	10	3	6	0	0
1993 Phi	15	1	0	0	0
NFL Total	137	30	241	1	1

HARRY HOPP Hopp, Harry 6'0", 209 **FB-DB-TB-LB**
(Hippity) *Col:* Nebraska *HS:* Hastings [NE] B: 12/13/1918, Hastings, NE D: 12/22/1964, Hastings, NE *Drafted:* 1941 Round 3 Det
AAFC **1946** BufA-MiaA: Pass 22-11 50.0%, 190 8.64; Rec 2-(-1) -0.5; KR 6-113 18.8; Punt 15-461 30.7. **1947** LA-A: Rec 3-59 19.7; KR 1-13 13.0; Int 1-16. **Total:** Pass 22-11 50.0%, 190 8.64; Rec 5-58 11.6; KR 7-126 18.0; Int 1-16; Punt 15-461 30.7.

		Rushing			
Year Team	G	Att	Yds	Avg	TD
1946 BufA-MiaA	13	61	218	3.6	3
1947 LA-A	9	10	52	5.2	0
AAFC Total	22	71	270	3.8	3

NFL **1941** Det: Rec 2-7 3.5; Int 1-3. **1942** Det: PR 9-98 10.9; KR 5-108 21.6; Int 1-0. **1943** Det: Rec 17-229 13.5 3 TD; PR 1-(-7) -7.0; KR 3-57 19.0; Int 2-40 **1** TD. **Total:** Rec 19-236 12.4 3 TD; PR 10-91 9.1; KR 8-165 20.6; Int 4-43 1 TD.

		Passing							
Year Team	G	Att	Comp	Comp%	Yds	YPA	TD	Int	Rating
1941 Det	10	3	0	0.0	0	0.00	0	1	0.0
1942 Det	10	68	20	29.4	258	3.79	0	13	3.3
1943 Det	10	8	5	62.5	60	7.50	0	0	85.4
NFL Total	30	79	25	31.6	318	4.03	0	14	5.6

	Rushing				Punting			Tot
Year Team	Att	Yds	Avg	TD	Punts	Yds	Avg	TD
1941 Det	69	202	2.9	1	2	84	42.0	1
1942 Det	66	230	3.5	0	27	1098	40.7	0
1943 Det	56	99	1.8	3	42	1643	39.1	9
NFL Total	191	531	2.8	4	71	2825	39.8	10

DARREL HOPPER Hopper, Darrel 6'1", 196 **DB**
Col: USC *HS:* Carson [CA] B: 3/14/1963, Los Angeles, CA
1987 SD: 4 G.

DOUG HOPPOCK Hoppock, Douglas Gene 6'4", 280 **OT-OG**
Col: Kansas State *HS:* Southeast [Wichita, KS] B: 1/30/1960, Wichita, KS
1987 KC: 3 G.

AL HOPTOWIT Hoptowit, Alphonse William 6′1″, 217 **T**
Col: Washington State *HS:* Wapato [WA] B: 9/7/1914, Yakima, WA D: 4/6/1981, Wapato, WA *Drafted:* 1938 Round 9 Cle
1942 ChiB: 11 G. **1943** ChiB: 10 G. **1944** ChiB: 10 G. **1945** ChiB: 10 G. **Total:** 41 G.

MIKE HORAN Horan, Michael William 5′11″, 192 **P**
Col: Fullerton Coll. CA (J.C.); Long Beach State *HS:* Sunny Hills [Fullerton, CA] B: 2/1/1959, Orange, CA *Drafted:* 1982 Round 9 Atl
1985 Phi: Rush 1-12 12.0. **1986** Den: Rush 1-0. **1991** Den: Rush 2-9 4.5. **1995** NYG: Rush 1-0. **1997** StL: Rush 1-(-3) -3.0. **1998** ChiB: Pass 2-1 50.0%, 18 9.00 1 TD. **Total:** Pass 2-1 50.0%, 18 9.00 1 TD; Rush 6-18 3.0.

		Punting			
Year Team	G	Punts	Yds	Avg	Fum
1984 Phi	16	92	3880	42.2	0
1985 Phi	16	91	3777	41.5	0
1986 Den	4	21	864	41.1	1
1987 Den	12	44	1807	41.1	0
1988 Den	16	65	2861	44.0	0
1989 Den	16	77	3111	40.4	0
1990 Den	15	58	2575	**44.4**	0
1991 Den	16	72	3012	41.8	0
1992 Den	7	37	1681	45.4	0
1993 NYG	8	44	1882	42.8	0
1994 NYG	16	85	3521	41.4	0
1995 NYG	16	72	3063	42.5	1
1996 NYG	16	**102**	**4289**	42.0	0
1997 StL	10	53	2272	42.9	0
1998 ChiB	13	64	2643	41.3	0
NFL Total	197	977	41238	42.2	2

ROY HORD Hord, Ambrose Roy Jr. 6′4″, 245 **OG**
Col: Duke *HS:* Harding University [Charlotte, NC] B: 12/25/1934, Charlotte, NC *Drafted:* 1957 Round 8 LARm
1960 LARm: 12 G. **1961** LARm: 14 G. **1962** LARm-Phi: 14 G. LARm: 3 G. Phi: 11 G. **1963** NYJ: 13 G. **Total:** 53 G.

ALVIN HORN Horn, Alvin Ramone Jr. 5′11″, 185 **DB**
Col: Coll. of the Sequoias CA (J.C.); Nevada-Las Vegas *HS:* Hanford [CA] B: 3/7/1965, Hanford, CA
1987 Cle: 3 G; Int 1-28.

DON HORN Horn, Donald Glenn 6′2″, 195 **QB**
Col: Los Angeles Harbor Coll. CA (J.C.); Washington State; San Diego State *HS:* Gardena [CA] B: 3/9/1945, South Gate, CA *Drafted:* 1967 Round 1 GB
1967 GB: Rush 1-(-2) -2.0. **1968** GB: Rush 3-(-7) -2.3. **1969** GB: Rush 3-(-7) -2.3 1 TD. **1970** GB: Rush 5-4 0.8. **1971** Den: Rush 6-15 2.5. **Total:** Rush 18-3 0.2 1 TD.

		Passing								
Year Team	G	Att	Comp	Comp%	Yds	YPA	TD	Int	Rating	Fum
1967 GB	3	24	12	50.0	171	7.13	1	1	70.0	1
1968 GB	1	16	10	62.5	187	11.69	2	0	142.4	1
1969 GB	9	168	89	53.0	1505	**8.96**	11	11	78.1	6
1970 GB	7	76	28	36.8	428	5.63	2	10	25.4	3
1971 Den	9	173	89	51.4	1056	6.10	3	14	42.4	4
1972 Den	2	0	0	—	0	—	0	0	—	0
1973 Cle	14	8	4	50.0	22	2.75	1	0	95.8	0
1974 SD	12	0	0	—	0	—	0	0	—	0
NFL Total	57	465	232	49.9	3369	7.25	20	36	55.9	15

JOE HORN Horn, Joseph 6′1″, 199 **WR**
Col: Itawamba CC MS *HS:* Douglas Byrd [Fayetteville, NC] B: 1/16/1972, Tupelo, MS *Drafted:* 1996 Round 5 KC
1996 KC: 9 G; Rush 1-8 8.0; Rec 2-30 15.0. **1997** KC: 8 G; Rec 2-65 32.5. **1998** KC: 16 G; Rush 1-0; Rec 14-198 14.1 1 TD; PR 1-6 6.0; KR 11-233 21.2; 6 Pt; 2 Fum. **Total:** 33 G; Rush 2-8 4.0; Rec 18-293 16.3 1 TD; PR 1-6 6.0; KR 11-233 21.2; 6 Pt; 2 Fum.

MARTY HORN Horn, Martin Louis 6′2″, 206 **QB**
Col: Lehigh *HS:* Millburn [NJ]; Milford Acad. [CT] B: 3/27/1963, Orange, NJ
1987 Phi: 1 G; Pass 11-5 45.5%, 68 6.18; Rush 1-0; 1 Fum.

DICK HORN Horn, Richard Henry 6′1″, 195 **QB**
Col: Stanford *HS:* Santa Monica [CA] B: 3/18/1930, Santa Monica, CA *Drafted:* 1952 Round 17 Dal
1958 Bal: 5 G; Punt 19-617 32.5.

BOB HORN Horn, Robert Allen 6′3″, 235 **LB**
Col: Oregon State *HS:* South Salem [Salem, OR] B: 2/6/1954, Salem, OR *Drafted:* 1976 Round 4 SD
1976 SD: 14 G; KR 1-7 7.0; Int 1-6. **1977** SD: 14 G; Int 1-12. **1978** SD: 16 G; KR 2-27 13.5; Int 1-0. **1979** SD: 16 G; Int 2-44. **1980** SD: 16 G; PR 1-0. **1981** SD: 16 G; Int 1-12. **1982** SF: 9 G; Int 1-19. **1983** SF: 8 G. **Total:** 109 G; PR 1-0; KR 3-34 11.3; Int 7-93.

ROD HORN Horn, Rodney Lee 6′4″, 268 **NT**
Col: Nebraska *HS:* Herbert Hoover [Fresno, CA] B: 11/23/1956, Fresno, CA *Drafted:* 1980 Round 3 Cin
1980 Cin: 7 G. **1981** Cin: 16 G. **Total:** 23 G.

JAY HORNBEAK Hornbeak, Jay William 5′11″, 185 **BB-DB**
Col: Washington *HS:* Corsicana [TX] B: 9/9/1911, Corsicana, TX D: 7/15/1990, Palm Springs, CA
1935 Bkn: 6 G; Rush 1-6 6.0; Rec 1-13 13.0.

GREG HORNE Horne, Gregory Lee 6′0″, 188 **P**
Col: Arkansas *HS:* Russellville [AR] B: 11/22/1964, Russellville, AR *Drafted:* 1987 Round 5 Cin
1988 Pho: Rush 3-20 6.7. **Total:** Rush 3-20 6.7.

		Punting			
Year Team	G	Punts	Yds	Avg	Fum
1987 Cin-StL	9	43	1730	40.2	0
1987 Cin	4	19	759	39.9	0
1987 StL	5	24	971	40.5	0
1988 Pho	16	79	3228	40.9	2
NFL Total	25	122	4958	40.6	2

DICK HORNE Horne, Richard Courtland 6′2″, 214 **DE-OE**
Col: Compton CC CA; Oregon *HS:* Woodrow Wilson [Long Beach, CA] B: 9/4/1918, Denver, CO D: 11/1964
AAFC **1946** MiaA: 10 G; Rec 5-48 9.6. **1947** SF-A: 10 G; Rec 3-69 23.0. **Total:** 20 G; Rec 8-117 14.6.

NFL **1941** NYG: 2 G.

TONY HORNE Horne, Tony Tremaine 5′9″, 173 **WR**
Col: Clemson *HS:* Richmond [Rockingham, NC] B: 3/21/1976, Montgomery Co., NC
1998 StL: PR 1-0.

		Kickoff Returns				
Year Team	G	Ret	Yds	Avg	TD	Fum
1998 StL	16	56	1306	23.3	1	1

SAM HORNER Horner, Samuel Watson III 6′0″, 198 **HB-DB-P**
Col: Virginia Military *HS:* Hill School [Pottstown, PA] B: 3/4/1938, Fort Sill, OK *Drafted:* 1960 Round 2 Was
1960 Was: Rec 7-106 15.1; PR 3-16 5.3. **1961** Was: Rec 10-113 11.3 1 TD. **1962** NYG: PR 3-3 1.0. **Total:** Rec 17-219 12.9 1 TD; PR 6-19 3.2.

		Rushing				Kickoff Returns			
Year Team	G	Att	Yds	Avg	TD	Ret	Yds	Avg	TD
1960 Was	10	22	80	3.6	0	24	511	21.3	0
1961 Was	14	96	275	2.9	0	4	75	18.8	0
1962 NYG	9	0	0	—	0	11	242	22.0	0
NFL Total	33	118	355	3.0	0	39	828	21.2	0

	Punting			
Year Team	Punts	Yds	Avg	Fum
1960 Was	1	48	48.0	2
1961 Was	63	2409	38.2	2
NFL Total	64	2457	38.4	4

BILL HORNICK Hornick, William Michael Thomas 6′1″, 207 **T**
Col: Tulane B: 2/13/1919 D: 5/3/1995, Taylorsville, MS
1947 Pit: 4 G.

STEAMER HORNING Horning, Clarence Edward 6′0″, 196 **T**
Col: Colgate *HS:* Caledonia [NY] B: 11/15/1892, Phoenix, NY D: 1/24/1982, Southfield, MI
1920 Det: 8 G. **1921** Det-Buf: 11 G; 6 Pt. Det: 7 G. Buf: 4 G; 6 Pt. **1922** Tol: 9 G; Rec 1 TD; 6 Pt. **1923** Tol: 8 G. **Total:** 36 G; Rec 1 TD; Tot TD 2; 12 Pt.

RON HORNSBY Hornsby, Ronald Joseph 6′3″, 232 **LB**
Col: Southeastern Louisiana *HS:* Greensburg [LA] B: 8/16/1949, Baton Rouge, LA *Drafted:* 1971 Round 3 NYG
1971 NYG: 14 G. **1972** NYG: 13 G. **1973** NYG: 13 G. **1974** NYG: 9 G; Int 1-2. **Total:** 49 G; Int 1-2.

PAUL HORNUNG Hornung, Paul Vernon 6′2″, 215 **HB-FB-QB**
(Golden Boy) *Col:* Notre Dame *HS:* Flaget [Louisville, KY] B: 12/23/1935, Louisville, KY *Drafted:* 1957 Round 1 GB *HOF:* 1986
1958 GB: KR 10-248 24.8. **Total:** KR 10-248 24.8.

		Passing							
Year Team	G	Att	Comp	Comp%	Yds	YPA	TD	Int	Rating
1957 GB	12	6	1	16.7	-1	-0.17	0	0	39.6
1958 GB	12	1	0	0.0	0	0.00	0	0	39.6
1959 GB	12	8	5	62.5	95	11.88	2	0	143.2
1960 GB	12	16	6	37.5	118	7.38	2	0	103.6
1961 GB	12	5	3	60.0	42	8.40	1	0	126.7
1962 GB	9	6	4	66.7	80	13.33	0	2	70.1
1964 GB	14	10	3	30.0	25	2.50	0	1	0.0
1965 GB	12	2	1	50.0	19	9.50	0	1	43.8

1966 GB	9	1	1	100.0	5	5.00	0	0	87.5
NFL Total	104	55	24	43.6	383	6.96	5	4	67.5

	Rushing				Receiving			
Year Team	**Att**	**Yds**	**Avg**	**TD**	**Rec**	**Yds**	**Avg**	**TD**
1957 GB	60	319	**5.3**	3	6	34	5.7	0
1958 GB	69	310	4.5	2	15	137	9.1	0
1959 GB	152	681	4.5	7	15	113	7.5	0
1960 GB	160	671	4.2	**13**	28	257	9.2	2
1961 GB	127	597	4.7	8	15	145	9.7	2
1962 GB	57	219	3.8	5	9	168	18.7	2
1964 GB	103	415	4.0	5	9	98	10.9	0
1965 GB	89	299	3.4	5	19	336	17.7	3
1966 GB	76	200	2.6	2	14	192	13.7	3
NFL Total	893	3711	4.2	50	130	1480	11.4	12

	Scoring								Tot
Year Team	**Pts**	**FG**	**FGA**	**FG%**	**XK**	**XKA**	**XK%**	**Fum**	**TD**
1957 GB	18	0	4	0.0	0	0	—	2	3
1958 GB	67	11	21	52.4	22	23	95.7	1	2
1959 GB	**94**	7	17	41.2	31	32	96.9	7	7
1960 GB	**176**	15	28	53.6	41	41	100.0	3	**15**
1961 GB	**146**	15	22	68.2	41	41	100.0	1	10
1962 GB	74	6	10	60.0	14	14	100.0	1	7
1964 GB	107	12	**38**	31.6	41	43	95.3	4	5
1965 GB	0	0	0	—	0	0	—	2	8
1966 GB	0	0	0	—	0	0	—	1	5
NFL Total	760	66	140	47.1	190	194	97.9	22	62

BILL HORRELL Horrell, William George 5'11", 222 **OG**
Col: Michigan State *HS:* New Kensington [PA] B: 3/15/1930, New Kensington, PA
1952 Phi: 4 G.

ROY HORSTMANN Horstmann, Roy Joseph 6'0", 188 **FB-LB-DB-WB**
Col: Purdue *HS:* Mishawaka [IN] B: 12/6/1910, Aurora, IL
1933 Bos: Pass 8-3 37.5%, 50 6.25 2 Int. **1934** ChiC: Pass 3-1 33.3%, 12 4.00. **Total:** Pass 11-4 36.4%, 62 5.64 2 Int.

		Rushing			
Year Team	**G**	**Att**	**Yds**	**Avg**	**TD**
1933 Bos	8	34	144	4.2	0
1934 ChiC	9	18	36	2.0	1
NFL Total	17	52	180	3.5	1

ETHAN HORTON Horton, Ethan Shane 6'4", 235 **TE-RB**
Col: North Carolina *HS:* A.L. Brown [Kannapolis, NC] B: 12/19/1962, Kannapolis, NC *Drafted:* 1985 Round 1 KC
1985 KC: Pass 1-0. **Total:** Pass 1-0.

		Rushing				Receiving					Tot
Year Team	**G**	**Att**	**Yds**	**Avg**	**TD**	**Rec**	**Yds**	**Avg**	**TD**	**Fum**	**TD**
1985 KC	16	48	146	3.0	3	28	185	6.6	1	2	4
1987 LARd	4	31	95	3.1	0	3	44	14.7	1	2	1
1989 LARd	16	0	0	—	0	4	44	11.0	1	0	1
1990 LARd	16	0	0	—	0	33	404	12.2	3	1	3
1991 LARd	16	0	0	—	0	53	650	12.3	5	1	5
1992 LARd	16	0	0	—	0	33	409	12.4	2	1	2
1993 LARd	16	0	0	—	0	43	467	10.9	1	0	1
1994 Was	16	0	0	—	0	15	157	10.5	3	0	3
NFL Total	116	79	241	3.1	3	212	2360	11.1	17	7	20

GREG HORTON Horton, Gregory Keith 6'4", 245 **OG-C**
Col: Colorado *HS:* Redlands [CA] B: 1/7/1951, San Bernardino, CA
Drafted: 1974 Round 3 ChiB
1976 LARm: 14 G. **1977** LARm: 14 G. **1978** LARm-TB: 16 G. LARm: 2 G. TB: 14 G. **1979** TB: 16 G. **1980** LARm: 3 G. **Total:** 63 G.

LARRY HORTON Horton, Lawrence 6'4", 248 **DE-DT**
Col: Indian Hills CC IA; Iowa *HS:* Froebel [Gary, IN] B: 4/29/1949, Gary, IN *Drafted:* 1972 Round 9 ChiB
1972 ChiB: 10 G; KR 1-3 3.0.

RAY HORTON Horton, Raymond Anthony 5'10", 189 **DB**
Col: Washington *HS:* Mount Tahoma [Tacoma, WA] B: 4/12/1960, Tacoma, WA *Drafted:* 1983 Round 2 Cin
1983 Cin: PR 1-10 10.0; KR 5-128 25.6. **1984** Cin: PR 2-(-1) -0.5; 1 Sac. **1986** Cin: PR 11-111 10.1. **1987** Cin: PR 1-0. **1988** Cin: 1 Sac. **1989** Dal: 1 Sac. **1991** Dal: PR 1-8 8.0; KR 1-0; 1 Fum TD. **1992** Dal: PR 1-1 1.0. **Total:** PR 17-129 7.6; KR 6-128 21.3; 1 Fum TD; 3 Sac.

		Interceptions				Tot
Year Team	**G**	**Int**	**Yds**	**TD**	**Fum**	**TD**
1983 Cin	16	5	121	1	1	1
1984 Cin	15	3	48	1	0	1
1985 Cin	16	2	3	0	1	0
1986 Cin	16	1	4	0	2	0
1987 Cin	12	0	0	0	0	0
1988 Cin	14	3	13	0	0	0
1989 Dal	16	1	0	0	0	0
1990 Dal	14	1	0	0	0	0
1991 Dal	16	1	65	1	1	2
1992 Dal	12	2	15	1	0	1
NFL Total	147	19	269	4	5	5

BOB HORTON Horton, Robert 6'2", 230 **LB**
Col: Boston U. *HS:* White Plains [NY] B: 9/15/1942, Chicago, IL
Drafted: 1964 Round 11 SD
1964 SD: 10 G. **1965** SD: 12 G. **Total:** 22 G.

LES HORVATH Horvath, Leslie 5'10", 173 **HB-DB**
Col: Ohio State *HS:* Parma [OH]; Rhodes HS [Cleveland, OH]
B: 10/12/1921, South Bend, IN D: 11/14/1995, Glendale, CA
Drafted: 1943 Round 6 Cle
AAFC **1949** CleA: 12 G; Rush 10-35 3.5 1 TD; Rec 2-71 35.5 1 TD; PR 3-19 6.3; Int 2-4; Tot TD 3; 18 Pt.

NFL **1947** LARm: Rec 3-29 9.7; PR 4-29 7.3; KR 3-58 19.3. **1948** LARm: Rec 4-42 10.5; PR 13-203 15.6; KR 2-31 15.5; Int 2-14. **Total:** Rec 7-71 10.1; PR 17-232 13.6; KR 5-89 17.8; Int 2-14.

		Rushing				
Year Team	**G**	**Att**	**Yds**	**Avg**	**TD**	**Fum**
1947 LARm	10	18	68	3.8	0	3
1948 LARm	12	30	118	3.9	0	2
NFL Total	22	48	186	3.9	0	5

ARNIE HORWEEN Horween, Arnold 5'11", 206 **BB-FB-TB**
(AKA Arnold Horowitz) *Col:* Harvard *HS:* Francis W. Parker [Chicago, IL] B: 7/7/1898, Chicago, IL D: 8/5/1985, Chicago, IL
1921 ChiC: 3 G. **1922** ChiC: 11 G; Pass 1 TD; Rush 4 TD; Scor 27, 1 FG. **1923** ChiC: 11 G; Pass 1 TD; Scor 9, 2 FG, 3 XK. **1924** ChiC: 7 G. **Total:** 32 G; Pass 2 TD; Rush 4 TD; Scor 36, 3 FG, 3 XK.

RALPH HORWEEN Horween, Ralph 5'10", 200 **FB-WB-BB-TB**
(AKA McMahon; Ralph Horowitz) *Col:* Harvard *HS:* Francis W. Parker [Chicago, IL] B: 8/3/1896, Chicago, IL D: 5/26/1997, Charlottesville, VA
1921 ChiC: 2 G; Scor 3, 1 FG. **1922** ChiC: 9 G; Scor 11, 3 FG, 2 XK. **1923** ChiC: 11 G; Rush 2 TD; 12 Pt. **Total:** 22 G; Rush 2 TD; Scor 26, 4 FG, 2 XK.

DERRICK HOSKINS Hoskins, Derrick Tremayne 6'2", 200 **DB**
Col: Southern Mississippi *HS:* Neshoba Central [Philadelphia, MS]
B: 11/14/1970, Meridian, MS *Drafted:* 1992 Round 5 LARd
1992 LARd: 16 G. **1993** LARd: 16 G; Int 2-34. **1994** LARd: 15 G. **1995** Oak: 13 G; Int 1-26. **1996** NO: 1 G. **Total:** 61 G; Int 3-60.

BOB HOSKINS Hoskins, Robert Juan 6'2", 251 **DT-OG**
Col: Wichita State *HS:* Edwardsville [IL] B: 9/16/1945, Highland, IL
D: 6/8/1980, Redwood City, CA *Drafted:* 1969 Round 16 SF
1970 SF: 14 G. **1971** SF: 7 G. **1972** SF: 14 G; KR 2-17 8.5. **1973** SF: 14 G. **1974** SF: 14 G. **1975** SF: 14 G. **Total:** 77 G; KR 2-17 8.5.

CLARENCE HOSMER Hosmer, Clarence 5'10", 205 **G**
Col: No College *HS:* Tonawanda [NY] B: 7/28/1891, NY D: 11/1968, Buffalo, NY
1921 Ton: 1 G.

CLARK HOSS Hoss, Clark 6'8", 235 **TE**
Col: Oregon State *HS:* West Linn [OR] B: 2/19/1949, Portland, OR
Drafted: 1972 Round 7 NE
1972 Phi: 4 G.

JEFF HOSTETLER Hostetler, William Jeffrey 6'3", 215 **QB**
Col: Penn State; West Virginia *HS:* Conemaugh Twp. [Davidsville, PA]
B: 4/22/1961, Hollsopple, PA *Drafted:* 1984 Round 3 NYG
1988 NYG: Rec 1-10 10.0. **Total:** Rec 1-10 10.0.

		Passing							
Year Team	**G**	**Att**	**Comp**	**Comp%**	**Yds**	**YPA**	**TD**	**Int**	**Rating**
1985 NYG	5	0	0	—	0	—	0	0	—
1986 NYG	13	0	0	—	0	—	0	0	—
1988 NYG	16	29	16	55.2	244	8.41	1	2	65.9
1989 NYG	16	39	20	51.3	294	7.54	3	2	80.5
1990 NYG	16	87	47	54.0	614	7.06	3	1	83.2
1991 NYG	12	285	179	62.8	2032	7.13	5	**4**	84.1
1992 NYG	13	192	103	53.6	1225	6.38	8	3	80.8
1993 LARd	15	419	236	56.3	3242	7.74	14	10	82.5
1994 LARd	16	455	263	57.8	3334	7.33	20	16	80.8
1995 Oak	11	286	172	60.1	1998	6.99	12	9	82.2
1996 Oak	13	402	242	60.2	2548	6.34	23	14	83.2
1997 Was	6	144	79	54.9	899	6.24	5	10	56.5
NFL Total	152	2338	1357	58.0	16430	7.03	94	71	80.5

	Rushing				
Year Team	**Att**	**Yds**	**Avg**	**TD**	**Fum**
1986 NYG	1	1	1.0	0	0
1988 NYG	5	-3	-0.6	0	1
1989 NYG	11	71	6.5	2	2
1990 NYG	39	190	4.9	2	4
1991 NYG	42	273	6.5	2	7

1992 NYG	35	172	4.9	3	6
1993 LARd	55	202	3.7	5	6
1994 LARd	46	159	3.5	2	10
1995 Oak	31	119	3.8	0	5
1996 Oak	37	179	4.8	1	4
1997 Was	14	28	2.0	0	3
NFL Total	316	1391	4.4	17	48

BABE HOUCK Houck, Orlan G 6'0", 275 **G**
Col: Bliss College *HS:* Gallia Acad. [Gallipolis, OH] B: 8/20/1897, Gallipolis, OH D: 7/6/1983, Athens, OH
1920 Col: 4 G. **1921** Col: 7 G. **Total:** 11 G.

JIM HOUGH Hough, James Husen 6'2", 267 **OG-C**
Col: Utah State *HS:* La Mirada [CA] B: 8/4/1956, Lynwood, CA
Drafted: 1978 Round 4 Min
1978 Min: 15 G. **1979** Min: 16 G. **1980** Min: 10 G. **1981** Min: 16 G. **1982** Min: 9 G. **1983** Min: 16 G. **1984** Min: 9 G. **1985** Min: 4 G. **1986** Min: 16 G. **Total:** 111 G.

JERRY HOUGHTON Houghton, Gerald Haines 6'2", 226 **LB-DT-OT**
Col: Washington State *HS:* Zillah [WA] B: 4/18/1926, Yakima, WA
Drafted: 1950 Round 7 Was
1950 Was: 12 G. **1951** ChiC: 2 G. **Total:** 14 G.

BILL HOULE Houle, Wilfred Theodore 5'8", 175 **BB**
Col: St. Thomas *HS:* White Bear Lake [MN] B: 7/14/1901
D: 12/26/1974, St. Paul, MN
1924 Min: 6 G.

KEVIN HOUSE House, Kevin Nathaniel 6'1", 181 **WR**
Col: Southern Illinois *HS:* University City [MO] B: 12/20/1957, St. Louis, MO *Drafted:* 1980 Round 2 TB
1980 TB: Rush 1-32 32.0. **1981** TB: Pass 1-0; Rush 2-9 4.5. **1982** TB: Rush 1-(-1) -1.0. **1983** TB: Rush 1-(-4) -4.0. **1986** TB-LARm: Rush 2-5 2.5. TB: Rush 2-5 2.5. **Total:** Pass 1-0; Rush 7-41 5.9.

		Receiving				
Year Team	**G**	**Rec**	**Yds**	**Avg**	**TD**	**Fum**
1980 TB	14	24	531	22.1	5	1
1981 TB	16	56	1176	21.0	9	2
1982 TB	9	28	438	15.6	2	1
1983 TB	16	47	769	16.4	5	0
1984 TB	16	76	1005	13.2	5	0
1985 TB	16	44	803	18.3	5	0
1986 TB-LARm	15	18	384	21.3	2	0
1986 TB	7	11	206	18.7	0	0
1986 LARm	8	7	178	25.4	2	0
1987 LARm	12	6	63	10.5	1	0
NFL Total	114	299	5169	17.3	34	4

JOHN HOUSER Houser, John Wesley Jr. 6'3", 238 **OG-C**
Col: Redlands *HS:* Boys Republic [Chino, CA] B: 6/21/1935, Oklahoma City, OK
1957 LARm: 12 G. **1958** LARm: 12 G. **1959** LARm: 12 G. **1960** Dal: 11 G. **1961** Dal: 14 G. **1963** StL: 7 G. **Total:** 68 G.

WALT HOUSMAN Housman, Walter Henry III 6'5", 285 **OT-OG**
Col: Iowa; Upsala *HS:* Merrimack [NH] B: 10/13/1962, Marshall, MO
1987 NO: 3 G.

BOBBY HOUSTON Houston, Bobby Darin 6'2", 242 **LB**
Col: North Carolina State *HS:* DeMatha [Hyattsville, MD]
B: 10/26/1967, Washington, DC *Drafted:* 1990 Round 3 GB
1990 GB: 1 G. **1991** NYJ: 14 G; 1 Sac. **1992** NYJ: 16 G; Int 1-20 1 TD; 6 Pt; 4 Sac. **1993** NYJ: 16 G; Int 1-0; 3 Sac. **1994** NYJ: 16 G; 3.5 Sac. **1995** NYJ: 16 G; 3 Sac. **1996** NYJ: 15 G; Int 2-3. **1997** KC-SD: 7 G. KC: 5 G. SD: 2 G. **1998** Min: 8 G. **Total:** 109 G; Int 4-23 1 TD; 6 Pt; 14.5 Sac.

JIM HOUSTON Houston, James Edward 6'3", 240 **LB-DE**
Col: Ohio State *HS:* Washington [Massillon, OH] B: 11/3/1937, Massillon, OH *Drafted:* 1960 Round 1 Cle
1966 Cle: Rec 1-10 10.0 1 TD; Scor **1** 1XP. **1968** Cle: KR 1-0. **1971** Cle: KR 1-21 21.0. **Total:** Rec 1-10 10.0 1 TD; KR 2-21 10.5; Scor 1 1XP.

		Interceptions			Tot
Year Team	**G**	**Int**	**Yds**	**TD**	**TD**
1960 Cle	12	0	0	0	0
1961 Cle	14	0	0	0	0
1962 Cle	14	0	0	0	0
1963 Cle	14	1	0	0	0
1964 Cle	14	2	86	1	1
1965 Cle	12	2	32	0	0
1966 Cle	14	2	27	0	1
1967 Cle	13	3	97	2	2
1968 Cle	14	3	11	0	0
1969 Cle	14	0	0	0	0
1970 Cle	14	1	25	0	0
1971 Cle	14	0	0	0	0
1972 Cle	14	0	0	0	0
NFL Total	177	14	278	3	4

KEN HOUSTON Houston, Kenneth Ray 6'3", 197 **DB**
Col: Prairie View A&M *HS:* Dunbar [Texarkana, TX] B: 11/12/1944, Lufkin, TX *Drafted:* 1967 Round 9 Hou *HOF:* 1986
1967 Hou: KR 2-40 20.0. **1968** Hou: KR 1-13 13.0. **1969** Hou: KR 0-27. **1971** Hou: **1** Fum TD. **Total:** KR 3-80 26.7; 1 Fum TD.

		Punt Returns				Interceptions				Tot
Year Team	**G**	**Ret**	**Yds**	**Avg**	**TD**	**Int**	**Yds**	**TD**	**Fum**	**TD**
1967 Hou	14	0	0	—	0	4	151	2	0	3
1968 Hou	14	0	0	—	0	5	160	**2**	0	2
1969 Hou	14	0	0	—	0	4	87	1	1	1
1970 Hou	14	4	13	3.3	0	3	32	0	0	0
1971 Hou	14	16	91	5.7	0	9	220	**4**	2	5
1972 Hou	14	25	148	5.9	0	0	0	0	2	0
1973 Was	14	0	0	—	0	6	32	0	0	0
1974 Was	14	6	81	13.5	1	2	40	0	1	1
1975 Was	14	0	0	—	0	4	33	0	0	0
1976 Was	14	0	0	—	0	4	25	0	1	0
1977 Was	14	0	0	—	0	5	69	0	3	0
1978 Was	16	0	0	—	0	2	29	0	0	0
1979 Was	13	0	0	—	0	1	20	0	0	0
1980 Was	13	0	0	—	0	0	0	0	0	0
NFL Total	196	51	333	6.5	1	49	898	**9**	10	12

LIN HOUSTON Houston, Lindell Lee 6'0", 235 **OG-DG**
Col: Michigan; Ohio State *HS:* Washington [Massillon, OH]
B: 1/11/1921, Carbondale, IL D: 9/8/1995, Canton, OH
AAFC **1946** CleA: 12 G. **1947** CleA: 14 G. **1948** CleA: 13 G. **1949** CleA: 12 G; Rec 0-19. **Total:** 51 G; Rec 0-19.

NFL **1950** Cle: 12 G. **1951** Cle: 11 G. **1952** Cle: 12 G. **1953** Cle: 12 G. **Total:** 47 G.

WALT HOUSTON Houston, Loren Walter 6'0", 217 **OG**
Col: Miami (Ohio); Purdue *HS:* Washington [Massillon, OH]
B: 10/26/1932, Wolf Lake, IL *Drafted:* 1955 Round 26 Was
1955 Was: 10 G.

RICH HOUSTON Houston, Richard Charles 6'2", 195 **WR**
Col: Texas A&M-Commerce *HS:* Dunbar [Texarkana, TX]
B: 11/16/1945, Texarkana, TX D: 12/11/1982 *Drafted:* 1969 Round 4 NYG
1969 NYG: Rush 1-11 11.0. **1971** NYG: Rush 2-2 1.0. **Total:** Rush 3-13 4.3.

		Receiving				Kickoff Returns				
Year Team	**G**	**Rec**	**Yds**	**Avg**	**TD**	**Ret**	**Yds**	**Avg**	**TD**	**Fum**
1969 NYG	6	2	69	34.5	0	12	252	21.0	0	0
1970 NYG	13	4	68	17.0	0	8	173	21.6	0	1
1971 NYG	13	24	426	17.8	4	0	0	—	0	0
1972 NYG	14	27	468	17.3	3	0	0	—	0	1
1973 NYG	14	8	90	11.3	0	15	375	25.0	0	0
NFL Total	60	65	1121	17.2	7	35	800	22.9	0	2

BILL HOUSTON Houston, William Glenn 6'3", 208 **WR**
Col: Northwest Mississippi CC; Jackson State *HS:* Central [Oxford, MS]
B: 8/22/1951, Oxford, MS
1974 Dal: 13 G; Rec 6-72 12.0.

DON HOVER Hover, Donald R 6'2", 225 **LB**
Col: Washington State *HS:* Issaquah [WA] B: 12/13/1954, Seattle, WA
Drafted: 1978 Round 8 Was
1978 Was: 16 G. **1979** Was: 16 G; **1** Fum TD; 6 Pt. **Total:** 32 G; 1 Fum TD; 6 Pt.

JUNIE HOVIOUS Hovious, John Alexander Jr. 5'8", 180 **QB-HB**
Col: Mississippi *HS:* Carr Central [Vicksburg, MS] B: 10/4/1919, Vicksburg, MS D: 5/7/1998, Oxford, MS *Drafted:* 1942 Round 16 NYG
1945 NYG: 6 G; Pass 46-22 47.8%, 373 8.11 4 TD 5 Int; Rush 22-(-7) -0.3; KR 1-20 20.0; 3 Fum.

RED HOWARD Howard, Albert Franklin 5'11", 192 **G**
Col: New Hampshire; Princeton *HS:* Haverhill [MA] B: 11/23/1900, Haverhill, MA D: 5/29/1973, Essex Falls, NJ
1926 Bkn: 3 G. **1927** NYG: 1 G. **Total:** 4 G.

ANTHONY HOWARD Howard, Anthony Craig 6'3", 267 **NT**
Col: Merritt Coll. CA (J.C.); Tennessee *HS:* Berkeley [CA]
B: 7/16/1960, Berkeley, CA
1987 NYG: 3 G.

BOBBY HOWARD Howard, Bobby Allen 6'0", 213 **RB**
Col: Indiana *HS:* Langley [Pittsburgh, PA] B: 6/1/1964, Pittsburgh, PA
Drafted: 1986 Round 12 Phi
1986 TB: Rec 5-60 12.0; KR 4-71 17.8. **1987** TB: Rec 10-123 12.3; KR 1-5 5.0. **Total:** Rec 15-183 12.2; KR 5-76 15.2.

		Rushing				
Year Team	**G**	**Att**	**Yds**	**Avg**	**TD**	**Fum**
1986 TB	7	30	110	3.7	1	1
1987 TB	12	30	100	3.3	1	1

1988 TB	1	0	0	—	0	0
NFL Total	20	60	210	3.5	2	2

BRYAN HOWARD Howard, Bryan Edward 6′0″, 200 **DB**
Col: Tennessee State *HS:* George Washington Carver [New Orleans, LA] B: 3/6/1959, New Orleans, LA *Drafted:* 1982 Round 9 Min
1982 Min: 2 G.

CARL HOWARD Howard, Carl Delano Jr. 6′2″, 188 **DB**
Col: Rutgers *HS:* Irvington Technical [NJ] B: 9/20/1961, Newark, NJ
1984 Dal: 10 G. **1985** TB-NYJ: 7 G. TB: 4 G. NYJ: 3 G. **1986** NYJ: 14 G. **1987** NYJ: 12 G; Int 3-29; 2 Sac. **1988** NYJ: 16 G; Int 2-0; 1 Sac. **1989** NYJ: 15 G. **1990** NYJ: 3 G. **Total:** 77 G; Int 5-29; 3 Sac.

CHRIS HOWARD Howard, Christopher L 5′10″, 223 **RB**
Col: Michigan *HS:* John Curtis [River Ridge, LA] B: 5/5/1975, Kenner, LA *Drafted:* 1998 Round 5 Den
1998 Jac: 8 G; Rush 7-16 2.3; Rec 1-3 3.0.

DANA HOWARD Howard, Dana Cortez 6′0″, 238 **LB**
Col: Illinois *HS:* East St. Louis [IL] B: 2/25/1972, East St. Louis, IL *Drafted:* 1995 Round 5 Dal
1995 StL: 16 G. **1996** ChiB: 3 G. **Total:** 19 G.

DAVID HOWARD Howard, David 6′1″, 231 **LB**
Col: Oregon State; Long Beach State *HS:* Long Beach Polytechnic [CA] B: 12/8/1961, Enterprise, AL *Drafted:* 1984 Supplemental Round 3 Min
1985 Min: 16 G. **1986** Min: 14 G; 2.5 Sac. **1987** Min: 10 G; Int 1-1. **1988** Min: 16 G; Int 3-16; 1 Sac. **1989** Min-Dal: 16 G. Min: 5 G. Dal: 11 G. **1990** Dal: 16 G. **1991** NE: 16 G; 1 Sac. **1992** NE: 16 G; Int 1-1; 1 Sac. **Total:** 120 G; Int 5-18; 5.5 Sac.

DESMOND HOWARD Howard, Desmond Kevin 5′10″, 185 **WR**
Col: Michigan *HS:* St. Joseph [Cleveland, OH] B: 5/15/1970, Cleveland, OH *Drafted:* 1992 Round 1 Was
1992 Was: Rush 3-14 4.7. **1993** Was: Rush 2-17 8.5. **1994** Was: Rush 1-4 4.0; Scor 1 2XP. **1995** Jac: Rush 1-8 8.0. **Total:** Rush 7-43 6.1; Scor 1 2XP.

		Receiving				Punt Returns			
Year Team	**G**	**Rec**	**Yds**	**Avg**	**TD**	**Ret**	**Yds**	**Avg**	**TD**
1992 Was	16	3	20	6.7	0	6	84	14.0	1
1993 Was	16	23	286	12.4	0	4	25	6.3	0
1994 Was	16	40	727	18.2	5	0	0	—	0
1995 Jac	13	26	276	10.6	1	24	246	10.3	0
1996 GB	16	13	95	7.3	0	**58**	**875**	**15.1**	**3**
1997 Oak	15	4	30	7.5	0	27	210	7.8	0
1998 Oak	15	2	16	8.0	0	45	541	12.0	**2**
NFL Total	107	111	1450	13.1	6	164	1981	12.1	6

	Kickoff Returns					Tot
Year Team	**Ret**	**Yds**	**Avg**	**TD**	**Fum**	**TD**
1992 Was	22	462	21.0	0	1	1
1993 Was	21	405	19.3	0	0	0
1994 Was	0	0	—	0	0	5
1995 Jac	10	178	17.8	0	0	1
1996 GB	22	460	20.9	0	2	3
1997 Oak	**61**	1318	21.6	0	2	0
1998 Oak	49	1040	21.2	0	4	2
NFL Total	185	3863	20.9	0	9	12

EDDIE HOWARD Howard, Eddie 6′1″, 203 **P**
Col: Mount San Antonio Coll. CA (J.C.); Idaho *HS:* West Covina [CA] B: 10/16/1972, Covina, CA
1998 SF: 2 G; Punt 9-324 36.0.

ERIK HOWARD Howard, Erik Matthew 6′4″, 270 **NT-DT-DE**
Col: Washington State *HS:* Bellarmine Prep [San Jose, CA] B: 11/12/1964, Pittsfield, MA *Drafted:* 1986 Round 2 NYG
1986 NYG: 8 G; 2 Sac. **1987** NYG: 12 G; 5.5 Sac. **1988** NYG: 16 G; 3 Sac. **1989** NYG: 16 G; 5.5 Sac. **1990** NYG: 16 G; 3 Sac. **1991** NYG: 6 G; 1.5 Sac. **1992** NYG: 16 G. **1993** NYG: 16 G; 3.5 Sac. **1994** NYG: 16 G; 6.5 Sac. **1995** NYJ: 16 G; Scor **1** Saf; 2 Pt; 2.5 Sac. **1996** NYJ: 1 G. **Total:** 139 G; Scor 1 Saf; 2 Pt; 33 Sac.

HARRY HOWARD Howard, Harry Jr. 6′1″, 189 **DB**
Col: Ohio State *HS:* Princeton [Cincinati, OH] B: 10/7/1949, Cincinnati, OH *Drafted:* 1972 Round 9 LARm
1976 NYJ: 1 G.

TOM HOWARD Howard, James Thomas 6′2″, 213 **LB**
Col: Texas Tech *HS:* Dunbar [Lubbock, TX] B: 8/18/1954, Lubbock, TX *Drafted:* 1977 Round 3 KC
1977 KC: 13 G; Int 1-0. **1978** KC: 16 G; Int 1-0. **1979** KC: 16 G; Int 1-19. **1980** KC: 16 G; **1** Fum TD; 6 Pt. **1981** KC: 9 G; 1 Fum TD; 6 Pt. **1982** KC: 9 G; Int 2-10; 3 Sac. **1983** KC: 16 G; 1 Sac. **1984** StL: 15 G; Int 2-(-4); **1** Fum TD; 6 Pt. **1985** StL: 3 G. **Total:** 113 G; Int 7-25; 3 Fum TD; 18 Pt; 4 Sac.

JOEY HOWARD Howard, Joseph Eissix 6′5″, 305 **OT**
Col: Northeastern Oklahoma A&M (J.C.); Tennessee *HS:* Springfield North [OH] B: 9/14/1965, Springfield, OH *Drafted:* 1988 Round 9 SD
1989 SD: 9 G.

LEROY HOWARD Howard, Leroy Jr. 5′11″, 175 **DB**
Col: Bishop *HS:* Lincoln [Port Arthur, TX] B: 6/16/1949, Port Arthur, TX
1971 Hou: 7 G.

TUBBY HOWARD Howard, Lynn Wales 5′10″, 210 **E-FB-BB**
Col: Ripon; Wisconsin; Indiana B: 6/10/1894, Bloomington, IN D: 5/1969, Prescott, AZ
1921 GB: 4 G; Rush 1 TD; 6 Pt. **1922** GB: 8 G. **Total:** 12 G; Rush 1 TD; 6 Pt.

PAUL HOWARD Howard, Paul Eugene 6′3″, 260 **OG**
Col: Brigham Young *HS:* Redding [CA] B: 9/12/1950, Redding, CA *Drafted:* 1973 Round 3 Den
1973 Den: 14 G. **1974** Den: 14 G. **1975** Den: 14 G. **1977** Den: 14 G. **1978** Den: 13 G. **1979** Den: 16 G. **1980** Den: 14 G. **1981** Den: 16 G. **1982** Den: 9 G. **1983** Den: 16 G. **1984** Den: 16 G. **1985** Den: 16 G. **1986** Den: 15 G. **Total:** 187 G.

PERCY HOWARD Howard, Percy Lenard 6′4″, 210 **WR**
Col: Isothermal CC NC; Austin Peay State *HS:* Dillard [Fort Lauderdale, FL] B: 1/21/1952, Savannah, GA
1975 Dal: 8 G; KR 2-51 25.5.

DOSEY HOWARD Howard, Robert Lee 6′0″, 225 **G-T**
Col: Marietta *HS:* Norman [OK] B: 8/26/1902, Norman, OK D: 5/15/1966, Alice, TX
1925 KC: 8 G. **1926** KC: 7 G. **1927** Cle: 12 G. **1928** Det: 9 G. **1929** NYG: 12 G. **1930** NYG: 16 G; Rec 1 TD; 6 Pt. **Total:** 64 G; Rec 1 TD; 6 Pt.

BOB HOWARD Howard, Robert Lee 6′2″, 174 **DB**
Col: Cal Poly-S.L.O.; San Diego State *HS:* San Bernardino [CA] B: 11/24/1944, Tallulah, LA *Drafted:* 1967 Round 2 SD

		Interceptions			
Year Team	**G**	**Int**	**Yds**	**TD**	**Fum**
1967 SD	14	0	0	0	0
1968 SD	14	1	0	0	0
1969 SD	14	6	50	0	1
1970 SD	14	2	19	0	0
1971 SD	14	4	47	0	0
1972 SD	5	0	0	0	0
1973 SD	13	5	25	0	0
1974 SD	14	3	52	0	0
1975 NE	14	3	52	1	0
1976 NE	14	3	28	0	0
1977 NE	13	4	10	0	0
1978 Phi	10	3	15	0	0
1979 Phi	16	3	34	0	0
NFL Total	169	37	332	1	1

RON HOWARD Howard, Ronald Ford 6′4″, 229 **TE**
Col: Seattle *HS:* Pasco [WA] B: 3/3/1951, Oakland, CA
1976 Sea: Rush 1-2 2.0. **Total:** Rush 1-2 2.0.

		Receiving				
Year Team	**G**	**Rec**	**Yds**	**Avg**	**TD**	**Fum**
1974 Dal	12	0	0	—	0	0
1975 Dal	10	0	0	—	0	0
1976 Sea	14	37	422	11.4	0	0
1977 Sea	12	17	177	10.4	1	0
1978 Sea	16	18	251	13.9	1	1
1979 Buf	1	0	0	—	0	0
NFL Total	65	72	850	11.8	2	1

SHERMAN HOWARD Howard, Sherman John 5′11″, 193 **HB-DB**
Col: Iowa; Nevada-Reno *HS:* Wendell Phillips [Chicago, IL] B: 11/28/1924, New Orleans, LA
AAFC **1949** NY-A: Rec 1-24 24.0; KR 4-95 23.8; Int 1-26.

		Rushing			
Year Team	**G**	**Att**	**Yds**	**Avg**	**TD**
1949 NY-A	12	117	459	3.9	3

NFL **1950** NYY: PR 1-12 12.0; KR 8-240 30.0 1 TD. **1952** Cle: KR 1-22 22.0. **1953** Cle: KR 1-6 6.0; Int 1-3. **Total:** PR 1-12 12.0; KR 10-268 26.8 1 TD; Int 1-3.

		Rushing				Receiving					Tot
Year Team	**G**	**Att**	**Yds**	**Avg**	**TD**	**Rec**	**Yds**	**Avg**	**TD**	**Fum**	**TD**
1950 NYY	12	71	362	5.1	3	12	278	23.2	5	3	9
1951 NYY	12	94	343	3.6	4	21	447	21.3	3	4	7
1952 Cle	5	34	95	2.8	0	11	219	19.9	3	0	3
1953 Cle	12	7	42	6.0	0	0	0	—	0	0	0
NFL Total	41	206	842	4.1	7	44	944	21.5	11	7	19

TY HOWARD Howard, Ty L 5′9″, 185 **DB**
Col: Ohio State *HS:* Briggs [Columbus, OH] B: 11/30/1973, Columbus, OH *Drafted:* 1997 Round 3 Ariz
1997 Ariz: 15 G; 1 Sac. **1998** Ariz: 9 G. **Total:** 24 G; 1 Sac.

TODD HOWARD Howard, Walter Lee 6'2", 235 **LB**
Col: Texas A&M *HS:* Bryan [TX] B: 2/18/1965, Bryan, TX
Drafted: 1987 Round 3 KC
1987 KC: 12 G. **1988** KC: 7 G. **Total:** 19 G.

BILLY HOWARD Howard, William 6'4", 252 **DT-DE**
Col: Alcorn State *HS:* Clarksdale [MS] B: 7/17/1950, Clarksdale, MS
Drafted: 1974 Round 2 Det
1974 Det: 12 G. **1975** Det: 13 G. **1976** Det: 13 G. **Total:** 38 G.

WILLIAM HOWARD Howard, William Dotson 6'0", 240 **RB**
Col: Tennessee *HS:* Lima [OH]; Tennessee Acad. [Sweetwater, TN]
B: 6/2/1964, Lima, OH *Drafted:* 1988 Round 5 TB
1988 TB: KR 2-21 10.5. **1989** TB: KR 5-82 16.4. **Total:** KR 7-103 14.7.

		Rushing				Receiving					Tot
Year Team	G	Att	Yds	Avg	TD	Rec	Yds	Avg	TD	Fum	TD
1988 TB	15	115	452	3.9	1	11	97	8.8	0	2	1
1989 TB	16	108	357	3.3	1	30	188	6.3	1	2	2
NFL Total	31	223	809	3.6	2	41	285	7.0	1	4	3

GENE HOWARD Howard, William Eugene 6'0", 190 **DB**
(Hog) *Col:* Langston *HS:* Scipio Jones [North Little Rock, AR]
B: 12/22/1946, Little Rock, AR *Drafted:* 1968 Round 7 NO
1968 NO: PR 8-42 5.3. **1969** NO: PR 9-73 8.1. **1970** NO: PR 5-14 2.8.
1971 LARm: **1** Fum TD. **Total:** PR 22-129 5.9; 1 Fum TD.

		Kickoff Returns				Interceptions				Tot
Year Team	G	Ret	Yds	Avg	TD	Int	Yds	TD	Fum	TD
1968 NO	14	23	533	23.2	0	3	51	0	2	0
1969 NO	14	9	227	25.2	0	2	0	0	2	0
1970 NO	8	0	0	—	0	0	0	0	0	0
1971 LARm	14	7	164	23.4	0	6	99	0	0	1
1972 LARm	13	2	51	25.5	0	3	26	1	0	1
NFL Total	63	41	975	23.8	0	14	176	1	4	2

GLEN HOWE Howe, Bobby Glen 6'7", 295 **OT**
Col: Southern Mississippi *HS:* W.P. Daniel [New Albany, MS]
B: 10/18/1961, New Albany, MS *Drafted:* 1984 Round 9 Atl
1985 Pit-Atl: 7 G. Pit: 2 G. Atl: 5 G. **1986** Atl: 7 G. **Total:** 14 G.

GARRY HOWE Howe, Garry William Jr. 6'1", 298 **NT**
Col: Colorado; Drake *HS:* Spencer [IA] B: 6/20/1968, Spencer, IA
1992 Pit: 11 G; 2 Sac. **1993** Cin: 1 G. **1994** Ind: 1 G. **Total:** 13 G; 2 Sac.

LANE HOWELL Howell, Autrey Lane 6'5", 257 **OT-DT**
Col: Grambling State *HS:* Carroll [Monroe, LA] B: 7/28/1941, Fomdale, LA *Drafted:* 1963 Round 15 NYG
1963 NYG: 14 G. **1964** NYG: 14 G. **1965** Phi: 14 G. **1966** Phi: 10 G.
1967 Phi: 11 G. **1968** Phi: 14 G. **1969** Phi: 14 G. **Total:** 91 G.

DELLES HOWELL Howell, Delles Ray 6'3", 200 **DB**
Col: Grambling State *HS:* Carroll [Monroe, LA] B: 8/22/1948, Vallejo, CA *Drafted:* 1970 Round 4 NO

		Interceptions			
Year Team	G	Int	Yds	TD	Fum
1970 NO	13	3	28	0	0
1971 NO	14	5	120	0	0
1972 NO	10	1	6	0	0
1973 NYJ	14	4	76	0	1
1974 NYJ	10	2	23	0	0
1975 NYJ	10	2	19	0	0
NFL Total	71	17	272	0	1

EARL HOWELL Howell, Earl Octo 5'10", 180 **HB**
(Dixie) *Col:* Mississippi *HS:* Talladega [AL] B: 9/28/1924, Talladega, AL
AAFC **1949** LA-A: Rec 5-11 2.2 1 TD; PR 1-7 7.0; KR 4-74 18.5.

		Rushing				Tot
Year Team	G	Att	Yds	Avg	TD	TD
1949 LA-A	12	31	116	3.7	1	2

FOSTER HOWELL Howell, Foster C 6'3", 215 **T**
Col: Texas Christian B: 2/8/1911, San Marcos, TX
1934 Cin: 6 G.

JIM LEE HOWELL Howell, James Lee 6'6", 220 **OE-DE**
Col: Arkansas *HS:* Lonoke [AR] B: 3/9/1915, Lonoke, AR
D: 1/4/1995, Lonoke, AR
1940 NYG: Int 1-0. **Total:** Int 1-0.

		Receiving			
Year Team	G	Rec	Yds	Avg	TD
1937 NYG	8	4	32	8.0	0
1938 NYG	10	12	163	13.6	2
1939 NYG	7	5	112	22.4	2
1940 NYG	11	14	255	18.2	2
1941 NYG	11	4	62	15.5	1
1942 NYG	10	10	115	11.5	0
1946 NYG	11	9	141	15.7	0
1947 NYG	6	3	41	13.7	0
NFL Total	74	61	921	15.1	7

CLARENCE HOWELL Howell, John Clarence Maurice 6'1", 188 **OE-DE**
(Cotton) *Col:* Texas A&M *HS:* Nacogdoches [TX] B: 4/7/1927
D: 10/6/1981, Houston, TX
AAFC **1948** SF-A: 12 G; Rec 1-9 9.0; Int 1-5.

NFL **1948** SF-A: 12 G.

JOHN HOWELL Howell, John Searl 5'10", 185 **FB-LB-BB**
Col: Nebraska *HS:* Central [Omaha, NE] B: 12/4/1915, Omaha, NE
Deceased *Drafted:* 1938 Round 7 GB
1938 GB: 6 G; Rush 7-7 1.0.

MIKE HOWELL Howell, Michael Lionel 6'1", 195 **DB**
Col: Grambling State *HS:* Carroll [Monroe, LA] B: 7/5/1943, West Monroe, LA *Drafted:* 1965 Round 8 Cle
1965 Cle: KR 2-3 1.5. **1968** Cle: KR 1-0. **1969** Cle: KR 1-0. **Total:** KR 4-3 0.8.

		Interceptions			
Year Team	G	Int	Yds	TD	Fum
1965 Cle	14	0	0	0	0
1966 Cle	14	8	62	0	0
1967 Cle	14	3	20	0	0
1968 Cle	14	6	55	0	0
1969 Cle	14	6	21	0	0
1970 Cle	14	1	0	0	0
1971 Cle	14	2	93	0	0
1972 Cle-Mia	5	1	1	0	1
1972 Cle	4	1	1	0	1
1972 Mia	1	0	0	0	0
NFL Total	103	27	252	0	1

DIXIE HOWELL Howell, Millard Fillmore 5'11", 175 **TB-DB**
Col: Alabama *HS:* Geneva Co. [Hartford, AL] B: 11/24/1912, Hartford, AL D: 3/2/1971, Los Angeles, CA
1937 Was: 5 G; Pass 6-1 16.7%, 14 2.33 3 Int; Rush 5-9 1.8.

PAT HOWELL Howell, Patrick Gerrad 6'5", 257 **OG**
Col: USC *HS:* Fresno [CA] B: 3/12/1957, Fresno, CA *Drafted:* 1979 Round 2 Atl
1979 Atl: 15 G. **1980** Atl: 5 G. **1981** Atl: 16 G. **1982** Atl: 9 G. **1983** Atl-Hou: 9 G. Atl: 2 G. Hou: 7 G. **1984** Hou: 11 G. **1985** Hou: 2 G. **Total:** 67 G.

STEVE HOWELL Howell, Stephen Glen 6'2", 227 **FB-TE**
Col: Baylor *HS:* Waxahachie [TX] B: 12/20/1956, Corsicana, TX
Drafted: 1979 Round 4 Mia
1979 Mia: Rec 3-23 7.7. **1980** Mia: Rec 5-38 7.6. **1981** Mia: Rec 2-9 4.5.
Total: Rec 10-70 7.0.

		Rushing				
Year Team	G	Att	Yds	Avg	TD	Fum
1979 Mia	16	3	8	2.7	0	0
1980 Mia	16	60	206	3.4	1	3
1981 Mia	10	5	21	4.2	0	0
NFL Total	42	68	235	3.5	1	3

BILL HOWELL Howell, Wilfred Daniel 5'11", 175 **OE**
Col: Catholic *HS:* Cony [Augusta, ME] B: 4/21/1904, Bath, Canada
D: 8/23/1981, Washington, DC
1929 Bost: 4 G.

KARL HOWER Hower, Karl **FB**
Col: No College B: 1902 Deceased
1921 Lou: 1 G.

IAN HOWFIELD Howfield, Ian Michael 6'2", 196 **K**
Col: Tennessee *HS:* Columbine [Littleton, CO] B: 6/4/1966, Watford, England
1991 Hou: 9 G; Scor 64, 13-18 72.2% FG, 25-29 86.2% XK.

BOBBY HOWFIELD Howfield, Robert Michael 5'9", 180 **K**
Col: No College B: 12/3/1936, Bushey, England

		Scoring						
Year Team	G	Pts	FG	FGA	FG%	XK	XKA	XK%
1968 Den	12	57	9	18	50.0	30	30	100.0
1969 Den	14	75	13	29	44.8	36	37	97.3
1970 Den	14	81	18	32	56.3	27	28	96.4
1971 NYJ	14	49	8	19	42.1	25	26	96.2
1972 NYJ	14	121	27	37	73.0	40	41	97.6
1973 NYJ	14	78	17	24	70.8	27	27	100.0
1974 NYJ	7	26	6	7	85.7	8	12	66.7
NFL Total	89	487	98	166	59.0	193	201	96.0

CHUCK HOWLEY Howley, Charles Louis 6′3″, 228 **LB**
Col: West Virginia *HS:* Warwood [Wheeling, WV] B: 6/28/1936, Wheeling, WV *Drafted:* 1958 Round 1 ChiB
1963 Dal: PR 1-2 2.0. **1964** Dal: Punt 1-37 37.0. **1966** Dal: PR 1-30 30.0; **1** Fum TD. **Total:** PR 2-32 16.0; Punt 1-37 37.0; 1 Fum TD.

Year Team	G	Interceptions Int	Yds	TD	Tot TD
1958 ChiB	12	1	4	0	0
1959 ChiB	3	0	0	0	0
1961 Dal	13	1	5	0	0
1962 Dal	14	2	33	0	0
1963 Dal	14	2	3	0	0
1964 Dal	12	2	27	0	0
1965 Dal	14	0	0	0	0
1966 Dal	14	0	0	0	1
1967 Dal	14	1	28	1	1
1968 Dal	14	6	115	1	1
1969 Dal	14	2	37	0	0
1970 Dal	14	2	18	0	0
1971 Dal	14	5	122	0	0
1972 Dal	13	1	7	0	0
1973 Dal	1	0	0	0	0
NFL Total	180	25	399	2	3

BILL HOWSER Howser, William A **T-G**
Col: No College B: 1900 Deceased
1921 Lou: 1 G.

BILLY HOWTON Howton, William Harris 6′2″, 191 **OE**
(Red) *Col:* Rice *HS:* Plainview [TX] B: 7/5/1930, Littlefield, TX
Drafted: 1952 Round 2 GB
1957 GB: Rush 4-20 5.0. **1961** Dal: Rush 1-9 9.0. **Total:** Rush 5-29 5.8.

Year Team	G	Receiving Rec	Yds	Avg	TD	Fum
1952 GB	12	53	**1231**	23.2	13	1
1953 GB	8	25	463	18.5	4	1
1954 GB	12	52	768	14.8	2	0
1955 GB	12	44	697	15.8	5	2
1956 GB	12	55	**1188**	21.6	**12**	0
1957 GB	12	38	727	19.1	5	1
1958 GB	12	36	507	14.1	2	0
1959 Cle	12	39	510	13.1	1	0
1960 Dal	11	23	363	15.8	4	0
1961 Dal	14	56	785	14.0	4	1
1962 Dal	14	49	706	14.4	6	0
1963 Dal	11	33	514	15.6	3	0
NFL Total	142	503	8459	16.8	61	6

LYNN HOYEM Hoyem, Lynn Douglas 6′4″, 253 **OG-C**
Col: El Camino Coll. CA (J.C.); Long Beach State *HS:* Redondo [Redondo Beach, CA] B: 6/27/1939, Fargo, ND D: 2/17/1973, Battle Ground, WA *Drafted:* 1961 Round 19 Dal
1962 Dal: 14 G. **1963** Dal: 14 G. **1964** Phi: 14 G. **1965** Phi: 14 G. **1966** Phi: 14 G. **1967** Phi: 14 G. **Total:** 84 G.

STEVE HOYEM Hoyem, Steven Randel 6′7″, 287 **OT**
Col: Stanford *HS:* Boise [ID] B: 11/12/1970, Boise, ID
1994 Buf: 6 G.

BOBBY HOYING Hoying, Robert Carl 6′3″, 221 **QB**
Col: Ohio State *HS:* St. Henry [OH] B: 9/20/1972, St. Henry, OH
Drafted: 1996 Round 3 Phi

Year Team	G	Passing Att	Comp	Comp%	Yds	YPA	TD	Int	Rating
1996 Phi	1	0	0	—	0	—	0	0	—
1997 Phi	7	225	128	56.9	1573	6.99	11	6	83.8
1998 Phi	8	224	114	50.9	961	4.29	0	9	45.6
NFL Total	16	449	242	53.9	2534	5.64	11	15	64.8

Year Team	Rushing Att	Yds	Avg	TD	Fum
1996 Phi	0	0	—	0	1
1997 Phi	16	78	4.9	0	7
1998 Phi	22	84	3.8	0	6
NFL Total	38	162	4.3	0	14

FRANK HRABETIN Hrabetin, Frank George 6′4″, 225 **T**
(Rab) *Col:* Loyola Marymount *HS:* George Washington [Cedar Rapids, IA] B: 12/1/1915, Cedar Rapids, IA
AAFC **1946** BknA-MiaA: 10 G; Rec 1-17 17.0.

NFL **1942** Phi: 7 G; KR 1-7 7.0.

GARY HRIVNAK Hrivnak, Gary Andrew 6′5″, 252 **DE**
Col: Purdue *HS:* Johnstown [PA] B: 3/3/1951, Johnstown, PA
Drafted: 1973 Round 2 ChiB
1973 ChiB: 13 G. **1974** ChiB: 14 G. **1975** ChiB: 14 G. **Total:** 41 G.

DAMON HUARD Huard, Damon Paul 6′3″, 215 **QB**
Col: Washington *HS:* Puyallup [WA] B: 7/9/1973, Yakima, WA
1998 Mia: 2 G; Pass 9-6 66.7%, 85 9.44 1 Int.

JOHN HUARD Huard, John Roland 6′0″, 228 **LB**
Col: Maine *HS:* Waterville [ME] B: 3/9/1944, Waterville, ME
Drafted: 1967 Round 5 Den
1967 Den: 14 G; PR 1-19 19.0; Int 2-12. **1968** Den: 14 G; Int 2-35. **1969** Den: 14 G; Int 2-18. **1971** NO: 1 G. **Total:** 43 G; PR 1-19 19.0; Int 6-65.

JOHN HUARTE Huarte, John Gregory 6′0″, 185 **QB**
Col: Notre Dame *HS:* Mater Dei [Santa Ana, CA] B: 4/6/1944, Anaheim, CA *Drafted:* 1965 Round 2 NYJ
1966 Bos: 14 G; Pass 11-5 45.5%, 63 5.73 1 Int; Rush 7-40 5.7. **1967** Bos: 4 G; Pass 9-3 33.3%, 25 2.78 1 Int; Rush 2-5 2.5. **1968** Phi: 2 G; Pass 15-7 46.7%, 110 7.33 1 TD 2 Int; Rush 2-9 4.5. **1970** KC: 1 G; Pass 2-0, 1 Int. **1971** KC: 1 G; Pass 6-2 33.3%, 18 3.00. **1972** ChiB: 2 G; Pass 5-2 40.0%, 14 2.80; Rush 1-(-2) -2.0; 1 Fum. **Total:** 24 G; Pass 48-19 39.6%, 230 4.79 1 TD 5 Int; Rush 12-52 4.3; 1 Fum.

MIKE HUBACH Hubach, Michael Andrew 5′10″, 185 **P**
Col: Kansas *HS:* West Tech [Cleveland, OH] B: 1/26/1958, Cleveland, OH *Drafted:* 1980 Round 11 NE
1980 NE: Rush 1-0. **Total:** Rush 1-0.

Year Team	G	Punting Punts	Yds	Avg
1980 NE	16	63	2392	38.0
1981 NE	5	19	726	38.2
NFL Total	21	82	3118	38.0

DAVE HUBBARD Hubbard, David Allen 6′7″, 270 **OT**
Col: Brigham Young *HS:* Vintage [Napa, CA] B: 9/29/1955, Napa, CA
Drafted: 1977 Round 5 NO
1977 NO: 5 G.

MARV HUBBARD Hubbard, Marvin Ronald 6′1″, 225 **RB**
Col: Colgate *HS:* Randolph [NY] B: 5/7/1946, Salamanca, NY
Drafted: 1968 Round 11 Oak
1970 Oak: KR 2-41 20.5. **1971** Oak: KR 3-46 15.3. **1977** Det: KR 1-18 18.0. **Total:** KR 6-105 17.5.

Year Team	G	Rushing Att	Yds	Avg	TD	Receiving Rec	Yds	Avg	TD	Fum	Tot TD
1969 Oak	14	21	119	5.7	0	2	30	15.0	0	1	0
1970 Oak	13	51	246	4.8	1	0	0	—	0	2	1
1971 Oak	14	181	867	4.8	5	22	167	7.6	1	4	6
1972 Oak	14	219	1100	5.0	4	22	103	4.7	0	5	4
1973 Oak	14	193	903	4.7	6	15	116	7.7	0	6	6
1974 Oak	14	188	865	4.6	4	11	95	8.6	0	6	4
1975 Oak	7	60	294	4.9	2	7	81	11.6	0	0	2
1977 Det	13	38	150	3.9	1	6	36	6.0	0	1	1
NFL Total	103	951	4544	4.8	23	85	628	7.4	1	25	24

CAL HUBBARD Hubbard, Robert Calvin 6′2″, 253 **T-DE-OE-G**
Col: Centenary; Geneva *HS:* Keytesville [MO] B: 10/31/1900, Keytesville, MO D: 10/17/1977, St.Petersburg, FL *HOF:* 1963
1927 NYG: 10 G. **1928** NYG: 13 G. **1929** GB: 12 G. **1930** GB: 14 G; Rec 1 TD; 6 Pt. **1931** GB: 12 G. **1932** GB: 13 G. **1933** GB: 13 G. **1935** GB: 11 G; Int **1** TD; 6 Pt. **1936** Pit-NYG: 7 G. Pit: 1 G. NYG: 6 G. **Total:** 105 G; Rec 1 TD; Int 1 TD; Tot TD 2; 12 Pt.

BUD HUBBARD Hubbard, Wesley L 6′0″, 190 **OE-DE**
Col: San Jose State B: 1/8/1911, San Jose, CA D: 6/8/1981, San Jose, CA
1935 Bkn: 10 G; Rush 1-1 1.0; Rec 3-99 33.0 1 TD; 6 Pt.

FRANK HUBBELL Hubbell, Franklin Sumner 6′2″, 222 **DE-OE**
Col: Tennessee *HS:* Central [Bridgeport, CT] B: 1/19/1922, Bridgeport, CT *Drafted:* 1944 Round 13 Cle
1947 LARm: 12 G; Rec 2-60 30.0 2 TD; 12 Pt. **1948** LARm: 12 G; Rec 10-134 13.4 1 TD; 6 Pt; 1 Fum. **1949** LARm: 12 G; Rec 3-32 10.7; Int 1-21 1 TD; 6 Pt. **Total:** 36 G; Rec 15-226 15.1 3 TD; Int 1-21 1 TD; Tot TD 4; 24 Pt; 1 Fum.

BRAD HUBBERT Hubbert, Bradley 6′1″, 235 **RB**
Col: Arizona *HS:* Greene Co. Training School [AL] B: 6/5/1941, Boligee, AL *Drafted:* 1966 Redshirt Round 8 SD
1969 SD: Pass 1-0. **Total:** Pass 1-0.

Year Team	G	Rushing Att	Yds	Avg	TD	Receiving Rec	Yds	Avg	TD	Fum	Tot TD
1967 SD	14	116	643	**5.5**	2	19	214	11.3	2	1	4
1968 SD	2	28	119	4.3	2	5	11	2.2	0	0	2
1969 SD	14	94	333	3.5	4	11	43	3.9	0	5	4
1970 SD	8	49	175	3.6	1	7	44	6.3	0	0	1
NFL Total	38	287	1270	4.4	9	42	312	7.4	2	6	11

GENE HUBKA Hubka, Eugene Lewis 5′11″, 175 **TB-DB**
Col: Temple; Bucknell *HS:* Perth Amboy [NJ] B: 5/18/1924, Perth Amboy, NJ
1947 Pit: 1 G; Rush 2-4 2.0.

HARLAN HUCKLEBY Huckleby, Harlan Charles 6′1″, 199 **RB**
Col: Michigan *HS:* Cass Tech [Detroit, MI] B: 12/30/1957, Detroit, MI
Drafted: 1979 Round 5 NO

		Rushing				Receiving			
Year Team	**G**	**Att**	**Yds**	**Avg**	**TD**	**Rec**	**Yds**	**Avg**	**TD**
1980 GB	16	6	11	1.8	1	3	11	3.7	0
1981 GB	16	139	381	2.7	5	27	221	8.2	3
1982 GB	9	4	19	4.8	0	0	0	—	0
1983 GB	16	50	182	3.6	4	10	87	8.7	0
1984 GB	16	35	145	4.1	0	8	65	8.1	0
1985 GB	11	8	41	5.1	0	5	27	5.4	0
NFL Total	84	242	779	3.2	10	53	411	7.8	3

	Kickoff Returns					Tot
Year Team	**Ret**	**Yds**	**Avg**	**TD**	**Fum**	**TD**
1980 GB	3	59	19.7	0	0	1
1981 GB	7	134	19.1	0	3	8
1982 GB	5	89	17.8	0	0	0
1983 GB	41	757	18.5	0	4	4
1984 GB	14	261	18.6	0	1	0
NFL Total	70	1300	18.6	0	8	13

JIM HUDDLESTON Huddleston, James Walden 6′4″, 280 **OG-OT**
Col: Virginia *HS:* Episcopal [Alexandria, VA] B: 9/22/1962, San Pedro, CA
1987 TB: 1 G.

JOHN HUDDLESTON Huddleston, John Charles 6′3″, 231 **LB**
Col: Utah *HS:* Jesuit [Sacramento, CA] B: 4/10/1954, Los Angeles, CA
Drafted: 1976 Round 16 Den
1978 Oak: 11 G. **1979** Oak: 16 G. **Total:** 27 G.

FLOYD HUDLOW Hudlow, Floyd Leroy 5′11″, 195 **DB**
(Buddy) *Col:* Arizona *HS:* West [Phoenix, AZ] B: 11/9/1943, Phoenix, AZ *Drafted:* 1965 Round 10 Buf
1965 Buf: 7 G; PR 1-12 12.0; KR 2-36 18.0; 1 Fum. **1967** Atl: 10 G; PR 1-2 2.0; KR 2-56 28.0; Int 2-25. **1968** Atl: 7 G. **Total:** 24 G; PR 2-14 7.0; KR 4-92 23.0; Int 2-25; 1 Fum.

MIKE HUDOCK Hudock, Michael Edward 6′2″, 245 **C**
Col: Miami (Fla.) *HS:* Tuckhannock [PA] B: 9/29/1934, Pittston, PA
Drafted: 1956 Round 11 GB
1960 NYT: 14 G. **1961** NYT: 11 G. **1962** NYT: 14 G. **1963** NYJ: 14 G. **1964** NYJ: 11 G. **1965** NYJ: 14 G. **1966** Mia: 14 G. **1967** KC: 4 G. **Total:** 96 G.

DOUG HUDSON Hudson, Benjamin Douglas 6′2″, 201 **QB**
Col: Nicholls State *HS:* Gulf Breeze [FL] B: 9/11/1964, Memphis, TX
Drafted: 1987 Round 7 KC
1987 KC: 1 G; Pass 1-0; Rush 1-0; 1 Fum.

CHRIS HUDSON Hudson, Christopher Resherd 5′10″, 199 **DB**
Col: Colorado *HS:* Evan E. Worthing [Houston, TX] B: 10/6/1971, Houston, TX *Drafted:* 1995 Round 3 Jac
1996 Jac: Int 2-25; 0.5 Sac. **1997** Jac: Int 3-26; 1 Fum TD. **1998** Jac: Int 3-10. **Total:** Int 8-61; 1 Fum TD; 0.5 Sac.

		Punt Returns					Tot
Year Team	**G**	**Ret**	**Yds**	**Avg**	**TD**	**Fum**	**TD**
1995 Jac	1	0	0	—	0	0	0
1996 Jac	16	32	348	10.9	0	3	0
1997 Jac	16	0	0	—	0	1	2
1998 Jac	13	0	0	—	0	0	0
NFL Total	46	32	348	10.9	0	4	2

GORDON HUDSON Hudson, Gordon Lynn 6′4″, 241 **TE**
Col: Brigham Young *HS:* Kennewick [WA] B: 6/22/1962, Kennewick, WA *Drafted:* 1984 Supplemental Round 1 Sea
1986 Sea: 16 G; Rec 13-131 10.1 1 TD; 6 Pt; 1 Fum.

JIM HUDSON Hudson, James Clark 6′2″, 210 **DB**
Col: Texas *HS:* La Feria [TX] B: 3/31/1943, Steubenville, OH
1965 NYJ: KR 1-0. **1966** NYJ: Pass 1-0; PR 1-18 18.0. **Total:** Pass 1-0; PR 1-18 18.0; KR 1-0.

		Interceptions		
Year Team	**G**	**Int**	**Yds**	**TD**
1965 NYJ	2	0	0	0
1966 NYJ	14	3	39	0
1967 NYJ	13	4	38	0
1968 NYJ	14	5	96	0
1969 NYJ	4	2	22	0
1970 NYJ	7	0	0	0
NFL Total	54	14	195	0

JOHN HUDSON Hudson, John Lewis 6′2″, 270 **OG-C**
Col: Auburn *HS:* Henry Co. [Paris, TN] B: 1/29/1968, Memphis, TN
Drafted: 1990 Round 11 Phi
1991 Phi: 16 G; 1 Fum. **1992** Phi: 3 G. **1993** Phi: 16 G; 1 Fum. **1994** Phi: 16 G. **1995** Phi: 16 G. **1996** NYJ: 16 G. **1997** NYJ: 16 G. **1998** NYJ: 16 G. **Total:** 115 G; 2 Fum.

JOHNNIE HUDSON Hudson, John Randolph 5′9″, 170 **WB-FB**
Col: North Carolina State *HS:* Shelby [NC] B: 10/7/1898, Shelby, NC Deceased
1921 Was: 3 G; Rec 1 TD; 6 Pt.

MIKE HUDSON Hudson, Michael Todd 6′0″, 202 **DB**
Col: Oklahoma State *HS:* Hominy [OK] B: 12/25/1963, Pawhuska, OK
1987 SD: 3 G.

NAT HUDSON Hudson, Nathaniel Lamar 6′3″, 268 **OG**
Col: Georgia *HS:* West [Rome, GA] B: 10/11/1957, Rome, GA
Drafted: 1981 Round 6 NO
1981 NO: 16 G. **1982** Bal: 2 G. **Total:** 18 G.

DICK HUDSON Hudson, Richard 182 **WB-FB**
(Super Six) *Col:* No College B: 10/7/1898 Deceased
1923 Min: 3 G. **1925** Ham: 3 G. **1926** Ham: 2 G. **Total:** 8 G.

DICK HUDSON Hudson, Richard Smith 6′3″, 272 **OT-OG**
Col: Memphis *HS:* Grove [Paris, TN] B: 7/30/1940, Memphis, TN
Drafted: 1962 Round 2 SD
1962 SD: 14 G. **1963** Buf: 2 G. **1964** Buf: 14 G; Rush 1-1 1.0. **1965** Buf: 14 G. **1966** Buf: 14 G. **1967** Buf: 8 G. **Total:** 66 G; Rush 1-1 1.0.

BOB HUDSON Hudson, Robert Dale 5′11″, 210 **RB**
Col: Northeastern State (Okla.) *HS:* Hominy [OK] B: 3/21/1948, Hominy, OK *Drafted:* 1972 Round 6 GB
1972 GB: Rush 15-62 4.1; PR 1-0. **1973** Oak: Rush 4-3 0.8; Rec 1-9 9.0. **1974** Oak: Rush 1-12 12.0. **Total:** Rush 20-77 3.9; Rec 1-9 9.0; PR 1-0.

		Kickoff Returns				
Year Team	**G**	**Ret**	**Yds**	**Avg**	**TD**	**Fum**
1972 GB	12	11	247	22.5	0	1
1973 Oak	14	14	350	25.0	0	0
1974 Oak	14	0	0	—	0	0
NFL Total	40	25	597	23.9	0	1

BOB HUDSON Hudson, Robert Willard 6′4″, 225 **LB-DB-OE**
Col: Clemson *HS:* North Charleston [SC] B: 4/5/1930, Lamar, SC
Drafted: 1951 Round 12 NYG
1951 NYG: Rec 4-122 30.5. **1952** NYG: Rec 4-40 10.0. **1953** Phi: PR 2-10 5.0; KR 1-0. **1955** Phi: PR 1-0. **Total:** Rec 8-162 20.3; PR 3-10 3.3; KR 1-0.

		Interceptions			
Year Team	**G**	**Int**	**Yds**	**TD**	**Fum**
1951 NYG	11	0	0	0	1
1952 NYG	12	0	0	0	0
1953 Phi	12	3	74	0	1
1954 Phi	12	8	89	0	0
1955 Phi	12	3	48	0	0
1957 Phi	12	0	0	0	0
1958 Phi	11	1	15	0	0
1959 Was	3	0	0	0	0
1960 DalT-Den	7	1	0	0	0
1960 DalT	5	1	0	0	0
1960 Den	2	0	0	0	0
1961 Den	14	3	16	0	0
NFL Total	106	19	242	0	2

BILL HUDSON Hudson, William Alex 6′4″, 270 **DT**
Col: Clemson *HS:* North Charleston [SC] B: 7/9/1935, Lamar, SC
Drafted: 1957 Round 3 ChiC
1961 SD: 14 G; Int 1-5 1 TD; 6 Pt. **1962** SD: 14 G. **1963** Bos: 4 G. **Total:** 32 G; Int 1-5 1 TD; 6 Pt.

JACK HUELLER Hueller, John C 5′10″, 200 **G**
Col: No College B: 9/29/1898, Milwaukee, WI D: 8/29/1993, Milwaukee, WI
1922 Rac: 9 G. **1923** Rac: 9 G. **1924** Rac: 4 G. **Total:** 22 G.

CARLOS HUERTA Huerta, Carlos Antonio 5′7″, 185 **K**
Col: Miami (Fla.) *HS:* Christopher Columbus [Miami, FL] B: 6/29/1969, Coral Gables, FL *Drafted:* 1992 Round 12 SD
1996 ChiB-StL: 4 G; Scor 17, 4-7 57.1% FG, 5-5 100.0% XK. ChiB: 3 G; Scor 15, 4-7 57.1% FG, 3-3 100.0% XK. StL: 1 G; Scor 2, 2-2 100.0% XK. **Total:** 4 G; Scor 17, 4-7 57.1% FG, 5-5 100.0% XK.

GENE HUEY Huey, Eugene Aaron 5′11″, 190 **DB**
Col: Wyoming *HS:* Uniontown [PA] B: 7/20/1947, Uniontown, PA
Drafted: 1969 Round 5 StL
1969 SD: 4 G; KR 1-0.

ALAN HUFF Huff, Alan Edward 6'4", 265 **NT**
Col: Marshall *HS:* Oak Glenn [New Cumberland, WV] B: 10/20/1963, East Liverpool, OH
1987 Pit: 2 G.

CHARLES HUFF Huff, Charles 5'11", 195 **DB**
Col: Presbyterian *HS:* Portal [GA] B: 2/24/1963, Statesboro, GA
1987 Atl: 3 G; Int 2-14.

GARY HUFF Huff, Gary Earl 6'1", 195 **QB**
Col: Florida State *HS:* Leto [Tampa FL] B: 4/27/1951, Natchez, MS
Drafted: 1973 Round 2 ChiB

		Passing							
Year Team	G	Att	Comp	Comp%	Yds	YPA	TD	Int	Rating
1973 ChiB	8	126	54	42.9	525	4.17	3	8	36.6
1974 ChiB	13	283	142	50.2	1663	5.88	6	17	50.4
1975 ChiB	14	205	114	55.6	1083	5.28	3	9	57.0
1976 ChiB	8	0	0	—	0	—	0	0	—
1977 TB	8	138	67	48.6	889	6.44	3	13	37.4
1978 TB	6	36	15	41.7	169	4.69	1	3	30.9
NFL Total	57	788	392	49.7	4329	5.49	16	50	46.8

	Rushing				
Year Team	Att	Yds	Avg	TD	Fum
1973 ChiB	11	22	2.0	0	1
1974 ChiB	23	37	1.6	2	**14**
1975 ChiB	5	7	1.4	0	4
1977 TB	8	10	1.3	0	2
1978 TB	3	10	3.3	0	2
NFL Total	50	86	1.7	2	23

KEN HUFF Huff, Kenneth Wayne 6'4", 260 **OG**
Col: North Carolina *HS:* Deerfield Academy [MA]; Coronado [CA]
B: 2/21/1953, Hutchinson, KS *Drafted:* 1975 Round 1 Bal
1975 Bal: 9 G. **1976** Bal: 8 G; KR 1-0. **1977** Bal: 14 G; KR 1-15 15.0. **1978** Bal: 16 G. **1979** Bal: 14 G. **1980** Bal: 16 G. **1981** Bal: 16 G; Rec 1-(-1) -1.0. **1982** Bal: 9 G. **1983** Was: 12 G. **1984** Was: 15 G. **1985** Was: 16 G. **Total:** 145 G; Rec 1-(-1) -1.0; KR 2-15 7.5.

MARTY HUFF Huff, Ralph Martin 6'2", 234 **LB**
Col: Michigan *HS:* St. Francis DeSales [Toledo, OH] B: 12/19/1948, Houston, TX *Drafted:* 1971 Round 5 SF
1972 SF: 3 G.

SAM HUFF Huff, Robert Lee 6'1", 230 **LB**
Col: West Virginia *HS:* Farmington [WV] B: 10/4/1934, Edna Gas, WV
Drafted: 1956 Round 3 NYG *HOF:* 1982
1959 NYG: **1** Fum TD. **1961** NYG: **1** Fum TD. **Total:** 2 Fum TD.

		Interceptions			Tot
Year Team	G	Int	Yds	TD	TD
1956 NYG	12	3	49	0	0
1957 NYG	12	1	6	0	1
1958 NYG	12	2	23	0	0
1959 NYG	12	1	21	0	1
1960 NYG	12	3	45	0	0
1961 NYG	14	3	13	0	1
1962 NYG	14	1	4	0	0
1963 NYG	14	4	47	1	1
1964 Was	14	4	34	0	0
1965 Was	14	2	49	0	0
1966 Was	14	1	17	0	0
1967 Was	10	2	8	0	0
1969 Was	14	3	65	1	1
NFL Total	168	30	381	2	5

KEN HUFFINE Huffine, Kenneth Wilbur 6'3", 208 **FB-T-G**
Col: Purdue *HS:* Kirklin [IN] B: 12/22/1897, Hammond, IN
D: 9/26/1977, Bradenton, FL
1920 Mun: 1 G. **1921** Sta: 10 G; Pass 1 TD; Rush 2 TD; 12 Pt. **1922** Day: 8 G; Rush 3 TD; 18 Pt. **1923** Day: 8 G. **1924** Day: 7 G. **1925** Day: 8 G. **Total:** 42 G; Pass 1 TD; Rush 5 TD; 30 Pt.

DARVELL HUFFMAN Huffman, Darvell Denario 5'8", 158 **WR**
Col: Boston U. *HS:* Newton South [MA] B: 5/5/1967, Boston, MA
Drafted: 1990 Round 9 Ind
1991 Ind: 3 G; Rush 1-(-8) -8.0; Rec 3-14 4.7.

DAVE HUFFMAN Huffman, David Lambert 6'6", 271 **OG-C-OT**
Col: Notre Dame *HS:* Thomas Jefferson [Dallas, TX] B: 4/4/1957, Canton, OH D: 11/27/1998, Lake Station, IN *Drafted:* 1979 Round 2 Min
1979 Min: 13 G. **1980** Min: 16 G. **1981** Min: 13 G. **1982** Min: 9 G. **1983** Min: 15 G; KR 3-42 14.0; 6 Pt. **1985** Min: 15 G; 1 Fum. **1986** Min: 16 G. **1987** Min: 12 G. **1988** Min: 2 G. **1989** Min: 16 G. **1990** Min: 1 G. **Total:** 128 G; KR 3-42 14.0; 6 Pt; 1 Fum.

FRANK HUFFMAN Huffman, Frank Jr. 6'2", 207 **G-LB**
Col: Marshall *HS:* Woodrow Wilson [Beckley, WV] B: 5/22/1915, Pittsburgh, PA D: 9/17/1980, Fayetteville, WV *Drafted:* 1939 Round 16 ChiC
1939 ChiC: 11 G. **1940** ChiC: 9 G. **1941** ChiC: 8 G. **Total:** 28 G.

IOLAS HUFFMAN Huffman, Iolas Melitus 5'11", 228 **T-G**
Col: Ohio State *HS:* Chandlersville [OH] B: 2/4/1898 D: 11/12/1989, Cleveland, OH
1923 Cle: 7 G. **1924** Buf: 6 G. **Total:** 13 G.

DICK HUFFMAN Huffman, Richard Maxwell 6'2", 255 **OT-DT**
Col: Tennessee *HS:* Charleston [WV] B: 3/27/1923, Charleston, WV
D: 9/13/1992, Big Chimney, WV *Drafted:* 1945 Round 9 Cle
1947 LARm: 11 G; 1 Fum TD; 6 Pt. **1948** LARm: 12 G. **1949** LARm: 12 G; Rec 2-36 18.0. **1950** LARm: 12 G; Int 0-6. **Total:** 47 G; Rec 2-36 18.0; Int 0-6; 1 Fum TD; 6 Pt.

TIM HUFFMAN Huffman, Timothy Patrick 6'5", 277 **OG-OT**
Col: Notre Dame *HS:* Thomas Jefferson [Dallas, TX] B: 8/31/1959, Canton, OH *Drafted:* 1981 Round 9 GB
1981 GB: 5 G. **1982** GB: 9 G. **1983** GB: 15 G. **1984** GB: 16 G. **1985** GB: 2 G. **Total:** 47 G.

VERN HUFFMAN Huffman, Vernon Richard 6'2", 220 **TB-DB-BB-WB**
Col: Indiana *HS:* New Castle [IN] B: 12/18/1914, Moreland, IN
D: 3/18/1995, Bloomington, IN *Drafted:* 1937 Round 3 Det
1937 Det: Rec 8-104 13.0; Int 1 TD. **1938** Det: Rec 1-17 17.0.
Total: Rec 9-121 13.4; Int 1 TD.

		Passing							
Year Team	G	Att	Comp	Comp%	Yds	YPA	TD	Int	Rating
1937 Det	11	23	5	21.7	102	4.43	1	6	20.5
1938 Det	11	85	27	31.8	382	4.49	2	8	15.9
NFL Total	22	108	32	29.6	484	4.48	3	14	15.4

	Rushing				Tot
Year Team	Att	Yds	Avg	TD	TD
1937 Det	35	187	5.3	0	1
1938 Det	69	181	2.6	1	1
NFL Total	104	368	3.5	1	2

DEL HUFFORD Hufford, Guy Darrell 5'11", 185 **E**
(Huf) *Col:* California *HS:* Manual Arts [Los Angeles, CA] B: 1/18/1901
D: 7/6/1984, Camarillo, CA
1926 LA: 10 G.

JOHN HUFNAGEL Hufnagel, John Coleman 6'1", 194 **QB**
Col: Penn State *HS:* Montour [McKees Rocks, PA] B: 9/13/1951, Pittsbugh, PA *Drafted:* 1973 Round 14 Den
1974 Den: Rush 2-22 11.0. **1975** Den: Rush 8-47 5.9. **Total:** Rush 10-69 6.9.

		Passing							
Year Team	G	Att	Comp	Comp%	Yds	YPA	TD	Int	Rating
1974 Den	4	10	6	60.0	70	7.00	0	1	41.7
1975 Den	5	51	16	31.4	287	5.63	1	8	18.6
NFL Total	9	61	22	36.1	357	5.85	1	9	22.4

HARRY HUGASIAN Hugasian, Harry 6'1", 192 **HB-DB**
Col: Stanford *HS:* Pasadena [CA]; South Milwaukee HS [WI]
B: 8/29/1929, Pasadena, CA *Drafted:* 1952 Round 22 Dal
1955 Bal-ChiB: 6 G; Rush 12-34 2.8; Rec 3-32 10.7; KR 1-0; 1 Fum. Bal: 2 G; Rush 12-34 2.8; Rec 3-32 10.7; 1 Fum. ChiB: 4 G; KR 1-0.
Total: 6 G; Rush 12-34 2.8; Rec 3-32 10.7; KR 1-0; 1 Fum.

ROY HUGGINS Huggins, Roy 5'11", 195 **FB-LB**
Col: Vanderbilt *HS:* George Peabody [Nashville, TN] B: 10/6/1918, Nashville, TN
1944 Cle: 5 G; Rush 12-41 3.4; Rec 1-0.

BERNIE HUGHES Hughes, Bernard Bill 6'1", 192 **C-LB**
Col: Oregon *HS:* Medford [OR] B: 1/9/1910, Dorris, CA
D: 12/26/1967, Medford, OR
1934 ChiC: 10 G. **1935** ChiC: 10 G. **1936** ChiC: 12 G. **Total:** 32 G.

BILL HUGHES Hughes, Bill Carter 6'1", 232 **G-C-LB**
(Hoss) *Col:* Texas *HS:* Van Alstyne [TX] B: 4/11/1915, Van Alstyne, TX D: 7/6/1978, Tampa, FL
1937 Phi: 11 G. **1938** Phi: 11 G. **1939** Phi: 11 G. **1940** Phi: 7 G.
1941 ChiB: 6 G; PR 1-6 6.0; Int 1-3. **Total:** 46 G; PR 1-6 6.0; Int 1-3.

CHUCK HUGHES Hughes, Charles Frederick 5'11", 175 **WR**
Col: Texas-El Paso *HS:* Abilene [TX] B: 3/24/1943, Philadelphia, PA
D: 10/24/1971, Detroit, MI *Drafted:* 1967 Round 4 Phi
1967 Phi: 9 G; PR 3-11 3.7; KR 7-126 18.0; 2 Fum. **1968** Phi: 6 G; Rec 3-39 13.0. **1969** Phi: 7 G; Rec 3-29 9.7; PR 1-0; 1 Fum. **1970** Det: 13 G; Rec 8-162 20.3. **1971** Det: 3 G; Rec 1-32 32.0. **Total:** 38 G; Rec 15-262 17.5; PR 4-11 2.8; KR 7-126 18.0; 3 Fum.

VAN HUGHES Hughes, Curtis Van 6'3", 280 **DE**
Col: Texas Tech; Southwest Texas State *HS:* Axtell [TX] B: 11/14/1960, Waco, TX *Drafted:* 1984 Round 5 Pit
1986 StL: 7 G. **1987** Sea: 1 G. **Total:** 8 G.

DAVID HUGHES Hughes, David Augustus III 6'0", 220 **RB**
Col: Boise State *HS:* Kamehameha School [Honolulu, HI] B: 6/1/1959, Honolulu, HI *Drafted:* 1981 Round 2 Sea

		Rushing				Receiving			
Year Team	**G**	**Att**	**Yds**	**Avg**	**TD**	**Rec**	**Yds**	**Avg**	**TD**
1981 Sea	16	47	135	2.9	0	35	263	7.5	2
1982 Sea	9	30	106	3.5	0	11	98	8.9	1
1983 Sea	16	83	313	3.8	1	10	100	10.0	1
1984 Sea	16	94	327	3.5	1	22	121	5.5	1
1985 Sea	12	40	128	3.2	0	19	184	9.7	0
1986 Pit	5	14	32	2.3	0	10	98	9.8	0
NFL Total	74	308	1041	3.4	2	107	864	8.1	5

	Kickoff Returns					Tot
Year Team	**Ret**	**Yds**	**Avg**	**TD**	**Fum**	**TD**
1981 Sea	0	0	—	0	4	2
1982 Sea	1	17	17.0	0	0	1
1983 Sea	12	282	23.5	0	2	2
1984 Sea	17	348	20.5	0	4	2
1985 Sea	0	0	—	0	2	0
1986 Pit	2	16	8.0	0	3	0
NFL Total	32	663	20.7	0	15	7

DENNIS HUGHES Hughes, Donald Dennis 6'1", 225 **TE**
Col: Georgia *HS:* Seneca [NC] B: 2/22/1948, Seneca, SC
1970 Pit: 11 G; Rush 1-(-8) -8.0; Rec 24-332 13.8 3 TD; 18 Pt; 1 Fum.
1971 Pit: 7 G. **Total:** 18 G; Rush 1-(-8) -8.0; Rec 24-332 13.8 3 TD; 18 Pt; 1 Fum.

ED HUGHES Hughes, Edward D 6'1", 184 **DB**
Col: Cameron; North Carolina State; Tulsa *HS:* Kensington [Buffalo, NY] B: 10/23/1927, Buffalo, NY *Drafted:* 1954 Round 10 LARm
1954 LARm: 11 G; PR 1-0; Int 2-24; 1 Fum. **1955** LARm: 12 G. **1956** NYG: 12 G; KR 1-27 27.0; Int 1-38. **1957** NYG: 8 G; 1 Fum. **1958** NYG: 10 G. **Total:** 53 G; PR 1-0; KR 1-27 27.0; Int 3-62; 2 Fum.

ERNIE HUGHES Hughes, Ernest Loyal Jr. 6'3", 259 **C-OG**
(The Enforcer) *Col:* Notre Dame *HS:* Capital [Boise, ID] B: 1/24/1955, Boise, ID *Drafted:* 1978 Round 3 SF
1978 SF: 15 G; KR 4-53 13.3. **1980** SF: 3 G; KR 1-10 10.0. **1981** NYG: 10 G; 2 Fum. **1982** NYG: 5 G; 1 Fum. **1983** NYG: 12 G; 1 Fum. **Total:** 45 G; KR 5-63 12.6; 4 Fum.

GEORGE HUGHES Hughes, George Samuel 6'1", 225 **OT-OG**
Col: William & Mary *HS:* Maury [Norfolk, VA] B: 8/19/1925, Norfolk, VA *Drafted:* 1950 Round 3 Pit
1950 Pit: 12 G. **1951** Pit: 12 G. **1952** Pit: 12 G; Rec 0-2. **1953** Pit: 12 G; KR 1-0; 1 Fum. **1954** Pit: 12 G. **Total:** 60 G; Rec 0-2; KR 1-0; 1 Fum.

HONOLULU HUGHES Hughes, Henry Thomas Jr. 5'10", 195 **BB-TB**
(Hula-Hula; Hank) *Col:* Oregon State *HS:* Punahou School [Honolulu, HI] B: 5/4/1907, Honolulu, HI D: 12/27/1963, Honolulu, HI
1932 Bos: Rush 14-28 2.0; Rec 2-35 17.5; Scor 5, 5 XK.

		Passing							
Year Team	**G**	**Att**	**Comp**	**Comp%**	**Yds**	**YPA**	**TD**	**Int**	**Rating**
1932 Bos	10	57	11	19.3	134	2.35	1	9	5.8

RANDY HUGHES Hughes, James Randell 6'4", 209 **DB**
Col: Oklahoma *HS:* Memorial [Tulsa, OK] B: 4/3/1953, Oklahoma City, OK *Drafted:* 1975 Round 4 Dal
1975 Dal: 14 G; Int 2-33 1 TD; 6 Pt. **1976** Dal: 14 G; Int 1-0. **1977** Dal: 13 G; Int 2-19. **1978** Dal: 16 G; Int 2-80. **1979** Dal: 15 G; Int 2-91. **1980** Dal: 5 G. **Total:** 77 G; Int 9-223 1 TD; 6 Pt.

DENNY HUGHES Hughes, Oliver Wendell Holmes 5'11", 185 **C**
(Dinty) *Col:* George Washington D: 1957
1925 Pott: 7 G; Scor 2, 2 XK.

DICK HUGHES Hughes, Richard 5'9", 185 **HB**
Col: Tulsa *HS:* Kensington [Buffalo, NY] B: 9/26/1932, Buffalo, NY *Drafted:* 1957 Round 11 Pit
1957 Pit: 1 G; Rush 2-6 3.0; PR 1-5 5.0; 1 Fum.

DANAN HUGHES Hughes, Robert Danan 6'2", 205 **WR**
Col: Iowa *HS:* Bayonne [NJ] B: 12/11/1970, Bayonne, NJ *Drafted:* 1993 Round 7 KC
1995 KC: Rush 1-5 5.0. **1996** KC: Pass 1-1 100.0%, 30 30.00. **1997** KC: 1 Fum TD. **1998** KC: Pass 1-1 100.0%, 25 25.00. **Total:** Pass 2-2 100.0%, 55 27.50; Rush 1-5 5.0; 1 Fum TD.

		Receiving				Punt Returns			
Year Team	**G**	**Rec**	**Yds**	**Avg**	**TD**	**Ret**	**Yds**	**Avg**	**TD**
1993 KC	6	0	0	—	0	3	49	16.3	0
1994 KC	16	7	80	11.4	0	27	192	7.1	0
1995 KC	16	14	103	7.4	1	3	9	3.0	0
1996 KC	15	17	167	9.8	1	0	0	—	0
1997 KC	16	7	65	9.3	2	0	0	—	0
1998 KC	16	1	10	10.0	0	2	10	5.0	0
NFL Total	85	46	425	9.2	4	35	260	7.4	0

	Kickoff Returns				Tot
Year Team	**Ret**	**Yds**	**Avg**	**TD**	**TD**
1993 KC	14	266	19.0	0	0
1994 KC	9	190	21.1	0	0
1995 KC	1	18	18.0	0	1
1996 KC	2	42	21.0	0	1
1997 KC	1	21	21.0	0	3
NFL Total	27	537	19.9	0	5

BOB HUGHES Hughes, Robert E 6'4", 236 **DE**
(Ox) *Col:* Rust Coll. MS (J.C.); Jackson State *HS:* R.E. Hunt [Columbus, MS] B: 11/17/1944, Columbus, MS *Drafted:* 1967 Round 6 Phi
1967 Atl: 2 G. **1969** Atl: 14 G. **Total:** 16 G.

TYRONE HUGHES Hughes, Tyrone Christopher 5'9", 175 **DB**
Col: Nebraska *HS:* St. Augustine [New Orleans, LA] B: 1/14/1970, New Orleans, LA *Drafted:* 1993 Round 5 NO
1994 NO: Rush 2-6 3.0; Int 2-31; **2** Fum TD. **1995** NO: Int 2-19. **1997** ChiB: Rush 1-3 3.0; Rec 8-68 8.5. **Total:** Rush 3-9 3.0; Rec 8-68 8.5; Int 4-50; 2 Fum TD.

		Punt Returns				Kickoff Returns					Tot
Year Team	**G**	**Ret**	**Yds**	**Avg**	**TD**	**Ret**	**Yds**	**Avg**	**TD**	**Fum**	**TD**
1993 NO	16	37	**503**	**13.6**	**2**	30	753	25.1	**1**	0	3
1994 NO	15	21	143	6.8	0	**63**	**1556**	24.7	2	7	4
1995 NO	16	28	262	9.4	0	**66**	**1617**	24.5	0	2	0
1996 NO	16	30	152	5.1	0	**70**	**1791**	25.6	0	2	0
1997 ChiB	14	36	258	7.2	0	43	1008	23.4	0	2	0
1998 Dal	4	10	93	9.3	0	11	274	24.9	0	1	0
NFL Total	81	162	1411	8.7	2	283	6999	24.7	3	14	7

PAT HUGHES Hughes, William Patrick 6'2", 240 **LB-C**
Col: Boston U. *HS:* Everett [MA] B: 6/2/1947, Everett, MA *Drafted:* 1970 Round 9 NYG
1970 NYG: KR 1-3 3.0. **Total:** KR 1-3 3.0.

		Interceptions		
Year Team	**G**	**Int**	**Yds**	**TD**
1970 NYG	14	0	0	0
1971 NYG	14	0	0	0
1972 NYG	14	2	4	0
1973 NYG	11	3	13	0
1974 NYG	14	2	4	0
1975 NYG	14	0	0	0
1976 NYG	14	1	5	0
1977 NO	14	1	2	0
1978 NO	16	2	11	0
1979 NO	16	4	62	0
NFL Total	141	15	101	0

TOMMY HUGHITT Hughitt, Ernest Frederick 5'8", 159 **BB-TB-WB-E**
Col: Michigan *HS:* Escanbia [MI] B: 12/27/1892, Genoa, Canada D: 12/27/1961, Bartow, FL
1920 Buf: 11 G. **1921** Buf: 12 G; Pass 2 TD; Rush 1 TD; Rec 2 TD; Scor 20, 2 XK; Tot TD 3. **1922** Buf: 10 G; Pass 2 TD; Rush 2 TD; 12 Pt. **1923** Buf: 12 G; Pass 1 TD; Rec 1 TD; Scor 9, 1 FG. **1924** Buf: 11 G. **Total:** 56 G; Pass 5 TD; Rush 3 TD; Rec 3 TD; Scor 41, 1 FG, 2 XK; Tot TD 6.

GEORGE HUGHLEY Hughley, George Charles 6'2", 223 **FB**
Col: Central Oklahoma *HS:* Santa Monica [CA] B: 6/26/1939, Los Angeles, CA
1965 Was: Rec 9-93 10.3 1 TD; PR 2-12 6.0; KR 13-295 22.7.

		Rushing				
Year Team	**G**	**Att**	**Yds**	**Avg**	**TD**	**Fum**
1965 Was	14	37	175	4.7	0	1

JOE HUGRET Hugret, Joseph Jon 6'2", 195 **OE-DE**
(Sugar) *Col:* New York U. *HS:* Bristol [CT] B: 4/11/1909, Torrington, CT D: 9/1977, Minot, ND
1934 Bkn: 2 G.

KENT HULL Hull, James Kent 6'5", 278 **C**
Col: Mississippi State *HS:* Greenwood [MS] B: 1/13/1961, Pontotoc, MS
1986 Buf: 16 G. **1987** Buf: 12 G. **1988** Buf: 16 G. **1989** Buf: 16 G. **1990** Buf: 16 G. **1991** Buf: 16 G. **1992** Buf: 16 G. **1993** Buf: 14 G. **1994** Buf: 16 G; 1 Fum. **1995** Buf: 16 G; 1 Fum. **1996** Buf: 16 G. **Total:** 170 G; 2 Fum.

MIKE HULL Hull, Michael Bruce 6'3", 220 **RB**
Col: Glendale CC CA; USC *HS:* Crescenta Valley [La Crescenta, CA] B: 1/2/1945, Glendale, CA *Drafted:* 1968 Round 1 ChiB

Year Team	G	Rushing Att	Yds	Avg	TD	Receiving Rec	Yds	Avg	TD	Fum
1968 ChiB	14	12	22	1.8	0	4	20	5.0	0	1
1969 ChiB	10	29	81	2.8	1	12	63	5.3	0	1
1970 ChiB	13	32	99	3.1	0	13	44	3.4	0	1
1971 Was	11	2	8	4.0	0	0	0	—	0	0
1972 Was	14	0	0	—	0	0	0	—	0	0
1973 Was	13	2	-3	-1.5	0	0	0	—	0	0
1974 Was	14	0	0	—	0	0	0	—	0	0
NFL Total	89	77	207	2.7	1	29	127	4.4	0	3

TOM HULL Hull, Thomas Michael 6′3″, 229 **LB**
Col: Penn State *HS:* Uniontown [PA] B: 6/30/1952, Cumberland, MD
Drafted: 1974 Round 12 SF
1974 SF: 13 G. **1975** GB: 12 G. **Total:** 25 G.

BILL HULL Hull, William Henry Jr. 6′6″, 245 **DE**
Col: Wake Forest *HS:* Tarboro [NC]; Virginia Episcopal HS [Alexandria, VA] B: 8/4/1940 *Drafted:* 1962 Round 5 DalT
1962 DalT: 14 G.

VIVIAN HULTMAN Hultman, Vivian Joseph 5′8″, 178 **OE-G**
Col: Michigan State B: 1/26/1903, Grand Rapids, MI D: 12/27/1987, Largo, FL
1925 Det: 11 G; Rec 1 TD; 6 Pt. **1926** Det: 10 G; Rec 1 TD; 6 Pt.
1927 Pott: 9 G; Rec 1 TD; 6 Pt. **Total:** 30 G; Rec 3 TD; 18 Pt.

GEORGE HULTZ Hultz, George A 6′4″, 250 **DT**
Col: Southern Mississippi *HS:* Grand Bay [AL] B: 3/7/1939, Moss Point, MS *Drafted:* 1961 Round 7 StL
1962 StL: 13 G.

DON HULTZ Hultz, William Donald 6′3″, 241 **DE-DT**
Col: Southern Mississippi *HS:* Grand Bay [AL] B: 12/16/1940, Moss Point, MS
1963 Min: 14 G; Int 1-35 1 TD; 6 Pt. **1964** Phi: 12 G; PR 1-2 2.0. **1965** Phi: 14 G; Int 1-6. **1966** Phi: 13 G. **1967** Phi: 13 G; Int 1-16 1 TD; 6 Pt.
1968 Phi: 10 G. **1969** Phi: 14 G. **1970** Phi: 12 G. **1971** Phi: 14 G; Int 1-4.
1972 Phi: 14 G. **1973** Phi: 3 G. **1974** ChiB: 8 G. **Total:** 141 G; PR 1-2 2.0; Int 4-61 2 TD; 12 Pt.

DICK HUMBERT Humbert, Richard Elmer 6′1″, 179 **OE-DE**
Col: Richmond *HS:* Reading [PA]; Suffolk HS [VA] B: 12/31/1918, Reading, PA
1941 Phi: KR 1-15 15.0. **1946** Phi: Rush 1-2 2.0; KR 1-18 18.0. **1948** Phi: PR 2-7 3.5. **Total:** Rush 1-2 2.0; PR 2-7 3.5; KR 2-33 16.5.

Year Team	G	Receiving Rec	Yds	Avg	TD	Interceptions Int	Yds	TD
1941 Phi	11	29	332	11.4	3	1	0	0
1945 Phi	4	6	53	8.8	0	0	0	0
1946 Phi	11	18	191	10.6	3	0	0	0
1947 Phi	11	13	139	10.7	0	2	12	0
1948 Phi	12	1	2	2.0	0	4	35	0
1949 Phi	11	1	14	14.0	0	7	69	0
NFL Total	60	68	731	10.8	6	14	116	0

WELDON HUMBLE Humble, Weldon Gaston 6′1″, 221 **OG-LB**
Col: Southwestern Louisiana; Rice *HS:* G. W. Brackenridge [San Antonio, TX] B: 4/24/1921, Nixon, TX *Drafted:* 1943 Round 24 ChiC
AAFC **1947** CleA: 12 G; Rush 1-0; Int 2-31. **1948** CleA: 13 G; Int 1-11.
1949 CleA: 10 G; Int 2-55. **Total:** 35 G; Rush 1-0; Int 5-97.

NFL **1950** Cle: 12 G; Rush 1-(-10) -10.0; 1 Fum. **1952** Dal: 11 G; KR 1-17 17.0. **Total:** 23 G; Rush 1-(-10) -10.0; KR 1-17 17.0; 1 Fum.

MIKE HUMISTON Humiston, Michael David 6′3″, 238 **LB**
Col: Shasta Coll. CA (J.C.); Weber State *HS:* Anderson [CA]
B: 1/8/1959, Oceanside, CA
1981 Buf: 16 G. **1982** Bal: 7 G. **1984** Ind: 16 G; Scor **1** Saf; 2 Pt. **1987** SD: 7 G. **Total:** 46 G; Scor 1 Saf; 2 Pt.

DAVID HUMM Humm, David Henry 6′2″, 188 **QB**
Col: Nebraska *HS:* Bishop Gorman [Las Vegas, NV] B: 4/2/1952, Las Vegas, NV *Drafted:* 1975 Round 5 Oak
1975 Oak: Rush 7-21 3.0. **1978** Oak: Rush 5-(-4) -0.8. **1980** Buf: Rush 1-5 5.0. **1983** LARd: Rush 1-(-1) -1.0. **1984** LARd: Rush 2-7 3.5.
Total: Rush 16-28 1.8.

Year Team	G	Passing Att	Comp	Comp%	Yds	YPA	TD	Int	Rating	Fum
1975 Oak	7	38	18	47.4	246	6.47	3	2	72.9	3
1976 Oak	14	5	3	60.0	41	8.20	0	0	86.3	0
1977 Oak	14	0	0	—	0	—	0	0	—	0
1978 Oak	16	26	14	53.8	151	5.81	0	1	55.1	1
1979 Oak	16	0	0	—	0	—	0	0	—	0
1980 Buf	16	14	4	28.6	39	2.79	0	1	9.8	1
1981 Bal	1	24	7	29.2	90	3.75	0	2	8.0	0
1982 Bal	2	23	13	56.5	130	5.65	0	1	54.6	0
1983 LARd	6	0	0	—	0	—	0	0	—	0
1984 LARd	3	7	4	57.1	56	8.00	0	1	43.5	2
NFL Total	95	137	63	46.0	753	5.50	3	8	46.3	7

SWEDE HUMMELL Hummell, Arthur Joseph 195 **WB**
Col: Lombard B: 5/30/1902, Belleville, IL D: 10/1964
1926 KC-Prov: 9 G. KC: 5 G. Prov: 4 G. **1927** ChiC: 8 G. **Total:** 17 G.

MACK HUMMON Hummon, John Mack 5′11″, 180 **E**
(Mousie) *Col:* Wittenberg *HS:* Leipsic [OH] B: 7/4/1901, Leipsic, OH
D: 2/27/1992, Oakwood, OH
1926 Day: 5 G. **1928** Day: 4 G. **Total:** 9 G.

BOBBY HUMPHERY Humphery, Robert Charles 5′10″, 178 **WR-DB**
Col: New Mexico State *HS:* Estacado [Lubbock, TX] B: 8/23/1961, Lubbock, TX *Drafted:* 1983 Round 9 NYJ
1984 NYJ: Rec 14-206 14.7 1 TD. **1985** NYJ: Rush 1-10 10.0; PR 1-0.
1986 NYJ: Scor **1** Saf; 4 Sac. **1987** NYJ: **1** Fum TD. **1988** NYJ: Int 1-0; 2 Sac. **1990** LARm: Int 4-52 1 TD. **Total:** Rush 1-10 10.0; Rec 14-206 14.7 1 TD; PR 1-0; Int 5-52 1 TD; Scor 1 Saf; 1 Fum TD; 6 Sac.

Year Team	G	Kickoff Returns Ret	Yds	Avg	TD	Fum	Tot TD
1984 NYJ	16	22	675	**30.7**	**1**	2	2
1985 NYJ	12	17	363	21.4	0	2	0
1986 NYJ	16	28	655	23.4	**1**	1	1
1987 NYJ	12	18	357	19.8	0	1	1
1988 NYJ	16	21	510	24.3	0	0	0
1989 NYJ	16	24	414	17.3	0	4	0
1990 LARm	16	0	0	—	0	0	1
NFL Total	104	130	2974	22.9	2	10	5

BOBBY HUMPHREY Humphrey, Bobby 6′1″, 201 **RB**
Col: Alabama *HS:* Glenn [Birmingham, AL] B: 10/11/1966, Birmingham, AL *Drafted:* 1989 Supplemental Round 1 Den
1989 Den: Pass 2-1 50.0%, 17 8.50 1 TD; KR 4-86 21.5. **1990** Den: Pass 2-0. **1992** Mia: KR 1-18 18.0. **Total:** Pass 4-1 25.0%, 17 4.25 1 TD; KR 5-104 20.8.

Year Team	G	Rushing Att	Yds	Avg	TD	Receiving Rec	Yds	Avg	TD	Fum	Tot TD
1989 Den	16	294	1151	3.9	7	22	156	7.1	1	4	8
1990 Den	15	288	1202	4.2	7	24	152	6.3	0	8	7
1991 Den	4	11	33	3.0	0	0	0	—	0	0	0
1992 Mia	16	102	471	4.6	1	54	507	9.4	1	2	2
NFL Total	51	695	2857	4.1	15	100	815	8.2	2	14	17

CLAUDE HUMPHREY Humphrey, Claude B 6′4″, 252 **DE**
Col: Tennessee State *HS:* Lester [Memphis, TN] B: 6/29/1944, Memphis, TN *Drafted:* 1968 Round 1 Atl
1968 Atl: 14 G. **1969** Atl: 14 G; **1** Fum TD; 6 Pt. **1970** Atl: 12 G; Int 1-5.
1971 Atl: 14 G. **1972** Atl: 14 G; Scor **1** Saf; 2 Pt. **1973** Atl: 14 G; Int 1-6.
1974 Atl: 14 G. **1976** Atl: 13 G; Scor **1** Saf; 2 Pt. **1977** Atl: 14 G. **1978** Atl: 4 G. **1979** Phi: 16 G. **1980** Phi: 16 G. **1981** Phi: 12 G. **Total:** 171 G; Int 2-11; Scor 2 Saf; 1 Fum TD; 10 Pt.

DONNIE HUMPHREY Humphrey, Donnie Ray 6′3″, 282 **DE**
Col: Auburn *HS:* J.O. Johnson [Huntsville, AL] B: 4/20/1961, Huntsville, AL *Drafted:* 1984 Round 3 GB
1984 GB: 16 G; 1 Sac. **1985** GB: 16 G; 2 Sac. **1986** GB: 16 G.
Total: 48 G; 3 Sac.

BUDDY HUMPHREY Humphrey, Loyie Nawlin 6′1″, 198 **QB**
Col: Baylor *HS:* Kilgore [TX] B: 9/29/1935, Dallas, TX D: 4/21/1988, Kilgore, TX *Drafted:* 1959 Round 2 LARm
1960 LARm: Rush 2-7 3.5. **1965** StL: Rush 2-4 2.0. **Total:** Rush 4-11 2.8.

Year Team	G	Passing Att	Comp	Comp%	Yds	YPA	TD	Int	Rating	Fum
1959 LARm	2	0	0	—	0	—	0	0	—	0
1960 LARm	4	24	9	37.5	78	3.25	0	2	12.2	0
1961 Dal	2	2	1	50.0	16	8.00	0	0	77.1	0
1963 StL	4	11	4	36.4	96	8.73	1	0	99.1	0
1964 StL	1	1	0	0.0	0	0.00	0	0	39.6	0
1965 StL	7	105	58	55.2	736	7.01	1	9	44.8	1
1966 Hou	6	32	15	46.9	168	5.25	2	1	70.8	0
NFL Total	26	175	87	49.7	1094	6.25	4	12	48.6	1

PAUL HUMPHREY Humphrey, Paul Eugene 6′0″, 210 **C-LB**
(Hump) *Col:* Purdue *HS:* Garfield [Terre Haute, IN] B: 7/18/1917, Terre Haute, IN *Drafted:* 1939 Round 11 Phi
1939 Bkn: 11 G.

RONALD HUMPHREY Humphrey, Ronald Lynn 5′10″, 211 **RB**
Col: Mississippi Valley State *HS:* Forest Brook [Houston, TX]
B: 3/3/1969, Marland, TX *Drafted:* 1992 Round 8 Ind
1994 Ind: Rush 18-85 4.7; Rec 3-19 6.3. **1995** Ind: Rush 2-6 3.0; Rec 2-11 5.5. **Total:** Rush 20-91 4.6; Rec 5-30 6.0.

Year Team	G	Kickoff Returns Ret	Yds	Avg	TD	Fum
1994 Ind	15	35	783	22.4	1	4

1995 Ind	11	21	453	21.6	0	1
NFL Total	26	56	1236	22.1	1	5

TOM HUMPHREY Humphrey, Thomas Franklin 6'3", 280 **OG-OT**
Col: Iowa *HS:* Amityville Memorial [NY] B: 12/16/1962, Huntington, NY
1987 NYJ: 3 G.

TOM HUMPHREY Humphrey, Thomas Gale 6'6", 260 **C**
Col: Abilene Christian *HS:* Comanche [TX] B: 3/24/1950, Comanche, TX *Drafted:* 1973 Round 10 Cle
1974 KC: 5 G; KR 1-7 7.0.

BOB HUMPHREYS Humphreys, Robert Keith 6'1", 240 **K**
Col: Long Beach City Coll. CA (J.C.); Wichita State *HS:* David Starr Jordan [Los Angeles, CA] B: 3/30/1940, Los Angeles, CA
1967 Den: 8 G; Scor 39, 7-15 46.7% FG, 18-19 94.7% XK. **1968** Den: 2 G; Scor 4, 1-5 20.0% FG, 1-1 100.0% XK. **Total:** 10 G; Scor 43, 8-20 40.0% FG, 19-20 95.0% XK.

LEONARD HUMPHRIES Humphries, Leonard Deshawn 5'9", 180 **DB**
Col: Penn State *HS:* North [Akron, OH] B: 6/19/1970, Akron, OH
Drafted: 1992 Round 8 Buf
1994 Ind: 13 G; Int 1-1.

STEFAN HUMPHRIES Humphries, Stefan Govan 6'3", 265 **OG**
Col: Michigan *HS:* St. Thomas Aquinas [Fort Lauderdale, FL]
B: 1/20/1962, Fort Lauderdale, FL *Drafted:* 1984 Round 3 ChiB
1984 ChiB: 10 G. **1985** ChiB: 11 G. **1986** ChiB: 4 G. **1987** Den: 7 G. **1988** Den: 1 G. **Total:** 33 G.

STAN HUMPHRIES Humphries, William Stanley 6'2", 223 **QB**
Col: Louisiana State; Northeast Louisiana *HS:* Southwood [Shreveport, LA] B: 4/14/1965, Shreveport, LA *Drafted:* 1988 Round 6 Was
1995 SD: Rec 1-(-4) -4.0. **Total:** Rec 1-(-4) -4.0.

		Passing							
Year Team	**G**	**Att**	**Comp**	**Comp%**	**Yds**	**YPA**	**TD**	**Int**	**Rating**
1989 Was	2	10	5	50.0	91	9.10	1	1	75.4
1990 Was	7	156	91	58.3	1015	6.51	3	10	57.5
1992 SD	16	454	263	57.9	3356	7.39	16	18	76.4
1993 SD	12	324	173	53.4	1981	6.11	12	10	71.5
1994 SD	15	453	264	58.3	3209	7.08	17	12	81.6
1995 SD	15	478	282	59.0	3381	7.07	17	14	80.4
1996 SD	13	416	232	55.8	2670	6.42	18	13	76.7
1997 SD	8	225	121	53.8	1488	6.61	5	6	70.8
NFL Total	88	2516	1431	56.9	17191	6.83	89	84	75.8

	Rushing				
Year Team	**Att**	**Yds**	**Avg**	**TD**	**Fum**
1989 Was	5	10	2.0	0	1
1990 Was	23	106	4.6	2	0
1992 SD	28	79	2.8	4	9
1993 SD	8	37	4.6	0	2
1994 SD	19	19	1.0	0	6
1995 SD	33	53	1.6	1	9
1996 SD	21	28	1.3	0	7
1997 SD	13	24	1.8	0	7
NFL Total	150	356	2.4	7	41

JAMES HUNDON Hundon, James Henry 6'1", 180 **WR**
Col: San Francisco City Coll. CA (J.C.); Portland State *HS:* Daly City [CA] B: 4/9/1971, San Francisco, CA
1996 Cin: PR 1-(-7) -7.0; KR 10-237 23.7. **1997** Cin: KR 10-169 16.9. **Total:** PR 1-(-7) -7.0; KR 20-406 20.3.

		Receiving				
Year Team	**G**	**Rec**	**Yds**	**Avg**	**TD**	**Fum**
1996 Cin	5	1	14	14.0	1	1
1997 Cin	16	16	285	17.8	2	1
1998 Cin	9	10	112	11.2	1	0
NFL Total	30	27	411	15.2	4	2

CHARLIE HUNEKE Huneke, Charles Franklyn 6'3", 225 **T**
(Chuck) *Col:* St. Mary's (Tex.); Benedictine *HS:* Cathedral Boys [Springfield, IL] B: 1/1/1921, Lincoln, IL D: 9/5/1990
AAFC **1946** ChiA: 14 G. **1947** ChiA-BknA: 13 G. **1948** BknA: 2 G. **Total:** 29 G.

LAMONTE HUNLEY Hunley, Kenneth Lamonte 6'2", 240 **LB**
Col: Arizona *HS:* Petersburg [VA] B: 1/31/1963, Richmond, VA
1985 Ind: 16 G. **1986** Ind: 6 G. **Total:** 22 G.

RICKY HUNLEY Hunley, Ricky Cardell 6'2", 242 **LB**
Col: Arizona *HS:* Petersburg [VA] B: 11/11/1961, Petersburg, VA
Drafted: 1984 Round 1 Cin
1984 Den: 8 G. **1985** Den: 16 G. **1986** Den: 16 G; KR 2-11 5.5; Int 1-22; 0.5 Sac. **1987** Den: 12 G; Int 2-64 1 TD; 6 Pt; 1 Sac. **1988** Pho: 16 G; PR 1-3 3.0; 1 Sac. **1989** LARd: 12 G. **1990** LARd: 11 G. **Total:** 91 G; PR 1-3 3.0; KR 2-11 5.5; Int 3-86 1 TD; 6 Pt; 2.5 Sac.

JIM HUNNICUTT Hunnicutt, James Edward 6'0", 175 **G**
Col: South Carolina B: 6/10/1923
1948 Det: 1 G.

CHUCK HUNSINGER Hunsinger, Charles Ray 6'0", 188 **HB**
Col: Florida *HS:* Harrisburg [IL] B: 7/25/1925, Harrisburg, IL
Drafted: 1950 Round 1 ChiB
1950 ChiB: Rec 1-20 20.0; PR 1-4 4.0. **1951** ChiB: Rec 6-59 9.8 1 TD; PR 1-7 7.0. **1952** ChiB: Rec 16-170 10.6 2 TD. **Total:** Rec 23-249 10.8 3 TD; PR 2-11 5.5.

		Rushing				Kickoff Returns					Tot
Year Team	**G**	**Ret**	**Yds**	**Avg**	**TD**	**Ret**	**Yds**	**Avg**	**TD**	**Fum**	**TD**
1950 ChiB	10	61	326	5.3	2	12	343	28.6	0	3	2
1951 ChiB	12	73	369	5.1	3	4	66	16.5	0	0	4
1952 ChiB	12	58	139	2.4	0	15	308	20.5	0	5	2
NFL Total	34	192	834	4.3	5	31	717	23.1	0	8	8

BEN HUNT Hunt, Ben 5'9", 185 **T**
Col: Alabama *HS:* Scottsboro [AL] B: 9/16/1900, Scottsboro, AL
D: 6/1981, Scottsboro, AL
1923 Tol: 3 G.

BYRON HUNT Hunt, Byron Ray 6'5", 238 **LB**
Col: Southern Methodist *HS:* White Oak [TX] B: 12/17/1958, Longview, TX *Drafted:* 1981 Round 9 NYG
1981 NYG: 16 G; Int 1-7. **1982** NYG: 9 G; 1.5 Sac. **1983** NYG: 16 G; 1 Sac. **1984** NYG: 13 G; Int 1-14; 1 Sac. **1985** NYG: 16 G; 1.5 Sac. **1986** NYG: 16 G. **1987** NYG: 12 G. **1988** NYG: 2 G. **Total:** 100 G; Int 2-21; 5 Sac.

CALVIN HUNT Hunt, Calvin Cornelius 6'3", 245 **C**
Col: Baylor *HS:* Edna [TX] B: 12/31/1947, Oceanside, CA
Drafted: 1970 Round 11 Pit
1970 Phi: 7 G. **1972** Hou: 10 G. **1973** Hou: 4 G. **Total:** 21 G.

CHARLIE HUNT Hunt, Charles Edward 6'2", 215 **LB**
Col: Florida State *HS:* Samuel W. Wolfson [Jacksonville, FL]
B: 2/1/1951, St. Augustine, FL *Drafted:* 1973 Round 10 SF
1973 SF: 8 G. **1976** TB: 5 G. **Total:** 13 G.

DARYL HUNT Hunt, Daryl Lynn 6'3", 229 **LB**
Col: Oklahoma *HS:* Permian [Odessa, TX] B: 11/3/1956, Odessa, TX
Drafted: 1979 Round 6 Hou
1979 Hou: 16 G. **1980** Hou: 16 G. **1981** Hou: 16 G; KR 3-19 6.3. **1982** Hou: 9 G; 1 Sac. **1983** Hou: 16 G; KR 1-12 12.0; 1 Sac. **1984** Hou: 5 G. **Total:** 78 G; KR 4-31 7.8; 2 Sac.

ERVIN HUNT Hunt, Ervin J 6'2", 190 **DB**
Col: Fresno State *HS:* Fresno [CA] B: 7/1/1947, Fowler, CA
Drafted: 1970 Round 6 GB
1970 GB: 6 G.

GARY HUNT Hunt, Gary Lynn 5'11", 175 **DB**
Col: Memphis *HS:* Liberty-Eylau [Texarkana, TX] B: 10/28/1963, Texarkana, TX *Drafted:* 1986 Round 6 Cin
1987 Cin: 3 G.

GEORGE HUNT Hunt, George Arthur 6'1", 215 **K**
Col: Tennessee *HS:* Clearwater [FL] B: 8/3/1949, Marietta, OK
Drafted: 1972 Round 5 Cle
1973 Bal: 14 G; Scor 70, 16-28 57.1% FG, 22-24 91.7% XK. **1975** NYG: 14 G; Punt 9-218 24.2; Scor 42, 6-11 54.5% FG, 24-29 82.8% XK. **Total:** 28 G; Punt 9-218 24.2; Scor 112, 22-39 56.4% FG, 46-53 86.8% XK.

JIM HUNT Hunt, James Lee 5'11", 250 **DT-DE**
(Earthquake) *Col:* Prairie View A&M *HS:* Booker T. Washington [Texarkana, TX] B: 10/5/1938, Atlanta, TX D: 11/22/1975, Philadelphia, PA *Drafted:* 1960 Round 2 NYT
1960 Bos: 6 G; KR 1-8 8.0; 1 Fum. **1961** Bos: 14 G. **1962** Bos: 14 G. **1963** Bos: 14 G; Int 1-78 1 TD; 6 Pt. **1964** Bos: 14 G. **1965** Bos: 14 G. **1966** Bos: 14 G; **1** Fum TD; 6 Pt. **1967** Bos: 14 G; Scor **1** Saf; 2 Pt. **1968** Bos: 14 G. **1969** Bos: 14 G. **1970** Bos: 14 G. **Total:** 146 G; KR 1-8 8.0; Int 1-78 1 TD; Scor 1 Saf; 1 Fum TD; Tot TD 2; 14 Pt; 1 Fum.

JACKIE HUNT Hunt, John Seva 6'0", 192 **HB-DB**
Col: Marshall *HS:* Huntington [WV] B: 2/17/1920, Huntington, WV
D: 6/21/1991, Huntiongton, WV *Drafted:* 1942 Round 11 ChiB
1945 ChiB: 4 G; Rush 1-1 1.0; Punt 2-54 27.0.

JOHN HUNT Hunt, John Stephen 6'4", 254 **OT-OG**
Col: Florida *HS:* Edgewater [Orlando, FL] B: 11/6/1962, Orlando, FL
Drafted: 1984 Round 9 Dal
1984 Dal: 2 G. **1987** TB: 1 G. **Total:** 3 G.

MIKE HUNT Hunt, Michael Anthony 6'2", 240 **LB**
Col: Minnesota *HS:* Ortonville [MN] B: 10/6/1956, Madison, MN
Drafted: 1978 Round 2 GB
1978 GB: 16 G; Int 1-10. **1979** GB: 3 G; Int 1-13. **1980** GB: 3 G. **Total:** 22 G; Int 2-23.

KEVIN HUNT Hunt, Richard Kevin 6'5", 260 **OT-OG**
Col: Doane *HS:* Burlington [VT] B: 11/29/1948, Farmington, MA
Drafted: 1971 Round 10 GB
1972 GB: 3 G. **1973** NE-Hou: 5 G. NE: 1 G. Hou: 4 G. **1974** Hou: 13 G. **1975** Hou: 13 G. **1976** Hou: 13 G. **1977** Hou: 13 G. **1978** NO: 10 G. **Total:** 70 G.

BOBBY HUNT Hunt, Robert Kenneth 6'1", 185 **DB**
Col: Auburn *HS:* Lanett [AL] B: 8/15/1940, Lanett, AL *Drafted:* 1962 Round 11 DalT
1968 Cin: Rush 1-5 5.0 1 TD. **Total:** Rush 1-5 5.0 1 TD.

		Interceptions			Tot
Year Team	G	Int	Yds	TD	TD
1962 DalT	14	8	101	0	0
1963 KC	14	6	228	0	0
1964 KC	14	7	133	**1**	1
1965 KC	14	1	28	0	0
1966 KC	14	**10**	113	0	0
1967 KC	14	5	71	0	0
1968 Cin	14	1	15	0	1
1969 Cin	14	4	66	0	0
NFL Total	112	42	755	1	2

BOB HUNT Hunt, Robert Steven 6'1", 210 **RB**
Col: Heidelberg *HS:* Columbian [Tiffin, OH] B: 9/3/1951, Toledo, OH
Drafted: 1974 Round 14 Cle
1974 Cle: 2 G.

RON HUNT Hunt, Ronald Michele 6'6", 261 **OT**
Col: Oregon *HS:* South Gate [CA] B: 1/27/1955, Los Angeles, CA
Drafted: 1976 Round 8 Cin
1976 Cin: 12 G; KR 2-24 12.0. **1977** Cin: 13 G. **1978** Cin: 3 G. **Total:** 28 G; KR 2-24 12.0.

SAM HUNT Hunt, Samuel Kay 6'1", 248 **LB**
Col: Stephen F. Austin St. *HS:* White Oak [TX] B: 8/6/1951, Longview, TX *Drafted:* 1974 Round 15 NE
1974 NE: 14 G; KR 1-21 21.0; Int 3-66. **1975** NE: 13 G. **1976** NE: 14 G; Int 2-106 1 TD; 6 Pt. **1977** NE: 13 G; Int 2-17. **1978** NE: 15 G. **1979** NE: 15 G. **Total:** 84 G; KR 1-21 21.0; Int 7-189 1 TD; 6 Pt.

AL HUNTER Hunter, Alfonse 5'11", 195 **RB**
Col: Notre Dame *HS:* J.H. Rose [Greenville, NC] B: 2/21/1955, Greenville, NC *Drafted:* 1977 Supplemental Round 1 Sea

		Rushing				Receiving			
Year Team	G	Att	Yds	Avg	TD	Rec	Yds	Avg	TD
1977 Sea	12	32	179	5.6	1	5	42	8.4	0
1978 Sea	16	105	348	3.3	2	12	172	14.3	0
1979 Sea	15	34	174	5.1	1	7	77	11.0	0
1980 Sea	9	9	14	1.6	0	3	40	13.3	0
NFL Total	52	180	715	4.0	4	27	331	12.3	0

	Kickoff Returns				
Year Team	Ret	Yds	Avg	TD	Fum
1977 Sea	36	820	22.8	0	2
1978 Sea	16	385	24.1	0	3
1979 Sea	15	299	19.9	0	1
1980 Sea	11	213	19.4	0	1
NFL Total	78	1717	22.0	0	7

TONY HUNTER Hunter, Anthony Fernando 5'9", 215 **RB**
Col: Minnesota *HS:* Tech [Memphis, TN] B: 2/24/1963, Memphis, TN
1987 GB: 1 G; Rush 1-0.

ART HUNTER Hunter, Arthur James 6'4", 245 **C-OT**
Col: Notre Dame *HS:* St. Vincent [Akron, OH] B: 4/24/1933, Fairport Harbor, OH *Drafted:* 1954 Round 1 GB
1954 GB: 12 G. **1956** Cle: 8 G. **1957** Cle: 12 G. **1958** Cle: 12 G. **1959** Cle: 12 G. **1960** LARm: 12 G. **1961** LARm: 14 G. **1962** LARm: 2 G. **1963** LARm: 12 G. **1964** LARm: 14 G. **1965** Pit: 9 G. **Total:** 119 G.

BRICE HUNTER Hunter, Brice 6'2", 206 **WR**
Col: Georgia *HS:* Valdosta [GA] B: 4/21/1974, Valdosta, GA
Drafted: 1996 Round 7 Mia
1997 TB: 3 G. **1998** TB: 10 G; Rec 4-73 18.3 1 TD; Scor 1 2XP; 8 Pt. **Total:** 13 G; Rec 4-73 18.3 1 TD; Scor 1 2XP; 8 Pt.

DANIEL HUNTER Hunter, Daniel Lewis 5'11", 178 **DB**
Col: Henderson State *HS:* Arkadelphia [AR] B: 9/1/1962, Arkadelphia, AR
1985 Den: 16 G; KR 2-33 16.5; Int 1-20. **1986** Den-SD: 15 G. Den: 10 G. SD: 5 G. **1987** SD: 12 G; KR 1-0; 1 Fum; 1 Sac. **Total:** 43 G; KR 3-33 11.0; Int 1-20; 1 Fum; 1 Sac.

EARNEST HUNTER Hunter, Earnest III 5'8", 201 **RB**
Col: Navarro Coll. TX (J.C.); Southeastern Oklahoma State
HS: Longview [TX] B: 12/21/1970, Longview, TX
1995 Cle: Rec 5-42 8.4; PR 3-40 13.3. **1996** Bal-NO: Pass 1-0; Rec 18-163 9.1. Bal: Rec 1-25 25.0. NO: Pass 1-0; Rec 17-138 8.1. **Total:** Pass 1-0; Rec 23-205 8.9; PR 3-40 13.3.

		Rushing				Kickoff Returns				
Year Team	G	Att	Yds	Avg	TD	Ret	Yds	Avg	TD	Fum
1995 Cle	10	30	100	3.3	0	23	508	22.1	0	4
1996 Bal-NO	11	15	44	2.9	0	10	198	19.8	0	4
1996 Bal	5	1	0	0.0	0	9	178	19.8	0	2
1996 NO	6	14	44	3.1	0	1	20	20.0	0	2
NFL Total	21	45	144	3.2	0	33	706	21.4	0	8

EDDIE HUNTER Hunter, Edward Lee 5'10", 205 **RB**
Col: Virginia Tech *HS:* Bishop McNamara [Forestville, MD]
B: 1/20/1965, Reno, NV *Drafted:* 1987 Round 8 NYJ
1987 NYJ-TB: Rec 7-28 4.0 2 TD; KR 8-123 15.4. NYJ: Rec 5-24 4.8 2 TD; KR 8-123 15.4. TB: Rec 2-4 2.0. **Total:** Rec 7-28 4.0 2 TD; KR 8-123 15.4.

		Rushing				
Year Team	G	Att	Yds	Avg	TD	Fum
1987 NYJ-TB	6	56	210	3.8	0	3
1987 NYJ	3	48	169	3.5	0	3
1987 TB	3	8	41	5.1	0	0
NFL Total	6	56	210	3.8	0	3

BILLY HUNTER Hunter, George William 6'1", 185 **WR-HB-DB**
Col: Syracuse *HS:* Delaware Twp. [South Merchantville, NJ]
B: 11/5/1942, Camden, NJ
1965 Was: 12 G; Rec 1-29 29.0 1 TD; KR 18-432 24.0; 6 Pt; 1 Fum. **1966** Mia: 4 G; KR 5-84 16.8; 1 Fum. **Total:** 16 G; Rec 1-29 29.0 1 TD; KR 23-516 22.4; 6 Pt; 2 Fum.

HERMAN HUNTER Hunter, Herman James 6'1", 197 **RB**
Col: Tennessee State *HS:* Hardaway [Columbus, GA] B: 2/14/1961, Columbus, GA *Drafted:* 1985 Round 11 Phi
1985 Phi: Pass 2-1 50.0%, 38 19.00 1 TD; PR 1-6 6.0. **Total:** Pass 2-1 50.0%, 38 19.00 1 TD; PR 1-6 6.0.

		Rushing				Receiving			
Year Team	G	Att	Yds	Avg	TD	Rec	Yds	Avg	TD
1985 Phi	16	27	121	4.5	1	28	405	14.5	1
1986 Det	16	3	22	7.3	0	25	218	8.7	1
1987 Hou	3	34	144	4.2	0	3	17	5.7	0
NFL Total	35	64	287	4.5	1	56	640	11.4	2

	Kickoff Returns					Tot
Year Team	Ret	Yds	Avg	TD	Fum	TD
1985 Phi	48	1047	21.8	0	4	2
1986 Det	**49**	**1007**	20.6	0	1	1
1987 Hou	4	79	19.8	0	1	0
NFL Total	101	2133	21.1	0	6	3

IVY JOE HUNTER Hunter, Ivy Joe 6'0", 237 **RB**
Col: Kentucky *HS:* F.W. Buchholz [Gainesville, FL] B: 11/16/1966, Gainesville, FL *Drafted:* 1989 Round 7 Ind
1989 Ind: KR 4-58 14.5. **1991** NE: Rec 11-97 8.8. **Total:** Rec 11-97 8.8; KR 4-58 14.5.

		Rushing			
Year Team	G	Att	Yds	Avg	TD
1989 Ind	16	13	47	3.6	0
1990 Ind	16	0	0	—	0
1991 NE	13	18	53	2.9	0
NFL Total	45	31	100	3.2	0

JAMES HUNTER Hunter, James Dale 6'5", 251 **NT-DE**
Col: USC *HS:* Santa Barbara [CA] B: 9/13/1957, Oklahoma City, OK
Drafted: 1981 Round 9 Pit
1982 Bal: 9 G; 1 Sac.

JAMES HUNTER Hunter, James Edward 6'3", 195 **DB**
Col: Grambling State *HS:* Silsbee [TX] B: 3/8/1954, Silsbee, TX
Drafted: 1976 Round 1 Det
1976 Det: PR 4-7 1.8; KR 14-375 26.8. **1977** Det: KR 4-95 23.8. **1978** Det: PR 2-21 10.5; KR 1-21 21.0. **1982** Det: 1 Sac. **Total:** PR 6-28 4.7; KR 19-491 25.8; 1 Sac.

		Interceptions			
Year Team	G	Int	Yds	TD	Fum
1976 Det	13	7	120	1	3
1977 Det	14	6	104	0	0
1978 Det	9	2	-4	0	0
1979 Det	15	3	6	0	0
1980 Det	16	6	20	0	0
1981 Det	12	1	-3	0	1
1982 Det	7	2	36	0	0
NFL Total	86	27	279	1	4

SCOTT HUNTER Hunter, James Scott 6'2", 205 **QB**
Col: Alabama *HS:* C.F. Vigor [Prichard, AL] B: 11/11/1947, Mobile, AL
Drafted: 1971 Round 6 GB

Year Team	G	Att	Comp	Comp%	Yds	YPA	TD	Int	Rating
		Passing							
1971 GB	13	163	75	46.0	1210	7.42	7	17	46.1
1972 GB	14	199	86	43.2	1252	6.29	6	9	55.5
1973 GB	8	84	35	41.7	442	5.26	2	4	46.8
1974 Buf	1	0	0	—	0	—	0	0	—
1976 Atl	8	110	51	46.4	633	5.75	5	4	64.7
1977 Atl	7	151	70	46.4	898	5.95	2	3	61.6
1979 Det	13	41	18	43.9	321	7.83	1	1	69.3
NFL Total	64	748	335	44.8	4756	6.36	23	38	55.0

Year Team	Att	Yds	Avg	TD	Fum
	Rushing				
1971 GB	21	50	2.4	4	7
1972 GB	22	37	1.7	5	5
1973 GB	8	3	0.4	1	1
1976 Atl	14	41	2.9	1	1
1977 Atl	28	70	2.5	1	3
1979 Det	2	3	1.5	1	0
NFL Total	95	204	2.1	13	17

JEFF HUNTER Hunter, Jeffrey Orlando 6'5", 286 **DE**
Col: Albany State (Ga.) *HS:* Hephzibah [GA] B: 4/12/1966, Hampton, VA *Drafted:* 1989 Round 11 Pho
1990 Buf-Det: 10 G; 3 Sac. Buf: 3 G. Det: 7 G; 3 Sac. **1991** Det: 16 G; 6 Sac. **1992** Det-Mia: 11 G. Det: 4 G. Mia: 7 G. **1993** Mia: 5 G; 3 Sac. **1994** TB: 1 G. **Total:** 43 G; 12 Sac.

JOHN HUNTER Hunter, John Rosel 6'8", 294 **OT**
Col: Brigham Young *HS:* North Bend [OR] B: 8/16/1965, Roseburg, OR *Drafted:* 1989 Round 3 Min
1989 Atl: 4 G. **1990** Atl: 15 G. **1991** Atl: 2 G. **1992** Sea: 5 G. **Total:** 26 G.

MERLE HUNTER Hunter, Merle Lucas 185 **T-G**
Col: No College *HS:* Brinkhaven [OH] B: 4/28/1906, Ossian, IN D: 7/15/1982, Ossian, IN
1925 Ham: 3 G. **1926** Ham: 1 G. **Total:** 4 G.

MONTY HUNTER Hunter, Orie Montgomery III 6'0", 202 **DB**
Col: Salem *HS:* Dover [OH] B: 1/21/1959, Dover, OH *Drafted:* 1982 Round 5 Dal
1982 Dal: 9 G; 1 Sac. **1983** StL: 5 G. **Total:** 14 G; 1 Sac.

PATRICK HUNTER Hunter, Patrick Edward 5'11", 186 **DB**
Col: Nevada-Reno *HS:* South San Francisco [CA] B: 10/24/1964, San Francisco, CA *Drafted:* 1986 Round 3 Sea
1988 Sea: PR 1-0. **1989** Sea: 1 Sac. **Total:** PR 1-0; 1 Sac.

Year Team	G	Int	Yds	TD	Fum
		Interceptions			
1986 Sea	16	0	0	0	0
1987 Sea	11	1	3	0	0
1988 Sea	10	0	0	0	1
1989 Sea	16	0	0	0	0
1990 Sea	16	1	0	0	0
1991 Sea	15	1	32	1	0
1992 Sea	16	2	0	0	0
1993 Sea	15	4	54	0	0
1994 Sea	5	3	85	0	0
1995 Ariz	5	2	21	0	0
NFL Total	125	14	195	1	1

RAMEY HUNTER Hunter, Raymond Q 6'0", 178 **E**
Col: Marshall *HS:* Huntington [WV] B: 8/26/1910, Huntington, WV D: 1/17/1992, Livingston, MT
1933 Port: 2 G.

STAN HUNTER Hunter, Stanford Keith 6'2", 184 **WR**
Col: Bowling Green State *HS:* Northmont [Clayton, OH] B: 11/29/1963, Dayton, OH
1987 NYJ: 3 G; Rec 6-50 8.3 1 TD; 6 Pt.

TONY HUNTER Hunter, Tony Wayne 6'4", 237 **TE**
Col: Notre Dame *HS:* Moeller [Cincinnati, OH] B: 5/22/1960, Cincinnati, OH *Drafted:* 1983 Round 1 Buf
1983 Buf: Rush 2-28 14.0. **1984** Buf: Rush 1-6 6.0. **1986** LARm: Rush 1-(-6) -6.0. **Total:** Rush 4-28 7.0.

Year Team	G	Rec	Yds	Avg	TD	Fum
		Receiving				
1983 Buf	13	36	402	11.2	3	1
1984 Buf	11	33	331	10.0	2	1
1985 LARm	16	50	562	11.2	4	3
1986 LARm	7	15	206	13.7	0	2
NFL Total	47	134	1501	11.2	9	7

TOREY HUNTER Hunter, Torey Hayward 5'9", 176 **DB**
Col: Washington State *HS:* Curtis [Tacoma, WA] B: 2/10/1972, Tacoma, WA *Drafted:* 1995 Round 3 Hou
1995 Hou: 12 G.

GREG HUNTINGTON Huntington, Gregory Gerard 6'3", 297 **C-OG**
Col: Penn State *HS:* Moeller [Cincinnati, OH] B: 9/22/1970, Morristown, NJ *Drafted:* 1993 Round 5 Was
1993 Was: 9 G. **1995** Jac: 4 G. **1996** Jac: 2 G. **1997** ChiB: 1 G. **1998** ChiB: 2 G. **Total:** 18 G.

RICHARD HUNTLEY Huntley, Richard Earl 5'11", 224 **RB**
Col: Winston-Salem State *HS:* Monroe [NC] B: 9/18/1972, Monroe, NC *Drafted:* 1996 Round 4 Atl
1996 Atl: Rec 1-14 14.0. **1998** Pit: Rec 3-18 6.0; KR 6-119 19.8. **Total:** Rec 4-32 8.0; KR 6-119 19.8.

Year Team	G	Att	Yds	Avg	TD	Fum
		Rushing				
1996 Atl	1	2	8	4.0	0	0
1998 Pit	16	55	242	4.4	1	5
NFL Total	17	57	250	4.4	1	5

TOM HUPKE Hupke, Thomas George 5'10", 192 **G-T**
Col: Alabama *HS:* Theodore Roosevelt [East Chicago, IL] B: 12/29/1910, East Chicago, IN D: 9/7/1959, Detroit, MI
1934 Det: 9 G. **1935** Det: 10 G. **1936** Det: 7 G. **1937** Det: 11 G; Int **1** TD; 6 Pt. **1938** Cle: 10 G. **1939** Cle: 8 G. **Total:** 55 G; Int 1 TD; 6 Pt.

JEFF HURD Hurd, Jeffrey Tonja 6'2", 245 **LB**
Col: Kansas State *HS:* Lincoln Prep [Kansas City, MO] B: 5/25/1964, Monroe, LA
1987 Dal: 5 G.

JOHN HURLBURT Hurlburt, John Blair 6'0", 175 **WB-BB**
Col: Chicago *HS:* Marshalltown, [IA] B: 7/23/1898, Burlington, IA D: 3/1968, Petrolia, CA
1924 ChiC: 9 G; Rush 2 TD; Rec 1 TD; Tot TD 3; 18 Pt. **1925** ChiC: 5 G. **Total:** 14 G; Rush 2 TD; Rec 1 TD; Tot TD 3; 18 Pt.

GEORGE HURLEY Hurley, George Frank 6'0", 200 **G**
Col: Washington State *HS:* Wilmerding [San Francisco, CA] B: 10/19/1909, San Francisco, CA D: 12/17/1989, Twain Harte, CA
1932 Bos: 10 G. **1933** Bos: 10 G. **Total:** 20 G.

JOHN HURLEY Hurley, John J 6'3", 192 **OE**
Col: Washington State *HS:* Wilmerding [San Francisco, CA] B: 1/9/1907, San Francisco, CA D: 1/1983, Santa Rosa, CA
1931 Cle: 10 G.

BILL HURLEY Hurley, William John Jr. 5'11", 195 **DB**
Col: Syracuse *HS:* St. Joseph's [Kenmore, NY] B: 6/15/1957, Kenmore, NY *Drafted:* 1980 Round 4 Pit
1982 NO: 9 G; Rec 1-39 39.0 1 TD; Int 1-26; 6 Pt. **1983** NO-Buf: 14 G; PR 1-0; 1 Fum. NO: 4 G. Buf: 10 G; PR 1-0; 1 Fum. **Total:** 23 G; Rec 1-39 39.0 1 TD; PR 1-0; Int 1-26; 6 Pt; 1 Fum.

MAURICE HURST Hurst, Maurice Roy 5'10", 185 **DB**
Col: Southern University *HS:* Alcee Fortier [New Orleans, LA] B: 9/17/1967, New Orleans, LA *Drafted:* 1989 Round 4 NE
1989 NE: PR 1-6 6.0. **1993** NE: 1 Sac. **1994** NE: 2 Sac. **Total:** PR 1-6 6.0; 3 Sac.

Year Team	G	Int	Yds	TD	Fum
		Interceptions			
1989 NE	16	5	31	1	0
1990 NE	16	4	61	0	1
1991 NE	15	3	21	0	0
1992 NE	16	3	29	0	0
1993 NE	16	4	53	0	0
1994 NE	16	7	68	0	0
1995 NE	10	1	0	0	0
NFL Total	105	27	263	1	1

BILL HURST Hurst, William Jr. 6'1", 195 **T**
(Pep) *Col:* No College B: 6/23/1903, Pendlebury, England D: 11/1966
1924 Ken: 5 G.

CHUCK HURSTON Hurston, Charles Frederick 6'6", 240 **DE-LB**
Col: Auburn *HS:* Jordan Vocational [Columbus, GA] B: 11/9/1942, Columbus, GA *Drafted:* 1965 Round 12 Buf
1965 KC: 14 G. **1966** KC: 14 G. **1967** KC: 14 G. **1968** KC: 14 G. **1969** KC: 14 G. **1970** KC: 14 G. **1971** Buf: 9 G. **Total:** 93 G.

ERIC HURT Hurt, Eric 5'11", 171 **DB**
Col: San Jose State *HS:* Compton [CA] B: 6/11/1957
1980 Dal: 4 G; KR 4-71 17.8.

ED HUSMANN Husmann, Edward Earl 6'2", 245 **DT-OG-LB-DE**
Col: Nebraska *HS:* Ogallala [NE] B: 8/6/1931, Schuyler, NE
1953 ChiC: 12 G. **1956** ChiC: 12 G. **1957** ChiC: 12 G. **1958** ChiC: 4 G. **1959** ChiC: 12 G. **1960** Dal: 12 G. **1961** Hou: 14 G. **1962** Hou: 14 G. **1963** Hou: 14 G. **1964** Hou: 14 G. **1965** Hou: 14 G. **Total:** 134 G.

AL HUST Hust, Albert 6′1″, 220 **DE-OE**
Col: Tennessee *HS:* West Tech [Cleveland, OH] B: 4/9/1921, Czechoslovakia D: 4/16/1984, Knoxville, TN *Drafted:* 1943 Round 4 ChiC
1946 ChiC: 10 G; Rec 1-9 9.0.

MICHAEL HUSTED Husted, Michael James 6′0″, 190 **K**
Col: Virginia *HS:* Hampton [VA] B: 6/16/1970, El Paso, TX
1994 TB: Punt 2-53 26.5. **1998** TB: Rush 1-20 20.0. **Total:** Rush 1-20 20.0; Punt 2-53 26.5.

		Scoring						
Year Team	**G**	**Pts**	**FG**	**FGA**	**FG%**	**XK**	**XKA**	**XK%**
1993 TB	16	75	16	22	72.7	27	27	100.0
1994 TB	16	89	23	35	65.7	20	20	100.0
1995 TB	16	82	19	26	73.1	25	25	100.0
1996 TB	16	93	25	32	78.1	18	19	94.7
1997 TB	16	71	13	17	76.5	32	35	91.4
1998 TB	16	92	21	28	75.0	29	30	96.7
NFL Total	96	502	117	160	73.1	151	156	96.8

KEN HUTCHERSON Hutcherson, Kenneth Lee 6′1″, 220 **LB**
Col: West Alabama *HS:* Anniston [AL] B: 7/14/1952, Anniston, AL *Drafted:* 1974 Round 4 Dal
1974 Dal: 14 G. **1975** SD: 8 G. **Total:** 22 G.

PAUL HUTCHINS Hutchins, Paul Andre 6′5″, 335 **OT**
(Hutch) *Col:* Western Michigan *HS:* Brother Rice [Chicago, IL] B: 2/11/1970, Chicago, IL *Drafted:* 1993 Round 6 GB
1993 GB: 1 G. **1994** GB: 16 G. **Total:** 17 G.

RALPH HUTCHINSON Hutchinson, Ralph 6′2″, 230 **T**
Col: Tennessee-Chattanooga *HS:* Southern Choctaw [Silas, AL] B: 5/2/1924, Silas, AL D: 1/10/1990 *Drafted:* 1948 Round 8 NYG
1949 NYG: 10 G.

SCOTT HUTCHINSON Hutchinson, Scott Rawls 6′4″, 246 **DE**
Col: Florida *HS:* Winter Park [FL] B: 5/27/1956, Winter Park, FL *Drafted:* 1978 Round 2 Buf
1978 Buf: 16 G; KR 1-8 8.0. **1979** Buf: 16 G. **1980** Buf: 16 G. **1981** TB: 16 G. **1983** Buf: 5 G. **Total:** 69 G; KR 1-8 8.0.

TOM HUTCHINSON Hutchinson, Thomas Edward 6′1″, 190 **WR**
Col: Kentucky *HS:* New Albany [IN] B: 6/15/1941, Stanford, KY *Drafted:* 1963 Round 1 Cle
1963 Cle: 14 G; Rec 9-244 27.1. **1964** Cle: 14 G; Rec 3-24 8.0. **1965** Cle: 14 G; Rec 6-113 18.8 2 TD; KR 2-0; 12 Pt. **1966** Atl: 5 G; Rec 1-28 28.0. **Total:** 47 G; Rec 19-409 21.5 2 TD; KR 2-0; 12 Pt.

BILL HUTCHINSON Hutchinson, William David 5′9″, 180 **QB-DB**
(Bombshell Bill) *Col:* Dartmouth *HS:* James Monroe [Bronx, NY] B: 3/9/1916, Bronx, NY
1942 NYG: 2 G; Pass 4-1 25.0%, -3 -0.75 2 Int; Rush 7-27 3.9; PR 1-1 1.0; Punt 2-65 32.5.

ANTHONY HUTCHISON Hutchison, Anthony LaRue 5′10″, 186 **RB**
Col: Texas Tech *HS:* Judson [Converse, TX] B: 2/4/1961, Houston, TX *Drafted:* 1983 Round 10 ChiB
1983 ChiB: Rush 6-13 2.2 1 TD. **1984** ChiB: Rush 14-39 2.8 1 TD; Rec 1-7 7.0. **1985** Buf: Rush 2-11 5.5. **Total:** Rush 22-63 2.9 2 TD; Rec 1-7 7.0.

		Kickoff Returns				
Year Team	**G**	**Ret**	**Yds**	**Avg**	**TD**	**Fum**
1983 ChiB	16	17	259	15.2	0	1
1984 ChiB	12	0	0	—	0	0
1985 Buf	5	12	239	19.9	0	0
NFL Total	33	29	498	17.2	0	1

CHUCK HUTCHISON Hutchison, Charles Arthur 6′3″, 250 **OG**
Col: Ohio State *HS:* Carrollton [OH] B: 11/17/1948, Canton, OH *Drafted:* 1970 Round 2 StL
1970 StL: 7 G. **1971** StL: 13 G. **1972** StL: 4 G. **1973** Cle: 2 G. **1974** Cle: 7 G. **1975** Cle: 14 G. **Total:** 47 G.

ELVIN HUTCHISON Hutchison, Elvin Clarence 5′11″, 210 **WB-DB**
(Red Oak Express) *Col:* Whittier *HS:* Red Oak [IA] B: 10/14/1912, Guthrie Center, IA
1939 Det: 2 G.

JERRY HUTH Huth, Gerald Bernard 6′0″, 226 **OG**
Col: Wake Forest *HS:* New Albany [IN] B: 7/23/1933, Floyds Knobs, IN *Drafted:* 1956 Round 24 NYG
1956 NYG: 11 G. **1959** Phi: 10 G; **1** Fum TD; 6 Pt. **1960** Phi: 12 G. **1961** Min: 14 G. **1962** Min: 14 G. **1963** Min: 13 G. **Total:** 74 G; 1 Fum TD; 6 Pt.

BRUCE HUTHER Huther, Bruce Albert 6′1″, 221 **LB**
Col: New Hampshire *HS:* Manchester [Haledon, NJ] B: 7/23/1954, Paterson, NJ
1977 Dal: 14 G. **1978** Dal: 16 G. **1979** Dal: 16 G; KR 1-8 8.0. **1980** Dal: 15 G. **1981** Cle: 16 G. **1982** ChiB: 4 G. **1983** Dal: 11 G; KR 1-0. **Total:** 92 G; KR 2-8 4.0.

BRIAN HUTSON Hutson, Brian Sinclair 6′1″, 198 **DB**
Col: Mississippi State *HS:* Brandon [MS] B: 2/20/1965, Jackson, MS
1990 NE: 2 G.

DON HUTSON Hutson, Donald Montgomery 6′1″, 183 **OE-DB-DE**
Col: Alabama *HS:* Pine Bluff [AR] B: 1/31/1913, Pine Bluff, AR D: 6/26/1997, Rancho Mirage, CA *HOF:* 1963
1935 GB: Scor 43, 1 XK. **1937** GB: Pass 4-0, 1 Int. **1938** GB: Scor 57, 3-3 100.0% XK. **1939** GB: Scor 38, 2-2 100.0% XK. **1940** GB: Scor **57**, 15-16 93.8% XK. **1941** GB: KR 1-8 8.0; Scor **95**, 1-1 100.0% FG, **20-24** 83.3% XK. **1942** GB: Scor **138**, 1-4 25.0% FG, **33-34** 97.1% XK. **1943** GB: Pass 4-1 25.0%, 38 9.50 1 TD 1 Int; Scor **117**, **3**-5 **60.0**% FG, 36-36 **100.0**% XK. **1944** GB: Pass 3-0; Scor **85**, 0-3 FG, 31-33 93.9% XK. **1945** GB: KR 4-37 9.3; Scor 97, 2-4 50.0% FG, **31-35** 88.6% XK. **Total:** Pass 11-1 9.1%, 38 3.45 1 TD 2 Int; KR 5-45 9.0; Scor 823, 7-17 41.2% FG, 172-183 93.4% XK.

		Rushing				Receiving			
Year Team	**G**	**Att**	**Yds**	**Avg**	**TD**	**Rec**	**Yds**	**Avg**	**TD**
1935 GB	9	6	22	3.7	0	18	420	23.3	**6**
1936 GB	12	1	-3	-3.0	0	**34**	**536**	15.8	**8**
1937 GB	11	14	26	1.9	0	**41**	552	13.5	**7**
1938 GB	10	3	-1	-0.3	0	32	**548**	17.1	**9**
1939 GB	11	5	26	5.2	0	**34**	**846**	24.9	6
1940 GB	11	0	0	—	0	45	664	14.8	**7**
1941 GB	11	4	22	5.5	2	**58**	**738**	12.7	**10**
1942 GB	11	3	4	1.3	0	**74**	**1211**	16.4	**17**
1943 GB	10	6	41	6.8	0	**47**	**776**	16.5	**11**
1944 GB	10	12	87	7.3	0	**58**	**866**	14.9	**9**
1945 GB	10	8	60	7.5	1	**47**	834	17.7	9
NFL Total	116	62	284	4.6	3	488	7991	16.4	99

	Interceptions				Tot
Year Team	**Int**	**Yds**	**TD**	**Fum**	**TD**
1935 GB	—	—	0	0	**7**
1936 GB	—	—	0	0	**9**
1937 GB	—	—	0	0	**7**
1938 GB	—	—	0	0	**9**
1939 GB	—	—	0	0	6
1940 GB	**6**	24	0	0	7
1941 GB	1	32	0	0	**12**
1942 GB	7	71	0	0	**17**
1943 GB	8	**197**	**1**	0	**12**
1944 GB	4	50	0	0	**9**
1945 GB	4	15	0	1	10
NFL Total	30	389	1	1	105

MERLE HUTSON Hutson, Merle 6′0″, 210 **G-T**
Col: Heidelberg B: 8/27/1908 Deceased
1931 Cle: 10 G.

TONY HUTSON Hutson, Tony 6′3″, 306 **OG**
Col: Kilgore Coll. TX (J.C.); Northeastern State (Okla.) *HS:* MacArthur [Houston, TX] B: 3/13/1974, Houston, TX
1997 Dal: 5 G. **1998** Dal: 10 G. **Total:** 15 G.

JACK HUTTON Hutton, Leon John H. 6′1″, 192 **OE-WB**
Col: Purdue *HS:* Emmerich Manual Training [Indianapolis, IN] B: 8/12/1906, Indianapolis, IN D: 1/2/1969, Bristol, PA
1930 Fra: 3 G.

TOM HUTTON Hutton, William Thomas 6′1″, 193 **P-K**
Col: Tennessee *HS:* Memphis University [Memphis, TN] B: 7/8/1972, Memphis, TN
1995 Phi: Rush 1-0. **1997** Phi: Rush 1-0. **Total:** Rush 2-0.

		Punting			
Year Team	**G**	**Punts**	**Yds**	**Avg**	**Fum**
1995 Phi	16	85	3682	43.3	1
1996 Phi	16	73	3107	42.6	0
1997 Phi	16	87	3660	42.1	1
1998 Phi	16	**104**	4339	41.7	0
NFL Total	64	349	14788	42.4	2

KEN HUXHOLD Huxhold, Kenneth Wayne 6′1″, 226 **OG**
Col: Wisconsin *HS:* Kenosha [WI] B: 8/10/1929, Kenosha, WI *Drafted:* 1951 Round 27 ChiC
1954 Phi: 11 G. **1955** Phi: 12 G. **1956** Phi: 12 G. **1957** Phi: 12 G. **1958** Phi: 12 G. **Total:** 59 G.

JOHN HUZVAR Huzvar, John Frank II 6′4″, 247 **FB**
(Jumbo) *Col:* North Carolina State; Pittsburgh *HS:* Milton S. Hershey [Hershey, PA] B: 8/6/1929, Carlisle, PA
1952 Phi: Rec 13-37 2.8. **1953** Bal: Rec 6-55 9.2 1 TD. **1954** Bal: KR 1-0. **Total:** Rec 19-92 4.8 1 TD; KR 1-0.

		Rushing					Tot
Year Team	**G**	**Att**	**Yds**	**Avg**	**TD**	**Fum**	**TD**
1952 Phi	12	105	349	3.3	2	9	2
1953 Bal	12	119	515	4.3	4	5	5

1954 Bal	8	19	29	1.5	0	3	0
NFL Total	32	243	893	3.7	6	17	7

FRED HYATT Hyatt, Frederick Phillip 6'3", 200 **WR**
Col: Auburn *HS:* Sylacauga [AL] B: 6/28/1946, Roanoke, AL
Drafted: 1968 Round 2 StL
1968 StL: 1 G. **1969** StL: 6 G. **1970** StL: 10 G. **1971** StL: 14 G; Rec 4-58 14.5. **1972** StL: 12 G; Rec 2-32 16.0; KR 1-41 41.0. **1973** NO-Was: 2 G. NO: 1 G. Was: 1 G. **Total:** 45 G; Rec 6-90 15.0; KR 1-41 41.0.

STEVE HYCHE Hyche, Steven Jay 6'3", 241 **LB**
Col: West Alabama *HS:* Cordova [AL] B: 6/12/1963, Jasper, AL
1989 ChiB: 6 G. **1991** Pho: 16 G. **1992** Pho: 16 G; 1 Sac. **1993** Pho: 2 G. **Total:** 40 G; 1 Sac.

GLENN HYDE Hyde, Glenn Thatcher 6'3", 253 **C-OT-OG**
Col: Pittsburgh *HS:* Lexington [MA] B: 3/14/1951, Boston, MA
1976 Den: 11 G; KR 1-17 17.0. **1977** Den: 14 G; KR 1-15 15.0. **1978** Den: 15 G. **1979** Den: 16 G. **1980** Den: 16 G. **1981** Den: 16 G. **1982** Bal: 5 G. **1985** Den: 11 G. **1986** Sea: 3 G. **1987** KC: 8 G; 1 Fum. **Total:** 115 G; KR 2-32 16.0; 1 Fum.

BOB HYLAND Hyland, Robert Joseph 6'5", 255 **C-OG**
Col: Boston College *HS:* Archbishop Stepinac [White Plains, NY]
B: 7/21/1945, White Plains, NY *Drafted:* 1967 Round 1 GB
1967 GB: 14 G. **1968** GB: 14 G. **1969** GB: 14 G; KR 1-0. **1970** ChiB: 14 G; 6 Fum. **1971** NYG: 14 G; 1 Fum. **1972** NYG: 10 G. **1973** NYG: 14 G; Rec 1-16 16.0. **1974** NYG: 11 G. **1975** NYG: 14 G. **1976** GB: 14 G; KR 3-31 10.3; 1 Fum. **1977** NE: 3 G. **Total:** 136 G; Rec 1-16 16.0; KR 4-31 7.8; 8 Fum.

PAUL HYNES Hynes, Paul Edward 6'1", 210 **DB**
Col: Louisiana Tech *HS:* Sulphur [LA] B: 9/9/1939, Sulphur, LA
Drafted: 1961 Round 12 DalT
1961 DalT-NYT: 10 G; KR 2-45 22.5. DalT: 1 G; KR 1-27 27.0. NYT: 9 G; KR 1-18 18.0. **1962** NYT: 13 G; Int 2-2. **Total:** 23 G; KR 2-45 22.5; Int 2-2.

HENRY HYNOSKI Hynoski, Henry Philip 6'0", 210 **RB**
Col: Temple *HS:* Mount Carmel [PA] B: 5/30/1953, Mount Carmel, PA
Drafted: 1975 Round 6 Cle
1975 Cle: 14 G; Pass 1-0; Rush 7-38 5.4; Rec 4-31 7.8; PR 2-16 8.0; KR 8-194 24.3; 1 Fum.

COSMO IACOVAZZI Iacovazzi, Cosmo Joseph 5'11", 209 **HB**
Col: Princeton *HS:* West Scranton [Scranton, PA] B: 8/18/1943, Scranton, PA *Drafted:* 1965 Round 20 Min
1965 NYJ: 2 G.

MIKE IAQUANIELLO Iaquaniello, Michael 6'3", 208 **DB**
Col: Michigan State *HS:* Fordson [Dearborn, MI] B: 2/13/1968, Detroit, MI
1991 Mia: 15 G.

MEKELI IEREMIA Ieremia, Mekeli Tolufale 6'2", 244 **DT**
Col: Brigham Young *HS:* Sleepy Hollow [North Tarrytown, NY]
B: 3/4/1954, Niosafutu, American Samoa *Drafted:* 1978 Round 6 ChiB
1978 Buf: 2 G.

ISRAEL IFEANYI Ifeanyi, Israel 6'3", 246 **DE**
(Nigerian Nightmare) *Col:* Orange Coast Coll. CA (J.C.); USC
HS: Government Sec. School [Lagos, Nigeria] B: 11/21/1970, Lagos, Nigeria *Drafted:* 1996 Round 2 SF
1996 SF: 3 G.

FLOYD IGLEHART Iglehart, Floyd Williams Jr. 6'4", 197 **DB**
Col: Wiley *HS:* Burnet [TX] B: 1/25/1934, Terrell, TX D: 9/5/1987, Dallas, TX *Drafted:* 1958 Round 6 LARm
1958 LARm: 1 G.

DONALD IGWEBUIKE Igwebuike, Donald Amechi 5'9", 181 **K**
Col: Clemson *HS:* Immaculate Conception School [Anambra, Nigeria]
B: 12/27/1960, Anambra, Nigeria *Drafted:* 1985 Round 10 TB

		Scoring						
Year Team	**G**	**Pts**	**FG**	**FGA**	**FG%**	**XK**	**XKA**	**XK%**
1985 TB	16	96	22	32	68.8	30	32	93.8
1986 TB	16	77	17	24	70.8	26	27	96.3
1987 TB	12	66	14	18	77.8	24	26	92.3
1988 TB	12	78	19	25	76.0	21	21	100.0
1989 TB	16	99	22	28	78.6	33	35	94.3
1990 Min	8	61	14	16	87.5	19	19	100.0
NFL Total	80	477	108	143	75.5	153	160	95.6

HANK ILESIC Ilesic, Henry 6'1", 210 **P**
Col: No College *HS:* St. Joseph's [Edmonton, Canada] B: 9/7/1959, Edmonton, Canada

		Punting		
Year Team	**G**	**Punts**	**Yds**	**Avg**
1989 SD	14	76	3049	40.1

RAY ILG Ilg, Raymond Arthur III 6'1", 220 **LB**
Col: Colgate *HS:* Wellesley [MA] B: 11/25/1945, Wellesley, MA
Drafted: 1967 Round 13 Bos
1967 Bos: 14 G; KR 1-10 10.0. **1968** Bos: 14 G. **Total:** 28 G; KR 1-10 10.0.

MARK ILGENFRITZ Ilgenfritz, Mark Monteith 6'4", 250 **DE**
Col: Vanderbilt *HS:* Sandy Springs [Atlanta, GA] B: 9/9/1952, Honolulu, HI *Drafted:* 1974 Round 5 Cle
1974 Cle: 14 G.

TUNCH ILKIN Ilkin, Tunch Ali 6'3", 263 **OT-OG-C**
Col: Indiana State *HS:* Highland Park [IL] B: 9/23/1957, Istanbul, Turkey *Drafted:* 1980 Round 6 Pit
1980 Pit: 10 G. **1981** Pit: 16 G. **1982** Pit: 8 G. **1983** Pit: 11 G. **1984** Pit: 16 G. **1985** Pit: 16 G. **1986** Pit: 15 G. **1987** Pit: 11 G. **1988** Pit: 16 G. **1989** Pit: 16 G. **1990** Pit: 13 G. **1991** Pit: 16 G. **1992** Pit: 12 G. **1993** GB: 1 G. **Total:** 177 G.

TED ILLMAN Illman, Edward Walter 6'0", 190 **WB-FB-TB-BB**
(Chief) *Col:* Montana *HS:* Glasgow [MT]; Powell Co. HS [Deer Lodge, MT]; Missoula HS [MT] B: 11/27/1900, Glasgow, MT D: 3/29/1962
1928 ChiC: 5 G.

ROY ILOWIT Ilowit, Roy 6'2", 220 **T**
(Baby LeRoy) *Col:* CCNY B: 4/3/1917, New York, NY D: 1/3/1990, Long Beach, NY
1937 Bkn: 4 G.

KEN IMAN Iman, Kenneth Charles 6'1", 240 **C**
Col: Southeast Missouri State *HS:* Beaumont [St. Louis, MO]
B: 2/8/1939, St. Louis, MO
1960 GB: 12 G. **1961** GB: 14 G. **1962** GB: 14 G. **1963** GB: 14 G. **1965** LARm: 14 G. **1966** LARm: 14 G; Rush 1-2 2.0. **1967** LARm: 14 G. **1968** LARm: 14 G. **1969** LARm: 14 G. **1970** LARm: 14 G. **1971** LARm: 14 G. **1972** LARm: 14 G. **1973** LARm: 14 G; 2 Fum. **1974** LARm: 14 G. **Total:** 194 G; Rush 1-2 2.0; 2 Fum.

MARTIN IMHOF Imhof, Martin Carl 6'6", 255 **DE-DT**
(Tree) *Col:* San Diego State *HS:* Blair [Pasadena, CA] B: 10/9/1949, Seattle, WA *Drafted:* 1972 Round 4 StL
1972 StL: 13 G. **1974** Was: 13 G. **1975** NE: 5 G. **1976** Den: 1 G. **Total:** 32 G.

TUT IMLAY Imlay, Talma W 5'8", 165 **TB-WB-BB**
Col: California *HS:* Boise [ID]; Salinas HS [CA] B: 3/20/1902, Panguitch, UT D: 3/20/1976, Monterey, CA
1926 LA: 10 G; Pass 1 TD; Rush 3 TD; Rec 1 TD; Tot TD 4; 24 Pt. **1927** NYG: 7 G. **Total:** 17 G; Pass 1 TD; Rush 3 TD; Rec 1 TD; Tot TD 4; 24 Pt.

BOB INGALLS Ingalls, Donald Robert 6'3", 200 **C-LB**
Col: Michigan *HS:* Marblehead [MA]; Kiski School [Saltsburg, PA]
B: 1/17/1919, Marblehead, MA D: 4/8/1970, Willimantic, CT
Drafted: 1942 Round 16 GB
1942 GB: 10 G; Int 1-23 **1** TD; 6 Pt.

MARK INGLE Ingle, Mark B 1 **G**
Col: No College B: 1891, OK Deceased
1921 Eva: 1 G.

TIM INGLIS Inglis, Timothy James 6'3", 232 **LB**
Col: Toledo *HS:* St. John's [Toledo, OH] B: 3/10/1964, Toledo, OH
1987 Cin: 8 G. **1988** Cin: 4 G. **Total:** 12 G.

BRIAN INGRAM Ingram, Brian DeWayne 6'4", 236 **LB**
Col: Tennessee *HS:* Hamilton [Memphis, TN] B: 10/31/1959, Memphis, TN *Drafted:* 1982 Round 4 NE
1982 NE: 8 G. **1983** NE: 4 G. **1984** NE: 12 G. **1985** NE: 15 G. **1987** SD: 1 G. **Total:** 40 G.

BYRON INGRAM Ingram, Byron Kimble 6'2", 295 **OG**
Col: Eastern Kentucky *HS:* Henry Clay [Lexington, KY] B: 11/17/1964, Lexington, KY
1987 KC: 1 G. **1988** KC: 12 G; KR 2-16 8.0. **Total:** 13 G; KR 2-16 8.0.

DARRYL INGRAM Ingram, Darryl 6'3", 240 **TE**
Col: California *HS:* William S. Hart [Newhall, CA] B: 5/2/1966, Lubbock, TX *Drafted:* 1989 Round 4 Min
1989 Min: 16 G; Rec 5-47 9.4 1 TD; 6 Pt. **1991** Cle: 2 G. **1992** GB: 16 G. **1993** GB: 2 G. **Total:** 36 G; Rec 5-47 9.4 1 TD; 6 Pt.

KEVIN INGRAM Ingram, Kevin 6'0", 178 **QB**
Col: East Carolina *HS:* Murrell Dobbins Area Vo-Tech [Philadelphia, PA]
B: 4/26/1962, Philadelphia, PA
1987 NO: 2 G; Pass 2-1 50.0%, 5 2.50 1 TD; Rush 2-14 7.0; 2 Fum.

MARK INGRAM Ingram, Mark V 5'10", 190 **WR**
Col: Michigan State *HS:* Northwestern [Flint, MI] B: 8/23/1965, Rockford, IL *Drafted:* 1987 Round 1 NYG
1989 NYG: Rush 1-1 1.0. **1990** NYG: Rush 1-4 4.0. **1991** NYG: Pass 1-0; PR 8-49 6.1. **1995** GB: Rush 1-(-3) -3.0; PR 1-0. **Total:** Pass 1-0; Rush 3-2 0.7; PR 9-49 5.4.

Year Team	G	Rec	Yds	Avg	TD	Ret	Yds	Avg	TD	Fum
		Receiving				Kickoff Returns				
1987 NYG	9	2	32	16.0	0	6	114	19.0	0	0
1988 NYG	7	13	158	12.2	1	8	129	16.1	0	0
1989 NYG	16	17	290	17.1	1	22	332	15.1	0	2
1990 NYG	16	26	499	19.2	5	3	42	14.0	0	1
1991 NYG	16	51	824	16.2	3	8	125	15.6	0	3
1992 NYG	12	27	408	15.1	1	0	0	—	0	0
1993 Mia	16	44	707	16.1	6	0	0	—	0	3
1994 Mia	15	44	506	11.5	6	1	0	0.0	0	1
1995 GB	16	39	469	12.0	3	0	0	—	0	1
1996 Phi	5	2	33	16.5	0	0	0	—	0	0
NFL Total	128	265	3926	14.8	26	48	742	15.5	0	11

STEVE INGRAM Ingram, Stephen Anthony 6′4″, 311 **OT-OG**
Col: Maryland *HS:* DuVal [Lanham, MD] B: 5/8/1971, Cheverly, MD
Drafted: 1995 Round 7 TB
1995 TB: 2 G.

BURT INGWERSEN Ingwersen, Burton Aherns 5′11″, 180 **T**
Col: Illinois *HS:* Clinton [IA] B: 8/29/1898, Fulton, IL D: 7/17/1969, Champaign, IL
1920 Sta: 13 G.

JERRY INMAN Inman, Jerald Franklin 6′2″, 256 **DT**
Col: Boise State; Oregon *HS:* Evergreen [Vancouver, WA] B: 2/4/1940, Manhattan, KS *Drafted:* 1965 Redshirt Round 6 Den
1966 Den: 14 G; KR 1-0. **1967** Den: 14 G. **1968** Den: 7 G. **1969** Den: 14 G. **1970** Den: 11 G. **1971** Den: 14 G. **1973** Den: 8 G. **Total:** 82 G; KR 1-0.

EARL INMON Inmon, Earl 6′1″, 215 **LB**
Col: Bethune-Cookman *HS:* Umatilla [FL] B: 3/21/1954, Umatilla, FL
Drafted: 1978 Round 7 Oak
1978 TB: 2 G.

DOU INNOCENT Innocent, Doudow 5′11″, 212 **RB**
Col: Mississippi *HS:* Ely [Pompano Beach, FL] B: 7/9/1972, Pompano Beach, FL
1996 Sea: 4 G.

MARNE INTRIERI Intrieri, Marino Charles 5′8″, 250 **G-T-C-LB**
Col: Loyola (Balt.) *HS:* Steelton [PA] B: 9/13/1907, Steelton, PA Deceased
1932 SI: 11 G. **1933** Bos: 3 G. **1934** Bos: 6 G. **Total:** 20 G.

TONY IPPOLITO Ippolito, Anthony Samuel 5′10″, 220 **G-LB**
Col: Purdue *HS:* St. Ignatius [Chicago, IL] B: 9/19/1917, Chicago, IL D: 11/12/1951, Evanston, IL *Drafted:* 1939 Round 7 Phi
1943 ChiB: 9 G; Int 1-5.

DARWIN IRELAND Ireland, Darwin Dawan 5′11″, 240 **LB**
Col: Arkansas *HS:* Dollarway [Pine Bluff, AR] B: 5/26/1971, Pine Bluff, AR
1994 ChiB: 2 G. **1995** ChiB: 1 G. **Total:** 3 G.

BILL IRGENS Irgens, Einer 5′8″, 175 **BB-WB-TB-OE**
Col: No College B: 6/1883, Norway Deceased
1921 Min: 2 G. **1922** Min: 4 G; Pass 1 TD; Scor 1, 1 XK. **1923** Min: 5 G; Pass 1 TD. **Total:** 11 G; Pass 2 TD.

GERALD IRONS Irons, Gerald Dwayne 6′2″, 230 **LB**
Col: Maryland East. Shore *HS:* Theodore Roosevelt [Gary, IN]
B: 5/2/1947, Gary, IN *Drafted:* 1970 Round 3 Oak

Year Team	G	Int	Yds	TD	Fum
		Interceptions			
1970 Oak	14	0	0	0	0
1971 Oak	7	0	0	0	0
1972 Oak	14	2	18	0	0
1973 Oak	14	2	19	0	0
1974 Oak	14	2	23	0	0
1975 Oak	14	1	9	0	0
1976 Cle	14	1	1	0	0
1977 Cle	14	3	99	**1**	0
1978 Cle	14	2	9	0	1
1979 Cle	16	0	0	0	0
NFL Total	135	13	178	1	1

BARLOW IRVIN Irvin, Barlow 5′10″, 225 **G-T**
(Bones) *Col:* Texas A&M B: 12/31/1903, Cotulla, TX D: 11/26/1985, Bryan, TX
1926 Buf: 10 G. **1927** Buf: 5 G. **Total:** 15 G.

TEX IRVIN Irvin, Cecil Paul 6′0″, 225 **T-FB-LB-G**
Col: Schreiner Coll.; Davis & Elkins *HS:* Cisco [TX] B: 10/9/1906, De Leon, TX D: 2/11/1978, DeLeon, TX
1931 Prov: 10 G. **1932** NYG: 10 G. **1933** NYG: 12 G; Rec 1-15 15.0 1 TD; 6 Pt. **1934** NYG: 12 G. **1935** NYG: 12 G. **Total:** 56 G; Rec 1-15 15.0 1 TD; 6 Pt.

DARRELL IRVIN Irvin, Darrell Bruce 6′4″, 259 **DE**
Col: Northeastern Oklahoma A&M (J.C.); Oklahoma *HS:* Pawhuska [OK]
B: 1/21/1957, Pawhuska, OK
1980 Buf: 7 G. **1981** Buf: 13 G. **1982** Buf: 9 G. **1983** Sea: 16 G.
Total: 45 G.

KEN IRVIN Irvin, Kenneth Pernell 5′10″, 186 **DB**
Col: Memphis *HS:* Pepperell [Lindale, GA] B: 7/11/1972, Lindale, GA
Drafted: 1995 Round 4 Buf
1995 Buf: 16 G; KR 1-12 12.0. **1996** Buf: 16 G; 2 Sac. **1997** Buf: 16 G; Int 2-28. **1998** Buf: 16 G; Int 1-43. **Total:** 64 G; KR 1-12 12.0; Int 3-71; 2 Sac.

LEROY IRVIN Irvin, LeRoy Jr. 5′11″, 184 **DB**
Col: Kansas *HS:* Glenn Hills [Augusta, GA] B: 9/15/1957, Fort Dix, NJ
Drafted: 1980 Round 3 LARm
1980 LARm: KR 1-5 5.0. **1983** LARm: KR 1-22 22.0; 1 Sac. **1984** LARm: KR 2-33 16.5. **1986** LARm: **1** Fum TD. **1988** LARm: 0.5 Sac.
Total: KR 4-60 15.0; 1 Fum TD; 1.5 Sac.

Year Team	G	Ret	Yds	Avg	TD	Int	Yds	TD	Fum	Tot TD
		Punt Returns				Interceptions				
1980 LARm	16	42	296	7.0	0	2	80	0	5	0
1981 LARm	16	46	**615**	**13.4**	**3**	3	18	0	3	3
1982 LARm	9	22	242	11.0	1	0	0	0	4	1
1983 LARm	15	25	212	8.5	0	4	42	0	4	0
1984 LARm	16	9	83	9.2	0	5	166	**2**	0	2
1985 LARm	16	0	0	—	0	6	83	**1**	0	1
1986 LARm	16	0	0	—	0	6	150	1	1	3
1987 LARm	10	1	0	0.0	0	2	47	1	0	1
1988 LARm	16	1	2	2.0	0	3	25	0	1	0
1989 LARm	13	1	7	7.0	0	3	43	0	0	0
1990 Det	16	0	0	—	0	1	22	0	0	0
NFL Total	159	147	1457	9.9	4	35	676	5	18	11

MARK IRVIN Irvin, Mark LuRue 5′10″, 190 **DB**
Col: Bethune-Cookman *HS:* Miami Northwestern [FL] B: 10/12/1964, Miami, FL
1987 Mia: 3 G.

MICHAEL IRVIN Irvin, Michael Jerome 6′2″, 207 **WR**
Col: Miami (Fla.) *HS:* St. Thomas Aquinas [Fort Lauderdale, FL]
B: 3/5/1966, Ft. Lauderdale, FL *Drafted:* 1988 Round 1 Dal
1988 Dal: Rush 1-2 2.0. **1989** Dal: Rush 1-6 6.0. **1992** Dal: Rush 1-(-9) -9.0. **1993** Dal: Rush 2-6 3.0. **1996** Dal: Scor 1 2XP. **1998** Dal: Rush 1-1 1.0. **Total:** Rush 6-6 1.0; Scor 1 2XP.

Year Team	G	Rec	Yds	Avg	TD	Fum
		Receiving				
1988 Dal	14	32	654	20.4	5	0
1989 Dal	6	26	378	14.5	2	0
1990 Dal	12	20	413	20.7	5	0
1991 Dal	16	93	**1523**	16.4	8	3
1992 Dal	16	78	1396	17.9	7	1
1993 Dal	16	88	1330	15.1	7	0
1994 Dal	16	79	1241	15.7	6	0
1995 Dal	16	111	1603	14.4	10	1
1996 Dal	11	64	962	15.0	2	1
1997 Dal	16	75	1180	15.7	9	0
1998 Dal	16	74	1057	14.3	1	1
NFL Total	155	740	11737	15.9	62	7

WILLIE IRVIN Irvin, Willie James 6′3″, 203 **DE-OE**
(Big Train) *Col:* Florida A&M *HS:* Excelsior [St. Augustine, FL]
B: 1/3/1930, St. Augustine, FL *Drafted:* 1953 Round 15 Phi
1953 Phi: 3 G; 1 Fum.

TERRY IRVING Irving, Terry Duane 6′2″, 230 **LB**
Col: McNeese State *HS:* Ball [Galveston, TX] B: 7/3/1971, Galveston, TX *Drafted:* 1994 Round 4 Ariz
1994 Ariz: 16 G. **1995** Ariz: 16 G; 1 Sac. **1996** Ariz: 16 G. **1997** Ariz: 16 G. **1998** Ariz: 6 G. **Total:** 70 G; 1 Sac.

DON IRWIN Irwin, Donald Emerson 6′1″, 196 **FB-DB-WB-TB**
(Bull) *Col:* Colgate *HS:* Utica Free Acad. [NY] B: 7/22/1913, New York, NY D: 6/8/1983, Detroit, MI *Drafted:* 1936 Round 7 Bos
1936 Bos: Pass 5-0, 1 Int. **1937** Was: Pass 3-0. **1938** Was: Pass 6-0, 2 Int; Scor 6, 0-1 XK. **Total:** Pass 14-0, 3 Int; Scor 36, 0-1 XK.

Year Team	G	Att	Yds	Avg	TD	Rec	Yds	Avg	TD
		Rushing				Receiving			
1936 Bos	2	17	78	4.6	2	2	31	15.5	0
1937 Was	10	89	315	3.5	2	8	112	14.0	0
1938 Was	10	56	130	2.3	1	16	138	8.6	0
1939 Was	7	10	63	6.3	1	1	8	8.0	0
NFL Total	29	172	586	3.4	6	27	289	10.7	0

DUTCH IRWIN Irwin, Harry Stratton 5′7″, 170 **WB**
Col: Mercer *HS:* East [Rochester, NY] B: 8/11/1889, Rochester, NY D: 6/6/1967, Fairport, NY
1920 Roch: 9 G.

HEATH IRWIN Irwin, Heath Spencer 6′4″, 300 **OG**
Col: Colorado *HS:* Boulder [CO] B: 6/27/1973, Boulder, CO
Drafted: 1996 Round 4 NE
1997 NE: 16 G. **1998** NE: 13 G. **Total:** 29 G.

JIM IRWIN Irwin, James C 5′7″, 165 **FB**
Col: No College *HS:* Anchorage [KY] B: 3/9/1897, Louisville, KY
D: 12/17/1965, Columbia, KY
1921 Lou: 1 G. **1922** Lou: 3 G. **Total:** 4 G.

TIM IRWIN Irwin, Timothy Edward 6′7″, 300 **OT**
Col: Tennessee *HS:* Central [Knoxville, TN] B: 12/13/1958, Knoxville, TN *Drafted:* 1981 Round 3 Min
1981 Min: 7 G. **1982** Min: 9 G. **1983** Min: 16 G. **1984** Min: 16 G. **1985** Min: 16 G. **1986** Min: 16 G; KR 1-0. **1987** Min: 12 G. **1988** Min: 16 G. **1989** Min: 16 G. **1990** Min: 16 G; 1 Fum. **1991** Min: 16 G. **1992** Min: 16 G. **1993** Min: 16 G. **1994** TB-Mia: 13 G. TB: 8 G. Mia: 5 G. **Total:** 201 G; KR 1-0; 1 Fum.

TED ISAACSON Isaacson, Theodore F 6′4″, 272 **T-C**
Col: Washington *HS:* James A. Garfield [Seattle, WA] B: 3/2/1912, Seattle, WA D: 3/1968
1934 ChiC: 10 G. **1935** ChiC: 12 G. **Total:** 22 G.

WILMER ISABEL Isabel, Wilmer Edward 6′0″, 180 **FB-BB-WB**
Col: Ohio State *HS:* East [Columbus, OH] B: 10/1/1899, Columbus, OH D: 9/9/1975, Columbus, OH
1923 Col: 10 G; Pass 1 TD; Rush 2 TD; 12 Pt. **1924** Col: 7 G. **Total:** 17 G; Pass 1 TD; Rush 2 TD; 12 Pt.

SALE ISAIA Isaia, Sale Jr. 6′5″, 315 **C-OT-OG**
Col: UCLA *HS:* Oceanside [CA] B: 6/13/1972, Honolulu, HI
1996 Bal: 9 G; KR 1-2 2.0; 1 Fum.

CECIL ISBELL Isbell, Cecil Frank 6′1″, 190 **TB-DB-HB**
Col: Purdue *HS:* Sam Houston [Houston, TX] B: 7/11/1915, Houston, TX D: 6/23/1985, Hammond, IN *Drafted:* 1938 Round 1 GB
1938 GB: Rec 5-104 20.8. **1939** GB: Rec 9-71 7.9; Punt 4-123 30.8; Scor 15, 3-3 100.0% XK. **1940** GB: Int 2-14; Punt 2-63 31.5. **1941** GB: Rec 1-(-1) -1.0; PR 3-19 6.3; KR 2-32 16.0; Int 1-0. **1942** GB: PR 1-14 14.0; KR 4-63 15.8; Int 6-47; Punt 4-141 35.3. **Total:** Rec 15-174 11.6; PR 4-33 8.3; KR 6-95 15.8; Int 9-61; Punt 10-327 32.7; Scor 63, 3-3 100.0% XK.

		Passing							
Year Team	**G**	**Att**	**Comp**	**Comp%**	**Yds**	**YPA**	**TD**	**Int**	**Rating**
1938 GB	11	91	37	40.7	659	7.24	8	10	55.9
1939 GB	11	103	43	41.7	749	7.27	6	5	66.4
1940 GB	10	150	68	45.3	1037	6.91	8	12	53.1
1941 GB	11	**206**	**117**	56.8	**1479**	7.18	**15**	11	81.4
1942 GB	11	268	**146**	54.5	**2021**	7.54	**24**	14	87.0
NFL Total	54	818	411	50.2	5945	7.27	61	52	72.6

	Rushing			
Year Team	**Att**	**Yds**	**Avg**	**TD**
1938 GB	85	445	**5.2**	2
1939 GB	132	407	3.1	2
1940 GB	97	270	2.8	4
1941 GB	72	317	4.4	1
1942 GB	36	83	2.3	1
NFL Total	422	1522	3.6	10

JOE BOB ISBELL Isbell, Joe Bob 6′1″, 243 **OG**
Col: Houston *HS:* Little Cypress [Orange, TX] B: 7/7/1940, Gorman, TX *Drafted:* 1962 Round 20 Hou
1962 Dal: 9 G. **1963** Dal: 8 G. **1964** Dal: 14 G. **1966** Cle: 14 G. **Total:** 45 G.

JOHN ISENBARGER Isenbarger, John Phillips 6′3″, 203 **RB-WR**
Col: Indiana *HS:* Muncie Central [IN] B: 1/5/1947, Muncie, IN
Drafted: 1970 Round 2 SF
1970 SF: Pass 1-0; Rec 8-158 19.8 1 TD. **1972** SF: Pass 1-0; Rec 3-66 22.0 1 TD. **1973** SF: Pass 1-1 100.0%, 48 48.00; Rec 10-67 6.7. **Total:** Pass 3-1 33.3%, 48 16.00; Rec 21-291 13.9 2 TD.

		Rushing			
Year Team	**G**	**Att**	**Yds**	**Avg**	**TD**
1970 SF	13	18	43	2.4	0
1971 SF	14	5	34	6.8	0
1972 SF	14	3	9	3.0	0
1973 SF	14	1	-6	-6.0	0
NFL Total	55	27	80	3.0	0

QADRY ISMAIL Ismail, Qadry Ramadan 6′0″, 196 **WR**
(Missle) *Col:* Syracuse *HS:* Elmer L. Myers [Wilkes-Barre, PA]
B: 11/8/1970, Newark, NJ *Drafted:* 1993 Round 2 Min
1993 Min: Rush 3-14 4.7. **1995** Min: Rush 1-7 7.0. **Total:** Rush 4-21 5.3.

		Receiving				Kickoff Returns				
Year Team	**G**	**Rec**	**Yds**	**Avg**	**TD**	**Ret**	**Yds**	**Avg**	**TD**	**Fum**
1993 Min	15	19	212	11.2	1	42	902	21.5	0	1
1994 Min	16	45	696	15.5	5	35	807	23.1	0	2
1995 Min	16	32	597	18.7	3	42	1037	24.7	0	3
1996 Min	16	22	351	16.0	3	28	527	18.8	0	2
1997 Mia	3	0	0	—	0	8	166	20.8	0	0
1998 NO	10	0	0	—	0	28	590	21.1	0	2
NFL Total	76	118	1856	15.7	12	183	4029	22.0	0	10

RAGHIB ISMAIL Ismail, Raghib Ramadan 5′11″, 180 **WR**
(Rocket) *Col:* Notre Dame *HS:* Elmer L. Myers [Wilkes-Barre, PA]
B: 11/18/1969, Elizabeth, NJ *Drafted:* 1991 Round 4 LARd

		Rushing				Receiving			
Year Team	**G**	**Att**	**Yds**	**Avg**	**TD**	**Rec**	**Yds**	**Avg**	**TD**
1993 LARd	13	4	-5	-1.3	0	26	353	13.6	1
1994 LARd	16	4	31	7.8	0	34	513	15.1	5
1995 Oak	16	6	29	4.8	0	28	491	17.5	3
1996 Car	13	8	80	10.0	1	12	214	17.8	0
1997 Car	13	4	32	8.0	0	36	419	11.6	2
1998 Car	16	3	42	14.0	0	69	1024	14.8	8
NFL Total	87	29	209	7.2	1	205	3014	14.7	19

	Kickoff Returns					Tot
Year Team	**Ret**	**Yds**	**Avg**	**TD**	**Fum**	**TD**
1993 LARd	25	605	24.2	0	0	1
1994 LARd	43	923	21.5	0	0	5
1995 Oak	36	706	19.6	0	4	3
1996 Car	5	100	20.0	0	0	1
1997 Car	0	0	—	0	0	2
1998 Car	0	0	—	0	2	8
NFL Total	109	2334	21.4	0	6	20

RAY ISOM Isom, Raymond Clinton 5′9″, 190 **DB**
Col: Penn State *HS:* Harrisburg [PA] B: 12/27/1965, Harrisburg, PA
1987 TB: 6 G; Int 2-67. **1988** TB: 2 G. **Total:** 8 G; Int 2-67.

RICKEY ISOM Isom, Rickey Lamarr 6′0″, 224 **RB**
Col: North Carolina State *HS:* Harrisburg [PA] B: 11/30/1963, Harrisburg, PA
1987 Mia: 3 G; Rush 9-41 4.6 1 TD; Rec 1-11 11.0; KR 1-11 11.0; 6 Pt.

STEVE ISRAEL Israel, Steven Douglas 5′11″, 194 **DB**
Col: Pittsburgh *HS:* Haddon Heights [NJ] B: 3/16/1969, Lawnside, NJ
Drafted: 1992 Round 2 LARm
1992 LARm: 16 G; KR 1-(-3) -3.0. **1993** LARm: 16 G; KR 5-92 18.4. **1994** LARm: 10 G. **1995** SF: 8 G. **1996** SF: 14 G; Int 1-3. **1997** NE: 5 G; 1 Sac. **1998** NE: 11 G; Int 3-13; 2 Sac. **Total:** 80 G; KR 6-89 14.8; Int 4-16; 3 Sac.

RALPH ISSELHARDT Isselhardt, Ralph L 6′1″, 205 **G**
Col: Franklin (Ohio) *HS:* Hillsboro [IL]; Marion HS [IN] B: 1/13/1910, Hillsboro, IL D: 10/24/1972, Grand Rapids, MI
1937 Det-Cle: 9 G. Det: 1 G. Cle: 8 G. **Total:** 9 G.

JACK ITZEL Itzel, John F Jr. 6′0″, 190 **FB-LB**
Col: Pittsburgh; Georgetown *HS:* Central Catholic [Pittsburgh, PA]
B: 11/12/1924 D: 12/21/1966, Wilkinsburg, PA *Drafted:* 1945 Round 17 Pit
1945 Pit: 10 G; Rush 4-11 2.8; Rec 1-4 4.0; Int 1-13.

DUKE IVERSON Iverson, Christopher Arnold 6′2″, 208 **DB-WB-HB-BB**
Col: Oregon *HS:* Petaluma [CA] B: 2/26/1920, Petaluma, CA
AAFC **1948** NY-A: 10 G; Rec 4-30 7.5; Int 1-1. **1949** NY-A: 12 G; Rush 6-50 8.3; KR 2-18 9.0; Int 1-8. **Total:** 22 G; Rush 6-50 8.3; Rec 4-30 7.5; KR 2-18 9.0; Int 2-9.

NFL **1947** NYG: 8 G; Rec 1-11 11.0; KR 1-16 16.0. **1950** NYY: 7 G; Int 3-26 1 TD; Scor **1** Saf; 8 Pt. **1951** NYY: 9 G; KR 1-14 14.0. **Total:** 24 G; Rec 1-11 11.0; KR 2-30 15.0; Int 3-26 1 TD; Scor 1 Saf; 8 Pt.

EDDIE LEE IVERY Ivery, Eddie Lee 6′0″, 210 **RB**
Col: Georgia Tech *HS:* Thomson [GA] B: 7/30/1957, McDuffie, GA
Drafted: 1979 Round 1 GB
1982 GB: Pass 1-0. **1983** GB: Pass 2-2 100.0%, 50 25.00; KR 1-17 17.0. **1985** GB: Pass 1-0. **Total:** Pass 4-2 50.0%, 50 12.50; KR 1-17 17.0.

		Rushing				Receiving					Tot
Year Team	**G**	**Att**	**Yds**	**Avg**	**TD**	**Rec**	**Yds**	**Avg**	**TD**	**Fum**	**TD**
1979 GB	1	3	24	8.0	0	0	0	—	0	1	0
1980 GB	16	202	831	4.1	3	50	481	9.6	1	3	4
1981 GB	1	14	72	5.1	1	2	10	5.0	0	0	1
1982 GB	9	127	453	3.6	9	16	186	11.6	1	2	10
1983 GB	8	86	340	4.0	2	16	139	8.7	1	1	3
1984 GB	10	99	552	5.6	6	19	141	7.4	1	1	7
1985 GB	15	132	636	4.8	2	28	270	9.6	2	1	4
1986 GB	12	4	25	6.3	0	31	385	12.4	1	0	1
NFL Total	72	667	2933	4.4	23	162	1612	10.0	7	9	30

JOHN IVLOW Ivlow, John David 5′11″, 226 **RB**
Col: Northwestern; Colorado State *HS:* Plainfield [IL] B: 1/26/1970, Joliet, IL
1993 ChiB: 2 G.

HORACE IVORY Ivory, Horace Orlando 6'0", 197 **RB**
Col: Navarro Coll. TX (J.C.); Oklahoma *HS:* Nolan [Fort Worth, TX]
B: 8/8/1954, Fort Worth, TX *Drafted:* 1977 Round 2 NE

		Rushing				Receiving			
Year Team	G	Att	Yds	Avg	TD	Rec	Yds	Avg	TD
1977 NE	5	3	10	3.3	0	0	0	—	0
1978 NE	15	141	693	4.9	11	14	122	8.7	0
1979 NE	11	143	522	3.7	1	23	216	9.4	2
1980 NE	14	42	111	2.6	2	12	95	7.9	0
1981 NE-Sea	7	9	38	4.2	0	0	0	—	0
1981 NE	1	0	0	—	0	0	0	—	0
1981 Sea	6	9	38	4.2	0	0	0	—	0
1982 Sea	6	13	51	3.9	1	5	38	7.6	0
NFL Total	58	351	1425	4.1	15	54	471	8.7	2

	Kickoff Returns					Tot
Year Team	Ret	Yds	Avg	TD	Fum	TD
1978 NE	7	165	23.6	0	5	11
1979 NE	1	15	15.0	0	4	3
1980 NE	36	992	**27.6**	**1**	3	3
1981 NE-Sea	16	300	18.8	0	1	0
1981 NE	1	19	19.0	0	0	0
1981 Sea	15	281	18.7	0	1	0
1982 Sea	10	224	22.4	0	0	1
NFL Total	70	1696	24.2	1	13	18

BOB IVORY Ivory, Robert James 6'2", 212 **G**
Col: Detroit Mercy *HS:* Catholic Central [Detroit, MI] B: 1/19/1924, Detroit, MI D: 2/25/1989, Detroit, MI *Drafted:* 1945 Round 24 Det
1947 Det: 3 G.

FRANK IVY Ivy, Lee Frank 6'3", 208 **E-K**
(Pop) *Col:* Oklahoma *HS:* Skiatook [OK] B: 1/25/1916, Skiatook, OK
Drafted: 1940 Round 4 Pit
1941 ChiC: Int 1-20 **1** TD; **1** Fum TD. **1942** ChiC: Scor 2, 2-2 100.0% XK. **1945** ChiC: Int 1-0. **1946** ChiC: Int 1-22. **1947** ChiC: Scor 0-1 FG.
Total: Int 3-42 1 TD; Scor 20, 0-1 FG, 2-2 100.0% XK; 1 Fum TD.

		Receiving					Tot
Year Team	G	Rec	Yds	Avg	TD	Fum	TD
1940 Pit-ChiC	9	2	32	16.0	0	0	0
1940 Pit	4	0	0	—	0	0	0
1940 ChiC	5	2	32	16.0	0	0	0
1941 ChiC	11	20	183	9.2	0	0	2
1942 ChiC	11	27	259	9.6	0	0	0
1945 ChiC	3	0	0	—	0	0	0
1946 ChiC	11	4	39	9.8	1	1	1
1947 ChiC	12	0	0	—	0	0	0
NFL Total	57	53	513	9.7	1	1	3

MARK IWANOWSKI Iwanowski, Mark David 6'4", 230 **TE**
Col: Pennsylvania *HS:* Kingsway Regional [Swedesboro, NJ]
B: 9/8/1955, Hazelton, PA
1978 NYJ: 5 G.

GEORGE IZO Izo, George William 6'4", 218 **QB**
Col: Notre Dame *HS:* Barberton [OH] B: 9/20/1937, Barberton, OH
Drafted: 1960 Round 1 StL
1961 Was: Rush 3-(-1) -0.3. **1962** Was: Rush 1-(-3) -3.0. **1963** Was: Rush 3-4 1.3. **1965** Det: Rush 1-(-5) -5.0. **1966** Pit: Rush 2-(-18) -9.0.
Total: Rush 10-(-23) -2.3.

		Passing								
Year Team	G	Att	Comp	Comp%	Yds	YPA	TD	Int	Rating	Fum
1960 StL	2	24	10	41.7	115	4.79	0	0	56.8	0
1961 Was	5	40	16	40.0	214	5.35	1	6	26.5	0
1962 Was	1	37	17	45.9	284	7.68	3	4	59.8	2
1963 Was	5	58	25	43.1	378	6.52	3	6	42.8	1
1964 Was	3	18	5	27.8	83	4.61	1	2	25.2	0
1965 Det	6	59	24	40.7	357	6.05	2	6	32.9	1
1966 Pit	4	81	35	43.2	360	4.44	2	8	25.3	2
NFL Total	26	317	132	41.6	1791	5.65	12	32	33.4	6

LARRY IZZO Izzo, Lawrence Alexander 5'10", 228 **LB**
Col: Rice *HS:* McCullough [The Woodlands, TX] B: 9/26/1974, Fort Belvior, VA
1996 Mia: 16 G; Rush 1-26 26.0. **1998** Mia: 13 G. **Total:** 29 G; Rush 1-26 26.0.

ERIC JACK Jack, Eric Demond 5'10", 177 **DB**
Col: New Mexico *HS:* Eastwood [Dallas, TX] B: 4/19/1972, Dallas, TX
1994 Atl: 16 G; 1 Fum TD; 6 Pt.

CHRIS JACKE Jacke, Christopher Lee 6'0", 205 **K**
Col: Texas-El Paso *HS:* J.J. Pearce [Richardson, TX] B: 3/12/1966, Richmond, VA *Drafted:* 1989 Round 6 GB

		Scoring						
Year Team	G	Pts	FG	FGA	FG%	XK	XKA	XK%
1989 GB	16	108	22	28	78.6	42	42	100.0
1990 GB	16	97	23	30	76.7	28	29	96.6
1991 GB	16	85	18	24	75.0	31	31	100.0
1992 GB	16	96	22	29	75.9	30	30	100.0
1993 GB	16	128	31	37	83.8	35	35	100.0
1994 GB	16	98	19	26	73.1	41	43	95.3
1995 GB	14	94	17	23	73.9	43	43	100.0
1996 GB	16	114	21	27	77.8	**51**	**53**	96.2
1997 Was	1	5	0	0	—	5	5	100.0
1998 Ariz	4	36	10	14	71.4	6	6	100.0
NFL Total	131	861	183	238	76.9	312	317	98.4

AL JACKSON Jackson, Alfonza 6'0", 182 **DB**
Col: Georgia *HS:* Pine Forest [Pensacola, FL] B: 9/7/1971, Pensacola, FL
1994 Phi: 11 G.

ALFRED JACKSON Jackson, Alfred 5'11", 176 **WR**
Col: Texas *HS:* Caldwell [TX] B: 8/3/1955, Cameron, TX
Drafted: 1978 Round 7 Atl
1978 Atl: PR 11-89 8.1; KR 11-225 20.5. **1979** Atl: KR 1-20 20.0. **1980** Atl: KR 3-70 23.3. **1981** Atl: Rush 2-5 2.5; 1 Fum TD. **1982** Atl: Rush 1-4 4.0.
Total: Rush 3-9 3.0; PR 11-89 8.1; KR 15-315 21.0; 1 Fum TD.

		Receiving					Tot
Year Team	G	Rec	Yds	Avg	TD	Fum	TD
1978 Atl	15	26	526	20.2	2	3	2
1979 Atl	12	11	156	14.2	0	0	0
1980 Atl	16	22	403	18.3	7	0	7
1981 Atl	16	37	604	16.3	6	0	7
1982 Atl	9	26	361	13.9	1	0	1
1983 Atl	4	13	220	16.9	3	0	3
1984 Atl	16	52	731	14.1	2	0	2
NFL Total	88	187	3001	16.0	21	3	22

ALFRED JACKSON Jackson, Alfred Melvin Jr. 6'0", 183 **WR**
Col: San Diego State *HS:* Tulare Western [CA] B: 7/10/1967, Tulare, CA *Drafted:* 1989 Round 5 LARm
1989 LARm: 7 G. **1990** LARm: 5 G. **1991** Cle: 6 G; Int 1-0. **1992** Cle: 5 G. **1995** Min: 8 G; Int 2-46 1 TD; 6 Pt. **1996** Min: 14 G; Int 2-4. **Total:** 45 G; Int 5-50 1 TD; 6 Pt.

ANDREW JACKSON Jackson, Andrew Leon 5'10", 190 **RB**
Col: El Camino Coll. CA (J.C.); USC; Iowa State *HS:* Manual Arts [Los Angeles, CA] B: 5/6/1964, Los Angeles, CA
1987 Hou: Rec 10-44 4.4.

		Rushing			
Year Team	G	Att	Yds	Avg	TD
1987 Hou	7	60	232	3.9	1

BERNARD JACKSON Jackson, Bernard Frank 6'0", 178 **DB**
Col: Pierce Coll. CA (J.C.); Washington State *HS:* Susan Miller Dorsey [Los Angeles, CA] B: 8/24/1950, Washington, DC D: 5/26/1997, Lompoc, CA *Drafted:* 1972 Round 4 Cin
1974 Cin: Rec 1-22 22.0. **Total:** Rec 1-22 22.0.

		Kickoff Returns				Interceptions			
Year Team	G	Ret	Yds	Avg	TD	Int	Yds	TD	Fum
1972 Cin	14	21	509	24.2	0	1	0	0	2
1973 Cin	14	21	520	24.8	0	1	0	0	0
1974 Cin	14	29	682	23.5	0	1	17	0	1
1975 Cin	14	25	587	23.5	0	5	97	0	0
1976 Cin	12	0	0	—	0	1	0	0	0
1977 Den	14	0	0	—	0	1	13	0	0
1978 Den	16	9	209	23.2	0	6	128	0	0
1979 Den	12	4	53	13.3	0	0	13	0	0
1980 Den-SD	8	9	149	16.6	0	1	11	0	1
1980 Den	4	0	0	—	0	1	11	0	0
1980 SD	4	9	149	16.6	0	0	0	0	1
NFL Total	118	118	2709	23.0	0	17	279	0	4

BILLY JACKSON Jackson, Billy Thurman 5'10", 217 **RB**
Col: Alabama *HS:* Central [Phenix City, AL] B: 9/13/1959, Phenix City, AL *Drafted:* 1981 Round 7 KC
1981 KC: KR 3-60 20.0. **Total:** KR 3-60 20.0.

		Rushing				Receiving					Tot
Year Team	G	Att	Yds	Avg	TD	Rec	Yds	Avg	TD	Fum	TD
1981 KC	16	111	398	3.6	10	6	31	5.2	1	1	11
1982 KC	9	86	243	2.8	3	5	41	8.2	0	1	3
1983 KC	16	152	499	3.3	2	32	243	7.6	0	3	2
1984 KC	16	50	225	4.5	1	15	101	6.7	1	2	2
NFL Total	57	399	1365	3.4	16	58	416	7.2	2	7	18

BOBBY JACKSON Jackson, Bobby Gerald 6′1″, 190 **DB**
Col: Alabama *HS:* S.S. Murphy [Mobile, AL] B: 1/10/1936, Geneva, AL
Drafted: 1959 Round 7 GB
1960 Phi: 12 G; PR 1-5 5.0. **1961** ChiB: 9 G. **Total:** 21 G; PR 1-5 5.0.

CALVIN JACKSON Jackson, Calvin Bernard 5′9″, 185 **DB**
Col: Auburn *HS:* Dillard [Fort Lauderdale, FL] B: 10/28/1972, Miami, FL
1994 Mia: 2 G. **1995** Mia: 9 G; Int 1-23. **1996** Mia: 16 G; Int 3-82 1 TD; 6 Pt; 1 Fum; 1.5 Sac. **1997** Mia: 16 G; 0.5 Sac. **1998** Mia: 16 G; 1 Sac. **Total:** 59 G; Int 4-105 1 TD; 6 Pt; 1 Fum; 3 Sac.

CEDRIC JACKSON Jackson, Cedric Anthony 5′11″, 229 **RB**
Col: Tyler JC TX; Texas Christian *HS:* Liberty-Eylau [Texarkana, TX] B: 1/13/1968, Texarkana, TX *Drafted:* 1991 Round 8 Det
1991 Det: 8 G; Rush 17-55 3.2; Rec 1-(-2) -2.0; KR 1-9 9.0; 1 Fum.

CHARLES JACKSON Jackson, Charles Edward 6′4″, 210 **DB**
Col: Texas Tech *HS:* North Miami [FL] B: 3/12/1962, Fort Gaines, GA
1987 Was: 1 G.

CHARLES JACKSON Jackson, Charles Melvin 6′2″, 225 **LB**
Col: Washington *HS:* Berkeley [CA] B: 3/22/1955, Los Angeles, CA
Drafted: 1977 Round 9 Den
1978 KC: 16 G. **1979** KC: 12 G. **1980** KC: 16 G. **1981** KC: 14 G. **1982** KC: 9 G; 1 Sac. **1983** KC: 15 G; 1 Fum TD; 6 Pt; 4 Sac. **1984** KC: 4 G; Int 1-16. **1985** NYJ: 16 G. **1986** NYJ: 15 G; 2 Sac. **Total:** 117 G; Int 1-16; 1 Fum TD; 6 Pt; 7 Sac.

CHARLIE JACKSON Jackson, Charles Robert 5′11″, 180 **DB**
Col: Southern Methodist *HS:* Paris [TX] B: 3/3/1936, Paris, TX
Drafted: 1958 Round 13 ChiC
1958 ChiC: 10 G; PR 2-10 5.0; Int 1-13; 1 Fum. **1960** DalT: 3 G. **Total:** 13 G; PR 2-10 5.0; Int 1-13; 1 Fum.

JAZZ JACKSON Jackson, Clarence Jr. 5′8″, 167 **RB**
Col: Western Kentucky *HS:* Austin-East [Knoxville, TN] B: 3/5/1952, Knoxville, TN *Drafted:* 1974 Round 16 NYJ
1974 NYJ: Rec 2-44 22.0 1 TD; PR 6-49 8.2; KR 4-100 25.0; 1 Fum TD. **1975** NYJ: Rec 5-54 10.8; PR 1-0; KR 2-52 26.0. **1976** NYJ: Rec 2-3 1.5; PR 6-(-1) -0.2; KR 10-207 20.7. **Total:** Rec 9-101 11.2 1 TD; PR 13-48 3.7; KR 16-359 22.4; 1 Fum TD.

		Rushing					Tot
Year Team	G	Att	Yds	Avg	TD	Fum	TD
1974 NYJ	13	20	74	3.7	0	2	2
1975 NYJ	13	6	11	1.8	0	0	0
1976 NYJ	7	1	6	6.0	0	1	0
NFL Total	33	27	91	3.4	0	3	2

CLEVELAND JACKSON Jackson, Cleveland Lee 6′4″, 230 **TE**
Col: Los Angeles Southwest Coll. CA (J.C.); Michigan State; Nevada-Las Vegas *HS:* Northwestern [Detroit, MI] B: 10/1/1956, Crossett, AR
Drafted: 1979 Round 5 NYG
1979 NYG: 2 G; Rec 1-7 7.0.

RED JACKSON Jackson, Colville Cameron 6′0″, 200 **T**
Col: Chicago *HS:* Evanston Twp. [Evanston, IL] B: 4/15/1897, Chicago, IL D: 11/1963, MS
1921 Eva-Ham: 2 G. Eva: 1 G. Ham: 1 G. **Total:** 2 G.

RUSTY JACKSON Jackson, Dalton Sharman 6′2″, 193 **P**
Col: Louisiana State *HS:* Washington Co. [Chatom, AL] B: 11/17/1950, Tuscaloosa, AL D: 4/14/1997, Chatom, WA
1978 Buf: Rush 1-(-13) -13.0. **Total:** Rush 1-(-13) -13.0.

		Punting		
Year Team	G	Punts	Yds	Avg
1976 LARm	14	77	3006	39.0
1978 Buf	16	87	3373	38.8
1979 Buf	16	96	3671	38.2
NFL Total	46	260	10050	38.7

DAVID JACKSON Jackson, David Leonard 5′8″, 175 **WR**
Col: Southeast Missouri State *HS:* Perry Hall [MD] B: 1/2/1965, Baltimore, MD
1987 TB: 1 G.

DON JACKSON Jackson, Donald Fletcher 5′11″, 184 **TB-DB**
Col: North Carolina *HS:* Seminole [Sanford, FL] B: 11/14/1913 D: 8/25/1946, Dallas, TX
1936 Phi: Pass 35-7 20.0%, 80 2.29 11 Int.

		Rushing			
Year Team	G	Att	Yds	Avg	TD
1936 Phi	10	46	76	1.7	0

ERNIE JACKSON Jackson, Earnest 5′10″, 173 **DB**
Col: Duke *HS:* Lower Richland [Hopkins, SC] B: 4/11/1950, Hopkins, SC *Drafted:* 1972 Round 7 NO
1972 NO: **1** Fum TD. **1973** NO: KR 1-0. **1974** NO: PR 2-3 1.5; KR 1-27 27.0. **Total:** PR 2-3 1.5; KR 2-27 13.5; 1 Fum TD.

		Interceptions		
Year Team	G	Int	Yds	TD
1972 NO	10	3	41	0
1973 NO	14	3	40	0
1974 NO	13	4	53	0
1975 NO	13	2	48	0
1976 NO	10	2	5	0
1977 NO	11	1	0	0
1978 Atl	16	0	0	0
1979 Det	2	0	0	0
NFL Total	89	15	187	0

EARNEST JACKSON Jackson, Earnest Jr. 5′9″, 213 **RB**
Col: Texas A&M *HS:* Lamar [Rosenberg, TX] B: 12/18/1959, Needville, TX *Drafted:* 1983 Round 8 SD
1983 SD: KR 11-201 18.3. **1984** SD: KR 1-10 10.0. **Total:** KR 12-211 17.6.

		Rushing				Receiving					Tot
Year Team	G	Att	Yds	Avg	TD	Rec	Yds	Avg	TD	Fum	TD
1983 SD	12	11	39	3.5	0	5	42	8.4	0	1	0
1984 SD	16	296	1179	4.0	8	39	222	5.7	1	3	9
1985 Phi	16	282	1028	3.6	5	10	126	12.6	1	3	6
1986 Pit	13	216	910	4.2	5	17	169	9.9	0	3	5
1987 Pit	12	180	696	3.9	1	7	52	7.4	0	2	1
1988 Pit	12	74	315	4.3	3	9	84	9.3	0	3	3
NFL Total	81	1059	4167	3.9	22	87	695	8.0	2	15	24

JACK JACKSON Jackson, Elliot Cornelius Jr. 5′8″, 174 **WR**
Col: Florida *HS:* Moss Point [MS] B: 11/11/1972, Moss Point, MS
Drafted: 1995 Round 4 ChiB
1996 ChiB: Rec 4-39 9.8.

		Kickoff Returns				
Year Team	G	Ret	Yds	Avg	TD	Fum
1996 ChiB	12	27	619	22.9	0	2

ENIS JACKSON Jackson, Enis 5′9″, 180 **DB**
Col: Memphis *HS:* Central [West Helena, AR] B: 5/16/1963, Helena, AR
1987 Cle: 1 G.

FRANK JACKSON Jackson, Frank Hardin 6′1″, 185 **WR-HB**
Col: Southern Methodist *HS:* Paris [TX] B: 4/14/1939, Levelland, TX
Drafted: 1961 Round 19 DalT
1961 DalT: Pass 2-1 50.0%, 9 4.50 1 Int. **Total:** Pass 2-1 50.0%, 9 4.50 1 Int.

		Rushing				Receiving			
Year Team	G	Att	Yds	Avg	TD	Rec	Yds	Avg	TD
1961 DalT	14	65	386	5.9	3	13	171	13.2	2
1962 DalT	14	47	251	5.3	3	10	177	17.7	1
1963 KC	14	3	52	17.3	1	50	785	15.7	8
1964 KC	14	2	5	2.5	0	62	943	15.2	9
1965 KC	14	1	26	26.0	0	28	440	15.7	1
1966 Mia	10	2	22	11.0	0	16	317	19.8	2
1967 Mia	10	1	48	48.0	0	9	122	13.6	1
NFL Total	90	121	790	6.5	7	188	2955	15.7	24

	Punt Returns				Kickoff Returns					Tot
Year Team	Ret	Yds	Avg	TD	Ret	Yds	Avg	TD	Fum	TD
1961 DalT	1	2	2.0	0	24	**645**	26.9	0	3	5
1962 DalT	11	117	10.6	0	10	254	25.4	0	2	4
1963 KC	11	95	8.6	0	1	20	20.0	0	3	9
1964 KC	11	103	9.4	0	0	0	—	0	2	9
1965 KC	13	163	12.5	0	9	260	28.9	0	2	1
1966 Mia	2	7	3.5	0	4	105	26.3	0	0	2
1967 Mia	0	0	—	0	0	0	—	0	0	1
NFL Total	49	487	9.9	0	48	1284	26.8	0	12	31

GERALD JACKSON Jackson, Gerald Eugene 6′1″, 195 **DB**
Col: Mississippi State *HS:* Moss Point [MS] B: 3/5/1956, Moss Point, MS *Drafted:* 1979 Round 10 KC
1979 KC: 16 G; Int 1-4; 1 Fum.

GRADY JACKSON Jackson, Grady 6′2″, 320 **DE**
Col: Hinds CC MS; Knoxville *HS:* Greensboro East [AL] B: 1/21/1973, Greensboro, AL *Drafted:* 1997 Round 6 Oak
1997 Oak: 5 G. **1998** Oak: 15 G; 3 Sac. **Total:** 20 G; 3 Sac.

GREG JACKSON Jackson, Greg Allen 6′1″, 205 **DB**
Col: Louisiana State *HS:* American Senior [Hialeah, FL] B: 8/20/1966, Hialeah, FL *Drafted:* 1989 Round 3 NYG
1990 NYG: 4 Sac. **1995** Phi: **1** Fum TD. **1997** SD: PR 1-0; 1 Fum TD. **Total:** PR 1-0; 2 Fum TD; 4 Sac.

		Interceptions				Tot
Year Team	G	Int	Yds	TD	Fum	TD
1989 NYG	16	0	0	0	0	0
1990 NYG	14	5	8	0	0	0

1991 NYG	13	1	3	0	1	0
1992 NYG	16	4	71	0	0	0
1993 NYG	16	4	32	0	0	0
1994 Phi	16	6	86	1	0	1
1995 Phi	16	1	18	0	0	1
1996 NO	16	3	24	0	1	0
1997 SD	13	2	37	1	0	2
1998 SD	16	6	50	0	0	0
NFL Total	152	32	329	2	2	4

HAROLD JACKSON Jackson, Harold 5'10", 175 **WR**
Col: Jackson State *HS:* Rowan [Hattiesburg, MS] B: 1/6/1946, Hattiesburg, MS *Drafted:* 1968 Round 12 LARm
1971 Phi: KR 2-48 24.0. **1979** NE: Pass 1-0. **1980** NE: Pass 2-2 100.0%, 35 17.50. **1981** NE: Pass 1-0. **Total:** Pass 4-2 50.0%, 35 8.75; KR 2-48 24.0.

		Rushing				Receiving				
Year Team	**G**	**Att**	**Yds**	**Avg**	**TD**	**Rec**	**Yds**	**Avg**	**TD**	**Fum**
1968 LARm	2	0	0	—	0	0	0	—	0	0
1969 Phi	14	2	10	5.0	0	65	**1116**	17.2	9	0
1970 Phi	14	1	-5	-5.0	0	41	613	15.0	5	0
1971 Phi	14	5	41	8.2	0	47	716	15.2	3	1
1972 Phi	14	9	76	8.4	0	**62**	**1048**	16.9	4	2
1973 LARm	14	2	-8	-4.0	0	40	874	**21.9**	**13**	0
1974 LARm	14	1	4	4.0	0	30	514	17.1	5	0
1975 LARm	14	0	0	—	0	43	786	18.3	7	1
1976 LARm	14	1	15	15.0	0	39	751	19.3	5	1
1977 LARm	14	1	6	6.0	0	48	666	13.9	6	0
1978 NE	16	1	7	7.0	0	37	743	20.1	6	0
1979 NE	16	3	12	4.0	0	45	1013	22.5	7	0
1980 NE	16	5	37	7.4	0	35	737	21.1	5	0
1981 NE	16	2	-14	-7.0	0	39	669	17.2	0	1
1982 Min	1	0	0	—	0	0	0	—	0	0
1983 Sea	15	0	0	—	0	8	126	15.8	1	1
NFL Total	208	33	181	5.5	0	579	10372	17.9	76	7

PETE JACKSON Jackson, Harry R 5'10", 200 **FB-BB-WB**
Col: Missouri *HS:* Central [St. Joseph, MO] B: 8/13/1904 D: 3/1967
1928 Det: 5 G; Rush 2 TD; 12 Pt.

HONOR JACKSON Jackson, Honor W 6'1", 195 **DB**
Col: Coll. of Marin CA (J.C.); U. of Pacific *HS:* Tamalpais [Mill Valley, CA] B: 11/21/1948, New Orleans, LA *Drafted:* 1971 Round 9 Dal
1972 NE: 13 G; Int 4-133. **1973** NE-NYG: 7 G; Int 1-0. NE: 4 G; Int 1-0. NYG: 3 G. **1974** NYG: 12 G. **Total:** 32 G; Int 5-133.

JIM JACKSON Jackson, James George 5'11", 193 **DB-HB**
Col: Western Illinois *HS:* Alton [IL] B: 4/19/1944, Alton, IL
Drafted: 1966 Round 13 SF
1966 SF: 10 G; Rush 4-7 1.8; Rec 1-63 63.0 1 TD; PR 2-0; KR 8-162 20.3; 6 Pt; 1 Fum. **1967** SF: 3 G; Int 1-22. **Total:** 13 G; Rush 4-7 1.8; Rec 1-63 63.0 1 TD; PR 2-0; KR 8-162 20.3; Int 1-22; 6 Pt; 1 Fum.

JEFF JACKSON Jackson, Jeffery Paul 6'1", 235 **LB**
Col: Auburn *HS:* Griffin [GA] B: 10/9/1961, Shreveport, LA
Drafted: 1984 Round 8 Atl
1984 Atl: 16 G; Int 1-35 1 TD; 6 Pt; 2 Sac. **1985** Atl: 11 G. **1987** SD: 11 G; 1 Sac. **1988** SD: 14 G. **Total:** 52 G; Int 1-35 1 TD; 6 Pt; 3 Sac.

JOHN JACKSON Jackson, John 6'6", 297 **OT**
Col: Eastern Kentucky *HS:* Woodward [Cincinnati, OH] B: 1/4/1965, Camp Kwe, Okinawa *Drafted:* 1988 Round 10 Pit
1988 Pit: 16 G; KR 1-10 10.0. **1989** Pit: 14 G. **1990** Pit: 16 G. **1991** Pit: 16 G. **1992** Pit: 16 G. **1993** Pit: 16 G. **1994** Pit: 16 G. **1995** Pit: 11 G. **1996** Pit: 16 G. **1997** Pit: 16 G. **1998** SD: 16 G. **Total:** 169 G; KR 1-10 10.0.

JOHN JACKSON Jackson, John 5'10", 175 **WR**
Col: USC *HS:* Bishop Amat [La Puente, CA] B: 1/2/1967, Brooklyn, NY
1991 Pho: Rec 8-108 13.5; KR 2-41 20.5. **1992** Pho: Rec 1-5 5.0 1 TD; KR 1-17 17.0. **Total:** Rec 9-113 12.6 1 TD; KR 3-58 19.3.

		Punt Returns				
Year Team	**G**	**Ret**	**Yds**	**Avg**	**TD**	**Fum**
1990 Pho	9	0	0	—	0	0
1991 Pho	16	31	244	7.9	0	3
1992 Pho	6	0	0	—	0	0
1996 ChiB	5	0	0	—	0	0
NFL Total	36	31	244	7.9	0	3

JOHNNY JACKSON Jackson, John 6'3", 250 **NT**
Col: Tennessee State; Southern University *HS:* Lima [OH] B: 7/1/1953, Lima, OH *Drafted:* 1977 Round 9 StL
1977 Phi: 2 G.

JOHNNIE JACKSON Jackson, Johnnie Bobby 6'1", 204 **DB**
Col: Houston *HS:* Harlingen [TX] B: 1/11/1967, Harlingen, TX
Drafted: 1989 Round 5 SF
1989 SF: 16 G; KR 1-0; Int 2-35; 6 Pt. **1990** SF: 16 G; 1 Sac. **1991** SF: 16 G; Int 1-11. **1992** SF-GB: 7 G; 1 Sac. SF: 5 G; 1 Sac. GB: 2 G. **Total:** 55 G; KR 1-0; Int 3-46; 6 Pt; 2 Sac.

JOE JACKSON Jackson, Joseph Loyd 6'1", 225 **LB**
Col: San Francisco State *HS:* Monterey [CA] B: 10/15/1962
1987 Sea: 3 G.

KEITH JACKSON Jackson, Keith Jerome 6'2", 250 **TE**
Col: Oklahoma *HS:* Parkview [Little Rock, AR] B: 4/19/1965, Little Rock, AR *Drafted:* 1988 Round 1 Phi
1994 Mia: Scor 1 2XP. **Total:** Scor 1 2XP.

		Receiving				
Year Team	**G**	**Rec**	**Yds**	**Avg**	**TD**	**Fum**
1988 Phi	16	81	869	10.7	6	3
1989 Phi	14	63	648	10.3	3	1
1990 Phi	14	50	670	13.4	6	1
1991 Phi	16	48	569	11.9	5	2
1992 Mia	13	48	594	12.4	5	2
1993 Mia	15	39	613	15.7	6	2
1994 Mia	16	59	673	11.4	7	2
1995 GB	9	13	142	10.9	1	0
1996 GB	16	40	505	12.6	10	0
NFL Total	129	441	5283	12.0	49	13

KENNY JACKSON Jackson, Kenneth 6'0", 180 **WR**
Col: Penn State *HS:* South River [NJ] B: 2/15/1962, Neptune, NJ
Drafted: 1984 Round 1 Phi
1986 Phi: Rush 1-6 6.0. **1987** Phi: Rush 6-27 4.5. **1990** Phi: KR 6-125 20.8. **1991** Phi: Rush 1-18 18.0. **Total:** Rush 8-51 6.4; KR 6-125 20.8.

		Receiving				
Year Team	**G**	**Rec**	**Yds**	**Avg**	**TD**	**Fum**
1984 Phi	11	26	398	15.3	1	0
1985 Phi	16	40	692	17.3	1	0
1986 Phi	16	30	506	16.9	6	0
1987 Phi	12	21	471	22.4	3	1
1988 Phi	7	0	0	—	0	0
1989 Hou	10	4	31	7.8	0	0
1990 Phi	14	1	43	43.0	0	0
1991 Phi	16	4	29	7.3	0	0
NFL Total	102	126	2170	17.2	11	1

KEN JACKSON Jackson, Kenneth Gene 6'2", 236 **OT-OG**
Col: Texas *HS:* Stephen F. Austin [Austin, TX] B: 4/26/1929, Austin, TX
Drafted: 1951 Round 2 NYY
1952 Dal: 12 G. **1953** Bal: 12 G; KR 3-37 12.3. **1954** Bal: 12 G. **1955** Bal: 8 G. **1956** Bal: 12 G. **1957** Bal: 12 G. **Total:** 68 G; KR 3-37 12.3.

KIRBY JACKSON Jackson, Kirby 5'10", 179 **DB**
Col: Mississippi State *HS:* Sturgis [MS] B: 2/2/1965, Sturgis, MS
Drafted: 1987 Round 5 NYJ
1989 Buf: KR 1-0. **1991** Buf: 1 Sac. **Total:** KR 1-0; 1 Sac.

		Interceptions			Tot
Year Team	**G**	**Int**	**Yds**	**TD**	**TD**
1987 LARm	5	1	36	0	1
1988 Buf	8	0	0	0	0
1989 Buf	14	2	43	1	1
1990 Buf	12	3	16	0	0
1991 Buf	16	4	31	0	0
1992 Buf	15	0	0	0	0
NFL Total	70	10	126	1	2

LARRON JACKSON Jackson, Larron Deonne 6'3", 270 **OG-OT**
Col: Missouri *HS:* Soldan [St. Louis, MO] B: 8/26/1949, St. Louis, MO
Drafted: 1971 Round 4 Hou
1971 Den: 14 G. **1972** Den: 14 G. **1973** Den: 13 G; Rec 1-(-2) -2.0. **1974** Den: 14 G. **1975** Atl: 14 G. **1976** Atl: 14 G. **Total:** 83 G; Rec 1-(-2) -2.0.

LAWRENCE JACKSON Jackson, Lawrence Dennell 6'1", 275 **OG**
Col: Presbyterian *HS:* North Fulton [Atlanta, GA] B: 8/10/1964, Jacksonville, FL
1987 Atl: 3 G.

LARRY JACKSON Jackson, Lawrence W 185 **C-TB**
Col: Loyola (Chicago) B: 11/4/1904 D: 3/1983, Princeton, IL
1926 Lou: 2 G.

LEONARD JACKSON Jackson, Leonard Maurice 6'0", 240 **LB**
Col: Oklahoma State *HS:* Pine Bluff [AR] B: 10/5/1964, Pine Bluff, AR
1987 LARd-ChiB: 2 G. LARd: 1 G. ChiB: 1 G. **Total:** 2 G.

LEROY JACKSON Jackson, Leroy 6'0", 198 **HB**
Col: Western Illinois *HS:* Bloom [Chicago Heights, IL] B: 12/8/1939, Chicago Heights, IL *Drafted:* 1962 Round 1 Cle
1962 Was: Rec 10-253 25.3 1 TD; KR 10-272 27.2. **1963** Was: KR 5-113 22.6. **Total:** Rec 10-253 25.3 1 TD; KR 15-385 25.7.

		Rushing				
Year Team	**G**	**Att**	**Yds**	**Avg**	**TD**	**Fum**
1962 Was	10	49	112	2.3	0	2

1963 Was	5	3	30	10.0	0	2
NFL Total	15	52	142	2.7	0	4

LOUIS JACKSON Jackson, Louis Bernard 5′11″, 195 **RB**
Col: Cal Poly-S.L.O. *HS:* Roosevelt [Fresno, CA] B: 1/27/1958, Fresno, CA *Drafted:* 1981 Round 7 NYG
1981 NYG: Rec 3-25 8.3.

		Rushing				
Year Team	**G**	**Att**	**Yds**	**Avg**	**TD**	**Fum**
1981 NYG	11	27	68	2.5	1	1

MARCUS JACKSON Jackson, Marcus Reginald 6′5″, 260 **DE-NT**
Col: Purdue *HS:* Lima [OH] B: 6/8/1957, Lima, OH
1987 Ind: 1 G.

MARK JACKSON Jackson, Mark Anthony 5′9″, 180 **WR**
Col: Purdue *HS:* South Vigo [Terre Haute, IN] B: 7/23/1963, Chicago, IL *Drafted:* 1986 Round 6 Den
1986 Den: Rush 2-6 3.0; PR 2-7 3.5; KR 1-16 16.0. **1988** Den: Rush 1-5 5.0. **1989** Den: Rush 5-13 2.6. **1990** Den: Rush 5-28 5.6 1 TD; KR 1-18 18.0. **1991** Den: Rush 2-18 9.0. **1992** Den: Rush 3-(-1) -0.3. **1993** NYG: Rush 3-25 8.3. **1994** NYG-Ind: KR 1-5 5.0. Ind: KR 1-5 5.0.
Total: Rush 21-94 4.5 1 TD; PR 2-7 3.5; KR 3-39 13.0.

		Receiving					Tot
Year Team	**G**	**Rec**	**Yds**	**Avg**	**TD**	**Fum**	**TD**
1986 Den	16	38	738	19.4	1	3	1
1987 Den	12	26	436	16.8	2	0	2
1988 Den	12	46	852	18.5	6	1	6
1989 Den	16	28	446	15.9	2	1	2
1990 Den	16	57	926	16.2	4	1	5
1991 Den	12	33	603	18.3	1	1	1
1992 Den	16	48	745	15.5	8	0	8
1993 NYG	16	58	708	12.2	4	1	4
1994 NYG-Ind	14	8	97	12.1	1	0	1
1994 NYG	2	0	0	—	0	0	0
1994 Ind	12	8	97	12.1	1	0	1
NFL Total	130	342	5551	16.2	29	8	30

MARK JACKSON Jackson, Mark Devalon 5′9″, 180 **DB**
Col: Abilene Christian *HS:* Tascosa [Amarillo, TX] B: 3/16/1962, Amarillo, TX
1987 StL: 11 G; **1** Fum TD; 6 Pt.

MELVIN JACKSON Jackson, Melvin Jr. 6′1″, 267 **OG**
Col: USC *HS:* Mount Carmel [Los Angeles, CA] B: 5/5/1954, Los Angeles, CA *Drafted:* 1976 Round 12 GB
1976 GB: 13 G; Rec 1-8 8.0. **1977** GB: 13 G. **1978** GB: 16 G. **1979** GB: 16 G. **1980** GB: 6 G. **Total:** 64 G; Rec 1-8 8.0.

MICHAEL JACKSON Jackson, Michael Anthony 6′1″, 220 **LB**
Col: Washington *HS:* Pasco [WA] B: 7/15/1957, Pasco, WA *Drafted:* 1979 Round 3 Sea
1979 Sea: 15 G. **1980** Sea: 15 G; Int 2-9. **1981** Sea: 16 G; Int 2-51. **1982** Sea: 8 G; Int 2-29. **1983** Sea: 11 G; 3 Sac. **1984** Sea: 8 G; 1 Sac. **1985** Sea: 16 G; 2 Sac. **1986** Sea: 16 G. **Total:** 105 G; Int 6-89; 6 Sac.

MICHAEL JACKSON Jackson, Michael Dwayne 6′4″, 195 **WR**
(AKA Michael Dyson) *Col:* Southern Mississippi *HS:* Kentwood [LA] B: 4/12/1969, Tangipahoa, LA *Drafted:* 1991 Round 6 Cle
1992 Cle: Rush 1-21 21.0. **1993** Cle: Pass 1-1 100.0%, 25 25.00; Rush 1-1 1.0. **1994** Cle: Pass 2-0. **1995** Cle: Pass 1-0, 1 Int. **1996** Bal: Scor 2 2XP. **1997** Bal: Scor 1 2XP. **Total:** Pass 4-1 25.0%, 25 6.25 1 Int; Rush 2-22 11.0; Scor 3 2XP.

		Receiving				
Year Team	**G**	**Rec**	**Yds**	**Avg**	**TD**	**Fum**
1991 Cle	16	17	268	15.8	2	0
1992 Cle	16	47	755	16.1	7	0
1993 Cle	15	41	756	18.4	8	1
1994 Cle	9	21	304	14.5	2	0
1995 Cle	13	44	714	16.2	9	1
1996 Bal	16	76	1201	15.8	**14**	0
1997 Bal	16	69	918	13.3	4	2
1998 Bal	13	38	477	12.6	0	1
NFL Total	114	353	5393	15.3	46	5

MONTE JACKSON Jackson, Monte Carl 5′11″, 193 **DB**
Col: San Diego Mesa Coll. CA (J.C.); San Diego State *HS:* St. Augustine [San Diego, CA] B: 7/14/1953, Sherman, TX *Drafted:* 1975 Round 2 LARm

		Interceptions			Tot
Year Team	**G**	**Int**	**Yds**	**TD**	**TD**
1975 LARm	14	2	13	0	1
1976 LARm	14	**10**	173	**3**	3
1977 LARm	14	5	73	0	0
1978 Oak	16	2	25	0	0
1979 Oak	8	2	5	0	0
1980 Oak	16	1	0	0	0
1981 Oak	16	0	0	0	0
1982 LARd	9	1	0	0	0
1983 LARm	5	0	0	0	0
NFL Total	112	23	289	3	4

NOAH JACKSON Jackson, Noah Dale 6′2″, 267 **OG**
Col: Tampa *HS:* Duncan U. Fletcher [Neptune Beach, FL] B: 4/14/1951, Jacksonville Beach, FL *Drafted:* 1974 Round 7 Bal
1975 ChiB: 14 G; Rec 1-17 17.0. **1976** ChiB: 12 G. **1977** ChiB: 14 G. **1978** ChiB: 16 G. **1979** ChiB: 15 G. **1980** ChiB: 16 G. **1981** ChiB: 16 G. **1982** ChiB: 9 G. **1983** ChiB: 13 G. **1984** TB: 6 G. **Total:** 131 G; Rec 1-17 17.0.

PERRY JACKSON Jackson, Perry 6′1″, 202 **T-OE**
(AKA Artha E. Shockley) *Col:* Southwestern Oklahoma State *HS:* Mountain View [OK] B: 8/31/1903, McKinley Twp., Douglas Co., MO D: 4/27/1988, Moutain View, OK
1928 Prov: 10 G. **1929** Prov: 7 G. **1930** Prov: 10 G. **Total:** 27 G.

RANDY JACKSON Jackson, Randall Belford 6′5″, 250 **OT**
Col: Florida *HS:* Columbia [Lake City, FL] B: 3/6/1944, Lake City, FL *Drafted:* 1966 Round 4 ChiB
1967 ChiB: 14 G; KR 1-0. **1968** ChiB: 14 G. **1969** ChiB: 14 G. **1970** ChiB: 10 G. **1971** ChiB: 14 G. **1972** ChiB: 14 G. **1973** ChiB: 14 G. **1974** ChiB: 11 G. **Total:** 105 G; KR 1-0.

RANDY JACKSON Jackson, Randy Joe 6′0″, 220 **RB**
Col: Texarkana Coll. TX (J.C.); Wichita State *HS:* Atlanta [TX] B: 11/13/1948, Atlanta, TX *Drafted:* 1972 Round 4 Buf
1972 Buf: Rec 2-21 10.5 1 TD. **1973** SF: Rec 1-20 20.0. **1974** Phi: Rec 2-17 8.5; KR 14-339 24.2. **Total:** Rec 5-58 11.6 1 TD; KR 14-339 24.2.

		Rushing				
Year Team	**G**	**Att**	**Yds**	**Avg**	**TD**	**Fum**
1972 Buf	5	17	57	3.4	0	0
1973 SF	2	6	10	1.7	0	0
1974 Phi	14	7	3	0.4	0	1
NFL Total	21	30	70	2.3	0	1

RAYMOND JACKSON Jackson, Raymond DeWayne 5′10″, 189 **DB**
Col: Colorado State *HS:* Montbello [Denver, CO] B: 2/17/1973, East Chicago, IN *Drafted:* 1996 Round 5 Buf
1996 Buf: 12 G; Int 1-0. **1997** Buf: 9 G; PR 1-0; 1 Fum. **1998** Buf: 14 G; Int 2-27. **Total:** 35 G; PR 1-0; Int 3-27; 1 Fum.

RICH JACKSON Jackson, Richard Samuel 6′3″, 255 **DE-LB**
(Tombstone) *Col:* Southern University *HS:* L.B. Landry [New Orleans, LA] B: 7/22/1941, New Orleans, LA
1966 Oak: 5 G. **1967** Den: 14 G; Scor **1** Saf; 2 Pt. **1968** Den: 14 G. **1969** Den: 14 G. **1970** Den: 14 G. **1971** Den: 7 G. **1972** Den-Cle: 14 G. Den: 4 G. Cle: 10 G. **Total:** 82 G; Scor 1 Saf; 2 Pt.

RICKEY JACKSON Jackson, Rickey Anderson 6′2″, 243 **LB**
Col: Pittsburgh *HS:* Pahokee [FL] B: 3/20/1958, Pahokee, FL *Drafted:* 1981 Round 2 NO
1981 NO: 16 G. **1982** NO: 9 G; Int 1-32; 4.5 Sac. **1983** NO: 16 G; Int 1-0; 1 Fum; 12 Sac. **1984** NO: 16 G; Int 1-14; 1 Fum; 12 Sac. **1985** NO: 16 G; 11 Sac. **1986** NO: 16 G; Int 1-1; 9 Sac. **1987** NO: 12 G; Int 2-4; 9.5 Sac. **1988** NO: 16 G; Int 1-16; Scor 1 Saf; 2 Pt; 7 Sac. **1989** NO: 14 G; 7.5 Sac. **1990** NO: 16 G; 6 Sac. **1991** NO: 16 G; 11.5 Sac. **1992** NO: 16 G; 13.5 Sac. **1993** NO: 16 G; 11.5 Sac. **1994** SF: 16 G; 3.5 Sac. **1995** SF: 16 G; Int 1-1; 9.5 Sac. **Total:** 227 G; Int 8-68; Scor 1 Saf; 2 Pt; 2 Fum; 128 Sac.

BOBBY JACKSON Jackson, Robert Charles 5′9″, 178 **DB**
Col: Florida State *HS:* Albany [GA] B: 12/23/1956, Albany, GA *Drafted:* 1978 Round 6 NYJ
1982 NYJ: 1 Fum TD. **Total:** 1 Fum TD.

		Interceptions			Tot
Year Team	**G**	**Int**	**Yds**	**TD**	**TD**
1978 NYJ	16	5	26	0	0
1979 NYJ	16	4	63	1	1
1980 NYJ	15	1	7	0	0
1981 NYJ	9	0	0	0	0
1982 NYJ	9	5	84	**1**	2
1983 NYJ	15	2	8	0	0
1984 NYJ	3	0	0	0	0
1985 NYJ	12	4	8	0	0
NFL Total	95	21	196	2	3

BOBBY JACKSON Jackson, Robert Dean 6′3″, 238 **FB**
Col: Riverside CC CA; New Mexico State *HS:* Turner [Carthage, TX]; Palm Springs HS [CA] B: 3/16/1940, Shreveport, LA *Drafted:* 1962 Round 7 SD
1962 SD: KR 1-16 16.0. **1963** SD: KR 1-16 16.0. **1964** Hou-Oak: PR 1-0; KR 2-32 16.0. Hou: KR 2-32 16.0. Oak: PR 1-0. **1965** Hou: KR 2-39 19.5. **Total:** PR 1-0; KR 6-103 17.2.

		Rushing				Receiving					Tot
Year Team	G	Att	Yds	Avg	TD	Rec	Yds	Avg	TD	Fum	TD
1962 SD	14	106	411	3.9	5	13	136	10.5	2	0	7
1963 SD	12	18	64	3.6	4	8	85	10.6	0	1	4
1964 Hou-Oak	14	23	64	2.8	3	10	81	8.1	0	1	3
1964 Hou	6	8	11	1.4	3	0	0	—	0	0	3
1964 Oak	8	15	53	3.5	0	10	81	8.1	0	1	0
1965 Hou	10	37	85	2.3	2	1	31	31.0	0	0	2
NFL Total	50	184	624	3.4	14	32	333	10.4	2	2	16

ROBERT JACKSON Jackson, Robert Edward 6′5″, 255 **OG-OT-C**
(Action Jackson) *Col:* Duke *HS:* North Mecklenburg [Huntersville, NC] B: 4/1/1953, Charlotte, NC
1975 Cle: 14 G. **1976** Cle: 14 G; KR 1-16 16.0. **1977** Cle: 14 G; KR 1-21 21.0. **1978** Cle: 16 G; KR 1-19 19.0. **1979** Cle: 16 G; KR 1-18 18.0. **1980** Cle: 14 G; KR 1-0. **1981** Cle: 16 G. **1982** Cle: 9 G. **1983** Cle: 16 G. **1984** Cle: 16 G. **1985** Cle: 15 G. **Total:** 160 G; KR 5-74 14.8.

BOB JACKSON Jackson, Robert Herman 5′11″, 210 **FB**
(Stonewall) *Col:* North Carolina A&T *HS:* Allentown [PA]
B: 10/26/1922, Mineral, VA D: 10/1971, Colonial Beach, VA
Drafted: 1950 Round 16 NYG
1950 NYG: 12 G; Rush 12-113 9.4 2 TD; 12 Pt. **1951** NYG: 12 G; Rush 5-9 1.8; KR 1-27 27.0. **Total:** 24 G; Rush 17-122 7.2 2 TD; KR 1-27 27.0; 12 Pt.

ROBERT JACKSON Jackson, Robert Lee 6′1″, 230 **LB**
Col: Trinity Valley CC TX; Texas A&M *HS:* M.B. Smiley [Houston, TX]
B: 8/7/1954, Houston, TX *Drafted:* 1977 Round 1 Cle
1978 Cle: 14 G. **1979** Cle: 16 G. **1980** Cle: 14 G; Int 2-15. **1981** Cle: 14 G. **1982** Atl: 4 G. **Total:** 62 G; Int 2-15.

ROBERT JACKSON Jackson, Robert Michael 5′10″, 184 **DB**
Col: Central Michigan *HS:* Allendale [MI] B: 10/10/1958, Grand Rapids, MI *Drafted:* 1981 Round 11 Cin

		Interceptions		
Year Team	G	Int	Yds	TD
1982 Cin	9	0	0	0
1983 Cin	16	2	21	0
1984 Cin	16	4	32	1
1985 Cin	16	6	100	**1**
1986 Cin	7	0	0	0
1987 Cin	12	3	49	0
1989 Cin	14	0	0	0
NFL Total	90	15	202	2

ROGER JACKSON Jackson, Roger 6′0″, 186 **DB**
Col: Bethune-Cookman *HS:* Central [Macon, GA] B: 2/28/1959, Macon, GA
1982 Den: 9 G. **1983** Den: 16 G; Int 1-15; 1 Fum; 1 Sac. **1984** Den: 16 G; Int 1-23. **1985** Den: 9 G. **1987** Den: 3 G. **Total:** 53 G; Int 2-38; 1 Fum; 1 Sac.

STEVE JACKSON Jackson, Stephan Loran 6′1″, 192 **DB**
Col: Louisiana State *HS:* Washington Co. [Chatom, AL] B: 4/6/1955, Chatom, AL
1977 Oak: 6 G; Int 1-33.

STEVE JACKSON Jackson, Stephen Franklin 6′1″, 225 **LB**
Col: Texas-Arlington *HS:* Arlington [TX] B: 12/8/1942, McKinney, TX
1966 Was: 14 G; KR 2-26 13.0; Int 1-0. **1967** Was: 11 G. **Total:** 25 G; KR 2-26 13.0; Int 1-0.

STEVE JACKSON Jackson, Steven Wayne 5′8″, 188 **DB**
Col: Purdue *HS:* Klein Forest [Houston, TX] B: 4/8/1969, Houston, TX
Drafted: 1991 Round 3 Hou
1991 Hou: PR 1-0; 1 Sac. **1992** Hou: 1 Sac. **1994** Hou: KR 14-285 20.4; 1 Sac. **1995** Hou: 1 Sac. **1996** Hou: Scor 1 Saf; 2 Sac. **1997** Ten: 1 Sac. **1998** Ten: 1.5 Sac. **Total:** PR 1-0; KR 14-285 20.4; Scor 1 Saf; 8.5 Sac.

		Interceptions			
Year Team	G	Int	Yds	TD	Fum
1991 Hou	15	0	0	0	1
1992 Hou	16	3	18	0	0
1993 Hou	16	5	54	1	0
1994 Hou	11	1	0	0	0
1995 Hou	10	2	0	0	0
1996 Hou	16	0	0	0	0
1997 Ten	12	0	0	0	0
1998 Ten	14	1	0	0	0
NFL Total	110	12	72	1	1

TERRY JACKSON Jackson, Terence Leon 5′10″, 197 **DB**
Col: San Diego City Coll. CA (J.C.); San Diego State *HS:* St. Augustine [San Diego, CA] B: 12/9/1955, Sherman, TX *Drafted:* 1978 Round 5 NYG
1978 NYG: PR 4-1 0.3. **1979** NYG: PR 1-5 5.0. **1981** NYG: PR 2-22 11.0. **1982** NYG: 1 Sac. **1983** NYG: 1 Fum TD. **1985** Sea: 4 Sac. **Total:** PR 7-28 4.0; 1 Fum TD; 5 Sac.

		Interceptions			Tot
Year Team	G	Int	Yds	TD	TD
1978 NYG	15	7	115	1	1
1979 NYG	16	3	10	0	1
1980 NYG	8	1	5	0	0
1981 NYG	16	3	57	1	1
1982 NYG	8	4	75	0	0
1983 NYG	12	6	20	0	1
1984 Sea	16	4	78	1	1
1985 Sea	16	0	0	0	0
NFL Total	107	28	360	3	5

TOM JACKSON Jackson, Thomas Louis 5′11″, 220 **LB**
Col: Louisville *HS:* John Adams [Cleveland, OH] B: 4/4/1951, Cleveland, OH *Drafted:* 1973 Round 4 Den
1982 Den: 1 Sac. **1983** Den: KR 1-2 2.0; 5.5 Sac. **1984** Den: 6 Sac. **1986** Den: 0.5 Sac. **Total:** KR 1-2 2.0; 13 Sac.

		Interceptions			
Year Team	G	Int	Yds	TD	Fum
1973 Den	8	0	0	0	0
1974 Den	13	1	39	0	0
1975 Den	14	2	0	0	0
1976 Den	14	7	136	1	1
1977 Den	13	4	95	**1**	1
1978 Den	16	3	28	1	0
1979 Den	13	1	34	0	0
1980 Den	16	0	0	0	0
1981 Den	16	0	0	0	0
1982 Den	9	1	8	0	0
1983 Den	15	1	0	0	0
1984 Den	16	0	0	0	0
1985 Den	12	0	0	0	0
1986 Den	16	0	0	0	0
NFL Total	191	20	340	3	2

ROLAND JACKSON Jackson, Thomas Roland 6′0″, 210 **FB-LB**
Col: Rice *HS:* Ruston [LA] B: 1/5/1940 *Drafted:* 1962 Round 21 Hou
1962 StL: 5 G.

TIM JACKSON Jackson, Timothy Gerrard 5′11″, 192 **DB**
Col: Kansas State; Nebraska *HS:* Skyline [Dallas, TX] B: 11/7/1965, Dallas, TX *Drafted:* 1989 Round 9 Dal
1989 Dal: 1 G.

T.J. JACKSON Jackson, Trenton James 6′0″, 180 **WR-DB**
Col: Illinois *HS:* Benjamin Franklin [Rochester, NY] B: 2/28/1943, Cordele, GA
1966 Phi: 3 G; KR 1-16 16.0. **1967** Was: 3 G; KR 7-131 18.7. **Total:** 6 G; KR 8-147 18.4.

TYOKA JACKSON Jackson, Tyoka 6′2″, 270 **DE-DT**
Col: Penn State *HS:* Bishop McNamara [Washington, DC]
B: 11/22/1971, Forestville, MD
1994 Mia: 1 G. **1996** TB: 13 G. **1997** TB: 12 G; 2.5 Sac. **1998** TB: 16 G; 3 Sac. **Total:** 42 G; 5.5 Sac.

VESTEE JACKSON Jackson, Vestee II 6′0″, 189 **DB**
Col: Washington *HS:* McLane [Fresno, CA] B: 8/14/1963, Fresno, CA
Drafted: 1986 Round 2 ChiB

		Interceptions		
Year Team	G	Int	Yds	TD
1986 ChiB	16	3	0	0
1987 ChiB	12	1	0	0
1988 ChiB	16	8	94	0
1989 ChiB	16	2	16	0
1990 ChiB	16	1	45	1
1991 Mia	16	0	0	0
1992 Mia	11	3	63	1
1993 Mia	16	0	0	0
NFL Total	119	18	218	2

VICTOR JACKSON Jackson, Victor Alan 6′0″, 205 **DB**
Col: Bowie State *HS:* Duval [Lanham, MD] B: 8/6/1959, Princess Anne, MD
1986 Ind: 2 G. **1987** LARd: 2 G. **Total:** 4 G.

BO JACKSON Jackson, Vincent Edward 6′1″, 227 **RB**
Col: Auburn *HS:* McAdory [McCalla, AL] B: 11/30/1962, Bessemer, AL
Drafted: 1987 Round 7 LARd

		Rushing				Receiving					Tot
Year Team	G	Att	Yds	Avg	TD	Rec	Yds	Avg	TD	Fum	TD
1987 LARd	7	81	554	6.8	4	16	136	8.5	2	2	6
1988 LARd	10	136	580	4.3	3	9	79	8.8	0	5	3
1989 LARd	11	173	950	5.5	4	9	69	7.7	0	1	4
1990 LARd	10	125	698	5.6	5	6	68	11.3	0	3	5
NFL Total	38	515	2782	5.4	16	40	352	8.8	2	11	18

WAVERLY JACKSON Jackson, Waverly Arthur Jr. 6'2", 310 **OT**
Col: Virginia Tech *HS:* Park View [South Hill, VA] B: 12/19/1972, South Hill, VA
1998 Ind: 6 G.

WILBUR JACKSON Jackson, Wilbur 6'1", 215 **RB**
Col: Alabama *HS:* Carroll [Ozark, AL] B: 11/19/1951, Ozark, AL
Drafted: 1974 Round 1 SF
1974 SF: KR 5-103 20.6. **1980** Was: KR 8-204 25.5. **1981** Was: KR 2-34 17.0. **Total:** KR 15-341 22.7.

		Rushing				Receiving					Tot
Year Team	**G**	**Att**	**Yds**	**Avg**	**TD**	**Rec**	**Yds**	**Avg**	**TD**	**Fum**	**TD**
1974 SF	14	174	705	4.1	0	23	190	8.3	2	4	2
1975 SF	14	78	303	3.9	0	17	128	7.5	0	8	0
1976 SF	14	200	792	4.0	1	33	324	9.8	1	3	2
1977 SF	14	179	780	4.4	7	22	169	7.7	0	3	7
1979 SF	16	114	375	3.3	2	53	422	8.0	0	6	2
1980 Was	16	176	708	4.0	3	27	279	10.3	1	10	4
1981 Was	5	46	183	4.0	0	7	51	7.3	0	2	0
1982 Was	1	4	6	1.5	0	1	9	9.0	0	0	0
NFL Total	94	971	3852	4.0	13	183	1572	8.6	4	36	17

JOEY JACKSON Jackson, William Joseph 6'4", 270 **DE-DT**
Col: New Mexico State *HS:* Withrow [Cincinnati, OH] B: 5/7/1949, Cincinnati, OH *Drafted:* 1972 Round 6 NYJ
1972 NYJ: 14 G. **1973** NYJ: 3 G. **1977** Min: 3 G. **Total:** 20 G.

BILL JACKSON Jackson, William Steven 6'1", 202 **DB**
Col: North Carolina *HS:* North Forsyth [Winston-Salem, NC]
B: 7/1/1960, Winston-Salem, NC *Drafted:* 1982 Round 8 Cle
1982 Cle: 9 G.

WILLIE JACKSON Jackson, Willie Bernard Jr. 6'1", 205 **WR**
Col: Florida *HS:* P.K. Yonge Lab [Gainesville, FL] B: 8/16/1971, Gainesville, FL *Drafted:* 1994 Round 4 Dal
1995 Jac: PR 1-(-2) -2.0; Scor 1 2XP. **1996** Jac: Rush 1-2 2.0; Scor 1 2XP. **1997** Jac: Rush 3-14 4.7; Scor 1 2XP. **Total:** Rush 4-16 4.0; PR 1-(-2) -2.0; Scor 3 2XP.

		Receiving				Kickoff Returns				
Year Team	**G**	**Rec**	**Yds**	**Avg**	**TD**	**Ret**	**Yds**	**Avg**	**TD**	**Fum**
1995 Jac	14	53	589	11.1	5	19	404	21.3	0	2
1996 Jac	16	33	486	14.7	3	7	149	21.3	0	0
1997 Jac	16	17	206	12.1	2	32	653	20.4	0	1
1998 Cin	8	7	165	23.6	0	0	0	—	0	0
NFL Total	54	110	1446	13.1	10	58	1206	20.8	0	3

FRANK JACKUNAS Jackunas, Frank Raymond 6'3", 225 **C**
Col: Detroit Mercy *HS:* Assumption [Windsor, Canada] B: 10/5/1940, Detroit, MI *Drafted:* 1961 Round 24 Buf
1962 Buf: 3 G.

ALLEN JACOBS Jacobs, Allen Winnitt 6'1", 215 **FB-HB**
Col: Glendale CC CA; Utah *HS:* Benjamin Franklin [Los Angeles, CA]
B: 5/19/1941, Los Angeles, CA *Drafted:* 1964 Round 10 GB
1966 NYG: Rec 10-69 6.9; KR 2-18 9.0. **Total:** Rec 10-69 6.9; KR 2-18 9.0.

		Rushing				
Year Team	**G**	**Att**	**Yds**	**Avg**	**TD**	**Fum**
1965 GB	14	3	5	1.7	0	0
1966 NYG	14	77	273	3.5	1	2
1967 NYG	6	11	23	2.1	0	0
NFL Total	34	91	301	3.3	1	2

DAVE JACOBS Jacobs, David Joseph 5'7", 151 **K**
Col: Syracuse *HS:* George Washington [Philadelphia, PA] B: 7/1/1957, Scranton, PA *Drafted:* 1979 Round 12 Den
1979 NYJ: 4 G; Scor 25, 5-9 55.6% FG, 10-11 90.9% XK. **1981** Cle: 5 G; Scor 21, 4-12 33.3% FG, 9-10 90.0% XK. **1987** Phi: 3 G; Punt 10-369 36.9; Scor 11, 3-5 60.0% FG, 2-4 50.0% XK. **Total:** 12 G; Punt 10-369 36.9; Scor 57, 12-26 46.2% FG, 21-25 84.0% XK.

HARRY JACOBS Jacobs, Harry Edward 6'1", 226 **LB-DE**
Col: Bradley *HS:* Canton [IL] B: 2/4/1937, Canton, IL *Drafted:* 1959 Round 11 Det
1962 Bos: KR 1-0. **Total:** KR 1-0.

		Interceptions		
Year Team	**G**	**Int**	**Yds**	**TD**
1960 Bos	14	4	26	0
1961 Bos	9	0	0	0
1962 Bos	14	0	0	0
1963 Buf	14	1	8	0
1964 Buf	14	2	13	0
1965 Buf	14	1	0	0
1966 Buf	14	2	15	0
1967 Buf	7	0	0	0
1968 Buf	14	0	0	0
1969 Buf	14	2	13	0
1970 NO	6	0	0	0
NFL Total	134	12	75	0

RAY JACOBS Jacobs, Hershel Ray 6'3", 285 **DT-DE**
Col: Navarro Coll. TX (J.C.); Howard Payne *HS:* Corsicana [TX]
B: 11/21/1938, Corsicana, TX *Drafted:* 1962 Round 1 Hou
1963 Den: 7 G. **1964** Den: 14 G. **1965** Den: 14 G. **1966** Den: 11 G. **1967** Mia: 14 G. **1968** Mia: 11 G. **1969** Bos: 8 G. **Total:** 79 G.

JACK JACOBS Jacobs, Jack 6'1", 186 **QB-DB-TB-HB**
(Indian Jack) *Col:* Oklahoma *HS:* Muskogee [OK] B: 8/7/1919, Holderville, OK D: 1/12/1974, Greensboro, NC *Drafted:* 1942 Round 2 Cle
1942 Cle: PR 8-63 7.9; KR 4-83 20.8. **1945** Cle: PR 1-6 6.0. **1946** Was: Rec 4-53 13.3; PR 2-23 11.5. **1947** GB: PR 1-4 4.0. **1948** GB: PR 1-3 3.0. **1949** GB: PR 1-9 9.0. **Total:** Rec 4-53 13.3; PR 14-108 7.7; KR 4-83 20.8.

		Passing							
Year Team	**G**	**Att**	**Comp**	**Comp%**	**Yds**	**YPA**	**TD**	**Int**	**Rating**
1942 Cle	8	93	43	46.2	640	6.88	6	6	63.9
1945 Cle	2	5	3	60.0	12	2.40	0	0	64.6
1946 Was	9	12	5	41.7	98	8.17	0	2	31.3
1947 GB	12	242	108	44.6	1615	6.67	16	17	59.8
1948 GB	12	184	82	44.6	848	4.61	5	21	27.9
1949 GB	12	16	3	18.8	55	3.44	0	3	1.8
NFL Total	55	552	244	44.2	3268	5.92	27	49	42.9

	Rushing				Interceptions		
Year Team	**Att**	**Yds**	**Avg**	**TD**	**Int**	**Yds**	**TD**
1942 Cle	32	-31	-1.0	0	4	22	0
1945 Cle	2	0	0.0	0	0	0	0
1946 Was	18	34	1.9	0	2	56	0
1947 GB	18	64	3.6	1	4	64	0
1948 GB	24	73	3.0	1	0	0	0
1949 GB	0	0	—	0	2	26	0
NFL Total	94	140	1.5	2	12	168	0

	Punting			
Year Team	**Punts**	**Yds**	**Avg**	**Fum**
1942 Cle	33	1395	42.3	0
1945 Cle	1	43	43.0	2
1946 Was	10	428	42.8	1
1947 GB	57	2481	43.5	5
1948 GB	**69**	**2782**	40.3	1
1949 GB	17	757	44.5	0
NFL Total	187	7886	42.2	9

MARV JACOBS Jacobs, Marvin Elzie 6'2", 235 **T**
Col: No College *HS:* Ellensburg [WA] B: 8/1/1925, Yakima, WA
1948 ChiC: 5 G.

PROVERB JACOBS Jacobs, Proverb Gabriel Jr. 6'4", 258 **DT-OT**
Col: Modesto JC CA; California *HS:* Oakland Technical [CA]
B: 5/25/1935, Marksville, LA *Drafted:* 1958 Round 2 Phi
1958 Phi: 12 G; KR 2-24 12.0. **1960** NYG: 8 G. **1961** NYT: 10 G. **1962** NYT: 4 G. **1963** Oak: 14 G. **1964** Oak: 6 G. **Total:** 54 G; KR 2-24 12.0.

RAY JACOBS Jacobs, Ray Anthony 6'2", 244 **LB**
Col: North Carolina *HS:* Topsail [Hamstead, NC] B: 8/18/1972, Hamstead, NC
1994 Den: 16 G. **1995** Den: 15 G. **Total:** 31 G.

STAN JACOBS Jacobs, Stanley 1 **TB**
Col: No College B: 4/15/1897 D: 4/1966, Inkster, MI
1920 Det: 3 G.

CAM JACOBS Jacobs, Thomas Cameron 6'2", 230 **LB**
Col: Kentucky *HS:* Coral Gables [FL] B: 3/10/1962, Oklahoma City, OK *Drafted:* 1985 Round 5 Pit
1987 TB: 3 G.

TIM JACOBS Jacobs, Timothy Jr. 5'10", 187 **DB**
Col: Delaware *HS:* Eleanor Roosevelt [Greenbelt, MD] B: 4/5/1970, Washington, DC
1993 Cle: 2 G. **1994** Cle: 9 G; Int 2-9. **1995** Cle: 14 G. **1996** Mia: 12 G. **1997** Mia: 16 G. **Total:** 53 G; Int 2-9.

JACK JACOBSON Jacobson, Jack Cliston 6'2", 200 **DB**
Col: Oklahoma State *HS:* Ardmore [OK] B: 6/23/1941, Stillwater, OK
Drafted: 1965 Round 13 Det
1965 SD: 3 G.

LARRY JACOBSON Jacobson, Larry Paul 6'6", 260 **DT-DE**
Col: Nebraska *HS:* O'Gorman [Sioux Falls, SD] B: 12/10/1949, Sioux Falls, SD *Drafted:* 1972 Round 1 NYG
1972 NYG: 14 G. **1973** NYG: 8 G. **1974** NYG: 11 G. **Total:** 33 G.

STEVE JACOBSON Jacobson, Stephen Dean 6'3", 255 **OG**
Col: Blinn Coll. TX (J.C.); Texas A&M; Abilene Christian *HS:* Ross S. Sterling [Houston, TX] B: 11/18/1962, Corpus Christi, TX
1987 Mia: 3 G.

JOE JACOBY Jacoby, Joseph Erwin 6′7″, 305 **OT-OG**
Col: Louisville *HS:* Western [Louisville, KY] B: 7/6/1959, Louisville, KY
1981 Was: 14 G. **1982** Was: 9 G. **1983** Was: 16 G. **1984** Was: 16 G; **1** Fum TD; 6 Pt. **1985** Was: 11 G. **1986** Was: 16 G. **1987** Was: 12 G. **1988** Was: 16 G. **1989** Was: 10 G. **1990** Was: 16 G. **1991** Was: 16 G. **1992** Was: 13 G. **1993** Was: 5 G. **Total:** 170 G; 1 Fum TD; 6 Pt.

MITCH JACOBY Jacoby, Mitchel Ray 6′4″, 260 **TE**
Col: Northern Illinois *HS:* Ozaukee [Fredonia, WI] B: 12/8/1973, Port Washington, WI
1997 StL: 14 G; Rec 2-10 5.0. **1998** StL: 5 G. **Total:** 19 G; Rec 2-10 5.0.

KENDYL JACOX Jacox, Kendyl LeMarc 6′2″, 330 **C**
Col: Kansas State *HS:* Davis W. Carter [Dallas, TX] B: 6/10/1975, Dallas, TX
1998 SD: 16 G; KR 1-0.

NATE JACQUET Jacquet, Nathaniel 6′0″, 173 **WR**
Col: Mount San Antonio Coll. CA (J.C.); San Diego State *HS:* Duarte [CA] B: 9/2/1975, Duarte, CA *Drafted:* 1997 Round 5 Ind
1997 Ind: 5 G; PR 13-96 7.4; KR 8-156 19.5; 1 Fum. **1998** Mia: 15 G; Rec 8-122 15.3; KR 4-103 25.8. **Total:** 20 G; Rec 8-122 15.3; PR 13-96 7.4; KR 12-259 21.6; 1 Fum.

JIM JACQUITH Jacquith, James M 5′9″, 175 **BB**
Col: Coll. of Emporia B: 4/1899, Council Grove, KS Deceased
1926 KC: 1 G.

HARRY JACUNSKI Jacunski, Harry Anthony 6′2″, 200 **OE-DE**
Col: Fordham *HS:* New Britain [CT] B: 10/20/1915, New Britain, CT
1943 GB: KR 1-33 33.0; Int 1-7. **Total:** KR 1-33 33.0; Int 1-7.

		Receiving			
Year Team	**G**	**Rec**	**Yds**	**Avg**	**TD**
1939 GB	11	5	104	20.8	2
1940 GB	10	2	29	14.5	0
1941 GB	10	4	48	12.0	0
1942 GB	5	8	125	15.6	1
1943 GB	10	24	528	22.0	3
1944 GB	9	9	151	16.8	0
NFL Total	55	52	985	18.9	6

JEFF JAEGER Jaeger, Jeff Todd 5′11″, 190 **K**
Col: Washington *HS:* Kent-Meridian [Kent, WA] B: 11/26/1964, Tacoma, WA *Drafted:* 1987 Round 3 Cle
1987 Cle: Pass 1-0. **1997** ChiB: Punt 1-18 18.0. **1998** ChiB: Punt 1-27 27.0. **Total:** Pass 1-0; Punt 2-45 22.5.

		Scoring						
Year Team	**G**	**Pts**	**FG**	**FGA**	**FG%**	**XK**	**XKA**	**XK%**
1987 Cle	10	75	14	22	63.6	33	33	100.0
1989 LARd	16	103	23	34	67.6	34	34	100.0
1990 LARd	16	85	15	20	75.0	40	42	95.2
1991 LARd	16	116	29	34	85.3	29	30	96.7
1992 LARd	16	73	15	26	57.7	28	28	100.0
1993 LARd	16	**132**	**35**	**44**	79.5	27	29	93.1
1994 LARd	16	97	22	28	78.6	31	31	100.0
1995 Oak	11	61	13	18	72.2	22	22	100.0
1996 ChiB	13	80	19	23	82.6	23	23	100.0
1997 ChiB	16	83	21	26	80.8	20	20	100.0
1998 ChiB	16	90	21	26	80.8	27	28	96.4
NFL Total	162	995	227	301	75.4	314	320	98.1

JOHNNY JAFFURS Jaffurs, John James III 5′10″, 200 **G**
Col: Penn State *HS:* Wilkinsburg [PA] B: 4/15/1923, Wilkinsburg, PA D: 12/28/1996, South Park, PA *Drafted:* 1943 Round 27 Was
1946 Was: 8 G.

CHICK JAGADE Jagade, Harry Charles 6′0″, 213 **FB-LB**
Col: Indiana *HS:* East Leyden [Franklin Park, IL] B: 12/9/1926, Chicago, IL D: 11/24/1968, Washington Island, WA *Drafted:* 1948 Round 12 Was
AAFC **1949** BalA: Rec 8-44 5.5; KR 6-75 12.5.

		Rushing			
Year Team	**G**	**Att**	**Yds**	**Avg**	**TD**
1949 BalA	10	33	174	5.3	2

NFL **1951** Cle: KR 2-36 18.0. **1952** Cle: KR 3-58 19.3. **1954** ChiB: KR 11-195 17.7. **1955** ChiB: KR 1-23 23.0. **Total:** KR 17-312 18.4.

		Rushing				Receiving					Tot
Year Team	**G**	**Att**	**Yds**	**Avg**	**TD**	**Rec**	**Yds**	**Avg**	**TD**	**Fum**	**TD**
1951 Cle	11	7	30	4.3	0	0	0	—	0	0	0
1952 Cle	12	57	373	6.5	2	9	203	22.6	1	1	3
1953 Cle	12	86	344	4.0	4	20	193	9.7	0	0	4
1954 ChiB	11	157	498	3.2	3	24	172	7.2	0	**12**	3
1955 ChiB	12	72	309	4.3	2	7	16	2.3	0	3	2
NFL Total	58	379	1554	4.1	11	60	584	9.7	1	16	12

HARRY JAGIELSKI Jagielski, Harry Anthony 6′0″, 257 **DT-OT**
(Moose) *Col:* Indiana *HS:* Tilden [Chicago, IL] B: 12/25/1931, Pittsburgh, PA D: 10/9/1993, Chicago, IL *Drafted:* 1954 Round 7 Was
1956 ChiC-Was: 9 G. ChiC: 4 G. Was: 5 G. **1960** Bos: 14 G. **1961** Bos-Oak: 13 G; Int 1-7. Bos: 5 G. Oak: 8 G; Int 1-7. **Total:** 36 G; Int 1-7.

VAN JAKES Jakes, Van Keith 6′0″, 188 **DB**
Col: Kent State *HS:* Seneca Vocational [Buffalo, NY] B: 5/10/1961, Phenix City, AL
1983 KC: 14 G. **1984** KC: 8 G. **1986** NO: 12 G; Int 2-6. **1987** NO: 12 G; Int 3-32. **1988** NO: 16 G; Int 3-61. **1989** GB: 16 G; Int 1-0. **Total:** 78 G; Int 9-99.

GEORGE JAKOWENKO Jakowenko, George 5′9″, 175 **K**
Col: Syracuse *HS:* Nyack [Upper Nyack, NY] B: 6/26/1948, Charleroi, Belgium
1974 Oak: 6 G. **1976** Buf: 11 G; Scor 57, 12-17 70.6% FG, 21-24 87.5% XK. **Total:** 17 G; Scor 57, 12-17 70.6% FG, 21-24 87.5% XK.

LEFTY JAMERSON Jamerson, Charles Dewey 6′1″, 195 **OE**
Col: Arkansas *HS:* Clarendon [AR] B: 1/26/1900, Enfield, IL D: 8/4/1980, Mocksville, NC
1926 Har: 3 G.

ARRIKE JAMES James, Arrike 6′4″, 238 **RB**
Col: Delta State *HS:* Dumas [AR] B: 12/31/1964, Dumas, AR
1987 Hou: 3 G; Rec 1-14 14.0.

CLAUDIS JAMES James, Claudis Ray 6′2″, 190 **WR-HB**
Col: Jackson State *HS:* Marion Central [Columbia, MS] B: 11/7/1943, Columbia, MS *Drafted:* 1967 Round 14 GB
1967 GB: 1 G. **1968** GB: 14 G; Rush 1-15 15.0; Rec 8-148 18.5 2 TD; 12 Pt; 2 Fum. **Total:** 15 G; Rush 1-15 15.0; Rec 8-148 18.5 2 TD; 12 Pt; 2 Fum.

DAN JAMES James, Daniel Anthony 6′4″, 250 **OT-C**
Col: Ohio State *HS:* Elder [Cincinnati, OH] B: 8/10/1937, Cincinnati, OH D: 7/4/1987, Harrison, OH *Drafted:* 1959 Round 1 SF
1960 Pit: 12 G. **1961** Pit: 14 G. **1962** Pit: 14 G. **1963** Pit: 14 G. **1964** Pit: 14 G. **1965** Pit: 13 G. **1966** Pit: 10 G. **1967** ChiB: 2 G. **Total:** 93 G.

GARRY JAMES James, Garry Malcolm 5′10″, 214 **RB**
Col: Louisiana State *HS:* West Jefferson [Harvey, LA] B: 9/4/1963, Marrero, LA *Drafted:* 1986 Round 2 Det

		Rushing				Receiving					Tot
Year Team	**G**	**Att**	**Yds**	**Avg**	**TD**	**Rec**	**Yds**	**Avg**	**TD**	**Fum**	**TD**
1986 Det	16	159	688	4.3	3	34	219	6.4	0	3	3
1987 Det	8	82	270	3.3	4	16	215	13.4	0	3	4
1988 Det	16	182	552	3.0	5	39	382	9.8	2	3	7
NFL Total	40	423	1510	3.6	12	89	816	9.2	2	9	14

JESSE JAMES James, Jesse 6′4″, 311 **C**
Col: Mississippi State *HS:* Lillie B. Williamson [Mobile, AL] B: 9/16/1971, Mobile, AL *Drafted:* 1995 Round 2 StL
1995 StL: 1 G. **1996** StL: 1 G. **Total:** 2 G.

CRAIG JAMES James, Jesse Craig 6′0″, 215 **RB**
Col: Southern Methodist *HS:* Stratford [TX] B: 1/2/1961, Jacksonville, TX *Drafted:* 1983 Round 7 NE
1985 NE: Pass 2-2 100.0%, 16 8.00 2 TD; KR 1-0. **1986** NE: Pass 4-1 25.0%, 10 2.50 1 TD 1 Int. **Total:** Pass 6-3 50.0%, 26 4.33 3 TD 1 Int; KR 1-0.

		Rushing				Receiving					Tot
Year Team	**G**	**Att**	**Yds**	**Avg**	**TD**	**Rec**	**Yds**	**Avg**	**TD**	**Fum**	**TD**
1984 NE	15	160	790	4.9	1	22	159	7.2	0	4	1
1985 NE	16	263	1227	4.7	5	27	360	13.3	2	8	7
1986 NE	13	154	427	2.8	4	18	129	7.2	0	5	4
1987 NE	2	4	10	2.5	0	0	0	—	0	0	0
1988 NE	6	4	15	3.8	1	14	171	12.2	0	0	1
NFL Total	52	585	2469	4.2	11	81	819	10.1	2	17	13

JOHN JAMES James, John Wilbur Jr. 6′3″, 197 **P**
Col: Florida *HS:* Gainesville [FL] B: 1/21/1949, Panama City, FL
1975 Atl: Pass 1-1 100.0%, 25 25.00. **1977** Atl: Pass 1-0. **1979** Atl: Pass 1-1 100.0%, 20 20.00; Rush 1-0. **1980** Atl: Pass 1-0, 1 Int; Rush 1-13 13.0. **1981** Atl: Pass 1-0; Rush 1-(7) -7.0. **1983** Hou: Pass 1-1 100.0%, 7 7.00; Rush 1-0. **Total:** Pass 6-3 50.0%, 52 8.67 1 Int; Rush 4-6 1.5.

		Punting		
Year Team	**G**	**Punts**	**Yds**	**Avg**
1972 Atl	14	61	2609	42.8
1973 Atl	14	63	2682	42.6
1974 Atl	14	**96**	**3891**	40.5
1975 Atl	14	89	3696	41.5
1976 Atl	14	**101**	**4253**	42.1
1977 Atl	14	**105**	**4349**	41.4
1978 Atl	16	**109**	**4227**	38.8
1979 Atl	16	83	3296	39.7

Year Team				
1980 Atl	16	79	3087	39.1
1981 Atl	16	87	3543	40.7
1982 Det-Hou	7	43	1741	40.5
1982 Det	2	12	481	40.1
1982 Hou	5	31	1260	40.6
1983 Hou	16	79	3136	39.7
1984 Hou	16	88	3482	39.6
NFL Total	187	1083	43992	40.6

JUNE JAMES James, June IV 6′1″, 227 **LB**
Col: Texas *HS:* Southeast [Kansas City, MO] B: 12/2/1962, Jennings, LA D: 5/8/1990, Ascension Parish, LA *Drafted:* 1985 Round 9 Det
1985 Det: 16 G. **1987** Ind: 11 G. **Total:** 27 G.

LIONEL JAMES James, Lionel 5′6″, 171 **RB-WR**
(Little Train) *Col:* Auburn *HS:* Dougherty [Albany, GA] B: 5/25/1962, Albany, GA *Drafted:* 1984 Round 5 SD
1984 SD: Pass 2-0, 1 Int. **Total:** Pass 2-0, 1 Int.

		Rushing				Receiving			
Year Team	G	Att	Yds	Avg	TD	Rec	Yds	Avg	TD
1984 SD	16	25	115	4.6	0	23	206	9.0	0
1985 SD	16	105	516	4.9	2	86	1027	11.9	6
1986 SD	7	51	224	4.4	0	23	173	7.5	0
1987 SD	12	27	102	3.8	2	41	593	14.5	3
1988 SD	16	23	105	4.6	0	36	279	7.8	1
NFL Total	67	231	1062	4.6	4	209	2278	10.9	10

	Punt Returns				Kickoff Returns					Tot
Year Team	Ret	Yds	Avg	TD	Ret	Yds	Avg	TD	Fum	TD
1984 SD	30	208	6.9	1	**43**	**959**	22.3	0	9	1
1985 SD	25	213	8.5	0	36	779	21.6	0	9	8
1986 SD	9	94	10.4	0	18	315	17.5	0	5	0
1987 SD	32	400	12.5	1	2	41	20.5	0	6	6
1988 SD	28	278	9.9	0	0	0	—	0	3	1
NFL Total	124	1193	9.6	2	99	2094	21.2	0	32	16

LYNN JAMES James, Lynn Fitzpatrick 6′0″, 191 **WR**
Col: Southern Methodist; Arizona State *HS:* Navasota [TX] B: 1/25/1965, Navasota, TX *Drafted:* 1990 Round 5 Cin
1990 Cin: 11 G; Pass 1-0; Rush 1-11 11.0; Rec 3-36 12.0; KR 1-43 43.0. **1991** Cin-Cle: 14 G; Rec 7-103 14.7 1 TD; PR 1-0; KR 11-192 17.5; 6 Pt; 1 Fum. Cin: 10 G; Rec 7-103 14.7 1 TD; PR 1-0; KR 8-143 17.9; 6 Pt; 1 Fum. Cle: 4 G; KR 3-49 16.3. **Total:** 25 G; Pass 1-0; Rush 1-11 11.0; Rec 10-139 13.9 1 TD; PR 1-0; KR 12-235 19.6; 6 Pt; 1 Fum.

ANGELO JAMES James, Michael Angelo 6′0″, 180 **DB**
Col: West Hills CC CA (J.C.); Sacramento State *HS:* S.S. Murphy [Mobile, AL] B: 6/13/1962, Mobile, AL
1987 Phi: 3 G.

NATE JAMES James, Nathaniel 6′1″, 195 **DB**
Col: Florida A&M *HS:* Union Acad. [Bartow, FL] B: 2/20/1945, Bartow, FL *Drafted:* 1968 Round 6 Cle
1968 Cle: 12 G; KR 8-166 20.8; 1 Fum.

PHILLIP JAMES James, Phillip Ray 6′2″, 265 **OG**
Col: Southern University *HS:* Jack Yates [Houston, TX] B: 12/3/1964, Atlanta, TX
1987 NO: 3 G.

DICK JAMES James, Richard Alwin 5′9″, 179 **HB-DB**
Col: Oregon *HS:* Grants Pass [OR] B: 5/22/1934, Grants Pass, OR *Drafted:* 1956 Round 8 Was
1960 Was: Pass 1-0. **1961** Was: Pass 4-1 25.0%, 15 3.75; Punt 6-210 35.0. **1963** Was: Pass 1-0. **1964** NYG: Pass 1-0, 1 Int; Punt 1-35 35.0. **Total:** Pass 7-1 14.3%, 15 2.14 1 Int; Punt 7-245 35.0.

		Rushing				Receiving			
Year Team	G	Att	Yds	Avg	TD	Rec	Yds	Avg	TD
1956 Was	10	58	280	4.8	1	7	127	18.1	2
1957 Was	11	7	19	2.7	0	0	0	—	0
1958 Was	12	24	88	3.7	1	2	33	16.5	0
1959 Was	12	100	384	3.8	3	13	192	14.8	1
1960 Was	12	73	199	2.7	4	16	243	15.2	2
1961 Was	14	71	374	5.3	3	20	298	14.9	2
1962 Was	14	9	13	1.4	0	19	373	19.6	5
1963 Was	14	105	384	3.7	4	15	302	20.1	2
1964 NYG	14	55	189	3.4	3	12	101	8.4	1
1965 Min	4	0	0	—	0	0	0	—	0
NFL Total	117	502	1930	3.8	19	104	1669	16.0	15

	Punt Returns				Kickoff Returns			
Year Team	Ret	Yds	Avg	TD	Ret	Yds	Avg	TD
1956 Was	6	84	14.0	0	9	181	20.1	0
1957 Was	11	83	7.5	0	12	259	21.6	0
1958 Was	6	37	6.2	0	9	212	23.6	0
1959 Was	21	95	4.5	0	23	503	21.9	0
1960 Was	7	46	6.6	0	19	458	24.1	0
1961 Was	12	90	7.5	0	21	617	29.4	0
1962 Was	19	145	7.6	0	32	889	27.8	0
1963 Was	16	214	**13.4**	0	30	830	27.7	0
1964 NYG	21	153	7.3	0	23	515	22.4	0
1965 Min	1	5	5.0	0	11	212	19.3	0
NFL Total	120	952	7.9	0	189	4676	24.7	0

	Interceptions				Tot
Year Team	Int	Yds	TD	Fum	TD
1956 Was	0	0	0	0	3
1957 Was	2	3	0	1	0
1958 Was	4	43	0	0	1
1959 Was	3	47	0	7	4
1960 Was	0	0	0	8	6
1961 Was	1	28	0	0	5
1962 Was	0	0	0	4	5
1963 Was	2	21	0	6	6
1964 NYG	0	0	0	7	4
1965 Min	0	0	0	1	0
NFL Total	12	142	0	34	34

ROBERT JAMES James, Robert Dematrice 6′1″, 184 **DB**
Col: Fisk *HS:* Holloway [Murfreesboro, TN] B: 7/7/1947, Murfreesboro, TN
1969 Buf: 14 G; Rec 1-19 19.0; PR 1-2 2.0. **1970** Buf: 14 G. **1971** Buf: 14 G; Int 4-25; **1** Fum TD; 6 Pt. **1972** Buf: 14 G; Int 1-0. **1973** Buf: 13 G; Int 1-0. **1974** Buf: 14 G; Int 3-13. **Total:** 83 G; Rec 1-19 19.0; PR 1-2 2.0; Int 9-38; 1 Fum TD; 6 Pt.

ROLAND JAMES James, Roland Orlando 6′2″, 191 **DB**
Col: Tennessee *HS:* Greenview [Jamestown, OH] B: 2/18/1958, Xenia, OH *Drafted:* 1980 Round 1 NE
1982 NE: 2 Sac. **1983** NE: 2 Sac. **1984** NE: Scor **1** Saf. **1986** NE: 1 Sac. **Total:** Scor 1 Saf; 5 Sac.

		Punt Returns				Interceptions			
Year Team	G	Ret	Yds	Avg	TD	Int	Yds	TD	Fum
1980 NE	16	33	331	10.0	1	4	32	0	2
1981 NE	16	7	56	8.0	0	2	29	0	1
1982 NE	7	0	0	—	0	3	12	0	1
1983 NE	16	0	0	—	0	5	99	0	0
1984 NE	15	0	0	—	0	2	14	0	0
1985 NE	16	2	13	6.5	0	4	51	0	1
1986 NE	15	0	0	—	0	2	39	0	0
1987 NE	9	0	0	—	0	1	27	0	0
1988 NE	15	0	0	—	0	4	30	0	0
1989 NE	14	0	0	—	0	2	50	0	0
1990 NE	6	0	0	—	0	0	0	0	0
NFL Total	145	42	400	9.5	1	29	383	0	5

PO JAMES James, Ronald 6′1″, 202 **RB**
Col: New Mexico State *HS:* New Brighton [PA] B: 3/19/1949, New Brighton, PA *Drafted:* 1972 Round 4 Phi

		Rushing				Receiving			
Year Team	G	Att	Yds	Avg	TD	Rec	Yds	Avg	TD
1972 Phi	14	182	565	3.1	0	20	156	7.8	1
1973 Phi	10	36	178	4.9	1	17	94	5.5	0
1974 Phi	11	67	276	4.1	2	33	230	7.0	0
1975 Phi	14	43	196	4.6	1	32	267	8.3	1
NFL Total	49	328	1215	3.7	4	102	747	7.3	2

	Kickoff Returns				Tot
Year Team	Ret	Yds	Avg	TD	Fum	TD
1972 Phi	0	0	—	0	6	1
1973 Phi	16	413	25.8	0	1	1
1974 Phi	12	238	19.8	0	2	2
1975 Phi	13	311	23.9	0	2	2
NFL Total	41	962	23.5	0	11	6

TED JAMES James, Theodore Lawrence 6′2″, 210 **G-C**
Col: Nebraska *HS:* Greeley Central [CO] B: 8/8/1906, Wymore, NE
1929 Fra: 10 G.

TOMMY JAMES James, Thomas Laverne Jr. 5′10″, 185 **DB-HB**
(Red) *Col:* Ohio State *HS:* Washington [Massillon, OH] B: 9/16/1923, Canton, OH *Drafted:* 1947 Round 17 Det
AAFC **1948** CleA: 14 G; Rush 1-8 8.0; Rec 1-44 44.0; PR 5-47 9.4; Int 4-37. **1949** CleA: 12 G; Rush 10-28 2.8; Int 4-64 1 TD; 6 Pt.
Total: 26 G; Rush 11-36 3.3; Rec 1-44 44.0; PR 5-47 9.4; Int 8-101 1 TD; 6 Pt.

NFL **1947** Det: Rush 2-(-1) -0.5; PR 1-2 2.0. **1950** Cle: Rush 1-(-1) -1.0; PR 0-15. **1953** Cle: **1** Fum TD. **1954** Cle: Rush 1-(-6) -6.0. **1955** Cle: Rush 1-2 2.0. **Total:** Rush 5-(-6) -1.2; PR 1-17 17.0; 1 Fum TD.

		Interceptions		
Year Team	G	Int	Yds	TD
1947 Det	2	0	0	0
1950 Cle	12	9	69	0
1951 Cle	12	2	1	0
1952 Cle	12	4	40	0

1953 Cle	12	5	21	0
1954 Cle	12	4	57	0
1955 Cle	8	2	20	0
1956 Bal	2	0	0	0
NFL Total	72	26	208	0

TORAN JAMES James, Toran Clay 6′3″, 240 **LB**
Col: North Carolina A&T *HS:* Hertford Co. [Ahoskie, NC] B: 3/8/1974, Richmond, VA *Drafted:* 1997 Round 7 SD
1997 SD: 14 G.

TORY JAMES James, Tory Steven 6′1″, 195 **DB**
Col: Louisiana State *HS:* Archbishop Shaw [Marrero, LA]
B: 5/18/1973, New Orleans, LA *Drafted:* 1996 Round 2 Den
1996 Den: 16 G; Int 2-15. **1998** Den: 16 G. **Total:** 32 G; Int 2-15.

LARRY JAMESON Jameson, George Larry 6′7″, 270 **DT**
Col: Indiana *HS:* Rantoul Twp. [Rantoul, IL] B: 2/1/1953, Washington, DC *Drafted:* 1975 Round 6 StL
1976 TB: 1 G.

DICK JAMIESON Jamieson, Richard Alexander 6′1″, 190 **QB**
Col: Bradley *HS:* Peoria [IL] B: 11/13/1937, Streator, IL
Drafted: 1959 Round 25 Phi
1960 NYT: Rush 2-10 5.0. **Total:** Rush 2-10 5.0.

		Passing								
Year Team	**G**	**Att**	**Comp**	**Comp%**	**Yds**	**YPA**	**TD**	**Int**	**Rating**	**Fum**
1960 NYT	11	70	35	50.0	586	8.37	6	2	95.3	1
1961 NYT	3	0	0	—	0	—	0	0	—	0
NFL Total	14	70	35	50.0	586	8.37	6	2	95.3	1

ROB JAMIESON Jamieson, Robert John 6′0″, 195 **C**
Col: Franklin & Marshall *HS:* Frankford [Philadelphia, PA] B: 1902
Deceased
1924 Fra: 3 G.

AL JAMISON Jamison, Alfred George 6′5″, 250 **OT**
Col: Colgate *HS:* Edward D. Libbey [Toledo, OH] B: 5/11/1937
1960 Hou: 14 G; KR 1-5 5.0; 1 Fum. **1961** Hou: 14 G. **1962** Hou: 14 G.
Total: 42 G; KR 1-5 5.0; 1 Fum.

GEORGE JAMISON Jamison, George R Jr. 6′1″, 232 **LB**
Col: Cincinnati *HS:* Bridgeton [NJ] B: 9/30/1962, Bridgeton, NJ
Drafted: 1984 Supplemental Round 2 Det
1987 Det: 12 G; Scor **1** Saf; 2 Pt; 1 Sac. **1988** Det: 16 G; Int 3-56 1 TD; **1** Fum TD; Tot TD 2; 12 Pt; 5.5 Sac. **1989** Det: 10 G; 2 Sac. **1990** Det: 14 G; 2 Sac. **1991** Det: 16 G; Int 3-52; 1 Fum; 4 Sac. **1992** Det: 16 G; 2 Sac. **1993** Det: 16 G; KR 1-0; Int 2-48 1 TD; 6 Pt; 2 Sac. **1994** KC: 13 G; 1 Sac. **1995** KC: 14 G. **1996** KC: 5 G. **1997** Det: 16 G; 1 Sac. **1998** Det: 14 G; Int 1-21. **Total:** 162 G; KR 1-0; Int 9-177 2 TD; Scor 1 Saf; 1 Fum TD; Tot TD 3; 20 Pt; 1 Fum; 20.5 Sac.

JOHN JANATA Janata, John Michael 6′7″, 274 **OT**
Col: Antelope Valley Coll. CA (J.C.); Illinois *HS:* Bonanza [Las Vegas, NV] B: 4/10/1961, Chicago, IL
1983 ChiB: 15 G; KR 1-2 2.0.

BOBBY JANCIK Jancik, Robert Lee Jr. 5′11″, 178 **DB-WR**
Col: Wharton Co. JC TX; Lamar *HS:* Lamar [Rosenberg, TX]
B: 2/9/1940, Houston, TX *Drafted:* 1962 Round 19 Hou
1964 Hou: Rec 1-14 14.0. **Total:** Rec 1-14 14.0.

		Punt Returns				Kickoff Returns			
Year Team	**G**	**Ret**	**Yds**	**Avg**	**TD**	**Ret**	**Yds**	**Avg**	**TD**
1962 Hou	14	14	116	8.3	0	24	726	**30.3**	0
1963 Hou	14	13	145	11.2	0	**45**	**1317**	**29.3**	0
1964 Hou	14	12	220	**18.3**	**1**	21	488	23.2	0
1965 Hou	14	12	85	7.1	0	18	430	23.9	0
1966 Hou	14	10	62	6.2	0	**34**	**875**	25.7	0
1967 Hou	11	6	19	3.2	0	16	349	21.8	0
NFL Total	81	67	647	9.7	1	158	4185	26.5	0

	Interceptions			
Year Team	**Int**	**Yds**	**TD**	**Fum**
1962 Hou	2	33	0	1
1963 Hou	3	31	0	3
1964 Hou	3	16	0	2
1965 Hou	4	90	0	3
1966 Hou	2	36	0	1
1967 Hou	1	4	0	1
NFL Total	15	210	0	11

CLARENCE JANECEK Janecek, Clarence Robert 6′0″, 200 **G**
(Janny) *Col:* Purdue *HS:* Harrison [Chicago, IL] B: 4/1/1911, Chicago, IL D: 1/16/1990
1933 Pit: 11 G.

CHUCK JANERETTE Janerette, Charles Fletcher Jr. 6′3″, 265 **DT-OT-OG**
Col: Penn State *HS:* Germantown [Philadelphia, PA] B: 12/1/1938, Philadelphia, PA D: 10/26/1984, Philadelphia, PA *Drafted:* 1960 Round 5 LARm
1960 LARm: 12 G. **1961** NYG: 14 G. **1962** NYG: 12 G. **1963** NYJ: 14 G; Int 1-6. **1964** Den: 14 G. **1965** Den: 14 G; Int 1-0. **Total:** 80 G; Int 2-6.

ERNIE JANET Janet, Ernest Jay 6′4″, 250 **OG**
Col: Washington *HS:* Glacier [Seattle, WA] B: 7/22/1949, Renton, WA
Drafted: 1971 Round 2 SF
1972 ChiB: 3 G. **1973** ChiB: 12 G. **1974** ChiB: 14 G. **1975** GB-Phi: 2 G. GB: 1 G. Phi: 1 G. **Total:** 31 G.

LEN JANIAK Janiak, Leonard Joseph 6′1″, 203 **DB-FB-BB-WB**
Col: Ohio U. *HS:* South [Cleveland, OH] B: 10/29/1915, Cleveland, OH
D: 5/22/1980, Cleveland, OH *Drafted:* 1939 Round 6 Bkn
1939 Bkn: Rec 2-6 3.0. **1940** Cle: Rec 1-3 3.0; Punt 1-30 30.0; Scor 0-1 XK. **1941** Cle: Rec 2-5 2.5; KR 2-27 13.5; Int 1-19. **1942** Cle: Pass 1-1 100.0%, 11 11.00; Rec 6-51 8.5 1 TD. **Total:** Pass 1-1 100.0%, 11 11.00; Rec 11-65 5.9 1 TD; KR 2-27 13.5; Int 1-19; Punt 1-30 30.0; Scor 6, 0-1 XK.

		Rushing			
Year Team	**G**	**Att**	**Yds**	**Avg**	**TD**
1939 Bkn	10	18	56	3.1	0
1940 Cle	11	19	44	2.3	0
1941 Cle	10	14	20	1.4	0
1942 Cle	9	34	109	3.2	0
NFL Total	40	85	229	2.7	0

TOM JANIK Janik, Thomas Alvin 6′3″, 190 **DB**
Col: Texas A&M; Texas A&M–Kingsville *HS:* Poth [TX] B: 9/6/1940, Poth, TX *Drafted:* 1963 Round 3 Den
1969 Bos: PR 1-0. **1971** NE: KR 1-0. **Total:** PR 1-0; KR 1-0.

		Interceptions			Punting			
Year Team	**G**	**Int**	**Yds**	**TD**	**Punts**	**Yds**	**Avg**	**Fum**
1963 Den	14	2	32	0	0	0	—	0
1964 Den	9	1	22	**1**	10	374	37.4	0
1965 Buf	10	0	0	0	0	0	—	0
1966 Buf	14	8	136	**2**	0	0	—	0
1967 Buf	14	**10**	222	2	0	0	—	0
1968 Buf	11	3	137	1	0	0	—	0
1969 Bos	14	1	8	0	70	2903	41.5	0
1970 Bos	14	0	0	0	86	3364	39.1	1
1971 NE	14	0	0	0	87	3249	37.3	1
NFL Total	114	25	557	6	253	9890	39.1	2

KEEVER JANKOVICH Jankovich, Keever David 6′0″, 215 **LB-DE**
Col: Rancho Santiago Coll. CA (J.C.); U. of Pacific *HS:* Tooele [UT]
B: 1/6/1928, Wilmington, NC D: 2/1979 *Drafted:* 1952 Round 5 Cle
1952 Dal: 10 G; KR 3-45 15.0. **1953** ChiC: 2 G. **Total:** 12 G; KR 3-45 15.0.

BRUCE JANKOWSKI Jankowski, Bruce David 5′11″, 185 **WR**
Col: Ohio State *HS:* Fair Lawn [NJ] B: 8/12/1949, Paterson, NJ
Drafted: 1971 Round 10 KC
1971 KC: 5 G. **1972** KC: 4 G; Rec 2-24 12.0. **Total:** 9 G; Rec 2-24 12.0.

ED JANKOWSKI Jankowski, Edward Joe 5′9″, 201 **FB-LB**
Col: Wisconsin *HS:* East Division [Milwaukee, WI]; [HS now Riverside]
B: 6/23/1913, Milwaukee, WI D: 7/20/1996, Madison, WI
Drafted: 1937 Round 1 GB
1937 GB: Rec 1-60 60.0 1 TD; Int 1 TD; Scor 25, 1 XK. **1938** GB: Scor 14, 2-3 66.7% XK. **1939** GB: Rec 1-5 5.0. **1941** GB: Int 1-33; Scor 4, 1-1 100.0% FG, 1-2 50.0% XK. **Total:** Rec 2-65 32.5 1 TD; Int 1-33 1 TD; Scor 67, 1-1 100.0% FG, 4-5 60.0% XK.

		Rushing				Tot
Year Team	**G**	**Att**	**Yds**	**Avg**	**TD**	**TD**
1937 GB	11	61	324	5.3	2	4
1938 GB	11	44	124	2.8	2	2
1939 GB	10	75	278	3.7	2	2
1940 GB	7	48	211	4.4	2	2
1941 GB	11	47	65	1.4	0	0
NFL Total	50	275	1002	3.6	8	10

VIC JANOWICZ Janowicz, Victor Felix 5′9″, 187 **HB**
Col: Ohio State *HS:* Elyria [OH] B: 2/26/1930, Elyria, OH
D: 2/27/1996, Columbus, OH *Drafted:* 1952 Round 7 Was
1954 Was: Pass 1-0; Rec 1-(-1) -1.0; KR 1-18 18.0; Punt 1-32 32.0; Scor 21, 4-8 50.0% FG, 9-9 100.0% XK. **1955** Was: Pass 5-0, 1 Int; Rec 11-149 13.5 3 TD; Scor 88, 6-20 30.0% FG, 28-31 90.3% XK.
Total: Pass 6-0, 1 Int; Rec 12-148 12.3 3 TD; KR 1-18 18.0; Punt 1-32 32.0; Scor 109, 10-28 35.7% FG, 37-40 92.5% XK.

		Rushing					Tot
Year Team	**G**	**Att**	**Yds**	**Avg**	**TD**	**Fum**	**TD**
1954 Was	10	6	13	2.2	0	0	0
1955 Was	12	93	397	4.3	4	2	7
NFL Total	22	99	410	4.1	4	2	7

VAL JANSANTE Jansante, Valerio Richard 6′1″, 190 **OE-DE**
(Blackie) *Col:* Duquesne; Villanova *HS:* Bentleyville [PA]
B: 9/27/1920, La Belle, PA *Drafted:* 1944 Round 10 Pit
1946 Pit: Rush 2-5 2.5. **1947** Pit: KR 2-42 21.0; Scor **1** Saf. **1948** Pit: Rush 1-(-3) -3.0. **1949** Pit: KR 3-46 15.3. **Total:** Rush 3-2 0.7; KR 5-88 17.6; Scor 1 Saf.

		Receiving				
Year Team	**G**	**Rec**	**Yds**	**Avg**	**TD**	**Fum**
1946 Pit	11	10	136	13.6	1	2
1947 Pit	12	35	599	17.1	5	1
1948 Pit	12	39	623	16.0	3	2
1949 Pit	12	29	445	15.3	4	0
1950 Pit	12	26	353	13.6	0	0
1951 Pit-GB	9	16	200	12.5	1	0
1951 Pit	6	15	194	12.9	1	0
1951 GB	3	1	6	6.0	0	0
NFL Total	68	155	2356	15.2	14	5

WHITEY JANSING Jansing, Lee Erwin 175 **FB**
Col: No College *HS:* St. Xavier [Louisville, KY] B: Louisville, KY
D: 7/21/1934, Louisville, KY
1922 Lou: 3 G.

MIKE JANUARY January, Michael Anthony 6′1″, 234 **LB**
Col: Texas *HS:* Westlake [LA] B: 6/30/1964, Lake Charles, LA
1987 ChiB: 3 G; 1 Sac.

PAUL JANUS Janus, Paul Scott 6′4″, 294 **OT**
Col: Northwestern *HS:* Edgerton [WI] B: 3/17/1975, Janesville, WI
1998 Car: 5 G.

PAUL JAPPE Jappe, Paul Eugene 6′1″, 195 **OE-G-T**
Col: Syracuse *HS:* Commercial [Brooklyn, NY] B: 1/16/1898, Union Hill, NJ D: 4/1/1989, Daytona Beach, FL
1925 NYG: 12 G. **1926** Bkn: 11 G. **1927** NYG: 13 G. **1928** NYG: 12 G. **Total:** 48 G.

JON JAQUA Jaqua, Jon V 6′0″, 190 **DB**
Col: Lewis & Clark *HS:* Eugene [OR] B: 9/10/1948, Eugene, OR
1970 Was: 14 G; Int 1-25. **1971** Was: 14 G; KR 6-78 13.0; 1 Fum. **1972** Was: 8 G. **Total:** 36 G; KR 6-78 13.0; Int 1-25; 1 Fum.

PETE JAQUESS Jaquess, Lindel Glenn 6′0″, 185 **DB**
Col: Eastern New Mexico *HS:* Roswell [NM] B: 12/25/1940, Earth, TX
Drafted: 1964 Round 20 Hou
1965 Hou: PR 4-17 4.3; KR 13-280 21.5. **1966** Mia: KR 5-77 15.4. **1968** Den: PR 2-5 2.5; KR 1-0. **1970** Den: PR 4-13 3.3. **Total:** PR 10-35 3.5; KR 19-357 18.8.

		Interceptions			
Year Team	**G**	**Int**	**Yds**	**TD**	**Fum**
1964 Hou	14	8	141	**1**	0
1965 Hou	14	0	0	0	0
1966 Mia	14	3	27	1	2
1967 Mia-Den	10	0	0	0	0
1967 Mia	7	0	0	0	0
1967 Den	3	0	0	0	0
1968 Den	13	5	64	0	1
1969 Den	7	0	0	0	0
1970 Den	13	0	0	0	0
NFL Total	85	16	232	2	3

MIKE JARMOLUK Jarmoluk, Michael Jr. 6′5″, 252 **DT-OT-DE-DG**
(Big Mike) *Col:* Temple *HS:* Frankford [Philadelphia, PA]; Bordentown Mil. Inst. [NJ] B: 10/22/1922, Philadelphia, PA *Drafted:* 1945 Round 5 Det
1946 ChiB: 11 G. **1947** ChiB: 12 G; Rec 2-33 16.5 1 TD; KR 1-0; 6 Pt. **1948** Bos: 12 G; Int 2-13. **1949** NYB-Phi: 11 G; Int 1-3. NYB: 2 G. Phi: 9 G; Int 1-3. **1950** Phi: 12 G. **1951** Phi: 12 G; Int 1-9; 1 Fum. **1952** Phi: 12 G; Int 2-48 1 TD; 1 Fum TD; Tot TD 2; 12 Pt. **1953** Phi: 12 G; Int 1-2. **1954** Phi: 12 G. **1955** Phi: 12 G. **Total:** 118 G; Rec 2-33 16.5 1 TD; KR 1-0; Int 7-75 1 TD; 1 Fum TD; Tot TD 3; 18 Pt; 1 Fum.

ILIA JAROSTCHUK Jarostchuk, Ilia 6′3″, 231 **LB**
Col: New Hampshire *HS:* Central [Whitesboro, NY] B: 8/1/1964, Utica, NY *Drafted:* 1987 Round 5 StL
1987 StL: 12 G. **1988** Mia: 6 G. **1989** Pho: 16 G. **1990** NE: 12 G. **Total:** 46 G.

TOIMI JARVI Jarvi, Toimi V 6′0″, 200 **DB-TB-HB**
Col: Northern Illinois *HS:* De Kalb [IL] B: 2/28/1920, DeKalb, IL
D: 11/18/1977, Chicago, IL
1944 Phi: 5 G; Rush 5-16 3.2; Rec 1-9 9.0; PR 2-22 11.0; Int 1-0. **1945** Pit: 1 G; Pass 10-4 40.0%, 50 5.00 3 Int; Rush 9-24 2.7; Punt 2-69 34.5. **Total:** 6 G; Pass 10-4 40.0%, 50 5.00 3 Int; Rush 14-40 2.9; Rec 1-9 9.0; PR 2-22 11.0; Int 1-0; Punt 2-69 34.5.

CURT JARVIS Jarvis, Curtis Versil Jr. 6′2″, 266 **NT-DE-DT**
Col: Alabama *HS:* Gardendale [AL] B: 1/28/1965, Birmingham, AL
Drafted: 1987 Round 7 TB
1987 TB: 2 G; 3 Sac. **1988** TB: 15 G; 2.5 Sac. **1989** TB: 14 G; 3 Sac. **1990** TB: 7 G. **Total:** 38 G; 8.5 Sac.

BRUCE JARVIS Jarvis, J. Bruce 6′7″, 250 **C**
Col: Washington *HS:* Franklin [Seattle, WA] B: 11/3/1948, Seattle, WA
Drafted: 1971 Round 3 Buf
1971 Buf: 14 G. **1972** Buf: 1 G. **1973** Buf: 8 G. **1974** Buf: 1 G. **Total:** 24 G.

RAY JARVIS Jarvis, Leon Raeminton 6′0″, 200 **WR**
Col: Norfolk State *HS:* Crestwood [Chesapeake, VA] B: 2/2/1949, Chesapeake, VA *Drafted:* 1971 Round 5 Atl
1971 Atl: Rush 1-13 13.0. **1973** Buf: KR 5-84 16.8. **1974** Det: PR 5-62 12.4; KR 5-90 18.0. **1975** Det: Rush 1-0. **Total:** Rush 2-13 6.5; PR 5-62 12.4; KR 10-174 17.4.

		Receiving				
Year Team	**G**	**Rec**	**Yds**	**Avg**	**TD**	**Fum**
1971 Atl	2	0	0	—	0	0
1972 Atl	4	1	18	18.0	0	0
1973 Buf	12	1	12	12.0	0	0
1974 Det	13	3	87	29.0	0	1
1975 Det	14	29	501	17.3	4	1
1976 Det	14	39	822	21.1	5	2
1977 Det	14	28	353	12.6	1	0
1978 Det	2	1	9	9.0	0	0
1979 NE	7	2	30	15.0	1	0
NFL Total	82	104	1832	17.6	11	4

RALPH JARVIS Jarvis, Ralph A 6′4″, 255 **DE**
Col: Temple *HS:* Glen Mills [PA] B: 6/1/1965, Philadelphia, PA
1990 Ind: 8 G; KR 1-0; 1 Fum.

EDWARD JASPER Jasper, Edward Vidal 6′2″, 295 **DT**
Col: Texas A&M *HS:* Troup [TX] B: 1/18/1973, Tyler, TX *Drafted:* 1997 Round 6 Phi
1997 Phi: 10 G; 1 Sac. **1998** Phi: 7 G. **Total:** 17 G; 1 Sac.

VINCE JASPER Jasper, Vincent Paul 6′4″, 270 **OG**
Col: Iowa State *HS:* Harry A. Burke [Omaha, NE] B: 11/30/1964, Hawarden, IA
1987 NYJ: 3 G.

FLOYD JASZEWSKI Jaszewski, Floyd Roman 6′4″, 230 **OT**
(Jazz) *Col:* Minnesota *HS:* Edison [Minneapolis, MN] B: 6/5/1927, Minneapolis, MN *Drafted:* 1950 Round 6 Det
1950 Det: 12 G. **1951** Det: 12 G. **Total:** 24 G.

DICK JAURON Jauron, Richard Manual 6′0″, 190 **DB**
Col: Yale *HS:* Swampscott [MA] B: 10/7/1950, Swampscott, MA
Drafted: 1973 Round 4 Det
1973 Det: KR 17-405 23.8. **1974** Det: KR 2-21 10.5. **Total:** KR 19-426 22.4.

		Punt Returns				Interceptions			
Year Team	**G**	**Ret**	**Yds**	**Avg**	**TD**	**Int**	**Yds**	**TD**	**Fum**
1973 Det	14	6	49	8.2	0	4	**208**	1	2
1974 Det	14	17	286	16.8	0	1	26	0	0
1975 Det	10	6	29	4.8	0	4	39	0	0
1976 Det	6	0	0	—	0	2	0	0	0
1977 Det	14	11	41	3.7	0	3	55	0	0
1978 Cin	16	3	32	10.7	0	4	52	1	0
1979 Cin	16	1	10	10.0	0	6	41	0	0
1980 Cin	10	0	0	—	0	1	11	0	0
NFL Total	100	44	447	10.2	0	25	432	2	2

HEINIE JAWISH Jawish, Henry King 5′8″, 210 **T-G**
(Hy) *Col:* George Washington; Georgetown *HS:* Emerson Inst. [Washington, DC] B: 2/15/1900, Syria D: 3/14/1941, Washington, DC
1926 Pott: 9 G.

MATT JAWORSKI Jaworski, Matthew Joseph 6′1″, 227 **LB**
Col: Colgate *HS:* St. Francis [Athol Springs, NY] B: 10/23/1967, Blasdell, NY
1991 Ind: 8 G.

RON JAWORSKI Jaworski, Ronald Vincent 6′2″, 196 **QB**
Col: Youngstown State *HS:* Lackawanna [NY] B: 3/23/1951, Lackawanna, NY *Drafted:* 1973 Round 2 LARm

		Passing							
Year Team	**G**	**Att**	**Comp**	**Comp%**	**Yds**	**YPA**	**TD**	**Int**	**Rating**
1974 LARm	5	24	10	41.7	144	6.00	0	1	44.4
1975 LARm	14	48	24	50.0	302	6.29	0	2	52.6
1976 LARm	5	52	20	38.5	273	5.25	1	5	22.8
1977 Phi	14	346	166	48.0	2183	6.31	18	21	60.4
1978 Phi	16	398	206	51.8	2487	6.25	16	16	67.9
1979 Phi	16	374	190	50.8	2669	7.14	18	12	76.8
1980 Phi	16	451	257	57.0	3529	7.82	27	12	91.0
1981 Phi	16	461	250	54.2	3095	6.71	23	20	73.8

1982 Phi	9	286	167	58.4	2076	7.26	12	12	77.5
1983 Phi	16	446	235	52.7	3315	7.43	20	18	75.1
1984 Phi	13	427	234	54.8	2754	6.45	16	14	73.5
1985 Phi	16	484	255	52.7	3450	7.13	17	20	70.2
1986 Phi	10	245	128	52.2	1405	5.73	8	**6**	70.2
1988 Mia	16	14	9	64.3	123	8.79	1	0	116.1
1989 KC	6	61	36	59.0	385	6.31	2	5	54.3
NFL Total	188	4117	2187	53.1	28190	6.85	179	164	72.8

	Rushing				
Year Team	**Att**	**Yds**	**Avg**	**TD**	**Fum**
1974 LARm	7	34	4.9	1	1
1975 LARm	12	33	2.8	2	1
1976 LARm	2	15	7.5	1	0
1977 Phi	40	127	3.2	5	6
1978 Phi	30	79	2.6	0	7
1979 Phi	43	119	2.8	2	12
1980 Phi	27	95	3.5	1	6
1981 Phi	22	128	5.8	0	3
1982 Phi	10	9	0.9	0	9
1983 Phi	25	129	5.2	1	11
1984 Phi	5	18	3.6	1	5
1985 Phi	17	35	2.1	2	5
1986 Phi	13	33	2.5	0	4
1989 KC	4	5	1.3	0	2
NFL Total	257	859	3.3	16	72

GARTH JAX Jax, James Garth 6′2″, 240 **LB**
Col: Florida State *HS:* Strake Jesuit Prep [Houston, TX] B: 9/16/1963, Houston, TX *Drafted:* 1986 Round 11 Dal
1986 Dal: 16 G. **1987** Dal: 3 G. **1988** Dal: 16 G. **1989** Pho: 16 G. **1990** Pho: 16 G; KR 2-17 8.5; Int 2-5; 3 Sac. **1991** Pho: 12 G. **1992** Pho: 16 G. **1993** Pho: 16 G. **1994** Ariz: 16 G. **1995** Ariz: 16 G. **Total:** 143 G; KR 2-17 8.5; Int 2-5; 3 Sac.

CRAIG JAY Jay, Craig Adam 6′4″, 257 **TE**
Col: Miami-Dade CC FL; Mount Senario *HS:* Miami Springs [FL]
B: 2/5/1963, Miami, FL
1987 GB: 3 G.

DAVID JAYNES Jaynes, David Duane 6′2″, 212 **QB**
Col: Kansas *HS:* Bonner Springs [KS] B: 12/12/1952, Kansas City, KS *Drafted:* 1974 Round 3 KC
1974 KC: 2 G; Pass 2-0, 1 Int; Rush 1-0; 1 Fum.

GARLAND JEAN-BATISTE Jean-Batiste, Garland Anthony 6′0″, 208 **RB**
Col: Louisiana State *HS:* St. Martinsville [LA] B: 4/2/1965, Lafayette, LA
1987 NO: 3 G; Rush 8-18 2.3.

RALPH JECHA Jecha, Ralph LeRoy 6′2″, 235 **OG-LB**
Col: Northwestern *HS:* Argo [Summit, IL] B: 12/1/1931, Chicago, IL *Drafted:* 1953 Round 15 ChiB
1955 ChiB: 12 G. **1956** Pit: 7 G. **Total:** 19 G.

JIM JEFFCOAT Jeffcoat, James Wilson Jr. 6′5″, 274 **DE**
Col: Arizona State *HS:* Matawan Regional [Aberdeen, NJ] B: 4/1/1961, Long Branch, NJ *Drafted:* 1983 Round 1 Dal
1983 Dal: 16 G; 2 Sac. **1984** Dal: 16 G; **1** Fum TD; 6 Pt; 11.5 Sac. **1985** Dal: 16 G; Int 1-65 **1** TD; 6 Pt; 12 Sac. **1986** Dal: 16 G; 14 Sac. **1987** Dal: 12 G; Int 1-26 1 TD; 6 Pt; 5 Sac. **1988** Dal: 16 G; 6.5 Sac. **1989** Dal: 16 G; 1 Fum TD; 6 Pt; 11.5 Sac. **1990** Dal: 16 G; 3.5 Sac. **1991** Dal: 16 G; 4 Sac. **1992** Dal: 16 G; 10.5 Sac. **1993** Dal: 16 G; 6 Sac. **1994** Dal: 16 G; 8 Sac. **1995** Buf: 16 G; 2.5 Sac. **1996** Buf: 16 G; 5 Sac. **1997** Buf: 7 G; 0.5 Sac. **Total:** 227 G; Int 2-91 2 TD; 2 Fum TD; Tot TD 4; 24 Pt; 102.5 Sac.

ED JEFFERS Jeffers, Edward Francis 6′3″, 215 **G**
Col: Oklahoma; Oklahoma State *HS:* McAlester [OK] B: 11/6/1921, Hartshorne, OK
AAFC **1947** BknA: 14 G.

PATRICK JEFFERS Jeffers, Patrick Christopher 6′3″, 217 **WR**
Col: Virginia *HS:* Fort Worth Country Day School [TX] B: 2/2/1973, Fort Campbell, KY *Drafted:* 1996 Round 5 Den
1996 Den: 4 G; KR 1-18 18.0. **1997** Den: 10 G; Rec 3-24 8.0. **1998** Dal: 8 G; Rec 18-330 18.3 2 TD; 12 Pt. **Total:** 22 G; Rec 21-354 16.9 2 TD; KR 1-18 18.0; 12 Pt.

CHARLES JEFFERSON Jefferson, Charles Ray 6′0″, 178 **DB**
Col: McNeese State *HS:* Capitol [Baton Rouge, LA] B: 5/5/1957, New Orleans, LA *Drafted:* 1979 Round 4 Den
1979 Hou: 5 G.

GREG JEFFERSON Jefferson, Greg Benton 6′3″, 263 **DE**
Col: Central Florida *HS:* Bartow [FL] B: 8/31/1971, Orlando, FL *Drafted:* 1995 Round 3 Phi
1995 Phi: 3 G. **1996** Phi: 11 G; 2.5 Sac. **1997** Phi: 12 G; 3 Sac. **1998** Phi: 15 G; 4 Sac. **Total:** 41 G; 9.5 Sac.

JAMES JEFFERSON Jefferson, James Andrew III 6′1″, 199 **DB**
Col: Texas A&M–Kingsville *HS:* H.M. King [Kingsville, TX]
B: 11/18/1963, Portsmouth, VA
1989 Sea: PR 12-87 7.3. **1990** Sea: PR 8-68 8.5; Int 1-0. **1991** Sea: 1 Sac. **1993** Sea: Int 1-12. **Total:** PR 20-155 7.8; Int 2-12; 1 Sac.

		Kickoff Returns				
Year Team	**G**	**Ret**	**Yds**	**Avg**	**TD**	**Fum**
1989 Sea	16	22	511	23.2	**1**	3
1990 Sea	15	4	96	24.0	0	1
1991 Sea	16	0	0	—	0	1
1992 Sea	1	0	0	—	0	0
1993 Sea	10	0	0	—	0	0
NFL Total	58	26	607	23.3	1	5

JOHN JEFFERSON Jefferson, John Larry 6′1″, 198 **WR**
(J.J.) *Col:* Arizona State *HS:* Franklin D. Roosevelt [Dallas, TX]
B: 2/3/1956, Dallas, TX *Drafted:* 1978 Round 1 SD
1978 SD: Rush 1-7 7.0. **1980** SD: Rush 1-16 16.0; KR 1-0. **1981** GB: Rush 2-22 11.0; KR 1-3 3.0. **1982** GB: Rush 2-16 8.0. **Total:** Rush 6-61 10.2; KR 2-3 1.5.

		Receiving				
Year Team	**G**	**Rec**	**Yds**	**Avg**	**TD**	**Fum**
1978 SD	14	56	1001	17.9	**13**	0
1979 SD	15	61	1090	17.9	10	0
1980 SD	16	82	**1340**	16.3	**13**	0
1981 GB	13	39	632	16.2	4	0
1982 GB	8	27	452	16.7	0	0
1983 GB	16	57	830	14.6	7	1
1984 GB	13	26	339	13.0	0	0
1985 Cle	7	3	30	10.0	0	0
NFL Total	102	351	5714	16.3	47	1

KEVIN JEFFERSON Jefferson, Kevin Howard 6′2″, 232 **LB**
Col: Lehigh *HS:* Hempfield Area [Greensburg, PA] B: 1/14/1974, Philadelphia, PA
1994 Cin: 6 G. **1995** Cin: 16 G. **Total:** 22 G.

NORMAN JEFFERSON Jefferson, Norman Jr. 5′10″, 183 **DB**
Col: Louisiana State *HS:* John Ehret [Marrero, LA] B: 8/7/1964, Marrero, LA *Drafted:* 1987 Round 12 GB
1987 GB: 12 G; KR 2-30 15.0; 2 Fum. **1988** GB: 2 G; PR 5-15 3.0; KR 4-116 29.0; 3 Fum. **Total:** 14 G; PR 5-15 3.0; KR 6-146 24.3; 5 Fum.

ROY JEFFERSON Jefferson, Roy Lee 6′2″, 195 **WR**
Col: Utah *HS:* Compton [CA] B: 11/9/1943, Texarkana, TX
Drafted: 1965 Round 2 Pit
1969 Pit: KR 4-80 20.0. **1970** Bal: KR 1-11 11.0. **Total:** KR 5-91 18.2.

		Rushing				Receiving			
Year Team	**G**	**Att**	**Yds**	**Avg**	**TD**	**Rec**	**Yds**	**Avg**	**TD**
1965 Pit	10	1	-1	-1.0	0	13	287	22.1	1
1966 Pit	14	2	36	18.0	0	32	772	24.1	4
1967 Pit	13	5	-11	-2.2	0	29	459	15.8	4
1968 Pit	14	6	57	9.5	0	58	**1074**	18.5	11
1969 Pit	14	4	46	11.5	0	67	1079	16.1	9
1970 Bal	14	4	47	11.8	0	44	749	17.0	7
1971 Was	14	2	13	6.5	0	47	701	14.9	4
1972 Was	14	0	0	—	0	35	550	15.7	3
1973 Was	14	1	1	1.0	0	41	595	14.5	1
1974 Was	14	0	0	—	0	43	654	15.2	4
1975 Was	13	0	0	—	0	15	255	17.0	2
1976 Was	14	0	0	—	0	27	364	13.5	2
NFL Total	162	25	188	7.5	0	451	7539	16.7	52

	Punt Returns					Tot
Year Team	**Ret**	**Yds**	**Avg**	**TD**	**Fum**	**TD**
1965 Pit	13	100	7.7	0	3	1
1966 Pit	12	29	2.4	0	3	4
1967 Pit	1	10	10.0	0	1	4
1968 Pit	**28**	274	9.8	1	3	12
1969 Pit	4	23	5.8	0	3	9
1970 Bal	0	0	—	0	1	7
1971 Was	0	0	—	0	0	4
1972 Was	0	0	—	0	1	3
1973 Was	0	0	—	0	0	1
1974 Was	0	0	—	0	1	4
1975 Was	0	0	—	0	1	2
1976 Was	0	0	—	0	1	2
NFL Total	58	436	7.5	1	18	53

THAD JEFFERSON Jefferson, Thaddius Eugene 5′11″, 225 **LB**
(Sweetness) *Col:* Hawaii *HS:* Ontario [CA] B: 3/11/1964
1987 Hou: 3 G.

SHAWN JEFFERSON Jefferson, Vanchi LaShawn 5'11", 180 **WR**
Col: Central Florida *HS:* William M. Raines [Jacksonville, FL]
B: 2/22/1969, Jacksonville, FL *Drafted:* 1991 Round 9 Hou
1991 SD: Rush 1-27 27.0. **1993** SD: Rush 5-53 10.6. **1994** SD: Rush 3-40 13.3. **1995** SD: Rush 2-1 0.5. **1996** NE: Rush 1-6 6.0. **1998** NE: Rush 1-15 15.0. **Total:** Rush 13-142 10.9.

		Receiving				
Year Team	**G**	**Rec**	**Yds**	**Avg**	**TD**	**Fum**
1991 SD	16	12	125	10.4	1	0
1992 SD	16	29	377	13.0	2	0
1993 SD	16	30	391	13.0	2	0
1994 SD	16	43	627	14.6	3	0
1995 SD	16	48	621	12.9	2	0
1996 NE	15	50	771	15.4	4	2
1997 NE	16	54	841	15.6	2	2
1998 NE	16	34	771	**22.7**	2	0
NFL Total	127	300	4524	15.1	18	4

BEN JEFFERSON Jefferson, Willam Benjamin 6'9", 330 **OG**
Col: Maryland *HS:* New Rochelle [NY] B: 1/15/1966, New Rochelle, NY
1990 Cle: 4 G.

BILLY JEFFERSON Jefferson, William C 6'2", 208 **TB-DB-HB**
Col: Mississippi State *HS:* Inverness [MS] B: 5/17/1918, Pheba, MS
D: 3/10/1974, Memphis, TN *Drafted:* 1941 Round 12 Det
1941 Det: Rec 2-14 7.0; PR 7-69 9.9; KR 3-142 47.3 **1** TD; Int 1-12; Punt 20-750 37.5. **1942** Phi-Bkn: KR 3-74 24.7; Punt 2-99 49.5. Phi: KR 3-74 24.7; Punt 1-50 50.0. Bkn: Punt 1-49 49.0. **Total:** Rec 2-14 7.0; PR 7-69 9.9; KR 6-216 36.0 1 TD; Int 1-12; Punt 22-849 38.6.

		Passing							
Year Team	**G**	**Att**	**Comp**	**Comp%**	**Yds**	**YPA**	**TD**	**Int**	**Rating**
1941 Det	11	72	18	25.0	181	2.51	0	9	0.0
1942 Phi-Bkn	8	4	1	25.0	11	2.75	0	0	39.6
1942 Phi	5	1	0	0.0	0	0.00	0	0	39.6
1942 Bkn	3	3	1	33.3	11	3.67	0	0	45.1
NFL Total	19	76	19	25.0	192	2.53	0	9	0.0

	Rushing				Tot
Year Team	**Att**	**Yds**	**Avg**	**TD**	**TD**
1941 Det	56	164	2.9	1	2
1942 Phi-Bkn	12	58	4.8	0	0
1942 Phi	11	57	5.2	0	0
1942 Bkn	1	1	1.0	0	0
NFL Total	68	222	3.3	1	2

TONY JEFFERY Jeffery, Tony Lorenzo 5'11", 208 **RB**
Col: Texas Christian *HS:* Gladewater [TX] B: 7/8/1964, Gladewater, TX
Drafted: 1988 Round 2 Pho
1988 Pho: 3 G; Rush 3-8 2.7; KR 1-11 11.0.

HAYWOOD JEFFIRES Jeffires, Haywood Franklin 6'2", 201 **WR**
Col: North Carolina State *HS:* Walter H. Page [Greensboro, NC]
B: 12/12/1964, Greensboro, NC *Drafted:* 1987 Round 1 Hou
1994 Hou: Scor **3** 2XP. **Total:** Scor 3 2XP.

		Receiving				
Year Team	**G**	**Rec**	**Yds**	**Avg**	**TD**	**Fum**
1987 Hou	9	7	89	12.7	0	0
1988 Hou	2	2	49	24.5	1	0
1989 Hou	16	47	619	13.2	2	0
1990 Hou	16	74	1048	14.2	8	0
1991 Hou	16	**100**	1181	11.8	7	3
1992 Hou	16	90	913	10.1	9	1
1993 Hou	16	66	753	11.4	6	5
1994 Hou	16	68	783	11.5	6	0
1995 Hou	16	61	684	11.2	8	0
1996 NO	9	20	215	10.8	3	1
NFL Total	132	535	6334	11.8	50	10

NEAL JEFFREY Jeffrey, James Neal 6'1", 180 **QB**
Col: Baylor *HS:* Shawnee Mission South [KS] B: 7/23/1953, Fort Worth, TX *Drafted:* 1975 Round 17 SD
1976 SD: 5 G; Pass 2-2 100.0%, 11 5.50; Rush 1-0; 1 Fum.

CURTIS JEFFRIES Jeffries, Curtis Anthony 6'4", 236 **TE**
Col: Louisville *HS:* Southern [Louisville, KY] B: 10/26/1964, Louisville, KY
1987 Cin: 3 G.

DAMEIAN JEFFRIES Jeffries, Dameian Vashun 6'4", 277 **DE**
Col: Alabama *HS:* B.B. Comer [Sylacauga, AL] B: 5/7/1973, Sylacauga, AL *Drafted:* 1995 Round 4 NO
1995 NO: 2 G.

ERIC JEFFRIES Jeffries, Eric Marcel 5'10", 161 **DB**
Col: Texas *HS:* Lyndon B. Johnson [Austin, TX] B: 7/25/1964, Springfield, MO *Drafted:* 1987 Round 12 ChiB
1987 ChiB: 1 G; PR 1-5 5.0.

GREG JEFFRIES Jeffries, Greg Lemont 5'9", 184 **DB**
Col: Virginia *HS:* T. Wingate Andrews [High Point, NC] B: 10/16/1971, High Point, NC *Drafted:* 1993 Round 6 Det
1993 Det: 7 G. **1994** Det: 16 G. **1995** Det: 14 G; 0.5 Sac. **1996** Det: 16 G; Int 1-0. **1997** Det: 15 G; Int 1-0; 1 Sac. **1998** Det: 15 G. **Total:** 83 G; Int 2-0; 1.5 Sac.

BOB JEFFRIES Jeffries, Robert James 6'2", 206 **G**
Col: Missouri *HS:* Central [Kansas City, MO] B: 8/19/1919, Kansas City, MO *Drafted:* 1942 Round 5 ChiB
1942 Bkn: 4 G.

JON JELACIC Jelacic, Jon Francis 6'3", 250 **DE-OG**
Col: Minnesota *HS:* Washington [Brainerd, MN] B: 12/19/1936, Brainerd, MN D: 9/17/1993, St. Paul, MN *Drafted:* 1958 Round 7 ChiC
1958 NYG: 9 G. **1961** Oak: 4 G. **1962** Oak: 14 G; Int 1-0. **1963** Oak: 14 G; Int 1-1 1 TD; **1** Fum TD; Tot TD 2; 12 Pt. **1964** Oak: 3 G. **Total:** 44 G; Int 2-1 1 TD; 1 Fum TD; Tot TD 2; 12 Pt.

TOM JELESKY Jelesky, Thomas John 6'6", 275 **OT**
Col: Purdue *HS:* Merrillville [IN] B: 10/4/1960, Merrillville, IN
1985 Phi: 16 G. **1986** Phi: 9 G. **Total:** 25 G.

TOM JELLEY Jelley, Thomas J 6'5", 225 **DE**
Col: Miami (Fla.) *HS:* Mount Lebanon [PA] B: 11/18/1926, Pittsburgh, PA *Drafted:* 1951 Round 4 ChiB
1951 Pit: 5 G; Rec 1-8 8.0.

DIETRICH JELLS Jells, Dietrich Davis 5'10", 186 **WR**
Col: Pittsburgh *HS:* Erie Tech [PA] B: 4/11/1972, Erie, PA
Drafted: 1996 Round 6 KC
1996 NE: 7 G; Rec 1-5 5.0. **1997** NE: 11 G; Rec 1-9 9.0. **1998** Phi: 9 G; Rush 2-9 4.5; Rec 2-53 26.5. **Total:** 27 G; Rush 2-9 4.5; Rec 4-67 16.8.

JIMMY JEMAIL Jemail, Manuel James 5'6", 165 **BB**
Col: Brown; Navy *HS:* Rogers [Newport, RI] B: 9/12/1893, Biblos, Lebanon D: 7/26/1978, New York, NY
1921 NYG: 1 G.

BOB JENCKS Jencks, Robert William 6'5", 227 **TE-K**
Col: Miami (Ohio) *HS:* Upper Arlington [OH] B: 7/15/1941, Columbus, OH *Drafted:* 1963 Round 2 ChiB
1963 ChiB: 14 G; Rec 1-6 6.0; Scor 38, 1-10 10.0% FG, 35-37 94.6% XK. **1964** ChiB: 14 G; Scor 38, 3-7 42.9% FG, 29-32 90.6% XK. **1965** Was: 14 G; Rec 2-20 10.0; Scor 59, 10-12 83.3% FG, 29-33 87.9% XK. **Total:** 42 G; Rec 3-26 8.7; Scor 135, 14-29 48.3% FG, 93-102 91.2% XK.

NOEL JENKE Jenke, Noel Charles 6'2", 221 **LB**
Col: Minnesota *HS:* Bloomington [MN] B: 12/17/1946, Owatonna, MN
Drafted: 1969 Round 12 Min
1971 Min: 14 G. **1972** Atl: 1 G. **1973** GB: 2 G. **1974** GB: 8 G. **Total:** 25 G.

A.J. JENKINS Jenkins, A.J. 6'2", 237 **LB-DE**
Col: Merced Coll. CA (J.C.); Cal State-Fullerton *HS:* Havelock [NC]
B: 4/12/1966, Havelock, NC *Drafted:* 1989 Round 9 Pit
1989 Pit: 16 G. **1990** Pit: 5 G; 2 Sac. **Total:** 21 G; 2 Sac.

ALFRED JENKINS Jenkins, Alfred Donell 5'10", 170 **WR**
Col: Morris Brown *HS:* Hogansville [GA] B: 1/25/1952, Hogansville, GA
1975 Atl: PR 6-38 6.3; KR 1-24 24.0. **1976** Atl: Pass 1-0, 1 Int. **1977** Atl: Rush 2-7 3.5. **Total:** Pass 1-0, 1 Int; Rush 2-7 3.5; PR 6-38 6.3; KR 1-24 24.0.

		Receiving				
Year Team	**G**	**Rec**	**Yds**	**Avg**	**TD**	**Fum**
1975 Atl	14	38	767	20.2	6	1
1976 Atl	14	41	710	17.3	6	0
1977 Atl	14	39	677	17.4	4	2
1978 Atl	1	2	28	14.0	0	0
1979 Atl	16	50	858	17.2	3	1
1980 Atl	16	58	1035	17.8	6	0
1981 Atl	16	70	**1358**	19.4	**13**	3
1982 Atl	9	24	347	14.5	1	0
1983 Atl	10	38	487	12.8	1	0
NFL Total	110	360	6267	17.4	40	7

AL JENKINS Jenkins, Alfred Joseph 6'2", 245 **OG-OT-DE-DT**
(Big Al) *Col:* Tulsa *HS:* St. Augustine [New Orleans, LA]
B: 7/15/1946, New Orleans, LA *Drafted:* 1969 Round 3 Cle
1969 Cle: 8 G; KR 1-0; 1 Fum. **1970** Cle: 5 G; PR 1-0; 1 Fum. **1972** Mia: 14 G. **1973** Hou: 13 G. **Total:** 40 G; PR 1-0; KR 1-0; 2 Fum.

BILLY JENKINS Jenkins, Billy Leon Jr. 5'10", 205 **DB**
Col: Howard *HS:* Albuquerque [NM] B: 7/8/1974, Albuquerque, NM
1997 StL: 16 G. **1998** StL: 16 G; Int 2-31; 3 Sac. **Total:** 32 G; Int 2-31; 3 Sac.

CARLOS JENKINS Jenkins, Carlos Edward 6'3", 220 **LB**
Col: Michigan State *HS:* Santaluces [Lantana, FL] B: 7/12/1968, Palm Beach, FL *Drafted:* 1991 Round 3 Min
1991 Min: 3 G. **1992** Min: 16 G; Int 1-19 1 TD; 1 Fum TD; Tot TD 2; 12 Pt; 4 Sac. **1993** Min: 16 G; Int 2-7; 2.5 Sac. **1994** Min: 16 G; 1 Sac. **1995** StL:

16 G; 1.5 Sac. **1996** StL: 13 G; Int 1-(-3). **Total:** 80 G; Int 4-23 1 TD; 1 Fum TD; Tot TD 2; 12 Pt; 9 Sac.

DERON JENKINS Jenkins, DeRon Charles 5'11", 190 **DB**
Col: Tennessee *HS:* Ritenour [St. Louis, MO] B: 11/14/1973, St. Louis, MO *Drafted:* 1996 Round 2 Bal
1996 Bal: 15 G. **1997** Bal: 16 G; Int 1-15. **1998** Bal: 16 G; Int 1-0. **Total:** 47 G; Int 2-15.

ED JENKINS Jenkins, Eddie Jay 6'2", 210 **RB**
Col: Holy Cross *HS:* St. Francis Prep [Brooklyn, NY] B: 8/31/1950, Jacksonville, FL *Drafted:* 1972 Round 11 Mia
1972 Mia: 3 G. **1974** NYG-Buf-NE: 11 G; Rec 1-12 12.0. NYG: 4 G. Buf: 4 G; Rec 1-12 12.0. NE: 3 G. **Total:** 14 G; Rec 1-12 12.0.

FLETCHER JENKINS Jenkins, Fletcher 6'2", 258 **DE-NT**
Col: Washington *HS:* Lakes [Tacoma, WA] B: 11/4/1959, Tacoma, WA *Drafted:* 1982 Round 7 Bal
1982 Bal: 9 G.

IZEL JENKINS Jenkins, Izel Jr. 5'10", 191 **DB**
Col: Taft Coll. CA (J.C.); North Carolina State *HS:* Ralph L. Fike [Wilson, NC] B: 5/27/1964, Wilson, NC *Drafted:* 1988 Round 11 Phi
1988 Phi: 16 G; KR 1-20 20.0; Scor 1 Saf; 2 Pt. **1989** Phi: 16 G; Int 4-58. **1990** Phi: 15 G; KR 1-14 14.0. **1991** Phi: 14 G; 1 Sac. **1992** Phi: 16 G. **1993** Min-NYG: 9 G. Min: 4 G. NYG: 5 G. **Total:** 86 G; KR 2-34 17.0; Int 4-58; Scor 1 Saf; 2 Pt; 1 Sac.

JACK JENKINS Jenkins, Jacque Sumpter 6'1", 206 **FB-LB**
Col: Vanderbilt *HS:* Texas [Texarkana] B: 5/6/1921, Texarkana, TX D: 4/30/1982, Florence, AL *Drafted:* 1943 Round 1 Was
1943 Was: Scor 1, 1-1 100.0% XK. **1946** Was: Rec 2-27 13.5; PR 2-14 7.0; Int 3-57. **1947** Was: Rec 5-96 19.2; Int 1-7. **Total:** Rec 7-123 17.6; PR 2-14 7.0; Int 4-64; Scor 7, 1-1 100.0% XK.

		Rushing				
Year Team	**G**	**Att**	**Yds**	**Avg**	**TD**	**Fum**
1943 Was	2	4	20	5.0	0	0
1946 Was	8	64	200	3.1	1	4
1947 Was	12	16	54	3.4	0	1
NFL Total	22	84	274	3.3	1	5

JAMES JENKINS Jenkins, James 6'2", 243 **TE**
Col: Rutgers *HS:* Staten Island Acad. [NY] B: 8/17/1967, Staten Island, NY
1991 Was: 4 G. **1992** Was: 5 G. **1993** Was: 15 G. **1994** Was: 16 G; Rec 8-32 4.0 4 TD; KR 1-4 4.0; 24 Pt. **1995** Was: 16 G; Rec 1-2 2.0; KR 1-12 12.0. **1996** Was: 16 G; Rec 1-7 7.0. **1997** Was: 16 G; Rec 4-43 10.8 3 TD; 18 Pt. **1998** Was: 16 G; KR 1-0. **Total:** 104 G; Rec 14-84 6.0 7 TD; KR 3-16 5.3; 42 Pt.

JOHN JENKINS Jenkins, John Eric 6'0", 188 **DB**
Col: Pittsburgh *HS:* East Allegheny [North Versailles, PA] B: 5/11/1975, East McKeesport, PA
1998 Pit: 1 G.

JON JENKINS Jenkins, Jonathan R 6'2", 225 **DT-OT**
Col: Dartmouth *HS:* St. Christopher's Acad. [Frostburg, MD] B: 6/17/1926, Frostburg, MD
AAFC **1949** BalA: 11 G.

NFL **1950** Bal-NYY: 4 G. Bal: 3 G. NYY: 1 G. **Total:** 4 G.

KEN JENKINS Jenkins, Kenneth Walton 5'8", 183 **RB**
Col: Bucknell *HS:* Landon [Bethesda, MD] B: 5/8/1959, Washington, DC
1984 Det: Pass 1-0; Rec 21-246 11.7. **Total:** Pass 1-0; Rec 21-246 11.7.

		Rushing				Punt Returns			
Year Team	**G**	**Att**	**Yds**	**Avg**	**TD**	**Ret**	**Yds**	**Avg**	**TD**
1983 Det	12	0	0	—	0	23	230	10.0	0
1984 Det	14	78	358	4.6	1	1	1	1.0	0
1985 Was	13	2	39	19.5	0	26	272	10.5	0
1986 Was	12	0	0	—	0	28	270	9.6	0
NFL Total	51	80	397	5.0	1	78	773	9.9	0

	Kickoff Returns				
Year Team	**Ret**	**Yds**	**Avg**	**TD**	**Fum**
1983 Det	22	459	20.9	0	2
1984 Det	18	396	22.0	0	0
1985 Was	41	1018	24.8	0	1
1986 Was	27	554	20.5	0	4
NFL Total	108	2427	22.5	0	7

KERRY JENKINS Jenkins, Kerry Cary 6'5", 310 **OT**
Col: Louisiana State; Troy State *HS:* Holt [AL] B: 9/6/1973, Birmingham, AL
1997 NYJ: 2 G. **1998** NYJ: 16 G. **Total:** 18 G.

KEYVAN JENKINS Jenkins, Keyvan Lewis 5'10", 190 **RB**
Col: Nevada-Las Vegas *HS:* Venice [Los Angeles, CA] B: 1/6/1961, Stockton, CA
1987 SD: 3 G; Rush 22-88 4.0; Rec 8-40 5.0; KR 2-46 23.0. **1988** KC: 2 G; KR 2-12 6.0; 1 Fum. **Total:** 5 G; Rush 22-88 4.0; Rec 8-40 5.0; KR 4-58 14.5; 1 Fum.

LEON JENKINS Jenkins, Leon 5'11", 165 **DB**
Col: West Virginia *HS:* Weir [Weirton, WV] B: 8/26/1950, Columbus, OH *Drafted:* 1972 Round 16 Det
1972 Det: 4 G.

MELVIN JENKINS Jenkins, Melvin 5'10", 172 **DB**
Col: Hinds CC MS; Cincinnati *HS:* Wingfield [Jackson, MS] B: 3/16/1962, Jackson, MS
1991 Det: PR 1-0; 1 Sac. **Total:** PR 1-0; 1 Sac.

		Interceptions			
Year Team	**G**	**Int**	**Yds**	**TD**	**Fum**
1987 Sea	12	3	46	0	1
1988 Sea	16	3	41	0	1
1989 Sea	16	0	0	0	0
1990 Sea	16	1	0	0	0
1991 Det	16	0	0	0	1
1992 Det	16	4	34	0	0
1993 Atl-Det	15	0	0	0	0
1993 Atl	14	0	0	0	0
1993 Det	1	0	0	0	0
NFL Total	107	11	121	0	3

MIKE JENKINS Jenkins, Michael 6'4", 200 **WR**
Col: Hampton *HS:* I.C. Norcom [Portsmouth, VA] B: 8/25/1974, Portsmouth, VA
1997 Cin: 4 G.

ROBERT JENKINS Jenkins, Robert Lloyd 6'5", 285 **OT**
(AKA Robert Lloyd Cox) *Col:* Chabot Coll. CA (J.C.); UCLA *HS:* Dublin [CA] B: 12/30/1963, San Francisco, CA *Drafted:* 1986 Round 6 LARm
1987 LARm: 10 G; KR 1-12 12.0. **1988** LARm: 16 G. **1989** LARm: 16 G. **1990** LARm: 11 G. **1991** LARm: 12 G. **1992** LARm: 9 G. **1993** LARm: 8 G. **1994** LARd: 10 G. **1995** Oak: 15 G. **1996** Oak: 10 G. **Total:** 117 G; KR 1-12 12.0.

TREZELLE JENKINS Jenkins, Trezelle Samuel 6'7", 317 **OT**
Col: Michigan *HS:* Morgan Park [Chicago, IL] B: 3/13/1973, Chicago, IL *Drafted:* 1995 Round 1 KC
1995 KC: 1 G. **1996** KC: 6 G. **1997** KC: 2 G. **Total:** 9 G.

WALT JENKINS Jenkins, Walter B 6'1", 223 **DE-DT**
(Kingfish) *Col:* Wayne State (Mich.) *HS:* Miller [Detroit, MI] B: 12/9/1930, Detroit, MI *Drafted:* 1955 Round 9 Det
1955 Det: 2 G.

DAVE JENNINGS Jennings, David Tuthill 6'4", 203 **P**
Col: St. Lawrence *HS:* Garden City [NY] B: 6/8/1952, New York, NY
1978 NYG: Pass 1-1 100.0%, -1 -1.00; Rush 1-0. **1979** NYG: Pass 2-2 100.0%, 48 24.00; Rush 2-11 5.5. **1983** NYG: Pass 1-0. **1986** NYJ: Rush 1-0. **1987** NYJ: Pass 1-1 100.0%, 16 16.00; Rush 2-5 2.5. **Total:** Pass 5-4 80.0%, 63 12.60; Rush 6-16 2.7.

		Punting			
Year Team	**G**	**Punts**	**Yds**	**Avg**	**Fum**
1974 NYG	14	68	2709	39.8	0
1975 NYG	14	76	3107	40.9	0
1976 NYG	14	74	3054	41.3	0
1977 NYG	14	100	3993	39.9	0
1978 NYG	16	95	3995	42.1	1
1979 NYG	16	**104**	**4445**	42.7	0
1980 NYG	16	94	**4211**	**44.8**	0
1981 NYG	16	97	4198	43.3	0
1982 NYG	9	49	2096	42.8	0
1983 NYG	16	84	3386	40.3	0
1984 NYG	16	90	3598	40.0	0
1985 NYJ	16	74	2978	40.2	0
1986 NYJ	16	85	3353	39.4	1
1987 NYJ	12	64	2444	38.2	0
NFL Total	205	**1154**	47567	41.2	2

JACK JENNINGS Jennings, Jack Weldon 6'4", 245 **T**
Col: Ohio State *HS:* North [Columbus, OH] B: 2/23/1926, Columbus, OH D: 6/11/1993, Rocky River, OH *Drafted:* 1950 Round 2 ChiC
1950 ChiC: 12 G. **1951** ChiC: 11 G; KR 1-16 16.0. **1952** ChiC: 7 G. **1953** ChiC: 12 G; KR 1-15 15.0. **1954** ChiC: 12 G; KR 1-10 10.0. **1955** ChiC: 12 G. **1956** ChiC: 12 G. **1957** ChiC: 12 G. **Total:** 90 G; KR 3-41 13.7.

JIM JENNINGS Jennings, James Benton 6'3", 195 **DE-OE**
Col: Missouri *HS:* Crystal City [MO] B: 11/14/1933, Crystal City, MO *Drafted:* 1955 Round 26 GB
1955 GB: 4 G.

KEITH JENNINGS Jennings, Keith O'Neal 6'4", 262 **TE**
Col: Clemson *HS:* Summerville [SC] B: 5/19/1966, Summerville, SC
Drafted: 1989 Round 5 Dal

		Receiving				
Year Team	G	Rec	Yds	Avg	TD	Fum
1989 Dal	10	6	47	7.8	0	0
1991 ChiB	10	8	109	13.6	0	0
1992 ChiB	16	23	264	11.5	1	0
1993 ChiB	13	14	150	10.7	0	1
1994 ChiB	9	11	75	6.8	3	0
1995 ChiB	16	25	217	8.7	6	0
1996 ChiB	6	6	56	9.3	0	0
1997 ChiB	12	14	164	11.7	0	0
NFL Total	92	107	1082	10.1	10	1

LOU JENNINGS Jennings, Louis Walter 6'3", 230 **C-OE**
(AKA Hawk Feather) *Col:* Haskell Indian; Centenary *HS:* Muskogee [OK]; Terrell Prep [TX] B: 1904 Deceased
1929 Prov: 2 G; Scor 4, 4 XK. **1930** Port: 9 G. **Total:** 11 G.

RICK JENNINGS Jennings, Richard T II 5'9", 180 **RB-WR**
Col: Maryland *HS:* Calvin Coolidge [Washington, DC] B: 4/17/1953, Houston, TX *Drafted:* 1976 Round 11 Oak
1976 Oak: 11 G; Rush 10-22 2.2; Rec 1-10 10.0; PR 1-20 20.0; KR 16-417 26.1. **1977** TB-SF-Oak: 5 G; PR 12-71 5.9; KR 7-153 21.9; 1 Fum. SF: 3 G; PR 7-32 4.6; KR 3-60 20.0. Oak: 2 G; PR 5-39 7.8; KR 4-93 23.3; 1 Fum. **Total:** 16 G; Rush 10-22 2.2; Rec 1-10 10.0; PR 13-91 7.0; KR 23-570 24.8; 1 Fum.

STANFORD JENNINGS Jennings, Stanford Jamison 6'1", 205 **RB**
Col: Furman *HS:* Summerville [SC] B: 3/12/1962, Summerville, SC
Drafted: 1984 Round 3 Cin

		Rushing				Receiving			
Year Team	G	Att	Yds	Avg	TD	Rec	Yds	Avg	TD
1984 Cin	15	79	379	4.8	2	35	346	9.9	3
1985 Cin	16	31	92	3.0	1	12	101	8.4	3
1986 Cin	16	16	54	3.4	1	6	86	14.3	0
1987 Cin	12	70	314	4.5	1	35	277	7.9	2
1988 Cin	16	17	47	2.8	1	5	75	15.0	0
1989 Cin	16	83	293	3.5	2	10	119	11.9	1
1990 Cin	16	12	46	3.8	1	4	23	5.8	0
1991 NO	5	0	0	—	0	0	0	—	0
1992 TB	11	5	25	5.0	0	9	69	7.7	1
NFL Total	123	313	1250	4.0	9	116	1096	9.4	10

	Kickoff Returns					Tot
Year Team	Ret	Yds	Avg	TD	Fum	TD
1984 Cin	22	452	20.5	0	3	5
1985 Cin	13	218	16.8	0	1	4
1986 Cin	12	257	21.4	0	0	1
1987 Cin	2	32	16.0	0	0	3
1988 Cin	32	684	21.4	**1**	1	2
1989 Cin	26	525	20.2	0	1	3
1990 Cin	29	584	20.1	0	2	1
1991 NO	12	213	17.8	0	1	0
1992 TB	0	0	—	0	1	1
NFL Total	148	2965	20.0	1	10	20

RAY JENNISON Jennison, Raymond Ellis 6'2", 224 **T**
Col: South Dakota State *HS:* Avon [SD] B: 1/19/1910, Oneida, SD
D: 5/13/1990, Bay Pines, FL
1931 GB: 2 G.

DERRICK JENSEN Jensen, Derrick 6'1", 221 **RB-TE**
Col: Texas-Arlington *HS:* Waukegan [IL]; Osawatomie HS [KS]
B: 4/27/1956, Waukegan, IL *Drafted:* 1978 Round 3 Oak
1979 Oak: KR 1-0. **1980** Oak: KR 1-33 33.0 **1** TD. **1982** LARd: KR 1-27 27.0. **1983** LARd: KR 1-0. **1984** LARd: KR 1-11 11.0. **Total:** KR 5-71 14.2 1 TD.

		Rushing				Receiving					Tot
Year Team	G	Att	Yds	Avg	TD	Rec	Yds	Avg	TD	Fum	TD
1979 Oak	16	73	251	3.4	0	7	23	3.3	1	6	1
1980 Oak	16	14	30	2.1	0	7	87	12.4	0	1	1
1981 Oak	16	117	456	3.9	4	28	271	9.7	0	0	4
1982 LARd	9	0	0	—	0	0	0	—	0	0	0
1983 LARd	16	1	5	5.0	0	1	2	2.0	1	1	1
1984 LARd	16	3	3	1.0	1	1	1	1.0	1	0	2
1985 LARd	16	16	35	2.2	0	0	0	—	0	0	0
1986 LARd	1	0	0	—	0	0	0	—	0	0	0
NFL Total	106	224	780	3.5	5	44	384	8.7	3	8	9

GREG JENSEN Jensen, Gregory George 6'3", 266 **C**
Col: No College *HS:* Sauk Prairie [Prairie du Sac, WI] B: 1/23/1962, Saux City, WI
1987 GB: 1 G.

JIM JENSEN Jensen, James Christopher 6'4", 215 **WR-QB-RB**
Col: Boston U. *HS:* Central Bucks West [Doylestown, PA]
B: 11/14/1958, Abington, PA *Drafted:* 1981 Round 11 Mia
1982 Mia: Pass 1-0. **1984** Mia: Pass 1-1 100.0%, 35 35.00 1 TD. **1986** Mia: Pass 2-0. **1989** Mia: Pass 1-1 100.0%, 19 19.00 1 TD. **1990** Mia: Pass 1-1 100.0%, 31 31.00. **1991** Mia: Pass 1-1 100.0%, 17 17.00. **Total:** Pass 7-4 57.1%, 102 14.57 2 TD.

		Rushing				Receiving				
Year Team	G	Att	Yds	Avg	TD	Rec	Yds	Avg	TD	Fum
1981 Mia	16	0	0	—	0	0	0	—	0	0
1982 Mia	6	0	0	—	0	0	0	—	0	0
1983 Mia	16	0	0	—	0	0	0	—	0	0
1984 Mia	16	0	0	—	0	13	139	10.7	2	0
1985 Mia	16	0	0	—	0	1	4	4.0	1	0
1986 Mia	16	0	0	—	0	5	50	10.0	1	0
1987 Mia	12	4	18	4.5	0	26	221	8.5	1	1
1988 Mia	16	10	68	6.8	0	58	652	11.2	5	2
1989 Mia	16	8	50	6.3	0	61	557	9.1	6	0
1990 Mia	15	4	6	1.5	0	44	365	8.3	1	1
1991 Mia	16	0	0	—	0	21	183	8.7	2	0
1992 Mia	3	0	0	—	0	0	0	—	0	0
NFL Total	164	26	142	5.5	0	229	2171	9.5	19	4

JIM JENSEN Jensen, James Douglas 6'3", 230 **RB-TE**
Col: Iowa *HS:* Central [Davenport, IA] B: 11/28/1953, Waterloo, IA
Drafted: 1976 Round 2 Dal
1976 Dal: KR 13-313 24.1. **1980** Den: KR 1-5 5.0. **1981** GB: KR 1-15 15.0. **Total:** KR 15-333 22.2.

		Rushing				Receiving					Tot
Year Team	G	Att	Yds	Avg	TD	Rec	Yds	Avg	TD	Fum	TD
1976 Dal	14	0	0	—	0	0	0	—	0	0	0
1977 Den	11	40	143	3.6	1	4	63	15.8	0	1	1
1979 Den	16	106	400	3.8	1	19	144	7.6	1	2	2
1980 Den	14	101	476	4.7	2	49	377	7.7	1	1	3
1981 GB	15	27	79	2.9	0	5	49	9.8	0	1	0
1982 GB	8	9	28	3.1	0	3	18	6.0	1	1	1
NFL Total	78	283	1126	4.0	4	80	651	8.1	3	6	7

JERRY JENSEN Jensen, Jerry Joe 6'0", 235 **LB**
Col: Washington *HS:* Cascade [Everett, WA] B: 2/26/1975, Downey, CA *Drafted:* 1998 Round 5 Car
1998 Car: 10 G; KR 1-9 9.0; 1 Fum.

BOB JENSEN Jensen, Robert Peter 6'2", 218 **DE-OE**
Col: Iowa State *HS:* Albert G. Lane Tech [Chicago, IL] B: 12/29/1925, Chicago, IL *Drafted:* 1948 Round 11 Bos
AAFC **1948** ChiA: 14 G; Rec 20-276 13.8 1 TD; KR 1-10 10.0; 6 Pt. **1949** ChiA: 11 G; Rec 2-14 7.0. **Total:** 25 G; Rec 22-290 13.2 1 TD; KR 1-10 10.0; 6 Pt.

NFL **1950** Bal: 9 G.

LEO JENSVOLD Jensvold, Leo Boyd 5'8", 173 **HB**
Col: Iowa *HS:* Emmetsburg [IA] B: 3/29/1908, Emmetsburg, IA
D: 5/30/1966
1931 ChiB-Cle: 8 G. ChiB: 1 G. Cle: 7 G. **Total:** 8 G.

LUTHER JERALDS Jeralds, Luther Reginald 6'3", 235 **DE**
Col: North Carolina Central *HS:* E.E. Smith [Fayetteville, NC]
B: 8/20/1938, Roberson Co., NC
1961 DalT: 9 G.

MARK JERUE Jerue, Mark Darrell 6'3", 229 **LB**
Col: Washington *HS:* Mercer Island [WA] B: 1/15/1960, Seattle, WA
Drafted: 1982 Round 5 NYJ
1983 LARm: 16 G. **1984** LARm: 16 G. **1985** LARm: 16 G. **1986** LARm: 16 G; Int 2-23 1 TD; 6 Pt; 1 Fum. **1987** LARm: 4 G. **1988** LARm: 12 G; Int 1-0. **1989** LARm: 6 G; 0.5 Sac. **Total:** 86 G; Int 3-23 1 TD; 6 Pt; 1 Fum; 0.5 Sac.

TRAVIS JERVEY Jervey, Travis Richard 6'0", 222 **RB**
(Flash) *Col:* The Citadel *HS:* Wando [Mount Pleasant, SC]
B: 5/5/1972, Columbia, SC *Drafted:* 1995 Round 5 GB
1995 GB: KR 8-165 20.6. **1996** GB: KR 1-17 17.0. **1998** GB: Rec 9-33 3.7. **Total:** Rec 9-33 3.7; KR 9-182 20.2.

		Rushing				
Year Team	G	Att	Yds	Avg	TD	Fum
1995 GB	16	0	0	—	0	0
1996 GB	16	26	106	4.1	0	4
1997 GB	16	0	0	—	0	0
1998 GB	8	83	325	3.9	1	0
NFL Total	56	109	431	4.0	1	4

ERNIE JESSEN Jessen, Ernest Robert 6'1", 250 **T**
Col: Iowa *HS:* Waseca [MN] B: 5/1/1905, Dickinson, ND
D: 9/23/1987, Cedar Rapids, IA
1931 Cle: 8 G.

RON JESSIE Jessie, Ronald Ray 6′0″, 185 **WR**
Col: Imperial Valley Coll. CA (J.C.); Kansas *HS:* Yuma [AZ]
B: 2/4/1948, Yuma, AZ *Drafted:* 1971 Round 8 Dal
1971 Det: Rush 1-0; Scor 1 Saf. **1972** Det: Pass 1-0. **1973** Det: Rush 5-31 6.2 1 TD. **1974** Det: Rush 6-17 2.8 1 TD. **1975** LARm: Rush 2-15 7.5. **1976** LARm: Rush 4-37 9.3. **1980** Buf: Rush 1-(-9) -9.0. **Total:** Pass 1-0; Rush 19-91 4.8 2 TD; Scor 1 Saf.

		Receiving				Kickoff Returns					Tot
Year Team	G	Rec	Yds	Avg	TD	Ret	Yds	Avg	TD	Fum	TD
1971 Det	14	4	87	21.8	0	16	470	29.4	**2**	3	2
1972 Det	14	24	424	17.7	4	23	558	24.3	0	2	4
1973 Det	14	20	364	18.2	3	6	154	25.7	0	1	4
1974 Det	12	54	761	14.1	3	2	55	27.5	0	3	4
1975 LARm	14	41	547	13.3	3	0	0	—	0	0	3
1976 LARm	14	34	779	22.9	6	0	0	—	0	1	6
1977 LARm	3	9	139	15.4	0	0	0	—	0	0	0
1978 LARm	16	49	752	15.3	4	0	0	—	0	0	4
1979 LARm	6	11	169	15.4	2	0	0	—	0	0	2
1980 Buf	16	4	56	14.0	1	0	0	—	0	0	1
1981 Buf	15	15	200	13.3	0	0	0	—	0	0	0
NFL Total	138	265	4278	16.1	26	47	1237	26.3	2	10	30

TIM JESSIE Jessie, Timothy LaWayne 5′11″, 190 **RB**
Col: Auburn *HS:* Opp [AL] B: 3/1/1963, Opp, AL *Drafted:* 1987 Round 11 ChiB
1987 Was: 3 G; Rush 10-37 3.7 1 TD; Rec 1-8 8.0; KR 4-73 18.3; 6 Pt.

BILL JESSUP Jessup, William Dean 6′1″, 195 **OE-FL**
(Rocky) *Col:* Long Beach City Coll. CA (J.C.); USC *HS:* Long Beach Polytechnic [CA] B: 3/17/1929, Wray, CO *Drafted:* 1951 Round 11 SF
1954 SF: Rush 1-(-5) -5.0. **1957** SF: KR 1-8 8.0. **1958** SF: Pass 1-0, 1 Int; PR 2-0. **Total:** Pass 1-0, 1 Int; Rush 1-(-5) -5.0; PR 2-0; KR 1-8 8.0.

		Receiving				Punting			
Year Team	G	Rec	Yds	Avg	TD	Punts	Yds	Avg	Fum
1951 SF	10	7	99	14.1	1	0	0	—	0
1952 SF	4	6	108	18.0	1	0	0	—	0
1954 SF	12	30	565	18.8	3	0	0	—	2
1956 SF	3	2	7	3.5	0	14	563	40.2	0
1957 SF	12	2	29	14.5	0	38	1656	43.6	0
1958 SF	12	5	66	13.2	1	23	856	37.2	0
1960 Den	9	9	120	13.3	1	0	0	—	0
NFL Total	62	61	994	16.3	7	75	3075	41.0	2

TONY JETER Jeter, Anthony John 6′3″, 223 **TE**
Col: Nebraska *HS:* Weir [Weirton, WV] B: 9/8/1944, Steubenville, OH *Drafted:* 1966 Round 3 GB
1966 Pit: 9 G; Rec 2-18 9.0. **1968** Pit: 2 G; Rec 1-9 9.0. **Total:** 11 G; Rec 3-27 9.0.

GENE JETER Jeter, Eugene 6′3″, 235 **LB**
(Bama Red) *Col:* Arkansas-Pine Bluff *HS:* Booker T. Washington [Montgomery, AL] B: 2/9/1942, Montgomery, AL *Drafted:* 1965 Round 10 Den
1965 Den: 14 G. **1966** Den: 14 G. **1967** Den: 2 G. **Total:** 30 G.

GARY JETER Jeter, Gary Michael 6′4″, 259 **DE-DT**
Col: USC *HS:* Cathedral Latin [Cleveland, OH] B: 1/24/1955, Weirton, WV *Drafted:* 1977 Round 1 NYG
1977 NYG: 14 G. **1978** NYG: 13 G. **1979** NYG: 16 G. **1980** NYG: 16 G. **1981** NYG: 12 G. **1982** NYG: 4 G. **1983** LARm: 16 G; 6.5 Sac. **1984** LARm: 5 G; 1 Sac. **1985** LARm: 16 G; 11 Sac. **1986** LARm: 15 G; Scor **1** Saf; 2 Pt; 8 Sac. **1987** LARm: 12 G; 7 Sac. **1988** LARm: 15 G; 11.5 Sac. **1989** NE: 14 G; 7 Sac. **Total:** 168 G; Scor 1 Saf; 2 Pt; 52.0 Sac.

PERRY JETER Jeter, Perry 5′7″, 178 **HB**
Col: San Bernardino Valley Coll. CA (J.C.); Cal Poly-S.L.O. *HS:* Steubenville [OH] B: 5/17/1931, Brevard, NC *Drafted:* 1955 Round 26 ChiB
1956 ChiB: Pass 1-0; Rec 5-52 10.4; PR 6-66 11.0 **1** TD; KR 5-105 21.0. **1957** ChiB: Rec 2-9 4.5; PR 2-3 1.5; KR 3-62 20.7. **Total:** Pass 1-0; Rec 7-61 8.7; PR 8-69 8.6 1 TD; KR 8-167 20.9.

		Rushing					Tot
Year Team	G	Att	Yds	Avg	TD	Fum	TD
1956 ChiB	7	60	316	5.3	2	2	3
1957 ChiB	9	10	11	1.1	0	2	0
NFL Total	16	70	327	4.7	2	4	3

BOB JETER Jeter, Robert DeLayafette Jr. 6′1″, 200 **DB-WR**
Col: Iowa *HS:* Dunbar [Weirton, WV]; Weir HS [Weirton, WV] B: 5/9/1937, Union, SC *Drafted:* 1960 Round 2 GB
1963 GB: Rec 1-2 2.0. **1964** GB: Rec 1-23 23.0. **Total:** Rec 2-25 12.5.

		Interceptions		
Year Team	G	Int	Yds	TD
1963 GB	13	0	0	0
1964 GB	13	0	0	0
1965 GB	13	1	21	0
1966 GB	14	5	142	**2**
1967 GB	14	8	78	0
1968 GB	12	3	35	0
1969 GB	14	3	30	0
1970 GB	14	3	27	0
1971 ChiB	9	1	0	0
1972 ChiB	10	2	0	0
1973 ChiB	13	0	0	0
NFL Total	139	26	333	2

TOMMY JETER Jeter, Thomas Melvin 6′5″, 285 **DT**
Col: Texas *HS:* Deer Park [TX] B: 9/20/1969, Nacogdoches, TX *Drafted:* 1992 Round 3 Phi
1992 Phi: 15 G. **1993** Phi: 7 G. **1994** Phi: 14 G; 1 Sac. **1996** Car: 1 G. **Total:** 37 G; 1 Sac.

CLIFF JETMORE Jetmore, Clifford **WB**
Col: No College B: 5/14/1895, Jackson Twp., Blackford Co., IN Deceased
1923 Tol: 1 G.

JAMES JETT Jett, James Sherman 5′10″, 165 **WR**
Col: West Virginia *HS:* Jefferson [Shenandoah Junction, WV] B: 12/28/1970, Charleston, WV
1993 LARd: Rush 1-0. **1998** Oak: Rush 1-3 3.0. **Total:** Rush 2-3 1.5.

		Receiving				
Year Team	G	Rec	Yds	Avg	TD	Fum
1993 LARd	16	33	771	**23.4**	3	1
1994 LARd	16	15	253	16.9	0	0
1995 Oak	16	13	179	13.8	1	1
1996 Oak	16	43	601	14.0	4	0
1997 Oak	16	46	804	17.5	12	2
1998 Oak	16	45	882	19.6	6	0
NFL Total	96	195	3490	17.9	26	4

JOHN JETT Jett, John 6′0″, 196 **P**
Col: East Carolina *HS:* Northumberland [Heathsville, VA] B: 11/11/1968, Richmond, VA
1996 Dal: Rush 1-(-23) -23.0. **1998** Det: Pass 1-0. **Total:** Pass 1-0; Rush 1-(-23) -23.0.

		Punting		
Year Team	G	Punts	Yds	Avg
1993 Dal	16	56	2342	41.8
1994 Dal	16	70	2935	41.9
1995 Dal	16	53	2166	40.9
1996 Dal	16	74	3150	42.6
1997 Det	16	84	3576	42.6
1998 Det	14	66	2892	43.8
NFL Total	94	403	17061	42.3

JOHN JETT Jett, John 6′7″, 225 **OE-DE**
Col: Wake Forest *HS:* West Union [WV] B: 2/9/1918, Canton, WV D: 8/3/1975 *Drafted:* 1941 Round 7 Det
1941 Det: 5 G; Rec 4-50 12.5; KR 2-24 12.0.

PAUL JETTON Jetton, Paul Ray 6′4″, 295 **OG-C**
Col: Texas *HS:* Jersey Village [Houston, TX] B: 10/6/1964, Houston, TX *Drafted:* 1988 Round 6 Cin
1989 Cin: 5 G. **1990** Cin: 15 G. **1991** Cin: 8 G. **1992** NO: 2 G. **Total:** 30 G.

BOB JEWETT Jewett, Robert Gary 6′2″, 198 **OE**
Col: Michigan State *HS:* Mason [MI] B: 11/14/1934, Mason, MI *Drafted:* 1958 Round 5 ChiB
1958 ChiB: 12 G; Rec 15-192 12.8 1 TD; 6 Pt.

DAN JIGGETTS Jiggetts, Daniel Marcellus 6′4″, 274 **OT-OG**
Col: Harvard *HS:* Westhampton Beach [NY] B: 3/10/1954, Brooklyn, NY *Drafted:* 1976 Round 6 ChiB
1976 ChiB: 14 G. **1977** ChiB: 12 G. **1978** ChiB: 16 G. **1979** ChiB: 16 G. **1980** ChiB: 15 G. **1981** ChiB: 16 G. **1982** ChiB: 9 G. **Total:** 98 G.

DAN JILEK Jilek, Daniel Douglas 6′2″, 220 **LB**
Col: Michigan *HS:* Sterling Heights [MI] B: 12/3/1953, Cedar Rapids, IA *Drafted:* 1976 Round 4 Buf
1976 Buf: 14 G; Int 2-33. **1977** Buf: 14 G. **1978** Buf: 15 G. **1979** Buf: 15 G. **Total:** 58 G; Int 2-33.

DWAYNE JILES Jiles, Dwayne Earl 6′4″, 242 **LB**
Col: Texas Tech *HS:* Linden-Kildare [Linden, TX] B: 11/23/1961, Linden, TX *Drafted:* 1985 Round 5 Phi
1985 Phi: 10 G. **1986** Phi: 16 G; 2 Sac. **1987** Phi: 9 G; 1.5 Sac. **1988** Phi: 16 G. **1989** Phi-NYG: 10 G. Phi: 1 G. NYG: 9 G. **Total:** 61 G; 3.5 Sac.

A.J. JIMERSON Jimerson, Arthur 6′3″, 233 **LB**
Col: Norfolk State *HS:* Deep Creek [Chesapeake, VA] B: 5/12/1968, Erie, PA *Drafted:* 1990 Round 8 LARd
1990 LARd: 4 G. **1991** LARd: 13 G. **Total:** 17 G.

STEVE JOACHIM Joachim, William Steven 6′3″, 215 **QB**
Col: Penn State; Temple *HS:* Haverford [Havertown, PA] B: 3/27/1952, Philadelphia, PA *Drafted:* 1975 Round 7 Bal
1976 NYJ: 1 G.

BILL JOBKO Jobko, William Kermit 6'2", 224 LB
(Jobo) *Col:* Ohio State *HS:* Martins Ferry [OH] B: 10/7/1935, Bridgeport, OH *Drafted:* 1958 Round 7 LARm
1958 LARm: 9 G. **1959** LARm: 12 G; Int 1-0. **1960** LARm: 12 G; Int 1-7. **1961** LARm: 11 G; Int 1-16. **1962** LARm: 13 G. **1963** Min: 13 G. **1964** Min: 9 G. **1965** Min: 14 G. **1966** Atl: 14 G; Int 2-5. **Total:** 107 G; Int 5-28.

ART JOCHER Jocher, Arthur Hamble 6'1", 205 G
(The Artful Dodger) *Col:* Manhattan *HS:* Belleville [NJ]
B: 10/19/1915, Philadelphia, PA *Drafted:* 1940 Round 9 Bkn
1940 Bkn: 10 G; Rec 1-2 2.0 1 TD; 6 Pt. **1942** Bkn: 11 G. **Total:** 21 G; Rec 1-2 2.0 1 TD; 6 Pt.

JIM JODAT Jodat, James Steven 5'11", 210 RB
Col: Carthage *HS:* Pio Nono [Milwaukee, WI] B: 3/3/1954, Milwaukee, WI *Drafted:* 1976 Round 12 LARm

		Rushing				Receiving			
Year Team	**G**	**Att**	**Yds**	**Avg**	**TD**	**Rec**	**Yds**	**Avg**	**TD**
1977 LARm	14	5	15	3.0	1	1	2	2.0	1
1978 LARm	16	26	100	3.8	0	3	21	7.0	0
1979 LARm	7	6	6	1.0	0	0	0	—	0
1980 Sea	16	155	632	4.1	5	26	190	7.3	1
1981 Sea	12	31	106	3.4	1	4	52	13.0	0
1982 SD	7	3	7	2.3	0	1	0	0.0	0
1983 SD	15	0	0	—	0	0	0	—	0
NFL Total	87	226	866	3.8	7	35	265	7.6	2

	Kickoff Returns					Tot
Year Team	**Ret**	**Yds**	**Avg**	**TD**	**Fum**	**TD**
1977 LARm	5	129	25.8	0	0	2
1978 LARm	22	447	20.3	0	5	0
1979 LARm	2	19	9.5	0	1	1
1980 Sea	0	0	—	0	3	6
1981 Sea	0	0	—	0	4	1
1982 SD	3	45	15.0	0	0	0
1983 SD	3	45	15.0	0	0	0
NFL Total	35	685	19.6	0	13	10

LARRY JOE Joe, Larry Edward 5'9", 190 RB
(AKA Lorenzo Giuseppe) *Col:* Penn State *HS:* Derry [PA]
B: 7/6/1923, New Derry, PA D: 4/1985
AAFC **1949** BufA: 1 G; Rush 2-18 9.0; Rec 2-52 26.0; KR 1-12 12.0.

BILLY JOE Joe, William 6'2", 235 RB
Col: Villanova *HS:* Scott [Coatesville, PA] B: 10/14/1940, Aynor, SC
Drafted: 1963 Round 11 Den
1964 Den: Scor 1 2XP. **1966** Mia: Scor **1** 2XP. **Total:** Scor 2 2XP.

		Rushing				Receiving					Tot
Year Team	**G**	**Att**	**Yds**	**Avg**	**TD**	**Rec**	**Yds**	**Avg**	**TD**	**Fum**	**TD**
1963 Den	14	154	646	4.2	4	15	90	6.0	1	3	5
1964 Den	14	112	415	3.7	2	12	16	1.3	0	2	2
1965 Buf	14	123	377	3.1	4	27	271	10.0	2	3	6
1966 Mia	14	71	232	3.3	0	13	116	8.9	1	3	1
1967 NYJ	11	37	154	4.2	2	8	85	10.6	0	0	2
1968 NYJ	10	42	186	4.4	3	2	11	5.5	0	1	3
1969 NYJ	1	0	0	—	0	0	0	—	0	0	0
NFL Total	78	539	2010	3.7	15	77	589	7.6	4	12	19

GREG JOELSON Joelson, Gregory Gordon 6'3", 270 DE
Col: Willamette; Arizona State *HS:* Marshfield [Coos Bay, OR]
B: 8/22/1966, Roseburg, OR
1991 SF: 4 G.

HERB JOESTING Joesting, Herbert Walter 6'2", 194 FB
(Owatonna Thunder) *Col:* Minnesota *HS:* Owatonna [MN]
B: 4/17/1905, Little Falls, MN D: 10/1/1963, St. Paul, MN
1929 Min: 10 G; Pass 2 TD; Rush 2 TD; 12 Pt. **1930** Min-Fra: 14 G. Min: 9 G; Rush 1 TD; 6 Pt. Fra: 5 G; Rush 2 TD; 12 Pt. **1931** Fra-ChiB: 14 G. Fra: 8 G; Rush 1 TD; 6 Pt. ChiB: 6 G; Rush 1 TD; 6 Pt. **1932** ChiB: 4 G; Pass 2-1 50.0%, 22 11.00; Rush 10-36 3.6. **Total:** 42 G; Pass 2-1 50.0%, 22 11.00 2 TD; Rush 10-36 3.6 7 TD; 42 Pt.

OVE JOHANSSON Johansson, Ove 5'10", 175 K
Col: Davis & Elkins; Abilene Christian *HS:* (in Gothenburg, Sweden)
B: 3/31/1948, Gothenburg, Sweden *Drafted:* 1977 Round 12 Hou
1977 Phi: 2 G; Scor 4, 1-4 25.0% FG, 1-3 33.3% XK.

FREEMAN JOHNS Johns, Freeman III 6'1", 175 WR
Col: Southern Methodist *HS:* S.H. Rider [Wichita Falls, TX]
B: 12/20/1953, Waco, TX *Drafted:* 1976 Round 10 LARm
1976 LARm: 2 G; PR 1-0; KR 2-56 28.0. **1977** LARm: 5 G. **Total:** 7 G; PR 1-0; KR 2-56 28.0.

ED JOHNS Johns, James Edmond 6'0", 175 G
Col: Michigan State; Michigan *HS:* Central [Lansing, MI] B: 2/22/1900
D: 12/1984, Marble Cliff, OH
1923 Cle: 4 G. **1924** Min: 2 G. **Total:** 6 G.

PAUL JOHNS Johns, Paul V 5'11", 173 WR
Col: Tyler JC TX; Tulsa *HS:* S.H. Rider [Wichita Falls, TX]
B: 11/14/1958, Waco, TX
1981 Sea: KR 5-81 16.2. **1982** Sea: Rush 1-(-1) -1.0; KR 3-57 19.0. **1983** Sea: Rush 2-12 6.0. **Total:** Rush 3-11 3.7; KR 8-138 17.3.

		Receiving				Punt Returns					Tot
Year Team	**G**	**Rec**	**Yds**	**Avg**	**TD**	**Ret**	**Yds**	**Avg**	**TD**	**Fum**	**TD**
1981 Sea	16	8	131	16.4	1	16	177	11.1	0	1	1
1982 Sea	9	15	234	15.6	1	19	210	11.1	0	2	1
1983 Sea	11	34	486	14.3	4	28	316	11.3	**1**	1	5
1984 Sea	4	17	207	12.2	1	11	140	12.7	1	2	2
NFL Total	40	74	1058	14.3	7	74	843	11.4	2	6	9

PETE JOHNS Johns, Peter Murray 6'2", 190 DB
Col: Tulane *HS:* Mayfield [OH] B: 8/14/1945, Cleveland, OH
Drafted: 1967 Round 5 Hou
1967 Hou: 13 G. **1968** Hou: 9 G. **Total:** 22 G.

AL JOHNSON Johnson, Albert Alphonso 6'0", 200 RB-DB
Col: Cincinnati *HS:* Frederick Douglass [Baltimore, MD] B: 6/17/1950, Baltimore, MD
1972 Hou: 14 G; Rush 11-13 1.2; Rec 6-24 4.0; PR 2-0; KR 7-154 22.0; 2 Fum. **1973** Hou: 5 G; Rush 1-(-3) -3.0. **1974** Hou: 14 G; KR 1-14 14.0. **1976** Hou: 14 G; KR 8-150 18.8. **1977** Hou: 14 G. **1978** Hou: 7 G. **Total:** 68 G; Rush 12-10 0.8; Rec 6-24 4.0; PR 2-0; KR 16-318 19.9; 2 Fum.

BERT JOHNSON Johnson, Albert Edward 6'0", 212 HB-P
(Man O' War) *Col:* Kentucky B: 2/18/1912, Ashland, KY
D: 8/10/1993, Lexington, KY *Drafted:* 1937 Round 5 Bkn
1937 Bkn: Rec 1-3 3.0. **1939** ChiB-ChiC: Rec 1-2 2.0; Punt 14-511 36.5. ChiC: Rec 1-2 2.0; Punt 14-511 36.5. **1940** ChiC: Rec 2-52 26.0; Int 2-49; Punt 1-19 19.0. **1941** ChiC: Rec 4-90 22.5 1 TD; KR 1-15 15.0; Int 1-30. **1942** Phi: Rec 9-123 13.7 2 TD; KR 2-40 20.0. **Total:** Rec 17-270 15.9 3 TD; KR 3-55 18.3; Int 3-79; Punt 15-530 35.3.

		Passing							
Year Team	**G**	**Att**	**Comp**	**Comp%**	**Yds**	**YPA**	**TD**	**Int**	**Rating**
1937 Bkn	10	11	0	0.0	0	0.00	0	1	1.7
1938 ChiB	9	2	1	50.0	4	2.00	0	0	56.3
1939 ChiB-ChiC	10	40	14	35.0	208	5.20	0	5	13.3
1939 ChiB	1	0	0	—	0	—	0	0	—
1939 ChiC	9	40	14	35.0	208	5.20	0	5	13.3
1940 ChiC	10	1	1	100.0	25	25.00	0	0	118.8
1941 ChiC	10	0	0	—	0	—	0	0	—
1942 Phi	7	0	0	—	0	—	0	0	—
NFL Total	56	54	16	29.6	237	4.39	0	6	5.8

	Rushing				Tot
Year Team	**Att**	**Yds**	**Avg**	**TD**	**TD**
1937 Bkn	41	59	1.4	0	0
1938 ChiB	37	138	3.7	2	2
1939 ChiB-ChiC	38	95	2.5	0	0
1939 ChiB	3	4	1.3	0	0
1939 ChiC	35	91	2.6	0	0
1940 ChiC	6	15	2.5	0	0
1941 ChiC	3	7	2.3	0	1
1942 Phi	27	54	2.0	0	2
NFL Total	152	368	2.4	2	5

ALEX JOHNSON Johnson, Alex Dexter 5'9", 167 WR
Col: Miami (Fla.) *HS:* Homestead [FL] B: 8/18/1968, Miami, FL
Drafted: 1991 Round 12 Hou
1991 Hou: 5 G.

ALONZO JOHNSON Johnson, Alonzo 5'11", 183 WR
(A.J.) *Col:* Central State (Ohio) *HS:* Mattie T. Blount [Prichard, AL]
B: 4/18/1973
1998 NO: 1 G.

ALONZO JOHNSON Johnson, Alonzo Al 6'3", 222 LB
Col: Florida *HS:* Rutherford [Panama City, FL] B: 4/4/1963, Panama City, FL *Drafted:* 1986 Round 2 Phi
1986 Phi: 15 G; Int 3-6; 1 Sac. **1987** Phi: 3 G; PR 1-0; 1 Fum. **Total:** 18 G; PR 1-0; Int 3-6; 1 Fum; 1 Sac.

ANDY JOHNSON Johnson, Anderson Sidney 6'0", 204 RB
Col: Georgia *HS:* Athens [GA] B: 10/18/1952, Athens, GA
Drafted: 1974 Round 5 NE
1975 NE: PR 6-60 10.0. **1976** NE: Pass 2-0. **1978** NE: Pass 2-0. **1981** NE: Pass 9-7 77.8%, 194 21.56 4 TD 1 Int. **Total:** Pass 13-7 53.8%, 194 14.92 4 TD 1 Int; PR 6-60 10.0.

		Rushing				Receiving			
Year Team	**G**	**Att**	**Yds**	**Avg**	**TD**	**Rec**	**Yds**	**Avg**	**TD**
1974 NE	14	2	-4	-2.0	0	8	147	18.4	0
1975 NE	14	117	488	4.2	3	26	294	11.3	1
1976 NE	14	169	699	4.1	6	29	343	11.8	4
1978 NE	15	147	675	4.6	3	26	267	10.3	0
1979 NE	5	43	132	3.1	1	9	68	7.6	0

1980 NE	16	11	26	2.4	0	24	259	10.8	3
1981 NE	16	2	1	0.5	0	39	429	11.0	1
NFL Total	94	491	2017	4.1	13	161	1807	11.2	9

	Kickoff Returns					Tot
Year Team	**Ret**	**Yds**	**Avg**	**TD**	**Fum**	**TD**
1974 NE	15	303	20.2	0	1	0
1975 NE	10	188	18.8	0	4	4
1976 NE	0	0	—	0	5	10
1978 NE	0	0	—	0	4	3
1979 NE	0	0	—	0	0	1
1980 NE	0	0	—	0	0	3
1981 NE	3	53	17.7	0	1	1
NFL Total	28	544	19.4	0	15	22

ANDRE JOHNSON Johnson, Andre T 6′5″, 314 **OT**
Col: Penn State *HS:* Southampton [NY] B: 8/25/1973, Southampton, NY *Drafted:* 1996 Round 1 Was
1997 Det: Postseason only. **1998** Det: 3 G.

ANTHONY JOHNSON Johnson, Anthony Scott 6′0″, 225 **RB**
Col: Notre Dame *HS:* John Adams [South Bend, IN] B: 10/25/1967, Indianapolis, IN *Drafted:* 1990 Round 2 Ind
1992 Ind: Pass 1-0. **1993** Ind: Pass 1-0, 1 Int. **1994** NYJ: PR 1-3 3.0. **1997** Car: Scor 1 2XP. **1998** Car: KR 2-12 6.0. **Total:** Pass 2-0, 1 Int; PR 1-3 3.0; KR 2-12 6.0; Scor 1 2XP.

		Rushing				Receiving					Tot
Year Team	**G**	**Att**	**Yds**	**Avg**	**TD**	**Rec**	**Yds**	**Avg**	**TD**	**Fum**	**TD**
1990 Ind	16	0	0	—	0	5	32	6.4	2	0	2
1991 Ind	9	22	94	4.3	0	42	344	8.2	0	2	0
1992 Ind	15	178	592	3.3	0	49	517	10.6	3	6	3
1993 Ind	13	95	331	3.5	1	55	443	8.1	0	5	1
1994 NYJ	15	5	12	2.4	0	5	31	6.2	0	0	0
1995 ChiB-Car	15	30	140	4.7	1	29	207	7.1	0	2	1
1995 ChiB	8	6	30	5.0	0	13	86	6.6	0	2	0
1995 Car	7	24	110	4.6	1	16	121	7.6	0	0	1
1996 Car	16	300	1120	3.7	6	26	192	7.4	0	2	6
1997 Car	16	97	358	3.7	0	21	158	7.5	1	2	1
1998 Car	16	36	135	3.8	0	27	242	9.0	1	3	1
NFL Total	131	763	2782	3.6	8	259	2166	8.4	7	22	15

A.J. JOHNSON Johnson, Anthony Sean 5′8″, 175 **DB**
Col: Southwest Texas State *HS:* Samuel Clemens [Schertz, TX] B: 6/22/1967, Lompoc, CA *Drafted:* 1989 Round 6 Was
1989 Was: 16 G; KR 24-504 21.0; Int 4-94 1 TD; 6 Pt. **1990** Was: 5 G; Int 1-0. **1991** Was: 11 G; 1 Sac. **1992** Was: 14 G; Int 3-38. **1993** Was: 13 G; Int 1-69 1 TD; 6 Pt. **1994** Was: 11 G. **1995** SD: 1 G. **Total:** 71 G; KR 24-504 21.0; Int 9-201 2 TD; 12 Pt; 1 Sac.

ART JOHNSON Johnson, Arthur H 5′11″, 189 **T-G**
Col: Fordham B: 1/14/1896, Duluth, MN D: 4/25/1972, Duluth, MN
1923 Dul: 7 G. **1924** Dul: 6 G. **1925** Dul: 3 G. **1926** Dul: 12 G. **Total:** 28 G.

BARRY JOHNSON Johnson, Barry Wayne 6′2″, 197 **WR**
Col: Maryland *HS:* Herndon [VA] B: 2/1/1968, Baltimore, MD
1991 Den: 4 G; Rec 1-13 13.0.

BENNY JOHNSON Johnson, Benny L 5′11″, 178 **DB**
Col: Johnson C. Smith *HS:* Jones [Orlando, FL] B: 6/29/1948, Fort Valley, GA *Drafted:* 1970 Round 6 Hou
1972 Hou: Int 1-34. **Total:** Int 1-34.

		Kickoff Returns				
Year Team	**G**	**Ret**	**Yds**	**Avg**	**TD**	**Fum**
1970 Hou	14	15	320	21.3	0	0
1971 Hou	10	0	0	—	0	0
1972 Hou	14	13	230	17.7	0	1
1973 Hou	13	0	0	—	0	0
1976 NO	9	0	0	—	0	0
NFL Total	60	28	550	19.6	0	1

BOBBY JOHNSON Johnson, Bobby Charles 6′0″, 191 **DB**
Col: Texas *HS:* La Grange [TX] B: 9/1/1960, La Grange, TX
1983 NO: 16 G; Int 2-80 1 TD; 6 Pt; 1 Fum. **1984** NO: 16 G; Int 1-7. **1985** StL: 11 G. **1986** StL-NO: 11 G. StL: 3 G. NO: 8 G. **Total:** 54 G; Int 3-87 1 TD; 6 Pt; 1 Fum.

BOBBY JOHNSON Johnson, Bobby Lee 5′11″, 170 **WR**
Col: Independence CC KS; Kansas *HS:* Assumption [East St. Louis, IL] B: 12/14/1961, East St. Louis, IL
1986 NYG: Rush 2-28 14.0. **Total:** Rush 2-28 14.0.

		Receiving				
Year Team	**G**	**Rec**	**Yds**	**Avg**	**TD**	**Fum**
1984 NYG	16	48	795	16.6	7	0
1985 NYG	16	33	533	16.2	8	0
1986 NYG	16	31	534	17.2	5	1
NFL Total	48	112	1862	16.6	20	1

BRENT JOHNSON Johnson, Brenton Howell 6′2″, 255 **C**
Col: Tennessee-Chattanooga B: 5/16/1963
1987 ChiB: 3 G.

BYRON JOHNSON Johnson, Byron Eugene 6′1″, 220 **DB**
Col: Baylor *HS:* Waller [TX] B: 10/21/1962, Bryan, TX
1987 Hou: 3 G; 2 Sac.

CARL JOHNSON Johnson, Carl Knud 6′3″, 248 **OT-OG**
Col: Phoenix Coll. AZ (J.C.); Nebraska *HS:* South Mountain [Phoenix, AZ] B: 12/26/1949, Phoenix, AZ *Drafted:* 1972 Round 5 NO
1972 NO: 14 G. **1973** NO: 14 G. **Total:** 28 G.

CARROLL JOHNSON Johnson, Carroll William 5′9″, 165 **OE**
Col: Northwestern B: 2/10/1894 D: 4/6/1974, Oak Brook, IL
1920 Ham: 7 G.

CECIL JOHNSON Johnson, Cecil Ellord 6′2″, 230 **LB**
Col: Pittsburgh *HS:* Miami Jackson [FL] B: 8/19/1955, Miami, FL
1977 TB: 13 G; Int 1-0; 1 Fum. **1978** TB: 13 G; Int 2-5. **1979** TB: 15 G. **1980** TB: 16 G. **1981** TB: 16 G; Int 5-84; 1 Fum. **1982** TB: 9 G. **1983** TB: 5 G. **1984** TB: 8 G. **1985** TB: 16 G; Int 1-12; 1 Sac. **Total:** 111 G; Int 9-101; 2 Fum; 1 Sac.

CECIL JOHNSON Johnson, Cecil Oran 5′11″, 197 **TB-DB-HB**
Col: Paris JC TX; Texas A&M-Commerce *HS:* Talco [TX] B: 9/3/1921, Franklin, TX D: 3/6/1961, Dallas, TX
1943 Bkn: Pass 8-4 50.0%, 16 2.00 1 Int; Rec 9-136 15.1 2 TD; KR 3-68 22.7; Int 1-14; Punt 10-349 34.9. **1944** Bkn: Pass 25-10 40.0%, 193 7.72 2 TD 4 Int; PR 7-102 14.6; Punt 23-981 **42.7**. **Total:** Pass 33-14 42.4%, 209 6.33 2 TD 5 Int; Rec 9-136 15.1 2 TD; PR 7-102 14.6; KR 3-68 22.7; Int 1-14; Punt 33-1330 40.3.

		Rushing			
Year Team	**G**	**Att**	**Yds**	**Avg**	**TD**
1943 Bkn	9	26	38	1.5	0
1944 Bkn	7	30	41	1.4	0
NFL Total	16	56	79	1.4	0

CHARLIE JOHNSON Johnson, Charles 6′3″, 266 **NT**
Col: Tyler JC TX; Colorado *HS:* Columbia [West Columbia, TX] B: 2/17/1952, West Columbia, TX *Drafted:* 1977 Round 7 Phi
1977 Phi: 12 G. **1978** Phi: 16 G. **1979** Phi: 16 G. **1980** Phi: 16 G; Int 3-9. **1981** Phi: 16 G; Int 1-0. **1982** Min: 9 G; 1 Fum TD; 6 Pt; 1 Sac. **1983** Min: 16 G; Int 1-2; 1 Fum TD; 6 Pt; 1 Sac. **1984** Min: 16 G; 4 Sac. **Total:** 117 G; Int 5-11; 2 Fum TD; 12 Pt; 6 Sac.

CHARLES JOHNSON Johnson, Charles 5′10″, 182 **DB**
Col: Grambling State *HS:* Mansfield [LA] B: 5/8/1956, Mansfield, LA *Drafted:* 1979 Round 4 Atl
1979 SF: 4 G. **1980** SF: 16 G; KR 2-10 5.0; Int 1-15; 1 Fum. **1981** StL: 5 G; Int 1-19; 1 Fum. **Total:** 25 G; KR 2-10 5.0; Int 2-34; 2 Fum.

CHARLES JOHNSON Johnson, Charles Adrian 6′1″, 262 **NT-DT**
Col: Maryland *HS:* Southwestern [Baltimore, MD] B: 6/29/1957, Baltimore, MD *Drafted:* 1979 Round 3 GB
1979 GB: 16 G; Int 1-0. **1980** GB: 15 G. **1983** GB: 14 G; 3.5 Sac. **Total:** 45 G; Int 1-0; 3.5 Sac.

CHARLES JOHNSON Johnson, Charles Everett 6′0″, 195 **WR**
Col: Colorado *HS:* Cajon [San Bernardino, CA] B: 1/3/1972, San Bernardino, CA *Drafted:* 1994 Round 1 Pit
1994 Pit: Rush 4-(-1) -0.3; PR 15-90 6.0; KR 16-345 21.6. **1995** Pit: Rush 1-(-10) -10.0; KR 2-47 23.5. **1996** Pit: KR 6-111 18.5; Scor 1 2XP. **1998** Pit: Rush 1-4 4.0; Scor **2** 2XP. **Total:** Rush 6-(-7) -1.2; PR 15-90 6.0; KR 24-503 21.0; Scor 3 2XP.

		Receiving				
Year Team	**G**	**Rec**	**Yds**	**Avg**	**TD**	**Fum**
1994 Pit	16	38	577	15.2	3	2
1995 Pit	15	38	432	11.4	0	0
1996 Pit	16	60	1008	16.8	3	1
1997 Pit	13	46	568	12.3	2	0
1998 Pit	16	65	815	12.5	7	0
NFL Total	76	247	3400	13.8	15	3

CHARLEY JOHNSON Johnson, Charles Lane 6′1″, 200 **QB**
Col: Schreiner Coll.; New Mexico State *HS:* Big Spring [TX] B: 11/22/1938, Big Spring, TX *Drafted:* 1960 Round 10 StL

		Passing							
Year Team	**G**	**Att**	**Comp**	**Comp%**	**Yds**	**YPA**	**TD**	**Int**	**Rating**
1961 StL	4	13	5	38.5	51	3.92	0	2	10.9
1962 StL	11	308	150	48.7	2440	7.92	16	20	65.9
1963 StL	14	**423**	222	52.5	3280	7.75	28	21	79.5
1964 StL	14	**420**	**223**	53.1	**3045**	7.25	21	24	69.4
1965 StL	11	322	155	48.1	2439	7.57	18	15	73.0
1966 StL	9	205	103	50.2	1334	6.51	10	11	65.0
1967 StL	5	29	12	41.4	162	5.59	1	3	31.8
1968 StL	7	67	29	43.3	330	4.93	1	1	57.4
1969 StL	12	260	131	50.4	1847	7.10	13	13	69.5
1970 Hou	10	281	144	51.2	1652	5.88	7	12	59.8

1971 Hou	14	94	46	48.9	592	6.30	3	7	48.7
1972 Den	12	238	132	55.5	1783	7.49	14	14	74.6
1973 Den	14	346	184	53.2	2465	7.12	20	17	74.9
1974 Den	14	244	136	55.7	1969	8.07	13	9	84.5
1975 Den	14	142	65	45.8	1021	7.19	5	12	46.7
NFL Total	165	3392	1737	51.2	24410	7.20	170	181	69.2

	Rushing				
Year Team	**Att**	**Yds**	**Avg**	**TD**	**Fum**
1961 StL	1	-3	-3.0	0	1
1962 StL	25	138	5.5	3	5
1963 StL	41	143	3.5	1	12
1964 StL	31	93	3.0	2	7
1965 StL	25	60	2.4	1	4
1966 StL	20	39	2.0	2	3
1967 StL	0	0	—	0	1
1968 StL	5	-1	-0.2	0	0
1969 StL	17	51	3.0	1	4
1970 Hou	5	3	0.6	0	3
1971 Hou	2	0	0.0	0	2
1972 Den	3	0	0.0	0	4
1973 Den	7	-2	-0.3	0	5
1974 Den	4	-3	-0.8	0	4
1975 Den	10	21	2.1	0	1
NFL Total	196	539	2.8	10	56

CHUCKIE JOHNSON Johnson, Charles Lewis 6′4″, 310 **DT**
Col: Auburn *HS:* 71st [Fayetteville, NC] B: 3/5/1969, Fayetteville, NC
1993 Pho: 5 G.

CHUCK JOHNSON Johnson, Charles Ray 6′5″, 275 **OT**
Col: Texas *HS:* Brazosport [Freeport, TX] B: 5/22/1969, Freeport, TX
Drafted: 1992 Round 4 Den
1992 Den: 16 G.

CHARLIE JOHNSON Johnson, Charles Wilbur 6′1″, 265 **DT**
Col: Louisville *HS:* William H. Spencer [Columbus, GA] B: 9/29/1944, Columbus, GA *Drafted:* 1966 Round 6 SF
1966 SF: 13 G. **1967** SF: 14 G. **1968** SF: 2 G. **Total:** 29 G.

CHRIS JOHNSON Johnson, Christopher T 6′4″, 225 **DB**
Col: Millersville *HS:* Carlisle [PA] B: 12/3/1960, Miami, FL
1987 Phi: 2 G.

CHRIS JOHNSON Johnson, Christopher T'Maul 6′0″, 205 **SAF**
Col: San Diego State *HS:* Crawford [San Diego, CA] B: 8/7/1971, San Diego, CA
1996 Min: 5 G.

CLYDE JOHNSON Johnson, Clyde A 5′10″, 191 **DB**
Col: Kansas State *HS:* Lyndon B. Johnson [Austin, TX] B: 5/22/1970, Austin, TX
1997 KC: 15 G.

CLYDE JOHNSON Johnson, Clyde Elmer 6′6″, 269 **T**
(Big Train; Big John) *Col:* Kentucky *HS:* Ashland [KY] B: 8/22/1917, Ashland, KY *Drafted:* 1943 Round 5 Cle
AAFC **1948** LA-A: 9 G.

NFL **1946** LARm: 11 G. **1947** LARm: 12 G. **Total:** 23 G.

CORNELIUS JOHNSON Johnson, Cornelius Otis 6′2″, 245 **OG**
(C.O.) *Col:* Virginia Union *HS:* Richmond [VA] B: 7/12/1943, Richmond, VA *Drafted:* 1967 Round 8 Bal
1968 Bal: 14 G. **1969** Bal: 14 G. **1970** Bal: 14 G. **1971** Bal: 7 G. **1972** Bal: 13 G. **1973** Bal: 12 G. **Total:** 74 G.

CURTIS JOHNSON Johnson, Curtis Wise 6′1″, 196 **DB**
Col: Toledo *HS:* Morrison R. Waite [Toledo, OH] B: 6/22/1948, Toledo, OH *Drafted:* 1970 Round 4 Mia
1973 Mia: Scor 1 Saf. **Total:** Scor 1 Saf.

		Interceptions		
Year Team	**G**	**Int**	**Yds**	**TD**
1970 Mia	14	3	29	0
1971 Mia	14	2	34	0
1972 Mia	14	3	20	0
1973 Mia	14	2	19	0
1974 Mia	13	0	0	0
1975 Mia	14	4	41	0
1976 Mia	13	1	14	0
1977 Mia	14	4	35	0
1978 Mia	15	3	-2	0
NFL Total	125	22	190	0

DAMIAN JOHNSON Johnson, Damian Curtis 6′5″, 290 **OT-OG**
Col: Kansas State *HS:* Great Bend [KS] B: 12/18/1962, Great Bend, KS
1986 NYG: 16 G. **1987** NYG: 12 G. **1988** NYG: 6 G. **1989** NYG: 4 G. **1990** NE: 16 G. **Total:** 54 G.

DAMONE JOHNSON Johnson, Damone 6′4″, 230 **TE**
Col: Cal Poly-S.L.O. *HS:* Santa Monica [CA] B: 3/2/1962, Los Angeles, CA *Drafted:* 1985 Round 6 LARm

		Receiving			
Year Team	**G**	**Rec**	**Yds**	**Avg**	**TD**
1986 LARm	5	0	0	—	0
1987 LARm	12	21	198	9.4	2
1988 LARm	16	42	350	8.3	6
1989 LARm	16	25	148	5.9	5
1990 LARm	13	12	66	5.5	3
1991 LARm	16	32	253	7.9	2
1992 LARm	4	0	0	—	0
NFL Total	82	132	1015	7.7	18

DANNY JOHNSON Johnson, Daniel 6′1″, 215 **LB**
Col: Tennessee State *HS:* Shelbyville [TN] B: 5/7/1955, Normandy, TN
Drafted: 1978 Round 4 KC
1978 GB: 3 G.

DAN JOHNSON Johnson, Daniel Jerome 6′3″, 240 **TE**
Col: Golden Valley Lutheran Coll. MN (J.C.); Iowa State *HS:* Cooper [New Hope, MN] B: 5/17/1960, Minneapolis, MN *Drafted:* 1982 Round 7 Mia
1986 Mia: KR 1-0. **1987** Mia: KR 2-13 6.5. **Total:** KR 3-13 4.3.

		Receiving				
Year Team	**G**	**Rec**	**Yds**	**Avg**	**TD**	**Fum**
1983 Mia	16	24	189	7.9	4	1
1984 Mia	16	34	426	12.5	3	0
1985 Mia	12	13	192	14.8	3	0
1986 Mia	15	19	170	8.9	4	0
1987 Mia	7	4	35	8.8	2	1
NFL Total	66	94	1012	10.8	16	2

DARRIUS JOHNSON Johnson, Darrius 5′9″, 185 **DB**
Col: Oklahoma *HS:* Terrell [TX] B: 9/17/1972, Terrell, TX
Drafted: 1996 Round 4 Den
1996 Den: 13 G. **1997** Den: 16 G; 1 Fum TD; 6 Pt. **1998** Den: 16 G; Int 2-79; 1 Sac. **Total:** 45 G; Int 2-79; 1 Fum TD; 6 Pt; 1 Sac.

DARYL JOHNSON Johnson, Daryl Evans 5′11″, 190 **DB**
Col: Morgan State *HS:* Richmond [VA] B: 8/11/1946, Richmond, VA
Drafted: 1968 Round 8 Bos
1968 Bos: 14 G; PR 1-5 5.0; KR 3-63 21.0; Int 1-11. **1969** Bos: 14 G; Int 2-23; Scor 1 Saf; **1** Fum TD; 8 Pt. **1970** Bos: 14 G; PR 2-6 3.0; Int 2-51. **Total:** 42 G; PR 3-11 3.7; KR 3-63 21.0; Int 5-85; Scor 1 Saf; 1 Fum TD; 8 Pt.

D.J. JOHNSON Johnson, David Allen 6′0″, 187 **DB**
Col: Kentucky *HS:* Male [Louisville, KY] B: 7/14/1966, Louisville, KY
Drafted: 1989 Round 7 Pit
1991 Pit: 1 Sac. **Total:** 1 Sac.

		Interceptions		
Year Team	**G**	**Int**	**Yds**	**TD**
1989 Pit	16	1	0	0
1990 Pit	16	2	60	1
1991 Pit	16	1	0	0
1992 Pit	15	5	67	0
1993 Pit	16	3	51	0
1994 Atl	16	5	0	0
1995 Atl	13	2	4	0
1996 Atl-Ariz	9	0	0	0
1996 Atl	2	0	0	0
1996 Ariz	7	0	0	0
NFL Total	117	19	182	1

HOSS JOHNSON Johnson, David G 6′4″, 295 **OT**
Col: Alabama *HS:* S.R. Butler [Huntsville, AL] B: 6/8/1963, Huntsville, AL
1987 TB: 1 G.

DEMETRIOUS JOHNSON Johnson, Demetrious 5′11″, 190 **DB**
Col: Missouri *HS:* McKinley [St. Louis, MO] B: 7/21/1961, St. Louis, MO *Drafted:* 1983 Round 5 Det
1983 Det: 14 G. **1984** Det: 16 G; PR 1-0. **1985** Det: 16 G; Int 3-39; 1 Fum; 3 Sac. **1986** Det: 16 G; Int 2-18. **1987** Mia: 3 G. **Total:** 65 G; PR 1-0; Int 5-57; 1 Fum; 3 Sac.

DENNIS JOHNSON Johnson, Dennis Craig 6′3″, 234 **LB**
Col: USC *HS:* Northwestern [Flint, MI] B: 6/19/1958, Flint, MI
Drafted: 1980 Round 4 Min
1980 Min: 12 G. **1981** Min: 16 G. **1982** Min: 9 G. **1983** Min: 16 G; 1 Sac. **1984** Min: 16 G. **1985** Min-TB: 16 G. Min: 8 G. TB: 8 G. **Total:** 85 G; 1 Sac.

DENNIS JOHNSON Johnson, Dennis D 6′3″, 220 **RB-TE**
Col: Mississippi State *HS:* Weir [MS] B: 2/26/1956, Weir, MS
Drafted: 1978 Round 3 Buf
1978 Buf: Rec 10-83 8.3; KR 10-204 20.4. **Total:** Rec 10-83 8.3; KR 10-204 20.4.

		Rushing				
Year Team	G	Att	Yds	Avg	TD	Fum
1978 Buf	16	55	222	4.0	2	2
1979 Buf	3	3	5	1.7	0	0
1980 NYG	2	0	0	—	0	0
NFL Total	21	58	227	3.9	2	2

DENNIS JOHNSON Johnson, Dennis Leroy 6′4″, 260 **DT-DE**
Col: Delaware *HS:* Passaic [NJ] B: 10/22/1951, Passaic, NJ
Drafted: 1973 Round 13 Was
1974 Was: 13 G. **1975** Was: 14 G; Int 1-57. **1976** Was: 13 G; Int 1-2. **1977** Was: 11 G. **1978** Buf: 14 G. **Total:** 65 G; Int 2-59.

DON JOHNSON Johnson, Donald Clifford 6′0″, 205 **C-LB**
Col: Northwestern *HS:* Austin [Chicago, IL] B: 9/14/1920, Chicago, IL
1942 Cle: 1 G.

DON JOHNSON Johnson, Donald Lee 6′0″, 187 **HB**
Col: Bakersfield Coll. CA (J.C.); California *HS:* Bakersfield [CA]
B: 10/31/1931, Bakersfield, CA *Drafted:* 1953 Round 3 Phi
1953 Phi: Rec 12-227 18.9 2 TD; PR 5-14 2.8; KR 4-69 17.3. **1954** Phi: Rec 1-20 20.0; KR 6-152 25.3. **Total:** Rec 13-247 19.0 2 TD; PR 5-14 2.8; KR 10-221 22.1.

		Rushing					Tot
Year Team	G	Att	Yds	Avg	TD	Fum	TD
1953 Phi	12	83	439	5.3	5	3	7
1954 Phi	6	7	16	2.3	0	1	0
1955 Phi	2	3	1	0.3	0	0	0
NFL Total	20	93	456	4.9	5	4	7

DONNELL JOHNSON Johnson, Donnell 6′7″, 310 **DE**
Col: Johnson C. Smith *HS:* Miami Northwestern [FL] B: 12/24/1969, Miami, FL
1993 Cin: 7 G.

EARL JOHNSON Johnson, Earl Jr. 6′0″, 195 **DB**
Col: South Carolina *HS:* Seabreeze [Daytona Beach, FL]
B: 10/20/1963, Daytona Beach, FL *Drafted:* 1985 Round 9 NO
1985 NO: 2 G. **1987** Den: 3 G. **Total:** 5 G.

EDDIE JOHNSON Johnson, Eddie L 6′1″, 220 **LB**
Col: Louisville *HS:* Dougherty [Albany, GA] B: 2/3/1959, Albany, GA
Drafted: 1981 Round 7 Cle
1981 Cle: 16 G; KR 1-7 7.0. **1982** Cle: 9 G. **1983** Cle: 16 G. **1984** Cle: 16 G; Int 2-3; 0.5 Sac. **1985** Cle: 16 G; Int 1-6; 0.5 Sac. **1986** Cle: 16 G. **1987** Cle: 12 G; Int 1-11; 1 Sac. **1988** Cle: 15 G; Int 2-0; 3 Sac. **1989** Cle: 16 G; KR 1-8 8.0. **1990** Cle: 16 G; KR 2-17 8.5. **Total:** 148 G; KR 4-32 8.0; Int 6-20; 5 Sac.

TRE' JOHNSON Johnson, Edward Stanton III 6′2″, 328 **OT-OG**
Col: Temple *HS:* Peekskill [NY] B: 8/30/1971, New York, NY
Drafted: 1994 Round 2 Was
1994 Was: 14 G; KR 0-4. **1995** Was: 10 G. **1996** Was: 15 G. **1997** Was: 11 G. **1998** Was: 10 G. **Total:** 60 G; KR 0-4.

ELLIS JOHNSON Johnson, Ellis Bernard 6′2″, 292 **DE-DT**
Col: Florida *HS:* Wildwood [FL] B: 10/30/1973, Wildwood, FL
Drafted: 1995 Round 1 Ind
1995 Ind: 16 G; 4.5 Sac. **1996** Ind: 12 G. **1997** Ind: 15 G; Int 1-18; 4.5 Sac. **1998** Ind: 16 G; 8 Sac. **Total:** 59 G; Int 1-18; 17 Sac.

ELLIS JOHNSON Johnson, Ellis Edward 6′0″, 195 **HB-WR**
Col: Southeastern Louisiana B: 7/9/1943, Baton Rouge, LA
Drafted: 1965 Round 4 Bos
1965 Bos: 14 G; Rush 19-29 1.5; Rec 4-29 7.3; KR 2-29 14.5; 2 Fum. **1966** Bos: 14 G; KR 2-45 22.5. **Total:** 28 G; Rush 19-29 1.5; Rec 4-29 7.3; KR 4-74 18.5; 2 Fum.

ERIC JOHNSON Johnson, Eric 6′1″, 192 **DB**
Col: Washington State *HS:* Moses Lake [WA] B: 7/23/1952, Ephrata, WA
1977 Phi: 14 G. **1978** Phi: 16 G. **1979** SF: 8 G. **Total:** 38 G.

ESSEX JOHNSON Johnson, Essex L 5′9″, 201 **RB**
Col: Grambling State *HS:* Shreveport [LA] B: 10/15/1946, Shreveport, LA *Drafted:* 1968 Round 6 Cin

		Rushing				Receiving			
Year Team	G	Att	Yds	Avg	TD	Rec	Yds	Avg	TD
1968 Cin	14	26	178	6.8	3	1	33	33.0	0
1969 Cin	12	15	54	3.6	0	1	3	3.0	0
1970 Cin	13	65	273	4.2	2	15	190	12.7	2
1971 Cin	14	85	522	6.1	4	14	258	18.4	2
1972 Cin	14	212	825	3.9	4	29	420	14.5	2
1973 Cin	14	195	997	5.1	4	28	356	12.7	3
1974 Cin	5	19	44	2.3	0	8	85	10.6	1
1975 Cin	12	58	177	3.1	1	25	196	7.8	1
1976 TB	14	47	166	3.5	1	25	201	8.0	1
NFL Total	112	722	3236	4.5	19	146	1742	11.9	12

	Punt Returns				Kickoff Returns					Tot
Year Team	Ret	Yds	Avg	TD	Ret	Yds	Avg	TD	Fum	TD
1968 Cin	22	111	5.0	0	14	266	19.0	0	4	3
1969 Cin	17	85	5.0	0	16	362	22.6	0	2	0
1970 Cin	7	72	10.3	0	3	68	22.7	0	1	4
1971 Cin	3	28	9.3	0	2	40	20.0	0	1	6
1972 Cin	2	7	3.5	0	1	13	13.0	0	4	6
1973 Cin	0	0	—	0	0	0	—	0	7	7
1974 Cin	0	0	—	0	0	0	—	0	1	1
1975 Cin	0	0	—	0	0	0	—	0	2	2
1976 TB	0	0	—	0	13	287	22.1	0	3	2
NFL Total	51	303	5.9	0	49	1036	21.1	0	25	31

EZRA JOHNSON Johnson, Ezra Ray 6′4″, 250 **DE**
Col: Morris Brown *HS:* Green Oaks [Shreveport, LA] B: 10/2/1955, Shreveport, LA *Drafted:* 1977 Round 1 GB
1977 GB: 14 G. **1978** GB: 16 G; KR 1-14 14.0. **1979** GB: 11 G. **1980** GB: 15 G. **1981** GB: 16 G. **1982** GB: 9 G; 5.5 Sac. **1983** GB: 16 G; 14.5 Sac. **1984** GB: 13 G; 7 Sac. **1985** GB: 16 G; 9.5 Sac. **1986** GB: 16 G; 3 Sac. **1987** GB: 6 G; 2 Sac. **1988** Ind: 10 G; 3 Sac. **1989** Ind: 16 G; 8.5 Sac. **1990** Hou: 16 G; 2.5 Sac. **1991** Hou: 2 G. **Total:** 192 G; KR 1-14 14.0; 55.5 Sac.

FARNHAM JOHNSON Johnson, Farnham James 6′0″, 215 **DE**
(Gunner) *Col:* Michigan; Wisconsin *HS:* St. Mary's [Menasha, WI]
B: 6/23/1924, St. Paul, MN
AAFC **1948** ChiA: 8 G; Scor 2, 2-2 100.0% XK.

FILMEL JOHNSON Johnson, Filmel C 5′10″, 187 **DB**
Col: Illinois *HS:* St. Mary's Prep [Orchard Lake, MI] B: 12/24/1970, Orchard Lake, MI *Drafted:* 1994 Round 7 Buf
1995 Buf: 2 G.

PIKE JOHNSON Johnson, Frank Leonard 5′11″, 185 **T-G**
Col: Washington & Lee *HS:* Everett [MA] B: 9/30/1896, Javla, Sweden
D: 4/13/1963, Boston, MA
1920 Akr: 10 G. **1921** Akr: 12 G. **Total:** 22 G.

FLIP JOHNSON Johnson, Fulton Frederick 5′10″, 185 **WR**
Col: McNeese State *HS:* Fannett [Hamshire, TX] B: 7/13/1963, Cheek, TX
1988 Buf: PR 16-72 4.5; KR 14-250 17.9. **1989** Buf: PR 1-7 7.0. **Total:** PR 17-79 4.6; KR 14-250 17.9.

		Receiving				
Year Team	G	Rec	Yds	Avg	TD	Fum
1988 Buf	11	9	170	18.9	1	1
1989 Buf	16	25	303	12.1	1	0
NFL Total	27	34	473	13.9	2	1

GARY JOHNSON Johnson, Gary Lynn 6′2″, 257 **DT-NT**
(Big Hands) *Col:* Grambling State *HS:* Mitchell [Bossier City, LA]
B: 8/31/1952, Shreveport, LA *Drafted:* 1975 Round 1 SD
1975 SD: 14 G. **1976** SD: 14 G. **1977** SD: 14 G. **1978** SD: 15 G; Int 1-52 1 TD; 6 Pt. **1979** SD: 16 G; 1 Fum. **1980** SD: 16 G. **1981** SD: 16 G; Int 1-41 1 TD; 6 Pt. **1982** SD: 9 G; Scor **1** Saf; 2 Pt; 4 Sac. **1983** SD: 16 G; 3 Sac. **1984** SD-SF: 16 G; Scor **1** Saf; **1** Fum TD; 8 Pt; 5 Sac. SD: 4 G. SF: 12 G; Scor 1 Saf; 1 Fum TD; 8 Pt; 5 Sac. **1985** SF: 11 G; 4 Sac. **Total:** 157 G; Int 2-93 2 TD; Scor 2 Saf; 1 Fum TD; Tot TD 3; 22 Pt; 1 Fum; 16 Sac.

GENE JOHNSON Johnson, Gene Paul 6′0″, 187 **DB**
Col: Cincinnati *HS:* Charleston [WV] B: 9/18/1935, Clay, WV
D: 8/4/1997, Union Twp., Butler Co., OH *Drafted:* 1959 Round 9 Phi
1959 Phi: 12 G; Int 1-22. **1960** Phi: 11 G; Int 3-34. **1961** Min-NYG: 7 G. Min: 4 G. NYG: 3 G. **Total:** 30 G; Int 4-56.

STAN JOHNSON Johnson, George Stanley 6′4″, 275 **NT**
Col: Tennessee State *HS:* Sandusky [OH] B: 6/18/1955, Sandusky, OH *Drafted:* 1978 Round 2 LARm
1978 KC: 10 G.

GIL JOHNSON Johnson, Gilbert 5′11″, 195 **QB**
Col: Southern Methodist *HS:* John Tyler [Tyler, TX] B: 12/4/1923, Tyler, TX
AAFC **1949** NY-A: 9 G; Pass 36-12 33.3%, 179 4.97 5 Int; Rush 3-21 7.0.

GILVANNI JOHNSON Johnson, Gilvanni Martinni 6′1″, 195 **WR**
Col: Michigan *HS:* Northern [Detroit, MI] B: 9/12/1963, Birmingham, AL
1987 Det: 3 G.

GLENN JOHNSON Johnson, Glenn Murray 6′4″, 263 **T**
(Rocky) *Col:* Arizona State *HS:* Mesa [AZ] B: 6/28/1922, Mesa, AZ
Drafted: 1948 Round 8 LARm
AAFC **1948** NY-A: 9 G.

NFL **1949** GB: 8 G; 6 Pt.

GREGG JOHNSON Johnson, Greggory Da-marr 6'1", 191 **DB**
Col: Oklahoma State *HS:* Ross S. Sterling [Houston, TX]
B: 10/20/1958, Houston, TX
1981 Sea: 16 G; PR 1-16 16.0; KR 13-235 18.1; 1 Fum TD; 6 Pt; 2 Fum. **1982** Sea: 9 G; PR 1-3 3.0. **1983** Sea: 16 G; PR 3-17 5.7; 1 Fum. **1986** Sea: 15 G; 1 Sac. **1987** StL: 8 G. **Total:** 64 G; PR 5-36 7.2; KR 13-235 18.1; 1 Fum TD; 6 Pt; 3 Fum; 1 Sac.

GREG JOHNSON Johnson, Gregory Devon 6'4", 240 **DT-NT-DE**
Col: Florida State *HS:* Leesburg [FL] B: 12/3/1953, Leesburg, FL
Drafted: 1976 Round 5 Phi
1977 Bal-TB-ChiB: 7 G; Int 1-0 **1** TD; 6 Pt. Bal: 2 G. TB: 5 G; Int 1-0 1 TD; 6 Pt. **Total:** 7 G; Int 1-0 1 TD; 6 Pt.

GREG JOHNSON Johnson, Gregory Kent 6'4", 295 **OT**
Col: Oklahoma *HS:* Moore [OK] B: 12/19/1964, Oklahoma City, OK
Drafted: 1988 Round 4 Mia
1988 Mia: 1 G.

HARVEY JOHNSON Johnson, Harvey Paul 5'11", 212 **LB-BB-FB-OG**
(Stud) *Col:* William & Mary *HS:* Bridgeton [NJ]; Staunton Mil. Acad. [VA] B: 6/22/1919, Bridgeton, NJ D: 8/8/1983, Orchard Park, NY
Drafted: 1943 Round 6 Bkn
AAFC **1946** NY-A: 13 G; Rush 16-63 3.9; Rec 2-19 9.5; Scor 54, 6-8 75.0% FG, 36-36 100.0% XK. **1947** NY-A: 14 G; Scor 70, 7-8 87.5% FG, 49-51 96.1% XK. **1948** NY-A: 14 G; Rec 1-6 6.0; Scor 43, 2-7 28.6% FG, 37-37 100.0% XK. **1949** NY-A: 12 G; Int 1-1; Scor 46, 7-15 46.7% FG, 25-25 100.0% XK. **Total:** 53 G; Rush 16-63 3.9; Rec 3-25 8.3; Int 1-1; Scor 213, 22-38 57.9% FG, 147-149 98.7% XK.

NFL **1951** NYY: 12 G; KR 1-4 4.0; Scor 49, 6-14 42.9% FG, 31-31 100.0% XK; 1 Fum.

HENRY JOHNSON Johnson, Henry William 6'1", 235 **LB**
Col: Georgia Tech *HS:* Wrens [GA] B: 3/20/1958, Wrens, GA
Drafted: 1980 Round 7 Min
1980 Min: 16 G. **1981** Min: 16 G. **1982** Min: 9 G. **1983** Min: 5 G. **Total:** 46 G.

HERBERT JOHNSON Johnson, Herbert Lewis 5'11", 182 **WR**
(Junebug) *Col:* Missouri *HS:* Fulton [MO] B: 10/13/1963, Fulton, MO
1987 ChiB: 3 G.

HERB JOHNSON Johnson, Herbert Lorch 5'10", 172 **HB**
Col: Army; Washington B: 7/10/1928
1954 NYG: Rec 10-89 8.9; PR 16-164 10.3 **1** TD; KR 10-251 25.1.

		Rushing					Tot
Year Team	**G**	**Att**	**Yds**	**Avg**	**TD**	**Fum**	**TD**
1954 NYG	11	42	168	4.0	1	2	2

HOLBERT JOHNSON Johnson, Holbert Dwayne 5'9", 180 **DB**
Col: Los Angeles Valley Coll. CA (J.C.); New Mexico State *HS:* Susan Miller Dorsey [Los Angeles, CA] B: 7/14/1960, Los Angeles, CA
1987 LARm: 3 G; Int 1-49.

SMILEY JOHNSON Johnson, Howard White 5'9", 198 **G-LB**
Col: Georgia *HS:* Clarksville [TN] B: 9/22/1916, Nashville, TN
D: 2/26/1945, Iwo Jima
1940 GB: 11 G. **1941** GB: 11 G; Int 1-10. **Total:** 22 G; Int 1-10.

JACK JOHNSON Johnson, Jack Connell 6'3", 198 **DB**
(High Stepper) *Col:* Miami (Fla.) *HS:* Carrick [Pittsburgh, PA]
B: 12/11/1933, Pittsburgh, PA Deceased *Drafted:* 1957 Round 4 ChiB
1957 ChiB: 11 G; Int 4-36; Punt 11-398 36.2. **1958** ChiB: 12 G; Int 1-5; Punt 18-627 34.8. **1959** ChiB: 6 G; Int 1-0; Punt 1-32 32.0. **1960** Buf: 12 G; Int 2-1. **1961** Buf-DalT: 4 G. Buf: 3 G. DalT: 1 G. **Total:** 45 G; Int 8-42; Punt 30-1057 35.2.

BRAD JOHNSON Johnson, James Bradley 6'5", 225 **QB**
Col: Florida State *HS:* Charles D. Owen [Black Mountain, NC]
B: 9/13/1968, Marietta, GA *Drafted:* 1992 Round 9 Min
1997 Min: Rec 1-3 3.0 1 TD; Scor 2 2XP. **Total:** Rec 1-3 3.0 1 TD; Scor 2 2XP.

		Passing							
Year Team	**G**	**Att**	**Comp**	**Comp%**	**Yds**	**YPA**	**TD**	**Int**	**Rating**
1994 Min	4	37	22	59.5	150	4.05	0	0	68.5
1995 Min	5	36	25	69.4	272	7.56	0	2	68.3
1996 Min	12	311	195	62.7	2258	7.26	17	10	89.4
1997 Min	13	452	275	60.8	3036	6.72	20	12	84.5
1998 Min	4	101	65	64.4	747	7.40	7	5	89.0
NFL Total	38	937	582	62.1	6463	6.90	44	29	85.3

	Rushing					Tot
Year Team	**Att**	**Yds**	**Avg**	**TD**	**Fum**	**TD**
1994 Min	2	-2	-1.0	0	0	0
1995 Min	9	-9	-1.0	0	2	0
1996 Min	34	90	2.6	1	5	1
1997 Min	35	139	4.0	0	4	1
1998 Min	12	15	1.3	0	1	0
NFL Total	92	233	2.5	1	12	2

JIM JOHNSON Johnson, James Earl 6'1", 195 **DB**
Col: South Carolina State B: 11/30/1945 *Drafted:* 1968 Round 6 Cin
1969 Cin: 11 G.

JIM JOHNSON Johnson, James Earl 6'2", 187 **DB**
Col: Santa Monica Coll. CA (J.C.); UCLA *HS:* Kingsburg [CA]
B: 3/31/1938, Dallas, TX *Drafted:* 1961 Round 1 SF *HOF:* 1994
1970 SF: Scor **1** Saf. **Total:** Scor 1 Saf.

		Receiving				Interceptions				Tot
Year Team	**G**	**Rec**	**Yds**	**Avg**	**TD**	**Int**	**Yds**	**TD**	**Fum**	**TD**
1961 SF	12	0	0	—	0	5	116	0	0	0
1962 SF	12	34	627	18.4	4	0	0	0	1	4
1963 SF	13	6	63	10.5	0	2	36	0	0	0
1964 SF	14	0	0	—	0	3	65	0	0	0
1965 SF	14	0	0	—	0	6	47	0	0	0
1966 SF	14	0	0	—	0	4	57	1	0	1
1967 SF	11	0	0	—	0	2	68	0	0	0
1968 SF	13	0	0	—	0	1	25	0	0	0
1969 SF	14	0	0	—	0	5	18	0	0	0
1970 SF	14	0	0	—	0	2	36	1	0	1
1971 SF	14	0	0	—	0	3	16	0	0	0
1972 SF	14	0	0	—	0	4	18	0	0	0
1973 SF	13	0	0	—	0	4	46	0	0	0
1974 SF	13	0	0	—	0	3	50	0	0	0
1975 SF	14	0	0	—	0	2	0	0	0	0
1976 SF	14	0	0	—	0	1	17	0	0	0
NFL Total	213	40	690	17.3	4	47	615	2	1	6

JAMES JOHNSON Johnson, James Lenord 6'2", 236 **LB**
Col: Orange Coast Coll. CA (J.C.); San Diego State *HS:* Lake Elsinore [CA] B: 6/21/1962, Los Angeles, CA *Drafted:* 1985 Round 3 Det
1986 Det: 11 G. **1987** SF-SD: 2 G. SF: 1 G. SD: 1 G. **Total:** 13 G.

JASON JOHNSON Johnson, Jason Joseph 6'3", 290 **C**
Col: Kansas State *HS:* Oak Park [Gladstone, MO] B: 2/6/1974, Gladstone, MO
1998 Ind: 14 G.

JASON JOHNSON Johnson, Jason Mansfield 5'10", 178 **WR**
Col: Illinois State *HS:* West Side [Gary, IN] B: 11/8/1965, Gary, IN
1988 Den: 8 G; Rush 1-3 3.0; Rec 1-6 6.0; PR 1-5 5.0; KR 14-292 20.9; 1 Fum. **1989** Pit: 14 G; PR 2-22 11.0; KR 3-43 14.3; 1 Fum. **Total:** 22 G; Rush 1-3 3.0; Rec 1-6 6.0; PR 3-27 9.0; KR 17-335 19.7; 2 Fum.

JERRY JOHNSON Johnson, Jerry 5'11", 195 **WB-TB-FB-BB**
Col: Morningside B: 1895 Deceased
1921 RI: 2 G. **1922** RI-Rac: 8 G; Rush 1 TD; Scor 15, 1 FG, 6 XK. RI: 5 G; Rush 1 TD; Scor 15, 1 FG, 6 XK. Rac: 3 G. **Total:** 10 G; Rush 1 TD; Scor 15, 1 FG, 6 XK.

JESSE JOHNSON Johnson, Jesse 6'3", 185 **DB**
Col: Colorado *HS:* East [Cheyenne, WY] B: 1/10/1958, Fort Collins, CO *Drafted:* 1980 Round 4 NYJ
1980 NYJ: 16 G. **1981** NYJ: 16 G. **1982** NYJ: 9 G. **1983** NYJ: 4 G. **Total:** 45 G.

JIMMIE JOHNSON Johnson, Jimmie Olden Jr. 6'2", 252 **TE**
Col: Howard *HS:* T.W. Josey [Augusta, GA] B: 10/6/1966, Augusta, GA *Drafted:* 1989 Round 12 Was
1992 Det: KR 1-0. **1997** Phi: KR 3-22 7.3. **Total:** KR 4-22 5.5.

		Receiving				
Year Team	**G**	**Rec**	**Yds**	**Avg**	**TD**	**Fum**
1989 Was	16	4	84	21.0	0	0
1990 Was	16	15	218	14.5	2	1
1991 Was	6	3	7	2.3	2	0
1992 Det	16	6	34	5.7	0	0
1993 Det	6	2	18	9.0	0	0
1994 KC	7	2	7	3.5	0	0
1995 Phi	16	6	37	6.2	0	0
1996 Phi	16	7	127	18.1	0	0
1997 Phi	16	14	177	12.6	1	1
1998 Phi	3	2	14	7.0	0	0
NFL Total	118	61	723	11.9	5	2

CURLEY JOHNSON Johnson, John Curley 6'0", 215 **RB-P-TE**
Col: Houston *HS:* Woodrow Wilson [Dallas, TX] B: 7/2/1935, Anna, TX
Drafted: 1957 Round 7 Pit
1960 DalT: KR 1-13 13.0; Scor 14, 0-1 FG, 1 2XP. **1961** NYT: KR 5-84 16.8. **1962** NYT: KR 1-14 14.0. **1963** NYJ: KR 6-77 12.8. **1964** NYJ: Pass 1-0; KR 4-62 15.5. **1966** NYJ: KR 1-4 4.0. **Total:** Pass 1-0; KR 18-254 14.1; Scor 26, 0-1 FG, 1 2XP.

		Rushing				Receiving			
Year Team	**G**	**Att**	**Yds**	**Avg**	**TD**	**Rec**	**Yds**	**Avg**	**TD**
1960 DalT	14	23	43	1.9	1	10	174	17.4	1
1961 NYT	12	1	3	3.0	0	1	32	32.0	0

1962 NYT	14	26	114	4.4	0	14	62	4.4	0
1963 NYJ	14	2	6	3.0	0	0	0	—	0
1964 NYJ	14	6	22	3.7	0	0	0	—	0
1965 NYJ	14	2	3	1.5	0	1	6	6.0	1
1966 NYJ	14	2	24	12.0	0	1	18	18.0	1
1967 NYJ	14	0	0	—	0	0	0	—	0
1968 NYJ	14	2	-6	-3.0	0	5	78	15.6	0
1969 NYG	5	0	0	—	0	0	0	—	0
NFL Total	129	64	209	3.3	1	32	370	11.6	3

	Punting				Tot
Year Team	Punts	Yds	Avg	Fum	TD
1960 DalT	3	110	36.7	1	2
1961 NYT	66	2821	42.7	0	0
1962 NYT	50	1998	40.0	3	0
1963 NYJ	72	3034	42.1	1	0
1964 NYJ	**79**	3261	41.3	0	0
1965 NYJ	72	3260	45.3	0	1
1966 NYJ	62	2633	42.5	2	1
1967 NYJ	65	2734	42.1	0	0
1968 NYJ	68	2977	43.8	1	0
1969 NYG	22	823	37.4	0	0
NFL Total	559	23651	42.3	8	4

JACK JOHNSON Johnson, John Denvil 6′4″, 216 **T**
Col: Utah *HS:* Grantsville [UT] B: 11/28/1909, Grantsville, UT
D: 10/27/1978, Tooele, UT
1934 Det: 13 G. **1935** Det: 10 G. **1936** Det: 11 G. **1937** Det: 11 G; 1 Fum TD; 6 Pt. **1938** Det: 10 G. **1939** Det: 10 G. **1940** Det: 11 G; Rec 1-48 48.0 1 TD; 6 Pt. **Total:** 76 G; Rec 1-48 48.0 1 TD; 1 Fum TD; Tot TD 2; 12 Pt.

JOHN HENRY JOHNSON Johnson, John Henry 6′2″, 210 **FB-HB-DB**
Col: St. Mary's (Cal.); Arizona State *HS:* Pittsburg [CA] B: 11/24/1929, Waterproof, LA *Drafted:* 1953 Round 2 Pit *HOF:* 1987
1954 SF: Pass 2-1 50.0%, 10 5.00 1 TD; KR 2-25 12.5. **1955** SF: PR 1-6 6.0; Int 1-29. **1956** SF: KR 1-23 23.0. **1960** Pit: Pass 1-1 100.0%, 15 15.00 1 TD. **1961** Pit: Pass 2-0, 1 Int; KR 1-11 11.0. **Total:** Pass 5-2 40.0%, 25 5.00 2 TD 1 Int; PR 1-6 6.0; KR 4-59 14.8; Int 1-29.

		Rushing				Receiving					Tot
Year Team	G	Att	Yds	Avg	TD	Rec	Yds	Avg	TD	Fum	TD
1954 SF	12	129	681	5.3	9	28	183	6.5	0	5	9
1955 SF	7	19	69	3.6	1	2	6	3.0	0	0	1
1956 SF	12	80	301	3.8	2	8	90	11.3	0	1	2
1957 Det	12	129	621	4.8	5	20	141	7.1	0	9	5
1958 Det	9	56	254	4.5	0	7	60	8.6	0	3	0
1959 Det	10	82	270	3.3	2	7	34	4.9	1	4	3
1960 Pit	12	118	621	5.3	2	12	112	9.3	1	5	3
1961 Pit	14	213	787	3.7	6	24	262	10.9	1	7	7
1962 Pit	14	251	1141	4.5	7	32	226	7.1	2	5	9
1963 Pit	12	186	773	4.2	4	21	145	6.9	1	5	5
1964 Pit	14	235	1048	4.5	7	17	69	4.1	1	4	8
1965 Pit	1	3	11	3.7	0	0	0	—	0	0	0
1966 Hou	14	70	226	3.2	3	8	150	18.8	0	0	3
NFL Total	143	1571	6803	4.3	48	186	1478	7.9	7	48	55

JOHN JOHNSON Johnson, John Howard 6′5″, 260 **DT**
Col: Indiana *HS:* Hobart [IN] B: 7/5/1941, Gary, IN *Drafted:* 1963 Round 6 ChiB
1963 ChiB: 12 G; KR 1-10 10.0. **1964** ChiB: 14 G. **1965** ChiB: 14 G. **1966** ChiB: 13 G. **1967** ChiB: 14 G. **1968** ChiB: 14 G. **1969** NYG: 4 G. **Total:** 85 G; KR 1-10 10.0.

PAT JOHNSON Johnson, John Patrick 6′1″, 204 **DB**
Col: Purdue *HS:* Potosi [MO] B: 6/10/1972, Mineral Point, MO
1995 Mia: 14 G; 1 Fum TD; 6 Pt.

JOHN JOHNSON Johnson, John Vernard 6′3″, 240 **LB**
Col: Clemson *HS:* La Grange [GA] B: 5/8/1968, La Grange, GA
Drafted: 1991 Round 2 SF
1991 SF: 9 G. **1992** SF: 16 G; Int 1-56 1 TD; 6 Pt; 1 Sac. **1993** SF: 15 G; Int 1-0; 2 Sac. **1994** Cin: 5 G. **1995** NO: 1 G. **Total:** 46 G; Int 2-56 1 TD; 6 Pt; 3 Sac.

JOHNNIE JOHNSON Johnson, Johnnie Junior 6′1″, 185 **DB**
Col: Texas *HS:* La Grange [TX] B: 10/8/1956, La Grange, TX
Drafted: 1980 Round 1 LARm
1980 LARm: PR 1-3 3.0. **1981** LARm: PR 1-39 39.0. **1982** LARm: 1 Sac. **1983** LARm: PR 14-109 7.8; 1 Sac. **1984** LARm: PR 1-3 3.0. **1987** LARm: PR 1-5 5.0. **1988** LARm: PR 2-4 2.0. **Total:** PR 20-163 8.2; 2 Sac.

		Interceptions				Tot
Year Team	G	Int	Yds	TD	Fum	TD
1980 LARm	16	3	102	1	0	1
1981 LARm	16	0	0	0	0	0
1982 LARm	9	1	7	0	0	0
1983 LARm	16	4	115	**2**	1	2
1984 LARm	9	2	21	0	0	0
1985 LARm	16	5	96	**1**	0	1
1986 LARm	16	1	13	0	0	0
1987 LARm	7	1	0	0	0	1
1988 LARm	16	4	18	0	1	0
1989 Sea	3	1	18	0	0	0
NFL Total	124	22	390	4	2	5

JOHNNY JOHNSON Johnson, Johnny Jr. 6′3″, 220 **RB**
Col: San Jose State *HS:* Santa Cruz [CA] B: 6/11/1968, Santa Clara, CA *Drafted:* 1990 Round 7 Pho
1990 Pho: Pass 1-0, 1 Int. **Total:** Pass 1-0, 1 Int.

		Rushing				Receiving					Tot
Year Team	G	Att	Yds	Avg	TD	Rec	Yds	Avg	TD	Fum	TD
1990 Pho	14	234	926	4.0	5	25	241	9.6	0	7	5
1991 Pho	15	196	666	3.4	4	29	225	7.8	2	2	6
1992 Pho	12	178	734	4.1	6	14	103	7.4	0	2	6
1993 NYJ	15	198	821	4.1	3	67	641	9.6	1	5	4
1994 NYJ	16	240	931	3.9	3	42	303	7.2	2	4	5
NFL Total	72	1046	4078	3.9	21	177	1513	8.5	5	20	26

JOE JOHNSON Johnson, Joseph 6′4″, 270 **DE-DT**
Col: Louisville *HS:* Jennings [MO] B: 7/11/1972, Cleveland, OH
Drafted: 1994 Round 1 NO
1994 NO: 15 G; 1 Sac. **1995** NO: 14 G; 5.5 Sac. **1996** NO: 13 G; 7.5 Sac. **1997** NO: 16 G; 8.5 Sac. **1998** NO: 16 G; 1 Fum TD; 6 Pt; 7 Sac. **Total:** 74 G; 1 Fum TD; 6 Pt; 29.5 Sac.

JOE JOHNSON Johnson, Joseph Cooper 6′2″, 195 **OE**
Col: Mississippi B: 9/15/1926
1948 NYG: 11 G; Rec 19-217 11.4 2 TD; 12 Pt.

JOE JOHNSON Johnson, Joseph F 6′0″, 185 **HB-OE-FL**
Col: Boston College *HS:* James Hillhouse [New Haven, CT]
B: 11/3/1929, New Haven, CT *Drafted:* 1953 Round 11 GB
1954 GB: PR 5-38 7.6; KR 4-91 22.8. **1955** GB: PR 1-5 5.0; KR 2-46 23.0. **1957** GB: PR 4-39 9.8. **Total:** PR 10-82 8.2; KR 6-137 22.8.

		Rushing				Receiving				
Year Team	G	Att	Yds	Avg	TD	Rec	Yds	Avg	TD	Fum
1954 GB	12	7	31	4.4	0	10	72	7.2	1	0
1955 GB	12	49	210	4.3	0	9	71	7.9	1	4
1956 GB	11	35	129	3.7	0	28	258	9.2	0	1
1957 GB	12	2	6	3.0	0	7	75	10.7	1	0
1958 GB	6	0	0	—	0	10	176	17.6	1	1
1960 Bos	7	0	0	—	0	11	186	16.9	3	0
1961 Bos	6	0	0	—	0	9	82	9.1	1	0
NFL Total	66	93	376	4.0	0	84	920	11.0	8	6

JOE JOHNSON Johnson, Joseph Pernell 5′8″, 170 **WR**
(AKA Joseph Pernell Howard) *Col:* Notre Dame *HS:* Archbishop Carroll [Washington, DC] B: 12/21/1962, Washington, DC
1990 Was: Rec 3-36 12.0. **1992** Min: Rush 4-26 6.5; Rec 21-211 10.0 1 TD. **Total:** Rush 4-26 6.5; Rec 24-247 10.3 1 TD.

		Punt Returns				Kickoff Returns					Tot
Year Team	G	Ret	Yds	Avg	TD	Ret	Yds	Avg	TD	Fum	TD
1989 Was	15	21	200	9.5	0	21	522	24.9	**1**	2	1
1990 Was	15	10	99	9.9	0	22	427	19.4	0	0	0
1991 Was	2	0	0	—	0	5	83	16.6	0	0	0
1992 Min	15	0	0	—	0	5	79	15.8	0	0	1
NFL Total	47	31	299	9.6	0	53	1111	21.0	1	2	2

KELLEY JOHNSON Johnson, Kelley Antonio 5′8″, 168 **WR**
Col: Los Angeles Valley Coll. CA (J.C.); Colorado *HS:* Carlsbad [NM]
B: 6/3/1962, Carlsbad, NM
1987 Ind: 3 G; Rec 1-15 15.0; PR 9-42 4.7; KR 6-98 16.3; 1 Fum.

KEN JOHNSON Johnson, Kenneth 6′2″, 220 **RB**
Col: Miami (Fla.) *HS:* Miami Jackson [FL] B: 11/27/1956, Miami, FL
Drafted: 1979 Round 11 NYG
1979 NYG: Rec 16-108 6.8 1 TD.

		Rushing				
Year Team	G	Att	Yds	Avg	TD	Fum
1979 NYG	9	62	168	2.7	0	3

KENNETH JOHNSON Johnson, Kenneth 6′0″, 185 **DB**
Col: Mississippi State *HS:* Weir [MS] B: 12/28/1963, Weir, MS
1987 GB: 12 G; Int 1-2; 1 Sac.

KEN JOHNSON Johnson, Kenneth Eugene 6′5″, 253 **DE**
Col: Knoxville *HS:* Stratford [Nashville, TN] B: 3/25/1955, Nashville, TN *Drafted:* 1979 Round 4 Buf
1979 Buf: 3 G. **1980** Buf: 16 G; Scor **1** Saf; 2 Pt. **1981** Buf: 16 G. **1982** Buf: 7 G. **1983** Buf: 16 G; 2 Sac. **1984** Buf: 16 G; 3.5 Sac. **1987** KC: 2 G. **Total:** 76 G; Scor 1 Saf; 2 Pt; 5.5 Sac.

KEN JOHNSON Johnson, Kenneth Lee 6′2″, 203 **DB**
Col: Florida A&M *HS:* Robert E. Lee Inst. [Thomaston, GA]
B: 9/14/1966, Thomaston, GA
1989 Min: 1 G. **1990** Min-NYJ: 8 G. Min: 4 G. NYJ: 4 G. **Total:** 9 G.

KENNY JOHNSON Johnson, Kenneth Ray 5'10", 176 **DB**
Col: Mississippi State *HS:* Moss Point [MS] B: 1/7/1958, Columbia, MS *Drafted:* 1980 Round 5 Atl
1981 Atl: **2** Fum TD. **1982** Atl: 1 Sac. **1984** Atl: 1 Sac. **Total:** 2 Fum TD; 2 Sac.

		Punt Returns				Kickoff Returns			
Year Team	G	Ret	Yds	Avg	TD	Ret	Yds	Avg	TD
1980 Atl	16	23	281	12.2	0	0	0	—	0
1981 Atl	16	4	6	1.5	0	0	0	—	0
1982 Atl	9	0	0	—	0	0	0	—	0
1983 Atl	16	0	0	—	0	11	224	20.4	0
1984 Atl	16	10	79	7.9	0	19	359	18.9	0
1985 Atl	5	0	0	—	0	1	20	20.0	0
1986 Atl-Hou	8	0	0	—	0	0	0	—	0
1986 Atl	7	0	0	—	0	0	0	—	0
1986 Hou	1	0	0	—	0	0	0	—	0
1987 Hou	12	24	196	8.2	0	2	24	12.0	0
1988 Hou	13	30	170	5.7	0	6	157	26.2	0
1989 Hou	16	19	122	6.4	0	21	372	17.7	0
NFL Total	127	110	854	7.8	0	60	1156	19.3	0

	Interceptions				Tot
Year Team	Int	Yds	TD	Fum	TD
1980 Atl	4	49	0	2	0
1981 Atl	3	35	0	1	2
1982 Atl	2	30	0	0	0
1983 Atl	2	57	**2**	1	2
1984 Atl	5	75	0	2	0
1987 Hou	0	0	0	3	0
1988 Hou	1	51	0	1	0
1989 Hou	0	0	0	4	0
NFL Total	17	297	2	14	4

KERMIT JOHNSON Johnson, Kermit DeKoven 6'1", 201 **RB**
Col: UCLA *HS:* Blair [Pasadena, CA] B: 2/22/1952, Los Angeles, CA *Drafted:* 1974 Round 7 SF
1975 SF: KR 6-135 22.5. **1976** SF: Rec 1-11 11.0; KR 4-114 28.5. **Total:** Rec 1-11 11.0; KR 10-249 24.9.

		Rushing				
Year Team	G	Att	Yds	Avg	TD	Fum
1975 SF	11	4	25	6.3	0	1
1976 SF	11	32	99	3.1	1	1
NFL Total	22	36	124	3.4	1	2

KESHON JOHNSON Johnson, Keshon Lorenzo 5'10", 180 **DB**
Col: Fresno City Coll. CA (J.C.); Arizona *HS:* Edison [Fresno, CA] B: 7/17/1970, Fresno, CA *Drafted:* 1993 Round 7 ChiB
1993 ChiB: 15 G. **1994** ChiB-GB: 13 G; Int 1-3. ChiB: 6 G. GB: 7 G; Int 1-3. **1995** ChiB: 12 G. **Total:** 40 G; Int 1-3.

KEVIN JOHNSON Johnson, Kevin Lanier 6'1", 305 **DT**
Col: Texas Southern *HS:* Westchester [Los Angeles, CA] B: 10/30/1970, Los Angeles, CA *Drafted:* 1993 Round 4 NE
1995 Phi: 11 G; **1** Fum TD; 6 Pt; 6 Sac. **1996** Phi: 12 G; 1 Sac. **1997** Oak: 15 G. **Total:** 38 G; 1 Fum TD; 6 Pt; 7 Sac.

KEYSHAWN JOHNSON Johnson, Keyshawn Joseph 6'3", 212 **WR**
Col: West Los Angeles Coll. CA (J.C.); USC *HS:* Susan Miller Dorsey [Los Angeles, CA] B: 7/22/1972, Los Angeles, CA *Drafted:* 1996 Round 1 NYJ
1996 NYJ: Scor 1 2XP. **1998** NYJ: Rush 2-60 30.0 1 TD. **Total:** Rush 2-60 30.0 1 TD; Scor 1 2XP.

		Receiving				Tot
Year Team	G	Rec	Yds	Avg	TD	TD
1996 NYJ	14	63	844	13.4	8	8
1997 NYJ	16	70	963	13.8	5	5
1998 NYJ	16	83	1131	13.6	10	11
NFL Total	46	216	2938	13.6	23	24

LARRY JOHNSON Johnson, Lawrence 6'3", 223 **LB-C-OE-DE**
(Chief) *Col:* Haskell Indian B: 3/28/1909, Odanah, WI
1933 Bos: 10 G. **1934** Bos: 12 G; Rec 2-25 12.5. **1935** Bos: 2 G. **1936** NYG: 5 G. **1937** NYG: 8 G. **1938** NYG: 10 G. **1939** NYG: 4 G. **1944** Was: 5 G. **Total:** 56 G; Rec 2-25 12.5.

LAWRENCE JOHNSON Johnson, Lawrence Wendell 5'11", 204 **DB**
Col: Wisconsin *HS:* Theodore Roosevelt [Gary, IN] B: 9/11/1957, Gary, IN *Drafted:* 1979 Round 2 Cle
1979 Cle: 16 G. **1980** Cle: 2 G; Int 1-3. **1981** Cle: 16 G. **1982** Cle: 8 G; Int 4-17. **1983** Cle: 16 G; Int 2-0. **1984** Cle-Buf: 16 G; Int 1-0. Cle: 6 G; Int 1-0. Buf: 10 G. **1985** Buf: 16 G; Int 1-0; 1.5 Sac. **1987** Buf: 6 G. **Total:** 96 G; Int 9-20; 1.5 Sac.

LEE JOHNSON Johnson, Leland Eric 6'2", 200 **P**
Col: Brigham Young *HS:* McCullough [The Woodlands, TX] B: 11/27/1961, Dallas, TX *Drafted:* 1985 Round 5 Hou
1985 Hou: Rush 1-0. **1988** Cle-Cin: Scor 3, 1-2 50.0% FG. Cin: Scor 3, 1-2 50.0% FG. **1989** Cin: Rush 1-(-7) -7.0; Scor 0-1 XK. **1990** Cin: Pass 1-1 100.0%, 4 4.00 1 TD; Scor 0-1 FG. **1991** Cin: Pass 1-1 100.0%, 3 3.00; Rush 1-(-2) -2.0; Scor 3, 1-3 33.3% FG. **1992** Cin: Scor 0-1 FG. **1993** Cin: Pass 1-0. **1994** Cin: Pass 1-1 100.0%, 7 7.00 1 TD. **1995** Cin: Pass 1-1 100.0%, 5 5.00; Rush 1-(-16) -16.0. **1997** Cin: Rush 1-0. **Total:** Pass 5-4 80.0%, 19 3.80 2 TD; Rush 5-(-25) -5.0; Scor 6, 2-7 28.6% FG, 0-1 XK.

		Punting			
Year Team	G	Punts	Yds	Avg	Fum
1985 Hou	16	83	3464	41.7	2
1986 Hou	16	88	3623	41.2	0
1987 Hou-Cle	12	50	1969	39.4	0
1987 Hou	9	41	1652	40.3	0
1987 Cle	3	9	317	35.2	0
1988 Cle-Cin	15	31	1237	39.9	0
1988 Cle	3	17	643	37.8	0
1988 Cin	12	14	594	42.4	0
1989 Cin	16	61	2446	40.1	0
1990 Cin	16	64	2705	42.3	0
1991 Cin	16	64	2795	43.7	1
1992 Cin	16	76	3196	42.1	0
1993 Cin	16	90	3954	43.9	0
1994 Cin	16	79	3461	43.8	0
1995 Cin	16	68	2861	42.1	1
1996 Cin	16	80	3630	45.4	0
1997 Cin	16	81	3471	42.9	0
1998 Cin	13	69	3083	44.7	0
NFL Total	216	984	41895	42.6	4

LEE JOHNSON Johnson, Leo Daniel 6'1", 200 **WR**
(Swamp Fox) *Col:* Tennessee State *HS:* Phillis Wheatley [Houston, TX] B: 10/1/1944, Houston, TX *Drafted:* 1968 Round 6 SF
1969 SF: 14 G; Rec 4-42 10.5. **1970** SF: 7 G. **Total:** 21 G; Rec 4-42 10.5.

LEON JOHNSON Johnson, Leon 5'11", 185 **E**
Col: Columbia *HS:* Kane [PA] B: 9/30/1906 D: 9/1978, Florence, NJ
1929 Ora: 5 G.

LEN JOHNSON Johnson, Leonard C **BB**
Col: Syracuse B: 11/15/1902 D: 4/1975, New York, NY
1926 Col: 1 G.

LEN JOHNSON Johnson, Leonard L Jr. 6'2", 250 **OG-C**
Col: St. Cloud State B: 1/26/1946, Worthington, MN
1970 NYG: 3 G.

LESHON JOHNSON Johnson, LeShon Eugene 6'0", 205 **RB**
Col: Northeastern Oklahoma A&M (J.C.); Northern Illinois *HS:* Haskell [OK] B: 1/15/1971, Tulsa, OK *Drafted:* 1994 Round 3 GB
1995 GB-Ariz: KR 11-259 23.5. Ariz: KR 11-259 23.5. **1996** Ariz: KR 10-198 19.8. **1997** Ariz: KR 0-26. **Total:** KR 21-483 23.0.

		Rushing				Receiving					Tot
Year Team	G	Att	Yds	Avg	TD	Rec	Yds	Avg	TD	Fum	TD
1994 GB	12	26	99	3.8	0	13	168	12.9	0	0	0
1995 GB-Ariz	5	2	-2	-1.0	0	0	0	—	0	1	0
1995 GB	2	2	-2	-1.0	0	0	0	—	0	0	0
1995 Ariz	3	0	0	—	0	0	0	—	0	1	0
1996 Ariz	15	141	634	4.5	3	15	176	11.7	1	5	4
1997 Ariz	14	23	81	3.5	0	3	4	1.3	0	0	0
NFL Total	46	192	812	4.2	3	31	348	11.2	1	6	4

LEVI JOHNSON Johnson, Levi 6'3", 196 **DB**
Col: Texas A&M–Kingsville *HS:* Roy Miller [Corpus Christi, TX] B: 10/30/1950, Corpus Christi, TX *Drafted:* 1973 Round 3 Det
1973 Det: KR 3-51 17.0. **1974** Det: KR 1-0. **Total:** KR 4-51 12.8.

		Interceptions				Tot
Year Team	G	Int	Yds	TD	Fum	TD
1973 Det	14	5	82	0	1	0
1974 Det	14	5	139	**2**	1	3
1975 Det	14	3	71	0	1	1
1976 Det	14	6	**206**	1	0	1
1977 Det	3	2	51	0	0	0
NFL Total	59	21	549	3	3	5

LONNIE JOHNSON Johnson, Lonnie Demetrius 6'3", 240 **TE**
Col: Florida State *HS:* Miami Senior [FL] B: 2/14/1971, Miami, FL *Drafted:* 1994 Round 2 Buf
1997 Buf: Rush 1-6 6.0. **1998** Buf: KR 3-18 6.0. **Total:** Rush 1-6 6.0; KR 3-18 6.0.

		Receiving				
Year Team	G	Rec	Yds	Avg	TD	Fum
1994 Buf	10	3	42	14.0	0	0
1995 Buf	16	49	504	10.3	1	0
1996 Buf	16	46	457	9.9	0	1
1997 Buf	16	41	340	8.3	2	2
1998 Buf	16	14	146	10.4	2	1
NFL Total	74	153	1489	9.7	5	4

LORNE JOHNSON Johnson, Lorne E 6'2", 195 **FB-LB**
Col: Temple *HS:* Classical [Lynn, MA] B: 4/19/1909, Orlando, FL
D: 3/11/1970, Lynn, MA
1934 Phi: 1 G; Rush 1-0.

MARIO JOHNSON Johnson, Mario Chavez Jr. 6'3", 292 **DT-OG**
Col: Missouri *HS:* Hazelwood Central [Florissant, MO] B: 1/30/1970, St. Louis, MO *Drafted:* 1992 Round 10 NYJ
1992 NYJ: 14 G; 2 Sac. **1993** NE: 6 G. **Total:** 20 G; 2 Sac.

MARK JOHNSON Johnson, Mark Anthony 6'1", 194 **DB**
Col: Cisco JC TX; Western Kentucky *HS:* M.B. Smiley [Houston, TX]
B: 3/20/1964, Houston, TX
1987 Cin: 3 G.

MARK JOHNSON Johnson, Mark Steven 6'2", 240 **DE-LB**
Col: Missouri *HS:* Riverdale [Port Byron, IL] B: 8/14/1953, Moline, IL
Drafted: 1975 Round 12 Buf
1975 Buf: 11 G. **1976** Buf: 13 G. **1977** Cle: 7 G. **Total:** 31 G.

MARSHALL JOHNSON Johnson, Marshall Donell 6'1", 191 **WR-RB**
Col: Houston *HS:* Douglass [Jacksonville, TX]; Jacksonville HS [TX]
B: 11/1/1952, Jacksonville, TX *Drafted:* 1975 Round 4 Bal
1975 Bal: Rec 4-115 28.8 2 TD. **1978** Bal: Rec 1-22 22.0.
Total: Rec 5-137 27.4 2 TD.

		Punt Returns				Kickoff Returns				
Year Team	**G**	**Ret**	**Yds**	**Avg**	**TD**	**Ret**	**Yds**	**Avg**	**TD**	**Fum**
1975 Bal	14	0	0	—	0	7	134	19.1	0	1
1977 Bal	3	0	0	—	0	1	15	15.0	0	0
1978 Bal	15	25	143	5.7	0	41	927	22.6	0	5
NFL Total	32	25	143	5.7	0	49	1076	22.0	0	6

MARVIN JOHNSON Johnson, Marvin L 5'11", 183 **DB-HB**
Col: San Jose State *HS:* Fremont [Sunnyvale, CA] B: 4/13/1927, San Francisco, CA D: 2/1981, Los Gatos, CA
1951 LARm: 9 G; Rec 2-38 19.0. **1952** LARm-GB: 10 G; Int 2-22. LARm: 5 G. GB: 5 G; Int 2-22. **1953** GB: 7 G; Int 4-39. **Total:** 26 G; Rec 2-38 19.0; Int 6-61.

MAURICE JOHNSON Johnson, Maurice Edward 6'2", 242 **TE**
Col: Temple *HS:* Roosevelt [Washington, DC] B: 1/9/1967, Washington, DC
1993 Phi: KR 1-7 7.0. **1994** Phi: KR 1-0. **Total:** KR 2-7 3.5.

		Receiving				
Year Team	**G**	**Rec**	**Yds**	**Avg**	**TD**	**Fum**
1991 Phi	12	6	70	11.7	2	0
1992 Phi	11	2	16	8.0	0	0
1993 Phi	16	10	81	8.1	0	1
1994 Phi	16	21	204	9.7	2	1
NFL Total	55	39	371	9.5	4	2

MELVIN JOHNSON Johnson, Melvin Carlton III 6'0", 198 **DB**
Col: Kentucky *HS:* Xavier [Cincinnati, OH] B: 4/15/1972, Cincinnati, OH *Drafted:* 1995 Round 2 TB
1995 TB: 11 G; Int 1-0. **1996** TB: 16 G; Int 2-24. **1997** TB: 16 G; Int 1-19. **1998** KC: 7 G; 1 Sac. **Total:** 50 G; Int 4-43; 1 Sac.

MIKE JOHNSON Johnson, Michael 6'5", 253 **DE**
Col: Illinois *HS:* South Shore [Chicago, IL] B: 4/24/1962, Chicago, IL
Drafted: 1984 Round 9 Hou
1984 Hou: 16 G; 0.5 Sac.

MIKE JOHNSON Johnson, Michael 6'1", 230 **LB**
Col: Virginia Tech *HS:* DeMatha [Hyattsville, MD] B: 11/26/1962, Southport, NC *Drafted:* 1984 Supplemental Round 1 Cle
1987 Cle: 2 Sac. **1989** Cle: 1 Sac. **1990** Cle: 2 Sac. **1992** Cle: 1 Fum TD; 2 Sac. **1993** Cle: 4 Sac. **1994** Det: 1.5 Sac. **1995** Det: 2 Sac.
Total: 1 Fum TD; 14.5 Sac.

		Interceptions			Tot
Year Team	**G**	**Int**	**Yds**	**TD**	**TD**
1986 Cle	16	0	0	0	0
1987 Cle	11	1	3	0	0
1988 Cle	16	2	36	0	0
1989 Cle	16	3	43	0	0
1990 Cle	16	1	64	1	1
1991 Cle	5	1	0	0	0
1992 Cle	16	1	0	0	1
1993 Cle	16	1	0	0	0
1994 Det	16	1	48	1	1
1995 Det	16	2	23	0	0
NFL Total	144	13	217	2	3

MIKE JOHNSON Johnson, Michael Alan 5'11", 184 **DB**
Col: Kansas *HS:* Garden City [KS] B: 10/7/1943, Denver, CO
1966 Dal: 14 G. **1967** Dal: 14 G; Int 5-88. **1968** Dal: 14 G; Int 3-3. **1969** Dal: 12 G; PR 1-0; KR 1-0; 2 Fum. **Total:** 54 G; PR 1-0; KR 1-0; Int 8-91; 2 Fum.

M.L. JOHNSON Johnson, Michael Lamarr 6'3", 228 **LB**
Col: Hawaii *HS:* Thomas Jefferson [Los Angeles, CA] B: 1/26/1964, New York, NY *Drafted:* 1987 Round 9 Sea
1987 Sea: 8 G. **1988** Sea: 16 G. **1989** Sea: 13 G. **Total:** 37 G.

BUTCH JOHNSON Johnson, Michael McColly 6'1", 187 **WR**
Col: California-Riverside *HS:* Susan Miller Dorsey [Los Angeles, CA]
B: 5/28/1954, Los Angeles, CA *Drafted:* 1976 Round 3 Dal
1977 Dal: Rush 1-(-3) -3.0. **1979** Dal: Rush 1-13 13.0. **1982** Dal: Rush 1-9 9.0. **1983** Dal: Rush 1-0. **1984** Den: Rush 1-3 3.0. **Total:** Rush 5-22 4.4.

		Receiving				Punt Returns			
Year Team	**G**	**Rec**	**Yds**	**Avg**	**TD**	**Ret**	**Yds**	**Avg**	**TD**
1976 Dal	14	5	84	16.8	2	45	489	10.9	0
1977 Dal	14	12	135	11.3	1	50	423	8.5	0
1978 Dal	16	12	155	12.9	0	51	401	7.9	0
1979 Dal	11	6	105	17.5	1	0	0	—	0
1980 Dal	16	19	263	13.8	4	0	0	—	0
1981 Dal	16	25	552	22.1	5	0	0	—	0
1982 Dal	9	12	269	22.4	3	0	0	—	0
1983 Dal	16	41	561	13.7	3	0	0	—	0
1984 Den	16	42	587	14.0	6	0	0	—	0
1985 Den	16	19	380	20.0	3	0	0	—	0
NFL Total	144	193	3091	16.0	28	146	1313	9.0	0

	Kickoff Returns				
Year Team	**Ret**	**Yds**	**Avg**	**TD**	**Fum**
1976 Dal	28	693	24.8	0	5
1977 Dal	22	536	24.4	0	4
1978 Dal	29	603	20.8	0	5
1984 Den	0	0	—	0	1
NFL Total	79	1832	23.2	0	15

MITCH JOHNSON Johnson, Mitchell Allen 6'4", 251 **OT-OG**
Col: Los Angeles State; UCLA *HS:* Centennial [Compton, CA]
B: 3/1/1942, Chicago, IL *Drafted:* 1965 Round 17 Dal
1965 Dal: 12 G. **1966** Was: 14 G; Rec 1-1 1.0; KR 2-22 11.0. **1967** Was: 14 G. **1969** LARm: 14 G. **1970** LARm: 14 G; Rush 1-1 1.0; KR 1-17 17.0. **1971** Cle: 11 G. **Total:** 79 G; Rush 1-1 1.0; Rec 1-1 1.0; KR 3-39 13.0.

MONTE JOHNSON Johnson, Monte Charles 6'4", 239 **LB**
Col: Nebraska *HS:* Lincoln [Bloomington, MN] B: 10/26/1951, Denver, CO *Drafted:* 1973 Round 2 Oak
1979 Oak: **1** Fum TD. **Total:** 1 Fum TD.

		Interceptions		
Year Team	**G**	**Int**	**Yds**	**TD**
1973 Oak	13	0	0	0
1974 Oak	14	1	17	0
1975 Oak	14	1	57	0
1976 Oak	14	4	40	0
1977 Oak	14	2	15	0
1978 Oak	14	1	6	0
1979 Oak	16	1	0	0
NFL Total	99	10	135	0

NATE JOHNSON Johnson, Nathan Elijah 6'3", 244 **DT-OT**
Col: Illinois *HS:* Benton [IL] B: 6/18/1920, Dale, IL
AAFC **1946** NY-A: 14 G. **1947** NY-A: 14 G. **1948** ChiA: 14 G. **1949** ChiA: 12 G. **Total:** 54 G.

NFL **1950** NYY: 11 G.

NATE JOHNSON Johnson, Nathaniel 5'11", 192 **WR**
Col: Charles Stewart Mott CC MI; Hillsdale *HS:* Dixie Hollins [St. Petersburg, FL] B: 5/12/1957, St. Petersburg, FL *Drafted:* 1980 Round 7 Pit
1980 NYG: 16 G; KR 5-89 17.8.

NATE JOHNSON Johnson, Nathaniel James 6'2", 224 **RB**
Col: Texas Southern *HS:* Dunbar [Fort Worth, TX] B: 10/25/1963, Fort Worth, TX
1987 NO: 1 G.

NORM JOHNSON Johnson, Norman Douglas 6'2", 196 **K**
Col: UCLA *HS:* Pacifica [Garden Grove, CA] B: 5/31/1960, Inglewood, CA
1982 Sea: Pass 1-1 100.0%, 27 27.00. **1991** Atl: Punt 1-21 21.0. **1992** Atl: Punt 1-37 37.0. **Total:** Pass 1-1 100.0%, 27 27.00; Punt 2-58 29.0.

		Scoring						
Year Team	**G**	**Pts**	**FG**	**FGA**	**FG%**	**XK**	**XKA**	**XK%**
1982 Sea	9	43	10	14	71.4	13	14	92.9
1983 Sea	16	103	18	25	72.0	49	50	98.0
1984 Sea	16	110	20	24	83.3	50	51	98.0
1985 Sea	16	82	14	25	56.0	40	41	97.6
1986 Sea	16	108	22	35	62.9	42	43	97.7
1987 Sea	13	85	15	20	75.0	40	40	100.0
1988 Sea	16	105	22	28	78.6	39	39	100.0
1989 Sea	16	72	15	25	60.0	27	27	100.0
1990 Sea	16	102	23	32	71.9	33	34	97.1

1991 Atl	14	95	19	23	82.6	38	39	97.4
1992 Atl	16	93	18	22	81.8	39	39	100.0
1993 Atl	15	112	26	27	**96.3**	34	34	**100.0**
1994 Atl	16	95	21	25	84.0	32	32	100.0
1995 Pit	16	141	**34**	**41**	82.9	39	39	100.0
1996 Pit	16	106	23	30	76.7	37	37	100.0
1997 Pit	16	106	22	25	88.0	40	40	100.0
1998 Pit	15	99	26	31	83.9	21	21	100.0
NFL Total	258	1657	348	452	77.0	613	620	98.9

JAY JOHNSON Johnson, Oliver Jay 6′3″, 230 **LB**
Col: Texas A&M-Commerce *HS:* Montclair [NJ] B: 10/8/1945, East Orange, NJ
1969 Phi: 3 G. **1970** Phi: 5 G. **Total:** 8 G.

OSCAR JOHNSON Johnson, Oscar Gotthard 5′10″, 199 **FB**
Col: Vermont *HS:* Lynn English [MA] B: 1901, Lynn, MA Deceased
1924 ChiB: 1 G.

PAT JOHNSON Johnson, Patrick Jevon 5′10″, 180 **WR**
Col: Oregon *HS:* Redlands [CA] B: 8/10/1976, Gainesville, GA
Drafted: 1998 Round 2 Bal
1998 Bal: 13 G; Rec 12-159 13.3 1 TD; PR 1-6 6.0; KR 16-399 24.9 1 TD; Tot TD 2; 12 Pt; 1 Fum.

PETE JOHNSON Johnson, Pete 6′0″, 252 **RB**
(AKA Willie James Hammock) *Col:* Ohio State *HS:* Peach Co. [Fort Valley, GA]; Long Beach HS [NY] B: 3/2/1954, Fort Valley, GA
Drafted: 1977 Round 2 Cin
1977 Cin: KR 1-11 11.0. **Total:** KR 1-11 11.0.

		Rushing				Receiving					Tot
Year Team	**G**	**Att**	**Yds**	**Avg**	**TD**	**Rec**	**Yds**	**Avg**	**TD**	**Fum**	**TD**
1977 Cin	14	153	585	3.8	4	5	49	9.8	0	1	4
1978 Cin	16	180	762	4.2	7	31	236	7.6	0	4	7
1979 Cin	16	243	865	3.6	14	24	154	6.4	1	6	15
1980 Cin	12	186	747	4.0	6	21	172	8.2	1	2	7
1981 Cin	16	274	1077	3.9	12	46	320	7.0	4	4	16
1982 Cin	9	156	622	4.0	7	31	267	8.6	0	1	7
1983 Cin	11	210	763	3.6	14	15	129	8.6	0	2	14
1984 SD-Mia	16	87	205	2.4	12	2	7	3.5	0	1	12
1984 SD	3	19	46	2.4	3	2	7	3.5	0	0	3
1984 Mia	13	68	159	2.3	9	0	0	—	0	1	9
NFL Total	110	1489	5626	3.8	76	175	1334	7.6	6	21	82

PETE JOHNSON Johnson, Peter Thomas Jr. 6′2″, 200 **DB**
Col: Virginia Military *HS:* William Fleming [Roanoke, VA] B: 8/9/1937, Bedford, VA *Drafted:* 1959 Round 3 ChiB
1959 ChiB: 7 G.

PRESTON JOHNSON Johnson, Preston 6′2″, 230 **RB**
Col: Florida A&M *HS:* Boston English [MA] B: 2/18/1945
1968 Bos: 3 G; Rush 2-6 3.0.

KEN JOHNSON Johnson, Ralph Kenneth 6′6″, 265 **DE-DT**
Col: Indiana *HS:* Anderson [IN] B: 3/12/1947, Anderson, IN
1971 Cin: 9 G. **1972** Cin: 11 G. **1973** Cin: 9 G. **1974** Cin: 13 G. **1975** Cin: 14 G. **1976** Cin: 13 G. **1977** Cin: 10 G. **Total:** 79 G.

RANDY JOHNSON Johnson, Randolph Klaus 6′3″, 205 **QB**
Col: Texas A&M–Kingsville *HS:* Sam Houston [San Antonio, TX]
B: 6/17/1944, San Antonio, TX *Drafted:* 1966 Round 1 Atl

		Passing							
Year Team	**G**	**Att**	**Comp**	**Comp%**	**Yds**	**YPA**	**TD**	**Int**	**Rating**
1966 Atl	14	295	129	43.7	1795	6.08	12	21	47.8
1967 Atl	14	288	142	49.3	1620	5.63	10	21	47.8
1968 Atl	8	156	73	46.8	892	5.72	2	10	42.5
1969 Atl	6	93	51	54.8	788	8.47	8	5	89.4
1970 Atl	4	72	40	55.6	443	6.15	2	8	43.7
1971 NYG	5	74	41	55.4	477	6.45	3	3	71.7
1972 NYG	4	17	10	58.8	230	13.53	3	3	103.2
1973 NYG	9	177	99	55.9	1279	7.23	7	8	73.2
1975 Was	8	79	41	51.9	556	7.04	4	10	52.0
1976 GB	3	35	21	60.0	249	7.11	0	1	69.8
NFL Total	75	1286	647	50.3	8329	6.48	51	90	55.1

	Rushing				
Year Team	**Att**	**Yds**	**Avg**	**TD**	**Fum**
1966 Atl	35	142	4.1	4	**13**
1967 Atl	24	144	6.0	1	4
1968 Atl	11	97	8.8	1	5
1969 Atl	11	55	5.0	1	3
1970 Atl	7	21	3.0	0	0
1971 NYG	6	29	4.8	0	4
1972 NYG	9	26	2.9	1	1
1973 NYG	4	24	6.0	1	2
1975 Was	2	10	5.0	0	2
1976 GB	5	25	5.0	1	2
NFL Total	114	573	5.0	10	36

RAYLEE JOHNSON Johnson, Raylee Terrell 6′3″, 265 **DE-DT**
Col: Arkansas *HS:* Fordyce [AR] B: 6/1/1970, Chicago, IL
Drafted: 1993 Round 4 SD
1993 SD: 9 G. **1994** SD: 15 G; 1.5 Sac. **1995** SD: 16 G; 3 Sac. **1996** SD: 16 G; 3 Sac. **1997** SD: 16 G; 2.5 Sac. **1998** SD: 16 G; 5.5 Sac.
Total: 88 G; 15.5 Sac.

RAY JOHNSON Johnson, Raymond Robert 6′1″, 195 **DB-TB-FB**
Col: Denver *HS:* Wheat Ridge [CO] B: 10/16/1914, Denver, CO
D: 8/20/1990, Topeka, KS *Drafted:* 1937 Round 9 Cle
1937 Cle: 2 G; Rush 7-28 4.0. **1938** Cle: 1 G; Pass 5-3 60.0%, 45 9.00 1 Int. **1940** ChiC: 1 G. **Total:** 4 G; Pass 5-3 60.0%, 45 9.00 1 Int; Rush 7-28 4.0.

REGGIE JOHNSON Johnson, Reginald Roosevelt 6′2″, 256 **TE**
Col: Florida State *HS:* Escambia [Pensacola, FL] B: 1/27/1968, Pensacola, FL *Drafted:* 1991 Round 2 Den
1992 Den: Rush 2-7 3.5; KR 2-47 23.5. **Total:** Rush 2-7 3.5; KR 2-47 23.5.

		Receiving				
Year Team	**G**	**Rec**	**Yds**	**Avg**	**TD**	**Fum**
1991 Den	16	6	73	12.2	1	0
1992 Den	15	10	139	13.9	1	0
1993 Den	13	20	243	12.2	1	1
1994 GB	9	7	79	11.3	0	0
1995 Phi	9	5	68	13.6	2	0
1996 KC	11	18	189	10.5	1	0
1997 GB	4	0	0	—	0	0
NFL Total	77	66	791	12.0	6	1

RICHARD JOHNSON Johnson, Richard James 6′1″, 195 **DB**
Col: Wisconsin *HS:* Thornton Twp. [Harvey, IL] B: 9/16/1963, Harvey, IL *Drafted:* 1985 Round 1 Hou
1986 Hou: 1 Sac. **1988** Hou: KR 1-2 2.0. **Total:** KR 1-2 2.0; 1 Sac.

		Interceptions		
Year Team	**G**	**Int**	**Yds**	**TD**
1985 Hou	16	0	0	0
1986 Hou	16	2	6	0
1987 Hou	5	1	0	0
1988 Hou	16	3	0	0
1989 Hou	14	1	0	0
1990 Hou	16	8	100	1
1991 Hou	14	0	0	0
1992 Hou	1	0	0	0
NFL Total	98	15	106	1

DICK JOHNSON Johnson, Richard John 6′4″, 220 **WR**
Col: Minnesota *HS:* Central [Red Wing, MN] B: 1939
1963 KC: 5 G; Rec 2-17 8.5 1 TD; 6 Pt.

RICH JOHNSON Johnson, Richard L 6′1″, 225 **RB**
Col: Illinois *HS:* Canton [IL] B: 5/13/1947, Canton, IL *Drafted:* 1969 Round 3 Hou
1969 Hou: 14 G; Rush 11-42 3.8; Rec 2-17 8.5 1 TD; 6 Pt.

RICHARD JOHNSON Johnson, Richard Lavon 5′7″, 182 **WR**
Col: Los Angeles Harbor Coll. CA (J.C.); Colorado *HS:* San Pedro [CA]
B: 10/19/1961, Los Angeles, CA
1989 Det: Rush 12-38 3.2. **Total:** Rush 12-38 3.2.

		Receiving				
Year Team	**G**	**Rec**	**Yds**	**Avg**	**TD**	**Fum**
1987 Was	1	1	5	5.0	0	0
1989 Det	16	70	1091	15.6	8	3
1990 Det	16	64	727	11.4	6	2
NFL Total	33	135	1823	13.5	14	5

RICK JOHNSON Johnson, Richard Lee Jr. 6′6″, 255 **OT**
Col: Grand Valley State *HS:* Ionia [MI] B: 12/12/1963, Greenville, MI
1987 Det: 1 G.

ROB JOHNSON Johnson, Rob Garland 6′4″, 217 **QB**
Col: USC *HS:* El Toro [CA] B: 3/18/1973, Newport Beach, CA
Drafted: 1995 Round 4 Jac

		Passing							
Year Team	**G**	**Att**	**Comp**	**Comp%**	**Yds**	**YPA**	**TD**	**Int**	**Rating**
1995 Jac	1	7	3	42.9	24	3.43	0	1	12.5
1996 Jac	2	0	0	—	0	—	0	0	—
1997 Jac	5	28	22	78.6	344	12.29	2	2	111.9
1998 Buf	8	107	67	62.6	910	8.50	8	3	102.9
NFL Total	16	142	92	64.8	1278	9.00	10	6	99.4

	Rushing				
Year Team	**Att**	**Yds**	**Avg**	**TD**	**Fum**
1995 Jac	3	17	5.7	0	0
1997 Jac	10	34	3.4	1	0
1998 Buf	24	123	5.1	1	2
NFL Total	37	174	4.7	2	2

SPIDER JOHNSON Johnson, Robert 6'4", 210 **T**
(Bob) *Col:* Tennessee-Chattanooga B: 1908 Deceased
1930 Port: 3 G.

BOB JOHNSON Johnson, Robert Douglas 6'5", 262 **C**
Col: Tennessee *HS:* Bradley Co. [Cleveland, TN] B: 8/19/1946, Gary, IN *Drafted:* 1968 Round 1 Cin
1968 Cin: 14 G. **1969** Cin: 14 G. **1970** Cin: 14 G. **1971** Cin: 14 G. **1972** Cin: 14 G; 1 Fum. **1973** Cin: 14 G. **1974** Cin: 10 G; Rec 1-3 3.0. **1975** Cin: 14 G; 2 Fum. **1976** Cin: 14 G; 1 Fum. **1977** Cin: 14 G; 3 Fum. **1978** Cin: 13 G. **1979** Cin: 5 G. **Total:** 154 G; Rec 1-3 3.0; 7 Fum.

RANDY JOHNSON Johnson, Robert Randall 6'2", 255 **OG**
Col: Georgia *HS:* Pepperell [Lindale, GA] B: 1/2/1953, Floyd Co., GA *Drafted:* 1976 Round 4 Sea
1977 TB: 12 G. **1978** TB: 10 G. **Total:** 22 G.

RON JOHNSON Johnson, Ronald 5'10", 200 **DB**
Col: Eastern Michigan *HS:* Northwestern [Detroit, MI] B: 6/8/1956, Detroit, MI *Drafted:* 1978 Round 1 Pit

		Interceptions		
Year Team	**G**	**Int**	**Yds**	**TD**
1978 Pit	16	4	24	0
1979 Pit	11	1	20	0
1980 Pit	16	1	19	0
1981 Pit	12	2	8	0
1982 Pit	9	2	5	0
1983 Pit	12	3	84	1
1984 Pit	15	0	0	0
NFL Total	91	13	160	1

RON JOHNSON Johnson, Ronald 6'3", 190 **WR**
Col: Long Beach State *HS:* Monterey [CA] B: 9/21/1958, Monterey, CA *Drafted:* 1981 Round 7 Sea
1989 Phi: Rush 1-3 3.0. **Total:** Rush 1-3 3.0.

		Receiving				
Year Team	**G**	**Rec**	**Yds**	**Avg**	**TD**	**Fum**
1985 Phi	8	11	186	16.9	0	0
1986 Phi	12	11	207	18.8	1	0
1987 Phi	3	0	0	—	0	0
1988 Phi	10	19	417	21.9	2	0
1989 Phi	14	20	295	14.8	1	2
NFL Total	47	61	1105	18.1	4	2

RON JOHNSON Johnson, Ronald Adolphus 6'1", 205 **RB**
Col: Michigan *HS:* Northwestern [Detroit, MI] B: 10/17/1947, Detroit, MI *Drafted:* 1969 Round 1 Cle
1969 Cle: Pass 1-0; KR 1-31 31.0. **1970** NYG: KR 5-140 28.0. **1972** NYG: Pass 1-0. **Total:** Pass 2-0; KR 6-171 28.5.

		Rushing				Receiving					Tot
Year Team	**G**	**Att**	**Yds**	**Avg**	**TD**	**Rec**	**Yds**	**Avg**	**TD**	**Fum**	**TD**
1969 Cle	14	138	472	3.4	7	24	164	6.8	0	4	7
1970 NYG	14	**263**	1027	3.9	8	48	487	10.1	4	5	12
1971 NYG	2	32	156	4.9	1	6	47	7.8	0	2	1
1972 NYG	14	**298**	1182	4.0	9	45	451	10.0	5	3	**14**
1973 NYG	12	260	902	3.5	6	32	377	11.8	3	4	9
1974 NYG	11	97	218	2.2	4	24	171	7.1	2	4	6
1975 NYG	14	116	351	3.0	5	34	280	8.2	1	5	6
NFL Total	81	1204	4308	3.6	40	213	1977	9.3	15	27	55

RUDY JOHNSON Johnson, Rudolph 5'11", 190 **HB**
Col: Nebraska *HS:* Aransas Pass [TX] B: 8/12/1941, Houston, TX *Drafted:* 1964 Round 5 SF
1964 SF: Rec 5-21 4.2. **1965** SF: Rec 3-49 16.3; KR 4-71 17.8. **Total:** Rec 8-70 8.8; KR 4-71 17.8.

		Rushing				
Year Team	**G**	**Att**	**Yds**	**Avg**	**TD**	**Fum**
1964 SF	5	16	48	3.0	1	1
1965 SF	14	6	9	1.5	0	1
1966 Atl	1	3	3	1.0	0	0
NFL Total	20	25	60	2.4	1	2

SAMUEL JOHNSON Johnson, Samuel 5'11", 180 **WR**
Col: Los Angeles Southwest Coll. CA (J.C.); Utah State; Prairie View A&M *HS:* South Gate [CA] B: 9/7/1964, East Los Angeles, CA
1987 LARm: 3 G; PR 4-(-4) -1.0; 2 Fum.

SAMMY JOHNSON Johnson, Samuel Lee 6'0", 223 **RB**
Col: North Carolina *HS:* High Point Central [NC] B: 9/22/1952, Burlington, NC *Drafted:* 1974 Round 4 SF
1974 SF: KR 2-31 15.5. **1975** SF: Pass 2-0; KR 17-400 23.5. **1976** SF-Min: KR 2-35 17.5. Min: KR 2-35 17.5. **1979** GB: KR 1-16 16.0. **Total:** Pass 2-0; KR 22-482 21.9.

		Rushing				Receiving				
Year Team	**G**	**Att**	**Yds**	**Avg**	**TD**	**Rec**	**Yds**	**Avg**	**TD**	**Fum**
1974 SF	14	44	237	5.4	2	11	106	9.6	0	1
1975 SF	14	55	185	3.4	3	23	177	7.7	0	3
1976 SF-Min	14	41	150	3.7	2	7	74	10.6	0	0
1976 SF	6	24	52	2.2	2	5	52	10.4	0	0
1976 Min	8	17	98	5.8	0	2	22	11.0	0	0
1977 Min	14	55	217	3.9	2	4	21	5.3	0	0
1978 Min	3	11	41	3.7	0	0	0	—	0	0
1979 GB	3	0	0	—	0	0	0	—	0	0
NFL Total	62	206	830	4.0	9	45	378	8.4	0	4

SIDNEY JOHNSON Johnson, Sidney 5'9", 175 **DB**
Col: Cerritos Coll. CA (J.C.); California *HS:* Cerritos [CA] B: 3/7/1965, Los Angeles, CA
1988 KC: 13 G. **1990** Was: 10 G. **1991** Was: 15 G; Int 2-5; 1 Sac. **1992** Was: 8 G; PR 1-0; Int 1-12; 1 Fum. **Total:** 46 G; PR 1-0; Int 3-17; 1 Fum; 1 Sac.

AL JOHNSON Johnson, Stephen Alvin 6'0", **QB-P**
Col: Hardin-Simmons *HS:* Hamlin [TX] B: 8/15/1922, Munday, TX
1948 Phi: 5 G; Punt 1-5 5.0.

STEVE JOHNSON Johnson, Steven Emil 6'6", 245 **TE**
Col: Virginia Tech *HS:* Oneonta [AL] B: 6/22/1965, Huntsville, AL *Drafted:* 1988 Round 6 NE
1988 NE: 14 G; Rec 1-5 5.0.

TED JOHNSON Johnson, Ted Curtis 6'3", 240 **LB**
Col: Colorado *HS:* Carlsbad [CA] B: 12/4/1972, Alameda, CA *Drafted:* 1995 Round 2 NE
1995 NE: 12 G; 0.5 Sac. **1996** NE: 16 G; Int 1-0. **1997** NE: 16 G; 4 Sac. **1998** NE: 13 G; 2 Sac. **Total:** 57 G; Int 1-0; 6.5 Sac.

PEPPER JOHNSON Johnson, Thomas 6'3", 250 **LB**
Col: Ohio State *HS:* MacKenzie [Detroit, MI] B: 7/29/1964, Detroit, MI *Drafted:* 1986 Round 2 NYG
1986 NYG: 2 Sac. **1987** NYG: 1 Sac. **1988** NYG: 4 Sac. **1989** NYG: 1 Sac. **1990** NYG: 3.5 Sac. **1991** NYG: 6.5 Sac. **1992** NYG: 1 Sac. **1993** Cle: 1 Sac. **1994** Cle: 2.5 Sac. **1995** Cle: 2 Sac. **1998** NYJ: 1 Sac. **Total:** 25.5 Sac.

		Interceptions			
Year Team	**G**	**Int**	**Yds**	**TD**	**Fum**
1986 NYG	16	1	13	0	0
1987 NYG	12	0	0	0	0
1988 NYG	16	1	33	1	0
1989 NYG	14	3	60	1	0
1990 NYG	16	1	0	0	0
1991 NYG	16	2	5	0	0
1992 NYG	16	2	42	0	1
1993 Cle	16	0	0	0	0
1994 Cle	16	0	0	0	0
1995 Cle	16	2	22	0	0
1996 Det	15	0	0	0	0
1997 NYJ	8	1	13	0	0
1998 NYJ	16	1	0	0	0
NFL Total	193	14	188	2	1

TOM JOHNSON Johnson, Thomas 6'2", 230 **DT**
Col: Michigan *HS:* Muskegon Heights [MI] B: 1/19/1931, Chicago, IL *Drafted:* 1952 Round 6 GB
1952 GB: 8 G.

TIM JOHNSON Johnson, Timothy 6'3", 275 **DE-DT**
Col: Penn State *HS:* Sarasota [FL] B: 1/29/1965, Sarasota, FL *Drafted:* 1987 Round 6 Pit
1987 Pit: 12 G. **1988** Pit: 15 G; 4 Sac. **1989** Pit: 14 G; 4.5 Sac. **1990** Was: 16 G; 3 Sac. **1991** Was: 16 G; Int 1-14; 3.5 Sac. **1992** Was: 16 G; 6 Sac. **1993** Was: 15 G; 4 Sac. **1994** Was: 14 G; 1 Sac. **1995** Was: 14 G; 3 Sac. **1996** Cin: 14 G; 2.5 Sac. **Total:** 146 G; Int 1-14; 31.5 Sac.

TOMMY JOHNSON Johnson, Tommy Postell 5'10", 183 **DB**
Col: Alabama *HS:* Niceville [FL] B: 12/5/1971, Rome, GA
1995 Jac: 1 G.

TONY JOHNSON Johnson, Tony Vincent 6'5", 255 **TE**
Col: Alabama *HS:* North Panola [Sardis, MS] B: 2/5/1972, Como, MS *Drafted:* 1996 Round 6 Phi
1996 NO: 9 G; Rec 7-76 10.9 1 TD; 6 Pt. **1997** NO: 7 G; Rec 1-13 13.0; 1 Fum. **1998** NO: 11 G; Rec 1-8 8.0. **Total:** 27 G; Rec 9-97 10.8 1 TD; 6 Pt; 1 Fum.

TRACY JOHNSON Johnson, Tracy Illya 6'0", 234 **RB**
Col: Clemson *HS:* A.L. Brown [Kannapolis, NC] B: 11/29/1966, Concord, NC *Drafted:* 1989 Round 10 Hou
1989 Hou: KR 13-224 17.2. **1990** Atl: KR 2-2 1.0. **1992** Sea: KR 1-15 15.0. **Total:** KR 16-241 15.1.

		Rushing				Receiving					Tot
Year Team	**G**	**Att**	**Yds**	**Avg**	**TD**	**Rec**	**Yds**	**Avg**	**TD**	**Fum**	**TD**
1989 Hou	16	4	16	4.0	0	1	8	8.0	0	1	0
1990 Atl	16	30	106	3.5	3	10	79	7.9	1	1	4
1991 Atl	16	8	26	3.3	0	3	27	9.0	0	0	0
1992 Sea	16	3	26	8.7	0	0	0	—	0	0	0
1993 Sea	16	2	8	4.0	0	3	15	5.0	1	0	1

1994 Sea	16	12	44	3.7	2	10	91	9.1	0	1	2
1995 Sea	15	1	2	2.0	1	1	-2	-2.0	0	0	1
1996 TB	10	0	0	—	0	0	0	—	0	0	0
NFL Total	121	60	228	3.8	6	28	218	7.8	2	3	8

TROY JOHNSON Johnson, Troy Antwain 6'2", 236 **LB-DE**
Col: Oklahoma *HS:* Hastings [Houston, TX] B: 11/10/1964, Houston, TX *Drafted:* 1988 Round 5 ChiB
1988 ChiB: 16 G; 1 Sac. **1989** ChiB: 7 G. **1990** NYJ: 16 G; 1 Sac. **1991** NYJ: 16 G. **1992** Det: 9 G. **Total:** 64 G; 2 Sac.

TROY JOHNSON Johnson, Troy Dwan 6'1", 180 **WR**
Col: Southeastern Louisiana; Southern University *HS:* South Terrebonne [Bourg, LA] B: 10/20/1962, New Orleans, LA
1986 StL: KR 3-46 15.3. **1987** StL: Rush 1-9 9.0. **Total:** Rush 1-9 9.0; KR 3-46 15.3.

		Receiving			
Year Team	**G**	**Rec**	**Yds**	**Avg**	**TD**
1986 StL	13	14	203	14.5	0
1987 StL	14	15	308	20.5	2
1988 Pit	14	10	237	23.7	0
1989 Det	9	2	29	14.5	0
NFL Total	50	41	777	19.0	2

TRUMAINE JOHNSON Johnson, Trumaine 6'1", 196 **WR**
Col: Grambling State *HS:* Baker [LA] B: 11/16/1960, Bogalusa, LA *Drafted:* 1983 Round 6 SD
1986 SD: KR 3-48 16.0. **Total:** KR 3-48 16.0.

		Receiving				
Year Team	**G**	**Rec**	**Yds**	**Avg**	**TD**	**Fum**
1985 SD	11	4	51	12.8	1	0
1986 SD	16	30	399	13.3	1	1
1987 Buf	12	15	186	12.4	2	0
1988 Buf	16	37	514	13.9	0	1
NFL Total	55	86	1150	13.4	4	2

TYRONE JOHNSON Johnson, Tyrone Benjamin 5'11", 171 **WR**
Col: Western State (Colo.) *HS:* Rangeview [Aurora, CO] B: 9/4/1971, Denver, CO
1994 NO: 1 G.

UNDRA JOHNSON Johnson, Undra Jerome 5'9", 199 **RB**
Col: West Virginia *HS:* Stranahan [Fort Lauderdale, FL] B: 1/8/1966, Valdosta, GA *Drafted:* 1989 Round 7 Atl
1989 NO-Dal-Atl: 6 G; KR 2-34 17.0. NO: 5 G; KR 2-34 17.0. Atl: 1 G. **Total:** 6 G; KR 2-34 17.0.

VANCE JOHNSON Johnson, Vance Edward 5'11", 185 **WR**
Col: Arizona *HS:* Cholla [Tucson, AZ] B: 3/13/1963, Trenton, NJ *Drafted:* 1985 Round 2 Den
1985 Den: Pass 1-0; Rush 10-36 3.6. **1986** Den: Pass 1-0; Rush 5-15 3.0. **1987** Den: Pass 1-0; Rush 1-(-8) -8.0. **1988** Den: Rush 1-1 1.0. **1989** Den: Pass 1-0. **Total:** Pass 4-0; Rush 17-44 2.6.

		Receiving				Punt Returns			
Year Team	**G**	**Rec**	**Yds**	**Avg**	**TD**	**Ret**	**Yds**	**Avg**	**TD**
1985 Den	16	51	721	14.1	3	30	260	8.7	0
1986 Den	12	31	363	11.7	2	3	36	12.0	0
1987 Den	11	42	684	16.3	7	1	9	9.0	0
1988 Den	16	68	896	13.2	5	0	0	—	0
1989 Den	16	76	1095	14.4	7	12	118	9.8	0
1990 Den	16	54	747	13.8	3	11	92	8.4	0
1991 Den	10	21	208	9.9	3	24	174	7.3	0
1992 Den	11	24	294	12.3	2	0	0	—	0
1993 Den	10	36	517	14.4	5	0	0	—	0
1995 Den	10	12	170	14.2	0	0	0	—	0
NFL Total	128	415	5695	13.7	37	81	689	8.5	0

	Kickoff Returns				
Year Team	**Ret**	**Yds**	**Avg**	**TD**	**Fum**
1985 Den	30	740	24.7	0	5
1986 Den	2	21	10.5	0	1
1987 Den	7	140	20.0	0	1
1990 Den	6	126	21.0	0	1
1991 Den	0	0	—	0	1
1992 Den	0	0	—	0	1
NFL Total	45	1027	22.8	0	10

VAUGHAN JOHNSON Johnson, Vaughan Monroe 6'3", 235 **LB**
Col: North Carolina State *HS:* West Cartaret [Morehead City, NJ] B: 3/24/1962, Morehead City, NC
1986 NO: 16 G; Int 1-15; 1 Sac. **1987** NO: 12 G; Int 1-0; 1 Sac. **1988** NO: 16 G; Int 1-34; 2 Sac. **1989** NO: 16 G; 1 Sac. **1990** NO: 16 G; 1 Sac. **1991** NO: 13 G; Int 1-19. **1992** NO: 16 G; 1 Sac. **1993** NO: 15 G; 5 Sac. **1994** Phi: 4 G. **Total:** 124 G; Int 4-68; 12 Sac.

WALTER JOHNSON Johnson, Walter 6'4", 265 **DT**
Col: New Mexico State; Los Angeles State *HS:* Robert A. Taft [Cincinnati, OH] B: 11/13/1942, Cincinnati, OH *Drafted:* 1965 Round 2 Cle
1965 Cle: 14 G. **1966** Cle: 14 G. **1967** Cle: 14 G. **1968** Cle: 14 G. **1969** Cle: 14 G; **1** Fum TD; 6 Pt. **1970** Cle: 14 G; Int 1-4; Scor **1** Saf; 2 Pt. **1971** Cle: 14 G; **1** Fum TD; 6 Pt. **1972** Cle: 14 G; KR 2-33 16.5; Int 1-1. **1973** Cle: 14 G. **1974** Cle: 14 G. **1975** Cle: 14 G. **1976** Cle: 14 G. **1977** Cin: 14 G. **Total:** 182 G; KR 2-33 16.5; Int 2-5; Scor 1 Saf; 2 Fum TD; 14 Pt.

WALT JOHNSON Johnson, Walter 6'1", 250 **DT**
Col: Pittsburgh *HS:* Pahokee [FL] B: 9/13/1965
1987 Dal: 1 G; 1 Sac.

WALTER JOHNSON Johnson, Walter Clarke 6'5", 235 **DE**
Col: Tuskegee *HS:* Bruce [Lithonia, GA]; Price HS [Atlanta, GA] B: 11/25/1943, Lithonia, GA *Drafted:* 1967 Round 8 SF
1967 SF: 1 G.

WALTER JOHNSON Johnson, Walter Ulysses Jr. 6'0", 241 **LB**
Col: Louisiana Tech *HS:* Ferriday [LA] B: 11/13/1963, Monroe, LA *Drafted:* 1987 Round 2 Hou
1987 Hou: 10 G. **1988** Hou: 16 G. **1989** NO: 15 G. **Total:** 41 G.

WILL JOHNSON Johnson, William Alexander 6'4", 245 **LB**
Col: Northeast Louisiana *HS:* Neville [Monroe, LA] B: 12/4/1964, Monroe, LA *Drafted:* 1987 Round 5 ChiB
1987 ChiB: 11 G.

BILLY JOHNSON Johnson, William Arthur 5'9", 170 **WR**
(White Shoes) *Col:* Widener *HS:* Chichester [Boothwyn, PA] B: 1/21/1952, Boothwyn, PA *Drafted:* 1974 Round 15 Hou
1983 Atl: Pass 1-0. **Total:** Pass 1-0.

		Rushing				Receiving			
Year Team	**G**	**Att**	**Yds**	**Avg**	**TD**	**Rec**	**Yds**	**Avg**	**TD**
1974 Hou	14	5	82	16.4	1	29	388	13.4	2
1975 Hou	14	5	17	3.4	0	37	393	10.6	1
1976 Hou	14	6	6	1.0	0	47	495	10.5	4
1977 Hou	14	6	102	17.0	1	20	412	20.6	3
1978 Hou	5	0	0	—	0	1	10	10.0	0
1979 Hou	2	0	0	—	0	6	108	18.0	1
1980 Hou	16	2	1	0.5	0	31	343	11.1	2
1982 Atl	9	0	0	—	0	2	11	5.5	0
1983 Atl	16	15	83	5.5	0	64	709	11.1	4
1984 Atl	6	3	8	2.7	0	24	371	15.5	3
1985 Atl	16	8	-8	-1.0	0	62	830	13.4	5
1986 Atl	4	6	25	4.2	0	6	57	9.5	0
1987 Atl	12	0	0	—	0	8	84	10.5	0
1988 Was	1	0	0	—	0	0	0	—	0
NFL Total	143	56	316	5.6	2	337	4211	12.5	25

	Punt Returns				Kickoff Returns					Tot
Year Team	**Ret**	**Yds**	**Avg**	**TD**	**Ret**	**Yds**	**Avg**	**TD**	**Fum**	**TD**
1974 Hou	30	409	13.6	0	29	785	27.1	0	1	3
1975 Hou	40	612	**15.3**	**3**	33	798	24.2	**1**	5	5
1976 Hou	38	403	10.6	0	26	579	22.3	0	3	4
1977 Hou	35	539	**15.4**	**2**	25	630	25.2	1	2	7
1978 Hou	8	60	7.5	0	4	73	18.3	0	0	0
1979 Hou	4	17	4.3	0	4	37	9.3	0	0	1
1980 Hou	0	0	—	0	0	0	—	0	1	2
1982 Atl	24	273	11.4	0	0	0	—	0	1	0
1983 Atl	46	489	10.6	**1**	0	0	—	0	4	5
1984 Atl	15	152	10.1	0	2	39	19.5	0	1	3
1985 Atl	10	82	8.2	0	0	0	—	0	4	5
1986 Atl	8	87	10.9	0	0	0	—	0	0	0
1987 Atl	21	168	8.0	0	0	0	—	0	2	0
1988 Was	3	26	8.7	0	0	0	—	0	0	0
NFL Total	282	3317	11.8	6	123	2941	23.9	2	24	35

BILL JOHNSON Johnson, William Edward 6'4", 305 **DT-DE**
Col: Michigan State *HS:* Neal F. Simeon [Chicago, IL] B: 12/9/1968, Chicago, IL *Drafted:* 1992 Round 3 Cle
1992 Cle: 16 G; 2 Sac. **1993** Cle: 10 G; 1 Sac. **1994** Cle: 14 G; 1 Sac. **1995** Pit: 9 G. **1996** Pit: 15 G; 1 Sac. **1997** StL: 16 G; 4 Sac. **1998** Phi: 13 G; 2.5 Sac. **Total:** 93 G; 11.5 Sac.

BILL JOHNSON Johnson, William Erick 6'1", 196 **DE**
Col: Minnesota *HS:* Slayton [MN] B: 10/4/1916, Larrabee, IA
1941 GB: 6 G.

BILL JOHNSON Johnson, William Henry III 6'2", 208 **P**
Col: West Alabama *HS:* Greene Co. [Eutaw, AL] B: 7/9/1944, Tuscaloosa, AL

		Punting			
Year Team	**G**	**Punts**	**Yds**	**Avg**	**Fum**
1970 NYG	11	43	1700	39.5	1

LEON JOHNSON Johnson, William Leon 6'0", 215 **RB**
(The Natural) *Col:* North Carolina *HS:* Freedom [Morganton, NC]
B: 7/13/1974, Morganton, NC *Drafted:* 1997 Round 4 NYJ
1997 NYJ: Pass 2-0, 1 Int. **Total:** Pass 2-0, 1 Int.

		Rushing				Receiving			
Year Team	G	Att	Yds	Avg	TD	Rec	Yds	Avg	TD
1997 NYJ	16	48	158	3.3	2	16	142	8.9	0
1998 NYJ	12	41	185	4.5	2	13	222	17.1	2
NFL Total	28	89	343	3.9	4	29	364	12.6	2

	Punt Returns				Kickoff Returns					Tot
Year Team	Ret	Yds	Avg	TD	Ret	Yds	Avg	TD	Fum	TD
1997 NYJ	51	**619**	12.1	1	12	319	26.6	1	5	4
1998 NYJ	29	203	7.0	0	16	366	22.9	0	3	4
NFL Total	80	822	10.3	1	28	685	24.5	1	8	8

BILL JOHNSON Johnson, William Levi Sr. 6'3", 228 **C-LB**
(Tiger) *Col:* Tyler JC TX; Texas A&M *HS:* John Tyler [Tyler, TX]
B: 7/14/1926, Tyler, TX
AAFC **1948** SF-A: 5 G; Int 1-0. **1949** SF-A: 12 G; Int 1-16 1 TD; 6 Pt.
Total: 17 G; Int 2-16 1 TD; 6 Pt.

NFL **1950** SF: 12 G. **1951** SF: 12 G; Rec 0-3. **1952** SF: 11 G. **1953** SF: 12 G. **1954** SF: 12 G. **1955** SF: 12 G. **1956** SF: 7 G. **Total:** 78 G; Rec 0-3.

BILL JOHNSON Johnson, William Orville 6'0", 210 **G-LB**
(Bull) *Col:* North Carolina; Southern Methodist *HS:* Bryan [TX]
B: 2/1/1921, Bryan, TX D: 4/8/1978, Dallas, TX
1947 ChiB: 6 G.

BILL JOHNSON Johnson, William Thomas 6'2", 230 **RB**
Col: Arkansas State *HS:* Arlington [Lagrangeville, NY] B: 10/31/1960, Poughkeepsie, NY *Drafted:* 1984 Supplemental Round 2 Cin
1986 Cin: Rec 13-103 7.9. **1987** Cin: Rec 3-19 6.3. **Total:** Rec 16-122 7.6.

		Rushing				
Year Team	G	Att	Yds	Avg	TD	Fum
1985 Cin	13	8	44	5.5	0	0
1986 Cin	14	39	226	5.8	0	2
1987 Cin	11	39	205	5.3	1	0
NFL Total	38	86	475	5.5	1	2

BILLY JOHNSON Johnson, William Walter 5'10", 180 **DB**
(B.J.) *Col:* Nebraska *HS:* Stanton [NE] B: 2/19/1943, Stanton, NE
Drafted: 1966 Round 6 Buf
1966 Bos: 12 G; PR 7-37 5.3; KR 1-2 2.0; 1 Fum. **1967** Bos: 6 G; PR 6-124 20.7; KR 1-9 9.0. **1968** Bos: 14 G; PR 10-34 3.4; KR 22-442 20.1; Int 2-33; 3 Fum. **Total:** 32 G; PR 23-195 8.5; KR 24-453 18.9; Int 2-33; 4 Fum.

LUKE JOHNSOS Johnsos, Luke Andrew 6'2", 195 **OE-DE**
Col: Northwestern *HS:* Carl Schurz [Chicago, IL] B: 12/6/1905, Chicago, IL D: 12/10/1984, Evanston, IL
1930 ChiB: Scor 28, 4 XK. **1931** ChiB: Scor 13, 1 FG, 4 XK. **1932** ChiB: Int **1** TD; Scor 26, 2 XK. **1933** ChiB: Scor 19, 1 XK. **1935** ChiB: Rush 1-4 4.0. **Total:** Rush 1-4 4.0; Int 1 TD; Scor 146, 1 FG, 11 XK.

		Receiving				Tot
Year Team	G	Rec	Yds	Avg	TD	TD
1929 ChiB	15	—	—	—	3	3
1930 ChiB	14	—	—	—	4	4
1931 ChiB	13	—	—	—	1	1
1932 ChiB	14	19	321	**16.9**	2	4
1933 ChiB	6	10	188	18.8	**3**	3
1934 ChiB	13	5	57	11.4	1	1
1935 ChiB	12	19	298	15.7	4	4
1936 ChiB	12	5	121	24.2	2	2
NFL Total	99	58	985	17.0	20	22

SWEDE JOHNSTON Johnston, Chester Arthur 5'8", 196 **FB-LB-DB-G**
Col: Elmhurst; Marquette *HS:* Appleton [WI] B: 3/7/1909, Appleton, WI
1934 GB-StL: Pass 4-3 75.0%, 17 4.25; Rec 1-25 25.0. StL: Pass 4-3 75.0%, 17 4.25; Rec 1-25 25.0. **1935** GB: Rec 6-59 9.8 1 TD. **1936** GB: Rec 2-11 5.5. **1939** Pit: Punt 10-372 37.2. **1940** Pit: Punt 8-321 40.1. **Total:** Pass 4-3 75.0%, 17 4.25; Rec 9-95 10.6 1 TD; Punt 18-693 38.5.

		Rushing				Tot
Year Team	G	Att	Yds	Avg	TD	TD
1931 GB	2	—	—	—	0	0
1933 ChiC	1	0	0	—	0	0
1934 GB-StL	4	42	107	2.5	1	1
1934 GB	1	7	23	3.3	0	0
1934 StL	3	35	84	2.4	1	1
1935 GB	11	52	176	3.4	0	1
1936 GB	9	42	110	2.6	1	1
1937 GB	1	0	0	—	0	0
1938 GB	2	0	0	—	0	0
1939 Pit	8	59	220	3.7	2	2
1940 Pit	10	41	113	2.8	0	0
NFL Total	48	236	726	3.1	4	5

DARYL JOHNSTON Johnston, Daryl Peter 6'2", 238 **RB**
(Moose) *Col:* Syracuse *HS:* Lewiston-Porter [Youngstown, NY]
B: 2/10/1966, Youngstown, NY *Drafted:* 1989 Round 2 Dal

		Rushing				Receiving					Tot
Year Team	G	Att	Yds	Avg	TD	Rec	Yds	Avg	TD	Fum	TD
1989 Dal	16	67	212	3.2	0	16	133	8.3	3	3	3
1990 Dal	16	10	35	3.5	1	14	148	10.6	1	1	2
1991 Dal	16	17	54	3.2	0	28	244	8.7	1	0	1
1992 Dal	16	17	61	3.6	0	32	249	7.8	2	0	2
1993 Dal	16	24	74	3.1	3	50	372	7.4	1	1	4
1994 Dal	16	40	138	3.5	2	44	325	7.4	2	2	4
1995 Dal	16	25	111	4.4	2	30	248	8.3	1	1	3
1996 Dal	16	22	48	2.2	0	43	278	6.5	1	1	1
1997 Dal	6	2	3	1.5	0	18	166	9.2	1	1	1
1998 Dal	16	8	17	2.1	0	18	60	3.3	1	0	1
NFL Total	150	232	753	3.2	8	293	2223	7.6	14	10	22

JIMMY JOHNSTON Johnston, James Everett 6'1", 193 **DB-FB-WB-HB**
Col: Washington *HS:* Caldwell [ID] B: 4/16/1917, Parma, ID
D: 11/27/1973, Caldwell, ID *Drafted:* 1939 Round 8 Was
1939 Was: Punt 8-311 38.9; Scor **1** 1XP. **1940** Was: Int 1-65 **1** TD; Punt 3-121 40.3. **1946** ChiC: KR 2-22 11.0; Int 1-20. **Total:** KR 2-22 11.0; Int 2-85 1 TD; Punt 11-432 39.3; Scor 1 1XP.

		Rushing				Receiving				Tot
Year Team	G	Att	Yds	Avg	TD	Rec	Yds	Avg	TD	TD
1939 Was	11	7	47	6.7	0	11	111	10.1	1	1
1940 Was	11	87	256	2.9	3	29	350	12.1	3	7
1946 ChiC	6	6	18	3.0	0	0	0	—	0	0
NFL Total	28	100	321	3.2	3	40	461	11.5	4	8

BRIAN JOHNSTON Johnston, Joseph Brian 6'3", 275 **C**
Col: North Carolina *HS:* Glenelg [MD] B: 11/26/1962, Highland, MD
Drafted: 1985 Round 3 NYG
1986 NYG: 4 G. **1987** NYG: 5 G. **Total:** 9 G.

PRES JOHNSTON Johnston, Luther Preston 6'0", 205 **FB-LB**
Col: Southern Methodist *HS:* Newcastle [TX] B: 10/12/1921, Newcastle, TX D: 1/15/1979, Lubbock, TX
AAFC **1946** MiaA-BufA: Pass 1-1 100.0%, 9 9.00; Rec 6-54 9.0 1 TD; KR 2-21 10.5; Int 1-15; Punt 28-1112 39.7; Scor 19, 1-1 100.0% XK.

		Rushing				Tot
Year Team	G	Att	Yds	Avg	TD	TD
1946 MiaA-BufA	11	45	218	4.8	2	3

MARK JOHNSTON Johnston, Mark Ronald 6'0", 203 **DB**
Col: Northwestern *HS:* Sycamore [IL] B: 3/4/1938, Sycamore, IL

		Interceptions				Tot
Year Team	G	Int	Yds	TD	Fum	TD
1960 Hou	14	4	42	0	0	0
1961 Hou	14	4	59	0	0	1
1962 Hou	14	4	31	0	1	0
1963 Hou	14	1	90	1	0	1
1964 Oak-NYJ	9	1	3	0	0	0
1964 Oak	1	0	0	0	0	0
1964 NYJ	8	1	3	0	0	0
NFL Total	65	14	225	1	1	2

REX JOHNSTON Johnston, Rex David 6'1", 195 **HB**
Col: USC *HS:* Compton [CA] B: 11/8/1937, Colton, CA
1960 Pit: 12 G; Rush 4-12 3.0; PR 12-45 3.8; KR 18-393 21.8; 5 Fum.

LANCE JOHNSTONE Johnstone, Lance 6'4", 250 **DE**
Col: Temple *HS:* Germantown [Philadelphia, PA] B: 6/11/1973, Philadelphia, PA *Drafted:* 1996 Round 2 Oak
1996 Oak: 16 G; **1** Fum TD; 6 Pt; 1 Sac. **1997** Oak: 14 G; 3.5 Sac. **1998** Oak: 16 G; 1 Fum TD; 6 Pt; 11 Sac. **Total:** 46 G; 2 Fum TD; 12 Pt; 15.5 Sac.

CHARLIE JOINER Joiner, Charles Jr. 5'11", 188 **WR**
Col: Grambling State *HS:* William Oscar Boston [Lake Charles, LA]
B: 10/14/1947, Many, LA *Drafted:* 1969 Round 4 Hou *HOF:* 1996
1969 Hou: KR 3-73 24.3. **1971** Hou: KR 1-25 25.0. **1972** Hou-Cin: Rush 3-14 4.7; KR 5-88 17.6. Hou: Rush 2-12 6.0. Cin: Rush 1-2 2.0; KR 5-88 17.6. **1974** Cin: Rush 4-20 5.0. **1976** SD: Pass 1-0. **1977** SD: KR 1-8 8.0. **1979** SD: Rush 1-(-12) -12.0. **Total:** Pass 1-0; Rush 8-22 2.8; KR 10-194 19.4.

		Receiving				
Year Team	G	Rec	Yds	Avg	TD	Fum
1969 Hou	7	7	77	11.0	0	0
1970 Hou	9	28	416	14.9	3	0
1971 Hou	14	31	681	22.0	7	1
1972 Hou-Cin	12	24	439	18.3	2	2

1972 Hou	6	16	306	19.1	2	1
1972 Cin	6	8	133	16.6	0	1
1973 Cin	5	13	214	16.5	0	1
1974 Cin	14	24	390	16.3	1	3
1975 Cin	14	37	726	19.6	5	1
1976 SD	14	50	1056	21.1	7	0
1977 SD	14	35	542	15.5	6	1
1978 SD	16	33	607	18.4	1	2
1979 SD	16	72	1008	14.0	4	1
1980 SD	16	71	1132	15.9	4	3
1981 SD	16	70	1188	17.0	7	2
1982 SD	9	36	545	15.1	0	1
1983 SD	16	65	960	14.8	3	2
1984 SD	16	61	793	13.0	6	0
1985 SD	16	59	932	15.8	7	1
1986 SD	15	34	440	12.9	2	0
NFL Total	239	750	12146	16.2	65	21

TIM JOINER Joiner, Timothy Lane 6′4″, 235 **LB**
Col: Louisiana State *HS:* Baton Rouge Catholic [LA] B: 1/7/1961, Monrovia, CA *Drafted:* 1983 Round 3 Hou
1983 Hou: 15 G. **1984** Hou: 11 G. **1987** Den: 3 G. **Total:** 29 G.

VERNON JOINES Joines, Vernon Willis 6′2″, 200 **WR**
Col: Maryland *HS:* Southwestern [Baltimore, MD] B: 6/20/1965, Charlotte, NC *Drafted:* 1989 Round 5 Cle
1989 Cle: 4 G; KR 1-12 12.0. **1990** Cle: 16 G; Rec 6-86 14.3. **Total:** 20 G; Rec 6-86 14.3; KR 1-12 12.0.

EVAN JOLITZ Jolitz, Evan C 6′2″, 225 **LB**
Col: Xavier (Ohio); Cincinnati *HS:* Memorial [St. Mary's, OH] B: 7/26/1951, St. Mary's, OH *Drafted:* 1974 Round 3 Cin
1974 Cin: 12 G.

AL JOLLEY Jolley, Alvin Jay 6′2″, 220 **T**
(Rocky) *Col:* Marietta; Tulsa; Kansas State *HS:* Manhattan [KS] B: 9/25/1899, Onago, KS D: 8/26/1948, Marietta, OH
1922 Akr: 10 G. **1923** Day-Oor: 4 G. Day: 1 G. Oor: 3 G. **1929** Buf: 7 G. **1930** Bkn: 8 G. **1931** Cle: 6 G. **Total:** 35 G.

GORDON JOLLEY Jolley, Gordon Harold 6′5″, 250 **OT-OG**
Col: Utah *HS:* Granite [Salt Lake City, UT] B: 5/22/1949, Provo, UT *Drafted:* 1971 Round 17 Det
1972 Det: 5 G. **1973** Det: 14 G; KR 1-15 15.0. **1974** Det: 11 G. **1975** Det: 2 G. **1976** Sea: 14 G. **1977** Sea: 13 G. **Total:** 59 G; KR 1-15 15.0.

LEWIS JOLLEY Jolley, Lewis Elman 5′11″, 210 **RB**
Col: North Carolina *HS:* East Rutherford [Forest City, NC] B: 11/15/1949, Bostic, NC *Drafted:* 1972 Round 3 Hou
1972 Hou: 7 G; KR 11-267 24.3. **1973** Hou: 10 G; Rush 7-6 0.9; Rec 3-56 18.7; KR 2-41 20.5; 2 Fum. **Total:** 17 G; Rush 7-6 0.9; Rec 3-56 18.7; KR 13-308 23.7; 2 Fum.

KEN JOLLY Jolly, Kenneth Clay 6′2″, 220 **LB**
Col: Dallas Co. CC TX; Johnson Co. CC KS; Park; MidAmerica Nazarene *HS:* Bryan Adams [Dallas, TX] B: 2/28/1962, Dallas, TX
1984 KC: 16 G. **1985** KC: 16 G. **Total:** 32 G.

MIKE JOLLY Jolly, Michael Anthony Joseph 6′3″, 188 **DB**
Col: Michigan *HS:* Aquinas [Southgate, MI] B: 3/19/1958, Detroit, MI *Drafted:* 1980 Round 4 NO
1980 GB: 16 G; Int 2-2. **1982** GB: 7 G. **1983** GB: 12 G; Int 1-0. **Total:** 35 G; Int 3-2.

DON JONAS Jonas, Donald Walter 5′11″, 195 **HB**
Col: Penn State *HS:* West Scranton [Scranton, PA] B: 12/3/1938, Scranton, PA *Drafted:* 1961 Round 13 Phi
1962 Phi: 1 G.

MARV JONAS Jonas, Marwin Frederick 5′11″, 186 **G**
Col: Utah B: 4/25/1909, Salt Lake City, UT D: 1/1987, Burbank, CA
1931 Bkn: 2 G.

CHARLIE JONASEN Jonasen, Charles **OE**
Col: No College *HS:* None B: 12/20/1892, Minneapolis, MN D: 3/9/1989, Minneapolis, MN
1921 Min: 1 G.

ERIC JONASSEN Jonassen, Eric Gustav 6′5″, 310 **OT**
Col: Penn State; Bloomsburg *HS:* Mount St. Joseph [Baltimore, MD] B: 8/16/1968, Baltimore, MD *Drafted:* 1992 Round 5 SD
1993 SD: 16 G. **1994** SD: 16 G. **Total:** 32 G.

JONES Jones **TB**
Col: No College
1921 Ham: 1 G.

AARON JONES Jones, Aaron Delmas II 6′5″, 261 **DE-LB**
Col: Eastern Kentucky *HS:* Apopka [FL] B: 12/18/1966, Orlando, FL *Drafted:* 1988 Round 1 Pit
1988 Pit: 15 G; 1.5 Sac. **1989** Pit: 16 G; 2 Sac. **1990** Pit: 7 G; Int 1-3; 2 Sac. **1991** Pit: 16 G; 2 Sac. **1992** Pit: 13 G; 2 Sac. **1993** NE: 11 G; 3.5 Sac. **1994** NE: 16 G; 1 Fum; 4 Sac. **1995** NE: 10 G; 1 Sac. **1996** Mia: 8 G. **Total:** 112 G; Int 1-3; 1 Fum; 18 Sac.

ANDRE JONES Jones, Andre Fitzgerald 6′2″, 245 **LB**
Col: Notre Dame *HS:* DeMatha [Hyattsville, MD] B: 5/15/1969, Washington, DC *Drafted:* 1991 Round 7 Pit
1992 Det: 6 G.

ANDREW JONES Jones, Andrew Lee 6′2″, 216 **RB**
Col: Washington State *HS:* East Tech [Cleveland, OH] B: 10/23/1951, Jackson, MS *Drafted:* 1975 Round 3 NO
1975 NO: Rec 10-52 5.2. **Total:** Rec 10-52 5.2.

		Rushing				
Year Team	**G**	**Att**	**Yds**	**Avg**	**TD**	**Fum**
1975 NO	13	42	108	2.6	1	1
1976 NO	2	1	2	2.0	0	0
NFL Total	15	43	110	2.6	1	1

SHAWN JONES Jones, Andrew Shawn 6′1″, 200 **DB**
Col: Georgia Tech *HS:* Thomasville [GA] B: 6/16/1970, Thomasville, GA
1993 Min: 1 G.

ANTHONY JONES Jones, Anthony Andrew 6′3″, 248 **TE**
Col: Maryland East. Shore; Wichita State *HS:* Patterson [Baltimore, MD] B: 5/16/1960, Baltimore, MD *Drafted:* 1984 Round 11 Was
1984 Was: 16 G; Rec 1-6 6.0. **1985** Was: 16 G; KR 1-0. **1986** Was: 15 G. **1987** Was: 2 G. **1988** Was-SD: 12 G; Rec 3-21 7.0; KR 1-13 13.0. Was: 8 G; Rec 2-10 5.0. SD: 4 G; Rec 1-11 11.0; KR 1-13 13.0. **Total:** 61 G; Rec 4-27 6.8; KR 2-13 6.5.

TONY JONES Jones, Anthony Bernard 5′7″, 142 **WR**
Col: Angelina Coll. TX (J.C.); Texas *HS:* Grapeland [TX] B: 12/30/1965, Grapeland, TX *Drafted:* 1990 Round 6 Hou
1990 Hou: Rush 1-(-2) -2.0. **Total:** Rush 1-(-2) -2.0.

		Receiving				
Year Team	**G**	**Rec**	**Yds**	**Avg**	**TD**	**Fum**
1990 Hou	15	30	409	13.6	6	0
1991 Hou	16	19	251	13.2	2	1
1992 Atl	10	14	138	9.9	1	0
1993 Hou	2	0	0	—	0	0
NFL Total	43	63	798	12.7	9	1

A.J. JONES Jones, Anthony Levine 6′1″, 202 **RB**
Col: Texas *HS:* North [Youngstown, OH] B: 5/30/1959, Youngstown, OH *Drafted:* 1982 Round 8 LARm
1982 LARm: 6 G. **1983** LARm: 9 G. **1984** LARm: 13 G. **1985** LARm-Det: 9 G; Rush 1-2 2.0; KR 10-226 22.6. LARm: 1 G. Det: 8 G; Rush 1-2 2.0; KR 10-226 22.6. **Total:** 37 G; Rush 1-2 2.0; KR 10-226 22.6.

LYNDELL JONES Jones, Anthony Lyndell 5′9″, 175 **DB**
Col: Columbia Basin Coll. WA (J.C.); Hawaii *HS:* James A. Garfield [Seattle, WA] B: 3/18/1959, Seattle, WA
1987 Atl: 3 G.

ARRINGTON JONES Jones, Arrington III 6′0″, 225 **KR**
Col: Winston-Salem State *HS:* John Marshall [Richmond, VA] B: 12/16/1959, Richmond, VA *Drafted:* 1981 Round 5 SF
1981 SF: 1 G; KR 3-43 14.3; 1 Fum.

ART JONES Jones, Arthur Edward Jr. 6′2″, 192 **DB-HB-TB**
(Artful Art) *Col:* Richmond *HS:* Suffolk [VA] B: 6/13/1919, Farmville, VA D: 8/29/1995, Suffolk, VA *Drafted:* 1941 Round 1 Phi
1941 Pit: Pass 23-6 26.1%, 86 3.74 3 Int; Rec 4-121 30.3 1 TD; PR 14-232 16.6; KR 7-122 17.4; Int 7-35. **1945** Pit: Rec 5-8 1.6; PR 5-62 12.4; KR 1-26 26.0; Int 1-17. **Total:** Pass 23-6 26.1%, 86 3.74 3 Int; Rec 9-129 14.3 1 TD; PR 19-294 15.5; KR 8-148 18.5; Int 8-52.

		Rushing				Punting				Tot
Year Team	**G**	**Att**	**Yds**	**Avg**	**TD**	**Punts**	**Yds**	**Avg**	**Fum**	**TD**
1941 Pit	11	62	239	3.9	4	47	1772	37.7	0	5
1945 Pit	7	16	64	4.0	0	0	0	—	1	0
NFL Total	18	78	303	3.9	4	47	1772	37.7	1	5

BEN JONES Jones, Benjamin F.H. 5′11″, 205 **FB-BB-WB**
Col: Indiana (Pa.); Grove City *HS:* Du Bois [PA] B: 1897, Du Bois, PA D: 5/17/1929, Grove City, PA
1923 Can: 11 G; Rush 6 TD; 36 Pt. **1924** Cle: 8 G; Rush 3 TD; Rec 1 TD; Scor 25, 1 XK; Tot TD 4. **1925** Can-Fra: 11 G. Can: 6 G; Rush 2 TD; 12 Pt. Fra: 5 G; Rush 1 TD; Rec 1 TD; Tot TD 2; 12 Pt. **1926** Fra: 14 G; Rush 7 TD; Rec 1 TD; 1 Fum TD; Tot TD 9; 54 Pt. **1927** ChiC: 9 G; Rush 2 TD; 12 Pt. **1928** ChiC: 5 G. **Total:** 58 G; Rush 21 TD; Rec 3 TD; 1 Fum TD; Tot TD 25.

BERT JONES Jones, Bertram Hays 6′3″, 210 **QB**
Col: Louisiana State *HS:* Ruston [LA] B: 9/7/1951, Ruston, LA *Drafted:* 1973 Round 1 Bal

		Passing							
Year Team	**G**	**Att**	**Comp**	**Comp%**	**Yds**	**YPA**	**TD**	**Int**	**Rating**
1973 Bal	8	108	43	39.8	539	4.99	4	12	28.8
1974 Bal	11	270	143	53.0	1610	5.96	8	12	62.4
1975 Bal	14	344	203	59.0	2483	7.22	18	8	89.1

1976 Bal	14	343	207	60.3	**3104**	9.05	24	9	102.5
1977 Bal	14	393	**224**	57.0	2686	6.83	17	11	80.8
1978 Bal	3	42	27	64.3	370	8.81	4	1	114.2
1979 Bal	4	92	43	46.7	643	6.99	3	3	67.4
1980 Bal	15	446	248	55.6	3134	7.03	23	21	75.3
1981 Bal	15	426	244	57.3	3094	7.26	21	20	76.9
1982 LARm	4	87	48	55.2	527	6.06	2	4	61.8
NFL Total	102	2551	1430	56.1	18190	7.13	124	101	78.2

	Rushing				
Year Team	**Att**	**Yds**	**Avg**	**TD**	**Fum**
1973 Bal	18	58	3.2	0	0
1974 Bal	39	279	7.2	4	4
1975 Bal	47	321	6.8	3	1
1976 Bal	38	214	5.6	2	4
1977 Bal	28	146	5.2	2	2
1978 Bal	9	38	4.2	0	1
1979 Bal	10	40	4.0	1	0
1980 Bal	27	175	6.5	2	1
1981 Bal	20	85	4.3	0	3
1982 LARm	11	73	6.6	0	0
NFL Total	247	1429	5.8	14	16

BOYD JONES Jones, Boyd Efram 6′3″, 265 **OT**
Col: Texas Southern B: 5/30/1961, Galveston, TX
1984 GB: 2 G.

BRENT JONES Jones, Brent Michael 6′4″, 230 **TE**
Col: Santa Clara *HS:* Leland [San Jose, CA] B: 2/12/1963, San Jose, CA *Drafted:* 1986 Round 5 Pit
1994 SF: Scor 1 2XP. **Total:** Scor 1 2XP.

		Receiving				
Year Team	**G**	**Rec**	**Yds**	**Avg**	**TD**	**Fum**
1987 SF	4	2	35	17.5	0	0
1988 SF	11	8	57	7.1	2	0
1989 SF	16	40	500	12.5	4	0
1990 SF	16	56	747	13.3	5	2
1991 SF	10	27	417	15.4	0	2
1992 SF	15	45	628	14.0	4	1
1993 SF	16	68	735	10.8	3	2
1994 SF	15	49	670	13.7	9	1
1995 SF	16	60	595	9.9	3	3
1996 SF	11	33	428	13.0	1	0
1997 SF	13	29	383	13.2	2	1
NFL Total	143	417	5195	12.5	33	12

BRIAN JONES Jones, Brian Keith 6′1″, 250 **LB**
Col: UCLA; Texas *HS:* Dunbar [Lubbock, TX] B: 1/22/1968, Iowa City, IA *Drafted:* 1991 Round 8 LARd
1991 Ind: 11 G. **1995** NO: 16 G; 1 Sac. **1996** NO: 16 G; **1** Fum TD; 6 Pt. **1998** NO: 1 G. **Total:** 44 G; 1 Fum TD; 6 Pt; 1 Sac.

RICKY JONES Jones, Broderick 6′1″, 211 **LB-DB**
Col: Tuskegee *HS:* Woodlawn [Birmingham, AL] B: 3/9/1955, Birmingham, AL
1977 Cle: 3 G. **1978** Cle: 15 G. **1979** Cle: 16 G. **1980** Bal: 12 G. **1981** Bal: 16 G. **1982** Bal: 9 G. **1983** Bal: 16 G. **Total:** 87 G.

BRUCE JONES Jones, Bruce Wayne 6′1″, 197 **DB**
Col: North Alabama *HS:* Courtland [AL] B: 12/26/1962, Courtland, AL *Drafted:* 1986 Round 7 ChiB
1987 Pit: 2 G; KR 2-38 19.0.

BRYANT JONES Jones, Bryant LyDell 5′11″, 186 **DB**
Col: Toledo *HS:* Northern [Detroit, MI] B: 12/5/1963, Detroit, MI
1987 Ind: 3 G; Int 2-26.

CALVIN JONES Jones, Calvin 5′7″, 170 **DB**
Col: Washington *HS:* Balboa [San Francisco, CA] B: 1/26/1951, San Francisco, CA *Drafted:* 1973 Round 15 Den
1976 Den: **1** Fum TD. **Total:** 1 Fum TD.

		Interceptions		
Year Team	**G**	**Int**	**Yds**	**TD**
1973 Den	14	4	69	0
1974 Den	14	5	19	0
1975 Den	8	1	0	0
1976 Den	10	2	7	0
NFL Total	46	12	95	0

CALVIN JONES Jones, Calvin D'Wayne 5′11″, 205 **RB**
Col: Nebraska *HS:* Central [Omaha, NE] B: 11/27/1970, Omaha, NE *Drafted:* 1994 Round 3 LARd
1994 LARd: Rec 2-6 3.0. **1995** Oak: KR 5-92 18.4. **Total:** Rec 2-6 3.0; KR 5-92 18.4.

		Rushing				
Year Team	**G**	**Att**	**Yds**	**Avg**	**TD**	**Fum**
1994 LARd	7	22	93	4.2	0	0
1995 Oak	8	5	19	3.8	0	1
1996 GB	1	0	0	—	0	0
NFL Total	16	27	112	4.1	0	1

CEDRIC JONES Jones, Cedric Decorrus 6′1″, 184 **WR**
Col: Duke *HS:* Weldon [NC] B: 6/1/1960, Norfolk, VA *Drafted:* 1982 Round 3 NE
1983 NE: KR 4-63 15.8. **1984** NE: KR 1-20 20.0; **1** Fum TD. **1985** NE: KR 3-37 12.3; **1** Fum TD. **1986** NE: Rush 1-(-7) -7.0; KR 4-63 15.8. **1987** NE: Pass 1-0. **1989** NE: Rush 1-3 3.0. **1990** NE: KR 2-24 12.0. **Total:** Pass 1-0; Rush 2-(-4) -2.0; KR 14-207 14.8; 2 Fum TD.

		Receiving					Tot
Year Team	**G**	**Rec**	**Yds**	**Avg**	**TD**	**Fum**	**TD**
1982 NE	2	1	5	5.0	0	0	0
1983 NE	15	20	323	16.2	1	1	1
1984 NE	14	19	244	12.8	2	1	3
1985 NE	16	21	237	11.3	2	0	3
1986 NE	16	14	222	15.9	1	1	1
1987 NE	12	25	388	15.5	3	0	3
1988 NE	16	22	313	14.2	1	1	1
1989 NE	15	48	670	14.0	6	1	6
1990 NE	14	21	301	14.3	0	0	0
NFL Total	120	191	2703	14.2	16	5	18

CEDRIC JONES Jones, Cedric L 6′4″, 275 **DE**
Col: Oklahoma *HS:* Mirabeau B. Lamar [Houston, TX] B: 4/30/1974, Houston, TX *Drafted:* 1996 Round 1 NYG
1996 NYG: 16 G. **1997** NYG: 9 G. **1998** NYG: 16 G; 4 Sac. **Total:** 41 G; 4 Sac.

CHARLIE JONES Jones, Charles Clifford 6′1″, 202 **DE**
Col: George Washington *HS:* Westville [OK] B: 1/24/1929, Summers, AR
1955 Was: 10 G; Rec 4-58 14.5; 1 Fum.

CHARLIE JONES Jones, Charlie Edward 5′8″, 175 **WR**
Col: Fresno State *HS:* Lemoore [CA] B: 12/1/1972, Hanford, CA *Drafted:* 1996 Round 4 SD
1996 SD: PR 1-21 21.0. **1997** SD: Rush 4-42 10.5. **1998** SD: Rush 4-39 9.8; KR 2-25 12.5. **Total:** Rush 8-81 10.1; PR 1-21 21.0; KR 2-25 12.5.

		Receiving				
Year Team	**G**	**Rec**	**Yds**	**Avg**	**TD**	**Fum**
1996 SD	14	41	524	12.8	4	0
1997 SD	16	32	423	13.2	1	0
1998 SD	16	46	699	15.2	3	1
NFL Total	46	119	1646	13.8	8	1

CHRIS JONES Jones, Chris Juan 6′3″, 263 **C**
Col: Delaware State *HS:* East Orange [NJ] B: 6/26/1964, Norfolk, VA
1987 NYG: 3 G; 1 Fum.

CHRIS T. JONES Jones, Christopher Todd 6′3″, 209 **WR**
Col: Miami (Fla.) *HS:* Cardinal Newman [West Palm Beach, FL] B: 8/7/1971, West Palm Beach, FL *Drafted:* 1995 Round 3 Phi
1995 Phi: KR 2-46 23.0. **Total:** KR 2-46 23.0.

		Receiving				
Year Team	**G**	**Rec**	**Yds**	**Avg**	**TD**	**Fum**
1995 Phi	12	5	61	12.2	0	0
1996 Phi	16	70	859	12.3	5	1
1997 Phi	4	5	73	14.6	0	0
NFL Total	32	80	993	12.4	5	1

CLARENCE JONES Jones, Clarence Thomas 6′6″, 280 **OT**
Col: Maryland *HS:* Central Islip [NY] B: 5/6/1968, Brooklyn, NY *Drafted:* 1991 Round 4 NYG
1991 NYG: 3 G. **1992** NYG: 3 G. **1993** NYG: 4 G. **1994** LARm: 16 G. **1995** StL: 13 G. **1996** NO: 16 G. **1997** NO: 15 G. **1998** NO: 14 G. **Total:** 84 G.

CLINT JONES Jones, Clinton 6′0″, 205 **RB**
(Clyde) *Col:* Michigan State *HS:* Cathedral Latin [Cleveland, OH] B: 5/24/1945, Cleveland, OH *Drafted:* 1967 Round 1 Min

		Rushing				Receiving			
Year Team	**G**	**Att**	**Yds**	**Avg**	**TD**	**Rec**	**Yds**	**Avg**	**TD**
1967 Min	14	13	23	1.8	0	0	0	—	0
1968 Min	12	128	536	4.2	1	4	26	6.5	0
1969 Min	14	54	241	4.5	3	3	23	7.7	0
1970 Min	14	120	369	3.1	9	9	117	13.0	0
1971 Min	14	180	675	3.8	4	9	98	10.9	0
1972 Min	7	52	164	3.2	2	6	42	7.0	0
1973 SD	12	55	170	3.1	1	7	125	17.9	0
NFL Total	87	602	2178	3.6	20	38	431	11.3	0

	Kickoff Returns					Tot
Year Team	**Ret**	**Yds**	**Avg**	**TD**	**Fum**	**TD**
1967 Min	25	597	23.9	1	3	1
1968 Min	4	60	15.0	0	1	1
1969 Min	17	444	26.1	0	0	3

1970 Min	19	452	23.8	0	5	9
1971 Min	12	329	27.4	0	7	4
1972 Min	12	327	27.3	0	1	2
1973 SD	10	217	21.7	0	2	1
NFL Total	99	2426	24.5	1	19	21

CODY JONES Jones, Cody C 6′5″, 243 **DE-DT**
Col: Trinidad State JC CO; San Jose State *HS:* Mission [San Francisco, CA] B: 5/3/1951, San Francisco, CA *Drafted:* 1973 Round 5 LARm
1974 LARm: 12 G. **1975** LARm: 14 G. **1976** LARm: 14 G. **1977** LARm: 14 G. **1978** LARm: 16 G. **1980** LARm: 15 G. **1981** LARm: 16 G. **1982** LARm: 9 G. **Total:** 110 G.

CURTIS JONES Jones, Curtis Warner 6′2″, 245 **LB**
Col: Missouri Southern State; Missouri *HS:* Sumner [St. Louis, MO] B: 12/20/1943, Stanton, TN D: 7/26/1998, Columbia, MO
1968 SD: 1 G.

DAMON JONES Jones, Damon 6′5″, 270 **TE**
Col: Michigan; Southern Illinois *HS:* Evanston Twp. [IL] B: 9/18/1974, Evanston, IL *Drafted:* 1997 Round 5 Jac
1997 Jac: 11 G; Rec 5-87 17.4 2 TD; 12 Pt. **1998** Jac: 16 G; Rec 8-90 11.3 4 TD; KR 2-(-1) -0.5; 24 Pt; 1 Fum. **Total:** 27 G; Rec 13-177 13.6 6 TD; KR 2-(-1) -0.5; 36 Pt; 1 Fum.

DAN JONES Jones, Daniel T 6′7″, 298 **OT**
Col: Maine *HS:* Malden [MA] B: 7/22/1970, Malden, MA
1993 Cin: 15 G. **1994** Cin: 14 G. **1995** Cin: 5 G. **Total:** 34 G.

DANTE JONES Jones, Dante Delaneo 6′1″, 235 **LB**
Col: Oklahoma *HS:* Skyline [Dallas, TX] B: 3/23/1965, Dallas, TX *Drafted:* 1988 Round 2 ChiB
1988 ChiB: 15 G. **1989** ChiB: 10 G. **1990** ChiB: 2 G; 2 Sac. **1991** ChiB: 16 G. **1992** ChiB: 13 G. **1993** ChiB: 16 G; Int 4-52; 1 Fum TD; 6 Pt; 1 Fum; 1 Sac. **1994** ChiB: 15 G. **1995** Den: 5 G. **Total:** 92 G; Int 4-52; 1 Fum TD; 6 Pt; 1 Fum; 3 Sac.

EARL JONES Jones, Darrel Earl 6′0″, 178 **DB**
Col: Norfolk State *HS:* Druid [Tuscaloosa, AL] B: 7/19/1957, Tuscaloosa, AL *Drafted:* 1980 Round 3 Atl
1980 Atl: 16 G; Int 1-0. **1981** Atl: 16 G; Int 2-42. **1982** Atl: 9 G. **1983** Atl: 16 G; Int 1-19. **Total:** 57 G; Int 4-61.

DARYLL JONES Jones, Daryll Keith 6′0″, 190 **DB**
Col: Georgia *HS:* Carver [Columbus, GA] B: 3/23/1962, Columbia, GA *Drafted:* 1984 Round 7 GB
1984 GB: 16 G; KR 1-19 19.0. **1985** GB: 8 G; KR 1-11 11.0. **1987** Den: 1 G. **Total:** 25 G; KR 2-30 15.0.

DEACON JONES Jones, David D 6′5″, 272 **DE**
Col: South Carolina State; Mississippi Valley State *HS:* Hungerford [Orlando, FL] B: 12/9/1938, Eatonville, FL *Drafted:* 1961 Round 14 LARm *HOF:* 1980
1961 LARm: 14 G; KR 1-12 12.0. **1962** LARm: 14 G; KR 1-0. **1963** LARm: 14 G; Int 1-0. **1964** LARm: 14 G. **1965** LARm: 14 G; Scor **1** Saf; 2 Pt. **1966** LARm: 14 G; Int 1-50. **1967** LARm: 14 G; Scor **1** Saf; 2 Pt. **1968** LARm: 14 G. **1969** LARm: 14 G. **1970** LARm: 14 G. **1971** LARm: 11 G. **1972** SD: 14 G. **1973** SD: 12 G. **1974** Was: 14 G; Scor 1, 1-1 100.0% XK. **Total:** 191 G; KR 2-12 6.0; Int 2-50; Scor 5, 1-1 100.0% XK, 2 Saf.

DAVID JONES Jones, David Dennison 6′2″, 220 **TE**
Col: Delaware State *HS:* Hillside [NJ] B: 11/9/1968, East Orange, NJ *Drafted:* 1991 Round 7 SD
1992 LARd: 16 G; Rec 2-29 14.5.

DAVID JONES Jones, David Jeffrey 6′3″, 262 **C-OG**
Col: Texas *HS:* David Crockett [Austin, TX] B: 10/25/1961, Taipei, Taiwan *Drafted:* 1984 Round 8 Det
1984 Det: 10 G. **1985** Det: 9 G. **1987** Den-Was: 8 G. Den: 3 G. Was: 5 G. **Total:** 27 G.

DAVE JONES Jones, David Ray 6′2″, 192 **WR**
Col: Kansas State *HS:* Goodland [KS] B: 8/10/1947, Goodland, KS *Drafted:* 1969 Round 11 Cle
1969 Cle: 13 G; Rec 2-33 16.5. **1970** Cle: 14 G. **1971** Cle: 14 G; Rec 4-66 16.5; PR 9-63 7.0. **Total:** 41 G; Rec 6-99 16.5; PR 9-63 7.0.

DON JONES Jones, Donald Ray 6′0″, 231 **LB**
Col: Washington *HS:* William Campbell [Naruna, VA] B: 3/26/1969, Lynchburg, VA *Drafted:* 1992 Round 9 NO
1992 NYJ: 2 G. **1993** NYJ: 6 G; 1 Sac. **Total:** 8 G; 1 Sac.

DOUG JONES Jones, Douglas Charles 6′2″, 202 **DB**
Col: San Diego City Coll. CA (J.C.); Arizona State; Cal State-Northridge *HS:* Abraham Lincoln [San Diego, CA] B: 5/31/1950, San Diego, CA *Drafted:* 1973 Round 6 KC
1973 KC: 4 G. **1974** KC: 14 G; KR 1-0; Int 1-13. **1976** Buf: 14 G; Int 3-5. **1977** Buf: 14 G; Int 2-30 **1** TD; 6 Pt. **1978** Buf: 12 G. **1979** Det: 10 G. **Total:** 68 G; KR 1-0; Int 6-48 1 TD; 6 Pt.

SEAN JONES Jones, Dwight Andre Sean-O'Neil 6′7″, 270 **DE**
Col: Northeastern *HS:* Montclair-Kimberly Acad. [Montclair, NJ] B: 12/19/1962, Kingston, Jamaica *Drafted:* 1984 Round 2 LARd
1984 LARd: 16 G; 1 Sac. **1985** LARd: 15 G; 8.5 Sac. **1986** LARd: 16 G; 15.5 Sac. **1987** LARd: 12 G; 6 Sac. **1988** Hou: 16 G; 7.5 Sac. **1989** Hou: 16 G; 6 Sac. **1990** Hou: 16 G; 12.5 Sac. **1991** Hou: 16 G; 10 Sac. **1992** Hou: 15 G; Int 1-0; 8.5 Sac. **1993** Hou: 16 G; 13 Sac. **1994** GB: 16 G; 10.5 Sac. **1995** GB: 16 G; **1** Fum TD; 6 Pt; 9 Sac. **1996** GB: 15 G; 5 Sac. **Total:** 201 G; Int 1-0; 1 Fum TD; 6 Pt; 113.0 Sac.

E.J. JONES Jones, Earnest Christopher 5′11″, 216 **RB**
Col: Kansas *HS:* Chicago Vocational [IL] B: 2/1/1962, Chicago, IL
1985 KC: 5 G; Rush 12-19 1.6; Rec 3-31 10.3. **1987** Dal: 3 G; Rush 2-7 3.5; Rec 3-16 5.3. **Total:** 8 G; Rush 14-26 1.9; Rec 6-47 7.8.

ED JONES Jones, Ed 6′0″, 185 **DB**
Col: Rutgers *HS:* Middletown Twp. [Navesink, NJ] B: 6/29/1952, Long Branch, NJ *Drafted:* 1975 Round 9 Dal
1975 Buf: 12 G; PR 1-9 9.0; Int 3-13.

SPECIAL DELIVERY JONES Jones, Edgar Francis 5′10″, 193 **HB-DB**
Col: Pittsburgh *HS:* Scranton [PA] B: 5/6/1920, Scranton, PA *Drafted:* 1942 Round 17 ChiB
AAFC **1946** CleA: Pass 4-1 25.0%, 4 1.00; PR 7-73 10.4; KR 12-307 25.6 1 TD; Int 2-16. **1947** CleA: Pass 3-2 66.7%, 79 26.33; PR 2-37 18.5; KR 2-48 24.0. **1949** CleA: Pass 1-0; KR 1-15 15.0. **Total:** Pass 8-3 37.5%, 83 10.38; PR 9-110 12.2; KR 15-370 24.7 1 TD; Int 2-16.

		Rushing				Receiving				Tot
Year Team	**G**	**Att**	**Yds**	**Avg**	**TD**	**Rec**	**Yds**	**Avg**	**TD**	**TD**
1946 CleA	14	77	539	7.0	4	4	120	30.0	1	6
1947 CleA	9	69	443	6.4	5	5	92	18.4	1	6
1948 CleA	13	100	400	4.0	5	14	293	20.9	5	10
1949 CleA	7	43	127	3.0	4	9	130	14.4	3	7
AAFC Total	43	289	1509	5.2	18	32	635	19.8	10	29

NFL **1945** ChiB: 1 G; Pass 1-0; Rush 8-41 5.1; Rec 1-0; KR 2-72 36.0.

TOO TALL JONES Jones, Edward Lee 6′9″, 271 **DE**
Col: Tennessee State *HS:* Merry [Jackson, TN] B: 2/23/1951, Jackson, TN *Drafted:* 1974 Round 1 Dal
1974 Dal: 14 G. **1975** Dal: 14 G; Int 1-2. **1976** Dal: 14 G. **1977** Dal: 14 G. **1978** Dal: 16 G. **1980** Dal: 16 G. **1981** Dal: 16 G. **1982** Dal: 9 G; Int 1-0; 6 Sac. **1983** Dal: 16 G; Int 1-12; 7 Sac. **1984** Dal: 16 G; 8 Sac. **1985** Dal: 16 G; 13 Sac. **1986** Dal: 16 G; 5.5 Sac. **1987** Dal: 15 G; 10 Sac. **1988** Dal: 16 G; 7 Sac. **1989** Dal: 16 G; 1 Sac. **Total:** 224 G; Int 3-14; 57.5 Sac.

ELLIS JONES Jones, Ellis Nathaniel 6′0″, 190 **G-LB**
(Bones; Lefty) *Col:* Tulsa *HS:* San Angelo [TX] B: 3/16/1921, Abilene, TX *Drafted:* 1945 Round 8 Bos
1945 Bos: 8 G.

ELMER JONES Jones, Elmer John 6′0″, 224 **G-LB**
(Buck) *Col:* Franklin & Marshall; Wake Forest *HS:* Tonawanda [NY] B: 8/4/1920, Buffalo, NY D: 2/21/1996, New Smyrna Beach, FL *Drafted:* 1946 Round 2 NYG
AAFC **1946** BufA: 12 G; Int 2-7.

NFL **1947** Det: 10 G. **1948** Det: 9 G. **Total:** 19 G.

ERNIE JONES Jones, Ernest 6′3″, 180 **DB**
Col: Miami-Dade CC North FL; Miami (Fla.) *HS:* Boca Raton [FL] B: 1/3/1953, Boca Raton, FL *Drafted:* 1976 Round 5 Sea
1976 Sea: 9 G. **1977** NYG: 14 G; Int 1-0; 1 Fum. **1978** NYG: 16 G; Int 3-100. **1979** NYG: 5 G; Int 2-42 1 TD; 6 Pt. **Total:** 44 G; Int 6-142 1 TD; 6 Pt; 1 Fum.

ERNEST JONES Jones, Ernest Lee 6′2″, 263 **DT-DE**
Col: Oregon *HS:* Utica Free Acad. [NY] B: 4/1/1971, Utica, NY *Drafted:* 1994 Round 3 LARm
1995 NO: 1 G. **1996** Den: 6 G. **1997** Den: 1 G. **1998** Den-NO-Car: 8 G; 1 Sac. Den: 1 G. Car: 7 G; 1 Sac. **Total:** 16 G; 1 Sac.

ERNIE JONES Jones, Ernest Lee 5′11″, 186 **WR**
Col: Indiana *HS:* Memorial [Elkhart, IN] B: 12/15/1964, Elkhart, IN *Drafted:* 1988 Round 7 Pho
1988 Pho: KR 11-147 13.4. **1989** Pho: Rush 1-18 18.0; PR 1-13 13.0; KR 7-124 17.7. **1990** Pho: Rush 4-33 8.3. **1991** Pho: Rush 5-24 4.8. **1992** Pho: Rush 2-(-3) -1.5. **1993** LARm: Rush 1-4 4.0. **Total:** Rush 13-76 5.8; PR 1-13 13.0; KR 18-271 15.1.

		Receiving				
Year Team	**G**	**Rec**	**Yds**	**Avg**	**TD**	**Fum**
1988 Pho	16	23	496	21.6	3	1
1989 Pho	15	45	838	18.6	3	3
1990 Pho	15	43	724	16.8	4	0
1991 Pho	16	61	957	15.7	4	1
1992 Pho	11	38	559	14.7	4	0
1993 LARm	10	5	56	11.2	2	0
NFL Total	83	215	3630	16.9	20	5

TYRONE JONES Jones, Ernest Tyrone 6′4″, 223 **DB**
Col: Mississippi Gulf Coast CC; Arkansas State *HS:* Ruston [LA]
B: 11/9/1966, Ruston, LA
1989 Phi: 3 G.

EZELL JONES Jones, Ezell M 6′4″, 255 **OT**
Col: Minnesota *HS:* Melrose [Memphis, TN]; John C. Fremont HS [Los Angeles, CA] B: 7/11/1947, Collierville, TN *Drafted:* 1969 Round 4 NYJ
1969 Bos: 14 G; Scor **1** Saf; 2 Pt. **1970** Bos: 4 G. **Total:** 18 G; Scor 1 Saf; 2 Pt.

FREDDIE JONES Jones, Freddie Ray Jr. 6′5″, 270 **TE**
Col: North Carolina *HS:* McKinley [Washington, DC] B: 9/16/1974, Cheverly, MD *Drafted:* 1997 Round 2 SD
1998 SD: Scor 1 2XP. **Total:** Scor 1 2XP.

		Receiving				
Year Team	G	Rec	Yds	Avg	TD	Fum
1997 SD	13	41	505	12.3	2	0
1998 SD	16	57	602	10.6	3	1
NFL Total	29	98	1107	11.3	5	1

FRED JONES Jones, Frederick Cornelius 5′9″, 175 **WR**
Col: Grambling State *HS:* Southwest De Kalb [Decatur, GA]
B: 3/6/1967, Atlanta, GA *Drafted:* 1990 Round 4 KC
1990 KC: Rush 1-(-1) -1.0; KR 9-175 19.4. **1991** KC: PR 12-108 9.0; KR 2-40 20.0. **1992** KC: KR 3-51 17.0. **1993** KC: Rush 5-34 6.8; KR 9-156 17.3. **Total:** Rush 6-33 5.5; PR 12-108 9.0; KR 23-422 18.3.

		Receiving				
Year Team	G	Rec	Yds	Avg	TD	Fum
1990 KC	6	1	5	5.0	0	1
1991 KC	11	8	85	10.6	0	3
1992 KC	14	18	265	14.7	0	0
1993 KC	10	9	111	12.3	0	1
NFL Total	41	36	466	12.9	0	5

FRED JONES Jones, Fredrick Daniel 6′3″, 240 **LB**
Col: Florida State *HS:* South Miami [Miami, FL] B: 9/2/1965, Miami, FL
1987 KC: 2 G.

GARY JONES Jones, Gary DeWayne 6′1″, 210 **DB**
Col: Texas A&M *HS:* John Tyler [Tyler, TX] B: 11/30/1967, San Augustine, TX *Drafted:* 1990 Round 9 Pit
1990 Pit: 16 G. **1991** Pit: 9 G; Int 1-0. **1993** Pit: 13 G; Int 2-11. **1994** Pit: 14 G; Int 1-0. **1995** NYJ: 11 G; Int 2-51 1 TD; 6 Pt. **1996** NYJ: 15 G. **Total:** 78 G; Int 6-62 1 TD; 6 Pt.

GEORGE JONES Jones, George Dee 5′9″, 204 **RB**
Col: Bakersfield Coll. CA (J.C.); San Diego State *HS:* Eastside [Taylors, SC] B: 12/31/1973, Greenville, SC *Drafted:* 1997 Round 5 Pit
1997 Pit: Rec 16-96 6.0 1 TD. **1998** Jac: Rec 1-9 9.0; KR 1-21 21.0. **Total:** Rec 17-105 6.2 1 TD; KR 1-21 21.0.

		Rushing					Tot
Year Team	G	Att	Yds	Avg	TD	Fum	TD
1997 Pit	16	72	235	3.3	1	3	2
1998 Jac	12	39	121	3.1	0	0	0
NFL Total	28	111	356	3.2	1	3	2

JERRY JONES Jones, Gerald Robert 6′4″, 260 **OT-DT-DE**
Col: Bowling Green State *HS:* Paul L. Dunbar [Dayton, OH]
B: 2/14/1944, Dayton, OH *Drafted:* 1966 Round 2 Atl
1966 Atl: 7 G. **1967** NO: 9 G. **1968** NO: 14 G; KR 1-5 5.0. **1969** NO: 14 G. **Total:** 44 G; KR 1-5 5.0.

GORDON JONES Jones, Gordon 6′0″, 190 **WR**
Col: Pittsburgh *HS:* East Allegheny [North Versailles, PA] B: 7/25/1957, Tampa, FL *Drafted:* 1979 Round 2 TB
1979 TB: Rush 1-12 12.0. **1980** TB: Rush 1-(-10) -10.0. **Total:** Rush 2-2 1.0.

		Receiving				
Year Team	G	Rec	Yds	Avg	TD	Fum
1979 TB	12	4	80	20.0	1	0
1980 TB	16	48	669	13.9	5	1
1981 TB	13	20	276	13.8	1	0
1982 TB	9	14	205	14.6	1	1
1983 LARm	11	11	172	15.6	0	0
NFL Total	61	97	1402	14.5	8	2

GREG JONES Jones, Gregory Martin 6′1″, 201 **RB**
Col: UCLA *HS:* South San Francisco [CA] B: 2/12/1948, San Francisco, CA *Drafted:* 1970 Round 5 Min
1970 Buf: Rec 8-89 11.1; KR 7-162 23.1 1 TD. **1971** Buf: Rec 16-113 7.1 1 TD; KR 1-24 24.0. **Total:** Rec 24-202 8.4 1 TD; KR 8-186 23.3 1 TD.

		Rushing					Tot
Year Team	G	Att	Yds	Avg	TD	Fum	TD
1970 Buf	10	31	113	3.6	1	0	2
1971 Buf	14	16	53	3.3	0	1	1
NFL Total	24	47	166	3.5	1	1	3

GREG JONES Jones, Gregory Phillip 6′4″, 238 **LB**
Col: Colorado *HS:* John F. Kennedy [Denver, CO] B: 5/22/1974, Denver, CO *Drafted:* 1997 Round 2 Was
1997 Was: 16 G; KR 1-6 6.0; 3.5 Sac. **1998** Was: 16 G; Int 1-9; 1 Sac. **Total:** 32 G; KR 1-6 6.0; Int 1-9; 4.5 Sac.

HARRIS JONES Jones, Harris J Jr. 6′5″, 255 **OG**
Col: Johnson C. Smith *HS:* Carver [Lake City, SC] B: 10/3/1945, Lake City, SC
1971 SD: 11 G. **1973** Hou: 5 G. **1974** Hou: 11 G; KR 1-0. **Total:** 27 G; KR 1-0.

HARRY JONES Jones, Harry Lee 6′2″, 205 **RB**
Col: Arkansas *HS:* Enid [OK] B: 7/25/1945, Huntington, WV
Drafted: 1967 Round 1 Phi
1967 Phi: Rec 3-32 10.7; KR 2-32 16.0. **1968** Phi: Rec 5-87 17.4; KR 1-18 18.0. **1970** Phi: Rec 1-12 12.0; KR 2-23 11.5. **Total:** Rec 9-131 14.6; KR 5-73 14.6.

		Rushing			
Year Team	G	Att	Yds	Avg	TD
1967 Phi	11	8	17	2.1	0
1968 Phi	4	22	24	1.1	0
1969 Phi	12	1	0	0.0	0
1970 Phi	2	13	44	3.4	0
NFL Total	29	44	85	1.9	0

HARVEY JONES Jones, Harvey Mabry 6′0″, 175 **DB-FB-HB**
Col: Baylor *HS:* Beaumont [TX] B: 4/15/1921, Beaumont, TX
D: 7/21/1993, Clarendon, TX
1944 Cle: Rec 6-59 9.8; PR 6-66 11.0; KR 1-33 33.0; Int 3-71. **1945** Cle: Rec 2-36 18.0 1 TD; Int 2-73. **1947** Was: KR 1-30 30.0. **Total:** Rec 8-95 11.9 1 TD; PR 6-66 11.0; KR 2-63 31.5; Int 5-144.

		Rushing				Tot
Year Team	G	Att	Yds	Avg	TD	TD
1944 Cle	10	38	133	3.5	1	1
1945 Cle	9	8	15	1.9	0	1
1947 Was	4	0	0	—	0	0
NFL Total	23	46	148	3.2	1	2

HASSAN JONES Jones, Hassan Ameer 6′0″, 198 **WR**
Col: Florida State *HS:* Clearwater [FL] B: 7/2/1964, Clearwater, FL
Drafted: 1986 Round 5 Min
1986 Min: Rush 1-14 14.0. **1988** Min: Rush 1-7 7.0. **1989** Min: Rush 1-37 37.0. **1990** Min: Rush 1-(-7) -7.0. **1992** Min: Pass 1-1 100.0%, 18 18.00; Rush 1-1 1.0. **Total:** Pass 1-1 100.0%, 18 18.00; Rush 5-52 10.4.

		Receiving				
Year Team	G	Rec	Yds	Avg	TD	Fum
1986 Min	16	28	570	20.4	4	1
1987 Min	12	7	189	27.0	2	0
1988 Min	16	40	778	19.5	5	0
1989 Min	16	42	694	16.5	1	2
1990 Min	15	51	810	15.9	7	0
1991 Min	16	32	384	12.0	1	1
1992 Min	9	22	308	14.0	4	0
1993 KC	8	7	91	13.0	0	0
NFL Total	108	229	3824	16.7	24	4

HENRY JONES Jones, Henry 5′11″, 197 **DB**
Col: Illinois *HS:* St. Louis University [MO] B: 12/29/1967, St. Louis, MO *Drafted:* 1991 Round 1 Buf
1993 Buf: Scor 1 Saf; 2 Sac. **1994** Buf: 1 Sac. **1997** Buf: PR 1-0; 2 Sac. **Total:** PR 1-0; Scor 1 Saf; 5 Sac.

		Interceptions			
Year Team	G	Int	Yds	TD	Fum
1991 Buf	15	0	0	0	0
1992 Buf	16	**8**	**263**	2	0
1993 Buf	16	2	92	1	0
1994 Buf	16	2	45	0	0
1995 Buf	13	1	10	0	0
1996 Buf	5	0	0	0	0
1997 Buf	15	0	0	0	1
1998 Buf	16	3	0	0	0
NFL Total	112	16	410	3	1

HENRY JONES Jones, Henry D 6′2″, 235 **RB**
(Juggie) *Col:* Grambling State *HS:* Scotlandville [Baton Rouge, LA]
B: 2/24/1946, Baton Rouge, LA *Drafted:* 1969 Round 9 Den
1969 Den: 2 G; Rush 1-3 3.0.

HOMER JONES Jones, Homer Carroll 6′2″, 215 **WR**
Col: Texas Southern *HS:* Frederick Douglass [Sherman, TX]
B: 2/18/1941, Pittsburg, TX *Drafted:* 1963 Round 20 NYG
1965 NYG: Rush 1-17 17.0. **1966** NYG: Rush 5-43 8.6. **1967** NYG: Rush 5-60 12.0 1 TD. **1968** NYG: Rush 3-18 6.0. **1969** NYG: Rush 3-8 2.7. **Total:** Rush 17-146 8.6 1 TD.

		Receiving				Kickoff Returns					Tot
Year Team	G	Rec	Yds	Avg	TD	Ret	Yds	Avg	TD	Fum	TD
1964 NYG	3	4	82	20.5	0	6	111	18.5	0	2	0
1965 NYG	14	26	709	27.3	6	0	0	—	0	0	6
1966 NYG	14	48	1044	21.8	8	0	0	—	0	1	8
1967 NYG	14	49	1209	**24.7**	**13**	2	38	19.0	0	1	**14**
1968 NYG	14	45	1057	**23.5**	7	0	0	—	0	0	7
1969 NYG	14	42	744	17.7	1	0	0	—	0	0	1
1970 Cle	14	10	141	14.1	1	29	739	25.5	1	1	2
NFL Total	87	224	4986	**22.3**	36	37	888	24.0	1	5	38

HORACE JONES Jones, Horace Arthur 6′3″, 255 **DE**
Col: Louisville *HS:* Washington [Pensacola, FL] B: 7/31/1949, Pensacola, FL *Drafted:* 1971 Round 12 Oak
1971 Oak: 14 G. **1972** Oak: 14 G. **1973** Oak: 14 G. **1974** Oak: 14 G. **1975** Oak: 14 G. **1977** Sea: 1 G. **Total:** 71 G.

BUCK JONES Jones, Horatio 6′0″, 210 **OE**
(AKA White Cloud) *Col:* Haskell Indian B: 10/23/1888, Cattaraugus Indian Reservation, NY D: 9/8/1975, Lewiston, NY
1922 Oor: 2 G.

JIM JONES Jones, James Alexander 6′0″, 175 **TE-DB**
(Casey) *Col:* Union (Tenn.) *HS:* Coffee [Florence, AL] B: 12/18/1920, Florence, AL D: 12/1979, Sneedville, TN *Drafted:* 1943 Round 6 Det
1946 Det: 2 G; Pass 4-0, 1 Int; Rush 3-3 1.0; KR 3-44 14.7; Punt 1-(-9) -9.0.

JAMES JONES Jones, James Alfie 6′2″, 290 **DT-NT**
Col: Northern Iowa *HS:* Central [Davenport, IA] B: 2/6/1969, Davenport, IA *Drafted:* 1991 Round 3 Cle
1991 Cle: 16 G; Int 1-20 1 TD; Scor 1 Saf; 8 Pt; 1 Sac. **1992** Cle: 16 G; Rec 1-1 1.0 1 TD; 6 Pt; 4 Sac. **1993** Cle: 16 G; Rush 2-2 1.0 1 TD; 6 Pt; 5.5 Sac. **1994** Cle: 16 G; Rush 1-0; Rec 1-1 1.0; 3 Sac. **1995** Den: 16 G; 1 Sac. **1996** Bal: 16 G; Rec 1-2 2.0 1 TD; 6 Pt; 1 Sac. **1997** Bal: 16 G; 6 Sac. **1998** Bal: 16 G; 5.5 Sac. **Total:** 128 G; Rush 3-2 0.7 1 TD; Rec 3-4 1.3 2 TD; Int 1-20 1 TD; Scor 1 Saf; Tot TD 4; 26 Pt; 27.0 Sac.

JIM JONES Jones, James Clyde 6′3″, 195 **WR**
Col: Wisconsin *HS:* Eastern [Washington, DC] B: 3/3/1941, Henderson, NC *Drafted:* 1964 Round 6 ChiB
1965 ChiB: Rush 2-13 6.5. **1966** ChiB: Rush 1-(-7) -7.0. **1967** ChiB: Rush 4-19 4.8. **1968** Den: Rush 1-(-1) -1.0. **Total:** Rush 8-24 3.0.

		Receiving				
Year Team	G	Rec	Yds	Avg	TD	Fum
1965 ChiB	13	21	350	16.7	4	0
1966 ChiB	14	28	504	18.0	5	1
1967 ChiB	14	7	138	19.7	0	0
1968 Den	13	13	190	14.6	2	0
NFL Total	54	69	1182	17.1	11	1

JAMES JONES Jones, James Jr. 5′10″, 200 **RB**
Col: Mississippi State *HS:* Vicksburg [MS] B: 12/6/1958, Starkville, MS *Drafted:* 1980 Round 3 Dal
1985 Dal: Pass 2-1 50.0%, 12 6.00 1 TD 1 Int. **Total:** Pass 2-1 50.0%, 12 6.00 1 TD 1 Int.

		Rushing				Receiving			
Year Team	G	Att	Yds	Avg	TD	Rec	Yds	Avg	TD
1980 Dal	16	41	135	3.3	0	5	39	7.8	0
1981 Dal	16	34	183	5.4	1	6	37	6.2	0
1982 Dal	5	0	0	—	0	0	0	—	0
1984 Dal	9	8	13	1.6	0	7	57	8.1	1
1985 Dal	16	1	0	0.0	0	24	179	7.5	0
NFL Total	62	84	331	3.9	1	42	312	7.4	1

	Punt Returns				Kickoff Returns					Tot
Year Team	Ret	Yds	Avg	TD	Ret	Yds	Avg	TD	Fum	TD
1980 Dal	54	548	10.1	0	32	720	22.5	0	5	0
1981 Dal	33	188	5.7	0	27	517	19.1	0	4	1
1982 Dal	0	0	—	0	2	46	23.0	0	0	0
1984 Dal	0	0	—	0	0	0	—	0	0	1
1985 Dal	0	0	—	0	9	161	17.9	0	0	0
NFL Total	87	736	8.5	0	70	1444	20.6	0	9	2

JIM JONES Jones, James Ray 6′1″, 204 **DB**
Col: Washington *HS:* Lincoln [Tacoma, WA] B: 5/6/1935 D: 10/1982 *Drafted:* 1958 Round 3 LARm
1958 LARm: 12 G. **1961** Oak: 1 G. **Total:** 13 G.

JAMES JONES Jones, James Roosevelt 6′2″, 229 **RB-TE**
Col: Florida *HS:* Ely [Pompano Beach, FL] B: 3/21/1961, Pompano Beach, FL *Drafted:* 1983 Round 1 Det
1983 Det: Pass 2-0. **1984** Det: Pass 5-3 60.0%, 62 12.40 1 TD. **1985** Det: Pass 1-0. **1987** Det: Pass 1-0, 1 Int. **1988** Det: Pass 1-0. **1990** Sea: KR 2-21 10.5. **1992** Sea: KR 1-16 16.0. **Total:** Pass 10-3 30.0%, 62 6.20 1 TD 1 Int; KR 3-37 12.3.

		Rushing				Receiving					Tot
Year Team	G	Att	Yds	Avg	TD	Rec	Yds	Avg	TD	Fum	TD
1983 Det	14	135	475	3.5	6	46	467	10.2	1	4	7
1984 Det	16	137	532	3.9	3	77	662	8.6	5	6	8
1985 Det	14	244	886	3.6	6	45	334	7.4	3	7	9
1986 Det	16	252	903	3.6	8	54	334	6.2	1	6	9
1987 Det	11	96	342	3.6	0	34	262	7.7	0	2	0
1988 Det	14	96	314	3.3	0	29	259	8.9	0	2	0
1989 Sea	2	0	0	—	0	1	8	8.0	0	0	0
1990 Sea	16	5	20	4.0	0	1	22	22.0	0	0	0
1991 Sea	16	45	154	3.4	3	10	103	10.3	0	2	3
1992 Sea	16	0	0	—	0	21	190	9.0	0	0	0
NFL Total	135	1010	3626	3.6	26	318	2641	8.3	10	29	36

JEFF JONES Jones, Jeffrey Raymond 6′6″, 310 **OT**
Col: Texas A&M *HS:* Killeen [TX] B: 5/30/1972, Killeen, TX
1995 Det: 1 G. **1996** Det: 7 G. **Total:** 8 G.

JERRY JONES Jones, Jerald Joseph 6′1″, 205 **G**
Col: Notre Dame *HS:* Sapulpa [OK] B: 1894 D: 6/2/1938, Rochester, MN
1920 Sta: 13 G. **1922** RI: 7 G. **1923** Tol: 8 G. **1924** Cle: 5 G. **Total:** 33 G.

JIMMIE JONES Jones, Jimmie Lee 6′5″, 220 **DE**
Col: Wichita State *HS:* Dwight Morrow [Englewood, NJ] B: 1/17/1947, Columbia, SC *Drafted:* 1969 Round 6 NYJ
1969 NYJ: 14 G. **1970** NYJ: 3 G. **1971** Was: 14 G. **1972** Was: 3 G. **1973** Was: 6 G. **Total:** 40 G.

JIMMIE JONES Jones, Jimmie Lee 5′10″, 205 **RB**
Col: East Los Angeles Coll. CA (J.C.); UCLA *HS:* Manual Arts [Los Angeles, CA] B: 6/15/1950, Los Angeles, CA
1974 Det: Rec 4-35 8.8.

		Rushing				Kickoff Returns				
Year Team	G	Att	Yds	Avg	TD	Ret	Yds	Avg	TD	Fum
1974 Det	14	32	147	4.6	1	38	927	24.4	0	4

JIMMIE JONES Jones, Jimmie Sims 6′4″, 285 **DT-DE**
Col: Miami (Fla.) *HS:* Okeechobee [FL] B: 1/9/1966, Lakeland, FL *Drafted:* 1990 Round 3 Dal
1990 Dal: 16 G; 7.5 Sac. **1991** Dal: 16 G; 2 Sac. **1992** Dal: 16 G; 4 Sac. **1993** Dal: 15 G; 5.5 Sac. **1994** LARm: 14 G; 5 Sac. **1995** StL: 16 G. **1996** StL: 14 G; 5.5 Sac. **1997** Phi: 14 G; 2.5 Sac. **Total:** 121 G; 32 Sac.

JOCK JONES Jones, Jock Stacy 6′2″, 235 **LB**
Col: Virginia Tech *HS:* Lee-Davis [Mechanicsville, VA] B: 3/13/1968, Ashland, VA *Drafted:* 1990 Round 8 Cle
1990 Cle: 11 G. **1991** Cle-Pho: 14 G. Cle: 9 G. Pho: 5 G. **1992** Pho: 14 G; Int 1-27; 1 Sac. **1993** Pho: 7 G. **Total:** 46 G; Int 1-27; 1 Sac.

SPIKE JONES Jones, John Amos 6′2″, 197 **P**
Col: Middle Georgia Coll. (J.C.); Georgia *HS:* Louisville Acad. [GA] B: 7/9/1947, Louisville, GA *Drafted:* 1970 Round 4 Hou
1972 Buf: Pass 2-1 50.0%, 4 2.00; Rush 2-18 9.0. **1973** Buf: Rush 1-0. **1975** Phi: Rush 1-(-1) -1.0. **1976** Phi: Pass 1-1 100.0%, -4 -4.00. **Total:** Pass 3-2 66.7%; Rush 4-17 4.3.

		Punting			
Year Team	G	Punts	Yds	Avg	Fum
1970 Hou	14	84	3559	42.4	0
1971 Buf	13	72	2966	41.2	0
1972 Buf	14	80	3104	38.8	1
1973 Buf	14	66	2660	40.3	1
1974 Buf	8	35	1305	37.3	0
1975 Phi	12	68	2742	40.3	1
1976 Phi	14	94	3445	36.6	1
1977 Phi	14	93	3463	37.2	1
NFL Total	103	592	23244	39.3	5

JOHN JONES Jones, John Eddie 6′1″, 190 **QB**
(J.J.) *Col:* Fisk *HS:* South Side [Memphis, TN] B: 4/16/1952, Memphis, TN
1975 NYJ: Rush 9-59 6.6.

		Passing								
Year Team	G	Att	Comp	Comp%	Yds	YPA	TD	Int	Rating	Fum
1975 NYJ	7	57	16	28.1	181	3.18	1	5	9.6	2

LAM JONES Jones, John Wesley 5′11″, 180 **WR**
Col: Texas *HS:* Lampasas [TX] B: 4/4/1958, Lawton, OK
Drafted: 1980 Round 1 NYJ
1980 NYJ: Rush 2-5 2.5; KR 4-67 16.8. **1981** NYJ: Rush 2-0; KR 1-6 6.0. **1982** NYJ: Rush 1-2 2.0. **1983** NYJ: Rush 4-10 2.5. **Total:** Rush 9-17 1.9; KR 5-73 14.6.

Year Team	G	Receiving Rec	Yds	Avg	TD	Fum
1980 NYJ	16	25	482	19.3	3	1
1981 NYJ	15	20	342	17.1	3	2
1982 NYJ	8	18	294	16.3	2	0
1983 NYJ	14	43	734	17.1	4	2
1984 NYJ	8	32	470	14.7	1	1
NFL Total	61	138	2322	16.8	13	6

JOE JONES Jones, Joseph 6′5″, 255 **TE**
Col: Virginia Tech *HS:* Forest Hill [Windber, PA] B: 6/26/1962, Windber, PA
1987 Ind: 3 G; Rec 3-25 8.3 1 TD; 6 Pt.

JOEY JONES Jones, Joseph Russell 5′8″, 165 **WR**
Col: Alabama *HS:* S.S. Murphy [Mobile, AL] B: 10/29/1962, Mobile, AL
Drafted: 1984 Supplemental Round 1 Atl
1986 Atl: 11 G; Rush 1-7 7.0; Rec 7-141 20.1; PR 7-36 5.1.

JOE JONES Jones, Joseph Willie 6′6″, 250 **DE**
(Turkey) *Col:* Tennessee State *HS:* Dalworth [Grand Prairie, TX]
B: 1/7/1948, Dallas, TX *Drafted:* 1970 Round 2 Cle
1970 Cle: 14 G. **1971** Cle: 14 G. **1973** Cle: 14 G. **1974** Phi: 14 G. **1975** Phi-Cle: 13 G. Phi: 7 G. Cle: 6 G. **1976** Cle: 14 G; **1** Fum TD; 6 Pt. **1977** Cle: 14 G; Int 1-0. **1978** Cle: 14 G. **1979** Was: 16 G. **1980** Was: 7 G. **Total:** 134 G; Int 1-0; 1 Fum TD; 6 Pt.

JUNE JONES Jones, June Sheldon III 6′4″, 200 **QB**
Col: Oregon; Hawaii; Portland State *HS:* U.S. Grant [Portland, OR]
B: 2/19/1953, Portland, OR
1978 Atl: Rush 10-(-3) -0.3. **1979** Atl: Rush 6-19 3.2. **1981** Atl: Rush 1-(-1) -1.0. **Total:** Rush 17-15 0.9.

Year Team	G	Passing Att	Comp	Comp%	Yds	YPA	TD	Int	Rating	Fum
1977 Atl	1	1	1	100.0	-1	-1.00	0	0	79.2	0
1978 Atl	7	79	34	43.0	394	4.99	1	4	41.9	4
1979 Atl	5	83	38	45.8	505	6.08	2	3	58.6	4
1981 Atl	4	3	2	66.7	25	8.33	0	0	92.4	0
NFL Total	17	166	75	45.2	923	5.56	3	7	51.4	8

KEITH JONES Jones, Keith 5′9″, 190 **RB**
Col: Nebraska *HS:* Central [Omaha, NE] B: 2/5/1966, Omaha, NE
Drafted: 1988 Round 6 LARm
1989 Cle: Rec 15-126 8.4; KR 4-42 10.5.

Year Team	G	Rushing Att	Yds	Avg	TD	Fum
1989 Cle	16	43	160	3.7	1	1

KEITH JONES Jones, Keith Lamar 6′1″, 210 **RB**
Col: Illinois *HS:* Webster Groves [MO] B: 3/20/1966, Rock Hill, MO
Drafted: 1989 Round 3 Atl
1989 Atl: Pass 1-0. **1990** Atl: Pass 1-1 100.0%, 37 37.00. **1992** Atl: Pass 1-0. **Total:** Pass 3-1 33.3%, 37 12.33.

Year Team	G	Rushing Att	Yds	Avg	TD	Receiving Rec	Yds	Avg	TD
1989 Atl	14	52	202	3.9	6	41	396	9.7	0
1990 Atl	15	49	185	3.8	0	13	103	7.9	0
1991 Atl	5	35	126	3.6	0	6	58	9.7	0
1992 Atl	16	79	278	3.5	0	12	94	7.8	0
NFL Total	50	215	791	3.7	6	72	651	9.0	0

Year Team	Kickoff Returns Ret	Yds	Avg	TD	Fum	Tot TD
1989 Atl	23	440	19.1	0	0	6
1990 Atl	8	236	29.5	1	2	1
1992 Atl	6	114	19.0	0	2	0
NFL Total	37	790	21.4	1	4	7

KEN JONES Jones, Kenneth A 6′3″, 185 **WB-E**
Col: Franklin & Marshall B: 9/2/1897 D: 1/3/1983, Solsville, NY
1924 Buf: 5 G.

KEN JONES Jones, Kenneth Eugene 6′5″, 260 **OT-DE**
Col: Arkansas State *HS:* Pattonville [Maryland Heights, MO]
B: 12/1/1952, St. Louis, MO *Drafted:* 1976 Round 2 Buf
1976 Buf: 12 G. **1977** Buf: 14 G. **1978** Buf: 16 G. **1979** Buf: 16 G. **1980** Buf: 16 G. **1981** Buf: 15 G. **1982** Buf: 9 G. **1983** Buf: 16 G. **1984** Buf: 16 G. **1985** Buf: 16 G. **1986** Buf: 12 G. **1987** NYJ: 5 G. **Total:** 163 G.

KIM JONES Jones, Kim Richard 6′4″, 238 **RB**
Col: Colorado State *HS:* Columbus [Waterloo, IA] B: 1/19/1952, Waterloo, IA *Drafted:* 1975 Round 7 Bal
1976 NO: Rec 1-14 14.0; KR 1-12 12.0. **1977** NO: Rec 1-9 9.0; KR 2-23 11.5. **1978** NO: Rec 2-10 5.0. **Total:** Rec 4-33 8.3; KR 3-35 11.7.

Year Team	G	Rushing Att	Yds	Avg	TD	Fum
1976 NO	11	6	21	3.5	0	0
1977 NO	14	8	23	2.9	0	0
1978 NO	16	9	31	3.4	0	1
1979 NO	2	3	5	1.7	0	0
NFL Total	43	26	80	3.1	0	1

LACURTIS JONES Jones, LaCurtis Burl 6′0″, 200 **LB**
Col: Baylor *HS:* Waco [TX] B: 6/23/1972, Waco, TX *Drafted:* 1996 Round 4 Mia
1996 TB: 10 G.

LARRY JONES Jones, Lawrance Allen 5′10″, 170 **WR-DB**
Col: Northeast Missouri State *HS:* Lemoore [CA] B: 3/4/1951, Lemoore, CA *Drafted:* 1974 Round 15 NYG
1975 Was: Rec 2-33 16.5. **1977** Was: Rush 1-1 1.0; Rec 5-55 11.0. **1978** SF: Rush 1-(-9) -9.0; Rec 1-21 21.0. **Total:** Rush 2-(-8) -4.0; Rec 8-109 13.6.

Year Team	G	Punt Returns Ret	Yds	Avg	TD	Kickoff Returns Ret	Yds	Avg	TD	Fum	Tot TD
1974 Was	13	8	54	6.8	0	23	672	29.2	**1**	1	1
1975 Was	14	**53**	407	7.7	1	**47**	**1086**	23.1	0	5	1
1976 Was	1	1	15	15.0	0	1	16	16.0	0	0	0
1977 Was	14	0	0	—	0	2	42	21.0	0	0	0
1978 SF	9	10	86	8.6	0	0	0	—	0	1	0
NFL Total	51	72	562	7.8	1	73	1816	24.9	1	7	2

LENOY JONES Jones, Lenoy 6′1″, 228 **LB**
Col: Texas Christian *HS:* Groesbeck [TX] B: 9/25/1974, Marlin, TX
1996 Hou: 11 G. **1997** Ten: 16 G; 1 Sac. **1998** Ten: 9 G. **Total:** 36 G; 1 Sac.

LEONARD JONES Jones, Leonard Dewayne 6′2″, 185 **DB**
Col: Texas Tech *HS:* O.D. Wyatt [Fort Worth, TX] B: 10/28/1964, St. Louis, MO *Drafted:* 1987 Round 9 Min
1987 Den: 2 G.

LEROY JONES Jones, Leroy 6′8″, 263 **DE**
Col: Norfolk State *HS:* Amanda Elzy [Greenwood, MS] B: 9/29/1950, Greenwood, MS *Drafted:* 1975 Round 2 LARm
1976 SD: 14 G; Int 1-11. **1977** SD: 14 G; Int 1-17 **1** TD; 6 Pt. **1978** SD: 16 G. **1979** SD: 16 G. **1980** SD: 15 G. **1981** SD: 16 G; Int 1-6. **1982** SD: 8 G; 1.5 Sac. **1983** SD: 12 G. **Total:** 111 G; Int 3-34 1 TD; 6 Pt; 1.5 Sac.

LEW JONES Jones, Lewis Norten 6′0″, 215 **G-LB**
Col: Weatherford Coll. TX (J.C.); Texas Tech B: 12/15/1912, Cleburne, TX
1943 Bkn: 10 G; KR 1-5 5.0; Int 1-4.

MARCUS JONES Jones, Marcus Edward 6′6″, 286 **DT**
Col: North Carolina *HS:* Southwest Onslow [Jacksonville, NC]
B: 8/15/1973, Jacksonville, NC *Drafted:* 1996 Round 1 TB
1996 TB: 16 G; 1 Sac. **1997** TB: 7 G. **1998** TB: 15 G. **Total:** 38 G; 1 Sac.

DONTA JONES Jones, Markeysia Donta 6′2″, 226 **LB**
Col: Nebraska *HS:* McDonough [Pomfret, MD] B: 8/27/1972, Washington, DC *Drafted:* 1995 Round 4 Pit
1995 Pit: 16 G. **1996** Pit: 15 G; PR 1-3 3.0; 1 Sac. **1997** Pit: 16 G. **1998** Pit: 16 G; 3 Sac. **Total:** 63 G; PR 1-3 3.0; 4 Sac.

MARLON JONES Jones, Marlon Anthony 6′4″, 263 **DE-DT**
Col: Central State (Ohio) *HS:* Milford Mill [Baltimore, MD] B: 7/1/1964, Baltimore, MD
1987 Cle: 1 G. **1988** Cle: 16 G; 1 Sac. **1989** Cle: 8 G. **Total:** 25 G; 1 Sac.

MARSHALL JONES Jones, Marshall Durell 5′11″, 165 **WB-TB-FB**
(Deacon) *Col:* North Dakota *HS:* Culver Mil. Acad. [IN]
B: 12/10/1894, Fargo, IN Deceased
1920 Ham-Det: 2 G. Ham: 1 G. Det: 1 G. **1921** Akr: 7 G. **Total:** 9 G.

DALE JONES Jones, Marvin Dale 6′1″, 234 **LB**
Col: Tennessee Mil. Acad. (J.C.); Tennessee *HS:* Bradley [Cleveland, TN] B: 3/8/1963, Cleveland, TN *Drafted:* 1987 Round 10 Dal
1987 Dal: 3 G.

MARVIN JONES Jones, Marvin Maurice 6′2″, 249 **LB**
(Shade Tree) *Col:* Florida State *HS:* Miami Northwestern [FL]
B: 6/28/1972, Miami, FL *Drafted:* 1993 Round 1 NYJ
1993 NYJ: 9 G. **1994** NYJ: 15 G; 0.5 Sac. **1995** NYJ: 10 G; 1.5 Sac. **1996** NYJ: 12 G; 1 Sac. **1997** NYJ: 16 G; 3 Sac. **Total:** 62 G; 6 Sac.

MELVIN JONES Jones, Melvin Curtis Jr. 6′2″, 260 **OG**
Col: Houston *HS:* Klein [TX] B: 2/27/1954, Houston, TX
Drafted: 1980 Round 7 Was
1981 Was: 11 G.

MIKE JONES Jones, Michael 6′4″, 224 **LB**
Col: Brockport State *HS:* Seward Park [New York, NY] B: 8/19/1964, New York, NY
1987 Buf: 1 G.

MIKE JONES Jones, Michael 6′3″, 224 **LB**
Col: Alcorn State; Jackson State *HS:* Male [Louisville, KY]
B: 7/12/1954, Chicago, IL
1977 Sea: 12 G.

MIKE JONES Jones, Michael Anthony 6′1″, 233 **LB**
Col: Missouri *HS:* Southwest [Kansas City, MO] B: 4/15/1969, Kansas City, MO
1991 LARd: 16 G. **1992** LARd: 16 G. **1993** LARd: 16 G. **1994** LARd: 16 G. **1995** Oak: 16 G; Int 1-23; **1** Fum TD; 6 Pt. **1996** Oak: 15 G; 1 Sac. **1997** StL: 16 G; Int 1-0; 2 Sac. **1998** StL: 16 G; Int 2-13; 3 Sac. **Total:** 127 G; Int 4-36; 1 Fum TD; 6 Pt; 6 Sac.

MIKE JONES Jones, Michael Anthony 5′11″, 181 **WR**
Col: Tennessee State *HS:* Riverside [Chattanooga, TN] B: 4/14/1960, Chattanooga, TN *Drafted:* 1983 Round 6 Min
1983 Min: Rush 1-9 9.0; KR 2-31 15.5. **1984** Min: Rush 4-45 11.3. **1985** Min: Rush 2-6 3.0. **Total:** Rush 7-60 8.6; KR 2-31 15.5.

		Receiving				
Year Team	**G**	**Rec**	**Yds**	**Avg**	**TD**	**Fum**
1983 Min	16	6	95	15.8	0	0
1984 Min	16	38	591	15.6	1	1
1985 Min	16	46	641	13.9	4	0
1986 NO	16	48	625	13.0	3	2
1987 NO	12	27	420	15.6	3	1
1989 NO	3	0	0	—	0	0
NFL Total	79	165	2372	14.4	11	4

MIKE JONES Jones, Michael David 6′4″, 290 **DE**
Col: North Carolina State *HS:* C.A. Johnson [Columbia, SC]
B: 8/25/1969, Columbia, SC *Drafted:* 1991 Round 2 Pho
1991 Pho: 16 G. **1992** Pho: 15 G; 6 Sac. **1993** Pho: 16 G; 3 Sac. **1994** NE: 16 G; 6 Sac. **1995** NE: 13 G; 3 Sac. **1996** NE: 16 G; 2 Sac. **1997** NE: 16 G; 4 Sac. **1998** StL: 16 G; KR 1-2 2.0; 2.5 Sac. **Total:** 124 G; KR 1-2 2.0; 26.5 Sac.

MIKE JONES Jones, Michael Lenere 6′3″, 255 **TE**
Col: Michigan; Texas A&M *HS:* Warren G. Harding [Bridgeport, CT]
B: 11/10/1966, Bridgeport, CT *Drafted:* 1990 Round 3 Min
1990 Min: 11 G. **1991** Min: 16 G; Rec 2-8 4.0 2 TD; 12 Pt. **1992** Sea: 4 G; Rec 3-18 6.0. **Total:** 31 G; Rec 5-26 5.2 2 TD; 12 Pt.

KIRK JONES Jones, Nolton Kirk 5′10″, 210 **RB**
Col: Nevada-Las Vegas *HS:* Long Beach Polytechnic [CA]
B: 1/5/1965, Long Beach, CA
1987 Cle: 1 G.

QUINTIN JONES Jones, Quintin Maurice 5′11″, 193 **DB**
Col: Pittsburgh *HS:* Ely [Pompano Beach, FL] B: 7/28/1966, Miami, FL
Drafted: 1988 Round 2 Hou
1988 Hou: 4 G. **1990** Hou: 1 G. **Total:** 5 G.

RALPH JONES Jones, Ralph Carroll 6′3″, 200 **OE-DE**
Col: Union (Tenn.); Alabama *HS:* Coffee [Florence, AL] B: 2/14/1922, Florence, AL D: 2/18/1995, Wilmington, NC
AAFC **1947** BalA: 6 G; Rec 3-23 7.7.

NFL **1946** Det: 11 G; Rec 4-84 21.0.

GENE JONES Jones, Ray Gene 6′0″, 200 **LB**
Col: Rice *HS:* Woodson [TX] B: 10/18/1936, Woodson, TX
Drafted: 1959 Round 13 ChiB
1961 Hou: 1 G.

RAY JONES Jones, Raymond 5′11″, 187 **DB**
Col: Southern University *HS:* Peabody [Alexandria, LA] B: 12/24/1947, Lufkin, TX *Drafted:* 1970 Round 2 Phi
1970 Phi: 12 G; KR 6-97 16.2; Int 2-17; 1 Fum. **1971** Mia: 2 G. **1972** SD: 14 G; KR 3-41 13.7; 2 Fum. **1973** NO: 2 G. **Total:** 30 G; KR 9-138 15.3; Int 2-17; 3 Fum.

TONY JONES Jones, Reginald Antonio 6′4″, 200 **DB**
Col: Syracuse *HS:* H.B. Plant [Tampa, FL] B: 2/16/1972, Tampa, FL
1995 Ariz: 2 G.

REGGIE JONES Jones, Reginald Moore 6′1″, 202 **DB**
Col: Memphis *HS:* West Memphis [AR] B: 1/11/1969, Memphis, TN
Drafted: 1991 Round 5 NO
1991 NO: 13 G; Int 3-61. **1992** NO: 15 G; Int 2-71 1 TD; 6 Pt. **1993** NO: 12 G; Int 1-12; 1 Sac. **1994** NO: 1 G. **Total:** 41 G; Int 6-144 1 TD; 6 Pt; 1 Sac.

REGGIE JONES Jones, Reginald Lee 6′0″, 175 **WR**
Col: Butler County CC KS; Louisiana State *HS:* Wyandotte [Kansas City, KS] B: 5/5/1971, Kansas City, KS
1995 Car: 1 G.

RENO JONES Jones, Reno Victor 6′0″, 195 **G**
Col: Cornell *HS:* Niles [OH] B: 2/20/1897, Niles, OH D: 1/7/1989, Wyckoff, NJ
1922 Tol: 4 G.

RICHARD JONES Jones, Richard B 5′9″, 183 **DB**
Col: Trinity Valley CC TX; Texas A&M–Kingsville *HS:* La Vega [Waco, TX]
B: 8/4/1973, Waco, TX
1996 Ind: 4 G.

BOB JONES Jones, Robert 6′1″, 194 **DB**
Col: Virginia Union *HS:* Fessenden [Martin, FL] B: 2/10/1951, Boardman, FL *Drafted:* 1973 Round 6 Cin
1973 Cin: 9 G. **1974** Cin: 14 G. **1975** Atl: 14 G; Rec 1-25 25.0. **1976** Atl: 14 G; PR 1-(-1) -1.0; KR 1-22 22.0. **Total:** 51 G; Rec 1-25 25.0; PR 1-(-1) -1.0; KR 1-22 22.0.

BRUCE JONES Jones, Robert Bruce 6′1″, 219 **G**
(Buck) *Col:* Alabama *HS:* Walker [Jasper, AL] B: 8/30/1904, Jasper, AL D: 12/1974, Evergreen, AL
1927 GB: 9 G. **1928** GB: 13 G; Int **1** TD; 6 Pt. **1930** Nwk: 2 G. **1932** Bkn: 12 G; Rec 1-10 10.0. **1933** Bkn: 8 G. **1934** Bkn: 10 G. **Total:** 54 G; Rec 1-10 10.0; Int 1 TD; 6 Pt.

BOB JONES Jones, Robert Dean 6′4″, 196 **WR**
Col: Mount San Antonio Coll. CA (J.C.); San Diego State *HS:* Claremont [CA] B: 8/25/1945, Warren, OH *Drafted:* 1967 Round 2 ChiB
1967 ChiB: 14 G; Rec 3-80 26.7 1 TD; 6 Pt. **1968** ChiB: 1 G. **Total:** 15 G; Rec 3-80 26.7 1 TD; 6 Pt.

BOBBY JONES Jones, Robert Ellis 5′11″, 180 **WR**
Col: Youngstown State; Millikin *HS:* Brookfield [OH] B: 7/12/1955, Sharon, PA
1979 NYJ: Rush 1-4 4.0; KR 7-140 20.0. **1980** NYJ: PR 1-0; KR 2-50 25.0. **1981** NYJ: PR 1-1 1.0; 1 Fum TD. **1983** Cle: Rush 1-19 19.0. **Total:** Rush 2-23 11.5; PR 2-1 0.5; KR 9-190 21.1; 1 Fum TD.

		Receiving					Tot
Year Team	**G**	**Rec**	**Yds**	**Avg**	**TD**	**Fum**	**TD**
1978 NYJ	16	1	18	18.0	0	0	0
1979 NYJ	10	19	379	19.9	1	2	1
1980 NYJ	15	14	193	13.8	0	0	0
1981 NYJ	16	16	239	14.9	1	0	2
1982 NYJ	9	3	32	10.7	0	0	0
1983 Cle	15	36	507	14.1	4	0	4
NFL Total	81	89	1368	15.4	6	2	7

BOBBY JONES Jones, Robert Irven 6′2″, 215 **G**
Col: Indiana *HS:* Wabash [IN] B: 3/28/1912, Wabash, IN
1934 GB: 12 G.

ROBERT JONES Jones, Robert Lee 6′3″, 244 **LB**
Col: East Carolina *HS:* Nottoway [VA]; Fork Union Mil. Acad. [VA]
B: 9/27/1969, Blackstone, VA *Drafted:* 1992 Round 1 Dal
1992 Dal: 15 G; 1 Sac. **1993** Dal: 13 G; KR 1-12 12.0. **1994** Dal: 16 G; KR 1-8 8.0. **1995** Dal: 12 G; 1 Sac. **1996** StL: 16 G; Int 1-0. **1997** StL: 16 G; 1 Sac. **1998** Mia: 16 G; Int 2-14 1 TD; 6 Pt; 5 Sac. **Total:** 104 G; KR 2-20 10.0; Int 3-14 1 TD; 6 Pt; 8 Sac.

SCOTT JONES Jones, Robert Scott 6′5″, 281 **OT**
Col: Washington *HS:* Clallam Bay [WA]; Port Angeles HS [WA]
B: 3/20/1966, Portland, OR *Drafted:* 1989 Round 12 Cin
1989 Cin: 15 G. **1990** NYJ: 3 G. **1991** GB-Cin: 4 G. GB: 2 G. Cin: 2 G. **Total:** 22 G.

ROBBIE JONES Jones, Robert Washington III 6′2″, 230 **LB**
Col: Alabama *HS:* Demopolis [AL] B: 12/25/1959, Demopolis, AL
Drafted: 1983 Round 12 NYG
1984 NYG: 16 G. **1985** NYG: 16 G. **1986** NYG: 16 G. **1987** NYG: 12 G. **Total:** 60 G.

ROD JONES Jones, Roderick Earl 6′4″, 240 **TE**
Col: Washington *HS:* El Cerrito [CA] B: 3/3/1964, Richmond, CA
Drafted: 1987 Round 8 NYG
1987 KC: 3 G; Rec 8-76 9.5 1 TD; 6 Pt; 1 Fum. **1988** KC: 2 G. **1989** Sea: 4 G. **Total:** 9 G; Rec 8-76 9.5 1 TD; 6 Pt; 1 Fum.

ROD JONES Jones, Roderick Wayne 6′0″, 185 **DB**
Col: Southern Methodist *HS:* South Oak Cliff [Dallas, TX]
B: 3/31/1964, Dallas, TX *Drafted:* 1986 Round 1 TB

		Interceptions		
Year Team	**G**	**Int**	**Yds**	**TD**
1986 TB	16	1	0	0
1987 TB	11	2	9	0
1988 TB	14	1	0	0
1989 TB	16	0	0	0
1990 Cin	16	0	0	0
1991 Cin	4	0	0	0
1992 Cin	16	2	14	0
1993 Cin	16	1	0	0
1994 Cin	16	0	0	0
1995 Cin	13	1	24	0

1996 Cin	6	2	2	0
NFL Total	144	10	49	0

ROD JONES Jones, Rodrek Edward 6′4″, 325 **OT**
Col: Kansas *HS:* Henry Ford [Detroit, MI] B: 1/11/1974, Detroit, MI *Drafted:* 1996 Round 7 Cin
1996 Cin: 5 G. **1997** Cin: 13 G. **1998** Cin: 6 G. **Total:** 24 G.

ROGER JONES Jones, Roger Carver 5′9″, 175 **DB**
Col: Tennessee State *HS:* Pearl-Cohn [Nashville, TN] B: 4/22/1969, Cleveland, TN
1991 TB: 6 G. **1992** TB: 9 G; 1 Fum TD; 6 Pt. **1993** TB: 16 G; 1 Sac. **1994** Cin: 16 G; PR 1-0; 1 Fum; 1.5 Sac. **1995** Cin: 16 G; Int 1-17 1 TD; 6 Pt; 2 Sac. **1996** Cin: 14 G; Int 1-30. **1997** Ten: 2 G; Int 1-24. **Total:** 79 G; PR 1-0; Int 3-71 1 TD; 1 Fum TD; Tot TD 2; 12 Pt; 1 Fum; 4.5 Sac.

RON JONES Jones, Ronald Gene 6′3″, 220 **TE**
Col: Trinity Valley CC TX; Texas-El Paso *HS:* W.W. Samuell [Dallas, TX] B: 10/7/1946, Dallas, TX *Drafted:* 1969 Round 6 GB
1969 GB: 6 G.

RONDELL JONES Jones, Rondell Tony 6′2″, 210 **DB**
Col: North Carolina *HS:* Northern [Owings, MD] B: 5/7/1971, Sunderland, MD *Drafted:* 1993 Round 3 Den
1993 Den: 16 G. **1994** Den: 16 G; Int 2-9. **1995** Den: 14 G. **1996** Den: 16 G. **1997** Bal: 14 G; Int 1-15. **Total:** 76 G; Int 3-24.

RULON JONES Jones, Rulon Kent 6′6″, 260 **DE**
Col: Utah State *HS:* Weber [Ogden, UT] B: 3/25/1958, Salt Lake City, UT *Drafted:* 1980 Round 2 Den
1980 Den: 16 G; Scor **1** Saf; 2 Pt. **1981** Den: 16 G. **1982** Den: 9 G; 2 Sac. **1983** Den: 12 G; Scor 1 Saf; 2 Pt; 4 Sac. **1984** Den: 16 G; **1** Fum TD; 6 Pt; 11 Sac. **1985** Den: 16 G; 10 Sac. **1986** Den: 16 G; Scor **1** Saf; 2 Pt; 13.5 Sac. **1987** Den: 12 G; 7 Sac. **1988** Den: 16 G; 5 Sac. **Total:** 129 G; Scor 3 Saf; 1 Fum TD; 12 Pt; 52.5 Sac.

SELWYN JONES Jones, Selwyn Aldridge 6′0″, 192 **DB**
Col: Colorado State *HS:* Willowridge [Sugar Land, TX] B: 5/13/1970, Houston, TX *Drafted:* 1992 Round 7 Cle
1993 Cle: 11 G; Int 3-0. **1994** NO: 5 G. **1995** Sea: 15 G; Int 1-0. **1996** Sea: 16 G. **Total:** 47 G; Int 4-0.

STAN JONES Jones, Stanley Paul 6′1″, 252 **OG-DT-OT**
Col: Maryland *HS:* Lemoyne [PA] B: 11/24/1931, Altoona, PA *Drafted:* 1953 Round 5 ChiB *HOF:* 1991
1954 ChiB: 12 G. **1955** ChiB: 12 G. **1956** ChiB: 11 G. **1957** ChiB: 12 G. **1958** ChiB: 12 G. **1959** ChiB: 12 G. **1960** ChiB: 12 G. **1961** ChiB: 14 G. **1962** ChiB: 14 G. **1963** ChiB: 13 G. **1964** ChiB: 14 G. **1965** ChiB: 6 G. **1966** Was: 13 G. **Total:** 157 G.

STEVE JONES Jones, Steven Hunter 6′0″, 200 **RB**
Col: Duke *HS:* Central [Sanford, NC] B: 3/6/1951, Sanford, NC *Drafted:* 1973 Round 5 LARm
1973 Buf: KR 6-116 19.3. **1975** StL: KR 1-18 18.0. **1977** StL: KR 8-132 16.5. **Total:** KR 15-266 17.7.

		Rushing				Receiving					Tot
Year Team	G	Att	Yds	Avg	TD	Rec	Yds	Avg	TD	Fum	TD
1973 Buf	11	3	9	3.0	0	0	0	—	0	0	0
1974 Buf-StL	8	0	0	—	0	0	0	—	0	0	0
1974 Buf	1	0	0	—	0	0	0	—	0	0	0
1974 StL	7	0	0	—	0	0	0	—	0	0	0
1975 StL	13	54	275	5.1	2	19	194	10.2	1	3	3
1976 StL	13	113	451	4.0	8	29	152	5.2	1	2	9
1977 StL	14	24	77	3.2	3	12	66	5.5	0	0	3
1978 StL	16	105	392	3.7	2	27	217	8.0	0	5	2
NFL Total	75	299	1204	4.0	15	87	629	7.2	2	10	17

TEBUCKY JONES Jones, Tebucky Shermaine 6′1″, 216 **DB**
Col: Syracuse *HS:* New Britain [CT] B: 10/6/1974, SC *Drafted:* 1998 Round 1 NE
1998 NE: 16 G.

TERRY JONES Jones, Terry Wayne 6′2″, 259 **NT-DT**
Col: Alabama *HS:* Washington Co. [Sandersville, GA] B: 11/8/1956, Sandersville, GA *Drafted:* 1978 Round 11 GB
1978 GB: 16 G. **1979** GB: 12 G. **1980** GB: 15 G. **1981** GB: 16 G. **1982** GB: 9 G; 3 Sac. **1983** GB: 1 G. **1984** GB: 16 G; 4 Sac. **Total:** 85 G; 7 Sac.

POTSY JONES Jones, Thomas Clinton 5′11″, 216 **G**
(Potsville) *Col:* Bucknell *HS:* Branch Twp. [Llewellyn, PA] B: 10/15/1909, Llewellyn, PA D: 7/3/1990, Lucama, NC
1930 Min: 2 G. Fra: 14 G. **1931** Fra: 8 G. **1932** NYG: 9 G; **1** Fum TD; 6 Pt. **1933** NYG: 7 G. **1934** NYG: 12 G. **1935** NYG: 9 G. **1936** NYG: 10 G. **1938** GB: 8 G. **Total:** 79 G; 1 Fum TD; 6 Pt.

TOM JONES Jones, Thomas Lee 6′6″, 300 **DT**
(Emporor) *Col:* Kentucky State; Miami (Ohio) *HS:* Cincinnati Central Voc. [OH] B: 6/22/1931, Cincinnati, OH D: 8/28/1978, Port Chevron, Canada *Drafted:* 1954 Round 9 Cle
1955 Cle: 2 G.

THURMAN JONES Jones, Thurman Lee 5′10″, 198 **FB-DB**
(Tugboat) *Col:* Abilene Christian *HS:* Gladewater [TX] B: 4/6/1918, Wilson, OK D: 1/16/1988, Tugwell, TX
1941 Bkn: 1 G; Rush 1-3 3.0. **1942** Bkn: 4 G; Rush 1-2 2.0; Scor 1, 1-1 100.0% XK. **Total:** 5 G; Rush 2-5 2.5; Scor 1, 1-1 100.0% XK.

TODD JONES Jones, Todd A 6′3″, 295 **OT**
Col: Arkansas; Henderson State *HS:* Little Rock Central [AR] B: 7/3/1967, Hope, AR *Drafted:* 1991 Round 11 Cle
1993 NE: 4 G.

TONY JONES Jones, Tony Edward 6′5″, 290 **OT-OG**
Col: Western Carolina *HS:* Franklin Co. [Carnesville, GA] B: 5/24/1966, Royston, GA
1988 Cle: 4 G. **1989** Cle: 9 G. **1990** Cle: 16 G. **1991** Cle: 16 G. **1992** Cle: 16 G. **1993** Cle: 16 G. **1994** Cle: 16 G. **1995** Cle: 16 G. **1996** Bal: 15 G. **1997** Den: 16 G. **1998** Den: 16 G. **Total:** 156 G.

TYRONE JONES Jones, Tyrone 6′0″, 220 **LB**
Col: Southern University *HS:* Camden Co. [St. Mary's, GA] B: 8/3/1961, St. Marys, GA
1988 Pho: 1 G.

VICTOR JONES Jones, Victor Pernell 6′2″, 250 **LB**
Col: Virginia Tech *HS:* Robert E. Peary [Rockville, MD] B: 10/19/1966, Rockville, MD *Drafted:* 1988 Round 12 TB
1988 TB: 8 G. **1989** Det: 11 G. **1990** Det: 16 G; Int 1-0; 1 Sac. **1991** Det: 10 G. **1992** Det: 16 G. **1993** Det: 16 G. **1994** Det: 16 G. **Total:** 93 G; Int 1-0; 1 Sac.

VICTOR JONES Jones, Victor Tyrone 5′8″, 212 **RB**
Col: Louisiana State *HS:* Zachary [LA] B: 12/5/1967, Zachary, LA
1990 Hou: 10 G; Rush 14-75 5.4; 1 Fum. **1991** Hou: 14 G; KR 1-7 7.0. **1992** Den: 16 G; Rec 3-17 5.7. **1993** Pit: 16 G. **1994** Pit-KC: 11 G. Pit: 10 G. KC: 1 G. **Total:** 67 G; Rush 14-75 5.4; Rec 3-17 5.7; KR 1-7 7.0; 1 Fum.

WALTER JONES Jones, Walter Junior 6′5″, 300 **OT**
Col: Holmes CC MS; Florida State *HS:* Aliceville [AL] B: 1/19/1974, Aliceville, AL *Drafted:* 1997 Round 1 Sea
1997 Sea: 12 G. **1998** Sea: 16 G. **Total:** 28 G.

WAYNE JONES Jones, Wayne Walter 6′4″, 270 **OG**
Col: Utah *HS:* Big Bear [Big Bear Lake, CA] B: 2/10/1960, Grand Island, NE *Drafted:* 1982 Round 10 Mia
1987 Min: 6 G.

DUB JONES Jones, William Augustus 6′4″, 202 **HB-DB-WB-TB**
Col: Tulane *HS:* Ruston [LA] B: 12/29/1924, Arcadia, LA *Drafted:* 1946 Round 1 ChiC
AAFC **1946** MiaA-BknA: Pass 2-1 50.0%, 1 Int; PR 1-6 6.0; KR 6-91 15.2. **1947** BknA: Pass 15-3 20.0%, 37 2.47 2 Int; PR 14-157 11.2; KR 7-121 17.3; Int 2-35. **1948** CleA: Rec 9-119 13.2 2 TD; KR 2-35 17.5. **1949** CleA: Rec 12-241 20.1 1 TD; KR 8-204 25.5. **Total:** Pass 17-4 23.5%, 37 2.18 3 Int; Rec 21-360 17.1 3 TD; PR 15-163 10.9; KR 23-451 19.6; Int 2-35.

		Rushing				Tot
Year Team	G	Att	Yds	Avg	TD	TD
1946 MiaA-BknA	11	43	163	3.8	0	0
1947 BknA	8	43	136	3.2	1	1
1948 CleA	12	33	149	4.5	1	3
1949 CleA	11	77	312	4.1	4	5
AAFC Total	42	196	760	3.9	6	9

NFL **1952** Cle: Pass 2-1 50.0%, 3 1.50 1 TD. **1953** Cle: Pass 1-0; PR 1-7 7.0. **Total:** Pass 3-1 33.3%, 3 1.00 1 TD; PR 1-7 7.0.

		Rushing				Receiving					Tot
Year Team	G	Att	Yds	Avg	TD	Rec	Yds	Avg	TD	Fum	TD
1950 Cle	12	83	384	4.6	6	31	458	14.8	5	1	11
1951 Cle	12	104	492	4.7	7	30	570	19.0	5	3	12
1952 Cle	12	65	270	4.2	2	43	651	15.1	4	2	6
1953 Cle	12	31	28	0.9	0	24	373	15.5	0	3	0
1954 Cle	12	51	231	4.5	0	19	347	18.3	2	1	2
1955 Cle	12	10	44	4.4	0	3	115	38.3	1	1	1
NFL Total	72	344	1449	4.2	15	150	2514	16.8	17	11	32

WILLIE JONES Jones, William D 5′11″, 208 **FB**
Col: Purdue *HS:* Robstown [TX] B: 8/30/1939, Angleton, TX *Drafted:* 1961 Round 17 Min
1962 Buf: 10 G; Rush 4-17 4.3; KR 14-287 20.5; 2 Fum.

BILLY JONES Jones, William H Jr. 6′0″, 220 **G**
Col: Charleston (WV); West Virginia Wesleyan *HS:* Mannington [WV] B: 1/30/1920, Mannington, WV D: 2/1988, Lexington, NC
AAFC **1947** BknA: 7 G.

BILL JONES Jones, William Jr. 5′11″, 228 **RB**
Col: Southern Methodist; Southwest Texas State *HS:* Corsicana [TX] B: 9/10/1966, Abilene, TX *Drafted:* 1989 Round 12 KC
1990 KC: Rush 10-47 4.7. **Total:** Rush 10-47 4.7.

Year Team	G	Receiving Rec	Yds	Avg	TD
1990 KC	16	19	137	7.2	5
1991 KC	15	14	97	6.9	1
1992 KC	7	2	6	3.0	0
NFL Total	38	35	240	6.9	6

WILLIE JONES Jones, Willie Lee 6′1″, 260 **DT-DE**
Col: Kansas State *HS:* McKinley [St. Louis, MO] B: 5/28/1942, Moro, AR *Drafted:* 1966 Round 18 StL
1967 Hou: 6 G. **1968** Cin: 1 G. **1970** Cin: 10 G. **1971** Cin: 5 G. **Total:** 22 G.

WILLIE JONES Jones, Willie Lorenzo 6′4″, 240 **DE**
Col: Florida State *HS:* South Dade [Homestead, FL] B: 11/22/1957, Dublin, GA *Drafted:* 1979 Round 2 Oak
1979 Oak: 16 G. **1980** Oak: 16 G; **1** Fum TD; 6 Pt. **1981** Oak: 8 G; 1 Fum TD; 6 Pt. **Total:** 40 G; 2 Fum TD; 12 Pt.

ANDREW JORDAN Jordan, Andrew 6′4″, 260 **TE**
Col: North Greenville Coll. SC (J.C.); Western Carolina *HS:* West Charlotte [Charlotte, NC] B: 6/21/1972, Charlotte, NC *Drafted:* 1994 Round 6 Min
1994 Min: KR 1-8 8.0; Scor 1 2XP. **1996** Min: Scor 1 2XP. **Total:** KR 1-8 8.0; Scor 2 2XP.

Year Team	G	Receiving Rec	Yds	Avg	TD	Fum
1994 Min	16	35	336	9.6	0	1
1995 Min	13	27	185	6.9	2	1
1996 Min	13	19	128	6.7	0	0
1997 Min-TB	4	1	0	0.0	0	0
1997 Min	2	0	0	—	0	0
1997 TB	2	1	0	0.0	0	0
1998 Phi	3	2	9	4.5	0	0
NFL Total	49	84	658	7.8	2	2

TONY JORDAN Jordan, Anthony T 6′2″, 220 **RB**
Col: Kansas State *HS:* East [Rochester, NY] B: 5/5/1965, Rochester, NY *Drafted:* 1988 Round 5 Pho
1988 Pho: Rec 4-24 6.0. **1989** Pho: Rec 6-20 3.3. **Total:** Rec 10-44 4.4.

Year Team	G	Rushing Att	Yds	Avg	TD	Fum
1988 Pho	9	61	160	2.6	3	1
1989 Pho	13	83	211	2.5	2	4
NFL Total	22	144	371	2.6	5	5

BRIAN JORDAN Jordan, Brian O'Neil 5′11″, 205 **DB**
Col: Richmond *HS:* Milford Mill [Baltimore, MD] B: 3/29/1967, Baltimore, MD *Drafted:* 1989 Round 7 Buf
1989 Atl: 4 G; PR 4-34 8.5; KR 3-27 9.0; 1 Fum. **1990** Atl: 16 G; PR 2-19 9.5; Int 3-14. **1991** Atl: 16 G; PR 14-116 8.3; KR 5-100 20.0; Int 2-3; Scor **2** Saf; 4 Pt; 4 Sac. **Total:** 36 G; PR 20-169 8.5; KR 8-127 15.9; Int 5-17; Scor 2 Saf; 4 Pt; 1 Fum; 4 Sac.

CHARLES JORDAN Jordan, Charles Alexander 5′11″, 182 **WR**
(CJ) *Col:* Long Beach City Coll. CA (J.C.) *HS:* Morningside [Inglewood, CA] B: 10/9/1969, Los Angeles, CA
1994 GB: Rush 1-5 5.0. **1997** Mia: Rush 3-12 4.0. **Total:** Rush 4-17 4.3.

Year Team	G	Receiving Rec	Yds	Avg	TD	Punt Returns Ret	Yds	Avg	TD
1994 GB	10	0	0	—	0	1	0	0.0	0
1995 GB	6	7	117	16.7	2	21	213	10.1	0
1996 Mia	6	7	152	21.7	0	0	0	—	0
1997 Mia	14	27	471	17.4	3	26	273	10.5	0
1998 Mia	3	2	17	8.5	0	5	47	9.4	0
NFL Total	39	43	757	17.6	5	53	533	10.1	0

Year Team	Kickoff Returns Ret	Yds	Avg	TD	Fum
1994 GB	5	115	23.0	0	1
1995 GB	21	444	21.1	0	1
1996 Mia	4	81	20.3	0	0
1997 Mia	1	6	6.0	0	2
1998 Mia	0	0	—	0	2
NFL Total	31	646	20.8	0	6

CURTIS JORDAN Jordan, Curtis Wayne 6′2″, 200 **DB**
Col: Texas Tech *HS:* Monterey [Lubbock, TX] B: 1/25/1954, Lubbock, TX *Drafted:* 1976 Round 6 TB
1980 TB: KR 1-0. **1984** Was: **1** Fum TD. **Total:** KR 1-0; 1 Fum TD.

Year Team	G	Interceptions Int	Yds	TD	Tot TD
1976 TB	11	2	10	0	0
1977 TB	12	1	0	0	0
1978 TB	16	3	23	0	0
1979 TB	16	0	0	0	0
1980 TB	16	0	0	0	0
1981 Was	2	0	0	0	0
1982 Was	9	0	0	0	1
1983 Was	15	1	20	0	0
1984 Was	16	2	18	0	1
1985 Was	16	5	88	0	0
1986 Was	16	3	46	0	0
NFL Total	145	17	205	0	2

DARIN JORDAN Jordan, Darin Godfrey 6′1″, 242 **LB-DE**
Col: Northeastern *HS:* Stoughton [MA] B: 12/4/1964, Boston, MA *Drafted:* 1988 Round 5 Pit
1988 Pit: 15 G; Int 1-28 1 TD; 6 Pt. **1990** LARd: Postseason only. **1991** SF: 15 G; Scor 1 Saf; 2 Pt. **1992** SF: 15 G. **1993** SF: 14 G. **1994** SF: Postseason only. **Total:** 59 G; Int 1-28 1 TD; Scor 1 Saf; 8 Pt.

DAVID JORDAN Jordan, David Turner 6′6″, 274 **OG**
Col: Auburn *HS:* Vestavia Hills [AL] B: 6/14/1962, Birmingham, AL *Drafted:* 1984 Round 10 NYG
1984 NYG: 14 G. **1985** NYG: 16 G. **1987** TB: 3 G. **Total:** 33 G.

DONALD JORDAN Jordan, Donald Ray 6′0″, 210 **RB**
Col: Houston *HS:* James Madison [Houston, TX] B: 2/9/1962, Houston, TX *Drafted:* 1984 Round 12 ChiB
1984 ChiB: 13 G; Rush 11-70 6.4; Rec 1-6 6.0; KR 5-62 12.4; 1 Fum.

FRANK JORDAN Jordan, Francis 168 **WB**
Col: Bucknell; Villanova B: 12/5/1897, Minneapolis, MN D: 9/1980, Tuscon, AZ
1920 RI: 3 G. **1923** Mil: 1 G. **Total:** 4 G.

HENRY JORDAN Jordan, Henry Wendell 6′2″, 248 **DT-DE**
Col: Virginia *HS:* Emporia [VA]; Warwick HS [Newport News, VA] B: 1/26/1935, Emporia, VA D: 2/21/1977, Milwaukee, WI *Drafted:* 1957 Round 5 Cle *HOF:* 1995
1957 Cle: 12 G. **1958** Cle: 12 G. **1959** GB: 12 G. **1960** GB: 12 G. **1961** GB: 14 G. **1962** GB: 14 G; Int 1-0. **1963** GB: 14 G. **1964** GB: 12 G; 1 Fum TD; 6 Pt. **1965** GB: 14 G. **1966** GB: 14 G. **1967** GB: 14 G. **1968** GB: 14 G. **1969** GB: 5 G. **Total:** 163 G; Int 1-0; 1 Fum TD; 6 Pt.

JIMMY JORDAN Jordan, James Andrew 6′1″, 200 **RB**
Col: Florida *HS:* Chamberlain [Tampa, FL] B: 8/11/1944, Glenville, GA *Drafted:* 1967 Round 3 Atl
1967 NO: 1 G; KR 3-56 18.7.

JEFF JORDAN Jordan, Jefferson Flynn 6′3″, 190 **DB**
Col: Tulsa *HS:* Bristow [OK] B: 11/23/1943, San Antonio, TX *Drafted:* 1965 Round 8 Min
1965 Min: 12 G; Int 4-45. **1966** Min: 14 G. **1967** Min: 11 G. **Total:** 37 G; Int 4-45.

JEFF JORDAN Jordan, Jeffrey Lincoln 6′1″, 215 **RB**
Col: Washington *HS:* Central Valley [Veradale, WA] B: 7/12/1945, St. Louis, MO
1970 LARm: 9 G; Rush 10-50 5.0; Rec 1-(-5) -5.0; 1 Fum. **1971** Was: 1 G. **1972** Was: 1 G. **Total:** 11 G; Rush 10-50 5.0; Rec 1-(-5) -5.0; 1 Fum.

KEN JORDAN Jordan, Kenneth Ray 6′2″, 235 **LB**
Col: Tuskegee *HS:* Jackson-Olin [Birmingham, AL] B: 4/29/1964, Birmingham, AL
1987 GB: 3 G; 1 Sac.

KEVIN JORDAN Jordan, Kevin Michael 6′2″, 197 **WR**
Col: UCLA *HS:* High Point [Beltsville, MD] B: 12/14/1972, Washington, DC
1996 Ariz: 1 G.

LARRY JORDAN Jordan, Lawrence Gene 6′6″, 230 **DE-LB**
Col: Youngstown State *HS:* South [Youngstown, OH] B: 4/18/1938, Youngstown, OH
1962 Den: 2 G. **1964** Den: 8 G; KR 1-0. **Total:** 10 G; KR 1-0.

LEE ROY JORDAN Jordan, Lee Roy 6′1″, 221 **LB**
Col: Alabama *HS:* Excel [AL] B: 4/27/1941, Excel, AL *Drafted:* 1963 Round 1 Dal
1967 Dal: Scor **1** Saf. **Total:** Scor 1 Saf.

Year Team	G	Interceptions Int	Yds	TD	Fum
1963 Dal	7	3	41	0	0
1964 Dal	12	1	3	0	0
1965 Dal	13	0	0	0	0
1966 Dal	14	1	49	1	0
1967 Dal	14	3	85	1	0
1968 Dal	14	3	17	0	0
1969 Dal	14	2	38	0	0
1970 Dal	14	1	6	0	0
1971 Dal	14	2	34	0	0
1972 Dal	14	2	18	0	0
1973 Dal	14	6	78	1	1
1974 Dal	14	2	23	0	0
1975 Dal	14	6	80	0	1
1976 Dal	14	0	0	0	0
NFL Total	186	32	472	3	2

BUFORD JORDAN Jordan, Paul Buford 6′0″, 222 **RB**
Col: McNeese State *HS:* Iota [LA] B: 6/26/1962, Lafayette, LA
Drafted: 1984 Supplemental Round 1 GB
1987 NO: PR 1-13 13.0; KR 2-28 14.0. **1988** NO: **1** Fum TD. **1991** NO: KR 2-18 9.0. **1992** NO: KR 1-18 18.0. **Total:** PR 1-13 13.0; KR 5-64 12.8; 1 Fum TD.

		Rushing				Receiving					Tot
Year Team	**G**	**Att**	**Yds**	**Avg**	**TD**	**Rec**	**Yds**	**Avg**	**TD**	**Fum**	**TD**
1986 NO	16	68	207	3.0	1	11	127	11.5	0	2	1
1987 NO	12	12	36	3.0	2	2	13	6.5	0	0	2
1988 NO	14	19	115	6.1	0	5	70	14.0	0	1	1
1989 NO	11	38	179	4.7	3	4	53	13.3	0	0	3
1990 NO	6	0	0	—	0	0	0	—	0	0	0
1991 NO	14	47	150	3.2	2	15	92	6.1	1	2	3
1992 NO	2	0	0	—	0	0	0	—	0	1	0
NFL Total	75	184	687	3.7	8	37	355	9.6	1	6	10

RANDY JORDAN Jordan, Randy Loment 5′10″, 207 **RB**
Col: North Carolina *HS:* Warren Co. [Warrenton, NC] B: 6/6/1970, Henderson, NC
1993 LARd: Rec 4-42 10.5. **1995** Jac: Rec 5-89 17.8 1 TD. **1998** Oak: Rec 3-2 0.7. **Total:** Rec 12-133 11.1 1 TD.

		Rushing				Kickoff Returns					Tot
Year Team	**G**	**Ret**	**Yds**	**Avg**	**TD**	**Ret**	**Yds**	**Avg**	**TD**	**Fum**	**TD**
1993 LARd	10	12	33	2.8	0	0	0	—	0	2	0
1995 Jac	12	21	62	3.0	0	2	41	20.5	0	0	1
1996 Jac	15	0	0	—	0	26	553	21.3	0	1	0
1997 Jac	7	1	2	2.0	0	0	0	—	0	0	0
1998 Oak	16	47	159	3.4	1	0	0	—	0	1	1
NFL Total	60	81	256	3.2	1	28	594	21.2	0	4	2

RICHARD JORDAN Jordan, Richard Lamont 6′1″, 245 **LB**
Col: Missouri Southern State *HS:* Vian [OK] B: 12/1/1974, Holdenville, OK
1997 Det: 10 G. **1998** Det: 16 G; Int 1-4. **Total:** 26 G; Int 1-4.

SHELBY JORDAN Jordan, Shelby Lewis 6′7″, 260 **OT**
Col: Washington-St. Louis *HS:* East St. Louis [IL] B: 1/23/1952, St. Louis, MO *Drafted:* 1973 Round 7 Hou
1975 NE: 14 G. **1977** NE: 10 G. **1978** NE: 16 G. **1979** NE: 14 G. **1980** NE: 16 G. **1981** NE: 16 G. **1982** NE: 9 G. **1983** LARd: 13 G. **1984** LARd: 11 G. **1985** LARd: 16 G. **1986** LARd: 16 G. **Total:** 151 G.

STEVE JORDAN Jordan, Stephen Bernard 5′10″, 205 **K**
Col: USC *HS:* Archbishop Riordan [San Francisco, CA] B: 3/20/1963, San Francisco, CA
1987 Ind: 3 G; Scor 16, 3-5 60.0% FG, 7-7 100.0% XK.

STEVE JORDAN Jordan, Steven Russell 6′3″, 236 **TE**
Col: Brown *HS:* South Mountain [Phoenix, AZ] B: 1/10/1961, Phoenix, AZ *Drafted:* 1982 Round 7 Min
1984 Min: Rush 1-4 4.0 1 TD. **1990** Min: KR 1-(-3) -3.0. **Total:** Rush 1-4 4.0 1 TD; KR 1-(-3) -3.0.

		Receiving					Tot
Year Team	**G**	**Rec**	**Yds**	**Avg**	**TD**	**Fum**	**TD**
1982 Min	9	3	42	14.0	0	0	0
1983 Min	13	15	212	14.1	2	0	2
1984 Min	14	38	414	10.9	2	0	3
1985 Min	16	68	795	11.7	0	2	0
1986 Min	16	58	859	14.8	6	0	6
1987 Min	12	35	490	14.0	2	1	2
1988 Min	16	57	756	13.3	5	2	5
1989 Min	16	35	506	14.5	3	1	3
1990 Min	16	45	636	14.1	3	3	3
1991 Min	16	57	638	11.2	2	2	2
1992 Min	14	28	394	14.1	2	0	2
1993 Min	14	56	542	9.7	1	0	1
1994 Min	4	3	23	7.7	0	0	0
NFL Total	176	498	6307	12.7	28	11	29

TIM JORDAN Jordan, Timothy Christopher 6′3″, 226 **LB**
Col: Wisconsin *HS:* Robert M. LaFollette [Madison, WI] B: 4/26/1964, Madison, WI *Drafted:* 1987 Round 4 NE
1987 NE: 5 G. **1988** NE: 16 G; Int 1-31; 3 Sac. **1989** NE: 9 G. **Total:** 30 G; Int 1-31; 3 Sac.

TIM JORDEN Jorden, Timothy Robert 6′3″, 235 **TE**
Col: Indiana *HS:* Fenwick [Middletown, OH] B: 10/30/1966, Lakewood, OH
1990 Pho: 16 G; Rec 2-10 5.0. **1991** Pho: 16 G; Rec 15-127 8.5. **1992** Pit: 15 G; Rec 6-28 4.7 2 TD; 12 Pt. **1993** Pit: 16 G; Rec 1-12 12.0. **Total:** 63 G; Rec 24-177 7.4 2 TD; 12 Pt.

ANTONY JORDON Jordon, Antony 6′2″, 234 **LB**
Col: Vanderbilt *HS:* Washington Twp. [Sewell, NJ] B: 12/19/1974, Sewell, NJ *Drafted:* 1998 Round 5 Ind
1998 Ind: 15 G.

BUD JORGENSEN Jorgensen, Carl A 6′0″, 205 **T**
Col: St. Mary's (Cal.) *HS:* San Mateo [CA] B: 2/5/1911, Denmark D: 7/2/1984, Arcadia, CA
1934 GB: 10 G. **1935** Phi: 11 G; Scor 4, 1 FG, 1 XK. **Total:** 21 G; Scor 4, 1 FG, 1 XK.

WAYNE JORGENSEN Jorgensen, Wagner 0 6′2″, 215 **C-LB**
Col: St. Mary's (Cal.) *HS:* San Mateo [CA] B: 7/31/1913, Denmark D: 7/24/1977, San Mateo, CA *Drafted:* 1936 Round 3 Bkn
1936 Bkn: 8 G. **1937** Bkn: 10 G. **Total:** 18 G.

RED JOSEPH Joseph, Chalmer Edward 6′3″, 188 **OE**
(Chal) *Col:* Miami (Ohio); Ohio State *HS:* East [Columbus, OH] B: 11/7/1905, OH D: 9/17/1983, Harlingen, TX
1927 Day: 8 G. **1930** Port: 12 G; Rec 1 TD; 6 Pt. **1931** Cle: 1 G. **Total:** 21 G; Rec 1 TD; 6 Pt.

DWAYNE JOSEPH Joseph, Dwayne Leonard 5′9″, 180 **DB**
Col: Syracuse *HS:* Miami Carol City [Miami, FL] B: 6/2/1972, Miami, FL
1995 ChiB: 16 G; Int 2-31.

JAMES JOSEPH Joseph, James Jr. 6′0″, 222 **RB**
Col: Auburn *HS:* Central [Phenix City, AL] B: 10/28/1967, Phenix City, AL *Drafted:* 1991 Round 7 Phi
1994 Phi: KR 1-11 11.0. **1995** Cin: KR 1-17 17.0. **Total:** KR 2-28 14.0.

		Rushing				Receiving					Tot
Year Team	**G**	**Att**	**Yds**	**Avg**	**TD**	**Rec**	**Yds**	**Avg**	**TD**	**Fum**	**TD**
1991 Phi	16	135	440	3.3	3	10	64	6.4	0	2	3
1992 Phi	16	0	0	—	0	0	0	—	0	0	0
1993 Phi	16	39	140	3.6	0	29	291	10.0	1	0	1
1994 Phi	14	60	203	3.4	1	43	344	8.0	2	1	3
1995 Cin	16	16	40	2.5	0	20	118	5.9	0	1	0
NFL Total	78	250	823	3.3	4	102	817	8.0	3	4	7

KERRY JOSEPH Joseph, Kerry Tremaine 6′1″, 205 **DB**
Col: McNeese State *HS:* New Iberia [LA] B: 10/4/1973, New Iberia, LA
1998 Sea: 16 G; PR 15-182 12.1; KR 2-49 24.5; 1 Fum.

VANCE JOSEPH Joseph, Vance Desmond 6′0″, 202 **DB**
Col: Colorado *HS:* Archbishop Shaw [Marrero, LA] B: 9/20/1972, Marrero, LA
1995 NYJ: 13 G; Int 2-39. **1996** Ind: 4 G. **Total:** 17 G; Int 2-39.

ZIP JOSEPH Joseph, Zern Carlton 6′2″, 183 **E-G-C-WB**
Col: Miami (Ohio) *HS:* East [Columbus, OH] B: 5/1903 D: 11/1977
1925 Day: 5 G. **1927** Day: 6 G. **Total:** 11 G.

LES JOSEPHSON Josephson, Lester Andrew 6′1″, 207 **RB**
Col: Augustana (S.D.) *HS:* Minneota [MN] B: 7/29/1942, Minneota, MN
1965 LARm: Pass 2-1 50.0%, 15 7.50 1 TD. **1967** LARm: Pass 5-2 40.0%, 47 9.40 1 Int; KR 5-91 18.2. **1970** LARm: Pass 1-1 100.0%, 25 25.00. **1971** LARm: KR 1-0. **Total:** Pass 8-4 50.0%, 87 10.88 1 TD 1 Int; KR 6-91 15.2.

		Rushing				Receiving					Tot
Year Team	**G**	**Att**	**Yds**	**Avg**	**TD**	**Rec**	**Yds**	**Avg**	**TD**	**Fum**	**TD**
1964 LARm	14	96	451	4.7	3	21	269	12.8	1	5	4
1965 LARm	13	71	225	3.2	0	18	169	9.4	0	1	0
1966 LARm	14	14	97	6.9	0	2	10	5.0	1	1	1
1967 LARm	14	178	800	4.5	4	37	400	10.8	4	4	8
1969 LARm	14	124	461	3.7	0	32	295	9.2	2	4	2
1970 LARm	12	150	640	4.3	5	44	427	9.7	0	3	5
1971 LARm	14	99	449	4.5	3	26	230	8.8	2	3	5
1972 LARm	8	18	75	4.2	0	14	170	12.1	1	1	1
1973 LARm	14	36	174	4.8	2	0	0	—	0	0	2
1974 LARm	12	11	35	3.2	0	0	0	—	0	0	0
NFL Total	129	797	3407	4.3	17	194	1970	10.2	11	22	28

BOB JOSWICK Joswick, Robert Leonard 6′5″, 250 **DE-DT**
Col: Tulsa *HS:* South Union [Uniontown, PA] B: 1/12/1946, Uniontown, PA *Drafted:* 1968 Round 13 Mia
1968 Mia: 1 G. **1969** Mia: 5 G. **Total:** 6 G.

YONEL JOURDAIN Jourdain, Yonel 5′11″, 204 **RB**
Col: Southern Illinois *HS:* Evanston Twp. [Evanston, IL] B: 4/20/1971, Brooklyn, NY
1994 Buf: Rec 10-56 5.6. **1995** Buf: Rec 1-7 7.0; PR 1-0. **Total:** Rec 11-63 5.7; PR 1-0.

		Rushing				Kickoff Returns				
Year Team	**G**	**Att**	**Yds**	**Avg**	**TD**	**Ret**	**Yds**	**Avg**	**TD**	**Fum**
1994 Buf	9	17	56	3.3	0	27	601	22.3	0	1
1995 Buf	8	8	31	3.9	0	19	348	18.3	0	2
NFL Total	17	25	87	3.5	0	46	949	20.6	0	3

DON JOYCE Joyce, Donald Gilbert 6′3″, 253 **DE-DT**
(Champ) *Col:* Tulane *HS:* Steubenville [OH] B: 10/8/1929, Steubenville, OH *Drafted:* 1951 Round 2 ChiC
1951 ChiC: 12 G. **1952** ChiC: 12 G. **1953** ChiC: 10 G; KR 1-7 7.0. **1954** Bal: 12 G; KR 1-13 13.0. **1955** Bal: 11 G. **1956** Bal: 12 G. **1957** Bal:

12 G; Int 1-0. **1958** Bal: 12 G. **1959** Bal: 11 G. **1960** Bal: 11 G. **1961** Min: 14 G. **1962** Den: 6 G. **Total:** 135 G; KR 2-20 10.0; Int 1-0.

MATT JOYCE Joyce, Matthew Lodge 6'7", 313 **OG**
Col: Richmond *HS:* Byram Hills [Armonk, NY]; New York Mil. Acad. [Cornwall-on-Hudson, NY] B: 3/30/1972, St. Petersburg, FL
1995 Sea: 16 G. **1996** Ariz: 2 G. **1997** Ariz: 9 G. **1998** Ariz: 11 G. **Total:** 38 G.

TERRY JOYCE Joyce, Terry Patrick 6'6", 230 **P-TE**
Col: Highland CC KS; Wichita State; Missouri Southern State *HS:* Knox Co. [Edina, MO] B: 7/18/1954, Kirksville, MO
1976 StL: Rush 1-0. **1977** StL: Pass 1-1 100.0%, 1 1.00; Rush 1-(-13) -13.0. **Total:** Pass 1-1 100.0%, 1 1.00; Rush 2-(-13) -6.5.

		Punting			
Year Team	**G**	**Punts**	**Yds**	**Avg**	**Fum**
1976 StL	14	64	2331	36.4	1
1977 StL	4	22	851	38.7	0
NFL Total	18	86	3182	37.0	1

BILL JOYCE Joyce, William Kelly 5'8", 180 **BB**
Col: Holy Cross; Catholic *HS:* Pittsfield [MA] B: 6/3/1895, Pittsfield, MA D: 8/29/1974, Camlachie, Canada
1920 Det: 1 G.

L.C. JOYNER Joyner, L. C 6'1", 187 **DB**
Col: No College *HS:* Pittsburg [CA] B: 1935 *Drafted:* 1956 Round 21 SF
1960 Oak: 2 G.

LARRY JOYNER Joyner, Larry Jr. 6'0", 207 **LB**
Col: Minnesota *HS:* Hamilton [Memphis, TN] B: 1/22/1964, Memphis, TN
1987 Hou: 1 G.

SETH JOYNER Joyner, Seth 6'2", 241 **LB**
Col: Texas-El Paso *HS:* Spring Valley [NY] B: 11/18/1964, Spring Valley, NY *Drafted:* 1986 Round 8 Phi
1986 Phi: 2 Sac. **1987** Phi: **1** Fum TD; 4 Sac. **1988** Phi: 3.5 Sac. **1989** Phi: 5 Sac. **1990** Phi: 7.5 Sac. **1991** Phi: **2** Fum TD; 6.5 Sac. **1992** Phi: 6.5 Sac. **1993** Phi: 2 Sac. **1994** Ariz: 6 Sac. **1995** Ariz: 1 Sac. **1996** Ariz: 5 Sac. **1997** GB: 3 Sac. **Total:** 3 Fum TD; 52.0 Sac.

		Interceptions				Tot
Year Team	**G**	**Int**	**Yds**	**TD**	**Fum**	**TD**
1986 Phi	14	1	4	0	0	0
1987 Phi	12	2	42	0	0	1
1988 Phi	16	4	96	0	1	0
1989 Phi	14	1	0	0	0	0
1990 Phi	16	1	9	0	1	0
1991 Phi	16	3	41	0	0	2
1992 Phi	16	4	88	2	0	2
1993 Phi	16	1	6	0	0	0
1994 Ariz	16	3	2	0	0	0
1995 Ariz	16	3	9	0	1	0
1996 Ariz	16	1	10	0	0	0
1997 GB	11	0	0	0	0	0
1998 Den	16	0	0	0	0	0
NFL Total	195	24	307	2	3	5

WILLIE JOYNER Joyner, Willie 5'10", 200 **RB**
Col: Maryland *HS:* Lafayette [Brooklyn, NY] B: 4/2/1962, Brooklyn, NY *Drafted:* 1984 Round 7 Hou
1984 Hou: 10 G; Rush 14-22 1.6; KR 3-57 19.0.

BRIAN JOZWIAK Jozwiak, Brian Joseph 6'5", 304 **OG-OT**
Col: West Virginia *HS:* Catonsville [MD] B: 6/20/1963, Baltimore, MD *Drafted:* 1986 Round 1 KC
1986 KC: 15 G. **1987** KC: 10 G. **1988** KC: 3 G. **Total:** 28 G.

SAXON JUDD Judd, Saxon Thomas 6'1", 190 **OE**
Col: Southwestern Louisiana; Tulsa B: 11/29/1919, Pottsboro, TX D: 3/31/1990, Tulsa, OK
AAFC **1946** BknA: KR 3-54 18.0. **1947** BknA: KR 2-5 2.5. **Total:** KR 5-59 11.8.

		Receiving				Tot
Year Team	**G**	**Rec**	**Yds**	**Avg**	**TD**	**TD**
1946 BknA	13	34	443	13.0	4	5
1947 BknA	14	18	204	11.3	1	1
1948 BknA	14	32	350	10.9	2	2
AAFC Total	41	84	997	11.9	7	8

ED JUDIE Judie, Edward Charles 6'2", 231 **LB**
Col: Northern Arizona *HS:* Tempe [AZ] B: 7/6/1959, Tyler, TX
1982 SF: 7 G. **1983** SF-TB: 15 G; 1 Sac. SF: 4 G. TB: 11 G; 1 Sac. **1984** Mia: 2 G. **Total:** 24 G; 1 Sac.

WILLIAM JUDSON Judson, William Thadius 6'1", 189 **DB**
Col: South Carolina State *HS:* Sylvan Hills [Atlanta, GA] B: 3/26/1959, Detroit, MI *Drafted:* 1981 Round 8 Mia

		Interceptions		
Year Team	**G**	**Int**	**Yds**	**TD**
1982 Mia	9	0	0	0
1983 Mia	16	6	60	0
1984 Mia	16	4	121	1
1985 Mia	16	4	88	**1**
1986 Mia	16	2	0	0
1987 Mia	12	2	11	0
1988 Mia	16	4	57	0
1989 Mia	14	2	31	0
NFL Total	115	24	368	2

DAVE JUENGER Juenger, David William 6'1", 195 **WR**
Col: Ohio U. *HS:* Unioto [Chillicothe, OH] B: 2/4/1951, Chillicothe, OH *Drafted:* 1973 Round 14 ChiB
1973 ChiB: 1 G.

FRED JULIAN Julian, Alfred J 5'9", 185 **DB**
Col: Michigan *HS:* Pershing [Detroit, MI] B: 1/27/1938, Detroit, MI
1960 NYT: 14 G; Int 6-27.

KEVIN JUMA Juma, Kevin Wade 6'2", 195 **WR**
Col: Walla Walla CC WA; Idaho *HS:* Fife [WA] B: 7/30/1962, Seattle, WA
1987 Sea: 3 G; Rec 7-95 13.6.

BUDDY JUNGMICHEL Jungmichel, Harold Neve 5'9", 200 **G**
Col: Kilgore Coll. TX (J.C.); Texas *HS:* Thorndale [TX] B: 10/18/1919, Gonzales, TX D: 8/28/1982, Austin, TX
AAFC **1946** MiaA: 14 G; Int 1-21.

E.J. JUNIOR Junior, Ester James III 6'3", 238 **LB**
Col: Alabama *HS:* Maplewood [Nashville, TN] B: 12/8/1959, Salisbury, NC *Drafted:* 1981 Round 1 StL
1982 StL: 1.5 Sac. **1983** StL: 7.5 Sac. **1984** StL: 9.5 Sac. **1985** StL: 2 Sac. **1987** StL: 2 Sac. **1988** Pho: **1** Fum TD; 2 Sac. **1989** Mia: 1 Sac. **1990** Mia: 6 Sac. **1991** Mia: PR 1-0; 5 Sac. **Total:** PR 1-0; 1 Fum TD; 36.5 Sac.

		Interceptions			
Year Team	**G**	**Int**	**Yds**	**TD**	**Fum**
1981 StL	16	1	5	0	0
1982 StL	9	0	0	0	0
1983 StL	12	3	27	0	0
1984 StL	16	1	18	0	0
1985 StL	16	5	109	0	0
1986 StL	13	0	0	0	0
1987 StL	13	1	25	0	1
1988 Pho	16	1	2	0	0
1989 Mia	16	0	0	0	0
1990 Mia	16	0	0	0	0
1991 Mia	16	0	0	0	0
1992 TB-Sea	7	0	0	0	0
1992 TB	2	0	0	0	0
1992 Sea	5	0	0	0	0
1993 Sea	4	0	0	0	0
NFL Total	170	12	186	0	1

STEVE JUNKER Junker, Steven Norbert 6'3", 217 **OE**
Col: Xavier (Ohio) *HS:* Elder [Cincinnati, OH] B: 5/22/1935, Cincinnati, OH *Drafted:* 1957 Round 4 Det
1961 Was: KR 1-0. **Total:** KR 1-0.

		Receiving			
Year Team	**G**	**Rec**	**Yds**	**Avg**	**TD**
1957 Det	12	22	305	13.9	4
1959 Det	6	0	0	—	0
1960 Det	12	6	55	9.2	0
1961 Was	11	9	130	14.4	0
1962 Was	14	11	149	13.5	2
NFL Total	55	48	639	13.3	6

TREY JUNKIN Junkin, Abner Kirk 6'2", 235 **TE-LB**
Col: Louisiana Tech *HS:* North Little Rock, East [AR] B: 1/23/1961, Conway, AR *Drafted:* 1983 Round 4 Buf
1983 Buf: 16 G. **1984** Buf-Was: 14 G. Buf: 2 G. Was: 12 G. **1985** LARd: 16 G; Rec 2-8 4.0 1 TD; 6 Pt. **1986** LARd: 3 G; Rec 2-38 19.0. **1987** LARd: 12 G; Rec 2-15 7.5. **1988** LARd: 16 G; Rec 4-25 6.3 2 TD; 12 Pt. **1989** LARd: 16 G; Rec 3-32 10.7 2 TD; KR 1-0; 12 Pt. **1990** Sea: 12 G. **1991** Sea: 16 G. **1992** Sea: 16 G; Rec 3-25 8.3 1 TD; 6 Pt. **1993** Sea: 16 G. **1994** Sea: 16 G; Rec 1-1 1.0 1 TD; 6 Pt. **1995** Sea: 16 G. **1996** Oak-Ariz: 16 G. Oak: 6 G. Ariz: 10 G. **1997** Ariz: 16 G. **1998** Ariz: 16 G. **Total:** 233 G; Rec 17-144 8.5 7 TD; KR 1-0; 42 Pt.

MIKE JUNKIN Junkin, Michael Wayne 6'3", 241 **LB**
Col: Duke *HS:* Belvidere [IL] B: 11/21/1964, North Little Rock, AR *Drafted:* 1987 Round 1 Cle
1987 Cle: 4 G. **1988** Cle: 11 G. **1989** KC: 5 G. **Total:** 20 G.

JOE JUREVICIUS Jurevicius, Joe Michael 6'5", 231 **WR**
Col: Penn State *HS:* Lake Catholic [Mentor, OH] B: 12/23/1974, Cleveland, OH *Drafted:* 1998 Round 2 NYG
1998 NYG: 14 G; Rec 9-146 16.2.

SONNY JURGENSEN Jurgensen, Christian Adolph III 5'11", 202 **QB**
Col: Duke *HS:* New Hanover [Wilmington, NC] B: 8/23/1934, Wilmington, NC *Drafted:* 1957 Round 4 Phi *HOF:* 1983
1973 Was: Rec 1-(-3) -3.0. **Total:** Rec 1-(-3) -3.0.

		Passing							
Year Team	G	Att	Comp	Comp%	Yds	YPA	TD	Int	Rating
1957 Phi	10	70	33	47.1	470	6.71	5	8	53.6
1958 Phi	12	22	12	54.5	259	11.77	0	1	77.7
1959 Phi	12	5	3	60.0	27	5.40	1	0	114.2
1960 Phi	12	44	24	54.5	486	11.05	5	1	122.0
1961 Phi	14	416	**235**	56.5	**3723**	8.95	**32**	24	88.1
1962 Phi	14	366	196	53.6	**3261**	**8.91**	22	26	74.3
1963 Phi	9	184	99	53.8	1413	7.68	11	13	69.4
1964 Was	14	385	207	53.8	2934	7.62	24	13	85.4
1965 Was	13	356	190	53.4	2367	6.65	15	16	69.6
1966 Was	14	**436**	**254**	58.3	**3209**	7.36	28	19	84.5
1967 Was	14	**508**	**288**	56.7	**3747**	7.38	**31**	16	87.3
1968 Was	12	292	167	57.2	1980	6.78	17	11	81.7
1969 Was	14	**442**	**274**	62.0	**3102**	7.02	22	15	85.4
1970 Was	14	337	202	**59.9**	2354	6.99	23	10	91.5
1971 Was	5	28	16	57.1	170	6.07	0	2	45.2
1972 Was	7	59	39	66.1	633	10.73	2	4	84.9
1973 Was	14	145	87	60.0	904	6.23	6	**5**	77.5
1974 Was	14	167	107	64.1	1185	7.10	11	**5**	94.5
NFL Total	218	4262	2433	57.1	32224	7.56	255	189	82.6

	Rushing				
Year Team	Att	Yds	Avg	TD	Fum
1957 Phi	10	-3	-0.3	2	0
1958 Phi	1	1	1.0	0	1
1960 Phi	4	5	1.3	0	3
1961 Phi	20	27	1.4	0	6
1962 Phi	17	44	2.6	2	4
1963 Phi	13	38	2.9	1	1
1964 Was	27	57	2.1	3	3
1965 Was	17	23	1.4	2	6
1966 Was	12	14	1.2	0	5
1967 Was	15	46	3.1	2	5
1968 Was	8	21	2.6	1	2
1969 Was	17	156	9.2	1	2
1970 Was	6	39	6.5	1	4
1971 Was	3	29	9.7	0	1
1972 Was	4	-5	-1.3	0	4
1973 Was	3	7	2.3	0	1
1974 Was	4	-6	-1.5	0	2
NFL Total	181	493	2.7	15	50

MIKE JURICH Jurich, Michael 6'1", 230 **T**
Col: Denver *HS:* Longmont [CO] B: 1/7/1919, Ruth, NV D: 1/5/1996, Denver, CO *Drafted:* 1941 Round 13 Bkn
1941 Bkn: 4 G. **1942** Bkn: 11 G. **Total:** 15 G.

TOM JURICH Jurich, Thomas N 5'10", 185 **K**
Col: Northern Arizona *HS:* Arcadia [CA] B: 7/26/1956, Alhambra, CA *Drafted:* 1978 Round 10 Pit
1978 NO: 1 G; Scor 2, 0-3 FG, 2-2 100.0% XK.

JIM JURIGA Juriga, James Allen 6'6", 269 **OT-OG**
Col: Illinois *HS:* North [Wheaton, IL] B: 9/12/1964, Fort Wayne, IN *Drafted:* 1986 Round 4 Den
1988 Den: 16 G. **1989** Den: 16 G. **1990** Den: 12 G. **Total:** 44 G.

WALT JURKIEWICZ Jurkiewicz, Walter Stephen 6'1", 220 **C-LB**
Col: Indiana *HS:* Hamtramck [MI] B: 2/16/1919, Scott Haven, PA
1946 Det: 11 G.

JOHN JURKOVIC Jurkovic, Ivan John 6'2", 301 **DT-NT**
Col: Eastern Illinois *HS:* Thornton Fractional North [Calumet City, IL] B: 8/18/1967, Friedrichshafen, Germany
1991 GB: 5 G. **1992** GB: 16 G; KR 3-39 13.0; 2 Sac. **1993** GB: 16 G; KR 2-22 11.0; 5.5 Sac. **1994** GB: 16 G; KR 4-57 14.3. **1995** GB: 16 G; KR 1-17 17.0. **1996** Jac: 16 G; 1 Sac. **1997** Jac: 3 G. **1998** Jac: 16 G; 0.5 Sac. **Total:** 104 G; KR 10-135 13.5; 9 Sac.

BOB JURY Jury, Robert Vincent 6'1", 188 **DB**
Col: Pittsburgh *HS:* South Park [Library, PA] B: 10/5/1955, Los Angeles, CA *Drafted:* 1978 Round 3 Sea
1978 SF: 15 G.

RUBE JUSTER Juster, Rubin J 6'2", 230 **T**
Col: Minnesota B: 9/9/1923 D: 1/1/1985, Chicago, IL
1946 Bos: 4 G.

CHARLIE JUSTICE Justice, Charles Ronald 5'10", 176 **HB**
(Choo Choo) *Col:* North Carolina *HS:* Lee H. Edwards [Asheville, NC] B: 5/18/1924, Asheville, NC *Drafted:* 1950 Round 16 Was
1950 Was: Pass 4-1 25.0%, 15 3.75; PR 7-46 6.6; KR 9-223 24.8. **1952** Was: Pass 1-0, 1 Int; PR 12-47 3.9; KR 10-209 20.9. **1953** Was: PR 4-6 1.5; KR 1-20 20.0. **1954** Was: Pass 2-0, 1 Int. **Total:** Pass 7-1 14.3%, 15 2.14 2 Int; PR 23-99 4.3; KR 20-452 22.6.

		Rushing				Receiving			
Year Team	G	Att	Yds	Avg	TD	Rec	Yds	Avg	TD
1950 Was	8	59	285	4.8	0	19	180	9.5	2
1952 Was	11	36	129	3.6	0	11	106	9.6	1
1953 Was	12	115	616	5.4	2	22	434	19.7	2
1954 Was	12	56	254	4.5	1	11	242	22.0	2
NFL Total	43	266	1284	4.8	3	63	962	15.3	7

	Punting				Tot
Year Team	Punts	Yds	Avg	Fum	TD
1950 Was	22	908	41.3	9	2
1952 Was	11	431	39.2	3	1
1953 Was	0	0	—	9	4
1954 Was	61	2461	40.3	6	3
NFL Total	94	3800	40.4	27	10

ED JUSTICE Justice, Edward S 6'1", 200 **WB-DB-OE**
(Chug) *Col:* Gonzaga *HS:* Clarkston [WA] B: 11/19/1912, Post Falls, ID D: 10/26/1991, Anacortes, WA
1939 Was: **1** Fum TD. **1940** Was: Int 1-14. **1941** Was: KR 2-49 24.5; Int 2-13. **1942** Was: Int 1-2. **Total:** KR 2-49 24.5; Int 4-29; 1 Fum TD.

		Rushing				Receiving				Tot
Year Team	G	Att	Yds	Avg	TD	Rec	Yds	Avg	TD	TD
1936 Bos	12	11	10	0.9	0	8	132	16.5	0	0
1937 Was	10	8	35	4.4	0	9	150	16.7	3	3
1938 Was	9	10	11	1.1	0	14	173	12.4	1	1
1939 Was	8	5	56	11.2	1	7	124	17.7	1	3
1940 Was	7	3	34	11.3	0	15	170	11.3	2	2
1941 Was	8	4	-8	-2.0	0	8	149	18.6	1	1
1942 Was	9	3	-1	-0.3	0	9	108	12.0	1	1
NFL Total	63	44	137	3.1	1	70	1006	14.4	9	11

KERRY JUSTIN Justin, Kerry August 5'11", 175 **DB**
Col: East Los Angeles Coll. CA (J.C.); Oregon State *HS:* Crenshaw [Los Angeles, CA] B: 5/3/1955, New Orleans, LA
1978 Sea: 16 G. **1979** Sea: 14 G; Int 1-0. **1980** Sea: 11 G; Int 1-0. **1981** Sea: 15 G. **1982** Sea: 9 G. **1983** Sea: 16 G; Int 1-2. **1986** Sea: 16 G; Int 4-29. **1987** Sea: 7 G. **Total:** 104 G; Int 7-31.

PAUL JUSTIN Justin, Paul Donald 6'4", 211 **QB**
Col: Arizona State *HS:* Schaumburg [IL] B: 5/19/1968, Schaumburg, IL *Drafted:* 1991 Round 7 ChiB
1995 Ind: Rush 3-1 0.3. **1996** Ind: Rush 2-7 3.5. **1997** Ind: Rush 6-2 0.3. **1998** Cin: Rush 1-2 2.0; Scor 1 2XP. **Total:** Rush 12-12 1.0; Scor 1 2XP.

		Passing								
Year Team	G	Att	Comp	Comp%	Yds	YPA	TD	Int	Rating	Fum
1995 Ind	3	36	20	55.6	212	5.89	0	2	49.8	1
1996 Ind	8	127	74	58.3	839	6.61	2	0	83.4	1
1997 Ind	8	140	83	59.3	1046	7.47	5	5	79.6	1
1998 Cin	5	63	34	54.0	426	6.76	1	3	60.7	0
NFL Total	24	366	211	57.7	2523	6.89	8	10	74.7	3

SIDNEY JUSTIN Justin, Sidney Arthur 5'10", 170 **DB**
Col: Los Angeles Southwest Coll. CA (J.C.); Long Beach State *HS:* Crenshaw [Los Angeles, CA] B: 8/14/1954, New Orleans, LA
1979 LARm: 13 G; PR 1-(-2) -2.0; Int 1-13; 6 Pt; 1 Fum. **1982** Bal: 5 G. **Total:** 18 G; PR 1-(-2) -2.0; Int 1-13; 6 Pt; 1 Fum.

STEVE JUZWIK Juzwik, Stephen Robert 5'8", 186 **HB-DB-FB**
Col: Notre Dame *HS:* DePaul Acad. [Chicago, IL] B: 6/18/1918, Gary, IN D: 6/6/1964, Chicago, IL *Drafted:* 1942 Round 19 Was
AAFC **1946** BufA: PR 11-135 12.3; KR 21-452 21.5; Int 5-108 1 TD. **1947** BufA: PR 4-36 9.0; KR 1-20 20.0; Scor 40, 2-3 66.7% FG, 28-32 87.5% XK. **1948** ChiA: Scor 5, 5-5 100.0% XK. **Total:** PR 15-171 11.4; KR 22-472 21.5; Int 5-108 1 TD; Scor 87, 2-3 66.7% FG, 33-37 89.2% XK.

		Rushing				Receiving				Tot
Year Team	G	Att	Yds	Avg	TD	Rec	Yds	Avg	TD	TD
1946 BufA	13	71	455	6.4	3	23	357	15.5	3	7
1947 BufA	10	26	130	5.0	0	5	35	7.0	1	1
1948 ChiA	4	13	19	1.5	0	1	5	5.0	0	0
AAFC Total	27	110	604	5.5	3	29	397	13.7	4	8

NFL **1942** Was: 2 G; Rush 15-75 5.0 2 TD; PR 3-33 11.0; KR 1-22 22.0; Scor 15, 3-3 100.0% XK.

VYTO KAB Kab, Vyto 6'5", 243 **TE**
Col: Penn State *HS:* DePaul [Wayne, NJ] B: 12/23/1959, Albany, GA *Drafted:* 1982 Round 3 Phi

Year Team	G	Receiving Rec	Yds	Avg	TD
1982 Phi	9	4	35	8.8	1
1983 Phi	14	18	195	10.8	1
1984 Phi	16	9	102	11.3	3
1985 Phi-NYG	12	0	0	—	0
1985 Phi	1	0	0	—	0
1985 NYG	11	0	0	—	0
1987 Det	7	5	54	10.8	0
NFL Total	58	36	386	10.7	5

MIKE KABEALO Kabealo, Michael T 5′8″, 185 **HB-DB**
Col: Ohio State *HS:* Chaney [Youngstown, OH] B: 10/1/1915, Youngstown, OH D: 9/24/1993, Centerville, OH
1944 Cle: Pass 1-1 100.0%, 54 54.00 1 TD; Rec 2-20 10.0; PR 7-64 9.1; KR 4-126 31.5; Int 2-9.

Year Team	G	Rushing Att	Yds	Avg	TD
1944 Cle	10	47	152	3.2	1

JOHN KACHERSKI Kacherski, John Richard 6′2″, 240 **LB**
Col: Ohio State *HS:* Riverhead [NY]; Milford Acad. [CT] B: 6/27/1967, Oceanside, NY
1992 Den: 7 G.

JEFF KACMAREK Kacmarek, Jeffrey Allen 6′2″, 240 **NT**
Col: Western Michigan *HS:* St. Laurence [Burbank, IL] B: 4/12/1963, Oaklawn, IL
1987 Det: 3 G.

MIKE KACZMAREK Kaczmarek, Michael Louis 6′4″, 235 **LB**
Col: Southern Illinois *HS:* Hobart [IN] B: 10/31/1951, Gary, IN
1973 Bal: 14 G; Int 1-2.

MAX KADESKY Kadesky, Max 5′11″, 175 **OE**
Col: Iowa *HS:* Dubuque [IA] B: 2/8/1901, Winsted, CT D: 8/14/1970, Dubuque, IA
1923 RI: 8 G.

MIKE KADISH Kadish, Michael Scott 6′5″, 270 **DT-NT**
Col: Notre Dame *HS:* Catholic Central [Grand Rapids, MI]
B: 5/27/1950, Grand Rapids, MI *Drafted:* 1972 Round 1 Mia
1973 Buf: 12 G. **1974** Buf: 14 G; Scor **1** Saf; 2 Pt. **1975** Buf: 14 G; **1** Fum TD; 6 Pt. **1976** Buf: 14 G. **1977** Buf: 14 G. **1978** Buf: 11 G. **1979** Buf: 16 G. **1980** Buf: 16 G. **1981** Buf: 16 G. **Total:** 127 G; Scor 1 Saf; 1 Fum TD; 8 Pt.

RON KADZIEL Kadziel, Ronald Dennis 6′4″, 230 **LB**
Col: Stanford *HS:* La Verne [CA]; Pomona Catholic HS [CA]
B: 2/27/1949, Pomona, CA *Drafted:* 1971 Round 5 Dal
1972 NE: 14 G.

MORT KAER Kaer, Morton Armour 5′11″, 167 **BB-TB**
(Devil May) *Col:* USC *HS:* Red Bluff [CA] B: 9/7/1902, Omaha, NE
D: 1/12/1992, Mount Shasta, CA
1931 Fra: 8 G; PR **1** TD; 6 Pt.

KURT KAFENTZIS Kafentzis, Kurt Michael 6′2″, 190 **DB**
Col: Hawaii *HS:* Columbia [Richland, WA] B: 12/31/1962, Richland, WA
1987 Hou: 2 G.

MARK KAFENTZIS Kafentzis, Mark Kevin 5′10″, 190 **DB**
Col: Columbia Basin Coll. WA (J.C.); Hawaii *HS:* Columbia [Richland, WA] B: 6/30/1958, Richland, WA *Drafted:* 1982 Round 8 Cle
1982 Cle: 9 G. **1983** Bal: 15 G. **1984** Ind: 16 G; KR 5-69 13.8; Int 1-59 1 TD; 6 Pt; 1 Fum. **Total:** 40 G; KR 5-69 13.8; Int 1-59 1 TD; 6 Pt; 1 Fum.

CY KAHL Kahl, Cyrus Paul 6′1″, 195 **BB-WB-FB-TB**
Col: North Dakota *HS:* Jefferson [Alexandria, MN] B: 11/29/1904, Heaton, ND D: 7/1971, Portsmouth, OH
1930 Port: 11 G. **1931** Port: 1 G. **Total:** 12 G.

BOB KAHLER Kahler, Robert William 6′3″, 201 **DB-HB**
Col: Nebraska *HS:* Grand Island [NE] B: 2/14/1917, Grand Island, NE
1942 GB: 7 G; Rush 8-4 0.5; Rec 2-21 10.5; PR 1-14 14.0. **1943** GB: 4 G; Rush 1-5 5.0. **1944** GB: 8 G. **Total:** 19 G; Rush 9-9 1.0; Rec 2-21 10.5; PR 1-14 14.0.

ROYAL KAHLER Kahler, Royal James 6′2″, 226 **T**
(King Kong) *Col:* Nebraska *HS:* Grand Island [NE] B: 3/22/1918, Grand Island, NE *Drafted:* 1941 Round 4 Phi
1941 Pit: 9 G; KR 1-3 3.0. **1942** GB: 7 G. **Total:** 16 G; KR 1-3 3.0.

EDDIE KAHN Kahn, Edwin Bernard 5′9″, 194 **G**
(King Kong) *Col:* North Carolina *HS:* Boston English [MA]
B: 11/9/1911, New York, NY D: 2/17/1945, during Leyte invasion
1935 Bos: 9 G. **1936** Bos: 5 G. **1937** Was: 10 G; 1 Fum TD; 6 Pt. **Total:** 24 G; 1 Fum TD; 6 Pt.

KARL KAIMER Kaimer, Karl Julius 6′3″, 230 **DE**
Col: Boston U. *HS:* Cranford [NJ] B: 11/12/1938, Elizabeth, NJ
1962 NYT: 8 G.

JASON KAISER Kaiser, Jason 6′0″, 190 **DB**
Col: Culver-Stockton *HS:* Highlands Ranch [CO] B: 11/9/1973, Denver, CO
1998 KC: 1 G.

JOHN KAISER Kaiser, John Frederick 6′3″, 227 **LB**
Col: Coll. of the Sequoias CA (J.C.); Arizona *HS:* Arrowhead [Hartland, WI] B: 6/6/1962, Oconomowoc, WI *Drafted:* 1984 Round 6 Sea
1984 Sea: 16 G. **1985** Sea: 16 G. **1986** Sea: 16 G. **1987** Buf: 12 G. **Total:** 60 G.

GEORGE KAKASIC Kakasic, George John 5′10″, 200 **G**
(Bunko AKA Kase) *Col:* Duquesne *HS:* Mingo Junction [OH]
B: 4/24/1912, Mingo Junction, OH D: 1/1973
1936 Pit: 12 G; Rush 1-(-8) -8.0; Scor 13, 2 FG, 1 XK; **1** Fum TD. **1937** Pit: 11 G; Scor 3, 3 XK. **1938** Pit: 4 G. **1939** Pit: 10 G. **Total:** 37 G; Rush 1-(-8) -8.0; Scor 16, 2 FG, 4 XK; 1 Fum TD.

IKE KAKELA Kakela, Wayne Erland 6′0″, 220 **C**
Col: Minnesota *HS:* Eveleth [MN] B: 7/16/1905, Eveleth, MN
D: 10/16/1981, Grand Forks, ND
1930 Min: 3 G.

JIM KALAFAT Kalafat, James William 6′0″, 235 **LB**
Col: Montana State *HS:* C.M. Russell [Great Falls, MT] B: 2/21/1962, Great Falls, MT
1987 LARm: 1 G.

DAVE KALINA Kalina, David 6′3″, 205 **WR**
Col: Coffeyville CC KS; Miami (Fla.) *HS:* Westinghouse [Pittsburgh, PA]
B: 9/2/1947, Braddock, PA
1970 Pit: 2 G.

TODD KALIS Kalis, Todd Alexander 6′6″, 288 **OG**
Col: Arizona State *HS:* Thunderbird [Phoenix, AZ] B: 5/10/1965, Stillwater, MN *Drafted:* 1988 Round 4 Min
1988 Min: 14 G. **1989** Min: 16 G. **1990** Min: 15 G. **1991** Min: 16 G. **1993** Min: 16 G. **1994** Pit: 11 G. **1995** Cin: 15 G. **Total:** 103 G.

ED KALLINA Kallina, Edward James 6′0″, 205 **T-G**
Col: Sam Houston State; Southwest Texas State *HS:* San Marcos [TX]
B: 10/28/1901, Nada, TX D: 5/15/1963, Houston, TX
1928 ChiB: 4 G.

TOM KALMANIR Kalmanir, Thomas J 5′8″, 171 **HB**
(Cricket) *Col:* Pittsburgh; Nevada-Reno *HS:* Conemaugh Twp. [Davidsville, PA] B: 3/30/1926, Jerome, PA *Drafted:* 1947 Round 23 Pit
1949 LARm: Rec 2-36 18.0. **1950** LARm: Rec 5-58 11.6 1 TD. **1951** LARm: Rec 6-91 15.2 1 TD. **1953** Bal: Rec 3-31 10.3 1 TD. **Total:** Rec 16-216 13.5 3 TD.

Year Team	G	Rushing Att	Yds	Avg	TD	Punt Returns Ret	Yds	Avg	TD
1949 LARm	12	29	218	7.5	1	14	164	11.7	1
1950 LARm	10	20	83	4.2	0	13	116	8.9	0
1951 LARm	12	16	61	3.8	0	5	86	17.2	1
1953 Bal	9	16	53	3.3	0	2	19	9.5	0
NFL Total	43	81	415	5.1	1	34	385	11.3	2

Year Team	Kickoff Returns Ret	Yds	Avg	TD	Fum	Tot TD
1949 LARm	18	403	22.4	0	1	2
1950 LARm	13	358	27.5	0	2	1
1951 LARm	6	120	20.0	0	0	2
1953 Bal	3	51	17.0	0	1	1
NFL Total	40	932	23.3	0	4	6

BOB KALSU Kalsu, James Robert 6′3″, 250 **OG**
Col: Oklahoma *HS:* Del City [OK] B: 4/13/1945, Oklahoma City, OK
D: 7/21/1970, Thua Thien, Vietnam *Drafted:* 1968 Round 8 Buf
1968 Buf: 14 G.

NDUKWE KALU Kalu, Ndukwe Dike 6′3″, 245 **DE**
Col: Rice *HS:* John Marshall [San Antonio, TX] B: 8/3/1975, Baltimore, MD *Drafted:* 1997 Round 5 Phi
1997 Phi: 3 G. **1998** Was: 13 G; 3 Sac. **Total:** 16 G; 3 Sac.

JOHN KAMANA Kamana, John Maia III 6′2″, 223 **TE-LB**
Col: USC *HS:* Punahou School [Honolulu, HI] B: 12/3/1961, Honolulu, HI
1984 LARm: 3 G. **1987** Atl: 2 G; Rec 7-51 7.3 1 TD; 6 Pt; 1 Fum. **Total:** 5 G; Rec 7-51 7.3 1 TD; 6 Pt; 1 Fum.

LEW KAMANU Kamanu, Lewellyn K 6′4″, 245 **DE**
Col: Wenatchee Valley Coll. WA (J.C.); Weber State *HS:* Farrington [Honolulu, HI] B: 4/9/1944, Honolulu, HI *Drafted:* 1967 Round 4 Det
1967 Det: 9 G. **1968** Det: 3 G. **Total:** 12 G.

LARRY KAMINSKI Kaminski, Lawrence Michael 6′2″, 245 C
Col: Purdue *HS:* Cathedral Latin [Cleveland, OH] B: 1/6/1945, Cleveland, OH
1966 Den: 14 G. **1967** Den: 14 G. **1968** Den: 14 G. **1969** Den: 14 G. **1970** Den: 14 G. **1971** Den: 3 G. **1972** Den: 11 G. **1973** Den: 12 G. **Total:** 96 G.

CARL KAMMERER Kammerer, Carlton Cordell 6′3″, 243 DE-LB
Col: San Francisco State; U. of Pacific *HS:* Lodi [CA] B: 3/20/1937, Stockton, CA *Drafted:* 1960 Round 2 SF
1961 SF: 14 G; KR 1-18 18.0. **1962** SF: 14 G; Int 1-13. **1963** Was: 14 G; Int 2-1. **1964** Was: 14 G; PR 1-0; 1 Fum. **1965** Was: 14 G; KR 1-14 14.0. **1966** Was: 14 G. **1967** Was: 11 G. **1968** Was: 14 G. **1969** Was: 14 G. **Total:** 123 G; PR 1-0; KR 2-32 16.0; Int 3-14; 1 Fum.

JIM KAMP Kamp, James 6′0″, 210 T-G
Col: Oklahoma City *HS:* Sacred Heart [El Reno, OK] B: 12/5/1907, El Reno, OK Deceased
1932 SI: 12 G. **1933** Bos: 10 G. **Total:** 22 G.

BOB KAMPA Kampa, Robert Eugene 6′4″, 252 DT
Col: Gavilan Coll. CA (J.C.); California *HS:* Gilroy [CA] B: 4/26/1951, San Francisco, CA *Drafted:* 1973 Round 3 Buf
1973 Buf: 7 G. **1974** Buf-Den: 6 G. Buf: 2 G. Den: 4 G. **Total:** 13 G.

CARL KANE Kane, Carl Everett 5′11″, 195 HB-DB
Col: St. Louis *HS:* Belleville [IL] B: 1/24/1913, Philadelphia, PA D: 9/5/1983, Vero Beach, FL
1936 Phi: 1 G.

GEORGE KANE Kane, George 5′9″, 190 G
Col: Fordham *HS:* Fordham Prep [Bronx, NY] B: NY Deceased
1921 NYG: 1 G.

JIM KANE Kane, Harold James G
Col: No College B: 11/28/1896, Rochester, NY D: 4/10/1976, Rochester, NY
1920 Roch: 6 G.

RICK KANE Kane, Richard James 5′11″, 200 RB
Col: Oregon; San Jose State *HS:* Amador Valley [Pleasanton, CA] B: 11/12/1954, Lincoln, NE *Drafted:* 1977 Round 3 Det
1977 Det: PR 1-13 13.0. **Total:** PR 1-13 13.0.

		Rushing				Receiving			
Year Team	G	Att	Yds	Avg	TD	Rec	Yds	Avg	TD
1977 Det	14	124	421	3.4	4	18	186	10.3	0
1978 Det	15	44	153	3.5	2	16	161	10.1	0
1979 Det	16	94	332	3.5	4	9	104	11.6	1
1980 Det	16	31	125	4.0	0	5	26	5.2	0
1981 Det	16	77	332	4.3	2	17	181	10.6	1
1982 Det	6	7	17	2.4	0	3	25	8.3	0
1983 Det	14	4	19	4.8	0	2	15	7.5	0
1984 Was	12	17	43	2.5	0	1	7	7.0	0
1985 Det	16	11	44	4.0	0	5	56	11.2	0
NFL Total	125	409	1486	3.6	12	76	761	10.0	2

	Kickoff Returns					Tot
Year Team	Ret	Yds	Avg	TD	Fum	TD
1977 Det	16	376	23.5	0	10	4
1978 Det	8	156	19.5	0	1	2
1979 Det	13	281	21.6	0	4	5
1980 Det	23	495	21.5	0	3	0
1981 Det	0	0	—	0	2	3
1982 Det	1	19	19.0	0	0	0
1984 Was	3	43	14.3	0	3	0
1985 Det	0	0	—	0	1	0
NFL Total	64	1370	21.4	0	24	14

HERB KANE Kane, Russell Herbert 6′1″, 216 T
Col: East Central (OK) *HS:* Ada [OK] B: 12/24/1920, Carroll, IA D: 4/19/1995, Las Vegas, NV *Drafted:* 1944 Round 4 NYG
1944 NYG: 6 G. **1945** NYG: 2 G. **Total:** 8 G.

TOMMY KANE Kane, Tommy Henry 5′11″, 180 WR
Col: Syracuse *HS:* Dawson Sec. School [Montreal, Canada] B: 1/14/1964, Montreal, Canada *Drafted:* 1988 Round 3 Sea

		Receiving				
Year Team	G	Rec	Yds	Avg	TD	Fum
1988 Sea	9	6	32	5.3	0	0
1989 Sea	5	7	94	13.4	0	0
1990 Sea	16	52	776	14.9	4	1
1991 Sea	16	50	763	15.3	2	1
1992 Sea	11	27	369	13.7	3	0
NFL Total	57	142	2034	14.3	9	2

DANNY KANELL Kanell, Daniel Paul 6′3″, 220 QB
Col: Florida State *HS:* Westminster Acad. [Fort Lauderdale, FL] B: 11/21/1973, Fort Lauderdale, FL *Drafted:* 1996 Round 4 NYG

		Passing							
Year Team	G	Att	Comp	Comp%	Yds	YPA	TD	Int	Rating
1996 NYG	4	60	23	38.3	227	3.78	1	1	48.4
1997 NYG	16	294	156	53.1	1740	5.92	11	9	70.7
1998 NYG	10	299	160	53.5	1603	5.36	11	10	67.3
NFL Total	30	653	339	51.9	3570	5.47	23	20	67.1

	Rushing				
Year Team	Att	Yds	Avg	TD	Fum
1996 NYG	7	6	0.9	0	2
1997 NYG	15	2	0.1	0	6
1998 NYG	15	36	2.4	0	6
NFL Total	37	44	1.2	0	14

JIM KANICKI Kanicki, James Henry 6′4″, 270 DT
(Smokey) *Col:* Michigan State *HS:* Central [Bay City, MI] B: 12/17/1941, Bay City, MI *Drafted:* 1963 Round 2 Cle
1963 Cle: 13 G. **1964** Cle: 14 G. **1965** Cle: 14 G. **1966** Cle: 14 G. **1967** Cle: 14 G. **1968** Cle: 13 G. **1969** Cle: 6 G; KR 1-0. **1970** NYG: 14 G. **1971** NYG: 14 G. **Total:** 116 G; KR 1-0.

JOE KANTOR Kantor, Joseph John Jr. 6′1″, 218 HB
Col: Notre Dame *HS:* St. Ignatius [Cleveland, OH] B: 12/17/1942, Parma Heights, OH
1966 Was: 4 G; Rush 1-2 2.0; KR 2-35 17.5.

AL KANYA Kanya, Albert Joseph 6′0″, 200 T-E
Col: Syracuse *HS:* Henry P. Becton [East Rutherford, NJ] B: 3/7/1908 D: 10/1985, Queens, NY
1931 SI: 11 G; 6 Pt. **1932** SI: 12 G. **Total:** 23 G; 6 Pt.

JOHN KAPELE Kapele, John Kamana 6′0″, 240 DE-DT-OT
Col: Utah; Brigham Young *HS:* James B. Castle [Kaneohe, HI] B: 10/19/1937, Honolulu, HI *Drafted:* 1960 Round 10 Pit
1960 Pit: 12 G. **1961** Pit: 14 G. **1962** Pit-Phi: 12 G. Pit: 6 G. Phi: 6 G. **Total:** 38 G.

BERNIE KAPITANSKY Kapitansky, Bernard 6′1″, 212 G
Col: Long Island University B: 1/1/1921, Brooklyn, NY
1942 Bkn: 7 G.

AVE KAPLAN Kaplan, Avold R 5′7″, 165 TB-WB-BB
Col: Hamline *HS:* Owatonna [MN] B: 11/16/1899, Owatonna, MN D: 12/28/1989, Birmingham, AL
1923 Min: 8 G; Pass 2 TD; Rec 1 TD; Scor 18, 3 FG, 3 XK.

BERNIE KAPLAN Kaplan, Bernard 6′0″, 208 G
(Champ AKA Karlan) *Col:* Western Maryland *HS:* Simon Gratz [Philadelphia, PA] B: 6/8/1913, Philadelphia, PA D: 6/14/1992
1935 NYG: 12 G. **1936** NYG: 7 G. **1942** Phi: 3 G. **Total:** 22 G.

KEN KAPLAN Kaplan, Kenneth Scott 6′4″, 270 OT
Col: New Hampshire *HS:* Brockton [MA] B: 1/12/1960, Boston, MA *Drafted:* 1983 Round 6 TB
1984 TB: 16 G. **1985** TB: 16 G. **1987** NO: 3 G. **Total:** 35 G.

SAM KAPLAN Kaplan, Samuel 166 E
Col: Lehigh *HS:* Central [Washington, DC] B: 1/1899, Washington, DC D: 6/29/1970
1921 Was: 1 G.

CARL KAPLANOFF Kaplanoff, Carl George 6′0″, 235 T-G
Col: Ohio State *HS:* Bucyrus [OH] B: 4/4/1917 D: 6/6/1991, CA *Drafted:* 1939 Round 10 Bkn
1939 Bkn: 11 G.

AL KAPORCH Kaporch, Albert John 5′10″, 215 T-G-LB
Col: St. Bonaventure *HS:* Pittston [PA] B: 10/6/1913, Jenkins Twp., PA Deceased
1943 Det: 10 G; Int 1-0. **1944** Det: 10 G; PR 1-14 14.0; Int 1-1. **1945** Det: 2 G; Int 1-14. **Total:** 22 G; PR 1-14 14.0; Int 3-15.

JOE KAPP Kapp, Joseph Robert 6′2″, 215 QB
Col: California *HS:* William S. Hart [Newhall, CA] B: 3/19/1938, Santa Fe, NM *Drafted:* 1959 Round 18 Was

		Passing							
Year Team	G	Att	Comp	Comp%	Yds	YPA	TD	Int	Rating
1967 Min	13	214	102	47.7	1386	6.48	8	17	48.2
1968 Min	14	248	129	52.0	1695	6.83	10	17	58.8
1969 Min	13	237	120	50.6	1726	7.28	19	13	78.5
1970 Bos	11	219	98	44.7	1104	5.04	3	17	32.6
NFL Total	51	918	449	48.9	5911	6.44	40	64	55.1

	Rushing				
Year Team	Att	Yds	Avg	TD	Fum
1967 Min	27	167	6.2	2	4
1968 Min	50	269	5.4	3	3
1969 Min	22	104	4.7	0	1
1970 Bos	20	71	3.6	0	1
NFL Total	119	611	5.1	5	9

ALEX KAPTER Kapter, Alexander Joe 6'0", 205 **G**
(Tata) *Col:* Northwestern *HS:* Waukegan [IL] B: 3/26/1922, Waukegan, IL
AAFC **1946** CleA: 6 G.

GEORGE KARAMATIC Karamatic, George 5'8", 187 **FB-DB**
(Automatic) *Col:* Gonzaga *HS:* J.M. Weatherwax [Aberdeen, WA] B: 2/22/1917, Seattle, WA *Drafted:* 1938 Round 1 NYG
1938 Was: Rec 4-99 24.8 1 TD; Scor 11, 1-2 50.0% FG, 2-3 66.7% XK.

		Rushing			
Year Team	**G**	**Att**	**Yds**	**Avg**	**TD**
1938 Was	10	50	185	3.7	0

EMIL KARAS Karas, Emil 6'3", 230 **LB-DE**
(Hands) *Col:* Dayton *HS:* Swissvale [PA] B: 12/13/1933, Pittsburgh, PA D: 11/25/1974, San Diego, CA *Drafted:* 1959 Round 3 Was
1959 Was: 11 G; Int 1-0. **1960** LAC: 12 G. **1961** SD: 14 G; KR 1-5 5.0; Int 3-21. **1962** SD: 14 G; Int 2-8. **1963** SD: 14 G; Int 2-30. **1964** SD: 4 G. **1966** SD: 2 G. **Total:** 71 G; KR 1-5 5.0; Int 8-59.

BOB KARCH Karch, Robert H 6'1", 220 **T**
Col: Ohio State *HS:* South [Columbus, OH] B: 7/4/1894, Columbus, OH D: 11/4/1958, Columbus, OH
1922 Col: 4 G. **1923** Lou: 2 G. **Total:** 6 G.

JIM KARCHER Karcher, James Norman 6'0", 205 **G**
(Doc) *Col:* Ohio State *HS:* Forest [OH] B: 5/2/1914, Forest, OH
1936 Bos: 10 G. **1937** Was: 11 G. **1938** Was: 10 G. **1939** Was: 11 G; Punt 8-311 38.9. **Total:** 42 G; Punt 8-311 38.9.

KEN KARCHER Karcher, Kenneth Paul 6'3", 205 **QB**
Col: Delgado CC LA; Notre Dame; Tulane *HS:* Shaler [Pittsburgh, PA] B: 7/1/1963, Pittsburgh, PA
1987 Den: Rush 9-3 0.3. **Total:** Rush 9-3 0.3.

		Passing								
Year Team	**G**	**Att**	**Comp**	**Comp%**	**Yds**	**YPA**	**TD**	**Int**	**Rating**	**Fum**
1987 Den	3	102	56	54.9	628	6.16	5	4	73.5	2
1988 Den	1	12	6	50.0	128	10.67	1	0	116.0	0
NFL Total	4	114	62	54.4	756	6.63	6	4	78.0	2

BULL KARCIS Karcis, John 5'9", 223 **FB-LB-BB**
(Five Yards) *Col:* Carnegie Mellon *HS:* Monaca [PA] B: 12/3/1908, Monaca, PA D: 9/4/1973, Pittsburgh, PA
1933 Bkn: Rec 1-4 4.0. **1935** Bkn: Pass 5-2 40.0%, 23 4.60; Rec 5-58 11.6. **1936** Pit: Pass 4-0, 2 Int; Rec 8-71 8.9; Scor **1** 1XP. **1937** Pit: Pass 3-1 33.3%, 2 0.67 1 TD 1 Int; Rec 2-18 9.0. **1938** Pit-NYG: **1** Fum TD. NYG: 1 Fum TD. **1943** NYG: Rec 1-1 1.0; KR 1-21 21.0. **Total:** Pass 12-3 25.0%, 25 2.08 1 TD 3 Int; Rec 17-152 8.9; KR 1-21 21.0; Scor 1 1XP; 1 Fum TD.

		Rushing				Tot
Year Team	**G**	**Att**	**Yds**	**Avg**	**TD**	**TD**
1932 Bkn	11	20	68	3.4	1	1
1933 Bkn	10	70	232	3.3	0	0
1934 Bkn	9	51	202	4.0	0	0
1935 Bkn	12	68	188	2.8	1	1
1936 Pit	12	89	272	3.1	2	2
1937 Pit	6	127	513	4.0	3	3
1938 Pit-NYG	11	89	212	2.4	4	5
1938 Pit	3	16	31	1.9	0	0
1938 NYG	8	73	181	2.5	4	5
1939 NYG	10	31	93	3.0	0	0
1943 NYG	8	12	19	1.6	0	0
NFL Total	89	557	1799	3.2	11	12

CARL KARILIVACZ Karilivacz, Carl E 6'0", 188 **DB**
Col: Syracuse *HS:* Glen Cove [NY] B: 11/20/1930, Glen Cove, NY D: 8/30/1969, Glen Cove, NY *Drafted:* 1953 Round 23 Det
1955 Det: PR 1-0. **1957** Det: PR 1-0. **1958** NYG: **1** Fum TD. **Total:** PR 2-0; 1 Fum TD.

		Interceptions				Tot
Year Team	**G**	**Int**	**Yds**	**TD**	**Fum**	**TD**
1953 Det	12	0	0	0	0	0
1954 Det	11	2	66	1	0	1
1955 Det	12	2	33	0	0	0
1956 Det	11	1	0	0	0	0
1957 Det	12	5	54	0	1	0
1958 NYG	12	3	15	0	0	1
1959 LARm	6	0	0	0	0	0
1960 LARm	9	0	0	0	0	0
NFL Total	85	13	168	1	1	2

RICH KARLIS Karlis, Richard John 6'0", 180 **K**
Col: Cincinnati *HS:* Salem [OH] B: 5/23/1959, Salem, OH

		Scoring						
Year Team	**G**	**Pts**	**FG**	**FGA**	**FG%**	**XK**	**XKA**	**XK%**
1982 Den	9	48	11	13	84.6	15	16	93.8
1983 Den	16	96	21	25	84.0	33	34	97.1
1984 Den	16	101	21	28	75.0	38	41	92.7
1985 Den	16	110	23	38	60.5	41	44	93.2
1986 Den	16	104	20	28	71.4	44	45	97.8
1987 Den	12	91	18	25	72.0	37	37	100.0
1988 Den	16	105	23	36	63.9	36	37	97.3
1989 Min	13	120	**31**	39	79.5	27	28	96.4
1990 Det	6	24	4	7	57.1	12	12	100.0
NFL Total	120	799	172	239	72.0	283	294	96.3

MIKE KARMAZIN Karmazin, Michael Laurence 5'11", 210 **G**
Col: Duke *HS:* Norwin [Irwin, PA] B: 7/16/1919, Manown, PA
AAFC **1946** NY-A: 10 G.

ABE KARNOFSKY Karnofsky, Abraham Sonny 5'10", 175 **HB-DB**
Col: Arizona *HS:* Phoenix Union [AZ] B: 9/22/1922, Oxnard, CA
1945 Phi: Rec 5-113 22.6; PR 7-103 14.7; Int 1-27. **1946** Bos: Rec 8-139 17.4 1 TD; PR 2-38 19.0. **Total:** Rec 13-252 19.4 1 TD; PR 9-141 15.7; Int 1-27.

		Rushing				Kickoff Returns					Tot
Year Team	**G**	**Ret**	**Yds**	**Avg**	**TD**	**Ret**	**Yds**	**Avg**	**TD**	**Fum**	**TD**
1945 Phi	8	41	134	3.3	2	6	164	27.3	0	3	2
1946 Bos	11	36	84	2.3	1	**21**	**599**	28.5	**1**	8	3
NFL Total	19	77	218	2.8	3	27	763	28.3	1	11	5

KEITH KARPINSKI Karpinski, Keith Carl 6'3", 255 **LB**
Col: Penn State *HS:* St. Ladislaus [Hamtramck, MI]; De La Salle Collegiate HS [Warren, MI] B: 10/12/1966, Southfield, MI
Drafted: 1989 Round 11 Det
1989 Det: 16 G.

ED KARPOWICH Karpowich, Edwin Walter 6'4", 220 **T**
Col: Catholic *HS:* Duquesne [PA]; Dickinson Sem. [Williamsport, PA] B: 9/28/1912, Duquesne, PA *Drafted:* 1936 Round 8 Pit
1936 Pit: 11 G; Rec 1-(-6) -6.0. **1937** Pit: 9 G; Rush 1-15 15.0. **1938** Pit: 8 G. **1939** Pit: 7 G. **1940** Pit: 1 G. **Total:** 36 G; Rush 1-15 15.0; Rec 1-(-6) -6.0.

BILL KARR Karr, William Morrison Jr. 6'1", 190 **OE-DE**
Col: West Virginia *HS:* Ripley [WV] B: 3/29/1911, Ripley, WV D: 10/29/1979, Clendenin, WV
1936 ChiB: Rush 4-11 2.8 1 TD. **1937** ChiB: Rush 1-10 10.0. **1938** ChiB: Rush 1-6 6.0. **Total:** Rush 6-27 4.5 1 TD.

		Receiving				Tot
Year Team	**G**	**Rec**	**Yds**	**Avg**	**TD**	**TD**
1933 ChiB	13	9	182	20.2	**3**	4
1934 ChiB	12	3	68	22.7	1	1
1935 ChiB	10	9	220	24.4	**6**	6
1936 ChiB	8	6	121	20.2	2	3
1937 ChiB	10	7	188	26.9	2	2
1938 ChiB	10	14	253	18.1	4	4
NFL Total	63	48	1032	21.5	18	20

ALEX KARRAS Karras, Alexander George 6'2", 248 **DT**
(The Mad Duck) *Col:* Iowa *HS:* Emerson [Gary, IN] B: 7/15/1935, Gary, IN *Drafted:* 1958 Round 1 Det
1958 Det: 12 G; KR 1-16 16.0. **1959** Det: 12 G. **1960** Det: 12 G. **1961** Det: 14 G. **1962** Det: 14 G; Int 1-28; Scor 1 Saf; 2 Pt. **1964** Det: 14 G; Int 2-7. **1965** Det: 14 G. **1966** Det: 14 G. **1967** Det: 14 G. **1968** Det: 14 G. **1969** Det: 14 G; Int 1-22. **1970** Det: 13 G. **Total:** 161 G; KR 1-16 16.0; Int 4-57; Scor 1 Saf; 2 Pt.

JOHNNY KARRAS Karras, John Bernard 5'11", 187 **HB**
(The Argo Express) *Col:* Illinois *HS:* Argo [Summit, IL] B: 1/29/1928, Chicago, IL *Drafted:* 1952 Round 2 ChiC
1952 ChiC: 10 G; Rush 24-42 1.8; Rec 5-63 12.6 1 TD; PR 4-47 11.8; KR 4-69 17.3; 6 Pt; 3 Fum.

LOU KARRAS Karras, Louis George 6'4", 241 **DT**
Col: Purdue *HS:* Emerson [Gary, IN] B: 9/19/1927, Gary, IN
Drafted: 1950 Round 3 Was
1950 Was: 12 G. **1951** Was: 12 G. **1952** Was: 2 G; Rec 1-(-2) -2.0. **Total:** 26 G; Rec 1-(-2) -2.0.

TED KARRAS Karras, Theodore George Jr. 6'2", 265 **DT**
Col: Northwestern *HS:* Hobart [IN] B: 12/10/1964, Gary, IN
1987 Was: 1 G; 1 Sac.

TED KARRAS Karras, Theodore George Sr. 6'1", 245 **OG-OT-LB**
Col: Indiana *HS:* Emerson [Gary, IN] B: 1/31/1934, Gary, IN
1958 Pit: 12 G; KR 1-6 6.0. **1959** Pit: 12 G. **1960** ChiB: 12 G. **1961** ChiB: 14 G. **1962** ChiB: 14 G. **1963** ChiB: 14 G. **1964** ChiB: 14 G. **1965** Det: 12 G. **1966** LARm: 4 G. **Total:** 108 G; KR 1-6 6.0.

JOHN KARRS Karrs, John Bernard 6'1", 210 **BB-LB**
Col: Duquesne B: 9/19/1915, Pittsburgh, PA
1944 Cle: 10 G; Pass 10-4 40.0%, 49 4.90 4 Int; Rush 7-0.

GEORGE KARSTENS Karstens, George Jacob 6'4", 205 **C**
Col: Indiana *HS:* Austin [Chicago, IL] B: 2/9/1924, Chicago, IL
1949 Det: 2 G.

KEITH KARTZ Kartz, Keith Leonard 6′4″, 270 **C-OT-OG**
Col: California *HS:* San Dieguito [Encinitas, CA] B: 5/5/1963, Las Vegas, NV
1987 Den: 12 G. **1988** Den: 13 G. **1989** Den: 16 G. **1990** Den: 16 G; 1 Fum. **1991** Den: 16 G. **1992** Den: 15 G. **1993** Den: 12 G; 2 Fum. **Total:** 100 G; 3 Fum.

JACK KARWALES Karwales, John Joseph 6′0″, 220 **OE**
Col: Michigan *HS:* Harrison [Chicago, IL] B: 6/22/1920, Chicago, IL
1947 ChiC: 2 G.

MIKE KASAP Kasap, Michael 6′2″, 255 **T**
(Cowboy; Battleship) *Col:* Purdue; Illinois *HS:* La Salle-Peru Twp. [La Salle, IL] B: 11/20/1922, Oglesby, IL D: 10/20/1994, La Salle, IL
AAFC **1947** BalA: 12 G.

JOHN KASAY Kasay, John David 5′10″, 193 **K**
Col: Georgia *HS:* Clarke Central [Athens, GA] B: 10/27/1969, Athens, GA *Drafted:* 1991 Round 4 Sea
1995 Car: Punt 1-32 32.0. **1996** Car: Punt 1-30 30.0. **Total:** Punt 2-62 31.0.

		Scoring						
Year Team	**G**	**Pts**	**FG**	**FGA**	**FG%**	**XK**	**XKA**	**XK%**
1991 Sea	16	102	25	31	80.6	27	28	96.4
1992 Sea	16	56	14	22	63.6	14	14	100.0
1993 Sea	16	98	23	28	82.1	29	29	100.0
1994 Sea	16	85	20	24	83.3	25	26	96.2
1995 Car	16	105	26	33	78.8	27	28	96.4
1996 Car	16	**145**	**37**	**45**	82.2	34	35	97.1
1997 Car	16	91	22	26	84.6	25	25	100.0
1998 Car	16	92	19	26	73.1	35	37	94.6
NFL Total	128	774	186	235	79.1	216	222	97.3

TONY KASKA Kaska, Anton 5′11″, 193 **FB-LB-BB-DB**
Col: Illinois Wesleyan *HS:* Johnston City [IL] B: 7/1/1911, Johnston City, IL
1935 Det: 2 G; Rush 5-15 3.0. **1936** Bkn: 12 G; Pass 1-0, 1 Int; Rush 9-29 3.2 1 TD; Rec 1-5 5.0; 6 Pt. **1937** Bkn: 10 G; Rush 1-4 4.0; Rec 4-84 21.0. **1938** Bkn: 11 G; Rush 2-1 0.5; Rec 2-77 38.5. **Total:** 35 G; Pass 1-0, 1 Int; Rush 17-49 2.9 1 TD; Rec 7-166 23.7; 6 Pt.

ED KASKY Kasky, Edward Thomas 6′1″, 220 **T**
Col: Villanova *HS:* Glen Cove [NY] B: 6/22/1919, Brooklyn, NY
1942 Phi: 10 G; Scor 0-1 FG.

CY KASPER Kasper, Thomas Cyril 5′10″, 170 **G-FB**
Col: Notre Dame *HS:* Faribault [MN]; Shattbuck Mil. Acad. [Faribault, MN] B: 5/27/1895, Faribault, MN D: 12/28/1991, Bismarck, ND
1923 Roch: 1 G.

DICK KASPEREK Kasperek, Dick Lee 6′3″, 225 **C**
Col: Iowa State *HS:* Le Sueur [MN] B: 2/6/1943, St. Peter, MN
Drafted: 1966 Round 16 StL
1966 StL: 4 G. **1967** StL: 2 G. **1968** StL: 14 G. **Total:** 20 G.

CHUCK KASSEL Kassel, Charles Edward 6′1″, 191 **OE-DE**
Col: Illinois *HS:* Proviso East [Maywood, IL] B: 11/20/1903, Chicago, IL D: 11/1977, Elgin, IL
1927 ChiB-Fra: 12 G; Rec 1 TD; 1 Fum TD; Tot TD 2; 12 Pt. ChiB: 1 G. Fra: 11 G; Rec 1 TD; 1 Fum TD; Tot TD 2; 12 Pt. **1928** Fra: 14 G; Rec 1 TD; 6 Pt. **1929** ChiC: 13 G; Rec 2 TD; 12 Pt. **1930** ChiC: 13 G. **1931** ChiC: 9 G; Rec 2 TD; 12 Pt. **1932** ChiC: 10 G; Rec 7-141 20.1 1 TD; 6 Pt. **1933** ChiC: 8 G; Rush 2-2 1.0; Rec 2-44 22.0. **Total:** 79 G; Rush 2-2 1.0; Rec 9-185 20.6 7 TD; 1 Fum TD; Tot TD 8; 48 Pt.

KARL KASSULKE Kassulke, Karl Otto 6′0″, 195 **DB**
Col: Drake *HS:* West Milwaukee [WI] B: 3/20/1941, Milwaukee, WI
Drafted: 1963 Round 11 Det
1963 Min: PR 1-31 31.0. **1964** Min: PR 1-0. **Total:** PR 2-31 15.5.

		Interceptions			
Year Team	**G**	**Int**	**Yds**	**TD**	**Fum**
1963 Min	14	0	0	0	0
1964 Min	14	3	4	0	1
1965 Min	14	2	31	0	0
1966 Min	14	2	30	0	0
1967 Min	14	2	10	0	0
1968 Min	14	1	0	0	0
1969 Min	13	2	36	0	0
1970 Min	14	3	22	0	0
1971 Min	12	2	29	0	0
1972 Min	8	2	25	0	0
NFL Total	131	19	187	0	1

LEO KATALINAS Katalinas, Leo John 6′2″, 240 **T**
Col: Catholic *HS:* J.W. Cooper [Shenandoah, PA] B: 2/4/1915, Shenandoah, PA D: 7/1977, Teaneck, NJ
1938 GB: 8 G.

JIM KATCAVAGE Katcavage, James Richard 6′3″, 237 **DE-DT**
Col: Dayton *HS:* Roman Catholic [Philadelphia, PA] B: 10/28/1934, Wilkes-Barre, PA D: 2/22/1995, Maple Glen, PA *Drafted:* 1956 Round 4 NYG
1956 NYG: 12 G. **1957** NYG: 10 G. **1958** NYG: 11 G; Scor **1** Saf; 2 Pt. **1959** NYG: 12 G. **1960** NYG: 8 G. **1961** NYG: 14 G; Scor **1** Saf; 2 Pt. **1962** NYG: 14 G; Int 1-4. **1963** NYG: 14 G; **1** Fum TD; 6 Pt. **1964** NYG: 14 G. **1965** NYG: 14 G; Scor **1** Saf; 2 Pt. **1966** NYG: 14 G. **1967** NYG: 14 G. **1968** NYG: 14 G. **Total:** 165 G; Int 1-4; Scor 3 Saf; 1 Fum TD; 12 Pt.

JOE KATCHIK Katchik, Joseph Jr. 6′9″, 290 **DT**
Col: Notre Dame *HS:* Plymouth [PA]; Wyoming Seminary [Kingston, PA] B: 1/9/1931, Plymouth, PA
1960 NYT: 2 G.

MIKE KATOLIN Katolin, Michael Ross 6′3″, 255 **C**
Col: Rio Hondo Coll. CA (J.C.); San Jose State *HS:* St. Paul [Whittier, CA] B: 1/30/1958, Pasadena, CA
1987 Cle: 3 G; Rush 1-0; 1 Fum.

MIKE KATRISHEN Katrishen, William Michael 6′1″, 214 **G**
Col: Southern Mississippi B: 5/7/1922, Hazleton, PA D: 3/1980
Drafted: 1948 Round 8 Was
1948 Was: 12 G. **1949** Was: 11 G. **Total:** 23 G.

ERIC KATTUS Kattus, John Eric 6′5″, 240 **TE**
Col: Michigan *HS:* Colerain [Cincinnati, OH] B: 3/4/1963, Cincinnati, OH *Drafted:* 1986 Round 4 Cin
1987 Cin: KR 2-22 11.0. **1990** Cin: KR 1-10 10.0. **Total:** KR 3-32 10.7.

		Receiving				
Year Team	**G**	**Rec**	**Yds**	**Avg**	**TD**	**Fum**
1986 Cin	16	11	99	9.0	1	0
1987 Cin	11	18	217	12.1	2	0
1988 Cin	4	2	8	4.0	0	1
1989 Cin	16	12	93	7.8	0	0
1990 Cin	16	11	145	13.2	2	0
1991 Cin	16	12	136	11.3	0	0
1992 NYJ	4	0	0	—	0	0
NFL Total	83	66	698	10.6	5	1

KANI KAUAHI Kauahi, Daniel Kani 6′2″, 268 **C**
Col: Arizona State; Hawaii *HS:* Kamehameha School [Honolulu, HI] B: 9/6/1959, Kekaha, HI
1982 Sea: 2 G. **1983** Sea: 10 G. **1984** Sea: 16 G. **1985** Sea: 16 G. **1986** Sea: 16 G. **1988** GB: 16 G. **1989** Pho: 16 G. **1990** Pho: 15 G. **1991** Pho: 16 G. **1992** KC: 16 G. **1993** Pho: 1 G; 1 Fum. **Total:** 140 G; 1 Fum.

JOHN KAUFFMAN Kauffman, John Richard 1 **T-G**
Col: No College *HS:* Miamisburg [OH] B: 11/27/1906, Miamisburg, OH D: 10/19/1982, Englewood, CO
1929 Day: 1 G.

MEL KAUFMAN Kaufman, Melvin 6′2″, 221 **LB**
Col: Cal Poly-S.L.O. *HS:* Santa Monica [CA] B: 2/24/1958, Los Angeles, CA
1981 Was: 11 G; Int 2-25. **1982** Was: 9 G; 1.5 Sac. **1983** Was: 16 G; Int 2-93 1 TD; 1 Fum TD; Tot TD 2; 12 Pt; 1.5 Sac. **1984** Was: 15 G; 5.5 Sac. **1985** Was: 15 G; Int 3-10; 4 Sac. **1986** Was: 2 G; 3 Sac. **1987** Was: 12 G; 2 Sac. **1988** Was: 11 G; 1 Sac. **Total:** 91 G; Int 7-128 1 TD; 1 Fum TD; Tot TD 2; 12 Pt; 18.5 Sac.

NAPOLEON KAUFMAN Kaufman, Napoleon 5′9″, 185 **RB**
Col: Washington *HS:* Lompoc [CA] B: 6/7/1973, Kansas City, MO
Drafted: 1995 Round 1 Oak
1997 Oak: Pass 1-0. **Total:** Pass 1-0.

		Rushing				Receiving			
Year Team	**G**	**Att**	**Yds**	**Avg**	**TD**	**Rec**	**Yds**	**Avg**	**TD**
1995 Oak	16	108	490	4.5	1	9	62	6.9	0
1996 Oak	16	150	874	**5.8**	1	22	143	6.5	1
1997 Oak	16	272	1294	4.8	6	40	403	10.1	2
1998 Oak	13	217	921	4.2	2	25	191	7.6	0
NFL Total	61	747	3579	4.8	10	96	799	8.3	3

	Kickoff Returns					Tot
Year Team	**Ret**	**Yds**	**Avg**	**TD**	**Fum**	**TD**
1995 Oak	22	572	26.0	1	0	2
1996 Oak	25	548	21.9	0	3	2
1997 Oak	0	0	—	0	7	8
1998 Oak	0	0	—	0	2	2
NFL Total	47	1120	23.8	1	12	14

STEVE KAUFUSI Kaufusi, Sitiveni P 6′4″, 274 **DE-DT**
Col: Brigham Young *HS:* South [Salt Lake City, UT] B: 10/17/1963, Nuku'Alofa, Tonga *Drafted:* 1988 Round 12 Phi
1989 Phi: 16 G. **1990** Phi: 16 G. **Total:** 32 G.

THOM KAUMEYER Kaumeyer, Thomas E Jr. 5′11″, 187 **DB**
Col: Palomar Coll. CA (J.C.); Oregon *HS:* San Dieguito [Encinitas, CA]
B: 3/17/1967, La Jolla, CA *Drafted:* 1989 Round 6 LARm
1989 Sea: 1 G. **1990** Sea: 7 G. **Total:** 8 G.

JERRY KAURIC Kauric, Jerry 6′0″, 210 **K**
Col: No College *HS:* Kennedy Collegiate School [Windsor, Canada]
B: 6/28/1963, Windsor, Canada
1990 Cle: 14 G; Rec 1-21 21.0; Scor 66, 14-20 70.0% FG, 24-27 88.9% XK.

KEN KAVANAUGH Kavanaugh, Kenneth William 6′3″, 207 **OE-DE**
Col: Louisiana State *HS:* Little Rock Central [AR] B: 11/23/1916, Little Rock, AR *Drafted:* 1940 Round 2 ChiB
1941 ChiB: KR 1-15 15.0; Int 1-6; Scor 37, 1-1 100.0% XK. **1945** ChiB: KR 1-7 7.0. **1948** ChiB: 1 Fum TD. **1950** ChiB: **1** Fum TD. **Total:** KR 2-22 11.0; Int 1-6; Scor 313, 1-1 100.0% XK; 2 Fum TD.

		Receiving					Tot
Year Team	G	Rec	Yds	Avg	TD	Fum	TD
1940 ChiB	11	12	276	23.0	3	0	3
1941 ChiB	11	11	314	**28.5**	6	0	6
1945 ChiB	10	25	543	21.7	6	0	6
1946 ChiB	10	18	337	18.7	5	1	5
1947 ChiB	12	32	818	25.6	**13**	0	13
1948 ChiB	12	18	352	19.6	6	0	7
1949 ChiB	12	29	655	22.6	**9**	0	9
1950 ChiB	12	17	331	19.5	2	1	3
NFL Total	90	162	3626	22.4	50	2	52

GEORGE KAVEL Kavel, George Charles 5′11″, 170 **HB-DB**
Col: Carnegie Mellon *HS:* Norwin [Irwin, PA] B: 5/3/1910, Wendel, PA
D: 7/17/1995, Sarasota, FL
1934 Pit-Phi: 2 G; Rush 7-10 1.4. Pit: 1 G; Rush 5-5 1.0. Phi: 1 G; Rush 2-5 2.5. **Total:** 2 G; Rush 7-10 1.4.

EDDIE KAW Kaw, Edgar Lawrence 5′11″, 185 **TB**
Col: Cornell *HS:* Principia School [Elsah, IL]; West [Minneapolis, MN]
B: 1/18/1897, Houston, TX D: 12/13/1971, Walnut Creek, CA
1924 Buf: 11 G; Pass 4 TD; Rec 2 TD; 12 Pt.

EDDIE KAWAL Kawal, Edward Joseph 6′2″, 200 **C-LB-G-T**
Col: Illinois; Widener *HS:* J. Sterling Morton [Cicero, IL] B: 10/13/1909, Cicero, IL D: 9/26/1960, Oak Park, IL
1931 ChiB: 1 G. **1934** ChiB: 13 G. **1935** ChiB: 12 G; Rec 1-11 11.0; Int **1** TD; 6 Pt. **1936** ChiB: 11 G. **1937** Was: 9 G. **Total:** 46 G; Rec 1-11 11.0; Int 1 TD; 6 Pt.

CLARENCE KAY Kay, Clarence Hubert 6′2″, 237 **TE**
Col: Georgia *HS:* Seneca [SC] B: 7/30/1961, Seneca, SC
Drafted: 1984 Round 7 Den
1990 Den: KR 2-10 5.0. **Total:** KR 2-10 5.0.

		Receiving				
Year Team	G	Rec	Yds	Avg	TD	Fum
1984 Den	16	16	136	8.5	3	1
1985 Den	16	29	339	11.7	3	1
1986 Den	13	15	195	13.0	1	0
1987 Den	12	31	440	14.2	0	3
1988 Den	14	34	352	10.4	4	1
1989 Den	16	21	197	9.4	2	0
1990 Den	16	29	282	9.7	0	0
1991 Den	16	11	139	12.6	0	0
1992 Den	16	7	56	8.0	0	0
NFL Total	135	193	2136	11.1	13	6

RICK KAY Kay, Richard Floyd 6′4″, 235 **LB**
Col: Colorado *HS:* Pacific [San Bernardino, CA] B: 11/10/1949, Henderson, NV
1973 LARm: 14 G. **1975** LARm: 14 G. **1976** LARm: 3 G; Int 1-0.
1977 LARm-Atl: 12 G. LARm: 5 G. Atl: 7 G. **Total:** 43 G; Int 1-0.

BILL KAY Kay, William Henry 6′1″, 190 **DB**
Col: Purdue *HS:* Proviso East [Maywood, IL] B: 1/10/1960, Detroit, MI
Drafted: 1981 Round 6 Hou
1981 Hou: 16 G; Int 2-47. **1982** Hou: 9 G. **1983** Hou: 16 G; Int 2-31.
1984 StL-SD: 15 G. StL: 10 G. SD: 5 G. **Total:** 56 G; Int 4-78.

MUADIANVITA KAZADI Kazadi, Muadianvita Matt 6′2″, 240 **LB**
Col: Tulsa *HS:* Newton [KS] B: 12/20/1973, Zaire *Drafted:* 1997 Round 6 StL
1997 StL: 12 G.

DUCE KEAHEY Keahey, Eulis Duce 6′2″, 215 **T-G**
Col: George Washington *HS:* Van [TX] B: 1/20/1917, Grand Saline, TX
1942 NYG-Bkn: 2 G. NYG: 1 G. Bkn: 1 G. **Total:** 2 G.

JIM KEANE Keane, James Patrick 6′4″, 217 **OE-DE**
Col: Iowa; Northwestern *HS:* Linsly Mil. Inst. [Wheeling, WV]
B: 1/11/1924, Bellaire, OH *Drafted:* 1945 Round 16 ChiB
1946 ChiB: PR 1-23 23.0; Punt 2-79 39.5. **Total:** PR 1-23 23.0; Punt 2-79 39.5.

		Receiving				
Year Team	G	Rec	Yds	Avg	TD	Fum
1946 ChiB	11	14	331	23.6	3	0
1947 ChiB	12	**64**	910	14.2	10	2
1948 ChiB	11	30	414	13.8	3	0
1949 ChiB	12	47	696	14.8	6	0
1950 ChiB	12	36	433	12.0	0	2
1951 ChiB	12	15	247	16.5	1	0
1952 GB	11	18	191	10.6	1	0
NFL Total	81	224	3222	14.4	24	4

TOM KEANE Keane, Thomas Lawrence 6′1″, 190 **DB**
Col: Ohio State; West Virginia *HS:* Linsly Mil. Inst. [Wheeling, WV]
B: 9/7/1926, Bellaire, OH *Drafted:* 1948 Round 2 LARm
1948 LARm: Rush 7-16 2.3. **1951** LARm: Pass 1-0, 1 Int. **1952** Dal: PR 1-8 8.0. **1953** Bal: PR 1-3 3.0; Punt 18-753 41.8. **1954** Bal: Pass 1-1 100.0%. **1955** ChiC: Scor 0-1 FG. **Total:** Pass 2-1 50.0%, 1 Int; Rush 7-16 2.3; PR 2-11 5.5; Punt 18-753 41.8; Scor 18, 0-1 FG.

		Receiving				Interceptions				Tot
Year Team	G	Rec	Yds	Avg	TD	Int	Yds	TD	Fum	TD
1948 LARm	11	11	195	17.7	2	0	0	0	1	2
1949 LARm	10	4	70	17.5	0	0	0	0	0	0
1950 LARm	9	1	19	19.0	0	6	50	1	0	1
1951 LARm	10	12	133	11.1	0	2	2	0	0	0
1952 Dal	12	3	73	24.3	0	10	93	0	0	0
1953 Bal	12	3	61	20.3	0	11	118	0	0	0
1954 Bal	12	0	0	—	0	5	22	0	0	0
1955 ChiC	11	0	0	—	0	6	64	0	0	0
NFL Total	87	34	551	16.2	2	40	349	1	1	3

JIM KEARNEY Kearney, James Lee 6′2″, 206 **DB**
Col: Prairie View A&M *HS:* Wharton Training [TX] B: 1/21/1943, Wharton, TX *Drafted:* 1965 Round 11 Det
1968 KC: KR 1-9 9.0. **1972** KC: KR 1-0. **Total:** KR 2-9 4.5.

		Interceptions			
Year Team	G	Int	Yds	TD	Fum
1965 Det	7	0	0	0	0
1966 Det	6	0	0	0	0
1967 KC	3	0	0	0	0
1968 KC	14	3	23	0	1
1969 KC	14	5	143	1	2
1970 KC	14	4	28	0	1
1971 KC	14	3	46	0	0
1972 KC	14	5	**192**	**4**	0
1973 KC	14	3	30	0	1
1974 KC	14	0	0	0	0
1975 KC	14	0	0	0	0
1976 NO	14	0	0	0	0
NFL Total	142	23	462	5	5

TIM KEARNEY Kearney, Timothy Edward 6′2″, 227 **LB**
Col: Northern Michigan *HS:* Kingsford [MI] B: 11/5/1950, Kingsford, MI *Drafted:* 1972 Round 4 Dal
1972 Cin: 1 G. **1973** Cin: 14 G. **1974** Cin: 12 G. **1975** KC: 14 G. **1976** StL: 12 G; Int 1-0. **1977** StL: 14 G. **1978** StL: 15 G; KR 1-22 22.0; Int 1-8. **1979** StL: 5 G. **1980** StL: 13 G; Int 1-22. **1981** StL: 6 G. **Total:** 106 G; KR 1-22 22.0; Int 3-30.

TOM KEARNS Kearns, Thomas 6′4″, 247 **T**
Col: Miami (Fla.) *HS:* Somerville [MA] B: 11/26/1920, Bedford, MA
Drafted: 1942 Round 6 NYG
1945 NYG: 3 G. **1946** ChiC: 9 G. **Total:** 12 G.

TIM KEARSE Kearse, Timothy Allynn 5′10″, 186 **WR**
Col: San Jose State *HS:* York [PA] B: 10/24/1959, York, PA
Drafted: 1983 Round 11 SD
1987 Ind: 3 G; Rec 3-56 18.7.

CHRIS KEATING Keating, Christopher Paul 6′2″, 223 **LB**
Col: Maine *HS:* Archbishop Williams [Cohasset, MA] B: 10/12/1957, Boston, MA
1979 Buf: 16 G; KR 1-14 14.0. **1980** Buf: 15 G; KR 3-38 12.7. **1981** Buf: 2 G. **1982** Buf: 9 G; KR 1-9 9.0; Int 1-14. **1983** Buf: 16 G; Int 2-20. **1984** Buf: 16 G; **1** Fum TD; 6 Pt; 2 Sac. **1985** Was: 10 G; KR 1-9 9.0. **Total:** 84 G; KR 6-70 11.7; Int 3-34; 1 Fum TD; 6 Pt; 2 Sac.

TOM KEATING Keating, Thomas Arthur 6′2″, 247 **DT**
Col: Michigan *HS:* St. Mel's [Chicago, IL] B: 9/2/1942, Chicago, IL
Drafted: 1964 Round 5 Buf
1964 Buf: 3 G. **1965** Buf: 6 G. **1966** Oak: 14 G. **1967** Oak: 14 G. **1969** Oak: 14 G. **1970** Oak: 13 G. **1971** Oak: 7 G. **1972** Oak: 8 G. **1973** Pit: 12 G. **1974** KC: 14 G; KR 1-10 10.0. **1975** KC: 9 G. **Total:** 114 G; KR 1-10 10.0.

BILL KEATING Keating, William Lawrence 6′2″, 242 **DT-OG**
Col: Michigan *HS:* St. Patrick [Chicago, IL] B: 11/22/1944, Chicago, IL
1966 Den: 14 G. **1967** Den-Mia: 8 G. Den: 6 G. Mia: 2 G. **Total:** 22 G.

STAN KECK Keck, James Stanton 5'11", 205 **T-G**
Col: Princeton *HS:* Kiski School [Saltsburg, PA]; Bellefonte Academy [PA] B: 9/11/1897, Greensburg, PA D: 1/20/1951, Pittsburgh, PA
1923 Cle: 3 G; Scor 7, 2 FG, 1 XK.

VAL KECKIN Keckin, Valdemar Christian 6'4", 215 **QB**
Col: Southern Mississippi *HS:* Alexander Hamilton [Los Angeles, CA] B: 2/12/1938, Los Angeles, CA *Drafted:* 1961 Round 11 GB
1962 SD: 6 G; Pass 9-5 55.6%, 64 7.11 1 Int; Rush 1-3 3.0; 2 Fum.

DAN KECMAN Kecman, Daniel S 6'2", 230 **LB**
Col: Maryland *HS:* North [West Mifflin, PA] B: 6/10/1948, Pittsburgh, PA
1970 Bos: 1 G.

JERRY KEEBLE Keeble, Jerry Anthony 6'3", 230 **LB**
Col: Arizona Western Coll. (J.C.); Minnesota *HS:* Hazelwood East [St. Louis, MO] B: 8/19/1963, St. Louis, MO
1987 SF: 3 G.

JOE KEEBLE Keeble, Joseph Bailey 6'0", 190 **TB-WB-DB**
(The Holtville Terror) *Col:* UCLA *HS:* Holtville [CA]; Oneonta Prep [South Pasadena, CA] B: 8/29/1909, Cleburne, TX D: 4/27/1984, Atascadero, CA
1937 Cle: 7 G; Pass 9-2 22.2%, 25 2.78 3 Int; Rush 12-40 3.3; Rec 1-42 42.0 1 TD; 6 Pt.

EMMETT KEEFE Keefe, Emmett Gerald 5'10", 195 **G**
Col: Notre Dame *HS:* Raub [IN] B: 4/28/1893, Raub, IN
D: 9/11/1965, Chicago, IL
1920 ChiT: 8 G. **1921** RI-GB: 8 G. RI: 7 G. GB: 1 G. **1922** RI-Mil: 7 G. RI: 5 G. Mil: 2 G. **Total:** 23 G.

JACK KEEFER Keefer, Jackson Milliman 5'9", 172 **TB**
Col: Michigan; Brown *HS:* Steele [Dayton, OH] B: 5/1/1900, Olney, IL
D: 8/3/1966, Dayton, OH
1926 Prov: 11 G; Pass 1 TD; Rush 2 TD; Scor 15, 3 XK. **1928** Day: 3 G. **Total:** 14 G; Pass 1 TD; Rush 2 TD.

MARK KEEL Keel, Mark Anthony 6'4", 228 **TE**
Col: Olympic Coll. WA (J.C.); Arizona *HS:* Clover Park [Tacoma, WA] B: 10/1/1961, Fort Worth, TX *Drafted:* 1983 Round 9 NE
1987 Sea-KC: 10 G; Rec 8-97 12.1 1 TD; 6 Pt. Sea: 3 G; Rec 6-88 14.7 1 TD; 6 Pt. KC: 7 G; Rec 2-9 4.5. **Total:** 10 G; Rec 8-97 12.1 1 TD; 6 Pt.

RAY KEELING Keeling, Raymond Grigsby 6'3", 259 **T**
(King Kong) *Col:* Texas B: 8/24/1915, Dallas, TX D: 4/1/1996, Littlefield, TX
1938 Phi: 9 G. **1939** Phi: 9 G. **Total:** 18 G.

REX KEELING Keeling, Rex George Jr. 6'4", 205 **P**
Col: Samford *HS:* Gadsden [AL] B: 9/9/1943, Dallas, TX
Drafted: 1967 Round 16 Hou
1968 Cin: 1 G; Pass 1-0; Rush 1-10 10.0; Punt 6-170 28.3.

RABBIT KEEN Keen, Delbert Allen 5'9", 170 **WB-DB-HB-TB**
Col: Arkansas *HS:* Henryetta [OK] B: 12/10/1914, Stillwell, OK
D: 6/4/1984, Overland Park, KS
1937 Phi: Pass 5-1 20.0%, 86 17.20 1 TD; Rec 5-45 9.0. **Total:** Pass 5-1 20.0%, 86 17.20 1 TD; Rec 5-45 9.0.

		Rushing			
Year Team	**G**	**Att**	**Yds**	**Avg**	**TD**
1937 Phi	8	34	154	4.5	0
1938 Phi	1	3	10	3.3	0
NFL Total	9	37	164	4.4	0

ED KEENAN Keenan, Edward F 6'4", 320 **G**
Col: Washington (Md) *HS:* Waterbury [CT] B: 10/30/1894
D: 1/28/1984, Waterbury, CT
1926 Har: 10 G.

JACK KEENAN Keenan, Jack Harvey 5'10", 214 **T-G**
Col: South Carolina B: 6/8/1919, Greensboro, NC D: 2/8/1977, Nash, NC
1944 Was: 10 G. **1945** Was: 3 G. **Total:** 13 G.

BOB KEENE Keene, Robert 5'10", 185 **WB-DB-HB-FB**
Col: Detroit Mercy *HS:* MacKenzie [Detroit, MI] B: 8/26/1919, Detroit, MI
1943 Det: 5 G; Rush 1-1 1.0; Rec 1-27 27.0; KR 1-12 12.0. **1944** Det: 10 G; Rush 9-26 2.9; Rec 5-91 18.2 2 TD; PR 7-128 **18.3**; KR 4-93 23.3; Int 2-14; Punt 1-30 30.0; 12 Pt. **1945** Det: 1 G; Rush 2-2 1.0; 1 Fum. **Total:** 16 G; Rush 12-29 2.4; Rec 6-118 19.7 2 TD; PR 7-128 18.3; KR 5-105 21.0; Int 2-14; Punt 1-30 30.0; 12 Pt; 1 Fum.

BRAD KEENEY Keeney, Brad O'Hara 6'3", 294 **DT**
Col: The Citadel *HS:* Hoggard [Wilmington, NC] B: 11/20/1973, Augusta, GA
1996 NYJ: 1 G.

DURWOOD KEETON Keeton, Durwood Lee 5'11", 178 **DB**
Col: Oklahoma *HS:* Bonham [TX] B: 8/14/1952, Bonham, TX
Drafted: 1974 Round 4 StL
1975 NE: 12 G.

CARL KEEVER Keever, Carl Richard 6'2", 236 **LB**
Col: Oregon State; Boise State *HS:* Boise [ID] B: 8/17/1961, Reno, NV
1987 SF: 3 G.

SCOTT KEHOE Kehoe, Scott Anton 6'4", 282 **OT**
Col: Illinois *HS:* Oak Lawn [IL] B: 9/20/1964, Oak Lawn, IL
1987 Mia: 3 G.

RICK KEHR Kehr, Karl Richard 6'3", 285 **OG**
Col: Carthage *HS:* Larkin [Elgin, IL] B: 6/18/1959, Phoenixville, PA
1987 Was: 5 G.

MIKE KEIM Keim, Karl Michael 6'7", 295 **OT**
Col: Mesa CC AZ; Brigham Young *HS:* Round Valley [Springerville, AZ] B: 11/12/1965, Anaheim, CA
1992 Sea: 1 G. **1993** Sea: 3 G. **1994** Sea: 16 G. **1995** Sea: 7 G. **Total:** 27 G.

CRAIG KEITH Keith, Craig Carlton 6'3", 262 **TE**
Col: Lenoir-Rhyne *HS:* Millbrook [Raleigh, NC] B: 4/27/1971, Raleigh, NC *Drafted:* 1993 Round 7 Pit
1993 Pit: 1 G. **1994** Pit: 16 G; Rec 1-2 2.0. **1995** Jac: 11 G; Rec 3-20 6.7. **Total:** 28 G; Rec 4-22 5.5.

GARY KEITHLEY Keithley, Gary Tom 6'3", 210 **QB**
Col: Alvin CC TX; Texas; Texas-El Paso *HS:* Alvin [TX] B: 1/11/1951, Alvin, TX *Drafted:* 1973 Round 2 StL
1973 StL: Rush 8-29 3.6.

		Passing							
Year Team	**G**	**Att**	**Comp**	**Comp%**	**Yds**	**YPA**	**TD**	**Int**	**Rating**
1973 StL	14	73	32	43.8	369	5.05	1	5	35.7

	Punting			
Year Team	**Punts**	**Yds**	**Avg**	**Fum**
1973 StL	66	2478	37.5	5

JIM KEKERIS Kekeris, James J 6'1", 257 **T**
Col: Missouri *HS:* McKinley [St. Louis, MO] B: 10/17/1923, St. Louis, MO D: 9/15/1997, Columbia, MO *Drafted:* 1947 Round 3 Det
1947 Phi: 10 G; Scor 2, 0-1 FG, 2-3 66.7% XK. **1948** GB: 5 G. **Total:** 15 G; Scor 2, 0-1 FG, 2-3 66.7% XK.

LOUIE KELCHER Kelcher, Louie James Jr. 6'5", 291 **DT-NT**
Col: Southern Methodist *HS:* French [Beaumont, TX] B: 8/23/1953, Beaumont, TX *Drafted:* 1975 Round 2 SD
1975 SD: 13 G. **1976** SD: 14 G. **1977** SD: 12 G. **1978** SD: 15 G; Int 1-0. **1979** SD: 1 G. **1980** SD: 15 G; Int 1-2. **1981** SD: 14 G. **1982** SD: 8 G; 2 Sac. **1983** SD: 8 G. **1984** SF: 16 G. **Total:** 116 G; Int 2-2; 2 Sac.

PAUL KELL Kell, Paul Ernest 6'2", 217 **T**
Col: Notre Dame *HS:* Niles [MI] B: 7/18/1915, Princeton, IL
D: 5/1977, Chippewa Falls, WI *Drafted:* 1939 Round 6 GB
1939 GB: 9 G. **1940** GB: 11 G. **Total:** 20 G.

BILL KELLAGHER Kellagher, William Michael 5'11", 205 **FB-LB-DB**
(Scrooge) *Col:* Fordham *HS:* Ashland [PA] B: 8/13/1920, Locust Gap, PA
AAFC **1946** ChiA: Pass 3-2 66.7%, 15 5.00 1 Int; Rec 2-36 18.0; KR 3-48 16.0; Punt 1-56 56.0. **1947** ChiA: Rec 3-22 7.3; Int 6-77. **1948** ChiA: KR 3-54 18.0. **Total:** Pass 3-2 66.7%, 15 5.00 1 Int; Rec 5-58 11.6; KR 6-102 17.0; Int 6-77; Punt 1-56 56.0.

		Rushing			
Year Team	**G**	**Att**	**Yds**	**Avg**	**TD**
1946 ChiA	12	49	178	3.6	3
1947 ChiA	14	42	243	5.8	0
1948 ChiA	12	33	97	2.9	1
AAFC Total	38	124	518	4.2	4

MARK KELLAR Kellar, Mark Peter 6'0", 225 **RB**
Col: Northern Illinois *HS:* Irving Crown [Carpentersville, IL] B: 7/17/1952, Chicago, IL *Drafted:* 1974 Round 6 Min
1976 Min: Rec 2-22 11.0; KR 1-22 22.0. **1977** Min: KR 3-37 12.3. **1978** Min: Rec 3-(-5) -1.7; KR 1-13 13.0. **Total:** Rec 5-17 3.4; KR 5-72 14.4.

		Rushing				
Year Team	**G**	**Att**	**Yds**	**Avg**	**TD**	**Fum**
1976 Min	3	7	25	3.6	0	0
1977 Min	14	7	15	2.1	0	0
1978 Min	16	11	34	3.1	0	1
NFL Total	33	25	74	3.0	0	1

SCOTT KELLAR Kellar, Scott Jeffery 6'3", 282 **NT**
Col: Northern Illinois *HS:* Lake Park [Roselle, IL] B: 12/31/1963, Elgin, IL *Drafted:* 1986 Round 5 Ind
1986 Ind: 14 G; 1 Sac. **1987** Ind: 3 G. **Total:** 17 G; 1 Sac.

BILL KELLAR Kellar, William Elden 5'11", 187 **WR**
Col: Stanford *HS:* Hillsboro [OR] B: 2/8/1956, Longview, WA
Drafted: 1978 Round 7 KC
1978 KC: 5 G.

KEN KELLER Keller, Kenneth Kay 5'11", 185 **HB**
(Little Man; Killer) *Col:* North Carolina *HS:* Bell Twp. [PA]
B: 9/12/1934, Salina, PA D: 12/10/1997, Youngstown, OH
Drafted: 1956 Round 11 Phi
1956 Phi: Rec 7-36 5.1; PR 15-146 9.7. **1957** Phi: Rec 4-31 7.8; PR 9-59 6.6. **Total:** Rec 11-67 6.1; PR 24-205 8.5.

		Rushing				Kickoff Returns				
Year Team	G	Att	Yds	Avg	TD	Ret	Yds	Avg	TD	Fum
1956 Phi	11	112	433	3.9	4	15	353	23.5	0	7
1957 Phi	12	57	195	3.4	0	15	320	21.3	0	3
NFL Total	23	169	628	3.7	4	30	673	22.4	0	10

LARRY KELLER Keller, Larry Ray 6'2", 223 **LB**
Col: Houston *HS:* Lutcher Stark [Orange, TX] B: 10/2/1953, San Benito, TX *Drafted:* 1975 Round 9 SD
1976 NYJ: 14 G; Int 1-31. **1977** NYJ: 14 G; Rush 1-25 25.0; Int 1-36.
1978 NYJ: 16 G; Int 1-4. **Total:** 44 G; Rush 1-25 25.0; Int 3-71.

MIKE KELLER Keller, Michael F 6'4", 221 **LB**
Col: Michigan *HS:* Catholic Central [Grand Rapids, MI] B: 12/13/1949, Chicago, IL *Drafted:* 1972 Round 3 Dal
1972 Dal: 5 G.

ERNIE KELLERMANN Kellermann, Ernest James 6'0", 183 **DB**
Col: Miami (Ohio) *HS:* Chanel [Bedford, OH] B: 12/17/1943, Cleveland, OH *Drafted:* 1965 Round 12 Dal
1971 Cle: PR 1-4 4.0; KR 1-5 5.0. **Total:** PR 1-4 4.0; KR 1-5 5.0.

		Interceptions			
Year Team	G	Int	Yds	TD	Fum
1966 Cle	14	3	23	0	0
1967 Cle	14	1	9	0	0
1968 Cle	14	6	29	0	1
1969 Cle	11	3	40	1	0
1970 Cle	14	1	18	0	0
1971 Cle	14	3	0	0	0
1972 Cin	14	0	0	0	0
1973 Buf	10	2	23	0	0
NFL Total	105	19	142	1	1

DOUG KELLERMEYER Kellermeyer, Douglas Arthur 6'3", 275 **OG-OT**
Col: Brigham Young *HS:* Coronado [Scottsdale, AZ] B: 6/1/1961, Bucyrus, OH
1987 Hou: 3 G.

DOC KELLEY Kelley, Albert James 5'10", 170 **TB-WB**
(Superior Tooth) *Col:* Northwestern *HS:* Central [Superior, WI]
B: 3/1/1902, Chicago, IL D: 7/5/1963
1924 Dul: 5 G. **1925** Dul: 3 G. **1926** Dul: 5 G. **Total:** 13 G.

BILL KELLEY Kelley, Billie Rex 6'2", 195 **E**
Col: Texas Tech *HS:* Idalou [TX] B: 8/23/1926, Becton, TX
Drafted: 1949 Round 23 GB
1949 GB: 12 G; Rec 17-222 13.1 1 TD; 6 Pt; 1 Fum.

BRIAN KELLEY Kelley, Brian Lee 6'3", 230 **LB**
Col: California Lutheran *HS:* Sunny Hills [Fullerton, CA] B: 9/1/1951, Dallas, TX *Drafted:* 1973 Round 14 NYG
1973 NYG: KR 2-30 15.0. **1974** NYG: KR 3-25 8.3. **1977** NYG: KR 1-20 20.0. **1978** NYG: Rush 1-2 2.0; Rec 1-(-1) -1.0. **1983** NYG: 1.5 Sac.
Total: Rush 1-2 2.0; Rec 1-(-1) -1.0; KR 6-75 12.5; 1.5 Sac.

		Interceptions			
Year Team	G	Int	Yds	TD	Fum
1973 NYG	14	0	0	0	0
1974 NYG	13	1	31	0	1
1975 NYG	14	3	30	0	0
1976 NYG	14	0	0	0	0
1977 NYG	13	1	17	0	0
1978 NYG	16	1	20	0	1
1979 NYG	16	3	41	0	0
1980 NYG	2	0	0	0	0
1981 NYG	16	2	43	0	0
1982 NYG	9	3	27	0	0
1983 NYG	16	1	17	0	0
NFL Total	143	15	226	0	2

CHRIS KELLEY Kelley, Christopher John 6'4", 240 **TE**
Col: Akron *HS:* Lorain Catholic [OH] B: 11/13/1964, Lorain, OH
Drafted: 1987 Round 7 Pit
1987 Cle: 2 G; Scor **1** 1XP; 1 Pt.

IKE KELLEY Kelley, Dwight Allen 5'11", 225 **LB**
Col: Ohio State *HS:* Bremen [OH] B: 7/14/1944, Ludington, MI
Drafted: 1966 Round 17 Phi
1966 Phi: 14 G. **1967** Phi: 14 G; KR 1-0; Int 1-18. **1969** Phi: 14 G.
1970 Phi: 11 G. **1971** Phi: 14 G. **Total:** 67 G; KR 1-0; Int 1-18.

ED KELLEY Kelley, Edward Allen 6'4", 230 **T**
Col: Texas *HS:* Jeff Davis [Houston, TX] B: 2/18/1924, Sugar Land, TX
AAFC **1949** LA-A: 12 G; Rush 1-(-2) -2.0.

EDWARD KELLEY Kelley, Edward Clemens Jr. 6'2", 195 **DB**
Col: Texas *HS:* Cuero [TX] B: 6/8/1933, Gonzales, TX *Drafted:* 1955 Round 5 LARm
1961 DalT: 13 G. **1962** DalT: 1 G. **Total:** 14 G.

FRANK KELLEY Kelley, Frank Edward 5'10", 165 **WB**
Col: South Dakota State *HS:* Bon Homme [Tyndall, SD] B: 10/1903, Tyndall, SD Deceased
1927 Cle: 7 G; Rush 2 TD; Rec 1 TD; Tot TD 3; 18 Pt.

GORDEN KELLEY Kelley, Gorden Bond 6'3", 231 **LB**
Col: Georgia *HS:* Decatur [GA] B: 6/11/1938, Decatur, GA
Drafted: 1960 Round 2 LAC
1960 SF: 12 G; Int 2-10. **1961** SF: 14 G; Int 1-0. **1962** Was: 11 G; Int 2-11.
1963 Was: 14 G. **Total:** 51 G; Int 5-21.

LES KELLEY Kelley, Leslie Howard 6'3", 233 **LB**
Col: Alabama *HS:* Cullman [AL] B: 12/9/1944, Decatur, AL
Drafted: 1967 Round 1 NO
1967 NO: 2 G. **1968** NO: 14 G; KR 1-20 20.0; Int 1-0. **1969** NO: 14 G.
Total: 30 G; KR 1-20 20.0; Int 1-0.

MIKE KELLEY Kelley, Michael Dennis 6'3", 195 **QB**
Col: Georgia Tech *HS:* Westside [Augusta, GA] B: 12/31/1959, Sonora, PA *Drafted:* 1982 Round 6 Atl
1987 SD: 3 G; Pass 29-17 58.6%, 305 10.52 1 TD; Rush 4-17 4.3.

MIKE KELLEY Kelley, Micheal Peter 6'5", 273 **C-OG-OT**
Col: Notre Dame *HS:* Westfield [MA] B: 2/27/1962, Westfield, MA
Drafted: 1985 Round 3 Hou
1985 Hou: 16 G. **1987** Hou: 1 G. **Total:** 17 G.

BOB KELLEY Kelley, Robert 6'2", 232 **C**
(Whitey) *Col:* West Texas A&M *HS:* Bovina [TX] B: 5/8/1930, Hereford, TX *Drafted:* 1952 Round 25 Phi
1955 Phi: 12 G. **1956** Phi: 12 G. **Total:** 24 G.

KEVIN KELLIN Kellin, Kevin Robert 6'6", 267 **DT**
Col: Minnesota *HS:* Grand Rapids [MN] B: 11/16/1959, Hampton, IA
1986 TB: 9 G; 2 Sac. **1987** TB: 7 G; 3.5 Sac. **1988** TB: 4 G. **Total:** 20 G; 5.5 Sac.

JOHN KELLISON Kellison, John Snowden 6'0", 210 **G-T**
(Honest John) *Col:* West Virginia Wesleyan *HS:* W.Va. Wesleyan Prep [Buckhannon, WV] B: 11/3/1886, Buckeye, WV D: 5/7/1971, Marlinton, WV
1920 Can: 3 G. **1921** Can: 4 G. **1922** Tol: 1 G. **Total:** 8 G.

KELLOGG Kellogg **TB**
Deceased
1921 Mun: 1 G.

CLARENCE KELLOGG Kellogg, Clarence 5'10", 205 **FB-DB**
Col: St. Mary's (Cal.) *HS:* Marseilles [IL] B: 9/8/1911 D: 9/3/1988, Denver, CO
1936 ChiC: Rec 4-11 2.8; Scor 9, 1 FG, 6 XK.

		Rushing			
Year Team	G	Att	Yds	Avg	TD
1936 ChiC	12	66	164	2.5	0

MIKE KELLOGG Kellogg, Michael Karl 6'0", 230 **RB**
Col: Santa Clara *HS:* Long Beach Polytechnic [CA] B: 10/28/1942, Tuscon, AZ
1966 Den: 8 G; Rush 6-3 0.5; Rec 1-5 5.0; 1 Fum. **1967** Den: 2 G.
Total: 10 G; Rush 6-3 0.5; Rec 1-5 5.0; 1 Fum.

BOB KELLOGG Kellogg, Robert Francis 5'10", 175 **TB-DB**
(Jitterbug) *Col:* Northeast Louisiana; Tulane *HS:* Wynne [AR]
B: 8/4/1917, Wynne, AR D: 5/9/1985, Columbus, MS
1940 ChiC: 3 G; Pass 18-6 33.3%, 42 2.33 4 Int; Rush 9-31 3.4; Punt 2-54 27.0.

BILL KELLOGG Kellogg, William J 5'10", 178 **FB-TB**
Col: Indiana (Pa.); Syracuse *HS:* Allegany [NY] B: 3/3/1897, Pittsburgh, PA D: 11/28/1969, Syracuse, NY
1924 Fra: 4 G; Rush 3 TD; 18 Pt. **1925** Roch: 5 G; Rush 1 TD; Rec 1 TD; Tot TD 2; 12 Pt. **Total:** 9 G; Rush 4 TD; Rec 1 TD; Tot TD 5; 30 Pt.

MARV KELLUM Kellum, Marvin Lee 6'2", 225 **LB**
Col: Wichita State *HS:* Lecompton [KS] B: 6/23/1952, Topeka, KS
1974 Pit: 14 G; Int 1-0. **1975** Pit: 14 G. **1976** Pit: 14 G. **1977** StL: 14 G; Int 1-14. **Total:** 56 G; Int 2-14.

BOB KELLY Kelly, Bob L 6′2″, 270 **OT-DT**
Col: New Mexico State *HS:* Carlsbad [NM] B: 8/18/1940, Carlsbad, NM *Drafted:* 1961 Round 22 Hou
1961 Hou: 14 G. **1962** Hou: 6 G. **1963** Hou: 11 G. **1964** Hou: 1 G. **1967** KC: 3 G. **1968** Cin: 4 G. **Total:** 39 G.

BRIAN KELLY Kelly, Brian 5′11″, 196 **DB**
Col: USC *HS:* Overland [Aurora, CO] B: 1/14/1976, Las Vegas, NV *Drafted:* 1998 Round 2 TB
1998 TB: 16 G; Int 1-4; 1 Fum.

TEX KELLY Kelly, Clarence A 6′3″, 220 **G-T-C-E**
(Clancy) *Col:* No College B: 10/29/1898, CO D: 2/1978, Shawnee, OK
1922 Tol: 7 G. **1923** Buf: 2 G. **1925** Roch: 6 G. **1926** Buf: 1 G. **1929** Ora: 1 G. **Total:** 17 G.

ELLISON KELLY Kelly, Ellison L 6′1″, 235 **OG**
Col: Michigan State *HS:* Sandusky [OH] B: 5/17/1935, Lake City, FL *Drafted:* 1959 Round 5 NYG
1959 NYG: 12 G.

ELMO KELLY Kelly, Elmo Lee 6′1″, 210 **DE**
Col: Wichita State *HS:* Laing No. 1 [Tillman Co., OK] B: 2/10/1917, Tipton, OK
1944 ChiB: 3 G.

JIM KELLY Kelly, James Edward 6′3″, 217 **QB**
Col: Miami (Fla.) *HS:* East Brady [PA] B: 2/14/1960, Pittsburgh, PA *Drafted:* 1983 Round 1 Buf
1987 Buf: Rec 1-35 35.0. **1988** Buf: Rec 1-5 5.0. **Total:** Rec 2-40 20.0.

		Passing							
Year Team	G	Att	Comp	Comp%	Yds	YPA	TD	Int	Rating
1986 Buf	16	480	285	59.4	3593	7.49	22	17	83.3
1987 Buf	12	419	250	59.7	2798	6.68	19	11	83.8
1988 Buf	16	452	269	59.5	3380	7.48	15	17	78.2
1989 Buf	13	391	228	58.3	3130	8.01	25	18	86.2
1990 Buf	14	346	219	**63.3**	2829	8.18	24	9	**101.2**
1991 Buf	15	474	304	64.1	3844	8.11	**33**	17	97.6
1992 Buf	16	462	269	58.2	3457	7.48	23	19	81.2
1993 Buf	16	470	288	61.3	3382	7.20	18	18	79.9
1994 Buf	14	448	285	63.6	3114	6.95	22	17	84.6
1995 Buf	15	458	255	55.7	3130	6.83	22	13	81.1
1996 Buf	13	379	222	58.6	2810	7.41	14	19	73.2
NFL Total	160	4779	2874	60.1	35467	7.42	237	175	84.4

	Rushing				
Year Team	Att	Yds	Avg	TD	Fum
1986 Buf	41	199	4.9	0	7
1987 Buf	29	133	4.6	0	6
1988 Buf	35	154	4.4	0	5
1989 Buf	29	137	4.7	2	6
1990 Buf	22	63	2.9	0	4
1991 Buf	20	45	2.3	1	6
1992 Buf	31	53	1.7	1	8
1993 Buf	36	102	2.8	0	7
1994 Buf	25	77	3.1	1	11
1995 Buf	17	20	1.2	0	7
1996 Buf	19	66	3.5	2	9
NFL Total	304	1049	3.5	7	76

JIM KELLY Kelly, James Harry 6′2″, 218 **TE**
Col: Notre Dame *HS:* Clairton [PA] B: 4/23/1942, McKeesport, PA *Drafted:* 1964 Round 2 Pit
1964 Pit: KR 1-12 12.0. **Total:** KR 1-12 12.0.

		Receiving				
Year Team	G	Rec	Yds	Avg	TD	Fum
1964 Pit	6	10	186	18.6	1	1
1965 Phi	1	0	0	—	0	0
1967 Phi	12	21	345	16.4	4	2
NFL Total	19	31	531	17.1	5	3

JIMMY KELLY Kelly, James J Jr. 5′9″, 160 **TB**
Col: St. Louis; Detroit Mercy B: 1890, MI Deceased
1920 Det: 6 G.

JIM KELLY Kelly, James William Jr. 6′4″, 212 **TE**
Col: Tennessee State *HS:* Columbia Central [TN] B: 8/7/1951, Columbia, TN
1974 ChiB: 14 G; Rec 8-100 12.5.

JOHN KELLY Kelly, John D 6′3″, 250 **OT**
Col: Florida A&M B: 3/31/1944, Fort Lauderdale, FL *Drafted:* 1966 Round 20 Was
1966 Was: 2 G. **1967** Was: 14 G; KR 2-19 9.5; 1 Fum. **Total:** 16 G; KR 2-19 9.5; 1 Fum.

SHIPWRECK KELLY Kelly, John Simms 6′2″, 190 **DB-TB-WB-FB**
Col: Kentucky *HS:* Springfield [KY] B: 7/8/1910, Simmstown, KY D: 8/17/1986, Lighthouse Point, FL
1933 Bkn: PR **2** TD; Scor 43, 1 XK. **Total:** PR 2 TD.

		Passing							
Year Team	G	Att	Comp	Comp%	Yds	YPA	TD	Int	Rating
1932 NYG	5	7	3	42.9	22	3.14	0	0	50.9
1933 Bkn	10	9	3	33.3	28	3.11	0	3	3.2
1934 Bkn	9	35	11	31.4	134	3.83	0	5	4.6
1937 Bkn	2	12	2	16.7	21	1.75	0	3	0.0
NFL Total	26	63	19	30.2	205	3.25	0	11	1.2

	Rushing				Receiving				Tot
Year Team	Att	Yds	Avg	TD	Rec	Yds	Avg	TD	TD
1932 NYG	32	133	4.2	0	7	49	7.0	0	0
1933 Bkn	85	274	3.2	2	**22**	246	11.2	**3**	**7**
1934 Bkn	29	96	3.3	1	0	0	—	0	1
1937 Bkn	16	29	1.8	0	1	7	7.0	0	0
NFL Total	162	532	3.3	3	30	302	10.1	3	8

JOE KELLY Kelly, Joseph Winston 6′2″, 235 **LB**
Col: Washington *HS:* Thomas Jefferson [Los Angeles, CA] B: 12/11/1964, Sun Valley, CA *Drafted:* 1986 Round 1 Cin
1986 Cin: 16 G; Int 1-6; 1 Sac. **1987** Cin: 10 G; 1 Sac. **1988** Cin: 16 G. **1989** Cin: 16 G; Int 1-25; 1 Sac. **1990** NYJ: 12 G. **1991** NYJ: 16 G; Int 2-6; 1 Fum. **1992** NYJ: 9 G. **1993** LARd: 16 G; 1 Sac. **1994** LARm: 16 G; Int 1-31; 2 Sac. **1995** GB: 13 G; Int 1-0. **1996** Phi: 16 G. **Total:** 156 G; Int 6-68; 1 Fum; 6 Sac.

LEROY KELLY Kelly, Leroy 6′0″, 202 **RB**
Col: Morgan State *HS:* Simon Gratz [Philadelphia, PA] B: 5/20/1942, Philadelphia, PA *Drafted:* 1964 Round 8 Cle *HOF:* 1994
1966 Cle: Pass 1-0. **1967** Cle: Pass 1-0; Punt 10-407 40.7. **1968** Cle: Pass 4-1 25.0%, 34 8.50 1 TD. **1969** Cle: Pass 5-1 20.0%, 36 7.20 1 TD. **1971** Cle: Pass 4-1 25.0%, 23 5.75. **1972** Cle: Pass 1-0. **Total:** Pass 16-3 18.8%, 93 5.81 2 TD; Punt 10-407 40.7.

		Rushing				Receiving			
Year Team	G	Att	Yds	Avg	TD	Rec	Yds	Avg	TD
1964 Cle	14	6	12	2.0	0	0	0	—	0
1965 Cle	13	37	139	3.8	0	9	122	13.6	0
1966 Cle	14	209	1141	**5.5**	**15**	32	366	11.4	1
1967 Cle	14	**235**	**1205**	**5.1**	**11**	20	282	14.1	2
1968 Cle	14	**248**	**1239**	5.0	**16**	22	297	13.5	4
1969 Cle	13	196	817	4.2	9	20	267	13.4	1
1970 Cle	13	206	656	3.2	6	24	311	13.0	2
1971 Cle	14	234	865	3.7	10	25	252	10.1	2
1972 Cle	14	224	811	3.6	4	23	204	8.9	1
1973 Cle	13	132	389	2.9	3	15	180	12.0	0
NFL Total	136	1727	7274	4.2	74	190	2281	12.0	13

	Punt Returns				Kickoff Returns					Tot
Year Team	Ret	Yds	Avg	TD	Ret	Yds	Avg	TD	Fum	TD
1964 Cle	9	171	19.0	1	24	582	24.3	0	0	1
1965 Cle	17	265	**15.6**	**2**	24	621	25.9	0	3	2
1966 Cle	13	104	8.0	0	19	403	21.2	0	1	**16**
1967 Cle	9	59	6.6	0	5	131	26.2	0	7	13
1968 Cle	1	9	9.0	0	1	10	10.0	0	6	**20**
1969 Cle	7	28	4.0	0	2	26	13.0	0	1	10
1970 Cle	2	15	7.5	0	0	0	—	0	3	8
1971 Cle	30	292	9.7	0	1	11	11.0	0	7	12
1972 Cle	5	40	8.0	0	0	0	—	0	4	5
1973 Cle	1	7	7.0	0	0	0	—	0	3	3
NFL Total	94	990	10.5	3	76	1784	23.5	0	35	90

MIKE KELLY Kelly, Michael Grey 6′4″, 215 **TE**
Col: Davidson *HS:* Davidson [NC] B: 1/14/1948, Davidson, NC
1970 Cin: 12 G. **1971** Cin: 14 G; Rec 1-9 9.0; KR 1-0. **1972** Cin: 13 G; KR 1-0; 1 Fum. **1973** NO: 1 G. **Total:** 40 G; Rec 1-9 9.0; KR 2-0; 1 Fum.

PATRICK KELLY Kelly, Patrick Joseph 6′6″, 252 **TE**
Col: Syracuse *HS:* R.L. Thomas [Webster, NY] B: 10/29/1965, Rochester, NY *Drafted:* 1988 Round 7 Den
1988 Den: 16 G; Rec 1-4 4.0; 1 Fum. **1989** Den: 16 G; Rec 3-13 4.3. **1990** NYJ: 1 G. **1991** NYJ: 8 G; KR 1-4 4.0. **Total:** 41 G; Rec 4-17 4.3; KR 1-4 4.0; 1 Fum.

ROB KELLY Kelly, Robert James 6′0″, 199 **DB**
Col: Ohio State *HS:* Newark Catholic [OH] B: 6/21/1974, Newark, OH *Drafted:* 1997 Round 2 NO
1997 NO: 16 G; Int 1-15. **1998** NO: 16 G; Int 2-104 1 TD; 6 Pt. **Total:** 32 G; Int 3-119 1 TD; 6 Pt.

BOB KELLY Kelly, Robert Joseph 5′10″, 190 **DB-HB**
Col: Notre Dame; Navy *HS:* Leo [Chicago, IL] B: 6/6/1925, Chicago, IL
AAFC **1947** LA-A: Rec 9-68 7.6 1 TD; PR 4-69 17.3; KR 3-61 20.3; Int 2-47. **1948** LA-A: Int 3-14. **1949** BalA: Rec 2-25 12.5; KR 2-31 15.5; Int 3-24. **Total:** Rec 11-93 8.5 1 TD; PR 4-69 17.3; KR 5-92 18.4; Int 8-85.

Year Team	G	Rushing Att	Yds	Avg	TD	Tot TD
1947 LA-A	12	51	205	4.0	2	3
1948 LA-A	13	3	10	3.3	0	0
1949 BalA	10	9	17	1.9	0	0
AAFC Total	35	63	232	3.7	2	3

TODD KELLY Kelly, Todd Eric 6'2", 259 **DE**
Col: Tennessee *HS:* Bethel [Hampton, VA] B: 11/27/1970, Hampton, VA *Drafted:* 1993 Round 1 SF
1993 SF: 14 G; 1 Sac. **1994** SF: 11 G; 3.5 Sac. **1995** Cin: 16 G; 1 Sac. **1996** Cin-Atl: 4 G. Cin: 2 G. Atl: 2 G. **Total:** 45 G; 5.5 Sac.

WILD BILL KELLY Kelly, William Carl 5'10", 184 **TB-BB-WB**
Col: Montana *HS:* Missoula [MT] B: 6/24/1905, Denver, CO D: 11/14/1931, New York, NY
1927 NYY: 12 G; Pass 5 TD; Rush 3 TD; 18 Pt. **1928** NYY: 12 G; Pass 7 TD; Rush 1 TD; Int **1** TD; Tot TD 2; 12 Pt. **1929** Fra: 17 G; Pass 4 TD; Rush 1 TD; 6 Pt. **1930** Bkn: 11 G; Pass 7 TD; Rush 1 TD; 6 Pt. **Total:** 52 G; Pass 23 TD; Rush 6 TD; Int 1 TD; Tot TD 7; 42 Pt.

LARRY KELM Kelm, Larry Dean 6'4", 236 **LB**
Col: Texas A&M *HS:* Richard King [Corpus Christi, TX] B: 11/29/1964, Corpus Christi, TX *Drafted:* 1987 Round 4 LARm
1987 LARm: 12 G. **1988** LARm: 16 G; Int 2-15. **1989** LARm: 7 G. **1990** LARm: 11 G. **1991** LARm: 16 G; 2 Sac. **1992** LARm: 16 G; Int 1-16. **1993** SF: 10 G; PR 1-0; KR 1-0; 1 Fum. **Total:** 88 G; PR 1-0; KR 1-0; Int 3-31; 1 Fum; 2 Sac.

MOSE KELSCH Kelsch, Christian 5'10", 235 **HB-FB-DB-LB**
Col: No College *HS:* Bellefonte Acad. [PA] B: 1/31/1897, Pittsburgh, PA D: 7/13/1935, Pittsburgh, PA
1933 Pit: 8 G; Rush 8-37 4.6; Scor 11, 3 FG, 2 XK. **1934** Pit: 8 G; Rush 3-11 3.7; Scor 5, 1 FG, 2 XK. **Total:** 16 G; Rush 11-48 4.4; Scor 16, 4 FG, 4 XK.

MATT KELSCH Kelsch, Matthew Leroy 5'11", 190 **OE**
Col: Iowa *HS:* Columbia Acad. [Mason City, IA] B: 10/4/1904, Dougherty, IA D: 8/8/1991, Owatonna, MN
1930 Bkn: 2 G.

MARK KELSO Kelso, Mark Alan 5'11", 181 **DB**
Col: William & Mary *HS:* North Hills [Pittsburgh, PA] B: 7/23/1963, Pittsburgh, PA *Drafted:* 1985 Round 10 Phi
1987 Buf: **1** Fum TD. **Total:** 1 Fum TD.

Year Team	G	Interceptions Int	Yds	TD	Tot TD
1986 Buf	3	0	0	0	0
1987 Buf	12	6	25	0	1
1988 Buf	16	7	**180**	1	1
1989 Buf	16	6	101	0	1
1990 Buf	6	2	0	0	0
1991 Buf	16	2	0	0	0
1992 Buf	16	7	21	0	0
1993 Buf	14	0	0	0	0
NFL Total	99	30	327	1	3

BOBBY KEMP Kemp, Bobby 6'0", 189 **DB**
Col: Taft Coll. CA (J.C.); Cal State-Fullerton *HS:* North Miami Beach [FL] B: 5/29/1959, Oakland, CA *Drafted:* 1981 Round 8 Cin
1981 Cin: KR 1-0. **1982** Cin: 1 Sac. **1983** Cin: 1 Sac. **1985** Cin: 1 Sac. **Total:** KR 1-0; 3 Sac.

Year Team	G	Interceptions Int	Yds	TD	Fum
1981 Cin	16	0	0	0	0
1982 Cin	9	1	0	0	0
1983 Cin	16	3	26	0	0
1984 Cin	10	4	27	0	1
1985 Cin	16	1	0	0	0
1986 Cin	16	0	0	0	0
1987 TB	12	1	11	0	0
NFL Total	95	10	64	0	1

JEFF KEMP Kemp, Jeffrey Allen 6'0", 201 **QB**
Col: Dartmouth *HS:* Winston Churchill [Potomac, MD] B: 7/11/1959, Santa Ana, CA

Year Team	G	Passing Att	Comp	Comp%	Yds	YPA	TD	Int	Rating
1981 LARm	1	6	2	33.3	25	4.17	0	1	7.6
1983 LARm	4	25	12	48.0	135	5.40	1	0	77.9
1984 LARm	14	284	143	50.4	2021	7.12	13	**7**	78.7
1985 LARm	5	38	16	42.1	214	5.63	0	1	49.7
1986 SF	10	200	119	59.5	1554	7.77	11	8	85.7
1987 Sea	13	33	23	69.7	396	12.00	5	1	137.1
1988 Sea	11	35	13	37.1	132	3.77	0	5	9.2
1989 Sea	9	0	0	—	0	—	0	0	—
1990 Sea	15	0	0	—	0	—	0	0	—
1991 Sea-Phi	14	295	151	51.2	1753	5.94	9	17	55.7
1991 Sea	7	181	94	51.9	1207	6.67	4	12	52.9
1991 Phi	7	114	57	50.0	546	4.79	5	5	60.1
NFL Total	96	916	479	52.3	6230	6.80	39	40	70.0

Year Team	Rushing Att	Yds	Avg	TD	Fum
1981 LARm	2	9	4.5	0	0
1983 LARm	3	-2	-0.7	0	2
1984 LARm	34	153	4.5	1	8
1985 LARm	5	0	0.0	0	2
1986 SF	15	49	3.3	0	3
1987 Sea	5	9	1.8	0	2
1988 Sea	6	51	8.5	0	0
1989 Sea	1	0	0.0	0	1
1991 Sea-Phi	38	179	4.7	0	5
1991 Sea	22	106	4.8	0	5
1991 Phi	16	73	4.6	0	0
NFL Total	109	448	4.1	1	23

JACK KEMP Kemp, John French 6'1", 201 **QB**
Col: Occidental *HS:* Fairfax [Los Angeles, CA] B: 7/13/1935, Los Angeles, CA *Drafted:* 1957 Round 17 Det
1957 Pit: Punt 2-55 27.5. **1965** Buf: Rec 1-(-9) -9.0. **1967** Buf: Scor 1 2XP. **Total:** Rec 1-(-9) -9.0; Punt 2-55 27.5; Scor 1 2XP.

Year Team	G	Passing Att	Comp	Comp%	Yds	YPA	TD	Int	Rating
1957 Pit	4	18	8	44.4	88	4.89	0	2	19.9
1960 LAC	14	406	211	52.0	3018	**7.43**	20	25	67.1
1961 SD	14	364	165	45.3	2686	7.38	15	22	59.2
1962 SD-Buf	6	139	64	46.0	928	6.68	5	6	62.3
1962 SD	2	45	13	28.9	292	6.49	2	2	50.4
1962 Buf	4	94	51	54.3	636	6.77	3	4	68.4
1963 Buf	14	384	193	50.3	2910	7.58	13	20	65.1
1964 Buf	14	269	119	44.2	2285	**8.49**	13	26	50.9
1965 Buf	14	391	179	45.8	2368	6.06	10	18	54.8
1966 Buf	14	389	166	42.7	2451	6.30	11	16	56.2
1967 Buf	14	369	161	43.6	2503	6.78	14	26	50.0
1969 Buf	14	344	170	49.4	1981	5.76	13	22	53.2
NFL Total	122	3073	1436	46.7	21218	6.90	114	183	57.3

Year Team	Rushing Att	Yds	Avg	TD	Fum
1957 Pit	3	-1	-0.3	0	1
1960 LAC	54	238	4.4	8	9
1961 SD	43	105	2.4	6	10
1962 SD-Buf	20	84	4.2	2	3
1962 SD	8	28	3.5	1	2
1962 Buf	12	56	4.7	1	1
1963 Buf	50	239	4.8	8	**10**
1964 Buf	37	124	3.4	5	7
1965 Buf	36	49	1.4	4	**9**
1966 Buf	40	130	3.3	5	7
1967 Buf	36	58	1.6	2	**14**
1969 Buf	37	124	3.4	0	8
NFL Total	356	1150	3.2	40	78

PERRY KEMP Kemp, Perry Commodore 5'11", 170 **WR**
Col: California (Pa.) *HS:* Fort Cherry [McDonald, PA] B: 12/31/1961, Canonsburg, PA
1989 GB: Rush 5-43 8.6. **1990** GB: Rush 1-(-1) -1.0. **Total:** Rush 6-42 7.0.

Year Team	G	Receiving Rec	Yds	Avg	TD	Fum
1987 Cle	3	12	224	18.7	2	0
1988 GB	16	48	620	12.9	0	3
1989 GB	14	48	611	12.7	2	3
1990 GB	16	44	527	12.0	2	2
1991 GB	16	42	583	13.9	2	2
NFL Total	65	194	2565	13.2	8	10

RAY KEMP Kemp, Raymond Howard 6'1", 215 **T**
Col: Duquesne *HS:* Cecil [PA] B: 4/7/1907, Cecil, PA
1933 Pit: 5 G.

FLORIAN KEMPF Kempf, Florian Gerard 5'9", 170 **K**
Col: Pennsylvania *HS:* Cardinal Dougherty [Philadelphia, PA] B: 5/25/1956, Philadelphia, PA
1983 Hou: Rec 1-7 7.0. **Total:** Rec 1-7 7.0.

Year Team	G	Scoring Pts	FG	FGA	FG%	XK	XKA	XK%
1982 Hou	9	28	4	6	66.7	16	18	88.9
1983 Hou	16	84	17	21	81.0	33	34	97.1
1984 Hou	9	26	4	6	66.7	14	14	100.0
1987 NO	1	13	4	5	80.0	1	1	100.0
NFL Total	35	151	29	38	76.3	64	67	95.5

CHARLIE KEMPINSKA Kempinska, Charles Conrad 6'0", 235 **OG**
(Butch) *Col:* Mississippi *HS:* Natchez [MS] B: 10/30/1938, Natchez, MS
1960 LAC: 10 G.

HERB KEMPTON Kempton, Herbert Mayberry 5'8", 155 **BB**
(Fido) *Col:* Yale *HS:* Malden [MA]; Phillips Exeter Acad. [Exeter, NH] B: 12/8/1892, Malden, MA D: 9/23/1970, Ocala, FL
1921 Can: 6 G.

CHARLIE KENDALL Kendall, Charles Barton Jr. 6'2", 185 **DB**
(Chuck) *Col:* Los Angeles Valley Coll. CA (J.C.); UCLA *HS:* Verdugo Hills [Tujunga, CA] B: 1/4/1935
1960 Hou: 14 G; Int 2-10.

PETE KENDALL Kendall, Peter Marcus 6'5", 292 **OG-C**
Col: Boston College *HS:* Archbishop Williams [Weymouth, MA] B: 7/9/1973, Weymouth, MA *Drafted:* 1996 Round 1 Sea
1996 Sea: 12 G. **1997** Sea: 16 G. **1998** Sea: 16 G. **Total:** 44 G.

JIM KENDRICK Kendrick, James Marcellus 6'0", 197 **OE-TB-HB-WB**
Col: Texas A&M; Centre *HS:* Douglas-Shuler Acad. [Waco, TX] B: 8/22/1893, Hillside, TX D: 11/17/1941, Waco, TX
1922 Can-Tol: 6 G. Can: 4 G. Tol: 2 G. **1923** Lou: 3 G. **1924** ChiB: 9 G. **1925** Ham-Buf-Roch-RI: 11 G; Pass 1 TD; Rush 1 TD; Scor 18, 3 FG, 3 XK. Ham: 2 G; Scor 4, 1 FG, 1 XK. Buf: 7 G; Pass 1 TD; Rush 1 TD; Scor 14, 2 FG, 2 XK. Roch: 1 G. RI: 1 G. **1926** Buf: 10 G; Pass 5 TD; Rush 2 TD; Scor 16, 4 XK. **1927** NYG: 8 G. **Total:** 47 G; Pass 6 TD; Rush 3 TD; Scor 34, 3 FG, 7 XK.

VINCE KENDRICK Kendrick, Vincent 6'0", 231 **RB**
Col: Florida *HS:* Miami Senior [FL] B: 3/18/1952, Miami, FL *Drafted:* 1974 Round 4 Atl
1974 Atl: 14 G; Rush 17-71 4.2; Rec 12-86 7.2 1 TD; 6 Pt. **1976** TB: 1 G; Rush 1-3 3.0. **Total:** 15 G; Rush 18-74 4.1; Rec 12-86 7.2 1 TD; 6 Pt.

JOHN KENERSON Kenerson, John D 6'3", 255 **DE-DT**
(Big John) *Col:* Kentucky State *HS:* Crane [Chicago, IL] B: 3/18/1938, Chicago, IL
1960 LARm: 7 G. **1962** Pit-NYT: 9 G. Pit: 1 G. NYT: 8 G. **Total:** 16 G.

MIKE KENN Kenn, Michael Lee 6'7", 273 **OT**
Col: Michigan *HS:* Evanston Twp. [Evanston, IL] B: 2/9/1956, Evanston, IL *Drafted:* 1978 Round 1 Atl
1978 Atl: 16 G. **1979** Atl: 16 G. **1980** Atl: 16 G. **1981** Atl: 16 G. **1982** Atl: 9 G. **1983** Atl: 16 G. **1984** Atl: 14 G. **1985** Atl: 11 G. **1986** Atl: 16 G. **1987** Atl: 12 G. **1988** Atl: 16 G. **1989** Atl: 15 G. **1990** Atl: 16 G. **1991** Atl: 15 G. **1992** Atl: 16 G. **1993** Atl: 16 G. **1994** Atl: 15 G. **Total:** 251 G.

DEREK KENNARD Kennard, Derek Craig 6'3", 303 **OG-C**
Col: Nevada-Reno *HS:* Edison [Stockton, CA] B: 9/9/1962, Stockton, CA *Drafted:* 1984 Supplemental Round 2 StL
1986 StL: 15 G. **1987** StL: 12 G; 2 Fum. **1988** Pho: 16 G. **1989** Pho: 14 G. **1990** Pho: 16 G. **1991** NO: 3 G. **1992** NO: 16 G; KR 1-11 11.0. **1993** NO: 16 G. **1994** Dal: 16 G; Rec 1-(-3) -3.0; 1 Fum. **1995** Dal: 9 G; 1 Fum. **1996** Dal: 1 G. **Total:** 134 G; Rec 1-(-3) -3.0; KR 1-11 11.0; 4 Fum.

GEORGE KENNARD Kennard, George Arthur 6'0", 210 **OG**
Col: Kansas *HS:* Paseo Acad. [Kansas City, MO] B: 1/8/1928, Kansas City, MO
1952 NYG: 12 G; KR 1-0. **1953** NYG: 12 G. **1954** NYG: 12 G; KR 1-16 16.0. **1955** NYG: 12 G; KR 3-36 12.0; 1 Fum. **Total:** 48 G; KR 5-52 10.4; 1 Fum.

KEN KENNARD Kennard, Kenneth Jerome 6'2", 248 **NT-DE**
Col: Angelo State *HS:* North Side [Fort Worth, TX] B: 10/4/1954, Fort Worth, TX
1977 Hou: 11 G; Scor 1 Saf; 2 Pt. **1978** Hou: 16 G. **1979** Hou: 16 G. **1980** Hou: 16 G. **1981** Hou: 16 G. **1982** Hou: 9 G; 3 Sac. **Total:** 84 G; Scor 1 Saf; 2 Pt; 3 Sac.

GEORGE KENNEALLY Kenneally, George Vincent 6'0", 180 **OE-DE-G**
(Gigi; Gus) *Col:* St. Bonaventure *HS:* Boston Latin [MA] B: 4/12/1902, South Boston, MA D: 9/3/1968, Boston, MA
1926 Pott: 11 G. **1927** Pott: 13 G; Rec 1 TD; 6 Pt. **1928** Pott: 9 G; Rec 1 TD; 6 Pt. **1929** Bost: 8 G; Scor **1** 1XP; 1 Pt. **1930** ChiC: 11 G. **1932** Bos: 10 G. **1933** Phi: 8 G; Rec 2-37 18.5. **1934** Phi: 11 G; Rec 1-12 12.0. **1935** Phi: 8 G; Rush 3-(-4) -1.3. **Total:** 89 G; Rush 3-(-4) -1.3; Rec 3-49 16.3 2 TD; Scor 1 1XP; 13 Pt.

ALLAN KENNEDY Kennedy, Allan Stephen 6'7", 273 **OT**
Col: Washington State *HS:* El Camino Real [Woodland Hills, CA] B: 1/8/1958, Vancouver, Canada *Drafted:* 1981 Round 10 Was
1981 SF: 3 G. **1983** SF: 16 G. **1984** SF: 15 G. **Total:** 34 G.

CORTEZ KENNEDY Kennedy, Cortez 6'3", 298 **DT**
Col: Northwest Mississippi CC; Miami (Fla.) *HS:* Rivercrest [Wilson, AR] B: 8/23/1968, Osceola, AR *Drafted:* 1990 Round 1 Sea
1990 Sea: 16 G; 1 Sac. **1991** Sea: 16 G; 6.5 Sac. **1992** Sea: 16 G; 1 Fum; 14 Sac. **1993** Sea: 16 G; 6.5 Sac. **1994** Sea: 16 G; 4 Sac. **1995** Sea: 16 G; 6.5 Sac. **1996** Sea: 16 G; 8 Sac. **1997** Sea: 8 G; 2 Sac. **1998** Sea: 15 G; 1 Fum TD; 6 Pt; 2 Sac. **Total:** 135 G; 1 Fum TD; 6 Pt; 1 Fum; 50.5 Sac.

JIMMIE KENNEDY Kennedy, James Dale 6'3", 231 **TE**
Col: Hiram; Colorado State *HS:* Perkins [Sandusky, OH] B: 7/30/1952, Laurel, MS *Drafted:* 1974 Round 9 Was
1975 Bal: 14 G; Rec 2-15 7.5 1 TD; KR 2-36 18.0; 6 Pt. **1976** Bal: 14 G; Rec 1-32 32.0; KR 4-64 16.0. **1977** Bal: 9 G; KR 1-9 9.0. **Total:** 37 G; Rec 3-47 15.7 1 TD; KR 7-109 15.6; 6 Pt.

JIMMY KENNEDY Kennedy, James David Jr. 5'9", 160 **FB**
Col: Boston College; Holy Cross *HS:* Somersworth [NH] B: 2/16/1901 D: 8/4/1968
1925 Buf: 1 G.

MIKE KENNEDY Kennedy, Michael Scott 6'0", 195 **DB**
Col: Toledo *HS:* St. Francis DeSales [Toledo, OH] B: 2/26/1959, Toledo, OH
1983 Buf: 12 G; Int 1-22 1 TD; 6 Pt. **1984** Hou: 11 G. **Total:** 23 G; Int 1-22 1 TD; 6 Pt.

BOB KENNEDY Kennedy, Robert Henry 5'11", 195 **FB-DB-LB-HB**
Col: Washington State *HS:* Sandpoint [ID] B: 6/29/1921, Sandpoint, ID
AAFC **1946** NY-A: Pass 6-2 33.3%, 45 7.50 3 Int; Rec 11-59 5.4; PR 3-20 6.7; KR 4-105 26.3; Punt 7-259 37.0. **1947** NY-A: Pass 3-2 66.7%, 56 18.67; PR 6-44 7.3; Punt 5-126 25.2. **1948** NY-A: Pass 1-0; Rec 5-23 4.6; PR 1-14 14.0; KR 2-20 10.0; Punt 7-237 33.9. **1949** NY-A: Pass 1-1 100.0%, 27 27.00; Rec 7-55 7.9 1 TD; KR 1-15 15.0. **Total:** Pass 11-5 45.5%, 128 11.64 3 Int; Rec 23-137 6.0 1 TD; PR 10-78 7.8; KR 7-140 20.0; Punt 19-622 32.7.

		Rushing				Interceptions			Tot
Year Team	**G**	**Att**	**Yds**	**Avg**	**TD**	**Int**	**Yds**	**TD**	**TD**
1946 NY-A	13	58	179	3.1	2	3	35	0	2
1947 NY-A	14	44	258	5.9	1	2	66	0	1
1948 NY-A	14	33	90	2.7	1	4	49	0	1
1949 NY-A	12	118	490	4.2	5	2	2	0	6
AAFC Total	53	253	1017	4.0	9	11	152	0	10

NFL **1950** NYY: 5 G; KR 1-15 15.0; Int 1-11.

BOB KENNEDY Kennedy, Robert Michael 6'0", 178 **DB-HB**
Col: North Carolina *HS:* Bergenfield [NJ] B: 9/16/1928, Weehauken, NJ
AAFC **1949** LA-A: 10 G; Rush 2-14 7.0; Int 1-33.

SAM KENNEDY Kennedy, Samuel Edward 6'3", 235 **LB**
Col: Cabrillo Coll. CA (J.C.); San Jose State *HS:* Aptos [CA] B: 7/10/1964, San Mateo, CA
1988 SF: 16 G.

LINCOLN KENNEDY Kennedy, Tamerlane Lincoln 6'6", 335 **OT-OG**
Col: Washington *HS:* Samuel F.B. Morse [San Diego, CA] B: 2/12/1971, York, PA *Drafted:* 1993 Round 1 Atl
1993 Atl: 16 G. **1994** Atl: 16 G. **1995** Atl: 16 G. **1996** Oak: 16 G. **1997** Oak: 16 G. **1998** Oak: 16 G. **Total:** 96 G.

TOM KENNEDY Kennedy, Thomas Joseph 6'0", 218 **T**
Col: Wayne State (Mich.) B: 6/4/1920, Pittsfield, MA
1944 Det: 2 G.

TOM KENNEDY Kennedy, Thomas Patrick 6'1", 210 **QB**
Col: Glendale CC CA; Los Angeles State *HS:* Pasadena [CA] B: 11/27/1939, Maywood, CA
1966 NYG: Rush 5-16 3.2.

		Passing								
Year Team	**G**	**Att**	**Comp**	**Comp%**	**Yds**	**YPA**	**TD**	**Int**	**Rating**	**Fum**
1966 NYG	6	100	55	55.0	748	7.48	7	6	77.4	5

BILL KENNEDY Kennedy, William James 6'0", 208 **DE-G**
(Wild Bill) *Col:* Michigan State *HS:* Northwestern [Detroit, MI] B: 3/13/1919, Lee, MA D: 12/29/1998, Southfield, MI
1942 Det: 11 G. **1947** Bos: 12 G. **Total:** 23 G.

STEVE KENNEY Kenney, Steven Faucette 6'4", 266 **OG-OT**
Col: Clemson *HS:* Sanderson [Raleigh, NC] B: 12/26/1955, Wilmington, NC
1980 Phi: 15 G. **1981** Phi: 13 G. **1982** Phi: 9 G. **1983** Phi: 16 G. **1984** Phi: 11 G. **1985** Phi: 16 G. **1986** Det: 9 G. **Total:** 89 G.

BILL KENNEY Kenney, William Patrick 6'4", 211 **QB**
Col: Saddleback Coll. CA (J.C.); Arizona State; Northern Colorado *HS:* San Clemente [CA] B: 1/20/1955, San Francisco, CA *Drafted:* 1978 Round 12 Mia
1983 KC: Rec 1-0. **1986** KC: Rec 1-0. **Total:** Rec 2-0.

		Passing							
Year Team	**G**	**Att**	**Comp**	**Comp%**	**Yds**	**YPA**	**TD**	**Int**	**Rating**
1980 KC	3	69	37	53.6	542	7.86	5	2	91.6
1981 KC	13	274	147	53.6	1983	7.24	9	16	63.6
1982 KC	7	169	95	56.2	1192	7.05	7	6	77.3
1983 KC	16	**603**	**346**	57.4	4348	7.21	24	18	80.8
1984 KC	9	282	151	53.5	2098	7.44	15	10	80.7
1985 KC	16	338	181	53.6	2536	7.50	17	9	83.6

Year Team									
1986 KC	15	308	161	52.3	1922	6.24	13	11	70.8
1987 KC	11	273	154	56.4	2107	7.72	15	9	85.8
1988 KC	16	114	58	50.9	549	4.82	0	5	46.3
NFL Total	106	2430	1330	54.7	17277	7.11	105	86	77.0

	Rushing				
Year Team	Att	Yds	Avg	TD	Fum
1980 KC	8	8	1.0	0	1
1981 KC	24	89	3.7	1	4
1982 KC	13	40	3.1	0	3
1983 KC	23	59	2.6	3	7
1984 KC	9	-8	-0.9	0	8
1985 KC	14	1	0.1	1	6
1986 KC	18	0	0.0	0	5
1987 KC	12	-2	-0.2	0	8
1988 KC	2	4	2.0	0	1
NFL Total	123	191	1.6	5	43

EDDIE KENNISON Kennison, Eddie Joseph III 6′0″, 195 **WR**
Col: Louisiana State *HS:* Washington-Marion [Lake Charles, LA]
B: 1/20/1973, Lake Charles, LA *Drafted:* 1996 Round 1 StL
1996 StL: KR 23-454 19.7. **1997** StL: Rush 3-13 4.3; KR 1-14 14.0. **1998** StL: Rush 2-9 4.5. **Total:** Rush 5-22 4.4; KR 24-468 19.5.

		Receiving				Punt Returns					Tot
Year Team	G	Rec	Yds	Avg	TD	Ret	Yds	Avg	TD	Fum	TD
1996 StL	15	54	924	17.1	9	29	423	14.6	2	5	11
1997 StL	14	25	404	16.2	0	34	247	7.3	0	2	0
1998 StL	16	17	234	13.8	1	40	415	10.4	1	4	2
NFL Total	45	96	1562	16.3	10	103	1085	10.5	3	11	13

GREG KENT Kent, Edward Greg 6′6″, 275 **OT-DE**
Col: Wisconsin; Utah *HS:* Whitewater [WI] B: 7/18/1943, Elkhorn, WI
Drafted: 1965 Redshirt Round 6 Oak
1966 Oak: 7 G. **1968** Det: 5 G. **Total:** 12 G.

JOEY KENT Kent, Joseph Edward III 6′1″, 191 **WR**
Col: Tennessee *HS:* J.O. Johnson [Huntsville, AL] B: 4/23/1974, Huntsville, AL *Drafted:* 1997 Round 2 Ten
1997 Ten: 12 G; Rec 6-55 9.2 1 TD; 6 Pt. **1998** Ten: 10 G; Rec 4-62 15.5. **Total:** 22 G; Rec 10-117 11.7 1 TD; 6 Pt.

BILL KENYON Kenyon, William Curtis 5′9″, 180 **TB**
Col: Georgetown *HS:* Manchester [NH]; Allen Mil. Sch. [West Newton, MA] B: 12/5/1898, Manchester, NH D: 5/6/1951, Orono, ME
1925 NYG: 1 G.

CRAWFORD KER Ker, Crawford Francis 6′3″, 288 **OG**
Col: Florida *HS:* Dunedin [FL] B: 5/5/1962, Philadelphia, PA
Drafted: 1985 Round 3 Dal
1985 Dal: 5 G. **1986** Dal: 16 G. **1987** Dal: 12 G. **1988** Dal: 16 G. **1989** Dal: 16 G. **1990** Dal: 15 G. **1991** Den: 12 G. **Total:** 92 G.

NICK KERASIOTIS Kerasiotis, Nicholas Peter 5′11″, 195 **G-LB**
Col: St. Ambrose; Iowa *HS:* Mooseheart Acad. [Chicago, IL]
B: 7/4/1918, Chicago, IL
1942 ChiB: 9 G. **1945** ChiB: 1 G. **Total:** 10 G.

RANDY KERBOW Kerbow, Randall Morris 6′1″, 190 **WR**
Col: Rice *HS:* Pasadena [TX] B: 12/19/1940, Paris, TX
1963 Hou: 8 G; Rec 5-61 12.2; 1 Fum.

DICK KERCHER Kercher, Richard S 6′2″, 205 **HB-DB**
Col: Tulsa *HS:* Central [Evansville, IN] B: 3/11/1932, Evansville, IN
Drafted: 1954 Round 6 Det
1954 Det: 7 G; Rush 3-1 0.3.

BOB KERCHER Kercher, Robert Fred 6′2″, 196 **DE**
Col: Georgetown *HS:* Central [Evansville, IN] B: 1/14/1918, Evansville, IN
1944 GB: 2 G.

RALPH KERCHEVAL Kercheval, Ralph Godfrey 6′1″, 190 **DB-HB-TB-WB**
Col: Kentucky *HS:* Henry Clay [Lexington, KY] B: 12/1/1911, Salt Lick, KY
1936 Bkn: Int 1 TD. **1939** Bkn: Punt 28-1081 38.6. **1940** Bkn: Punt 8-369 46.1. **Total:** Int 1 TD; Punt 36-1450 40.3.

		Passing							
Year Team	G	Att	Comp	Comp%	Yds	YPA	TD	Int	Rating
1934 Bkn	11	12	3	25.0	17	1.42	0	3	0.0
1935 Bkn	12	33	13	39.4	203	6.15	1	**1**	58.0
1936 Bkn	12	25	6	24.0	92	3.68	0	3	2.8
1937 Bkn	9	19	11	57.9	154	8.11	1	1	79.7
1938 Bkn	11	9	3	33.3	98	10.89	0	1	35.6
1939 Bkn	9	1	1	100.0	7	7.00	0	0	95.8
1940 Bkn	10	7	4	57.1	38	5.43	1	0	111.9
NFL Total	74	106	41	38.7	609	5.75	3	9	32.3

	Rushing				Receiving			
Year Team	Att	Yds	Avg	TD	Rec	Yds	Avg	TD
1934 Bkn	33	128	3.9	0	8	166	20.8	3
1935 Bkn	34	89	2.6	0	7	130	18.6	2
1936 Bkn	66	261	4.0	2	7	63	9.0	0
1937 Bkn	48	84	1.8	1	5	57	11.4	0
1938 Bkn	51	86	1.7	1	11	136	12.4	0
1939 Bkn	34	99	2.9	0	3	8	2.7	0
1940 Bkn	11	19	1.7	0	1	17	17.0	0
NFL Total	277	766	2.8	4	42	577	13.7	5

	Scoring							Tot
Year Team	Pts	FG	FGA	FG%	XK	XKA	XK%	TD
1934 Bkn	37	4	—	—	7	—	—	3
1935 Bkn	35	5	—	—	8	—	—	2
1936 Bkn	37	5	—	—	4	—	—	3
1937 Bkn	13	2	—	—	1	—	—	1
1938 Bkn	28	**5**	**13**	38.5	7	9	77.8	1
1939 Bkn	21	6	13	46.2	3	3	100.0	0
1940 Bkn	15	4	11	36.4	3	3	100.0	0
NFL Total	186	31	37	40.5	33	15	86.7	10

GARY KERKORIAN Kerkorian, Gary Ray 5′11″, 185 **QB**
Col: Stanford *HS:* Inglewood [CA] B: 1/14/1930, Los Angeles, CA
Drafted: 1952 Round 19 Pit
1952 Pit: Scor 47, 4-9 44.4% FG, 35-41 85.4% XK. **1954** Bal: Scor 32, 5-10 50.0% FG, 11-12 91.7% XK. **1955** Bal: Scor 9, 1-2 50.0% FG. **1956** Bal: Scor 1, 1-2 50.0% XK. **Total:** Scor 89, 10-21 47.6% FG, 47-55 85.5% XK.

		Passing							
Year Team	G	Att	Comp	Comp%	Yds	YPA	TD	Int	Rating
1952 Pit	12	11	5	45.5	79	7.18	1	3	60.6
1954 Bal	10	217	117	53.9	1515	6.98	9	12	66.9
1955 Bal	7	29	15	51.7	209	7.21	1	3	47.1
1956 Bal	3	2	2	100.0	59	29.50	1	0	158.3
NFL Total	32	259	139	53.7	1862	7.19	12	18	63.2

	Rushing				
Year Team	Att	Yds	Avg	TD	Fum
1952 Pit	2	20	10.0	0	1
1954 Bal	22	36	1.6	1	6
1955 Bal	6	20	3.3	1	1
NFL Total	30	76	2.5	2	8

DON KERN Kern, Donald Emit III 6′4″, 228 **TE**
Col: West Valley Coll. CA (J.C.); Arizona State *HS:* Saratoga [CA]
B: 8/25/1962, Los Gatos, CA *Drafted:* 1984 Round 6 Cin
1984 Cin: 16 G; Rec 2-14 7.0. **1985** Cin: 8 G. **1986** Buf: 1 G. **Total:** 25 G; Rec 2-14 7.0.

REX KERN Kern, Rex William 5′11″, 190 **DB**
Col: Ohio State *HS:* Lancaster [OH] B: 5/28/1949, Lancaster, OH
Drafted: 1971 Round 10 Bal
1971 Bal: 14 G; PR 3-19 6.3; 1 Fum. **1972** Bal: 5 G. **1973** Bal: 14 G; PR 2-12 6.0; Int 2-22; 1 Fum. **1974** Buf: 8 G; PR 1-1 1.0. **Total:** 41 G; PR 6-32 5.3; Int 2-22; 2 Fum.

BILL KERN Kern, William Franklin 6′0″, 187 **T**
Col: Pittsburgh *HS:* Wyoming Seminary [Kingston, PA] B: 9/2/1906, Kingston, PA D: 4/5/1985, Pittsburgh, PA
1929 GB: 12 G. **1930** GB: 6 G. **Total:** 18 G.

MARLON KERNER Kerner, Marlon Lavalle 5′10″, 187 **DB**
Col: Ohio State *HS:* Brookhaven [Columbus, OH] B: 3/18/1973, Columbus, OH *Drafted:* 1995 Round 3 Buf
1995 Buf: 14 G. **1996** Buf: 15 G; Int 1-6; 1 Sac. **1997** Buf: 13 G; Int 2-20. **1998** Buf: 1 G. **Total:** 43 G; Int 3-26; 1 Sac.

JOHN KERNS Kerns, John Emery 6′3″, 243 **T**
(Moose) *Col:* Ohio U.; Duke; North Carolina *HS:* Geneva [OH]
B: 6/17/1923, Ashtabula, OH D: 6/1988, Leesburg, FL
AAFC **1947** BufA: 14 G. **1948** BufA: 14 G; PR 0-2; KR 1-3 3.0. **1949** BufA: 12 G. **Total:** 40 G; PR 0-2; KR 1-3 3.0.

GRAHAM KERNWEIN Kernwein, Graham A 5′11″, 175 **TB**
Col: Chicago *HS:* Wenona [IL] B: 10/23/1904, Claremont, IL
D: 1/25/1983, Rochester, MN
1926 Rac: 5 G.

GEORGE KERR Kerr, George Ropes 6′1″, 211 **T-G**
Col: Catholic *HS:* Medford [MA] B: 8/28/1893, Medford, MA
D: 10/1977, Frazeysburg, OH
1920 Cle: 2 G. **1921** NYG: 1 G. **Total:** 3 G.

JIM KERR Kerr, James Norman 6′0″, 195 **DB**
Col: Penn State *HS:* Richland [St. Clairsville, OH] B: 7/23/1939, Colver, PA *Drafted:* 1961 Round 7 Was
1961 Was: 13 G; PR 5-23 4.6; KR 14-385 27.5; Int 7-93; 1 Fum. **1962** Was: 11 G; PR 1-2 2.0; Int 1-12. **Total:** 24 G; PR 6-25 4.2; KR 14-385 27.5; Int 8-105; 1 Fum.

BILL KERR Kerr, William Howard 6'0", 220 **OE-DE**
(Bud) *Col:* Notre Dame *HS:* Newburgh Free Acad. [NY]
B: 11/10/1915, Tarrytown, NY D: 4/9/1964, San Mateo, CA
AAFC **1946** LA-A: 11 G; Rush 1-10 10.0; Rec 7-122 17.4; Int 1-34.

MIKE KERRIGAN Kerrigan, Michael Joseph 6'3", 205 **QB**
Col: Northwestern *HS:* Mount Carmel [Chicago, IL] B: 4/27/1960, Chicago, IL
1983 NE: 1 G; Pass 14-6 42.9%, 72 5.14 1 Int; Rush 1-14 14.0. **1984** NE: 1 G; Pass 1-1 100.0%, 13 13.00. **Total:** 2 G; Pass 15-7 46.7%, 85 5.67 1 Int; Rush 1-14 14.0.

TOM KERRIGAN Kerrigan, Thomas Martin 6'2", 200 **G**
Col: Columbia *HS:* Evander Childs [Bronx, NY] B: 7/7/1906, New York, NY D: 7/29/1979, Stamford, CT
1929 Ora: 1 G. **1930** Nwk: 4 G. **Total:** 5 G.

MERRITT KERSEY Kersey, Merritt Warren 6'1", 205 **P-RB**
Col: West Chester *HS:* Henderson [PA] B: 2/22/1950, Alexandria, VA
1974 Phi: Rush 1-2 2.0. **Total:** Rush 1-2 2.0.

		Punting		
Year Team	**G**	**Punts**	**Yds**	**Avg**
1974 Phi	14	82	2959	36.1
1975 Phi	2	15	489	32.6
NFL Total	16	97	3448	35.5

GEORGE KERSHAW Kershaw, George Alfred 6'4", 210 **DE**
Col: Colgate *HS:* Oneonta [NY] B: 3/13/1927
1949 NYG: 9 G.

WALLY KERSTEN Kersten, Wallace Todd 6'5", 270 **OT**
Col: Normandale CC MN; Minnesota *HS:* Roosevelt [Minneapolis, MN]
B: 12/8/1959, Minneapolis, MN *Drafted:* 1982 Round 5 LARm
1982 LARm: 3 G.

BOB KESEDAY Keseday, Robert John 6'4", 225 **TE**
Col: Texas-El Paso *HS:* Park Ridge [NJ] B: 1/9/1965, Bayonne, NJ
1987 StL: 3 G.

ALEX KETZKO Ketzko, Alexander Gregorieff 5'11", 215 **T**
Col: Michigan State *HS:* Mattawan [MI] B: 11/19/1919
D: 12/23/1944, France
1943 Det: 9 G.

KEN KEUPER Keuper, Kenneth Erwin 6'0", 207 **DB-BB-HB-DE**
(Red) *Col:* Georgia *HS:* Waukesha [WI] B: 11/14/1918, Waukesha, WI
1945 GB: 9 G; Punt 1-12 12.0. **1946** GB: 10 G; KR 1-6 6.0; Int 3-22.
1947 GB: 12 G; Rush 6-14 2.3; Rec 2-37 18.5; Int 2-41. **1948** NYG: 7 G; Int 1-30; 1 Fum. **Total:** 38 G; Rush 6-14 2.3; Rec 2-37 18.5; KR 1-6 6.0; Int 6-93; Punt 1-12 12.0; 1 Fum.

WADE KEY Key, Allan Wade 6'5", 245 **OG-OT**
Col: Texas; Southwest Texas State *HS:* Thomas Edison [San Antonio, TX] B: 10/14/1946, San Antonio, TX *Drafted:* 1969 Round 13 Phi
1970 Phi: 14 G. **1971** Phi: 14 G. **1972** Phi: 13 G. **1973** Phi: 12 G. **1974** Phi: 14 G. **1975** Phi: 2 G. **1976** Phi: 13 G. **1977** Phi: 14 G. **1978** Phi: 13 G.
1979 Phi: 12 G. **Total:** 121 G.

DAVID KEY Key, David Russell 5'10", 190 **DB**
Col: Michigan *HS:* Bishop Hartley [Columbus, OH] B: 3/27/1968, Columbus, OH *Drafted:* 1991 Round 6 NE
1991 NE: 3 G.

JIMMY KEYES Keyes, James Elton 6'2", 225 **LB-K**
Col: Mississippi *HS:* Laurel [MS] B: 6/16/1944, Laurel, MS
Drafted: 1968 Round 2 Mia
1968 Mia: 12 G; Scor 51, 7-16 43.8% FG, 30-30 100.0% XK. **1969** Mia: 5 G. **Total:** 17 G; Scor 51, 7-16 43.8% FG, 30-30 100.0% XK.

LEROY KEYES Keyes, Marvin Leroy 6'3", 208 **RB-DB**
Col: Purdue *HS:* George Washington Carver [Newport News, VA]
B: 2/18/1947, Newport News, VA *Drafted:* 1969 Round 1 Phi
1969 Phi: Pass 2-1 50.0%, 14 7.00; KR 9-200 22.2. **1971** Phi: Int 6-31.
1972 Phi: Int 2-0. **1973** KC: Pass 1-0. **Total:** Pass 3-1 33.3%, 14 4.67; KR 9-200 22.2; Int 8-31.

		Rushing				Receiving				
Year Team	**G**	**Att**	**Yds**	**Avg**	**TD**	**Rec**	**Yds**	**Avg**	**TD**	**Fum**
1969 Phi	14	121	361	3.0	3	29	276	9.5	0	3
1970 Phi	3	2	7	3.5	0	0	0	—	0	0
1971 Phi	14	0	0	—	0	0	0	—	0	0
1972 Phi	14	0	0	—	0	0	0	—	0	0
1973 KC	3	2	1	0.5	0	1	-6	-6.0	0	1
NFL Total	48	125	369	3.0	3	30	270	9.0	0	4

BOB KEYES Keyes, Robert 5'10", 183 **HB**
Col: San Diego State B: 1936
1960 Oak: 4 G; Rush 1-7 7.0; Rec 1-19 19.0; PR 1-5 5.0.

MARCUS KEYES Keyes, Willis Marcus 6'3", 303 **DT**
Col: Jones Co. JC MS; North Alabama *HS:* Taylorsville [MS]
B: 10/20/1973, Taylorsville, MS *Drafted:* 1996 Round 7 ChiB
1996 ChiB: 2 G.

BRADY KEYS Keys, Brady Jr. 6'0", 185 **DB-HB**
Col: East Los Angeles Coll. CA (J.C.); Colorado State *HS:* Anderson [Austin, TX]; Los Angeles Polytechnic HS [CA] B: 5/19/1936, Austin, TX
Drafted: 1960 Round 14 Pit
1961 Pit: Rush 6-14 2.3. **Total:** Rush 6-14 2.3.

		Punt Returns				Kickoff Returns			
Year Team	**G**	**Ret**	**Yds**	**Avg**	**TD**	**Ret**	**Yds**	**Avg**	**TD**
1961 Pit	12	9	135	15.0	0	2	41	20.5	0
1962 Pit	14	7	46	6.6	0	28	667	23.8	0
1963 Pit	11	13	198	15.2	0	9	219	24.3	0
1964 Pit	14	14	172	12.3	0	7	168	24.0	0
1965 Pit	14	10	77	7.7	0	0	0	—	0
1966 Pit	14	5	11	2.2	0	1	18	18.0	0
1967 Pit-Min	14	7	7	1.0	0	0	0	—	0
1967 Pit	6	2	5	2.5	0	0	0	—	0
1967 Min	8	5	2	0.4	0	0	0	—	0
1968 StL	7	0	0	—	0	0	0	—	0
NFL Total	100	65	646	9.9	0	47	1113	23.7	0

	Interceptions			
Year Team	**Int**	**Yds**	**TD**	**Fum**
1961 Pit	2	21	0	2
1962 Pit	3	16	0	0
1963 Pit	0	0	0	1
1964 Pit	2	11	0	2
1965 Pit	1	20	0	1
1966 Pit	4	0	0	2
1967 Pit-Min	3	38	0	2
1967 Pit	2	8	0	1
1967 Min	1	30	0	1
1968 StL	1	8	0	0
NFL Total	16	114	0	10

HOWARD KEYS Keys, Howard Newton 6'3", 240 **C-OT-OG**
(Sonny) *Col:* Oklahoma State *HS:* Stillwater [OK] B: 1/24/1935, Orlando, OK D: 10/21/1971, Philadelphia, PA *Drafted:* 1959 Round 12 Phi
1960 Phi: 12 G. **1961** Phi: 14 G. **1962** Phi: 13 G. **1963** Phi: 2 G.
Total: 41 G.

TYRONE KEYS Keys, Tyrone Paree 6'7", 272 **DE**
Col: Mississippi State *HS:* Callaway [Jackson, MS] B: 10/24/1959, Jackson, MS *Drafted:* 1981 Round 5 NYJ
1983 ChiB: 14 G; 1 Sac. **1984** ChiB: 14 G; 2.5 Sac. **1985** ChiB: 16 G; 2 Sac. **1986** TB: 14 G. **1987** TB: 3 G; 0.5 Sac. **1988** SD: 13 G; 3 Sac.
Total: 74 G; 9 Sac.

JON KEYWORTH Keyworth, Jonathan Kimball 6'3", 230 **RB**
Col: Colorado *HS:* Chaffey [Ontario, CA] B: 12/15/1950, San Diego, CA *Drafted:* 1974 Round 6 Was
1974 Den: KR 4-85 21.3. **1977** Den: KR 1-15 15.0. **1978** Den: KR 2-24 12.0. **1979** Den: Pass 1-1 100.0%, 32 32.00 1 TD. **Total:** Pass 1-1 100.0%, 32 32.00 1 TD; KR 7-124 17.7.

		Rushing				Receiving					Tot
Year Team	**G**	**Att**	**Yds**	**Avg**	**TD**	**Rec**	**Yds**	**Avg**	**TD**	**Fum**	**TD**
1974 Den	14	81	374	4.6	10	12	109	9.1	0	1	10
1975 Den	14	182	725	4.0	3	42	314	7.5	1	4	4
1976 Den	14	122	349	2.9	3	22	201	9.1	1	1	4
1977 Den	11	83	311	3.7	1	11	48	4.4	0	2	1
1978 Den	16	112	444	4.0	3	21	166	7.9	1	2	4
1979 Den	16	81	323	4.0	1	18	132	7.3	0	4	1
1980 Den	10	38	127	3.3	1	15	87	5.8	0	2	1
NFL Total	95	699	2653	3.8	22	141	1057	7.5	3	16	25

ED KHAYAT Khayat, Edward Michel 6'3", 240 **DT-DE-OT**
Col: Mississippi Gulf Coast CC; Millsaps; Tulane *HS:* Moss Point [MS]
B: 9/14/1935, Moss Point, MS
1957 Was: 12 G; KR 1-12 12.0. **1958** Phi: 5 G. **1959** Phi: 9 G; Int 1-0.
1960 Phi: 12 G. **1961** Phi: 14 G. **1962** Was: 14 G. **1963** Was: 10 G.
1964 Phi: 13 G. **1965** Phi: 14 G. **1966** Bos: 14 G. **Total:** 117 G; KR 1-12 12.0; Int 1-0.

BOB KHAYAT Khayat, Robert Conrad 6'2", 230 **OG-K-C**
Col: Mississippi *HS:* Moss Point [MS] B: 4/18/1938, Moss Point, MS
Drafted: 1960 Round 6 Cle

		Scoring						
Year Team	**G**	**Pts**	**FG**	**FGA**	**FG%**	**XK**	**XKA**	**XK%**
1960 Was	12	64	15	23	65.2	19	19	100.0
1962 Was	14	71	11	25	44.0	38	38	100.0
1963 Was	14	69	12	26	46.2	33	35	94.3
NFL Total	40	204	38	74	51.4	90	92	97.8

BILL KIBLER Kibler, William F 5′11″, 180 **TB**
HS: Tonawanda [NY] B: 11/3/1901, Tonowanda, NY D: 3/1983, Tonawanda, NY
1922 Buf: 2 G.

WALT KICHEFSKI Kichefski, Walter Raymond 6′1″, 212 **OE-DE**
(Ski; Vatz) *Col:* Miami (Fla.) *HS:* Rhinelander [WI] B: 6/17/1916, Rhinelander, WI D: 1/9/1992, Miami, FL *Drafted:* 1940 Round 20 ChiB
1941 Pit: KR 1-18 18.0. **Total:** KR 1-18 18.0.

		Receiving			
Year Team	**G**	**Rec**	**Yds**	**Avg**	**TD**
1940 Pit	11	4	26	6.5	0
1941 Pit	11	5	111	22.2	1
1942 Pit	11	15	189	12.6	0
1944 ChPt	10	6	85	14.2	0
NFL Total	43	30	411	13.7	1

CARL KIDD Kidd, Carl Edward 6′1″, 205 **DB**
Col: Northeastern Oklahoma A&M (J.C.); Arkansas *HS:* Dollarway [Pine Bluff, AR] B: 6/14/1973, Pine Bluff, AR
1996 Oak: PR 0-47; Int 1-1. **Total:** PR 0-47; Int 1-1.

		Kickoff Returns				
Year Team	**G**	**Ret**	**Yds**	**Avg**	**TD**	**Fum**
1995 Oak	13	0	0	—	0	0
1996 Oak	16	29	622	21.4	0	2
NFL Total	29	29	622	21.4	0	2

KEITH KIDD Kidd, Keith Darryl 6′1″, 195 **WR**
Col: Arkansas *HS:* Crossett [AR] B: 9/10/1962, Crossett, AR
1987 Min: 1 G.

JOHN KIDD Kidd, Max John 6′3″, 210 **P**
Col: Northwestern *HS:* Findley [OH] B: 8/22/1961, Springfield, IL
Drafted: 1984 Round 5 Buf
1986 Buf: Rush 1-0. **1987** Buf: Pass 1-0. **1992** SD: Rush 2-(-13) -6.5. **1993** SD: Rush 3-(-13) -4.3 1 TD. **1996** Mia: Rush 1-3 3.0. **1997** Mia: Rush 1-4 4.0. **Total:** Pass 1-0; Rush 8-(-19) -2.4 1 TD.

		Punting			
Year Team	**G**	**Punts**	**Yds**	**Avg**	**Fum**
1984 Buf	16	88	3696	42.0	0
1985 Buf	16	92	3818	41.5	0
1986 Buf	16	75	3031	40.4	0
1987 Buf	12	64	2495	39.0	0
1988 Buf	16	62	2451	39.5	0
1989 Buf	16	65	2564	39.4	0
1990 SD	16	61	2442	40.0	1
1991 SD	16	76	3064	40.3	0
1992 SD	16	68	2899	42.6	1
1993 SD	14	57	2431	42.6	0
1994 SD-Mia	6	21	848	40.4	0
1994 SD	2	7	246	35.1	0
1994 Mia	4	14	602	43.0	0
1995 Mia	16	57	2433	42.7	0
1996 Mia	16	78	3611	**46.3**	0
1997 Mia	13	52	2247	43.2	0
1998 Det-NYJ	10	41	1686	41.1	0
1998 Det	2	13	520	40.0	0
1998 NYJ	8	28	1166	41.6	0
NFL Total	215	957	39716	41.5	2

BILLY KIDD Kidd, William Wayne Jr. 6′4″, 270 **C**
Col: Houston *HS:* Keller [TX] B: 11/28/1959, Dallas, TX
1987 Hou: 7 G.

BLAIR KIEL Kiel, Blair Armstrong 6′0″, 209 **QB**
Col: Notre Dame *HS:* East [Columbus, IN] B: 11/29/1961, Columbus, IN *Drafted:* 1984 Round 11 TB
1986 Ind: Rush 3-20 6.7; Punt 5-190 38.0. **1987** Ind: Rush 4-30 7.5; Punt 12-440 36.7. **1990** GB: Rush 5-9 1.8 1 TD. **1991** GB: Rush 4-46 11.5. **Total:** Rush 16-105 6.6 1 TD; Punt 17-630 37.1.

		Passing								
Year Team	**G**	**Att**	**Comp**	**Comp%**	**Yds**	**YPA**	**TD**	**Int**	**Rating**	**Fum**
1984 TB	10	0	0	—	0	—	0	0	—	0
1986 Ind	3	25	11	44.0	236	9.44	2	0	104.8	0
1987 Ind	4	33	17	51.5	195	5.91	1	3	41.9	0
1988 GB	1	0	0	—	0	—	0	0	—	0
1990 GB	3	85	51	60.0	504	5.93	2	2	74.8	2
1991 GB	4	50	29	58.0	361	7.22	3	2	83.8	2
NFL Total	25	193	108	56.0	1296	6.72	8	7	75.4	4

MAX KIELBASA Kielbasa, Maxmillian 6′1″, 185 **HB-DB**
Col: Duquesne *HS:* Brownsville [PA] B: 8/23/1921 D: 1/12/1980, Pittsburgh, PA *Drafted:* 1943 Round 14 Pit
1946 Pit: 2 G; Rush 2-(-2) -1.0; 1 Fum.

HOWARD KIELEY Kieley, Howard 5′8″, 208 **T-G**
Col: No College *HS:* Cathedral [Duluth, MN] B: 8/1896, MI Deceased
1923 Dul: 7 G. **1924** Dul: 6 G. **1925** Dul: 2 G. **1926** ChiC: 6 G. **Total:** 21 G.

WALT KIESLING Kiesling, Walter Andrew 6′2″, 249 **G-T**
(Babe) *Col:* St. Thomas *HS:* Cretin [St. Paul, MN] B: 3/27/1903, St. Paul, MN D: 3/2/1962, Pittsburgh, PA *HOF:* 1966
1926 Dul: 14 G. **1927** Dul: 6 G. **1928** Pott: 10 G. **1929** ChiC: 12 G. **1930** ChiC: 11 G. **1931** ChiC: 9 G. **1932** ChiC: 10 G. **1933** ChiC: 10 G. **1934** ChiB: 13 G. **1935** GB: 10 G. **1936** GB: 8 G. **1937** Pit: 6 G. **1938** Pit: 6 G. **Total:** 125 G.

JEFF KIEWEL Kiewel, Jeffrey Clayton 6′4″, 270 **OG**
Col: Arizona *HS:* Sabino [Tucson, AZ] B: 9/27/1960, Tucson, AZ
1985 Atl: 16 G. **1987** Atl: 12 G. **Total:** 28 G.

GEORGE KIICK Kiick, George Herman 6′0″, 198 **DB-FB-HB-LB**
Col: Bucknell *HS:* Ephrata [PA] B: 9/5/1917, Hanover, PA
Drafted: 1940 Round 3 Pit
1940 Pit: Pass 2-0, 1 Int; Rec 3-22 7.3. **1945** Pit: Rec 1-(-2) -2.0; KR 1-19 19.0. **Total:** Pass 2-0, 1 Int; Rec 4-20 5.0; KR 1-19 19.0.

		Rushing			
Year Team	**G**	**Att**	**Yds**	**Avg**	**TD**
1940 Pit	11	66	212	3.2	0
1945 Pit	6	15	45	3.0	1
NFL Total	17	81	257	3.2	1

JIM KIICK Kiick, James Forrest 5′11″, 214 **RB**
(The Sundance Kid) *Col:* Wyoming *HS:* Lincoln Park [NJ]
B: 8/9/1946, Lincoln Park, NJ *Drafted:* 1968 Round 5 Mia
1968 Mia: Pass 1-0; KR 1-28 28.0. **1970** Mia: Pass 1-1 100.0%, 25 25.00. **1974** Mia: Pass 1-1 100.0%, 13 13.00. **Total:** Pass 3-2 66.7%, 38 12.67; KR 1-28 28.0.

		Rushing				Receiving					Tot
Year Team	**G**	**Att**	**Yds**	**Avg**	**TD**	**Rec**	**Yds**	**Avg**	**TD**	**Fum**	**TD**
1968 Mia	14	165	621	3.8	4	44	422	9.6	0	2	4
1969 Mia	14	180	575	3.2	**9**	29	443	15.3	1	2	10
1970 Mia	14	191	658	3.4	6	42	497	11.8	0	4	6
1971 Mia	13	162	738	4.6	3	40	338	8.5	0	1	3
1972 Mia	14	137	521	3.8	5	21	147	7.0	1	3	6
1973 Mia	14	76	257	3.4	0	27	208	7.7	0	3	0
1974 Mia	14	86	274	3.2	1	18	155	8.6	1	0	2
1976 Den	14	31	114	3.7	1	10	78	7.8	1	0	2
1977 Den-Was	4	1	1	1.0	0	2	14	7.0	0	0	0
1977 Den	3	1	1	1.0	0	2	14	7.0	0	0	0
1977 Was	1	0	0	—	0	0	0	—	0	0	0
NFL Total	115	1029	3759	3.7	29	233	2302	9.9	4	15	33

WALLY KILBOURNE Kilbourne, Warren William 6′3″, 240 **T**
(Cleats) *Col:* Minnesota B: 6/20/1916, St. Paul, MN Deceased
1939 GB: 4 G.

BOB KILCULLEN Kilcullen, Robert Brian 6′3″, 245 **DE-OT-DT**
Col: Texas Tech *HS:* Southwest [St. Louis, MO] B: 5/13/1936, St. Louis, MO *Drafted:* 1957 Round 8 ChiB
1957 ChiB: 12 G. **1958** ChiB: 12 G. **1960** ChiB: 4 G. **1961** ChiB: 14 G. **1962** ChiB: 14 G. **1963** ChiB: 14 G. **1964** ChiB: 12 G. **1965** ChiB: 8 G. **1966** ChiB: 14 G. **Total:** 104 G.

ROGER KILEY Kiley, Roger Joseph 6′0″, 180 **E**
(Rodge) *Col:* Notre Dame *HS:* St.Phillip [Chicago, IL] B: 10/23/1900, Chicago, IL D: 9/9/1974, River Forest, IL
1923 ChiC: 11 G; Rec 1 TD; 6 Pt.

JON KILGORE Kilgore, Jon Wilton 6′1″, 205 **P**
Col: Auburn *HS:* North Fulton [Atlanta, GA] B: 12/3/1943, Fort Jackson, SC
1966 LARm: Pass 1-1 100.0%, 47 47.00. **1968** ChiB: Pass 1-0. **Total:** Pass 2-1 50.0%, 47 23.50.

		Punting			
Year Team	**G**	**Punts**	**Yds**	**Avg**	**Fum**
1965 LARm	5	24	999	41.6	0
1966 LARm	14	71	3037	42.8	0
1967 LARm	14	68	2872	42.2	1
1968 ChiB	7	35	1231	35.2	0
1969 SF	7	36	1451	40.3	0
NFL Total	47	234	9590	41.0	1

TERRY KILLENS Killens, Terry Deleon 6′1″, 235 **LB**
Col: Penn State *HS:* Purcell [Cincinnati, OH] B: 3/24/1974, Cincinnati, OH *Drafted:* 1996 Round 3 Hou
1996 Hou: 14 G. **1997** Ten: 16 G. **1998** Ten: 16 G. **Total:** 46 G.

CHARLIE KILLETT Killett, Charles William 6′1″, 205 **HB**
Col: Memphis *HS:* Central [West Helena, AR] B: 11/8/1940, Helena, AR *Drafted:* 1963 Round 16 NYG
1963 NYG: 13 G; Rush 11-36 3.3; KR 14-332 23.7; 2 Fum.

GENE KILLIAN Killian, Lowell Eugene 6′4″, 250 **OG**
Col: Tennessee *HS:* Brandon [FL] B: 9/22/1952, Tampa, FL
Drafted: 1974 Round 16 Dal
1974 Dal: 7 G.

LYONS KILLIHER Killiher, Lyons 1 **G**
Col: No College B: 1903, IL Deceased
1928 ChiC: 1 G.

GLENN KILLINGER Killinger, William Glenn 5′9″, 162 **TB**
Col: Penn State *HS:* Harrisburg Tech [PA] B: 9/13/1898, Harrisburg, PA D: 1/25/1988, Stanton, DE
1921 Can: 1 G; Pass 1 TD. **1926** NYG: 1 G. **Total:** 2 G; Pass 1 TD.

PAT KILLORIN Killorin, Patrick Michael 6′2″, 220 **C**
Col: Syracuse *HS:* Watertown [NY] B: 6/11/1944, Watertown, NY
Drafted: 1966 Round 3 Pit
1966 Pit: 5 G.

BILLY KILMER Kilmer, William Orland Jr. 6′0″, 204 **QB**
Col: UCLA *HS:* Citrus [Azusa, CA] B: 9/5/1939, Topeka, KS
Drafted: 1961 Round 1 SF
1961 SF: Punt 9-364 40.4. **1966** SF: Punt 7-234 33.4. **Total:** Punt 16-598 37.4.

		Passing							
Year Team	**G**	**Att**	**Comp**	**Comp%**	**Yds**	**YPA**	**TD**	**Int**	**Rating**
1961 SF	11	34	19	55.9	286	8.41	0	4	44.1
1962 SF	12	13	8	61.5	191	14.69	1	3	91.5
1964 SF	10	14	8	57.1	92	6.57	1	1	71.1
1966 SF	6	16	5	31.3	84	5.25	0	1	24.0
1967 NO	10	204	97	47.5	1341	6.57	6	11	56.4
1968 NO	12	315	167	53.0	2060	6.54	15	17	66.9
1969 NO	14	360	193	53.6	2532	7.03	20	17	74.9
1970 NO	13	237	135	57.0	1557	6.57	6	17	55.5
1971 Was	14	306	166	54.2	2221	7.26	13	13	74.0
1972 Was	12	225	120	53.3	1648	7.32	**19**	11	84.8
1973 Was	10	227	122	53.7	1656	7.30	14	9	81.3
1974 Was	11	234	137	58.5	1632	6.97	10	6	83.5
1975 Was	12	346	178	51.4	2440	7.05	23	16	77.2
1976 Was	10	206	108	52.4	1252	6.08	12	10	70.3
1977 Was	8	201	99	49.3	1187	5.91	8	7	66.5
1978 Was	5	46	23	50.0	316	6.87	4	3	74.2
NFL Total	170	2984	1585	53.1	20495	6.87	152	146	71.6

	Rushing				Receiving					Tot
Year Team	**Att**	**Yds**	**Avg**	**TD**	**Rec**	**Yds**	**Avg**	**TD**	**Fum**	**TD**
1961 SF	96	509	5.3	10	0	0	—	0	8	10
1962 SF	93	478	5.1	5	16	152	9.5	1	5	6
1964 SF	36	113	3.1	0	11	136	12.4	0	3	0
1966 SF	3	23	7.7	0	0	0	—	0	0	0
1967 NO	20	142	7.1	1	0	0	—	0	5	1
1968 NO	21	97	4.6	2	0	0	—	0	5	2
1969 NO	11	18	1.6	0	0	0	—	0	5	0
1970 NO	12	42	3.5	0	0	0	—	0	4	0
1971 Was	17	5	0.3	2	0	0	—	0	2	2
1972 Was	3	-3	-1.0	0	0	0	—	0	1	0
1973 Was	9	10	1.1	0	0	0	—	0	6	0
1974 Was	6	27	4.5	0	0	0	—	0	3	0
1975 Was	11	34	3.1	1	0	0	—	0	3	1
1976 Was	13	-7	-0.5	0	0	0	—	0	3	0
1977 Was	10	20	2.0	0	0	0	—	0	4	0
1978 Was	1	1	1.0	0	0	0	—	0	1	0
NFL Total	362	1509	4.2	21	27	288	10.7	1	58	22

BUCKO KILROY Kilroy, Francis Joseph 6′2″, 243 **DG-OT-DT-OG**
Col: Notre Dame; Temple *HS:* Northeast Catholic [Philadelphia, PA]
B: 5/30/1921, Philadelphia, PA
1943 PhPt: 9 G. **1944** Phi: 10 G. **1945** Phi: 9 G; KR 1-7 7.0. **1946** Phi: 9 G; Int 1-0. **1947** Phi: 12 G. **1948** Phi: 12 G. **1949** Phi: 12 G. **1950** Phi: 12 G. **1951** Phi: 12 G; KR 1-18 18.0. **1952** Phi: 12 G; 1 Fum. **1953** Phi: 12 G. **1954** Phi: 12 G; Int 4-29. **1955** Phi: 1 G. **Total:** 134 G; KR 2-25 12.5; Int 5-29; 1 Fum.

DAVE KILSON Kilson, David Wayne 6′1″, 200 **DB**
Col: Sacramento City Coll. CA (J.C.); Nevada-Reno *HS:* Grant Union [Sacramento, CA] B: 8/11/1960, San Francisco, CA
1983 Buf: 16 G; 1 Fum TD; 6 Pt.

BRUCE KIMBALL Kimball, Bruce Michael 6′2″, 260 **OG**
Col: Massachusetts *HS:* Triton [Byfield, MA]; Bridgeton Academy [MA]
B: 8/19/1959, Beverly, MA *Drafted:* 1979 Round 7 Pit
1982 NYG: 1 G. **1983** Was: 16 G. **1984** Was: 8 G. **Total:** 25 G.

BOBBY KIMBALL Kimball, Robert Lund 6′1″, 190 **WR**
Col: Ventura Coll. CA (J.C.); Oklahoma *HS:* Camarillo [CA]
B: 3/12/1957, Camarillo, CA
1979 GB: 7 G. **1980** GB: 1 G. **Total:** 8 G.

BILL KIMBER Kimber, William Lee 6′2″, 192 **DE**
Col: Florida State *HS:* Winter Park [FL] B: 1/31/1936, Winter Park, FL
1959 NYG: 1 G. **1960** NYG: 3 G; Rec 2-48 24.0. **1961** Bos: 4 G.
Total: 8 G; Rec 2-48 24.0.

FRANK KIMBLE Kimble, Frank 6′5″, 205 **OE-DE**
(Duke) *Col:* West Virginia *HS:* Williamson [WV] B: 11/9/1917, Williamson, WV
1945 Pit: 9 G; Rec 2-16 8.0.

GARRY KIMBLE Kimble, Garry Lynn 5′11″, 184 **DB**
Col: Cisco JC TX; Sam Houston State *HS:* James Madison [Houston, TX] B: 4/5/1963, Lake Charles, LA *Drafted:* 1985 Round 11 Was
1987 Was: 3 G.

TONY KIMBROUGH Kimbrough, Antonius 6′2″, 192 **WR**
Col: Jackson State *HS:* Weir [MS] B: 9/17/1970, Weir, MS
Drafted: 1993 Round 7 Den
1993 Den: 15 G; Rec 8-79 9.9. **1994** Den: 12 G; Rec 2-20 10.0.
Total: 27 G; Rec 10-99 9.9.

ELBERT KIMBROUGH Kimbrough, Elbert Leon 5′11″, 196 **DB**
(E) *Col:* Northwestern *HS:* Galesburg [IL] B: 3/24/1938, Galesburg, IL
Drafted: 1961 Round 2 LARm
1961 LARm: 5 G. **1962** SF: 14 G. **1963** SF: 14 G; Int 1-45. **1964** SF: 14 G; Int 2-3. **1965** SF: 14 G; Int 2-5. **1966** SF: 14 G; Int 3-60; 1 Fum. **1968** NO: 10 G; Int 1-15. **Total:** 85 G; Int 9-128; 1 Fum.

JOHN KIMBROUGH Kimbrough, John 5′10″, 165 **WR**
Col: St. Cloud State *HS:* Citronelle [AL] B: 8/12/1954, Mount Vernon, AL *Drafted:* 1977 Round 3 Buf
1977 Buf: 14 G; Rec 10-207 20.7 2 TD; PR 16-184 11.5 1 TD; KR 15-346 23.1; Tot TD 3; 18 Pt.

JOHN KIMBROUGH Kimbrough, John Alec 6′2″, 210 **FB-LB**
(Jarrin' John) *Col:* Texas A&M *HS:* Haskell [TX]; Abilene HS [TX]
B: 6/14/1918, Haskell, TX
AAFC **1946** LA-A: KR 5-111 22.2. **1947** LA-A: KR 4-96 24.0. **1948** LA-A: KR 4-54 13.5. **Total:** KR 13-261 20.1.

		Rushing				Receiving				Tot
Year Team	**G**	**Att**	**Yds**	**Avg**	**TD**	**Rec**	**Yds**	**Avg**	**TD**	**TD**
1946 LA-A	14	122	473	3.9	6	9	162	18.0	1	7
1947 LA-A	14	131	562	4.3	8	16	281	17.6	3	11
1948 LA-A	10	76	189	2.5	3	10	131	13.1	2	5
AAFC Total	38	329	1224	3.7	17	35	574	16.4	6	23

JAMIE KIMMEL Kimmel, James L 6′3″, 235 **LB**
Col: Syracuse *HS:* Susquuehanna Valley [Conklin, NY] B: 3/28/1962, Johnson City, NY *Drafted:* 1985 Round 4 LARd
1986 LARd: 16 G. **1987** LARd: 15 G. **Total:** 31 G.

JERRY KIMMEL Kimmel, Jerry M 6′2″, 240 **LB**
Col: Syracuse *HS:* Susquuehanna Valley [Conklin, NY] B: 7/18/1963, Johnson City, NY
1987 NYG: 2 G.

J.D. KIMMEL Kimmel, John D 6′4″, 248 **DT**
Col: Army; Houston *HS:* Texas [Texarkana, TX] B: 9/30/1929, Omaha, TX *Drafted:* 1952 Round 11 SF
1955 Was: 12 G. **1956** Was: 12 G; KR 1-12 12.0. **1958** GB: 12 G.
Total: 36 G; KR 1-12 12.0.

JON KIMMEL Kimmel, Jon Joseph 6′4″, 240 **LB**
Col: Colgate *HS:* Susquuehanna Valley [Conklin, NY] B: 7/21/1960, Binghamton, NY
1985 Phi: 4 G. **1987** Was: 1 G. **Total:** 5 G.

TERRY KINARD Kinard, Alfred Terance 6′1″, 199 **DB**
Col: Clemson *HS:* Sumter [SC] B: 11/24/1959, Bitburg, Germany
Drafted: 1983 Round 1 NYG
1983 NYG: 1 Sac. **1984** NYG: PR 1-0. **1985** NYG: 1 Sac. **1986** NYG: 1 Sac. **1988** NYG: PR 1-8 8.0. **1990** Hou: 1 Fum TD. **Total:** PR 2-8 4.0; 1 Fum TD; 3 Sac.

		Interceptions				Tot
Year Team	**G**	**Int**	**Yds**	**TD**	**Fum**	**TD**
1983 NYG	16	3	49	0	0	0
1984 NYG	15	2	29	0	1	0
1985 NYG	16	5	100	0	0	0
1986 NYG	14	4	52	0	0	0
1987 NYG	12	5	163	1	0	1
1988 NYG	16	3	46	0	0	0
1989 NYG	16	5	135	1	0	1
1990 Hou	16	4	75	0	0	1
NFL Total	121	31	649	2	1	3

BILLY KINARD Kinard, Billy Russell 6′0″, 189 **DB-HB**
Col: Mississippi *HS:* Rolling Fork [MS]; Central HS [Jackson, MS]
B: 12/16/1933, Jackson, MS *Drafted:* 1956 Round 2 Cle
1956 Cle: 7 G; Rush 1-27 27.0 1 TD; KR 7-196 28.0; 6 Pt. **1957** GB: 12 G; PR 3-19 6.3; 2 Fum. **1958** GB: 12 G. **1960** Buf: 14 G; KR 1-39 39.0;

Int 4-29. **Total:** 45 G; Rush 1-27 27.0 1 TD; PR 3-19 6.3; KR 8-235 29.4; Int 4-29; 6 Pt; 2 Fum.

BRUISER KINARD Kinard, Frank Manning 6′1″, 216 **T**
Col: Mississippi *HS:* Central [Jackson, MS] B: 10/23/1914, Pelahatchie, MS D: 9/7/1985, Jackson, MS *Drafted:* 1938 Round 2 Bkn *HOF:* 1971
AAFC **1946** NY-A: 14 G. **1947** NY-A: 14 G. **Total:** 28 G.

NFL **1938** Bkn: 11 G. **1939** Bkn: 11 G; Scor 7, 7-7 100.0% XK. **1940** Bkn: 9 G. **1941** Bkn: 11 G; KR 1-14 14.0; Scor 9, 3-5 60.0% XK; **1** Fum TD. **1942** Bkn: 11 G. **1943** Bkn: 10 G; Rec 5-62 12.4 1 TD; Scor 17, 1-1 100.0% FG, 8-9 88.9% XK. **1944** Bkn: 10 G; KR 1-22 22.0; Int 1-26; Scor 9, 9-9 100.0% XK. **Total:** 73 G; Rec 5-62 12.4 1 TD; KR 2-36 18.0; Int 1-26; Scor 42, 1-1 100.0% FG, 27-30 90.0% XK; 1 Fum TD; Tot TD 2.

GEORGE KINARD Kinard, George Truitt 6′1″, 202 **G-LB**
Col: Mississippi *HS:* Central [Jackson, MS] B: 10/9/1916, Crystal Spring, MS *Drafted:* 1941 Round 11 Bkn
AAFC **1946** NY-A: 11 G.

NFL **1941** Bkn: 11 G. **1942** Bkn: 7 G. **Total:** 18 G.

JIM KINCAID Kincaid, James Davis 5′11″, 180 **DB**
(Blackie) *Col:* South Carolina B: 8/11/1930, Ansted, WV
Drafted: 1954 Round 3 LARm
1954 Was: 2 G; Scor 1, 1-1 100.0% XK.

BRIAN KINCHEN Kinchen, Brian Douglas 6′2″, 240 **TE**
Col: Louisiana State *HS:* University [Baton Rouge, LA] B: 8/6/1965, Baton Rouge, LA *Drafted:* 1988 Round 12 Mia
1989 Mia: KR 2-26 13.0. **1990** Mia: KR 1-16 16.0. **1993** Cle: KR 1-0. **1994** Cle: KR 3-38 12.7. **1996** Bal: KR 1-19 19.0. **1998** Bal: KR 2-33 16.5. **Total:** KR 10-132 13.2.

		Receiving				
Year Team	G	Rec	Yds	Avg	TD	Fum
1988 Mia	16	1	3	3.0	0	0
1989 Mia	16	1	12	12.0	0	2
1990 Mia	4	0	0	—	0	0
1991 Cle	14	0	0	—	0	1
1992 Cle	16	0	0	—	0	0
1993 Cle	16	29	347	12.0	2	1
1994 Cle	16	24	232	9.7	1	1
1995 Cle	13	20	216	10.8	0	1
1996 Bal	16	55	581	10.6	1	1
1997 Bal	16	11	95	8.6	1	0
1998 Bal	16	13	110	8.5	0	0
NFL Total	159	154	1596	10.4	5	7

TODD KINCHEN Kinchen, Todd Whittington 5′11″, 187 **WR**
Col: Louisiana State *HS:* Trafton Acad. [Baton Rouge, LA]
B: 1/7/1969, Baton Rouge, LA *Drafted:* 1992 Round 3 LARm
1993 LARm: Rush 2-10 5.0. **1994** LARm: Rush 1-44 44.0 1 TD. **1995** StL: Pass 1-0; Rush 4-16 4.0. **Total:** Pass 1-0; Rush 7-70 10.0 1 TD.

		Receiving				Punt Returns			
Year Team	G	Rec	Yds	Avg	TD	Ret	Yds	Avg	TD
1992 LARm	14	0	0	—	0	4	103	25.8	**2**
1993 LARm	6	8	137	17.1	1	7	32	4.6	0
1994 LARm	13	23	352	15.3	3	16	158	9.9	0
1995 StL	16	36	419	11.6	4	**53**	416	7.8	0
1996 Den	7	1	27	27.0	0	26	300	11.5	0
1997 Atl	16	16	266	16.6	1	**52**	446	8.6	0
1998 Atl	11	11	157	14.3	1	6	38	6.3	0
NFL Total	83	95	1358	14.3	10	164	1493	9.1	2

	Kickoff Returns					Tot
Year Team	Ret	Yds	Avg	TD	Fum	TD
1992 LARm	4	63	15.8	0	0	2
1993 LARm	6	96	16.0	0	1	1
1994 LARm	21	510	24.3	0	5	4
1995 StL	35	743	21.2	0	8	4
1996 Den	0	0	—	0	5	0
1997 Atl	1	18	18.0	0	5	1
1998 Atl	0	0	—	0	2	1
NFL Total	67	1430	21.3	0	26	13

RANDY KINDER Kinder, Randolph Samuel 6′1″, 213 **RB**
Col: Notre Dame *HS:* East Lansing [MI] B: 4/4/1975, Washington, DC
1997 GB-Phi: 12 G. GB: 6 G. Phi: 6 G. **Total:** 12 G.

HOBBY KINDERDINE Kinderdine, George 5′11″, 183 **C**
Col: No College *HS:* Miamisburg [OH] B: 8/13/1891, Miamisburg, OH D: 6/22/1967, Kettering, OH
1920 Day: 8 G. **1921** Day: 9 G. **1922** Day: 8 G. **1923** Day: 8 G. **1924** Day: 8 G. **1925** Day: 8 G. **1926** Day: 6 G. **1927** Day: 8 G. **1928** Day: 7 G. **1929** Day: 6 G. **Total:** 76 G.

SHINE KINDERDINE Kinderdine, Harry R 6′0″, 195 **G**
Col: No College *HS:* Miamisburg [OH] B: 3/1893, Miamisburg, OH D: 2/17/1947, Dayton, OH
1924 Day: 1 G.

WALT KINDERDINE Kinderdine, Walter 1 **WB-FB-TB**
(Babe) *Col:* No College *HS:* Miamisburg [OH] B: 8/1899, Miamisburg, OH D: 7/25/1964
1923 Day: 5 G. **1924** Day: 4 G. **1925** Day: 2 G. **Total:** 11 G.

KEITH KINDERMAN Kinderman, Keith John 6′0″, 221 **FB-DB**
Col: Florida State *HS:* Crystal Lake [IL] B: 4/16/1940, Chicago, IL
Drafted: 1963 Round 3 SD
1963 SD: 3 G. **1964** SD: 8 G; Pass 1-0; Rush 24-111 4.6; Rec 3-21 7.0. **1965** Hou: 4 G; KR 4-72 18.0. **Total:** 15 G; Pass 1-0; Rush 24-111 4.6; Rec 3-21 7.0; KR 4-72 18.0.

HOWARD KINDIG Kindig, Howard Wayne Jr. 6′6″, 265 **DE-OT**
(Adam) *Col:* Moberly Area CC; Los Angeles State *HS:* Mexico [MO]
B: 6/22/1941, Mexico, MO *Drafted:* 1964 Round 14 SD
1965 SD: 14 G. **1966** SD: 14 G; Int 1-0. **1967** SD-Buf: 12 G. SD: 7 G. Buf: 5 G. **1968** Buf: 14 G. **1969** Buf: 12 G. **1970** Buf: 10 G. **1971** Buf: 14 G; KR 2-16 8.0. **1972** Mia: 14 G. **1974** NYJ: 8 G; 1 Fum. **Total:** 112 G; KR 2-16 8.0; Int 1-0; 1 Fum.

GREG KINDLE Kindle, Gregory Lamarr 6′4″, 265 **OT-OG**
Col: Tennessee State *HS:* Weavey [Houston, TX] B: 9/16/1950, Houston, TX *Drafted:* 1974 Round 2 StL
1974 StL: 10 G. **1975** StL: 14 G. **1976** Atl: 10 G. **1977** Atl: 1 G. **Total:** 35 G.

BILL KINDRICKS Kindricks, William Alfred 6′3″, 268 **DT**
(Bruiser) *Col:* Alabama A&M *HS:* J.W. Darden [Opelika, AL]
B: 7/24/1946, Tuskegee, AL *Drafted:* 1968 Round 6 Cin
1968 Cin: 9 G.

DON KINDT Kindt, Donald John Jr. 6′6″, 242 **TE**
Col: Wis.-La Crosse B: 5/9/1961, Milwaukee, WI
1987 ChiB: 3 G; Rec 5-34 6.8 1 TD; 6 Pt.

DON KINDT Kindt, Donald John Sr. 6′1″, 207 **HB-DB**
Col: Wisconsin *HS:* Washington [Milwaukee, WI] B: 7/2/1925, Milwaukee, WI *Drafted:* 1947 Round 1 ChiB
1947 ChiB: KR 10-220 22.0. **1950** ChiB: PR 1-4 4.0; KR 2-33 16.5. **1952** ChiB: PR 1-7 7.0; Scor **1** Saf. **1954** ChiB: PR 1-1 1.0; KR 1-10 10.0. **1955** ChiB: PR 1-0. **Total:** PR 4-12 3.0; KR 13-263 20.2; Scor 1 Saf.

		Rushing				Receiving			
Year Team	G	Att	Yds	Avg	TD	Rec	Yds	Avg	TD
1947 ChiB	12	61	266	4.4	2	2	24	12.0	0
1948 ChiB	12	54	189	3.5	2	11	137	12.5	0
1949 ChiB	12	41	118	2.9	0	12	118	9.8	0
1950 ChiB	12	1	4	4.0	0	3	72	24.0	1
1951 ChiB	12	2	5	2.5	0	4	39	9.8	1
1952 ChiB	12	3	13	4.3	0	0	0	—	0
1953 ChiB	12	0	0	—	0	0	0	—	0
1954 ChiB	12	10	-9	-0.9	0	9	101	11.2	0
1955 ChiB	12	0	0	—	0	2	15	7.5	0
NFL Total	108	172	586	3.4	4	43	506	11.8	2

	Interceptions				Tot
Year Team	Int	Yds	TD	Fum	TD
1947 ChiB	3	19	0	6	2
1948 ChiB	1	21	0	0	2
1949 ChiB	2	3	0	3	0
1950 ChiB	0	0	0	0	1
1951 ChiB	4	56	0	0	1
1952 ChiB	3	49	0	1	0
1953 ChiB	6	172	**1**	0	1
1954 ChiB	2	28	0	0	0
NFL Total	21	348	1	10	7

GEORGE KINEK Kinek, George 6′2″, 190 **DB-OE**
Col: Tulane *HS:* Central Catholic [Allentown, PA] B: 1/13/1929, Palmerton, PA D: 1/21/1995, Salisbury Twp., PA *Drafted:* 1951 Round 4 LARm
1954 ChiC: 12 G; Int 2-0.

MIKE KINEK Kinek, Michael Kenneth 6′1″, 200 **DE-OE**
Col: Michigan State *HS:* Whiting [IN] B: 8/11/1917, Akron, OH
1940 Cle: 2 G.

STEVE KINER Kiner, Steven Albert 6′1″, 220 **LB**
Col: Tennessee *HS:* Hillsborough [Tampa, FL] B: 6/12/1947, Sandstone, MN *Drafted:* 1970 Round 3 Dal
1970 Dal: Rec 1-14 14.0; KR 3-50 16.7. **1973** NE: Scor 1 Saf.
Total: Rec 1-14 14.0; KR 3-50 16.7; Scor 1 Saf.

		Interceptions			
Year Team	G	Int	Yds	TD	Fum
1970 Dal	14	1	28	0	0
1971 NE	14	4	25	0	1

1973 NE	14	0	0	0	0
1974 Hou	14	1	34	0	0
1975 Hou	14	2	7	0	0
1976 Hou	14	0	0	0	0
1977 Hou	14	1	17	0	0
1978 Hou	16	1	3	0	0
NFL Total	114	10	114	0	1

KING King **TB**
Col: No College
1920 Det: 1 G.

GUS KING King, Alexander Cook 5′11″, 180 **OE**
Col: Centre *HS:* Fleming Co. [Flemingsburg, KY] B: 1/11/1900, Flemingsburg, KY D: 7/1955
1922 Tol: 3 G.

RIP KING King, Andrew V 6′1″, 205 **TB-WB-FB**
Col: West Virginia *HS:* Tennessee Acad. [Sweetwater, TN]
B: 10/25/1895, Franklin, TN D: 5/4/1950, Reno, NV
1920 Akr: 11 G. **1921** Akr: 11 G; Pass 3 TD; Rush 2 TD; Scor 15, 3 XK. **1922** Akr: 6 G; Pass 2 TD; Rush 2 TD; Int 1 TD; Scor 21, 3 XK; Tot TD 3. **1923** ChiC: 11 G; Rush 1 TD; Scor 7, 1 XK. **1924** ChiC: 2 G. **1925** Ham: 2 G. **Total:** 43 G; Pass 5 TD; Rush 5 TD; Int 1 TD; Tot TD 6.

ANGELO KING King, Angelo Tyrone 6′1″, 224 **LB**
Col: South Carolina State *HS:* Columbia [SC] B: 2/10/1958, Columbia, SC
1981 Dal: 15 G. **1982** Dal: 9 G. **1983** Dal: 16 G. **1984** Det: 16 G. **1985** Det: 16 G; 4 Sac. **1986** Det: 11 G; 2 Sac. **1987** Det: 1 G; **1** Fum TD; 6 Pt. **Total:** 84 G; 1 Fum TD; 6 Pt; 6 Sac.

BRUCE KING King, Bruce Eric 6′1″, 219 **RB**
Col: Purdue *HS:* Heritage Hills [Lincoln City, IN] B: 1/7/1963, Clarksville, IN *Drafted:* 1985 Round 5 KC
1985 KC: Rec 7-45 6.4; KR 1-13 13.0. **1987** Buf: Rec 1-3 3.0. **Total:** Rec 8-48 6.0; KR 1-13 13.0.

		Rushing			
Year Team	**G**	**Att**	**Yds**	**Avg**	**TD**
1985 KC	16	28	83	3.0	0
1986 KC-Buf	9	4	10	2.5	0
1986 KC	4	0	0	—	0
1986 Buf	5	4	10	2.5	0
1987 Buf	3	9	28	3.1	0
NFL Total	28	41	121	3.0	0

CARLOS KING King, Carlos Jermaine 6′0″, 230 **RB**
Col: North Carolina State *HS:* Starmount [Boonville, NC]; Hargrave Mil. Acad. [Chatham, VA] B: 11/25/1973, Yadkinville, NC *Drafted:* 1998 Round 4 Pit
1998 Pit: 1 G.

CHARLIE KING King, Charles Ronnie 6′0″, 184 **DB**
Col: Purdue *HS:* Alliance [OH] B: 1/7/1943, Canton, OH
Drafted: 1965 Redshirt Round 8 Buf
1966 Buf: 14 G; Int 1-0. **1967** Buf: 14 G; PR 1-12 12.0; KR 12-316 26.3. **1968** Cin: 14 G; PR 1-3 3.0; Int 1-32 1 TD; 6 Pt. **1969** Cin: 9 G; PR 0-35. **Total:** 51 G; PR 2-50 25.0; KR 12-316 26.3; Int 2-32 1 TD; 6 Pt.

CLAUDE KING King, Claude Robert 5′11″, 185 **HB**
Col: Houston *HS:* Vicksburg [MS] B: 12/3/1938 *Drafted:* 1960 Round 1 Den
1961 Hou: Rec 3-83 27.7 1 TD; PR 7-32 4.6; KR 8-190 23.8. **1962** Bos: Rec 5-42 8.4; KR 9-177 19.7. **Total:** Rec 8-125 15.6 1 TD; PR 7-32 4.6; KR 17-367 21.6.

		Rushing					Tot
Year Team	**G**	**Att**	**Yds**	**Avg**	**TD**	**Fum**	**TD**
1961 Hou	11	12	50	4.2	2	2	3
1962 Bos	14	21	144	6.9	1	2	1
NFL Total	25	33	194	5.9	3	4	4

DAVID KING King, David Joel 5′8″, 176 **DB**
Col: Auburn *HS:* Fairhope [AL] B: 5/19/1963, Mobile, AL
Drafted: 1985 Round 10 SD
1985 SD: 1 G. **1987** GB: 3 G. **Total:** 4 G.

DON KING King, Donald Erwin 6′0″, 200 **DB**
Col: Southern Methodist *HS:* Justin F. Kimball [Dallas,TX]
B: 2/10/1964, Dallas, TX
1987 GB: 1 G.

DON KING King, Donald William 6′3″, 260 **DT**
Col: Kentucky *HS:* Union [Turtle Creek, PA] B: 3/11/1929, McBee, SC
1954 Cle: 8 G. **1956** Phi-GB: 9 G. Phi: 3 G. GB: 6 G. **1960** Den: 14 G; Int 2-18. **Total:** 31 G; Int 2-18.

ED KING King, Ed E'Dainia 6′4″, 300 **OG-OT**
Col: Auburn *HS:* Central [Phenix City, AL] B: 12/3/1969, Fort Benning, GA *Drafted:* 1991 Round 2 Cle
1991 Cle: 16 G. **1992** Cle: 16 G. **1993** Cle: 6 G. **1995** NO: 1 G. **1996** NO: 16 G. **1997** NO: 2 G. **Total:** 57 G.

ED KING King, Edward Joseph 6′0″, 217 **OG-DE-DG**
Col: Boston College *HS:* Boston College [MA] B: 5/10/1925, Chelsea, MA
AAFC **1948** BufA: 14 G. **1949** BufA: 5 G. **Total:** 19 G.

NFL **1950** Bal: 12 G.

EMANUEL KING King, Emanuel 6′4″, 250 **LB**
Col: Alabama *HS:* Leroy [AL] B: 8/15/1963, Leroy, AL *Drafted:* 1985 Round 1 Cin
1985 Cin: 16 G; 2 Sac. **1986** Cin: 16 G; 9 Sac. **1987** Cin: 12 G; 4 Sac. **1988** Cin: 7 G. **1989** LARd: 16 G. **Total:** 67 G; 15 Sac.

EMMETT KING King, Emmett Eugene 5′9″, 195 **HB**
Col: No College *HS:* Hallettsville [TX] B: 5/8/1933, Hallettsville, TX
1954 ChiC: Rec 6-43 7.2 1 TD; KR 1-19 19.0.

		Rushing				
Year Team	**G**	**Att**	**Yds**	**Avg**	**TD**	**Fum**
1954 ChiC	12	57	167	2.9	0	1

FRED KING King, Frederick James 6′2″, 205 **BB-LB**
Col: Hobart *HS:* Frank H. Morrell [Irvington, NJ] B: 6/3/1913, New York, NY D: 3/12/1987, Reading, MA
1937 Bkn: 1 G.

STEVE KING King, George Stephen 6′4″, 232 **LB**
Col: Tulsa *HS:* Quinton [OK] B: 6/10/1951, McAlester, OK
1973 NE: 7 G. **1974** NE: 14 G; Int 1-9. **1975** NE: 14 G. **1976** NE: 11 G. **1977** NE: 14 G. **1978** NE: 16 G. **1979** NE: 16 G. **1980** NE: 16 G. **1981** NE: 16 G. **Total:** 124 G; Int 1-9.

GORDON KING King, Gordon David 6′6″, 275 **OT-OG**
Col: Stanford *HS:* Bella Vista [Fair Oaks, CA] B: 2/3/1956, Madison, WI *Drafted:* 1978 Round 1 NYG
1978 NYG: 11 G. **1979** NYG: 7 G. **1980** NYG: 12 G. **1981** NYG: 16 G. **1982** NYG: 9 G. **1983** NYG: 14 G. **1985** NYG: 15 G. **1986** NYJ: 11 G. **1987** NYJ: 2 G. **Total:** 97 G.

HENRY KING King, Henry Louis 6′4″, 205 **DB**
Col: San Francisco City Coll. CA (J.C.); Utah State *HS:* San Francisco Polytechnic [CA] B: 1/25/1945, San Francisco, CA *Drafted:* 1967 Round 3 NYJ
1967 NYJ: 13 G.

HORACE KING King, Horace Edward 5′10″, 208 **RB**
Col: Georgia *HS:* Clarke Central [Athens, GA] B: 3/5/1953, Athens, GA
Drafted: 1975 Round 6 Det
1975 Det: Pass 1-0; KR 6-117 19.5. **1976** Det: KR 3-63 21.0. **1979** Det: KR 2-36 18.0. **1981** Det: KR 3-33 11.0. **1982** Det: KR 2-23 11.5. **1983** Det: KR 1-11 11.0. **Total:** Pass 1-0; KR 17-283 16.6.

		Rushing				Receiving					Tot
Year Team	**G**	**Att**	**Yds**	**Avg**	**TD**	**Rec**	**Yds**	**Avg**	**TD**	**Fum**	**TD**
1975 Det	14	61	260	4.3	2	13	81	6.2	0	1	2
1976 Det	7	93	325	3.5	0	21	163	7.8	0	4	0
1977 Det	14	155	521	3.4	1	40	238	6.0	0	2	1
1978 Det	15	155	660	4.3	4	48	396	8.3	2	3	6
1979 Det	16	39	160	4.1	1	18	150	8.3	0	1	1
1980 Det	16	18	57	3.2	1	19	184	9.7	1	1	2
1981 Det	16	7	25	3.6	0	21	217	10.3	1	0	1
1982 Det	9	18	67	3.7	0	9	74	8.2	1	0	1
1983 Det	16	3	6	2.0	0	9	76	8.4	0	0	0
NFL Total	123	549	2081	3.8	9	198	1579	8.0	5	12	14

JEROME KING King, Jerome Manual 5′10″, 175 **DB**
Col: Purdue *HS:* Lincoln [Jersey City, NJ] B: 1/4/1955, Jersey City, NJ
1979 Atl: 1 G. **1980** Atl-NYG: 3 G. Atl: 2 G. NYG: 1 G. **Total:** 4 G.

JOE KING King, Joe Derek 6′2″, 200 **DB**
Col: Oklahoma State *HS:* South Oak Cliff [Dallas, TX] B: 5/7/1968, Dallas, TX
1991 Cin-Cle: 13 G; KR 3-34 11.3. Cin: 6 G; KR 3-34 11.3. Cle: 7 G. **1992** TB: 14 G; Int 2-24. **1993** TB: 15 G; Int 3-29. **1995** Oak: 16 G. **Total:** 58 G; KR 3-34 11.3; Int 5-53.

KENNY KING King, Kenneth Leon 5′11″, 203 **RB**
Col: Oklahoma *HS:* Clarendon [TX] B: 3/7/1957, Clarendon, TX
Drafted: 1979 Round 3 Hou
1979 Hou: KR 1-17 17.0. **Total:** KR 1-17 17.0.

		Rushing				Receiving					Tot
Year Team	**G**	**Att**	**Yds**	**Avg**	**TD**	**Rec**	**Yds**	**Avg**	**TD**	**Fum**	**TD**
1979 Hou	12	3	9	3.0	0	0	0	—	0	0	0
1980 Oak	15	172	761	4.4	4	22	145	6.6	0	6	4
1981 Oak	14	170	828	4.9	0	27	216	8.0	0	10	0
1982 LARd	9	69	264	3.8	2	9	57	6.3	0	1	2
1983 LARd	15	82	294	3.6	1	14	149	10.6	1	1	2
1984 LARd	16	67	254	3.8	0	14	99	7.1	0	3	0
1985 LARd	16	16	67	4.2	0	3	49	16.3	0	1	0
NFL Total	97	579	2477	4.3	7	89	715	8.0	1	22	8

FAY KING King, LaFayette Henry 6′3″, 195 **OE**
(Dolly) *Col:* Georgia *HS:* Lanier [Macon, GA] B: 3/7/1922, Dothan, AL
AAFC **1948** ChiA: KR 1-11 11.0. **1949** ChiA: KR 1-13 13.0. **Total:** KR 2-24 12.0.

		Receiving			
Year Team	**G**	**Rec**	**Yds**	**Avg**	**TD**
1946 BufA	14	30	466	15.5	6
1947 BufA	14	26	382	14.7	6
1948 ChiA	14	50	647	12.9	7
1949 ChiA	8	9	88	9.8	1
AAFC Total	50	115	1583	13.8	20

LINDEN KING King, Linden Keith 6′4″, 241 **LB**
Col: Colorado State *HS:* Air Force Academy Prep [Colorado Springs, CO] B: 6/28/1955, Memphis, TN *Drafted:* 1977 Round 3 SD
1978 SD: 14 G; Int 1-3. **1979** SD: 16 G. **1980** SD: 5 G. **1981** SD: 16 G; Int 1-28. **1982** SD: 9 G; 1 Sac. **1983** SD: 16 G; Int 1-19; 8 Sac. **1984** SD: 16 G; Int 2-52; 1 Fum; 4 Sac. **1985** SD: 16 G; Int 2-8; 6 Sac. **1986** LARd: 16 G. **1987** LARd: 12 G; Int 1-8; 4.5 Sac. **1988** LARd: 14 G; 1 Sac. **1989** LARd: 14 G; 1 Fum TD; 6 Pt. **Total:** 164 G; Int 8-118; 1 Fum TD; 6 Pt; 1 Fum; 24.5 Sac.

PHIL KING King, Phillip Edgar 6′4″, 223 **HB-FB**
(Chief) *Col:* Vanderbilt *HS:* Dyersburg [TN] B: 6/22/1936, Nashville, TN D: 1/18/1973, Memphis, TN *Drafted:* 1958 Round 1 NYG
1966 Min: Pass 1-1 100.0%, 9 9.00. **Total:** Pass 1-1 100.0%, 9 9.00.

		Rushing				Receiving			
Year Team	**G**	**Att**	**Yds**	**Avg**	**TD**	**Rec**	**Yds**	**Avg**	**TD**
1958 NYG	12	83	316	3.8	1	11	132	12.0	0
1959 NYG	12	72	232	3.2	0	7	98	14.0	1
1960 NYG	10	26	97	3.7	0	3	6	2.0	0
1961 NYG	5	4	7	1.8	0	0	0	—	0
1962 NYG	14	108	460	4.3	2	15	186	12.4	0
1963 NYG	14	161	613	3.8	3	32	377	11.8	5
1964 Pit	8	26	71	2.7	1	4	32	8.0	1
1965 Min	14	72	356	4.9	0	12	96	8.0	1
1966 Min	14	17	40	2.4	0	2	24	12.0	1
NFL Total	103	569	2192	3.9	7	86	951	11.1	9

	Kickoff Returns					Tot
Year Team	**Ret**	**Yds**	**Avg**	**TD**	**Fum**	**TD**
1958 NYG	13	279	21.5	0	5	1
1959 NYG	4	84	21.0	0	3	1
1960 NYG	2	73	36.5	0	2	0
1962 NYG	2	37	18.5	0	3	2
1963 NYG	0	0	—	0	4	8
1964 Pit	2	27	13.5	0	0	2
1965 Min	1	14	14.0	0	3	1
1966 Min	6	78	13.0	0	0	1
NFL Total	30	592	19.7	0	20	16

RALPH KING King, Ralph Warren 6′0″, 250 **G-C**
Col: Chicago *HS:* University [Chicago, IL] B: 11/2/1901, Chicago, IL D: 2/1978, Fairhope, AL
1924 Rac: 9 G. **1925** ChiB: 2 G. **Total:** 11 G.

DICK KING King, Richard Stewart Cutter 5′8″, 175 **FB-WB**
Col: Harvard *HS:* Boston Latin [MA] B: 2/9/1895, Boston, MA D: 10/16/1930, Bogota, Colombia
1921 Ham: 5 G. **1922** Mil-Roch: 7 G. Mil: 4 G. Roch: 3 G. **1923** StL: 7 G; Scor 2, 2 XK. **Total:** 19 G.

SHAWN KING King, Shawn 6′3″, 278 **DE**
Col: Louisiana State; Northeast Louisiana *HS:* West Monroe [LA] B: 6/24/1972, West Monroe, LA *Drafted:* 1995 Round 2 Car
1995 Car: 14 G; 2 Sac. **1996** Car: 16 G; Int 1-1; **1** Fum TD; 6 Pt; 3 Sac. **1997** Car: 9 G; 2 Sac. **Total:** 39 G; Int 1-1; 1 Fum TD; 6 Pt; 7 Sac.

TIM KING King, Timothy 6′2″, 190 **DB**
Col: Delaware State *HS:* Fort Meade [FL] B: 3/7/1960, New York, NY
1987 TB: 3 G.

TONY KING King, Tony Emanuel 6′1″, 197 **DB**
Col: Findlay *HS:* Alliance [OH] B: 5/6/1944, Canton, OH
Drafted: 1966 Redshirt Round 3 Buf
1967 Buf: 7 G.

ELLSWORTH KINGERY Kingery, Ellsworth Lee 5′11″, 180 **DB**
Col: Tulane *HS:* Lake Charles [LA] B: 8/6/1929, Lake Charles, LA
1954 ChiC: 9 G; Int 1-19.

WAYNE KINGERY Kingery, Wayne 5′11″, 175 **HB-DB**
Col: Louisiana State; McNeese State *HS:* Lake Charles [LA] B: 6/5/1927, Lake Charles, LA
AAFC **1949** BalA: 9 G; Rush 3-3 1.0; Rec 1-(-2) -2.0; PR 2-19 9.5; Int 1-0; Punt 3-109 36.3.

RICK KINGREA Kingrea, Richard Owen 6′1″, 233 **LB**
Col: Tulane *HS:* Baton Rouge [LA] B: 7/18/1949, Pearisburg, VA
Drafted: 1971 Round 14 Cle
1971 Cle: 14 G. **1972** Cle: 7 G. **1973** Buf-NO: 13 G. Buf: 4 G. NO: 9 G. **1974** NO: 14 G; KR 1-22 22.0. **1975** NO: 14 G; Int 1-14. **1976** NO: 14 G. **1977** NO: 14 G; KR 2-21 10.5. **1978** NO: 1 G. **Total:** 91 G; KR 3-43 14.3; Int 1-14.

DOUG KINGSRITER Kingsriter, Douglas James 6′2″, 222 **TE**
Col: Minnesota *HS:* Richfield [MN] B: 1/29/1950, Little Falls, MN
Drafted: 1973 Round 6 Min
1973 Min: 11 G; Rec 2-27 13.5. **1974** Min: 14 G; Rec 5-89 17.8. **1975** Min: 3 G. **Total:** 28 G; Rec 7-116 16.6.

REGGIE KINLAW Kinlaw, Reginald 6′2″, 245 **NT**
Col: Oklahoma *HS:* Miami Springs [FL] B: 1/9/1957, Miami, FL
Drafted: 1979 Round 12 Oak
1979 Oak: 16 G. **1980** Oak: 14 G. **1981** Oak: 1 G. **1982** LARd: 8 G; 1 Sac. **1983** LARd: 16 G; 1 Sac. **1984** LARd: 13 G. **1985** Sea: 16 G. **1986** Sea: 14 G. **Total:** 98 G; 2 Sac.

LARRY KINNEBREW Kinnebrew, Lawrence D 6′1″, 255 **RB**
Col: Tennessee State *HS:* East [Rome, GA] B: 6/11/1959, Rome, GA
Drafted: 1983 Round 6 Cin
1984 Cin: KR 1-7 7.0. **Total:** KR 1-7 7.0.

		Rushing				Receiving					Tot
Year Team	**G**	**Att**	**Yds**	**Avg**	**TD**	**Rec**	**Yds**	**Avg**	**TD**	**Fum**	**TD**
1983 Cin	16	39	156	4.0	3	2	4	2.0	0	3	3
1984 Cin	16	154	623	4.0	9	19	159	8.4	1	4	10
1985 Cin	12	170	714	4.2	9	22	187	8.5	1	4	10
1986 Cin	16	131	519	4.0	8	13	136	10.5	1	6	9
1987 Cin	11	145	570	3.9	8	9	114	12.7	0	1	8
1989 Buf	15	131	533	4.1	6	5	60	12.0	0	3	6
1990 Buf	2	9	18	2.0	1	0	0	—	0	0	1
NFL Total	88	779	3133	4.0	44	70	660	9.4	3	21	47

GEORGE KINNEY Kinney, George Raynard 6′4″, 250 **DE**
Col: Wiley *HS:* W.H. Lanier [Jackson, MS] B: 11/13/1942, Jackson, MS *Drafted:* 1965 Round 9 Hou
1965 Hou: 1 G.

JEFF KINNEY Kinney, Jeffrey Bruce 6′2″, 215 **RB**
Col: Nebraska *HS:* McCook [NE] B: 11/1/1949, Oxford, NE
Drafted: 1972 Round 1 KC
1972 KC: KR 4-63 15.8. **1973** KC: KR 5-130 26.0. **1975** KC: KR 2-39 19.5. **Total:** KR 11-232 21.1.

		Rushing				Receiving					Tot
Year Team	**G**	**Att**	**Yds**	**Avg**	**TD**	**Rec**	**Yds**	**Avg**	**TD**	**Fum**	**TD**
1972 KC	9	38	122	3.2	1	4	45	11.3	0	2	1
1973 KC	14	50	128	2.6	1	11	126	11.5	0	2	1
1974 KC	13	63	249	4.0	0	18	105	5.8	1	0	1
1975 KC	13	85	304	3.6	2	21	148	7.0	0	1	2
1976 KC-Buf	13	117	482	4.1	1	14	78	5.6	0	3	1
1976 KC	1	1	7	7.0	0	0	0	—	0	0	0
1976 Buf	12	116	475	4.1	1	14	78	5.6	0	3	1
NFL Total	62	353	1285	3.6	5	68	502	7.4	1	8	6

KELVIN KINNEY Kinney, Kelvin Lamonta 6′6″, 264 **DE**
Col: Virginia State *HS:* Dupont [Belle, WV] B: 12/31/1972, Montgomery, WV *Drafted:* 1996 Round 6 Was
1997 Was: 4 G. **1998** Was: 14 G; 1 Sac. **Total:** 18 G; 1 Sac.

STEVE KINNEY Kinney, Steven Arthur 6′5″, 255 **OT**
Col: San Jose City Coll. CA (J.C.); Utah State *HS:* Willow Glen [San Jose, CA] B: 6/27/1949, San Jose, CA
1973 ChiB: 2 G. **1974** ChiB: 10 G; KR 1-0. **Total:** 12 G; KR 1-0.

VINCE KINNEY Kinney, Vincent Marc 6′2″, 190 **WR**
Col: Maryland *HS:* Calvert Hall [Baltimore, MD] B: 3/17/1956, Baltimore, MD *Drafted:* 1978 Round 10 Den
1978 Den: 8 G; Rec 1-23 23.0. **1979** Den: 15 G; KR 1-14 14.0. **Total:** 23 G; Rec 1-23 23.0; KR 1-14 14.0.

CARL KINSCHERF Kinscherf, Carl Raymond 6′1″, 188 **FB-DB**
Col: Colgate *HS:* Morristown [NJ] B: 10/20/1919, Brooklyn, NY
1943 NYG: Rec 2-4 2.0; KR 2-57 28.5; Punt 32-1303 40.7. **1944** NYG: Rec 1-9 9.0; Int 1-3. **Total:** Rec 3-13 4.3; KR 2-57 28.5; Int 1-3; Punt 32-1303 40.7.

		Rushing			
Year Team	**G**	**Att**	**Yds**	**Avg**	**TD**
1943 NYG	8	49	77	1.6	1
1944 NYG	7	9	21	2.3	0
NFL Total	15	58	98	1.7	1

MATT KINZER Kinzer, Matthew Roy 6′3″, 225 **P**
Col: Purdue *HS:* Norwell [Ossian, IN] B: 6/17/1963, Indianapolis, IN
1987 Det: 1 G; Punt 7-238 34.0.

JACK KIRBY Kirby, Jack Evans 5′11″, 185 **HB-DB**
(Rabbit) *Col:* USC *HS:* Susan Miller Dorsey [Los Angeles, CA]
B: 9/21/1923, Los Angeles, CA
1949 GB: 6 G; Rush 3-6 2.0; PR 8-48 6.0; KR 14-315 22.5; 3 Fum.

JOHN KIRBY Kirby, John Patrick 6′3″, 230 **LB**
(Kirk) *Col:* Nebraska *HS:* St. Mary's [David City, NE] B: 5/30/1942, David City, NE *Drafted:* 1964 Round 5 Min
1964 Min: 14 G. **1965** Min: 14 G. **1966** Min: 10 G. **1967** Min: 14 G. **1968** Min: 14 G. **1969** Min-NYG: 14 G. Min: 2 G. NYG: 12 G. **1970** NYG: 14 G. **Total:** 94 G.

TERRY KIRBY Kirby, Terry Gayle 6′1″, 221 **RB**
Col: Virginia *HS:* Tabb [Yorktown, VA] B: 1/20/1970, Hampton, VA
Drafted: 1993 Round 3 Mia
1994 Mia: Scor 1 2XP. **1995** Mia: Pass 1-1 100.0%, 31 31.00 1 TD. **1996** SF: Pass 2-1 50.0%, 24 12.00 1 TD; PR 1-3 3.0. **1997** SF: Scor 2 2XP. **1998** SF: Pass 1-1 100.0%, 28 28.00 1 TD. **Total:** Pass 4-3 75.0%, 83 20.75 3 TD; PR 1-3 3.0; Scor 3 2XP.

		Rushing				Receiving			
Year Team	G	Att	Yds	Avg	TD	Rec	Yds	Avg	TD
1993 Mia	16	119	390	3.3	3	75	874	11.7	3
1994 Mia	4	60	233	3.9	2	14	154	11.0	0
1995 Mia	16	108	414	3.8	4	66	618	9.4	3
1996 SF	14	134	559	4.2	3	52	439	8.4	1
1997 SF	16	125	418	3.3	6	23	279	12.1	1
1998 SF	9	48	258	5.4	3	16	134	8.4	0
NFL Total	75	594	2272	3.8	21	246	2498	10.2	8

	Kickoff Returns					Tot
Year Team	Ret	Yds	Avg	TD	Fum	TD
1993 Mia	4	85	21.3	0	5	6
1994 Mia	0	0	—	0	2	2
1995 Mia	0	0	—	0	2	7
1996 SF	1	22	22.0	0	1	4
1997 SF	3	124	41.3	1	3	8
1998 SF	17	340	20.0	0	0	3
NFL Total	25	571	22.8	1	13	30

KELLY KIRCHBAUM Kirchbaum, Kelly 6′2″, 240 **LB**
Col: Kentucky *HS:* North Hardin [Radcliff, KY] B: 6/14/1957, Fort Knox, KY *Drafted:* 1979 Round 5 NYJ
1980 KC: 1 G. **1987** Phi: 3 G. **Total:** 4 G.

BILL KIRCHIRO Kirchiro, William John 6′1″, 235 **OG**
Col: Maryland *HS:* Bernards [Bernardsville, NJ] B: 6/29/1940, Bernardsville, NJ *Drafted:* 1962 Round 7 StL
1962 Bal: 8 G.

MARK KIRCHNER Kirchner, Mark Steven 6′3″, 261 **OG-OT**
Col: Baylor *HS:* Deer Park [TX] B: 10/19/1959, Pasadena, TX
Drafted: 1983 Round 7 Pit
1983 Pit-KC: 8 G. Pit: 3 G. KC: 5 G. **1984** Ind: 11 G. **1986** Ind: 13 G. **Total:** 32 G.

ERNEST KIRK Kirk, Ernest 6′2″, 265 **DE**
Col: Howard Payne B: 4/14/1952, Marin, TX
1977 Hou: 14 G; Int 1-2.

GEORGE KIRK Kirk, George Asa 6′0″, 205 **C**
Col: Baylor *HS:* Ballinger [TX] B: 9/21/1901, Ballinger, TX
D: 3/20/1996, Austin, TX
1926 Buf: 7 G.

KEN KIRK Kirk, Kenneth Henry 6′2″, 230 **LB**
Col: Mississippi *HS:* Tupelo [MS] B: 2/26/1938, Tupelo, MS
Drafted: 1960 Round 9 ChiB
1960 ChiB: 12 G. **1961** ChiB: 10 G. **1962** Pit: 14 G. **1963** LARm: 8 G. **Total:** 44 G.

RANDY KIRK Kirk, Randall Scott 6′2″, 232 **LB**
Col: De Anza Coll. CA (J.C.); San Diego State *HS:* Bellarmine Prep [San Jose, CA] B: 12/27/1964, San Jose, CA
1987 SD: 13 G; KR 3-15 5.0; 1 Fum; 1 Sac. **1988** SD: 16 G. **1989** Pho: 6 G. **1990** Was: 1 G. **1991** Cle-SD: 7 G. Cle: 2 G. SD: 5 G. **1992** Cin: 15 G. **1993** Cin: 16 G. **1994** Ariz: 16 G. **1995** Ariz: 16 G. **1996** SF: 16 G. **1997** SF: 16 G. **1998** SF: 16 G; 1 Fum. **Total:** 154 G; KR 3-15 5.0; 2 Fum; 1 Sac.

HEINIE KIRKGARD Kirkgard, Henry Gotlieb 165 **WB**
Col: Trinity (Tex.); Centre; Southern Methodist B: 9/2/1898, Danevang, TX D: 2/26/1967, Dallas, TX
1923 Tol: 5 G.

BO KIRKLAND Kirkland, B'Ho 6′0″, 215 **G**
Col: Alabama *HS:* Dothan [AL] B: 4/9/1912, Columbia, GA
1935 Bkn: 11 G. **1936** Bkn: 12 G. **Total:** 23 G.

LEVON KIRKLAND Kirkland, Lorenzo Levon 6′1″, 260 **LB**
Col: Clemson *HS:* Lamar [SC] B: 2/17/1969, Lamar, SC
Drafted: 1992 Round 2 Pit
1992 Pit: 16 G. **1993** Pit: 16 G; 1 Fum TD; 6 Pt; 1 Sac. **1994** Pit: 16 G; Int 2-0; 3 Sac. **1995** Pit: 16 G; 1 Sac. **1996** Pit: 16 G; Int 4-12; 4 Sac. **1997** Pit: 16 G; Int 2-14; 5 Sac. **1998** Pit: 16 G; Int 1-1; 2.5 Sac. **Total:** 112 G; Int 9-27; 1 Fum TD; 6 Pt; 16.5 Sac.

MIKE KIRKLAND Kirkland, Michael Albert 6′1″, 195 **QB**
Col: Arkansas *HS:* Pasadena [TX] B: 6/29/1954, Pasadena, TX
Drafted: 1976 Round 5 Bal
1978 Bal: 16 G; Pass 41-19 46.3%, 211 5.15 1 TD 8 Int; Rush 8-35 4.4.

FRANK KIRKLESKI Kirkleski, Frank William 5′10″, 179 **TB-BB**
Col: Lafayette *HS:* Nutley [NJ] B: 5/19/1904, Nutley, NJ D: 5/6/1980, Chatham, NJ
1927 Pott: 12 G; Pass 3 TD; Rush 1 TD; 1 Fum TD; Tot TD 2; 12 Pt. **1929** Ora: 12 G; Pass 1 TD; Rush 1 TD; Rec 1 TD; Tot TD 2; 12 Pt. **1930** Nwk: 12 G; Pass 3 TD; Rush 1 TD; 6 Pt. **1931** Bkn: 3 G. **Total:** 39 G; Pass 7 TD; Rush 3 TD; Rec 1 TD; 1 Fum TD; Tot TD 5; 30 Pt.

RED KIRKMAN Kirkman, Roger Randolph 6′1″, 195 **BB-DB-TB**
Col: Case Western Reserve; Washington & Jefferson *HS:* Central [Akron, OH] B: 10/17/1905, Woodland, WV D: 11/30/1973, Columbus, OH
1933 Phi: Rec 4-84 21.0 1 TD; Scor 8, 2 XK. **1934** Phi: Rec 8-114 14.3 1 TD; Scor 11, 5 XK. **1935** Phi: Scor 1, 1 XK. **Total:** Rec 12-198 16.5 2 TD.

		Passing							
Year Team	G	Att	Comp	Comp%	Yds	YPA	TD	Int	Rating
1933 Phi	9	73	22	30.1	354	4.85	2	13	17.0
1934 Phi	10	23	7	30.4	38	1.65	1	2	18.2
1935 Phi	1	1	1	100.0	1	1.00	1	0	118.8
NFL Total	20	97	30	30.9	393	4.05	4	15	18.9

	Rushing			
Year Team	Att	Yds	Avg	TD
1933 Phi	22	43	2.0	0
1934 Phi	6	12	2.0	0
NFL Total	28	55	2.0	0

JON KIRKSEY Kirksey, Jonathan O'Neal 6′4″, 350 **DE-DT**
Col: Bakersfield Coll. CA (J.C.); Arizona State; Sacramento State
HS: Riverside [Greer, SC] B: 2/21/1970, Greenville, SC *Drafted:* 1993 Round 8 NO
1996 StL: 11 G.

ROY KIRKSEY Kirksey, Roy Lewis 6′1″, 270 **OG-OT**
Col: Maryland East. Shore *HS:* Washington [Greenville, SC]
B: 9/18/1947, Greenville, SC D: 9/5/1981, Paris Mountain, SC
Drafted: 1971 Round 8 NYJ
1971 NYJ: 4 G. **1972** NYJ: 10 G; KR 2-33 16.5; 1 Fum. **1973** Phi: 7 G. **1974** Phi: 13 G; KR 1-19 19.0. **Total:** 34 G; KR 3-52 17.3; 1 Fum.

WILLIAM KIRKSEY Kirksey, William W Jr. 6′2″, 221 **LB**
Col: Southern Mississippi *HS:* Leeds [AL] B: 1/29/1966, Birmingham, AL
1990 Min: 9 G.

GARY KIRNER Kirner, Gary Burgess 6′3″, 255 **OT-OG**
Col: Santa Monica Coll. CA (J.C.); USC *HS:* Alexander Hamilton [Los Angeles, CA] B: 6/22/1942, Los Angeles, CA *Drafted:* 1964 Round 5 SD
1964 SD: 14 G. **1965** SD: 14 G; KR 1-0. **1966** SD: 14 G. **1967** SD: 14 G. **1968** SD: 14 G. **1969** SD: 7 G. **Total:** 77 G; KR 1-0.

LOU KIROUAC Kirouac, Louis 6′3″, 248 **OG-OT-K**
Col: Boston College *HS:* Bishop Bradley [Manchester, NH]
B: 5/17/1940, Manchester, NH
1963 NYG: 14 G. **1964** Bal: 14 G. **1966** Atl: 14 G; Scor 46, 9-18 50.0% FG, 19-24 79.2% XK. **1967** Atl: 8 G. **Total:** 50 G; Scor 46, 9-18 50.0% FG, 19-24 79.2% XK.

TRAVIS KIRSCHKE Kirschke, Travis 6′3″, 286 **DT**
Col: UCLA *HS:* Esperanza [Anaheim, CA] B: 9/6/1974, Fullerton, CA
1997 Det: 3 G.

MIKE KISELAK Kiselak, Michael John 6′3″, 295 **OG**
Col: Maryland *HS:* Pine Bush [NY] B: 3/9/1967, North Tarrytown, NY
1998 Dal: 15 G.

PAUL KISER Kiser, Paul David 6′4″, 272 **OG**
Col: Wake Forest *HS:* East Burke [Icard, NC] B: 11/19/1963, Valdese, NC *Drafted:* 1987 Round 6 Atl
1987 Det: 1 G.

BEN KISH Kish, Benjamin Ernest 6′0″, 207 **LB-FB-BB-DB**
Col: Pittsburgh *HS:* North Tonawanda [NY] B: 3/31/1917, Tonawanda, NY D: 2/24/1989, Philadelphia, PA *Drafted:* 1940 Round 8 ChiC
1940 Bkn: Punt 3-133 44.3. **1941** Bkn: Punt 1-35 35.0. **1943** PhPt: Punt 1-42 42.0. **1944** Phi: KR 2-36 18.0; Punt 4-182 45.5; Scor 7, 1-1 100.0% XK. **1946** Phi: Punt 4-163 40.8. **1947** Phi: KR 1-10 10.0;

Punt 8-301 37.6. **1948** Phi: PR 1-0. **Total:** PR 1-0; KR 3-46 15.3; Punt 21-856 40.8; Scor 25, 1-1 100.0% XK.

Year Team	G	Rushing Att	Yds	Avg	TD	Receiving Rec	Yds	Avg	TD
1940 Bkn	11	0	0	—	0	9	124	13.8	0
1941 Bkn	5	0	0	—	0	4	50	12.5	0
1943 PhPt	10	22	50	2.3	0	8	67	8.4	1
1944 Phi	10	22	96	4.4	0	5	73	14.6	1
1945 Phi	9	9	82	9.1	0	8	78	9.8	0
1946 Phi	10	6	13	2.2	0	3	16	5.3	0
1947 Phi	12	3	-1	-0.3	0	1	12	12.0	0
1948 Phi	9	10	106	10.6	1	0	0	—	0
1949 Phi	7	2	-2	-1.0	0	0	0	—	0
NFL Total	83	74	344	4.6	1	38	420	11.1	2

Year Team	Interceptions Int	Yds	TD	Fum	Tot TD
1940 Bkn	2	0	0	0	0
1941 Bkn	1	9	0	0	0
1943 PhPt	5	114	**1**	0	2
1944 Phi	4	52	0	0	1
1945 Phi	1	0	0	0	0
1946 Phi	1	13	0	1	0
1947 Phi	1	37	0	3	0
1948 Phi	3	32	0	0	1
NFL Total	18	257	1	4	4

GEORGE KISIDAY Kisiday, George John 6′1″, 220 **T**
Col: Duquesne; Columbia *HS:* Ambridge [PA] B: 4/16/1923, Ambridge, PA D: 11/9/1970
AAFC **1948** BufA: 14 G; Rec 1-20 20.0.

ADOLPH KISSELL Kissell, Adolph J Jr. 5′11″, 190 **HB-DB**
(Butch) *Col:* Boston College *HS:* Nashua [NH] B: 9/11/1920, Nashua, NH D: 8/7/1983, Wareham, MA *Drafted:* 1942 Round 19 ChiB
1942 ChiB: 4 G; Rush 2-(-1) -0.5; KR 2-63 31.5.

ED KISSELL Kissell, Edward John Julius 6′1″, 193 **DB**
Col: Wake Forest *HS:* Nashua [NH]; Marianapolis Acad. [Thompson, CT] B: 9/29/1929, Nashua, NH *Drafted:* 1952 Round 30 Pit
1952 Pit: 6 G; Int 5-71; Scor 0-2 FG. **1954** Pit: 7 G; Int 1-15; Scor 14, 2-4 50.0% FG, 8-9 88.9% XK. **Total:** 13 G; Int 6-86; Scor 14, 2-6 33.3% FG, 8-9 88.9% XK.

JOHN KISSELL Kissell, John Jay 6′3″, 245 **DT-OT**
Col: Boston College *HS:* Nashua [NH];La Salle Mil. Acad. [Oakdale, NY] B: 5/14/1923, Nashua, NH D: 4/9/1992, Nashua, NH *Drafted:* 1947 Round 12 LARm
AAFC **1948** BufA: 14 G. **1949** BufA: 12 G. **Total:** 26 G.

NFL **1950** Cle: 12 G; Scor **1** Saf; 2 Pt. **1951** Cle: 12 G. **1952** Cle: 12 G. **1954** Cle: 12 G. **1955** Cle: 12 G. **1956** Cle: 12 G. **Total:** 72 G; Scor 1 Saf; 2 Pt.

VITO KISSELL Kissell, Vito Joseph 5′10″, 205 **LB-FB**
Col: Holy Cross *HS:* Nashua [NH] B: 6/13/1927, Nashua, NH
Drafted: 1949 Round 17 Pit
AAFC **1949** BufA: 9 G; Rush 10-19 1.9; Rec 3-37 12.3; KR 1-1 1.0; Int 1-14.

NFL **1950** Bal: 11 G; Rush 2-6 3.0; KR 2-19 9.5; Int 2-7; Scor 11, 0-1 FG, 11-11 100.0% XK.

JON KITNA Kitna, Jon 6′2″, 217 **QB**
Col: Central Washington *HS:* Lincoln [Tacoma, WA] B: 9/21/1972, Tacoma, WA

Year Team	G	Passing Att	Comp	Comp%	Yds	YPA	TD	Int	Rating
1997 Sea	3	45	31	68.9	371	8.24	1	2	82.7
1998 Sea	6	172	98	57.0	1177	6.84	7	8	72.3
NFL Total	9	217	129	59.4	1548	7.13	8	10	74.4

Year Team	Rushing Att	Yds	Avg	TD	Fum
1997 Sea	10	9	0.9	1	1
1998 Sea	20	67	3.4	1	6
NFL Total	30	76	2.5	2	7

SYD KITSON Kitson, Sydney William 6′4″, 258 **OG-OT**
Col: Wake Forest *HS:* New Providence [NJ] B: 9/27/1958, Orange, NJ
Drafted: 1980 Round 3 GB
1980 GB: 14 G. **1981** GB: 11 G. **1983** GB: 16 G; Rec 1-9 9.0; KR 1-0. **1984** GB-Dal: 9 G. GB: 8 G. Dal: 1 G. **Total:** 50 G; Rec 1-9 9.0; KR 1-0.

PAUL KITTREDGE Kittredge, Paul John 5′10″, 170 **HB-BB-TB**
Col: Holy Cross *HS:* Clinton [MA] B: 10/9/1904, Clinton, MA D: 3/2/1947, Groton, CT
1929 Bost: 7 G; Rush 1 TD; Int **1** TD; Tot TD 2; 12 Pt.

JIM KITTS Kitts, James Matthew 6′2″, 248 **RB**
Col: Ferrum *HS:* Great Bridge [Chesapeake, VA] B: 12/28/1972, Portsmouth, VA
1997 Mia: 10 G. **1998** Mia-Was-GB: 5 G. Was: 3 G. GB: 2 G. **Total:** 15 G.

DUTCH KITZMILLER Kitzmiller, John Wesley 5′11″, 170 **FB**
Col: Oregon *HS:* Harrisburg Tech [PA]; New York Mil. Acad. [Cornwall-on-Hudson, NY] B: 11/25/1904, Harrisburg, PA D: 4/26/1986, Dallas, OR
1931 NYG: 14 G; Rush 4 TD; Scor 27, 3 XK.

LEE KIZZIRE Kizzire, William Lee 6′0″, 200 **FB-LB**
Col: Wyoming *HS:* Greybull [WY] B: 1915 D: 12/5/1943, KIA near New Guinea
1937 Det: 7 G; Rush 7-20 2.9.

EARL KLAPSTEIN Klapstein, Earl Loren 6′0″, 220 **T**
(Elk) *Col:* U. of Pacific *HS:* Lodi [CA] B: 3/8/1922, Lodi, CA
Drafted: 1944 Round 22 Phi
1946 Pit: 9 G.

JOHN KLASNIC Klasnic, John 6′0″, 185 **WB-DB**
Col: Auburn *HS:* McKeesport [PA] B: 2/23/1927, Port View, PA
AAFC **1948** BknA: 1 G.

FEE KLAUS Klaus, Feryl J 5′9″, 190 **C**
Col: No College *HS:* Green Bay West [WI] B: 9/26/1902, Green Bay, WI D: 2/14/1951, Green Bay, WI
1921 GB: 4 G.

DICK KLAWITTER Klawitter, Richard Dominic 6′7″, 270 **C**
Col: South Dakota State *HS:* Bowen [Chicago, IL] B: 6/29/1929, Chicago, IL D: 12/11/1977, Waterloo, IA *Drafted:* 1956 Round 8 ChiB
1956 ChiB: 5 G.

JOE KLECKO Klecko, Joseph Edward 6′3″, 263 **DE-DT-NT**
Col: Temple *HS:* St. James [Chester, PA] B: 10/15/1953, Chester, PA
Drafted: 1977 Round 6 NYJ
1977 NYJ: 13 G. **1978** NYJ: 16 G. **1979** NYJ: 16 G. **1980** NYJ: 15 G. **1981** NYJ: 16 G. **1982** NYJ: 2 G; 2 Sac. **1983** NYJ: 16 G; 6.5 Sac. **1984** NYJ: 12 G; 3 Sac. **1985** NYJ: 16 G; 7.5 Sac. **1986** NYJ: 11 G; 4 Sac. **1987** NYJ: 7 G; 1 Sac. **1988** Ind: 15 G. **Total:** 155 G; 24.0 Sac.

PERRY KLEIN Klein, Perry Sandor 6′2″, 218 **QB**
Col: California; C.W. Post *HS:* Carson [CA]; Pacific Palisades HS [CA] B: 3/25/1971, Santa Monica, CA *Drafted:* 1994 Round 4 Atl
1994 Atl: 2 G; Pass 1-0.

DICK KLEIN Klein, Richard James 6′4″, 254 **OT**
Col: Georgia; Iowa *HS:* Schlarman [Danville, IL] B: 2/11/1934, Pana, IL
Drafted: 1955 Round 29 ChiB
1958 ChiB: 12 G. **1959** ChiB: 12 G; 1 Fum. **1960** Dal: 7 G. **1961** Pit-Bos: 12 G. Pit: 2 G. Bos: 10 G. **1962** Bos: 14 G. **1963** Oak: 14 G; KR 1-7 7.0. **1964** Oak: 14 G; KR 1-0. **Total:** 85 G; KR 2-7 3.5; 1 Fum.

BOB KLEIN Klein, Robert Owen 6′5″, 235 **TE**
Col: USC *HS:* St. Monica's [Santa Monica, CA] B: 7/27/1947, South Gate, CA *Drafted:* 1969 Round 1 LARm
1969 LARm: KR 1-0. **1971** LARm: Rush 3-21 7.0. **1972** LARm: Rush 1-(-7) -7.0. **1973** LARm: KR 1-0. **1978** SD: KR 1-13 13.0. **Total:** Rush 4-14 3.5; KR 3-13 4.3.

Year Team	G	Receiving Rec	Yds	Avg	TD	Fum
1969 LARm	14	2	17	8.5	1	0
1970 LARm	7	2	20	10.0	0	0
1971 LARm	14	14	160	11.4	4	0
1972 LARm	14	29	330	11.4	1	1
1973 LARm	14	21	277	13.2	2	0
1974 LARm	14	24	336	14.0	4	1
1975 LARm	11	16	237	14.8	2	0
1976 LARm	14	20	229	11.5	1	0
1977 SD	12	20	244	12.2	1	0
1978 SD	16	34	413	12.1	2	0
1979 SD	15	37	424	11.5	5	0
NFL Total	145	219	2687	12.3	23	2

QUENTIN KLENK Klenk, Quentin Earl 6′2″, 225 **T**
Col: USC *HS:* Long Beach Polytechnic [CA] B: 2/13/1919, Long Beach, CA D: 1/4/1979, San Mateo, CA
AAFC **1946** BufA-ChiA: 10 G.

ROCKY KLEVER Klever, Victor Kenneth 6′3″, 225 **TE-RB**
Col: Montana *HS:* West [Anchorage, AK] B: 7/10/1959, Portland, OR
Drafted: 1982 Round 9 NYJ
1985 NYJ: KR 1-3 3.0. **1987** NYJ: KR 5-85 17.0. **Total:** KR 6-88 14.7.

Year Team	G	Receiving Rec	Yds	Avg	TD
1983 NYJ	5	0	0	—	0
1984 NYJ	16	3	29	9.7	1
1985 NYJ	16	14	183	13.1	2
1986 NYJ	16	15	150	10.0	0

1987 NYJ	12	14	152	10.9	0
NFL Total	65	46	514	11.2	3

ED KLEWICKI Klewicki, Edward Leonard 5'10", 209 **OE-DE-WB**
Col: Michigan State *HS:* Hamtramck [MI] B: 5/4/1911, Pittsburgh, PA D: 7/20/1997, East Lansing, MI
1935 Det: 11 G; Rec 4-112 28.0 2 TD; 12 Pt. **1936** Det: 11 G; Rec 4-90 22.5. **1937** Det: 11 G; Rush 10-53 5.3; Rec 8-134 16.8; 1 Fum TD; 6 Pt. **1938** Det: 10 G; Rush 10-76 7.6; Rec 3-57 19.0. **Total:** 43 G; Rush 20-129 6.5; Rec 19-393 20.7 2 TD; 1 Fum TD; Tot TD 3; 18 Pt.

ADOLPH KLIEBHAN Kliebhan, Adolph **BB**
(AKA Adolph Kliephahn) *Col:* No College B: 8/14/1897, Milwaukee, WI D: 3/1963, WI
1921 GB: 1 G.

TONY KLIMEK Klimek, Anthony Francis 5'11", 200 **DE**
Col: Illinois *HS:* Carl Schurz [Chicago, IL] B: 11/24/1925, Chicago, IL *Drafted:* 1949 Round 14 ChiC
1951 ChiC: 12 G; Int 3-39. **1952** ChiC: 12 G; Int 2-5. **Total:** 24 G; Int 5-44.

ALAN KLINE Kline, Alan Nathan 6'5", 290 **OT**
Col: Ohio State *HS:* Columbian [Tiffin, OH] B: 5/25/1971, Tiffin, OH
1995 NO: 3 G.

JIGGS KLINE Kline, Harry Smethers 6'1", 196 **DE-OE**
Col: Emporia State *HS:* Elmdale [KS] B: 10/22/1913, Elmdale, KS D: 7/27/1995, Great Bend, KS
1939 NYG: 9 G; Rec 4-44 11.0 1 TD; 6 Pt. **1940** NYG: 6 G. **1942** NYG: 10 G. **Total:** 25 G; Rec 4-44 11.0 1 TD; 6 Pt.

CHUCK KLINGBEIL Klingbeil, Charles E 6'1", 288 **NT**
Col: Northern Michigan *HS:* Houghton [MI] B: 11/2/1965, Houghton, MI
1991 Mia: 15 G; 1 Fum TD; 6 Pt; 5 Sac. **1992** Mia: 15 G; 1 Sac. **1993** Mia: 16 G; 1.5 Sac. **1994** Mia: 16 G. **1995** Mia: 16 G. **Total:** 78 G; 1 Fum TD; 6 Pt; 7.5 Sac.

JOHN KLINGEL Klingel, John 6'3", 267 **DE**
Col: Eastern Kentucky *HS:* Cardington-Lincoln [Cardington, OH] B: 12/21/1963, Marion, OH
1987 Phi: 5 G. **1988** Phi: 16 G. **Total:** 21 G.

DAVID KLINGLER Klingler, David R 6'3", 210 **QB**
Col: Houston *HS:* Stratford [TX] B: 2/17/1969, Houston, TX *Drafted:* 1992 Round 1 Cin
1994 Cin: Rec 1-(-6) -6.0. **Total:** Rec 1-(-6) -6.0.

		Passing							
Year Team	**G**	**Att**	**Comp**	**Comp%**	**Yds**	**YPA**	**TD**	**Int**	**Rating**
1992 Cin	4	98	47	48.0	530	5.41	3	2	66.3
1993 Cin	14	343	190	55.4	1935	5.64	6	9	66.6
1994 Cin	10	231	131	56.7	1327	5.74	6	9	65.7
1995 Cin	3	15	7	46.7	88	5.87	1	1	59.9
1996 Oak	1	24	10	41.7	87	3.63	0	0	51.9
1997 Oak	1	7	4	57.1	27	3.86	0	1	26.2
NFL Total	33	718	389	54.2	3994	5.56	16	22	65.1

	Rushing				
Year Team	**Att**	**Yds**	**Avg**	**TD**	**Fum**
1992 Cin	11	53	4.8	0	3
1993 Cin	41	282	6.9	0	7
1994 Cin	17	85	5.0	0	7
1996 Oak	4	36	9.0	0	1
1997 Oak	1	0	0.0	0	1
NFL Total	74	456	6.2	0	19

HARRY KLOPPENBERG Kloppenberg, William Harry 6'1", 210 **OE-DE-G**
Col: Fordham *HS:* Xavier [New York, NY] B: 8/30/1908, Bronx, NY
1930 SI: 9 G. **1931** Bkn: 2 G. **1933** Bkn: 1 G. **1934** Bkn: 7 G; Rec 3-18 6.0. **Total:** 19 G; Rec 3-18 6.0.

BRUCE KLOSTERMAN Klosterman, Bruce Donald 6'4", 230 **LB**
Col: Waldorf Coll. IA (J.C.); Iowa; South Dakota State *HS:* Beckman [Dyersville, IA] B: 4/17/1963, Dubuque, IA *Drafted:* 1986 Round 8 Den
1987 Den: 9 G. **1988** Den: 12 G. **1989** Den: 16 G. **1990** LARm: 5 G. **Total:** 42 G.

DON KLOSTERMAN Klosterman, Donald Clement 5'10", 180 **QB**
(Duke) *Col:* Loyola Marymount *HS:* Compton [CA] B: 1/18/1930, Le Mars, IA *Drafted:* 1952 Round 3 Cle
1952 LARm: 2 G; Pass 10-3 30.0%, 47 4.70 3 Int; Rush 1-(-9) -9.0; 1 Fum.

MIKE KLOTOVICH Klotovich, Michael Joseph 5'10", 180 **WB-DB**
(Yotz) *Col:* St. Mary's (Cal.) *HS:* Mission [San Francisco, CA] B: 8/15/1917, San Francisco, CA
1945 NYG: 6 G; Rush 5-26 5.2; Rec 1-7 7.0; Punt 11-423 38.5; 2 Fum.

JACK KLOTZ Klotz, John Stephen 6'4", 260 **OT**
Col: Widener *HS:* PMC Prep [Chester, PA] B: 12/5/1932, Chester, PA *Drafted:* 1956 Round 18 LARm
1960 NYT: 14 G; Rec 0-5; KR 1-8 8.0. **1961** NYT: 14 G. **1962** NYT-SD: 6 G; KR 1-15 15.0; 1 Fum. NYT: 3 G; 1 Fum. SD: 3 G; KR 1-15 15.0. **1963** NYJ: 13 G. **1964** Hou: 8 G. **Total:** 55 G; Rec 0-5; KR 2-23 11.5; 1 Fum.

AL KLUG Klug, Alfred W 6'1", 215 **G-T**
Col: Marquette *HS:* Bay View [Milwaukee, WI] B: 6/1/1920, Milwaukee, WI Deceased
AAFC **1946** BufA: 12 G. **1947** BalA: 11 G. **1948** BalA: 13 G. **Total:** 36 G.

DAVE KLUG Klug, David John 6'4", 230 **LB**
Col: Concordia (Minn.) *HS:* Litchfield [MN] B: 5/17/1958, Litchfield, MN *Drafted:* 1980 Round 4 KC
1981 KC: 16 G. **1982** KC: 9 G; 6 Pt. **1983** KC: 1 G. **Total:** 26 G; 6 Pt.

JOHN KLUMB Klumb, John James 6'3", 200 **OE-DE**
(Sticky Fingers) *Col:* Washington State *HS:* Stadium [Tacoma, WA] B: 1/22/1916, Aurora, NE
1939 ChiC: 3 G; Rec 4-21 5.3. **1940** ChiC-Pit: 10 G; Rec 3-76 25.3. ChiC: 6 G. Pit: 4 G; Rec 3-76 25.3. **Total:** 13 G; Rec 7-97 13.9.

NICK KLUTKA Klutka, Nicholas 5'11", 200 **OE-DE**
Col: Florida *HS:* New Brighton [PA] B: 1/21/1921, New Brighton, PA
AAFC **1946** BufA: 11 G; Rec 1-9 9.0.

PETE KMETOVIC Kmetovic, Peter George 5'9", 175 **HB-DB**
Col: Stanford *HS:* San Jose [CA] B: 12/27/1919, San Jose, CA D: 2/8/1990, Palo Alto, CA *Drafted:* 1942 Round 1 Phi
1946 Phi: 5 G; Rush 5-30 6.0; Rec 4-68 17.0; 1 Fum. **1947** Det: 11 G; Rush 14-23 1.6; Rec 6-143 23.8 2 TD; PR 3-26 8.7; KR 4-62 15.5; 12 Pt. **Total:** 16 G; Rush 19-53 2.8; Rec 10-211 21.1 2 TD; PR 3-26 8.7; KR 4-62 15.5; 12 Pt; 1 Fum.

SHINER KNAB Knab, Stanley S 6'1", 190 **WB-FB-BB**
Col: No College *HS:* Hughes [Cincinnati, OH] B: 3/25/1894, OH D: 11/28/1974, Clermont, FL
1921 Cin: 4 G.

GLENN KNACK Knack, Glenn **G**
Col: No College B: 3/29/1901 D: 9/1983, Niagara Falls, NY
1922 Buf: 1 G. **1924** Buf: 1 G. **Total:** 2 G.

GARY KNAFELC Knafelc, Gary Lee 6'4", 217 **OE**
Col: Colorado *HS:* Central [Pueblo, CO] B: 1/2/1932, Pueblo, CO *Drafted:* 1954 Round 2 ChiC

		Receiving			
Year Team	**G**	**Rec**	**Yds**	**Avg**	**TD**
1954 ChiC-GB	10	5	48	9.6	0
1954 ChiC	1	2	11	5.5	0
1954 GB	9	3	37	12.3	0
1955 GB	12	40	613	15.3	8
1956 GB	12	30	418	13.9	6
1957 GB	3	9	164	18.2	2
1958 GB	6	8	118	14.8	1
1959 GB	12	27	384	14.2	4
1960 GB	12	14	164	11.7	0
1961 GB	13	3	32	10.7	0
1962 GB	11	0	0	—	0
1963 SF	10	18	221	12.3	2
NFL Total	101	154	2162	14.0	23

GREG KNAFELC Knafelc, Gregory Kurt 6'4", 220 **QB**
Col: Notre Dame *HS:* Premontre [Green Bay, WI] B: 2/20/1959, Green Bay, WI
1983 NO: 6 G.

KEN KNAPCZYK Knapczyk, Kenneth John 5'11", 190 **WR**
Col: Joliet JC IL; Northern Iowa *HS:* Lincoln-Way [New Lenox, IL] B: 4/21/1963, Mokena, IL
1987 ChiB: 3 G; Rec 4-62 15.5; KR 1-14 14.0.

LINDSAY KNAPP Knapp, Lindsay Haines 6'6", 290 **OT-OG**
Col: Notre Dame *HS:* Deerfield [IL] B: 2/25/1970, Arlington Heights, IL *Drafted:* 1993 Round 5 KC
1994 KC: 2 G. **1996** GB: 9 G. **Total:** 11 G.

JACK KNAPPER Knapper, Jack Freeman 6'3", 190 **FB-LB-HB-DB**
Col: Ottawa (Ks) B: 1/12/1910, Kansas City, MO D: 4/1953
1934 Phi: 2 G; Pass 7-0, 3 Int; Rush 10-19 1.9.

JEFF KNAPPLE Knapple, Jeffrey Scott 6'2", 200 **QB**
Col: UCLA; Colorado; Northern Colorado *HS:* Fairview [Boulder, CO] B: 8/27/1956, Wurzburg, Germany
1980 Den: 2 G; Pass 4-1 25.0%, 15 3.75; Rush 6-0.

BILL KNECHT Knecht, William George 6'0", 188 **T**
Col: Xavier (Ohio) *HS:* East Side [Cincinnati, OH] B: 7/1899, Cincinnati, OH Deceased
1925 Day: 3 G.

GAYLE KNIEF Knief, Gayle C 6'3", 205 **WR**
Col: Morningside *HS:* Schleswig [IA] B: 12/28/1946, Denison, IA
1970 Bos: 3 G; Rec 3-39 13.0 1 TD; 6 Pt.

CHARLIE KNIGHT Knight, Charles Edward 6'2", 200 **T**
Col: Loyola (Chicago) *HS:* Evanston Twp. [Evanston, IL] B: 10/1/1899, Chicago, IL D: 3/12/1979, Miami, FL
1920 ChiC: 6 G. **1921** ChiC: 4 G. **Total:** 10 G.

DAVID KNIGHT Knight, David Randle 6'1", 182 **WR**
Col: William & Mary *HS:* Mount Vernon [Alexandria, VA] B: 2/1/1951, Trieste, Italy *Drafted:* 1973 Round 11 NYJ
1974 NYJ: KR 2-0. **Total:** KR 2-0.

		Receiving			
Year Team	G	Rec	Yds	Avg	TD
1973 NYJ	14	6	78	13.0	1
1974 NYJ	14	40	579	14.5	4
1975 NYJ	6	0	0	—	0
1976 NYJ	14	20	403	20.2	2
1977 NYJ	10	7	129	18.4	0
NFL Total	58	73	1189	16.3	7

GEORGE KNIGHT Knight, George F 180 **T**
Col: Loyola (Chicago) *HS:* St. Rita [Chicago, IL] B: 1898 Deceased
1920 ChiC: 2 G.

PAT KNIGHT Knight, Jon Patrick 6'2", 207 **LB**
Col: Southern Methodist *HS:* Thomas Jefferson [San Antonio, TX] B: 5/14/1929, San Antonio, TX *Drafted:* 1952 Round 10 NYG
1952 NYG: 2 G. **1954** NYG: 10 G; Int 3-41. **1955** NYG: 8 G; Int 2-29. **Total:** 20 G; Int 5-70.

LEANDER KNIGHT Knight, Leander Jr. 6'1", 193 **DB**
Col: Hudson Valley CC NY; Ferrum; Montclair State *HS:* East Orange [NJ] B: 2/16/1963, Newark, NJ
1987 Atl: 1 G. **1988** Atl: 2 G. **1989** NYJ: 13 G. **1990** Hou: 16 G; Int 1-0. **Total:** 32 G; Int 1-0.

CURT KNIGHT Knight, Luther Curtis Jr. 6'2", 190 **K**
Col: North Texas; Texas; Coast Guard *HS:* Mineral Wells [TX] B: 4/14/1943, Gulfport, MS
1969 Was: Pass 1-0, 1 Int. **Total:** Pass 1-0, 1 Int.

		Scoring						
Year Team	G	Pts	FG	FGA	FG%	XK	XKA	XK%
1969 Was	14	83	16	27	59.3	35	36	97.2
1970 Was	14	93	20	27	74.1	33	34	97.1
1971 Was	14	114	**29**	**49**	59.2	27	27	100.0
1972 Was	14	82	14	30	46.7	40	41	97.6
1973 Was	14	103	22	42	52.4	37	37	100.0
NFL Total	70	475	101	175	57.7	172	175	98.3

SUGE KNIGHT Knight, Marion H 6'2", 265 **DE**
(Sugar Bear) *Col:* El Camino Coll. CA (J.C.); Nevada-Las Vegas *HS:* Lynwood [CA] B: 4/19/1965
1987 LARm: 2 G.

SAMMY KNIGHT Knight, Sammy Dee 6'0", 205 **DB**
Col: USC *HS:* Rubidoux [Riverside, CA] B: 9/10/1975, Fontana, CA

		Interceptions		
Year Team	G	Int	Yds	TD
1997 NO	16	5	75	0
1998 NO	14	6	171	2
NFL Total	30	11	246	2

SHAWN KNIGHT Knight, Shawn Matthew 6'6", 290 **DE**
Col: Brigham Young *HS:* Edward C. Reed [Sparks, NV] B: 6/4/1964, Provo, UT *Drafted:* 1987 Round 1 NO
1987 NO: 10 G. **1988** Den: 14 G. **1989** Pho: 7 G. **Total:** 31 G.

STEVE KNIGHT Knight, Steven Paul 6'4", 298 **OG**
Col: Tennessee *HS:* Abingdon [VA] B: 3/13/1961, Abingdon, VA
1987 Ind: 3 G.

TOM KNIGHT Knight, Thomas Lorenzo 5'11", 196 **DB**
Col: Iowa *HS:* Cherokee [Marlton, NJ] B: 12/29/1974, Summitt, NJ *Drafted:* 1997 Round 1 Ariz
1997 Ariz: 15 G. **1998** Ariz: 8 G; 1 Sac. **Total:** 23 G; 1 Sac.

KURT KNOFF Knoff, Kurt Leroy 6'2", 191 **DB**
Col: Kansas *HS:* East Grand Forks [MN] B: 4/6/1954, East Grand Forks, MN *Drafted:* 1976 Round 2 Den
1982 Min: 1 Sac. **Total:** 1 Sac.

		Interceptions		
Year Team	G	Int	Yds	TD
1977 Hou	3	0	0	0
1978 Hou	16	1	6	0
1979 Min	10	2	25	0
1980 Min	16	3	87	1
1981 Min	16	3	24	0
1982 Min	9	1	4	0
NFL Total	70	10	146	1

JOHNNY KNOLLA Knolla, John Alexander 5'10", 180 **DB-HB-TB-WB**
Col: Creighton *HS:* Harrison [Chicago, IL] B: 3/19/1919, Chicago, IL D: 1/13/1992 *Drafted:* 1941 Round 2 Pit
1942 ChiC: Pass 6-1 16.7%, 16 2.67; Rec 8-48 6.0; PR 6-64 10.7; KR 1-24 24.0; Int 1-28. **1945** ChiC: Pass 1-0; Rec 1-15 15.0; PR 3-43 14.3; KR 6-114 19.0; Punt 2-66 33.0. **Total:** Pass 7-1 14.3%, 16 2.29; Rec 9-63 7.0; PR 9-107 11.9; KR 7-138 19.7; Int 1-28; Punt 2-66 33.0.

		Rushing				
Year Team	G	Att	Yds	Avg	TD	Fum
1942 ChiC	11	15	43	2.9	0	0
1945 ChiC	7	15	36	2.4	0	2
NFL Total	18	30	79	2.6	0	2

OSCAR KNOP Knop, Robert Oscar 6'0", 191 **FB-WB-E-QB**
Col: Illinois *HS:* Albert G. Lane Tech [Chicago, IL] B: 9/5/1896, Chicago, IL D: 11/5/1952, Chicago, IL
1920 ChiT: 8 G. **1921** Ham: 5 G. **1922** Ham: 5 G. **1923** Ham-ChiB: 17 G; Rush 1 TD; Int **1** TD; Tot TD 2; 12 Pt. Ham: 4 G. ChiB: 13 G; Rush 1 TD; Int 1 TD; Tot TD 2; 12 Pt. **1924** ChiB: 11 G; Rush 1 TD; 6 Pt. **1925** ChiB: 17 G; Rush 1 TD; Rec 1 TD; Tot TD 2; 12 Pt. **1926** ChiB: 13 G; Rush 1 TD; 6 Pt. **1927** ChiB: 10 G; Rec 1 TD; 6 Pt. **Total:** 86 G; Rush 4 TD; Rec 2 TD; Int 1 TD; Tot TD 7; 42 Pt.

LARRY KNORR Knorr, Lawrence Frank 6'2", 194 **OE-DE-DB**
(Soupie) *Col:* Alabama; Dayton *HS:* Stivers [Dayton, OH] B: 4/22/1917, New York, NY
1942 Det: 8 G; Rec 2-18 9.0. **1945** Det: 2 G. **Total:** 10 G; Rec 2-18 9.0.

CHARLIE KNOX Knox, Charles 5'11", 185 **T**
Col: St. Edmonds
1937 Phi: 1 G.

DARYL KNOX Knox, Daryl A 6'3", 220 **LB**
Col: Santa Monica Coll. CA (J.C.); Nevada-Las Vegas *HS:* Susan Miller Dorsey [Los Angeles, CA] B: 9/3/1962
1987 Pit: 3 G.

SAM KNOX Knox, Frank Samuel 6'0", 213 **G-T**
Col: Illinois; New Hampshire *HS:* Concord [NH]; Philips Exeter Acad. [Exeter, NH]; Clark School [Hanover, NH] B: 3/29/1910, Bow, NH D: 5/1981, Bradenton, FL
1934 Det: 11 G. **1935** Det: 9 G. **1936** Det: 11 G. **Total:** 31 G.

KEVIN KNOX Knox, Kevin DeVon 6'3", 195 **WR**
Col: Florida State *HS:* Niceville [FL] B: 1/30/1971, Niceville, FL *Drafted:* 1994 Round 6 Buf
1994 Ariz: 2 G.

MIKE KNOX Knox, Michael Alan 6'2", 240 **LB**
Col: Nebraska *HS:* Douglas Co. [Castle Rock, CO] B: 11/21/1962, Boulder, CO
1987 Den: 3 G.

RONNIE KNOX Knox, Ronald 6'1", 198 **QB**
Col: California; UCLA *HS:* Beverly Hills [CA]; Inglewood HS [CA];Santa Monica HS [CA] B: 2/14/1935, Santa Monica, CA *Drafted:* 1957 Round 3 ChiB
1957 ChiB: 1 G.

BILL KNOX Knox, William Robert 5'9", 190 **DB**
Col: Purdue *HS:* Theodore Roosevelt [East Chicago, IL] B: 6/19/1951, Elba, AL
1974 ChiB: 14 G; PR 5-35 7.0; Int 2-26. **1975** ChiB: 14 G; PR 1-0; KR 4-67 16.8. **1976** ChiB: 14 G; PR 1-0; 1 Fum. **Total:** 42 G; PR 7-35 5.0; KR 4-67 16.8; Int 2-26; 1 Fum.

GENE KNUTSON Knutson, Eugene Peter 6'2", 218 **DE**
Col: Michigan *HS:* Beloit [WI] B: 11/10/1932, Beloit, WI *Drafted:* 1954 Round 10 GB
1954 GB: 12 G. **1956** GB: 6 G. **Total:** 18 G.

STEVE KNUTSON Knutson, Steven Craig 6'3", 254 **OG-OT**
Col: East Los Angeles Coll. CA (J.C.); USC *HS:* South Gate [CA] B: 10/5/1951, Bagley, MN *Drafted:* 1975 Round 16 Atl
1976 GB: 12 G. **1977** GB: 13 G. **1978** SF: 15 G. **Total:** 40 G.

MATT KOART Koart, Matthew 6'5", 257 **DE**
Col: USC *HS:* Dos Pueblos [Goleta, CA] B: 9/28/1963, CA *Drafted:* 1986 Round 5 GB
1986 GB: 6 G.

STEVE KOBOLINSKI Kobolinski, Stephen A 5'8", 170 **C**
Col: Boston College *HS:* South Boston [MA] B: 11/19/1903, Boston, MA D: 10/11/1976, Fall River, MA
1926 Bkn: 1 G.

MICKEY KOBROSKY Kobrosky, Milton Leonard 6'0", 187 **QB-DB**
Col: Trinity (Conn.) *HS:* Springfield Central [MA] B: 2/22/1915, Springfield, MA *Drafted:* 1937 Round 5 NYG
1937 NYG: 7 G; Pass 13-2 15.4%, 18 1.38 2 Int; Rush 13-41 3.2.

GEORGE KOCH Koch, George Theodore 6'0", 200 **HB-DB**
Col: Baylor; St. Mary's (Tex.) *HS:* Temple [TX] B: 7/2/1919, Temple, TX D: 9/5/1966, Temple, TX
AAFC **1947** BufA: Rec 1-10 10.0; PR 4-84 21.0; KR 1-12 12.0; Int 3-24.

		Rushing			
Year Team	**G**	**Att**	**Yds**	**Avg**	**TD**
1947 BufA	13	37	149	4.0	1

NFL **1945** Cle: 5 G; Rush 12-101 8.4; KR 1-7 7.0.

GREG KOCH Koch, Gregory Michael 6'4", 270 **OT-OG**
Col: Arkansas *HS:* Spring Woods [Houston, TX] B: 6/14/1955, Bethesda, MD *Drafted:* 1977 Round 2 GB
1977 GB: 14 G. **1978** GB: 16 G. **1979** GB: 16 G. **1980** GB: 16 G. **1981** GB: 16 G. **1982** GB: 9 G. **1983** GB: 15 G. **1984** GB: 15 G. **1985** GB: 16 G. **1986** Mia: 16 G. **1987** Mia-Min: 10 G. Mia: 1 G. Min: 9 G. **Total:** 159 G.

MARKUS KOCH Koch, Markus 6'5", 270 **DE**
Col: Boise State *HS:* Eastwood Collegiate School [Kitchener, Canada] B: 2/13/1963, Niedermarsberg, Germany *Drafted:* 1986 Round 2 Was
1986 Was: 16 G. **1987** Was: 12 G; 2 Sac. **1988** Was: 11 G; 3.5 Sac. **1989** Was: 10 G; 2 Sac. **1990** Was: 13 G; 2 Sac. **1991** Was: 6 G; 1 Sac. **Total:** 68 G; 10.5 Sac.

PETE KOCH Koch, Peter Alan 6'6", 270 **NT-DT**
Col: Maryland *HS:* Memorial [New Hyde Park, NY] B: 1/23/1962, Nassau Co., NY *Drafted:* 1984 Round 1 Cin
1984 Cin: 16 G. **1985** KC: 16 G; 2 Sac. **1986** KC: 16 G; 5.5 Sac. **1987** KC: 6 G; 0.5 Sac. **1989** LARd: 4 G. **Total:** 58 G; 8 Sac.

POLLY KOCH Koch, Walter Henry 5'11", 180 **T-G**
Col: Wisconsin *HS:* North Division [Milwaukee, WI] B: 1/27/1895, Fond du Lac, WI D: 6/22/1976, Hartford, WI
1920 RI: 4 G.

MIKE KOCHEL Kochel, Michael Joseph 5'11", 195 **G-LB**
Col: Fordham *HS:* Bloomfield [NJ] B: 3/6/1916, Bloomfield, NJ D: 8/18/1994, Bellevue, NE *Drafted:* 1939 Round 17 ChiC
1939 ChiC: 8 G.

ROGER KOCHMAN Kochman, Roger 6'2", 205 **HB**
Col: Penn State *HS:* Wilkinsburg [PA] B: 6/16/1941, Pittsburgh, PA *Drafted:* 1962 Round 15 Buf
1963 Buf: Rec 4-148 37.0 1 TD; PR 1-11 11.0.

		Rushing			
Year Team	**G**	**Att**	**Yds**	**Avg**	**TD**
1963 Buf	5	47	232	4.9	0

DAVE KOCOUREK Kocourek, David Allen 6'5", 240 **TE**
Col: Wisconsin *HS:* J. Sterling Morton [Cicero, IL] B: 8/20/1937, Chicago, IL *Drafted:* 1959 Round 19 Pit
1962 SD: Scor **1** 2XP. **1963** SD: Scor **1** 2XP. **1967** Oak: Scor 1 2XP. **Total:** Scor 3 2XP.

		Receiving				
Year Team	**G**	**Rec**	**Yds**	**Avg**	**TD**	**Fum**
1960 LAC	14	40	662	16.6	1	1
1961 SD	14	55	1055	19.2	4	1
1962 SD	14	39	688	17.6	4	0
1963 SD	14	23	359	15.6	5	0
1964 SD	14	33	593	18.0	5	0
1965 SD	14	28	363	13.0	2	0
1966 Mia	14	27	320	11.9	2	0
1967 Oak	10	1	4	4.0	0	0
1968 Oak	7	3	46	15.3	1	0
NFL Total	115	249	4090	16.4	24	2

JOE KODBA Kodba, Joespeh Stephen 5'11", 190 **C-LB**
(Jolting Joe) *Col:* Butler; Purdue *HS:* Michael Washington [South Bend, IN] B: 2/27/1922, Yugoslavia
AAFC **1947** BalA: 13 G; Int 1-2.

VIC KOEGEL Koegel, Victor Aloysius 6'0", 215 **LB**
Col: Ohio State *HS:* Moeller [Cincinnati, OH] B: 11/2/1952, Cincinnati, OH *Drafted:* 1974 Round 12 Atl
1974 Cin: 6 G.

WARREN KOEGEL Koegel, Warren Dewitt 6'3", 253 **C**
Col: Penn State *HS:* Seaford [NY] B: 11/1/1949, Mineola, NY *Drafted:* 1971 Round 3 Oak
1971 Oak: 1 G. **1973** StL: 3 G. **1974** NYJ: 2 G. **Total:** 6 G.

BOB KOEHLER Koehler, Robert Adam Charles 5'11", 185 **FB-WB**
Col: Northwestern *HS:* Wendell Phillips [Chicago, IL] B: 4/7/1894, Chicago, IL D: 7/1/1949, Sister Lake, MI
1920 Sta: 10 G. **1921** ChiC: 8 G; Pass 1 TD; Rush 1 TD; Scor 8, 2 XK. **1922** ChiC: 10 G; Rush 2 TD; 12 Pt. **1923** ChiC: 11 G; Rush 1 TD; 6 Pt. **1924** ChiC: 10 G; Rush 1 TD; 6 Pt. **1925** ChiC: 12 G; Rush 4 TD; 24 Pt. **1926** ChiC: 10 G. **Total:** 71 G; Pass 1 TD; Rush 9 TD.

ART KOENINGER Koeninger, Arthur Frank 6'1", 202 **C-LB-T**
Col: Tennessee-Chattanooga *HS:* California [Coal Center, PA] B: 11/1/1906, Roscoe, PA D: 12/16/1990, Chattanooga, TN
1931 Fra: 2 G. **1932** SI: 10 G; Rec 1-17 17.0. **1933** Phi: 1 G. **Total:** 13 G; Rec 1-17 17.0.

DICK KOEPER Koeper, Richard Manfred 6'4", 260 **OT**
Col: Oregon State *HS:* Sequoia [Redwood City, CA] B: 7/23/1943, San Francisco, CA *Drafted:* 1965 Round 6 GB
1966 Atl: 3 G.

KARL KOEPFER Koepfer, Karl Justin 6'2", 230 **OG**
Col: Bowling Green State *HS:* Swanton [OH] B: 10/7/1934, Swanton, OH *Drafted:* 1958 Round 8 Det
1958 Det: 1 G.

MATT KOFLER Kofler, Matthew Joseph 6'3", 192 **QB**
Col: San Diego Mesa Coll. CA (J.C.); San Diego State *HS:* Patrick Henry [San Diego, CA] B: 8/30/1959, Longview, WA *Drafted:* 1982 Round 2 Buf
1982 Buf: Rush 2-21 10.5. **1983** Buf: Rush 4-25 6.3. **1984** Buf: Rush 10-80 8.0. **1985** Ind: Rush 4-33 8.3 1 TD. **Total:** Rush 20-159 8.0 1 TD.

		Passing								
Year Team	**G**	**Att**	**Comp**	**Comp%**	**Yds**	**YPA**	**TD**	**Int**	**Rating**	**Fum**
1982 Buf	4	0	0	—	0	—	0	0	—	0
1983 Buf	16	61	35	57.4	440	7.21	4	3	81.3	0
1984 Buf	16	93	33	35.5	432	4.65	2	5	35.8	1
1985 Ind	5	48	23	47.9	284	5.92	1	3	47.6	0
NFL Total	41	202	91	45.0	1156	5.72	7	11	52.3	1

DUTCH KOHL Kohl, George H **OE**
Col: No College B: 9/1893, Hammond, IN Deceased
1920 Ham: 5 G. **1922** Ham: 5 G. **Total:** 10 G.

JOE KOHLBRAND Kohlbrand, Joseph 6'4", 242 **LB**
Col: Miami (Fla.) *HS:* Merritt Island [FL] B: 3/18/1963, Merritt Island, FL *Drafted:* 1985 Round 8 NO
1985 NO: 12 G. **1986** NO: 16 G. **1987** NO: 12 G. **1988** NO: 16 G; 2 Sac. **1989** NO: 16 G. **Total:** 72 G; 2 Sac.

BOB KOHRS Kohrs, Robert Henry 6'3", 240 **LB-DE**
Col: Arizona State *HS:* Brophy Prep [Phoenix, AZ] B: 11/8/1958, Phoenix, AZ *Drafted:* 1980 Round 2 Pit
1981 Pit: 16 G. **1982** Pit: 9 G; 2 Sac. **1983** Pit: 9 G; KR 1-6 6.0; Scor 1 Saf; 2 Pt; 1.5 Sac. **1984** Pit: 10 G. **1985** Pit: 11 G. **Total:** 55 G; KR 1-6 6.0; Scor 1 Saf; 2 Pt; 3.5 Sac.

MIKE KOKEN Koken, Michael Richard 5'11", 180 **TB-DB-BB**
Col: Notre Dame *HS:* South [Youngstown, OH] B: 4/6/1909, Butler, PA D: 4/15/1962, South Bend, IN
1933 ChiC: Pass 26-9 34.6%, 74 2.85 1 TD 2 Int; Rec 2-44 22.0; Scor 1, 1 XK.

		Rushing			
Year Team	**G**	**Att**	**Yds**	**Avg**	**TD**
1933 ChiC	9	27	65	2.4	0

JON KOLB Kolb, Jon Paul 6'2", 262 **OT-C**
Col: Oklahoma State *HS:* Owasso [OK] B: 8/30/1947, Ponca City, OK *Drafted:* 1969 Round 3 Pit
1969 Pit: 14 G; KR 1-0. **1970** Pit: 14 G. **1971** Pit: 14 G. **1972** Pit: 14 G. **1973** Pit: 14 G. **1974** Pit: 14 G. **1975** Pit: 14 G. **1976** Pit: 14 G. **1977** Pit: 13 G. **1978** Pit: 16 G. **1979** Pit: 14 G. **1980** Pit: 7 G. **1981** Pit: 15 G. **Total:** 177 G; KR 1-0.

ELMER KOLBERG Kolberg, Elmer Frank 6'4", 199 **OE-DB-DE-HB**
Col: Oregon State *HS:* Lincoln [Portland, OR] B: 1/21/1916, Orange, CA D: 9/30/1994, Portland, OR *Drafted:* 1938 Round 7 Phi
1939 Phi: 8 G; Rec 3-33 11.0. **1940** Phi: 10 G; Rec 6-43 7.2; Int 1-15; Punt 10-401 40.1. **1941** Pit: 4 G; Rec 1-2 2.0. **Total:** 22 G; Rec 10-78 7.8; Int 1-15; Punt 10-401 40.1.

MIKE KOLEN Kolen, John Michael 6'2", 220 **LB**
Col: Auburn *HS:* W.A. Berry [Birmingham, AL] B: 1/31/1948, Opelika, AL *Drafted:* 1970 Round 12 Mia
1970 Mia: 14 G. **1971** Mia: 14 G. **1972** Mia: 13 G; Int 1-14. **1973** Mia: 14 G; Int 2-54. **1974** Mia: 14 G; Int 1-3; 1 Fum. **1975** Mia: 9 G; Int 1-14. **1977** Mia: 6 G. **Total:** 84 G; Int 5-85; 1 Fum.

BOB KOLESAR Kolesar, Robert C 5'10", 200 **G**
(Doc) *Col:* Michigan *HS:* John Adams [Cleveland, OH] B: 4/5/1921, Cleveland, OH
AAFC **1946** CleA: 2 G.

LARRY KOLIC Kolic, Lawrence Vincent 6'1", 242 **LB**
Col: Ohio State *HS:* Smithville [OH] B: 8/31/1963, Cleveland, OH
Drafted: 1986 Round 7 Mia
1986 Mia: 2 G. **1987** Mia: 7 G. **1988** Mia: 7 G. **Total:** 16 G.

BILL KOLLAR Kollar, William Wallace 6'3", 255 **DT-DE-NT**
Col: Montana State *HS:* Warren G. Harding [Warren, OH]
B: 11/27/1952, Warren, OH *Drafted:* 1974 Round 1 Cin
1974 Cin: 14 G. **1975** Cin: 14 G. **1976** Cin: 9 G. **1977** TB: 14 G. **1978** TB: 16 G. **1979** TB: 15 G. **1980** TB: 15 G. **1981** TB: 12 G. **Total:** 109 G.

LOUIS KOLLS Kolls, Louis C 6'1", 203 **C-OE-G**
Col: St. Ambrose B: 12/15/1892, IL D: 2/23/1941, Yorktown Twp., Henry Co., IL
1920 ChiC-Ham: 6 G. ChiC: 1 G. Ham: 4 G. **1922** RI: 6 G. **1923** RI: 6 G. **1924** RI: 9 G. **1925** RI: 11 G. **1927** NYY: 2 G. **Total:** 39 G.

ED KOLMAN Kolman, Edward Victor 6'2", 232 **T**
(Big Ed) *Col:* Temple *HS:* Stuyvesant [New York, NY]; Boys HS [Brooklyn, NY] B: 10/21/1915, Brooklyn, NY D: 7/31/1985, New Hyde Park, NY *Drafted:* 1940 Round 3 ChiB
1940 ChiB: 10 G. **1941** ChiB: 11 G. **1942** ChiB: 11 G. **1946** ChiB: 11 G. **1947** ChiB: 12 G. **1949** NYG: 11 G; KR 2-24 12.0. **Total:** 66 G; KR 2-24 12.0.

CHRIS KOLODZIEJSKI Kolodziejski, Christopher James 6'3", 231 **TE**
Col: Wyoming *HS:* Santa Monica [CA] B: 2/5/1961, Augsburg, Germany *Drafted:* 1984 Round 2 Pit
1984 Pit: 7 G; Rec 5-59 11.8.

BILL KOMAN Koman, William John 6'2", 229 **LB**
Col: North Carolina *HS:* Hopewell [Aliquippa, PA] B: 9/16/1934, Ambridge, PA *Drafted:* 1956 Round 8 Bal
1956 Bal: 12 G. **1957** Phi: 11 G. **1958** Phi: 12 G; PR 1-5 5.0; KR 1-7 7.0; Int 1-5; 1 Fum. **1959** ChiC: 11 G. **1960** StL: 12 G; Int 1-5. **1961** StL: 14 G; Int 1-8. **1962** StL: 14 G; Int 1-6. **1963** StL: 14 G. **1964** StL: 14 G; Int 2-1. **1965** StL: 14 G; KR 1-0; Int 1-2. **1966** StL: 14 G. **1967** StL: 14 G; 1 Fum. **Total:** 156 G; PR 1-5 5.0; KR 2-7 3.5; Int 7-27; 2 Fum.

JEFF KOMLO Komlo, William Jeffrey 6'2", 200 **QB**
Col: Delaware *HS:* DeMatha [Hyattsville, MD] B: 7/30/1956, Cleverly, MD *Drafted:* 1979 Round 9 Det

		Passing							
Year Team	**G**	**Att**	**Comp**	**Comp%**	**Yds**	**YPA**	**TD**	**Int**	**Rating**
1979 Det	16	368	183	49.7	2238	6.08	11	23	52.8
1980 Det	4	4	2	50.0	26	6.50	0	1	31.3
1981 Det	3	57	29	50.9	290	5.09	1	3	49.6
1983 TB	2	8	4	50.0	49	6.13	0	1	29.7
NFL Total	25	437	218	49.9	2603	5.96	12	28	50.9

	Rushing				
Year Team	**Att**	**Yds**	**Avg**	**TD**	**Fum**
1979 Det	30	107	3.6	2	11
1981 Det	6	3	0.5	0	2
1983 TB	2	11	5.5	0	2
NFL Total	38	121	3.2	2	15

JOHN KOMPARA Kompara, John Joseph 6'2", 245 **DT**
Col: South Carolina *HS:* McKinley [Canton, OH] B: 4/12/1936, Canton, OH *Drafted:* 1959 Round 13 NYG
1960 LAC: 7 G.

MARK KONCAR Koncar, Mark 6'5", 271 **OT**
(Claw) *Col:* Colorado *HS:* Murray [UT] B: 5/5/1953, Murray, UT
Drafted: 1976 Round 1 GB
1976 GB: 14 G. **1977** GB: 13 G. **1979** GB: 12 G. **1980** GB: 1 G. **1981** GB: 13 G. **1982** Hou: 5 G. **Total:** 58 G.

JOHN KONDRLA Kondrla, John Joseph 6'2", 195 **T**
(Ace; Hungry John) *Col:* St. Vincent *HS:* Georges Twp. [York Run, PA]
B: 2/23/1921, Republic, PA *Drafted:* 1945 Round 30 Pit
1945 Pit: 1 G.

MARK KONECNY Konecny, Mark William 5'11", 197 **RB**
Col: Alma *HS:* Mona Shores [Muskegon, MI] B: 4/2/1963, Chicago, IL
1987 Mia: Rush 6-46 7.7; Rec 6-26 4.3. **1988** Phi: Rec 1-18 18.0; KR 17-276 16.2. **Total:** Rush 6-46 7.7; Rec 7-44 6.3; KR 17-276 16.2.

		Punt Returns				
Year Team	**G**	**Ret**	**Yds**	**Avg**	**TD**	**Fum**
1987 Mia	3	0	0	—	0	0
1988 Phi	16	33	233	7.1	0	3
NFL Total	19	33	233	7.1	0	3

FLOYD KONETSKY Konetsky, Floyd Walter 6'0", 197 **DE**
Col: Florida *HS:* German Twp. [McClellandtown, PA] B: 5/26/1920, Marianna, PA Deceased *Drafted:* 1943 Round 29 Cle
AAFC **1947** BalA: 6 G; Int 1-15.
NFL **1944** Cle: 8 G. **1945** Cle: 10 G. **Total:** 18 G.

JOHN KONISZEWSKI Koniszewski, John Edward 6'3", 243 **T**
(Big John) *Col:* George Washington *HS:* Dickson City [PA]
B: 8/29/1921, Dickson City, PA
1945 Was: 8 G. **1946** Was: 9 G. **1948** Was: 12 G; Scor **1** Saf; 2 Pt.
Total: 29 G; Scor 1 Saf; 2 Pt.

ED KONOPASEK Konopasek, Edward Steven 6'6", 289 **OT**
Col: Ball State *HS:* Griffith [IN] B: 4/12/1964, Gary, IN
1987 GB: 3 G.

BOB KONOVSKY Konovsky, Robert Erwin 6'2", 246 **OG**
Col: Wisconsin *HS:* J. Sterling Morton [Cicero, IL] B: 8/19/1934, Cicero, IL D: 3/6/1982, Chicago, IL *Drafted:* 1956 Round 7 ChiC
1956 ChiC: 12 G. **1957** ChiC: 12 G. **1958** ChiC: 12 G. **1961** Den: 13 G. **Total:** 49 G.

KEN KONZ Konz, Kenneth Earl 5'10", 184 **DB**
Col: Louisiana State *HS:* Weimar [TX] B: 9/25/1928, Weimar, TX
Drafted: 1951 Round 1 Cle
1954 Cle: KR 2-53 26.5; Scor 15, 3-3 100.0% XK. **1955** Cle: KR 3-66 22.0. **Total:** KR 5-119 23.8; Scor 33, 3-3 100.0% XK.

		Punt Returns				Interceptions		
Year Team	**G**	**Ret**	**Yds**	**Avg**	**TD**	**Int**	**Yds**	**TD**
1953 Cle	12	1	4	4.0	0	5	15	0
1954 Cle	12	7	37	5.3	0	7	133	**2**
1955 Cle	12	17	138	8.1	0	5	32	1
1956 Cle	12	13	187	**14.4**	**1**	4	34	0
1957 Cle	12	3	13	4.3	0	4	20	0
1958 Cle	12	18	143	7.9	0	4	123	1
1959 Cle	12	9	34	3.8	0	1	35	0
NFL Total	84	68	556	8.2	1	30	392	4

	Punting				Tot
Year Team	**Punts**	**Yds**	**Avg**	**Fum**	**TD**
1953 Cle	0	0	—	1	0
1954 Cle	0	0	—	0	2
1955 Cle	0	0	—	0	1
1956 Cle	0	0	—	0	1
1957 Cle	61	2396	39.3	1	0
1958 Cle	0	0	—	0	1
NFL Total	61	2396	39.3	2	5

GEORGE KOONCE Koonce, George Earl Jr. 6'1", 245 **LB**
Col: Chowan Coll. NC; East Carolina *HS:* West Craven [Vanceboro, NC]
B: 10/15/1968, New Bern, NC
1992 GB: 16 G; 1.5 Sac. **1993** GB: 15 G; 3 Sac. **1994** GB: 16 G; 1 Sac. **1995** GB: 16 G; Int 1-12; 1 Sac. **1996** GB: 16 G; Int 3-84 1 TD; 6 Pt. **1997** GB: 4 G. **1998** GB: 14 G; 1 Sac. **Total:** 97 G; Int 4-96 1 TD; 6 Pt; 7.5 Sac.

JOE KOONS Koons, Joseph Leo Jr. 6'2", 195 **C-LB**
Col: Scranton B: 1/12/1915, Wilkes-Barre, PA D: 10/20/1993, Shelby Twp., MI
1941 Bkn: 6 G.

ED KOONTZ Koontz, Edward Larry 6'2", 230 **LB**
Col: Catawba *HS:* Littletown [PA] B: 6/11/1946, Hanover, PA
Drafted: 1968 Round 17 Bos
1968 Bos: 6 G.

JOE KOONTZ Koontz, Joseph William 6'1", 192 **WR**
Col: Contra Costa Coll. CA (J.C.); San Francisco State *HS:* De Anza [Richmond, CA] B: 8/13/1945, Visalia, CA *Drafted:* 1968 Round 9 NYG
1968 NYG: 14 G; KR 1-13 13.0.

DAVE KOPAY Kopay, David Marquette 6'0", 218 **RB**
Col: Washington *HS:* Notre Dame [Los Angeles, CA] B: 6/28/1942, Chicago, IL
1964 SF: Pass 1-0; KR 2-30 15.0. **1965** SF: KR 1-21 21.0; **1** Fum TD. **1966** SF: PR 4-28 7.0; KR 2-20 10.0. **1967** SF: KR 1-21 21.0. **1968** Det: KR 2-29 14.5. **1969** Was: KR 9-187 20.8. **1970** Was: PR 1-0.
Total: Pass 1-0; PR 5-28 5.6; KR 17-308 18.1; 1 Fum TD.

		Rushing				Receiving					Tot
Year Team	**G**	**Att**	**Yds**	**Avg**	**TD**	**Rec**	**Yds**	**Avg**	**TD**	**Fum**	**TD**
1964 SF	14	75	271	3.6	0	20	135	6.8	2	3	2
1965 SF	12	28	81	2.9	2	11	147	13.4	1	1	4
1966 SF	14	47	204	4.3	1	10	67	6.7	1	1	2
1967 SF	8	6	21	3.5	0	2	11	5.5	0	0	0
1968 Det	14	53	207	3.9	0	18	130	7.2	0	1	0
1969 Was	13	3	4	1.3	0	6	60	10.0	0	0	0
1970 Was	12	13	49	3.8	0	7	24	3.4	0	0	0
1971 NO	10	0	0	—	0	0	0	—	0	0	0
1972 GB	14	10	39	3.9	0	3	19	6.3	0	1	0
NFL Total	111	235	876	3.7	3	77	593	7.7	4	7	8

JOE KOPCHA Kopcha, Joseph Edwards 6'0", 221 **G-T**
(Doc; Big Boy) *Col:* Tennessee-Chattanooga *HS:* Whiting [IN]
B: 12/23/1905, Whiting, IN D: 7/29/1986, Hobart, IN
1929 ChiB: 12 G. **1932** ChiB: 12 G. **1933** ChiB: 13 G. **1934** ChiB: 11 G; Rec 2-24 12.0. **1935** ChiB: 12 G; Pass 1-0; Scor 3, 1 FG. **1936** Det: 12 G. **Total:** 72 G; Pass 1-0; Rec 2-24 12.0; Scor 3, 1 FG.

LOU KOPLOW Koplow, Louis H 6'3", 235 **T**
Col: Boston U. B: 2/1/1904 D: 8/12/1988, Brookline, MA
1926 Prov: 1 G.

JEFF KOPP Kopp, Jeffrey Blair 6'3", 244 **LB**
Col: USC *HS:* San Ramon Valley [Danville, CA] B: 7/8/1971, Danville, CA *Drafted:* 1995 Round 6 Mia
1995 Mia: 16 G. **1996** Jac: 12 G. **1997** Jac: 16 G; Int 1-9; 1 Sac. **1998** Jac-Bal: 13 G. Jac: 6 G. Bal: 7 G. **Total:** 57 G; Int 1-9; 1 Sac.

WALT KOPPISCH Koppisch, Walter Frederick 5'10", 180 **TB-WB-FB**
Col: Columbia *HS:* Masten Park [Buffalo, NY] B: 1901, Buffalo, NY D: 11/5/1953, New York, NY
1925 Buf: 6 G. **1926** NYG: 9 G; Pass 1 TD. **Total:** 15 G; Pass 1 TD.

MARK KORFF Korff, Mark Curtis 6'1", 230 **LB**
Col: Pasadena City Coll. CA (J.C.); Florida *HS:* John F. Kennedy [Los Angeles, CA] B: 4/5/1963, Canoga Park, CA
1987 SF: 2 G; 1.5 Sac.

ED KORISKY Korisky, Edward Andrew 6'1", 210 **C-LB**
Col: Villanova *HS:* Bulkeley [Hartford, CT] B: 8/23/1918, Hartford, CT D: 7/13/1992, Hartford, CT
1944 Bos: 9 G; Int 1-1.

R.J. KORS Kors, Richard James 6'0", 195 **DB**
Col: Taft Coll. CA (J.C.); USC; Long Beach State *HS:* El Camino Real [Woodland Hills, CA] B: 6/27/1966, Santa Monica, CA *Drafted:* 1989 Round 12 Sea
1991 NYJ: 16 G; Int 1-0. **1992** NYJ: 14 G; Int 1-16. **1993** Cin: 7 G. **Total:** 37 G; Int 2-16.

KEN KORTAS Kortas, Kenneth Conrad 6'4", 280 **DT**
(Founder) *Col:* Louisville *HS:* Taft [Chicago, IL] B: 5/17/1942, Chicago, IL *Drafted:* 1964 Round 1 StL
1964 StL: 14 G. **1965** Pit: 14 G. **1966** Pit: 14 G. **1967** Pit: 14 G; **1** Fum TD; 6 Pt. **1968** Pit: 14 G. **1969** ChiB: 3 G. **Total:** 73 G; 1 Fum TD; 6 Pt.

STEVE KORTE Korte, Steven Jeffrey 6'3", 265 **OG-C**
Col: Arkansas *HS:* Arapahoe [Littleton, CO] B: 1/15/1960, Denver, CO *Drafted:* 1983 Round 2 NO
1983 NO: 16 G; 1 Fum TD; 6 Pt. **1984** NO: 15 G. **1985** NO: 12 G; 1 Fum. **1986** NO: 16 G. **1987** NO: 3 G. **1988** NO: 16 G. **1989** NO: 5 G. **Total:** 83 G; 1 Fum TD; 6 Pt; 1 Fum.

KELVIN KORVER Korver, Kelvin Mitchell 6'6", 267 **DT**
Col: Texas A&M; Northwestern (Ia) *HS:* Irving [TX] B: 2/21/1949, Dallas, TX *Drafted:* 1972 Round 2 Oak
1973 Oak: 14 G; Int 1-12. **1974** Oak: 9 G. **1975** Oak: 1 G. **Total:** 24 G; Int 1-12.

BERNIE KOSAR Kosar, Bernie Joseph Jr. 6'5", 214 **QB**
Col: Miami (Fla.) *HS:* Boardman [Youngstown, OH] B: 11/25/1963, Boardman, OH *Drafted:* 1985 Supplemental Round 1 Cle
1986 Cle: Rec 1-1 1.0. **1989** Cle: Rec 1-(-7) -7.0. **1991** Cle: Rec 1-1 1.0. **Total:** Rec 3-(-5) -1.7.

		Passing							
Year Team	**G**	**Att**	**Comp**	**Comp%**	**Yds**	**YPA**	**TD**	**Int**	**Rating**
1985 Cle	12	248	124	50.0	1578	6.36	8	**7**	69.3
1986 Cle	16	531	310	58.4	3854	7.26	17	10	83.8
1987 Cle	12	389	241	62.0	3033	7.80	22	9	95.4
1988 Cle	9	259	156	60.2	1890	7.30	10	**7**	84.3
1989 Cle	16	513	303	59.1	3533	6.89	18	14	80.3
1990 Cle	13	423	230	54.4	2562	6.06	10	15	65.7
1991 Cle	16	494	307	62.1	3487	7.06	18	9	87.8
1992 Cle	7	155	103	66.5	1160	7.48	8	7	87.0
1993 Cle-Dal	11	201	115	57.2	1217	6.05	8	3	82.0
1993 Cle	7	138	79	57.2	807	5.85	5	3	77.2
1993 Dal	4	63	36	57.1	410	6.51	3	0	92.7
1994 Mia	2	12	7	58.3	80	6.67	1	1	71.5
1995 Mia	9	108	74	68.5	699	6.47	3	5	76.1
1996 Mia	3	32	24	75.0	208	6.50	1	0	102.1
NFL Total	126	3365	1994	59.3	23301	6.92	124	87	81.8

	Rushing				
Year Team	**Att**	**Yds**	**Avg**	**TD**	**Fum**
1985 Cle	26	-12	-0.5	1	14
1986 Cle	24	19	0.8	0	7
1987 Cle	15	22	1.5	1	2
1988 Cle	12	-1	-0.1	1	0
1989 Cle	30	70	2.3	1	2
1990 Cle	10	13	1.3	0	6
1991 Cle	26	74	2.8	0	10
1992 Cle	5	12	2.4	0	1
1993 Cle-Dal	23	26	1.1	0	6
1993 Cle	14	19	1.4	0	4
1993 Dal	9	7	0.8	0	2
1994 Mia	1	17	17.0	0	0
1995 Mia	7	19	2.7	1	3
1996 Mia	1	6	6.0	0	0
NFL Total	180	265	1.5	5	51

STAN KOSEL Kosel, Stanley Joseph 5'11", 190 **FB-DB-BB-LB**
Col: Albright *HS:* Carteret [NJ] B: 8/19/1916, Carteret, NJ D: 5/1982, Carteret, NJ
1938 Bkn: 8 G; Pass 1-0; Rush 13-43 3.3. **1939** Bkn: 5 G; Rush 2-6 3.0; Rec 2-40 20.0 1 TD; 6 Pt. **Total:** 13 G; Pass 1-0; Rush 15-49 3.3; Rec 2-40 20.0 1 TD; 6 Pt.

TERRY KOSENS Kosens, Theodore James 6'3", 195 **DB**
Col: Hofstra *HS:* Chaminade [Mineola, NY] B: 10/3/1941, Brooklyn, NY *Drafted:* 1963 Round 10 Min
1963 Min: 8 G.

JULIE KOSHLAP Koshlap, Julius Michael 5'11", 180 **HB-DB**
Col: Georgetown *HS:* Garfield [NJ] B: 12/25/1917, Wallington, NJ
1945 Pit: 1 G.

FRANK KOSIKOWSKI Kosikowski, Frank Leon 6'1", 200 **DE**
Col: Marquette; Notre Dame *HS:* Cudahy [WI] B: 7/23/1926, Cudahy, WI D: 11/17/1991, Milwaukee, WI
AAFC **1948** CleA: 12 G.

GARY KOSINS Kosins, Gary James 6'1", 215 **RB**
Col: Dayton *HS:* Chaminade [Dayton, OH] B: 1/21/1949, Warsaw, IN *Drafted:* 1972 Round 3 Mia
1972 ChiB: Rec 2-15 7.5 1 TD. **1973** ChiB: Rec 4-8 2.0. **1974** ChiB: Rec 1-3 3.0. **Total:** Rec 7-26 3.7 1 TD.

		Rushing					Tot
Year Team	**G**	**Att**	**Yds**	**Avg**	**TD**	**Fum**	**TD**
1972 ChiB	14	3	5	1.7	0	1	1
1973 ChiB	12	24	65	2.7	0	0	0
1974 ChiB	14	8	30	3.8	1	1	1
NFL Total	40	35	100	2.9	1	2	2

STEIN KOSS Koss, Stein Jeffrey 6'2", 225 **TE**
Col: Arizona State *HS:* Durango [CO] B: 8/21/1963, Durango, CO
1987 KC: 2 G; Rec 2-25 12.5.

RON KOSTELNIK Kostelnik, Ronald Michael 6'4", 260 **DT**
Col: Cincinnati *HS:* Central Catholic [Ebensburg, PA] B: 1/14/1940, Colver, PA D: 1/29/1993, Scott Co., KY *Drafted:* 1961 Round 2 GB
1961 GB: 14 G. **1962** GB: 14 G; PR 1-0. **1963** GB: 13 G. **1964** GB: 14 G. **1965** GB: 14 G. **1966** GB: 14 G. **1967** GB: 14 G. **1968** GB: 13 G. **1969** Bal: 10 G. **Total:** 120 G; PR 1-0.

MICHAEL KOSTIUK Kostiuk, Michael A 6'0", 212 **T**
Col: Detroit Tech *HS:* Hamtramck [MI] B: 8/1/1919, Krydor, Canada Deceased
1941 Cle: 1 G. **1945** Det: 6 G. **Total:** 7 G.

STAN KOSTKA Kostka, Stanislaus Clarence 5'11", 225 **FB-LB**
(King Kong) *Col:* Oregon; Minnesota *HS:* South St. Paul [MN] B: 7/8/1912, St.Paul, MN D: 2/3/1997, Fargo, ND
1935 Bkn: Pass 6-0, 2 Int; Rec 1-9 9.0.

		Rushing		
Year Team	**G**	**Att**	**Yds**	**Avg**	**TD**
1935 Bkn	9	63	249	4.0	0

TONY KOSTOS Kostos, Anthony Joseph 5'11", 191 **OE-C-G-T**
Col: Bucknell *HS:* Mount Carmel [PA] B: 6/12/1905 D: 11/16/1984, New Brunswick, NJ
1927 Fra: 7 G. **1928** Fra: 16 G; Scor 2 1XP; 2 Pt. **1929** Fra: 19 G; Rec 1 TD; 6 Pt. **1930** Fra-Min: 18 G. Fra: 16 G; Rec 1 TD; Scor 1 1XP; 7 Pt. Min: 2 G. **1931** Fra: 6 G. **Total:** 66 G; Rec 2 TD; Scor **3** 1XP; 15 Pt.

MARTY KOSTOS Kostos, Martin V 5'11", 185 **OE-WB-BB**
Col: Schuylkill *HS:* Mount Carmel [PA] B: 11/11/1901 D: 9/1961, Sunbury, PA
1929 Fra: 6 G.

EDDIE KOTAL Kotal, Edward Louis 5'8", 170 **HB-TB-BB-E**
(Lawrence Flash) *Col:* Illinois; Lawrence *HS:* Bloom [Chicago Heights, IL] B: 9/1/1902 D: 1/27/1973, North Hollywood, CA
1925 GB: 5 G; Int 1 TD; 6 Pt. **1926** GB: 10 G; Pass 1 TD; Rush 1 TD; Rec 1 TD; Tot TD 2; 12 Pt. **1927** GB: 8 G; Rush 1 TD; 6 Pt. **1928** GB: 12 G; Pass 1 TD; Rush 2 TD; Rec 1 TD; Tot TD 3; 18 Pt. **1929** GB: 11 G; Rec 3 TD; 18 Pt. **Total:** 46 G; Pass 2 TD; Rush 4 TD; Rec 5 TD; Int 1 TD; Tot TD 10; 60 Pt.

DOUG KOTAR Kotar, Douglas Allan 5'11", 205 **RB**
Col: Kentucky *HS:* Canon-McMillan [Canonsburg, PA] B: 6/11/1951, Canonsburg, PA D: 12/16/1983, Pittsburgh, PA
1974 NYG: PR 3-14 4.7. **1975** NYG: PR 1-5 5.0. **Total:** PR 4-19 4.8.

Year Team	G	Rushing Att	Yds	Avg	TD	Receiving Rec	Yds	Avg	TD
1974 NYG	12	106	396	3.7	4	10	57	5.7	0
1975 NYG	14	122	378	3.1	6	9	86	9.6	0
1976 NYG	14	185	731	4.0	3	36	319	8.9	0
1977 NYG	12	132	480	3.6	2	15	73	4.9	0
1978 NYG	15	149	625	4.2	1	22	225	10.2	1
1979 NYG	16	160	616	3.9	3	25	230	9.2	0
1981 NYG	7	46	154	3.3	1	9	32	3.6	0
NFL Total	90	900	3380	3.8	20	126	1022	8.1	1

Year Team	Kickoff Returns Ret	Yds	Avg	TD	Fum	Tot TD
1974 NYG	15	350	23.3	0	4	4
1975 NYG	17	405	23.8	0	4	6
1976 NYG	3	39	13.0	0	3	3
1977 NYG	2	36	18.0	0	1	2
1978 NYG	3	51	17.0	0	1	2
1979 NYG	2	39	19.5	0	3	3
1981 NYG	0	0	—	0	0	1
NFL Total	42	920	21.9	0	16	21

RICH KOTITE Kotite, Richard Edward 6'3", 230 **TE**
Col: Miami (Fla.); Wagner *HS:* Poly Prep [Brooklyn, NY] B: 10/13/1942, Brooklyn, NY
1967 NYG: 4 G. **1968** Pit: 12 G; Rec 6-65 10.8 2 TD; 12 Pt. **1969** NYG: 3 G; Rec 1-2 2.0 1 TD; 6 Pt. **1971** NYG: 14 G; Rec 10-146 14.6 2 TD; 12 Pt. **1972** NYG: 2 G. **Total:** 35 G; Rec 17-213 12.5 5 TD; 30 Pt.

MARTY KOTTLER Kottler, Martin Albert 5'9", 180 **FB-LB**
(Butch) *Col:* Centre *HS:* Carnegie [PA] B: 5/1/1910, Carnegie, PA D: 6/10/1989, Centerbrook, CT
1933 Pit: 3 G; Int **1** TD; 6 Pt.

ED KOVAC Kovac, Edward William 6'0", 195 **HB**
Col: Cincinnati B: 4/22/1938, McKeesport, PA *Drafted:* 1960 Round 6 ChiB
1960 Bal: 12 G; Rush 4-1 0.3; Rec 2-27 13.5; KR 1-8 8.0; 1 Fum. **1962** NYT: 3 G; Rush 3-5 1.7; Rec 1-3 3.0; KR 4-72 18.0; Int 1-21. **Total:** 15 G; Rush 7-6 0.9; Rec 3-30 10.0; KR 5-80 16.0; Int 1-21; 1 Fum.

JIM KOVACH Kovach, James Joseph 6'2", 230 **LB**
Col: Kentucky *HS:* Valley Forge [Parma Heights, OH] B: 5/1/1956, Parma Heights, OH *Drafted:* 1979 Round 4 NO
1979 NO: 16 G; KR 1-10 10.0. **1980** NO: 11 G; Int 1-0. **1981** NO: 15 G; Int 1-13. **1982** NO: 8 G; 2.5 Sac. **1983** NO: 16 G; 3 Sac. **1984** NO: 15 G; Int 1-16; 1 Sac. **1985** NO-SF: 6 G; Int 1-53; 1 Sac. NO: 2 G; Int 1-53; 1 Sac. SF: 4 G. **Total:** 87 G; KR 1-10 10.0; Int 4-82; 7.5 Sac.

BILL KOVACSY Kovacsy, William George 5'10", 195 **G**
Col: Illinois *HS:* Hammond [IN] B: 2/15/1901, Bridgeport, CT D: 5/30/1980, Crown Point, IN
1923 Ham: 4 G.

MIKE KOVALESKI Kovaleski, Michael Aaron 6'2", 225 **LB**
Col: Notre Dame *HS:* New Castle [IN] B: 1/30/1965, Union City, NJ
1987 Cle: 1 G.

JOHN KOVATCH Kovatch, John George Jr. 6'3", 197 **DE-OE**
Col: Notre Dame *HS:* Michael Washington [South Bend, IN] B: 7/21/1920, South Bend, IN *Drafted:* 1942 Round 11 Was
1942 Was: 8 G; Rec 12-90 7.5 1 TD; KR 1-13 13.0; 6 Pt. **1946** Was: 10 G; Rec 6-67 11.2; 1 Fum. **1947** GB: 3 G. **Total:** 21 G; Rec 18-157 8.7 1 TD; KR 1-13 13.0; 6 Pt; 1 Fum.

JOHNNY KOVATCH Kovatch, John Paul 5'11", 172 **E**
Col: Northwestern *HS:* South Bend Central [IN] B: 6/24/1912, South Bend, IN *Drafted:* 1938 Round 5 GB
1938 Cle: 6 G; Rec 8-97 12.1 1 TD; 6 Pt.

WALT KOWALCZYK Kowalczyk, Walter Joseph 6'0", 208 **FB-DB**
(Red) *Col:* Michigan State *HS:* Westfield [MA] B: 4/17/1935, Westfield, MA *Drafted:* 1958 Round 1 Phi
1958 Phi: Int 1-2. **1960** Dal: KR 1-0. **1961** Oak: KR 1-19 19.0. **Total:** KR 2-19 9.5; Int 1-2.

Year Team	G	Rushing Att	Yds	Avg	TD	Receiving Rec	Yds	Avg	TD	Fum	Tot TD
1958 Phi	12	17	43	2.5	1	8	72	9.0	0	2	1
1959 Phi	12	26	37	1.4	0	9	33	3.7	0	0	0
1960 Dal	12	50	156	3.1	1	14	143	10.2	1	2	2
1961 Oak	4	10	28	2.8	0	3	8	2.7	0	0	0
NFL Total	40	103	264	2.6	2	34	256	7.5	1	4	3

BOB KOWALKOWSKI Kowalkowski, Robert 6'3", 240 **OG**
Col: Virginia *HS:* Arnold [PA] B: 11/5/1943, Upper Darby, PA *Drafted:* 1965 Round 7 Det
1966 Det: 14 G. **1967** Det: 14 G. **1968** Det: 14 G. **1969** Det: 2 G. **1970** Det: 10 G. **1971** Det: 14 G. **1972** Det: 14 G. **1973** Det: 14 G. **1974** Det: 14 G. **1975** Det: 14 G. **1976** Det: 14 G. **1977** GB: 4 G. **Total:** 142 G.

SCOTT KOWALKOWSKI Kowalkowski, Scott Thomas 6'2", 228 **LB**
Col: Notre Dame *HS:* St. Mary's Prep [Orchard Lake, MI] B: 8/23/1968, Royal Oak, MI *Drafted:* 1991 Round 8 Phi
1991 Phi: 16 G. **1992** Phi: 16 G. **1994** Det: 16 G. **1995** Det: 16 G. **1996** Det: 16 G. **1997** Det: 16 G. **1998** Det: 15 G. **Total:** 111 G.

ADOLPH KOWALSKI Kowalski, Adolph Ernest 6'3", 205 **BB-DB**
Col: Tulsa *HS:* Central [Bridgeport, CT] B: 1921
AAFC **1947** BknA: 10 G.

ANDY KOWALSKI Kowalski, Anthony Joseph 6'1", 199 **DE-OE**
Col: Mississippi State *HS:* Gloucester City [NJ] B: 6/2/1920, Gloucester City, NJ D: 12/3/1983, Clinton, MS
1943 Bkn: 8 G; Rec 11-145 13.2; Int 1-9. **1944** Bkn: 10 G; Rec 9-155 17.2 1 TD; 6 Pt. **1945** Bos: 3 G. **Total:** 21 G; Rec 20-300 15.0 1 TD; Int 1-9; 6 Pt.

GARY KOWALSKI Kowalski, Gary Stuart 6'6", 280 **OT-OG**
Col: Boston College *HS:* The Morgan School [Clinton, CT] B: 7/2/1960, New Haven, CT *Drafted:* 1983 Round 6 LARm
1983 LARm: 15 G. **1985** SD: 13 G. **1986** SD: 16 G. **1987** SD: 12 G. **1988** SD: 2 G. **Total:** 58 G.

NICK KOWGIOS Kowgios, Nicholas 6'0", 216 **RB**
Col: Lafayette *HS:* Hackley School [Tarrytown, NY] B: 11/19/1962, Yonkers, NY
1987 Det: 3 G; Rush 1-2 2.0; Rec 1-3 3.0.

ERNIE KOY Koy, Ernest Melvin 6'3", 230 **RB-P**
Col: Texas *HS:* Bellville [TX] B: 10/22/1942, Bellville, TX *Drafted:* 1965 Round 11 NYG
1965 NYG: Pass 2-0, 1 Int. **1966** NYG: Pass 2-0. **1967** NYG: Pass 4-3 75.0%, 101 25.25 1 TD. **1968** NYG: Pass 3-2 66.7%, 13 4.33. **1969** NYG: Pass 1-1 100.0%, 15 15.00. **Total:** Pass 12-6 50.0%, 129 10.75 1 TD 1 Int.

Year Team	G	Rushing Att	Yds	Avg	TD	Receiving Rec	Yds	Avg	TD
1965 NYG	13	35	174	5.0	0	4	22	5.5	0
1966 NYG	13	66	146	2.2	0	8	43	5.4	0
1967 NYG	14	146	704	4.8	4	32	212	6.6	1
1968 NYG	13	89	394	4.4	3	12	59	4.9	1
1969 NYG	14	76	300	3.9	2	19	152	8.0	4
1970 NYG	12	2	5	2.5	0	1	10	10.0	0
NFL Total	79	414	1723	4.2	9	76	498	6.6	6

Year Team	Kickoff Returns Ret	Yds	Avg	TD	Punting Punts	Yds	Avg	Fum	Tot TD
1965 NYG	21	401	19.1	0	55	2268	41.2	2	0
1966 NYG	3	20	6.7	0	49	1932	39.4	3	0
1967 NYG	1	18	18.0	0	40	1509	37.7	3	5
1968 NYG	0	0	—	0	44	1649	37.5	1	4
1969 NYG	0	0	—	0	24	856	35.7	1	6
1970 NYG	0	0	—	0	11	369	33.5	0	0
NFL Total	25	439	17.6	0	223	8583	38.5	10	15

TED KOY Koy, James Theodore 6'2", 212 **TE-RB-LB**
Col: Texas *HS:* Bellville [TX] B: 9/15/1947, Bellville, TX *Drafted:* 1970 Round 2 Oak
1970 Oak: 14 G. **1971** Buf: 14 G; Rec 10-133 13.3 1 TD; 6 Pt. **1972** Buf: 14 G; Rush 1-9 9.0; Rec 1-9 9.0; KR 5-63 12.6. **1973** Buf: 13 G. **1974** Buf: 12 G. **Total:** 67 G; Rush 1-9 9.0; Rec 11-142 12.9 1 TD; KR 5-63 12.6; 6 Pt.

SCOTT KOZAK Kozak, Scott Allen 6'3", 226 **LB**
Col: Oregon *HS:* Colton [OR] B: 11/28/1965, Hillsboro, OR *Drafted:* 1989 Round 2 Hou
1989 Hou: 16 G. **1990** Hou: 16 G. **1991** Hou: 16 G; 0.5 Sac. **1992** Hou: 16 G. **1993** Hou: 16 G. **Total:** 80 G; 0.5 Sac.

CHET KOZEL Kozel, Chester Richard 6'2", 211 **G-T**
Col: Mississippi *HS:* Kenosha [WI] B: 10/15/1919, Kenosha, WI D: 6/27/1982, Kenosha, WI
AAFC **1947** BufA: 12 G; KR 1-11 11.0. **1948** BufA-ChiA: 7 G. **Total:** 19 G; KR 1-11 11.0.

BRUCE KOZERSKI Kozerski, Bruce W 6'4", 281 **C-OG-OT**
Col: Holy Cross *HS:* James M. Coughlin [Wilkes-Barre, PA] B: 4/2/1962, Plains, PA *Drafted:* 1984 Round 9 Cin
1984 Cin: 16 G. **1985** Cin: 14 G. **1986** Cin: 16 G. **1987** Cin: 8 G. **1988** Cin: 16 G. **1989** Cin: 15 G. **1990** Cin: 16 G. **1991** Cin: 16 G. **1992** Cin: 16 G. **1993** Cin: 15 G; 3 Fum. **1994** Cin: 16 G. **1995** Cin: 8 G. **Total:** 172 G; 3 Fum.

MIKE KOZIAK Koziak, Michael 5'9", 185 **G**
Col: No College B: 1892 Deceased
1925 Dul: 1 G.

BRIAN KOZLOWSKI Kozlowski, Brian Scott 6'3", 255 **TE**
Col: Connecticut *HS:* Webster [NY] B: 10/4/1970, Rochester, NY
1994 NYG: 16 G; Rec 1-5 5.0; KR 2-21 10.5. **1995** NYG: 16 G; Rec 2-17 8.5; KR 5-75 15.0; 1 Fum. **1996** NYG: 5 G; Rec 1-4 4.0 1 TD; KR 1-16 16.0; 6 Pt. **1997** Atl: 16 G; Rec 7-99 14.1 1 TD; KR 2-49 24.5; 6 Pt.

1998 Atl: 16 G; Rec 10-103 10.3 1 TD; KR 1-12 12.0; 6 Pt. **Total:** 69 G; Rec 21-228 10.9 3 TD; KR 11-173 15.7; 18 Pt; 1 Fum.

GLEN KOZLOWSKI Kozlowski, Glen Allen 6'1", 200 **WR**
Col: Brigham Young *HS:* Carlsbad [CA] B: 12/31/1962, Honolulu, HI
Drafted: 1986 Round 11 ChiB
1987 ChiB: KR 3-72 24.0. **1988** ChiB: Rush 1-3 3.0; PR 1-0; KR 2-37 18.5. **1989** ChiB: PR 4-(-2) -0.5; KR 1-12 12.0. **Total:** Rush 1-3 3.0; PR 5-(-2) -0.4; KR 6-121 20.2.

		Receiving				
Year Team	**G**	**Rec**	**Yds**	**Avg**	**TD**	**Fum**
1987 ChiB	3	15	199	13.3	3	0
1988 ChiB	16	3	92	30.7	0	1
1989 ChiB	15	3	74	24.7	0	1
1990 ChiB	12	7	83	11.9	0	0
1991 ChiB	16	2	16	8.0	0	0
1992 ChiB	4	1	7	7.0	0	0
NFL Total	66	31	471	15.2	3	2

MIKE KOZLOWSKI Kozlowski, Michael John 6'0", 196 **DB**
Col: Mira Costa Coll. CA (J.C.); San Diego State; Brigham Young; Colorado *HS:* San Dieguito [Encinitas, CA] B: 2/24/1956, Newark, NJ
Drafted: 1979 Round 10 Mia
1979 Mia: 16 G; PR 3-21 7.0; KR 4-85 21.3. **1981** Mia: 14 G; PR 1-9 9.0; KR 1-40 40.0; Int 3-37; 1 Fum TD; 6 Pt. **1982** Mia: 9 G; KR 1-10 10.0; Int 1-36; 1 Sac. **1983** Mia: 16 G; PR 2-12 6.0; KR 4-50 12.5; Int 2-73 **2** TD; 12 Pt; 2 Fum; 1 Sac. **1984** Mia: 16 G; PR 4-41 10.3; KR 2-23 11.5; Int 1-26. **1985** Mia: 5 G; PR 7-65 9.3; KR 0-32. **1986** Mia: 15 G; Int 1-0. **Total:** 91 G; PR 17-148 8.7; KR 12-240 20.0; Int 8-172 2 TD; 1 Fum TD; Tot TD 3; 18 Pt; 2 Fum; 2 Sac.

STAN KOZLOWSKI Kozlowski, Stanley J 6'1", 200 **FB**
Col: Holy Cross *HS:* St. Raphael Acad. [East Providence, RI]
B: 2/5/1924, Rumford, RI D: 8/23/1972, Boxboro, MA
AAFC **1946** MiaA: 5 G; Rush 18-61 3.4; Rec 2-27 13.5; PR 1-4 4.0; KR 3-72 24.0.

JOE KOZLOWSKY Kozlowsky, Joseph Alexander 5'10", 199 **T-G-E**
Col: Boston College *HS:* Cambridge Latin [MA] B: 8/9/1901, Cambridge, MA D: 12/22/1970, Boston, MA
1925 Prov: 11 G. **1926** Prov: 10 G. **1927** Prov: 12 G. **1929** Bost: 8 G. **1930** Prov: 8 G. **Total:** 49 G.

DAVE KRAAYEVELD Kraayeveld, David Ray 6'5", 255 **DE-DT**
Col: Wis.-Whitewater; Milton *HS:* Delavan-Darien [Delavan, WI]
B: 10/26/1955, Elkhorn, WI
1978 Sea: 12 G.

GEORGE KRACUM Kracum, George Vince 6'1", 212 **FB-DB**
Col: Pittsburgh *HS:* Hazleton [PA] B: 1/24/1918, Tresckow, PA
D: 6/7/1981, Minneapolis, MN *Drafted:* 1941 Round 8 ChiC
1941 Bkn: Rec 2-17 8.5; KR 1-20 20.0; Int 1-27.

		Rushing			
Year Team	**G**	**Att**	**Yds**	**Avg**	**TD**
1941 Bkn	11	52	169	3.3	3

OLLIE KRAEHE Kraehe, Oliver Robert 5'10", 180 **G-C-OE**
Col: Washington-St. Louis *HS:* Cleveland Acad. [St. Louis, MO]
B: 8/22/1898, St.Louis, MO D: 11/2/1969, St. Louis, MO
1922 RI: 3 G. **1923** StL: 7 G. **Total:** 10 G.

ELDRED KRAEMER Kraemer, Eldred John 6'2", 225 **OG**
Col: Pittsburgh *HS:* Clear Lake [MN] B: 10/2/1929, St. Cloud, MN
D: 9/16/1992, Pittsburgh, PA *Drafted:* 1955 Round 5 SF
1955 SF: 12 G.

REN KRAFT Kraft, Reynold Rudolph 5'11", 170 **E**
(Dolly) *Col:* Illinois *HS:* Oak Park [IL] B: 3/29/1895, Menomonie, WI
D: 11/7/1951, Chicago, IL
1922 Min: 2 G.

RUDY KRAFT Kraft, Rudolph George 5'10", 190 **G-C**
Col: Penn State *HS:* Wilkes-Barre [PA] B: 10/21/1896, Wilkes-Barre, PA D: 11/20/1978, Buffalo, NY
1921 Ton: 1 G.

GREG KRAGEN Kragen, Greg John 6'3", 263 **NT-DT**
Col: Utah State *HS:* Amador Valley [Pleasanton, CA] B: 3/4/1962, Chicago, IL
1985 Den: 16 G; 2 Sac. **1986** Den: 16 G. **1987** Den: 12 G; 2 Sac. **1988** Den: 16 G; 2.5 Sac. **1989** Den: 14 G; 1 Fum TD; 6 Pt; 2 Sac. **1990** Den: 16 G; 2 Sac. **1991** Den: 16 G; 3.5 Sac. **1992** Den: 16 G; 5.5 Sac. **1993** Den: 14 G; 3 Sac. **1994** KC: 16 G. **1995** Car: 16 G; Int 1-29; **1** Fum TD; 6 Pt; 1 Sac. **1996** Car: 16 G; 3 Sac. **1997** Car: 16 G; 2 Sac. **Total:** 200 G; Int 1-29; 2 Fum TD; 12 Pt; 28.5 Sac.

JIM KRAHL Krahl, James Kenneth 6'5", 252 **DT**
Col: Texas Tech *HS:* Westbury [Houston, TX] B: 11/19/1953, Houston, TX *Drafted:* 1978 Round 5 NYG
1978 NYG: 16 G. **1979** Bal: 1 G. **1980** Bal-SF: 4 G. Bal: 2 G. SF: 2 G. **Total:** 21 G.

MERV KRAKAU Krakau, Mervin Floyd 6'2", 242 **LB**
Col: Iowa State *HS:* Guthrie Center [IA] B: 5/16/1951, Jefferson, IA
Drafted: 1973 Round 14 Buf
1973 Buf: 14 G. **1974** Buf: 11 G; Int 1-37. **1975** Buf: 14 G; Int 1-2. **1976** Buf: 14 G; Int 1-0. **1977** Buf: 13 G. **1978** Buf-NE: 6 G. Buf: 5 G. NE: 1 G. **Total:** 72 G; Int 3-39.

JOE KRAKER Kraker, Joseph 6'1", 190 **G**
Col: Saskatchewan (Canada) *HS:* Roosevelt [Virginia, MN] B: 1895 Deceased
1924 RI: 5 G.

JOE KRAKOSKI Krakoski, Joseph Andrew Jr. 6'2", 195 **DB**
Col: Illinois *HS:* Westville [IL] B: 12/18/1937, Danville, IL
Drafted: 1961 Round 6 Was
1961 Was: 11 G; Int 4-13. **1963** Oak: 14 G; PR 4-10 2.5; Int 4-39. **1964** Oak: 14 G; PR 1-8 8.0. **1965** Oak: 12 G; PR 2-5 2.5; 1 Fum. **1966** Oak: 11 G; PR 2-19 9.5; 1 Fum. **Total:** 62 G; PR 9-42 4.7; Int 8-52; 2 Fum.

JOE KRAKOSKI Krakoski, Joseph Joshua 6'1", 224 **LB**
Col: Washington *HS:* Mission San Jose [Fremont, NE] B: 11/11/1962, Aurora, IL *Drafted:* 1985 Round 6 Hou
1986 Was: 8 G; KR 1-8 8.0.

GERRY KRALL Krall, Gerald Stanley 5'10", 185 **HB-DB**
Col: Ohio State *HS:* Edward D. Libbey [Toledo, OH] B: 4/19/1927, Toledo, OH *Drafted:* 1949 Round 6 ChiB
1950 Det: 7 G; Rush 3-0; Rec 2-61 30.5; PR 1-9 9.0; 1 Fum.

FRITZ KRAMER Kramer, Fred F 6'0", 191 **G-BB**
Col: Washington State *HS:* Pendleton [OR] B: 5/27/1903
D: 1/20/1992, Orange, CA
1927 NYY: 10 G.

GEORGE KRAMER Kramer, George Lambert 6'2", 240 **G-T**
Col: No College B: 6/2/1895, Joliet, IL D: 9/1974, Chicago, IL
1921 Min: 3 G. **1922** Min: 3 G. **1923** Min: 7 G. **1924** Min: 6 G. **Total:** 19 G.

JERRY KRAMER Kramer, Gerald Louis 6'3", 245 **OG**
Col: Idaho *HS:* Sandpoint [ID] B: 1/23/1936, Jordan, MT
Drafted: 1958 Round 4 GB
1958 GB: KR 1-0. **1963** GB: KR 1-0. **Total:** KR 2-0.

		Scoring						
Year Team	**G**	**Pts**	**FG**	**FGA**	**FG%**	**XK**	**XKA**	**XK%**
1958 GB	12	0	0	0	—	0	0	—
1959 GB	12	0	0	0	—	0	0	—
1960 GB	12	0	0	0	—	0	0	—
1961 GB	8	0	0	0	—	0	0	—
1962 GB	14	65	9	11	81.8	38	39	97.4
1963 GB	14	91	16	34	47.1	43	46	93.5
1964 GB	2	0	0	0	—	0	0	—
1965 GB	14	0	0	0	—	0	0	—
1966 GB	14	0	0	0	—	0	0	—
1967 GB	14	0	0	0	—	0	0	—
1968 GB	14	21	4	9	44.4	9	10	90.0
NFL Total	130	177	29	54	53.7	90	95	94.7

JACK KRAMER Kramer, John Francis 6'0", 220 **T**
Col: Marquette *HS:* Solomon Juneau [Milwaukee, WI] B: 7/26/1919, Milwaukee, WI D: 12/15/1978, Milwaukee, WI
AAFC **1946** BufA: 13 G.

KENT KRAMER Kramer, Kent Devlin 6'4", 235 **TE**
Col: Minnesota *HS:* Temple City [CA] B: 7/21/1944, Los Angeles, CA
Drafted: 1966 Round 9 SF
1971 Phi: KR 1-0. **1974** Phi: KR 2-39 19.5. **Total:** KR 3-39 13.0.

		Receiving				
Year Team	**G**	**Rec**	**Yds**	**Avg**	**TD**	**Fum**
1966 SF	14	5	81	16.2	3	0
1967 NO	10	20	207	10.4	2	0
1969 Min	13	2	37	18.5	1	0
1970 Min	11	1	10	10.0	0	0
1971 Phi	10	6	65	10.8	1	0
1972 Phi	14	11	176	16.0	1	1
1973 Phi	11	0	0	—	0	0
1974 Phi	14	0	0	—	0	0
NFL Total	97	45	576	12.8	8	1

KYLE KRAMER Kramer, Kyle Mevoy 6'3", 190 **DB**
Col: Bowling Green State *HS:* Fairmont [Kettering, OH] B: 1/12/1967, Kansas City, MO *Drafted:* 1989 Round 5 Cle
1989 Cle: 14 G; Int 1-12.

RON KRAMER Kramer, Ronald John 6'3", 234 **OE-TE**
Col: Michigan *HS:* East Detroit [Eastpointe, MI] B: 6/24/1935, Girard, KS *Drafted:* 1957 Round 1 GB
1957 GB: Pass 1-0, 1 Int. **1961** GB: Rush 5-13 2.6. **1962** GB: Rush 1-(-4) -4.0. **Total:** Pass 1-0, 1 Int; Rush 6-9 1.5.

Year Team	G	Receiving Rec	Yds	Avg	TD	Fum
1957 GB	11	28	337	12.0	0	1
1959 GB	12	0	0	—	0	0
1960 GB	12	4	55	13.8	0	0
1961 GB	14	35	559	16.0	4	0
1962 GB	14	37	555	15.0	7	0
1963 GB	12	32	537	16.8	4	1
1964 GB	14	34	551	16.2	0	1
1965 Det	14	18	206	11.4	1	0
1966 Det	14	37	432	11.7	0	0
1967 Det	11	4	40	10.0	0	0
NFL Total	128	229	3272	14.3	16	3

TOMMY KRAMER Kramer, Thomas Francis 6'2", 200 **QB**
Col: Rice *HS:* Robert E. Lee [San Antonio, TX] B: 3/7/1955, San Antonio, TX *Drafted:* 1977 Round 1 Min
1979 Min: Rec 0-3. **1984** Min: Rec 1-20 20.0 1 TD. **Total:** Rec 1-23 23.0 1 TD.

Year Team	G	Passing Att	Comp	Comp%	Yds	YPA	TD	Int	Rating
1977 Min	6	57	30	52.6	425	7.46	5	4	77.0
1978 Min	4	16	5	31.3	50	3.13	0	1	15.1
1979 Min	16	566	315	55.7	3397	6.00	23	24	69.3
1980 Min	15	522	299	57.3	3582	6.86	19	23	72.2
1981 Min	14	593	322	54.3	3912	6.60	26	24	72.6
1982 Min	9	308	176	57.1	2037	6.61	15	12	77.3
1983 Min	3	82	55	67.1	550	6.71	3	4	77.8
1984 Min	9	236	124	52.5	1678	7.11	9	10	70.6
1985 Min	15	506	277	54.7	3522	6.96	19	26	67.8
1986 Min	13	372	208	55.9	3000	8.06	24	10	**92.6**
1987 Min	6	81	40	49.4	452	5.58	4	3	67.5
1988 Min	10	173	83	48.0	1264	7.31	5	9	60.5
1989 Min	8	136	77	56.6	906	6.66	7	7	72.7
1990 NO	1	3	1	33.3	2	0.67	0	1	2.8
NFL Total	129	3651	2012	55.1	24777	6.79	159	158	72.8

Year Team	Rushing Att	Yds	Avg	TD	Fum	Tot TD
1977 Min	10	3	0.3	0	3	0
1978 Min	1	10	10.0	0	0	0
1979 Min	32	138	4.3	1	9	1
1980 Min	31	115	3.7	1	2	1
1981 Min	10	13	1.3	0	8	0
1982 Min	21	77	3.7	3	3	3
1983 Min	8	3	0.4	0	2	0
1984 Min	15	9	0.6	0	10	1
1985 Min	27	54	2.0	0	9	0
1986 Min	23	48	2.1	1	7	1
1987 Min	10	44	4.4	2	2	2
1988 Min	14	8	0.6	0	3	0
1989 Min	12	9	0.8	0	1	0
NFL Total	214	531	2.5	8	59	9

ERIK KRAMER Kramer, William Erik 6'1", 200 **QB**
Col: Pierce Coll. CA (J.C.); North Carolina State *HS:* Canoga Park [CA] B: 11/6/1964, Encino, CA

Year Team	G	Passing Att	Comp	Comp%	Yds	YPA	TD	Int	Rating
1987 Atl	3	92	45	48.9	559	6.08	4	5	60.0
1991 Det	13	265	136	51.3	1635	6.17	11	8	71.8
1992 Det	7	106	58	54.7	771	7.27	4	8	59.1
1993 Det	5	138	87	63.0	1002	7.26	8	3	95.1
1994 ChiB	6	158	99	62.7	1129	7.15	8	8	79.9
1995 ChiB	16	522	315	60.3	3838	7.35	29	10	93.5
1996 ChiB	4	150	73	48.7	781	5.21	3	6	54.3
1997 ChiB	15	477	275	57.7	3011	6.31	14	14	74.0
1998 ChiB	8	250	151	60.4	1823	7.29	9	7	83.1
NFL Total	77	2158	1239	57.4	14549	6.74	90	69	78.6

Year Team	Rushing Att	Yds	Avg	TD	Fum
1987 Atl	2	10	5.0	0	0
1991 Det	35	26	0.7	1	8
1992 Det	12	34	2.8	0	4
1993 Det	10	5	0.5	0	1
1994 ChiB	6	-2	-0.3	0	3
1995 ChiB	35	39	1.1	1	6
1996 ChiB	8	4	0.5	0	1
1997 ChiB	27	83	3.1	2	11
1998 ChiB	13	17	1.3	1	3
NFL Total	148	216	1.5	5	37

KEN KRANZ Kranz, Kenneth Andrew 5'10", 190 **DB**
Col: Wis.-Milwaukee *HS:* Custer [Milwaukee, WI] B: 9/12/1923, Milwaukee, WI *Drafted:* 1949 Round 21 GB
1949 GB: 7 G.

BOB KRATCH Kratch, Robert Anthony 6'3", 288 **OG-OT**
Col: Iowa *HS:* Mahwah [NJ] B: 1/6/1966, Brooklyn, NY *Drafted:* 1989 Round 3 NYG
1989 NYG: 4 G. **1990** NYG: 14 G. **1991** NYG: 15 G. **1992** NYG: 16 G. **1993** NYG: 16 G. **1994** NE: 16 G. **1995** NE: 16 G. **1996** NE: 8 G. **Total:** 105 G.

DAN KRATZER Kratzer, Daniel Leon 6'3", 192 **WR**
Col: Northern Arizona; Missouri Valley *HS:* Lathrop [MO] B: 7/7/1949, Kearney, MO *Drafted:* 1972 Round 8 Cin
1973 KC: 1 G.

BABE KRAUS Kraus, Francis Lucius 6'2", 220 **T-G**
Col: Colgate; Hobart B: 9/2/1899 D: 9/5/1966, Geneva, NY
1924 Buf: 7 G.

HENRY KRAUSE Krause, Henry J Jr. 6'1", 212 **C-LB-G**
Col: St. Louis *HS:* Roosevelt [St. Louis, MO] B: 8/28/1913, St.Louis, MO D: 2/20/1987, Beltsville, MD
1936 Bkn: 12 G. **1937** Bkn-Was: 8 G. Bkn: 5 G. Was: 3 G. **1938** Was: 9 G. **Total:** 29 G.

LARRY KRAUSE Krause, Lawrence James 6'0", 208 **RB**
Col: St. Norbert *HS:* Greenwood [WI] B: 4/22/1948, Stanley, WI *Drafted:* 1970 Round 17 GB
1970 GB: Rush 2-13 6.5; Rec 2-22 11.0. **1971** GB: Rush 3-(-6) -2.0. **1973** GB: Rush 1-8 8.0. **Total:** Rush 6-15 2.5; Rec 2-22 11.0.

Year Team	G	Kickoff Returns Ret	Yds	Avg	TD	Fum
1970 GB	14	18	513	28.5	1	2
1971 GB	9	5	101	20.2	0	0
1973 GB	14	11	244	22.2	0	1
1974 GB	14	1	6	6.0	0	0
NFL Total	51	35	864	24.7	1	3

MAX KRAUSE Krause, Max Joseph 5'10", 202 **BB-DB-LB-FB**
(Bananas) *Col:* Gonzaga *HS:* Gonzaga Prep [Spokane, WA] B: 4/5/1909, Spokane, WA D: 7/11/1984, Spokane, WA
1933 NYG: Rec 2-28 14.0 1 TD; Scor 7, 1 XK. **1934** NYG: Rec 1-4 4.0. **1935** NYG: Rec 1-5 5.0. **1936** NYG: Rec 5-47 9.4 1 TD. **1937** Was: Rec 2-13 6.5. **1938** Was: Rec 2-62 31.0 1 TD. **Total:** Rec 13-159 12.2 3 TD.

Year Team	G	Rushing Att	Yds	Avg	TD	Tot TD
1933 NYG	5	16	61	3.8	0	1
1934 NYG	12	26	89	3.4	0	0
1935 NYG	6	32	121	3.8	0	0
1936 NYG	9	11	37	3.4	0	1
1937 Was	8	21	47	2.2	1	1
1938 Was	6	25	214	8.6	2	3
1939 Was	2	3	23	7.7	0	0
1940 Was	9	4	21	5.3	0	0
NFL Total	57	138	613	4.4	3	6

PAUL KRAUSE Krause, Paul James 6'3", 200 **DB-WR**
Col: Iowa *HS:* Bendle [Burton, MI] B: 2/19/1942, Flint, MI *Drafted:* 1964 Round 2 Was *HOF:* 1998
1965 Was: Rec 2-17 8.5; **1** Fum TD. **1972** Min: Pass 1-0; Rush 1-0; **1** Fum TD. **1975** Min: **1** Fum TD. **1977** Min: Pass 1-1 100.0%, 11 11.00 1 TD. **Total:** Pass 2-1 50.0%, 11 5.50 1 TD; Rush 1-0; Rec 2-17 8.5; 3 Fum TD.

Year Team	G	Interceptions Int	Yds	TD	Fum	Tot TD
1964 Was	14	**12**	140	1	0	1
1965 Was	14	6	118	0	1	1
1966 Was	13	2	0	0	0	0
1967 Was	13	8	75	0	0	0
1968 Min	14	7	82	0	0	0
1969 Min	14	5	82	1	0	1
1970 Min	14	6	90	0	1	0
1971 Min	14	6	112	0	0	0
1972 Min	14	6	109	1	1	2
1973 Min	14	4	28	0	0	0
1974 Min	14	2	53	0	0	0
1975 Min	14	10	**201**	0	0	1
1976 Min	14	2	21	0	0	0
1977 Min	14	2	25	0	0	0
1978 Min	16	0	0	0	0	0
1979 Min	16	3	49	0	0	0
NFL Total	226	**81**	1185	3	3	6

BILL KRAUSE Krause, William Edward 6'0", 210 **T**
Col: Baldwin-Wallace *HS:* Aurora [OH] B: 7/9/1914 D: 7/1971 *Drafted:* 1938 Round 9 Pit
1938 Cle: 2 G.

BARRY KRAUSS Krauss, Richard Barry 6′3″, 245 **LB**
Col: Alabama *HS:* Pompano Beach [FL] B: 3/17/1957, Pompano Beach, FL *Drafted:* 1979 Round 1 Bal
1979 Bal: 15 G. **1980** Bal: 16 G. **1981** Bal: 16 G; Int 1-10. **1982** Bal: 9 G; Rec 1-5 5.0 1 TD; 6 Pt; 2 Sac. **1983** Bal: 16 G; Rush 1-(-1) -1.0; 1 Sac. **1984** Ind: 16 G; Int 3-20; 1 Fum; 1 Sac. **1985** Ind: 16 G; Int 1-0; 1 Sac. **1986** Ind: 4 G. **1987** Ind: 12 G; 2 Sac. **1988** Ind: 16 G; Int 1-3. **1989** Mia: 16 G; 1 Sac. **Total:** 152 G; Rush 1-(-1) -1.0; Rec 1-5 5.0 1 TD; Int 6-33; 6 Pt; 1 Fum; 8 Sac.

RICH KRAYNAK Kraynak, Richard Bernard 6′1″, 227 **LB**
Col: Pittsburgh *HS:* Phoenixville [PA] B: 1/20/1961, Phoenixville, PA *Drafted:* 1983 Round 8 Phi
1983 Phi: 16 G. **1984** Phi: 14 G; 6 Pt. **1985** Phi: 16 G; Int 1-26. **1986** Phi: 6 G. **1987** Atl: 9 G. **Total:** 61 G; Int 1-26; 6 Pt.

JOHN KREAMCHECK Kreamcheck, John Joseph 6′5″, 255 **DT**
(Big John) *Col:* William & Mary *HS:* Centerville [PA] B: 1/7/1926, Vestaburg, PA *Drafted:* 1953 Round 8 ChiB
1953 ChiB: 12 G. **1954** ChiB: 12 G. **1955** ChiB: 12 G. **Total:** 36 G.

STEVE KREIDER Kreider, Steven Kenneth 6′3″, 192 **WR**
Col: Lehigh *HS:* Schuylkill Valley [Leesport, PA] B: 5/12/1958, Reading, PA *Drafted:* 1979 Round 6 Cin
1979 Cin: Rush 2-0. **1980** Cin: Pass 1-0; KR 1-19 19.0. **1981** Cin: Pass 3-1 33.3%, 13 4.33; Rush 1-21 21.0. **1982** Cin: Scor **1** 1XP. **1983** Cin: Pass 1-0; Rush 1-2 2.0. **1985** Cin: Pass 1-1 100.0%, 1 1.00; Scor **1** 1XP. **1986** Cin: Pass 1-0, 1 Int. **Total:** Pass 7-2 28.6%, 14 2.00 1 Int; Rush 4-23 5.8; KR 1-19 19.0; Scor 2 1XP.

		Receiving				
Year Team	**G**	**Rec**	**Yds**	**Avg**	**TD**	**Fum**
1979 Cin	15	3	20	6.7	0	1
1980 Cin	16	17	272	16.0	0	1
1981 Cin	16	37	520	14.1	5	2
1982 Cin	9	16	230	14.4	1	0
1983 Cin	16	42	554	13.2	1	0
1984 Cin	16	20	243	12.2	1	1
1985 Cin	16	10	184	18.4	1	0
1986 Cin	10	5	96	19.2	0	0
NFL Total	114	150	2119	14.1	9	5

WALT KREINHEDER Kreinheder, Walter Roswell 6′2″, 208 **C-G-BB**
Col: Michigan *HS:* East Tech [Cleveland, OH] B: 9/8/1901, Buffalo, NY D: 10/12/1960, Boerne, TX
1922 Akr: 5 G; Scor 4, 1 FG, 1 XK. **1923** StL: 6 G. **1925** Cle: 5 G. **Total:** 16 G; Scor 4, 1 FG, 1 XK.

RICH KREITLING Kreitling, Richard Allen 6′2″, 208 **OE**
Col: Auburn; Illinois *HS:* Fenger [Chicago, IL] B: 3/13/1936, Chicago, IL *Drafted:* 1959 Round 1 Cle
1960 Cle: Rush 2-(-17) -8.5. **1961** Cle: Rush 0-4. **Total:** Rush 2-(-13) -6.5.

		Receiving				
Year Team	**G**	**Rec**	**Yds**	**Avg**	**TD**	**Fum**
1959 Cle	12	0	0	—	0	0
1960 Cle	12	16	316	19.8	3	0
1961 Cle	13	21	229	10.9	3	2
1962 Cle	14	44	659	15.0	3	0
1963 Cle	14	22	386	17.5	6	0
1964 ChiB	14	20	185	9.3	2	0
NFL Total	79	123	1775	14.4	17	2

JOE KREJCI Krejci, Joe Albert 6′0″, 190 **OE-DE**
Col: Peru State *HS:* Plattsmouth [NE] B: 3/16/1906, Plattsmouth, NE D: 8/10/1992, Fort Myers, FL
1934 ChiC: 1 G.

KEN KREMER Kremer, James Kendall 6′4″, 250 **NT-DE**
Col: Ball State *HS:* Thornton Fractional South [Lansing, IL] B: 7/16/1957, Hammond, IN *Drafted:* 1979 Round 7 KC
1979 KC: 16 G. **1980** KC: 14 G. **1981** KC: 16 G. **1982** KC: 9 G; 1 Sac. **1983** KC: 16 G; 2 Sac. **1984** KC: 16 G; Int 1-1; 2.5 Sac. **Total:** 87 G; Int 1-1; 5.5 Sac.

KARL KREMSER Kremser, Karl Friedrich 6′0″, 175 **K**
Col: Army; Tennessee *HS:* Woodrow Wilson [Levittown, PA] B: 8/3/1945, Salzwedel, Germany *Drafted:* 1969 Round 5 Mia
1969 Mia: 14 G; Scor 65, 13-22 59.1% FG, 26-27 96.3% XK. **1970** Mia: 1 G; Scor 2, 0-1 FG, 2-2 100.0% XK. **Total:** 15 G; Scor 67, 13-23 56.5% FG, 28-29 96.6% XK.

MITCH KRENK Krenk, Mitchell James 6′2″, 225 **TE**
Col: Nebraska *HS:* Nebraska City [NE] B: 11/19/1959, Crete, NE
1984 ChiB: 8 G; Rec 2-31 15.5.

TY KRENTLER Krentler, Walter L 160 **FB-TB**
Col: Western Michigan; Detroit Mercy *HS:* East Detroit [Eastpointe, MI] B: 4/21/1896, Detroit, MI D: 11/30/1971, St. Clair Shores, MI
1920 Det: 5 G.

KEITH KREPFLE Krepfle, Keith Robert 6′3″, 227 **TE**
Col: Iowa State *HS:* Potosi [WI] B: 2/4/1952, Dubuque, IA *Drafted:* 1974 Round 5 Phi
1980 Phi: Rush 1-2 2.0. **Total:** Rush 1-2 2.0.

		Receiving				
Year Team	**G**	**Rec**	**Yds**	**Avg**	**TD**	**Fum**
1975 Phi	14	1	16	16.0	0	0
1976 Phi	10	6	80	13.3	1	1
1977 Phi	14	27	530	19.6	3	1
1978 Phi	10	26	374	14.4	3	1
1979 Phi	16	41	760	18.5	3	1
1980 Phi	13	30	450	15.0	4	0
1981 Phi	16	20	210	10.5	5	0
1982 Atl	4	1	5	5.0	0	0
NFL Total	97	152	2425	16.0	19	4

MARK KREROWICZ Krerowicz, Mark Thomas 6′3″, 285 **OG**
Col: Ohio State *HS:* St. John's [Toledo, OH] B: 3/1/1963, Toledo, OH *Drafted:* 1985 Round 6 Cle
1987 Cle: 3 G.

JOE KRESKY Kresky, Joseph Lawrence 6′0″, 215 **G-T**
(Mink) *Col:* Wisconsin *HS:* Marinette [WI] B: 4/27/1906, Marinette, WI D: 12/24/1988, Naples, FL
1932 Bos: 8 G. **1933** Phi: 9 G. **1934** Phi: 10 G. **1935** Pit-Phi: 10 G. Pit: 1 G. Phi: 9 G. **Total:** 37 G.

ERIC KRESSER Kresser, Eric Joel 6′2″, 209 **QB**
Col: Marshall *HS:* Palm Beach Gardens [FL] B: 2/6/1973, Cincinnati, OH
1998 Cin: 2 G; Pass 21-10 47.6%, 164 7.81 1 TD 2 Int; Rush 1-(-1) -1.0.

OLIN KREUTZ Kreutz, Olin George 6′2″, 300 **C**
Col: Washington *HS:* St. Louis [Honolulu, HI] B: 6/9/1977, Honolulu, HI *Drafted:* 1998 Round 3 ChiB
1998 ChiB: 9 G.

AL KREVIS Krevis, Albert Raymond 6′5″, 263 **OT**
Col: Boston College *HS:* Morris Catholic [Denville, NJ] B: 7/9/1952, Providence, RI *Drafted:* 1975 Round 2 Cin
1975 Cin: 3 G. **1976** NYJ: 10 G. **Total:** 13 G.

DAVE KRIEG Krieg, David Michael 6′1″, 193 **QB**
Col: Milton *HS:* D.C. Everest [Schofield, WI] B: 10/20/1958, Iola, WI
1983 Sea: Rec 1-11 11.0. **1990** Sea: Rec 1-(-6) -6.0. **1996** ChiB: Rec 1-5 5.0. **Total:** Rec 3-10 3.3.

		Passing							
Year Team	**G**	**Att**	**Comp**	**Comp%**	**Yds**	**YPA**	**TD**	**Int**	**Rating**
1980 Sea	1	2	0	0.0	0	0.00	0	0	39.6
1981 Sea	7	112	64	57.1	843	7.53	7	5	83.3
1982 Sea	3	78	49	62.8	501	6.42	2	2	79.1
1983 Sea	9	243	147	60.5	2139	8.80	18	11	95.0
1984 Sea	16	480	276	57.5	3671	7.65	32	24	83.3
1985 Sea	16	532	285	53.6	3602	6.77	27	20	76.2
1986 Sea	15	375	225	60.0	2921	7.79	21	11	91.0
1987 Sea	12	294	178	60.5	2131	7.25	23	15	87.6
1988 Sea	9	228	134	58.8	1741	7.64	18	8	94.6
1989 Sea	15	499	286	57.3	3309	6.63	21	20	74.8
1990 Sea	16	448	265	59.2	3194	7.13	15	20	73.6
1991 Sea	10	285	187	**65.6**	2080	7.30	11	12	82.5
1992 KC	16	413	230	55.7	3115	7.54	15	12	79.9
1993 KC	12	189	105	55.6	1238	6.55	7	3	81.4
1994 Det	14	212	131	61.8	1629	7.68	14	3	101.7
1995 Ariz	16	521	304	58.3	3554	6.82	16	21	72.6
1996 ChiB	13	377	226	59.9	2278	6.04	14	12	76.3
1997 Ten	8	2	1	50.0	2	1.00	0	0	56.3
1998 Ten	5	21	12	57.1	199	9.48	0	0	89.2
NFL Total	213	5311	3105	58.5	38147	7.18	261	199	81.5

	Rushing				
Year Team	**Att**	**Yds**	**Avg**	**TD**	**Fum**
1981 Sea	11	56	5.1	1	4
1982 Sea	6	-3	-0.5	0	5
1983 Sea	16	55	3.4	2	10
1984 Sea	46	186	4.0	3	11
1985 Sea	35	121	3.5	1	11
1986 Sea	35	122	3.5	1	10
1987 Sea	36	155	4.3	2	11
1988 Sea	24	64	2.7	0	6
1989 Sea	40	160	4.0	0	**18**
1990 Sea	32	115	3.6	0	16
1991 Sea	13	59	4.5	0	6
1992 KC	37	74	2.0	2	10
1993 KC	21	24	1.1	0	6
1994 Det	23	35	1.5	0	4
1995 Ariz	19	29	1.5	0	**16**
1996 ChiB	16	12	0.8	1	6
1997 Ten	4	-2	-0.5	0	0

1998 Ten	3	-1	-0.3	0	3
NFL Total	417	1261	3.0	13	153

JIM KRIEG Krieg, James Leo 5′9″, 172 **WR**
Col: Taft Coll. CA (J.C.); Washington *HS:* Kenmore East [Tonawanda, NY] B: 5/29/1949, Buffalo, NY *Drafted:* 1972 Round 5 Den
1972 Den: 6 G; Rush 1-63 63.0; Rec 4-99 24.8; PR 1-3 3.0; KR 1-18 18.0.

EARL KRIEGER Krieger, Earl C 5′11″, 185 **HB**
(Irish) *Col:* Ohio U. *HS:* North [Columbus, OH] B: 8/31/1896, Columbus, OH D: 11/10/1960, Bexley, OH
1921 Det: 5 G. **1922** Col: 4 G. **Total:** 9 G.

BOB KRIEGER Krieger, Robert Emery 6′1″, 190 **OE**
Col: Dartmouth *HS:* West [Minneapolis, MN] B: 5/2/1920, Minneapolis, MN D: 10/17/1980, Minneapolis, MN
1941 Phi: 11 G; Rec 19-240 12.6 2 TD; 12 Pt. **1946** Phi: 7 G; Rec 2-47 23.5. **Total:** 18 G; Rec 21-287 13.7 2 TD; 12 Pt.

EMMETT KRIEL Kriel, Emmett Karl 6′2″, 200 **G**
(Sally) *Col:* Baylor *HS:* Taylor [TX] B: 5/12/1916, Coupland, TX D: 11/26/1984, Houston, TX *Drafted:* 1938 Round 8 Phi
1939 Phi: 1 G.

DOUG KRIEWALD Kriewald, Douglas Clark 6′4″, 245 **OG**
Col: West Texas A&M *HS:* William B. Travis [Austin, TX] B: 8/30/1945, Seguin, TX *Drafted:* 1967 Round 6 ChiB
1967 ChiB: 2 G; KR 1-0. **1968** ChiB: 13 G. **Total:** 15 G; KR 1-0.

JOHN KRIMM Krimm, John Joseph Jr. 6′2″, 190 **DB**
Col: Notre Dame *HS:* Bishop Watterson [Columbus, OH] B: 5/30/1960, Philadelphia, PA *Drafted:* 1982 Round 3 NO
1982 NO: 9 G.

FRANK KRING Kring, Frank H 6′0″, 190 **LB**
Col: Texas Christian B: 12/21/1918, Lampasas, TX
1945 Det: 4 G.

BILLY KRISHER Krisher, William Irwin 6′1″, 233 **OG**
Col: Oklahoma *HS:* Midwest City [OK] B: 9/18/1935, Perry, OK *Drafted:* 1958 Round 3 Pit
1958 Pit: 8 G. **1960** DalT: 13 G. **1961** DalT: 14 G. **Total:** 35 G.

HOWIE KRISS Kriss, Howard Edwin 5′9″, 175 **HB**
(Buckeye Bullet) *Col:* Ohio State *HS:* East [Cleveland, OH] B: 6/2/1907, Cleveland, OH D: 6/13/1992, El Paso, TX
1931 Cle: 2 G.

FRANK KRISTUFEK Kristufek, Frank Charles 6′0″, 209 **T**
Col: Pittsburgh *HS:* McKeesport [PA] B: 12/12/1915, McKees Rocks, PA
1940 Bkn: 11 G. **1941** Bkn: 11 G. **Total:** 22 G.

JOE KRIVONAK Krivonak, Joseph 6′2″, 230 **G**
Col: South Carolina *HS:* Erie Tech [PA] B: 1918
AAFC **1946** MiaA: 4 G.

JOE KROL Krol, Joseph 6′1″, 210 **DB**
(King) *Col:* Western Ontario (Canada) *HS:* in Canada B: 2/20/1919
1945 Det: 2 G; Punt 2-74 37.0.

ALEX KROLL Kroll, Alexander Stanley 6′3″, 230 **OT-C**
Col: Yale; Rutgers *HS:* Leechburg [PA] B: 11/23/1937, Leechburg, PA *Drafted:* 1962 Round 2 NYT
1962 NYT: 14 G.

BOB KROLL Kroll, Robert Lee 6′1″, 195 **DB**
Col: Northern Michigan *HS:* Preble [Green Bay, WI] B: 6/9/1950, Green Bay, WI
1972 GB: 5 G; KR 1-23 23.0.

GARY KRONER Kroner, Gary Lee 6′1″, 200 **DB-K**
Col: Wisconsin *HS:* Premontre [Green Bay, WI] B: 11/6/1940, Green Bay, WI *Drafted:* 1963 Round 19 NYJ

		Scoring						
Year Team	G	Pts	FG	FGA	FG%	XK	XKA	XK%
1965 Den	14	71	13	29	44.8	32	32	100.0
1966 Den	14	62	14	25	56.0	20	20	100.0
1967 Den	3	11	2	2	100.0	5	6	83.3
NFL Total	31	144	29	56	51.8	57	58	98.3

RAY KROUSE Krouse, Raymond Francis 6′3″, 263 **DT-DE-OT**
Col: Maryland *HS:* Western [Washington, DC] B: 3/21/1927, Washington, DC D: 4/7/1966, Bethesda, MD *Drafted:* 1951 Round 2 NYG
1951 NYG: 12 G. **1952** NYG: 12 G. **1953** NYG: 10 G. **1954** NYG: 12 G. **1955** NYG: 12 G. **1956** Det: 12 G. **1957** Det: 12 G. **1958** Bal: 12 G. **1959** Bal: 12 G. **1960** Was: 12 G. **Total:** 118 G.

MIKE KRUCZEK Kruczek, Michael Francis 6′1″, 202 **QB**
Col: Boston College *HS:* St. John's [Fairfax, VA] B: 3/15/1953, Washington, DC *Drafted:* 1976 Round 2 Pit

		Passing							
Year Team	G	Att	Comp	Comp%	Yds	YPA	TD	Int	Rating
1976 Pit	10	85	51	60.0	758	8.92	0	3	74.5
1977 Pit	2	7	2	28.6	19	2.71	0	0	39.6
1978 Pit	9	11	5	45.5	46	4.18	0	2	17.8
1979 Pit	8	20	13	65.0	153	7.65	0	1	67.3
1980 Was	7	31	22	71.0	209	6.74	0	2	62.4
NFL Total	36	154	93	60.4	1185	7.69	0	8	62.8

	Rushing				
Year Team	Att	Yds	Avg	TD	Fum
1976 Pit	18	106	5.9	2	2
1977 Pit	1	0	0.0	0	1
1978 Pit	5	7	1.4	0	1
1979 Pit	4	20	5.0	0	1
1980 Was	9	5	0.6	0	3
NFL Total	37	138	3.7	2	8

AL KRUEGER Krueger, Albert Leroy 5′10″, 180 **T**
Col: Drake *HS:* East [Des Moines, IA] B: 8/18/1901, Wellman, IA D: 2/25/1976
1924 KC: 7 G.

AL KRUEGER Krueger, Alvin John 6′1″, 188 **OE-DE-DB**
(Antelope Al) *Col:* USC *HS:* Antelope Valley [Lancaster, CA] B: 4/3/1919, Orange, CA D: 2/20/1999, Lancaster, PA *Drafted:* 1941 Round 5 Was
AAFC **1946** LA-A: 10 G; Rec 19-213 11.2 1 TD; 6 Pt.

NFL **1941** Was: 7 G; Rec 7-123 17.6 1 TD; KR 1-23 23.0; Int 1-12; 6 Pt. **1942** Was: 11 G; Rec 9-65 7.2; KR 1-19 19.0. **Total:** 18 G; Rec 16-188 11.8 1 TD; KR 2-42 21.0; Int 1-12; 6 Pt.

CHARLIE KRUEGER Krueger, Charles Andrew 6′4″, 256 **DT-DE**
Col: Texas A&M *HS:* Caldwell [TX] B: 1/28/1937, Caldwell, TX *Drafted:* 1958 Round 1 SF
1959 SF: 12 G; Scor **1** Saf; 2 Pt. **1960** SF: 12 G; Scor **1** Saf; 2 Pt. **1961** SF: 14 G; Scor **1** Saf; 2 Pt. **1962** SF: 14 G. **1963** SF: 7 G. **1964** SF: 14 G. **1965** SF: 14 G; **1** Fum TD; 6 Pt. **1966** SF: 14 G. **1967** SF: 13 G. **1968** SF: 14 G. **1969** SF: 14 G; Int 1-0. **1970** SF: 14 G. **1971** SF: 14 G. **1972** SF: 14 G. **1973** SF: 14 G. **Total:** 198 G; Int 1-0; Scor 3 Saf; 1 Fum TD; 12 Pt.

ROLF KRUEGER Krueger, Rolf Frank 6′4″, 253 **DE-DT**
Col: Texas A&M *HS:* Stephen F. Austin [Bryan, TX] B: 12/8/1946, Caldwell, TX *Drafted:* 1969 Round 2 StL
1969 StL: 14 G. **1970** StL: 14 G. **1971** StL: 14 G. **1972** SF: 4 G. **1973** SF: 14 G. **1974** SF: 9 G. **Total:** 69 G.

TODD KRUMM Krumm, Todd Alan 6′0″, 189 **DB**
Col: Michigan State *HS:* West Bloomfield [MI] B: 12/18/1965, Royal Oak, MI
1988 ChiB: 15 G; Int 2-14.

TIM KRUMRIE Krumrie, Timothy Allen 6′2″, 270 **NT-DT**
Col: Wisconsin *HS:* Mondovi [WI] B: 5/20/1960, Eau Claire, WI *Drafted:* 1983 Round 10 Cin
1983 Cin: 16 G; 1.5 Sac. **1984** Cin: 16 G; 5 Sac. **1985** Cin: 16 G; 3.5 Sac. **1986** Cin: 16 G; 1 Sac. **1987** Cin: 12 G; 3.5 Sac. **1988** Cin: 16 G; 3 Sac. **1989** Cin: 16 G; 3 Sac. **1990** Cin: 16 G; 2 Sac. **1991** Cin: 16 G; 4 Sac. **1992** Cin: 16 G; 4 Sac. **1993** Cin: 16 G; 3 Sac. **1994** Cin: 16 G; 1 Sac. **Total:** 188 G; 34.5 Sac.

JOE KRUPA Krupa, Joseph Steven 6′2″, 232 **DT**
Col: Purdue *HS:* Weber [Chicago, IL] B: 7/6/1933, Chicago, IL *Drafted:* 1956 Round 2 Pit
1956 Pit: 12 G. **1957** Pit: 12 G. **1958** Pit: 12 G. **1959** Pit: 9 G. **1960** Pit: 12 G. **1961** Pit: 14 G. **1962** Pit: 14 G. **1963** Pit: 14 G. **1964** Pit: 11 G. **Total:** 110 G.

BOB KRUSE Kruse, Robert Anthony 6′2″, 259 **OG-DT**
Col: Colorado State; Wayne State (Neb.) *HS:* East Leyden [Franklin Park, IL] B: 2/10/1942, Franklin Park, IL *Drafted:* 1967 Round 12 Oak
1967 Oak: 13 G. **1968** Oak: 12 G; KR 1-1 1.0. **1969** Buf: 3 G. **Total:** 28 G; KR 1-1 1.0.

LARRY KRUTKO Krutko, Lawrence Leroy 6′0″, 220 **FB**
Col: West Virginia *HS:* Cumberland Twp. [Carmichaels, PA] B: 6/27/1935, Carmichaels, PA *Drafted:* 1958 Round 2 Pit
1959 Pit: Rec 13-100 7.7. **1960** Pit: Rec 1-8 8.0. **Total:** Rec 14-108 7.7.

		Rushing				
Year Team	G	Att	Yds	Avg	TD	Fum
1958 Pit	6	4	6	1.5	0	1
1959 Pit	12	75	226	3.0	4	4
1960 Pit	7	17	99	5.8	0	0
NFL Total	25	96	331	3.4	4	5

JERRY KRYSL Krysl, Gerald Charles 5′11″, 200 **T**
Col: Kansas State B: 1/26/1905
1927 Cle: 8 G.

JOHN KSIONZYK Ksionzyk, John Lawrence 5'10", 190 **QB**
Col: St. Bonaventure *HS:* Binghamton [NY] B: 1/28/1919, Binghamton, NY
1947 LARm: 3 G; Pass 7-1 14.3%, 17 2.43 2 Int.

RAY KUBALA Kubala, Raymond George 6'5", 265 **C**
Col: Texas A&M *HS:* West [TX] B: 10/26/1942, West, TX
Drafted: 1964 Round 7 Den
1964 Den: 8 G. **1965** Den: 14 G. **1966** Den: 14 G. **1967** Den: 5 G. **Total:** 41 G.

BOB KUBERSKI Kuberski, Robert Kenneth Jr. 6'4", 298 **DT**
(Scooby) *Col:* Navy *HS:* Ridley [Folsom, PA] B: 4/5/1971, Chester, PA *Drafted:* 1993 Round 7 GB
1995 GB: 9 G; 2 Sac. **1996** GB: 1 G. **1997** GB: 11 G. **1998** GB: 16 G. **Total:** 37 G; 2 Sac.

GARY KUBIAK Kubiak, Gary Wayne 6'0", 192 **QB**
Col: Texas A&M *HS:* St. Pius X [Houston, TX] B: 8/15/1961, Houston, TX *Drafted:* 1983 Round 8 Den
1984 Den: Rec 1-20 20.0. **1989** Den: Punt 2-43 21.5. **Total:** Rec 1-20 20.0; Punt 2-43 21.5.

		Passing							
Year Team	**G**	**Att**	**Comp**	**Comp%**	**Yds**	**YPA**	**TD**	**Int**	**Rating**
1983 Den	4	22	12	54.5	186	8.45	1	1	79.0
1984 Den	7	75	44	58.7	440	5.87	4	1	87.6
1985 Den	16	5	2	40.0	61	12.20	1	0	125.8
1986 Den	16	38	23	60.5	249	6.55	1	3	55.7
1987 Den	12	7	3	42.9	25	3.57	0	2	13.1
1988 Den	16	69	43	62.3	497	7.20	5	3	90.1
1989 Den	16	55	32	58.2	284	5.16	2	2	69.1
1990 Den	16	22	11	50.0	145	6.59	0	4	31.6
1991 Den	16	5	3	60.0	33	6.60	0	0	79.6
NFL Total	119	298	173	58.1	1920	6.44	14	16	70.6

	Rushing				
Year Team	**Att**	**Yds**	**Avg**	**TD**	**Fum**
1983 Den	4	17	4.3	1	0
1984 Den	9	27	3.0	1	1
1985 Den	1	6	6.0	0	0
1986 Den	6	22	3.7	0	0
1987 Den	1	3	3.0	0	0
1988 Den	17	65	3.8	0	3
1989 Den	15	35	2.3	0	2
1990 Den	9	52	5.8	0	2
1991 Den	3	11	3.7	0	1
NFL Total	65	238	3.7	2	9

LARRY KUBIN Kubin, Lawrence William 6'2", 234 **LB**
Col: Penn State *HS:* Union [NJ] B: 2/26/1959, Union, NJ
Drafted: 1981 Round 6 Was
1982 Was: 9 G; 0.5 Sac. **1983** Was: 12 G. **1984** Was: 16 G. **1985** Buf-TB: 6 G. Buf: 2 G. TB: 4 G. **Total:** 43 G; 0.5 Sac.

TED KUCHARSKI Kucharski, Theodore Michael 6'1", 185 **E**
Col: Holy Cross *HS:* Exeter [NH]; St.Anselm Prep [Manchester, NH]
B: 8/26/1907, Exeter, NH D: 10/7/1992, Mesa, AZ
1930 Prov: 8 G.

FRANK KUCHTA Kuchta, Frank William 6'2", 225 **C-LB**
Col: Notre Dame *HS:* Benedictine [Cleveland, OH] B: 9/18/1936, Cleveland, OH *Drafted:* 1958 Round 9 Was
1958 Was: 2 G. **1959** Was: 12 G. **1960** Den: 12 G. **Total:** 26 G.

PAUL KUCZO Kuczo, Paul James 5'9", 165 **TB-BB**
Col: Villanova *HS:* Stamford [CT] B: 2/4/1903, Stamford, CT
D: 12/4/1970, Stamford, CT
1929 SI: 4 G.

BERT KUCZYNSKI Kuczynski, Bernard Carl 6'0", 196 **E**
Col: Pennsylvania *HS:* Northeast [Philadelphia, PA] B: 1/8/1920, Philadelphia, PA D: 1/19/1997, Allentown, PA *Drafted:* 1943 Round 19 Det
1943 Det: 2 G; Rec 1-4 4.0. **1946** Phi: 3 G; Rec 1-9 9.0 1 TD; 6 Pt. **Total:** 5 G; Rec 2-13 6.5 1 TD; 6 Pt.

BOB KUECHENBERG Kuechenberg, Robert John 6'2", 253 **OG-OT-C**
Col: Notre Dame *HS:* Hobart [IN] B: 10/14/1947, Gary, IN
Drafted: 1969 Round 4 Phi
1970 Mia: 14 G. **1971** Mia: 14 G. **1972** Mia: 14 G. **1973** Mia: 13 G. **1974** Mia: 14 G. **1975** Mia: 14 G. **1976** Mia: 10 G. **1977** Mia: 14 G. **1978** Mia: 16 G. **1979** Mia: 16 G. **1980** Mia: 16 G. **1981** Mia: 16 G. **1982** Mia: 9 G. **1983** Mia: 16 G; 1 Fum. **Total:** 196 G; 1 Fum.

RUDY KUECHENBERG Kuechenberg, Rudolph Bernard 6'0", 215 **LB**
Col: Indiana *HS:* Hobart [IN] B: 2/7/1943, Hobart, IN
1967 ChiB: 14 G; KR 1-0. **1968** ChiB: 14 G; KR 1-0. **1969** ChiB: 14 G; KR 1-0. **1970** Cle-GB: 9 G. Cle: 3 G. GB: 6 G. **1971** Atl: 3 G. **Total:** 54 G; KR 3-0.

WADDY KUEHL Kuehl, Ray Otto 5'9", 170 **WB-TB-OE-FB**
(Babe) *Col:* St. Ambrose *HS:* Central [Davenport, IA] B: 2/12/1893, Davenport, IA D: 7/24/1967, Venice, FL
1920 RI: 10 G. **1921** Det-Buf: 8 G; Rush 1 TD; Rec 1 TD; Tot TD 2; 12 Pt. Det: 6 G; Rush 1 TD; 6 Pt. Buf: 2 G; Rec 1 TD; 6 Pt. **1922** Buf: 10 G; Pass 1 TD; Rush 2 TD; Rec 1 TD; Scor **1** 1XP; Tot TD 3; 19 Pt. **1923** RI: 8 G; Rush 2 TD; Rec 2 TD; Tot TD 4; 24 Pt. **1924** Day: 3 G. **Total:** 39 G; Pass 1 TD; Rush 5 TD; Rec 4 TD; Scor 1 1XP; Tot TD 9; 55 Pt.

RYAN KUEHL Kuehl, Ryan Philip 6'4", 289 **DT**
Col: Virginia *HS:* Walt Whitman [Bethesda, MD] B: 1/18/1972, Washington, DC
1996 Was: 2 G. **1997** Was: 12 G. **Total:** 14 G.

ART KUEHN Kuehn, Arthur Bert 6'3", 257 **C**
Col: San Jose State; UCLA *HS:* Cubberley [Palo Alto, CA]
B: 2/12/1953, Victoria, Canada *Drafted:* 1975 Round 15 Was
1976 Sea: 14 G. **1977** Sea: 14 G; 1 Fum. **1978** Sea: 16 G; 1 Fum. **1979** Sea: 16 G. **1980** Sea: 16 G; 1 Fum. **1981** Sea: 16 G. **1982** Sea: 6 G. **1983** NE: 2 G. **Total:** 100 G; 3 Fum.

OSCAR KUEHNER Kuehner, Oscar 6'0", 200 **T-G-E**
Col: No College B: 1889, OH Deceased
1920 Col: 10 G. **1921** Col: 7 G. **Total:** 17 G.

RAY KUFFEL Kuffel, Raymond Francis 6'3", 213 **OE-DE**
Col: Notre Dame; Marquette *HS:* Messmer [Milwaukee, WI]
B: 12/9/1921, Milwaukee, WI D: 12/12/1974, Brookfield, WI
AAFC **1947** BufA: 7 G; Rec 3-37 12.3. **1948** ChiA: 14 G; Rec 19-365 19.2 3 TD; KR 1-16 16.0; 18 Pt. **1949** ChiA: 2 G. **Total:** 23 G; Rec 22-402 18.3 3 TD; KR 1-16 16.0; 18 Pt.

PETE KUGLER Kugler, Peter David 6'4", 255 **NT-DE**
Col: Penn State *HS:* Cherry Hill [NJ] B: 8/9/1959, Philadelphia, PA
Drafted: 1981 Round 6 SF
1981 SF: 13 G. **1982** SF: 7 G; 2 Sac. **1983** SF: 16 G; 3 Sac. **1986** SF: 3 G. **1987** SF: 11 G; 4.5 Sac. **1988** SF: 6 G. **1989** SF: 14 G; 3 Sac. **1990** SF: 11 G. **Total:** 81 G; 12.5 Sac.

JOE KUHARICH Kuharich, Joseph Lawrence 5'11", 195 **G-LB**
Col: Notre Dame *HS:* James Whitcomb Riley [South Bend, IN]
B: 4/14/1917, South Bend, IN D: 1/25/1981, Philadelphia, PA
Drafted: 1938 Round 10 Pit
1940 ChiC: 11 G; Int 2-9; Scor 0-1 FG. **1941** ChiC: 10 G; Int 1-20; Punt 1-45 45.0. **1945** ChiC: 6 G; Scor 12, 0-3 FG, 12-13 92.3% XK. **Total:** 27 G; Int 3-29; Punt 1-45 45.0; Scor 12, 0-4 FG, 12-13 92.3% XK.

GEORGE KUHRT Kuhrt, George 5'11", 185 **T**
Col: No College *HS:* Tonawanda [NY] B: 7/1896, Tonawanda, NY Deceased
1921 Ton: 1 G.

STAN KUICK Kuick, Stanley Jacob 5'10", 192 **G**
Col: Beloit *HS:* Kewuanee [WI] B: 4/24/1904, Kewaunee, WI
D: 8/26/1977, Orlando, FL
1926 Mil: 9 G.

JOE KULBACKI Kulbacki, Joseph Vincent 6'0", 185 **HB**
Col: Purdue *HS:* Youngsville [PA] B: 3/1/1938, Ridgway, PA
Drafted: 1960 Round 1 Bos
1960 Buf: Rec 2-9 4.5; PR 12-100 8.3; KR 13-226 17.4.

		Rushing				
Year Team	**G**	**Att**	**Yds**	**Avg**	**TD**	**Fum**
1960 Buf	14	41	108	2.6	1	4

VIC KULBITSKI Kulbitski, Victor John 5'11", 205 **FB-LB-G-C**
Col: Notre Dame; Minnesota *HS:* Central [Duluth, MN] B: 6/15/1921, Virginia, MN D: 5/23/1998, West St. Paul, MN
AAFC **1946** BufA: Rec 1-0; KR 5-81 16.2; Int 1-20. **1947** BufA: Rec 9-117 13.0 4 TD; PR 1-13 13.0; KR 1-19 19.0; Int 1-14; Scor 31, 1-1 100.0% XK. **1948** BufA: Rec 3-37 12.3; KR 1-18 18.0; Scor 14, 8-10 80.0% XK. **Total:** Rec 13-154 11.8 4 TD; PR 1-13 13.0; KR 7-118 16.9; Int 2-34; Scor 57, 9-11 81.8% XK.

		Rushing				Tot
Year Team	**G**	**Att**	**Yds**	**Avg**	**TD**	**TD**
1946 BufA	13	97	605	6.2	2	2
1947 BufA	13	56	249	4.4	1	5
1948 BufA	14	40	152	3.8	0	1
AAFC Total	40	193	1006	5.2	3	8

MICHAEL KULLMAN Kullman, Michael 6'1", 185 **DB**
Col: Kutztown *HS:* Archbishop Ryan [Philadelphia, PA] B: 1/22/1962, Frankfurt, Germany
1987 Phi: 3 G; Int 2-25.

ERIC KUMEROW Kumerow, Eric Palmer 6'7", 264 **DE-LB**
Col: Ohio State *HS:* River Forest [Oak Park, IL] B: 4/17/1965, Chicago, IL *Drafted:* 1988 Round 1 Mia
1988 Mia: 14 G; 3 Sac. **1989** Mia: 12 G; 2 Sac. **1990** Mia: 16 G; Int 1-5. **Total:** 42 G; Int 1-5; 5 Sac.

GEORGE KUNZ Kunz, George James 6'5", 257 **OT**
Col: Notre Dame *HS:* Loyola [Los Angeles, CA] B: 7/5/1947, Fort Sheridan, IL *Drafted:* 1969 Round 1 Atl
1969 Atl: 14 G; KR 1-13 13.0. **1970** Atl: 9 G. **1971** Atl: 14 G; Rec 1-2 2.0. **1972** Atl: 14 G. **1973** Atl: 14 G. **1974** Atl: 14 G. **1975** Bal: 12 G. **1976** Bal: 14 G. **1977** Bal: 14 G. **1978** Bal: 1 G. **1980** Bal: 9 G. **Total:** 129 G; Rec 1-2 2.0; KR 1-13 13.0.

LEE KUNZ Kunz, Lee Roy 6'2", 226 **LB**
Col: Nebraska *HS:* Wheat Ridge [CO] B: 4/21/1957, Golden, CO *Drafted:* 1979 Round 7 ChiB
1979 ChiB: 16 G. **1980** ChiB: 16 G. **1981** ChiB: 16 G. **Total:** 48 G.

TERRY KUNZ Kunz, Terry Tim 6'1", 215 **RB**
Col: Colorado *HS:* Wheat Ridge [CO] B: 10/26/1952, Denver, CO *Drafted:* 1976 Round 8 Oak
1976 Oak: 7 G; Rush 4-33 8.3.

IRV KUPCINET Kupcinet, Irving 6'1", 190 **BB-DB**
Col: Northwestern; North Dakota *HS:* Harrison [Chicago, IL] B: 7/31/1912, Chicago, IL
1935 Phi: 2 G; Pass 5-1 20.0%, 6 1.20.

CRAIG KUPP Kupp, Craig Marion 6'4", 215 **QB**
Col: Montana Tech; Pacific Lutheran *HS:* Selah [WA] B: 4/14/1967, Sunnyside, WA *Drafted:* 1990 Round 5 NYG
1991 Pho: 1 G; Pass 7-3 42.9%, 23 3.29; Rush 1-5 5.0; 1 Fum.

JAKE KUPP Kupp, Jacob Ralph 6'3", 248 **TE-OG**
Col: Washington *HS:* Sunnyside [WA] B: 3/12/1941, Pasadena, CA *Drafted:* 1964 Round 9 Dal
1964 Dal: 14 G. **1965** Dal: 14 G. **1966** Was: 14 G; Rec 4-28 7.0. **1967** NO-Atl: 11 G. NO: 5 G. Atl: 6 G. **1968** NO: 14 G. **1969** NO: 14 G. **1970** NO: 14 G. **1971** NO: 14 G. **1972** NO: 3 G. **1973** NO: 14 G. **1974** NO: 14 G. **1975** NO: 14 G. **Total:** 154 G; Rec 4-28 7.0.

RALPH KUREK Kurek, Ralph Eamer 6'2", 210 **RB**
(Bullet) *Col:* Wisconsin *HS:* Watertown [WI] B: 2/23/1943, Milwaukee, WI *Drafted:* 1965 Round 20 ChiB
1965 ChiB: KR 1-11 11.0. **1967** ChiB: KR 5-81 16.2. **1968** ChiB: KR 4-48 12.0. **1969** ChiB: KR 4-66 16.5. **Total:** KR 14-206 14.7.

		Rushing				Receiving				
Year Team	G	Att	Yds	Avg	TD	Rec	Yds	Avg	TD	Fum
1965 ChiB	14	1	0	0.0	0	0	0	—	0	0
1966 ChiB	14	52	179	3.4	1	10	178	17.8	0	1
1967 ChiB	14	37	112	3.0	0	5	30	6.0	0	2
1968 ChiB	14	17	95	5.6	1	4	50	12.5	0	2
1969 ChiB	14	8	24	3.0	0	4	30	7.5	0	0
1970 ChiB	11	6	24	4.0	0	3	11	3.7	0	0
NFL Total	81	121	434	3.6	2	26	299	11.5	0	5

JAMIE KURISKO Kurisko, Jamie A 6'4", 236 **TE**
Col: Allentown College; Southern Connecticut State *HS:* Nanuet [NY] B: 12/22/1963, Nyack, NY
1987 NYJ: 3 G; Rec 1-41 41.0 1 TD; 6 Pt.

HOWIE KURNICK Kurnick, Howard Raymond 6'2", 219 **LB**
Col: Cincinnati *HS:* South [Willoughby, OH] B: 5/13/1957, Cleveland, OH *Drafted:* 1979 Round 8 Cin
1979 Cin: 15 G; KR 4-60 15.0; **1** Fum TD; 6 Pt.

ROY KURRASCH Kurrasch, Roy William 6'2", 195 **DE-OE**
(Crash) *Col:* UCLA *HS:* Hollywood [Los Angeles, CA] B: 10/8/1922, Toledo, OH
AAFC **1947** NY-A: 10 G; Rec 2-53 26.5.

NFL **1948** Pit: 9 G.

JOE KURTH Kurth, Joseph James 6'1", 202 **T**
Col: Wisconsin; Notre Dame *HS:* East [Madison, WI] B: 3/27/1914, Madison, WI D: 1/13/1987, Plano, TX
1933 GB: 13 G. **1934** GB: 7 G. **Total:** 20 G.

ROD KUSH Kush, Rodney Randle 6'0", 188 **DB**
Col: Nebraska-Omaha *HS:* Harry A. Burke [Omaha, NE] B: 12/29/1956, Omaha, NE *Drafted:* 1979 Round 5 Buf
1980 Buf: 5 G. **1981** Buf: 16 G; Rush 1-(-6) -6.0; Int 1-19; 1 Fum. **1982** Buf: 9 G. **1983** Buf: 4 G. **1984** Buf: 16 G; Int 1-15; 1 Fum; 2 Sac. **1985** Hou: 16 G; Int 2-6; 5 Sac. **Total:** 66 G; Rush 1-(-6) -6.0; Int 4-40; 2 Fum; 7 Sac.

JOHN KUSKO Kusko, John 5'11", 194 **FB-LB-DB-BB**
Col: Temple B: 3/27/1914, Nesquehoning, PA D: 7/1974
1936 Phi: Pass 27-6 22.2%, 108 4.00 8 Int. **1937** Phi: Pass 7-2 28.6%, 11 1.57 2 Int; Rec 2-47 23.5. **Total:** Pass 34-8 23.5%, 119 3.50 10 Int; Rec 2-47 23.5.

		Rushing			
Year Team	G	Att	Yds	Avg	TD
1936 Phi	12	49	209	4.3	1
1937 Phi	10	17	27	1.6	0
1938 Phi	1	0	0	—	0
NFL Total	23	66	236	3.6	1

LOU KUSSEROW Kusserow, Louis Joseph 6'1", 200 **FB-LB**
Col: Columbia *HS:* Glassport [PA] B: 9/6/1927, Braddock, PA
AAFC **1949** NY-A: Pass 1-0; KR 6-136 22.7.

		Rushing			
Year Team	G	Att	Yds	Avg	TD
1949 NY-A	11	39	136	3.5	0

NFL **1950** NYY: 11 G; Rush 1-6 6.0.

RUDY KUTLER Kutler, Rudolph John 5'9", 190 **G**
Col: Ohio State *HS:* West Tech [Cleveland, OH] B: 11/14/1901 D: 3/20/1974, Brecksville, OH
1925 Cle: 1 G.

MAL KUTNER Kutner, Malcolm James 6'2", 197 **OE-DB**
Col: Texas *HS:* Woodrow Wilson [Dallas, TX] B: 3/27/1921, Dallas, TX *Drafted:* 1942 Round 4 Pit
1946 ChiC: Rush 1-(-1) -1.0; KR 3-30 10.0. **1948** ChiC: Rush 5-50 10.0 1 TD. **1949** ChiC: Rush 5-10 2.0. **Total:** Rush 11-59 5.4 1 TD; KR 3-30 10.0.

		Receiving				Interceptions				Tot
Year Team	G	Rec	Yds	Avg	TD	Int	Yds	TD	Fum	TD
1946 ChiC	11	27	634	23.5	5	5	29	0	1	5
1947 ChiC	12	43	**944**	22.0	7	3	56	1	2	8
1948 ChiC	12	41	**943**	23.0	**14**	2	35	0	0	**15**
1949 ChiC	12	30	465	15.5	5	0	0	0	0	5
1950 ChiC	9	4	74	18.5	0	3	31	0	0	0
NFL Total	56	145	3060	21.1	31	13	151	1	3	33

BILL KUUSISTO Kuusisto, William 6'0", 228 **G**
Col: Minnesota *HS:* Roosevelt [Virginia, MN] B: 4/26/1918, Herman, MI D: 5/28/1973, Paynesville, MN *Drafted:* 1941 Round 6 GB
1941 GB: 9 G. **1942** GB: 11 G. **1943** GB: 10 G. **1944** GB: 10 G. **1945** GB: 10 G. **1946** GB: 4 G. **Total:** 54 G.

FULTON KUYKENDALL Kuykendall, Fulton Gerald 6'4", 225 **LB**
(Captain Crazy) *Col:* UCLA *HS:* St. Patrick's [Vallejo, CA] B: 6/10/1953, Coronado, CA *Drafted:* 1975 Round 6 Atl
1975 Atl: 14 G. **1976** Atl: 7 G. **1977** Atl: 5 G. **1978** Atl: 16 G. **1979** Atl: 16 G. **1980** Atl: 10 G. **1981** Atl: 16 G; Int 1-20 1 TD; 6 Pt. **1982** Atl: 9 G; Int 2-22. **1983** Atl: 14 G; 1 Sac. **1984** Atl: 16 G; 1 Sac. **1985** SF: 1 G. **Total:** 124 G; Int 3-42 1 TD; 6 Pt; 2 Sac.

BOB KUZIEL Kuziel, Robert Charles 6'4", 255 **C-OT**
Col: Pittsburgh *HS:* Manlius [NY] B: 7/24/1950, New Haven, CT *Drafted:* 1972 Round 3 NO
1972 NO: 1 G. **1975** Was: 14 G. **1976** Was: 14 G. **1977** Was: 14 G. **1978** Was: 16 G. **1979** Was: 16 G. **1980** Was: 15 G. **Total:** 90 G.

JOHN KUZMAN Kuzman, John 6'1", 232 **T**
(Chief) *Col:* Fordham *HS:* Coaldale [PA]; Bordentown Mil. Acad. [NJ] B: 6/29/1915, Coaldale, PA *Drafted:* 1941 Round 7 ChiC
AAFC **1946** SF-A: 11 G; 6 Pt. **1947** ChiA: 13 G; KR 1-7 7.0. **Total:** 24 G; KR 1-7 7.0; 6 Pt.

NFL **1941** ChiC: 5 G.

ZVONIMIR KVATERNIK Kvaternik, Zvonimir 5'11", 210 **G**
Col: Kansas *HS:* Wyandotte [Kansas City, KS] B: 10/18/1911, Kansas City, KS D: 10/19/1994, Kansas City, KS
1934 Pit: 1 G.

JOHN KVIST Kvist, John L **T**
Col: No College B: 9/13/1899 D: 7/1972, South Amboy, NJ
1920 Roch: 1 G.

TED KWALICK Kwalick, Thaddeus John Jr. 6'4", 226 **TE**
Col: Penn State *HS:* McKees Rocks [PA] B: 4/15/1947, Pittsburgh, PA *Drafted:* 1969 Round 1 SF
1969 SF: KR 1-0. **1970** SF: Rush 3-65 21.7. **1971** SF: Rush 6-62 10.3; KR 2-9 4.5. **1972** SF: Rush 5-11 2.2. **1973** SF: Rush 5-37 7.4. **Total:** Rush 19-175 9.2; KR 3-9 3.0.

		Receiving				
Year Team	G	Rec	Yds	Avg	TD	Fum
1969 SF	13	2	32	16.0	1	0
1970 SF	14	10	148	14.8	1	0
1971 SF	14	52	664	12.8	5	2
1972 SF	14	40	751	18.8	9	2
1973 SF	14	47	729	15.5	5	1
1974 SF	14	13	231	17.8	2	0
1975 Oak	6	0	0	—	0	0
1976 Oak	7	4	15	3.8	0	0
1977 Oak	12	0	0	—	0	0
NFL Total	108	168	2570	15.3	23	5

AARON KYLE Kyle, Aaron Douglas 5′11″, 185 **DB**
Col: Wyoming *HS:* Detroit Tech [MI] B: 4/6/1954, Detroit, MI
Drafted: 1976 Round 1 Dal
1976 Dal: Scor **1** Saf. **1981** Den: PR 1-0. **Total:** PR 1-0; Scor 1 Saf.

		Interceptions		
Year Team	**G**	**Int**	**Yds**	**TD**
1976 Dal	14	0	0	0
1977 Dal	14	1	9	0
1978 Dal	16	3	20	0
1979 Dal	16	2	0	0
1980 Den	10	0	0	0
1981 Den	16	2	40	0
1982 Den	9	3	26	0
NFL Total	95	11	95	0

RIP KYLE Kyle, James William Jr. 6′0″, 240 **C-T-G**
Col: Gettysburg *HS:* Mifflintown [PA] B: 8/20/1899, Mifflintown, PA
Deceased
1925 Can: 4 G. **1926** Can: 11 G. **Total:** 15 G.

JASON KYLE Kyle, Jason C 6′3″, 242 **LB**
Col: Arizona State *HS:* McClintock [Tempe, AZ] B: 5/12/1972, Mesa, AZ *Drafted:* 1995 Round 4 Sea
1995 Sea: 16 G. **1996** Sea: 16 G. **1998** Sea: 16 G. **Total:** 48 G.

JOHNNY KYLE Kyle, John William 5′9″, 214 **FB**
Col: Indiana *HS:* Emerson [Gary, IN] B: 9/12/1898, Gary, IN
D: 5/1974, Valparaiso, IN
1923 Cle: 7 G; Rush 1 TD; 6 Pt.

TROY KYLES Kyles, Troy Thomas 6′1″, 185 **WR**
Col: Howard *HS:* St. Martin de Porres [Detroit, MI] B: 8/13/1968, Lorain, OH
1990 NYG: 9 G; Rec 4-77 19.3.

JEFF KYSAR Kysar, Jeffrey John-Charles 6′7″, 325 **OT**
Col: Arizona State *HS:* Serra [San Diego, CA] B: 6/14/1972, Norman, OK *Drafted:* 1995 Round 5 Oak
1995 Oak: 1 G.

GALEN LAACK Laack, Galen William 6′0″, 230 **OG**
Col: U. of Pacific *HS:* Abbotsford [WI] B: 4/3/1931, Abbotsford, WI
D: 12/31/1958, Livermore, CA *Drafted:* 1957 Round 9 Was
1958 Phi: 8 G.

ERIC LAAKSO Laakso, Eric Henry 6′4″, 265 **OT-OG**
Col: Tulane *HS:* Killingly [Danielson, CT] B: 11/29/1956, New York, NY
Drafted: 1978 Round 4 Mia
1978 Mia: 16 G. **1979** Mia: 10 G. **1980** Mia: 16 G. **1981** Mia: 16 G. **1982** Mia: 9 G. **1983** Mia: 15 G. **1984** Mia: 4 G. **Total:** 86 G.

PAUL LAAVEG Laaveg, Paul Martin 6′4″, 245 **OG**
Col: Iowa *HS:* Belmond [IA] B: 10/1/1948, Sioux Falls, SD
Drafted: 1970 Round 4 Was
1970 Was: 11 G. **1971** Was: 14 G. **1972** Was: 14 G. **1973** Was: 14 G. **1974** Was: 14 G. **1975** Was: 5 G. **Total:** 72 G.

SANDY LABEAUX LaBeaux, Sandy Jr. 6′3″, 210 **DB**
Col: Cal State-Hayward *HS:* California [San Ramon, CA] B: 8/22/1961, San Antonio, TX
1983 TB: 3 G.

TONY LABISSONIERE LaBissoniere, Horace C 5′9″, 185 **C**
Col: St. Thomas; Michigan *HS:* Mechanical Arts [St. Paul, MN]
B: 9/13/1896, St. Paul, MN D: 1/1972, St. Paul, MN
1922 Ham: 2 G.

MATT LABOUNTY LaBounty, Matthew James 6′4″, 271 **DE-DT**
Col: Oregon *HS:* San Marin [Novato, CA] B: 1/3/1969, San Francisco, CA *Drafted:* 1992 Round 12 SF
1993 SF: 6 G. **1995** GB: 14 G; 3 Sac. **1996** Sea: 3 G. **1997** Sea: 16 G; 3 Sac. **1998** Sea: 16 G; 1 Fum; 6 Sac. **Total:** 55 G; 1 Fum; 12 Sac.

BOB LACEY Lacey, Robert Reavil 6′3″, 205 **WR**
Col: North Carolina *HS:* Trinity Pawling Prep [Pawling, NY]
B: 3/30/1942, New York, NY *Drafted:* 1964 Round 6 Min
1964 Min: 1 G.

STEVE LACH Lach, Stephen John 6′2″, 207 **FB-WB**
Col: Duke *HS:* Altoona [PA] B: 8/6/1920, Altoona, PA D: 7/12/1961, Altoona, PA *Drafted:* 1942 Round 1 ChiC
1942 ChiC: PR 13-178 13.7; KR 7-164 23.4; Int 4-52; Punt 31-1245 40.2; Scor 25, 1-1 100.0% XK. **1946** Pit: Pass 1-0; Int 1-10. **1947** Pit: Pass 5-2 40.0%, 12 2.40 1 TD; KR 3-59 19.7. **Total:** Pass 6-2 33.3%, 12 2.00 1 TD; PR 13-178 13.7; KR 10-223 22.3; Int 5-62; Punt 31-1245 40.2; Scor 109, 1-1 100.0% XK.

		Rushing				Receiving					Tot
Year Team	**G**	**Att**	**Yds**	**Avg**	**TD**	**Rec**	**Yds**	**Avg**	**TD**	**Fum**	**TD**
1942 ChiC	9	30	97	3.2	0	18	261	14.5	4	0	4
1946 Pit	11	42	111	2.6	5	3	22	7.3	0	4	5
1947 Pit	12	120	372	3.1	8	11	77	7.0	1	1	9
NFL Total	32	192	580	3.0	13	32	360	11.3	5	5	18

SEAN LACHAPELLE LaChapelle, Sean Paul Richard 6′3″, 205 **WR**
Col: UCLA *HS:* Vintage [Napa, CA] B: 7/29/1970, Sacramento, CA
Drafted: 1993 Round 5 LARm

		Receiving			
Year Team	**G**	**Rec**	**Yds**	**Avg**	**TD**
1993 LARm	10	2	23	11.5	0
1996 KC	12	27	422	15.6	2
NFL Total	22	29	445	15.3	2

JIM LACHEY Lachey, James Michael 6′6″, 290 **OT**
Col: Ohio State *HS:* St. Henry [OH] B: 6/4/1963, St. Henry, OH
Drafted: 1985 Round 1 SD
1985 SD: 16 G. **1986** SD: 16 G. **1987** SD: 12 G. **1988** LARd-Was: 16 G. LARd: 1 G. Was: 15 G. **1989** Was: 14 G. **1990** Was: 16 G. **1991** Was: 15 G. **1992** Was: 10 G. **1994** Was: 13 G. **1995** Was: 3 G. **Total:** 131 G.

CORBIN LACINA Lacina, Corbin James 6′4″, 300 **OT-OG**
Col: Augustana (S.D.) *HS:* Cretin-Derham Hall [St. Paul, MN]
B: 11/2/1970, Woodbury, MN *Drafted:* 1993 Round 6 Buf
1994 Buf: 11 G. **1995** Buf: 16 G. **1996** Buf: 12 G. **1997** Buf: 16 G. **1998** Car: 10 G. **Total:** 65 G.

RICK LACKMAN Lackman, Richard H 5′11″, 186 **HB-DB-TB**
Col: No College *HS:* Germantown [Philadelphia, PA] B: 9/20/1910, Philadelphia, PA D: 3/12/1990
1933 Phi: Pass 1-0, 1 Int. **1934** Phi: Rec 4-83 20.8. **1935** Phi: Rec 5-49 9.8. **Total:** Pass 1-0, 1 Int; Rec 9-132 14.7.

		Rushing			
Year Team	**G**	**Att**	**Yds**	**Avg**	**TD**
1933 Phi	4	17	59	3.5	0
1934 Phi	8	4	9	2.3	0
1935 Phi	11	22	56	2.5	0
NFL Total	23	43	124	2.9	0

DAVE LACROSSE LaCrosse, David Joseph 6′3″, 210 **LB**
Col: Wake Forest *HS:* Archbishop Kennedy [Conshohocken, PA]
B: 12/22/1955, Philadelphia, PA *Drafted:* 1977 Round 10 Pit
1977 Pit: 14 G.

KEN LACY Lacy, Kenneth Wayne Jr. 6′0″, 222 **RB**
Col: Tulsa *HS:* Justin F. Kimball [Dallas, TX] B: 11/1/1960, Waco, TX
1984 KC: Rec 13-87 6.7 2 TD. **1987** KC: KR 4-44 11.0. **Total:** Rec 13-87 6.7 2 TD; KR 4-44 11.0.

		Rushing					Tot
Year Team	**G**	**Att**	**Yds**	**Avg**	**TD**	**Fum**	**TD**
1984 KC	15	46	165	3.6	2	2	4
1985 KC	2	6	21	3.5	0	1	0
1987 KC	3	14	49	3.5	0	2	0
NFL Total	20	66	235	3.6	2	5	4

ANTHONY LADD Ladd, Anthony 6′1″, 188 **WR**
(Amp) *Col:* Cincinnati *HS:* Homestead [FL] B: 12/23/1973, Miami, FL
1998 NE: 3 G.

ERNIE LADD Ladd, Ernest 6′9″, 290 **DT**
(The Big Cat) *Col:* Grambling State *HS:* Wallace [Orange, TX]
B: 11/28/1938, Rayville, LA *Drafted:* 1961 Round 15 SD
1961 SD: 14 G. **1962** SD: 14 G. **1963** SD: 14 G. **1964** SD: 14 G. **1965** SD: 14 G. **1966** Hou: 14 G. **1967** Hou-KC: 14 G. Hou: 4 G. KC: 10 G. **1968** KC: 14 G; Int 1-3. **Total:** 112 G; Int 1-3.

JIM LADD Ladd, James W 6′4″, 205 **OE**
Col: Bowling Green State *HS:* Put-in-Bay [OH] B: 7/29/1932, Put-in-Bay, OH D: 11/13/1996, Indianapolis, IN *Drafted:* 1954 Round 20 ChiB
1954 ChiC: 11 G; Rec 22-254 11.5.

DOC LADORUM Ladorum, ? **FB**
Col: No College Deceased
1921 Mun: 1 G.

WALLY LADROW Ladrow, Walter 5′9″, 180 **HB**
Col: No College B: 10/16/1895, Brookside, WI D: 7/22/1974, Green Bay, WI
1921 GB: 1 G.

TINY LADSON Ladson, Glessie Merritt 254 **G**
Col: No College B: 12/17/1895, Sullivan Co., IN D: 11/28/1978, Hanover, IN
1922 Eva: 3 G.

PETE LADYGO Ladygo, Peter Glenn 6′2″, 218 **OG-LB**
Col: Potomac State Coll. WV (J.C.); Maryland *HS:* Allegheny Prep [Pittsburgh, PA] B: 6/23/1925, West Brownsville, PA *Drafted:* 1952 Round 16 Pit
1952 Pit: 12 G; KR 1-4 4.0. **1954** Pit: 12 G. **Total:** 24 G; KR 1-4 4.0.

DAVE LAFARY Lafary, David Walter 6′7″, 280 **OT-OG**
Col: Purdue *HS:* La Salle [Cincinnati, OH] B: 1/13/1955, Cincinnati, OH *Drafted:* 1977 Round 5 NO
1977 NO: 10 G. **1978** NO: 15 G. **1979** NO: 16 G. **1980** NO: 15 G. **1981** NO: 16 G; Rec 1-5 5.0. **1982** NO: 9 G. **1983** NO: 16 G. **1984** NO: 1 G. **1985** NO: 11 G. **Total:** 109 G; Rec 1-5 5.0.

BILL LAFITTE LaFitte, William Sorrells 6′1″, 170 **OE**
Col: Ouachita Baptist *HS:* Pine Bluff [AR] B: 1/23/1926, Stonewall, LA Deceased
1944 Bkn: 3 G; Rec 1-15 15.0.

DAVID LAFLEUR LaFleur, David Alan 6′7″, 272 **TE**
Col: Louisiana State *HS:* Westlake [LA] B: 1/29/1974, Lake Charles, LA *Drafted:* 1997 Round 1 Dal
1998 Dal: KR 1-12 12.0. **Total:** KR 1-12 12.0.

		Receiving				
Year Team	**G**	**Rec**	**Yds**	**Avg**	**TD**	**Fum**
1997 Dal	16	18	122	6.8	2	1
1998 Dal	13	20	176	8.8	2	1
NFL Total	29	38	298	7.8	4	2

GREG LAFLEUR LaFleur, Gregory Louis 6′4″, 236 **TE**
Col: Louisiana State *HS:* Ville Platte [LA] B: 9/16/1958, Lafayette, LA *Drafted:* 1981 Round 3 Phi

		Receiving				
Year Team	**G**	**Rec**	**Yds**	**Avg**	**TD**	**Fum**
1981 StL	16	14	190	13.6	2	0
1982 StL	9	5	67	13.4	1	0
1983 StL	16	12	99	8.3	0	3
1984 StL	16	17	198	11.6	0	0
1985 StL	16	9	119	13.2	0	0
1986 StL-Ind	13	7	56	8.0	0	0
1986 StL	4	0	0	—	0	0
1986 Ind	9	7	56	8.0	0	0
NFL Total	86	64	729	11.4	3	3

JOE LAFLEUR LaFleur, Harry Joseph 6′0″, 223 **G-FB-C-HB**
(Frenchy) *Col:* St. Norbert; Marquette *HS:* Escanaba [MI]; Worcester Acad. [MA] B: 3/3/1896, DePere, WI D: 10/5/1973, La Crosse, WI
1922 ChiB: 10 G. **1923** ChiB: 10 G. **1924** ChiB: 7 G. **Total:** 27 G.

DICK LAGE Lage, Richard Lloyd 6′4″, 228 **OE**
Col: Lenoir-Rhyne *HS:* Repogle [New Enterprise, PA] B: 8/9/1939, Omaha, NE *Drafted:* 1961 Round 12 Cle
1961 StL: 1 G.

JEFF LAGEMAN Lageman, Jeffrey David 6′6″, 266 **DE-LB**
Col: Virginia *HS:* Park View [Sterling, VA] B: 7/18/1967, Fairfax, VA *Drafted:* 1989 Round 1 NYJ
1989 NYJ: 16 G; Rush 1-(-5) -5.0; 4.5 Sac. **1990** NYJ: 16 G; 4 Sac. **1991** NYJ: 16 G; 10 Sac. **1992** NYJ: 2 G; 1 Sac. **1993** NYJ: 16 G; Int 1-15; 8.5 Sac. **1994** NYJ: 16 G; 6.5 Sac. **1995** Jac: 11 G; 3 Sac. **1996** Jac: 12 G; 4.5 Sac. **1997** Jac: 16 G; 5 Sac. **1998** Jac: 1 G. **Total:** 122 G; Rush 1-(-5) -5.0; Int 1-15; 47.0 Sac.

CHET LAGOD Lagod, Chester Joseph 6′2″, 220 **OG**
Col: Tennessee-Chattanooga *HS:* St. Clairsville [OH] B: 1/8/1928, Fairpoint, OH *Drafted:* 1951 Round 25 NYG
1953 NYG: 11 G.

MORRIS LAGRAND LaGrand, James Morris 6′1″, 220 **RB**
Col: Tampa *HS:* T.R. Robinson [Tampa, FL] B: 2/9/1953, Tampa, FL *Drafted:* 1975 Round 6 KC
1975 KC-NO: 13 G; Rush 13-38 2.9 1 TD; Rec 1-(-1) -1.0; 6 Pt; 1 Fum. KC: 11 G; Rush 13-38 2.9 1 TD; Rec 1-(-1) -1.0; 6 Pt; 1 Fum. NO: 2 G. **Total:** 13 G; Rush 13-38 2.9 1 TD; Rec 1-(-1) -1.0; 6 Pt; 1 Fum.

HAL LAHAR Lahar, Harold Wade 6′0″, 221 **G**
Col: Oklahoma *HS:* Central [Oklahoma City, OK] B: 7/14/1919, Durant, OK *Drafted:* 1941 Round 11 ChiB
AAFC **1946** BufA: 12 G. **1947** BufA: 14 G. **1948** BufA: 13 G. **Total:** 39 G.

NFL **1941** ChiB: 8 G; Scor 4, 1-1 100.0% FG, 1-3 33.3% XK.

PAT LAHEY Lahey, Thomas Patrick 6′2″, 218 **OE-DE**
Col: John Carroll *HS:* Bowling Green [OH] B: 10/21/1919, Dunbridge, OH
AAFC **1946** ChiA: Rush 1-(-2) -2.0; KR 1-5 5.0; Int 1-4. **1947** ChiA: KR 2-18 9.0. **Total:** Rush 1-(-2) -2.0; KR 3-23 7.7; Int 1-4.

		Receiving			
Year Team	**G**	**Rec**	**Yds**	**Avg**	**TD**
1946 ChiA	13	17	203	11.9	0
1947 ChiA	13	13	148	11.4	0
AAFC Total	26	30	351	11.7	0

MIKE LAHOOD LaHood, Michael James 6′3″, 250 **OG**
Col: Wyoming *HS:* Spaulding Inst. [Peoria, IL] B: 12/11/1944, Peoria, IL *Drafted:* 1968 Round 2 LARm
1969 LARm: 14 G. **1970** StL: 14 G. **1971** LARm: 9 G; KR 1-25 25.0. **1972** LARm: 14 G. **Total:** 51 G; KR 1-25 25.0.

WARREN LAHR Lahr, Warren Emmett 5′11″, 185 **DB**
Col: Case Western Reserve *HS:* West Wyoming [PA] B: 9/5/1923, Mount Zion, PA D: 1/19/1969, Cleveland, OH *Drafted:* 1947 Round 30 Pit
AAFC **1949** CleA: 11 G; Rush 9-36 4.0 1 TD; Rec 1-20 20.0; PR 6-83 13.8; Int 4-32; Punt 4-125 31.3; 6 Pt.

NFL **1954** Cle: Pass 1-0, 1 Int; Rush 3-18 6.0. **Total:** Pass 1-0, 1 Int; Rush 3-18 6.0.

		Interceptions			
Year Team	**G**	**Int**	**Yds**	**TD**	**Fum**
1950 Cle	12	8	99	**2**	0
1951 Cle	12	5	95	**2**	0
1952 Cle	12	5	51	0	0
1953 Cle	12	5	119	0	0
1954 Cle	12	5	44	1	0
1955 Cle	12	5	52	0	1
1956 Cle	12	3	33	0	0
1957 Cle	11	2	12	0	0
1958 Cle	7	1	25	0	0
1959 Cle	12	1	0	0	0
NFL Total	114	40	530	5	1

SCOTT LAIDLAW Laidlaw, Robert Scott 6′0″, 206 **RB**
Col: Stanford *HS:* Hawthorne [CA] B: 2/17/1953, Hawthorne, CA *Drafted:* 1975 Round 14 Dal
1980 NYG: KR 1-18 18.0. **Total:** KR 1-18 18.0.

		Rushing				Receiving					Tot
Year Team	**G**	**Att**	**Yds**	**Avg**	**TD**	**Rec**	**Yds**	**Avg**	**TD**	**Fum**	**TD**
1975 Dal	8	3	10	3.3	0	11	100	9.1	0	1	0
1976 Dal	13	94	424	4.5	3	38	325	8.6	1	5	4
1977 Dal	14	9	15	1.7	0	5	60	12.0	1	0	1
1978 Dal	16	75	312	4.2	3	6	108	18.0	1	3	4
1979 Dal	16	69	236	3.4	3	12	59	4.9	0	5	3
1980 NYG	7	5	10	2.0	0	2	16	8.0	0	0	0
NFL Total	74	255	1007	3.9	9	74	668	9.0	3	14	12

AARON LAING Laing, Aaron Matthew 6′3″, 260 **TE**
Col: New Mexico State *HS:* Sharpstown [Houston, TX] B: 7/19/1971, Houston, TX *Drafted:* 1994 Round 5 SD
1994 SD: 5 G. **1996** StL: 12 G; Rec 13-116 8.9; KR 1-15 15.0. **1997** StL: 15 G; Rec 5-31 6.2 1 TD; 6 Pt. **Total:** 32 G; Rec 18-147 8.2 1 TD; KR 1-15 15.0; 6 Pt.

PORTER LAINHART Lainhart, Porter Ward 6′0″, 180 **BB-DB**
Col: Washington State *HS:* Goldendale [WA] B: 11/6/1907 D: 8/1991, Coquille, OR
1933 Phi: 1 G; Rec 1-20 20.0.

BRUCE LAIRD Laird, Bruce Allan 6′0″, 193 **DB**
Col: American International *HS:* Scituate [MA] B: 5/23/1950, Lowell, MA *Drafted:* 1972 Round 6 Bal
1975 Bal: Scor **1** Saf. **Total:** Scor 1 Saf.

		Punt Returns				Kickoff Returns			
Year Team	**G**	**Ret**	**Yds**	**Avg**	**TD**	**Ret**	**Yds**	**Avg**	**TD**
1972 Bal	14	**34**	**303**	8.9	0	29	843	29.1	0
1973 Bal	12	15	72	4.8	0	24	547	22.8	0
1974 Bal	14	11	30	2.7	0	19	499	26.3	0
1975 Bal	14	0	0	—	0	31	799	25.8	0
1976 Bal	14	0	0	—	0	7	143	20.4	0
1977 Bal	14	0	0	—	0	24	541	22.5	0
1978 Bal	14	0	0	—	0	0	0	—	0
1979 Bal	15	0	0	—	0	3	34	11.3	0
1980 Bal	15	0	0	—	0	0	0	—	0
1981 Bal	15	0	0	—	0	0	0	—	0
1982 SD	9	0	0	—	0	0	0	—	0
1983 SD	14	1	0	0.0	0	15	342	22.8	0
NFL Total	164	61	405	6.6	0	152	3748	24.7	0

	Interceptions			
Year Team	**Int**	**Yds**	**TD**	**Fum**
1972 Bal	1	31	0	8
1973 Bal	0	0	0	4
1974 Bal	1	15	0	4
1975 Bal	3	46	0	2
1977 Bal	3	56	0	0
1979 Bal	3	101	0	1
1980 Bal	5	71	0	0
1981 Bal	3	59	0	0
1983 SD	0	0	0	1
NFL Total	19	379	0	20

JIM LAIRD Laird, James Tyler 6′0″, 194 **FB-G-WB-T**
Col: Colgate *HS:* Holderness School [Plymouth, NH] B: 9/10/1897, Montpelier, VT D: 8/16/1970, Lebanon, CT
1920 Roch-Buf: 10 G. Roch: 9 G. Buf: 1 G. **1921** Buf-Roch-Can: 8 G; Rush 5 TD; Rec 1 TD; Tot TD 6; 36 Pt. Buf: 1 G. Roch: 6 G; Rush 3 TD; Rec 1 TD; Tot TD 4; 24 Pt. Can: 1 G; Rush 2 TD; 12 Pt. **1922** Buf: 10 G; Rush 3 TD; Rec 1 TD; Tot TD 4; 24 Pt. **1925** Prov: 11 G; Rush 3 TD; Scor 29, 3 FG, 2 XK. **1926** Prov: 9 G. **1927** Prov: 14 G. **1928** Prov: 8 G. **1931** SI: 9 G. **Total:** 79 G; Rush 11 TD; Rec 2 TD; Scor 89, 3 FG, 2 XK; Tot TD 13.

BILL LAJOUSKY Lajousky, William 5′11″, 200 **G**
Col: Catholic *HS:* Worcester Classical [MA] B: 4/18/1913, Vilna, Lithuania D: 1/7/1973, Waterville, ME
1936 Pit: 11 G; Rush 1-1 1.0.

CARNELL LAKE Lake, Carnell Augustino 6′1″, 210 **DB**
Col: UCLA *HS:* Culver City [CA] B: 7/15/1967, Salt Lake City, UT
Drafted: 1989 Round 2 Pit
1989 Pit: 1 Sac. **1990** Pit: 1 Sac. **1991** Pit: 1 Sac. **1992** Pit: 2 Sac. **1993** Pit: 5 Sac. **1994** Pit: 1 Sac. **1995** Pit: 1.5 Sac. **1996** Pit: **1** Fum TD; 2 Sac. **1997** Pit: 1 Fum TD; 6 Sac. **1998** Pit: 1 Sac. **Total:** 2 Fum TD; 21.5 Sac.

		Interceptions			Tot
Year Team	**G**	**Int**	**Yds**	**TD**	**TD**
1989 Pit	15	1	0	0	0
1990 Pit	16	1	0	0	0
1991 Pit	16	0	0	0	0
1992 Pit	16	0	0	0	0
1993 Pit	14	4	31	0	0
1994 Pit	16	1	2	0	0
1995 Pit	16	1	32	1	1
1996 Pit	13	1	47	1	2
1997 Pit	16	3	16	0	1
1998 Pit	16	4	33	1	1
NFL Total	154	16	161	3	5

ROLAND LAKES Lakes, Roland Hayes 6′4″, 279 **DT-DE-OT**
Col: Wichita State *HS:* Parsons [KS] B: 12/25/1939, Vicksburg, MS
Drafted: 1961 Round 2 SF
1961 SF: 14 G. **1962** SF: 14 G. **1963** SF: 14 G. **1964** SF: 14 G. **1965** SF: 14 G. **1966** SF: 14 G. **1967** SF: 14 G. **1968** SF: 14 G. **1969** SF: 14 G; **1** Fum TD; 6 Pt. **1970** SF: 14 G. **1971** NYG: 14 G. **Total:** 154 G; 1 Fum TD; 6 Pt.

BOB LALLY Lally, Robert Michael 6′2″, 230 **LB**
Col: Cornell *HS:* Bergen Catholic [Oradell, NJ] B: 2/12/1952, Hoboken, NJ *Drafted:* 1974 Round 9 Mia
1976 GB: 2 G.

ROGER LALONDE LaLonde, Roger Fredrick 6′3″, 255 **DT**
Col: Muskingum *HS:* Van Wert [OH] B: 1/6/1942, Antwerp, NY
Drafted: 1964 Round 15 Det
1964 Det: 14 G. **1965** NYG: 11 G. **Total:** 25 G.

PETE LAMANA Lamana, Peter Charles 5′11″, 210 **LB-C-FB**
Col: Boston U. *HS:* Cathedral [Springfield, MA] B: 5/15/1921, Bristol, CT
AAFC **1946** ChiA: 10 G; Rush 6-21 3.5; PR 0-20 1 TD; KR 1-18 18.0; Int 1-16; 6 Pt. **1947** ChiA: 12 G. **1948** ChiA: 13 G; Int 1-0. **Total:** 35 G; Rush 6-21 3.5; PR 0-20 1 TD; KR 1-18 18.0; Int 2-16; 6 Pt.

KEVIN LAMAR Lamar, Kevin Thomas 6′4″, 260 **OG**
Col: Stanford *HS:* St. Xavier [Louisville, KY] B: 11/29/1961, Louisville, KY
1987 Buf: 1 G.

JOE LAMAS Lamas, Joseph Francis 5′10″, 216 **G**
(Lawless Lamas) *Col:* Mount St. Mary's *HS:* Straubenmuller Textile [New York, NY] B: 1/10/1916, Havana, Cuba
1942 Pit: 8 G; **1** Fum TD; 6 Pt.

BRAD LAMB Lamb, Bradley 5′10″, 171 **WR**
Col: Anderson (Ind.) *HS:* Springboro [OH] B: 10/7/1967, Springboro, OH *Drafted:* 1991 Round 8 Buf
1992 Buf: 7 G; Rec 7-139 19.9; KR 5-97 19.4. **1993** Buf: 1 G; KR 2-40 20.0. **Total:** 8 G; Rec 7-139 19.9; KR 7-137 19.6.

MACK LAMB Lamb, Mack Edward 6′1″, 188 **DB**
Col: Tennessee State *HS:* Booker T. Washington [Miami, FL]
B: 5/9/1944, Miami, FL
1967 Mia: 2 G. **1968** Mia: 13 G; KR 1-24 24.0; Int 1-0. **Total:** 15 G; KR 1-24 24.0; Int 1-0.

RON LAMB Lamb, Ronald 6′2″, 225 **RB**
Col: South Carolina *HS:* McCormick [SC] B: 2/3/1944, New London, CT *Drafted:* 1966 Round 13 Dal
1968 Den-Cin: Rec 7-87 12.4. Den: Rec 3-10 3.3. Cin: Rec 4-77 19.3. **1969** Cin: KR 5-64 12.8; Punt 1-29 29.0. **1970** Cin: KR 2-41 20.5. **1971** Cin: KR 2-42 21.0. **1972** Atl: Rec 1-10 10.0. **Total:** Rec 8-97 12.1; KR 9-147 16.3; Punt 1-29 29.0.

		Rushing				
Year Team	**G**	**Att**	**Yds**	**Avg**	**TD**	**Fum**
1968 Den-Cin	9	39	107	2.7	0	2
1968 Den	3	22	63	2.9	0	1
1968 Cin	6	17	44	2.6	0	1
1969 Cin	14	5	8	1.6	0	0
1970 Cin	14	6	35	5.8	0	1
1971 Cin	12	5	13	2.6	0	0
1972 Atl	7	0	0	—	0	0
NFL Total	56	55	163	3.0	0	3

RODDY LAMB Lamb, Roy Elmer 5′6″, 160 **TB-DB-BB-WB**
(Roy) *Col:* Lombard B: 8/20/1899, Garrison, NE D: 12/21/1995, Philomath, OR
1925 RI: 9 G; Pass 3 TD; Rush 2 TD; Rec 1 TD; PR **1** TD; Scor 27, 1 XK, 2 1XP; Tot TD 4. **1926** ChiC: 10 G; Rush 1 TD; Scor 7, 1 XK. **1927** ChiC: 9 G; Rush 1 TD; 6 Pt. **1933** ChiC: 4 G; Pass 5-1 20.0%, 8 1.60 1 Int; Rush 19-46 2.4. **Total:** 32 G; Pass 5-1 20.0%, 8 1.60 3 TD 1 Int; Rush 19-46 2.4 4 TD; Rec 1 TD; PR 1 TD; Scor 2 1XP; Tot TD 6.

WALT LAMB Lamb, Walter G 6′1″, 195 **DE-OE**
(Dub) *Col:* Oklahoma *HS:* Ardmore [OK] B: 12/21/1920, Ardmore, OK D: 1/5/1991 *Drafted:* 1943 Round 8 ChiB
1946 ChiB: 11 G; Rec 1-10 10.0.

CURLY LAMBEAU Lambeau, Earl Louis 5′10″, 187 **TB-BB-FB-E**
Col: Wisconsin; Notre Dame *HS:* Green Bay East [WI] B: 4/9/1898, Green Bay, WI D: 6/1/1965, Sturgeon Bay, WI
1921 GB: 6 G; Pass 1 TD; Rush 2 TD; Scor 28, 3 FG, 7 XK. **1922** GB: 8 G; Pass 2 TD; Rush 3 TD; Scor 30, 1 FG, 3 XK; Tot TD 4. **1923** GB: 10 G; Pass 3 TD; Rush 1 TD; Rec 2 TD; Tot TD 3; 18 Pt. **1924** GB: 11 G; Pass 8 TD; Rec 1 TD; Scor 10, 1 FG, **1** 1XP. **1925** GB: 11 G; Pass 5 TD; Scor 8, 1 FG, 5 XK. **1926** GB: 12 G; Pass 3 TD; Scor 4, 4 XK. **1927** GB: 10 G; Pass 1 TD; Rush 2 TD; 12 Pt. **1928** GB: 8 G; Pass 1 TD. **1929** GB: 1 G. **Total:** 77 G; Pass 24 TD; Rush 8 TD; Rec 3 TD; Scor 110, 6 FG, 19 XK, 1 1XP; Tot TD 12.

DION LAMBERT Lambert, Dion Adrian 6′0″, 190 **DB**
Col: UCLA *HS:* John F. Kennedy [Los Angeles, CA] B: 2/12/1969, Lakeview Terrace, CA *Drafted:* 1992 Round 4 NE
1992 NE: 16 G; PR 1-0; 1 Sac. **1993** NE: 14 G; Int 1-0. **1994** Sea: 1 G. **Total:** 31 G; PR 1-0; Int 1-0; 1 Sac.

FRANK LAMBERT Lambert, Franklin Talley 6′3″, 200 **P**
Col: Mississippi *HS:* Hattiesburg [MS] B: 4/17/1943, Hattiesburg, MS
Drafted: 1965 Round 5 NYG

		Punting			
Year Team	**G**	**Punts**	**Yds**	**Avg**	**Fum**
1965 Pit	14	**78**	**3518**	45.1	1
1966 Pit	14	78	3284	42.1	0
NFL Total	28	156	6802	43.6	1

GORDON LAMBERT Lambert, Gordon Olaf 6′5″, 245 **LB**
Col: West Virginia; Tennessee-Martin *HS:* Gary [WV] B: 7/5/1945, Leckie, WV *Drafted:* 1968 Round 4 Den
1968 Den: 10 G. **1969** Den: 4 G. **Total:** 14 G.

JACK LAMBERT Lambert, John Harold 6′4″, 220 **LB**
Col: Kent State *HS:* Mantua [OH] B: 7/8/1952, Mantua, OH
Drafted: 1974 Round 2 Pit *HOF:* 1990
1982 Pit: 4 Sac. **1983** Pit: 4 Sac. **Total:** 8 Sac.

		Interceptions			
Year Team	**G**	**Int**	**Yds**	**TD**	**Fum**
1974 Pit	14	2	19	0	1
1975 Pit	14	2	35	0	0
1976 Pit	14	2	32	0	0
1977 Pit	11	1	5	0	0
1978 Pit	16	4	41	0	0
1979 Pit	16	6	29	0	0
1980 Pit	14	2	1	0	0
1981 Pit	16	6	76	0	0
1982 Pit	8	1	6	0	0
1983 Pit	15	2	-1	0	0
1984 Pit	8	0	0	0	0
NFL Total	146	28	243	0	1

PAT LAMBERTI Lamberti, Pasquale C Jr. 6′2″, 225 **LB**
Col: Richmond *HS:* Woodbridge [NJ] B: 9/1/1937, Woodbridge, NJ
Drafted: 1959 Round 13 ChiC
1961 NYT-Den: 12 G; Int 1-5. NYT: 5 G. Den: 7 G; Int 1-5. **Total:** 12 G; Int 1-5.

MIKE LAMBRECHT Lambrecht, Michael James 6′1″, 271 **DT**
Col: St. Cloud State *HS:* Watertown [MN] B: 5/2/1963, Watertown, MN
1987 Mia: 5 G; 1.5 Sac. **1988** Mia: 8 G. **1989** Mia: 6 G. **Total:** 19 G; 1.5 Sac.

BUCK LAMME Lamme, Emerald Ford 6′2″, 180 **E**
Col: Ohio Wesleyan *HS:* Ostrander [OH] B: 7/2/1905 D: 9/4/1957, Columbus, OH
1931 Cle: 1 G.

PETE LAMMONS Lammons, Peter Spencer Jr. 6′3″, 230 **TE**
Col: Texas *HS:* Jacksonville [TX] B: 10/20/1943, Crockett, TX
Drafted: 1966 Round 8 NYJ
1971 NYJ: Rush 0-3. **Total:** Rush 0-3.

		Receiving				
Year Team	G	Rec	Yds	Avg	TD	Fum
1966 NYJ	14	41	565	13.8	4	2
1967 NYJ	14	45	515	11.4	2	1
1968 NYJ	13	32	400	12.5	3	0
1969 NYJ	14	33	400	12.1	2	1
1970 NYJ	14	25	316	12.6	2	1
1971 NYJ	14	8	149	18.6	1	1
1972 GB	12	1	19	19.0	0	0
NFL Total	95	185	2364	12.8	14	6

DARYLE LAMONICA Lamonica, Daryle Patrick 6′3″, 215 **QB**
(The Mad Bomber) *Col:* Notre Dame *HS:* Clovis [CA] B: 7/17/1941, Fresno, CA *Drafted:* 1963 Round 24 Buf
1963 Buf: Scor **1** 2XP. **1964** Buf: Scor **2** 2XP. **Total:** Scor 3 2XP.

		Passing							
Year Team	G	Att	Comp	Comp%	Yds	YPA	TD	Int	Rating
1963 Buf	14	71	33	46.5	437	6.15	3	4	57.1
1964 Buf	14	128	55	43.0	1137	8.88	6	8	64.5
1965 Buf	14	70	29	41.4	376	5.37	3	6	37.6
1966 Buf	14	84	33	39.3	549	6.54	4	5	53.1
1967 Oak	14	425	220	51.8	3228	7.60	**30**	20	80.8
1968 Oak	13	416	206	49.5	3245	7.80	25	15	80.9
1969 Oak	14	**426**	**221**	51.9	**3302**	7.75	**34**	25	79.8
1970 Oak	14	356	179	50.3	2516	7.07	22	15	76.5
1971 Oak	14	242	118	48.8	1717	7.10	16	16	66.8
1972 Oak	14	281	149	53.0	1998	7.11	18	12	79.5
1973 Oak	8	93	42	45.2	614	6.60	2	8	38.6
1974 Oak	4	9	3	33.3	35	3.89	1	4	43.5
NFL Total	151	2601	1288	49.5	19154	7.36	164	138	72.9

	Rushing				Punting			
Year Team	Att	Yds	Avg	TD	Punts	Yds	Avg	Fum
1963 Buf	9	8	0.9	0	52	2086	40.1	1
1964 Buf	55	289	5.3	**6**	0	0	—	6
1965 Buf	10	30	3.0	1	0	0	—	2
1966 Buf	9	6	0.7	1	0	0	—	2
1967 Oak	22	110	5.0	4	0	0	—	3
1968 Oak	19	98	5.2	1	0	0	—	4
1969 Oak	13	36	2.8	1	0	0	—	1
1970 Oak	8	24	3.0	0	0	0	—	0
1971 Oak	4	16	4.0	0	0	0	—	3
1972 Oak	10	33	3.3	0	0	0	—	5
1973 Oak	5	-7	-1.4	0	0	0	—	3
1974 Oak	2	-3	-1.5	0	0	0	—	2
NFL Total	166	640	3.9	14	52	2086	40.1	32

CHUCK LAMSON Lamson, Charles Watt 6′0″, 190 **DB**
Col: Iowa State; Wyoming *HS:* Ames [IA] B: 3/14/1939, Webster City, IA *Drafted:* 1961 Round 4 Min
1966 LARm: KR 1-3 3.0. **Total:** KR 1-3 3.0.

		Interceptions			
Year Team	G	Int	Yds	TD	Fum
1962 Min	14	1	0	0	0
1963 Min	12	1	7	0	0
1965 LARm	13	2	0	0	0
1966 LARm	14	5	59	1	0
1967 LARm	14	2	18	0	1
NFL Total	67	11	84	1	1

DAN LAND Land, Daniel 6′0″, 195 **DB-RB**
Col: Albany State (Ga.) *HS:* Seminole Co. [Donalsonville, GA]
B: 7/3/1965, Donalsonville, GA
1987 TB: 3 G; Rush 9-20 2.2. **1989** LARd: 10 G. **1990** LARd: 16 G. **1991** LARd: 16 G. **1992** LARd: 16 G; KR 2-27 13.5; Int 1-0; 1 Fum. **1993** LARd: 15 G. **1994** LARd: 16 G. **1995** Oak: 16 G. **1996** Oak: 16 G. **1997** Oak: 16 G; Int 1-13. **Total:** 140 G; Rush 9-20 2.2; KR 2-27 13.5; Int 2-13; 1 Fum.

FRED LAND Land, Frederick N 6′1″, 220 **T-G**
Col: Louisiana State *HS:* Little Rock Central [AR] B: 5/8/1925, North Little Rock, AR D: 3/19/1992, Baton Rouge, LA
AAFC **1948** SF-A: 2 G.

MEL LAND Land, Melvin 6′3″, 243 **LB-DE**
Col: Michigan State *HS:* Memorial [Campbell, OH] B: 11/30/1955, Youngstown, OH *Drafted:* 1979 Round 3 Mia
1979 Mia: 16 G. **1980** SF: 3 G. **Total:** 19 G.

LOWELL LANDER Lander, Lowell Ken 6′0″, 195 **DB**
Col: Westminster *HS:* Avonworth [Pittsburgh, PA] B: 9/12/1932, Pittsburgh, PA
1958 ChiC: 1 G.

WALT LANDERS Landers, Walter James 6′0″, 214 **RB**
(Brick) *Col:* Clark Atlanta B: 7/4/1953, Lanett, AL
1978 GB: 4 G; Rush 7-40 5.7; KR 1-0; 6 Pt. **1979** GB: 9 G; Rush 17-41 2.4; Rec 5-60 12.0 1 TD; 6 Pt. **Total:** 13 G; Rush 24-81 3.4; Rec 5-60 12.0 1 TD; KR 1-0; Tot TD 2; 12 Pt.

SEAN LANDETA Landeta, Sean Edward 6′0″, 210 **P**
Col: Towson State *HS:* Loch Raven [Baltimore, MD] B: 1/6/1962, Baltimore, MD
1985 NYG: Pass 1-0. **1996** StL: Rush 2-0. **Total:** Pass 1-0; Rush 2-0.

		Punting			
Year Team	G	Punts	Yds	Avg	Fum
1985 NYG	16	81	3472	42.9	0
1986 NYG	16	79	3539	44.8	0
1987 NYG	12	65	2773	42.7	0
1988 NYG	1	6	222	37.0	0
1989 NYG	16	70	3019	43.1	0
1990 NYG	16	75	3306	44.1	0
1991 NYG	15	64	2768	43.3	0
1992 NYG	11	53	2317	43.7	0
1993 NYG-LARm	16	75	3215	42.9	0
1993 NYG	8	33	1390	42.1	0
1993 LARm	8	42	1825	43.5	0
1994 LARm	16	78	3494	**44.8**	0
1995 StL	16	83	3679	44.3	0
1996 StL	16	78	3491	44.8	1
1997 TB	10	54	2274	42.1	0
1998 GB	16	65	2788	42.9	0
NFL Total	193	926	40357	43.6	1

JIM LANDRIGAN Landrigan, James Montague 6′4″, 235 **T**
(Big Jim) *Col:* Dartmouth; Holy Cross *HS:* Wakefield [MA]
B: 5/31/1923, Everett, MA D: 6/24/1974, San Diego, CA
AAFC **1947** BalA: 5 G.

MIKE LANDRUM Landrum, Michael Geddie 6′2″, 231 **TE**
Col: Southern Mississippi *HS:* Columbia [MS] B: 11/6/1961, Laurel, MS
1984 Atl: 15 G; Rec 6-66 11.0.

GREG LANDRY Landry, Gregory Paul 6′4″, 210 **QB**
Col: Massachusetts *HS:* Nashua [NH] B: 12/18/1946, Nashua, NH
Drafted: 1968 Round 1 Det
1981 Bal: 1 Fum TD. **Total:** 1 Fum TD.

		Passing							
Year Team	G	Att	Comp	Comp%	Yds	YPA	TD	Int	Rating
1968 Det	4	48	23	47.9	338	7.04	2	7	45.7
1969 Det	10	160	80	50.0	853	5.33	4	10	48.3
1970 Det	12	136	83	61.0	1072	7.88	9	5	92.5
1971 Det	14	261	136	52.1	2237	8.57	16	13	80.9
1972 Det	14	268	134	50.0	2066	7.71	18	17	71.8
1973 Det	7	128	70	54.7	908	7.09	3	10	52.5
1974 Det	5	82	49	59.8	572	6.98	3	3	77.9
1975 Det	6	56	31	55.4	403	7.20	1	0	84.2
1976 Det	14	291	168	57.7	2191	7.53	17	8	89.6
1977 Det	11	240	135	56.3	1359	5.66	6	7	68.7
1978 Det	5	77	48	62.3	452	5.87	1	1	77.4
1979 Bal	16	457	270	59.1	2932	6.42	15	15	75.3
1980 Bal	16	47	24	51.1	275	5.85	2	3	56.6
1981 Bal	11	29	14	48.3	195	6.72	0	1	56.0
1984 ChiB	1	20	11	55.0	199	9.95	1	3	66.5
NFL Total	146	2300	1276	55.5	16052	6.98	98	103	72.9

	Rushing					Tot
Year Team	Att	Yds	Avg	TD	Fum	TD
1968 Det	7	39	5.6	1	0	1
1969 Det	33	243	7.4	1	2	1
1970 Det	35	350	10.0	1	3	1
1971 Det	76	530	7.0	3	5	3
1972 Det	81	524	6.5	9	3	9
1973 Det	42	267	6.4	2	2	2
1974 Det	22	95	4.3	1	2	1
1975 Det	20	92	4.6	0	4	0
1976 Det	43	234	5.4	1	5	1
1977 Det	25	99	4.0	0	2	0
1978 Det	5	29	5.8	0	3	0
1979 Bal	31	115	3.7	0	8	0
1980 Bal	7	26	3.7	1	0	1
1981 Bal	1	11	11.0	0	2	1
1984 ChiB	2	1	0.5	1	0	1
NFL Total	430	2655	6.2	21	41	22

TOM LANDRY Landry, Thomas Wade 6′1″, 195 **DB-HB-QB**
Col: Texas *HS:* Mission [TX] B: 9/11/1924, Mission, TX *Drafted:* 1947 Round 18 NYG
AAFC **1949** NY-A: Rec 6-109 18.2; PR 3-52 17.3; KR 2-39 19.5; Int 1-44.

		Rushing				Punting		
Year Team	G	Att	Yds	Avg	TD	Punts	Yds	Avg
1949 NY-A	12	29	91	3.1	0	51	2249	44.1

NFL **1950** NYG: **1** Fum TD. **1951** NYG: PR 1-0; KR 1-0; 1 Fum TD. **1952** NYG: Pass 47-11 23.4%, 172 3.66 1 TD 7 Int; Rush 7-40 5.7 1 TD; PR 10-88 8.8; KR 1-20 20.0. **1953** NYG: PR 1-5 5.0; KR 2-38 19.0. **Total:** Pass 47-11 23.4%, 172 3.66 1 TD 7 Int; Rush 7-40 5.7 1 TD; PR 12-93 7.8; KR 4-58 14.5; 2 Fum TD.

		Interceptions			Punting				Tot
Year Team	G	Int	Yds	TD	Punts	Yds	Avg	Fum	TD
1950 NYG	12	2	0	0	58	2136	36.8	0	1
1951 NYG	10	8	121	**2**	15	638	42.5	0	3
1952 NYG	12	8	99	1	82	**3363**	41.0	5	2
1953 NYG	12	3	55	0	44	1772	40.3	1	0
1954 NYG	12	8	71	0	64	2720	42.5	1	0
1955 NYG	12	2	14	0	**75**	**3022**	40.3	0	0
NFL Total	70	31	360	3	338	13651	40.4	7	6

MORT LANDSBERG Landsberg, Mortimer William Jr. 5′11″, 180 **HB-DB**
Col: Cornell *HS:* Lawrenceville School [NJ] B: 7/25/1919, New York, NY D: 12/31/1970, New York, NY *Drafted:* 1941 Round 20 Pit
AAFC **1947** LA-A: 6 G; Rush 2-(-11) -5.5; Rec 1-0.

NFL **1941** Phi: 11 G; Rush 23-69 3.0; Rec 5-51 10.2; PR 2-15 7.5; KR 2-49 24.5; Int 2-45.

BOB LANDSEE Landsee, Robert John 6′4″, 273 **C-OG**
Col: Wisconsin *HS:* Iron Mountain [MI] B: 3/21/1964, Iron Mountain, MI *Drafted:* 1986 Round 6 Phi
1986 Phi: 7 G. **1987** Phi: 2 G. **Total:** 9 G.

BOBBY LANE Lane, Bobby Allen 6′2″, 222 **LB**
Col: Cerritos Coll. CA (J.C.); Baylor *HS:* Bellflower [CA] B: 10/30/1939, Wagoner, OK
1963 SD: 7 G. **1964** SD: 1 G. **Total:** 8 G.

CLAYTON LANE Lane, Clayton Harold 6′0″, 215 **T**
(Clayt) *Col:* New Hampshire *HS:* Brattleboro [VT] B: 11/23/1922, Worcester, MA
AAFC **1948** NY-A: 1 G.

ERIC LANE Lane, Eric 6′2″, 240 **RB**
Col: Tennessee *HS:* Bergen Catholic [Oradell, NJ] B: 3/17/1974, East Orange, NJ
1997 NYG: 15 G; Rush 5-13 2.6.

ERIC LANE Lane, Eric T 6′0″, 195 **RB**
Col: Chabot Coll. CA (J.C.); Brigham Young *HS:* Hayward [CA] B: 1/6/1959, Oakland, CA *Drafted:* 1981 Round 8 Sea
1982 Sea: Pass 1-0. **Total:** Pass 1-0.

		Rushing				Receiving			
Year Team	G	Att	Yds	Avg	TD	Rec	Yds	Avg	TD
1981 Sea	14	8	22	2.8	0	7	58	8.3	0
1982 Sea	9	0	0	—	0	0	0	—	0
1983 Sea	16	3	1	0.3	0	2	9	4.5	0
1984 Sea	15	80	299	3.7	4	11	101	9.2	1
1985 Sea	16	14	32	2.3	0	15	153	10.2	0
1986 Sea	15	6	11	1.8	0	3	6	2.0	1
1987 Sea	12	13	40	3.1	0	4	30	7.5	0
NFL Total	97	124	405	3.3	4	42	357	8.5	2

	Kickoff Returns					Tot
Year Team	Ret	Yds	Avg	TD	Fum	TD
1981 Sea	10	208	20.8	0	0	0
1982 Sea	11	172	15.6	0	1	0
1983 Sea	4	58	14.5	0	2	0
1984 Sea	0	0	—	0	1	5
1985 Sea	1	1	1.0	0	0	0
1986 Sea	1	3	3.0	0	0	2
1987 Sea	2	34	17.0	0	0	0
NFL Total	29	476	16.4	0	4	7

OXIE LANE Lane, Francis Charles 6′4″, 220 **T**
Col: Marquette *HS:* Merrill [WI] B: 1/2/1905, Merrill, WI D: 8/19/1977, Merrill, WI
1926 Mil: 9 G.

FRED LANE Lane, Freddie Brown Jr. 5′10″, 205 **RB**
Col: Lane *HS:* Franklin [TN] B: 9/6/1975, Nashville, TN
1997 Car: Rec 8-27 3.4. **1998** Car: Rec 12-85 7.1. **Total:** Rec 20-112 5.6.

		Rushing				
Year Team	G	Att	Yds	Avg	TD	Fum
1997 Car	13	182	809	4.4	7	4
1998 Car	14	205	717	3.5	5	4
NFL Total	27	387	1526	3.9	12	8

GARCIA LANE Lane, Garcia R 5′9″, 180 **DB**
Col: Ohio State *HS:* South [Youngstown, OH] B: 12/31/1961, Youngstown, OH *Drafted:* 1984 Supplemental Round 3 KC
1985 KC: KR 13-269 20.7; 0.5 Sac. **1987** KC: KR 2-37 18.5. **Total:** KR 15-306 20.4; 0.5 Sac.

		Punt Returns				
Year Team	G	Ret	Yds	Avg	TD	Fum
1985 KC	16	43	381	8.9	0	3
1987 KC	1	0	0	—	0	0
NFL Total	17	43	381	8.9	0	3

GARY LANE Lane, Gary Owen 6′1″, 210 **QB**
Col: Missouri *HS:* Wood River [IL] B: 12/21/1942, Alton, IL *Drafted:* 1965 Round 9 Cle
1966 Cle: 8 G. **1967** Cle: 3 G; Pass 43-21 48.8%, 254 5.91 2 TD 1 Int; Rush 2-21 10.5. **1968** NYG: 7 G. **Total:** 18 G; Pass 43-21 48.8%, 254 5.91 2 TD 1 Int; Rush 2-21 10.5.

LES LANE Lane, Leslie Willard 6′3″, 193 **G**
Col: South Dakota B: 4/18/1916, Walthill, NE
1939 Bkn: 2 G.

LEW LANE Lane, Lindley Roedesto 5′10″, 180 **TB-WB-BB**
Col: St. Mary's (Kansas) *HS:* Bucklin [KS] B: 1/28/1898, Bucklin, KS D: 8/1963
1924 KC: 5 G.

MACARTHUR LANE Lane, MacArthur 6′1″, 220 **RB**
Col: Merritt Coll. CA (J.C.); Utah State *HS:* Fremont [Oakland, CA] B: 3/16/1942, Oakland, CA *Drafted:* 1968 Round 1 StL
1969 StL: KR 20-523 26.2. **1972** GB: Pass 2-2 100.0%, 19 9.50. **1973** GB: Pass 2-1 50.0%, 23 11.50 1 TD; KR 2-31 15.5. **1974** GB: Pass 1-0. **Total:** Pass 5-3 60.0%, 42 8.40 1 TD; KR 22-554 25.2.

		Rushing				Receiving					Tot
Year Team	G	Att	Yds	Avg	TD	Rec	Yds	Avg	TD	Fum	TD
1968 StL	14	23	74	3.2	0	0	0	—	0	0	0
1969 StL	9	25	93	3.7	1	9	61	6.8	0	2	1
1970 StL	14	206	977	4.7	**11**	32	365	11.4	2	2	**13**
1971 StL	13	150	592	3.9	3	29	298	10.3	0	2	3
1972 GB	14	177	821	4.6	3	26	285	11.0	0	6	3
1973 GB	13	170	528	3.1	1	27	255	9.4	1	4	2
1974 GB	14	137	362	2.6	3	34	315	9.3	3	3	6
1975 KC	9	79	311	3.9	2	25	202	8.1	0	5	2
1976 KC	14	162	542	3.3	5	**66**	686	10.4	1	9	6
1977 KC	3	25	79	3.2	1	3	40	13.3	0	0	1
1978 KC	16	52	277	5.3	0	36	279	7.8	0	1	0
NFL Total	133	1206	4656	3.9	30	287	2786	9.7	7	34	37

MAX LANE Lane, Max Aaron 6′6″, 301 **OT-OG**
Col: Navy *HS:* Norbone [MO]; Naval Academy Prep [Newport, RI] B: 2/22/1971, Norbone, MO *Drafted:* 1994 Round 6 NE
1994 NE: 14 G. **1995** NE: 16 G. **1996** NE: 16 G. **1997** NE: 16 G. **1998** NE: 16 G. **Total:** 78 G.

SKIP LANE Lane, Paul John Jr. 6′1″, 210 **DB**
Col: Mississippi *HS:* Staples [Westport, CT] B: 1/30/1960, Norwalk, CT
1984 NYJ-KC: 4 G. NYJ: 3 G. KC: 1 G. **1987** Was: 3 G. **Total:** 7 G.

NIGHT TRAIN LANE Lane, Richard 6′1″, 194 **DB-OE**
Col: Western Nebraska CC-Scottsbluff *HS:* L. C. Anderson [Austin, TX] B: 4/16/1927, Austin, TX *HOF:* 1974
1952 LARm: Scor **1** Saf. **1953** LARm: **1** Fum TD. **1954** ChiC: Rec 4-58 14.5. **1955** ChiC: Rec 2-110 55.0 1 TD. **1956** ChiC: Rec 1-75 75.0; PR 2-0. **1957** ChiC: PR 1-8 8.0. **1958** ChiC: Rec 1-10 10.0. **1961** Det: PR 1-6 6.0. **Total:** Rec 8-253 31.6 1 TD; PR 4-14 3.5; Scor 1 Saf; 1 Fum TD.

		Interceptions				Tot
Year Team	G	Int	Yds	TD	Fum	TD
1952 LARm	12	**14**	**298**	**2**	0	2
1953 LARm	11	3	9	0	0	2
1954 ChiC	12	**10**	**181**	0	1	0
1955 ChiC	12	6	69	0	0	1
1956 ChiC	12	7	206	1	2	1
1957 ChiC	8	2	47	0	0	0
1958 ChiC	12	2	0	0	0	0
1959 ChiC	12	3	125	**1**	0	1
1960 Det	12	5	102	1	0	1
1961 Det	14	6	73	0	0	0
1962 Det	14	4	16	0	1	0
1963 Det	12	5	70	0	0	0
1964 Det	7	1	11	0	0	0

1965 Det	7	0	0	0	0	0
NFL Total	157	68	1207	5	4	8

DAVID LANG Lang, David 5'11", 210 **RB**
Col: Northern Arizona *HS:* Eisenhower [Rialto, CA] B: 3/28/1967, San Bernardino, CA *Drafted:* 1990 Round 12 LARm

		Rushing				Receiving			
Year Team	G	Att	Yds	Avg	TD	Rec	Yds	Avg	TD
1991 LARm	16	0	0	—	0	0	0	—	0
1992 LARm	16	33	203	6.2	5	18	283	15.7	1
1993 LARm	6	9	29	3.2	0	4	45	11.3	0
1994 LARm	13	6	34	5.7	0	8	60	7.5	0
1995 Dal	16	1	7	7.0	0	0	0	—	0
NFL Total	67	49	273	5.6	5	30	388	12.9	1

	Kickoff Returns					Tot
Year Team	Ret	Yds	Avg	TD	Fum	TD
1991 LARm	12	194	16.2	0	1	0
1992 LARm	13	228	17.5	0	5	6
1994 LARm	27	626	23.2	0	2	0
NFL Total	52	1048	20.2	0	8	6

GENE LANG Lang, Gene Eric 5'10", 196 **RB**
Col: Louisiana State *HS:* Pass Christian [MS] B: 3/15/1962, Pass Christian, MS *Drafted:* 1984 Round 11 Den
1987 Den: Pass 1-0. **Total:** Pass 1-0.

		Rushing				Receiving			
Year Team	G	Att	Yds	Avg	TD	Rec	Yds	Avg	TD
1984 Den	16	8	42	5.3	2	4	24	6.0	1
1985 Den	12	84	318	3.8	5	23	180	7.8	2
1986 Den	15	29	94	3.2	1	13	105	8.1	2
1987 Den	12	89	303	3.4	2	17	130	7.6	2
1988 Atl	16	53	191	3.6	0	37	398	10.8	1
1989 Atl	15	47	176	3.7	1	39	436	11.2	1
1990 Atl	3	9	24	2.7	0	1	7	7.0	0
NFL Total	89	319	1148	3.6	11	134	1280	9.6	9

	Kickoff Returns					Tot
Year Team	Ret	Yds	Avg	TD	Fum	TD
1984 Den	19	404	21.3	0	0	3
1985 Den	17	361	21.2	0	3	7
1986 Den	21	480	22.9	0	0	3
1987 Den	4	78	19.5	0	0	4
1988 Atl	1	12	12.0	0	3	1
1989 Atl	0	0	—	0	1	2
1990 Atl	1	18	18.0	0	0	0
NFL Total	63	1353	21.5	0	7	20

IZZY LANG Lang, Israel Alvin 6'1", 232 **RB**
Col: Tennessee State *HS:* Middleton [Tampa, FL] B: 2/2/1942, Tampa, FL *Drafted:* 1964 Round 18 Phi
1964 Phi: PR 6-26 4.3; KR 13-352 27.1. **1965** Phi: KR 3-36 12.0. **1966** Phi: Pass 3-2 66.7%, 51 17.00. **1967** Phi: Pass 1-1 100.0%, 26 26.00. **1969** LARm: KR 4-70 17.5. **Total:** Pass 4-3 75.0%, 77 19.25; PR 6-26 4.3; KR 20-458 22.9.

		Rushing				Receiving					Tot
Year Team	G	Att	Yds	Avg	TD	Rec	Yds	Avg	TD	Fum	TD
1964 Phi	12	12	37	3.1	0	6	69	11.5	0	7	0
1965 Phi	14	10	25	2.5	1	2	30	15.0	0	0	1
1966 Phi	14	52	239	4.6	1	12	107	8.9	0	2	1
1967 Phi	14	101	336	3.3	2	26	201	7.7	3	4	5
1968 Phi	11	69	235	3.4	0	17	147	8.6	1	1	1
1969 LARm	12	1	1	1.0	0	0	0	—	0	0	0
NFL Total	77	245	873	3.6	4	63	554	8.8	4	14	8

CHICK LANG Lang, James H 195 **T**
Col: No College *HS:* Harrison [Chicago, IL] B: 10/7/1900, Fort William, Scotland D: 10/25/1976, Mount Aukum, CA
1927 Dul: 2 G. **1929** ChiC: 3 G. **Total:** 5 G.

KENARD LANG Lang, Kenard Dushun 6'4", 277 **DE**
(Shaq) *Col:* Miami (Fla.) *HS:* Maynard Evans [Orlando, FL] B: 1/31/1975, Orlando, FL *Drafted:* 1997 Round 1 Was
1997 Was: 11 G; 1.5 Sac. **1998** Was: 16 G; 7 Sac. **Total:** 27 G; 8.5 Sac.

LE-LO LANG Lang, Le-Lo 5'11", 185 **DB**
Col: Washington *HS:* David Starr Jordan [Los Angeles, CA] B: 1/23/1967, Los Angeles, CA *Drafted:* 1990 Round 5 Den
1990 Den: 6 G; Int 1-5. **1991** Den: 16 G; Int 1-30. **1992** Den: 16 G; Int 1-26; 1 Sac. **1993** Den: 16 G; Int 2-4. **Total:** 54 G; Int 5-65; 1 Sac.

BOB LANGAS Langas, Robert Frederick 6'4", 230 **DE**
(Hooks) *Col:* Wayne State (Mich.) *HS:* Cooley [Detroit, MI] B: 1/22/1930, Detroit, MI
1954 Bal: 8 G; KR 1-18 18.0.

BILL LANGE Lange, William Henry 6'1", 239 **OG-LB**
Col: Dayton *HS:* St. Rose [Lima, OH] B: 1/12/1928, Delphos, OH D: 4/5/1995, Dayton, OH *Drafted:* 1950 Round 30 LARm
1951 LARm: 12 G. **1952** LARm: 10 G. **1953** Bal: 12 G. **1954** ChiC: 10 G. **1955** ChiC: 12 G; KR 2-0. **Total:** 56 G; KR 2-0.

JIM LANGER Langer, James John 6'2", 250 **C-OG**
Col: South Dakota State *HS:* Royalton [MN] B: 5/16/1948, Little Falls, MN *HOF:* 1987
1970 Mia: 6 G. **1971** Mia: 14 G. **1972** Mia: 14 G. **1973** Mia: 14 G. **1974** Mia: 14 G. **1975** Mia: 14 G. **1976** Mia: 14 G. **1977** Mia: 14 G. **1978** Mia: 16 G. **1979** Mia: 9 G. **1980** Min: 13 G. **1981** Min: 9 G. **Total:** 151 G.

JEVON LANGFORD Langford, Jevon Dicorious 6'3", 290 **DE**
Col: Oklahoma State *HS:* Archbishop Carroll [Washington, DC] B: 2/16/1974, Washington, DC *Drafted:* 1996 Round 4 Cin
1996 Cin: 12 G; Int 1-0; 2 Sac. **1997** Cin: 14 G; 1 Sac. **1998** Cin: 14 G; 0.5 Sac. **Total:** 40 G; Int 1-0; 3.5 Sac.

ANTONIO LANGHAM Langham, Collie Antonio 6'0", 181 **DB**
Col: Alabama *HS:* Hazelwood [Town Creek, AL] B: 7/31/1972, Town Creek, AL *Drafted:* 1994 Round 1 Cle
1997 Bal: 1 Sac. **Total:** 1 Sac.

		Interceptions			
Year Team	G	Int	Yds	TD	Fum
1994 Cle	16	2	2	0	1
1995 Cle	16	2	29	0	0
1996 Bal	15	5	59	0	0
1997 Bal	16	3	40	1	0
1998 SF	11	1	0	0	0
NFL Total	74	13	130	1	1

IRV LANGHOFF Langhoff, Irvin John 5'8", 155 **WB-BB-TB**
(Oofie) *Col:* Marquette *HS:* Marquette Acad. [Milwaukee, WI] B: 8/1897, Milwaukee, WI D: 1/12/1952, Milwaukee, WI
1922 Rac: 11 G; Rush 1 TD; Scor 8, 1 XK, **1** 1XP. **1923** Rac: 4 G. **Total:** 15 G; Rush 1 TD; Scor 1 1XP.

REGGIE LANGHORNE Langhorne, Reginald Devan 6'2", 200 **WR**
Col: Elizabeth City State *HS:* Smithfield [VA] B: 4/7/1963, Suffolk, VA *Drafted:* 1985 Round 7 Cle
1985 Cle: KR 3-46 15.3. **1986** Cle: Rush 1-(-11) -11.0; KR 4-57 14.3. **1987** Cle: KR 1-8 8.0. **1988** Cle: Rush 2-26 13.0 1 TD. **1989** Cle: Rush 5-19 3.8. **1992** Ind: Rush 1-(-7) -7.0. **Total:** Rush 9-27 3.0 1 TD; KR 8-111 13.9.

		Receiving					Tot
Year Team	G	Rec	Yds	Avg	TD	Fum	TD
1985 Cle	16	1	12	12.0	0	1	0
1986 Cle	16	39	678	17.4	1	2	1
1987 Cle	12	20	288	14.4	1	0	1
1988 Cle	16	57	780	13.7	7	3	8
1989 Cle	16	60	749	12.5	2	3	2
1990 Cle	12	45	585	13.0	2	2	2
1991 Cle	14	39	505	12.9	2	0	2
1992 Ind	16	65	811	12.5	1	0	1
1993 Ind	16	85	1038	12.2	3	4	3
NFL Total	134	411	5446	13.3	19	15	20

CHARLIE LANHAM Lanham, Charles T 170 **T**
Col: No College *HS:* Male [Louisville, KY] B: 6/1/1891 D: 5/10/1971, Danville, KY
1922 Lou: 1 G. **1923** Lou: 1 G. **Total:** 2 G.

KEN LANIER Lanier, Kenneth Wayne 6'3", 281 **OT**
Col: Florida State *HS:* Marion-Franklin [Columbus, OH] B: 7/8/1959, Columbus, OH *Drafted:* 1981 Round 5 Den
1981 Den: 8 G. **1982** Den: 9 G. **1983** Den: 16 G. **1984** Den: 16 G. **1985** Den: 16 G. **1986** Den: 16 G. **1987** Den: 12 G. **1988** Den: 16 G. **1989** Den: 16 G. **1990** Den: 16 G; Rec 1-(-4) -4.0. **1991** Den: 16 G. **1992** Den: 16 G. **1993** LARd: 2 G. **1994** Den: 4 G. **Total:** 179 G; Rec 1-(-4) -4.0.

WILLIE LANIER Lanier, Willie Edward 6'1", 245 **LB**
Col: Morgan State *HS:* Maggie L. Walker [Richmond, VA] B: 8/21/1945, Clover, VA *Drafted:* 1967 Round 2 KC *HOF:* 1986
1967 KC: KR 1-1 1.0. **1974** KC: Scor **1** Saf. **Total:** KR 1-1 1.0; Scor 1 Saf.

		Interceptions		
Year Team	G	Int	Yds	TD
1967 KC	10	0	0	0
1968 KC	14	4	120	1
1969 KC	14	4	70	0
1970 KC	14	2	2	0
1971 KC	14	2	38	0
1972 KC	13	2	2	0
1973 KC	14	3	47	1
1974 KC	14	2	28	0
1975 KC	14	5	105	0

1976 KC	14	3	28	0
1977 KC	14	0	0	0
NFL Total	149	27	440	2

JIM LANKAS Lankas, James 6'2", 220 **FB-LB**
Col: St. Mary's (Cal.) *HS:* Abbey School [Canon City, CO]
B: 8/26/1918, Stratton, NE D: 8/9/1978, Earlton, KS
1942 Phi: 1 G. **1943** GB: 3 G; Rush 2-2 1.0. **Total:** 4 G; Rush 2-2 1.0.

PAUL LANKFORD Lankford, Paul Jay 6'1", 185 **DB**
Col: Penn State *HS:* Farmingdale [NY] B: 6/15/1958, New York, NY
Drafted: 1982 Round 3 Mia
1985 Mia: 1 Sac. **1988** Mia: 1 Sac. **1989** Mia: 1 Sac. **Total:** 3 Sac.

		Interceptions		
Year Team	**G**	**Int**	**Yds**	**TD**
1982 Mia	7	0	0	0
1983 Mia	16	1	10	0
1984 Mia	16	3	25	0
1985 Mia	16	4	10	0
1986 Mia	12	0	0	0
1987 Mia	12	3	44	0
1988 Mia	13	1	0	0
1989 Mia	16	1	0	0
1990 Mia	7	0	0	0
1991 Mia	15	0	0	0
NFL Total	130	13	89	0

DAN LANPHEAR Lanphear, George Daniel 6'2", 230 **DE**
Col: Wisconsin *HS:* West [Madison, WI] B: 1/24/1938, Madison, WI
Drafted: 1960 Round 8 Pit
1960 Hou: 14 G. **1962** Hou: 2 G. **Total:** 16 G.

GRENNY LANSDELL Lansdell, Grenville A Jr. 6'0", 190 **QB-DB**
Col: USC *HS:* Pasadena [CA] B: 7/16/1918 D: 5/14/1984, Newport Beach, CA *Drafted:* 1940 Round 1 NYG
1940 NYG: 2 G; Pass 3-2 66.7%, 23 7.67; Rush 7-9 1.3.

BUCK LANSFORD Lansford, Alex John 6'2", 232 **OG-OT**
Col: Texas *HS:* Carrizo Springs [TX] B: 11/4/1933, Catarina, TX
Drafted: 1955 Round 2 Phi
1955 Phi: 12 G. **1956** Phi: 12 G. **1957** Phi: 10 G. **1958** LARm: 12 G. **1959** LARm: 4 G. **1960** LARm: 11 G. **Total:** 61 G.

JIM LANSFORD Lansford, James Albert 6'3", 235 **OT**
Col: Texas *HS:* Carrizo Springs [TX] B: 8/19/1930, Jackson Co., TX
D: 1/17/1989 *Drafted:* 1952 Round 9 Dal
1952 Dal: 12 G.

MIKE LANSFORD Lansford, Michael John 6'0", 183 **K**
Col: Pasadena City Coll. CA (J.C.); Washington *HS:* Arcadia [CA]
B: 7/20/1958, Monterey Park, CA *Drafted:* 1980 Round 12 NYG

		Scoring						
Year Team	**G**	**Pts**	**FG**	**FGA**	**FG%**	**XK**	**XKA**	**XK%**
1982 LARm	9	50	9	15	60.0	23	24	95.8
1983 LARm	4	27	6	9	66.7	9	9	100.0
1984 LARm	16	112	25	33	75.8	37	38	97.4
1985 LARm	16	104	22	29	75.9	38	39	97.4
1986 LARm	16	85	17	24	70.8	34	35	97.1
1987 LARm	15	87	17	21	81.0	36	38	94.7
1988 LARm	16	117	24	32	75.0	45	48	93.8
1989 LARm	16	120	23	30	76.7	**51**	**51**	100.0
1990 LARm	16	87	15	24	62.5	42	43	97.7
NFL Total	124	789	158	217	72.8	315	325	96.9

MOSE LANTZ Lantz, Montgomery Stoffal 5'11", 185 **C-LB**
Col: Grove City *HS:* Westinghouse [Pittsburgh, PA] B: 11/24/1903, Pittsburgh, PA D: 11/2/1969, Pittsburgh, PA
1933 Pit: 10 G.

JAKE LANUM Lanum, Ralph Lewis 5'11", 190 **HB-FB**
Col: Illinois; Millikin *HS:* Urbana [IL]; Champaign HS [IL]; Decatur HS [IL]
B: 9/13/1896, Champaign, IL D: 3/19/1968, Homewood, IL
1920 Sta: 12 G. **1921** Sta: 7 G. **1922** ChiB: 12 G. **1923** ChiB: 10 G; Rush 1 TD; 6 Pt. **1924** ChiB: 7 G. **Total:** 48 G; Rush 1 TD; 6 Pt.

CHUCK LANZA Lanza, Charles Louis 6'2", 263 **C**
Col: Notre Dame *HS:* Christian Brothers [Memphis, TN] B: 9/20/1964, Coraopolis, PA *Drafted:* 1988 Round 3 Pit
1988 Pit: 16 G. **1989** Pit: 11 G. **Total:** 27 G.

DAVE LAPHAM Lapham, David Allan 6'4", 259 **OG-OT-C**
Col: Syracuse *HS:* Wakefield [MA] B: 6/24/1952, Melrose, MA
Drafted: 1974 Round 3 Cin
1974 Cin: 14 G. **1975** Cin: 13 G. **1976** Cin: 14 G. **1977** Cin: 13 G. **1978** Cin: 16 G. **1979** Cin: 16 G. **1980** Cin: 16 G. **1981** Cin: 13 G. **1982** Cin: 9 G. **1983** Cin: 16 G. **Total:** 140 G.

BILL LAPHAM Lapham, William Gaius 6'3", 238 **C**
Col: Drake; Iowa *HS:* Lincoln [Des Moines, IA] B: 2/2/1934, Des Moines, IA *Drafted:* 1958 Round 14 Phi
1960 Phi: 12 G. **1961** Min: 14 G. **Total:** 26 G.

MYRON LAPKA Lapka, Myron Lynn 6'4", 258 **NT-DE-DT**
Col: USC *HS:* Chatsworth [CA] B: 5/10/1956, Van Nuys, CA
Drafted: 1980 Round 3 NYG
1980 NYG: 10 G; KR 1-3 3.0. **1982** LARm: 2 G. **1983** LARm: 4 G. **Total:** 16 G; KR 1-3 3.0.

TED LAPKA Lapka, Theodore Aloysius 6'1", 193 **OE-DE**
Col: DePaul; St. Ambrose *HS:* St. Ignatius [Chicago, IL] B: 4/20/1920, Hawthorne, IL
1943 Was: 7 G; Rec 2-39 19.5. **1944** Was: 5 G; Rec 4-61 15.3 1 TD; 6 Pt. **1946** Was: 7 G; Rec 3-28 9.3; **1** Fum TD; 6 Pt. **Total:** 19 G; Rec 9-128 14.2 1 TD; 1 Fum TD; Tot TD 2; 12 Pt.

RON LAPOINTE LaPointe, Ronald Arthur 6'2", 235 **TE**
Col: Penn State *HS:* Holliston [MA] B: 2/28/1957, Framingham, MA
1980 Bal: 2 G; KR 1-18 18.0.

PHIL LAPORTA LaPorta, Philip Francis Jr. 6'4", 256 **OT**
Col: Penn State *HS:* Valley Stream Central [NY] B: 5/4/1952, Oceanside, NY *Drafted:* 1974 Round 9 NO
1974 NO: 6 G. **1975** NO: 14 G. **Total:** 20 G.

BENNY LAPRESTA LaPresta, Benjamin 5'9", 185 **BB-LB-DB**
Col: St. Louis *HS:* Crystal City [MO] B: 1/22/1909 D: 8/11/1975, St.Louis, MO
1933 Bos: 8 G; Pass 4-2 50.0%, 50 12.50; Rush 11-62 5.6; Rec 1-23 23.0; Scor 1, 1 XK. **1934** StL: 1 G; Pass 1-0; Rec 1-4 4.0. **Total:** 9 G; Pass 5-2 40.0%, 50 10.00; Rush 11-62 5.6; Rec 2-27 13.5.

BOB LARABA Laraba, Robert Edward 6'3", 216 **QB-LB**
Col: Texas-El Paso B: 5/30/1933, Sheldon, VT D: 2/16/1962, San Diego, CA *Drafted:* 1959 Round 8 GB
1960 LAC: 14 G; Pass 7-2 28.6%, 23 3.29 2 Int; Rush 3-13 4.3; Int 1-17; Punt 15-558 37.2; 2 Fum. **1961** SD: 14 G; Rush 5-5 1.0 1 TD; Int 5-151 2 TD; Scor 19, 1-2 50.0% XK; Tot TD 3. **Total:** 28 G; Pass 7-2 28.6%, 23 3.29 2 Int; Rush 8-18 2.3 1 TD; Int 6-168 2 TD; Punt 15-558 37.2; Scor 19, 1-2 50.0% XK; Tot TD 3; 2 Fum.

JACK LARAWAY Laraway, Jack Duane 6'1", 220 **LB**
Col: Purdue *HS:* Erie Acad. [PA] B: 9/20/1935, Erie, PA *Drafted:* 1959 Round 10 Det
1960 Buf: 12 G. **1961** Hou: 10 G; KR 1-22 22.0; Int 1-30. **Total:** 22 G; KR 1-22 22.0; Int 1-30.

STEVE LARGENT Largent, Stephen Michael 5'11", 187 **WR**
Col: Tulsa *HS:* Putnam City [Oklahoma City, OK] B: 9/28/1954, Tulsa, OK *Drafted:* 1976 Round 4 Hou *HOF:* 1995
1976 Sea: Pass 1-0; Rush 4-(-14) -3.5; PR 4-36 9.0; KR 8-156 19.5. **1977** Sea: PR 4-32 8.0. **1980** Sea: Rush 1-2 2.0. **1981** Sea: Pass 1-0; Rush 6-47 7.8 1 TD. **1982** Sea: Rush 1-8 8.0. **1983** Sea: Pass 1-1 100.0%, 11 11.00. **1984** Sea: Rush 2-10 5.0. **1985** Sea: Pass 1-0; Scor **1** 1XP. **1986** Sea: Pass 1-1 100.0%, 18 18.00. **1987** Sea: Pass 2-0; Rush 2-33 16.5. **1988** Sea: Rush 1-(-3) -3.0. **1989** Sea: Scor **1** 1XP. **Total:** Pass 7-2 28.6%, 29 4.14; Rush 17-83 4.9 1 TD; PR 8-68 8.5; KR 8-156 19.5; Scor 2 1XP.

		Receiving					Tot
Year Team	**G**	**Rec**	**Yds**	**Avg**	**TD**	**Fum**	**TD**
1976 Sea	14	54	705	13.1	4	2	4
1977 Sea	14	33	643	19.5	10	0	10
1978 Sea	16	71	1168	16.5	8	0	8
1979 Sea	15	66	**1237**	18.7	9	0	9
1980 Sea	16	66	1064	16.1	6	1	6
1981 Sea	16	75	1224	16.3	9	2	10
1982 Sea	8	34	493	14.5	3	0	3
1983 Sea	15	72	1074	14.9	11	3	11
1984 Sea	16	74	1164	15.7	12	1	12
1985 Sea	16	79	**1287**	16.3	6	0	6
1986 Sea	16	70	1070	15.3	9	3	9
1987 Sea	13	58	912	15.7	8	2	8
1988 Sea	15	39	645	16.5	2	3	2
1989 Sea	10	28	403	14.4	3	0	3
NFL Total	200	819	13089	16.0	100	17	101

ERIC LARKIN Larkin, Eric Lenell 6'4", 265 **DE**
Col: Miami (Fla.) B: 5/14/1962
1987 Hou: 1 G.

GORDON LARO Laro, Gordon Edward 6'3", 253 **TE**
Col: Michigan; Boston College *HS:* Lynn English [MA] B: 4/17/1972, Lynn, MA
1995 Jac: 2 G; Rec 1-6 6.0.

PAUL LAROSA LaRosa, Paul 5'11", 175 **E**
Col: No College B: 1890 Deceased
1920 ChiC: 9 G. **1921** ChiC: 2 G. **Total:** 11 G.

DAN LAROSE LaRose, Marvin Daniel 6'5", 250 **DE-OT-OG**
Col: Missouri *HS:* Crystal City [MO] B: 2/8/1939, Cystal City, MO
Drafted: 1961 Round 2 Det
1961 Det: 14 G. **1962** Det: 14 G. **1963** Det: 9 G. **1964** Pit: 12 G. **1965** SF: 5 G. **1966** Den: 11 G. **Total:** 65 G.

CARL LARPENTER Larpenter, Carl James 6′4″, 235 **OG-OT**
Col: Texas *HS:* Thomas Jefferson [Port Arthur, TX] B: 7/1/1936, Port Arthur, TX
1960 Den: 14 G. **1961** Den: 14 G. **1962** DalT: 2 G. **Total:** 30 G.

JACK LARSCHEID Larscheid, Phillip John 5′6″, 162 **HB**
Col: Los Medanos Coll. CA (J.C.); U. of Pacific *HS:* Riverside [Milwaukee, WI] B: 5/10/1933, Whitefish Bay, WI D: 2/5/1970, Sacramento, CA
1960 Oak: Pass 6-3 50.0%, 71 11.83 2 Int; Rec 22-187 8.5 1 TD; PR 12-106 8.8. **1961** Oak: Pass 1-0, 1 Int; Rec 2-11 5.5. **Total:** Pass 7-3 42.9%, 71 10.14 3 Int; Rec 24-198 8.3 1 TD; PR 12-106 8.8.

		Rushing				Kickoff Returns					Tot
Year Team	G	Ret	Yds	Avg	TD	Ret	Yds	Avg	TD	Fum	TD
1960 Oak	14	94	397	4.2	1	**30**	852	28.4	0	11	2
1961 Oak	2	6	3	0.5	0	9	254	28.2	0	2	0
NFL Total	16	100	400	4.0	1	39	1106	28.4	0	13	2

GARY LARSEN Larsen, Gary Lee 6′5″, 261 **DT**
Col: Concordia (Ill.) *HS:* Moorhead College [MN] B: 3/13/1940, Fargo, ND *Drafted:* 1964 Round 10 LARm
1964 LARm: 14 G; KR 2-14 7.0. **1965** Min: 12 G. **1966** Min: 14 G. **1967** Min: 14 G. **1968** Min: 14 G. **1969** Min: 14 G. **1970** Min: 14 G. **1971** Min: 14 G. **1972** Min: 14 G. **1973** Min: 14 G. **1974** Min: 11 G. **Total:** 149 G; KR 2-14 7.0.

OJAY LARSON Larson, Frederic Adolphus 6′1″, 199 **C-LB**
Col: Notre Dame *HS:* Calumet [MI] B: 10/15/1897, Calumet, MI D: 5/1/1977, Milwaukee, WI
1922 ChiB: 10 G. **1923** Mil: 12 G. **1924** Mil: 8 G. **1925** GB: 13 G. **1929** ChiB-ChiC: 10 G. ChiB: 1 G. ChiC: 9 G. **Total:** 53 G.

GREG LARSON Larson, Gregory Kenneth 6′3″, 250 **C-OG-OT**
Col: Minnesota *HS:* Roosevelt [Minneapolis, MN] B: 11/15/1939, Minneapolis, MN *Drafted:* 1961 Round 6 NYG
1961 NYG: 14 G. **1962** NYG: 14 G. **1963** NYG: 14 G. **1964** NYG: 13 G. **1965** NYG: 12 G. **1966** NYG: 14 G. **1967** NYG: 14 G. **1968** NYG: 14 G; Rec 0-1. **1969** NYG: 14 G. **1970** NYG: 14 G; 2 Fum. **1971** NYG: 14 G. **1972** NYG: 14 G. **1973** NYG: 14 G. **Total:** 179 G; Rec 0-1; 2 Fum.

PETE LARSON Larson, Harry Peter III 6′1″, 200 **RB**
Col: Cornell *HS:* Paxton [IL] B: 5/30/1944, Wilmington, DE *Drafted:* 1967 Round 9 Was
1967 Was: Rec 8-45 5.6. **1968** Was: Rec 12-146 12.2 1 TD; KR 6-151 25.2. **Total:** Rec 20-191 9.6 1 TD; KR 6-151 25.2.

		Rushing				Tot
Year Team	G	Att	Yds	Avg	TD	TD
1967 Was	8	25	84	3.4	1	1
1968 Was	14	44	132	3.0	1	2
NFL Total	22	69	216	3.1	2	3

KURT LARSON Larson, Kurt Arvin 6′4″, 236 **LB**
Col: Michigan State *HS:* North [Waukesha, WI] B: 2/25/1966, Waukesha, WI *Drafted:* 1989 Round 8 Ind
1989 Ind: 13 G; 1 Sac. **1990** Ind: 16 G. **1991** GB: 13 G. **Total:** 42 G; 1 Sac.

LOUIE LARSON Larson, Louis Peter 168 **WB-BB-OE-FB**
Col: No College B: 1/5/1898, Reynolds, ND D: 5/28/1982, Fort Worth, TX
1926 Dul: 7 G. **1929** ChiC: 3 G. **Total:** 10 G.

LYNN LARSON Larson, Lyndon Arthur 6′4″, 254 **OT**
Col: Phoenix Coll. AZ (J.C.); Kansas State *HS:* Alhambra [Phoenix, AZ] B: 3/9/1948, Phoenix, AZ *Drafted:* 1970 Round 4 ChiB
1971 Bal: 1 G.

PAUL LARSON Larson, Paul Leroy 5′11″, 185 **QB**
Col: California *HS:* Turlock [CA] B: 3/19/1932 *Drafted:* 1954 Round 8 ChiC
1957 ChiC: 5 G; Pass 14-6 42.9%, 61 4.36 1 Int; Rush 8-12 1.5. **1960** Oak: 1 G. **Total:** 6 G; Pass 14-6 42.9%, 61 4.36 1 Int; Rush 8-12 1.5.

SWEDE LARSON Larson, Swede **HB**
Col: No College Deceased
1920 Ham: 1 G. **1923** Ham: 3 G. **Total:** 4 G.

BILL LARSON Larson, William 5′10″, 190 **FB**
Col: Illinois Wesleyan B: 1939
1960 Bos: 1 G.

BILL LARSON Larson, William Harry 6′4″, 225 **TE**
Col: Pratt CC KS; Colorado State *HS:* West [Wichita, KS] B: 10/7/1953, Greenfield, IA
1975 SF: 14 G; Rec 5-64 12.8. **1977** Was-Det: 13 G. Was: 1 G. Det: 12 G. **1978** Phi: 5 G. **1980** Den-GB: 11 G; Rec 5-44 8.8 1 TD; 6 Pt. Den: 2 G; Rec 1-7 7.0. GB: 9 G; Rec 4-37 9.3 1 TD; 6 Pt. **Total:** 43 G; Rec 10-108 10.8 1 TD; 6 Pt.

YALE LARY Lary, Robert Yale Jr. 5′11″, 185 **DB**
Col: Texas A&M *HS:* North Side [Fort Worth, TX] B: 11/24/1930, Fort Worth, TX *Drafted:* 1952 Round 3 Det *HOF:* 1979
1952 Det: KR 12-303 25.3. **1953** Det: Rush 1-21 21.0; KR 6-116 19.3. **1956** Det: Rush 1-10 10.0; KR 4-76 19.0. **1957** Det: Pass 1-0; Rush 1-32 32.0. **1958** Det: Pass 1-0; Rush 1-2 2.0. **1959** Det: Pass 1-0; Rush 1-18 18.0; **1** Fum TD. **1960** Det: Rush 1-19 19.0. **1961** Det: Rush 1-14 14.0. **1962** Det: Pass 1-0. **1963** Det: Rush 1-26 26.0. **1964** Det: Rush 2-11 5.5. **Total:** Pass 4-0; Rush 10-153 15.3; KR 22-495 22.5; 1 Fum TD.

		Punt Returns				Interceptions		
Year Team	G	Ret	Yds	Avg	TD	Int	Yds	TD
1952 Det	12	16	182	11.4	1	4	61	0
1953 Det	11	13	115	8.8	**1**	5	98	0
1956 Det	12	22	70	3.2	0	8	182	1
1957 Det	12	25	139	5.6	0	2	64	0
1958 Det	12	27	196	7.3	**1**	3	70	0
1959 Det	10	21	43	2.0	0	3	0	0
1960 Det	12	1	5	5.0	0	3	44	0
1961 Det	14	1	8	8.0	0	6	95	0
1962 Det	14	0	0	—	0	8	51	0
1963 Det	10	0	0	—	0	2	21	1
1964 Det	14	0	0	—	0	6	101	0
NFL Total	133	126	758	6.0	3	50	787	2

	Punting				Tot
Year Team	Punts	Yds	Avg	Fum	TD
1952 Det	5	181	36.2	0	1
1953 Det	28	1112	39.7	1	1
1956 Det	42	1698	40.4	0	1
1957 Det	54	2156	39.9	2	0
1958 Det	59	2524	42.8	3	1
1959 Det	45	2121	**47.1**	2	1
1960 Det	**64**	2802	43.8	0	0
1961 Det	52	2519	**48.4**	0	0
1962 Det	52	2354	45.3	0	0
1963 Det	35	1713	**48.9**	0	1
1964 Det	67	3099	46.3	0	0
NFL Total	503	22279	44.3	8	6

JOHN LASCARI Lascari, John Albert 6′2″, 210 **OE-DE**
Col: Georgetown B: 3/5/1918, Lodi, NJ D: 7/1971
1942 NYG: 10 G; Rec 3-38 12.7 1 TD; Scor 6, 0-1 FG; 6 Pt.

JIM LASH Lash, James Verle 6′1″, 200 **WR**
Col: Northwestern *HS:* Garfield [Akron, OH] B: 11/12/1951, Akron, OH *Drafted:* 1973 Round 3 Min
1975 Min: Pass 1-0; **1** Fum TD. **1976** Min-SF: Rush 3-5 1.7. SF: Rush 3-5 1.7. **Total:** Pass 1-0; Rush 3-5 1.7; 1 Fum TD.

		Receiving					Tot
Year Team	G	Rec	Yds	Avg	TD	Fum	TD
1973 Min	9	2	34	17.0	0	0	0
1974 Min	14	32	631	19.7	0	2	0
1975 Min	14	37	535	14.5	3	0	4
1976 Min-SF	13	17	242	14.2	0	0	0
1976 Min	5	4	52	13.0	0	0	0
1976 SF	8	13	190	14.6	0	0	0
1977 SF	10	3	22	7.3	0	1	0
NFL Total	60	91	1464	16.1	3	3	4

TIM LASHAR Lashar, Timothy Alan 5′9″, 160 **K**
Col: Oklahoma *HS:* Barrington [IL]; Plano HS [TX] B: 9/5/1964, Santa Monica, CA
1987 ChiB: 3 G; Scor 19, 3-4 75.0% FG, 10-10 100.0% XK.

GREG LASKER Lasker, Gregory Cephus 6′0″, 200 **DB**
Col: Arkansas *HS:* Conway [AR] B: 9/28/1964, St. Louis, MO *Drafted:* 1986 Round 2 NYG
1986 NYG: 16 G; KR 1-0; Int 1-0; 1 Sac. **1987** NYG: 11 G; 1.5 Sac. **1988** NYG-ChiB-Pho: 6 G. NYG: 4 G. ChiB: 1 G. Pho: 1 G. **Total:** 33 G; KR 1-0; Int 1-0; 2.5 Sac.

BILL LASKEY Laskey, William Grant 6′3″, 235 **LB**
Col: Michigan *HS:* Milan [MI] B: 2/10/1943, Ann Arbor, MI
1965 Buf: 14 G. **1966** Oak: 14 G. **1967** Oak: 13 G. **1969** Oak: 12 G; Int 3-66. **1970** Oak: 14 G; Int 1-0. **1971** Bal: 13 G. **1972** Bal: 14 G. **1973** Den: 11 G; Int 2-3; 1 Fum. **1974** Den: 14 G; Int 1-3. **Total:** 119 G; Int 7-72; 1 Fum.

FRANK LASKY Lasky, Francis Joseph 6′2″, 265 **OT**
Col: Northeastern Oklahoma A&M (J.C.); Florida *HS:* Coral Gables [FL] B: 10/4/1941, New York, NY *Drafted:* 1963 Round 2 NYG
1964 NYG: 4 G. **1965** NYG: 14 G. **Total:** 18 G.

JIM LASLAVIC Laslavic, James Edward 6′2″, 237 **LB**
Col: Penn State *HS:* Etna [PA] B: 10/24/1951, Pittsburgh, PA *Drafted:* 1973 Round 3 Det
1973 Det: 14 G. **1974** Det: 14 G; Int 1-14. **1975** Det: 14 G; Int 2-12. **1976** Det: 12 G; Int 2-13. **1977** Det: 14 G; Int 1-14. **1978** SD: 16 G.

1980 SD: 16 G; KR 2-26 13.0; Int 2-11. **1981** SD: 16 G. **1982** GB: 8 G. **Total:** 124 G; KR 2-26 13.0; Int 8-64.

NICK LASSA Lassa, Niccola 5'10", 205 **T-G-C-OE**
(AKA Niccola Lassaw) *Col:* Carlisle; Haskell Indian *HS:* Carlisle Indian School [PA] B: 7/11/1898, Flathead Indian Reservation, MT D: 9/1964
1922 Oor: 9 G. **1923** Oor: 11 G. **Total:** 20 G.

LOU LASSAHN Lassahn, Louis Kenneth 6'0", 205 **T-DE**
Col: Western Maryland *HS:* Baltimore Polytechnic Inst. [MD]
B: 10/1/1915 D: 10/27/1987, Baltimore, MD
1938 Pit: 2 G.

DICK LASSE Lasse, Richard Stephen 6'2", 222 **LB**
Col: Syracuse *HS:* Weymouth [MA]; Worcester Acad. [MA]
B: 11/13/1935, Quincy, MA *Drafted:* 1958 Round 6 Pit
1958 Pit: 12 G. **1959** Pit: 12 G. **1960** Was: 12 G; Int 3-17. **1961** Was: 14 G. **1962** NYG: 4 G. **Total:** 54 G; Int 3-17.

DERRICK LASSIC Lassic, Derrick Owens 5'10", 188 **RB**
Col: Alabama *HS:* North Rockland [Thiells, NY] B: 1/26/1970, Haverstraw, NY *Drafted:* 1993 Round 4 Dal
1993 Dal: Rec 9-37 4.1.

		Rushing				
Year Team	G	Att	Yds	Avg	TD	Fum
1993 Dal	10	75	269	3.6	3	2

IKE LASSITER Lassiter, Isaac Thomas 6'5", 270 **DE-DT**
Col: St. Augustine's *HS:* Charles H. Darden [Wilson, NC]
B: 11/15/1940, Wilson, NC *Drafted:* 1962 Round 9 LARm
1962 Den: 14 G. **1963** Den: 7 G. **1964** Den: 2 G. **1965** Oak: 14 G. **1966** Oak: 14 G; Int 1-10. **1967** Oak: 14 G. **1968** Oak: 14 G. **1969** Oak: 14 G. **1970** Bos: 5 G. **1971** NE: 14 G. **Total:** 112 G; Int 1-10.

KWAMIE LASSITER Lassiter, Kwamie Jerome 6'0", 191 **DB**
Col: Butler County CC KS; Kansas *HS:* Menchville [Newport News, VA]
B: 12/3/1969, Hampton, VA
1995 Ariz: Rush 1-1 1.0. **1997** Ariz: 3 Sac. **Total:** Rush 1-1 1.0; 3 Sac.

		Interceptions		
Year Team	G	Int	Yds	TD
1995 Ariz	5	0	0	0
1996 Ariz	14	1	20	0
1997 Ariz	16	1	10	0
1998 Ariz	16	8	80	0
NFL Total	51	10	110	0

DON LASTER Laster, Anthony Donald 6'5", 285 **OT**
Col: Tennessee State *HS:* Dougherty [Albany, GA] B: 12/13/1958, Albany, GA *Drafted:* 1982 Round 12 Was
1982 Was: 8 G. **1984** Det: 14 G. **Total:** 22 G.

ART LASTER Laster, Arthur L 6'5", 280 **OT**
Col: Maryland East. Shore *HS:* Tolleston [Gary, IN] B: 3/2/1948, Gary, IN *Drafted:* 1970 Round 5 Oak
1970 Buf: 14 G; KR 2-8 4.0.

GREG LATHAN Lathan, Gregory R 6'1", 195 **WR**
Col: San Diego Mesa Coll. CA (J.C.); Cincinnati *HS:* Monte Vista [Cupertino, CA] B: 9/2/1964, San Diego, CA
1987 LARd: 3 G; Rec 5-98 19.6.

LAMAR LATHON Lathon, Lamar Lavantha 6'3", 260 **LB-DE**
Col: Houston *HS:* Wharton [TX] B: 12/23/1967, Wharton, TX
Drafted: 1990 Round 1 Hou
1990 Hou: 11 G. **1991** Hou: 16 G; Int 3-77 1 TD; 6 Pt; 2 Sac. **1992** Hou: 11 G; 1.5 Sac. **1993** Hou: 13 G; 2 Sac. **1994** Hou: 16 G; Scor **1** Saf; 2 Pt; 8.5 Sac. **1995** Car: 15 G; 8 Sac. **1996** Car: 16 G; 13.5 Sac. **1997** Car: 15 G; Int 1-1; 2 Sac. **1998** Car: 2 G. **Total:** 115 G; Int 4-78 1 TD; Scor 1 Saf; 8 Pt; 37.5 Sac.

KIT LATHROP Lathrop, Kit Douglas 6'5", 255 **DE-NT**
Col: West Valley Coll. CA (J.C.); Arizona State *HS:* Leigh [San Jose, CA]
B: 5/10/1956, San Jose, CA
1979 Den-GB: 11 G. Den: 9 G. GB: 2 G. **1980** GB: 15 G. **1986** KC: 16 G. **1987** Was: 1 G. **Total:** 43 G.

AL LATIMER Latimer, Albert 5'11", 176 **DB**
Col: Ferrum; Clemson *HS:* Lyman [Longwood, FL] B: 10/14/1957, Winter Park, FL
1979 Phi: 13 G; KR 1-18 18.0. **1982** Det: 4 G. **1983** Det: 8 G; Int 1-0. **1984** Det: 15 G. **Total:** 40 G; KR 1-18 18.0; Int 1-0.

DON LATIMER Latimer, Donald B 6'3", 259 **NT**
Col: Miami (Fla.) *HS:* Fort Pierce Central [FL] B: 3/1/1955, Fort Pierce, FL *Drafted:* 1978 Round 1 Den
1978 Den: 14 G. **1979** Den: 15 G. **1980** Den: 14 G; Int 1-15 1 TD; 6 Pt. **1981** Den: 16 G. **1982** Den: 9 G; 1 Sac. **1983** Den: 12 G; 0.5 Sac. **Total:** 80 G; Int 1-15 1 TD; 6 Pt; 1.5 Sac.

JERRY LATIN Latin, Jerry Louis 5'10", 190 **RB**
Col: Northern Illinois *HS:* Rockford East [IL] B: 8/25/1953, Prescott, AR *Drafted:* 1975 Round 11 StL
1975 StL: Rec 2-25 12.5. **1976** StL: Rec 4-35 8.8. **1977** StL: Rec 9-89 9.9. **1978** StL-LARm: Rec 1-3 3.0. StL: Rec 1-3 3.0. **Total:** Rec 16-152 9.5.

		Rushing				Kickoff Returns				
Year Team	G	Att	Yds	Avg	TD	Ret	Yds	Avg	TD	Fum
1975 StL	10	35	165	4.7	1	0	0	—	0	2
1976 StL	11	25	115	4.6	1	16	357	22.3	0	3
1977 StL	14	56	208	3.7	2	3	79	26.3	0	6
1978 StL-LARm	16	24	72	3.0	0	24	515	21.5	0	5
1978 StL	2	6	8	1.3	0	2	48	24.0	0	1
1978 LARm	14	18	64	3.6	0	22	467	21.2	0	4
NFL Total	51	140	560	4.0	4	43	951	22.1	0	16

TONY LATONE Latone, Anthony J 5'11", 195 **FB-WB-TB**
Col: No College *HS:* No High School B: 4/18/1897, Spring Valley, IL
D: 11/24/1975, Detroit, MI
1925 Pott: 12 G; Rush **7** TD; Int 1 TD; Tot TD **8**; 48 Pt. **1926** Pott: 12 G; Rush 4 TD; 24 Pt. **1927** Pott: 12 G. **1928** Pott: 10 G; Pass 1 TD; Rush 3 TD; 18 Pt. **1929** Bost: 8 G; Rush 9 TD; 54 Pt. **1930** Prov: 11 G; Rush 3 TD; 18 Pt. **Total:** 65 G; Pass 1 TD; Rush 26 TD; Int 1 TD; Tot TD 27; 162 Pt.

CHUCK LATOURETTE Latourette, Charles Pierre 6'0", 190 **DB-P-WR**
Col: Rice *HS:* Jonesboro [AR] B: 7/21/1945, San Antonio, TX
D: 12/22/1982, West University Place, TX
1967 StL: Rush 2-23 11.5. **1968** StL: Pass 1-0; Rush 1-15 15.0. **1970** StL: Rush 2-38 19.0; 1 Fum TD. **1971** StL: Rush 3-19 6.3. **Total:** Pass 1-0; Rush 8-95 11.9; 1 Fum TD.

		Punt Returns				Kickoff Returns			
Year Team	G	Ret	Yds	Avg	TD	Ret	Yds	Avg	TD
1967 StL	14	6	21	3.5	0	0	0	—	0
1968 StL	14	**28**	**345**	12.3	1	**46**	**1237**	26.9	0
1970 StL	14	30	171	5.7	0	13	254	19.5	0
1971 StL	13	0	0	—	0	0	0	—	0
NFL Total	55	64	537	8.4	1	59	1491	25.3	0

	Punting				Tot
Year Team	Punts	Yds	Avg	Fum	TD
1967 StL	62	2532	40.8	0	0
1968 StL	65	2701	41.6	3	1
1970 StL	65	2659	40.9	8	1
1971 StL	56	2157	38.5	1	0
NFL Total	248	10049	40.5	12	2

GREG LATTA Latta, Gregory Edwin 6'3", 226 **TE**
Col: Morgan State *HS:* South Side [Newark, NJ] B: 10/13/1952, Newark, NJ *Drafted:* 1974 Round 8 Bal
1976 ChiB: Rush 2-(-8) -4.0. **1978** ChiB: KR 2-14 7.0. **1979** ChiB: KR 1-8 8.0. **Total:** Rush 2-(-8) -4.0; KR 3-22 7.3.

		Receiving				
Year Team	G	Rec	Yds	Avg	TD	Fum
1975 ChiB	14	16	202	12.6	3	1
1976 ChiB	14	18	254	14.1	0	0
1977 ChiB	14	26	335	12.9	4	0
1978 ChiB	16	15	159	10.6	0	0
1979 ChiB	15	15	131	8.7	0	0
NFL Total	73	90	1081	12.0	7	1

BRIAN LATTIMORE Lattimore, Brian Keith 6'1", 202 **RB**
Col: Southeast Missouri State *HS:* Osceola [Largo, FL] B: 10/29/1966, St. Petersburg, FL
1991 Ind: 3 G.

JOHNNY LATTNER Lattner, John Joseph 6'1", 195 **HB**
Col: Notre Dame *HS:* Fenwick [Chicago, IL] B: 10/24/1932, Chicago, IL *Drafted:* 1954 Round 1 Pit
1954 Pit: PR 17-73 4.3; KR 16-413 25.8.

		Rushing				Receiving					Tot
Year Team	G	Att	Yds	Avg	TD	Rec	Yds	Avg	TD	Fum	TD
1954 Pit	12	69	237	3.4	5	25	305	12.2	2	4	7

PAUL LATZKE Latzke, Pete Lewis 6'4", 240 **C**
Col: U. of Pacific *HS:* Gilroy [CA] B: 3/22/1942, Los Angeles, CA
1966 SD: 2 G. **1967** SD: 13 G. **1968** SD: 7 G; KR 1-0; 1 Fum. **Total:** 22 G; KR 1-0; 1 Fum.

PETE LAUER Lauer, Albert Lee 5'6", 150 **TB**
Col: Iowa B: 10/14/1897, Muncie, IN D: 7/9/1950, Evansville, IN
1922 Eva: 1 G.

DUTCH LAUER Lauer, Harold Sebastian 5'10", 183 **WB-BB-OE-FB**
(Hal) *Col:* Detroit Mercy *HS:* James Monroe [Detroit, MI] B: 1/8/1898, Monroe, MI D: 8/9/1978, Southfield, MI
1922 RI-GB: 9 G; Rush 4 TD; Rec 1 TD; Scor 31, 1 XK; Tot TD 5. RI: 7 G; Rush 4 TD; Rec 1 TD; Scor 31, 1 XK; Tot TD 5. GB: 2 G. **1923** Tol: 7 G; Pass 1 TD. **1925** Det: 11 G. **1926** Det: 10 G; Rec 1 TD; 6 Pt. **Total:** 37 G; Pass 1 TD; Rush 4 TD; Rec 2 TD; Tot TD 6.

LARRY LAUER Lauer, Lawrence Gene 6'3", 235 **C**
(Moose) *Col:* Alabama *HS:* New Trier Twp. [Winnetka, IL] B: 8/27/1927, Chicago, IL D: 1/3/1992, Las Vegas, NV *Drafted:* 1951 Round 8 NYY
1956 GB: 6 G. **1957** GB: 12 G. **Total:** 18 G.

BABE LAUFENBERG Laufenberg, Hugh Brandon 6'2", 198 **QB**
Col: Pierce Coll. CA (J.C.); Stanford; Missouri; Indiana *HS:* Crespi [Encino, CA] B: 12/5/1959, Burbank, CA *Drafted:* 1983 Round 6 Was

		Passing							
Year Team	**G**	**Att**	**Comp**	**Comp%**	**Yds**	**YPA**	**TD**	**Int**	**Rating**
1986 NO	1	0	0	—	0	—	0	0	—
1988 SD	8	144	69	47.9	778	5.40	4	5	59.3
1989 Dal	3	0	0	—	0	—	0	0	—
1990 Dal	4	67	24	35.8	279	4.16	1	6	16.9
NFL Total	16	211	93	44.1	1057	5.01	5	11	45.9

	Rushing				
Year Team	**Att**	**Yds**	**Avg**	**TD**	**Fum**
1988 SD	31	120	3.9	0	2
1990 Dal	2	6	3.0	0	1
NFL Total	33	126	3.8	0	3

BUD LAUGHLIN Laughlin, Henry James 6'1", 200 **FB**
Col: Kansas *HS:* Southeast [Kansas City, MO] B: 1/15/1931, Kansas City, MO D: 3/20/1986, Shawnee Mission, KS *Drafted:* 1952 Round 25 SF
1955 SF: 10 G; Rush 20-58 2.9; Rec 8-54 6.8; KR 1-25 25.0; 4 Fum.

JIM LAUGHLIN Laughlin, James David 6'0", 222 **LB**
Col: Ohio State *HS:* Charles F. Brush [Lyndhurst, OH] B: 7/5/1958, Euclid, OH *Drafted:* 1980 Round 4 Atl
1980 Atl: 16 G; Int 1-7. **1981** Atl: 14 G. **1982** Atl: 9 G; KR 1-10 10.0. **1983** GB: 15 G; Int 1-22. **1984** LARm: 3 G. **1985** LARm: 10 G. **1986** LARm: 16 G. **1987** Atl: 5 G. **Total:** 88 G; KR 1-10 10.0; Int 2-29.

JIM LAUGHTON Laughton, James Edward 6'5", 225 **TE**
Col: San Diego State *HS:* Salinas [CA] B: 1/18/1960, Salinas, CA
1986 Sea: 6 G.

HANK LAURICELLA Lauricella, Francis Edward 5'11", 175 **HB**
Col: Tennessee *HS:* Holy Cross [New Orleans, LA] B: 10/9/1930, Harahan, LA *Drafted:* 1952 Round 17 Det
1952 Dal: Pass 22-11 50.0%, 177 8.05 4 TD 2 Int; Rush 19-55 2.9; KR 1-26 26.0.

		Punting			
Year Team	**G**	**Punts**	**Yds**	**Avg**	**Fum**
1952 Dal	11	58	2036	35.1	1

FRANK LAURINAITIS Laurinaitis, Francis Ignatius 5'10", 200 **LB**
(Fritz) *Col:* Richmond *HS:* Blythe Twp. [Cumbola, PA] B: 12/20/1922, New Philidelphia, PA
AAFC **1947** BknA: 8 G.

LINDY LAURO Lauro, Lindoro L 5'10", 195 **DB**
Col: Pittsburgh *HS:* New Castle [PA] B: 6/3/1921, New Castle, PA
1951 ChiC: 1 G.

TED LAUX Laux, Theodore 5'10", 185 **HB-DB**
Col: St. Joseph's (Pa) *HS:* Collingswood [NJ] B: 3/1/1918, Swedesboro, NJ
1943 PhPt: 4 G; Rush 9-23 2.6; Rec 2-19 9.5; PR 1-11 11.0; Int 1-24; Scor 2, 2-2 100.0% XK. **1944** Phi: 1 G; Rush 2-(-1) -0.5; Rec 1-6 6.0; Punt 1-18 18.0. **Total:** 5 G; Rush 11-22 2.0; Rec 3-25 8.3; PR 1-11 11.0; Int 1-24; Punt 1-18 18.0; Scor 2, 2-2 100.0% XK.

AL LAVAN Lavan, Alton 6'1", 202 **DB**
Col: Colorado State *HS:* South Side [Newark, NJ]; Union Acad. [Bartow, FL] B: 9/13/1946, Pierce, FL *Drafted:* 1968 Round 8 Phi
1969 Atl: 11 G; Int 2-0; 1 Fum. **1970** Atl: 13 G; KR 1-10 10.0; Int 3-11. **Total:** 24 G; KR 1-10 10.0; Int 5-11; 1 Fum.

DANTE LAVELLI Lavelli, Dante Bert Joseph 6'0", 191 **OE-DE**
(Gluefingers) *Col:* Ohio State *HS:* Hudson [OH] B: 2/23/1923, Hudson, OH *Drafted:* 1947 Round 10 LARm *HOF:* 1975
AAFC **1946** CleA: Rush 1-14 14.0. **1947** CleA: KR 1-10 10.0. **1948** CleA: Rush 1-9 9.0; KR 1-0. **Total:** Rush 2-23 11.5; KR 2-10 5.0.

		Receiving			
Year Team	**G**	**Rec**	**Yds**	**Avg**	**TD**
1946 CleA	14	40	843	21.1	8
1947 CleA	13	49	799	16.3	9
1948 CleA	8	25	463	18.5	5
1949 CleA	9	28	475	17.0	7
AAFC Total	44	142	2580	18.2	29

NFL Statistics

		Receiving				
Year Team	**G**	**Rec**	**Yds**	**Avg**	**TD**	**Fum**
1950 Cle	12	37	565	15.3	5	2
1951 Cle	12	43	586	13.6	6	0
1952 Cle	8	21	336	16.0	4	0
1953 Cle	12	45	783	17.4	6	1
1954 Cle	12	47	802	17.1	7	0
1955 Cle	12	31	492	15.9	4	0
1956 Cle	11	20	344	17.2	1	1
NFL Total	79	244	3908	16.0	33	4

JOE LAVENDER Lavender, Joseph 6'4", 190 **DB**
(Big Bird) *Col:* Imperial Valley Coll. CA (J.C.); San Diego State *HS:* Central [El Centro, CA] B: 2/10/1949, Rayville, LA *Drafted:* 1973 Round 12 Phi
1974 Phi: 1 Fum TD. **Total:** 1 Fum TD.

		Interceptions			Tot
Year Team	**G**	**Int**	**Yds**	**TD**	**TD**
1973 Phi	13	0	0	0	0
1974 Phi	14	1	37	1	2
1975 Phi	13	3	59	1	1
1976 Was	14	8	77	0	0
1977 Was	14	4	36	0	0
1978 Was	16	1	0	0	0
1979 Was	16	6	77	0	0
1980 Was	16	6	96	1	1
1981 Was	16	4	52	0	0
1982 Was	7	0	0	0	0
NFL Total	139	33	434	3	4

ROBERT LAVETTE Lavette, Robert Lee 5'11", 190 **RB**
Col: Georgia Tech *HS:* Cartersville [GA] B: 9/8/1963, Cartersville, GA *Drafted:* 1985 Round 4 Dal
1985 Dal: Rush 13-34 2.6; Rec 1-8 8.0. **1986** Dal: Rush 10-6 0.6; Rec 5-31 6.2 1 TD; PR 18-92 5.1. **1987** Dal-Phi: Rec 1-6 6.0. Dal: Rec 1-6 6.0. **Total:** Rush 23-40 1.7; Rec 7-45 6.4 1 TD; PR 18-92 5.1.

		Kickoff Returns				
Year Team	**G**	**Ret**	**Yds**	**Avg**	**TD**	**Fum**
1985 Dal	12	34	682	20.1	0	0
1986 Dal	16	36	699	19.4	0	3
1987 Dal-Phi	5	6	109	18.2	0	0
1987 Dal	4	4	72	18.0	0	0
1987 Phi	1	2	37	18.5	0	0
NFL Total	33	76	1490	19.6	0	3

PAUL LAVINE Lavine, Paul III 6'2", 207 **LB**
Col: San Bernardino Valley Coll. CA (J.C.); Utah State *HS:* Highland [Bakersfield, CA] B: 5/1/1962, San Bernardino, CA
1987 Sea: 3 G.

HUBBARD LAW Law, Hubbard Paul 6'1", 210 **G-LB**
(Red) *Col:* Sam Houston State *HS:* Willis [TX] B: 1/27/1921, Houston, TX D: 3/29/1995, Mesa, AZ *Drafted:* 1942 Round 15 Pit
1942 Pit: 11 G; Rush 1-6 6.0; Int 1-13. **1945** Pit: 6 G. **Total:** 17 G; Rush 1-6 6.0; Int 1-13.

JOHN LAW Law, John Brendon 5'9", 180 **T**
Col: Notre Dame *HS:* Yonkers [NY]; Hamilton Inst. [New York, NY] B: 2/13/1905, Yonkers, NY D: 10/14/1962, Tarrytown, NY
1930 Nwk: 1 G.

DENNIS LAW Law, Raymond Dennis 6'1", 179 **WR**
Col: East Tennessee State *HS:* Jefferson [GA] B: 4/4/1955, Commerce, GA *Drafted:* 1978 Round 4 Cin
1978 Cin: Rush 1-(-1) -1.0; Rec 5-81 16.2; KR 2-30 15.0.

		Punt Returns				
Year Team	**G**	**Ret**	**Yds**	**Avg**	**TD**	**Fum**
1978 Cin	14	25	106	4.2	0	1

TY LAW Law, Taujan Edward 5'11", 200 **DB**
Col: Michigan *HS:* Aliquippa [PA] B: 2/10/1974, Aliquippa, PA *Drafted:* 1995 Round 1 NE
1995 NE: 1 Sac. **1997** NE: 0.5 Sac. **Total:** 1.5 Sac.

		Interceptions			
Year Team	**G**	**Int**	**Yds**	**TD**	**Fum**
1995 NE	14	3	47	0	0
1996 NE	13	3	45	1	0
1997 NE	16	3	70	0	1
1998 NE	16	**9**	133	1	0
NFL Total	59	18	295	2	1

AL LAWLER Lawler, Allen Gilbert 5′10″, 175 **HB-DB**
Col: Texas *HS:* Arkansas [Texarkana, AR] B: 6/23/1922, Malta, TX
Drafted: 1947 Round 21 ChiB
1948 ChiB: 7 G; Rush 9-44 4.9; Rec 3-40 13.3; PR 5-81 16.2; KR 3-85 28.3; Scor 6, 1-1 100.0% FG, 3-3 100.0% XK; 2 Fum.

BURTON LAWLESS Lawless, Richard Burton 6′4″, 253 **OG**
Col: Florida *HS:* Punta Gorda [FL] B: 11/1/1953, Dothan, AL
Drafted: 1975 Round 2 Dal
1975 Dal: 14 G. **1976** Dal: 14 G. **1977** Dal: 14 G. **1978** Dal: 16 G; KR 1-10 10.0. **1979** Dal: 15 G. **1980** Det: 9 G. **Total:** 82 G; KR 1-10 10.0.

AMOS LAWRENCE Lawrence, Amos Jr. 5′11″, 181 **RB**
(Famous Amos) *Col:* North Carolina *HS:* Lake Taylor [Norfolk, VA]
B: 1/9/1958, Norfolk, VA *Drafted:* 1981 Round 4 SD
1981 SF: Rush 13-48 3.7 1 TD; Rec 3-10 3.3. **1982** SF: Rush 5-7 1.4; Rec 2-12 6.0. **Total:** Rush 18-55 3.1 1 TD; Rec 5-22 4.4.

		Kickoff Returns					Tot
Year Team	**G**	**Ret**	**Yds**	**Avg**	**TD**	**Fum**	**TD**
1981 SF	13	17	437	25.7	**1**	3	2
1982 SF	8	9	190	21.1	0	1	0
NFL Total	21	26	627	24.1	1	4	2

BEN LAWRENCE Lawrence, Benjamin J 6′1″, 325 **OG**
Col: Indiana (Pa.) *HS:* Waynesboro [PA] B: 9/19/1961, Sparta, WI
1987 Pit: 1 G.

DON LAWRENCE Lawrence, Donald Jerome 6′1″, 245 **DT-OG-OT**
Col: Notre Dame *HS:* Cathedral Latin [Cleveland, OH] B: 6/4/1937, Cleveland, OH *Drafted:* 1959 Round 7 Was
1959 Was: 12 G. **1960** Was: 12 G; KR 1-10 10.0. **1961** Was: 11 G. **Total:** 35 G; KR 1-10 10.0.

ED LAWRENCE Lawrence, Edward James 5′8″, 170 **HB-TB-FB-OE**
Col: Brown *HS:* Fitchburg [MA] B: 7/14/1905, Fitchburg, MA
D: 11/21/1961, North Las Vegas, NV
1929 Bost: 6 G. **1930** SI: 4 G. **Total:** 10 G.

HENRY LAWRENCE Lawrence, Henry 6′4″, 272 **OT-OG**
Col: Florida A&M *HS:* Lincoln [Palmetto, FL]; Manatee HS [Brandenton, FL]; Central HS [Wyoming, NY] B: 9/26/1951, Danville, PA
Drafted: 1974 Round 1 Oak
1974 Oak: 14 G. **1975** Oak: 14 G. **1976** Oak: 8 G. **1977** Oak: 14 G. **1978** Oak: 16 G. **1979** Oak: 16 G. **1980** Oak: 16 G. **1981** Oak: 16 G. **1982** LARd: 9 G. **1983** LARd: 16 G. **1984** LARd: 16 G. **1985** LARd: 16 G. **1986** LARd: 16 G. **Total:** 187 G.

JIMMY LAWRENCE Lawrence, James Boydston 5′11″, 190 **WB-DB-TB**
Col: Texas Christian *HS:* Harlingen [TX] B: 3/15/1913, Dawson, TX
D: 5/17/1990, Harlingen, TX *Drafted:* 1936 Round 1 ChiC
1936 ChiC: Pass 2-0, 1 Int. **1937** ChiC: Pass 3-0. **1938** ChiC: Pass 11-3 27.3%, 65 5.91 4 Int. **1939** ChiC-GB: Pass 4-1 25.0%, 15 3.75 1 Int; Punt 3-115 38.3. ChiC: Punt 3-115 38.3. GB: Pass 4-1 25.0%, 15 3.75 1 Int. **Total:** Pass 20-4 20.0%, 80 4.00 6 Int; Punt 3-115 38.3.

		Rushing				Receiving			
Year Team	**G**	**Att**	**Yds**	**Avg**	**TD**	**Rec**	**Yds**	**Avg**	**TD**
1936 ChiC	7	26	84	3.2	0	8	98	12.3	0
1937 ChiC	11	19	60	3.2	1	3	32	10.7	0
1938 ChiC	11	78	207	2.7	3	14	105	7.5	0
1939 ChiC-GB	4	7	6	0.9	0	3	39	13.0	0
1939 ChiC	1	3	6	2.0	0	2	18	9.0	0
1939 GB	3	4	0	0.0	0	1	21	21.0	0
NFL Total	33	130	357	2.7	4	28	274	9.8	0

LARRY LAWRENCE Lawrence, Larry Robert 6′1″, 208 **QB**
Col: Iowa; Miami (Fla.) *HS:* Thomas Jefferson [Cedar Rapids, IA]
B: 4/11/1949, Mount Pleasant, IA
1974 Oak: 7 G; Pass 11-4 36.4%, 29 2.64 1 Int; Rush 4-39 9.8. **1975** Oak: 1 G; Pass 15-5 33.3%, 50 3.33 1 Int; Rush 2-(-3) -1.5. **1976** TB: 1 G; Pass 5-0, 2 Int. **Total:** 9 G; Pass 31-9 29.0%, 79 2.55 4 Int; Rush 6-36 6.0.

KENT LAWRENCE Lawrence, Norman Kent 6′0″, 180 **WR**
Col: Georgia *HS:* D.W. Daniel [Central, SC] B: 6/3/1946, Anderson, SC
Drafted: 1969 Round 9 Phi
1969 Phi: 9 G; Rec 1-10 10.0; PR 2-26 13.0; KR 5-97 19.4. **1970** Atl: 1 G. **Total:** 10 G; Rec 1-10 10.0; PR 2-26 13.0; KR 5-97 19.4.

REGGIE LAWRENCE Lawrence, Reginald James 6′0″, 178 **WR**
Col: North Carolina State *HS:* Camden [NJ] B: 9/4/1969, Camden, NJ
1993 Phi: 1 G; Rec 1-5 5.0.

ROLLAND LAWRENCE Lawrence, Rolland Derenfro 5′10″, 179 **DB**
Col: Tabor *HS:* Franklin [PA] B: 3/24/1951, Franklin, PA

		Punt Returns				Kickoff Returns			
Year Team	**G**	**Ret**	**Yds**	**Avg**	**TD**	**Ret**	**Yds**	**Avg**	**TD**
1973 Atl	14	0	0	—	0	3	71	23.7	0
1974 Atl	14	0	0	—	0	0	0	—	0
1975 Atl	14	0	0	—	0	4	80	20.0	0
1976 Atl	14	**54**	372	6.9	0	21	521	24.8	0
1977 Atl	14	51	352	6.9	0	1	13	13.0	0
1978 Atl	16	1	17	17.0	0	0	0	—	0
1979 Atl	16	0	0	—	0	0	0	—	0
1980 Atl	16	3	-7	-2.3	0	0	0	—	0
NFL Total	118	109	734	6.7	0	29	685	23.6	0

	Interceptions				Tot
Year Team	**Int**	**Yds**	**TD**	**Fum**	**TD**
1973 Atl	1	81	0	0	0
1974 Atl	1	0	0	0	0
1975 Atl	9	163	1	0	1
1976 Atl	6	43	0	5	0
1977 Atl	7	138	0	3	0
1978 Atl	6	76	0	1	0
1979 Atl	6	120	0	0	1
1980 Atl	3	37	0	2	0
NFL Total	39	658	1	11	2

JOE LAWS Laws, Joseph Roy 5′9″, 186 **HB-DB-BB**
(Lefty; Tiger) *Col:* Iowa *HS:* Colfax [IA] B: 6/16/1911, Colfax, IA
D: 8/24/1979, Green Bay, WI
1934 GB: Pass 4-0, 1 Int. **1935** GB: Pass 1-1 100.0%, 8 8.00. **1936** GB: Pass 4-1 25.0%, 22 5.50 1 TD. **1937** GB: Pass 11-5 45.5%, 42 3.82 1 TD 2 Int. **1938** GB: Pass 5-0, 2 Int. **1939** GB: Pass 1-0. **1941** GB: KR 3-75 25.0. **1942** GB: Pass 3-2 66.7%, 76 25.33 1 TD; KR 2-36 18.0. **1943** GB: KR 2-47 23.5. **1944** GB: Pass 4-1 25.0%, 15 3.75 1 Int; KR 8-132 16.5. **1945** GB: KR 4-72 18.0. **Total:** Pass 33-10 30.3%, 163 4.94 3 TD 6 Int; KR 19-362 19.1.

		Rushing				Receiving			
Year Team	**G**	**Att**	**Yds**	**Avg**	**TD**	**Rec**	**Yds**	**Avg**	**TD**
1934 GB	13	46	155	3.4	1	9	165	18.3	1
1935 GB	11	24	63	2.6	1	4	82	20.5	0
1936 GB	11	50	296	5.9	1	10	132	13.2	2
1937 GB	11	74	310	4.2	1	10	121	12.1	0
1938 GB	10	60	253	4.2	0	6	55	9.2	1
1939 GB	10	55	162	2.9	2	11	177	16.1	1
1940 GB	3	7	21	3.0	0	5	60	12.0	1
1941 GB	11	21	58	2.8	0	4	48	12.0	1
1942 GB	10	29	100	3.4	0	6	96	16.0	1
1943 GB	10	43	232	5.4	0	5	33	6.6	0
1944 GB	10	45	200	4.4	3	7	61	8.7	1
1945 GB	10	16	82	5.1	0	2	11	5.5	0
NFL Total	120	470	1932	4.1	9	79	1041	13.2	9

	Punt Returns				Interceptions				Tot
Year Team	**Ret**	**Yds**	**Avg**	**TD**	**Int**	**Yds**	**TD**	**Fum**	**TD**
1934 GB	—	—	—	0	—	—	0	0	2
1935 GB	—	—	—	0	—	—	0	0	1
1936 GB	—	—	—	0	—	—	0	0	3
1937 GB	—	—	—	0	—	—	0	0	2
1938 GB	—	—	—	0	—	—	**1**	0	2
1939 GB	—	—	—	**1**	—	—	0	0	4
1940 GB	—	—	—	0	0	0	0	0	1
1941 GB	2	3	1.5	0	2	36	0	0	1
1942 GB	7	56	8.0	0	3	67	0	0	1
1943 GB	10	84	8.4	0	7	67	0	0	0
1944 GB	15	118	7.9	0	3	36	0	0	4
1945 GB	12	78	6.5	0	3	60	0	2	0
NFL Total	46	339	7.4	1	18	266	1	2	21

AL LAWSON Lawson, Alphonzo 5′11″, 190 **WR**
Col: Delaware State *HS:* Spingarn [Washington, DC] B: 6/6/1941, Washington, DC
1964 NYJ: 1 G.

JIM LAWSON Lawson, James Wilmer 5′11″, 190 **OE-WB**
Col: Stanford *HS:* Long Beach Polytechnic [CA] B: 3/11/1902, Long Beach, CA D: 1/3/1989, Carmel by the Sea, CA
1927 NYY: 11 G.

JAMIE LAWSON Lawson, Jamie Lee 5′10″, 240 **RB**
Col: Louisiana State; Nicholls State *HS:* Central Lafourche [Mathews, LA] B: 10/2/1965, New Orleans, LA *Drafted:* 1989 Round 5 TB
1989 TB: 5 G. **1990** TB-NE: 7 G. TB: 6 G. NE: 1 G. **Total:** 12 G.

JERRY LAWSON Lawson, Jerome Lee 5′11″, 192 **DB**
Col: Rancho Santiago Coll. CA (J.C.); Utah *HS:* Santa Ana [CA]
B: 10/30/1944, Bakersfield, CA *Drafted:* 1968 Round 10 Buf
1968 Buf: 1 G.

ODELL LAWSON Lawson, Odell 6′2″, 218 **RB**
Col: Langston *HS:* Ponca City [OK] B: 12/20/1948, Ponca City, OK
Drafted: 1970 Round 7 Bos
1970 Bos: Rec 11-113 10.3; PR 1-0. **1973** NO: Rec 2-(-5) -2.5. **Total:** Rec 13-108 8.3; PR 1-0.

Year Team	G	Rushing				Kickoff Returns				Fum
		Att	Yds	Avg	TD	Ret	Yds	Avg	TD	
1970 Bos	14	56	99	1.8	0	25	546	21.8	0	2
1971 NE	2	8	8	1.0	0	2	47	23.5	0	0
1973 NO	12	6	23	3.8	0	7	118	16.9	0	0
1974 NO	9	0	0	—	0	1	20	20.0	0	0
NFL Total	37	70	130	1.9	0	35	731	20.9	0	2

ROGER LAWSON Lawson, Roger Alan 6′2″, 215 **RB**
Col: Western Michigan *HS:* Southwestern [Detroit, MI] B: 9/28/1949, Detroit, MI *Drafted:* 1972 Round 15 ChiB
1972 ChiB: Rec 8-120 15.0. **1973** ChiB: Rec 9-60 6.7. **Total:** Rec 17-180 10.6.

Year Team	G	Rushing				Fum
		Att	Yds	Avg	TD	
1972 ChiB	12	33	106	3.2	1	2
1973 ChiB	10	24	70	2.9	0	1
NFL Total	22	57	176	3.1	1	3

STEVE LAWSON Lawson, Stephen Wendell 6′3″, 265 **OG**
Col: Kansas *HS:* Mount Carmel [Chicago, IL] B: 1/4/1949, Atlanta, GA *Drafted:* 1971 Round 2 Cin
1971 Cin: 7 G. **1972** Cin: 3 G. **1973** Min: 2 G. **1974** Min: 13 G. **1975** Min: 11 G. **1976** SF: 14 G. **1977** SF: 14 G. **Total:** 64 G.

RUSS LAY Lay, Russell M 5′11″, 198 **G**
Col: Michigan State *HS:* Williamston [MI] B: 1/11/1907, Williamston, MI D: 11/8/1971, Milwaukee, WI
1934 Det-Cin-StL: 5 G. Det: 2 G. Cin: 2 G. StL: 1 G. **Total:** 5 G.

PETE LAYDEN Layden, Peter John Jr. 5′11″, 192 **DB-TB-HB**
(Pistol Pete) *Col:* Texas *HS:* W.H. Adamson [Dallas, TX] B: 12/30/1919, Dallas, TX D: 7/18/1982, Edna, TX
AAFC **1948** NY-A: KR 8-211 26.4; Punt 21-884 42.1. **1949** NY-A: Rec 1-0; KR 1-28 28.0; Punt 15-626 41.7. **Total:** Rec 1-0; KR 9-239 26.6; Punt 36-1510 41.9.

Year Team	G	Passing							
		Att	Comp	Comp%	Yds	YPA	TD	Int	Rating
1948 NY-A	9	105	43	41.0	816	7.77	9	8	65.4
1949 NY-A	12	10	2	20.0	25	2.50	0	1	0.0
AAFC Total	21	115	45	39.1	841	7.31	9	9	58.6

Year Team	Rushing				Punt Returns			
	Att	Yds	Avg	TD	Ret	Yds	Avg	TD
1948 NY-A	95	576	6.1	3	7	64	9.1	0
1949 NY-A	19	96	5.1	0	29	287	9.9	0
AAFC Total	114	672	5.9	3	36	351	9.8	0

Year Team	Interceptions			Tot TD
	Int	Yds	TD	
1948 NY-A	3	63	0	3
1949 NY-A	7	137	1	1
AAFC Total	10	200	1	4

NFL **1950** NYY: 10 G; Int 3-40; Scor 3, 3-3 100.0% XK.

BOB LAYDEN Layden, Robert 6′2″, 215 **DE**
Col: Cowley Co. CC KS; Southwestern (Ks) *HS:* Frontenac [KS] B: 1/21/1920 D: 3/14/1988
1943 Det: 4 G.

JASON LAYMAN Layman, Jason Todd 6′5″, 310 **OT**
Col: Tennessee *HS:* Sevier Co. [Sevierville, TN] B: 7/29/1973, Sevierville, TN *Drafted:* 1996 Round 2 Hou
1996 Hou: 16 G. **1997** Ten: 14 G; KR 1-5 5.0. **1998** Ten: 16 G. **Total:** 46 G; KR 1-5 5.0.

BOBBY LAYNE Layne, Robert Lawrence 6′1″, 201 **QB**
Col: Texas *HS:* Highland Park [Dallas, TX] B: 12/19/1926, Santa Ana, TX D: 12/1/1986, Lubbock, TX *Drafted:* 1948 Round 1 ChiB
HOF: 1967
1948 ChiB: Punt 1-24 24.0. **Total:** Punt 1-24 24.0.

Year Team	G	Passing							
		Att	Comp	Comp%	Yds	YPA	TD	Int	Rating
1948 ChiB	11	52	16	30.8	232	4.46	3	2	49.5
1949 NYB	12	299	155	51.8	1796	6.01	9	18	55.3
1950 Det	12	**336**	152	45.2	**2323**	6.91	16	18	62.1
1951 Det	12	**332**	**152**	45.8	**2403**	7.24	**26**	23	67.6
1952 Det	12	287	139	48.4	1999	6.97	19	20	64.5
1953 Det	12	273	125	45.8	2088	7.65	16	21	59.6
1954 Det	12	246	135	54.9	1818	7.39	14	12	77.3
1955 Det	12	270	143	53.0	1830	6.78	11	17	61.8
1956 Det	12	244	129	52.9	1909	7.82	9	17	62.0
1957 Det	11	179	87	48.6	1169	6.53	6	12	53.0
1958 Det-Pit	12	294	145	49.3	2510	8.54	14	12	77.6
1958 Det	2	26	12	46.2	171	6.58	1	2	48.7
1958 Pit	10	268	133	49.6	2339	8.73	13	10	80.4
1959 Pit	12	297	142	47.8	1986	6.69	20	21	62.8
1960 Pit	12	209	103	49.3	1814	8.68	13	17	66.2
1961 Pit	8	149	75	50.3	1205	8.09	11	16	62.8
1962 Pit	13	233	116	49.8	1686	7.24	9	17	56.2
NFL Total	175	3700	1814	49.0	26768	7.23	196	243	63.4

Year Team	Rushing			
	Att	Yds	Avg	TD
1948 ChiB	13	80	6.2	1
1949 NYB	54	196	3.6	3
1950 Det	56	250	4.5	4
1951 Det	61	290	4.8	1
1952 Det	94	411	4.4	1
1953 Det	87	343	3.9	0
1954 Det	30	119	4.0	2
1955 Det	31	111	3.6	0
1956 Det	46	169	3.7	5
1957 Det	24	99	4.1	0
1958 Det-Pit	40	154	3.9	3
1958 Det	3	1	0.3	0
1958 Pit	37	153	4.1	3
1959 Pit	33	181	5.5	2
1960 Pit	19	12	0.6	2
1961 Pit	8	11	1.4	0
1962 Pit	15	25	1.7	1
NFL Total	611	2451	4.0	25

Year Team	Scoring							Fum
	Pts	FG	FGA	FG%	XK	XKA	XK%	
1948 ChiB	6	0	1	0.0	0	0	—	3
1949 NYB	0	0	0	—	0	0	—	**10**
1950 Det	25	0	0	—	1	2	50.0	**13**
1951 Det	0	0	0	—	0	0	—	8
1952 Det	8	0	0	—	2	2	100.0	5
1953 Det	0	0	0	—	0	0	—	8
1954 Det	0	0	0	—	0	0	—	2
1955 Det	0	0	0	—	0	0	—	4
1956 Det	**99**	12	15	**80.0**	33	33	**100.0**	3
1957 Det	43	6	11	54.5	25	25	100.0	3
1958 Det-Pit	19	0	0	—	1	3	33.3	7
1958 Det	1	0	0	—	1	3	33.3	2
1958 Pit	0	0	0	—	0	0	—	5
1959 Pit	77	11	17	64.7	32	32	100.0	2
1960 Pit	48	5	6	83.3	21	22	95.5	1
1961 Pit	5	0	0	—	5	5	100.0	4
1962 Pit	0	0	0	—	0	0	—	7
NFL Total	372	34	50	68.0	120	124	96.8	80

JOHNNIE LAYPORT Layport, John Evans 5′9″, 200 **G-T**
Col: Wooster *HS:* East [Cincinnati, OH]; Loveland HS [OH] B: 3/19/1901, Pataskala, OH D: 11/4/1986, Hendersonville, NC
1924 Col: 5 G. **1925** Day: 4 G. **1926** Day: 4 G. **Total:** 13 G.

MIKE LAZETICH Lazetich, Milan 6′1″, 211 **OG-LB**
(Sheriff) *Col:* Montana; Michigan *HS:* Anaconda [MT] B: 8/27/1921, Anaconda, MT D: 7/9/1969 *Drafted:* 1945 Round 2 Cle
1945 Cle: 10 G. **1946** LARm: 10 G. **1947** LARm: 11 G; KR 1-1 1.0. **1948** LARm: 12 G. **1949** LARm: 7 G; Int 2-47. **1950** LARm: 9 G. **Total:** 59 G; KR 1-1 1.0; Int 2-47.

PETE LAZETICH Lazetich, Peter Gary 6′3″, 245 **DE-LB-DT-NT**
Col: Stanford *HS:* Billings [MT] B: 2/4/1950, Billings, MT *Drafted:* 1972 Round 2 SD
1972 SD: 14 G. **1973** SD: 12 G. **1974** SD: 9 G. **1976** Phi: 13 G. **1977** Phi: 14 G. **Total:** 62 G.

BILL LAZETICH Lazetich, William Valdemere 6′0″, 195 **WB-DB**
Col: Montana *HS:* Anaconda [MT] B: 10/16/1916, Anaconda, MT *Drafted:* 1939 Round 14 Det
1939 Cle: 6 G; Rush 6-23 3.8; Rec 8-44 5.5 1 TD; 6 Pt. **1942** Cle: 9 G; Rush 3-19 6.3 1 TD; Rec 6-65 10.8 1 TD; KR 1-27 27.0; Tot TD 2; 12 Pt. **Total:** 15 G; Rush 9-42 4.7 1 TD; Rec 14-109 7.8 2 TD; KR 1-27 27.0; Tot TD 3; 18 Pt.

PAUL LEA Lea, Paul Addison 6′2″, 240 **OT-DT**
Col: Tulane *HS:* New London [TX] B: 2/19/1929, New Orleans, LA *Drafted:* 1951 Round 7 ChiB
1951 Pit: 9 G.

SCOTT LEACH Leach, Scott Haywood 6′2″, 221 **LB**
Col: Ohio State *HS:* Bassick [White Plains, NY] B: 9/18/1963, Bridgeport, CT *Drafted:* 1987 Round 9 NO
1987 NO: 3 G; Int 1-10; 1.5 Sac.

BILL LEACH Leach, William Kenneth 6′5″, 280 **OG-OT**
Col: Kentucky; North Carolina State *HS:* Perry Hall [MD] B: 7/2/1964, Baltimore, MD
1987 NO: 1 G.

GAR LEAF Leaf, Garfield Robert 6′1″, 195 **T**
(Sock) *Col:* Lake Forest; Syracuse *HS:* Highland Park [IL]
B: 5/26/1902, Waukegan, IL D: 3/20/1990, Colorado Springs, CO
1926 Lou: 3 G.

RYAN LEAF Leaf, Ryan David 6′5″, 245 **QB**
Col: Washington State *HS:* C.M. Russell [Great Falls, MT]
B: 5/15/1976, Great Falls, MT *Drafted:* 1998 Round 1 SD

		Passing							
Year Team	**G**	**Att**	**Comp**	**Comp%**	**Yds**	**YPA**	**TD**	**Int**	**Rating**
1998 SD	10	245	111	45.3	1289	5.26	2	15	39.0

	Rushing				
Year Team	**Att**	**Yds**	**Avg**	**TD**	**Fum**
1998 SD	27	80	3.0	0	8

BERNIE LEAHY Leahy, Bernard Philip 5′11″, 185 **HB**
Col: Notre Dame *HS:* St. Mel's [Chicago, IL] B: 8/15/1908
D: 3/12/1978, Walnut Creek, CA
1932 ChiB: 1 G; Rush 1-1 1.0.

JERRY LEAHY Leahy, Gerald Leo 6′2″, 220 **OT**
Col: Colorado *HS:* St. Joseph's [Bay City, MI] B: 10/15/1934, Bay City, MI *Drafted:* 1957 Round 7 Det
1957 Pit: 1 G.

PAT LEAHY Leahy, Patrick Joseph 6′0″, 194 **K**
Col: St. Louis *HS:* Augustinian Acad. [St. Louis, MO] B: 3/19/1951, St. Louis, MO
1988 NYJ: Rush 1-10 10.0. **1990** NYJ: Punt 1-12 12.0. **Total:** Rush 1-10 10.0; Punt 1-12 12.0.

		Scoring						
Year Team	**G**	**Pts**	**FG**	**FGA**	**FG%**	**XK**	**XKA**	**XK%**
1974 NYJ	6	36	6	11	54.5	18	19	94.7
1975 NYJ	14	66	13	21	61.9	27	30	90.0
1976 NYJ	14	49	11	16	68.8	16	20	80.0
1977 NYJ	14	63	15	25	60.0	18	21	85.7
1978 NYJ	16	107	22	30	73.3	41	42	97.6
1979 NYJ	6	36	8	13	61.5	12	15	80.0
1980 NYJ	16	78	14	22	63.6	36	36	100.0
1981 NYJ	16	113	25	36	69.4	38	39	97.4
1982 NYJ	9	59	11	17	64.7	26	31	83.9
1983 NYJ	16	84	16	24	66.7	36	37	97.3
1984 NYJ	16	89	17	24	70.8	38	39	97.4
1985 NYJ	16	121	26	34	76.5	43	45	95.6
1986 NYJ	16	92	16	19	84.2	44	44	100.0
1987 NYJ	12	85	18	22	81.8	31	31	100.0
1988 NYJ	16	112	23	28	82.1	43	43	100.0
1989 NYJ	16	71	14	21	66.7	29	30	96.7
1990 NYJ	16	101	23	26	88.5	32	32	100.0
1991 NYJ	15	108	26	37	70.3	30	30	100.0
NFL Total	250	1470	304	426	71.4	558	584	95.5

BOB LEAHY Leahy, Robert V 6′2″, 205 **QB**
Col: Connecticut; Emporia State *HS:* Lindenhurst [NY] B: 9/5/1947, Lindenhurst, NY
1971 Pit: 1 G; Pass 11-3 27.3%, 18 1.64 1 Int; Rush 1-(-6) -6.0; 2 Fum.

ROOSEVELT LEAKS Leaks, Roosevelt Jr. 5′10″, 225 **RB**
Col: Texas *HS:* Brenham [TX] B: 1/31/1953, Brenham, TX
Drafted: 1975 Round 5 Bal
1981 Buf: Pass 1-0. **Total:** Pass 1-0.

		Rushing				Receiving					Tot
Year Team	**G**	**Att**	**Yds**	**Avg**	**TD**	**Rec**	**Yds**	**Avg**	**TD**	**Fum**	**TD**
1975 Bal	11	41	175	4.3	1	1	5	5.0	0	2	1
1976 Bal	13	118	445	3.8	7	8	43	5.4	0	3	7
1977 Bal	11	59	237	4.0	3	3	39	13.0	1	3	4
1978 Bal	12	83	266	3.2	2	9	111	12.3	2	3	4
1979 Bal	7	49	145	3.0	1	14	119	8.5	0	2	1
1980 Buf	16	67	219	3.3	2	8	57	7.1	1	1	3
1981 Buf	16	91	357	3.9	6	7	51	7.3	0	1	6
1982 Buf	9	97	405	4.2	5	13	91	7.0	0	2	5
1983 Buf	12	58	157	2.7	1	8	74	9.3	0	0	1
NFL Total	107	663	2406	3.6	28	71	590	8.3	4	17	32

WES LEAPER Leaper, Wesley Stuart 5′11″, 175 **OE**
Col: Wisconsin *HS:* Green Bay West [WI] B: 10/23/1900, Green Bay, WI D: 1/30/1958, Cleveland, OH
1923 GB: 2 G.

LES LEAR Lear, Leslie 5′11″, 225 **G**
(Butch) *Col:* Manitoba (Canada) *HS:* HS in Canada B: 8/22/1918, Grafton, ND D: 1/5/1979, Hollywood, FL
1944 Cle: 10 G. **1945** Cle: 9 G. **1946** LARm: 11 G; Int 1-0. **1947** Det: 10 G. **Total:** 40 G; Int 1-0.

TOM LEARY Leary, Thomas John 6′0″, 180 **OE**
(Goof) *Col:* Fordham *HS:* Westbrook Seminary [ME] B: 4/15/1904, Springfield, MA D: 8/6/1976, Springfield, MA
1927 Fra: 1 G. **1929** SI: 10 G; Rec 2 TD; 12 Pt. **1930** Nwk: 8 G; Int **2** TD; 12 Pt. **1931** Fra: 7 G. **Total:** 26 G; Rec 2 TD; Int 2 TD; Tot TD 4; 24 Pt.

WESLEY LEASY Leasy, Wesley 6′3″, 235 **LB**
Col: Mississippi State *HS:* Greenville [MS] B: 9/7/1971, Vicksburg, MS
Drafted: 1995 Round 7 Ariz
1995 Ariz: 12 G. **1996** Ariz: 16 G. **Total:** 28 G.

PAUL LEATHERMAN Leatherman, Paul Christian 5′9″, 200 **G**
Col: Chicago *HS:* Garfield [Terre Haute, IN] B: 8/9/1897, Terre Haute, IN Deceased
1922 Ham: 4 G.

MILT LEATHERS Leathers, Leon Milton Jr. 5′11″, 198 **G**
(Red) *Col:* Georgia *HS:* Clarke Central [Athens, GA] B: 12/16/1908, Winder, GA
1933 Phi: 4 G.

ALLAN LEAVITT Leavitt, Allan James 5′11″, 176 **K**
Col: Georgia *HS:* Hernando [Brooksville, FL]; Lakewood HS [St. Petersburg, FL] B: 10/22/1955, St. Petersburg, FL *Drafted:* 1977 Round 4 Atl
1977 TB: 8 G; Scor 20, 5-10 50.0% FG, 5-5 100.0% XK.

FRANK LEAVITT Leavitt, Frank Simmons 270 **G**
(Soldier AKA Man Mountain Dean) *Col:* No College B: 6/30/1891, New York, NY D: 5/29/1953, Norcross, GA
1921 NYG: 2 G.

EDDIE LEBARON LeBaron, Edward Wayne Jr. 5′9″, 168 **QB**
Col: U. of Pacific *HS:* Oakdale [CA] B: 1/7/1930, San Rafael, CA
Drafted: 1950 Round 10 Was
1952 Was: Scor 18, 6-7 85.7% XK. **Total:** Scor 60, 6-7 85.7% XK.

		Passing							
Year Team	**G**	**Att**	**Comp**	**Comp%**	**Yds**	**YPA**	**TD**	**Int**	**Rating**
1952 Was	12	194	96	49.5	1420	7.32	14	15	65.7
1953 Was	12	149	62	41.6	874	5.87	3	17	28.3
1955 Was	12	178	79	44.4	1270	7.13	9	15	50.5
1956 Was	10	98	47	48.0	554	5.65	3	10	36.2
1957 Was	12	167	99	59.3	1508	9.03	11	10	86.1
1958 Was	12	145	79	54.5	1365	**9.41**	11	10	83.3
1959 Was	12	173	77	44.5	1077	6.23	8	11	54.0
1960 Dal	11	225	111	49.3	1736	7.72	12	25	53.5
1961 Dal	14	236	120	50.8	1741	7.38	14	16	66.7
1962 Dal	14	166	95	57.2	1436	8.65	16	9	95.4
1963 Dal	13	65	33	50.8	418	6.43	3	3	67.3
NFL Total	134	1796	898	50.0	13399	7.46	104	141	61.4

	Rushing				Punting			
Year Team	**Att**	**Yds**	**Avg**	**TD**	**Punts**	**Yds**	**Avg**	**Fum**
1952 Was	43	164	3.8	2	51	2150	42.2	7
1953 Was	21	95	4.5	2	51	2004	39.3	2
1955 Was	37	190	5.1	4	62	2581	41.6	5
1956 Was	11	6	0.5	0	4	161	40.3	4
1957 Was	20	-12	-0.6	0	0	0	—	7
1958 Was	12	30	2.5	0	0	0	—	2
1959 Was	13	7	0.5	0	0	0	—	5
1960 Dal	17	94	5.5	1	3	99	33.0	4
1961 Dal	20	72	3.6	0	0	0	—	7
1962 Dal	6	-1	-0.2	0	0	0	—	1
1963 Dal	2	5	2.5	0	0	0	—	0
NFL Total	202	650	3.2	9	171	6995	40.9	44

DICK LEBEAU LeBeau, Charles Richard 6′1″, 185 **DB**
Col: Ohio State *HS:* London [OH] B: 9/9/1937, London, OH
Drafted: 1959 Round 5 Cle
1960 Det: KR 2-16 8.0. **1962** Det: **1** Fum TD. **Total:** KR 2-16 8.0; 1 Fum TD.

		Interceptions			Tot
Year Team	**G**	**Int**	**Yds**	**TD**	**TD**
1959 Det	6	0	0	0	0
1960 Det	12	4	58	0	0
1961 Det	14	3	45	0	0
1962 Det	14	4	67	**1**	2
1963 Det	14	5	158	1	1
1964 Det	14	5	45	0	0
1965 Det	14	7	84	1	1
1966 Det	14	4	66	0	0
1967 Det	14	4	29	0	0
1968 Det	14	5	23	0	0
1969 Det	14	6	15	0	0
1970 Det	14	9	96	0	0
1971 Det	13	6	76	0	0
1972 Det	14	0	0	0	0
NFL Total	185	62	762	3	4

HARPER LEBEL LeBel, Brian Harper 6'4", 250 **TE**
Col: Colorado State *HS:* Notre Dame [Los Angeles, CA] B: 7/14/1963, Granada Hills, CA *Drafted:* 1985 Round 12 KC
1989 Sea: 16 G; 1 Fum. **1990** Phi: 16 G; Rec 1-9 9.0; 1 Fum. **1991** Atl: 3 G. **1992** Atl: 16 G; 1 Fum. **1993** Atl: 16 G; 1 Fum. **1994** Atl: 16 G; 1 Fum. **1995** Atl: 16 G; 1 Fum. **1996** Atl: 16 G. **1997** ChiB: 16 G; Rush 1-0; 1 Fum. **1998** Bal: 5 G; 1 Fum. **Total:** 136 G; Rush 1-0; Rec 1-9 9.0; 8 Fum.

FUNGY LEBENGOOD Lebengood, Howard Edward 5'11", 175 **WB**
Col: Villanova *HS:* Pottsville [PA] B: 4/23/1902, Pottsville, PA D: 1/20/1980, Lakeland, FL
1925 Pott: 5 G.

BOB LEBERMAN Leberman, Robert W 6'1", 180 **DB**
Col: Syracuse *HS:* Hamburg [NY] B: 2/10/1932 *Drafted:* 1954 Round 11 Bal
1954 Bal: 12 G; Int 2-0; 1 Fum.

MICHAEL LEBLANC LeBlanc, Michael Keith 5'11", 199 **RB**
Col: Stephen F. Austin St. *HS:* Willowridge [Sugar Land, TX] B: 5/5/1962, Missouri City, TX
1987 NE: Rec 2-3 1.5; KR 2-31 15.5.

		Rushing				
Year Team	**G**	**Att**	**Yds**	**Avg**	**TD**	**Fum**
1987 NE	4	49	170	3.5	1	2

BOB LEBLANC LeBlanc, Robert Leron 6'2", 243 **LB**
Col: Coffeyville CC KS; Elon *HS:* Shawnee Mission South [KS] B: 11/5/1962, Panama City, FL
1987 Buf: 3 G.

ED LECHNER Lechner, Edgar Henry 6'1", 200 **G-T**
Col: Minnesota *HS:* Fessenden [ND] B: 12/14/1919, Fessenden, ND
1942 NYG: 4 G.

ROY LECHTHALER Lechthaler, Roy Melvin 5'10", 198 **G**
Col: Lebanon Valley *HS:* Mercersburg Acad. [PA] B: 4/1/1908 D: 12/16/1980, Harrisburg, PA
1933 Phi: 4 G.

BILL LECKONBY Leckonby, William Bader 6'1", 185 **TB-DB**
(Wild Bill) *Col:* St. Lawrence *HS:* Troy [NY] B: 9/16/1917, Greenville, OH
1940 Bkn: Rec 1-8 8.0 1 TD; KR **1** TD; Int 3-29; Punt 2-54 27.0. **1941** Bkn: Rec 1-9 9.0 1 TD; PR 15-119 7.9; KR 2-76 38.0; Int 3-22; Punt 15-588 39.2. **Total:** Rec 2-17 8.5 2 TD; PR 15-119 7.9; KR 2-76 38.0 1 TD; Int 6-51; Punt 17-642 37.8.

		Passing							
Year Team	**G**	**Att**	**Comp**	**Comp%**	**Yds**	**YPA**	**TD**	**Int**	**Rating**
1939 Bkn	5	1	0	0.0	0	0.00	0	0	39.6
1940 Bkn	11	13	7	53.8	74	5.69	0	0	70.7
1941 Bkn	11	64	25	39.1	299	4.67	1	5	26.8
NFL Total	27	78	32	41.0	373	4.78	1	5	33.8

	Rushing				Tot
Year Team	**Att**	**Yds**	**Avg**	**TD**	**TD**
1939 Bkn	4	-1	-0.3	0	0
1940 Bkn	19	53	2.8	0	2
1941 Bkn	54	202	3.7	0	1
NFL Total	77	254	3.3	0	3

JIM LECLAIR LeClair, James Michael 6'3", 234 **LB**
Col: North Dakota *HS:* South St. Paul [MN] B: 10/30/1950, St. Paul, MN *Drafted:* 1972 Round 3 Cin
1979 Cin: **1** Fum TD. **1982** Cin: 2.5 Sac. **1983** Cin: 1 Sac. **Total:** 1 Fum TD; 3.5 Sac.

		Interceptions		
Year Team	**G**	**Int**	**Yds**	**TD**
1972 Cin	14	0	0	0
1973 Cin	10	0	0	0
1974 Cin	8	0	0	0
1975 Cin	14	3	25	0
1976 Cin	14	1	9	0
1977 Cin	14	2	8	0
1978 Cin	16	1	11	0
1979 Cin	16	1	0	0
1980 Cin	16	0	0	0
1981 Cin	14	1	0	0
1982 Cin	8	1	11	0
1983 Cin	14	0	0	0
NFL Total	158	10	64	0

JIM LECLAIR LeClair, James Michael 6'1", 200 **QB**
Col: C.W. Post *HS:* Archbishop Molloy [Queens, NY] B: 3/23/1944, Mount Vernon, NY *Drafted:* 1966 Round 16 SF
1967 Den: Rush 8-6 0.8 1 TD. **1968** Den: Rush 12-40 3.3. **Total:** Rush 20-46 2.3 1 TD.

		Passing								
Year Team	**G**	**Att**	**Comp**	**Comp%**	**Yds**	**YPA**	**TD**	**Int**	**Rating**	**Fum**
1967 Den	5	45	19	42.2	275	6.11	1	1	60.9	3
1968 Den	3	54	27	50.0	401	7.43	1	5	42.3	5
NFL Total	8	99	46	46.5	676	6.83	2	6	50.7	8

ROGER LECLERC LeClerc, Roger Alvin 6'3", 235 **LB-K-C**
Col: Trinity (Conn.) *HS:* Agawam [MA] B: 10/1/1936, Springfield, MA *Drafted:* 1959 Round 15 ChiB
1963 ChiB: Pass 1-0; Int 1-2. **1965** ChiB: KR 1-0. **Total:** Pass 1-0; KR 1-0; Int 1-2.

		Scoring						
Year Team	**G**	**Pts**	**FG**	**FGA**	**FG%**	**XK**	**XKA**	**XK%**
1960 ChiB	12	0	0	0	—	0	0	—
1961 ChiB	14	70	10	24	41.7	40	41	97.6
1962 ChiB	14	75	13	27	48.1	36	40	90.0
1963 ChiB	14	39	13	23	56.5	0	0	—
1964 ChiB	14	30	10	16	62.5	0	0	—
1965 ChiB	14	85	11	26	42.3	**52**	52	100.0
1966 ChiB	14	78	18	30	60.0	24	25	96.0
1967 Den	8	5	1	6	16.7	2	2	100.0
NFL Total	104	382	76	152	50.0	154	160	96.3

TERRY LECOUNT LeCount, Terry Jerome 5'10", 178 **WR**
Col: Florida *HS:* William M. Raines [Jacksonville, FL] B: 7/9/1956, Jacksonville, FL *Drafted:* 1978 Round 4 SF
1978 SF: KR 5-91 18.2. **1981** Min: Rush 3-51 17.0. **1982** Min: Rush 1-(-3) -3.0. **1983** Min: Pass 1-0; Rush 2-42 21.0. **Total:** Pass 1-0; Rush 6-90 15.0; KR 5-91 18.2.

		Receiving				
Year Team	**G**	**Rec**	**Yds**	**Avg**	**TD**	**Fum**
1978 SF	3	10	131	13.1	0	0
1979 SF-Min	14	6	119	19.8	2	0
1979 SF	2	0	0	—	0	0
1979 Min	12	6	119	19.8	2	0
1980 Min	16	13	168	12.9	0	0
1981 Min	16	24	425	17.7	2	0
1982 Min	9	14	179	12.8	1	0
1983 Min	11	21	318	15.1	2	1
1984 Min	2	1	14	14.0	0	0
1987 Min	1	0	0	—	0	0
NFL Total	72	89	1354	15.2	7	1

JIM LECTURE Lecture, James Wayne Jr. 5'10", 220 **G**
Col: Washington-St. Louis; Northwestern *HS:* St. George [Evanston, IL] B: 10/29/1924, Chiacgo, IL
AAFC **1946** BufA: 1 G.

DOC LEDBETTER Ledbetter, Homer Carroll 5'10", 190 **FB-LB-WB-DB**
Col: Arkansas *HS:* Springdale [AR] B: 1/25/1910, Huntsville, AR D: 1995
1932 SI-ChiC: Rec 2-37 18.5. SI: Rec 2-37 18.5. **1933** ChiC: Pass 4-2 50.0%, 12 3.00 2 Int. **Total:** Pass 4-2 50.0%, 12 3.00 2 Int; Rec 2-37 18.5.

		Rushing			
Year Team	**G**	**Att**	**Yds**	**Avg**	**TD**
1932 SI-ChiC	10	52	149	2.9	2
1932 SI	8	41	114	2.8	2
1932 ChiC	2	11	35	3.2	0
1933 ChiC	7	15	21	1.4	0
NFL Total	17	67	170	2.5	2

MONTE LEDBETTER Ledbetter, Monte Richards 6'2", 185 **WR**
Col: Northwestern State-Louisiana *HS:* Roanoke [LA] B: 8/13/1943, Jennings, LA *Drafted:* 1966 Round 11 Hou
1967 Hou-Buf: 10 G; Rec 13-204 15.7 2 TD; 12 Pt. Hou: 5 G; Rec 4-43 10.8 1 TD; 6 Pt. Buf: 5 G; Rec 9-161 17.9 1 TD; 6 Pt. **1968** Buf: 7 G; Rec 4-94 23.5 1 TD; KR 0-18; 6 Pt. **1969** Buf-Atl: 4 G; Rec 1-16 16.0. Buf: 2 G. Atl: 2 G; Rec 1-16 16.0. **Total:** 21 G; Rec 18-314 17.4 3 TD; KR 0-18; 18 Pt.

TOY LEDBETTER Ledbetter, Toy W 5'10", 198 **HB-DB**
Col: Oklahoma State *HS:* Durant [OK] B: 10/30/1927, Morris, OK D: 7/25/1995, Denver, CO
1954 Phi: KR 8-175 21.9. **1955** Phi: KR 1-21 21.0. **Total:** KR 9-196 21.8.

		Rushing				Receiving					Tot
Year Team	**G**	**Att**	**Yds**	**Avg**	**TD**	**Rec**	**Yds**	**Avg**	**TD**	**Fum**	**TD**
1950 Phi	10	67	320	4.8	1	4	81	20.3	2	2	3
1953 Phi	10	41	120	2.9	1	13	137	10.5	2	5	3
1954 Phi	12	81	241	3.0	1	15	192	12.8	3	7	4
1955 Phi	8	21	48	2.3	0	7	88	12.6	1	0	1
NFL Total	40	210	729	3.5	3	39	498	12.8	8	14	11

HAL LEDYARD Ledyard, Harold 6'0", 185 QB
Col: Tennessee-Chattanooga *HS:* Chattanooga [TN] B: 7/7/1931, Montgomery, AL D: 4/21/1973, Big Sur, CA *Drafted:* 1953 Round 9 SF
1953 SF: 10 G; Pass 9-0, 1 Int; Rush 1-3 3.0.

AMP LEE Lee, Anthonia Wayne 5'11", 200 RB
Col: Florida State *HS:* Chipley [FL] B: 10/1/1971, Chipley, FL
Drafted: 1992 Round 2 SF
1995 Min: PR 5-50 10.0. **1996** Min: PR 10-84 8.4. **1998** StL: Scor 1 2XP. **Total:** PR 15-134 8.9; Scor 1 2XP.

		Rushing				Receiving			
Year Team	G	Att	Yds	Avg	TD	Rec	Yds	Avg	TD
1992 SF	16	91	362	4.0	2	20	102	5.1	2
1993 SF	15	72	230	3.2	1	16	115	7.2	2
1994 Min	13	29	104	3.6	0	45	368	8.2	2
1995 Min	16	69	371	5.4	2	71	558	7.9	1
1996 Min	16	51	161	3.2	0	54	422	7.8	2
1997 StL	16	28	104	3.7	0	61	825	13.5	3
1998 StL	14	44	175	4.0	2	64	667	10.4	2
NFL Total	106	384	1507	3.9	7	331	3057	9.2	14

	Kickoff Returns					Tot
Year Team	Ret	Yds	Avg	TD	Fum	TD
1992 SF	14	276	19.7	0	1	4
1993 SF	10	160	16.0	0	1	3
1994 Min	3	42	14.0	0	1	2
1995 Min	5	100	20.0	0	3	3
1996 Min	5	85	17.0	0	2	2
1997 StL	4	71	17.8	0	0	3
1998 StL	0	0	—	0	3	4
NFL Total	41	734	17.9	0	11	21

BERNIE LEE Lee, Bernard Michael 5'11", 190 BB-LB
Col: Villanova *HS:* Canonsburg [PA] B: 10/25/1912, Broughton, PA D: 5/19/1990, Las Vegas, NV
1938 Phi-Pit: 5 G. Phi: 1 G. Pit: 4 G. **Total:** 5 G.

BIVIAN LEE Lee, Bivian Lewis Jr. 6'3", 200 DB
Col: Prairie View A&M *HS:* Emile [Bastrop, TX] B: 8/3/1948, Austin, TX D: 11/12/1984 *Drafted:* 1971 Round 3 NO
1971 NO: 14 G. **1972** NO: 13 G; Int 4-65. **1973** NO: 14 G; Int 3-23. **1974** NO: 13 G. **1975** NO: 11 G; Int 2-22; 1 Fum. **Total:** 65 G; Int 9-110; 1 Fum.

BOBBY LEE Lee, Bobby Dale 6'3", 200 WR
Col: Minnesota *HS:* Booker T. Washington [Montgomery, AL] B: 8/26/1945, Montgomery, AL *Drafted:* 1968 Round 17 StL
1968 StL: 2 G. **1969** Atl: 4 G. **Total:** 6 G.

BYRON LEE Lee, Byron Keith 6'2", 230 LB
Col: Ohio State *HS:* Eastmoor [Columbus, OH] B: 9/8/1964, Columbus, OH *Drafted:* 1986 Round 7 Phi
1986 Phi: 3 G. **1987** Phi: 3 G; 1 Sac. **Total:** 6 G; 1 Sac.

CARL LEE Lee, Carl III 5'11", 185 DB
Col: Marshall *HS:* South Charleston [WV] B: 2/6/1961, South Charleston, WV *Drafted:* 1983 Round 7 Min

		Interceptions		
Year Team	G	Int	Yds	TD
1983 Min	16	1	31	0
1984 Min	16	1	0	0
1985 Min	15	3	68	0
1986 Min	16	3	10	0
1987 Min	12	3	53	0
1988 Min	16	8	118	**2**
1989 Min	16	2	0	0
1990 Min	16	2	29	0
1991 Min	14	1	0	0
1992 Min	16	2	20	0
1993 Min	16	3	20	0
1994 NO	12	2	3	0
NFL Total	181	31	352	2

DANZELL LEE Lee, Danzell Ivan 6'2", 235 TE
Col: Lamar *HS:* Corsicana [TX] B: 3/16/1963, Corsicana, TX
Drafted: 1985 Round 6 Was
1987 Pit: 13 G; Rec 12-124 10.3. **1988** Atl: 5 G. **Total:** 18 G; Rec 12-124 10.3.

DAVID LEE Lee, David Allen 6'4", 230 P
Col: Louisiana Tech *HS:* Minden [LA] B: 11/8/1943, Shreveport, LA
1968 Bal: Rush 3-12 4.0. **1973** Bal: Rush 2-(-16) -8.0. **1976** Bal: Rush 1-(-12) -12.0. **1977** Bal: Rush 2-(-2) -1.0. **Total:** Rush 8-(-18) -2.3.

		Punting			
Year Team	G	Punts	Yds	Avg	Fum
1966 Bal	14	49	2233	**45.6**	0
1967 Bal	14	49	2075	42.3	0
1968 Bal	14	49	1935	39.5	0
1969 Bal	14	57	2580	**45.3**	0
1970 Bal	14	63	2819	44.7	0
1971 Bal	14	62	2542	41.0	0
1972 Bal	14	57	2400	42.1	0
1973 Bal	14	62	2402	38.7	1
1974 Bal	14	71	2634	37.1	0
1975 Bal	14	86	3402	39.6	0
1976 Bal	14	59	2342	39.7	0
1977 Bal	14	82	3142	38.3	1
1978 Bal	16	92	3513	38.2	0
NFL Total	184	838	34019	40.6	2

BIFF LEE Lee, David Hilary 6'0", 226 G
Col: Missouri; Oklahoma *HS:* Charleston [MO] B: 1/11/1905, Wolf Island, MO D: 5/1981, Troy, AL
1931 Port-Cle: 8 G. Port: 1 G. Cle: 7 G. **1933** Cin: 9 G; Scor 3, 1 FG. **1934** Cin: 8 G; Scor 1, 1 XK. **Total:** 25 G; Scor 4, 1 FG, 1 XK.

DWIGHT LEE Lee, Dwight Lionel 6'2", 190 RB
(Big D) *Col:* Michigan State *HS:* New Haven [MI] B: 9/3/1945, Mount Clemens, MI *Drafted:* 1968 Round 5 SF
1968 SF-Atl: 13 G; Rush 6-7 1.2; KR 3-63 21.0. SF: 2 G; Rush 2-1 0.5; KR 2-43 21.5. Atl: 11 G; Rush 4-6 1.5; KR 1-20 20.0. **Total:** 13 G; Rush 6-7 1.2; KR 3-63 21.0.

EDWARD LEE Lee, Edward Preston 5'11", 182 WR
Col: South Carolina State *HS:* Woodrow Wilson [Washington, DC] B: 12/8/1959, Washington, DC *Drafted:* 1982 Round 11 Det
1982 Det: Postseason only.

GENE LEE Lee, Eugene Orson 6'3", 226 C-LB
Col: Florida *HS:* Elbert Co. [Elberton, GA] B: 4/21/1922, Covington, GA *Drafted:* 1943 Round 25 Bkn
1946 Bos: 11 G; KR 1-0; Int 1-31.

GARY LEE Lee, Gary DeWayne 6'1", 202 WR
Col: Georgia Tech *HS:* Westover [Albany, GA] B: 2/12/1965, Albany, GA *Drafted:* 1987 Round 12 Det

		Receiving				Kickoff Returns				
Year Team	G	Rec	Yds	Avg	TD	Ret	Yds	Avg	TD	Fum
1987 Det	12	19	308	16.2	0	32	719	22.5	0	1
1988 Det	14	22	261	11.9	1	18	355	19.7	0	2
NFL Total	26	41	569	13.9	1	50	1074	21.5	0	3

GREG LEE Lee, Gregory Lamont 6'1", 207 DB
Col: Arkansas State *HS:* Dollarway [Pine Bluff, AR] B: 1/15/1965, Pine Bluff, AR
1988 Pit: 16 G.

JACKY LEE Lee, Jack Ross 6'1", 189 QB
Col: Cincinnati *HS:* Ellet [Akron, OH] B: 7/11/1939, Minneapolis, MN
Drafted: 1960 Round 1 Hou
1967 Hou-KC: Rec 1-(-1) -1.0. Hou: Rec 1-(-1) -1.0. **Total:** Rec 1-(-1) -1.0.

		Passing							
Year Team	G	Att	Comp	Comp%	Yds	YPA	TD	Int	Rating
1960 Hou	14	77	41	53.2	842	10.94	5	6	81.2
1961 Hou	14	127	66	52.0	1205	9.49	12	6	96.7
1962 Hou	14	50	26	52.0	433	8.66	4	5	68.6
1963 Hou	14	75	37	49.3	475	6.33	2	8	38.9
1964 Den	14	265	133	50.2	1611	6.08	11	20	51.6
1965 Den	4	80	44	55.0	692	8.65	5	3	89.2
1966 Hou	8	8	4	50.0	27	3.38	0	1	18.2
1967 Hou-KC	9	91	42	46.2	414	4.55	3	6	43.0
1967 Hou	4	72	36	50.0	309	4.29	2	4	47.7
1967 KC	5	19	6	31.6	105	5.53	1	2	29.4
1968 KC	6	45	25	55.6	383	8.51	3	1	96.8
1969 KC	3	20	12	60.0	109	5.45	1	1	70.6
NFL Total	100	838	430	51.3	6191	7.39	46	57	65.6

	Rushing				
Year Team	Att	Yds	Avg	TD	Fum
1960 Hou	6	11	1.8	0	4
1961 Hou	8	36	4.5	0	3
1962 Hou	4	1	0.3	0	1
1963 Hou	2	9	4.5	0	2
1964 Den	42	163	3.9	3	3
1965 Den	2	1	0.5	0	1
1966 Hou	1	-3	-3.0	0	1
1967 Hou-KC	6	-3	-0.5	0	1
1967 Hou	5	0	0.0	0	0
1967 KC	1	-3	-3.0	0	1
1969 KC	1	3	3.0	0	0
NFL Total	72	218	3.0	3	16

JEFF LEE Lee, Jeffrey Leroy 6'2", 195 WR
Col: Nebraska *HS:* Horlick [Racine, WI] B: 5/23/1955, Racine, WI
1980 StL: 4 G; Rec 2-19 9.5.

JACK LEE Lee, John 5′10″, 205 **BB-LB**
(Whitey) *Col:* Carnegie Mellon *HS:* Coneburg [Ellsworth, PA]
B: 3/28/1917 D: 7/1972 *Drafted:* 1939 Round 10 Pit
1939 Pit: 5 G; Pass 1-0; Rush 1-(-11) -11.0; Punt 1-44 44.0.

JOHN LEE Lee, John Dana 6′2″, 255 **DE**
Col: Nebraska *HS:* Red Bank [NJ] B: 2/17/1953, Fort Monmouth, NJ
Drafted: 1976 Round 13 SD
1976 SD: 14 G. **1977** SD: 12 G. **1978** SD: 1 G. **1979** SD: 10 G. **1980** SD: 11 G. **1981** NE: 4 G. **Total:** 52 G.

KEITH LEE Lee, Keith Lamar 5′11″, 192 **DB**
Col: Santa Monica Coll. CA (J.C.); Colorado State *HS:* Gardena [CA]
B: 12/22/1957, San Antonio, TX *Drafted:* 1980 Round 5 Buf
1981 NE: 15 G; KR 2-20 10.0; Int 1-0. **1982** NE: 9 G; KR 1-14 14.0. **1983** NE: 15 G; PR 1-0; KR 4-40 10.0; 1 Fum. **1984** NE: 15 G; KR 3-43 14.3. **1985** Ind: 14 G; KR 1-6 6.0; 1 Sac. **Total:** 68 G; PR 1-0; KR 11-123 11.2; Int 1-0; 1 Fum; 1 Sac.

KEN LEE Lee, Kenneth Alan 6′4″, 230 **LB**
Col: Washington *HS:* Oak Harbor [WA] B: 9/3/1948, Honolulu, HI
Drafted: 1971 Round 8 Det
1971 Det: 1 G. **1972** Buf: 12 G; Int 6-155 1 TD; 6 Pt. **Total:** 13 G; Int 6-155 1 TD; 6 Pt.

KEVIN LEE Lee, Kevin DeWayne 6′1″, 194 **WR**
Col: Alabama *HS:* C.F. Vigor [Prichard, AL] B: 1/1/1971, Mobile, AL
Drafted: 1994 Round 2 NE
1995 NE: 7 G; Rush 1-4 4.0; Rec 8-107 13.4; KR 1-14 14.0. **1996** SF: 2 G. **Total:** 9 G; Rush 1-4 4.0; Rec 8-107 13.4; KR 1-14 14.0.

LARRY LEE Lee, Larry Dwayne 6′2″, 265 **OG-C**
Col: UCLA *HS:* Nettie Lee Roth [Dayton, OH] B: 9/10/1959, Dayton, OH *Drafted:* 1981 Round 5 Det
1981 Det: 16 G; KR 1-0. **1982** Det: 9 G; KR 1-14 14.0. **1983** Det: 16 G; KR 1-11 11.0. **1984** Det: 15 G; 2 Fum. **1985** Det-Mia: 11 G. Det: 6 G. Mia: 5 G. **1986** Mia: 16 G; KR 1-5 5.0; 1 Fum. **1987** Den: 9 G. **1988** Den: 4 G. **Total:** 96 G; KR 4-30 7.5; 3 Fum.

LLOYD LEE Lee, Lloyd Ceyoung 6′1″, 210 **DB**
Col: Dartmouth *HS:* Thomas Jefferson [Bloomington, MN]
B: 8/10/1976, Minneapolis, MN
1998 SD: 8 G.

MARK LEE Lee, Mark Anthony 5′11″, 187 **DB**
Col: Washington *HS:* Hanford [CA] B: 3/20/1958, Hanford, CA
Drafted: 1980 Round 2 GB

		Punt Returns				Kickoff Returns			
Year Team	**G**	**Ret**	**Yds**	**Avg**	**TD**	**Ret**	**Yds**	**Avg**	**TD**
1980 GB	15	5	32	6.4	0	30	589	19.6	0
1981 GB	16	20	187	9.4	1	14	270	19.3	0
1982 GB	9	0	0	—	0	0	0	—	0
1983 GB	16	1	-4	-4.0	0	1	0	0.0	0
1984 GB	16	0	0	—	0	0	0	—	0
1985 GB	14	0	0	—	0	0	0	—	0
1986 GB	16	0	0	—	0	0	0	—	0
1987 GB	12	0	0	—	0	0	0	—	0
1988 GB	15	0	0	—	0	0	0	—	0
1989 GB	12	0	0	—	0	0	0	—	0
1990 GB	16	0	0	—	0	0	0	—	0
1991 SF-NO	8	0	0	—	0	0	0	—	0
1991 SF	5	0	0	—	0	0	0	—	0
1991 NO	3	0	0	—	0	0	0	—	0
NFL Total	165	26	215	8.3	1	45	859	19.1	0

	Interceptions			
Year Team	**Int**	**Yds**	**TD**	**Fum**
1980 GB	0	0	0	1
1981 GB	6	50	0	0
1982 GB	1	40	0	0
1983 GB	4	23	0	1
1984 GB	3	33	0	0
1985 GB	1	23	0	0
1986 GB	9	33	0	0
1987 GB	1	0	0	0
1988 GB	3	37	0	0
1989 GB	2	10	0	0
1990 GB	1	0	0	0
1991 SF-NO	1	5	0	0
1991 SF	1	5	0	0
NFL Total	32	254	0	2

MIKE LEE Lee, Michael 6′0″, 232 **LB**
Col: Nevada-Las Vegas *HS:* Abraham Lincoln [San Diego, CA]
B: 8/31/1951, San Diego, CA
1974 SD: 7 G.

JOHN LEE Lee, Min Jong 5′11″, 182 **K**
Col: UCLA *HS:* Downey [CA] B: 5/19/1964, Seoul, South Korea
Drafted: 1986 Round 2 StL
1986 StL: 11 G; Scor 38, 8-13 61.5% FG, 14-17 82.4% XK.

MONTE LEE Lee, Monte Vern 6′4″, 225 **LB**
Col: Texas *HS:* Hale Center [TX] B: 7/11/1938, Ballinger, TX
Drafted: 1960 Round 8 Phi
1961 StL: 12 G; KR 1-12 12.0; Int 1-7. **1963** Det: 8 G. **1964** Det: 14 G; KR 1-25 25.0. **1965** Bal: 5 G. **Total:** 39 G; KR 2-37 18.5; Int 1-7.

OUDIOUS LEE Lee, Oudious Jr. 6′1″, 253 **NT**
Col: Nebraska *HS:* Omaha South [NE] B: 6/14/1956, Omaha, NE
1980 StL: 1 G.

BOB LEE Lee, Robert Edward 6′1″, 245 **OG**
Col: Missouri *HS:* Hickman [Columbia, MO] B: 7/4/1935
1960 Bos: 8 G.

BOB LEE Lee, Robert Melville 6′2″, 195 **QB-P**
Col: San Francisco City Coll. CA (J.C.); Arizona State; U. of Pacific
HS: Lowell [San Francisco, CA] B: 8/7/1945, Columbus, OH
Drafted: 1968 Round 17 Min

		Passing							
Year Team	**G**	**Att**	**Comp**	**Comp%**	**Yds**	**YPA**	**TD**	**Int**	**Rating**
1969 Min	14	11	7	63.6	79	7.18	1	0	115.3
1970 Min	6	79	40	50.6	610	7.72	5	5	71.2
1971 Min	14	90	45	50.0	598	6.64	2	4	60.3
1972 Min	2	6	3	50.0	75	12.50	1	0	135.4
1973 Atl	12	230	120	52.2	1786	7.77	10	8	77.9
1974 Atl	9	172	78	45.3	852	4.95	3	14	32.4
1975 Min	4	14	5	35.7	103	7.36	2	1	72.3
1976 Min	4	30	15	50.0	156	5.20	0	2	37.6
1977 Min	5	72	42	58.3	522	7.25	4	4	76.3
1978 Min	3	4	2	50.0	10	2.50	0	1	16.7
1979 LARm	3	22	11	50.0	243	11.05	2	1	101.1
1980 LARm	1	0	0	—	0	—	0	0	—
NFL Total	77	730	368	50.4	5034	6.90	30	40	63.7

	Rushing				Punting			
Year Team	**Att**	**Yds**	**Avg**	**TD**	**Punts**	**Yds**	**Avg**	**Fum**
1969 Min	3	9	3.0	0	67	2680	40.0	2
1970 Min	10	20	2.0	1	0	0	—	2
1971 Min	11	14	1.3	1	**89**	**3515**	39.5	2
1973 Atl	29	67	2.3	0	0	0	—	6
1974 Atl	19	99	5.2	1	0	0	—	4
1975 Min	1	0	0.0	0	0	0	—	1
1976 Min	2	2	1.0	0	0	0	—	3
1977 Min	12	-8	-0.7	0	0	0	—	1
1979 LARm	4	-5	-1.3	0	0	0	—	1
1980 LARm	1	-1	-1.0	0	0	0	—	0
NFL Total	92	197	2.1	3	156	6195	39.7	22

RONNIE LEE Lee, Ronald Van 6′3″, 265 **OT-TE-OG**
Col: Baylor *HS:* John Tyler [Tyler, TX] B: 12/24/1956, Pine Bluff, AR
Drafted: 1979 Round 3 Mia

		Receiving			
Year Team	**G**	**Rec**	**Yds**	**Avg**	**TD**
1979 Mia	16	2	14	7.0	0
1980 Mia	16	7	83	11.9	2
1981 Mia	16	14	64	4.6	1
1982 Mia	9	2	6	3.0	0
1983 Atl	14	0	0	—	0
1984 Mia	16	0	0	—	0
1985 Mia	15	0	0	—	0
1986 Mia	10	0	0	—	0
1987 Mia	9	0	0	—	0
1988 Mia	16	0	0	—	0
1989 Mia	15	0	0	—	0
1990 Sea	15	0	0	—	0
1991 Sea	10	0	0	—	0
1992 Sea	9	0	0	—	0
NFL Total	186	25	167	6.7	3

RON LEE Lee, Ronnell 6′4″, 226 **RB**
Col: West Virginia *HS:* Bellaire [OH] B: 9/17/1953, Bellaire, OH
Drafted: 1976 Round 3 Bal
1976 Bal: Rec 1-(-9) -9.0; PR 1-0; KR 3-24 8.0. **1977** Bal: Rec 10-60 6.0. **1978** Bal: Rec 13-109 8.4 1 TD. **Total:** Rec 24-160 6.7 1 TD; PR 1-0; KR 3-24 8.0.

		Rushing					Tot
Year Team	**G**	**Att**	**Yds**	**Avg**	**TD**	**Fum**	**TD**
1976 Bal	14	41	220	5.4	1	1	1
1977 Bal	13	84	346	4.1	3	1	3
1978 Bal	15	81	374	4.6	1	3	2
NFL Total	42	206	940	4.6	5	5	6

SHAWN LEE Lee, Shawn Swaboda 6′2″, 300 **NT-DT**
Col: North Alabama *HS:* Erasmus Hall [Brooklyn, NY] B: 10/24/1966, Brooklyn, NY *Drafted:* 1988 Round 6 TB
1988 TB: 15 G; 2 Sac. **1989** TB: 15 G; 1 Sac. **1990** Mia: 13 G; 1.5 Sac. **1991** Mia: 3 G; Int 1-14. **1992** SD: 9 G; 0.5 Sac. **1993** SD: 16 G; 3 Sac.

1994 SD: 15 G; 6.5 Sac. **1995** SD: 16 G; 8 Sac. **1996** SD: 15 G; Int 1-(-1); 1 Sac. **1997** SD: 16 G; 3 Sac. **1998** ChiB: 15 G; 1 Fum TD; 6 Pt; 2 Sac. **Total:** 148 G; Int 2-13; 1 Fum TD; 6 Pt; 28.5 Sac.

BILL LEE Lee, William Earl 6′2″, 231 **T**
Col: Alabama *HS:* Greene Co. [Eutaw, AL] B: 10/19/1911, Eutaw, AL
1935 Bkn: 12 G. **1936** Bkn: 12 G. **1937** Bkn-GB: 9 G. Bkn: 5 G. GB: 4 G. **1938** GB: 11 G. **1939** GB: 11 G. **1940** GB: 11 G; Int 1-14. **1941** GB: 11 G. **1942** GB: 1 G. **1946** GB: 4 G. **Total:** 82 G; Int 1-14.

WILLIE LEE Lee, Willie 6′5″, 249 **DT**
Col: Bethune-Cookman *HS:* Seabreeze [Daytona Beach, FL]
B: 7/13/1950, Daytona Beach, FL *Drafted:* 1976 Round 5 KC
1976 KC: 14 G. **1977** KC: 14 G; 1 Fum TD; 6 Pt. **Total:** 28 G; 1 Fum TD; 6 Pt.

HERMAN LEE Lee, Willie Herman 6′4″, 244 **OT-OG**
Col: Florida A&M *HS:* Central [Phenix City, AL] B: 8/29/1931, Phenix City, AL *Drafted:* 1954 Round 23 ChiB
1957 Pit: 8 G. **1958** ChiB: 12 G. **1959** ChiB: 12 G. **1960** ChiB: 12 G; Rec 1-16 16.0. **1961** ChiB: 14 G. **1962** ChiB: 14 G. **1963** ChiB: 14 G. **1964** ChiB: 14 G. **1965** ChiB: 14 G. **1966** ChiB: 13 G. **Total:** 127 G; Rec 1-16 16.0.

ZEPH LEE Lee, Zephrini 6′3″, 208 **RB**
Col: USC *HS:* Abraham Lincoln [San Francisco, CA] B: 6/17/1963, San Francisco, CA *Drafted:* 1986 Round 9 LARd
1987 Den-LARd: 3 G. Den: 1 G. LARd: 2 G. **1988** LARd: 8 G; KR 1-0; Int 1-20. **1989** LARd: 13 G; KR 1-0; 1 Fum. **Total:** 24 G; KR 2-0; Int 1-20; 1 Fum.

TUFFY LEEMANS Leemans, Alphonse Emil 6′0″, 195 **FB-DB-QB**
Col: Oregon; George Washington *HS:* Central [Superior, WI]
B: 11/12/1912, Superior, WI D: 1/19/1979, Hillsboro Beach, FL
Drafted: 1936 Round 2 NYG *HOF:* 1978
1940 NYG: Int 1-0. **1941** NYG: PR 14-170 12.1; KR 3-48 16.0; Int 3-35. **1942** NYG: PR 2-26 13.0. **1943** NYG: PR 3-66 22.0; KR 2-29 14.5. **Total:** PR 19-262 13.8; KR 5-77 15.4; Int 4-35.

		Passing							
Year Team	**G**	**Att**	**Comp**	**Comp%**	**Yds**	**YPA**	**TD**	**Int**	**Rating**
1936 NYG	12	42	13	31.0	258	6.14	3	6	37.7
1937 NYG	9	20	5	25.0	64	3.20	1	1	36.3
1938 NYG	10	42	19	45.2	249	5.93	3	6	48.7
1939 NYG	10	26	12	46.2	198	7.62	0	2	40.2
1940 NYG	10	31	15	48.4	159	5.13	2	3	45.7
1941 NYG	11	66	31	47.0	475	7.20	4	5	59.8
1942 NYG	8	69	35	50.7	555	8.04	7	4	87.5
1943 NYG	10	87	37	42.5	360	4.14	5	5	50.0
NFL Total	80	383	167	43.6	2318	6.05	25	32	50.6

	Rushing				Receiving				Tot
Year Team	**Att**	**Yds**	**Avg**	**TD**	**Rec**	**Yds**	**Avg**	**TD**	**TD**
1936 NYG	**206**	**830**	4.0	2	4	22	5.5	0	2
1937 NYG	144	429	3.0	0	11	157	14.3	1	1
1938 NYG	121	463	3.8	4	4	68	17.0	0	4
1939 NYG	128	429	3.4	3	8	185	23.1	2	5
1940 NYG	132	474	3.6	1	0	0	—	0	1
1941 NYG	100	332	3.3	4	0	0	—	0	4
1942 NYG	51	116	2.3	3	1	-10	-10.0	0	3
1943 NYG	37	59	1.6	0	0	0	—	0	0
NFL Total	919	3132	3.4	17	28	422	15.1	3	20

MAX LEETZOW Leetzow, Max Arthur 6′4″, 240 **DE-DT**
Col: Idaho *HS:* Los Altos [CA] B: 9/17/1943, Lodi, CA *Drafted:* 1965 Round 5 Den
1965 Den: 14 G. **1966** Den: 14 G. **Total:** 28 G.

JAY LEEUWENBURG Leeuwenburg, Jay Robert 6′3″, 294 **OG-C-OT**
Col: Colorado *HS:* Kirkwood [MO] B: 6/18/1969, St. Louis, MO
Drafted: 1992 Round 9 KC
1992 ChiB: 12 G; KR 1-7 7.0. **1993** ChiB: 16 G. **1994** ChiB: 16 G. **1995** ChiB: 16 G. **1996** Ind: 15 G. **1997** Ind: 16 G; 1 Fum. **1998** Ind: 16 G. **Total:** 107 G; KR 1-7 7.0; 1 Fum.

DICK LEEUWENBURG Leeuwenburg, Richard Peter 6′5″, 242 **OT**
Col: Stanford *HS:* Olympus [Salt Lake City, UT] B: 3/26/1942, Salt Lake City, UT *Drafted:* 1964 Round 11 ChiB
1965 ChiB: 9 G.

BILLY LEFEAR Lefear, William Ray 5′11″, 197 **RB-WR**
Col: Henderson State *HS:* Washington [El Dorado, AR] B: 2/12/1950, Magnolia, AR *Drafted:* 1972 Round 9 Cle
1973 Cle: Rec 5-38 7.6; PR 7-51 7.3. **1974** Cle: Rec 4-21 5.3; PR 2-1 0.5. **1975** Cle: Rec 1-14 14.0; PR 1-14 14.0. **Total:** Rec 10-73 7.3; PR 10-66 6.6.

		Rushing				Kickoff Returns				
Year Team	**G**	**Att**	**Yds**	**Avg**	**TD**	**Ret**	**Yds**	**Avg**	**TD**	**Fum**
1972 Cle	9	3	6	2.0	0	6	138	23.0	0	0
1973 Cle	13	26	135	5.2	0	15	337	22.5	0	3
1974 Cle	11	6	2	0.3	0	26	574	22.1	0	5
1975 Cle	10	0	0	—	0	13	412	31.7	0	0
NFL Total	43	35	143	4.1	0	60	1461	24.4	0	8

GIL LEFEBVRE LeFebvre, Gilbert 5′6″, 155 **TB-WB-DB**
(Frenchy) *Col:* No College *HS:* Manual Arts [Los Angeles, CA]
B: 3/10/1910, Douglas, AZ D: 5/7/1987, Bellflower, CA
1933 Cin: Pass 14-5 35.7%, 75 5.36 2 Int; Rec 2-20 10.0; PR 1 TD. **1934** Cin: Pass 9-1 11.1%, 22 2.44. **Total:** Pass 23-6 26.1%, 97 4.22 2 Int; Rec 2-20 10.0; PR 1 TD.

		Rushing			
Year Team	**G**	**Att**	**Yds**	**Avg**	**TD**
1933 Cin	10	64	155	2.4	0
1934 Cin	4	13	136	10.5	0
1935 Det	1	4	4	1.0	0
NFL Total	15	81	295	3.6	0

CLYDE LEFORCE LeForce, Clyde J Jr. 5′11″, 176 **QB-DB-WB**
Col: Tulsa *HS:* Bristow [OK] B: 6/4/1923, Pawnee, OK *Drafted:* 1945 Round 17 Det
1947 Det: PR 6-78 13.0; KR 4-98 24.5; Int 3-13. **1948** Det: Rec 8-122 15.3 3 TD; PR 1-9 9.0; KR 1-10 10.0; Int 1-0. **Total:** Rec 8-122 15.3 3 TD; PR 7-87 12.4; KR 5-108 21.6; Int 4-13.

		Passing							
Year Team	**G**	**Att**	**Comp**	**Comp%**	**Yds**	**YPA**	**TD**	**Int**	**Rating**
1947 Det	9	175	94	53.7	1384	7.91	13	20	65.0
1948 Det	12	101	50	49.5	912	9.03	9	8	77.7
1949 Det	11	112	53	47.3	665	5.94	3	9	41.7
NFL Total	32	388	197	50.8	2961	7.63	25	37	58.1

	Rushing					Tot
Year Team	**Att**	**Yds**	**Avg**	**TD**	**Fum**	**TD**
1947 Det	18	143	7.9	0	7	0
1948 Det	28	86	3.1	0	3	5
1949 Det	13	58	4.5	1	1	1
NFL Total	59	287	4.9	1	11	6

DICK LEFTRIDGE Leftridge, Jack Richard 6′2″, 240 **FB**
Col: West Virginia *HS:* Hinton [WV] B: 4/14/1944, Hinton, WV
Drafted: 1966 Round 1 Pit
1966 Pit: 4 G; Rush 8-17 2.1 2 TD; KR 1-10 10.0; 12 Pt; 1 Fum.

BURNIE LEGETTE Legette, Burnie A 6′1″, 243 **RB**
Col: Michigan *HS:* General William Mitchell [Colorado Springs, CO]
B: 12/5/1970, Colorado Springs, CO
1993 NE: 7 G. **1994** NE: 3 G. **Total:** 10 G.

TYRONE LEGETTE Legette, Tyrone Christopher 5′9″, 179 **DB**
Col: Nebraska *HS:* Spring Valley [Columbia, SC] B: 2/15/1970, Marion, SC *Drafted:* 1992 Round 3 NO
1992 NO: 8 G. **1993** NO: 14 G. **1994** NO: 15 G; PR 1-0; 1 Fum; 1 Sac. **1995** NO: 16 G; PR 1-6 6.0; Int 1-43; 1 Sac. **1996** TB: 15 G. **1997** TB: 16 G; Int 1-0. **1998** SF: 7 G. **Total:** 91 G; PR 2-6 3.0; Int 2-43; 1 Fum; 2 Sac.

BRAD LEGGETT Leggett, Brad 6′4″, 270 **C**
Col: USC *HS:* Fountain Valley [CA] B: 1/16/1966, Vicksburg, MS
Drafted: 1990 Round 8 Den
1991 NO: 4 G.

EARL LEGGETT Leggett, Earl Franklin 6′3″, 265 **DT**
Col: Hinds CC MS; Louisiana State *HS:* Robert E. Lee [Jacksonville, FL]; Raymond HS [MS] B: 3/5/1933, Palatka, FL *Drafted:* 1957 Round 1 ChiB
1957 ChiB: 12 G. **1958** ChiB: 12 G. **1959** ChiB: 12 G; Scor **1** Saf; 2 Pt. **1960** ChiB: 12 G; Int 1-11. **1962** ChiB: 14 G. **1963** ChiB: 12 G. **1964** ChiB: 14 G. **1965** ChiB: 14 G. **1966** LARm: 10 G. **1967** NO: 6 G. **1968** NO: 14 G. **Total:** 132 G; Int 1-11; Scor 1 Saf; 2 Pt.

SCOTT LEGGETT Leggett, Scott Curtis 6′3″, 285 **OG-OT**
Col: Oklahoma; Central Oklahoma *HS:* Muskogee [OK] B: 9/2/1962, Muskogee, OK
1987 Phi: 2 G.

DAVE LEGGETT Leggett, William David 6′2″, 198 **QB-DB**
Col: Ohio State *HS:* New Philadelphia [OH] B: 9/18/1933, New Philadelphia, OH *Drafted:* 1955 Round 7 ChiC
1955 ChiC: 4 G; Pass 1-0.

CHRIS LEHRER Lehrer, Christopher 185 **WB**
Col: No College Deceased
1922 Roch: 2 G.

JAKE LEICHT Leicht, Jake 5′9″, 170 **DB-HB**
Col: Pasadena City Coll. CA (J.C.); Oregon *HS:* Stockton [CA]
B: 10/1/1920, Jamestown, ND
AAFC **1948** BalA: Rec 12-134 11.2 1 TD; PR 8-139 17.4; KR 4-83 20.8; Int 5-91. **1949** BalA: Rec 1-12 12.0; PR 9-109 12.1; KR 8-171 21.4; Int 1-0. **Total:** Rec 13-146 11.2 1 TD; PR 17-248 14.6; KR 12-254 21.2; Int 6-91.

Year Team	G	Rushing Att	Yds	Avg	TD	Tot TD
1948 BalA	14	20	88	4.4	1	2
1949 BalA	12	6	-7	-1.2	0	0
AAFC Total	26	26	81	3.1	1	2

JEFF LEIDING Leiding, Jeffrey James 6'3", 232 **LB**
Col: Texas *HS:* Hickman Mills [Kansas City, MO]; Union HS [Tulsa OK] B: 10/28/1961, Kansas City, MO *Drafted:* 1984 Round 5 StL
1986 Ind: 12 G; Scor **1** Saf; 2 Pt. **1987** Ind: 9 G; Scor **1** Saf; 2 Pt; 1 Sac. **Total:** 21 G; Scor 2 Saf; 4 Pt; 1 Sac.

CHARLIE LEIGH Leigh, Charles Irving 5'11", 206 **RB**
Col: No College *HS:* Albany [NY] B: 10/29/1945, Halifax, VA
1968 Cle: Rec 3-(-4) -1.3. **1969** Cle: Rec 2-(-9) -4.5. **1973** Mia: Rec 4-9 2.3. **Total:** Rec 9-(-4) -0.4.

Year Team	G	Rushing Att	Yds	Avg	TD	Punt Returns Ret	Yds	Avg	TD
1968 Cle	14	23	144	6.3	1	14	76	5.4	0
1969 Cle	13	0	0	—	0	5	18	3.6	0
1971 Mia	14	5	15	3.0	0	0	0	—	0
1972 Mia	14	21	79	3.8	0	22	210	9.5	0
1973 Mia	14	22	134	6.1	1	9	64	7.1	0
1974 Mia-GB	11	1	0	0.0	0	0	0	—	0
1974 Mia	1	0	0	—	0	0	0	—	0
1974 GB	10	1	0	0.0	0	0	0	—	0
NFL Total	80	72	372	5.2	2	50	368	7.4	0

Year Team	Kickoff Returns Ret	Yds	Avg	TD	Fum
1968 Cle	14	322	23.0	0	1
1969 Cle	2	6	3.0	0	2
1971 Mia	4	99	24.8	0	0
1972 Mia	6	153	25.5	0	4
1973 Mia	9	251	27.9	0	3
1974 Mia-GB	11	251	22.8	0	1
1974 Mia	2	50	25.0	0	1
1974 GB	9	201	22.3	0	0
NFL Total	46	1082	23.5	0	11

DUTCH LEIGHTY Leighty, Orland Freed 5'11", 168 **BB-TB**
Col: Georgetown *HS:* Connellsville [PA] B: 12/1894, Connellsville, PA Deceased
1921 Was: 2 G.

TONY LEIKER Leiker, Anthony Wade 6'5", 250 **DE**
Col: Coffeyville CC KS; Stanford *HS:* Silver Lake [KS] B: 9/26/1964, Hays, KS *Drafted:* 1987 Round 7 GB
1987 GB: 1 G.

RUBE LEISK Leisk, C. Wardell 6'0", 195 **G**
Col: Louisiana State *HS:* C.E. Byrd [Shreveport, LA] B: 7/12/1915, Shreveport, LA
1937 Bkn: 11 G.

AL LEITH Leith, Alfred 5'9", 175 **BB-WB**
(AKA Alfred Leth) *Col:* Pennsylvania *HS:* Erasmus Hall [Brooklyn, NY] B: 3/14/1903, Brooklyn, NY D: 4/12/1969, Media, PA
1926 Bkn: 7 G.

WALT LEJEUNE LeJeune, Walter 6'0", 231 **G-C-T-WB**
(AKA Walt Jean) *Col:* Heidelberg; Bethany (W.V.) *HS:* Chillicothe [OH] B: 1900 Deceased
1922 Akr: 8 G; Rush 3 TD; Rec 1 TD; Tot TD 4; 24 Pt. **1923** Akr: 7 G. **1924** Mil: 10 G. **1925** GB-Fra: 12 G. GB: 9 G. Fra: 3 G. **1926** GB: 10 G. **1927** Pott: 3 G. **Total:** 50 G; Rush 3 TD; Rec 1 TD; Tot TD 4; 24 Pt.

FRANK LEMASTER LeMaster, Frank Preston 6'2", 232 **LB**
Col: Kentucky *HS:* Bryan Station [Lexington, KY] B: 3/12/1952, Lexington, KY *Drafted:* 1974 Round 4 Phi
1976 Phi: Rec 1-(-4) -4.0. **1977** Phi: Rush 1-30 30.0. **1978** Phi: Rush 2-29 14.5. **1979** Phi: Rush 1-15 15.0. **1980** Phi: Rush 2-21 10.5. **1981** Phi: Rush 1-7 7.0; 1 Fum TD. **1982** Phi: Rush 1-(-1) -1.0; 2 Sac. **Total:** Rush 8-101 12.6; Rec 1-(-4) -4.0; 1 Fum TD; 2 Sac.

Year Team	G	Interceptions Int	Yds	TD	Tot TD
1974 Phi	14	0	0	0	0
1975 Phi	14	4	133	1	1
1976 Phi	14	0	0	0	0
1977 Phi	14	0	0	0	0
1978 Phi	16	3	22	1	1
1979 Phi	16	0	0	0	0
1980 Phi	16	1	7	0	0
1981 Phi	16	2	28	0	1
1982 Phi	9	0	0	0	0
NFL Total	129	10	190	2	3

RAY LEMEK Lemek, Raymond Edward 6'0", 238 **OT-OG**
Col: Notre Dame *HS:* Heelan [Sioux City, IA] B: 6/28/1934, Sioux City, IA *Drafted:* 1956 Round 19 Was
1957 Was: 12 G. **1958** Was: 12 G. **1959** Was: 11 G. **1960** Was: 12 G. **1961** Was: 14 G. **1962** Pit: 14 G. **1963** Pit: 14 G. **1964** Pit: 14 G; KR 1-19 19.0. **1965** Pit: 14 G. **Total:** 117 G; KR 1-19 19.0.

BRUCE LEMMERMAN Lemmerman, Bruce 6'1", 206 **QB**
Col: Cal State-Northridge *HS:* Westchester [Los Angeles, CA] B: 10/4/1945, Los Angeles, CA
1968 Atl: Rush 1-0. **1969** Atl: Rush 10-57 5.7 1 TD. **Total:** Rush 11-57 5.2 1 TD.

Year Team	G	Passing Att	Comp	Comp%	Yds	YPA	TD	Int	Rating	Fum
1968 Atl	4	15	3	20.0	40	2.67	0	1	11.8	1
1969 Atl	7	62	25	40.3	330	5.32	1	4	36.4	4
NFL Total	11	77	28	36.4	370	4.81	1	5	29.7	5

JIM LEMOINE LeMoine, James Douglas 6'2", 250 **TE-OG**
Col: Chabot Coll. CA (J.C.); Utah State *HS:* Alameda [CA] B: 4/29/1945, Alameda, CA *Drafted:* 1967 Round 2 Buf
1967 Buf: 8 G. **1968** Hou: 13 G. **1969** Hou: 14 G. **Total:** 35 G.

CLIFF LEMON Lemon, Clifton Wilson 5'10", 190 **OE**
Col: Centre *HS:* Mayfield [KY] B: 4/15/1901, Paducah, KY D: 11/9/1955, Louisville, KY
1926 ChiB: 2 G.

MIKE LEMON Lemon, Michael Donald 6'2", 218 **LB**
Col: Ellsworth CC IA; Kansas *HS:* Heelan [Sioux City, IA] B: 2/26/1951, Topeka, KS *Drafted:* 1975 Round 6 NO
1975 NO-Den: 3 G. NO: 2 G. Den: 1 G. **1976** TB: 5 G; KR 1-2 2.0. **1977** TB: 14 G. **Total:** 22 G; KR 1-2 2.0.

GEORGE LENC Lenc, George C 6'3", 204 **OE-DE**
(Chili) *Col:* Augustana (Ill.) *HS:* United Twp. [East Moline, IL] B: 3/17/1917, Chicago, IL D: 11/16/1942, Pasco, WA *Drafted:* 1939 Round 11 Bkn
1939 Bkn: 2 G.

BILL LENKAITIS Lenkaitis, William Edward 6'4", 255 **C-OG**
Col: Penn State *HS:* South [Youngstown, OH] B: 6/30/1946, Cleveland, OH *Drafted:* 1968 Round 2 SD
1968 SD: 6 G. **1969** SD: 14 G. **1970** SD: 9 G. **1971** NE: 14 G. **1972** NE: 12 G. **1973** NE: 12 G. **1974** NE: 14 G. **1975** NE: 11 G; 1 Fum. **1976** NE: 14 G. **1977** NE: 14 G. **1978** NE: 16 G. **1979** NE: 16 G. **1980** NE: 16 G. **1981** NE: 12 G. **Total:** 180 G; 1 Fum.

REID LENNAN Lennan, Reid Burgess 6'0", 232 **G**
Col: No College *HS:* Baltimore City College [MD] B: 8/17/1922, Baltimore, MD
AAFC **1947** LA-A: 7 G.

NFL **1945** Was: 10 G.

GREG LENS Lens, Gregory Joseph 6'5", 261 **DT**
Col: Trinity (Tex.) *HS:* Central Catholic [Marshall, MN] B: 3/11/1945, Marshall, MN *Drafted:* 1970 Round 4 StL
1970 Atl: 14 G. **1971** Atl: 7 G. **Total:** 21 G.

VINCE LENSING Lensing, Vincent H 6'0", 200 **G-T**
Col: General Motors Inst *HS:* Central [Evansville, IN]; St. Meinrad Seminary [Evansville, IN] B: 1/26/1901, Evansville, IN D: 8/26/1951, Evansville, IN
1921 Eva: 5 G.

JACK LENTZ Lentz, Henry Edgar Jr. 6'0", 190 **DB**
Col: Holy Cross *HS:* Loyola [Baltimore, MD] B: 2/22/1945, Baltimore, MD *Drafted:* 1967 Round 16 Den
1967 Den: 14 G; Int 4-72. **1968** Den: 12 G; Int 1-0. **Total:** 26 G; Int 5-72.

PESTY LENTZ Lentz, Lawrence H 5'10", 175 **FB-TB**
Col: Wittenberg *HS:* North Central [Spokane, WA] B: 10/11/1897 D: 5/30/1966, Baltimore, MD
1920 Day: 2 G.

CHUCK LEO Leo, Charles James 6'0", 240 **OG**
Col: Indiana *HS:* Bishop Duffy [Niagara Falls, NY] B: 8/29/1934, Niagara Falls, NY
1960 Bos: 13 G. **1961** Bos: 14 G. **1962** Bos: 7 G. **1963** Buf: 4 G. **Total:** 38 G.

JIM LEO Leo, James Phillip 6'1", 225 **LB-DE**
Col: Cincinnati *HS:* Bishop Duffy [Niagara Falls, NY] B: 6/18/1937, Niagara Falls, NY *Drafted:* 1960 Round 3 NYG
1960 NYG: 12 G. **1961** Min: 14 G; KR 3-9 3.0. **1962** Min: 14 G; Scor 1 Saf; 2 Pt. **Total:** 40 G; KR 3-9 3.0; Scor 1 Saf; 2 Pt.

BOBBY LEO Leo, Robert Samuel 5'10", 180 **RB-WR**
Col: Harvard *HS:* Everett [MA] B: 1/19/1945, Everett, MA *Drafted:* 1967 Round 7 Bos
1967 Bos: 2 G; Rush 1-7 7.0; Rec 1-25 25.0 1 TD; PR 5-54 10.8; KR 11-232 21.1; 6 Pt; 3 Fum. **1968** Bos: 1 G; PR 2-12 6.0. **Total:** 3 G;

Rush 1-7 7.0; Rec 1-25 25.0 1 TD; PR 7-66 9.4; KR 11-232 21.1; 6 Pt; 3 Fum.

TONY LEON Leon, Anthony David 5'9", 203 **G-LB**
Col: Alabama *HS:* Weir [Weirton, WV] B: 2/18/1917, Follansbee, WV
Drafted: 1943 Round 6 Was
1943 Was: 6 G. **1944** Bkn: 10 G; Int 1-14. **1945** Bos: 10 G. **1946** Bos: 10 G; KR 1-6 6.0; 1 Fum. **Total:** 36 G; KR 1-6 6.0; Int 1-14; 1 Fum.

TONY LEONARD Leonard, Anthony 5'11", 170 **DB**
Col: Virginia Union *HS:* Maggie L. Walker [Richmond, VA]
B: 2/28/1953, Richmond, VA *Drafted:* 1976 Round 5 SF
1977 SF: Int 1-0. **1978** SF-Det: Int 4-44 1 TD. SF: Int 4-44 1 TD.
Total: Int 5-44 1 TD.

		Punt Returns				Kickoff Returns					Tot
Year Team	G	Ret	Yds	Avg	TD	Ret	Yds	Avg	TD	Fum	TD
1976 SF	14	35	293	8.4	1	26	553	21.3	0	5	1
1977 SF	13	22	154	7.0	0	1	68	68.0	0	0	0
1978 SF-Det	15	18	140	7.8	0	0	0	—	0	1	1
1978 SF	12	8	26	3.3	0	0	0	—	0	1	1
1978 Det	3	10	114	11.4	0	0	0	—	0	0	0
1979 Det	1	1	7	7.0	0	3	70	23.3	0	1	0
NFL Total	43	76	594	7.8	1	30	691	23.0	0	7	2

CECIL LEONARD Leonard, Cecil 5'11", 160 **DB**
Col: Tuskegee *HS:* Sylacauga [AL] B: 7/20/1946, Sylacauga, AL
Drafted: 1969 Round 8 NYJ
1969 NYJ: 8 G; PR 1-0; KR 7-120 17.1. **1970** NYJ: 5 G; KR 1-35 35.0.
Total: 13 G; PR 1-0; KR 8-155 19.4.

JIM LEONARD Leonard, James Francis 6'3", 258 **C-OG**
Col: Santa Clara *HS:* Harbor [Santa Cruz, CA] B: 10/19/1957, Santa Cruz, CA *Drafted:* 1980 Round 7 TB
1980 TB: 16 G. **1981** TB: 16 G; 1 Fum. **1982** TB: 9 G. **1983** TB: 15 G. **1985** SF-SD: 16 G; 1 Fum. SF: 9 G; 1 Fum. SD: 7 G. **1986** SD: 15 G.
Total: 87 G; 2 Fum.

JIM LEONARD Leonard, James Michael 6'0", 205 **G**
Col: Geneseo State; Colgate *HS:* Geneseo [NY] B: 1/2/1899, Geneseo, NY D: 2/2/1979, Naples, FL
1923 Roch: 3 G.

JIM LEONARD Leonard, James Raymond 6'0", 202 **BB-FB-DB-LB**
Col: Notre Dame *HS:* St. Joseph's Prep [Philadelphia, PA]
B: 2/14/1910, Pedricktown, NJ D: 11/28/1993, Woodbury, NJ
1934 Phi: Pass 10-2 20.0%, 29 2.90; Rec 3-7 2.3. **1935** Phi: Pass 32-11 34.4%, 119 3.72 3 Int. **1936** Phi: Pass 6-2 33.3%, 45 7.50 2 Int; Rec 5-46 9.2 1 TD. **Total:** Pass 48-15 31.3%, 193 4.02 5 Int; Rec 8-53 6.6 1 TD.

		Rushing				Tot
Year Team	G	Att	Yds	Avg	TD	TD
1934 Phi	9	55	207	3.8	1	1
1935 Phi	11	74	171	2.3	1	1
1936 Phi	10	33	72	2.2	0	1
1937 Phi	2	0	0	—	0	0
NFL Total	32	162	450	2.8	2	3

JOHN LEONARD Leonard, John Edward 6'2", 200 **T**
Col: Indiana *HS:* Englewood [Chicago, IL] B: 5/13/1896, Bloomington, IN D: 10/2/1980, Neshanic, NJ
1922 ChiC: 5 G. **1923** ChiC: 6 G. **Total:** 11 G.

BILL LEONARD Leonard, William George Jr. 6'2", 200 **DE**
(Hoppy) *Col:* Notre Dame *HS:* East [Youngstown, OH] B: 4/27/1927, Youngstown, OH
AAFC **1949** BalA: 11 G; KR 1-25 25.0; Int 1-7.

BOB LEONETTI Leonetti, Robert Phillip 6'0", 230 **G**
Col: Wake Forest *HS:* Mount Carmel [PA] B: 1/1/1923, Mount Carmel, PA D: 8/1973
AAFC **1948** BufA-BknA: 11 G.

BOBBY LEOPOLD Leopold, Leroy Joseph Jr. 6'1", 215 **LB**
Col: Notre Dame *HS:* Lincoln [Port Arthur, TX] B: 10/18/1957, Port Arthur, TX *Drafted:* 1980 Round 8 SF
1980 SF: 16 G; Int 2-23. **1981** SF: 16 G. **1982** SF: 6 G. **1983** SF: 16 G; Int 2-13; 1 Sac. **1986** GB: 12 G; Int 1-21; 1.5 Sac. **Total:** 66 G; Int 5-57; 2.5 Sac.

BARNEY LEPPER Lepper, Bernard 5'10", 185 **T**
Col: No College *HS:* Lafayette [Buffalo, NY] B: 9/1895, Auburn, NY Deceased
1920 Buf: 5 G.

MATT LEPSIS Lepsis, Matthew 6'4", 290 **OT**
Col: Colorado *HS:* Frisco [TX] B: 1/13/1974, Conroe, TX
1998 Den: 16 G.

JIMMY LESANE Lesane, James Edwin 5'10", 176 **DB-HB**
Col: The Citadel; Virginia *HS:* Needham B. Broughton [Raleigh, NC]
B: 3/8/1930, Raleigh, NC *Drafted:* 1952 Round 20 ChiB
1952 ChiB: 10 G; Pass 1-0; Rush 1-5 5.0; PR 9-25 2.8. **1954** ChiB-Bal: 7 G; Pass 1-0; PR 6-13 2.2; KR 4-91 22.8. ChiB: 3 G; Pass 1-0; PR 6-13 2.2; KR 4-91 22.8. Bal: 4 G. **Total:** 17 G; Pass 2-0; Rush 1-5 5.0; PR 15-38 2.5; KR 4-91 22.8.

DARRELL LESTER Lester, Darrell George 6'3", 220 **C-LB**
Col: Texas Christian *HS:* Jacksboro [TX] B: 4/29/1914, Jack Co., TX
D: 7/30/1993, Temple, TX *Drafted:* 1936 Round 5 GB
1937 GB: 8 G. **1938** GB: 8 G. **Total:** 16 G.

PINKY LESTER Lester, Harold William 5'6", 160 **E**
Col: No College *HS:* East Providence [RI] B: 3/13/1900, New London, CT D: 1/1/1972, Providence, RI
1926 Prov: 8 G.

KEITH LESTER Lester, Keith 6'5", 235 **TE**
Col: Florida State; Murray State *HS:* Clearwater [FL] B: 5/28/1962
Drafted: 1985 Round 6 Cin
1987 Ind: 1 G.

DARRELL LESTER Lester, Marcus Darrell 6'2", 228 **FB**
Col: Louisiana State; McNeese State *HS:* Lake Charles [LA]
B: 11/6/1940, Lake Charles, LA *Drafted:* 1964 Round 9 Min
1966 Den: Rec 2-26 13.0 1 TD; PR 1-1 1.0; KR 1-11 11.0. **Total:** Rec 2-26 13.0 1 TD; PR 1-1 1.0; KR 1-11 11.0.

		Rushing				
Year Team	G	Att	Yds	Avg	TD	Fum
1964 Min	6	4	18	4.5	0	0
1965 Den	12	0	0	—	0	0
1966 Den	11	34	84	2.5	0	3
NFL Total	29	38	102	2.7	0	3

TIM LESTER Lester, Timothy Lee 5'10", 233 **RB**
Col: Eastern Kentucky *HS:* Miami Southridge [FL] B: 6/15/1968, Miami, FL *Drafted:* 1992 Round 10 LARm
1994 LARm: KR 1-8 8.0. **Total:** KR 1-8 8.0.

		Rushing				Receiving				
Year Team	G	Att	Yds	Avg	TD	Rec	Yds	Avg	TD	Fum
1992 LARm	11	0	0	—	0	0	0	—	0	0
1993 LARm	16	11	74	6.7	0	18	154	8.6	0	0
1994 LARm	14	7	14	2.0	0	1	1	1.0	0	1
1995 Pit	6	5	9	1.8	1	0	0	—	0	0
1996 Pit	16	8	20	2.5	1	7	70	10.0	0	1
1997 Pit	16	2	9	4.5	0	10	51	5.1	0	0
1998 Pit	9	0	0	—	0	9	46	5.1	0	0
NFL Total	88	33	126	3.8	2	45	322	7.2	0	2

RUSS LETLOW Letlow, Willard Russell 6'0", 214 **G**
Col: San Francisco *HS:* Taft Union [CA] B: 10/5/1913, Dinuba, CA
Deceased *Drafted:* 1936 Round 1 GB
1936 GB: 8 G. **1937** GB: 11 G. **1938** GB: 11 G. **1939** GB: 10 G. **1940** GB: 11 G. **1941** GB: 4 G. **1942** GB: 11 G. **1946** GB: 5 G. **Total:** 71 G.

COTTON LETNER Letner, Robert Gene 6'1", 215 **LB**
Col: Tennessee *HS:* Meigs Co. [Decatur, TN] B: 1/26/1937, Ten Mile, TN
1961 Buf: 5 G.

JIM LETSINGER Letsinger, John Howard 5'10", 190 **G**
Col: Purdue B: 11/17/1911 Deceased
1933 Pit: 1 G.

LEON LETT Lett, Leon Jr. 6'6", 290 **DE**
(Big Cat) *Col:* Hinds CC MS; Emporia State *HS:* Fairhope [AL]
B: 10/12/1968, Mobile, AL *Drafted:* 1991 Round 7 Dal
1991 Dal: 5 G. **1992** Dal: 16 G; 3.5 Sac. **1993** Dal: 11 G; 1 Fum. **1994** Dal: 16 G; 4 Sac. **1995** Dal: 12 G; 3 Sac. **1996** Dal: 13 G; 3.5 Sac. **1997** Dal: 3 G; 0.5 Sac. **1998** Dal: 16 G; 4 Sac. **Total:** 92 G; 1 Fum; 18.5 Sac.

STEVE LEVANITIS Levanitis, Steven Joseph 6'1", 220 **T**
(Big Steve) *Col:* Boston College *HS:* Rindge Tech [Cambridge, MA]
B: 3/26/1920, Cambridge, MA D: 3/28/1996, North Easton, MA
1942 Phi: 5 G.

LOU LEVANTI Levanti, Louis Michael 6'1", 215 **C-OG-LB**
Col: Illinois *HS:* Frankfort [West Frankfort, IL] B: 4/4/1923, West Frankfort, IL *Drafted:* 1947 Round 21 LARm
1952 Pit: 6 G.

JACK LEVECK LeVeck, John Charles 6'0", 225 **LB**
Col: Ohio U. *HS:* Watkins Memorial [Pataskala, OH] B: 2/3/1950, Columbus, OH
1973 StL: 11 G. **1974** StL: 13 G; KR 2-32 16.0. **1975** Cle: 7 G. **Total:** 31 G; KR 2-32 16.0.

DAVE LEVENICK Levenick, David John 6'3", 222 **LB**
Col: Wisconsin *HS:* Grafton [WI] B: 5/28/1959, Milwaukee, WI
Drafted: 1982 Round 12 Atl
1983 Atl: 16 G. **1984** Atl: 8 G. **Total:** 24 G.

DORSEY LEVENS Levens, Herbert Dorsey 6'1", 233 **RB**
(Horse) *Col:* Notre Dame; Georgia Tech *HS:* Nottingham [Syracuse, NY] B: 5/21/1970, Syracuse, NY *Drafted:* 1994 Round 5 GB
1994 GB: KR 2-31 15.5. **1996** GB: KR 5-84 16.8. **1997** GB: Scor 1 2XP.
Total: KR 7-115 16.4; Scor 1 2XP.

		Rushing				Receiving					Tot
Year Team	**G**	**Att**	**Yds**	**Avg**	**TD**	**Rec**	**Yds**	**Avg**	**TD**	**Fum**	**TD**
1994 GB	14	5	15	3.0	0	1	9	9.0	0	0	0
1995 GB	15	36	120	3.3	3	48	434	9.0	4	0	7
1996 GB	16	121	566	4.7	5	31	226	7.3	5	2	10
1997 GB	16	329	1435	4.4	7	53	370	7.0	5	5	12
1998 GB	7	115	378	3.3	1	27	162	6.0	0	0	1
NFL Total	68	606	2514	4.1	16	160	1201	7.5	14	7	30

MIKE LEVENSELLER Levenseller, Michael Thomas 6'1", 180 **WR**
Col: Washington State *HS:* Curtis [Tacoma, WA] B: 2/21/1956, Bremerton, WA *Drafted:* 1978 Round 6 Oak
1978 Buf-TB: 4 G; PR 3-35 11.7. Buf: 2 G; PR 3-35 11.7. TB: 2 G.
1979 Cin: 12 G; PR 8-46 5.8; 1 Fum. **1980** Cin: 8 G; Rush 1-6 6.0; Rec 2-30 15.0. **Total:** 24 G; Rush 1-6 6.0; Rec 2-30 15.0; PR 11-81 7.4; 1 Fum.

JIM LEVEY Levey, James Julius 5'10", 163 **HB-DB-TB**
Col: No College *HS:* Peabody [Pittsburgh, PA] B: 9/13/1906, Pittsburgh, PA D: 3/14/1970, Dallas, TX
1935 Pit: Pass 4-1 25.0%, 4 1.00; Rec 7-112 16.0 2 TD. **Total:** Pass 4-1 25.0%, 4 1.00; Rec 7-112 16.0 2 TD.

		Rushing				Tot
Year Team	**G**	**Att**	**Yds**	**Avg**	**TD**	**TD**
1934 Pit	1	9	69	7.7	0	0
1935 Pit	8	42	61	1.5	2	4
1936 Pit	4	4	3	0.8	0	0
NFL Total	13	55	133	2.4	2	4

JERRY LEVIAS LeVias, Jerry 5'9", 177 **WR**
Col: Southern Methodist *HS:* Hebert [Beaumont, TX] B: 9/5/1946, Beaumont, TX *Drafted:* 1969 Round 2 Hou
1969 Hou: Pass 2-0; Rush 6-18 3.0. **1970** Hou: Pass 1-0, 1 Int; Rush 7-37 5.3. **1971** SD: Rush 4-73 18.3. **1973** SD: Rush 2-33 16.5. **Total:** Pass 3-0, 1 Int; Rush 19-161 8.5.

		Receiving				Punt Returns			
Year Team	**G**	**Rec**	**Yds**	**Avg**	**TD**	**Ret**	**Yds**	**Avg**	**TD**
1969 Hou	14	42	696	16.6	5	**35**	**292**	8.3	0
1970 Hou	14	41	529	12.9	5	25	213	8.5	0
1971 SD	14	21	265	12.6	1	22	145	6.6	0
1972 SD	1	1	8	8.0	0	1	-4	-4.0	0
1973 SD	14	30	536	17.9	3	0	0	—	0
1974 SD	13	9	105	11.7	0	5	41	8.2	0
NFL Total	70	144	2139	14.9	14	88	687	7.8	0

	Kickoff Returns				
Year Team	**Ret**	**Yds**	**Avg**	**TD**	**Fum**
1969 Hou	38	940	24.7	0	5
1970 Hou	26	598	23.0	0	2
1971 SD	24	559	23.3	0	3
1972 SD	0	0	—	0	1
1974 SD	6	116	19.3	0	1
NFL Total	94	2213	23.5	0	12

CHAD LEVITT Levitt, Chad Aaron 6'1", 231 **RB**
Col: Cornell *HS:* Cheltenham [Wyncote, PA] B: 11/21/1975, Melrose Park, PA *Drafted:* 1997 Round 4 Oak
1997 Oak: 10 G; Rush 2-3 1.5; Rec 2-24 12.0; KR 1-12 12.0.

CHUCK LEVY Levy, Charles 6'0", 200 **RB-WR**
Col: Arizona *HS:* Lynwood [CA] B: 1/7/1972, Torrance, CA
Drafted: 1994 Round 2 Ariz
1994 Ariz: Rec 4-35 8.8. **1997** SF: Rec 5-68 13.6; PR 6-109 18.2 1 TD.
1998 SF: Rec 15-64 4.3. **Total:** Rec 24-167 7.0; PR 6-109 18.2 1 TD.

		Rushing				Kickoff Returns					Tot
Year Team	**G**	**Ret**	**Yds**	**Avg**	**TD**	**Ret**	**Yds**	**Avg**	**TD**	**Fum**	**TD**
1994 Ariz	11	3	15	5.0	0	26	513	19.7	0	0	0
1997 SF	14	16	90	5.6	0	36	793	22.0	0	1	1
1998 SF	12	25	112	4.5	1	22	383	17.4	0	0	1
NFL Total	37	44	217	4.9	1	84	1689	20.1	0	1	2

HARVEY LEVY Levy, Harvey Sherwin 5'10", 212 **T-G**
Col: Syracuse *HS:* Central [Syracuse, NY]; St. John's Prep [Manlius, NY] B: 6/8/1902, Syracuse, NY D: 9/29/1986, North Olmsted, OH
1928 NYY: 12 G.

LEN LEVY Levy, Leonard Bernard 6'0", 256 **G-T**
(Butch) *Col:* Minnesota *HS:* West [Minneapolis, MN] B: 2/19/1921, Minneapolis, MN *Drafted:* 1942 Round 4 Cle
AAFC **1947** LA-A: 11 G. **1948** LA-A: 14 G. **Total:** 25 G.

NFL **1945** Cle: 7 G. **1946** LARm: 10 G; 6 Pt. **Total:** 17 G; 6 Pt.

VERNE LEWELLEN Lewellen, Verne Clark 6'1", 180 **HB-TB-WB-BB**
Col: Nebraska *HS:* Lincoln [NE] B: 9/29/1901, Garland, NE
D: 4/16/1980, Rockville, MD
1925 GB: Rec 3 TD; Scor 25, 1 XK. **1926** GB: Rec 3 TD; 1 Fum TD.
1927 GB-NYY: Pass 1 TD. NYY: Pass 1 TD. **1928** GB: Pass 1 TD; Rec 3 TD. **1929** GB: Pass 4 TD; Rec 1 TD; Int **1** TD. **1930** GB: Pass 3 TD; Rec 1 TD. **1932** GB: Pass 13-3 23.1%, 67 5.15 2 Int; Rec 3-33 11.0 1 TD.
Total: Pass 13-3 23.1%, 67 5.15 9 TD 2 Int; Rec 3-33 11.0 12 TD; Int 1 TD; 1 Fum TD.

		Rushing				Tot
Year Team	**G**	**Att**	**Yds**	**Avg**	**TD**	**TD**
1924 GB	8	—	—	—	2	2
1925 GB	10	—	—	—	1	4
1926 GB	13	—	—	—	3	7
1927 GB-NYY	13	—	—	—	5	5
1927 GB	10	—	—	—	5	5
1927 NYY	3	—	—	—	0	0
1928 GB	13	—	—	—	**6**	**9**
1929 GB	13	—	—	—	6	8
1930 GB	14	—	—	—	**8**	**9**
1931 GB	7	—	—	—	6	6
1932 GB	14	44	115	2.6	0	1
NFL Total	105	44	115	2.6	37	51

ALBERT LEWIS Lewis, Albert Ray 6'2", 196 **DB**
Col: Grambling State *HS:* DeSoto [Mansfield, LA] B: 10/6/1960, Mansfield, LA *Drafted:* 1983 Round 3 KC
1984 KC: 1 Sac. **1985** KC: **1** Fum TD; 1.5 Sac. **1986** KC: 1 Sac. **1988** KC: Scor 1 Saf. **1989** KC: 1 Sac. **1994** LARd: 1 Sac. **1995** Oak: 1 Sac.
1996 Oak: 3 Sac. **1997** Oak: 2 Sac. **1998** Oak: 1 Sac. **Total:** Scor 1 Saf; 1 Fum TD; 12.5 Sac.

		Interceptions			Tot
Year Team	**G**	**Int**	**Yds**	**TD**	**TD**
1983 KC	16	4	42	0	0
1984 KC	15	4	57	0	0
1985 KC	16	8	59	0	1
1986 KC	15	4	18	0	0
1987 KC	12	1	0	0	0
1988 KC	14	1	19	0	0
1989 KC	16	4	37	0	0
1990 KC	15	2	15	0	0
1991 KC	8	3	21	0	0
1992 KC	9	1	0	0	0
1993 KC	14	6	61	0	1
1994 LARd	14	0	0	0	0
1995 Oak	16	0	0	0	0
1996 Oak	16	2	0	0	0
1997 Oak	14	0	0	0	0
1998 Oak	15	2	74	1	1
NFL Total	225	42	403	1	3

ART LEWIS Lewis, Arthur 6'1", **T**
Col: No College B: 1891, IN Deceased
1921 Cin: 3 G; Scor 1, 1 XK.

ART LEWIS Lewis, Arthur Everett 6'3", 226 **T**
(Pappy) *Col:* Ohio U. *HS:* Middleport [OH] B: 2/18/1911, Pomeroy, OH D: 6/13/1962, Pittsburgh, PA *Drafted:* 1936 Round 1 NYG
1936 NYG: 12 G; **1** Fum TD; 6 Pt. **1938** Cle: 9 G. **1939** Cle: 7 G.
Total: 28 G; 1 Fum TD; 6 Pt.

CHAD LEWIS Lewis, Chad Wayne 6'6", 253 **TE**
Col: Utah Valley State (J.C.); Brigham Young *HS:* Orem [UT]
B: 10/5/1971, Fort Dix, NJ
1997 Phi: 16 G; Rec 12-94 7.8 4 TD; KR 1-11 11.0; 24 Pt. **1998** Phi: 2 G.
Total: 18 G; Rec 12-94 7.8 4 TD; KR 1-11 11.0; 24 Pt.

MAC LEWIS Lewis, Charles Mac 6'6", 290 **OT**
Col: Iowa *HS:* Morgan Park [Chicago, IL] B: 8/28/1937, Pittsburgh, PA
Drafted: 1959 Round 6 ChiC
1959 ChiC: 8 G.

CLIFF LEWIS Lewis, Clifford Allen 5'11", 167 **DB-QB**
Col: Duke *HS:* Lakewood [OH]; Staunton Mil. Acad. [VA] B: 3/22/1923, Lakewood, OH
AAFC **1946** CleA: KR 3-70 23.3. **1947** CleA: KR 4-71 17.8. **1948** CleA: KR 7-147 21.0; Punt 1-18 18.0. **Total:** KR 14-288 20.6; Punt 1-18 18.0.

		Passing							
Year Team	**G**	**Att**	**Comp**	**Comp%**	**Yds**	**YPA**	**TD**	**Int**	**Rating**
1946 CleA	10	30	11	36.7	125	4.17	1	1	47.2
1947 CleA	13	11	5	45.5	70	6.36	1	1	58.9

1948 CleA	14	8	4	50.0	69	8.63	1	0	119.3
1949 CleA	11	10	5	50.0	144	14.40	2	2	95.8
AAFC Total	48	59	25	42.4	408	6.92	5	4	66.2

	Rushing				Punt Returns			
Year Team	Att	Yds	Avg	TD	Ret	Yds	Avg	TD
1946 CleA	24	-34	-1.4	0	8	133	16.6	0
1947 CleA	11	66	6.0	0	7	84	12.0	0
1948 CleA	5	44	8.8	0	26	258	9.9	0
1949 CleA	9	-17	-1.9	1	20	174	8.7	0
AAFC Total	49	59	1.2	1	61	649	10.6	0

	Interceptions		
Year Team	Int	Yds	TD
1946 CleA	5	41	0
1947 CleA	4	19	0
1948 CleA	9	103	0
1949 CleA	6	53	0
AAFC Total	24	216	0

NFL **1950** Cle: 11 G; Pass 4-1 25.0%, 38 9.50 1 TD; Rush 2-(-1) -0.5; PR 2-13 6.5; Int 1-4. **1951** Cle: 12 G; Pass 6-4 66.7%, 68 11.33 1 TD 1 Int; Rush 3-(-10) -3.3; PR 14-48 3.4; Int 5-46; 3 Fum. **Total:** 23 G; Pass 10-5 50.0%, 106 10.60 2 TD 1 Int; Rush 5-(-11) -2.2; PR 16-61 3.8; Int 6-50; 3 Fum.

CLIFF LEWIS Lewis, Clifford Sylvester 6′1″, 226 **LB**
Col: Southern Mississippi *HS:* Fort Walton Beach [FL] B: 11/9/1959, Brewton, AL *Drafted:* 1981 Round 12 GB
1981 GB: 16 G. **1982** GB: 9 G; KR 1-4 4.0. **1983** GB: 16 G; PR 1-0; 2 Sac. **1984** GB: 16 G. **Total:** 57 G; PR 1-0; KR 1-4 4.0; 2 Sac.

DAN LEWIS Lewis, Daniel Nathan 6′1″, 199 **HB**
Col: Wisconsin *HS:* Freehold Twp. [Freehold, NJ] B: 2/14/1936, Freehold, NJ *Drafted:* 1958 Round 6 Det
1962 Det: Pass 1-0. **1964** Det: Pass 1-0. **1965** Was: Pass 2-1 50.0%, 26 13.00 1 TD. **1966** NYG: Pass 1-1 100.0%, 4 4.00. **Total:** Pass 5-2 40.0%, 30 6.00 1 TD.

		Rushing				Receiving			
Year Team	G	Att	Yds	Avg	TD	Rec	Yds	Avg	TD
1958 Det	11	25	131	5.2	0	1	12	12.0	0
1959 Det	11	49	199	4.1	2	5	75	15.0	0
1960 Det	12	92	438	4.8	1	12	192	16.0	1
1961 Det	13	110	451	4.1	4	8	118	14.8	0
1962 Det	12	120	488	4.1	6	16	158	9.9	1
1963 Det	14	133	528	4.0	2	15	115	7.7	0
1964 Det	11	122	463	3.8	1	11	129	11.7	1
1965 Was	13	117	343	2.9	2	25	276	11.0	2
1966 NYG	13	32	164	5.1	1	6	87	14.5	0
NFL Total	110	800	3205	4.0	19	99	1162	11.7	5

	Kickoff Returns					Tot
Year Team	Ret	Yds	Avg	TD	Fum	TD
1958 Det	6	110	18.3	0	5	0
1959 Det	1	9	9.0	0	3	2
1960 Det	10	202	20.2	0	2	2
1961 Det	0	0	—	0	4	4
1962 Det	0	0	—	0	5	7
1963 Det	0	0	—	0	2	2
1964 Det	0	0	—	0	1	2
1965 Was	0	0	—	0	4	4
1966 NYG	13	214	16.5	0	1	1
NFL Total	30	535	17.8	0	27	24

DARREN LEWIS Lewis, Darren 5′10″, 230 **RB**
Col: Texas A&M *HS:* David W. Carter [Dallas, TX] B: 11/7/1968, Dallas, TX *Drafted:* 1991 Round 6 ChiB
1992 ChiB: Rec 18-175 9.7. **1993** ChiB: Rec 4-26 6.5. **Total:** Rec 22-201 9.1.

		Rushing				Kickoff Returns					Tot
Year Team	G	Ret	Yds	Avg	TD	Ret	Yds	Avg	TD	Fum	TD
1991 ChiB	15	15	36	2.4	0	2	13	6.5	0	0	0
1992 ChiB	16	90	382	4.2	4	23	511	22.2	1	4	5
1993 ChiB	2	7	13	1.9	0	0	0	—	0	0	0
NFL Total	33	112	431	3.8	4	25	524	21.0	1	4	5

DARRYL LEWIS Lewis, Darryl Gerard 6′6″, 232 **TE**
Col: Texas-Arlington *HS:* Daingerfield [TX] B: 4/16/1961, Mount Pleasant, TX *Drafted:* 1983 Round 5 NE
1984 Cle: 2 G.

DARRYLL LEWIS Lewis, Darryll Lamont 5′9″, 188 **DB**
Col: Arizona *HS:* Nogales [West Covina, CA] B: 12/16/1968, Bellflower, CA *Drafted:* 1991 Round 2 Hou
1991 Hou: 1 Sac. **1992** Hou: KR 8-171 21.4; 1 Sac. **1995** Hou: 1 Sac. **1998** Ten: 1 Sac. **Total:** KR 8-171 21.4; 4 Sac.

		Interceptions			
Year Team	G	Int	Yds	TD	Fum
1991 Hou	16	1	33	1	0
1992 Hou	13	0	0	0	0
1993 Hou	4	1	47	1	0
1994 Hou	16	5	57	0	0
1995 Hou	16	6	145	1	0
1996 Hou	16	5	103	1	0
1997 Ten	16	5	115	1	1
1998 Ten	16	4	40	0	0
NFL Total	113	27	540	5	1

DAVE LEWIS Lewis, David Ray 6′2″, 216 **QB-P**
Col: Stanford *HS:* Clovis [CA] B: 10/16/1945, Clovis, CA *Drafted:* 1967 Round 5 NYG
1970 Cin: Pass 4-3 75.0%, 39 9.75; Rush 2-8 4.0. **1971** Cin: Pass 10-3 30.0%, 18 1.80; Rush 6-6 1.0. **1972** Cin: Rush 1-15 15.0; KR 1-15 15.0. **1973** Cin: Rush 3-(-7) -2.3; PR 1-2 2.0; KR 2-40 20.0. **Total:** Pass 14-6 42.9%, 57 4.07; Rush 12-22 1.8; PR 1-2 2.0; KR 3-55 18.3.

		Punting			
Year Team	G	Punts	Yds	Avg	Fum
1970 Cin	14	79	3651	**46.2**	0
1971 Cin	14	72	3229	**44.8**	2
1972 Cin	14	66	2777	42.1	0
1973 Cin	14	68	2790	41.0	2
NFL Total	56	285	12447	43.7	4

DAVE LEWIS Lewis, David Rodney 6′4″, 240 **LB**
Col: San Diego City Coll. CA (J.C.); USC *HS:* Abraham Lincoln [San Diego, CA] B: 10/15/1954, San Diego, CA *Drafted:* 1977 Round 2 TB
1979 TB: **1** Fum TD. **Total:** 1 Fum TD.

		Interceptions		
Year Team	G	Int	Yds	TD
1977 TB	14	2	55	0
1978 TB	16	3	24	0
1979 TB	16	2	19	0
1980 TB	16	1	0	0
1981 TB	13	2	12	0
1982 SD	9	0	0	0
1983 LARm	13	0	0	0
NFL Total	97	10	110	0

DAVID LEWIS Lewis, David Wayne 6′3″, 234 **TE**
Col: California *HS:* U.S. Grant [Portland, OR] B: 6/8/1961, Portland, OR *Drafted:* 1984 Round 1 Det
1987 Mia: KR 1-0. **Total:** KR 1-0.

		Receiving				
Year Team	G	Rec	Yds	Avg	TD	Fum
1984 Det	16	16	236	14.8	3	2
1985 Det	15	28	354	12.6	3	1
1986 Det	11	10	88	8.8	1	0
1987 Mia	5	6	53	8.8	1	0
NFL Total	47	60	731	12.2	8	3

D.D. LEWIS Lewis, Dwight Douglas 6′1″, 225 **LB**
Col: Mississippi State *HS:* Fulton [Knoxville, TN] B: 10/16/1945, Knoxville, TN *Drafted:* 1968 Round 6 Dal
1968 Dal: 14 G. **1970** Dal: 12 G. **1971** Dal: 14 G; KR 1-15 15.0; Int 1-0. **1972** Dal: 12 G; Int 1-15; 1 Fum. **1973** Dal: 14 G; 6 Pt. **1974** Dal: 14 G; Int 2-45. **1975** Dal: 14 G. **1976** Dal: 14 G. **1977** Dal: 14 G; Int 1-29. **1978** Dal: 16 G. **1979** Dal: 16 G; Int 2-8. **1980** Dal: 16 G. **1981** Dal: 16 G; Int 1-0; 1 Fum. **Total:** 186 G; KR 1-15 15.0; Int 8-97; 6 Pt; 2 Fum.

EDDIE LEWIS Lewis, Edward Lee 6′0″, 177 **DB**
Col: Kansas *HS:* Toulminville [Mobile, AL] B: 12/15/1953, Mobile, AL *Drafted:* 1976 Round 2 SF
1976 SF: 14 G. **1977** SF: 14 G. **1978** SF: 16 G; Int 3-17. **1979** SF-Det: 15 G; PR 1-(-1) -1.0. SF: 7 G. Det: 8 G; PR 1-(-1) -1.0. **1980** Det: 14 G. **Total:** 73 G; PR 1-(-1) -1.0; Int 3-17.

ERNIE LEWIS Lewis, Ernest Clayton 6′1″, 211 **FB-LB**
(Big Swink; Tiny) *Col:* Colorado *HS:* Swink [CO] B: 11/20/1923, Boonville, MO
AAFC **1946** ChiA: Pass 8-4 50.0%, 17 2.13 1 Int; Rec 2-26 13.0; KR 2-22 11.0; Int 1-10. **1948** ChiA: Rec 1-6 6.0. **Total:** Pass 8-4 50.0%, 17 2.13 1 Int; Rec 3-32 10.7; KR 2-22 11.0; Int 1-10.

		Rushing				Punting		
Year Team	G	Att	Yds	Avg	TD	Punts	Yds	Avg
1946 ChiA	12	57	164	2.9	1	50	2085	41.7
1947 ChiA	14	13	47	3.6	0	65	2549	39.2
1948 ChiA	14	13	54	4.2	0	60	2680	44.7
1949 ChiA	6	11	43	3.9	1	16	680	42.5
AAFC Total	46	94	308	3.3	2	191	7994	41.9

FRANK LEWIS Lewis, Frank Douglas 6'1", 196 **WR**
Col: Grambling State *HS:* Southtown [Houma, LA] B: 7/4/1947, Houma, LA *Drafted:* 1971 Round 1 Pit
1972 Pit: Rush 3-68 22.7; PR 5-56 11.2. **1973** Pit: Rush 1-(-1) -1.0. **1974** Pit: Rush 2-25 12.5. **1975** Pit: Rush 2-36 18.0. **1976** Pit: Rush 2-24 12.0 1 TD. **1979** Buf: Rush 2-(-6) -3.0. **Total:** Rush 12-146 12.2 1 TD; PR 5-56 11.2.

		Receiving					Tot
Year Team	**G**	**Rec**	**Yds**	**Avg**	**TD**	**Fum**	**TD**
1971 Pit	9	3	44	14.7	0	1	0
1972 Pit	13	27	391	14.5	5	1	5
1973 Pit	9	23	409	17.8	3	0	3
1974 Pit	12	30	365	12.2	4	1	4
1975 Pit	10	17	308	18.1	2	0	2
1976 Pit	12	17	306	18.0	1	0	2
1977 Pit	10	11	263	23.9	1	0	1
1978 Buf	15	41	735	17.9	7	0	7
1979 Buf	15	54	1082	20.0	2	1	2
1980 Buf	15	40	648	16.2	6	0	6
1981 Buf	16	70	1244	17.8	4	1	4
1982 Buf	8	28	443	15.8	2	0	2
1983 Buf	11	36	486	13.5	3	0	3
NFL Total	155	397	6724	16.9	40	5	41

FRANKLIN LEWIS Lewis, Franklin A **FB**
1931 Cle: 1 G.

GARRY LEWIS Lewis, Garry 5'11", 185 **DB**
Col: Alcorn State *HS:* Walter L. Cohen [New Orleans, LA] B: 8/25/1967, New Orleans, LA *Drafted:* 1990 Round 7 LARd
1990 LARd: 12 G. **1991** LARd: 16 G. **1992** TB: 16 G; Int 1-0. **1993** KC: 1 G. **Total:** 45 G; Int 1-0.

GARY LEWIS Lewis, Gary L 6'3", 260 **NT**
Col: Oklahoma State *HS:* Millwood [Oklahoma City, OK] B: 1/14/1961, Oklahoma City, OK *Drafted:* 1983 Round 4 NO
1983 NO: 6 G.

GARY LEWIS Lewis, Gary Rogers 6'3", 225 **RB**
Col: San Francisco City Coll. CA (J.C.); Washington State; Arizona State *HS:* San Francisco Polytechnic [CA] B: 2/22/1942, New Orleans, LA D: 12/12/1986, Daly City, CA *Drafted:* 1964 Round 6 SF
1965 SF: PR 1-3 3.0. **Total:** PR 1-3 3.0.

		Rushing				Receiving			
Year Team	**G**	**Att**	**Yds**	**Avg**	**TD**	**Rec**	**Yds**	**Avg**	**TD**
1964 SF	8	43	115	2.7	1	7	73	10.4	0
1965 SF	14	52	256	4.9	3	10	25	2.5	0
1966 SF	14	36	130	3.6	2	7	44	6.3	1
1967 SF	13	67	342	5.1	6	21	218	10.4	1
1968 SF	14	141	573	4.1	1	27	244	9.0	3
1969 SF	9	4	5	1.3	0	0	0	—	0
1970 NO	1	0	0	—	0	0	0	—	0
NFL Total	73	343	1421	4.1	13	72	604	8.4	5

	Kickoff Returns					Tot
Year Team	**Ret**	**Yds**	**Avg**	**TD**	**Fum**	**TD**
1964 SF	1	0	0.0	0	3	1
1965 SF	15	355	23.7	0	3	3
1966 SF	3	65	21.7	0	1	3
1967 SF	9	190	21.1	0	2	7
1968 SF	0	0	—	0	3	4
1969 SF	5	155	31.0	0	0	0
1970 NO	1	19	19.0	0	0	0
NFL Total	34	784	23.1	0	12	18

GARY LEWIS Lewis, Gary Wayne 6'5", 234 **TE-WR**
Col: Texas-Arlington *HS:* Daingerfield [TX] B: 12/30/1958, Mount Pleasant, TX *Drafted:* 1981 Round 2 GB
1981 GB: 16 G; Rec 3-31 10.3. **1982** GB: 9 G; Rec 3-21 7.0. **1983** GB: 16 G; Rush 4-16 4.0 1 TD; Rec 11-204 18.5 1 TD; Tot TD 2; 12 Pt. **1984** GB: 3 G; Rec 4-29 7.3. **Total:** 44 G; Rush 4-16 4.0 1 TD; Rec 21-285 13.6 1 TD; Tot TD 2; 12 Pt.

GREG LEWIS Lewis, Gregory Alan 5'10", 214 **RB**
Col: Washington *HS:* Ingraham [Seattle, WA] B: 8/10/1969, Port St. Joe, FL *Drafted:* 1991 Round 5 Den
1991 Den: Rec 2-9 4.5; KR 1-20 20.0. **1992** Den: Pass 1-0; Rec 4-30 7.5. **Total:** Pass 1-0; Rec 6-39 6.5; KR 1-20 20.0.

		Rushing				
Year Team	**G**	**Att**	**Yds**	**Avg**	**TD**	**Fum**
1991 Den	16	99	376	3.8	4	3
1992 Den	16	73	268	3.7	4	2
NFL Total	32	172	644	3.7	8	5

H. LEWIS Lewis, H. 5'8", 175 **G**
Col: No College *HS:* Male [Louisville, KY] B: 1896 Deceased
1921 Lou: 1 G.

HAL LEWIS Lewis, Harold DeWitt 6'0", 185 **DB**
Col: Arizona State *HS:* Oakland [CA] B: 8/1/1944, Memphis, TN
1968 Den: 1 G.

HAL LEWIS Lewis, Harold Lee 6'0", 200 **HB-DB**
Col: Houston *HS:* Pampa [TX] B: 9/22/1935, Houston, TX *Drafted:* 1959 Round 7 Bal
1959 Bal: 12 G; Rush 4-2 0.5; Rec 3-54 18.0; KR 2-31 15.5; 1 Fum. **1960** Buf: 3 G; PR 1-2 2.0; KR 4-97 24.3. **1962** Oak: 11 G; Rush 9-18 2.0; Rec 7-53 7.6; PR 9-65 7.2; KR 3-65 21.7; 2 Fum. **Total:** 26 G; Rush 13-20 1.5; Rec 10-107 10.7; PR 10-67 6.7; KR 9-193 21.4; 3 Fum.

JEFF LEWIS Lewis, Jeffrey Scott 6'2", 211 **QB**
Col: Northern Arizona *HS:* Horizon [Scottsdale, AZ] B: 4/17/1973, Columbus, OH *Drafted:* 1996 Round 4 Den
1996 Den: 2 G; Pass 17-9 52.9%, 58 3.41 1 Int; Rush 4-39 9.8. **1997** Den: 3 G; Pass 2-1 50.0%, 21 10.50; Rush 5-2 0.4. **Total:** 5 G; Pass 19-10 52.6%, 79 4.16 1 Int; Rush 9-41 4.6.

JERMAINE LEWIS Lewis, Jermaine Edward 5'7", 172 **WR**
Col: Maryland *HS:* Eleanor Roosevelt [Greenbelt, MD] B: 10/16/1974, Lanham, MD *Drafted:* 1996 Round 5 Bal
1996 Bal: Rush 1-(-3) -3.0. **1997** Bal: Rush 3-35 11.7. **1998** Bal: Rush 5-20 4.0. **Total:** Rush 9-52 5.8.

		Receiving				Punt Returns			
Year Team	**G**	**Rec**	**Yds**	**Avg**	**TD**	**Ret**	**Yds**	**Avg**	**TD**
1996 Bal	16	5	78	15.6	1	36	339	9.4	0
1997 Bal	14	42	648	15.4	6	28	437	**15.6**	2
1998 Bal	13	41	784	19.1	6	32	405	12.7	**2**
NFL Total	43	88	1510	17.2	13	96	1181	12.3	4

	Kickoff Returns					Tot
Year Team	**Ret**	**Yds**	**Avg**	**TD**	**Fum**	**TD**
1996 Bal	41	883	21.5	0	4	1
1997 Bal	41	905	22.1	0	3	8
1998 Bal	6	145	24.2	0	3	8
NFL Total	88	1933	22.0	0	10	17

JESS LEWIS Lewis, Jess T 6'1", 230 **LB**
Col: Oregon State *HS:* Cascade [Aumsville, OR] B: 7/28/1947, Aumsville, OR *Drafted:* 1970 Round 13 Hou
1970 Hou: 10 G; KR 1-15 15.0.

JOHN LEWIS Lewis, John R 5'10", 175 **DB**
Col: Pittsburgh *HS:* Woodrow Wilson [Levittown, PA] B: 3/8/1962, Levittown, PA
1987 Buf: 3 G.

JOE LEWIS Lewis, Joseph 6'2", 256 **DT**
Col: Compton CC CA *HS:* David Starr Jordan [Los Angeles, CA] B: 1/23/1936, Los Angeles, CA *Drafted:* 1958 Round 17 Pit
1958 Pit: 12 G; Int 1-8. **1959** Pit: 5 G. **1960** Pit: 12 G; **1** Fum TD; 6 Pt. **1961** Bal: 11 G; KR 1-14 14.0. **1962** Phi: 13 G. **Total:** 53 G; KR 1-14 14.0; Int 1-8; 1 Fum TD; 6 Pt.

KENNY LEWIS Lewis, Kenneth 6'0", 190 **RB**
Col: Virginia Tech *HS:* George Washington [Danville, VA] B: 10/2/1957, Danville, VA *Drafted:* 1980 Round 5 Oak
1980 NYJ: 7 G; Rec 1-6 6.0. **1981** NYJ: 5 G; Rush 6-18 3.0; Rec 2-14 7.0; KR 5-108 21.6. **1983** NYJ: 7 G; Rush 5-25 5.0; Rec 6-62 10.3. **Total:** 19 G; Rush 11-43 3.9; Rec 9-82 9.1; KR 5-108 21.6.

KEVIN LEWIS Lewis, Kevin 5'11", 173 **DB**
Col: Northwestern State-Louisiana *HS:* Alcee Fortier [New Orleans, LA] B: 11/14/1966, New Orleans, LA
1990 SF: 10 G; Int 1-28. **1991** SF: 16 G; PR 1-0; Int 2-20; 1 Fum. **Total:** 26 G; PR 1-0; Int 3-48; 1 Fum.

LEO LEWIS Lewis, Leo Everett III 5'8", 170 **WR**
Col: Missouri *HS:* Hickman [Columbia, MO] B: 9/17/1956, Columbia, MO
1981 Min: Rush 1-16 16.0. **1983** Min: Rush 1-2 2.0; KR 1-25 25.0. **1984** Min: Rush 2-11 5.5; KR 1-31 31.0. **1985** Min: Rush 1-2 2.0. **1986** Min: Rush 3-(-16) -5.3. **1987** Min: Rush 5-(-7) -1.4. **1988** Min: KR 1-12 12.0. **1989** Min: Rush 1-11 11.0; KR 2-30 15.0. **1990** Cle-Min: KR 3-39 13.0. Min: KR 3-39 13.0. **Total:** Rush 14-19 1.4; KR 8-137 17.1.

		Receiving				Punt Returns					Tot
Year Team	**G**	**Rec**	**Yds**	**Avg**	**TD**	**Ret**	**Yds**	**Avg**	**TD**	**Fum**	**TD**
1981 Min	4	2	58	29.0	0	0	0	—	0	0	0
1982 Min	9	8	150	18.8	3	0	0	—	0	0	3
1983 Min	14	12	127	10.6	0	3	52	17.3	0	0	0
1984 Min	16	47	830	17.7	4	4	31	7.8	0	1	4
1985 Min	10	29	442	15.2	3	0	0	—	0	1	3
1986 Min	16	32	600	18.8	2	7	53	7.6	0	3	2
1987 Min	12	24	383	16.0	2	22	275	12.5	1	1	3
1988 Min	16	11	141	12.8	1	**58**	550	9.5	0	2	1
1989 Min	16	12	148	12.3	1	44	446	10.1	0	4	1
1990 Cle-Min	14	1	9	9.0	0	33	236	7.2	0	1	0
1990 Cle	3	0	0	—	0	8	56	7.0	0	0	0
1990 Min	11	1	9	9.0	0	25	180	7.2	0	1	0

1991 Min	16	4	36	9.0	0	30	225	7.5	0	3	0
NFL Total	143	182	2924	16.1	16	201	1868	9.3	1	16	17

TINY LEWIS Lewis, Loren Leland 6'2", 210 **FB-WB-BB**
Col: Northwestern *HS:* Carlinville [IL] B: 10/18/1906, Foosland, IL D: 1/17/1954, Michigan City, IN
1930 Port: 13 G; Rush 2 TD; Scor 22, 10 XK. **1931** Cle: 1 G. **Total:** 14 G; Rush 2 TD.

MARK LEWIS Lewis, Mark Joseph 6'2", 239 **TE**
Col: Texas A&M *HS:* Kashmere [Houston, TX] B: 5/5/1961, Houston, TX *Drafted:* 1985 Round 6 GB
1985 GB: 1 G. **1986** GB: 16 G; Rec 2-7 3.5 2 TD; 12 Pt. **1987** GB-Det: 10 G. GB: 1 G. Det: 9 G. **1988** Det: 3 G; Rec 3-32 10.7 1 TD; 6 Pt. **Total:** 30 G; Rec 5-39 7.8 3 TD; 18 Pt.

MARVIN LEWIS Lewis, Marvin Victor 6'3", 208 **RB**
Col: Tyler JC TX; Tulane *HS:* Liberty-Eylau [Texarkana, TX] B: 1/15/1960, Texarkana, TX *Drafted:* 1982 Round 6 NO
1982 NO: 1 G.

MIKE LEWIS Lewis, Michael Henry 6'4", 261 **DT-DE-NT**
Col: Wiley; Arkansas-Pine Bluff *HS:* Jack Yates [Houston, TX] B: 7/14/1949, Houston, TX D: 1995
1971 Atl: 9 G. **1972** Atl: 14 G; Int 1-3; Scor **1** Saf; 2 Pt. **1973** Atl: 14 G. **1974** Atl: 14 G. **1975** Atl: 14 G. **1976** Atl: 12 G. **1977** Atl: 14 G. **1978** Atl: 16 G. **1979** Atl: 13 G; Scor **1** Saf; 2 Pt. **1980** GB: 10 G. **Total:** 130 G; Int 1-3; Scor 2 Saf; 4 Pt.

MO LEWIS Lewis, Morris Clyde 6'3", 255 **LB**
Col: Georgia *HS:* J.C. Murphy [Atlanta, GA] B: 10/21/1969, Atlanta, GA *Drafted:* 1991 Round 3 NYJ
1991 NYJ: 1 Sac. **1992** NYJ: 2 Sac. **1993** NYJ: 4 Sac. **1994** NYJ: 6 Sac. **1995** NYJ: 5 Sac. **1996** NYJ: 0.5 Sac. **1997** NYJ: 8 Sac. **1998** NYJ: 7 Sac. **Total:** 33.5 Sac.

		Interceptions			
Year Team	**G**	**Int**	**Yds**	**TD**	**Fum**
1991 NYJ	16	0	0	0	0
1992 NYJ	16	1	1	0	0
1993 NYJ	16	2	4	0	0
1994 NYJ	16	4	106	2	0
1995 NYJ	16	2	22	1	0
1996 NYJ	9	0	0	0	0
1997 NYJ	16	1	43	1	0
1998 NYJ	16	1	11	0	1
NFL Total	121	11	187	4	1

NATE LEWIS Lewis, Nathaniel 5'11", 198 **WR**
Col: Northeastern Oklahoma A&M (J.C.); Georgia; Oregon Tech *HS:* Colquitt Co. [Moultrie, GA] B: 10/19/1966, Moultrie, GA *Drafted:* 1990 Round 7 SD
1990 SD: Rush 4-25 6.3 1 TD. **1991** SD: Rush 3-10 3.3. **1992** SD: Rush 2-7 3.5. **1993** SD: Rush 3-2 0.7. **Total:** Rush 12-44 3.7 1 TD.

		Receiving				Punt Returns			
Year Team	**G**	**Rec**	**Yds**	**Avg**	**TD**	**Ret**	**Yds**	**Avg**	**TD**
1990 SD	12	14	192	13.7	1	13	117	9.0	**1**
1991 SD	16	42	554	13.2	3	5	59	11.8	0
1992 SD	15	34	580	17.1	4	13	127	9.8	0
1993 SD	15	38	463	12.2	4	3	17	5.7	0
1994 ChiB	13	2	13	6.5	1	1	7	7.0	0
1995 ChiB	11	0	0	—	0	0	0	—	0
NFL Total	82	130	1802	13.9	13	35	327	9.3	1

	Kickoff Returns					Tot
Year Team	**Ret**	**Yds**	**Avg**	**TD**	**Fum**	**TD**
1990 SD	17	383	22.5	0	3	3
1991 SD	23	578	25.1	**1**	0	4
1992 SD	19	402	21.2	0	1	4
1993 SD	33	684	20.7	0	2	4
1994 ChiB	35	874	25.0	0	1	1
1995 ChiB	42	904	21.5	0	0	0
NFL Total	169	3825	22.6	1	7	16

RAY LEWIS Lewis, Raymond Anthony 6'1", 240 **LB**
Col: Miami (Fla.) *HS:* Kathleen [Lakeland, FL] B: 5/15/1975, Lakeland, FL *Drafted:* 1996 Round 1 Bal
1996 Bal: 14 G; Int 1-0; 2.5 Sac. **1997** Bal: 16 G; Int 1-18; 4 Sac. **1998** Bal: 14 G; Int 2-25; 3 Sac. **Total:** 44 G; Int 4-43; 9.5 Sac.

REGGIE LEWIS Lewis, Reginald Anthony 6'2", 252 **DE**
Col: Oregon; San Diego State *HS:* Crenshaw [Los Angeles, CA] B: 1/20/1954, New Orleans, LA *Drafted:* 1976 Round 16 SF
1982 NO: 9 G; 3 Sac. **1983** NO: 12 G; Int 1-27 1 TD; 6 Pt; 6.5 Sac. **1984** NO: 13 G; 2 Sac. **Total:** 34 G; Int 1-27 1 TD; 6 Pt; 11.5 Sac.

REGGIE LEWIS Lewis, Reginald Paul 6'3", 260 **DE-NT**
Col: North Texas *HS:* Lincoln [Port Arthur, TX] B: 5/6/1956, Port Arthur, TX *Drafted:* 1979 Round 3 TB
1979 TB: 12 G. **1980** TB: 10 G. **Total:** 22 G.

RICH LEWIS Lewis, Richard L 6'3", 220 **LB**
Col: Portland State *HS:* U.S. Grant [Portland, OR] B: 6/8/1950, Portland, OR
1972 Hou: 10 G. **1973** Buf: 10 G. **1974** Buf: 2 G; Int 1-33. **1975** NYJ: 11 G. **Total:** 33 G; Int 1-33.

RODERICK LEWIS Lewis, Roderick Albert 6'5", 254 **TE**
Col: Arizona *HS:* Bishop Dunne [Dallas, TX] B: 6/9/1971, Washington, DC *Drafted:* 1994 Round 5 Hou
1995 Hou: KR 1-5 5.0. **Total:** KR 1-5 5.0.

		Receiving			
Year Team	**G**	**Rec**	**Yds**	**Avg**	**TD**
1994 Hou	3	4	48	12.0	0
1995 Hou	16	16	116	7.3	0
1996 Hou	16	7	50	7.1	0
1997 Ten	10	1	7	7.0	0
NFL Total	45	28	221	7.9	0

RODNEY LEWIS Lewis, Rodney Earl 5'11", 190 **DB**
Col: Nebraska *HS:* Central [Minneapolis, MN] B: 4/2/1959, Minneapolis, MN *Drafted:* 1982 Round 3 NO
1982 NO: 9 G; Int 1-12. **1983** NO: 2 G. **1984** NO: 16 G. **Total:** 27 G; Int 1-12.

RON LEWIS Lewis, Ronald Alexander 5'11", 185 **WR**
Col: Florida State *HS:* William M. Raines [Jacksonville, FL] B: 3/25/1968, Jacksonville, FL *Drafted:* 1990 Round 3 SF
1992 SF-GB: PR 4-23 5.8. SF: PR 4-23 5.8. **Total:** PR 4-23 5.8.

		Receiving				
Year Team	**G**	**Rec**	**Yds**	**Avg**	**TD**	**Fum**
1990 SF	8	5	44	8.8	0	0
1992 SF-GB	11	13	152	11.7	0	2
1992 SF	5	0	0	—	0	2
1992 GB	6	13	152	11.7	0	0
1993 GB	9	2	21	10.5	0	0
1994 GB	6	7	108	15.4	0	0
NFL Total	34	27	325	12.0	0	2

RON LEWIS Lewis, Ronald Mack II 6'3", 299 **OG**
Col: West Los Angeles Coll. CA (J.C.); Washington State *HS:* Susan Miller Dorsey [Los Angeles, CA] B: 11/17/1972, Los Angeles, CA
1995 Was: 4 G.

SHERMAN LEWIS Lewis, Sherman Paul 5'9", 158 **DB**
Col: Michigan State *HS:* Manual [Louisville, KY] B: 6/29/1942, Louisville, KY *Drafted:* 1964 Round 9 NYJ
1966 NYJ: 5 G; PR 7-76 10.9; KR 5-121 24.2; 2 Fum. **1967** NYJ: 5 G; PR 7-24 3.4; KR 1-22 22.0; 1 Fum. **Total:** 10 G; PR 14-100 7.1; KR 6-143 23.8; 3 Fum.

SID LEWIS Lewis, Sidney Scot 5'11", 180 **DB**
Col: Penn State *HS:* McKinley [Canton, OH] B: 5/30/1964, Canton, OH *Drafted:* 1987 Round 10 NYJ
1987 NYJ: 2 G.

STAN LEWIS Lewis, Stanley 6'4", 240 **DE**
Col: Wayne State (Neb.) *HS:* Fenger [Chicago, IL] B: 9/11/1953, Chicago, IL *Drafted:* 1975 Round 10 Cle
1975 Cle: 6 G.

TAHAUN LEWIS Lewis, Tahaun 5'10", 175 **DB**
Col: Nebraska *HS:* Thomas B. Doherty [Colorado Springs, CO] B: 9/29/1968, Los Angeles, CA *Drafted:* 1991 Round 9 LARd
1992 KC: 9 G.

TERRY LEWIS Lewis, Terence L 5'11", 193 **DB**
Col: Michigan State *HS:* Highland Park [MI] B: 12/9/1962, Detroit, MI *Drafted:* 1985 Round 6 SD
1985 SD: 10 G.

THOMAS LEWIS Lewis, Thomas A 6'1", 191 **WR**
Col: Indiana *HS:* Garfield [Akron, OH] B: 1/10/1972, Akron, OH *Drafted:* 1994 Round 1 NYG
1994 NYG: PR 5-64 12.8. **1995** NYG: PR 6-46 7.7. **1996** NYG: PR 10-36 3.6. **Total:** PR 21-146 7.0.

		Receiving				Kickoff Returns					Tot
Year Team	**G**	**Rec**	**Yds**	**Avg**	**TD**	**Ret**	**Yds**	**Avg**	**TD**	**Fum**	**TD**
1994 NYG	9	4	46	11.5	0	26	509	19.6	0	2	0
1995 NYG	8	12	208	17.3	1	9	257	28.6	1	1	2
1996 NYG	13	53	694	13.1	4	4	107	26.8	0	0	4
1997 NYG	4	5	84	16.8	0	14	364	26.0	0	0	0
NFL Total	34	74	1032	13.9	5	53	1237	23.3	1	3	6

TIM LEWIS Lewis, Timothy Jay 5'11", 194 **DB**
Col: Pittsburgh *HS:* Pennridge [Perkasie, PA] B: 12/18/1961, Quakertown, PA *Drafted:* 1983 Round 1 GB
1983 GB: KR 20-358 17.9. **1985** GB: **1** Fum TD. **Total:** KR 20-358 17.9; 1 Fum TD.

Year Team	G	Interceptions Int	Yds	TD	Fum	Tot TD
1983 GB	16	5	111	0	3	0
1984 GB	16	7	151	1	0	1
1985 GB	16	4	4	0	0	1
1986 GB	3	0	0	0	0	0
NFL Total	51	16	266	1	3	2

VERNON LEWIS Lewis, Vernon Jr. 5′10″, 192 **DB**
Col: Pittsburgh *HS:* Kashmere [Houston, TX] B: 10/27/1970, Houston, TX
1993 NE: 10 G. **1994** NE: 11 G. **1995** NE: 16 G; 1.5 Sac. **1996** NE: 7 G. **Total:** 44 G; 1.5 Sac.

BILL LEWIS Lewis, William Glenn 6′6″, 285 **C**
Col: Nebraska *HS:* East [Sioux City, IA] B: 7/12/1963, Sioux City, IA *Drafted:* 1986 Round 7 LARd
1986 LARd: 4 G. **1987** LARd: 8 G. **1988** LARd: 14 G. **1990** Pho: 16 G. **1991** Pho: 16 G. **1992** Pho: 6 G. **1993** NE: 7 G; 2 Fum. **Total:** 71 G; 2 Fum.

WILL LEWIS Lewis, William L 5′9″, 185 **DB**
Col: Millersville *HS:* Pennridge [Perkasie, PA] B: 1/16/1958, Quakertown, PA

Year Team	G	Punt Returns Ret	Yds	Avg	TD	Kickoff Returns Ret	Yds	Avg	TD	Fum
1980 Sea	16	41	349	8.5	1	25	585	23.4	0	7
1981 Sea	10	15	100	6.7	0	20	378	18.9	0	5
NFL Total	26	56	449	8.0	1	45	963	21.4	0	12

BILL LEWIS Lewis, Wilton 5′11″, 186 **BB-DB**
Col: No College
1934 Cin: 2 G; Rush 3-(-4) -1.3.

WOODLEY LEWIS Lewis, Woodley Carl Jr. 6′0″, 185 **DB-OE**
Col: Los Angeles City Coll. CA (J.C.); Oregon *HS:* Manual Arts [Los Angeles, CA] B: 6/14/1925, Los Angeles, CA *Drafted:* 1950 Round 8 LARm
1950 LARm: **1** Fum TD. **Total:** 1 Fum TD.

Year Team	G	Rushing Att	Yds	Avg	TD	Receiving Rec	Yds	Avg	TD
1950 LARm	12	0	0	—	0	0	0	—	0
1951 LARm	12	0	0	—	0	0	0	—	0
1952 LARm	12	19	114	6.0	0	0	0	—	0
1953 LARm	12	2	2	1.0	0	0	0	—	0
1954 LARm	12	26	72	2.8	0	2	19	9.5	0
1955 LARm	12	0	0	—	0	19	199	10.5	0
1956 ChiC	12	0	0	—	0	0	0	—	0
1957 ChiC	12	0	0	—	0	21	424	20.2	5
1958 ChiC	12	0	0	—	0	46	690	15.0	4
1959 ChiC	12	0	0	—	0	34	534	15.7	3
1960 Dal	6	0	0	—	0	1	19	19.0	0
NFL Total	126	47	188	4.0	0	123	1885	15.3	12

Year Team	Punt Returns Ret	Yds	Avg	TD	Kickoff Returns Ret	Yds	Avg	TD
1950 LARm	1	0	0.0	0	2	47	23.5	0
1951 LARm	1	12	12.0	0	4	67	16.8	0
1952 LARm	19	351	18.5	**2**	16	345	21.6	0
1953 LARm	35	**267**	7.6	**1**	**32**	**830**	25.9	0
1954 LARm	22	82	3.7	0	**34**	**836**	24.6	1
1955 LARm	29	105	3.6	0	20	450	22.5	0
1956 ChiC	5	22	4.4	0	1	22	22.0	0
1957 ChiC	24	175	7.3	0	26	682	26.2	0
1958 ChiC	2	12	6.0	0	2	46	23.0	0
NFL Total	138	1026	7.4	3	137	3325	24.3	1

Year Team	Interceptions Int	Yds	TD	Fum	Tot TD
1950 LARm	12	**275**	0	0	1
1951 LARm	3	34	0	0	0
1952 LARm	1	20	0	2	2
1953 LARm	7	87	**1**	2	2
1954 LARm	0	0	0	1	1
1955 LARm	0	0	0	2	0
1956 ChiC	1	0	0	0	0
1957 ChiC	2	34	0	2	5
1958 ChiC	0	0	0	0	4
1959 ChiC	0	0	0	2	3
NFL Total	26	450	1	11	18

TEX LEYENDECKER Leyendecker, Charles B 6′1″, 235 **T-C-LB**
Col: Vanderbilt *HS:* Waco [TX] B: 2/3/1906 D: 6/24/1988, Columbus, TX
1933 Phi: 2 G.

JOHN LEYPOLDT Leypoldt, John Howard 6′2″, 229 **K**
Col: Northern Virginia CC *HS:* Washington Lee [Arlington, VA] B: 3/31/1946, Washington, DC D: 2/7/1987

Year Team	G	Scoring Pts	FG	FGA	FG%	XK	XKA	XK%
1971 Buf	8	39	9	15	60.0	12	12	100.0
1972 Buf	14	77	16	24	66.7	29	30	96.7
1973 Buf	14	90	21	30	70.0	27	27	100.0
1974 Buf	14	82	19	33	57.6	25	29	86.2
1975 Buf	14	78	9	16	56.3	**51**	**57**	89.5
1976 Buf-Sea	12	46	8	15	53.3	22	25	88.0
1976 Buf	1	3	0	3	0.0	3	3	100.0
1976 Sea	11	43	8	12	66.7	19	22	86.4
1977 Sea	13	60	9	18	50.0	33	37	89.2
1978 NO-Sea	3	10	2	3	66.7	4	5	80.0
1978 NO	2	10	2	3	66.7	4	5	80.0
1978 Sea	1	0	0	0	—	0	0	—
NFL Total	92	482	93	154	60.4	203	222	91.4

DENNIS LICK Lick, Dennis Allen 6′3″, 266 **OT**
Col: Wisconsin *HS:* St. Rita [Chicago, IL] B: 4/26/1954, Chicago, IL *Drafted:* 1976 Round 1 ChiB
1976 ChiB: 14 G. **1977** ChiB: 14 G. **1978** ChiB: 16 G. **1979** ChiB: 16 G. **1980** ChiB: 16 G. **1981** ChiB: 3 G. **Total:** 79 G.

CULLY LIDBERG Lidberg, Carl Leroy 5′9″, 190 **FB**
Col: Hamline; Minnesota *HS:* Red Wing [MI] B: 8/25/1900, Red Wing, MN D: 6/26/1987, Minneapolis, MN
1926 GB: 11 G; Rush 4 TD; 24 Pt. **1929** GB: 10 G; Rush 2 TD; 12 Pt. **1930** GB: 5 G; Rush 1 TD; 6 Pt. **Total:** 26 G; Rush 7 TD; 42 Pt.

DAVE LIDDICK Liddick, David LeRoy 6′2″, 240 **DT**
Col: George Washington *HS:* Millersburg [PA] B: 12/10/1935, Harrisburg, PA *Drafted:* 1957 Round 8 Det
1957 Pit: 4 G.

FRANK LIEBEL Liebel, Frank Edward 6′1″, 211 **OE-DE-DB**
Col: Norwich *HS:* Erie Acad. [PA] B: 11/19/1919, Erie, PA D: 12/26/1996, Erie, PA
1944 NYG: Int 1-8; 1 Fum TD. **1945** NYG: Int 1-17. **1946** NYG: Int 5-117. **1947** NYG: KR 1-12 12.0. **Total:** KR 1-12 12.0; Int 7-142; 1 Fum TD.

Year Team	G	Receiving Rec	Yds	Avg	TD	Fum	Tot TD
1942 NYG	5	2	51	25.5	0	0	0
1943 NYG	10	11	199	18.1	3	0	3
1944 NYG	10	13	292	22.5	5	0	6
1945 NYG	10	22	593	**27.0**	**10**	0	10
1946 NYG	11	20	360	18.0	4	1	4
1947 NYG	11	16	258	16.1	1	1	1
1948 ChiC	5	0	0	—	0	0	0
NFL Total	62	84	1753	20.9	23	2	24

TODD LIEBENSTEIN Liebenstein, Todd E 6′6″, 253 **DE**
Col: Nevada-Las Vegas *HS:* Valley [Las Vegas, NV] B: 1/9/1960, Las Vegas, NV *Drafted:* 1982 Round 4 Was
1982 Was: 9 G; 1 Sac. **1983** Was: 15 G; 1.5 Sac. **1984** Was: 1 G. **1985** Was: 4 G. **Total:** 29 G; 2.5 Sac.

DON LIEBERUM Lieberum, Donald 6′0″, 175 **WB-DB**
Col: Manchester *HS:* North Side [Fort Wayne, IN] B: 7/3/1918, Pittsburgh, PA D: 11/7/1982, Fort Wayne, IN
1942 NYG: 11 G; Rush 11-29 2.6; Rec 6-65 10.8; PR 1-0; KR 1-12 12.0.

BOB LIGGETT Liggett, Robert Ellsworth 6′2″, 255 **DT**
Col: Nebraska *HS:* Aliquippa [PA] B: 12/8/1946, Aliquippa, PA *Drafted:* 1970 Round 15 KC
1970 KC: 7 G.

ALVA LILES Liles, Alva Edison 6′3″, 255 **NT-DT**
Col: Boise State *HS:* Sacremento [CA] B: 3/6/1956, Oklahoma City, OK
1980 Oak-Det: 3 G. Oak: 2 G. Det: 1 G. **Total:** 3 G.

SONNY LILES Liles, Elvin Merle 5′8″, 188 **G-LB**
Col: Oklahoma State *HS:* Clinton [OK] B: 8/9/1919, Marlow, OK
1943 Det: 5 G. **1944** Det: 9 G; PR 1-5 5.0; Int 1-14. **1945** Det-Cle: 9 G; Int 1-6. Det: 1 G. Cle: 8 G; Int 1-6. **Total:** 23 G; PR 1-5 5.0; Int 2-20.

GEORGE LILJA Lilja, George Vincent 6′4″, 264 **C-OG-OT**
Col: Michigan *HS:* Carl Sandburg [Orland Park, IL] B: 3/3/1958, Evergreen Park, IL *Drafted:* 1981 Round 4 LARm
1982 LARm: 9 G. **1983** NYJ: 1 G. **1984** NYJ-Cle: 7 G. NYJ: 3 G. Cle: 4 G. **1985** Cle: 16 G. **1986** Cle: 16 G. **1987** Dal: 5 G; 1 Fum. **Total:** 54 G; 1 Fum.

JOE LILLARD Lillard, Joseph 6′0″, 185 **TB-DB**
(Midnight Express) *Col:* Oregon *HS:* Mason City [IA] B: 6/15/1905, Tulsa, OK D: 9/18/1978, New York, NY
1932 ChiC: Rec 1-10 10.0; Scor 2, 2 XK. **1933** ChiC: Rec 1-19 19.0; PR 1 TD; Scor 19, 2 FG, 1 XK. **Total:** Rec 2-29 14.5; PR 1 TD; Scor 21, 2 FG, 3 XK.

Year Team	G	Passing Att	Comp	Comp%	Yds	YPA	TD	Int	Rating
1932 ChiC	7	28	9	32.1	103	3.68	0	3	4.6
1933 ChiC	11	67	18	26.9	269	4.01	2	16	14.2
NFL Total	18	95	27	28.4	372	3.92	2	19	10.8

Year Team	Rushing Att	Yds	Avg	TD	Tot TD
1932 ChiC	52	121	2.3	0	0
1933 ChiC	119	373	3.1	1	2
NFL Total	171	494	2.9	1	2

KEVIN LILLY Lilly, Kevin Paschal 6′4″, 265 DE-NT-DT
Col: Tulsa *HS:* Memorial [Tulsa, OK] B: 5/14/1963, Tulsa, OK
1988 SF: 9 G. **1989** SF-Dal: 2 G. SF: 1 G. Dal: 1 G. **Total:** 11 G.

TONY LILLY Lilly, Robert Anthoney 6′0″, 199 DB
Col: Florida *HS:* Woodbridge [VA] B: 2/16/1962, Alexandria, VA
Drafted: 1984 Round 3 Den
1984 Den: 13 G; Int 1-5; 1 Fum. **1985** Den: 16 G; Int 2-4. **1986** Den: 16 G; Int 3-22; 1 Sac. **1987** Den: 13 G; PR 2-6 3.0; Int 3-29. **Total:** 58 G; PR 2-6 3.0; Int 9-60; 1 Fum; 1 Sac.

BOB LILLY Lilly, Robert Lewis 6′5″, 260 DT
Col: Texas Christian *HS:* Throckmorton [TX]; Pendleton HS [OR]
B: 7/26/1939, Olney, TX *Drafted:* 1961 Round 1 Dal *HOF:* 1980
1961 Dal: 14 G. **1962** Dal: 14 G. **1963** Dal: 14 G; **1** Fum TD; 6 Pt.
1964 Dal: 14 G; 1 Fum. **1965** Dal: 14 G; Int 1-17 1 TD; 6 Pt. **1966** Dal: 14 G. **1967** Dal: 14 G. **1968** Dal: 14 G. **1969** Dal: 14 G; **1** Fum TD; 6 Pt.
1970 Dal: 14 G. **1971** Dal: 14 G; **1** Fum TD; 6 Pt. **1972** Dal: 14 G.
1973 Dal: 14 G. **1974** Dal: 14 G. **Total:** 196 G; Int 1-17 1 TD; 3 Fum TD; Tot TD 4; 24 Pt; 1 Fum.

SAMMY LILLY Lilly, Samuel Julius IV 5′9″, 178 DB
Col: Georgia Tech *HS:* George P. Butler [Augusta, GA] B: 2/12/1965, Anchorage, AK *Drafted:* 1988 Round 8 NYG
1989 Phi: 15 G. **1990** Phi-SD: 10 G. Phi: 8 G. SD: 2 G. **1991** LARm: 16 G.
1992 LARm: 9 G. **Total:** 50 G.

VERL LILLYWHITE Lillywhite, Verl Thomas 5′10″, 185 HB-DB
(Giant Wallet) *Col:* Modesto JC CA; USC *HS:* Inglewood [CA]
B: 12/5/1926, Garland, UT
AAFC **1948** SF-A: Pass 1-0, 1 Int; Rec 1-(-1) -1.0; PR 3-41 13.7; Int 3-26; Punt 3-76 25.3. **1949** SF-A: Rec 8-82 10.3 2 TD; KR 1-16 16.0; Int 1-9; Punt 4-202 50.5. **Total:** Pass 1-0, 1 Int; Rec 9-81 9.0 2 TD; PR 3-41 13.7; KR 1-16 16.0; Int 4-35; Punt 7-278 39.7.

Year Team	G	Rushing Att	Yds	Avg	TD	Tot TD
1948 SF-A	14	53	340	6.4	3	3
1949 SF-A	12	69	263	3.8	2	4
AAFC Total	26	122	603	4.9	5	7

NFL **1950** SF: Rec 1-6 6.0; KR 2-36 18.0; Int 1-11. **1951** SF: Rec 11-125 11.4 1 TD; Int 3-47. **Total:** Rec 12-131 10.9 1 TD; KR 2-36 18.0; Int 4-58.

Year Team	G	Rushing Att	Yds	Avg	TD	Punting Punts	Yds	Avg	Fum	Tot TD
1950 SF	9	7	4	0.6	0	26	1016	39.1	1	0
1951 SF	12	67	397	5.9	1	20	847	42.4	3	2
NFL Total	21	74	401	5.4	1	46	1863	40.5	4	2

GARRETT LIMBRICK Limbrick, Garrett IV 6′2″, 240 RB
Col: Oklahoma State *HS:* Northbrook [Houston, TX] B: 11/6/1965, Houston, TX
1990 Mia: 7 G; Rush 5-14 2.8; Rec 4-23 5.8; 1 Fum.

DAVE LINCE Lince, David LeRoy 6′7″, 265 TE
(Butch) *Col:* North Dakota *HS:* Lincoln [Mott, ND] B: 5/17/1944, Fargo, ND *Drafted:* 1966 Round 7 Phi
1966 Phi: 4 G; KR 1-13 13.0. **1967** Phi: 14 G; PR 1-0; KR 3-46 15.3.
Total: 18 G; PR 1-0; KR 4-59 14.8.

JEREMY LINCOLN Lincoln, Jeremy Arlo 5′10″, 180 DB
Col: Tennessee *HS:* Thomas DeVilbiss [Toldeo, OH] B: 4/7/1969, Toledo, OH *Drafted:* 1992 Round 3 ChiB
1993 ChiB: 16 G; Int 3-109 1 TD; 6 Pt. **1994** ChiB: 15 G; Int 1-5.
1995 ChiB: 16 G; Int 1-32; 1 Sac. **1996** StL: 13 G; Int 1-3. **1997** Sea: 12 G.
1998 NYG: 16 G; Int 1-0. **Total:** 88 G; Int 7-149 1 TD; 6 Pt; 1 Sac.

KEITH LINCOLN Lincoln, Keith Payson 6′1″, 215 FB-K
Col: Washington State *HS:* Monrovia [CA] B: 5/8/1939, Reading, MI
Drafted: 1961 Round 2 SD
1962 SD: Pass 5-2 40.0%, 43 8.60 2 TD. **1963** SD: Pass 1-0. **1964** SD: Pass 4-2 50.0%, 61 15.25 1 TD; Scor 67, 5-12 41.7% FG, 16-17 94.1% XK. **1965** SD: Pass 3-2 66.7%, 65 21.67 1 TD 1 Int. **1966** SD: Pass 4-2 50.0%, 71 17.75 1 TD. **Total:** Pass 17-8 47.1%, 240 14.12 5 TD 1 Int; Scor 271, 5-12 41.7% FG, 16-17 94.1% XK.

Year Team	G	Rushing Att	Yds	Avg	TD	Receiving Rec	Yds	Avg	TD
1961 SD	14	41	150	3.7	0	12	208	17.3	2
1962 SD	14	117	574	4.9	2	16	214	13.4	1
1963 SD	14	128	826	**6.5**	5	24	325	13.5	3
1964 SD	14	155	632	4.1	4	34	302	8.9	2
1965 SD	10	74	302	4.1	3	23	376	16.3	4
1966 SD	14	58	214	3.7	1	14	264	18.9	2
1967 Buf	14	159	601	3.8	4	41	558	13.6	5
1968 Buf-SD	5	26	84	3.2	0	1	3	3.0	0
1968 Buf	4	26	84	3.2	0	1	3	3.0	0
1968 SD	1	0	0	—	0	0	0	—	0
NFL Total	99	758	3383	4.5	19	165	2250	13.6	19

Year Team	Punt Returns Ret	Yds	Avg	TD	Kickoff Returns Ret	Yds	Avg	TD	Fum	Tot TD
1961 SD	7	150	21.4	1	4	98	24.5	0	0	3
1962 SD	11	94	8.5	0	14	398	28.4	**1**	1	4
1963 SD	7	98	14.0	0	17	439	25.8	0	5	8
1964 SD	0	0	—	0	0	0	—	0	1	6
1965 SD	0	0	—	0	2	46	23.0	0	0	7
1966 SD	0	0	—	0	0	0	—	0	1	3
1967 Buf	0	0	—	0	0	0	—	0	3	9
1968 Buf-SD	0	0	—	0	2	37	18.5	0	1	0
1968 Buf	0	0	—	0	0	0	—	0	1	0
1968 SD	0	0	—	0	2	37	18.5	0	0	0
NFL Total	25	342	13.7	1	39	1018	26.1	1	12	40

MIKE LIND Lind, Harry Norman 6′2″, 225 FB
Col: Notre Dame *HS:* Calumet [Chicago, IL] B: 2/2/1940, Chicago, IL
Drafted: 1962 Round 5 SF
1964 SF: Pass 1-1 100.0%, 69 69.00 1 TD. **1966** Pit: KR 1-15 15.0.
Total: Pass 1-1 100.0%, 69 69.00 1 TD; KR 1-15 15.0.

Year Team	G	Rushing Att	Yds	Avg	TD	Receiving Rec	Yds	Avg	TD	Fum	Tot TD
1963 SF	11	8	26	3.3	0	2	13	6.5	0	0	0
1964 SF	13	100	256	2.6	7	25	178	7.1	0	3	7
1965 Pit	14	111	375	3.4	1	25	236	9.4	1	3	2
1966 Pit	6	3	4	1.3	0	0	0	—	0	0	0
NFL Total	44	222	661	3.0	8	52	427	8.2	1	6	9

JOE LINDAHL Lindahl, Virgil Youngquist 6′1″, 197 G-LB-OE
Col: Wayne State (Neb.); Kentucky *HS:* Elkhorn Valley [Tilden, NE]
B: 3/14/1919, Tilden, NE
1945 NYG: 2 G; Rec 1-32 32.0.

ERROL LINDEN Linden, Errol Joseph 6′5″, 260 OT
(Moose) *Col:* Houston *HS:* De La Salle [New Orleans, LA]
B: 10/21/1937, New Orleans, LA D: 3/10/1983, New Orleans, LA
Drafted: 1961 Round 10 Det
1961 Cle: 10 G; KR 1-5 5.0. **1962** Min: 12 G. **1963** Min: 14 G. **1964** Min: 14 G. **1965** Min: 14 G. **1966** Atl: 14 G. **1967** Atl: 14 G; KR 3-37 12.3.
1968 Atl: 14 G. **1969** NO: 14 G. **1970** NO: 14 G. **Total:** 134 G; KR 4-42 10.5.

LUKE LINDON Lindon, Luther W 5′10″, 243 T
Col: Kentucky B: 6/23/1915, Salyersville, KY D: 4/21/1988, Blacksburg, VA
1944 Det: 10 G. **1945** Det: 4 G. **Total:** 14 G.

AL LINDOW Lindow, Allen Lapham 6′0″, 165 HB-DB
Col: Washington-St. Louis *HS:* University [Milwaukee, WI]
B: 7/9/1919, Milwaukee, WI D: 1/18/1989, Fort Lauderdale, FL
1945 ChiC: 1 G; PR 1-18 18.0; KR 1-13 13.0.

PAUL LINDQUIST Lindquist, Paul August 6′3″, 265 DT
Col: New Hampshire *HS:* Abington [MA] B: 4/30/1939, Brockton, MA
Drafted: 1961 Round 8 Min
1961 Bos: 2 G.

EVERETT LINDSAY Lindsay, Everett Eric 6′4″, 297 OG-C-OT
Col: Mississippi *HS:* Millbrook [Raleigh, NC] B: 9/18/1970, Burlington, IA *Drafted:* 1993 Round 5 Min
1993 Min: 12 G. **1995** Min: 16 G. **1997** Min: 16 G. **1998** Min: 16 G.
Total: 60 G.

MENZ LINDSEY Lindsey, Ellis Menzies 5′6″, 165 BB-TB
Col: Wabash *HS:* Central [Evansville, IN] B: 7/25/1898, Boonville, IN
D: 9/20/1961, Evansville, IN
1921 Eva: 5 G; Rush 2 TD; 12 Pt.

HUB LINDSEY Lindsey, Hubert Allen 5′11″, 196 RB
Col: Wyoming *HS:* Steubenville [OH] B: 3/17/1945, Steubenville, OH
1968 Den: 3 G; Rush 4-17 4.3; KR 3-72 24.0; 1 Fum.

JIM LINDSEY Lindsey, James Edgar 6′2″, 210 RB
Col: Arkansas *HS:* Forrest City [AR] B: 11/24/1944, Caldwell, AR
Drafted: 1966 Round 2 Min
1966 Min: PR 2-4 2.0; KR 4-79 19.8. **1967** Min: KR 3-71 23.7. **1968** Min: KR 1-7 7.0. **1969** Min: KR 2-26 13.0. **1971** Min: **1** Fum TD. **1972** Min: KR 1-17 17.0. **Total:** PR 2-4 2.0; KR 11-200 18.2; 1 Fum TD.

Year Team	G	Rushing Att	Yds	Avg	TD	Receiving Rec	Yds	Avg	TD	Fum	Tot TD
1966 Min	14	57	146	2.6	1	20	250	12.5	2	3	3
1967 Min	8	4	10	2.5	0	4	36	9.0	0	0	0
1968 Min	14	53	152	2.9	4	15	148	9.9	0	3	4
1969 Min	10	6	21	3.5	1	2	45	22.5	1	0	2
1970 Min	11	11	47	4.3	0	4	94	23.5	1	0	1
1971 Min	14	46	182	4.0	0	8	31	3.9	0	1	1
1972 Min	13	1	8	8.0	0	3	28	9.3	0	0	0
NFL Total	84	178	566	3.2	6	56	632	11.3	4	7	11

DALE LINDSEY Lindsey, Phillip Dale 6′2″, 223 **LB**
Col: Kentucky; Western Kentucky *HS:* Bowling Green [KY]
B: 1/18/1943, Bedford, IN *Drafted:* 1965 Round 7 Cle
1965 Cle: 14 G; KR 1-0; Int 1-11. **1966** Cle: 13 G. **1967** Cle: 14 G; Int 1-5. **1968** Cle: 12 G; Int 1-0. **1969** Cle: 14 G; Int 1-3. **1970** Cle: 14 G; Int 2-65 1 TD; 6 Pt. **1971** Cle: 14 G; Int 2-50. **1972** Cle: 11 G. **1973** NO: 5 G. **Total:** 111 G; KR 1-0; Int 8-134 1 TD; 6 Pt.

VIC LINDSKOG Lindskog, Victor Junior 6′1″, 203 **C-LB**
Col: Rancho Santiago Coll. CA (J.C.); Stanford *HS:* Roundup [MT]
B: 12/3/1914, Roundup, MT *Drafted:* 1942 Round 2 Phi
1944 Phi: 7 G; Int 1-65 1 TD; 6 Pt. **1945** Phi: 10 G; Int 1-22. **1946** Phi: 11 G; Int 1-10. **1947** Phi: 10 G; Int 1-15. **1948** Phi: 12 G. **1949** Phi: 5 G. **1950** Phi: 12 G. **1951** Phi: 11 G; Rec 0-21. **Total:** 78 G; Rec 0-21; Int 4-112 1 TD; 6 Pt.

CHRIS LINDSTROM Lindstrom, Christopher Richard 6′7″, 260 **DE**
Col: Boston U. *HS:* South [Weymouth, MA] B: 8/3/1960, Weymouth, MA *Drafted:* 1982 Round 8 StL
1983 Cin: 1 G. **1985** TB: 15 G. **1987** KC: 3 G. **Total:** 19 G.

DAVE LINDSTROM Lindstrom, David Alan 6′6″, 255 **DE**
Col: Boston U. *HS:* South [Weymouth, MA] B: 11/16/1954, Cambridge, MA *Drafted:* 1977 Round 6 SD
1978 KC: 16 G. **1979** KC: 13 G. **1980** KC: 16 G. **1981** KC: 16 G. **1982** KC: 9 G; KR 1-1 1.0; 3 Sac. **1983** KC: 16 G; KR 1-0; 1 Sac. **1984** KC: 16 G; 2 Sac. **1985** KC: 16 G; 1.5 Sac. **Total:** 118 G; KR 2-1 0.5; 7.5 Sac.

BILL LINE Line, Billie Boyd Jr. 6′7″, 260 **DT**
Col: Air Force; Southern Methodist *HS:* L.D. Bell [Hurst, TX]
B: 8/11/1948, San Angelo, TX
1972 ChiB: 13 G.

BOB LINGENFELTER Lingenfelter, Robert Newton 6′7″, 277 **OT-OG**
Col: Nebraska *HS:* Plainview [NE] B: 9/1/1954, Norfolk, NE
Drafted: 1977 Round 7 Cle
1977 Cle: 14 G. **1978** Min: 5 G. **Total:** 19 G.

GORAN LINGMERTH Lingmerth, Goran R 5′8″, 160 **K**
Col: Kings River CC CA; Northern Arizona *HS:* Kingsburg [CA]
B: 11/11/1964, Nassjo, Sweden
1987 Cle: 1 G.

ADAM LINGNER Lingner, Adam James 6′4″, 264 **C-OG**
Col: Illinois *HS:* Alleman [Rock Island, IL] B: 11/2/1960, Indianapolis, IN *Drafted:* 1983 Round 9 KC
1983 KC: 16 G. **1984** KC: 16 G. **1985** KC: 16 G. **1986** KC: 12 G. **1987** Buf: 12 G. **1988** KC: 16 G. **1989** Buf: 16 G. **1990** Buf: 16 G. **1991** Buf: 16 G. **1992** Buf: 16 G. **1993** Buf: 16 G. **1994** Buf: 16 G. **1995** Buf: 16 G. **Total:** 200 G.

CHIM LINGREL Lingrel, Chalmers 6′2″, 200 **WB-FB**
(Tomahawk) *Col:* No College B: 1/1899, Ridgeway, OH Deceased
1923 Oor: 6 G.

TONI LINHART Linhart, Anton Hansjorg 6′0″, 178 **K**
Col: Austria Tech School *HS:* Modlina School [Vienna, Austria]
B: 7/24/1942, Donawitz, Austria

Year Team	G	Scoring Pts	FG	FGA	FG%	XK	XKA	XK%
1972 NO	2	11	2	5	40.0	5	5	100.0
1974 Bal	14	58	12	20	60.0	22	22	100.0
1975 Bal	14	81	10	18	55.6	**51**	52	98.1
1976 Bal	14	**109**	20	27	74.1	**49**	**50**	98.0
1977 Bal	14	83	17	26	65.4	32	35	91.4
1978 Bal	16	51	8	17	47.1	27	31	87.1
1979 Bal-NYJ	8	32	6	14	42.9	14	18	77.8
1979 Bal	3	12	3	8	37.5	3	4	75.0
1979 NYJ	5	20	3	6	50.0	11	14	78.6
NFL Total	82	425	75	127	59.1	200	213	93.9

JACK LININGER Lininger, Raymond Jack 5′11″, 217 **LB-C**
Col: Ohio State *HS:* Van Wert [OH] B: 6/27/1927, Van Wert, OH
Drafted: 1949 Round 21 Det
1950 Det: 12 G; Int 3-20; 1 Fum. **1951** Det: 12 G. **Total:** 24 G; Int 3-20; 1 Fum.

JACK LINN Linn, Jack Laroy Jr. 6′5″, 295 **OT-OG**
Col: West Virginia *HS:* Freedom [PA] B: 6/10/1967, Sewickley, PA
Drafted: 1990 Round 9 Det
1991 Ind: 1 G. **1992** Det: 4 G. **1993** Det-Cin: 6 G. Det: 3 G. Cin: 3 G. **Total:** 11 G.

FRANK LINNAN Linnan, Michael Francis 6′2″, 202 **T**
Col: Marquette *HS:* Sacred Heart [Pocahontas, IA] B: 2/20/1895, Pocahontas, IA D: 6/2/1981, Tequesta, FL
1922 Rac: 3 G. **1926** Rac: 2 G. **Total:** 5 G.

AUBREY LINNE Linne, Aubrey Arthur Jr. 6′7″, 235 **TE**
Col: Texas Christian *HS:* Hobbs [NM] B: 4/19/1939
1961 Bal: 1 G.

LARRY LINNE Linne, Larry Glen 6′1″, 185 **WR**
Col: Midland Coll. TX (J.C.); Texas; Texas-El Paso *HS:* Robert E. Lee [Midland, TX] B: 7/20/1962, Baltimore, MD
1987 NE: 3 G; Rec 11-158 14.4 2 TD; PR 5-22 4.4; 12 Pt; 1 Fum.

CHRIS LINNIN Linnin, Christopher Bennett 6′4″, 255 **DE**
Col: Washington *HS:* Arcadia [CA] B: 5/4/1957, Pasadena, CA
Drafted: 1980 Round 7 NYG
1980 NYG: 10 G.

JONATHAN LINTON Linton, Jonathan C 6′0″, 248 **RB**
Col: North Carolina *HS:* Catasauqua [PA] B: 10/7/1974, Catasauqua, PA *Drafted:* 1998 Round 5 Buf
1998 Buf: Rec 1-10 10.0.

Year Team	G	Rushing Att	Yds	Avg	TD
1998 Buf	14	45	195	4.3	1

JOE LINTZENICH Lintzenich, Joseph Francis 5′11″, 187 **HB-FB**
Col: St. Louis *HS:* Webster Groves [MO] B: 3/26/1908, Webster Grove, MO D: 6/23/1985, Creve Coeur, MO
1930 ChiB: 13 G. **1931** ChiB: 11 G; Pass 2 TD; Rec 2 TD; 12 Pt.
Total: 24 G; Pass 2 TD; Rec 2 TD; 12 Pt.

AUGIE LIO Lio, Augostino Salvatore 6′0″, 234 **G-LB**
Col: Georgetown *HS:* Passaic [NJ] B: 4/30/1918, East Boston, MA
D: 9/3/1989, Clifton, NJ *Drafted:* 1941 Round 4 Det
AAFC **1947** BalA: 10 G; Scor 28, 3-8 37.5% FG, 19-20 95.0% XK.

NFL **1941** Det: Rush 1-(-4) -4.0; KR 1-7 7.0; Punt 1-28 28.0; Scor 18, 0-5 FG, 12-13 92.3% XK. **1942** Det: KR 1-4 4.0; Scor 5, 0-4 FG, 5-5 100.0% XK. **1943** Det: Scor 27, 2-**11** 18.2% FG, 21-23 91.3% XK. **1944** Bos: Scor 16, 2-8 25.0% FG, 10-11 90.9% XK. **1945** Bos: Scor 27, 4-5 **80.0**% FG, 15-16 **93.8**% XK. **1946** Phi: Scor 51, 6-11 54.5% FG, 27-27 100.0% XK. **Total:** Rush 1-(-4) -4.0; KR 2-11 5.5; Punt 1-28 28.0; Scor 144, 14-44 31.8% FG, 90-95 94.7% XK.

Year Team	G	Interceptions Int	Yds	TD	Tot TD
1941 Det	11	3	12	0	1
1942 Det	10	1	9	0	0
1943 Det	10	1	-2	0	0
1944 Bos	10	2	13	0	0
1945 Bos	10	3	42	0	0
1946 Phi	11	0	0	0	1
NFL Total	62	10	74	0	2

JIM LIPINSKI Lipinski, James Victor 6′4″, 238 **OT-DT**
Col: Fairmont State *HS:* Monongah [WV] B: 2/25/1927, Monongah, WV *Drafted:* 1950 Round 22 ChiC
1950 ChiC: 1 G.

RONNIE LIPPETT Lippett, Ronnie Leon 5′11″, 180 **DB**
Col: Miami (Fla.) *HS:* Sebring [FL] B: 12/10/1960, Melbourne, FL
Drafted: 1983 Round 8 NE
1987 NE: 1 Sac. **Total:** 1 Sac.

Year Team	G	Interceptions Int	Yds	TD	Fum
1983 NE	16	0	0	0	0
1984 NE	16	3	23	0	1
1985 NE	16	3	93	0	0
1986 NE	15	8	76	0	0
1987 NE	12	3	103	**2**	0
1988 NE	15	1	4	0	0
1990 NE	16	4	94	0	0
1991 NE	16	2	27	0	0
NFL Total	122	24	420	2	1

LOUIS LIPPS Lipps, Louis Adams Jr. 5′10″, 190 **WR**
Col: Southern Mississippi *HS:* East St. John [Reserve, LA]
B: 8/9/1962, New Orleans, LA *Drafted:* 1984 Round 1 Pit
1985 Pit: KR 13-237 18.2. **1988** Pit: Pass 2-1 50.0%, 13 6.50 1 TD 1 Int. **1990** Pit: KR 1-9 9.0. **Total:** Pass 2-1 50.0%, 13 6.50 1 TD 1 Int; KR 14-246 17.6.

Year Team	G	Rushing Att	Yds	Avg	TD	Receiving Rec	Yds	Avg	TD
1984 Pit	14	3	71	23.7	1	45	860	19.1	9
1985 Pit	16	2	16	8.0	1	59	1134	19.2	12
1986 Pit	13	4	-3	-0.8	0	38	590	15.5	3
1987 Pit	4	0	0	—	0	11	164	14.9	0
1988 Pit	16	6	129	21.5	1	50	973	19.5	5
1989 Pit	16	13	180	13.8	1	50	944	18.9	5
1990 Pit	14	1	-5	-5.0	0	50	682	13.6	3
1991 Pit	15	0	0	—	0	55	671	12.2	2
1992 NO	2	0	0	—	0	1	1	1.0	0
NFL Total	110	29	388	13.4	4	359	6019	16.8	39

Year Team	Punt Returns Ret	Yds	Avg	TD	Fum	Tot TD
1984 Pit	53	**656**	12.4	1	8	11
1985 Pit	36	437	12.1	**2**	5	15
1986 Pit	3	16	5.3	0	2	3
1987 Pit	7	46	6.6	0	0	0
1988 Pit	4	30	7.5	0	2	6
1989 Pit	4	27	6.8	0	2	6
1990 Pit	0	0	—	0	1	3
1991 Pit	0	0	—	0	1	2
1992 NO	5	22	4.4	0	1	0
NFL Total	112	1234	11.0	3	22	46

GENE LIPSCOMB Lipscomb, Eugene Allen 6'6", 284 **DT-DE**
(Big Daddy) *Col:* No College *HS:* Miller [Detroit, MI] B: 8/9/1931, Detroit, MI D: 5/10/1963, Baltimore, MD
1953 LARm: 2 G. **1954** LARm: 11 G; KR 1-6 6.0. **1955** LARm: 12 G; KR 2-32 16.0. **1956** Bal: 11 G. **1957** Bal: 12 G. **1958** Bal: 12 G. **1959** Bal: 12 G; Int 1-49. **1960** Bal: 12 G; Scor **1** Saf; 2 Pt. **1961** Pit: 14 G. **1962** Pit: 14 G. **Total:** 112 G; KR 3-38 12.7; Int 1-49; Scor 1 Saf; 2 Pt.

PAUL LIPSCOMB Lipscomb, Paul Edward 6'5", 246 **DT-OT**
(Lippy) *Col:* Tennessee *HS:* Benton [IL] B: 1/13/1923, Benton, IL D: 8/20/1964, Elm Grove, TN
1945 GB: 10 G. **1946** GB: 11 G. **1947** GB: 12 G; KR 1-1 1.0. **1948** GB: 12 G. **1949** GB: 12 G. **1950** Was: 12 G. **1951** Was: 12 G; KR 2-27 13.5; Int 1-0; 1 Fum. **1952** Was: 12 G; KR 1-5 5.0; Int 1-7; 1 Fum. **1953** Was: 12 G; KR 1-8 8.0. **1954** Was-ChiB: 12 G. Was: 1 G. ChiB: 11 G. **Total:** 117 G; KR 5-41 8.2; Int 2-7; 2 Fum.

JOHN LIPSKI Lipski, John J 5'11", 200 **C-LB**
(Bull) *Col:* Temple *HS:* Larksville [PA] D: 1/22/1963, Philadelphia, PA
1933 Phi: 8 G. **1934** Phi: 10 G. **Total:** 18 G.

DON LISBON Lisbon, Donald 5'10", 197 **HB**
Col: Bowling Green State *HS:* South [Youngstown, OH] B: 1/15/1941, Youngstown, OH *Drafted:* 1963 Round 3 SF
1963 SF: Pass 2-1 50.0%, 45 22.50 1 TD. **Total:** Pass 2-1 50.0%, 45 22.50 1 TD.

Year Team	G	Rushing Att	Yds	Avg	TD	Receiving Rec	Yds	Avg	TD	Fum
1963 SF	14	109	399	3.7	0	21	259	12.3	2	4
1964 SF	6	55	162	2.9	0	13	104	8.0	1	2
NFL Total	20	164	561	3.4	0	34	363	10.7	3	6

RUSTY LISCH Lisch, Russell John 6'3", 213 **QB**
Col: Notre Dame *HS:* West [Belleville, IL] B: 12/21/1956, Belleville, IL *Drafted:* 1980 Round 4 StL
1983 StL: Rush 2-9 4.5. **1984** ChiB: Rush 18-121 6.7. **Total:** Rush 20-130 6.5.

Year Team	G	Passing Att	Comp	Comp%	Yds	YPA	TD	Int	Rating	Fum
1980 StL	2	17	6	35.3	68	4.00	0	3	8.6	0
1981 StL	9	0	0	—	0	—	0	0	—	0
1982 StL	8	0	0	—	0	—	0	0	—	0
1983 StL	4	13	6	46.2	66	5.08	1	2	47.8	1
1984 ChiB	7	85	43	50.6	413	4.86	0	6	35.1	5
NFL Total	30	115	55	47.8	547	4.76	1	11	25.1	6

TONY LISCIO Liscio, Anthony Fred 6'5", 264 **OT-OG**
Col: Tulsa *HS:* Westinghouse [Pittsburgh, PA] B: 7/2/1940, Pittsburgh, PA *Drafted:* 1963 Round 3 GB
1963 Dal: 7 G. **1964** Dal: 10 G. **1966** Dal: 14 G. **1967** Dal: 14 G. **1968** Dal: 14 G. **1969** Dal: 14 G. **1970** Dal: 11 G. **1971** Dal: 5 G. **Total:** 89 G.

PETE LISKE Liske, Peter Adrian 6'3", 200 **QB**
Col: Penn State *HS:* Plainfield [NJ] B: 5/24/1942, Plainfield, NJ *Drafted:* 1963 Round 15 NYJ

Year Team	G	Passing Att	Comp	Comp%	Yds	YPA	TD	Int	Rating
1964 NYJ	2	18	9	50.0	55	3.06	0	2	16.9
1969 Den	7	115	61	53.0	845	7.35	9	11	63.4
1970 Den	11	238	112	47.1	1340	5.63	7	11	55.3
1971 Phi	14	269	143	53.2	1957	7.28	11	15	67.1
1972 Phi	14	138	71	51.4	973	7.05	3	7	60.4
NFL Total	48	778	396	50.9	5170	6.65	30	46	60.4

Year Team	Rushing Att	Yds	Avg	TD	Fum
1964 NYJ	1	0	0.0	0	0
1969 Den	10	50	5.0	0	1
1970 Den	7	42	6.0	1	3
1971 Phi	13	29	2.2	1	5
1972 Phi	7	20	2.9	0	3
NFL Total	38	141	3.7	2	12

PAUL LISTON Liston, Edward Paul Jones Jr. 5'11", 185 **G**
Col: Georgetown *HS:* Washington [PA] B: 1906, PA Deceased
1930 Nwk: 1 G.

ED LISTOPAD Listopad, Edward George 6'1", 230 **OG**
Col: Wake Forest *HS:* Patterson [Baltimore, MD] B: 8/28/1929, Baltimore, MD *Drafted:* 1952 Round 19 ChiC
1952 ChiC: 4 G.

GREG LITER Liter, Gregory Paul 6'6", 275 **DE**
Col: Iowa State *HS:* Mosinee [WI] B: 12/31/1963, Wausau, WI
1987 SF-Phi: 2 G. SF: 1 G. Phi: 1 G. **Total:** 2 G.

RED LITKUS Litkus, Bernard Howard 187 **T-E**
Col: No College B: 1894, PA Deceased
1921 Was: 3 G.

DAVE LITTLE Little, David Gene 6'2", 233 **TE**
Col: Middle Tennessee State *HS:* Roosevelt [Fresno, CA] B: 4/18/1961, Selma, CA *Drafted:* 1981 Round 7 Pit
1985 Phi: **1** Fum TD. **1989** Phi: KR 2-14 7.0. **Total:** KR 2-14 7.0; 1 Fum TD.

Year Team	G	Receiving Rec	Yds	Avg	TD	Fum	Tot TD
1984 KC	10	1	13	13.0	0	0	0
1985 Phi	15	7	82	11.7	0	0	1
1986 Phi	16	14	132	9.4	0	1	0
1987 Phi	12	1	8	8.0	0	0	0
1988 Phi	10	0	0	—	0	0	0
1989 Phi	16	2	8	4.0	1	1	1
1990 Pho	11	0	0	—	0	0	0
1991 Det	2	0	0	—	0	0	0
NFL Total	92	25	243	9.7	1	2	2

DAVID LITTLE Little, David Lamar 6'1", 232 **LB**
Col: Florida *HS:* Miami Jackson [FL] B: 1/3/1959, Miami, FL
1984 Pit: 1 Sac. **1985** Pit: 1 Sac. **1986** Pit: 0.5 Sac. **1987** Pit: 1.5 Sac. **1989** Pit: 2 Sac. **1992** Pit: 3 Sac. **Total:** 9 Sac.

Year Team	G	Interceptions Int	Yds	TD
1981 Pit	16	0	0	0
1982 Pit	9	0	0	0
1983 Pit	16	0	0	0
1984 Pit	16	0	0	0
1985 Pit	16	2	0	0
1986 Pit	16	0	0	0
1987 Pit	12	0	0	0
1988 Pit	16	1	0	0
1989 Pit	16	3	23	0
1990 Pit	16	1	35	0
1991 Pit	14	1	5	0
1992 Pit	16	2	6	0
NFL Total	179	10	69	0

EARL LITTLE Little, Earl Jerome 6'0", 191 **DB**
Col: Michigan; Miami (Fla.) *HS:* North Miami [FL] B: 3/10/1973, Miami, FL
1998 NO: 16 G; KR 4-64 16.0.

EVERETT LITTLE Little, Everett Charles 6'4", 265 **OG**
Col: Houston *HS:* Lufkin [TX] B: 6/12/1954, Lufkin, TX *Drafted:* 1976 Round 4 TB
1976 TB: 10 G.

FLOYD LITTLE Little, Floyd Douglas 5'10", 196 **RB**
Col: Syracuse *HS:* James Hillhouse [New Haven, CT] Bordentown Mil. Acad. [NJ] B: 7/4/1942, New Haven, CT *Drafted:* 1967 Round 1 Den
1968 Den: Pass 2-0. **1969** Den: Pass 2-0. **1970** Den: Pass 2-0. **1971** Den: Pass 1-0. **1972** Den: Pass 2-2 100.0%, 43 21.50 1 TD. **Total:** Pass 9-2 22.2%, 43 4.78 1 TD.

Year Team	G	Rushing Att	Yds	Avg	TD	Receiving Rec	Yds	Avg	TD
1967 Den	13	130	381	2.9	1	7	11	1.6	0
1968 Den	11	158	584	3.7	3	19	331	17.4	1
1969 Den	9	146	729	5.0	6	19	218	11.5	1
1970 Den	14	209	901	4.3	3	17	161	9.5	0

1971 Den	14	**284**	**1133**	4.0	6	26	255	9.8	0
1972 Den	14	216	859	4.0	9	28	367	13.1	4
1973 Den	14	256	979	3.8	**12**	41	423	10.3	1
1974 Den	14	117	312	2.7	1	29	344	11.9	0
1975 Den	14	125	445	3.6	2	29	308	10.6	2
NFL Total	117	1641	6323	3.9	43	215	2418	11.2	9

	Punt Returns				Kickoff Returns					Tot
Year Team	Ret	Yds	Avg	TD	Ret	Yds	Avg	TD	Fum	TD
1967 Den	16	270	**16.9**	**1**	35	942	26.9	0	3	2
1968 Den	24	261	10.9	1	26	649	25.0	0	6	5
1969 Den	6	70	11.7	0	3	81	27.0	0	2	7
1970 Den	22	187	8.5	0	6	126	21.0	0	6	3
1971 Den	0	0	—	0	7	199	28.4	0	4	6
1972 Den	8	64	8.0	0	3	48	16.0	0	4	13
1973 Den	1	7	7.0	0	0	0	—	0	3	13
1974 Den	4	34	8.5	0	8	171	21.4	0	2	1
1975 Den	0	0	—	0	16	307	19.2	0	2	4
NFL Total	81	893	11.0	2	104	2523	24.3	0	32	54

GEORGE LITTLE Little, George Willard 6'4", 278 **DE-NT**
Col: Iowa *HS:* Duquesne [PA] B: 6/27/1963, Duquesne, PA
Drafted: 1985 Round 3 Mia
1985 Mia: 14 G; 1 Sac. **1986** Mia: 16 G; 4 Sac. **1987** Mia: 9 G. **Total:** 39 G; 5 Sac.

JACK LITTLE Little, Jack Harold 6'4", 235 **OT**
Col: Texas A&M *HS:* Corpus Christi [TX] B: 12/31/1931, Corpus Christi, TX *Drafted:* 1953 Round 5 Bal
1953 Bal: 9 G. **1954** Bal: 11 G. **Total:** 20 G.

JIM LITTLE Little, James W 6'1", 200 **T**
Col: Kentucky B: 3/18/1920
1945 NYG: 3 G.

JOHN LITTLE Little, John David Jr. 6'3", 250 **DT-DE-NT**
Col: Oklahoma State *HS:* Langston [Hot Springs, AR] B: 5/3/1947, Tallulah, LA D: 7/9/1997, Hot Coffee, MS *Drafted:* 1970 Round 14 NYJ
1970 NYJ: 14 G. **1971** NYJ: 14 G. **1972** NYJ: 14 G. **1973** NYJ: 14 G. **1974** NYJ: 14 G. **1975** Hou: 14 G. **1976** Hou: 14 G. **1977** Buf: 12 G. **Total:** 110 G.

LARRY LITTLE Little, Lawrence Chatmon 6'1", 265 **OG-OT**
Col: Bethune-Cookman *HS:* Booker T. Washington [Miami, FL] B: 11/2/1945, Groveland, GA *HOF:* 1993
1967 SD: 10 G. **1968** SD: 14 G. **1969** Mia: 12 G. **1970** Mia: 14 G. **1971** Mia: 14 G. **1972** Mia: 14 G. **1973** Mia: 13 G. **1974** Mia: 14 G. **1975** Mia: 14 G. **1976** Mia: 14 G. **1977** Mia: 14 G. **1978** Mia: 16 G. **1979** Mia: 15 G. **1980** Mia: 5 G. **Total:** 183 G.

LEONARD LITTLE Little, Leonard Antonio 6'3", 237 **LB**
Col: Coffeyville CC KS; Tennessee *HS:* Asheville [NC] B: 10/19/1974, Asheville, NC *Drafted:* 1998 Round 3 StL
1998 StL: 6 G; 0.5 Sac.

LOU LITTLE Little, Louis Lawrence 6'0", 205 **T**
Col: Vermont; Pennsylvania *HS:* Leominster [MA]; Worcester Acad. [MA] B: 12/6/1891, Boston, MA D: 5/28/1979, Delray Beach, FL
1920 Buf: 11 G. **1921** Buf: 6 G. **Total:** 17 G.

STEVE LITTLE Little, Steven Richard 6'0", 180 **P-K**
Col: Arkansas *HS:* Shawnee Mission South [KS] B: 2/19/1956, Springfield, IL *Drafted:* 1978 Round 1 StL
1978 StL: Rush 1-0. **1979** StL: Pass 3-2 66.7%, 31 10.33; Rush 2-0; Scor 54, 10-19 52.6% FG, 24-32 75.0% XK. **1980** StL: Scor 26, 3-8 37.5% FG, 17-19 89.5% XK. **Total:** Pass 3-2 66.7%, 31 10.33; Rush 3-0; Scor 80, 13-27 48.1% FG, 41-51 80.4% XK.

		Punting			
Year Team	G	Punts	Yds	Avg	Fum
1978 StL	11	46	1749	38.0	1
1979 StL	16	79	3060	38.7	0
1980 StL	6	0	0	—	0
NFL Total	33	125	4809	38.5	1

CARL LITTLEFIELD Littlefield, Carl Lester 6'0", 200 **DB-FB-TB**
(Moon Eyes) *Col:* Sacramento City Coll. CA (J.C.); Washington State *HS:* Sutter Creek [CA] B: 8/6/1916, Plymouth, CA D: 5/23/1988, Plymouth, CA
1938 Cle: Pass 15-1 6.7%, 23 1.53 5 Int; Rec 1-9 9.0; **1** Fum TD. **1939** Pit: Rec 1-18 18.0. **Total:** Pass 15-1 6.7%, 23 1.53 5 Int; Rec 2-27 13.5; 1 Fum TD.

		Rushing			
Year Team	G	Att	Yds	Avg	TD
1938 Cle	9	19	69	3.6	0
1939 Pit	10	39	141	3.6	0
1940 Pit	1	0	0	—	0
NFL Total	20	58	210	3.6	0

JOE LITTLE TWIG Little Twig, Joseph 5'11", 183 **E**
(AKA Joseph Johnson) *Col:* Carlisle D: 1937
1922 Oor: 2 G. **1923** Oor: 11 G; Scor **1** 1XP; 1 Pt. **1924** RI: 7 G; 1 Fum TD; 6 Pt. **1925** RI: 10 G; Rec 1 TD; 6 Pt. **1926** Can-Akr: 7 G. Can: 6 G. Akr: 1 G. **Total:** 37 G; Rec 1 TD; Scor 1 1XP; 1 Fum TD; Tot TD 2; 13 Pt.

MICKEY LIVERS Livers, Harold Irving 5'10", 175 **FB**
Col: Georgetown B: 11/30/1895 D: 9/1977, Hampton, VA
1921 Was: 1 G.

VIRGIL LIVERS Livers, Virgil Chester Jr. 5'8", 176 **DB**
Col: Western Kentucky *HS:* Nelson Co. [Bardstown, KY] B: 3/26/1952, Fairfield, KY *Drafted:* 1975 Round 4 ChiB

		Punt Returns				Kickoff Returns			
Year Team	G	Ret	Yds	Avg	TD	Ret	Yds	Avg	TD
1975 ChiB	14	42	456	10.9	0	26	529	20.3	0
1976 ChiB	14	28	205	7.3	0	1	14	14.0	0
1977 ChiB	14	6	46	7.7	0	0	0	—	0
1978 ChiB	13	10	31	3.1	0	0	0	—	0
1979 ChiB	13	0	0	—	0	0	0	—	0
NFL Total	68	86	738	8.6	0	27	543	20.1	0

	Interceptions			
Year Team	Int	Yds	TD	Fum
1975 ChiB	2	40	1	5
1976 ChiB	3	34	0	3
1977 ChiB	2	29	0	1
1978 ChiB	3	86	1	0
1979 ChiB	2	41	0	0
NFL Total	12	230	2	9

ANDY LIVINGSTON Livingston, Andrew Leon 6'1", 235 **RB**
Col: Phoenix Coll. AZ (J.C.) *HS:* Mesa [AZ] B: 10/21/1944, Eufaula, OK
1964 ChiB: KR 6-167 27.8 **1** TD. **1965** ChiB: KR 2-66 33.0. **1969** NO: Pass 4-3 75.0%, 38 9.50 1 TD 1 Int. **Total:** Pass 4-3 75.0%, 38 9.50 1 TD 1 Int; KR 8-233 29.1 1 TD.

		Rushing				Receiving					Tot
Year Team	G	Att	Yds	Avg	TD	Rec	Yds	Avg	TD	Fum	TD
1964 ChiB	2	2	-3	-1.5	0	1	0	0.0	0	1	1
1965 ChiB	14	63	363	5.8	2	12	134	11.2	0	2	2
1967 ChiB	12	28	41	1.5	0	5	62	12.4	0	3	0
1968 ChiB	4	7	25	3.6	0	0	0	—	0	1	0
1969 NO	14	181	761	4.2	5	28	278	9.9	3	2	8
1970 NO	1	10	29	2.9	0	0	0	—	0	0	0
NFL Total	47	291	1216	4.2	7	46	474	10.3	3	9	11

BRUCE LIVINGSTON Livingston, Bruce 5'10", 169 **DB**
Col: Arkansas Tech *HS:* Sarasota [FL] B: 8/7/1963
1987 Dal: 3 G; PR 1-0; 1 Fum.

CLIFF LIVINGSTON Livingston, Clifford Lyman 6'3", 218 **LB**
(Livy; Tongue) *Col:* Orange Coast Coll. CA (J.C.); UCLA *HS:* Montebello [CA] B: 7/2/1930, Compton, CA
1954 NYG: 12 G. **1955** NYG: 4 G; **1** Fum TD; 6 Pt. **1956** NYG: 12 G. **1957** NYG: 10 G. **1958** NYG: 12 G. **1959** NYG: 12 G; Int 2-25. **1960** NYG: 11 G; Int 1-0. **1961** NYG: 13 G; Int 3-0. **1962** Min: 12 G. **1963** LARm: 14 G; Int 1-13. **1964** LARm: 14 G. **1965** LARm: 10 G; Int 1-8. **Total:** 136 G; Int 8-46; 1 Fum TD; 6 Pt.

DALE LIVINGSTON Livingston, Dale Roger 6'0", 210 **K**
Col: Eastern Michigan; Western Michigan *HS:* Plymouth [MI] B: 3/12/1945, Plymouth, MI *Drafted:* 1968 Round 3 Cin
1968 Cin: Rush 1-11 11.0. **1969** Cin: Pass 2-2 100.0%, 15 7.50; Rush 1-18 18.0. **1970** GB: Rush 1-1 1.0. **Total:** Pass 2-2 100.0%, 15 7.50; Rush 3-30 10.0.

		Punting		
Year Team	G	Punts	Yds	Avg
1968 Cin	12	70	3036	43.4
1969 Cin	12	70	2769	39.6
1970 GB	14	6	199	33.2
NFL Total	38	146	6004	41.1

	Scoring						
Year Team	Pts	FG	FGA	FG%	XK	XKA	XK%
1968 Cin	59	13	26	50.0	20	20	100.0
1970 GB	64	15	28	53.6	19	21	90.5
NFL Total	123	28	54	51.9	39	41	95.1

HOWIE LIVINGSTON Livingston, Howard 6'1", 193 **DB-FB-WB-HB**
Col: Fullerton Coll. CA (J.C.) *HS:* Montebello [CA] B: 5/15/1922, Los Angeles, CA D: 7/16/1994, Yorba Linda, CA
1944 NYG: Pass 1-0, 1 Int; PR 4-44 11.0; KR 4-114 28.5; Punt 2-79 39.5. **1945** NYG: PR 13-106 8.2; KR 4-104 26.0; Punt 13-481 37.0. **1946** NYG: KR 1-30 30.0; **1** Fum TD. **1947** NYG: KR 9-203 22.6. **1950** Was-SF: PR 2-3 1.5. Was: PR 2-3 1.5. **Total:** Pass 1-0, 1 Int; PR 19-153 8.1; KR 18-451 25.1; Punt 15-560 37.3; 1 Fum TD.

Year Team	G	Rushing Att	Yds	Avg	TD	Receiving Rec	Yds	Avg	TD
1944 NYG	10	84	313	3.7	1	1	12	12.0	1
1945 NYG	10	40	109	2.7	3	14	250	17.9	2
1946 NYG	10	10	38	3.8	0	2	36	18.0	1
1947 NYG	10	19	87	4.6	0	12	273	22.8	3
1948 Was	7	0	0	—	0	0	0	—	0
1949 Was	12	1	1	1.0	1	3	41	13.7	0
1950 Was-SF	11	1	0	0.0	0	5	156	31.2	2
1950 Was	4	1	0	0.0	0	5	156	31.2	2
1950 SF	7	0	0	—	0	0	0	—	0
1953 ChiB	2	0	0	—	0	0	0	—	0
NFL Total	72	155	548	3.5	5	37	768	20.8	9

Year Team	Interceptions Int	Yds	TD	Fum	Tot TD
1944 NYG	**9**	**172**	1	0	3
1945 NYG	3	65	0	3	5
1946 NYG	4	69	0	4	3
1947 NYG	4	69	0	2	3
1949 Was	4	53	0	0	1
1950 Was-SF	5	126	1	0	3
1950 Was	1	27	0	0	2
1950 SF	4	99	1	0	1
NFL Total	29	554	2	9	18

MIKE LIVINGSTON Livingston, Michael Paul 6'4", 212 **QB**
Col: Southern Methodist *HS:* South Oak Cliff [Dallas, TX]
B: 11/14/1945, Dallas, TX *Drafted:* 1968 Round 2 KC
1975 KC: **1** Fum TD. **Total:** 1 Fum TD.

Year Team	G	Passing Att	Comp	Comp%	Yds	YPA	TD	Int	Rating
1968 KC	1	0	0	—	0	—	0	0	—
1969 KC	9	161	84	52.2	1123	6.98	4	**6**	67.4
1970 KC	4	22	11	50.0	122	5.55	0	1	47.9
1971 KC	3	28	12	42.9	130	4.64	0	0	57.1
1972 KC	5	78	41	52.6	480	6.15	7	8	61.9
1973 KC	8	145	75	51.7	916	6.32	6	7	65.2
1974 KC	8	141	66	46.8	732	5.19	4	10	42.6
1975 KC	7	176	88	50.0	1245	7.07	8	6	74.2
1976 KC	14	338	189	55.9	2682	7.93	12	13	77.6
1977 KC	13	282	143	50.7	1823	6.46	9	15	59.8
1978 KC	14	290	159	54.8	1573	5.42	5	13	57.4
1979 KC	5	90	44	48.9	469	5.21	1	4	49.7
NFL Total	91	1751	912	52.1	11295	6.45	56	83	63.3

Year Team	Rushing Att	Yds	Avg	TD	Fum	Tot TD
1968 KC	2	2	1.0	0	2	0
1969 KC	15	102	6.8	0	4	0
1970 KC	3	26	8.7	0	0	0
1971 KC	5	11	2.2	0	1	0
1972 KC	14	133	9.5	0	0	0
1973 KC	19	94	4.9	2	4	2
1974 KC	9	28	3.1	0	1	0
1975 KC	13	68	5.2	1	6	2
1976 KC	31	89	2.9	2	4	2
1977 KC	19	78	4.1	1	7	1
1978 KC	23	49	2.1	1	8	1
1979 KC	3	2	0.7	0	2	0
NFL Total	156	682	4.4	7	39	8

TED LIVINGSTON Livingston, Theodore Alfred 6'3", 219 **T-G**
Col: Kansas State; Indiana *HS:* Geneseo [KS] B: 2/18/1913, Ellsworth, KS D: 6/8/1984, Cleveland, OH
1937 Cle: 11 G. **1938** Cle: 10 G. **1939** Cle: 11 G. **1940** Cle: 9 G. **Total:** 41 G.

WALT LIVINGSTON Livingston, Walter 6'0", 185 **HB**
Col: Heidelberg *HS:* Ravenna [OH] B: 9/12/1934, Ravenna, OH
Drafted: 1957 Round 20 Bal
1960 Bos: 3 G; Rush 10-16 1.6 1 TD; Rec 1-0; KR 1-3 3.0; 6 Pt; 1 Fum.

WARREN LIVINGSTON Livingston, Warren 5'10", 192 **DB**
Col: Arizona *HS:* Mesa [AZ] B: 7/5/1938, Eufaula, OK
1961 Dal: PR 6-20 3.3. **1964** Dal: 1 Fum TD. **Total:** PR 6-20 3.3; 1 Fum TD.

Year Team	G	Interceptions Int	Yds	TD	Fum
1961 Dal	8	1	3	0	1
1962 Dal	3	0	0	0	0
1963 Dal	14	3	31	0	0
1964 Dal	14	1	27	0	0
1965 Dal	14	3	5	0	0
1966 Dal	14	2	13	0	0
NFL Total	67	10	79	0	1

BOB LIVINGSTONE Livingstone, Robert Edward 6'0", 173 **DB-HB**
Col: Notre Dame *HS:* Hammond [IN] B: 5/11/1922, Hammond, IN
Drafted: 1945 Round 20 ChiB
AAFC **1948** ChiA: Rec 15-240 16.0 2 TD; PR 3-24 8.0; KR 9-211 23.4. **1949** ChiA-BufA: Rec 3-80 26.7; PR 17-292 17.2 1 TD; KR 6-85 14.2; Int 1-6. **Total:** Rec 18-320 17.8 2 TD; PR 20-316 15.8 1 TD; KR 15-296 19.7; Int 1-6.

Year Team	G	Rushing Att	Yds	Avg	TD	Tot TD
1948 ChiA	13	55	174	3.2	0	2
1949 ChiA-BufA	11	1	0	0.0	0	1
AAFC Total	24	56	174	3.1	0	3

NFL **1950** Bal: 11 G; Rush 1-(-3) -3.0; PR 3-33 11.0; KR 1-11 11.0; Int 3-61; 1 Fum.

CHRIS LIWIENSKI Liwienski, Chris 6'5", 303 **OT**
Col: Indiana *HS:* Adlai Stevenson [Sterling Heights, MI] B: 8/2/1975, Sterling Heights, MI *Drafted:* 1998 Round 7 Det
1998 Min: 1 G.

DAN LLOYD Lloyd, Daniel B 6'2", 225 **LB**
Col: Washington *HS:* Hames Lick [San Jose, CA] B: 11/9/1953, Heber, UT *Drafted:* 1976 Round 6 NYG
1976 NYG: 14 G. **1977** NYG: 14 G. **1978** NYG: 16 G. **1979** NYG: 13 G; KR 1-0; Int 2-10. **Total:** 57 G; KR 1-0; Int 2-10.

DAVE LLOYD Lloyd, David Allen 6'3", 247 **LB-C**
Col: Texas Tech; Georgia *HS:* Staunton Mil. Acad. [VA]; Darlington School [Rome, GA] B: 11/9/1936, Sapulpa, OK *Drafted:* 1959 Round 4 Cle
1965 Phi: Scor 10, 1-2 50.0% FG, 7-7 100.0% XK. **Total:** Scor 10, 1-2 50.0% FG, 7-7 100.0% XK.

Year Team	G	Interceptions Int	Yds	TD
1959 Cle	12	0	0	0
1960 Cle	12	0	0	0
1961 Cle	14	0	0	0
1962 Det	14	0	0	0
1963 Phi	14	3	30	0
1964 Phi	11	3	68	0
1965 Phi	13	2	35	0
1966 Phi	14	3	46	0
1967 Phi	14	1	1	0
1968 Phi	13	0	0	0
1969 Phi	14	2	22	0
1970 Phi	12	0	0	0
NFL Total	157	14	202	0

DOUG LLOYD Lloyd, Douglas G 6'1", 220 **RB**
Col: North Dakota State *HS:* River Falls [WI] B: 8/31/1965, Beaver Dam, IL *Drafted:* 1989 Round 6 LARd
1991 LARd: 1 G.

GREG LLOYD Lloyd, Gregory Lenard 6'2", 228 **LB**
Col: Fort Valley State *HS:* Peach Co. [Fort Valley, GA] B: 5/26/1965, Miami, FL *Drafted:* 1987 Round 6 Pit
1988 Pit: 0.5 Sac. **1989** Pit: 7 Sac. **1990** Pit: 4.5 Sac. **1991** Pit: 8 Sac. **1992** Pit: 6.5 Sac. **1993** Pit: 6 Sac. **1994** Pit: 10 Sac. **1995** Pit: 6.5 Sac. **1996** Pit: 1 Sac. **1997** Pit: 3.5 Sac. **1998** Car: 1 Sac. **Total:** 54.5 Sac.

Year Team	G	Interceptions Int	Yds	TD	Fum
1988 Pit	9	0	0	0	0
1989 Pit	16	3	49	0	1
1990 Pit	15	1	9	0	0
1991 Pit	16	1	0	0	1
1992 Pit	16	1	35	0	1
1993 Pit	15	0	0	0	0
1994 Pit	15	1	8	0	0
1995 Pit	16	3	85	0	0
1996 Pit	1	0	0	0	0
1997 Pit	12	0	0	0	1
1998 Car	16	1	3	0	0
NFL Total	147	11	189	0	4

JEFF LLOYD Lloyd, Jeffery John 6'6", 255 **DE-NT**
Col: West Texas A&M *HS:* Cameron Co. [Emporium, PA] B: 3/14/1954, St. Mary's, PA *Drafted:* 1976 Round 3 Sea
1976 Buf: 9 G. **1978** KC: 16 G. **Total:** 25 G.

BILL LOBENSTEIN Lobenstein, William Joseph 6'3", 261 **DE**
Col: Coll. of DuPage IL (J.C.); Wisconsin; Wis.-Whitewater *HS:* Deerfield [WI] B: 5/11/1961, Mauston, WI
1987 Den: 3 G.

GREG LOBERG Loberg, Gregory Scott 6′4″, 264 **OG-OT**
Col: California *HS:* Terra Linda [San Rafael, CA] B: 12/7/1961, San Rafael, CA
1987 NO: 3 G.

CHARLES LOCKETT Lockett, Charles Edward 6′0″, 178 **WR**
Col: Long Beach State *HS:* Crenshaw [Los Angeles, CA] B: 10/1/1965, Los Angeles, CA *Drafted:* 1987 Round 3 Pit
1987 Pit: PR 2-3 1.5. **Total:** PR 2-3 1.5.

		Receiving				
Year Team	**G**	**Rec**	**Yds**	**Avg**	**TD**	**Fum**
1987 Pit	11	7	116	16.6	1	1
1988 Pit	16	22	365	16.6	1	0
NFL Total	27	29	481	16.6	2	1

DANNY LOCKETT Lockett, Danny Key 6′2″, 239 **LB**
Col: Coll. of the Sequoias CA (J.C.); Arizona *HS:* Peach Co. [Fort Valley, GA] B: 7/11/1964, Fort Valley, GA *Drafted:* 1987 Round 6 Det
1987 Det: 13 G; 1 Sac. **1988** Det: 16 G; 1 Sac. **Total:** 29 G; 2 Sac.

FRANK LOCKETT Lockett, Frank Arthur 6′0″, 200 **WR**
Col: Contra Costa Coll. CA (J.C.); Nebraska *HS:* De Anza [Richmond, CA] B: 6/1/1957, Independance, LA *Drafted:* 1979 Round 10 GB
1985 Mia: 3 G; PR 5-23 4.6.

J.W. LOCKETT Lockett, J.W. 6′2″, 226 **FB**
Col: Central Oklahoma *HS:* Booker T. Washington [Tulsa, OK]
B: 3/23/1937, Bardwell, TX
1961 SF-Dal: Pass 2-0; KR 5-61 12.2. SF: KR 1-15 15.0. Dal: Pass 2-0; KR 4-46 11.5. **1962** Dal: Pass 1-0; PR 8-45 5.6; KR 6-130 21.7. **1963** Bal: KR 3-52 17.3. **1964** Was: KR 3-72 24.0. **Total:** Pass 3-0; PR 8-45 5.6; KR 17-315 18.5.

		Rushing				Receiving					Tot
Year Team	**G**	**Att**	**Yds**	**Avg**	**TD**	**Rec**	**Yds**	**Avg**	**TD**	**Fum**	**TD**
1961 SF-Dal	14	77	298	3.9	1	19	149	7.8	2	8	3
1961 SF	2	11	18	1.6	1	4	35	8.8	0	1	1
1961 Dal	12	66	280	4.2	0	15	114	7.6	2	7	2
1962 Dal	14	8	24	3.0	1	7	78	11.1	2	4	3
1963 Bal	12	81	273	3.4	0	16	158	9.9	1	2	1
1964 Was	14	63	175	2.8	1	20	204	10.2	2	1	3
NFL Total	54	229	770	3.4	3	62	589	9.5	7	15	10

KEVIN LOCKETT Lockett, Kevin 6′0″, 188 **WR**
Col: Kansas State *HS:* Booker T. Washington [Tulsa, OK] B: 9/8/1974, Tulsa, OK *Drafted:* 1997 Round 2 KC
1997 KC: 9 G; Rec 1-35 35.0. **1998** KC: 13 G; Rec 19-281 14.8; PR 7-36 5.1; 2 Fum. **Total:** 22 G; Rec 20-316 15.8; PR 7-36 5.1; 2 Fum.

WADE LOCKETT Lockett, Milton Wade 6′1″, 190 **WR**
Col: Cal State-Fullerton *HS:* Sweetwater [National City, CA]
B: 2/13/1964, AL
1987 LARd: 2 G.

CARL LOCKHART Lockhart, Carl Ford 6′2″, 175 **DB**
(Spider) *Col:* North Texas *HS:* Hamilton Park [Dallas, TX]
B: 4/6/1943, Dallas, TX D: 7/8/1986, Hackensack, NJ *Drafted:* 1965 Round 13 NYG
1965 NYG: Punt 6-267 44.5. **1966** NYG: Punt 4-131 32.8. **1968** NYG: Punt 3-110 36.7. **1969** NYG: KR 1-19 19.0. **Total:** KR 1-19 19.0; Punt 13-508 39.1.

		Punt Returns				Interceptions			
Year Team	**G**	**Ret**	**Yds**	**Avg**	**TD**	**Int**	**Yds**	**TD**	**Fum**
1965 NYG	14	2	-6	-3.0	0	4	117	0	0
1966 NYG	14	17	113	6.6	0	6	20	0	1
1967 NYG	12	7	54	7.7	0	5	38	0	2
1968 NYG	14	13	69	5.3	0	8	130	**2**	2
1969 NYG	11	10	29	2.9	0	2	0	0	2
1970 NYG	14	9	31	3.4	0	4	51	0	1
1971 NYG	13	4	24	6.0	0	3	60	0	1
1972 NYG	13	0	0	—	0	4	56	1	0
1973 NYG	14	0	0	—	0	2	3	0	0
1974 NYG	14	0	0	—	0	2	0	0	0
1975 NYG	12	2	14	7.0	0	1	0	0	0
NFL Total	145	64	328	5.1	0	41	475	3	9

EUGENE LOCKHART Lockhart, Eugene Jr. 6′2″, 234 **LB**
Col: Houston *HS:* David Crockett [Austin, TX] B: 3/8/1961, Crockett, TX *Drafted:* 1984 Round 6 Dal
1984 Dal: 15 G; Int 1-32; 2.5 Sac. **1985** Dal: 16 G; Int 1-19 **1** TD; 6 Pt; 3.5 Sac. **1986** Dal: 16 G; Int 1-5; 5 Sac. **1987** Dal: 9 G; Int 1-13; 2 Sac. **1988** Dal: 16 G. **1989** Dal: 16 G; Int 2-14; 1 Fum TD; 6 Pt; 2 Sac. **1990** Dal: 16 G; 1 Sac. **1991** NE: 16 G. **1992** NE: 16 G. **Total:** 136 G; Int 6-83 1 TD; 1 Fum TD; Tot TD 2; 12 Pt; 16 Sac.

BILLY LOCKLIN Locklin, Billy Ray 6′2″, 225 **LB**
Col: New Mexico State *HS:* Rockdale [TX] B: 8/13/1937, Rockdale, TX *Drafted:* 1960 Round 1 LAC
1960 Oak: 2 G.

KERRY LOCKLIN Locklin, Kerry Barth 6′3″, 230 **TE**
Col: New Mexico State *HS:* Rockdale [TX] B: 9/9/1959, Las Cruces, NM *Drafted:* 1982 Round 6 LARm
1982 LARm: 6 G. **1987** Den: 3 G. **Total:** 9 G.

SCOTT LOCKWOOD Lockwood, Scott Nelson 5′10″, 196 **RB**
Col: USC *HS:* Fairview [Boulder, CO] B: 3/23/1968, Los Angeles, CA *Drafted:* 1992 Round 8 NE
1992 NE: KR 11-233 21.2. **Total:** KR 11-233 21.2.

		Rushing				
Year Team	**G**	**Att**	**Yds**	**Avg**	**TD**	**Fum**
1992 NE	4	35	162	4.6	0	1
1993 NE	2	0	0	—	0	0
NFL Total	6	35	162	4.6	0	1

MIKE LODISH Lodish, Michael Timothy 6′3″, 275 **NT-DE**
Col: UCLA *HS:* Brother Rice [Birmingham, MI] B: 8/11/1967, Detroit, MI *Drafted:* 1990 Round 10 Buf
1990 Buf: 12 G; 2 Sac. **1991** Buf: 16 G; 1.5 Sac. **1992** Buf: 16 G; 1 Fum TD; 6 Pt. **1993** Buf: 15 G; 0.5 Sac. **1994** Buf: 15 G; 1 Fum TD; 6 Pt. **1995** Den: 16 G. **1996** Den: 16 G; 1.5 Sac. **1997** Den: 16 G; 1 Sac. **1998** Den: 15 G; 2 Sac. **Total:** 137 G; 2 Fum TD; 12 Pt; 8.5 Sac.

DICK LOEPFE Loepfe, Richard 6′2″, 230 **T**
Col: Wisconsin *HS:* East Division [Milwaukee, WI] B: 1/1/1922, Milwaukee, WI *Drafted:* 1946 Round 11 ChiC
1948 ChiC: 7 G. **1949** ChiC: 6 G. **Total:** 13 G.

CHUCK LOEWEN Loewen, Charles Duane 6′3″, 263 **OT-OG**
Col: South Dakota State *HS:* Mountain Lake [MN] B: 1/23/1957, Mountain Lake, MN *Drafted:* 1980 Round 7 SD
1980 SD: 16 G. **1981** SD: 9 G. **1982** SD: 9 G. **1984** SD: 13 G. **Total:** 47 G.

JAMES LOFTON Lofton, James David 6′3″, 192 **WR**
Col: Stanford *HS:* George Washington [Los Angeles, CA] B: 7/5/1956, Fort Ord, CA *Drafted:* 1978 Round 1 GB
1978 GB: Pass 2-0; KR 1-0. **1979** GB: Pass 1-0. **1982** GB: Pass 1-1 100.0%, 43 43.00. **1986** GB: Pass 1-0. **Total:** Pass 5-1 20.0%, 43 8.60; KR 1-0.

		Rushing				Receiving					Tot
Year Team	**G**	**Att**	**Yds**	**Avg**	**TD**	**Rec**	**Yds**	**Avg**	**TD**	**Fum**	**TD**
1978 GB	16	3	13	4.3	0	46	818	17.8	6	2	6
1979 GB	16	1	-1	-1.0	0	54	968	17.9	4	5	4
1980 GB	16	0	0	—	0	71	1226	17.3	4	0	4
1981 GB	16	0	0	—	0	71	1294	18.2	8	0	8
1982 GB	9	4	101	25.3	1	35	696	19.9	4	0	5
1983 GB	16	9	36	4.0	0	58	1300	**22.4**	8	0	8
1984 GB	16	10	82	8.2	0	62	1361	**22.0**	7	1	7
1985 GB	16	4	14	3.5	0	69	1153	16.7	4	3	4
1986 GB	15	0	0	—	0	64	840	13.1	4	3	4
1987 LARd	12	1	1	1.0	0	41	880	21.5	5	0	5
1988 LARd	16	0	0	—	0	28	549	19.6	0	0	0
1989 Buf	12	0	0	—	0	8	166	20.8	3	0	3
1990 Buf	16	0	0	—	0	35	712	20.3	4	0	4
1991 Buf	15	0	0	—	0	57	1072	18.8	8	2	8
1992 Buf	16	0	0	—	0	51	786	15.4	6	0	6
1993 LARm-Phi	10	0	0	—	0	14	183	13.1	0	0	0
1993 LARm	1	0	0	—	0	1	16	16.0	0	0	0
1993 Phi	9	0	0	—	0	13	167	12.8	0	0	0
NFL Total	233	32	246	7.7	1	764	14004	18.3	75	16	76

OSCAR LOFTON Lofton, Oscar W 6′6″, 218 **OE**
Col: Southeastern Louisiana *HS:* Istrouma [Baton Rouge, LA]
B: 4/2/1938, McCall Creek, MS
1960 Bos: 14 G; Rec 19-360 18.9 4 TD; 24 Pt.

STEVE LOFTON Lofton, Steven Lynn 5′9″, 180 **DB**
Col: Texas A&M *HS:* Alto [TX] B: 11/26/1968, Jacksonville, TX
1991 Pho: 11 G. **1992** Pho: 4 G. **1993** Pho: 13 G; KR 1-18 18.0. **1995** Car: 10 G. **1996** Car: 11 G; Int 1-42. **1997** NE: 4 G. **1998** NE-Car: 16 G. NE: 6 G. Car: 10 G. **Total:** 69 G; KR 1-18 18.0; Int 1-42.

ANDY LOGAN Logan, Andrew L 6′0″, 222 **T**
Col: Case Western Reserve B: 2/17/1918, Connorville, OH
1941 Det: 9 G.

CHUCK LOGAN Logan, Charles Russell 6′4″, 210 **TE**
Col: Northwestern *HS:* Albert G. Lane Tech [Chicago, IL]
B: 4/10/1943, Chicago, IL *Drafted:* 1964 Round 7 ChiB
1964 Pit: 14 G; Rec 1-7 7.0. **1965** StL: 4 G. **1967** StL: 14 G. **1968** StL: 14 G. **Total:** 46 G; Rec 1-7 7.0.

DAVID LOGAN Logan, David 6′2″, 250 **NT-DE**
Col: Pittsburgh *HS:* Peabody [Pittsburgh, PA] B: 10/25/1956, Pittsburgh, PA D: 1/12/1998, Tampa, FL *Drafted:* 1979 Round 12 TB
1979 TB: 5 G. **1980** TB: 16 G; **1** Fum TD; 6 Pt. **1981** TB: 16 G; 1 Fum TD; 6 Pt. **1982** TB: 9 G; 4.8 Sac. **1983** TB: 16 G; 1 Fum TD; 6 Pt; 9.5 Sac. **1984** TB: 16 G; Int 1-27 1 TD; 6 Pt; 5.5 Sac. **1985** TB: 16 G; 6.5 Sac.

1986 TB: 16 G; 2 Sac. **1987** GB: 2 G. **Total:** 112 G; Int 1-27 1 TD; 3 Fum TD; Tot TD 4; 24 Pt; 28.3 Sac.

DAVE LOGAN Logan, David Russell 6'4", 219 **WR-DB**
Col: Colorado *HS:* Wheat Ridge [CO] B: 2/2/1954, Fargo, ND
Drafted: 1976 Round 3 Cle
1977 Cle: Pass 2-0. **1981** Cle: Int 1-0. **Total:** Pass 2-0; Int 1-0.

		Receiving				
Year Team	G	Rec	Yds	Avg	TD	Fum
1976 Cle	14	5	104	20.8	0	0
1977 Cle	14	19	284	14.9	1	0
1978 Cle	16	37	585	15.8	4	0
1979 Cle	16	59	982	16.6	7	1
1980 Cle	16	51	822	16.1	4	0
1981 Cle	14	31	497	16.0	4	0
1982 Cle	9	23	346	15.0	2	0
1983 Cle	16	37	627	16.9	2	1
1984 Den	4	1	3	3.0	0	0
NFL Total	119	263	4250	16.2	24	2

ERNIE LOGAN Logan, Ernest Edward II 6'3", 283 **DE-DT**
Col: East Carolina *HS:* Pine Forest [Fayetteville, NC] B: 5/18/1968, Fort Bragg, NC *Drafted:* 1991 Round 9 Atl
1991 Cle: 15 G; 0.5 Sac. **1992** Cle: 16 G; 1 Sac. **1993** Atl: 8 G; 1 Sac. **1995** Jac: 15 G; 3 Sac. **1996** Jac: 4 G. **1997** NYJ: 15 G. **1998** NYJ: 16 G; 2.5 Sac. **Total:** 89 G; 8 Sac.

JAMES LOGAN Logan, James Eddie 6'2", 222 **LB**
Col: Jones Co. JC MS; Memphis *HS:* Opp [AL] B: 12/6/1972, Opp, AL
1995 Hou-Cin-Sea: 10 G. Hou: 3 G. Cin: 1 G. Sea: 6 G. **1996** Sea: 6 G. **1997** Sea: 14 G. **1998** Sea: 4 G; 1 Sac. **Total:** 34 G; 1 Sac.

JIM LOGAN Logan, James Zimmerman 5'11", 190 **G**
Col: Indiana *HS:* Morton [Richmond, IN] B: 12/22/1916, Richmond, IN
1943 ChiB: 9 G; KR 1-2 2.0.

JERRY LOGAN Logan, Jerry Don 6'1", 185 **DB**
Col: West Texas A&M *HS:* Graham [TX] B: 8/27/1941, Graham, TX
Drafted: 1963 Round 4 Bal
1963 Bal: KR 8-170 21.3; Punt 4-121 30.3. **1967** Bal: KR 2-17 8.5. **1968** Bal: KR 1-14 14.0. **1971** Bal: KR 1-16 16.0. **Total:** KR 12-217 18.1; Punt 4-121 30.3.

		Punt Returns				Interceptions				Tot
Year Team	G	Ret	Yds	Avg	TD	Int	Yds	TD	Fum	TD
1963 Bal	14	28	279	10.0	0	1	15	0	2	0
1964 Bal	14	13	111	8.5	0	6	91	1	2	1
1965 Bal	14	0	0	—	0	2	74	2	0	2
1966 Bal	14	1	3	3.0	0	3	13	0	0	0
1967 Bal	14	5	80	16.0	**1**	4	22	0	1	1
1968 Bal	14	1	27	27.0	0	3	9	0	0	0
1969 Bal	14	8	41	5.1	0	1	6	0	1	0
1970 Bal	14	2	4	2.0	0	6	92	**2**	0	2
1971 Bal	14	1	12	12.0	0	4	28	0	0	0
1972 Bal	14	4	20	5.0	0	4	47	0	2	0
NFL Total	140	63	577	9.2	1	34	397	5	8	6

MARC LOGAN Logan, Marc Anthony 6'0", 217 **RB**
Col: Kentucky *HS:* Bryan Station [Lexington, KY] B: 5/9/1965, Lexington, KY *Drafted:* 1987 Round 5 Cin

		Rushing				Receiving			
Year Team	G	Att	Yds	Avg	TD	Rec	Yds	Avg	TD
1987 Cin	3	37	203	5.5	1	3	14	4.7	0
1988 Cin	9	2	10	5.0	0	2	20	10.0	0
1989 Mia	10	57	201	3.5	0	5	34	6.8	0
1990 Mia	16	79	317	4.0	2	7	54	7.7	0
1991 Mia	16	4	5	1.3	0	0	0	—	0
1992 SF	16	8	44	5.5	1	2	17	8.5	0
1993 SF	14	58	280	4.8	7	37	348	9.4	0
1994 SF	10	33	143	4.3	1	16	97	6.1	1
1995 Was	16	23	72	3.1	1	25	276	11.0	2
1996 Was	14	20	111	5.6	2	23	269	11.7	0
1997 Was	15	4	5	1.3	0	3	6	2.0	0
NFL Total	139	325	1391	4.3	15	123	1135	9.2	3

	Kickoff Returns					Tot
Year Team	Ret	Yds	Avg	TD	Fum	TD
1987 Cin	3	31	10.3	0	0	1
1988 Cin	4	80	20.0	0	1	0
1989 Mia	24	613	25.5	**1**	1	2
1990 Mia	20	367	18.4	0	4	2
1991 Mia	12	191	15.9	0	1	0
1992 SF	22	478	21.7	0	0	1
1993 SF	0	0	—	0	2	7
1994 SF	0	0	—	0	0	2
1995 Was	0	0	—	0	1	3
1996 Was	0	0	—	0	1	2
1997 Was	4	70	17.5	0	1	0
NFL Total	89	1830	20.6	1	12	20

MIKE LOGAN Logan, Michael Victor 6'0", 207 **DB**
Col: West Virginia *HS:* McKeesport [PA] B: 9/15/1974, Pittsburgh, PA
Drafted: 1997 Round 2 Jac
1998 Jac: PR 2-26 13.0. **Total:** PR 2-26 13.0.

		Kickoff Returns				
Year Team	G	Ret	Yds	Avg	TD	Fum
1997 Jac	11	10	236	23.6	0	0
1998 Jac	15	18	414	23.0	0	1
NFL Total	26	28	650	23.2	0	1

OBERT LOGAN Logan, Obert Clark 5'10", 182 **DB**
Col: Trinity (Tex.) *HS:* Gonzales [TX] B: 12/6/1941, Yoakum, TX
1965 Dal: 14 G; Int 3-5; 6 Pt. **1966** Dal: 14 G; Int 2-44. **1967** NO: 13 G; KR 1-0; Int 3-21. **Total:** 41 G; KR 1-0; Int 8-70; 6 Pt.

RANDY LOGAN Logan, Randolph 6'1", 195 **DB**
Col: Michigan *HS:* Northern [Detroit, MI] B: 5/1/1951, Detroit, MI
Drafted: 1973 Round 3 Phi
1983 Phi: PR 1-0. **Total:** PR 1-0.

		Interceptions			
Year Team	G	Int	Yds	TD	Fum
1973 Phi	14	5	38	0	0
1974 Phi	14	2	2	0	0
1975 Phi	14	1	4	0	0
1976 Phi	14	1	38	0	0
1977 Phi	14	5	124	0	0
1978 Phi	16	2	15	0	0
1979 Phi	16	3	57	0	0
1980 Phi	16	1	16	0	0
1981 Phi	16	2	-1	0	0
1982 Phi	9	0	0	0	0
1983 Phi	16	1	0	0	1
NFL Total	159	23	293	0	1

DICK LOGAN Logan, Richard L 6'2", 228 **OG-DT**
Col: Ohio State *HS:* Mansfield [OH] B: 5/4/1930, Mansfield, OH
Drafted: 1952 Round 11 Cle
1952 GB: 7 G. **1953** GB: 12 G. **Total:** 19 G.

BOB LOGEL Logel, Robert James 6'3", 210 **DE**
Col: Sampson CC NC *HS:* East Aurora [NY] B: 7/29/1928, East Aurora, NY
AAFC **1949** BufA: 1 G.

JOHN LOHMEYER Lohmeyer, John Carl 6'4", 229 **DE-DT**
Col: Emporia State *HS:* Emporia [KS] B: 1/15/1951, Emporia, KS
Drafted: 1973 Round 4 KC
1973 KC: 7 G; **1** Fum TD; 6 Pt. **1975** KC: 7 G. **1976** KC: 13 G; Scor **1** Saf; 2 Pt. **1977** KC: 14 G. **Total:** 41 G; Scor 1 Saf; 1 Fum TD; 8 Pt.

CHIP LOHMILLER Lohmiller, John McLeod 6'3", 215 **K**
Col: Minnesota *HS:* Woodbury [MN] B: 7/16/1966, Woodbury, MN
Drafted: 1988 Round 2 Was
1988 Was: Punt 6-208 34.7. **Total:** Punt 6-208 34.7.

		Scoring						
Year Team	G	Pts	FG	FGA	FG%	XK	XKA	XK%
1988 Was	16	97	19	26	73.1	40	41	97.6
1989 Was	16	128	29	**40**	72.5	41	41	100.0
1990 Was	16	131	30	**40**	75.0	41	41	100.0
1991 Was	16	**149**	**31**	**43**	72.1	**56**	56	100.0
1992 Was	16	120	**30**	**40**	75.0	30	30	100.0
1993 Was	16	72	16	28	57.1	24	26	92.3
1994 Was	16	90	20	28	71.4	30	32	93.8
1995 NO	8	35	8	14	57.1	11	13	84.6
1996 StL	15	91	21	25	84.0	28	29	96.6
NFL Total	135	913	204	284	71.8	301	309	97.4

JOE LOKANC Lokanc, Joseph Andrew 5'11", 205 **G-LB**
Col: Northwestern *HS:* Theodore Roosevelt [East Chicago, IL] B: 3/11/1917, East Chicago, IN *Drafted:* 1941 Round 14 ChiC
1941 ChiC: 9 G; Rec 1-2 2.0.

SLICK LOLLAR Lollar, John Hope 5'11", 200 **FB**
Col: Samford *HS:* Walker [Jasper, AL] B: 1906
1928 GB: 3 G.

AL LOLOTAI Lolotai, Albert 6'0", 224 **G-T**
Col: Weber State *HS:* Iolani [Honolulu, HI] B: 6/22/1920, Western Samoa D: 9/30/1990, Pago Pago, American Samoa
AAFC **1946** LA-A: 14 G. **1947** LA-A: 13 G. **1948** LA-A: 14 G. **1949** LA-A: 8 G. **Total:** 49 G.

NFL **1945** Was: 10 G; KR 1-15 15.0; Int 1-0.

TONY LOMACK Lomack, Thomas Jerome 5'8", 180 **WR**
Col: Florida *HS:* Leon [Tallahassee, FL] B: 4/27/1968, Tallahassee, FL
Drafted: 1990 Round 9 LARm
1990 LARm: 3 G. **1991** Pho: 1 G; KR 1-19 19.0. **Total:** 4 G; KR 1-19 19.0.

JOHN LOMAKOSKI Lomakoski, John A 6′4″, 250 **OT**
Col: Western Michigan *HS:* Romeo [MI] B: 11/11/1940, Washington, MI D: 2/16/1999, Munising, MI *Drafted:* 1962 Round 4 Det
1962 Det: 3 G.

MARK LOMAS Lomas, Mark Arnold 6′4″, 250 **DE-DT**
Col: Golden West Coll. CA (J.C.); Northern Arizona *HS:* Garden Grove [CA] B: 6/8/1948, Los Angeles, CA *Drafted:* 1970 Round 8 NYJ
1970 NYJ: 14 G. **1971** NYJ: 14 G. **1972** NYJ: 14 G. **1973** NYJ: 14 G. **1974** NYJ: 11 G. **Total:** 67 G.

TOM LOMASNEY Lomasney, Thomas Martin 6′0″, 180 **E-BB**
(Lope) *Col:* Villanova *HS:* Salem [MA] B: 5/11/1906, Salem, MA D: 12/29/1976, Salem, MA
1929 SI: 4 G.

NEIL LOMAX Lomax, Neil Vincent 6′3″, 215 **QB**
Col: Portland State *HS:* Lake Oswego [OR] B: 2/17/1959, Portland, OR *Drafted:* 1981 Round 2 StL
1982 StL: Rec 1-10 10.0. **Total:** Rec 1-10 10.0.

		Passing							
Year Team	G	Att	Comp	Comp%	Yds	YPA	TD	Int	Rating
1981 StL	14	236	119	50.4	1575	6.67	4	10	59.9
1982 StL	9	205	109	53.2	1367	6.67	5	6	70.1
1983 StL	13	354	209	59.0	2636	7.45	24	11	92.0
1984 StL	16	560	345	61.6	4614	8.24	28	16	92.5
1985 StL	16	471	265	56.3	3214	6.82	18	12	79.5
1986 StL	14	421	240	57.0	2583	6.14	13	12	73.6
1987 StL	12	**463**	**275**	59.4	**3387**	7.32	24	12	88.5
1988 Pho	14	443	255	57.6	3395	7.66	20	11	86.7
NFL Total	108	3153	1817	57.6	22771	7.22	136	90	82.7

	Rushing				
Year Team	Att	Yds	Avg	TD	Fum
1981 StL	19	104	5.5	2	6
1982 StL	28	119	4.3	1	8
1983 StL	27	127	4.7	2	9
1984 StL	35	184	5.3	3	11
1985 StL	32	125	3.9	0	10
1986 StL	35	148	4.2	1	7
1987 StL	29	107	3.7	0	7
1988 Pho	17	55	3.2	1	5
NFL Total	222	969	4.4	10	63

ANTONIO LONDON London, Antonio Monte 6′2″, 238 **LB**
Col: Alabama *HS:* Tullahoma [TN] B: 4/14/1971, Tullahoma, TN *Drafted:* 1993 Round 3 Det
1993 Det: 14 G; 1 Sac. **1994** Det: 16 G. **1995** Det: 15 G; 7 Sac. **1996** Det: 14 G; 3 Sac. **1997** Det: 16 G; 2 Sac. **1998** GB: 1 G. **Total:** 76 G; 13 Sac.

MIKE LONDON London, Michael David 6′2″, 230 **LB**
Col: Wisconsin *HS:* Central [Madison, WI] B: 12/31/1944, Madison, WI *Drafted:* 1966 Round 14 SD
1966 SD: 3 G.

TOM LONDON London, Tommy 6′1″, 197 **DB**
Col: North Carolina State *HS:* Shelby [NC] B: 6/15/1954, Shelby, NC
1978 Cle: 15 G.

KEITH LONEKER Loneker, Keith Joseph 6′3″, 330 **OG**
Col: Kansas *HS:* Roselle Park [NJ] B: 6/21/1971, Roselle Park, NJ
1993 LARm: 4 G. **1994** LARm: 2 G. **1995** StL: 13 G. **Total:** 19 G.

FRANK LONE STAR Lone Star, Frank 5′11″, 200 **G-T**
Col: Carlisle *HS:* Carlisle Indian School [PA] B: 1891 Deceased
1920 Col: 3 G.

TED LONE WOLF Lone Wolf, Ted 6′2″, 207 **G-T-WB**
Col: No College Deceased
1922 Oor: 5 G. **1923** Oor: 4 G. **Total:** 9 G.

BUFORD LONG Long, Buford Eugene 6′1″, 195 **HB-DB-OE**
Col: Florida *HS:* Lake Wales [FL] B: 12/14/1931, Lake Wales, FL *Drafted:* 1953 Round 5 NYG
1953 NYG: KR 7-198 28.3; Int 3-59; Scor **1** Saf. **1954** NYG: PR 6-54 9.0; KR 10-237 23.7. **1955** NYG: KR 6-172 28.7. **Total:** PR 6-54 9.0; KR 23-607 26.4; Int 3-59; Scor 1 Saf.

		Rushing				Receiving					Tot
Year Team	G	Att	Yds	Avg	TD	Rec	Yds	Avg	TD	Fum	TD
1953 NYG	10	20	58	2.9	0	14	220	15.7	2	0	2
1954 NYG	12	32	106	3.3	1	13	178	13.7	1	2	2
1955 NYG	4	0	0	—	0	6	64	10.7	1	0	1
NFL Total	26	52	164	3.2	1	33	462	14.0	4	2	5

CARSON LONG Long, Carson Gerald 5′10″, 210 **K**
Col: Pittsburgh *HS:* North Schuylkill [Ashland, PA] B: 12/16/1954, Pottsville, PA *Drafted:* 1977 Round 11 LARm
1977 Buf: 9 G; Scor 34, 7-11 63.6% FG, 13-14 92.9% XK.

CHARLEY LONG Long, Charles B 6′4″, 260 **OT-OG**
(Choo-Choo) *Col:* Tennessee-Chattanooga *HS:* Fyffe [AL] B: 4/6/1938, DeKalb, AL D: 12/16/1989, Framingham, MA *Drafted:* 1961 Round 8 Bos
1961 Bos: 14 G; KR 4-24 6.0. **1962** Bos: 14 G. **1963** Bos: 14 G. **1964** Bos: 14 G. **1965** Bos: 14 G. **1966** Bos: 14 G. **1967** Bos: 14 G. **1968** Bos: 13 G; KR 2-20 10.0. **1969** Bos: 13 G. **Total:** 124 G; KR 6-44 7.3.

CHUCK LONG Long, Charles Franklin II 6′4″, 217 **QB**
Col: Iowa *HS:* North [Wheaton, IL] B: 2/18/1963, Norman, OK *Drafted:* 1986 Round 1 Det
1991 Det: Postseason only.

		Passing							
Year Team	G	Att	Comp	Comp%	Yds	YPA	TD	Int	Rating
1986 Det	3	40	21	52.5	247	6.18	2	2	67.4
1987 Det	12	416	232	55.8	2598	6.25	11	20	63.4
1988 Det	7	141	75	53.2	856	6.07	6	6	68.2
1989 Det	1	5	2	40.0	42	8.40	0	0	70.4
1990 LARm	4	5	1	20.0	4	0.80	0	0	39.6
NFL Total	27	607	331	54.5	3747	6.17	19	28	64.5

	Rushing				
Year Team	Att	Yds	Avg	TD	Fum
1986 Det	2	0	0.0	0	1
1987 Det	22	64	2.9	0	8
1988 Det	7	22	3.1	0	4
1989 Det	3	2	0.7	0	0
NFL Total	34	88	2.6	0	13

DARREN LONG Long, Darren Murrell 6′3″, 240 **TE**
Col: Coll. of the Sequoias CA (J.C.); Long Beach State *HS:* Exeter [CA] B: 7/12/1959, Exeter, CA
1986 LARm: 4 G; Rec 5-47 9.4.

DAVE LONG Long, David Frank 6′4″, 245 **DE-DT**
Col: Iowa *HS:* Thomas Jefferson [Cedar Rapids, IA] B: 9/6/1944, Jefferson, IA *Drafted:* 1966 Round 3 StL
1966 StL: 14 G; KR 1-9 9.0. **1967** StL: 14 G. **1968** StL: 14 G; KR 1-0; 1 Fum. **1969** NO: 14 G. **1970** NO: 12 G. **1971** NO: 14 G. **1972** NO: 14 G. **Total:** 96 G; KR 2-9 4.5; 1 Fum.

DOUG LONG Long, Douglas 6′0″, 189 **DB**
Col: Whitworth *HS:* Shelton [WA] B: 5/24/1955, Spokane, WA
1977 Sea: 1 G. **1978** Sea: 15 G; KR 4-35 8.8. **Total:** 16 G; KR 4-35 8.8.

HARVEY LONG Long, Harvey John 6′0″, 198 **T-G**
Col: Detroit Mercy *HS:* Sheboygan [WI] B: 1906, WI Deceased
1929 ChiB: 4 G. **1930** Fra: 1 G. **Total:** 5 G.

HOWIE LONG Long, Howard Michael 6′5″, 268 **DE-NT**
Col: Villanova *HS:* Milford [MA] B: 1/6/1960, Somerville, MA *Drafted:* 1981 Round 2 Oak
1981 Oak: 16 G. **1982** LARd: 9 G; 5.5 Sac. **1983** LARd: 16 G; 13 Sac. **1984** LARd: 16 G; 12 Sac. **1985** LARd: 16 G; 10 Sac. **1986** LARd: 13 G; 7.5 Sac. **1987** LARd: 14 G; 4 Sac. **1988** LARd: 7 G; Int 1-73; 3 Sac. **1989** LARd: 14 G; 5 Sac. **1990** LARd: 12 G; 6 Sac. **1991** LARd: 14 G; Int 1-11; 3 Sac. **1992** LARd: 16 G; 9 Sac. **1993** LARd: 16 G; 6 Sac. **Total:** 179 G; Int 2-84; 84 Sac.

JOHNNY LONG Long, John Anton 6′0″, 185 **QB-DB**
Col: Colgate *HS:* Columbia [South Orange, NJ] B: 12/13/1914, South Orange, NJ D: 2/3/1975, Pemberton, NJ
1944 ChiB: Pass 14-9 64.3%, 128 9.14 1 TD 1 Int; PR 2-14 7.0; KR 1-14 14.0; Punt 7-249 35.6. **1945** ChiB: PR 1-12 12.0; Punt 1-42 42.0. **Total:** Pass 14-9 64.3%, 128 9.14 1 TD 1 Int; PR 3-26 8.7; KR 1-14 14.0; Punt 8-291 36.4.

		Rushing				
Year Team	G	Att	Yds	Avg	TD	Fum
1944 ChiB	9	24	2	0.1	0	0
1945 ChiB	3	2	3	1.5	0	1
NFL Total	12	26	5	0.2	0	1

KEN LONG Long, Kenneth Donald 6′3″, 265 **OG**
Col: Purdue *HS:* Ravenna [OH] B: 7/24/1953, Pittsburgh, PA *Drafted:* 1976 Round 2 Det
1976 Det: 13 G; KR 2-18 9.0.

KEVIN LONG Long, Kevin Dale 6′5″, 296 **C**
Col: Florida State *HS:* Summerville [SC] B: 5/2/1975, Summerville, SC *Drafted:* 1998 Round 7 Ten
1998 Ten: 16 G.

KEVIN LONG Long, Kevin Fernando 6′1″, 212 **RB**
Col: South Carolina *HS:* Clinton [SC] B: 1/20/1955, Clinton, SC *Drafted:* 1977 Round 7 NYJ

		Rushing				Receiving					Tot
Year Team	G	Att	Yds	Avg	TD	Rec	Yds	Avg	TD	Fum	TD
1977 NYJ	14	56	170	3.0	0	5	17	3.4	0	1	0
1978 NYJ	16	214	954	4.5	10	26	204	7.8	0	4	10

1979 NYJ	12	116	442	3.8	7	10	115	11.5	0	3	7
1980 NYJ	15	115	355	3.1	6	20	137	6.9	0	3	6
1981 NYJ	16	73	269	3.7	2	13	66	5.1	3	2	5
NFL Total	73	574	2190	3.8	25	74	539	7.3	3	13	28

LOUIE LONG Long, Louis Charles 6′0″, 185 **OE**
Col: Texas; Southern Methodist *HS:* Talyor [TX] B: 1/6/1909, Chicago, IL D: 4/23/1974, Richmond, VA
1931 Port: 13 G; 6 Pt.

MATT LONG Long, Matthew Scott 6′3″, 270 **C**
Col: San Diego State *HS:* Buena [Ventura, CA] B: 3/16/1961, Glendale, CA
1987 Phi: 3 G.

MEL LONG Long, Melvin M 6′0″, 228 **LB**
Col: Toledo *HS:* Macomber [Toledo, OH] B: 11/22/1946, Toledo, OH
Drafted: 1972 Round 11 Cle
1972 Cle: 14 G. **1973** Cle: 14 G; KR 6-87 14.5. **1974** Cle: 14 G.
Total: 42 G; KR 6-87 14.5.

MIKE LONG Long, Michael Stanford 6′0″, 188 **OE**
Col: Brandeis *HS:* Marlboro [MA] B: 10/29/1938
1960 Bos: 2 G; Rec 2-10 5.0.

BOB LONG Long, Robert Albert 5′10″, 190 **HB-DB**
Col: Tennessee *HS:* Peabody [Trenton, TN] B: 4/9/1922, Trenton, TN
Drafted: 1946 Round 26 Phi
1947 Bos: 2 G.

BOB LONG Long, Robert Andrew 6′3″, 205 **WR**
Col: Wichita State *HS:* Washington Twp. [Apollo, PA] B: 6/16/1942, McKeesport, PA *Drafted:* 1964 Round 4 GB

		Receiving			
Year Team	**G**	**Rec**	**Yds**	**Avg**	**TD**
1964 GB	7	1	19	19.0	0
1965 GB	13	13	304	23.4	4
1966 GB	5	3	68	22.7	0
1967 GB	10	8	96	12.0	0
1968 Atl	9	22	484	22.0	4
1969 Was	14	48	533	11.1	1
1970 LARm	3	3	35	11.7	1
NFL Total	61	98	1539	15.7	10

BOB LONG Long, Robert Wendell 6′3″, 232 **LB**
Col: UCLA *HS:* South Pasadena [CA] B: 2/24/1934, South Pasadena, CA *Drafted:* 1955 Round 2 LARm
1955 LARm-Det: 11 G; Scor **1** Saf; 2 Pt. LARm: 1 G. Det: 10 G; Scor 1 Saf; 2 Pt. **1956** Det: 12 G; Int 2-47. **1957** Det: 12 G; Int 1-3. **1958** Det: 12 G; Int 2-28; 1 Fum. **1959** Det: 12 G. **1960** LARm: 9 G; Int 1-23. **1961** LARm: 13 G; Int 1-10. **1962** Dal: 8 G. **Total:** 89 G; Int 7-111; Scor 1 Saf; 2 Pt; 1 Fum.

TERRY LONG Long, Terry Luther 5′11″, 272 **OG**
Col: East Carolina *HS:* Eau Claire [Columbia, SC] B: 7/21/1959, Columbia, SC *Drafted:* 1984 Round 4 Pit
1984 Pit: 12 G; PR 1-0; 1 Fum. **1985** Pit: 15 G. **1986** Pit: 16 G. **1987** Pit: 13 G. **1988** Pit: 12 G. **1989** Pit: 13 G. **1990** Pit: 16 G. **1991** Pit: 8 G.
Total: 105 G; PR 1-0; 1 Fum.

TOM LONG Long, Thomas Noble 6′0″, 205 **G**
Col: Ohio State B: 8/7/1899 D: 7/23/1969, Columbus, OH
1925 Col: 7 G.

TIM LONG Long, Timothy Joe 6′6″, 295 **C**
Col: Memphis *HS:* Bradley [Cleveland, TN] B: 4/20/1963, Cleveland, TN *Drafted:* 1985 Round 3 Min
1987 SF: 2 G.

BILL LONG Long, William Gene 6′1″, 200 **OE-DE**
Col: Oklahoma State *HS:* Hominy [OK] B: 9/11/1926, Lenapah, OK Deceased *Drafted:* 1949 Round 5 Pit
1949 Pit: 10 G; Rush 2-6 3.0; Rec 2-21 10.5; Punt 30-1127 37.6; 1 Fum.

KEN LONGENECKER Longenecker, Kenneth Allen 6′4″, 285 **DT**
Col: Lebanon Valley B: 4/23/1938
1960 Pit: 4 G.

CLINT LONGLEY Longley, Howard Clinton Jr. 6′1″, 193 **QB**
Col: Abilene Christian *HS:* Littleton [CO] B: 7/28/1952, Wichita Falls, TX *Drafted:* 1974 Supplemental Round 1 Cin
1974 Dal: Rush 4-(-13) -3.3. **1975** Dal: Rush 3-12 4.0. **1976** SD: Rush 4-22 5.5. **Total:** Rush 11-21 1.9.

		Passing							
Year Team	**G**	**Att**	**Comp**	**Comp%**	**Yds**	**YPA**	**TD**	**Int**	**Rating**
1974 Dal	2	21	12	57.1	209	9.95	2	0	122.9
1975 Dal	4	23	7	30.4	102	4.43	1	1	42.3
1976 SD	3	24	12	50.0	130	5.42	2	3	54.5
NFL Total	9	68	31	45.6	441	6.49	5	4	67.1

SAM LONGMIRE Longmire, Samuel Robert 6′3″, 195 **DB-WR**
Col: Purdue *HS:* Alliance [OH] B: 1/3/1943, Birmingham, AL
1967 KC: 3 G. **1968** KC: 2 G. **Total:** 5 G.

TOM LONGO Longo, Thomas Victor 6′1″, 200 **DB**
Col: Notre Dame *HS:* Lyndhurst [NJ] B: 2/21/1942, Lyndhurst, NJ
Drafted: 1965 Round 14 Phi
1969 NYG: 13 G; KR 2-31 15.5; Int 2-31. **1970** NYG: 14 G; Int 2-33.
1971 StL: 2 G. **Total:** 29 G; KR 2-31 15.5; Int 4-64.

ROY LONGSTREET Longstreet, Roy William 5′11″, 185 **C**
(Shorty) *Col:* Iowa State *HS:* Sioux Falls [SD] B: 2/24/1901, Sioux Falls, SD D: 1/9/1991
1926 Rac: 1 G.

PAUL LONGUA Longua, Paul J 5′10″, 175 **OE**
Col: Villanova *HS:* St. John's Prep [Brooklyn, NY] B: 4/17/1903, Brooklyn, NY D: 6/13/1983, Hightstown, NJ
1929 Ora: 11 G; Rec 1 TD; 6 Pt. **1930** Nwk: 6 G. **Total:** 17 G; Rec 1 TD; 6 Pt.

RYAN LONGWELL Longwell, Ryan Walker 6′0″, 192 **K**
Col: California *HS:* Bend [OR] B: 8/16/1974, Seattle, WA

		Scoring						
Year Team	**G**	**Pts**	**FG**	**FGA**	**FG%**	**XK**	**XKA**	**XK%**
1997 GB	16	120	24	30	80.0	**48**	**48**	100.0
1998 GB	16	128	29	33	87.9	41	43	95.3
NFL Total	32	248	53	63	84.1	89	91	97.8

DEAN LOOK Look, Dean Zachary 5′11″, 185 **QB**
Col: Michigan State *HS:* Everett [Lansing, MI] B: 7/23/1937, Lansing, MI *Drafted:* 1960 Round 1 Den
1962 NYT: 1 G; Pass 1-0, 1 Int; Rush 2-9 4.5.

JOHN LOOKABAUGH Lookabaugh, John Ellsworth 6′4″, 216 **OE-DE**
Col: Maryland *HS:* Ridgeley [WV] B: 9/13/1922, Ridgeley, WV D: 5/16/1993, Millville, NJ
1946 Was: 3 G; Rec 6-67 11.2. **1947** Was: 6 G; Rec 6-78 13.0 1 TD; 6 Pt.
Total: 9 G; Rec 12-145 12.1 1 TD; 6 Pt.

ACE LOOMIS Loomis, Ace Darl 6′1″, 195 **DB-HB**
Col: Wis.-La Crosse *HS:* Merrillan [WI] B: 6/12/1928, Dubuque, IA
1951 GB: Rec 1-9 9.0. **1952** GB: PR 8-83 10.4; KR 10-207 20.7.
1953 GB: KR 1-19 19.0. **Total:** Rec 1-9 9.0; PR 8-83 10.4; KR 11-226 20.5.

		Interceptions			
Year Team	**G**	**Int**	**Yds**	**TD**	**Fum**
1951 GB	12	4	103	0	0
1952 GB	11	4	115	1	2
1953 GB	10	4	39	0	0
NFL Total	33	12	257	1	2

JIM LOONEY Looney, James Jr. 6′0″, 225 **LB**
Col: Purdue *HS:* Crenshaw [Los Angeles, CA] B: 8/18/1957, Bastrop, LA
1981 SF: 1 G.

JOE DON LOONEY Looney, Joe Don 6′1″, 230 **FB-P**
Col: Cameron; Texas; Texas Christian; Oklahoma *HS:* Admiral Farragut Acad. [St. Petersburg, FL]; R.L. Paschal [Fort Worth, TX] B: 10/10/1942, San Angelo, TX D: 9/24/1988, Studt Butte, TX *Drafted:* 1964 Round 1 NYG
1964 Bal: Punt 32-1358 42.4. **1969** NO: Pass 1-0. **Total:** Pass 1-0; Punt 32-1358 42.4.

		Rushing				Receiving			
Year Team	**G**	**Att**	**Yds**	**Avg**	**TD**	**Rec**	**Yds**	**Avg**	**TD**
1964 Bal	13	23	127	5.5	1	1	1	1.0	1
1965 Det	9	114	356	3.1	5	12	109	9.1	1
1966 Det-Was	13	63	220	3.5	4	12	49	4.1	0
1966 Det	3	8	42	5.3	1	4	24	6.0	0
1966 Was	10	55	178	3.2	3	8	25	3.1	0
1967 Was	4	11	26	2.4	1	1	12	12.0	0
1969 NO	3	3	-5	-1.7	0	0	0	—	0
NFL Total	42	214	724	3.4	11	26	171	6.6	2

	Kickoff Returns					Tot
Year Team	**Ret**	**Yds**	**Avg**	**TD**	**Fum**	**TD**
1964 Bal	14	345	24.6	0	0	2
1965 Det	0	0	—	0	7	6
1966 Det-Was	13	265	20.4	0	3	4
1966 Det	3	75	25.0	0	0	1
1966 Was	10	190	19.0	0	3	3
1967 Was	2	42	21.0	0	0	1
NFL Total	29	652	22.5	0	10	13

DON LOONEY Looney, John Don 6′2″, 182 **OE-DE**
Col: Texas Christian *HS:* Sulphur Springs [TX] B: 9/2/1917, Saltillo, TX
Drafted: 1940 Round 8 Phi
1940 Phi: Rush 2-(-4) -2.0; **1** Fum TD. **1941** Pit: KR 1-16 16.0.
Total: Rush 2-(-4) -2.0; KR 1-16 16.0; 1 Fum TD.

		Receiving				Tot
Year Team	G	Rec	Yds	Avg	TD	TD
1940 Phi	11	**58**	**707**	12.2	4	5
1941 Pit	9	10	186	18.6	1	1
1942 Pit	3	7	59	8.4	1	1
NFL Total	23	75	952	12.7	6	7

BILL LOPASKY Lopasky, William Joseph 6′2″, 235 **OG**
Col: West Virginia *HS:* Lehman [PA] B: 1/29/1937, Trucksville, PA
Drafted: 1960 Round 1 LAC
1961 SF: 10 G.

KARL LORCH Lorch, Karl P Jr. 6′3″, 258 **DE-DT**
Col: Arizona Western Coll. (J.C.); USC *HS:* Kamehameha School [Honolulu, HI] B: 6/14/1950, Honolulu, HI *Drafted:* 1973 Round 9 Mia
1976 Was: 13 G; KR 1-0; 1 Fum. **1977** Was: 14 G. **1978** Was: 16 G.
1979 Was: 15 G; Int 1-31 1 TD; 6 Pt. **1980** Was: 16 G. **1981** Was: 16 G.
Total: 90 G; KR 1-0; Int 1-31 1 TD; 6 Pt; 1 Fum.

JACK LORD Lord, John Warner 6′0″, 195 **G-T**
Col: Rutgers *HS:* Erasmus Hall [Brooklyn, NY] B: 9/23/1904, Avon, NJ
D: 3/11/1958, Rye, NY
1929 SI: 6 G.

TONY LORICK Lorick, William Anthony 6′1″, 217 **RB**
Col: East Los Angeles Coll. CA (J.C.); Arizona State *HS:* John C. Fremont [Los Angeles, CA] B: 5/25/1941, Los Angeles, CA
Drafted: 1964 Round 2 Bal
1968 NO: Punt 1-36 36.0. **Total:** Punt 1-36 36.0.

		Rushing				Receiving			
Year Team	G	Att	Yds	Avg	TD	Rec	Yds	Avg	TD
1964 Bal	14	100	513	5.1	4	11	164	14.9	0
1965 Bal	14	63	296	4.7	1	15	184	12.3	2
1966 Bal	14	143	524	3.7	3	12	81	6.8	0
1967 Bal	14	133	436	3.3	6	22	189	8.6	0
1968 NO	13	104	344	3.3	0	26	272	10.5	3
1969 NO	14	5	11	2.2	0	0	0	—	0
NFL Total	83	548	2124	3.9	14	86	890	10.3	5

	Kickoff Returns					Tot
Year Team	Ret	Yds	Avg	TD	Fum	TD
1964 Bal	13	385	29.6	0	5	4
1965 Bal	9	211	23.4	0	3	3
1966 Bal	10	214	21.4	0	2	3
1967 Bal	8	212	26.5	0	2	6
1968 NO	0	0	—	0	3	3
1969 NO	0	0	—	0	1	0
NFL Total	40	1022	25.6	0	16	19

JACK LOSCH Losch, John Lee 6′1″, 205 **HB**
Col: Miami (Fla.) *HS:* Williamsport [PA] B: 8/13/1934, New York, NY
Drafted: 1956 Round 1 GB
1956 GB: 12 G; Pass 1-1 100.0%, 63 63.00 1 TD; Rush 19-43 2.3; Rec 7-85 12.1; PR 8-74 9.3; KR 15-390 26.0; 3 Fum.

ED LOTHAMER Lothamer, Edward Dewey 6′5″, 270 **DT-DE**
Col: Michigan State *HS:* St. Mary's of Redford [Detroit, MI]
B: 5/20/1942, Detroit, MI *Drafted:* 1964 Round 4 KC
1964 KC: 11 G; KR 1-0. **1965** KC: 14 G. **1966** KC: 7 G. **1967** KC: 13 G; KR 1-0. **1968** KC: 14 G. **1969** KC: 13 G. **1971** KC: 14 G. **1972** KC: 2 G.
Total: 88 G; KR 2-0.

BILLY LOTHRIDGE Lothridge, Billy Lamar 6′2″, 194 **QB-DB-P**
Col: Georgia Tech *HS:* Gainesville [GA] B: 1/1/1942, Cleveland, GA
D: 2/23/1996, Pensacola, FL *Drafted:* 1964 Round 6 Dal
1964 Dal: Pass 9-2 22.2%, 24 2.67 2 Int; Rush 2-(-6) -3.0 1 TD. **1966** Atl: Pass 1-0; Rush 1-22 22.0. **1967** Atl: Rush 1-16 16.0. **1968** Atl: Rush 1-(-16) -16.0; Int 3-76. **1969** Atl: Pass 1-1 100.0%, 9 9.00. **1971** Atl: Pass 1-1 100.0%, 27 27.00. **Total:** Pass 12-4 33.3%, 60 5.00 2 Int; Rush 5-16 3.2 1 TD; Int 3-76.

		Punting			
Year Team	G	Punts	Yds	Avg	Fum
1964 Dal	14	62	2501	40.3	1
1965 LARm	9	42	1619	38.5	0
1966 Atl	14	73	2968	40.7	0
1967 Atl	14	**87**	**3801**	**43.7**	0
1968 Atl	14	75	**3324**	**44.3**	1
1969 Atl	14	69	2846	41.2	0
1970 Atl	14	76	2944	38.7	0
1971 Atl	9	44	1639	37.3	0
1972 Mia	2	4	150	37.5	0
NFL Total	104	532	21792	41.0	2

ANTHONE LOTT Lott, Anthone Vouchan 5′9″, 194 **DB**
Col: Florida *HS:* William M. Raines [Jacksonville, FL] B: 7/22/1974, Gainesville, FL
1997 Cin: 5 G.

BILLY LOTT Lott, Billy Rex 6′0″, 203 **FB**
Col: Mississippi *HS:* Sumrall [MS] B: 11/8/1934, Sumrall, MS
D: 1995 *Drafted:* 1958 Round 6 NYG
1958 NYG: KR 5-78 15.6. **1960** Oak: Scor 1 2XP. **1961** Bos: PR 1-8 8.0.
Total: PR 1-8 8.0; KR 5-78 15.6; Scor 1 2XP.

		Rushing				Receiving					Tot
Year Team	G	Att	Yds	Avg	TD	Rec	Yds	Avg	TD	Fum	TD
1958 NYG	12	4	30	7.5	0	0	0	—	0	0	0
1960 Oak	14	99	520	5.3	5	49	524	10.7	1	2	6
1961 Bos	14	100	461	4.6	5	32	333	10.4	6	3	11
1962 Bos	7	8	34	4.3	0	1	1	1.0	0	1	0
1963 Bos	14	35	78	2.2	2	3	61	20.3	1	1	3
NFL Total	61	246	1123	4.6	12	85	919	10.8	8	7	20

JOHN LOTT Lott, John **T**
HS: Lawrenceville School [NJ] B: 1906, NJ Deceased
1929 Ora: 2 G. **1930** Bkn: 2 G. **Total:** 4 G.

JOHN LOTT Lott, John Randall 6′2″, 260 **C-OG**
Col: North Texas *HS:* Denton [TX] B: 5/9/1964, Denton, TX
1987 Pit: 1 G.

RONNIE LOTT Lott, Ronald Mandel 6′0″, 203 **DB**
Col: USC *HS:* Eisenhower [Rialto, CA] B: 5/8/1959, Albuquerque, NM
Drafted: 1981 Round 1 SF
1981 SF: KR 7-111 15.9. **1983** SF: 1 Sac. **1984** SF: 1 Sac. **1985** SF: KR 1-2 2.0; 1.5 Sac. **1986** SF: 2 Sac. **1991** LARd: 1 Sac. **1993** NYJ: 1 Sac. **1994** NYJ: 1 Sac. **Total:** KR 8-113 14.1; 8.5 Sac.

		Interceptions			
Year Team	G	Int	Yds	TD	Fum
1981 SF	16	7	117	**3**	1
1982 SF	9	2	95	**1**	0
1983 SF	15	4	22	0	0
1984 SF	12	4	26	0	0
1985 SF	16	6	68	0	0
1986 SF	14	**10**	134	1	0
1987 SF	12	5	62	0	0
1988 SF	13	5	59	0	0
1989 SF	11	5	34	0	0
1990 SF	11	3	26	0	0
1991 LARd	16	**8**	52	0	0
1992 LARd	16	1	0	0	0
1993 NYJ	16	3	35	0	0
1994 NYJ	15	0	0	0	0
NFL Total	192	63	730	5	1

THOMAS LOTT Lott, Thomas Willie Jr. 5′11″, 205 **RB**
Col: Oklahoma *HS:* John Jay [San Antonio, TX] B: 8/1/1957, San Antonio, TX *Drafted:* 1979 Round 6 StL
1979 StL: 10 G; Rush 11-50 4.5; Rec 2-8 4.0; PR 4-33 8.3; KR 1-19 19.0; 2 Fum.

RON LOU Lou, Ronald Wayne 6′2″, 240 **C**
Col: Arizona State *HS:* Montebello [CA] B: 7/24/1951, Los Angeles, CA *Drafted:* 1973 Round 14 Hou
1973 Hou: 9 G. **1975** Phi: 14 G. **1976** Hou: 14 G. **Total:** 37 G.

FLETCHER LOUALLEN Louallen, Fletcher Allison 6′0″, 195 **DB**
Col: West Alabama *HS:* Central [Pageland, SC] B: 9/12/1962, Jefferson, SC
1987 Min: 3 G; Int 1-16.

COREY LOUCHIEY Louchiey, Corey 6′8″, 305 **OT**
Col: Tennessee; South Carolina *HS:* Carolina [Greenville, SC]
B: 10/10/1971, Greenville, SC *Drafted:* 1994 Round 3 Buf
1995 Buf: 13 G; KR 1-13 13.0. **1996** Buf: 16 G; Rec 1-0. **1997** Buf: 16 G.
Total: 45 G; Rec 1-0; KR 1-13 13.0.

ALVIN LOUCKS Loucks, Alvin E 170 **G**
Col: Michigan *HS:* Grand Rapids Union [MI] B: 6/15/1895 D: 4/1973, Hopkins, MN
1920 Det: 1 G.

ED LOUCKS Loucks, Edwin Earl 5′9″, 180 **E**
Col: Washington & Jefferson *HS:* Scottsdale [PA] B: 9/15/1895
D: 9/14/1959
1925 Cle: 6 G.

KAMIL LOUD Loud, Kamil Kassam 6′0″, 190 **WR**
Col: Cal Poly-S.L.O. *HS:* Salesian [Richmond, CA]; El Cerrito HS [CA]
B: 6/25/1976, Richmond, CA *Drafted:* 1998 Round 7 Buf
1998 Buf: 5 G.

ROMMIE LOUDD Loudd, Rommie Lee 6′3″, 226 **LB**
Col: UCLA *HS:* Thomas Jefferson [Los Angeles, CA] B: 6/8/1933, Madisonville, TX D: 5/9/1998, Miami, FL *Drafted:* 1956 Round 26 SF
1960 LAC: 14 G; Int 3-17; **1** Fum TD; 6 Pt. **1961** Bos: 13 G; Int 1-12. **1962** Bos: 14 G; KR 1-15 15.0; 1 Fum. **Total:** 41 G; KR 1-15 15.0; Int 4-29; 1 Fum TD; 6 Pt; 1 Fum.

TOM LOUDERBACK Louderback, Thomas Franklin Jr. 6′2″, 235 **LB-C-OG**
Col: Santa Rosa JC CA; San Jose State *HS:* Petaluma [CA]
B: 3/5/1933, Petaluma, CA *Drafted:* 1955 Round 10 Was
1958 Phi: 12 G. **1959** Phi: 12 G. **1960** Oak: 14 G; Int 2-7. **1961** Oak: 14 G; Int 1-46 1 TD; 6 Pt. **1962** Buf: 2 G. **Total:** 54 G; Int 3-53 1 TD; 6 Pt.

ANGELO LOUKAS Loukas, Angelo Cous 6′3″, 250 **OG-OT**
Col: Northwestern *HS:* Bowen [Chicago, IL] B: 2/25/1947, Corinth, Greece
1969 Buf: 13 G. **1970** Bos: 2 G. **Total:** 15 G.

CLARENCE LOVE Love, Clarence Eugene 5′10″, 181 **DB**
Col: Toledo *HS:* Jackson [MI] B: 6/16/1976, Jackson, MI
Drafted: 1998 Round 4 Phi
1998 Phi: 6 G.

DUVAL LOVE Love, Duval Lee 6′3″, 288 **OG-OT**
Col: USC; UCLA *HS:* Fountain Valley [CA] B: 6/24/1963, Los Angeles, CA *Drafted:* 1985 Round 10 LARm
1985 LARm: 6 G. **1986** LARm: 16 G; KR 1-(-6) -6.0; 1 Fum. **1987** LARm: 10 G. **1988** LARm: 15 G. **1989** LARm: 15 G. **1990** LARm: 16 G. **1991** LARm: 16 G. **1992** Pit: 16 G. **1993** Pit: 16 G. **1994** Pit: 16 G. **1995** Ariz: 16 G. **1996** Ariz: 9 G. **Total:** 167 G; KR 1-(-6) -6.0; 1 Fum.

JOHN LOVE Love, John Louis 5′11″, 185 **WR-K**
Col: Cisco JC TX; North Texas *HS:* Booker T. Washington [Mawlin, TX]
B: 2/24/1944, Linden, TX *Drafted:* 1967 Round 7 Was
1967 Was: Rec 17-248 14.6 1 TD; PR 11-(-5) -0.5; Scor 34, 2-7 28.6% FG, 10-11 90.9% XK; **1** Fum TD. **1972** LARm: Rec 1-19 19.0 1 TD; PR 10-39 3.9. **Total:** Rec 18-267 14.8 2 TD; PR 21-34 1.6; Scor 40, 2-7 28.6% FG, 10-11 90.9% XK; 1 Fum TD.

		Kickoff Returns					Tot
Year Team	**G**	**Ret**	**Yds**	**Avg**	**TD**	**Fum**	**TD**
1967 Was	13	17	422	24.8	1	6	3
1972 LARm	5	8	167	20.9	0	2	1
NFL Total	18	25	589	23.6	1	8	4

RANDY LOVE Love, Randy Louis 6′1″, 208 **RB**
Col: Houston *HS:* Garland [TX] B: 9/30/1956, Garland, TX
Drafted: 1979 Round 8 NE
1980 StL: KR 3-46 15.3. **1981** StL: KR 3-46 15.3. **1982** StL: KR 4-69 17.3. **1983** StL: Rec 6-58 9.7 1 TD; KR 3-71 23.7. **1984** StL: Rec 7-33 4.7 1 TD; KR 1-1 1.0. **1985** StL: Rec 2-4 2.0. **Total:** Rec 15-95 6.3 2 TD; KR 14-233 16.6.

		Rushing					Tot
Year Team	**G**	**Att**	**Yds**	**Avg**	**TD**	**Fum**	**TD**
1979 StL	4	0	0	—	0	0	0
1980 StL	16	1	3	3.0	0	3	0
1981 StL	16	3	11	3.7	0	0	0
1982 StL	9	0	0	—	0	1	0
1983 StL	16	35	103	2.9	2	4	3
1984 StL	16	25	90	3.6	1	1	2
1985 StL	12	1	4	4.0	0	0	0
NFL Total	89	65	211	3.2	3	9	5

SEAN LOVE Love, Sean Fitzgerald 6′3″, 295 **OG**
Col: Penn State *HS:* Marian [Tamaqua, PA] B: 9/6/1968, Coaldale, PA
Drafted: 1991 Round 10 Dal
1993 TB: 2 G. **1994** TB: 6 G. **1995** Car: 11 G. **Total:** 19 G.

TERRY LOVE Love, Terry Lee 6′2″, 205 **DB**
Col: Coll. of the Canyons CA (J.C.); Murray State *HS:* Proviso East [Maywood, IL] B: 8/25/1958, Forrest City, AR
1987 Min: 1 G.

WALT LOVE Love, Walter James 5′9″, 180 **WR**
Col: Westminster (Ut.) *HS:* John F. Kennedy [Cleveland, OH]
B: 6/4/1950, Cleveland, OH *Drafted:* 1973 Round 10 NYG
1973 NYG: 12 G; KR 18-396 22.0; 1 Fum.

CALVIN LOVEALL Loveall, Calvin Earl 5′9″, 180 **DB**
Col: Idaho *HS:* Kennewick [WA] B: 7/23/1962, Kennewick, WA
1988 Hou-KC-Atl: 11 G. Hou: 3 G. KC: 4 G. Atl: 4 G. **Total:** 11 G.

EDWIN LOVELADY Lovelady, Edwin Patrick 5′9″, 180 **WR**
Col: Memphis *HS:* Brainerd [Chattanooga, TN] B: 4/23/1963, Chattanooga, TN
1987 NYG: 3 G; Rush 2-11 5.5; Rec 10-125 12.5 2 TD; PR 10-38 3.8; 12 Pt; 5 Fum.

FRITZ LOVEN Loven, Fred Oscar 200 **G**
Col: No College B: 6/11/1894, Minneapolis, MN D: 10/1975, Brainerd, MN
1929 Min: 8 G; 6 Pt.

JOHN LOVETERE LoVetere, John Manning 6′4″, 280 **DT**
Col: Compton CC CA *HS:* Paramount [CA] B: 5/31/1936, Boston, MA
1959 LARm: 12 G. **1960** LARm: 12 G; PR 1-6 6.0 **1** TD; 6 Pt. **1961** LARm: 13 G. **1962** LARm: 14 G. **1963** NYG: 14 G. **1964** NYG: 8 G. **1965** NYG: 4 G. **Total:** 77 G; PR 1-6 6.0 1 TD; 6 Pt.

DEREK LOVILLE Loville, Derek Kevin 5′10″, 203 **RB**
Col: Oregon *HS:* Archbishop Riordan [San Francisco, CA]
B: 7/4/1968, San Francisco, CA
1991 Sea: PR 3-16 5.3. **1995** SF: Scor 1 2XP. **Total:** PR 3-16 5.3; Scor 1 2XP.

		Rushing				Receiving			
Year Team	**G**	**Att**	**Yds**	**Avg**	**TD**	**Rec**	**Yds**	**Avg**	**TD**
1990 Sea	11	7	12	1.7	0	0	0	—	0
1991 Sea	16	22	69	3.1	0	0	0	—	0
1994 SF	14	31	99	3.2	0	2	26	13.0	0
1995 SF	16	218	723	3.3	10	87	662	7.6	3
1996 SF	12	70	229	3.3	2	16	138	8.6	2
1997 Den	16	25	124	5.0	1	2	10	5.0	0
1998 Den	16	53	161	3.0	2	2	29	14.5	0
NFL Total	101	426	1417	3.3	15	109	865	7.9	5

	Kickoff Returns					Tot
Year Team	**Ret**	**Yds**	**Avg**	**TD**	**Fum**	**TD**
1990 Sea	18	359	19.9	0	1	0
1991 Sea	18	412	22.9	0	0	0
1994 SF	2	34	17.0	0	0	0
1995 SF	0	0	—	0	1	13
1996 SF	10	229	22.9	0	0	4
1997 Den	5	136	27.2	0	1	1
1998 Den	6	105	17.5	0	0	2
NFL Total	59	1275	21.6	0	3	20

WARREN LOVING Loving, Warren Eric 6′1″, 230 **RB**
Col: William Penn *HS:* James J. Ferris [Jersey City, NJ] B: 11/12/1960, Jersey City, NJ
1987 Buf: 2 G.

FRANK LOVUOLO LoVuolo, Frank Anthony 6′2″, 210 **OE-DE**
Col: St. Bonaventure *HS:* North [Binghamton, NY] B: 5/1/1924, Binghamton, NY *Drafted:* 1949 Round 7 NYG
1949 NYG: 11 G; Rec 2-37 18.5; **1** Fum TD; 6 Pt.

KIRK LOWDERMILK Lowdermilk, Robert Kirk 6′3″, 273 **C**
Col: Ohio State *HS:* Salem [OH] B: 4/10/1963, Canton, OH
Drafted: 1985 Round 3 Min
1985 Min: 16 G. **1986** Min: 11 G. **1987** Min: 12 G. **1988** Min: 12 G. **1989** Min: 16 G. **1990** Min: 15 G. **1991** Min: 16 G; 1 Fum. **1992** Min: 16 G. **1993** Ind: 16 G. **1994** Ind: 16 G; 1 Fum. **1995** Ind: 16 G. **1996** Ind: 16 G. **Total:** 178 G; 2 Fum.

GARY LOWE Lowe, Gary Richard 5′11″, 196 **DB-HB**
Col: Michigan State *HS:* Trenton [MI] B: 5/4/1934, Trenton, MI
Drafted: 1956 Round 5 Was
1956 Was: PR 1-0. **1959** Det: PR 6-8 1.3. **1961** Det: Scor **1** Saf. **1964** Det: Pass 1-0, 1 Int. **Total:** Pass 1-0, 1 Int; PR 7-8 1.1; Scor 1 Saf.

		Interceptions			
Year Team	**G**	**Int**	**Yds**	**TD**	**Fum**
1956 Was	11	1	30	0	0
1957 Was-Det	8	1	3	0	1
1957 Was	1	0	0	0	0
1957 Det	7	1	3	0	1
1958 Det	12	2	25	0	0
1959 Det	12	5	**130**	0	1
1960 Det	11	2	49	0	0
1961 Det	14	5	16	0	0
1962 Det	13	2	20	0	0
1963 Det	3	2	14	0	0
1964 Det	13	0	0	0	1
NFL Total	97	20	287	0	3

BULL LOWE Lowe, Henry Bulger Jr. 5′11″, 180 **E-T**
Col: Lafayette; Fordham *HS:* Arlington [MA]; Phillips Exeter Acad. [Exeter, NH] B: 6/21/1895, Arlington, MA D: 2/18/1939, Arlington, MA
1920 Can: 10 G. **1921** Cle: 7 G. **1925** Prov-Fra: 10 G. Prov: 2 G. Fra: 8 G. **1926** Fra: 2 G. **1927** Prov: 11 G. **Total:** 40 G.

LLOYD LOWE Lowe, Lloyd Alvie 5′10″, 155 **DB-HB**
Col: North Texas *HS:* Mart [TX] B: 12/18/1928, Prairie Hill, TX
1953 ChiB: 7 G; Rec 4-34 8.5; PR 15-51 3.4; KR 1-26 26.0; Int 1-6; 1 Fum. **1954** ChiB: 1 G; PR 2-4 2.0; KR 1-0. **Total:** 8 G; Rec 4-34 8.5; PR 17-55 3.2; KR 2-26 13.0; Int 1-6; 1 Fum.

PAUL LOWE Lowe, Paul Edward 6'0", 205 HB
Col: Compton CC CA; Oregon State *HS:* Centennial [Compton, CA]
B: 9/27/1936, Homer, LA
1960 LAC: Pass 3-1 33.3%, 24 8.00; PR 1-0. **1961** SD: Pass 4-2 50.0%, 70 17.50; PR 1-0. **1963** SD: Pass 4-2 50.0%, 100 25.00 1 TD 1 Int. **1964** SD: Pass 2-0. **1965** SD: Pass 4-3 75.0%, 81 20.25; **1** Fum TD. **1966** SD: Pass 3-1 33.3%, 25 8.33. **1967** SD: Pass 1-1 100.0%, 26 26.00. **Total:** Pass 21-10 47.6%, 326 15.52 1 TD 1 Int; PR 2-0; 1 Fum TD.

		Rushing				Receiving			
Year Team	G	Att	Yds	Avg	TD	Rec	Yds	Avg	TD
1960 LAC	14	136	855	**6.3**	8	23	377	16.4	2
1961 SD	14	175	767	4.4	**9**	17	103	6.1	0
1963 SD	14	177	1010	5.7	8	26	191	7.3	2
1964 SD	14	130	496	3.8	3	14	182	13.0	2
1965 SD	14	222	**1121**	**5.0**	**6**	17	126	7.4	1
1966 SD	14	146	643	4.4	3	12	41	3.4	0
1967 SD	7	28	71	2.5	1	2	25	12.5	0
1968 SD-KC	2	2	-1	-0.5	0	0	0	—	0
1968 SD	1	1	9	9.0	0	0	0	—	0
1968 KC	1	1	-10	-10.0	0	0	0	—	0
1969 KC	7	10	33	3.3	0	0	0	—	0
NFL Total	100	1026	4995	4.9	38	111	1045	9.4	7

	Kickoff Returns					Tot
Year Team	Ret	Yds	Avg	TD	Fum	TD
1960 LAC	28	611	21.8	0	2	10
1961 SD	10	240	24.0	0	6	9
1963 SD	5	132	26.4	0	7	10
1964 SD	0	0	—	0	2	5
1965 SD	0	0	—	0	2	8
1966 SD	7	167	23.9	0	3	3
1967 SD	8	145	18.1	0	0	1
1969 KC	5	116	23.2	0	1	0
NFL Total	63	1411	22.4	0	23	46

REGGIE LOWE Lowe, Reginald James 6'2", 250 DE
Col: Troy State *HS:* Central [Phenix City, AL] B: 6/14/1975, Phenix City, AL
1998 Jac: 4 G.

WALTER LOWE Lowe, Walter 5'11", 180 FB-WB-TB
(Bull) *Col:* Dubuque; Georgetown B: 3/6/1899, Blackhawk Co., IA
D: 3/1978, Painesville, OH
1923 RI: 5 G.

WOODROW LOWE Lowe, Woodrow 6'0", 227 LB
(Woody) *Col:* Alabama *HS:* Phenix City Central [AL] B: 6/9/1954, Columbus, GA *Drafted:* 1976 Round 5 SD
1982 SD: 2 Sac. **1983** SD: 4.5 Sac. **1984** SD: 3 Sac. **1985** SD: 5.5 Sac. **Total:** 15 Sac.

		Interceptions			
Year Team	G	Int	Yds	TD	Fum
1976 SD	14	1	8	0	0
1977 SD	14	1	28	0	0
1978 SD	16	1	16	0	0
1979 SD	16	5	150	**2**	0
1980 SD	16	3	72	1	0
1981 SD	16	3	0	0	0
1982 SD	9	1	2	0	0
1983 SD	16	0	0	0	0
1984 SD	15	3	61	1	1
1985 SD	16	3	6	0	0
1986 SD	16	0	0	0	0
NFL Total	164	21	343	4	1

DARBY LOWERY Lowery, Darby 6'0", 203 G-E-T
Col: No College Deceased
1920 Roch: 9 G. **1921** Roch: 4 G. **1922** Roch: 5 G. **1923** Roch: 4 G. **1924** Roch: 7 G. **1925** Roch: 7 G. **Total:** 36 G.

NICK LOWERY Lowery, Dominic Gerald 6'4", 197 K
Col: Dartmouth *HS:* St. Albans [Washington, DC] B: 5/27/1956, Munich, Germany
1992 KC: Punt 4-141 35.3. **Total:** Punt 4-141 35.3.

		Scoring						
Year Team	G	Pts	FG	FGA	FG%	XK	XKA	XK%
1978 NE	2	7	0	1	0.0	7	7	100.0
1980 KC	16	97	20	26	76.9	37	37	100.0
1981 KC	16	115	26	36	72.2	37	38	97.4
1982 KC	9	74	19	**24**	79.2	17	17	100.0
1983 KC	16	116	24	30	80.0	44	45	97.8
1984 KC	16	104	23	33	69.7	35	35	100.0
1985 KC	16	107	24	27	**88.9**	35	35	**100.0**
1986 KC	16	100	19	26	73.1	43	43	100.0
1987 KC	12	83	19	23	82.6	26	26	100.0
1988 KC	16	104	27	32	84.4	23	23	100.0
1989 KC	16	106	24	33	72.7	34	35	97.1
1990 KC	16	**139**	**34**	37	**91.9**	37	38	**97.4**
1991 KC	16	110	25	30	83.3	35	35	100.0
1992 KC	15	105	22	24	**91.7**	39	39	**100.0**
1993 KC	16	106	23	29	79.3	37	37	100.0
1994 NYJ	16	86	20	23	87.0	26	27	96.3
1995 NYJ	14	75	17	21	81.0	24	24	100.0
1996 NYJ	16	77	17	24	70.8	26	27	96.3
NFL Total	260	1711	383	479	80.0	562	568	98.9

HUGH LOWERY Lowery, Hugh 6'0", 220 T
(Huge) *Col:* Indiana; Franklin (Ind.) *HS:* Cutler [IN] B: 7/19/1892, Cutler, IN D: 9/5/1972, Bradenton, FL
1920 Det: 7 G.

MICHAEL LOWERY Lowery, Michael Zantel 6'0", 232 LB
Col: Mississippi *HS:* South Pike [Magnolia, MS] B: 2/14/1974, McComb, MS
1996 ChiB: 16 G; **1** Fum TD; 6 Pt. **1997** ChiB: 16 G. **Total:** 32 G; 1 Fum TD; 6 Pt.

ORLANDO LOWRY Lowry, Orlando Dewey 6'4", 237 LB
Col: Ohio State *HS:* Shaker Heights [OH] B: 8/14/1961, Cleveland, OH
1985 Ind: 16 G; PR 1-0. **1986** Ind: 16 G. **1987** Ind: 8 G. **1988** Ind: 16 G. **1989** Ind-NE: 11 G. Ind: 9 G. NE: 2 G. **Total:** 67 G; PR 1-0.

QUENTIN LOWRY Lowry, Quentin Ivory 6'2", 232 LB
Col: Youngstown State *HS:* Shaker Heights [OH] B: 11/11/1957, Cleveland, OH *Drafted:* 1979 Round 12 Dal
1981 Was: 9 G. **1982** Was: 9 G. **1983** Was-TB: 9 G. Was: 3 G. TB: 6 G. **Total:** 27 G.

JACKIE LOWTHER Lowther, Russell Jack 5'8", 165 TB-DB
Col: Detroit Mercy *HS:* East Detroit [Eastpointe, MI] B: 12/27/1922, Detroit, MI D: 9/29/1952, Livonia, MI *Drafted:* 1945 Round 6 Det
1944 Det: 8 G; Pass 10-7 70.0%, 54 5.40 2 Int; Rush 9-18 2.0; PR 2-28 14.0; Int 1-32; Punt 5-205 41.0. **1945** Pit: 2 G; Pass 4-0, 1 Int; Rush 15-54 3.6; PR 2-35 17.5; KR 1-20 20.0; Punt 1-35 35.0; Scor 0-1 XK. **Total:** 10 G; Pass 14-7 50.0%, 54 3.86 3 Int; Rush 24-72 3.0; PR 4-63 15.8; KR 1-20 20.0; Int 1-32; Punt 6-240 40.0; Scor 0-1 XK.

MIKE LOYD Loyd, Charles Michael 6'2", 216 QB
Col: Kansas; Tulsa; Missouri Southern State *HS:* Memorial [Joplin, MO] B: 5/6/1956, Joplin, MO
1980 StL: 5 G; Pass 28-5 17.9%, 49 1.75 1 Int; Rush 6-2 0.3; 1 Fum.

ALEX LOYD Loyd, Edgar Alex 6'4", 198 OE
Col: Oklahoma State *HS:* Stigler [OK] B: 8/7/1927, Stigler, OK
D: 5/25/1976, Dallas, TX *Drafted:* 1950 Round 15 Was

		Receiving				
Year Team	G	Rec	Yds	Avg	TD	Fum
1950 SF	12	32	402	12.6	0	2

STEVE LUBISCHER Lubischer, Stephen Anthony 6'3", 240 LB
Col: Boston College *HS:* Shore Regional [West Long Branch, NJ]
B: 6/29/1962, Long Branch, NJ
1987 Mia: 1 G.

LOU LUBRATOVICH Lubratovich, Milo Milan 6'2", 230 T
Col: Wisconsin *HS:* Central [Duluth, MN] B: 5/30/1907, Indian Harbor, IN
1931 Bkn: 14 G. **1932** Bkn: 12 G. **1933** Bkn: 10 G. **1934** Bkn: 10 G. **1935** Bkn: 7 G. **Total:** 53 G.

JEFF LUCAS Lucas, Jeffrey Alan 6'7", 288 OT
Col: West Virginia *HS:* Hackensack [NJ] B: 5/30/1964, Hackensack, NJ
1987 Pit: 3 G.

RAY LUCAS Lucas, Ray 6'3", 214 WR-QB
Col: Rutgers *HS:* Harrison [NJ] B: 8/6/1972, Harrison, NJ
1996 NE: 2 G. **1997** NYJ: 5 G; Pass 4-3 75.0%, 28 7.00 1 Int; Rush 6-55 9.2. **1998** NYJ: 15 G; Pass 3-1 33.3%, 27 9.00; Rush 5-23 4.6. **Total:** 22 G; Pass 7-4 57.1%, 55 7.86 1 Int; Rush 11-78 7.1.

DICK LUCAS Lucas, Richard Albert 6'2", 213 OE
Col: Boston College *HS:* South Boston [MA] B: 1/9/1934, South Boston, MA *Drafted:* 1956 Round 10 ChiB
1960 Phi: KR 1-5 5.0. **Total:** KR 1-5 5.0.

		Receiving				
Year Team	G	Rec	Yds	Avg	TD	Fum
1958 Pit	4	4	47	11.8	0	0
1960 Phi	12	3	34	11.3	0	0
1961 Phi	14	8	67	8.4	5	0
1962 Phi	9	19	236	12.4	1	1
1963 Phi	3	0	0	—	0	0
NFL Total	42	34	384	11.3	6	1

RICHIE LUCAS Lucas, Richard John 6'0", 190 QB-DB-HB
Col: Penn State *HS:* Glassport [PA] B: 4/15/1938, Glassport, PA
Drafted: 1960 Round 1 Buf
1960 Buf: Rec 5-58 11.6 1 TD; PR 4-3 0.8. **1961** Buf: Rec 6-69 11.5; KR 7-126 18.0; Int 2-0; Scor **3** 2XP; 1 Fum TD. **Total:** Rec 11-127 11.5 1 TD; PR 4-3 0.8; KR 7-126 18.0; Int 2-0; Scor 3 2XP; 1 Fum TD.

		Passing							
Year Team	G	Att	Comp	Comp%	Yds	YPA	TD	Int	Rating
1960 Buf	14	49	23	46.9	314	6.41	2	3	56.0
1961 Buf	8	50	20	40.0	282	5.64	2	4	38.9
NFL Total	22	99	43	43.4	596	6.02	4	7	47.4

	Rushing					Tot
Year Team	Att	Yds	Avg	TD	Fum	TD
1960 Buf	38	138	3.6	2	2	3
1961 Buf	10	15	1.5	0	1	1
NFL Total	48	153	3.2	2	3	4

TIM LUCAS Lucas, Timothy Brian 6'3", 230 LB
Col: California *HS:* Rio Vista [CA] B: 4/3/1961, Stockton, CA
Drafted: 1983 Round 10 StL
1987 Den: 11 G; Int 1-11; 2 Sac. **1988** Den: 16 G. **1989** Den: 16 G; 2 Sac. **1990** Den: 11 G; 1 Sac. **1991** Den: 5 G. **1992** Den: 9 G. **1993** Den: 7 G. **Total:** 75 G; Int 1-11; 5 Sac.

MIKE LUCCI Lucci, Michael Gene 6'2", 230 LB
Col: Pittsburgh; Tennessee *HS:* Ambridge [PA] B: 12/29/1939, Ambridge, PA *Drafted:* 1961 Round 5 Cle
1965 Det: KR 1-0. **Total:** KR 1-0.

		Interceptions			
Year Team	G	Int	Yds	TD	Fum
1962 Cle	13	0	0	0	0
1963 Cle	10	0	0	0	0
1964 Cle	14	0	0	0	0
1965 Det	11	0	0	0	0
1966 Det	13	5	118	1	0
1967 Det	14	2	47	1	0
1968 Det	12	1	1	0	0
1969 Det	14	0	0	0	0
1970 Det	14	2	18	0	0
1971 Det	14	5	74	2	1
1972 Det	14	2	0	0	0
1973 Det	11	4	50	0	0
NFL Total	154	21	308	4	1

DERREL LUCE Luce, Derrel Joe 6'3", 226 LB
Col: Baylor *HS:* Brazoswood [Freeport, TX] B: 9/29/1952, Lake Jackson, TX *Drafted:* 1975 Round 7 Bal
1975 Bal: 14 G. **1976** Bal: 14 G; Int 2-7; **1** Fum TD; 6 Pt. **1977** Bal: 12 G. **1978** Bal: 16 G; Int 1-15; 1 Fum TD; 6 Pt. **1979** Min: 16 G. **1980** Min-Det: 13 G. Min: 4 G. Det: 9 G. **Total:** 85 G; Int 3-22; 2 Fum TD; 12 Pt.

LEW LUCE Luce, Llewellyn Attsett Jr. 6'1", 187 HB
Col: Penn State *HS:* Woodrow Wilson [Washington, DC] B: 4/3/1938, Washington, DC
1961 Was: 2 G; Rush 3-1 0.3; PR 1-0; KR 4-77 19.3; 1 Fum.

JOHN LUCENTE Lucente, John 5'9", 200 FB-LB
Col: West Virginia *HS:* Notre Dame [Clarksburg, WV] B: 11/4/1922, Clarksburg, WV
1945 Pit: Rec 11-45 4.1; KR 5-102 20.4.

		Rushing					Tot
Year Team	G	Att	Yds	Avg	TD	Fum	TD
1945 Pit	10	82	242	3.0	1	8	2

OLIVER LUCK Luck, Oliver Francis 6'2", 196 QB
Col: West Virginia *HS:* St. Ignatius [Cleveland, OH] B: 4/5/1960, Cleveland, OH *Drafted:* 1982 Round 2 Hou

		Passing							
Year Team	G	Att	Comp	Comp%	Yds	YPA	TD	Int	Rating
1983 Hou	7	217	124	57.1	1375	6.34	8	13	63.4
1984 Hou	4	36	22	61.1	256	7.11	2	1	89.6
1985 Hou	5	100	56	56.0	572	5.72	2	2	70.9
1986 Hou	4	60	31	51.7	341	5.68	1	5	39.7
NFL Total	20	413	233	56.4	2544	6.16	13	21	64.1

	Rushing				
Year Team	Att	Yds	Avg	TD	Fum
1983 Hou	17	55	3.2	0	5
1984 Hou	10	75	7.5	1	2
1985 Hou	15	95	6.3	0	9
1986 Hou	2	12	6.0	0	0
NFL Total	44	237	5.4	1	16

TERRY LUCK Luck, Terry Lee 6'3", 205 QB
Col: Nebraska *HS:* Massey Hill [Fayetteville, NC] B: 12/14/1952, Fayetteville, NC
1977 Cle: Rush 3-(-2) -0.7; Rec 1-4 4.0 1 TD.

		Passing								
Year Team	G	Att	Comp	Comp%	Yds	YPA	TD	Int	Rating	Fum
1977 Cle	4	50	25	50.0	316	6.32	1	7	37.2	1

MICK LUCKHURST Luckhurst, Michael Christopher Wilbert 6'1", 180 K
Col: St. Cloud State; California *HS:* St. Columbus Coll. [Redbourn, England] B: 3/31/1958, Redbourn, England
1985 Atl: Punt 1-26 26.0. **1987** Atl: Punt 1-37 37.0. **Total:** Punt 2-63 31.5.

		Scoring						
Year Team	G	Pts	FG	FGA	FG%	XK	XKA	XK%
1981 Atl	16	114	21	33	63.6	51	51	100.0
1982 Atl	9	51	10	14	71.4	21	22	95.5
1983 Atl	16	94	17	22	77.3	43	45	95.6
1984 Atl	16	91	20	27	74.1	31	31	100.0
1985 Atl	16	101	24	31	77.4	29	29	100.0
1986 Atl	10	63	14	24	58.3	21	21	100.0
1987 Atl	12	44	9	13	69.2	17	17	100.0
NFL Total	95	558	115	164	70.1	213	216	98.6

SID LUCKMAN Luckman, Sidney 6'0", 197 QB-DB-HB
Col: Columbia *HS:* Erasmus Hall [Brooklyn, NY] B: 11/21/1916, Brooklyn, NY D: 7/5/1998, Aventura, FL *Drafted:* 1939 Round 1 ChiB
HOF: 1965
1941 ChiB: KR 2-29 14.5. **1942** ChiB: PR 6-55 9.2. **1943** ChiB: PR 4-46 11.5; KR 1-7 7.0. **1944** ChiB: PR 1-6 6.0. **1945** ChiB: KR 2-31 15.5. **1947** ChiB: Rec 1-15 15.0; Scor **1** 1XP. **Total:** Rec 1-15 15.0; PR 11-107 9.7; KR 5-67 13.4; Scor 1 1XP.

		Passing							
Year Team	G	Att	Comp	Comp%	Yds	YPA	TD	Int	Rating
1939 ChiB	11	51	23	45.1	636	**12.47**	5	4	91.6
1940 ChiB	11	105	48	45.7	941	**8.96**	4	9	54.5
1941 ChiB	11	119	68	**57.1**	1181	**9.92**	9	6	95.3
1942 ChiB	11	105	57	54.3	1024	9.75	10	13	80.1
1943 ChiB	10	202	110	54.5	**2194**	**10.86**	**28**	12	107.5
1944 ChiB	7	143	71	49.7	1018	7.12	11	12	63.8
1945 ChiB	10	217	117	53.9	**1727**	7.96	**14**	10	82.5
1946 ChiB	11	229	110	48.0	**1826**	7.97	**17**	16	71.0
1947 ChiB	12	323	176	54.5	2712	8.40	24	31	67.7
1948 ChiB	12	163	89	54.6	1047	6.42	13	14	65.1
1949 ChiB	11	50	22	44.0	200	4.00	1	3	37.1
1950 ChiB	11	37	13	35.1	180	4.86	1	2	38.1
NFL Total	128	1744	904	51.8	14686	8.42	137	132	75.0

	Rushing				Interceptions		
Year Team	Att	Yds	Avg	TD	Int	Yds	TD
1939 ChiB	24	42	1.8	0	—	—	**1**
1940 ChiB	23	-65	-2.8	0	3	17	0
1941 ChiB	18	18	1.0	1	3	52	0
1942 ChiB	13	-6	-0.5	0	4	96	**1**
1943 ChiB	22	-40	-1.8	1	4	85	0
1944 ChiB	20	-96	-4.8	1	2	36	0
1945 ChiB	36	-118	-3.3	0	0	0	0
1946 ChiB	25	-76	-3.0	0	1	24	0
1947 ChiB	10	86	8.6	1	0	0	0
1948 ChiB	8	11	1.4	0	0	0	0
1949 ChiB	3	4	1.3	0	0	0	0
1950 ChiB	2	1	0.5	0	0	0	0
NFL Total	204	-239	-1.2	4	17	310	2

	Punting				Tot
Year Team	Punts	Yds	Avg	Fum	TD
1939 ChiB	27	1199	44.4	0	1
1940 ChiB	27	1147	42.5	0	0
1941 ChiB	13	534	41.1	0	1
1942 ChiB	24	976	40.7	0	1
1943 ChiB	34	1220	35.9	0	1
1944 ChiB	20	685	34.3	0	1
1945 ChiB	36	1299	36.1	4	0
1946 ChiB	33	1235	37.4	7	0
1947 ChiB	5	177	35.4	2	1
1948 ChiB	10	384	38.4	1	0
1949 ChiB	1	16	16.0	1	0
NFL Total	230	8872	38.6	15	6

BILL LUCKY Lucky, William Henry Jr. 6'3", 250 DT
Col: Baylor *HS:* Temple [TX] B: 8/24/1931, Temple, TX *Drafted:* 1954 Round 5 Cle
1955 GB: 12 G.

BILL LUECK Lueck, William Melville 6'3", 250 **OG**
Col: Arizona *HS:* Agua Fria Union [Avondale, AZ] B: 4/7/1946, Buckeye, AZ *Drafted:* 1968 Round 1 GB
1968 GB: 11 G. **1969** GB: 14 G. **1970** GB: 14 G. **1971** GB: 14 G. **1972** GB: 14 G. **1973** GB: 14 G. **1974** GB: 9 G. **1975** Phi: 11 G. **Total:** 101 G.

DON LUFT Luft, Donald Richard 6'5", 220 **DE-OE**
Col: Indiana *HS:* South [Sheboygan, WI] B: 2/14/1930, Fisk, WI
1954 Phi: 12 G; Rec 3-59 19.7.

NOLAN LUHN Luhn, Nolan Harry 6'3", 200 **OE-DE**
Col: Kilgore Coll. TX (J.C.); Tulsa *HS:* Belville [TX] B: 7/27/1921, Kenney, TX *Drafted:* 1945 Round 23 GB
1946 GB: KR 2-28 14.0; Scor **1** Saf. **1947** GB: KR 2-30 15.0. **1948** GB: KR 3-18 6.0. **Total:** KR 7-76 10.9; Scor 1 Saf.

		Receiving				
Year Team	G	Rec	Yds	Avg	TD	Fum
1945 GB	9	10	151	15.1	1	0
1946 GB	11	16	224	14.0	2	1
1947 GB	12	42	696	16.6	7	1
1948 GB	12	17	285	16.8	2	0
1949 GB	12	15	169	11.3	1	0
NFL Total	56	100	1525	15.3	13	2

JOHNNY LUJACK Lujack, John Christopher Jr. 6'0", 186 **QB-DB**
Col: Notre Dame *HS:* Connellsville [PA] B: 1/4/1925, Connellsville, PA *Drafted:* 1946 Round 1 ChiB
1948 ChiB: Scor 50, 0-3 FG, 44-46 95.7% XK. **1949** ChiB: Punt 3-123 41.0; Scor 57, 1-1 100.0% FG, 42-44 95.5% XK. **1950** ChiB: Rec 1-16 16.0; Scor 109, 3-5 60.0% FG, 34-35 97.1% XK. **1951** ChiB: Scor 52, 10-11 90.9% XK. **Total:** Rec 1-16 16.0; Punt 3-123 41.0; Scor 268, 4-9 44.4% FG, 130-136 95.6% XK.

		Passing							
Year Team	G	Att	Comp	Comp%	Yds	YPA	TD	Int	Rating
1948 ChiB	9	66	36	54.5	611	**9.26**	6	3	97.5
1949 ChiB	12	**312**	**162**	51.9	**2658**	8.52	**23**	22	76.0
1950 ChiB	12	254	121	47.6	1731	6.81	4	21	41.0
1951 ChiB	12	176	85	48.3	1295	7.36	8	**8**	69.2
NFL Total	45	808	404	50.0	6295	7.79	41	54	65.3

	Rushing				Interceptions			
Year Team	Att	Yds	Avg	TD	Int	Yds	TD	Fum
1948 ChiB	15	110	7.3	1	8	131	0	1
1949 ChiB	8	64	8.0	2	0	0	0	2
1950 ChiB	63	397	**6.3**	**11**	1	15	0	2
1951 ChiB	47	171	3.6	7	3	44	0	2
NFL Total	133	742	5.6	21	12	190	0	7

STEVE LUKE Luke, Steven Norman 6'2", 205 **DB**
Col: Ohio State *HS:* Washington [Massillon, OH] B: 9/4/1953, Massillon, OH *Drafted:* 1975 Round 4 GB
1975 GB: KR 6-91 15.2. **Total:** KR 6-91 15.2.

		Interceptions			
Year Team	G	Int	Yds	TD	Fum
1975 GB	14	0	0	0	1
1976 GB	14	2	30	0	0
1977 GB	14	4	9	0	0
1978 GB	16	2	91	1	0
1979 GB	16	1	10	0	0
1980 GB	16	1	9	0	0
NFL Total	90	10	149	1	1

TOMMY LUKE Luke, Tommy Junior 6'0", 190 **DB**
Col: Mississippi *HS:* Nanih Waiya [Louisville, MS] B: 1/26/1944, Louisville, MS *Drafted:* 1967 Round 8 Buf
1968 Den: 7 G; PR 3-13 4.3; KR 2-34 17.0.

TOM LUKEN Luken, Thomas James 6'3", 253 **OG**
Col: Purdue *HS:* La Salle [Cincinnati, OH] B: 6/15/1950, Cincinnati, OH *Drafted:* 1972 Round 3 Phi
1972 Phi: 12 G. **1973** Phi: 3 G. **1974** Phi: 14 G. **1975** Phi: 5 G. **1977** Phi: 14 G. **1978** Phi: 16 G. **Total:** 64 G.

JIM LUKENS Lukens, James Willie Jr. 6'4", 205 **OE**
Col: Washington & Lee *HS:* Swarthmore [PA] B: 9/6/1924, Chester, PA
AAFC **1949** BufA: 11 G; Rec 24-249 10.4 2 TD; 12 Pt.

JACK LUMMUS Lummus, Jack Jr. 6'3", 194 **OE-DE**
Col: Baylor *HS:* Ennis [TX] B: 10/22/1915, Ennis, TX D: 3/8/1945, Iwo Jima
1941 NYG: 9 G; Rec 1-5 5.0.

JOEY LUMPKIN Lumpkin, Joseph Lynn 6'2", 230 **LB**
Col: Arizona State *HS:* Scottsdale [AZ] B: 2/19/1960, Ardmore, OK
1982 Buf: 6 G. **1983** Buf: 14 G. **Total:** 20 G.

RON LUMPKIN Lumpkin, Ronald 6'2", 205 **DB**
Col: Arizona State *HS:* Mount Carmel [Los Angeles, CA] B: 6/22/1951, Los Angeles, CA *Drafted:* 1973 Round 12 NYG
1973 NYG: 1 G.

FATHER LUMPKIN Lumpkin, Roy Lee 6'2", 211 **BB-DB-LB-FB**
Col: Georgia Tech *HS:* Oak Cliff [Dallas, TX] B: 1/27/1907, Jefferson, TX D: 3/31/1974, Dallas, TX
1930 Port: Pass 3 TD. **1933** Port: Pass 1-0. **1934** Det: Int **1** TD. **1935** Bkn: Pass 6-3 50.0%, 58 9.67 1 Int. **Total:** Pass 7-3 42.9%, 58 8.29 3 TD 1 Int; Int 1 TD.

		Rushing				Receiving				Tot
Year Team	G	Att	Yds	Avg	TD	Rec	Yds	Avg	TD	TD
1930 Port	14	—	—	—	3	—	—	—	0	3
1931 Port	14	—	—	—	1	—	—	—	0	1
1932 Port	12	25	47	1.9	0	6	80	13.3	1	1
1933 Port	11	7	26	3.7	0	10	191	19.1	1	1
1934 Det	13	6	44	7.3	1	4	24	6.0	0	2
1935 Bkn	12	11	26	2.4	0	4	26	6.5	0	0
1936 Bkn	12	11	29	2.6	0	6	34	5.7	0	0
1937 Bkn	5	0	0	—	0	0	0	—	0	0
NFL Total	93	60	172	2.9	5	30	355	11.8	2	8

SEAN LUMPKIN Lumpkin, Sean Franklin 6'0", 206 **DB**
Col: Minnesota *HS:* Benilde-St. Margaret [St. Louis Park, MN] B: 1/4/1970, Minneapolis, MN *Drafted:* 1992 Round 4 NO
1992 NO: 16 G. **1993** NO: 12 G. **1994** NO: 16 G; Int 1-1. **1995** NO: 16 G; Int 1-47 1 TD; 6 Pt. **1996** NO: 7 G. **Total:** 67 G; Int 2-48 1 TD; 6 Pt.

BOBBY LUNA Luna, Robert Kendal 5'11", 187 **DB**
Col: Alabama *HS:* Huntsville [AL] B: 3/25/1933, Lewisburg, TN *Drafted:* 1955 Round 6 SF
1955 SF: Int 2-0. **1959** Pit: Pass 1-1 100.0%, 55 55.00; Rush 3-3 1.0; PR 2-13 6.5; Int 3-53. **Total:** Pass 1-1 100.0%, 55 55.00; Rush 3-3 1.0; PR 2-13 6.5; Int 5-53.

		Punting			
Year Team	G	Punts	Yds	Avg	Fum
1955 SF	12	63	2558	40.6	0
1959 Pit	12	63	2563	40.7	1
NFL Total	24	126	5121	40.6	1

DAVE LUNCEFORD Lunceford, David Glenn 6'4", 240 **DT**
Col: Tyler JC TX; Baylor *HS:* Van [TX] B: 5/6/1934, Canton, TX *Drafted:* 1956 Round 8 ChiC
1957 ChiC: 12 G.

BILL LUND Lund, William Harold 5'10", 180 **HB-DB**
Col: Case Western Reserve *HS:* Cuyahoga Falls [OH] B: 10/27/1924, Akron, OH
AAFC **1946** CleA: Rec 4-64 16.0 2 TD; PR 2-30 15.0; KR 1-32 32.0; Int 1-12. **1947** CleA: Rec 6-110 18.3 1 TD; KR 2-37 18.5; Int 2-36 1 TD. **Total:** Rec 10-174 17.4 3 TD; PR 2-30 15.0; KR 3-69 23.0; Int 3-48 1 TD.

		Rushing				Tot
Year Team	G	Att	Yds	Avg	TD	TD
1946 CleA	10	23	72	3.1	1	3
1947 CleA	8	14	105	7.5	1	3
AAFC Total	18	37	177	4.8	2	6

KAYO LUNDAY Lunday, Levin Kenneth 6'3", 217 **LB-G-C**
Col: Arkansas *HS:* Cleora [OK] B: 8/13/1912, Cleora, OK
1937 NYG: 11 G. **1938** NYG: 11 G. **1939** NYG: 11 G. **1940** NYG: 10 G. **1941** NYG: 11 G; Int 1-5. **1946** NYG: 7 G. **1947** NYG: 6 G. **Total:** 67 G; Int 1-5.

BOB LUNDELL Lundell, Wilbur Harvey 6'4", 215 **E**
(Gloom) *Col:* Gustavus Adolphus *HS:* Edison [Minneapolis, MN] B: 6/21/1907, Pueblo, CO D: 7/7/1993, McAllen, TX
1929 Min: 10 G. **1930** Min-Sl: 10 G; Int 1 TD; 6 Pt. Min: 4 G. Sl: 6 G; Int 1 TD; 6 Pt. **Total:** 20 G; Int 1 TD; 6 Pt.

DENNIS LUNDY Lundy, Dennis Leonard 5'9", 190 **RB**
Col: Northwestern *HS:* Chamberlain [Tampa, FL] B: 7/6/1972, Tampa, FL
1995 Hou-ChiB: 9 G; Rec 1-11 11.0; PR 1-(-4) -4.0; KR 3-39 13.0; 1 Fum. Hou: 7 G; Rec 1-11 11.0; KR 2-28 14.0. ChiB: 2 G; PR 1-(-4) -4.0; KR 1-11 11.0; 1 Fum. **Total:** 9 G; Rec 1-11 11.0; PR 1-(-4) -4.0; KR 3-39 13.0; 1 Fum.

LAMAR LUNDY Lundy, Lamar Jr. 6'7", 245 **DE-OE**
Col: Purdue *HS:* Richmond [IN] B: 4/17/1935, Richmond, IN *Drafted:* 1957 Round 4 LARm
1957 LARm: KR 1-0. **1960** LARm: Int 1-25 1 TD. **1964** LARm: Int 1-14 1 TD. **1966** LARm: Int 1-33 1 TD. **Total:** KR 1-0; Int 3-72 3 TD.

		Receiving					Tot
Year Team	G	Rec	Yds	Avg	TD	Fum	TD
1957 LARm	12	6	114	19.0	3	0	3
1958 LARm	12	25	396	15.8	3	1	3

1959 LARm	12	4	74	18.5	0	0	0
1960 LARm	12	0	0	—	0	0	1
1961 LARm	14	0	0	—	0	0	0
1962 LARm	14	0	0	—	0	0	0
1963 LARm	14	0	0	—	0	0	0
1964 LARm	13	0	0	—	0	0	1
1965 LARm	12	0	0	—	0	0	0
1966 LARm	14	0	0	—	0	0	1
1967 LARm	14	0	0	—	0	0	0
1968 LARm	5	0	0	—	0	0	0
1969 LARm	4	0	0	—	0	0	0
NFL Total	152	35	584	16.7	6	1	9

CHARLIE LUNGREN Lungren, Charles Howard Jr. 5′8″, 158 **BB-WB**
Col: Swarthmore *HS:* Germantown [Philadelphia, PA]; Swarthmore Prep [PA] B: 6/23/1894 D: 3/21/1972, Milwaukee, WI
1923 RI: 4 G.

MEL LUNSFORD Lunsford, Melvin T 6′3″, 256 **DT-DE-NT**
Col: Central State (Ohio) *HS:* Lockland [OH] B: 6/13/1950, Cincinnati, OH *Drafted:* 1972 Round 3 Oak
1973 NE: 4 G. **1974** NE: 13 G. **1975** NE: 4 G. **1976** NE: 14 G. **1977** NE: 13 G. **1978** NE: 16 G. **1979** NE: 16 G. **1980** NE: 12 G. **Total:** 92 G.

JERRY LUNZ Lunz, Gerald A 6′3″, 210 **G-T**
Col: Marquette *HS:* Marquette Acad. [Milwaukee, WI] B: 3/13/1903, Milwaukee, WI D: 1/11/1974, Milwaukee, WI
1925 ChiC: 14 G. **1926** ChiC: 12 G; 6 Pt. **1930** Fra: 1 G. **Total:** 27 G; 6 Pt.

LADUE LURTH Lurth, Charles Andrew LaDue 6′0″, 180 **TB**
Col: Gustavus Adolphus *HS:* St. Peter [MN] B: 2/23/1905, LeSueur Co, MN D: 10/2/1991, Moab, UT
1929 Min: 1 G.

BOB LURTSEMA Lurtsema, Robert Ross 6′6″, 250 **DE-DT**
(Lurtz) *Col:* Grand Rapids CC MI; Michigan Tech; Western Michigan *HS:* Ottawa Hills [Grand Rapids, MI] B: 3/29/1942, Grand Rapids, MI
1967 NYG: 14 G; KR 1-7 7.0. **1968** NYG: 14 G; KR 1-11 11.0; Int 1-39. **1969** NYG: 13 G. **1970** NYG: 14 G. **1971** NYG: 7 G. **1972** Min: 14 G. **1973** Min: 14 G. **1974** Min: 12 G. **1975** Min: 14 G. **1976** Min-Sea: 14 G. Min: 1 G. Sea: 13 G. **1977** Sea: 14 G. **Total:** 144 G; KR 2-18 9.0; Int 1-39.

VAUGHN LUSBY Lusby, Alawndra Vaughn 5′10″, 178 **DB**
Col: Arkansas *HS:* MacArthur [Lawton, OK] B: 8/23/1956, Fort Polk, LA *Drafted:* 1979 Round 4 Cin
1979 Cin: KR 6-92 15.3. **Total:** KR 6-92 15.3.

		Punt Returns				
Year Team	**G**	**Ret**	**Yds**	**Avg**	**TD**	**Fum**
1979 Cin	16	32	260	8.1	0	2
1980 ChiB	2	4	14	3.5	0	1
NFL Total	18	36	274	7.6	0	3

JIM LUSCINSKI Luscinski, James V 6′5″, 275 **OT-OG**
Col: Norwich *HS:* Hanover [MA] B: 12/16/1958, Arlington, MA
1982 NYJ: 6 G.

MIKE LUSH Lush, Michael Stephen 6′2″, 195 **DB**
Col: East Stroudsburg *HS:* William Allen [Allentown, PA] B: 4/18/1958, Allentown, PA
1986 Ind-Min: 10 G. Ind: 4 G. Min: 6 G. **1987** Atl: 3 G. **Total:** 13 G.

HENRY LUSK Lusk, Hendrick Hamilton 6′2″, 245 **TE**
Col: Utah *HS:* Monterey [CA] B: 5/8/1972, Seaside, CA *Drafted:* 1996 Round 7 NO
1996 NO: KR 1-16 16.0. **1998** Mia: Rush 1-7 7.0. **Total:** Rush 1-7 7.0; KR 1-16 16.0.

		Receiving				
Year Team	**G**	**Rec**	**Yds**	**Avg**	**TD**	**Fum**
1996 NO	16	27	210	7.8	0	1
1998 Mia	3	0	0	—	0	0
NFL Total	19	27	210	7.8	0	1

HERB LUSK Lusk, Herbert H 6′0″, 190 **RB**
Col: Monterey Peninsula Coll. CA (J.C.); Long Beach State *HS:* Seaside [CA] B: 2/19/1953, Memphis, TN *Drafted:* 1976 Round 10 Phi
1976 Phi: Rec 13-119 9.2; KR 7-155 22.1. **1977** Phi: Rec 5-102 20.4 1 TD; KR 1-23 23.0. **1978** Phi: KR 3-61 20.3. **Total:** Rec 18-221 12.3 1 TD; KR 11-239 21.7.

		Rushing					Tot
Year Team	**G**	**Att**	**Yds**	**Avg**	**TD**	**Fum**	**TD**
1976 Phi	14	61	254	4.2	0	1	0
1977 Phi	11	52	229	4.4	2	1	3
1978 Phi	3	0	0	—	0	0	0
NFL Total	28	113	483	4.3	2	2	3

BOB LUSK Lusk, Robert Arlen 6′1″, 222 **C**
Col: William & Mary *HS:* Williamson [WV] B: 5/18/1932, Williamson, WV *Drafted:* 1956 Round 6 Det
1956 Det: 5 G.

BOOTH LUSTEG Lusteg, Gerald Booth 5′11″, 190 **K**
Col: Connecticut *HS:* New Haven [CT] B: 5/8/1939, New Haven, CT
1967 Mia: Pass 1-0. **Total:** Pass 1-0.

		Scoring						
Year Team	**G**	**Pts**	**FG**	**FGA**	**FG%**	**XK**	**XKA**	**XK%**
1966 Buf	14	98	19	**38**	50.0	**41**	**42**	97.6
1967 Mia	8	39	7	12	58.3	18	18	100.0
1968 Pit	13	50	8	20	40.0	26	29	89.7
1969 GB	4	15	1	5	20.0	12	12	100.0
NFL Total	39	202	35	75	46.7	97	101	96.0

ED LUTHER Luther, Edward Augustine 6′3″, 206 **QB**
Col: San Jose State *HS:* St. Paul [Santa Fe Springs, CA] B: 1/2/1957, Gardena, CA *Drafted:* 1980 Round 4 SD
1980 SD: Rush 3-5 1.7. **1981** SD: Rush 3-(-8) -2.7. **1982** SD: Rush 1-(-13) -13.0. **1983** SD: Rush 9-(-14) -1.6. **1984** SD: Rush 4-11 2.8. **Total:** Rush 20-(-19) -1.0.

		Passing								
Year Team	**G**	**Att**	**Comp**	**Comp%**	**Yds**	**YPA**	**TD**	**Int**	**Rating**	**Fum**
1980 SD	5	3	2	66.7	26	8.67	0	1	54.2	0
1981 SD	16	15	7	46.7	68	4.53	0	1	32.1	0
1982 SD	9	4	2	50.0	55	13.75	0	1	56.3	1
1983 SD	16	287	151	52.6	1875	6.53	7	17	56.6	6
1984 SD	15	151	83	55.0	1163	7.70	5	3	82.7	2
NFL Total	61	460	245	53.3	3187	6.93	12	23	63.2	9

DAVE LUTZ Lutz, David Graham 6′6″, 297 **OT-OG**
Col: Georgia Tech *HS:* Bowman [Wadesboro, NC] B: 12/20/1959, Monroe, NC *Drafted:* 1983 Round 2 KC
1983 KC: 16 G. **1984** KC: 7 G. **1985** KC: 16 G. **1986** KC: 9 G. **1987** KC: 12 G. **1988** KC: 15 G. **1989** KC: 16 G. **1990** KC: 16 G. **1991** KC: 16 G. **1992** KC: 16 G. **1993** Det: 16 G. **1994** Det: 16 G. **1995** Det: 16 G. **Total:** 187 G.

ALLEN LYDAY Lyday, Allen Clark 5′10″, 190 **DB**
Col: Texas Southern; Nebraska *HS:* South [Wichita, KS] B: 9/16/1960, Wichita, KS
1984 Hou: 4 G; Int 1-12. **1985** Hou: 13 G; KR 1-6 6.0; 1 Fum. **1986** Hou: 12 G; Int 3-24. **1987** Hou: 7 G. **Total:** 36 G; KR 1-6 6.0; Int 4-36; 1 Fum.

TODD LYGHT Lyght, Todd William 6′0″, 190 **DB**
Col: Notre Dame *HS:* Luke M. Powers [Flint, MI] B: 2/9/1969, Kwajalein, Marshall Islands *Drafted:* 1991 Round 1 LARm
1994 LARm: PR 1-29 29.0; 1 Fum TD. **1995** StL: PR 0-16. **1997** StL: 1 Sac. **1998** StL: 1.5 Sac. **Total:** PR 1-45 45.0; 1 Fum TD; 2.5 Sac.

		Interceptions				Tot
Year Team	**G**	**Int**	**Yds**	**TD**	**Fum**	**TD**
1991 LARm	12	1	0	0	1	0
1992 LARm	12	3	80	0	0	0
1993 LARm	9	2	0	0	0	0
1994 LARm	16	1	14	0	0	1
1995 StL	16	4	34	1	0	1
1996 StL	16	5	43	1	1	1
1997 StL	16	4	25	0	0	0
1998 StL	16	3	30	0	0	0
NFL Total	113	23	226	2	2	3

DEWEY LYLE Lyle, Dewitt W 5′11″, 196 **G-T-OE**
Col: Minnesota *HS:* Central [Minneapolis, MN] B: 3/23/1891 D: 11/27/1980, Paso Robles, CA
1920 RI: 8 G. **1921** RI: 7 G. **1922** RI-GB: 8 G. RI: 6 G. GB: 2 G. **1923** GB: 9 G. **Total:** 32 G.

GARRY LYLE Lyle, Garry Thomas 6′2″, 198 **DB-RB**
Col: George Washington *HS:* Verona [PA] B: 10/20/1945, New Martinsville, WV *Drafted:* 1967 Round 3 ChiB
1968 ChiB: Rush 4-28 7.0; Rec 5-32 6.4; Punt 4-134 33.5. **1969** ChiB: Rec 1-11 11.0; PR 12-78 6.5; KR 11-248 22.5. **1970** ChiB: Rec 1-5 5.0; PR 9-37 4.1; Punt 1-29 29.0. **1971** ChiB: PR 1-5 5.0. **Total:** Rush 4-28 7.0; Rec 7-48 6.9; PR 22-120 5.5; KR 11-248 22.5; Punt 5-163 32.6.

		Interceptions			
Year Team	**G**	**Int**	**Yds**	**TD**	**Fum**
1968 ChiB	12	0	0	0	1
1969 ChiB	13	1	10	0	2
1970 ChiB	14	0	0	0	1
1971 ChiB	14	1	29	0	0
1972 ChiB	3	2	52	0	0
1973 ChiB	14	5	62	0	0
1974 ChiB	14	3	57	0	0
NFL Total	84	12	210	0	4

KEITH LYLE Lyle, Keith Allen 6′2″, 210 **DB**
Col: Virginia *HS:* Mendon [NY]; George C. Marshall HS [Falls Church, VA] B: 4/17/1972, Washington, DC *Drafted:* 1994 Round 3 LARm
1995 StL: Rush 1-4 4.0. **1996** StL: Rush 3-39 13.0. **1997** StL: 2 Sac. **1998** StL: 1 Sac. **Total:** Rush 4-43 10.8; 3 Sac.

Year Team	G	Interceptions Int	Yds	TD	Fum
1994 LARm	16	2	1	0	0
1995 StL	16	3	42	0	0
1996 StL	16	**9**	152	0	1
1997 StL	16	8	102	0	0
1998 StL	16	3	20	0	0
NFL Total	80	25	317	0	1

RICK LYLE Lyle, Rick James Earl 6'5", 283 **DE**
Col: Missouri *HS:* Hickman Mills [Kansas City, MO] B: 2/26/1971, Monroe, LA
1994 Cle: 3 G. **1996** Bal: 11 G; 1 Sac. **1997** NYJ: 16 G; 3 Sac. **1998** NYJ: 16 G; 1.5 Sac. **Total:** 46 G; 5.5 Sac.

LENNY LYLES Lyles, Leonard Everett 6'2", 202 **DB-HB**
Col: Louisville *HS:* Central [Louisville, KY] B: 1/26/1936, Nashville, TN
Drafted: 1958 Round 1 Bal
1958 Bal: Rec 5-24 4.8 1 TD. **1959** SF: Rec 3-33 11.0. **Total:** Rec 8-57 7.1 1 TD.

Year Team	G	Rushing Att	Yds	Avg	TD	Kickoff Returns Ret	Yds	Avg	TD
1958 Bal	12	22	41	1.9	1	11	398	36.2	**2**
1959 SF	12	13	28	2.2	1	**25**	**565**	22.6	0
1960 SF	12	0	0	—	0	17	526	30.9	**1**
1961 Bal	14	0	0	—	0	28	672	24.0	0
1962 Bal	6	0	0	—	0	0	0	—	0
1963 Bal	14	0	0	—	0	0	0	—	0
1964 Bal	14	0	0	—	0	0	0	—	0
1965 Bal	11	0	0	—	0	0	0	—	0
1966 Bal	14	0	0	—	0	0	0	—	0
1967 Bal	12	0	0	—	0	0	0	—	0
1968 Bal	14	0	0	—	0	0	0	—	0
1969 Bal	14	0	0	—	0	0	0	—	0
NFL Total	149	35	69	2.0	2	81	2161	26.7	3

Year Team	Interceptions Int	Yds	TD	Fum	Tot TD
1958 Bal	0	0	0	4	4
1959 SF	0	0	0	1	1
1960 SF	0	0	0	0	1
1961 Bal	0	0	0	1	0
1963 Bal	2	36	1	0	1
1964 Bal	2	40	0	0	0
1965 Bal	1	28	0	0	0
1966 Bal	1	6	0	0	0
1967 Bal	5	59	1	0	1
1968 Bal	5	32	0	0	0
NFL Total	16	201	2	6	8

LESTER LYLES Lyles, Lester Everett 6'3", 209 **DB-LB**
Col: Virginia *HS:* St. Albans [Washington, DC] B: 12/27/1962, Washington, DC *Drafted:* 1985 Round 2 NYJ
1985 NYJ: 3 Sac. **1986** NYJ: 1 Sac. **1989** SD: PR 1-0; 1 Sac. **1990** SD: PR 1-0. **Total:** PR 2-0; 5 Sac.

Year Team	G	Interceptions Int	Yds	TD	Fum
1985 NYJ	6	0	0	0	0
1986 NYJ	16	5	36	0	0
1987 NYJ	4	0	0	0	0
1988 Pho	6	2	0	0	0
1989 SD	16	2	28	0	1
1990 SD	15	1	19	0	0
NFL Total	63	10	83	0	1

ROBERT LYLES Lyles, Robert Damon 6'1", 226 **LB**
Col: Texas Christian *HS:* Belmont [Los Angeles, CA] B: 3/21/1961, Los Angeles, CA *Drafted:* 1984 Round 5 Hou
1986 Hou: **1** Fum TD; 3 Sac. **1987** Hou: **1** Fum TD; 2 Sac. **1988** Hou: 1.5 Sac. **1989** Hou: KR 1-0; 2 Sac. **1990** Hou-Atl: 1.5 Sac. Atl: 1.5 Sac. **Total:** KR 1-0; 2 Fum TD; 10 Sac.

Year Team	G	Interceptions Int	Yds	TD
1984 Hou	6	0	0	0
1985 Hou	16	0	0	0
1986 Hou	16	2	0	0
1987 Hou	12	2	42	0
1988 Hou	16	2	3	0
1989 Hou	13	4	66	0
1990 Hou-Atl	14	0	0	0
1990 Hou	3	0	0	0
1990 Atl	11	0	0	0
1991 Atl	16	0	0	0
NFL Total	109	10	111	0

JEFF LYMAN Lyman, Jeffrey Borden 6'3", 235 **LB**
Col: Brigham Young *HS:* Skyline [Salt Lake City, UT] B: 8/21/1950, Salt Lake City, UT *Drafted:* 1972 Round 4 StL
1972 StL-Buf: 3 G. StL: 2 G. Buf: 1 G. **Total:** 3 G.

DEL LYMAN Lyman, Marion Dell 6'3", 223 **T**
Col: UCLA *HS:* Fairfax [Los Angeles, CA] B: 7/9/1918, Aberdeen, WA
D: 12/19/1986, Ojai, CA *Drafted:* 1941 Round 12 GB
1941 GB-Cle: 9 G. GB: 5 G. Cle: 4 G. **1944** Cle: 2 G. **Total:** 11 G.

LINK LYMAN Lyman, William Roy 6'2", 233 **T**
Col: Nebraska *HS:* McDonald Rural [KS] B: 11/30/1898, Table Rock, NE D: 12/28/1972, Barstow, CA *HOF:* 1964
1922 Can: 12 G. **1923** Can: 12 G; Rec 1 TD; 6 Pt. **1924** Cle: 9 G; Rec 1 TD; Scor 25, 1 XK; 3 Fum TD; Tot TD 4. **1925** Can-Fra: 11 G. Can: 7 G. Fra: 4 G. **1926** ChiB: 15 G. **1927** ChiB: 14 G. **1928** ChiB: 13 G. **1930** ChiB: 11 G. **1931** ChiB: 11 G; 1 Fum TD; 6 Pt. **1933** ChiB: 13 G. **1934** ChiB: 12 G. **Total:** 133 G; Rec 2 TD; 4 Fum TD; Tot TD 6.

LYNCH Lynch **G**
Deceased
1921 Cin: 1 G.

PAUL LYNCH Lynch, E. Paul 6'1", 190 **WB-BB**
(Deac) *Col:* Ohio Northern D: 9/25/1961
1925 Col: 7 G.

ED LYNCH Lynch, Edward James 5'11", 190 **E-T**
(Ace) *Col:* Catholic *HS:* St. Michael's [Northampton, MA]
B: 10/4/1896, Northampton, MA D: 8/24/1967, Dearborn, MI
1925 Roch: 6 G. **1926** Har: 1 G. Det: 12 G. **1927** Prov: 11 G; Rec 1 TD; 6 Pt. **1929** Ora: 5 G. **Total:** 35 G; Rec 1 TD; 6 Pt.

ERIC LYNCH Lynch, Eric 5'10", 224 **RB**
Col: Grand Valley State *HS:* Woodhaven [Flat Rock, MI] B: 5/16/1970, Woodhaven, MI
1993 Det: Rec 13-82 6.3; KR 1-22 22.0. **1994** Det: Rec 2-18 9.0; KR 9-105 11.7. **1996** Det: KR 1-15 15.0. **Total:** Rec 15-100 6.7; KR 11-142 12.9.

Year Team	G	Rushing Att	Yds	Avg	TD	Fum
1992 Det	1	0	0	—	0	0
1993 Det	4	53	207	3.9	2	1
1994 Det	12	1	0	0.0	0	0
1995 Det	4	0	0	—	0	0
1996 Det	16	2	2	1.0	0	1
NFL Total	37	56	209	3.7	2	2

FRAN LYNCH Lynch, Francis Xavier 6'1", 205 **RB**
Col: Oklahoma Mil. Acad. (J.C.); Hofstra *HS:* Fairfield [CT]
B: 12/3/1945, Bridgeport, CT *Drafted:* 1967 Round 5 Den
1967 Den: KR 1-27 27.0. **1968** Den: Pass 2-1 50.0%, 4 2.00. **1970** Den: KR 0-11. **1971** Den: KR 0-19; Scor 1 Saf. **1972** Den: KR 3-45 15.0. **1973** Den: KR 1-14 14.0. **1975** Den: PR 1-0. **Total:** Pass 2-1 50.0%, 4 2.00; PR 1-0; KR 5-116 23.2; Scor 1 Saf.

Year Team	G	Rushing Att	Yds	Avg	TD	Receiving Rec	Yds	Avg	TD	Fum	Tot TD
1967 Den	6	2	7	3.5	0	0	0	—	0	0	0
1968 Den	9	66	221	3.3	4	4	52	13.0	0	1	4
1969 Den	11	96	407	4.2	2	9	86	9.6	0	1	2
1970 Den	14	20	81	4.1	1	7	69	9.9	0	1	1
1971 Den	10	26	162	6.2	0	2	42	21.0	1	0	1
1972 Den	14	34	164	4.8	2	7	75	10.7	0	2	2
1973 Den	9	0	0	—	0	0	0	—	0	0	0
1974 Den	12	3	-2	-0.7	0	0	0	—	0	0	0
1975 Den	14	57	218	3.8	3	6	33	5.5	1	1	4
NFL Total	99	304	1258	4.1	12	35	357	10.2	2	6	14

JIM LYNCH Lynch, James Robert 6'1", 235 **LB**
Col: Notre Dame *HS:* Central Catholic [Lima, OH] B: 8/28/1945, Lima, OH *Drafted:* 1967 Round 2 KC

Year Team	G	Interceptions Int	Yds	TD
1967 KC	14	1	26	0
1968 KC	14	3	73	1
1969 KC	14	3	18	0
1970 KC	14	3	40	0
1971 KC	14	1	10	0
1972 KC	14	0	0	0
1973 KC	14	1	9	0
1974 KC	14	0	0	0
1975 KC	14	0	0	0
1976 KC	14	2	7	0
1977 KC	11	3	8	0
NFL Total	151	17	191	1

JOHN LYNCH Lynch, John Terrence 6′2″, 214 **DB**
Col: Stanford *HS:* Torrey Pines [Encinitas, CA] B: 9/25/1971, Hinsdale, IL *Drafted:* 1993 Round 3 TB
1996 TB: Rush 1-40 40.0; 1 Sac. **1998** TB: 2 Sac. **Total:** Rush 1-40 40.0; 3 Sac.

		Interceptions			
Year Team	**G**	**Int**	**Yds**	**TD**	**Fum**
1993 TB	15	0	0	0	0
1994 TB	16	0	0	0	0
1995 TB	9	3	3	0	0
1996 TB	16	3	26	0	1
1997 TB	16	2	28	0	0
1998 TB	15	2	29	0	0
NFL Total	87	10	86	0	1

LORENZO LYNCH Lynch, Lorenzo 5′11″, 200 **DB**
Col: Chabot Coll. CA (J.C.); Sacramento State *HS:* Oakland [CA] B: 4/6/1963, Oakland, CA
1987 ChiB: KR 3-66 22.0. **1993** Pho: 1 Fum TD; 1 Sac. **1994** Ariz: 0.5 Sac. **1995** Ariz: 1 Sac. **1997** Oak: 1 Sac. **Total:** KR 3-66 22.0; 1 Fum TD; 3.5 Sac.

		Interceptions			Tot
Year Team	**G**	**Int**	**Yds**	**TD**	**TD**
1987 ChiB	2	0	0	0	0
1988 ChiB	9	0	0	0	0
1989 ChiB	16	3	55	0	0
1990 Pho	16	0	0	0	0
1991 Pho	16	3	59	1	1
1992 Pho	16	0	0	0	0
1993 Pho	16	3	13	0	1
1994 Ariz	15	2	35	0	0
1995 Ariz	12	1	72	1	1
1996 Oak	16	3	75	0	0
1997 Oak	15	2	6	0	0
NFL Total	149	17	315	2	3

LYNN LYNCH Lynch, Lynn E 6′2″, 225 **OG**
Col: Illinois *HS:* Indianapolis Tech [IN] B: 8/10/1928, Indianapolis, IN *Drafted:* 1951 Round 5 ChiC
1951 ChiC: 3 G.

DICK LYNCH Lynch, Richard Dennis 6′1″, 202 **DB**
Col: Notre Dame *HS:* Cathedral [Phillipsburg, NJ] B: 4/29/1936, Oceanside, NY *Drafted:* 1958 Round 6 Was
1965 NYG: **1** Fum TD. **Total:** 1 Fum TD.

		Interceptions				Tot
Year Team	**G**	**Int**	**Yds**	**TD**	**Fum**	**TD**
1958 Was	12	2	24	0	0	0
1959 NYG	12	1	0	0	0	0
1960 NYG	12	3	61	1	0	1
1961 NYG	14	**9**	60	0	2	0
1962 NYG	13	5	90	0	0	2
1963 NYG	14	**9**	**251**	**3**	1	3
1964 NYG	10	4	68	0	0	0
1965 NYG	14	4	38	0	0	1
1966 NYG	8	0	0	0	0	0
NFL Total	109	37	592	4	3	7

TOM LYNCH Lynch, Thomas Frank 6′5″, 256 **OG**
Col: Boston College *HS:* Whitman-Hanson [Whitman, MA] B: 5/24/1955, Chicago, IL *Drafted:* 1977 Round 2 Sea
1977 Sea: 14 G. **1978** Sea: 16 G. **1979** Sea: 15 G. **1980** Sea: 16 G. **1981** Buf: 5 G. **1982** Buf: 8 G. **1983** Buf: 15 G. **1984** Buf: 16 G. **Total:** 105 G.

ANTHONY LYNN Lynn, Anthony Ray 6′3″, 230 **RB**
Col: Texas Tech *HS:* Celina [TX] B: 12/21/1968, McKinney, TX
1996 SF: Rec 2-14 7.0. **1997** Den: Rec 1-21 21.0. **Total:** Rec 3-35 11.7.

		Rushing			
Year Team	**G**	**Att**	**Yds**	**Avg**	**TD**
1993 Den	13	0	0	—	0
1995 SF	6	2	11	5.5	0
1996 SF	16	24	164	6.8	0
1997 Den	16	0	0	—	0
1998 Den	16	0	0	—	0
NFL Total	67	26	175	6.7	0

JOHNNY LYNN Lynn, Johnny Ross 6′0″, 196 **DB**
Col: UCLA *HS:* John Muir [Pasadena, CA] B: 12/19/1956, Los Angeles, CA *Drafted:* 1979 Round 4 NYJ
1986 NYJ: KR 1-0. **Total:** KR 1-0.

		Interceptions			Tot
Year Team	**G**	**Int**	**Yds**	**TD**	**TD**
1979 NYJ	16	2	46	0	1
1981 NYJ	13	3	76	0	0
1982 NYJ	8	1	3	0	0
1983 NYJ	16	3	70	1	1
1984 NYJ	14	2	16	0	0
1985 NYJ	14	1	24	0	0
1986 NYJ	16	5	36	0	0
NFL Total	97	17	271	1	2

BABE LYON Lyon, George Cardinal 6′2″, 235 **T-G**
Col: Kansas State B: 3/30/1907, Jamestown, KS D: 12/22/1970, Manhattan, KS
1929 NYG: 1 G. **1930** Port: 10 G. **1931** ChiB-Cle: 8 G. ChiB: 1 G. Cle: 7 G. **1932** Bkn: 10 G. **1934** StL: 3 G. **Total:** 32 G.

BILLY LYON Lyon, William Morton 6′5″, 295 **DE**
Col: Marshall *HS:* Lloyd Memorial [Erlanger, KY] B: 12/10/1973, Ashland, KY
1998 GB: 4 G; 1 Sac.

JOHN LYONS Lyons, John Stacy 6′1″, 185 **OE-DE**
Col: Tulsa B: 9/10/1911, Coronado, CA D: 11/1981, Bonita, CA
1933 Bkn: 2 G.

LAMAR LYONS Lyons, Lamar Kahlil-Kasim II 6′3″, 210 **DB**
Col: Washington *HS:* University [Los Angeles, CA]; St. Monica's HS [Santa Monica, CA] B: 3/25/1973, Los Angeles, CA
1996 Oak: 6 G. **1997** Bal: 1 G. **Total:** 7 G.

MARTY LYONS Lyons, Martin Anthony 6′5″, 269 **DT-DE-NT**
Col: Alabama *HS:* St. Petersburg Catholic [FL] B: 1/5/1957, Takoma Park, MD *Drafted:* 1979 Round 1 NYJ
1979 NYJ: 16 G. **1980** NYJ: 16 G. **1981** NYJ: 12 G. **1982** NYJ: 7 G; 1.5 Sac. **1983** NYJ: 16 G; 4 Sac. **1984** NYJ: 13 G; 2 Sac. **1985** NYJ: 16 G; 6.5 Sac. **1986** NYJ: 12 G; 3 Sac. **1987** NYJ: 13 G; Scor **1** Saf; 2 Pt; 3.5 Sac. **1988** NYJ: 16 G; Scor 1 Saf; 2 Pt; 7.5 Sac. **1989** NYJ: 10 G; 1 Sac. **Total:** 147 G; Scor 2 Saf; 4 Pt; 29.0 Sac.

MITCH LYONS Lyons, Mitchell Warren 6′5″, 265 **TE**
Col: Michigan State *HS:* Forest Hills Northern [Grand Rapids, MI] B: 5/13/1970, Grand Rapids, MI *Drafted:* 1993 Round 6 Atl
1998 Pit: KR 2-(-4) -2.0. **Total:** KR 2-(-4) -2.0.

		Receiving			
Year Team	**G**	**Rec**	**Yds**	**Avg**	**TD**
1993 Atl	16	8	63	7.9	0
1994 Atl	7	7	54	7.7	0
1995 Atl	14	5	83	16.6	0
1996 Atl	14	4	16	4.0	1
1997 Pit	10	4	29	7.3	0
1998 Pit	15	3	19	6.3	0
NFL Total	76	31	264	8.5	1

PRATT LYONS Lyons, Pratt Gilbert Jr. 6′5″, 295 **DE**
Col: Utah State; Troy State *HS:* Trimble Tech [Fort Worth, TX] B: 9/17/1974, Fort Worth, TX *Drafted:* 1997 Round 4 Ten
1997 Ten: 16 G; 2.5 Sac. **1998** Ten: 16 G; 2 Sac. **Total:** 32 G; 4.5 Sac.

DICKY LYONS Lyons, Richard 6′0″, 191 **DB**
Col: Kentucky *HS:* St. Xavier [Louisville, KY] B: 8/11/1947, Louisville, KY
1970 NO: 4 G; PR 5-34 6.8; KR 1-20 20.0; Int 1-12; 1 Fum.

ROBERT LYONS Lyons, Robert Louis 6′2″, 200 **DB**
Col: Akron *HS:* St. Clairsville [OH] B: 5/16/1966, Wheeling, WV
1989 Cle: 9 G; Int 1-0.

TOMMY LYONS Lyons, Thomas Lewis 6′2″, 230 **OG-C**
Col: Georgia *HS:* Georgia Mil. Coll. [Milledgeville, GA] B: 8/7/1948, Atlanta, GA *Drafted:* 1971 Round 14 Den
1971 Den: 11 G. **1972** Den: 10 G. **1973** Den: 14 G. **1974** Den: 14 G. **1975** Den: 10 G. **1976** Den: 14 G; Rec 1-(-1) -1.0. **Total:** 73 G; Rec 1-(-1) -1.0.

ROB LYTLE Lytle, Robert William 6′1″, 198 **RB**
Col: Michigan *HS:* Ross [Fremont, OH] B: 11/12/1954, Fremont, OH *Drafted:* 1977 Round 2 Den
1980 Den: KR 1-19 19.0. **1981** Den: KR 5-80 16.0. **Total:** KR 6-99 16.5.

		Rushing				Receiving					Tot
Year Team	**G**	**Att**	**Yds**	**Avg**	**TD**	**Rec**	**Yds**	**Avg**	**TD**	**Fum**	**TD**
1977 Den	14	104	408	3.9	1	17	198	11.6	1	2	2
1978 Den	13	81	341	4.2	2	6	37	6.2	0	0	2
1979 Den	15	102	371	3.6	4	13	93	7.2	0	1	4
1980 Den	16	57	223	3.9	1	18	177	9.8	0	1	1
1981 Den	16	30	106	3.5	4	6	47	7.8	1	1	5
1982 Den	9	2	2	1.0	0	1	10	10.0	0	0	0
1983 Den	4	0	0	—	0	0	0	—	0	0	0
NFL Total	87	376	1451	3.9	12	61	562	9.2	2	5	14

HERB MAACK Maack, Herbert Henry 6′2″, 210 **T**
Col: Columbia *HS:* Hun School [West New York, NJ] B: 4/6/1917, Union City, NJ
AAFC **1946** BknA: 7 G.

J.D. MAARLEVELD Maarleveld, John David 6′6″, 300 **OT**
Col: Notre Dame; Maryland *HS:* St. Joseph of the Palisades [West New York, NJ] B: 10/24/1961, Jersey City, NJ *Drafted:* 1986 Round 5 TB
1986 TB: 14 G. **1987** TB: 11 G. **Total:** 25 G.

BILL MAAS Maas, William Thomas 6′5″, 271 **NT-DE**
Col: Pittsburgh *HS:* Marple Newtown [Newtown Square, PA] B: 3/2/1962, Newton Square, PA *Drafted:* 1984 Round 1 KC
1984 KC: 14 G; 5 Sac. **1985** KC: 16 G; 7 Sac. **1986** KC: 16 G; 7 Sac. **1987** KC: 11 G; **1** Fum TD; 6 Pt; 6 Sac. **1988** KC: 8 G; Scor 1 Saf; 2 Pt; 4 Sac. **1989** KC: 10 G; 1 Fum TD; 6 Pt. **1990** KC: 16 G; Scor **1** Saf; 2 Pt; 5.5 Sac. **1991** KC: 16 G; 4 Sac. **1992** KC: 9 G; 1.5 Sac. **1993** GB: 14 G. **Total:** 130 G; Scor 2 Saf; 2 Fum TD; 16 Pt; 40 Sac.

RON MABRA Mabra, Ronald Edwin 5′10″, 166 **DB**
Col: Howard *HS:* Westside [Talladega, AL] B: 6/4/1951, Talladega, AL
1975 Atl: 8 G; PR 4-20 5.0. **1976** Atl: 8 G; PR 1-0; KR 3-61 20.3. **1977** NYJ: 3 G. **Total:** 19 G; PR 5-20 4.0; KR 3-61 20.3.

KEN MACAFEE MacAfee, Kenneth Adams II 6′4″, 250 **TE**
Col: Notre Dame *HS:* Brockton [MA] B: 1/9/1956, Portland, OR
Drafted: 1978 Round 1 SF

		Receiving			
Year Team	**G**	**Rec**	**Yds**	**Avg**	**TD**
1978 SF	13	22	205	9.3	1
1979 SF	16	24	266	11.1	4
NFL Total	29	46	471	10.2	5

KEN MACAFEE MacAfee, Kenneth Adams Sr. 6′2″, 212 **OE**
Col: Alabama *HS:* Oliver Ames [North Easton, MA] B: 8/31/1929, North Easton, MA
1959 Phi-Was: KR 1-12 12.0. Was: KR 1-12 12.0. **Total:** KR 1-12 12.0.

		Receiving				
Year Team	**G**	**Rec**	**Yds**	**Avg**	**TD**	**Fum**
1954 NYG	11	24	438	18.3	8	0
1955 NYG	8	11	170	15.5	1	0
1956 NYG	12	14	184	13.1	4	0
1957 NYG	11	16	229	14.3	2	2
1958 NYG	10	5	52	10.4	2	0
1959 Phi-Was	11	9	87	9.7	1	0
1959 Phi	4	5	48	9.6	0	0
1959 Was	7	4	39	9.8	1	0
NFL Total	63	79	1160	14.7	18	2

JOHN MACAULAY Macaulay, John Dunn 6′3″, 254 **C**
Col: Stanford *HS:* Bonita Vista [Chula Vista, CA] B: 4/27/1959, San Diego, CA *Drafted:* 1982 Round 11 GB
1984 SF: 3 G.

MAX MACCOLLUM MacCollum, Maxwell Speers 5′11″, 165 **OE**
(Red) *Col:* Centre *HS:* Male [Louisville, KY] B: 2/22/1900, Marietta, OH D: 9/25/1943, Indianapolis, IN
1922 Lou: 1 G.

ALLEN MACDONALD MacDonald, Allen J 5′10″, 170 **WB-FB**
Col: No College B: 3/1896, Duluth, MN Deceased
1924 Dul: 6 G.

DAN MACDONALD MacDonald, Dante J 6′2″, 230 **LB**
Col: Golden West Coll. CA (J.C.); Idaho State *HS:* Kennewick [WA] B: 9/2/1962, San Bernardino, CA
1987 Den: 3 G.

BUCK MACDONALD MacDonald, George Glover 5′10″, 180 **G-BB**
Col: Lehigh B: 5/5/1894, Nova Scotia, Canada D: 3/1/1985, Miami Springs, FL
1920 Can: 2 G. **1921** Ton-NYG: 2 G. Ton: 1 G. NYG: 1 G. **Total:** 4 G.

MARK MACDONALD MacDonald, Mark Goodwin 6′4″, 267 **OG**
Col: Boston College *HS:* Catholic Memorial [Boston, MA] B: 4/30/1961, West Roxbury, MA *Drafted:* 1985 Round 5 Min
1985 Min: 16 G. **1986** Min: 10 G. **1987** Min: 12 G. **1988** Min-Pho: 6 G. Min: 5 G. Pho: 1 G. **Total:** 44 G.

MICKEY MACDONNELL MacDonnell, John D 5′8″, 159 **WB-TB-BB**
Col: No College B: 1904 Deceased
1923 Dul: 1 G. **1925** Dul-ChiC: 5 G; Rec 1 TD; 6 Pt. Dul: 3 G; Rec 1 TD; 6 Pt. ChiC: 2 G. **1926** ChiC: 11 G; Rush 1 TD; Rec 1 TD; Tot TD 2; 12 Pt. **1927** ChiC: 9 G; Pass 1 TD. **1928** ChiC: 1 G. **1929** ChiC: 13 G; Rec 1 TD; PR **1** TD; Tot TD 2; 12 Pt. **1930** ChiC: 8 G. **1931** Fra: 3 G. **Total:** 51 G; Pass 1 TD; Rush 1 TD; Rec 3 TD; PR 1 TD; Tot TD 5; 30 Pt.

JAY MACDOWELL MacDowell, Jay Sidney 6′2″, 217 **DT-OT-DE-OE**
Col: Washington *HS:* Oak Park [IL] B: 9/14/1919, Oak Park, IL D: 6/15/1992, Springfield, DE *Drafted:* 1941 Round 3 Cle
1946 Phi: 6 G; Rec 1-28 28.0; Scor **1** Saf; 2 Pt. **1947** Phi: 12 G. **1948** Phi: 12 G. **1949** Phi: 8 G. **1950** Phi: 12 G. **1951** Phi: 12 G. **Total:** 62 G; Rec 1-28 28.0; Scor 1 Saf; 2 Pt.

MEL MACEAU Maceau, Melvin Anthony 6′0″, 203 **C-LB**
Col: Marquette *HS:* Rufus King [Milwaukee, WI] B: 12/25/1921, Milwaukee, WI D: 2/1981, Rudolph, OH
AAFC **1946** CleA: 12 G. **1947** CleA: 14 G. **1948** CleA: 11 G. **Total:** 37 G.

DON MACEK Macek, Donald Matthew 6′3″, 261 **C-OG**
Col: Boston College *HS:* Manchester Central [NH] B: 7/21/1954, Manchester, NH *Drafted:* 1976 Round 2 SD
1976 SD: 14 G. **1977** SD: 14 G. **1978** SD: 14 G; KR 1-6 6.0; 1 Fum. **1979** SD: 10 G. **1980** SD: 16 G; 2 Fum. **1981** SD: 15 G. **1982** SD: 9 G; 1 Fum. **1983** SD: 11 G. **1984** SD: 13 G. **1985** SD: 15 G. **1986** SD: 13 G. **1987** SD: 11 G; 1 Fum. **1988** SD: 5 G; 1 Fum. **1989** SD: 2 G. **Total:** 162 G; KR 1-6 6.0; 6 Fum.

JOHN MACERELLI Macerelli, John Edward 6′2″, 230 **OG-OT**
Col: St. Vincent *HS:* Cecil Twp. [Venice, PA] B: 11/2/1930, Muse, PA D: 10/12/1984, Canonsburg, PA
1956 Cle: 12 G.

MIKE MACHUREK Machurek, Michael Bruce 6′1″, 205 **QB**
Col: San Diego City Coll. CA (J.C.); Idaho State *HS:* Madison [San Diego, CA] B: 7/22/1960, Las Vegas, NV *Drafted:* 1982 Round 6 Det
1984 Det: 4 G; Pass 43-14 32.6%, 193 4.49 6 Int; Rush 1-9 9.0.

ART MACIOSZCZYK Macioszczyk, Arthur A 5′9″, 208 **FB-LB**
(Choo-Choo) *Col:* Western Michigan *HS:* Hamtramck [MI] B: 10/19/1920, Hamtramack, MI D: 5/6/1982, Detroit, MI
Drafted: 1943 Round 27 Phi
1944 Phi: Rec 3-28 9.3; PR 1-14 14.0; KR 1-4 4.0. **1947** Phi: Rec 3-20 6.7; KR 2-36 18.0. **Total:** Rec 6-48 8.0; PR 1-14 14.0; KR 3-40 13.3.

		Rushing				
Year Team	**G**	**Att**	**Yds**	**Avg**	**TD**	**Fum**
1944 Phi	10	16	55	3.4	0	0
1947 Phi	11	30	104	3.5	0	2
1948 Was	1	0	0	—	0	0
NFL Total	22	46	159	3.5	0	2

CEDRIC MACK Mack, Cedric Manuel 6′0″, 193 **DB**
Col: Baylor *HS:* Brazosport [Freeport, TX] B: 9/14/1960, Freeport, TX
Drafted: 1983 Round 2 StL
1984 StL: Rec 5-61 12.2. **1985** StL: Rec 1-16 16.0. **1987** StL: 1 Sac. **1988** Pho: **1** Fum TD. **1989** Pho: 1 Sac. **1990** Pho: 1 Sac. **Total:** Rec 6-77 12.8; 1 Fum TD; 3 Sac.

		Interceptions		
Year Team	**G**	**Int**	**Yds**	**TD**
1983 StL	16	3	25	0
1984 StL	12	0	0	0
1985 StL	16	2	10	0
1986 StL	15	4	42	0
1987 StL	10	2	0	0
1988 Pho	16	3	33	0
1989 Pho	16	4	15	0
1990 Pho	16	2	53	0
1991 SD	7	0	0	0
1992 KC-NO	15	0	0	0
1992 KC	1	0	0	0
1992 NO	14	0	0	0
1993 NO	1	0	0	0
NFL Total	140	20	178	0

KEVIN MACK Mack, James Kevin 6′0″, 224 **RB**
Col: Clemson *HS:* Kings Mountain [NC] B: 8/9/1962, Kings Mountain, NC *Drafted:* 1984 Supplemental Round 1 Cle

		Rushing				Receiving					Tot
Year Team	**G**	**Att**	**Yds**	**Avg**	**TD**	**Rec**	**Yds**	**Avg**	**TD**	**Fum**	**TD**
1985 Cle	16	222	1104	5.0	7	29	297	10.2	3	4	10
1986 Cle	12	174	665	3.8	10	28	292	10.4	0	6	10
1987 Cle	12	201	735	3.7	5	32	223	7.0	1	6	6
1988 Cle	11	123	485	3.9	3	11	87	7.9	0	5	3
1989 Cle	4	37	130	3.5	1	2	7	3.5	0	1	1
1990 Cle	14	158	702	4.4	5	42	360	8.6	2	6	7
1991 Cle	14	197	726	3.7	8	40	255	6.4	2	1	10
1992 Cle	12	169	543	3.2	6	13	81	6.2	0	1	6
1993 Cle	4	10	33	3.3	1	0	0	—	0	0	1
NFL Total	99	1291	5123	4.0	46	197	1602	8.1	8	30	54

KIM MACK Mack, Kimbeflu Evanda 6′0″, 190 **DB**
Col: Florida State *HS:* Spruce Creek [Port Orange, FL] B: 10/29/1961
1987 Sea: 1 G.

MILTON MACK Mack, Milton Jerome 5′11″, 188 **DB**
Col: Alcorn State *HS:* Callaway [Jackson, MS] B: 9/20/1963, Jackson, MS *Drafted:* 1987 Round 5 NO
1988 NO: 1 Sac. **1989** NO: 1 Sac. **1990** NO: KR 1-17 17.0. **Total:** KR 1-17 17.0; 2 Sac.

Year Team	G	Interceptions Int	Yds	TD
1987 NO	13	4	32	0
1988 NO	14	1	19	0
1989 NO	16	2	0	0
1990 NO	16	0	0	0
1991 NO	8	0	0	0
1992 TB	16	3	0	0
1993 TB	12	1	27	1
1994 Det	16	1	0	0
NFL Total	111	12	78	1

RICO MACK Mack, Rico Rodrigus 6′4″, 239 **LB**
Col: Appalachian State *HS:* Winder-Barrow [Winder, GA]
B: 2/22/1971, Stratham, GA
1993 Pit: 8 G.

TERENCE MACK Mack, Terence Bernard 6′3″, 240 **LB**
Col: Clemson *HS:* Winnsboro [SC] B: 7/9/1964, Winnsboro, SC
1987 StL: 5 G.

TOM MACK Mack, Thomas Lee 6′3″, 250 **OG**
Col: Michigan *HS:* Cleveland Heights [OH] B: 11/1/1943, Cleveland, OH *Drafted:* 1966 Round 1 LARm *HOF:* 1999
1966 LARm: 14 G. **1967** LARm: 14 G. **1968** LARm: 14 G. **1969** LARm: 14 G. **1970** LARm: 14 G. **1971** LARm: 14 G. **1972** LARm: 14 G. **1973** LARm: 14 G. **1974** LARm: 14 G. **1975** LARm: 14 G. **1976** LARm: 14 G. **1977** LARm: 14 G. **1978** LARm: 16 G. **Total:** 184 G.

TREMAIN MACK Mack, Tremain F 6′0″, 193 **DB**
(T-Mack) *Col:* Miami (Fla.) *HS:* Chapel Hill [Tyler, TX] B: 11/21/1974, Atlanta, TX *Drafted:* 1997 Round 4 Cin
1997 Cin: Int 1-29. **Total:** Int 1-29.

Year Team	G	Kickoff Returns Ret	Yds	Avg	TD	Fum
1997 Cin	4	0	0	—	0	0
1998 Cin	12	45	1165	25.9	1	2
NFL Total	16	45	1165	25.9	1	2

RED MACK Mack, William Richard 5′10″, 180 **WR-HB**
Col: Notre Dame *HS:* Hampton [Allison Park, PA] B: 6/19/1937, Oconto, WI *Drafted:* 1961 Round 10 Pit
1962 Pit: Rush 2-(-2) -1.0. **1963** Pit: Rush 2-1 0.5. **1964** Phi: PR 1-0. **Total:** Rush 4-(-1) -0.3; PR 1-0.

Year Team	G	Receiving Rec	Yds	Avg	TD	Fum
1961 Pit	11	8	128	16.0	2	1
1962 Pit	14	8	203	25.4	2	1
1963 Pit	14	25	618	24.7	3	0
1964 Phi	8	8	169	21.1	1	1
1965 Pit	2	3	41	13.7	0	0
1966 Atl-GB	9	0	0	—	0	0
1966 Atl	1	0	0	—	0	0
1966 GB	8	0	0	—	0	0
NFL Total	58	52	1159	22.3	8	3

EARSELL MACKBEE Mackbee, James Earsell 6′1″, 195 **DB**
Col: Vallejo JC CA; Utah State *HS:* Vallejo [CA] B: 1/15/1941, Brookhaven, MS
1967 Min: **1** Fum TD. **Total:** 1 Fum TD.

Year Team	G	Interceptions Int	Yds	TD	Tot TD
1965 Min	10	0	0	0	0
1966 Min	14	2	27	0	0
1967 Min	14	5	98	1	2
1968 Min	14	2	55	0	0
1969 Min	14	6	100	0	0
NFL Total	66	15	280	1	2

JACK MACKENROTH Mackenroth, Jack Dakota 6′2″, 215 **C-LB**
Col: North Dakota *HS:* Minot [ND] B: 6/29/1916, Minot, ND
1938 Det: 2 G.

ROY MACKERT Mackert, Charles Leroy 6′2″, 202 **C-T**
Col: Lebanon Valley; Maryland *HS:* Conway Hall [Carlisle, PA]
B: 2/2/1894, Sunbury, PA Deceased
1925 Roch: 2 G.

DEE MACKEY Mackey, Dee Elbert 6′5″, 235 **TE**
Col: Tyler JC TX; Texas A&M-Commerce *HS:* Union Grove [Gladewater, TX] B: 10/16/1934, Gilmer, TX *Drafted:* 1958 Round 24 SF
1961 Bal: KR 1-6 6.0. **1963** NYJ: KR 1-0. **1965** NYJ: Scor 1 2XP.
Total: KR 2-6 3.0; Scor 1 2XP.

Year Team	G	Receiving Rec	Yds	Avg	TD	Fum
1960 SF	12	12	159	13.3	0	0
1961 Bal	14	4	66	16.5	0	0
1962 Bal	14	25	396	15.8	4	1
1963 NYJ	14	23	263	11.4	3	1
1964 NYJ	14	14	213	15.2	0	0
1965 NYJ	10	16	255	15.9	1	2
NFL Total	78	94	1352	14.4	8	4

JOHN MACKEY Mackey, John 6′2″, 224 **TE**
Col: Syracuse *HS:* Hempstead [NY] B: 9/24/1941, Queens, NY
Drafted: 1963 Round 2 Bal *HOF:* 1992
1963 Bal: Rush 1-3 3.0; KR 9-271 30.1. **1964** Bal: Rush 1-(-1) -1.0. **1965** Bal: Rush 1-7 7.0. **1966** Bal: Rush 1-(-6) -6.0. **1968** Bal: Rush 10-103 10.3. **1969** Bal: Rush 2-3 1.5. **1971** Bal: Rush 3-18 6.0.
Total: Rush 19-127 6.7; KR 9-271 30.1.

Year Team	G	Receiving Rec	Yds	Avg	TD	Fum
1963 Bal	14	35	726	20.7	7	2
1964 Bal	14	22	406	18.5	2	1
1965 Bal	14	40	814	20.4	7	2
1966 Bal	14	50	829	16.6	9	0
1967 Bal	14	55	686	12.5	3	1
1968 Bal	14	45	644	14.3	5	1
1969 Bal	14	34	443	13.0	2	1
1970 Bal	14	28	435	15.5	3	1
1971 Bal	14	11	143	13.0	0	1
1972 SD	13	11	110	10.0	0	1
NFL Total	139	331	5236	15.8	38	11

KYLE MACKEY Mackey, Kyle Erickson 6′3″, 220 **QB**
Col: Texas A&M-Commerce *HS:* Alpine [TX] B: 3/2/1962, Gladewater, TX *Drafted:* 1984 Round 11 StL
1987 Mia: Rush 17-98 5.8 2 TD. **1989** NYJ: Rush 2-3 1.5.
Total: Rush 19-101 5.3 2 TD.

Year Team	G	Passing Att	Comp	Comp%	Yds	YPA	TD	Int	Rating	Fum
1987 Mia	3	109	57	52.3	604	5.54	3	5	58.8	3
1989 NYJ	4	25	11	44.0	125	5.00	0	1	42.9	1
NFL Total	7	134	68	50.7	729	5.44	3	6	55.8	4

DOUG MACKIE Mackie, Douglas Brian 6′4″, 280 **OT**
Col: Ohio State *HS:* Saugus [MA] B: 2/18/1957, Malden, MA
1987 Atl: 3 G.

JACQUE MACKINNON MacKinnon, Jacque Harold 6′4″, 235 **TE-RB**
Col: Colgate *HS:* Dover [NJ] B: 11/10/1938, Dover, NJ D: 3/6/1975, San Diego, CA
1965 SD: KR 1-0. **1968** SD: Scor **1** 2XP. **Total:** KR 1-0; Scor 1 2XP.

Year Team	G	Rushing Att	Yds	Avg	TD	Receiving Rec	Yds	Avg	TD	Fum	Tot TD
1961 SD	9	0	0	—	0	3	58	19.3	0	0	0
1962 SD	14	59	240	4.1	0	9	125	13.9	2	2	2
1963 SD	14	0	0	—	0	11	262	23.8	4	0	4
1964 SD	14	24	124	5.2	2	10	177	17.7	0	0	2
1965 SD	14	3	17	5.7	0	6	106	17.7	0	0	0
1966 SD	14	0	0	—	0	26	477	18.3	6	0	6
1967 SD	14	0	0	—	0	7	176	25.1	2	0	2
1968 SD	14	0	0	—	0	33	646	19.6	6	0	6
1969 SD	7	0	0	—	0	7	82	11.7	0	0	0
1970 Oak	4	0	0	—	0	0	0	—	0	0	0
NFL Total	118	86	381	4.4	2	112	2109	18.8	20	2	22

JOHNNY MACKORELL Mackorell, John Campbell 5′10″, 178 **TB-DB**
Col: Davidson *HS:* Hickory [NC] B: 11/3/1912, York, SC
D: 4/28/1980, Morganton, NC
1935 NYG: 2 G; Rush 2-6 3.0.

BILL MACKRIDES Mackrides, William 5′11″, 182 **QB**
Col: Nevada-Reno *HS:* West Philadelphia [Philadelphia, PA]
B: 7/8/1925, Philadelphia, PA *Drafted:* 1947 Round 2 Phi

Year Team	G	Passing Att	Comp	Comp%	Yds	YPA	TD	Int	Rating
1947 Phi	8	17	8	47.1	58	3.41	2	3	55.1
1948 Phi	10	53	18	34.0	276	5.21	2	4	33.2
1949 Phi	7	36	14	38.9	182	5.06	2	**2**	50.9
1950 Phi	8	46	14	30.4	228	4.96	4	6	37.5
1951 Phi	6	54	23	42.6	333	6.17	3	5	43.2
1953 NYG-Pit	7	109	54	49.5	506	4.64	2	**8**	38.2
1953 NYG	3	15	6	40.0	53	3.53	1	3	32.8
1953 Pit	4	94	48	51.1	453	4.82	1	5	46.1
NFL Total	46	315	131	41.6	1583	5.03	15	28	36.5

Year Team	Rushing Att	Yds	Avg	TD	Fum
1947 Phi	7	-15	-2.1	1	3
1948 Phi	7	4	0.6	0	0
1949 Phi	14	17	1.2	1	2
1950 Phi	21	82	3.9	0	2

1951 Phi	7	9	1.3	0	0
1953 NYG-Pit	14	27	1.9	1	3
1953 NYG	1	2	2.0	0	0
1953 Pit	13	25	1.9	1	3
NFL Total	70	124	1.8	3	10

BOB MACLEOD MacLeod, Robert Frederick 6'0", 190 **HB-DB**
(Wildfire) *Col:* Dartmouth *HS:* Glenbard [Glen Ellyn, IL]
B: 10/15/1917, Glen Ellyn, IL *Drafted:* 1939 Round 1 Bkn
1939 ChiB: 9 G; Rush 17-88 5.2 1 TD; Rec 10-231 23.1 3 TD; Int **1** TD; Tot TD 5; 30 Pt.

TOM MACLEOD MacLeod, Thomas William 6'3", 225 **LB**
Col: Minnesota *HS:* Proctor [MN] B: 1/10/1951, Proctor, MN
Drafted: 1973 Round 3 GB
1973 GB: 10 G; Int 2-8. **1974** Bal: 14 G. **1975** Bal: 14 G; Int 1-50. **1977** Bal: 14 G; Int 2-37. **1978** Bal: 12 G. **Total:** 64 G; Int 5-95.

STU MACMILLAN MacMillan, Charles Stuart 5'9", 175 **C-G**
Col: North Dakota *HS:* University [Grand Forks, ND] B: 2/13/1908, McVille, ND D: 1/13/1992, Seattle, WA
1931 Cle: 2 G.

JIM MACMURDO MacMurdo, James Edward 6'1", 209 **T**
(Big Jim) *Col:* Pittsburgh *HS:* Ellwood City [PA]; Kiski School [Saltsburg, PA] B: 9/2/1909, Ellwood City, PA D: 8/10/1981, Darby, PA
1932 Bos: 10 G. **1933** Bos: 10 G; Rush 1-2 2.0. **1934** Phi: 11 G. **1935** Phi: 4 G. **1936** Phi: 9 G. **1937** Phi: 3 G. **Total:** 47 G; Rush 1-2 2.0.

RAY MACMURRAY MacMurray, Raymond Stuart **G**
Col: Lincoln College; Dartmouth B: 7/3/1889, Tuscarawas Co., OH
D: 2/21/1966, Huntington, IN
1921 Mun: 1 G.

EDDIE MACON Macon, Edwin Donald 6'0", 177 **HB-DB**
Col: U. of Pacific *HS:* Stockton [CA] B: 3/7/1927, Stockton, CA
Drafted: 1952 Round 2 ChiB
1952 ChiB: Rec 8-25 3.1; PR 7-74 10.6; KR 9-299 33.2 1 TD. **1953** ChiB: Pass 1-0; Rec 6-24 4.0 2 TD; PR 17-68 4.0; KR 13-373 28.7. **1960** Oak: Int 9-105 1 TD. **Total:** Pass 1-0; Rec 14-49 3.5 2 TD; PR 24-142 5.9; KR 22-672 30.5 1 TD; Int 9-105 1 TD.

		Rushing					Tot
Year Team	**G**	**Att**	**Yds**	**Avg**	**TD**	**Fum**	**TD**
1952 ChiB	11	30	194	6.5	1	8	2
1953 ChiB	12	40	130	3.3	1	2	3
1960 Oak	14	0	0	—	0	1	1
NFL Total	37	70	324	4.6	2	11	6

WADDY MACPHEE MacPhee, Walter Scott 5'8", 160 **WB-TB**
Col: Brooklyn College; Princeton *HS:* Erasmus Hall [Brooklyn, NY]
B: 12/23/1899, Brooklyn, NY D: 1/20/1980, Charlotte, NC
1926 Prov: 10 G.

KILE MACWHERTER MacWherter, William Kile 5'9", 210 **FB**
Col: Millikin; Bethany (W.V.) *HS:* Stephen Decatur [Decatur, IL]
B: 7/19/1892, Decatur, IL D: 12/1977, Greeley, CO
1920 Sta: 4 G.

JOHN MACZUZAK Maczuzak, John A 6'5", 250 **DT**
Col: Pittsburgh *HS:* Ellsworth [PA] B: 4/4/1941 *Drafted:* 1963 Round 22 KC
1964 KC: 1 G.

ELMER MADAR Madar, Elmer F 5'11", 185 **OE-DB**
Col: Michigan *HS:* Northeastern [Detroit, MI] B: 11/28/1920, Sykesville, PA D: 2/9/1972, Detroit, MI
AAFC **1947** BalA: 9 G; Rec 8-53 6.6; KR 1-14 14.0.

ELMER MADARIK Madarik, Elmer Laurence 5'11", 200 **DB-HB-WB-TB**
(Tippy) *Col:* Detroit Mercy *HS:* Joliet Catholic [IL] B: 7/15/1922, Joliet, IL D: 2/3/1974 *Drafted:* 1944 Round 18 Det
1945 Det: Int 1-40. **1946** Det: Pass 14-7 50.0%, 104 7.43 1 TD; Rec 6-38 6.3; PR 5-71 14.2; KR 5-131 26.2; Int 3-75. **1947** Det: Rec 4-75 18.8; PR 1-7 7.0; KR 3-49 16.3. **1948** Det-Was: KR 1-20 20.0. Det: KR 1-20 20.0. **Total:** Pass 14-7 50.0%, 104 7.43 1 TD; Rec 10-113 11.3; PR 6-78 13.0; KR 9-200 22.2; Int 4-115.

		Rushing			
Year Team	**G**	**Att**	**Yds**	**Avg**	**TD**
1945 Det	1	2	5	2.5	0
1946 Det	10	8	7	0.9	0
1947 Det	8	19	29	1.5	1
1948 Det-Was	4	2	7	3.5	0
1948 Det	3	2	7	3.5	0
1948 Was	1	0	0	—	0
NFL Total	23	31	48	1.5	1

LLOYD MADDEN Madden, Lloyd Willis 6'1", 195 **WB-DB**
Col: Colorado Mines B: 8/27/1918, Dodge City, KS *Drafted:* 1940 Round 3 ChiC
1940 ChiC: Rec 4-90 22.5 1 TD.

		Rushing				Tot
Year Team	**G**	**Att**	**Yds**	**Avg**	**TD**	**TD**
1940 ChiC	9	29	186	6.4	2	3

BOB MADDOCK Maddock, Robert Charles 6'0", 200 **G-LB**
Col: Notre Dame *HS:* Santa Ana [CA] B: 8/6/1920, Santa Ana, CA
1942 ChiC: 2 G. **1946** ChiC: 7 G. **Total:** 9 G.

BUSTER MADDOX Maddox, George Woodrow 6'3", 240 **T**
Col: Kansas State *HS:* Greenville [TX] B: 11/4/1911, Greenville, TX
D: 3/14/1956, McKinney, TX
1935 GB: 1 G.

MARK MADDOX Maddox, Mark Anthony 6'1", 233 **LB**
Col: Northern Michigan *HS:* James Madison [Milwaukee, WI]
B: 3/23/1968, Milwaukee, WI *Drafted:* 1991 Round 9 Buf
1992 Buf: 15 G. **1993** Buf: 11 G. **1994** Buf: 15 G; Int 1-11. **1995** Buf: 4 G. **1996** Buf: 14 G. **1997** Buf: 8 G; Int 1-25. **1998** Ariz: 14 G; 1 Sac. **Total:** 81 G; Int 2-36; 1 Sac.

BOB MADDOX Maddox, Robert Earl 6'5", 237 **DE-DT**
Col: Frostburg State *HS:* Thomas Jefferson [Frederick, MD]
B: 5/2/1949, Frederick, MD *Drafted:* 1973 Round 7 Cin
1974 Cin: 14 G; 6 Pt. **1975** KC: 6 G. **1976** KC: 8 G. **Total:** 28 G; 6 Pt.

TOMMY MADDOX Maddox, Thomas Alfred 6'4", 205 **QB**
Col: UCLA *HS:* L.D. Bell [Hurst, TX] B: 9/2/1971, Shreveport, LA
Drafted: 1992 Round 1 Den
1992 Den: Rush 9-20 2.2. **1993** Den: Rush 2-(-2) -1.0. **1994** LARm: Rush 1-1 1.0. **1995** NYG: Rush 1-4 4.0. **Total:** Rush 13-23 1.8.

		Passing								
Year Team	**G**	**Att**	**Comp**	**Comp%**	**Yds**	**YPA**	**TD**	**Int**	**Rating**	**Fum**
1992 Den	13	121	66	54.5	757	6.26	5	9	56.4	4
1993 Den	16	1	1	100.0	1	1.00	1	0	118.8	0
1994 LARm	5	19	10	52.6	141	7.42	0	2	37.3	0
1995 NYG	16	23	6	26.1	49	2.13	0	3	0.0	1
NFL Total	50	164	83	50.6	948	5.78	6	14	45.0	5

GEORGE MADEROS Maderos, George 6'1", 187 **DB**
(Chico) *Col:* Cal State-Chico *HS:* Chico [CA] B: 11/3/1933, Chico, CA *Drafted:* 1955 Round 21 SF
1955 SF: 8 G; Int 2-23. **1956** SF: 12 G; KR 2-21 10.5; Int 2-2; 1 Fum. **Total:** 20 G; KR 2-21 10.5; Int 4-25; 1 Fum.

JOHN MADIGAN Madigan, John A 6'0", 185 **C**
Col: St. Mary's (Minn.); St. Thomas *HS:* Mankato [MN] B: 3/12/1899, Madison Lake, MN D: 1/5/1976, St. Paul, MN
1922 Min: 2 G. **1923** Dul: 7 G. **1924** Min: 6 G. **Total:** 15 G.

SAM MADISON Madison, Samuel Adolphus Jr. 5'11", 185 **DB**
Col: Louisville *HS:* Florida A&M University [Tallahassee, FL]
B: 4/23/1974, Thomasville, GA *Drafted:* 1997 Round 2 Mia
1997 Mia: 14 G; Int 1-21. **1998** Mia: 16 G; Int 8-114; 1 Sac. **Total:** 30 G; Int 9-135; 1 Sac.

LYNN MADSEN Madsen, Lynn Thomas 6'4", 260 **DT**
Col: Washington *HS:* Vista [CA] B: 8/8/1960, Blair, NE *Drafted:* 1984 Supplemental Round 3 Hou
1986 Hou: 15 G; KR 1-0; 1 Fum; 1 Sac.

CHET MAEDA Maeda, Chester A 5'10", 187 **HB-DB**
Col: Colorado State B: 10/2/1918, Los Angeles, CA *Drafted:* 1943 Round 18 Det
1945 ChiC: 1 G; Pass 1-0; 1 Fum.

AL MAEDER Maeder, Albert Raymond 5'9", 185 **T**
Col: Minnesota *HS:* East [Minneapolis, MN]; North HS [Minneapolis, MN] B: 1/25/1906, Minneapolis, MN D: 8/25/1984, Eden Prairie, MN
1929 Min: 9 G.

MIKE MAGAC Magac, Michael Stephen 6'3", 240 **OG**
Col: Missouri *HS:* Assumption [East St. Louis, IL] B: 5/25/1938, East St. Louis, IL *Drafted:* 1960 Round 2 SF
1960 SF: 12 G. **1961** SF: 6 G. **1962** SF: 14 G. **1963** SF: 10 G. **1964** SF: 14 G. **1965** Pit: 8 G. **1966** Pit: 14 G. **Total:** 78 G.

CALVIN MAGEE Magee, Calvin 6'3", 240 **TE**
Col: Southern University *HS:* Booker T. Washington [New Orleans, LA]
B: 4/23/1963, New Orleans, LA
1985 TB: KR 2-20 10.0. **1986** TB: KR 2-21 10.5. **Total:** KR 4-41 10.3.

		Receiving				
Year Team	**G**	**Rec**	**Yds**	**Avg**	**TD**	**Fum**
1985 TB	16	26	288	11.1	3	1
1986 TB	16	45	564	12.5	5	1
1987 TB	11	34	424	12.5	3	0
1988 TB	13	9	103	11.4	0	0
NFL Total	56	114	1379	12.1	11	2

JIM MAGEE Magee, James J Jr. 6'1", 202 **C-LB**
Col: Georgia; Villanova *HS:* West Catholic [Philadelphia, PA]
B: 11/27/1920, Philadelphia, PA D: 3/1970
1944 Bos: 10 G. **1945** Bos: 9 G; Int 1-6. **1946** Bos: 11 G. **Total:** 30 G; Int 1-6.

JOHN MAGEE Magee, John Wesley Jr. 5'10", 220 **OG-DG-LB**
(Maggie; Hog Jaw) *Col:* Southwestern Louisiana; Rice *HS:* Robstown [TX] B: 7/21/1923, Robstown, TX D: 11/26/1991, Kaplan, LA
Drafted: 1945 Round 20 Phi
1948 Phi: 12 G. **1949** Phi: 12 G. **1950** Phi: 12 G. **1951** Phi: 12 G; Rec 0-7. **1952** Phi: 12 G. **1953** Phi: 12 G. **1954** Phi: 12 G. **1955** Phi: 7 G. **Total:** 91 G; Rec 0-7.

GEORGE MAGERKURTH Magerkurth, George Levi 6'3", 210 **T**
Col: No College B: 12/30/1888, KS D: 10/7/1966, Rock Island, IL
1920 RI: 1 G.

CHICK MAGGIOLI Maggioli, Achille Fred 5'11", 178 **DB-HB**
Col: Indiana; Notre Dame; Illinois *HS:* Mishawaka [IN] B: 5/17/1922, Mishawaka, IN *Drafted:* 1946 Round 9 Was
AAFC **1948** BufA: 7 G; Pass 1-1 100.0%; Rush 11-27 2.5; Rec 3-23 7.7; PR 1-0; KR 2-38 19.0; Int 1-7; Punt 2-95 47.5.

NFL **1949** Det: Rec 1-9 9.0; **1** Fum TD. **Total:** Rec 1-9 9.0; 1 Fum TD.

		Interceptions		
Year Team	**G**	**Int**	**Yds**	**TD**
1949 Det	12	3	46	0
1950 Bal	8	8	165	0
NFL Total	20	11	211	0

DON MAGGS Maggs, Donald James 6'5", 290 **OT-OG**
Col: Tulane *HS:* Cardinal Mooney [Youngstown, OH] B: 11/1/1961, Youngstown, OH *Drafted:* 1984 Supplemental Round 2 Hou
1986 Hou: 14 G. **1988** Hou: 16 G. **1989** Hou: 16 G. **1990** Hou: 16 G. **1991** Hou: 16 G. **1992** Hou: 16 G. **1993** Den: 7 G. **1994** Den: 9 G. **Total:** 110 G.

AL MAGINNES Maginnes, Albert Bristol 6'1", 188 **G-C**
Col: Lehigh *HS:* Boston English [MA] B: 4/5/1897, Boston, MA
D: 1/30/1966, New York, NY
1920 Can: 1 G. **1921** NYG: 2 G. **Total:** 3 G.

DAVE MAGINNES Maginnes, William David 5'10", 165 **TB**
Col: Lehigh *HS:* Boston English [MA]; Phillips Exeter Acad. [Exeter, NH]
B: 11/29/1894, Boston, MA D: 7/26/1981, Exeter, NH
1921 NYG: 2 G.

JOE MAGLIOLO Magliolo, Joseph Jr. 6'0", 210 **LB**
Col: Texas *HS:* Ball [Galveston, TX] B: 10/17/1922, Galveston, TX
AAFC **1948** NY-A: 13 G; Int 1-12.

AL MAGLISCEAU Maglisceau, Albert Samuel 6'1", 210 **T-G**
Col: Geneva *HS:* Parnassus [PA] B: 5/21/1904, Pittsburgh, PA
D: 11/5/1985, Sun City Center, FL
1929 Fra: 5 G.

DANTE MAGNANI Magnani, Dante A 5'10", 182 **HB-DB-WB**
Col: St. Mary's (Cal.) *HS:* St. Vincent's [Vallejo, CA]; St. Mary's Prep [Berkeley, CA] B: 3/16/1917, Dalzell, IL D: 12/22/1985, Vallejo, CA
Drafted: 1940 Round 19 Cle
1940 Cle: Int 3-59; Punt 1-33 33.0. **1941** Cle: PR 5-54 10.8; Int 2-6. **1942** Cle: Pass 1-0; PR 2-27 13.5. **1943** ChiB: PR 4-40 10.0; Int 2-23. **1946** ChiB: Int 1-35. **Total:** Pass 1-0; PR 11-121 11.0; Int 8-123; Punt 1-33 33.0.

		Rushing				Receiving			
Year Team	**G**	**Att**	**Yds**	**Avg**	**TD**	**Rec**	**Yds**	**Avg**	**TD**
1940 Cle	11	7	19	2.7	0	11	119	10.8	1
1941 Cle	9	24	128	5.3	0	14	189	13.5	1
1942 Cle	11	59	344	5.8	1	24	276	11.5	4
1943 ChiB	10	51	310	6.1	2	6	88	14.7	1
1946 ChiB	10	68	277	4.1	0	14	156	11.1	1
1947 LARm	12	48	178	3.7	0	4	57	14.3	1
1948 LARm	8	38	144	3.8	0	3	28	9.3	1
1949 ChiB	6	33	59	1.8	0	3	29	9.7	0
1950 Det	7	3	7	2.3	0	0	0	—	0
NFL Total	84	331	1466	4.4	3	79	942	11.9	10

	Kickoff Returns					Tot
Year Team	**Ret**	**Yds**	**Avg**	**TD**	**Fum**	**TD**
1940 Cle	—	—	—	0	0	1
1941 Cle	8	241	30.1	**1**	0	2
1942 Cle	11	250	22.7	0	0	5
1943 ChiB	6	171	28.5	**1**	0	4
1946 ChiB	3	50	16.7	0	2	1
1947 LARm	6	186	31.0	0	2	1
1948 LARm	3	49	16.3	0	2	1
1949 ChiB	0	0	—	0	1	0
NFL Total	37	947	25.6	2	7	15

JIM MAGNER Magner, James Edward 6'0", 165 **TB-BB**
Col: Widener; North Carolina *HS:* St. Joseph's Prep [Philadelphia, PA]
B: 7/22/1903, Philadelphia, PA D: 9/20/1977, Philadelphia, PA
1931 Fra: 2 G.

GLEN MAGNUSSON Magnusson, Glen Edward 5'11", 225 **G-C**
(Ole) *Col:* Northwestern *HS:* La Porte [IN] B: 7/30/1899, Salt Lake City, UT D: 1/7/1945, Chicago, IL
1925 Ham: 1 G.

PAUL MAGUIRE Maguire, Paul Leo 6'0", 228 **LB-P**
Col: The Citadel *HS:* Ursuline [Youngstown, OH] B: 8/22/1938, Youngstown, OH *Drafted:* 1960 Round 1 LAC
1960 LAC: Int 3-37. **1961** SD: Rush 1-(-11) -11.0; Int 1-2. **1962** SD: Int 1-13. **1963** SD: KR 1-5 5.0; Int 4-47. **1964** Buf: KR 1-0. **1965** Buf: Rush 1-21 21.0; KR 1-5 5.0. **1966** Buf: KR 1-0. **1968** Buf: Rush 1-6 6.0; KR 1-5 5.0. **1969** Buf: Pass 1-1 100.0%, 19 19.00. **Total:** Pass 1-1 100.0%, 19 19.00; Rush 3-16 5.3; KR 5-15 3.0; Int 9-99.

		Punting			
Year Team	**G**	**Punts**	**Yds**	**Avg**	**Fum**
1960 LAC	11	43	1743	**40.5**	0
1961 SD	14	63	2615	41.5	0
1962 SD	14	**79**	**3289**	41.6	0
1963 SD	14	58	2241	38.6	0
1964 Buf	14	65	2777	42.7	0
1965 Buf	14	80	3437	43.0	1
1966 Buf	14	69	2841	41.2	0
1967 Buf	14	77	3320	43.1	0
1968 Buf	14	**100**	**4175**	41.8	0
1969 Buf	14	78	**3471**	44.5	0
1970 Buf	14	83	3228	38.9	0
NFL Total	151	795	33137	41.7	1

GEORGE MAGULICK Magulick, George 5'9", 150 **HB-DB**
Col: St. Francis (Pa.) *HS:* Spangler [PA] B: 1/10/1919, Spangler, PA
Deceased
1944 ChPt: 9 G; Rush 17-102 6.0; Rec 6-50 8.3; PR 7-86 12.3; KR 5-101 20.2; Int 2-12.

DREW MAHALIC Mahalic, Drew Alan 6'4", 225 **LB**
Col: Notre Dame *HS:* North Farmington [Farmington, MI]
B: 5/22/1953, Albany, NY *Drafted:* 1975 Round 3 Den
1975 SD: 13 G; Int 1-3. **1976** Phi: 13 G. **1977** Phi: 14 G. **1978** Phi: 9 G; Int 1-5; 1 Fum. **Total:** 49 G; Int 2-8; 1 Fum.

BOB MAHAN Mahan, Robert Cullen 5'9", 178 **FB-E-WB-HB**
Col: Drake; Washington-St. Louis B: 2/6/1904 D: 8/1990, Sun City, AZ
1929 Buf: 9 G. **1930** Bkn: 11 G. **Total:** 20 G.

WALTER MAHAN Mahan, Walter Everett 5'10", 210 **G**
Col: West Virginia *HS:* Follansbee [WV]; Steubenville HS [OH]
B: 6/23/1902, Follansbee, WV D: 5/10/1990, Wheeling, WV
1926 Fra: 1 G.

BRUCE MAHER Maher, Bruce David 5'11", 190 **DB**
Col: Detroit Mercy *HS:* University of Detroit [MI] B: 7/25/1937, Detroit, MI *Drafted:* 1959 Round 15 Det
1960 Det: PR 1-10 10.0; KR 10-214 21.4; Scor **1** Saf. **1961** Det: KR 1-19 19.0. **1962** Det: Rush 3-8 2.7; PR 2-3 1.5; KR 7-141 20.1. **1963** Det: PR 1-3 3.0; Scor **1** Saf. **1964** Det: PR 0-9. **1967** Det: Scor **1** Saf. **Total:** Rush 3-8 2.7; PR 4-25 6.3; KR 18-374 20.8; Scor 3 Saf.

		Interceptions			
Year Team	**G**	**Int**	**Yds**	**TD**	**Fum**
1960 Det	12	1	19	0	0
1961 Det	12	1	8	0	0
1962 Det	14	0	0	0	1
1963 Det	14	1	0	0	0
1964 Det	14	2	28	0	0
1965 Det	14	4	76	0	0
1966 Det	14	5	90	0	0
1967 Det	14	2	14	0	0
1968 NYG	14	1	89	0	0
1969 NYG	14	5	112	0	0
NFL Total	136	22	436	0	1

FRANK MAHER Maher, Francis Xavier 6'1", 195 **DB**
Col: Toledo B: 5/8/1918, Detroit, MI Deceased *Drafted:* 1940 Round 10 Phi
1941 Pit-Cle: 4 G. Pit: 2 G. Cle: 2 G. **Total:** 4 G.

BIRDIE MAHER Maher, Gilbert Thomas 5'8", 180 **E**
Col: Detroit Mercy *HS:* No High School B: 12/16/1892, County Mayo, Ireland D: 12/8/1980, Detroit, MI
1920 Det: 2 G.

ERIC MAHLUM Mahlum, Eric Arnold 6'4", 285 **OG**
Col: California *HS:* Pacific Grove [CA] B: 12/6/1970, San Diego, CA
Drafted: 1994 Round 2 Ind
1994 Ind: 16 G. **1995** Ind: 7 G. **1996** Ind: 13 G. **Total:** 36 G.

IKE MAHONEY Mahoney, Frank John 6′0″, 173 **BB-WB-E**
Col: Creighton *HS:* Omaha Tech [NE] B: 10/25/1901, Omaha, NE D: 5/1963
1925 ChiC: 7 G; Rec 1 TD; Scor 7, 1 XK. **1926** ChiC: 11 G; Rush 1 TD; 1 Fum TD; Tot TD 2; 12 Pt. **1927** ChiC: 9 G; Pass 1 TD. **1928** ChiC: 5 G. **1931** ChiC: 1 G. **Total:** 33 G; Pass 1 TD; Rush 1 TD; Rec 1 TD; 1 Fum TD; Tot TD 3.

JOHN MAHONEY Mahoney, John J 6′0″, 183 **WB-FB-OE**
(Buck) *Col:* Canisius *HS:* Canisius Prep [Buffalo, NY] B: 10/16/1899 D: 9/23/1980, Clarence, NY
1923 Buf: 7 G.

ROGER MAHONEY Mahoney, Roger Sylvis 6′0″, 205 **C-G-OE**
Col: Penn State *HS:* Northeast [Philadelphia, PA] B: 7/19/1906 D: 3/12/1981, Reading, PA
1928 Fra: 14 G. **1929** Fra: 17 G. **1930** Fra-Min: 11 G. Fra: 10 G. Min: 1 G. **Total:** 42 G.

AL MAHRT Mahrt, Alphonse H 5′11″, 168 **BB**
(Marty) *Col:* Dayton *HS:* U. of Dayton Prep [OH] B: 10/11/1893, Dayton, OH D: 6/24/1970, Chillicothe, OH
1920 Day: 9 G. **1921** Day: 7 G; Pass 2 TD; Rec 1 TD; 6 Pt. **1922** Day: 8 G; Pass 1 TD; Rec 1 TD; 6 Pt. **Total:** 24 G; Pass 3 TD; Rec 2 TD; 12 Pt.

ARMIN MAHRT Mahrt, Armin Richard 5′11″, 182 **TB-WB-BB-OE**
Col: Dayton; West Virginia *HS:* U. of Dayton Prep [OH]; Phillips Andover Acad. [Andover, MA] B: 11/1897, Dayton, OH Deceased
1924 Day: 7 G; Rush 1 TD; 6 Pt. **1925** Day-Pott: 10 G; Rush 1 TD; 6 Pt. Day: 8 G. Pott: 2 G; Rush 1 TD; 6 Pt. **1926** Day: 4 G. **Total:** 21 G; Rush 2 TD; 12 Pt.

JOHNNY MAHRT Mahrt, C. John 5′9″, 180 **OE**
Col: Dayton *HS:* U. of Dayton Prep [OH] B: 12/22/1899, Dayton, OH D: 8/24/1967, Dayton, OH
1925 Day: 1 G.

LOU MAHRT Mahrt, Louis Richard 5′11″, 178 **TB**
Col: Dayton *HS:* U. of Dayton Prep [OH] B: 7/30/1904 D: 8/7/1982, Dayton, OH
1926 Day: 6 G; Pass 2 TD. **1927** Day: 2 G. **Total:** 8 G; Pass 2 TD.

STEVE MAIDLOW Maidlow, Steven Kenneth 6′2″, 234 **LB**
Col: Michigan State *HS:* East Lansing [MI] B: 6/6/1960, Lansing, MI *Drafted:* 1983 Round 4 Cin
1983 Cin: 16 G. **1984** Cin: 16 G. **1985** Buf: 16 G. **1987** Buf: 2 G. **Total:** 50 G.

RALPH MAILLARD Maillard, Ralph Jacob 6′2″, 190 **T**
(Mall) *Col:* Creighton *HS:* Randolph [NE] B: 10/10/1905, Randolph, NE D: 5/9/1990, Omaha, NE
1929 ChiB: 4 G.

GIL MAINS Mains, Gilbert Lee 6′2″, 243 **DT-DE**
(Wild Hoss) *Col:* Murray State *HS:* Mount Carmel [IL] B: 12/17/1929, Mount Carmel, IL *Drafted:* 1952 Round 20 Det
1953 Det: 3 G. **1954** Det: 12 G; KR 1-3 3.0. **1955** Det: 12 G; **1** Fum TD; 6 Pt. **1956** Det: 8 G. **1957** Det: 12 G. **1958** Det: 11 G. **1959** Det: 12 G; 1 Fum. **1960** Det: 12 G. **1961** Det: 3 G. **Total:** 85 G; KR 1-3 3.0; 1 Fum TD; 6 Pt; 1 Fum.

JACK MAITLAND Maitland, John Frederick 6′2″, 211 **RB**
Col: Williams *HS:* Upper St. Clair [Pittsburgh, PA] B: 2/8/1948, Pittsburgh, PA *Drafted:* 1970 Round 16 Bal
1970 Bal: Rec 9-67 7.4 1 TD; KR 1-28 28.0. **1971** NE: Rec 1-6 6.0; KR 2-40 20.0. **1972** NE: Rec 4-33 8.3; KR 3-48 16.0. **Total:** Rec 14-106 7.6 1 TD; KR 6-116 19.3.

		Rushing					Tot
Year Team	**G**	**Att**	**Yds**	**Avg**	**TD**	**Fum**	**TD**
1970 Bal	14	74	209	2.8	1	3	2
1971 NE	14	13	25	1.9	1	0	1
1972 NE	13	13	33	2.5	0	2	0
NFL Total	41	100	267	2.7	2	5	3

DON MAJKOWSKI Majkowski, Donald Vincent 6′2″, 200 **QB**
Col: Virginia *HS:* Depew [NY]; Fork Union Mil. Acad. [VA] B: 2/25/1964, Buffalo, NY *Drafted:* 1987 Round 10 GB

		Passing							
Year Team	**G**	**Att**	**Comp**	**Comp%**	**Yds**	**YPA**	**TD**	**Int**	**Rating**
1987 GB	7	127	55	43.3	875	6.89	5	3	70.2
1988 GB	13	336	178	53.0	2119	6.31	9	11	67.8
1989 GB	16	**599**	**353**	58.9	**4318**	7.21	27	20	82.3
1990 GB	9	264	150	56.8	1925	7.29	10	12	73.5
1991 GB	9	226	115	50.9	1362	6.03	3	8	59.3
1992 GB	14	55	38	69.1	271	4.93	2	2	77.2
1993 Ind	3	24	13	54.2	105	4.38	0	1	48.1
1994 Ind	9	152	84	55.3	1010	6.64	6	7	69.8
1995 Det	5	20	15	75.0	161	8.05	1	0	114.8
1996 Det	5	102	55	53.9	554	5.43	3	3	67.2
NFL Total	90	1905	1056	55.4	12700	6.67	66	67	72.9

	Rushing				
Year Team	**Att**	**Yds**	**Avg**	**TD**	**Fum**
1987 GB	15	127	8.5	0	5
1988 GB	47	225	4.8	1	8
1989 GB	75	358	4.8	5	15
1990 GB	29	186	6.4	1	6
1991 GB	25	108	4.3	2	10
1992 GB	8	33	4.1	0	4
1993 Ind	2	4	2.0	0	1
1994 Ind	24	34	1.4	3	5
1995 Det	9	1	0.1	0	0
1996 Det	14	38	2.7	0	5
NFL Total	248	1114	4.5	12	59

JOE MAJORS Majors, Joe Inman 6′1″, 190 **DB**
Col: Florida State *HS:* Huntland [TN] B: 12/25/1936, Lynchburg, TN
1960 Hou: 1 G.

BOBBY MAJORS Majors, Robert Owen 6′1″, 193 **DB**
Col: Tennessee *HS:* Franklin Co. [Winchester, TN] B: 7/7/1949, Lynchburg, TN *Drafted:* 1972 Round 3 Phi
1972 Cle: 9 G; PR 16-96 6.0; KR 10-222 22.2; 1 Fum.

BILLY MAJORS Majors, William Bobo 6′0″, 175 **DB**
Col: Tennessee *HS:* Huntland [TN] B: 11/7/1938, Lynchburg, TN *Drafted:* 1961 Round 9 Buf
1961 Buf: 1 G.

SIUPELI MALAMALA Malamala, Siupeli 6′5″, 310 **OT-OG**
Col: Washington *HS:* Kalahoe [Kailua, HI] B: 1/15/1969, Tofoa, Tonga *Drafted:* 1992 Round 3 NYJ
1992 NYJ: 9 G. **1993** NYJ: 15 G. **1994** NYJ: 12 G. **1995** NYJ: 6 G. **1996** NYJ: 4 G. **1997** NYJ: 10 G. **Total:** 56 G.

RYDELL MALANCON Malancon, Rydell Joseph 6′2″, 227 **LB**
Col: Louisiana State *HS:* St. James [LA] B: 1/10/1962, New Orleans, LA *Drafted:* 1984 Round 4 Atl
1984 Atl: 7 G; KR 1-0. **1987** GB: 3 G. **Total:** 10 G; KR 1-0.

HARRY MALCOLM Malcolm, Harry Elmer 6′0″, 195 **T**
Col: Indiana (Pa.); Washington & Jefferson *HS:* Indiana [PA] B: 11/25/1905, Indiana Co., PA D: 9/15/1987, Springfield, PA
1929 Fra: 14 G.

HOWIE MALEY Maley, Howard Edward 5′11″, 187 **QB-HB-DB**
(Red) *Col:* Texas-Arlington; Southern Methodist B: 12/6/1921 D: 6/20/1987, Dallas, TX *Drafted:* 1944 Round 17 Bkn
1946 Bos: Pass 8-3 37.5%, 71 8.88 1 TD 2 Int; Rec 2-35 17.5; PR 3-12 4.0; KR 1-3 3.0. **1947** Bos: Pass 12-6 50.0%, 144 12.00 1 TD 1 Int; KR 1-23 23.0. **Total:** Pass 20-9 45.0%, 215 10.75 2 TD 3 Int; Rec 2-35 17.5; PR 3-12 4.0; KR 2-26 13.0.

		Rushing				Punting			
Year Team	**G**	**Att**	**Yds**	**Avg**	**TD**	**Punts**	**Yds**	**Avg**	**Fum**
1946 Bos	11	13	67	5.2	0	60	2373	39.6	1
1947 Bos	12	32	132	4.1	0	**92**	**3731**	40.6	0
NFL Total	23	45	199	4.4	0	152	6104	40.2	1

BILL MALINCHAK Malinchak, William John 6′1″, 200 **WR**
Col: Indiana *HS:* Monessen [PA] B: 4/2/1944, Charleroi, PA *Drafted:* 1966 Round 3 Det
1969 Det: Punt 5-184 36.8. **1972** Was: Scor **1** Saf. **Total:** Punt 5-184 36.8; Scor 1 Saf.

		Receiving				Tot
Year Team	**G**	**Rec**	**Yds**	**Avg**	**TD**	**TD**
1966 Det	14	5	34	6.8	0	0
1967 Det	14	26	397	15.3	4	4
1968 Det	14	1	41	41.0	0	0
1969 Det	6	2	24	12.0	0	0
1970 Was	9	0	0	—	0	0
1971 Was	13	0	0	—	0	0
1972 Was	6	0	0	—	0	1
1973 Was	14	0	0	—	0	0
1974 Was	13	0	0	—	0	0
1976 Was	3	1	12	12.0	0	0
NFL Total	106	35	508	14.5	4	5

GENE MALINOWSKI Malinowski, Eugene Paul 6′1″, 210 **TB-DB**
Col: Georgia; Detroit Mercy *HS:* Hamtramck [MI] B: 9/26/1923, Hamtramck, MI D: 11/24/1993, Clinton Twp., MI *Drafted:* 1947 Round 9 Bos
1948 Bos: Rush 11-21 1.9; Rec 3-(-10) -3.3; Int 1-9.

		Passing								
Year Team	**G**	**Att**	**Comp**	**Comp%**	**Yds**	**YPA**	**TD**	**Int**	**Rating**	**Fum**
1948 Bos	12	54	15	27.8	218	4.04	3	7	22.8	3

JOE MALKOVICH Malkovich, Joseph N 6′3″, 205 **C-LB**
(Hunk) *Col:* Duquesne *HS:* Chisholm [MN] B: 1/17/1912, Calumet, MI D: 2/17/1981, Camarillo, CA
1935 Pit: 2 G.

FRAN MALLICK Mallick, Francis J 6′2″, 245 **DE-DT**
Col: No College B: 2/25/1941
1965 Pit: 6 G.

IRVIN MALLORY Mallory, Irvin M 6′1″, 196 **DB**
Col: Virginia Union B: 2/10/1949, Glen Allen, VA *Drafted:* 1971 Round 14 Cin
1971 NE: 2 G; KR 1-19 19.0.

JOHN MALLORY Mallory, John 6′0″, 184 **DB**
Col: West Virginia *HS:* Summit [NJ] B: 7/24/1946, Summit, NJ
Drafted: 1968 Round 10 Phi
1968 Phi: Rec 1-58 58.0 1 TD; KR 6-94 15.7. **1969** Atl: Int 1-22. **1970** Atl: Int 1-9; 1 Fum TD. **1971** Atl: Rec 1-27 27.0; **1** Fum TD. **Total:** Rec 2-85 42.5 1 TD; KR 6-94 15.7; Int 2-31; 2 Fum TD.

		Punt Returns					Tot
Year Team	**G**	**Ret**	**Yds**	**Avg**	**TD**	**Fum**	**TD**
1968 Phi	14	4	46	11.5	0	1	1
1969 Atl	13	13	42	3.2	0	1	0
1970 Atl	14	17	203	11.9	**1**	1	2
1971 Atl	14	5	3	0.6	0	1	1
NFL Total	55	39	294	7.5	1	4	4

LARRY MALLORY Mallory, Larry Montel 5′11″, 185 **DB**
Col: Tennessee State *HS:* Melrose [Memphis, TN] B: 7/21/1952, Memphis, TN
1976 NYG: 14 G; Rush 1-0; Int 1-0; 1 Fum. **1977** NYG: 14 G; KR 1-0; Int 1-9; 1 Fum. **1978** NYG: 16 G; Pass 1-1 100.0%, 35 35.00. **Total:** 44 G; Pass 1-1 100.0%, 35 35.00; Rush 1-0; KR 1-0; Int 2-9; 2 Fum.

RICK MALLORY Mallory, Ricke Leroy 6′2″, 265 **OG**
Col: Washington *HS:* Lindbergh [Renton, WA] B: 10/21/1960, Seattle, WA *Drafted:* 1984 Round 9 TB
1985 TB: 13 G. **1986** TB: 16 G; Rec 1-9 9.0. **1987** TB: 12 G. **1988** TB: 16 G. **Total:** 57 G; Rec 1-9 9.0.

RAY MALLOUF Mallouf, Raymond Lucian 5′11″, 180 **QB-DB-TB**
(Slingin' Syrian) *Col:* Southern Methodist *HS:* Sayre [OK]
B: 7/11/1918, Sayre, OK *Drafted:* 1941 Round 10 ChiC
1941 ChiC: PR 4-11 2.8; KR 2-31 15.5. **1946** ChiC: Int 1-15. **1949** NYG: Int 1-0. **Total:** PR 4-11 2.8; KR 2-31 15.5; Int 2-15.

		Passing							
Year Team	**G**	**Att**	**Comp**	**Comp%**	**Yds**	**YPA**	**TD**	**Int**	**Rating**
1941 ChiC	9	96	48	50.0	725	7.55	2	4	64.8
1946 ChiC	5	34	14	41.2	260	7.65	4	**2**	83.0
1947 ChiC	11	36	21	58.3	340	**9.44**	1	**2**	76.2
1948 ChiC	12	143	73	51.0	1160	8.11	13	6	91.2
1949 NYG	11	16	3	18.8	19	1.19	0	2	0.0
NFL Total	48	325	159	48.9	2504	7.70	20	16	75.0

	Rushing				Punting			
Year Team	**Att**	**Yds**	**Avg**	**TD**	**Punts**	**Yds**	**Avg**	**Fum**
1941 ChiC	43	104	2.4	0	28	1150	41.1	0
1946 ChiC	4	6	1.5	0	15	520	34.7	3
1947 ChiC	5	13	2.6	0	43	1717	39.9	2
1948 ChiC	13	17	1.3	1	45	1754	39.0	4
1949 NYG	1	-1	-1.0	0	57	2129	37.4	2
NFL Total	66	139	2.1	1	188	7270	38.7	11

LES MALLOY Malloy, Leslie A 6′0″, 200 **BB-DB-WB-TB**
Col: Loyola (Chicago) *HS:* St. Ignatius [Chicago, IL] B: 12/8/1907
D: 7/1982, Downers Grove, IL
1931 ChiC: 8 G; Rec 1 TD; 6 Pt. **1932** ChiC: 8 G; Pass 11-2 18.2%, 22 2.00; Rush 9-32 3.6; Rec 3-57 19.0. **1933** ChiC: 10 G; Rush 9-20 2.2. **Total:** 26 G; Pass 11-2 18.2%, 22 2.00; Rush 18-52 2.9; Rec 3-57 19.0 1 TD; 6 Pt.

ART MALONE Malone, Arthur Lee 5′11″, 211 **RB**
Col: Arizona State *HS:* Santa Cruz Valley Union [Eloy, AZ]
B: 3/20/1948, Tyler, TX *Drafted:* 1970 Round 2 Atl
1970 Atl: KR 5-66 13.2. **1972** Atl: KR 2-37 18.5. **Total:** KR 7-103 14.7.

		Rushing				Receiving					Tot
Year Team	**G**	**Att**	**Yds**	**Avg**	**TD**	**Rec**	**Yds**	**Avg**	**TD**	**Fum**	**TD**
1970 Atl	14	40	136	3.4	0	9	38	4.2	1	0	1
1971 Atl	13	120	438	3.7	6	34	380	11.2	2	5	8
1972 Atl	14	180	798	4.4	8	50	585	11.7	2	**10**	10
1973 Atl	10	76	336	4.4	2	19	177	9.3	1	2	3
1974 Atl	13	116	410	3.5	2	28	168	6.0	0	1	2
1975 Phi	13	101	325	3.2	0	20	120	6.0	0	2	0
1976 Phi	3	2	14	7.0	1	1	-3	-3.0	0	0	1
NFL Total	80	635	2457	3.9	19	161	1465	9.1	6	20	25

BENNY MALONE Malone, Ben Jr. 5′10″, 193 **RB**
Col: Arizona State *HS:* Santa Cruz Valley Union [Eloy, AZ] B: 2/3/1952, Tyler, TX *Drafted:* 1974 Round 2 Mia
1974 Mia: KR 6-159 26.5. **1975** Mia: KR 1-18 18.0. **Total:** KR 7-177 25.3.

		Rushing				Receiving					Tot
Year Team	**G**	**Att**	**Yds**	**Avg**	**TD**	**Rec**	**Yds**	**Avg**	**TD**	**Fum**	**TD**
1974 Mia	13	117	479	4.1	3	2	26	13.0	0	2	3
1975 Mia	10	65	220	3.4	3	2	47	23.5	0	0	3
1976 Mia	14	186	797	4.3	4	9	103	11.4	0	3	4
1977 Mia	14	129	615	4.8	5	4	58	14.5	0	4	5
1978 Mia-Was	15	33	110	3.3	1	3	29	9.7	0	0	1
1978 Mia	6	6	18	3.0	1	0	0	—	0	0	1
1978 Was	9	27	92	3.4	0	3	29	9.7	0	0	0
1979 Was	16	176	472	2.7	3	13	137	10.5	1	1	4
NFL Total	82	706	2693	3.8	19	33	400	12.1	1	10	20

CHUCK MALONE Malone, Charles T 6′4″, 206 **OE-DE**
Col: Texas A&M B: 6/18/1910, Hillsboro, TX D: 5/1992, Lake San Marcos, CA
1934 Bos: Rush 1-30 30.0. **1939** Was: Scor 18, 0-1 XK. **Total:** Rush 1-30 30.0; Scor 78, 0-1 XK.

		Receiving			
Year Team	**G**	**Rec**	**Yds**	**Avg**	**TD**
1934 Bos	12	11	131	11.9	2
1935 Bos	11	22	**433**	19.7	2
1936 Bos	12	11	167	15.2	1
1937 Was	11	28	419	15.0	4
1938 Was	11	24	257	10.7	1
1939 Was	11	18	274	15.2	3
1940 Was	11	20	222	11.1	0
1942 Was	5	3	29	9.7	0
NFL Total	84	137	1932	14.1	13

DARRELL MALONE Malone, Darrell Kenyatta 5′10″, 177 **DB**
Col: Jacksonville State *HS:* Jacksonville [AL] B: 11/23/1967, Mobile, AL *Drafted:* 1991 Round 6 KC
1992 KC-Mia: 8 G. KC: 4 G. Mia: 4 G. **1993** Mia: 16 G. **1994** Mia: 5 G; Int 1-0. **Total:** 29 G; Int 1-0.

GROVER MALONE Malone, John Grover 5′8″, 185 **WB-HB-OE-TB**
(Molly) *Col:* Notre Dame *HS:* La Salle-Peru Twp. [La Salle, IL]
B: 11/12/1895, Chicago, IL D: 11/26/1985, West Allis, WI
1920 ChiT: 6 G. **1921** GB-RI: 9 G. GB: 6 G. RI: 3 G. **1923** Akr: 2 G.
Total: 17 G.

MARK MALONE Malone, Mark M 6′4″, 223 **QB-WR**
Col: Arizona State *HS:* Valley [El Cajon, CA] B: 11/22/1958, San Diego, CA *Drafted:* 1980 Round 1 Pit
1981 Pit: Rec 1-90 90.0 1 TD; KR 1-3 3.0. **Total:** Rec 1-90 90.0 1 TD; KR 1-3 3.0.

		Passing							
Year Team	**G**	**Att**	**Comp**	**Comp%**	**Yds**	**YPA**	**TD**	**Int**	**Rating**
1980 Pit	1	0	0	—	0	—	0	0	—
1981 Pit	8	88	45	51.1	553	6.28	3	5	58.6
1983 Pit	2	20	9	45.0	124	6.20	1	2	42.5
1984 Pit	13	272	147	54.0	2137	7.86	16	17	73.4
1985 Pit	10	233	117	50.2	1428	6.13	13	**7**	75.5
1986 Pit	14	425	216	50.8	2444	5.75	15	18	62.5
1987 Pit	12	336	156	46.4	1896	5.64	6	19	46.7
1988 SD	12	272	147	54.0	1580	5.81	6	13	58.8
1989 NYJ	1	2	2	100.0	13	6.50	0	0	93.8
NFL Total	73	1648	839	50.9	10175	6.17	60	81	61.9

	Rushing					Tot
Year Team	**Att**	**Yds**	**Avg**	**TD**	**Fum**	**TD**
1981 Pit	16	68	4.3	2	2	3
1984 Pit	25	42	1.7	3	4	3
1985 Pit	15	80	5.3	1	3	1
1986 Pit	31	107	3.5	5	7	5
1987 Pit	34	162	4.8	3	10	3
1988 SD	37	169	4.6	4	6	4
1989 NYJ	1	0	0.0	0	1	0
NFL Total	159	628	3.9	18	33	19

RALPH MALONE Malone, Ralph DeVaughn 6′5″, 225 **DE**
Col: Georgia Tech *HS:* Bob Jones [Madison, AL] B: 1/12/1964, Huntsville, AL
1986 Cle: 16 G.

VAN MALONE Malone, Van Buren 5′11″, 189 **DB**
Col: Texas *HS:* Waltrip [Houston, TX] B: 7/1/1970, Houston, TX
Drafted: 1994 Round 2 Det
1994 Det: 16 G; KR 3-38 12.7; 1 Fum. **1995** Det: 16 G; Int 1-0. **1996** Det: 15 G; Int 1-5. **1997** Det: 8 G; Int 1-(-5); 1 Fum. **Total:** 55 G; KR 3-38 12.7; Int 3-0; 2 Fum.

RED MALONEY Maloney, Gerald Stack 5'11", 181 **E-WB**
Col: Dartmouth *HS:* Worcester [MA] B: 9/5/1901, Ware, MA
D: 5/16/1976, Waban, MA
1925 Prov: 12 G; Scor 19, 3 FG, 4 XK; 1 Fum TD. **1927** NYY: 12 G; Rec 1 TD; 6 Pt. **1929** Bost: 8 G. **Total:** 32 G; Rec 1 TD; Scor 25, 3 FG, 4 XK; 1 Fum TD; Tot TD 2.

NED MALONEY Maloney, Norman Edward 6'1", 190 **OE-DE**
Col: Purdue *HS:* Fenwick [Chicago, IL] B: 4/21/1923, Chicago, IL
AAFC **1948** SF-A: 14 G; Rec 1-29 29.0 1 TD; Scor 7, 1-1 100.0% XK.
1949 SF-A: 12 G; PR 1-5 5.0. **Total:** 26 G; Rec 1-29 29.0 1 TD; PR 1-5 5.0; Scor 7, 1-1 100.0% XK.

MIKE MAMULA Mamula, Michael David 6'4", 252 **DE-LB**
Col: Boston College *HS:* Lackawanna [NY] B: 8/14/1973, Lackawanna, NY *Drafted:* 1995 Round 1 Phi
1995 Phi: 14 G; 5.5 Sac. **1996** Phi: 16 G; **1** Fum TD; 6 Pt; 8 Sac. **1997** Phi: 16 G; 4 Sac. **Total:** 46 G; 1 Fum TD; 6 Pt; 17.5 Sac.

MASSIMO MANCA Manca, Massimo 5'10", 211 **K**
Col: Penn State *HS:* Reno [NV] B: 3/18/1964, Sassari, Italy
1987 Cin: 3 G; Scor 6, 1-2 50.0% FG, 3-3 100.0% XK.

VAUGHN MANCHA Mancha, Vaughn Hall 6'1", 230 **C-LB**
Col: Alabama *HS:* Ramsey [Birmingham, AL] B: 10/7/1921, Sugar Valley, GA *Drafted:* 1948 Round 1 Bos
1948 Bos: 12 G.

TONY MANDARICH Mandarich, Ante Josip 6'5", 311 **OT**
Col: Michigan State *HS:* White Oaks Sec. School [Oakville, Canada]; Roosevelt [Kent, OH] B: 9/23/1966, Oakville, Canada *Drafted:* 1989 Round 1 GB
1989 GB: 14 G; KR 1-0. **1990** GB: 16 G. **1991** GB: 15 G. **1996** Ind: 15 G. **1997** Ind: 16 G. **1998** Ind: 10 G. **Total:** 86 G; KR 1-0.

MIKE MANDARINO Mandarino, Michael Pascol 5'11", 240 **C**
Col: La Salle *HS:* West Catholic [Philadelphia, PA] B: 3/16/1921, Philadelphia, PA D: 12/7/1985, Media, PA
1944 Phi: 8 G. **1945** Phi: 5 G. **Total:** 13 G.

PUG MANDERS Manders, Clarence Edward 6'0", 202 **FB-LB-DB-BB**
Col: Drake *HS:* Milbank [SD] B: 5/5/1913, Milbank, SD D: 1/20/1985, Des Moines, IA *Drafted:* 1939 Round 2 Bkn
AAFC **1946** NY-A: Pass 3-2 66.7%, 14 4.67; Rec 3-49 16.3; KR 1-26 26.0. **Total:** Pass 3-2 66.7%, 14 4.67; Rec 3-49 16.3; KR 1-26 26.0.

		Rushing			
Year Team	**G**	**Att**	**Yds**	**Avg**	**TD**
1946 NY-A	13	49	168	3.4	3
1947 BufA	3	3	15	5.0	0
AAFC Total	16	52	183	3.5	3

NFL **1944** Bkn: Scor 30, 0-1 FG. **Total:** Scor 216, 0-1 FG.

		Passing							
Year Team	**G**	**Att**	**Comp**	**Comp%**	**Yds**	**YPA**	**TD**	**Int**	**Rating**
1939 Bkn	11	0	0	—	0	—	0	0	—
1940 Bkn	11	1	0	0.0	0	0.00	0	0	39.6
1941 Bkn	11	0	0	—	0	—	0	0	—
1942 Bkn	11	1	0	0.0	0	0.00	0	0	39.6
1943 Bkn	10	5	4	80.0	31	6.20	1	0	132.1
1944 Bkn	10	34	9	26.5	96	2.82	0	4	0.0
1945 Bos	10	9	5	55.6	42	4.67	0	1	28.2
NFL Total	74	50	18	36.0	169	3.38	1	5	13.3

	Rushing				Receiving			
Year Team	**Att**	**Yds**	**Avg**	**TD**	**Rec**	**Yds**	**Avg**	**TD**
1939 Bkn	114	482	4.2	2	3	22	7.3	0
1940 Bkn	80	311	3.9	5	1	38	38.0	1
1941 Bkn	111	**486**	4.4	5	6	67	11.2	0
1942 Bkn	93	316	3.4	6	4	53	13.3	0
1943 Bkn	89	266	3.0	3	5	68	13.6	1
1944 Bkn	127	430	3.4	5	6	78	13.0	0
1945 Bos	76	238	3.1	6	0	0	—	0
NFL Total	690	2529	3.7	32	25	326	13.0	2

	Kickoff Returns				Interceptions				Tot
Year Team	**Ret**	**Yds**	**Avg**	**TD**	**Int**	**Yds**	**TD**	**Fum**	**TD**
1939 Bkn	—	—	—	0	—	—	0	0	2
1940 Bkn	—	—	—	0	1	15	0	0	6
1941 Bkn	7	128	18.3	0	4	73	**1**	0	7
1942 Bkn	9	210	23.3	0	2	23	0	0	6
1943 Bkn	1	19	19.0	0	0	0	0	0	4
1944 Bkn	11	227	20.6	0	1	4	0	0	5
1945 Bos	2	10	5.0	0	3	5	0	6	6
NFL Total	30	594	19.8	0	11	120	1	6	36

DAVE MANDERS Manders, David Francis 6'2", 250 **C**
Col: Michigan State *HS:* Kingsford [MI] B: 2/20/1941, Milwaukee, WI
1964 Dal: 14 G. **1965** Dal: 14 G. **1966** Dal: 14 G. **1968** Dal: 14 G. **1969** Dal: 14 G. **1970** Dal: 14 G. **1971** Dal: 14 G. **1972** Dal: 14 G. **1973** Dal: 13 G. **1974** Dal: 14 G. **Total:** 139 G.

JACK MANDERS Manders, John Albert 6'0", 203 **FB-LB-HB-DB**
(Automatic Jack) *Col:* Minnesota *HS:* Milbank [SD] B: 1/13/1909, Milbank, SD D: 1/28/1977, Chicago, IL
1933 ChiB: Pass 15-6 40.0%, 57 3.80 3 Int; Rec 1-9 9.0. **1934** ChiB: Pass 3-2 66.7%, 14 4.67; Rec 1-12 12.0; Int **1** TD. **1935** ChiB: Pass 9-1 11.1%, 10 1.11 1 Int; Rec 2-16 8.0. **1936** ChiB: Pass 3-2 66.7%, 52 17.33; Rec 1-4 4.0. **1937** ChiB: Rec 7-163 23.3 4 TD; Int **1** TD. **1938** ChiB: Pass 1-0; Rec 2-27 13.5 1 TD. **1939** ChiB: Rec 1-29 29.0 1 TD.
1940 ChiB: Int 1-27. **Total:** Pass 31-11 35.5%, 133 4.29 4 Int; Rec 15-260 17.3 6 TD; Int 1-27 2 TD.

		Rushing			
Year Team	**G**	**Att**	**Yds**	**Avg**	**TD**
1933 ChiB	13	65	234	3.6	0
1934 ChiB	13	57	184	3.2	2
1935 ChiB	12	93	296	3.2	0
1936 ChiB	12	63	207	3.3	4
1937 ChiB	11	73	319	4.4	0
1938 ChiB	11	67	263	3.9	2
1939 ChiB	11	25	63	2.5	3
1940 ChiB	10	8	20	2.5	0
NFL Total	93	451	1586	3.5	11

	Scoring							Tot
Year Team	**Pts**	**FG**	**FGA**	**FG%**	**XK**	**XKA**	**XK%**	**TD**
1933 ChiB	31	**6**	—	—	**13**	—	—	0
1934 ChiB	**76**	**10**	—	—	**28**	—	—	3
1935 ChiB	19	1	—	—	**16**	—	—	0
1936 ChiB	62	**7**	—	—	17	—	—	4
1937 ChiB	**69**	**8**	—	—	15	—	—	5
1938 ChiB	37	3	9	33.3	10	12	83.3	3
1939 ChiB	50	3	7	42.9	17	**20**	85.0	4
1940 ChiB	23	2	3	66.7	17	18	94.4	0
NFL Total	367	40	19	42.1	133	50	88.0	19

CHRIS MANDEVILLE Mandeville, Christopher Scott 6'1", 213 **DB**
Col: California-Davis *HS:* Irvine [CA] B: 2/1/1965, Santa Barbara, CA
1987 GB: 4 G. **1988** GB: 2 G. **1989** Was: 1 G; KR 1-10 10.0. **Total:** 7 G; KR 1-10 10.0.

JIM MANDICH Mandich, James Michael 6'2", 224 **TE-WB**
Col: Michigan *HS:* Solon [OH] B: 7/30/1948, Cleveland, OH
Drafted: 1970 Round 2 Mia
1970 Mia: KR 2-0. **Total:** KR 2-0.

		Receiving				
Year Team	**G**	**Rec**	**Yds**	**Avg**	**TD**	**Fum**
1970 Mia	14	1	3	3.0	1	1
1971 Mia	11	3	19	6.3	1	0
1972 Mia	14	11	168	15.3	3	0
1973 Mia	14	24	302	12.6	4	0
1974 Mia	14	33	374	11.3	6	0
1975 Mia	14	21	217	10.3	4	0
1976 Mia	14	22	260	11.8	4	0
1977 Mia	14	6	63	10.5	0	0
1978 Pit	10	0	0	—	0	0
NFL Total	119	121	1406	11.6	23	1

PETE MANDLEY Mandley, William Henry 5'10", 191 **WR**
Col: Northern Arizona *HS:* Westwood [Mesa, AZ] B: 7/29/1961, Phoenix, AZ *Drafted:* 1984 Round 2 Det
1987 Det: Rush 1-3 3.0. **1988** Det: Rush 6-44 7.3 1 TD. **1989** KC: Rush 2-1 0.5. **Total:** Rush 9-48 5.3 1 TD.

		Receiving				Punt Returns			
Year Team	**G**	**Rec**	**Yds**	**Avg**	**TD**	**Ret**	**Yds**	**Avg**	**TD**
1984 Det	15	3	38	12.7	0	2	0	0.0	0
1985 Det	16	18	316	17.6	0	38	403	10.6	1
1986 Det	16	7	106	15.1	0	43	420	9.8	1
1987 Det	12	58	720	12.4	7	23	250	10.9	0
1988 Det	15	44	617	14.0	4	37	287	7.8	0
1989 KC	13	35	476	13.6	1	19	151	7.9	0
1990 KC	5	7	97	13.9	0	0	0	—	0
NFL Total	92	172	2370	13.8	12	162	1511	9.3	2

	Kickoff Returns					Tot
Year Team	**Ret**	**Yds**	**Avg**	**TD**	**Fum**	**TD**
1984 Det	22	390	17.7	0	2	0
1985 Det	6	152	25.3	0	3	1
1986 Det	2	37	18.5	0	3	1
1987 Det	0	0	—	0	0	7
1988 Det	0	0	—	0	3	5
1989 KC	1	0	0.0	0	1	1

1990 KC	4	51	12.8	0	1	0
NFL Total	35	630	18.0	0	13	15

JAMES MANESS Maness, James Lynn 6′1″, 174 **WR**
Col: Texas Christian *HS:* Decatur [TX] B: 5/1/1963, Decatur, TX
Drafted: 1985 Round 3 ChiB
1985 ChiB: 8 G; Rec 1-34 34.0; PR 2-9 4.5.

TONY MANFREDA Manfreda, Anthony Richard 5′8″, 172 **WB-TB**
Col: Holy Cross *HS:* Sanborn Seminary [Kingston, NH] B: 2/19/1904, Meriden, CT D: 10/9/1988, Brooksville, FL
1930 Nwk: 2 G.

MARK MANGES Manges, Mark Roy 6′2″, 210 **QB**
Col: Maryland *HS:* Fort Hill [Cumberland, MD] B: 1/10/1956, Cumberland, MD *Drafted:* 1978 Round 4 LARm
1978 StL: 1 G.

DINO MANGIERO Mangiero, Dino M 6′2″, 265 **NT-DE**
Col: Rutgers *HS:* Curtis [Staten Island, NY] B: 12/19/1958, New York, NY
1980 KC: 16 G; Int 1-0. **1981** KC: 9 G. **1982** KC: 6 G; KR 1-8 8.0; 1 Sac. **1983** KC: 16 G; 5 Sac. **1984** Sea: 15 G; 1 Sac. **1987** NE: 2 G; 1 Sac. **Total:** 64 G; KR 1-8 8.0; Int 1-0; 8 Sac.

PETE MANGUM Mangum, Ernest Glynde 6′0″, 219 **LB**
Col: Mississippi *HS:* Rolling Fork [MS] B: 1/17/1931, Forest, LA
Drafted: 1954 Round 23 NYG
1954 NYG: 2 G. **1960** Den: 14 G. **Total:** 16 G.

JOHN MANGUM Mangum, John Wayne Jr. 5′10″, 187 **DB**
Col: Alabama *HS:* Magee [MS] B: 3/16/1967, Magee, MS
Drafted: 1990 Round 6 ChiB
1990 ChiB: 10 G. **1991** ChiB: 16 G; Int 1-5; 1 Sac. **1992** ChiB: 5 G. **1993** ChiB: 12 G; KR 1-0; Int 1-0. **1994** ChiB: 16 G; 0.5 Sac. **1995** ChiB: 11 G; Int 1-2; 1 Sac. **1996** ChiB: 16 G; 1 Sac. **1997** ChiB: 16 G; Int 2-4; 1 Sac. **1998** ChiB: 3 G. **Total:** 105 G; KR 1-0; Int 5-11; 4.5 Sac.

JOHN MANGUM Mangum, John Wayne Sr. 6′1″, 270 **DT**
Col: Mississippi; Southern Mississippi *HS:* Magee [MS] B: 9/30/1942, Magee, MS Deceased *Drafted:* 1966 Round 5 Bos
1966 Bos: 14 G; KR 1-8 8.0. **1967** Bos: 14 G. **Total:** 28 G; KR 1-8 8.0.

KRIS MANGUM Mangum, Kris Thomas 6′4″, 249 **TE**
Col: Alabama; Mississippi *HS:* Magee [MS] B: 8/15/1973, Magee, MS
Drafted: 1997 Round 7 Car
1997 Car: 2 G; Rec 4-56 14.0. **1998** Car: 6 G; Rec 1-5 5.0. **Total:** 8 G; Rec 5-61 12.2.

JOE MANIACI Maniaci, Joseph Gene 6′1″, 212 **FB-LB-HB-DB**
Col: Fordham *HS:* Hasbrouck Heights [NJ] B: 1/23/1914, New York, NY *Drafted:* 1936 Round 6 Bkn
1936 Bkn: Pass 4-1 25.0%, 1 0.25; Rec 1-30 30.0. **1937** Bkn: Pass 4-1 25.0%, 2 Int; Rec 3-11 3.7; Scor 23, 2 FG, 5 XK. **1938** Bkn-ChiB: Pass 2-1 50.0%, 19 9.50 1 TD; Rec 9-127 14.1; Scor 32, 1-3 33.3% FG, 11-11 100.0% XK. Bkn: Pass 2-1 50.0%, 19 9.50 1 TD; Rec 3-55 18.3. ChiB: Rec 6-72 12.0; Scor 32, 1-3 33.3% FG, 11-11 100.0% XK. **1939** ChiB: Pass 2-1 50.0%, 10 5.00; Scor 37, 1-2 50.0% FG, 4-8 50.0% XK; **1** Fum TD. **1940** ChiB: Rec 1-(-5) -5.0; Int 2-38; Scor 19, 1-2 50.0% XK. **1941** ChiB: Rec 2-21 10.5; Scor 29, 1-1 100.0% FG, 8-8 100.0% XK. **Total:** Pass 12-4 33.3%, 30 2.50 1 TD 2 Int; Rec 16-184 11.5; Int 2-38; Scor 140, 5-6 50.0% FG, 29-29 82.8% XK; 1 Fum TD.

		Rushing				Tot
Year Team	**G**	**Att**	**Yds**	**Avg**	**TD**	**TD**
1936 Bkn	11	35	70	2.0	0	0
1937 Bkn	11	92	433	4.7	2	2
1938 Bkn-ChiB	11	88	345	3.9	3	3
1938 Bkn	2	17	57	3.4	0	0
1938 ChiB	9	71	288	4.1	3	3
1939 ChiB	9	77	544	**7.1**	4	5
1940 ChiB	11	84	368	4.4	2	3
1941 ChiB	7	28	95	3.4	3	3
NFL Total	60	404	1855	4.6	14	16

JASON MANIECKI Maniecki, Jason Zbiyniew 6′4″, 291 **DT**
Col: Wisconsin *HS:* Wisconsin Dells [WI] B: 8/15/1972, Rabka, Poland
Drafted: 1996 Round 5 TB
1996 TB: 5 G. **1997** TB: 10 G; 1 Sac. **1998** TB: 3 G. **Total:** 18 G; 1 Sac.

JIMMY MANION Manion, James H 5′9″, 178 **G-C**
(Skipper) *Col:* St. Thomas *HS:* St. Mary's [Winona, MN]
B: 9/20/1904, Jasper, MN D: 7/11/1978, Pipestone, MN
1926 Dul: 11 G. **1927** Dul: 6 G. **Total:** 17 G.

CARL MANKAT Mankat, Carl Robert 6′3″, 208 **E-T-G**
Col: Colgate *HS:* Steele [Dayton, OH] B: 1/13/1904, Dayton, OH
D: 11/21/1963, Dayton, OH
1928 Day: 6 G. **1929** Day: 6 G. **Total:** 12 G.

JIM MANKINS Mankins, James Frank 6′1″, 215 **RB**
(Cowboy) *Col:* Hartnell Coll. CA (J.C.); Oklahoma; Florida State
HS: King City [CA] B: 6/23/1944, Chino, CA *Drafted:* 1966 Round 12 GB
1967 Atl: 11 G; Rush 2-7 3.5; Rec 1-11 11.0; KR 1-12 12.0.

DEXTER MANLEY Manley, Dexter Keith 6′3″, 253 **DE**
Col: Oklahoma State *HS:* Jack Yates [Houston, TX] B: 7/2/1959, Houston, TX *Drafted:* 1981 Round 5 Was
1981 Was: 16 G. **1982** Was: 9 G; Int 1-(-2); 6.5 Sac. **1983** Was: 16 G; Int 1-1; 11 Sac. **1984** Was: 15 G; 13.5 Sac. **1985** Was: 16 G; 15 Sac. **1986** Was: 16 G; **1** Fum TD; 6 Pt; 18.5 Sac. **1987** Was: 11 G; 8.5 Sac. **1988** Was: 16 G; 9 Sac. **1989** Was: 10 G; Scor **1** Saf; 2 Pt; 9 Sac. **1990** Pho: 4 G. **1991** TB: 14 G; 6.5 Sac. **Total:** 143 G; Int 2-(-1); Scor 1 Saf; 1 Fum TD; 8 Pt; 97.5 Sac.

JAMES MANLEY Manley, James O III 6′2″, 316 **DT**
Col: Vanderbilt *HS:* Huffman [Birmingham, AL] B: 7/11/1974, Birmingham, AL *Drafted:* 1996 Round 2 Min
1996 Min: Postseason only.

JACK MANLEY Manley, Joseph Jackson 6′3″, 215 **C-LB**
Col: Mississippi State *HS:* Hazelwood [Town Creek, OK] B: 9/20/1929, Town Creek, AL
1953 SF: 12 G.

LEON MANLEY Manley, William Leon 6′2″, 218 **OG-OT**
(Willie) *Col:* Oklahoma *HS:* Hollis [OK] B: 5/20/1926, Hollis, OK
Drafted: 1950 Round 7 GB
1950 GB: 12 G; Rec 5-66 13.2. **1951** GB: 12 G. **Total:** 24 G; Rec 5-66 13.2.

CHARLES MANN Mann, Charles Andre 6′6″, 268 **DE**
Col: Nevada-Reno *HS:* Valley [Sacramento, CA] B: 4/12/1961, Sacramento, CA *Drafted:* 1983 Round 3 Was
1983 Was: 16 G; Scor 1 Saf; 2 Pt; 3 Sac. **1984** Was: 16 G; 7 Sac. **1985** Was: 16 G; 14.5 Sac. **1986** Was: 15 G; 10 Sac. **1987** Was: 12 G; 9.5 Sac. **1988** Was: 14 G; 5.5 Sac. **1989** Was: 16 G; 10 Sac. **1990** Was: 15 G; 5.5 Sac. **1991** Was: 15 G; 11.5 Sac. **1992** Was: 16 G; 4.5 Sac. **1993** Was: 12 G; 1 Sac. **1994** SF: 14 G; 1 Sac. **Total:** 177 G; Scor 1 Saf; 2 Pt; 83 Sac.

DAVE MANN Mann, David Carl 6′1″, 190 **HB-OE**
Col: Oregon State *HS:* Castlemont [Oakland, CA] B: 6/2/1932, Berkeley, CA *Drafted:* 1954 Round 7 ChiC
1955 ChiC: Pass 10-5 50.0%, 53 5.30 2 TD; KR 6-136 22.7; Scor 33, 1-1 100.0% FG, 0-2 XK. **1956** ChiC: Pass 2-0, 1 Int; KR 7-131 18.7. **1957** ChiC: Pass 1-0; PR 1-0; KR 1-23 23.0. **Total:** Pass 13-5 38.5%, 53 4.08 2 TD 1 Int; PR 1-0; KR 14-290 20.7; Scor 39, 1-1 100.0% FG, 0-2 XK.

		Rushing				Receiving			
Year Team	**G**	**Att**	**Yds**	**Avg**	**TD**	**Rec**	**Yds**	**Avg**	**TD**
1955 ChiC	12	87	336	3.9	4	16	137	8.6	1
1956 ChiC	12	45	116	2.6	0	13	170	13.1	1
1957 ChiC	12	22	92	4.2	0	8	137	17.1	0
NFL Total	36	154	544	3.5	4	37	444	12.0	2

	Punting				Tot
Year Team	**Punts**	**Yds**	**Avg**	**Fum**	**TD**
1955 ChiC	43	1723	40.1	6	5
1956 ChiC	36	1346	37.4	1	1
1957 ChiC	59	2509	42.5	1	0
NFL Total	138	5578	40.4	8	6

ERROL MANN Mann, Errol Denis 6′0″, 200 **K**
Col: North Dakota *HS:* Campbell [MN] B: 6/27/1941, Breckenridge, MN
1974 Det: Punt 1-18 18.0. **1975** Det: Punt 1-34 34.0. **Total:** Punt 2-52 26.0.

		Scoring						
Year Team	**G**	**Pts**	**FG**	**FGA**	**FG%**	**XK**	**XKA**	**XK%**
1968 GB	2	4	0	3	0.0	4	4	100.0
1969 Det	14	101	25	37	67.6	26	26	100.0
1970 Det	14	101	20	29	69.0	**41**	**41**	100.0
1971 Det	14	103	22	37	59.5	37	37	100.0
1972 Det	14	98	20	29	69.0	38	39	97.4
1973 Det	8	53	13	19	68.4	14	14	100.0
1974 Det	14	92	23	32	71.9	23	26	88.5
1975 Det	14	67	14	21	66.7	25	29	86.2
1976 Det-GB-Oak	13	59	8	21	38.1	35	37	94.6
1976 Det	6	21	4	10	40.0	9	10	90.0
1976 Oak	7	38	4	11	36.4	26	27	96.3
1977 Oak	14	**99**	20	28	71.4	**39**	**42**	92.9
1978 Oak	16	69	12	20	60.0	33	38	86.8
NFL Total	137	846	177	276	64.1	315	333	94.6

BOB MANN Mann, Robert 5′11″, 172 **OE**
Col: Michigan *HS:* J.T. Barber [New Bern, NC] B: 4/8/1924, New Bern, NC
1948 Det: Rush 6-46 7.7; KR 1-16 16.0. **1951** GB: Rush 2-9 4.5.
Total: Rush 8-55 6.9; KR 1-16 16.0.

		Receiving				
Year Team	G	Rec	Yds	Avg	TD	Fum
1948 Det	12	33	560	17.0	3	4
1949 Det	12	66	**1014**	15.4	4	0
1950 GB	3	6	89	14.8	1	0
1951 GB	11	50	696	13.9	8	0
1952 GB	12	30	517	17.2	6	0
1953 GB	10	23	327	14.2	2	0
1954 GB	2	0	0	—	0	0
NFL Total	62	208	3203	15.4	24	4

PATRICK MANNELLY Mannelly, James Patrick 6′5″, 286 **OT**
Col: Duke *HS:* Marist [Atlanta, GA] B: 4/18/1975, Atlanta, GA
Drafted: 1998 Round 6 ChiB
1998 ChiB: 16 G.

AARON MANNING Manning, Aaron K 5′10″, 178 **DB**
Col: Hutchinson CC KS; Iowa State *HS:* James J. Ferris [Jersey City, NJ] B: 8/26/1961, Jersey City, NJ
1987 Cin: 3 G.

BRIAN MANNING Manning, Brian Keith 5′11″, 188 **WR**
Col: Stanford *HS:* Ruskin [Kansas City, MO] B: 4/22/1975, Kansas City, KS *Drafted:* 1997 Round 6 Mia
1997 Mia: 7 G; Rec 7-85 12.1. **1998** GB: 3 G. **Total:** 10 G; Rec 7-85 12.1.

ARCHIE MANNING Manning, Elisha Archie III 6′3″, 212 **QB**
Col: Mississippi *HS:* Drew [MS] B: 5/19/1949, Cleveland, MS
Drafted: 1971 Round 1 NO
1971 NO: Rec 1-(-7) -7.0. **Total:** Rec 1-(-7) -7.0.

		Passing							
Year Team	G	Att	Comp	Comp%	Yds	YPA	TD	Int	Rating
1971 NO	12	177	86	48.6	1164	6.58	6	9	60.1
1972 NO	14	**448**	**230**	51.3	2781	6.21	18	21	64.6
1973 NO	13	267	140	52.4	1642	6.15	10	12	65.2
1974 NO	11	261	134	51.3	1429	5.48	6	16	49.8
1975 NO	13	338	159	47.0	1683	4.98	7	20	44.3
1977 NO	10	205	113	55.1	1284	6.26	8	9	68.8
1978 NO	16	471	291	61.8	3416	7.25	17	16	81.7
1979 NO	16	420	252	60.0	3169	7.55	15	20	75.6
1980 NO	16	509	309	60.7	3716	7.30	23	20	81.8
1981 NO	12	232	134	57.8	1447	6.24	5	11	63.6
1982 NO-Hou	7	132	67	50.8	880	6.67	6	8	62.1
1982 NO	1	7	1	14.3	3	0.43	0	2	0.0
1982 Hou	6	125	66	52.8	877	7.02	6	6	71.3
1983 Hou-Min	5	88	44	50.0	755	8.58	2	8	49.2
1983 Hou	3	88	44	50.0	755	8.58	2	8	49.2
1983 Min	2	0	0	—	0	—	0	0	—
1984 Min	6	94	52	55.3	545	5.80	2	3	66.1
NFL Total	151	3642	2011	55.2	23911	6.57	125	173	67.1

	Rushing				
Year Team	Att	Yds	Avg	TD	Fum
1971 NO	33	172	5.2	4	7
1972 NO	63	351	5.6	2	9
1973 NO	63	293	4.7	2	9
1974 NO	28	204	7.3	1	4
1975 NO	33	186	5.6	1	7
1977 NO	39	270	6.9	5	5
1978 NO	38	202	5.3	1	8
1979 NO	35	186	5.3	2	4
1980 NO	23	166	7.2	0	6
1981 NO	2	28	14.0	0	3
1982 NO-Hou	13	85	6.5	0	5
1982 Hou	13	85	6.5	0	5
1983 Hou-Min	3	12	4.0	0	2
1983 Hou	2	13	6.5	0	2
1983 Min	1	-1	-1.0	0	0
1984 Min	11	42	3.8	0	4
NFL Total	384	2197	5.7	18	73

JIM MANNING Manning, James Joseph 5′11″, 195 **TB-FB**
Col: Fordham *HS:* Xavier [New York, NY] B: 11/20/1900, Holyoke, MA
D: 8/5/1973, Springfield, MA
1926 Har-Prov: 7 G. Har: 6 G; Rush 2 TD; Rec 1 TD; Tot TD 3; 18 Pt. Prov: 1 G. **Total:** 7 G; Rush 2 TD; Rec 1 TD; Tot TD 3; 18 Pt.

PETE MANNING Manning, Peter Jonathan 6′3″, 208 **DB**
Col: Wake Forest *HS:* Hudson [MA] B: 8/11/1937, Hudson, MA
Drafted: 1960 Round 8 ChiB
1960 ChiB: 6 G. **1961** ChiB: 3 G. **Total:** 9 G.

PEYTON MANNING Manning, Peyton Williams 6′5″, 230 **QB**
Col: Tennessee *HS:* Isidore Newman [New Orleans, LA] B: 3/24/1976, New Orleans, LA *Drafted:* 1998 Round 1 Ind
1998 Ind: Rush 15-62 4.1.

		Passing								
Year Team	G	Att	Comp	Comp%	Yds	YPA	TD	Int	Rating	Fum
1998 Ind	16	**575**	326	56.7	3739	6.50	26	**28**	71.2	3

ROSIE MANNING Manning, Roosevelt Jr. 6′5″, 256 **DT**
Col: Northeastern State (Okla.) *HS:* Washington [Wichita Falls, TX]
B: 5/31/1950, Wichita Falls, TX *Drafted:* 1972 Round 2 Atl
1972 Atl: 3 G. **1973** Atl: 1 G. **1974** Atl: 8 G. **1975** Atl-Phi: 12 G. Atl: 2 G. Phi: 10 G. **Total:** 24 G.

WADE MANNING Manning, Wade Ronald Arthur 5′11″, 190 **WR-DB**
Col: Ohio State *HS:* Shaker Heights [OH] B: 7/25/1955, Meadville, PA
1981 Den: Rec 3-49 16.3. **1982** Den: Rec 3-46 15.3. **Total:** Rec 6-95 15.8.

		Punt Returns				Kickoff Returns				
Year Team	G	Ret	Yds	Avg	TD	Ret	Yds	Avg	TD	Fum
1979 Dal	9	10	55	5.5	0	7	145	20.7	0	1
1981 Den	16	41	378	9.2	0	26	514	19.8	0	3
1982 Den	9	0	0	—	0	15	346	23.1	0	0
NFL Total	34	51	433	8.5	0	48	1005	20.9	0	4

TIM MANOA Manoa, Timote Taliai 6′1″, 227 **RB**
Col: Penn State *HS:* Kahuku [HI]; Shawman HS [Medford Lakes, NJ]; North Allegheny HS [Wexford, PA] B: 9/9/1964, Tonga *Drafted:* 1987 Round 3 Cle
1987 Cle: KR 2-14 7.0. **Total:** KR 2-14 7.0.

		Rushing				Receiving					Tot
Year Team	G	Att	Yds	Avg	TD	Rec	Yds	Avg	TD	Fum	TD
1987 Cle	12	23	116	5.0	0	1	8	8.0	0	1	0
1988 Cle	16	99	389	3.9	2	10	54	5.4	0	4	2
1989 Cle	16	87	289	3.3	3	27	241	8.9	2	2	5
1991 Ind	9	27	144	5.3	1	2	5	2.5	0	1	1
NFL Total	53	236	938	4.0	6	40	308	7.7	2	8	8

BRISON MANOR Manor, Brison Jr. 6′4″, 247 **DE**
Col: Pratt CC KS; Arkansas *HS:* Bridgeton [NJ] B: 8/10/1952, Bridgeton, NJ *Drafted:* 1975 Round 15 NYJ
1977 Den: 13 G. **1978** Den: 16 G. **1979** Den: 16 G. **1980** Den: 16 G. **1981** Den: 16 G; Int 1-16. **1982** Den: 9 G; 2 Sac. **1983** Den: 16 G; 3 Sac. **1984** TB-Den: 11 G; 1 Sac. TB: 6 G; 1 Sac. Den: 5 G. **Total:** 113 G; Int 1-16; 6 Sac.

SAM MANOS Manos, Samuel John 6′3″, 265 **C**
Col: Marshall *HS:* New Castle [PA]; Massanutten Mil. Acad. [Woodstock, VA] B: 10/2/1962, New Castle, PA
1987 Cin: 3 G.

DON MANOUKIAN Manoukian, Donald 5′9″, 242 **OG**
Col: Stanford *HS:* Reno [NV] B: 6/9/1934, Merced, CA
1960 Oak: 14 G.

VON MANSFIELD Mansfield, Edward Von 5′11″, 185 **DB**
Col: Wisconsin *HS:* University [Milwaukee, WI] B: 7/12/1960, Anderson, IN *Drafted:* 1982 Round 5 Atl
1982 Phi: 7 G. **1987** GB: 3 G; Int 1-14; 1 Fum. **Total:** 10 G; Int 1-14; 1 Fum.

JERRY MANSFIELD Mansfield, James R 5′8″, 160 **FB-E-WB-TB**
Col: No College *HS:* Rock Island [IL] B: IA D: 10/27/1960
1920 RI: 8 G. **1921** RI: 1 G. **Total:** 9 G.

RAY MANSFIELD Mansfield, James Raymond 6′3″, 250 **C-DT**
Col: Washington *HS:* Kennewick [WA] B: 1/21/1941, Bakersfield, CA
D: 11/2/1996, Grand Canyon National Park, AZ *Drafted:* 1963 Round 2 Phi
1963 Phi: 14 G. **1964** Pit: 14 G. **1965** Pit: 14 G. **1966** Pit: 14 G; 1 Fum. **1967** Pit: 14 G; 2 Fum. **1968** Pit: 14 G. **1969** Pit: 14 G. **1970** Pit: 14 G. **1971** Pit: 14 G. **1972** Pit: 14 G. **1973** Pit: 14 G; KR 1-0. **1974** Pit: 14 G. **1975** Pit: 14 G. **1976** Pit: 14 G. **Total:** 196 G; KR 1-0; 3 Fum.

EGGS MANSKE Manske, Edgar John 6′0″, 185 **OE-DE-HB-DB**
Col: Northwestern *HS:* Nekoosa [WI] B: 7/4/1912, Nekoosa, WI
1935 Phi: Rush 3-9 3.0. **1937** ChiB: Int **1** TD. **1938** Pit-ChiB: Rush 5-29 5.8; **1** Fum TD. Pit: Rush 5-29 5.8; 1 Fum TD. **Total:** Rush 8-38 4.8; Int 1 TD; 1 Fum TD.

		Receiving				Tot
Year Team	G	Rec	Yds	Avg	TD	TD
1935 Phi	10	9	205	22.8	4	4
1936 Phi	12	17	325	19.1	0	0
1937 ChiB	11	9	225	25.0	3	4
1938 Pit-ChiB	12	19	310	16.3	2	3
1938 Pit	6	9	113	12.6	1	2
1938 ChiB	6	10	197	19.7	1	1
1939 ChiB	11	10	321	**32.1**	2	2

1940 ChiB	9	6	81	13.5	0	0
NFL Total	65	70	1467	21.0	11	13

JOE MANTELL Mantell, Joseph 1 **G**
Col: No College
1924 Col: 1 G.

TILLY MANTON Manton, Taldon 5′11″, 188 **BB-LB-DB**
Col: Louisiana State; Texas Christian B: 8/24/1909, Ryan, OK
D: 2/15/1991, Bellaire, TX
1936 NYG: Pass 5-3 60.0%, 27 5.40; Rec 5-81 16.2 1 TD; Scor 21, 15 XK. **1937** NYG: Pass 1-1 100.0%, 14 14.00; Rec 3-15 5.0; Scor 27, 5 FG, 12 XK. **1938** NYG-Was: Scor 5, 1-4 25.0% FG, 2-3 66.7% XK. NYG: Scor 0-1 XK. Was: Scor 5, 1-4 25.0% FG, 2-2 100.0% XK. **1943** Bkn: Pass 4-2 50.0%, 26 6.50; Rec 6-26 4.3; Scor 0-1 FG. **Total:** Pass 10-6 60.0%, 67 6.70; Rec 14-122 8.7 1 TD; Scor 53, 6-5 20.0% FG, 29-3 66.7% XK.

		Rushing			
Year Team	**G**	**Att**	**Yds**	**Avg**	**TD**
1936 NYG	12	30	86	2.9	0
1937 NYG	10	8	16	2.0	0
1938 NYG-Was	8	2	3	1.5	0
1938 NYG	1	0	0	—	0
1938 Was	7	2	3	1.5	0
1943 Bkn	10	2	-7	-3.5	0
NFL Total	40	42	98	2.3	0

DAN MANUCCI Manucci, Daniel Joseph 6′2″, 196 **QB**
Col: Mesa CC AZ; Kansas State *HS:* McClintock [Tempe, AZ]
B: 9/3/1957, Erie, PA *Drafted:* 1979 Round 5 Buf
1979 Buf: 14 G. **1980** Buf: 2 G; Pass 6-5 83.3%, 64 10.67; Rush 3-29 9.7. **1987** Buf: 3 G; Pass 21-7 33.3%, 68 3.24 2 Int; Rush 4-6 1.5; 1 Fum. **Total:** 19 G; Pass 27-12 44.4%, 132 4.89 2 Int; Rush 7-35 5.0; 1 Fum.

LIONEL MANUEL Manuel, Lionel Jr. 5′11″, 178 **WR**
Col: Citrus Coll. CA (J.C.); U. of Pacific *HS:* Bassett [La Puente, CA]
B: 4/13/1962, Rancho Cucamonga, CA *Drafted:* 1984 Round 7 NYG
1984 NYG: Rush 3-2 0.7; PR 8-62 7.8. **1986** NYG: Rush 1-25 25.0; PR 3-22 7.3. **1987** NYG: Rush 1-(-10) -10.0. **1988** NYG: Rush 4-27 6.8. **Total:** Rush 9-44 4.9; PR 11-84 7.6.

		Receiving				
Year Team	**G**	**Rec**	**Yds**	**Avg**	**TD**	**Fum**
1984 NYG	16	33	619	18.8	4	2
1985 NYG	12	49	859	17.5	5	1
1986 NYG	4	11	181	16.5	3	0
1987 NYG	12	30	545	18.2	6	1
1988 NYG	16	65	1029	15.8	4	1
1989 NYG	16	33	539	16.3	1	0
1990 NYG	14	11	169	15.4	0	0
NFL Total	90	232	3941	17.0	23	5

ROD MANUEL Manuel, Roderick Demond 6′5″, 290 **DE**
Col: Oklahoma *HS:* Western Hills [Fort Worth, TX] B: 10/8/1974, Fort Worth, TX *Drafted:* 1997 Round 6 Pit
1997 Pit: 1 G. **1998** Pit: 2 G. **Total:** 3 G.

SEAN MANUEL Manuel, Sandor Lorene 6′2″, 245 **TE**
Col: Laney Coll. CA (J.C.); New Mexico State *HS:* Pinole Valley [Pinole, CA] B: 12/1/1973, Los Gatos, CA *Drafted:* 1996 Round 7 SF
1996 SF: 11 G; Rec 3-18 6.0.

FRANK MANUMALEUGA Manumaleuga, Toto'a Frank 6′2″, 245 **LB**
Col: De Anza Coll. CA (J.C.); UCLA; San Jose State *HS:* Phineas Banning [Los Angeles, CA] B: 5/9/1956, Salelavalu, Western Samoa
Drafted: 1979 Round 4 KC
1979 KC: 15 G; Rush 1-(-3) -3.0; Int 1-17. **1980** KC: 16 G; Int 3-44 1 TD; 6 Pt. **1981** KC: 4 G; Int 2-17; 1 Fum. **Total:** 35 G; Rush 1-(-3) -3.0; Int 6-78 1 TD; 6 Pt; 1 Fum.

GREG MANUSKY Manusky, Gregory 6′1″, 238 **LB**
Col: Colgate *HS:* Dallas [PA] B: 8/12/1966, Wilkes-Barre, PA
1988 Was: 7 G. **1989** Was: 16 G. **1990** Was: 16 G. **1991** Min: 16 G. **1992** Min: 11 G. **1993** Min: 16 G. **1994** KC: 16 G. **1995** KC: 16 G. **1996** KC: 16 G; KR 2-32 16.0; 1 Fum. **1997** KC: 16 G; KR 1-16 16.0. **1998** KC: 16 G; KR 3-20 6.7. **Total:** 162 G; KR 6-68 11.3; 1 Fum.

BAP MANZINI Manzini, Baptiste John 5′11″, 195 **C-LB**
Col: St. Vincent *HS:* Monongahela [PA] B: 8/27/1920, Treveskyn, PA
Drafted: 1943 Round 21 Phi
1944 Phi: 10 G; Int 1-16. **1945** Phi: 9 G. **1948** Phi-Det: 4 G. Phi: 3 G. Det: 1 G. **Total:** 23 G; Int 1-16.

JOE MANZO Manzo, Joseph M 6′1″, 220 **T**
Col: Boston College *HS:* Medford [MA]; St. John's Prep [Danvers, MA]
B: 2/3/1917, Medford, MA *Drafted:* 1941 Round 8 Det
1945 Det: 3 G.

HOWIE MAPLE Maple, Howard Albert 5′7″, 175 **WB**
Col: Oregon State *HS:* Peoria [IL]; Salem HS [OR] B: 7/20/1903, Adrian, MO D: 11/9/1970, Portland, OR
1930 ChiC: 8 G.

BOBBY MAPLES Maples, Bobby Ray 6′3″, 250 **C-LB**
Col: Baylor *HS:* Mount Vernon [TX] B: 12/28/1942, Mount Vernon, TX
D: 2/16/1991, Sugar Land, TX *Drafted:* 1965 Round 4 Hou
1965 Hou: 14 G; KR 1-15 15.0; Int 1-0. **1966** Hou: 13 G. **1967** Hou: 14 G. **1968** Hou: 14 G. **1969** Hou: 14 G. **1970** Hou: 14 G; 1 Fum. **1971** Pit: 3 G. **1972** Den: 12 G. **1973** Den: 14 G. **1974** Den: 14 G. **1975** Den: 14 G; KR 1-15 15.0. **1976** Den: 14 G; 1 Fum. **1977** Den: 14 G; 1 Fum. **1978** Den: 16 G. **Total:** 184 G; KR 2-30 15.0; Int 1-0; 3 Fum.

BUTCH MAPLES Maples, James Harold 6′4″, 225 **LB**
Col: Baylor *HS:* Mount Vernon [TX] B: 1/28/1941, Mount Vernon, TX
Drafted: 1963 Round 12 Bal
1963 Bal: 5 G.

TAL MAPLES Maples, Talmadge Robert 6′0″, 195 **C-LB**
(Sheriff) *Col:* Tennessee *HS:* Knoxville [TN] B: 12/3/1910, Knoxville, TN D: 4/19/1975, Pompano Beach, FL
1934 Cin: 4 G.

GARY MARANGI Marangi, Gary Angelo 6′1″, 201 **QB**
Col: Boston College *HS:* Memorial [Elmont, NY] B: 7/29/1952, Rockville Centre, NY *Drafted:* 1974 Round 3 Buf

		Passing							
Year Team	**G**	**Att**	**Comp**	**Comp%**	**Yds**	**YPA**	**TD**	**Int**	**Rating**
1974 Buf	3	18	9	50.0	140	7.78	2	3	73.6
1975 Buf	5	33	13	39.4	235	7.12	3	2	69.6
1976 Buf	11	232	82	35.3	998	4.30	7	16	30.8
NFL Total	19	283	104	36.7	1373	4.85	12	21	36.1

	Rushing				
Year Team	**Att**	**Yds**	**Avg**	**TD**	**Fum**
1974 Buf	4	20	5.0	0	2
1975 Buf	7	78	11.1	0	0
1976 Buf	39	230	5.9	2	12
NFL Total	50	328	6.6	2	14

JOE MARAS Maras, Joseph Thomas 6′1″, 203 **C-LB-T**
Col: Hibbing CC MN; Duquesne *HS:* Hibbing [MN] B: 1/19/1916, Hibbing, MN *Drafted:* 1938 Round 8 Cle
1938 Pit: 5 G. **1939** Pit: 10 G. **1940** Pit: 2 G. **Total:** 17 G.

GINO MARCHETTI Marchetti, Gino John 6′4″, 244 **DE-OT-DT**
Col: Modesto JC CA; San Francisco *HS:* Antioch [CA] B: 1/2/1927, Smithers, WV *Drafted:* 1952 Round 2 Dal *HOF:* 1972
1952 Dal: 12 G; Rec 1-17 17.0 1 TD; 6 Pt. **1953** Bal: 11 G; Rec 0-19. **1954** Bal: 10 G. **1955** Bal: 8 G. **1956** Bal: 12 G. **1957** Bal: 12 G; 1 Fum TD; 6 Pt. **1958** Bal: 12 G. **1959** Bal: 12 G; Int 1-1. **1960** Bal: 12 G. **1961** Bal: 14 G; Scor **1** Saf; 2 Pt. **1962** Bal: 14 G. **1963** Bal: 14 G; **1** Fum TD; 6 Pt. **1964** Bal: 14 G. **1966** Bal: 4 G. **Total:** 161 G; Rec 1-36 36.0 1 TD; Int 1-1; Scor 1 Saf; 2 Fum TD; Tot TD 3; 20 Pt.

BASILIO MARCHI Marchi, Basilio 6′2″, 220 **G-C-LB**
Col: New York U. *HS:* Parkersburg [WV] B: 7/14/1909, Middleport, OH
Deceased
1934 Pit: 5 G. **1942** Phi: 7 G. **Total:** 12 G.

TED MARCHIBRODA Marchibroda, Theodore Joseph 5′10″, 178 **QB**
Col: St. Bonaventure; Detroit Mercy *HS:* Franklin [PA] B: 3/15/1931, Franklin, PA *Drafted:* 1953 Round 1 Pit
1953 Pit: KR 1-25 25.0. **Total:** KR 1-25 25.0.

		Passing							
Year Team	**G**	**Att**	**Comp**	**Comp%**	**Yds**	**YPA**	**TD**	**Int**	**Rating**
1953 Pit	4	22	9	40.9	66	3.00	1	2	25.9
1955 Pit	7	43	24	55.8	280	6.51	2	3	62.2
1956 Pit	12	275	124	45.1	1585	5.76	12	19	49.4
1957 ChiC	7	45	15	33.3	238	5.29	1	5	19.7
NFL Total	30	385	172	44.7	2169	5.63	16	29	45.3

	Rushing				
Year Team	**Att**	**Yds**	**Avg**	**TD**	**Fum**
1953 Pit	1	15	15.0	0	0
1955 Pit	6	-1	-0.2	1	3
1956 Pit	39	152	3.9	2	3
1957 ChiC	4	10	2.5	0	0
NFL Total	50	176	3.5	3	6

KEN MARCHIOL Marchiol, Kenneth J 6′2″, 248 **LB**
Col: Adams State; Mesa *HS:* Trinidad [CO] B: 8/27/1965, Las Vegas, NV
1987 NO: 3 G.

FRANK MARCHLEWSKI Marchlewski, Frank Charles 6′2″, 240 **C**
Col: Minnesota *HS:* Plum [Pittsburgh, PA] B: 10/14/1943, New Kensington, PA *Drafted:* 1965 Round 5 LARm
1965 LARm: 14 G. **1966** Atl: 14 G; Rec 0-1. **1967** Atl: 14 G. **1968** Atl-LARm: 14 G. Atl: 1 G. LARm: 13 G. **1969** LARm: 5 G. **1970** Buf: 13 G; 1 Fum. **Total:** 74 G; Rec 0-1; 1 Fum.

RON MARCINIAK Marciniak, Ronald Joseph 6′1″, 218 **OG**
Col: Kansas State *HS:* St. Justin's [Pittsburgh, PA] B: 7/16/1932, Pittsburgh, PA *Drafted:* 1955 Round 7 Was
1955 Was: 12 G; KR 1-0.

CHESTER MARCOL Marcol, Czeslaw Boleslaw 6′0″, 190 **K**
Col: Hillsdale *HS:* Imlay City [MI] B: 10/24/1949, Opole, Poland
Drafted: 1972 Round 2 GB
1980 GB-Hou: Punt 1-33 33.0. GB: Punt 1-33 33.0. **Total:** Punt 1-33 33.0.

		Scoring						
Year Team	G	Pts	FG	FGA	FG%	XK	XKA	XK%
1972 GB	14	**128**	**33**	**48**	68.8	29	29	100.0
1973 GB	14	82	21	35	60.0	19	20	95.0
1974 GB	14	**94**	**25**	**39**	64.1	19	19	100.0
1975 GB	1	3	1	1	100.0	0	0	—
1976 GB	14	54	10	19	52.6	24	27	88.9
1977 GB	14	50	13	21	61.9	11	14	78.6
1978 GB	16	63	11	19	57.9	30	30	100.0
1979 GB	10	28	4	10	40.0	16	18	88.9
1980 GB-Hou	6	23	3	4	75.0	8	10	80.0
1980 GB	5	19	2	3	66.7	7	7	100.0
1980 Hou	1	4	1	1	100.0	1	3	33.3
NFL Total	103	525	121	196	61.7	156	167	93.4

HUGO MARCOLINI Marcolini, Hugo Francis 6′0″, 203 **WB-DB**
Col: St. Bonaventure *HS:* St. Joseph's [Canada] B: 4/7/1923, Brooklyn, NY D: 9/22/1963, Upper Saddle River, NJ
AAFC **1948** BknA: 10 G; Rush 5-11 2.2; Rec 2-38 19.0; KR 2-33 16.5.

JOE MARCONI Marconi, Joseph George 6′2″, 225 **FB-HB**
Col: West Virginia *HS:* Fredericktown [PA] B: 2/6/1934, Fredericktown, PA D: 8/24/1992, Chicago, IL *Drafted:* 1956 Round 1 LARm
1959 LARm: Punt 2-81 40.5. **1960** LARm: Punt 10-408 40.8. **1961** LARm: Punt 6-265 44.2. **1962** ChiB: KR 2-30 15.0. **1963** ChiB: KR 2-15 7.5. **1964** ChiB: KR 2-12 6.0. **Total:** KR 6-57 9.5; Punt 18-754 41.9.

		Rushing				Receiving					Tot
Year Team	G	Att	Yds	Avg	TD	Rec	Yds	Avg	TD	Fum	TD
1956 LARm	12	75	298	4.0	7	12	70	5.8	0	4	7
1957 LARm	10	104	481	4.6	3	16	171	10.7	1	1	4
1958 LARm	12	89	428	4.8	1	10	87	8.7	0	2	1
1959 LARm	12	52	176	3.4	4	10	81	8.1	1	2	5
1960 LARm	12	42	240	5.7	3	9	32	3.6	0	0	3
1961 LARm	13	36	146	4.1	3	4	20	5.0	1	0	4
1962 ChiB	13	89	406	4.6	5	23	306	13.3	1	0	6
1963 ChiB	14	118	446	3.8	2	28	335	12.0	2	1	4
1964 ChiB	13	46	98	2.1	2	20	181	9.1	3	0	5
1965 ChiB	14	19	47	2.5	0	4	43	10.8	0	0	0
1966 ChiB	10	3	5	1.7	0	0	0	—	0	0	0
NFL Total	135	673	2771	4.1	30	136	1326	9.8	9	10	39

ED MARCONTELL Marcontell, Edmon Dwight 6′0″, 240 **OG**
Col: Lamar *HS:* West Hardin Co. [Saratoga, TX] B: 7/10/1945, Liberty, TX *Drafted:* 1967 Round 11 StL
1967 StL-Hou: 4 G. StL: 2 G. Hou: 2 G. **Total:** 4 G.

PETE MARCUS Marcus, Peter 6′2″, 200 **DE**
Col: Kentucky B: 12/17/1918, Rilton, PA
1944 Was: 3 G.

GREG MARDERIAN Marderian, Gregory John 6′4″, 250 **DT**
Col: USC *HS:* Granada Hills [Los Angeles, CA] B: 1/15/1952, Burbank, CA
1976 Atl: 1 G.

OLINDO MARE Mare, Olindo Franco 5′10″, 190 **K**
Col: Valencia CC FL; MacMurray; Syracuse *HS:* Cooper City [FL]
B: 6/6/1973, Hollywood, FL
1997 Mia: Punt 5-235 47.0. **1998** Mia: Punt 3-115 38.3. **Total:** Punt 8-350 43.8.

		Scoring						
Year Team	G	Pts	FG	FGA	FG%	XK	XKA	XK%
1997 Mia	16	117	28	36	77.8	33	33	100.0
1998 Mia	16	99	22	27	81.5	33	34	97.1
NFL Total	32	216	50	63	79.4	66	67	98.5

ANDY MAREFOS Marefos, Andrew Gust 6′0″, 223 **FB-DB-QB-LB**
(Anvil Andy) *Col:* St. Mary's (Cal.) *HS:* Mission [San Francisco, CA]
B: 7/16/1917, San Francisco, CA D: 2/18/1996, Marysville, CA
Drafted: 1941 Round 10 NYG
AAFC **1946** LA-A: Rec 1-13 13.0; Scor 26, 2-2 100.0% XK.

		Rushing		
Year Team	G	Att	Yds	Avg	TD
1946 LA-A	13	30	93	3.1	4

NFL **1941** NYG: Pass 8-2 25.0%, 69 8.63 1 TD 1 Int; Rec 1-5 5.0; Int 2-48; Scor 30, 4-5 **80.0%** FG, 6-6 **100.0%** XK. **1942** NYG: Pass 29-11 37.9%, 176 6.07 1 TD 5 Int; Int 1-11; Scor 6, 0-2 FG. **Total:** Pass 37-13 35.1%, 245 6.62 2 TD 6 Int; Rec 1-5 5.0; Int 3-59; Scor 36, 4-7 57.1% FG, 6-6 100.0% XK.

		Rushing			
Year Team	G	Att	Yds	Avg	TD
1941 NYG	10	60	153	2.6	2
1942 NYG	11	48	138	2.9	1
NFL Total	21	108	291	2.7	3

JODIE MAREK Marek, Joseph Lee 5′11″, 182 **FB-LB**
Col: Texas Tech *HS:* Temple [TX] B: 3/7/1916, Temple, TX
D: 11/19/1986, Temple, TX
1943 Bkn: 8 G; Rush 6-9 1.5; Scor 0-1 FG.

RAY MARELLI Marelli, Raymond Charles 5′10″, 190 **G**
Col: Notre Dame *HS:* Rockford Central [IL] B: 1/23/1901, Rockford, IL
D: 12/1/1976, Rockford, IL
1928 ChiC: 2 G.

BOB MARGARITA Margarita, Henry Robert 5′11″, 178 **HB-DB**
(Hank) *Col:* Brown *HS:* Scarborough [Medford, MA] B: 11/3/1920, Boston, MA *Drafted:* 1944 Round 19 ChiB
1944 ChiB: PR 5-9 1.8; KR 12-279 23.3; Int 3-34; Punt 1-34 34.0.
1945 ChiB: PR 6-51 8.5; KR 10-155 15.5; Int 6-79; Punt 1-29 29.0.
Total: PR 11-60 5.5; KR 22-434 19.7; Int 9-113; Punt 2-63 31.5.

		Rushing				Receiving					Tot
Year Team	G	Att	Yds	Avg	TD	Rec	Yds	Avg	TD	Fum	TD
1944 ChiB	10	88	463	5.3	4	15	130	8.7	0	0	4
1945 ChiB	10	112	497	4.4	3	23	394	17.1	2	4	5
1946 ChiB	1	4	0	0.0	0	0	0	—	0	0	0
NFL Total	21	204	960	4.7	7	38	524	13.8	2	4	9

KEN MARGERUM Margerum, Kenneth 6′0″, 175 **WR**
Col: Stanford *HS:* Fountain Valley [CA] B: 10/5/1958, Fountain Valley, CA *Drafted:* 1981 Round 3 ChiB
1981 ChiB: Rush 1-11 11.0. **1983** ChiB: Rush 1-7 7.0. **1985** ChiB: Rush 1-(-7) -7.0. **Total:** Rush 3-11 3.7.

		Receiving			
Year Team	G	Rec	Yds	Avg	TD	Fum
1981 ChiB	16	39	584	15.0	1	0
1982 ChiB	9	14	207	14.8	3	1
1983 ChiB	15	21	336	16.0	2	1
1985 ChiB	16	17	190	11.2	2	1
1986 ChiB-SF	6	2	12	6.0	0	0
1986 ChiB	1	0	0	—	0	0
1986 SF	5	2	12	6.0	0	0
1987 SF	2	1	7	7.0	0	0
NFL Total	64	94	1336	14.2	8	3

JOE MARGUCCI Margucci, Joseph Americus 5′10″, 182
WB-QB-HB-DB
(White Britches) *Col:* Rancho Santiago Coll. CA (J.C.); USC
HS: Benjamin Franklin [Los Angeles, CA] B: 9/5/1921, Brooklyn, NY
D: 4/27/1996, Encino, CA
1947 Det: Pass 31-13 41.9%, 171 5.52 1 TD 5 Int; PR 2-23 11.5; KR 5-94 18.8. **1948** Det: PR 10-100 10.0; KR 10-199 19.9. **Total:** Pass 31-13 41.9%, 171 5.52 1 TD 5 Int; PR 12-123 10.3; KR 15-293 19.5.

		Rushing				Receiving					Tot
Year Team	G	Att	Yds	Avg	TD	Rec	Yds	Avg	TD	Fum	TD
1947 Det	11	26	97	3.7	1	10	125	12.5	1	1	2
1948 Det	11	34	14	0.4	3	36	450	12.5	2	4	5
NFL Total	22	60	111	1.9	4	46	575	12.5	3	5	7

ED MARINARO Marinaro, Edward Francis 6′2″, 212 **RB**
Col: Cornell *HS:* New Milford [NJ] B: 3/31/1950, New York, NY
Drafted: 1972 Round 2 Min
1974 Min: KR 1-5 5.0. **1975** Min: KR 5-71 14.2. **Total:** KR 6-76 12.7.

		Rushing				Receiving					Tot
Year Team	G	Att	Yds	Avg	TD	Rec	Yds	Avg	TD	Fum	TD
1972 Min	10	66	223	3.4	0	28	218	7.8	1	4	1
1973 Min	13	95	302	3.2	2	26	196	7.5	2	3	4
1974 Min	14	44	124	2.8	1	17	132	7.8	1	3	2
1975 Min	14	101	358	3.5	1	54	462	8.6	3	3	4
1976 NYJ	6	77	312	4.1	2	21	168	8.0	0	1	2
1977 Sea	1	0	0	—	0	0	0	—	0	0	0
NFL Total	58	383	1319	3.4	6	146	1176	8.1	7	14	13

DAN MARINO Marino, Daniel Constantine Jr. 6′4″, 218 **QB**
Col: Pittsburgh *HS:* Central Catholic [Pittsburgh, PA] B: 9/15/1961, Pittsburgh, PA *Drafted:* 1983 Round 1 Mia
1995 Mia: Rec 1-(-6) -6.0. **Total:** Rec 1-(-6) -6.0.

		Passing							
Year Team	G	Att	Comp	Comp%	Yds	YPA	TD	Int	Rating
1983 Mia	11	296	173	58.4	2210	7.47	20	6	96.0
1984 Mia	16	**564**	**362**	64.2	**5084**	**9.01**	**48**	17	**108.9**

1985 Mia	16	567	**336**	59.3	**4137**	7.30	**30**	21	84.1
1986 Mia	16	**623**	**378**	60.7	**4746**	7.62	**44**	23	92.5
1987 Mia	12	444	263	59.2	3245	7.31	26	13	89.2
1988 Mia	16	**606**	**354**	58.4	**4434**	7.32	28	23	80.8
1989 Mia	16	550	308	56.0	3997	7.27	24	22	76.9
1990 Mia	16	531	306	57.6	3563	6.71	21	11	82.6
1991 Mia	16	549	318	57.9	3970	7.23	25	13	85.8
1992 Mia	16	**554**	**330**	59.6	**4116**	7.43	24	16	85.1
1993 Mia	5	150	91	60.7	1218	8.12	8	3	95.9
1994 Mia	16	615	385	62.6	4453	7.24	30	17	89.2
1995 Mia	14	482	309	64.1	3668	7.61	24	15	90.8
1996 Mia	13	373	221	59.2	2795	7.49	17	9	87.8
1997 Mia	16	**548**	**319**	58.2	3780	6.90	16	11	80.7
1998 Mia	16	537	310	57.7	3497	6.51	23	15	80.0
NFL Total	231	**7989**	**4763**	59.6	**58913**	7.37	**408**	235	87.3

	Rushing				
Year Team	**Att**	**Yds**	**Avg**	**TD**	**Fum**
1983 Mia	28	45	1.6	2	5
1984 Mia	28	-7	-0.3	0	6
1985 Mia	26	-24	-0.9	0	9
1986 Mia	12	-3	-0.3	0	8
1987 Mia	12	-5	-0.4	1	5
1988 Mia	20	-17	-0.9	0	10
1989 Mia	14	-7	-0.5	2	7
1990 Mia	16	29	1.8	0	3
1991 Mia	27	32	1.2	1	6
1992 Mia	20	66	3.3	0	5
1993 Mia	9	-4	-0.4	1	4
1994 Mia	22	-6	-0.3	1	9
1995 Mia	11	14	1.3	0	7
1996 Mia	11	-3	-0.3	0	4
1997 Mia	18	-14	-0.8	0	8
1998 Mia	21	-3	-0.1	1	9
NFL Total	295	93	0.3	9	105

VIC MARINO Marino, Victor Irving 5′8″, 205 **G**
(Sub Marino) *Col:* Ohio State *HS:* Rayen [Youngstown, OH]
B: 10/2/1918, Columbus, OH
AAFC **1947** BalA: 13 G.

MARV MARINOVICH Marinovich, Marvin Jack 6′3″, 250 **OG**
Col: Santa Monica Coll. CA (J.C.); USC *HS:* Watsonville [CA]
B: 8/6/1939, Watsonville, CA *Drafted:* 1962 Round 28 Oak
1965 Oak: 1 G.

TODD MARINOVICH Marinovich, Todd Marvin 6′4″, 215 **QB**
Col: USC *HS:* Mater Dei [Santa Ana, CA]; Capistrano Valley HS [Mission Viejo, CA] B: 7/4/1969, San Leandro, CA *Drafted:* 1991 Round 1 LARd
1991 LARd: Rush 3-14 4.7. **1992** LARd: Rush 9-30 3.3. **Total:** Rush 12-44 3.7.

		Passing								
Year Team	**G**	**Att**	**Comp**	**Comp%**	**Yds**	**YPA**	**TD**	**Int**	**Rating**	**Fum**
1991 LARd	1	40	23	57.5	243	6.08	3	0	100.3	0
1992 LARd	7	165	81	49.1	1102	6.68	5	9	58.2	4
NFL Total	8	205	104	50.7	1345	6.56	8	9	66.4	4

BROCK MARION Marion, Brock Elliot 5′11″, 194 **DB**
Col: Nevada-Reno *HS:* West [Bakersfield, CA] B: 6/11/1970, Bakersfield, CA *Drafted:* 1993 Round 7 Dal
1993 Dal: 15 G; Int 1-2. **1994** Dal: 14 G; KR 2-39 19.5; Int 1-11; 1 Sac. **1995** Dal: 16 G; KR 1-16 16.0; Int 6-40 1 TD; 6 Pt. **1996** Dal: 10 G; KR 3-68 22.7; 1 Fum. **1997** Dal: 16 G; KR 10-311 31.1. **1998** Mia: 16 G; KR 6-109 18.2. **Total:** 87 G; KR 22-543 24.7; Int 8-53 1 TD; 6 Pt; 1 Fum; 1 Sac.

FRANK MARION Marion, Frank N II 6′3″, 227 **LB**
Col: Florida A&M *HS:* Lincoln [Gainesville, FL]; Gainesville HS [FL]
B: 3/16/1951, Mount Brook, FL
1977 NYG: 3 G. **1978** NYG: 16 G; KR 1-12 12.0. **1979** NYG: 16 G; KR 1-14 14.0. **1980** NYG: 11 G; Int 1-7. **1981** NYG: 16 G. **1982** NYG: 9 G; 0.5 Sac. **1983** NYG: 10 G. **Total:** 81 G; KR 2-26 13.0; Int 1-7; 0.5 Sac.

FRED MARION Marion, Fred Donald 6′2″, 192 **DB**
Col: Miami (Fla.) *HS:* F.W. Buchholz [Gainesville, FL] B: 1/2/1959, Gainesville, FL *Drafted:* 1982 Round 5 NE
1984 NE: 1 Sac. **1986** NE: PR 1-12 12.0. **1987** NE: PR 1-0. **Total:** PR 2-12 6.0; 1 Sac.

		Interceptions		
Year Team	**G**	**Int**	**Yds**	**TD**
1982 NE	9	0	0	0
1983 NE	16	2	4	0
1984 NE	16	2	39	0
1985 NE	16	7	**189**	0
1986 NE	16	2	56	1
1987 NE	12	4	53	0
1988 NE	16	4	47	0
1989 NE	16	2	19	0
1990 NE	16	4	17	0
1991 NE	11	2	33	0
NFL Total	144	29	457	1

JERRY MARION Marion, Jerry Richard 5′10″, 175 **WR**
Col: Wyoming *HS:* Bakersfield [CA] B: 8/7/1944, Bakersfield, CA
Drafted: 1966 Round 10 Pit
1967 Pit: 7 G; Rec 1-16 16.0; PR 1-2 2.0.

DUTCH MARION Marion, Phillip Eugene 5′9″, 180 **FB**
Col: Washington & Jefferson; Michigan *HS:* Northwestern [Detroit, MI]
B: 6/18/1902 D: 6/23/1985, Dearborn, MI
1925 Det: 10 G; Rush 4 TD; 24 Pt. **1926** Det: 12 G. **Total:** 22 G; Rush 4 TD; 24 Pt.

GREG MARK Mark, Greg 6′3″, 252 **DE-LB**
Col: Miami (Fla.) *HS:* Pennsauken [NJ] B: 7/7/1967, Cherry Hill, NJ
Drafted: 1990 Round 3 NYG
1990 Mia-Phi: 6 G. Mia: 4 G. Phi: 2 G. **Total:** 6 G.

LOU MARK Mark, Louis 6′1″, 210 **LB-OE-DE**
Col: North Carolina State *HS:* White Plains [NY] B: 12/21/1914, New York, NY *Drafted:* 1938 Round 10 Bkn
1938 Bkn: 11 G. **1939** Bkn: 11 G. **1940** Bkn: 11 G. **1945** Bos: 6 G. **Total:** 39 G.

CLIFF MARKER Marker, Clifford Norwell 5′10″, 190 **OE-BB-FB-TB**
Col: Washington State *HS:* Stadium [Tacoma, WA] B: 6/13/1903, Tacoma, WA D: 7/17/1972, Tacoma, WA
1926 Can: 12 G; 1 Fum TD; 6 Pt. **1927** Fra-NYG: 4 G. Fra: 2 G. NYG: 2 G. **Total:** 16 G; 1 Fum TD; 6 Pt.

HARRY MARKER Marker, Harry Joseph 5′6″, 155 **BB-DB**
Col: West Virginia *HS:* Ligonier [PA] B: 9/17/1910, Ligonier, PA
D: 4/19/1989, Patrick AFB, FL
1934 Pit: 1 G.

DALE MARKHAM Markham, Dale Jon 6′8″, 280 **OT-DE**
Col: North Dakota *HS:* Whitewater [WI] B: 7/24/1957, Whitewater, WI
Drafted: 1980 Round 11 KC
1980 NYG: 1 G. **1981** StL: 2 G. **Total:** 3 G.

JEFF MARKLAND Markland, Jeffrey Stuart 6′3″, 245 **TE**
Col: Pierce Coll. CA (J.C.); Illinois *HS:* John Burroughs [Burbank, CA]
B: 11/16/1965, Los Angeles, CA
1988 Pit: 1 G.

STEVE MARKO Marko, Stephen 6′0″, 200 **TB-DB**
(AKA Markoe) *Col:* No College B: 5/26/1924, Philadelphia, PA
D: 5/1985, Cherry Hill, NJ
1944 Bkn: 4 G; Pass 7-1 14.3%, 2 0.29 2 Int; Rush 6-10 1.7; KR 3-80 26.7.

VIC MARKOV Markov, Victor William 6′0″, 215 **G-T**
Col: Washington *HS:* Lindblom [Chicago, IL] B: 12/28/1915, Chicago, IL D: 12/7/1998, Fort Lauderdale, FL *Drafted:* 1938 Round 2 Cle
1938 Cle: 10 G.

MARK MARKOVICH Markovich, Mark James 6′5″, 256 **C-OG**
Col: Penn State *HS:* Central Catholic [Greensburg, PA] B: 11/7/1952, Latrobe, PA *Drafted:* 1974 Round 2 SD
1974 SD: 9 G. **1975** SD: 14 G; KR 1-0. **1976** Det: 14 G; 1 Fum. **1977** Det: 4 G; 1 Fum. **Total:** 41 G; KR 1-0; 2 Fum.

LARRY MARKS Marks, Lawrence Eugene 5′11″, 185 **WB-HB-TB-FB**
Col: Indiana *HS:* Wabash [IN] B: 12/20/1902, Wabash, IN
D: 1/19/1974, Kalamazoo, MI
1927 NYY: 13 G; Pass 1 TD. **1928** GB: 11 G; Rec 2 TD; 12 Pt. **Total:** 24 G; Pass 1 TD; Rec 2 TD; 12 Pt.

SAL MARONE Marone, Salvatore John 5′10″, 195 **G**
Col: Manhattan *HS:* Poughkeepsie [NY] B: 8/10/1917, Highland Falls, NJ D: 1/12/1975, Walden, NY
1943 NYG: 8 G.

DUKE MARONIC Maronic, Dusan J 5′9″, 209 **OG-DG**
Col: No College *HS:* Steelton [PA] B: 7/13/1921, Steelton, PA
D: 7/1/1996, Harrisburg, PA
1944 Phi: 9 G; Int 1-32. **1945** Phi: 8 G. **1946** Phi: 11 G; Int 1-7. **1947** Phi: 4 G. **1948** Phi: 12 G. **1949** Phi: 11 G. **1950** Phi: 12 G; KR 1-4 4.0. **1951** NYG: 10 G. **Total:** 77 G; KR 1-4 4.0; Int 2-39.

STEVE MARONIC Maronic, Steven Jesse 6′0″, 225 **T**
Col: North Carolina *HS:* Steelton [PA] B: 5/30/1917, PA D: 5/7/1980, Durham, NC *Drafted:* 1939 Round 3 Det
1939 Det: 10 G. **1940** Det: 5 G; Scor 0-1 FG. **Total:** 15 G; Scor 0-1 FG.

LOU MAROTTI Marotti, Louis 5′10″, 210 **G**
Col: Toledo *HS:* Hibbing [MN]; Whitmer HS [Toledo, OH] B: 3/28/1918, Chisolm, MN
1943 ChiC: 6 G. **1944** ChPt: 8 G; KR 1-2 2.0. **1945** ChiC: 1 G. **Total:** 15 G; KR 1-2 2.0.

RUBE MARQUARDT Marquardt, Reuben Allen 5'9", 155 **E**
Col: Northwestern *HS:* Evanston Twp. [Evanston, IL] B: 3/7/1898, Evanston, IL D: 2/15/1973, Fort Lauderdale, FL
1921 ChiC: 3 G; Rec 1 TD; 6 Pt.

BOB MARQUES Marques, Robert 6'0", 220 **LB**
Col: Boston U. *HS:* Everett [MA] B: 5/1/1935
1960 NYT: 6 G.

DOUG MARRONE Marrone, Douglas Charles 6'5", 269 **OG-C-OT**
Col: Syracuse *HS:* Herbert H. Lehman [Bronx, NY] B: 7/25/1964, Bronx, NY *Drafted:* 1986 Round 6 LARd
1987 Mia: 4 G. **1989** NO: 1 G. **Total:** 5 G.

JOHN MARROW Marrow, Herbert John 5'11", 230 **G-T**
Col: Nebraska-Kearney *HS:* College View [Lincoln, NE] B: 7/8/1914, Lincoln, NE
1937 ChiC: 11 G. **1938** ChiC: 5 G. **Total:** 16 G.

VINCE MARROW Marrow, Vincent Charles 6'3", 251 **TE**
Col: Youngstown State; Toledo *HS:* Cardinal Mooney [Youngstown, OH] B: 8/17/1968, Youngstown, OH *Drafted:* 1992 Round 11 Buf
1994 Buf: 10 G; Rec 5-44 8.8.

JIM MARSALIS Marsalis, James J Jr. 5'11", 194 **DB**
Col: Tennessee State *HS:* Carver [Pascagoula, MS] B: 10/10/1945, Pascagoula, MS *Drafted:* 1969 Round 1 KC

		Interceptions		
Year Team	**G**	**Int**	**Yds**	**TD**
1969 KC	14	2	33	0
1970 KC	14	4	26	0
1971 KC	14	3	0	0
1972 KC	14	2	20	0
1973 KC	10	2	36	0
1974 KC	2	0	0	0
1975 KC	10	1	1	0
1977 NO	12	1	0	0
NFL Total	90	15	116	0

AARON MARSH Marsh, Aaron Washington 6'1", 190 **WR**
Col: Eastern Kentucky *HS:* Springfield [OH] B: 7/27/1945, Dayton, OH *Drafted:* 1968 Round 3 Bos
1968 Bos: Rush 4-8 2.0; KR 4-74 18.5. **1969** Bos: KR 6-136 22.7. **Total:** Rush 4-8 2.0; KR 10-210 21.0.

		Receiving			
Year Team	**G**	**Rec**	**Yds**	**Avg**	**TD**
1968 Bos	14	19	331	17.4	4
1969 Bos	14	8	108	13.5	0
NFL Total	28	27	439	16.3	4

AMOS MARSH Marsh, Amos Jr. 6'0", 220 **HB**
Col: Oregon State *HS:* Wallowa [OR] B: 5/7/1939, Williams, AZ D: 11/2/1992, San Jose, CA
1961 Dal: PR 14-71 5.1. **1962** Dal: PR 3-4 1.3. **1965** Det: Pass 1-0. **Total:** Pass 1-0; PR 17-75 4.4.

		Rushing				Receiving			
Year Team	**G**	**Att**	**Yds**	**Avg**	**TD**	**Rec**	**Yds**	**Avg**	**TD**
1961 Dal	14	84	379	4.5	1	21	189	9.0	2
1962 Dal	14	144	802	**5.6**	6	35	467	13.3	2
1963 Dal	14	99	483	4.9	5	26	224	8.6	0
1964 Dal	12	100	401	4.0	2	15	131	8.7	0
1965 Det	13	131	495	3.8	6	17	159	9.4	2
1966 Det	14	134	433	3.2	3	12	111	9.3	0
1967 Det	14	58	229	3.9	2	7	103	14.7	1
NFL Total	95	750	3222	4.3	25	133	1384	10.4	7

	Kickoff Returns					Tot
Year Team	**Ret**	**Yds**	**Avg**	**TD**	**Fum**	**TD**
1961 Dal	26	667	25.7	0	12	3
1962 Dal	29	725	25.0	**1**	6	9
1963 Dal	9	167	18.6	0	6	5
1964 Dal	1	2	2.0	0	2	2
1965 Det	0	0	—	0	4	8
1966 Det	0	0	—	0	5	3
1967 Det	0	0	—	0	0	3
NFL Total	65	1561	24.0	1	35	33

CURTIS MARSH Marsh, Curtis Joseph 6'2", 201 **WR**
Col: Moorpark Coll. CA (J.C.); Utah *HS:* Simi Valley [CA] B: 11/24/1970, Simi Valley, CA *Drafted:* 1995 Round 7 Jac
1995 Jac: 9 G; Rec 7-127 18.1; KR 15-323 21.5; 2 Fum. **1996** Jac: 1 G. **1997** Pit: 5 G; Rush 1-2 2.0; Rec 2-14 7.0. **Total:** 15 G; Rush 1-2 2.0; Rec 9-141 15.7; KR 15-323 21.5; 2 Fum.

CURT MARSH Marsh, Curtiss Lane 6'5", 273 **OG**
Col: Washington *HS:* Snohomish [WA] B: 8/25/1959, Tacoma, WA *Drafted:* 1981 Round 1 Oak
1981 Oak: 11 G. **1982** LARd: 9 G. **1984** LARd: 16 G. **1985** LARd: 7 G. **1986** LARd: 2 G. **Total:** 45 G.

DOUG MARSH Marsh, Douglas Walter 6'3", 236 **TE**
Col: Michigan *HS:* Central [Akron, OH] B: 6/18/1958, Akron, OH *Drafted:* 1980 Round 2 StL
1984 StL: Rush 1-(-5) -5.0. **1986** StL: Rush 1-5 5.0. **Total:** Rush 2-0.

		Receiving				
Year Team	**G**	**Rec**	**Yds**	**Avg**	**TD**	**Fum**
1980 StL	16	22	269	12.2	4	1
1981 StL	4	6	80	13.3	1	1
1982 StL	8	6	94	15.7	0	0
1983 StL	16	32	421	13.2	8	1
1984 StL	16	39	608	15.6	5	0
1985 StL	16	37	355	9.6	1	0
1986 StL	16	25	313	12.5	0	0
NFL Total	92	167	2140	12.8	19	3

FRANK MARSH Marsh, Frank Wayne 6'2", 205 **DB**
Col: Oregon State *HS:* Wallowa [OR] B: 6/19/1940, La Grande, OR
1967 SD: 1 G.

DICK MARSH Marsh, Victor Burton 6'2", 210 **G**
Col: Oklahoma; Phillips *HS:* Sayre [OK] B: 8/29/1906, Sayre, OK D: 1/1968
1933 NYG: 1 G.

AL MARSHALL Marshall, Albert Calvin 6'2", 190 **WR**
Col: Boise State *HS:* Santa Cruz [CA] B: 1/7/1951, Monroe, LA *Drafted:* 1973 Round 10 Den
1974 NE: 4 G; Rec 1-17 17.0 1 TD; 6 Pt.

ANTHONY MARSHALL Marshall, Anthony Dewayne 6'1", 212 **DB**
Col: Louisiana State *HS:* John L. LeFlore [Mobile, AL] B: 9/16/1970, Mobile, AL
1994 ChiB: 3 G. **1995** ChiB: 16 G; Int 1-0; 6 Pt. **1996** ChiB: 13 G; KR 0-75; Int 2-20. **1997** ChiB: 14 G; KR 0-3; Int 2-0; 1 Fum; 3 Sac. **1998** Phi: 16 G. **Total:** 62 G; KR 0-78; Int 5-20; 6 Pt; 1 Fum; 3 Sac.

ARTHUR MARSHALL Marshall, Arthur James Jr. 5'11", 175 **WR**
Col: Georgia *HS:* Hephzibah [GA] B: 4/29/1969, Fort Gordon, GA
1992 Den: Pass 1-1 100.0%, 81 81.00 1 TD; Rush 11-56 5.1; KR 8-132 16.5. **1993** Den: Pass 1-1 100.0%, 30 30.00 1 TD. **1994** NYG: Rush 2-8 4.0; KR 15-249 16.6. **1995** NYG: Rush 1-1 1.0. **Total:** Pass 2-2 100.0%, 111 55.50 2 TD; Rush 14-65 4.6; KR 23-381 16.6.

		Receiving				Punt Returns				
Year Team	**G**	**Rec**	**Yds**	**Avg**	**TD**	**Ret**	**Yds**	**Avg**	**TD**	**Fum**
1992 Den	16	26	493	19.0	1	33	349	10.6	0	3
1993 Den	16	28	360	12.9	2	0	0	—	0	0
1994 NYG	16	16	219	13.7	0	1	1	1.0	0	1
1995 NYG	15	17	195	11.5	1	12	96	8.0	0	1
1996 NYG	5	0	0	—	0	13	144	11.1	0	0
NFL Total	68	87	1267	14.6	4	59	590	10.0	0	5

TANK MARSHALL Marshall, Charles 6'4", 245 **DT**
Col: Texas A&M *HS:* Franklin D. Roosevelt [Dallas, TX] B: 1/6/1955, Dallas, TX *Drafted:* 1977 Round 3 NYJ
1977 NYJ: 5 G.

CHUCK MARSHALL Marshall, Charles Edward 6'0", 180 **DB**
Col: Oregon State *HS:* Mission [San Francisco, CA] B: 2/13/1939, Hickory, MS
1962 Den: 5 G.

CHARLEY MARSHALL Marshall, Charles Fred 6'0", 193 **OE**
Col: New York U. *HS:* Sherrill [NY] B: 10/17/1906, Richford, NY D: 11/1986, Staten Island, NY
1931 SI: 10 G. **1932** SI: 8 G. **Total:** 18 G.

DAVID MARSHALL Marshall, David Mark 6'3", 220 **LB**
Col: Eastern Michigan *HS:* Benedictine [Cleveland, OH] B: 1/3/1961, Cleveland, OH
1984 Cle: 16 G. **1987** Mia: 2 G. **Total:** 18 G.

ED MARSHALL Marshall, Edward L Jr. 6'4", 199 **WR**
Col: Ranger Coll. TX (J.C.); Cameron *HS:* Roy Miller [Corpus Christi, TX] B: 9/23/1947, Corpus Christi, TX *Drafted:* 1971 Round 11 Cin
1971 Cin: 13 G; Rec 2-18 9.0; 1 Fum. **1976** NYG: 6 G; Rec 8-166 20.8 3 TD; 18 Pt. **1977** NYG: 14 G; Rec 7-178 25.4. **Total:** 33 G; Rec 17-362 21.3 3 TD; 18 Pt; 1 Fum.

GREG MARSHALL Marshall, Gregory Edward 6'3", 255 **DT**
Col: Oregon State *HS:* Lakeridge [Lake Oswego, OR] B: 9/9/1956, Beverly, MA *Drafted:* 1978 Round 7 Phi
1978 Bal: 2 G.

HENRY MARSHALL Marshall, Henry Howard 6′2″, 214 **WR**
Col: Missouri *HS:* Hillcrest [Dalzell, SC] B: 8/9/1954, Broxton, GA
Drafted: 1976 Round 3 KC
1976 KC: Rush 5-101 20.2 1 TD; KR 1-0. **1977** KC: Rush 7-11 1.6. **1978** KC: Rush 1-(-5) -5.0. **1979** KC: Rush 2-34 17.0 1 TD. **1980** KC: Rush 3-22 7.3. **1981** KC: Pass 1-0, 1 Int; Rush 3-69 23.0. **1982** KC: Pass 1-0; Rush 3-25 8.3. **1986** KC: Pass 1-0. **Total:** Pass 3-0, 1 Int; Rush 24-257 10.7 2 TD; KR 1-0.

		Receiving					Tot
Year Team	G	Rec	Yds	Avg	TD	Fum	TD
1976 KC	14	28	443	15.8	2	1	3
1977 KC	14	23	445	19.3	4	2	4
1978 KC	16	26	433	16.7	2	0	2
1979 KC	16	21	332	15.8	1	0	2
1980 KC	16	47	799	17.0	6	0	6
1981 KC	12	38	620	16.3	4	2	4
1982 KC	9	40	549	13.7	3	0	3
1983 KC	13	50	788	15.8	6	0	6
1984 KC	16	62	912	14.7	4	2	4
1985 KC	11	25	446	17.8	0	1	0
1986 KC	16	46	652	14.2	1	0	1
1987 KC	12	10	126	12.6	0	0	0
NFL Total	165	416	6545	15.7	33	8	35

JAMES MARSHALL Marshall, James Carl 6′0″, 187 **DB**
Col: Jackson State *HS:* Eva Gorden [Magnolia, MS] B: 9/8/1952, Magnolia, MS
1980 NO: 16 G; Int 2-17.

JIM MARSHALL Marshall, James Lawrence 6′4″, 248 **DE**
Col: Ohio State *HS:* East [Columbus, OH] B: 12/30/1937, Danville, KY
Drafted: 1960 Round 4 Cle
1960 Cle: 12 G. **1961** Min: 14 G. **1962** Min: 14 G. **1963** Min: 14 G; **1** Fum TD; 6 Pt; 1 Fum. **1964** Min: 14 G. **1965** Min: 14 G. **1966** Min: 14 G. **1967** Min: 14 G. **1968** Min: 14 G; Scor **1** Saf; 2 Pt. **1969** Min: 14 G; Int 1-30. **1970** Min: 14 G. **1971** Min: 14 G. **1972** Min: 14 G. **1973** Min: 14 G; 1 Fum. **1974** Min: 14 G. **1975** Min: 14 G; 1 Fum. **1976** Min: 14 G. **1977** Min: 14 G. **1978** Min: 16 G. **1979** Min: 16 G. **Total:** 282 G; Int 1-30; Scor 1 Saf; 1 Fum TD; 8 Pt; 3 Fum.

LARRY MARSHALL Marshall, Lawrence Eugene 5′10″, 195 **DB-RB**
Col: Maryland *HS:* Bishop Egan [Levittown, PA] B: 3/2/1950, Levittown, PA *Drafted:* 1972 Round 15 KC

		Punt Returns				Kickoff Returns				
Year Team	G	Ret	Yds	Avg	TD	Ret	Yds	Avg	TD	Fum
1972 KC	11	18	103	5.7	0	23	651	28.3	0	3
1973 KC	10	29	180	6.2	0	14	391	27.9	0	3
1974 Min-Phi	13	13	118	9.1	0	20	468	23.4	0	2
1974 Min	5	5	46	9.2	0	4	56	14.0	0	1
1974 Phi	8	8	72	9.0	0	16	412	25.8	0	1
1975 Phi	10	23	235	10.2	0	22	557	25.3	0	4
1976 Phi	12	27	290	10.7	0	30	651	21.7	0	3
1977 Phi	14	46	489	10.6	0	20	455	22.8	0	3
1978 KC-LARm	5	6	51	8.5	0	9	223	24.8	0	2
1978 KC	2	6	51	8.5	0	7	173	24.7	0	2
1978 LARm	3	0	0	—	0	2	50	25.0	0	0
NFL Total	75	162	1466	9.0	0	138	3396	24.6	0	20

LEONARD MARSHALL Marshall, Leonard Allen 6′3″, 288 **DE**
Col: Louisiana State *HS:* Franklin [LA] B: 10/22/1961, Franklin, LA
Drafted: 1983 Round 2 NYG
1983 NYG: 14 G; Scor 1 Saf; 2 Pt; 0.5 Sac. **1984** NYG: 16 G; 6.5 Sac. **1985** NYG: 16 G; Int 1-3; 15.5 Sac. **1986** NYG: 16 G; Int 1-0; 12 Sac. **1987** NYG: 10 G; 8 Sac. **1988** NYG: 15 G; 8 Sac. **1989** NYG: 16 G; Scor **1** Saf; 2 Pt; 9.5 Sac. **1990** NYG: 16 G; 4.5 Sac. **1991** NYG: 16 G; 11 Sac. **1992** NYG: 14 G; 4 Sac. **1993** NYJ: 12 G; 2 Sac. **1994** Was: 16 G; 2 Sac. **Total:** 177 G; Int 2-3; Scor 2 Saf; 4 Pt; 83.5 Sac.

MARVIN MARSHALL Marshall, Marvin Ali 5′10″, 162 **WR**
Col: South Carolina State *HS:* Butler [Augusta, GA] B: 6/21/1972, Aschaffenburg, Germany
1996 TB: 5 G; Rec 2-27 13.5; PR 13-95 7.3; KR 12-264 22.0; 1 Fum.

PHIL MARSHALL Marshall, Philip Pence 5′8″, 165 **OE**
Col: Carnegie Mellon *HS:* Peabody [Pittsburgh, PA] B: 3/28/1895, Pittsburgh, PA D: 8/9/1962, Kittanning, PA
1920 Cle: 1 G.

RANDY MARSHALL Marshall, Randall Donn 6′5″, 237 **DE**
Col: Linfield *HS:* Santiam [Mill City, OR] B: 12/14/1946, Oregon City, OR *Drafted:* 1970 Round 6 Atl
1970 Atl: 9 G; 1 Fum TD; 6 Pt. **1971** Atl: 6 G. **Total:** 15 G; 1 Fum TD; 6 Pt.

BUD MARSHALL Marshall, Richard Arlen 6′4″, 270 **DT-DE**
Col: Baylor; Stephen F. Austin St. *HS:* Carthage [TX] B: 9/12/1941, Carthage, TX *Drafted:* 1965 Round 10 GB
1965 GB: 14 G. **1966** Was-Atl: 12 G. Was: 6 G. Atl: 6 G. **1967** Hou: 11 G. **1968** Hou: 11 G. **Total:** 48 G.

BOBBY MARSHALL Marshall, Robert Walls 6′2″, 195 **E**
(Rube) *Col:* Minnesota *HS:* Central [Minneapolis, MN] B: 3/12/1880, Milwaukee, WI D: 8/27/1958, Minneapolis, MN
1920 RI: 9 G. **1925** Dul: 3 G. **Total:** 12 G.

WHIT MARSHALL Marshall, Thomas Whitfield 6′2″, 245 **LB**
Col: Georgia *HS:* The Lovett School [Atlanta, GA] B: 1/6/1973, Atlanta, GA *Drafted:* 1996 Round 5 Phi
1996 Phi: 1 G.

WARREN MARSHALL Marshall, Warren Keith 6′0″, 218 **RB**
Col: James Madison *HS:* T. Wingate Andrews [High Point, NC]
B: 7/24/1964, High Point, NC *Drafted:* 1987 Round 6 Den
1987 Den: 1 G.

WILBER MARSHALL Marshall, Wilber Buddyhia 6′1″, 231 **LB**
Col: Florida *HS:* Astronaut [Titusville, FL] B: 4/18/1962, Titusville, FL
Drafted: 1984 Round 1 ChiB
1985 ChiB: KR 0-2; 6 Sac. **1986** ChiB: **1** Fum TD; 5.5 Sac. **1987** ChiB: Rush 1-1 1.0; 5 Sac. **1988** Was: 4 Sac. **1989** Was: 4 Sac. **1990** Was: 5 Sac. **1991** Was: 5.5 Sac. **1992** Was: 6 Sac. **1993** Hou: 2 Sac. **1994** Ariz: 1 Sac. **1995** NYJ: 1 Sac. **Total:** Rush 1-1 1.0; KR 0-2; 1 Fum TD; 45 Sac.

		Interceptions			Tot
Year Team	G	Int	Yds	TD	TD
1984 ChiB	15	0	0	0	0
1985 ChiB	16	4	23	0	0
1986 ChiB	16	5	68	1	2
1987 ChiB	12	0	0	0	0
1988 Was	16	3	61	0	0
1989 Was	16	1	18	0	0
1990 Was	16	1	6	0	0
1991 Was	16	5	75	1	1
1992 Was	16	2	20	1	1
1993 Hou	10	0	0	0	0
1994 Ariz	15	0	13	0	0
1995 NYJ	15	2	20	0	0
NFL Total	179	23	304	3	4

RALPH MARSTON Marston, Ralph Fulsom 5′9″, 170 **BB**
Col: Boston U. *HS:* Malden [MA] B: 2/16/1907, Malden, MA
D: 12/1967
1929 Bost: 1 G.

HERM MARTELL Martell, Herman Joseph 5′8″, 155 **OE**
Col: No College *HS:* Green Bay West [WI] B: 12/8/1900, Crystal Falls, MI D: 10/27/1957, Green Bay, WI
1921 GB: 1 G.

PAUL MARTHA Martha, John Paul 6′0″, 187 **DB-WR-HB**
Col: Pittsburgh *HS:* Redstone Twp. [PA]; Shady Side Acad. [Pittsburgh, PA] B: 6/22/1942, Pittsburgh, PA *Drafted:* 1964 Round 1 Pit
1964 Pit: Rush 4-12 3.0; Rec 6-145 24.2; PR 13-64 4.9; KR 1-26 26.0. **1965** Pit: Rush 2-3 1.5; Rec 11-171 15.5. **1966** Pit: KR 2-39 19.5. **1967** Pit: KR 18-403 22.4. **1968** Pit: **1** Fum TD. **1969** Pit: PR 3-0. **Total:** Rush 6-15 2.5; Rec 17-316 18.6; PR 16-64 4.0; KR 21-468 22.3; 1 Fum TD.

		Interceptions			
Year Team	G	Int	Yds	TD	Fum
1964 Pit	14	0	0	0	5
1965 Pit	12	0	0	0	0
1966 Pit	12	3	44	0	0
1967 Pit	14	4	41	0	1
1968 Pit	9	3	43	0	0
1969 Pit	14	5	37	0	3
1970 Den	13	6	99	0	1
NFL Total	88	21	264	0	10

AARON MARTIN Martin, Aaron Beamon 6′0″, 190 **DB**
(Pete) *Col:* North Carolina Central *HS:* J.T. Barber [New Bern, NC]
B: 2/10/1942, New Bern, NC
1964 LARm: KR 2-18 9.0. **1966** Phi: KR 4-132 33.0. **1968** Was: KR 7-146 20.9. **Total:** KR 13-296 22.8.

		Punt Returns				Interceptions				Tot
Year Team	G	Ret	Yds	Avg	TD	Int	Yds	TD	Fum	TD
1964 LARm	14	0	0	—	0	2	107	1	2	1
1965 LARm	4	0	0	—	0	2	60	1	0	1
1966 Phi	14	11	118	10.7	**1**	1	47	0	3	1
1967 Phi	14	20	128	6.4	0	2	8	0	0	0
1968 Was	14	2	12	6.0	0	4	23	0	0	0
NFL Total	60	33	258	7.8	1	11	245	2	5	3

AMOS MARTIN Martin, Anthony Irl 6′3″, 228 **LB**
Col: Louisville *HS:* Bardstown [KY] B: 1/30/1949, Indianapolis, IN
Drafted: 1972 Round 6 Min
1972 Min: 5 G. **1973** Min: 14 G. **1974** Min: 14 G; Int 3-39; 1 Fum TD; 6 Pt. **1975** Min: 5 G. **1976** Min: 14 G. **1977** Sea: 2 G. **Total:** 54 G; Int 3-39; 1 Fum TD; 6 Pt.

BLANCHE MARTIN Martin, Blanche 6'0", 195 **FB**
Col: Michigan State *HS:* River Rouge [MI] B: 1/16/1937, GA
Drafted: 1960 Round 1 NYT
1960 NYT-LAC: 13 G; Rush 18-58 3.2; Rec 4-23 5.8 1 TD; 6 Pt; 1 Fum. NYT: 4 G; Rush 12-35 2.9; Rec 2-5 2.5. LAC: 9 G; Rush 6-23 3.8; Rec 2-18 9.0 1 TD; 6 Pt; 1 Fum. **Total:** 13 G; Rush 18-58 3.2; Rec 4-23 5.8 1 TD; 6 Pt; 1 Fum.

CALEB MARTIN Martin, Caleb Snyder 6'4", 245 **T**
Col: Louisiana Tech *HS:* Winnsboro [LA] B: 2/10/1924, Winnsboro, LA D: 9/10/1994, Winnsboro, LA
1947 ChiC: 10 G.

CHARLES MARTIN Martin, Charles Milton 6'4", 276 **NT-DE**
Col: West Alabama *HS:* Cherokee [Canton, GA] B: 8/31/1959, Canton, GA
1984 GB: 16 G; 3 Sac. **1985** GB: 16 G; 3 Sac. **1986** GB: 14 G; 1 Sac. **1987** GB-Hou: 14 G; 4 Sac. GB: 2 G; 1 Sac. Hou: 12 G; 3 Sac. **1988** Atl: 16 G. **Total:** 76 G; 11 Sac.

CHRIS MARTIN Martin, Christopher 6'2", 236 **LB**
Col: Auburn *HS:* J.O. Johnson [Huntsville, AL] B: 12/19/1960, Huntsville, AL
1983 NO: 15 G. **1984** Min: 16 G; **1** Fum TD; 6 Pt; 1 Sac. **1985** Min: 12 G; 3.5 Sac. **1986** Min: 16 G. **1987** Min: 12 G. **1988** Min-KC: 15 G; **1** Fum TD; 6 Pt; 1 Sac. Min: 9 G; 1 Fum TD; 6 Pt; 1 Sac. KC: 6 G. **1989** KC: 16 G; 4 Sac. **1990** KC: 16 G; 6 Pt; 5.5 Sac. **1991** KC: 16 G; Int 1-0; 1 Fum TD; 6 Pt; 5 Sac. **1992** KC: 14 G; 0.5 Sac. **1993** LARm: 16 G. **1994** LARm: 14 G. **Total:** 178 G; Int 1-0; 3 Fum TD; Tot TD 4; 24 Pt; 20.5 Sac.

CURTIS MARTIN Martin, Curtis James Jr. 5'11", 207 **RB**
Col: Pittsburgh *HS:* Allderdice [Pittsburgh, PA] B: 5/1/1973, Pittsburgh, PA *Drafted:* 1995 Round 3 NE
1995 NE: Scor 1 2XP. **1996** NE: Scor 1 2XP. **Total:** Scor 2 2XP.

		Rushing				Receiving					Tot
Year Team	**G**	**Att**	**Yds**	**Avg**	**TD**	**Rec**	**Yds**	**Avg**	**TD**	**Fum**	**TD**
1995 NE	16	368	1487	4.0	14	30	261	8.7	1	5	15
1996 NE	16	316	1152	3.6	14	46	333	7.2	3	4	17
1997 NE	13	274	1160	4.2	4	41	296	7.2	1	3	5
1998 NYJ	15	369	1287	3.5	8	43	365	8.5	1	5	9
NFL Total	60	1327	5086	3.8	40	160	1255	7.8	6	17	46

DEE MARTIN Martin, D'Artagnan Athos 6'1", 190 **DB**
Col: Kentucky State *HS:* George Washington Carver [New Orleans, LA] B: 3/28/1949, New Orleans, LA *Drafted:* 1971 Round 4 NO
1971 NO: 14 G; Int 3-51; 1 Fum.

DAVID MARTIN Martin, David Earl 5'9", 191 **DB**
Col: Villanova *HS:* John Bartram [Philadelphia, PA] B: 3/15/1959, Philadelphia, PA *Drafted:* 1981 Round 9 Det
1986 SD: 4 G. **1987** Buf: 3 G; 1 Sac. **Total:** 7 G; 1 Sac.

DAVE MARTIN Martin, David Kenneth 6'0", 225 **LB**
Col: Notre Dame *HS:* Bishop Miege [Shawnee Mission, KS] B: 10/23/1946, Kansas City, KS *Drafted:* 1968 Round 6 Phi
1968 KC: 2 G. **1969** ChiB: 8 G. **Total:** 10 G.

DERRICK MARTIN Martin, Derrick Roy 6'0", 185 **DB**
Col: Arizona State; San Jose State *HS:* Compton [CA] B: 5/31/1957, Los Angeles, CA
1987 SF: 3 G; PR 2-12 6.0; Int 1-12; 1 Fum.

DON MARTIN Martin, Donald Joe 5'11", 187 **DB**
Col: Yale *HS:* Carrollton [MO] B: 9/17/1949, Carrollton, MO
Drafted: 1971 Round 7 Oak
1973 NE: 14 G. **1975** KC: 14 G. **1976** TB: 1 G. **Total:** 29 G.

DOUG MARTIN Martin, Douglas 6'3", 260 **DE-NT**
Col: Washington *HS:* Armijo [Farifield, CA] B: 5/22/1957, Fairfield, CA
Drafted: 1980 Round 1 Min
1980 Min: 11 G. **1981** Min: 16 G. **1982** Min: 9 G; Int 1-0; **11.5** Sac. **1983** Min: 16 G; 13 Sac. **1984** Min: 13 G; 1 Sac. **1985** Min: 16 G; 4 Sac. **1986** Min: 15 G; 9 Sac. **1987** Min: 12 G; 9 Sac. **1988** Min: 11 G; 3 Sac. **1989** Min: 7 G. **Total:** 126 G; Int 1-0; 50.5 Sac.

EMANUEL MARTIN Martin, Emanuel C 5'11", 184 **DB**
Col: Alabama State *HS:* Miami Central [FL] B: 7/31/1969, Miami, FL
1993 Hou: 1 G. **1996** Buf: 16 G; Int 2-35. **1997** Buf: 16 G; Int 1-12. **1998** Buf: 14 G; Int 1-23. **Total:** 47 G; Int 4-70.

EMERSON MARTIN Martin, Emerson Floyd 6'2", 300 **OG**
Col: Catawba; Hampton *HS:* East Bladen [Elizabethtown, NC] B: 5/6/1970, Elizabethtown, NC
1995 Car: 2 G.

ERIC MARTIN Martin, Eric Wayne 6'1", 207 **WR**
Col: Louisiana State *HS:* Van Vleck [TX] B: 11/8/1961, Van Vleck, TX
Drafted: 1985 Round 7 NO
1985 NO: Rush 2-(-1) -0.5; KR 15-384 25.6. **1986** NO: KR 3-64 21.3. **1987** NO: KR 1-15 15.0. **1988** NO: Rush 2-12 6.0; KR 3-32 10.7. **Total:** Rush 4-11 2.8; KR 22-495 22.5.

		Receiving				Punt Returns				
Year Team	**G**	**Rec**	**Yds**	**Avg**	**TD**	**Ret**	**Yds**	**Avg**	**TD**	**Fum**
1985 NO	16	35	522	14.9	4	8	53	6.6	0	1
1986 NO	16	37	675	18.2	5	24	227	9.5	0	5
1987 NO	15	44	778	17.7	7	14	88	6.3	0	3
1988 NO	16	85	1083	12.7	7	0	0	—	0	2
1989 NO	16	68	1090	16.0	8	0	0	—	0	1
1990 NO	16	63	912	14.5	5	0	0	—	0	3
1991 NO	16	66	803	12.2	4	0	0	—	0	2
1992 NO	16	68	1041	15.3	5	0	0	—	0	1
1993 NO	16	66	950	14.4	3	0	0	—	0	0
1994 KC	10	21	307	14.6	1	0	0	—	0	0
NFL Total	153	553	8161	14.8	49	46	368	8.0	0	18

FRANK MARTIN Martin, Frank Hayes 5'10", 177 **DB-HB-WB**
Col: Alabama *HS:* Shelby Co. [Columbiana, AL] B: 6/13/1919, Calera, AL D: 11/1981, Birmingham, AL
1943 Bkn: Pass 4-2 50.0%, 15 3.75; Rec 13-152 11.7; PR 5-38 7.6; Int 2-22. **1944** Bkn: Pass 1-1 100.0%, 7 7.00; Rec 3-15 5.0; PR 3-16 5.3; Int 1-0; Punt 1-2 2.0. **1945** Bos-NYG: Rec 4-67 16.8 1 TD; PR 1-10 10.0; KR 1-18 18.0; Int 1-0. Bos: Rec 1-53 53.0 1 TD. NYG: Rec 3-14 4.7; PR 1-10 10.0; KR 1-18 18.0; Int 1-0. **Total:** Pass 5-3 60.0%, 22 4.40; Rec 20-234 11.7 1 TD; PR 9-64 7.1; KR 1-18 18.0; Int 4-22; Punt 1-2 2.0.

		Rushing			
Year Team	**G**	**Att**	**Yds**	**Avg**	**TD**
1943 Bkn	10	25	50	2.0	0
1944 Bkn	6	11	18	1.6	0
1945 Bos-NYG	6	3	11	3.7	0
1945 Bos	3	2	10	5.0	0
1945 NYG	3	1	1	1.0	0
NFL Total	22	39	79	2.0	0

GEORGE MARTIN Martin, George Dwight 6'4", 245 **DE-TE**
Col: Oregon *HS:* Armijo [Fairfield, CA] B: 2/16/1953, Greenville, SC
Drafted: 1975 Round 11 NYG
1975 NYG: 14 G. **1976** NYG: 14 G. **1977** NYG: 10 G; Int 1-30 **1** TD; 6 Pt. **1978** NYG: 16 G; 6 Pt. **1979** NYG: 16 G. **1980** NYG: 16 G; Rec 1-4 4.0 1 TD; 6 Pt. **1981** NYG: 16 G; **2** Fum TD; 12 Pt. **1982** NYG: 9 G; 6 Sac. **1983** NYG: 14 G; 9 Sac. **1984** NYG: 16 G; 5.5 Sac. **1985** NYG: 16 G; Int 1-56 **1** TD; 6 Pt; 10 Sac. **1986** NYG: 16 G; Int 1-78 1 TD; 6 Pt; 3 Sac. **1987** NYG: 12 G; 5 Sac. **1988** NYG: 16 G; 7.5 Sac. **Total:** 201 G; Rec 1-4 4.0 1 TD; Int 3-164 3 TD; 2 Fum TD; Tot TD 7; 42 Pt; 46.0 Sac.

WAYNE MARTIN Martin, Gerald Wayne 6'5", 275 **DE-DT**
Col: Arkansas *HS:* Cross Co. [Cherry Valley, AR] B: 10/26/1965, Forrest City, AR *Drafted:* 1989 Round 1 NO
1989 NO: 16 G; 2.5 Sac. **1990** NO: 11 G; 4 Sac. **1991** NO: 16 G; 3.5 Sac. **1992** NO: 16 G; 15.5 Sac. **1993** NO: 16 G; 5 Sac. **1994** NO: 16 G; 10 Sac. **1995** NO: 16 G; Int 1-12; 13 Sac. **1996** NO: 16 G; 11 Sac. **1997** NO: 16 G; 10.5 Sac. **1998** NO: 16 G; Scor **1** Saf; 2 Pt; 3 Sac. **Total:** 155 G; Int 1-12; Scor 1 Saf; 2 Pt; 78 Sac.

HARVEY MARTIN Martin, Harvey Banks 6'5", 262 **DE**
Col: Texas A&M-Commerce *HS:* South Oak Cliff [Dallas, TX] B: 11/16/1950, Dallas, TX *Drafted:* 1973 Round 3 Dal
1973 Dal: 14 G. **1974** Dal: 14 G. **1975** Dal: 13 G. **1976** Dal: 14 G; Int 1-0. **1977** Dal: 14 G. **1978** Dal: 16 G; Int 1-7. **1979** Dal: 16 G; Scor **1** Saf; 2 Pt. **1980** Dal: 16 G. **1981** Dal: 16 G; Scor **1** Saf; 2 Pt. **1982** Dal: 9 G; 8 Sac. **1983** Dal: 16 G; 2 Sac. **Total:** 158 G; Int 2-7; Scor 2 Saf; 4 Pt; 10 Sac.

HERSH MARTIN Martin, Herschel Herbert 5'11", 180 **FB-WB-HB-BB**
(Jack; Buzz Saw) *Col:* No College *HS:* Manual [Kansas City, MO] B: 7/16/1906, Springfield, MO D: 6/1975, Fort Lauderdale, FL
1929 SI: 8 G. **1930** Nwk: 7 G. **Total:** 15 G.

IKE MARTIN Martin, Isaac Roy 5'11", 190 **HB**
Col: William Jewell *HS:* Liberty [MO] B: 7/15/1887, Liberty, MO D: 7/20/1979, Aurora, OH
1920 Can: 7 G.

BILLY MARTIN Martin, Jake William 6'4", 235 **TE**
Col: Georgia Tech *HS:* Gainesville [GA] B: 10/27/1942, Gainesville, GA
1966 Atl: KR 1-0. **1967** Atl: KR 1-0. **1968** Min: KR 1-0; Punt 28-1046 37.4. **Total:** KR 3-0; Punt 28-1046 37.4.

		Receiving				
Year Team	**G**	**Rec**	**Yds**	**Avg**	**TD**	**Fum**
1964 ChiB	14	3	93	31.0	0	0
1965 ChiB	14	1	-1	-1.0	0	0
1966 Atl	14	29	330	11.4	0	0
1967 Atl	14	15	182	12.1	3	0
1968 Min	14	10	101	10.1	1	1
NFL Total	70	58	705	12.2	4	1

CHRIS MARTIN Martin, James Christopher 5'9", 184 **DB**
Col: Northwestern *HS:* Jesuit [Tampa, FL] B: 9/1/1974, Tampa, FL
1996 ChiB: 1 G.

JIM MARTIN Martin, James Richard 6'2", 227 **LB**
(Jungle Jim) *Col:* Notre Dame *HS:* East Tech [Cleveland, OH]
B: 4/8/1924, Cleveland, OH *Drafted:* 1950 Round 2 Cle
1950 Cle: KR 1-14 14.0; Int 2-15. **1951** Det: Rec 0-10. **1953** Det: Int 1-0. **1955** Det: KR 1-14 14.0. **1957** Det: Int 1-22. **1959** Det: KR 1-0; Int 2-33.
Total: Rec 0-10; KR 3-28 9.3; Int 6-70.

		Scoring						
Year Team	G	Pts	FG	FGA	FG%	XK	XKA	XK%
1950 Cle	12	0	0	0	—	0	0	—
1951 Det	12	0	0	0	—	0	0	—
1952 Det	12	0	0	0	—	0	0	—
1953 Det	8	10	2	4	50.0	4	4	100.0
1954 Det	12	3	1	6	16.7	0	0	—
1955 Det	9	0	0	1	0.0	0	0	—
1956 Det	12	15	4	10	40.0	3	3	100.0
1957 Det	12	26	7	14	50.0	5	5	100.0
1958 Det	12	49	7	19	36.8	28	28	100.0
1959 Det	12	21	7	17	41.2	0	1	0.0
1960 Det	12	65	13	24	54.2	26	28	92.9
1961 Det	13	70	15	30	50.0	25	26	96.2
1963 Bal	14	104	**24**	39	61.5	32	35	91.4
1964 Was	14	71	12	28	42.9	35	39	89.7
NFL Total	166	434	92	192	47.9	158	169	93.5

JAMIE MARTIN Martin, Jamie Blane 6'2", 212 **QB**
Col: Weber State *HS:* Arroyo Grande [CA] B: 2/8/1970, Orange, CA
1996 StL: Rush 7-14 2.0. **1998** Jac: Rush 5-8 1.6. **Total:** Rush 12-22 1.8.

		Passing								
Year Team	G	Att	Comp	Comp%	Yds	YPA	TD	Int	Rating	Fum
1996 StL	6	34	23	67.6	241	7.09	3	2	92.9	2
1998 Jac	4	45	27	60.0	355	7.89	2	0	99.8	0
NFL Total	10	79	50	63.3	596	7.54	5	2	96.8	2

JOHNNY MARTIN Martin, John Jay 6'1", 195 **DB-WB-HB**
Col: Oklahoma *HS:* Broken Bow [OK] B: 1/8/1918, Nashville, AR
Deceased *Drafted:* 1941 Round 16 ChiB
1942 ChiC: PR 4-50 12.5. **1943** ChiC: PR 9-95 10.6. **1944** ChPt-Bos: PR 3-50 16.7. Bos: PR 3-50 16.7. **1945** Bos: PR 4-7 1.8.
Total: PR 20-202 10.1.

		Rushing				Receiving			
Year Team	G	Att	Yds	Avg	TD	Rec	Yds	Avg	TD
1941 ChiC	9	25	56	2.2	1	4	53	13.3	1
1942 ChiC	11	30	10	0.3	0	22	312	14.2	0
1943 ChiC	10	30	98	3.3	0	7	138	19.7	0
1944 ChPt-Bos	9	19	-7	-0.4	0	6	56	9.3	0
1944 ChPt	1	0	0	—	0	0	0	—	0
1944 Bos	8	19	-7	-0.4	0	6	56	9.3	0
1945 Bos	6	39	191	4.9	1	2	20	10.0	0
NFL Total	45	143	348	2.4	2	41	579	14.1	1

	Kickoff Returns				Interceptions		
Year Team	Ret	Yds	Avg	TD	Int	Yds	TD
1941 ChiC	3	86	28.7	0	1	2	0
1942 ChiC	8	202	25.3	0	6	45	0
1943 ChiC	7	130	18.6	0	1	35	0
1944 ChPt-Bos	8	265	33.1	0	3	46	0
1944 Bos	8	265	33.1	0	3	46	0
1945 Bos	13	302	23.2	0	1	10	0
NFL Total	39	985	25.3	0	12	138	0

	Punting				Tot
Year Team	Punts	Yds	Avg	Fum	TD
1941 ChiC	24	959	40.0	0	2
1942 ChiC	36	1417	39.4	0	0
1943 ChiC	30	1187	39.6	0	0
1944 ChPt-Bos	41	1457	35.5	0	0
1944 ChPt	6	184	30.7	0	0
1944 Bos	35	1273	36.4	0	0
1945 Bos	14	575	41.1	4	2
NFL Total	145	5595	38.6	4	4

JACK MARTIN Martin, John Taber 6'3", 238 **C**
Col: Princeton; Navy *HS:* Morrison R. Waite [Toledo, OH]
B: 4/10/1922, Flint, MI
1947 LARm: 11 G; Int 1-0. **1948** LARm: 12 G. **1949** LARm: 12 G.
Total: 35 G; Int 1-0.

JOE MARTIN Martin, Joseph Peter **WB**
Col: No College *HS:* North Side [Fort Worth, TX] B: 2/5/1895, Nashville, TN D: 5/6/1965, Louisville, KY
1921 Lou: 1 G.

KELVIN MARTIN Martin, Kelvin Brian 5'9", 162 **WR**
(K-Mart) *Col:* Boston College *HS:* Jean Ribault [Jacksonville, FL]
B: 5/14/1965, San Diego, CA *Drafted:* 1987 Round 4 Dal
1988 Dal: Rush 4-(-4) -1.0. **1990** Dal: Rush 4-(-2) -0.5. **1992** Dal: Rush 2-13 6.5. **1993** Sea: Rush 1-0. **Total:** Rush 11-7 0.6.

		Receiving				Punt Returns			
Year Team	G	Rec	Yds	Avg	TD	Ret	Yds	Avg	TD
1987 Dal	7	5	103	20.6	0	22	216	9.8	0
1988 Dal	16	49	622	12.7	3	44	360	8.2	0
1989 Dal	11	46	644	14.0	2	4	32	8.0	0
1990 Dal	16	64	732	11.4	0	5	46	9.2	0
1991 Dal	16	16	243	15.2	0	21	244	11.6	1
1992 Dal	16	32	359	11.2	3	42	**532**	12.7	**2**
1993 Sea	16	57	798	14.0	5	32	270	8.4	0
1994 Sea	16	56	681	12.2	1	33	280	8.5	0
1995 Phi	9	17	206	12.1	0	17	214	12.6	0
1996 Dal	16	25	380	15.2	1	41	373	9.1	0
NFL Total	139	367	4768	13.0	15	261	2567	9.8	3

	Kickoff Returns					Tot
Year Team	Ret	Yds	Avg	TD	Fum	TD
1987 Dal	12	237	19.8	0	1	0
1988 Dal	12	210	17.5	0	2	3
1989 Dal	0	0	—	0	0	2
1990 Dal	0	0	—	0	2	0
1991 Dal	3	47	15.7	0	2	1
1992 Dal	24	503	21.0	0	2	5
1993 Sea	3	38	12.7	0	1	5
1994 Sea	2	30	15.0	0	2	1
1995 Phi	20	388	19.4	0	2	0
1996 Dal	0	0	—	0	1	1
NFL Total	76	1453	19.1	0	15	18

LARRY MARTIN Martin, Larry L 6'2", 270 **DT**
Col: San Diego State *HS:* North [Bakersfield, CA] B: 4/9/1941
Drafted: 1965 Redshirt Round 2 SD
1966 SD: 1 G.

MIKE MARTIN Martin, Michael 5'10", 186 **WR**
Col: Illinois *HS:* Eastern [Washington, DC] B: 11/18/1960, Washington, DC *Drafted:* 1983 Round 8 Cin
1983 Cin: Rush 2-21 10.5. **1984** Cin: Rush 1-3 3.0. **Total:** Rush 3-24 8.0.

		Receiving				Punt Returns			
Year Team	G	Rec	Yds	Avg	TD	Ret	Yds	Avg	TD
1983 Cin	10	2	22	11.0	0	23	227	9.9	0
1984 Cin	15	11	164	14.9	0	24	376	**15.7**	0
1985 Cin	16	14	187	13.4	0	32	268	8.4	0
1986 Cin	7	3	68	22.7	0	13	96	7.4	0
1987 Cin	12	20	394	19.7	3	28	277	9.9	0
1988 Cin	4	2	22	11.0	1	5	30	6.0	0
1989 Cin	12	15	160	10.7	2	15	107	7.1	0
NFL Total	76	67	1017	15.2	6	140	1381	9.9	0

	Kickoff Returns				
Year Team	Ret	Yds	Avg	TD	Fum
1983 Cin	1	19	19.0	0	2
1984 Cin	19	386	20.3	0	4
1985 Cin	48	1104	23.0	0	4
1986 Cin	4	83	20.8	0	0
1987 Cin	3	51	17.0	0	1
1989 Cin	0	0	—	0	1
NFL Total	75	1643	21.9	0	12

ABE MARTIN Martin, Morris Glenn 6'0", 185 **WB-FB-BB**
Col: Southern Illinois *HS:* Carbondale [IL] B: 1/19/1906, Burnt Prairie, IL D: 4/17/1997, Springfield, IL
1932 ChiC: Rec 3-99 33.0 1 TD.

		Rushing				Tot
Year Team	G	Att	Yds	Avg	TD	TD
1932 ChiC	9	40	152	3.8	1	2

ROBBIE MARTIN Martin, Robbie Lance 5'8", 179 **WR**
Col: Cal Poly-S.L.O. *HS:* Villa Park [CA] B: 12/3/1958, Los Angeles, CA *Drafted:* 1981 Round 4 Pit
1982 Det: Rec 1-18 18.0. **1984** Det: Rush 1-14 14.0; Rec 1-9 9.0.
1985 Ind: Rush 1-23 23.0; Rec 10-128 12.8. **1986** Ind: Rec 1-41 41.0.
Total: Rush 2-37 18.5; Rec 13-196 15.1.

		Punt Returns				Kickoff Returns				
Year Team	G	Ret	Yds	Avg	TD	Ret	Yds	Avg	TD	Fum
1981 Det	16	52	450	8.7	1	25	509	20.4	0	3
1982 Det	9	26	275	10.6	0	16	268	16.8	0	3
1983 Det	10	15	183	12.2	**1**	8	140	17.5	0	3
1984 Det	14	25	210	8.4	0	10	144	14.4	0	5
1985 Ind	16	40	443	11.1	1	32	638	19.9	0	5
1986 Ind	7	17	109	6.4	0	21	385	18.3	0	4
NFL Total	72	175	1670	9.5	3	112	2084	18.6	0	23

BOB MARTIN Martin, Robert A 6'1", 217 **LB**
Col: Nebraska *HS:* David City [NE] B: 11/14/1953, David City, NE
Drafted: 1976 Round 6 NYJ
1976 NYJ: 13 G; Int 2-15. **1977** NYJ: 5 G; Int 1-0. **1978** NYJ: 16 G; Int 2-32. **1979** NYJ-SF: 15 G. NYJ: 2 G. SF: 13 G. **Total:** 49 G; Int 5-47.

ROD MARTIN Martin, Roderick Darryl 6'2", 218 **LB**
Col: Los Angeles City Coll. CA (J.C.); USC *HS:* Alexander Hamilton [Los Angeles, CA] B: 4/7/1954, Welch, WV *Drafted:* 1977 Round 12 Oak
1980 Oak: **1** Fum TD. **1982** LARd: 1 Sac. **1983** LARd: KR 1-0; 6 Sac.
1984 LARd: Scor **1** Saf; **1** Fum TD; 11 Sac. **1985** LARd: 7 Sac.
1986 LARd: 5 Sac. **1987** LARd: 3.5 Sac. **Total:** KR 1-0; Scor 1 Saf; 2 Fum TD; 33.5 Sac.

		Interceptions				Tot
Year Team	**G**	**Int**	**Yds**	**TD**	**Fum**	**TD**
1977 Oak	1	0	0	0	0	0
1978 Oak	15	0	0	0	0	0
1979 Oak	16	0	0	0	0	0
1980 Oak	16	2	15	0	0	1
1981 Oak	16	1	7	0	0	0
1982 LARd	9	3	60	**1**	0	1
1983 LARd	16	4	81	**2**	0	2
1984 LARd	16	2	31	1	0	2
1985 LARd	16	1	16	0	1	0
1986 LARd	16	1	15	0	0	0
1987 LARd	12	0	0	0	0	0
1988 LARd	16	0	0	0	0	0
NFL Total	165	14	225	4	1	6

SALADIN MARTIN Martin, Saladin 6'0", 180 **DB**
Col: San Diego City Coll. CA (J.C.); San Diego State *HS:* Abraham Lincoln [San Diego, CA] B: 1/17/1956, San Diego, CA
1980 NYJ: 3 G. **1981** SF: 15 G; Int 1-0. **Total:** 18 G; Int 1-0.

SAMMY MARTIN Martin, Samson Joseph 5'11", 175 **WR**
Col: Louisiana State *HS:* De La Salle [New Orleans, LA] B: 8/21/1965, Gretna, LA *Drafted:* 1988 Round 4 NE
1989 NE: Rush 2-20 10.0; PR 19-164 8.6. **1990** NE: PR 1-1 1.0.
Total: Rush 2-20 10.0; PR 20-165 8.3.

		Receiving				Kickoff Returns					Tot
Year Team	**G**	**Rec**	**Yds**	**Avg**	**TD**	**Ret**	**Yds**	**Avg**	**TD**	**Fum**	**TD**
1988 NE	16	4	51	12.8	0	31	735	23.7	**1**	0	1
1989 NE	10	13	229	17.6	0	24	584	24.3	0	1	0
1990 NE	10	4	65	16.3	1	25	515	20.6	0	0	1
1991 NE-Ind	12	5	79	15.8	0	20	483	24.2	0	1	0
1991 NE	4	0	0	—	0	8	178	22.3	0	0	0
1991 Ind	8	5	79	15.8	0	12	305	25.4	0	1	0
NFL Total	48	26	424	16.3	1	100	2317	23.2	1	2	2

STEVE MARTIN Martin, Steven 6'3", 260 **DE**
Col: Jackson State *HS:* Varnado [LA] B: 12/24/1964, Angie, LA
1987 Was: 3 G; 5 Sac.

STEVE MARTIN Martin, Steven Albert 6'4", 303 **DT**
Col: Missouri *HS:* Jefferson City [MO] B: 5/31/1974, St. Paul, MN
Drafted: 1996 Round 5 Ind
1996 Ind: 14 G; 1 Sac. **1997** Ind: 12 G. **1998** Ind-Phi: 13 G; 1 Sac. Ind: 4 G. Phi: 9 G; 1 Sac. **Total:** 39 G; 2 Sac.

TONY MARTIN Martin, Tony Derrick 6'0", 181 **WR**
Col: Bishop; Mesa *HS:* Miami Northwestern [FL] B: 9/5/1965, Miami, FL *Drafted:* 1989 Round 5 NYJ
1990 Mia: Rush 1-8 8.0. **1992** Mia: Pass 1-0; Rush 1-(-2) -2.0. **1993** Mia: Rush 1-6 6.0. **1994** SD: Pass 1-0, 1 Int; Rush 2-(-9) -4.5; KR 8-167 20.9.
1995 SD: Pass 1-0. **1998** Atl: Pass 1-0. **Total:** Pass 4-0, 1 Int; Rush 5-3 0.6; KR 8-167 20.9.

		Receiving				Punt Returns				
Year Team	**G**	**Rec**	**Yds**	**Avg**	**TD**	**Ret**	**Yds**	**Avg**	**TD**	**Fum**
1990 Mia	16	29	388	13.4	2	26	140	5.4	0	4
1991 Mia	16	27	434	16.1	2	1	10	10.0	0	2
1992 Mia	16	33	553	16.8	2	1	0	0.0	0	2
1993 Mia	12	20	347	17.4	3	0	0	—	0	1
1994 SD	16	50	885	17.7	7	0	0	—	0	2
1995 SD	16	90	1224	13.6	6	0	0	—	0	3
1996 SD	16	85	1171	13.8	**14**	0	0	—	0	0
1997 SD	16	63	904	14.3	6	0	0	—	0	0
1998 Atl	16	66	1181	17.9	6	0	0	—	0	0
NFL Total	140	463	7087	15.3	48	28	150	5.4	0	14

TRACY MARTIN Martin, Tracy Aaron 6'3", 205 **WR**
Col: North Dakota *HS:* Brooklyn Center [MN] B: 12/4/1964, Minneapolis, MN *Drafted:* 1987 Round 6 NYJ
1987 NYJ: 12 G; KR 8-180 22.5.

VERN MARTIN Martin, Vernon Lewis 5'10", 195 **BB-LB**
Col: Texas *HS:* Amarillo [TX] B: 5/2/1920, Amarillo, TX *Drafted:* 1942 Round 2 Pit
1942 Pit: 11 G; Rec 7-64 9.1 1 TD; Tot TD 2; 12 Pt.

BILLY MARTIN Martin, William Vance 5'11", 197 **HB**
Col: Minnesota *HS:* Wendell Phillips [Chicago, IL] B: 6/6/1938, Chicago, IL D: 11/10/1976 *Drafted:* 1960 Round 4 ChiB
1962 ChiB: Rush 9-28 3.1 1 TD; Rec 1-8 8.0. **1964** ChiB: Rec 1-9 9.0.
Total: Rush 9-28 3.1 1 TD; Rec 2-17 8.5.

		Punt Returns				Kickoff Returns				
Year Team	**G**	**Ret**	**Yds**	**Avg**	**TD**	**Ret**	**Yds**	**Avg**	**TD**	**Fum**
1962 ChiB	14	17	62	3.6	0	25	515	20.6	0	3
1963 ChiB	4	2	62	31.0	0	4	99	24.8	0	0
1964 ChiB	14	11	31	2.8	0	24	534	22.3	0	1
NFL Total	32	30	155	5.2	0	53	1148	21.7	0	4

ROY MARTINEAU Martineau, Daniel Roy 6'0", 210 **G-FB-T**
Col: Buffalo; Syracuse *HS:* Solvay [NY] B: 1900, Syracuse, NY
D: 10/25/1961, Syracuse, NY
1923 Buf: 5 G; Rush 1 TD; 6 Pt. **1924** Roch: 5 G. **1925** Roch: 7 G.
Total: 17 G; Rush 1 TD; 6 Pt.

PATSY MARTINELLI Martinelli, Pasquale Joseph 6'0", 227 **C-LB**
Col: Scranton *HS:* Dunmore [PA] B: 7/27/1919 D: 9/7/1992, Rockville, MD
AAFC **1946** BufA: 3 G; Int 1-12.

RICH MARTINI Martini, Richard William 6'2", 185 **WR**
Col: California-Davis *HS:* Ygnacio Valley [Concord, CA]
B: 11/19/1955, Berkeley, CA *Drafted:* 1977 Round 7 Oak

		Receiving			
Year Team	**G**	**Rec**	**Yds**	**Avg**	**TD**
1979 Oak	16	24	259	10.8	2
1980 Oak	16	1	36	36.0	0
1981 NO	12	8	72	9.0	0
NFL Total	44	33	367	11.1	2

JOHN MARTINKOVIC Martinkovic, John George 6'3", 241 **DE-DT**
Col: Xavier (Ohio) *HS:* Catholic [Hamilton, OH] B: 2/4/1927, Hamilton, OH *Drafted:* 1951 Round 6 Was
1951 GB: 12 G; KR 2-34 17.0. **1952** GB: 12 G; KR 1-0; 1 Fum TD; Tot TD 2; 12 Pt. **1953** GB: 12 G; KR 2-12 6.0. **1954** GB: 12 G. **1955** GB: 12 G. **1956** GB: 12 G. **1957** NYG: 12 G. **Total:** 84 G; KR 5-46 9.2; 1 Fum TD; Tot TD 2; 12 Pt.

PHIL MARTINOVICH Martinovich, Philip Joseph 5'10", 220 **G**
(Iron Mike) *Col:* U. of Pacific *HS:* El Dorado [Placentia, CA]
B: 2/9/1915, Diamond Springs, CA D: 9/22/1964, West Sacramento, CA
AAFC **1946** BknA: 10 G; Scor 36, 5-10 50.0% FG, 21-22 95.5% XK.
1947 BknA: 14 G; Scor 31, 3-20 15.0% FG, 22-25 88.0% XK. **Total:** 24 G; Scor 67, 8-30 26.7% FG, 43-47 91.5% XK.

NFL **1939** Det: 4 G; Scor 9, 3-6 50.0% FG. **1940** ChiB: 2 G; Scor 6, 2-2 100.0% FG. **Total:** 6 G; Scor 15, 5-8 62.5% FG.

LONNIE MARTS Marts, Lonnie Jr. 6'2", 240 **LB**
Col: Tulane *HS:* St. Augustine [New Orleans, LA] B: 11/10/1968, New Orleans, LA
1991 KC: 16 G; 1 Sac. **1992** KC: 15 G; Int 1-36 1 TD; 6 Pt. **1993** KC: 16 G; KR 1-0; Int 1-20; 2 Sac. **1994** TB: 16 G. **1995** TB: 15 G; Int 1-8. **1996** TB: 16 G; 7 Sac. **1997** Ten: 14 G; 1 Sac. **1998** Ten: 16 G; Int 1-27 1 TD; 6 Pt; 4 Sac. **Total:** 124 G; KR 1-0; Int 4-91 2 TD; 12 Pt; 15 Sac.

TOMMY MARVASO Marvaso, Thomas Michael 6'1", 190 **DB**
Col: Cincinnati *HS:* St. John's [Washington, DC] B: 10/2/1953, Washington, DC *Drafted:* 1976 Round 6 Was
1976 NYJ: 12 G; PR 1-0; 2 Fum. **1977** NYJ: 2 G; KR 2-36 18.0.
Total: 14 G; PR 1-0; KR 2-36 18.0; 2 Fum.

EUGENE MARVE Marve, Eugene Raymond 6'2", 237 **LB**
Col: Saginaw Valley State *HS:* Northern [Flint, MI] B: 8/14/1960, Flint, MI *Drafted:* 1982 Round 3 Buf
1982 Buf: 9 G; Int 1-0. **1983** Buf: 16 G; 2 Sac. **1984** Buf: 16 G. **1985** Buf: 14 G. **1986** Buf: 16 G; 2.5 Sac. **1987** Buf: 5 G. **1988** TB: 16 G; Int 1-29; 1.5 Sac. **1989** TB: 16 G. **1990** TB: 16 G; 2 Sac. **1991** TB: 16 G; Int 1-1.
1992 SD: 16 G. **Total:** 156 G; Int 3-30; 8 Sac.

MICKEY MARVIN Marvin, Phillip Michael 6'4", 270 **OG**
Col: Tennessee *HS:* Brevard [NC] B: 10/5/1955, Pisgah Forest, NC
Drafted: 1977 Round 4 Oak
1977 Oak: 8 G. **1978** Oak: 14 G. **1979** Oak: 2 G. **1980** Oak: 16 G.
1981 Oak: 16 G. **1982** LARd: 9 G. **1983** LARd: 14 G. **1984** LARd: 9 G.
1985 LARd: 15 G. **1986** LARd: 16 G. **1987** LARd: 1 G. **Total:** 120 G.

GREG MARX Marx, Gregory Allen 6'4", 260 **DE**
Col: Notre Dame *HS:* Catholic Central [Detroit, MI] B: 7/18/1950, Detroit, MI *Drafted:* 1973 Round 2 Atl
1973 Atl: 14 G.

RUSSELL MARYLAND Maryland, Russell 6'1", 285 **DT**
Col: Miami (Fla.) *HS:* Whitney-Young [Chicago, IL] B: 3/22/1969, Chicago, IL *Drafted:* 1991 Round 1 Dal
1991 Dal: 16 G; 4.5 Sac. **1992** Dal: 14 G; 1 Fum TD; 6 Pt; 2.5 Sac.
1993 Dal: 16 G; 2.5 Sac. **1994** Dal: 16 G; 3 Sac. **1995** Dal: 13 G; 2 Sac.

1996 Oak: 16 G; 2 Sac. **1997** Oak: 16 G; 4.5 Sac. **1998** Oak: 15 G; 2 Sac. **Total:** 122 G; 1 Fum TD; 6 Pt; 23.0 Sac.

LEN MASINI Masini, Leonard Leory 6'0", 225 **FB-LB**
(Mickey) *Col:* Fresno State *HS:* Technical [Fresno, CA] B: 10/6/1922, Firebaugh, CA
AAFC **1947** SF-A: Int 1-0. **1948** SF-A-LA-A: Rec 1-(-1) -1.0.
Total: Rec 1-(-1) -1.0; Int 1-0.

Year Team	G	Rushing Att	Yds	Avg	TD
1947 SF-A	11	38	167	4.4	2
1948 SF-A-LA-A	13	3	12	4.0	0
AAFC Total	24	41	179	4.4	2

JOHN MASKAS Maskas, John Demitrious 5'11", 212 **G-T**
Col: North Carolina; Virginia Tech *HS:* Monessen [PA] B: 8/15/1920, Chios, Greece D: 2/9/1983, Manahawkin, NJ
AAFC **1947** BufA: 7 G. **1949** BufA: 11 G. **Total:** 18 G.

MATT MASLOWSKI Maslowski, Matthew Anthony 6'3", 210 **WR**
Col: San Diego *HS:* Mission Bay [San Diego, CA] B: 9/10/1949, Chicago, IL
1971 LARm: 14 G; Rec 3-82 27.3 1 TD; 6 Pt. **1972** ChiB: 1 G. **Total:** 15 G; Rec 3-82 27.3 1 TD; 6 Pt.

DAVE MASON Mason, David Clayton 6'0", 199 **DB**
Col: Nebraska *HS:* Green Bay West [WI] B: 11/2/1949, Menominee, MI
Drafted: 1973 Round 10 Min
1973 NE: 7 G. **1974** GB: 12 G. **Total:** 19 G.

DERRICK MASON Mason, Derrick James 5'10", 187 **WR**
Col: Michigan State *HS:* Mumphord [Detroit, MI] B: 1/17/1974, Detroit, MI *Drafted:* 1997 Round 4 Ten
1997 Ten: Rush 1-(-7) -7.0. **Total:** Rush 1-(-7) -7.0.

Year Team	G	Receiving Rec	Yds	Avg	TD	Punt Returns Ret	Yds	Avg	TD
1997 Ten	16	14	186	13.3	0	13	95	7.3	0
1998 Ten	16	25	333	13.3	3	31	228	7.4	0
NFL Total	32	39	519	13.3	3	44	323	7.3	0

Year Team	Kickoff Returns Ret	Yds	Avg	TD	Fum
1997 Ten	26	551	21.2	0	5
1998 Ten	8	154	19.3	0	1
NFL Total	34	705	20.7	0	6

EDDIE MASON Mason, Eddie Lee 6'0", 245 **LB**
Col: North Carolina *HS:* Jordan Matthews [Siler City, NC] B: 1/9/1972, Siler City, NC *Drafted:* 1995 Round 6 NYJ
1995 NYJ: 15 G. **1998** Jac: 4 G. **Total:** 19 G.

JOEL MASON Mason, Joel Gregory 6'0", 199 **OE-DE-DB**
(AKA Joel Gregory Muleski) *Col:* Western Michigan *HS:* Stambaugh [MI] B: 3/12/1912, Iron River, MI D: 10/31/1995, Detroit, MI
1945 GB: PR 1-20 20.0; KR 1-15 15.0. **Total:** PR 1-20 20.0; KR 1-15 15.0.

Year Team	G	Receiving Rec	Yds	Avg	TD
1939 ChiC	9	18	188	10.4	0
1942 GB	11	7	86	12.3	0
1943 GB	10	8	107	13.4	2
1944 GB	10	1	9	9.0	0
1945 GB	10	0	0	—	0
NFL Total	50	34	390	11.5	2

LARRY MASON Mason, Larry Darnell 5'11", 205 **RB**
Col: Southern Mississippi; Troy State *HS:* McAdory [McCalla, AL] B: 3/21/1961, Birmingham, AL
1987 Cle: Rec 5-26 5.2 1 TD; KR 1-0. **1988** GB: Rec 8-84 10.5 1 TD. **Total:** Rec 13-110 8.5 2 TD; KR 1-0.

Year Team	G	Rushing Att	Yds	Avg	TD	Fum	Tot TD
1987 Cle	3	56	207	3.7	2	4	3
1988 GB	15	48	194	4.0	0	0	1
NFL Total	18	104	401	3.9	2	4	4

LINDSEY MASON Mason, Lindsey Michael 6'5", 265 **OT**
Col: Kansas *HS:* Carver [Baltimore, MD] B: 8/1/1955, Baltimore, MD
Drafted: 1978 Round 3 Oak
1978 Oak: 16 G; KR 1-12 12.0. **1980** Oak: 16 G. **1981** Oak: 11 G. **1982** SF: 9 G. **1983** Bal: 5 G. **Total:** 57 G; KR 1-12 12.0.

SAM MASON Mason, Samuel Anthony II 5'8", 175 **FB**
Col: Virginia Military *HS:* Episcopal [Hampton, VA] B: 7/21/1899, Hampton, VA D: 3/7/1971, Richmond, VA
1922 Min: 2 G. **1925** Mil: 6 G; Scor 1, 1 XK. **Total:** 8 G.

TOMMY MASON Mason, Thomas Cyril 6'1", 196 **RB**
Col: Tulane *HS:* Lake Charles [LA] B: 7/8/1939, Lake Charles, LA
Drafted: 1961 Round 1 Min
1961 Min: Pass 1-0. **1962** Min: Pass 1-0, 1 Int. **1964** Min: Pass 1-1 100.0%, 30 30.00 1 TD. **1965** Min: Pass 1-0, 1 Int. **1967** LARm: Pass 3-2 66.7%, 65 21.67 1 TD. **1968** LARm: Pass 2-0. **Total:** Pass 9-3 33.3%, 95 10.56 2 TD 2 Int.

Year Team	G	Rushing Att	Yds	Avg	TD	Receiving Rec	Yds	Avg	TD
1961 Min	13	60	226	3.8	3	20	122	6.1	0
1962 Min	14	167	740	4.4	2	36	603	16.8	6
1963 Min	13	166	763	4.6	7	40	365	9.1	2
1964 Min	13	169	691	4.1	4	26	239	9.2	1
1965 Min	10	141	597	4.2	10	22	321	14.6	1
1966 Min	7	58	235	4.1	2	7	39	5.6	1
1967 LARm	13	63	213	3.4	0	13	70	5.4	0
1968 LARm	12	108	395	3.7	3	15	144	9.6	0
1969 LARm	13	33	135	4.1	1	11	185	16.8	1
1970 LARm	6	44	123	2.8	0	12	127	10.6	1
1971 Was	10	31	85	2.7	0	12	109	9.1	0
NFL Total	124	1040	4203	4.0	32	214	2324	10.9	13

Year Team	Punt Returns Ret	Yds	Avg	TD	Kickoff Returns Ret	Yds	Avg	TD	Fum	Tot TD
1961 Min	14	146	10.4	0	25	603	24.1	0	7	3
1962 Min	6	52	8.7	0	12	301	25.1	0	9	8
1963 Min	4	63	15.8	0	3	61	20.3	0	**14**	9
1964 Min	10	150	15.0	0	2	36	18.0	0	9	5
1965 Min	9	63	7.0	0	3	66	22.0	0	9	11
1966 Min	3	9	3.0	0	0	0	—	0	6	3
1967 LARm	0	0	—	0	0	0	—	0	2	0
1968 LARm	0	0	—	0	0	0	—	0	2	3
1969 LARm	0	0	—	0	0	0	—	0	0	2
1970 LARm	0	0	—	0	0	0	—	0	1	1
1971 Was	0	0	—	0	0	0	—	0	2	0
NFL Total	46	483	10.5	0	45	1067	23.7	0	61	45

WAYNE MASS Mass, Wayne 6'4", 240 **OT**
Col: Clemson *HS:* Edmonds [Sumter, SC] B: 3/11/1946, Portales, NM
Drafted: 1968 Round 4 ChiB
1968 ChiB: 14 G. **1969** ChiB: 11 G. **1970** ChiB: 14 G. **1971** Mia: 11 G. **1972** NE-Phi: 9 G. NE: 6 G. Phi: 3 G. **Total:** 59 G.

CARLTON MASSEY Massey, Carlton William 6'2", 221 **DE**
Col: Southwestern (Tex.); Texas *HS:* Rockwall [TX] B: 1/17/1930, Rockwall, TX D: 5/22/1989, Dilley, TX *Drafted:* 1953 Round 8 Cle
1954 Cle: 11 G; KR 1-10 10.0. **1955** Cle: 12 G; Int 1-24. **1956** Cle: 12 G. **1957** GB: 12 G. **1958** GB: 2 G; KR 1-10 10.0. **Total:** 49 G; KR 2-20 10.0; Int 1-24.

JIM MASSEY Massey, James Lee 5'11", 198 **DB**
Col: Linfield *HS:* Neah-Kah-Nie [Rockaway, OR] B: 4/24/1948, McMinnville, OR *Drafted:* 1972 Round 10 LARm
1974 NE: 1 G. **1975** NE: 14 G. **Total:** 15 G.

ROBERT MASSEY Massey, Robert Lee 5'11", 200 **DB**
Col: North Carolina Central *HS:* Garinger [Charlotte, NC]
B: 2/27/1967, Rock Hill, SC *Drafted:* 1989 Round 2 NO
1989 NO: PR 0-54. **1994** Det: PR 1-3 3.0. **Total:** PR 1-57 57.0.

Year Team	G	Interceptions Int	Yds	TD	Fum
1989 NO	16	5	26	0	0
1990 NO	16	0	0	0	0
1991 Pho	12	0	0	0	0
1992 Pho	15	5	147	**3**	0
1993 Pho	10	0	0	0	0
1994 Det	16	4	25	0	1
1995 Det	16	0	0	0	0
1996 Jac	16	0	0	0	0
1997 NYG	16	0	0	0	0
NFL Total	133	14	198	3	1

RICK MASSIE Massie, Richard Ray 6'1", 190 **WR**
Col: Kentucky *HS:* Bourbon Co. [Paris, KY] B: 1/16/1960, Paris, KY
Drafted: 1984 Supplemental Round 2 Den
1987 Den: 9 G; Rec 13-244 18.8 4 TD; 24 Pt. **1988** Den: 4 G; Rec 3-39 13.0. **Total:** 13 G; Rec 16-283 17.7 4 TD; 24 Pt.

BOB MASTERS Masters, George Robert 5'11", 200 **HB**
(Chief) *Col:* Baylor *HS:* Comanche [TX] B: 1/16/1913, Comanche, TX
D: 2/9/1987, Hurst, TX
1937 Phi: Rec 4-60 15.0. **1939** Pit: Pass 3-1 33.3%, 9 3.00 1 Int; Rec 2-12 6.0. **1943** PhPt-ChiB: KR 2-37 18.5. PhPt: KR 2-37 18.5.
Total: Pass 3-1 33.3%, 9 3.00 1 Int; Rec 6-72 12.0; KR 2-37 18.5.

Year Team	G	Rushing Att	Yds	Avg	TD
1937 Phi	9	9	32	3.6	0

1938 Phi	1	0	0	—	0
1939 Pit	4	9	39	4.3	0
1942 Phi	3	1	3	3.0	0
1943 PhPt-ChiB	5	4	16	4.0	0
1943 PhPt	3	2	6	3.0	0
1943 ChiB	2	2	10	5.0	0
1944 ChiB	10	11	9	0.8	0
NFL Total	32	34	99	2.9	0

NORM MASTERS Masters, Norman Donald 6'2", 249 **OT**
Col: Michigan State *HS:* St. Mary's of Redford [Detroit, MI]
B: 9/19/1933, Detroit, MI *Drafted:* 1956 Round 2 ChiC
1957 GB: 12 G. **1958** GB: 12 G. **1959** GB: 12 G. **1960** GB: 12 G. **1961** GB: 14 G. **1962** GB: 14 G. **1963** GB: 14 G. **1964** GB: 14 G. **Total:** 104 G.

WALT MASTERS Masters, Walter Thomas 5'10", 192 **TB-QB-HB**
Col: Pennsylvania *HS:* Haverford School [PA] B: 3/28/1907, Pen Argyl, PA D: 7/10/1992, Ottawa, Canada
1936 Phi: Rush 7-18 2.6. **1943** ChiC: Rush 14-(-17) -1.2; PR 1-13 13.0; KR 2-39 19.5; Punt 10-368 36.8. **1944** ChPt: Rush 1-(-14) -14.0; Punt 2-91 45.5. **Total:** Rush 22-(-13) -0.6; PR 1-13 13.0; KR 2-39 19.5; Punt 12-459 38.3.

		Passing							
Year Team	**G**	**Att**	**Comp**	**Comp%**	**Yds**	**YPA**	**TD**	**Int**	**Rating**
1936 Phi	2	6	1	16.7	11	1.83	0	1	0.0
1943 ChiC	7	45	17	37.8	249	5.53	2	7	31.9
1944 ChPt	3	7	1	14.3	13	1.86	0	2	0.0
NFL Total	12	58	19	32.8	273	4.71	2	10	20.9

BILLY MASTERS Masters, William Joel 6'5", 240 **TE**
Col: Louisiana State *HS:* La Salle [Olla, LA] B: 3/15/1944, Grayson, LA
Drafted: 1967 Round 3 KC
1968 Buf: Rush 6-70 11.7. **1969** Buf: Rush 1-(-3) -3.0. **1971** Den: Rush 7-71 10.1. **1972** Den: Rush 3-(-15) -5.0. **1973** Den: Rush 1-(-9) -9.0. **Total:** Rush 18-114 6.3.

		Receiving				
Year Team	**G**	**Rec**	**Yds**	**Avg**	**TD**	**Fum**
1967 Buf	14	20	274	13.7	2	0
1968 Buf	14	8	101	12.6	0	0
1969 Buf	14	33	387	11.7	1	1
1970 Den	14	9	83	9.2	2	0
1971 Den	14	27	382	14.1	1	1
1972 Den	14	25	393	15.7	3	1
1973 Den	11	5	65	13.0	0	1
1974 Den	13	0	0	—	0	0
1975 KC	14	24	314	13.1	3	1
1976 KC	10	18	269	14.9	3	0
NFL Total	132	169	2268	13.4	15	5

BERNIE MASTERSON Masterson, Bernard Edward 6'3", 195 **QB-DB**
Col: Nebraska *HS:* Lincoln [NE] B: 8/10/1911, Shenandoah, IA
D: 5/16/1963, Chicago, IL
1934 ChiB: Rec 5-89 17.8 1 TD; Scor 7, 1 XK. **1935** ChiB: Rec 7-99 14.1 1 TD. **1936** ChiB: Rec 1-28 28.0. **1938** ChiB: Rec 1-4 4.0. **1939** ChiB: Rec 2-37 18.5. **1940** ChiB: Scor 7, 1-1 100.0% XK. **Total:** Rec 16-257 16.1 2 TD; Scor 50, 2-1 100.0% XK.

		Passing							
Year Team	**G**	**Att**	**Comp**	**Comp%**	**Yds**	**YPA**	**TD**	**Int**	**Rating**
1934 ChiB	9	3	3	100.0	39	13.00	1	0	158.3
1935 ChiB	12	44	18	40.9	446	**10.14**	6	4	80.1
1936 ChiB	12	42	10	23.8	292	6.95	3	6	40.3
1937 ChiB	10	72	26	36.1	615	**8.54**	**9**	7	67.8
1938 ChiB	11	112	46	41.1	848	7.57	5	9	49.3
1939 ChiB	11	113	44	38.9	914	8.09	8	9	58.6
1940 ChiB	7	23	9	39.1	212	9.22	2	3	62.5
NFL Total	72	409	156	38.1	3366	8.23	34	38	57.2

	Rushing				Tot
Year Team	**Att**	**Yds**	**Avg**	**TD**	**TD**
1934 ChiB	4	11	2.8	0	1
1935 ChiB	21	2	0.1	0	1
1936 ChiB	9	-7	-0.8	2	2
1937 ChiB	30	-21	-0.7	1	1
1938 ChiB	13	-16	-1.2	0	0
1939 ChiB	21	-31	-1.5	2	2
1940 ChiB	10	-7	-0.7	1	1
NFL Total	108	-69	-0.6	6	8

FORREST MASTERSON Masterson, Forrest Joseph 6'3", 246 **C-G**
Col: Iowa *HS:* Louisville [OH] B: 4/2/1922, Alliance, OH
Drafted: 1945 Round 3 ChiB
1945 ChiB: 6 G.

BOB MASTERSON Masterson, Robert Patrick 6'1", 213 **OE-DE**
Col: Miami (Fla.) *HS:* North Branch [NJ] B: 1/5/1915, North Branch, NJ
D: 7/1/1994, Miami, FL *Drafted:* 1938 Round 4 ChiB
AAFC **1946** NY-A: 14 G; Rec 10-119 11.9; KR 5-55 11.0; Int 1-0; Scor 0-1 FG.

NFL **1938** Was: Rush 3-89 29.7; Scor 14, 1-1 100.0% FG, 5-6 83.3% XK. **1939** Was: Scor 15, 1-6 16.7% FG, 6-8 75.0% XK. **1940** Was: Rush 1-0; Scor 42, 1-2 50.0% FG, 15-16 93.8% XK. **1941** Was: Rush 1-3 3.0; KR 2-20 10.0; Int 1-0; Scor 23, 3-6 50.0% FG, 8-8 100.0% XK. **1942** Was: Pass 1-0; Rush 3-12 4.0; KR 3-45 15.0; Scor 32, 1-5 20.0% FG, 17-19 89.5% XK. **1943** Was: KR 2-66 33.0; Scor 41, 1-5 20.0% FG, 20-21 95.2% XK. **1944** Bkn: Pass 1-1 100.0%, 1 1.00; Punt 4-136 34.0; Scor 6, 0-5 FG. **1945** Bos: Scor 0-1 FG. **Total:** Pass 2-1 50.0%, 1 0.50; Rush 8-104 13.0; KR 7-131 18.7; Int 1-0; Punt 4-136 34.0; Scor 173, 8-31 25.8% FG, 71-78 91.0% XK.

		Receiving			
Year Team	**G**	**Rec**	**Yds**	**Avg**	**TD**
1938 Was	11	10	213	**21.3**	1
1939 Was	10	10	114	11.4	1
1940 Was	11	18	283	15.7	4
1941 Was	11	11	135	12.3	1
1942 Was	11	22	308	14.0	2
1943 Was	10	16	200	12.5	3
1944 Bkn	10	24	258	10.8	1
1945 Bos	10	15	186	12.4	0
NFL Total	84	126	1697	13.5	13

LE'SHAI MASTON Maston, Le'Shai Edwoin 6'0", 227 **RB**
Col: Baylor *HS:* David W. Carter [Dallas, TX] B: 10/7/1970, Dallas, TX
1995 Jac: KR 1-5 5.0. **Total:** KR 1-5 5.0.

		Rushing				Receiving				
Year Team	**G**	**Att**	**Yds**	**Avg**	**TD**	**Rec**	**Yds**	**Avg**	**TD**	**Fum**
1993 Hou	10	1	10	10.0	0	1	14	14.0	0	1
1994 Hou	5	0	0	—	0	2	12	6.0	0	0
1995 Jac	16	41	186	4.5	0	18	131	7.3	0	3
1996 Jac	15	8	22	2.8	0	6	54	9.0	0	0
1998 Was	1	0	0	—	0	0	0	—	0	0
NFL Total	47	50	218	4.4	0	27	211	7.8	0	4

JOHN MASTRANGELO Mastrangelo, John Battista 6'1", 228 **OG-DG-OT-DT**
Col: Notre Dame *HS:* Vandergrift [PA] B: 3/10/1926, Vandergrift, PA
D: 10/2/1987, Vandergrift, PA *Drafted:* 1947 Round 2 Pit
AAFC **1949** NY-A: 12 G.

NFL **1947** Pit: 11 G; 6 Pt. **1948** Pit: 12 G. **1950** NYG: 9 G. **Total:** 32 G; 6 Pt.

GUS MASTROGANY Mastrogany, August Nicholas 6'0", 180 **OE**
Col: Iowa *HS:* Central [Davenport, IA] B: 10/25/1907, Davenport, IA
D: 5/12/1992, Northbrook, IL
1931 ChiB: 1 G.

STAN MATAELE Mataele, Stanley 6'2", 278 **NT**
Col: Sacramento City Coll. CA (J.C.); Arizona *HS:* Kahuku [HI]
B: 6/24/1963, Tonga
1987 GB: 2 G.

BILL MATAN Matan, William Douglas 6'4", 240 **DE**
Col: Kansas State *HS:* Cleveland Acad. [St. Louis, MO] B: 12/6/1943, St. Louis, MO *Drafted:* 1966 Round 8 NYG
1966 NYG: 3 G.

CHRIS MATAU Matau, Christopher Volaga 6'3", 310 **OG**
Col: Long Beach City Coll. CA (J.C.); Brigham Young *HS:* Carson [CA]
B: 1/22/1964, Torrance, CA
1987 LARm: 3 G.

ED MATESIC Matesic, Edward J 6'1", 198 **TB-DB**
(Dick; Lefty) *Col:* Pittsburgh B: 11/6/1907, Union District, Marshall Co., WV D: 6/4/1988, Wheeling, WV
1934 Phi: Rec 3-38 12.7 1 TD. **1936** Pit: Rec 1-13 13.0. **Total:** Rec 4-51 12.8 1 TD.

		Passing							
Year Team	**G**	**Att**	**Comp**	**Comp%**	**Yds**	**YPA**	**TD**	**Int**	**Rating**
1934 Phi	11	60	20	33.3	278	4.63	2	5	25.6
1935 Phi	11	64	15	23.4	284	4.44	2	13	16.4
1936 Pit	12	138	64	46.4	850	6.16	4	16	36.5
NFL Total	34	262	99	37.8	1412	5.39	8	34	26.6

	Rushing				Tot
Year Team	**Att**	**Yds**	**Avg**	**TD**	**TD**
1934 Phi	63	181	2.9	0	1
1935 Phi	50	138	2.8	1	1
1936 Pit	46	58	1.3	0	0
NFL Total	159	377	2.4	1	2

JOE MATESIC Matesic, Joseph Thomas 6'4", 250 **DT-OT**
Col: Indiana; Arizona State B: 11/10/1927, Rankin, PA D: 8/19/1989, Burgettstown, PA *Drafted:* 1953 Round 12 NYG
1954 Pit: 1 G.

JACK MATHESON Matheson, Jack Kenneth 6'2", 221 **OE-DE**
Col: Western Michigan *HS:* Lake View [St. Clair Shores, MI]
B: 6/9/1920, Detroit, MI
1943 Det: KR 1-19 19.0. **1944** Det: Int 1-21. **1945** Det: PR 1-10 10.0 **1** TD; Scor **1** Saf. **1946** Det: KR 1-17 17.0; Int 1-8. **Total:** PR 1-10 10.0 1 TD; KR 2-36 18.0; Int 2-29; Scor 1 Saf.

		Receiving					Tot
Year Team	G	Rec	Yds	Avg	TD	Fum	TD
1943 Det	9	13	156	12.0	1	0	1
1944 Det	10	23	361	15.7	3	0	3
1945 Det	9	19	241	12.7	1	1	2
1946 Det	11	17	178	10.5	0	0	0
1947 ChiB	3	1	8	8.0	0	0	0
NFL Total	42	73	944	12.9	5	1	6

RILEY MATHESON Matheson, Riley 6'2", 207 **G-LB**
(Rattlesnake) *Col:* Cameron; Texas-El Paso *HS:* Hedrick [OK]
B: 12/6/1914, Shannon, TX D: 6/1987, Paraguay
AAFC **1948** SF-A: 14 G; Int 2-4.

NFL **1945** Cle: PR 1-5 5.0. **Total:** PR 1-5 5.0.

		Interceptions		
Year Team	G	Int	Yds	TD
1939 Cle	2	—	—	0
1940 Cle	11	0	0	0
1941 Cle	9	1	1	0
1942 Cle	10	1	13	0
1943 Det	10	0	0	0
1944 Cle	9	3	12	0
1945 Cle	10	2	49	0
1946 LARm	11	4	21	0
1947 LARm	11	1	5	0
NFL Total	83	12	101	0

BOB MATHESON Matheson, Robert Edward 6'4", 235 **LB-DE**
Col: Duke *HS:* Appalachian [Boone, NC] B: 11/25/1944, Boone, NC
D: 9/5/1994, Durham, NC *Drafted:* 1967 Round 1 Cle
1969 Cle: KR 1-0. **1970** Cle: KR 2-21 10.5. **1971** Mia: KR 3-32 10.7. **1972** Mia: KR 2-34 17.0. **1974** Mia: KR 5-65 13.0. **Total:** KR 13-152 11.7.

		Interceptions			
Year Team	G	Int	Yds	TD	Fum
1967 Cle	14	1	0	0	0
1968 Cle	14	2	44	0	0
1969 Cle	14	0	0	0	0
1970 Cle	13	1	11	0	0
1971 Mia	14	0	0	0	0
1972 Mia	14	0	0	0	0
1973 Mia	14	0	0	0	0
1974 Mia	14	1	10	0	1
1975 Mia	14	3	32	0	0
1976 Mia	13	2	34	0	0
1977 Mia	14	1	7	0	0
1978 Mia	12	0	0	0	0
1979 Mia	16	1	28	0	0
NFL Total	180	12	166	0	1

BARNEY MATHEWS Mathews, Frank E 5'8", 185 **OE**
Col: Northwestern *HS:* Central [St. Louis, MO] B: 7/1/1903, St.Louis, MO D: 4/17/1970, St.Louis, MO
1926 Rac: 5 G.

NED MATHEWS Mathews, Ned Alfred 5'10", 187 **HB**
Col: UCLA *HS:* Manual Arts [Los Angeles, CA] B: 8/11/1918, Provo, UT
AAFC **1946** ChiA-SF-A: Pass 1-1 100.0%, 26 26.00; Rec 6-100 16.7 2 TD; KR 6-118 19.7; Int 2-8. **1947** SF-A: Pass 2-0; Rec 6-51 8.5 2 TD; PR 4-44 11.0; KR 2-46 23.0; Int 4-149 1 TD. **Total:** Pass 3-1 33.3%, 26 8.67; Rec 12-151 12.6 4 TD; PR 4-44 11.0; KR 8-164 20.5; Int 6-157 1 TD.

		Rushing				Tot
Year Team	G	Att	Yds	Avg	TD	TD
1946 ChiA-SF-A	14	30	109	3.6	1	3
1947 SF-A	12	39	238	6.1	2	5
AAFC Total	26	69	347	5.0	3	8

NFL **1941** Det: Pass 8-3 37.5%, 59 7.38 1 TD; Rec 6-56 9.3; PR 1-3 3.0; Punt 1-26 26.0. **1942** Det: Pass 22-6 27.3%, 53 2.41 1 TD 2 Int; Rec 3-38 12.7; PR 7-82 11.7. **1943** Det: Pass 12-4 33.3%, 76 6.33 1 TD; Rec 9-193 21.4 1 TD; PR 4-37 9.3. **1945** Bos: Pass 1-0; Rec 4-56 14.0 1 TD. **Total:** Pass 43-13 30.2%, 188 4.37 3 TD 2 Int; Rec 22-343 15.6 2 TD; PR 12-122 10.2; Punt 1-26 26.0.

		Rushing				Kickoff Returns			
Year Team	G	Att	Yds	Avg	TD	Ret	Yds	Avg	TD
1941 Det	9	31	56	1.8	0	9	233	25.9	0
1942 Det	9	21	79	3.8	0	5	97	19.4	0
1943 Det	10	38	124	3.3	1	7	246	**35.1**	**1**
1945 Bos	9	27	146	5.4	0	4	108	27.0	0
NFL Total	37	117	405	3.5	1	25	684	27.4	1

	Interceptions				Tot
Year Team	Int	Yds	TD	Fum	TD
1941 Det	5	128	**1**	0	1
1943 Det	4	44	0	0	3
1945 Bos	3	42	0	3	1
NFL Total	12	214	1	3	5

NEIL MATHEWS Mathews, Neilson Murray 6'0", 200 **T**
Col: Pennsylvania *HS:* Hyde Park [Chicago, IL] B: 9/13/1893, Chicago, IL D: 7/21/1965, Bryn Mawr, PA
1920 ChiT: 6 G.

RAY MATHEWS Mathews, Raymond Dyral 6'0", 185 **OE-HB**
Col: Clemson *HS:* McKeesport [PA] B: 2/26/1929, Dayton, PA
Drafted: 1951 Round 7 Pit
1951 Pit: Int 1-0. **1952** Pit: Scor 43, 1-1 100.0% XK. **1953** Pit: Int 1-17; Scor **1** Saf; **1** Fum TD. **Total:** Int 2-17; Scor 261, 1-1 100.0% XK, 1 Saf; 1 Fum TD.

		Passing							
Year Team	G	Att	Comp	Comp%	Yds	YPA	TD	Int	Rating
1951 Pit	12	31	15	48.4	208	6.71	2	0	91.9
1952 Pit	12	13	3	23.1	104	8.00	0	1	28.4
1953 Pit	12	2	0	0.0	0	0.00	0	0	39.6
1954 Pit	12	4	0	0.0	0	0.00	0	1	0.0
1955 Pit	12	0	0	—	0	—	0	0	—
1956 Pit	12	0	0	—	0	—	0	0	—
1957 Pit	12	0	0	—	0	—	0	0	—
1958 Pit	12	0	0	—	0	—	0	0	—
1959 Pit	12	1	1	100.0	38	38.00	0	0	118.8
1960 Dal	6	0	0	—	0	—	0	0	—
NFL Total	114	51	19	37.3	350	6.86	2	2	58.5

	Rushing				Receiving			
Year Team	Att	Yds	Avg	TD	Rec	Yds	Avg	TD
1951 Pit	21	37	1.8	0	0	0	—	0
1952 Pit	66	315	4.8	0	33	543	16.5	5
1953 Pit	65	260	4.0	2	27	346	12.8	4
1954 Pit	80	242	3.0	2	44	652	14.8	6
1955 Pit	57	187	3.3	1	42	762	18.1	6
1956 Pit	3	-11	-3.7	0	31	540	17.4	5
1957 Pit	3	-1	-0.3	0	15	369	24.6	4
1958 Pit	4	24	6.0	0	25	525	21.0	4
1959 Pit	1	4	4.0	0	13	182	14.0	0
1960 Dal	0	0	—	0	3	44	14.7	0
NFL Total	300	1057	3.5	5	233	3963	17.0	34

	Punt Returns				Kickoff Returns					Tot
Year Team	Ret	Yds	Avg	TD	Ret	Yds	Avg	TD	Fum	TD
1951 Pit	15	231	15.4	1	13	327	25.2	0	3	1
1952 Pit	26	397	15.3	**2**	14	367	26.2	0	6	7
1953 Pit	16	128	8.0	0	10	261	26.1	0	5	7
1954 Pit	2	6	3.0	0	4	88	22.0	0	5	8
1955 Pit	0	0	—	0	0	0	—	0	1	7
1956 Pit	0	0	—	0	1	26	26.0	0	0	5
1957 Pit	0	0	—	0	0	0	—	0	3	4
1958 Pit	0	0	—	0	0	0	—	0	0	4
1959 Pit	2	17	8.5	0	0	0	—	0	0	0
NFL Total	61	779	12.8	3	42	1069	25.5	0	23	43

JASON MATHEWS Mathews, Samuel Jason 6'5", 291 **OT**
Col: Brigham Young; Texas A&M *HS:* Bridge City [TX] B: 2/9/1971, Orange, TX *Drafted:* 1994 Round 3 Ind
1994 Ind: 10 G. **1995** Ind: 16 G. **1996** Ind: 16 G. **1997** Ind: 16 G. **1998** Ten: 3 G. **Total:** 61 G.

MATHEWSON Mathewson **WB**
Col: No College Deceased
1920 Ham: 1 G.

RIC MATHIAS Mathias, Ric 5'10", 180 **DB**
Col: Wis.-La Crosse B: 12/10/1975, Monroe, WI
1998 Cin: 3 G.

DEDRIC MATHIS Mathis, Dedric Ronshell 5'10", 188 **DB**
Col: Houston *HS:* Cuero [TX] B: 9/26/1973, Cuero, TX *Drafted:* 1996 Round 2 Ind
1996 Ind: 16 G. **1997** Ind: 13 G; Int 1-31. **Total:** 29 G; Int 1-31.

KEVIN MATHIS Mathis, Kevin 5'9", 179 **DB**
Col: Texas A&M-Commerce *HS:* Gainesville [TX] B: 4/29/1974, Kansas City, MO
1997 Dal: PR 11-91 8.3. **1998** Dal: PR 2-3 1.5; Int 2-0; 1 Sac.
Total: PR 13-94 7.2; Int 2-0; 1 Sac.

		Kickoff Returns				
Year Team	**G**	**Ret**	**Yds**	**Avg**	**TD**	**Fum**
1997 Dal	16	0	0	—	0	2
1998 Dal	13	25	621	24.8	0	2
NFL Total	29	25	621	24.8	0	4

MARK MATHIS Mathis, Mark E 5'9", 178 **DB**
Col: Liberty *HS:* Marietta [GA] B: 8/23/1965, Mount Clemens, MI
1987 StL: 2 G; Int 1-4.

REGGIE MATHIS Mathis, Reginald Levi 6'2", 220 **LB**
Col: Navarro Coll. TX (J.C.); Oklahoma *HS:* Notre Dame [Chattanooga, TN] B: 3/18/1956, Chattanooga, TN *Drafted:* 1979 Round 2 NO
1979 NO: 16 G. **1980** NO: 16 G; Int 1-15. **Total:** 32 G; Int 1-15.

TERANCE MATHIS Mathis, Terance Paul 5'10", 177 **WR**
Col: New Mexico *HS:* Redan [Stone Mountain, GA] B: 6/7/1967, Detroit, MI *Drafted:* 1990 Round 6 NYJ
1990 NYJ: Rush 2-9 4.5. **1991** NYJ: Rush 1-19 19.0. **1992** NYJ: Rush 3-25 8.3 1 TD. **1993** NYJ: Rush 2-20 10.0 1 TD. **1994** Atl: Scor 2 2XP. **1995** Atl: Scor **3** 2XP. **1996** Atl: Scor 1 2XP. **1997** Atl: Rush 3-35 11.7. **1998** Atl: Rush 1-(-6) -6.0. **Total:** Rush 12-102 8.5 2 TD; Scor **6** 2XP.

		Receiving				Punt Returns			
Year Team	**G**	**Rec**	**Yds**	**Avg**	**TD**	**Ret**	**Yds**	**Avg**	**TD**
1990 NYJ	16	19	245	12.9	0	11	165	15.0	**1**
1991 NYJ	16	28	329	11.8	1	23	157	6.8	0
1992 NYJ	16	22	316	14.4	3	2	24	12.0	0
1993 NYJ	16	24	352	14.7	0	14	99	7.1	0
1994 Atl	16	111	1342	12.1	11	0	0	—	0
1995 Atl	14	78	1039	13.3	9	0	0	—	0
1996 Atl	16	69	771	11.2	7	3	19	6.3	0
1997 Atl	16	62	802	12.9	6	0	0	—	0
1998 Atl	16	64	1136	17.8	11	1	0	0.0	0
NFL Total	142	477	6332	13.3	48	54	464	8.6	1

	Kickoff Returns					Tot
Year Team	**Ret**	**Yds**	**Avg**	**TD**	**Fum**	**TD**
1990 NYJ	43	787	18.3	0	1	1
1991 NYJ	29	599	20.7	0	4	1
1992 NYJ	28	492	17.6	0	2	4
1993 NYJ	7	102	14.6	0	5	1
1994 Atl	0	0	—	0	0	11
1995 Atl	0	0	—	0	1	9
1996 Atl	0	0	—	0	0	7
1997 Atl	0	0	—	0	0	6
1998 Atl	0	0	—	0	0	11
NFL Total	107	1980	18.5	0	13	51

BILL MATHIS Mathis, William Hart 6'1", 220 **FB**
Col: Clemson *HS:* Manchester [GA] B: 12/10/1938, Rocky Mount, NC *Drafted:* 1960 Round 1 Den
1963 NYJ: KR 1-11 11.0. **1964** NYJ: KR 1-0. **1967** NYJ: Scor **2** 2XP. **1968** NYJ: Scor **1** 2XP. **Total:** KR 2-11 5.5; Scor 3 2XP.

		Rushing				Receiving					Tot
Year Team	**G**	**Att**	**Yds**	**Avg**	**TD**	**Rec**	**Yds**	**Avg**	**TD**	**Fum**	**TD**
1960 NYT	14	92	307	3.3	2	18	103	5.7	0	2	2
1961 NYT	14	**202**	846	4.2	7	12	42	3.5	1	3	8
1962 NYT	11	71	245	3.5	3	6	32	5.3	0	1	3
1963 NYJ	14	107	268	2.5	1	18	177	9.8	1	1	2
1964 NYJ	14	105	305	2.9	4	4	39	9.8	0	0	4
1965 NYJ	14	147	604	4.1	5	17	242	14.2	1	2	6
1966 NYJ	14	72	208	2.9	2	22	379	17.2	1	2	3
1967 NYJ	14	78	243	3.1	4	25	429	17.2	3	1	7
1968 NYJ	14	74	208	2.8	5	9	149	16.6	1	1	6
1969 NYJ	14	96	355	3.7	4	18	183	10.2	1	0	5
NFL Total	137	1044	3589	3.4	37	149	1775	11.9	9	13	46

BRUCE MATHISON Mathison, Bruce Martin 6'3", 205 **QB**
Col: Nebraska *HS:* Superior [WI] B: 4/25/1959, Superior, WI
Drafted: 1983 Round 10 SD

		Passing							
Year Team	**G**	**Att**	**Comp**	**Comp%**	**Yds**	**YPA**	**TD**	**Int**	**Rating**
1983 SD	1	5	3	60.0	41	8.20	0	1	46.7
1984 SD	2	0	0	—	0	—	0	0	—
1985 Buf	10	228	113	49.6	1635	7.17	4	14	53.5
1986 SD	2	0	0	—	0	—	0	0	—
1987 Sea	3	76	36	47.4	501	6.59	3	5	54.8
NFL Total	18	309	152	49.2	2177	7.05	7	20	53.0

	Rushing				
Year Team	**Att**	**Yds**	**Avg**	**TD**	**Fum**
1983 SD	1	0	0.0	0	1
1985 Buf	27	231	8.6	1	8
1986 SD	1	-1	-1.0	0	0
1987 Sea	5	15	3.0	0	0
NFL Total	34	245	7.2	1	9

CHARLIE MATHYS Mathys, Charles Peter 5'10", 165 **BB**
Col: Ripon; Indiana *HS:* Green Bay West [WI] B: 6/20/1897, Green Bay, WI D: 1/18/1983, Ashwaubenon, WI
1921 Ham: 5 G; Scor 3, 1 FG. **1922** GB: 10 G; Rec **2** TD; Scor 15, 1 FG. **1923** GB: 10 G; Pass 2 TD; Rush 1 TD; 6 Pt. **1924** GB: 11 G; Rec 2 TD; 12 Pt. **1925** GB: 12 G; Pass 6 TD. **1926** GB: 4 G; Pass 2 TD. **Total:** 52 G; Pass 10 TD; Rush 1 TD; Rec 4 TD; Scor 36, 2 FG; Tot TD 5.

TREVOR MATICH Matich, Trevor Anthony 6'4", 282 **C-OG-OT-TE**
Col: Brigham Young *HS:* Rio Americano [Sacramento, CA]
B: 10/9/1961, Sacramento, CA *Drafted:* 1985 Round 1 NE
1985 NE: 1 G. **1986** NE: 11 G. **1987** NE: 6 G. **1988** NE: 8 G. **1989** Det: 11 G. **1990** NYJ: 16 G. **1991** NYJ: 15 G; Rec 3-23 7.7 1 TD; 6 Pt. **1992** Ind: 16 G. **1993** Ind: 16 G. **1994** Was: 16 G. **1995** Was: 16 G; 1 Fum. **1996** Was: 16 G. **Total:** 148 G; Rec 3-23 7.7 1 TD; 6 Pt; 1 Fum.

TONY MATISI Matisi, Anthony Francis 6'2", 230 **T**
Col: Pittsburgh *HS:* Union Endicott [NY] B: 8/23/1914, New York, NY D: 8/26/1969, Endicott, NY *Drafted:* 1938 Round 2 Pit
1938 Det: 5 G.

JOHN MATISI Matisi, John Bernard 6'2", 218 **T**
Col: Duquesne *HS:* Union Endicott [NY] B: 11/2/1920, New York, NY
Drafted: 1943 Round 7 Bkn
AAFC **1946** BufA: 12 G.

NFL **1943** Bkn: 4 G; Int 1-13.

JOHN MATLOCK Matlock, John James 6'4", 249 **C**
Col: Miami (Fla.) *HS:* St. Edward [Cleveland, OH] B: 10/19/1944, Louisville, KY
1967 NYJ: 10 G. **1968** Cin: 12 G. **1970** Atl: 14 G. **1971** Atl: 12 G; KR 1-4 4.0. **1972** Buf: 11 G. **Total:** 59 G; KR 1-4 4.0.

OLLIE MATSON Matson, Ollie Genoa 6'2", 220 **RB-FL**
Col: San Francisco City Coll. CA (J.C.); San Francisco *HS:* George Washington [San Francisco, CA] B: 5/1/1930, Trinity, TX
Drafted: 1952 Round 1 ChiC *HOF:* 1972
1952 ChiC: Int 2-51; 1 Fum TD. **1954** ChiC: Pass 2-0; Int 1-0. **1955** ChiC: Pass 1-1 100.0%, 43 43.00. **1956** ChiC: Pass 3-0. **1957** ChiC: Pass 5-2 40.0%, 59 11.80. **1958** ChiC: Pass 2-1 50.0%, 4 2.00. **1959** LARm: Pass 1-0, 1 Int. **1962** LARm: Pass 1-1 100.0%, 13 13.00.
Total: Pass 15-5 33.3%, 119 7.93 1 Int; Int 3-51; 1 Fum TD.

		Rushing				Receiving			
Year Team	**G**	**Att**	**Yds**	**Avg**	**TD**	**Rec**	**Yds**	**Avg**	**TD**
1952 ChiC	12	96	344	3.6	3	11	187	17.0	3
1954 ChiC	12	101	506	5.0	4	34	611	18.0	3
1955 ChiC	12	109	475	4.4	1	17	237	13.9	2
1956 ChiC	12	192	924	4.8	5	15	199	13.3	2
1957 ChiC	12	134	577	4.3	6	20	451	22.6	3
1958 ChiC	12	129	505	3.9	5	33	465	14.1	3
1959 LARm	12	161	863	5.4	6	18	130	7.2	0
1960 LARm	12	61	170	2.8	1	15	98	6.5	0
1961 LARm	14	24	181	7.5	2	29	537	18.5	3
1962 LARm	13	3	0	0.0	0	3	49	16.3	1
1963 Det	8	13	20	1.5	0	2	20	10.0	0
1964 Phi	12	96	404	4.2	4	17	242	14.2	1
1965 Phi	14	22	103	4.7	2	2	29	14.5	1
1966 Phi	14	29	101	3.5	1	6	30	5.0	1
NFL Total	171	1170	5173	4.4	40	222	3285	14.8	23

	Punt Returns				Kickoff Returns					Tot
Year Team	**Ret**	**Yds**	**Avg**	**TD**	**Ret**	**Yds**	**Avg**	**TD**	**Fum**	**TD**
1952 ChiC	9	86	9.6	0	20	624	31.2	**2**	8	9
1954 ChiC	11	100	9.1	**1**	17	449	26.4	1	7	9
1955 ChiC	13	**245**	**18.8**	**2**	15	368	24.5	0	7	5
1956 ChiC	5	39	7.8	0	13	362	27.8	**1**	6	8
1957 ChiC	10	54	5.4	0	7	154	22.0	0	6	9
1958 ChiC	0	0	—	0	14	497	**35.5**	**2**	10	10
1959 LARm	14	61	4.4	0	16	367	22.9	0	9	6
1960 LARm	1	0	0.0	0	9	216	24.0	0	3	1
1961 LARm	0	0	—	0	0	0	—	0	0	5
1962 LARm	0	0	—	0	0	0	—	0	0	1
1963 Det	0	0	—	0	3	61	20.3	0	0	0
1964 Phi	2	10	5.0	0	3	104	34.7	0	7	5
1965 Phi	0	0	—	0	0	0	—	0	0	3
1966 Phi	0	0	—	0	26	544	20.9	0	3	2
NFL Total	65	595	9.2	3	143	3746	26.2	**6**	66	73

PAT MATSON Matson, Patrick William 6'1", 245 **OG**
(Lon) *Col:* Oregon *HS:* Lakewood [CO] B: 7/22/1944, Laramie, WY
1966 Den: 14 G. **1967** Den: 14 G. **1968** Cin: 14 G. **1969** Cin: 6 G.
1970 Cin: 14 G. **1971** Cin: 14 G. **1972** Cin: 14 G. **1973** Cin: 14 G.
1974 Cin: 14 G. **1975** GB: 14 G. **Total:** 132 G.

ARCHIE MATSOS Matsos, Emil George 6'0", 217 **LB**
Col: Michigan State *HS:* St. Mary's of Redford [Detroit, MI]
B: 11/22/1934, Detroit, MI *Drafted:* 1958 Round 16 Bal
1960 Buf: PR 1-20 20.0. **Total:** PR 1-20 20.0.

		Interceptions			
Year Team	G	Int	Yds	TD	Fum
1960 Buf	14	8	142	1	0
1961 Buf	14	2	12	0	1
1962 Buf	14	0	0	0	0
1963 Oak	14	4	39	0	0
1964 Oak	14	2	50	0	0
1965 Oak	12	3	52	0	0
1966 Den-SD	13	3	16	0	0
1966 Den	9	2	10	0	0
1966 SD	4	1	6	0	0
NFL Total	95	22	311	1	1

ART MATSU Matsu, Arthur A 5'7", 168 **BB**
(AKA Ichya Matsu) *Col:* William & Mary *HS:* East [Cleveland, OH]
B: 4/30/1904, Glasgow, Scotland D: 5/28/1987, Prescott, AZ
1928 Day: 2 G.

TOM MATTE Matte, Thomas Roland 6'0", 214 **RB-QB**
(Kid) *Col:* Ohio State *HS:* Shaw [East Cleveland, OH] B: 6/14/1939, Pittsburgh, PA *Drafted:* 1961 Round 1 Bal
1962 Bal: Pass 13-5 38.5%, 85 6.54 1 TD. **1963** Bal: Pass 5-1 20.0%, 20 4.00. **1964** Bal: Pass 4-3 75.0%, 58 14.50 1 TD. **1965** Bal: Pass 7-1 14.3%, 19 2.71 1 Int. **1966** Bal: Pass 3-0, 1 Int; PR 1-0. **1967** Bal: Pass 5-1 20.0%, 18 3.60. **1968** Bal: Pass 1-0. **1969** Bal: Pass 3-1 33.3%, 46 15.33. **1971** Bal: Pass 1-0. **Total:** Pass 42-12 28.6%, 246 5.86 2 TD 2 Int; PR 1-0.

		Rushing				Receiving			
Year Team	G	Att	Yds	Avg	TD	Rec	Yds	Avg	TD
1961 Bal	8	13	54	4.2	0	1	8	8.0	0
1962 Bal	14	74	226	3.1	2	8	81	10.1	1
1963 Bal	14	133	541	4.1	4	48	466	9.7	1
1964 Bal	14	42	215	5.1	1	10	169	16.9	0
1965 Bal	14	69	235	3.4	1	12	131	10.9	0
1966 Bal	14	86	381	4.4	0	23	307	13.3	3
1967 Bal	14	147	636	4.3	9	35	496	14.2	3
1968 Bal	14	183	662	3.6	9	25	275	11.0	1
1969 Bal	14	235	909	3.9	**11**	43	513	11.9	2
1970 Bal	2	12	43	3.6	0	1	2	2.0	0
1971 Bal	14	173	607	3.5	8	29	239	8.2	0
1972 Bal	6	33	137	4.2	0	14	182	13.0	1
NFL Total	142	1200	4646	3.9	45	249	2869	11.5	12

	Kickoff Returns					Tot
Year Team	Ret	Yds	Avg	TD	Fum	TD
1961 Bal	2	50	25.0	0	0	0
1962 Bal	27	613	22.7	0	2	3
1963 Bal	16	331	20.7	0	2	5
1964 Bal	3	71	23.7	0	0	1
1965 Bal	8	211	26.4	0	2	1
1966 Bal	3	55	18.3	0	2	3
1967 Bal	1	14	14.0	0	1	12
1968 Bal	1	22	22.0	0	2	10
1969 Bal	0	0	—	0	4	**13**
1971 Bal	1	0	0.0	0	4	8
1972 Bal	0	0	—	0	2	1
NFL Total	62	1367	22.0	0	21	57

FRANK MATTEO Matteo, Francis Pasquale 5'11", 194 **T-G**
Col: Syracuse *HS:* North [Syracuse, NY] B: 4/2/1896, Syracuse, NY
D: 12/19/1983, Oneida, NY
1922 Roch: 4 G. **1923** Roch: 4 G. **1924** Roch: 5 G. **1925** Roch: 4 G.
Total: 17 G.

JOE MATTERN Mattern, Joseph Peter 155 **BB-TB**
Col: Minnesota; Lehigh B: 9/9/1892 Deceased
1920 Cle: 1 G. **1922** Min: 1 G. **Total:** 2 G.

RON MATTES Mattes, Ronald Anthony 6'6", 309 **OT**
Col: Virginia *HS:* North Schuylkill [Ashland, PA] B: 8/8/1963, Shenandoah, PA *Drafted:* 1985 Round 7 Sea
1986 Sea: 16 G. **1987** Sea: 12 G. **1988** Sea: 16 G. **1989** Sea: 16 G.
1990 Sea: 15 G. **1991** ChiB: 15 G. **1992** Ind: 5 G. **Total:** 95 G.

ALLAMA MATTHEWS Matthews, Allama 6'3", 230 **TE-RB**
Col: Vanderbilt *HS:* Andrew Jackson [Jacksonville, FL] B: 8/24/1961, Jacksonville, FL *Drafted:* 1983 Round 12 Atl
1983 Atl: 16 G; Rec 3-37 12.3. **1984** Atl: 6 G; Rec 1-7 7.0; KR 1-3 3.0.
1985 Atl: 15 G; Rec 7-57 8.1 1 TD; KR 1-11 11.0; 6 Pt. **Total:** 37 G; Rec 11-101 9.2 1 TD; KR 2-14 7.0; 6 Pt.

AL MATTHEWS Matthews, Alvin Leon 5'11", 190 **DB**
Col: Texas A&M–Kingsville *HS:* Stephen F. Austin [Austin, TX]
B: 11/7/1947, Austin, TX *Drafted:* 1970 Round 2 GB

		Interceptions		
Year Team	G	Int	Yds	TD
1970 GB	14	0	0	0
1971 GB	14	1	20	0
1972 GB	14	2	8	0
1973 GB	14	2	58	1
1974 GB	14	3	41	0
1975 GB	14	2	42	0
1976 Sea	14	3	60	1
1977 SF	1	0	0	0
NFL Total	99	13	229	2

AUBREY MATTHEWS Matthews, Aubrey Derron 5'7", 165 **WR**
Col: Mississippi Gulf Coast CC; Delta State *HS:* Moss Point [MS]
B: 9/15/1962, Pascagoula, MS
1986 Atl: Rush 1-12 12.0; KR 3-42 14.0. **1987** Atl: Rush 1-(-4) -4.0.
1988 Atl-GB: Rush 3-3 1.0; PR 6-26 4.3. Atl: PR 6-26 4.3. GB: Rush 3-3 1.0. **1993** Det: Rush 2-7 3.5. **1996** Det: KR 1-10 10.0. **Total:** Rush 7-18 2.6; PR 6-26 4.3; KR 4-52 13.0.

		Receiving				
Year Team	G	Rec	Yds	Avg	TD	Fum
1986 Atl	4	1	25	25.0	0	0
1987 Atl	12	32	537	16.8	3	2
1988 Atl-GB	11	20	231	11.6	2	2
1988 Atl	4	5	64	12.8	0	2
1988 GB	7	15	167	11.1	2	0
1989 GB	13	18	200	11.1	0	0
1990 Det	13	30	349	11.6	1	2
1991 Det	1	3	21	7.0	0	0
1992 Det	13	9	137	15.2	0	0
1993 Det	14	11	171	15.5	0	0
1994 Det	14	29	359	12.4	3	1
1995 Det	11	4	41	10.3	0	0
1996 Det	16	3	41	13.7	0	0
NFL Total	122	160	2112	13.2	9	7

BRUCE MATTHEWS Matthews, Bruce Rankin 6'5", 289 **C-OT-OG**
Col: USC *HS:* Arcadia [CA] B: 8/8/1961, Raleigh, NC *Drafted:* 1983 Round 1 Hou
1983 Hou: 16 G. **1984** Hou: 16 G. **1985** Hou: 16 G. **1986** Hou: 16 G.
1987 Hou: 8 G. **1988** Hou: 16 G. **1989** Hou: 16 G; 2 Fum. **1990** Hou: 16 G.
1991 Hou: 16 G; 1 Fum. **1992** Hou: 16 G. **1993** Hou: 16 G. **1994** Hou: 16 G; 2 Fum. **1995** Hou: 16 G. **1996** Hou: 16 G. **1997** Ten: 16 G. **1998** Ten: 16 G. **Total:** 248 G; 5 Fum.

IRA MATTHEWS Matthews, Ira Richard III 5'8", 175 **RB-WR**
Col: Wisconsin *HS:* Rockford East [IL] B: 8/23/1957, Rockford, IL
Drafted: 1979 Round 6 Oak
1979 Oak: Rush 2-3 1.5. **1980** Oak: Rush 5-11 2.2; Rec 3-33 11.0.
Total: Rush 7-14 2.0; Rec 3-33 11.0.

		Punt Returns				Kickoff Returns				
Year Team	G	Ret	Yds	Avg	TD	Ret	Yds	Avg	TD	Fum
1979 Oak	16	32	165	5.2	0	35	873	24.9	**1**	4
1980 Oak	16	48	421	8.8	0	29	585	20.2	0	7
1981 Oak	5	15	92	6.1	0	7	144	20.6	0	5
NFL Total	37	95	678	7.1	0	71	1602	22.6	1	16

HENRY MATTHEWS Matthews, John Henry Jr. 6'3", 203 **RB**
Col: Michigan State *HS:* South [Akron, OH] B: 3/17/1949, Akron, OH
1972 NE: 3 G; KR 3-74 24.7. **1973** NO-Atl: 9 G; Rush 4-4 1.0; Rec 2-19 9.5. NO: 6 G; Rush 4-4 1.0; Rec 2-19 9.5. Atl: 3 G. **Total:** 12 G; Rush 4-4 1.0; Rec 2-19 9.5; KR 3-74 24.7.

SHANE MATTHEWS Matthews, Michael Shane 6'3", 196 **QB**
Col: William Rainey Harper Coll. IL (J.C.); Florida *HS:* Pascagoula [MS]
B: 6/1/1970, Pascagoula, MS
1996 ChiB: 2 G; Pass 17-13 76.5%, 158 9.29 1 TD; Rush 1-2 2.0 1 TD; 6 Pt.

STEVE MATTHEWS Matthews, Stephen Keith 6'3", 222 **QB**
Col: William Rainey Harper Coll. IL (J.C.); Tennessee; Memphis
HS: Tullahoma [TN] B: 10/13/1970, Tullahoma, TN *Drafted:* 1994 Round 7 KC
1997 Jac: 2 G; Pass 40-26 65.0%, 275 6.88; Rush 1-10 10.0; 1 Fum.
1998 Ten: 1 G; Pass 3-2 66.7%, 24 8.00. **Total:** 3 G; Pass 43-28 65.1%, 299 6.95; Rush 1-10 10.0; 1 Fum.

WES MATTHEWS Matthews, Wesley Carroll 5'10", 180 **WR**
Col: Oklahoma State; Northeastern State (Okla.) *HS:* Muskogee [OK]
B: 10/10/1943, San Antonio, TX
1966 Mia: 4 G; Rec 1-20 20.0; PR 4-38 9.5; KR 5-109 21.8; 1 Fum.

CLAY MATTHEWS Matthews, William Clay Jr. 6'2", 238 **LB**
Col: USC *HS:* Arcadia [CA]; New Trier East HS [Wilmette IL]
B: 3/15/1956, Palo Alto, CA *Drafted:* 1978 Round 1 Cle
1983 Cle: 6 Sac. **1984** Cle: 12 Sac. **1985** Cle: 6 Sac. **1986** Cle: 1 Sac. **1987** Cle: 2.5 Sac. **1988** Cle: 6 Sac. **1989** Cle: 1 Fum TD; 4 Sac. **1990** Cle: 3.5 Sac. **1991** Cle: 6.5 Sac. **1992** Cle: 9 Sac. **1993** Cle: 5.5 Sac. **1994** Atl: 1 Sac. **1996** Atl: 6.5 Sac. **Total:** 1 Fum TD; 69.5 Sac.

		Interceptions				Tot
Year Team	**G**	**Int**	**Yds**	**TD**	**Fum**	**TD**
1978 Cle	15	1	5	0	0	0
1979 Cle	16	1	30	0	0	0
1980 Cle	14	1	6	0	0	0
1981 Cle	16	2	14	0	0	0
1982 Cle	2	0	0	0	0	0
1983 Cle	16	0	0	0	0	0
1984 Cle	16	0	0	0	0	0
1985 Cle	14	0	0	0	0	0
1986 Cle	16	2	12	0	0	0
1987 Cle	12	3	62	1	0	1
1988 Cle	16	0	0	0	0	0
1989 Cle	16	1	25	0	1	1
1990 Cle	16	0	0	0	0	0
1991 Cle	15	1	35	0	0	0
1992 Cle	16	1	6	0	0	0
1993 Cle	16	1	10	0	0	0
1994 Atl	15	0	0	0	0	0
1995 Atl	16	2	1	0	0	0
1996 Atl	15	0	0	0	0	0
NFL Total	278	16	206	1	1	2

CLAY MATTHEWS Matthews, William Clay Sr. 6'3", 219 **DE-DT**
Col: Georgia Tech *HS:* Charleston [SC] B: 8/1/1928, Charleston, SC
Drafted: 1949 Round 25 LARm
1950 SF: 12 G; KR 1-10 10.0. **1953** SF: 9 G. **1954** SF: 12 G. **1955** SF: 12 G; Int 1-19. **Total:** 45 G; KR 1-10 10.0; Int 1-19.

BILL MATTHEWS Matthews, William Marvin 6'2", 235 **LB**
Col: South Dakota State *HS:* Wessington [SD] B: 3/12/1956, Santa Monica, CA *Drafted:* 1978 Round 5 NE
1979 NE: 16 G. **1980** NE: 16 G; Int 1-5. **1981** NE: 16 G; KR 1-5 5.0.
Total: 48 G; KR 1-5 5.0; Int 1-5.

BO MATTHEWS Matthews, William Pierce 6'4", 230 **RB**
Col: Colorado *HS:* S.R. Butler [Huntsville, AL] B: 11/15/1951, Huntsville, AL *Drafted:* 1974 Round 1 SD
1976 SD: KR 1-19 19.0; **1** Fum TD. **1979** SD: KR 1-4 4.0. **Total:** KR 2-23 11.5; 1 Fum TD.

		Rushing				Receiving					Tot
Year Team	**G**	**Att**	**Yds**	**Avg**	**TD**	**Rec**	**Yds**	**Avg**	**TD**	**Fum**	**TD**
1974 SD	14	95	328	3.5	4	12	90	7.5	0	2	4
1975 SD	13	71	254	3.6	3	9	59	6.6	0	6	3
1976 SD	12	46	199	4.3	3	12	81	6.8	0	3	4
1977 SD	12	43	193	4.5	0	3	41	13.7	0	0	0
1978 SD	11	71	286	4.0	0	11	78	7.1	0	5	0
1979 SD	16	30	112	3.7	1	7	40	5.7	0	1	1
1980 NYG	15	64	180	2.8	0	19	86	4.5	0	2	0
1981 NYG-Mia	8	4	14	3.5	0	2	13	6.5	0	0	0
1981 NYG	5	4	14	3.5	0	2	13	6.5	0	0	0
1981 Mia	3	0	0	—	0	0	0	—	0	0	0
NFL Total	101	424	1566	3.7	11	75	488	6.5	0	19	12

FRANK MATTIACE Mattiace, Frank Louis 6'1", 264 **DE-NT**
Col: Holy Cross *HS:* Montville [NJ] B: 1/20/1961, Patterson, NJ
1987 Ind: 3 G; 1 Sac.

JACK MATTIFORD Mattiford, John Blaker 5'10", 216 **G**
Col: Marshall *HS:* Clarksburg [WV] B: 6/24/1916, Peora, WV
D: 4/6/1960, Guilford, CT
1941 Det: 10 G; Rec 1-21 21.0.

FRAN MATTINGLY Mattingly, Francis Edward 5'11", 212 **G-LB**
(Sax) *Col:* Texas A&M B: 12/4/1919 D: 9/1988, Sand Springs, OK
AAFC **1947** ChiA: 1 G; Int 1-1.

FRANK MATTIOLI Mattioli, Francis A 6'0", 210 **G-LB**
Col: Pittsburgh B: 2/20/1921 D: 6/17/1993, Vincentown, NJ
Drafted: 1945 Round 12 ChiB
1946 Pit: 11 G.

HARRY MATTOS Mattos, Harry N 6'0", 198 **TB-DB**
(The Horse; The Toe) *Col:* St. Mary's (Cal.) *HS:* Castlemont [Oakland, CA] B: 4/7/1911, Oakland, CA D: 2/5/1992, San Jose, CA
1936 GB: Pass 12-4 33.3%, 32 2.67 2 Int. **1937** Cle: Pass 22-5 22.7%, 94 4.27 1 TD 4 Int; Scor 8, 2 XK. **Total:** Pass 34-9 26.5%, 126 3.71 1 TD 6 Int.

		Rushing			
Year Team	**G**	**Att**	**Yds**	**Avg**	**TD**
1936 GB	2	1	2	2.0	0
1937 Cle	6	26	16	0.6	1
NFL Total	8	27	18	0.7	1

JACK MATTOX Mattox, John V 6'4", 240 **DT**
Col: Fresno State *HS:* Clovis [CA] B: 8/3/1938, Fresno, CA
1961 Den: 8 G.

MARV MATTOX Mattox, Marvin Bruce 5'9", 170 **BB-G**
(Monk) *Col:* Washington & Lee *HS:* Fishburne Mil. Acad. [Waynesboro, VA] B: 2/11/1900, Leesville, VA D: 2/5/1996, Salisbury, NC
1923 Mil: 5 G.

RILEY MATTSON Mattson, Riley Carl 6'4", 248 **OT**
Col: Oregon *HS:* U.S. Grant [Portland, OR] B: 12/18/1938, Portland, OR *Drafted:* 1961 Round 11 Was
1961 Was: 14 G. **1962** Was: 14 G. **1963** Was: 14 G. **1964** Was: 14 G; KR 3-30 10.0; 2 Fum. **1966** ChiB: 12 G. **Total:** 68 G; KR 3-30 10.0; 2 Fum.

JOHN MATUSZAK Matuszak, John Daniel 6'8", 282 **DE-DT**
(Tooz) *Col:* Iowa Central CC; Missouri; Tampa *HS:* Oak Creek [WI]
B: 10/25/1950, Milwaukee, WI D: 6/17/1989 *Drafted:* 1973 Round 1 Hou
1973 Hou: 14 G. **1974** KC: 8 G. **1975** KC: 14 G; **1** Fum TD; 6 Pt.
1976 Oak: 13 G. **1977** Oak: 14 G. **1978** Oak: 16 G. **1979** Oak: 12 G.
1980 Oak: 16 G. **1981** Oak: 16 G. **Total:** 123 G; 1 Fum TD; 6 Pt.

MARV MATUSZAK Matuszak, Marvin H 6'3", 232 **LB-OG**
Col: Tulsa *HS:* Michael Washington [South Bend, IN] B: 9/12/1931, South Bend, IN *Drafted:* 1953 Round 3 Pit
1955 Pit: KR 1-0. **1956** Pit: KR 1-5 5.0. **1961** Bal: KR 1-14 14.0. **1963** Buf: KR 1-0. **Total:** KR 4-19 4.8.

		Interceptions			
Year Team	**G**	**Int**	**Yds**	**TD**	**Fum**
1953 Pit	12	1	0	0	0
1955 Pit	4	1	7	0	1
1956 Pit	9	2	28	0	1
1957 SF	12	0	0	0	0
1958 SF-GB	7	1	0	0	0
1958 SF	4	1	0	0	0
1958 GB	3	0	0	0	0
1959 Bal	11	1	23	0	0
1960 Bal	12	0	0	0	0
1961 Bal	14	0	0	0	0
1962 Buf	14	6	46	0	0
1963 Buf	14	0	0	0	0
1964 Den	14	2	16	0	0
NFL Total	123	14	120	0	2

AL MATUZA Matuza, Albert Charles 6'2", 200 **C-LB**
Col: Georgetown *HS:* Shenandoah [PA]; Staunton Mil. Acad. [VA]
B: 9/11/1918, Shenandoah, PA *Drafted:* 1941 Round 10 ChiB
1941 ChiB: 10 G; Int 2-9. **1942** ChiB: 11 G; Int 2-8. **1943** ChiB: 10 G.
Total: 31 G; Int 4-17.

CARL MAUCK Mauck, Carl Frey 6'4", 243 **C**
Col: Southern Illinois *HS:* McLeansboro [IL] B: 7/7/1947, McLeansboro, IL *Drafted:* 1969 Round 13 Bal
1969 Bal: 4 G. **1970** Mia: 3 G. **1971** SD: 13 G. **1972** SD: 14 G; **1** Fum TD; 6 Pt; 2 Fum. **1973** SD: 14 G. **1974** SD: 14 G. **1975** Hou: 14 G. **1976** Hou: 14 G; 1 Fum. **1977** Hou: 14 G. **1978** Hou: 16 G. **1979** Hou: 16 G.
1980 Hou: 16 G. **1981** Hou: 14 G. **Total:** 166 G; 1 Fum TD; 6 Pt; 3 Fum.

TUFFY MAUL Maul, Elmo Alvin 5'11", 200 **FB**
Col: St. Mary's (Cal.) B: 6/20/1902 D: 3/16/1974, Fresno, CA
1926 LA: 10 G; Pass 1 TD; Rush 2 TD; Scor 21, 2 FG, 3 XK.

STAN MAULDIN Mauldin, Stanley Hubert 6'2", 225 **T**
Col: Texas *HS:* Amarillo [TX] B: 12/27/1920, Amarillo, TX
D: 9/25/1948, Chicago, IL *Drafted:* 1943 Round 7 ChiC
1946 ChiC: 6 G; KR 1-16 16.0. **1947** ChiC: 12 G; Int 1-11. **1948** ChiC: 1 G. **Total:** 19 G; KR 1-16 16.0; Int 1-11.

CHRIS MAUMALANGA Maumalanga, Christian Netane 6'2", 288 **DT**
Col: Kansas *HS:* Bishop Montgomery [Redondo Beach, CA]
B: 12/15/1971, Redwood City, CA *Drafted:* 1994 Round 4 NYG
1994 NYG: 7 G. **1995** Ariz: 6 G. **1996** Ariz: 1 G. **Total:** 14 G.

ANDY MAURER Maurer, Andrew Lee 6′3″, 265 **OG-OT**
Col: Oregon *HS:* Prospect [OR] B: 9/30/1948, Silverton, OR
Drafted: 1970 Round 3 Atl
1970 Atl: 14 G. **1971** Atl: 14 G. **1972** Atl: 14 G. **1973** Atl: 14 G. **1974** NO-Min: 12 G. NO: 4 G. Min: 8 G. **1975** Min: 14 G. **1976** SF: 13 G. **1977** Den: 13 G. **Total:** 108 G.

RICH MAUTI Mauti, Richard Dominic 6′0″, 190 **WR**
Col: Nassau CC NY; Penn State *HS:* East Meadow [NY] B: 5/25/1954, Queens, NY
1977 NO: Rec 4-71 17.8. **1978** NO: Rec 8-69 8.6 2 TD. **1979** NO: Rec 2-64 32.0. **1980** NO: Rush 1-2 2.0; Rec 1-10 10.0. **1982** NO: Rec 4-70 17.5. **1983** NO: Rec 2-30 15.0. **Total:** Rush 1-2 2.0; Rec 21-314 15.0 2 TD.

		Punt Returns				Kickoff Returns				
Year Team	**G**	**Ret**	**Yds**	**Avg**	**TD**	**Ret**	**Yds**	**Avg**	**TD**	**Fum**
1977 NO	14	37	281	7.6	0	27	609	22.6	0	2
1978 NO	16	0	0	—	0	17	388	22.8	0	0
1979 NO	15	27	218	8.1	0	36	801	22.3	0	3
1980 NO	9	11	111	10.1	0	31	798	25.7	0	0
1982 NO	9	0	0	—	0	5	93	18.6	0	0
1983 NO	16	0	0	—	0	8	147	18.4	0	0
1984 Was	16	1	2	2.0	0	1	16	16.0	0	0
NFL Total	95	76	612	8.1	0	125	2852	22.8	0	5

EARL MAVES Maves, Earl Clifford 5′9″, 180 **WB-DB**
(Steamer) *Col:* Michigan; Wisconsin *HS:* Stanley [WI] B: 4/8/1923, Ladysmith, WI D: 3/1952, Korea *Drafted:* 1947 Round 26 Det
1948 Det: 1 G.

MENIL MAVRAIDES Mavraides, Menil 6′1″, 235 **OG**
(Minnie) *Col:* Notre Dame *HS:* Lowell [MA] B: 11/17/1931, Lowell, MA
1954 Phi: 12 G. **1957** Phi: 12 G. **Total:** 24 G.

KEVIN MAWAE Mawae, Kevin James 6′4″, 299 **OG**
Col: Louisiana State *HS:* Leesville [LA] B: 1/23/1971, Savannah, GA
Drafted: 1994 Round 2 Sea
1994 Sea: 14 G. **1995** Sea: 16 G. **1996** Sea: 16 G. **1997** Sea: 16 G. **1998** NYJ: 16 G. **Total:** 78 G.

CURTIS MAXEY Maxey, Curtis Wilson 6′3″, 298 **DE-DT**
Col: Grambling State *HS:* Broad Ripple [Indianapolis, IN]
B: 6/28/1965, Indianapolis, IN *Drafted:* 1988 Round 8 Cin
1988 Cin: 3 G. **1989** Atl: 2 G. **Total:** 5 G.

BRETT MAXIE Maxie, Brett Derrell 6′2″, 194 **DB**
Col: Texas Southern *HS:* James Madison [Dallas, TX] B: 1/13/1962, Dallas, TX
1987 NO: PR 1-12 12.0; Scor **1** Saf; 2 Sac. **1992** NO: 1 Sac. **1997** SF: 1 Sac. **Total:** PR 1-12 12.0; Scor 1 Saf; 4 Sac.

		Interceptions		
Year Team	**G**	**Int**	**Yds**	**TD**
1985 NO	16	0	0	0
1986 NO	15	2	15	0
1987 NO	12	3	17	0
1988 NO	16	0	0	0
1989 NO	16	3	41	1
1990 NO	16	2	88	1
1991 NO	16	3	33	1
1992 NO	10	2	12	0
1993 NO	1	0	0	0
1994 Atl	4	0	0	0
1995 Car	16	6	59	0
1996 Car	13	1	35	0
1997 SF	2	1	0	0
NFL Total	153	23	300	3

ALVIN MAXSON Maxson, Alvin Earl 5′11″, 205 **RB**
Col: Southern Methodist *HS:* Hebert [Beaumont, TX] B: 11/12/1951, Beaumont, TX *Drafted:* 1974 Round 8 NO

		Rushing				Receiving			
Year Team	**G**	**Att**	**Yds**	**Avg**	**TD**	**Rec**	**Yds**	**Avg**	**TD**
1974 NO	14	165	714	4.3	2	42	294	7.0	1
1975 NO	13	139	371	2.7	3	41	234	5.7	0
1976 NO	14	34	120	3.5	1	7	21	3.0	0
1977 Pit	7	18	56	3.1	0	5	70	14.0	0
1978 ChiB-Pit-TB-Hou-NYG	8	4	9	2.3	0	0	0	—	0
1978 Pit	5	4	9	2.3	0	0	0	—	0
1978 TB	1	0	0	—	0	0	0	—	0
1978 Hou	1	0	0	—	0	0	0	—	0
1978 NYG	1	0	0	—	0	0	0	—	0
NFL Total	56	360	1270	3.5	6	95	619	6.5	1

	Kickoff Returns					Tot
Year Team	**Ret**	**Yds**	**Avg**	**TD**	**Fum**	**TD**
1974 NO	0	0	—	0	4	3
1975 NO	6	103	17.2	0	4	3
1976 NO	11	191	17.4	0	3	1
1977 Pit	5	120	24.0	0	1	0
1978 ChiB-Pit-TB-Hou-NYG	3	50	16.7	0	2	0
1978 Pit	2	33	16.5	0	2	0
1978 TB	1	17	17.0	0	0	0
NFL Total	25	464	18.6	0	14	7

BRUCE MAXWELL Maxwell, Donald Bruce 6′1″, 220 **RB**
Col: Arkansas *HS:* Pine Bluff [AR] B: 3/23/1947, Crossett, AR
Drafted: 1970 Round 10 Det
1970 Det: 11 G; Rush 1-9 9.0; KR 1-20 20.0.

JOEY MAXWELL Maxwell, Joseph William 6′2″, 197 **C-E**
Col: Notre Dame *HS:* Central Catholic [Philadelphia, PA] B: 11/5/1904, Cincinnati, OH D: 2/21/1983, Ardsley, PA
1927 Fra: 18 G. **1928** Fra: 8 G. **1929** Fra: 12 G. **Total:** 38 G.

TOMMY MAXWELL Maxwell, Thomas Marshall Jr. 6′2″, 195 **DB**
Col: Texas A&M *HS:* Jesse H. Jones [Houston, TX] B: 5/5/1947, Houston, TX *Drafted:* 1969 Round 2 Bal
1969 Bal: 13 G; Int 3-37. **1970** Bal: 14 G; Int 0-9. **1971** Oak: 13 G; PR 6-21 3.5; 2 Fum. **1972** Oak: 7 G; PR 2-12 6.0; KR 1-26 26.0. **1973** Oak: 8 G; PR 4-8 2.0; 2 Fum. **1974** Hou: 13 G; Int 2-30. **Total:** 68 G; PR 12-41 3.4; KR 1-26 26.0; Int 5-76; 4 Fum.

VERNON MAXWELL Maxwell, Vernon Leroy 6′2″, 233 **LB**
Col: Arizona State *HS:* Verbum Dei [Los Angeles, CA] B: 10/25/1961, Birmingham, AL *Drafted:* 1983 Round 2 Bal
1983 Bal: 16 G; Int 1-31; 11 Sac. **1984** Ind: 16 G; 8.5 Sac. **1985** Det: 9 G. **1986** Det: 15 G; 2 Sac. **1987** Det: 12 G. **1989** Sea: 9 G. **Total:** 77 G; Int 1-31; 21.5 Sac.

ART MAY May, Arthur Lee 6′3″, 255 **DE**
(Pop) *Col:* Tuskegee *HS:* Abrams [Bessemer, AL] B: 11/16/1948, Bessemer, AL *Drafted:* 1971 Round 5 Cin
1971 NE: 11 G.

DEEMS MAY May, Bert Deems Jr. 6′4″, 263 **TE**
Col: North Carolina *HS:* Lexington [NC] B: 3/6/1969, Lexington, NC
Drafted: 1992 Round 7 SD
1997 Sea: KR 1-8 8.0. **Total:** KR 1-8 8.0.

		Receiving			
Year Team	**G**	**Rec**	**Yds**	**Avg**	**TD**
1992 SD	16	0	0	—	0
1993 SD	15	0	0	—	0
1994 SD	5	2	22	11.0	0
1995 SD	5	0	0	—	0
1996 SD	16	19	188	9.9	0
1997 Sea	16	2	21	10.5	0
1998 Sea	16	3	7	2.3	1
NFL Total	89	26	238	9.2	1

DEAN MAY May, Dean Curtis 6′5″, 220 **QB**
Col: Louisville *HS:* Trinity [Louisville, KY]; Chamberlain HS [Tampa, FL]
B: 5/26/1962, Orlando, FL *Drafted:* 1984 Round 5 Mia
1984 Phi: 2 G; Pass 1-1 100.0%, 33 33.00. **1987** Den: 3 G; Pass 5-0, 1 Int; Rush 2-(-4) -2.0. **Total:** 5 G; Pass 6-1 16.7%, 33 5.50 1 Int; Rush 2-(-4) -2.0.

JACK MAY May, Francis John 5′10″, 210 **C-LB**
Col: Centenary *HS:* Harrisburg [AR] B: 4/6/1915
1938 Cle: 9 G.

MARC MAY May, Marc Edward 6′4″, 230 **TE**
Col: Purdue B: 1/1/1958, Chicago, IL
1987 Min: 3 G; Rec 1-22 22.0; 1 Fum.

MARK MAY May, Mark Eric 6′6″, 295 **OT-OG-C**
Col: Pittsburgh *HS:* Oneonta [NY] B: 11/2/1959, Oneonta, NY
Drafted: 1981 Round 1 Was
1981 Was: 16 G. **1982** Was: 9 G. **1983** Was: 15 G. **1984** Was: 16 G. **1985** Was: 16 G. **1986** Was: 16 G. **1987** Was: 10 G. **1988** Was: 16 G. **1989** Was: 9 G. **1991** SD: 9 G. **1992** Pho: 16 G. **1993** Pho: 11 G. **Total:** 159 G.

RAY MAY May, Reginald Raymond 6′1″, 230 **LB**
Col: Los Angeles City Coll. CA (J.C.); USC *HS:* Los Angeles [CA]
B: 6/4/1945, Los Angeles, CA *Drafted:* 1967 Round 4 Pit
1967 Pit: KR 1-0. **Total:** KR 1-0.

		Interceptions			
Year Team	**G**	**Int**	**Yds**	**TD**	**Fum**
1967 Pit	14	0	0	0	0
1968 Pit	12	3	31	1	0
1969 Pit	14	2	4	0	0
1970 Bal	14	1	18	0	0
1971 Bal	14	1	46	0	0
1972 Bal	14	2	43	0	0
1973 Bal-Den	14	1	1	0	0
1973 Bal	3	0	0	0	0

1973 Den	11	1	1	0	0
1974 Den	14	2	40	0	0
1975 Den	8	1	0	0	1
NFL Total	118	13	183	1	1

SHERRIDEN MAY May, Sherriden Allen 6′0″, 220 **RB**
Col: Idaho *HS:* Spanaway Lake [Spanaway, WA] B: 8/10/1973, Tacoma, WA
1995 NYJ: 5 G; Rush 2-5 2.5. **1996** NYJ: 8 G. **Total:** 13 G; Rush 2-5 2.5.

WALT MAY May, Walter 0 6′1″, 205 **G**
(Red) *Col:* No College *HS:* Taylorville [IL] B: 2/27/1894, Taylorville, IL D: 8/11/1934, Peoria, IL
1920 Sta: 4 G.

BILL MAY May, William 5′11″, 188 **BB-LB**
Col: Louisiana State *HS:* El Dorado [AR] B: 2/4/1913
1937 ChiC: 9 G; Rush 4-16 4.0; Scor 10, 2 FG, 4 XK. **1938** ChiC: 1 G; Rec 1-16 16.0; Scor 0-1 FG, 0-2 XK. **Total:** 10 G; Rush 4-16 4.0; Rec 1-16 16.0; Scor 10, 2-1 FG, 4-2 XK.

DOUG MAYBERRY Mayberry, Douglas Clark 6′1″, 220 **FB**
(Horse) *Col:* Yuba Coll. CA (J.C.); California; Utah State *HS:* Colusa [CA] B: 3/23/1937, Arbuckle, CA *Drafted:* 1961 Round 10 Min
1961 Min: Rec 2-18 9.0. **1962** Min: Rec 11-100 9.1 1 TD.
Total: Rec 13-118 9.1 1 TD.

		Rushing					Tot
Year Team	**G**	**Att**	**Yds**	**Avg**	**TD**	**Fum**	**TD**
1961 Min	4	13	40	3.1	0	0	0
1962 Min	13	74	274	3.7	1	5	2
1963 Oak	2	0	0	—	0	0	0
NFL Total	19	87	314	3.6	1	5	2

TONY MAYBERRY Mayberry, Eino Anthony 6′4″, 293 **C**
Col: Wake Forest *HS:* Hayfield [Alexandria, VA] B: 12/8/1967, Wurzburg, Germany *Drafted:* 1990 Round 4 TB
1990 TB: 16 G. **1991** TB: 16 G; 3 Fum. **1992** TB: 16 G. **1993** TB: 16 G; 1 Fum. **1994** TB: 16 G. **1995** TB: 16 G. **1996** TB: 16 G. **1997** TB: 16 G. **1998** TB: 16 G. **Total:** 144 G; 4 Fum.

JAMES MAYBERRY Mayberry, James Loyd 5′11″, 210 **RB**
Col: Colorado *HS:* Tascosa [Amarillo, TX] B: 11/5/1957, Amarillo, TX *Drafted:* 1979 Round 3 Atl
1979 Atl: Rec 7-48 6.9; KR 4-49 12.3; Int 1-6 1 TD. **1980** Atl: Rec 3-1 0.3. **1981** Atl: Rec 3-4 1.3; KR 2-23 11.5. **Total:** Rec 13-53 4.1; KR 6-72 12.0; Int 1-6 1 TD.

		Rushing					Tot
Year Team	**G**	**Att**	**Yds**	**Avg**	**TD**	**Fum**	**TD**
1979 Atl	16	45	193	4.3	1	1	2
1980 Atl	16	18	88	4.9	0	0	0
1981 Atl	16	18	66	3.7	0	1	0
NFL Total	48	81	347	4.3	1	2	2

JERMANE MAYBERRY Mayberry, Jermane Timothy 6′4″, 325 **OT-OG**
Col: Texas A&M–Kingsville *HS:* Floresville [TX] B: 8/29/1973, Floresville, TX *Drafted:* 1996 Round 1 Phi
1996 Phi: 3 G. **1997** Phi: 16 G. **1998** Phi: 15 G. **Total:** 34 G.

EMIL MAYER Mayer, Emil Leroy 6′0″, 190 **OE-T**
(Puss) *Col:* Bethany (W.V.); Catholic *HS:* East Liverpool [OH] B: East Liverpool, OH Deceased
1927 Pott: 1 G. **1930** Port: 10 G. **Total:** 11 G.

FRANK MAYER Mayer, Francis George 5′11″, 215 **G-T**
Col: Iowa State; Notre Dame *HS:* Glencoe [MN] B: 6/18/1902, Glencoe, MN D: 3/1960
1927 GB: 10 G.

ALONZO MAYES Mayes, Alonzo Lewis Jr. 6′4″, 259 **TE**
Col: Rose State Coll. OK (J.C.); Oklahoma State *HS:* Frederick Douglass [Oklahoma City, OK] B: 6/4/1975, Oklahoma City, OK *Drafted:* 1998 Round 4 ChiB
1998 ChiB: 16 G; Rec 21-217 10.3; 2 Fum.

TONY MAYES Mayes, Anthony Curtis 6′0″, 200 **DB**
Col: Kentucky *HS:* Paintsville [KY] B: 5/19/1964, Tazewell, TN
1987 StL: 3 G.

BEN MAYES Mayes, Benjamin Clayton 6′5″, 265 **DE-DT**
Col: Duke *HS:* Gibbs [St. Petersburg, FL] B: 3/16/1945, St. Petersburg, FL *Drafted:* 1969 Round 5 Buf
1969 Hou: 5 G.

CARL MAYES Mayes, Carlton Hazen 6′0″, 190 **HB**
Col: Texas *HS:* Pampa [TX] B: 3/31/1930, Austin, TX
1952 LARm: 7 G; Rush 5-2 0.4.

DERRICK MAYES Mayes, Derrick Binet 6′0″, 205 **WR**
(A-Mayes-ing) *Col:* Notre Dame *HS:* North Central [Indianapolis, IN] B: 1/28/1974, Indianapolis, IN *Drafted:* 1996 Round 2 GB
1997 GB: PR 14-141 10.1. **1998** GB: PR 1-9 9.0. **Total:** PR 15-150 10.0.

		Receiving				
Year Team	**G**	**Rec**	**Yds**	**Avg**	**TD**	**Fum**
1996 GB	7	6	46	7.7	2	0
1997 GB	12	18	290	16.1	0	0
1998 GB	10	30	394	13.1	3	1
NFL Total	29	54	730	13.5	5	1

MICHAEL MAYES Mayes, Michael Oneal 5′10″, 182 **DB**
Col: Louisiana State *HS:* DeRidder [LA] B: 8/17/1966, DeRidder, LA *Drafted:* 1989 Round 4 NO
1989 NO: 2 G. **1990** NYJ: 16 G; Int 1-0. **1991** Min: 9 G; 1 Sac. **Total:** 27 G; Int 1-0; 1 Sac.

RUEBEN MAYES Mayes, Rueben A 5′11″, 201 **RB**
Col: Washington State *HS:* Comprehensive Secondary School [North Battlefield, Canada] B: 6/6/1963, North Battleford, Canada *Drafted:* 1986 Round 3 NO

		Rushing				Receiving			
Year Team	**G**	**Att**	**Yds**	**Avg**	**TD**	**Rec**	**Yds**	**Avg**	**TD**
1986 NO	16	286	1353	4.7	8	17	96	5.6	0
1987 NO	12	243	917	3.8	5	15	68	4.5	0
1988 NO	16	170	628	3.7	3	11	103	9.4	0
1990 NO	15	138	510	3.7	7	12	121	10.1	0
1992 Sea	16	28	74	2.6	0	2	13	6.5	0
1993 Sea	1	1	2	2.0	0	0	0	—	0
NFL Total	76	866	3484	4.0	23	57	401	7.0	0

	Kickoff Returns				
Year Team	**Ret**	**Yds**	**Avg**	**TD**	**Fum**
1986 NO	10	213	21.3	0	4
1987 NO	0	0	—	0	8
1988 NO	7	132	18.9	0	1
1990 NO	2	39	19.5	0	1
1992 Sea	19	311	16.4	0	1
NFL Total	38	695	18.3	0	15

RUFUS MAYES Mayes, Rufus Lee 6′5″, 260 **OT**
Col: Ohio State *HS:* Macomber [Toledo, OH] B: 12/5/1947, Clarksdale, AR D: 1/9/1990, Bellevue, WA *Drafted:* 1969 Round 1 ChiB
1969 ChiB: 13 G. **1970** Cin: 14 G. **1971** Cin: 14 G. **1972** Cin: 6 G. **1973** Cin: 13 G. **1974** Cin: 14 G. **1975** Cin: 14 G. **1976** Cin: 14 G. **1977** Cin: 12 G. **1978** Cin: 9 G. **1979** Phi: 16 G. **Total:** 139 G.

COREY MAYFIELD Mayfield, Arthur Corey 6′3″, 280 **NT**
Col: Oklahoma *HS:* Robert E. Lee [Tyler, TX] B: 2/25/1970, Tyler, TX *Drafted:* 1992 Round 10 SF
1992 TB: 11 G; KR 2-22 11.0. **1995** Jac: 16 G; 1.5 Sac. **Total:** 27 G; KR 2-22 11.0; 1.5 Sac.

LINDY MAYHEW Mayhew, Hayden L 6′1″, 223 **G-T**
Col: Texas-El Paso B: 8/24/1907 D: 2/21/1990, Lilburn, GA
1936 Pit: 12 G. **1937** Pit: 9 G. **1938** Pit: 6 G. **Total:** 27 G.

MARTIN MAYHEW Mayhew, Martin Ronz 5′8″, 175 **DB**
Col: Florida State *HS:* Florida [Tallahassee, FL] B: 10/8/1965, Daytona Beach, FL *Drafted:* 1988 Round 10 Buf
1989 Was: PR 1-0. **1995** TB: **1** Fum TD. **1996** TB: 1 Sac. **Total:** PR 1-0; 1 Fum TD; 1 Sac.

		Interceptions				Tot
Year Team	**G**	**Int**	**Yds**	**TD**	**Fum**	**TD**
1989 Was	16	0	0	0	1	0
1990 Was	16	7	20	0	0	0
1991 Was	16	3	31	1	0	1
1992 Was	10	3	58	0	0	0
1993 TB	15	0	0	0	0	0
1994 TB	16	2	4	0	0	0
1995 TB	13	5	81	0	0	1
1996 TB	16	1	5	0	0	0
NFL Total	118	21	199	1	1	2

GENE MAYL Mayl, Eugene Aloysius 6′2″, 198 **OE**
(Moose) *Col:* Notre Dame *HS:* St. Mary's Inst. [Dayton, OH] B: 10/23/1901, Dayton, OH D: 7/12/1986, Dayton, OH
1925 Day: 8 G. **1926** Day: 4 G; Rec 2 TD; 12 Pt. **Total:** 12 G; Rec 2 TD; 12 Pt.

BRAD MAYNARD Maynard, Bradley Alan 6′1″, 190 **P**
Col: Ball State *HS:* Marion-Adams [Sheridan, IN] B: 2/9/1974, Tipton, IN *Drafted:* 1997 Round 3 NYG
1998 NYG: Pass 1-0; Rush 1-(-5) -5.0. **Total:** Pass 1-0; Rush 1-(-5) -5.0.

		Punting		
Year Team	**G**	**Punts**	**Yds**	**Avg**
1997 NYG	16	**111**	**4531**	40.8
1998 NYG	16	101	**4566**	45.2
NFL Total	32	212	9097	42.9

DON MAYNARD Maynard, Donald Rogers 6′0″, 180 **FL-WB-OE-HB**
Col: Rice; Texas-El Paso *HS:* Colorado [Colorado City, TX]
B: 1/25/1935, Crosbyton, TX *Drafted:* 1957 Round 9 NYG *HOF:* 1987
1958 NYG: Rush 12-45 3.8; KR 11-284 25.8. **1960** NYT: KR 3-59 19.7. **1963** NYJ: Rush 2-6 3.0. **1964** NYJ: Rush 3-3 1.0. **1965** NYJ: Rush 1-2 2.0. **1967** NYJ: Rush 4-18 4.5; Scor 1 2XP. **1969** NYJ: Rush 1-(-6) -6.0; Scor **1** 2XP. **1971** NYJ: Rush 1-2 2.0. **Total:** Rush 24-70 2.9; KR 14-343 24.5; Scor 2 2XP.

		Receiving				Punt Returns					Tot
Year Team	G	Rec	Yds	Avg	TD	Ret	Yds	Avg	TD	Fum	TD
1958 NYG	12	5	84	16.8	0	24	117	4.9	0	3	0
1960 NYT	14	72	1265	17.6	6	0	0	—	0	0	6
1961 NYT	14	43	629	14.6	8	1	9	9.0	0	1	8
1962 NYT	14	56	1041	18.6	8	0	0	—	0	0	8
1963 NYJ	12	38	780	**20.5**	9	1	6	6.0	0	0	9
1964 NYJ	14	46	847	18.4	8	0	0	—	0	1	8
1965 NYJ	14	68	1218	17.9	**14**	0	0	—	0	1	**14**
1966 NYJ	14	48	840	17.5	5	0	0	—	0	0	5
1967 NYJ	14	71	**1434**	20.2	10	0	0	—	0	1	10
1968 NYJ	13	57	1297	**22.8**	10	0	0	—	0	0	10
1969 NYJ	11	47	938	20.0	6	0	0	—	0	0	6
1970 NYJ	10	31	525	16.9	0	0	0	—	0	1	0
1971 NYJ	14	21	408	19.4	2	0	0	—	0	0	2
1972 NYJ	14	29	510	17.6	2	0	0	—	0	0	2
1973 StL	2	1	18	18.0	0	0	0	—	0	0	0
NFL Total	186	633	11834	18.7	88	26	132	5.1	0	8	88

LES MAYNARD Maynard, Lester 6′3″, 210 **E**
Col: Rider B: 1911
1932 SI: 8 G; Rec 3-67 22.3.

LEW MAYNE Mayne, Lewis Elwood 6′1″, 190 **HB-TB-DB**
(Mickey) *Col:* Texas *HS:* Cuero [TX] B: 3/21/1920, Cuero, TX
AAFC **1946** BknA: Pass 25-14 56.0%, 219 8.76 3 TD 4 Int; Rec 5-9 1.8; PR 6-47 7.8; KR 4-90 22.5; Punt 3-79 26.3. **1947** CleA: Rec 6-238 39.7 3 TD; KR 5-102 20.4. **1948** BalA: Rec 2-33 16.5; PR 2-24 12.0; KR 3-61 20.3. **Total:** Pass 25-14 56.0%, 219 8.76 3 TD 4 Int; Rec 13-280 21.5 3 TD; PR 8-71 8.9; KR 12-253 21.1; Punt 3-79 26.3.

		Rushing				Tot
Year Team	G	Att	Yds	Avg	TD	TD
1946 BknA	13	70	191	2.7	1	2
1947 CleA	13	41	75	1.8	0	3
1948 BalA	8	14	26	1.9	0	0
AAFC Total	34	125	292	2.3	1	5

RON MAYO Mayo, Ronald 6′2″, 222 **TE**
Col: Morgan State *HS:* Spingarn [Washington, DC] B: 10/11/1950, Washington, DC *Drafted:* 1973 Round 6 Hou
1973 Hou: 13 G. **1974** Bal: 9 G; KR 2-23 11.5. **Total:** 22 G; KR 2-23 11.5.

MIKE MAYOCK Mayock, Michael Francis Jr. 6′2″, 195 **DB**
Col: Boston College *HS:* Haverford [Havertown, PA] B: 8/14/1958, Phildelphia, PA *Drafted:* 1981 Round 10 Pit
1982 NYG: 3 G. **1983** NYG: 6 G; KR 1-9 9.0; 1 Fum. **Total:** 9 G; KR 1-9 9.0; 1 Fum.

ALVOID MAYS Mays, Alvoid Wilson 5′9″, 180 **DB**
Col: West Virginia *HS:* Manatee [Bradenton, FL] B: 7/10/1966, Palmetto, FL *Drafted:* 1989 Round 8 Hou
1990 Was: 15 G. **1991** Was: 13 G; Int 1-0. **1992** Was: 16 G; Int 2-18; 1 Sac. **1993** Was: 15 G; PR 1-0; 1 Fum. **1994** Was: 2 G. **1995** Pit: 13 G; Int 2-35 1 TD; 6 Pt. **Total:** 74 G; PR 1-0; Int 5-53 1 TD; 6 Pt; 1 Fum; 1 Sac.

DAMON MAYS Mays, Damon Jr. 5′9″, 170 **WR**
Col: Glendale CC AZ; Missouri *HS:* Central [Phoenix, AZ]
B: 5/20/1968, Phoenix, AZ *Drafted:* 1991 Round 9 Dal
1992 Hou: 1 G. **1993** Hou: 1 G. **Total:** 2 G.

DAVE MAYS Mays, David 6′1″, 204 **QB**
Col: Texas Southern *HS:* Southern U. Lab [Baton Rouge, LA]
B: 6/20/1949, Pine Bluff, AR
1976 Cle: Rush 5-14 2.8; Punt 2-91 45.5. **1977** Cle: Rush 4-2 0.5. **Total:** Rush 9-16 1.8; Punt 2-91 45.5.

		Passing								
Year Team	G	Att	Comp	Comp%	Yds	YPA	TD	Int	Rating	Fum
1976 Cle	4	20	9	45.0	101	5.05	0	1	39.8	1
1977 Cle	7	121	67	55.4	797	6.59	6	10	57.8	3
1978 Buf	1	15	4	26.7	39	2.60	1	0	61.8	2
NFL Total	12	156	80	51.3	937	6.01	7	11	55.4	6

JERRY MAYS Mays, Gerald Avery 6′4″, 252 **DE-DT**
Col: Southern Methodist *HS:* Sunset [Dallas, TX] B: 11/24/1939, Dallas, TX D: 7/17/1994, Lake Lewisville, TX *Drafted:* 1961 Round 5 DalT
1961 DalT: 14 G; KR 1-13 13.0; Int 1-7; 1 Fum. **1962** DalT: 14 G. **1963** KC: 14 G; **1** Fum TD; 6 Pt. **1964** KC: 14 G. **1965** KC: 14 G; KR 2-3 1.5. **1966** KC: 14 G. **1967** KC: 14 G. **1968** KC: 14 G. **1969** KC: 14 G. **1970** KC: 14 G. **Total:** 140 G; KR 3-16 5.3; Int 1-7; 1 Fum TD; 6 Pt; 1 Fum.

JERRY MAYS Mays, Jerry Dewayne 5′7″, 176 **RB**
Col: Georgia Tech *HS:* Thomson [GA] B: 12/8/1967, Augusta, GA
1990 SD: 2 G; PR 7-30 4.3; 1 Fum.

KIVUUSAMA MAYS Mays, Kivuusama 6′3″, 247 **LB**
Col: North Carolina *HS:* Cole [San Antonio, TX]; Anniston HS [AL]
B: 1/7/1975, Anniston, AL *Drafted:* 1998 Round 4 Min
1998 Min: 16 G.

STAFFORD MAYS Mays, Stafford Earl 6′2″, 252 **DE-NT**
Col: Mount Hood CC OR; Washington *HS:* Lincoln [Tacoma, WA]
B: 3/13/1958, Lawrence, KS *Drafted:* 1980 Round 9 StL
1980 StL: 16 G. **1981** StL: 16 G. **1982** StL: 8 G. **1983** StL: 16 G; 2.5 Sac. **1984** StL: 16 G; 3.5 Sac. **1985** StL: 16 G; 2 Sac. **1986** StL: 16 G. **1987** Min: 12 G; 7 Sac. **1988** Min: 3 G. **Total:** 119 G; 15 Sac.

FRANK MAZNICKI Maznicki, Francis Stanley 5′9″, 181 **HB-DB**
(Monk) *Col:* Boston College *HS:* West Warwick [RI] B: 7/19/1920, West Warwick, RI *Drafted:* 1942 Round 6 ChiB
1942 ChiB: Pass 1-0; Rec 2-17 8.5 1 TD; PR 6-50 8.3; KR 1-33 33.0; Scor 45, 4-5 **80.0**% FG, 21-22 **95.5**% XK. **1946** ChiB: Rec 2-38 19.0; PR 1-12 12.0; KR 2-65 32.5; Scor 37, 4-9 44.4% FG, 25-26 96.2% XK. **1947** Bos: Pass 1-0, 1 Int; Rec 6-76 12.7; PR 2-48 24.0; Scor 37, 2-2 100.0% FG, 19-21 90.5% XK; **2** Fum TD. **Total:** Pass 2-0, 1 Int; Rec 10-131 13.1 1 TD; PR 9-110 12.2; KR 3-98 32.7; Scor 119, 10-16 62.5% FG, 65-69 94.2% XK; 2 Fum TD.

		Rushing				Interceptions				Tot
Year Team	G	Att	Yds	Avg	TD	Int	Yds	TD	Fum	TD
1942 ChiB	11	54	343	**6.4**	1	4	13	0	0	2
1946 ChiB	4	19	43	2.3	0	2	17	0	0	0
1947 Bos	12	34	77	2.3	0	4	46	0	1	2
NFL Total	27	107	463	4.3	1	10	76	0	1	4

FRED MAZUREK Mazurek, Frederick Henry 5′11″, 192 **WR**
Col: Catholic; Pittsburgh *HS:* Redstone [PA] B: 3/21/1943, Uniontown, PA
1965 Was: 1 G; PR 1-0. **1966** Was: 12 G; Rec 2-28 14.0; PR 2-9 4.5; KR 21-505 24.0. **Total:** 13 G; Rec 2-28 14.0; PR 3-9 3.0; KR 21-505 24.0.

VINCE MAZZA Mazza, Vincent Leonard 6′1″, 216 **DE-OE**
Col: No College *HS:* Trott Vocational [Niagara Falls, NY] B: 3/25/1925, Niagara Falls, NY D: 12/5/1993, Winona, Canada
AAFC **1947** BufA: 13 G; Rec 2-11 5.5; Int 1-26. **1948** BufA: 14 G; Int 0-5 1 TD; 6 Pt. **1949** BufA: 12 G. **Total:** 39 G; Rec 2-11 5.5; Int 1-31 1 TD; 6 Pt.

NFL **1945** Det: 5 G. **1946** Det: 1 G. **Total:** 6 G.

GENO MAZZANTI Mazzanti, Geno 5′11″, 190 **HB**
Col: Arkansas *HS:* Lakeside [Lake Village, AR] B: 4/1/1929, Lake Village, AR *Drafted:* 1950 Round 26 Bal
1950 Bal: 4 G; Rush 7-22 3.1 1 TD; Rec 1-11 11.0; 6 Pt.

JERRY MAZZANTI Mazzanti, Jerry Edward 6′3″, 240 **DE**
Col: Arkansas *HS:* Lakeside [Lake Village, AR] B: 7/13/1940, Lake Village, AR *Drafted:* 1962 Round 16 Phi
1963 Phi: 5 G. **1966** Det: 13 G; KR 1-8 8.0. **1967** Pit: 12 G. **Total:** 30 G; KR 1-8 8.0.

TIM MAZZETTI Mazzetti, Timothy Alan 6′1″, 175 **K**
Col: Pennsylvania *HS:* Escola Graduada [San Paulo, Brazil]
B: 2/1/1956, San Paulo, Brazil

		Scoring						
Year Team	G	Pts	FG	FGA	FG%	XK	XKA	XK%
1978 Atl	10	57	13	16	81.3	18	18	100.0
1979 Atl	16	70	13	25	52.0	31	37	83.8
1980 Atl	16	103	19	27	70.4	46	49	93.9
NFL Total	42	230	45	68	66.2	95	104	91.3

CARL MCADAMS McAdams, Carl Lee 6′3″, 240 **DT-LB-DE**
Col: Oklahoma *HS:* White Deer [TX] B: 4/26/1944, Dumas, TX
Drafted: 1966 Round 3 NYJ
1967 NYJ: 8 G; KR 1-16 16.0. **1968** NYJ: 14 G. **1969** NYJ: 4 G. **Total:** 26 G; KR 1-16 16.0.

DEAN MCADAMS McAdams, Dean LeRoy 6′1″, 193 **TB-DB-HB**
Col: Washington *HS:* Caldwell [ID] B: 10/3/1917, Caldwell, ID
D: 1/10/1996, Seattle, WA *Drafted:* 1941 Round 1 Bkn
1941 Bkn: Rec 7-94 13.4; PR 2-11 5.5; Int 1-0; Scor 9, 2-3 66.7% FG, 3-3 100.0% XK. **1942** Bkn: Rec 3-11 3.7; PR 7-95 13.6; KR 7-165 23.6; Scor 2, 2-2 100.0% XK. **1943** Bkn: Rec 2-6 3.0; PR 4-54 13.5; KR 5-102 20.4; Int 3-34. **Total:** Rec 12-111 9.3; PR 13-160 12.3; KR 12-267 22.3; Int 4-34; Scor 11, 2-3 66.7% FG, 5-5 100.0% XK.

		Passing							
Year Team	G	Att	Comp	Comp%	Yds	YPA	TD	Int	Rating
1941 Bkn	11	27	12	44.4	176	6.52	2	3	51.4
1942 Bkn	11	89	35	39.3	441	4.96	2	15	23.4
1943 Bkn	8	75	37	49.3	315	4.20	0	7	21.8
NFL Total	30	191	84	44.0	932	4.88	4	25	26.5

	Rushing				Punting		
Year Team	Att	Yds	Avg	TD	Punts	Yds	Avg
1941 Bkn	38	99	2.6	0	16	761	47.6
1942 Bkn	110	314	2.9	0	**52**	**2158**	41.5
1943 Bkn	40	-38	-1.0	0	36	1354	37.6
NFL Total	188	375	2.0	0	104	4273	41.1

BOB MCADAMS McAdams, Robert Louis 6′3″, 250 **DT**
Col: North Carolina Central *HS:* Hillside [Durham, NC] B: 11/1/1939, Durham, NC *Drafted:* 1963 Round 17 NYG
1963 NYJ: 12 G. **1964** NYJ: 14 G. **Total:** 26 G.

DERRICK MCADOO McAdoo, Derrick Mark 5′10″, 198 **RB**
Col: Baylor *HS:* Northwest Acad. [Houston, TX] B: 4/2/1965, Pensacola, FL
1987 StL: Rec 2-12 6.0; **1** Fum TD. **1988** TB-Pho: PR 1-0. Pho: PR 1-0. **Total:** Rec 2-12 6.0; PR 1-0; 1 Fum TD.

		Rushing				Kickoff Returns					Tot
Year Team	G	Ret	Yds	Avg	TD	Ret	Yds	Avg	TD	Fum	TD
1987 StL	15	53	230	4.3	3	23	444	19.3	0	2	4
1988 TB-Pho	9	0	0	—	0	13	311	23.9	0	0	0
1988 TB	5	0	0	—	0	4	108	27.0	0	0	0
1988 Pho	4	0	0	—	0	9	203	22.6	0	0	0
NFL Total	24	53	230	4.3	3	36	755	21.0	0	2	4

FRED MCAFEE McAfee, Fred Lee 5′10″, 193 **RB**
Col: Mississippi College *HS:* Philadelphia [MS] B: 6/20/1968, Philadelphia, MS *Drafted:* 1991 Round 6 NO

		Rushing				Receiving			
Year Team	G	Att	Yds	Avg	TD	Rec	Yds	Avg	TD
1991 NO	9	109	494	4.5	2	1	8	8.0	0
1992 NO	14	39	114	2.9	1	1	16	16.0	0
1993 NO	15	51	160	3.1	1	1	3	3.0	0
1994 Ariz-Pit	13	18	51	2.8	2	1	4	4.0	0
1994 Ariz	7	2	-5	-2.5	1	1	4	4.0	0
1994 Pit	6	16	56	3.5	1	0	0	—	0
1995 Pit	16	39	156	4.0	1	15	88	5.9	0
1996 Pit	14	7	17	2.4	0	5	21	4.2	0
1997 Pit	14	13	41	3.2	0	2	44	22.0	0
1998 Pit	14	18	111	6.2	0	9	27	3.0	0
NFL Total	109	294	1144	3.9	7	35	211	6.0	0

	Kickoff Returns					Tot
Year Team	Ret	Yds	Avg	TD	Fum	TD
1991 NO	1	14	14.0	0	2	2
1992 NO	19	393	20.7	0	0	1
1993 NO	28	580	20.7	0	3	1
1994 Ariz-Pit	7	113	16.1	0	1	2
1994 Ariz	7	113	16.1	0	1	1
1994 Pit	0	0	—	0	0	1
1995 Pit	5	56	11.2	0	0	1
1997 Pit	0	0	—	0	1	0
1998 Pit	1	10	10.0	0	0	1
NFL Total	61	1166	19.1	0	7	8

GEORGE MCAFEE McAfee, George Anderson 6′0″, 178 **HB-DB**
(One-Play) *Col:* Duke *HS:* Ironton [OH] B: 3/13/1918, Corbin, KY *Drafted:* 1940 Round 1 Phi *HOF:* 1966
1940 ChiB: Pass 11-4 36.4%, 50 4.55 2 TD; KR **1** TD; Punt 22-851 38.7. **1941** ChiB: Pass 3-1 33.3%, 44 14.67 1 TD; KR 7-223 **31.9** **1** TD; Punt 12-430 35.8; **1** Fum TD. **1945** ChiB: Pass 1-0; KR 5-98 19.6; Punt 2-62 31.0. **1946** ChiB: Pass 2-1 50.0%; KR 3-96 32.0. **1947** ChiB: KR 1-23 23.0; Punt 2-71 35.5. **1948** ChiB: Pass 4-0; KR 1-25 25.0; Punt 1-18 18.0. **1950** ChiB: Pass 1-0, 1 Int; KR 1-23 23.0.
Total: Pass 22-6 27.3%, 94 4.27 3 TD 1 Int; KR 18-488 27.1 2 TD; Punt 39-1432 36.7; 1 Fum TD.

		Rushing				Receiving			
Year Team	G	Att	Yds	Avg	TD	Rec	Yds	Avg	TD
1940 ChiB	10	47	253	5.4	2	7	117	16.7	0
1941 ChiB	11	65	474	**7.3**	5	7	144	20.6	3
1945 ChiB	3	16	139	8.7	3	3	85	28.3	1
1946 ChiB	3	14	53	3.8	0	10	137	13.7	3
1947 ChiB	12	63	209	3.3	3	32	492	15.4	1
1948 ChiB	12	92	392	4.3	5	17	227	13.4	2
1949 ChiB	12	42	161	3.8	3	9	157	17.4	1
1950 ChiB	12	2	4	2.0	0	0	0	—	0
NFL Total	75	341	1685	4.9	21	85	1359	16.0	11

	Punt Returns				Interceptions				Tot
Year Team	Ret	Yds	Avg	TD	Int	Yds	TD	Fum	TD
1940 ChiB	—	—	—	0	4	50	0	0	3
1941 ChiB	5	158	31.6	**1**	6	78	0	0	**12**
1945 ChiB	1	8	8.0	0	1	13	0	1	4
1946 ChiB	1	24	24.0	0	3	18	0	0	3
1947 ChiB	18	261	14.5	0	1	49	0	3	4
1948 ChiB	**30**	**417**	13.9	1	2	35	0	**11**	8
1949 ChiB	24	279	11.6	0	6	76	1	2	5
1950 ChiB	**33**	284	8.6	0	2	31	0	0	0
NFL Total	112	1431	12.8	2	25	350	1	17	39

WES MCAFEE McAfee, Wesley Taylor 5′11″, 175 **HB-DB**
(Rebel) *Col:* Duke *HS:* Ironton [OH] B: 10/20/1918, Corbin, KY D: 1/1984, Myrtle Beach, SC *Drafted:* 1941 Round 14 Pit
1941 Phi: 8 G; Pass 4-1 25.0%, 4 1.00; Rush 9-6 0.7; Rec 3-30 10.0 1 TD; PR 3-21 7.0; KR 2-64 32.0; Punt 1-32 32.0; Scor 8, 2-2 100.0% XK.

ED MCALENEY McAleney, Edward P 6′2″, 235 **DE**
Col: Massachusetts *HS:* South Portland [ME] B: 9/21/1953, Portland, ME *Drafted:* 1976 Round 8 Pit
1976 TB: 2 G.

JAMES MCALISTER McAlister, James Edward 6′1″, 205 **RB**
Col: UCLA *HS:* Blair [Pasadena, CA] B: 9/5/1951, Little Rock, AR *Drafted:* 1974 Round 6 Oak

		Rushing				Receiving			
Year Team	G	Att	Yds	Avg	TD	Rec	Yds	Avg	TD
1975 Phi	14	103	335	3.3	1	17	134	7.9	2
1976 Phi	13	68	265	3.9	0	12	72	6.0	0
1978 NE	16	19	77	4.1	2	1	12	12.0	0
NFL Total	43	190	677	3.6	3	30	218	7.3	2

	Kickoff Returns					Tot
Year Team	Ret	Yds	Avg	TD	Fum	TD
1975 Phi	12	278	23.2	0	5	3
1976 Phi	9	172	19.1	0	4	0
1978 NE	10	186	18.6	0	3	2
NFL Total	31	636	20.5	0	12	5

KEN MCALISTER McAlister, Kenneth H 6′5″, 220 **LB-DB**
Col: San Francisco *HS:* Oakland [CA] B: 4/15/1960, Oakland, CA
1982 Sea: 9 G; KR 2-41 20.5. **1983** Sea-SF: 6 G; KR 3-59 19.7. Sea: 2 G; KR 3-59 19.7. SF: 4 G. **1984** KC: 15 G; Int 2-33; 4 Sac. **1986** KC: 3 G; 1 Sac. **1987** KC: 1 G. **Total:** 34 G; KR 5-100 20.0; Int 2-33; 5 Sac.

JACK MCARTHUR McArthur, Jackson 5′11″, 211 **C-T-G-E**
Col: St. Mary's (Cal.) B: 1904
1926 LA: 10 G. **1927** Buf-NYY: 13 G. Buf: 5 G. NYY: 8 G. **1928** NYY: 13 G. **1929** Ora: 10 G. **1930** Nwk-Prov-Fra-Bkn: 12 G. Nwk: 1 G. Prov: 4 G. Fra: 2 G. Bkn: 5 G. **1931** Prov: 9 G. **Total:** 67 G.

KEVIN MCARTHUR McArthur, Kevin Lee 6′2″, 244 **LB**
Col: Lamar *HS:* Lake Charles [LA] B: 5/11/1962, Cameron, LA
1986 NYJ: 8 G; 1 Sac. **1987** NYJ: 12 G. **1988** NYJ: 16 G; Int 1-3; 2 Sac. **1989** NYJ: 9 G. **Total:** 45 G; Int 1-3; 3 Sac.

JACK MCAULIFFE McAuliffe, John Theodore 5′7″, 155 **HB**
Col: Montana; Beloit *HS:* Butte [MT] B: 5/21/1901, Butte, MT D: 12/17/1971, Butte, MT
1926 GB: 8 G; Pass 1 TD.

MIKE MCBATH McBath, Michael Strickler 6′4″, 251 **DE-OT-DT**
Col: Penn State *HS:* Woodbury [NJ] B: 5/29/1946, Woodbury, NJ *Drafted:* 1968 Round 5 Buf
1968 Buf: 9 G. **1969** Buf: 14 G. **1970** Buf: 12 G; KR 1-7 7.0. **1971** Buf: 13 G. **1972** Buf: 2 G. **Total:** 50 G; KR 1-7 7.0.

CHARLIE MCBRIDE McBride, Charles Harold 5′10″, 185 **BB-LB**
Col: Washington State *HS:* Puyallup [WA] B: 7/6/1914 D: 4/1972
1936 ChiC: 1 G; Rush 2-1 0.5; Rec 1-38 38.0 1 TD; 6 Pt.

RON MCBRIDE McBride, James Ronald 6′0″, 202 **RB**
Col: Missouri *HS:* Fulton [MO] B: 10/12/1948, Fulton, MO
1973 GB: 1 G.

JACK MCBRIDE McBride, John F 5′11″, 185 **DB-FB-TB-BB**
Col: Syracuse *HS:* Conshohocken [PA]; Bellefonte Acad. [PA] B: 11/30/1901, Conshohocken, PA D: 10/1966, Conshohocken, PA
1925 NYG: Scor 25, 2 FG, 7 XK. **1926** NYG: Scor 48, 1 FG, **15** XK. **1927** NYG: Scor **57**, 2 FG, **15** XK. **1928** NYG: Scor 8, 2 XK. **1929** Prov: Scor 6, 6 XK. **1930** Bkn: Scor **56**, 8 XK. **1931** Bkn: Scor 19, 1 XK. **1933** NYG: Scor 7, 7 XK. **1934** NYG: Scor 1, 1 XK. **Total:** Scor 233, 5 FG, 62 XK.

		Passing							
Year Team	G	Att	Comp	Comp%	Yds	YPA	TD	Int	Rating
1925 NYG	12	—	—	—	—	—	6	—	—
1926 NYG	13	—	—	—	—	—	3	—	—
1927 NYG	12	—	—	—	—	—	7	—	—
1928 NYG	9	—	—	—	—	—	0	—	—
1929 Prov	12	—	—	—	—	—	2	—	—
1930 Bkn	11	—	—	—	—	—	2	—	—
1931 Bkn	13	—	—	—	—	—	2	—	—
1932 Bkn-NYG	12	74	36	48.6	363	4.91	6	9	50.5
1932 Bkn	3	0	0	—	0	—	0	0	—
1932 NYG	9	74	36	48.6	363	4.91	6	9	50.5
1933 NYG	11	24	11	45.8	138	5.75	2	2	57.3

1934 NYG	1	3	3	100.0	37	12.33	1	0	157.6
NFL Total	106	101	50	49.5	538	5.33	31	11	65.5

	Rushing				Tot
Year Team	Att	Yds	Avg	TD	TD
1925 NYG	—	—	—	2	2
1926 NYG	—	—	—	5	5
1927 NYG	—	—	—	**6**	**6**
1928 NYG	—	—	—	1	1
1930 Bkn	—	—	—	**8**	8
1931 Bkn	—	—	—	3	3
1932 Bkn-NYG	87	325	3.7	1	1
1932 Bkn	3	23	7.7	0	0
1932 NYG	84	302	3.6	1	1
1933 NYG	33	87	2.6	0	0
1934 NYG	4	14	3.5	0	0
NFL Total	124	426	3.4	26	26

NORM MCBRIDE McBride, Norman 6'3", 245 **DE**
Col: East Los Angeles Coll. CA (J.C.); Utah *HS:* John C. Fremont [Los Angeles, CA] B: 2/21/1947, Los Angeles, CA *Drafted:* 1969 Round 4 Mia
1969 Mia: 8 G. **1970** Mia: 2 G. **Total:** 10 G.

OSCAR MCBRIDE McBride, Oscar Bernard 6'5", 266 **TE**
Col: Notre Dame *HS:* Chiefland [FL] B: 7/23/1972, Gainesville, FL
1995 Ariz: 16 G; Rec 13-112 8.6 2 TD; 12 Pt. **1996** Ariz: 2 G. **Total:** 18 G; Rec 13-112 8.6 2 TD; 12 Pt.

ADRIAN MCBRIDE McBride, Richard Adrian 6'0", 195 **WR**
Col: Tennessee; Missouri *HS:* Zanesville [OH] B: 3/23/1963, Zanesville, OH
1987 StL: 3 G.

GERALD MCBURROWS McBurrows, Gerald Lance 5'11", 205 **DB**
Col: Kansas *HS:* Martin Luther King [Detroit, MI] B: 10/7/1973, Detroit, MI *Drafted:* 1995 Round 7 StL
1995 StL: 14 G; 1 Sac. **1996** StL: 16 G; Int 1-3. **1997** StL: 8 G. **1998** StL: 10 G. **Total:** 48 G; Int 1-3; 1 Sac.

JERRY MCCABE McCabe, Jerome Francis 6'1", 225 **LB**
Col: Holy Cross *HS:* De La Salle Collegiate [Warren, MI] B: 1/25/1965, Detroit, MI
1987 NE: 3 G; 1 Sac. **1988** KC: 3 G. **Total:** 6 G; 1 Sac.

RICHIE MCCABE McCabe, Richard Paul 6'1", 185 **DB**
Col: Pittsburgh *HS:* North Catholic [Pittsburgh, PA] B: 3/12/1933, Pittsburgh, PA D: 1/4/1983, Denver, CO *Drafted:* 1955 Round 22 Pit
1955 Pit: 12 G; Int 3-29; **1** Fum TD; 6 Pt. **1957** Pit: 2 G. **1958** Pit: 5 G. **1959** Was: 10 G; Int 1-8. **1960** Buf: 14 G; Int 4-0. **1961** Buf: 9 G; Int 1-17. **Total:** 52 G; Int 9-54; 1 Fum TD; 6 Pt.

DON MCCAFFERTY McCafferty, Donald William 6'4", 220 **OE-DE**
Col: Ohio State *HS:* James Ford Rhodes [Cleveland, OH]
B: 3/12/1921, Cleveland, OH D: 7/28/1974, West Bloomfield Hills, MI
Drafted: 1943 Round 11 NYG
1946 NYG: 9 G; Rec 3-38 12.7 1 TD; 6 Pt.

ART MCCAFFRAY McCaffray, Arthur Joseph 5'11", 190 **T**
Col: Santa Clara; U. of Pacific *HS:* Seattle Prep [WA] B: 12/26/1921, Seattle, WA D: 12/5/1994, Seattle, WA *Drafted:* 1944 Round 4 Pit
1946 Pit: 11 G.

ED MCCAFFREY McCaffrey, Edward Thomas 6'5", 215 **WR**
Col: Stanford *HS:* Central Catholic [Allentown, PA] B: 8/17/1968, Waynesboro, PA *Drafted:* 1991 Round 3 NYG
1995 Den: Rush 1-(-1) -1.0; Scor 1 2XP. **1998** Den: Scor 1 2XP. **Total:** Rush 1-(-1) -1.0; Scor 2 2XP.

		Receiving				
Year Team	G	Rec	Yds	Avg	TD	Fum
1991 NYG	16	16	146	9.1	0	0
1992 NYG	16	49	610	12.4	5	2
1993 NYG	16	27	335	12.4	2	0
1994 SF	16	11	131	11.9	2	0
1995 Den	16	39	477	12.2	2	1
1996 Den	15	48	553	11.5	7	0
1997 Den	15	45	590	13.1	8	0
1998 Den	15	64	1053	16.5	10	1
NFL Total	125	299	3895	13.0	36	4

MIKE MCCAFFREY McCaffrey, Michael James 6'3", 235 **LB**
Col: California *HS:* Garces Memorial [Bakersfield, CA] B: 4/11/1946, Bakersfield, CA *Drafted:* 1969 Round 4 Min
1970 Buf: 12 G; KR 2-15 7.5.

BOB MCCAFFREY McCaffrey, Robert Alan 6'2", 245 **C**
Col: USC *HS:* Garces Memorial [Bakersfield, CA] B: 4/16/1952, Bakersfield, CA *Drafted:* 1975 Round 16 GB
1975 GB: 11 G.

BOB MCCAIN McCain, Robert Floyd 5'11", 195 **OE-DE**
Col: Mississippi *HS:* Greenville [MS] B: 8/15/1922
AAFC **1946** BknA: 11 G; Rec 3-27 9.0.

DON MCCALL McCall, Donald Charles 5'11", 195 **RB**
Col: Los Angeles City Coll. CA (J.C.); USC *HS:* John C. Fremont [Los Angeles, CA] B: 9/21/1944, Birmingham, AL *Drafted:* 1967 Round 5 NO
1968 NO: Pass 1-0. **Total:** Pass 1-0.

		Rushing				Receiving			
Year Team	G	Att	Yds	Avg	TD	Rec	Yds	Avg	TD
1967 NO	14	21	86	4.1	1	4	75	18.8	1
1968 NO	13	155	637	4.1	4	26	270	10.4	2
1969 Pit	13	30	98	3.3	0	2	2	1.0	0
1970 NO	2	23	63	2.7	1	5	43	8.6	0
NFL Total	42	229	884	3.9	6	37	390	10.5	3

	Kickoff Returns					Tot
Year Team	Ret	Yds	Avg	TD	Fum	TD
1967 NO	7	198	28.3	0	0	2
1968 NO	0	0	—	0	4	6
1969 Pit	21	532	25.3	**1**	1	1
1970 NO	1	26	26.0	0	1	1
NFL Total	29	756	26.1	1	6	10

ED MCCALL McCall, Edward 6'3", 205 **WR**
Col: Miles B: 12/19/1943
1968 Cin: 1 G.

JOE MCCALL McCall, Joseph Shepard 5'11", 205 **RB**
Col: Pittsburgh *HS:* Miami Jackson [FL] B: 2/17/1962, Miami, FL
Drafted: 1984 Round 3 LARd
1984 LARd: 3 G; Rush 1-3 3.0.

REESE MCCALL McCall, Reese Jr. 6'6", 239 **TE**
Col: Auburn *HS:* Jess Lanier [Bessemer, AL] B: 6/16/1956, Bessemer, AL *Drafted:* 1978 Round 1 Bal
1978 Bal: PR 1-37 37.0. **Total:** PR 1-37 37.0.

		Receiving					Tot
Year Team	G	Rec	Yds	Avg	TD	Fum	TD
1978 Bal	16	11	160	14.5	1	1	2
1979 Bal	14	37	536	14.5	4	1	4
1980 Bal	16	18	322	17.9	5	1	5
1981 Bal	16	21	314	15.0	2	0	2
1982 Bal	7	2	6	3.0	0	0	0
1983 Det	16	1	6	6.0	0	0	0
1984 Det	16	3	15	5.0	0	0	0
1985 Det	16	1	7	7.0	0	0	0
NFL Total	117	94	1366	14.5	12	3	13

BOB MCCALL McCall, Robert Henry 6'0", 205 **RB**
Col: Arizona *HS:* Centennial [Compton, CA] B: 4/26/1950, Sarasota, FL *Drafted:* 1973 Round 5 Cin
1973 NE: 8 G; Rush 10-15 1.5; Rec 3-18 6.0; KR 2-17 8.5; 4 Fum.

RON MCCALL McCall, Ronald George 6'2", 240 **LB**
Col: Dixie Coll. UT (J.C.); Utah State; Weber State *HS:* Clearfield [UT]
B: 7/11/1944, San Bernardino, CA *Drafted:* 1967 Round 2 SD
1967 SD: 2 G. **1968** SD: 3 G. **Total:** 5 G.

FRED MCCALLISTER McCallister, Frederick Milton 6'1", 250 **LB**
Col: Florida *HS:* Palm Bay [FL] B: 2/17/1962, Melbourne, FL
1987 TB: 3 G; 1 Sac.

NAPOLEON MCCALLUM McCallum, Napoleon Ardel 6'2", 220 **RB**
Col: Navy *HS:* Milford [OH] B: 10/6/1963, Milford, OH *Drafted:* 1986 Round 4 LARd
1986 LARd: Rec 13-103 7.9; PR 7-44 6.3. **1992** LARd: Rec 2-13 6.5; PR 4-19 4.8. **1993** LARd: Rec 2-5 2.5. **Total:** Rec 17-121 7.1; PR 11-63 5.7.

		Rushing				Kickoff Returns				
Year Team	G	Att	Yds	Avg	TD	Ret	Yds	Avg	TD	Fum
1986 LARd	15	142	536	3.8	1	8	183	22.9	0	5
1990 LARd	16	10	25	2.5	0	1	0	0.0	0	0
1991 LARd	16	31	110	3.5	1	5	105	21.0	0	1
1992 LARd	13	0	0	—	0	14	274	19.6	0	0
1993 LARd	13	37	114	3.1	3	1	12	12.0	0	1
1994 LARd	1	3	5	1.7	1	0	0	—	0	0
NFL Total	74	223	790	3.5	6	29	574	19.8	0	7

JOHN MCCAMBRIDGE McCambridge, John Raymond 6'4", 245 **DE**
Col: Northwestern *HS:* Rockhurst [Kansas City, MO] B: 8/30/1944, Klamath Falls, OR *Drafted:* 1967 Round 6 Det
1967 Det: 6 G.

JIM MCCANLESS McCanless, James Robert 6'2", 240 **OG**
Col: Clemson *HS:* Lee H. Edwards [Asheville, NC] B: 1/1/1936
1960 Hou: 1 G.

ERNIE MCCANN McCann, Ernest Harmer 5'11", 188 **T-OE-G**
(Blondy) *Col:* Penn State *HS:* Cheltenham [Wyncote, PA] B: 8/5/1902
D: 11/25/1971, Acton, CA
1926 Har: 9 G.

JIM MCCANN McCann, James William 6'2", 163 **P**
Col: Phoenix Coll. AZ (J.C.); Arizona State *HS:* North [Phoenix, AZ]
B: 3/29/1949, Phoenix, AZ *Drafted:* 1971 Round 8 SF
1971 SF: Rush 2-(-15) -7.5. **Total:** Rush 2-(-15) -7.5.

		Punting			
Year Team	G	Punts	Yds	Avg	Fum
1971 SF	13	49	1897	38.7	3
1972 SF	13	64	2542	39.7	0
1973 NYG	2	12	294	24.5	0
1975 KC	3	14	493	35.2	1
NFL Total	31	139	5226	37.6	4

TIM MCCANN McCann, Timothy John 6'5", 265 **DT**
Col: Princeton *HS:* Central Catholic [San Antonio, TX] B: 5/15/1947, Milwaukee, WI
1969 NYG: 1 G.

KEITH MCCANTS McCants, Alvin Keith 6'3", 265 **DE-LB**
Col: Alabama *HS:* S.S. Murphy [Mobile, AL] B: 4/19/1968, Mobile, AL
Drafted: 1990 Round 1 TB
1990 TB: 15 G; 2 Sac. **1991** TB: 16 G; 5 Sac. **1992** TB: 16 G; 5 Sac.
1993 Hou: 13 G. **1994** Hou-Ariz: 12 G; Int 1-46 1 TD; 6 Pt; 1 Sac. Hou: 4 G. Ariz: 8 G; Int 1-46 1 TD; 6 Pt; 1 Sac. **1995** Ariz: 16 G; **1** Fum TD; 6 Pt; 0.5 Sac. **Total:** 88 G; Int 1-46 1 TD; 1 Fum TD; Tot TD 2; 12 Pt; 13.5 Sac.

KEENAN MCCARDELL McCardell, Keenan Wayne 6'1", 188 **WR**
Col: Nevada-Las Vegas *HS:* Waltrip [Houston, TX] B: 1/6/1970, Houston, TX *Drafted:* 1991 Round 12 Was
1995 Cle: PR 13-93 7.2; KR 9-161 17.9. **1996** Jac: PR 1-2 2.0; Scor 2 2XP. **1998** Jac: KR 1-15 15.0; Scor 1 2XP. **Total:** PR 14-95 6.8; KR 10-176 17.6; Scor 3 2XP.

		Receiving				
Year Team	G	Rec	Yds	Avg	TD	Fum
1992 Cle	2	1	8	8.0	0	0
1993 Cle	6	13	234	18.0	4	0
1994 Cle	13	10	182	18.2	0	0
1995 Cle	16	56	709	12.7	4	0
1996 Jac	16	85	1129	13.3	3	1
1997 Jac	16	85	1164	13.7	5	0
1998 Jac	15	64	892	13.9	6	0
NFL Total	84	314	4318	13.8	22	1

LARRY MCCARREN McCarren, Laurence Anthony 6'3", 246 **C**
Col: Illinois *HS:* Park Forest [IL] B: 11/9/1951, Park Forest, IL
Drafted: 1973 Round 12 GB
1973 GB: 5 G. **1974** GB: 14 G. **1975** GB: 14 G. **1976** GB: 14 G. **1977** GB: 14 G. **1978** GB: 16 G. **1979** GB: 16 G. **1980** GB: 16 G; 1 Fum. **1981** GB: 16 G; 1 Fum. **1982** GB: 9 G. **1983** GB: 16 G. **1984** GB: 12 G. **Total:** 162 G; 2 Fum.

BRENDAN MCCARTHY McCarthy, Brendan Barrett 6'3", 220 **RB**
Col: Boston College *HS:* DeMatha [Hyattsville, MD] B: 8/6/1945, Boston, MA *Drafted:* 1968 Round 4 GB
1968 Atl-Den: Rec 20-188 9.4 2 TD. Atl: Rec 13-119 9.2. Den: Rec 7-69 9.9 2 TD. **Total:** Rec 20-188 9.4 2 TD.

		Rushing					Tot
Year Team	G	Att	Yds	Avg	TD	Fum	TD
1968 Atl-Den	14	59	175	3.0	1	3	3
1968 Atl	7	31	86	2.8	1	1	1
1968 Den	7	28	89	3.2	0	2	2
1969 Den	1	0	0	—	0	0	0
NFL Total	15	59	175	3.0	1	3	3

DON MCCARTHY McCarthy, Donald 5'10", 172 **E**
Col: Lehigh B: 1897 Deceased
1921 Was: 3 G.

JIM MCCARTHY McCarthy, James Patrick 6'1", 205 **OE-DE**
(Red) *Col:* Illinois *HS:* Lockport [IL] B: 11/28/1920, Lockport, IL
D: 12/2/1991, Orland Park, IL
AAFC **1946** BknA: KR 1-8 8.0; Int 1-3; Scor 23, 0-1 FG, 5-7 71.4% XK.
1947 BknA: Pass 2-1 50.0%, 17 8.50 1 Int. **1948** ChiA: Scor 27, 2-3 66.7% FG, 21-21 100.0% XK. **1949** ChiA: Scor 39, 6-13 46.2% FG, 21-23 91.3% XK. **Total:** Pass 2-1 50.0%, 17 8.50 1 Int; KR 1-8 8.0; Int 1-3; Scor 89, 8-17 47.1% FG, 47-51 92.2% XK.

		Receiving			
Year Team	G	Rec	Yds	Avg	TD
1946 BknA	14	11	296	26.9	3
1947 BknA	14	10	147	14.7	0
1948 ChiA	14	3	30	10.0	0
1949 ChiA	12	4	58	14.5	0
AAFC Total	54	28	531	19.0	3

JACK MCCARTHY McCarthy, John Lacey 186 **T**
Col: California
1927 Dul: 8 G.

JOHN MCCARTHY McCarthy, John Patrick 5'8", 155 **QB-DB**
Col: St. Francis (Pa.) *HS:* Camden Catholic [NJ] B: 8/9/1916, Philadelphia, PA
1944 ChPt: Rush 6-(-49) -8.2; PR 1-9 9.0; Punt 24-801 33.4.

		Passing							
Year Team	G	Att	Comp	Comp%	Yds	YPA	TD	Int	Rating
1944 ChPt	7	67	20	29.9	250	3.73	0	13	3.0

SHAWN MCCARTHY McCarthy, Shawn Michael 6'6", 227 **P**
Col: Purdue *HS:* Ross [Fremont, OH] B: 2/22/1968, Fremont, OH
Drafted: 1990 Round 12 Atl
1991 NE: Pass 1-1 100.0%, 11 11.00. **1992** NE: Rush 3-(-10) -3.3.
Total: Pass 1-1 100.0%, 11 11.00; Rush 3-(-10) -3.3.

		Punting			
Year Team	G	Punts	Yds	Avg	Fum
1991 NE	13	66	2650	40.2	0
1992 NE	16	103	4227	41.0	1
NFL Total	29	169	6877	40.7	1

VINCE MCCARTHY McCarthy, Vincent John 5'10", 155 **WB-BB-OE**
Col: St. Viator *HS:* Rock Island [IL] B: 11/3/1899, IL D: 11/25/1968, Fort Lauderdale, FL
1924 RI: 2 G; Rush 1 TD; Scor 7, 1 XK. **1925** RI: 4 G; Pass 1 TD; Rush 1 TD; Rec 1 TD; Tot TD 2; 12 Pt. **Total:** 6 G; Pass 1 TD; Rush 2 TD; Rec 1 TD; Tot TD 3.

PETE MCCARTNEY McCartney, Peter Daniel 6'6", 260 **OT**
Col: Louisville *HS:* East Rockaway [NY] B: 6/15/1962
1987 NYJ: 3 G.

RONNIE MCCARTNEY McCartney, Ronnie L 6'1", 220 **LB**
Col: Tennessee *HS:* Stonewall Jackson [Charleston, WV]
B: 7/20/1954, Charleston, WV *Drafted:* 1976 Round 2 LARm
1977 Atl: 14 G. **1978** Atl: 15 G. **1979** Atl: 16 G. **Total:** 45 G.

MICKEY MCCARTY McCarty, Robert Mickey 6'5", 255 **TE**
Col: Texas Christian *HS:* Pasadena [TX] B: 11/15/1946, Jonesboro, AR
Drafted: 1968 Round 4 KC
1969 KC: 3 G.

DON MCCAULEY McCauley, Donald Frederick Jr. 6'1", 211 **RB**
Col: North Carolina *HS:* Garden City [NY] B: 5/12/1949, Worcester, MA *Drafted:* 1971 Round 1 Bal
1974 Bal: Pass 2-1 50.0%, 11 5.50 1 TD. **Total:** Pass 2-1 50.0%, 11 5.50 1 TD.

		Rushing				Receiving			
Year Team	G	Att	Yds	Avg	TD	Rec	Yds	Avg	TD
1971 Bal	13	58	246	4.2	2	3	6	2.0	0
1972 Bal	14	178	675	3.8	2	30	256	8.5	2
1973 Bal	13	144	514	3.6	2	25	186	7.4	0
1974 Bal	13	30	90	3.0	0	17	112	6.6	1
1975 Bal	14	60	196	3.3	10	14	93	6.6	1
1976 Bal	13	69	227	3.3	9	34	347	10.2	2
1977 Bal	14	83	234	2.8	6	51	495	9.7	2
1978 Bal	15	44	107	2.4	5	34	296	8.7	0
1979 Bal	15	59	168	2.8	3	55	575	10.5	3
1980 Bal	16	35	133	3.8	1	34	313	9.2	4
1981 Bal	16	10	37	3.7	0	36	347	9.6	2
NFL Total	156	770	2627	3.4	40	333	3026	9.1	17

	Kickoff Returns					Tot
Year Team	Ret	Yds	Avg	TD	Fum	TD
1971 Bal	8	194	24.3	0	0	2
1972 Bal	13	377	29.0	**1**	2	5
1973 Bal	1	12	12.0	0	3	2
1974 Bal	1	17	17.0	0	0	1
1975 Bal	4	86	21.5	0	1	11
1976 Bal	1	17	17.0	0	2	11
1977 Bal	5	67	13.4	0	2	8
1978 Bal	7	150	21.4	0	2	5
1979 Bal	2	29	14.5	0	3	6
1980 Bal	1	18	18.0	0	1	5
1981 Bal	0	0	—	0	0	2
NFL Total	43	967	22.5	1	16	58

TOM MCCAULEY McCauley, Thomas Michael 6'3", 193 **DB**
Col: North Carolina *HS:* Garden City [NY] B: 5/3/1947, Worcester, MA
Drafted: 1969 Round 10 Min
1969 Atl: 14 G; Rush 2-49 24.5; PR 4-(-11) -2.8; 1 Fum. **1970** Atl: 14 G; PR 14-138 9.9 **1** TD; Int 1-32; 6 Pt. **1971** Atl: 4 G; PR 1-8 8.0; Int 1-0.
Total: 32 G; Rush 2-49 24.5; PR 19-135 7.1 1 TD; Int 2-32; 6 Pt; 1 Fum.

LEO MCCAUSLAND McCausland, Leo Joseph 6'0", 195 **C-G-T-E**
(Mac) *Col:* Detroit Mercy *HS:* Campion [Akron, OH] B: 6/14/1895
D: 9/1968, Akron, OH
1922 Akr: 4 G.

BILL MCCAW McCaw, William Glass 6'2", 194 **OE**
Col: Indiana *HS:* Bloomington [IN] B: 2/6/1898, St. Paul, MN
D: 4/19/1942, Bloomington, IN
1923 Rac: 3 G. **1926** Lou: 4 G. **Total:** 7 G.

BOB MCCHESNEY McChesney, Robert Edward 6'2", 195 **E**
Col: UCLA *HS:* Benjamin Franklin [Los Angeles, CA] B: 7/12/1912, Los Angeles, CA D: 9/1986, Silver City, NM
1939 Was: Rush 1-5 5.0. **1942** Was: Rush 2-22 11.0. **Total:** Rush 3-27 9.0.

		Receiving				Tot
Year Team	G	Rec	Yds	Avg	TD	TD
1936 Bos	9	5	62	12.4	0	0
1937 Was	10	6	50	8.3	0	0
1938 Was	10	3	49	16.3	1	1
1939 Was	8	9	86	9.6	0	1
1940 Was	11	9	119	13.2	1	1
1941 Was	11	19	213	11.2	2	2
1942 Was	10	8	100	12.5	1	2
NFL Total	69	59	679	11.5	5	7

BOB MCCHESNEY McChesney, Robert Eugene 6'2", 190 **OE**
Col: Hardin-Simmons *HS:* Van Nuys [CA] B: 10/27/1926, Van Nuys, CA *Drafted:* 1950 Round 4 Phi
1952 NYG: Rush 2-2 1.0; KR 3-28 9.3. **Total:** Rush 2-2 1.0; KR 3-28 9.3.

		Receiving			
Year Team	G	Rec	Yds	Avg	TD
1950 NYG	12	19	380	20.0	6
1951 NYG	12	14	230	16.4	2
1952 NYG	12	21	430	20.5	6
NFL Total	36	54	1040	19.3	14

CLIFF MCCLAIN McClain, Clifford 6'0", 217 **RB**
Col: South Carolina State *HS:* Orlando [FL] B: 12/29/1947, Orlando, FL *Drafted:* 1970 Round 5 NYJ
1970 NYJ: Rec 1-11 11.0; KR 4-70 17.5. **1971** NYJ: KR 1-11 11.0.
1972 NYJ: Pass 1-0; Rec 6-88 14.7; KR 2-45 22.5. **1973** NYJ: Rec 6-52 8.7; KR 5-89 17.8. **Total:** Pass 1-0; Rec 13-151 11.6; KR 12-215 17.9.

		Rushing				
Year Team	G	Att	Yds	Avg	TD	Fum
1970 NYJ	10	0	0	—	0	1
1971 NYJ	11	12	108	9.0	2	1
1972 NYJ	13	59	305	5.2	0	5
1973 NYJ	12	8	32	4.0	0	1
NFL Total	46	79	445	5.6	2	8

CLINT MCCLAIN McClain, Clinton 5'9", 182 **FB-DB**
(Red) *Col:* Southern Methodist *HS:* Waco [TX] B: 6/18/1918, Lufkin, TX D: 12/11/1994, Dallas, TX
1941 NYG: 6 G; Rush 9-36 4.0 2 TD; Int 1-34; 12 Pt.

DEWEY MCCLAIN McClain, Dewey Loren 6'3", 236 **LB**
Col: East Central (OK) *HS:* Okmulgee [OK] B: 4/25/1954, Okmulgee, OK
1976 Atl: 14 G; Int 1-13. **1977** Atl: 13 G. **1978** Atl: 16 G; Scor **1** Saf; 2 Pt.
1979 Atl: 15 G; PR 1-2 2.0. **1980** Atl: 15 G. **Total:** 73 G; PR 1-2 2.0; Int 1-13; Scor 1 Saf; 2 Pt.

JOE MCCLAIN McClain, Joseph T 6'0", 200 **T**
Col: St. John's (N.Y.); Canisius *HS:* Shenandoah [PA] B: 4/5/1905
D: 4/14/1967, Pottsville, PA
1928 NYY: 7 G.

JACK MCCLAIREN McClairen, Jack Forsyth 6'4", 213 **OE**
(Goose; Cy) *Col:* Bethune-Cookman *HS:* Rosenwald [Panama City, FL] B: 3/2/1931, Panama City, FL *Drafted:* 1953 Round 26 Pit
1958 Pit: KR 1-0. **1960** Pit: KR 1-1 1.0. **Total:** KR 2-1 0.5.

		Receiving				
Year Team	G	Rec	Yds	Avg	TD	Fum
1955 Pit	12	1	13	13.0	0	0
1956 Pit	7	5	56	11.2	0	0
1957 Pit	12	46	630	13.7	2	0
1958 Pit	12	29	491	16.9	1	1
1959 Pit	1	3	46	15.3	1	0
1960 Pit	1	1	17	17.0	0	0
NFL Total	45	85	1253	14.7	3	1

BRENT MCCLANAHAN McClanahan, Brent Anthony 5'10", 202 **RB**
Col: Arizona State *HS:* South [Bakersfield, CA] B: 9/21/1951, Bakersfield, CA *Drafted:* 1973 Round 5 Min

		Rushing				Receiving			
Year Team	G	Att	Yds	Avg	TD	Rec	Yds	Avg	TD
1973 Min	13	17	69	4.1	0	0	0	—	0
1974 Min	14	9	41	4.6	1	3	35	11.7	0
1975 Min	12	92	336	3.7	0	18	141	7.8	1
1976 Min	13	130	382	2.9	4	40	252	6.3	1
1977 Min	14	95	324	3.4	1	34	276	8.1	2
1978 Min	13	10	26	2.6	0	2	11	5.5	0
1979 Min	16	14	29	2.1	0	10	57	5.7	0
NFL Total	95	367	1207	3.3	6	107	772	7.2	4

	Kickoff Returns					Tot
Year Team	Ret	Yds	Avg	TD	Fum	TD
1973 Min	16	410	25.6	0	2	0
1974 Min	23	549	23.9	0	1	1
1975 Min	17	360	21.2	0	0	1
1976 Min	0	0	—	0	5	5
1977 Min	4	90	22.5	0	7	3
1978 Min	3	38	12.7	0	1	0
1979 Min	3	53	17.7	0	0	0
NFL Total	66	1500	22.7	0	16	10

RANDY MCCLANAHAN McClanahan, Randy Duane 6'5", 225 **LB**
Col: Glendale CC AZ; Southwestern Louisiana *HS:* Moon Valley [Phoenix, AZ] B: 12/12/1954, Lincoln, NE
1977 Oak: 14 G. **1978** Buf: 16 G. **1980** Oak: 14 G; Int 1-7. **1981** Oak: 16 G. **1982** LARd: 1 G. **Total:** 61 G; Int 1-7.

BILL MCCLARD McClard, William Wayne 5'10", 202 **K**
Col: Arkansas *HS:* Norman [OK] B: 10/15/1949, Purcell, OK
Drafted: 1972 Round 3 SD
1974 NO: Pass 1-0, 1 Int. **Total:** Pass 1-0, 1 Int.

		Scoring						
Year Team	G	Pts	FG	FGA	FG%	XK	XKA	XK%
1972 SD	9	11	3	6	50.0	2	2	100.0
1973 NO	8	48	13	24	54.2	9	9	100.0
1974 NO	14	46	9	16	56.3	19	20	95.0
1975 NO	3	4	1	5	20.0	1	1	100.0
NFL Total	34	109	26	51	51.0	31	32	96.9

MIKE MCCLELLAN McClellan, William Michael 6'1", 185 **DB**
Col: Oklahoma *HS:* Stamford [TX] B: 10/10/1939, Stamford, TX
Drafted: 1961 Round 6 SF
1962 Phi: 14 G; Int 3-2. **1963** Phi: 10 G; Int 1-0. **Total:** 24 G; Int 4-2.

SKIP MCCLENDON McClendon, Kenneth Christopher 6'6", 282 **DE**
Col: Butler County CC KS; Northwestern; Arizona State *HS:* Redford [Detroit, MI] B: 4/9/1964, Detroit, MI *Drafted:* 1987 Round 3 Cin
1987 Cin: 12 G. **1988** Cin: 16 G; 2 Sac. **1989** Cin: 16 G; 1.5 Sac.
1990 Cin: 15 G; 2 Sac. **1991** Cin-SD: 7 G. Cin: 5 G. SD: 2 G.
1992 Min-Ind: 10 G; 1 Sac. Min: 3 G. Ind: 7 G; 1 Sac. **1993** Ind: 16 G; 1.5 Sac. **Total:** 92 G; 8 Sac.

WILLIE MCCLENDON McClendon, Willie Edward 6'1", 205 **RB**
Col: Georgia *HS:* Glynn Acad. [Brunswick, GA] B: 9/13/1957, Brunswick, GA *Drafted:* 1979 Round 3 ChiB
1979 ChiB: Rec 6-27 4.5; KR 1-12 12.0. **1980** ChiB: KR 1-11 11.0.
1981 ChiB: Rec 2-4 2.0. **1982** ChiB: Rec 1-7 7.0. **Total:** Rec 9-38 4.2; KR 2-23 11.5.

		Rushing			
Year Team	G	Att	Yds	Avg	TD
1979 ChiB	16	37	160	4.3	1
1980 ChiB	16	10	88	8.8	1
1981 ChiB	16	30	74	2.5	0
1982 ChiB	9	17	47	2.8	0
NFL Total	57	94	369	3.9	2

DEXTER MCCLEON McCleon, Dexter Keith 5'10", 195 **DB**
Col: Clemson *HS:* Meridian [MS] B: 10/9/1973, Meridian, MS
Drafted: 1997 Round 2 StL
1997 StL: 16 G; Int 1-0; 1 Sac. **1998** StL: 15 G; Int 2-29. **Total:** 31 G; Int 3-29; 1 Sac.

J.J. MCCLESKEY McCleskey, Thomas Joseph Jr. 5'8", 180 **CB**
Col: Tennessee *HS:* Karns [Knoxville, TN] B: 4/10/1970, Knoxville, TN
1994 NO: 13 G. **1995** NO: 14 G; KR 1-0; Int 1-0. **1996** NO-Ariz: 10 G; KR 1-18 18.0. NO: 5 G; KR 1-18 18.0. Ariz: 5 G. **1997** Ariz: 13 G; Int 1-15; 1 Sac. **1998** Ariz: 12 G; Int 1-1. **Total:** 62 G; KR 2-18 9.0; Int 3-16; 1 Sac.

CURTIS MCCLINTON McClinton, Curtis Realious Jr. 6'3", 227 **FB-TE**
(Count) *Col:* Kansas *HS:* North [Wichita, KS] B: 6/25/1939, Muskogee, OK *Drafted:* 1961 Round 14 DalT
1962 DalT: KR 2-32 16.0. **1963** KC: Pass 3-1 33.3%, 33 11.00 1 TD.
1964 KC: Scor 1 2XP. **1965** KC: Pass 1-0. **1967** KC: Scor 1 2XP.
Total: Pass 4-1 25.0%, 33 8.25 1 TD; KR 2-32 16.0; Scor 2 2XP.

Year Team	G	Rushing Att	Yds	Avg	TD	Receiving Rec	Yds	Avg	TD	Fum	Tot TD
1962 DalT	14	111	604	**5.4**	2	29	333	11.5	0	5	2
1963 KC	14	142	568	4.0	3	27	301	11.1	3	4	6
1964 KC	14	73	252	3.5	1	13	221	17.0	2	5	3
1965 KC	14	175	661	3.8	**6**	37	590	15.9	3	**9**	9
1966 KC	14	140	540	3.9	4	19	285	15.0	5	2	9
1967 KC	14	97	392	4.0	2	26	219	8.4	1	2	3
1968 KC	9	24	107	4.5	0	3	-4	-1.3	0	0	0
1969 KC	14	0	0	—	0	0	0	—	0	0	0
NFL Total	107	762	3124	4.1	18	154	1945	12.6	14	27	32

MIKE MCCLOSKEY McCloskey, Michael James 6'5", 244 **TE**
Col: Penn State *HS:* Father Judge [Philadelphia, PA] B: 2/2/1961, Philadelphia, PA *Drafted:* 1983 Round 4 Hou
1983 Hou: KR 1-11 11.0. **Total:** KR 1-11 11.0.

Year Team	G	Receiving Rec	Yds	Avg	TD
1983 Hou	16	16	137	8.6	1
1984 Hou	15	9	152	16.9	1
1985 Hou	16	4	29	7.3	1
1987 Phi	1	0	0	—	0
NFL Total	48	29	318	11.0	3

TYRUS MCCLOUD McCloud, Tyrus Kamall 6'1", 250 **LB**
Col: Louisville *HS:* Nova [Davie, FL] B: 11/23/1974, Fort Lauderdale, FL *Drafted:* 1997 Round 4 Bal
1997 Bal: 16 G; KR 1-0; 1 Fum. **1998** Bal: 7 G. **Total:** 23 G; KR 1-0; 1 Fum.

DAVE MCCLOUGHAN McCloughan, David Kent 6'1", 186 **DB**
Col: Colorado *HS:* Loveland [CO] B: 11/20/1966, San Leandro, CA *Drafted:* 1991 Round 3 Ind
1991 Ind: 15 G; KR 2-35 17.5. **1992** GB: 5 G. **1993** Sea: 15 G; PR 1-10 10.0. **1994** Sea: 13 G; PR 3-26 8.7. **Total:** 48 G; PR 4-36 9.0; KR 2-35 17.5.

KENT MCCLOUGHAN McCloughan, Kent Auburn 6'1", 190 **DB**
Col: Nebraska *HS:* Broken Bow [NE] B: 2/12/1940, Scottsbluff, NE *Drafted:* 1965 Round 11 Hou

Year Team	G	Interceptions Int	Yds	TD
1965 Oak	14	3	22	0
1966 Oak	14	4	62	0
1967 Oak	14	2	7	0
1968 Oak	8	1	0	0
1969 Oak	4	0	0	0
1970 Oak	13	5	5	0
NFL Total	67	15	96	0

WILLIE MCCLUNG McClung, William Albert 6'2", 250 **OT-DT**
Col: Florida A&M *HS:* Edward Bok Area Vo-Tech [Philadelphia, PA] B: 5/9/1930, Marion, AL
1955 Pit: 12 G. **1956** Pit: 12 G. **1957** Pit: 12 G. **1958** Cle: 12 G; KR 1-0. **1959** Cle: 12 G. **1960** Det: 11 G. **1961** Det: 3 G. **Total:** 74 G; KR 1-0.

BRIAN MCCLURE McClure, Brian Scott 6'6", 222 **QB**
Col: Bowling Green State *HS:* Rootstown [OH] B: 12/28/1963, Ravenna, OH *Drafted:* 1986 Round 12 Buf
1987 Buf: 1 G; Pass 38-20 52.6%, 181 4.76 3 Int; Rush 2-4 2.0.

BOB MCCLURE McClure, Robert D 6'1", 224 **G**
(Buster) *Col:* Drake; Nevada-Reno *HS:* Russellville [AR]; Flora HS [IL] B: 7/8/1924, Dardanelle, AR *Drafted:* 1946 Round 3 Bos
1947 Bos: 10 G; KR 1-12 12.0. **1948** Bos: 12 G; KR 2-14 7.0. **Total:** 22 G; KR 3-26 8.7.

WAYNE MCCLURE McClure, Wayne Leroy 6'1", 225 **LB**
Col: Mississippi *HS:* Hattiesburg [MS] B: 7/2/1942, Merryville, TN *Drafted:* 1968 Round 9 KC
1968 Cin: 13 G; KR 1-11 11.0. **1970** Cin: 14 G. **Total:** 27 G; KR 1-11 11.0.

DAVID MCCLUSKEY McCluskey, David Eugene 6'1", 227 **RB**
(Davie) *Col:* Georgia *HS:* West Rome [Rome, GA] B: 11/5/1963, Rome, GA *Drafted:* 1987 Round 10 Cin
1987 Cin: Rec 1-8 8.0.

Year Team	G	Rushing Att	Yds	Avg	TD	Fum
1987 Cin	3	29	94	3.2	1	2

MILT MCCOLL McColl, Milton Bird 6'6", 248 **LB**
Col: Stanford *HS:* South Hills [Covina, CA] B: 8/28/1959, Oak Park, IL
1981 SF: 16 G; Int 1-22. **1982** SF: 9 G; 0.5 Sac. **1983** SF: 12 G; 1 Sac. **1984** SF: 16 G; 4 Sac. **1985** SF: 16 G; **1** Fum TD; 6 Pt. **1986** SF: 16 G; 2 Sac. **1987** SF: 12 G; Int 1-0; 1 Sac. **1988** LARd: 15 G. **Total:** 112 G; Int 2-22; 1 Fum TD; 6 Pt; 8.5 Sac.

BILL MCCOLL McColl, William Frazer Jr. 6'4", 230 **OE**
Col: Stanford *HS:* Herbert Hoover [San Diego, CA] B: 4/2/1930, San Diego, CA *Drafted:* 1952 Round 3 ChiB
1952 ChiB: KR 1-0. **1953** ChiB: **1** Fum TD. **1955** ChiB: Pass 2-1 50.0%, 59 29.50. **1956** ChiB: Pass 4-1 25.0%, 79 19.75 1 TD 2 Int; KR 2-4 2.0. **Total:** Pass 6-2 33.3%, 138 23.00 1 TD 2 Int; KR 3-4 1.3; 1 Fum TD.

Year Team	G	Receiving Rec	Yds	Avg	TD	Fum	Tot TD
1952 ChiB	12	20	277	13.9	2	0	2
1953 ChiB	12	36	453	12.6	4	2	5
1954 ChiB	12	24	368	15.3	2	0	2
1955 ChiB	12	35	502	14.3	4	0	4
1956 ChiB	12	24	322	13.4	4	0	4
1957 ChiB	12	19	282	14.8	1	0	1
1958 ChiB	12	35	517	14.8	8	1	8
1959 ChiB	12	8	94	11.8	0	0	0
NFL Total	96	201	2815	14.0	25	3	26

ANDY MCCOLLUM McCollum, Andrew Jon 6'4", 295 **C-OG**
Col: Toledo *HS:* Revere [Richfield, OH] B: 6/2/1970, Akron, OH
1995 NO: 11 G. **1996** NO: 16 G. **1997** NO: 16 G. **1998** NO: 16 G. **Total:** 59 G.

HARLEY MCCOLLUM McCollum, Harley Raymond 6'4", 245 **T**
Col: Tulane *HS:* Stillwell [OK]; Wagoner HS [OK] B: 2/28/1916 D: 6/1984, Palm Springs, CA
AAFC **1946** NY-A: 10 G. **1947** ChiA: 13 G; KR 1-9 9.0. **Total:** 23 G; KR 1-9 9.0.

BUBBA MCCOLLUM McCollum, James Henry 6'0", 250 **DT**
Col: Kentucky *HS:* Male [Louisville, KY] B: 9/13/1952, Louisville, KY
1974 Hou: 11 G.

DON MCCOMB McComb, Donald H 6'4", 240 **DE**
Col: Villanova *HS:* Camden Catholic [NJ] B: 3/24/1934 *Drafted:* 1956 Round 21 NYG
1960 Bos: 1 G.

TONY MCCOMBS McCombs, Antonias Orlando 6'2", 246 **LB**
Col: Eastern Kentucky *HS:* Christian Co. [Hopkinsville, KY] B: 8/24/1974, Hopkinsville, KY *Drafted:* 1997 Round 6 Ariz
1997 Ariz: 12 G. **1998** Ariz: 14 G; Int 1-14. **Total:** 26 G; Int 1-14.

NAT MCCOMBS McCombs, Nathaniel Hawthorne 5'11", 226 **G-OE-T-C**
(AKA Chief Big Twig) *Col:* Haskell Indian *HS:* Eufaula [OK] B: 12/18/1904, Eufaula, OK D: 7/1965, OK
1926 Akr: 8 G; Rec 1 TD; 6 Pt. **1929** Buf: 9 G. **Total:** 17 G; Rec 1 TD; 6 Pt.

PHIL MCCONKEY McConkey, Philip Joseph 5'10", 170 **WR**
Col: Navy *HS:* Canisius Prep [Buffalo, NY] B: 2/24/1957, Buffalo, NY

Year Team	G	Receiving Rec	Yds	Avg	TD	Punt Returns Ret	Yds	Avg	TD
1984 NYG	13	8	154	19.3	0	46	306	6.7	0
1985 NYG	16	25	404	16.2	1	53	442	8.3	0
1986 GB-NYG	16	16	279	17.4	1	32	253	7.9	0
1986 GB	4	0	0	—	0	0	0	—	0
1986 NYG	12	16	279	17.4	1	32	253	7.9	0
1987 NYG	12	11	186	16.9	0	42	394	9.4	0
1988 NYG	16	5	72	14.4	0	40	313	7.8	0
1989 Pho-SD	11	2	18	9.0	0	15	124	8.3	0
1989 Pho	6	2	18	9.0	0	1	13	13.0	0
1989 SD	5	0	0	—	0	14	111	7.9	0
NFL Total	84	67	1113	16.6	2	228	1832	8.0	0

Year Team	Kickoff Returns Ret	Yds	Avg	TD	Fum	Tot TD
1984 NYG	28	541	19.3	0	2	1
1985 NYG	12	234	19.5	0	1	1
1986 GB-NYG	24	471	19.6	0	1	1
1986 NYG	24	471	19.6	0	1	1
1987 NYG	1	8	8.0	0	2	0
1988 NYG	2	30	15.0	0	2	0
1989 Pho-SD	2	40	20.0	0	1	0
1989 Pho	2	40	20.0	0	0	0
1989 SD	0	0	—	0	1	0
NFL Total	69	1324	19.2	0	9	3

BRIAN MCCONNELL McConnell, Brian Thomas 6'4", 220 **LB**
Col: Michigan State *HS:* Peddie School [Highstown, NJ] B: 1/21/1950, Smoke Rise, NJ *Drafted:* 1973 Round 7 Buf
1973 Buf-Hou: 8 G. Buf: 1 G. Hou: 7 G. **Total:** 8 G.

DEWEY MCCONNELL McConnell, Dewey L 6'0", 190 **DB-DE**
Col: Wyoming *HS:* Laramie [WY] B: 1/26/1930, Laramie, WY D: 2/19/1984, Laramie, WY *Drafted:* 1952 Round 3 LARm
1954 Pit: 9 G; Rec 1-2 2.0; Int 3-117.

FRANK MCCONNELL McConnell, William Felton 6'0", 195 **G**
Col: Virginia; Georgia Tech *HS:* Commerce [GA] B: 8/23/1900
D: 11/26/1985
1927 Buf: 5 G.

DARRIS MCCORD McCord, Darris Paul 6'4", 250 **DE-DT-OT**
(Cody; Dakota) *Col:* Tennessee *HS:* Cass Tech [Detroit, MI]; Franklin HS [TN] B: 1/4/1933, Detroit, MI *Drafted:* 1955 Round 3 Det
1955 Det: 12 G. **1956** Det: 12 G. **1957** Det: 12 G; Scor **1** Saf; 2 Pt. **1958** Det: 12 G. **1959** Det: 12 G. **1960** Det: 12 G. **1961** Det: 14 G; Int 1-11. **1962** Det: 14 G; Scor 1 Saf; 2 Pt. **1963** Det: 13 G; Int 1-5; **1** Fum TD; 6 Pt. **1964** Det: 14 G. **1965** Det: 14 G. **1966** Det: 13 G. **1967** Det: 14 G; Int 1-15. **Total:** 168 G; Int 3-31; Scor 2 Saf; 1 Fum TD; 10 Pt.

HURVIN MCCORMACK McCormack, Hurvin Michael 6'5", 281 **DT**
Col: Indiana *HS:* New Dorp [Staten Island, NY] B: 4/6/1972, Brooklyn, NY
1994 Dal: 4 G. **1995** Dal: 15 G; 2 Sac. **1996** Dal: 16 G; 2.5 Sac. **1997** Dal: 13 G; 0.5 Sac. **1998** Dal: 16 G; 5 Sac. **Total:** 64 G; 10 Sac.

MIKE MCCORMACK McCormack, Michael Joseph Jr. 6'4", 246 **OT-DG-DT**
Col: Kansas *HS:* De La Salle [Kansas City, KS] B: 6/21/1930, Chicago, IL *Drafted:* 1951 Round 3 NYY *HOF:* 1984
1951 NYY: 12 G; KR 1-0. **1954** Cle: 12 G; Int 1-14. **1955** Cle: 12 G. **1956** Cle: 12 G. **1957** Cle: 12 G; Rush 0-4. **1958** Cle: 9 G. **1959** Cle: 10 G. **1960** Cle: 12 G. **1961** Cle: 14 G; Rush 0-4. **1962** Cle: 14 G. **Total:** 119 G; Rush 0-8; KR 1-0; Int 1-14.

DAVE MCCORMICK McCormick, David Oliver 6'6", 250 **OT**
Col: Louisiana State *HS:* Rayville [LA] B: 7/10/1943, Winnsboro, LA
D: 3/17/1986, Rayville, LA *Drafted:* 1965 Round 5 SF
1966 SF: 14 G. **1967** NO: 2 G. **Total:** 16 G.

ELMER MCCORMICK McCormick, Elmer Francis 5'7", 220 **G-C-T-WB**
(Moose) *Col:* Detroit Mercy; Canisius *HS:* St. John's Prep [Danvers, MA] B: 10/1898, Holyoke, MA Deceased
1923 Buf: 8 G. **1924** Buf: 3 G. **1925** Buf-Fra: 16 G. Buf: 8 G. Fra: 8 G. **1926** Har: 3 G. **Total:** 30 G.

FELIX MCCORMICK McCormick, Felix John 5'7", 185 **FB-G-TB**
Col: Bucknell *HS:* Bloomfield [NJ] B: 5/21/1905, Newark, NJ
D: 3/30/1971, Glen Ridge, NJ
1929 Ora: 10 G; Scor 3, 1 FG. **1930** Nwk: 3 G. **Total:** 13 G; Scor 3, 1 FG.

FRANK MCCORMICK McCormick, Frank G 5'11", 190 **FB**
Col: South Dakota *HS:* Wagner [SD] B: 11/5/1894, Genoa, NE
D: 3/24/1976, Fullerton, CA
1920 Akr: 11 G. **1921** Akr-Cin: 3 G; Rush 3 TD; 18 Pt. Akr: 2 G; Rush 3 TD; 18 Pt. Cin: 1 G. **Total:** 14 G; Rush 3 TD; 18 Pt.

LEN MCCORMICK McCormick, Gardner Len 6'3", 232 **C-LB**
(Tuffy) *Col:* Schreiner Coll.; Southwestern (Tex.); Baylor *HS:* Eldorado [TX] B: 10/28/1922, Eldorado, TX
AAFC **1948** BalA: 11 G; Int 1-5.

JOHN MCCORMICK McCormick, John Joseph Jr. 6'1", 208 **QB-P**
Col: Massachusetts *HS:* Belmont [MA] B: 5/26/1937, Boston, MA
1962 Min: Rush 2-4 2.0. **1963** Den: Rush 3-(-5) -1.7. **1965** Den: Rush 1-(-2) -2.0. **1966** Den: Rush 4-2 0.5. **Total:** Rush 10-(-1) -0.1.

		Passing							
Year Team	**G**	**Att**	**Comp**	**Comp%**	**Yds**	**YPA**	**TD**	**Int**	**Rating**
1962 Min	13	18	7	38.9	104	5.78	0	5	19.0
1963 Den	9	72	28	38.9	417	5.79	4	3	59.8
1965 Den	14	253	103	40.7	1292	5.11	7	14	43.5
1966 Den	14	193	68	35.2	993	5.15	6	15	30.9
1968 Den	1	19	8	42.1	89	4.68	0	1	34.8
NFL Total	51	555	214	38.6	2895	5.22	17	38	37.6

	Punting			
Year Team	**Punts**	**Yds**	**Avg**	**Fum**
1962 Min	46	1795	39.0	1
1963 Den	0	0	—	2
1965 Den	1	45	45.0	2
1966 Den	0	0	—	3
NFL Total	47	1840	39.1	8

TOM MCCORMICK McCormick, Thomas 5'11", 185 **HB**
Col: Menlo Coll. CA (J.C.); U. of Pacific *HS:* Sam Francisco Polytechnic [CA] B: 5/16/1930, Waco, TX *Drafted:* 1952 Round 8 LARm
1953 LARm: Rec 5-72 14.4; PR 2-2 1.0; KR 5-134 26.8. **1954** LARm: Rec 3-58 19.3; PR 7-8 1.1; KR 3-49 16.3. **1955** LARm: Rec 3-(-1) -0.3; KR 2-42 21.0. **1956** SF: KR 1-18 18.0. **Total:** Rec 11-129 11.7; PR 9-10 1.1; KR 11-243 22.1.

		Rushing				
Year Team	**G**	**Att**	**Yds**	**Avg**	**TD**	**Fum**
1953 LARm	11	20	29	1.5	0	3
1954 LARm	9	48	173	3.6	0	1
1955 LARm	6	16	66	4.1	1	0
1956 SF	6	2	4	2.0	0	0
NFL Total	32	86	272	3.2	1	4

WALT MCCORMICK McCormick, Walter Kendell 6'1", 215 **C-LB**
(Mac) *Col:* Washington; USC *HS:* Visalia [CA] B: 1927
AAFC **1948** SF-A: 9 G.

KEZ MCCORVEY McCorvey, Kezarrick Montines 6'0", 184 **WR**
Col: Florida State *HS:* Gautier [MS] B: 1/23/1972, Gautier, MS
Drafted: 1995 Round 5 Det
1995 Det: 1 G. **1996** Det: 1 G. **1997** Det: 7 G; Rec 2-9 4.5. **Total:** 9 G; Rec 2-9 4.5.

MCCOY McCoy 175 **T**
Col: No College Deceased
1920 Det: 1 G.

TONY MCCOY McCoy, Anthony Bernard 6'0", 282 **DT-NT**
Col: Florida *HS:* Maynard Evans [Orlando, FL] B: 6/10/1969, Orlando, FL *Drafted:* 1992 Round 4 Ind
1992 Ind: 16 G; 1 Sac. **1993** Ind: 6 G. **1994** Ind: 15 G; 6 Sac. **1995** Ind: 16 G; 2.5 Sac. **1996** Ind: 15 G; 5 Sac. **1997** Ind: 16 G; 2.5 Sac. **1998** Ind: 14 G; 6 Sac. **Total:** 98 G; 23.0 Sac.

JOEL MCCOY McCoy, Joel Lawson Jr. 5'10", 170 **TB-DB**
(Real) *Col:* Alabama *HS:* Shades Valley [Birmingham, AL]
B: 8/22/1920, Birmingham, AL
1946 Det: 10 G; Pass 18-6 33.3%, 72 4.00 4 Int; Rush 19-(-29) -1.5; PR 1-8 8.0; KR 1-7 7.0; 2 Fum.

LARRY MCCOY McCoy, Larry Joe 6'2", 240 **LB**
Col: Lamar *HS:* Madison [Madisonville, TX] B: 8/12/1961, Madisonville, TX
1984 LARd: 4 G. **1987** NO: 3 G; 2 Sac. **Total:** 7 G; 2 Sac.

LLOYD MCCOY McCoy, Lloyd 6'1", 245 **OG**
Col: San Diego State *HS:* Kennewick [WA] B: 1942
1964 SD: 1 G.

MIKE MCCOY McCoy, Michael Charles 5'11", 183 **DB**
(M.C.) *Col:* West Los Angeles Coll. CA (J.C.); Colorado *HS:* West Memphis [AR] B: 8/16/1953, West Memphis, AR *Drafted:* 1976 Round 3 GB

		Kickoff Returns				Interceptions			
Year Team	**G**	**Ret**	**Yds**	**Avg**	**TD**	**Int**	**Yds**	**TD**	**Fum**
1976 GB	14	18	457	25.4	0	0	0	0	1
1977 GB	14	0	0	—	0	4	2	0	0
1978 GB	16	0	0	—	0	3	34	0	2
1979 GB	16	11	248	22.5	0	3	60	0	1
1980 GB	16	14	261	18.6	0	1	0	0	1
1981 GB	16	11	221	20.1	0	2	20	0	1
1982 GB	9	0	0	—	0	0	0	0	0
1983 GB	9	0	0	—	0	0	0	0	0
NFL Total	110	54	1187	22.0	0	13	116	0	6

MIKE MCCOY McCoy, Michael Patrick 6'5", 284 **DT-NT**
Col: Notre Dame *HS:* Cathedral Prep [Erie, PA] B: 9/6/1948, Erie, PA
Drafted: 1970 Round 1 GB
1970 GB: 14 G; KR 3-22 7.3; 1 Fum. **1971** GB: 12 G. **1972** GB: 12 G. **1973** GB: 14 G. **1974** GB: 14 G; Int 1-5. **1975** GB: 14 G; **1** Fum TD; 6 Pt. **1976** GB: 14 G. **1977** Oak: 14 G; KR 1-0. **1978** Oak: 15 G. **1979** NYG: 3 G. **1980** NYG-Det: 6 G. NYG: 2 G. Det: 4 G. **Total:** 132 G; KR 4-22 5.5; Int 1-5; 1 Fum TD; 6 Pt; 1 Fum.

FRED MCCRARY McCrary, Freddy Demetrius 6'0", 226 **RB**
Col: Mississippi State *HS:* Naples [FL] B: 9/19/1972, Naples, FL
Drafted: 1995 Round 6 Phi
1995 Phi: 13 G; Rush 3-1 0.3 1 TD; Rec 9-60 6.7; KR 1-1 1.0; 6 Pt. **1997** NO: 7 G; Rush 8-15 1.9; Rec 4-17 4.3; KR 2-26 13.0. **Total:** 20 G; Rush 11-16 1.5 1 TD; Rec 13-77 5.9; KR 3-27 9.0; 6 Pt.

GREG MCCRARY McCrary, Gregory Alonza 6'1", 233 **TE**
Col: Clark Atlanta *HS:* Griffin [GA] B: 3/24/1952, Griffin, GA
Drafted: 1975 Round 5 Atl
1975 Atl: 13 G; KR 3-48 16.0. **1977** Atl: 13 G; Rec 2-48 24.0 1 TD; 6 Pt. **1978** Was-SD: 13 G; Rush 2-18 9.0; Rec 1-29 29.0 1 TD; 6 Pt. Was: 5 G. SD: 8 G; Rush 2-18 9.0; Rec 1-29 29.0 1 TD; 6 Pt. **1979** SD: 14 G; Rec 5-32 6.4; Scor **1** Saf; 2 Pt. **1980** SD: 16 G; Rec 11-106 9.6 2 TD; 12 Pt. **1981** Was: 5 G; Rec 3-13 4.3. **Total:** 74 G; Rush 2-18 9.0; Rec 22-228 10.4 4 TD; KR 3-48 16.0; Scor 1 Saf; 26 Pt.

HERDIS MCCRARY McCrary, Herdis William 6'0", 207 **FB-LB-HB-DB**
Col: Georgia *HS:* Bicknell [IN] B: 6/9/1904, Bicknell, IN D: 5/11/1981, Green Bay, WI
1929 GB: Pass 1 TD; Rec 2 TD; Int **1** TD. **1930** GB: Rec 2 TD.
Total: Pass 1 TD; Rec 4 TD; Int 1 TD.

		Rushing				Tot
Year Team	**G**	**Att**	**Yds**	**Avg**	**TD**	**TD**
1929 GB	13	—	—	—	1	4
1930 GB	14	—	—	—	4	6
1931 GB	12	—	—	—	1	1

1932 GB	11	42	152	3.6	1	1
1933 GB	2	6	10	1.7	0	0
NFL Total	52	48	162	3.4	7	12

MICHAEL MCCRARY McCrary, Michael Curtis 6′4″, 266 **DE**
Col: Wake Forest *HS:* George C. Marshall [Falls Church, VA]
B: 7/7/1970, Vienna, VA *Drafted:* 1993 Round 7 Sea
1993 Sea: 15 G; 4 Sac. **1994** Sea: 16 G; 1.5 Sac. **1995** Sea: 11 G; 1 Sac. **1996** Sea: 16 G; 13.5 Sac. **1997** Bal: 15 G; 9 Sac. **1998** Bal: 16 G; 14.5 Sac. **Total:** 89 G; 43.5 Sac.

BRUCE MCCRAY McCray, Bruce Edward 5′9″, 181 **DB**
Col: Independence CC KS; Western Illinois *HS:* East [Wichita, KS]
B: 10/27/1963
1987 ChiB: 3 G; Int 1-23 1 TD; 6 Pt.

PRENTICE MCCRAY McCray, Prentice Jr. 6′1″, 188 **DB**
Col: Arizona State *HS:* Edison [Stockton, CA] B: 3/1/1951, Los Angeles, CA *Drafted:* 1973 Round 8 Det

		Interceptions		
Year Team	G	Int	Yds	TD
1974 NE	14	3	61	0
1975 NE	14	0	0	0
1976 NE	14	5	182	2
1977 NE	14	4	61	0
1978 NE	8	0	0	0
1979 NE	14	3	48	0
1980 NE-Det	10	0	0	0
1980 NE	3	0	0	0
1980 Det	7	0	0	0
NFL Total	88	15	352	2

WILLIE MCCRAY McCray, Willie Lee Jr. 6′5″, 234 **DE**
Col: Alabama; Troy State *HS:* Hopewell [VA]; Laurinburg Inst. [NC]
B: 7/17/1953, Fort Lee, VA *Drafted:* 1978 Round 11 SF
1978 SF: 16 G.

LOAIRD MCCREARY McCreary, Loaird Arthur 6′5″, 227 **TE-WR**
Col: Tennessee State *HS:* Walter F. George [Atlanta, GA]
B: 3/15/1953, Crawfordville, GA *Drafted:* 1976 Round 2 Mia
1976 Mia: 14 G; Rec 2-51 25.5. **1977** Mia: 14 G; Rec 2-10 5.0 1 TD; KR 1-30 30.0; 6 Pt. **1978** Mia: 16 G; Rec 3-27 9.0 2 TD; 12 Pt. **1979** NYG: 11 G; Rec 1-7 7.0. **Total:** 55 G; Rec 8-95 11.9 3 TD; KR 1-30 30.0; 18 Pt.

BOB MCCREARY McCreary, Robert Joe 6′5″, 256 **OT**
Col: Wake Forest *HS:* Hudson [NC] B: 6/20/1939, Lenoir, NC
Drafted: 1961 Round 5 SF
1961 Dal: 9 G.

ED MCCRILLIS McCrillis, Edgar Vincent Frederick 6′0″, 205 **G**
Col: Brown *HS:* Classical [Providence, RI] B: 9/7/1904, New York, NY
D: 9/1/1940, Warwick, RI
1926 Prov: 1 G. **1929** Bost: 7 G. **Total:** 8 G.

JOHN MCCRUMBLY McCrumbly, John Paul 6′1″, 245 **LB**
Col: Tyler JC TX; Texas A&M *HS:* Woodrow Wilson [Dallas, TX]
B: 7/28/1952, Dallas, TX *Drafted:* 1975 Round 5 Buf
1975 Buf: 13 G.

DALE MCCULLERS McCullers, Dale Green 6′1″, 215 **LB**
Col: Florida State *HS:* Suwannee [Live Oak, FL] B: 10/11/1947, Lake City, FL *Drafted:* 1969 Round 12 Mia
1969 Mia: 14 G; PR 1-0; 1 Fum.

EARL MCCULLOUCH McCullouch, Earl Raymond 5′11″, 175 **WR**
Col: USC *HS:* Long Beach Polytechnic [CA] B: 1/10/1946, Clarksville, TX *Drafted:* 1968 Round 1 Det
1968 Det: Rush 3-13 4.3. **1969** Det: Rush 1-4 4.0. **1970** Det: Rush 1-7 7.0. **1971** Det: Rush 1-(-7) -7.0. **1972** Det: Pass 1-1 100.0%, 23 23.00. **1973** Det: Rush 2-12 6.0. **Total:** Pass 1-1 100.0%, 23 23.00; Rush 8-29 3.6.

		Receiving				
Year Team	G	Rec	Yds	Avg	TD	Fum
1968 Det	14	40	680	17.0	5	1
1969 Det	14	33	529	16.0	5	0
1970 Det	10	15	278	18.5	4	0
1971 Det	13	21	552	26.3	3	0
1972 Det	10	5	96	19.2	1	0
1973 Det	11	9	179	19.9	1	0
1974 NO	3	1	5	5.0	0	0
NFL Total	75	124	2319	18.7	19	1

GEORGE MCCULLOUGH McCullough, George Wayne Jr. 5′10″, 187 **DB**
Col: Baylor *HS:* Ball [Galveston, TX] B: 2/18/1975, Galveston, TX
Drafted: 1997 Round 5 Ten
1997 Ten: 2 G. **1998** Ten: 7 G. **Total:** 9 G.

HAL MCCULLOUGH McCullough, Harold Francis 5′11″, 170 **TB-DB**
Col: Cornell *HS:* Boys [Brooklyn, NY] B: 4/4/1918, New York, NY
D: 2/13/1991, Doylestown, PA
1942 Bkn: 9 G; Pass 38-12 31.6%, 211 5.55 1 TD **3** Int; Rush 21-(-17) -0.8; PR 1-0; Punt 12-462 38.5.

HUGH MCCULLOUGH McCullough, Hugh Warner 6′0″, 185 **DB-TB-QB**
Col: Oklahoma *HS:* Central [Oklahoma City, OK] B: 5/18/1916, Anadarko, OK *Drafted:* 1939 Round 4 Pit
1939 Pit: Rec 4-57 14.3. **1940** ChiC: Int 5-68; Scor 19, 0-1 FG, 1-3 33.3% XK. **1941** ChiC: PR 3-35 11.7; KR 1-23 23.0. **1945** Bos: Rec 1-17 17.0. **Total:** Rec 5-74 14.8; PR 3-35 11.7; KR 1-23 23.0; Int 5-68; Scor 25, 0-1 FG, 1-3 33.3% XK.

		Passing							
Year Team	G	Att	Comp	Comp%	Yds	YPA	TD	Int	Rating
1939 Pit	10	100	32	32.0	443	4.43	2	12	14.3
1940 ChiC	11	116	43	37.1	529	4.56	4	21	23.9
1941 ChiC	7	32	12	37.5	133	4.16	0	5	11.1
1943 PhPt	1	0	0	—	0	—	0	0	—
1945 Bos	7	6	0	0.0	0	0.00	0	3	0.0
NFL Total	36	254	87	34.3	1105	4.35	6	41	17.0

	Rushing				Punting		
Year Team	Att	Yds	Avg	TD	Punts	Yds	Avg
1939 Pit	60	96	1.6	1	31	1006	32.5
1940 ChiC	57	278	4.9	3	30	1215	40.5
1941 ChiC	15	22	1.5	0	3	122	40.7
1945 Bos	2	1	0.5	0	2	64	32.0
NFL Total	134	397	3.0	4	66	2407	36.5

JAKE MCCULLOUGH McCullough, Richard Charles 6′5″, 270 **DE**
Col: Clemson *HS:* Loris [SC] B: 7/23/1965, Loris, SC *Drafted:* 1989 Round 4 Den
1989 Den: 10 G. **1990** Den: 6 G. **Total:** 16 G.

BOB MCCULLOUGH McCullough, Robert Vernon 6′2″, 245 **OG**
Col: Colorado *HS:* Helena [MT] B: 11/18/1940, Helena, MT
1962 Den: 14 G. **1963** Den: 14 G. **1964** Den: 14 G. **1965** Den: 14 G; Rec 1-1 1.0. **Total:** 56 G; Rec 1-1 1.0.

SAM MCCULLUM McCullum, Samuel Charles 6′2″, 203 **WR**
(Sudden-Sam) *Col:* Montana State *HS:* Flathead [Kalispell, MT]
B: 11/30/1952, McComb, MS *Drafted:* 1974 Round 9 Min
1974 Min: PR 12-85 7.1; KR 12-300 25.0. **1975** Min: PR 12-22 1.8; KR 9-221 24.6. **Total:** PR 24-107 4.5; KR 21-521 24.8.

		Receiving				
Year Team	G	Rec	Yds	Avg	TD	Fum
1974 Min	12	7	138	19.7	3	1
1975 Min	9	2	25	12.5	0	2
1976 Sea	14	32	506	15.8	4	0
1977 Sea	13	9	198	22.0	1	0
1978 Sea	16	37	525	14.2	3	0
1979 Sea	16	46	739	16.1	4	2
1980 Sea	16	62	874	14.1	6	0
1981 Sea	16	46	567	12.3	3	1
1982 Min	6	12	131	10.9	0	1
1983 Min	11	21	314	15.0	2	0
NFL Total	129	274	4017	14.7	26	7

DAVE MCCURRY McCurry, David Gene 6′1″, 187 **DB**
Col: Iowa State *HS:* Grinnell [IA] B: 2/23/1951, Grinnell, IA
Drafted: 1973 Round 5 Mia
1974 NE: 2 G.

MIKE MCCURRY McCurry, Michael Lee 6′3″, 258 **OG**
Col: Indiana *HS:* Marshall [Indianapolis, IN] B: 3/26/1963, Indianapolis, IN
1987 Min: 3 G.

JIM MCCUSKER McCusker, James Brian 6′2″, 246 **OT**
(Mac) *Col:* Pittsburgh *HS:* Jamestown [NY] B: 5/19/1936, Jamestown, NY *Drafted:* 1958 Round 2 ChiC
1958 ChiC: 11 G. **1959** Phi: 12 G. **1960** Phi: 12 G. **1961** Phi: 13 G. **1962** Phi: 14 G. **1963** Cle: 7 G. **1964** NYJ: 14 G; KR 1-0. **Total:** 83 G; KR 1-0.

LAWRENCE MCCUTCHEON McCutcheon, Lawrence 6′1″, 205 **RB**
Col: Colorado State *HS:* Plainview [TX] B: 6/2/1950, Plainview, TX
Drafted: 1972 Round 3 LARm
1973 LARm: KR 1-6 6.0. **1975** LARm: Pass 1-0. **1978** LARm: Pass 1-0. **1980** Den-Sea: Pass 2-1 50.0%, 12 6.00. Sea: Pass 2-1 50.0%, 12 6.00. **Total:** Pass 4-1 25.0%, 12 3.00; KR 1-6 6.0.

		Rushing				Receiving					Tot
Year Team	G	Att	Yds	Avg	TD	Rec	Yds	Avg	TD	Fum	TD
1972 LARm	3	0	0	—	0	0	0	—	0	0	0
1973 LARm	12	210	1097	5.2	2	30	289	9.6	3	4	5
1974 LARm	14	236	1109	4.7	3	39	408	10.5	2	7	5

1975 LARm	13	213	911	4.3	2	31	230	7.4	1	4	3
1976 LARm	14	291	1168	4.0	9	28	305	10.9	2	10	11
1977 LARm	14	294	1238	4.2	7	25	274	11.0	2	6	9
1978 LARm	8	118	420	3.6	0	12	76	6.3	2	4	2
1979 LARm	11	73	243	3.3	0	19	101	5.3	0	1	0
1980 Den-Sea	14	52	254	4.9	3	9	76	8.4	1	4	4
1980 Den	6	12	52	4.3	0	1	12	12.0	0	1	0
1980 Sea	8	40	202	5.1	3	8	64	8.0	1	3	4
1981 Buf	6	34	138	4.1	0	5	40	8.0	0	1	0
NFL Total	109	1521	6578	4.3	26	198	1799	9.1	13	41	39

KARL MCDADE McDade, Karl Vautrain 6′3″, 195 **C-LB**
Col: Portland *HS:* U.S. Grant [Portland, OR] B: 3/27/1915, Madras, OR
1938 Pit: 6 G.

ED MCDANIEL McDaniel, Edward 5′11″, 230 **LB**
Col: Clemson *HS:* Batesburg-Leesville [Batesburg, SC] B: 3/23/1969, Batesburg, SC *Drafted:* 1992 Round 5 Min
1992 Min: 8 G. **1993** Min: 7 G. **1994** Min: 16 G; Int 1-0; 1.5 Sac. **1995** Min: 16 G; Int 1-3; 4.5 Sac. **1997** Min: 16 G; Int 1-18; 1.5 Sac. **1998** Min: 16 G; 7 Sac. **Total:** 79 G; Int 3-21; 14.5 Sac.

WAHOO MCDANIEL McDaniel, Edward Wahoo 6′1″, 235 **LB-OG-P**
Col: Oklahoma *HS:* Midland [TX] B: 6/19/1938, Bernice, LA
Drafted: 1960 Round 1 LAC
1962 Den: Punt 5-173 34.6. **1965** NYJ: Rush 1-13 13.0. **1966** Mia: Punt 33-1222 37.0. **Total:** Rush 1-13 13.0; Punt 38-1395 36.7.

		Interceptions		
Year Team	**G**	**Int**	**Yds**	**TD**
1960 Hou	7	0	0	0
1961 Den	14	0	0	0
1962 Den	14	4	37	0
1963 Den	14	2	12	0
1964 NYJ	12	3	60	**1**
1965 NYJ	14	1	7	0
1966 Mia	12	2	20	0
1967 Mia	14	1	15	0
1968 Mia	4	0	0	0
NFL Total	105	13	151	1

EMMANUEL MCDANIEL McDaniel, Emmanuel 5′9″, 180 **DB**
Col: East Carolina *HS:* Jonesboro [GA] B: 7/27/1972, Griffin, GA
Drafted: 1996 Round 4 Car
1996 Car: 2 G. **1997** Ind: 3 G. **Total:** 5 G.

JOHNNIE MCDANIEL McDaniel, Johnnie 6′1″, 193 **WR**
Col: Lincoln (Mo.) *HS:* Wenonah [Birmingham, AL] B: 9/23/1951, Birmingham, AL *Drafted:* 1974 Round 8 Cin
1974 Cin: Rush 1-5 5.0; KR 3-64 21.3. **1975** Cin: Rush 1-(-2) -2.0; KR 3-69 23.0. **1978** Was: Rush 2-25 12.5. **Total:** Rush 4-28 7.0; KR 6-133 22.2.

		Receiving				
Year Team	**G**	**Rec**	**Yds**	**Avg**	**TD**	**Fum**
1974 Cin	14	2	79	39.5	0	0
1975 Cin	14	0	0	—	0	1
1976 Cin	14	12	232	19.3	1	0
1977 Cin	14	12	148	12.3	0	0
1978 Was	15	34	577	17.0	4	1
1979 Was	15	25	357	14.3	2	0
1980 Was	10	14	154	11.0	0	0
NFL Total	96	99	1547	15.6	7	2

LECHARLS MCDANIEL McDaniel, LeCharls Barnet 5′9″, 183 **DB**
Col: Cal Poly-S.L.O. *HS:* Seaside [CA] B: 10/15/1958, Fort Bragg, NC
1981 Was: 6 G. **1982** Was: 8 G; Int 1-7. **1983** NYG: 9 G. **Total:** 23 G; Int 1-7.

ORLANDO MCDANIEL McDaniel, Orlando Keith 6′0″, 180 **WR**
Col: Louisiana State *HS:* Lake Charles [LA] B: 12/1/1960, Shreveport, LA *Drafted:* 1982 Round 2 Den
1982 Den: 3 G.

RANDALL MCDANIEL McDaniel, Randall Cornell 6′3″, 276 **OG**
Col: Arizona State *HS:* Agua Fria Union [Avondale, AZ] B: 12/19/1964, Phoenix, AZ *Drafted:* 1988 Round 1 Min
1988 Min: 16 G. **1989** Min: 14 G. **1990** Min: 16 G. **1991** Min: 16 G. **1992** Min: 16 G. **1993** Min: 16 G. **1994** Min: 16 G. **1995** Min: 16 G. **1996** Min: 16 G; Rush 2-1 0.5. **1997** Min: 16 G. **1998** Min: 16 G. **Total:** 174 G; Rush 2-1 0.5.

TERRY MCDANIEL McDaniel, Terence Lee 5′10″, 180 **DB**
Col: Tennessee *HS:* Saginaw [MI] B: 2/8/1965, Mansfield, OH
Drafted: 1988 Round 1 LARd
1989 LARd: 1 Sac. **1990** LARd: 1 Fum TD; 2 Sac. **1994** LARd: 1 Fum TD. **Total:** 2 Fum TD; 3 Sac.

		Interceptions				Tot
Year Team	**G**	**Int**	**Yds**	**TD**	**Fum**	**TD**
1988 LARd	2	0	0	0	0	0
1989 LARd	16	3	21	0	0	0
1990 LARd	16	3	20	0	0	1
1991 LARd	16	0	0	0	0	0
1992 LARd	16	4	180	0	0	0
1993 LARd	16	5	87	1	0	1
1994 LARd	16	7	103	2	0	3
1995 Oak	16	6	46	1	0	1
1996 Oak	16	5	150	1	0	1
1997 Oak	13	1	17	0	1	0
1998 Sea	9	1	43	1	0	1
NFL Total	152	35	667	6	1	8

DAVE MCDANIELS McDaniels, David 6′4″, 200 **WR**
Col: Mississippi Valley State *HS:* Miami Northwestern [FL]
B: 4/9/1945, Miami, FL *Drafted:* 1968 Round 2 Dal
1968 Dal: 4 G.

PELLOM MCDANIELS McDaniels, Pellom III 6′3″, 284 **DE**
Col: Oregon State *HS:* Silver Creek [San Jose, CA] B: 2/21/1968, San Jose, CA
1993 KC: 10 G. **1994** KC: 12 G; 2 Sac. **1995** KC: 16 G; KR 1-0; 2 Sac. **1996** KC: 9 G. **1997** KC: 16 G; 3.5 Sac. **1998** KC: 11 G. **Total:** 74 G; KR 1-0; 7.5 Sac.

GARY MCDERMOTT McDermott, Gary Don 6′1″, 211 **RB**
Col: Tulsa *HS:* Judson [Converse, TX] B: 6/9/1946, Longview, TX
Drafted: 1968 Round 9 Buf
1968 Buf: Pass 3-2 66.7%, 35 11.67; Rec 20-115 5.8 1 TD; KR 1-16 16.0; Scor **1** 2XP. **Total:** Pass 3-2 66.7%, 35 11.67; Rec 20-115 5.8 1 TD; KR 1-16 16.0; Scor 1 2XP.

		Rushing					Tot
Year Team	**G**	**Att**	**Yds**	**Avg**	**TD**	**Fum**	**TD**
1968 Buf	14	47	102	2.2	3	2	4
1969 Atl	4	7	6	0.9	0	0	0
NFL Total	18	54	108	2.0	3	2	4

LLOYD MCDERMOTT McDermott, Lloyd Ivan 6′3″, 240 **DT**
(Big Mac) *Col:* Kentucky *HS:* Holmes [Covington, KY] B: 12/20/1925, Covington, KY D: 1/16/1964, Covington, KY *Drafted:* 1950 Round 6 Phi
1950 Det-ChiC: 12 G. Det: 1 G. ChiC: 11 G. **1951** ChiC: 12 G; Int 1-5. **Total:** 24 G; Int 1-5.

MARDYE MCDOLE McDole, Mardye Kepez 5′11″, 198 **WR**
Col: Mississippi State *HS:* S.S. Murphy [Mobile, AL] B: 5/1/1959, Pensacola, FL *Drafted:* 1981 Round 2 Min
1981 Min: 9 G; KR 11-170 15.5; 1 Fum. **1982** Min: 2 G; KR 1-26 26.0. **1983** Min: 15 G; Rec 3-29 9.7; 1 Fum. **Total:** 26 G; Rec 3-29 9.7; KR 12-196 16.3; 2 Fum.

RON MCDOLE McDole, Roland Owen 6′4″, 265 **DE-DT**
(The Dancing Bear) *Col:* Nebraska *HS:* Thomas DeVilbiss [Toldeo, OH]
B: 9/9/1939, Chester, OH *Drafted:* 1961 Round 4 StL
1964 Buf: Scor **2** Saf. **1975** Was: **1** Fum TD. **1976** Was: Scor **1** Saf. **Total:** Scor 3 Saf; 1 Fum TD.

		Interceptions			Tot
Year Team	**G**	**Int**	**Yds**	**TD**	**TD**
1961 StL	13	0	0	0	0
1962 Hou	4	0	0	0	0
1963 Buf	12	0	0	0	0
1964 Buf	14	1	0	0	0
1965 Buf	14	1	24	0	0
1966 Buf	14	1	4	0	0
1967 Buf	13	1	5	0	0
1968 Buf	14	2	47	0	0
1969 Buf	14	0	0	0	0
1970 Buf	14	0	0	0	0
1971 Was	14	3	18	1	1
1972 Was	14	0	0	0	0
1973 Was	14	0	0	0	0
1974 Was	14	0	0	0	0
1975 Was	14	0	0	0	1
1976 Was	14	0	0	0	0
1977 Was	14	2	15	0	0
1978 Was	16	1	2	0	0
NFL Total	240	12	115	1	2

MCDONALD McDonald 165 **E-G**
1925 Ham: 4 G.

MCDONALD McDonald **WB**
1926 Det: 1 G.

CY MCDONALD McDonald, Cyril 6′1″, 197 **G**
Col: No College *HS:* Business [Washington, DC] Deceased
1921 Was: 3 G.

DEVON MCDONALD McDonald, Devon Linton 6'4", 244 **LB**
Col: Notre Dame *HS:* John F. Kennedy [Paterson, NJ] B: 11/8/1969, Kingston, Jamaica *Drafted:* 1993 Round 4 Ind
1993 Ind: 16 G. **1994** Ind: 16 G; 1 Sac. **1995** Ind: 15 G. **1996** Ariz: 16 G; KR 1-16 16.0. **Total:** 63 G; KR 1-16 16.0; 1 Sac.

DON MCDONALD McDonald, Don Kay 5'11", 185 **DB**
Col: Houston *HS:* Sherman [TX] B: 2/5/1937, Sherman, TX
Drafted: 1958 Round 29 Phi
1961 Buf: 11 G; 1 Fum TD; 6 Pt.

FLIP MCDONALD McDonald, Donald Gene 6'2", 200 **OE-DB-DE**
Col: Oklahoma *HS:* Commerce [OK] B: 2/12/1921, Webb City, MO
AAFC **1948** NY-A: 2 G; Rec 3-30 10.0.

NFL **1944** Bkn-Phi: 7 G; Rec 4-26 6.5 1 TD; Int 1-14; 6 Pt. Bkn: 2 G. Phi: 5 G; Rec 4-26 6.5 1 TD; Int 1-14; 6 Pt. **1945** Phi: 9 G; Rec 8-75 9.4 1 TD; 6 Pt. **1946** Phi: 1 G. **Total:** 17 G; Rec 12-101 8.4 2 TD; Int 1-14; 12 Pt.

DUSTIN MCDONALD McDonald, Dustin C 6'4", 205 **G**
Col: Indiana B: 10/3/1908
1935 GB: 1 G.

DWIGHT MCDONALD McDonald, Dwight Vinson 6'3", 185 **WR**
Col: San Diego City Coll. CA (J.C.); U.S. International; San Diego State
HS: Kearny [San Diego, CA] B: 5/24/1951, Nixon, TX

		Receiving			
Year Team	G	Rec	Yds	Avg	TD
1975 SD	14	19	298	15.7	3
1976 SD	12	11	161	14.6	4
1977 SD	11	13	174	13.4	0
1978 SD	12	3	84	28.0	1
NFL Total	49	46	717	15.6	8

JIM MCDONALD McDonald, Edward 6'0", 195 **HB-DB**
Col: Duquesne B: 2/27/1911 D: 2/18/1980, Homestead, PA
1936 Pit: 5 G; Rush 9-18 2.0; Rec 1-8 8.0.

JIM MCDONALD McDonald, James Allen 6'1", 193 **DB-WB-BB-FB**
Col: Ohio State *HS:* Springfield [OH] B: 6/9/1915, Springfield, OH
D: 5/1/1997, Knoxville, TN *Drafted:* 1938 Round 1 Phi
1938 Det: Rec 2-41 20.5. **1939** Det: Rec 5-71 14.2. **Total:** Rec 7-112 16.0.

		Rushing			
Year Team	G	Att	Yds	Avg	TD
1938 Det	11	0	0	—	0
1939 Det	9	25	80	3.2	0
NFL Total	20	25	80	3.2	0

JAMES MCDONALD McDonald, James Zell 6'5", 234 **TE**
Col: USC *HS:* Long Beach Polytechnic [CA] B: 3/29/1961, Long Beach, CA
1983 LARm: 16 G; Rec 1-1 1.0 1 TD; 6 Pt. **1984** LARm: 16 G; Rec 4-55 13.8. **1985** Det-LARm: 15 G; Rec 5-81 16.2. Det: 6 G; Rec 3-23 7.7. LARm: 9 G; Rec 2-58 29.0. **1987** LARm: 5 G; Rec 4-31 7.8 2 TD; 12 Pt. **Total:** 52 G; Rec 14-168 12.0 3 TD; 18 Pt.

JOHN MCDONALD McDonald, John 6'0", 195 **T-G**
Col: Lawrence B: 3/20/1900 Deceased
1921 Eva: 1 G. **1926** Lou: 2 G. **Total:** 3 G.

LES MCDONALD McDonald, Lester Bruce 6'4", 202 **OE-DE**
Col: Nebraska *HS:* Grand Island [NE] B: 9/19/1914, Grand Island, NE
D: 7/26/1971, Grand Island, NE *Drafted:* 1937 Round 1 ChiB
1938 ChiB: Rush 1-0; Scor **1** 1XP. **1939** ChiB: Rush 1-(-2) -2.0.
1940 Phi-Det: Rush 2-(-2) -1.0. Phi: Rush 2-(-2) -1.0. **Total:** Rush 4-(-4) -1.0; Scor 1 1XP.

		Receiving			
Year Team	G	Rec	Yds	Avg	TD
1937 ChiB	8	11	179	16.3	4
1938 ChiB	10	9	175	19.4	1
1939 ChiB	11	16	261	16.3	3
1940 Phi-Det	10	15	309	20.6	0
1940 Phi	9	14	289	20.6	0
1940 Det	1	1	20	20.0	0
NFL Total	39	51	924	18.1	8

MIKE MCDONALD McDonald, Michael 6'2", 215 **LB**
Col: Catawba *HS:* Fort Lauderdale [FL] B: 6/20/1953, St. Augustine, FL *Drafted:* 1975 Round 16 NO
1976 StL: 4 G.

MIKE MCDONALD McDonald, Michael Jr. 6'1", 238 **LB**
Col: USC *HS:* John Burroughs [Burbank, CA] B: 6/22/1958, North Hollywood, CA
1984 LARm: 16 G. **1986** LARm: 13 G. **1987** LARm: 10 G; KR 3-31 10.3. **1988** LARm: 16 G; KR 3-34 11.3; 1 Fum. **1989** LARm: 16 G; KR 2-22 11.0. **1990** LARm: 16 G; KR 1-15 15.0. **1991** LARm: 16 G; KR 3-32 10.7. **1992** Det: 1 G. **Total:** 104 G; KR 12-134 11.2; 1 Fum.

PAUL MCDONALD McDonald, Paul Brian 6'2", 185 **QB**
Col: USC *HS:* Bishop Amat [La Puente, CA] B: 2/23/1958, Montebello, CA *Drafted:* 1980 Round 4 Cle
1984 Cle: Rec 1-(-4) -4.0. **Total:** Rec 1-(-4) -4.0.

		Passing							
Year Team	G	Att	Comp	Comp%	Yds	YPA	TD	Int	Rating
1980 Cle	15	0	0	—	0	—	0	0	—
1981 Cle	12	57	35	61.4	463	8.12	4	2	95.9
1982 Cle	9	149	73	49.0	993	6.66	5	8	59.5
1983 Cle	16	68	32	47.1	341	5.01	1	4	42.6
1984 Cle	16	493	271	55.0	3472	7.04	14	23	67.3
1985 Cle	16	0	0	—	0	—	0	0	—
1986 Dal	1	0	0	—	0	—	0	0	—
NFL Total	85	767	411	53.6	5269	6.87	24	37	65.7

	Rushing				
Year Team	Att	Yds	Avg	TD	Fum
1980 Cle	3	-2	-0.7	0	2
1981 Cle	2	0	0.0	0	4
1982 Cle	7	-13	-1.9	0	3
1983 Cle	3	17	5.7	0	1
1984 Cle	22	4	0.2	1	16
NFL Total	37	6	0.2	1	26

QUINTUS MCDONALD McDonald, Quintus Alonzo 6'3", 259 **LB**
Col: Penn State *HS:* Montclair [NJ] B: 12/14/1966, Rockingham, NC
Drafted: 1989 Round 6 Ind
1989 Ind: 15 G; 2 Sac. **1990** Ind: 9 G. **1991** Ind: 16 G; KR 1-3 3.0.
Total: 40 G; KR 1-3 3.0; 2 Sac.

RAMOS MCDONALD McDonald, Ramos 5'11", 195 **DB**
Col: Navarro Coll. TX (J.C.); New Mexico *HS:* Liberty-Eylau [Texarkana, TX] B: 4/30/1976, Dallas, TX *Drafted:* 1998 Round 3 Min
1998 Min: 15 G.

RAY MCDONALD McDonald, Raymond Douglas 6'4", 248 **RB**
Col: Idaho *HS:* Caldwell [ID] B: 5/7/1944, McKinney, TX D: 5/4/1993, Houston, TX *Drafted:* 1967 Round 1 Was
1967 Was: Rec 10-60 6.0; KR 1-0. **Total:** Rec 10-60 6.0; KR 1-0.

		Rushing				
Year Team	G	Att	Yds	Avg	TD	Fum
1967 Was	12	52	223	4.3	4	1
1968 Was	1	0	0	—	0	0
NFL Total	13	52	223	4.3	4	1

RICARDO MCDONALD McDonald, Ricardo Milton 6'2", 240 **LB**
Col: Pittsburgh *HS:* Eastside [Paterson, NJ] B: 11/8/1969, Kingston, Jamaica *Drafted:* 1992 Round 4 Cin
1992 Cin: 16 G; Int 1-0. **1993** Cin: 14 G; 1 Sac. **1994** Cin: 13 G; 1 Sac. **1995** Cin: 16 G; 5 Sac. **1996** Cin: 16 G; 5 Sac. **1997** Cin: 13 G; 1 Sac. **1998** ChiB: 15 G; 1 Sac. **Total:** 103 G; Int 1-0; 14 Sac.

KEITH MCDONALD McDonald, R. Keith 5'9", 170 **WR**
Col: Santa Monica Coll. CA (J.C.); San Jose State *HS:* Phineas Banning [Los Angeles, CA] B: 11/7/1963, Los Angeles, CA
1987 Hou: 3 G; Rec 4-56 14.0 1 TD; 6 Pt. **1989** Det: 6 G; Rush 1-(-2) -2.0; Rec 12-138 11.5. **Total:** 9 G; Rush 1-(-2) -2.0; Rec 16-194 12.1 1 TD; 6 Pt.

TOMMY MCDONALD McDonald, Thomas Franklin 5'9", 176 **WR**
Col: Oklahoma *HS:* Roy [NM];Highland HS [Albuquerque, NM]
B: 7/26/1934, Roy, NM *Drafted:* 1957 Round 3 Phi *HOF:* 1998
1957 Phi: Pass 1-1 100.0%, 11 11.00; Rush 12-36 3.0. **1958** Phi: Rush 3-(-4) -1.3. **1959** Phi: Rush 2-(-10) -5.0. **1962** Phi: Pass 1-1 100.0%, 10 10.00 1 TD. **Total:** Pass 2-2 100.0%, 21 10.50 1 TD; Rush 17-22 1.3.

		Receiving				Punt Returns			
Year Team	G	Rec	Yds	Avg	TD	Ret	Yds	Avg	TD
1957 Phi	12	9	228	25.3	3	**26**	127	4.9	0
1958 Phi	10	29	603	20.8	**9**	18	135	7.5	0
1959 Phi	12	47	846	18.0	10	21	115	5.5	1
1960 Phi	12	39	801	20.5	13	1	2	2.0	0
1961 Phi	14	64	**1144**	17.9	**13**	0	0	—	0
1962 Phi	14	58	1146	19.8	10	5	8	1.6	0
1963 Phi	14	41	731	17.8	8	0	0	—	0
1964 Dal	14	46	612	13.3	2	2	17	8.5	0
1965 LARm	14	67	1036	15.5	9	0	0	—	0
1966 LARm	13	55	714	13.0	2	0	0	—	0
1967 Atl	14	33	436	13.2	4	0	0	—	0
1968 Cle	9	7	113	16.1	1	0	0	—	0
NFL Total	152	495	8410	17.0	84	73	404	5.5	1

	Kickoff Returns					Tot
Year Team	Ret	Yds	Avg	TD	Fum	TD
1957 Phi	11	304	27.6	0	5	3
1958 Phi	14	262	18.7	0	4	9
1959 Phi	24	444	18.5	0	4	11
1960 Phi	2	45	22.5	0	1	13

1961 Phi	0	0	—	0	1	13
1962 Phi	0	0	—	0	1	10
1963 Phi	0	0	—	0	3	8
1964 Dal	0	0	—	0	1	2
1965 LARm	0	0	—	0	2	9
1966 LARm	0	0	—	0	2	2
1967 Atl	0	0	—	0	0	4
1968 Cle	0	0	—	0	0	1
NFL Total	51	1055	20.7	0	24	85

TIM MCDONALD McDonald, Timothy 6′2″, 215 **DB**
Col: USC *HS:* Edison [Fresno, CA] B: 1/6/1965, Fresno, CA
Drafted: 1987 Round 2 StL
1988 Pho: 2 Sac. **1992** Pho: 0.5 Sac. **1994** SF: 1 Fum TD. **1996** SF: 1 Sac. **1998** SF: 4 Sac. **Total:** 1 Fum TD; 7.5 Sac.

		Interceptions			Tot
Year Team	**G**	**Int**	**Yds**	**TD**	**TD**
1987 StL	3	0	0	0	0
1988 Pho	16	2	11	0	0
1989 Pho	16	7	170	1	1
1990 Pho	16	4	63	0	0
1991 Pho	13	5	36	0	0
1992 Pho	16	2	35	0	0
1993 SF	16	3	23	0	0
1994 SF	16	2	79	1	2
1995 SF	16	4	135	**2**	2
1996 SF	16	2	14	0	0
1997 SF	15	3	34	0	0
1998 SF	16	4	22	0	0
NFL Total	175	38	622	4	5

WALT MCDONALD McDonald, Walter 5′10″, 210 **C-LB**
Col: Utah *HS:* Worland [WY] B: 10/22/1911, Worland, WY
1935 Bkn: 11 G.

WALT MCDONALD McDonald, Walter Vincent 6′1″, 210 **BB-DB-QB**
Col: Tulane *HS:* Struthers [OH] B: 11/5/1920, Lowellville, OH
AAFC **1946** BknA-MiaA: 13 G; Pass 3-1 33.3%, 24 8.00 1 Int; Rush 4-(-11) -2.8; Rec 12-126 10.5; KR 3-32 10.7; Int 2-31. **1947** BknA: 12 G; Rush 1-1 1.0; Rec 3-30 10.0; PR 1-19 19.0. **1948** BknA: 12 G; Rush 6-15 2.5; Rec 7-41 5.9 1 TD; Int 3-21. **1949** ChiA: 9 G; Rush 1-0. **Total:** 46 G; Pass 3-1 33.3%, 24 8.00 1 Int; Rush 12-5 0.4; Rec 22-197 9.0 1 TD; PR 1-19 19.0; KR 3-32 10.7; Int 5-52; 6 Pt.

COLEY MCDONOUGH McDonough, Coleman Regis 6′1″, 189 **TB-DB-QB**
Col: Dayton *HS:* Scott Twp. [North Braddock, PA] B: 10/10/1915, North Braddock, PA D: 7/6/1965, Pittsburgh, PA
1939 ChiC-Pit: Rec 1-3 3.0 1 TD; Punt 10-368 36.8. ChiC: Punt 1-43 43.0. Pit: Rec 1-3 3.0 1 TD; Punt 9-325 36.1. **1940** Pit: Punt 4-160 40.0. **1941** Pit: PR 2-28 14.0; KR 4-77 19.3; Punt 7-260 37.1. **Total:** Rec 1-3 3.0 1 TD; PR 2-28 14.0; KR 4-77 19.3; Punt 21-788 37.5.

		Passing							
Year Team	**G**	**Att**	**Comp**	**Comp%**	**Yds**	**YPA**	**TD**	**Int**	**Rating**
1939 ChiC-Pit	11	47	17	36.2	365	7.77	2	8	39.2
1939 ChiC	4	9	2	22.2	73	8.11	0	2	21.3
1939 Pit	7	38	15	39.5	292	7.68	2	6	45.0
1940 Pit	4	14	8	57.1	92	6.57	0	3	37.5
1941 Pit	6	41	12	29.3	200	4.88	1	7	16.0
1944 ChPt	2	23	10	43.5	208	9.04	2	4	65.4
NFL Total	23	125	47	37.6	865	6.92	5	22	36.0

	Rushing				Tot
Year Team	**Att**	**Yds**	**Avg**	**TD**	**TD**
1939 ChiC-Pit	29	75	2.6	0	1
1939 ChiC	6	12	2.0	0	0
1939 Pit	23	63	2.7	0	1
1940 Pit	15	33	2.2	1	1
1941 Pit	20	64	3.2	0	0
1944 ChPt	3	7	2.3	0	0
NFL Total	67	179	2.7	1	2

PAUL MCDONOUGH McDonough, Paul Roy 6′4″, 222 **OE-DE-DB**
Col: Utah *HS:* East [Salt Lake City, UT] B: 12/14/1916, Salt Lake City, UT D: 8/11/1960, Salt Lake City, UT *Drafted:* 1938 Round 7 Pit
1940 Cle: Rush 2-5 2.5. **1941** Cle: KR 1-9 9.0. **Total:** Rush 2-5 2.5; KR 1-9 9.0.

		Receiving			
Year Team	**G**	**Rec**	**Yds**	**Avg**	**TD**
1938 Pit	6	6	86	14.3	0
1939 Cle	10	8	73	9.1	1
1940 Cle	11	12	315	**26.3**	1
1941 Cle	11	14	198	14.1	2
NFL Total	38	40	672	16.8	4

BOB MCDONOUGH McDonough, Robert E 6′1″, 170 **DB**
Col: California (Pa.) *HS:* Perry [Pittsburgh, PA] B: 3/7/1963, Pittsburgh, PA
1987 Det: 3 G.

BOB MCDONOUGH McDonough, Robert Walter 5′11″, 205 **G**
(Red) *Col:* Duke *HS:* The Hun School [Princeton, NJ] B: 5/31/1919, Orange, NJ
1946 Phi: 10 G.

BOB MCDOUGAL McDougal, Robert Joseph 6′2″, 205 **LB-FB**
Col: Duke; Miami (Fla.) *HS:* Oconto [WI] B: 3/19/1921, Oconto, WI
Drafted: 1947 Round 7 GB
1947 GB: 1 G.

DOUG MCDOUGALD McDougald, Douglas Elaine 6′5″, 271 **DE**
Col: Virginia Tech *HS:* 71st [Fayetteville, NC] B: 2/6/1957, Fayetteville, NC *Drafted:* 1980 Round 5 NE
1980 NE: 8 G.

GERRY MCDOUGALL McDougall, Gerald Gordon 6′3″, 225 **FB**
Col: Long Beach City Coll. CA (J.C.); UCLA *HS:* Long Beach Polytechnic [CA] B: 3/21/1935, Long Beach, CA
1962 SD: Rec 4-27 6.8; KR 3-71 23.7. **1963** SD: Pass 1-1 100.0%, 11 11.00 1 TD; Rec 10-115 11.5; KR 3-77 25.7. **1964** SD: Rec 8-106 13.3; Scor 1 2XP. **Total:** Pass 1-1 100.0%, 11 11.00 1 TD; Rec 22-248 11.3; KR 6-148 24.7; Scor 1 2XP.

		Rushing				
Year Team	**G**	**Att**	**Yds**	**Avg**	**TD**	**Fum**
1962 SD	4	43	197	4.6	3	1
1963 SD	14	39	201	5.2	1	1
1964 SD	7	23	73	3.2	2	2
NFL Total	25	105	471	4.5	6	4

ANTHONY MCDOWELL McDowell, Anthony Lequinn 5′11″, 235 **RB**
Col: Texas Tech *HS:* Killeen [TX] B: 11/12/1968, Augsburg, Germany
Drafted: 1992 Round 8 TB

		Rushing				Receiving				
Year Team	**G**	**Att**	**Yds**	**Avg**	**TD**	**Rec**	**Yds**	**Avg**	**TD**	**Fum**
1992 TB	12	14	81	5.8	0	27	258	9.6	2	1
1993 TB	4	2	6	3.0	0	8	26	3.3	1	2
1994 TB	14	21	58	2.8	0	29	193	6.7	1	0
NFL Total	30	37	145	3.9	0	64	477	7.5	4	3

JOHN MCDOWELL McDowell, John Bernard 6′3″, 260 **OT-OG**
Col: St. John's (Minn.) *HS:* St. Thomas Acad. [St. Paul, MN]
B: 2/12/1942, St. Paul, MN *Drafted:* 1964 Round 9 GB
1964 GB: 12 G. **1965** NYG: 14 G. **1966** StL: 1 G. **Total:** 27 G.

BUBBA MCDOWELL McDowell, Leonard 6′1″, 196 **DB**
Col: Miami (Fla.) *HS:* Merritt Island [FL] B: 11/4/1966, Fort Gaines, GA
Drafted: 1989 Round 3 Hou
1989 Hou: Scor **1** Saf; 1 Sac. **1990** Hou: 0.5 Sac. **1991** Hou: 1 Sac. **1992** Hou: 1.5 Sac. **1993** Hou: 1 Sac. **Total:** Scor 1 Saf; 5 Sac.

		Interceptions				Tot
Year Team	**G**	**Int**	**Yds**	**TD**	**Fum**	**TD**
1989 Hou	16	4	65	0	1	0
1990 Hou	15	2	11	0	0	0
1991 Hou	16	4	31	0	0	1
1992 Hou	16	3	52	1	0	1
1993 Hou	14	3	31	0	0	0
1994 Hou	9	0	0	0	0	0
1995 Car	16	1	33	0	0	0
NFL Total	102	17	223	1	1	2

GEORGE MCDUFFIE McDuffie, George Allen 6′6″, 270 **DE**
Col: Waldorf Coll. IA (J.C.); Salem (NC); Findlay *HS:* Lima [OH]
B: 1/20/1963, Vicksburg, MS
1987 Det: 3 G; 2 Sac.

O.J. MCDUFFIE McDuffie, Otis James 5′10″, 194 **WR**
Col: Penn State *HS:* Hawken [Gates Mills, OH] B: 12/2/1969, Marion, OH *Drafted:* 1993 Round 1 Mia
1993 Mia: Rush 1-(-4) -4.0. **1994** Mia: Rush 5-32 6.4. **1995** Mia: Rush 3-6 2.0; Scor 1 2XP. **1996** Mia: Rush 2-7 3.5. **1997** Mia: 1 Fum TD. **1998** Mia: Rush 3-11 3.7. **Total:** Rush 14-52 3.7; Scor 1 2XP; 1 Fum TD.

		Receiving				Punt Returns			
Year Team	**G**	**Rec**	**Yds**	**Avg**	**TD**	**Ret**	**Yds**	**Avg**	**TD**
1993 Mia	16	19	197	10.4	0	28	317	11.3	**2**
1994 Mia	15	37	488	13.2	3	32	228	7.1	0
1995 Mia	16	62	819	13.2	8	24	163	6.8	0
1996 Mia	16	74	918	12.4	8	22	212	9.6	0
1997 Mia	16	76	943	12.4	1	2	4	2.0	0
1998 Mia	16	**90**	1050	11.7	7	12	141	11.8	0
NFL Total	95	358	4415	12.3	27	120	1065	8.9	2

Year Team	Kickoff Returns Ret	Yds	Avg	TD	Fum	Tot TD
1993 Mia	32	755	23.6	0	4	2
1994 Mia	36	767	21.3	0	3	3
1995 Mia	23	564	24.5	0	4	8
1996 Mia	0	0	—	0	6	8
1997 Mia	0	0	—	0	0	2
1998 Mia	0	0	—	0	0	7
NFL Total	91	2086	22.9	0	17	30

HUGH MCELHENNY McElhenny, Hugh Edward Jr. 6′1″, 195 **HB**
(The King) *Col:* Compton CC CA; Washington *HS:* George Washington [Los Angeles, CA] B: 12/31/1928, Los Angeles, CA *Drafted:* 1952 Round 1 SF *HOF:* 1970
1953 SF: Pass 3-2 66.7%, 13 4.33 1 TD. **1956** SF: Pass 1-0, 1 Int. **1958** SF: Pass 2-0. **1961** Min: Pass 1-0. **Total:** Pass 7-2 28.6%, 13 1.86 1 TD 1 Int.

Year Team	G	Rushing Att	Yds	Avg	TD	Receiving Rec	Yds	Avg	TD
1952 SF	12	98	684	**7.0**	6	26	367	14.1	3
1953 SF	12	112	503	4.5	3	30	474	15.8	2
1954 SF	6	64	515	**8.0**	6	8	162	20.3	0
1955 SF	12	90	327	3.6	4	11	203	18.5	2
1956 SF	12	185	916	5.0	8	16	193	12.1	0
1957 SF	12	102	478	4.7	1	37	458	12.4	2
1958 SF	12	113	451	4.0	6	31	366	11.8	2
1959 SF	10	18	67	3.7	1	22	329	15.0	3
1960 SF	9	95	347	3.7	0	14	114	8.1	1
1961 Min	13	120	570	4.8	3	37	283	7.6	3
1962 Min	11	50	200	4.0	0	16	191	11.9	0
1963 NYG	14	55	175	3.2	0	11	91	8.3	2
1964 Det	8	22	48	2.2	0	5	16	3.2	0
NFL Total	143	1124	5281	4.7	38	264	3247	12.3	20

Year Team	Punt Returns Ret	Yds	Avg	TD	Kickoff Returns Ret	Yds	Avg	TD	Fum	Tot TD
1952 SF	20	284	14.2	1	18	396	22.0	0	5	10
1953 SF	15	104	6.9	0	15	368	24.5	0	6	5
1954 SF	8	78	9.8	0	8	210	26.3	0	4	6
1955 SF	7	10	1.4	0	9	189	21.0	0	3	6
1956 SF	15	38	2.5	0	13	300	23.1	0	4	8
1957 SF	10	41	4.1	0	0	0	—	0	8	3
1958 SF	24	93	3.9	0	2	31	15.5	0	10	8
1959 SF	0	0	—	0	0	0	—	0	1	4
1960 SF	0	0	—	0	0	0	—	0	2	1
1961 Min	8	155	19.4	1	2	59	29.5	0	8	7
1962 Min	5	43	8.6	0	7	160	22.9	0	3	0
1963 NYG	13	74	5.7	0	6	136	22.7	0	3	2
1964 Det	1	0	0.0	0	3	72	24.0	0	0	0
NFL Total	126	920	7.3	2	83	1921	23.1	0	57	60

BLAINE MCELMURRY McElmurry, Blaine 6′0″, 188 **DB**
Col: Montana *HS:* Troy [MT] B: 10/23/1973
1997 GB: 1 G. **1998** Jac: 2 G. **Total:** 3 G.

LEELAND MCELROY McElroy, Leeland Anthony 5′9″, 212 **RB**
Col: Texas A&M *HS:* Central [Beaumont, TX] B: 6/25/1974, Beaumont, TX *Drafted:* 1996 Round 2 Ariz
1996 Ariz: Rec 5-41 8.2 1 TD. **1997** Ariz: Rec 7-32 4.6. **Total:** Rec 12-73 6.1 1 TD.

Year Team	G	Rushing Ret	Yds	Avg	TD	Kickoff Returns Ret	Yds	Avg	TD	Fum	Tot TD
1996 Ariz	16	89	305	3.4	1	54	1148	21.3	0	3	2
1997 Ariz	14	135	424	3.1	2	0	0	—	0	3	2
NFL Total	30	224	729	3.3	3	54	1148	21.3	0	6	4

RAY MCELROY McElroy, Raymond Edward 5′11″, 207 **DB**
Col: Eastern Illinois *HS:* Proviso West [Hillside, IL] B: 7/31/1972, Bellwood, IL *Drafted:* 1995 Round 4 Ind
1995 Ind: 16 G. **1996** Ind: 16 G. **1997** Ind: 16 G; 6 Pt. **1998** Ind: 16 G. **Total:** 64 G; 6 Pt.

REGGIE MCELROY McElroy, Reginald Lee 6′6″, 290 **OT-OG**
Col: West Texas A&M *HS:* Charlton-Pollard [Beaumont, TX]
B: 3/4/1960, Beaumont, TX *Drafted:* 1982 Round 2 NYJ
1983 NYJ: 16 G; KR 1-7 7.0. **1984** NYJ: 16 G. **1985** NYJ: 13 G. **1986** NYJ: 8 G. **1987** NYJ: 8 G. **1988** NYJ: 16 G. **1989** NYJ: 15 G. **1991** LARd: 16 G. **1992** LARd: 16 G. **1993** KC: 8 G. **1994** Min: 10 G. **1995** Den: 16 G. **1996** Den: 7 G. **Total:** 165 G; KR 1-7 7.0.

VANN MCELROY McElroy, Vann William 6′2″, 193 **DB**
Col: Baylor *HS:* Uvalde [TX] B: 1/13/1960, Birmingham, AL
Drafted: 1982 Round 3 LARd
1990 LARd-Sea: 1 Sac. Sea: 1 Sac. **Total:** 1 Sac.

Year Team	G	Interceptions Int	Yds	TD
1982 LARd	7	1	0	0
1983 LARd	16	8	68	0
1984 LARd	16	4	42	0
1985 LARd	12	2	23	0
1986 LARd	16	7	105	0
1987 LARd	12	4	41	1
1988 LARd	12	3	17	0
1989 LARd	7	2	0	0
1990 LARd-Sea	13	0	0	0
1990 LARd	3	0	0	0
1990 Sea	10	0	0	0
NFL Total	111	31	296	1

BUCKY MCELROY McElroy, William Murry Jr. 5′11″, 195 **HB**
Col: Hinds CC MS; Southern Mississippi *HS:* Monroe [LA]
B: 1/23/1929, Monroe, LA *Drafted:* 1953 Round 7 ChiB
1954 ChiB: 1 G; KR 1-21 21.0.

BILL MCELWAIN McElwain, William Thompson 5′10″, 175 **WB-TB-BB**
Col: Northwestern *HS:* Evanston Twp. [Evanston, IL] B: 5/14/1903, Chicago, IL
1924 ChiC: 3 G. **1926** ChiC: 8 G; Rush 1 TD; 6 Pt. **Total:** 11 G; Rush 1 TD; 6 Pt.

JASON MCENDOO McEndoo, Jason Howard 6′5″, 307 **C**
Col: Washington State *HS:* Weatherwax [Aberdeen, WA] B: 2/25/1975, San Diego, CA *Drafted:* 1998 Round 7 Sea
1998 Sea: 1 G; 1 Fum.

DOUG MCENULTY McEnulty, Douglas Michael 6′3″, 221 **HB-DB**
Col: Wichita State *HS:* East [Wichita, KS] B: 1/16/1922, Tonganozie, KS
1943 ChiB: 8 G; Rush 16-45 2.8; Rec 1-10 10.0 1 TD; Int 1-11; Punt 4-187 46.8; 6 Pt. **1944** ChiB: 10 G; Rush 8-11 1.4; Rec 2-10 5.0 1 TD; Int 1-34; Punt 25-993 39.7; 6 Pt. **Total:** 18 G; Rush 24-56 2.3; Rec 3-20 6.7 2 TD; Int 2-45; Punt 29-1180 40.7; 12 Pt.

ED MCEVOY McEvoy, Edward Clarence 5′11″, 190 **WB**
Col: Spring Hill *HS:* Spring Hill [Mobile, AL] B: 11/6/1903, Mobile, AL
D: 8/7/1976, Houston, TX
1926 Har: 7 G.

CRAIG MCEWEN McEwen, Craig Eugene 6′1″, 220 **TE**
Col: Rancho Santiago Coll. CA (J.C.); Utah *HS:* Northport [NY]
B: 12/16/1965, Northport, NY

Year Team	G	Receiving Rec	Yds	Avg	TD	Fum
1987 Was	4	12	164	13.7	0	0
1988 Was	14	23	323	14.0	0	0
1989 SD	4	7	99	14.1	0	0
1990 SD	16	29	325	11.2	3	1
1991 SD	16	37	399	10.8	3	0
NFL Total	54	108	1310	12.1	6	1

BANKS MCFADDEN McFadden, James Banks 6′2″, 180 **HB-DB**
Col: Clemson *HS:* Great Falls [SC] B: 2/7/1917, Fort Lawn, SC
Drafted: 1940 Round 1 Bkn
1940 Bkn: Pass 8-3 37.5%, 103 12.88 1 TD 1 Int; Rec 9-97 10.8 2 TD; Int 2-40.

Year Team	G	Rushing Att	Yds	Avg	TD	Tot TD
1940 Bkn	11	85	411	4.8	1	3

MARV MCFADDEN McFadden, Marvin G 6′0″, 223 **OG**
Col: Michigan State *HS:* Eastern [Lansing, MI] B: 1/18/1930, Columbus Junction, MI *Drafted:* 1952 Round 12 Pit
1953 Pit: 12 G. **1956** Pit: 12 G. **Total:** 24 G.

PAUL MCFADDEN McFadden, Paul Joseph 5′11″, 163 **K**
Col: Youngstown State *HS:* Euclid [OH] B: 9/24/1961, Cleveland, OH
Drafted: 1984 Round 12 Phi

Year Team	G	Scoring Pts	FG	FGA	FG%	XK	XKA	XK%
1984 Phi	16	116	**30**	**37**	81.1	26	27	96.3
1985 Phi	16	104	25	30	83.3	29	29	100.0
1986 Phi	16	86	20	31	64.5	26	27	96.3
1987 Phi	12	84	16	26	61.5	36	36	100.0
1988 NYG	10	67	14	19	73.7	25	27	92.6
1989 Atl	9	63	15	20	75.0	18	18	100.0
NFL Total	79	520	120	163	73.6	160	164	97.6

THAD MCFADDEN McFadden, Thaddeus Dwayne 6′2″, 200 **WR**
Col: Wisconsin *HS:* Beecher [Flint, MI] B: 8/14/1962, Flint, MI
1987 Buf: 3 G; Rec 4-41 10.3 1 TD; PR 8-83 10.4; KR 7-121 17.3; 6 Pt.

BUD MCFADIN McFadin, Lewis Pate 6′3″, 260 **DT-DG-OG-LB**
Col: Texas *HS:* Iraan [TX] B: 8/21/1928, Rankin, TX *Drafted:* 1951 Round 1 LARm
1952 LARm: Postseason only. **1953** LARm: 7 G; KR 1-5 5.0; Int 1-0. **1954** LARm: 12 G. **1955** LARm: 12 G; Scor 3, 1-5 20.0% FG. **1956** LARm:

12 G; Scor 9, 1-4 25.0% FG; **1** Fum TD; 1 Fum. **1960** Den: 14 G. **1961** Den: 14 G. **1962** Den: 14 G; **1** Fum TD; 6 Pt. **1963** Den: 14 G; **1** Fum TD; 6 Pt. **1964** Hou: 14 G. **1965** Hou: 12 G. **Total:** 125 G; KR 1-5 5.0; Int 1-0; Scor 24, 2-9 22.2% FG; 3 Fum TD; 1 Fum.

JIM MCFARLAND McFarland, James Darrell 6'5", 225 **TE**
Col: Nebraska *HS:* North Platte [NE] B: 10/4/1947, North Platte, NE
Drafted: 1970 Round 7 StL
1970 Buf-StL: 10 G. Buf: 1 G. StL: 9 G. **1971** StL: 14 G; Rec 5-54 10.8 2 TD; 12 Pt. **1972** StL: 10 G. **1973** StL: 14 G; Rec 2-10 5.0; KR 3-57 19.0; **1** Fum TD; 6 Pt. **1974** StL: 14 G. **1975** Mia: 6 G. **Total:** 68 G; Rec 7-64 9.1 2 TD; KR 3-57 19.0; 1 Fum TD; Tot TD 3; 18 Pt.

KAY MCFARLAND McFarland, Russel Kay 6'2", 186 **WR**
Col: Colorado State *HS:* Englewood [CO] B: 4/10/1938, Quincy, IL
Drafted: 1961 Round 18 SF

		Receiving			
Year Team	G	Rec	Yds	Avg	TD
1962 SF	6	3	24	8.0	0
1963 SF	12	11	126	11.5	1
1964 SF	12	5	67	13.4	0
1965 SF	12	8	106	13.3	1
1966 SF	12	13	219	16.8	1
1968 SF	9	5	140	28.0	1
NFL Total	63	45	682	15.2	4

NYLE MCFARLANE McFarlane, Hardy Nyle 6'2", 205 **HB**
Col: Brigham Young *HS:* Jordan [Sandy, UT] B: 11/25/1935, Lehi, UT
1960 Oak: 13 G; Rush 4-52 13.0; Rec 5-89 17.8 2 TD; KR 5-71 14.2; 12 Pt.

SCOTT MCGARRAHAN McGarrahan, John Scott 6'1", 197 **DB**
Col: New Mexico *HS:* Lamar [Arlington, TX] B: 2/12/1974, Dallas, TX
Drafted: 1998 Round 6 GB
1998 GB: 15 G.

BARNEY MCGARRY McGarry, Bernard Duane 6'1", 203 **G-LB**
Col: Utah *HS:* Park City [UT] B: 12/24/1917, Park City, UT
Drafted: 1939 Round 6 Cle
1939 Cle: 11 G. **1940** Cle: 11 G. **1941** Cle: 11 G. **1942** Cle: 4 G. **Total:** 37 G.

JOHN MCGARRY McGarry, John Thomas 6'5", 288 **OG**
Col: St. Joseph's (Ind.) *HS:* Marian Catholic [Chicago Heights, IL]
B: 11/24/1963, Chicago, IL
1987 GB: 2 G.

WALT MCGAW McGaw, Raymond Peter 195 **G**
Col: Beloit *HS:* Rockford Central [IL] B: 12/27/1899, Rockford, IL
D: 10/8/1979, Trego, WI
1926 GB: 1 G.

CLARENCE MCGEARY McGeary, Clarence Valentine Jr. 6'5", 250 **DT**
(Clink) *Col:* Minnesota; North Dakota State *HS:* White Bear Lake [MN]
B: 8/8/1926, St. Paul, MN D: 4/6/1993, Salt Lake City, UT
Drafted: 1948 Round 28 GB
1950 GB: 12 G.

TONY MCGEE McGee, Anthony Eugene 6'4", 250 **DE-DT**
Col: Wyoming; Bishop *HS:* Battle Creek Central [MI] B: 1/18/1949, Battle Creek, MI *Drafted:* 1971 Round 3 ChiB
1971 ChiB: 14 G. **1972** ChiB: 14 G. **1973** ChiB: 14 G. **1974** NE: 14 G. **1975** NE: 13 G. **1976** NE: 14 G. **1977** NE: 14 G. **1978** NE: 16 G. **1979** NE: 16 G. **1980** NE: 16 G. **1981** NE: 16 G. **1982** Was: 9 G; 6.5 Sac. **1983** Was: 16 G; 10 Sac. **1984** Was: 16 G; 4.5 Sac. **Total:** 202 G; 21 Sac.

DELL MCGEE McGee, Antonio Deleon 5'8", 180 **DB**
Col: Auburn *HS:* Kendrick [Columbia, GA] B: 9/7/1973, Columbus, GA
Drafted: 1996 Round 5 Ariz
1998 Ariz: 3 G.

BEN MCGEE McGee, Benjamin Jr. 6'3", 250 **DE-DT**
(Big Ben) *Col:* Jackson State *HS:* Henderson [Starkville, MS]
B: 1/26/1939, Starkville, MS *Drafted:* 1964 Round 4 Pit
1964 Pit: 14 G. **1965** Pit: 13 G. **1966** Pit: 14 G. **1967** Pit: 10 G; Int 1-21 1 TD; 6 Pt. **1968** Pit: 14 G. **1969** Pit: 14 G. **1970** Pit: 14 G. **1971** Pit: 13 G. **1972** Pit: 14 G. **Total:** 120 G; Int 1-21 1 TD; 6 Pt.

BUFORD MCGEE McGee, Buford Lamar 6'0", 206 **RB**
Col: Mississippi *HS:* Durant [MS] B: 8/16/1960, Durant, MS
Drafted: 1984 Round 11 SD
1984 SD: KR 14-315 22.5. **1985** SD: KR 7-135 19.3. **1986** SD: Pass 1-1 100.0%, 1 1.00; KR 1-15 15.0. **1988** LARm: KR 1-0. **1990** LARm: Pass 2-2 100.0%, 23 11.50 1 TD. **Total:** Pass 3-3 100.0%, 24 8.00 1 TD; KR 23-465 20.2.

		Rushing				Receiving					Tot
Year Team	G	Att	Yds	Avg	TD	Rec	Yds	Avg	TD	Fum	TD
1984 SD	16	67	226	3.4	4	9	76	8.4	2	1	6
1985 SD	11	42	181	4.3	3	3	15	5.0	0	4	3
1986 SD	9	63	187	3.0	7	10	105	10.5	0	4	7
1987 LARm	3	3	6	2.0	1	7	40	5.7	0	0	1
1988 LARm	16	22	69	3.1	0	16	117	7.3	3	0	3
1989 LARm	16	21	99	4.7	1	37	303	8.2	4	2	5
1990 LARm	16	44	234	5.3	1	47	388	8.3	4	0	5
1991 LARm	16	19	65	3.4	0	20	160	8.0	0	1	0
1992 GB	4	8	19	2.4	0	6	60	10.0	0	0	0
NFL Total	107	289	1086	3.8	17	155	1264	8.2	13	12	30

CARL MCGEE McGee, Carl Demetrius 6'3", 228 **LB**
Col: Duke *HS:* Woodward [Cincinnati, OH] B: 7/15/1956, Cincinnati, OH *Drafted:* 1979 Round 9 Cle
1980 SD: 6 G.

ED MCGEE McGee, Edward D 6'1", 224 **T**
Col: Temple *HS:* Fort Edward [NY] B: 2/26/1916, Fort Edward, NY
D: 12/1995, Glens Falls, NY *Drafted:* 1940 Round 10 NYG
1940 NYG: 3 G. **1944** Bos: 10 G; Int 1-15. **1945** Bos: 8 G. **1946** Bos: 11 G. **Total:** 32 G; Int 1-15.

GEORGE MCGEE McGee, George 6'2", 255 **OT**
Col: Southern University *HS:* Southern U. Lab [Baton Rouge, LA]
B: 10/7/1935, Baton Rouge, LA *Drafted:* 1959 Round 16 Det
1960 Bos: 14 G.

HARRY MCGEE McGee, Harry Loyd 6'1", 198 **C-G**
Col: Kansas State B: 4/27/1905 D: 10/1983, FL
1927 Cle: 2 G. **1929** SI: 10 G. **1930** Nwk: 1 G. **1932** SI: 1 G. **Total:** 14 G.

MIKE MCGEE McGee, Michael Burnette 6'1", 230 **OG**
Col: Duke *HS:* Elizabeth City [NC] B: 12/1/1938, Washington, DC
Drafted: 1960 Round 2 StL
1960 StL: 11 G. **1961** StL: 13 G. **1962** StL: 13 G. **Total:** 37 G.

BOB MCGEE McGee, Robert Joseph 6'0", 210 **T**
(Bus) *Col:* Santa Clara *HS:* Mission [San Francisco, CA]
B: 7/28/1912, San Fransisco, CA D: 9/1/1963, Burlingame, CA
1938 ChiC: 1 G.

MOLLY MCGEE McGee, Sylvester 5'10", 184 **RB**
Col: Rhode Island *HS:* North Rockland [Thiells, NY] B: 8/26/1952, Haverstraw, NY *Drafted:* 1974 Round 16 Atl
1974 Atl: 10 G; Rush 7-30 4.3; KR 8-167 20.9.

TIM MCGEE McGee, Timothy Dwayne Hatchett 5'10", 183 **WR**
Col: Tennessee *HS:* John Hay [Cleveland, OH] B: 8/7/1964, Cleveland, OH *Drafted:* 1986 Round 1 Cin
1986 Cin: Rush 4-10 2.5; PR 3-21 7.0. **1987** Cin: Rush 1-(-10) -10.0. **1989** Cin: Rush 2-36 18.0. **1994** Cin: Rush 1-(-18) -18.0. **Total:** Rush 8-18 2.3; PR 3-21 7.0.

		Receiving				Kickoff Returns				
Year Team	G	Rec	Yds	Avg	TD	Ret	Yds	Avg	TD	Fum
1986 Cin	16	16	276	17.3	1	43	**1007**	23.4	0	0
1987 Cin	11	23	408	17.7	1	15	242	16.1	0	0
1988 Cin	16	36	686	19.1	6	0	0	—	0	0
1989 Cin	16	65	1211	18.6	8	0	0	—	0	0
1990 Cin	16	43	737	17.1	1	0	0	—	0	1
1991 Cin	16	51	802	15.7	4	0	0	—	0	1
1992 Cin	16	35	408	11.7	3	0	0	—	0	0
1993 Was	13	39	500	12.8	3	0	0	—	0	0
1994 Cin	14	13	175	13.5	1	0	0	—	0	0
NFL Total	134	321	5203	16.2	28	58	1249	21.5	0	2

TONY MCGEE McGee, Tony Lamont 6'3", 247 **TE**
Col: Michigan *HS:* South Vigo [Terre Haute, IN] B: 4/21/1971, Terre Haute, IN *Drafted:* 1993 Round 2 Cin
1994 Cin: KR 1-4 4.0. **1997** Cin: Scor 1 2XP. **Total:** KR 1-4 4.0; Scor 1 2XP.

		Receiving				
Year Team	G	Rec	Yds	Avg	TD	Fum
1993 Cin	15	44	525	11.9	0	1
1994 Cin	16	40	492	12.3	1	0
1995 Cin	16	55	754	13.7	4	2
1996 Cin	16	38	446	11.7	4	0
1997 Cin	16	34	414	12.2	6	0
1998 Cin	16	22	363	16.5	1	0
NFL Total	95	233	2994	12.8	16	3

MAX MCGEE McGee, William Max 6'3", 205 **OE**
Col: Tulane *HS:* White Oak [TX] B: 7/16/1932, Saxon City, NV
Drafted: 1954 Round 5 GB
1954 GB: Rush 1-9 9.0. **1957** GB: Rush 5-40 8.0; KR 4-69 17.3. **1958** GB: Pass 1-0; Rush 1-9 9.0. **1960** GB: Rush 2-11 5.5. **1962** GB: Pass 1-0, 1 Int; Rush 3-52 17.3. **1964** GB: 1 Fum TD. **Total:** Pass 2-0, 1 Int; Rush 12-121 10.1; KR 4-69 17.3; 1 Fum TD.

		Receiving				Punting				Tot
Year Team	G	Rec	Yds	Avg	TD	Punts	Yds	Avg	Fum	TD
1954 GB	12	36	614	17.1	9	72	**2999**	41.7	0	9
1957 GB	12	17	273	16.1	1	0	0	—	0	1
1958 GB	12	37	655	17.7	7	62	2625	42.3	1	7
1959 GB	12	30	695	**23.2**	5	**64**	**2716**	42.4	0	5

1960 GB	12	38	787	20.7	4	31	1291	41.6	1	4
1961 GB	13	51	883	17.3	7	13	520	40.0	1	7
1962 GB	14	49	820	16.7	3	14	496	35.4	2	3
1963 GB	14	39	749	19.2	6	0	0	—	0	6
1964 GB	13	31	592	19.1	6	0	0	—	1	7
1965 GB	12	10	154	15.4	1	0	0	—	0	1
1966 GB	12	4	91	22.8	1	0	0	—	0	1
1967 GB	10	3	33	11.0	0	0	0	—	0	0
NFL Total	148	345	6346	18.4	50	256	10647	41.6	6	51

WILLIE MCGEE McGee, Willie 5′11″, 179 **WR**
Col: Alcorn State *HS:* Rowan [Hattiesburg, MS] B: 5/14/1950, New Orleans, LA *Drafted:* 1973 Round 5 SD
1973 SD: Rec 3-67 22.3; PR 6-56 9.3. **1975** LARm: Rec 6-83 13.8. **1976** SF: Rush 3-12 4.0; Rec 13-269 20.7 4 TD. **1977** SF: Rush 1-(-3) -3.0; Rec 2-27 13.5. **Total:** Rush 4-9 2.3; Rec 24-446 18.6 4 TD; PR 6-56 9.3.

		Kickoff Returns				
Year Team	**G**	**Ret**	**Yds**	**Avg**	**TD**	**Fum**
1973 SD	11	20	423	21.2	0	4
1974 LARm	14	12	288	24.0	0	0
1975 LARm	14	17	404	23.8	0	1
1976 SF	6	0	0	—	0	0
1977 SF	7	0	0	—	0	0
1978 Det	4	1	0	0.0	0	0
NFL Total	56	50	1115	22.3	0	5

JOHN MCGEEVER McGeever, John 6′1″, 195 **DB**
Col: Auburn *HS:* John Carroll [Birmingham, AL] B: 2/14/1939, Bogalusa, LA *Drafted:* 1962 Round 7 Den
1962 Den: KR 5-143 28.6. **Total:** KR 5-143 28.6.

		Interceptions			
Year Team	**G**	**Int**	**Yds**	**TD**	**Fum**
1962 Den	14	2	63	**1**	1
1963 Den	13	0	18	0	1
1964 Den	14	6	60	0	0
1965 Den	14	1	36	0	0
1966 Mia	12	2	15	0	0
NFL Total	67	11	192	1	2

RICH MCGEORGE McGeorge, Richard Eugene 6′4″, 235 **TE**
Col: Elon *HS:* Jefferson [Roanoke, VA] B: 9/14/1948, Roanoke, VA *Drafted:* 1970 Round 1 GB
1970 GB: Rush 1-3 3.0. **1975** GB: KR 1-17 17.0. **1978** GB: KR 1-0. **Total:** Rush 1-3 3.0; KR 2-17 8.5.

		Receiving				
Year Team	**G**	**Rec**	**Yds**	**Avg**	**TD**	**Fum**
1970 GB	14	2	32	16.0	2	0
1971 GB	14	27	463	17.1	4	0
1972 GB	2	4	50	12.5	2	0
1973 GB	14	16	260	16.3	1	0
1974 GB	14	30	440	14.7	0	0
1975 GB	14	32	458	14.3	1	1
1976 GB	14	24	278	11.6	1	0
1977 GB	14	17	142	8.4	1	1
1978 GB	16	23	247	10.7	1	0
NFL Total	116	175	2370	13.5	13	2

KANAVIS MCGHEE McGhee, Kanavis 6′4″, 257 **LB**
Col: Colorado *HS:* Phillis Wheatley [Houston, TX] B: 10/4/1968, Houston, TX *Drafted:* 1991 Round 2 NYG
1991 NYG: 16 G. **1992** NYG: 14 G. **1993** NYG: 10 G; 1.5 Sac. **1994** Cin: 1 G. **1995** Hou: 9 G; 1.5 Sac. **Total:** 50 G; 3 Sac.

CHARLIE MCGIBBONY McGibbony, Charles William 5′10″, 160 **TB-DB**
Col: Alabama; Central Arkansas *HS:* Pine Bluff [AR] B: 10/23/1915, Pine Bluff, AR
1944 Bkn: Pass 48-18 37.5%, 262 5.46 1 TD 10 Int; PR 5-66 13.2; KR 2-40 20.0; Int 1-6; Punt 8-294 36.8.

		Rushing			
Year Team	**G**	**Att**	**Yds**	**Avg**	**TD**
1944 Bkn	7	26	81	3.1	0

FIRPO MCGILBRA McGilbra, L. Vance 6′1″, 210 **T-G**
Col: Haskell Indian *HS:* Muskogee [OK] B: 1906
1926 Buf: 4 G.

LENNY MCGILL McGill, Charles Leonard III 6′1″, 195 **DB**
Col: Arizona State *HS:* Orange Glen [Escondido, CA] B: 5/31/1971, Long Beach, CA
1994 GB: 6 G; Int 2-16. **1995** GB: 15 G. **1996** Atl: 16 G. **1997** Atl: 15 G; Int 1-7. **1998** Car: 10 G; Int 1-6; 1 Sac. **Total:** 62 G; Int 4-29; 1 Sac.

EDDIE MCGILL McGill, Edward Hoyt 6′6″, 225 **TE**
Col: Western Carolina *HS:* Enka [NC] B: 7/5/1960, Asheville, NC *Drafted:* 1982 Round 10 StL
1982 StL: 9 G. **1983** StL: 2 G; Rec 1-11 11.0. **Total:** 11 G; Rec 1-11 11.0.

GEORGE MCGILL McGill, George 5′10″, 180 **G**
(Mickey) *Col:* Marquette *HS:* Winona [MN] B: 9/17/1897, Winona, MN D: 1/1966, FL
1922 Rac: 3 G.

KARMEELEYAH MCGILL McGill, Karmeeleyah 6′3″, 224 **LB**
Col: Notre Dame *HS:* Dunedin [FL] B: 1/11/1971, Clearwater, FL
1993 Cin: 4 G.

MIKE MCGILL McGill, Michael Ray 6′2″, 235 **LB**
Col: Notre Dame *HS:* Bishop Noll [Hammond, IN] B: 11/21/1946, Hammond, IN *Drafted:* 1968 Round 3 Min
1968 Min: 14 G. **1969** Min: 10 G. **1970** Min: 14 G; 1 Fum TD; 6 Pt. **1971** StL: 11 G; Int 1-19. **1972** StL: 4 G; Int 2-28. **Total:** 53 G; Int 3-47; 1 Fum TD; 6 Pt.

RALPH MCGILL McGill, Ralph Louis 5′11″, 183 **DB**
Col: Northeastern Oklahoma A&M (J.C.); Tulsa *HS:* Sebring [FL] B: 4/28/1950, Thomasville, GA *Drafted:* 1972 Round 2 SF
1974 SF: Int 5-71. **1975** SF: Int 1-27; **1** Fum TD. **1977** SF: Int 1-30. **1979** NO: Int 1-6. **Total:** Int 8-134; 1 Fum TD.

		Punt Returns				Kickoff Returns					Tot
Year Team	**G**	**Ret**	**Yds**	**Avg**	**TD**	**Ret**	**Yds**	**Avg**	**TD**	**Fum**	**TD**
1972 SF	11	22	219	10.0	0	10	192	19.2	0	4	0
1973 SF	14	22	186	8.5	0	17	374	22.0	0	3	0
1974 SF	13	20	166	8.3	0	0	0	—	0	1	0
1975 SF	9	31	290	9.4	0	0	0	—	0	5	1
1976 SF	10	10	103	10.3	1	0	0	—	0	1	1
1977 SF	13	0	0	—	0	0	0	—	0	0	0
1978 NO	16	1	5	5.0	0	0	0	—	0	0	0
1979 NO	13	0	0	—	0	0	0	—	0	0	0
NFL Total	99	106	969	9.1	1	27	566	21.0	0	14	2

WILLIE MCGINEST McGinest, William Lee 6′5″, 255 **DE**
Col: USC *HS:* Long Beach Polytechnic [CA] B: 12/11/1971, Long Beach, CA *Drafted:* 1994 Round 1 NE
1994 NE: 16 G; 4.5 Sac. **1995** NE: 16 G; 11 Sac. **1996** NE: 16 G; Int 1-46 1 TD; **1** Fum TD; Tot TD 2; 12 Pt; 9.5 Sac. **1997** NE: 11 G; 2 Sac. **1998** NE: 9 G; 3.5 Sac. **Total:** 68 G; Int 1-46 1 TD; 1 Fum TD; Tot TD 2; 12 Pt; 30.5 Sac.

ED MCGINLEY McGinley, Edward Francis Jr. 5′11″, 185 **T**
Col: Pennsylvania *HS:* Swarthmore Prep [PA] B: 8/9/1899, Chester, PA D: 4/16/1985, Point Pleasant, NJ
1925 NYG: 2 G.

LARRY MCGINNIS McGinnis, James Laurence 6′1″, 210 **G-OE-C**
Col: Washburn; Marquette *HS:* Topeka Catholic [KS] B: 7/16/1899, Topeka, KS D: 3/1948
1923 Mil: 8 G. **1924** Mil: 13 G. **Total:** 21 G.

LEN MCGIRL McGirl, Leonard Edward 6′2″, 206 **G**
Col: Missouri *HS:* Odessa [MO] B: 1909, Washington Twp., Lafayette Co., MO Deceased
1934 StL: 3 G.

ED MCGLASSON McGlasson, Edward Tandy 6′4″, 248 **C**
Col: Maryland; Youngstown State *HS:* Bullis Prep [Potomac, MD] B: 7/11/1956, Annapolis, MD *Drafted:* 1979 Round 10 NYJ
1979 NYJ: 7 G. **1980** LARm: 1 G. **1981** NYG: 16 G. **Total:** 24 G.

CHESTER MCGLOCKTON McGlockton, Chester Morris 6′4″, 320 **DT**
Col: Clemson *HS:* Whiteville [NC] B: 9/16/1969, Whiteville, NC *Drafted:* 1992 Round 1 LARd
1992 LARd: 10 G; 3 Sac. **1993** LARd: 16 G; Int 1-19; 7 Sac. **1994** LARd: 16 G; 9.5 Sac. **1995** Oak: 16 G; 7.5 Sac. **1996** Oak: 16 G; 8 Sac. **1997** Oak: 16 G; 4.5 Sac. **1998** KC: 10 G; 1 Sac. **Total:** 100 G; Int 1-19; 40.5 Sac.

JOE MCGLONE McGlone, Joseph Carlton 5′7″, 150 **BB**
Col: Harvard *HS:* Natick [MA]; Phillips Exeter Acad. [Exeter, NH] B: 9/12/1896, Natick, MA D: 1/25/1963, New York, NY
1926 Prov: 1 G.

HUGH MCGOLDRICK McGoldrick, Hugh Francis 5′10″, 180 **T-E**
Col: Lehigh *HS:* Medford [MA]; Dean Acad. [Franklin, MA] B: 11/22/1900, Boston, MA D: 10/7/1965, Cotuit, MA
1925 Prov: 1 G.

BRUCE MCGONNIGAL McGonnigal, Joseph Bruce 6′4″, 229 **TE**
Col: Virginia *HS:* Loyola [Towson, MD] B: 5/1/1968, Cambridge, MA *Drafted:* 1991 Round 9 Pit
1991 Cle: 2 G.

ROB MCGOVERN McGovern, Robert Patrick 6'2", 225 **LB**
Col: Holy Cross *HS:* Bergen Catholic [Oradell, NJ] B: 10/1/1966, Teaneck, NJ *Drafted:* 1989 Round 10 KC
1989 KC: 16 G; Scor 1 Saf; 2 Pt. **1990** KC: 11 G. **1991** Pit: 15 G; KR 1-0. **1992** NE: 4 G. **Total:** 46 G; KR 1-0; Scor 1 Saf; 2 Pt.

REGGIE MCGOWAN McGowan, Reginald 5'8", 165 **WR**
Col: Abilene Christian B: 9/25/1964
1987 NYG: 3 G; Rec 4-111 27.8 1 TD; 6 Pt.

JOE MCGRAIL McGrail, Joseph John 6'3", 280 **NT**
Col: Delaware *HS:* Pope Paul VI [Glendora, NJ] B: 6/6/1964, Philadelphia, PA *Drafted:* 1987 Round 12 Buf
1987 Buf: 2 G.

BRIAN MCGRATH McGrath, Brian Patrick 245 **G**
Col: No College B: 3/18/1901, Ireland D: 1/1985, Bronx, NY
1922 Lou: 1 G.

FRANK MCGRATH McGrath, Frank LeDuke 5'11", 192 **OE**
Col: Georgetown *HS:* St.James [Bay City, MI] B: 3/13/1904 D: 3/4/1990, Essexville, MI
1927 Fra: 12 G. **1928** NYY: 12 G. **Total:** 24 G.

MARK MCGRATH McGrath, Mark Allen 5'11", 175 **WR**
Col: Montana State *HS:* Shorecrest [Seattle, WA] B: 12/17/1957, San Diego, CA
1981 Sea: 6 G; Rec 4-47 11.8. **1983** Was: 2 G; Rec 1-6 6.0. **1984** Was: 13 G; Rec 10-118 11.8 1 TD; 6 Pt. **1985** Was: 5 G. **Total:** 26 G; Rec 15-171 11.4 1 TD; 6 Pt.

DICK MCGRATH McGrath, Richard James 5'10", 190 **T-C**
Col: Holy Cross *HS:* Seton Hall Prep [South Orange, NJ]; St. John's Prep [Brooklyn, NY] B: 6/30/1901, Winthrop, MA D: 10/23/1965, Virginia Beach, VA
1926 Bkn: 10 G.

MIKE MCGRAW McGraw, Michael Shane 6'2", 225 **LB**
Col: Wyoming *HS:* Poudre [Fort Collins, CO] B: 12/27/1953, Denver, CO *Drafted:* 1975 Round 10 StL
1976 StL: 4 G; KR 1-13 13.0. **1977** Det: 1 G. **Total:** 5 G; KR 1-13 13.0.

THURMAN MCGRAW McGraw, Thurman Fay 6'5", 235 **DT-OT**
(Fum) *Col:* Colorado State *HS:* Paonia [CO] B: 7/17/1927, Garden City, KS *Drafted:* 1950 Round 2 Det
1950 Det: 12 G; Int 1-4. **1951** Det: 8 G. **1952** Det: 12 G. **1953** Det: 11 G; Int 1-2. **1954** Det: 6 G. **Total:** 49 G; Int 2-6.

KELI MCGREGOR McGregor, Keli Scott 6'6", 250 **TE**
Col: Colorado State *HS:* Lakewood [CO] B: 1/23/1963, Primghar, IA *Drafted:* 1985 Round 4 Den
1985 Den-Ind: 8 G. Den: 2 G. Ind: 6 G. **Total:** 8 G.

DAN MCGREW McGrew, Daniel Atwood 6'2", 250 **C**
Col: Purdue *HS:* Martins Ferry [OH] B: 4/7/1937, Martins Ferry, OH *Drafted:* 1959 Round 20 Det
1960 Buf: 14 G.

LARRY MCGREW McGrew, Lawrence 6'5", 233 **LB**
Col: Contra Costa Coll. CA (J.C.); USC *HS:* Berkeley [CA] B: 7/23/1957, Berkeley, CA *Drafted:* 1980 Round 2 NE
1980 NE: 11 G. **1982** NE: 8 G; 1.5 Sac. **1983** NE: 16 G; Int 1-3; 2 Sac. **1984** NE: 16 G; 0.5 Sac. **1985** NE: 13 G; Int 1-0; 1 Sac. **1986** NE: 14 G; Int 2-44; 1 Sac. **1987** NE: 12 G; 1 Sac. **1988** NE: 16 G; Int 1-6; 2 Sac. **1989** NE: 16 G; Int 1-(-4); 4.5 Sac. **1990** NYG: 11 G. **Total:** 133 G; Int 6-49; 13.5 Sac.

SYLVESTER MCGREW McGrew, Sylvester Lee 6'4", 257 **DE**
Col: Tulane *HS:* West Jefferson [Harvey, LA] B: 2/27/1960, New Orleans, LA
1987 GB: 3 G.

CURTIS MCGRIFF McGriff, Curtis 6'5", 270 **DE-NT**
Col: Alabama *HS:* Cottonwood [AL] B: 5/17/1958, Donaldsonville, GA
1980 NYG: 13 G. **1981** NYG: 14 G. **1982** NYG: 9 G. **1983** NYG: 8 G. **1984** NYG: 16 G. **1985** NYG: 16 G. **1987** Was: 1 G. **Total:** 77 G.

LEE MCGRIFF McGriff, Lee Colson 5'9", 165 **WR**
Col: Florida *HS:* H.B. Plant [Tampa, FL] B: 10/3/1953, Tampa, FL
1976 TB: 6 G; Pass 1-1 100.0%, 39 39.00.

TYRONE MCGRIFF McGriff, Tyrone Keith 6'0", 269 **OG**
Col: Florida A&M *HS:* Vero Beach [FL] B: 1/13/1958, Vero Beach, FL *Drafted:* 1980 Round 12 Pit
1980 Pit: 16 G. **1981** Pit: 12 G. **1982** Pit: 8 G. **Total:** 36 G.

LAMAR MCGRIGGS McGriggs, Lamar V 6'3", 213 **DB**
Col: Arizona Western Coll. (J.C.); Oklahoma State; Western Illinois *HS:* Thornton Twp. [Harvey, IL] B: 5/9/1968, Chicago, IL *Drafted:* 1991 Round 8 NYG
1991 NYG: 16 G. **1992** NYG: 16 G. **1993** Min: 9 G; Int 1-63 1 TD; 6 Pt. **1994** Min: 16 G; Int 1-1. **Total:** 57 G; Int 2-64 1 TD; 6 Pt.

MIKE MCGRUDER McGruder, Michael J.P. 5'11", 185 **DB**
(Scooter) *Col:* Kent State *HS:* Cleveland Heights [OH] B: 5/6/1964, Cleveland, OH
1989 GB: 2 G. **1990** Mia: 1 G. **1991** Mia: 16 G. **1992** SF: 9 G. **1993** SF: 16 G; Int 5-89 1 TD; 6 Pt. **1994** TB: 15 G; Int 1-0. **1995** TB: 16 G. **1996** NE: 14 G; 0.5 Sac. **1997** NE: 3 G; 1 Sac. **Total:** 92 G; Int 6-89 1 TD; 6 Pt; 1.5 Sac.

MONTE MCGUIRE McGuire, Monte Lin 6'4", 202 **QB**
Col: Texas Tech *HS:* Monahans [TX] B: 5/7/1964, Abilene, TX
1987 Den: 2 G; Pass 3-2 66.7%, 23 7.67.

KAIPO MCGUIRE McGuire, Roy Kaiponohea 5'10", 182 **WR**
Col: Brigham Young *HS:* St. Louis [Honolulu, HI] B: 1/16/1974, Honolulu, HI
1997 Ind: 3 G. **1998** Ind: 1 G; PR 2-4 2.0; KR 4-75 18.8. **Total:** 4 G; PR 2-4 2.0; KR 4-75 18.8.

GENE MCGUIRE McGuire, Walter Eugene Jr. 6'2", 284 **C**
Col: Notre Dame *HS:* A. Crawford Mosley [Lynn Haven, FL] B: 7/17/1970, Fort Dix, NJ *Drafted:* 1992 Round 4 NO
1993 ChiB: 9 G. **1996** GB: 8 G. **Total:** 17 G.

WARREN MCGUIRK McGuirk, Warren Pierce 5'11", 200 **T**
Col: Boston College *HS:* Dorchester [Boston, MA]; St. Anselm's Prep [Manchester, NH] B: 1/2/1906, Boston, MA D: 2/19/1981, Boston, MA
1929 Prov: 12 G. **1930** Prov: 11 G. **Total:** 23 G.

DAN MCGWIRE McGwire, Daniel Scott 6'8", 243 **QB**
Col: San Diego State; Iowa *HS:* Claremont [CA] B: 12/18/1967, Ponoma, CA *Drafted:* 1991 Round 1 Sea
1992 Sea: Rush 3-13 4.3. **1993** Sea: Rush 1-(-1) -1.0. **1994** Sea: Rush 10-(-6) -0.6. **Total:** Rush 14-6 0.4.

		Passing								
Year Team	G	Att	Comp	Comp%	Yds	YPA	TD	Int	Rating	Fum
1991 Sea	1	7	3	42.9	27	3.86	0	1	14.3	0
1992 Sea	2	30	17	56.7	116	3.87	0	3	25.8	1
1993 Sea	2	5	3	60.0	24	4.80	1	0	111.7	0
1994 Sea	7	105	51	48.6	578	5.50	1	2	60.7	9
1995 Mia	1	1	0	0.0	0	0.00	0	0	39.6	0
NFL Total	13	148	74	50.0	745	5.03	2	6	52.3	10

JOE MCHALE McHale, Joseph T 6'2", 227 **LB**
Col: Delaware *HS:* Morris Catholic [Denville, NJ] B: 9/26/1963, Passaic, NJ
1987 NE: 3 G.

TOM MCHALE McHale, Thomas 6'4", 284 **OG-OT-DE**
Col: Maryland; Cornell *HS:* Gaithersburg [MD]; Wyoming Seminary [Kingston, PA] B: 2/25/1963, Gaithersburg, MD
1987 TB: 3 G. **1988** TB: 10 G; 1 Fum. **1989** TB: 15 G. **1990** TB: 7 G. **1991** TB: 15 G. **1992** TB: 9 G. **1993** Phi: 8 G. **1994** Phi: 13 G. **1995** Mia: 7 G. **Total:** 87 G; 1 Fum.

LAMAR MCHAN McHan, Clarence Lamar 6'1", 201 **QB**
Col: Arkansas *HS:* Lakeside [Lake Village, AR] B: 12/16/1932, Lake Village, AR D: 11/23/1998, New Orleans, LA *Drafted:* 1954 Round 1 ChiC
1954 ChiC: Punt 4-159 39.8. **1955** ChiC: Scor 12, 0-2 XK. **1956** ChiC: Punt 8-285 35.6. **1958** ChiC: Rec 0-1; Punt 2-65 32.5. **1962** Bal: Punt 1-22 22.0. **Total:** Rec 0-1; Punt 15-531 35.4; Scor 72, 0-2 XK.

		Passing							
Year Team	G	Att	Comp	Comp%	Yds	YPA	TD	Int	Rating
1954 ChiC	12	255	105	41.2	1475	5.78	6	22	32.4
1955 ChiC	12	207	78	37.7	1085	5.24	11	19	34.8
1956 ChiC	12	152	72	47.4	1159	7.63	10	8	73.3
1957 ChiC	12	200	87	43.5	1568	7.84	11	15	58.1
1958 ChiC	12	198	91	46.0	1291	6.52	12	13	60.4
1959 GB	12	108	48	44.4	805	7.45	8	9	60.1
1960 GB	12	91	33	36.3	517	5.68	3	5	44.1
1961 Bal	7	15	3	20.0	28	1.87	1	4	22.2
1962 Bal	10	20	10	50.0	278	13.90	3	2	95.8
1963 Bal-SF	12	196	83	42.3	1243	6.34	8	11	54.0
1963 Bal	1	1	0	0.0	0	0.00	0	0	39.6
1963 SF	11	195	83	42.6	1243	6.37	8	11	54.3
NFL Total	113	1442	610	42.3	9449	6.55	73	108	50.3

	Rushing				
Year Team	Att	Yds	Avg	TD	Fum
1954 ChiC	34	152	4.5	1	3
1955 ChiC	56	194	3.5	2	3
1956 ChiC	58	161	2.8	5	2
1957 ChiC	25	82	3.3	2	1
1958 ChiC	17	65	3.8	1	4
1959 GB	16	64	4.0	0	3
1960 GB	8	67	8.4	1	0
1961 Bal	4	1	0.3	0	0
1962 Bal	4	4	1.0	0	1
1963 Bal-SF	17	59	3.5	0	3

1963 SF	17	59	3.5	0	3
NFL Total	239	849	3.6	12	20

PAT MCHUGH McHugh, William Patrick 5′11″, 185 **DB-HB**
Col: Georgia Tech *HS:* Keith [Orville, AL]; Notre Dame HS [Chattanooga, TN] B: 12/21/1919, Selma, AL *Drafted:* 1946 Round 10 Phi
1947 Phi: Rec 2-16 8.0; KR 3-50 16.7. **1950** Phi: KR 2-45 22.5.
Total: Rec 2-16 8.0; KR 5-95 19.0.

		Rushing				Punt Returns			
Year Team	**G**	**Att**	**Yds**	**Avg**	**TD**	**Ret**	**Yds**	**Avg**	**TD**
1947 Phi	9	22	171	7.8	1	10	156	15.6	**1**
1948 Phi	10	4	12	3.0	0	18	220	12.2	0
1949 Phi	12	2	5	2.5	0	3	26	8.7	0
1950 Phi	12	4	14	3.5	0	0	0	—	0
1951 Phi	8	0	0	—	0	0	0	—	0
NFL Total	51	32	202	6.3	1	31	402	13.0	1

	Interceptions				Tot
Year Team	**Int**	**Yds**	**TD**	**Fum**	**TD**
1947 Phi	3	52	0	7	2
1948 Phi	2	27	0	3	0
1949 Phi	6	89	1	2	1
1950 Phi	4	34	0	0	0
1951 Phi	1	19	0	0	0
NFL Total	16	221	1	12	3

DANNY MCILHANY McIlhany, Joseph Daniel 6′1″, 195 **DB**
Col: Texas A&M *HS:* South Houston [TX] B: 1/12/1943, Brownwood, TX
1965 LARm: 10 G; Int 2-7; 1 Fum.

DON MCILHENNY McIlhenny, Donald Brookes 6′0″, 197 **HB**
Col: Southern Methodist *HS:* South Houston [TX] B: 11/22/1934, Cleveland, OH *Drafted:* 1956 Round 3 Det
1956 Det: Pass 1-0. **1958** GB: PR 1-0. **Total:** Pass 1-0; PR 1-0.

		Rushing				Receiving			
Year Team	**G**	**Att**	**Yds**	**Avg**	**TD**	**Rec**	**Yds**	**Avg**	**TD**
1956 Det	9	87	372	4.3	3	8	70	8.8	2
1957 GB	12	100	384	3.8	1	18	210	11.7	2
1958 GB	12	74	239	3.2	1	20	154	7.7	1
1959 GB	12	47	231	4.9	1	8	95	11.9	1
1960 Dal	11	96	321	3.3	1	15	120	8.0	1
1961 Dal-SF	8	10	34	3.4	0	1	6	6.0	0
1961 Dal	3	2	4	2.0	0	1	6	6.0	0
1961 SF	5	8	30	3.8	0	0	0	—	0
NFL Total	64	414	1581	3.8	7	70	655	9.4	7

	Kickoff Returns					Tot
Year Team	**Ret**	**Yds**	**Avg**	**TD**	**Fum**	**TD**
1956 Det	0	0	—	0	0	5
1957 GB	14	362	25.9	0	4	3
1958 GB	7	146	20.9	0	8	2
1959 GB	3	50	16.7	0	1	2
1960 Dal	0	0	—	0	0	2
1961 Dal-SF	6	189	31.5	0	0	0
1961 SF	6	189	31.5	0	0	0
NFL Total	30	747	24.9	0	13	14

WALLY MCILWAIN McIlwain, Wallace Wesley 5′9″, 173 **WB**
Col: Illinois *HS:* Highland Park [IL] B: 1/20/1903, Chicago, IL D: 6/30/1963, Evanston, IL
1926 Rac: 5 G.

PAT MCINALLY McInally, Patrick J 6′6″, 210 **WR-P**
Col: Harvard *HS:* Villa Park [CA] B: 5/7/1953, Villa Park, CA *Drafted:* 1975 Round 5 Cin
1977 Cin: Pass 1-1 100.0%, 4 4.00; Rush 1-4 4.0. **1979** Cin: Rush 1-18 18.0. **1980** Cin: Rush 1-0. **1981** Cin: Rush 1-(-27) -27.0. **1984** Cin: Pass 2-2 100.0%, 77 38.50. **1985** Cin: Pass 1-0; Rush 1-(-2) -2.0.
Total: Pass 4-3 75.0%, 81 20.25; Rush 5-(-7) -1.4.

		Receiving				Punting			
Year Team	**G**	**Rec**	**Yds**	**Avg**	**TD**	**Punts**	**Yds**	**Avg**	**Fum**
1976 Cin	14	0	0	—	0	76	2999	39.5	0
1977 Cin	14	17	258	15.2	3	67	2802	41.8	1
1978 Cin	16	15	189	12.6	0	91	3919	**43.1**	0
1979 Cin	16	1	24	24.0	0	89	3678	41.3	0
1980 Cin	16	18	269	14.9	2	83	3390	40.8	2
1981 Cin	16	6	68	11.3	0	72	3272	**45.4**	0
1982 Cin	9	0	0	—	0	31	1201	38.7	0
1983 Cin	16	0	0	—	0	67	2804	41.9	0
1984 Cin	16	0	0	—	0	67	2832	42.3	0
1985 Cin	16	0	0	—	0	57	2410	42.3	0
NFL Total	149	57	808	14.2	5	700	29307	41.9	3

MAC MCINDOE McIndoe, George R **OE**
Col: No College *HS:* Wilkinsburg [PA] B: 12/6/1896, Pitcairn, PA D: 1/1958
1921 Mun: 2 G.

NICK MCINERNEY McInerney, Nicholas 6′2″, 201 **C-T-E-G**
(Bull) *Col:* No College Deceased
1920 ChiC: 8 G. **1921** ChiC: 6 G. **1922** ChiC: 11 G. **1923** ChiC: 11 G. **1924** ChiC: 9 G. **1925** ChiC: 10 G. **1926** ChiC: 11 G. **1927** ChiC: 8 G.
Total: 74 G.

SEAN MCINERNEY McInerney, Sean Mallan 6′3″, 255 **DE**
Col: Frostburg State *HS:* Langley [McLean, VA] B: 12/27/1960
1987 ChiB: 3 G; 6.5 Sac.

HUGH MCINNIS McInnis, Hugh Allen 6′3″, 228 **TE**
(Sonny) *Col:* Southern Mississippi *HS:* Greene Co. HS [Leakesville, MS] B: 9/18/1938, Mobile, AL *Drafted:* 1960 Round 3 StL
1960 StL: 12 G; Rec 13-260 20.0. **1961** StL: 3 G; Rush 4-30 7.5; Rec 7-107 15.3. **1962** StL: 9 G; Rec 1-10 10.0; 1 Fum. **1964** Det: 14 G; Rec 1-15 15.0. **Total:** 38 G; Rush 4-30 7.5; Rec 22-392 17.8; 1 Fum.

AL MCINTOSH McIntosh, Ira Daniel 5′9″, 180 **WB**
(Chick) *Col:* Rhode Island *HS:* Tech [Providence, RI] B: 4/12/1903, Providence, RI D: 10/13/1973, CA
1925 Prov: 9 G. **1926** Prov: 2 G. **Total:** 11 G.

JOE MCINTOSH McIntosh, Joseph Ellison 5′10″, 192 **RB**
Col: North Carolina State *HS:* Lexington [NC] B: 12/9/1962, Lexington, NC
1987 Atl: 2 G; Rush 5-11 2.2; Rec 3-15 5.0 1 TD; KR 3-108 36.0; 6 Pt.

TODDRICK MCINTOSH McIntosh, Toddrick Poole 6′3″, 277 **DT-DE**
Col: Florida State *HS:* L.V. Berkner [Richardson, TX] B: 1/22/1972, Tallahassee, FL *Drafted:* 1994 Round 7 Dal
1994 TB: 4 G. **1995** TB: 11 G; 2 Sac. **Total:** 15 G; 2 Sac.

GUY MCINTYRE McIntyre, Guy Maurice 6′3″, 275 **OG**
Col: Georgia *HS:* Thomasville [GA] B: 2/17/1961, Thomasville, GA *Drafted:* 1984 Round 3 SF
1984 SF: 15 G; KR 1-0. **1985** SF: 15 G; **1** Fum TD; 6 Pt. **1986** SF: 16 G. **1987** SF: 3 G. **1988** SF: 16 G; Rec 1-17 17.0 1 TD; 6 Pt. **1989** SF: 16 G. **1990** SF: 16 G. **1991** SF: 16 G. **1992** SF: 16 G. **1993** SF: 16 G. **1994** GB: 10 G. **1995** Phi: 16 G. **1996** Phi: 15 G; Rec 1-4 4.0. **Total:** 186 G; Rec 2-21 10.5 1 TD; KR 1-0; 1 Fum TD; Tot TD 2; 12 Pt.

JEFF MCINTYRE McIntyre, Jeffrey Glenn 6′3″, 232 **LB**
Col: Los Angeles Southwest Coll. CA (J.C.); Arizona State *HS:* Mount Carmel [Los Angeles, CA] B: 9/20/1955, Beaumont, TX *Drafted:* 1979 Round 6 Den
1979 SF: 14 G. **1980** StL: 10 G. **Total:** 24 G.

SECDRICK MCINTYRE McIntyre, Secdrick 5′10″, 190 **RB**
Col: Auburn *HS:* Robert E. Lee [Montgomery, AL] B: 6/2/1954, Montgomery, AL
1977 Atl: 6 G; Rush 13-65 5.0; Rec 1-27 27.0 1 TD; KR 1-15 15.0; 6 Pt.

EVERETT MCIVER McIver, Everett Allen 6′5″, 318 **OG**
Col: Elizabeth City State *HS:* 71st [Fayetteville, NC] B: 8/5/1970, Cumberland, NC
1994 NYJ: 4 G. **1995** NYJ: 14 G. **1996** Mia: 7 G. **1997** Mia: 14 G. **1998** Dal: 6 G. **Total:** 45 G.

RICK MCIVOR McIvor, Richard E 6′4″, 210 **QB**
Col: Texas *HS:* Fort Stockton [TX] B: 9/26/1960, Fort Davis, TX *Drafted:* 1984 Round 3 StL
1984 StL: 4 G; Pass 4-0; Rush 3-5 1.7. **1985** StL: 2 G. **Total:** 6 G; Pass 4-0; Rush 3-5 1.7.

PAUL MCJULIEN McJulien, Paul Dorien 5′10″, 190 **P**
Col: Jackson State *HS:* Baker [LA] B: 2/24/1965, Chicago, IL
1991 GB: Rush 1-0. **1992** GB: Pass 1-0. **Total:** Pass 1-0; Rush 1-0.

		Punting			
Year Team	**G**	**Punts**	**Yds**	**Avg**	**Fum**
1991 GB	16	86	3473	40.4	1
1992 GB	9	36	1386	38.5	0
1993 LARm	5	21	795	37.9	0
NFL Total	30	143	5654	39.5	1

BILL MCKALIP McKalip, William Ward 6′10″, 160 **OE-DE-WB-DB**
(Wild Bill) *Col:* Oregon State *HS:* Oakland Technical [CA] B: 6/5/1907, Pittsburgh, PA D: 7/11/1993, Corvallis, OR
1931 Port: Rec 4 TD. **1932** Port: Rec 5-105 21.0. **1934** Det: Rec 6-97 16.2. **1936** Det: Rec 1-10 10.0. **Total:** Rec 12-212 17.7 4 TD.

		Rushing			
Year Team	**G**	**Att**	**Yds**	**Avg**	**TD**
1931 Port	14	—	—	—	0
1932 Port	12	0	0	—	0
1934 Det	13	19	63	3.3	0
1936 Det	10	7	39	5.6	0
NFL Total	49	26	102	3.9	0

JOHN MCKAY McKay, John Kenneth 5′11″, 182 **WR**
(J.K.) *Col:* USC *HS:* Bishop Amat [La Puente, CA] B: 3/28/1953, Eugene, OR *Drafted:* 1975 Round 16 Cle

		Receiving			
Year Team	G	Rec	Yds	Avg	TD
1976 TB	14	20	302	15.1	1
1977 TB	14	12	164	13.7	0
1978 TB	15	9	166	18.4	1
NFL Total	43	41	632	15.4	2

BOB MCKAY McKay, Robert Charles 6′5″, 260 **OT-OG**
Col: Texas *HS:* Crane [TX] B: 12/27/1947, Seminole, TX
Drafted: 1970 Round 1 Cle
1970 Cle: 8 G. **1971** Cle: 14 G. **1972** Cle: 10 G. **1973** Cle: 14 G. **1974** Cle: 14 G. **1975** Cle: 7 G. **1976** NE: 14 G; KR 1-23 23.0. **1977** NE: 12 G; KR 1-16 16.0. **1978** NE: 12 G. **Total:** 105 G; KR 2-39 19.5.

ROY MCKAY McKay, Roy Dale 6′0″, 193 **DB-TB-FB-HB**
(Tex) *Col:* Texas *HS:* Junction [TX] B: 2/2/1920, Mason, TX
D: 5/29/1969, Sonora, TX *Drafted:* 1943 Round 3 GB
1944 GB: PR 2-19 9.5. **1945** GB: PR 7-66 9.4; KR 4-67 16.8; Int 3-33. **1946** GB: KR 2-41 20.5; Int 1-20; Scor 8, 2-2 100.0% XK. **1947** GB: Scor 1, 1-1 100.0% XK. **Total:** PR 9-85 9.4; KR 6-108 18.0; Int 4-53; Scor 21, 3-3 100.0% XK.

		Passing							
Year Team	G	Att	Comp	Comp%	Yds	YPA	TD	Int	Rating
1944 GB	3	14	6	42.9	72	5.14	1	2	43.5
1945 GB	10	89	32	36.0	520	5.84	5	9	35.5
1946 GB	11	0	0	—	0	—	0	0	—
1947 GB	11	0	0	—	0	—	0	0	—
NFL Total	35	103	38	36.9	592	5.75	6	11	36.6

	Rushing				Punting			
Year Team	Att	Yds	Avg	TD	Punts	Yds	Avg	Fum
1944 GB	5	12	2.4	0	8	297	37.1	0
1945 GB	71	231	3.3	2	44	1814	41.2	4
1946 GB	21	34	1.6	1	**64**	**2735**	42.7	2
1947 GB	3	11	3.7	0	8	350	43.8	0
NFL Total	100	288	2.9	3	124	5196	41.9	6

PAUL MCKEE McKee, Paul Melvin 6′3″, 217 **OE-DE**
(Beaver) *Col:* Rochester; Syracuse *HS:* Beaver Falls [PA]
B: 4/26/1923, Beaver Falls, PA *Drafted:* 1945 Round 10 Was

		Receiving				
Year Team	G	Rec	Yds	Avg	TD	Fum
1947 Was	11	16	242	15.1	2	1
1948 Was	12	14	171	12.2	0	0
NFL Total	23	30	413	13.8	2	1

JAMES MCKEEHAN McKeehan, James Bell 6′3″, 251 **TE**
Col: Texas A&M *HS:* Willis [TX] B: 8/9/1973, Houston, TX
1996 Hou: 14 G; KR 2-6 3.0. **1997** Ten: 10 G. **Total:** 24 G; KR 2-6 3.0.

VITO MCKEEVER McKeever, Juan Devito 6′0″, 180 **DB**
Col: Florida *HS:* Dunnellon [FL] B: 10/8/1961, Inverness, FL
1986 TB: 16 G; Int 3-12. **1987** TB: 1 G. **Total:** 17 G; Int 3-12.

MARLIN MCKEEVER McKeever, Marlin Thomas 6′1″, 235 **LB-TE**
Col: USC *HS:* Mount Carmel [Los Angeles, CA] B: 1/1/1940, Cheyenne, WY *Drafted:* 1961 Round 1 LARm
1962 LARm: Int 2-1. **1963** LARm: KR 2-8 4.0. **1966** LARm: KR 1-8 8.0. **1968** Was: KR 1-0. **1969** Was: KR 2-31 15.5; Int 1-3. **1970** Was: KR 1-21 21.0. **1971** LARm: Int 4-38. **1972** LARm: Int 2-8. **Total:** KR 7-68 9.7; Int 9-50.

		Receiving				
Year Team	G	Rec	Yds	Avg	TD	Fum
1961 LARm	3	0	0	—	0	0
1962 LARm	14	0	0	—	0	0
1963 LARm	13	11	152	13.8	0	0
1964 LARm	14	41	582	14.2	1	1
1965 LARm	12	44	542	12.3	4	4
1966 LARm	11	23	277	12.0	1	2
1967 Min	14	14	184	13.1	0	0
1968 Was	14	0	0	—	0	0
1969 Was	12	0	0	—	0	0
1970 Was	14	0	0	—	0	0
1971 LARm	14	0	0	—	0	0
1972 LARm	14	0	0	—	0	0
1973 Phi	13	0	0	—	0	0
NFL Total	162	133	1737	13.1	6	7

KEITH MCKELLER McKeller, Terrell Keith 6′6″, 240 **TE**
Col: Jacksonville State *HS:* Fairfield [AL] B: 7/9/1964, Birmingham, AL
Drafted: 1987 Round 9 Buf

		Receiving				
Year Team	G	Rec	Yds	Avg	TD	Fum
1987 Buf	1	9	80	8.9	0	0
1988 Buf	12	0	0	—	0	0
1989 Buf	16	20	341	17.1	2	1
1990 Buf	16	34	464	13.6	5	1
1991 Buf	16	44	434	9.9	3	0
1992 Buf	11	14	110	7.9	0	1
1993 Buf	8	3	35	11.7	1	0
NFL Total	80	124	1464	11.8	11	3

KEITH MCKENZIE McKenzie, Keith Derrick 6′3″, 248 **LB-DE**
Col: Ball State *HS:* Highland Park [MI] B: 10/17/1973, Detroit, MI
Drafted: 1996 Round 7 GB
1996 GB: 10 G; 1 Sac. **1997** GB: 16 G; 1.5 Sac. **1998** GB: 16 G; KR 1-17 17.0; Int 1-33 1 TD; 1 Fum TD; Tot TD 2; 12 Pt; 8 Sac. **Total:** 42 G; KR 1-17 17.0; Int 1-33 1 TD; 1 Fum TD; Tot TD 2; 12 Pt; 10.5 Sac.

RALEIGH MCKENZIE McKenzie, Raleigh 6′2″, 283 **OG-C-OT**
Col: Tennessee *HS:* Austin-East [Knoxville, TN] B: 2/8/1963, Knoxville, TN *Drafted:* 1985 Round 11 Was
1985 Was: 6 G. **1986** Was: 15 G. **1987** Was: 12 G. **1988** Was: 16 G. **1989** Was: 15 G. **1990** Was: 16 G. **1991** Was: 16 G. **1992** Was: 16 G. **1993** Was: 16 G. **1994** Was: 16 G. **1995** Phi: 16 G. **1996** Phi: 16 G. **1997** SD: 16 G. **1998** SD: 16 G. **Total:** 208 G.

REGGIE MCKENZIE McKenzie, Reginald 6′4″, 255 **OG**
Col: Michigan *HS:* Highland Park [MI] B: 7/27/1950, Detroit, MI
Drafted: 1972 Round 2 Buf
1972 Buf: 14 G. **1973** Buf: 14 G. **1974** Buf: 14 G. **1975** Buf: 14 G; KR 1-15 15.0. **1976** Buf: 14 G. **1977** Buf: 14 G. **1978** Buf: 16 G. **1979** Buf: 16 G. **1980** Buf: 16 G; 1 Fum. **1981** Buf: 6 G. **1982** Buf: 9 G. **1983** Sea: 14 G. **1984** Sea: 10 G. **Total:** 171 G; KR 1-15 15.0; 1 Fum.

REGGIE MCKENZIE McKenzie, Reginald 6′1″, 240 **LB**
Col: Tennessee *HS:* Austin-East [Knoxville, TN] B: 2/8/1963, Knoxville, TN *Drafted:* 1985 Round 10 LARd
1985 LARd: 16 G; 1 Sac. **1986** LARd: 16 G; Int 1-9; 1 Sac. **1987** LARd: 10 G. **1988** LARd: 16 G; Int 1-26; 1 Sac. **1992** SF: 2 G. **Total:** 60 G; Int 2-35; 3 Sac.

RICH MCKENZIE McKenzie, Richard Anthony 6′2″, 258 **LB**
Col: Penn State *HS:* Boyd H. Anderson [Lauderdale Lakes, FL]
B: 4/15/1971, Fort Lauderdale, FL *Drafted:* 1993 Round 6 Cle
1995 Cle: 8 G; 1.5 Sac.

JACK MCKETES McKetes, Jack 1 **BB**
Col: No College
1926 Ham: 1 G.

MIKE MCKIBBEN McKibben, Michael Wayne 6′3″, 228 **LB**
Col: Kent State *HS:* Lewis Co. [Weston, WV] B: 9/3/1956, Mount Carmel, IL
1979 NYJ: 16 G; Int 1-5. **1980** NYJ: 9 G. **Total:** 25 G; Int 1-5.

BILL MCKINLEY McKinley, William James 6′2″, 240 **DE-LB**
Col: Arizona *HS:* Pueblo [Tucson, AZ] B: 1/14/1949, Vincennes, IN
Drafted: 1971 Round 6 Buf
1971 Buf: 7 G.

PHIL MCKINNELY McKinnely, Philip Byron 6′4″, 248 **OT-OG-TE**
Col: UCLA *HS:* St. Mary's Prep [Berkeley, CA] B: 7/8/1954, Oakland, CA *Drafted:* 1976 Round 9 Atl
1976 Atl: 12 G. **1977** Atl: 14 G. **1978** Atl: 14 G. **1979** Atl: 15 G. **1980** Atl: 7 G. **1981** LARm: 7 G. **1982** ChiB: 8 G. **Total:** 77 G.

ODIS MCKINNEY McKinney, Odis Jr. 6′2″, 187 **DB**
Col: Los Angeles Valley Coll. CA (J.C.); Colorado *HS:* Reseda [Los Angeles, CA] B: 5/19/1957, Detroit, MI *Drafted:* 1978 Round 2 NYG
1980 Oak: PR 1-0. **1982** LARd: 1 Sac. **1984** LARd: KR 1-0; 1 Sac.
Total: PR 1-0; KR 1-0; 2 Sac.

		Interceptions			
Year Team	G	Int	Yds	TD	Fum
1978 NYG	14	1	11	0	0
1979 NYG	15	1	25	0	1
1980 Oak	16	3	22	0	1
1981 Oak	16	3	38	0	0
1982 LARd	9	0	0	0	0
1983 LARd	16	1	0	0	0
1984 LARd	16	1	0	0	1
1985 KC-LARd	15	1	22	0	0
1985 KC	5	0	0	0	0
1985 LARd	10	1	22	0	0
1986 LARd	2	0	0	0	0
NFL Total	119	11	118	0	3

ROYCE MCKINNEY McKinney, Royce William 6′1″, 190 **DB**
Col: Kentucky State *HS:* River Rouge [MI] B: 11/3/1953, River Rouge, MI *Drafted:* 1975 Round 9 Bal
1975 Buf: 9 G; KR 6-151 25.2.

STEVE MCKINNEY McKinney, Stephen Michael 6′4″, 297 **OG**
Col: Texas A&M *HS:* Clear Lake [Houston, TX] B: 10/15/1975, Houston, TX *Drafted:* 1998 Round 4 Ind
1998 Ind: 16 G.

BILL MCKINNEY McKinney, William C 6′1″, 226 **LB**
Col: West Texas A&M *HS:* Borger [TX] B: 7/14/1945, Borger, TX *Drafted:* 1972 Round 16 ChiB
1972 ChiB: 8 G.

ZION MCKINNEY McKinney, Zion Bailus 6′0″, 200 **WR**
Col: South Carolina *HS:* Pickens [SC] B: 2/10/1958, Pickens, SC
1980 Was: 10 G; KR 2-48 24.0.

HUGH MCKINNIS McKinnis, Hugh Lee Jr. 6′0″, 225 **RB**
Col: Arizona State *HS:* Farrell [PA] B: 6/9/1948, Sharon, PA *Drafted:* 1972 Round 8 Cle
1975 Cle: KR 3-39 13.0. **Total:** KR 3-39 13.0.

		Rushing				Receiving				
Year Team	G	Att	Yds	Avg	TD	Rec	Yds	Avg	TD	Fum
1973 Cle	14	28	77	2.8	0	3	11	3.7	0	1
1974 Cle	13	124	519	4.2	2	32	258	8.1	0	1
1975 Cle	14	71	259	3.6	4	17	155	9.1	0	2
1976 Sea	11	46	105	2.3	4	13	148	11.4	0	1
NFL Total	52	269	960	3.6	10	65	572	8.8	0	5

DENNIS MCKINNON McKinnon, Dennis Lewis 6′1″, 185 **WR**
Col: Florida State *HS:* South Miami [Miami, FL] B: 8/22/1961, Quitman, GA
1983 ChiB: KR 2-42 21.0. **1984** ChiB: Rush 2-12 6.0. **1985** ChiB: Rush 1-0; KR 1-16 16.0. **1988** ChiB: Rush 3-25 8.3 1 TD. **1989** ChiB: Rush 3-5 1.7. **1990** Dal: Rush 1-(-8) -8.0. **Total:** Rush 10-34 3.4 1 TD; KR 3-58 19.3.

		Receiving				Punt Returns					Tot
Year Team	G	Rec	Yds	Avg	TD	Ret	Yds	Avg	TD	Fum	TD
1983 ChiB	16	20	326	16.3	4	34	316	9.3	**1**	2	5
1984 ChiB	12	29	431	14.9	3	5	62	12.4	0	1	3
1985 ChiB	14	31	555	17.9	7	4	44	11.0	0	1	7
1987 ChiB	12	27	406	15.0	1	40	405	10.1	**2**	6	3
1988 ChiB	15	45	704	15.6	3	34	277	8.1	0	3	4
1989 ChiB	16	28	418	14.9	3	10	67	6.7	0	3	3
1990 Dal	9	14	172	12.3	1	2	20	10.0	0	1	1
NFL Total	94	194	3012	15.5	22	129	1191	9.2	3	17	26

DON MCKINNON McKinnon, Donald Bruce 6′3″, 230 **LB-C**
Col: Dartmouth *HS:* Matignon [Cambridge, MA] B: 8/28/1941, Arlington, MA *Drafted:* 1963 Round 10 Bos
1963 Bos: 14 G. **1964** Bos: 3 G. **Total:** 17 G.

RONALD MCKINNON McKinnon, Ronald 6′0″, 240 **LB**
Col: North Alabama *HS:* Elba [AL] B: 9/20/1973, Fort Rucker, AL
1996 Ariz: 16 G; Rush 1-(-4) -4.0. **1997** Ariz: 16 G; Rush 1-3 3.0; Int 3-40; 1 Sac. **1998** Ariz: 13 G; Int 5-25; 1 Fum; 2 Sac. **Total:** 45 G; Rush 2-(-1) -0.5; Int 8-65; 1 Fum; 3 Sac.

DICK MCKISSACK McKissack, James Richard 6′2″, 208 **DB**
Col: Southern Methodist *HS:* Thomas Jefferson [San Antonio, TX] B: 2/10/1926, San Antonio, TX D: 8/28/1982, Dallas, TX *Drafted:* 1950 Round 5 LARm
1952 Dal: 1 G.

DENNIS MCKNIGHT McKnight, Dennis Neal 6′3″, 273 **OG-C**
Col: Drake *HS:* Susan E. Wagner [Staten Island, NY] B: 9/12/1959, Dallas, TX
1982 SD: 7 G. **1983** SD: 16 G. **1984** SD: 16 G. **1985** SD: 16 G. **1986** SD: 16 G. **1987** SD: 12 G. **1988** SD: 16 G. **1990** Det: 14 G; KR 1-0. **1991** Phi: 16 G; 1 Fum. **1992** Det: 12 G. **Total:** 141 G; KR 1-0; 1 Fum.

JAMES MCKNIGHT McKnight, James 6′1″, 195 **WR**
Col: Liberty *HS:* Apopka [FL] B: 6/17/1972, Orlando, FL
1995 Sea: KR 1-4 4.0. **1996** Sea: KR 3-86 28.7. **1997** Sea: KR 1-14 14.0. **Total:** KR 5-104 20.8.

		Receiving				
Year Team	G	Rec	Yds	Avg	TD	Fum
1994 Sea	2	1	25	25.0	1	0
1995 Sea	16	6	91	15.2	0	1
1996 Sea	16	1	73	73.0	0	0
1997 Sea	12	34	637	**18.7**	6	1
1998 Sea	14	21	346	16.5	2	0
NFL Total	60	63	1172	18.6	9	2

TED MCKNIGHT McKnight, Theodore Robert 6′1″, 209 **RB**
Col: Minnesota-Duluth *HS:* Central [Duluth, MN] B: 2/26/1954, Duluth, MN *Drafted:* 1977 Round 2 Oak
1977 KC: KR 12-305 25.4. **1978** KC: KR 3-65 21.7. **1979** KC: KR 2-34 17.0. **1982** Buf: KR 3-34 11.3. **Total:** KR 20-438 21.9.

		Rushing				Receiving					Tot
Year Team	G	Att	Yds	Avg	TD	Rec	Yds	Avg	TD	Fum	TD
1977 KC	13	11	74	6.7	0	1	11	11.0	0	1	0
1978 KC	16	104	627	**6.0**	6	14	83	5.9	1	2	7
1979 KC	15	153	755	4.9	8	38	226	5.9	0	5	8
1980 KC	16	206	693	3.4	3	38	320	8.4	0	5	3
1981 KC	5	54	195	3.6	5	8	77	9.6	0	2	5
1982 Buf	3	0	0	—	0	0	0	—	0	1	0
NFL Total	68	528	2344	4.4	22	99	717	7.2	1	16	23

BILL MCKOY McKoy, William Edmond 6′3″, 235 **LB**
Col: Purdue *HS:* Atkins [Winston-Salem, NC] B: 7/17/1948, Winston-Salem, NC *Drafted:* 1970 Round 5 Den
1970 Den: 2 G. **1971** Den: 14 G. **1972** Den: 14 G. **1974** SF: 14 G. **Total:** 44 G.

TIM MCKYER McKyer, Timothy Bernard 6′0″, 174 **DB**
Col: Texas-Arlington *HS:* Lincoln [Port Arthur, TX] B: 9/5/1963, Orlando, FL *Drafted:* 1986 Round 3 SF
1986 SF: PR 1-5 5.0; KR 1-15 15.0. **1992** Atl: 1 Sac. **1996** Atl: 1 Sac. **1997** Den: 1 Sac. **Total:** PR 1-5 5.0; KR 1-15 15.0; 3 Sac.

		Interceptions		
Year Team	G	Int	Yds	TD
1986 SF	16	6	33	1
1987 SF	12	2	0	0
1988 SF	16	7	11	0
1989 SF	7	1	18	0
1990 Mia	16	4	40	0
1991 Atl	16	6	24	0
1992 Atl	16	1	0	0
1993 Det	15	2	10	0
1994 Pit	16	0	0	0
1995 Car	16	3	99	1
1996 Atl	8	0	0	0
1997 Den	16	1	0	0
NFL Total	170	33	235	2

KEVIN MCLAIN McLain, Kevin Wayne 6′2″, 230 **LB**
Col: Fullerton Coll. CA (J.C.); Colorado State *HS:* Loara [Anaheim, CA] B: 9/15/1954, Tulsa, OK *Drafted:* 1976 Round 1 LARm
1976 LARm: 14 G. **1977** LARm: 8 G. **1978** LARm: 16 G. **1979** LARm: 10 G. **Total:** 48 G.

CHIEF MCLAIN McLain, Mayes Watt 6′3″, 225 **HB**
Col: Haskell Indian; Iowa *HS:* Pryor [OK] B: 4/16/1905, Pryor, OK D: 3/6/1983, Marietta, GA
1930 Port: 14 G; Rush 4 TD; Rec 3 TD; Tot TD 7; 42 Pt. **1931** Port-SI: 10 G. Port: 1 G. SI: 9 G; Rec 2 TD; 12 Pt. **Total:** 24 G; Rush 4 TD; Rec 5 TD; Tot TD 9; 54 Pt.

CHARLIE MCLAUGHLIN McLaughlin, Charles Edward 6′0″, 183 **TB-DB**
Col: Wichita State *HS:* Peabody [KS] B: 3/11/1910 D: 2/1983, Pamplin, VA
1934 StL: 1 G; Pass 4-2 50.0%, 18 4.50 1 Int; Rush 6-22 3.7.

JOE MCLAUGHLIN McLaughlin, Joseph James 6′1″, 235 **LB**
Col: Massachusetts *HS:* Stoneham [MA] B: 7/1/1957, Stoneham, MA
1979 GB: 3 G. **1980** NYG: 8 G; KR 2-27 13.5; 1 Fum. **1981** NYG: 16 G; KR 2-9 4.5. **1982** NYG: 8 G; KR 1-14 14.0. **1983** NYG: 7 G; KR 1-8 8.0. **1984** NYG: 16 G; KR 2-18 9.0. **Total:** 58 G; KR 8-76 9.5; 1 Fum.

LEE MCLAUGHLIN McLaughlin, Lee Massey 6′1″, 226 **G**
Col: Virginia *HS:* Thomas Jefferson [Richmond, VA] B: 2/28/1917, Brownsburg, VA D: 8/13/1968, Lexington, VA
1941 GB: 8 G.

LEON MCLAUGHLIN McLaughlin, Leon C 6′2″, 228 **C**
Col: UCLA *HS:* Santa Monica [CA] B: 5/30/1925, San Diego, CA *Drafted:* 1947 Round 19 LARm
1951 LARm: 12 G. **1952** LARm: 12 G. **1953** LARm: 12 G. **1954** LARm: 12 G. **1955** LARm: 12 G. **Total:** 60 G.

STEVE MCLAUGHLIN McLaughlin, Steven John 6′0″, 176 **K**
Col: Arizona *HS:* Sahuaro [Tucson, AZ] B: 10/2/1971, Tucson, AZ *Drafted:* 1995 Round 3 StL
1995 StL: 8 G; Scor 41, 8-16 50.0% FG, 17-17 100.0% XK.

TOM MCLAUGHLIN McLaughlin, Thomas Flynn 5′10″, 185 **FB**
Col: Notre Dame B: 1/22/1889, Ireland D: 6/1964, NY
1921 Ton: 1 G.

JOHN MCLAUGHRY McLaughry, John Jackson 6′1″, 205 **BB-LB**
(Tuss) *Col:* Brown *HS:* Moses Brown School [Providence, RI]; Phillips Andover Acad. [Andover, MA] B: 4/8/1917, New Wilmington, PA *Drafted:* 1940 Round 2 NYG
1940 NYG: 9 G; Rec 1-(-1) -1.0.

RAY MCLEAN McLean, Raymond 5′7″, 155 **FB-BB**
(Toody) *Col:* No College *HS:* Green Bay West [WI] B: 9/13/1897 D: 10/1967, Detroit, MI
1921 GB: 3 G.

RAY MCLEAN McLean, Raymond Tuttle 5'10", 167 **HB**
(Scooter) *Col:* St. Anselm *HS:* Cushing Acad. [Ashburnham, MA]
B: 12/6/1915, Lowell, MA D: 3/4/1964, Ann Arbor, MI
1940 ChiB: Scor 25, 1-1 100.0% XK. **1941** ChiB: KR 2-31 15.5. **1942** ChiB: KR 3-62 20.7. **1943** ChiB: KR 4-105 26.3; Scor 18, 0-1 XK. **1944** ChiB: KR 4-102 25.5. **1945** ChiB: KR 3-60 20.0. **1946** ChiB: KR 3-53 17.7. **1947** ChiB: KR 2-35 17.5; Scor 50, 0-1 FG, **44-52** 84.6% XK.
Total: KR 21-448 21.3; Scor 225, 0-1 FG, 45-54 83.3% XK.

		Rushing				Receiving			
Year Team	G	Att	Yds	Avg	TD	Rec	Yds	Avg	TD
1940 ChiB	10	14	10	0.7	1	6	138	23.0	2
1941 ChiB	10	13	78	6.0	1	5	84	16.8	1
1942 ChiB	11	26	63	2.4	0	19	571	30.1	8
1943 ChiB	10	35	127	3.6	1	18	435	24.2	2
1944 ChiB	8	29	25	0.9	1	19	414	21.8	5
1945 ChiB	5	9	22	2.4	0	8	117	14.6	0
1946 ChiB	10	16	29	1.8	1	17	348	20.5	2
1947 ChiB	12	10	58	5.8	0	11	125	11.4	1
NFL Total	76	152	412	2.7	5	103	2232	21.7	21

	Punt Returns				Interceptions				Tot
Year Team	Ret	Yds	Avg	TD	Int	Yds	TD	Fum	TD
1940 ChiB	—	—	—	**1**	1	5	0	0	4
1941 ChiB	3	99	33.0	**1**	3	79	0	0	3
1942 ChiB	6	118	19.7	**1**	3	74	0	0	9
1943 ChiB	7	94	13.4	0	4	20	0	0	3
1944 ChiB	8	79	9.9	0	3	42	0	0	7
1945 ChiB	6	87	14.5	0	1	0	0	1	0
1946 ChiB	7	87	12.4	0	2	26	0	2	3
1947 ChiB	5	58	11.6	0	1	12	0	0	1
NFL Total	42	622	14.8	3	18	258	0	3	30

SCOTT MCLEAN McLean, Robert Scott 6'4", 231 **LB**
Col: Florida State *HS:* Clermont [FL] B: 12/16/1960, Clermont, FL
1983 Dal: 4 G.

RON MCLEAN McLean, Ronald James 6'3", 270 **NT-DE**
Col: Cal State-Fullerton *HS:* Ernest Righetti [Santa Maria, CA]
B: 4/13/1963, Everett, WA *Drafted:* 1987 Round 9 NYJ
1987 Den: 3 G. **1988** KC: 6 G. **Total:** 9 G.

CHRIS MCLEMORE McLemore, Christopher Clark 6'1", 232 **RB**
Col: Colorado; Arizona *HS:* Valley [Las Vegas, NV] B: 12/31/1963, Las Vegas, NV *Drafted:* 1987 Round 11 LARd
1987 Ind-LARd: 5 G; Rush 17-58 3.4; Rec 2-9 4.5; 1 Fum. Ind: 2 G; Rush 17-58 3.4; Rec 2-9 4.5; 1 Fum. LARd: 3 G. **1988** LARd: 7 G.
Total: 12 G; Rush 17-58 3.4; Rec 2-9 4.5; 1 Fum.

DANA MCLEMORE McLemore, Dana 5'10", 183 **DB**
Col: Hawaii *HS:* Venice [Los Angeles, CA] B: 7/1/1960, Los Angeles, CA *Drafted:* 1982 Round 10 SF
1984 SF: Int 2-54 1 TD. **1985** SF: Int 1-0. **1987** SF: Int 2-35.
Total: Int 5-89 1 TD.

		Punt Returns				Kickoff Returns					Tot
Year Team	G	Ret	Yds	Avg	TD	Ret	Yds	Avg	TD	Fum	TD
1982 SF	8	7	156	22.3	1	16	353	22.1	0	0	1
1983 SF	14	31	331	10.7	**1**	30	576	19.2	0	0	1
1984 SF	16	45	521	11.6	1	3	80	26.7	0	1	2
1985 SF	16	38	258	6.8	0	4	76	19.0	0	5	0
1986 SF-NO	6	10	67	6.7	0	2	39	19.5	0	0	0
1986 SF	3	0	0	—	0	0	0	—	0	0	0
1986 NO	3	10	67	6.7	0	2	39	19.5	0	0	0
1987 SF	12	21	265	12.6	1	1	23	23.0	0	1	1
NFL Total	72	152	1598	10.5	4	56	1147	20.5	0	7	5

EMMETT MCLEMORE McLemore, Emmett 5'7", 163 **BB**
(Red Fox) *Col:* Haskell Indian; Pittsburg State B: 9/12/1899, Lyons, OK D: 5/1973, Stilwell, OK
1923 Oor: 9 G; Pass 1 TD; Rec 1 TD; Scor 8, 1 XK, **1** 1XP. **1924** KC: 4 G.
Total: 13 G; Pass 1 TD; Rec 1 TD; Scor 1 1XP.

THOMAS MCLEMORE McLemore, Thomas Tyree 6'5", 245 **TE**
Col: Southern University *HS:* Huntington [Shreveport, LA]
B: 3/14/1970, Shreveport, LA *Drafted:* 1992 Round 3 Det
1992 Det: 11 G; Rec 2-12 6.0. **1993** Cle: 4 G. **1994** Cle: 2 G. **1995** Ind: 1 G. **Total:** 18 G; Rec 2-12 6.0.

BRUCE MCLENNA McLenna, Bruce Oliver 6'3", 225 **HB**
(Spike) *Col:* Michigan; Hillsdale *HS:* Fenton [MI] B: 12/23/1941, Holly, MI D: 6/18/1968, Urbana, MO *Drafted:* 1965 Round 9 Det
1966 Det: 9 G; Rush 16-51 3.2; Rec 3-13 4.3.

MIKE MCLEOD McLeod, Michael James 6'0", 180 **DB**
Col: Montana State *HS:* East [Cheyenne, WY] B: 5/4/1958, Bozeman, MT
1984 GB: 12 G; Int 1-0. **1985** GB: 8 G. **Total:** 20 G; Int 1-0.

BOB MCLEOD McLeod, Robert Don 6'4", 240 **TE**
Col: Abilene Christian *HS:* Merkel [TX] B: 11/10/1938, Sweetwater, TX
Drafted: 1961 Round 12 Hou
1961 Hou: KR 1-13 13.0. **1962** Hou: KR 1-0. **Total:** KR 2-13 6.5.

		Receiving				
Year Team	G	Rec	Yds	Avg	TD	Fum
1961 Hou	14	14	172	12.3	2	0
1962 Hou	14	33	578	17.5	6	0
1963 Hou	14	33	530	16.1	5	0
1964 Hou	14	8	81	10.1	2	0
1965 Hou	14	15	226	15.1	1	1
1966 Hou	14	23	339	14.7	3	0
NFL Total	84	126	1926	15.3	19	1

RUSS MCLEOD McLeod, Russell Ferguson 6'0", 190 **C-LB**
Col: St. Louis *HS:* Calumet [MI] B: 7/29/1906, Cypress River, Canada
D: 4/4/1977, Los Angeles, CA
1934 StL: 3 G.

HAROLD MCLINTON McLinton, Harold Lucious 6'2", 235 **LB**
Col: Southern University *HS:* C.L. Harper [Atlanta, GA] B: 7/1/1947, Fort Valley, GA D: 10/31/1980, Washington, DC *Drafted:* 1969 Round 6 Was
1969 Was: 7 G. **1970** Was: 14 G. **1971** Was: 14 G; KR 5-46 9.2. **1972** Was: 13 G; KR 1-15 15.0; Int 2-22. **1973** Was: 8 G. **1974** Was: 13 G; Int 1-14 1 TD; 6 Pt. **1975** Was: 14 G. **1976** Was: 14 G; Int 1-8. **1977** Was: 14 G. **1978** Was: 16 G. **Total:** 127 G; KR 6-61 10.2; Int 4-44 1 TD; 6 Pt.

ART MCMAHON McMahon, Arthur John 6'0", 190 **DB**
Col: North Carolina State *HS:* Carteret [NJ] B: 2/24/1946, Newark, NJ
Drafted: 1968 Round 15 Bos
1968 Bos: 12 G; Int 2-27. **1969** Bos: 10 G. **1970** Bos: 7 G; Int 1-72. **1972** NE: 14 G. **Total:** 43 G; Int 3-99.

HARRY MCMAHON McMahon, Harry John 5'7", 150 **BB**
(Shorty) *Col:* Holy Cross *HS:* Staunton Mil. Acad. [VA]
B: 10/25/1898, Tampa, FL D: 1/12/1984, Southbridge, MA
1926 Har: 2 G.

JIM MCMAHON McMahon, James Robert 6'1", 195 **QB**
(Jimmy Mac) *Col:* Brigham Young *HS:* Roy [UT] B: 8/21/1959, Jersey City, NJ *Drafted:* 1982 Round 1 ChiB
1982 ChiB: Punt 1-59 59.0. **1983** ChiB: Rec 1-18 18.0 1 TD; Punt 1-36 36.0. **1984** ChiB: Rec 1-42 42.0. **1985** ChiB: Rec 1-13 13.0 1 TD.
1989 SD: Rec 1-4 4.0. **1991** Phi: Rec 1-(-5) -5.0. **Total:** Rec 5-72 14.4 2 TD; Punt 2-95 47.5.

		Passing							
Year Team	G	Att	Comp	Comp%	Yds	YPA	TD	Int	Rating
1982 ChiB	8	210	120	57.1	1501	7.15	9	7	79.9
1983 ChiB	14	295	175	59.3	2184	7.40	12	13	77.6
1984 ChiB	9	143	85	59.4	1146	8.01	8	2	97.8
1985 ChiB	13	313	178	56.9	2392	7.64	15	11	82.6
1986 ChiB	6	150	77	51.3	995	6.63	5	8	61.4
1987 ChiB	7	210	125	59.5	1639	7.80	12	8	87.4
1988 ChiB	9	192	114	59.4	1346	7.01	6	7	76.0
1989 SD	12	318	176	55.3	2132	6.70	10	10	73.5
1990 Phi	5	9	6	66.7	63	7.00	0	0	86.8
1991 Phi	12	311	187	60.1	2239	7.20	12	11	80.3
1992 Phi	4	43	22	51.2	279	6.49	1	2	60.1
1993 Min	12	331	200	60.4	1968	5.95	9	8	76.2
1994 Ariz	2	43	23	53.5	219	5.09	1	3	46.6
1995 GB	1	1	1	100.0	6	6.00	0	0	91.7
1996 GB	5	4	3	75.0	39	9.75	0	0	105.2
NFL Total	119	2573	1492	58.0	18148	7.05	100	90	78.2

	Rushing					Tot
Year Team	Att	Yds	Avg	TD	Fum	TD
1982 ChiB	24	105	4.4	1	1	1
1983 ChiB	55	307	5.6	2	4	3
1984 ChiB	39	276	7.1	2	1	2
1985 ChiB	47	252	5.4	3	4	4
1986 ChiB	22	152	6.9	1	1	1
1987 ChiB	22	88	4.0	2	2	2
1988 ChiB	26	104	4.0	4	6	4
1989 SD	29	141	4.9	0	3	0
1990 Phi	3	1	0.3	0	0	0
1991 Phi	22	55	2.5	1	2	1
1992 Phi	6	23	3.8	0	0	0
1993 Min	33	96	2.9	0	4	0
1994 Ariz	6	32	5.3	0	1	0
1996 GB	4	-1	-0.3	0	1	0
NFL Total	338	1631	4.8	16	30	18

TOMMY MCMAHON McMahon, Thomas Francis 5'11", 200 **HB**
(Gig) *Col:* Denison *HS:* Doane Acad. [Granville, OH] B: 5/19/1891
D: 11/22/1962, Newark, OH
1921 Cin: 3 G.

JOHN MCMAKIN McMakin, John Garvin 6'3", 232 **TE**
Col: Clemson *HS:* Tucker [GA] B: 9/24/1950, Spartanburg, SC
Drafted: 1972 Round 3 Pit
1972 Pit: Rush 1-0; KR 1-0. **Total:** Rush 1-0; KR 1-0.

		Receiving			
Year Team	**G**	**Rec**	**Yds**	**Avg**	**TD**
1972 Pit	14	21	277	13.2	1
1973 Pit	14	13	195	15.0	1
1974 Pit	8	0	0	—	0
1975 Det	11	2	43	21.5	0
1976 Sea	13	9	158	17.6	2
NFL Total	60	45	673	15.0	4

TOM MCMANUS McManus, Thomas Edward 6'2", 252 **LB**
Col: Boston College *HS:* Wheeling [IL] B: 7/30/1970, Buffalo Grove, IL
1995 Jac: 14 G. **1996** Jac: 16 G. **1998** Jac: 16 G. **Total:** 46 G.

HERB MCMATH McMath, Herbert Louis 6'4", 248 **DT-DE**
Col: Ellsworth CC IA; Morningside *HS:* Springfield Southeast [IL]
B: 9/6/1954, Coahoma, MS *Drafted:* 1976 Round 4 Oak
1976 Oak: 14 G. **1977** GB: 8 G. **Total:** 22 G.

STEVE MCMICHAEL McMichael, Steve Douglas 6'2", 270 **DT-NT**
(Mongo) *Col:* Texas *HS:* Freer [TX] B: 10/17/1957, Houston, TX
Drafted: 1980 Round 3 NE
1980 NE: 6 G. **1981** ChiB: 10 G. **1982** ChiB: 9 G; 2.5 Sac. **1983** ChiB: 16 G; 8.5 Sac. **1984** ChiB: 16 G; 10 Sac. **1985** ChiB: 16 G; Scor 1 Saf; 2 Pt; 8 Sac. **1986** ChiB: 16 G; Int 1-5; Scor **1** Saf; 2 Pt; 8 Sac. **1987** ChiB: 12 G; 7 Sac. **1988** ChiB: 16 G; Scor 1 Saf; 2 Pt; 11.5 Sac. **1989** ChiB: 16 G; 7.5 Sac. **1990** ChiB: 16 G; 4 Sac. **1991** ChiB: 16 G; 9 Sac. **1992** ChiB: 16 G; 10.5 Sac. **1993** ChiB: 16 G; Int 1-0; 6 Sac. **1994** GB: 16 G; 2.5 Sac. **Total:** 213 G; Int 2-5; Scor 3 Saf; 6 Pt; 95.0 Sac.

JOHN MCMICHAELS McMichaels, John Richard 5'11", 190 **TB-DB**
Col: Birmingham-Southern *HS:* Cordova [AL] B: 12/14/1917, Cordova, AL D: 12/25/1991, Birmingham, AL
1944 Bkn: 1 G; Pass 1-0, 1 Int; Rush 3-1 0.3; PR 1-5 5.0; Punt 2-85 42.5.

CHUCK MCMILLAN McMillan, Charles David 6'3", 175 **DB**
Col: John Carroll *HS:* East Tech [Cleveland, OH] B: 11/16/1931, Cleveland, OH *Drafted:* 1954 Round 13 Bal
1954 Bal: 6 G; KR 1-5 5.0.

EDDIE MCMILLAN McMillan, Eddie Alexander 6'0", 189 **DB**
Col: Florida State *HS:* Howard W. Blake [Tampa, FL] B: 11/25/1951, Tampa, FL *Drafted:* 1973 Round 4 LARm
1976 Sea: PR 1-(-1) -1.0. **Total:** PR 1-(-1) -1.0.

		Interceptions		
Year Team	**G**	**Int**	**Yds**	**TD**
1973 LARm	14	4	20	0
1974 LARm	14	0	0	0
1975 LARm	14	3	64	0
1976 Sea	14	1	0	0
1977 Sea	14	4	157	0
1978 Buf	14	0	0	0
NFL Total	84	12	241	0

ERIK MCMILLAN McMillan, Erik Charles 6'2", 200 **DB**
Col: Missouri *HS:* John F. Kennedy [Silver Spring, MD] B: 5/3/1965, St. Louis, MO *Drafted:* 1988 Round 3 NYJ
1989 NYJ: **2** Fum TD; 2 Sac. **1991** NYJ: 1 Sac. **1992** NYJ: KR 22-420 19.1; 2 Sac. **Total:** KR 22-420 19.1; 2 Fum TD; 5 Sac.

		Interceptions				Tot
Year Team	**G**	**Int**	**Yds**	**TD**	**Fum**	**TD**
1988 NYJ	13	8	168	**2**	1	2
1989 NYJ	16	6	180	1	0	3
1990 NYJ	16	5	92	0	3	0
1991 NYJ	16	3	168	**2**	0	2
1992 NYJ	15	0	0	0	1	0
1993 Phi-Cle-KC	10	0	0	0	0	0
1993 Phi	6	0	0	0	0	0
1993 Cle	3	0	0	0	0	0
1993 KC	1	0	0	0	0	0
NFL Total	86	22	608	5	5	7

ERNIE MCMILLAN McMillan, Ernest Charles 6'5", 275 **OT**
Col: Illinois *HS:* DuSable [Chicago, IL] B: 2/21/1938, Chicago Heights, IL *Drafted:* 1961 Round 13 StL
1961 StL: 6 G. **1962** StL: 14 G. **1963** StL: 14 G. **1964** StL: 14 G. **1965** StL: 14 G. **1966** StL: 14 G. **1967** StL: 14 G. **1968** StL: 14 G. **1969** StL: 14 G. **1970** StL: 14 G. **1971** StL: 14 G. **1972** StL: 14 G. **1973** StL: 7 G. **1974** StL: 11 G. **1975** GB: 12 G. **Total:** 190 G.

RANDY MCMILLAN McMillan, Lewis Lorando 6'0", 219 **RB**
Col: Harford CC MD; Pittsburgh *HS:* North Harford [Pylesville, MD]
B: 12/17/1958, Havre de Grace, MD *Drafted:* 1981 Round 1 Bal

		Rushing				Receiving					Tot
Year Team	**G**	**Att**	**Yds**	**Avg**	**TD**	**Rec**	**Yds**	**Avg**	**TD**	**Fum**	**TD**
1981 Bal	16	149	597	4.0	3	50	466	9.3	1	1	4
1982 Bal	9	101	305	3.0	1	15	90	6.0	0	1	1
1983 Bal	16	198	802	4.1	5	24	195	8.1	1	5	6
1984 Ind	16	163	705	4.3	5	19	201	10.6	0	1	5
1985 Ind	15	190	858	4.5	7	22	115	5.2	0	0	7
1986 Ind	16	189	609	3.2	3	34	289	8.5	0	5	3
NFL Total	88	990	3876	3.9	24	164	1356	8.3	2	13	26

DAN MCMILLEN McMillen, Daniel A 6'4", 240 **DE**
Col: Colorado *HS:* Wasson [Colorado Springs, CO] B: 2/23/1964, Weisbaden, Germany *Drafted:* 1986 Round 5 Phi
1987 LARd-Phi: 2 G; 1 Sac. LARd: 1 G; 1 Sac. Phi: 1 G. **Total:** 2 G; 1 Sac.

JIM MCMILLEN McMillen, James Willard 6'1", 215 **G**
(Mac) *Col:* Illinois *HS:* Libertyville [IL] B: 10/23/1902, Grays Lake, IL
D: 1/28/1984, Antioch, IL
1924 ChiB: 10 G. **1925** ChiB: 17 G. **1926** ChiB: 16 G. **1927** ChiB: 13 G. **1928** ChiB: 13 G. **Total:** 69 G.

AUDRAY MCMILLIAN McMillian, Audray Glenn 5'11", 190 **DB**
Col: Houston *HS:* Carthage [TX] B: 8/13/1962, Carthage, TX
Drafted: 1985 Round 3 NE
1993 Min: KR 1-0. **Total:** KR 1-0.

		Interceptions		
Year Team	**G**	**Int**	**Yds**	**TD**
1985 Hou	16	0	0	0
1986 Hou	16	0	0	0
1987 Hou	12	0	0	0
1989 Min	16	0	0	0
1990 Min	15	3	20	0
1991 Min	16	4	5	0
1992 Min	16	**8**	157	2
1993 Min	16	4	45	1
NFL Total	123	19	227	3

HENRY MCMILLIAN McMillian, Henry James 6'3", 275 **DT**
Col: Florida *HS:* Charlton Co. [Folkston, GA] B: 10/17/1971, Folkston, GA *Drafted:* 1995 Round 6 Sea
1995 Sea: 1 G. **1996** Sea: 3 G. **Total:** 4 G.

MARK MCMILLIAN McMillian, Mark D 5'7", 154 **DB**
Col: Alabama *HS:* John F. Kennedy [Los Angeles, CA] B: 4/29/1970, Los Angeles, CA *Drafted:* 1992 Round 10 Phi

		Interceptions			
Year Team	**G**	**Int**	**Yds**	**TD**	**Fum**
1992 Phi	16	1	0	0	0
1993 Phi	16	2	25	0	1
1994 Phi	16	2	2	0	0
1995 Phi	16	3	27	0	0
1996 NO	16	2	4	0	0
1997 KC	16	8	**274**	**3**	0
1998 KC	16	3	48	0	0
NFL Total	112	21	380	3	1

BO MCMILLIN McMillin, Alvin Nugent 5'9", 163 **TB-BB**
Col: Centre *HS:* North Side [Fort Worth, TX]; Somerset HS [KY]
B: 1/12/1895, Prairie Hill, TX D: 3/31/1952, Bloomington, IN
1922 Mil: 2 G; Pass 1 TD; Rec 1 TD; 6 Pt. **1923** Mil-Cle: 4 G; Pass 1 TD. Mil: 3 G; Pass 1 TD. Cle: 1 G. **Total:** 6 G; Pass 2 TD; Rec 1 TD; 6 Pt.

JIM MCMILLIN McMillin, James Robert 6'0", 190 **DB**
Col: Diablo Valley Coll. CA (J.C.); Colorado State *HS:* Pleasant Hill [CA]
B: 9/18/1939, Pleasant Hill, CA
1962 Den: KR 1-6 6.0; **1** Fum TD. **1963** Oak: KR 1-23 23.0.
1964 Oak-Den: **1** Fum TD. Den: 1 Fum TD. **Total:** KR 2-29 14.5; 2 Fum TD.

		Interceptions			Tot
Year Team	**G**	**Int**	**Yds**	**TD**	**TD**
1961 Den	14	5	56	0	0
1962 Den	14	4	117	**1**	2
1963 Oak	14	4	62	1	1
1964 Oak-Den	8	1	3	0	1
1964 Oak	1	0	0	0	0
1964 Den	7	1	3	0	1
1965 Den	12	0	0	0	0
NFL Total	62	14	238	2	4

JOHN MCMULLAN McMullan, John Gerald Jr. 6'0", 245 **OG**
Col: Notre Dame *HS:* Demarest [NJ] B: 6/28/1933, Brooklyn, NY
D: 4/1/1994 *Drafted:* 1956 Round 14 NYG
1960 NYT: 14 G. **1961** NYT: 14 G. **Total:** 28 G.

DANNY MCMULLEN McMullen, Daniel Edward 5'8", 231 G
(Wild Man) *Col:* Nebraska *HS:* Belleville [KS] B: 5/8/1906, Belleville, KS D: 8/22/1983, St. Francis, KS
1929 NYG: 7 G. **1930** ChiB: 10 G. **1931** ChiB: 11 G. **1932** Port: 2 G. **Total:** 30 G.

CHUCK MCMURTRY McMurtry, Charles 6'0", 280 DT
Col: Fullerton Coll. CA (J.C.); Whittier *HS:* Whittier [CA] B: 2/15/1937, Chaneller, OK *Drafted:* 1960 Round 1 Buf
1960 Buf: 14 G. **1961** Buf: 14 G. **1962** Oak: 11 G. **1963** Oak: 14 G. **Total:** 53 G.

GREG MCMURTRY McMurtry, Gregory Wendell 6'2", 207 WR
Col: Michigan *HS:* Brockton [MA] B: 10/15/1967, Brockton, MA *Drafted:* 1990 Round 3 NE
1992 NE: Pass 1-0; Rush 2-3 1.5. **Total:** Pass 1-0; Rush 2-3 1.5.

		Receiving				
Year Team	G	Rec	Yds	Avg	TD	Fum
1990 NE	13	22	240	10.9	0	1
1991 NE	15	41	614	15.0	2	1
1992 NE	16	35	424	12.1	1	0
1993 NE	14	22	241	11.0	1	1
1994 ChiB	9	8	112	14.0	1	0
NFL Total	67	128	1631	12.7	5	3

DEXTER MCNABB McNabb, Dexter Eugene 6'1", 245 FB
Col: Florida *HS:* Walton [De Funiak Springs, FL] B: 7/9/1969, De Funiak Springs, FL *Drafted:* 1992 Round 5 GB
1992 GB: 16 G; Rush 2-11 5.5; KR 1-15 15.0. **1993** GB: 16 G. **1995** Phi: 1 G. **Total:** 33 G; Rush 2-11 5.5; KR 1-15 15.0.

STEVE MCNAIR McNair, Steve LaTreal 6'2", 224 QB
(Air) *Col:* Alcorn State *HS:* Mount Olive [MS] B: 2/14/1973, Mount Olive, MS *Drafted:* 1995 Round 1 Hou

		Passing							
Year Team	G	Att	Comp	Comp%	Yds	YPA	TD	Int	Rating
1995 Hou	4	80	41	51.3	569	7.11	3	1	81.7
1996 Hou	9	143	88	61.5	1197	8.37	6	4	90.6
1997 Ten	16	415	216	52.0	2665	6.42	14	13	70.4
1998 Ten	16	492	289	58.7	3228	6.56	15	10	80.1
NFL Total	45	1130	634	56.1	7659	6.78	38	28	78.0

	Rushing				
Year Team	Att	Yds	Avg	TD	Fum
1995 Hou	11	38	3.5	0	3
1996 Hou	31	169	5.5	2	7
1997 Ten	101	674	**6.7**	8	**16**
1998 Ten	77	559	7.3	4	5
NFL Total	220	1440	6.5	14	31

TODD MCNAIR McNair, Todd Darren 6'1", 196 RB
Col: Temple *HS:* Pennsauken [NJ] B: 10/7/1965, Camden, NJ *Drafted:* 1989 Round 8 KC

		Rushing				Receiving			
Year Team	G	Att	Yds	Avg	TD	Rec	Yds	Avg	TD
1989 KC	14	23	121	5.3	0	34	372	10.9	1
1990 KC	15	14	61	4.4	0	40	507	12.7	2
1991 KC	14	10	51	5.1	0	37	342	9.2	1
1992 KC	16	21	124	5.9	1	44	380	8.6	1
1993 KC	15	51	278	5.5	2	10	74	7.4	0
1994 Hou	16	0	0	—	0	8	78	9.8	0
1995 Hou	15	19	136	7.2	0	60	501	8.4	1
1996 KC	16	9	32	3.6	0	21	181	8.6	1
NFL Total	121	147	803	5.5	3	254	2435	9.6	7

	Kickoff Returns					Tot
Year Team	Ret	Yds	Avg	TD	Fum	TD
1989 KC	13	257	19.8	0	1	1
1990 KC	14	227	16.2	0	1	2
1991 KC	4	66	16.5	0	2	1
1992 KC	2	20	10.0	0	1	2
1993 KC	1	28	28.0	0	2	2
1994 Hou	23	481	20.9	0	0	0
1995 Hou	0	0	—	0	1	1
1996 KC	2	21	10.5	0	0	1
NFL Total	59	1100	18.6	0	8	10

FRANK MCNALLY McNally, Frank James 6'1", 203 C-LB-T-G
Col: St. Mary's (Cal.) *HS:* Madera [CA] B: 3/19/1907, NV D: 2/5/1993, Delray Beach, FL
1931 ChiC: 8 G. **1932** ChiC: 7 G; Scor 1 Saf; 2 Pt. **1933** ChiC: 11 G; Int **1** TD; 6 Pt. **1934** ChiC: 10 G. **Total:** 36 G; Int 1 TD; Scor 1 Saf; 8 Pt.

ED MCNAMARA McNamara, Edmund Leo 6'2", 225 T
(Big Ed) *Col:* Holy Cross *HS:* Clinton [MA] B: 4/13/1920, Clinton, MA *Drafted:* 1943 Round 25 NYG
1945 Pit: 1 G.

TOM MCNAMARA McNamara, Edward A 5'10", 210 G-FB
Col: Tufts; Detroit Mercy *HS:* Clinton [MA] B: 8/31/1897, Worcester, MA D: 3/13/1966, Worcester, MA
1923 Tol: 8 G; Scor 3, 1 FG. **1925** Det: 12 G. **1926** Det: 11 G. **Total:** 31 G; Scor 3, 1 FG.

BOB MCNAMARA McNamara, Robert John 6'0", 190 DB-HB
Col: Minnesota *HS:* Hastings [MN] B: 8/12/1931, Hastings, MN
1960 Den: 14 G; Rush 17-33 1.9 1 TD; Rec 7-143 20.4 1 TD; PR 11-68 6.2; KR 9-192 21.3; Int 4-63; Tot TD 2; 12 Pt; 2 Fum. **1961** Den: 14 G; PR 4-17 4.3; Int 3-85. **Total:** 28 G; Rush 17-33 1.9 1 TD; Rec 7-143 20.4 1 TD; PR 15-85 5.7; KR 9-192 21.3; Int 7-148; Tot TD 2; 12 Pt; 2 Fum.

SEAN MCNANIE McNanie, Sean Lawrence 6'5", 265 DE
Col: Arizona State; San Diego State *HS:* Mundelein [IL] B: 9/9/1961, Rockford, IL *Drafted:* 1984 Round 3 Buf
1984 Buf: 15 G; 3 Sac. **1985** Buf: 16 G; 3 Sac. **1986** Buf: 16 G; 6.5 Sac. **1987** Buf: 12 G; **1** Fum TD; 6 Pt; 2.5 Sac. **1988** Pho: 12 G. **1990** Ind: 1 G. **Total:** 72 G; 1 Fum TD; 6 Pt; 15 Sac.

DON MCNEAL McNeal, Donald 5'11", 190 DB
Col: Alabama *HS:* Escambia Co. [Altmore, AL] B: 5/6/1958, Atmore, AL *Drafted:* 1980 Round 1 Mia

		Interceptions		
Year Team	G	Int	Yds	TD
1980 Mia	13	5	17	0
1981 Mia	12	0	0	0
1982 Mia	9	4	42	**1**
1984 Mia	11	3	41	1
1985 Mia	10	0	0	0
1986 Mia	15	2	46	0
1987 Mia	12	0	0	0
1988 Mia	16	1	23	0
1989 Mia	12	3	-6	0
NFL Total	110	18	163	2

TRAVIS MCNEAL McNeal, Travis S 6'3", 248 TE
Col: Tennessee-Chattanooga *HS:* West End [Birmingham, AL] B: 1/10/1967, Birmingham, AL *Drafted:* 1989 Round 4 Sea
1989 Sea: KR 1-17 17.0. **1990** Sea: Rush 1-2 2.0; KR 2-29 14.5. **1991** Sea: KR 4-30 7.5. **Total:** Rush 1-2 2.0; KR 7-76 10.9.

		Receiving				
Year Team	G	Rec	Yds	Avg	TD	Fum
1989 Sea	16	9	147	16.3	0	0
1990 Sea	16	10	143	14.3	0	0
1991 Sea	16	17	208	12.2	1	1
1992 LARm	12	4	79	19.8	0	0
1993 LARm	16	8	75	9.4	1	0
NFL Total	76	48	652	13.6	2	1

CHARLIE MCNEIL McNeil, Charles Edis 5'11", 180 DB
Col: Compton CC CA *HS:* Centennial [Compton, CA] B: 8/8/1936, Caldwell, TX D: 1/7/1994, Houston, TX

		Interceptions			
Year Team	G	Int	Yds	TD	Fum
1960 LAC	9	3	47	0	0
1961 SD	14	9	**349**	2	1
1962 SD	4	1	36	0	0
1963 SD	10	4	40	0	0
1964 SD	6	2	30	0	0
NFL Total	43	19	502	2	1

CLIFTON MCNEIL McNeil, Clifton Anthony 6'2", 187 WR
(Sticks; Spider) *Col:* Grambling State *HS:* Central [Mobile, AL] B: 5/25/1940, Mobile, AL *Drafted:* 1962 Round 11 Cle
1968 SF: Pass 2-1 50.0%, 43 21.50 1 TD 1 Int; Rush 1-(-1) -1.0. **1970** NYG: Rush 4-7 1.8; 1 Fum TD. **Total:** Pass 2-1 50.0%, 43 21.50 1 TD 1 Int; Rush 5-6 1.2; 1 Fum TD.

		Receiving					Tot
Year Team	G	Rec	Yds	Avg	TD	Fum	TD
1964 Cle	14	4	69	17.3	1	0	1
1965 Cle	13	3	69	23.0	0	0	0
1966 Cle	14	2	94	47.0	2	0	2
1967 Cle	2	3	33	11.0	2	0	2
1968 SF	14	**71**	994	14.0	7	1	7
1969 SF	11	17	255	15.0	3	1	3
1970 NYG	14	50	764	15.3	4	0	5
1971 NYG-Was	14	30	453	15.1	3	1	3
1971 NYG	6	16	209	13.1	1	0	1
1971 Was	8	14	244	17.4	2	1	2
1972 Was	6	0	0	—	0	0	0
1973 Hou	3	1	3	3.0	0	0	0
NFL Total	105	181	2734	15.1	22	3	23

EMANUEL MCNEIL McNeil, Emanuel 6'3", 285 **NT**
Col: Tennessee-Martin *HS:* Highland Springs [VA] B: 6/9/1967, Richmond, VA *Drafted:* 1989 Round 10 NE
1989 NE: 1 G. **1990** NYJ: 2 G. **Total:** 3 G.

FRANK MCNEIL McNeil, Francis Kenneth 6'0", 185 **E**
Col: Washington & Jefferson B: 12/23/1909 D: 10/1971
1932 Bkn: 7 G; Rec 3-18 6.0.

FREEMAN MCNEIL McNeil, Freeman 5'11", 216 **RB**
Col: UCLA *HS:* Phineas Banning [Los Angeles, CA] B: 4/22/1959, Jackson, MS *Drafted:* 1981 Round 1 NYJ
1983 NYJ: Pass 1-1 100.0%, 5 5.00 1 TD. **Total:** Pass 1-1 100.0%, 5 5.00 1 TD.

		Rushing				Receiving					Tot
Year Team	**G**	**Att**	**Yds**	**Avg**	**TD**	**Rec**	**Yds**	**Avg**	**TD**	**Fum**	**TD**
1981 NYJ	11	137	623	4.5	2	18	171	9.5	1	5	3
1982 NYJ	9	151	**786**	**5.2**	6	16	187	11.7	1	7	7
1983 NYJ	9	160	654	4.1	1	21	172	8.2	3	4	4
1984 NYJ	12	229	1070	4.7	5	25	294	11.8	1	4	6
1985 NYJ	14	294	1331	4.5	3	38	427	11.2	2	9	5
1986 NYJ	12	214	856	4.0	5	49	410	8.4	1	8	6
1987 NYJ	9	121	530	4.4	0	24	262	10.9	1	1	1
1988 NYJ	16	219	944	4.3	6	34	288	8.5	1	3	7
1989 NYJ	11	80	352	4.4	2	31	310	10.0	1	1	3
1990 NYJ	16	99	458	4.6	6	16	230	14.4	0	1	6
1991 NYJ	13	51	300	5.9	2	7	56	8.0	0	1	2
1992 NYJ	12	43	170	4.0	0	16	154	9.6	0	1	0
NFL Total	144	1798	8074	4.5	38	295	2961	10.0	12	45	50

GERALD MCNEIL McNeil, Gerald Lynn 5'7", 145 **WR**
(Ice Cube) *Col:* Baylor *HS:* Killeen [TX] B: 3/27/1962, Frankfurt, Germany *Drafted:* 1984 Supplemental Round 2 Cle
1986 Cle: Rush 1-12 12.0. **1987** Cle: Rush 1-17 17.0. **1989** Cle: Rush 2-32 16.0. **Total:** Rush 4-61 15.3.

		Receiving				Punt Returns			
Year Team	**G**	**Rec**	**Yds**	**Avg**	**TD**	**Ret**	**Yds**	**Avg**	**TD**
1986 Cle	16	1	9	9.0	0	40	348	8.7	1
1987 Cle	12	8	120	15.0	2	34	386	11.4	0
1988 Cle	16	5	74	14.8	0	38	315	8.3	0
1989 Cle	16	10	114	11.4	0	**49**	496	10.1	0
1990 Hou	16	5	63	12.6	0	30	172	5.7	0
NFL Total	76	29	380	13.1	2	191	1717	9.0	1

	Kickoff Returns					Tot
Year Team	**Ret**	**Yds**	**Avg**	**TD**	**Fum**	**TD**
1986 Cle	47	997	21.2	**1**	3	2
1987 Cle	11	205	18.6	0	2	2
1988 Cle	2	38	19.0	0	3	0
1989 Cle	4	61	15.3	0	0	0
1990 Hou	27	551	20.4	0	4	0
NFL Total	91	1852	20.4	1	12	4

PAT MCNEIL McNeil, Patrick Lamott 5'9", 208 **RB**
Col: Baylor *HS:* Killeen [TX] B: 2/28/1954, Pittsburg, CA *Drafted:* 1976 Round 17 KC
1976 KC: 12 G; Rush 8-26 3.3; Rec 2-33 16.5; KR 2-21 10.5; 1 Fum. **1977** KC: 1 G. **Total:** 13 G; Rush 8-26 3.3; Rec 2-33 16.5; KR 2-21 10.5; 1 Fum.

RYAN MCNEIL McNeil, Ryan Darrell 6'2", 192 **DB**
Col: Miami (Fla.) *HS:* Fort Pierce Westwood [FL] B: 10/4/1970, Fort Pierce, FL *Drafted:* 1993 Round 2 Det

		Interceptions			
Year Team	**G**	**Int**	**Yds**	**TD**	**Fum**
1993 Det	16	2	19	0	0
1994 Det	14	1	14	0	0
1995 Det	16	2	26	0	0
1996 Det	16	5	14	0	0
1997 StL	16	**9**	127	1	1
1998 StL	16	1	37	1	0
NFL Total	94	20	237	2	1

FRED MCNEILL McNeill, Frederick Arnold 6'2", 230 **LB**
Col: UCLA *HS:* Baldwin Park [CA] B: 5/6/1952, Durham, NC *Drafted:* 1974 Round 1 Min
1974 Min: 14 G. **1975** Min: 14 G; Int 1-0. **1976** Min: 13 G. **1977** Min: 14 G; Int 1-0. **1978** Min: 16 G; Int 2-1; 6 Pt. **1979** Min: 16 G. **1980** Min: 16 G. **1981** Min: 16 G; Int 2-26. **1982** Min: 9 G. **1983** Min: 16 G; 0.5 Sac. **1984** Min: 13 G; Int 1-0; 1 Sac. **1985** Min: 10 G. **Total:** 167 G; Int 7-27; 6 Pt; 1.5 Sac.

ROD MCNEILL McNeill, Rodney Carlyle 6'2", 219 **RB**
Col: USC *HS:* Baldwin Park [CA] B: 3/26/1951, Durham, NC *Drafted:* 1974 Round 4 NO
1974 NO: PR 1-0. **Total:** PR 1-0.

		Rushing				Receiving			
Year Team	**G**	**Att**	**Yds**	**Avg**	**TD**	**Rec**	**Yds**	**Avg**	**TD**
1974 NO	11	22	90	4.1	1	5	64	12.8	0
1975 NO	14	61	206	3.4	2	18	138	7.7	2
1976 TB	11	27	135	5.0	0	7	33	4.7	0
NFL Total	36	110	431	3.9	3	30	235	7.8	2

	Kickoff Returns					Tot
Year Team	**Ret**	**Yds**	**Avg**	**TD**	**Fum**	**TD**
1974 NO	0	0	—	0	1	1
1975 NO	10	276	27.6	0	6	4
1976 TB	17	384	22.6	0	3	0
NFL Total	27	660	24.4	0	10	5

TOM MCNEILL McNeill, Thomas Gregg 6'1", 195 **P**
Col: Wharton Co. JC TX; Stephen F. Austin St. *HS:* Spring Branch [Houston, TX] B: 8/12/1942, Rockford, IL
1967 NO: Pass 1-1 100.0%, 24 24.00; Rush 4-38 9.5. **1968** NO: Rush 2-1 0.5. **Total:** Pass 1-1 100.0%, 24 24.00; Rush 6-39 6.5.

		Punting		
Year Team	**G**	**Punts**	**Yds**	**Avg**
1967 NO	14	74	3174	42.9
1968 NO	10	49	2009	41.0
1969 NO	2	7	312	44.6
1970 Min	14	61	2309	37.9
1971 Phi	14	73	3063	42.0
1972 Phi	2	7	290	41.4
1973 Phi	10	46	1881	40.9
NFL Total	66	317	13038	41.1

BILL MCNELLIS McNellis, William 5'11", 177 **WB**
Col: St. Mary's (Minn.) *HS:* Denfeld [Duluth, MN] B: 1902, Duluth, MN D: 1942
1927 Dul: 2 G.

BRUCE MCNORTON McNorton, Bruce Edward 5'11", 175 **DB**
Col: Georgetown (Ky.) *HS:* Spruce Creek [Port Orange, FL] B: 2/28/1959, Daytona Beach, FL *Drafted:* 1982 Round 4 Det
1989 Det: 1 Sac. **Total:** 1 Sac.

		Interceptions		
Year Team	**G**	**Int**	**Yds**	**TD**
1982 Det	4	0	0	0
1983 Det	16	7	30	0
1984 Det	16	2	0	0
1985 Det	16	2	14	0
1986 Det	16	4	10	0
1987 Det	12	3	20	0
1988 Det	16	1	4	0
1989 Det	8	0	0	0
1990 Det	12	1	33	0
NFL Total	116	20	111	0

PAUL MCNULTY McNulty, Paul Davis 6'0", 180 **E**
Col: Michigan; Notre Dame *HS:* Loyola Acad. [Chicago, IL] B: 8/9/1902, Chicago, IL D: 9/27/1985, Chicago, IL
1924 ChiC: 9 G. **1925** ChiC: 1 G; Int 1 TD; 6 Pt. **Total:** 10 G; Int 1 TD; 6 Pt.

BILL MCPEAK McPeak, William Patrick 6'1", 208 **DE**
Col: Notre Dame; Pittsburgh *HS:* New Castle [PA] B: 7/24/1926, New Castle, PA D: 5/7/1991, Foxboro, MA *Drafted:* 1948 Round 14 Pit
1949 Pit: 12 G. **1950** Pit: 11 G. **1951** Pit: 12 G; KR 3-10 3.3. **1952** Pit: 12 G. **1953** Pit: 12 G. **1954** Pit: 12 G; Scor **1** Saf; 2 Pt. **1955** Pit: 10 G. **1956** Pit: 12 G; Scor 1 Saf; 2 Pt. **1957** Pit: 12 G; Scor **1** Saf; 2 Pt. **Total:** 105 G; KR 3-10 3.3; Scor 3 Saf; 6 Pt.

BUCK MCPHAIL McPhail, Coleman Howard 6'1", 195 **FB-K**
Col: Oklahoma *HS:* Central [Oklahoma City, OK] B: 12/25/1929, Oklahoma City, OK *Drafted:* 1953 Round 3 Bal
1953 Bal: Rec 10-38 3.8; Scor 27, 2-5 40.0% FG, 21-23 91.3% XK.

		Rushing				
Year Team	**G**	**Att**	**Yds**	**Avg**	**TD**	**Fum**
1953 Bal	12	53	138	2.6	0	1

HAL MCPHAIL McPhail, Harold Thomas 6'1", 230 **FB-DB**
(Bumper) *Col:* Army; Xavier (Ohio) *HS:* Aquinas [Columbus, OH] B: 10/26/1912, Columbus, OH D: 8/30/1977, Newport, KY
1934 Bos: Pass 22-9 40.9%, 96 4.36; Scor 22, 4 XK; **2** Fum TD. **1935** Bos: Pass 2-0, 1 Int. **Total:** Pass 24-9 37.5%, 96 4.00 1 Int; 2 Fum TD.

		Rushing				Tot
Year Team	**G**	**Att**	**Yds**	**Avg**	**TD**	**TD**
1934 Bos	12	94	356	3.8	1	3
1935 Bos	7	45	105	2.3	0	0
NFL Total	19	139	461	3.3	1	3

JERRIS MCPHAIL McPhail, Jerris Cornelius 5'11", 198 RB
Col: Wake Forest; Mount Olive Coll. NC (J.C.); East Carolina *HS:* Clinton [NC] B: 6/26/1972, Clinton, NC *Drafted:* 1996 Round 5 Mia
1996 Mia: Rush 6-28 4.7. **1997** Mia: Rush 17-146 8.6 1 TD.
Total: Rush 23-174 7.6 1 TD.

		Receiving				Kickoff Returns					Tot
Year Team	G	Rec	Yds	Avg	TD	Ret	Yds	Avg	TD	Fum	TD
1996 Mia	9	20	282	14.1	0	15	335	22.3	0	2	0
1997 Mia	14	34	262	7.7	1	15	314	20.9	0	1	2
1998 Det	3	0	0	—	0	6	71	11.8	0	0	0
NFL Total	26	54	544	10.1	1	36	720	20.0	0	3	2

FRANK MCPHEE McPhee, Frank Melvin 6'3", 195 DB-OE
(Mickey) *Col:* Princeton *HS:* Chaney [Youngstown, OH] B: 3/19/1931, Youngstown, OH *Drafted:* 1953 Round 13 ChiC
1955 ChiC: 7 G.

FORREST MCPHERSON McPherson, Forrest Winfield 5'11", 233 C-G-T-LB
(Aimee) *Col:* Nebraska *HS:* Fairbury [NE] B: 10/22/1911, Fairbury, NE D: 10/7/1989, Centralia, WA
1935 ChiB-Phi: 8 G. ChiB: 1 G. Phi: 7 G. **1936** Phi: 12 G. **1937** Phi: 3 G. **1943** GB: 5 G. **1944** GB: 4 G. **1945** GB: 5 G. **Total:** 37 G.

MILES MCPHERSON McPherson, Miles Gregory 5'11", 184 DB
Col: New Haven *HS:* Malverne [NY] B: 3/30/1960, Queens, NY *Drafted:* 1982 Round 10 LARm
1982 SD: 6 G. **1983** SD: 11 G; KR 5-77 15.4; Int 1-0; 1 Fum; 1 Sac. **1984** SD: 9 G. **1985** SD: 9 G; Int 1-30. **Total:** 35 G; KR 5-77 15.4; Int 2-30; 1 Fum; 1 Sac.

JOHNNY MCQUADE McQuade, John Doyle 5'10", 176 WB-BB
Col: Georgetown *HS:* Manchester [NH]; Cushing Acad. [Ashburnham, MA] B: 6/4/1895 D: 12/24/1980, Bradford Woods, PA
1922 Can: 5 G.

DAN MCQUAID McQuaid, Daniel James 6'7", 278 OT-OG
Col: Nevada-Las Vegas *HS:* Delta [Clarksburg, CA] B: 10/4/1960, Cortland, CA
1985 Was: 16 G. **1986** Was: 13 G. **1987** Was: 1 G. **1988** Min-Ind: 4 G. Min: 3 G. Ind: 1 G. **Total:** 34 G.

ED MCQUARTERS McQuarters, Eddie Lee 6'1", 255 DT
Col: Oklahoma *HS:* Booker T. Washington [Tulsa, OK] B: 4/16/1943, Tulsa, OK *Drafted:* 1965 Round 18 StL
1965 StL: 1 G.

R.W. MCQUARTERS McQuarters, Robert William II 5'9", 198 DB
Col: Oklahoma State *HS:* Booker T. Washington [Tulsa, OK] B: 12/21/1976, Tulsa, OK *Drafted:* 1998 Round 1 SF
1998 SF: KR 17-339 19.9.

		Punt Returns				
Year Team	G	Ret	Yds	Avg	TD	Fum
1998 SF	16	**47**	406	8.6	1	4

JACK MCQUARY McQuary, John Edward 6'1", 208 HB-DB
Col: California *HS:* Alexander Hamilton [Los Angeles, CA] B: 6/20/1920, Tacoma, WA D: 12/20/1986, Monterey, CA
AAFC **1946** LA-A: 1 G.

LEON MCQUAY McQuay, Leon 5'9", 200 RB
Col: Tampa *HS:* Howard W. Blake [Tampa, FL] B: 3/19/1950, Tampa, FL D: 11/29/1995, Tampa, FL *Drafted:* 1973 Round 5 NYG
1974 NYG: Rec 5-59 11.8; PR 7-81 11.6. **1975** NE: Rec 4-27 6.8. **1976** NO: PR 2-5 2.5. **Total:** Rec 9-86 9.6; PR 9-86 9.6.

		Rushing				Kickoff Returns				
Year Team	G	Att	Yds	Avg	TD	Ret	Yds	Avg	TD	Fum
1974 NYG	13	55	240	4.4	1	25	689	27.6	0	3
1975 NE	13	33	47	1.4	0	15	252	16.8	0	3
1976 NO	4	0	0	—	0	8	151	18.9	0	1
NFL Total	30	88	287	3.3	1	48	1092	22.8	0	7

KIM MCQUILKEN McQuilken, Kim Evan 6'2", 203 QB
Col: Lehigh *HS:* William Allen [Allentown, PA] B: 2/26/1951, Allentown, PA *Drafted:* 1974 Round 3 Atl
1974 Atl: Rush 2-1 0.5. **1975** Atl: Rush 4-26 6.5. **1976** Atl: Rush 9-26 2.9. **1977** Atl: Rush 2-(-1) -0.5. **1979** Was: Rush 2-(-3) -1.5. **Total:** Rush 19-49 2.6.

		Passing								
Year Team	G	Att	Comp	Comp%	Yds	YPA	TD	Int	Rating	Fum
1974 Atl	5	79	34	43.0	373	4.72	0	9	18.0	0
1975 Atl	3	61	20	32.8	253	4.15	1	9	12.6	3
1976 Atl	8	121	48	39.7	450	3.72	2	10	21.7	6
1977 Atl	7	7	5	71.4	47	6.71	1	0	129.2	0
1979 Was	3	4	1	25.0	12	3.00	0	1	0.0	0
NFL Total	26	272	108	39.7	1135	4.17	4	29	17.9	9

BENNIE MCRAE McRae, Benjamin Prince 6'0", 180 DB
Col: Michigan *HS:* Huntington [Newport News, VA] B: 12/8/1939, Pinehurst, NC *Drafted:* 1962 Round 2 ChiB

		Interceptions		
Year Team	G	Int	Yds	TD
1962 ChiB	14	1	47	0
1963 ChiB	14	6	90	1
1964 ChiB	14	2	44	0
1965 ChiB	14	4	116	1
1966 ChiB	14	3	53	0
1967 ChiB	14	5	94	2
1968 ChiB	14	4	41	0
1969 ChiB	14	1	0	0
1970 ChiB	13	1	0	0
1971 NYG	8	0	0	0
NFL Total	133	27	485	4

CHARLES MCRAE McRae, Charles Edward 6'7", 299 OT-OG
Col: Tennessee *HS:* Clinton [TN] B: 9/16/1968, Oscowda, MI *Drafted:* 1991 Round 1 TB
1991 TB: 16 G. **1992** TB: 16 G. **1993** TB: 13 G. **1994** TB: 15 G. **1995** TB: 11 G. **1996** Oak: 13 G. **Total:** 84 G.

FRANK MCRAE McRae, Franklin 6'7", 270 DT
Col: Tennessee State *HS:* Manassas [Memphis, TN] B: 3/18/1944, Memphis, TN *Drafted:* 1966 Round 6 ChiB
1967 ChiB: 6 G.

JERROLD MCRAE McRae, Jerrold Elisha 6'1", 194 WR
Col: Tennessee State *HS:* R.H. Watkins [Laurel, MS] B: 4/9/1955, Laurel, MS *Drafted:* 1978 Round 5 KC
1978 KC: 4 G. **1979** Phi: 5 G; Rec 1-(-2) -2.0. **Total:** 9 G; Rec 1-(-2) -2.0.

BILL MCRAVEN McRaven, Claude Coy 5'11", 170 WB-DB
(Bullet Bill) *Col:* Murray State *HS:* Portageville [MO] B: 2/23/1914, East St.Louis, IL
1939 Cle: 9 G; Rush 7-29 4.1; Rec 2-14 7.0.

BOB MCROBERTS McRoberts, Robert Allen 5'11", 190 HB-DB
Col: Wis.-Stout *HS:* Durand [WI] B: 4/28/1924, Eau Galle, WI
1944 Bos: 1 G.

WADE MCROBERTS McRoberts, Wade Edward 6'0", 210 C
Col: Westminster (Pa.) *HS:* Niles [OH] B: 1/7/1901, Niles, OH D: 11/1941
1925 Can: 4 G. **1926** Can: 8 G. **Total:** 12 G.

CHARLES MCSHANE McShane, Charles Dean 6'3", 230 LB
Col: Long Beach City Coll. CA (J.C.); California Lutheran *HS:* R.A. Millikan [Long Beach, CA] B: 1/4/1954, Long Beach, CA *Drafted:* 1976 Round 12 Dal
1977 Sea: 14 G. **1978** Sea: 14 G. **1979** Sea: 1 G. **Total:** 29 G.

JOE MCSHEA McShea, Joseph Maurice 5'8", 185 G
Col: Rochester *HS:* Charlotte [NY] B: 12/13/1899 D: 12/21/1985, Rochester, NY
1923 Roch: 1 G.

CHUCK MCSWAIN McSwain, Anthony 6'0", 193 RB
Col: Clemson *HS:* Chase [Forest City, NC] B: 2/21/1961, Rutherford, NC *Drafted:* 1983 Round 5 Dal
1983 Dal: 1 G; KR 1-17 17.0. **1984** Dal: 15 G; KR 20-403 20.2; 2 Fum. **1987** NE: 3 G; Rush 9-23 2.6; KR 2-32 16.0; 1 Fum. **Total:** 19 G; Rush 9-23 2.6; KR 23-452 19.7; 3 Fum.

ROD MCSWAIN McSwain, Rodney 6'1", 198 DB
Col: Clemson *HS:* Chase [Forest City, NC] B: 1/28/1962, Caroleen, NC *Drafted:* 1984 Round 3 Atl
1984 NE: 15 G. **1985** NE: 16 G; Int 1-0. **1986** NE: 9 G; Int 1-3; 6 Pt. **1987** NE: 12 G; Int 1-17. **1988** NE: 16 G; Int 2-51. **1989** NE: 9 G; Int 1-18. **1990** NE: 13 G; KR 1-0; 2 Sac. **Total:** 90 G; KR 1-0; Int 6-89; 6 Pt; 2 Sac.

TIM MCTYER McTyer, Timothy Thomas 5'11", 181 DB
Col: Los Angeles Southwest Coll. CA (J.C.); Brigham Young *HS:* George Washington [Los Angeles, CA] B: 12/14/1975, Los Angeles, CA
1997 Phi: 10 G. **1998** Phi: 16 G; Int 1-18; 0.5 Sac. **Total:** 26 G; Int 1-18; 0.5 Sac.

WARREN MCVEA McVea, Warren Douglas 5'9", 182 RB-WR
Col: Houston *HS:* G. W. Brackenridge [San Antonio, TX] B: 7/30/1946, San Antonio, TX *Drafted:* 1968 Round 4 Cin
1969 KC: Pass 3-1 33.3%, 50 16.67 1 TD. **1970** KC: Pass 1-0. **Total:** Pass 4-1 25.0%, 50 12.50 1 TD.

		Rushing				Receiving			
Year Team	G	Att	Yds	Avg	TD	Rec	Yds	Avg	TD
1968 Cin	12	9	133	14.8	1	21	264	12.6	2
1969 KC	11	106	500	4.7	7	7	71	10.1	0
1970 KC	14	61	260	4.3	0	5	26	5.2	0
1971 KC	12	68	288	4.2	3	5	-3	-0.6	0
1973 KC	7	4	5	1.3	0	0	0	—	0
NFL Total	56	248	1186	4.8	11	38	358	9.4	2

Year Team	Kickoff Returns Ret	Yds	Avg	TD	Fum	Tot TD
1968 Cin	14	310	22.1	0	1	3
1969 KC	13	318	24.5	0	1	7
1970 KC	3	57	19.0	0	2	0
1971 KC	9	177	19.7	0	1	3
1973 KC	8	146	18.3	0	1	0
NFL Total	47	1008	21.4	0	6	13

JOHN MCVEIGH McVeigh, John Bosco 6′1″, 226 **LB**
Col: Miami (Fla.); Kentucky *HS:* Christopher Columbus [Miami, FL]
B: 10/19/1962
1987 Sea: 3 G.

BILL MCWATTERS McWatters, Billie Pittman 6′0″, 225 **FB**
Col: North Texas *HS:* Teague [TX] B: 8/1/1942, Donie, TX
Drafted: 1964 Round 8 Min
1964 Min: 11 G; Rush 14-60 4.3 1 TD; Rec 2-(-1) -0.5; KR 1-7 7.0; 6 Pt; 2 Fum.

JOHNNY MCWILLIAMS McWilliams, Johnny E 6′4″, 271 **TE**
Col: USC *HS:* Pomona [CA] B: 12/14/1972, Ontario, CA
Drafted: 1996 Round 3 Ariz

Year Team	G	Receiving Rec	Yds	Avg	TD
1996 Ariz	12	7	80	11.4	1
1997 Ariz	16	7	75	10.7	0
1998 Ariz	16	26	284	10.9	4
NFL Total	44	40	439	11.0	5

SHORTY MCWILLIAMS McWilliams, Thomas Edward 6′3″, 185 **DB-TB-HB**
Col: Army; Mississippi State *HS:* Meridian [MS] B: 5/12/1926, Newton, MS D: 1/9/1997, Meridian, MS *Drafted:* 1948 Round 6 ChiB
AAFC **1949** LA-A: 12 G; Pass 2-0; Rush 3-15 5.0; PR 8-112 14.0; Int 2-35.

NFL **1950** Pit: 10 G; Pass 8-5 62.5%, 113 14.13 1 Int; Rush 10-39 3.9; PR 11-139 12.6; KR 2-47 23.5; Int 2-31; Punt 3-135 45.0; 1 Fum.

BILL MCWILLIAMS McWilliams, William Henry 6′1″, 205 **WB-DB**
Col: Iowa *HS:* DePaul Acad. [Chicago, IL] B: 11/28/1910, Dubuque, IA
1934 Det: 5 G; Rush 6-16 2.7.

JACK MEAD Mead, John Michael 6′3″, 213 **OE-DB-DE**
Col: Wisconsin *HS:* West Division [Milwaukee, WI] B: 4/18/1921, Appleton, WI *Drafted:* 1945 Round 5 NYG
1946 NYG: 10 G; Rec 3-36 12.0; Int 1-33. **1947** NYG: 10 G; Rec 6-91 15.2. **Total:** 20 G; Rec 9-127 14.1; Int 1-33.

JIM MEADE Meade, James Gordon Jr. 6′1″, 197 **DB-WB-FB**
Col: Maryland *HS:* The Tome School [North East, MD] B: 2/28/1914, Philadelphia, PA D: 8/7/1977, Peachtree City, GA
1939 Was: Rec 1-1 1.0; Punt 8-297 37.1. **1940** Was: Rec 4-39 9.8; Int 1-0; Punt 9-358 39.8. **Total:** Rec 5-40 8.0; Int 1-0; Punt 17-655 38.5.

Year Team	G	Rushing Att	Yds	Avg	TD
1939 Was	8	13	34	2.6	0
1940 Was	10	48	115	2.4	0
NFL Total	18	61	149	2.4	0

MIKE MEADE Meade, Michael Lee 5′11″, 228 **RB**
Col: Penn State *HS:* Dover [DE] B: 2/12/1960, Dover, DE
Drafted: 1982 Round 5 GB
1982 GB: Rec 3-(-5) -1.7; KR 2-31 15.5. **1983** GB: Rec 16-110 6.9 2 TD. **1984** Det: KR 4-32 8.0. **1985** Det: Rec 2-21 10.5. **Total:** Rec 21-126 6.0 2 TD; KR 6-63 10.5.

Year Team	G	Rushing Att	Yds	Avg	TD	Fum	Tot TD
1982 GB	2	14	42	3.0	0	0	0
1983 GB	16	55	201	3.7	1	2	3
1984 Det	15	0	0	—	0	1	0
1985 Det	16	3	18	6.0	0	0	0
NFL Total	49	72	261	3.6	1	3	3

ED MEADOR Meador, Edward Doyle 5′11″, 193 **DB**
Col: Arkansas Tech *HS:* Russellville [AR] B: 8/10/1937, Dallas, TX
Drafted: 1959 Round 7 LARm
1963 LARm: Rush 1-1 1.0. **1964** LARm: Pass 1-0; KR 6-148 24.7. **1965** LARm: Pass 1-0; Rush 2-35 17.5 1 TD. **1966** LARm: Pass 1-0; Rush 1-7 7.0. **1967** LARm: Pass 1-1 100.0%, 18 18.00 1 TD. **1968** LARm: Rush 1-11 11.0; KR 1-20 20.0. **1969** LARm: Pass 1-0; Rush 1-5 5.0. **Total:** Pass 5-1 20.0%, 18 3.60 1 TD; Rush 6-59 9.8 1 TD; KR 7-168 24.0.

Year Team	G	Punt Returns Ret	Yds	Avg	TD	Interceptions Int	Yds	TD	Fum	Tot TD
1959 LARm	12	1	0	0.0	0	3	3	0	2	0
1960 LARm	12	1	0	0.0	0	4	46	1	0	1
1961 LARm	14	0	0	—	0	1	34	0	0	0
1962 LARm	14	0	0	—	0	1	0	0	0	0
1963 LARm	14	0	0	—	0	6	38	0	0	0
1964 LARm	14	2	9	4.5	0	3	50	0	1	0
1965 LARm	14	0	0	—	0	2	57	0	0	1
1966 LARm	14	0	0	—	0	5	60	0	0	0
1967 LARm	14	21	131	6.2	0	8	103	2	1	2
1968 LARm	14	17	136	8.0	0	6	37	0	3	0
1969 LARm	14	1	-1	-1.0	0	5	97	**2**	0	2
1970 LARm	13	0	0	—	0	2	22	0	0	0
NFL Total	163	43	275	6.4	0	46	547	5	7	6

RALPH MEADOW Meadow, Ralph 6′2″, 195 **E**
Col: No College Deceased
1920 Can: 1 G.

DARRYL MEADOWS Meadows, Darryl Scott 6′1″, 202 **DB**
Col: Toledo *HS:* La Salle [Cincinnati, OH] B: 2/15/1961, Cincinnati, OH
1983 Hou: 16 G. **1984** Hou: 13 G. **Total:** 29 G.

ED MEADOWS Meadows, Edward Allen 6′2″, 221 **DE**
(Country) *Col:* Duke *HS:* Oxford [NC] B: 2/19/1932, Oxford, NC
D: 10/22/1974, Morehead, NC *Drafted:* 1954 Round 3 ChiB
1954 ChiB: 12 G; KR 1-17 17.0; 1 Fum. **1955** Pit: 12 G. **1956** ChiB: 12 G. **1957** ChiB: 12 G. **1958** Phi: 12 G. **1959** Was: 5 G. **Total:** 65 G; KR 1-17 17.0; 1 Fum.

ADAM MEADOWS Meadows, Jonathan Adam 6′5″, 299 **OT**
Col: Georgia *HS:* McEachern [Powder Springs, GA] B: 1/25/1974, Powder Springs, GA *Drafted:* 1997 Round 2 Ind
1997 Ind: 16 G. **1998** Ind: 14 G. **Total:** 30 G.

JOHNNY MEADS Meads, Johnny Sand 6′2″, 231 **LB**
Col: Nicholls State *HS:* Assumption [Napoleonville, LA] B: 6/25/1961, Labadieville, LA *Drafted:* 1984 Round 3 Hou
1984 Hou: 16 G. **1985** Hou: 5 G; 1.5 Sac. **1986** Hou: 16 G; 3.5 Sac. **1987** Hou: 12 G; 4 Sac. **1988** Hou: 16 G; 8 Sac. **1989** Hou: 16 G; 4 Sac. **1990** Hou: 16 G; Int 1-32; 2.5 Sac. **1991** Hou: 16 G. **1992** Hou-Was: 6 G; 1 Fum TD; 6 Pt. Hou: 4 G; 1 Fum TD; 6 Pt. Was: 2 G. **Total:** 119 G; Int 1-32; 1 Fum TD; 6 Pt; 23.5 Sac.

JACK MEAGHER Meagher, John Francis 5′10″, 178 **E**
Col: Notre Dame *HS:* Elgin [IL] B: 10/1/1896, Chicago, IL
D: 11/7/1968, San Francisco, CA
1920 ChiT: 4 G.

TIM MEAMBER Meamber, Timothy Frederick 6′3″, 231 **LB**
Col: Washington *HS:* Yreka [CA] B: 10/29/1962, Yreka, CA
Drafted: 1985 Round 3 Min
1985 Min: 4 G.

DAVE MEANS Means, David Mitchell 6′4″, 235 **DE**
Col: Southeast Missouri State *HS:* Hopkinsville [KY] B: 1/23/1952, Hopkinsville, KY *Drafted:* 1974 Round 12 Buf
1974 Buf: 9 G.

NATRONE MEANS Means, Natrone Jermaine 5′10″, 245 **RB**
Col: North Carolina *HS:* Central Cabarrus [Concord, NC]
B: 4/26/1972, Harrisburg, NC *Drafted:* 1993 Round 2 SD
1993 SD: Pass 1-0; KR 2-22 11.0. **1994** SD: Pass 1-0. **Total:** Pass 2-0; KR 2-22 11.0.

Year Team	G	Rushing Att	Yds	Avg	TD	Receiving Rec	Yds	Avg	TD	Fum	Tot TD
1993 SD	16	160	645	4.0	8	10	59	5.9	0	1	8
1994 SD	16	343	1350	3.9	12	39	235	6.0	0	5	12
1995 SD	10	186	730	3.9	5	7	46	6.6	0	2	5
1996 Jac	14	152	507	3.3	2	7	45	6.4	1	3	3
1997 Jac	14	244	823	3.4	9	15	104	6.9	0	5	9
1998 SD	10	212	883	4.2	5	16	91	5.7	0	2	5
NFL Total	80	1297	4938	3.8	41	94	580	6.2	1	18	42

CURT MECHAM Mecham, Curtis William 6′0″, 180 **TB-DB**
Col: Oregon *HS:* Bakersfield [CA] B: 3/2/1920, Bakersfield, CA
Drafted: 1942 Round 2 Bkn
1942 Bkn: 6 G; Pass 4-1 25.0%, 9 2.25 1 Int; Rush 3-0.

KARL MECKLENBURG Mecklenburg, Karl Bernard 6′3″, 240 **LB-DE**
(The Albino Rhino) *Col:* Augustana (S.D.); Minnesota *HS:* Edina West [Edina, MN] B: 9/1/1960, Seattle, WA *Drafted:* 1983 Round 12 Den
1983 Den: 16 G; 2 Sac. **1984** Den: 16 G; Int 2-105; 7 Sac. **1985** Den: 16 G; 13 Sac. **1986** Den: 16 G; 9.5 Sac. **1987** Den: 12 G; Int 3-23; 7 Sac. **1988** Den: 9 G; 1 Sac. **1989** Den: 15 G; 1 Fum TD; 6 Pt; 7.5 Sac. **1990** Den: 16 G; Scor **1** Saf; 1 Fum TD; 8 Pt; 5 Sac. **1991** Den: 16 G; 9 Sac. **1992** Den: 16 G; 7.5 Sac. **1993** Den: 16 G; 9 Sac. **1994** Den: 16 G; 1.5 Sac. **Total:** 180 G; Int 5-128; Scor 1 Saf; 2 Fum TD; 14 Pt; 79 Sac.

DAN MEDLIN Medlin, Daniel Ellis 6′3″, 260 **OG**
Col: North Carolina State *HS:* Thomasville [NC] B: 10/12/1949, High Point, NC *Drafted:* 1972 Round 6 Oak
1974 Oak: 6 G. **1975** Oak: 14 G. **1976** Oak: 13 G. **1977** TB: 14 G. **1978** TB: 14 G. **1979** Oak: 15 G. **Total:** 76 G.

RON MEDVED Medved, Ronald George 6′1″, 210 **DB**
Col: Washington *HS:* Bellarmine [Tacoma, WA] B: 5/27/1944, Tacoma, WA *Drafted:* 1966 Round 14 Phi
1966 Phi: 14 G; KR 2-10 5.0. **1967** Phi: 8 G; KR 1-7 7.0; Int 2-23. **1968** Phi: 14 G; Int 1-0. **1969** Phi: 3 G. **1970** Phi: 12 G. **Total:** 51 G; KR 3-17 5.7; Int 3-23.

GREG MEEHAN Meehan, Gregory Allen 6′0″, 191 **WR**
Col: Scottsdale CC AZ; Bowling Green State *HS:* Shadow Mountain [Phoenix, AZ] B: 4/27/1963, Otis AFB, MA
1987 Cin: 3 G; Rush 4-19 4.8; Rec 3-25 8.3; KR 1-9 9.0; 1 Fum.

BUTCH MEEKER Meeker, Herbert Lawerence 5′3″, 143 **BB-TB**
(Shorty) *Col:* Washington State *HS:* Lewis and Clark [Spokane, WA]
1930 Prov: 11 G; Rec 1 TD; KR **1** TD; Scor 16, 1 FG, 1 XK; Tot TD 2. **1931** Prov: 9 G; Scor 1, 1 XK. **Total:** 20 G; Rec 1 TD; KR 1 TD; Scor 17, 1 FG, 2 XK; Tot TD 2.

BRYANT MEEKS Meeks, Bryant Adams Jr. 6′2″, 193 **C-LB**
(Meatball) *Col:* Georgia; South Carolina *HS:* Deland [FL] B: 1/16/1926, Jacksonville, FL *Drafted:* 1947 Round 5 Pit
1947 Pit: 8 G. **1948** Pit: 10 G. **Total:** 18 G.

EDDIE MEEKS Meeks, John Edward 5′7″, 155 **WB**
Col: Louisville *HS:* Manual [Louisville, KY] B: 9/30/1897, Louisville, KY D: 10/15/1963, Louisville, KY
1922 Lou: 3 G.

BOB MEEKS Meeks, Robert Earl Jr. 6′2″, 279 **C**
Col: Auburn *HS:* Hillcrest [Evergreen, AL] B: 5/28/1969, Andalusia, AL *Drafted:* 1992 Round 10 Den
1993 Den: 8 G; KR 1-9 9.0.

WARD MEESE Meese, Ward King 5′10″, 175 **E**
Col: Wabash *HS:* Huntington [IN] B: 7/28/1898 Deceased
1922 Mil: 4 G. **1923** StL: 5 G. **1924** Ham: 1 G. **1925** Ham: 1 G. **Total:** 11 G.

DAVE MEGGETT Meggett, David Lee 5′7″, 190 **RB**
Col: Morgan State; Towson State *HS:* Bonds-Wilson [North Charleston, SC] B: 4/30/1966, Charleston, SC *Drafted:* 1989 Round 5 NYG
1991 NYG: Pass 1-0. **1993** NYG: Pass 2-2 100.0%, 63 31.50 2 TD. **1994** NYG: Pass 2-1 50.0%, 16 8.00 1 TD. **1995** NE: Pass 1-0; Scor 2 2XP. **1996** NE: Pass 1-0. **1997** NE: Pass 1-1 100.0%, 35 35.00 1 TD. **Total:** Pass 8-4 50.0%, 114 14.25 4 TD; Scor 2 2XP.

		Rushing				Receiving			
Year Team	**G**	**Att**	**Yds**	**Avg**	**TD**	**Rec**	**Yds**	**Avg**	**TD**
1989 NYG	16	28	117	4.2	0	34	531	15.6	4
1990 NYG	16	22	164	7.5	0	39	410	10.5	1
1991 NYG	16	29	153	5.3	1	50	412	8.2	3
1992 NYG	16	32	167	5.2	0	38	229	6.0	2
1993 NYG	16	69	329	4.8	0	38	319	8.4	0
1994 NYG	16	91	298	3.3	4	32	293	9.2	0
1995 NE	16	60	250	4.2	2	52	334	6.4	0
1996 NE	16	40	122	3.1	0	33	292	8.8	0
1997 NE	16	20	60	3.0	1	19	203	10.7	1
1998 NYJ	2	7	24	3.4	0	1	15	15.0	0
NFL Total	146	398	1684	4.2	8	336	3038	9.0	11

	Punt Returns				Kickoff Returns					Tot
Year Team	**Ret**	**Yds**	**Avg**	**TD**	**Ret**	**Yds**	**Avg**	**TD**	**Fum**	**TD**
1989 NYG	46	**582**	12.7	**1**	27	577	21.4	0	8	5
1990 NYG	**43**	**467**	10.9	**1**	21	492	23.4	0	3	2
1991 NYG	28	287	10.3	1	25	514	20.6	0	8	5
1992 NYG	27	240	8.9	0	20	455	22.8	1	5	3
1993 NYG	32	331	10.3	1	24	403	16.8	0	1	1
1994 NYG	26	323	12.4	**2**	29	548	18.9	0	6	6
1995 NE	45	383	8.5	0	38	964	25.4	0	5	2
1996 NE	52	588	11.3	1	34	781	23.0	0	7	1
1997 NE	45	467	10.4	0	33	816	24.7	0	2	2
1998 NYJ	5	40	8.0	0	1	16	16.0	0	0	0
NFL Total	**349**	**3708**	10.6	7	252	5566	22.1	1	45	27

DAVE MEGGYESY Meggyesy, David Michael 6′2″, 220 **LB**
Col: Syracuse *HS:* Solon [OH] B: 11/1/1941, Cleveland, OH *Drafted:* 1963 Round 17 StL
1963 StL: 6 G. **1964** StL: 14 G. **1965** StL: 14 G. **1966** StL: 14 G. **1967** StL: 14 G. **1968** StL: 12 G. **1969** StL: 8 G. **Total:** 82 G.

CHARLEY MEHELICH Mehelich, Charles J 6′1″, 199 **DE-OE**
(Iron Man) *Col:* Duquesne *HS:* Verona [PA] B: 8/4/1922, Oakmont, PA D: 12/2/1984, Abington, PA *Drafted:* 1945 Round 5 Pit
1946 Pit: 10 G; Rec 10-116 11.6. **1947** Pit: 11 G; Rec 3-38 12.7. **1948** Pit: 12 G; Pass 2-0; KR 1-2 2.0. **1949** Pit: 9 G. **1950** Pit: 12 G; Rec 2-18 9.0; KR 2-16 8.0. **1951** Pit: 5 G; Scor **1** Saf; 2 Pt. **Total:** 59 G; Pass 2-0; Rec 15-172 11.5; KR 3-18 6.0; Scor 1 Saf; 2 Pt.

TONY MEHELICH Mehelich, Thomas Tony 5′11″, 185 **G-C**
Col: St. Mary's (Minn.) *HS:* Greenway [Coleraine, MN] B: 8/4/1906, Grand Rapids, MN D: 5/20/1972, Coleraine, MN
1929 Min: 8 G.

LANCE MEHL Mehl, Lance Alan 6′3″, 235 **LB**
Col: Penn State *HS:* Bellaire [OH] B: 2/14/1958, Bellaire, OH *Drafted:* 1980 Round 3 NYJ
1983 NYJ: 2.5 Sac. **1984** NYJ: 5 Sac. **1985** NYJ: 5.5 Sac. **1986** NYJ: 1 Sac. **Total:** 14 Sac.

		Interceptions			
Year Team	**G**	**Int**	**Yds**	**TD**	**Fum**
1980 NYJ	14	0	0	0	0
1981 NYJ	15	3	17	0	0
1982 NYJ	9	2	38	0	0
1983 NYJ	16	7	57	1	0
1984 NYJ	16	0	0	0	0
1985 NYJ	16	3	33	0	1
1986 NYJ	8	0	0	0	0
1987 NYJ	3	0	0	0	0
NFL Total	97	15	145	1	1

HARRY MEHRE Mehre, Harry James 6′1″, 190 **C**
(Red) *Col:* Notre Dame *HS:* Huntington [IN] B: 9/18/1901, Huntington, IN D: 9/27/1978, Atlanta, GA
1922 Min: 3 G. **1923** Min: 9 G. **Total:** 12 G.

PETE MEHRINGER Mehringer, Peter Joseph 6′2″, 206 **T-G**
(Champ) *Col:* Kansas *HS:* Kinsley [KS] B: 7/15/1910, Jetmore, KS D: 8/27/1987, Pullman, WA
1934 ChiC: 8 G. **1935** ChiC: 8 G. **1936** ChiC: 3 G. **Total:** 19 G.

STEVE MEILINGER Meilinger, Stephen Frank 6′2″, 227 **OE**
Col: Kentucky *HS:* Bethlehem [PA]; Fork Union Mil. Acad. [VA] B: 12/12/1930, Bethlehem, PA *Drafted:* 1954 Round 1 Was
1960 GB: KR 1-0. **1961** Pit: Rush 1-6 6.0. **Total:** Rush 1-6 6.0; KR 1-0.

		Receiving				
Year Team	**G**	**Rec**	**Yds**	**Avg**	**TD**	**Fum**
1956 Was	12	24	395	16.5	5	1
1957 Was	12	13	183	14.1	2	0
1958 GB	12	13	139	10.7	1	0
1960 GB	12	2	43	21.5	0	0
1961 Pit	4	8	103	12.9	0	0
NFL Total	52	60	863	14.4	8	1

DALE MEINERT Meinert, Dale Herman 6′2″, 220 **LB**
Col: Oklahoma State *HS:* Lone Wolf [OK] B: 12/18/1933, Lone Wolf, OK *Drafted:* 1955 Round 8 Bal
1958 ChiC: 12 G. **1959** ChiC: 12 G. **1960** StL: 12 G; Int 3-17. **1961** StL: 14 G; Int 2-68. **1962** StL: 5 G; Int 1-12. **1963** StL: 14 G. **1964** StL: 14 G; Int 2-24 1 TD; 6 Pt. **1965** StL: 14 G. **1966** StL: 14 G. **1967** StL: 14 G; Int 1-5. **Total:** 125 G; Int 9-126 1 TD; 6 Pt.

GEORGE MEINHARDT Meinhardt, George Michael 5′9″, 200 **C-G**
Col: St. Louis *HS:* Yeatman [St. Louis, MO] B: 11/24/1897, St. Louis, MO D: 4/1/1971, St. Louis, MO
1923 StL: 6 G.

DARREL MEISENHEIMER Meisenheimer, Darrel David 5′10″, 195 **DB**
Col: Oklahoma State *HS:* Attica [KS] B: 4/30/1927, Wellsford, KS *Drafted:* 1951 Round 17 Det
1951 NYY: 9 G; Int 3-26.

GREG MEISNER Meisner, Gregory Paul 6′3″, 257 **NT-DE**
Col: Pittsburgh *HS:* Valley [New Kensington, PA] B: 4/23/1959, New Kensington, PA *Drafted:* 1981 Round 3 LARm
1981 LARm: 9 G; KR 1-17 17.0. **1982** LARm: 6 G; 1 Sac. **1983** LARm: 16 G. **1984** LARm: 16 G; 3.5 Sac. **1985** LARm: 14 G. **1986** LARm: 15 G; 2 Sac. **1987** LARm: 15 G; 3 Sac. **1988** LARm: 12 G; Int 1-20; 1 Sac. **1989** KC: 12 G; 0.5 Sac. **1990** KC: 16 G; 1 Sac. **1991** NYG: 4 G. **Total:** 135 G; KR 1-17 17.0; Int 1-20; 12 Sac.

BILL MEISNER Meisner, William L 5′11″, 185 **WB**
Col: Syracuse *HS:* Tonawanda [NY] B: 2/19/1893 D: 2/1968, North Tonawanda, NY
1921 Ton: 1 G.

ED MEIXLER Meixler, Edward 6′3″, 245 **LB**
Col: Boston U. *HS:* Saratoga Springs [NY] B: 10/11/1943 *Drafted:* 1965 Round 18 Bos
1965 Bos: 4 G.

JON MELANDER Melander, Jon James 6′7″, 280 **OG-OT**
Col: Minnesota *HS:* Fridley [MN] B: 12/27/1966, Fridley, MN *Drafted:* 1990 Round 5 NE
1991 NE: 10 G. **1992** Cin: 15 G. **1993** Den: 14 G. **1994** Den: 15 G. **Total:** 54 G.

MIKE MELINKOVICH Melinkovich, Michael Joseph 6′4″, 245 **DE**
Col: Grays Harbor Coll. WA (J.C.); Washington *HS:* J.M. Weatherwax [Aberdeen, WA] B: 1/7/1942, Tonasket, WA *Drafted:* 1965 Round 17 StL
1965 StL: 14 G. **1966** StL: 10 G; KR 1-2 2.0. **1967** Det: 7 G. **Total:** 31 G; KR 1-2 2.0.

JAMES MELKA Melka, James David 6′1″, 235 **LB**
Col: Wisconsin *HS:* Central [West Alilis, WI] B: 1/15/1962, West Allis, WI
1987 GB: 1 G; Int 1-0.

JOHN MELLEKAS Mellekas, John Stavros 6′3″, 255 **C-DT-OT**
(Golden Greek) *Col:* Arizona *HS:* Rogers [Newport, RI] B: 6/14/1933, Newport, RI *Drafted:* 1956 Round 4 ChiB
1956 ChiB: 12 G. **1958** ChiB: 12 G. **1959** ChiB: 12 G. **1960** ChiB: 12 G. **1961** ChiB: 14 G. **1962** SF: 11 G. **1963** Phi: 11 G. **Total:** 84 G.

JIM MELLO Mello, James Anthony 5′10″, 190 **DB-FB-LB**
Col: Notre Dame *HS:* West Warwick [RI] B: 11/8/1920, Warwick, RI
Drafted: 1945 Round 6 Bos
AAFC **1948** ChiA: Rec 3-38 12.7; KR 2-30 15.0.

		Rushing			
Year Team	G	Att	Yds	Avg	TD
1948 ChiA	6	50	243	4.9	1

NFL **1947** Bos: Rec 2-26 13.0; Int 1-0. **1948** LARm: Rec 1-17 17.0. **1949** Det: KR 3-37 12.3; Int 3-61. **Total:** Rec 3-43 14.3; KR 3-37 12.3; Int 4-61.

		Rushing				
Year Team	G	Att	Yds	Avg	TD	Fum
1947 Bos	9	33	62	1.9	0	1
1948 LARm	3	7	3	0.4	0	0
1949 Det	10	0	0	—	0	0
NFL Total	22	40	65	1.6	0	1

DUTCH MELLODY Mellody, Walter 5′8″, 188 **WB-C**
Col: No College Deceased
1920 Roch: 4 G.

JOHN MELLUS Mellus, John G 6′0″, 214 **T**
Col: Villanova *HS:* Hanover Area [Wilkes-Barre, PA] B: 6/16/1917, Plymouth, PA *Drafted:* 1938 Round 7 NYG
AAFC **1946** SF-A: 14 G; Scor 1, 0-1 FG, 1-2 50.0% XK. **1947** BalA: 14 G; Rec 0-5. **1948** BalA: 14 G. **1949** BalA: 12 G. **Total:** 54 G; Rec 0-5; Scor 1, 0-1 FG, 1-2 50.0% XK.

NFL **1938** NYG: 11 G. **1939** NYG: 11 G. **1940** NYG: 8 G; **1** Fum TD; 6 Pt. **1941** NYG: 11 G. **Total:** 41 G; 1 Fum TD; 6 Pt.

ANDREW MELONTREE Melontree, Andrew Richard 6′4″, 228 **LB**
Col: Tyler JC TX; Baylor *HS:* John Tyler [Tyler, TX] B: 12/1/1957, Tyler, TX *Drafted:* 1980 Round 6 Cin
1980 Cin: 16 G.

DAN MELVILLE Melville, Daniel Lee 6′0″, 185 **P**
Col: Grossmont Coll. CA (J.C.); California *HS:* El Capital [San Diego, CA] B: 3/4/1956, San Diego, CA
1979 SF: Rush 3-0.

		Punting			
Year Team	G	Punts	Yds	Avg	Fum
1979 SF	16	71	2626	37.0	1

TOM MELVIN Melvin, Thomas 6′1″, 185 **E-WB**
Col: No College Deceased
1921 Cin: 3 G; Rec 1 TD; 6 Pt.

DALE MEMMELAAR Memmelaar, Dale Edward 6′2″, 247 **OG-OT**
Col: Wyoming *HS:* Goshen [NY] B: 1/15/1937, Goshen, NY
Drafted: 1959 Round 21 ChiC
1959 ChiC: 12 G. **1960** StL: 12 G; KR 1-8 8.0. **1961** StL: 8 G. **1962** Dal: 14 G; KR 1-0; 1 Fum. **1963** Dal: 14 G. **1964** Cle: 14 G. **1965** Cle: 14 G. **1966** Bal: 12 G. **1967** Bal: 7 G. **Total:** 107 G; KR 2-8 4.0; 1 Fum.

DON MENASCO Menasco, Donald Dean 6′0″, 185 **DB**
Col: Texas *HS:* Longview [TX] B: 10/18/1929, Hyman, TX
Drafted: 1952 Round 4 NYG
1952 NYG: 12 G; Int 4-5. **1953** NYG: 8 G; Int 1-5. **1954** Was: 6 G. **Total:** 26 G; Int 5-10.

JOHN MENDENHALL Mendenhall, John Rufus 6′1″, 255 **DT**
Col: Grambling State *HS:* Charles Brown [Springhill, LA] B: 12/3/1948, Cullen, LA *Drafted:* 1972 Round 3 NYG
1972 NYG: 14 G; PR 1-0; 1 Fum. **1973** NYG: 8 G. **1974** NYG: 13 G. **1975** NYG: 9 G. **1976** NYG: 14 G; Int 1-3. **1977** NYG: 14 G. **1978** NYG: 16 G. **1979** NYG: 13 G. **1980** Det: 15 G. **Total:** 116 G; PR 1-0; Int 1-3; 1 Fum.

KEN MENDENHALL Mendenhall, Kenneth Ernest 6′3″, 242 **C**
Col: Oklahoma *HS:* Enid [OK] B: 8/11/1948, Enid, OK *Drafted:* 1970 Round 5 Atl
1971 Bal: 14 G. **1972** Bal: 12 G. **1973** Bal: 13 G. **1974** Bal: 14 G. **1975** Bal: 14 G. **1976** Bal: 14 G. **1977** Bal: 14 G. **1978** Bal: 16 G. **1979** Bal: 16 G. **1980** Bal: 16 G. **Total:** 143 G.

MAT MENDENHALL Mendenhall, Mathew W 6′6″, 254 **DE**
Col: Brigham Young *HS:* East [Salt Lake City, UT] B: 5/14/1957, Salt Lake City, UT *Drafted:* 1980 Round 2 Was
1981 Was: 14 G. **1982** Was: 9 G; 1 Sac. **Total:** 23 G; 1 Sac.

TERRY MENDENHALL Mendenhall, Terry T 6′1″, 210 **LB**
Col: El Camino Coll. CA (J.C.); San Diego State *HS:* Aviation [Manhattan Beach, CA] B: 4/16/1949, Los Angeles, CA
1971 Oak: 14 G. **1972** Oak: 3 G. **Total:** 17 G.

MARIO MENDEZ Mendez, Mario 5′11″, 200 **HB**
Col: San Diego State *HS:* Santa Fe [Santa Fe Springs, CA] B: 1942
1964 SD: 1 G.

RUBEN MENDOZA Mendoza, Ruben Edward 6′4″, 290 **OG**
Col: Yankton; Wayne State (Neb.) *HS:* Milwaukee Tech [WI]
B: 5/10/1963, Crystal City, TX
1986 GB: 6 G.

PEP MENEFEE Menefee, Hartwell 6′1″, 198 **WR**
Col: Cameron; New Mexico State *HS:* Lawton [OK] B: 1/1/1943, Fort Worth, TX *Drafted:* 1966 Round 7 Hou
1966 NYG: 7 G; Rec 1-11 11.0.

VIC MENEFEE Menefee, Victor E 6′0″, 185 **OE**
(Bud) *Col:* Morningside *HS:* Sioux City [IA] B: 1898 Deceased
1921 RI: 2 G.

CHUCK MERCEIN Mercein, Charles Schley 6′2″, 225 **RB**
Col: Yale *HS:* New Trier Twp. [Winnetka, IL] B: 4/9/1943, Milwaukee, WI *Drafted:* 1965 Round 3 NYG
1965 NYG: KR 1-4 4.0; Scor 12, 0-2 FG. **1967** NYG-GB: Scor 8, 0-1 FG, 2-3 66.7% XK. NYG: Scor 2, 0-1 FG, 2-3 66.7% XK. **1968** GB: Scor 19, 2-5 40.0% FG, 7-7 100.0% XK. **1970** NYJ: KR 4-32 8.0. **Total:** KR 5-36 7.2; Scor 45, 2-8 25.0% FG, 9-10 90.0% XK.

		Rushing				Receiving					Tot
Year Team	G	Att	Yds	Avg	TD	Rec	Yds	Avg	TD	Fum	TD
1965 NYG	13	18	55	3.1	2	3	14	4.7	0	0	2
1966 NYG	13	94	327	3.5	0	27	152	5.6	0	3	0
1967 NYG-GB	7	14	56	4.0	1	1	6	6.0	0	1	1
1967 NYG	1	0	0	—	0	0	0	—	0	0	0
1967 GB	6	14	56	4.0	1	1	6	6.0	0	1	1
1968 GB	11	17	49	2.9	1	3	6	2.0	0	0	1
1969 GB	5	0	0	—	0	0	0	—	0	0	0
1970 NYJ	9	20	44	2.2	0	3	27	9.0	1	1	1
NFL Total	58	163	531	3.3	4	37	205	5.5	1	5	5

KEN MERCER Mercer, Kenneth Ernest 5′11″, 183 **TB-BB-WB-FB**
(Moco) *Col:* Simpson *HS:* Albia [IA] B: 6/9/1903, Albia, IA
D: 2/1970, Asbury, IA
1927 Fra: 17 G; Pass 4 TD; Rush 3 TD; Scor 39, **5** FG, 6 XK. **1928** Fra: 14 G; Pass 5 TD; Rush 5 TD; Rec 1 TD; Scor 38, 2 XK; Tot TD 6. **1929** Fra: 13 G; Pass 3 TD; Rec 1 TD; Scor 18, 2 FG, 6 XK. **Total:** 44 G; Pass 12 TD; Rush 8 TD; Rec 2 TD; Scor 95, 7 FG, 14 XK; Tot TD 10.

MIKE MERCER Mercer, Michael 6′0″, 220 **K**
Col: Minnesota; Florida State; Hardin-Simmons; Arizona State
HS: Dubuque [IA] B: 11/21/1935, Algona, IA *Drafted:* 1961 Round 15 Min
1961 Min: Rush 1-(-32) -32.0. **1963** Oak: Rush 1-(-5) -5.0. **1965** Oak: Pass 1-1 100.0%, 14 14.00; Rush 1-(-1) -1.0. **Total:** Pass 1-1 100.0%, 14 14.00; Rush 3-(-38) -12.7.

		Punting		
Year Team	G	Punts	Yds	Avg
1961 Min	14	63	2458	39.0
1962 Min	4	19	827	43.5
1963 Oak	14	75	3007	40.1
1964 Oak	14	59	2446	41.5
1965 Oak	14	75	3079	41.1
1966 Oak-KC	12	9	373	41.4
1966 Oak	2	9	373	41.4
1966 KC	10	0	0	—
1967 Buf	14	0	0	—
1968 Buf-GB	9	0	0	—
1968 Buf	3	0	0	—
1968 GB	6	0	0	—
1969 GB	10	0	0	—
1970 SD	14	8	283	35.4
NFL Total	119	308	12473	40.5

	Scoring						
Year Team	Pts	FG	FGA	FG%	XK	XKA	XK%
1961 Min	63	9	21	42.9	36	37	97.3
1962 Min	3	0	5	0.0	3	3	100.0
1963 Oak	71	8	19	42.1	**47**	47	100.0
1964 Oak	79	15	24	62.5	34	34	100.0
1965 Oak	62	9	15	60.0	35	35	100.0
1966 Oak-KC	98	**21**	30	**70.0**	35	38	**92.1**

1966 Oak	5	1	4	25.0	2	3	66.7
1966 KC	93	20	26	76.9	33	35	94.3
1967 Buf	73	16	27	59.3	25	25	100.0
1968 Buf-GB	37	7	16	43.8	16	18	88.9
1968 Buf	4	0	4	0.0	4	4	100.0
1968 GB	33	7	12	58.3	12	14	85.7
1969 GB	38	5	17	29.4	23	23	100.0
1970 SD	70	12	19	63.2	34	35	97.1
NFL Total	594	102	193	52.8	288	295	97.6

DUDLEY MEREDITH Meredith, Cecil Dudley 6′4″, 290 **DT**
Col: Del Mar Coll. TX (J.C.); Florida; Midwestern State; Lamar
HS: Burnet [TX] B: 1/16/1935, Smithwick, TX D: 12/22/1987
Drafted: 1957 Round 21 Det
1963 Hou: 14 G. **1964** Buf: 11 G. **1965** Buf: 14 G. **1966** Buf: 14 G. **1967** Buf: 14 G; KR 3-0; Int 1-8; 1 Fum. **1968** Buf-Hou: 10 G. Buf: 5 G. Hou: 5 G. **Total:** 77 G; KR 3-0; Int 1-8; 1 Fum.

DON MEREDITH Meredith, Joseph Donald 6′3″, 210 **QB**
(Dandy Don) *Col:* Southern Methodist *HS:* Mount Vernon [TX]
B: 4/10/1938, Mount Vernon, TX *Drafted:* 1960 Round 3 ChiB

		Passing							
Year Team	**G**	**Att**	**Comp**	**Comp%**	**Yds**	**YPA**	**TD**	**Int**	**Rating**
1960 Dal	6	68	29	42.6	281	4.13	2	5	34.0
1961 Dal	8	182	94	51.6	1161	6.38	9	11	63.0
1962 Dal	13	212	105	49.5	1679	7.92	15	8	84.2
1963 Dal	14	310	167	53.9	2381	7.68	17	18	73.1
1964 Dal	12	323	158	48.9	2143	6.63	9	16	59.1
1965 Dal	14	305	141	46.2	2415	7.92	22	13	79.9
1966 Dal	13	344	177	51.5	2805	8.15	24	12	87.7
1967 Dal	11	255	128	50.2	1834	7.19	16	16	68.7
1968 Dal	13	309	171	55.3	2500	8.09	21	12	88.4
NFL Total	104	2308	1170	50.7	17199	7.45	135	111	74.8

	Rushing				
Year Team	**Att**	**Yds**	**Avg**	**TD**	**Fum**
1960 Dal	3	4	1.3	0	2
1961 Dal	22	176	8.0	1	9
1962 Dal	21	74	3.5	0	10
1963 Dal	41	185	4.5	3	7
1964 Dal	32	81	2.5	4	**16**
1965 Dal	35	247	7.1	1	11
1966 Dal	38	242	6.4	5	8
1967 Dal	28	84	3.0	0	6
1968 Dal	22	123	5.6	1	2
NFL Total	242	1216	5.0	15	71

RUSS MEREDITH Meredith, Russell Delmar 5′11″, 200 **G-T**
Col: West Virginia *HS:* Fairmont [WV] B: 6/27/1897, Fairmont, WV
D: 5/22/1989, Fairmont, WV
1923 Lou: 1 G. **1925** Cle: 9 G. **Total:** 10 G.

MIKE MERGEN Mergen, Michael John 6′5″, 245 **DT**
Col: Illinois Wesleyan; San Francisco *HS:* McHenry [IL] B: 2/13/1929, Cicero, IL *Drafted:* 1952 Round 16 ChiC
1952 ChiC: 12 G; KR 1-13 13.0.

ART MERGENTHAL Mergenthal, Arthur Louis 5′11″, 215 **G-LB**
Col: Tennessee; Xavier (Ohio); Bowling Green State; Notre Dame
HS: Bellevue [KY] B: 3/21/1921, Bellevue, KY
1945 Cle: 10 G. **1946** LARm: 9 G. **Total:** 19 G.

LOU MERILLAT Merillat, Louis Alfred Jr. 5′9″, 165 **E**
Col: Illinois Tech; Army *HS:* Armour Scientific Acad. [Chicago, IL]
B: 6/9/1892, Chicago, IL D: 4/26/1948, Chicago, IL
1925 Can: 6 G.

MONTE MERKEL Merkel, Monte John 5′10″, 215 **G**
Col: Kansas *HS:* St. John's Mil. Acad. [Delafield, WI] B: 11/6/1916, Keystone, IA D: 6/1981, Missoula, MT
1943 ChiB: 1 G.

GUIDO MERKENS Merkens, Guido Albert Jr. 6′1″, 200 **QB-WR-DB**
Col: Sam Houston State *HS:* Edison [San Antonio, CA] B: 8/14/1955, San Antonio, TX
1978 Hou: PR 13-132 10.2. **1979** Hou: PR 2-6 3.0; KR 2-22 11.0. **1981** NO: Rush 2-(-1) -0.5; PR 1-(-12) -12.0; KR 2-38 19.0. **1982** NO: Rush 9-30 3.3. **1983** NO: Rush 1-16 16.0; Punt 4-144 36.0. **1985** NO: Rush 1-(-2) -2.0; KR 1-0. **1987** Phi: Rush 3-(-8) -2.7; Punt 2-61 30.5. **Total:** Rush 16-35 2.2; PR 16-126 7.9; KR 5-60 12.0; Punt 6-205 34.2.

		Passing							
Year Team	**G**	**Att**	**Comp**	**Comp%**	**Yds**	**YPA**	**TD**	**Int**	**Rating**
1978 Hou	12	0	0	—	0	—	0	0	—
1979 Hou	16	0	0	—	0	—	0	0	—
1980 Hou-NO	4	0	0	—	0	—	0	0	—
1980 Hou	3	0	0	—	0	—	0	0	—
1980 NO	1	0	0	—	0	—	0	0	—
1981 NO	16	2	1	50.0	20	10.00	0	0	85.4
1982 NO	9	49	18	36.7	186	3.80	1	2	38.3
1983 NO	16	0	0	—	0	—	0	0	—
1984 NO	16	0	0	—	0	—	0	0	—
1985 NO	16	1	1	100.0	7	7.00	1	0	135.4
1987 Phi	3	14	7	50.0	70	5.00	0	0	64.6
NFL Total	108	66	27	40.9	283	4.29	2	2	51.5

	Receiving				
Year Team	**Rec**	**Yds**	**Avg**	**TD**	**Fum**
1978 Hou	1	6	6.0	0	3
1979 Hou	3	44	14.7	1	1
1981 NO	29	458	15.8	1	1
1982 NO	0	0	—	0	1
1985 NO	3	61	20.3	1	0
1987 Phi	0	0	—	0	3
NFL Total	36	569	15.8	3	9

ED MERKLE Merkle, Edward L 5′10″, 215 **G-LB**
Col: Oklahoma State B: 7/3/1917, Windsor, MO
1944 Was: 10 G.

ELMER MERKOVSKY Merkovsky, Albert J 6′1″, 239 **T-G**
Col: Pittsburgh *HS:* Scott Twp. [North Braddock, PA] B: 4/13/1917, North Braddock, PA D: 6/28/1982, Long Beach, CA
1944 ChPt: 9 G. **1945** Pit: 10 G. **1946** Pit: 4 G. **Total:** 23 G.

ED MERLIN Merlin, Edward 5′10″, 210 **G**
Col: Vanderbilt *HS:* Riverside Mil. Acad. [Gainesville, GA]
B: 12/31/1916, Spartanburg, SC *Drafted:* 1938 Round 3 Bkn
1938 Bkn: 11 G. **1939** Bkn: 5 G. **Total:** 16 G.

JIM MERLO Merlo, James Louis 6′1″, 221 **LB**
Col: Fresno City Coll. CA (J.C.); Stanford *HS:* Sanger [CA]
B: 10/3/1951, Sanger, CA *Drafted:* 1973 Round 4 NO
1973 NO: 14 G; Int 3-25; 1 Fum. **1974** NO: 14 G. **1976** NO: 14 G; Int 4-142 2 TD; 12 Pt; 1 Fum. **1977** NO: 14 G; Int 1-57 **1** TD; 6 Pt. **1978** NO: 16 G. **1979** NO: 16 G. **Total:** 88 G; Int 8-224 3 TD; 18 Pt; 2 Fum.

MARK MERRILL Merrill, Mark Christopher 6′4″, 237 **LB**
Col: Minnesota *HS:* Kellogg [St. Paul, MN] B: 5/5/1955, St. Paul, MN
Drafted: 1978 Round 2 NYJ
1978 NYJ: 16 G. **1979** NYJ-ChiB: 15 G. NYJ: 6 G. ChiB: 9 G. **1981** Den: 15 G. **1982** Den-GB: 6 G. Den: 2 G. GB: 4 G. **1983** Buf: 12 G. **1984** Buf-LARd: 4 G. Buf: 2 G. LARd: 2 G. **Total:** 68 G.

CASEY MERRILL Merrill, Richard Casey 6′4″, 254 **DE-DT**
Col: California-Davis *HS:* Monte Vista [Danville, CA] B: 7/16/1957, Oakland, CA *Drafted:* 1979 Round 5 Cin
1979 GB: 13 G. **1980** GB: 16 G. **1981** GB: 16 G. **1982** GB: 9 G; 4 Sac. **1983** GB-NYG: 15 G; 3 Sac. GB: 5 G. NYG: 10 G; 3 Sac. **1984** NYG: 16 G; 8.5 Sac. **1985** NYG: 11 G; 3 Sac. **1986** NO: 1 G. **Total:** 97 G; 18.5 Sac.

WALT MERRILL Merrill, Walter 0 6′2″, 217 **T**
Col: Alabama *HS:* Andalusia [AL] B: 8/7/1917, Andalusia, AL
Deceased *Drafted:* 1940 Round 5 Bkn
1940 Bkn: 11 G. **1941** Bkn: 6 G. **1942** Bkn: 11 G. **Total:** 28 G.

SAM MERRIMAN Merriman, Samuel Wheeler 6′3″, 229 **LB**
Col: Idaho *HS:* Amphitheater [Tucson, AZ] B: 5/5/1961, Tucson, AZ
Drafted: 1983 Round 7 Sea
1983 Sea: 16 G. **1984** Sea: 16 G. **1985** Sea: 14 G; 6 Pt. **1986** Sea: 16 G; 2 Sac. **1987** Sea: 9 G. **Total:** 71 G; 6 Pt; 2 Sac.

DAVID MERRITT Merritt, David Lee 6′1″, 237 **LB**
Col: North Carolina State *HS:* Millbrook [Raleigh, NC] B: 9/8/1971, Raleigh, NC *Drafted:* 1993 Round 7 Mia
1993 Mia-Pho: 7 G. Mia: 4 G. Pho: 3 G. **1994** Ariz: 16 G. **1995** Ariz: 15 G. **Total:** 38 G.

JIM MERRITTS Merritts, James Clystis 6′3″, 255 **DE-NT**
Col: Connecticut; West Virginia *HS:* Hollidaysburg [PA] B: 3/22/1961, Roaring Springs, PA
1987 Ind: 1 G.

MIKE MERRIWEATHER Merriweather, Michael Lamar 6′2″, 230 **LB**
Col: U. of Pacific *HS:* Vallejo [CA] B: 11/26/1960, Albany, NY
Drafted: 1982 Round 3 Pit
1982 Pit: PR 1-3 3.0. **1983** Pit: 0.5 Sac. **1984** Pit: 15 Sac. **1985** Pit: 4 Sac. **1986** Pit: KR 1-27 27.0; 6 Sac. **1987** Pit: 5.5 Sac. **1989** Min: Scor **1** Saf; 3.5 Sac. **1990** Min: 1 Fum TD; 2.5 Sac. **1991** Min: 1 Sac. **1992** Min: 3 Sac. **Total:** PR 1-3 3.0; KR 1-27 27.0; Scor 1 Saf; 1 Fum TD; 41 Sac.

		Interceptions				Tot
Year Team	**G**	**Int**	**Yds**	**TD**	**Fum**	**TD**
1982 Pit	9	0	0	0	0	0
1983 Pit	16	3	55	1	0	1
1984 Pit	16	2	9	0	0	0
1985 Pit	16	2	36	**1**	1	1
1986 Pit	16	2	14	0	0	0
1987 Pit	12	2	26	0	0	0
1989 Min	15	3	29	1	0	1
1990 Min	16	3	108	0	0	1
1991 Min	16	1	22	1	0	1
1992 Min	16	0	0	0	0	0

1993 NYJ	1	0	0	0	0	0
NFL Total	149	18	299	4	1	5

JEFF MERROW Merrow, Jeffrey Colin 6′4″, 236 **DE-DT-LB**
Col: West Virginia *HS:* Firestone [Akron, OH] B: 7/12/1953, Akron, OH
Drafted: 1975 Round 11 Atl
1975 Atl: 12 G. **1976** Atl: 14 G. **1977** Atl: 14 G. **1978** Atl: 14 G. **1979** Atl: 3 G. **1980** Atl: 16 G. **1981** Atl: 11 G. **1982** Atl: 8 G; 2.5 Sac. **1983** Atl: 16 G; 3 Sac. **Total:** 108 G; 5.5 Sac.

SCOTT MERSEREAU Mersereau, Scott Robert 6′4″, 275 **DT-NT-DE**
Col: Southern Connecticut State *HS:* Riverside [Buffalo, NY]
B: 4/8/1965, Riverhead, NY *Drafted:* 1987 Round 5 LARm
1987 NYJ: 13 G; 1.5 Sac. **1988** NYJ: 16 G; 4.5 Sac. **1989** NYJ: 16 G; Int 1-4; 0.5 Sac. **1990** NYJ: 16 G; 4.5 Sac. **1991** NYJ: 13 G; Int 2-0; 2 Sac. **1992** NYJ: 15 G; 5 Sac. **1993** NYJ: 13 G; 1 Sac. **Total:** 102 G; Int 3-4; 19 Sac.

JIM MERTENS Mertens, James Frederick 6′3″, 240 **TE**
Col: Fairmont State *HS:* Fort Hill [Cumberland, MD] B: 5/25/1947, Cumberland, MD *Drafted:* 1969 Round 10 Mia
1969 Mia: 14 G; Rec 2-26 13.0; KR 2-1 0.5.

JERRY MERTENS Mertens, Jerome William 6′0″, 184 **DB**
Col: Drake *HS:* St. Catherine's [Racine, WI] B: 11/12/1934, Racine, WI
Drafted: 1958 Round 20 SF
1958 SF: 12 G; Int 2-16. **1959** SF: 12 G; Int 2-56 **1** TD; 6 Pt. **1960** SF: 12 G; Int 2-0. **1961** SF: 14 G. **1962** SF: 14 G; Int 2-0. **1964** SF: 14 G. **1965** SF: 13 G. **Total:** 91 G; Int 8-72 1 TD; 6 Pt.

BUS MERTES Mertes, Bernard James 6′0″, 201 **FB-HB-DB**
Col: Iowa *HS:* Albert G. Lane Tech [Chicago, IL] B: 10/6/1921, Chicago, IL
AAFC **1946** LA-A: Rec 5-61 12.2 1 TD; KR 2-35 17.5; Int 1-14. **1947** BalA: Rec 2-28 14.0. **1948** BalA: Rec 6-56 9.3; KR 1-15 15.0. **Total:** Rec 13-145 11.2 1 TD; KR 3-50 16.7; Int 1-14.

		Rushing				Tot
Year Team	**G**	**Att**	**Yds**	**Avg**	**TD**	**TD**
1946 LA-A	9	40	111	2.8	0	1
1947 BalA	14	95	321	3.4	2	2
1948 BalA	14	155	680	4.4	4	4
AAFC Total	37	290	1112	3.8	6	7

NFL **1945** ChiC: Rec 2-1 0.5; PR 1-7 7.0; KR 1-12 12.0. **1949** NYG: Rec 2-14 7.0. **Total:** Rec 4-15 3.8; PR 1-7 7.0; KR 1-12 12.0.

		Rushing				
Year Team	**G**	**Att**	**Yds**	**Avg**	**TD**	**Fum**
1945 ChiC	8	24	111	4.6	0	1
1949 NYG	8	16	46	2.9	0	3
NFL Total	16	40	157	3.9	0	4

CURT MERZ Merz, Curtis Carl 6′4″, 267 **OG-DE**
Col: Iowa *HS:* Jonathon Dayton Regional [Springfield, NJ]
B: 4/17/1938, Newark, NJ *Drafted:* 1960 Round 1 NYT
1962 DalT: 14 G. **1963** KC: 14 G. **1964** KC: 14 G. **1965** KC: 14 G. **1966** KC: 14 G. **1967** KC: 8 G. **1968** KC: 14 G. **Total:** 92 G.

DICK MESAK Mesak, Richard H 6′2″, 225 **T**
Col: St. Mary's (Cal.) *HS:* Mission [San Francisco, CA]; St. Mary's HS [Berkeley, CA] B: 3/1/1919, San Francisco, CA
1945 Det: 6 G.

MARK MESEROLL Meseroll, Mark Steven 6′5″, 270 **OT**
Col: Wesley; Middlesex Co. Coll. NJ (J.C.); Florida State
HS: Piscataway [NJ] B: 7/22/1955, Piscataway, NJ
1978 NO: 16 G; 3 Fum.

BRUCE MESNER Mesner, Bruce M 6′5″, 280 **NT**
Col: Maryland *HS:* Harrison [NY] B: 3/21/1964, New York, NY
Drafted: 1987 Round 8 Buf
1987 Buf: 11 G.

DALE MESSER Messer, Lyndy Dale 5′10″, 175 **HB-WR-DB**
Col: Fresno State *HS:* Lemoore [CA] B: 8/6/1937, Lenmoore, CA
Drafted: 1961 Round 4 SF
1961 SF: 4 G; Rush 3-13 4.3; Rec 3-33 11.0; PR 2-11 5.5; KR 3-36 12.0. **1962** SF: 13 G; Rec 3-30 10.0; PR 3-7 2.3; KR 4-112 28.0; Int 1-35; 2 Fum. **1963** SF: 14 G; PR 5-4 0.8; 1 Fum. **1964** SF: 6 G; Rec 4-72 18.0. **1965** SF: 9 G; Rec 2-41 20.5; KR 1-27 27.0. **Total:** 46 G; Rush 3-13 4.3; Rec 12-176 14.7; PR 10-22 2.2; KR 8-175 21.9; Int 1-35; 3 Fum.

MARK MESSNER Messner, Mark W 6′2″, 256 **LB**
Col: Michigan *HS:* Catholic Central [Redford, MI] B: 12/29/1965, Riverview, MI *Drafted:* 1989 Round 6 LARm
1989 LARm: 4 G.

MAX MESSNER Messner, Max Carlton 6′3″, 225 **LB**
Col: Cincinnati *HS:* Ashland [OH] B: 10/13/1938, Ashland, OH
D: 3/13/1996, Ashland, OH *Drafted:* 1960 Round 9 Det
1960 Det: 1 G; Int 1-26. **1961** Det: 14 G. **1962** Det: 14 G. **1963** Det: 14 G. **1964** NYG-Pit: 13 G. NYG: 6 G. Pit: 7 G. **1965** Pit: 14 G; Int 1-14. **Total:** 70 G; Int 2-40.

FRANK MESTNIK Mestnik, Frank Gerald 6′2″, 200 **FB**
Col: Marquette *HS:* Maple Heights [OH] B: 2/23/1938, Cleveland, OH
Drafted: 1960 Round 15 StL
1960 StL: Rec 3-24 8.0; KR 3-39 13.0. **1961** StL: Rec 12-29 2.4 1 TD; KR 2-27 13.5. **1963** GB: KR 1-0. **Total:** Rec 15-53 3.5 1 TD; KR 6-66 11.0.

		Rushing					Tot
Year Team	**G**	**Att**	**Yds**	**Avg**	**TD**	**Fum**	**TD**
1960 StL	9	104	429	4.1	3	3	3
1961 StL	13	95	334	3.5	1	6	2
1963 GB	11	1	4	4.0	0	0	0
NFL Total	33	200	767	3.8	4	9	5

ERIC METCALF Metcalf, Eric Quinn 5′10″, 188 **WR-RB**
Col: Texas *HS:* Bishop Dennis J. O'Connell [Arlington, VA]
B: 1/23/1968, Seattle, WA *Drafted:* 1989 Round 1 Cle
1989 Cle: Pass 2-1 50.0%, 32 16.00 1 TD. **1992** Cle: Pass 1-0. **1994** Cle: Pass 1-0. **1995** Atl: Pass 1-0. **Total:** Pass 5-1 20.0%, 32 6.40 1 TD.

		Rushing				Receiving			
Year Team	**G**	**Att**	**Yds**	**Avg**	**TD**	**Rec**	**Yds**	**Avg**	**TD**
1989 Cle	16	187	633	3.4	6	54	397	7.4	4
1990 Cle	16	80	248	3.1	1	57	452	7.9	1
1991 Cle	8	30	107	3.6	0	29	294	10.1	0
1992 Cle	16	73	301	4.1	1	47	614	13.1	5
1993 Cle	16	129	611	4.7	1	63	539	8.6	2
1994 Cle	16	93	329	3.5	2	47	436	9.3	3
1995 Atl	16	28	133	4.8	1	104	1189	11.4	8
1996 Atl	16	3	8	2.7	0	54	599	11.1	6
1997 SD	16	3	-5	-1.7	0	40	576	14.4	2
1998 Ariz	16	0	0	—	0	31	324	10.5	0
NFL Total	152	626	2365	3.8	12	526	5420	10.3	31

	Punt Returns				Kickoff Returns					Tot
Year Team	**Ret**	**Yds**	**Avg**	**TD**	**Ret**	**Yds**	**Avg**	**TD**	**Fum**	**TD**
1989 Cle	0	0	—	0	31	718	23.2	0	5	10
1990 Cle	0	0	—	0	**52**	**1052**	20.2	**2**	8	4
1991 Cle	12	100	8.3	0	23	351	15.3	0	1	0
1992 Cle	**44**	429	9.8	1	9	157	17.4	0	6	7
1993 Cle	36	464	12.9	**2**	15	318	21.2	0	4	5
1994 Cle	35	348	9.9	**2**	9	210	23.3	0	6	7
1995 Atl	39	383	9.8	**1**	12	278	23.2	0	4	10
1996 Atl	27	296	11.0	0	49	1034	21.1	0	3	6
1997 SD	45	489	10.9	**3**	16	355	22.2	0	4	5
1998 Ariz	43	295	6.9	0	57	1218	21.4	0	5	0
NFL Total	281	2804	10.0	**9**	273	5691	20.8	2	46	54

BO METCALF Metcalf, Isaac Scott 6′2″, 193 **DB**
Col: Baylor *HS:* Richfield [Waco, TX] B: 4/18/1961, Waco, TX
Drafted: 1983 Round 4 Pit
1984 Ind: 1 G.

TERRY METCALF Metcalf, Terrance Randolph 5′10″, 185 **RB-WR**
Col: Everett CC WA; Long Beach State *HS:* Franklin [Seattle, WA]
B: 9/24/1951, Seattle, WA *Drafted:* 1973 Round 3 StL
1974 StL: Pass 2-0. **1975** StL: Pass 2-1 50.0%, 51 25.50 1 TD. **1976** StL: Pass 1-0. **1977** StL: Pass 5-3 60.0%, 27 5.40 1 TD 1 Int. **Total:** Pass 10-4 40.0%, 78 7.80 2 TD 1 Int.

		Rushing				Receiving			
Year Team	**G**	**Att**	**Yds**	**Avg**	**TD**	**Rec**	**Yds**	**Avg**	**TD**
1973 StL	12	148	628	4.2	2	37	316	8.5	0
1974 StL	14	152	718	4.7	6	50	377	7.5	1
1975 StL	13	165	816	4.9	9	43	378	8.8	2
1976 StL	12	134	537	4.0	3	33	388	11.8	4
1977 StL	14	149	739	5.0	4	34	403	11.9	2
1981 Was	16	18	60	3.3	0	48	595	12.4	0
NFL Total	81	766	3498	4.6	24	245	2457	10.0	9

	Punt Returns				Kickoff Returns					Tot
Year Team	**Ret**	**Yds**	**Avg**	**TD**	**Ret**	**Yds**	**Avg**	**TD**	**Fum**	**TD**
1973 StL	0	0	—	0	4	124	31.0	0	9	2
1974 StL	26	340	13.1	0	20	623	**31.2**	**1**	**14**	8
1975 StL	23	285	12.4	1	35	960	27.4	**1**	8	13
1976 StL	17	188	11.1	0	16	325	20.3	0	**15**	7
1977 StL	14	108	7.7	0	32	772	24.1	0	10	6
1981 Was	4	15	3.8	0	14	283	20.2	0	6	0
NFL Total	84	936	11.1	1	121	3087	25.5	2	62	36

RUSS METHOD Method, Russell 5'10", 192 **WB-BB-FB-OE**
(Cuss) *Col:* No College *HS:* Denfeld [Duluth, MN] B: 6/27/1897, Duluth, MN D: 9/17/1971, Two Harbors, MN
1923 Dul: 7 G. **1924** Dul: 5 G; Rush 1 TD; 6 Pt. **1925** Dul: 3 G. **1926** Dul: 12 G; Int **1** TD; 6 Pt. **1927** Dul: 8 G; Rec 1 TD; 6 Pt. **1929** ChiC: 10 G.
Total: 45 G; Rush 1 TD; Rec 1 TD; Int 1 TD; Tot TD 3; 18 Pt.

PETE METZELAARS Metzelaars, Peter Henry 6'7", 254 **TE**
Col: Wabash *HS:* Central [Portage, MI] B: 5/24/1960, Three Rivers, MI
Drafted: 1982 Round 3 Sea
1983 Sea: KR 1-0. **1986** Buf: **1** Fum TD. **1996** Det: KR 1-1 1.0.
Total: KR 2-1 0.5; 1 Fum TD.

Year Team	G	Receiving Rec	Yds	Avg	TD	Fum	Tot TD
1982 Sea	9	15	152	10.1	0	2	0
1983 Sea	16	7	72	10.3	1	0	1
1984 Sea	9	5	80	16.0	0	1	0
1985 Buf	16	12	80	6.7	1	0	1
1986 Buf	16	49	485	9.9	3	2	4
1987 Buf	12	28	290	10.4	0	3	0
1988 Buf	16	33	438	13.3	1	0	1
1989 Buf	16	18	179	9.9	2	0	2
1990 Buf	16	10	60	6.0	1	1	1
1991 Buf	16	5	54	10.8	2	0	2
1992 Buf	16	30	298	9.9	6	0	6
1993 Buf	16	68	609	9.0	4	1	4
1994 Buf	16	49	428	8.7	5	0	5
1995 Car	14	20	171	8.6	3	0	3
1996 Det	15	17	146	8.6	0	0	0
1997 Det	16	17	144	8.5	0	0	0
NFL Total	235	383	3686	9.6	29	10	30

LOU METZGER Metzger, Louis Eugene 5'9", 170 **FB-WB**
Col: Georgetown *HS:* Loyola Acad. [Chicago, IL] B: 2/13/1904, Chicago, IL D: 5/25/1953, Evanston, IL
1926 Lou: 3 G.

KEVIN MEUTH Meuth, Kevin Karl 6'5", 270 **OT**
Col: Southwest Texas State *HS:* Needville [TX] B: 5/4/1964, Richmond, TX
1987 NYG: 3 G.

EDDIE MEYER Meyer, Clarence Edwin 6'2", 240 **OT**
Col: West Texas A&M *HS:* Borger [TX] B: 10/17/1936 *Drafted:* 1960 Round 1 NYT
1960 Buf: 9 G.

ERNIE MEYER Meyer, Ernest Henry 6'2", 200 **G**
(Puss; Egg) *Col:* Geneva *HS:* Borger [TX] B: 6/23/1904, West Bridgewater, PA D: 1/23/1979, Paoli, PA
1930 Port: 9 G.

FRED MEYER Meyer, Frederic D 6'2", 190 **OE-DE**
Col: Stanford *HS:* Classen [Oklahoma City, OK] B: 9/29/1919, Mount Sterling, IL D: 7/10/1996, Fort Morgan, AL *Drafted:* 1942 Round 12 Phi
1942 Phi: Rush 2-13 6.5; KR 1-14 14.0. **Total:** Rush 2-13 6.5; KR 1-14 14.0.

Year Team	G	Receiving Rec	Yds	Avg	TD
1942 Phi	10	16	324	20.3	1
1945 Phi	8	11	135	12.3	1
NFL Total	18	27	459	17.0	2

GIL MEYER Meyer, Gilbert P 6'2", 200 **OE-DE**
Col: Wake Forest *HS:* Baltimore City College [MD] B: 11/25/1920, Baltimore, MD D: 1/6/1995, Baltimore, MD
AAFC **1947** BalA: 13 G; Rec 1-3 3.0.

JIM MEYER Meyer, James David 6'5", 290 **OT**
Col: Illinois State *HS:* Brodhead [WI] B: 6/9/1963, Glenview, IL
1987 GB: 2 G.

DENNIS MEYER Meyer, John Dennis 5'11", 186 **DB**
Col: Arkansas State *HS:* Jefferson City [MO] B: 4/8/1950, Jefferson City, MO *Drafted:* 1972 Round 6 Pit
1973 Pit: 11 G; PR 18-80 4.4; 1 Fum.

JOHN MEYER Meyer, John Edwin 6'1", 225 **LB**
Col: Notre Dame *HS:* Brother Rice [Chicago, IL] B: 2/20/1942, Chicago, IL *Drafted:* 1965 Round 15 Buf
1966 Hou: 14 G.

RON MEYER Meyer, Ronald Allen 6'4", 205 **QB**
Col: South Dakota State *HS:* Wells [MN] B: 8/27/1944, Austin, MN
Drafted: 1966 Round 7 ChiB
1966 Pit: 4 G; Pass 19-7 36.8%, 59 3.11 1 Int; Rush 1-(-2) -2.0; 1 Fum.

JERRY MEYERS Meyers, Jerry Edward 6'4", 249 **DE-DT**
Col: Northern Illinois *HS:* Lake View [Chicago, IL] B: 2/21/1954, Chicago, IL *Drafted:* 1976 Round 15 ChiB
1976 ChiB: 12 G. **1977** ChiB: 13 G. **1978** ChiB: 16 G. **1979** ChiB: 6 G. **1980** KC: 2 G. **Total:** 49 G.

JOHN MEYERS Meyers, John Douglas 6'6", 276 **DT**
(Big John) *Col:* Washington *HS:* Columbia [Richland, WA]
B: 1/16/1940, Forest City, IA *Drafted:* 1962 Round 3 LARm
1962 Dal: 14 G. **1963** Dal: 14 G. **1964** Phi: 14 G. **1965** Phi: 14 G; Int 2-12. **1966** Phi: 14 G. **1967** Phi: 14 G. **Total:** 84 G; Int 2-12.

PAUL MEYERS Meyers, Paul Duncan 5'11", 170 **OE**
(Chief) *Col:* Wis.-Milwaukee; Wisconsin *HS:* East Division [Milwaukee, WI] B: 12/3/1894 D: 10/1970, Akron, OH
1921 NYG: 1 G. **1922** Roch: 1 G. **1923** Rac: 9 G; Rec 1 TD; 6 Pt.
Total: 11 G; Rec 1 TD; 6 Pt.

BOB MEYERS Meyers, Robert Ellis Jr. 6'2", 184 **HB**
Col: Pasadena City Coll. CA (J.C.); Stanford *HS:* Van Nuys [CA]
B: 10/12/1930, Los Angeles, CA D: 4/19/1993, Morro Bay, CA
Drafted: 1952 Round 16 SF
1952 SF: 1 G; Rush 1-2 2.0.

KLINKS MEYERS Meyers, Stanton Wade **BB**
Col: No College B: 10/23/1893, Indianapolis, IN D: 10/1964
1920 Ham: 3 G.

WAYNE MEYLAN Meylan, Wayne Alfred 6'0", 235 **LB**
Col: Nebraska *HS:* Central [Bay City, MI] B: 3/2/1946, Bay City, MI
D: 6/26/1987, Ludington, MI *Drafted:* 1968 Round 4 Cle
1968 Cle: 14 G. **1969** Cle: 13 G. **1970** Min: 2 G. **Total:** 29 G.

LARRY MIALIK Mialik, Lawrence George 6'2", 226 **TE**
Col: Wisconsin *HS:* Clifton [NJ] B: 5/15/1950, Passaic, NJ
Drafted: 1972 Round 12 Atl
1972 Atl: 14 G. **1973** Atl: 14 G; Rec 2-30 15.0. **1974** Atl: 14 G. **1976** SD: 7 G. **Total:** 49 G; Rec 2-30 15.0.

RICH MIANO Miano, Richard James 6'1", 200 **DB**
Col: Hawaii *HS:* Kaiser [Honolulu, HI] B: 9/3/1962, Newton, MA
Drafted: 1985 Round 6 NYJ
1988 NYJ: 0.5 Sac. **Total:** 0.5 Sac.

Year Team	G	Interceptions Int	Yds	TD
1985 NYJ	16	2	9	0
1986 NYJ	14	0	0	0
1987 NYJ	12	3	24	0
1988 NYJ	16	2	0	0
1989 NYJ	2	0	0	0
1991 Phi	16	3	30	0
1992 Phi	16	1	39	0
1993 Phi	16	4	26	0
1994 Phi	16	0	0	0
1995 Atl	11	0	0	0
NFL Total	135	15	128	0

PHIL MICECH Micech, Philip John 6'5", 265 **DE**
Col: Wis.-Platteville B: 8/11/1961, Milwaukee, WI
1987 Min: 3 G.

BILL MICHAEL Michael, Paul William 6'2", 240 **OG**
Col: Ohio State *HS:* Fairfield [Hamilton, OH] B: 12/24/1935
Drafted: 1957 Round 2 Pit
1957 Pit: 3 G.

RICH MICHAEL Michael, Richard John 6'3", 242 **OT**
Col: Ohio State *HS:* Fairfield [OH] B: 11/15/1938, Hamilton, OH
1960 Hou: 10 G. **1961** Hou: 14 G. **1962** Hou: 14 G. **1963** Hou: 14 G; KR 1-3 3.0. **1965** Hou: 14 G. **1966** Hou: 14 G. **Total:** 80 G; KR 1-3 3.0.

AL MICHAELS Michaels, Alton Court 6'0", 190 **TB**
Col: Heidelberg; Ohio State *HS:* Tiffin [OH] B: 4/1/1900
D: 10/21/1972, Gadsden, AL
1923 Akr: 7 G; Scor 3, 1 FG. **1924** Akr: 7 G; Rush 1 TD; 6 Pt. **1925** Cle: 14 G; Pass 3 TD. **Total:** 28 G; Pass 3 TD; Rush 1 TD; Scor 9, 1 FG.

EDDIE MICHAELS Michaels, Edward Joseph 5'11", 205 **G**
(Whitey AKA Edward Joesph Mikolajewski) *Col:* Villanova
HS: Salesianum [Wilmington, DE] B: 6/11/1915, Wilmington, DE
D: 1/21/1976, Wilmington, DE *Drafted:* 1936 Round 2 ChiB
1936 ChiB: 12 G. **1937** Was: 11 G. **1943** PhPt: 10 G. **1944** Phi: 10 G. **1945** Phi: 9 G. **1946** Phi: 10 G. **Total:** 62 G.

LOU MICHAELS Michaels, Louis Andrew 6'2", 243 **DE-K**
Col: Kentucky *HS:* Swoyersville [PA];Staunton Mil.Acad. [Front Royal, VA] B: 9/28/1935, Swoyersville, PA *Drafted:* 1958 Round 1 LARm
1958 LARm: Int 2-6 1 TD. **1960** LARm: KR 1-15 15.0. **1961** Pit: Int 1-30. **1962** Pit: KR 2-15 7.5; Scor 1 1XP. **1963** Pit: Int 1-0. **1965** Bal: Scor **1** Saf.
Total: KR 3-30 10.0; Int 4-36 1 TD; Scor 1 Saf, 1 1XP.

Year Team	G	Scoring Pts	FG	FGA	FG%	XK	XKA	XK%	Fum
1958 LARm	12	0	0	0	—	0	0	—	0
1959 LARm	12	36	8	17	47.1	12	14	85.7	0
1960 LARm	11	7	2	3	66.7	1	1	100.0	0
1961 Pit	14	72	15	26	57.7	27	29	93.1	0
1962 Pit	14	110	**26**	**42**	61.9	31	32	96.9	1
1963 Pit	14	95	21	**41**	51.2	32	35	91.4	0
1964 Bal	14	104	17	35	48.6	**53**	**54**	98.1	0
1965 Bal	14	101	17	28	60.7	48	48	100.0	0
1966 Bal	14	98	21	39	53.8	35	36	97.2	0
1967 Bal	14	106	20	37	54.1	46	**48**	95.8	0
1968 Bal	14	102	18	28	64.3	48	50	96.0	0
1969 Bal	14	75	14	31	45.2	33	34	97.1	0
1971 GB	10	43	8	14	57.1	19	20	95.0	0
NFL Total	171	955	187	341	54.8	385	401	96.0	1

WALT MICHAELS Michaels, Walter Edward 6'0", 231 **LB**
Col: Washington & Lee *HS:* Swoyersville [PA] B: 10/16/1929, Swoyersville, PA *Drafted:* 1951 Round 7 Cle
1951 GB: KR 5-86 17.2; Scor 0-1 FG. **1952** Cle: KR 1-16 16.0. **1953** Cle: KR 2-40 20.0. **1955** Cle: KR 3-45 15.0. **Total:** KR 11-187 17.0; Scor 12, 0-1 FG.

Year Team	G	Interceptions Int	Yds	TD	Fum
1951 GB	12	0	0	0	0
1952 Cle	11	4	26	0	1
1953 Cle	12	1	34	**1**	1
1954 Cle	12	1	20	0	0
1955 Cle	12	1	25	1	0
1956 Cle	12	0	0	0	0
1957 Cle	12	1	10	0	0
1958 Cle	12	0	0	0	0
1959 Cle	12	1	7	0	0
1960 Cle	11	0	0	0	0
1961 Cle	14	2	17	0	0
1963 NYJ	1	0	0	0	0
NFL Total	133	11	139	2	2

ART MICHALIK Michalik, Arthur E 6'2", 229 **LB-OG**
(Automatic Art) *Col:* St. Ambrose *HS:* Weber [Chicago, IL] B: 1/31/1930 *Drafted:* 1951 Round 17 SF
1953 SF: 12 G. **1954** SF: 2 G. **1955** Pit: 12 G; Scor 12, 1-12 8.3% FG, 9-15 60.0% XK. **1956** Pit: 12 G; Scor 0-1 FG. **Total:** 38 G; Scor 12, 1-13 7.7% FG, 9-15 60.0% XK.

MIKE MICHALSKE Michalske, August Mike 6'0", 210 **G-T-LB-BB**
Col: Penn State *HS:* West Tech [Cleveland, OH] B: 4/24/1903, Cleveland, OH D: 10/26/1983, Green Bay, WI *HOF:* 1964
1927 NYY: 14 G. **1928** NYY: 13 G. **1929** GB: 13 G. **1930** GB: 14 G. **1931** GB: 13 G; Int **1** TD; 6 Pt. **1932** GB: 13 G; Scor 1 Saf; **1** Fum TD; 8 Pt. **1933** GB: 13 G. **1934** GB: 13 G. **1935** GB: 10 G. **1937** GB: 6 G. **Total:** 122 G; Int 1 TD; Scor 1 Saf; 1 Fum TD; Tot TD 2; 14 Pt.

MIKE MICHEL Michel, Michael Walter 5'10", 177 **P-K**
Col: Ventura Coll. CA (J.C.); Stanford *HS:* Buena [CA] B: 8/4/1954, Ventura, CA *Drafted:* 1977 Round 5 Mia
1977 Mia: Rush 1-(-2) -2.0; Scor 0-1 XK. **1978** Phi: Rush 1-0; Scor 9, 9-12 75.0% XK. **Total:** Rush 2-(-2) -1.0; Scor 9, 9-13 69.2% XK.

Year Team	G	Punting Punts	Yds	Avg	Fum
1977 Mia	13	35	1338	38.2	0
1978 Phi	10	58	2078	35.8	1
NFL Total	23	93	3416	36.7	1

TOM MICHEL Michel, William Thomas 6'0", 215 **HB**
Col: East Carolina *HS:* Wakefield [Arlington, VA] B: 12/7/1940, Oakland, CA *Drafted:* 1964 Round 14 Min
1964 Min: Rec 1-14 14.0; KR 8-192 24.0.

Year Team	G	Rushing Att	Yds	Avg	TD	Fum
1964 Min	11	39	129	3.3	0	3

JOHN MICHELS Michels, John Joseph 5'11", 200 **OG**
Col: Tennessee *HS:* West Catholic [Philadelphia, PA] B: 2/15/1931, Philadelphia, PA *Drafted:* 1953 Round 25 Phi
1953 Phi: 11 G.

JOHN MICHELS Michels, John Spiegel 6'7", 300 **OT**
Col: USC *HS:* La Jolla [CA] B: 3/19/1973, La Jolla, CA *Drafted:* 1996 Round 1 GB
1996 GB: 15 G. **1997** GB: 9 G. **Total:** 24 G.

BOBBY MICHO Micho, Robert Anthony 6'3", 236 **TE-FB**
Col: Texas *HS:* L.C. Anderson [Austin, TX] B: 3/7/1962, Omaha, NE *Drafted:* 1984 Round 10 Den
1987 Den: Rush 4-8 2.0. **Total:** Rush 4-8 2.0.

Year Team	G	Receiving Rec	Yds	Avg	TD	Fum
1984 SD	6	0	0	—	0	0
1986 Den	5	0	0	—	0	0
1987 Den	15	25	242	9.7	2	1
NFL Total	26	25	242	9.7	2	1

MIKE MICKA Micka, Michael 6'0", 188 **DB-HB-FB-LB**
Col: Colgate *HS:* Clairton [PA] B: 6/18/1921, Clairton, PA D: 1/4/1989, Gaithersburg, MD *Drafted:* 1944 Round 1 Was
1944 Was: Rec 2-16 8.0; Int 1-5; Punt 2-35 17.5. **1945** Was-Bos: Rec 2-74 37.0; KR 2-31 15.5; Int 1-0. Was: Rec 2-74 37.0; KR 1-10 10.0. Bos: KR 1-21 21.0; Int 1-0. **1946** Bos: Int 2-40 **1** TD. **1947** Bos: Rec 2-11 5.5; Int 2-46. **1948** Bos: Int 3-9. **Total:** Rec 6-101 16.8; KR 2-31 15.5; Int 9-100 1 TD; Punt 2-35 17.5.

Year Team	G	Rushing Att	Yds	Avg	TD
1944 Was	10	25	94	3.8	0
1945 Was-Bos	9	19	62	3.3	0
1945 Was	6	18	57	3.2	0
1945 Bos	3	1	5	5.0	0
1946 Bos	11	20	76	3.8	0
1947 Bos	12	1	-4	-4.0	0
1948 Bos	12	4	3	0.8	0
NFL Total	54	69	231	3.3	0

JEFF MICKEL Mickel, Arthur Jeffery 6'6", 300 **OT**
Col: Eastern Washington *HS:* Woodway [Edmonds, WA] B: 8/4/1966, Limestone, ME *Drafted:* 1989 Round 6 Min
1990 LARm: 1 G.

DARREN MICKELL Mickell, Darren 6'4", 285 **DE**
Col: Florida *HS:* Miami Senior [FL] B: 8/3/1970, Miami, FL *Drafted:* 1992 Supplemental Round 2 KC
1992 KC: 1 G. **1993** KC: 16 G; 1 Sac. **1994** KC: 16 G; 7 Sac. **1995** KC: 12 G; 5.5 Sac. **1996** NO: 12 G; 3 Sac. **1997** NO: 14 G; 3.5 Sac. **Total:** 71 G; 20 Sac.

ARNOLD MICKENS Mickens, Arnold Lee Jr. 5'11", 220 **RB**
Col: Indiana; Butler *HS:* Broad Ripple [Indianapolis, IN] B: 10/12/1972, Indianapolis, IN
1996 Ind: 3 G.

TERRY MICKENS Mickens, Terry KaJuan 6'0", 201 **WR**
(T-Mick) *Col:* Florida A&M *HS:* Leon [Tallahassee, FL] B: 2/21/1971, Tallahassee, FL *Drafted:* 1994 Round 5 GB
1995 GB: KR 1-0. **1997** GB: KR 1-0. **Total:** KR 2-0.

Year Team	G	Receiving Rec	Yds	Avg	TD	Fum
1994 GB	12	4	31	7.8	0	0
1995 GB	16	3	50	16.7	0	0
1996 GB	8	18	161	8.9	2	1
1997 GB	11	1	2	2.0	1	0
1998 Oak	16	24	346	14.4	1	0
NFL Total	63	50	590	11.8	4	1

RAY MICKENS Mickens, William Ray 5'8", 184 **DB**
Col: Texas A&M *HS:* Andress [El Paso, TX] B: 1/4/1973, Frankfurt, Germany *Drafted:* 1996 Round 3 NYJ
1996 NYJ: 15 G. **1997** NYJ: 16 G; Int 4-2; 6 Pt; 1 Sac. **1998** NYJ: 16 G; Int 3-10. **Total:** 47 G; Int 7-12; 6 Pt; 1 Sac.

JOEY MICKEY Mickey, Joey 6'5", 274 **TE**
Col: Oklahoma *HS:* Millwood [Oklahoma City, OK] B: 11/29/1970, Oklahoma City, OK *Drafted:* 1993 Round 7 Phi
1993 Dal: 5 G.

JOE MICKLES Mickles, Joseph Nathan 5'10", 221 **RB**
Col: Mississippi *HS:* Gardendale [AL] B: 12/25/1965, Birmingham, AL *Drafted:* 1989 Round 12 Was
1989 Was: 9 G. **1990** SD: 1 G. **Total:** 10 G.

DAVE MIDDENDORF Middendorf, David Warren 6'3", 260 **OG**
Col: Washington State *HS:* Ingraham [Seattle, WA] B: 11/23/1945, Seattle, WA *Drafted:* 1968 Round 5 Cin
1968 Cin: 14 G. **1969** Cin: 12 G. **1970** NYJ: 8 G. **Total:** 34 G.

OREN MIDDLEBROOK Middlebrook, Oren James 6'2", 185 **WR**
Col: Itawamba CC MS; Arkansas State *HS:* Aberdeen [MS] B: 1/23/1953, Aberdeen, MS *Drafted:* 1977 Round 10 Den
1978 Phi: 16 G.

DAVE MIDDLETON Middleton, David Hinton 6'1", 194 **OE-HB-FL**
(Hoppy) *Col:* Auburn *HS:* Ensley [Birmingham, AL] B: 11/23/1933, Birmingham, AL *Drafted:* 1955 Round 1 Det
1955 Det: KR 11-188 17.1. **1958** Det: KR 1-15 15.0. **1959** Det: PR 3-30 10.0. **Total:** PR 3-30 10.0; KR 12-203 16.9.

		Rushing				Receiving				Tot
Year Team	**G**	**Att**	**Yds**	**Avg**	**TD**	**Rec**	**Yds**	**Avg**	**TD**	**TD**
1955 Det	12	59	201	3.4	2	44	663	15.1	3	5
1956 Det	12	3	9	3.0	0	39	606	15.5	5	5
1957 Det	8	0	0	—	0	18	294	16.3	2	2
1958 Det	12	2	1	0.5	0	29	506	17.4	3	3
1959 Det	12	0	0	—	0	18	402	22.3	2	2
1960 Det	7	3	-1	-0.3	0	5	51	10.2	0	0
1961 Min	12	0	0	—	0	30	444	14.8	2	2
NFL Total	75	67	210	3.1	2	183	2966	16.2	17	19

FRANK MIDDLETON Middleton, Frank Jr. 6′3″, 340 **OG**
Col: Fort Scott CC KS; Arizona *HS:* West Brook [Beaumont, TX]
B: 10/25/1974, Beaumont, TX *Drafted:* 1997 Round 3 TB
1997 TB: 15 G. **1998** TB: 16 G. **Total:** 31 G.

FRANK MIDDLETON Middleton, Franklin Jr. 5′11″, 205 **RB**
Col: Florida A&M *HS:* Sol C. Johnson [Savannah, GA] B: 10/28/1960, Savannah, GA
1984 Ind: KR 1-11 11.0. **1985** Ind: KR 1-20 20.0. **Total:** KR 2-31 15.5.

		Rushing				Receiving					Tot
Year Team	**G**	**Att**	**Yds**	**Avg**	**TD**	**Rec**	**Yds**	**Avg**	**TD**	**Fum**	**TD**
1984 Ind	16	92	275	3.0	1	15	112	7.5	1	2	2
1985 Ind	5	13	35	2.7	1	5	54	10.8	0	0	1
1987 SD	3	28	74	2.6	1	8	43	5.4	0	0	1
NFL Total	24	133	384	2.9	3	28	209	7.5	1	2	4

KELVIN MIDDLETON Middleton, Kelvin Bernard 6′0″, 186 **DB**
Col: Wichita State *HS:* Southwest [Macon, GA] B: 9/8/1961, Macon, GA
1987 Pit: 2 G.

RICK MIDDLETON Middleton, Richard Ray 6′2″, 228 **LB**
Col: Ohio State *HS:* Rutherford B. Hayes [Delaware, OH]
B: 11/28/1951, Columbus, OH *Drafted:* 1974 Round 1 NO
1974 NO: 14 G; KR 2-18 9.0. **1975** NO: 14 G; Int 1-0. **1976** SD: 10 G; KR 1-21 21.0. **1977** SD: 14 G; KR 1-20 20.0. **1978** SD: 12 G; KR 1-5 5.0; Int 1-2. **Total:** 64 G; KR 5-64 12.8; Int 2-2.

RON MIDDLETON Middleton, Ronald Allen 6′2″, 262 **TE**
Col: Auburn *HS:* Escambia Co. [Altmore, AL] B: 7/17/1965, Atmore, AL
1990 Was: KR 1-7 7.0. **Total:** KR 1-7 7.0.

		Receiving			
Year Team	**G**	**Rec**	**Yds**	**Avg**	**TD**
1986 Atl	16	6	31	5.2	0
1987 Atl	12	1	1	1.0	0
1988 Was	2	0	0	—	0
1989 Cle	9	1	5	5.0	1
1990 Was	16	0	0	—	0
1991 Was	12	3	25	8.3	0
1992 Was	16	7	50	7.1	0
1993 Was	16	24	154	6.4	2
1994 LARm	16	0	0	—	0
1995 SD	3	0	0	—	0
NFL Total	118	42	266	6.3	3

TERDELL MIDDLETON Middleton, Terdell 6′0″, 198 **RB**
Col: Memphis *HS:* South Side [Memphis, TN] B: 4/8/1955, Memphis, TN *Drafted:* 1977 Round 3 StL
1977 GB: KR 4-141 35.3 1 TD. **1978** GB: KR 1-22 22.0. **1981** GB: KR 6-100 16.7. **1983** TB: KR 1-10 10.0. **Total:** KR 12-273 22.8 1 TD.

		Rushing				Receiving					Tot
Year Team	**G**	**Att**	**Yds**	**Avg**	**TD**	**Rec**	**Yds**	**Avg**	**TD**	**Fum**	**TD**
1977 GB	14	35	97	2.8	0	1	27	27.0	0	4	1
1978 GB	16	284	1116	3.9	11	34	332	9.8	1	8	12
1979 GB	14	131	495	3.8	2	18	155	8.6	1	3	3
1980 GB	13	56	155	2.8	2	13	59	4.5	0	1	2
1981 GB	14	53	181	3.4	0	12	86	7.2	1	2	1
1982 TB	2	0	0	—	0	0	0	—	0	0	0
1983 TB	7	2	4	2.0	0	0	0	—	0	0	0
NFL Total	80	561	2048	3.7	15	78	659	8.4	3	18	19

LOU MIDLER Midler, Louis Thomas 6′1″, 223 **G-T**
Col: Minnesota *HS:* Washington [St. Paul, MN] B: 7/21/1915, St. Paul, MN D: 8/29/1992, Marine on St.Croix, MN *Drafted:* 1938 Round 3 Pit
1939 Pit: 11 G. **1940** GB: 7 G. **Total:** 18 G.

SAUL MIELZINER Mielziner, Saul Robert 6′1″, 245 **C-T-G-LB**
Col: Carnegie Mellon *HS:* Glenville [Cleveland, OH]; Kiski School [Saltsburg, PA] B: 6/1/1905, Cleveland, OH D: 10/13/1985, Levittown, PA
1929 NYG: 12 G. **1930** NYG: 16 G. **1931** Bkn: 9 G. **1932** Bkn: 11 G. **1933** Bkn: 7 G. **1934** Bkn: 5 G. **Total:** 60 G.

ED MIESZKOWSKI Mieszkowski, Edward Thomas 6′2″, 220 **T**
Col: Notre Dame *HS:* Tilden [Chicago, IL] B: 10/14/1925, Chicago, IL
AAFC **1946** BknA: 13 G. **1947** BknA: 10 G. **Total:** 23 G.

PAUL MIGLIAZZO Migliazzo, Paul Salvatore 6′1″, 228 **LB**
Col: Oklahoma *HS:* Rockhurst [Kansas City, MO] B: 3/11/1964, Kansas City, MO *Drafted:* 1987 Round 8 ChiB
1987 ChiB: 3 G.

LOU MIHAJLOVICH Mihajlovich, Louis 5′11″, 175 **DE**
Col: Indiana *HS:* James Whitcomb Riley [South Bend, IN]
B: 2/19/1925, Detroit, MI D: 12/11/1994, Scottsdale, AZ
AAFC **1948** LA-A: 9 G; Rec 4-42 10.5.

NFL **1954** GB: 3 G.

JOE MIHAL Mihal, Joseph C 6′3″, 240 **T**
Col: Purdue *HS:* Emerson [Gary, IN] B: 4/2/1916, Homestead, PA
D: 9/18/1979, Dallas, TX *Drafted:* 1939 Round 3 Phi
AAFC **1946** LA-A: 12 G. **1947** ChiA: 1 G. **Total:** 13 G.

NFL **1940** ChiB: 11 G. **1941** ChiB: 9 G. **Total:** 20 G.

BOB MIKE Mike, Robert Melvin 6′1″, 220 **T**
Col: Florida A&M; UCLA *HS:* Steubenville [OH] B: 10/29/1923
AAFC **1948** SF-A: 4 G. **1949** SF-A: 12 G. **Total:** 16 G.

NFL **1948** SF-A: 14 G.

STEVE MIKE-MAYER Mike-Mayer, Istvan 6′0″, 180 **K**
Col: Maryland *HS:* in [Bologna, Italy] B: 9/8/1947, Budapest, Hungary
Drafted: 1975 Round 3 SF

		Scoring						
Year Team	**G**	**Pts**	**FG**	**FGA**	**FG%**	**XK**	**XKA**	**XK%**
1975 SF	14	69	14	28	50.0	27	31	87.1
1976 SF	14	74	16	28	57.1	26	30	86.7
1977 Det	14	43	8	19	42.1	19	21	90.5
1978 NO	9	36	6	13	46.2	18	18	100.0
1979 Bal	13	61	11	20	55.0	28	29	96.6
1980 Bal	16	79	12	23	52.2	43	46	93.5
NFL Total	80	362	67	131	51.1	161	175	92.0

NICK MIKE-MAYER Mike-Mayer, Nicholas 5′8″, 186 **K**
Col: Temple *HS:* Passaic [NJ] B: 3/1/1950, Bologna, Italy
Drafted: 1973 Round 10 Atl
1977 Atl-Phi: Punt 1-23 23.0. Atl: Punt 1-23 23.0. **1979** Buf: Rush 1-4 4.0. **1981** Buf: Pass 1-0. **Total:** Pass 1-0; Rush 1-4 4.0; Punt 1-23 23.0.

		Scoring						
Year Team	**G**	**Pts**	**FG**	**FGA**	**FG%**	**XK**	**XKA**	**XK%**
1973 Atl	14	112	26	38	68.4	34	34	100.0
1974 Atl	14	39	9	16	56.3	12	12	100.0
1975 Atl	14	42	4	10	40.0	30	33	90.9
1976 Atl	14	50	10	21	47.6	20	20	100.0
1977 Atl-Phi	10	44	10	22	45.5	14	14	100.0
1977 Atl	7	28	7	19	36.8	7	7	100.0
1977 Phi	3	16	3	3	100.0	7	7	100.0
1978 Phi	12	45	8	17	47.1	21	22	95.5
1979 Buf	13	77	20	29	69.0	17	18	94.4
1980 Buf	16	76	13	23	56.5	37	39	94.9
1981 Buf	16	79	14	24	58.3	37	37	100.0
1982 Buf	2	7	1	4	25.0	4	5	80.0
NFL Total	125	571	115	204	56.4	226	234	96.6

RUSS MIKESKA Mikeska, Russell E 6′3″, 225 **TE**
Col: Texas A&M *HS:* Temple [TX] B: 9/10/1955, Temple, TX
1979 Atl: 16 G; Rec 1-14 14.0. **1980** Atl: 16 G; Rec 1-4 4.0. **1981** Atl: 16 G; Rec 2-16 8.0. **1982** Atl: 5 G; Rec 2-19 9.5. **Total:** 53 G; Rec 6-53 8.8.

ANDY MIKETA Miketa, Andrew John 6′2″, 210 **C**
Col: North Carolina *HS:* Ambridge [PA] B: 11/1/1929, Girard, OH
1954 Det: 12 G. **1955** Det: 12 G. **Total:** 24 G.

BILL MIKLICH Miklich, William John 6′0″, 208 **LB-BB-C**
Col: Idaho *HS:* Central [West Allis, WI] B: 4/3/1919, Greenwood, WI
1947 NYG: 7 G; Rec 1-(-5) -5.0; KR 1-3 3.0. **1948** NYG-Det: 11 G. NYG: 4 G. Det: 7 G. **Total:** 18 G; Rec 1-(-5) -5.0; KR 1-3 3.0.

RON MIKOLAJCZYK Mikolajczyk, Ronald 6′3″, 275 **OT-OG**
Col: Marshall; Tampa *HS:* Passaic [NJ] B: 6/2/1950, Passaic, NJ
Drafted: 1973 Round 5 Oak
1976 NYG: 9 G. **1977** NYG: 14 G. **1978** NYG: 8 G. **1979** NYG: 1 G. **Total:** 32 G.

PETE MIKOLAJEWSKI Mikolajewski, Peter James 6′1″, 210 **QB**
Col: Kent State *HS:* Piqua Catholic [OH] B: 2/26/1943, Portsmouth, VA
1969 SD: 1 G; 1 Fum.

DOUG MIKOLAS Mikolas, Douglas Adolph 6′1″, 270 **NT**
Col: Portland State *HS:* Scio [OR] B: 6/7/1962, Manteca, CA
1987 SF: 8 G. **1988** SF-Hou: 2 G; 1 Sac. SF: 1 G. Hou: 1 G; 1 Sac. **Total:** 10 G; 1 Sac.

TOM MIKULA Mikula, Thomas Michael 5′10″, 200 **FB-LB**
Col: William & Mary *HS:* Johnstown Central [PA] B: 9/26/1926, Johnstown, PA
AAFC **1948** BknA: 1 G.

MIKE MIKULAK Mikulak, Michael Nicholas 6′1″, 210 **FB-LB-BB-WB**
(Iron Mike) *Col:* Oregon *HS:* Edison [Minneapolis, MN] B: 12/2/1912, Minneapolis, MN
1934 ChiC: Pass 10-2 20.0%, 21 2.10 2 Int; Rec 5-47 9.4. **1935** ChiC: Rec 8-93 11.6. **1936** ChiC: Rec 6-62 10.3. **Total:** Pass 10-2 20.0%, 21 2.10 2 Int; Rec 19-202 10.6.

		Rushing			
Year Team	G	Att	Yds	Avg	TD
1934 ChiC	11	74	308	4.2	3
1935 ChiC	11	68	82	1.2	1
1936 ChiC	12	24	56	2.3	0
NFL Total	34	166	446	2.7	4

BARNES MILAM Milam, Israel Barnes 6′2″, 190 **G-T**
Col: Austin *HS:* Sherman [TX];Denison HS [TX] B: 3/4/1906, Hagerman, TX D: 12/18/1979, Austin, TX
1934 Phi: 2 G.

JOE MILAM Milam, Joseph Baker 5′11″, 180 **G-E-T**
Col: Phillips *HS:* Cherokee [OK] B: 3/13/1899, Amorita, OK D: 11/25/1971, Victoria, TX
1925 KC: 7 G.

DON MILAN Milan, Donald Lee 6′3″, 200 **QB**
Col: Cal Poly-S.L.O. *HS:* Santa Ynez [CA] B: 1/12/1949, Glendale, CA
1975 GB: 7 G; Pass 32-15 46.9%, 181 5.66 1 TD 1 Int; Rush 4-41 10.3; 1 Fum.

ARCHIE MILANO Milano, Archie 6′0″, 197 **OE-DE**
Col: St. Francis (Pa.) B: 5/26/1918 D: 8/12/1991
1945 Det: 1 G.

SCOTT MILANOVICH Milanovich, Scott Stewart 6′3″, 220 **QB**
Col: Maryland *HS:* Butler [PA] B: 1/25/1973, Butler, PA
1996 TB: 1 G; Pass 3-2 66.7%, 9 3.00.

DARRYL MILBURN Milburn, Darryl Wayne 6′3″, 260 **DE**
Col: Grambling State *HS:* Baton Rouge [LA] B: 10/25/1968, Baton Rouge, LA *Drafted:* 1991 Round 9 Det
1991 Det: 2 G.

GLYN MILBURN Milburn, Glyn Curt 5′8″, 177 **RB-WR**
Col: Oklahoma; Stanford *HS:* Santa Monica [CA] B: 2/19/1971, Santa Monica, CA *Drafted:* 1993 Round 2 Den

		Rushing				Receiving			
Year Team	G	Att	Yds	Avg	TD	Rec	Yds	Avg	TD
1993 Den	16	52	231	4.4	0	38	300	7.9	3
1994 Den	16	58	201	3.5	1	77	549	7.1	3
1995 Den	16	49	266	5.4	0	22	191	8.7	0
1996 Det	16	0	0	—	0	0	0	—	0
1997 Det	16	0	0	—	0	5	77	15.4	0
1998 ChiB	16	4	8	2.0	0	4	37	9.3	0
NFL Total	96	163	706	4.3	1	146	1154	7.9	6

	Punt Returns				Kickoff Returns					Tot
Year Team	Ret	Yds	Avg	TD	Ret	Yds	Avg	TD	Fum	TD
1993 Den	40	425	10.6	0	12	188	15.7	0	9	3
1994 Den	41	379	9.2	0	37	793	21.4	0	4	4
1995 Den	31	354	11.4	0	47	1269	27.0	0	2	0
1996 Det	34	284	8.4	0	64	1627	25.4	0	0	0
1997 Det	47	433	9.2	0	55	1315	23.9	0	3	0
1998 ChiB	25	291	11.6	1	**62**	**1550**	25.0	**2**	1	3
NFL Total	218	2166	9.9	1	277	6742	24.3	2	19	10

JACK MILDREN Mildren, Larry Jack Jr. 6′1″, 200 **DB**
Col: Oklahoma *HS:* Cooper [Abilene, TX] B: 10/16/1949, Kingsville, TX *Drafted:* 1972 Round 2 Bal
1972 Bal: 14 G; Pass 1-0; Rush 3-8 2.7; KR 1-1 1.0; 1 Fum. **1973** Bal: 14 G; Rush 2-14 7.0; 1 Fum. **1974** NE: 14 G; Int 3-51. **Total:** 42 G; Pass 1-0; Rush 5-22 4.4; KR 1-1 1.0; Int 3-51; 2 Fum.

EDDIE MILES Miles, Eddie 6′1″, 233 **LB**
Col: Minnesota *HS:* Miami Springs [FL] B: 9/13/1968, Miami, FL *Drafted:* 1990 Round 10 Pit
1990 Pit: 1 G.

LEO MILES Miles, Leo Fidelis 6′0″, 200 **DB**
Col: Virginia State *HS:* Cardozo [Washington, DC] B: 5/21/1931, Washington, DC D: 9/21/1995, Washington, DC
1953 NYG: 3 G.

BUCK MILES Miles, Mark Robert 195 **FB**
Col: Washington & Lee *HS:* Erasmus Hall [Brooklyn, NY] B: 12/1888, Brooklyn, NY Deceased
1920 Akr: 1 G.

OSTELL MILES Miles, Ostell Shawn 6′0″, 236 **RB**
Col: Pasadena City Coll. CA (J.C.); Houston *HS:* George Washington [Denver, CO] B: 8/6/1970, Denver, CO *Drafted:* 1992 Round 9 Cin
1992 Cin: KR 8-128 16.0. **1993** Cin: Rec 6-89 14.8; KR 4-65 16.3. **Total:** Rec 6-89 14.8; KR 12-193 16.1.

		Rushing			
Year Team	G	Att	Yds	Avg	TD
1992 Cin	11	8	22	2.8	0
1993 Cin	15	22	56	2.5	1
NFL Total	26	30	78	2.6	1

ITULA MILI Mili, Itula 6′4″, 265 **TE**
Col: Brigham Young *HS:* Kahuku [HI] B: 4/20/1973, Kahuku, HI *Drafted:* 1997 Round 6 Sea
1998 Sea: 7 G; Rec 1-20 20.0.

JOE MILINICHIK Milinichik, Joseph Michael 6′5″, 290 **OG-OT**
Col: North Carolina State *HS:* Emmaus [PA] B: 3/30/1963, Allentown, PA *Drafted:* 1986 Round 3 Det
1987 Det: 11 G. **1988** Det: 15 G. **1989** Det: 15 G. **1990** LARm: 8 G. **1991** LARm: 5 G. **1992** LARm: 16 G. **1993** SD: 10 G. **1994** SD: 16 G. **Total:** 96 G.

JOHN MILKS Milks, John 6′0″, 222 **LB**
Col: San Diego State *HS:* Excelsior [Norwalk, CA] B: 10/17/1943
1966 SD: 3 G; Int 1-13.

BRYAN MILLARD Millard, Bryan James 6′5″, 282 **OG-OT**
Col: Texas *HS:* Dumas [TX] B: 12/2/1960, Sioux City, IA
1984 Sea: 14 G. **1985** Sea: 16 G. **1986** Sea: 16 G. **1987** Sea: 12 G; Rec 1-(-5) -5.0. **1988** Sea: 15 G. **1989** Sea: 16 G. **1990** Sea: 16 G. **1991** Sea: 16 G. **Total:** 121 G; Rec 1-(-5) -5.0.

KEITH MILLARD Millard, Keith Joseph 6′6″, 260 **DT-DE**
Col: Washington State *HS:* Foothill [Pleasanton, CA] B: 3/18/1962, Pleasanton, CA *Drafted:* 1984 Round 1 Min
1985 Min: 16 G; 11 Sac. **1986** Min: 15 G; Int 1-17; 10.5 Sac. **1987** Min: 9 G; 3.5 Sac. **1988** Min: 15 G; 8 Sac. **1989** Min: 16 G; Int 1-48; 1 Fum TD; 6 Pt; 18 Sac. **1990** Min: 4 G; 2 Sac. **1992** Sea-GB: 4 G; 1 Sac. Sea: 2 G; 1 Sac. GB: 2 G. **1993** Phi: 14 G; 4 Sac. **Total:** 93 G; Int 2-65; 1 Fum TD; 6 Pt; 58.0 Sac.

HUGH MILLEN Millen, Hugh B 6′5″, 216 **QB**
Col: Santa Rosa JC CA; Washington *HS:* Roosevelt [Seattle, WA] B: 11/22/1963, Des Moines, IA *Drafted:* 1986 Round 3 LARm

		Passing							
Year Team	G	Att	Comp	Comp%	Yds	YPA	TD	Int	Rating
1987 LARm	1	1	1	100.0	0	0.00	0	0	79.2
1988 Atl	3	31	17	54.8	215	6.94	0	2	49.8
1989 Atl	5	50	31	62.0	432	8.64	1	2	79.8
1990 Atl	3	63	34	54.0	427	6.78	1	0	80.6
1991 NE	13	409	246	60.1	3073	7.51	9	18	72.5
1992 NE	7	203	124	61.1	1203	5.93	8	10	70.3
1994 Den	5	131	81	61.8	893	6.82	2	3	77.6
1995 Den	3	40	26	65.0	197	4.93	1	0	85.1
NFL Total	40	928	560	60.3	6440	6.94	22	35	73.5

	Rushing				
Year Team	Att	Yds	Avg	TD	Fum
1987 LARm	0	0	—	0	1
1988 Atl	1	7	7.0	0	1
1989 Atl	1	0	0.0	0	2
1990 Atl	7	-12	-1.7	0	3
1991 NE	31	92	3.0	1	10
1992 NE	17	108	6.4	0	8
1994 Den	5	57	11.4	0	2
1995 Den	3	8	2.7	0	1
NFL Total	65	260	4.0	1	28

MATT MILLEN Millen, Matthew George 6′2″, 250 **LB**
Col: Penn State *HS:* Whitehall [PA] B: 3/12/1958, Hokendauqua, PA *Drafted:* 1980 Round 2 Oak
1980 Oak: 16 G; Int 2-17. **1981** Oak: 16 G. **1982** LARd: 9 G; KR 1-13 13.0; Int 3-77; 2.5 Sac. **1983** LARd: 16 G; KR 2-19 9.5; Int 1-14; 2 Sac. **1984** LARd: 16 G; 2.5 Sac. **1985** LARd: 16 G; 1 Sac. **1986** LARd: 16 G; KR 3-40 13.3; 1 Sac. **1987** LARd: 12 G; KR 1-0; Int 1-6; 1 Fum; 1 Sac. **1988** LARd: 16 G; 1 Sac. **1989** SF: 15 G; Int 1-10. **1990** SF: 16 G; Int 1-8. **1991** Was: 16 G. **Total:** 180 G; KR 7-72 10.3; Int 9-132; 1 Fum; 11 Sac.

ALAN MILLER Miller, Alan Roger 6′0″, 219 **FB**
Col: Boston College *HS:* Milford [CT] B: 6/19/1937, Mount Kisco, NY *Drafted:* 1959 Round 19 Phi
1961 Oak: KR 6-66 11.0. **1962** Oak: KR 6-45 7.5. **Total:** KR 12-111 9.3.

		Rushing				Receiving					Tot
Year Team	G	Att	Yds	Avg	TD	Rec	Yds	Avg	TD	Fum	TD
1960 Bos	14	101	416	4.1	2	29	284	9.8	2	6	4
1961 Oak	14	85	255	3.0	3	36	315	8.8	4	2	7
1962 Oak	14	65	182	2.8	1	20	259	13.0	0	4	1

1963 Oak	14	62	270	4.4	3	34	404	11.9	2	0	5
1965 Oak	14	73	272	3.7	1	21	208	9.9	3	2	4
NFL Total	70	386	1395	3.6	10	140	1470	10.5	11	14	21

AL MILLER Miller, Alfred Henry 5′11″, 210 **HB-FB-BB**
(Truck) *Col:* Harvard *HS:* Boston English [MA]; Worcester Acad. [MA]
B: 3/17/1904, Boston, MA D: 12/20/1967, Detroit, MI
1929 Bost: 7 G.

AL MILLER Miller, Allen 6′0″, 228 **LB**
Col: Ohio U. *HS:* Canal Winchester [OH]; Groveport HS [OH]
B: 4/18/1940, Fostoria, OH *Drafted:* 1962 Round 17 Was
1962 Was: 14 G; KR 1-0; 1 Fum. **1963** Was: 11 G. **Total:** 25 G; KR 1-0; 1 Fum.

BLAKE MILLER Miller, Blake Randolph 6′1″, 282 **C**
Col: Louisiana State *HS:* Alexandria [LA] B: 8/23/1968, Alexandria, LA
1992 Det: 14 G.

BRETT MILLER Miller, Brett Kolste 6′7″, 293 **OT**
Col: Glendale CC CA; Iowa *HS:* Glendale [CA] B: 10/2/1958, Lynwood, CA *Drafted:* 1983 Round 5 Atl
1983 Atl: 16 G. **1984** Atl: 15 G. **1985** Atl: 12 G. **1986** Atl: 8 G. **1987** Atl: 2 G. **1988** Atl: 15 G. **1989** SD: 14 G. **1990** NYJ: 16 G. **1991** NYJ: 15 G. **1992** NYJ: 5 G. **Total:** 118 G.

BRONZELL MILLER Miller, Bronzell LaJames 6′4″, 247 **DE**
Col: Eastern Arizona Coll. (J.C.); Utah *HS:* Federal Way [WA]
B: 10/12/1971, Federal Way, WA *Drafted:* 1995 Round 7 StL
1995 Jac: 3 G.

CALVIN MILLER Miller, Calvin 6′2″, 260 **NT-DT-DE**
Col: Mississippi Gulf Coast CC; Oklahoma State *HS:* Harrison Central [Gulfport, MS] B: 8/31/1953, Gulfport, MS
1979 NYG: 11 G. **1980** Atl: 2 G. **Total:** 13 G.

CHUCKIE MILLER Miller, Charles Elliot 5′8″, 180 **DB**
Col: UCLA *HS:* Long Beach Polytechnic [CA] B: 5/9/1965, Anniston, AL *Drafted:* 1987 Round 8 Ind
1988 Ind: 3 G.

OOKIE MILLER Miller, Charles Lewis 6′0″, 209 **C-LB-G**
Col: Purdue *HS:* Marion [IN] B: 11/12/1909, Marion, IN
1932 ChiB: 13 G. **1933** ChiB: 13 G. **1934** ChiB: 12 G. **1935** ChiB: 11 G. **1936** ChiB: 11 G; **1** Fum TD; 6 Pt. **1937** Cle: 11 G. **1938** GB: 11 G. **Total:** 82 G; 1 Fum TD; 6 Pt.

CHRIS MILLER Miller, Christopher James 6′2″, 204 **QB**
Col: Oregon *HS:* Henry D. Sheldon [Eugene, OR] B: 8/9/1965, Pomona, CA *Drafted:* 1987 Round 1 Atl
1989 Atl: Scor 3, 1-1 100.0% FG. **Total:** Scor 15, 1-1 100.0% FG.

		Passing							
Year Team	**G**	**Att**	**Comp**	**Comp%**	**Yds**	**YPA**	**TD**	**Int**	**Rating**
1987 Atl	3	92	39	42.4	552	6.00	1	9	26.4
1988 Atl	13	351	184	52.4	2133	6.08	11	12	67.3
1989 Atl	15	526	280	53.2	3459	6.58	16	10	76.1
1990 Atl	12	388	222	57.2	2735	7.05	17	14	78.7
1991 Atl	15	413	220	53.3	3103	7.51	26	18	80.6
1992 Atl	8	253	152	60.1	1739	6.87	15	**6**	90.7
1993 Atl	3	66	32	48.5	345	5.23	1	3	50.4
1994 LARm	13	317	173	54.6	2104	6.64	16	14	73.6
1995 StL	13	405	232	57.3	2623	6.48	18	15	76.2
NFL Total	95	2811	1534	54.6	18793	6.69	121	101	74.8

	Rushing				
Year Team	**Att**	**Yds**	**Avg**	**TD**	**Fum**
1987 Atl	4	21	5.3	0	0
1988 Atl	31	138	4.5	1	2
1989 Atl	10	20	2.0	0	13
1990 Atl	26	99	3.8	1	11
1991 Atl	32	229	7.2	0	5
1992 Atl	23	89	3.9	0	6
1993 Atl	2	11	5.5	0	2
1994 LARm	20	100	5.0	0	7
1995 StL	22	67	3.0	0	4
NFL Total	170	774	4.6	2	50

CLAY MILLER Miller, Clay 6′4″, 275 **OT-OG**
Col: Michigan *HS:* Norman [OK] B: 8/27/1963, Columbus, OH
Drafted: 1986 Round 12 TB
1987 Hou: 3 G.

CLEO MILLER Miller, Cleophus Jr. 5′11″, 207 **RB**
Col: Arkansas-Pine Bluff *HS:* Merrill [Pine Bluff, AR] B: 9/5/1952, Gould, AR

		Rushing				Receiving			
Year Team	**G**	**Att**	**Yds**	**Avg**	**TD**	**Rec**	**Yds**	**Avg**	**TD**
1974 KC	14	40	186	4.7	0	14	149	10.6	0
1975 KC-Cle	11	13	23	1.8	1	2	20	10.0	0
1975 KC	6	7	20	2.9	0	0	0	—	0
1975 Cle	5	6	3	0.5	1	2	20	10.0	0
1976 Cle	12	153	613	4.0	4	16	145	9.1	0
1977 Cle	14	163	756	4.6	4	41	291	7.1	1
1978 Cle	15	89	336	3.8	1	20	152	7.6	0
1979 Cle	16	39	213	5.5	1	26	251	9.7	0
1980 Cle	16	28	139	5.0	3	2	8	4.0	0
1981 Cle	12	52	165	3.2	2	16	139	8.7	0
1982 Cle	5	16	61	3.8	0	3	20	6.7	0
NFL Total	115	593	2492	4.2	16	140	1175	8.4	1

	Kickoff Returns					Tot
Year Team	**Ret**	**Yds**	**Avg**	**TD**	**Fum**	**TD**
1974 KC	14	310	22.1	0	4	0
1975 KC-Cle	12	241	20.1	0	2	1
1975 KC	9	171	19.0	0	1	0
1975 Cle	3	70	23.3	0	1	1
1976 Cle	1	23	23.0	0	8	4
1977 Cle	0	0	—	0	5	5
1978 Cle	1	15	15.0	0	2	1
1979 Cle	1	14	14.0	0	1	1
1980 Cle	2	22	11.0	0	2	3
1981 Cle	3	35	11.7	0	0	2
1982 Cle	0	0	—	0	1	0
NFL Total	34	660	19.4	0	25	17

COREY MILLER Miller, Corey James 6′2″, 252 **LB**
Col: South Carolina *HS:* Central [Pageland, SC] B: 10/25/1968, Pageland, SC *Drafted:* 1991 Round 6 NYG
1991 NYG: 16 G; 2.5 Sac. **1992** NYG: 16 G; Int 2-10; 2 Sac. **1993** NYG: 16 G; Int 2-18; 1 Fum; 6.5 Sac. **1994** NYG: 15 G; Int 2-6. **1995** NYG: 14 G. **1996** NYG: 14 G; 2 Sac. **1997** NYG: 14 G; 1 Sac. **Total:** 105 G; Int 6-34; 1 Fum; 14 Sac.

DANNY MILLER Miller, Daniel Scott 5′10″, 172 **K**
Col: Miami (Fla.) *HS:* Clewiston [FL] B: 12/30/1960, West Palm Beach, FL *Drafted:* 1982 Round 11 Was
1982 NE-Bal: 5 G; Scor 27, 6-11 54.5% FG, 9-10 90.0% XK. NE: 2 G; Scor 10, 2-3 66.7% FG, 4-5 80.0% XK. Bal: 3 G; Scor 17, 4-8 50.0% FG, 5-5 100.0% XK. **Total:** 5 G; Scor 27, 6-11 54.5% FG, 9-10 90.0% XK.

DARRIN MILLER Miller, Darrin James 6′1″, 227 **LB**
Col: Tennessee *HS:* Hunterdon Central [Flemington, NJ] B: 3/24/1965, Flemington, NJ
1988 Sea: 16 G; Int 1-7. **1989** Sea: 16 G. **Total:** 32 G; Int 1-7.

DON MILLER Miller, Don Jack 6′2″, 195 **HB**
Col: Southern Methodist *HS:* Opelousas [LA] B: 5/24/1932, Houston, TX *Drafted:* 1954 Round 7 Cle
1954 GB-Phi: 3 G. GB: 1 G. Phi: 2 G. **Total:** 3 G.

DONALD MILLER Miller, Donald 6′2″, 223 **LB**
Col: Coll. of Eastern Utah (J.C.); Utah State; Idaho State *HS:* Fenger [Chicago, IL] B: 4/9/1964, Chicago, IL
1990 Sea: 7 G.

DON MILLER Miller, Donald Charles 5′11″, 170 **HB**
Col: Notre Dame *HS:* Defiance [OH] B: 3/29/1902, Defiance, OH
D: 7/28/1979, Cleveland, OH
1925 Prov: 1 G.

DOUG MILLER Miller, Doug Alan 6′3″, 237 **LB**
Col: South Dakota State *HS:* Brown [Sturgis, SD] B: 10/29/1969, Cheyenne, WY D: 7/21/1998, Dotsero, CO *Drafted:* 1993 Round 7 SD
1993 SD: 8 G. **1994** SD: 15 G. **Total:** 23 G.

EDDIE MILLER Miller, Edward 5′10″, 165 **QB-DB**
(Muscles) *Col:* New Mexico Mil. Inst. (J.C.); New Mexico State B: 1918
1939 NYG: Punt 5-183 36.6. **1940** NYG: Int 2-5; Punt 19-731 38.5. **Total:** Int 2-5; Punt 24-914 38.1.

		Passing							
Year Team	**G**	**Att**	**Comp**	**Comp%**	**Yds**	**YPA**	**TD**	**Int**	**Rating**
1939 NYG	8	23	13	56.5	195	8.48	2	2	77.3
1940 NYG	8	73	35	47.9	505	6.92	4	7	49.5
NFL Total	16	96	48	50.0	700	7.29	6	9	55.9

	Rushing			
Year Team	**Att**	**Yds**	**Avg**	**TD**
1939 NYG	30	99	3.3	1
1940 NYG	65	206	3.2	1
NFL Total	95	305	3.2	2

EDDIE MILLER Miller, Edward Jr. 6′0″, 185 **WR**
Col: South Carolina *HS:* Southwest De Kalb [Decatur, GA]
B: 6/20/1969, Tumison, GA *Drafted:* 1992 Round 9 Ind
1992 Ind: 14 G. **1993** Ind: 1 G. **Total:** 15 G.

CLARK MILLER Miller, Franklin Clark 6′5″, 245 **DE**
Col: Merritt Coll. CA (J.C.); Utah State *HS:* Oakland [CA] B: 8/11/1938, Oakland, CA *Drafted:* 1961 Round 5 SF
1962 SF: 10 G. **1963** SF: 14 G. **1964** SF: 14 G. **1965** SF: 14 G; **1** Fum TD; 6 Pt. **1966** SF: 14 G. **1967** SF: 13 G; Int 1-3. **1968** SF: 10 G. **1969** Was: 2 G. **1970** LARm: 6 G. **Total:** 97 G; Int 1-3; 1 Fum TD; 6 Pt.

FRED MILLER Miller, Fred Junior 6′7″, 315 **OT**
Col: Baylor *HS:* Eisenhower [Houston, TX] B: 2/6/1973, Aldine, TX *Drafted:* 1996 Round 5 StL
1996 StL: 14 G. **1997** StL: 15 G. **1998** StL: 15 G. **Total:** 44 G.

FRED MILLER Miller, Frederick David 6′3″, 250 **DT**
Col: Louisiana State *HS:* Homer [LA] B: 8/8/1940, Homer, LA *Drafted:* 1962 Round 7 Bal
1963 Bal: 13 G. **1964** Bal: 14 G. **1965** Bal: 12 G. **1966** Bal: 14 G. **1967** Bal: 14 G. **1968** Bal: 14 G. **1969** Bal: 14 G. **1970** Bal: 12 G. **1971** Bal: 14 G. **1972** Bal: 12 G. **Total:** 133 G.

FRED MILLER Miller, Frederick Louis 6′3″, 225 **OT**
Col: Santa Monica Coll. CA (J.C.); U. of Pacific *HS:* Venice [Los Angeles, CA] B: 8/30/1931, San Francisco, CA
1955 Was: 12 G.

HAL MILLER Miller, Hal Maurice 6′4″, 230 **OT**
Col: Georgia Tech *HS:* Kingsport [TN] B: 2/4/1930, Kingsport, TN *Drafted:* 1953 Round 5 SF
1953 SF: 12 G.

JIM MILLER Miller, Henry F 5′11″, 195 **HB**
Col: West Virginia Wesleyan *HS:* Sharpsburg [PA] B: 2/19/1908, Sharpsburg, PA D: 2/10/1965, Pittsburg, PA
1930 Bkn: 4 G; Rec 1 TD; 6 Pt.

HEINIE MILLER Miller, Henry John 5′10″, 185 **E-G**
Col: Pennsylvania *HS:* Mercersburg Acad. [PA]; Haverford School [PA] B: 1/1/1893, Williamsport, PA D: 6/9/1964, Longport, NJ
1920 Buf: 11 G. **1921** Buf: 7 G; Rec **3** TD; 18 Pt. **1925** Mil: 1 G. **Total:** 19 G; Rec 3 TD; 18 Pt.

JIM MILLER Miller, James Donald 6′2″, 226 **QB**
Col: Michigan State *HS:* Kettering [Waterford, MI] B: 2/9/1971, Grosse Pointe, MI *Drafted:* 1994 Round 6 Pit
1995 Pit: Rush 1-2 2.0. **1996** Pit: Rush 2-(-4) -2.0. **Total:** Rush 3-(-2) -0.7.

		Passing								
Year Team	**G**	**Att**	**Comp**	**Comp%**	**Yds**	**YPA**	**TD**	**Int**	**Rating**	**Fum**
1995 Pit	3	56	32	57.1	397	7.09	2	5	53.9	1
1996 Pit	2	25	13	52.0	123	4.92	0	0	65.9	1
NFL Total	5	81	45	55.6	520	6.42	2	5	57.6	2

JIM MILLER Miller, James Gordon 5′11″, 183 **P**
Col: Mississippi *HS:* Ripley [MS] B: 7/5/1957, Ripley, MS *Drafted:* 1980 Round 3 SF
1980 SF: Rush 2-(-12) -6.0. **Total:** Rush 2-(-12) -6.0.

		Punting		
Year Team	**G**	**Punts**	**Yds**	**Avg**
1980 SF	16	77	3152	40.9
1981 SF	16	93	3858	41.5
1982 SF	9	44	1676	38.1
1983 Dal	2	5	178	35.6
1984 Dal	1	5	173	34.6
1987 NYG	1	10	345	34.5
NFL Total	45	234	9382	40.1

JIM MILLER Miller, James Robert 6′3″, 240 **OG**
Col: Iowa *HS:* Regina [Iowa City, IA] B: 7/24/1949, Iowa City, IA
1971 Atl: 14 G. **1972** Atl: 2 G. **1974** Atl: 14 G. **Total:** 30 G.

JAMIR MILLER Miller, Jamir Malik 6′5″, 252 **LB**
Col: UCLA *HS:* El Cerrito [CA] B: 11/19/1973, Philadelphia, PA *Drafted:* 1994 Round 1 Ariz
1994 Ariz: 16 G; 3 Sac. **1995** Ariz: 10 G; 1 Fum; 1 Sac. **1996** Ariz: 16 G; **1** Fum TD; 6 Pt; 1 Sac. **1997** Ariz: 16 G; 5.5 Sac. **1998** Ariz: 16 G; 3 Sac. **Total:** 74 G; 1 Fum TD; 6 Pt; 1 Fum; 13.5 Sac.

BING MILLER Miller, John Edward 6′1″, 188 **T**
Col: New York U. *HS:* Blodgett Voc. [Syracuse, NY]; Dean Acad. [Franklin, MA] B: 12/6/1903, Syracuse, NY D: 10/12/1964, Bronx, NY
1929 SI: 10 G. **1930** SI: 10 G. **1931** SI: 9 G. **Total:** 29 G.

JOHN MILLER Miller, John Frank 6′2″, 218 **LB**
Col: Mississippi State *HS:* Cedar Shoals [Athens, GA] B: 9/22/1960, Oberlin, OH
1987 GB: 1 G.

JOHNNY MILLER Miller, John Joseph 6′5″, 253 **OT-DT-DE**
Col: Boston College *HS:* Keith Acad. [Lowell, MA] B: 2/1/1934, Lowell, MA *Drafted:* 1955 Round 9 Was
1956 Was: 12 G; Scor **1** Saf; 2 Pt. **1958** Was: 12 G; KR 1-15 15.0. **1959** Was: 12 G. **1960** GB: 5 G. **Total:** 41 G; KR 1-15 15.0; Scor 1 Saf; 2 Pt.

JOHN MILLER Miller, John Milton 6′0″, 188 **FB**
Col: Notre Dame *HS:* Clinton [IL] B: 3/31/1893 Deceased
1921 Day: 1 G.

DUTCH MILLER Miller, John Robert 6′1″, 212 **C**
Col: Wittenberg *HS:* Dover [OH] B: 2/23/1906, Dover, OH D: 7/6/1987, Roswell, NM
1931 Port: 1 G.

JOHN MILLER Miller, John Thomas 6′1″, 195 **DB**
Col: Michigan State *HS:* Harrison [Farmington Hills, MI] B: 6/22/1966, Detroit, MI
1989 Det: 9 G. **1990** Det: 4 G. **Total:** 13 G.

JOHNNY MILLER Miller, Johnny 6′1″, 247 **OG**
Col: Livingstone B: 2/3/1954, Ellerbe, NC *Drafted:* 1976 Round 14 SF
1977 SF: 6 G.

JOSH MILLER Miller, Joshua Harris 6′3″, 215 **P**
Col: Scottsdale CC AZ; Arizona *HS:* East Brunswick [NJ] B: 7/14/1970, Queens, NY
1997 Pit: Rush 1-(-7) -7.0. **Total:** Rush 1-(-7) -7.0.

		Punting		
Year Team	**G**	**Punts**	**Yds**	**Avg**
1996 Pit	12	55	2256	41.0
1997 Pit	16	64	2729	42.6
1998 Pit	16	81	3530	43.6
NFL Total	44	200	8515	42.6

KEVIN MILLER Miller, Kevin Von 5′10″, 180 **WR**
Col: Louisville *HS:* Weir [Weirton, WV] B: 3/21/1955, Weirton, WV
1978 Min: Rec 1-35 35.0 1 TD. **Total:** Rec 1-35 35.0 1 TD.

		Punt Returns				Kickoff Returns				
Year Team	**G**	**Ret**	**Yds**	**Avg**	**TD**	**Ret**	**Yds**	**Avg**	**TD**	**Fum**
1978 Min	16	48	239	5.0	0	40	854	21.4	0	3
1979 Min	3	18	85	4.7	0	0	0	—	0	1
1980 Min	4	0	0	—	0	0	0	—	0	0
NFL Total	23	66	324	4.9	0	40	854	21.4	0	4

LARRY MILLER Miller, Lawrence 6′4″, 220 **QB**
Col: Northern Iowa B: 2/8/1962, Chicago, IL
1987 Min: 2 G; Pass 6-1 16.7%, 2 0.33 1 Int; Rush 1-(-1) -1.0.

ANTHONY MILLER Miller, Lawrence Anthony 5′11″, 190 **WR**
Col: Pasadena City Coll. CA (J.C.); San Diego State; Tennessee *HS:* John Muir [Pasadena, CA] B: 4/15/1965, Los Angeles, CA *Drafted:* 1988 Round 1 SD
1988 SD: Rush 7-45 6.4. **1989** SD: Rush 4-21 5.3. **1990** SD: Rush 3-13 4.3. **1992** SD: Rush 1-(-1) -1.0; 1 Fum TD. **1993** SD: Rush 1-0. **1994** Den: Rush 1-3 3.0; Scor 1 2XP. **1995** Den: Rush 1-5 5.0. **1996** Den: Rush 3-39 13.0 1 TD. **1997** Dal: Rush 1-6 6.0. **Total:** Rush 22-131 6.0 1 TD; Scor 1 2XP; 1 Fum TD.

		Receiving				Kickoff Returns					Tot
Year Team	**G**	**Rec**	**Yds**	**Avg**	**TD**	**Ret**	**Yds**	**Avg**	**TD**	**Fum**	**TD**
1988 SD	16	36	526	14.6	3	25	648	25.9	**1**	1	4
1989 SD	16	75	1252	16.7	10	21	533	25.4	**1**	1	11
1990 SD	16	63	933	14.8	7	1	13	13.0	0	2	7
1991 SD	13	44	649	14.8	3	0	0	—	0	1	3
1992 SD	16	72	1060	14.7	7	1	33	33.0	0	0	8
1993 SD	16	84	1162	13.8	7	2	42	21.0	0	0	7
1994 Den	16	60	1107	18.5	5	0	0	—	0	0	5
1995 Den	14	59	1079	18.3	14	0	0	—	0	1	14
1996 Den	16	56	735	13.1	3	0	0	—	0	0	4
1997 Dal	16	46	645	14.0	4	0	0	—	0	1	4
NFL Total	155	595	9148	15.4	63	50	1269	25.4	2	7	67

PAT MILLER Miller, Leon Patrick 6′1″, 206 **LB**
Col: Florida *HS:* A. Crawford Mosley [Lynn Haven, FL] B: 6/24/1964, Panama City, FL *Drafted:* 1986 Round 5 SF
1987 SD: 1 G. **1988** SD: 8 G; 1 Sac. **Total:** 9 G; 1 Sac.

LES MILLER Miller, Leslie Paul 6′7″, 292 **DT**
Col: Kansas State; Fort Hays State *HS:* Arkansas City [KS] B: 3/1/1965, Arkansas City, KS
1987 SD: 9 G; **1** Fum TD; 6 Pt; 3 Sac. **1988** SD: 13 G. **1989** SD: 14 G; 2.5 Sac. **1990** SD: 14 G; **2** Fum TD; 12 Pt; 1 Sac. **1991** NO: 16 G; 1 Sac. **1992** NO: 16 G; 1 Sac. **1993** NO: 13 G; 2.5 Sac. **1994** NO-SD: 12 G; 0.5 Sac. NO: 8 G. SD: 4 G; 0.5 Sac. **1996** Car: 15 G; 3 Sac. **1997** Car: 16 G; 5.5 Sac. **1998** Car: 14 G; 1 Fum. **Total:** 152 G; 3 Fum TD; 18 Pt; 1 Fum; 20 Sac.

MARK MILLER Miller, Mark Allen 6′2″, 210 **QB**
Col: Colorado State; Mesa *HS:* Grand Junction [CO] B: 11/6/1962, Grand Junction, CO
1987 Buf: 1 G; Pass 3-1 33.3%, 9 3.00 1 Int.

MARK MILLER Miller, Mark George 6'2", 176 QB
Col: Bowling Green State *HS:* Canton South [OH] B: 8/13/1956, Canton, OH *Drafted:* 1978 Round 3 Cle
1978 Cle: 8 G; Pass 39-13 33.3%, 212 5.44 1 TD 4 Int; Rush 7-63 9.0 1 TD; 6 Pt; 1 Fum. **1979** Cle: 2 G; Pass 8-2 25.0%, 31 3.88 1 Int; Rush 1-(-2) -2.0. **Total:** 10 G; Pass 47-15 31.9%, 243 5.17 1 TD 5 Int; Rush 8-61 7.6 1 TD; 6 Pt; 1 Fum.

MATT MILLER Miller, Matthew Peter 6'6", 270 OT-OG
Col: Colorado *HS:* Durango [CO] B: 7/30/1956, Durango, CO *Drafted:* 1979 Round 4 Cle
1979 Cle: 16 G; KR 1-0. **1981** Cle: 16 G; KR 1-6 6.0. **1982** Cle: 9 G. **Total:** 41 G; KR 2-6 3.0.

MIKE MILLER Miller, Michael Duane 5'11", 182 WR
Col: Tennessee *HS:* Northern [Flint, MI] B: 12/29/1959, Flint, MI *Drafted:* 1983 Round 4 GB
1983 NYG: 13 G; Rush 1-2 2.0; Rec 7-170 24.3; KR 2-31 15.5. **1985** NO: 3 G. **Total:** 16 G; Rush 1-2 2.0; Rec 7-170 24.3; KR 2-31 15.5.

DUB MILLER Miller, Milford William 6'0", 218 G-T
Col: Chadron State *HS:* Crawford [NE] B: 9/28/1911, Litchfield, NE D: 4/8/1981, Chadron, NE
1935 ChiB: 11 G. **1936** ChiC: 4 G. **1937** ChiC: 8 G. **Total:** 23 G.

NATE MILLER Miller, Nathan Udell 6'3", 310 OG
Col: Louisiana State *HS:* Central East [Tuscaloosa, AL] B: 10/8/1971, Tuscaloosa, AL
1997 Atl: 13 G.

NICK MILLER Miller, Nicholas Galen 6'2", 238 LB
Col: Arkansas *HS:* Brazoswood [Freeport, TX] B: 10/26/1963, Brunswick, ME *Drafted:* 1986 Round 5 Cle
1987 Cle: 9 G.

PAUL MILLER Miller, Paul William 5'11", 180 HB
Col: South Dakota State *HS:* Platte [SD] B: 1/23/1913, Platte, SD D: 6/2/1994, Tucson, AZ
1936 GB: Pass 1-0, 1 Int; Rec 8-113 14.1 2 TD. **1937** GB: Rec 6-66 11.0 1 TD. **1938** GB: Rec 4-36 9.0. **Total:** Pass 1-0, 1 Int; Rec 18-215 11.9 3 TD.

		Rushing				Tot
Year Team	**G**	**Att**	**Yds**	**Avg**	**TD**	**TD**
1936 GB	12	52	227	4.4	1	3
1937 GB	10	71	262	3.7	0	1
1938 GB	10	20	48	2.4	0	0
NFL Total	32	143	537	3.8	1	4

PAUL MILLER Miller, Paul William Jr. 6'2", 226 DE
Col: Louisiana State *HS:* Istrouma [Baton Rouge, LA] B: 11/8/1930
1954 LARm: 12 G; Int 1-0. **1955** LARm: 12 G. **1956** LARm: 12 G. **1957** LARm: 12 G. **1960** DalT: 14 G. **1961** DalT: 14 G; PR 1-0; 1 Fum. **1962** SD: 2 G. **Total:** 78 G; PR 1-0; Int 1-0; 1 Fum.

RALPH MILLER Miller, Ralph 6'3", 260 OG
Col: California Lutheran; Alabama State B: 8/13/1948, Hartford, AL
1972 Hou: 6 G. **1973** Hou: 1 G. **Total:** 7 G.

PRIMO MILLER Miller, Ralph Edward 6'2", 220 T
Col: Rice B: 1916, San Antonio, TX Deceased
1937 Cle: 11 G; 6 Pt. **1938** Cle: 8 G. **Total:** 19 G; 6 Pt.

CANDY MILLER Miller, Raymond Frederick 6'3", 215 OE-T
Col: Purdue *HS:* Rochester [IN] B: 6/7/1898, Fulton Co., IN D: 11/3/1986, Frankfort, IN
1922 Can-Rac: 11 G; Rush 1 TD; 6 Pt. Can: 3 G; Rush 1 TD; 6 Pt. Rac: 8 G. **1923** Rac: 6 G. **Total:** 17 G; Rush 1 TD; 6 Pt.

ROBERT MILLER Miller, Robert Laverne 5'11", 204 RB
Col: Kansas *HS:* Jack Yates [Houston, TX] B: 1/9/1953, Houston, TX *Drafted:* 1975 Round 5 Min
1975 Min: KR 5-93 18.6. **1976** Min: KR 5-77 15.4. **1977** Min: KR 5-66 13.2. **1978** Min: KR 2-23 11.5. **1979** Min: KR 3-38 12.7. **1980** Min: KR 1-23 23.0. **Total:** KR 21-320 15.2.

		Rushing				Receiving					Tot
Year Team	**G**	**Att**	**Yds**	**Avg**	**TD**	**Rec**	**Yds**	**Avg**	**TD**	**Fum**	**TD**
1975 Min	14	30	93	3.1	1	4	35	8.8	0	1	1
1976 Min	14	67	286	4.3	0	23	181	7.9	1	2	1
1977 Min	14	46	152	3.3	0	27	246	9.1	0	2	0
1978 Min	15	70	213	3.0	3	22	230	10.5	0	2	3
1979 Min	16	35	109	3.1	2	9	60	6.7	0	1	2
1980 Min	16	27	98	3.6	1	10	19	1.9	0	0	1
NFL Total	89	275	951	3.5	7	95	771	8.1	1	8	8

BOB MILLER Miller, Robert Marguese 6'3", 242 DT-OT
Col: Virginia *HS:* Norwalk [CT] B: 12/11/1929, Norwalk, CT *Drafted:* 1952 Round 5 Det
1952 Det: 11 G; KR 1-0. **1953** Det: 12 G; Int 1-0. **1954** Det: 12 G. **1955** Det: 12 G. **1956** Det: 12 G. **1957** Det: 12 G. **1958** Det: 10 G. **Total:** 81 G; KR 1-0; Int 1-0.

TERRY MILLER Miller, Robert Terry 6'2", 225 LB
Col: Illinois *HS:* Arcola [IL] B: 4/11/1946, Mattoon, IL *Drafted:* 1968 Round 8 Det
1970 Det: 1 G. **1971** StL: 9 G. **1972** StL: 12 G. **1973** StL: 14 G. **1974** StL: 5 G. **Total:** 41 G.

RON MILLER Miller, Ronald Rudolph 6'0", 190 QB
Col: Wisconsin *HS:* Morton [IL] B: 8/19/1939, Lyons, IL *Drafted:* 1961 Round 3 LARm
1962 LARm: 6 G; Pass 43-17 39.5%, 250 5.81 1 TD 1 Int; Rush 3-27 9.0; 1 Fum.

RON MILLER Miller, Ronald William 6'4", 200 OE
Col: USC *HS:* John C. Fremont [Los Angeles, CA] B: 4/17/1933
1956 LARm: 7 G; Rec 11-129 11.7.

SCOTT MILLER Miller, Scott Patrick 5'11", 181 WR
Col: Saddleback Coll. CA (J.C.); UCLA *HS:* El Toro [CA] B: 10/20/1968, Phoenix, AZ *Drafted:* 1991 Round 9 Mia
1991 Mia: Rec 4-49 12.3. **1993** Mia: Rec 2-15 7.5; KR 2-22 11.0. **1994** Mia: Rec 6-94 15.7 1 TD; KR 1-13 13.0. **1996** Mia: Rec 9-116 12.9; 1 Fum TD. **Total:** Rec 21-274 13.0 1 TD; KR 3-35 11.7; 1 Fum TD.

		Punt Returns					Tot
Year Team	**G**	**Ret**	**Yds**	**Avg**	**TD**	**Fum**	**TD**
1991 Mia	16	28	248	8.9	0	4	0
1992 Mia	15	24	175	7.3	0	2	0
1993 Mia	3	0	0	—	0	0	0
1994 Mia	9	1	13	13.0	0	0	1
1996 Mia	12	1	15	15.0	0	0	1
NFL Total	55	54	451	8.4	0	6	2

JUNIOR MILLER Miller, Selvia Jr. 6'4", 239 TE
Col: Nebraska *HS:* Robert E. Lee [Midland, TX] B: 11/26/1957, Midland, TX *Drafted:* 1980 Round 1 Atl
1980 Atl: Rush 2-(-2) -1.0. **1983** Atl: Rush 1-2 2.0. **Total:** Rush 3-0.

		Receiving				
Year Team	**G**	**Rec**	**Yds**	**Avg**	**TD**	**Fum**
1980 Atl	16	46	584	12.7	9	2
1981 Atl	16	32	398	12.4	3	0
1982 Atl	9	20	221	11.1	1	1
1983 Atl	15	16	125	7.8	0	1
1984 NO	15	8	81	10.1	1	0
NFL Total	71	122	1409	11.5	14	4

SHAWN MILLER Miller, Shawn Vernon 6'4", 255 NT-DE-DT
Col: Utah State *HS:* Weber [Ogden, UT] B: 3/14/1961, Ogden, UT
1984 LARm: 8 G. **1985** LARm: 16 G; KR 1-10 10.0; 5 Sac. **1986** LARm: 16 G; 5 Sac. **1987** LARm: 6 G; 6 Sac. **1988** LARm: 16 G; 4 Sac. **1989** LARm: 16 G; Int 1-3; 1 Sac. **Total:** 78 G; KR 1-10 10.0; Int 1-3; 21 Sac.

SOLOMON MILLER Miller, Solomon 6'1", 185 WR
Col: Compton CC CA; Utah State *HS:* Carson [CA] B: 12/6/1964, Los Angeles, CA *Drafted:* 1986 Round 6 NYG
1986 NYG: 16 G; Rush 1-3 3.0; Rec 9-144 16.0 2 TD; KR 7-111 15.9; 12 Pt; 1 Fum. **1987** TB: 8 G; Rec 5-97 19.4; KR 3-68 22.7. **Total:** 24 G; Rush 1-3 3.0; Rec 14-241 17.2 2 TD; KR 10-179 17.9; 12 Pt; 1 Fum.

BUBBA MILLER Miller, Stephen DeJuan 6'1", 305 C
Col: Tennessee *HS:* Brentwood Acad. [TN] B: 1/24/1973, Nashville, TN
1997 Phi: 13 G. **1998** Phi: 15 G; Rec 1-11 11.0. **Total:** 28 G; Rec 1-11 11.0.

TERRY MILLER Miller, Terry 5'10", 196 RB
(T.M.) *Col:* Oklahoma State *HS:* General William Mitchell [Colorado Springs, CO] B: 1/7/1956, Columbus, GA *Drafted:* 1978 Round 1 Buf

		Rushing				Receiving			
Year Team	**G**	**Att**	**Yds**	**Avg**	**TD**	**Rec**	**Yds**	**Avg**	**TD**
1978 Buf	16	238	1060	4.5	7	22	246	11.2	0
1979 Buf	16	139	484	3.5	1	10	111	11.1	0
1980 Buf	15	12	35	2.9	0	3	25	8.3	0
1981 Sea	1	2	4	2.0	0	0	0	—	0
NFL Total	48	391	1583	4.0	8	35	382	10.9	0

	Kickoff Returns				
Year Team	**Ret**	**Yds**	**Avg**	**TD**	**Fum**
1978 Buf	1	17	17.0	0	8
1979 Buf	8	160	20.0	0	2
1980 Buf	16	303	18.9	0	0
NFL Total	25	480	19.2	0	10

TOM MILLER Miller, Thomas Marshall 6'2", 202 DE-OE
Col: Hampden-Sydney *HS:* Fork Union Mil. Acad. [VA] B: 5/23/1918, Milton, PA
1943 PhPt: 8 G; Rec 3-60 20.0 1 TD; Int 1-0; 6 Pt. **1944** Phi: 10 G; Rush 1-(-2) -2.0; Rec 8-135 16.9; KR 1-8 8.0; Int 1-35 1 TD; 6 Pt.

1945 Was: 9 G; Rec 11-84 7.6. **1946** GB: 2 G. **Total:** 29 G; Rush 1-(-2) -2.0; Rec 22-279 12.7 1 TD; KR 1-8 8.0; Int 2-35 1 TD; Tot TD 2; 12 Pt.

VERNE MILLER Miller, Verne L 5'8", 152 **HB**
Col: Carleton; St. Mary's (Minn.) B: 5/11/1908, Grand Rapids, MN D: 10/8/1982, Milltown, WI
1930 Min: 5 G.

BLAKE MILLER Miller, William Blake 5'7", 170 **WB-E**
Col: Michigan State *HS:* Tonawanda [NY] B: 5/3/1889, Tonawanda, NY D: 1/9/1987, Lansing, MI
1920 Det: 2 G. **1921** Det: 3 G. **Total:** 5 G.

BILL MILLER Miller, William C 6'4", 270 **DT**
Col: New Mexico Highlands *HS:* Stoco [Coal City, PA] B: WV
Drafted: 1958 Round 21 ChiB
1962 Hou: 4 G.

BILL MILLER Miller, William Joseph 6'1", 195 **WR**
Col: Miami (Fla.) *HS:* McKeesport [PA] B: 4/17/1940, McKeesport, PA
Drafted: 1962 Round 2 DalT

		Receiving			
Year Team	G	Rec	Yds	Avg	TD
1962 DalT	14	23	277	12.0	0
1963 Buf	14	69	860	12.5	3
1964 Oak	12	2	29	14.5	0
1966 Oak	5	0	0	—	0
1967 Oak	12	38	537	14.1	6
1968 Oak	9	9	176	19.6	1
NFL Total	66	141	1879	13.3	10

WILLIE MILLER Miller, Willie T 5'9", 172 **WR**
Col: Colorado State *HS:* Hooper City [Sayreton, AL] B: 4/26/1947, Birmingham, AL *Drafted:* 1975 Round 12 Hou
1975 Cle: Pass 1-1 100.0%, 26 26.00 1 TD; Rush 1-(-2) -2.0; PR 10-47 4.7; KR 4-94 23.5; **1** Fum TD. **1976** Cle: PR 5-22 4.4; KR 1-0. **1978** LARm: Rush 1-(-7) -7.0. **1979** LARm: Rush 1-4 4.0. **1980** LARm: Rush 1-(-2) -2.0. **1982** LARm: Rush 1-5 5.0. **Total:** Pass 1-1 100.0%, 26 26.00 1 TD; Rush 5-(-2) -0.4; PR 15-69 4.6; KR 5-94 18.8; 1 Fum TD.

		Receiving					Tot
Year Team	G	Rec	Yds	Avg	TD	Fum	TD
1975 Cle	14	7	57	8.1	0	0	1
1976 Cle	6	0	0	—	0	1	0
1978 LARm	16	50	767	15.3	5	1	5
1979 LARm	3	8	111	13.9	1	0	1
1980 LARm	16	22	358	16.3	8	1	8
1981 LARm	13	10	147	14.7	0	0	0
1982 LARm	9	15	346	23.1	1	0	1
NFL Total	77	112	1786	15.9	15	3	16

BERT MILLING Milling, Bert William 5'10", 185 **G**
Col: Richmond *HS:* University Mil. Sch. [Mobile, AL] B: 11/4/1921, Mobile, AL
1942 Phi: 2 G.

JAMES MILLING Milling, James Thomas Jr. 5'9", 156 **WR**
Col: Maryland *HS:* Potomac [Oxon Hill, MD] B: 2/14/1965, Winnsboro, SC *Drafted:* 1988 Round 11 Atl

		Receiving			
Year Team	G	Rec	Yds	Avg	TD
1988 Atl	6	5	66	13.2	0
1990 Atl	13	18	161	8.9	1
1992 Atl	5	3	25	8.3	0
NFL Total	24	26	252	9.7	1

TED MILLION Million, Tedder Clark 6'4", 260 **OG**
Col: Duke *HS:* Norman [OK] B: 5/9/1963
1987 Min: 1 G.

BOB MILLMAN Millman, Robert Dent 5'11", 178 **WB-BB**
Col: Lafayette *HS:* Kiski School [Saltsburg, PA] B: 5/17/1903, Cumberland, MD D: 3/19/1963, Trenton, NJ
1925 Pott: 2 G. **1926** Pott: 7 G; Rec 1 TD; 6 Pt. **1927** Pott: 3 G. **Total:** 12 G; Rec 1 TD; 6 Pt.

WAYNE MILLNER Millner, Wayne Vernal 6'1", 189 **OE-DE**
Col: Notre Dame *HS:* Salem [MA]; Malvern Prep [MA]; Devitt Prep [MA] B: 1/31/1913, Boston, MA D: 11/19/1976, Arlington, VA *Drafted:* 1936 Round 8 Bos *HOF:* 1968
1937 Was: Rush 2-6 3.0. **1938** Was: Rush 3-5 1.7. **1939** Was: Rush 4-12 3.0. **1940** Was: Rush 3-31 10.3. **1941** Was: Rush 2-8 4.0. **Total:** Rush 14-62 4.4.

		Receiving				Tot
Year Team	G	Rec	Yds	Avg	TD	TD
1936 Bos	12	18	211	11.7	0	0
1937 Was	11	14	216	15.4	2	3
1938 Was	11	18	232	12.9	1	1
1939 Was	11	19	294	15.5	4	4
1940 Was	10	22	233	10.6	3	3
1941 Was	11	20	262	13.1	0	0
1945 Was	10	13	130	10.0	2	2
NFL Total	76	124	1578	12.7	12	13

LAWYER MILLOY Milloy, Lawyer Marzell 6'0", 208 **DB**
Col: Washington *HS:* Lincoln [Tacoma, WA] B: 11/14/1973, St. Louis, MO *Drafted:* 1996 Round 2 NE
1996 NE: 1 Sac. **1998** NE: 1 Sac. **Total:** 2 Sac.

		Interceptions		
Year Team	G	Int	Yds	TD
1996 NE	16	2	14	0
1997 NE	16	3	15	0
1998 NE	16	6	54	1
NFL Total	48	11	83	1

CHARLIE MILLS Mills, Charles 1 **FB-BB**
Col: Maryland Deceased
1920 Buf: 5 G.

DENVER MILLS Mills, Denver Burton 6'3", 225 **LB**
Col: William & Mary *HS:* George Wythe [Wytheville, VA] B: 8/29/1925, Crockett, VA D: 11/4/1997, Richmond, VA
1952 ChiC: 1 G.

ERNIE MILLS Mills, Ernest Lee III 5'11", 192 **WR**
Col: Florida *HS:* Dunnellon [FL] B: 10/28/1968, Dunnellon, FL
Drafted: 1991 Round 3 Pit
1991 Pit: PR 1-0 1 TD. **1992** Pit: Rush 1-20 20.0. **1993** Pit: Rush 3-12 4.0. **1994** Pit: Rush 3-18 6.0. **1995** Pit: Rush 5-39 7.8. **1996** Pit: Rush 2-24 12.0. **1998** Dal: Rush 3-9 3.0. **Total:** Rush 17-122 7.2; PR 1-0 1 TD.

		Receiving				Kickoff Returns					Tot
Year Team	G	Rec	Yds	Avg	TD	Ret	Yds	Avg	TD	Fum	TD
1991 Pit	16	3	79	26.3	1	11	284	25.8	0	0	2
1992 Pit	16	30	383	12.8	3	1	11	11.0	0	2	3
1993 Pit	14	29	386	13.3	1	0	0	—	0	0	1
1994 Pit	15	19	384	20.2	1	2	6	3.0	0	1	1
1995 Pit	16	39	679	17.4	8	54	1306	24.2	0	2	8
1996 Pit	9	7	92	13.1	1	8	146	18.3	0	0	1
1997 Car	10	11	127	11.5	1	4	65	16.3	0	0	1
1998 Dal	11	28	479	17.1	4	0	0	—	0	0	4
NFL Total	107	166	2609	15.7	20	80	1818	22.7	0	5	21

LAMAR MILLS Mills, Franciscus Lamar 6'5", 270 **DE**
Col: Indiana *HS:* St. Martin de Porres [Detroit, MI] B: 1/26/1971, Detroit, MI
1994 Was: 13 G.

JIM MILLS Mills, James Anthony 6'9", 276 **OT**
Col: Hawaii *HS:* Richmond [Canada] B: 9/23/1961, Vancouver, Canada *Drafted:* 1983 Round 9 Bal
1983 Bal: 7 G. **1984** Ind: 14 G. **Total:** 21 G.

JIM MILLS Mills, James Gary 6'4", 290 **OG-OT**
Col: Idaho *HS:* Marysville [WA] B: 3/30/1973, Everett, WA
Drafted: 1996 Round 6 SD
1996 SD: 1 G. **1997** SD: 1 G. **Total:** 2 G.

JEFF MILLS Mills, Jeff Jonathan 6'3", 244 **LB**
Col: Nebraska *HS:* Montclair [NJ] B: 10/8/1968, Montclair, NJ
Drafted: 1990 Round 3 SD
1990 SD-Den: 7 G. SD: 5 G. Den: 2 G. **1991** Den: 12 G; 3 Sac. **1992** Den: 14 G; 2 Sac. **1993** Den: 13 G. **Total:** 46 G; 5 Sac.

JOHN HENRY MILLS Mills, John Henry 6'0", 226 **LB**
Col: Wake Forest *HS:* Amos P. Godby [Tallahassee, FL]
B: 10/31/1969, Jacksonville, FL *Drafted:* 1993 Round 5 Hou
1994 Hou: Rec 1-4 4.0. **Total:** Rec 1-4 4.0.

		Kickoff Returns				
Year Team	G	Ret	Yds	Avg	TD	Fum
1993 Hou	16	11	230	20.9	0	0
1994 Hou	16	15	282	18.8	0	1
1995 Hou	16	0	0	—	0	0
1996 Hou	16	0	0	—	0	0
1997 Oak	16	0	0	—	0	0
1998 Oak	5	0	0	—	0	0
NFL Total	85	26	512	19.7	0	1

JOE MILLS Mills, Joseph Edward 6'3", 212 **C-G-WB-OE**
Col: Carnegie Mellon *HS:* Alliance [OH] B: 9/3/1897, Knoxville, OH D: 5/31/1967, Alliance, OH
1922 Akr: 7 G; Rush 1 TD; Scor **1** 1XP; 7 Pt. **1923** Akr: 6 G. **1924** Akr: 4 G. **1925** Akr: 5 G. **1926** Akr: 6 G. **Total:** 28 G; Rush 1 TD; Scor 1 1XP; 7 Pt.

DICK MILLS Mills, Richard J 6'3", 240 **OG**
Col: Pittsburgh *HS:* Beaver [PA] B: 3/6/1939, Indiana, PA
Drafted: 1961 Round 3 Det
1961 Det: 14 G. **1962** Det: 8 G. **Total:** 22 G.

SAM MILLS Mills, Samuel Davis Jr. 5'9", 229 **LB**
Col: Montclair State *HS:* Long Branch [NJ] B: 6/3/1959, Neptune, NJ
1989 NO: 3 Sac. **1990** NO: 0.5 Sac. **1991** NO: 1 Sac. **1992** NO: 1 Fum TD; 3 Sac. **1993** NO: 1 Fum TD; 2 Sac. **1994** NO: 1 Sac. **1995** Car: 4.5 Sac. **1996** Car: **1** Fum TD; 5.5 Sac. **1997** Car: KR 2-12 6.0. **Total:** KR 2-12 6.0; 3 Fum TD; 20.5 Sac.

		Interceptions				Tot
Year Team	G	Int	Yds	TD	Fum	TD
1986 NO	16	0	0	0	0	0
1987 NO	12	0	0	0	0	0
1988 NO	16	0	0	0	0	0
1989 NO	16	0	0	0	0	0
1990 NO	16	0	0	0	0	0
1991 NO	16	2	13	0	0	0
1992 NO	16	1	10	0	0	1
1993 NO	9	0	0	0	0	1
1994 NO	16	1	10	0	0	0
1995 Car	16	5	58	1	0	1
1996 Car	16	1	10	0	0	1
1997 Car	16	1	18	0	1	0
NFL Total	181	11	119	1	1	4

STAN MILLS Mills, Stanley Jr. 5'9", 180 **FB-HB-OE**
Col: Penn State *HS:* Peddie School [Hightstown, NJ] B: 1893 Deceased
1922 GB: 8 G. **1923** GB: 9 G; Rush 1 TD; Rec 2 TD; Tot TD 3; 18 Pt. **1924** Akr: 5 G; Int 1 TD; 6 Pt. **Total:** 22 G; Rush 1 TD; Rec 2 TD; Int 1 TD; Tot TD 4; 24 Pt.

PETE MILLS Mills, Sullivan 5'10", 180 **WR**
Col: Coffeyville CC KS; Wichita State B: 5/29/1942, Calvert, TX
Drafted: 1965 Round 12 Buf
1965 Buf: 2 G; Rec 1-43 43.0. **1966** Buf: 1 G; KR 4-76 19.0; 2 Fum. **Total:** 3 G; Rec 1-43 43.0; KR 4-76 19.0; 2 Fum.

BRIAN MILNE Milne, Brian Fitzsimons 6'3", 255 **RB**
Col: Penn State *HS:* Fort Le Boeuf [Waterford, PA] B: 1/7/1973, Waterford, PA *Drafted:* 1996 Round 4 Ind

		Rushing				Receiving			
Year Team	G	Att	Yds	Avg	TD	Rec	Yds	Avg	TD
1996 Cin	6	8	22	2.8	1	3	29	9.7	0
1997 Cin	16	13	32	2.5	2	23	138	6.0	0
1998 Cin	14	10	41	4.1	1	26	124	4.8	0
NFL Total	36	31	95	3.1	4	52	291	5.6	0

BILL MILNER Milner, Charles Edgar 6'1", 228 **LB-OG-DG-DE**
Col: South Carolina; Duke *HS:* Waynesville [NC] B: 3/7/1919, Waynesville, NC
1947 ChiB: 12 G; Int 1-7. **1948** ChiB: 12 G. **1949** ChiB: 12 G. **1950** NYG: 12 G. **Total:** 48 G; Int 1-7.

BILLY MILNER Milner, Willie Perry 6'5", 293 **OT**
Col: Southwest Mississippi CC; Houston *HS:* Northside [Atlanta, GA] B: 6/21/1972, Atlanta, GA *Drafted:* 1995 Round 1 Mia
1995 Mia: 16 G; KR 1-13 13.0. **1996** Mia-StL: 14 G. Mia: 4 G. StL: 10 G. **Total:** 30 G; KR 1-13 13.0.

RAY MILO Milo, Raymond Wesley 5'11", 178 **DB**
Col: New Mexico State *HS:* Conroe [TX] B: 2/19/1954, Conroe, TX
Drafted: 1978 Round 11 KC
1978 KC: 1 G.

RICH MILOT Milot, Richard Paul 6'4", 234 **LB**
Col: Penn State *HS:* Moon [Coraopolis, PA] B: 5/28/1957, Coraopolis, PA *Drafted:* 1979 Round 7 Was
1982 Was: 3 Sac. **1983** Was: 1.5 Sac. **1984** Was: 4 Sac. **1985** Was: 3 Sac. **1986** Was: PR 1-3 3.0; 2 Sac. **1987** Was: 1 Sac. **Total:** PR 1-3 3.0; 14.5 Sac.

		Interceptions			
Year Team	G	Int	Yds	TD	Fum
1979 Was	14	0	0	0	0
1980 Was	16	4	-8	0	0
1981 Was	11	0	0	0	1
1982 Was	9	0	0	0	0
1983 Was	16	2	20	0	0
1984 Was	14	3	42	0	0
1985 Was	16	2	33	0	0
1986 Was	16	2	33	0	1
1987 Was	9	0	0	0	0
NFL Total	121	13	120	0	2

CENTURY MILSTEAD Milstead, Century Allen 6'1", 213 **T**
(Wally) *Col:* Wabash; Yale *HS:* Rock Island [IL] B: 1/1/1900, Rock Island, IL D: 6/1/1963, Pleasantville, NY
1925 NYG: 12 G. **1927** NYG: 7 G. **1928** NYG: 11 G. **Total:** 30 G.

CHARLIE MILSTEAD Milstead, Charles Frank 6'2", 190 **QB-DB**
Col: Texas A&M *HS:* John Tyler [Tyler, TX] B: 11/21/1937, Tyler, TX
Drafted: 1960 Round 1 LAC
1960 Hou: Pass 7-4 57.1%, 43 6.14; Rush 3-3 1.0. **1961** Hou: Int 2-25; Scor 1, 1-1 100.0% XK. **Total:** Pass 7-4 57.1%, 43 6.14; Rush 3-3 1.0; Int 2-25; Scor 1, 1-1 100.0% XK.

		Punting		
Year Team	G	Punts	Yds	Avg
1960 Hou	14	66	2365	35.8
1961 Hou	8	0	0	—
NFL Total	22	66	2365	35.8

ROD MILSTEAD Milstead, Roderick Leon Jr. 6'2", 290 **OG**
Col: Delaware State *HS:* Lackey [Indian Head, MD] B: 11/10/1969, Washington, DC *Drafted:* 1992 Round 5 Dal
1994 SF: 5 G. **1995** SF: 16 G. **1996** SF: 11 G. **1997** SF: 4 G. **1998** Was: 14 G. **Total:** 50 G.

ELDRIDGE MILTON Milton, Eldridge Dennis 6'1", 235 **LB**
Col: Clemson *HS:* Charleston Co. [Folkston, GA] B: 12/8/1962, Folkston, CA
1987 ChiB: 3 G; KR 1-10 10.0.

GENE MILTON Milton, Eugene 5'10", 185 **WR**
Col: Florida A&M *HS:* Howard [Ocala, FL] B: 9/28/1944, Ocala, FL
1968 Mia: Rush 2-46 23.0; Rec 9-143 15.9 1 TD; PR 6-55 9.2. **1969** Mia: Rush 7-62 8.9; Rec 12-179 14.9; PR 1-4 4.0; **1** Fum TD. **Total:** Rush 9-108 12.0; Rec 21-322 15.3 1 TD; PR 7-59 8.4; 1 Fum TD.

		Kickoff Returns					Tot
Year Team	G	Ret	Yds	Avg	TD	Fum	TD
1968 Mia	13	18	408	22.7	0	4	1
1969 Mia	14	8	166	20.8	0	2	1
NFL Total	27	26	574	22.1	0	6	2

JOHNNY MILTON Milton, John William 5'8", 175 **OE-WB-BB**
Col: USC *HS:* South Division [Milwaukee, WI] B: 1899 Deceased
1923 Mil-StL: 7 G. Mil: 1 G. StL: 6 G. **1924** KC: 8 G. **Total:** 15 G.

CHRIS MIMS Mims, Christopher Eddie 6'5", 288 **DE-DT**
Col: Pierce Coll. CA (J.C.); Los Angeles Southwest Coll. CA (J.C.); Tennessee *HS:* Susan Miller Dorsey [Los Angeles, CA] B: 9/29/1970, Los Angeles, CA *Drafted:* 1992 Round 1 SD
1992 SD: 16 G; Scor 1 Saf; 2 Pt; 10 Sac. **1993** SD: 16 G; 7 Sac. **1994** SD: 16 G; 11 Sac. **1995** SD: 15 G; 2 Sac. **1996** SD: 15 G; 6 Sac. **1997** Was: 11 G; 4 Sac. **1998** SD: 6 G; 2 Sac. **Total:** 95 G; Scor 1 Saf; 2 Pt; 42 Sac.

DAVID MIMS Mims, David James 5'8", 191 **WR**
Col: Baylor *HS:* Daingerfield [TX] B: 7/7/1970, Daingerfield, TX
1993 Atl: 15 G; Rush 1-3 3.0; Rec 12-107 8.9 1 TD; KR 1-22 22.0; 6 Pt. **1994** Atl: 2 G; Rec 3-14 4.7. **Total:** 17 G; Rush 1-3 3.0; Rec 15-121 8.1 1 TD; KR 1-22 22.0; 6 Pt.

HENRY MINARIK Minarik, Henry John 6'2", 200 **OE**
(Hank) *Col:* Michigan State *HS:* Central [Flint, MI] B: 9/1/1927, Flint, MI *Drafted:* 1951 Round 8 Pit

		Receiving			
Year Team	G	Rec	Yds	Avg	TD
1951 Pit	11	35	459	13.1	1

CHARLES MINCY Mincy, Charles Anthony 6'0", 195 **DB**
Col: Washington *HS:* Susan Miller Dorsey [Los Angeles, CA]
B: 12/16/1969, Los Angeles, CA *Drafted:* 1991 Round 5 KC
1991 KC: Postseason only. **1992** KC: PR 1-4 4.0; 1 Fum TD. **1993** KC: PR 2-9 4.5. **1995** Min: PR 4-22 5.5. **Total:** PR 7-35 5.0; 1 Fum TD.

		Interceptions			Tot
Year Team	G	Int	Yds	TD	TD
1992 KC	16	4	128	2	3
1993 KC	16	5	44	0	0
1994 KC	16	3	49	0	0
1995 Min	16	3	37	0	0
1996 TB	2	1	26	0	0
1997 TB	16	1	14	0	0
1998 TB	16	4	58	1	1
NFL Total	98	21	356	3	4

TOM MINER Miner, Thomas Earl 6'4", 235 **K-LB**
Col: Tulsa *HS:* Checotah [OK] B: 5/14/1932, Checotah, OK
D: 1/1/1988, Tucson, AZ *Drafted:* 1954 Round 3 Pit
1958 Pit: 12 G; Scor 73, **14-28** 50.0% FG, 31-31 100.0% XK.

GENE MINGO Mingo, Eugene 6'2", 216 **HB-K**
(The Golden Toe) *Col:* No College *HS:* South [Akron, OH]
B: 9/22/1938, Akron, OH
1960 Den: Pass 7-1 14.3%, 46 6.57; PR 3-92 30.7 **1** TD. **1961** Den: Pass 8-4 50.0%, 136 17.00 2 TD; PR 1-1 1.0. **1962** Den: Pass 2-1 50.0%, 18 9.00 1 Int; PR 7-36 5.1. **1963** Den: Pass 1-0; PR 7-85 12.1. **Total:** Pass 18-6 33.3%, 200 11.11 2 TD 1 Int; PR 18-214 11.9 1 TD.

Year Team	G	Rushing Att	Rushing Yds	Rushing Avg	Rushing TD	Receiving Rec	Receiving Yds	Receiving Avg	Receiving TD
1960 Den	14	83	323	3.9	4	19	156	8.2	1
1961 Den	10	18	51	2.8	0	8	110	13.8	2
1962 Den	14	54	287	5.3	4	14	107	7.6	0
1963 Den	14	24	90	3.8	0	3	11	3.7	0
1964 Den-Oak	14	6	26	4.3	0	4	25	6.3	1
1964 Den	7	6	26	4.3	0	3	15	5.0	0
1964 Oak	7	0	0	—	0	1	10	10.0	1
1965 Oak	14	0	0	—	0	1	5	5.0	0
1966 Mia	14	0	0	—	0	3	40	13.3	0
1967 Mia-Was	12	0	0	—	0	0	0	—	0
1967 Mia	6	0	0	—	0	0	0	—	0
1967 Was	6	0	0	—	0	0	0	—	0
1969 Pit	14	0	0	—	0	0	0	—	0
1970 Pit	10	0	0	—	0	0	0	—	0
NFL Total	130	185	777	4.2	8	52	454	8.7	4

Year Team	Kickoff Returns Ret	Yds	Avg	TD
1960 Den	9	209	23.2	0
1961 Den	4	120	30.0	0
1962 Den	6	99	16.5	0
1963 Den	7	151	21.6	0
1964 Den-Oak	8	163	20.4	0
1964 Den	8	163	20.4	0
NFL Total	34	742	21.8	0

Year Team	Scoring Pts	FG	FGA	FG%	XK	XKA	XK%	Fum	Tot TD
1960 Den	**123**	**18**	28	**64.3**	33	36	**91.7**	3	6
1961 Den	32	3	10	30.0	11	11	100.0	2	2
1962 Den	**137**	**27**	**39**	69.2	32	34	94.1	3	4
1963 Den	83	16	29	55.2	35	35	100.0	0	0
1964 Den-Oak	39	8	12	66.7	9	10	90.0	0	1
1964 Den	33	8	12	66.7	9	10	90.0	0	0
1964 Oak	0	0	0	—	0	0	—	0	1
1965 Oak	24	8	19	42.1	0	0	—	0	0
1966 Mia	53	10	22	45.5	23	23	100.0	0	0
1967 Mia-Was	44	5	16	31.3	29	31	93.5	0	0
1967 Mia	12	1	6	16.7	9	9	100.0	0	0
1967 Was	32	4	10	40.0	20	22	90.9	0	0
1969 Pit	62	12	26	46.2	26	26	100.0	0	0
1970 Pit	32	5	18	27.8	17	17	100.0	0	0
NFL Total	629	112	219	51.1	215	223	96.4	8	13

PAUL MINICK Minick, Paul Daniel 6'0", 195 **G-E**
Col: Iowa *HS:* West [Des Moines, IA] B: 12/17/1899, Villisca, IA
D: 12/22/1978, Springfield, MO
1927 Buf: 5 G. **1928** GB: 12 G. **1929** GB: 6 G. **Total:** 23 G.

KEVIN MINIEFIELD Miniefield, Kevin Lamar 5'9", 182 **DB**
Col: Arizona State *HS:* Camelback [Phoenix, AZ] B: 3/2/1970, Phoenix, AZ *Drafted:* 1993 Round 8 Det
1993 ChiB: 8 G. **1994** ChiB: 12 G. **1995** ChiB: 15 G; Int 3-37. **1996** ChiB: 13 G; 1.5 Sac. **1997** Ariz: 3 G. **Total:** 51 G; Int 3-37; 1.5 Sac.

FRANK MININI Minini, Frank David 6'1", 209 **HB-BB-DB**
Col: San Jose State *HS:* Paso Robles [CA] B: 12/23/1921, Paso Robles, CA *Drafted:* 1947 Round 2 ChiB
1947 ChiB: Rec 2-23 11.5; Int 1-3. **1948** ChiB: Rec 1-14 14.0 1 TD; 1 Fum TD. **Total:** Rec 3-37 12.3 1 TD; Int 1-3; 1 Fum TD.

Year Team	G	Rushing Ret	Rushing Yds	Rushing Avg	Rushing TD	Kickoff Returns Ret	Kickoff Returns Yds	Kickoff Returns Avg	Kickoff Returns TD	Fum	Tot TD
1947 ChiB	12	26	132	5.1	2	11	261	23.7	0	3	2
1948 ChiB	12	24	79	3.3	2	12	370	**30.8**	**1**	2	5
1949 Pit	12	1	5	5.0	0	16	390	24.4	0	1	0
NFL Total	36	51	216	4.2	4	39	1021	26.2	1	6	7

SKIPPY MINISI Minisi, Anthony Salvatore 5'11", 190 **HB-DB**
Col: Navy; Pennsylvania *HS:* Newark Acad. [NJ] B: 9/18/1926, Newark, NJ *Drafted:* 1948 Round 1 NYG
1948 NYG: Pass 3-0, 2 Int; Rec 13-123 9.5 1 TD; PR 3-25 8.3; KR 4-82 20.5; Int 2-10.

Year Team	G	Rushing Att	Rushing Yds	Rushing Avg	Rushing TD	Fum	Tot TD
1948 NYG	12	36	160	4.4	1	2	2

RANDY MINNIEAR Minniear, Randall Harry 6'1", 210 **RB**
Col: Purdue *HS:* Broad Ripple [Indianapolis, IN] B: 12/27/1943, Indianapolis, IN *Drafted:* 1966 Round 20 NYG
1967 NYG: Rec 8-49 6.1 1 TD; PR 4-13 3.3; KR 6-98 16.3. **1968** NYG: Rec 4-32 8.0. **1969** NYG: Rec 6-68 11.3; PR 3-15 5.0; KR 5-83 16.6; Punt 2-77 38.5. **1970** Cle: Rec 1-(-1) -1.0. **Total:** Rec 19-148 7.8 1 TD; PR 7-28 4.0; KR 11-181 16.5; Punt 2-77 38.5.

Year Team	G	Rushing Att	Rushing Yds	Rushing Avg	Rushing TD	Fum	Tot TD
1967 NYG	6	35	98	2.8	1	0	2
1968 NYG	2	14	38	2.7	2	1	2
1969 NYG	11	35	141	4.0	1	2	1
1970 Cle	8	12	39	3.3	1	0	1
NFL Total	27	96	316	3.3	5	3	6

FRANK MINNIFIELD Minnifield, Frank LyDale 5'9", 180 **DB**
Col: Louisville *HS:* Henry Clay [Lexington, KY] B: 1/1/1960, Lexington, KY
1991 Cle: PR 0-28. **Total:** PR 0-28.

Year Team	G	Interceptions Int	Yds	TD
1984 Cle	15	1	26	0
1985 Cle	16	1	3	0
1986 Cle	15	3	20	0
1987 Cle	12	4	24	0
1988 Cle	15	4	16	0
1989 Cle	16	3	29	0
1990 Cle	9	2	0	0
1991 Cle	14	0	0	0
1992 Cle	10	2	6	0
NFL Total	122	20	124	0

CLAUDIE MINOR Minor, Claudie Dee Jr. 6'4", 280 **OT**
Col: Mount San Antonio Coll. CA (J.C.); San Diego City Coll. CA (J.C.); San Diego Sta *HS:* Garey [Pomona, CA] B: 4/21/1951, Pomona, CA
Drafted: 1974 Round 3 Den
1974 Den: 14 G. **1975** Den: 14 G. **1976** Den: 14 G. **1977** Den: 14 G. **1978** Den: 16 G. **1979** Den: 16 G. **1980** Den: 15 G. **1981** Den: 13 G. **1982** Den: 9 G. **Total:** 125 G.

LINCOLN MINOR Minor, Lincoln 6'2", 211 **RB**
Col: New Mexico State *HS:* Ravenswood [Palo Alto, CA]
B: 1/22/1950, New Orleans, LA
1973 NO: 9 G; Rush 3-10 3.3; Rec 1-5 5.0.

VIC MINOR Minor, Victor Wayne 6'0", 198 **DB**
Col: Northeast Louisiana *HS:* Woodlawn [Shreveport, LA]
B: 11/28/1958, Shreveport, LA *Drafted:* 1980 Round 8 Sea
1980 Sea: 16 G; Int 1-0. **1981** Sea: 4 G. **Total:** 20 G; Int 1-0.

BARRY MINTER Minter, Barry Antoine 6'2", 242 **LB**
Col: Tulsa *HS:* Mount Pleasant [TX] B: 1/28/1970, Mount Pleasant, TX
Drafted: 1993 Round 6 Dal
1993 ChiB: 2 G. **1994** ChiB: 13 G. **1995** ChiB: 16 G; Int 1-2 1 TD; 6 Pt. **1996** ChiB: 16 G; Int 1-5; 1.5 Sac. **1997** ChiB: 16 G; 6 Sac. **1998** ChiB: 16 G; Int 1-17; 1 Sac. **Total:** 79 G; Int 3-24 1 TD; 6 Pt; 8.5 Sac.

CEDRIC MINTER Minter, Cedric Alwyn 5'10", 200 **RB**
Col: Boise State *HS:* Borah [Boise, ID] B: 11/13/1958, Charleston, SC
1984 NYJ: Rec 10-109 10.9 1 TD; PR 4-44 11.0; KR 10-224 22.4.
1985 NYJ: Rec 1-13 13.0; PR 2-25 12.5; KR 1-14 14.0. **Total:** Rec 11-122 11.1 1 TD; PR 6-69 11.5; KR 11-238 21.6.

Year Team	G	Rushing Att	Rushing Yds	Rushing Avg	Rushing TD	Fum	Tot TD
1984 NYJ	8	34	136	4.0	1	1	2
1985 NYJ	3	8	23	2.9	0	0	0
NFL Total	11	42	159	3.8	1	1	2

MIKE MINTER Minter, Michael Christopher 5'10", 188 **DB**
Col: Nebraska *HS:* Lawton [OK] B: 1/15/1974, Cleveland, OH
Drafted: 1997 Round 2 Car
1997 Car: 16 G; 3.5 Sac. **1998** Car: 6 G; Int 1-7. **Total:** 22 G; Int 1-7; 3.5 Sac.

MICHAEL MINTER Minter, Michael Jerome 6'3", 275 **NT**
Col: North Texas *HS:* Mount Pleasant [TX] B: 8/13/1965, Mount Pleasant, TX
1987 Pit: 3 G.

TOM MINTER Minter, Tommie Earl 5'10", 178 **DB**
Col: Baylor *HS:* Gladewater [TX] B: 7/18/1939, Henderson, TX
Drafted: 1962 Round 9 SD
1962 Den-Buf: 12 G; PR 2-1 0.5; KR 10-227 22.7; 3 Fum. Den: 7 G; PR 2-1 0.5; KR 10-227 22.7; 3 Fum. Buf: 5 G. **Total:** 12 G; PR 2-1 0.5; KR 10-227 22.7; 3 Fum.

JAKE MINTUN Mintun, John F 5'11", 191 **C**
Col: No College *HS:* Cambridge [NE] B: 7/12/1894 D: 2/25/1976, Decatur, IL
1920 Sta: 5 G. **1921** Sta: 3 G. **1922** Rac: 7 G. **1923** Rac: 10 G. **1924** Rac: 10 G. **1925** KC: 8 G. **1926** Rac: 2 G. **Total:** 45 G.

ED MIODUSZEWSKI Mioduszewski, Edward Thomas 5'10", 185 **QB-DB**
(AKA Ed Meadows) *Col:* William & Mary *HS:* Cliffside Park [NJ]
B: 10/28/1931, Cliffside Park, NJ *Drafted:* 1953 Round 18 Det
1953 Bal: 12 G; Pass 30-11 36.7%, 113 3.77 2 TD 2 Int; Rush 3-33 11.0; PR 4-13 3.3; KR 1-25 25.0; Int 1-0; 1 Fum.

FRANK MIOTKE Miotke, Frank 6'0", 175 **WR**
Col: Grand Valley State *HS:* Hartland [MI] B: 12/22/1965, Dearborn, MI
1991 Hou: 8 G.

GEORGE MIRA Mira, George Ignacio 6'0", 190 **QB**
Col: Miami (Fla.) *HS:* Key West [FL] B: 1/11/1942, Key West, FL
Drafted: 1964 Round 2 SF

		Passing							
Year Team	**G**	**Att**	**Comp**	**Comp%**	**Yds**	**YPA**	**TD**	**Int**	**Rating**
1964 SF	7	53	23	43.4	331	6.25	2	5	37.5
1965 SF	10	58	28	48.3	460	7.93	4	3	76.8
1966 SF	14	53	22	41.5	284	5.36	5	2	74.7
1967 SF	3	65	35	53.8	592	9.11	5	3	91.3
1968 SF	13	11	4	36.4	44	4.00	1	1	41.5
1969 Phi	7	76	25	32.9	240	3.16	1	5	19.6
1971 Mia	6	30	11	36.7	159	5.30	1	1	51.9
NFL Total	60	346	148	42.8	2110	6.10	19	20	57.4

	Rushing				
Year Team	**Att**	**Yds**	**Avg**	**TD**	**Fum**
1964 SF	18	177	9.8	0	7
1965 SF	5	64	12.8	0	2
1966 SF	10	103	10.3	0	3
1967 SF	7	23	3.3	0	4
1968 SF	1	5	5.0	0	1
1969 Phi	3	16	5.3	0	0
1971 Mia	6	-9	-1.5	0	1
NFL Total	50	379	7.6	0	18

DEAN MIRALDI Miraldi, Dean Martin 6'5", 266 **OG-OT**
Col: Long Beach State; Utah *HS:* Rosemead [CA] B: 4/8/1958, Culver City, CA *Drafted:* 1981 Round 2 Phi
1982 Phi: 1 G. **1983** Phi: 13 G. **1984** Phi: 16 G. **1985** Den: 10 G.
1987 LARd: 10 G. **Total:** 50 G.

RICK MIRER Mirer, Rick Franklin 6'2", 214 **QB**
Col: Notre Dame *HS:* Goshen [IN] B: 3/19/1970, Goshen, IN
Drafted: 1993 Round 1 Sea
1997 ChiB: Scor 1 2XP. **Total:** Scor 1 2XP.

		Passing							
Year Team	**G**	**Att**	**Comp**	**Comp%**	**Yds**	**YPA**	**TD**	**Int**	**Rating**
1993 Sea	16	486	274	56.4	2833	5.83	12	17	67.0
1994 Sea	13	381	195	51.2	2151	5.65	11	**7**	70.2
1995 Sea	15	391	209	53.5	2564	6.56	13	20	63.7
1996 Sea	11	265	136	51.3	1546	5.83	5	12	56.6
1997 ChiB	7	103	53	51.5	420	4.08	0	6	37.7
NFL Total	62	1626	867	53.3	9514	5.85	41	62	63.4

	Rushing				
Year Team	**Att**	**Yds**	**Avg**	**TD**	**Fum**
1993 Sea	68	343	5.0	3	13
1994 Sea	34	153	4.5	0	2
1995 Sea	43	193	4.5	1	5
1996 Sea	33	191	5.8	2	4
1997 ChiB	20	78	3.9	1	4
NFL Total	198	958	4.8	7	28

REX MIRICH Mirich, Rex L 6'4", 250 **DT-DE**
Col: Arizona State *HS:* San Manuel [AZ] B: 3/11/1941, Florence, AZ
Drafted: 1963 Round 20 Oak
1964 Oak: 14 G. **1965** Oak: 14 G. **1966** Oak: 14 G; KR 2-0. **1967** Den: 13 G. **1968** Den: 14 G. **1969** Den: 7 G. **1970** Bos: 7 G. **Total:** 83 G; KR 2-0.

BOB MISCHAK Mischak, Robert Michael 6'0", 237 **OG**
Col: Army *HS:* Union [NJ] B: 10/25/1932, Newark, NJ *Drafted:* 1954 Round 23 Cle
1958 NYG: 12 G; Rec 1-27 27.0. **1960** NYT: 4 G. **1961** NYT: 14 G.
1962 NYT: 14 G. **1963** Oak: 14 G; Rec 2-25 12.5. **1964** Oak: 13 G.
1965 Oak: 8 G. **Total:** 79 G; Rec 3-52 17.3.

DAVE MISHEL Mishel, David 5'9", 179 **TB-QB-WB-FB**
Col: Brown *HS:* Classical [Lynn, MA] B: 7/6/1905, Lynn, MA
D: 3/11/1975, Newton, MA
1927 Prov: 4 G. **1931** Cle: 6 G; Pass 1 TD; Scor 1, 1 XK. **Total:** 10 G; Pass 1 TD.

JOHN MISKO Misko, John Charles 6'5", 207 **P**
Col: Porterville Coll. CA (J.C.); Oregon State *HS:* Porterville [CA]
B: 10/1/1954, Highland Park, MI

		Punting		
Year Team	**G**	**Punts**	**Yds**	**Avg**
1982 LARm	9	45	1961	43.6
1983 LARm	16	82	3301	40.3
1984 LARm	16	74	2866	38.7
1987 Det	1	6	242	40.3
NFL Total	42	207	8370	40.4

JOHN MISTLER Mistler, John Andrew 6'2", 186 **WR**
Col: Arizona State *HS:* Sahuaro [Tucson, AZ] B: 10/28/1958, Columbia, MO *Drafted:* 1981 Round 3 NYG
1983 NYG: Pass 1-0. **Total:** Pass 1-0.

		Receiving				
Year Team	**G**	**Rec**	**Yds**	**Avg**	**TD**	**Fum**
1981 NYG	16	8	119	14.9	1	0
1982 NYG	9	18	191	10.6	2	0
1983 NYG	16	45	422	9.4	0	1
1984 Buf-NYG	4	1	5	5.0	0	0
1984 Buf	3	0	0	—	0	0
1984 NYG	1	1	5	5.0	0	0
NFL Total	45	72	737	10.2	3	1

GENE MITCHAM Mitcham, Eugene Gale 6'2", 206 **OE**
Col: Arizona State *HS:* North [Phoenix, AZ] B: 5/18/1932, Phoenix, AZ
Drafted: 1955 Round 17 LARm
1958 Phi: 2 G; Rec 3-39 13.0 1 TD; 6 Pt.

AARON MITCHELL Mitchell, Aaron Templeton Jr. 6'1", 196 **DB**
Col: Coll. of the Canyons CA (J.C.); Morris Brown; Nevada-Las Vegas
HS: North Hollywood [CA] B: 12/15/1956, Los Angeles, CA
Drafted: 1979 Round 2 Dal
1979 Dal: 16 G; Int 1-36. **1980** Dal: 15 G; Int 3-56. **1981** TB: 13 G.
Total: 44 G; Int 4-92.

AL MITCHELL Mitchell, Albert Edwin 6'1", 180 **T-C-G**
(Tally) *Col:* Thiel *HS:* Greenville [PA] B: 8/30/1897, Greenville, PA
D: 5/12/1967, Livonia, NY
1924 Buf: 6 G.

ALVIN MITCHELL Mitchell, Alvin Eugene 6'3", 195 **DB**
(Wild Man) *Col:* Morgan State *HS:* Simon Gratz [Philadelphia, PA]
B: 10/18/1943, Philadelphia, PA *Drafted:* 1968 Round 10 Cle
1968 Cle: 12 G. **1969** Cle: 14 G; KR 1-0. **1970** Den: 2 G. **Total:** 28 G; KR 1-0.

ALVIN MITCHELL Mitchell, Alvin Jerome 6'0", 235 **RB**
Col: Auburn *HS:* Venice [FL] B: 8/20/1964, Venice, FL
1989 TB: 5 G; Rec 1-11 11.0.

BRANDON MITCHELL Mitchell, Brandon Paul 6'3", 289 **DE-DT**
Col: Texas A&M *HS:* Abbeville [LA] B: 6/19/1975, Abbeville, LA
Drafted: 1997 Round 2 NE
1997 NE: 12 G. **1998** NE: 7 G; 2 Sac. **Total:** 19 G; 2 Sac.

BRIAN MITCHELL Mitchell, Brian Keith 5'10", 211 **RB**
Col: Southwestern Louisiana *HS:* Plaquemine [LA] B: 8/18/1968, Fort Polk, LA *Drafted:* 1990 Round 5 Was
1990 Was: Pass 6-3 50.0%, 40 6.67. **1992** Was: Pass 1-0. **1993** Was: Pass 2-1 50.0%, 50 25.00 1 Int. **1994** Was: Pass 1-0, 1 Int; Scor 1 2XP.
1996 Was: Pass 1-0. **1998** Was: Pass 2-1 50.0%. **Total:** Pass 13-5 38.5%, 90 6.92 2 Int; Scor 1 2XP.

		Rushing				Receiving			
Year Team	**G**	**Att**	**Yds**	**Avg**	**TD**	**Rec**	**Yds**	**Avg**	**TD**
1990 Was	15	15	81	5.4	1	2	5	2.5	0
1991 Was	16	3	14	4.7	0	0	0	—	0
1992 Was	16	6	70	11.7	0	3	30	10.0	0
1993 Was	16	63	246	3.9	3	20	157	7.9	0
1994 Was	16	78	311	4.0	0	26	236	9.1	1
1995 Was	16	46	301	6.5	1	38	324	8.5	1
1996 Was	16	39	193	4.9	0	32	286	8.9	0
1997 Was	16	23	107	4.7	1	36	438	12.2	1
1998 Was	16	39	208	5.3	2	44	306	7.0	0
NFL Total	143	312	1531	4.9	8	201	1782	8.9	3

	Punt Returns				Kickoff Returns					Tot
Year Team	**Ret**	**Yds**	**Avg**	**TD**	**Ret**	**Yds**	**Avg**	**TD**	**Fum**	**TD**
1990 Was	12	107	8.9	0	18	365	20.3	0	2	1
1991 Was	45	**600**	13.3	**2**	29	583	20.1	0	8	2
1992 Was	29	271	9.3	1	23	492	21.4	0	4	1
1993 Was	29	193	6.7	0	33	678	20.5	0	3	3
1994 Was	32	452	**14.1**	**2**	58	1478	25.5	0	4	3
1995 Was	25	315	12.6	**1**	55	1408	25.6	0	2	3
1996 Was	23	258	11.2	0	56	1258	22.5	0	1	0
1997 Was	38	442	11.6	1	47	1094	23.3	1	3	4
1998 Was	44	506	11.5	0	59	1337	22.7	1	3	3
NFL Total	277	3144	11.4	7	378	8693	23.0	2	30	20

BRIAN MITCHELL Mitchell, Brian Keith 5′9″, 164 **DB**
Col: Brigham Young *HS:* Waco [TX] B: 12/13/1968, Indianapolis, IN
Drafted: 1991 Round 7 Atl
1991 Atl: 15 G; 2 Sac. **1992** Atl: 16 G; Int 1-0. **1993** Atl: 5 G. **Total:** 36 G; Int 1-0; 2 Sac.

CHARLIE MITCHELL Mitchell, Charles E Jr. 6′0″, 188 **DB**
(Mitch) *Col:* Southwest Missouri State; Tulsa *HS:* Neosho [MO]
B: 12/28/1920, Oilton, OK *Drafted:* 1944 Round 26 ChiB
1945 ChiB: 8 G. **1946** GB: 2 G; Int 1-18. **Total:** 10 G; Int 1-18.

CHARLEY MITCHELL Mitchell, Charles Howard 5′11″, 185 **HB-DB**
Col: Washington *HS:* James A. Garfield [Seattle, WA] B: 5/25/1940, McNary, AZ *Drafted:* 1963 Round 18 Den
1963 Den: PR 12-141 11.8; Int 1-0. **1964** Den: Pass 1-0; PR 9-110 12.2.
Total: Pass 1-0; PR 21-251 12.0; Int 1-0.

		Rushing				Receiving			
Year Team	**G**	**Att**	**Yds**	**Avg**	**TD**	**Rec**	**Yds**	**Avg**	**TD**
1963 Den	14	24	41	1.7	0	8	71	8.9	0
1964 Den	14	177	590	3.3	5	33	225	6.8	1
1965 Den	1	0	0	—	0	0	0	—	0
1966 Den	13	70	199	2.8	0	14	239	17.1	2
1967 Den	14	82	308	3.8	0	7	15	2.1	0
1968 Buf	3	0	0	—	0	0	0	—	0
NFL Total	59	353	1138	3.2	5	62	550	8.9	3

	Kickoff Returns					Tot
Year Team	**Ret**	**Yds**	**Avg**	**TD**	**Fum**	**TD**
1963 Den	37	954	25.8	**1**	2	1
1964 Den	10	221	22.1	0	3	6
1966 Den	3	55	18.3	0	3	2
1967 Den	8	164	20.5	0	2	0
1968 Buf	5	98	19.6	0	0	0
NFL Total	63	1492	23.7	1	10	9

KEITH MITCHELL Mitchell, Clarence Marquis 6′2″, 240 **LB**
Col: Texas A&M *HS:* Lakeview [Garland, TX] B: 7/24/1974, Garland, TX
1997 NO: 16 G; 4 Sac. **1998** NO: 16 G; 1 Fum TD; 6 Pt; 2.5 Sac.
Total: 32 G; 1 Fum TD; 6 Pt; 6.5 Sac.

DALE MITCHELL Mitchell, Dale James 6′3″, 223 **LB**
Col: USC *HS:* Carlsbad [CA] B: 9/1/1953, Oceanside, CA
Drafted: 1975 Round 13 SF
1976 SF: 13 G. **1977** SF: 4 G. **Total:** 17 G.

DERRELL MITCHELL Mitchell, Derrell Lavoice 5′9″, 189 **WR**
Col: Joliet JC IL; Texas Tech *HS:* Miami Northwestern [FL]
B: 9/16/1971, Miami, FL *Drafted:* 1994 Round 6 NO
1994 NO: 14 G; Rec 1-13 13.0; PR 3-9 3.0; KR 6-129 21.5.

DEVON MITCHELL Mitchell, Devon Dermott 6′1″, 194 **DB**
Col: Iowa *HS:* Samuel J. Tilden [Brooklyn, NY] B: 12/30/1962, Kingston, Jamaica *Drafted:* 1986 Round 4 Det
1986 Det: 16 G; Int 5-41. **1988** Det: 10 G; Int 3-107 1 TD; 6 Pt.
Total: 26 G; Int 8-148 1 TD; 6 Pt.

ED MITCHELL Mitchell, Edward Levine 6′2″, 285 **OG**
(Earthquake) *Col:* Southern University *HS:* Galveston Central [TX]
B: 9/5/1942, Galveston, TX *Drafted:* 1964 Round 15 SD
1965 SD: 3 G. **1966** SD: 14 G. **1967** SD: 4 G. **Total:** 21 G.

FONDREN MITCHELL Mitchell, Fondren Lack 6′0″, 185 **HB-DB**
Col: Florida *HS:* Leon [Tallahassee, FL] B: 6/19/1921, Tallahassee, FL
D: 9/24/1952, Tampa, FL
AAFC **1946** MiaA: 7 G; Rush 5-17 3.4; Rec 8-131 16.4; KR 4-52 13.0; Int 1-2.

TED MITCHELL Mitchell, Frederick Brice 5′10″, 195 **C**
Col: Bucknell *HS:* Madison [NJ] B: 8/4/1905, Madison, NJ
D: 10/11/1985, Toms River, NJ
1929 Ora: 12 G. **1930** Nwk: 11 G. **Total:** 23 G.

BUSTER MITCHELL Mitchell, Granville Myrick 6′0″, 205 **OE-DE-T**
(Tex) *Col:* Cisco JC TX; Davis & Elkins *HS:* Sweetwater [TX]
B: 2/16/1906, Irene, TX D: 3/4/1964, Sweetwater, TX
1931 Port: 13 G. **1932** Port: 10 G; Rec 2-31 15.5. **1933** Port: 11 G.
1934 Det: 13 G; Rush 7-48 6.9. **1935** Det-NYG: 5 G; Rec 1-11 11.0. Det: 3 G. NYG: 2 G; Rec 1-11 11.0. **1936** NYG: 8 G; Rec 2-10 5.0. **1937** Bkn: 11 G; Rush 2-4 2.0; Rec 8-115 14.4 1 TD; 6 Pt. **Total:** 71 G; Rush 9-52 5.8; Rec 13-167 12.8 1 TD; 6 Pt.

HAL MITCHELL Mitchell, Harold Dwayne 6′1″, 225 **OT-OG**
Col: UCLA *HS:* Leuzinger [Lawndale, CA] B: 8/11/1930
Drafted: 1952 Round 14 NYG
1952 NYG: 11 G.

JIM MITCHELL Mitchell, James Halcot 6′3″, 245 **DE-DT**
Col: Virginia State *HS:* John M. Langston [Danville, VA] B: 9/15/1948, Danville, VA *Drafted:* 1970 Round 3 Det
1970 Det: 14 G. **1971** Det: 13 G; 1 Fum. **1972** Det: 14 G; Int 1-0; 1 Fum.
1973 Det: 9 G. **1974** Det: 14 G; Scor **1** Saf; 2 Pt. **1975** Det: 14 G.
1976 Det: 14 G. **1977** Det: 9 G. **Total:** 101 G; Int 1-0; Scor 1 Saf; 2 Pt; 2 Fum.

JIM MITCHELL Mitchell, James Robert 6′1″, 234 **TE**
Col: Prairie View A&M *HS:* Harris [Shelbyville, TN] B: 10/19/1947, Shelbyville, TN *Drafted:* 1969 Round 4 Atl
1971 Atl: **1** Fum TD. **1975** Atl: **1** Fum TD. **1978** Atl: KR 1-14 14.0.
Total: KR 1-14 14.0; 2 Fum TD.

		Rushing				Receiving					Tot
Year Team	**G**	**Att**	**Yds**	**Avg**	**TD**	**Rec**	**Yds**	**Avg**	**TD**	**Fum**	**TD**
1969 Atl	14	5	77	15.4	0	22	339	15.4	4	1	4
1970 Atl	14	5	23	4.6	1	44	650	14.8	6	0	7
1971 Atl	13	4	25	6.3	0	33	593	18.0	5	3	6
1972 Atl	14	2	19	9.5	0	28	470	16.8	4	0	4
1973 Atl	14	5	34	6.8	0	32	420	13.1	0	0	0
1974 Atl	14	3	21	7.0	0	30	479	16.0	1	1	1
1975 Atl	14	0	0	—	0	34	536	15.8	4	0	5
1976 Atl	14	1	-6	-6.0	0	17	209	12.3	0	0	0
1977 Atl	12	1	-6	-6.0	0	17	178	10.5	0	0	0
1978 Atl	16	0	0	—	0	32	366	11.4	2	2	2
1979 Atl	16	0	0	—	0	16	118	7.4	2	0	2
NFL Total	155	26	187	7.2	1	305	4358	14.3	28	7	31

JEFF MITCHELL Mitchell, Jeffrey Clay 6′4″, 300 **C**
Col: Florida *HS:* Countryside [Clearwater, FL] B: 1/29/1974, Clearwater, FL *Drafted:* 1997 Round 5 Bal
1998 Bal: 11 G; 1 Fum.

JOHNNY MITCHELL Mitchell, Johnnie Jr. 6′3″, 247 **TE**
Col: Nebraska *HS:* Neal F. Simeon [Chicago, IL] B: 1/20/1971, Chicago, IL *Drafted:* 1992 Round 1 NYJ

		Receiving				
Year Team	**G**	**Rec**	**Yds**	**Avg**	**TD**	**Fum**
1992 NYJ	11	16	210	13.1	1	0
1993 NYJ	14	39	630	16.2	6	0
1994 NYJ	16	58	749	12.9	4	1
1995 NYJ	12	45	497	11.0	5	2
1996 Dal	4	1	17	17.0	0	0
NFL Total	57	159	2103	13.2	16	3

KEN MITCHELL Mitchell, Kenneth Wayne 6′2″, 224 **LB**
Col: Nevada-Las Vegas *HS:* Lutheran [Inglewood, CA] B: 11/14/1948, Denio, NV
1973 Atl: 14 G. **1974** Atl: 14 G; KR 4-36 9.0. **Total:** 28 G; KR 4-36 9.0.

KEVIN MITCHELL Mitchell, Kevin Danyelle 6′1″, 255 **LB**
Col: Syracuse *HS:* John Harris [Harrisburg, PA] B: 1/1/1971, Harrisburg, PA *Drafted:* 1994 Round 2 SF
1994 SF: 16 G. **1995** SF: 15 G. **1996** SF: 12 G; 1 Sac. **1997** SF: 16 G.
1998 NO: 8 G; 2.5 Sac. **Total:** 67 G; 3.5 Sac.

LEONARD MITCHELL Mitchell, Leonard Boyd 6′7″, 290 **DE**
Col: Houston *HS:* Booker T. Washington [Houston, TX] B: 10/12/1958, Houston, TX *Drafted:* 1981 Round 1 Phi
1981 Phi: 16 G. **1982** Phi: 9 G. **1983** Phi: 10 G. **1984** Phi: 16 G. **1985** Phi: 16 G. **1986** Phi: 10 G. **1987** Atl: 12 G. **Total:** 89 G.

LEROY MITCHELL Mitchell, Leroy 6′1″, 190 **DB**
(Baby Face) *Col:* Texas Southern *HS:* Wharton Training [TX]
B: 9/22/1944, Wharton, TX *Drafted:* 1967 Round 11 Bos
1971 Den: PR 1-0. **1973** Den: PR 1-0. **Total:** PR 2-0.

		Interceptions			
Year Team	**G**	**Int**	**Yds**	**TD**	**Fum**
1967 Bos	14	3	9	0	0
1968 Bos	14	7	41	0	0
1970 Hou	14	2	35	0	0
1971 Den	14	2	0	0	1
1972 Den	14	3	27	0	0
1973 Den	12	2	43	1	0
NFL Total	82	19	155	1	1

LYDELL MITCHELL Mitchell, Lydell Douglas 5′11″, 204 **RB**
Col: Penn State *HS:* Salem [NJ] B: 5/30/1949, Salem, NJ
Drafted: 1972 Round 2 Bal
1979 SD: KR 1-15 15.0. **Total:** KR 1-15 15.0.

		Rushing				Receiving					Tot
Year Team	**G**	**Att**	**Yds**	**Avg**	**TD**	**Rec**	**Yds**	**Avg**	**TD**	**Fum**	**TD**
1972 Bal	11	45	215	4.8	1	18	147	8.2	1	3	2
1973 Bal	14	253	963	3.8	2	17	113	6.6	0	2	2
1974 Bal	14	214	757	3.5	5	**72**	544	7.6	2	6	7
1975 Bal	14	289	1193	4.1	11	60	544	9.1	4	5	15
1976 Bal	14	289	1200	4.2	5	60	555	9.3	3	4	8
1977 Bal	14	301	1159	3.9	3	**71**	620	8.7	4	5	7
1978 SD	16	214	820	3.8	3	57	500	8.8	2	2	5
1979 SD	12	63	211	3.3	0	19	159	8.4	1	2	1
1980 LARm	2	7	16	2.3	0	2	21	10.5	0	0	0
NFL Total	111	1675	6534	3.9	30	376	3203	8.5	17	29	47

STUMP MITCHELL Mitchell, Lyvonia Albert 5′9″, 188 **RB**
Col: The Citadel *HS:* Camden Co. [St. Mary's, GA] B: 3/15/1959, St. Mary's, GA *Drafted:* 1981 Round 9 StL
1984 StL: Pass 1-1 100.0%, 20 20.00. **1985** StL: Pass 2-1 50.0%, 31 15.50. **1986** StL: Pass 3-1 33.3%, 15 5.00 1 TD. **1987** StL: Pass 3-1 33.3%, 17 5.67. **Total:** Pass 9-4 44.4%, 83 9.22 1 TD.

		Rushing				Receiving			
Year Team	G	Att	Yds	Avg	TD	Rec	Yds	Avg	TD
1981 StL	16	31	175	5.6	0	6	35	5.8	1
1982 StL	9	39	189	4.8	1	11	149	13.5	0
1983 StL	15	68	373	5.5	3	7	54	7.7	0
1984 StL	16	81	434	5.4	9	26	318	12.2	2
1985 StL	16	183	1006	**5.5**	7	47	502	10.7	3
1986 StL	15	174	800	4.6	5	41	276	6.7	0
1987 StL	12	203	781	3.8	3	45	397	8.8	2
1988 Pho	14	164	726	4.4	4	25	214	8.6	1
1989 Pho	3	43	165	3.8	0	1	10	10.0	0
NFL Total	116	986	4649	4.7	32	209	1955	9.4	9

	Punt Returns				Kickoff Returns					Tot
Year Team	Ret	Yds	Avg	TD	Ret	Yds	Avg	TD	Fum	TD
1981 StL	42	445	10.6	1	55	**1292**	23.5	0	3	2
1982 StL	27	165	6.1	0	16	364	22.8	0	3	1
1983 StL	38	337	8.9	0	36	778	21.6	0	5	3
1984 StL	38	333	8.8	0	35	804	23.0	0	6	11
1985 StL	11	97	8.8	0	19	345	18.2	0	6	10
1986 StL	0	0	—	0	6	203	33.8	0	4	5
1987 StL	0	0	—	0	0	0	—	0	3	5
1988 Pho	0	0	—	0	10	221	22.1	0	6	5
NFL Total	156	1377	8.8	1	177	4007	22.6	0	36	42

MACK MITCHELL Mitchell, Mack Henry 6′8″, 246 **DE**
Col: Houston *HS:* Diboll [TX] B: 8/16/1952, Diboll, TX *Drafted:* 1975 Round 1 Cle
1975 Cle: 14 G. **1976** Cle: 14 G; Scor **1** Saf; 2 Pt. **1977** Cle: 14 G. **1978** Cle: 14 G. **1979** Cin: 13 G. **Total:** 69 G; Scor 1 Saf; 2 Pt.

MARK MITCHELL Mitchell, Martin 6′1″, 180 **DB**
Col: Tulane *HS:* Marion [Lake Charles, LA] B: 1/10/1954, Lake Charles, LA *Drafted:* 1977 Round 6 Phi
1977 Phi: 14 G; PR 2-4 2.0; 2 Fum.

MEL MITCHELL Mitchell, Melvin 6′3″, 260 **OG-C-OT**
Col: Tennessee State *HS:* Lincoln [Dallas, TX] B: 2/21/1953, Dallas, TX *Drafted:* 1976 Round 4 Mia
1976 Mia: 12 G. **1977** Mia-Det: 12 G. Mia: 3 G. Det: 9 G. **1978** Mia: 4 G. **1980** Min: 6 G. **Total:** 34 G.

MICHAEL MITCHELL Mitchell, Michael George 5′10″, 180 **DB**
Col: Howard Payne *HS:* Richfield [Waco, TX] B: 10/18/1961, Waco, TX
1987 Was: 3 G; Int 1-17. **1989** NYJ: 5 G. **Total:** 8 G; Int 1-17.

PAUL MITCHELL Mitchell, Paul Anthony 6′3″, 235 **DT-OT**
Col: Minnesota *HS:* Edison [Minneapolis, MN] B: 8/10/1920, Minneapolis, MN
AAFC **1946** LA-A: 10 G. **1947** LA-A: 11 G. **1948** LA-A-NY-A: 12 G. **1949** NY-A: 12 G; PR 1-15 15.0. **Total:** 45 G; PR 1-15 15.0.

NFL **1950** NYY: 12 G. **1951** NYY: 12 G; KR 1-11 11.0. **Total:** 24 G; KR 1-11 11.0.

PETE MITCHELL Mitchell, Peter Clark 6′2″, 243 **TE**
Col: Boston College *HS:* Brother Rice [Birmingham, MI] B: 10/9/1971, Royal Oak, MI *Drafted:* 1995 Round 4 Mia
1997 Jac: KR 2-17 8.5. **1998** Jac: KR 2-27 13.5. **Total:** KR 4-44 11.0.

		Receiving				
Year Team	G	Rec	Yds	Avg	TD	Fum
1995 Jac	16	41	527	12.9	2	0
1996 Jac	16	52	575	11.1	1	1
1997 Jac	16	35	380	10.9	4	0
1998 Jac	16	38	363	9.6	2	0
NFL Total	64	166	1845	11.1	9	1

RANDALL MITCHELL Mitchell, Randall Evans 6′1″, 275 **NT**
Col: Tennessee-Chattanooga *HS:* Herschel V. Jenkins [Savannah, GA] B: 9/19/1963, Savannah, GA
1987 Phi: 3 G; 1 Sac.

BOBBY MITCHELL Mitchell, Robert Cornelius 6′0″, 192 **FL-HB-WR**
Col: Illinois *HS:* Langston [Hot Springs, AR] B: 6/6/1935, Hot Springs, AR *Drafted:* 1958 Round 7 Cle *HOF:* 1983
1960 Cle: Pass 1-1 100.0%, 23 23.00 1 TD. **1966** Was: Pass 1-1 100.0%, 21 21.00. **1967** Was: Pass 1-1 100.0%, 17 17.00. **Total:** Pass 3-3 100.0%, 61 20.33 1 TD.

		Rushing				Receiving			
Year Team	G	Att	Yds	Avg	TD	Rec	Yds	Avg	TD
1958 Cle	12	80	500	6.3	1	16	131	8.2	3
1959 Cle	12	131	743	5.7	5	35	351	10.0	4
1960 Cle	12	111	506	4.6	5	45	612	13.6	6
1961 Cle	14	101	548	**5.4**	5	32	368	11.5	3
1962 Was	14	1	5	5.0	0	**72**	**1384**	19.2	11
1963 Was	14	3	24	8.0	0	69	**1436**	20.8	7
1964 Was	14	2	33	16.5	0	60	904	15.1	**10**
1965 Was	14	0	0	—	0	60	867	14.5	6
1966 Was	14	13	141	10.8	1	58	905	15.6	9
1967 Was	14	61	189	3.1	1	60	866	14.4	6
1968 Was	14	10	46	4.6	0	14	130	9.3	0
NFL Total	148	513	2735	5.3	18	521	7954	15.3	65

	Punt Returns				Kickoff Returns					Tot
Year Team	Ret	Yds	Avg	TD	Ret	Yds	Avg	TD	Fum	TD
1958 Cle	14	165	11.8	**1**	18	454	25.2	1	2	6
1959 Cle	17	177	10.4	1	11	236	21.5	0	2	10
1960 Cle	9	101	11.2	0	17	432	25.4	**1**	4	12
1961 Cle	14	164	11.7	1	16	428	26.8	**1**	6	10
1962 Was	3	7	2.3	0	12	398	33.2	**1**	5	12
1963 Was	6	49	8.2	0	9	343	38.1	1	7	8
1964 Was	0	0	—	0	3	58	19.3	0	2	10
1965 Was	1	15	15.0	0	5	106	21.2	0	1	6
1966 Was	4	21	5.3	0	0	0	—	0	0	10
1967 Was	0	0	—	0	0	0	—	0	2	7
1968 Was	1	0	0.0	0	11	235	21.4	0	1	0
NFL Total	69	699	10.1	3	102	2690	26.4	5	32	91

BOB MITCHELL Mitchell, Robert Stanley 5′11″, 195 **DB-HB-BB-QB**
Col: Stanford *HS:* Turlock [CA] B: 1/27/1921, Turlock, CA D: 7/17/1997, Silver Lake, CA
AAFC **1946** LA-A: Pass 10-3 30.0%, 19 1.90 2 Int; Rec 1-1 1.0; Int 1-32; Punt 1-44 44.0. **1947** LA-A: Rec 3-36 12.0 1 TD; KR 6-119 19.8; Int 2-24. **1948** LA-A: Pass 2-1 50.0%, 15 7.50 1 Int; Int 3-1. **Total:** Pass 12-4 33.3%, 34 2.83 3 Int; Rec 4-37 9.3 1 TD; KR 6-119 19.8; Int 6-57; Punt 1-44 44.0.

		Rushing			
Year Team	G	Att	Yds	Avg	TD
1946 LA-A	11	8	-12	-1.5	0
1947 LA-A	12	32	85	2.7	0
1948 LA-A	4	2	-2	-1.0	0
AAFC Total	27	42	71	1.7	0

ROLAND MITCHELL Mitchell, Roland Earl 5′11″, 195 **DB**
Col: Texas Tech *HS:* Bay City [TX] B: 3/15/1964, Columbus, TX *Drafted:* 1987 Round 2 Buf
1987 Buf: 11 G. **1988** Buf-Pho: 14 G; Int 1-0. Buf: 3 G. Pho: 11 G; Int 1-0. **1989** Pho: 3 G. **1990** Atl: 13 G; PR 1-0; Int 2-16; 1 Fum. **1991** GB: 16 G; 1 Sac. **1992** GB: 15 G; Int 2-40. **1993** GB: 16 G; Int 1-0. **1994** GB: 1 G. **Total:** 89 G; PR 1-0; Int 6-56; 1 Fum; 1 Sac.

RUSSELL MITCHELL Mitchell, Russell Bryan 6′5″, 288 **C**
Col: Mississippi *HS:* Slidell [LA] B: 12/28/1960, El Campo, TX
1987 NYG: 3 G.

SHANNON MITCHELL Mitchell, Shannon Lamont 6′2″, 245 **TE**
Col: Georgia *HS:* Alcoa [TN] B: 3/28/1972, Alcoa, TN
1994 SD: KR 1-18 18.0. **Total:** KR 1-18 18.0.

		Receiving				
Year Team	G	Rec	Yds	Avg	TD	Fum
1994 SD	16	11	105	9.5	0	0
1995 SD	16	3	31	10.3	1	0
1996 SD	16	10	57	5.7	0	1
1997 SD	4	1	14	14.0	0	0
NFL Total	52	25	207	8.3	1	1

STAN MITCHELL Mitchell, Stanton Earl 6′2″, 210 **RB**
(Bronk) *Col:* Tennessee *HS:* Sparta [TN] B: 8/17/1944, Wayne, MI *Drafted:* 1966 Round 8 Was
1967 Mia: KR 2-57 28.5. **1970** Mia: KR 4-35 8.8. **Total:** KR 6-92 15.3.

		Rushing				Receiving					Tot
Year Team	G	Att	Yds	Avg	TD	Rec	Yds	Avg	TD	Fum	TD
1966 Mia	2	0	0	—	0	0	0	—	0	0	0
1967 Mia	14	83	269	3.2	3	18	133	7.4	1	4	4
1968 Mia	9	54	176	3.3	1	8	190	23.8	3	0	4
1969 Mia	3	28	80	2.9	0	10	125	12.5	0	1	0
1970 Mia	14	8	23	2.9	0	6	85	14.2	1	0	1
NFL Total	42	173	548	3.2	4	42	533	12.7	5	5	9

TOM MITCHELL Mitchell, Thomas Gordon 6′2″, 215 **TE-WR**
Col: Bucknell *HS:* Plymouth-Whitemarsh [Plymouth Meeting, PA] B: 8/22/1944, Newport, RI *Drafted:* 1966 Round 3 Oak
1971 Bal: Rush 2-9 4.5; KR 1-0. **1972** Bal: Rush 0-7. **1974** SF: Rush 1-(-2) -2.0. **1976** SF: KR 2-7 3.5. **Total:** Rush 3-14 4.7; KR 3-7 2.3.

		Receiving				
Year Team	G	Rec	Yds	Avg	TD	Fum
1966 Oak	14	23	301	13.1	1	0
1968 Bal	14	6	117	19.5	4	0

Year Team						
1969 Bal	8	9	199	22.1	3	0
1970 Bal	14	20	261	13.1	4	0
1971 Bal	14	33	402	12.2	0	0
1972 Bal	14	40	494	12.4	4	1
1973 Bal	13	25	313	12.5	4	0
1974 SF	14	19	262	13.8	0	0
1975 SF	13	25	366	14.6	3	2
1976 SF	14	20	240	12.0	1	1
1977 SF	13	19	226	11.9	0	0
NFL Total	145	239	3181	13.3	24	4

WILLIE MITCHELL Mitchell, William Anderson 6′0″, 185 **DB**
(Top Cat) *Col:* Tennessee State *HS:* Phillis Wheatley [Houston, TX] B: 8/28/1940, San Antonio, TX
1969 KC: KR 7-178 25.4. **Total:** KR 7-178 25.4.

		Punt Returns				Interceptions				Tot
Year Team	**G**	**Ret**	**Yds**	**Avg**	**TD**	**Int**	**Yds**	**TD**	**Fum**	**TD**
1964 KC	9	18	160	8.9	0	1	0	0	1	0
1965 KC	14	19	242	12.7	1	2	44	1	3	2
1966 KC	14	1	7	7.0	0	3	97	1	0	1
1967 KC	9	0	0	—	0	4	88	1	0	1
1968 KC	13	1	21	21.0	0	5	46	0	0	0
1969 KC	14	13	101	7.8	0	1	27	0	4	0
1970 KC	14	4	33	8.3	0	0	0	0	1	0
NFL Total	87	56	564	10.1	1	16	302	3	9	4

SCOTT MITCHELL Mitchell, William Scott 6′6″, 230 **QB**
Col: Utah *HS:* Springville [UT] B: 1/2/1968, Salt Lake City, UT
Drafted: 1990 Round 4 Mia

		Passing							
Year Team	**G**	**Att**	**Comp**	**Comp%**	**Yds**	**YPA**	**TD**	**Int**	**Rating**
1991 Mia	2	0	0	—	0	—	0	0	—
1992 Mia	16	8	2	25.0	32	4.00	0	1	4.2
1993 Mia	13	233	133	57.1	1773	7.61	12	8	84.2
1994 Det	9	246	119	48.4	1456	5.92	10	11	62.0
1995 Det	16	583	346	59.3	4338	7.44	32	12	92.3
1996 Det	14	437	253	57.9	2917	6.68	17	17	74.9
1997 Det	16	509	293	57.6	3484	6.84	19	14	79.6
1998 Det	2	75	38	50.7	452	6.03	1	3	57.2
NFL Total	88	2091	1184	56.6	14452	6.91	91	66	79.4

	Rushing				
Year Team	**Att**	**Yds**	**Avg**	**TD**	**Fum**
1992 Mia	8	10	1.3	0	1
1993 Mia	21	89	4.2	0	3
1994 Det	15	24	1.6	1	8
1995 Det	36	104	2.9	4	8
1996 Det	37	83	2.2	4	9
1997 Det	37	83	2.2	1	15
1998 Det	7	30	4.3	0	1
NFL Total	161	423	2.6	10	45

BOB MITINGER Mitinger, Robert Bray 6′2″, 230 **LB**
Col: Penn State *HS:* Salem [Greensburg, PA] B: 2/13/1940, Greensburg, PA *Drafted:* 1962 Round 5 SD
1962 SD: 14 G. **1963** SD: 14 G; Int 3-26. **1964** SD: 9 G. **1966** SD: 2 G. **1968** SD: 3 G. **Total:** 42 G; Int 3-26.

ALONZO MITZ Mitz, Alonzo Loqwone 6′3″, 275 **DE-LB**
Col: Florida *HS:* Fort Pierce Central [FL] B: 6/5/1963, Henderson, NC
Drafted: 1986 Round 8 Sea
1986 Sea: 6 G; 1 Sac. **1987** Sea: 6 G. **1988** Sea: 16 G; 3 Sac. **1989** Sea: 12 G; 1 Sac. **1991** Cin: 15 G; Int 1-8. **1992** Cin: 16 G; Int 1-3; 3 Sac. **Total:** 71 G; Int 2-11; 8 Sac.

BRYANT MIX Mix, Bryant Lee 6′3″, 291 **DE**
(Big Mix) *Col:* Northwest Mississippi CC; Alcorn State *HS:* Water Valley [MS] B: 7/28/1972, Water Valley, MS *Drafted:* 1996 Round 2 Hou
1996 Hou: 6 G; 1 Sac. **1997** Ten: 1 G. **Total:** 7 G; 1 Sac.

RON MIX Mix, Ronald Jack 6′4″, 250 **OT-OG**
Col: USC *HS:* Hawthorne [CA] B: 3/10/1938, Los Angeles, CA
Drafted: 1960 Round 1 Bos *HOF:* 1979
1960 LAC: 14 G. **1961** SD: 10 G; KR 1-0. **1962** SD: 14 G. **1963** SD: 14 G. **1964** SD: 14 G. **1965** SD: 14 G. **1966** SD: 14 G. **1967** SD: 14 G. **1968** SD: 14 G. **1969** SD: 8 G. **1971** Oak: 12 G. **Total:** 142 G; KR 1-0.

BILLY MIXON Mixon, Billy Raymond 5′11″, 191 **HB-DB**
Col: Georgia *HS:* Tift Co. [Tifton, GA] B: 5/24/1929, Tifton, GA
Drafted: 1951 Round 3 SF
1953 SF: Rec 1-7 7.0. **1954** SF: Int 2-6. **Total:** Rec 1-7 7.0; Int 2-6.

		Rushing			
Year Team	**G**	**Att**	**Yds**	**Avg**	**TD**
1953 SF	12	25	176	7.0	1
1954 SF	10	7	19	2.7	0
NFL Total	22	32	195	6.1	1

KENNY MIXON Mixon, Kenneth Jermaine 6′4″, 273 **DE**
Col: Louisiana State *HS:* Pineville [LA] B: 5/31/1975, Los Angeles, CA
Drafted: 1998 Round 2 Mia
1998 Mia: 16 G; 2 Sac.

WARNER MIZELL Mizell, Lawrence Warner 5′10″, 188 **WB-FB-TB**
Col: Georgia Tech *HS:* Miami Senior [FL] Deceased
1931 Bkn-Fra: 8 G. Bkn: 5 G. Fra: 3 G. **Total:** 8 G.

KELLY MOAN Moan, Emmett Auto 6′0″, 193 **TB-DB**
Col: West Virginia *HS:* Long Beach Polytechnic [CA] B: 10/20/1912, Long Beach, CA D: 8/3/1954, Wheeling, WV *Drafted:* 1938 Round 5 NYG
1939 Cle: 2 G; Pass 9-3 33.3%, 77 8.56 1 TD 2 Int; Rush 2-(-15) -7.5; Punt 1-30 30.0; Scor 1, 1-1 100.0% XK.

JOHN MOBLEY Mobley, John Ulysses 6′1″, 236 **LB**
Col: Kutztown *HS:* Chichester [Boothwyn, PA] B: 10/10/1973, Chester, PA *Drafted:* 1996 Round 1 Den
1996 Den: 16 G; Int 1-8; 1.5 Sac. **1997** Den: 16 G; Int 1-13 1 TD; 6 Pt; 4 Sac. **1998** Den: 16 G; Int 1-(-2); 1 Sac. **Total:** 48 G; Int 3-19 1 TD; 6 Pt; 6.5 Sac.

ORSON MOBLEY Mobley, Orson Odell 6′5″, 256 **TE**
Col: Florida State; Salem *HS:* Miami Palmetto [FL] B: 3/4/1963, Brookeville, FL *Drafted:* 1986 Round 6 Den
1986 Den: Rush 1-(-1) -1.0. **1990** Den: KR 1-9 9.0. **Total:** Rush 1-(-1) -1.0; KR 1-9 9.0.

		Receiving				
Year Team	**G**	**Rec**	**Yds**	**Avg**	**TD**	**Fum**
1986 Den	14	22	332	15.1	1	1
1987 Den	10	16	228	14.3	1	1
1988 Den	16	21	218	10.4	2	1
1989 Den	12	17	200	11.8	0	0
1990 Den	9	8	41	5.1	0	1
NFL Total	61	84	1019	12.1	4	4

RUDY MOBLEY Mobley, Rudolph Hamilton 5′7″, 155 **HB-DB**
Col: Hardin-Simmons *HS:* Paducah [TX] B: 12/8/1921, Paducah, TX
AAFC **1947** BalA: Rec 11-121 11.0 1 TD; PR 5-74 14.8; KR 1-18 18.0; Int 2-8.

		Rushing				Tot
Year Team	**G**	**Att**	**Yds**	**Avg**	**TD**	**TD**
1947 BalA	14	26	90	3.5	1	2

SINGOR MOBLEY Mobley, Singor A 5′11″, 195 **DB**
Col: Washington State *HS:* Curtis [Tacoma, WA] B: 10/12/1972, Tacoma, WA
1997 Dal: 12 G. **1998** Dal: 16 G. **Total:** 28 G.

STACEY MOBLEY Mobley, Stacey Lance 5′8″, 168 **WR**
Col: Jackson State *HS:* Spruce Creek [Port Orange, FL] B: 9/15/1965, Daytona Beach, FL
1987 LARm: 3 G; Rec 8-107 13.4 1 TD; PR 1-12 12.0; 6 Pt. **1989** Det: 10 G; Rec 13-158 12.2. **Total:** 13 G; Rec 21-265 12.6 1 TD; PR 1-12 12.0; 6 Pt.

MIKE MOCK Mock, Michael Earl 6′1″, 225 **LB**
Col: Texas Tech *HS:* Longview [TX] B: 2/25/1955, Trondheim, Norway
Drafted: 1978 Round 8 NYJ
1978 NYJ: 15 G.

CHARLIE MOCKMORE Mockmore, Charles A 5′11″, 192 **G**
Col: Iowa *HS:* Wilton [IA] B: 11/7/1891, Platte Co., NE D: 4/1953
1920 RI: 7 G.

JEFF MODESITT Modesitt, Jeffrey A 6′5″, 245 **TE**
Col: Delaware *HS:* Yorktown [Yorktown Heights, NY] B: 1/1/1964, Terre Haute, IN D: 8/3/1990, Atlanta, GA
1987 TB: 1 G.

ED MODZELEWSKI Modzelewski, Edward Walter 6′0″, 217 **FB**
(Big Mo) *Col:* Maryland *HS:* Har-Brack Union [Brackenridge, PA] B: 1/13/1929, West Natrona, PA *Drafted:* 1952 Round 1 Pit
1957 Cle: KR 5-74 14.8. **1959** Cle: KR 4-37 9.3. **Total:** KR 9-111 12.3.

		Rushing				Receiving					Tot
Year Team	**G**	**Att**	**Yds**	**Avg**	**TD**	**Rec**	**Yds**	**Avg**	**TD**	**Fum**	**TD**
1952 Pit	10	82	195	2.4	3	11	109	9.9	0	2	3
1955 Cle	12	185	619	3.3	6	13	113	8.7	2	3	8
1956 Cle	8	107	431	4.0	2	10	27	2.7	0	0	2
1957 Cle	12	10	21	2.1	0	0	0	—	0	0	0
1958 Cle	12	3	8	2.7	0	1	10	10.0	0	0	0
1959 Cle	12	6	18	3.0	0	3	18	6.0	1	0	1
NFL Total	66	393	1292	3.3	11	38	277	7.3	3	5	14

DICK MODZELEWSKI Modzelewski, Richard Blair 6′0″, 250 **DT**
(Little Mo) *Col:* Maryland *HS:* Har-Brack Union [Brackenridge, PA] B: 2/16/1931, West Natrona, PA *Drafted:* 1953 Round 2 Was
1953 Was: 12 G. **1954** Was: 12 G; Scor **1** Saf; 2 Pt. **1955** Pit: 12 G. **1956** NYG: 12 G. **1957** NYG: 12 G. **1958** NYG: 12 G. **1959** NYG: 12 G.

1960 NYG: 12 G. **1961** NYG: 14 G; Scor **1** Saf; 2 Pt. **1962** NYG: 14 G. **1963** NYG: 14 G. **1964** Cle: 14 G. **1965** Cle: 14 G. **1966** Cle: 14 G. **Total:** 180 G; Scor 2 Saf; 4 Pt.

HAL MOE Moe, Harold William 5′10″, 182 **WB-DB**
Col: Oregon State *HS:* Great Falls [MT] B: 3/28/1910, Spokane, WA
1933 ChiC: Pass 1-0; Rec 7-95 13.6 2 TD.

		Rushing			
Year Team	G	Att	Yds	Avg	TD
1933 ChiC	10	27	48	1.8	0

EDDIE MOEGLE Moegle, Edgar L 5′9″, 186 **WB**
Col: Detroit Mercy *HS:* Central [Detroit, MI] B: 7/11/1896 D: 6/1983, Romeo, MI
1920 Det: 1 G.

DICKY MOEGLE Moegle, Richard Lee 6′0″, 195 **DB-HB**
Col: Rice *HS:* Taylor [TX] B: 9/14/1934, Taylor, TX *Drafted:* 1955 Round 1 SF
1955 SF: Pass 1-0; Rec 4-94 23.5; PR 8-36 4.5; KR 10-249 24.9. **1956** SF: Rec 3-79 26.3; PR 1-5 5.0; KR 2-39 19.5. **1957** SF: PR 1-0. **1959** SF: Pass 1-0; Rec 1-12 12.0. **1960** Pit: PR 3-15 5.0; KR 7-174 24.9. **Total:** Pass 2-0; Rec 8-185 23.1; PR 13-56 4.3; KR 19-462 24.3.

		Rushing				Interceptions				Tot
Year Team	G	Att	Yds	Avg	TD	Int	Yds	TD	Fum	TD
1955 SF	11	41	235	5.7	5	6	50	0	2	5
1956 SF	12	7	18	2.6	0	6	75	1	0	1
1957 SF	12	9	48	5.3	1	8	107	0	0	1
1958 SF	4	0	0	—	0	0	0	0	0	0
1959 SF	8	3	9	3.0	0	0	0	0	0	0
1960 Pit	12	0	0	—	0	6	49	0	0	0
1961 Dal	14	0	0	—	0	2	31	0	0	0
NFL Total	73	60	310	5.2	6	28	312	1	2	7

TIM MOFFETT Moffett, Timothy 6′2″, 180 **WR**
Col: Mississippi *HS:* Taylorsville [MS] B: 2/8/1962, Laurel, MS *Drafted:* 1985 Round 3 LARd
1985 LARd: 13 G; Rec 5-90 18.0; 1 Fum. **1986** LARd: 16 G; Rec 6-77 12.8. **1987** SD: 3 G; Rush 1-1 1.0; Rec 5-80 16.0 1 TD; 6 Pt. **Total:** 32 G; Rush 1-1 1.0; Rec 16-247 15.4 1 TD; 6 Pt; 1 Fum.

MIKE MOFFITT Moffitt, Michael Jerome 6′4″, 215 **TE**
Col: Fresno State *HS:* Los Angeles [CA] B: 7/28/1963, Los Angeles, CA
1986 GB: 4 G; Rec 4-87 21.8.

JOHNNY MOHARDT Mohardt, John Henry 5′10″, 166 **TB-WB-HB**
Col: Notre Dame *HS:* Emerson [Gary, IN]; Notre Dame Prep [South Bend, IN] B: 1/21/1898, Pittsburgh, PA D: 11/24/1961, La Jolla, CA
1922 ChiC: 10 G; Pass 1 TD; Rec 1 TD; 6 Pt. **1923** ChiC: 10 G; Pass 1 TD; Rush 1 TD; 6 Pt. **1924** Rac: 8 G; Pass 1 TD. **1925** ChiB: 14 G; Pass 1 TD; Rec 1 TD; 6 Pt. **Total:** 42 G; Pass 4 TD; Rush 1 TD; Rec 2 TD; Tot TD 3; 18 Pt.

CHRIS MOHR Mohr, Christopher Garrett 6′5″, 215 **P**
Col: Alabama *HS:* Briarwood Acad. [Thomson, GA] B: 5/11/1966, Atlanta, GA *Drafted:* 1989 Round 6 TB
1989 TB: Scor **1** 1XP. **1991** Buf: Pass 1-1 100.0%, -9 -9.00. **1992** Buf: Rush 1-11 11.0. **1994** Buf: Rush 1-(-9) -9.0. **1997** Buf: Pass 1-1 100.0%, 29 29.00; Rush 1-0. **Total:** Pass 2-2 100.0%, 20 10.00; Rush 3-2 0.7; Scor 1 1XP.

		Punting			
Year Team	G	Punts	Yds	Avg	Fum
1989 TB	16	84	3311	39.4	0
1991 Buf	16	54	2085	38.6	0
1992 Buf	15	60	2531	42.2	0
1993 Buf	16	74	2991	40.4	1
1994 Buf	16	67	2799	41.8	0
1995 Buf	16	86	3473	40.4	0
1996 Buf	16	101	4194	41.5	0
1997 Buf	16	90	3764	41.8	1
1998 Buf	16	69	2882	41.8	0
NFL Total	143	685	28030	40.9	2

JOHN MOHRING Mohring, John Dennis 6′3″, 240 **LB**
Col: C.W. Post *HS:* Locust Valley [NY] B: 11/14/1956, Glen Cove, NY *Drafted:* 1979 Round 8 Det
1980 Det-Cle: 15 G. Det: 1 G. Cle: 14 G. **Total:** 15 G.

MIKE MOHRING Mohring, Michael Joseph 6′5″, 295 **DT**
Col: Pittsburgh *HS:* East [West Chester, PA] B: 3/22/1974, Glen Cove, NY
1997 SD: 2 G. **1998** SD: 10 G; 1 Sac. **Total:** 12 G; 1 Sac.

LOUIE MOHS Mohs, Louis M 6′2″, 220 **E-G-T**
Col: St. Thomas *HS:* St. John's Univ. Prep [Collegeville, MN] B: 1/1896, St. Cloud, MN D: 8/1967
1922 Min: 1 G. **1923** Min: 9 G; Rec 1 TD; 6 Pt. **1924** Min: 5 G. **Total:** 15 G; Rec 1 TD; 6 Pt.

DICK MOJE Moje, Richard L 6′2″, 210 **DE**
Col: Glendale CC CA; Loyola Marymount *HS:* Benjamin Franklin [Los Angeles, CA] B: 5/8/1927, Los Angeles, CA
1951 GB: 2 G; Rec 1-11 11.0.

RALF MOJSIEJENKO Mojsiejenko, Ralf 6′3″, 209 **P**
Col: Michigan State *HS:* Bridgman [MI] B: 1/28/1963, Salzgitter, Germany *Drafted:* 1985 Round 4 SD
1985 SD: Rush 1-0. **1990** Was: Rush 1-0. **Total:** Rush 2-0.

		Punting			
Year Team	G	Punts	Yds	Avg	Fum
1985 SD	16	68	2881	42.4	1
1986 SD	16	72	3026	42.0	0
1987 SD	12	67	2875	42.9	0
1988 SD	16	85	3745	44.1	0
1989 Was	16	62	2663	43.0	0
1990 Was	12	43	1687	39.2	0
1991 SF	5	16	656	41.0	0
NFL Total	93	413	17533	42.5	1

ALEX MOLDEN Molden, Alex Monroe 5′10″, 190 **DB**
Col: Oregon *HS:* Sierra [Colorado Springs, CO] B: 8/4/1973, Detroit, MI *Drafted:* 1996 Round 1 NO
1996 NO: 14 G; Int 2-2; 2 Sac. **1997** NO: 16 G; 4 Sac. **1998** NO: 16 G; Int 2-35. **Total:** 46 G; Int 4-37; 6 Sac.

FRED MOLDEN Molden, Frederick 6′2″, 272 **DT**
Col: Southern Mississippi; Jackson State *HS:* Moss Point [MS] B: 8/12/1963, Singing River, MS
1987 Min: 2 G; 1 Sac.

FRANK MOLDEN Molden, William Francis 6′5″, 276 **DT**
(Bruno) *Col:* Jackson State *HS:* Magnolia [Moss Point, MS] B: 7/28/1942, Town, MS *Drafted:* 1965 Round 11 Pit
1965 LARm: 11 G; Int 1-59; **1** Fum TD; 6 Pt. **1968** Phi: 13 G. **1969** NYG: 7 G. **Total:** 31 G; Int 1-59; 1 Fum TD; 6 Pt.

BO MOLENDA Molenda, John J 5′10″, 210 **FB-LB-BB**
Col: Michigan *HS:* Northeastern [Detroit, MI] B: 2/20/1905, Oglesby, IL D: 7/20/1986, Banning, CA
1927 NYY: Rec 1 TD; Scor 7, 1 XK. **1928** NYY-GB: Pass 1 TD; Scor 3, 3 XK. NYY: Pass 1 TD; Scor 3, 3 XK. **1929** GB: Pass 1 TD; Scor 21, 3 XK. **1930** GB: Scor 22, 4 XK. **1931** GB: Pass 4 TD; Scor 21, 3 XK. **1932** GB-NYG: Pass 15-7 46.7%, 106 7.07 1 TD 1 Int; Rec 1-15 15.0; Scor 3, 3 XK. NYG: Pass 15-7 46.7%, 106 7.07 1 TD 1 Int; Rec 1-15 15.0; Scor 3, 3 XK. **1933** NYG: Pass 2-1 50.0%, 8 4.00. **1934** NYG: Rec 3-55 18.3; Scor 2, 2 XK. **1935** NYG: Int **1** TD; Scor 11, 5 XK. **Total:** Pass 17-8 47.1%, 114 6.71 7 TD 1 Int; Rec 4-70 17.5 1 TD; Int 1 TD.

		Rushing				Tot
Year Team	G	Att	Yds	Avg	TD	TD
1927 NYY	10	—	—	—	0	1
1928 NYY-GB	12	—	—	—	0	0
1928 NYY	8	—	—	—	0	0
1928 GB	4	—	—	—	0	0
1929 GB	12	—	—	—	3	3
1930 GB	13	—	—	—	3	3
1931 GB	14	—	—	—	3	3
1932 GB-NYG	12	34	66	1.9	0	0
1932 GB	2	10	20	2.0	0	0
1932 NYG	10	24	46	1.9	0	0
1933 NYG	13	77	240	3.1	3	3
1934 NYG	13	28	99	3.5	0	0
1935 NYG	12	4	23	5.8	0	1
NFL Total	111	143	428	3.0	12	14

KEITH MOLESWORTH Molesworth, Keith Frank 5′9″, 167 **DB-HB-QB**
(Rabbit) *Col:* Monmouth (Ill.) *HS:* Washington [IA] B: 10/20/1905, Washington, IA D: 3/12/1966, Baltimore, MD
1937 ChiB: Scor 1, 1 XK.

		Passing							
Year Team	G	Att	Comp	Comp%	Yds	YPA	TD	Int	Rating
1931 ChiB	11	—	—	—	—	—	1	—	—
1932 ChiB	14	64	25	39.1	346	5.41	3	4	46.7
1933 ChiB	13	50	19	38.0	433	**8.66**	4	4	63.2
1934 ChiB	12	39	13	33.3	249	6.38	3	4	42.5
1935 ChiB	11	36	13	36.1	266	7.39	3	3	56.0
1936 ChiB	11	31	15	48.4	188	6.06	4	4	67.7
1937 ChiB	9	6	1	16.7	4	0.67	0	0	39.6
NFL Total	81	226	86	38.1	1486	6.58	18	19	52.7

	Rushing				Receiving				Tot
Year Team	Att	Yds	Avg	TD	Rec	Yds	Avg	TD	TD
1931 ChiB	—	—	—	1	—	—	—	0	1
1932 ChiB	65	213	3.3	2	3	19	6.3	1	3
1933 ChiB	61	145	2.4	0	11	118	10.7	1	1
1934 ChiB	61	125	2.0	1	1	6	6.0	0	1

1935 ChiB	81	293	3.6	4	7	154	22.0	0	4
1936 ChiB	60	276	4.6	0	9	146	16.2	0	0
1937 ChiB	20	53	2.7	0	4	21	5.3	0	0
NFL Total	348	1105	3.2	8	35	464	13.3	2	10

LOU MOLINET Molinet, Ignacio Saturnino 5′11″, 195 **FB**
Col: Cornell *HS:* Peddie School [Highstown, NJ] B: 11/30/1904, Chaparra, Cuba D: 8/27/1977, West Palm Beach, FL
1927 Fra: 9 G; Rush 1 TD; 6 Pt.

TONY MOMSEN Momsen, Anton Jr. 6′1″, 215 **C**
Col: Michigan *HS:* Edward D. Libbey [Toledo, OH] B: 1/29/1928, Toledo, OH D: 3/6/1994, Columbus, OH *Drafted:* 1951 Round 5 LARm
1951 Pit: 11 G. **1952** Was: 2 G. **Total:** 13 G.

BOB MOMSEN Momsen, Robert Edward 6′3″, 225 **OG-LB**
Col: Ohio State *HS:* Edward D. Libbey [Toledo, OH] B: 5/28/1929, Toledo, OH *Drafted:* 1951 Round 7 Det
1951 Det: 12 G. **1952** SF: 10 G; Scor **1** Saf; 2 Pt. **Total:** 22 G; Scor 1 Saf; 2 Pt.

JIM MONACHINO Monachino, James 5′10″, 187 **HB-FB-DB**
Col: California *HS:* Redondo [Redondo Beach, CA] B: 7/9/1929, Cleveland, OH *Drafted:* 1951 Round 12 SF
1951 SF: Rec 1-6 6.0. **1953** SF: Rec 2-9 4.5. **1955** Was: Rec 8-74 9.3; PR 6-26 4.3. **Total:** Rec 11-89 8.1; PR 6-26 4.3.

		Rushing				
Year Team	**G**	**Att**	**Yds**	**Avg**	**TD**	**Fum**
1951 SF	8	21	74	3.5	2	2
1953 SF	5	4	10	2.5	0	1
1955 Was	7	46	207	4.5	2	1
NFL Total	20	71	291	4.1	4	4

RAY MONACO Monaco, Raymond William 5′10″, 212 **G-LB**
(Piano Legs) *Col:* Holy Cross *HS:* Central [Providence, RI]; Massanupten Mil. Acad. [Woodstock, VA] B: 2/10/1918, Providence, RI
1944 Was: 5 G. **1945** Cle: 1 G. **Total:** 6 G.

ROB MONACO Monaco, Robin Gabriel 6′3″, 283 **C**
Col: Vanderbilt *HS:* Hamden [CT] B: 9/5/1961, Hamden, CT
Drafted: 1985 Round 8 StL
1985 StL: 6 G.

RON MONACO Monaco, Ronnie Carl 6′1″, 225 **LB**
Col: South Carolina *HS:* Hamden [CT] B: 5/3/1963, New Haven, CT
1986 StL: 15 G. **1987** GB: 2 G. **Total:** 17 G.

REGIS MONAHAN Monahan, John Regis 5′10″, 216 **G-T**
(Monty; Tim) *Col:* Ohio State *HS:* St.Rosalia's [Pittsburgh, PA]; Kiski School [Saltsburg, PA] B: 11/15/1908, Pittsburgh, PA D: 4/23/1979, Detroit, MI
1935 Det: 12 G. **1936** Det: 10 G; 6 Pt. **1937** Det: 11 G; Scor 20, 5 FG, 5 XK. **1938** Det: 9 G; Scor 14, 4-5 **80.0**% FG, 2-4 **50.0**% XK. **1939** ChiC: 2 G; Scor 4, 1-1 100.0% FG, 1-1 100.0% XK. **Total:** 44 G; Scor 44, 10-6 83.3% FG, 8-5 60.0% XK.

WONDER MONDS Monds, Wonderful Jr. 6′3″, 215 **DB**
Col: Indian Hills CC IA; Nebraska *HS:* Fort Pierce Central [FL]
B: 5/3/1952, Fort Pierce, FL *Drafted:* 1976 Round 4 Pit
1978 SF: 16 G.

AVERY MONFORT Monfort, William Avery 5′10″, 178 **WB-DB**
(Lefty; Monty) *Col:* San Bernardino Valley Coll. CA (J.C.); New Mexico *HS:* San Bernardino [CA] B: 12/19/1918, Copan, OK
1941 ChiC: 4 G; Rush 3-8 2.7.

MATT MONGER Monger, Matthew L 6′1″, 235 **LB**
Col: Oklahoma State *HS:* Miami [OK] B: 11/15/1961, Denver, CO
Drafted: 1985 Round 8 NYJ
1985 NYJ: 15 G. **1986** NYJ: 16 G. **1987** NYJ: 12 G. **1989** Buf: 9 G. **1990** Buf: 4 G. **Total:** 56 G.

ART MONK Monk, James Arthur 6′3″, 210 **WR**
Col: Syracuse *HS:* White Plains [NY] B: 12/5/1957, White Plains, NY
Drafted: 1980 Round 1 Was
1980 Was: KR 1-10 10.0. **1983** Was: Pass 1-1 100.0%, 46 46.00. **1988** Was: Pass 1-0. **Total:** Pass 2-1 50.0%, 46 23.00; KR 1-10 10.0.

		Rushing				Receiving				
Year Team	**G**	**Att**	**Yds**	**Avg**	**TD**	**Rec**	**Yds**	**Avg**	**TD**	**Fum**
1980 Was	16	0	0	—	0	58	797	13.7	3	0
1981 Was	16	1	-5	-5.0	0	56	894	16.0	6	0
1982 Was	9	7	21	3.0	0	35	447	12.8	1	3
1983 Was	12	3	-19	-6.3	0	47	746	15.9	5	0
1984 Was	16	2	18	9.0	0	**106**	1372	12.9	7	1
1985 Was	15	7	51	7.3	0	91	1226	13.5	2	2
1986 Was	16	4	27	6.8	0	73	1068	14.6	4	2
1987 Was	9	6	63	10.5	0	38	483	12.7	6	0
1988 Was	16	7	46	6.6	0	72	946	13.1	5	0
1989 Was	16	3	8	2.7	0	86	1186	13.8	8	2
1990 Was	16	7	59	8.4	0	68	770	11.3	5	0
1991 Was	16	9	19	2.1	0	71	1049	14.8	8	2
1992 Was	16	6	45	7.5	0	46	644	14.0	3	1
1993 Was	16	1	-1	-1.0	0	41	398	9.7	2	0
1994 NYJ	16	0	0	—	0	46	581	12.6	3	0
1995 Phi	3	0	0	—	0	6	114	19.0	0	0
NFL Total	224	63	332	5.3	0	940	12721	13.5	68	13

BOB MONNETT Monnett, Robert C 5′9″, 182 **TB-DB-HB**
Col: Michigan State *HS:* Bucyrus [OH] B: 2/27/1910, Bucyrus, OH D: 8/1/1978, Galion, OH
1933 GB: PR 1 TD; Scor 34, 9 XK, 1 1XP. **1934** GB: Scor 29, 4 FG, 5 XK. **1935** GB: Scor 11, 1 FG, 2 XK. **1936** GB: Scor 3, 3 XK. **1938** GB: Scor 7, 7-7 100.0% XK. **Total:** PR 1 TD; Scor 90, 5 FG, 26-7 100.0% XK, 1 1XP.

		Passing							
Year Team	**G**	**Att**	**Comp**	**Comp%**	**Yds**	**YPA**	**TD**	**Int**	**Rating**
1933 GB	10	46	23	50.0	325	7.07	3	**3**	67.8
1934 GB	11	43	16	37.2	223	5.19	2	4	31.4
1935 GB	11	65	31	47.7	354	5.45	2	5	42.7
1936 GB	12	52	20	38.5	280	5.38	4	**2**	66.2
1937 GB	10	73	37	**50.7**	580	7.95	8	8	74.4
1938 GB	8	57	31	**54.4**	465	**8.16**	**9**	4	91.7
NFL Total	62	336	158	47.0	2227	6.63	28	26	64.4

	Rushing				Receiving				Tot
Year Team	**Att**	**Yds**	**Avg**	**TD**	**Rec**	**Yds**	**Avg**	**TD**	**TD**
1933 GB	108	413	3.8	3	6	44	7.3	0	4
1934 GB	68	129	1.9	2	2	27	13.5	0	2
1935 GB	68	336	4.9	1	1	8	8.0	0	1
1936 GB	104	224	2.2	0	13	169	13.0	0	0
1937 GB	87	161	1.9	1	4	32	8.0	0	1
1938 GB	75	225	3.0	0	1	23	23.0	0	0
NFL Total	510	1488	2.9	7	27	303	11.2	0	8

CARL MONROE Monroe, Carl 5′8″, 166 **RB-WR**
Col: Gavilan Coll. CA (J.C.); Utah *HS:* William C. Overfelt [San Jose, CA] B: 2/20/1960, Pittsburgh, PA D: 4/26/1989, San Jose, CA
1983 SF: Rush 10-23 2.3. **1984** SF: Rush 3-13 4.3. **1987** SF: Rush 2-26 13.0. **Total:** Rush 15-62 4.1.

		Receiving				Kickoff Returns					Tot
Year Team	**G**	**Rec**	**Yds**	**Avg**	**TD**	**Ret**	**Yds**	**Avg**	**TD**	**Fum**	**TD**
1983 SF	5	2	61	30.5	0	8	152	19.0	0	0	0
1984 SF	16	11	139	12.6	1	27	561	20.8	0	2	1
1985 SF	14	10	51	5.1	0	28	717	25.6	1	0	1
1986 SF	5	2	6	3.0	0	8	139	17.4	0	1	0
1987 SF	3	3	66	22.0	1	5	91	18.2	0	1	1
NFL Total	43	28	323	11.5	2	76	1660	21.8	1	4	3

HENRY MONROE Monroe, Henry Evans 5′11″, 180 **DB**
Col: Mississippi State *HS:* Benjamin C. Rain [Mobile, AL]
B: 12/30/1956, Mobile, AL *Drafted:* 1979 Round 7 GB
1979 GB-Phi: 6 G. GB: 3 G. Phi: 3 G. **Total:** 6 G.

TOMMY MONT Mont, Thomas Allison Jr. 6′0″, 194 **QB-DB-HB**
(Tossin' Tommy) *Col:* Maryland *HS:* Allegany [Cumberland, MD]
B: 6/20/1922, Mount Savage, MD *Drafted:* 1944 Round 12 NYG
1947 Was: Rec 2-14 7.0; PR 3-37 12.3; Int 1-7. **1948** Was: Pass 28-12 42.9%, 157 5.61 2 TD 2 Int; Int 2-21. **1949** Was: Pass 7-3 42.9%, 44 6.29; Rec 8-105 13.1 2 TD; KR 1-22 22.0. **Total:** Pass 35-15 42.9%, 201 5.74 2 TD 2 Int; Rec 10-119 11.9 2 TD; PR 3-37 12.3; KR 1-22 22.0; Int 3-28.

		Rushing				Tot
Year Team	**G**	**Att**	**Yds**	**Avg**	**TD**	**TD**
1947 Was	4	1	7	7.0	0	0
1948 Was	11	11	103	9.4	1	1
1949 Was	12	14	75	5.4	0	2
NFL Total	27	26	185	7.1	1	3

DAVID MONTAGNE Montagne, David Andrew 6′2″, 184 **WR**
Col: Oregon State *HS:* Miramonte [Orinda, CA] B: 4/18/1964, Berkeley, CA
1987 KC: 3 G; Rec 5-47 9.4; PR 1-8 8.0.

MEL MONTALBO Montalbo, Melvin James 6′1″, 190 **DB**
Col: Utah State *HS:* San Lorenzo [CA] B: 3/29/1938
1962 Oak: 2 G.

JOE MONTANA Montana, Joseph Clifford Jr. 6′2″, 200 **QB**
Col: Notre Dame *HS:* Ringgold [Monongahela, PA] B: 6/11/1956, New Eagle, PA *Drafted:* 1979 Round 3 SF

		Passing							
Year Team	**G**	**Att**	**Comp**	**Comp%**	**Yds**	**YPA**	**TD**	**Int**	**Rating**
1979 SF	16	23	13	56.5	96	4.17	1	0	81.1
1980 SF	15	273	176	**64.5**	1795	6.58	15	**9**	87.8
1981 SF	16	488	311	**63.7**	3565	7.31	19	12	88.4
1982 SF	9	**346**	213	61.6	2613	7.55	**17**	11	88.0
1983 SF	16	515	332	64.5	3910	7.59	26	12	94.6
1984 SF	16	432	279	64.6	3630	8.40	28	10	102.9

1985 SF	15	494	303	**61.3**	3653	7.39	27	13	91.3
1986 SF	8	307	191	62.2	2236	7.28	8	9	80.7
1987 SF	13	398	266	**66.8**	3054	7.67	**31**	13	**102.1**
1988 SF	14	397	238	59.9	2981	7.51	18	10	87.9
1989 SF	13	386	271	**70.2**	3521	**9.12**	26	**8**	**112.4**
1990 SF	15	520	321	61.7	3944	7.58	26	16	89.0
1992 SF	1	21	15	71.4	126	6.00	2	0	118.4
1993 KC	11	298	181	60.7	2144	7.19	13	7	87.4
1994 KC	14	493	299	60.6	3283	6.66	16	9	83.6
NFL Total	192	5391	3409	63.2	40551	7.52	273	139	92.3

	Rushing				
Year Team	**Att**	**Yds**	**Avg**	**TD**	**Fum**
1979 SF	3	22	7.3	0	1
1980 SF	32	77	2.4	2	4
1981 SF	25	95	3.8	2	2
1982 SF	30	118	3.9	1	4
1983 SF	61	284	4.7	2	3
1984 SF	39	118	3.0	2	4
1985 SF	42	153	3.6	3	5
1986 SF	17	38	2.2	0	3
1987 SF	35	141	4.0	1	3
1988 SF	38	132	3.5	3	3
1989 SF	49	227	4.6	3	9
1990 SF	40	162	4.1	1	4
1992 SF	3	28	9.3	0	0
1993 KC	25	64	2.6	0	1
1994 KC	18	17	0.9	0	7
NFL Total	457	1676	3.7	20	53

ALTON MONTGOMERY Montgomery, Alton 6′0″, 200 **DB**
Col: Northwest Mississippi CC; Houston *HS:* Griffin [GA]
B: 6/16/1968, Griffin, GA *Drafted:* 1990 Round 2 Den
1990 Den: Int 2-43. **1995** Atl: Int 1-71 1 TD; 3 Sac. **Total:** Int 3-114 1 TD; 3 Sac.

		Kickoff Returns				
Year Team	**G**	**Ret**	**Yds**	**Avg**	**TD**	**Fum**
1990 Den	15	14	286	20.4	0	1
1991 Den	16	26	488	18.8	0	1
1992 Den	12	21	466	22.2	0	1
1993 Atl	8	2	53	26.5	0	0
1994 Atl	2	2	58	29.0	0	0
1995 Atl	15	0	0	—	0	0
NFL Total	68	65	1351	20.8	0	3

BLANCHARD MONTGOMERY Montgomery, Blanchard III 6′2″, 236 **LB**
Col: UCLA *HS:* Granada Hills [Los Angeles, CA] B: 2/17/1961, Los Angeles, CA *Drafted:* 1983 Round 3 SF
1983 SF: 11 G. **1984** SF: 16 G. **Total:** 27 G.

CLEO MONTGOMERY Montgomery, Cleotha 5′8″, 183 **WR**
Col: Abilene Christian *HS:* Greenville [MS] B: 7/1/1955, Greenville, MS
1980 Cin: Rush 1-12 12.0. **1983** LARd: Rush 2-7 3.5; Rec 2-29 14.5.
1984 LARd: Rush 1-1 1.0. **Total:** Rush 4-20 5.0; Rec 2-29 14.5.

		Punt Returns				Kickoff Returns				
Year Team	**G**	**Ret**	**Yds**	**Avg**	**TD**	**Ret**	**Yds**	**Avg**	**TD**	**Fum**
1980 Cin	14	31	223	7.2	0	44	843	19.2	0	3
1981 Cle-Oak	5	17	121	7.1	0	17	382	22.5	0	2
1981 Cle	4	17	121	7.1	0	14	334	23.9	0	2
1981 Oak	1	0	0	—	0	3	48	16.0	0	0
1982 LARd	9	0	0	—	0	17	312	18.4	0	0
1983 LARd	14	0	0	—	0	21	464	22.1	0	1
1984 LARd	16	14	194	13.9	1	26	555	21.3	0	1
1985 LARd	4	8	84	10.5	0	7	150	21.4	0	0
NFL Total	62	70	622	8.9	1	132	2706	20.5	0	7

CLIFF MONTGOMERY Montgomery, Clifford Earl 5′9″, 165 **TB-DB**
Col: Columbia *HS:* Har-brack Union [Brackenridge, PA]; Kiski School [Saltsburg, PA] B: 9/17/1910, Pittsburgh, PA
1934 Bkn: Pass 32-7 21.9%, 93 2.91 1 TD 6 Int; Rec 2-21 10.5.

		Rushing			
Year Team	**G**	**Att**	**Yds**	**Avg**	**TD**
1934 Bkn	11	47	70	1.5	0

MONTY MONTGOMERY Montgomery, Delmonico 5′11″, 197 **DB**
Col: Houston *HS:* Gladewater [TX] B: 12/8/1973, Dallas, TX
Drafted: 1997 Round 4 Ind
1997 Ind: 16 G; 1 Sac. **1998** Ind: 16 G; Int 1-22; 2 Sac. **Total:** 32 G; Int 1-22; 3 Sac.

GLENN MONTGOMERY Montgomery, Glenn Steven 6′0″, 280 **NT-DT**
Col: Houston *HS:* West Jefferson [Harvey, LA] B: 3/31/1967, New Orleans, LA D: 6/28/1998, Dallas, TX *Drafted:* 1989 Round 5 Hou
1989 Hou: 15 G; KR 1-0; 1.5 Sac. **1990** Hou: 15 G; 0.5 Sac. **1991** Hou: 16 G. **1992** Hou: 16 G; KR 1-13 13.0; 0.5 Sac. **1993** Hou: 16 G; 6 Sac. **1994** Hou: 14 G; 3 Sac. **1995** Hou: 15 G; 2 Sac. **1996** Sea: 7 G. **Total:** 114 G; KR 2-13 6.5; 13.5 Sac.

GREG MONTGOMERY Montgomery, Gregory Hugh Jr. 6′4″, 215 **P**
Col: Penn State; Michigan State *HS:* Red Bank Regional [Little Silver, NJ] B: 10/29/1964, Morristown, NJ *Drafted:* 1988 Round 3 Hou
1989 Hou: Rush 3-17 5.7. **1992** Hou: Rush 2-(-14) -7.0. **1996** Bal: Rush 1-0. **1997** Bal: Rush 1-11 11.0. **Total:** Rush 7-14 2.0.

		Punting			
Year Team	**G**	**Punts**	**Yds**	**Avg**	**Fum**
1988 Hou	16	65	2523	38.8	0
1989 Hou	16	56	2422	43.3	1
1990 Hou	16	34	1530	45.0	0
1991 Hou	15	48	2105	43.9	0
1992 Hou	16	53	2487	**46.9**	1
1993 Hou	15	54	2462	**45.6**	0
1994 Det	16	63	2782	44.2	0
1996 Bal	16	68	2980	43.8	1
1997 Bal	16	83	3540	42.7	0
NFL Total	142	524	22831	43.6	3

JIM MONTGOMERY Montgomery, James Brown Jr. 6′4″, 235 **T**
Col: Texas A&M *HS:* Moran [TX] B: 3/18/1922, Breckenridge, TX
D: 8/14/1992, Dallas, TX
1946 Det: 11 G.

MIKE MONTGOMERY Montgomery, James Michael 6′2″, 210 **RB-WR**
Col: Kansas State *HS:* Dodge City [KS] B: 7/10/1949, Wichita Falls, TX
Drafted: 1971 Round 3 SD
1971 SD: Pass 6-3 50.0%, 80 13.33 1 TD. **1972** Dal: Pass 3-1 33.3%, 31 10.33; KR 1-15 15.0; **1** Fum TD. **1973** Dal: Pass 1-0; PR 2-2 1.0; KR 6-175 29.2; Punt 4-158 39.5. **Total:** Pass 10-4 40.0%, 111 11.10 1 TD; PR 2-2 1.0; KR 7-190 27.1; Punt 4-158 39.5; 1 Fum TD.

		Rushing				Receiving					Tot
Year Team	**G**	**Att**	**Yds**	**Avg**	**TD**	**Rec**	**Yds**	**Avg**	**TD**	**Fum**	**TD**
1971 SD	11	60	226	3.8	1	28	361	12.9	2	4	3
1972 Dal	12	35	81	2.3	1	8	131	16.4	1	1	3
1973 Dal	9	1	-10	-10.0	0	14	164	11.7	3	0	3
1974 Hou	5	0	0	—	0	9	179	19.9	1	0	1
NFL Total	37	96	297	3.1	2	59	835	14.2	7	5	10

SULLY MONTGOMERY Montgomery, James Ralph 6′3″, 213 **T-C**
Col: Centre *HS:* North Side [Fort Worth, TX] B: 1/12/1901, TX
D: 9/5/1970, Fort Worth, TX
1923 ChiC: 11 G. **1927** Fra: 4 G. **Total:** 15 G.

MARV MONTGOMERY Montgomery, Marvin 6′6″, 255 **OT**
Col: Los Angeles Valley Coll. CA (J.C.); USC *HS:* Sylmar [CA]
B: 2/8/1948, Torrance, CA *Drafted:* 1971 Round 1 Den
1971 Den: 12 G. **1972** Den: 14 G. **1973** Den: 10 G. **1974** Den: 4 G. **1975** Den: 14 G. **1976** Den-NO: 12 G. Den: 3 G. NO: 9 G. **1977** NO: 14 G. **1978** Atl: 1 G. **Total:** 81 G.

RANDY MONTGOMERY Montgomery, Randle John 5′11″, 182 **DB**
Col: Everett CC WA; Weber State *HS:* Cleveland [Seattle, WA]
B: 8/12/1947, Houston, TX *Drafted:* 1970 Round 7 Den
1972 Den: Int 1-20. **1974** ChiB: Int 2-56. **Total:** Int 3-76.

		Kickoff Returns				
Year Team	**G**	**Ret**	**Yds**	**Avg**	**TD**	**Fum**
1971 Den	3	4	80	20.0	0	0
1972 Den	14	29	756	26.1	**1**	2
1973 Den	9	1	22	22.0	0	0
1974 ChiB	14	0	0	—	0	0
NFL Total	40	34	858	25.2	1	2

ROSS MONTGOMERY Montgomery, Ross Elliott 6′3″, 220 **RB**
Col: Texas Christian *HS:* Midland [TX] B: 12/10/1946, Detroit, MI
Drafted: 1969 Round 3 ChiB
1969 ChiB: Rec 2-8 4.0. **1970** ChiB: Rec 14-75 5.4; KR 4-69 17.3.
Total: Rec 16-83 5.2; KR 4-69 17.3.

		Rushing			
Year Team	**G**	**Att**	**Yds**	**Avg**	**TD**
1969 ChiB	12	15	52	3.5	0
1970 ChiB	14	62	229	3.7	0
NFL Total	26	77	281	3.6	0

TYRONE MONTGOMERY Montgomery, Tyrone 6′0″, 190 **RB**
Col: Tyler JC TX; Mississippi *HS:* Greenville [MS] B: 8/3/1970, Greenville, MS
1993 LARd: Rec 10-43 4.3. **1994** LARd: Rec 8-126 15.8 1 TD.
Total: Rec 18-169 9.4 1 TD.

		Rushing				
Year Team	**G**	**Att**	**Yds**	**Avg**	**TD**	**Fum**
1993 LARd	12	37	106	2.9	0	2
1994 LARd	6	36	97	2.7	0	2
NFL Total	18	73	203	2.8	0	4

WILBERT MONTGOMERY Montgomery, Wilbert 5'10", 195 **RB**
Col: Jackson State; Abilene Christian *HS:* Greenville [MS]
B: 9/16/1954, Greenville, MS *Drafted:* 1977 Round 6 Phi
1980 Phi: Pass 1-0. **1984** Phi: Pass 2-0. **Total:** Pass 3-0.

		Rushing				Receiving			
Year Team	G	Att	Yds	Avg	TD	Rec	Yds	Avg	TD
1977 Phi	14	45	183	4.1	2	3	18	6.0	0
1978 Phi	14	259	1220	4.7	9	34	195	5.7	1
1979 Phi	16	338	1512	4.5	9	41	494	12.0	5
1980 Phi	12	193	778	4.0	8	50	407	8.1	2
1981 Phi	15	286	1402	4.9	8	49	521	10.6	2
1982 Phi	8	114	515	4.5	7	20	258	12.9	2
1983 Phi	5	29	139	4.8	0	9	53	5.9	0
1984 Phi	16	201	789	3.9	2	60	501	8.4	0
1985 Det	7	75	251	3.3	0	7	55	7.9	0
NFL Total	107	1540	6789	4.4	45	273	2502	9.2	12

	Kickoff Returns					Tot
Year Team	Ret	Yds	Avg	TD	Fum	TD
1977 Phi	23	619	26.9	1	4	3
1978 Phi	6	154	25.7	0	6	10
1979 Phi	1	6	6.0	0	**14**	14
1980 Phi	1	23	23.0	0	3	10
1981 Phi	0	0	—	0	6	10
1982 Phi	1	12	12.0	0	3	9
1983 Phi	0	0	—	0	1	0
1984 Phi	0	0	—	0	5	2
NFL Total	32	814	25.4	1	42	58

BILL MONTGOMERY Montgomery, William A Jr. 5'9", 200 **T**
Col: St. Louis *HS:* St. Louis University [MO] B: 5/4/1909, St. Louis, MO D: 7/1978, Camdenton, MO
1934 StL: 3 G.

BILL MONTGOMERY Montgomery, William N 6'0", 205 **HB**
Col: Louisiana State *HS:* Murphysboro [IL] B: 1923 *Drafted:* 1945 Round 13 Phi
1946 ChiC: 3 G; Rush 8-11 1.4.

MIKE MONTLER Montler, Michael Russel 6'5", 254 **C-OT-OG**
Col: Colorado *HS:* St. Mary's [Columbus, OH] B: 1/10/1944, Columbus, OH *Drafted:* 1969 Round 2 Bos
1969 Bos: 14 G. **1970** Bos: 11 G. **1971** NE: 14 G. **1972** NE: 14 G. **1973** Buf: 10 G. **1974** Buf: 14 G. **1975** Buf: 14 G. **1976** Buf: 14 G; Rec 1-6 6.0. **1977** Den: 14 G. **1978** Det: 4 G. **Total:** 123 G; Rec 1-6 6.0.

SANKAR MONTOUTE Montoute, Sankar Jerome 6'3", 230 **LB**
Col: Wisconsin; St. Leo *HS:* St. John's Mil. Acad. [Delafield, WI]
B: 2/2/1961, Trinidad
1987 TB: 3 G; Int 1-0; 1.5 Sac.

MAX MONTOYA Montoya, Max Jr. 6'5", 282 **OG**
Col: Mount San Jacinto Coll. CA (J.C.); UCLA *HS:* La Puente [CA]
B: 5/12/1956, Montebello, CA *Drafted:* 1979 Round 7 Cin
1979 Cin: 11 G. **1980** Cin: 16 G. **1981** Cin: 16 G. **1982** Cin: 9 G. **1983** Cin: 16 G. **1984** Cin: 16 G. **1985** Cin: 16 G. **1986** Cin: 16 G. **1987** Cin: 10 G. **1988** Cin: 15 G. **1989** Cin: 16 G. **1990** LARd: 16 G. **1991** LARd: 11 G. **1992** LARd: 10 G. **1993** LARd: 16 G. **1994** LARd: 13 G. **Total:** 223 G.

MARK MONTREUIL Montreuil, Mark Allen 6'2", 200 **DB**
Col: Concordia (Quebec) *HS:* Beaconsfield Secondary Sch. [Montreal, Canada] B: 12/29/1971, Montreal, Canada *Drafted:* 1995 Round 7 SD
1995 SD: 16 G. **1996** SD: 13 G. **1997** SD: 6 G. **Total:** 35 G.

PETE MONTY Monty, Peter Charles 6'2", 250 **LB**
Col: Wisconsin *HS:* Fort Collins [CO] B: 7/13/1974, Ft. Collins, CO
Drafted: 1997 Round 4 NYG
1997 NYG: 3 G. **1998** NYG: 11 G. **Total:** 14 G.

KEITH MOODY Moody, Keith M 5'11", 171 **DB**
Col: Syracuse *HS:* Nottingham [Syracuse, NY] B: 6/13/1953, Salisbury, NC *Drafted:* 1976 Round 10 Buf
1976 Buf: Int 3-63. **Total:** Int 3-63.

		Punt Returns				Kickoff Returns				
Year Team	G	Ret	Yds	Avg	TD	Ret	Yds	Avg	TD	Fum
1976 Buf	14	16	166	10.4	1	26	605	23.3	0	3
1977 Buf	14	15	196	13.1	1	30	636	21.2	0	2
1978 Buf	14	19	240	12.6	**1**	18	371	20.6	0	1
1979 Buf	16	38	318	8.4	0	27	556	20.6	0	4
1980 Oak	5	0	0	—	0	8	150	18.8	0	1
NFL Total	63	88	920	10.5	3	109	2318	21.3	0	11

WILKIE MOODY Moody, Wilkie Osgood 5'7", 183 **WB-BB-TB**
Col: Linfield; Denison *HS:* Grand Island [NE]; Colby Acad. [NH]
B: 5/12/1897, Irabo, Congo D: 2/22/1976, Granville, OH
1920 Col: 9 G. **1921** Day: 1 G. **1924** Col: 3 G. **1925** Col: 2 G. **Total:** 15 G.

DOUG MOOERS Mooers, Douglas F 6'6", 265 **DE**
Col: Whittier *HS:* Western [Anaheim, CA] B: 3/11/1947, Seattle, WA
1971 NO: 4 G. **1972** NO: 14 G. **Total:** 18 G.

AARON MOOG Moog, Aaron John 6'4", 260 **DE**
Col: Nevada-Las Vegas *HS:* Chaffey [Ontario, Canada] B: 2/3/1962, Loma Linda, CA
1987 Cle: 3 G.

WARREN MOON Moon, Harold Warren 6'3", 212 **QB**
Col: Washington *HS:* Alexander Hamilton [Los Angeles, CA]
B: 11/18/1956, Los Angeles, CA

		Passing							
Year Team	G	Att	Comp	Comp%	Yds	YPA	TD	Int	Rating
1984 Hou	16	450	259	57.6	3338	7.42	12	14	76.9
1985 Hou	14	377	200	53.1	2709	7.19	15	19	68.5
1986 Hou	15	488	256	52.5	3489	7.15	13	26	62.3
1987 Hou	12	368	184	50.0	2806	7.63	21	18	74.2
1988 Hou	11	294	160	54.4	2327	7.91	17	8	88.4
1989 Hou	16	464	280	60.3	3631	7.83	23	14	88.9
1990 Hou	15	**584**	**362**	62.0	**4689**	8.03	**33**	13	96.8
1991 Hou	16	**655**	**404**	61.7	**4690**	7.16	23	21	81.7
1992 Hou	11	346	224	64.7	2521	7.29	18	12	89.3
1993 Hou	15	520	303	58.3	3485	6.70	21	21	75.2
1994 Min	15	601	371	61.7	4264	7.09	18	19	79.9
1995 Min	16	606	**377**	62.2	4228	6.98	33	14	91.5
1996 Min	8	247	134	54.3	1610	6.52	7	9	68.7
1997 Sea	15	528	313	59.3	3678	6.97	25	16	83.7
1998 Sea	10	258	145	56.2	1632	6.33	11	8	76.6
NFL Total	205	6786	3972	58.5	49097	7.24	290	232	81.0

	Rushing				
Year Team	Att	Yds	Avg	TD	Fum
1984 Hou	58	211	3.6	1	**17**
1985 Hou	39	130	3.3	0	12
1986 Hou	42	157	3.7	2	11
1987 Hou	34	112	3.3	3	8
1988 Hou	33	88	2.7	5	8
1989 Hou	70	268	3.8	4	11
1990 Hou	55	215	3.9	2	**18**
1991 Hou	33	68	2.1	2	11
1992 Hou	27	147	5.4	1	7
1993 Hou	48	145	3.0	1	13
1994 Min	27	55	2.0	0	9
1995 Min	33	82	2.5	0	13
1996 Min	9	6	0.7	0	7
1997 Sea	17	40	2.4	1	7
1998 Sea	16	10	0.6	0	8
NFL Total	541	1734	3.2	22	**160**

TIPP MOONEY Mooney, Bow Tipp 6'0", 187 **HB-DB**
Col: Abilene Christian *HS:* Shamrock [TX] B: 4/19/1919, Shamrock, TX Deceased
1944 ChiB: Rec 2-74 37.0 1 TD; PR 1-46 46.0; KR 3-65 21.7; Int 1-35. **1945** ChiB: Rec 2-10 5.0; KR 3-51 17.0. **Total:** Rec 4-84 21.0 1 TD; PR 1-46 46.0; KR 6-116 19.3; Int 1-35.

		Rushing				
Year Team	G	Att	Yds	Avg	TD	Fum
1944 ChiB	10	29	88	3.0	0	0
1945 ChiB	7	17	105	6.2	0	1
NFL Total	17	46	193	4.2	0	1

ED MOONEY Mooney, Edward John 6'2", 225 **LB**
Col: Western Nebraska CC-Scottsbluff; Texas Tech *HS:* Walkill [NY]
B: 2/26/1945, Brooklyn, NY *Drafted:* 1968 Round 4 Det
1968 Det: 14 G; KR 1-11 11.0. **1969** Det: 14 G; KR 2-12 6.0. **1970** Det: 14 G; KR 1-12 12.0. **1971** Det: 14 G; KR 2-8 4.0. **1973** Bal: 13 G. **Total:** 69 G; KR 6-43 7.2.

GEORGE MOONEY Mooney, George 5'8", 163 **WB-OE-BB-FB**
B: 2/22/1896, Chicago, IL D: 2/10/1985, Glendale, CA
1922 Mil: 5 G. **1923** Mil: 8 G. **1924** Mil: 5 G. **Total:** 18 G.

JIM MOONEY Mooney, James L Jr. 5'11", 200 **OE-DE-T-G**
Col: Georgetown *HS:* Loyola Acad. [Wilmette, IL] B: 9/16/1907, Chicago, IL D: 8/12/1944, France
1930 Nwk-Bkn: 15 G; Scor 2, 2 XK. Nwk: 12 G; Scor 2, 2 XK. Bkn: 3 G. **1931** Bkn: 14 G; Scor 1, 1 XK. **1933** Cin: 7 G; Rush 3-27 9.0; Rec 3-47 15.7; Scor 1 Saf; 2 Pt. **1934** Cin: 8 G; Pass 6-4 66.7%, 27 4.50; Rush 2-(-7) -3.5; Rec 6-36 6.0. **1935** ChiC: 4 G. **Total:** 48 G; Pass 6-4 66.7%, 27 4.50; Rush 5-20 4.0; Rec 9-83 9.2; Scor 1 Saf.

MIKE MOONEY Mooney, Michael Paul 6'6", 320 **OT**
Col: Georgia Tech *HS:* South Carroll [Sykesville, MD] B: 5/31/1969, Baltimore, MD *Drafted:* 1992 Round 4 Hou
1993 SD: 1 G.

TEX MOONEY Mooney, Orrin T Jr. 6'5", 280 **T**
(AKA Orrin T. Schupbach Jr.) *Col:* West Texas A&M *HS:* Sanderson [TX] B: 3/8/1917, El Paso, TX
1942 Cle: 1 G. **1943** Bkn: 2 G. **Total:** 3 G.

TIM MOONEY Mooney, Timothy Michael 6'2", 265 DE
Col: Anderson (Ind.); Western Kentucky *HS:* Central [Evansville, IN]
B: 1/25/1962, Evansville, IN
1987 Phi: 2 G.

BUDDY MOOR Moor, Morris Howard 6'5", 250 DE
Col: Eastern Kentucky *HS:* Lowndes [Valdosta, GA] B: 12/1/1958, Greenville, MS
1987 Atl: 3 G; 4 Sac.

MOORE Moore T
1921 Cle: 1 G.

AL MOORE Moore, Albert Bennett 5'9", 185 HB
Col: Northwestern *HS:* Washington [Portland, OR] B: 4/17/1908, Portland, OR D: 3/23/1991, Crawford, CO
1932 ChiB: 2 G; Rush 6-17 2.8.

ALEX MOORE Moore, Alexander Lee 6'0", 195 RB
Col: Norfolk State *HS:* East [Colombus, OH] B: 5/22/1945, West Point, GA *Drafted:* 1968 Round 14 SF
1968 Den: 3 G; Rush 4-22 5.5; Rec 3-35 11.7; KR 4-74 18.5; 1 Fum.

AL MOORE Moore, Allen A 6'2", 218 DE
Col: Texas A&M B: 3/12/1909, Burkburnett, TX D: 9/1968
1939 GB: 5 G.

ALVIN MOORE Moore, Alvin 6'0", 194 RB
Col: Arizona State *HS:* Coolidge [AZ] B: 5/3/1959, Randolph, AZ
Drafted: 1983 Round 7 Bal
1983 Bal: KR 2-40 20.0. **1984** Ind: Pass 1-0; KR 2-19 9.5. **1985** Det: Pass 1-0; KR 13-230 17.7. **Total:** Pass 2-0; KR 17-289 17.0.

		Rushing				Receiving					Tot
Year Team	G	Att	Yds	Avg	TD	Rec	Yds	Avg	TD	Fum	TD
1983 Bal	15	57	205	3.6	1	6	38	6.3	0	0	1
1984 Ind	13	38	127	3.3	2	9	52	5.8	0	3	2
1985 Det	16	80	221	2.8	4	19	154	8.1	1	5	5
1986 Det	13	19	73	3.8	0	8	47	5.9	0	2	0
1987 Sea	1	3	15	5.0	0	0	0	—	0	0	0
NFL Total	58	197	641	3.3	7	42	291	6.9	1	10	8

ART MOORE Moore, Arthur Clark 6'5", 253 NT-DT
Col: Tulsa *HS:* Daingerfield [TX] B: 4/4/1951, Daingerfield, TX
Drafted: 1973 Round 6 SF
1973 NE: 13 G. **1974** NE: 11 G. **1976** NE: 4 G. **1977** NE: 1 G. **Total:** 29 G.

BOOKER MOORE Moore, Booker Thomas 5'11", 224 RB
Col: Penn State *HS:* Southwestern [Flint, MI] B: 6/23/1959, Flint, MI
Drafted: 1981 Round 1 Buf
1985 Buf: KR 3-31 10.3. **Total:** KR 3-31 10.3.

		Rushing				Receiving					Tot
Year Team	G	Att	Yds	Avg	TD	Rec	Yds	Avg	TD	Fum	TD
1982 Buf	5	16	38	2.4	0	1	8	8.0	0	2	0
1983 Buf	15	60	275	4.6	0	34	199	5.9	1	1	1
1984 Buf	15	24	84	3.5	0	33	172	5.2	0	4	0
1985 Buf	16	15	23	1.5	1	7	44	6.3	0	1	1
NFL Total	51	115	420	3.7	1	75	423	5.6	1	8	2

BRANDON MOORE Moore, Brandon Christopher 6'6", 290 OT
Col: Duke *HS:* Archbishop Carroll [Radnor, PA] B: 6/21/1970, Ardmore, PA
1993 NE: 16 G. **1994** NE: 4 G. **1995** NE: 6 G. **Total:** 26 G.

BRENT MOORE Moore, Brent Allen 6'5", 242 LB
Col: USC *HS:* San Marin [Novato, CA] B: 1/9/1963, Novato, CA
Drafted: 1986 Round 9 GB
1987 GB: 4 G.

CHARLIE MOORE Moore, Charles Dewell 6'5", 237 OG
Col: Arkansas *HS:* Robert E. Lee [Marianna, AR] B: 1/3/1940, Marianna, AR
1962 Was: 14 G.

CLIFF MOORE Moore, Clifford 6'1", 202 WB-DB
Col: No College
1934 Cin: 1 G.

DANA MOORE Moore, Dana Earl 5'11", 180 P
Col: Mississippi State *HS:* Belaire [Baton Rouge, LA] B: 9/7/1961, Baton Rouge, LA
1987 NYG: 2 G; Punt 14-486 34.7.

DARRYL MOORE Moore, Darryl Jerome 6'2", 292 OG
Col: Tyler JC TX; Texas-El Paso *HS:* Minden [LA] B: 1/27/1969, Minden, LA *Drafted:* 1992 Round 8 Was
1993 Was: 12 G.

DAVE MOORE Moore, David Edward 6'2", 242 TE
Col: Pittsburgh *HS:* Roxbury [Succasunna, NJ] B: 11/11/1969, Morristown, NJ *Drafted:* 1992 Round 7 Mia
1993 TB: Pass 1-0. **1994** TB: KR 2-27 13.5. **1995** TB: Rush 1-4 4.0.
Total: Pass 1-0; Rush 1-4 4.0; KR 2-27 13.5.

		Receiving				
Year Team	G	Rec	Yds	Avg	TD	Fum
1992 Mia-TB	5	1	10	10.0	0	0
1992 Mia	1	0	0	—	0	0
1992 TB	4	1	10	10.0	0	0
1993 TB	15	4	47	11.8	1	0
1994 TB	15	4	57	14.3	0	0
1995 TB	16	13	102	7.8	0	0
1996 TB	16	27	237	8.8	3	0
1997 TB	16	19	217	11.4	4	0
1998 TB	16	24	255	10.6	4	1
NFL Total	99	92	925	10.1	12	1

DERLAND MOORE Moore, Derland Paul 6'4", 250 DT-NT-DE
Col: Oklahoma *HS:* Poplar Bluff [MO] B: 10/7/1951, Minden, MO
Drafted: 1973 Round 2 NO
1973 NO: 13 G; KR 1-14 14.0; Int 1-0. **1974** NO: 14 G. **1975** NO: 14 G. **1976** NO: 14 G. **1977** NO: 10 G. **1978** NO: 15 G. **1979** NO: 15 G. **1980** NO: 16 G. **1981** NO: 16 G. **1982** NO: 9 G; 4 Sac. **1983** NO: 16 G; 6 Sac. **1984** NO: 12 G; 2 Sac. **1985** NO: 6 G. **1986** NYJ: 1 G.
Total: 171 G; KR 1-14 14.0; Int 1-0; 12 Sac.

DERRICK MOORE Moore, Derrick 6'0", 229 RB
Col: Darton Coll. GA (J.C.); Troy State; Northeastern State (Okla.)
HS: Monroe [Albany, GA] B: 10/13/1967, Albany, GA *Drafted:* 1992 Round 8 Atl
1993 Det: KR 1-68 68.0. **1994** Det: KR 10-113 11.3. **Total:** KR 11-181 16.5.

		Rushing				Receiving					Tot
Year Team	G	Att	Yds	Avg	TD	Rec	Yds	Avg	TD	Fum	TD
1993 Det	13	88	405	4.6	3	21	169	8.0	1	4	4
1994 Det	16	27	52	1.9	4	1	10	10.0	0	2	4
1995 Car	13	195	740	3.8	4	4	12	3.0	0	4	4
NFL Total	42	310	1197	3.9	11	26	191	7.3	1	10	12

BLAKE MOORE Moore, Edward Blake Jr. 6'5", 267 C-OG-OT
Col: Wooster *HS:* Baylor Prep [Chattanooga, TN] B: 5/8/1958, Durham, NC
1980 Cin: 16 G. **1981** Cin: 14 G. **1982** Cin: 4 G. **1983** Cin: 16 G. **1984** GB: 11 G; Rec 1-3 3.0 1 TD; 6 Pt. **1985** GB: 16 G; Rec 1-3 3.0 1 TD; 6 Pt; 1 Fum. **Total:** 77 G; Rec 2-6 3.0 2 TD; 12 Pt; 1 Fum.

ERIC MOORE Moore, Eric Patrick 6'5", 293 OT-OG
Col: Northeastern Oklahoma A&M (J.C.); Indiana *HS:* Berkeley [MO]
B: 1/21/1965, Berkeley, MO *Drafted:* 1988 Round 1 NYG
1988 NYG: 11 G. **1989** NYG: 16 G. **1990** NYG: 15 G. **1991** NYG: 16 G. **1992** NYG: 10 G. **1993** NYG: 7 G. **1994** Cin: 6 G. **1995** Cle-Mia: 3 G. Cle: 1 G. Mia: 2 G. **Total:** 84 G.

MCNEIL MOORE Moore, Ernest McNeil 6'0", 185 DB
Col: Rice; Sam Houston State *HS:* Center [TX] B: 6/26/1933, Center, TX *Drafted:* 1954 Round 18 ChiB
1954 ChiB: 12 G; PR 11-80 7.3; KR 8-156 19.5; Int 3-76; 1 Fum.
1956 ChiB: 11 G; PR 3-28 9.3; KR 1-19 19.0; Int 3-30. **1957** ChiB: 12 G; Int 2-28. **Total:** 35 G; PR 14-108 7.7; KR 9-175 19.4; Int 8-134; 1 Fum.

GENE MOORE Moore, Eugene Ralph III 6'1", 208 RB
Col: Occidental *HS:* Los Angeles [CA] B: 5/12/1947, San Diego, CA
Drafted: 1969 Round 4 SF
1969 SF: 5 G; Rush 2-4 2.0; Rec 2-28 14.0.

GENE MOORE Moore, Eugene Robert 6'3", 205 C-LB
Col: Colorado B: 12/16/1912 *Drafted:* 1938 Round 2 Bkn
1938 Bkn: 7 G.

ZEKE MOORE Moore, Ezekiel Jr. 6'3", 198 DB
Col: Lincoln (Mo.) *HS:* Booker T. Washington [Tuskegee, AL]
B: 12/2/1943, Tuskegee, AL *Drafted:* 1967 Round 5 Hou
1967 Hou: PR 5-82 16.4. **1968** Hou: PR 1-11 11.0. **1972** Hou: PR 7-15 2.1. **1977** Hou: 1 Fum TD. **Total:** PR 13-108 8.3; 1 Fum TD.

		Kickoff Returns				Interceptions				Tot
Year Team	G	Ret	Yds	Avg	TD	Int	Yds	TD	Fum	TD
1967 Hou	14	14	405	**28.9**	**1**	0	0	0	4	1
1968 Hou	14	32	787	24.6	0	0	0	0	1	0
1969 Hou	13	0	0	—	0	4	71	1	0	1
1970 Hou	14	7	190	27.1	0	6	85	0	1	0
1971 Hou	13	10	214	21.4	0	3	29	0	0	0
1972 Hou	8	1	22	22.0	0	0	0	0	3	0
1973 Hou	13	0	0	—	0	0	0	0	0	0
1974 Hou	14	0	0	—	0	2	38	1	0	1
1975 Hou	14	0	0	—	0	5	137	0	0	0
1976 Hou	14	0	0	—	0	1	28	0	0	0
1977 Hou	14	0	0	—	0	3	56	0	1	1
NFL Total	145	64	1618	25.3	1	24	444	2	10	4

FRED MOORE Moore, Frederick Wallace 6'3", 255 DT-DE
Col: Memphis *HS:* Sulligent [AL]; Florence Central HS [AL]
B: 12/18/1939, Sulligent, AL *Drafted:* 1962 Round 15 SD
1964 SD: 4 G. **1965** SD: 12 G. **1966** SD: 13 G. **Total:** 29 G.

GREG MOORE Moore, Gregory Herring 6'1", 240 **LB**
Col: Tennessee-Chattanooga *HS:* Walton [Cartersville, GA]
B: 3/28/1965, Cartersville, GA
1987 NE: 3 G.

HENRY MOORE Moore, Henry Dewell 6'1", 195 **DB-HB**
Col: Arkansas *HS:* Little Rock Central [AR] B: 4/3/1934, Little Rock, AR *Drafted:* 1956 Round 2 NYG
1956 NYG: 5 G; Rush 2-(-2) -1.0. **1957** Bal: 11 G; KR 1-16 16.0; Int 1-0.
Total: 16 G; Rush 2-(-2) -1.0; KR 1-16 16.0; Int 1-0.

HERMAN MOORE Moore, Herman Joseph 6'4", 210 **WR**
Col: Virginia *HS:* George Washington [Danville, VA] B: 10/20/1969, Danville, VA *Drafted:* 1991 Round 1 Det
1996 Det: Scor 1 2XP. **1997** Det: Scor 1 2XP. **Total:** Scor 2 2XP.

		Receiving				
Year Team	**G**	**Rec**	**Yds**	**Avg**	**TD**	**Fum**
1991 Det	13	11	135	12.3	0	0
1992 Det	12	51	966	18.9	4	0
1993 Det	15	61	935	15.3	6	2
1994 Det	16	72	1173	16.3	11	1
1995 Det	16	**123**	1686	13.7	14	2
1996 Det	16	106	1296	12.2	9	0
1997 Det	16	**104**	1293	12.4	8	0
1998 Det	15	82	983	12.0	5	0
NFL Total	119	610	8467	13.9	57	5

DEAN MOORE Moore, Irvin Dean 6'2", 210 **LB**
Col: Iowa *HS:* East [Akron, OH] B: 1/26/1955, Birmingham, AL
Drafted: 1978 Round 9 SF
1978 SF: 16 G.

DENIS MOORE Moore, James Denis III 6'5", 255 **DT-DE**
Col: USC *HS:* Westchester [Los Angeles, CA] B: 7/18/1944, Berkeley, CA D: 5/27/1995, Spokane, WA *Drafted:* 1966 Round 14 Det
1967 Det: 5 G. **1968** Det: 12 G. **1969** Det: 14 G. **1970** Phi: 2 G.
Total: 33 G.

JEFF MOORE Moore, Jeffrey Bernard 6'1", 194 **WR**
Col: Tennessee *HS:* Fairley [Memphis, TN] B: 3/2/1957, Memphis, TN
Drafted: 1979 Round 3 LARm
1980 LARm: 14 G; Rec 10-168 16.8 1 TD; 6 Pt. **1981** LARm: 10 G; Rec 7-105 15.0. **Total:** 24 G; Rec 17-273 16.1 1 TD; 6 Pt.

JEFF MOORE Moore, Jeffrey Dwayne 6'0", 195 **RB**
Col: Jackson State *HS:* Kosciusko [MS] B: 8/20/1956, Kosciusko, MS
Drafted: 1979 Round 12 Sea
1979 Sea: PR 10-90 9.0. **Total:** PR 10-90 9.0.

		Rushing				Receiving			
Year Team	**G**	**Att**	**Yds**	**Avg**	**TD**	**Rec**	**Yds**	**Avg**	**TD**
1979 Sea	16	44	168	3.8	2	14	128	9.1	0
1980 Sea	14	60	202	3.4	0	25	231	9.2	0
1981 Sea	2	1	15	15.0	0	3	18	6.0	0
1982 SF	9	85	281	3.3	4	37	405	10.9	4
1983 SF	15	15	43	2.9	1	19	206	10.8	0
1984 Was	7	3	13	4.3	0	17	115	6.8	2
NFL Total	63	208	722	3.5	7	115	1103	9.6	6

	Kickoff Returns					Tot
Year Team	**Ret**	**Yds**	**Avg**	**TD**	**Fum**	**TD**
1979 Sea	31	641	20.7	0	5	2
1980 Sea	1	11	11.0	0	4	0
1982 SF	1	15	15.0	0	4	8
1983 SF	7	117	16.7	0	0	1
1984 Was	0	0	—	0	1	2
NFL Total	40	784	19.6	0	14	13

JERALD MOORE Moore, Jerald Christopher 5'9", 225 **RB**
Col: Oklahoma *HS:* Jack Yates [Houston, TX] B: 11/20/1974, Houston, TX *Drafted:* 1996 Round 3 StL
1996 StL: Rec 3-13 4.3. **1997** StL: Rec 8-69 8.6. **1998** StL: Rec 9-60 6.7.
Total: Rec 20-142 7.1.

		Rushing				
Year Team	**G**	**Att**	**Yds**	**Avg**	**TD**	**Fum**
1996 StL	11	11	32	2.9	0	0
1997 StL	9	104	380	3.7	3	4
1998 StL	11	55	137	2.5	2	3
NFL Total	31	170	549	3.2	5	7

JERRY MOORE Moore, Jerry Porter 6'3", 208 **DB**
Col: Arkansas *HS:* Belleville [IL] B: 3/16/1949, Belleville, IL
Drafted: 1971 Round 4 ChiB
1971 ChiB: 11 G. **1972** ChiB: 13 G; Int 1-5. **1973** NO: 10 G. **1974** NO: 9 G; Int 1-0. **Total:** 43 G; Int 2-5.

JIMMY MOORE Moore, Jimmy Lee 6'5", 268 **OG**
Col: Ohio State *HS:* Marcos de Niza [Tempe, AZ] B: 1/28/1957, Pittsburgh, PA *Drafted:* 1979 Round 6 Bal
1981 Bal: 4 G.

JOE MOORE Moore, Joseph Lee Jr. 6'1", 205 **RB**
Col: Missouri *HS:* Beaumont [St. Louis, MO] B: 6/29/1949, St. Louis, MO *Drafted:* 1971 Round 1 ChiB
1971 ChiB: Rec 2-22 11.0. **1973** ChiB: Rec 3-17 5.7; PR 1-0.
Total: Rec 5-39 7.8; PR 1-0.

		Rushing				
Year Team	**G**	**Att**	**Yds**	**Avg**	**TD**	**Fum**
1971 ChiB	9	29	90	3.1	0	2
1973 ChiB	14	58	191	3.3	0	1
NFL Total	23	87	281	3.2	0	3

KELVIN MOORE Moore, Kelvin 6'0", 210 **DB**
Col: Santa Monica Coll. CA (J.C.); Morgan State *HS:* Alexander Hamilton [Los Angeles, CA] B: 3/7/1975, Los Angeles, CA
1998 Cin: 4 G.

KEN MOORE Moore, Kenneth Charles 6'0", 212 **G**
Col: West Virginia Wesleyan *HS:* Washington Irving [Clarksburg, WV]
B: 5/22/1917, Clarksburg, WV
1940 NYG: 8 G.

KEN MOORE Moore, Kenneth Earl 6'4", 232 **TE**
Col: Northern Illinois *HS:* South Shore [Chicago, IL] B: 7/25/1954, Merigold, MS *Drafted:* 1977 Round 5 Min
1978 Atl: 6 G.

LARRY MOORE Moore, Larry Maceo Jr. 6'3", 301 **OG**
Col: Grossmont Coll. CA (J.C.); Brigham Young *HS:* Monte Vista [Spring Valley, CA] B: 6/1/1975, San Diego, CA
1998 Ind: 6 G.

LEONARD MOORE Moore, Leonard Calvin 6'0", 222 **RB**
Col: Jackson State *HS:* Walton [Cartersville, GA] B: 1/27/1963, Cartersville, GA
1987 Min: 1 G; Rush 4-11 2.8; Rec 1-8 8.0.

LENNY MOORE Moore, Leonard Edward 6'1", 191 **HB-FL**
(Spats; The Reading Rocket) *Col:* Penn State *HS:* Reading [PA]
B: 11/25/1933, Reading, PA *Drafted:* 1956 Round 1 Bal *HOF:* 1975
1956 Bal: Pass 4-1 25.0%, 8 2.00 1 TD 1 Int; PR 8-38 4.8. **1957** Bal: Pass 2-0; PR 2-0. **1958** Bal: PR 2-11 5.5. **1959** Bal: Pass 3-2 66.7%, 25 8.33 1 TD. **1960** Bal: Pass 1-0. **1961** Bal: Pass 2-0, 1 Int. **1963** Bal: PR 2-7 3.5. **1964** Bal: 1 Fum TD. **Total:** Pass 12-3 25.0%, 33 2.75 2 TD 2 Int; PR 14-56 4.0; 1 Fum TD.

		Rushing				Receiving			
Year Team	**G**	**Att**	**Yds**	**Avg**	**TD**	**Rec**	**Yds**	**Avg**	**TD**
1956 Bal	12	86	649	**7.5**	8	11	102	9.3	1
1957 Bal	12	98	488	5.0	3	40	687	17.2	7
1958 Bal	12	82	598	**7.3**	7	50	938	18.8	7
1959 Bal	12	92	422	4.6	2	47	846	18.0	6
1960 Bal	12	91	374	4.1	4	45	936	20.8	9
1961 Bal	13	92	648	7.0	7	49	728	14.9	8
1962 Bal	10	106	470	4.4	2	18	215	11.9	2
1963 Bal	7	27	136	5.0	2	21	288	13.7	2
1964 Bal	14	157	584	3.7	**16**	21	472	22.5	3
1965 Bal	12	133	464	3.5	5	27	414	15.3	3
1966 Bal	13	63	209	3.3	3	21	260	12.4	0
1967 Bal	14	42	132	3.1	4	13	153	11.8	0
NFL Total	143	1069	5174	4.8	63	363	6039	16.6	48

	Kickoff Returns					Tot
Year Team	**Ret**	**Yds**	**Avg**	**TD**	**Fum**	**TD**
1956 Bal	10	129	12.9	0	5	9
1957 Bal	0	92	—	**1**	6	**11**
1958 Bal	4	91	22.8	0	5	14
1959 Bal	0	0	—	0	4	8
1960 Bal	1	23	23.0	0	3	13
1961 Bal	0	0	—	0	1	15
1962 Bal	0	0	—	0	1	4
1963 Bal	0	0	—	0	2	4
1964 Bal	0	0	—	0	8	**20**
1965 Bal	0	0	—	0	3	8
1966 Bal	18	453	25.2	0	2	3
1967 Bal	16	392	24.5	0	1	4
NFL Total	49	1180	24.1	1	41	113

LEROY MOORE Moore, Leroy Franklin 6'2", 240 **DE**
(Sweetpea) *Col:* Fort Valley State *HS:* Pontiac Central [MI]
B: 9/16/1935, Pontiac, MI
1960 Buf: 1 G. **1961** Bos: 14 G; 6 Pt. **1962** Bos-Buf: 11 G; Int 1-3 **1** TD; 6 Pt. Bos: 5 G. Buf: 6 G; Int 1-3 1 TD; 6 Pt. **1963** Buf: 2 G. **1964** Den: 12 G; Int 1-70. **1965** Den: 14 G. **Total:** 54 G; Int 2-73 1 TD; Tot TD 2; 12 Pt.

MACK MOORE Moore, Mack Henry 6'4", 258 DE
Col: San Francisco City Coll. CA (J.C.); Texas A&M *HS:* Monroe [LA]
B: 3/4/1959, Monroe, LA *Drafted:* 1981 Round 6 Mia
1985 Mia: 16 G; 5.5 Sac. **1986** Mia-SD: 10 G; 1 Sac. Mia: 7 G; 1 Sac. SD: 3 G. **Total:** 26 G; 6.5 Sac.

MALCOLM MOORE Moore, Malcolm Grady 6'3", 240 WR
Col: USC *HS:* San Fernando [CA] B: 6/24/1961, Los Angeles, CA
Drafted: 1984 Supplemental Round 2 Dal
1987 LARm: 3 G; Rec 6-107 17.8 1 TD; 6 Pt.

MANFRED MOORE Moore, Manfred 6'1", 197 RB
Col: USC *HS:* San Fernando [CA] B: 12/22/1950, Martinez, CA
Drafted: 1974 Round 9 SF
1974 SF: Rush 10-24 2.4 1 TD; Rec 2-29 14.5. **1975** SF: Rush 3-10 3.3; Rec 1-11 11.0. **1976** TB-Oak: Rush 7-4 0.6; Rec 6-54 9.0. TB: Rush 7-4 0.6; Rec 6-54 9.0. **Total:** Rush 20-38 1.9 1 TD; Rec 9-94 10.4.

		Punt Returns				Kickoff Returns					Tot
Year Team	G	Ret	Yds	Avg	TD	Ret	Yds	Avg	TD	Fum	TD
1974 SF	14	5	149	29.8	1	18	398	22.1	0	4	2
1975 SF	14	16	160	10.0	0	26	650	25.0	0	2	0
1976 TB-Oak	11	20	184	9.2	0	8	162	20.3	0	3	0
1976 TB	10	14	106	7.6	0	7	134	19.1	0	3	0
1976 Oak	1	6	78	13.0	0	1	28	28.0	0	0	0
1977 Min	12	47	277	5.9	0	24	524	21.8	0	3	0
NFL Total	51	88	770	8.8	1	76	1734	22.8	0	12	2

MARK MOORE Moore, Mark Quentin 6'0", 194 DB
Col: Oklahoma State *HS:* Nacogdoches [Tx] B: 9/3/1964, Nacogdoches, TX *Drafted:* 1987 Round 4 Sea
1987 Sea: 5 G.

MARTY MOORE Moore, Martin Neff 6'1", 244 LB
Col: Kentucky *HS:* Highlands [Fort Thomas, KY] B: 3/19/1971, Phoenix, AZ *Drafted:* 1994 Round 7 NE
1994 NE: 16 G. **1995** NE: 16 G. **1996** NE: 16 G. **1997** NE: 16 G; Int 2-7. **1998** NE: 14 G. **Total:** 78 G; Int 2-7.

MAULTY MOORE Moore, Maulty James 6'5", 265 DT
Col: Bethune-Cookman *HS:* Moton [Brooksville, FL] B: 8/12/1946, Milligan, FL
1972 Mia: 14 G. **1973** Mia: 12 G. **1974** Mia: 14 G. **1975** Cin: 13 G. **1976** TB: 5 G. **Total:** 58 G.

NAT MOORE Moore, Nathaniel 5'9", 184 WR-RB
Col: Miami-Dade CC North FL; Florida *HS:* Miami Edison [FL]
B: 9/19/1951, Tallahassee, FL *Drafted:* 1974 Round 3 Mia
1974 Mia: Pass 1-1 100.0%, 31 31.00. **1980** Mia: Pass 1-0.
Total: Pass 2-1 50.0%, 31 15.50.

		Rushing				Receiving			
Year Team	G	Att	Yds	Avg	TD	Rec	Yds	Avg	TD
1974 Mia	13	3	16	5.3	0	37	605	16.4	2
1975 Mia	14	8	69	8.6	0	40	705	17.6	4
1976 Mia	9	4	36	9.0	0	33	625	18.9	4
1977 Mia	14	14	89	6.4	1	52	765	14.7	**12**
1978 Mia	16	4	-3	-0.8	0	48	645	13.4	10
1979 Mia	16	3	22	7.3	0	48	840	17.5	6
1980 Mia	16	1	3	3.0	0	47	564	12.0	7
1981 Mia	13	1	3	3.0	0	26	452	17.4	2
1982 Mia	9	0	0	—	0	8	82	10.3	1
1983 Mia	16	0	0	—	0	39	558	14.3	6
1984 Mia	16	1	3	3.0	0	43	573	13.3	6
1985 Mia	15	1	11	11.0	0	51	701	13.7	7
1986 Mia	16	0	0	—	0	38	431	11.3	7
NFL Total	183	40	249	6.2	1	510	7546	14.8	74

	Punt Returns				Kickoff Returns					Tot
Year Team	Ret	Yds	Avg	TD	Ret	Yds	Avg	TD	Fum	TD
1974 Mia	9	136	15.1	0	22	587	26.7	0	1	2
1975 Mia	8	80	10.0	0	9	243	27.0	0	1	4
1976 Mia	8	72	9.0	0	2	28	14.0	0	1	4
1977 Mia	0	0	—	0	0	0	—	0	0	13
1978 Mia	1	11	11.0	0	0	0	—	0	1	10
1979 Mia	0	0	—	0	0	0	—	0	1	6
1980 Mia	0	0	—	0	0	0	—	0	1	7
1981 Mia	0	0	—	0	0	0	—	0	0	2
1982 Mia	0	0	—	0	0	0	—	0	0	1
1983 Mia	0	0	—	0	0	0	—	0	1	6
1984 Mia	0	0	—	0	0	0	—	0	2	6
1985 Mia	0	0	—	0	0	0	—	0	0	7
1986 Mia	1	-2	-2.0	0	0	0	—	0	0	7
NFL Total	27	297	11.0	0	33	858	26.0	0	9	75

PAUL MOORE Moore, Paul Neely 5'9", 208 BB-LB
(June) *Col:* Presbyterian *HS:* York [SC] B: 1/23/1918, York, SC
D: 5/7/1975, Okeechobee, FL
1940 Det: 7 G; Rush 2-4 2.0; Rec 4-29 7.3 1 TD; 6 Pt. **1941** Det: 8 G.
Total: 15 G; Rush 2-4 2.0; Rec 4-29 7.3 1 TD; 6 Pt.

RANDY MOORE Moore, Randall Kay 6'2", 241 DT
Col: Arizona State *HS:* Richland [Johnstown, PA] B: 4/5/1954, Johnstown, PA *Drafted:* 1976 Round 12 Den
1976 Den: 8 G.

REYNAUD MOORE Moore, Reynaud Eric 6'2", 190 DB
Col: UCLA *HS:* Susan Miller Dorsey [Los Angeles, CA] B: 10/17/1949, Los Angeles, CA
1971 NO: 14 G; PR 2-12 6.0; KR 11-246 22.4; 1 Fum.

RICH MOORE Moore, Richard Clifton 6'6", 280 DT
Col: Villanova *HS:* St. Joseph [Cleveland, OH] B: 4/26/1947, Cleveland, OH *Drafted:* 1969 Round 1 GB
1969 GB: 14 G. **1970** GB: 6 G. **Total:** 20 G.

RICKY MOORE Moore, Ricky Delano 5'11", 234 RB
Col: Alabama *HS:* Robert E. Lee [Huntsville, AL] B: 4/7/1963, Huntsville, AL *Drafted:* 1985 Round 3 SF

		Rushing				Receiving				
Year Team	G	Att	Yds	Avg	TD	Rec	Yds	Avg	TD	Fum
1986 Buf	11	33	104	3.2	1	23	184	8.0	0	2
1987 Hou	3	7	22	3.1	0	3	21	7.0	0	0
1988 Pho	8	0	0	—	0	1	15	15.0	0	0
NFL Total	22	40	126	3.2	1	27	220	8.1	0	2

ROBERT MOORE Moore, Robert Anthony 5'11", 190 DB
Col: Northwestern State-Louisiana *HS:* Captain Shreve [Shreveport, LA]
B: 8/15/1964, Shreveport, LA
1986 Atl: 16 G; Int 1-0; 1 Sac. **1987** Atl: 12 G; Int 2-23; **1** Fum TD; 6 Pt. **1988** Atl: 16 G; Int 5-56 1 TD; 6 Pt. **1989** Atl: 16 G. **Total:** 60 G; Int 8-79 1 TD; 1 Fum TD; Tot TD 2; 12 Pt; 1 Sac.

BOB MOORE Moore, Robert Rory 6'3", 220 TE
Col: Stanford *HS:* Klamath Falls [OR] B: 2/12/1949, Baltimore, MD
Drafted: 1971 Round 5 Oak
1976 TB: Rush 2-23 11.5. **Total:** Rush 2-23 11.5.

		Receiving				
Year Team	G	Rec	Yds	Avg	TD	Fum
1971 Oak	14	2	26	13.0	0	0
1972 Oak	14	6	49	8.2	1	0
1973 Oak	14	34	375	11.0	4	0
1974 Oak	14	30	356	11.9	2	1
1975 Oak	14	19	175	9.2	0	0
1976 TB	12	23	281	12.2	0	0
1977 TB	3	0	0	—	0	0
1978 Den	8	0	0	—	0	0
NFL Total	93	114	1262	11.1	7	1

ROB MOORE Moore, Robert Sean 6'3", 203 WR
Col: Syracuse *HS:* Hempstead [NY] B: 9/27/1968, New York, NY
Drafted: 1990 Supplemental Round 1 NYJ
1990 NYJ: Rush 2-(-4) -2.0. **1992** NYJ: Rush 1-21 21.0. **1993** NYJ: Rush 1-(-6) -6.0. **1994** NYJ: Rush 1-(-3) -3.0; Scor 2 2XP. **1995** Ariz: Pass 2-1 50.0%, 33 16.50 1 Int; Scor 1 2XP. **1996** Ariz: Scor 1 2XP. **1997** Ariz: Scor 1 2XP. **Total:** Pass 2-1 50.0%, 33 16.50 1 Int; Rush 5-8 1.6; Scor 5 2XP.

		Receiving				
Year Team	G	Rec	Yds	Avg	TD	Fum
1990 NYJ	15	44	692	15.7	6	1
1991 NYJ	16	70	987	14.1	5	2
1992 NYJ	16	50	726	14.5	4	0
1993 NYJ	13	64	843	13.2	1	2
1994 NYJ	16	78	1010	12.9	6	0
1995 Ariz	15	63	907	14.4	5	0
1996 Ariz	16	58	1016	17.5	4	0
1997 Ariz	16	97	**1584**	16.3	8	0
1998 Ariz	16	67	982	14.7	5	0
NFL Total	139	591	8747	14.8	44	5

ROCCO MOORE Moore, Rocco Ray 6'5", 276 OG-OT
Col: Western Michigan *HS:* Charlotte [MI] B: 3/31/1955, Charlotte, MI
Drafted: 1977 Round 11 Phi
1980 ChiB: 7 G.

RONALD MOORE Moore, Ronald Lynn 5'10", 220 RB
Col: Pittsburg State *HS:* Star Spencer [Spencer, OK] B: 1/26/1970, Spencer, OK *Drafted:* 1993 Round 4 Pho
1993 Pho: Rec 3-16 5.3; KR 1-9 9.0. **1994** Ariz: Pass 1-0; Rec 8-52 6.5 1 TD; Scor 1 2XP. **1995** NYJ: Rec 8-50 6.3; KR 8-166 20.8. **1996** NYJ: KR 8-118 14.8. **1997** StL-Ariz: Rec 4-34 8.5; KR 1-17 17.0. StL: Rec 4-34 8.5; KR 1-17 17.0. **1998** Mia: Rec 1-1 1.0. **Total:** Pass 1-0; Rec 24-153 6.4 1 TD; KR 18-310 17.2; Scor 1 2XP.

		Rushing					Tot
Year Team	G	Att	Yds	Avg	TD	Fum	TD
1993 Pho	16	263	1018	3.9	9	3	9
1994 Ariz	16	232	780	3.4	4	2	5
1995 NYJ	15	43	121	2.8	0	3	0

1996 NYJ	16	1	1	1.0	0	0	0
1997 StL-Ariz	13	81	278	3.4	1	0	1
1997 StL	7	24	103	4.3	1	0	1
1997 Ariz	6	57	175	3.1	0	0	0
1998 Mia	1	4	12	3.0	0	1	0
NFL Total	77	624	2210	3.5	14	9	15

SHAWN MOORE Moore, Shawn Levique 6′2″, 213 **QB**
Col: Virginia *HS:* Martinsville [VA] B: 4/4/1968, Martinsville, VA
Drafted: 1991 Round 11 Den
1992 Den: 3 G; Pass 34-17 50.0%, 232 6.82 3 Int; Rush 8-39 4.9; 3 Fum.

WAYNE MOORE Moore, Solomon Wayne 6′6″, 265 **OT**
Col: Lamar *HS:* Charlton-Pollard [Beaumont, TX] B: 8/17/1945, Beaumont, TX D: 8/19/1989, Miami, FL
1970 Mia: 14 G. **1971** Mia: 1 G. **1972** Mia: 9 G. **1973** Mia: 13 G. **1974** Mia: 3 G. **1975** Mia: 14 G. **1976** Mia: 14 G. **1977** Mia: 14 G. **1978** Mia: 16 G. **Total:** 98 G.

STEVE MOORE Moore, Stephen Elliott 6′4″, 293 **OT**
(Big House) *Col:* Tennessee State *HS:* Fairley [Memphis, TN]
B: 10/1/1960, Memphis, TN D: 10/25/1989, Memphis, TN
Drafted: 1983 Round 3 NE
1983 NE: 4 G. **1984** NE: 16 G. **1985** NE: 16 G. **1986** NE: 11 G. **1987** NE: 5 G. **Total:** 52 G.

STEVON MOORE Moore, Stevon Nathaniel 5′11″, 210 **DB**
Col: Mississippi *HS:* Stone [Wiggins, MS] B: 2/9/1967, Wiggins, MS
Drafted: 1989 Round 7 NYJ
1992 Cle: 1 Fum TD; 2 Sac. **1993** Cle: 1 Fum TD. **1995** Cle: 1 Sac.
Total: 2 Fum TD; 3 Sac.

		Interceptions		
Year Team	**G**	**Int**	**Yds**	**TD**
1990 Mia	7	0	0	0
1992 Cle	14	0	0	0
1993 Cle	16	0	0	0
1994 Cle	16	0	0	0
1995 Cle	16	5	55	0
1996 Bal	16	1	10	0
1997 Bal	13	4	56	0
1998 Bal	16	0	0	0
NFL Total	114	10	121	0

TOM MOORE Moore, Thomas Marshall 6′2″, 215 **HB**
Col: Vanderbilt *HS:* Goodlettsville [TN] B: 7/17/1938, Goodlettsville, TN *Drafted:* 1960 Round 1 GB
1961 GB: Pass 2-2 100.0%, 42 21.00 1 TD. **1962** GB: Pass 5-2 40.0%, 70 14.00 2 TD 1 Int. **1963** GB: Pass 4-3 75.0%, 99 24.75 1 TD. **1964** GB: Pass 3-1 33.3%, 28 9.33. **1965** GB: Pass 2-2 100.0%, 22 11.00.
1966 LARm: Pass 1-1 100.0%, 20 20.00. **1967** Atl: Pass 2-2 100.0%, 102 51.00 1 TD. **Total:** Pass 19-13 68.4%, 383 20.16 5 TD 1 Int.

		Rushing				Receiving			
Year Team	**G**	**Att**	**Yds**	**Avg**	**TD**	**Rec**	**Yds**	**Avg**	**TD**
1960 GB	12	45	237	5.3	4	5	40	8.0	1
1961 GB	13	61	302	5.0	1	8	41	5.1	1
1962 GB	14	112	377	3.4	7	11	100	9.1	0
1963 GB	12	132	658	5.0	6	23	237	10.3	2
1964 GB	14	102	371	3.6	2	17	140	8.2	2
1965 GB	13	51	124	2.4	0	7	87	12.4	1
1966 LARm	14	104	272	2.6	1	60	433	7.2	3
1967 Atl	10	53	104	2.0	0	10	74	7.4	0
NFL Total	102	660	2445	3.7	21	141	1152	8.2	10

	Kickoff Returns					Tot
Year Team	**Ret**	**Yds**	**Avg**	**TD**	**Fum**	**TD**
1960 GB	12	397	**33.1**	0	0	5
1961 GB	15	409	27.3	0	2	2
1962 GB	13	284	21.8	0	4	7
1963 GB	0	0	—	0	2	8
1964 GB	16	431	26.9	0	0	4
1965 GB	15	361	24.1	0	4	1
1966 LARm	0	0	—	0	1	4
1967 Atl	0	0	—	0	1	0
NFL Total	71	1882	26.5	0	14	31

DINTY MOORE Moore, Walter Stanley 5′8″, 160 **WB-BB**
Col: Lafayette *HS:* Irving Prep [Tarrytown, NY] B: 9/30/1903, New York, NY
1927 Pott: 7 G; Rush 1 TD; Rec 1 TD; Tot TD 2; 12 Pt.

WILBUR MOORE Moore, Wilbur John 5′11″, 187 **DB-WB-HB-FB**
(Little Indian) *Col:* Minnesota *HS:* Austin [MN] B: 4/22/1916, Austin, MN D: 8/9/1965, Takoma Park, MD *Drafted:* 1939 Round 7 Was
1941 Was: KR 1-21 21.0. **1942** Was: PR 1-3 3.0; KR 1-24 24.0. **1943** Was: PR 2-2 1.0; KR 1-18 18.0. **1944** Was: PR 1-12 12.0; KR 8-143 17.9. **1945** Was: PR 1-10 10.0. **1946** Was: PR 1-2 2.0. **Total:** PR 6-29 4.8; KR 11-206 18.7.

		Rushing				Receiving			
Year Team	**G**	**Att**	**Yds**	**Avg**	**TD**	**Rec**	**Yds**	**Avg**	**TD**
1939 Was	10	27	100	3.7	0	1	2	2.0	0
1940 Was	10	15	89	5.9	2	2	26	13.0	1
1941 Was	6	10	48	4.8	1	2	6	3.0	0
1942 Was	11	10	25	2.5	0	10	114	11.4	2
1943 Was	9	40	231	5.8	2	30	537	17.9	7
1944 Was	10	37	140	3.8	2	33	424	12.8	5
1945 Was	7	29	206	7.1	1	13	115	8.8	1
1946 Was	9	15	62	4.1	0	0	0	—	0
NFL Total	72	183	901	4.9	8	91	1224	13.5	16

	Interceptions			Tot
Year Team	**Int**	**Yds**	**TD**	**TD**
1940 Was	1	0	0	3
1941 Was	0	0	0	1
1942 Was	3	23	0	2
1943 Was	2	46	0	9
1944 Was	5	53	0	7
1945 Was	0	0	0	2
1946 Was	2	45	0	0
NFL Total	13	167	0	24

WILL MOORE Moore, Will Henry III 6′1″, 184 **WR**
Col: Texas Southern *HS:* David W. Carter [Dallas, TX] B: 2/21/1970, Dallas, TX
1997 Jac: KR 1-36 36.0. **1998** Jac: KR 0-10. **Total:** KR 1-46 46.0.

		Receiving			
Year Team	**G**	**Rec**	**Yds**	**Avg**	**TD**
1995 NE	14	43	502	11.7	1
1996 NE	2	3	37	12.3	0
1997 Jac	11	1	10	10.0	0
1998 Jac	16	1	9	9.0	0
NFL Total	43	48	558	11.6	1

BUCKY MOORE Moore, William 5′11″, 185 **DB-HB-WB**
(The Dixie Flyer) *Col:* Loyola (N.O.) B: 1906 Deceased
1932 ChiC: Rec 2-8 4.0. **Total:** Rec 2-8 4.0.

		Rushing			
Year Team	**G**	**Att**	**Yds**	**Avg**	**TD**
1932 ChiC	4	21	42	2.0	1
1933 Pit	5	16	42	2.6	0
NFL Total	9	37	84	2.3	1

BILL MOORE Moore, William Julius 6′1″, 195 **OE-DE**
Col: North Carolina *HS:* Kiski School [Saltsburg, PA] B: 2/4/1912 D: 5/25/1973
1939 Det: 9 G; Rush 1-7 7.0; Rec 6-82 13.7 1 TD; 6 Pt.

RED MOORE Moore, William Roy 5′11″, 218 **G**
Col: Penn State *HS:* Rochester [PA] B: 12/14/1922, Pittsburgh, PA
Drafted: 1947 Round 12 Pit
1947 Pit: 12 G. **1948** Pit: 12 G. **1949** Pit: 12 G. **Total:** 36 G.

EMERY MOOREHEAD Moorehead, Emery Matthew 6′2″, 218 **TE-WR-RB**
Col: Colorado *HS:* Evanston Twp. [Evanston, IL] B: 3/22/1954, Evanston, IL *Drafted:* 1977 Round 6 NYG

		Rushing				Receiving			
Year Team	**G**	**Att**	**Yds**	**Avg**	**TD**	**Rec**	**Yds**	**Avg**	**TD**
1977 NYG	13	1	5	5.0	0	12	143	11.9	1
1978 NYG	10	0	0	—	0	3	45	15.0	0
1979 NYG	13	36	95	2.6	0	9	62	6.9	0
1980 Den	16	2	7	3.5	0	0	0	—	0
1981 ChiB	9	0	0	—	0	0	0	—	0
1982 ChiB	9	2	3	1.5	0	30	363	12.1	5
1983 ChiB	16	5	6	1.2	0	42	597	14.2	3
1984 ChiB	16	1	-2	-2.0	0	29	497	17.1	1
1985 ChiB	15	0	0	—	0	35	481	13.7	1
1986 ChiB	16	0	0	—	0	26	390	15.0	1
1987 ChiB	12	0	0	—	0	24	269	11.2	1
1988 ChiB	13	0	0	—	0	14	133	9.5	2
NFL Total	158	47	114	2.4	0	224	2980	13.3	15

	Kickoff Returns				
Year Team	**Ret**	**Yds**	**Avg**	**TD**	**Fum**
1977 NYG	4	65	16.3	0	0
1978 NYG	2	52	26.0	0	0
1979 NYG	1	16	16.0	0	0
1980 Den	1	18	18.0	0	0
1981 ChiB	23	476	20.7	0	0
1986 ChiB	0	0	—	0	1
1987 ChiB	0	0	—	0	1
NFL Total	31	627	20.2	0	2

JOHN MOORING Mooring, John Franklin 6′6″, 255 **OT-C**
Col: Tampa *HS:* Falfurrias [TX] B: 5/8/1947, Falfurrias, TX
Drafted: 1971 Round 2 NYJ
1971 NYJ: 14 G. **1972** NYJ: 14 G. **1973** NYJ: 14 G. **1974** NO: 11 G.
Total: 53 G.

MO MOORMAN Moorman, Maurice F Jr. 6′5″, 252 **OG**
Col: Kentucky; Texas A&M *HS:* St. Xavier [Louisville, KY]
B: 7/24/1944, Louisville, KY *Drafted:* 1968 Round 1 KC
1968 KC: 13 G. **1969** KC: 11 G. **1970** KC: 13 G. **1971** KC: 9 G. **1972** KC: 13 G. **1973** KC: 13 G; Rec 1-(-1) -1.0. **Total:** 72 G; Rec 1-(-1) -1.0.

JIM MOOTY Mooty, James W 5′11″, 177 **DB**
Col: Arkansas *HS:* El Dorado [AR] B: 6/15/1937 *Drafted:* 1960 Round 1 NYT
1960 Dal: 7 G; PR 8-37 4.6; KR 12-210 17.5; 2 Fum.

TIM MORABITO Morabito, Timothy Robert 6′3″, 296 **DT-NT**
Col: Boston College *HS:* St. Joseph's Regional [Montvale, NJ]
B: 10/12/1973, West Haverstraw, NY
1996 Cin: 7 G; 0.5 Sac. **1997** Car: 8 G. **1998** Car: 8 G. **Total:** 23 G; 0.5 Sac.

GONZALO MORALES Morales, Gonzalo 6′0″, 185 **TB-DB**
(Gonzie) *Col:* St. Mary's (Cal.) *HS:* Mission [San Francisco, CA]
B: 6/10/1922, San Francisco, CA
1947 Pit: Pass 27-8 29.6%, 78 2.89 1 TD 4 Int; PR 6-88 14.7; KR 5-113 22.6; Int 1-5. **1948** Pit: Pass 4-3 75.0%, 30 7.50; PR 8-83 10.4; KR 3-62 20.7; Int 1-11; 1 Fum TD. **Total:** Pass 31-11 35.5%, 108 3.48 1 TD 4 Int; PR 14-171 12.2; KR 8-175 21.9; Int 2-16; 1 Fum TD.

		Rushing				
Year Team	G	Att	Yds	Avg	TD	Fum
1947 Pit	8	29	96	3.3	0	1
1948 Pit	10	13	29	2.2	0	0
NFL Total	18	42	125	3.0	0	1

ERIC MORAN Moran, Eric Michael 6′5″, 285 **OT-OG**
Col: Washington *HS:* Foothill [Pleasanton, CA] B: 6/10/1960, Spokane, WA *Drafted:* 1983 Round 10 Dal
1984 Hou: 8 G. **1985** Hou: 15 G. **1986** Hou: 14 G. **Total:** 37 G.

HAP MORAN Moran, Francis Dale 6′1″, 190 **DB-TB-WB-LB**
Col: Grinnell; Carnegie Mellon *HS:* Boone [IA] B: 7/31/1901, Belle Plaine, IA D: 12/30/1994, New Milford, CT
1926 Fra: Rec 1 TD; Scor 33, 3 XK. **1927** Fra-ChiC: Scor 27, 3 FG, 6 XK. Fra: Scor 21, 3 FG, 6 XK. **1928** Pott-NYG: Pass 3 TD. Pott: Pass 3 TD. **1929** NYG: Pass 2 TD; Rec 5 TD. **1930** NYG: Pass 2 TD; Scor 27, 3 XK. **1931** NYG: Rec 2 TD; Scor 35, 1 FG, 8 XK. **1932** NYG: Pass 20-12 60.0%, 91 4.55; Rec 6-47 7.8; Scor 8, 2 XK. **1933** NYG: Pass 1-0; Rec 3-114 38.0 1 TD. **Total:** Pass 21-12 57.1%, 91 4.33 7 TD; Rec 9-161 17.9 9 TD; Scor 166, 4 FG, 22 XK.

		Rushing				Tot
Year Team	G	Att	Yds	Avg	TD	TD
1926 Fra	14	—	—	—	4	5
1927 Fra-ChiC	10	—	—	—	2	2
1927 Fra	6	—	—	—	1	1
1927 ChiC	4	—	—	—	1	1
1928 Pott-NYG	11	—	—	—	0	0
1928 Pott	10	—	—	—	0	0
1928 NYG	1	—	—	—	0	0
1929 NYG	14	—	—	—	0	5
1930 NYG	16	—	—	—	4	4
1931 NYG	14	—	—	—	2	4
1932 NYG	11	82	262	3.2	1	1
1933 NYG	9	4	8	2.0	0	1
NFL Total	99	86	270	3.1	13	22

FRANK MORAN Moran, Frank 6′4″, 285 **C-T**
Col: No College B: 1891 Deceased
1920 Ham-Akr: 3 G. Ham: 2 G. Akr: 1 G. **Total:** 3 G.

JIM MORAN Moran, James Harry 6′5″, 275 **DT**
(Farmer) *Col:* Idaho *HS:* Gonzaga Prep [Spokane, WA] B: 5/4/1942, Spokane, WA *Drafted:* 1964 Round 10 NYG
1964 NYG: 8 G. **1966** NYG: 10 G. **1967** NYG: 10 G. **Total:** 28 G.

JIM MORAN Moran, James Patrick 6′1″, 208 **G**
Col: Holy Cross *HS:* Boston College [MA] B: 9/27/1912, Boston, MA
D: 8/18/1983, Natick, MA
1935 Bos: 11 G. **1936** Bos: 5 G. **Total:** 16 G.

RICH MORAN Moran, Richard James 6′3″, 276 **OG-C**
Col: San Diego State *HS:* Foothill [Pleasanton, CA] B: 3/19/1962, Boise, ID *Drafted:* 1985 Round 3 GB
1985 GB: 16 G. **1986** GB: 5 G. **1987** GB: 12 G; 1 Fum. **1988** GB: 16 G. **1989** GB: 16 G. **1990** GB: 16 G. **1991** GB: 16 G. **1992** GB: 8 G. **1993** GB: 3 G. **Total:** 108 G; 1 Fum.

SEAN MORAN Moran, Sean Farrell 6′3″, 275 **DE**
Col: Colorado State *HS:* Overland [Aurora, CO] B: 6/5/1973, Denver, CO *Drafted:* 1996 Round 4 Buf
1996 Buf: 16 G. **1997** Buf: 16 G; Int 2-12; 4.5 Sac. **1998** Buf: 9 G.
Total: 41 G; Int 2-12; 4.5 Sac.

TOM MORAN Moran, Tom McGee 5′8″, 175 **BB**
Col: Centre *HS:* Horse Cave [KY] B: 1898 Deceased
1925 NYG: 1 G.

DOUG MOREAU Moreau, Douglas Paul 6′1″, 215 **TE-K**
Col: Louisiana State *HS:* University [Baton Rouge, LA] B: 2/15/1945, Thibodaux, LA *Drafted:* 1966 Round 19 Mia
1967 Mia: Rush 1-(-2) -2.0. **1968** Mia: Scor 27, 1-3 33.3% FG, 6-6 100.0% XK. **Total:** Rush 1-(-2) -2.0; Scor 45, 1-3 33.3% FG, 6-6 100.0% XK.

		Receiving			
Year Team	G	Rec	Yds	Avg	TD
1966 Mia	3	2	15	7.5	0
1967 Mia	14	34	410	12.1	3
1968 Mia	11	27	365	13.5	3
1969 Mia	5	10	136	13.6	0
NFL Total	33	73	926	12.7	6

JOE MOREINO Moreino, Joseph P Jr. 6′6″, 246 **NT-DE**
Col: Idaho State *HS:* Central Islip [NY] B: 4/4/1955, Providence, RI
1978 NYJ: 1 G.

FRAN MORELLI Morelli, Francis Paul 6′2″, 258 **OT**
Col: Colgate *HS:* Manlius Mil. Acad. [NY] B: 1/15/1939, Medford, MA
1962 NYT: 12 G.

JOHN MORELLI Morelli, John 5′10″, 191 **G-LB**
Col: Georgetown *HS:* Revere [MA] B: 6/11/1923, Revere, MA
Drafted: 1945 Round 28 Bos
1944 Bos: 10 G; **2** Fum TD; 12 Pt. **1945** Bos: 9 G; Int 1-10. **Total:** 19 G; Int 1-10; 2 Fum TD; 12 Pt.

MOSES MORENO Moreno, Moses Nathaniel 6′1″, 205 **QB**
Col: Colorado State *HS:* Castle Park [Chula Vista, CA] B: 9/5/1975, Chula Vista, CA *Drafted:* 1998 Round 7 ChiB
1998 ChiB: 2 G; Pass 43-19 44.2%, 166 3.86 1 TD; Rush 4-9 2.3; 2 Fum.

TIM MORESCO Moresco, Timothy John 5′11″, 176 **DB**
Col: Syracuse *HS:* Ithaca [NY] B: 10/3/1954, Ithaca, NY
Drafted: 1977 Round 6 GB
1977 GB: 14 G; KR 1-15 15.0. **1978** NYJ: 11 G. **1979** NYJ: 16 G; Scor **1** Saf; 2 Pt. **1980** NYJ: 11 G. **Total:** 52 G; KR 1-15 15.0; Scor 1 Saf; 2 Pt.

ARNOLD MORGADO Morgado, Arnold Theodore Jr. 6′0″, 210 **RB**
Col: Michigan State; Hawaii *HS:* Punahou School [Honolulu, HI]
B: 3/27/1952, Honolulu, HI
1977 KC: Rec 2-21 10.5. **1978** KC: Rec 7-47 6.7; KR 5-100 20.0. **1979** KC: Rec 5-55 11.0; KR 1-0. **1980** KC: Rec 5-27 5.4 1 TD; KR 2-33 16.5. **Total:** Rec 19-150 7.9 1 TD; KR 8-133 16.6.

		Rushing					Tot
Year Team	G	Att	Yds	Avg	TD	Fum	TD
1977 KC	14	3	12	4.0	0	0	0
1978 KC	16	160	593	3.7	7	2	7
1979 KC	11	75	231	3.1	4	1	4
1980 KC	11	47	120	2.6	4	0	5
NFL Total	52	285	956	3.4	15	3	16

ANTHONY MORGAN Morgan, Anthony Eugene 6′1″, 195 **WR**
(A.M.) *Col:* Tennessee *HS:* John Adams [Cleveland, OH]
B: 11/15/1967, Cleveland, OH *Drafted:* 1991 Round 5 ChiB
1991 ChiB: Rush 3-18 6.0; PR 3-19 6.3; KR 8-133 16.6. **1992** ChiB: Rush 3-68 22.7; PR 3-21 7.0; KR 4-71 17.8. **1995** GB: KR 3-46 15.3.
Total: Rush 6-86 14.3; PR 6-40 6.7; KR 15-250 16.7.

		Receiving				
Year Team	G	Rec	Yds	Avg	TD	Fum
1991 ChiB	14	13	211	16.2	2	1
1992 ChiB	12	14	323	23.1	2	0
1993 ChiB-GB	3	1	8	8.0	0	0
1993 ChiB	1	0	0	—	0	0
1993 GB	2	1	8	8.0	0	0
1994 GB	16	28	397	14.2	4	1
1995 GB	16	31	344	11.1	4	0
1996 GB	3	0	0	—	0	0
NFL Total	64	87	1283	14.7	12	2

BOYD MORGAN Morgan, Boyd F 6′0″, 198 **BB-LB-WB-DB**
(Red) *Col:* USC *HS:* Holtville [CA] B: 10/24/1915, Comanche, OK
D: 6/8/1988, Los Angeles, CA *Drafted:* 1939 Round 16 Was
1939 Was: 5 G; Rush 1-0; Rec 1-4 4.0. **1940** Was: 6 G. **Total:** 11 G; Rush 1-0; Rec 1-4 4.0.

DAN MORGAN Morgan, Daniel Scott 6'6", 285 **OG**
Col: Penn State *HS:* St. Clairsville [OH] B: 2/2/1964, Wheeling, WV
1987 NYG: 2 G.

DENNIS MORGAN Morgan, Dennis 5'11", 200 **RB**
Col: Western Illinois *HS:* White Plains [NY] B: 6/26/1952, White Plains, NY *Drafted:* 1974 Round 10 Dal

		Punt Returns				Kickoff Returns				
Year Team	G	Ret	Yds	Avg	TD	Ret	Yds	Avg	TD	Fum
1974 Dal	13	19	287	15.1	1	35	823	23.5	0	2
1975 Phi	4	8	60	7.5	0	7	170	24.3	0	0
NFL Total	17	27	347	12.9	1	42	993	23.6	0	2

BILL MORGAN Morgan, Elmer William 6'2", 232 **T**
Col: Oregon *HS:* Medford [OR] B: 5/8/1910, Portland, OR
D: 7/10/1985, Canby, OR
1933 NYG: 13 G. **1934** NYG: 13 G. **1935** NYG: 12 G. **1936** NYG: 10 G.
Total: 48 G.

JOE MORGAN Morgan, Joe Winfred 6'1", 245 **T**
Col: McNeese State; Southern Mississippi *HS:* DeRidder [LA]
B: 10/23/1928, DeRidder, LA
AAFC **1949** SF-A: 8 G.

MELVIN MORGAN Morgan, Melvin 6'0", 183 **DB**
Col: Mississippi Gulf Coast CC; Mississippi Valley State *HS:* Harrison Central [Gulfport, MS] B: 3/31/1953, Gulfport, MS *Drafted:* 1976 Round 11 Cin
1976 Cin: 14 G; KR 1-14 14.0; **1** Fum TD; 6 Pt; 1 Fum. **1977** Cin: 12 G; Int 1-0. **1978** Cin: 15 G; Int 1-64. **1979** SF: 8 G; Int 1-0. **1980** SF: 6 G.
Total: 55 G; KR 1-14 14.0; Int 3-64; 1 Fum TD; 6 Pt; 1 Fum.

KARL MORGAN Morgan, Michael Karl 6'1", 255 **NT**
Col: UCLA *HS:* Vandebilt Catholic [Houma, LA] B: 2/23/1961, Houma, LA
1984 TB: 13 G. **1985** TB: 16 G; 4 Sac. **1986** TB-Hou: 13 G. TB: 12 G. Hou: 1 G. **Total:** 42 G; 4 Sac.

MIKE MORGAN Morgan, Michael Lee 6'4", 242 **LB**
Col: Louisiana State *HS:* Natchez [MS] B: 1/31/1942, Shreveport, LA
D: 12/2/1996, Baker, LA *Drafted:* 1964 Round 17 Phi
1964 Phi: 14 G; KR 2-0; 1 Fum TD; 6 Pt; 1 Fum. **1965** Phi: 14 G; KR 1-3 3.0; Int 1-1. **1966** Phi: 9 G; Int 1-5. **1967** Phi: 13 G; Int 1-0. **1968** Was: 14 G; Int 2-23. **1969** NO: 14 G. **1970** NO: 9 G; Int 1-7; 1 Fum TD; 6 Pt.
Total: 87 G; KR 3-3 1.0; Int 6-36; 2 Fum TD; 12 Pt; 1 Fum.

MIKE MORGAN Morgan, Michael Lee 5'11", 207 **RB**
Col: Wisconsin *HS:* Albert G. Lane Tech [Chicago, IL] B: 1/19/1956, Tallassee, AL
1978 ChiB: 5 G; KR 5-110 22.0.

BOBBY MORGAN Morgan, Robert Bernard 6'0", 205 **DB**
Col: Independence CC KS; New Mexico *HS:* Wamego [KS]
B: 8/7/1940, Wamego, KS
1967 Pit: 5 G.

BOB MORGAN Morgan, Robert Francis 6'0", 235 **DT**
Col: Maryland *HS:* Freeport [PA] B: 6/28/1930, Freeport, PA
D: 10/10/1991, Westminster, CO *Drafted:* 1953 Round 8 LARm
1954 Was: 10 G.

STANLEY MORGAN Morgan, Stanley Douglas 5'11", 181 **WR**
Col: Tennessee *HS:* Easley [SC] B: 2/17/1955, Easley, SC
Drafted: 1977 Round 1 NE
1977 NE: Rush 1-10 10.0. **1978** NE: Rush 2-11 5.5; KR 1-17 17.0.
1979 NE: Rush 7-39 5.6; KR 1-12 12.0. **1980** NE: Rush 4-36 9.0.
1981 NE: Rush 2-21 10.5. **1982** NE: Rush 2-3 1.5. **1983** NE: Rush 1-13 13.0. **1985** NE: Rush 1-0. **1988** NE: Rush 1-(-6) -6.0. **Total:** Rush 21-127 6.0; KR 2-29 14.5.

		Receiving				Punt Returns					Tot
Year Team	G	Rec	Yds	Avg	TD	Ret	Yds	Avg	TD	Fum	TD
1977 NE	14	21	443	21.1	3	16	220	13.8	0	0	3
1978 NE	16	34	820	24.1	5	32	335	10.5	0	6	5
1979 NE	16	44	1002	**22.8**	**12**	29	289	10.0	1	1	13
1980 NE	16	45	991	**22.0**	6	0	0	—	0	0	6
1981 NE	13	44	1029	**23.4**	6	15	116	7.7	0	2	6
1982 NE	9	28	584	20.9	3	0	0	—	0	0	3
1983 NE	16	58	863	14.9	2	0	0	—	0	5	2
1984 NE	13	38	709	18.7	5	0	0	—	0	0	5
1985 NE	15	39	760	19.5	5	0	0	—	0	1	5
1986 NE	16	84	1491	17.8	10	0	0	—	0	0	10
1987 NE	10	40	672	16.8	3	0	0	—	0	0	3
1988 NE	16	31	502	16.2	4	0	0	—	0	1	4
1989 NE	10	28	486	17.4	3	0	0	—	0	0	3
1990 Ind	16	23	364	15.8	5	0	0	—	0	1	5
NFL Total	196	557	10716	19.2	72	92	960	10.4	1	17	73

LARRY MORIARTY Moriarty, Larry Scott 6'1", 240 **RB**
Col: Santa Barbara City Coll. CA (J.C.); Notre Dame *HS:* Dos Pueblos [Goleta, CA] B: 4/24/1958, Santa Barbara, CA *Drafted:* 1983 Round 5 Hou
1983 Hou: KR 2-25 12.5. **1984** Hou: Pass 1-1 100.0%, 16 16.00.
1986 Hou-KC: KR 4-80 20.0. KC: KR 4-80 20.0. **1987** KC: KR 6-102 17.0.
Total: Pass 1-1 100.0%, 16 16.00; KR 12-207 17.3.

		Rushing				Receiving					Tot
Year Team	G	Att	Yds	Avg	TD	Rec	Yds	Avg	TD	Fum	TD
1983 Hou	16	65	321	4.9	3	4	32	8.0	0	1	3
1984 Hou	14	189	785	4.2	6	31	206	6.6	1	5	7
1985 Hou	15	106	381	3.6	3	17	112	6.6	0	2	3
1986 Hou-KC	15	90	252	2.8	1	9	67	7.4	0	2	1
1986 Hou	5	55	137	2.5	1	2	16	8.0	0	1	1
1986 KC	10	35	115	3.3	0	7	51	7.3	0	1	0
1987 KC	12	30	107	3.6	0	10	37	3.7	1	0	1
1988 KC	9	20	62	3.1	0	6	40	6.7	0	0	0
NFL Total	81	500	1908	3.8	13	77	494	6.4	2	10	15

PAT MORIARTY Moriarty, Patrick John 6'0", 195 **RB**
Col: Georgia Tech *HS:* Benedictine [Cleveland, OH] B: 5/19/1955, Cleveland, OH
1979 Cle: 16 G; Rush 14-11 0.8 2 TD; Rec 1-17 17.0; KR 1-0; 12 Pt.

TOM MORIARTY Moriarty, Thomas E Jr. 6'0", 185 **DB**
Col: Bowling Green State *HS:* Benedictine [Cleveland, OH]
B: 4/7/1953, Lima, OH
1977 Atl: 14 G; KR 8-136 17.0. **1978** Atl: 14 G; 6 Pt. **1979** Atl: 16 G.
1980 Pit: 4 G. **1981** Atl: 9 G. **Total:** 57 G; KR 8-136 17.0; 6 Pt.

MILT MORIN Morin, Milton Denis 6'4", 236 **TE**
Col: Massachusetts *HS:* St. Bernard's [Fitchburg, MA] B: 10/15/1942, Leominster, MA *Drafted:* 1966 Round 1 Cle
1968 Cle: Rush 1-8 8.0. **1969** Cle: Rush 2-30 15.0. **1970** Cle: Rush 1-2 2.0; KR 1-0. **1971** Cle: Rush 1-1 1.0. **Total:** Rush 5-41 8.2; KR 1-0.

		Receiving				
Year Team	G	Rec	Yds	Avg	TD	Fum
1966 Cle	11	23	333	14.5	3	3
1967 Cle	6	7	90	12.9	0	0
1968 Cle	14	43	792	18.4	5	0
1969 Cle	14	37	495	13.4	0	1
1970 Cle	14	37	611	16.5	1	1
1971 Cle	14	40	581	14.5	2	2
1972 Cle	14	30	540	18.0	1	0
1973 Cle	14	26	417	16.0	1	0
1974 Cle	14	27	330	12.2	3	0
1975 Cle	14	1	19	19.0	0	0
NFL Total	129	271	4208	15.5	16	7

BRETT MORITZ Moritz, Brett I 6'5", 250 **OG**
Col: Army; Nebraska *HS:* Osmond [NE] B: 7/15/1955, Lincoln, NE
Drafted: 1978 Round 2 TB
1978 TB: 6 G.

SAM MORLEY Morley, Samuel Robertson 6'2", 182 **OE**
Col: Yuba Coll. CA (J.C.); Stanford *HS:* San Marino [CA] B: 5/12/1932, Pasadena, CA *Drafted:* 1954 Round 20 Was
1954 Was: 1 G.

JACK MORLOCK Morlock, Jack 5'10", 165 **WB-DB**
Col: Marshall *HS:* Moundsville [WV] B: 4/7/1916, McKeesport, PA
D: 1/7/1976, Huntington, WV *Drafted:* 1940 Round 12 Det
1940 Det: 4 G; Rush 1-0.

MIKE MOROSKI Moroski, Michael Henry 6'4", 200 **QB**
Col: California-Davis *HS:* Novato [CA] B: 9/4/1957, Bakersfield, CA
Drafted: 1979 Round 6 Atl

		Passing							
Year Team	G	Att	Comp	Comp%	Yds	YPA	TD	Int	Rating
1979 Atl	2	15	8	53.3	97	6.47	0	0	73.5
1980 Atl	3	3	2	66.7	24	8.00	0	0	91.0
1981 Atl	3	26	12	46.2	132	5.08	0	1	45.7
1982 Atl	9	13	10	76.9	87	6.69	1	0	119.7
1983 Atl	16	70	45	64.3	575	8.21	2	4	75.6
1984 Atl	16	191	102	53.4	1207	6.32	2	9	56.8
1985 Hou	5	34	20	58.8	249	7.32	1	1	79.2
1986 SF	15	73	42	57.5	493	6.75	2	3	70.2
NFL Total	69	425	241	56.7	2864	6.74	8	18	66.0

	Rushing				
Year Team	Att	Yds	Avg	TD	Fum
1979 Atl	3	31	10.3	1	1
1981 Atl	3	17	5.7	0	0
1983 Atl	2	12	6.0	0	2
1984 Atl	21	98	4.7	0	6
1985 Hou	2	2	1.0	0	0
1986 SF	6	22	3.7	1	3
NFL Total	37	182	4.9	2	12

EARL MORRALL Morrall, Earl Edwin 6′1″, 205 **QB**
Col: Michigan State *HS:* Muskegon [MI] B: 5/17/1934, Muskegon, MI
Drafted: 1956 Round 1 SF

		Passing							
Year Team	G	Att	Comp	Comp%	Yds	YPA	TD	Int	Rating
1956 SF	12	78	38	48.7	621	7.96	1	6	48.1
1957 Pit	12	289	139	48.1	1900	6.57	11	12	64.9
1958 Pit-Det	11	78	25	32.1	463	5.94	5	9	35.3
1958 Pit	2	46	16	34.8	275	5.98	1	7	23.6
1958 Det	9	32	9	28.1	188	5.88	4	2	65.1
1959 Det	12	137	65	47.4	1102	8.04	5	6	69.1
1960 Det	12	49	32	65.3	423	8.63	4	3	94.2
1961 Det	13	150	69	46.0	909	6.06	7	9	56.2
1962 Det	14	52	32	61.5	449	8.63	4	4	82.9
1963 Det	14	328	174	53.0	2621	7.99	24	14	86.2
1964 Det	6	91	50	54.9	588	6.46	4	3	75.7
1965 NYG	14	302	155	51.3	2446	8.10	22	12	86.3
1966 NYG	7	151	71	47.0	1105	7.32	7	12	54.1
1967 NYG	8	24	13	54.2	181	7.54	3	1	100.9
1968 Bal	14	317	182	57.4	2909	9.18	**26**	17	93.2
1969 Bal	9	99	46	46.5	755	7.63	5	7	60.0
1970 Bal	14	93	51	54.8	792	8.52	9	4	97.6
1971 Bal	14	167	84	50.3	1210	7.25	7	12	58.2
1972 Mia	14	150	83	55.3	1360	**9.07**	11	7	91.0
1973 Mia	14	38	17	44.7	253	6.66	0	4	27.5
1974 Mia	14	27	17	63.0	301	11.15	2	3	86.1
1975 Mia	13	43	26	60.5	273	6.35	3	2	82.8
1976 Mia	14	26	10	38.5	148	5.69	1	1	54.6
NFL Total	255	2689	1379	51.3	20809	7.74	161	148	74.1

	Rushing				Punting			
Year Team	Att	Yds	Avg	TD	Punts	Yds	Avg	Fum
1956 SF	6	10	1.7	0	45	1705	37.9	1
1957 Pit	41	81	2.0	2	0	0	—	**12**
1958 Pit-Det	11	80	7.3	0	1	25	25.0	1
1958 Pit	4	39	9.8	0	0	0	—	1
1958 Det	7	41	5.9	0	1	25	25.0	0
1959 Det	26	112	4.3	0	11	481	43.7	7
1960 Det	10	37	3.7	1	0	0	—	3
1961 Det	20	86	4.3	0	3	113	37.7	6
1962 Det	17	65	3.8	1	1	48	48.0	1
1963 Det	26	105	4.0	1	29	1143	39.4	5
1964 Det	10	70	7.0	0	1	8	8.0	3
1965 NYG	17	52	3.1	0	0	0	—	5
1966 NYG	5	12	2.4	0	0	0	—	3
1967 NYG	4	11	2.8	1	15	472	31.5	0
1968 Bal	11	18	1.6	1	0	0	—	7
1970 Bal	2	6	3.0	0	0	0	—	2
1971 Bal	6	13	2.2	0	0	0	—	3
1972 Mia	17	67	3.9	1	0	0	—	3
1973 Mia	1	9	9.0	0	0	0	—	0
1974 Mia	1	11	11.0	0	0	0	—	0
1975 Mia	4	33	8.3	0	0	0	—	1
NFL Total	235	878	3.7	8	106	3995	37.7	63

KYLE MORRELL Morrell, Kyle Douglas 6′1″, 190 **DB**
Col: Brigham Young *HS:* Viewmont [Bountiful, UT] B: 10/9/1963, Scottsdale, AZ *Drafted:* 1985 Round 4 Min
1986 Min: 5 G.

BAM MORRIS Morris, Byron 6′0″, 244 **RB**
Col: Texas Tech *HS:* Cooper [Abilene, TX] B: 1/13/1972, Cooper, TX
Drafted: 1994 Round 3 Pit
1994 Pit: KR 4-114 28.5. **1996** Bal: KR 1-3 3.0. **1997** Bal: KR 1-23 23.0. **Total:** KR 6-140 23.3.

		Rushing				Receiving					Tot
Year Team	G	Att	Yds	Avg	TD	Rec	Yds	Avg	TD	Fum	TD
1994 Pit	15	198	836	4.2	7	22	204	9.3	0	3	7
1995 Pit	13	148	559	3.8	9	8	36	4.5	0	3	9
1996 Bal	11	172	737	4.3	4	25	242	9.7	1	0	5
1997 Bal	11	204	774	3.8	4	29	176	6.1	0	4	4
1998 ChiB-KC	12	132	489	3.7	8	12	95	7.9	0	3	8
1998 ChiB	2	3	8	2.7	0	0	0	—	0	0	0
1998 KC	10	129	481	3.7	8	12	95	7.9	0	3	8
NFL Total	62	854	3395	4.0	32	96	753	7.8	1	13	33

LARRY MORRIS Morris, Calvin Larry 5′7″, 207 **RB**
Col: Syracuse *HS:* Ayer [MA] B: 2/27/1962, NC
1987 GB: 2 G; Rush 8-18 2.3.

CHRIS MORRIS Morris, Christopher Steven 6′3″, 250 **OT**
Col: Indiana *HS:* Southport [Indianapolis, IN] B: 10/7/1949, Indianapolis, IN *Drafted:* 1971 Round 10 Min
1972 Cle: 14 G. **1973** Cle: 2 G. **1975** NO: 6 G. **Total:** 22 G.

DENNIT MORRIS Morris, Dennit Elton 6′1″, 228 **LB**
Col: Oklahoma *HS:* Webster [Tulsa, OK] B: 4/15/1936, Hanna, OK
Drafted: 1958 Round 18 SF
1958 SF: 12 G. **1960** Hou: 14 G; Int 4-32. **1961** Hou: 14 G; Int 1-31. **Total:** 40 G; Int 5-63.

DONNIE JOE MORRIS Morris, Donnie Joe 5′11″, 195 **RB**
Col: North Texas B: 2/16/1950, Amarillo, TX
1974 KC: 3 G; PR 1-0; KR 1-17 17.0.

DWAINE MORRIS Morris, Dwaine 6′2″, 260 **NT-DT**
Col: Southwestern Louisiana *HS:* Greensburg [LA] B: 8/24/1963, Independence, LA
1985 Phi: 1 G. **1987** Atl: 3 G; 0.5 Sac. **Total:** 4 G; 0.5 Sac.

MERCURY MORRIS Morris, Eugene E 5′10″, 190 **RB**
Col: West Texas A&M *HS:* Avonworth [Pittsburgh, PA] B: 1/5/1947, Pittsburgh, PA *Drafted:* 1969 Round 3 Mia

		Rushing				Receiving			
Year Team	G	Att	Yds	Avg	TD	Rec	Yds	Avg	TD
1969 Mia	14	23	110	4.8	1	6	65	10.8	0
1970 Mia	12	60	409	6.8	0	12	149	12.4	0
1971 Mia	14	57	315	5.5	1	5	16	3.2	0
1972 Mia	14	190	1000	5.3	**12**	15	168	11.2	0
1973 Mia	13	149	954	**6.4**	10	4	51	12.8	0
1974 Mia	5	56	214	3.8	1	2	27	13.5	1
1975 Mia	14	219	875	4.0	4	2	15	7.5	0
1976 SD	13	50	256	5.1	2	8	52	6.5	0
NFL Total	99	804	4133	5.1	31	54	543	10.1	1

	Punt Returns				Kickoff Returns					Tot
Year Team	Ret	Yds	Avg	TD	Ret	Yds	Avg	TD	Fum	TD
1969 Mia	25	172	6.9	0	**43**	**1136**	26.4	**1**	4	2
1970 Mia	2	-1	-0.5	0	28	812	29.0	1	6	1
1971 Mia	0	0	—	0	15	423	28.2	1	1	2
1972 Mia	0	0	—	0	14	334	23.9	0	8	12
1973 Mia	0	0	—	0	11	242	22.0	0	3	10
1974 Mia	0	0	—	0	0	0	—	0	4	2
1975 Mia	0	0	—	0	0	0	—	0	5	4
1976 SD	0	0	—	0	0	0	—	0	1	2
NFL Total	27	171	6.3	0	111	2947	26.5	3	32	35

FRANK MORRIS Morris, Francis Michael 6′2″, 214 **FB-LB**
Col: Boston U. *HS:* Our Lady [Newton, MA] B: 5/25/1918, Newton, MA
D: 10/16/1988, North Kingstown, RI
1942 ChiB: 6 G; Rush 3-7 2.3; Rec 3-24 8.0.

GEORGE MORRIS Morris, George Augustus Jr. 6′2″, 220 **C-LB**
Col: Georgia Tech *HS:* Carr Central [Vicksburg, MS] B: 3/19/1931, Vicksburg, MS
1956 SF: 12 G.

GEORGE MORRIS Morris, George William 5′11″, 188 **HB**
Col: Baldwin-Wallace *HS:* East Palestine [OH] B: 2/24/1919, East Palestine, OH
1941 Cle: Rec 9-17 1.9; PR 5-33 6.6; KR 8-118 14.8. **1942** Cle: PR 1-2 2.0; KR 1-15 15.0; Int 2-7. **Total:** Rec 9-17 1.9; PR 6-35 5.8; KR 9-133 14.8; Int 2-7.

		Rushing			
Year Team	G	Att	Yds	Avg	TD
1941 Cle	10	24	69	2.9	0
1942 Cle	9	22	65	3.0	0
NFL Total	19	46	134	2.9	0

GLEN MORRIS Morris, Glen Edgar 6′0″, 200 **OE-DE**
Col: Colorado State *HS:* Simla [CO] B: 6/8/1912, St. Louis, MO
D: 1/31/1974, San Mateo, CA
1940 Det: 4 G; Int 1-20.

MAX MORRIS Morris, Glen Max 6′2″, 200 **OE-DE**
Col: Illinois; Northwestern *HS:* Frankfort [West Frankfort, IL]
B: 3/14/1925, Norris City, IL
AAFC **1946** ChiA: Rush 1-20 20.0. **1947** ChiA: KR 1-13 13.0. **1948** BknA: KR 1-14 14.0. **Total:** Rush 1-20 20.0; KR 2-27 13.5.

		Receiving				Tot
Year Team	G	Rec	Yds	Avg	TD	TD
1946 ChiA	11	3	66	22.0	0	0
1947 ChiA	14	22	239	10.9	1	2
1948 BknA	13	28	372	13.3	1	1
AAFC Total	38	53	677	12.8	2	3

JIM BOB MORRIS Morris, James Robert 6′3″, 211 **DB**
Col: Coffeyville CC KS; Kansas State *HS:* Hamilton [KS] B: 5/17/1961, Burbank, CA
1987 GB: 11 G; Int 3-135; 1 Sac.

JAMIE MORRIS Morris, James Walter 5′7″, 188 **RB**
Col: Michigan *HS:* Ayer [MA] B: 6/6/1965, Southern Pines, NC
Drafted: 1988 Round 4 Was
1988 Was: Rec 1-3 3.0. **1989** Was: Rec 8-65 8.1. **Total:** Rec 9-68 7.6.

		Rushing				Kickoff Returns				
Year Team	**G**	**Att**	**Yds**	**Avg**	**TD**	**Ret**	**Yds**	**Avg**	**TD**	**Fum**
1988 Was	16	126	437	3.5	2	21	413	19.7	0	3
1989 Was	12	124	336	2.7	2	0	0	—	0	3
1990 NE	5	2	4	2.0	0	11	202	18.4	0	1
NFL Total	33	252	777	3.1	4	32	615	19.2	0	7

JACK MORRIS Morris, John Bradley 6′0″, 189 **DB**
Col: Oregon *HS:* Medford [OR] B: 11/1/1931, White City, KS
Drafted: 1956 Round 7 LARm
1958 LARm: 12 G; PR 8-9 1.1; KR 2-37 18.5; Int 6-152 1 TD; 6 Pt.
1959 LARm: 12 G; Scor 24, 3-8 37.5% FG, 15-15 100.0% XK.
1960 LARm-Pit: 7 G. LARm: 3 G. Pit: 4 G. **1961** Min: 14 G; Int 2-90.
Total: 45 G; PR 8-9 1.1; KR 2-37 18.5; Int 8-242 1 TD; Scor 30, 3-8 37.5% FG, 15-15 100.0% XK.

JOHNNY MORRIS Morris, John Edward 5′10″, 180 **FL-HB**
Col: California-Santa Barbara *HS:* Long Beach Polytechnic [CA]
B: 9/26/1935, Long Beach, CA *Drafted:* 1958 Round 12 ChiB

		Rushing				Receiving			
Year Team	**G**	**Att**	**Yds**	**Avg**	**TD**	**Rec**	**Yds**	**Avg**	**TD**
1958 ChiB	12	52	239	4.6	2	11	170	15.5	0
1959 ChiB	12	87	312	3.6	0	13	197	15.2	2
1960 ChiB	12	73	417	5.7	3	20	224	11.2	3
1961 ChiB	14	8	49	6.1	0	36	548	15.2	4
1962 ChiB	14	2	7	3.5	0	58	889	15.3	5
1963 ChiB	13	1	10	10.0	0	47	705	15.0	2
1964 ChiB	14	0	0	—	0	**93**	**1200**	12.9	**10**
1965 ChiB	14	0	0	—	0	53	846	16.0	4
1966 ChiB	2	0	0	—	0	5	49	9.8	0
1967 ChiB	14	1	6	6.0	0	20	231	11.6	1
NFL Total	121	224	1040	4.6	5	356	5059	14.2	31

	Punt Returns				Kickoff Returns					Tot
Year Team	**Ret**	**Yds**	**Avg**	**TD**	**Ret**	**Yds**	**Avg**	**TD**	**Fum**	**TD**
1958 ChiB	14	96	6.9	0	16	399	24.9	0	4	2
1959 ChiB	14	171	**12.2**	1	17	438	25.8	0	3	3
1960 ChiB	13	75	5.8	0	19	384	20.2	0	2	6
1961 ChiB	23	155	6.7	0	2	46	23.0	0	2	4
1962 ChiB	20	208	10.4	0	0	0	—	0	2	5
1963 ChiB	16	164	10.3	0	0	0	—	0	2	2
1964 ChiB	0	0	—	0	0	0	—	0	1	10
1965 ChiB	0	0	—	0	0	0	—	0	0	4
1967 ChiB	4	24	6.0	0	0	0	—	0	0	1
NFL Total	104	893	8.6	1	54	1267	23.5	0	16	37

JON MORRIS Morris, Jon Nicholson 6′4″, 254 **C**
Col: Holy Cross *HS:* Gonzaga [Washington, DC] B: 4/5/1942, Washington, DC *Drafted:* 1964 Round 4 Bos
1964 Bos: 14 G. **1965** Bos: 14 G. **1966** Bos: 14 G. **1967** Bos: 14 G; 3 Fum. **1968** Bos: 14 G. **1969** Bos: 14 G. **1970** Bos: 14 G. **1971** NE: 14 G; 1 Fum. **1972** NE: 13 G. **1973** NE: 2 G. **1974** NE: 3 G. **1975** Det: 14 G. **1976** Det: 14 G. **1977** Det: 14 G; 1 Fum. **1978** ChiB: 10 G; 2 Fum.
Total: 182 G; 7 Fum.

JOE MORRIS Morris, Joseph Edward 5′7″, 195 **RB**
Col: Syracuse *HS:* Southern Pines [NC]; Ayer HS [MA] B: 9/15/1960, Fort Bragg, NC *Drafted:* 1982 Round 2 NYG

		Rushing				Receiving			
Year Team	**G**	**Att**	**Yds**	**Avg**	**TD**	**Rec**	**Yds**	**Avg**	**TD**
1982 NYG	5	15	48	3.2	1	8	34	4.3	0
1983 NYG	15	35	145	4.1	0	2	1	0.5	1
1984 NYG	16	133	510	3.8	4	12	124	10.3	0
1985 NYG	16	294	1336	4.5	**21**	22	212	9.6	0
1986 NYG	15	341	1516	4.4	14	21	233	11.1	1
1987 NYG	11	193	658	3.4	3	11	114	10.4	0
1988 NYG	16	307	1083	3.5	5	22	166	7.5	0
1991 Cle	16	93	289	3.1	2	13	76	5.8	0
NFL Total	110	1411	5585	4.0	50	111	960	8.6	2

	Kickoff Returns					Tot
Year Team	**Ret**	**Yds**	**Avg**	**TD**	**Fum**	**TD**
1982 NYG	0	0	—	0	1	1
1983 NYG	14	255	18.2	0	2	1
1984 NYG	6	69	11.5	0	1	4
1985 NYG	2	25	12.5	0	6	**21**
1986 NYG	0	0	—	0	6	15
1987 NYG	0	0	—	0	2	3
1988 NYG	0	0	—	0	7	5
1991 Cle	18	310	17.2	0	2	2
NFL Total	40	659	16.5	0	27	52

LARRY MORRIS Morris, Lawrence Cleo 6′2″, 226 **LB-HB**
Col: Georgia Tech *HS:* Boys [Decatur, GA] B: 12/10/1933, Decatur, GA *Drafted:* 1955 Round 1 LARm
1957 LARm: Int 1-0. **1959** ChiB: Int 1-14; **1** Fum TD. **1960** ChiB: Int 1-5. **1961** ChiB: PR 1-2 2.0; Int 1-25. **1962** ChiB: Int 2-9. **1966** Atl: KR 5-50 10.0. **Total:** PR 1-2 2.0; KR 5-50 10.0; Int 6-53; 1 Fum TD.

		Rushing				Tot
Year Team	**G**	**Att**	**Yds**	**Avg**	**TD**	**TD**
1955 LARm	12	40	148	3.7	1	1
1956 LARm	7	0	0	—	0	0
1957 LARm	6	0	0	—	0	0
1959 ChiB	12	0	0	—	0	1
1960 ChiB	12	0	0	—	0	0
1961 ChiB	14	0	0	—	0	0
1962 ChiB	14	0	0	—	0	0
1963 ChiB	14	0	0	—	0	0
1964 ChiB	9	0	0	—	0	0
1965 ChiB	12	0	0	—	0	0
1966 Atl	12	0	0	—	0	0
NFL Total	124	40	148	3.7	1	2

LEE MORRIS Morris, Lee A Jr. 5′11″, 180 **WR**
Col: Oklahoma *HS:* Del City [OK] B: 7/14/1964, Oklahoma City, OK
1987 GB: 5 G; Rush 2-2 1.0; Rec 16-259 16.2 1 TD; PR 1-1 1.0; KR 6-104 17.3; 6 Pt; 1 Fum.

MIKE MORRIS Morris, Michael Stephen 6′5″, 276 **C-OG**
Col: Northeast Missouri State *HS:* Centerville [IA] B: 2/22/1961, Centerville, IA
1987 StL: 14 G. **1989** KC-NE: 16 G. KC: 5 G. NE: 11 G. **1990** Sea-Cle: 14 G; 1 Fum. Sea: 4 G. Cle: 10 G; 1 Fum. **1991** Min: 16 G. **1992** Min: 16 G. **1993** Min: 16 G. **1994** Min: 16 G. **1995** Min: 16 G. **1996** Min: 16 G. **1997** Min: 16 G. **1998** Min: 16 G. **Total:** 172 G; 1 Fum.

RANDALL MORRIS Morris, Randall 6′0″, 195 **RB**
Col: Tennessee *HS:* Long Beach Polytechnic [CA] B: 4/22/1961, Anniston, AL *Drafted:* 1984 Round 10 Sea
1984 Sea: Rec 9-61 6.8. **1985** Sea: Pass 1-0; Rec 6-14 2.3. **1986** Sea: Pass 1-0. **Total:** Pass 2-0; Rec 15-75 5.0.

		Rushing				Kickoff Returns				
Year Team	**G**	**Att**	**Yds**	**Avg**	**TD**	**Ret**	**Yds**	**Avg**	**TD**	**Fum**
1984 Sea	10	58	189	3.3	0	8	153	19.1	0	2
1985 Sea	16	55	236	4.3	0	31	636	20.5	0	4
1986 Sea	16	19	149	7.8	1	23	465	20.2	0	2
1987 Sea	10	21	71	3.4	0	9	149	16.6	0	0
1988 Sea-Det	12	3	6	2.0	0	13	259	19.9	0	0
1988 Sea	9	3	6	2.0	0	11	218	19.8	0	0
1988 Det	3	0	0	—	0	2	41	20.5	0	0
NFL Total	64	156	651	4.2	1	84	1662	19.8	0	8

RAYMOND MORRIS Morris, Raymond Willie 5′10″, 222 **LB**
Col: Texas-El Paso *HS:* Ector [TX] B: 6/8/1961, Crane, TX
1987 ChiB: 3 G; 1 Sac.

RILEY MORRIS Morris, Riley D 6′2″, 230 **LB-DE**
Col: Florida A&M B: 3/22/1935
1960 Oak: 14 G; KR 1-3 3.0. **1961** Oak: 14 G; Int 3-79 1 TD; 6 Pt.
1962 Oak: 4 G. **Total:** 32 G; KR 1-3 3.0; Int 3-79 1 TD; 6 Pt.

BOB MORRIS Morris, Robert 5′10″, 200 **G**
Col: Cornell *HS:* Erasmus Hall [Brooklyn, NY] B: 12/15/1903, Newark, NJ D: 11/1985, North Miami Beach, FL
1926 Bkn: 6 G.

BOB MORRIS Morris, Robert William 5′11″, 180 **HB**
Col: USC *HS:* Monrovia [CA] B: 3/9/1925
1947 NYG: 1 G; Int 1-0.

RON MORRIS Morris, Ronald Wayne 6′1″, 190 **WR**
Col: Southern Methodist *HS:* Cooper [Abilene, TX] B: 11/4/1964, Cooper, TX *Drafted:* 1987 Round 2 ChiB
1988 ChiB: Rush 3-40 13.3. **1989** ChiB: Rush 1-(-14) -14.0. **1990** ChiB: Rush 2-26 13.0. **Total:** Rush 6-52 8.7.

		Receiving				
Year Team	**G**	**Rec**	**Yds**	**Avg**	**TD**	**Fum**
1987 ChiB	12	20	379	19.0	1	0
1988 ChiB	16	28	498	17.8	4	0
1989 ChiB	16	30	486	16.2	1	1
1990 ChiB	15	31	437	14.1	3	0
1991 ChiB	3	8	147	18.4	0	0
1992 ChiB	4	4	44	11.0	0	0
NFL Total	66	121	1991	16.5	9	1

TOM MORRIS Morris, Thomas Lewis 5′11″, 175 **DB**
Col: Cypress Coll. CA (J.C.); Golden West Coll. CA (J.C.); Michigan State *HS:* R.A. Millikan [Long Beach, CA] B: 4/2/1960, Anniston, AL
Drafted: 1982 Round 7 TB
1982 TB: 8 G. **1983** TB: 12 G. **Total:** 20 G.

VICTOR MORRIS Morris, Victor Fitzgerald 6'1", 243 **LB**
Col: Miami (Fla.) *HS:* Ely [Pompano Beach, FL] B: 1/25/1964, Boynton Beach, FL
1987 Mia: 3 G.

WAYNE MORRIS Morris, Wayne Lee 6'0", 207 **RB**
Col: Southern Methodist *HS:* South Oak Cliff [Dallas, TX] B: 5/3/1954, Dallas, TX *Drafted:* 1976 Round 5 StL
1976 StL: KR 9-181 20.1. **1977** StL: KR 2-39 19.5. **1978** StL: KR 3-66 22.0. **1982** StL: KR 1-14 14.0. **Total:** KR 15-300 20.0.

		Rushing				Receiving					Tot
Year Team	G	Att	Yds	Avg	TD	Rec	Yds	Avg	TD	Fum	TD
1976 StL	14	64	292	4.6	3	8	75	9.4	1	4	4
1977 StL	12	165	661	4.0	8	24	222	9.3	1	5	9
1978 StL	13	174	631	3.6	1	33	298	9.0	1	1	2
1979 StL	15	106	387	3.7	8	35	237	6.8	1	2	9
1980 StL	16	117	456	3.9	6	15	110	7.3	1	0	7
1981 StL	16	109	417	3.8	5	19	165	8.7	0	0	5
1982 StL	9	84	274	3.3	4	3	8	2.7	0	1	4
1983 StL	15	75	257	3.4	2	14	55	3.9	0	2	2
1984 SD	10	5	12	2.4	1	5	20	4.0	0	0	1
NFL Total	120	899	3387	3.8	38	156	1190	7.6	5	15	43

DARRYL MORRISON Morrison, Darryl Lamon 5'11", 185 **DB**
Col: Phoenix Coll. AZ (J.C.); Arizona *HS:* Central [Phoenix, AZ]; Camelback HS [Phoenix, AZ] B: 5/19/1971, Phoenix, AZ
Drafted: 1993 Round 6 Was
1993 Was: 4 G. **1994** Was: 16 G; 1 Fum TD; 6 Pt. **1995** Was: 16 G. **1996** Was: 12 G; Int 1-4. **Total:** 48 G; Int 1-4; 1 Fum TD; 6 Pt.

DENNIS MORRISON Morrison, Dennis Charles 6'3", 211 **QB**
Col: Kansas State *HS:* Pico Rivera [CA] B: 5/18/1951, Pico Rivera, CA
Drafted: 1973 Round 14 SF
1974 SF: Rush 1-0.

		Passing								
Year Team	G	Att	Comp	Comp%	Yds	YPA	TD	Int	Rating	Fum
1974 SF	3	51	21	41.2	227	4.45	1	5	21.9	1

DON MORRISON Morrison, Don Alan 6'5", 255 **OT-C**
Col: Texas-Arlington *HS:* Forney [TX] B: 12/16/1949, Fort Worth, TX
Drafted: 1971 Round 4 NO
1971 NO: 14 G. **1972** NO: 14 G. **1973** NO: 14 G. **1974** NO: 11 G. **1975** NO: 13 G. **1976** NO: 14 G. **1977** NO: 14 G. **1978** Bal: 14 G; KR 1-6 6.0. **1979** Det: 15 G. **Total:** 123 G; KR 1-6 6.0.

FRED MORRISON Morrison, Fred Liew 6'2", 215 **FB-HB**
(Curly) *Col:* Ohio State *HS:* Upper Arlington [OH] B: 10/7/1926, Columbus, OH *Drafted:* 1950 Round 1 ChiB
1951 ChiB: Pass 1-1 100.0%, 7 7.00. **Total:** Pass 1-1 100.0%, 7 7.00.

		Rushing				Receiving			
Year Team	G	Att	Yds	Avg	TD	Rec	Yds	Avg	TD
1950 ChiB	12	66	252	3.8	1	13	86	6.6	0
1951 ChiB	12	29	96	3.3	0	1	-3	-3.0	0
1952 ChiB	12	95	367	3.9	3	10	129	12.9	1
1953 ChiB	12	95	307	3.2	2	16	214	13.4	0
1954 Cle	12	54	234	4.3	2	12	81	6.8	0
1955 Cle	12	156	824	5.3	3	9	185	20.6	0
1956 Cle	12	83	340	4.1	1	6	29	4.8	1
NFL Total	84	578	2420	4.2	12	67	721	10.8	2

	Kickoff Returns				Punting				Tot
Year Team	Ret	Yds	Avg	TD	Punts	Yds	Avg	Fum	TD
1950 ChiB	10	261	26.1	0	57	2470	**43.3**	3	1
1951 ChiB	13	353	27.2	0	57	2227	39.1	2	0
1952 ChiB	4	41	10.3	0	64	2707	42.3	4	4
1953 ChiB	4	43	10.8	0	65	2766	42.6	2	2
1954 Cle	1	8	8.0	0	0	0	—	6	2
1955 Cle	0	0	—	0	0	0	—	5	3
1956 Cle	1	17	17.0	0	38	1561	41.1	2	2
NFL Total	33	723	21.9	0	281	11731	41.7	24	14

JOE MORRISON Morrison, Joseph R 6'1", 210 **HB-FL-WR-FB**
Col: Cincinnati *HS:* South [Lima, OH] B: 8/21/1937, Lima, OH
D: 2/5/1989, Columbia, SC *Drafted:* 1959 Round 3 NYG
1959 NYG: Pass 2-1 50.0%, 14 7.00; PR 15-51 3.4. **1960** NYG: Pass 1-0, 1 Int. **1961** NYG: PR 3-6 2.0; Int 2-30. **1962** NYG: PR 5-22 4.4. **1963** NYG: Pass 2-1 50.0%, 18 9.00. **1967** NYG: Pass 1-1 100.0%, 12 12.00. **Total:** Pass 6-3 50.0%, 44 7.33 1 Int; PR 23-79 3.4; Int 2-30.

		Rushing				Receiving			
Year Team	G	Att	Yds	Avg	TD	Rec	Yds	Avg	TD
1959 NYG	12	62	165	2.7	1	17	183	10.8	1
1960 NYG	12	103	346	3.4	2	29	367	12.7	3
1961 NYG	13	33	48	1.5	1	11	67	6.1	1
1962 NYG	14	35	146	4.2	1	6	107	17.8	2
1963 NYG	14	119	568	4.8	3	31	284	9.2	7
1964 NYG	14	45	138	3.1	1	40	505	12.6	2
1965 NYG	13	3	20	6.7	1	41	574	14.0	4
1966 NYG	14	67	275	4.1	2	46	724	15.7	6
1967 NYG	13	36	161	4.5	2	37	524	14.2	7
1968 NYG	14	9	28	3.1	0	37	425	11.5	6
1969 NYG	14	107	387	3.6	4	44	647	14.7	7
1970 NYG	10	11	25	2.3	0	11	136	12.4	0
1971 NYG	13	38	131	3.4	0	40	411	10.3	1
1972 NYG	14	9	36	4.0	0	5	39	7.8	0
NFL Total	184	677	2474	3.7	18	395	4993	12.6	47

	Kickoff Returns					Tot
Year Team	Ret	Yds	Avg	TD	Fum	TD
1959 NYG	15	345	23.0	0	5	2
1960 NYG	0	0	—	0	7	5
1961 NYG	2	32	16.0	0	4	2
1962 NYG	5	113	22.6	0	1	3
1963 NYG	4	75	18.8	0	3	10
1964 NYG	4	75	18.8	0	2	3
1965 NYG	0	0	—	0	1	5
1966 NYG	0	0	—	0	1	8
1967 NYG	0	0	—	0	0	9
1968 NYG	0	0	—	0	1	6
1969 NYG	0	0	—	0	0	11
1970 NYG	0	0	—	0	1	0
1971 NYG	0	0	—	0	1	1
1972 NYG	0	0	—	0	1	0
NFL Total	30	640	21.3	0	28	65

DOC MORRISON Morrison, Maynard Davis 5'11", 210 **C-LB**
Col: Michigan *HS:* Royal Oak [MI] B: 6/17/1909 D: 10/20/1993, Monrovia, CA
1933 Bkn: 10 G. **1934** Bkn: 11 G. **Total:** 21 G.

PAT MORRISON Morrison, Patrick Anthony 6'2", 194 **DB**
Col: Southern Connecticut State *HS:* New Rochelle [NY]
B: 3/21/1965, London, England
1987 NYG: 1 G.

REECE MORRISON Morrison, Reece Earsal 6'0", 207 **RB**
Col: Southwest Texas State *HS:* San Marcos [TX] B: 10/21/1945, Tulsa, OK *Drafted:* 1968 Round 3 Cle
1968 Cle: Rec 2-40 20.0 1 TD. **1969** Cle: Pass 1-1 100.0%, 16 16.00; Rec 6-71 11.8. **1970** Cle: Rec 5-95 19.0 1 TD. **1973** Cin: Rec 1-4 4.0. **Total:** Pass 1-1 100.0%, 16 16.00; Rec 14-210 15.0 2 TD.

		Rushing				Punt Returns			
Year Team	G	Att	Yds	Avg	TD	Ret	Yds	Avg	TD
1968 Cle	14	18	39	2.2	1	0	0	—	0
1969 Cle	14	59	300	5.1	1	11	49	4.5	0
1970 Cle	14	73	175	2.4	0	15	133	8.9	0
1971 Cle	8	5	-2	-0.4	0	0	0	—	0
1972 Cle-Cin	10	1	2	2.0	0	0	0	—	0
1972 Cle	4	0	0	—	0	0	0	—	0
1972 Cin	6	1	2	2.0	0	0	0	—	0
1973 Cin	3	3	11	3.7	0	0	0	—	0
NFL Total	63	159	525	3.3	2	26	182	7.0	0

	Kickoff Returns					Tot
Year Team	Ret	Yds	Avg	TD	Fum	TD
1968 Cle	4	85	21.3	0	0	2
1969 Cle	9	155	17.2	0	2	1
1970 Cle	7	153	21.9	0	0	1
1971 Cle	9	267	29.7	0	0	0
1972 Cle-Cin	3	67	22.3	0	0	0
1972 Cle	3	67	22.3	0	0	0
NFL Total	32	727	22.7	0	2	4

RON MORRISON Morrison, Ronald Vern 6'4", 250 **DT**
Col: New Mexico *HS:* Albuquerque [NM] B: 9/10/1938, Lansing, MI
Drafted: 1960 Round 2 Hou
1960 Hou: 1 G.

STEVE MORRISON Morrison, Steven Craig 6'3", 246 **LB**
Col: Michigan *HS:* Brother Rice [Birmingham, MI] B: 12/28/1971, Birmingham, MI
1995 Ind: 10 G; KR 2-6 3.0. **1996** Ind: 16 G; Int 1-20. **1997** Ind: 16 G; Int 1-2; 1 Sac. **1998** Ind: 16 G; KR 1-2 2.0; 1 Sac. **Total:** 58 G; KR 3-8 2.7; Int 2-22; 2 Sac.

POP MORRISON Morrison, Stewart E 6'3", 205 **T**
Col: No College *HS:* West Side [Rochester, NY] B: 3/2/1892
D: 4/28/1980, Rochester, NY
1920 Roch: 2 G.

TIM MORRISON Morrison, Timothy 6'1", 195 **DB**
Col: North Carolina *HS:* Terry Sanford [Fayetteville, NC] B: 4/3/1963, Raeford, NC
1986 Was: 16 G. **1987** Was: 7 G. **Total:** 23 G.

GUY MORRISS Morriss, Guy Walker 6'4", 255 **C**
Col: Texas Christian *HS:* Sam Houston [Arlington, TX] B: 5/13/1951, Colorado City, TX *Drafted:* 1973 Round 2 Phi
1973 Phi: 14 G. **1974** Phi: 14 G; 2 Fum. **1975** Phi: 14 G; 2 Fum. **1976** Phi: 14 G. **1977** Phi: 13 G; 1 Fum. **1978** Phi: 16 G. **1979** Phi: 16 G. **1980** Phi: 16 G. **1981** Phi: 16 G; 2 Fum. **1982** Phi: 9 G. **1983** Phi: 16 G; 1 Fum. **1984** NE: 16 G. **1985** NE: 16 G. **1986** NE: 16 G. **1987** NE: 11 G; 1 Fum. **Total:** 217 G; 9 Fum.

FRANK MORRISSEY Morrissey, Francis J 6'1", 203 **T-G**
Col: Boston College *HS:* Medford [MA] B: 3/11/1899 D: 11/19/1968, Wynnewood, PA
1921 Roch: 5 G. **1922** Buf: 10 G; Scor 14, 2 FG, **8** XK. **1923** Buf: 12 G; Scor 31, 8 FG, 7 XK. **1924** Buf-Mil: 4 G; Scor 6, 2 FG. Buf: 2 G; Scor 6, 2 FG. Mil: 2 G. **Total:** 31 G; Scor 51, 12 FG, 15 XK.

JIM MORRISSEY Morrissey, James Michael 6'3", 223 **LB**
Col: Michigan State *HS:* Powers [Flint, MI] B: 12/24/1962, Flint, MI *Drafted:* 1985 Round 11 ChiB
1985 ChiB: 15 G. **1986** ChiB: 16 G. **1987** ChiB: 10 G. **1988** ChiB: 11 G; Int 3-13. **1989** ChiB: 6 G; Int 2-0. **1990** ChiB: 16 G; Int 2-12. **1991** ChiB: 16 G; Int 1-5. **1992** ChiB: 16 G; Int 1-22; 1 Sac. **1993** ChiB-GB: 8 G. ChiB: 2 G. GB: 6 G. **Total:** 114 G; Int 9-52; 1 Sac.

HAROLD MORROW Morrow, Harold Jr. 5'11", 221 **RB**
Col: Auburn *HS:* Maplesville [AL] B: 2/24/1973, Maplesville, AL
1996 Min: 8 G; KR 6-117 19.5. **1997** Min: 16 G; KR 5-99 19.8. **1998** Min: 11 G; Rush 3-7 2.3. **Total:** 35 G; Rush 3-7 2.3; KR 11-216 19.6.

JIM MORROW Morrow, James Thomas 5'10", 170 **TB-WB-BB**
Col: Pittsburgh *HS:* Carnegie [PA] B: 2/5/1895, Crafton, PA D: 8/9/1975, Fort Lauderdale, FL
1921 Can: 5 G; Int **1** TD; Scor 7, 1 XK. **1922** Buf: 1 G. **Total:** 6 G; Int 1 TD.

JOHN MORROW Morrow, John Melville Jr. 6'3", 244 **C-OG-DE**
Col: Michigan *HS:* Ann Arbor [MI]; Staunton Mil. Acad. [VA] B: 4/27/1933, Port Huron, MI *Drafted:* 1956 Round 28 LARm
1956 LARm: 12 G. **1958** LARm: 12 G. **1959** LARm: 11 G. **1960** Cle: 12 G. **1961** Cle: 14 G. **1962** Cle: 14 G. **1963** Cle: 14 G; KR 1-4 4.0. **1964** Cle: 14 G. **1965** Cle: 14 G. **1966** Cle: 8 G. **Total:** 125 G; KR 1-4 4.0.

BOB MORROW Morrow, Robert Edward 6'0", 222 **FB-DB-BB-LB**
Col: Illinois Wesleyan *HS:* Bloom [Chicago Heights, IL] B: 5/5/1918, Madison, WI *Drafted:* 1941 Round 14 ChiB
AAFC **1946** NY-A: 13 G; Rush 8-54 6.8; Rec 1-6 6.0.

NFL **1941** ChiC: Int 1-0. **1943** ChiC: Rec 3-20 6.7; KR 3-66 22.0; Int 2-49. **Total:** Rec 3-20 6.7; KR 3-66 22.0; Int 3-49.

		Rushing			
Year Team	**G**	**Att**	**Yds**	**Avg**	**TD**
1941 ChiC	9	37	128	3.5	1
1942 ChiC	10	45	145	3.2	1
1943 ChiC	10	38	129	3.4	2
1945 NYG	1	0	0	—	0
NFL Total	30	120	402	3.4	4

RUSS MORROW Morrow, Russell Lee 6'7", 210 **LB-C-DE-OE**
Col: Tennessee *HS:* Roosevelt [St. Louis, MO] B: 9/7/1924, St. Louis, MO D: 7/1980, Blue Jay, WV
AAFC **1946** BknA: 9 G; Rush 0-22 1 TD; Rec 1-8 8.0 1 TD; Tot TD 2; 12 Pt. **1947** BknA: 1 G. **Total:** 10 G; Rush 0-22 1 TD; Rec 1-8 8.0 1 TD; Tot TD 2; 12 Pt.

TOMMY MORROW Morrow, Thomas Alvin 6'0", 187 **DB-P**
Col: Southern Mississippi *HS:* Georgiana [AL] B: 6/3/1938, Georgiana, AL
1962 Oak: PR 2-13 6.5. **1964** Oak: PR 1-0. **Total:** PR 3-13 4.3.

		Interceptions			Punting			
Year Team	**G**	**Int**	**Yds**	**TD**	**Punts**	**Yds**	**Avg**	**Fum**
1962 Oak	14	10	141	0	45	1654	36.8	1
1963 Oak	14	9	104	0	0	0	—	1
1964 Oak	14	4	101	0	0	0	—	1
NFL Total	42	23	346	0	45	1654	36.8	3

BUTCH MORSE Morse, Raymond Joseph 6'2", 199 **OE-DE**
Col: Oregon *HS:* Benson Polytechnic [Portland, OR] B: 12/5/1910, Cleveland, OH D: 5/22/1995, Corvallis, OR
1935 Det: 12 G; Rec 6-63 10.5. **1936** Det: 12 G; Rec 5-83 16.6. **1937** Det: 10 G; Rush 1-(-3) -3.0; Rec 8-131 16.4 1 TD; 6 Pt. **1938** Det: 8 G; Rec 3-55 18.3. **1940** Det: 2 G; Rec 1-13 13.0. **Total:** 44 G; Rush 1-(-3) -3.0; Rec 23-345 15.0 1 TD; 6 Pt.

BOBBY MORSE Morse, Robert J 5'10", 207 **RB**
Col: Michigan State *HS:* Catholic Central [Muskegon, MI] B: 10/3/1965, Muskegon, MI *Drafted:* 1987 Round 12 Phi
1987 Phi: Rush 6-14 2.3; Rec 1-8 8.0. **1989** NO: Rush 2-43 21.5. **1991** NO: Rush 3-7 2.3. **Total:** Rush 11-64 5.8; Rec 1-8 8.0.

		Punt Returns				Kickoff Returns				
Year Team	**G**	**Ret**	**Yds**	**Avg**	**TD**	**Ret**	**Yds**	**Avg**	**TD**	**Fum**
1987 Phi	11	20	121	6.1	0	24	386	16.1	0	1
1989 NO	11	10	29	2.9	0	10	278	27.8	**1**	0
1990 NO	10	8	95	11.9	0	4	56	14.0	0	1
1991 NO	6	1	2	2.0	0	3	60	20.0	0	0
NFL Total	38	39	247	6.3	0	41	780	19.0	1	2

STEVE MORSE Morse, Steven Bryan 5'11", 211 **RB**
Col: Virginia *HS:* John S. Shaw [Mobile, AL] B: 5/28/1963, Mobile, AL
1985 Pit: 16 G; Rush 8-17 2.1.

RED MORSE Morse, Wilbur 5'10", 198 **G**
Col: No College B: 1899, MN Deceased
1923 Dul: 1 G.

EMMETT MORTELL Mortell, Emmett Francis 6'1", 181 **TB-DB-QB**
Col: Notre Dame; Wisconsin *HS:* Appleton [WI] B: 4/8/1916, Appleton, WI
1937 Phi: Rec 1-0. **1939** Phi: Punt 23-907 39.4. **Total:** Rec 1-0; Punt 23-907 39.4.

		Passing							
Year Team	**G**	**Att**	**Comp**	**Comp%**	**Yds**	**YPA**	**TD**	**Int**	**Rating**
1937 Phi	11	71	18	25.4	320	4.51	2	8	15.7
1938 Phi	11	57	12	21.1	201	3.53	6	7	37.3
1939 Phi	8	41	12	29.3	134	3.27	1	**0**	48.8
NFL Total	30	169	42	24.9	655	3.88	9	15	24.0

	Rushing			
Year Team	**Att**	**Yds**	**Avg**	**TD**
1937 Phi	100	312	3.1	0
1938 Phi	110	296	2.7	0
1939 Phi	37	88	2.4	0
NFL Total	247	696	2.8	0

DAVE MORTON Morton, David Byron 6'2", 224 **LB**
Col: Kings River CC CA; UCLA *HS:* Fresno [CA] B: 5/13/1955, Fresno, CA
1979 SF: 3 G.

GREG MORTON Morton, Gregory Alan 6'1", 230 **DE**
Col: Michigan *HS:* Central-Hower [Akron, OH] B: 10/8/1953, Akron, OH *Drafted:* 1977 Round 8 Buf
1977 Buf: 9 G.

JOHN MORTON Morton, John Jay 6'2", 220 **LB**
Col: Compton CC CA; Texas Christian *HS:* Compton [CA] B: 9/1/1929, Compton, CA
1953 SF: 10 G; Int 2-16.

JACK MORTON Morton, John Joseph 6'0", 197 **OE-DE-DB**
Col: Missouri; Purdue *HS:* East St. Louis [IL]; Maryland Heights HS [MO] B: 7/22/1922, East St. Louis, IL D: 12/17/1983, Manteno, IL *Drafted:* 1944 Round 7 ChiB
AAFC **1946** LA-A: 12 G; Rec 4-44 11.0 1 TD; Int 1-11. **1947** BufA: 2 G. **Total:** 14 G; Rec 4-44 11.0 1 TD; Int 1-11; 6 Pt.

NFL **1945** ChiB: 8 G; Rec 1-18 18.0.

JOHNNIE MORTON Morton, Johnnie James 6'0", 190 **WR**
Col: USC *HS:* South [Torrance, CA] B: 10/7/1971, Inglewood, CA *Drafted:* 1994 Round 1 Det
1994 Det: KR 4-143 35.8 1 TD. **1995** Det: Rush 3-33 11.0; PR 7-48 6.9; KR 18-390 21.7. **1996** Det: Rush 9-35 3.9. **1997** Det: Rush 3-33 11.0. **1998** Det: Rush 1-11 11.0. **Total:** Rush 16-112 7.0; PR 7-48 6.9; KR 22-533 24.2 1 TD.

		Receiving					Tot
Year Team	**G**	**Rec**	**Yds**	**Avg**	**TD**	**Fum**	**TD**
1994 Det	14	3	39	13.0	1	1	2
1995 Det	16	44	590	13.4	8	1	8
1996 Det	16	55	714	13.0	6	1	6
1997 Det	16	80	1057	13.2	6	2	6
1998 Det	16	69	1028	14.9	2	0	2
NFL Total	78	251	3428	13.7	23	5	24

CRAIG MORTON Morton, Larry Craig 6'4", 214 **QB**
Col: California *HS:* Campbell [CA] B: 2/5/1943, Flint, MI *Drafted:* 1965 Round 1 Dal

		Passing							
Year Team	**G**	**Att**	**Comp**	**Comp%**	**Yds**	**YPA**	**TD**	**Int**	**Rating**
1965 Dal	4	34	17	50.0	173	5.09	2	4	45.0
1966 Dal	6	27	13	48.1	225	8.33	3	1	98.5
1967 Dal	9	137	69	50.4	978	7.14	10	10	67.7
1968 Dal	13	85	44	51.8	752	8.85	4	6	68.4
1969 Dal	13	302	162	53.6	2619	8.67	21	15	85.4
1970 Dal	12	207	102	49.3	1819	**8.79**	15	7	89.8
1971 Dal	10	143	78	54.5	1131	7.91	7	8	73.5
1972 Dal	14	339	185	54.6	2396	7.07	15	21	65.9

1973 Dal	14	32	13	40.6	174	5.44	3	1	76.8
1974 Dal-NYG	10	239	124	51.9	1522	6.37	9	13	61.7
1974 Dal	2	2	2	100.0	12	6.00	0	0	91.7
1974 NYG	8	237	122	51.5	1510	6.37	9	13	61.3
1975 NYG	14	363	186	51.2	2359	6.50	11	16	63.6
1976 NYG	12	284	153	53.9	1865	6.57	9	20	55.6
1977 Den	14	254	131	51.6	1929	7.59	14	8	82.0
1978 Den	14	267	146	54.7	1802	6.75	11	**8**	77.0
1979 Den	14	370	204	55.1	2626	7.10	16	19	70.6
1980 Den	12	301	183	60.8	2150	7.14	12	13	77.8
1981 Den	15	376	225	59.8	3195	8.50	21	14	90.5
1982 Den	3	26	18	69.2	193	7.42	0	3	51.1
NFL Total	203	3786	2053	54.2	27908	7.37	183	187	73.5

	Rushing				
Year Team	Att	Yds	Avg	TD	Fum
1965 Dal	3	-8	-2.7	0	2
1966 Dal	7	50	7.1	0	0
1967 Dal	15	42	2.8	0	5
1968 Dal	4	28	7.0	2	1
1969 Dal	16	62	3.9	1	4
1970 Dal	16	37	2.3	0	1
1971 Dal	4	9	2.3	1	1
1972 Dal	8	26	3.3	2	4
1973 Dal	1	0	0.0	0	1
1974 Dal-NYG	4	5	1.3	0	4
1974 NYG	4	5	1.3	0	4
1975 NYG	22	72	3.3	0	9
1976 NYG	15	48	3.2	0	7
1977 Den	31	125	4.0	4	7
1978 Den	17	71	4.2	0	6
1979 Den	23	13	0.6	1	9
1980 Den	21	29	1.4	1	4
1981 Den	8	18	2.3	0	2
1982 Den	0	0	—	0	1
NFL Total	215	627	2.9	12	68

MIKE MORTON Morton, Michael Anthony Jr. 6′4″, 235 **LB**
Col: North Carolina *HS:* A.L. Brown [Kannapolis, NC] B: 3/28/1972, Kannapolis, NC *Drafted:* 1995 Round 4 Oak
1995 Oak: 12 G. **1996** Oak: 16 G; Int 2-13; 1 Sac. **1997** Oak: 11 G; KR 1-14 14.0. **1998** Oak: 16 G; KR 1-3 3.0. **Total:** 55 G; KR 2-17 8.5; Int 2-13; 1 Sac.

MICHAEL MORTON Morton, Michael Da'mond 5′8″, 180 **RB**
Col: Nevada-Las Vegas *HS:* Inglewood [CA] B: 2/6/1960, Birmingham, AL *Drafted:* 1982 Round 12 TB
1982 TB: Rec 1-5 5.0. **1983** TB: Rec 1-9 9.0. **Total:** Rec 2-14 7.0.

		Rushing				Kickoff Returns				
Year Team	G	Att	Yds	Avg	TD	Ret	Yds	Avg	TD	Fum
1982 TB	9	2	3	1.5	0	21	361	17.2	0	1
1983 TB	16	13	28	2.2	0	30	689	23.0	0	5
1984 TB	16	16	27	1.7	0	38	835	22.0	0	3
1985 Was	1	0	0	—	0	6	131	21.8	0	0
1987 Sea	2	19	52	2.7	1	0	0	—	0	1
NFL Total	44	50	110	2.2	1	95	2016	21.2	0	10

FRANK MORZE Morze, Frank Joseph Jr. 6′4″, 270 **C-OT**
Col: Boston College *HS:* Gardner [MA] B: 3/21/1933, Gardner, MA *Drafted:* 1955 Round 2 SF
1957 SF: 12 G. **1958** SF: 4 G. **1959** SF: 12 G. **1960** SF: 12 G. **1961** SF: 14 G. **1962** Cle: 2 G. **1963** Cle: 14 G. **1964** SF: 14 G. **Total:** 84 G.

MONK MOSCRIP Moscrip, James Henderson 6′0″, 195 **OE-DE**
Col: Stanford *HS:* Adena [OH]; Kiski School [Saltsburg, PA] B: 9/17/1913, Adena, OH D: 10/11/1980, Atherton, CA *Drafted:* 1936 Round 9 Bkn
1938 Det: 11 G; Rec 6-118 19.7 1 TD; Scor 12, 0-1 FG, 6-6 100.0% XK. **1939** Det: 11 G; Rush 1-8 8.0; Rec 14-176 12.6; Scor 15, 0-1 FG, 9-12 75.0% XK; **1** Fum TD. **Total:** 22 G; Rush 1-8 8.0; Rec 20-294 14.7 1 TD; Scor 27, 0-2 FG, 15-18 83.3% XK; 1 Fum TD; Tot TD 2.

DON MOSEBAR Mosebar, Donald Howard 6′6″, 285 **C-OT-OG**
Col: USC *HS:* Mount Whitney [Visalia, CA] B: 9/11/1961, Yakima, WA *Drafted:* 1983 Round 1 LARd
1983 LARd: 14 G. **1984** LARd: 10 G. **1985** LARd: 16 G. **1986** LARd: 16 G; 1 Fum. **1987** LARd: 12 G. **1988** LARd: 13 G. **1989** LARd: 12 G. **1990** LARd: 16 G. **1991** LARd: 16 G. **1992** LARd: 16 G. **1993** LARd: 16 G. **1994** LARd: 16 G. **Total:** 173 G; 1 Fum.

MARK MOSELEY Moseley, Mark Dewayne 5′11″, 202 **K**
Col: Texas A&M; Stephen F. Austin St. *HS:* Livingston [TX] B: 3/12/1948, Laneville, TX *Drafted:* 1970 Round 14 Phi
1970 Phi: Punt 10-350 35.0. **Total:** Punt 10-350 35.0.

		Scoring						
Year Team	G	Pts	FG	FGA	FG%	XK	XKA	XK%
1970 Phi	14	67	14	25	56.0	25	28	89.3
1971 Hou	12	73	16	26	61.5	25	27	92.6
1972 Hou	1	5	1	2	50.0	2	2	100.0
1974 Was	13	81	18	30	60.0	27	29	93.1
1975 Was	14	85	16	25	64.0	37	39	94.9
1976 Was	14	97	**22**	34	64.7	31	32	96.9
1977 Was	14	82	**21**	**37**	56.8	19	19	100.0
1978 Was	16	87	19	30	63.3	30	31	96.8
1979 Was	16	114	**25**	**33**	75.8	39	39	100.0
1980 Was	16	81	18	33	54.5	27	30	90.0
1981 Was	16	95	19	30	63.3	38	42	90.5
1982 Was	9	76	**20**	21	**95.2**	16	19	**84.2**
1983 Was	16	**161**	33	**47**	70.2	**62**	**63**	98.4
1984 Was	16	120	24	31	77.4	48	51	94.1
1985 Was	16	97	22	34	64.7	31	33	93.9
1986 Was-Cle	10	61	12	19	63.2	25	28	89.3
1986 Was	6	30	6	12	50.0	12	14	85.7
1986 Cle	4	31	6	7	85.7	13	14	92.9
NFL Total	213	1382	300	457	65.6	482	512	94.1

DOM MOSELLE Moselle, Dominic Angelo 6′0″, 192 **DB-HB**
Col: Wis.-Superior *HS:* Hurley [WI] B: 6/3/1926, Gile, WI *Drafted:* 1950 Round 23 Cle
1950 Cle: PR 7-126 18.0. **1951** GB: PR 9-80 8.9; Int 1-0. **1952** GB: PR 7-77 11.0; Int 3-2. **Total:** PR 23-283 12.3; Int 4-2.

		Rushing				Receiving			
Year Team	G	Att	Yds	Avg	TD	Rec	Yds	Avg	TD
1950 Cle	11	5	39	7.8	0	0	0	—	0
1951 GB	12	12	23	1.9	1	14	233	16.6	2
1952 GB	8	0	0	—	0	0	0	—	0
1954 Phi	12	29	114	3.9	1	17	242	14.2	2
NFL Total	43	46	176	3.8	2	31	475	15.3	4

	Kickoff Returns					Tot
Year Team	Ret	Yds	Avg	TD	Fum	TD
1950 Cle	5	107	21.4	0	1	0
1951 GB	20	547	27.4	0	4	3
1952 GB	5	83	16.6	0	0	0
1954 Phi	7	149	21.3	0	2	3
NFL Total	37	886	23.9	0	7	6

RICK MOSER Moser, Richard Avery 6′0″, 210 **RB**
Col: Rhode Island *HS:* Scarsdale [NY] B: 12/18/1956, White Plains, NY *Drafted:* 1978 Round 8 Pit
1978 Pit: Rec 1-(-1) -1.0; KR 1-8 8.0. **1979** Pit: Rec 1-6 6.0; KR 1-6 6.0. **1981** KC-Pit: Rec 1-5 5.0 1 TD; KR 3-76 25.3. Pit: Rec 1-5 5.0 1 TD; KR 3-76 25.3. **1982** Pit-TB: KR 1-18 18.0. Pit: KR 1-18 18.0. **Total:** Rec 3-10 3.3 1 TD; KR 6-108 18.0.

		Rushing					Tot
Year Team	G	Att	Yds	Avg	TD	Fum	TD
1978 Pit	15	42	153	3.6	0	3	0
1979 Pit	16	11	33	3.0	1	0	1
1980 Mia	4	0	0	—	0	0	0
1981 KC-Pit	7	1	4	4.0	0	0	1
1981 KC	1	0	0	—	0	0	0
1981 Pit	6	1	4	4.0	0	0	1
1982 Pit-TB	7	0	0	—	0	0	0
1982 Pit	6	0	0	—	0	0	0
1982 TB	1	0	0	—	0	0	0
NFL Total	49	54	190	3.5	1	3	2

BOB MOSER Moser, Robert Joseph 6′3″, 240 **C**
Col: U. of Pacific *HS:* Oakdale [CA] B: 12/26/1928, Modesto, CA Deceased *Drafted:* 1951 Round 4 ChiB
1951 ChiB: 12 G. **1952** ChiB: 12 G. **1953** ChiB: 6 G. **Total:** 30 G.

TED MOSER Moser, Theodore F 5′9″, 195 **G**
(Doc) *Col:* No College *HS:* Manual [Louisville, KY]; Male HS [Louisville, KY] B: 6/14/1897, Louisville, KY D: 8/1986, Dayton, OH
1921 Lou: 1 G.

DON MOSES Moses, Donald Clyde 5′11″, 185 **BB-DB**
Col: USC *HS:* Los Angeles [CA] B: 1906 D: 6/15/1965, Arcadia, CA
1933 Cin: 3 G; Rush 7-20 2.9.

HAVEN MOSES Moses, Haven Christopher 6′2″, 208 **WR**
(Heavenly) *Col:* Los Angeles Harbor Coll. CA (J.C.); San Diego State *HS:* Fermin Lasuen [San Pedro, CA] B: 7/27/1946, Los Angeles, CA *Drafted:* 1968 Round 1 Buf
1968 Buf: Rush 5-(-4) -0.8. **1972** Buf-Den: Rush 2-11 5.5. Den: Rush 2-11 5.5. **1973** Den: Rush 3-25 8.3 1 TD. **1974** Den: Rush 2-16 8.0. **1976** Den: Rush 1-(-4) -4.0. **1977** Den: Rush 5-(-1) -0.2. **Total:** Rush 18-43 2.4 1 TD.

		Receiving					Tot
Year Team	G	Rec	Yds	Avg	TD	Fum	TD
1968 Buf	14	42	633	15.1	2	0	2
1969 Buf	14	39	752	19.3	5	0	5
1970 Buf	14	39	726	18.6	2	0	2
1971 Buf	12	23	470	20.4	2	0	2
1972 Buf-Den	13	18	284	15.8	6	0	6
1972 Buf	5	3	60	20.0	1	0	1
1972 Den	8	15	224	14.9	5	0	5

1973 Den	14	28	518	18.5	8	1	9
1974 Den	13	34	559	16.4	2	1	2
1975 Den	14	29	505	17.4	2	1	2
1976 Den	14	25	498	19.9	7	0	7
1977 Den	14	27	539	20.0	4	1	4
1978 Den	16	37	744	20.1	5	1	5
1979 Den	16	54	943	17.5	6	0	6
1980 Den	15	38	674	17.7	4	1	4
1981 Den	16	15	246	16.4	1	1	1
NFL Total	199	448	8091	18.1	56	7	57

CLURE MOSHER Mosher, Clure Harrison 6'1", 215 **C-G-LB**
Col: Louisville B: 1/11/1920, Fort Worth, TX D: 7/23/1966, New York, NY *Drafted:* 1942 Round 14 Pit
1942 Pit: 2 G.

JOHN MOSIER Mosier, John Paul 6'3", 220 **TE**
Col: Kansas *HS:* West [Wichita, KS] B: 3/1/1948, Wichita Falls, TX *Drafted:* 1970 Round 6 Den
1971 Den: 11 G; Rush 4-31 7.8; Rec 3-36 12.0. **1972** Bal: 14 G; Rec 1-53 53.0. **Total:** 25 G; Rush 4-31 7.8; Rec 4-89 22.3.

ANTHONY MOSLEY Mosley, Anthony Lewis 5'9", 205 **RB**
Col: Fresno City Coll. CA (J.C.); Fresno State *HS:* Selma [CA] B: 6/17/1965, Selma, CA
1987 ChiB: 2 G; Rush 18-80 4.4; Rec 2-16 8.0; KR 1-17 17.0; 6 Pt.

HENRY MOSLEY Mosley, Henry 6'2", 210 **HB**
Col: Morris Brown *HS:* Brooks Co. [Quitman, GA] B: 2/10/1931, Chattanooga, TN D: 12/24/1994, Chicago, IL *Drafted:* 1955 Round 6 ChiB
1955 ChiB: 1 G; Rush 3-10 3.3; KR 1-14 14.0.

MIKE MOSLEY Mosley, Michael Gene 6'2", 192 **WR**
Col: Texas A&M *HS:* Humble [TX] B: 6/6/1958, Hillsboro, TX *Drafted:* 1981 Round 3 Buf
1982 Buf: PR 11-61 5.5. **1984** Buf: Pass 1-0. **Total:** Pass 1-0; PR 11-61 5.5.

		Receiving				Kickoff Returns				
Year Team	**G**	**Rec**	**Yds**	**Avg**	**TD**	**Ret**	**Yds**	**Avg**	**TD**	**Fum**
1982 Buf	9	9	96	10.7	0	18	487	**27.1**	0	3
1983 Buf	7	14	180	12.9	3	9	236	26.2	0	1
1984 Buf	4	4	38	9.5	0	0	0	—	0	0
NFL Total	20	27	314	11.6	3	27	723	26.8	0	4

NORMAN MOSLEY Mosley, Norman S 5'9", 185 **TB-DB**
Col: Alabama *HS:* Blytheville [AR] B: 1/4/1922, Blytheville, AR *Drafted:* 1945 Round 21 Phi
1948 Pit: 5 G; Pass 2-0; Rush 13-39 3.0 1 TD; PR 7-52 7.4; KR 1-31 31.0; 6 Pt; 1 Fum.

RUSS MOSLEY Mosley, Russell Clinton 5'10", 170 **DB-HB**
Col: Alabama *HS:* Blytheville [AR] B: 7/22/1918, Puxico, MO
1945 GB: 6 G; Pass 1-0, 1 Int; Rush 16-49 3.1; Rec 1-10 10.0; PR 1-13 13.0; Int 1-20. **1946** GB: 2 G; Int 1-20. **Total:** 8 G; Pass 1-0, 1 Int; Rush 16-49 3.1; Rec 1-10 10.0; PR 1-13 13.0; Int 2-40.

WAYNE MOSLEY Mosley, Wayne 6'0", 190 **RB**
Col: Alabama A&M B: 10/6/1952, Decatur, AL
1974 Buf: 3 G; Rush 2-6 3.0.

BRENT MOSS Moss, Brent 5'8", 211 **RB**
Col: Wisconsin *HS:* Washington Park [Racine, WI] B: 1/30/1972, Racine, WI
1995 StL: 4 G; Rush 22-90 4.1; Rec 1-(-3) -3.0.

EDDIE MOSS Moss, Eddie B 6'0", 215 **RB**
Col: Indian Hills CC IA; Southeast Missouri State *HS:* Poplar Bluff [MO] B: 9/27/1948, Dell, AR *Drafted:* 1972 Round 13 Buf
1973 StL: 5 G; Rush 14-41 2.9; KR 4-78 19.5; 2 Fum. **1974** StL: 11 G; Rush 4-13 3.3; KR 8-133 16.6. **1975** StL: 8 G; Rush 4-12 3.0 1 TD; KR 1-21 21.0; 6 Pt. **1976** StL: 2 G. **1977** Was: 9 G; KR 2-35 17.5. **Total:** 35 G; Rush 22-66 3.0 1 TD; KR 15-267 17.8; 6 Pt; 2 Fum.

GARY MOSS Moss, Gary James 5'10", 192 **DB**
Col: Georgia *HS:* White Co. [Cleveland, GA] B: 7/18/1964, Habersham Co., GA
1987 Atl: 3 G; PR 3-15 5.0; KR 1-23 23.0; Int 1-18.

JOE MOSS Moss, Joseph Charles 6'1", 221 **OT**
Col: Maryland *HS:* Ridgeley [WV] B: 4/9/1930, Elkins, WV
1952 Was: 12 G.

MARTIN MOSS Moss, Martin 6'4", 250 **DE**
Col: UCLA *HS:* Abraham Lincoln [San Diego, CA] B: 12/16/1958, San Diego, CA *Drafted:* 1982 Round 8 Det
1982 Det: 5 G. **1983** Det: 15 G; 0.5 Sac. **1984** Det: 16 G. **1985** Det: 6 G. **Total:** 42 G; 0.5 Sac.

PAUL MOSS Moss, Paul 6'2", 200 **OE-DE**
Col: Purdue *HS:* Gerstmeyer [Terre Haute, IN] B: 10/2/1908, Brazil, IN
1933 Pit: 10 G; Rec 13-**283 21.8** 2 TD; 12 Pt. **1934** StL: 3 G; Rec 6-131 21.8 1 TD; 6 Pt. **Total:** 13 G; Rec 19-414 21.8 3 TD; 18 Pt.

PERRY MOSS Moss, Perry Lee 5'10", 170 **QB**
Col: Tulsa; Illinois *HS:* Central [Tulsa, OK] B: 8/4/1926, Tulsa, OK *Drafted:* 1948 Round 11 GB
1948 GB: 6 G; Pass 17-4 23.5%, 20 1.18; Rush 5-2 0.4; 3 Fum.

RANDY MOSS Moss, Randy Gene 6'4", 197 **WR**
(The Freak) *Col:* Florida State; Marshall *HS:* Dupont [Belle, WV] B: 2/13/1977, Rand, WV *Drafted:* 1998 Round 1 Min
1998 Min: Rush 1-4 4.0; PR 1-0; Scor **2** 2XP.

		Receiving				
Year Team	**G**	**Rec**	**Yds**	**Avg**	**TD**	**Fum**
1998 Min	16	69	1313	19.0	**17**	2

ROLAND MOSS Moss, Roland Jr. 6'3", 215 **TE**
Col: Toledo *HS:* Passaic [NJ] B: 9/20/1946, St. Matthews, SC *Drafted:* 1969 Round 7 Bal
1969 Bal: 6 G. **1970** SD-Buf: 6 G; Rec 2-31 15.5; KR 7-131 18.7. SD: 2 G; KR 1-0. Buf: 4 G; Rec 2-31 15.5; KR 6-131 21.8. **1971** NE: 14 G; Rec 9-124 13.8 1 TD; Tot TD 2; 12 Pt. **Total:** 26 G; Rec 11-155 14.1 1 TD; KR 7-131 18.7; Tot TD 2; 12 Pt.

WINSTON MOSS Moss, Winston N 6'3", 245 **LB**
Col: Miami (Fla.) *HS:* Miami Southridge [FL] B: 12/24/1965, Miami, FL *Drafted:* 1987 Round 2 TB
1987 TB: 12 G; **1** Fum TD; 6 Pt; 1.5 Sac. **1988** TB: 16 G. **1989** TB: 16 G; 5.5 Sac. **1990** TB: 16 G; Int 1-31; 3.5 Sac. **1991** LARd: 16 G; 3 Sac. **1992** LARd: 15 G; 2 Sac. **1993** LARd: 16 G. **1994** LARd: 16 G; 2 Sac. **1995** Sea: 16 G; Int 1-0; 2 Sac. **1996** Sea: 16 G; Int 1-1; 1 Sac. **1997** Sea: 14 G. **Total:** 169 G; Int 3-32; 1 Fum TD; 6 Pt; 20.5 Sac.

ZEFROSS MOSS Moss, Zefross 6'6", 325 **OT**
Col: Alabama State *HS:* Holt [AL] B: 8/17/1966, Tuscaloosa, AL
1989 Ind: 16 G. **1990** Ind: 16 G. **1991** Ind: 11 G. **1992** Ind: 13 G. **1993** Ind: 16 G. **1994** Ind: 11 G. **1995** Det: 14 G. **1996** Det: 15 G. **1997** NE: 15 G. **1998** NE: 14 G. **Total:** 141 G.

RICH MOSTARDO Mostardo, Richard Albert 5'11", 188 **DB**
Col: Charleston (WV); Kent State *HS:* Upper Darby [PA] B: 7/1/1938, Bryn Mawr, PA *Drafted:* 1960 Round 12 Cle
1960 Cle: 10 G. **1961** Min: 11 G; Int 2-22. **1962** Oak: 5 G. **Total:** 26 G; Int 2-22.

KELLEY MOTE Mote, Kelley Henry 6'2", 189 **OE-DE-DB**
(Feets) *Col:* South Carolina; Duke *HS:* Hapeville [GA] B: 4/27/1923, Hapeville, GA *Drafted:* 1946 Round 14 Det
1947 Det: KR 1-17 17.0; Int 1-0. **1948** Det: KR 3-27 9.0. **1950** NYG: Int 1-10. **Total:** KR 4-44 11.0; Int 2-10.

		Receiving				
Year Team	**G**	**Rec**	**Yds**	**Avg**	**TD**	**Fum**
1947 Det	12	16	180	11.3	1	1
1948 Det	12	13	212	16.3	0	0
1949 Det	12	4	58	14.5	0	0
1950 NYG	9	4	72	18.0	1	0
1951 NYG	12	11	187	17.0	4	0
1952 NYG	12	4	45	11.3	0	0
NFL Total	69	52	754	14.5	6	1

ERIC MOTEN Moten, Eric Dean 6'2", 306 **OG**
Col: Michigan State *HS:* Shaw [East Cleveland, OH] B: 4/11/1968, Cleveland, OH *Drafted:* 1991 Round 2 SD
1991 SD: 16 G. **1992** SD: 16 G. **1993** SD: 4 G. **1995** SD: 16 G. **1996** SD: 15 G. **Total:** 67 G.

GARY MOTEN Moten, Gary Kim 6'1", 210 **LB**
Col: Southern Methodist *HS:* Brazoswood [Freeport, TX] B: 4/3/1961, Galveston, TX *Drafted:* 1983 Round 7 SF
1983 SF: 6 G. **1987** KC: 1 G. **Total:** 7 G.

MIKE MOTEN Moten, Michael Edward 6'5", 266 **DT**
Col: Florida *HS:* Mainland [Daytona Beach, FL] B: 3/12/1974, Daytona Beach, FL
1998 Ariz: 1 G.

BOBBY MOTEN Moten, Robert Earl 6'4", 212 **WR**
Col: Bishop *HS:* Cheatham [Clarksville, TX] B: 1/29/1943, Clarksville, TX *Drafted:* 1967 Round 9 Atl
1968 Den: 3 G.

BOB MOTL Motl, Robert Joseph 6'3", 195 **OE-DE**
Col: Northwestern *HS:* Austin [Chicago, IL] B: 7/26/1920, Chicago, IL
AAFC **1946** ChiA: 14 G; Rec 9-124 13.8 1 TD; 6 Pt.

MARION MOTLEY Motley, Marion 6'1", 232 **FB-LB**
Col: South Carolina State; Nevada-Reno *HS:* McKinley [Canton, OH] B: 6/5/1920, Leesburg, GA *HOF:* 1968
AAFC **1946** CleA: PR 1-0; Int 1-0. **1947** CleA: Int 1-48 1 TD. **1948** CleA: Pass 1-0. **Total:** Pass 1-0; PR 1-0; Int 2-48 1 TD.

		Rushing				Receivinc	
Year Team	**G**	**Att**	**Yds**	**Avg**	**TD**	**Rec**	**Yds**
1946 CleA	13	73	601	8.2	5	10	

1947 CleA	14	146	889	6.1	8	7	73	10.4	1
1948 CleA	14	157	964	6.1	5	13	192	14.8	2
1949 CleA	11	113	570	5.0	8	15	191	12.7	0
AAFC Total	52	489	3024	6.2	26	45	644	14.3	4

	Kickoff Returns				Tot
Year Team	Ret	Yds	Avg	TD	TD
1946 CleA	3	53	17.7	0	6
1947 CleA	13	322	24.8	0	10
1948 CleA	14	337	24.1	0	7
1949 CleA	12	262	21.8	0	8
AAFC Total	42	974	23.2	0	31

NFL **1952** Cle: Pass 2-0; KR 3-88 29.3. **1953** Cle: KR 3-60 20.0. **Total:** Pass 2-0; KR 6-148 24.7.

		Rushing				Receiving					Tot
Year Team	G	Att	Yds	Avg	TD	Rec	Yds	Avg	TD	Fum	TD
1950 Cle	12	140	**810**	5.8	3	11	151	13.7	1	5	4
1951 Cle	11	61	273	4.5	1	10	52	5.2	0	1	1
1952 Cle	12	104	444	4.3	1	13	213	16.4	2	2	3
1953 Cle	12	32	161	5.0	0	6	47	7.8	0	1	0
1955 Pit	7	2	8	4.0	0	0	0	—	0	0	0
NFL Total	54	339	1696	5.0	5	40	463	11.6	3	9	8

JOE MOTT Mott, John Christopher 6′4″, 253 **LB**
Col: Iowa *HS:* Union Endicott [NY] B: 10/6/1965, Endicott, NY
Drafted: 1989 Round 3 NYJ
1989 NYJ: 16 G. **1990** NYJ: 16 G. **1993** GB: 2 G. **Total:** 34 G.

BUSTER MOTT Mott, Norman Howard 5′8″, 193 **DB-BB-HB-FB**
Col: Georgia *HS:* Tech [Atlanta, GA] B: 6/21/1909, Atlanta, GA
Deceased
1933 GB: 3 G; Rush 5-13 2.6. **1934** Cin-Pit: 2 G; Rush 5-24 4.8; Rec 1-12 12.0. Cin: 1 G; Rec 1-12 12.0. Pit: 1 G; Rush 5-24 4.8. **Total:** 5 G; Rush 10-37 3.7; Rec 1-12 12.0.

STEVE MOTT Mott, Walter Stephen III 6′3″, 266 **C**
Col: Alabama *HS:* Archbishop Shaw [Marrero, LA] B: 3/24/1961, New Orleans, LA *Drafted:* 1983 Round 5 Det
1983 Det: 13 G; 1 Fum. **1984** Det: 6 G. **1985** Det: 16 G. **1986** Det: 14 G. **1987** Det: 11 G. **1988** Det: 16 G; 3 Fum. **Total:** 76 G; 4 Fum.

ERIC MOULDS Moulds, Eric Shannon 6′0″, 204 **WR**
Col: Mississippi State *HS:* George Co. [Lucedale, MS] B: 7/17/1973, Lucedale, MS *Drafted:* 1996 Round 1 Buf
1996 Buf: Rush 12-44 3.7. **1997** Buf: Rush 4-59 14.8; PR 2-20 10.0; Scor 1 2XP. **Total:** Rush 16-103 6.4; PR 2-20 10.0; Scor 1 2XP.

		Receiving				Kickoff Returns					Tot
Year Team	G	Rec	Yds	Avg	TD	Ret	Yds	Avg	TD	Fum	TD
1996 Buf	16	20	279	14.0	2	52	1205	23.2	1	1	3
1997 Buf	16	29	294	10.1	0	43	921	21.4	0	3	0
1998 Buf	16	67	1368	20.4	9	0	0	—	0	0	9
NFL Total	48	116	1941	16.7	11	95	2126	22.4	1	4	12

ZEKE MOWATT Mowatt, Ezekiel 6′3″, 238 **TE**
Col: Florida State *HS:* Hardee [Wauchula, FL] B: 3/5/1961, Wauchula, FL

		Receiving				
Year Team	G	Rec	Yds	Avg	TD	Fum
1983 NYG	16	21	280	13.3	1	0
1984 NYG	16	48	698	14.5	6	0
1986 NYG	16	10	119	11.9	2	1
1987 NYG	12	3	39	13.0	1	0
1988 NYG	16	15	196	13.1	1	2
1989 NYG	16	27	288	10.7	0	1
1990 NE	10	6	67	11.2	0	1
1991 NYG	16	5	78	15.6	1	0
NFL Total	118	135	1765	13.1	12	5

ALEX MOYER Moyer, Alexander III 6′1″, 221 **LB**
Col: Northwestern *HS:* St. John's Mil. Acad. [Delafield, WI]
B: 10/25/1963, Detroit, MI *Drafted:* 1985 Round 3 Mia
1985 Mia: 10 G; Int 1-4. **1986** Mia: 3 G. **Total:** 13 G; Int 1-4.

KEN... Moyer, Kenneth Wayne 6′7″, 297 **OG-OT-C**
...: Bedford [Temperance, MI] B: 11/19/1966, Canoga
...
...**90** Cin: 16 G. **1991** Cin: 15 G. **1993** Cin: 16 G. **1994** Cin:
...

... Moyer, Paul Stewart 6′1″, 201 **DB**
...ton; Arizona State *HS:* Villa Park [CA]
...ark, CA
...**5** Sea: 1 Sac. **1986** Sea: 1 Sac. **1987** Sea: 1 Sac.

		Interceptions			Tot
Year Team	G	Int	Yds	TD	TD
1983 Sea	16	1	19	1	1
1984 Sea	16	0	0	0	0
1985 Sea	11	0	0	0	0
1986 Sea	16	3	38	0	1
1987 Sea	12	1	0	0	0
1988 Sea	16	6	79	0	0
1989 Sea	11	0	0	0	0
NFL Total	98	11	136	1	2

DICK MOYNIHAN Moynihan, Richard A 5′8″, 160 **BB-FB**
Col: Villanova *HS:* St. James [Haverhill, MA] B: 1/9/1902, Haverhill, MA D: 10/8/1991, Haverhill, MA
1927 Fra: 9 G; Scor 3, 1 FG.

TIM MOYNIHAN Moynihan, Timothy Anthony 6′1″, 204 **C-LB-G**
Col: Notre Dame *HS:* Rawlings [WY]; St. Mel's HS [Chicago, IL]
B: 9/21/1906, Chicago, IL D: 4/3/1952, Orange, CA
1932 ChiC: 10 G; 12 Pt. **1933** ChiC: 8 G. **Total:** 18 G; 12 Pt.

MARK MRAZ Mraz, Mark David 6′4″, 258 **DE**
Col: Utah State *HS:* Glendora [CA] B: 2/9/1965, Glendale, CA
Drafted: 1987 Round 5 Atl
1987 Atl: 11 G. **1989** LARd: 11 G; 0.5 Sac. **Total:** 22 G; 0.5 Sac.

GEORGE MRKONIC Mrkonic, George Ralph 6′2″, 225 **OT-DT**
Col: Kansas *HS:* McKeesport Tech [PA] B: 12/17/1929, McKeesport, PA *Drafted:* 1953 Round 4 Phi
1953 Phi: 10 G.

BOB MROSKO Mrosko, Robert Allen 6′6″, 265 **TE**
Col: Penn State *HS:* Wickliffe [OH] B: 11/13/1965, Cleveland, OH
Drafted: 1989 Round 9 Hou
1989 Hou: 15 G; Rec 3-28 9.3; KR 3-46 15.3. **1990** NYG: 16 G; Rec 3-27 9.0 1 TD; 6 Pt. **1991** Ind: 11 G; Rec 8-90 11.3; KR 1-9 9.0. **Total:** 42 G; Rec 14-145 10.4 1 TD; KR 4-55 13.8; 6 Pt.

RUDY MUCHA Mucha, Rudolph John 6′1″, 236 **G-LB-BB**
(Moose) *Col:* Washington *HS:* Fenger [Chicago, IL] B: 7/22/1918, Chicago, IL D: 9/7/1982, Dolton, IL *Drafted:* 1941 Round 1 Cle
1941 Cle: 10 G; Rush 1-0; Rec 1-3 3.0; Punt 11-488 44.4. **1945** Cle-ChiB: 7 G. Cle: 3 G. ChiB: 4 G. **1946** ChiB: 5 G; Rush 1-(-1) -1.0; Punt 23-896 39.0. **Total:** 22 G; Rush 2-(-1) -0.5; Rec 1-3 3.0; Punt 34-1384 40.7.

JERRY MUCKENSTURM Muckensturm, Jerry Ray 6′4″, 223 **LB**
Col: Arkansas State *HS:* Althoff [Belleville, IL] B: 10/13/1953, Belleville, IL *Drafted:* 1976 Round 7 ChiB
1976 ChiB: 13 G. **1977** ChiB: 14 G. **1978** ChiB: 16 G; KR 1-6 6.0. **1979** ChiB: 16 G; Int 1-5. **1980** ChiB: 15 G; Int 2-2. **1982** ChiB: 6 G; KR 1-5 5.0. **1983** ChiB: 1 G. **Total:** 81 G; KR 2-11 5.5; Int 3-7.

LARRY MUCKER Mucker, Larry Donnell 5′11″, 190 **WR**
Col: Arizona State *HS:* McLane [Fresno, CA] B: 12/15/1954, Fresno, CA *Drafted:* 1977 Round 9 TB
1978 TB: Rush 5-35 7.0; PR 7-49 7.0; KR 2-9 4.5. **1979** TB: Rush 4-16 4.0. **Total:** Rush 9-51 5.7; PR 7-49 7.0; KR 2-9 4.5.

		Receiving				
Year Team	G	Rec	Yds	Avg	TD	Fum
1977 TB	14	4	59	14.8	0	0
1978 TB	16	13	271	20.8	0	2
1979 TB	16	14	268	19.1	5	1
1980 TB	7	2	37	18.5	0	0
NFL Total	53	33	635	19.2	5	3

HOWARD MUDD Mudd, Howard Edward 6′2″, 254 **OG**
Col: Michigan State; Hillsdale *HS:* Midland [MI] B: 2/10/1942, Midland, MI *Drafted:* 1964 Round 9 SF
1964 SF: 14 G. **1965** SF: 14 G. **1966** SF: 14 G. **1967** SF: 14 G. **1968** SF: 14 G. **1969** SF-ChiB: 13 G. SF: 5 G. ChiB: 8 G. **1970** ChiB: 10 G. **Total:** 93 G.

FRANK MUEHLHEUSER Muehlheuser, Frank Paul 6′2″, 215 **FB-LB**
(Moose) *Col:* Colgate *HS:* Bloomfield [NJ] B: 7/2/1926, Irvington, NJ
Drafted: 1947 Round 6 NYG
1948 Bos: Rec 3-19 6.3; KR 1-27 27.0; Punt 1-46 46.0. **1949** NYB: Rec 2-26 13.0; KR 1-40 40.0. **Total:** Rec 5-45 9.0; KR 2-67 33.5; Punt 1-46 46.0.

		Rushing				
Year Team	G	Att	Yds	Avg	TD	Fum
1948 Bos	12	38	169	4.4	1	3
1949 NYB	8	9	10	1.1	1	2
NFL Total	20	47	179	3.8	2	5

CHUCK MUELHAUPT Muelhaupt, Edward Charles Jr. 6′3″, 230 **OG**
Col: Iowa State *HS:* Dowling [West Des Moines, IA] B: 12/11/1935, Canton, OH *Drafted:* 1957 Round 26 Det
1960 Buf: 14 G. **1961** Buf: 14 G; 1 Fum TD; 6 Pt. **Total:** 28 G; 1 Fum TD; 6 Pt.

JAMIE MUELLER Mueller, Jamie F 6′1″, 225 RB
Col: Benedictine *HS:* Fairview [Fairview Park, OH] B: 10/4/1964, Cleveland, OH *Drafted:* 1987 Round 3 Buf
1987 Buf: KR 5-74 14.8. **1989** Buf: KR 1-19 19.0. **Total:** KR 6-93 15.5.

		Rushing				Receiving					Tot
Year Team	G	Att	Yds	Avg	TD	Rec	Yds	Avg	TD	Fum	TD
1987 Buf	12	82	354	4.3	2	3	13	4.3	0	5	2
1988 Buf	15	81	296	3.7	0	8	42	5.3	0	2	0
1989 Buf	14	16	44	2.8	0	1	8	8.0	0	1	0
1990 Buf	16	59	207	3.5	2	16	106	6.6	1	1	3
NFL Total	57	238	901	3.8	4	28	169	6.0	1	9	5

VANCE MUELLER Mueller, Vance Alan 6′0″, 210 RB
Col: Occidental *HS:* Jackson [CA] B: 5/5/1964, Tucson, AZ
Drafted: 1986 Round 4 LARd

		Rushing				Receiving			
Year Team	G	Att	Yds	Avg	TD	Rec	Yds	Avg	TD
1986 LARd	15	13	30	2.3	0	6	54	9.0	0
1987 LARd	12	37	175	4.7	1	11	95	8.6	0
1988 LARd	14	17	60	3.5	0	5	63	12.6	0
1989 LARd	16	48	161	3.4	2	18	240	13.3	2
1990 LARd	16	13	43	3.3	0	0	0	—	0
NFL Total	73	128	469	3.7	3	40	452	11.3	2

	Kickoff Returns					Tot
Year Team	Ret	Yds	Avg	TD	Fum	TD
1986 LARd	2	73	36.5	0	1	0
1987 LARd	27	588	21.8	0	3	1
1988 LARd	5	97	19.4	0	1	0
1989 LARd	5	120	24.0	0	0	4
NFL Total	39	878	22.5	0	5	5

BILL MUELLNER Muellner, William Clarence 5′11″, 175 OE-DE
Col: DePaul *HS:* DePaul Acad. [Chicago, IL] B: 9/30/1914, Chicago, IL
1937 ChiC: 1 G.

GARVIN MUGG Mugg, Garvin Bray 6′1″, 215 T
Col: North Texas *HS:* Anna [TX] B: 2/19/1918, Weston, TX
D: 10/27/1990, Tallapoosa, GA
1945 Det: 3 G.

JOE MUHA Muha, Joseph George 6′1″, 205 FB-LB
Col: Virginia Military *HS:* Sto-Rox [McKees Rocks, PA] B: 4/28/1921, Central City, PA D: 3/31/1993, Hemet, CA *Drafted:* 1943 Round 1 Phi
1946 Phi: KR 1-23 23.0; Int 1-8. **1947** Phi: Rec 1-10 10.0; KR 3-55 18.3; Scor 15, 1-5 20.0% FG; 1 Fum TD. **1948** Phi: Rec 2-22 11.0 1 TD; Scor 6, 0-5 FG. **1949** Phi: Rec 1-10 10.0; PR 1-2 2.0; KR 1-20 20.0; Int 2-31 1 TD; Scor 11, 0-1 FG, 5-5 100.0% XK. **1950** Phi: KR 2-28 14.0; Int 2-40 1 TD; Scor 6, 0-5 FG. **Total:** Rec 4-42 10.5 1 TD; PR 1-2 2.0; KR 7-126 18.0; Int 5-79 2 TD; Scor 38, 1-16 6.3% FG, 5-5 100.0% XK; 1 Fum TD.

		Rushing				Punting				Tot
Year Team	G	Att	Yds	Avg	TD	Punts	Yds	Avg	Fum	TD
1946 Phi	10	12	41	3.4	0	22	843	38.3	4	0
1947 Phi	12	27	107	4.0	1	53	2303	43.5	1	2
1948 Phi	11	25	90	3.6	0	57	2694	**47.3**	1	1
1949 Phi	12	3	19	6.3	0	45	1800	40.0	1	1
1950 Phi	11	0	0	—	0	2	48	24.0	0	1
NFL Total	56	67	257	3.8	1	179	7688	42.9	7	5

CALVIN MUHAMMAD Muhammad, Calvin Saleem 5′11″, 190 WR
(CNN AKA Calvin Vincent Rainey) *Col:* Texas Southern *HS:* William M. Raines [Jacksonville, FL] B: 12/10/1958, Jacksonville, FL
Drafted: 1980 Round 12 Oak

		Receiving				
Year Team	G	Rec	Yds	Avg	TD	Fum
1982 LARd	8	3	92	30.7	1	0
1983 LARd	15	13	252	19.4	2	2
1984 Was	10	42	729	17.4	4	1
1985 Was	12	9	116	12.9	1	0
1987 SD	2	2	87	43.5	0	0
NFL Total	47	69	1276	18.5	8	3

MUHSIN MUHAMMAD Muhammad, Muhsin II 6′2″, 217 WR
Col: Michigan State *HS:* Waverly [Lansing, MI] B: 5/5/1973, Lansing, MI *Drafted:* 1996 Round 2 Car
1996 Car: Rush 1-(-1) -1.0. **1997** Car: Scor 1 2XP. **1998** Car: Scor 1 2XP.
Total: Rush 1-(-1) -1.0; Scor 2 2XP.

		Receiving				
Year Team	G	Rec	Yds	Avg	TD	Fum
1996 Car	9	25	407	16.3	1	0
1997 Car	13	27	317	11.7	0	0
1998 Car	16	68	941	13.8	6	2
NFL Total	38	120	1665	13.9	7	2

HORST MUHLMANN Muhlmann, Horst Herbert Erich 6′1″, 219 K
Col: No College B: 1/2/1940, Dortmund, Germany
1969 Cin: Punt 2-38 19.0. **Total:** Punt 2-38 19.0.

		Scoring						
Year Team	G	Pts	FG	FGA	FG%	XK	XKA	XK%
1969 Cin	14	80	16	24	66.7	32	33	97.0
1970 Cin	14	108	25	37	67.6	33	33	100.0
1971 Cin	14	91	20	36	55.6	31	31	100.0
1972 Cin	14	111	27	40	67.5	30	31	96.8
1973 Cin	14	94	21	31	67.7	31	32	96.9
1974 Cin	14	65	11	18	61.1	32	35	91.4
1975 Phi	14	81	20	29	69.0	21	24	87.5
1976 Phi	14	51	11	16	68.8	18	19	94.7
1977 Phi	9	26	3	8	37.5	17	19	89.5
NFL Total	121	707	154	239	64.4	245	257	95.3

STAN MUIRHEAD Muirhead, Stanley Nelson 6′0″, 180 G-T
Col: Michigan *HS:* Central [Detroit, MI]; Northern HS [Detroit,MI]
B: 8/29/1902, Calumet, MI D: 9/14/1992, Detroit, MI
1924 Day-Cle: 8 G. Day: 5 G. Cle: 3 G. **Total:** 8 G.

MIKE MULARKEY Mularkey, Michael Rene 6′4″, 245 TE
Col: Florida *HS:* Northeast [Fort Lauderdale, FL] B: 11/19/1961, Miami, FL *Drafted:* 1983 Round 9 SF
1985 Min: KR 0-9. **1987** Min: KR 1-16 16.0. **1988** Min: Rush 1-(-6) -6.0.
Total: Rush 1-(-6) -6.0; KR 1-25 25.0.

		Receiving				
Year Team	G	Rec	Yds	Avg	TD	Fum
1983 Min	3	0	0	—	0	0
1984 Min	16	14	134	9.6	2	1
1985 Min	15	13	196	15.1	1	0
1986 Min	16	11	89	8.1	2	0
1987 Min	9	1	6	6.0	0	0
1988 Min	16	3	39	13.0	0	0
1989 Pit	14	22	326	14.8	1	0
1990 Pit	16	32	365	11.4	3	1
1991 Pit	9	6	67	11.2	0	0
NFL Total	114	102	1222	12.0	9	2

JOE MULBARGER Mulbarger, Joseph G 5′9″, 221 T-G
(Dutch; Tiny) *Col:* No College *HS:* East [Columbus, OH] B: 1895, OH
Deceased
1920 Col: 9 G. **1921** Col: 8 G; Rec 1 TD; 6 Pt. **1922** Col: 8 G. **1923** Col: 10 G. **1924** Col: 8 G. **1925** Col: 9 G. **1926** Col: 7 G. **Total:** 59 G; Rec 1 TD; 6 Pt.

HERB MUL-KEY Mul-key, Herbert Felton 6′0″, 190 RB
Col: No College *HS:* Charles Harper [Atlanta, GA] B: 11/15/1949, Atlanta, GA
1972 Was: Rec 4-66 16.5. **1973** Was: PR 11-103 9.4. **1974** Was: PR 13-140 10.8. **Total:** Rec 4-66 16.5; PR 24-243 10.1.

		Rushing				Kickoff Returns					Tot
Year Team	G	Ret	Yds	Avg	TD	Ret	Yds	Avg	TD	Fum	TD
1972 Was	2	33	155	4.7	1	8	209	26.1	0	1	1
1973 Was	14	8	20	2.5	0	36	1011	28.1	1	4	1
1974 Was	7	1	3	3.0	0	10	285	28.5	0	0	0
NFL Total	23	42	178	4.2	1	54	1505	27.9	1	5	2

TOM MULLADY Mullady, Thomas Francis 6′3″, 232 WR
Col: Rhodes *HS:* McCallie School [Chattanooga, TN] B: 1/30/1957, Dayton, OH *Drafted:* 1979 Round 7 Buf

		Receiving				
Year Team	G	Rec	Yds	Avg	TD	Fum
1979 NYG	2	0	0	—	0	0
1980 NYG	16	28	391	14.0	2	0
1981 NYG	16	14	136	9.7	1	1
1982 NYG	9	27	287	10.6	0	1
1983 NYG	16	13	184	14.2	1	0
1984 NYG	16	2	35	17.5	0	0
NFL Total	75	84	1033	12.3	4	2

MARK MULLANEY Mullaney, Mark Alan 6′6″, 242 DE
Col: Colorado State *HS:* George Washington [Denver, CO]
B: 4/30/1953, Denver, CO *Drafted:* 1975 Round 1 Min
1975 Min: 14 G. **1976** Min: 12 G. **1977** Min: 14 G. **1978** Min: 15 G.
1979 Min: 16 G. **1980** Min: 16 G. **1981** Min: 15 G. **1982** Min: 9 G; 5 Sac.
1983 Min: 7 G; 2.5 Sac. **1984** Min: 7 G; 2 Sac. **1985** Min: 15 G; Int 1-15; 2 Sac. **1986** Min: 11 G; 2 Sac. **Total:** 151 G; Int 1-15; 13.5 Sac.

DAVLIN MULLEN Mullen, Davlin 6′1″, 175 DB
Col: Western Kentucky *HS:* Clairton [PA] B: 2/17/1960, McKeesport, PA *Drafted:* 1983 Round 8 NYJ
1983 NYJ: 11 G; PR 2-13 6.5; KR 3-57 19.0; 1 Fum. **1984** NYJ: 15 G; PR 1-8 8.0; KR 2-34 17.0; Int 1-25. **1985** NYJ: 11 G; Int 3-14. **1986** NYJ: 5 G. **Total:** 42 G; PR 3-21 7.0; KR 5-91 18.2; Int 4-39; 1 Fum.

GARY MULLEN Mullen, Gary 5'11", 174 **WR**
Col: West Virginia *HS:* Clairton [PA] B: 2/1/1963, McKeesport, PA
1987 ChiB: 3 G; Rec 2-33 16.5.

RODERICK MULLEN Mullen, Roderick Louis 6'1", 202 **DB**
(Muney) *Col:* Grambling State *HS:* West Felencia [St. Francisville, LA]
B: 12/5/1972, Baton Rouge, LA *Drafted:* 1995 Round 5 NYG
1995 GB: 8 G. **1996** GB: 14 G. **1997** GB: 16 G; Int 1-17. **Total:** 38 G; Int 1-17.

CHIEF MULLEN Mullen, Samuel 165 **WB**
Col: Haskell Indian *HS:* Lawton [OK] B: 1/9/1894, Lawton, OK
D: 5/25/1976, Lawton, OK
1921 Eva: 2 G.

TOM MULLEN Mullen, Thomas Patrick 6'3", 248 **OG-OT**
Col: Southwest Missouri State *HS:* Vianney [Kirkwood, MO]
B: 11/11/1951, St. Louis, MO *Drafted:* 1974 Round 2 NYG
1974 NYG: 11 G. **1975** NYG: 12 G. **1976** NYG: 12 G. **1977** NYG: 8 G.
1978 StL: 7 G. **Total:** 50 G.

VERN MULLEN Mullen, Vern Elmo 6'0", 186 **E-HB**
(Moon) *Col:* Illinois; West Virginia Wesleyan *HS:* Taylorville [IL]
B: 2/27/1900, Taylorville, IL D: 9/14/1980, Taft, CA
1923 Can: 4 G. **1924** ChiB: 11 G. **1925** ChiB: 16 G. **1926** ChiB: 16 G; Rec 1 TD; 6 Pt. **1927** ChiC-Pott: 9 G. ChiC: 1 G. Pott: 8 G. **Total:** 56 G; Rec 1 TD; 6 Pt.

CARL MULLENEAUX Mulleneaux, Carl Kenneth 6'3", 209 **DE-OE**
(Moose) *Col:* Utah State *HS:* Phoenix Union [AZ] B: 9/16/1914, Phoenix, AZ D: 1/23/1995, Chico, CA
1940 GB: **1** Fum TD. **Total:** 1 Fum TD.

		Receiving				Tot
Year Team	**G**	**Rec**	**Yds**	**Avg**	**TD**	**TD**
1938 GB	9	4	97	24.3	2	2
1939 GB	11	12	218	18.2	1	1
1940 GB	10	16	288	18.0	6	7
1941 GB	10	9	216	24.0	2	2
1945 GB	5	3	31	10.3	0	0
1946 GB	1	0	0	—	0	0
NFL Total	46	44	850	19.3	11	12

LEE MULLENEAUX Mulleneaux, Cecil Lee 6'2", 221 **LB-C-DB-WB**
(Brute) *Col:* Northern Arizona *HS:* Phoenix Union [AZ] B: 4/1/1908
D: 11/14/1985, Whittier, CA
1933 Cin: Rec 2-13 6.5. **1934** Cin-StL: Rec 1-5 5.0. Cin: Rec 1-5 5.0.
Total: Rec 3-18 6.0.

		Rushing			
Year Team	**G**	**Att**	**Yds**	**Avg**	**TD**
1932 NYG	6	3	1	0.3	0
1933 Cin	9	19	62	3.3	0
1934 Cin-StL	10	3	7	2.3	0
1934 Cin	8	3	7	2.3	0
1934 StL	2	0	0	—	0
1935 Pit	7	0	0	—	0
1936 Pit	12	0	0	—	0
1938 ChiC-GB	9	0	0	—	0
1938 ChiC	4	0	0	—	0
1938 GB	5	0	0	—	0
NFL Total	53	25	70	2.8	0

BRICK MULLER Muller, Harold Powers 6'2", 195 **E**
Col: California *HS:* Oakland Tech [CA]; San Diego HS [CA]
B: 6/12/1901, Dunsmuir, CA D: 5/17/1962, Berkeley, CA
1926 LA: 10 G; Rec 1 TD; 6 Pt.

GEORGE MULLIGAN Mulligan, George Edward 6'1", 198 **OE-DE-LB**
Col: Catholic *HS:* Crosby [Waterbury, CT] B: 6/7/1914, Waterbury, CT
Deceased
1936 Phi: 9 G; Rec 1-3 3.0.

WAYNE MULLIGAN Mulligan, Wayne Eugene 6'3", 250 **C**
Col: Clemson *HS:* Calvert Hall [Towson, MD] B: 5/5/1947, Baltimore, MD *Drafted:* 1969 Round 8 StL
1969 StL: 14 G. **1970** StL: 14 G. **1971** StL: 7 G. **1972** StL: 12 G. **1973** StL: 13 G. **1974** NYJ: 13 G. **1975** NYJ: 14 G. **Total:** 87 G.

DON MULLINS Mullins, Don Ray 6'1", 195 **DB**
Col: Houston *HS:* Fair Park [Shreveport, LA] B: 3/31/1939, Shreveport, LA
1961 ChiB: 4 G. **1962** ChiB: 9 G. **Total:** 13 G.

ERIC MULLINS Mullins, Eric Dwayne 5'11", 181 **WR**
Col: Stanford *HS:* Strake Jesuit Prep [Houston, TX] B: 7/30/1962, Houston, TX *Drafted:* 1984 Round 6 Hou
1984 Hou: 13 G; Rush 1-0; Rec 6-85 14.2 1 TD; 6 Pt.

GERRY MULLINS Mullins, Gerald Blaine 6'3", 244 **OG-OT**
Col: USC *HS:* Anaheim [CA] B: 8/24/1949, Fullerton, CA
Drafted: 1971 Round 4 Pit
1971 Pit: 14 G. **1972** Pit: 14 G; Rec 1-3 3.0 1 TD; 6 Pt. **1973** Pit: 13 G.
1974 Pit: 12 G; Rec 1-7 7.0 1 TD; 6 Pt. **1975** Pit: 14 G; **1** Fum TD; 6 Pt.
1976 Pit: 14 G. **1977** Pit: 12 G. **1978** Pit: 16 G; KR 1-0. **1979** Pit: 15 G.
Total: 124 G; Rec 2-10 5.0 2 TD; KR 1-0; 1 Fum TD; Tot TD 3; 18 Pt.

NOAH MULLINS Mullins, Noah Walker 5'11", 182 **DB-HB**
(Moon) *Col:* Kentucky *HS:* Woodford Co. [Versailles, KY]
B: 5/23/1918, Midway, KY *Drafted:* 1942 Round 8 ChiB
1946 ChiB: Pass 1-1 100.0%, 16 16.00; PR 4-50 12.5; KR 1-22 22.0.
1947 ChiB: Rec 1-4 4.0; PR 13-153 11.8. **1948** ChiB: Pass 1-0; Rec 9-127 14.1 4 TD; PR 3-33 11.0; KR 1-41 41.0; Punt 2-88 44.0.
1949 NYG: Rec 2-45 22.5 1 TD. **Total:** Pass 2-1 50.0%, 16 8.00; Rec 12-176 14.7 5 TD; PR 20-236 11.8; KR 2-63 31.5; Punt 2-88 44.0.

		Rushing				Interceptions				Tot
Year Team	**G**	**Att**	**Yds**	**Avg**	**TD**	**Int**	**Yds**	**TD**	**Fum**	**TD**
1946 ChiB	10	20	102	5.1	0	3	96	0	4	0
1947 ChiB	12	9	55	6.1	0	6	113	0	3	0
1948 ChiB	12	36	208	5.8	1	7	99	1	4	6
1949 NYG	11	2	-3	-1.5	0	3	26	0	0	1
NFL Total	45	67	362	5.4	1	19	334	1	11	7

JERRY MULREADY Mulready, John Jerome 6'1", 205 **OE-DE**
Col: Minnesota; North Dakota State *HS:* Central [Fargo, ND]
B: 1/5/1923, Fargo, ND D: 6/3/1976, Fargo, ND
AAFC **1947** ChiA: 9 G; Rec 7-108 15.4.

VINCE MULVEY Mulvey, Vincent J 155 **FB**
Col: Syracuse B: 10/6/1891, Geneva, NY D: 2/25/1988
1923 Buf: 3 G.

TONY MUMFORD Mumford, Anthony Vincent 6'0", 215 **RB**
Col: Penn State *HS:* Overbrook Regional [Pine Hill, NJ] B: 6/14/1963, Philadelphia, PA *Drafted:* 1985 Round 12 NE
1985 StL: 2 G; KR 1-19 19.0; 1 Fum.

NICK MUMLEY Mumley, Nicholas Jr. 6'4", 255 **DE-OT**
Col: Purdue *HS:* Wheeling [WV] B: 1/26/1937, Wheeling, WV
Drafted: 1959 Round 5 Phi
1960 NYT: 14 G; Int 1-26 1 TD; 6 Pt. **1961** NYT: 14 G. **1962** NYT: 14 G.
Total: 42 G; Int 1-26 1 TD; 6 Pt.

LLOYD MUMPHORD Mumphord, Lloyd N 5'10", 176 **DB**
Col: Texas Southern *HS:* Middleton [Tampa, FL] B: 12/20/1946, Los Angeles, CA *Drafted:* 1969 Round 16 Mia
1969 Mia: KR 1-0. **Total:** KR 1-0.

		Interceptions			Tot
Year Team	**G**	**Int**	**Yds**	**TD**	**TD**
1969 Mia	11	5	102	0	0
1970 Mia	14	5	35	1	2
1971 Mia	14	0	0	0	0
1972 Mia	14	4	50	1	1
1973 Mia	11	0	0	0	0
1974 Mia	13	0	0	0	0
1975 Bal	14	4	58	0	0
1976 Bal	13	1	22	0	0
1977 Bal	2	0	0	0	0
1978 Bal	16	2	20	0	0
NFL Total	122	21	287	2	3

LLOYD MUMPHREY Mumphrey, Lloyd Ellis 6'3", 260 **DE-LB**
Col: Mississippi Valley State *HS:* Westwood [Memphis, TN]
B: 2/14/1961, Memphis, TN
1987 KC: 3 G.

MIKE MUNCHAK Munchak, Michael Anthony 6'3", 281 **OG**
Col: Penn State *HS:* Scranton [PA] B: 3/5/1960, Scranton, PA
Drafted: 1982 Round 1 Hou
1982 Hou: 4 G. **1983** Hou: 16 G. **1984** Hou: 16 G. **1985** Hou: 16 G.
1986 Hou: 6 G; **1** Fum TD; 6 Pt. **1987** Hou: 12 G. **1988** Hou: 16 G.
1989 Hou: 16 G. **1990** Hou: 16 G. **1991** Hou: 13 G. **1992** Hou: 15 G.
1993 Hou: 13 G. **Total:** 159 G; 1 Fum TD; 6 Pt.

CHUCK MUNCIE Muncie, Harry Vance 6'3", 227 **RB**
Col: Arizona Western Coll. (J.C.); California *HS:* Uniontown [PA]
B: 3/17/1953, Uniontown, PA *Drafted:* 1976 Round 1 NO
1976 NO: KR 3-69 23.0. **1977** NO: KR 1-19 19.0. **1978** NO: Pass 1-0.
1979 NO: Pass 2-1 50.0%, 40 20.00 1 TD. **1980** NO-SD: KR 16-344 21.5.
SD: KR 16-344 21.5. **1981** SD: Pass 1-1 100.0%, 3 3.00 1 TD. **1982** SD: Pass 3-2 66.7%, 83 27.67 2 TD. **Total:** Pass 7-4 57.1%, 126 18.00 4 TD; KR 20-432 21.6.

		Rushing				Receiving					Tot
Year Team	**G**	**Att**	**Yds**	**Avg**	**TD**	**Rec**	**Yds**	**Avg**	**TD**	**Fum**	**TD**
1976 NO	12	149	659	4.4	2	31	272	8.8	0	6	2
1977 NO	14	201	811	4.0	6	21	248	11.8	1	3	7
1978 NO	13	160	557	3.5	7	26	233	9.0	0	7	7
1979 NO	16	238	1198	5.0	11	40	308	7.7	0	8	11

1980 NO-SD	15	175	827	4.7	6	31	259	8.4	0	11	6
1980 NO	4	40	168	4.2	2	7	25	3.6	0	1	2
1980 SD	11	135	659	4.9	4	24	234	9.8	0	10	4
1981 SD	15	251	1144	4.6	**19**	43	362	8.4	0	9	**19**
1982 SD	9	138	569	4.1	8	25	207	8.3	1	4	9
1983 SD	15	235	886	3.8	12	42	396	9.4	1	8	13
1984 SD	1	14	51	3.6	0	4	38	9.5	0	1	0
NFL Total	110	1561	6702	4.3	71	263	2323	8.8	3	57	74

GEORGE MUNDAY Munday, George 6′2″, 215 **T-G**
(Sunny) *Col:* Emporia State B: 6/13/1907, Climax, KS D: 10/17/1975, Miami Beach, FL
1931 Cle-NYG: 2 G. Cle: 1 G. NYG: 1 G. **1932** NYG: 4 G. **1933** Cin: 10 G. **1934** Cin-StL: 10 G. Cin: 8 G. StL: 2 G. **Total:** 26 G.

FRED MUNDEE Mundee, Frederick William 6′1″, 220 **C-LB**
Col: Notre Dame *HS:* South [Youngstown, OH] B: 5/20/1913, Youngstown, OH D: 1/15/1990, Chicago, IL
1943 ChiB: 5 G; Int 1-8. **1944** ChiB: 10 G; Int 1-0. **1945** ChiB: 6 G. **Total:** 21 G; Int 2-8.

MARC MUNFORD Munford, Marc Christopher 6′2″, 231 **LB**
Col: Nebraska *HS:* Heritage [Littleton, CO] B: 2/14/1965, Lincoln, NE *Drafted:* 1987 Round 4 Den
1987 Den: 12 G. **1988** Den: 7 G. **1989** Den: 16 G; Int 2-16; 1 Sac. **1990** Den: 13 G. **Total:** 48 G; Int 2-16; 1 Sac.

JOCK MUNGAVIN Mungavin, James Francis 5′10″, 175 **OE**
Col: Wis.-Superior; Wisconsin *HS:* Superior [WI] B: 9/12/1893, Superior, WI D: 10/26/1977, Washburn, WI
1920 ChiT: 3 G.

MUNGER Munger **T**
1924 ChiC: 1 G.

LYLE MUNN Munn, Lyle Smith 6′0″, 186 **OE**
(Doc) *Col:* Kansas State *HS:* Norton [KS] B: 4/13/1902, Fairbury, NE D: 1/12/1984, Topeka, KS
1925 KC: 7 G. **1926** KC: 11 G; Int **1** TD; 6 Pt. **1927** Cle: 10 G. **1928** Det: 10 G. **1929** NYG: 15 G; Scor **1** 1XP; 1 Pt. **Total:** 53 G; Int 1 TD; Scor 1 1XP; 7 Pt.

GEORGE MUNNS Munns, George Francis 5′9″, 170 **TB**
(Yats) *Col:* Miami (Ohio) *HS:* McGuffey [Oxford, OH] B: 6/1898, Oxford, OH D: 1/1972
1921 Cin: 4 G; Pass 2 TD; Scor 1, 1 XK.

ANTHONY MUNOZ Munoz, Michael Anthony 6′6″, 278 **OT**
Col: USC *HS:* Chaffey [Ontario, Canada] B: 8/19/1958, Ontario, CA *Drafted:* 1980 Round 1 Cin *HOF:* 1998
1980 Cin: 16 G; Rec 1-(-6) -6.0. **1981** Cin: 16 G. **1982** Cin: 9 G. **1983** Cin: 16 G. **1984** Cin: 16 G; Rec 1-1 1.0 1 TD; 6 Pt. **1985** Cin: 16 G; Rec 1-1 1.0. **1986** Cin: 16 G; Rec 2-7 3.5 2 TD; 12 Pt. **1987** Cin: 11 G; Rec 2-15 7.5 1 TD; 6 Pt. **1988** Cin: 16 G. **1989** Cin: 16 G. **1990** Cin: 16 G. **1991** Cin: 13 G. **1992** Cin: 8 G. **Total:** 185 G; Rec 7-18 2.6 4 TD; 24 Pt.

NELSON MUNSEY Munsey, Nelson Emory 6′1″, 188 **DB**
Col: Wyoming *HS:* Uniontown [PA] B: 7/2/1948, Uniontown, PA
1972 Bal: 9 G; **1** Fum TD; 6 Pt. **1973** Bal: 14 G; KR 1-13 13.0. **1974** Bal: 14 G. **1975** Bal: 14 G; Int 3-36 1 TD; 6 Pt. **1976** Bal: 8 G; Int 1-10. **1977** Bal: 13 G; Int 3-25. **Total:** 72 G; KR 1-13 13.0; Int 7-71 1 TD; 1 Fum TD; Tot TD 2; 12 Pt.

BILL MUNSON Munson, William Alan 6′2″, 210 **QB**
Col: Foothill Coll. CA (J.C.); Utah State *HS:* Lodi [CA] B: 8/11/1941, Sacramento, CA *Drafted:* 1964 Round 1 LARm
1974 Det: Rec 1-(-6) -6.0. **Total:** Rec 1-(-6) -6.0.

		Passing							
Year Team	**G**	**Att**	**Comp**	**Comp%**	**Yds**	**YPA**	**TD**	**Int**	**Rating**
1964 LARm	11	223	108	48.4	1533	6.87	9	15	56.5
1965 LARm	10	267	144	53.9	1701	6.37	10	14	64.2
1966 LARm	5	50	30	60.0	284	5.68	2	1	80.8
1967 LARm	5	10	5	50.0	38	3.80	1	2	53.3
1968 Det	12	329	181	55.0	2311	7.02	15	**8**	82.3
1969 Det	8	166	84	50.6	1062	6.40	7	8	64.9
1970 Det	8	158	84	53.2	1049	6.64	10	7	76.7
1971 Det	4	38	21	55.3	216	5.68	1	1	69.6
1972 Det	2	35	20	57.1	194	5.54	1	1	70.4
1973 Det	10	187	95	50.8	1129	6.04	9	8	67.8
1974 Det	11	292	166	56.8	1874	6.42	8	7	75.3
1975 Det	5	109	65	59.6	626	5.74	5	2	83.4
1976 Sea	5	37	20	54.1	295	7.97	1	3	55.6
1977 SD	4	31	20	64.5	225	7.26	1	1	83.4
1978 Buf	4	43	24	55.8	328	7.63	4	2	92.0
1979 Buf	3	7	3	42.9	31	4.43	0	0	56.3
NFL Total	107	1982	1070	54.0	12896	6.51	84	80	71.5

	Rushing				
Year Team	**Att**	**Yds**	**Avg**	**TD**	**Fum**
1964 LARm	19	150	7.9	0	7
1965 LARm	26	157	6.0	1	9
1966 LARm	4	3	0.8	0	0
1967 LARm	2	-22	-11.0	0	2
1968 Det	25	109	4.4	1	5
1969 Det	7	31	4.4	0	3
1970 Det	9	33	3.7	0	1
1971 Det	3	9	3.0	0	0
1972 Det	1	0	0.0	0	1
1973 Det	10	33	3.3	0	3
1974 Det	18	40	2.2	1	2
1975 Det	4	-3	-0.8	0	2
1976 Sea	1	6	6.0	0	0
1977 SD	1	2	2.0	0	2
NFL Total	130	548	4.2	3	37

ART MURAKOWSKI Murakowski, Arthur Raymond 6′0″, 195 **FB-LB**
Col: Northwestern *HS:* Washington [East Chicago, IN] B: 5/15/1925, East Chicago, IN D: 9/13/1985, Hammond, IN *Drafted:* 1950 Round 3 Det
1951 Det: 12 G; KR 1-0.

ED MURANSKY Muransky, Edward William 6′7″, 277 **OT**
Col: Michigan *HS:* Cardinal Mooney [Youngstown, OH] B: 1/20/1960, Youngstown, OH *Drafted:* 1982 Round 4 LARd
1982 LARd: 5 G. **1983** LARd: 16 G. **1984** LARd: 3 G. **Total:** 24 G.

LEE MURCHISON Murchison, Ola Lee 6′3″, 205 **WR**
Col: U. of Pacific *HS:* Washington [CA]; Placer HS [Auburn, CA] B: 4/16/1938, AR *Drafted:* 1960 Round 6 SF
1961 Dal: 14 G.

GUY MURDOCK Murdock, Guy Boyd 6′2″, 245 **C**
Col: Michigan *HS:* Barrington [IL] B: 6/27/1950, Chicago, IL *Drafted:* 1972 Round 16 Hou
1972 Hou: 14 G.

JESSE MURDOCK Murdock, Jesse 6′2″, 203 **HB**
Col: California Western *HS:* Alameda [CA] B: 9/17/1938, Oakland, CA
1963 Oak-Buf: 7 G; KR 1-17 17.0. Oak: 1 G; KR 1-17 17.0. Buf: 6 G. **Total:** 7 G; KR 1-17 17.0.

LES MURDOCK Murdock, Leslie Ray 6′3″, 245 **K**
Col: Florida State *HS:* South Broward [Hollywood, FL] B: 6/6/1941, Boston, MA
1967 NYG: 4 G; Scor 25, 4-9 44.4% FG, 13-15 86.7% XK.

DICK MURLEY Murley, Richard Allen 6′0″, 247 **OT**
Col: Purdue *HS:* Richmond [IN] B: 8/1/1933, Richmond, IN *Drafted:* 1956 Round 4 Pit
1956 Pit-Phi: 7 G. Pit: 2 G. Phi: 5 G. **Total:** 7 G.

DENNIS MURPHY Murphy, Alvin Dennis 6′2″, 250 **DT**
Col: Florida *HS:* Cairo [GA] B: 3/9/1943, Cairo, GA *Drafted:* 1965 Round 10 ChiB
1965 ChiB: 2 G.

FRED MURPHY Murphy, Fred Joe 6′3″, 205 **OE**
Col: Georgia Tech *HS:* Fulton [Atlanta, GA] B: 2/20/1938, Atlanta, GA
1960 Cle: 9 G; Rec 2-36 18.0. **1961** Min: 13 G. **Total:** 22 G; Rec 2-36 18.0.

GEORGE MURPHY Murphy, George Patrick Jr. 6′0″, 200 **BB**
Col: USC *HS:* Loyola [Los Angeles, CA] B: 5/10/1927, Santa Monica, CA D: 8/25/1987, Chula Vista, CA
AAFC **1949** LA-A: 11 G; Rush 1-0; Rec 1-17 17.0.

HARVEY MURPHY Murphy, Harvey Allen 5′10″, 194 **OE-DE**
Col: Mississippi *HS:* Forrest Co. [Brooklyn, MS] B: 8/24/1915 D: 5/25/1992, Harvey, LA
1940 Cle: 2 G.

JAMES MURPHY Murphy, James Jessie 5′10″, 177 **WR**
Col: Utah State *HS:* Deland [FL] B: 10/10/1959, Deland, FL *Drafted:* 1981 Round 10 Min
1981 KC: 10 G; Rec 2-36 18.0; KR 20-457 22.9.

JIM MURPHY Murphy, James Thomas 6′0″, 184 **WB-OE-C-BB**
Col: St. Thomas *HS:* Russell [MN] B: 11/3/1904, Russell, MN D: 12/17/1993, Denton, TX
1926 Rac-Dul: 7 G. Rac: 5 G. Dul: 2 G. **1928** ChiC: 1 G. **Total:** 8 G.

JOE MURPHY Murphy, Joseph Thomas 5′9″, 215 **G**
(Cuddy) *Col:* Harvard; Dartmouth *HS:* Worcester Acad. [MA]; Hebron Acad. [MA]; Keewatin Acad. [Prarie du Chien, WI] B: 5/15/1897, Concord, NH D: 5/21/1940, Manchester, NH
1920 Can: 2 G. **1921** Cle: 6 G. **Total:** 8 G.

KEVIN MURPHY Murphy, Kevin Dion 6′2″, 233 **LB**
Col: Oklahoma *HS:* L.V. Berkner [Richardson, TX] B: 9/8/1963, Plano, TX *Drafted:* 1986 Round 2 TB
1986 TB: 16 G. **1987** TB: 9 G. **1988** TB: 16 G; Int 1-35 1 TD; 6 Pt; 1 Sac. **1989** TB: 16 G; 6 Sac. **1990** TB: 15 G; 4 Sac. **1991** TB: 16 G; 1 Sac. **1992** SD: 14 G. **1993** Sea: 14 G. **Total:** 116 G; Int 1-35 1 TD; 6 Pt; 12 Sac.

MARK MURPHY Murphy, Mark Hodge 6'4", 210 **DB**
Col: Colgate *HS:* Clarence Central [Williamsville, NY] B: 7/13/1955, Fulton, NY
1977 Was: KR 3-44 14.7. **1978** Was: Rec 1-13 13.0. **1982** Was: 1 Sac. **1983** Was: 1 Sac. **Total:** Rec 1-13 13.0; KR 3-44 14.7; 2 Sac.

		Interceptions			
Year Team	G	Int	Yds	TD	Fum
1977 Was	14	0	0	0	0
1978 Was	16	0	0	0	0
1979 Was	16	3	29	0	0
1980 Was	16	6	58	0	1
1981 Was	16	7	68	0	0
1982 Was	9	2	0	0	0
1983 Was	15	**9**	127	0	0
1984 Was	7	0	0	0	0
NFL Total	109	27	282	0	1

MARK MURPHY Murphy, Mark Steven 6'2", 200 **DB**
Col: West Liberty State *HS:* Glenoak [Canton, OH] B: 4/22/1958, Canton, OH
1984 GB: 2 Sac. **1985** GB: PR 1-4 4.0; 4 Sac. **1987** GB: 2 Sac. **1989** GB: 1 Sac. **1990** GB: 1 Sac. **1991** GB: 1 Sac. **Total:** PR 1-4 4.0; 11 Sac.

		Interceptions			
Year Team	G	Int	Yds	TD	Fum
1980 GB	1	0	0	0	0
1981 GB	16	3	57	0	0
1982 GB	9	0	0	0	0
1983 GB	16	0	0	0	0
1984 GB	16	1	4	0	1
1985 GB	15	2	50	**1**	0
1987 GB	12	0	0	0	0
1988 GB	14	5	19	0	0
1989 GB	16	3	31	0	0
1990 GB	16	3	6	0	0
1991 GB	16	3	27	0	0
NFL Total	147	20	194	1	1

MIKE MURPHY Murphy, Michael William 6'2", 222 **LB**
Col: Southwest Missouri State *HS:* St. Mary's [St. Louis, MO] B: 1/14/1957, St. Louis, MO *Drafted:* 1979 Round 6 Hou
1979 Hou: 3 G.

PHIL MURPHY Murphy, Philip John 6'5", 290 **DT**
Col: South Carolina State *HS:* Xavier [Middletown, CT] B: 9/26/1957, New London, CT *Drafted:* 1980 Round 3 LARm
1980 LARm: 16 G. **1981** LARm: 16 G. **Total:** 32 G.

TOM MURPHY Murphy, Thomas 5'8", 165 **TB-HB**
Col: Wis.-Superior *HS:* Cathedral [Duluth, MN] B: 1/22/1900, Minneapolis, MN D: 12/1986, Tacoma, WA
1926 Mil: 8 G.

TOMMY MURPHY Murphy, Thomas B 5'10", 187 **HB**
Col: St. Mary's (Kansas) B: 5/2/1899, Norwood, OH D: 4/29/1961, Cleveland, OH
1926 KC-Col: 7 G. KC: 1 G. Col: 6 G. **Total:** 7 G.

TOM MURPHY Murphy, Thomas Benjamin 5'11", 170 **BB-DB-FB-LB**
(Smiling Tom; Red) *Col:* Arkansas *HS:* Batesville [AR] B: 12/7/1906, Jonesboro, AR D: 10/19/1981, Dallas, TX
1934 ChiC: 5 G; Pass 9-3 33.3%, 8 0.89 1 Int; Rush 12-37 3.1; Rec 1-(-2) -2.0.

BILL MURPHY Murphy, William Joseph Jr. 6'1", 185 **WR**
Col: Cornell *HS:* Glen Ridge [NJ] B: 3/26/1946, Montclair, NJ
1968 Bos: 6 G; Rec 18-268 14.9.

BILL MURPHY Murphy, William Leslie 6'0", 203 **G**
Col: Washington-St. Louis *HS:* Mount Carmel [IL] B: 4/7/1914, Owensboro, KY D: 1/1985, Forrest, IL
1940 ChiC: 8 G. **1941** ChiC: 4 G. **Total:** 12 G.

CAP MURRAH Murrah, William Ervin 5'10", 215 **C-G**
Col: Texas A&M *HS:* Plano [TX] B: 9/5/1900, Plano, TX Deceased
1922 Can: 6 G. **1923** StL: 7 G. **Total:** 13 G.

DAN MURRAY Murray, Daniel Francis 6'1", 240 **LB**
Col: East Stroudsburg *HS:* Vernon Township [Vernon, NJ] B: 10/20/1966, Teaneck, NJ *Drafted:* 1988 Round 6 Buf
1989 Ind: 2 G. **1990** NYJ: 2 G. **Total:** 4 G.

BILL MURRAY Murray, Earl William 6'2", 240 **OG**
(Moose) *Col:* Purdue *HS:* Dayton [KY] B: 7/16/1926, Dayton, KY D: 7/14/1994, Midlothian, VA *Drafted:* 1950 Round 4 Bal
1950 Bal: 12 G. **1951** NYG: 12 G; Rec 1-(-4) -4.0; KR 1-0. **1952** Pit: 11 G; KR 1-14 14.0. **Total:** 35 G; Rec 1-(-4) -4.0; KR 2-14 7.0.

EDDIE MURRAY Murray, Edward Peter 5'10", 177 **K**
Col: Tulane *HS:* Spectrum [Victoria, Canada] B: 8/29/1956, Halifax, Canada *Drafted:* 1980 Round 7 Det
1986 Det: Punt 1-37 37.0. **1987** Det: Punt 4-155 38.8. **Total:** Punt 5-192 38.4.

		Scoring						
Year Team	G	Pts	FG	FGA	FG%	XK	XKA	XK%
1980 Det	16	116	**27**	**42**	64.3	35	36	97.2
1981 Det	16	**121**	25	35	71.4	46	46	100.0
1982 Det	7	49	11	12	91.7	16	16	100.0
1983 Det	16	113	25	32	78.1	38	38	100.0
1984 Det	16	91	20	27	74.1	31	31	100.0
1985 Det	16	109	26	31	83.9	31	33	93.9
1986 Det	16	85	18	25	72.0	31	32	96.9
1987 Det	12	81	20	32	62.5	21	21	100.0
1988 Det	16	82	20	21	**95.2**	22	23	**95.7**
1989 Det	16	96	20	21	**95.2**	36	36	**100.0**
1990 Det	11	73	13	19	68.4	34	34	100.0
1991 Det	16	97	19	28	67.9	40	40	100.0
1992 KC-TB	8	28	5	9	55.6	13	13	100.0
1992 KC	1	3	1	1	100.0	0	0	—
1992 TB	7	25	4	8	50.0	13	13	100.0
1993 Dal	14	122	28	33	84.8	38	38	100.0
1994 Phi	16	96	21	25	84.0	33	33	100.0
1995 Was	16	114	27	36	75.0	33	33	100.0
1997 Min	12	59	12	17	70.6	23	24	95.8
NFL Total	240	1532	337	445	75.7	521	527	98.9

FRANNY MURRAY Murray, Francis Thomas 6'0", 200 **DB-WB-HB**
Col: Pennsylvania *HS:* St. Joseph's Prep [Philadelphia, PA] B: 7/21/1915, Glenolden, PA D: 6/28/1998, Boca Raton, FL *Drafted:* 1937 Round 2 Phi
1939 Phi: Scor 26, 2-4 50.0% FG, 8-12 66.7% XK. **1940** Phi: Int 2-10; Scor 6, 0-1 FG, 6-8 75.0% XK. **Total:** Int 2-10; Scor 32, 2-5 40.0% FG, 14-20 70.0% XK.

		Rushing				Receiving			
Year Team	G	Att	Yds	Avg	TD	Rec	Yds	Avg	TD
1939 Phi	11	49	137	2.8	1	13	144	11.1	1
1940 Phi	11	8	7	0.9	0	12	125	10.4	0
NFL Total	22	57	144	2.5	1	25	269	10.8	1

	Punting			Tot
Year Team	Punts	Yds	Avg	TD
1939 Phi	33	1220	37.0	2
1940 Phi	30	1098	36.6	0
NFL Total	63	2318	36.8	2

JOCK MURRAY Murray, John T 6'1", 210 **OE-G**
Col: St. Thomas *HS:* Cathedral [Duluth, MN] B: 2/19/1904, Duluth, MN D: 7/17/1969, Minneapolis, MN
1926 Dul: 7 G.

JOE MURRAY Murray, Joseph Andrew 6'4", 265 **OG**
Col: USC *HS:* Loyola [Los Angeles, CA] B: 11/7/1960, Los Angeles, CA
1987 LARm: 3 G.

CALVIN MURRAY Murray, Leon Calvin 5'11", 185 **RB**
Col: Ohio State *HS:* Millville [NJ] B: 10/18/1958, Middle Twp., NJ *Drafted:* 1981 Round 4 Phi
1981 Phi: 7 G; Rush 23-134 5.8; Rec 1-7 7.0; KR 1-14 14.0. **1982** Phi: 1 G; KR 3-42 14.0. **Total:** 8 G; Rush 23-134 5.8; Rec 1-7 7.0; KR 4-56 14.0.

MARK MURRAY Murray, Mark Allan 6'2", 240 **LB**
Col: Florida *HS:* Apopka [FL] B: 10/15/1967, Orlando, FL
1991 Den: 6 G.

JAB MURRAY Murray, Richard John 6'1", 219 **T-E-C**
Col: Marquette *HS:* Marinette [WI] B: 10/28/1892, Oconto, WI Deceased
1921 GB: 6 G. **1922** GB-Rac: 11 G; Scor 1, 1 XK. GB: 3 G. Rac: 8 G; Scor 1, 1 XK. **1923** GB: 9 G. **1924** GB: 4 G. **Total:** 30 G.

WALTER MURRAY Murray, Walter Clyde Jr. 6'4", 200 **WR**
Col: Hawaii *HS:* Berkeley [CA] B: 12/13/1962, Berkeley, CA *Drafted:* 1986 Round 2 Was
1986 Ind: 5 G; Rec 2-34 17.0. **1987** Ind: 14 G; Rec 20-339 17.0 3 TD; 18 Pt. **Total:** 19 G; Rec 22-373 17.0 3 TD; 18 Pt.

ADRIAN MURRELL Murrell, Adrian Bryan 5'11", 214 **RB**
Col: West Virginia *HS:* Leilehua [Wahiawa, HI] B: 10/16/1970, Lafayette, LA *Drafted:* 1993 Round 5 NYJ

		Rushing				Receiving			
Year Team	G	Att	Yds	Avg	TD	Rec	Yds	Avg	TD
1993 NYJ	16	34	157	4.6	1	5	12	2.4	0
1994 NYJ	10	33	160	4.8	0	7	76	10.9	0
1995 NYJ	15	192	795	4.1	1	71	465	6.5	2

1996 NYJ	16	301	1249	4.1	6	17	81	4.8	1
1997 NYJ	16	300	1086	3.6	7	27	106	3.9	0
1998 Ariz	15	274	1042	3.8	8	18	169	9.4	2
NFL Total	88	1134	4489	4.0	23	145	909	6.3	5

	Kickoff Returns					Tot
Year Team	**Ret**	**Yds**	**Avg**	**TD**	**Fum**	**TD**
1993 NYJ	23	342	14.9	0	4	1
1994 NYJ	14	268	19.1	0	1	0
1995 NYJ	1	5	5.0	0	2	3
1996 NYJ	0	0	—	0	6	7
1997 NYJ	0	0	—	0	4	7
1998 Ariz	0	0	—	0	6	10
NFL Total	38	615	16.2	0	23	28

BILL MURRELL Murrell, William Ellis 6′3″, 220 **TE**
Col: Winston-Salem State *HS:* South Stokes [Walnut Cove, NC]
B: 6/14/1956, Walnut Cove, NC *Drafted:* 1979 Round 6 Pit
1979 StL: 12 G; Rec 2-20 10.0.

DON MURRY Murry, Donald Franklin 6′2″, 191 **T-E-G**
Col: Wisconsin *HS:* Taylorville, [IL]; Elderton HS [WI] B: 1900, Taylorville, IL D: 7/1951
1922 Rac: 4 G. **1924** Rac: 10 G. **1925** ChiB: 17 G; 6 Pt. **1926** ChiB: 15 G. **1927** ChiB: 11 G. **1928** ChiB: 12 G. **1929** ChiB: 14 G. **1930** ChiB: 11 G. **1931** ChiB: 13 G. **1932** ChiB: 5 G. **Total:** 112 G; 6 Pt.

MICKEY MURTAGH Murtagh, George Augustus 6′1″, 189 **C-G-E-BB**
Col: Georgetown *HS:* St. Peter's Prep [Jersey City, NJ] B: 4/8/1904, Jersey City, NJ D: 2/10/1993, Richmond, VA
1926 NYG: 11 G. **1927** NYG: 13 G. **1928** NYG: 10 G. **1929** NYG: 13 G; Rush 1 TD; 6 Pt. **1930** NYG: 11 G. **1931** NYG: 7 G. **1932** NYG: 6 G. **Total:** 71 G; Rush 1 TD; 6 Pt.

GREG MURTHA Murtha, Gregory Thomas 6′6″, 268 **OT**
Col: Minnesota *HS:* Southwest [Minneapolis, MN] B: 4/23/1957, Minneapolis, MN *Drafted:* 1980 Round 6 Phi
1982 Bal: 5 G.

TED MURTHA Murtha, Ted 5′11″, 205 **G-FB**
Col: No College *HS:* Aquinas [Columbus, OH] B: 1901 Deceased
1921 Col: 2 G.

BILL MUSGRAVE Musgrave, William Scott 6′2″, 199 **QB**
Col: Oregon *HS:* Grand Junction [CO] B: 11/11/1967, Grand Junction, CO *Drafted:* 1991 Round 4 Dal
1993 SF: Rush 3-(-3) -1.0. **1994** SF: Postseason only. **1995** Den: Rush 4-(-4) -1.0. **1996** Den: Rush 12-(-4) -0.3. **Total:** Rush 19-(-11) -0.6.

		Passing								
Year Team	**G**	**Att**	**Comp**	**Comp%**	**Yds**	**YPA**	**TD**	**Int**	**Rating**	**Fum**
1991 SF	1	5	4	80.0	33	6.60	1	0	133.8	0
1993 SF	1	0	0	—	0	—	0	0	—	0
1995 Den	4	12	8	66.7	93	7.75	0	0	89.9	1
1996 Den	6	52	31	59.6	276	5.31	0	2	57.9	3
NFL Total	12	69	43	62.3	402	5.83	1	2	71.0	4

SPAIN MUSGROVE Musgrove, Spain 6′4″, 275 **DT-DE**
Col: Bakersfield Coll. CA (J.C.); Utah State *HS:* Bakersfield [CA]
B: 7/30/1945, Kansas City, MO *Drafted:* 1967 Round 2 Was
1967 Was: 6 G. **1968** Was: 14 G. **1969** Was: 10 G. **1970** Hou: 7 G. **Total:** 37 G.

JIM MUSICK Musick, James Andrew 5′11″, 205 **FB-DB**
(Sweet) *Col:* USC *HS:* Santa Ana [CA] B: 5/5/1910, Kirksville, MO
D: 12/15/1992, Santa Ana, CA
1932 Bos: Pass 2-1 50.0%, 7 3.50 1 Int. **1933** Bos: Pass 36-11 30.6%, 151 4.19 14 Int; Rec 3-78 26.0; Scor 45, 1 FG, 12 XK. **1935** Bos: Pass 1-0; Scor 14, 2 XK. **1936** Bos: Pass 1-1 100.0%, 9 9.00. **Total:** Pass 40-13 32.5%, 167 4.18 15 Int; Rec 3-78 26.0; Scor 65, 1 FG, 14 XK.

		Rushing			
Year Team	**G**	**Att**	**Yds**	**Avg**	**TD**
1932 Bos	10	88	316	3.6	1
1933 Bos	12	**173**	**809**	4.7	5
1935 Bos	5	60	174	2.9	2
1936 Bos	6	6	14	2.3	0
NFL Total	33	327	1313	4.0	8

NEAL MUSSER Musser, James Neal 6′2″, 220 **LB**
Col: North Carolina State *HS:* Western Alamance [Elon, NC]
B: 3/20/1957, Elon, NC
1981 Atl: 7 G; Int 1-0. **1982** Atl: 8 G. **Total:** 15 G; Int 1-0.

GEORGE MUSSO Musso, George Francis 6′2″, 262 **G-T**
(Moose) *Col:* Millikin *HS:* Collinsville [IL] B: 4/8/1910, Collinsville, IL
HOF: 1982
1933 ChiB: 12 G; Scor **1** Saf; 2 Pt. **1934** ChiB: 12 G. **1935** ChiB: 12 G. **1936** ChiB: 12 G. **1937** ChiB: 11 G. **1938** ChiB: 11 G. **1939** ChiB: 11 G. **1940** ChiB: 6 G. **1941** ChiB: 10 G. **1942** ChiB: 11 G. **1943** ChiB: 10 G. **1944** ChiB: 10 G. **Total:** 128 G; Scor 1 Saf; 2 Pt.

JOHNNY MUSSO Musso, John Jr. 5′11″, 201 **RB**
(The Italian Stallion) *Col:* Alabama *HS:* Banks [Birmingham, AL]
B: 3/6/1950, Birmingham, AL *Drafted:* 1972 Round 3 ChiB
1976 ChiB: Rec 4-26 6.5; KR 2-18 9.0; Scor **1** Saf. **1977** ChiB: Rec 3-13 4.3; KR 5-100 20.0. **Total:** Rec 7-39 5.6; KR 7-118 16.9; Scor 1 Saf.

		Rushing				
Year Team	**G**	**Att**	**Yds**	**Avg**	**TD**	**Fum**
1975 ChiB	2	6	33	5.5	0	0
1976 ChiB	14	57	200	3.5	4	1
1977 ChiB	14	37	132	3.6	2	0
NFL Total	30	100	365	3.7	6	1

NAJEE MUSTAFAA Mustafaa, Najee 6′1″, 190 **DB**
(AKA Reginald Bernard Rutland) *Col:* Georgia Tech *HS:* Russell [East Point, GA] B: 6/20/1964, East Point, GA *Drafted:* 1987 Round 4 Min
1989 Min: 1 Fum TD. **Total:** 1 Fum TD.

		Interceptions				Tot
Year Team	**G**	**Int**	**Yds**	**TD**	**Fum**	**TD**
1987 Min	7	0	0	0	0	0
1988 Min	16	3	63	0	1	0
1989 Min	16	2	7	0	0	1
1990 Min	16	2	21	0	0	0
1991 Min	13	3	104	1	0	1
1993 Cle	14	1	97	1	0	1
1995 Oak	15	0	0	0	0	0
NFL Total	97	11	292	2	1	3

BRAD MUSTER Muster, Brad William 6′3″, 235 **RB**
Col: Stanford *HS:* San Marin [Novato, CA] B: 4/11/1965, Novato, CA
Drafted: 1988 Round 1 ChiB
1988 ChiB: KR 3-33 11.0. **1992** ChiB: Pass 1-0, 1 Int. **Total:** Pass 1-0, 1 Int; KR 3-33 11.0.

		Rushing				Receiving					Tot
Year Team	**G**	**Att**	**Yds**	**Avg**	**TD**	**Rec**	**Yds**	**Avg**	**TD**	**Fum**	**TD**
1988 ChiB	16	44	197	4.5	0	21	236	11.2	1	1	1
1989 ChiB	16	82	327	4.0	5	32	259	8.1	3	2	8
1990 ChiB	16	141	664	4.7	6	47	452	9.6	0	3	6
1991 ChiB	11	90	412	4.6	6	35	287	8.2	1	0	7
1992 ChiB	16	98	414	4.2	3	34	389	11.4	2	2	5
1993 NO	13	64	214	3.3	3	23	195	8.5	0	0	3
1994 NO	7	1	3	3.0	1	10	88	8.8	0	0	1
NFL Total	95	520	2231	4.3	24	202	1906	9.4	7	8	31

CHET MUTRYN Mutryn, Chester A 5′9″, 179 **HB-DB**
Col: Xavier (Ohio) *HS:* Cathedral Latin [Cleveland, OH] B: 3/12/1921, Cleveland, OH D: 3/24/1995, Cleveland, OH *Drafted:* 1943 Round 20 Phi
AAFC **1947** BufA: Int 1-11; Scor 73, 1-2 50.0% XK. **1948** BufA: Pass 6-2 33.3%, 21 3.50. **Total:** Pass 6-2 33.3%, 21 3.50; Int 1-11; Scor 229, 1-2 50.0% XK.

		Rushing				Receiving			
Year Team	**G**	**Att**	**Yds**	**Avg**	**TD**	**Rec**	**Yds**	**Avg**	**TD**
1946 BufA	14	57	289	5.1	1	7	168	24.0	3
1947 BufA	14	140	868	6.2	9	10	176	17.6	2
1948 BufA	14	147	823	5.6	10	39	794	20.4	5
1949 BufA	11	131	696	5.3	5	29	333	11.5	0
AAFC Total	53	475	2676	5.6	25	85	1471	17.3	10

	Punt Returns				Kickoff Returns				Tot
Year Team	**Ret**	**Yds**	**Avg**	**TD**	**Ret**	**Yds**	**Avg**	**TD**	**TD**
1946 BufA	5	57	11.4	0	4	79	19.8	0	5
1947 BufA	13	187	14.4	0	21	691	32.9	1	12
1948 BufA	10	171	17.1	1	19	500	26.3	0	16
1949 BufA	7	77	11.0	0	10	224	22.4	0	5
AAFC Total	35	492	14.1	1	54	1494	27.7	1	38

NFL **1950** Bal: Pass 1-1 100.0%, 4 4.00; PR 6-45 7.5; KR 19-408 21.5.

		Rushing				Receiving					Tot
Year Team	**G**	**Att**	**Yds**	**Avg**	**TD**	**Rec**	**Yds**	**Avg**	**TD**	**Fum**	**TD**
1950 Bal	12	108	355	3.3	2	36	379	10.5	2	5	4

JIM MUTSCHELLER Mutscheller, James Francis 6′1″, 205 **OE-DE**
Col: Notre Dame *HS:* Beaver Falls [PA] B: 3/31/1930, Beaver Falls, PA
Drafted: 1952 Round 12 Dal

		Receiving				
Year Team	**G**	**Rec**	**Yds**	**Avg**	**TD**	**Fum**
1954 Bal	12	1	49	49.0	0	0
1955 Bal	12	33	518	15.7	7	0
1956 Bal	12	44	715	16.3	6	1
1957 Bal	12	32	558	17.4	**8**	1
1958 Bal	12	28	504	18.0	7	0
1959 Bal	12	44	699	15.9	8	2
1960 Bal	11	18	271	15.1	2	0

1961 Bal	12	20	370	18.5	2	0
NFL Total	95	220	3684	16.7	40	4

STEVE MYER Myer, Steven Paul 6′2″, 191 **QB**
Col: Mount San Antonio Coll. CA (J.C.); New Mexico *HS:* West Covina [CA] B: 7/17/1954, Covina, CA *Drafted:* 1976 Round 4 Sea
1977 Sea: Rush 6-1 0.2. **1978** Sea: Rush 2-10 5.0. **1979** Sea: Rush 1-0. **Total:** Rush 9-11 1.2.

		Passing								
Year Team	**G**	**Att**	**Comp**	**Comp%**	**Yds**	**YPA**	**TD**	**Int**	**Rating**	**Fum**
1977 Sea	7	130	70	53.8	729	5.61	6	12	47.2	3
1978 Sea	4	22	11	50.0	94	4.27	0	2	23.7	0
1979 Sea	1	8	2	25.0	28	3.50	0	0	41.7	0
NFL Total	12	160	83	51.9	851	5.32	6	14	43.5	3

BRAD MYERS Myers, Bradford James 6′1″, 197 **HB-FB-OE-DB**
(Rookie) *Col:* Bucknell *HS:* Quarryville [PA]; Mercerberg Acad. [PA] B: 2/14/1929, Lancaster, PA *Drafted:* 1953 Round 9 LARm
1953 LARm: Rec 4-13 3.3; PR 1-1 1.0. **1956** LARm: PR 1-26 26.0; KR 3-57 19.0. **1958** Phi: Rec 4-25 6.3. **Total:** Rec 8-38 4.8; PR 2-27 13.5; KR 3-57 19.0.

		Rushing				
Year Team	**G**	**Att**	**Yds**	**Avg**	**TD**	**Fum**
1953 LARm	12	40	124	3.1	3	1
1956 LARm	5	6	33	5.5	0	1
1958 Phi	9	9	23	2.6	0	1
NFL Total	26	55	180	3.3	3	3

TRUCK MYERS Myers, Cyril Edward 6′0″, 177 **OE-T**
Col: Ohio State *HS:* Bucyrus [OH] B: 4/16/1897, Bucyrus, OH D: 7/19/1969, Winter Garden, FL
1922 Tol: 9 G; Scor 1, 1 XK. **1923** Cle: 5 G. **1925** Cle: 2 G. **Total:** 16 G.

DAVE MYERS Myers, David W 5′11″, 177 **G-BB-WB**
Col: New York U. *HS:* Stuyvesant [New York, NY] B: 11/11/1906, Brooklyn, NY D: 3/1972, New York, NY
1930 SI: 6 G. **1931** Bkn: 7 G. **Total:** 13 G.

DENNY MYERS Myers, Dennis Edward 6′1″, 206 **G**
Col: Iowa *HS:* Algona [IA] B: 11/10/1905, Algona, IA D: 5/30/1957, Newton, MA
1931 ChiB: 2 G.

FRANK MYERS Myers, Frank 6′5″, 255 **OT**
Col: Texas A&M *HS:* Central [San Angelo, TX] B: 1/4/1956, San Bernardino, CA *Drafted:* 1978 Round 5 Bal
1978 Min: 12 G. **1979** Min: 14 G. **Total:** 26 G.

GREG MYERS Myers, Gregory Jay 6′1″, 202 **DB**
Col: Colorado State *HS:* Windsor [CO] B: 9/30/1972, Tampa, FL *Drafted:* 1996 Round 5 Cin
1996 Cin: Int 2-10. **1997** Cin: Int 1-25. **Total:** Int 3-35.

		Punt Returns				
Year Team	**G**	**Ret**	**Yds**	**Avg**	**TD**	**Fum**
1996 Cin	14	9	51	5.7	0	1
1997 Cin	16	26	201	7.7	0	3
1998 Cin	16	0	0	—	0	0
NFL Total	46	35	252	7.2	0	4

JACK MYERS Myers, John Melvin 6′2″, 200 **FB-LB**
(Moose) *Col:* UCLA *HS:* Ventura [CA] B: 10/8/1924, St.Louis, MO *Drafted:* 1948 Round 3 Phi
1948 Phi: Int 2-9. **1949** Phi: KR 2-27 13.5. **1950** Phi: KR 2-25 12.5. **Total:** KR 4-52 13.0; Int 2-9.

		Rushing				Receiving				
Year Team	**G**	**Att**	**Yds**	**Avg**	**TD**	**Rec**	**Yds**	**Avg**	**TD**	**Fum**
1948 Phi	12	21	118	5.6	1	7	57	8.1	0	2
1949 Phi	12	48	182	3.8	1	7	98	14.0	0	1
1950 Phi	12	29	159	5.5	0	12	204	17.0	0	0
1952 LARm	12	27	82	3.0	1	2	1	0.5	0	1
NFL Total	48	125	541	4.3	3	28	360	12.9	0	4

MICHAEL MYERS Myers, Michael DeWayne 6′2″, 285 **DT**
Col: Hinds CC MS; Alabama *HS:* Vicksburg [MS] B: 1/20/1976, Vicksburg, MS *Drafted:* 1998 Round 4 Dal
1998 Dal: 16 G; 3 Sac.

CHIP MYERS Myers, Philip Leon III 6′5″, 210 **WR**
Col: Northwestern Okla. State *HS:* C.E. Donart [Stillwater, OK] B: 8/9/1945, Panama City, FL D: 2/22/1999, Long Lake, MN *Drafted:* 1967 Round 10 SF

		Receiving				
Year Team	**G**	**Rec**	**Yds**	**Avg**	**TD**	**Fum**
1967 SF	12	2	13	6.5	0	0
1969 Cin	14	10	205	20.5	2	0
1970 Cin	14	32	542	16.9	1	0
1971 Cin	10	27	286	10.6	1	1
1972 Cin	14	57	792	13.9	3	0
1973 Cin	5	7	77	11.0	0	0
1974 Cin	14	32	383	12.0	1	0
1975 Cin	13	36	527	14.6	3	0
1976 Cin	12	17	267	15.7	1	0
NFL Total	108	220	3092	14.1	12	1

BOB MYERS Myers, Robert Clarence 6′0″, 260 **DT**
Col: Ohio State *HS:* Springfield [OH] B: 1/31/1933, Springfield, OH *Drafted:* 1955 Round 28 Bal
1955 Bal: 1 G.

TOMMY MYERS Myers, Thomas Edward 5′8″, 170 **BB-WB**
Col: Fordham *HS:* Mahanoy City [PA] B: 2/9/1901, New Britain, CT D: 7/1/1944
1925 NYG: 2 G. **1926** Bkn: 2 G. **Total:** 4 G.

TOM MYERS Myers, Thomas Patrick 5′11″, 184 **DB**
Col: Syracuse *HS:* Pulaski [New Britain, CT] B: 10/24/1950, Cohoes, NY *Drafted:* 1972 Round 3 NO
1972 NO: PR 9-43 4.8. **1973** NO: Rush 1-8 8.0. **1975** NO: PR 10-70 7.0; **1** Fum TD. **1976** NO: PR 2-22 11.0; **1** Fum TD. **1981** NO: Pass 2-1 50.0%, 8 4.00 1 TD; Rush 2-(-3) -1.5. **Total:** Pass 2-1 50.0%, 8 4.00 1 TD; Rush 3-5 1.7; PR 21-135 6.4; 2 Fum TD.

		Interceptions				Tot
Year Team	**G**	**Int**	**Yds**	**TD**	**Fum**	**TD**
1972 NO	13	3	0	0	1	0
1973 NO	13	3	33	0	0	0
1974 NO	12	3	43	0	0	0
1975 NO	9	5	83	0	2	1
1976 NO	14	1	0	0	1	1
1977 NO	12	1	2	0	0	1
1978 NO	16	6	167	1	0	1
1979 NO	15	7	127	1	0	1
1980 NO	16	5	96	0	0	0
1981 NO	16	2	70	0	1	0
NFL Total	136	36	621	2	5	5

TOM MYERS Myers, Thomas William 6′1″, 188 **QB**
Col: Northwestern *HS:* Troy [OH] B: 8/13/1943, Piqua, OH *Drafted:* 1965 Round 4 Det
1965 Det: 1 G; Pass 5-3 60.0%, 16 3.20 1 Int. **1966** Det: 1 G; Pass 1-0, 1 Int. **Total:** 2 G; Pass 6-3 50.0%, 16 2.67 2 Int.

WILBUR MYERS Myers, Wilbur Lee 5′11″, 195 **DB**
Col: Delta State *HS:* Bassfield [MS] B: 8/17/1961, Bassfield, MS
1983 Den: 16 G.

STEVE MYHRA Myhra, Steven Murray 6′1″, 237 **OG-LB**
Col: Minnesota; North Dakota *HS:* Wahpeton [ND] B: 4/2/1934, Wahpeton, ND D: 8/4/1994, Detroit Lakes, MN *Drafted:* 1956 Round 12 Bal
1957 Bal: Rush 1-1 1.0; KR 1-19 19.0. **Total:** Rush 1-1 1.0; KR 1-19 19.0.

		Scoring						
Year Team	**G**	**Pts**	**FG**	**FGA**	**FG%**	**XK**	**XKA**	**XK%**
1957 Bal	12	26	4	6	66.7	14	16	87.5
1958 Bal	12	60	4	10	40.0	**48**	**51**	94.1
1959 Bal	12	68	6	17	35.3	**50**	**51**	98.0
1960 Bal	12	62	9	19	47.4	35	37	94.6
1961 Bal	14	96	**21**	**39**	53.8	33	34	97.1
NFL Total	62	312	44	91	48.4	180	189	95.2

DESHONE MYLES Myles, DeShone 6′2″, 235 **LB**
Col: Nevada-Reno *HS:* Cheyenne [North Las Vegas, NV] B: 10/31/1974, Las Vegas, NV *Drafted:* 1998 Round 4 Sea
1998 Sea: 12 G.

GODFREY MYLES Myles, Godfrey Clarence 6′1″, 240 **LB**
Col: Florida *HS:* Miami Carol City [Miami, FL] B: 9/22/1968, Miami, FL *Drafted:* 1991 Round 3 Dal
1991 Dal: 3 G. **1992** Dal: 16 G; Int 1-13. **1993** Dal: 10 G. **1994** Dal: 15 G. **1995** Dal: 16 G; Int 1-15. **1996** Dal: 16 G. **Total:** 76 G; Int 2-28.

HARRY MYLES Myles, Harry Seig 6′0″, 190 **OE-T-G**
Col: Hampden-Sydney *HS:* Greenbrier Mil. Acad. [Lewisburg, WV] B: 9/1/1904, Lewisburg, WV D: 11/30/1978, Orange Park, FL
1929 Buf: 5 G.

JESSE MYLES Myles, Jesse James 5′10″, 210 **RB**
Col: Louisiana State *HS:* H.L. Bourgeois [Gray, LA] B: 9/28/1960, New Orleans, LA
1983 Den: 16 G; Rush 8-52 6.5; Rec 7-119 17.0 1 TD; 6 Pt. **1984** Den: 7 G; Rush 5-7 1.4; Rec 2-22 11.0. **Total:** 23 G; Rush 13-59 4.5; Rec 9-141 15.7 1 TD; 6 Pt.

CHIP MYRTLE Myrtle, Charles Joseph Jr. 6′2″, 225 **LB**
Col: Maryland *HS:* John Carroll [Washington, DC] B: 2/6/1945, Hyattsville, MD
1967 Den: 14 G; Int 1-1. **1968** Den: 13 G; Rec 1-18 18.0; Scor **1** Saf; 2 Pt. **1969** Den: 12 G; KR 1-0. **1970** Den: 14 G; KR 1-1 1.0. **1971** Den: 14 G;

Int 3-64. **1972** Den: 14 G. **1974** SD: 8 G. **Total:** 89 G; Rec 1-18 18.0; KR 2-1 0.5; Int 4-65; Scor 1 Saf; 2 Pt.

TOM MYSLINSKI Myslinski, Thomas Joseph Jr. 6'3", 293 **OG**
Col: Tennessee *HS:* Rome Free Acad. [NY] B: 12/7/1968, Rome, NY
Drafted: 1992 Round 4 Dal
1992 Was: 1 G. **1993** Buf-ChiB: 2 G. Buf: 1 G. ChiB: 1 G. **1994** ChiB: 4 G. **1995** Jac: 9 G. **1996** Pit: 8 G. **1997** Pit: 16 G. **1998** Ind: 4 G. **Total:** 44 G.

ROLAND NABORS Nabors, Roland Richard 6'2", 200 **LB-C**
(Tuffy) *Col:* Texas Tech *HS:* Lubbock [TX] B: 7/22/1924, Meadow, TX
AAFC **1948** NY-A: 10 G; Int 1-10.

ANDY NACRELLI Nacrelli, Andrew Frank 6'1", 190 **OE**
Col: Fordham *HS:* St. James [Chester, PA] B: 8/15/1933, Chester, PA
D: 9/23/1991, Lake Oswego, OR *Drafted:* 1955 Round 12 Phi
1958 Phi: 2 G; Rec 2-15 7.5.

PEACHES NADOLNEY Nadolney, Romanus Frank 5'11", 211 **G-T**
Col: Notre Dame *HS:* Ironwood [MI] B: 5/23/1899, WI D: 2/21/1963, Houston, TX
1922 GB: 8 G. **1923** Mil: 3 G. **1924** Mil: 3 G. **1925** Mil: 6 G. **Total:** 20 G.

CHRIS NAEOLE Naeole, Chris Kealoha 6'3", 313 **OG**
Col: Colorado *HS:* Kahuka [Kaaawa, HI] B: 12/25/1974, Kailua, HI
Drafted: 1997 Round 1 NO
1997 NO: 4 G. **1998** NO: 16 G. **Total:** 20 G.

DANA NAFZIGER Nafziger, Dana Albert 6'1", 220 **LB-TE**
Col: Cal Poly-S.L.O. *HS:* Western [Anaheim, CA] B: 10/26/1953, Woodstock, IL
1977 TB: 14 G; Rec 9-119 13.2; KR 1-4 4.0. **1978** TB: 14 G. **1979** TB: 16 G; KR 2-36 18.0. **1981** TB: 16 G. **1982** TB: 8 G. **Total:** 68 G; Rec 9-119 13.2; KR 3-40 13.3.

RAY NAGEL Nagel, Raymond Robert 5'11", 177 **QB**
Col: UCLA *HS:* Los Angeles [CA] B: 5/18/1927, Los Angeles, CA
1953 ChiC: Rush 4-8 2.0.

		Passing								
Year Team	**G**	**Att**	**Comp**	**Comp%**	**Yds**	**YPA**	**TD**	**Int**	**Rating**	**Fum**
1953 ChiC	4	62	30	48.4	192	3.10	0	5	21.7	2

ROSS NAGEL Nagel, Ross Otto 6'4", 234 **DT-OT**
Col: St. Louis *HS:* Maplewood [MO] B: 6/12/1923, St.Louis, MO
D: 2/12/1997, Waco, TX
1942 ChiC: 1 G. **1951** NYY: 9 G; Int 1-27. **Total:** 10 G; Int 1-27.

BILL NAGIDA Nagida, William 180 **BB**
Col: No College
1926 Ham: 1 G.

BROWNING NAGLE Nagle, Browning Kenneth 6'3", 225 **QB**
Col: West Virginia; Louisville *HS:* Pinellas Park [Largo, FL]
B: 4/29/1968, Philadelphia, PA *Drafted:* 1991 Round 2 NYJ

		Passing							
Year Team	**G**	**Att**	**Comp**	**Comp%**	**Yds**	**YPA**	**TD**	**Int**	**Rating**
1991 NYJ	1	2	1	50.0	10	5.00	0	0	64.6
1992 NYJ	14	387	192	49.6	2280	5.89	7	17	55.7
1993 NYJ	3	14	6	42.9	71	5.07	0	0	58.9
1994 Ind	1	21	8	38.1	69	3.29	0	1	27.7
1996 Atl	5	13	6	46.2	59	4.54	1	2	45.5
NFL Total	24	437	213	48.7	2489	5.70	8	20	53.5

	Rushing				
Year Team	**Att**	**Yds**	**Avg**	**TD**	**Fum**
1991 NYJ	1	-1	-1.0	0	0
1992 NYJ	24	57	2.4	0	12
1994 Ind	1	12	12.0	0	2
1996 Atl	0	0	—	0	1
NFL Total	26	68	2.6	0	15

JOHNNY NAGLE Nagle, John C 5'9", 175 **OE**
Col: No College B: 8/4/1893, Reading, PA D: 11/5/1974, Emmaus, PA
1921 NYG: 1 G.

GERN NAGLER Nagler, Robert Gern 6'2", 190 **OE**
Col: Santa Clara *HS:* Marysville [CA] B: 2/23/1932, Yuba City, CA

		Receiving				
Year Team	**G**	**Rec**	**Yds**	**Avg**	**TD**	**Fum**
1953 ChiC	11	43	610	14.2	6	0
1955 ChiC	11	7	218	31.1	3	0
1956 ChiC	8	14	268	19.1	4	1
1957 ChiC	12	27	475	17.6	4	0
1958 ChiC	12	36	469	13.0	5	1
1959 Pit	12	14	222	15.9	2	0
1960 Cle	12	36	616	17.1	3	1
1961 Cle	13	19	241	12.7	1	0
NFL Total	91	196	3119	15.9	28	3

BRONKO NAGURSKI Nagurski, Bronislaw 6'2", 226 **FB-LB-T**
Col: Minnesota *HS:* Bemidji [MN]; Falls HS [International Falls, MN]
B: 11/3/1908, Rainy River, Canada D: 1/7/1990, International Falls, MN
HOF: 1963
1932 ChiB: Rec 6-67 11.2. **1933** ChiB: Rec 1-23 23.0; Scor 7, 1 XK. **1934** ChiB: Rec 3-32 10.7; Scor 44, 2 XK. **1936** ChiB: Rec 1-12 12.0; Scor 19, 1 XK. **Total:** Rec 11-134 12.2.

		Passing							
Year Team	**G**	**Att**	**Comp**	**Comp%**	**Yds**	**YPA**	**TD**	**Int**	**Rating**
1930 ChiB	13	—	—	—	—	—	0	—	—
1931 ChiB	10	—	—	—	—	—	0	—	—
1932 ChiB	14	26	11	42.3	150	5.77	3	2	67.8
1933 ChiB	13	27	14	51.9	233	8.63	0	3	41.7
1934 ChiB	13	14	5	35.7	48	3.43	2	1	56.0
1935 ChiB	5	3	0	0.0	0	0.00	0	1	0.0
1936 ChiB	11	5	1	20.0	8	1.60	1	2	39.6
1937 ChiB	10	2	1	50.0	35	17.50	1	0	135.4
1943 ChiB	8	0	0	—	0	—	0	0	—
NFL Total	97	77	32	41.6	474	6.16	7	9	53.1

	Rushing			
Year Team	**Att**	**Yds**	**Avg**	**TD**
1930 ChiB	—	—	—	5
1931 ChiB	—	—	—	2
1932 ChiB	121	533	4.4	**4**
1933 ChiB	128	533	4.2	1
1934 ChiB	123	586	4.8	7
1935 ChiB	50	170	3.4	1
1936 ChiB	122	529	4.3	3
1937 ChiB	73	343	4.7	1
1943 ChiB	16	84	5.3	1
NFL Total	633	2778	4.4	25

JAMIE NAILS Nails, Jamie Marcellus 6'6", 354 **OT**
Col: Florida A&M *HS:* Appling Co. [Baxley, GA] B: 6/3/1975, Baxley, GA *Drafted:* 1997 Round 4 Buf
1997 Buf: 2 G. **1998** Buf: 15 G. **Total:** 17 G.

JOHN NAIOTI Naioti, John F 5'10", 180 **DB-HB**
(Tim) *Col:* St. Francis (Pa.) *HS:* Fulton [NY] B: 11/6/1921, Fulton, NY
D: 9/5/1990
1942 Pit: 1 G. **1945** Pit: 6 G; Rush 1-(-17) -17.0; Rec 2-14 7.0; Scor 4, 4-4 100.0% XK; 1 Fum. **Total:** 7 G; Rush 1-(-17) -17.0; Rec 2-14 7.0; Scor 4, 4-4 100.0% XK; 1 Fum.

RALPH NAIRAN Nairan, Roger 5'11", 185 **E-WB**
Col: Trinity (Tex.) B: 1902
1926 Buf: 3 G.

ROB NAIRNE Nairne, Robert Carlton 6'4", 223 **LB**
Col: Oregon State *HS:* Ferndale [CA] B: 3/24/1954, Redding, CA
1977 Den: 13 G; KR 1-1 1.0. **1978** Den: 16 G. **1979** Den: 10 G; 6 Pt. **1980** Den: 16 G; Int 1-2. **1981** NO: 16 G; Int 1-18. **1982** NO: 9 G; Int 1-1; 1 Sac. **1983** NO: 16 G; 2 Sac. **Total:** 96 G; KR 1-1 1.0; Int 3-21; 6 Pt; 3 Sac.

PETE NAJARIAN Najarian, Peter Michael 6'2", 233 **LB**
Col: Minnesota *HS:* Central [Minneapolis, MN] B: 12/22/1963, San Francisco, CA
1987 Min: 5 G. **1988** TB: 1 G. **1989** TB: 12 G. **Total:** 18 G.

TOM NALEN Nalen, Thomas Andrew 6'2", 286 **C-OG**
Col: Boston College *HS:* Foxboro [MA] B: 5/13/1971, Boston, MA
Drafted: 1994 Round 7 Den
1994 Den: 7 G. **1995** Den: 15 G. **1996** Den: 16 G. **1997** Den: 16 G; Rec 1-(-1) -1.0. **1998** Den: 16 G. **Total:** 70 G; Rec 1-(-1) -1.0.

JOE NAMATH Namath, Joseph William 6'2", 200 **QB**
(Broadway Joe) *Col:* Alabama *HS:* Beaver Falls [PA] B: 5/31/1943, Beaver Falls, PA *Drafted:* 1965 Round 1 NYJ *HOF:* 1985
1967 NYJ: **1** Fum TD. **Total:** 1 Fum TD.

		Passing							
Year Team	**G**	**Att**	**Comp**	**Comp%**	**Yds**	**YPA**	**TD**	**Int**	**Rating**
1965 NYJ	13	340	164	48.2	2220	6.53	18	15	68.8
1966 NYJ	14	**471**	**232**	49.3	**3379**	7.17	19	27	62.6
1967 NYJ	14	**491**	**258**	52.5	**4007**	**8.16**	26	28	73.8
1968 NYJ	14	380	187	49.2	3147	8.28	15	17	72.1
1969 NYJ	14	361	185	51.2	2734	7.57	19	17	74.3
1970 NYJ	5	179	90	50.3	1259	7.03	5	12	54.7
1971 NYJ	4	59	28	47.5	537	9.10	5	6	68.2
1972 NYJ	13	324	162	50.0	**2816**	8.69	**19**	21	72.5
1973 NYJ	6	133	68	51.1	966	7.26	5	6	68.7
1974 NYJ	14	361	191	52.9	2616	7.25	20	22	69.4
1975 NYJ	14	326	157	48.2	2286	7.01	15	28	51.0
1976 NYJ	11	230	114	49.6	1090	4.74	4	16	39.9
1977 LARm	4	107	50	46.7	606	5.66	3	5	54.5
NFL Total	140	3762	1886	50.1	27663	7.35	173	220	65.5

Year Team	Rushing Att	Yds	Avg	TD	Fum	Tot TD
1965 NYJ	8	19	2.4	0	6	0
1966 NYJ	6	42	7.0	2	1	2
1967 NYJ	6	14	2.3	0	2	1
1968 NYJ	5	11	2.2	2	1	2
1969 NYJ	11	33	3.0	2	3	2
1970 NYJ	1	-1	-1.0	0	1	0
1971 NYJ	3	-1	-0.3	0	0	0
1972 NYJ	6	8	1.3	0	3	0
1973 NYJ	1	-2	-2.0	0	1	0
1974 NYJ	8	1	0.1	1	6	1
1975 NYJ	10	6	0.6	0	4	0
1976 NYJ	2	5	2.5	0	3	0
1977 LARm	4	5	1.3	0	2	0
NFL Total	71	140	2.0	7	33	8

JIM NANCE Nance, James Solomon 6′1″, 235 **RB**
Col: Syracuse *HS:* Indiana [PA] B: 12/30/1942, Indiana, PA
D: 6/16/1992, Quincy, MA *Drafted:* 1965 Round 19 Bos
1965 Bos: PR 1-16 16.0; KR 3-40 13.3. **Total:** PR 1-16 16.0; KR 3-40 13.3.

Year Team	G	Rushing Att	Yds	Avg	TD	Receiving Rec	Yds	Avg	TD	Fum	Tot TD
1965 Bos	14	111	321	2.9	5	12	83	6.9	0	2	5
1966 Bos	14	**299**	**1458**	4.9	**11**	8	103	12.9	0	7	11
1967 Bos	14	**269**	**1216**	4.5	7	22	196	8.9	1	10	8
1968 Bos	12	177	593	3.4	4	14	51	3.6	0	2	4
1969 Bos	14	**193**	750	3.9	6	29	168	5.8	0	1	6
1970 Bos	13	145	522	3.6	7	26	148	5.7	0	6	7
1971 NE	13	129	463	3.6	5	18	95	5.3	0	2	5
1973 NYJ	7	18	78	4.3	0	4	26	6.5	0	0	0
NFL Total	101	1341	5401	4.0	45	133	870	6.5	1	30	46

WALTER NAPIER Napier, Walter 6′4″, 270 **DT**
Col: Paul Quinn *HS:* A.J. Moore [Waco, TX] B: 8/27/1932, Waco, TX
1960 DalT: 14 G. **1961** DalT: 6 G. **Total:** 20 G.

BOB NAPONIC Naponic, Robert Andrew 6′0″, 190 **QB**
Col: Illinois *HS:* Hempfield Area [Greensburg, PA] B: 3/9/1947, Greensburg, PA *Drafted:* 1969 Round 10 Hou
1970 Hou: 2 G; Pass 20-6 30.0%, 85 4.25 2 Int; Rush 3-12 4.0; 1 Fum.

ERIC NAPOSKI Naposki, Eric Andrew 6′2″, 230 **LB**
Col: Connecticut *HS:* Eastchester [NY] B: 12/20/1966, New York, NY
1988 NE: 3 G. **1989** NE-Ind: 2 G. NE: 1 G. Ind: 1 G. **Total:** 5 G.

NICK NARDACCI Nardacci, Nicholas James 5′10″, 160 **TB-WB**
Col: West Virginia *HS:* Rayen [Youngstown, OH] B: 1903, Youngstown, OH D: 8/30/1961, Youngstown, OH
1925 Cle: 2 G.

DICK NARDI Nardi, Richard Louis 5′10″, 200 **DB-WB-HB-TB**
Col: Ohio State *HS:* Collinwood [Cleveland, OH] B: 9/25/1915, Cleveland, OH D: 12/1972 *Drafted:* 1938 Round 6 Det
1939 Pit-Bkn: Pass 5-2 40.0%, 12 2.40 1 Int; Rec 1-3 3.0; Punt 1-19 19.0. Pit: Pass 5-2 40.0%, 12 2.40 1 Int; Punt 1-19 19.0. Bkn: Rec 1-3 3.0. **Total:** Pass 5-2 40.0%, 12 2.40 1 Int; Rec 1-3 3.0; Punt 1-19 19.0.

Year Team	G	Rushing Att	Yds	Avg	TD
1938 Det	8	20	109	5.5	0
1939 Pit-Bkn	6	10	15	1.5	0
1939 Pit	3	8	10	1.3	0
1939 Bkn	3	2	5	2.5	0
NFL Total	14	30	124	4.1	0

JOE NASH Nash, Joseph Andrew 6′3″, 267 **NT-DT**
Col: Boston College *HS:* Boston College [MA] B: 10/11/1960, Boston, MA
1982 Sea: 7 G; 1 Sac. **1983** Sea: 16 G; 3 Sac. **1984** Sea: 16 G; **1** Fum TD; 6 Pt; 7 Sac. **1985** Sea: 16 G; 9 Sac. **1986** Sea: 16 G; 5 Sac. **1987** Sea: 12 G; 3.5 Sac. **1988** Sea: 15 G; 2 Sac. **1989** Sea: 16 G; 8 Sac. **1990** Sea: 16 G; 1 Sac. **1991** Sea: 16 G. **1992** Sea: 16 G; 4.5 Sac. **1993** Sea: 16 G; Int 1-13 1 TD; 6 Pt; 0.5 Sac. **1994** Sea: 16 G; 2 Sac. **1995** Sea: 16 G; 1 Sac. **1996** Sea: 8 G. **Total:** 218 G; Int 1-13 1 TD; 1 Fum TD; Tot TD 2; 12 Pt; 47.5 Sac.

KENNY NASH Nash, Kenneth 6′2″, 193 **WR**
Col: San Jose State *HS:* Esperanza [Anaheim, CA] B: 10/28/1962, Los Angeles, CA
1987 KC: 1 G; Rec 2-22 11.0.

MARCUS NASH Nash, Marcus DeLando 6′3″, 195 **WR**
Col: Tennessee *HS:* Edmond Memorial [OK] B: 2/1/1976, Tulsa, OK
Drafted: 1998 Round 1 Den
1998 Den: 8 G; Rec 4-76 19.0.

BOB NASH Nash, Robert Arthur 6′1″, 205 **T-OE**
(Nasty) *Col:* Cornell; Rutgers *HS:* Bernards [Bernardsville, NJ]
B: 12/16/1892, County Meathe, Ireland D: 2/1/1977, Winsted, CT
1920 Akr: 9 G. **1921** Buf: 11 G; 1 Fum TD; 6 Pt. **1922** Buf: 2 G. **1923** Buf: 6 G. **1924** Roch: 2 G. **1925** NYG: 3 G. **Total:** 33 G; 1 Fum TD; 6 Pt.

TOM NASH Nash, Thomas Acton Jr. 6′3″, 208 **E**
Col: Georgia *HS:* Washington [GA] B: 11/21/1905, Lincoln Co., GA
D: 8/24/1972, Washington, GA
1928 GB: 8 G. **1929** GB: 10 G; Rec 1 TD; 6 Pt. **1930** GB: 12 G; Rec 1 TD; 6 Pt. **1931** GB: 13 G; 6 Pt. **1932** GB: 10 G; Rec 3-50 16.7; Scor 1 Saf; 2 Pt. **1933** Bkn: 9 G; Rec 9-184 20.4 2 TD; 12 Pt. **1934** Bkn: 3 G. **Total:** 65 G; Rec 12-234 19.5 4 TD; Scor 1 Saf; Tot TD 5; 32 Pt.

ED NASON Nason, Edward Earl 5′8″, 185 **T-WB**
(AKA Running Deer) *Col:* No College B: 4/8/1899 D: 3/9/1977, Wichita, KS
1922 Oor: 4 G. **1923** Oor: 6 G. **Total:** 10 G.

TONY NATHAN Nathan, Tony Curtis 6′0″, 206 **RB**
Col: Alabama *HS:* Woodlawn [Birmingham, AL] B: 12/14/1956, Birmingham, AL *Drafted:* 1979 Round 3 Mia
1980 Mia: Pass 1-0. **1981** Mia: Pass 1-0. **1982** Mia: Pass 2-1 50.0%, 15 7.50 1 TD. **1983** Mia: Pass 4-3 75.0%, 46 11.50. **Total:** Pass 8-4 50.0%, 61 7.63 1 TD.

Year Team	G	Rushing Att	Yds	Avg	TD	Receiving Rec	Yds	Avg	TD
1979 Mia	16	16	68	4.3	0	17	213	12.5	2
1980 Mia	16	60	327	5.5	1	57	588	10.3	5
1981 Mia	13	147	782	**5.3**	5	50	452	9.0	3
1982 Mia	8	66	233	3.5	1	16	114	7.1	0
1983 Mia	16	151	685	4.5	3	52	461	8.9	1
1984 Mia	16	118	558	4.7	1	61	579	9.5	2
1985 Mia	16	143	667	4.7	5	72	651	9.0	1
1986 Mia	16	27	203	7.5	0	48	457	9.5	2
1987 Mia	6	4	20	5.0	0	10	77	7.7	0
NFL Total	123	732	3543	4.8	16	383	3592	9.4	16

Year Team	Punt Returns Ret	Yds	Avg	TD	Kickoff Returns Ret	Yds	Avg	TD	Fum	Tot TD
1979 Mia	28	306	10.9	1	45	1016	22.6	0	8	3
1980 Mia	23	178	7.7	0	5	102	20.4	0	9	6
1981 Mia	0	0	—	0	0	0	—	0	2	8
1982 Mia	0	0	—	0	0	0	—	0	2	1
1983 Mia	0	0	—	0	3	15	5.0	0	2	4
1984 Mia	0	0	—	0	0	0	—	0	3	3
1985 Mia	0	0	—	0	0	0	—	0	7	6
1986 Mia	0	0	—	0	0	0	—	0	0	2
1987 Mia	0	0	—	0	0	0	—	0	1	0
NFL Total	51	484	9.5	1	53	1133	21.4	0	34	33

ANDY NATOWICH Natowich, Andrew 5′10″, 175 **HB-DB**
(Bubby) *Col:* Holy Cross *HS:* Ansonia [CT] B: 12/11/1918, Derby, CT
1944 Was: 1 G; KR 1-16 16.0.

RICKY NATTIEL Nattiel, Ricky Rennard 5′9″, 180 **WR**
Col: Florida *HS:* Newberry [FL] B: 1/25/1966, Gainesville, FL
Drafted: 1987 Round 1 Den
1987 Den: Rush 2-13 6.5; KR 4-78 19.5. **1988** Den: Pass 1-0; Rush 5-51 10.2; KR 6-124 20.7. **1990** Den: KR 1-0. **Total:** Pass 1-0; Rush 7-64 9.1; KR 11-202 18.4.

Year Team	G	Receiving Rec	Yds	Avg	TD	Punt Returns Ret	Yds	Avg	TD	Fum
1987 Den	12	31	630	20.3	2	12	73	6.1	0	2
1988 Den	15	46	574	12.5	1	23	223	9.7	0	3
1989 Den	8	10	183	18.3	1	9	77	8.6	0	2
1990 Den	15	18	297	16.5	2	1	5	5.0	0	0
1991 Den	16	16	288	18.0	2	10	43	4.3	0	2
1992 Den	4	0	0	—	0	0	0	—	0	0
NFL Total	70	121	1972	16.3	8	55	421	7.7	0	9

FRED NAUMETZ Naumetz, Frederick 6′1″, 222 **C-LB**
Col: Boston College *HS:* Newburyport [MA] B: 3/28/1922, Newburyport, MA D: 1/2/1998, Thousand Oaks, CA
1946 LARm: 11 G; Int 1-1. **1947** LARm: 12 G; KR 1-0; Int 1-9. **1948** LARm: 11 G; Int 4-75. **1949** LARm: 12 G. **1950** LARm: 12 G; Int 1-13. **Total:** 58 G; KR 1-0; Int 7-98.

PAUL NAUMOFF Naumoff, Paul Peter 6′1″, 215 **LB**
Col: Tennessee *HS:* Eastmoor [Columbus, OH] B: 7/3/1945, Columbus, OH *Drafted:* 1967 Round 3 Det
1967 Det: 14 G. **1968** Det: 14 G; Int 1-3. **1969** Det: 14 G. **1970** Det: 14 G; KR 2-6 3.0. **1971** Det: 14 G. **1972** Det: 14 G; Int 1-4. **1973** Det: 14 G. **1974** Det: 14 G; Int 1-8. **1975** Det: 14 G; Int 2-11. **1976** Det: 14 G. **1977** Det: 13 G. **1978** Det: 15 G; Int 1-12. **Total:** 168 G; KR 2-6 3.0; Int 6-38.

JOHNNY NAUMU Naumu, John Punualii 5'8", 175 **HB**
Col: Hawaii; USC *HS:* McKinley [Honolulu, HI] B: 9/30/1919, Hooehva, HI
AAFC **1948** LA-A: 9 G; Rush 1-0; KR 6-131 21.8; Punt 1-34 34.0.

STEVE NAVE Nave, Stevan Lewis 6'2", 250 **LB**
Col: Kansas *HS:* Field Kindley [Coffeyville, KS] B: 8/29/1963, Nowata, OK
1987 Cle: 2 G.

CLEM NEACY Neacy, Clement Francis 6'3", 206 **E-T**
Col: Wis.-Milwaukee; Colgate *HS:* South Division [Milwaukee, WI] B: 7/19/1898, Milwaukee, WI D: 3/19/1968, Palos Verdes Estates, CA
1924 Mil: 13 G; Rec 2 TD; 12 Pt. **1925** Mil: 6 G; 1 Fum TD; 6 Pt. **1926** Mil: 9 G. **1927** Dul-ChiB: 8 G. Dul: 6 G. ChiB: 2 G. **1928** ChiC: 6 G. **Total:** 42 G; Rec 2 TD; 1 Fum TD; Tot TD 3; 18 Pt.

FRANKIE NEAL Neal, Frankie Leon 6'1", 202 **WR**
Col: Florida; Fort Hays State *HS:* Okeechobee [FL] B: 10/1/1965, Sebring, FL *Drafted:* 1987 Round 3 GB
1987 GB: Pass 1-0; Rush 1-0; KR 4-44 11.0.

		Receiving				
Year Team	**G**	**Rec**	**Yds**	**Avg**	**TD**	**Fum**
1987 GB	12	36	420	11.7	3	1

LEON NEAL Neal, Leon Kamli 5'9", 185 **RB**
Col: Washington *HS:* Paramount [CA] B: 9/11/1972, St. Paul, MN *Drafted:* 1996 Round 6 Buf
1997 Ind: 1 G; KR 1-23 23.0.

LORENZO NEAL Neal, Lorenzo LaVonne 5'11", 240 **RB**
Col: Fresno State *HS:* Lemoore [CA] B: 12/27/1970, Hanford, CA *Drafted:* 1993 Round 4 NO
1994 NO: KR 1-17 17.0. **1995** NO: KR 2-28 14.0. **1997** NYJ: KR 2-22 11.0. **Total:** KR 5-67 13.4.

		Rushing				Receiving					Tot
Year Team	**G**	**Att**	**Yds**	**Avg**	**TD**	**Rec**	**Yds**	**Avg**	**TD**	**Fum**	**TD**
1993 NO	2	21	175	8.3	1	0	0	—	0	1	1
1994 NO	16	30	90	3.0	1	2	9	4.5	0	1	1
1995 NO	16	5	3	0.6	0	12	123	10.3	1	2	1
1996 NO	16	21	58	2.8	1	31	194	6.3	1	1	2
1997 NYJ	16	10	28	2.8	0	8	40	5.0	1	0	1
1998 TB	16	5	25	5.0	0	5	14	2.8	1	0	1
NFL Total	82	92	379	4.1	3	58	380	6.6	4	5	7

LOUIS NEAL Neal, Louis Charles 6'4", 215 **WR**
Col: Prairie View A&M *HS:* Woodrow Wilson [San Francisco, CA] B: 1/10/1951, San Francisco, CA *Drafted:* 1973 Round 5 Oak
1973 Atl: 5 G; Rec 5-131 26.2 1 TD; 6 Pt. **1974** Atl: 10 G; Rush 1-(-1) -1.0; Rec 8-99 12.4; 1 Fum. **Total:** 15 G; Rush 1-(-1) -1.0; Rec 13-230 17.7 1 TD; 6 Pt; 1 Fum.

RANDY NEAL Neal, Randy Peter 6'3", 236 **LB**
Col: Virginia *HS:* Hackensack [NJ] B: 12/29/1972, Hackensack, NJ
1995 Cin: 2 G. **1996** Cin: 1 G. **1998** SF: 1 G. **Total:** 4 G.

RAY NEAL Neal, Raymond Robert 5'9", 211 **T-G**
(Gaumy) *Col:* Wabash; Washington & Jefferson *HS:* Mellott [IN]; Wingate HS [IN] B: 11/1/1897, Mellott, IN D: 11/25/1977, Greencastle, IN
1922 Akr: 10 G. **1924** Ham: 5 G. **1925** Ham: 5 G; 1 Fum TD; 6 Pt. **1926** Ham: 2 G. **Total:** 22 G; 1 Fum TD; 6 Pt.

RICHARD NEAL Neal, Richard 6'3", 260 **DE-DT**
Col: Southern University *HS:* Booker T. Washington [Shreveport, LA] B: 9/2/1947, Minden, LA D: 4/3/1983, St. Louis, MO *Drafted:* 1969 Round 2 NO
1969 NO: 14 G. **1970** NO: 12 G. **1971** NO: 14 G. **1972** NO: 14 G; 6 Pt. **1973** NYJ: 14 G. **1974** NYJ: 14 G. **1975** NYJ: 9 G. **1976** NYJ: 13 G. **1977** NYJ: 14 G. **1978** NO: 2 G. **Total:** 120 G; 6 Pt.

SPEEDY NEAL Neal, Robert 6'2", 254 **RB**
Col: Miami (Fla.) *HS:* Key West [FL] B: 8/26/1962, Key West, FL *Drafted:* 1984 Round 3 Buf
1984 Buf: Rec 9-76 8.4.

		Rushing			
Year Team	**G**	**Att**	**Yds**	**Avg**	**TD**
1984 Buf	12	49	175	3.6	1

DAN NEAL Neal, Thomas Daniel 6'4", 250 **C-OG**
Col: Kentucky *HS:* Atherton [Louisville, KY] B: 8/30/1949, Corbin, KY *Drafted:* 1973 Round 11 Bal
1973 Bal: 5 G. **1974** Bal: 14 G. **1975** ChiB: 6 G. **1976** ChiB: 14 G. **1977** ChiB: 14 G. **1978** ChiB: 16 G. **1979** ChiB: 16 G. **1980** ChiB: 16 G. **1981** ChiB: 16 G; Rush 1-(-6) -6.0; 2 Fum. **1982** ChiB: 9 G. **1983** ChiB: 8 G. **Total:** 134 G; Rush 1-(-6) -6.0; 2 Fum.

ED NEAL Neal, William Henry Edward 6'4", 285 **DG-DT-OT-OG**
Col: Tulane; Louisiana State; Ouachita Baptist B: 12/30/1918, Wichita Falls, TX D: 12/27/1984, Euless, TX
1945 GB: 9 G. **1946** GB: 10 G. **1947** GB: 12 G; 6 Pt. **1948** GB: 12 G. **1949** GB: 12 G; 1 Fum. **1950** GB: 12 G. **1951** GB-ChiB: 5 G. GB: 1 G. ChiB: 4 G. **Total:** 72 G; 6 Pt; 1 Fum.

RAY NEALY Nealy, Ray T 5'11", 220 **RB**
Col: Arkansas-Pine Bluff *HS:* Little Rock Central [AR] B: 4/30/1975, Little Rock, AR
1997 Mia: 1 G; Rush 1-2 2.0.

MIKE NEASE Nease, Michael Ray 6'3", 272 **OG**
Col: Tennessee-Chattanooga *HS:* South Greene [Greeneville, TN] B: 10/30/1961, Morristown, TN
1987 Phi: 2 G.

TOMMY NECK Neck, Thomas Ulric 5'11", 190 **DB**
Col: Louisiana State *HS:* Marksville [LA] B: 1/10/1939, Marksville, LA *Drafted:* 1962 Round 18 ChiB
1962 ChiB: 1 G.

DERRICK NED Ned, Derrick Deyone 6'1", 220 **RB**
Col: Grambling State *HS:* Eunice [LA] B: 1/5/1969, Eunice, LA
1993 NO: Rush 9-71 7.9 1 TD. **1994** NO: Rush 11-36 3.3; KR 7-77 11.0. **1995** NO: Rush 3-1 0.3; KR 2-33 16.5. **Total:** Rush 23-108 4.7 1 TD; KR 9-110 12.2.

		Receiving				
Year Team	**G**	**Rec**	**Yds**	**Avg**	**TD**	**Fum**
1993 NO	14	9	54	6.0	0	1
1994 NO	16	13	86	6.6	0	1
1995 NO	12	3	9	3.0	0	1
NFL Total	42	25	149	6.0	0	3

JOE NEDNEY Nedney, Joseph Thomas 6'4", 215 **K**
Col: San Jose State *HS:* Santa Teresa [San Jose, CA] B: 3/22/1973, San Jose, CA

		Scoring						
Year Team	**G**	**Pts**	**FG**	**FGA**	**FG%**	**XK**	**XKA**	**XK%**
1996 Mia	16	89	18	29	62.1	35	36	97.2
1997 Ariz	10	52	11	17	64.7	19	19	100.0
1998 Ariz	12	69	13	19	68.4	30	30	100.0
NFL Total	38	210	42	65	64.6	84	85	98.8

RALPH NEELY Neely, Ralph Eugene 6'6", 265 **OT**
Col: Oklahoma *HS:* Farmington [NM] B: 9/12/1943, Little Rock, AR *Drafted:* 1965 Round 2 Bal
1965 Dal: 14 G; KR 2-13 6.5. **1966** Dal: 14 G; KR 2-18 9.0; 1 Fum. **1967** Dal: 14 G. **1968** Dal: 14 G; KR 3-17 5.7. **1969** Dal: 12 G. **1970** Dal: 14 G. **1971** Dal: 7 G. **1972** Dal: 13 G; Rush 1-10 10.0. **1973** Dal: 14 G. **1974** Dal: 14 G. **1975** Dal: 14 G. **1976** Dal: 14 G. **1977** Dal: 14 G. **Total:** 172 G; Rush 1-10 10.0; KR 7-48 6.9; 1 Fum.

BOBBY NEELY Neely, Robert Lee Jr. 6'3", 251 **TE**
Col: Virginia *HS:* Mays [Atlanta, GA] B: 3/22/1974, Atlanta, GA
1996 ChiB: 11 G; Rec 9-92 10.2.

BOB NEFF Neff, Robert Milan 5'11", 180 **DB**
Col: Stephen F. Austin St. *HS:* Hearne [TX] B: 3/5/1944, Hearne, TX
1966 Mia: PR 10-60 6.0; Int 1-22. **1967** Mia: PR 6-34 5.7; Int 1-32. **1968** Mia: PR 8-71 8.9. **Total:** PR 24-165 6.9; Int 2-54.

		Kickoff Returns				
Year Team	**G**	**Ret**	**Yds**	**Avg**	**TD**	**Fum**
1966 Mia	14	15	376	25.1	0	3
1967 Mia	14	15	351	23.4	0	1
1968 Mia	5	5	190	38.0	0	0
NFL Total	33	35	917	26.2	0	4

FRED NEGUS Negus, Frederick Wilson 6'1", 208 **LB-C**
(Father) *Col:* Michigan; Wisconsin *HS:* Martins Ferry [OH]; Kiski School [Saltsburg, PA] B: 11/7/1923, Colerain, OH
AAFC **1947** ChiA: 12 G. **1948** ChiA: 14 G; Int 5-30; 6 Pt. **1949** ChiA: 12 G; Int 2-28; 6 Pt. **Total:** 38 G; Int 7-58; 12 Pt.

NFL **1950** ChiB: 11 G.

RENALDO NEHEMIAH Nehemiah, Renaldo 6'1", 181 **WR**
(Skeets) *Col:* Maryland *HS:* Fanwood [NJ] B: 3/24/1959, Newark, NJ
1982 SF: Rush 1-(-1) -1.0. **Total:** Rush 1-(-1) -1.0.

		Receiving				
Year Team	**G**	**Rec**	**Yds**	**Avg**	**TD**	**Fum**
1982 SF	8	8	161	20.1	1	0
1983 SF	16	17	236	13.9	1	1
1984 SF	16	18	357	19.8	2	0
NFL Total	40	43	754	17.5	4	1

JOHN NEIDERT Neidert, John Thomas 6'2", 230 LB
Col: Louisville *HS:* Archbishop Hoban [Akron, OH] B: 6/18/1946, Akron, OH *Drafted:* 1968 Round 6 Cin
1968 Cin-NYJ: 13 G; KR 1-0. Cin: 8 G. NYJ: 5 G; KR 1-0. **1969** NYJ: 14 G. **1970** ChiB: 3 G. **Total:** 30 G; KR 1-0.

BILLY NEIGHBORS Neighbors, William Wesley 6'0", 250 OG
Col: Alabama *HS:* Tuscaloosa Co. [Northport, AL] B: 2/4/1940, Tuscaloosa, AL *Drafted:* 1962 Round 6 Bos
1962 Bos: 14 G. **1963** Bos: 14 G. **1964** Bos: 14 G. **1965** Bos: 14 G. **1966** Mia: 14 G. **1967** Mia: 14 G. **1968** Mia: 14 G. **1969** Mia: 14 G. **Total:** 112 G.

DAN NEIL Neil, Daniel Patrick 6'2", 281 OG
(Stump) *Col:* Texas *HS:* Cypress Creek [Houston, TX] B: 10/21/1973, Houston, TX *Drafted:* 1997 Round 3 Den
1997 Den: 3 G. **1998** Den: 16 G. **Total:** 19 G.

KENNY NEIL Neil, Kenny 6'4", 244 DE-DT
Col: Iowa State *HS:* Aiken [Cincinnati, OH] B: 1/8/1959, Cincinnati, OH *Drafted:* 1981 Round 7 NYJ
1981 NYJ: 16 G. **1982** NYJ: 9 G; 4 Sac. **1983** NYJ: 16 G; 5.5 Sac. **1987** Hou: 1 G. **Total:** 42 G; 9.5 Sac.

JIM NEILL Neill, James Hubert 6'2", 190 DB-FB-WB
Col: Texas Tech *HS:* Brownfield [TX] B: 5/9/1913, Brownfield, TX D: 7/1988
1937 NYG: 3 G; Pass 3-1 33.3%, 1 Int; Rush 7-55 7.9. **1939** ChiC: 1 G. **Total:** 4 G; Pass 3-1 33.3%, 1 Int; Rush 7-55 7.9.

BILL NEILL Neill, William M 6'4", 258 NT
Col: Pittsburgh *HS:* Perkiomen Valley [Greaterford, PA] B: 3/15/1959, Graterford, PA *Drafted:* 1981 Round 5 NYG
1981 NYG: 16 G. **1982** NYG: 7 G; 2 Sac. **1983** NYG: 1 G. **1984** GB: 16 G; 1 Sac. **Total:** 40 G; 3 Sac.

STEVE NEILS Neils, Steven Lynn 6'2", 217 LB
Col: Minnesota *HS:* St. Peter [MN] B: 5/2/1951, St. Peter, MN *Drafted:* 1974 Round 5 StL
1974 StL: 14 G. **1975** StL: 14 G. **1976** StL: 7 G; PR 1-0; 1 Fum. **1977** StL: 14 G. **1978** StL: 16 G; Int 1-18. **1979** StL: 9 G; **1** Fum TD; 6 Pt. **1980** StL: 14 G. **Total:** 88 G; PR 1-0; Int 1-18; 1 Fum TD; 6 Pt; 1 Fum.

MIKE NELMS Nelms, Michael Craig 6'1", 188 DB
Col: Tarrant Co. JC TX; Sam Houston State; Baylor *HS:* O.D. Wyatt [Fort Worth, TX] B: 4/8/1955, Fort Worth, TX *Drafted:* 1977 Round 7 Buf
1981 Was: Int 1-3. **Total:** Int 1-3.

		Punt Returns				Kickoff Returns				
Year Team	**G**	**Ret**	**Yds**	**Avg**	**TD**	**Ret**	**Yds**	**Avg**	**TD**	**Fum**
1980 Was	16	48	487	10.1	0	38	810	21.3	0	1
1981 Was	16	45	492	10.9	2	37	1099	**29.7**	0	2
1982 Was	8	32	252	7.9	0	23	557	24.2	0	3
1983 Was	12	38	289	7.6	0	35	802	22.9	0	0
1984 Was	16	49	428	8.7	0	42	860	20.5	0	1
NFL Total	68	212	1948	9.2	2	175	4128	23.6	0	7

BILL NELSEN Nelsen, William Keith 6'0", 195 QB
Col: Cerritos Coll. CA (J.C.); USC *HS:* El Rancho [Pico Rivera, CA] B: 1/29/1941, Los Angeles, CA *Drafted:* 1963 Round 10 Pit
1965 Pit: Rec 1-(-5) -5.0. **Total:** Rec 1-(-5) -5.0.

		Passing							
Year Team	**G**	**Att**	**Comp**	**Comp%**	**Yds**	**YPA**	**TD**	**Int**	**Rating**
1963 Pit	2	2	0	0.0	0	0.00	0	0	39.6
1964 Pit	5	42	16	38.1	276	6.57	2	3	47.3
1965 Pit	12	270	121	44.8	1917	7.10	8	17	52.7
1966 Pit	5	112	63	56.3	1122	10.02	7	1	107.8
1967 Pit	8	165	74	44.8	1125	6.82	10	9	65.3
1968 Cle	14	293	152	51.9	2366	8.08	19	10	86.4
1969 Cle	14	352	190	54.0	2743	7.79	23	19	78.8
1970 Cle	12	313	159	50.8	2156	6.89	16	16	68.9
1971 Cle	14	325	174	53.5	2319	7.14	13	23	60.3
1972 Cle	4	31	14	45.2	141	4.55	0	3	19.1
NFL Total	90	1905	963	50.6	14165	7.44	98	101	70.2

	Rushing				
Year Team	**Att**	**Yds**	**Avg**	**TD**	**Fum**
1963 Pit	1	-6	-6.0	0	1
1964 Pit	3	17	5.7	0	0
1965 Pit	26	84	3.2	1	6
1966 Pit	6	18	3.0	0	1
1967 Pit	9	-19	-2.1	0	7
1968 Cle	13	30	2.3	1	2
1969 Cle	5	-11	-2.2	0	**8**
1970 Cle	7	-4	-0.6	0	6
1971 Cle	13	-18	-1.4	0	10
1972 Cle	1	-2	-2.0	0	0
NFL Total	84	89	1.1	2	41

AL NELSON Nelson, Albert 5'11", 186 DB
(Pete) *Col:* Cincinnati *HS:* Robert A. Taft [Cincinnati, OH] B: 10/27/1943, Cincinnati, OH *Drafted:* 1965 Round 3 Phi
1966 Phi: PR 1-3 3.0. **Total:** PR 1-3 3.0.

		Kickoff Returns				Interceptions				Tot
Year Team	**G**	**Ret**	**Yds**	**Avg**	**TD**	**Int**	**Yds**	**TD**	**Fum**	**TD**
1965 Phi	14	26	683	26.3	0	2	23	0	1	0
1966 Phi	13	2	34	17.0	0	1	0	0	0	1
1967 Phi	1	0	0	—	0	0	0	0	0	0
1968 Phi	14	11	308	28.0	0	3	7	0	0	0
1969 Phi	14	3	63	21.0	0	3	10	0	0	0
1970 Phi	13	10	187	18.7	0	2	45	0	0	0
1971 Phi	14	13	358	27.5	0	2	63	1	0	2
1972 Phi	14	25	728	29.1	0	0	0	0	1	0
1973 Phi	8	11	264	24.0	0	0	0	0	0	0
NFL Total	105	101	2625	26.0	0	13	148	1	2	3

ANDY NELSON Nelson, Andrew vaughan 6'1", 180 DB
(Bones) *Col:* Memphis *HS:* Athens [AL] B: 5/27/1933, Athens, AL *Drafted:* 1957 Round 11 Bal
1960 Bal: PR 3-1 0.3. **1961** Bal: PR 4-19 4.8. **1962** Bal: PR 2-22 11.0. **Total:** PR 9-42 4.7.

		Interceptions			
Year Team	**G**	**Int**	**Yds**	**TD**	**Fum**
1957 Bal	12	5	29	0	0
1958 Bal	12	8	**199**	1	0
1959 Bal	12	6	33	**1**	0
1960 Bal	12	6	47	0	0
1961 Bal	14	0	0	0	0
1962 Bal	14	4	20	0	1
1963 Bal	13	3	37	1	0
1964 NYG	14	1	13	0	0
NFL Total	103	33	378	3	1

CHUCK NELSON Nelson, Charles LaVerne 5'11", 175 K
Col: Washington *HS:* Everett [WA] B: 2/23/1960, Seattle, WA *Drafted:* 1983 Round 4 LARm
1986 Min: Punt 3-72 24.0. **Total:** Punt 3-72 24.0.

		Scoring						
Year Team	**G**	**Pts**	**FG**	**FGA**	**FG%**	**XK**	**XKA**	**XK%**
1983 LARm	12	48	5	11	45.5	33	37	89.2
1984 Buf	7	23	3	5	60.0	14	14	100.0
1986 Min	16	110	22	28	78.6	44	47	93.6
1987 Min	12	75	13	24	54.2	36	37	97.3
1988 Min	16	108	20	25	80.0	48	49	98.0
NFL Total	63	364	63	93	67.7	175	184	95.1

SHANE NELSON Nelson, Curtis Shane 6'1", 226 LB
Col: Blinn Coll. TX (J.C.); Baylor *HS:* Mathis [TX] B: 5/25/1955, Mathis, TX
1977 Buf: 14 G. **1978** Buf: 16 G; Int 3-69. **1979** Buf: 16 G; Int 1-13. **1980** Buf: 16 G. **1981** Buf: 10 G; Int 1-9. **1982** Buf: 1 G. **Total:** 73 G; Int 5-91.

DARRELL NELSON Nelson, Darrell Maurice 6'2", 235 TE
Col: Memphis *HS:* Mitchell [Memphis, TN] B: 10/27/1961, Memphis, TN
1984 Pit: 11 G; Rec 2-31 15.5. **1985** Pit: 5 G. **Total:** 16 G; Rec 2-31 15.5.

DARRIN NELSON Nelson, Darrin Milo 5'9", 184 RB
Col: Stanford *HS:* Pius X [Downey, CA] B: 1/2/1959, Sacramento, CA *Drafted:* 1982 Round 1 Min
1991 Min: Pass 1-1 100.0%, 25 25.00 1 TD. **Total:** Pass 1-1 100.0%, 25 25.00 1 TD.

		Rushing				Receiving			
Year Team	**G**	**Att**	**Yds**	**Avg**	**TD**	**Rec**	**Yds**	**Avg**	**TD**
1982 Min	7	44	136	3.1	0	9	100	11.1	0
1983 Min	15	154	642	4.2	1	51	618	12.1	0
1984 Min	15	80	406	5.1	3	27	162	6.0	1
1985 Min	16	200	893	4.5	5	43	301	7.0	1
1986 Min	16	191	793	4.2	4	53	593	11.2	3
1987 Min	10	131	642	**4.9**	2	26	129	5.0	0
1988 Min	13	112	380	3.4	1	16	105	6.6	0
1989 Min-Dal-SD	14	67	321	4.8	0	38	380	10.0	0
1989 Min	5	31	124	4.0	0	7	52	7.4	0
1989 SD	9	36	197	5.5	0	31	328	10.6	0
1990 SD	14	3	14	4.7	0	4	29	7.3	0
1991 Min	16	28	210	7.5	2	19	142	7.5	0
1992 Min	16	10	5	0.5	0	0	0	—	0
NFL Total	152	1020	4442	4.4	18	286	2559	8.9	5

	Punt Returns				Kickoff Returns					Tot
Year Team	**Ret**	**Yds**	**Avg**	**TD**	**Ret**	**Yds**	**Avg**	**TD**	**Fum**	**TD**
1982 Min	0	0	—	0	6	132	22.0	0	2	0
1983 Min	0	0	—	0	18	445	24.7	0	5	1

Year Team										
1984 Min	23	180	7.8	0	39	891	22.8	0	4	4
1985 Min	16	133	8.3	0	3	51	17.0	0	7	6
1986 Min	0	0	—	0	3	105	35.0	0	3	7
1987 Min	0	0	—	0	7	164	23.4	0	2	2
1988 Min	0	0	—	0	9	210	23.3	0	3	1
1989 Min-Dal-SD	0	0	—	0	14	317	22.6	0	1	0
1989 Min	0	0	—	0	14	317	22.6	0	0	0
1989 SD	0	0	—	0	0	0	—	0	1	0
1990 SD	3	44	14.7	0	4	36	9.0	0	1	0
1991 Min	0	0	—	0	31	682	22.0	0	2	2
1992 Min	0	0	—	0	29	626	21.6	0	2	0
NFL Total	42	357	8.5	0	163	3659	22.4	0	32	23

DAVID NELSON Nelson, David Leon 6'2", 230 **RB**
Col: Taft Coll. CA (J.C.); Heidelberg *HS:* North Miami Beach [FL]
B: 11/23/1963, Miami, FL
1984 Min: 2 G; Rush 1-3 3.0; KR 1-0.

DENNIS NELSON Nelson, Dennis Ray 6'5", 260 **OT**
Col: Illinois State *HS:* Wethersfield [Kewanee, IL] B: 2/2/1946, Kewanee, IL *Drafted:* 1969 Round 3 Bal
1970 Bal: 6 G. **1971** Bal: 14 G. **1972** Bal: 13 G. **1973** Bal: 14 G; Rush 0-3. **1974** Bal: 14 G. **1976** Phi: 14 G. **1977** Phi: 2 G. **Total:** 77 G; Rush 0-3.

DERRIE NELSON Nelson, Derald Lawrence 6'2", 236 **LB**
Col: Nebraska *HS:* Fairmont [NE] B: 2/8/1958, York, NE
Drafted: 1981 Round 4 Dal
1983 SD: 15 G; 6 Pt. **1984** SD: 6 G. **1985** SD: 16 G. **1986** SD: 11 G. **Total:** 48 G; 6 Pt.

FRANK NELSON Nelson, Dewey Frank 5'9", 167 **HB**
Col: Utah B: 5/28/1923, Salt Lake City, UT *Drafted:* 1948 Round 18 Bos
1948 Bos: Pass 17-8 47.1%, 71 4.18 2 Int; Rec 1-10 10.0; PR 2-27 13.5; KR 3-34 11.3; Int 1-28. **1949** NYB: PR 3-14 4.7; KR 3-52 17.3; Int 1-10. **Total:** Pass 17-8 47.1%, 71 4.18 2 Int; Rec 1-10 10.0; PR 5-41 8.2; KR 6-86 14.3; Int 2-38.

		Rushing				
Year Team	**G**	**Att**	**Yds**	**Avg**	**TD**	**Fum**
1948 Bos	12	18	60	3.3	0	2
1949 NYB	4	8	26	3.3	0	2
NFL Total	16	26	86	3.3	0	4

DON NELSON Nelson, Donald Fritz 5'10", 200 **G**
Col: Iowa *HS:* Rockford Central [IL] B: 5/12/1915, Moline, IL
D: 10/25/1996, Ames, IA
1937 Bkn: 11 G.

DON NELSON Nelson, Donald Roswell 6'1", 210 **T-C**
Col: Ohio Wesleyan *HS:* Washington [Massillon, OH] B: 2/10/1903, Cambridge, MA D: 10/26/1980, Larkspur, CA
1926 Ham-Can: 7 G. Ham: 1 G. Can: 6 G. **Total:** 7 G.

ED NELSON Nelson, Edmund Clau-Von 6'3", 272 **DE-NT-DT**
Col: Auburn *HS:* C. Leon King [Tampa, FL] B: 4/30/1960, Live Oak, FL
Drafted: 1982 Round 7 Pit
1982 Pit: 8 G. **1983** Pit: 16 G; 3 Sac. **1984** Pit: 16 G; 7 Sac. **1985** Pit: 6 G; 1 Sac. **1986** Pit: 16 G; 5 Sac. **1987** Pit: 10 G. **1988** NE: 12 G. **Total:** 84 G; 16 Sac.

PACKIE NELSON Nelson, Everett Fritchof 5'11", 205 **T**
Col: Illinois *HS:* New Trier Twp. [Winnetka, IL] B: 2/18/1907, Chicago, IL D: 12/1/1992, Gaithersburg, MD
1929 ChiB: 7 G.

HERB NELSON Nelson, Herbert Russell 6'4", 219 **DE-OE-T**
Col: Pennsylvania *HS:* William Hall [West Hartford, CT] B: 4/25/1921, Hartford, CT
AAFC **1946** BufA: 12 G; Rush 1-1 1.0; Rec 4-47 11.8. **1947** BknA: 14 G; Rec 2-17 8.5. **1948** BknA: 4 G. **Total:** 30 G; Rush 1-1 1.0; Rec 6-64 10.7.

BENNY NELSON Nelson, James Benny 6'0", 185 **DB**
Col: Alabama *HS:* Huntsville [AL] B: 4/1/1941, Gadsden, AL
Drafted: 1964 Round 12 Hou
1964 Hou: 14 G; KR 13-304 23.4; Int 1-45 **1** TD; 6 Pt.

JIM NELSON Nelson, James Robert 6'1", 235 **LB**
Col: Penn State *HS:* McDonogh School [MD] B: 4/16/1975, Riverside, CA
1998 GB: Postseason only.

JIMMY NELSON Nelson, Jimmy Guess 5'11", 180 **HB-QB-DB**
Col: Alabama *HS:* Suwannee [Live Oak, FL] B: 7/26/1919, Live Oak, FL D: 12/24/1986, Encinitas, CA
AAFC **1946** MiaA: Pass 24-8 33.3%, 135 5.63 4 Int; Rec 4-20 5.0; PR 7-71 10.1; KR 10-192 19.2; Int 2-8; Punt 16-635 39.7.

		Rushing			
Year Team	**G**	**Att**	**Yds**	**Avg**	**TD**
1946 MiaA	14	39	163	4.2	2

KARL NELSON Nelson, Karl Stuart 6'6", 285 **OT**
Col: Iowa State *HS:* De Kalb [IL] B: 6/14/1960, DeKalb, IL
Drafted: 1983 Round 3 NYG
1984 NYG: 16 G. **1985** NYG: 16 G. **1986** NYG: 16 G. **1988** NYG: 9 G. **Total:** 57 G.

LEE NELSON Nelson, Lee Martin 5'10", 185 **DB**
Col: Pensacola JC FL; Florida State *HS:* Melbourne [FL] B: 1/30/1954, Kissimmee, FL *Drafted:* 1976 Round 15 StL
1976 StL: 9 G; KR 1-43 43.0. **1977** StL: 10 G; PR 1-4 4.0; KR 3-68 22.7; Int 4-37. **1978** StL: 16 G; KR 3-58 19.3; Int 1-(-3). **1979** StL: 16 G; PR 4-88 22.0. **1980** StL: 16 G; PR 1-5 5.0; KR 1-29 29.0. **1981** StL: 15 G. **1982** StL: 8 G; Int 1-7. **1983** StL: 16 G; Int 1-8; 1 Fum TD; 6 Pt; 2 Sac. **1984** StL: 16 G; 3 Sac. **1985** StL: 13 G; PR 2-14 7.0; KR 3-49 16.3; 1 Fum. **Total:** 135 G; PR 8-111 13.9; KR 11-247 22.5; Int 7-49; 1 Fum TD; 6 Pt; 1 Fum; 5 Sac.

MARK NELSON Nelson, Mark David 6'4", 270 **OT**
Col: Normandale CC MN; Iowa State; Bowling Green State *HS:* Thomas Jefferson [Bloomington, MN] B: 6/22/1964, Grand Forks, ND
1987 KC: 1 G.

RALPH NELSON Nelson, Ralph 6'2", 195 **RB**
Col: No College *HS:* Centennial [Stockton, CA] B: 1/23/1953, Los Angeles, CA
1975 Was: Rec 5-58 11.6 1 TD; KR 5-107 21.4. **1976** Sea: Rec 12-96 8.0. **Total:** Rec 17-154 9.1 1 TD; KR 5-107 21.4.

		Rushing					Tot
Year Team	**G**	**Att**	**Yds**	**Avg**	**TD**	**Fum**	**TD**
1975 Was	14	31	139	4.5	0	3	1
1976 Sea	8	52	173	3.3	1	2	1
NFL Total	22	83	312	3.8	1	5	2

ROBERT NELSON Nelson, Robert Cole 6'1", 214 **C-LB-OT-DT**
Col: Baylor *HS:* Bryan [TX] B: 1/30/1920, Paris, TX D: 11/3/1986, Granbury, TX *Drafted:* 1941 Round 5 Det
AAFC **1946** LA-A: 10 G; KR 1-0; Int 1-5; Scor 9, 2-6 33.3% FG, 3-5 60.0% XK. **1947** LA-A: 14 G; Rec 3-61 20.3 1 TD; Int 2-52 1 TD; Tot TD 2; 12 Pt. **1948** LA-A: 14 G; Rush 1-(-7) -7.0; Int 1-0. **1949** LA-A: 12 G; Scor 43, 3-6 50.0% FG, 34-35 97.1% XK. **Total:** 50 G; Rush 1-(-7) -7.0; Rec 3-61 20.3 1 TD; KR 1-0; Int 4-57 1 TD; Scor 64, 5-12 41.7% FG, 37-40 92.5% XK; Tot TD 2.

NFL **1941** Det: 9 G; Int 1-41. **1945** Det: 9 G; Int 1-0; Scor 3, 1-4 25.0% FG. **1950** Bal: 3 G. **Total:** 21 G; Int 2-41; Scor 3, 1-4 25.0% FG.

BOB NELSON Nelson, Robert Lee 6'4", 232 **LB**
Col: Nebraska *HS:* Stillwater [MN] B: 6/30/1953, Stillwater, MN
Drafted: 1975 Round 2 Buf
1976 Buf: 14 G. **1977** Buf: 11 G; KR 1-10 10.0. **1979** SF: 1 G. **1980** Oak: 9 G; Int 1-0. **1982** LARd: 9 G; 1 Sac. **1983** LARd: 16 G; 2 Sac. **1984** LARd: 12 G; 1.5 Sac. **Total:** 72 G; KR 1-10 10.0; Int 1-0; 4.5 Sac.

BOB NELSON Nelson, Robert William 6'4", 272 **NT**
Col: Miami (Fla.) *HS:* Patapsco [Baltimore, MD] B: 3/3/1959, Baltimore, MD *Drafted:* 1982 Round 5 Mia
1986 TB: 16 G; 1 Sac. **1988** GB: 14 G. **1989** GB: 16 G; 1 Sac. **1990** GB: 16 G; 1 Sac. **Total:** 62 G; 3 Sac.

STEVE NELSON Nelson, Steven Lee 6'2", 230 **LB**
Col: Augsburg; North Dakota State *HS:* Anoka [MN] B: 4/26/1951, Farmington, MN *Drafted:* 1974 Round 2 NE
1983 NE: 1 Sac. **1984** NE: 4 Sac. **1985** NE: 2 Sac. **1986** NE: 1 Sac. **Total:** 8 Sac.

		Interceptions		
Year Team	**G**	**Int**	**Yds**	**TD**
1974 NE	11	0	0	0
1975 NE	14	2	8	0
1976 NE	10	2	32	0
1977 NE	13	0	0	0
1978 NE	14	5	104	0
1979 NE	15	1	18	0
1980 NE	16	3	37	0
1981 NE	12	0	0	0
1982 NE	9	0	0	0
1983 NE	8	1	6	0
1984 NE	16	1	0	0
1985 NE	15	0	0	0
1986 NE	10	2	21	0
1987 NE	11	0	0	0
NFL Total	174	17	226	0

TERRY NELSON Nelson, Terry Louis 6'2", 233 **TE**
Col: Arkansas-Pine Bluff *HS:* Peake [Arkadelphia, AR] B: 5/20/1951, Arkadelphia, AR *Drafted:* 1973 Round 4 LARm
1974 LARm: Rush 1-3 3.0. **1976** LARm: KR 0-1. **1977** LARm: Rush 3-31 10.3. **1978** LARm: Rush 6-67 11.2 1 TD. **1979** LARm: Rush 2-(-16) -8.0. **Total:** Rush 12-85 7.1 1 TD; KR 0-1.

Year Team	G	Receiving Rec	Yds	Avg	TD	Fum	Tot TD
1973 LARm	2	0	0	—	0	0	0
1974 LARm	10	0	0	—	0	0	0
1975 LARm	14	1	5	5.0	0	0	0
1976 LARm	14	4	48	12.0	0	0	0
1977 LARm	14	31	401	12.9	3	2	3
1978 LARm	13	23	344	15.0	0	2	1
1979 LARm	16	25	293	11.7	3	1	3
1980 LARm	4	3	22	7.3	0	0	0
NFL Total	87	87	1113	12.8	6	5	7

TED NELSON Nelson, Theodore R III 5'10", 203 **DB**
Col: Nevada-Las Vegas *HS:* Peabody [Pittsburgh, PA] B: 1/1/1965, Pittsburgh, PA
1987 KC: 3 G.

BILL NELSON Nelson, William Howard 6'7", 270 **DT**
Col: Oregon State *HS:* El Cerrito [CA] B: 3/9/1948, Berkeley, CA
Drafted: 1970 Round 7 LARm
1971 LARm: 6 G. **1972** LARm: 7 G. **1973** LARm: 12 G. **1974** LARm: 14 G. **1975** LARm: 8 G. **Total:** 47 G.

ANDY NEMECEK Nemecek, Andrew James 6'4", 215 **C-G-T**
Col: Ohio State *HS:* Lorain [OH] B: 5/6/1896, Lorain, OH
D: 5/8/1984, Mayfield Heights, OH
1923 Col: 10 G. **1924** Col: 8 G. **1925** Col: 9 G. **Total:** 27 G.

JERRY NEMECEK Nemecek, Jerald Cyrill 6'0", 185 **OE**
Col: New York U. *HS:* East Syracuse [NY]; Bellefonte Acad. [PA]
B: 1/1/1907, New York, NY D: 5/5/1987, Pittsford, NY
1931 Bkn: 9 G; Rec 1 TD; 6 Pt.

STEVE NEMETH Nemeth, Steven Joseph 5'10", 174 **QB-TB-DB**
Col: Notre Dame *HS:* James Whitcomb Riley [South Bend, IN]
B: 12/10/1922, South Bend, IN D: 3/27/1998, South Bend, IN
AAFC **1946** ChiA: 13 G; Pass 23-5 21.7%, 68 2.96; Rush 4-10 2.5; PR 1-14 14.0; Punt 2-92 46.0; Scor 59, 9-12 75.0% FG, 32-33 97.0% XK. **1947** BalA: 4 G; Pass 6-2 33.3%, 18 3.00 2 Int; Rush 1-1 1.0; Punt 3-126 42.0; Scor 1, 0-1 FG, 1-1 100.0% XK. **Total:** 17 G; Pass 29-7 24.1%, 86 2.97 2 Int; Rush 5-11 2.2; PR 1-14 14.0; Punt 5-218 43.6; Scor 60, 9-13 69.2% FG, 33-34 97.1% XK.

NFL **1945** Cle: 9 G; Pass 1-0.

TED NEMZEK Nemzek, Theodore C 205 **T**
Col: Moorhead State *HS:* Moorhead [MN] B: 2/11/1906, Moorhead, MN Deceased
1930 Min: 4 G.

CARL NERY Nery, Carl N 6'0", 214 **G**
Col: Duquesne *HS:* Springdale [PA] B: 6/17/1917, Lawrenceville, PA
Drafted: 1940 Round 8 Pit
1940 Pit: 11 G. **1941** Pit: 11 G. **Total:** 22 G.

RON NERY Nery, Ronald Duane 6'6", 247 **DE**
Col: Kansas State *HS:* New Kensington [PA] B: 12/30/1934, New Kensington, PA *Drafted:* 1956 Round 7 NYG
1960 LAC: 14 G. **1961** SD: 14 G. **1962** SD: 14 G. **1963** Den-Hou: 8 G. Den: 4 G. Hou: 4 G. **Total:** 50 G.

DICK NESBITT Nesbitt, Richard Jackson 6'0", 204 **HB-DB-FB-LB**
Col: Drake *HS:* Roosevelt [Des Moines, IA]; Kemper Mil. School [Boonville, MO] B: 11/12/1907, Des Moines, IA D: 3/5/1962, Minneapolis, MN
1931 ChiB: Pass 1 TD; Int **1** TD. **1932** ChiB: Pass 4-2 50.0%, 14 3.50; Rec 2-5 2.5. **1933** ChiB-ChiC: Pass 18-2 11.1%, 34 1.89 4 Int; Rec 6-36 6.0; Scor **1** Saf. ChiB: Pass 3-1 33.3%, 23 7.67; Rec 1-15 15.0. ChiC: Pass 15-1 6.7%, 11 0.73 4 Int; Rec 5-21 4.2; Scor 1 Saf. **1934** Bkn: Pass 1-1 100.0%, 46 46.00. **Total:** Pass 23-5 21.7%, 94 4.09 1 TD 4 Int; Rec 8-41 5.1; Int 1 TD; Scor 1 Saf.

Year Team	G	Rushing Att	Yds	Avg	TD	Tot TD
1930 ChiB	8	—	—	—	1	1
1931 ChiB	13	—	—	—	1	2
1932 ChiB	14	92	295	3.2	2	2
1933 ChiB-ChiC	9	88	251	2.9	1	1
1933 ChiB	4	21	78	3.7	0	0
1933 ChiC	5	67	173	2.6	1	1
1934 Bkn	9	25	58	2.3	0	0
NFL Total	53	205	604	2.9	5	6

AL NESSER Nesser, Alfred L 6'0", 195 **G-OE-C**
(Nappy; Whitey) *Col:* No College *HS:* None B: 6/6/1893, Columbus, OH D: 3/11/1967, Akron, OH
1920 Akr: 11 G. **1921** Akr: 12 G; 1 Fum TD; 6 Pt. **1922** Akr: 9 G; 6 Pt. **1923** Akr: 7 G; Int **1** TD; 6 Pt. **1924** Akr: 7 G. **1925** Akr-Cle: 13 G; 1 Fum TD; 6 Pt. Akr: 6 G. Cle: 7 G; 1 Fum TD; 6 Pt. **1926** Akr-NYG: 8 G. Akr: 3 G. NYG: 5 G. **1927** NYG: 13 G. **1928** NYG: 4 G. **1931** Cle: 9 G. **Total:** 93 G; Int 1 TD; 2 Fum TD; Tot TD 4; 24 Pt.

CHARLIE NESSER Nesser, Charles T 6'2", 195 **TB**
Col: No College B: 1902, Columbus, OH Deceased
1921 Col: 9 G.

FRANK NESSER Nesser, Frank B 6'1", 245 **FB-G-T**
Col: No College *HS:* None B: 6/3/1889, Columbus, OH D: 1/1/1953, Columbus, OH
1920 Col: 10 G. **1921** Col: 9 G; Pass 3 TD; Rush 1 TD; Scor 7, 1 XK. **1922** Col: 8 G; Rec 1 TD; 6 Pt. **1925** Col: 6 G. **1926** Col: 7 G. **Total:** 40 G; Pass 3 TD; Rush 1 TD; Rec 1 TD; Tot TD 2.

FRED NESSER Nesser, Frederick W 6'5", 250 **T-OE-FB**
Col: No College *HS:* None B: 9/10/1887, Columbus, OH
D: 7/2/1967, Columbus, OH
1921 Col: 7 G.

JOHN NESSER Nesser, John 5'11", 195 **G-T**
(The Wolf) *Col:* No College *HS:* None B: 4/25/1876, Triere, Germany
D: Columbus, OH
1921 Col: 2 G.

PHIL NESSER Nesser, Phillip G 6'0", 225 **G-T-WB**
Col: No College *HS:* None B: 12/10/1880, Triere, Germany
D: 5/9/1959, Columbus, OH
1920 Col: 1 G. **1921** Col: 6 G. **Total:** 7 G.

TED NESSER Nesser, Theodore Jr. 5'10", 230 **C-T-G**
Col: No College *HS:* None B: 4/5/1883, Denison, OH D: 6/7/1941, Columbus, OH
1920 Col: 5 G. **1921** Col: 9 G. **Total:** 14 G.

BILL NETHERTON Netherton, William Jackson 5'11", 180 **OE**
Col: Kentucky *HS:* Male [Louisville, KY] B: 3/2/1898, Worthington, KY
D: 8/9/1984, Louisville, KY
1921 Lou: 1 G. **1922** Lou: 1 G. **Total:** 2 G.

DOUG NETTLES Nettles, Gordon Douglas 6'0", 179 **DB**
Col: Vanderbilt *HS:* Rutherford [Panama City, FL] B: 8/13/1951, Panama City, FL *Drafted:* 1974 Round 5 Bal
1974 Bal: 13 G; Int 1-0. **1975** Bal: 13 G. **1977** Bal: 14 G; Int 1-30; Scor 1 Saf; 2 Pt. **1978** Bal: 16 G; Int 1-0. **1979** Bal: 15 G; Int 2-30. **1980** NYG: 2 G. **Total:** 73 G; Int 5-60; Scor 1 Saf; 2 Pt.

JIM NETTLES Nettles, James Arthur 5'10", 177 **DB**
Col: Wisconsin *HS:* Muncie Central [IN] B: 2/15/1942, Muncie, IN
1970 LARm: PR 2-4 2.0. **Total:** PR 2-4 2.0.

Year Team	G	Interceptions Int	Yds	TD	Tot TD
1965 Phi	14	3	84	1	1
1966 Phi	14	3	57	1	1
1967 Phi	12	4	52	0	1
1968 Phi	14	0	0	0	0
1969 LARm	13	2	37	0	0
1970 LARm	14	3	54	0	0
1971 LARm	14	5	97	1	1
1972 LARm	14	6	168	0	0
NFL Total	109	26	549	3	4

KEITH NEUBERT Neubert, Keith Robert 6'5", 250 **TE**
Col: Nebraska *HS:* Fort Atkinson [WI] B: 9/13/1964, Fort Atkinson, WI
Drafted: 1988 Round 8 NYJ

Year Team	G	Receiving Rec	Yds	Avg	TD	Fum
1988 NYJ	1	0	0	—	0	0
1989 NYJ	16	28	302	10.8	1	2
NFL Total	17	28	302	10.8	1	2

RICK NEUHEISEL Neuheisel, Richard Gerald 6'1", 190 **QB**
Col: UCLA *HS:* McClintock [Tempe, AZ] B: 2/7/1961, Madison, WI
1987 SD: Rush 6-41 6.8 1 TD; Scor **1** 1XP.

Year Team	G	Passing Att	Comp	Comp%	Yds	YPA	TD	Int	Rating	Fum
1987 SD	3	59	40	67.8	367	6.22	1	1	83.1	1

QUENTIN NEUJAHR Neujahr, Quentin Troy 6'4", 297 **C**
Col: Kansas State *HS:* Centennial [Ulysses, NE] B: 1/30/1971, Seward, NE
1996 Bal: 5 G. **1997** Bal: 9 G. **1998** Jac: 16 G. **Total:** 30 G.

BOB NEUMAN Neuman, Robert John 6'0", 198 **OE-DE**
Col: Illinois Wesleyan *HS:* Mendota Twp. [Mendota, IL] B: 1/18/1912, Mendota, IL D: 1/17/1984, Normal, IL
1934 ChiC: 5 G; Rush 1-0. **1935** ChiC: 11 G; Rec 3-52 17.3; 6 Pt. **1936** ChiC: 8 G; Rush 1-3 3.0; Rec 3-41 13.7. **Total:** 24 G; Rush 2-3 1.5; Rec 6-93 15.5; 6 Pt.

TOM NEUMANN Neumann, Thomas James 5'11", 205 **HB**
Col: Wisconsin; Northern Michigan *HS:* Peshtigo [WI] B: 3/4/1940, Menominee, WI *Drafted:* 1963 Round 17 Bos
1963 Bos: Rec 10-48 4.8 1 TD.

Year Team	G	Rushing Att	Yds	Avg	TD	Fum
1963 Bos	10	44	148	3.4	0	1

ERNIE NEVERS Nevers, Ernest Alonzo 6'0", 204 **FB**
Col: Stanford *HS:* Superior Central [WI]; Santa Rosa HS [CA]
B: 6/11/1903, Willow River, MN D: 5/3/1976, San Rafael, CA
HOF: 1963
1926 Dul: 14 G; Pass 3 TD; Rush 8 TD; Scor 71, 4 FG, 11 XK. **1927** Dul: 9 G; Pass 5 TD; Rush 4 TD; Scor 31, 7 XK. **1929** ChiC: 11 G; Pass 6 TD; Rush **12** TD; Scor **85**, 1 FG, 10 XK; Tot TD **12**. **1930** ChiC: 11 G; Pass 5 TD; Rush 6 TD; Scor 48, 1 FG, 9 XK. **1931** ChiC: 9 G; Pass 6 TD; Rush 8 TD; Scor 66, 1 FG, **15** XK. **Total:** 54 G; Pass 25 TD; Rush 38 TD; Scor 301, 7 FG, 52 XK.

ELIJAH NEVETT Nevett, Elijah 6'0", 185 **DB-WR**
Col: Clark Atlanta *HS:* Brighton [AL] B: 4/28/1944, Bessemer, AL
1967 NO: 2 G; KR 1-0; 1 Fum. **1968** NO: 10 G; PR 3-(-9) -3.0; KR 2-94 47.0; 1 Fum. **1969** NO: 14 G; KR 2-53 26.5; Int 3-20; 1 Fum. **1970** NO: 11 G; Int 3-49. **Total:** 37 G; PR 3-(-9) -3.0; KR 5-147 29.4; Int 6-69; 3 Fum.

TOM NEVILLE Neville, Thomas Lee 6'5", 300 **OG-OT**
Col: Weber State; Fresno State *HS:* Ben Eielson [Fairbanks, AK]
B: 9/4/1961, Great Falls, MT D: 5/9/1998, Fresno, CA
1986 GB: 16 G. **1987** GB: 12 G. **1988** GB: 2 G. **1991** SF: 12 G. **1992** GB: 8 G. **Total:** 50 G.

TOM NEVILLE Neville, Thomas Oliver Jr. 6'4", 260 **OT**
Col: Mississippi State *HS:* Sidney Lanier [Montgomery, AL]
B: 8/12/1943, Montgomery, AL *Drafted:* 1965 Round 7 Bos
1965 Bos: 14 G. **1966** Bos: 14 G. **1967** Bos: 14 G. **1968** Bos: 14 G. **1969** Bos: 14 G. **1970** Bos: 13 G. **1971** NE: 14 G. **1972** NE: 13 G. **1973** NE: 8 G. **1974** NE: 14 G. **1976** NE: 14 G. **1977** NE: 14 G. **1978** Den: 16 G. **1979** NYG: 14 G. **Total:** 190 G.

BILL NEWASHE Newashe, William 5'11", 200 **T**
Col: Carlisle *HS:* Carlisle Indian School [PA] B: 1890 Deceased
1923 Oor: 5 G.

TOM NEWBERRY Newberry, Thomas J 6'2", 285 **OG-C**
Col: Wis.-La Crosse *HS:* Onalaska [WI] B: 12/20/1962, Onalaska, WI
Drafted: 1986 Round 2 LARm
1986 LARm: 16 G; **1** Fum TD; 6 Pt. **1987** LARm: 12 G. **1988** LARm: 16 G. **1989** LARm: 16 G. **1990** LARm: 15 G. **1991** LARm: 16 G. **1992** LARm: 16 G. **1993** LARm: 9 G. **1994** LARm: 15 G. **1995** Pit: 16 G. **Total:** 147 G; 1 Fum TD; 6 Pt.

RICHARD NEWBILL Newbill, Richard Arthur 6'1", 240 **LB**
Col: Bakersfield Coll. CA (J.C.); Miami (Fla.) *HS:* Clearview Regional [Mullica Hill, NJ] B: 2/8/1968, Camden, NJ *Drafted:* 1990 Round 5 Hou
1990 Min-Sea: 3 G. Min: 2 G. Sea: 1 G. **1991** Sea: 1 G. **1992** Sea: 7 G. **Total:** 11 G.

STEVE NEWELL Newell, Stephen Eugene 6'1", 186 **WR**
Col: Long Beach State *HS:* Culver City [CA] B: 12/27/1944, Springfield, IL *Drafted:* 1967 Round 9 SD
1967 SD: 7 G; Rec 7-68 9.7.

ROBERT NEWHOUSE Newhouse, Robert Fulton 5'10", 209 **RB**
Col: Houston *HS:* Galilee [Hallsville, TX] B: 1/9/1950, Longview, TX
Drafted: 1972 Round 2 Dal
1972 Dal: KR 18-382 21.2. **1973** Dal: KR 3-62 20.7. **1975** Dal: Pass 2-1 50.0%, 46 23.00 1 TD. **1981** Dal: KR 3-34 11.3. **1983** Dal: PR 1-0. **Total:** Pass 2-1 50.0%, 46 23.00 1 TD; PR 1-0; KR 24-478 19.9.

		Rushing				Receiving					Tot
Year Team	G	Att	Yds	Avg	TD	Rec	Yds	Avg	TD	Fum	TD
1972 Dal	14	28	116	4.1	1	1	8	8.0	0	1	1
1973 Dal	14	84	436	5.2	1	9	87	9.7	1	3	2
1974 Dal	14	124	501	4.0	3	9	67	7.4	0	1	3
1975 Dal	14	209	930	4.4	2	34	275	8.1	0	5	2
1976 Dal	14	116	450	3.9	3	15	86	5.7	0	2	3
1977 Dal	14	180	721	4.0	3	16	106	6.6	1	2	4
1978 Dal	13	140	584	4.2	8	20	176	8.8	2	1	10
1979 Dal	14	124	449	3.6	3	7	55	7.9	1	2	4
1980 Dal	16	118	451	3.8	6	8	75	9.4	0	3	6
1981 Dal	16	14	33	2.4	0	1	21	21.0	0	0	0
1982 Dal	9	14	79	5.6	1	0	0	—	0	0	1
1983 Dal	16	9	34	3.8	0	0	0	—	0	3	0
NFL Total	168	1160	4784	4.1	31	120	956	8.0	5	23	36

HARRY NEWLAND Newland, Harry Edward 1 **OE**
Col: No College *HS:* Lincoln Co. [Stanford, KY] B: 3/12/1892, Stanford, KY D: 10/17/1974, Brownsville, OR
1921 Lou: 1 G.

BOB NEWLAND Newland, Robert Vaughn 6'2", 190 **WR**
Col: Oregon *HS:* North Eugene [OR] B: 10/27/1948, Medford, OR
Drafted: 1971 Round 7 NO
1972 NO: KR 1-6 6.0. **1973** NO: Rush 1-6 6.0. **Total:** Rush 1-6 6.0; KR 1-6 6.0.

		Receiving				
Year Team	G	Rec	Yds	Avg	TD	Fum
1971 NO	14	21	319	15.2	0	0
1972 NO	14	47	579	12.3	2	1
1973 NO	14	29	489	16.9	4	0
1974 NO	14	27	490	18.1	2	0
NFL Total	56	124	1877	15.1	8	1

ANTHONY NEWMAN Newman, Anthony Q 6'0", 203 **DB**
Col: Oregon *HS:* Beaverton [OR] B: 11/21/1965, Bellingham, WA
Drafted: 1988 Round 2 LARm
1991 LARm: 1 Fum TD; 1 Sac. **1995** NO: Rec 1-18 18.0. **Total:** Rec 1-18 18.0; 1 Fum TD; 1 Sac.

		Interceptions			Tot
Year Team	G	Int	Yds	TD	TD
1988 LARm	16	2	27	0	0
1989 LARm	15	0	0	0	0
1990 LARm	16	2	0	0	0
1991 LARm	16	1	58	0	1
1992 LARm	16	4	33	0	0
1993 LARm	16	0	0	0	0
1994 LARm	16	2	46	1	1
1995 NO	12	0	0	0	0
1996 NO	16	3	40	0	0
1997 NO	12	3	19	0	0
1998 Oak	11	2	17	0	0
NFL Total	162	19	240	1	2

ED NEWMAN Newman, Edward Kenneth 6'2", 245 **OG**
Col: Florida Atlantic; Duke *HS:* Syosset [NY] B: 6/4/1951, New York, NY *Drafted:* 1973 Round 6 Mia
1973 Mia: 11 G. **1974** Mia: 14 G. **1975** Mia: 14 G. **1976** Mia: 14 G. **1977** Mia: 14 G. **1978** Mia: 12 G. **1979** Mia: 16 G. **1980** Mia: 16 G. **1981** Mia: 16 G. **1982** Mia: 8 G. **1983** Mia: 16 G. **1984** Mia: 16 G. **Total:** 167 G.

PAT NEWMAN Newman, Edward Patrick 5'11", 189 **WR**
Col: Utah State *HS:* Abraham Lincoln [San Diego, CA] B: 9/10/1968, Memphis, TN *Drafted:* 1990 Round 10 Min
1991 NO: 7 G; Rec 3-33 11.0. **1992** NO: 10 G; Rec 3-21 7.0; PR 23-158 6.9; KR 3-62 20.7; 2 Fum. **1993** NO: 16 G; Rec 8-121 15.1 1 TD; PR 1-14 14.0; 6 Pt. **1994** Cle: 1 G. **Total:** 34 G; Rec 14-175 12.5 1 TD; PR 24-172 7.2; KR 3-62 20.7; 6 Pt; 2 Fum.

HARRY NEWMAN Newman, Harry F 5'6", 150 **G-T**
Col: Ohio U. *HS:* Logan [OH] B: 1/24/1897 D: 12/10/1973, Shaker Heights, OH
1924 Akr: 6 G.

HARRY NEWMAN Newman, Harry Lawrence 5'8", 179 **TB-DB**
Col: Michigan *HS:* Northern [Detroit, MI] B: 9/5/1909, Detroit, MI
1933 NYG: Rec 4-136 34.0 1 TD; Scor 33, 1 FG, 6 XK. **1934** NYG: Rec 4-55 13.8; KR **1** TD; Scor 37, 3 FG, 4 XK. **1935** NYG: Rec 2-12 6.0; Scor 9, 2 FG, 3 XK. **Total:** Rec 10-203 20.3 1 TD; KR 1 TD; Scor 79, 6 FG, 13 XK.

		Passing							
Year Team	G	Att	Comp	Comp%	Yds	YPA	TD	Int	Rating
1933 NYG	14	**136**	**53**	39.0	**973**	7.15	**11**	17	51.7
1934 NYG	10	93	35	37.6	391	4.20	1	12	15.0
1935 NYG	8	29	9	31.0	132	4.55	0	7	7.3
NFL Total	32	258	97	37.6	1496	5.80	12	36	33.5

	Rushing				Tot
Year Team	Att	Yds	Avg	TD	TD
1933 NYG	130	437	3.4	3	4
1934 NYG	141	483	3.4	3	4
1935 NYG	65	166	2.6	0	0
NFL Total	336	1086	3.2	6	8

OBIE NEWMAN Newman, Olin Berris Jr. 6'2", 199 **WB-OE-TB**
Col: Carnegie Mellon *HS:* Central [Birmingham, AL] B: 1900 D: 6/4/1949
1925 Akr: 8 G; Rec 1 TD; Scor 7, 1 XK. **1926** Akr-Ham: 9 G. Akr: 8 G. Ham: 1 G. **Total:** 17 G; Rec 1 TD.

TIM NEWMAN Newman, Timothy 6'0", 220 **RB**
Col: Johnson C. Smith *HS:* Olympic [Charlotte, NC] B: 6/11/1964, Charlotte, NC
1987 NYJ: 1 G.

DON NEWMEYER Newmeyer, Donald 6'2", 205 **T**
Col: California *HS:* Berkeley [CA] B: 2/13/1902, Cleveland, OH D: 6/25/1992, Napa, CA
1926 LA: 10 G; Scor 2, 2 XK.

TONY NEWSOM Newsom, Anthony Edwin 5'8", 175 **DB**
Col: Stephen F. Austin St. *HS:* John Tyler [Tyler, TX] B: 7/20/1965, Jacksonville, FL
1987 Hou: 5 G; Int 1-(-3); 1 Sac.

CRAIG NEWSOME Newsome, Craig 6'0", 190 **DB**
(C-New) *Col:* San Bernardino Valley Coll. CA (J.C.); Arizona State
HS: Eisenhower [Rialto, CA] B: 8/10/1971, San Bernardino, CA
Drafted: 1995 Round 1 GB
1995 GB: 16 G; Int 1-3. **1996** GB: 16 G; Int 2-22. **1997** GB: 1 G. **1998** GB: 13 G; Int 1-26. **Total:** 46 G; Int 4-51.

HARRY NEWSOME Newsome, Harry Kent Jr. 6'0", 192 **P**
Col: Wake Forest *HS:* Cheraw [SC] B: 1/25/1963, Cheraw, SC
Drafted: 1985 Round 8 Pit
1986 Pit: Pass 2-1 50.0%, 12 6.00 1 TD. **1987** Pit: Rush 2-16 8.0. **1988** Pit: Rush 2-0. **1989** Pit: Rush 2-(-8) -4.0. **1990** Min: Rush 2-(-2) -1.0. **1992** Min: Pass 1-0. **Total:** Pass 3-1 33.3%, 12 4.00 1 TD; Rush 8-6 0.8.

		Punting			
Year Team	**G**	**Punts**	**Yds**	**Avg**	**Fum**
1985 Pit	16	78	3088	39.6	0
1986 Pit	16	86	3447	40.1	0
1987 Pit	12	64	2678	41.8	1
1988 Pit	16	65	2950	**45.4**	0
1989 Pit	16	82	3368	41.1	1
1990 Min	16	78	3299	42.3	1
1991 Min	16	68	3095	45.5	0
1992 Min	16	72	3243	45.0	0
1993 Min	16	90	3862	42.9	0
NFL Total	140	683	29030	42.5	3

OZZIE NEWSOME Newsome, Ozzie Jr. 6'2", 232 **TE**
Col: Alabama *HS:* Colbert Co. [Leighton, AL] B: 3/15/1956, Muscle Shoals, AL *Drafted:* 1978 Round 1 Cle *HOF:* 1999
1978 Cle: Rush 13-96 7.4 2 TD; PR 2-29 14.5. **1979** Cle: Rush 1-6 6.0. **1980** Cle: Rush 2-13 6.5. **1981** Cle: Rush 2-20 10.0. **Total:** Rush 18-135 7.5 2 TD; PR 2-29 14.5.

		Receiving					Tot
Year Team	**G**	**Rec**	**Yds**	**Avg**	**TD**	**Fum**	**TD**
1978 Cle	16	38	589	15.5	2	1	4
1979 Cle	16	55	781	14.2	9	0	9
1980 Cle	16	51	594	11.6	3	2	3
1981 Cle	16	69	1002	14.5	6	0	6
1982 Cle	9	49	633	12.9	3	0	3
1983 Cle	16	89	970	10.9	6	0	6
1984 Cle	16	89	1001	11.2	5	0	5
1985 Cle	16	62	711	11.5	5	0	5
1986 Cle	16	39	417	10.7	3	0	3
1987 Cle	13	34	375	11.0	0	0	0
1988 Cle	16	35	343	9.8	2	0	2
1989 Cle	16	29	324	11.2	1	0	1
1990 Cle	16	23	240	10.4	2	0	2
NFL Total	198	662	7980	12.1	47	3	49

TIMMY NEWSOME Newsome, Timothy Arthur 6'1", 232 **RB**
Col: Winston-Salem State *HS:* Ahoskie [NC] B: 5/17/1958, Ahoskie, NC *Drafted:* 1980 Round 6 Dal

		Rushing				Receiving			
Year Team	**G**	**Att**	**Yds**	**Avg**	**TD**	**Rec**	**Yds**	**Avg**	**TD**
1980 Dal	16	25	79	3.2	2	4	43	10.8	0
1981 Dal	15	13	38	2.9	0	0	0	—	0
1982 Dal	9	15	98	6.5	1	6	118	19.7	1
1983 Dal	16	44	185	4.2	2	18	250	13.9	4
1984 Dal	15	66	268	4.1	5	26	263	10.1	0
1985 Dal	14	88	252	2.9	2	46	361	7.8	1
1986 Dal	16	34	110	3.2	2	48	421	8.8	3
1987 Dal	11	25	121	4.8	2	34	274	8.1	2
1988 Dal	9	32	75	2.3	3	30	236	7.9	0
NFL Total	121	342	1226	3.6	19	212	1966	9.3	11

	Kickoff Returns					Tot
Year Team	**Ret**	**Yds**	**Avg**	**TD**	**Fum**	**TD**
1980 Dal	12	293	24.4	0	0	2
1981 Dal	12	228	19.0	0	1	0
1982 Dal	5	74	14.8	0	1	2
1983 Dal	1	28	28.0	0	0	6
1984 Dal	0	0	—	0	3	5
1985 Dal	0	0	—	0	2	3
1986 Dal	2	32	16.0	0	2	5
1987 Dal	2	22	11.0	0	1	4
1988 Dal	0	0	—	0	1	3
NFL Total	34	677	19.9	0	11	30

VINCE NEWSOME Newsome, Vincent Karl 6'1", 180 **DB**
Col: Washington *HS:* Vacaville [CA] B: 1/22/1961, Braintree, England
Drafted: 1983 Round 4 LARm
1984 LARm: 1 Sac. **1985** LARm: 1 Sac. **1991** Cle: 1 Fum TD. **1992** Cle: 2 Sac. **Total:** 1 Fum TD; 4 Sac.

		Interceptions			Tot
Year Team	**G**	**Int**	**Yds**	**TD**	**TD**
1983 LARm	16	0	0	0	0
1984 LARm	16	1	31	0	0
1985 LARm	16	3	20	0	0
1986 LARm	16	3	45	0	0
1987 LARm	8	0	0	0	0
1988 LARm	6	0	3	0	0
1989 LARm	16	1	81	1	1
1990 LARm	16	4	47	0	0
1991 Cle	15	1	31	0	1
1992 Cle	16	3	55	0	0
NFL Total	141	16	313	1	2

BILLY NEWSOME Newsome, William Ray 6'4", 250 **DE**
Col: Grambling State *HS:* Frederick Douglass [Jacksonville, TX]
B: 3/2/1948, Jacksonville, TX *Drafted:* 1970 Round 5 Bal
1970 Bal: 14 G; KR 1-0. **1971** Bal: 14 G; Int 2-19 1 TD; 6 Pt. **1972** Bal: 14 G. **1973** NO: 14 G; Int 1-1. **1974** NO: 13 G. **1975** NYJ: 14 G. **1976** NYJ: 2 G. **1977** ChiB: 14 G. **Total:** 99 G; KR 1-0; Int 3-20 1 TD; 6 Pt.

CHUCK NEWTON Newton, Charles Edward 6'0", 205 **DB-BB-HB-FB**
Col: Washington *HS:* Jefferson [Lafayette, IN] B: 11/15/1916, Randolph Twp., Tippecanoe Co., IN D: 4/1984, Glen Burnie, MD
Drafted: 1939 Round 2 Phi
1939 Phi: 9 G; Rush 1-0; Rec 9-123 13.7 1 TD; 6 Pt. **1940** Phi: 3 G; Rec 1-22 22.0; Int 1-12. **Total:** 12 G; Rush 1-0; Rec 10-145 14.5 1 TD; Int 1-12; 6 Pt.

NATE NEWTON Newton, Nathaniel Jr. 6'3", 318 **OG-OT**
Col: Florida A&M *HS:* Jones [Orlando, FL] B: 12/20/1961, Orlando, FL
1986 Dal: 11 G. **1987** Dal: 11 G. **1988** Dal: 15 G; Rec 1-2 2.0. **1989** Dal: 16 G. **1990** Dal: 16 G. **1991** Dal: 14 G. **1992** Dal: 15 G. **1993** Dal: 16 G. **1994** Dal: 16 G. **1995** Dal: 16 G. **1996** Dal: 16 G. **1997** Dal: 13 G. **1998** Dal: 16 G. **Total:** 191 G; Rec 1-2 2.0.

BOB NEWTON Newton, Robert Lee 6'4", 257 **OG-OT**
Col: Cerritos Coll. CA (J.C.); Nebraska *HS:* John Glenn [Norwalk, CA]
B: 8/16/1949, Pomona, CA *Drafted:* 1971 Round 3 ChiB
1971 ChiB: 12 G. **1972** ChiB: 14 G. **1973** ChiB: 13 G. **1974** ChiB: 14 G. **1975** ChiB: 6 G. **1976** Sea: 12 G. **1977** Sea: 13 G. **1978** Sea: 16 G. **1979** Sea: 11 G. **1980** Sea: 16 G. **1981** Sea: 15 G. **Total:** 142 G.

TOM NEWTON Newton, Thomas Richard 6'0", 212 **RB**
Col: San Jose City Coll. CA (J.C.); California *HS:* William C. Overfelt [San Jose, CA] B: 3/8/1954, Carmel, FL
1979 NYJ: KR 1-0. **Total:** KR 1-0.

		Rushing				Receiving				
Year Team	**G**	**Att**	**Yds**	**Avg**	**TD**	**Rec**	**Yds**	**Avg**	**TD**	**Fum**
1977 NYJ	14	8	39	4.9	0	5	33	6.6	0	0
1978 NYJ	16	11	45	4.1	2	5	48	9.6	0	1
1979 NYJ	16	37	145	3.9	6	4	33	8.3	0	0
1980 NYJ	16	59	299	5.1	0	20	144	7.2	0	0
1981 NYJ	16	73	244	3.3	1	17	104	6.1	0	2
1982 NYJ	9	0	0	—	0	1	7	7.0	0	0
NFL Total	87	188	772	4.1	9	52	369	7.1	0	3

TIM NEWTON Newton, Timothy Reginald 6'0", 280 **DT-NT**
Col: Florida *HS:* Jones [Orlando, FL] B: 3/23/1963, Orlando, FL
Drafted: 1985 Round 6 Min
1985 Min: 16 G; Int 2-63; 1 Fum; 2 Sac. **1986** Min: 14 G; 5 Sac. **1987** Min: 9 G. **1988** Min: 14 G; 1 Sac. **1989** Min: 9 G; 1 Fum TD; 6 Pt. **1990** TB: 14 G; 3 Sac. **1991** TB: 16 G; 5 Sac. **1993** KC: 16 G; 1 Sac. **Total:** 108 G; Int 2-63; 1 Fum TD; 6 Pt; 1 Fum; 17 Sac.

ARMAND NICCOLAI Niccolai, Armand 6'2", 226 **T-G-DE-OE**
(Nick) *Col:* Duquesne *HS:* Monessen [PA] B: 11/8/1911, Vesta, PA
D: 12/2/1988, Pittsburgh, PA
1935 Pit: Rec 1-0. **1940** Pit: Int 1-5. **Total:** Rec 1-0; Int 1-5.

		Scoring						
Year Team	**G**	**Pts**	**FG**	**FGA**	**FG%**	**XK**	**XKA**	**XK%**
1934 Pit	12	10	3	—	—	1	—	—
1935 Pit	12	28	**6**	—	—	10	—	—
1936 Pit	11	28	**7**	—	—	7	—	—
1937 Pit	11	17	4	—	—	5	—	—
1938 Pit	11	13	1	5	20.0	10	10	100.0
1939 Pit	11	24	3	8	37.5	15	15	100.0
1940 Pit	11	24	6	**14**	42.9	6	6	100.0
1941 Pit	8	14	2	4	50.0	8	9	88.9
1942 Pit	10	15	2	**14**	14.3	9	9	100.0
NFL Total	97	173	34	45	31.1	71	49	98.0

JIM NICELY Nicely, James Harris 5'10", 185 **T**
Col: Gettysburg *HS:* Harrisburg [PA] B: 10/7/1898, Montoursville, PA
Deceased
1930 SI: 1 G.

AL NICHELINI Nichelini, Allen James 6'2", 207 **WB-DB**
Col: St. Mary's (Cal.) *HS:* St. Helena [CA] B: 11/23/1909, St. Helena, CA D: 1/3/1992, Fresno, CA
1935 ChiC: Pass 1-1 100.0%, 16 16.00; Rec 1-0. **1936** ChiC: Rec 9-133 14.8. **Total:** Pass 1-1 100.0%, 16 16.00; Rec 10-133 13.3.

Year Team	G	Rushing Att	Yds	Avg	TD	Tot TD
1935 ChiC	11	94	234	2.5	4	4
1936 ChiC	12	55	189	3.4	0	1
NFL Total	23	149	423	2.8	4	5

CALVIN NICHOLAS Nicholas, Calvin Lewis 6'4", 208 **WR**
Col: Grambling State *HS:* McKinley [Baton Rouge, LA] B: 6/11/1964, Baton Rouge, LA *Drafted:* 1987 Round 11 SF
1988 SF: 7 G; Rec 1-14 14.0.

ALLEN NICHOLS Nichols, Allen 5'10", 205 **FB-LB**
Col: Temple *HS:* Avalon [Bellview, PA] B: 10/28/1916 D: 6/1981
1945 Pit: 1 G; Rush 10-5 0.5.

GERALD NICHOLS Nichols, Gerald William 6'2", 261 **DT-NT-DE**
Col: Florida State *HS:* Hazelwood East [St. Louis, MO] B: 2/10/1964, St. Louis, MO *Drafted:* 1987 Round 7 NYJ
1987 NYJ: 13 G; 2.5 Sac. **1988** NYJ: 16 G; 1.5 Sac. **1989** NYJ: 16 G; KR 2-9 4.5; 4 Sac. **1990** NYJ: 15 G; KR 2-3 1.5; 3.5 Sac. **1991** TB: 16 G; 1 Sac. **1993** Phi-Was: 9 G. Phi: 7 G. Was: 2 G. **Total:** 85 G; KR 4-12 3.0; 12.5 Sac.

HAMILTON NICHOLS Nichols, Hamilton James Jr. 5'11", 209 **OG-LB**
Col: Rice *HS:* Mirabeau B. Lamar [Houston, TX] B: 10/18/1924, Houston, TX *Drafted:* 1946 Round 4 ChiC
1947 ChiC: 11 G; Int 1-41. **1948** ChiC: 12 G. **1949** ChiC: 11 G. **1951** GB: 9 G. **Total:** 43 G; Int 1-41.

JOHN NICHOLS Nichols, John Howard 6'0", 200 **G-T**
Col: Ohio State *HS:* Lyons Twp. [La Grange, IL] B: 7/30/1904 D: 6/16/1978, Cleveland, OH
1926 Can: 13 G.

MIKE NICHOLS Nichols, Lee Michael 6'3", 225 **C**
Col: Arkansas-Monticello *HS:* Monticello [AR] B: 7/29/1938, College Heights, AR
1960 Den: 14 G; Rush 0-3. **1961** Den: 14 G. **Total:** 28 G; Rush 0-3.

MARK NICHOLS Nichols, Mark Robe 6'3", 225 **LB**
Col: Golden West Coll. CA (J.C.); Colorado State *HS:* Marina [Huntington Beach, CA] B: 10/23/1956, Columbus, OH *Drafted:* 1978 Round 8 Oak
1978 SF: 15 G; KR 3-39 13.0; Int 1-0.

MARK NICHOLS Nichols, Mark Stephen 6'2", 210 **WR**
Col: Bakersfield Coll. CA (J.C.); San Jose State *HS:* Bakersfield [CA] B: 10/29/1959, Bakersfield, CA *Drafted:* 1981 Round 1 Det
1981 Det: Rush 3-50 16.7; KR 4-74 18.5. **1982** Det: Rush 1-3 3.0. **1983** Det: Rush 1-13 13.0. **1984** Det: Rush 3-27 9.0. **1985** Det: Rush 1-15 15.0. **Total:** Rush 9-108 12.0; KR 4-74 18.5.

Year Team	G	Receiving Rec	Yds	Avg	TD	Fum
1981 Det	12	10	222	22.2	1	1
1982 Det	7	8	153	19.1	2	0
1983 Det	16	29	437	15.1	1	2
1984 Det	15	34	744	21.9	1	0
1985 Det	14	36	592	16.4	4	1
1987 Det	12	7	87	12.4	0	0
NFL Total	76	124	2235	18.0	9	4

RALPH NICHOLS Nichols, Ralph Dale 6'0", 210 **T-G**
Col: Kansas State B: 8/2/1899 Deceased
1926 Har: 10 G.

RICKY NICHOLS Nichols, Ricky Antonio 5'10", 176 **WR**
Col: East Carolina *HS:* Great Bridge [Chesapeake, VA] B: 7/27/1962, Norfolk, VA *Drafted:* 1985 Round 8 Ind
1985 Ind: 3 G.

ROBBIE NICHOLS Nichols, Robert B 6'3", 220 **LB**
Col: Tulsa *HS:* Cleveland [OK] B: 11/17/1946, Cleveland, OK
1970 Bal: 14 G. **1971** Bal: 4 G. **Total:** 18 G.

BOB NICHOLS Nichols, Robert Gordon 6'3", 250 **OT**
Col: Stanford *HS:* Nathaniel Narbonne [Los Angeles, CA] B: 7/18/1943, Los Angeles, CA *Drafted:* 1964 Round 9 Pit
1965 Pit: 14 G. **1966** LARm: 13 G. **1967** LARm: 14 G; **4** Sac. **Total:** 41 G; 4 Sac.

BOBBY NICHOLS Nichols, Robert P 6'2", 220 **TE**
Col: Boston U. *HS:* South Boston [MA] B: 1/30/1943 *Drafted:* 1967 Round 17 Bos
1967 Bos: 9 G; Rec 1-19 19.0. **1968** Bos: 6 G. **Total:** 15 G; Rec 1-19 19.0.

SID NICHOLS Nichols, Sidney Warren 5'7", 177 **BB**
Col: Illinois *HS:* Des Moines West [IA] B: 4/15/1895, Creston, IA D: 3/23/1971, Paso Robles, CA
1920 RI: 7 G. **1921** RI: 7 G; Rush 1 TD; 6 Pt. **Total:** 14 G; Rush 1 TD; 6 Pt.

CALVIN NICHOLSON Nicholson, Calvin T 5'9", 183 **DB**
Col: West Los Angeles Coll. CA (J.C.); Oregon State *HS:* El Camino Real [Woodland Hills, CA] B: 7/9/1967, Los Angeles, CA *Drafted:* 1989 Round 11 NO
1989 NO: 1 G. **1991** NO: 8 G. **Total:** 9 G.

FRANK NICHOLSON Nicholson, Frank 6'2", 205 **LB**
Col: Delaware State B: 3/6/1961
1987 NYG: 3 G.

JIM NICHOLSON Nicholson, James Burton Jr. 6'6", 269 **OT**
Col: Michigan State *HS:* St. Louis [Honolulu, HI] B: 2/28/1949, Honolulu, HI *Drafted:* 1973 Round 9 LARm
1974 KC: 13 G. **1975** KC: 12 G. **1976** KC: 14 G. **1977** KC: 12 G. **1978** KC: 6 G. **1979** KC: 15 G. **Total:** 72 G.

ELBIE NICKEL Nickel, Elbert Everett 6'1", 196 **OE-DE**
Col: Cincinnati *HS:* Chillicothe [OH] B: 12/28/1922, Fullerton, KY *Drafted:* 1947 Round 15 Pit
1949 Pit: KR 1-20 20.0. **Total:** KR 1-20 20.0.

Year Team	G	Receiving Rec	Yds	Avg	TD	Fum
1947 Pit	11	1	10	10.0	0	0
1948 Pit	12	22	324	14.7	1	2
1949 Pit	12	26	633	**24.3**	3	0
1950 Pit	12	22	527	24.0	4	0
1951 Pit	12	28	447	16.0	3	0
1952 Pit	12	55	884	16.1	9	1
1953 Pit	12	62	743	12.0	4	1
1954 Pit	12	40	584	14.6	5	1
1955 Pit	12	36	488	13.6	2	0
1956 Pit	12	27	376	13.9	5	0
1957 Pit	12	10	115	11.5	1	0
NFL Total	131	329	5131	15.6	37	5

HARDY NICKERSON Nickerson, Hardy Otto 6'2", 230 **LB**
Col: California *HS:* Verbum Dei [Los Angeles, CA] B: 9/1/1965, Compton, CA *Drafted:* 1987 Round 5 Pit
1987 Pit: 12 G. **1988** Pit: 15 G; Int 1-0; 3.5 Sac. **1989** Pit: 10 G; 1 Sac. **1990** Pit: 16 G; 2 Sac. **1991** Pit: 16 G; 1 Sac. **1992** Pit: 15 G; 2 Sac. **1993** TB: 16 G; Int 1-6; 1 Sac. **1994** TB: 14 G; Int 2-9; 1 Sac. **1995** TB: 16 G; 1.5 Sac. **1996** TB: 16 G; Int 2-24; 3 Sac. **1997** TB: 16 G; 1 Sac. **1998** TB: 10 G; 1 Sac. **Total:** 172 G; Int 6-39; 18 Sac.

ED NICKLA Nickla, Edward Michael 6'3", 240 **OT**
Col: Tennessee; Maryland *HS:* Merrick [NY] B: 8/11/1933, New York, NY *Drafted:* 1955 Round 14 ChiB
1959 ChiB: 12 G.

PETE NICKLAS Nicklas, Peter Lawrence 6'4", 240 **OT**
Col: Cerritos Coll. CA (J.C.); Baylor *HS:* Whittier [CA] B: 7/24/1939 *Drafted:* 1961 Round 9 Bal
1962 Oak: 14 G.

GEORGE NICKSICH Nicksich, George 6'0", 225 **LB-OG**
Col: St. Bonaventure *HS:* Monessen [PA] B: 5/5/1928, Monessen, PA D: 1/1985, Greensburg, PA
1950 Pit: 12 G; Int 3-31.

SCOTT NICOLAS Nicolas, Scott Stephen 6'3", 226 **LB**
Col: Miami (Fla.) *HS:* Clearwater [FL] B: 8/7/1960, Wichita Falls, TX *Drafted:* 1982 Round 12 Cle
1982 Cle: 9 G; KR 2-16 8.0; 1 Fum. **1983** Cle: 16 G; KR 2-29 14.5. **1984** Cle: 16 G; KR 1-12 12.0. **1985** Cle: 16 G; KR 1-9 9.0; 1 Sac. **1986** Cle: 16 G; KR 3-28 9.3. **1987** Mia: 12 G. **Total:** 85 G; KR 9-94 10.4; 1 Fum; 1 Sac.

BRUNO NIEDZIELA Niedziela, Bruno Joseph 6'2", 225 **T**
Col: Iowa *HS:* Crane [Chicago, IL] B: 4/12/1923, Chicago, IL
AAFC **1947** ChiA: 12 G.

FANNY NIEHAUS Niehaus, Francis W 6'0", 170 **WB-BB**
Col: Washington & Jefferson *HS:* West [Akron, OH] B: 3/16/1902 D: 3/1985, Wadsworth, OH
1925 Akr: 7 G; Rush 1 TD; 6 Pt. **1926** Pott: 4 G. **Total:** 11 G; Rush 1 TD; 6 Pt.

RALPH NIEHAUS Niehaus, Ralph H 6'4", 220 **T**
(Biff) *Col:* Dayton *HS:* Roger Bacon [Cincinnati, OH] B: 11/19/1917, Cincinnati, OH *Drafted:* 1939 Round 15 Det
1939 Cle: 6 G.

STEVE NIEHAUS Niehaus, Steven Gerard 6'4", 263 **DT-DE**
Col: Notre Dame *HS:* Moeller [Cincinnati, OH] B: 9/25/1954, Cincinnati, OH *Drafted:* 1976 Round 1 Sea
1976 Sea: 14 G. **1977** Sea: 8 G. **1978** Sea: 14 G. **1979** Min: 3 G. **Total:** 39 G.

ROB NIEHOFF Niehoff, Robert Thomas 6'2", 205 **DB**
Col: Cincinnati *HS:* Roger Bacon [Cincinnati, OH] B: 5/9/1964, Cincinnati, OH
1987 Cin: 3 G; Int 1-19.

HANS NIELSEN Nielsen, Hans Jorgen 5′11″, 165 K
Col: Michigan State *HS:* Manistee [Vejle, Denmark] B: 11/18/1952, Vejle, Denmark
1981 ChiB: 3 G; Scor 8, 0-2 FG, 8-8 100.0% XK.

GIFFORD NIELSEN Nielsen, Stanley Gifford 6′4″, 205 QB
Col: Brigham Young *HS:* Provo [UT] B: 10/25/1954, Provo, UT
Drafted: 1978 Round 3 Hou

		Passing							
Year Team	G	Att	Comp	Comp%	Yds	YPA	TD	Int	Rating
1978 Hou	2	4	2	50.0	0	0.00	0	0	56.3
1979 Hou	16	61	32	52.5	404	6.62	3	3	69.3
1980 Hou	16	4	2	50.0	12	3.00	1	0	95.8
1981 Hou	5	93	60	64.5	709	7.62	5	3	92.1
1982 Hou	9	161	87	54.0	1005	6.24	6	8	64.8
1983 Hou	7	175	90	51.4	1125	6.43	5	8	62.2
NFL Total	55	498	273	54.8	3255	6.54	20	22	70.0

	Rushing				
Year Team	Att	Yds	Avg	TD	Fum
1978 Hou	0	0	—	0	1
1979 Hou	5	7	1.4	0	1
1980 Hou	1	0	0.0	0	1
1981 Hou	6	2	0.3	0	3
1982 Hou	9	37	4.1	0	4
1983 Hou	8	43	5.4	0	6
NFL Total	29	89	3.1	0	16

WALT NIELSEN Nielsen, Walter Ring 6′3″, 220 FB-DB
(Hoss) *Col:* Arizona *HS:* Redondo [Redondo Beach, CA] B: 2/4/1917
Drafted: 1939 Round 1 NYG
1940 NYG: Pass 1-0; Rec 2-17 8.5; Punt 1-42 42.0.

		Rushing			
Year Team	G	Att	Yds	Avg	TD
1940 NYG	9	73	269	3.7	1

NIELSON Nielson WB
Col: No College
1924 Roch: 1 G.

WALLY NIEMANN Niemann, Walter Albright 5′11″, 180 C
Col: Michigan *HS:* Hermansville [MI] B: 4/21/1894, Hermansville, MI
D: 12/5/1967, Menominee, MI
1922 GB: 8 G. **1923** GB: 10 G. **1924** GB: 4 G. **Total:** 22 G.

LAURIE NIEMI Niemi, Laurie Jack 6′1″, 251 OT-DT
Col: Washington State *HS:* Clarkston [WA] B: 3/19/1925, Red Lodge, MT D: 2/19/1968, Spokane, WA *Drafted:* 1949 Round 2 Was
1949 Was: 12 G. **1950** Was: 8 G. **1951** Was: 12 G. **1952** Was: 12 G.
1953 Was: 12 G; **1** Fum TD; 6 Pt. **Total:** 56 G; 1 Fum TD; 6 Pt.

JOHN NIES Nies, John Richard 6′2″, 199 P
Col: Nassau CC NY; Arizona *HS:* Ocean Twp. [Oakhurst, NJ]
B: 2/13/1967, Jersey City, NJ *Drafted:* 1990 Round 6 Buf
1990 Buf: 4 G; Punt 5-174 34.8.

NICK NIGHSWANDER Nighswander, Nicholas M 6′0″, 232 C
Col: Morehead State B: 11/3/1952
1974 Buf: 7 G.

JOHN NILAND Niland, John Hugh 6′3″, 245 OG
(Big John) *Col:* Iowa *HS:* Amityville Memorial [NY] B: 2/29/1944, Quincy, MA *Drafted:* 1966 Round 1 Dal
1966 Dal: 13 G. **1967** Dal: 14 G. **1968** Dal: 14 G. **1969** Dal: 14 G.
1970 Dal: 14 G. **1971** Dal: 14 G. **1972** Dal: 14 G; **1** Fum TD; 6 Pt.
1973 Dal: 13 G. **1974** Dal: 14 G. **1975** Phi: 14 G. **Total:** 138 G; 1 Fum TD; 6 Pt.

JERRY NILES Niles, Jerry Maynard Jr. 6′1″, 195 QB
Col: Iowa *HS:* Clinton [IA] B: 5/1/1919, East Moline, IL D: 12/27/1950
1947 NYG: Rush 8-24 3.0; KR 1-12 12.0.

		Passing								
Year Team	G	Att	Comp	Comp%	Yds	YPA	TD	Int	Rating	Fum
1947 NYG	4	57	19	33.3	269	4.72	1	7	15.8	2

REED NILSEN Nilsen, Reed Elfin 6′0″, 230 C
Col: Brigham Young *HS:* Provo [UT] B: 1/13/1921, Provo, UT
1947 Det: 2 G.

JIM NINOWSKI Ninowski, James 6′1″, 206 QB
Col: Michigan State *HS:* Pershing [Detroit, MI] B: 3/26/1936, Detroit, MI *Drafted:* 1958 Round 4 Cle

		Passing							
Year Team	G	Att	Comp	Comp%	Yds	YPA	TD	Int	Rating
1958 Cle	4	17	8	47.1	139	8.18	1	3	55.4
1959 Cle	2	10	3	30.0	41	4.10	0	1	4.6
1960 Det	11	283	134	47.3	1599	5.65	2	18	40.9
1961 Det	13	247	117	47.4	1921	7.78	7	18	53.0
1962 Cle	7	173	87	50.3	1178	6.81	7	8	66.6
1963 Cle	4	61	29	47.5	423	6.93	2	6	41.9
1964 Cle	3	9	6	66.7	125	13.89	2	0	149.3
1965 Cle	6	83	40	48.2	549	6.61	4	3	70.8
1966 Cle	14	18	11	61.1	175	9.72	4	1	110.0
1967 Was	14	18	12	66.7	123	6.83	0	1	63.0
1968 Was	7	95	49	51.6	633	6.66	4	6	60.5
1969 NO	4	34	17	50.0	227	6.68	1	2	56.9
NFL Total	89	1048	513	49.0	7133	6.81	34	67	55.4

	Rushing				
Year Team	Att	Yds	Avg	TD	Fum
1958 Cle	2	1	0.5	0	0
1959 Cle	1	11	11.0	0	0
1960 Det	32	81	2.5	5	2
1961 Det	33	238	7.2	5	4
1962 Cle	9	15	1.7	0	2
1963 Cle	5	-19	-3.8	0	2
1964 Cle	1	-8	-8.0	0	1
1965 Cle	4	46	11.5	0	0
1966 Cle	3	-11	-3.7	0	3
1968 Was	2	13	6.5	0	1
NFL Total	92	367	4.0	10	15

MAURY NIPP Nipp, Maurice Herman 6′0″, 219 OG
Col: Loyola Marymount *HS:* Excelsior [Norwalk, CA] B: 3/21/1930, Yankton, SD *Drafted:* 1952 Round 9 Phi
1952 Phi: 10 G. **1953** Phi: 12 G. **1956** Phi: 3 G. **Total:** 25 G.

DAVE NISBET Nisbet, David McLean 6′1″, 190 OE-DE
Col: Washington *HS:* Chehalis [WA] B: 8/29/1910 D: 12/1976, Seattle, WA
1933 ChiC: 10 G; Pass 3-1 33.3%, 36 12.00 1 Int; Rec 1-25 25.0.

JOHN NISBY Nisby, John Edward 6′1″, 235 OG
Col: U. of Pacific *HS:* Stockton [CA] B: 9/9/1936, San Francisco, CA
Drafted: 1957 Round 6 GB
1957 Pit: 11 G. **1958** Pit: 12 G. **1959** Pit: 12 G. **1960** Pit: 12 G. **1961** Pit: 13 G. **1962** Was: 14 G. **1963** Was: 14 G. **1964** Was: 14 G. **Total:** 102 G.

RAY NITSCHKE Nitschke, Raymond Ernest 6′3″, 235 LB
Col: Illinois *HS:* Proviso East [Maywood, IL] B: 12/29/1936, Elmwood Park, IL D: 3/8/1998, Venice, FL *Drafted:* 1958 Round 3 GB
HOF: 1978
1958 GB: KR 1-0. **1959** GB: KR 2-13 6.5. **1960** GB: KR 2-33 16.5.
1962 GB: KR 1-7 7.0. **1972** GB: Rec 1-34 34.0. **Total:** Rec 1-34 34.0; KR 6-53 8.8.

		Interceptions			
Year Team	G	Int	Yds	TD	Fum
1958 GB	12	1	2	0	0
1959 GB	12	0	0	0	0
1960 GB	12	3	90	1	0
1961 GB	12	2	41	0	0
1962 GB	14	4	56	0	1
1963 GB	12	2	8	0	1
1964 GB	14	2	36	0	0
1965 GB	12	1	21	0	0
1966 GB	14	2	44	0	0
1967 GB	14	3	35	1	0
1968 GB	14	2	20	0	0
1969 GB	14	2	32	0	0
1970 GB	14	0	0	0	0
1971 GB	9	1	0	0	0
1972 GB	11	0	0	0	0
NFL Total	190	25	385	2	2

BJORN NITTMO Nittmo, Bjorn Arne 5′11″, 185 K
Col: Appalachian State *HS:* Enterprise [AL] B: 7/26/1966, Lomma, Sweden
1989 NYG: 6 G; Scor 39, 9-12 75.0% FG, 12-13 92.3% XK.

KENT NIX Nix, Alvin Kent 6′2″, 195 QB
Col: Texas Christian *HS:* W.B. Ray [Corpus Christi, TX] B: 3/12/1944, Corpus Christi, TX

		Passing							
Year Team	G	Att	Comp	Comp%	Yds	YPA	TD	Int	Rating
1967 Pit	12	268	136	50.7	1587	5.92	8	19	49.5
1968 Pit	8	130	56	43.1	720	5.54	4	8	45.7
1969 Pit	5	53	25	47.2	290	5.47	2	6	37.2
1970 ChiB	1	1	0	0.0	0	0.00	0	0	39.6
1971 ChiB	8	137	51	37.2	760	5.55	6	10	40.4
1972 Hou	12	63	33	52.4	287	4.56	3	6	41.0
NFL Total	46	652	301	46.2	3644	5.59	23	49	44.3

	Rushing				
Year Team	Att	Yds	Avg	TD	Fum
1967 Pit	15	45	3.0	2	2
1968 Pit	6	15	2.5	0	4

1969 Pit	10	70	7.0	0	1
1971 ChiB	9	12	1.3	0	3
1972 Hou	3	3	1.0	0	3
NFL Total	43	145	3.4	2	13

DOYLE NIX Nix, Doyle Edward 6'1", 191 **DB**
Col: Southern Methodist *HS:* Texas [Texarkana, TX] B: 5/30/1933, Texarkana, TX *Drafted:* 1955 Round 18 GB
1958 Was: PR 1-12 12.0. **Total:** PR 1-12 12.0.

		Interceptions		
Year Team	**G**	**Int**	**Yds**	**TD**
1955 GB	12	5	33	0
1958 Was	11	3	5	0
1959 Was	8	1	19	0
1960 LAC	12	4	30	1
1961 DalT	11	3	58	0
NFL Total	54	16	145	1

GEORGE NIX Nix, George Augustus 5'11", 195 **G**
(Chief) *Col:* Haskell Indian B: 3/18/1895, Howkan, AK D: 10/5/1978, Tacoma, WA
1926 Buf: 2 G.

JACK NIX Nix, Jack Clarence 6'0", 175 **WB-DB**
Col: Mississippi State *HS:* Pachuta [MS] B: 11/9/1917, Moselle, MS D: 12/29/1990, Starkville, MS *Drafted:* 1940 Round 17 Cle
1940 Cle: 1 G.

JACK NIX Nix, Jack Louis 6'2", 200 **OE**
Col: Pasadena City Coll. CA (J.C.); USC *HS:* Susan Miller Dorsey [Los Angeles, CA] B: 5/7/1928, Gary, IN *Drafted:* 1950 Round 20 SF
1950 SF: 9 G; Rec 9-114 12.7; Scor **1** 1XP; 1 Pt.

EMERY NIX Nix, Kenneth Emery 5'11", 180 **QB**
Col: Texas Christian *HS:* Corpus Christi [TX] B: 12/1/1919, Chillicothe, TX
1943 NYG: PR 4-50 12.5; KR 1-12 12.0; Int 2-13. **Total:** PR 4-50 12.5; KR 1-12 12.0; Int 2-13.

		Passing							
Year Team	**G**	**Att**	**Comp**	**Comp%**	**Yds**	**YPA**	**TD**	**Int**	**Rating**
1943 NYG	10	53	24	45.3	396	7.47	3	3	66.2
1946 NYG	4	19	10	52.6	156	8.21	2	0	115.2
NFL Total	14	72	34	47.2	552	7.67	5	3	79.2

	Rushing				
Year Team	**Att**	**Yds**	**Avg**	**TD**	**Fum**
1943 NYG	19	26	1.4	0	0
1946 NYG	8	-25	-3.1	0	1
NFL Total	27	1	0.0	0	1

ROOSEVELT NIX Nix, Roosevelt 6'6", 299 **DE**
Col: Coll. of DuPage IL (J.C.); Central State (Ohio) *HS:* V. W. Scott [Toledo, OH] B: 4/17/1967, Toledo, OH *Drafted:* 1992 Round 8 Cin
1992 Cin: 6 G; 1 Sac. **1993** Cin: 10 G. **1994** Min: 2 G. **Total:** 18 G; 1 Sac.

FRED NIXON Nixon, Frederick Lenar 5'11", 191 **WR**
Col: Oklahoma *HS:* Miami Carol City [Miami, FL] B: 9/22/1958, Camila, GA *Drafted:* 1980 Round 4 GB
1980 GB: Rec 4-78 19.5; KR 6-160 26.7. **1981** GB: Rec 2-27 13.5; KR 12-222 18.5. **Total:** Rec 6-105 17.5; KR 18-382 21.2.

		Punt Returns				
Year Team	**G**	**Ret**	**Yds**	**Avg**	**TD**	**Fum**
1980 GB	15	11	85	7.7	0	1
1981 GB	8	15	118	7.9	0	2
NFL Total	23	26	203	7.8	0	3

JEFF NIXON Nixon, Jeffrey Allen 6'3", 190 **DB**
Col: Richmond *HS:* Gar-Field [Woodbridge, VA] B: 10/13/1956, Furstenfeldbruck, Germany *Drafted:* 1979 Round 4 Buf

		Interceptions		
Year Team	**G**	**Int**	**Yds**	**TD**
1979 Buf	16	6	81	0
1980 Buf	7	5	81	1
1981 Buf	13	0	0	0
1982 Buf	7	0	0	0
NFL Total	43	11	162	1

MIKE NIXON Nixon, Michael Regis 5'11", 181 **HB**
(AKA Michael Regis Nicksick) *Col:* Pittsburgh *HS:* Burgettstown [PA] B: 11/21/1911, Masontown, PA
1935 Pit: 3 G; Pass 3-0, 1 Int; Rush 7-5 0.7. **1942** Bkn: 3 G. **Total:** 6 G; Pass 3-0, 1 Int; Rush 7-5 0.7.

TORY NIXON Nixon, Torran Blake 5'11", 186 **DB**
Col: Phoenix Coll. AZ (J.C.); Arizona; San Diego State *HS:* Shadow Mountain [Phoenix, AZ] B: 2/24/1962, Eugene, OR *Drafted:* 1985 Round 2 Was
1985 SF: 16 G. **1986** SF: 16 G; Int 2-106 1 TD; 6 Pt. **1987** SF: 12 G; Int 1-5. **1988** SF: 6 G. **Total:** 50 G; Int 3-111 1 TD; 6 Pt.

BOB NIZIOLEK Niziolek, Robert Craig 6'4", 220 **TE**
Col: Colorado *HS:* Weber [Chicago, IL] B: 6/30/1958, Chicago, IL *Drafted:* 1981 Round 8 Det
1981 Det: 4 G.

LEO NOBILE Nobile, Leo Anthony 5'10", 213 **G-LB**
Col: Penn State *HS:* Ambridge [PA] B: 9/22/1922, Ambridge, PA
1947 Was: 9 G. **1948** Pit: 12 G. **1949** Pit: 12 G; Int 1-7. **Total:** 33 G; Int 1-7.

TOMMY NOBIS Nobis, Thomas Henry Jr. 6'2", 240 **LB**
Col: Texas *HS:* Thomas Jefferson [San Antonio, TX] B: 9/20/1943, San Antonio, TX *Drafted:* 1966 Round 1 Atl

		Interceptions			
Year Team	**G**	**Int**	**Yds**	**TD**	**Fum**
1966 Atl	14	0	0	0	0
1967 Atl	14	3	57	1	0
1968 Atl	14	1	0	0	0
1969 Atl	5	1	0	0	0
1970 Atl	14	2	36	0	0
1971 Atl	4	0	0	0	0
1972 Atl	14	3	74	1	1
1973 Atl	14	0	0	0	0
1974 Atl	14	1	10	0	0
1975 Atl	13	0	0	0	0
1976 Atl	13	1	5	0	0
NFL Total	133	12	182	2	1

BRIAN NOBLE Noble, Brian David 6'3", 250 **LB**
Col: Fullerton Coll. CA (J.C.); Arizona State *HS:* Anaheim [CA] B: 9/6/1962, Anaheim, CA *Drafted:* 1985 Round 5 GB
1985 GB: 16 G; 3 Sac. **1986** GB: 16 G; KR 1-1 1.0; 2 Sac. **1987** GB: 12 G; Int 1-10; 1 Sac. **1988** GB: 12 G; 0.5 Sac. **1989** GB: 16 G; Int 2-10; 2 Sac. **1990** GB: 14 G; 1 Sac. **1991** GB: 16 G; 1 Fum TD; 6 Pt; 2.5 Sac. **1992** GB: 13 G; 2 Sac. **1993** GB: 2 G. **Total:** 117 G; KR 1-1 1.0; Int 3-20; 1 Fum TD; 6 Pt; 14 Sac.

DAVE NOBLE Noble, David Gordon 6'2", 195 **WB**
(Big Moose) *Col:* Wisconsin; Nebraska *HS:* Central [Omaha, NE] B: 7/29/1900, Omaha, NE D: 1/24/1983, Omaha, NE
1924 Cle: 9 G; Rush 4 TD; Rec 2 TD; Tot TD 6; 36 Pt. **1925** Cle: 13 G; Rush 3 TD; Rec 3 TD; Tot TD 6; 36 Pt. **Total:** 22 G; Rush 7 TD; Rec 5 TD; Tot TD 12; 72 Pt.

DON NOBLE Noble, Donald LaWayne 6'2", 253 **TE**
Col: California *HS:* Pius X [Downey, CA] B: 10/11/1965, Los Angeles, CA
1987 LARm: 2 G.

JAMES NOBLE Noble, James Brown Jr. 6'0", 193 **WR**
Col: Stephen F. Austin St. *HS:* Jacksonville [TX] B: 8/14/1963, Jacksonville, TX
1986 Was: 6 G. **1987** Ind: 3 G; Rec 10-78 7.8 2 TD; KR 2-35 17.5; 12 Pt; 2 Fum. **Total:** 9 G; Rec 10-78 7.8 2 TD; KR 2-35 17.5; 12 Pt; 2 Fum.

JIM NOBLE Noble, James E 6'1", 190 **E**
Col: Syracuse *HS:* East [Cleveland, OH] B: 10/10/1901 D: 9/30/1959, Willowick, OH
1925 Buf: 9 G.

MIKE NOBLE Noble, Michael Wayne 6'4", 220 **LB**
Col: Stanford *HS:* Monte Vista [Cupertino, CA] B: 10/31/1963, Santa Ana, CA
1987 LARd: 1 G.

DICK NOBLE Noble, Richard Brown 178 **G**
Col: Trinity (Conn.) *HS:* Cushing Acad. [Ashburnham, MA] B: 12/4/1902, Hatford, CT D: 5/14/1973, Milford, CT
1926 Har: 1 G.

JOHN NOCERA Nocera, John Stanley 6'1", 220 **LB**
Col: Iowa *HS:* Rayen [Youngstown, OH] B: 5/4/1934, Youngstown, OH D: 5/17/1981, Youngstown, OH *Drafted:* 1957 Round 16 Phi
1959 Phi: 12 G; KR 1-15 15.0. **1960** Phi: 10 G. **1961** Phi: 12 G; Int 0-3; 1 Fum. **1962** Phi: 14 G; Int 1-0. **1963** Den: 9 G. **Total:** 57 G; KR 1-15 15.0; Int 1-3; 1 Fum.

GEORGE NOCK Nock, George Verdell 5'11", 200 **RB**
Col: Morgan State *HS:* Benjamin Franklin [Philadelphia, PA] B: 3/4/1946, Baltimore, MD *Drafted:* 1969 Round 16 NYJ
1970 NYJ: Rec 18-146 8.1 1 TD; KR 1-18 18.0. **1971** NYJ: Rec 6-44 7.3 2 TD; KR 5-71 14.2. **Total:** Rec 24-190 7.9 3 TD; KR 6-89 14.8.

Year Team	G	Rushing Att	Yds	Avg	TD	Fum	Tot TD
1969 NYJ	2	3	-5	-1.7	0	1	0
1970 NYJ	14	135	402	3.0	5	4	6
1971 NYJ	14	48	137	2.9	3	4	5
1972 Was	7	6	22	3.7	0	1	0
NFL Total	37	192	556	2.9	8	10	11

TERRY NOFSINGER Nofsinger, William Terry 6′4″, 215 **QB**
Col: Utah *HS:* South [Salt Lake City, UT] B: 7/13/1938, Salt Lake City, UT *Drafted:* 1961 Round 17 Pit

Year Team	G	Passing Att	Comp	Comp%	Yds	YPA	TD	Int	Rating
1961 Pit	5	11	7	63.6	78	7.09	0	0	84.7
1962 Pit	1	0	0	—	0	—	0	0	—
1963 Pit	2	3	2	66.7	46	15.33	0	0	109.7
1964 Pit	1	4	3	75.0	35	8.75	0	1	61.5
1965 StL	1	20	8	40.0	47	2.35	1	1	43.8
1966 StL	7	162	68	42.0	799	4.93	2	8	41.2
1967 Atl	7	60	30	50.0	352	5.87	1	2	59.9
NFL Total	24	260	118	45.4	1357	5.22	4	12	47.5

Year Team	Rushing Att	Yds	Avg	TD	Fum
1961 Pit	6	6	1.0	0	0
1965 StL	4	1	0.3	1	0
1966 StL	18	25	1.4	2	8
1967 Atl	3	33	11.0	0	0
NFL Total	31	65	2.1	3	8

AL NOGA Noga, Alapati 6′1″, 265 **DE-DT**
Col: Hawaii *HS:* Farrington [Honolulu, HI] B: 9/16/1965, American Samoa *Drafted:* 1988 Round 3 Min
1988 Min: 9 G. **1989** Min: 16 G; 11.5 Sac. **1990** Min: 16 G; Int 1-26 1 TD; 1 Fum TD; Tot TD 2; 12 Pt; 6 Sac. **1991** Min: 16 G; 3 Sac. **1992** Min: 16 G; 9 Sac. **1993** Was: 16 G; 4 Sac. **1994** Ind: 4 G; 1 Sac. **Total:** 93 G; Int 1-26 1 TD; 1 Fum TD; Tot TD 2; 12 Pt; 34.5 Sac.

NIKO NOGA Noga, Falaniko 6′1″, 234 **LB**
Col: Hawaii *HS:* Farrington [Honolulu, HI] B: 3/1/1962, American Samoa *Drafted:* 1984 Round 8 StL
1984 StL: 16 G. **1985** StL: 16 G; 1 Sac. **1986** StL: 16 G; 2 Sac. **1987** StL: 12 G; **1** Fum TD; 6 Pt; 3 Sac. **1988** Pho: 16 G; 1 Sac. **1989** Det: 14 G; Int 1-0. **1990** Det: 16 G. **1991** Det: 16 G. **Total:** 122 G; Int 1-0; 1 Fum TD; 6 Pt; 7 Sac.

PETER NOGA Noga, Petelo 6′0″, 212 **LB**
Col: Hawaii *HS:* Farrington [Honolulu, HI] B: 6/24/1964, American Samoa
1987 StL: 3 G; Int 1-60 1 TD; 6 Pt.

JOHN NOLAN Nolan, John Ervin 5′10″, 185 **G**
Col: Santa Clara *HS:* Gardena [CA] B: 7/10/1900, Los Angeles, CA D: 10/21/1971, San Diego, CA
1926 LA: 10 G.

JOHN NOLAN Nolan, John Joseph Jr. 6′2″, 232 **OT-DT**
Col: Holy Cross; Penn State *HS:* St. Mary's Acad. [Glens Falls, NY] B: 2/26/1926, Glens Falls, NY D: 7/14/1996, Glens Falls, NY
1948 Bos: 12 G. **1949** NYB: 12 G. **1950** NYY: 12 G. **Total:** 36 G.

EARL NOLAN Nolan, Michael Earl 6′1″, 205 **T**
Col: Arizona *HS:* Tucson [AZ] B: 3/8/1914 D: 3/23/1981, Long Beach, CA
1937 ChiC: 8 G. **1938** ChiC: 4 G. **Total:** 12 G.

DICK NOLAN Nolan, Richard Charles 6′1″, 185 **DB**
Col: Maryland *HS:* White Plains [NY] B: 3/26/1932, Pittsburgh, PA *Drafted:* 1954 Round 4 NYG
1954 NYG: Scor **1** Saf. **1958** ChiC: PR 1-2 2.0. **Total:** PR 1-2 2.0; Scor 1 Saf.

Year Team	G	Interceptions Int	Yds	TD	Fum
1954 NYG	12	6	48	0	0
1955 NYG	10	1	20	0	0
1956 NYG	12	2	17	0	0
1957 NYG	11	1	12	0	0
1958 ChiC	12	5	30	0	1
1959 NYG	12	5	57	0	0
1960 NYG	10	3	32	0	0
1961 NYG	9	0	0	0	0
1962 Dal	11	0	0	0	0
NFL Total	99	23	216	0	1

DON NOLANDER Nolander, Donald Austin 6′1″, 210 **C-LB**
Col: Minnesota *HS:* Roosevelt [Minneapolis, MN] B: 9/14/1921, Minneapolis, MN
AAFC **1946** LA-A: 11 G; Int 1-13.

CHUCK NOLL Noll, Charles Henry 6′1″, 220 **LB-OG-C**
Col: Dayton *HS:* Benedictine [Cleveland, OH] B: 1/5/1932, Cleveland, OH *Drafted:* 1953 Round 20 Cle
1953 Cle: 12 G; KR 1-2 2.0. **1954** Cle: 12 G. **1955** Cle: 12 G; Int 5-74 1 TD; Scor **1** Saf; 8 Pt. **1956** Cle: 12 G; Int 1-13; **1** Fum TD; 6 Pt. **1957** Cle: 5 G. **1958** Cle: 12 G. **1959** Cle: 12 G; KR 1-20 20.0; Int 2-5. **Total:** 77 G; KR 2-22 11.0; Int 8-92 1 TD; Scor 1 Saf; 1 Fum TD; Tot TD 2; 14 Pt.

RAY NOLTING Nolting, Raymond Albert 5′11″, 188 **HB-DB**
Col: Cincinnati *HS:* Hughes [Cincinnati, OH] B: 11/8/1913, Cincinnati, OH D: 7/5/1995, Cincinnati, OH
1936 ChiB: Pass 13-3 23.1%, 30 2.31 2 TD 1 Int. **1937** ChiB: Pass 4-0, 1 Int. **1938** ChiB: Pass 11-0, 3 Int. **1939** ChiB: Int **1** TD; Punt 12-463 38.6. **1940** ChiB: Pass 2-1 50.0%, 38 19.00; KR **1** TD; Int 3-18; Punt 2-68 34.0. **1941** ChiB: Pass 5-3 60.0%, 71 14.20 1 TD; PR 4-50 12.5; KR 4-73 18.3. **1942** ChiB: PR 3-23 7.7; KR 1-10 10.0; **1** Fum TD. **1943** ChiB: PR 2-13 6.5; KR 2-40 20.0; Int 1-5. **Total:** Pass 35-7 20.0%, 139 3.97 3 TD 5 Int; PR 9-86 9.6; KR 7-123 17.6 1 TD; Int 4-23 1 TD; Punt 14-531 37.9; 1 Fum TD.

Year Team	G	Rushing Att	Yds	Avg	TD	Receiving Rec	Yds	Avg	TD	Tot TD
1936 ChiB	11	76	352	4.6	0	2	50	25.0	1	1
1937 ChiB	11	106	424	4.0	2	4	64	16.0	0	2
1938 ChiB	11	63	297	4.7	1	4	90	22.5	1	2
1939 ChiB	11	50	216	4.3	2	6	87	14.5	1	4
1940 ChiB	11	78	373	4.8	1	3	36	12.0	0	2
1941 ChiB	9	40	169	4.2	1	4	68	17.0	0	1
1942 ChiB	11	57	245	4.3	2	2	23	11.5	0	3
1943 ChiB	7	38	209	5.5	1	5	90	18.0	0	1
NFL Total	82	508	2285	4.5	10	30	508	16.9	3	16

LEO NOMELLINI Nomellini, Leo Joseph 6′3″, 259 **DT-OT**
(The Lion) *Col:* Minnesota *HS:* Crane [Chicago, IL] B: 6/19/1924, Lucca, Italy *Drafted:* 1950 Round 1 SF *HOF:* 1969
1950 SF: 12 G. **1951** SF: 12 G; PR 1-20 20.0 1 TD; KR 2-27 13.5; 6 Pt. **1952** SF: 12 G; Rush 1-5 5.0; KR 1-18 18.0; 1 Fum. **1953** SF: 12 G; KR 1-5 5.0. **1954** SF: 12 G. **1955** SF: 12 G. **1956** SF: 12 G. **1957** SF: 12 G; Scor **1** Saf; 2 Pt. **1958** SF: 12 G. **1959** SF: 12 G. **1960** SF: 12 G; Scor **1** Saf; 2 Pt. **1961** SF: 14 G. **1962** SF: 14 G. **1963** SF: 14 G. **Total:** 174 G; Rush 1-5 5.0; PR 1-20 20.0 1 TD; KR 4-50 12.5; Scor 2 Saf; 10 Pt; 1 Fum.

TOM NOMINA Nomina, Thomas John 6′3″, 260 **DT-OG**
Col: Miami (Ohio) *HS:* St. John's [Delphos, OH] B: 12/27/1941, Delphos, OH *Drafted:* 1963 Round 2 Den
1963 Den: 14 G. **1964** Den: 11 G. **1965** Den: 12 G. **1966** Mia: 11 G. **1967** Mia: 5 G. **1968** Mia: 14 G. **Total:** 67 G.

IKE NONNENMAKER Nonnenmaker, Clarence Frederick 5′8″, 175 **OE-BB**
Col: Ohio State; Wittenberg *HS:* Aquinas [Columbus, OH] B: 12/11/1901, Columbus, OH D: 11/29/1988, Lockbourne, OH
1926 Col: 7 G.

DANNY NOONAN Noonan, Daniel Nicholas 6′4″, 270 **DT**
Col: Nebraska *HS:* Lincoln Northeast [NE] B: 7/14/1965, Lincoln, NE *Drafted:* 1987 Round 1 Dal
1987 Dal: 11 G; 1 Sac. **1988** Dal: 16 G; Int 1-17 1 TD; Scor 1 Saf; 8 Pt; 7.5 Sac. **1989** Dal: 7 G; 1 Sac. **1990** Dal: 16 G; 4.5 Sac. **1991** Dal: 15 G; 1 Sac. **1992** Dal-GB: 8 G. Dal: 2 G. GB: 6 G. **Total:** 73 G; Int 1-17 1 TD; Scor 1 Saf; 8 Pt; 15 Sac.

JERRY NOONAN Noonan, Gerald Michael 6′1″, 189 **BB-WB-OE**
Col: Notre Dame; Fordham B: 1898 Deceased
1921 Roch-NYG: 6 G; Pass 1 TD; Rec 2 TD; 12 Pt. Roch: 5 G; Pass 1 TD; Rec 2 TD; 12 Pt. NYG: 1 G. **1923** Roch: 1 G. **1924** Roch: 5 G; Rush 1 TD; 6 Pt. **Total:** 12 G; Pass 1 TD; Rush 1 TD; Rec 2 TD; Tot TD 3; 18 Pt.

KARL NOONAN Noonan, Karl Paul 6′2″, 198 **WR**
Col: Iowa *HS:* Assumption [Dubuque, IA] B: 2/17/1944, Dubuque, IA
1966 Mia: KR 0-23. **1969** Mia: Rush 1-(-11) -11.0. **1970** Mia: Rush 1-(-9) -9.0. **Total:** Rush 2-(-20) -10.0; KR 0-23.

Year Team	G	Receiving Rec	Yds	Avg	TD	Fum
1966 Mia	14	17	224	13.2	1	0
1967 Mia	14	12	141	11.8	1	1
1968 Mia	14	58	760	13.1	**11**	1
1969 Mia	14	29	307	10.6	3	0
1970 Mia	14	10	186	18.6	1	1
1971 Mia	14	10	180	18.0	0	0
NFL Total	84	136	1798	13.2	17	3

JOHN NOPPENBERG Noppenberg, John Louis 6′0″, 196 **DB-HB-FB-TB**
Col: Miami (Fla.) *HS:* Menominee [MI] B: 9/8/1917, Wallace, MI *Drafted:* 1940 Round 13 Pit
1940 Pit: 9 G; Rush 2-4 2.0; Rec 4-74 18.5; Int 1-27; Punt 4-136 34.0. **1941** Pit-Det: 6 G; Pass 3-0; Rush 11-16 1.5; KR 1-24 24.0; Punt 7-270 38.6. Pit: 4 G; Pass 3-0; Rush 10-21 2.1; KR 1-24 24.0; Punt 7-270 38.6.

Det: 2 G; Rush 1-(-5) -5.0. **Total:** 15 G; Pass 3-0; Rush 13-20 1.5; Rec 4-74 18.5; KR 1-24 24.0; Int 1-27; Punt 11-406 36.9.

JOHN NORBECK Norbeck, John W 195 **G-BB**
Col: No College B: 7/25/1898, Minneapolis, MN D: 10/23/1984, Santa Ana, CA
1921 Min: 2 G.

HANK NORBERG Norberg, Henry Francis Jr. 6'2", 225 **DE-OE**
Col: Stanford *HS:* Palo Alto [CA] B: 12/22/1920 D: 12/4/1974
Drafted: 1943 Round 16 ChiB
AAFC **1946** SF-A: 14 G; Rec 3-29 9.7; Int 1-22. **1947** SF-A: 11 G; Rec 2-31 15.5. **Total:** 25 G; Rec 5-60 12.0; Int 1-22.

NFL **1948** ChiB: 10 G; Rec 1-4 4.0.

JOHN NORBY Norby, John Heyerdahl 6'0", 195 **DB-WB-BB-HB**
Col: Idaho *HS:* Rupert [ID] B: 8/30/1910, Rupert, ID
1934 NYG-Phi-StL: 5 G; Rush 2-5 2.5; Rec 2-40 20.0. NYG: 3 G; Rush 1-4 4.0; Rec 1-6 6.0. Phi: 1 G. StL: 1 G; Rush 1-1 1.0; Rec 1-34 34.0. **1935** Bkn: 6 G; Rec 1-3 3.0. **Total:** 11 G; Rush 2-5 2.5; Rec 3-43 14.3.

KEITH NORD Nord, Keith Sterling 6'0", 197 **DB**
Col: St. Cloud State *HS:* Minnetonka [MN] B: 3/3/1957, Minneapolis, MN
1979 Min: 16 G; PR 3-11 3.7; 1 Fum. **1980** Min: 16 G; KR 1-70 70.0 **1** TD; 6 Pt. **1981** Min: 16 G; KR 14-229 16.4; 2 Fum. **1982** Min: 9 G; KR 3-43 14.3. **1983** Min: 3 G; Int 1-0; 1 Sac. **1985** Min: 16 G. **Total:** 76 G; PR 3-11 3.7; KR 18-342 19.0 1 TD; Int 1-0; 6 Pt; 3 Fum; 1 Sac.

FRED NORDGREN Nordgren, Frederick Marvin 6'0", 240 **NT**
Col: Portland State *HS:* Hillsboro [OR] B: 12/11/1959, Hillsboro, OR
1987 TB: 3 G; 1 Sac.

MARK NORDQUIST Nordquist, Mark Allan 6'4", 246 **OG-C**
Col: Pierce Coll. CA (J.C.); U. of Pacific *HS:* Reseda [Los Angeles, CA]
B: 11/3/1945, Long Beach, CA *Drafted:* 1968 Round 5 Phi
1968 Phi: 14 G. **1969** Phi: 14 G. **1970** Phi: 14 G. **1971** Phi: 14 G. **1972** Phi: 14 G. **1973** Phi: 14 G. **1974** Phi: 12 G. **1975** ChiB: 14 G. **1976** ChiB: 1 G. **Total:** 111 G.

SWEDE NORDSTROM Nordstrom, Harry William 6'2", 238 **G-T**
(Tiny) *Col:* Trinity (Conn.) *HS:* Bay Ridge [Brooklyn, NY]
B: 10/11/1896, Brooklyn, NY D: 2/13/1963, Toms River, NJ
1925 NYG: 4 G. **1926** Bkn: 4 G. **Total:** 8 G.

AL NORGARD Norgard, Alvar Alfred 6'1", 194 **OE-DE**
Col: Stanford *HS:* Eureka [CA] B: 11/3/1907, Fort Bragg, CA
D: 11/20/1975, Aptos, CA
1934 GB: 10 G; Rec 3-29 9.7.

ERIK NORGARD Norgard, Erik Christian 6'1", 282 **OG-C**
Col: Colorado *HS:* Arlington [WA] B: 11/4/1965, Bellevue, WA
1990 Hou: 16 G; KR 2-0. **1992** Hou: 15 G. **1993** Hou: 16 G; Rec 1-13 13.0. **1994** Hou: 16 G. **1995** Hou: 15 G. **1996** Hou: 13 G; Rec 1-1 1.0 1 TD; 6 Pt. **1997** Ten: 16 G; Rec 1-2 2.0 1 TD; 6 Pt. **1998** Ten: 1 G. **Total:** 108 G; Rec 3-16 5.3 2 TD; KR 2-0; 12 Pt.

REINO NORI Nori, Reino Oscar 5'8", 167 **TB-DB-QB**
Col: Northern Illinois *HS:* De Kalb [IL] B: 2/26/1913, DeKalb, IL
D: 10/8/1988, DeKalb, IL
1937 Bkn: Pass 23-11 47.8%, 168 7.30 1 TD 3 Int. **Total:** Pass 23-11 47.8%, 168 7.30 1 TD 3 Int.

		Rushing			
Year Team	G	Att	Yds	Avg	TD
1937 Bkn	6	26	81	3.1	0
1938 ChiB	1	1	1	1.0	0
NFL Total	7	27	82	3.0	0

TONY NORMAN Norman, Anthony Alexander 6'5", 270 **DE**
Col: Iowa State *HS:* George Washington Carver [Atlanta, GA]
B: 1/27/1955, Atlanta, GA
1987 Min: 2 G.

BEN NORMAN Norman, Benjamin Lee 6'1", 212 **RB**
Col: Colorado State *HS:* North Surry [Mount Airy, NC] B: 12/16/1955, Elkin, NC
1980 Den: 3 G.

CHRIS NORMAN Norman, Christopher Cooper 6'2", 198 **P**
Col: South Carolina *HS:* Dougherty [Albany, GA] B: 5/25/1962, Albany, GA
1985 Den: Pass 1-0; Rush 1-0. **1986** Den: Pass 1-1 100.0%, 43 43.00 1 TD; Rush 1-(-11) -11.0. **Total:** Pass 2-1 50.0%, 43 21.50 1 TD; Rush 2-(-11) -5.5.

		Punting			
Year Team	G	Punts	Yds	Avg	Fum
1984 Den	16	96	3850	40.1	1
1985 Den	16	92	3764	40.9	1
1986 Den	6	30	1168	38.9	1
NFL Total	38	218	8782	40.3	3

JIM NORMAN Norman, James Thomas 6'2", 248 **DT-OT**
Col: No College *HS:* York [NE] B: 1/2/1934, Fortress Monroe, VA
1955 Was: 7 G.

JOE NORMAN Norman, Josef Dennison 6'1", 220 **LB**
Col: Indiana *HS:* West Holmes [Millersburg, OH] B: 10/15/1956, Millersburg, OH *Drafted:* 1979 Round 2 Sea
1979 Sea: 15 G. **1980** Sea: 16 G; Int 1-0. **1981** Sea: 8 G. **1983** Sea: 11 G. **Total:** 50 G; Int 1-0.

PETTIS NORMAN Norman, Pettis Burch 6'3", 222 **TE**
Col: Johnson C. Smith *HS:* West Charlotte [Charlotte, NC]
B: 1/4/1939, Lincolnton, GA *Drafted:* 1962 Round 16 DalT
1962 Dal: KR 2-5 2.5. **1963** Dal: PR 1-0. **1967** Dal: Rush 9-91 10.1. **1968** Dal: Rush 4-51 12.8; KR 1-0. **1969** Dal: Rush 5-20 4.0. **1970** Dal: Rush 2-16 8.0. **1971** SD: Rush 1-1 1.0. **1972** SD: Rush 1-9 9.0. **1973** SD: Rush 1-10 10.0. **Total:** Rush 23-198 8.6; PR 1-0; KR 3-5 1.7.

		Receiving				
Year Team	G	Rec	Yds	Avg	TD	Fum
1962 Dal	14	2	34	17.0	0	1
1963 Dal	14	18	341	18.9	3	0
1964 Dal	14	24	311	13.0	2	1
1965 Dal	14	11	110	10.0	3	1
1966 Dal	14	12	144	12.0	0	0
1967 Dal	14	20	220	11.0	2	1
1968 Dal	13	18	204	11.3	1	1
1969 Dal	10	13	238	18.3	3	1
1970 Dal	14	6	70	11.7	0	0
1971 SD	14	27	358	13.3	1	0
1972 SD	13	19	262	13.8	0	2
1973 SD	14	13	200	15.4	0	0
NFL Total	162	183	2492	13.6	15	8

DICK NORMAN Norman, Richard Michael 6'3", 209 **QB**
Col: Stanford *HS:* Lynwood [CA] B: 9/14/1938, Downey, CA
Drafted: 1960 Round 5 ChiB
1961 ChiB: 3 G.

BOB NORMAN Norman, Robert H 6'1", 185 **C-LB**
Col: No College *HS:* Marion [IL] B: 4/23/1919, Marion, IL
D: 4/25/1982, Marion, IL
1945 ChiC: 1 G.

TIM NORMAN Norman, Timothy Scott 6'6", 270 **OT**
Col: Illinois *HS:* West Chicago [IL] B: 7/10/1959, Winfield, IL
1983 ChiB: 1 G.

WILL NORMAN Norman, Willard Patterson 6'0", 175 **WB-TB**
(Toad) *Col:* Washington & Jefferson B: 9/22/1903 D: 7/1964, WA
1928 Pott: 10 G; Rec 1 TD; 6 Pt.

DAVID NORRIE Norrie, David Doherty 6'4", 220 **QB**
Col: UCLA *HS:* Jesuit [Portland, OR] B: 11/30/1963, Boston, MA
1987 NYJ: Rush 5-5 1.0.

		Passing								
Year Team	G	Att	Comp	Comp%	Yds	YPA	TD	Int	Rating	Fum
1987 NYJ	2	68	35	51.5	376	5.53	1	4	48.4	4

HAL NORRIS Norris, Harold 5'11", 194 **LB-DB**
Col: California *HS:* Grossmont [La Mesa, CA] B: 11/4/1931, Baton Rouge, LA *Drafted:* 1955 Round 16 Was
1955 Was: 12 G. **1956** Was: 1 G. **Total:** 13 G.

JIM NORRIS Norris, James Arthur 6'4", 238 **DT-OT**
Col: Houston *HS:* Mercedes [TX] B: 10/14/1939, Houston, TX
Drafted: 1962 Round 7 Oak
1962 Oak: 7 G; KR 1-2 2.0. **1963** Oak: 14 G. **1964** Oak: 1 G. **Total:** 22 G; KR 1-2 2.0.

JIMMY NORRIS Norris, James Najee 5'11", 188 **DB**
Col: Upsala *HS:* Vailsburg [Newark, NJ] B: 3/12/1964, Asheville, NC
1987 NYG: 3 G; KR 4-70 17.5.

JEROME NORRIS Norris, Jerome 6'0", 187 **DB**
Col: Furman *HS:* Crescent [Iva, SC] B: 1/31/1964
1987 Atl: 3 G.

JACK NORRIS Norris, John Clayton 6'3", 185 **OE**
Col: Western Maryland; Maryland B: 5/18/1909, Lancaster, PA
1932 SI: 2 G.

JON NORRIS Norris, Jonathan Clayton 6'3", 260 **DE-DT**
Col: American International B: 11/1/1962, Lancaster, Wales
1987 ChiB: 3 G; Int 1-6; 2 Sac.

TRUSSE NORRIS Norris, Trusse Rupert Brown 6'1", 194 **OE**
Col: UCLA *HS:* Phillis Wheatley [Houston, TX] B: 8/10/1937, Houston, TX
1960 LAC: 2 G.

ULYSSES NORRIS Norris, Ulysses Jr. 6'4", 230 **TE**
Col: Georgia *HS:* Monticello [GA] B: 1/15/1957, Monticello, GA
Drafted: 1979 Round 4 Det
1983 Det: KR 1-0. **Total:** KR 1-0.

		Receiving				
Year Team	G	Rec	Yds	Avg	TD	Fum
1979 Det	16	4	43	10.8	1	0
1980 Det	16	0	0	—	0	0
1981 Det	12	8	132	16.5	0	0
1982 Det	9	3	44	14.7	0	1
1983 Det	15	26	291	11.2	7	0
1984 Buf	14	0	0	—	0	0
1985 Buf	2	2	30	15.0	0	1
NFL Total	84	43	540	12.6	8	2

MIKE NORSETH Norseth, Michael Adam 6'2", 200 **QB**
Col: Snow Coll. UT (J.C.); Kansas *HS:* Valley [La Crescenta, CA]
B: 8/22/1964, Los Angeles, CA *Drafted:* 1986 Round 7 Cle
1988 Cin: 1 G; Rush 1-5 5.0.

JIM NORTH North, James Morris 6'3", 235 **T**
Col: Central Washington *HS:* Foster [Seattle, WA] B: 8/11/1919, Tuckwila, WA
1944 Was: 7 G.

JOHN NORTH North, John Puckett 6'2", 199 **OE-DB**
Col: Vanderbilt *HS:* Castle Heights Mil. Acad. [TN] B: 6/17/1921, Gilliam, LA *Drafted:* 1945 Round 4 Was
AAFC **1948** BalA: Int 1-25. **Total:** Int 1-25.

		Receiving				Tot
Year Team	G	Rec	Yds	Avg	TD	TD
1948 BalA	14	8	204	25.5	1	2
1949 BalA	11	25	490	19.6	4	4
AAFC Total	25	33	694	21.0	5	6

NFL **1950** Bal: 4 G; Rec 5-90 18.0.

GABE NORTHERN Northern, Gabriel O'Kara 6'2", 240 **DE-LB**
Col: Louisiana State *HS:* Glen Oaks [Baton Rouge, LA] B: 6/8/1974, Baton Rouge, LA *Drafted:* 1996 Round 2 Buf
1996 Buf: 16 G; 6 Pt; 5 Sac. **1997** Buf: 16 G. **1998** Buf: 16 G; Int 1-40 1 TD; 6 Pt; 2 Sac. **Total:** 48 G; Int 1-40 1 TD; Tot TD 2; 12 Pt; 7 Sac.

DON NORTON Norton, Donald Farris 6'1", 195 **WR**
Col: Iowa *HS:* Anamosa [IA] B: 3/3/1938, Iowa City, IA D: 6/23/1997, Cedar Rapids, IA *Drafted:* 1960 Round 1 Oak
1960 LAC: Rush 1-2 2.0; KR 8-153 19.1. **1963** SD: Pass 1-1 100.0%, 15 15.00. **1964** SD: KR 1-0. **1965** SD: Rush 1-(-5) -5.0. **Total:** Pass 1-1 100.0%, 15 15.00; Rush 2-(-3) -1.5; KR 9-153 17.0.

		Receiving				
Year Team	G	Rec	Yds	Avg	TD	Fum
1960 LAC	14	25	414	16.6	5	1
1961 SD	14	47	816	17.4	6	0
1962 SD	14	48	771	16.1	7	1
1963 SD	7	21	281	13.4	1	0
1964 SD	14	49	669	13.7	6	1
1965 SD	14	34	485	14.3	2	2
1966 SD	14	4	50	12.5	0	0
NFL Total	91	228	3486	15.3	27	5

JIM NORTON Norton, James Alfred 6'4", 254 **DT-OT-DE**
Col: Washington *HS:* Wenatchee [WA] B: 11/18/1942, Wilmington, NC
Drafted: 1965 Round 3 SF
1965 SF: 14 G. **1966** SF: 14 G. **1967** Atl: 14 G; Int 1-0. **1968** Atl-Phi: 13 G. Atl: 7 G. Phi: 6 G. **1969** Was: 5 G. **1970** NYG: 4 G. **Total:** 64 G; Int 1-0.

JIM NORTON Norton, James Charles 6'3", 190 **DB-P**
(Blade) *Col:* Idaho *HS:* Fullerton [CA] B: 10/20/1938, Glendale, CA
Drafted: 1960 Round 1 DalT
1960 Hou: Rec 1-5 5.0. **1963** Hou: Rush 1-15 15.0. **1967** Hou: Rush 1-(-7) -7.0. **1968** Hou: Rush 1-20 20.0. **Total:** Rush 3-28 9.3; Rec 1-5 5.0.

		Interceptions			Punting			
Year Team	G	Int	Yds	TD	Punts	Yds	Avg	Fum
1960 Hou	13	1	0	0	0	0	—	0
1961 Hou	14	9	150	0	48	1952	40.7	0
1962 Hou	14	8	75	0	56	2298	41.0	0
1963 Hou	14	6	86	0	65	2792	43.0	0
1964 Hou	14	2	31	0	55	2267	41.2	0
1965 Hou	14	7	52	0	**85**	**3711**	43.7	0
1966 Hou	14	4	125	0	69	2908	42.1	1
1967 Hou	14	6	73	1	71	3025	42.6	1
1968 Hou	14	2	0	0	73	3008	41.2	0
NFL Total	125	45	592	1	522	21961	42.1	2

JERRY NORTON Norton, Jerry Ray 5'11", 195 **DB-HB**
Col: Southern Methodist *HS:* Texas [Texarkana, TX] B: 5/16/1931, Gilmer, TX *Drafted:* 1954 Round 7 Phi
1955 Phi: Pass 1-0; Rec 11-125 11.4 1 TD; KR 8-281 35.1 **1** TD.
1956 Phi: KR 1-31 31.0. **1957** Phi: Pass 1-0; KR 2-33 16.5. **1959** ChiC: KR 3-70 23.3. **Total:** Pass 2-0; Rec 11-125 11.4 1 TD; KR 14-415 29.6 1 TD.

		Rushing				Punt Returns			
Year Team	G	Att	Yds	Avg	TD	Ret	Yds	Avg	TD
1954 Phi	12	1	-3	-3.0	0	21	89	4.2	0
1955 Phi	12	36	144	4.0	1	20	33	1.7	0
1956 Phi	6	0	0	—	0	0	0	—	0
1957 Phi	12	2	73	36.5	0	1	13	13.0	0
1958 Phi	9	0	0	—	0	1	8	8.0	0
1959 ChiC	12	2	41	20.5	0	3	4	1.3	0
1960 StL	12	2	47	23.5	0	0	0	—	0
1961 StL	14	1	15	15.0	0	0	0	—	0
1962 Dal	14	0	0	—	0	0	0	—	0
1963 GB	14	2	0	0.0	0	0	0	—	0
1964 GB	14	1	24	24.0	0	0	0	—	0
NFL Total	131	47	341	7.3	1	46	147	3.2	0

	Interceptions			Punting				Tot
Year Team	Int	Yds	TD	Punts	Yds	Avg	Fum	TD
1954 Phi	5	110	1	0	0	—	2	1
1955 Phi	1	0	0	0	0	—	6	3
1956 Phi	2	34	0	0	0	—	0	0
1957 Phi	4	155	1	**68**	**2798**	41.1	0	1
1958 Phi	1	0	0	0	0	—	0	0
1959 ChiC	3	35	0	59	2650	44.9	0	0
1960 StL	**10**	96	0	39	1777	**45.6**	0	0
1961 StL	7	136	**2**	**85**	**3802**	44.7	0	2
1962 Dal	2	21	0	0	0	—	0	1
1963 GB	0	0	0	51	2279	44.7	0	0
1964 GB	0	0	0	56	2365	42.2	0	0
NFL Total	35	587	4	358	15671	43.8	8	8

KEN NORTON Norton, Kenneth Howard Jr. 6'2", 241 **LB**
Col: UCLA *HS:* Westchester [Los Angeles, CA] B: 9/29/1966, Lincoln, IL *Drafted:* 1988 Round 2 Dal
1988 Dal: 3 G. **1989** Dal: 13 G; 2.5 Sac. **1990** Dal: 15 G; 2.5 Sac.
1991 Dal: 16 G. **1992** Dal: 16 G. **1993** Dal: 16 G; Int 1-25; 2 Sac. **1994** SF: 16 G; Int 1-0. **1995** SF: 16 G; Int 3-102 **2** TD; 12 Pt; 1 Sac. **1996** SF: 16 G. **1997** SF: 16 G; 1.5 Sac. **1998** SF: 16 G; 2 Sac. **Total:** 159 G; Int 5-127 2 TD; 12 Pt; 11.5 Sac.

MARTY NORTON Norton, Martin 5'6", 178 **TB-HB-WB**
Col: Hamline *HS:* Central [Minneapolis, MN] B: 1903 Deceased
1922 Min: 3 G; Rush 2 TD; 12 Pt. **1924** Min: 6 G; Rush 2 TD; 12 Pt.
1925 GB: 10 G; Rush 1 TD; Rec **4** TD; Int 1 TD; Tot TD 6; 36 Pt.
Total: 19 G; Rush 5 TD; Rec 4 TD; Int 1 TD; Tot TD 10; 60 Pt.

RAY NORTON Norton, Raymond 1 **WB**
(Nick) *Col:* No College B: 1900, NY Deceased
1925 Cle: 1 G.

RAY NORTON Norton, Raymond 6'2", 184 **HB**
Col: San Jose State *HS:* McClymonds [Oakland, CA] B: 9/22/1937
Drafted: 1960 Round 4 SF
1960 SF: 3 G; Rush 2-2 1.0. **1961** SF: 6 G; Rush 2-(-2) -1.0; KR 1-60 60.0; 1 Fum. **Total:** 9 G; Rush 4-0; KR 1-60 60.0; 1 Fum.

RICK NORTON Norton, Richard Eugene 6'2", 200 **QB**
Col: Kentucky *HS:* Flaget [Louisville, KY] B: 11/16/1943, Louisville, KY
Drafted: 1966 Round 1 Mia
1966 Mia: Rush 3-2 0.7. **1967** Mia: Rush 7-14 2.0. **1968** Mia: Rush 1-9 9.0. **1969** Mia: Rush 8-16 2.0. **Total:** Rush 19-41 2.2.

		Passing								
Year Team	G	Att	Comp	Comp%	Yds	YPA	TD	Int	Rating	Fum
1966 Mia	7	55	21	38.2	192	3.49	3	6	27.0	3
1967 Mia	14	133	53	39.8	596	4.48	1	9	28.3	5
1968 Mia	3	41	17	41.5	254	6.20	0	4	22.9	1
1969 Mia	7	148	65	43.9	709	4.79	2	11	32.2	6
1970 GB	1	5	3	60.0	64	12.80	1	0	143.8	0
NFL Total	32	382	159	41.6	1815	4.75	7	30	30.0	15

JAY NORVELL Norvell, Merritt Jay 6'2", 232 **LB**
Col: Iowa *HS:* James Madison Memorial [Madison, WI] B: 3/28/1963, Madison, WI
1987 ChiB: 6 G; 4 Sac.

RALPH NORWOOD Norwood, Ralph E 6'7", 285 **OT**
Col: Louisiana State *HS:* O. Perry Walker [New Orleans, LA]
B: 1/23/1966, New Orleans, LA D: 11/24/1989, Suwanee, GA
Drafted: 1989 Round 2 Atl
1989 Atl: 11 G.

SCOTT NORWOOD Norwood, Scott Allan 6′0″, 207 **K**
Col: James Madison *HS:* Thomas Jefferson [Alexandria, VA]
B: 7/17/1960, Alexandria, VA

		Scoring						
Year Team	**G**	**Pts**	**FG**	**FGA**	**FG%**	**XK**	**XKA**	**XK%**
1985 Buf	16	62	13	17	76.5	23	23	100.0
1986 Buf	16	83	17	27	63.0	32	34	94.1
1987 Buf	12	61	10	15	66.7	31	31	100.0
1988 Buf	16	**129**	**32**	37	86.5	33	33	100.0
1989 Buf	16	115	23	30	76.7	46	47	97.9
1990 Buf	16	110	20	29	69.0	**50**	**52**	96.2
1991 Buf	16	110	18	29	62.1	**56**	**58**	96.6
NFL Total	108	670	133	184	72.3	271	278	97.5

JOHN NOSICH Nosich, John Anthony 6′3″, 230 **T**
Col: Duquesne *HS:* Clairton [PA] B: 10/12/1915, Clairton, PA
D: 7/24/1985, McKeesport, PA
1938 Pit: 2 G.

DOUG NOTT Nott, Douglas N 5′11″, 195 **TB-DB**
Col: Detroit Mercy *HS:* Ann Arbor [MI] B: 6/14/1911, Pontiac, MI
D: 5/25/1991, Detroit, MI
1935 Bos-Det: Pass 34-9 26.5%, 169 4.97 1 TD 5 Int. Bos: Pass 24-7 29.2%, 134 5.58 1 TD 3 Int. Det: Pass 10-2 20.0%, 35 3.50 2 Int.
Total: Pass 34-9 26.5%, 169 4.97 1 TD 5 Int.

		Rushing			
Year Team	**G**	**Att**	**Yds**	**Avg**	**TD**
1935 Bos-Det	9	48	98	2.0	0
1935 Bos	4	45	95	2.1	0
1935 Det	5	3	3	1.0	0
NFL Total	9	48	98	2.0	0

MIKE NOTT Nott, Wesley Michael 6′3″, 203 **QB**
Col: Santa Clara *HS:* Analy [Sebastopol, CA] B: 5/19/1952, Eureka, CA
1976 KC: 1 G; Pass 10-4 40.0%, 46 4.60; Punt 1-35 35.0.

DEXTER NOTTAGE Nottage, Dexter Alexander 6′4″, 287 **DE**
Col: Florida A&M *HS:* Hollywood Hills [Hollywood, FL] B: 11/14/1970, Miami, FL *Drafted:* 1994 Round 6 Was
1994 Was: 15 G; 1 Sac. **1995** Was: 16 G. **1996** Was: 16 G; 5 Sac.
1997 KC: 1 G. **Total:** 48 G; 6 Sac.

DON NOTTINGHAM Nottingham, Don Ray 5′10″, 210 **RB**
Col: Kent State *HS:* Ravenna [OH] B: 6/28/1949, Widen, WV
Drafted: 1971 Round 17 Bal
1972 Bal: KR 2-38 19.0. **1973** Bal-Mia: KR 1-17 17.0. Bal: KR 1-17 17.0.
1975 Mia: KR 3-80 26.7. **1976** Mia: KR 6-107 17.8. **1977** Mia: KR 2-36 18.0. **Total:** KR 14-278 19.9.

		Rushing				Receiving					Tot
Year Team	**G**	**Att**	**Yds**	**Avg**	**TD**	**Rec**	**Yds**	**Avg**	**TD**	**Fum**	**TD**
1971 Bal	14	95	388	4.1	5	15	88	5.9	0	2	6
1972 Bal	14	123	466	3.8	3	25	191	7.6	0	6	3
1973 Bal-Mia	14	52	252	4.8	1	3	26	8.7	0	1	1
1973 Bal	3	28	118	4.2	1	2	10	5.0	0	0	1
1973 Mia	11	24	134	5.6	0	1	16	16.0	0	1	0
1974 Mia	14	66	273	4.1	8	3	40	13.3	0	2	8
1975 Mia	14	168	718	4.3	12	9	66	7.3	0	5	12
1976 Mia	14	63	185	2.9	3	4	33	8.3	0	1	3
1977 Mia	14	44	214	4.9	2	8	58	7.3	0	1	2
NFL Total	98	611	2496	4.1	34	67	502	7.5	0	18	35

JAY NOVACEK Novacek, Jay McKinley 6′4″, 234 **TE-WR**
Col: Wyoming *HS:* Gothenburg [WY] B: 10/24/1962, Martin, SD
Drafted: 1985 Round 6 StL
1985 StL: KR 1-20 20.0. **1988** Pho: Rush 1-10 10.0. **1993** Dal: Rush 1-2 2.0 1 TD; KR 1-(-1) -1.0. **1995** Dal: Scor 1 2XP. **Total:** Rush 2-12 6.0 1 TD; KR 2-19 9.5; Scor 1 2XP.

		Receiving					Tot
Year Team	**G**	**Rec**	**Yds**	**Avg**	**TD**	**Fum**	**TD**
1985 StL	16	1	4	4.0	0	0	0
1986 StL	8	1	2	2.0	0	0	0
1987 StL	7	20	254	12.7	3	1	3
1988 Pho	16	38	569	15.0	4	0	4
1989 Pho	16	23	225	9.8	1	0	1
1990 Dal	16	59	657	11.1	4	1	4
1991 Dal	16	59	664	11.3	4	3	4
1992 Dal	16	68	630	9.3	6	0	6
1993 Dal	16	44	445	10.1	1	3	2
1994 Dal	16	47	475	10.1	2	0	2
1995 Dal	15	62	705	11.4	5	1	5
NFL Total	158	422	4630	11.0	30	9	31

JACK NOVAK Novak, Clarence John 6′4″, 242 **TE**
Col: Wisconsin *HS:* Kewaunee [WI] B: 6/6/1953, Kewaunee, WI
Drafted: 1975 Round 12 Cin
1975 Cin: 14 G; Rec 2-34 17.0. **1976** TB: 12 G; Rec 8-130 16.3 1 TD; 6 Pt. **1977** TB: 9 G; Rec 2-24 12.0. **Total:** 35 G; Rec 12-188 15.7 1 TD; 6 Pt.

EDDIE NOVAK Novak, Edward 5′9″, 175 **WB-FB-TB-BB**
(Five Yards) *Col:* No College *HS:* Central [Minneapolis, MN]
B: 8/3/1897 D: 7/1984, Webster, MN
1920 RI: 9 G. **1921** RI: 7 G; Pass 1 TD; 1 Fum TD; 6 Pt. **1922** RI: 1 G.
1924 Min: 5 G; Scor 1, 1 XK. **1925** RI: 11 G; Rush 1 TD; 6 Pt. **Total:** 33 G; Pass 1 TD; Rush 1 TD; 1 Fum TD; Tot TD 2.

JEFF NOVAK Novak, Jeffrey Ladd 6′6″, 297 **OG-OT**
Col: Southwest Texas State *HS:* Clear Lake [Houston, TX]
B: 7/27/1967, Arlington Heights, IL *Drafted:* 1990 Round 7 SD
1994 Mia: 6 G. **1995** Jac: 16 G. **1996** Jac: 5 G. **1997** Jac: 7 G. **1998** Jac: 4 G. **Total:** 38 G.

KEN NOVAK Novak, Kenneth 6′7″, 268 **DT**
Col: Purdue *HS:* St. Joseph [Cleveland, OH] B: 7/3/1954, Willowick, OH *Drafted:* 1976 Round 1 Bal
1976 Bal: 11 G; KR 1-12 12.0. **1977** Bal: 12 G. **Total:** 23 G; KR 1-12 12.0.

CRAIG NOVITSKY Novitsky, Craig Aaron 6′5″, 295 **OT-OG-C**
Col: UCLA *HS:* Potomac School [Dumfries, VA] B: 5/12/1971, Washington, DC *Drafted:* 1994 Round 5 NO
1994 NO: 9 G. **1995** NO: 16 G. **1996** NO: 16 G. **Total:** 41 G.

BRENT NOVOSELSKY Novoselsky, Brent Howard 6′2″, 232 **TE**
Col: Pennsylvania *HS:* Niles North [Skokie, IL] B: 1/8/1966, Skokie, IL
1988 ChiB: 8 G. **1989** Min: 15 G; Rec 4-11 2.8 2 TD; 12 Pt. **1990** Min: 16 G. **1991** Min: 16 G; Rec 4-27 6.8. **1992** Min: 16 G; Rec 4-63 15.8.
1993 Min: 15 G. **1994** Min: 12 G; Rec 2-7 3.5; KR 2-10 5.0. **Total:** 98 G; Rec 14-108 7.7 2 TD; KR 2-10 5.0; 12 Pt.

RAY NOVOTNY Novotny, Raymond John 5′10″, 165 **TB-HB-WB-BB**
Col: Ashland *HS:* West Tech [Cleveland, OH] B: 10/12/1907, Cleveland, OH D: 5/30/1995, Welches, OR
1930 Port: 11 G; Pass 1 TD; Rush 1 TD; 6 Pt. **1931** Cle: 10 G. **1932** Bkn: 10 G; Pass 15-5 33.3%, 50 3.33 1 Int; Rush 6-4 0.7; Rec 3-72 24.0.
Total: 31 G; Pass 15-5 33.3%, 50 3.33 1 TD 1 Int; Rush 6-4 0.7 1 TD; Rec 3-72 24.0; 6 Pt.

JOE NOVSEK Novsek, Joseph John 6′4″, 237 **DE**
Col: Tulsa *HS:* Redstone [PA] B: 5/29/1939 *Drafted:* 1961 Round 17 Oak
1962 Oak: 14 G; KR 1-0.

GARY NOWAK Nowak, Gary William 6′5″, 258 **DT**
Col: Michigan State *HS:* St. Ambrose [Detroit, MI] B: 12/8/1948, St. Clair Shores, MI *Drafted:* 1971 Round 10 SD
1971 SD: 6 G.

WALT NOWAK Nowak, Walter Ignatius 5′11″, 185 **OE-DB**
Col: Villanova *HS:* Camden [NJ] B: 6/2/1915, Camden, NJ
D: 11/12/1993, Westmont, NJ
1944 Phi: 2 G.

BOB NOWASKEY Nowaskey, Robert John 6′0″, 205 **DE-OE**
Col: George Washington *HS:* Scottsdale [PA] B: 2/3/1918, Everson, PA D: 3/21/1971, Arlington Heights, IL *Drafted:* 1940 Round 7 Cle
AAFC **1946** LA-A: Rush 3-14 4.7; PR 1-5 5.0; Int 1-35 1 TD. **1947** LA-A: PR 1-22 22.0; Int 2-15. **1949** BalA: Int 1-9. **Total:** Rush 3-14 4.7; PR 2-27 13.5; Int 4-59 1 TD.

		Receiving				Tot
Year Team	**G**	**Rec**	**Yds**	**Avg**	**TD**	**TD**
1946 LA-A	14	19	198	10.4	3	4
1947 LA-A	14	8	106	13.3	0	0
1948 LA-A-BalA	14	1	31	31.0	0	0
1949 BalA	12	0	0	—	0	0
AAFC Total	54	28	335	12.0	3	4

NFL **1940** ChiB: 10 G; Rush 1-4 4.0; Rec 5-105 21.0 2 TD; 12 Pt.
1941 ChiB: 11 G; Rush 3-5 1.7; Rec 12-199 16.6 1 TD; Scor 13, 1-2 50.0% XK; **1** Fum TD; Tot TD 2. **1942** ChiB: 11 G; Rush 1-3 3.0; Rec 6-128 21.3. **1950** Bal: 9 G. **Total:** 41 G; Rush 5-12 2.4; Rec 23-432 18.8 3 TD; Scor 25, 1-2 50.0% XK; 1 Fum TD; Tot TD 4.

TOM NOWATZKE Nowatzke, Thomas Matthew 6′3″, 230 **FB-LB**
Col: Indiana *HS:* Michigan City [IN] B: 9/30/1942, La Porte, IN
Drafted: 1965 Round 1 Det
1965 Det: KR 2-12 6.0. **1968** Det: KR 3-34 11.3. **1969** Det: KR 1-14 14.0.
1970 Bal: KR 7-93 13.3. **1971** Bal: KR 1-1 1.0; Int 1-29. **Total:** KR 14-154 11.0; Int 1-29.

		Rushing				Receiving					Tot
Year Team	**G**	**Att**	**Yds**	**Avg**	**TD**	**Rec**	**Yds**	**Avg**	**TD**	**Fum**	**TD**
1965 Det	14	27	73	2.7	1	5	45	9.0	1	1	2
1966 Det	14	151	512	3.4	6	54	316	5.9	1	6	7

1967 Det	14	70	288	4.1	4	21	145	6.9	2	3	6
1968 Det	14	36	116	3.2	1	4	6	1.5	0	2	1
1969 Det	9	0	0	—	0	0	0	—	0	0	0
1970 Bal	11	73	248	3.4	1	16	93	5.8	0	3	1
1971 Bal	14	1	1	1.0	0	0	0	—	0	0	0
1972 Bal	6	3	11	3.7	0	0	0	—	0	0	0
NFL Total	96	361	1249	3.5	13	100	605	6.1	4	15	17

LEN NOYES Noyes, Leonard William 6′0″, 214 **G**
Col: Montana *HS:* Butte [MT] B: 7/12/1914, Butte, MT
D: 12/24/1985, Winston-Salem, NC *Drafted:* 1938 Round 6 Bkn
1938 Bkn: 5 G.

DAN NUGENT Nugent, Daniel Lawrence 6′3″, 250 **OG**
Col: Auburn *HS:* Pompano Beach [FL] B: 8/22/1953, Mount Clemenms, MI *Drafted:* 1975 Round 3 LARm
1976 Was: 14 G. **1977** Was: 14 G. **1978** Was: 16 G. **1980** Was: 14 G. **Total:** 58 G.

CLEM NUGENT Nugent, Earl Clement 5′9″, 155 **FB-WB**
Col: Iowa *HS:* Algona [IA] B: 11/9/1899, Algona, IA Deceased
1924 Roch: 1 G.

PHIL NUGENT Nugent, Philip Harper 6′2″, 195 **DB**
Col: Tulane *HS:* Lafayette [LA] B: 8/16/1939, Lafayette, LA
Drafted: 1961 Round 9 Den
1961 Den: 12 G; Int 7-77.

TERRY NUGENT Nugent, Terence John 6′4″, 218 **QB**
Col: Colorado State *HS:* Elk Grove [CA] B: 12/5/1961, Merced, CA
Drafted: 1984 Round 6 Cle
1987 Ind: 1 G; Pass 5-3 60.0%, 47 9.40; Rush 2-1 0.5.

JULIAN NUNAMAKER Nunamaker, Julian Francis 6′3″, 252 **DE-DT**
Col: Tennessee-Martin *HS:* Charleston [SC] B: 2/13/1946, Charleston, SC D: 2/25/1995, Jackson, TN *Drafted:* 1969 Round 3 Buf
1969 Buf: 10 G. **1970** Buf: 8 G. **Total:** 18 G.

FRANK NUNLEY Nunley, Frank Hembre 6′2″, 229 **LB**
(Fudgehammer) *Col:* Michigan *HS:* Belleville [MI] B: 10/1/1945, Florence, AL *Drafted:* 1967 Round 3 SF
1967 SF: KR 2-0. **1968** SF: KR 2-0. **1972** SF: KR 1-21 21.0.
Total: KR 5-21 4.2.

		Interceptions			
Year Team	**G**	**Int**	**Yds**	**TD**	**Fum**
1967 SF	14	1	7	0	0
1968 SF	14	0	0	0	1
1969 SF	14	1	7	0	0
1970 SF	14	3	42	0	0
1971 SF	14	1	7	0	0
1972 SF	13	1	12	0	0
1973 SF	14	1	13	0	0
1974 SF	13	4	30	0	0
1975 SF	14	1	6	0	0
1976 SF	13	1	12	0	0
NFL Total	137	14	136	0	1

JEREMY NUNLEY Nunley, Jody Jeremy 6′5″, 278 **DE**
Col: Alabama *HS:* Franklin Co. [Winchester, TN] B: 9/19/1971, Winchester, TN *Drafted:* 1994 Round 2 Hou
1994 Hou: 12 G.

FREDDIE JOE NUNN Nunn, Fred Joe 6′4″, 249 **DE-LB**
Col: Mississippi *HS:* Nanih Waiya [Louisville, MS] B: 4/9/1962, Noxubee Co., MS *Drafted:* 1985 Round 1 StL
1985 StL: 16 G; 3 Sac. **1986** StL: 16 G; 7 Sac. **1987** StL: 12 G; 11 Sac. **1988** Pho: 16 G; 14 Sac. **1989** Pho: 12 G; 5 Sac. **1990** Pho: 16 G; 9 Sac. **1991** Pho: 16 G; 7 Sac. **1992** Pho: 11 G; 4 Sac. **1993** Pho: 16 G; 6.5 Sac. **1994** Ind: 11 G; 1 Sac. **1995** Ind: 10 G. **1996** Ind: 5 G. **Total:** 157 G; 67.5 Sac.

R.B. NUNNERY Nunnery, Robert Brock 6′4″, 275 **OT**
(Bob) *Col:* Louisiana State *HS:* Summit [MS] B: 12/28/1933, McComb, MS *Drafted:* 1956 Round 12 Det
1960 DalT: 6 G.

BOB NUSSBAUMER Nussbaumer, Robert John 5′11″, 172 **DB-HB**
Col: Michigan *HS:* Oak Park [IL] B: 4/23/1924, Oak Park, IL
D: 7/26/1997, Moreland Hills, OH *Drafted:* 1946 Round 2 GB
1946 GB: Pass 1-1 100.0%, 10 10.00; PR 12-98 8.2; KR 6-148 24.7. **1947** Was: PR 2-15 7.5; KR 8-154 19.3. **1948** Was: PR 1-(8) -8.0; KR 2-38 19.0. **1949** ChiC: PR 1-16 16.0. **1951** GB: PR 1-3 3.0.
Total: Pass 1-1 100.0%, 10 10.00; PR 17-124 7.3; KR 16-340 21.3.

		Rushing				Receiving			
Year Team	**G**	**Att**	**Yds**	**Avg**	**TD**	**Rec**	**Yds**	**Avg**	**TD**
1946 GB	10	29	43	1.5	0	10	143	14.3	0
1947 Was	12	43	136	3.2	0	47	597	12.7	4
1948 Was	10	23	59	2.6	0	19	252	13.3	1
1949 ChiC	12	0	0	—	0	0	0	—	0
1950 ChiC	1	0	0	—	0	0	0	—	0
1951 GB	4	0	0	—	0	0	0	—	0
NFL Total	49	95	238	2.5	0	76	992	13.1	5

	Interceptions			
Year Team	**Int**	**Yds**	**TD**	**Fum**
1946 GB	3	31	0	1
1947 Was	1	0	0	2
1948 Was	0	0	0	5
1949 ChiC	**12**	157	0	0
NFL Total	16	188	0	8

DOUG NUSSMEIER Nussmeier, Douglas Keith 6′3″, 211 **QB**
Col: Idaho *HS:* Lakeridge [Lake Oswego, OR] B: 12/11/1970, Portland, OR *Drafted:* 1994 Round 4 NO
1996 NO: Rush 3-6 2.0. **1997** NO: Rush 8-30 3.8. **Total:** Rush 11-36 3.3.

		Passing								
Year Team	**G**	**Att**	**Comp**	**Comp%**	**Yds**	**YPA**	**TD**	**Int**	**Rating**	**Fum**
1996 NO	2	50	28	56.0	272	5.44	1	1	69.8	2
1997 NO	3	32	18	56.3	183	5.72	0	3	33.7	1
NFL Total	5	82	46	56.1	455	5.55	1	4	55.7	3

TOM NUTTEN Nutten, Thomas R 6′4″, 280 **C-OG**
Col: Western Michigan *HS:* Champlain Regional School [Lennoxville, Canada] B: 6/8/1971, Magog, Canada *Drafted:* 1995 Round 7 Buf
1995 Buf: 1 G. **1998** StL: 5 G. **Total:** 6 G.

BUZZ NUTTER Nutter, Madison Moore 6′4″, 230 **C-LB**
Col: Virginia Tech *HS:* Vinson [Huntington, WV] B: 2/16/1931, Summersville, WV *Drafted:* 1953 Round 12 Was
1954 Bal: 12 G. **1955** Bal: 12 G. **1956** Bal: 12 G. **1957** Bal: 12 G. **1958** Bal: 12 G. **1959** Bal: 12 G. **1960** Bal: 12 G. **1961** Pit: 14 G. **1962** Pit: 14 G. **1963** Pit: 14 G. **1964** Pit: 14 G. **1965** Bal: 13 G. **Total:** 153 G.

ED NUTTING Nutting, John Edward 6′4″, 246 **OT**
Col: Georgia Tech *HS:* Northside [Atlanta, GA] B: 2/8/1939, Washington, DC *Drafted:* 1961 Round 2 Cle
1961 Cle: 4 G. **1963** Dal: 14 G. **Total:** 18 G.

RICK NUZUM Nuzum, Frederick Merril 6′4″, 238 **C**
Col: Kentucky *HS:* Marietta [OH] B: 6/30/1952, Charleston, WV
Drafted: 1975 Round 5 LARm
1977 LARm: 14 G. **1978** GB: 16 G. **Total:** 30 G.

JERRY NUZUM Nuzum, Jerry Hanson 6′1″, 198 **HB-DB**
(Bruiser) *Col:* Cameron; New Mexico State *HS:* Clovis [NM]
B: 9/8/1923, Clovis, NM D: 4/23/1997, Monroeville, PA *Drafted:* 1948 Round 2 Pit
1948 Pit: Rec 2-37 18.5; PR 1-7 7.0; KR 6-122 20.3; Int 1-3. **1949** Pit: Pass 1-1 100.0%, 21 21.00; Rec 4-81 20.3 2 TD; KR 1-17 17.0. **1950** Pit: Rec 6-142 23.7 1 TD; KR 3-45 15.0. **1951** Pit: Rec 2-43 21.5.
Total: Pass 1-1 100.0%, 21 21.00; Rec 14-303 21.6 3 TD; PR 1-7 7.0; KR 10-184 18.4; Int 1-3.

		Rushing					Tot
Year Team	**G**	**Att**	**Yds**	**Avg**	**TD**	**Fum**	**TD**
1948 Pit	10	26	109	4.2	0	4	0
1949 Pit	12	139	611	4.4	5	5	7
1950 Pit	12	57	154	2.7	1	7	2
1951 Pit	11	27	56	2.1	1	2	1
NFL Total	45	249	930	3.7	7	18	10

CHIP NUZZO Nuzzo, Anthony Chris 5′11″, 190 **DB**
Col: Princeton *HS:* Corry Area [PA] B: 7/26/1965, Olean, NY
1987 Buf: 3 G.

MALLY NYDALL Nydall, Malvin John 5′11″, 163 **TB-HB-BB-WB**
Col: Minnesota *HS:* South [Minneapolis, MN] B: 11/24/1906, Minneapolis, MN D: 5/1979, Sun City, AZ
1929 Min: 10 G; Rush 2 TD; Scor 14, 2 XK. **1930** Min-Fra: 13 G; Rush 2 TD; Scor 13, 1 XK. Min: 9 G; Scor 1, 1 XK. Fra: 4 G; Rush 2 TD; 12 Pt. **1931** Fra: 4 G. **Total:** 27 G; Rush 4 TD.

BLAINE NYE Nye, Blaine Francis 6′4″, 251 **OG**
Col: Stanford *HS:* Servite [Anaheim, CA] B: 3/29/1946, Ogden, UT
Drafted: 1968 Round 5 Dal
1968 Dal: 13 G. **1969** Dal: 14 G. **1970** Dal: 14 G. **1971** Dal: 14 G. **1972** Dal: 14 G. **1973** Dal: 14 G. **1974** Dal: 14 G. **1975** Dal: 14 G. **1976** Dal: 14 G. **Total:** 125 G.

DICK NYERS Nyers, Charles Richard 5′11″, 177 **DB-HB**
(Dickie) *Col:* Indianapolis *HS:* Emmerich Manual Training [Indianapolis, IN] B: 9/8/1934, Indianapolis, IN
1956 Bal: 5 G; PR 2-16 8.0; KR 3-69 23.0. **1957** Bal: 7 G; Rush 1-(-4) -4.0; KR 17-350 20.6; 1 Fum. **Total:** 12 G; Rush 1-(-4) -4.0; PR 2-16 8.0; KR 20-419 21.0; 1 Fum.

BERNIE NYGREN Nygren, Bernard Clifford 5′9″, 193 **HB-DB**
(Bud) *Col:* Gustavus Adolphus; San Jose State *HS:* Forest Lake [MN]
B: 11/14/1918, Minneapolis, MN D: 12/26/1984, San Jose, CA
AAFC **1946** LA-A: Rec 13-170 13.1 1 TD; KR 4-88 22.0; Int 2-30.
Total: Rec 13-170 13.1 1 TD; KR 4-88 22.0; Int 2-30.

Year Team	G	Rushing Att	Yds	Avg	TD
1946 LA-A	14	26	111	4.3	0
1947 BknA	1	0	0	—	0
AAFC Total	15	26	111	4.3	0

LEE NYSTROM Nystrom, Lee Allen 6′5″, 260 **OT**
Col: Macalester *HS:* Worthington [MN] B: 10/30/1951, Worthington, MN
1974 GB: 13 G.

VIC NYVALL Nyvall, Victor A 5′10″, 185 **RB**
Col: Northwestern State-Louisiana B: 4/29/1948
1970 NO: 2 G; Rush 5-6 1.2; Rec 2-(-1) -0.5.

DON OAKES Oakes, Donald Sherman 6′4″, 255 **OT-DT**
(Tree) *Col:* Virginia Tech *HS:* Andrew Lewis [Salem, VA] B: 7/22/1938, Roanoke, VA *Drafted:* 1961 Round 3 Phi
1961 Phi: 13 G. **1962** Phi: 8 G. **1963** Bos: 14 G. **1964** Bos: 14 G; KR 1-0; 1 Fum. **1965** Bos: 14 G. **1966** Bos: 14 G. **1967** Bos: 14 G. **1968** Bos: 13 G. **Total:** 104 G; KR 1-0; 1 Fum.

CHARLEY OAKLEY Oakley, Charles Lynn 5′10″, 170 **DB**
Col: Louisiana State *HS:* Lake Charles [LA] B: 7/7/1931, Montgomery, AL *Drafted:* 1954 Round 23 ChiC
1954 ChiC: 1 G.

BEN OAS Oas, Bernard 6′0″, 195 **C-BB**
Col: St. Mary's (Minn.) *HS:* Greenway [Coleraine, MN] B: 4/27/1901, MN D: 2/1976, Chicago, IL
1929 Min: 7 G.

BART OATES Oates, Bart Steven 6′3″, 270 **C**
Col: Brigham Young *HS:* Albany [GA] B: 12/16/1958, Mesa, AZ
1985 NYG: 16 G. **1986** NYG: 16 G; 1 Fum. **1987** NYG: 12 G. **1988** NYG: 16 G; 1 Fum. **1989** NYG: 16 G; 1 Fum. **1990** NYG: 16 G; 1 Fum. **1991** NYG: 16 G. **1992** NYG: 16 G; 2 Fum. **1993** NYG: 16 G. **1994** SF: 16 G. **1995** SF: 16 G. **Total:** 172 G; 6 Fum.

BRAD OATES Oates, Robert Bradley 6′6″, 274 **OT-OG**
Col: Duke; Brigham Young *HS:* Albany [GA] B: 9/30/1953, Mesa, AZ *Drafted:* 1976 Round 3 StL
1976 StL: 14 G; KR 1-12 12.0. **1977** StL: 9 G; KR 1-11 11.0. **1978** Det: 16 G. **1979** StL: 11 G. **1980** StL-KC: 11 G. StL: 10 G. KC: 1 G. **1981** Cin-GB: 6 G. Cin: 5 G. GB: 1 G. **Total:** 67 G; KR 2-23 11.5.

VICTOR OATIS Oatis, Victor Hugo 6′0″, 177 **WR**
Col: Northwestern State-Louisiana *HS:* Winnsboro [LA] B: 1/6/1959, Monroe, LA *Drafted:* 1983 Round 6 Phi
1983 Bal: 9 G; Rec 6-93 15.5.

CARLETON OATS Oats, Carleton 6′3″, 260 **DE-DT**
(Ron) *Col:* Florida A&M *HS:* Middleton [Tampa, FL] B: 4/24/1942, Tampa, FL *Drafted:* 1964 Round 21 Oak
1965 Oak: 14 G. **1966** Oak: 14 G. **1967** Oak: 9 G; **1** Fum TD; 6 Pt. **1968** Oak: 14 G. **1969** Oak: 13 G. **1970** Oak: 13 G. **1971** Oak: 12 G. **1972** Oak: 14 G. **1973** GB: 8 G. **Total:** 111 G; 1 Fum TD; 6 Pt.

RONNIE O'BARD O'Bard, Ronald Alexander 5′9″, 190 **DB**
Col: Grossmont Coll. CA (J.C.); Idaho; Brigham Young *HS:* Monte Vista [Spring Valley, CA] B: 6/11/1958, San Diego, CA
1985 SD: 16 G.

VIC OBECK Obeck, Victor Francis Joseph 6′0″, 225 **G**
Col: Springfield *HS:* Audubon [NJ] B: 3/28/1917, Audubon, NJ D: 4/21/1979, New York, NY
AAFC **1946** BknA: 12 G; PR 1-3 3.0.

NFL **1945** ChiC: 10 G.

DUNC OBEE Obee, Duncan Francis 5′11″, 200 **C-LB**
Col: Dayton *HS:* Central Catholic [Toledo, OH] B: 7/9/1918, Battle Creek, MI
1941 Det: 3 G.

TERRY OBEE Obee, Terry Lamar 5′10″, 190 **WR**
Col: Oregon *HS:* John F. Kennedy [Richmond, CA] B: 6/15/1968, Vallejo, CA
1993 ChiB: KR 9-159 17.7. **Total:** KR 9-159 17.7.

Year Team	G	Receiving Rec	Yds	Avg	TD	Punt Returns Ret	Yds	Avg	TD	Fum
1991 Min	1	0	0	—	0	0	0	—	0	0
1993 ChiB	16	26	351	13.5	3	35	289	8.3	0	1
NFL Total	17	26	351	13.5	3	35	289	8.3	0	1

ROMAN OBEN Oben, Roman Dissake 6′4″, 310 **OT**
Col: Louisville *HS:* Gonzaga [Washington, DC]; Fork Union Mil. Acad. [VA] B: 10/9/1972, Cameroon *Drafted:* 1996 Round 3 NYG
1996 NYG: 2 G. **1997** NYG: 16 G. **1998** NYG: 16 G. **Total:** 34 G.

RAY OBERBROEKLING Oberbroekling, Raymond Joseph 5′8″, 198 **T**
Col: Loras B: 12/31/1898, New Vienna, IA D: 3/1972, New Vienna, IA
1924 Ken: 2 G.

TOM OBERG Oberg, Thomas Harvey 6′0″, 185 **DB**
Col: Oregon State; Portland State *HS:* Clackamas [Milwaukie, OR] B: 8/7/1945, Portland, OR
1968 Den: 9 G; Int 3-17. **1969** Den: 7 G. **Total:** 16 G; Int 3-17.

HERMAN O'BERRY O'Berry, Herman Lee 5′9″, 182 **DB**
Col: Oregon *HS:* Highlands [North Highlands, CA] B: 7/11/1971, Sacramento, CA *Drafted:* 1995 Round 7 StL
1996 StL: 9 G; PR 5-16 3.2; 1 Fum.

HARRY O'BOYLE O'Boyle, Harry William 5′9″, 178 **BB-DB-FB-LB**
Col: Notre Dame *HS:* East [Des Moines, IA] B: 10/31/1904, Des Moines, IA D: 5/5/1994, Wheeling, IL
1928 GB: 10 G; Rush 1 TD; Scor 23, **3** FG, 8 XK. **1932** GB: 11 G; Pass 7-1 14.3%, 8 1.14 2 Int; Rush 9-14 1.6; Scor 7, 7 XK. **1933** Phi: 2 G; Pass 2-0, 1 Int; Rush 2-4 2.0. **Total:** 23 G; Pass 9-1 11.1%, 8 0.89 3 Int; Rush 11-18 1.6 1 TD; Scor 30, 3 FG, 15 XK.

ED O'BRADOVICH O'Bradovich, Edward 6′3″, 255 **DE**
Col: Illinois *HS:* Proviso East [Maywood, IL] B: 5/21/1940, Hillside, IL *Drafted:* 1962 Round 7 ChiB
1962 ChiB: 14 G; KR 1-8 8.0. **1963** ChiB: 6 G. **1964** ChiB: 7 G. **1965** ChiB: 13 G. **1966** ChiB: 14 G; **1** Fum TD; 6 Pt. **1967** ChiB: 14 G. **1968** ChiB: 14 G. **1969** ChiB: 14 G; Scor **1** Saf; 2 Pt. **1970** ChiB: 14 G. **1971** ChiB: 14 G. **Total:** 124 G; KR 1-8 8.0; Scor 1 Saf; 1 Fum TD; 8 Pt.

JIM OBRADOVICH Obradovich, James Robert 6′2″, 225 **TE**
Col: El Camino Coll. CA (J.C.); USC *HS:* El Segundo [CA] B: 4/2/1953, Los Angeles, CA *Drafted:* 1975 Round 7 NYG
1975 NYG: KR 2-38 19.0. **1977** SF: KR 1-9 9.0. **1978** TB: KR 3-48 16.0. **1980** TB: KR 5-46 9.2. **1981** TB: KR 1-14 14.0. **1982** TB: KR 1-12 12.0. **1983** TB: KR 1-0. **Total:** KR 14-167 11.9.

Year Team	G	Receiving Rec	Yds	Avg	TD	Fum
1975 NYG	14	7	65	9.3	1	1
1976 SF	14	1	11	11.0	0	0
1977 SF	12	2	16	8.0	0	0
1978 TB	16	14	219	15.6	3	0
1979 TB	16	6	63	10.5	1	0
1980 TB	16	11	152	13.8	0	1
1981 TB	16	4	42	10.5	1	0
1982 TB	9	2	22	11.0	0	0
1983 TB	16	9	71	7.9	1	1
NFL Total	129	56	661	11.8	7	3

CON O'BRIEN O'Brien, Cornelius 6′2″, 195 **T**
Col: Boston College *HS:* Commerce [Boston, MA] B: 2/13/1898, Ireland D: 5/9/1973, Medford, MA
1921 NYG: 1 G.

DAVE O'BRIEN O'Brien, David Hyde 6′3″, 247 **OT-DT-OG**
Col: Boston College *HS:* Watertown [MA] B: 6/13/1941, Cambridge, MA *Drafted:* 1963 Round 13 Min
1963 Min: 14 G. **1964** Min: 14 G. **1965** NYG: 10 G. **1966** StL: 14 G. **1967** StL: 8 G. **Total:** 60 G.

FRAN O'BRIEN O'Brien, Francis Joseph 6′1″, 253 **OT-OG-DE**
Col: Michigan State *HS:* Holyoke [MA] B: 4/17/1936, Springfield, MA *Drafted:* 1959 Round 3 Cle
1959 Cle: 12 G; 1 Fum. **1960** Was: 12 G; KR 1-16 16.0. **1961** Was: 14 G. **1962** Was: 14 G. **1963** Was: 13 G. **1964** Was: 14 G. **1965** Was: 14 G. **1966** Was-Pit: 13 G. Was: 2 G. Pit: 11 G. **1967** Pit: 4 G. **1968** Pit: 14 G. **Total:** 124 G; KR 1-16 16.0; 1 Fum.

JACK O'BRIEN O'Brien, Jack Edward 6′2″, 213 **OE-DE**
Col: Florida *HS:* Jeannette [PA] B: 10/21/1932, Jeannette, PA *Drafted:* 1954 Round 7 Pit
1954 Pit: 7 G; Rec 1-9 9.0. **1955** Pit: 12 G; Rec 9-105 11.7 2 TD; 12 Pt. **1956** Pit: 12 G; Rec 6-71 11.8. **Total:** 31 G; Rec 16-185 11.6 2 TD; 12 Pt.

JIM O'BRIEN O'Brien, James Eugene 6′0″, 195 **WR-K**
Col: Cincinnati *HS:* Aiken [Cincinnati, OH] B: 2/2/1947, El Paso, TX *Drafted:* 1970 Round 3 Bal
1970 Bal: Rec 1-28 28.0. **1972** Bal: Rush 3-9 3.0; Rec 11-263 23.9 2 TD. **1973** Det: Rec 2-14 7.0. **Total:** Rush 3-9 3.0; Rec 14-305 21.8 2 TD.

Year Team	G	Scoring Pts	FG	FGA	FG%	XK	XKA	XK%
1970 Bal	14	93	19	34	55.9	36	38	94.7
1971 Bal	14	95	20	29	69.0	35	36	97.2
1972 Bal	14	75	13	31	41.9	24	24	100.0
1973 Det	10	38	8	14	57.1	14	14	100.0
NFL Total	52	301	60	108	55.6	109	112	97.3

JACK O'BRIEN O'Brien, John Joseph 5′10″, 170 **HB**
Col: Minnesota *HS:* De La Salle [Minneapolis, MN] B: 8/8/1899, Minneapolis, MN D: 1971
1929 Min: 1 G.

GAIL O'BRIEN O'Brien, Joseph Gail 6'1", 219 T
(Obie) *Col:* Nebraska *HS:* Omaha South [NE] B: 11/14/1911, Cheyenne, WY D: 7/7/1978, Los Angeles Co., CA
1934 Bos: 10 G. **1935** Bos: 11 G. **1936** Bos: 11 G. **Total:** 32 G.

KEN O'BRIEN O'Brien, Kenneth John Jr. 6'4", 210 QB
Col: Sacramento State; California-Davis *HS:* Jesuit [Sacramento, CA] B: 11/27/1960, Rockville Centre, NY *Drafted:* 1983 Round 1 NYJ
1990 NYJ: Punt 1-23 23.0. **1991** NYJ: Rec 1-27 27.0. **Total:** Rec 1-27 27.0; Punt 1-23 23.0.

		Passing							
Year Team	G	Att	Comp	Comp%	Yds	YPA	TD	Int	Rating
1984 NYJ	10	203	116	57.1	1402	6.91	6	7	74.0
1985 NYJ	16	488	297	60.9	3888	7.97	25	8	**96.2**
1986 NYJ	15	482	300	62.2	3690	7.66	25	20	85.8
1987 NYJ	12	393	234	59.5	2696	6.86	13	8	82.8
1988 NYJ	14	424	236	55.7	2567	6.05	15	**7**	78.6
1989 NYJ	15	477	288	60.4	3346	7.01	12	18	74.3
1990 NYJ	16	411	226	55.0	2855	6.95	13	10	77.3
1991 NYJ	16	489	287	58.7	3300	6.75	10	11	76.6
1992 NYJ	10	98	55	56.1	642	6.55	5	6	67.6
1993 Phi	5	137	71	51.8	708	5.17	4	3	67.4
NFL Total	129	3602	2110	58.6	25094	6.97	128	98	80.4

	Rushing				
Year Team	Att	Yds	Avg	TD	Fum
1984 NYJ	16	29	1.8	0	4
1985 NYJ	25	58	2.3	0	14
1986 NYJ	17	46	2.7	0	10
1987 NYJ	30	61	2.0	0	8
1988 NYJ	21	25	1.2	0	11
1989 NYJ	9	18	2.0	0	10
1990 NYJ	21	72	3.4	0	5
1991 NYJ	23	60	2.6	0	6
1992 NYJ	8	8	1.0	0	0
1993 Phi	4	17	4.3	0	4
NFL Total	174	394	2.3	0	72

MIKE O'BRIEN O'Brien, Michael Patrick 6'1", 195 DB
Col: California *HS:* Shorecrest [Seattle, WA]; West Bremerton HS [Bremerton, WA] B: 4/25/1956, Kirkland, WA
1979 Sea: 3 G.

DAVEY O'BRIEN O'Brien, Robert David 5'7", 151 QB-DB-TB
(Slingshot) *Col:* Texas Christian *HS:* Woodrow Wilson [Dallas, TX] B: 6/22/1917, Dallas, TX D: 11/18/1977, Ft. Worth, TX *Drafted:* 1939 Round 1 Phi
1939 Phi: Punt 3-120 40.0. **1940** Phi: Int 4-92; Punt 6-246 41.0. **Total:** Int 4-92; Punt 9-366 40.7.

		Passing							
Year Team	G	Att	Comp	Comp%	Yds	YPA	TD	Int	Rating
1939 Phi	11	201	99	49.3	**1324**	6.59	6	17	45.3
1940 Phi	11	**277**	**124**	44.8	1290	4.66	5	17	39.2
NFL Total	22	478	223	46.7	2614	5.47	11	34	41.8

	Rushing			
Year Team	Att	Yds	Avg	TD
1939 Phi	108	-14	-0.1	1
1940 Phi	100	-180	-1.8	1
NFL Total	208	-194	-0.9	2

BILL O'BRIEN O'Brien, William George 6'0", 180 HB-DB
Col: No College *HS:* University of Detroit [MI] B: 8/25/1924, Detroit, MI
1947 Det: 9 G; Rush 1-2 2.0.

MIKE OBROVAC Obrovac, Michael Louis 6'6", 275 OT-OG
Col: Bowling Green State *HS:* McKinley [Canton, OH] B: 10/11/1955, Canton, OH
1981 Cin: 6 G. **1982** Cin: 9 G. **1983** Cin: 10 G. **Total:** 25 G.

HENRY OBST Obst, Henry D 5'11", 192 G
Col: Syracuse *HS:* Textile [New York, NY] B: 12/23/1906 D: 8/27/1975, Brooklyn, NY
1931 SI: 2 G. **1933** Phi: 1 G. **Total:** 3 G.

JOHN O'CALLAGHAN O'Callaghan, John James 6'4", 245 TE
Col: Long Beach State; San Diego State *HS:* Edison [Huntington Beach, CA] B: 5/15/1964
1987 Sea: 1 G.

HARRY O'CONNELL O'Connell, Harold F 6'1", 190 T
Col: Chicago *HS:* Loyola Acad. [Chicago, IL] B: 2/13/1904, Chicago, IL D: 5/1965, IL
1924 ChiB: 1 G.

GRAT O'CONNELL O'Connell, John Grattan 5'11", 185 E
Col: Boston College *HS:* Bristol [CT]; Dean Academy [Franklin, MA] B: 10/27/1902, Thomaston, CT D: 3/14/1942, Simsbury, CT
1926 Har: 10 G; Int 1 TD; 6 Pt. **1927** Prov: 2 G. **Total:** 12 G; Int 1 TD; 6 Pt.

MILT O'CONNELL O'Connell, Milton Timothy 6'0", 175 E
Col: Lafayette *HS:* Easton [PA] B: 11/12/1900, Nutley, NJ D: 5/18/1928, Wilmington, DE
1924 Fra: 13 G; Rec 1 TD; 6 Pt. **1925** Fra: 2 G. **Total:** 15 G; Rec 1 TD; 6 Pt.

TOMMY O'CONNELL O'Connell, Thomas Bernard 5'11", 187 QB
Col: Notre Dame; Illinois *HS:* South Shore [Chicago, IL] B: 9/26/1930, Chicago, IL *Drafted:* 1952 Round 18 ChiB
1960 Buf: Scor 8, 0-1 FG, 1 2XP. **Total:** Scor 26, 0-1 FG, 1 2XP.

		Passing							
Year Team	G	Att	Comp	Comp%	Yds	YPA	TD	Int	Rating
1953 ChiB	12	67	33	49.3	437	6.52	1	4	50.4
1956 Cle	7	96	42	43.8	551	5.74	4	8	41.6
1957 Cle	11	110	63	57.3	1229	**11.17**	9	**8**	93.3
1960 Buf	14	145	65	44.8	1033	7.12	7	13	47.9
1961 Buf	1	5	1	20.0	11	2.20	0	1	0.0
NFL Total	45	423	204	48.2	3261	7.71	21	34	57.5

	Rushing				
Year Team	Att	Yds	Avg	TD	Fum
1953 ChiB	7	16	2.3	0	3
1956 Cle	24	40	1.7	2	1
1957 Cle	14	-5	-0.4	1	0
1960 Buf	16	21	1.3	1	2
NFL Total	61	72	1.2	4	6

DAN O'CONNOR O'Connor, Daniel Gerald 6'2", 210 G-T
Col: Boston College; Georgetown B: 1/1894, Manchester, NH D: 6/9/1964, Boston, MA
1920 Can: 10 G. **1921** Cle: 7 G. **Total:** 17 G.

FRANK O'CONNOR O'Connor, Francis Stephen 6'0", 210 T
Col: Holy Cross *HS:* Framingham [MA]; Horbitts Prep B: 12/14/1897, Melrose, MA D: 12/15/1965, Worcester, MA
1926 Har: 2 G.

PAUL O'CONNOR O'Connor, Paul 6'3", 270 OG
Col: Miami (Fla.) *HS:* Gov. Livingston Regional [Berkeley Heights, NJ]; Worcester Prep [MA] B: 11/7/1962, Summit, NJ *Drafted:* 1987 Round 5 NYG
1987 TB: 2 G.

RED O'CONNOR O'Connor, Red 5'8", 170 E
Col: DePaul Deceased
1920 ChiC: 3 G. **1921** ChiC: 5 G. **1922** ChiC: 5 G. **1924** ChiC: 3 G. **Total:** 16 G.

BOB O'CONNOR O'Connor, Robert Charles 6'1", 220 G-T-DE-BB
Col: Stanford *HS:* Schenectady [NY] B: 1/27/1910, Elmira, NY
1935 GB: 7 G.

TOM O'CONNOR O'Connor, Thomas L 6'1", 190 P
Col: Nassau CC NY; South Carolina *HS:* Medford [NY] B: 11/8/1963, Patchogue, NY
1987 NYJ: 3 G; Punt 18-602 33.4; 1 Fum.

BILL O'CONNOR O'Connor, William Francis Jr. 6'4", 220 OE-DE
(Zeke) *Col:* Notre Dame *HS:* Mount St. Michael's [Bronx, NY] B: 5/2/1926, New York, NY *Drafted:* 1948 Round 16 LARm
AAFC **1948** BufA: KR 1-0. **Total:** KR 1-0.

		Receiving			
Year Team	G	Rec	Yds	Avg	TD
1948 BufA	14	31	301	9.7	2
1949 CleA	9	0	0	—	0
AAFC Total	23	31	301	9.7	2

NFL **1951** NYY: 12 G; Rec 14-192 13.7; KR 1-10 10.0.

DON ODEGARD Odegard, Don Boyd 6'0", 180 DB
Col: Oregon State; Nevada-Las Vegas *HS:* Kennewick [WA] B: 11/22/1966, Seattle, WA *Drafted:* 1990 Round 6 Cin
1990 NYJ: 14 G; PR 1-0; KR 5-89 17.8. **1991** NYJ: 16 G; KR 6-106 17.7; 1 Fum. **Total:** 30 G; PR 1-0; KR 11-195 17.7; 1 Fum.

STU O'DELL O'Dell, Stewart Harry 6'1", 220 LB
Col: Indiana *HS:* Mooresville [IN] B: 11/27/1951, Linton, IN *Drafted:* 1974 Round 13 Was
1974 Was: 8 G. **1976** Was: 14 G. **1977** Was: 3 G. **1978** Bal: 14 G; KR 0-10; 1 Fum. **Total:** 39 G; KR 0-10; 1 Fum.

MEL O'DELLI O'Delli, Melvin J 5'8", 176 HB-DB
Col: Duquesne *HS:* South Huntington [Smithton, PA] B: 1923
1945 Pit: 2 G.

DERRICK ODEN Oden, Derrick 5'11", 230 LB
Col: Alabama *HS:* Hillcrest [Evergreen, AL] B: 9/29/1970, Los Angeles, CA *Drafted:* 1993 Round 6 Phi
1993 Phi: 12 G. **1994** Phi: 11 G. **1995** Phi: 12 G. **Total:** 35 G.

MCDONALD ODEN Oden, McDonald 6'4", 234 **TE**
Col: Tennessee State *HS:* Spring Hill [Columbia, TN] B: 3/28/1958, Franklin, TN
1980 Cle: 16 G; Rec 3-18 6.0. **1981** Cle: 16 G; Rec 1-6 6.0. **1982** Cle: 9 G; Rec 1-4 4.0. **Total:** 41 G; Rec 5-28 5.6.

CURLY ODEN Oden, Olof Gustave Hazard 5'6", 163 **BB-WB-TB**
(Swede) *Col:* Brown *HS:* Classical [Providence, RI] B: 5/10/1899, Stockholm, Sweden D: 8/31/1978, Cranston, RI
1925 Prov: 8 G. **1926** Prov: 13 G; Rush 6 TD; Rec 1 TD; PR **3** TD; Tot TD **10**; 60 Pt. **1927** Prov: 13 G; Pass 1 TD; Rush 1 TD; PR **1** TD; Tot TD 2; 12 Pt. **1928** Prov: 11 G; Rush 1 TD; Rec 3 TD; Scor 27, 2 XK, **1** 1XP; Tot TD 4. **1930** Prov: 10 G; Pass 1 TD; Scor 1, 1 XK. **1931** Prov: 11 G; Pass 1 TD; PR 1 TD; 6 Pt. **1932** Bos: 1 G. **Total:** 67 G; Pass 3 TD; Rush 8 TD; Rec 4 TD; PR 5 TD; Scor 1 1XP; Tot TD 17.

PHIL ODLE Odle, Philip Morris 5'11", 195 **WR**
Col: Brigham Young *HS:* Elgin [IL] B: 11/23/1942, Macdonia, IL
Drafted: 1968 Round 5 Det
1968 Det: 14 G; Rec 6-71 11.8. **1969** Det: 13 G; Rec 2-24 12.0. **1970** Det: 4 G. **Total:** 31 G; Rec 8-95 11.9.

CLIFF ODOM Odom, Clifton Louis 6'2", 237 **LB**
Col: Texas-Arlington *HS:* French [Beaumont, TX] B: 8/15/1958, Beaumont, TX *Drafted:* 1980 Round 3 Cle
1980 Cle: 8 G. **1982** Bal: 8 G. **1983** Bal: 15 G; 1 Sac. **1984** Ind: 16 G; 3 Sac. **1985** Ind: 16 G; 2 Sac. **1986** Ind: 16 G; 1 Sac. **1987** Ind: 12 G. **1988** Ind: 13 G; 2 Sac. **1989** Ind: 16 G. **1990** Mia: 16 G; 1 Fum TD; 6 Pt; 1 Sac. **1991** Mia: 14 G; Int 1-0; 1 Sac. **1992** Mia: 3 G. **1993** Mia: 14 G. **Total:** 167 G; Int 1-0; 1 Fum TD; 6 Pt; 11 Sac.

HENRY ODOM Odom, Henry Collins 5'10", 200 **RB**
Col: South Carolina State *HS:* Olar [Denmark, SC] B: 2/12/1959, Bamberg, SC *Drafted:* 1983 Round 8 Pit
1983 Pit: Rush 2-7 3.5.

		Kickoff Returns				
Year Team	**G**	**Ret**	**Yds**	**Avg**	**TD**	**Fum**
1983 Pit	16	39	756	19.4	0	2

JASON ODOM Odom, Jason Brian 6'5", 307 **OT**
Col: Florida *HS:* Bartow [FL] B: 3/31/1974, Winter Haven, FL
Drafted: 1996 Round 4 TB
1996 TB: 12 G. **1997** TB: 16 G. **1998** TB: 15 G. **Total:** 43 G.

RICKY ODOM Odom, Ricky L 6'0", 183 **DB**
Col: USC *HS:* Los Angeles [CA] B: 9/16/1956, Jonesboro, LA
Drafted: 1978 Round 7 KC
1978 KC-SF: 11 G; Int 2-19. KC: 8 G. SF: 3 G; Int 2-19. **1979** LARm: 3 G. **Total:** 14 G; Int 2-19.

SAMMY ODOM Odom, Sammy Joe 6'2", 235 **LB**
(Sonny) *Col:* Northwestern State-Louisiana *HS:* Minden [LA]
B: 11/13/1941, Shreveport, LA *Drafted:* 1964 Round 10 Hou
1964 Hou: 14 G; Int 2-22.

STEVE ODOM Odom, Stephen Talmage 5'8", 173 **WR**
Col: Utah *HS:* Berkeley [CA] B: 9/5/1952, Oakland, CA *Drafted:* 1974 Round 5 GB
1974 GB: Rush 6-66 11.0 1 TD. **1975** GB: Rush 5-55 11.0. **1976** GB: Rush 4-78 19.5. **1977** GB: Rush 1-6 6.0. **Total:** Rush 16-205 12.8 1 TD.

		Receiving				Punt Returns			
Year Team	**G**	**Rec**	**Yds**	**Avg**	**TD**	**Ret**	**Yds**	**Avg**	**TD**
1974 GB	14	15	249	16.6	1	15	191	12.7	1
1975 GB	14	15	299	19.9	4	1	0	0.0	0
1976 GB	12	23	456	19.8	2	0	0	—	0
1977 GB	14	27	549	20.3	3	0	0	—	0
1978 GB	12	4	60	15.0	1	33	298	9.0	0
1979 GB-NYG	15	0	0	—	0	24	106	4.4	0
1979 GB	9	0	0	—	0	15	80	5.3	0
1979 NYG	6	0	0	—	0	9	26	2.9	0
NFL Total	81	84	1613	19.2	11	73	595	8.2	1

	Kickoff Returns					Tot
Year Team	**Ret**	**Yds**	**Avg**	**TD**	**Fum**	**TD**
1974 GB	31	713	23.0	0	5	3
1975 GB	42	1034	24.6	**1**	2	5
1976 GB	29	610	21.0	0	2	2
1977 GB	23	468	20.3	0	0	3
1978 GB	25	677	**27.1**	**1**	2	2
1979 GB-NYG	44	949	21.6	0	8	0
1979 GB	29	622	21.4	0	4	0
1979 NYG	15	327	21.8	0	4	0
NFL Total	194	4451	22.9	2	19	15

NATE ODOMES Odomes, Nathaniel Bernard 5'10", 188 **DB**
Col: Wisconsin *HS:* Carver [Columbus, GA] B: 8/25/1965, Columbus, GA *Drafted:* 1987 Round 2 Buf
1989 Buf: 1 Sac. **1990** Buf: PR 1-9 9.0; 1 Fum TD. **1991** Buf: PR 1-9 9.0; 1 Sac. **1992** Buf: 1 Sac. **1993** Buf: 1 Fum TD. **Total:** PR 2-18 9.0; 2 Fum TD; 3 Sac.

		Interceptions				Tot
Year Team	**G**	**Int**	**Yds**	**TD**	**Fum**	**TD**
1987 Buf	12	0	0	0	0	0
1988 Buf	16	1	0	0	0	0
1989 Buf	16	5	20	0	0	0
1990 Buf	16	1	0	0	0	1
1991 Buf	16	5	120	1	1	1
1992 Buf	16	5	19	0	0	0
1993 Buf	16	**9**	65	0	0	1
1996 Atl	7	0	0	0	0	0
NFL Total	115	26	224	1	1	3

RILEY ODOMS Odoms, Riley Mackey 6'4", 230 **TE**
Col: Houston *HS:* West Oso [Corpus Christi, TX] B: 3/1/1950, Luling, TX *Drafted:* 1972 Round 1 Den
1975 Den: **1** Fum TD. **Total:** 1 Fum TD.

		Rushing				Receiving					Tot
Year Team	**G**	**Att**	**Yds**	**Avg**	**TD**	**Rec**	**Yds**	**Avg**	**TD**	**Fum**	**TD**
1972 Den	14	5	72	14.4	0	21	320	15.2	1	1	1
1973 Den	14	5	53	10.6	0	43	629	14.6	7	1	7
1974 Den	14	4	25	6.3	0	42	639	15.2	6	0	6
1975 Den	14	5	27	5.4	0	40	544	13.6	3	2	4
1976 Den	14	3	36	12.0	2	30	477	15.9	3	0	5
1977 Den	14	0	0	—	0	37	429	11.6	3	1	3
1978 Den	16	2	5	2.5	0	54	829	15.4	6	2	6
1979 Den	13	1	-7	-7.0	0	40	638	16.0	1	0	1
1980 Den	15	0	0	—	0	39	590	15.1	6	0	6
1981 Den	15	0	0	—	0	38	516	13.6	5	1	5
1982 Den	8	0	0	—	0	8	82	10.3	0	0	0
1983 Den	2	0	0	—	0	4	62	15.5	0	0	0
NFL Total	153	25	211	8.4	2	396	5755	14.5	41	8	44

PAT O'DONAHUE O'Donahue, James Patrick Michael 6'1", 215 **DE**
Col: Wisconsin *HS:* Regis [Eau Claire, WI] B: 10/7/1930, Eau Claire, WI
Drafted: 1952 Round 5 SF
1952 SF: 8 G; PR 1-23 23.0 1 TD; KR 2-17 8.5; Scor 7, 1-1 100.0% XK. **1955** GB: 12 G. **Total:** 20 G; PR 1-23 23.0 1 TD; KR 2-17 8.5; Scor 7, 1-1 100.0% XK.

JOE O'DONNELL O'Donnell, Joseph Raymond 6'2", 262 **OG-OT**
Col: Michigan *HS:* Milan [MI] B: 8/31/1941, Ann Arbor, MI
Drafted: 1964 Round 13 Buf
1964 Buf: 14 G. **1965** Buf: 14 G. **1966** Buf: 14 G; Rec 1-2 2.0; KR 0-3. **1967** Buf: 14 G. **1969** Buf: 14 G. **1970** Buf: 14 G. **1971** Buf: 7 G. **Total:** 91 G; Rec 1-2 2.0; KR 0-3.

NEIL O'DONNELL O'Donnell, Neil Kennedy 6'3", 228 **QB**
Col: Maryland *HS:* Madison [NJ] B: 7/3/1966, Morristown, NJ
Drafted: 1990 Round 3 Pit

		Passing							
Year Team	**G**	**Att**	**Comp**	**Comp%**	**Yds**	**YPA**	**TD**	**Int**	**Rating**
1991 Pit	12	286	156	54.5	1963	6.86	11	7	78.8
1992 Pit	12	313	185	59.1	2283	7.29	13	9	83.6
1993 Pit	16	486	270	55.6	3208	6.60	14	7	79.5
1994 Pit	14	370	212	57.3	2443	6.60	13	9	78.9
1995 Pit	12	416	246	59.1	2970	7.14	17	7	87.7
1996 NYJ	6	188	110	58.5	1147	6.10	4	7	67.8
1997 NYJ	15	460	259	56.3	2796	6.08	17	7	80.3
1998 Cin	13	343	212	61.8	2216	6.46	15	4	90.2
NFL Total	100	2862	1650	57.7	19026	6.65	104	57	81.6

	Rushing				
Year Team	**Att**	**Yds**	**Avg**	**TD**	**Fum**
1991 Pit	18	82	4.6	1	11
1992 Pit	27	5	0.2	1	6
1993 Pit	26	111	4.3	0	5
1994 Pit	31	80	2.6	1	4
1995 Pit	24	45	1.9	0	2
1996 NYJ	6	30	5.0	0	2
1997 NYJ	32	36	1.1	1	9
1998 Cin	13	34	2.6	0	6
NFL Total	177	423	2.4	4	45

DICK O'DONNELL O'Donnell, Richard 6'0", 190 **E**
Col: Minnesota *HS:* Denfeld [Duluth, MN] B: 1900 Deceased
1923 Dul: 7 G; Rec 1 TD; 6 Pt. **1924** GB: 9 G. **1925** GB: 12 G; Rec 1 TD; 6 Pt. **1926** GB: 11 G; Rec 2 TD; 12 Pt. **1927** GB: 9 G. **1928** GB: 13 G; Rec 1 TD; 6 Pt. **1929** GB: 10 G. **1930** GB: 10 G. **1931** Bkn: 11 G; Rec 1 TD; 6 Pt. **Total:** 92 G; Rec 6 TD; 36 Pt.

NEIL O'DONOGHUE O'Donoghue, Cornelius Joseph Dennis 6'6", 208 **K**
Col: St. Bernard; Auburn *HS:* in Dublin, Ireland B: 1/18/1953, Dublin, Ireland *Drafted:* 1977 Round 5 Buf

		Scoring						
Year Team	**G**	**Pts**	**FG**	**FGA**	**FG%**	**XK**	**XKA**	**XK%**
1977 Buf	5	10	2	6	33.3	4	5	80.0
1978 TB	15	64	13	23	56.5	25	29	86.2

1979 TB	16	63	11	19	57.9	30	35	85.7
1980 StL	10	51	11	15	73.3	18	18	100.0
1981 StL	16	93	19	32	59.4	36	37	97.3
1982 StL	8	39	8	13	61.5	15	16	93.8
1983 StL	16	90	15	28	53.6	45	47	95.7
1984 StL	16	117	23	35	65.7	48	51	94.1
1985 StL	8	49	10	18	55.6	19	19	100.0
NFL Total	110	576	112	189	59.3	240	257	93.4

URBAN ODSON Odson, Urban Leroy 6'3", 251 **T**
Col: Minnesota *HS:* Clark [SD] B: 11/17/1918, Clark, SD
D: 6/22/1986, Rapid City, SD *Drafted:* 1942 Round 1 GB
1946 GB: 6 G; Scor **1** Saf; 2 Pt. **1947** GB: 11 G. **1948** GB: 12 G. **1949** GB: 10 G. **Total:** 39 G; Scor 1 Saf; 2 Pt.

MATT O'DWYER O'Dwyer, Matthew Phillip 6'5", 300 **OG**
Col: Northwestern *HS:* Adlai E. Stevenson [Lincolnshire, IL]
B: 9/1/1972, Lincolnshire, IL *Drafted:* 1995 Round 2 NYJ
1995 NYJ: 12 G. **1996** NYJ: 16 G. **1997** NYJ: 16 G. **1998** NYJ: 16 G. **Total:** 60 G.

VERN OECH Oech, Vernon Milton 6'1", 207 **G**
Col: Montana; Minnesota *HS:* Winona [MN] B: 5/31/1913, Beach, ND
D: 12/1972 *Drafted:* 1936 Round 5 ChiB
1936 ChiB: 7 G. **1937** ChiB: 1 G. **Total:** 8 G.

CAP OEHLER Oehler, John Walter 6'0", 204 **C-LB**
Col: Purdue *HS:* Staunton [IL] B: 8/5/1910, Queens, NY
D: 5/12/1983, Pinehurst, NC
1933 Pit: 11 G; Scor **1** Saf; 2 Pt. **1934** Pit: 12 G; Rush 2-14 7.0. **1935** Bkn: 12 G. **1936** Bkn: 5 G. **Total:** 40 G; Rush 2-14 7.0; Scor 1 Saf; 2 Pt.

ARNIE OEHLRICH Oehlrich, Arnold Henry 5'11", 190 **WB-BB**
Col: Nebraska *HS:* Columbus [NE] B: 11/24/1905, Clarks, NE
D: 6/27/1965, Omaha, NE
1928 Fra: 16 G; Rec 2 TD; 12 Pt. **1929** Fra: 17 G; Rec 1 TD; 6 Pt. **Total:** 33 G; Rec 3 TD; 18 Pt.

JOHN OELERICH Oelerich, John Herman 6'0", 192 **HB-DB**
Col: St. Ambrose *HS:* St. Ambrose [Davenport, IA] B: 2/7/1916, Davenport, IA D: 2/9/1989, Pensacola, FL
1938 ChiB-Pit: 5 G; Pass 1-1 100.0%, 10 10.00; Rush 14-23 1.6; Rec 2-23 11.5. ChiB: 2 G; Pass 1-1 100.0%, 10 10.00; Rush 2-2 1.0. Pit: 3 G; Rush 12-21 1.8; Rec 2-23 11.5. **Total:** 5 G; Pass 1-1 100.0%, 10 10.00; Rush 14-23 1.6; Rec 2-23 11.5.

JOHN OFFERDAHL Offerdahl, John Arnold 6'3", 232 **LB**
Col: Western Michigan *HS:* Fort Atkinson [WI] B: 8/17/1964, Wisconsin Rapids, WI *Drafted:* 1986 Round 2 Mia
1986 Mia: 15 G; Int 1-14; 2 Sac. **1987** Mia: 9 G; 1.5 Sac. **1988** Mia: 16 G; Int 2-2; 0.5 Sac. **1989** Mia: 10 G; 1.5 Sac. **1990** Mia: 16 G; Int 1-28; 1 Sac. **1991** Mia: 6 G; 1.5 Sac. **1992** Mia: 8 G; 1.5 Sac. **1993** Mia: 9 G. **Total:** 89 G; Int 4-44; 9.5 Sac.

TONY OFFICE Office, Anthony Lee 6'2", 250 **LB**
Col: Illinois State *HS:* Fort Meade [FL] B: 2/24/1960, Tifton, GA
1987 Det: 3 G.

A.J. OFODILE Ofodile, Anselm Aniagboso Jr. 6'6", 260 **TE**
Col: Missouri *HS:* Cass Tech [Detroit, MI] B: 10/9/1973, Detroit, MI
Drafted: 1994 Round 5 Buf
1997 Bal: 12 G. **1998** Bal: 5 G. **Total:** 17 G.

DAVE OGAS Ogas, David H 6'1", 225 **LB**
Col: San Diego State *HS:* La Habra [CA] B: 7/23/1946, Silver City, NM
1968 Oak: 6 G. **1969** Buf: 14 G. **Total:** 20 G.

ERIC OGBOGU Ogbogu, Eric 6'4", 280 **DE**
Col: Maryland *HS:* Archbishop Stepinac [White Plains, NY]
B: 7/18/1975, Irvington, NY *Drafted:* 1998 Round 6 NYJ
1998 NYJ: 12 G.

JEFF OGDEN Ogden, Jeffrey Matthew 6'0", 190 **WR**
Col: Eastern Washington *HS:* Snohomish [WA] B: 2/22/1975, Tacoma, WA
1998 Dal: 16 G; Rush 1-12 12.0; Rec 8-63 7.9; KR 3-65 21.7; 1 Fum.

JONATHAN OGDEN Ogden, Jonathan Phillip 6'8", 318 **OT-OG**
Col: UCLA *HS:* St. Albans [Washington, DC] B: 7/31/1974, Washington, DC *Drafted:* 1996 Round 1 Bal
1996 Bal: 16 G; Rec 1-1 1.0 1 TD; 6 Pt. **1997** Bal: 16 G. **1998** Bal: 13 G. **Total:** 45 G; Rec 1-1 1.0 1 TD; 6 Pt.

RAY OGDEN Ogden, Raymond Douglas 6'5", 225 **TE**
Col: Alabama *HS:* Jesup [GA] B: 9/2/1942, Jesup, GA *Drafted:* 1965 Round 3 StL
1965 StL: KR 2-55 27.5. **1966** StL: KR 1-0. **1967** NO-Atl: KR 3-41 13.7. Atl: KR 3-41 13.7. **1968** Atl: Rush 1-12 12.0. **Total:** Rush 1-12 12.0; KR 6-96 16.0.

		Receiving			
Year Team	**G**	**Rec**	**Yds**	**Avg**	**TD**
1965 StL	3	0	0	—	0
1966 StL	14	0	0	—	0
1967 NO-Atl	13	20	327	16.4	1
1967 NO	2	1	19	19.0	0
1967 Atl	11	19	308	16.2	1
1968 Atl	14	25	452	18.1	2
1969 ChiB	11	7	100	14.3	0
1970 ChiB	9	1	6	6.0	1
1971 ChiB	6	0	0	—	0
NFL Total	70	53	885	16.7	4

RICK OGLE Ogle, Richard James 6'3", 230 **LB**
Col: Colorado *HS:* Bozeman [MT] B: 1/14/1949, Bozeman, MT
Drafted: 1971 Round 11 StL
1971 StL: 6 G. **1972** Det: 4 G. **Total:** 10 G.

ALFRED OGLESBY Oglesby, Alfred Lee 6'3", 280 **NT-DT-DE**
Col: Houston *HS:* Weimar [TX] B: 1/27/1967, Weimar, TX
Drafted: 1990 Round 3 Mia
1990 Mia: 13 G; 2.5 Sac. **1991** Mia: 12 G. **1992** Mia-GB: 13 G. Mia: 6 G. GB: 7 G. **1994** NYJ: 15 G; 0.5 Sac. **1995** Cin: 6 G; 1 Sac. **Total:** 59 G; 4 Sac.

PAUL OGLESBY Oglesby, Paul William 6'4", 235 **DT**
Col: UCLA *HS:* Riverside [CA] B: 1/9/1939 *Drafted:* 1960 Round 2 Hou
1960 Oak: 14 G.

CRAIG OGLETREE Ogletree, Craig Algernon 6'2", 236 **LB**
Col: Auburn *HS:* Lamar Co. [Barnesville, GA] B: 4/2/1968, Barnesville, GA *Drafted:* 1990 Round 7 Cin
1990 Cin: 11 G.

PAT OGRIN Ogrin, Patrick John 6'5", 265 **DT**
Col: Wyoming *HS:* Butte [MT] B: 2/10/1958, Butte, MT
1981 Was: 5 G. **1982** Was: 3 G. **Total:** 8 G.

ROSS O'HANLEY O'Hanley, Ross A 6'0", 180 **DB**
Col: Boston College *HS:* Christopher Columbus [Everett, MA]
B: 2/16/1939, Everett, MA D: 4/2/1972, Needham, MA

		Interceptions		
Year Team	**G**	**Int**	**Yds**	**TD**
1960 Bos	14	3	1	0
1961 Bos	7	0	0	0
1962 Bos	14	5	83	0
1963 Bos	14	3	79	0
1964 Bos	14	3	120	**1**
1965 Bos	14	1	5	0
NFL Total	77	15	288	1

ED O'HEARN O'Hearn, Edmund Francis 5'10", 185 **G-T**
Col: Boston College; Lehigh *HS:* Brookline [MA] B: 12/1/1898, Brookline, MA D: 4/25/1972, Boston, MA
1920 Cle: 2 G. **1921** NYG: 2 G. **Total:** 4 G.

JACK O'HEARN O'Hearn, John Ewing 5'10", 180 **WB**
Col: Cornell *HS:* Brookline [MA] B: 7/28/1893, Brookline, MA
D: 7/22/1977, Boston, MA
1920 Cle: 5 G. **1921** Buf: 2 G. **Total:** 7 G.

EARL OHLGREN Ohlgren, Earl August 6'2", 210 **DE**
Col: Minnesota *HS:* Cokato [MN] B: 2/21/1918, Cokato, MN
D: 1/1963
1942 GB: 2 G.

OHMER Ohmer **WB**
Col: No College Deceased
1921 Cin: 1 G.

STEVE OKONIEWSKI Okoniewski, John Stephen 6'3", 257 **DE**
Col: Everett CC WA; Washington; Montana *HS:* Central Kitsap [Silverdale, WA] B: 8/22/1949, Bremerton, WA *Drafted:* 1972 Round 2 Atl
1972 Buf: 10 G. **1973** Buf: 5 G. **1974** GB: 14 G; KR 2-11 5.5. **1975** GB: 14 G. **1976** StL: 8 G; KR 1-12 12.0. **1977** StL: 1 G. **Total:** 52 G; KR 3-23 7.7.

CHRISTIAN OKOYE Okoye, Christian Emeka 6'1", 253 **RB**
(Nigerian Nightmare) *Col:* Azusa Pacific *HS:* Uwani Secondary School [Enugu, Nigeria] B: 8/16/1961, Enugu, Nigeria *Drafted:* 1987 Round 2 KC

		Rushing				Receiving				
Year Team	**G**	**Att**	**Yds**	**Avg**	**TD**	**Rec**	**Yds**	**Avg**	**TD**	**Fum**
1987 KC	12	157	660	4.2	3	24	169	7.0	0	5
1988 KC	9	105	473	4.5	3	8	51	6.4	0	1
1989 KC	15	**370**	**1480**	4.0	12	2	12	6.0	0	8
1990 KC	14	245	805	3.3	7	4	23	5.8	0	6
1991 KC	14	225	1031	4.6	9	3	34	11.3	0	5
1992 KC	15	144	448	3.1	6	1	5	5.0	0	2
NFL Total	79	1246	4897	3.9	40	42	294	7.0	0	27

CLIFF OLANDER Olander, Clifford Valmore 6'5", 191 **QB**
Col: New Mexico State *HS:* League City [TX]; Clear Creek HS [CO]; Arvada HS [CO] B: 5/15/1955, Hartford, CT *Drafted:* 1977 Round 5 SD
1977 SD: 2 G; Pass 16-7 43.8%, 76 4.75 2 Int; Rush 7-30 4.3. **1978** SD: 9 G; Pass 8-5 62.5%, 49 6.13 1 Int; Rush 1-(-3) -3.0. **1979** SD: 4 G; Scor 1, 0-1 FG, 1-1 100.0% XK. **Total:** 15 G; Pass 24-12 50.0%, 125 5.21 3 Int; Rush 8-27 3.4; Scor 1, 0-1 FG, 1-1 100.0% XK.

BOB OLDERMAN Olderman, Robert Bruce 6'5", 262 **OG**
Col: Virginia *HS:* Marist [Atlanta, GA] B: 6/5/1962, Brookville, PA D: 10/20/1993, Atlanta, GA *Drafted:* 1985 Round 4 KC
1985 KC: 16 G.

DOUG OLDERSHAW Oldershaw, Douglas C 6'0", 195 **G-LB-DE-OE**
Col: California-Santa Barbara B: 7/6/1915, Bakersfield, CA D: 10/30/1995, Laguna Beach, CA *Drafted:* 1938 Round 9 NYG
1939 NYG: 10 G. **1940** NYG: 11 G; Int 4-48. **1941** NYG: 10 G; Int 1-26 **1** TD; 6 Pt. **Total:** 31 G; Int 5-74 1 TD; 6 Pt.

CHRIS OLDHAM Oldham, Christopher Martin 5'9", 193 **DB**
Col: Oregon *HS:* O. Perry Walker [New Orleans, LA] B: 10/26/1968, Sacramento, CA *Drafted:* 1990 Round 4 Det
1990 Det: 16 G; KR 13-234 18.0; Int 1-28; 2 Fum. **1991** Buf-Pho: 4 G. Buf: 2 G. Pho: 2 G. **1992** Pho: 1 G. **1993** Pho: 16 G; Int 1-0; 1 Sac. **1994** Ariz: 11 G. **1995** Pit: 15 G; Int 1-12; **1** Fum TD; 6 Pt. **1996** Pit: 16 G; 2 Sac. **1997** Pit: 16 G; Int 2-16; 4 Sac. **1998** Pit: 16 G; Int 1-14; 1 Fum TD; 6 Pt; 0.5 Sac. **Total:** 111 G; KR 13-234 18.0; Int 6-70; 2 Fum TD; Tot TD 2; 12 Pt; 2 Fum; 7.5 Sac.

RAY OLDHAM Oldham, Donnil Ray 6'0", 200 **DB**
Col: Middle Tennessee State *HS:* Gallatin [TN] B: 2/23/1951, Gallatin, TN *Drafted:* 1973 Round 8 Bal
1974 Bal: KR 1-0. **1977** Bal: PR 1-0. **1982** Det: 1 Sac. **Total:** PR 1-0; KR 1-0; 1 Sac.

		Interceptions		
Year Team	**G**	**Int**	**Yds**	**TD**
1973 Bal	11	2	10	0
1974 Bal	14	1	3	0
1975 Bal	14	2	23	0
1976 Bal	14	2	40	0
1977 Bal	14	0	0	0
1978 Bal-Pit	6	0	0	0
1978 Bal	2	0	0	0
1978 Pit	4	0	0	0
1979 NYG	15	2	4	0
1980 Det	16	3	39	1
1981 Det	16	1	10	0
1982 Det	5	1	35	**1**
NFL Total	125	14	164	2

JIM OLDHAM Oldham, James R 5'10", 183 **OE-WB-BB-FB**
(Red; Brute) *Col:* Arizona *HS:* Phoenix Union [AZ] Deceased
1926 Rac: 5 G; Rec 1 TD; 6 Pt.

BILL OLDS Olds, William Henry 6'1", 224 **RB**
Col: Nebraska *HS:* Sumner [Kansas City, KS] B: 2/21/1951, Kansas City, KS *Drafted:* 1973 Round 3 Bal
1973 Bal: KR 3-14 4.7. **1976** Sea-Phi: KR 1-11 11.0. Phi: KR 1-11 11.0. **Total:** KR 4-25 6.3.

		Rushing				Receiving					Tot
Year Team	**G**	**Att**	**Yds**	**Avg**	**TD**	**Rec**	**Yds**	**Avg**	**TD**	**Fum**	**TD**
1973 Bal	13	26	100	3.8	2	2	-4	-2.0	0	0	2
1974 Bal	13	129	475	3.7	1	21	153	7.3	2	3	3
1975 Bal	14	94	281	3.0	2	30	194	6.5	2	1	4
1976 Sea-Phi	12	38	129	3.4	1	9	29	3.2	0	1	1
1976 Sea	1	2	9	4.5	0	0	0	—	0	0	0
1976 Phi	11	36	120	3.3	1	9	29	3.2	0	1	1
NFL Total	52	287	985	3.4	6	62	372	6.0	4	5	10

STAN OLEJNICZAK Olejniczak, Stanley Joseph 6'0", 220 **T**
Col: Pittsburgh *HS:* Bellaire [OH] B: 5/31/1912, Neffs, OH D: 3/11/1982, Buffalo, NY
1935 Pit: 12 G; 6 Pt.

JOHN OLENCHALK Olenchalk, John Hunt 6'0", 228 **LB-C**
Col: Stanford *HS:* Antioch [CA] B: 11/27/1955, Stockton, CA
1981 KC: 1 G. **1982** KC: 9 G. **Total:** 10 G.

MITCH OLENSKI Olenski, Mitchell Joseph 6'3", 222 **T**
Col: Alabama *HS:* Union Endicott [NY] B: 1/13/1921, Benton, IL *Drafted:* 1944 Round 9 Bkn
AAFC **1946** MiaA: 14 G; KR 1-2 2.0.

NFL **1947** Det: 12 G.

DAVE OLERICH Olerich, David Byron 6'1", 220 **LB-TE**
Col: San Francisco *HS:* Menlo-Atherton [Atherton, CA] B: 11/14/1944, Elmhurst, IL
1967 SF: 6 G; Rec 1-2 2.0; 1 Fum. **1968** SF: 14 G; KR 1-4 4.0. **1969** StL: 14 G; KR 2-2 1.0; 1 Fum. **1970** StL: 11 G. **1971** Hou: 14 G. **1972** SF: 12 G. **1973** SF: 14 G; KR 2-17 8.5. **Total:** 85 G; Rec 1-2 2.0; KR 5-23 4.6; 2 Fum.

AARON OLIKER Oliker, Aaron Earl 5'11", 170 **E**
Col: West Virginia *HS:* Clarksburg [WV] B: 12/5/1903, Clarksburg, WV D: 9/8/1965, Clarksburg, WV
1926 Pott: 1 G.

ELMER OLIPHANT Oliphant, Elmer Quillen 5'7", 175 **WB-TB**
(Ollie) *Col:* Purdue; Army *HS:* Washington [IN]; Linton HS [IN] B: 7/9/1892, Bloomfield, IN D: 7/3/1975, New Canaan, CT
1920 Roch: 1 G. **1921** Buf: 10 G; Pass **7** TD; Rush 1 TD; Scor **47**, **5** FG, **26** XK. **Total:** 11 G; Pass 7 TD; Rush 1 TD; Scor 47, 5 FG, 26 XK.

MIKE OLIPHANT Oliphant, Michael Nathaniel 5'10", 183 **RB**
Col: Puget Sound *HS:* Federal Way [WA] B: 5/19/1963, Jacksonville, FL *Drafted:* 1988 Round 3 Was
1988 Was: 8 G; Rush 8-30 3.8; Rec 15-111 7.4; PR 7-24 3.4; KR 7-127 18.1; 2 Fum. **1989** Cle: 14 G; Rush 15-97 6.5 1 TD; Rec 3-22 7.3; KR 5-69 13.8; 6 Pt; 3 Fum. **1991** Cle: 4 G. **Total:** 26 G; Rush 23-127 5.5 1 TD; Rec 18-133 7.4; PR 7-24 3.4; KR 12-196 16.3; 6 Pt; 5 Fum.

BOBBY OLIVE Olive, Bobby Leo Jr. 6'0", 167 **WR**
Col: Ohio State *HS:* Frederick Douglass [Atlanta, GA] B: 4/22/1969, Paris, TN *Drafted:* 1991 Round 11 KC
1995 Ind: 1 G. **1996** Ind: 1 G. **Total:** 2 G.

CLANCY OLIVER Oliver, Clarence H 6'1", 183 **DB**
Col: Orange Coast Coll. CA (J.C.); San Diego State *HS:* Laguna Beach [CA] B: 11/17/1947, Bakersfield, CA
1969 Pit: 9 G. **1970** Pit: 14 G. **1973** StL: 2 G. **Total:** 25 G.

DARRYL OLIVER Oliver, Darryl Hiram 5'10", 195 **RB**
Col: Miami (Fla.) *HS:* Palatka [FL] B: 7/13/1964, Palatka, FL *Drafted:* 1987 Round 11 Sea
1987 Atl: 2 G; Rush 1-0; Rec 1-2 2.0; KR 5-90 18.0.

FRANK OLIVER Oliver, Franklin Justice 6'1", 194 **DB**
Col: Kentucky State *HS:* St. Jude [Montgomery, AL] B: 3/3/1952, Wetumpka, AL *Drafted:* 1975 Round 4 SF
1975 Buf: 14 G. **1976** TB: 4 G. **Total:** 18 G.

GREG OLIVER Oliver, Gregory Curtis 6'0", 192 **RB**
Col: Ranger Coll. TX (J.C.); Trinity (Tex.) *HS:* G.W. Brackenridge [San Antonio, TX] B: 1/15/1949, San Antonio, TX *Drafted:* 1973 Round 17 Phi
1973 Phi: 11 G; Rush 1-6 6.0; Rec 1-9 9.0; KR 1-17 17.0. **1974** Phi: 14 G; Rush 7-19 2.7. **Total:** 25 G; Rush 8-25 3.1; Rec 1-9 9.0; KR 1-17 17.0.

HUBIE OLIVER Oliver, Hubert 5'10", 215 **RB**
Col: Arizona *HS:* Elyria [OH] B: 11/12/1957, Elyria, OH *Drafted:* 1981 Round 10 Phi

		Rushing				Receiving					Tot
Year Team	**G**	**Att**	**Yds**	**Avg**	**TD**	**Rec**	**Yds**	**Avg**	**TD**	**Fum**	**TD**
1981 Phi	13	75	329	4.4	1	10	37	3.7	0	1	1
1983 Phi	16	121	434	3.6	1	49	421	8.6	2	5	3
1984 Phi	16	72	263	3.7	0	32	142	4.4	0	0	0
1985 Phi	1	1	3	3.0	0	1	4	4.0	0	0	0
1986 Ind-Hou	6	1	1	1.0	0	1	-2	-2.0	0	0	0
1986 Ind	4	0	0	—	0	0	0	—	0	0	0
1986 Hou	2	1	1	1.0	0	1	-2	-2.0	0	0	0
NFL Total	52	270	1030	3.8	2	93	602	6.5	2	6	4

JEFF OLIVER Oliver, Jeffrey Peter 6'4", 292 **OT-OG**
Col: Boston College *HS:* Delaware Acad. [Delhi, NY] B: 7/28/1965, Delhi, NY
1989 NYJ: 1 G.

JACK OLIVER Oliver, John Gerald 6'3", 281 **OT**
Col: Texas-El Paso; Memphis *HS:* Pensacola Catholic [Pensacola, FL] B: 2/3/1962, Washington, DC *Drafted:* 1985 Round 6 NYG
1987 ChiB: 3 G.

MAURICE OLIVER Oliver, Julius Maurice 6'3", 235 **LB**
Col: Southern Mississippi *HS:* Vestavia Hills [AL] B: 6/14/1967, Birmingham, AL
1991 TB: 3 G.

LOUIS OLIVER Oliver, Louis III 6'2", 224 **DB**
Col: Florida *HS:* Glades Central [Belle Glade, FL] B: 3/9/1966, Belle Glade, FL *Drafted:* 1989 Round 1 Mia
1990 Mia: 1 Sac. **1994** Cin: 1 Sac. **Total:** 2 Sac.

		Interceptions			
Year Team	**G**	**Int**	**Yds**	**TD**	**Fum**
1989 Mia	15	4	32	0	0
1990 Mia	16	5	87	0	0
1991 Mia	16	5	80	0	0
1992 Mia	16	5	200	1	0
1993 Mia	11	2	60	1	0
1994 Cin	12	3	36	0	1

1995 Mia	15	0	0	0	0
1996 Mia	16	3	110	0	1
NFL Total	117	27	605	2	2

MUHAMMAD OLIVER Oliver, Muhammad Ramadan 5'11", 179 **DB**
Col: Glendale CC AZ; Oregon *HS:* North [Phoenix, AZ] B: 3/12/1969, Brooklyn, NY *Drafted:* 1992 Round 9 Den
1992 Den: 3 G; KR 1-20 20.0. **1993** KC-GB-Mia: 4 G. KC: 2 G. GB: 2 G. **1994** Mia: 13 G; Int 1-0. **1995** Was: 1 G. **Total:** 21 G; KR 1-20 20.0; Int 1-0.

CHIP OLIVER Oliver, Ralph 6'2", 220 **LB**
Col: San Diego City Coll. CA (J.C.); USC *HS:* Herbert Hoover [San Diego, CA]; Centralia HS [WA] B: 4/24/1944, Winona, MS
Drafted: 1968 Round 11 Oak
1968 Oak: 14 G. **1969** Oak: 14 G; Int 1-29 1 TD; 6 Pt. **Total:** 28 G; Int 1-29 1 TD; 6 Pt.

BOB OLIVER Oliver, Robert Lee 6'3", 240 **DE**
Col: Abilene Christian *HS:* Albany [TX] B: 6/17/1947, Olney, TX
Drafted: 1969 Round 17 Cle
1969 Cle: 8 G.

VINCE OLIVER Oliver, Vincent James 5'11", 180 **QB**
Col: Indiana *HS:* Whiting [IN] B: 12/28/1915, Whiting, IN
D: 8/28/1985, Chicago, IL
1945 ChiC: 3 G; Pass 10-4 40.0%, 22 2.20; Rush 11-(-3) -0.3; 1 Fum.

BILL OLIVER Oliver, William Seth Jr. 5'11", 180 **G**
(Country) *Col:* Alabama *HS:* Marion Mil. Inst. [AL] B: 2/16/1902, Panola, AL D: 5/1/1932, Birmingham, AL
1927 NYY: 13 G.

WINSLOW OLIVER Oliver, Winslow Paul 5'7", 180 **RB**
Col: New Mexico *HS:* Clements [Sugar Land, TX]; Kempner HS [Houston, TX] B: 3/3/1973, Houston, TX *Drafted:* 1996 Round 3 Car
1996 Car: Rec 15-144 9.6; KR 7-160 22.9. **1997** Car: Rec 6-47 7.8. **1998** Car: KR 2-43 21.5. **Total:** Rec 21-191 9.1; KR 9-203 22.6.

		Rushing				Punt Returns				
Year Team	**G**	**Att**	**Yds**	**Avg**	**TD**	**Ret**	**Yds**	**Avg**	**TD**	**Fum**
1996 Car	16	47	183	3.9	0	52	598	11.5	1	4
1997 Car	6	1	0	0.0	0	14	111	7.9	0	2
1998 Car	16	0	0	—	0	44	464	10.5	0	1
NFL Total	38	48	183	3.8	0	110	1173	10.7	1	7

BROCK OLIVO Olivo, Brock 6'0", 226 **RB**
Col: Missouri *HS:* St. Francis Borgia [Washington, MO] B: 6/24/1976, St. Louis, MO
1998 Det: 1 G.

NEAL OLKEWICZ Olkewicz, Neal 6'0", 230 **LB**
Col: Maryland *HS:* Phoenixville [PA] B: 1/30/1957, Phoenixville, PA
1979 Was: 16 G; Int 1-4. **1980** Was: 12 G. **1981** Was: 14 G; Int 2-22 1 TD; 6 Pt. **1982** Was: 9 G; 3 Sac. **1983** Was: 16 G; Int 1-14; 2 Sac. **1984** Was: 16 G; 1 Sac. **1985** Was: 16 G; Int 1-21. **1986** Was: 16 G; Int 1-15; 2 Sac. **1987** Was: 10 G; 2 Sac. **1988** Was: 16 G; 2 Sac. **1989** Was: 9 G. **Total:** 150 G; Int 6-76 1 TD; 6 Pt; 12 Sac.

CHARLIE OLMSTEAD Olmstead, Charles Howard 1 **G**
Col: No College B: 3/21/1898, Louisville, KY D: 12/16/1970, Louisville, KY
1922 Lou: 3 G. **1923** Lou: 3 G. **Total:** 6 G.

JERRY OLSAVSKY Olsavsky, Jerome Donald 6'1", 221 **LB**
Col: Pittsburgh *HS:* Chaney [Youngstown, OH] B: 3/29/1967, Youngstown, OH *Drafted:* 1989 Round 10 Pit
1989 Pit: 16 G; 1 Sac. **1990** Pit: 15 G. **1991** Pit: 16 G. **1992** Pit: 7 G. **1993** Pit: 7 G. **1994** Pit: 1 G. **1995** Pit: 15 G; 1 Sac. **1996** Pit: 15 G; Int 1-5; 0.5 Sac. **1997** Pit: 16 G. **1998** Bal: 9 G. **Total:** 117 G; Int 1-5; 2.5 Sac.

MERLIN OLSEN Olsen, Merlin Jay 6'5", 270 **DT**
Col: Utah State *HS:* James Logan [Logan, UT] B: 9/15/1940, Logan, UT *Drafted:* 1962 Round 1 LARm *HOF:* 1982
1962 LARm: 12 G; Int 1-20 **1** TD; 6 Pt. **1963** LARm: 14 G; KR 1-0; 1 Fum. **1964** LARm: 14 G. **1965** LARm: 14 G. **1966** LARm: 14 G; 1 Fum. **1967** LARm: 14 G. **1968** LARm: 14 G. **1969** LARm: 14 G. **1970** LARm: 14 G. **1971** LARm: 14 G. **1972** LARm: 14 G. **1973** LARm: 14 G. **1974** LARm: 14 G. **1975** LARm: 14 G. **1976** LARm: 14 G. **Total:** 208 G; KR 1-0; Int 1-20 1 TD; 6 Pt; 2 Fum.

NORM OLSEN Olsen, Norman E 6'2", 220 **T**
Col: Alabama B: 12/1/1921, New York, NY
1944 Cle: 10 G; KR 1-19 19.0.

ORRIN OLSEN Olsen, Orrin James 6'1", 245 **C**
Col: Brigham Young *HS:* Orem [UT] B: 7/7/1953, Logan, UT
Drafted: 1976 Round 8 KC
1976 KC: 14 G.

PHIL OLSEN Olsen, Phillip Vernor 6'5", 265 **DT-C**
Col: Utah State *HS:* James Logan [Logan, UT] B: 4/26/1948, Logan, UT *Drafted:* 1970 Round 1 Bos
1971 LARm: 10 G. **1972** LARm: 14 G. **1973** LARm: 14 G. **1974** LARm: 14 G. **1975** Den: 14 G. **1976** Den: 13 G. **Total:** 79 G.

RALPH OLSEN Olsen, Ralph Kenneth 6'4", 220 **DE**
Col: Utah *HS:* West [Salt Lake City, UT] B: 4/10/1924, Salt Lake City, UT D: 11/28/1994, Fruit Heights, UT *Drafted:* 1947 Round 30 GB
1949 GB: 4 G.

BENJI OLSON Olson, Benjamin Dempsey 6'3", 315 **OG**
Col: Washington *HS:* South Kitsap [Port Orchard, WA] B: 6/5/1975, Bremerton, WA *Drafted:* 1998 Round 5 Ten
1998 Ten: 13 G.

CARL OLSON Olson, Carl Virgil 6'2", 206 **T**
Col: UCLA *HS:* John C. Fremont [Los Angeles, CA] B: 1/16/1917, San Francisco, CA
1942 ChiC: 2 G.

FORREST OLSON Olson, Forrest Morten 6'0", 200 **G-FB**
Col: Iowa *HS:* Sioux City [IA] B: 11/15/1902, Vermillion, SD
D: 12/13/1970, Sioux City, IA
1927 NYY: 3 G.

GLENN OLSON Olson, Glenn Earl 6'0", 195 **BB-DB**
Col: Iowa *HS:* Colo [IA] B: 3/14/1915, Colo, IA D: 5/1973
1940 Cle: 2 G.

HAROLD OLSON Olson, Harold Vincent 6'2", 255 **OT**
Col: Clemson *HS:* Southwest De Kalb [Decatur, GA] B: 1/19/1938, Asheville, NC *Drafted:* 1960 Round 1 Buf
1960 Buf: 14 G. **1961** Buf: 14 G. **1962** Buf: 14 G. **1963** Den: 14 G; KR 2-0. **1964** Den: 14 G; KR 2-27 13.5. **Total:** 70 G; KR 4-27 6.8.

LARRY OLSONOSKI Olsonoski, Lawrence Rodney 6'2", 214 **G**
Col: Minnesota *HS:* Lancaster [MN] B: 9/10/1925, Lancaster, MN
D: 3/6/1991, Edina, MN *Drafted:* 1948 Round 4 GB
1948 GB: 12 G. **1949** GB-NYB: 12 G. GB: 4 G. NYB: 8 G. **Total:** 24 G.

LANCE OLSSEN Olssen, Lance Everett 6'5", 257 **OT-C**
Col: Purdue *HS:* Stuyvesant [New York, NY] B: 4/17/1947, Boston, MA
Drafted: 1968 Round 3 SF
1968 SF: 7 G. **1969** SF: 2 G. **Total:** 9 G.

LES OLSSON Olsson, Carl Lester 6'0", 232 **G**
(Swede) *Col:* Mercer *HS:* Central [Akron, OH] B: 8/18/1909, Akron, OH D: 7/3/1972, Barberton, OH
1934 Bos: 12 G. **1935** Bos: 11 G. **1936** Bos: 12 G. **1937** Was: 11 G. **1938** Was: 11 G. **Total:** 57 G.

AL OLSZEWSKI Olszewski, Albert Frank 6'2", 185 **OE-DB**
Col: Penn State; Pittsburgh *HS:* Connellsville [PA] B: 11/14/1920
1945 Pit: 1 G; Rec 2-28 14.0.

JOHNNY OLSZEWSKI Olszewski, John Peter 5'11", 200 **FB-HB**
(Johnny O) *Col:* California *HS:* St.Anthony's [Long Beach, CA]
B: 12/21/1929, Washington, DC D: 12/8/1996, Long Beach, CA
Drafted: 1953 Round 1 ChiC
1953 ChiC: Pass 1-0, 1 Int; PR 1-0; KR 1-17 17.0. **1954** ChiC: KR 1-21 21.0. **1955** ChiC: KR 2-26 13.0. **1956** ChiC: KR 3-25 8.3. **1957** ChiC: KR 0-13. **1958** Was: PR 2-0; KR 1-2 2.0. **1959** Was: PR 1-0. **1960** Was: PR 1-0; KR 5-119 23.8. **1961** Det: KR 4-59 14.8. **1962** Den: KR 3-66 22.0. **Total:** Pass 1-0, 1 Int; PR 5-0; KR 20-348 17.4.

		Rushing				Receiving					Tot
Year Team	**G**	**Att**	**Yds**	**Avg**	**TD**	**Rec**	**Yds**	**Avg**	**TD**	**Fum**	**TD**
1953 ChiC	12	106	386	3.6	4	21	210	10.0	1	6	5
1954 ChiC	11	106	352	3.3	1	12	133	11.1	1	5	2
1955 ChiC	11	84	326	3.9	1	9	37	4.1	0	9	1
1956 ChiC	11	157	598	3.8	2	17	182	10.7	0	**13**	2
1957 ChiC	11	83	271	3.3	2	3	36	12.0	0	5	2
1958 Was	10	98	505	5.2	2	11	102	9.3	0	6	2
1959 Was	10	65	432	**6.6**	1	7	62	8.9	0	3	1
1960 Was	11	75	227	3.0	3	10	62	6.2	0	3	3
1961 Det	14	30	109	3.6	0	1	14	14.0	0	0	0
1962 Den	12	33	114	3.5	0	13	150	11.5	1	3	1
NFL Total	113	837	3320	4.0	16	104	988	9.5	3	53	19

RUSS OLTZ Oltz, Russell Manning 6'0", 210 **C-G-T-FB**
(Fat) *Col:* Illinois *HS:* Hammond [IN] B: 3/19/1899, Beloit, WI
D: 6/2/1956
1920 Ham: 5 G. **1921** Ham: 5 G; 6 Pt. **1923** Ham: 7 G. **1924** Ham: 5 G. **1925** Ham: 5 G. **Total:** 27 G; 6 Pt.

JIM O'MAHONEY O'Mahoney, James John 6'1", 228 **LB**
Col: Miami (Fla.) *HS:* Schenley [Pittsburgh, PA] B: 3/29/1941, Pittsburgh, PA *Drafted:* 1963 Round 8 Min
1965 NYJ: 14 G; KR 1-15 15.0. **1966** NYJ: 12 G. **Total:** 26 G; KR 1-15 15.0.

JIM O'MALLEY O'Malley, James John 6'1", 229 **LB**
Col: Notre Dame *HS:* Chaney [Youngstown, OH] B: 7/24/1951, Youngstown, OH *Drafted:* 1973 Round 12 Den
1973 Den: 12 G. **1974** Den: 14 G. **1975** Den: 14 G; Int 1-38. **Total:** 40 G; Int 1-38.

JOE O'MALLEY O'Malley, Joseph Patrick 6'2", 218 **DE**
Col: Georgia *HS:* Scranton Technical [PA] B: 1/1/1933, Scranton, PA
Drafted: 1955 Round 4 ChiB
1955 Pit: 10 G; 6 Pt. **1956** Pit: 12 G. **Total:** 22 G; 6 Pt.

TOM O'MALLEY O'Malley, Thomas Louis 5'11", 185 **QB**
Col: Cincinnati *HS:* Hughes [Cincinnati, OH] B: 7/23/1925
1950 GB: 1 G; Pass 15-4 26.7%, 31 2.07 6 Int; Rush 1-(-9) -9.0.

OMENSKY Omensky **G**
Col: No College
1926 Lou: 1 G.

BRIAN O'NEAL O'Neal, Brian Louis 6'0", 233 **RB**
Col: Penn State *HS:* Purcell Marian [Cincinnati, OH] B: 2/25/1970, Cincinnati, OH
1994 Phi: 14 G; PR 1-0; KR 1-0; 1 Fum. **1995** SF: 3 G. **Total:** 17 G; PR 1-0; KR 1-0; 1 Fum.

CALVIN O'NEAL O'Neal, Calvin 6'1", 235 **LB**
Col: Michigan *HS:* Saginaw [MI] B: 10/6/1954, Oceola, AR
Drafted: 1977 Round 6 Bal
1978 Bal: 15 G.

JIM O'NEAL O'Neal, James C. Summer 6'1", 230 **G**
(Chief) *Col:* Texas Christian; Texas-El Paso; Southwestern (Tex.)
HS: Anna [TX] B: 2/13/1924, Anna, TX
AAFC **1946** ChiA: 12 G. **1947** ChiA: 12 G. **Total:** 24 G.

KEN O'NEAL O'Neal, Kenneth Adrian 6'3", 240 **TE**
Col: Chabot Coll. CA (J.C.); Idaho State *HS:* Berkeley [CA]
B: 6/21/1962, San Francisco, CA
1987 NO: 2 G; Rec 3-10 3.3 1 TD; 6 Pt.

LESLIE O'NEAL O'Neal, Leslie Claudis 6'4", 264 **DE-LB**
Col: Oklahoma State *HS:* Hall [Little Rock, AR] B: 5/7/1964, Pulaski Co., AR *Drafted:* 1986 Round 1 SD
1986 SD: 13 G; Int 2-22 1 TD; 6 Pt; 12.5 Sac. **1988** SD: 9 G; 4 Sac. **1989** SD: 16 G; 12.5 Sac. **1990** SD: 16 G; 1 Fum; 13.5 Sac. **1991** SD: 16 G; 9 Sac. **1992** SD: 15 G; 17 Sac. **1993** SD: 16 G; 12 Sac. **1994** SD: 16 G; 12.5 Sac. **1995** SD: 16 G; 12.5 Sac. **1996** StL: 16 G; 7 Sac. **1997** StL: 15 G; Int 1-5; 1 Fum TD; 6 Pt; 10 Sac. **1998** KC: 16 G; 4.5 Sac. **Total:** 180 G; Int 3-27 1 TD; 1 Fum TD; Tot TD 2; 12 Pt; 1 Fum; 127.0 Sac.

ROBERT O'NEAL O'Neal, Robert Oliver 6'1", 199 **DB**
Col: Clemson *HS:* Clarkston [GA] B: 2/1/1971, Atlanta, GA
Drafted: 1993 Round 6 Mia
1994 Ind: 2 G.

STEVE O'NEAL O'Neal, Stephen James 6'3", 185 **P**
Col: Texas A&M *HS:* Hearne [TX] B: 2/4/1946, Hearne, TX
Drafted: 1969 Round 13 NYJ
1970 NYJ: Pass 1-1 100.0%, 2 2.00; Rush 1-16 16.0. **1971** NYJ: Pass 1-0. **1973** NO: Rush 2-(-1) -0.5. **Total:** Pass 2-1 50.0%, 2 1.00; Rush 3-15 5.0.

		Punting			
Year Team	**G**	**Punts**	**Yds**	**Avg**	**Fum**
1969 NYJ	14	54	2393	44.3	0
1970 NYJ	14	73	2925	40.1	0
1971 NYJ	14	78	3026	38.8	2
1972 NYJ	14	51	2006	39.3	1
1973 NO	14	81	3375	41.7	0
NFL Total	70	337	13725	40.7	3

RED O'NEIL O'Neil, Charles 5'10", 190 **C**
Col: Connecticut B: 12/1899, New Haven, CT D: 1955
1926 Har: 9 G; 1 Fum TD; 6 Pt.

CHUCK O'NEIL O'Neil, Charles Leo 5'10", 180 **E-WB-BB-FB**
Col: Phillips *HS:* Michigan Mil. Acad. [Ann Arbor, MI] B: 3/25/1898
D: 11/1951
1921 Eva: 5 G; Pass 1 TD. **1922** Tol-Eva: 2 G. Tol: 1 G. Eva: 1 G. **1923** Tol: 2 G. **Total:** 9 G; Pass 1 TD.

ED O'NEIL O'Neil, Edward William 6'3", 236 **LB**
Col: Penn State *HS:* Warren [PA] B: 9/8/1952, Warren, PA
Drafted: 1974 Round 1 Det
1974 Det: 14 G. **1975** Det: 14 G; **1** Fum TD; 6 Pt. **1976** Det: 14 G; Rec 1-32 32.0 1 TD; Int 1-16; 6 Pt. **1977** Det: 14 G; 1 Fum TD; 6 Pt. **1978** Det: 16 G; Rush 1-25 25.0; Int 4-49. **1979** Det: 16 G; Rush 1-0. **1980** GB: 12 G. **Total:** 100 G; Rush 2-25 12.5; Rec 1-32 32.0 1 TD; Int 5-65; 2 Fum TD; Tot TD 3; 18 Pt.

BOB O'NEIL O'Neil, Robert Maioli 6'1", 229 **LB-OG**
Col: Duquesne; Notre Dame *HS:* Bridgeville [PA] B: 2/21/1931
1956 Pit: 12 G. **1957** Pit: 12 G; 6 Pt. **1961** NYT: 14 G; Rec 1-(-13) -13.0; 1 Fum. **Total:** 38 G; Rec 1-(-13) -13.0; 6 Pt; 1 Fum.

TIP O'NEILL O'Neill, Gerald Raphael 5'10", 170 **WB**
(Jerry) *Col:* St. Norbert; Detroit Mercy *HS:* St. Joseph [Detroit, MI]
B: 10/24/1898, Sault Ste. Marie, MI D: 12/6/1984, Boynton Beach, FL
1922 Day: 4 G; Rush 1 TD; 6 Pt.

KEVIN O'NEILL O'Neill, Kevin Christopher 6'2", 239 **LB**
Col: Bowling Green State *HS:* Walsh Jesuit [Akron, OH] B: 4/14/1975, Allen Park, MI
1998 Det: 11 G.

PAT O'NEILL O'Neill, Patrick James 6'1", 200 **P-K**
Col: Syracuse *HS:* Red Land [Lewisberry, PA] B: 2/9/1971, Scott AFB, IL *Drafted:* 1994 Round 5 NE
1994 NE: Scor 0-1 FG. **Total:** Scor 0-1 FG.

		Punting		
Year Team	**G**	**Punts**	**Yds**	**Avg**
1994 NE	16	69	2841	41.2
1995 NE-ChiB-NYJ	9	44	1603	36.4
1995 NE	8	41	1514	36.9
1995 ChiB	1	3	89	29.7
NFL Total	25	113	4444	39.3

WALLY O'NEILL O'Neill, Richard Wallace 6'0", 195 **OE-G-T**
Col: Wis.-Superior *HS:* Central [Duluth, MN] B: 3/27/1899, MI
D: 1/1973, Aberdeen, SD
1925 Dul: 3 G.

BILL O'NEILL O'Neill, William James 6'0", 187 **TB-DB-WB**
(Speedy; Sidecar) *Col:* Detroit Mercy *HS:* Quigley Prep [Chicago, IL]
B: 4/25/1910, Chicago, IL D: 4/1971
1935 Det: 1 G. **1937** Cle: 1 G; Pass 2-1 50.0%, 20 10.00 1 Int; Rush 4-12 3.0. **Total:** 2 G; Pass 2-1 50.0%, 20 10.00 1 Int; Rush 4-12 3.0.

LARRY ONESTI Onesti, Lawrence Joseph 6'0", 195 **LB**
Col: Northwestern *HS:* Assumption [Windsor, Canada] B: 11/12/1938, Chicago, IL *Drafted:* 1962 Round 9 Hou
1962 Hou: 4 G. **1963** Hou: 14 G. **1964** Hou: 6 G. **1965** Hou: 14 G; 6 Pt. **Total:** 38 G; 6 Pt.

DENNIS ONKOTZ Onkotz, Dennis Henry 6'1", 220 **LB**
Col: Penn State *HS:* Northampton [PA] B: 2/6/1948, Northampton, PA
Drafted: 1970 Round 3 NYJ
1970 NYJ: 9 G; KR 1-0.

BOB ONTKO Ontko, Robert Paul 6'3", 237 **LB**
Col: Penn State *HS:* Wyoming Valley West [Plymouth, PA]
B: 3/21/1964, Kingston, PA *Drafted:* 1987 Round 9 Ind
1987 Ind: 3 G.

ED OPALEWSKI Opalewski, Edward L Jr. 6'3", 230 **T**
(Big Ed) *Col:* Eastern Michigan *HS:* Pershing [Detroit, MI]
B: 11/11/1919, Detroit, MI D: 3/4/1993, Novi, MI
1943 Det: 2 G. **1944** Det: 9 G. **Total:** 11 G.

DAVE OPFAR Opfar, David Louis 6'4", 270 **NT**
Col: Penn State *HS:* South Allegheny [McKeesport, PA] B: 1/16/1960, McKeesport, PA
1987 Pit: 3 G.

JIM OPPERMAN Opperman, James Jay 6'3", 220 **LB**
Col: Colorado State *HS:* Lakewood [CO] B: 12/18/1953, Waterbury, CT
1975 Phi: 10 G; KR 1-15 15.0.

RED O'QUINN O'Quinn, John William Jr. 6'2", 195 **DB-OE-DE**
Col: Wake Forest *HS:* Asheboro [NC] B: 9/7/1925, Bluett Falls, NC
Drafted: 1949 Round 3 ChiB
1950 ChiB: 12 G; Int 3-73 1 TD; 6 Pt. **1951** Phi-ChiB: 7 G; Rec 3-58 19.3. Phi: 5 G; Rec 3-58 19.3. ChiB: 2 G. **Total:** 19 G; Rec 3-58 19.3; Int 3-73 1 TD; 6 Pt.

JOE ORDUNA Orduna, Joseph Manuel 6'0", 195 **RB**
Col: Nebraska *HS:* Central [Omaha, NE] B: 11/6/1948, Omaha, NE
Drafted: 1971 Round 2 SF
1972 NYG: Rec 4-6 1.5 1 TD; KR 12-244 20.3. **1973** NYG: Rec 6-44 7.3; KR 6-104 17.3. **1974** Bal: Rec 1-8 8.0; KR 3-68 22.7. **Total:** Rec 11-58 5.3 1 TD; KR 21-416 19.8.

		Rushing					Tot
Year Team	**G**	**Att**	**Yds**	**Avg**	**TD**	**Fum**	**TD**
1972 NYG	11	36	129	3.6	1	1	2
1973 NYG	14	36	104	2.9	1	0	1
1974 Bal	14	2	3	1.5	1	0	1
NFL Total	39	74	236	3.2	3	1	4

FRANK ORI Ori, Frank 6'2", 255 **OG**
Col: Garden City CC KS; Northern Iowa B: 3/20/1964, Highland Park, IL
1987 Min: 3 G.

MIKE ORIARD Oriard, Michael Vincent 6′4″, 223 **C-OG**
Col: Notre Dame *HS:* Gonzaga Prep [Spokane, WA] B: 5/26/1948, Spokane, WA *Drafted:* 1970 Round 5 KC
1970 KC: 1 G. **1971** KC: 14 G. **1972** KC: 14 G. **1973** KC: 13 G.
Total: 42 G.

BOB ORISTAGLIO Oristaglio, Robert Peter 6′2″, 214 **DE-OE**
Col: Pennsylvania *HS:* Southeast Catholic [Philadelphia, PA]
B: 4/6/1924, Philadelphia, PA D: 2/14/1995, York, PA
AAFC **1949** BufA: 12 G; Rec 1-14 14.0.

NFL **1950** Bal: 12 G; Rec 14-134 9.6; KR 2-32 16.0. **1951** Cle: 12 G; Rec 1-20 20.0 1 TD; 6 Pt. **1952** Phi: 4 G. **Total:** 28 G; Rec 15-154 10.3 1 TD; KR 2-32 16.0; 6 Pt.

BO ORLANDO Orlando, Joseph John 5′10″, 180 **DB**
Col: West Virginia *HS:* Berwick [PA] B: 4/3/1966, Berwick, PA
Drafted: 1989 Round 6 Hou
1996 Cin: 1 Sac. **1997** Cin: 1 Sac. **Total:** 2 Sac.

		Interceptions		
Year Team	**G**	**Int**	**Yds**	**TD**
1990 Hou	16	0	0	0
1991 Hou	16	4	18	0
1992 Hou	6	0	0	0
1993 Hou	16	3	68	1
1994 Hou	16	0	0	0
1995 SD	16	0	37	0
1996 Cin	16	2	0	0
1997 Cin	16	1	3	0
1998 Pit	11	0	0	0
NFL Total	129	10	126	1

DAN ORLICH Orlich, Dan 6′5″, 215 **DE-OE**
Col: Compton CC CA; Northwestern; Penn State; Nevada-Reno
HS: Chisholm [MN] B: 12/21/1924, Chisholm, MN *Drafted:* 1949 Round 8 GB
1949 GB: 12 G; Rec 4-39 9.8. **1950** GB: 12 G; Int 1-0; **1** Fum TD; 6 Pt. **1951** GB: 12 G; Rec 1-9 9.0. **Total:** 36 G; Rec 5-48 9.6; Int 1-0; 1 Fum TD; 6 Pt.

ELLIOTT ORMSBEE Ormsbee, Ezra Elliott 5′11″, 185 **HB-DB**
(Bus) *Col:* Bradley *HS:* Hamilton [IL] B: 9/19/1921, Hamilton, IL
Drafted: 1944 Round 9 Phi
1946 Phi: 4 G; Rush 4-12 3.0; KR 1-5 5.0; 1 Fum.

FRED ORNS Orns, Frederick Karl 6′2″, 230 **LB**
Col: Chapman *HS:* Shorewood [Seattle, WA] B: 5/24/1962
1987 Sea: 2 G.

TOM OROSZ Orosz, Thomas Paul 6′1″, 204 **P**
Col: Ohio State *HS:* Harding [Fairport Harbor, OH] B: 9/26/1959, Painesville, OH
1981 Mia: Rush 1-13 13.0. **1983** SF: Rush 2-39 19.5. **Total:** Rush 3-52 17.3.

		Punting			
Year Team	**G**	**Punts**	**Yds**	**Avg**	**Fum**
1981 Mia	16	83	3386	40.8	0
1982 Mia	9	35	1353	38.7	0
1983 SF	16	65	2552	39.3	1
1984 SF	2	5	195	39.0	0
NFL Total	43	188	7486	39.8	1

CHARLIE O'ROURKE O'Rourke, Charles Christopher 5′11″, 175 **QB-DB**
Col: Boston College *HS:* Malden [MA] B: 5/10/1917, Montreal, Canada *Drafted:* 1941 Round 5 ChiB
AAFC **1946** LA-A: KR 1-28 28.0; Int 0-7. **1947** LA-A: KR 1-24 24.0.
Total: KR 2-52 26.0; Int 0-7.

		Passing							
Year Team	**G**	**Att**	**Comp**	**Comp%**	**Yds**	**YPA**	**TD**	**Int**	**Rating**
1946 LA-A	14	182	105	57.7	1250	6.87	12	14	68.7
1947 LA-A	14	178	89	50.0	1449	8.14	13	16	64.6
1948 BalA	14	51	24	47.1	377	7.39	3	4	59.0
1949 BalA	5	7	1	14.3	12	1.71	0	1	0.0
AAFC Total	47	418	219	52.4	3088	7.39	28	35	64.0

	Rushing				Punting		
Year Team	**Att**	**Yds**	**Avg**	**TD**	**Punts**	**Yds**	**Avg**
1946 LA-A	47	50	1.1	1	8	312	39.0
1947 LA-A	24	55	2.3	1	0	0	—
1948 BalA	7	15	2.1	1	66	2546	38.6
1949 BalA	0	0	—	0	28	1098	39.2
AAFC Total	78	120	1.5	3	102	3956	38.8

NFL **1942** ChiB: Rush 18-(-17) -0.9 1 TD; PR 2-8 4.0; Int 3-15; Punt 23-817 35.5.

		Passing							
Year Team	**G**	**Att**	**Comp**	**Comp%**	**Yds**	**YPA**	**TD**	**Int**	**Rating**
1942 ChiB	11	88	37	42.0	951	**10.81**	11	16	82.1

JIMMY ORR Orr, James Edward Jr. 5′11″, 185 **FL-OE-WR**
Col: Wake Forest; Clemson; Georgia *HS:* Seneca [SC] B: 10/4/1935, Seneca, SC *Drafted:* 1957 Round 25 LARm
1958 Pit: Rush 1-8 8.0. **1959** Pit: Pass 1-0; Rush 5-43 8.6. **1960** Pit: Rush 8-57 7.1. **1962** Bal: Rush 1-14 14.0. **Total:** Pass 1-0; Rush 15-122 8.1.

		Receiving				Punting			
Year Team	**G**	**Rec**	**Yds**	**Avg**	**TD**	**Punts**	**Yds**	**Avg**	**Fum**
1958 Pit	12	33	910	**27.6**	7	51	2023	39.7	1
1959 Pit	12	35	604	17.3	5	8	302	37.8	1
1960 Pit	12	29	541	18.7	4	0	0	—	2
1961 Bal	13	18	357	19.8	4	0	0	—	0
1962 Bal	14	55	974	17.7	11	0	0	—	0
1963 Bal	12	41	708	17.3	5	0	0	—	1
1964 Bal	14	40	867	**21.7**	6	0	0	—	2
1965 Bal	14	45	847	18.8	10	0	0	—	1
1966 Bal	13	37	618	16.7	3	0	0	—	0
1967 Bal	5	3	72	24.0	1	0	0	—	0
1968 Bal	13	29	743	25.6	6	0	0	—	0
1969 Bal	7	25	474	19.0	2	0	0	—	0
1970 Bal	8	10	199	19.9	2	0	0	—	0
NFL Total	149	400	7914	19.8	66	59	2325	39.4	8

TERRY ORR Orr, Terrance 6′3″, 231 **TE**
Col: Texas *HS:* Cooper [Abilene, TX] B: 9/27/1961, Savannah, GA
Drafted: 1985 Round 10 Was
1986 Was: KR 2-31 15.5. **1987** Was: KR 4-62 15.5. **1988** Was: PR 2-10 5.0; KR 1-6 6.0. **1989** Was: KR 1-0. **1990** Was-SD: KR 1-13 13.0. SD: KR 1-13 13.0. **1992** Was: KR 1-3 3.0. **Total:** PR 2-10 5.0; KR 10-115 11.5.

		Receiving				
Year Team	**G**	**Rec**	**Yds**	**Avg**	**TD**	**Fum**
1986 Was	16	3	45	15.0	1	0
1987 Was	10	3	35	11.7	0	0
1988 Was	16	11	222	20.2	2	0
1989 Was	16	3	80	26.7	0	0
1990 Was-SD	11	0	0	—	0	0
1990 Was	2	0	0	—	0	0
1990 SD	9	0	0	—	0	0
1991 Was	16	10	201	20.1	4	0
1992 Was	16	22	356	16.2	3	1
1993 Was	4	0	0	—	0	0
NFL Total	105	52	939	18.1	10	1

RALPH ORTEGA Ortega, Ralph 6′2″, 220 **LB**
Col: Florida *HS:* Coral Gables [FL] B: 7/6/1953, Havana, Cuba
Drafted: 1975 Round 2 Atl
1975 Atl: 14 G. **1976** Atl: 14 G; KR 1-9 9.0. **1977** Atl: 14 G; Int 4-15; 1 Fum TD; 6 Pt. **1978** Atl: 15 G. **1979** Mia: 8 G. **1980** Mia: 16 G; Int 1-17.
Total: 81 G; KR 1-9 9.0; Int 5-32; 1 Fum TD; 6 Pt.

KEITH ORTEGO Ortego, Bryant Keith 6′0″, 180 **WR**
Col: McNeese State *HS:* Eunice [LA] B: 8/30/1963, Eunice, LA
1985 ChiB: 7 G; PR 17-158 9.3. **1986** ChiB: 16 G; Rec 23-430 18.7 2 TD; 12 Pt; 1 Fum. **1987** ChiB: 8 G. **Total:** 31 G; Rec 23-430 18.7 2 TD; PR 17-158 9.3; 12 Pt; 1 Fum.

HENRY ORTH Orth, Henry William 6′0″, 180 **G**
Col: Miami (Ohio) *HS:* Chillicothe [OH] B: 11/20/1897, Chillicothe, OH
D: 3/25/1980, Zanesville, OH
1921 Cin: 1 G.

CHUCK ORTMANN Ortmann, Charles H 6′1″, 190 **TB-DB-QB**
Col: Michigan *HS:* Riverside [Milwaukee, WI] B: 6/1/1929, Milwaukee, WI *Drafted:* 1951 Round 2 Pit
1951 Pit: Rec 4-62 15.5; Int 1-62; Punt 7-302 43.1. **Total:** Rec 4-62 15.5; Int 1-62; Punt 7-302 43.1.

		Passing							
Year Team	**G**	**Att**	**Comp**	**Comp%**	**Yds**	**YPA**	**TD**	**Int**	**Rating**
1951 Pit	12	139	56	40.3	671	4.83	3	13	24.0
1952 Dal	3	15	5	33.3	73	4.87	0	1	22.4
NFL Total	15	154	61	39.6	744	4.83	3	14	23.8

	Rushing				
Year Team	**Att**	**Yds**	**Avg**	**TD**	**Fum**
1951 Pit	59	327	5.5	0	5
1952 Dal	8	24	3.0	0	0
NFL Total	67	351	5.2	0	5

GREG ORTON Orton, Gregory Jay 6′1″, 265 **OG**
Col: Nebraska *HS:* Nebraska City [NE] B: 8/9/1962, Nebraska City, NE
1987 Det: 3 G.

HERB ORVIS Orvis, Herbert Vaughn 6'5", 248 **DE-DT**
Col: Colorado *HS:* Beecher [Flint, MI] B: 10/17/1946, Petoskey, MI
Drafted: 1972 Round 1 Det
1972 Det: 14 G; KR 1-5 5.0. **1973** Det: 14 G. **1974** Det: 14 G. **1975** Det: 14 G. **1976** Det: 2 G. **1977** Det: 14 G. **1978** Bal: 2 G. **1979** Bal: 16 G. **1980** Bal: 16 G. **1981** Bal: 16 G. **Total:** 122 G; KR 1-5 5.0.

OSSIE ORWOLL Orwoll, Oswald Christian 5'11", 165 **HB**
Col: Luther *HS:* Toronto [SD] B: 11/17/1900, Portland, OR
D: 5/8/1967, Decorah, IA
1926 Mil: 3 G.

DAVE OSBORN Osborn, David Vance 6'0", 208 **RB**
(Rocky) *Col:* North Dakota *HS:* Cando [ND] B: 3/18/1943, Everett, WA *Drafted:* 1965 Round 13 Min
1965 Min: KR 18-422 23.4. **1966** Min: KR 1-19 19.0. **1974** Min: KR 1-14 14.0. **1975** Min: KR 1-38 38.0. **1976** GB: KR 3-19 6.3. **Total:** KR 24-512 21.3.

		Rushing				Receiving					Tot
Year Team	**G**	**Att**	**Yds**	**Avg**	**TD**	**Rec**	**Yds**	**Avg**	**TD**	**Fum**	**TD**
1965 Min	14	20	106	5.3	2	1	4	4.0	0	2	2
1966 Min	14	87	344	4.0	1	15	141	9.4	2	2	3
1967 Min	14	215	972	4.5	2	34	272	8.0	1	3	3
1968 Min	4	42	140	3.3	0	0	0	—	0	1	0
1969 Min	14	186	643	3.5	7	22	236	10.7	1	3	8
1970 Min	14	207	681	3.3	5	23	202	8.8	1	5	6
1971 Min	11	123	349	2.8	5	25	195	7.8	1	3	6
1972 Min	14	82	261	3.2	2	20	166	8.3	1	3	3
1973 Min	11	48	216	4.5	0	3	4	1.3	0	2	0
1974 Min	13	131	514	3.9	4	29	196	6.8	0	1	4
1975 Min	14	32	94	2.9	1	1	-4	-4.0	0	2	1
1976 GB	6	6	16	2.7	0	0	0	—	0	0	0
NFL Total	143	1179	4336	3.7	29	173	1412	8.2	7	27	36

MIKE OSBORN Osborn, Michael Joseph 6'5", 235 **LB**
Col: Kansas State *HS:* Shawnee Mission South [KS] B: 11/19/1955, San Antonio, TX
1978 Phi: 16 G.

DUKE OSBORN Osborn, Robert Duke 5'10", 188 **G-C**
(Ossey) *Col:* Penn State *HS:* Du Bois [PA] B: 2/1/1897, Falls Creek, PA D: 11/2/1976, Lansing, MI
1921 Can: 10 G. **1922** Can: 12 G. **1923** Can: 10 G. **1924** Cle: 9 G. **1925** Pott: 11 G. **1926** Pott: 14 G. **1927** Pott: 8 G. **1928** Pott: 8 G. **Total:** 82 G.

CHUCK OSBORNE Osborne, Charles Wayne Jr. 6'2", 290 **DT**
Col: Arizona *HS:* Canyon [Canyon County, CA] B: 11/2/1973, Los Angeles, CA *Drafted:* 1996 Round 7 StL
1996 StL: 15 G; 1 Sac. **1998** Oak: 6 G. **Total:** 21 G; 1 Sac.

CLANCY OSBORNE Osborne, Clarence Dewitt 6'3", 218 **LB**
Col: Arizona State *HS:* Palo Verde [Blythe, CA] B: 11/23/1934, Lubbock, TX *Drafted:* 1957 Round 27 LARm
1959 SF: 8 G. **1960** SF: 8 G. **1961** Min: 14 G; Int 4-35. **1962** Min: 14 G. **1963** Oak: 14 G; Int 2-64; 1 Fum. **1964** Oak: 14 G; Int 2-50. **Total:** 72 G; Int 8-149; 1 Fum.

ELDONTA OSBORNE Osborne, Eldonta R 6'0", 226 **LB**
Col: Louisiana Tech *HS:* Jonesboro-Hodge [Jonesboro, LA]
B: 8/12/1967
1990 Pho: 12 G; 1 Sac.

JIM OSBORNE Osborne, James Henry 6'3", 250 **DT**
Col: Southern University *HS:* Dillard [Fort Lauderdale, FL] B: 9/7/1949, Sylvania, GA *Drafted:* 1972 Round 7 ChiB
1972 ChiB: 14 G. **1973** ChiB: 14 G; KR 1-0; 1 Fum. **1974** ChiB: 14 G. **1975** ChiB: 12 G; KR 1-0. **1976** ChiB: 14 G. **1977** ChiB: 14 G. **1978** ChiB: 15 G. **1979** ChiB: 16 G. **1980** ChiB: 16 G. **1981** ChiB: 16 G. **1982** ChiB: 9 G; Scor **1** Saf; 2 Pt; 4.5 Sac. **1983** ChiB: 16 G; 5 Sac. **1984** ChiB: 16 G; 1 Sac. **Total:** 186 G; KR 2-0; Scor 1 Saf; 2 Pt; 1 Fum; 10.5 Sac.

RICHARD OSBORNE Osborne, Richard Arlen 6'3", 230 **TE**
Col: Texas A&M *HS:* Lee [San Antonio, KS] B: 10/31/1953, Wichita, KS *Drafted:* 1976 Round 9 Phi
1976 Phi-NYJ: 13 G; Rec 2-9 4.5 1 TD; KR 1-8 8.0; 6 Pt; 1 Fum. Phi: 4 G. NYJ: 9 G; Rec 2-9 4.5 1 TD; KR 1-8 8.0; 6 Pt; 1 Fum. **1977** Phi: 14 G; Rec 1-6 6.0. **1978** Phi: 16 G; Rec 13-145 11.2. **1979** StL: 7 G; Rec 7-37 5.3. **Total:** 50 G; Rec 23-197 8.6 1 TD; KR 1-8 8.0; 6 Pt; 1 Fum.

TOM OSBORNE Osborne, Thomas William 6'3", 190 **WR**
Col: Hastings *HS:* Hastings [NE] B: 2/23/1937, Hastings, NE
Drafted: 1959 Round 19 SF

		Receiving			
Year Team	**G**	**Rec**	**Yds**	**Avg**	**TD**
1960 Was	10	7	46	6.6	0
1961 Was	14	22	297	13.5	2
NFL Total	24	29	343	11.8	2

VINCE OSBY Osby, Vincent Lee 5'11", 220 **LB**
Col: Pasadena City Coll. CA (J.C.); Illinois *HS:* Lynwood [CA]
B: 7/8/1961, Los Angeles, CA
1984 SD: 16 G. **1985** SD: 7 G. **Total:** 23 G.

TERRY O'SHEA O'Shea, Terence William 6'4", 236 **TE**
Col: California (Pa.) *HS:* Seton-La Salle [Pittsburgh, PA] B: 12/3/1966, Pittsburgh, PA
1989 Pit: 16 G; Rec 1-8 8.0. **1990** Pit: 16 G; Rec 1-13 13.0. **Total:** 32 G; Rec 2-21 10.5.

WILLIE OSHODIN Oshodin, William Ehizela 6'4", 265 **DE**
Col: Villanova *HS:* Georgetown Prep [Rockville, MD] B: 9/16/1969, Benin City, Nigeria
1993 Den: 15 G; 1 Sac. **1994** Den: 13 G. **1995** Den: 2 G. **Total:** 30 G; 1 Sac.

SANDY OSIECKI Osiecki, Stanley Eugene 6'5", 202 **QB**
Col: Arizona State *HS:* Ansonia [CT] B: 5/18/1960, Ansonia, CT
1984 KC: 4 G; Pass 17-7 41.2%, 64 3.76 1 Int; Rush 1-(-2) -2.0.

WILLIE OSLEY Osley, Willie Glenn 6'0", 195 **DB**
Col: Illinois *HS:* Edwin Denby [Detroit, MI] B: 4/10/1951, Detroit, MI
Drafted: 1973 Round 10 KC
1974 NE-KC: 10 G. NE: 7 G. KC: 3 G. **Total:** 10 G.

JOE OSMANSKI Osmanski, Joseph Charles 6'2", 218 **FB-LB**
(Little Joe) *Col:* Holy Cross *HS:* Central [Providence, RI]
B: 12/26/1917, Providence, RI D: 7/24/1993, Chicago, IL
Drafted: 1941 Round 16 Was
1946 ChiB: KR 3-54 18.0. **1948** ChiB: KR 2-26 13.0. **1949** ChiB-NYB: KR 4-46 11.5. NYB: KR 4-46 11.5. **Total:** KR 9-126 14.0.

		Rushing				Receiving				
Year Team	**G**	**Att**	**Yds**	**Avg**	**TD**	**Rec**	**Yds**	**Avg**	**TD**	**Fum**
1946 ChiB	8	55	201	3.7	2	2	14	7.0	0	3
1947 ChiB	12	64	328	5.1	1	7	134	19.1	0	0
1948 ChiB	12	74	341	4.6	1	9	43	4.8	0	0
1949 ChiB-NYB	10	81	312	3.9	2	18	138	7.7	0	0
1949 ChiB	2	9	37	4.1	0	1	3	3.0	0	0
1949 NYB	8	72	275	3.8	2	17	135	7.9	0	0
NFL Total	42	274	1182	4.3	6	36	329	9.1	0	3

BILL OSMANSKI Osmanski, William Thomas 5'11", 197 **FB-LB**
Col: Holy Cross *HS:* Central [Providence, RI] B: 12/29/1915, Providence, RI D: 12/25/1996, Chicago, IL *Drafted:* 1939 Round 1 ChiB
1939 ChiB: Rec 3-65 21.7 1 TD. **1940** ChiB: Rec 1-13 13.0. **1941** ChiB: Pass 1-0; Rec 4-52 13.0; KR 1-15 15.0; Int 3-19. **1946** ChiB: Rec 4-40 10.0; PR 1-10 10.0; KR 8-203 25.4; Int 1-13. **1947** ChiB: KR 3-67 22.3. **Total:** Pass 1-0; Rec 12-170 14.2 1 TD; PR 1-10 10.0; KR 12-285 23.8; Int 4-32.

		Rushing					Tot
Year Team	**G**	**Att**	**Yds**	**Avg**	**TD**	**Fum**	**TD**
1939 ChiB	10	121	**699**	5.8	7	0	8
1940 ChiB	8	50	192	3.8	3	0	3
1941 ChiB	10	70	371	5.3	4	0	4
1942 ChiB	1	2	9	4.5	0	0	0
1943 ChiB	4	37	102	2.8	1	0	1
1946 ChiB	9	78	343	4.4	5	5	5
1947 ChiB	4	10	37	3.7	0	0	0
NFL Total	46	368	1753	4.8	20	5	21

TED OSSOWSKI Ossowski, Theodore Leory 6'0", 218 **T**
Col: USC; Oregon State *HS:* Beatrice [NE] B: 5/12/1922, Beatrice, NE
Deceased
AAFC **1947** NY-A: 3 G.

DWAYNE O'STEEN O'Steen, Dwayne Philip 6'1", 193 **DB**
Col: California; San Jose State *HS:* Manual Arts [Los Angeles, CA]
B: 12/20/1954, Los Angeles, CA
1978 LARm: 13 G. **1979** LARm: 16 G; Int 4-42. **1980** Oak: 15 G; Int 3-10. **1981** Oak: 16 G; Int 1-2. **1982** Bal: 3 G. **1983** TB-GB: 10 G; KR 2-30 15.0. TB: 3 G; KR 2-30 15.0. GB: 7 G. **1984** GB: 4 G. **Total:** 77 G; KR 2-30 15.0; Int 8-54.

JIM OSTENDARP Ostendarp, James Elmore 5'8", 178 **HB**
(Smokey) *Col:* Bucknell *HS:* Baltimore Polytechnic Inst. [MD]
B: 2/15/1923, Baltimore, MD
1950 NYG: 7 G; Rush 18-144 8.0 2 TD; PR 7-60 8.6; KR 3-68 22.7; 12 Pt; 3 Fum. **1951** NYG: 2 G; PR 2-57 28.5; KR 1-15 15.0; 1 Fum. **Total:** 9 G; Rush 18-144 8.0 2 TD; PR 9-117 13.0; KR 4-83 20.8; 12 Pt; 4 Fum.

JERRY OSTROSKI Ostroski, Gerald Jr. 6'4", 310 **OG**
Col: Tulsa *HS:* Owen J. Roberts [Pottstown, PA] B: 7/12/1970, Collegeville, PA *Drafted:* 1992 Round 10 KC
1994 Buf: 4 G. **1995** Buf: 16 G. **1996** Buf: 16 G. **1997** Buf: 16 G. **1998** Buf: 16 G. **Total:** 68 G.

CHET OSTROWSKI Ostrowski, Chester Casmir 6′1″, 232 **DE-DT**
Col: Notre Dame *HS:* Weber [Chicago, IL] B: 4/8/1930, Chicago, IL
Drafted: 1952 Round 10 Was
1954 Was: 12 G; KR 3-9 3.0; Int 1-5. **1955** Was: 11 G. **1956** Was: 12 G; Int 1-2. **1957** Was: 12 G. **1958** Was: 12 G. **1959** Was: 9 G. **Total:** 68 G; KR 3-9 3.0; Int 2-7.

PAUL OSWALD Oswald, Paul Eugene 6′3″, 273 **C-OG**
Col: Kansas *HS:* Hayden [Topeka, KS] B: 4/9/1964, Topeka, KS
Drafted: 1987 Round 11 Pit
1987 Pit: 2 G. **1988** Dal-Atl: 4 G. Dal: 1 G. Atl: 3 G. **Total:** 6 G.

JIM OTIS Otis, James Lloyd 6′0″, 220 **RB**
Col: Ohio State *HS:* Celina [OH] B: 4/29/1948, Celina, OH
Drafted: 1970 Round 9 NO
1970 NO: KR 2-22 11.0. **1977** StL: KR 1-16 16.0. **Total:** KR 3-38 12.7.

		Rushing				Receiving					Tot
Year Team	G	Att	Yds	Avg	TD	Rec	Yds	Avg	TD	Fum	TD
1970 NO	13	71	211	3.0	0	20	124	6.2	0	4	0
1971 KC	13	49	184	3.8	0	13	81	6.2	2	1	2
1972 KC	10	29	92	3.2	0	12	76	6.3	0	1	0
1973 StL	10	55	234	4.3	1	2	19	9.5	0	3	1
1974 StL	14	158	664	4.2	1	19	109	5.7	0	2	1
1975 StL	14	269	1076	4.0	5	12	69	5.8	1	5	6
1976 StL	14	233	891	3.8	2	2	15	7.5	0	7	2
1977 StL	13	99	334	3.4	2	2	18	9.0	0	2	2
1978 StL	15	197	664	3.4	8	8	38	4.8	0	4	8
NFL Total	116	1160	4350	3.8	19	90	549	6.1	3	29	22

BILL O'TOOLE O'Toole, Milton Timothy 1 **G**
Col: No College *HS:* Cathedral [Duluth, MN] B: 1898, MN Deceased
1924 Dul: 1 G.

LOWELL OTTE Otte, Frederic Lowell 6′2″, 188 **OE-T**
Col: Iowa *HS:* Sidney [IA] B: 9/20/1903, IA Deceased
1927 Buf: 5 G.

DICK OTTELE Ottele, Ricard G 6′3″, 210 **BB-DB**
Col: Washington *HS:* Woodrow Wilson [Long Beach, CA]
B: 12/8/1926, Yuma, CO D: 9/20/1985, Bremerton, WA
AAFC **1948** LA-A: 8 G; Rush 2-11 5.5; KR 3-47 15.7.

BRAD OTTIS Ottis, Brad Allen 6′5″, 281 **DE**
Col: Wayne State (Neb.) *HS:* Bergan [Fremont, NE] B: 8/2/1972, Wahoo, NE *Drafted:* 1994 Round 2 LARm
1994 LARm: 13 G; 1 Sac. **1995** StL: 12 G. **1996** Ariz: 11 G; 1 Sac. **1997** Ariz: 16 G. **Total:** 52 G; 2 Sac.

BO OTTO Otto, Albert Henry 182 **C-G-T**
Col: No College B: 10/15/1901, Louisville, KY D: 11/18/1981, Huntingburg, IN
1922 Lou: 4 G. **1923** Lou: 3 G. **Total:** 7 G.

GUS OTTO Otto, August Joseph 6′1″, 220 **LB**
Col: Missouri *HS:* McBride [St. Louis, MO] B: 12/8/1943, St. Louis, MO *Drafted:* 1965 Round 4 Oak
1965 Oak: 14 G; Int 3-131 **2** TD; 12 Pt. **1966** Oak: 14 G. **1967** Oak: 14 G; Int 1-0. **1968** Oak: 13 G; KR 1-0. **1969** Oak: 14 G; Int 2-4. **1970** Oak: 14 G. **1971** Oak: 8 G. **1972** Oak: 11 G. **Total:** 102 G; KR 1-0; Int 6-135 2 TD; 12 Pt.

JIM OTTO Otto, James Edwin 6′2″, 255 **C**
Col: Miami (Fla.) *HS:* Wausau [WI] B: 1/5/1938, Wausau, WI
Drafted: 1960 Round 1 Oak *HOF:* 1980
1960 Oak: 14 G. **1961** Oak: 14 G. **1962** Oak: 14 G. **1963** Oak: 14 G. **1964** Oak: 14 G. **1965** Oak: 14 G; 1 Fum. **1966** Oak: 14 G. **1967** Oak: 14 G. **1968** Oak: 14 G. **1969** Oak: 14 G. **1970** Oak: 14 G. **1971** Oak: 14 G; 1 Fum. **1972** Oak: 14 G. **1973** Oak: 14 G; 1 Fum. **1974** Oak: 14 G. **Total:** 210 G; 3 Fum.

BOB OTTO Otto, Robert 6′6″, 251 **DE**
Col: Idaho State *HS:* Foothill [Pleasanton, CA] B: 12/16/1962, Sacramento, CA *Drafted:* 1985 Round 9 Sea
1986 Dal: 4 G. **1987** Hou: 3 G. **Total:** 7 G.

LOUIS OUBRE Oubre, Louis Byron 6′4″, 268 **OG**
Col: Oklahoma *HS:* St. Augustine [New Orleans, LA] B: 5/15/1958, New Orleans, LA *Drafted:* 1981 Round 5 NO
1982 NO: 9 G. **1983** NO: 16 G. **1984** NO: 12 G. **1987** Mia: 3 G. **Total:** 40 G.

GREG OURS Ours, Gregory William 6′5″, 279 **C**
Col: Muskingum *HS:* Lakewood [OH] B: 10/29/1963, Hebron, OH
1987 Mia: 3 G.

JOHN OUTLAW Outlaw, John L 5′10″, 180 **DB**
Col: Jackson State *HS:* Higgins [Clarksdale, MS] B: 1/8/1945, Clarksdale, MS *Drafted:* 1968 Round 10 Bos

		Interceptions			
Year Team	G	Int	Yds	TD	Fum
1969 Bos	9	0	0	0	0
1970 Bos	5	0	0	0	0
1971 NE	14	3	89	1	0
1972 NE	6	0	0	0	0
1973 Phi	7	2	48	1	0
1974 Phi	14	2	22	0	0
1975 Phi	14	5	23	0	1
1976 Phi	13	2	19	0	0
1977 Phi	14	2	41	0	0
1978 Phi	14	0	0	0	0
NFL Total	110	16	242	2	1

BILL OVERMYER Overmyer, William Lee 6′3″, 220 **LB**
Col: Ashland *HS:* St. Joseph's [Fremont, OH] B: 6/16/1949, Fremont, OH *Drafted:* 1972 Round 14 Phi
1972 Phi: 6 G; KR 1-0.

DAVID OVERSTREET Overstreet, David Arthur 5′11″, 208 **RB**
Col: Oklahoma *HS:* Big Sandy [TX] B: 9/20/1958, Big Sandy, TX
D: 6/24/1984, Winona, TX *Drafted:* 1981 Round 1 Mia
1983 Mia: Rec 8-55 6.9 2 TD.

		Rushing					Tot
Year Team	G	Att	Yds	Avg	TD	Fum	TD
1983 Mia	14	85	392	4.6	1	2	3

DON OVERTON Overton, Donald Eugene 6′0″, 221 **RB**
Col: Fairmont State *HS:* Whitehall [OH] B: 9/24/1967, Columbus, OH
1990 NE: 7 G; Rush 5-8 1.6; Rec 2-19 9.5; KR 10-188 18.8. **1991** Det: 14 G; Rush 14-59 4.2; Rec 4-38 9.5; KR 4-71 17.8; 1 Fum. **1992** Det: 1 G. **Total:** 22 G; Rush 19-67 3.5; Rec 6-57 9.5; KR 14-259 18.5; 1 Fum.

JERRY OVERTON Overton, Jerry Lee 6′2″, 190 **DB**
Col: Utah *HS:* Mar Vista [Imperial Beach, CA] B: 1/24/1941, El Dorado Springs, MO *Drafted:* 1963 Round 15 Dal
1963 Dal: 10 G; PR 5-32 6.4; 1 Fum.

AL OWEN Owen, Alton 6′0″, 194 **BB-LB-FB-DB**
Col: Mercer *HS:* Leonia [NJ] B: 2/16/1913, Glen Ridge, NJ D: 6/1992
1939 NYG: 6 G; Rush 8-11 1.4; Rec 2-45 22.5 1 TD; 6 Pt. **1940** NYG: 5 G; Rush 2-10 5.0; Rec 1-5 5.0. **1942** NYG: 7 G; Rush 8-27 3.4; Rec 1-20 20.0; PR 2-20 10.0. **Total:** 18 G; Rush 18-48 2.7; Rec 4-70 17.5 1 TD; PR 2-20 10.0; 6 Pt.

STEVE OWEN Owen, Stephen Joseph 5′10″, 237 **T**
(Stout Steve) *Col:* Phillips *HS:* Aline [OK] B: 4/21/1898, Cleo Springs, OK D: 5/17/1964, New York, NY
1924 KC: 9 G. **1925** KC-Cle: 9 G. KC: 8 G. Cle: 1 G. **1926** NYG: 13 G. **1927** NYG: 13 G. **1928** NYG: 12 G. **1929** NYG: 15 G. **1930** NYG: 17 G. **1931** NYG: 8 G. **1933** NYG: 1 G. **Total:** 97 G.

BILL OWEN Owen, William Criswell 6′0″, 211 **T-G**
(Red) *Col:* Oklahoma State; Phillips *HS:* Aline [OK] B: 9/29/1903, Aline, OK D: 3/1975, Kinsley, KS
1926 KC: 11 G. **1927** Cle: 13 G. **1928** Det: 10 G. **1929** NYG: 15 G. **1930** NYG: 16 G. **1931** NYG: 14 G. **1932** NYG: 11 G. **1933** NYG: 13 G. **1934** NYG: 12 G. **1935** NYG: 12 G. **1936** NYG: 11 G. **Total:** 138 G.

TOM OWEN Owen, Willis Thomas 6′1″, 195 **QB**
Col: Wichita State *HS:* Turner [Kansas City, KS] B: 9/1/1952, Shreveport, LA *Drafted:* 1974 Round 13 SF
1974 SF: Rush 16-36 2.3 1 TD. **1975** SF: Rush 1-1 1.0. **1979** NE: Rush 2-(-1) -0.5. **Total:** Rush 19-36 1.9 1 TD.

		Passing								
Year Team	G	Att	Comp	Comp%	Yds	YPA	TD	Int	Rating	Fum
1974 SF	10	184	88	47.8	1327	7.21	10	15	56.1	4
1975 SF	4	51	24	47.1	318	6.24	1	2	57.5	1
1976 NE	2	5	1	20.0	7	1.40	0	0	39.6	0
1978 NE	2	26	15	57.7	182	7.00	0	2	47.3	0
1979 NE	6	47	27	57.4	248	5.28	2	3	59.5	1
1981 NE	2	36	15	41.7	218	6.06	1	4	31.7	1
NFL Total	26	349	170	48.7	2300	6.59	14	26	52.5	7

ARTIE OWENS Owens, Arthur Gene 5′10″, 176 **WR-RB**
Col: West Virginia *HS:* Stroudsburg [PA] B: 1/14/1953, Montgomery, AL *Drafted:* 1976 Round 4 SD
1978 SD: PR 1-20 20.0. **Total:** PR 1-20 20.0.

		Rushing				Receiving			
Year Team	G	Att	Yds	Avg	TD	Rec	Yds	Avg	TD
1976 SD	14	0	0	—	0	3	54	18.0	1
1977 SD	14	1	3	3.0	0	0	0	—	0
1978 SD	13	0	0	—	0	9	188	20.9	0
1979 SD	16	40	151	3.8	1	15	176	11.7	1
1980 Buf-NO	7	0	0	—	0	0	0	—	0
1980 Buf	4	0	0	—	0	0	0	—	0
1980 NO	3	0	0	—	0	0	0	—	0
NFL Total	64	41	154	3.8	1	27	418	15.5	2

Year Team	Kickoff Returns Ret	Yds	Avg	TD	Fum	Tot TD
1976 SD	25	551	22.0	0	1	1
1977 SD	8	132	16.5	0	2	0
1978 SD	20	524	26.2	0	0	0
1979 SD	35	791	22.6	0	1	2
1980 Buf-NO	8	157	19.6	0	0	0
1980 Buf	8	157	19.6	0	0	0
NFL Total	96	2155	22.4	0	4	3

BILLY OWENS Owens, Billy Joe Jr. 6′1″, 207 **DB**
Col: Pittsburgh *HS:* Christian Brothers Acad. [Syracuse, NY]
B: 12/2/1965, Syracuse, NY *Drafted:* 1988 Round 10 Dal
1988 Dal: 16 G; 1 Sac.

BRIG OWENS Owens, Brigman 5′11″, 190 **DB**
Col: Fullerton Coll. CA (J.C.); Cincinnati *HS:* Fullerton [CA]
B: 2/16/1943, Linden, TX *Drafted:* 1965 Round 7 Dal
1966 Was: **1** Fum TD. **1967** Was: Scor 8, 0-2 FG, 2-3 66.7% XK.
1968 Was: PR 1-0. **1973** Was: **1** Fum TD. **1976** Was: KR 1-15 15.0.
Total: PR 1-0; KR 1-15 15.0; Scor 32, 0-2 FG, 2-3 66.7% XK; 2 Fum TD.

Year Team	G	Interceptions Int	Yds	TD	Fum	Tot TD
1966 Was	14	7	165	1	0	2
1967 Was	14	1	68	1	0	1
1968 Was	14	8	109	0	1	0
1969 Was	14	3	24	0	0	0
1970 Was	14	4	86	0	0	0
1971 Was	14	2	27	0	0	0
1972 Was	14	1	0	0	0	0
1973 Was	14	5	123	1	0	2
1974 Was	14	4	59	0	0	0
1975 Was	14	1	25	0	0	0
1976 Was	14	0	0	0	0	0
1977 Was	4	0	0	0	0	0
NFL Total	158	36	686	3	1	5

TINKER OWENS Owens, Charles Wayne 5′11″, 170 **WR**
Col: Oklahoma *HS:* Miami [OK] B: 10/3/1954, Miami, OK
Drafted: 1976 Round 4 NO
1979 NO: KR 1-10 10.0. **Total:** KR 1-10 10.0.

Year Team	G	Receiving Rec	Yds	Avg	TD	Fum
1976 NO	14	12	241	20.1	1	0
1978 NO	14	40	446	11.2	2	1
1979 NO	13	7	72	10.3	1	0
1980 NO	7	1	26	26.0	0	0
NFL Total	48	60	785	13.1	4	1

BURGESS OWENS Owens, Clarence Burgess Jr. 6′2″, 200 **DB**
Col: Miami (Fla.) *HS:* James S. Rickards [Tallahassee, FL] B: 8/2/1951, Columbus, OH *Drafted:* 1973 Round 1 NYJ
1973 NYJ: KR 2-103 51.5 1 TD. **1974** NYJ: KR 3-35 11.7. **Total:** KR 5-138 27.6 1 TD.

Year Team	G	Interceptions Int	Yds	TD	Fum	Tot TD
1973 NYJ	14	1	27	0	0	1
1974 NYJ	14	3	68	1	1	2
1975 NYJ	11	3	3	0	0	0
1976 NYJ	14	0	0	0	0	0
1977 NYJ	14	3	18	0	0	0
1978 NYJ	14	5	156	1	0	1
1979 NYJ	16	6	41	0	0	0
1980 Oak	16	3	59	1	0	1
1981 Oak	16	2	30	1	0	1
1982 LARd	8	4	56	0	0	0
NFL Total	137	30	458	4	1	6

DAN OWENS Owens, Daniel William 6′3″, 280 **DE**
Col: USC *HS:* La Habra [CA] B: 3/16/1967, Whittier, CA
Drafted: 1990 Round 2 Det
1990 Det: 16 G; 3 Sac. **1991** Det: 16 G; 5.5 Sac. **1992** Det: 16 G; 2 Sac. **1993** Det: 15 G; Int 1-1; 3 Sac. **1994** Det: 16 G; 3 Sac. **1995** Det: 16 G; KR 1-9 9.0. **1996** Atl: 16 G; 5.5 Sac. **1997** Atl: 15 G; KR 1-9 9.0; Int 1-14; 1 Fum; 8 Sac. **1998** Det: 11 G; 2.5 Sac. **Total:** 137 G; KR 2-18 9.0; Int 2-15; 1 Fum; 32.5 Sac.

DARRICK OWENS Owens, Darrick Alfred 6′2″, 195 **WR**
Col: Northeastern Oklahoma A&M (J.C.); Mississippi *HS:* Florida [Tallahassee, FL] B: 11/5/1970, Boynton Beach, FL
1992 Pit: 3 G.

DENNIS OWENS Owens, Dennis Ray 6′1″, 257 **NT**
Col: North Carolina State *HS:* Clinton [NC] B: 2/24/1960, Clinton, NC
1982 NE: 9 G. **1983** NE: 16 G; 4 Sac. **1984** NE: 16 G; 6.5 Sac. **1985** NE: 14 G. **1986** NE: 16 G; 1 Sac. **Total:** 71 G; 11.5 Sac.

DON OWENS Owens, Donald Fred 6′5″, 255 **DT-OT**
Col: Southern Mississippi *HS:* St.Mark's [St.Louis, MO] B: 4/3/1932, St. Louis, MO D: 8/17/1997, Jefferson City, MO *Drafted:* 1957 Round 3 Pit
1957 Was: 10 G. **1958** Phi: 12 G. **1959** Phi: 12 G; **1** Fum TD; 6 Pt. **1960** Phi-StL: 12 G. Phi: 3 G. StL: 9 G. **1961** StL: 14 G. **1962** StL: 14 G. **1963** StL: 13 G. **Total:** 87 G; 1 Fum TD; 6 Pt.

PETE OWENS Owens, Floyd Russell 5′11″, 205 **G-C-LB**
Col: Texas Tech *HS:* Littlefield [TX] B: 2/11/1917, Littlefield, TX
D: 11/3/1962, Fort Worth, TX
1943 Bkn: 5 G.

IKE OWENS Owens, Isiah Hudson 6′1″, 190 **DE**
Col: Illinois *HS:* Theodore Roosevelt [Gary, IN] B: 1/8/1920, Columbus, GA D: 1/14/1980, Gary, IN
AAFC **1948** ChiA: 8 G.

JIM OWENS Owens, James Donald 6′3″, 205 **OE-DE**
Col: Oklahoma *HS:* Classen [Oklahoma City, OK] B: 3/6/1927, Oklahoma City, OK *Drafted:* 1949 Round 23 Pit
1950 Bal: 9 G; Rec 19-188 9.9; KR 2-29 14.5; Int 1-25 1 TD; 6 Pt; 1 Fum.

JAMES OWENS Owens, James Earl 5′11″, 192 **RB-WR-DB**
Col: UCLA *HS:* Norte del Rio [Sacramento, CA] B: 7/5/1955, Sacramento, CA *Drafted:* 1979 Round 2 SF

Year Team	G	Rushing Att	Yds	Avg	TD	Receiving Rec	Yds	Avg	TD
1979 SF	16	7	33	4.7	0	10	121	12.1	0
1980 SF	14	0	0	—	0	9	133	14.8	0
1981 TB	16	91	406	4.5	3	12	145	12.1	0
1982 TB	8	76	238	3.1	0	8	42	5.3	1
1983 TB	12	96	266	2.8	5	15	81	5.4	1
1984 TB	4	1	1	1.0	0	2	13	6.5	1
NFL Total	70	271	944	3.5	8	56	535	9.6	3

Year Team	Kickoff Returns Ret	Yds	Avg	TD	Fum	Tot TD
1979 SF	41	1002	24.4	**1**	4	1
1980 SF	31	726	23.4	**1**	3	1
1981 TB	24	473	19.7	0	1	3
1982 TB	3	52	17.3	0	2	1
1983 TB	20	380	19.0	0	0	6
1984 TB	8	168	21.0	0	0	1
NFL Total	127	2801	22.1	2	10	13

JOE OWENS Owens, Joseph T 6′2″, 245 **DE**
Col: Alcorn State *HS:* Jefferson [Columbia, MS] B: 11/8/1946, Columbia, MS *Drafted:* 1969 Round 9 NO
1970 SD: 14 G; Scor **1** Saf; 2 Pt. **1971** NO: 14 G. **1972** NO: 14 G; Scor **1** Saf; 2 Pt. **1973** NO: 14 G; Int 1-3. **1974** NO: 14 G. **1975** NO: 14 G. **1976** Hou: 3 G. **Total:** 87 G; Int 1-3; Scor 2 Saf; 4 Pt.

STEVE OWENS Owens, Loren Everett 6′2″, 215 **RB**
Col: Oklahoma *HS:* Miami [OK] B: 12/9/1947, Gore, OK
Drafted: 1970 Round 1 Det
1970 Det: KR 1-26 26.0. **Total:** KR 1-26 26.0.

Year Team	G	Rushing Att	Yds	Avg	TD	Receiving Rec	Yds	Avg	TD	Fum	Tot TD
1970 Det	6	36	122	3.4	2	4	21	5.3	0	2	2
1971 Det	14	246	1035	4.2	8	32	350	10.9	2	5	10
1972 Det	10	143	519	3.6	4	15	100	6.7	0	0	4
1973 Det	12	113	401	3.5	3	24	232	9.7	0	2	3
1974 Det	11	97	374	3.9	3	24	158	6.6	0	2	3
NFL Total	53	635	2451	3.9	20	99	861	8.7	2	11	22

LUKE OWENS Owens, Luke 6′2″, 254 **DE-DT-OT**
Col: Kent State *HS:* John Adams [Cleveland, OH] B: 10/19/1933, Cleveland, OH *Drafted:* 1957 Round 3 Bal
1957 Bal: 11 G; KR 1-23 23.0. **1958** ChiC: 11 G. **1959** ChiC: 12 G. **1960** StL: 12 G; Scor **1** Saf; 2 Pt. **1961** StL: 14 G. **1962** StL: 14 G. **1963** StL: 14 G. **1964** StL: 14 G. **1965** StL: 13 G. **Total:** 115 G; KR 1-23 23.0; Scor 1 Saf; 2 Pt.

MARV OWENS Owens, Marvin Duane 5′11″, 203 **WR**
Col: San Diego State *HS:* Fullerton [CA] B: 6/16/1950, Orange, CA
Drafted: 1972 Round 14 Min
1973 StL: 8 G; KR 1-19 19.0. **1974** NYJ: 2 G. **Total:** 10 G; KR 1-19 19.0.

MEL OWENS Owens, Mel Tyrae 6′2″, 224 **LB**
Col: Michigan *HS:* De Kalb [IL] B: 12/7/1958, Detroit, MI
Drafted: 1981 Round 1 LARm
1981 LARm: 16 G. **1982** LARm: 7 G. **1983** LARm: 16 G; 4 Sac. **1984** LARm: 16 G; Int 1-(-4); 3.5 Sac. **1985** LARm: 16 G; 9 Sac. **1986** LARm: 16 G; 4 Sac. **1987** LARm: 12 G; Int 1-26; 1 Sac. **1988** LARm: 7 G; Int 1-11; 5 Sac. **1989** LARm: 16 G; Int 1-4. **Total:** 122 G; Int 4-37; 26.5 Sac.

MORRIS OWENS Owens, Morris Lamar 6′0″, 190 **WR**
Col: Arizona State *HS:* Chowchilla [CA] B: 2/14/1953, Oakland, CA
Drafted: 1975 Round 5 Mia
1976 Mia-TB: Rush 2-2 1.0. TB: Rush 2-2 1.0. **1977** TB: Rush 2-(-2) -1.0. **Total:** Rush 4-0.

		Receiving				
Year Team	G	Rec	Yds	Avg	TD	Fum
1975 Mia	2	0	0	—	0	0
1976 Mia-TB	14	30	390	13.0	6	1
1976 Mia	2	0	0	—	0	0
1976 TB	12	30	390	13.0	6	1
1977 TB	14	34	655	19.3	3	1
1978 TB	16	32	640	20.0	5	1
1979 TB	16	20	377	18.9	0	1
NFL Total	62	116	2062	17.8	14	4

R.C. OWENS Owens, Raleigh C 6′3″, 197 **OE-FL**
(Alley Oop) *Col:* Coll. of Idaho *HS:* Santa Monica [CA] B: 11/12/1933, Shreveport, LA *Drafted:* 1956 Round 14 SF
1959 SF: Rush 1-0. **1961** SF: Rush 0-23 1 TD. **Total:** Rush 1-23 23.0 1 TD.

		Receiving					Tot
Year Team	G	Rec	Yds	Avg	TD	Fum	TD
1957 SF	12	27	395	14.6	5	0	5
1958 SF	12	40	620	15.5	1	1	1
1959 SF	12	17	347	20.4	3	0	3
1960 SF	12	37	532	14.4	6	1	6
1961 SF	14	55	1032	18.8	5	1	6
1962 Bal	14	25	307	12.3	2	1	2
1963 Bal	3	1	7	7.0	0	0	0
1964 NYG	11	4	45	11.3	0	0	0
NFL Total	90	206	3285	15.9	22	4	23

RIP OWENS Owens, Ralph B 5′10″, 220 **G**
(Brick) *Col:* Nebraska; Lawrence *HS:* Waukegan [IL] B: 12/9/1894, WI D: 8/1970, Lakeview, AR
1922 GB: 3 G.

RICH OWENS Owens, Ritchie Darryl 6′6″, 274 **DE-DT**
Col: Lehigh *HS:* Abraham Lincoln [Philadelphia, PA] B: 5/22/1972, Philadelphia, PA *Drafted:* 1995 Round 5 Was
1995 Was: 10 G; 3 Sac. **1996** Was: 16 G; 11 Sac. **1997** Was: 16 G; 2.5 Sac. **Total:** 42 G; 16.5 Sac.

TERRELL OWENS Owens, Terrell Eldorado 6′3″, 217 **WR**
Col: Tennessee-Chattanooga *HS:* Benjamin Russell [Alexander City, AL] B: 12/7/1973, Alexander City, AL *Drafted:* 1996 Round 3 SF
1996 SF: KR 3-47 15.7. **1997** SF: KR 2-31 15.5. **1998** SF: Rush 4-53 13.3 1 TD; Scor 1 2XP. **Total:** Rush 4-53 13.3 1 TD; KR 5-78 15.6; Scor 1 2XP.

		Receiving					Tot
Year Team	G	Rec	Yds	Avg	TD	Fum	TD
1996 SF	16	35	520	14.9	4	1	4
1997 SF	16	60	936	15.6	8	1	8
1998 SF	16	67	1097	16.4	14	1	15
NFL Total	48	162	2553	15.8	26	3	27

TERRY OWENS Owens, Terry Woodrow 6′6″, 260 **OT**
Col: Jacksonville State *HS:* Samson [AL] B: 7/5/1944, Jasper, AL
Drafted: 1966 Round 11 SD
1966 SD: 14 G. **1967** SD: 14 G. **1968** SD: 14 G. **1969** SD: 14 G. **1970** SD: 14 G; KR 1-0. **1971** SD: 14 G. **1972** SD: 14 G. **1973** SD: 14 G. **1974** SD: 13 G. **1975** SD: 7 G. **Total:** 132 G; KR 1-0.

KEN OXENDINE Oxendine, Ken Qwarious 6′0″, 228 **RB**
Col: Virginia Tech *HS:* Thomas Dale [Chester, VA] B: 10/4/1975, Richmond, VA *Drafted:* 1998 Round 7 Atl
1998 Atl: 9 G; Rush 18-50 2.8; Rec 1-11 11.0; 1 Fum.

MIKE OZDOWSKI Ozdowski, Michael Thomas 6′5″, 243 **DE**
Col: Virginia *HS:* Parma [OH] B: 9/24/1955, Cleveland, OH
Drafted: 1977 Round 2 Bal
1978 Bal: 16 G. **1979** Bal: 11 G. **1980** Bal: 15 G. **1981** Bal: 12 G. **Total:** 54 G.

JAMES PACE Pace, James E 6′0″, 195 **HB**
Col: Michigan *HS:* Dunbar [Little Rock, AR] B: 1/1/1936, Little Rock, AR D: 3/4/1983, Culver City, CA *Drafted:* 1958 Round 1 SF
1958 SF: Rec 10-59 5.9; PR 2-0; KR 8-134 16.8.

		Rushing			
Year Team	G	Att	Yds	Avg	TD
1958 SF	12	52	161	3.1	2

ORLANDO PACE Pace, Orlando Lamar 6′7″, 320 **OT**
Col: Ohio State *HS:* Sandusky [OH] B: 11/4/1975, Sandusky, OH
Drafted: 1997 Round 1 StL
1997 StL: 13 G. **1998** StL: 16 G. **Total:** 29 G.

DAVE PACELLA Pacella, David Wade 6′2″, 266 **C-OG**
Col: Maryland *HS:* Reading [PA] B: 2/7/1960, Sewickley, PA
1984 Phi: 16 G.

VINCE PACEWIC Pacewic, Vincent C 6′1″, 205 **HB-DB**
Col: Loyola Marymount; San Francisco *HS:* Gillepie [IL] B: 5/28/1920, Collinsville, IL D: 4/1/1990, Los Angeles, CA *Drafted:* 1943 Round 25 Was
1947 Was: 2 G; Rec 5-42 8.4.

CHRIS PACHECO Pacheco, Christopher Luis 6′0″, 250 **NT**
Col: Cerritos Coll. CA (J.C.); Cal State-Northridge; Fresno State
HS: Earl Warren [Downey, CA] B: 1/22/1964, Los Angeles, CA
1987 LARm: 3 G.

WALTER PACKER Packer, Walter 5′10″, 174 **DB**
Col: Mississippi State *HS:* Greene Co. HS [Leakesville, MS]
B: 11/7/1955, Leakesville, MS *Drafted:* 1977 Round 8 Atl
1977 Sea-TB: 11 G; PR 20-131 6.6; KR 13-280 21.5; 2 Fum. Sea: 10 G; PR 20-131 6.6; KR 13-280 21.5; 2 Fum. TB: 1 G. **Total:** 11 G; PR 20-131 6.6; KR 13-280 21.5; 2 Fum.

BOB PADAN Padan, Robert Samuel 165 **WB-TB**
Col: Ohio State; Otterbein *HS:* Martins Ferry [OH] B: 8/1893, Portsmouth, OH Deceased
1922 Lou: 3 G.

GARY PADJEN Padjen, Gary Anthony 6′2″, 244 **LB**
Col: Arizona State *HS:* Kearns [UT] B: 7/2/1958, Salt Lake City, UT
1982 Bal: 8 G. **1983** Bal: 16 G. **1984** Ind: 16 G; PR 1-0; 1 Fum. **1987** Ind: 1 G. **Total:** 41 G; PR 1-0; 1 Fum.

MAX PADLOW Padlow, Max 6′1″, 199 **OE-DE**
Col: Ohio State *HS:* Stivers [Dayton, OH] B: 8/15/1912, Russia
D: 8/8/1971, Dayton, OH
1935 Phi: 4 G. **1936** Phi: 1 G. **Total:** 5 G.

BOB PAFFRATH Paffrath, Robert William 5′8″, 190 **HB-DB-BB**
Col: Minnesota *HS:* Redwood Valley [Redwood Falls, MN]
B: 7/3/1918, Mankato, MN
AAFC **1946** BknA-MiaA: Pass 1-0; Rec 4-(-6) -1.5; PR 1-1 1.0; KR 4-76 19.0; Punt 1-50 50.0.

		Rushing			
Year Team	G	Att	Yds	Avg	TD
1946 BknA-MiaA	11	31	100	3.2	2

FRED PAGAC Pagac, Frederick 6′0″, 222 **TE**
Col: Ohio State *HS:* Bethlehem Center [Fredericktown, PA]
B: 4/26/1952, Brownsville, PA
1974 ChiB: 14 G; Rush 1-(-1) -1.0; Rec 6-79 13.2; KR 3-53 17.7. **1976** TB: 14 G; Rush 1-4 4.0; Rec 2-15 7.5; KR 1-20 20.0. **Total:** 28 G; Rush 2-3 1.5; Rec 8-94 11.8; KR 4-73 18.3.

ALAN PAGE Page, Alan Cedric 6′4″, 245 **DT**
Col: Notre Dame *HS:* Central Catholic [Canton, OH] B: 8/7/1945, Canton, OH *Drafted:* 1967 Round 1 Min *HOF:* 1988
1967 Min: 14 G. **1968** Min: 14 G. **1969** Min: 14 G; Int 0-15 1 TD; 6 Pt. **1970** Min: 14 G; Int 1-27; 1 Fum TD; 6 Pt. **1971** Min: 14 G; Scor **2** Saf; 4 Pt. **1972** Min: 14 G. **1973** Min: 14 G. **1974** Min: 14 G. **1975** Min: 14 G. **1976** Min: 14 G. **1977** Min: 14 G. **1978** Min-ChiB: 16 G. Min: 6 G. ChiB: 10 G. **1979** ChiB: 16 G. **1980** ChiB: 16 G; Int 1-0; Scor **1** Saf; **1** Fum TD; 8 Pt. **1981** ChiB: 16 G. **Total:** 218 G; Int 2-42 1 TD; Scor 3 Saf; 2 Fum TD; Tot TD 3; 24 Pt.

PAUL PAGE Page, Paul Eugene 6′0″, 180 **HB-DB**
Col: Southern Methodist *HS:* Eldorado [TX] B: 9/16/1927, Eldorado, TX
AAFC **1949** BalA: Rec 4-62 15.5; PR 1-16 16.0; KR 4-108 27.0.

		Rushing			
Year Team	G	Att	Yds	Avg	TD
1949 BalA	8	25	81	3.2	0

MIKE PAGEL Pagel, Michael Jonathan 6′2″, 206 **QB**
Col: Arizona State *HS:* Washington [Phoenix, AZ] B: 9/13/1960, Douglas, AZ *Drafted:* 1982 Round 4 Bal
1985 Ind: Rec 1-6 6.0. **Total:** Rec 1-6 6.0.

		Passing							
Year Team	G	Att	Comp	Comp%	Yds	YPA	TD	Int	Rating
1982 Bal	9	221	111	50.2	1281	5.80	5	7	62.4
1983 Bal	15	328	163	49.7	2353	7.17	12	17	64.0
1984 Ind	11	212	114	53.8	1426	6.73	8	8	71.8
1985 Ind	16	393	199	50.6	2414	6.14	14	15	65.8
1986 Cle	1	3	2	66.7	53	17.67	0	0	109.7
1987 Cle	4	0	0	—	0	—	0	0	—
1988 Cle	5	134	71	53.0	736	5.49	3	4	64.1
1989 Cle	16	14	5	35.7	60	4.29	1	1	43.8
1990 Cle	16	148	69	46.6	819	5.53	3	8	48.2
1991 LARm	16	27	11	40.7	150	5.56	2	0	83.9
1992 LARm	16	20	8	40.0	99	4.95	1	2	33.1

1993 LARm	7	9	3	33.3	23	2.56	0	1	2.8
NFL Total	132	1509	756	50.1	9414	6.24	49	63	63.3

	Rushing				
Year Team	Att	Yds	Avg	TD	Fum
1982 Bal	19	82	4.3	1	9
1983 Bal	54	441	8.2	0	4
1984 Ind	26	149	5.7	1	4
1985 Ind	25	160	6.4	2	6
1986 Cle	2	0	0.0	0	2
1988 Cle	4	1	0.3	0	0
1989 Cle	2	-1	-0.5	0	0
1990 Cle	3	-1	-0.3	0	3
1992 LARm	1	0	0.0	0	1
NFL Total	136	831	6.1	4	29

JOE PAGLIEI Pagliei, Joseph Anthony 6'0", 220 **FB**
Col: Clemson *HS:* Clairton [PA] B: 4/12/1934, Clairton, PA
1959 Phi: Rush 2-(-5) -2.5; Rec 2-9 4.5. **1960** NYT: Rush 17-69 4.1 1 TD; Rec 1-13 13.0. **Total:** Rush 19-64 3.4 1 TD; Rec 3-22 7.3.

		Punting			
Year Team	G	Punts	Yds	Avg	Fum
1959 Phi	7	1	45	45.0	0
1960 NYT	11	48	1779	37.1	3
NFL Total	18	49	1824	37.2	3

LOUIE PAHL Pahl, Louis 5'8", 185 **WB-FB**
Col: No College *HS:* Central [St. Paul, MN] B: 1897 Deceased
1923 Min: 8 G; Rush 1 TD; 6 Pt. **1924** Min: 3 G. **Total:** 11 G; Rush 1 TD; 6 Pt.

JEFF PAHUKOA Pahukoa, Jeff Kalani 6'2", 298 **OG-OT**
Col: Washington *HS:* Marysville-Pitchuk [Marysville, WA] B: 2/9/1969, Vancouver, WA *Drafted:* 1991 Round 12 LARm
1991 LARm: 7 G. **1992** LARm: 16 G. **1993** LARm: 16 G. **1995** Atl: 6 G. **1996** Atl: 14 G. **Total:** 59 G.

SHANE PAHUKOA Pahukoa, Shane Kapualani 6'2", 202 **DB**
Col: Washington *HS:* Marysville-Pitchuk [Marysville, WA]
B: 11/25/1970, Vancouver, WA
1995 NO: 15 G; Int 2-12.

TONY PAIGE Paige, Anthony Ricardo 5'10", 225 **RB**
(Spike) *Col:* Virginia Tech *HS:* DeMatha [Hyattsville, MD]
B: 10/14/1962, Washington, DC *Drafted:* 1984 Round 6 NYJ
1984 NYJ: KR 3-7 2.3. **1990** Mia: KR 1-18 18.0. **1991** Mia: KR 2-31 15.5. **1992** Mia: KR 2-29 14.5. **Total:** KR 8-85 10.6.

		Rushing				Receiving					Tot
Year Team	G	Att	Yds	Avg	TD	Rec	Yds	Avg	TD	Fum	TD
1984 NYJ	16	35	130	3.7	7	6	31	5.2	1	1	8
1985 NYJ	16	55	158	2.9	8	18	120	6.7	2	1	10
1986 NYJ	16	47	109	2.3	2	18	121	6.7	0	2	2
1987 Det	5	4	13	3.3	0	2	1	0.5	0	0	0
1988 Det	16	52	207	4.0	0	11	100	9.1	0	1	0
1989 Det	16	30	105	3.5	0	2	27	13.5	0	1	0
1990 Mia	13	32	95	3.0	2	35	247	7.1	4	1	6
1991 Mia	16	10	25	2.5	0	57	469	8.2	1	1	1
1992 Mia	16	7	11	1.6	1	48	399	8.3	1	1	2
NFL Total	130	272	853	3.1	20	197	1515	7.7	9	9	29

LEE PAIGE Paige, Lee E 6'0", 197 **DB**
Col: Florida State *HS:* Winter Haven [FL] B: 10/16/1960, Jackson, MS
1987 TB: 3 G.

STEPHONE PAIGE Paige, Stephone 6'2", 184 **WR**
Col: Saddleback Coll. CA (J.C.); Fresno State *HS:* Long Beach Polytechnic [CA] B: 10/15/1961, Long Beach, CA
1984 KC: Rush 3-19 6.3. **1985** KC: Rush 1-15 15.0. **1986** KC: Rush 2-(-2) -1.0. **Total:** Rush 6-32 5.3.

		Receiving				Kickoff Returns				
Year Team	G	Rec	Yds	Avg	TD	Ret	Yds	Avg	TD	Fum
1983 KC	16	30	528	17.6	6	0	0	—	0	1
1984 KC	16	30	541	18.0	4	27	544	20.1	0	0
1985 KC	16	43	943	**21.9**	10	2	36	18.0	0	0
1986 KC	16	52	829	15.9	11	0	0	—	0	0
1987 KC	12	43	707	16.4	4	0	0	—	0	0
1988 KC	16	61	902	14.8	7	0	0	—	0	2
1989 KC	14	44	759	17.3	2	0	0	—	0	3
1990 KC	16	65	1021	15.7	5	0	0	—	0	3
1991 KC	3	9	111	12.3	0	0	0	—	0	0
NFL Total	125	377	6341	16.8	49	29	580	20.0	0	9

HOMER PAINE Paine, Homer 6'0", 235 **T**
Col: Tulsa; Oklahoma *HS:* Enid [OK] B: 9/20/1923, Hennessey, OK
AAFC **1949** ChiA: 12 G.

JEFF PAINE Paine, Jeffrey Franklin 6'2", 224 **LB**
Col: Texas A&M *HS:* Richardson [TX] B: 8/19/1961, Garland, TX
Drafted: 1984 Round 5 KC
1984 KC: 14 G. **1985** KC: 12 G; 1 Sac. **1986** Was: 2 G. **1987** StL: 1 G. **Total:** 29 G; 1 Sac.

CARL PAINTER Painter, Carl Drew 5'9", 184 **RB**
Col: Hampton *HS:* Booker T. Washington [Norfolk, VA] B: 5/10/1964, Norfolk, VA *Drafted:* 1988 Round 6 Det
1988 Det: Rec 1-1 1.0; KR 17-347 20.4. **1989** Det: Rec 3-41 13.7; KR 1-14 14.0. **Total:** Rec 4-42 10.5; KR 18-361 20.1.

		Rushing				
Year Team	G	Att	Yds	Avg	TD	Fum
1988 Det	12	17	42	2.5	0	1
1989 Det	15	15	64	4.3	0	1
NFL Total	27	32	106	3.3	0	2

LOU PALATELLA Palatella, Louis 6'2", 230 **OG-LB**
Col: Pittsburgh *HS:* Vandergrift [PA] B: 7/28/1933, Vandergrift, PA
Drafted: 1955 Round 12 SF
1955 SF: 9 G; KR 1-1 1.0. **1956** SF: 10 G. **1957** SF: 12 G; KR 0-30. **1958** SF: 12 G. **Total:** 43 G; KR 1-31 31.0.

LOU PALAZZI Palazzi, Louis Joseph 6'0", 198 **C-LB**
Col: Penn State *HS:* Dunmore [PA] B: 6/26/1921, Groton, CT
Drafted: 1943 Round 5 NYG
1946 NYG: 5 G. **1947** NYG: 11 G. **Total:** 16 G.

LONNIE PALELEI Palelei, Si'ulagi Jack 6'3", 310 **OG-OT**
Col: Purdue; Nevada-Las Vegas *HS:* Blue Springs [MO]
B: 10/15/1970, Nu'uuli, American Samoa *Drafted:* 1993 Round 5 Pit
1993 Pit: 3 G. **1995** Pit: 1 G. **1997** NYJ: 15 G. **1998** NYG: 9 G; KR 3-14 4.7; 1 Fum. **Total:** 28 G; KR 3-14 4.7; 1 Fum.

JIM PALERMO Palermo, James Vincent 5'9", 180 **G-C**
Col: Missouri B: 3/31/1902, Kansas City, KS D: 10/26/1983, Shawnee Mission, KS
1925 KC: 2 G. **1926** KC: 1 G. **Total:** 3 G.

AL PALEWICZ Palewicz, Albert Paul 6'1", 215 **LB**
(Chuck) *Col:* Miami (Fla.) *HS:* Miami Palmetto [FL] B: 3/23/1950, Fort Worth, TX *Drafted:* 1973 Round 8 KC
1973 KC: 14 G. **1974** KC: 13 G. **1975** KC: 9 G. **1977** NYJ: 14 G. **Total:** 50 G.

MIKE PALM Palm, Myron Herrick 5'10", 170 **DB-BB-WB**
Col: Penn State *HS:* Carlisle [PA] B: 11/26/1899, St. James, MN
D: 4/8/1974, Washington, DC
1925 NYG: 2 G. **1926** NYG: 1 G; Rush 1 TD; 6 Pt. **1933** Cin: 6 G; Pass 8-3 37.5%, 51 6.38 2 Int; Rush 14-6 0.4. **Total:** 9 G; Pass 8-3 37.5%, 51 6.38 2 Int; Rush 14-6 0.4 1 TD; 6 Pt.

CHUCK PALMER Palmer, Charles William 5'10", 185 **BB-WB**
Col: Northwestern *HS:* Englewood [Chicago, IL] B: 2/15/1901, Chicago, IL D: 2/10/1974, Littleton, CO
1924 Rac: 3 G. **1926** Lou: 4 G. **Total:** 7 G.

DAVID PALMER Palmer, David Lee 5'8", 173 **WR**
Col: Alabama *HS:* Jackson-Olin [Birmingham, AL] B: 11/19/1972, Birmingham, AL *Drafted:* 1994 Round 2 Min

		Rushing				Receiving			
Year Team	G	Att	Yds	Avg	TD	Rec	Yds	Avg	TD
1994 Min	13	1	1	1.0	0	6	90	15.0	0
1995 Min	14	7	15	2.1	0	12	100	8.3	0
1996 Min	11	2	9	4.5	0	6	40	6.7	0
1997 Min	16	11	36	3.3	1	26	193	7.4	1
1998 Min	16	10	52	5.2	0	18	185	10.3	0
NFL Total	70	31	113	3.6	1	68	608	8.9	1

	Punt Returns				Kickoff Returns					Tot
Year Team	Ret	Yds	Avg	TD	Ret	Yds	Avg	TD	Fum	TD
1994 Min	30	193	6.4	0	0	0	—	0	2	0
1995 Min	26	342	**13.2**	**1**	17	354	20.8	0	1	1
1996 Min	22	216	9.8	1	13	292	22.5	0	3	1
1997 Min	34	444	13.1	0	32	711	22.2	0	2	2
1998 Min	28	289	10.3	0	50	1176	23.5	1	2	1
NFL Total	140	1484	10.6	2	112	2533	22.6	1	10	5

DERRELL PALMER Palmer, Derrell Franklin 6'2", 240 **DT**
Col: Texas Christian *HS:* Albany [TX] B: 8/27/1922, Breckenridge, TX
Drafted: 1943 Round 4 ChiB
AAFC **1946** NY-A: 13 G. **1947** NY-A: 14 G. **1948** NY-A: 14 G. **1949** CleA: 11 G. **Total:** 52 G.

NFL **1950** Cle: 12 G. **1951** Cle: 10 G. **1952** Cle: 11 G. **1953** Cle: 11 G. **Total:** 44 G.

SCOTT PALMER Palmer, Derrell Scott 6′3″, 245 DT
Col: Texas *HS:* Westbury [Houston, TX] B: 9/15/1948, Cleburne, TX
Drafted: 1971 Round 7 NYJ
1971 NYJ: 2 G. **1972** StL: 5 G. **Total:** 7 G.

EMILE PALMER Palmer, Emile 6′3″, 320 DT
Col: Syracuse *HS:* Fairmont Heights [Capitol Heights, MD]
B: 4/5/1973, Cheverly, MD
1996 NO: 1 G.

GERY PALMER Palmer, Gery Dean 6′4″, 255 OT
Col: Kansas *HS:* Central [Kansas City, MO] B: 12/25/1950, Weimar, TX *Drafted:* 1973 Round 4 Bal
1975 KC: 2 G.

LES PALMER Palmer, Leslie Hatfield Jr. 6′0″, 180 DB-HB
(Footsie) *Col:* North Carolina State *HS:* East Bank [WV]
B: 12/15/1923, Cedar Grove, WV
1948 Phi: 5 G; PR 1-8 8.0; KR 1-20 20.0; Punt 4-148 37.0.

MIKE PALMER Palmer, Major 0 5′10″, 203 T
Col: No College *HS:* None B: 2/2/1890, WI D: 3/16/1972, Ceylon, MN
1921 Min: 4 G.

PAUL PALMER Palmer, Paul Woodrow 5′9″, 184 RB
Col: Temple *HS:* Winston Churchill [Potomac, MD] B: 10/14/1964, Bethesda, MD *Drafted:* 1987 Round 1 KC
1987 KC: Pass 1-0. **Total:** Pass 1-0.

		Rushing				Receiving			
Year Team	G	Att	Yds	Avg	TD	Rec	Yds	Avg	TD
1987 KC	12	24	155	6.5	0	4	27	6.8	0
1988 KC	15	134	452	3.4	2	53	611	11.5	4
1989 Det-Dal	14	112	446	4.0	2	17	93	5.5	0
1989 Det	5	0	0	—	0	0	0	—	0
1989 Dal	9	112	446	4.0	2	17	93	5.5	0
NFL Total	41	270	1053	3.9	4	74	731	9.9	4

	Kickoff Returns					Tot
Year Team	Ret	Yds	Avg	TD	Fum	TD
1987 KC	**38**	**923**	24.3	**2**	2	2
1988 KC	23	364	15.8	0	7	6
1989 Det-Dal	11	255	23.2	0	3	2
1989 Det	11	255	23.2	0	0	0
1989 Dal	0	0	—	0	3	2
NFL Total	72	1542	21.4	2	12	10

DICK PALMER Palmer, Richard Harry 6′2″, 232 LB
Col: Kentucky *HS:* Kubasaki [Okinawa] B: 4/9/1947, Lexington, KY
Drafted: 1970 Round 10 Bal
1970 Mia: 9 G. **1972** Buf-NO: 10 G. Buf: 4 G. NO: 6 G. **1973** NO: 10 G. **1974** Atl: 14 G. **Total:** 43 G.

MITCH PALMER Palmer, Richard Mitchell 6′4″, 245 LB
Col: Colorado State *HS:* Poway [San Diego, CA] B: 9/2/1973, Oceanside, CA
1998 TB: 16 G.

STERLING PALMER Palmer, Sterling Lanard 6′5″, 272 DE
Col: Florida State *HS:* St. Thomas Aquinas [Fort Lauderdale, FL]
B: 2/4/1971, Fort Lauderdale, FL *Drafted:* 1993 Round 4 Was
1993 Was: 14 G; 4.5 Sac. **1994** Was: 16 G; 1 Sac. **1995** Was: 13 G; 4.5 Sac. **1996** Was: 6 G; 1 Sac. **Total:** 49 G; 11 Sac.

TOM PALMER Palmer, Thomas 6′2″, 240 DT
Col: Wake Forest *HS:* Collingswood [NJ] B: 8/12/1929 D: 2/1980, Kingsport, TN *Drafted:* 1950 Round 17 ChiC
1953 Pit: 11 G. **1954** Pit: 7 G. **Total:** 18 G.

JOHN PALUCK Paluck, John J 6′2″, 241 DE-OT
Col: Pittsburgh *HS:* Swoyersville [PA] B: 5/23/1935, Swoyersville, PA
Drafted: 1956 Round 2 Was
1956 Was: 12 G; **1** Fum TD; 6 Pt. **1959** Was: 12 G. **1960** Was: 12 G. **1961** Was: 13 G; Int 1-0. **1962** Was: 14 G. **1963** Was: 14 G; Int 1-23. **1964** Was: 14 G; Scor **1** Saf; 2 Pt. **1965** Was: 14 G. **Total:** 105 G; Int 2-23; Scor 1 Saf; 1 Fum TD; 8 Pt.

SAM PALUMBO Palumbo, Samuel Frank 6′2″, 226 LB-C
Col: Notre Dame *HS:* Collinwood [Cleveland, OH] B: 6/7/1932, Cleveland, OH *Drafted:* 1955 Round 4 Cle
1955 Cle: 9 G. **1956** Cle: 12 G. **1957** GB: 9 G; Int 1-11. **1960** Buf: 1 G. **Total:** 31 G; Int 1-11.

TONY PANACCION Panaccion, Victor Samuel 6′1″, 212 T
(Toots) *Col:* Penn State *HS:* Jenkintown [PA] B: 9/11/1908
D: 3/26/1986, Bryn Mawr, PA
1930 Fra: 4 G.

DON PANCIERA Panciera, Donald Matthew 6′1″, 192 QB-DB
Col: San Francisco *HS:* La Salle [Providence, RI] B: 6/23/1927, Westerly, RI *Drafted:* 1949 Round 4 Phi
AAFC **1949** NY-A: Rush 10-(-4) -0.4.

		Passing							
Year Team	G	Att	Comp	Comp%	Yds	YPA	TD	Int	Rating
1949 NY-A	12	150	51	34.0	801	5.34	5	16	24.2

NFL **1950** Det: Int 1-1. **1952** ChiC: Rush 4-6 1.5. **Total:** Rush 4-6 1.5; Int 1-1.

		Passing								
Year Team	G	Att	Comp	Comp%	Yds	YPA	TD	Int	Rating	Fum
1950 Det	4	0	0	—	0	—	0	0	—	0
1952 ChiC	10	96	35	36.5	582	6.06	5	9	36.0	4
NFL Total	14	96	35	36.5	582	6.06	5	9	36.0	4

CHRIS PANE Pane, Chris Albert 5′11″, 184 DB
Col: Cal State-Chico *HS:* Livermore [CA] B: 5/19/1953, Berkeley, CA
1976 Den: 4 G. **1977** Den: 11 G; PR 6-48 8.0; KR 1-16 16.0; 1 Fum. **1978** Den: 5 G; PR 1-(-2) -2.0; KR 1-29 29.0. **1979** Den: 16 G; PR 5-20 4.0; KR 18-354 19.7; 1 Fum. **Total:** 36 G; PR 12-66 5.5; KR 20-399 20.0; 2 Fum.

JOHN PANELLI Panelli, John Rocco 5′11″, 200 LB-FB
(Pep; Babe) *Col:* Notre Dame *HS:* Morristown [NJ]; Cheshire Acad. [CT] B: 5/7/1926, Morristown, NJ *Drafted:* 1949 Round 2 Det
1949 Det: Rec 1-13 13.0; KR 1-16 16.0; Int 1-2. **1950** Det: Rec 2-9 4.5; KR 2-48 24.0. **1951** ChiC: Rec 1-5 5.0; KR 2-57 28.5. **1952** ChiC: Int 3-5. **1953** ChiC: Int 1-22. **Total:** Rec 4-27 6.8; KR 5-121 24.2; Int 5-29.

		Rushing				
Year Team	G	Att	Yds	Avg	TD	Fum
1949 Det	11	10	37	3.7	0	1
1950 Det	8	32	82	2.6	0	1
1951 ChiC	12	13	38	2.9	0	1
1952 ChiC	9	0	0	—	0	0
1953 ChiC	11	0	0	—	0	0
NFL Total	51	55	157	2.9	0	3

MIKE PANEPINTO Panepinto, Michael Gino 5′7″, 180 RB
Col: Canisius *HS:* Kenmore West [NY] B: 11/17/1965, Buffalo, NY
1987 Buf: 1 G.

KEN PANFIL Panfil, Kenneth Charles 6′6″, 262 OT-DT
Col: Purdue *HS:* Gage Park [Chicago, IL] B: 9/16/1930, Chicago, IL
Drafted: 1954 Round 6 LARm
1956 LARm: 6 G; KR 1-0. **1957** LARm: 12 G. **1958** LARm: 12 G. **1959** ChiC: 12 G; KR 1-0. **1960** StL: 12 G. **1961** StL: 3 G. **1962** StL: 1 G. **Total:** 58 G; KR 2-0.

HAL PANGLE Pangle, Harold James 5′10″, 200 FB-DB-LB-BB
Col: Oregon State *HS:* Santa Ana [CA] B: 5/4/1912, Huntington Beach, CA D: 1/1/1968, Los Angeles Co., CA
1935 ChiC: Pass 4-1 25.0%, 15 3.75 2 Int; Rec 1-5 5.0. **1936** ChiC: Pass 2-0; Rec 9-195 21.7. **1937** ChiC: Pass 2-0, 1 Int; Rec 5-58 11.6. **1938** ChiC: Rec 2-14 7.0. **Total:** Pass 8-1 12.5%, 15 1.88 3 Int; Rec 17-272 16.0.

		Rushing			
Year Team	G	Att	Yds	Avg	TD
1935 ChiC	9	18	50	2.8	0
1936 ChiC	12	38	101	2.7	1
1937 ChiC	11	61	203	3.3	2
1938 ChiC	4	2	3	1.5	0
NFL Total	36	119	357	3.0	3

IRVIN PANKEY Pankey, Irvin Lee 6′4″, 277 OT
Col: Penn State *HS:* Aberdeen [MD] B: 2/15/1958, Aberdeen, MD
Drafted: 1980 Round 2 LARm
1980 LARm: 16 G. **1981** LARm: 13 G; KR 1-0. **1982** LARm: 9 G. **1984** LARm: 16 G. **1985** LARm: 16 G. **1986** LARm: 16 G. **1987** LARm: 12 G. **1988** LARm: 16 G. **1989** LARm: 14 G. **1990** LARm: 16 G. **1991** Ind: 3 G. **1992** Ind: 3 G. **Total:** 150 G; KR 1-0.

ERNIE PANNELL Pannell, Ernest Woodrow 6′2″, 220 T
(Bulldog) *Col:* Texas A&M *HS:* State Home Sch. [Corsicana, TX]
B: 2/2/1917, Manor, TX *Drafted:* 1941 Round 14 GB
1941 GB: 10 G; Int 1-0; **1** Fum TD; 6 Pt. **1942** GB: 5 G. **1945** GB: 7 G; KR 1-10 10.0. **Total:** 22 G; KR 1-10 10.0; Int 1-0; 1 Fum TD; 6 Pt.

JOE PANOS Panos, Zois 6′2″, 293 OG-C
(AKA Zois Panagiotopoulos) *Col:* Wis.-Whitewater; Wisconsin
HS: East [Brookfield, WI] B: 1/24/1971, Brookfield, WI *Drafted:* 1994 Round 3 Phi
1994 Phi: 16 G. **1995** Phi: 9 G. **1996** Phi: 16 G. **1997** Phi: 13 G. **1998** Buf: 16 G. **Total:** 70 G.

BEN PAOLUCCI Paolucci, Ben John 6′2″, 240 DT
Col: Wayne State (Mich.) *HS:* Cass Tech [Detroit, MI] B: 3/5/1937, Cleveland, OH *Drafted:* 1958 Round 9 Det
1959 Det: 4 G.

NICK PAPAC Papac, Nicholas Robert 5′11″, 190 **QB**
Col: Fresno State *HS:* Sanger [CA] B: 5/18/1935, Fresno, CA
1961 Oak: 14 G; Pass 44-13 29.5%, 173 3.93 2 TD 7 Int; Rush 6-28 4.7 1 TD; 6 Pt; 1 Fum.

GEORGE PAPACH Papach, George Martin 6′2″, 208 **FB-DB**
Col: Purdue *HS:* Chaney [Youngstown, OH] B: 4/27/1925, Youngstown, OH *Drafted:* 1948 Round 10 Pit
1948 Pit: Rec 4-72 18.0 1 TD; KR 1-16 16.0. **1949** Pit: Pass 1-0; Rec 6-18 3.0; KR 3-57 19.0. **Total:** Pass 1-0; Rec 10-90 9.0 1 TD; KR 4-73 18.3.

		Rushing					Tot
Year Team	G	Att	Yds	Avg	TD	Fum	TD
1948 Pit	10	60	324	**5.4**	2	0	3
1949 Pit	12	99	407	4.1	0	3	0
NFL Total	22	159	731	4.6	2	3	3

VINCE PAPALE Papale, Vincent Francis 6′2″, 195 **WR**
Col: St. Joseph's (Pa) *HS:* Interboro [Prospect Park, PA] B: 2/9/1946, Chester, PA
1976 Phi: 14 G. **1977** Phi: 14 G; Rec 1-15 15.0. **1978** Phi: 13 G. **Total:** 41 G; Rec 1-15 15.0.

ORAN PAPE Pape, Oran Henry 5′11″, 180 **TB-WB-HB-BB**
(Nanny) *Col:* Iowa *HS:* Dubuque [IA] B: 3/10/1904, Waupeton, IA D: 4/29/1936, Muscatine, IA
1930 Min-GB: 8 G; Rush 2 TD; 12 Pt. Min: 6 G; Rush 2 TD; 12 Pt. GB: 2 G. **1931** Prov: 11 G; Rush 1 TD; Rec 2 TD; Tot TD 3; 18 Pt. **1932** Bos-SI: 7 G; Pass 9-2 22.2%, 31 3.44 1 TD 2 Int; Rush 15-160 10.7; KR **1** TD; 6 Pt. Bos: 5 G; Pass 2-1 50.0%, 5 2.50 1 Int; Rush 9-148 16.4; KR 1 TD; 6 Pt. SI: 2 G; Pass 7-1 14.3%, 26 3.71 1 TD 1 Int; Rush 6-12 2.0. **Total:** 26 G; Pass 9-2 22.2%, 31 3.44 1 TD 2 Int; Rush 15-160 10.7 3 TD; Rec 2 TD; KR 1 TD; Tot TD 6; 36 Pt.

JOHNNY PAPIT Papit, John Michael 6′0″, 190 **HB**
Col: Virginia *HS:* Northeast [Philadelphia, PA] B: 7/25/1928, Philadelphia, PA *Drafted:* 1951 Round 7 Was
1951 Was: Rec 3-43 14.3. **1952** Was: Rec 3-71 23.7 1 TD; KR 1-25 25.0. **1953** GB-Was: Rec 1-9 9.0; KR 2-38 19.0. GB: KR 2-38 19.0. Was: Rec 1-9 9.0. **Total:** Rec 7-123 17.6 1 TD; KR 3-63 21.0.

		Rushing					Tot
Year Team	G	Att	Yds	Avg	TD	Fum	TD
1951 Was	11	44	175	4.0	0	0	0
1952 Was	11	34	102	3.0	0	1	1
1953 GB-Was	7	17	102	6.0	1	1	1
1953 GB	4	6	44	7.3	1	0	1
1953 Was	3	11	58	5.3	0	1	0
NFL Total	29	95	379	4.0	1	2	2

JOE PAPPIO Pappio, Joseph 6′0″, 189 **G-E-T-BB**
Col: Haskell Indian B: 1903
1923 Oor: 1 G. **1930** ChiC: 4 G. **Total:** 5 G.

JACK PARDEE Pardee, John Perry 6′2″, 225 **LB**
(Gabby) *Col:* Texas A&M *HS:* Cristoval [TX] B: 4/19/1936, Exira, IA *Drafted:* 1957 Round 2 LARm
1957 LARm: KR 3-21 7.0. **1962** LARm: Scor 1 Saf; **1** Fum TD. **Total:** KR 3-21 7.0; Scor 1 Saf; 1 Fum TD.

		Interceptions				Tot
Year Team	G	Int	Yds	TD	Fum	TD
1957 LARm	12	0	0	0	0	0
1958 LARm	12	0	0	0	0	0
1959 LARm	12	0	0	0	1	0
1960 LARm	8	1	10	0	0	0
1961 LARm	13	1	2	0	0	0
1962 LARm	14	0	0	0	0	1
1963 LARm	14	2	5	0	0	0
1964 LARm	14	1	32	0	0	0
1966 LARm	14	2	0	0	0	0
1967 LARm	14	6	95	2	0	2
1968 LARm	14	2	75	**2**	0	2
1969 LARm	14	1	19	0	0	0
1970 LARm	14	1	9	0	0	0
1971 Was	14	5	58	1	0	1
1972 Was	13	0	0	0	0	0
NFL Total	196	22	305	5	1	6

PAUL PARDONNER Pardonner, Paul F 5′8″, 170 **BB-DB**
(Pudge) *Col:* Purdue *HS:* Middletown [OH]; Roxbury Prep [Cheshire, CT] B: 4/29/1910, Ingomar, OH D: 2/14/1989, Columbus, OH
1934 ChiC: 6 G; Rec 1-1 1.0; Scor 3, 1 FG. **1935** ChiC: 9 G; Pass 5-1 20.0%, 6 1.20 3 Int; Rush 4-(-14) -3.5; Rec 2-44 22.0; Scor 4, 1 FG, 1 XK. **Total:** 15 G; Pass 5-1 20.0%, 6 1.20 3 Int; Rush 4-(-14) -3.5; Rec 3-45 15.0; Scor 7, 2 FG, 1 XK.

CURT PARDRIDGE Pardridge, Curtis Lynn 5′10″, 175 **WR**
Col: Northern Illinois *HS:* De Kalb [IL] B: 3/12/1964, De Kalb, IL
1987 Sea: 3 G; Rec 8-145 18.1 1 TD; KR 2-29 14.5; 6 Pt.

BOB PAREMORE Paremore, Robert Cero 5′11″, 190 **HB**
Col: Florida A&M *HS:* Lincoln [Tallahassee, FL] B: 12/5/1939, Tallahassee, FL *Drafted:* 1963 Round 6 StL
1963 StL: Rec 6-89 14.8 1 TD; PR 4-23 5.8; KR 12-292 24.3; **1** Fum TD. **1964** StL: KR 9-192 21.3. **Total:** Rec 6-89 14.8 1 TD; PR 4-23 5.8; KR 21-484 23.0; 1 Fum TD.

		Rushing					Tot
Year Team	G	Att	Yds	Avg	TD	Fum	TD
1963 StL	14	36	107	3.0	0	1	2
1964 StL	4	0	0	—	0	0	0
NFL Total	18	36	107	3.0	0	1	2

BABE PARILLI Parilli, Vito 6′1″, 196 **QB**
Col: Kentucky *HS:* Rochester [PA] B: 5/7/1930, Rochester, PA *Drafted:* 1952 Round 1 GB
1960 Oak: Rec 1-0. **1961** Bos: Scor 1 2XP; 1 Fum TD. **Total:** Rec 1-0; Scor 1 2XP; 1 Fum TD.

		Passing							
Year Team	G	Att	Comp	Comp%	Yds	YPA	TD	Int	Rating
1952 GB	12	177	77	43.5	1416	8.00	13	17	56.6
1953 GB	12	166	74	44.6	830	5.00	4	19	28.5
1956 Cle	5	49	24	49.0	409	8.35	3	7	58.5
1957 GB	12	102	39	38.2	669	6.56	4	12	34.8
1958 GB	12	157	68	43.3	1068	6.80	10	13	53.3
1960 Oak	14	187	87	46.5	1003	5.36	5	11	47.6
1961 Bos	14	198	104	**52.5**	1314	6.64	13	**9**	76.5
1962 Bos	10	253	140	55.3	1988	7.86	18	**8**	91.5
1963 Bos	14	337	153	45.4	2345	6.96	13	24	52.1
1964 Bos	14	473	228	48.2	**3465**	7.33	**31**	27	70.8
1965 Bos	14	426	173	40.6	2597	6.10	18	26	50.0
1966 Bos	14	382	181	47.4	2721	7.12	20	20	66.9
1967 Bos	14	344	161	46.8	2317	6.74	19	24	58.5
1968 NYJ	14	55	29	52.7	401	7.29	5	2	91.6
1969 NYJ	14	24	14	58.3	138	5.75	2	1	85.1
NFL Total	189	3330	1552	46.6	22681	6.81	178	220	59.6

	Rushing				Punting				Tot
Year Team	Att	Yds	Avg	TD	Punts	Yds	Avg	Fum	TD
1952 GB	32	106	3.3	1	65	2645	40.7	4	1
1953 GB	42	171	4.1	4	19	685	36.1	8	4
1956 Cle	18	65	3.6	0	0	0	—	4	0
1957 GB	24	83	3.5	2	0	0	—	3	2
1958 GB	8	15	1.9	0	0	0	—	4	0
1960 Oak	21	131	6.2	1	0	0	—	3	1
1961 Bos	38	183	4.8	4	0	0	—	2	5
1962 Bos	28	169	6.0	2	0	0	—	6	2
1963 Bos	36	126	3.5	5	0	0	—	7	5
1964 Bos	34	168	4.9	2	5	180	36.0	7	2
1965 Bos	50	200	4.0	0	0	0	—	8	0
1966 Bos	28	42	1.5	1	0	0	—	8	1
1967 Bos	14	61	4.4	0	0	0	—	4	0
1968 NYJ	7	-2	-0.3	1	0	0	—	3	1
1969 NYJ	3	4	1.3	0	0	0	—	0	0
NFL Total	383	1522	4.0	23	89	3510	39.4	71	24

BUBBA PARIS Paris, William H 6′6″, 300 **OT**
Col: Michigan *HS:* DeSales [Louisville, KY] B: 10/6/1960, Louisville, KY *Drafted:* 1982 Round 2 SF
1983 SF: 16 G. **1984** SF: 16 G. **1985** SF: 16 G. **1986** SF: 10 G. **1987** SF: 11 G. **1988** SF: 16 G. **1989** SF: 16 G. **1990** SF: 16 G. **1991** Ind: 13 G. **Total:** 130 G.

DON PARISH Parish, Donald Edward 6′1″, 220 **LB**
Col: Stanford *HS:* Paso Robles [CA] B: 1/4/1948, Paso Robles, CA *Drafted:* 1970 Round 4 StL
1970 StL: 14 G; Int 1-41 1 TD; 6 Pt. **1971** StL-LARm: 2 G. StL: 1 G. LARm: 1 G. **1972** StL-Den: 3 G. StL: 2 G. Den: 1 G. **Total:** 19 G; Int 1-41 1 TD; 6 Pt.

ERNIE PARK Park, Ernest Carol 6′3″, 253 **OT-OG**
Col: McMurry *HS:* Wylie [Abilene, TX] B: 10/22/1940, San Angelo, TX *Drafted:* 1963 Round 19 SD
1963 SD: 7 G. **1964** SD: 14 G. **1965** SD: 14 G. **1966** Mia: 14 G. **1967** Den: 14 G. **1969** Cin: 11 G. **Total:** 74 G.

KAULANA PARK Park, Kaulana Hnr 6′2″, 230 **RB**
Col: Menlo Coll. CA (J.C.); Stanford *HS:* Kamehameha School [Honolulu, HI] B: 6/16/1962, Honolulu, HI
1987 NYG: 2 G; Rush 6-11 1.8; Rec 1-6 6.0.

ANDY PARKER Parker, Andrew James 6′5″, 244 **TE**
Col: Utah *HS:* Dana Hills [Dana Point, CA]; San Dieguito HS [Encinitas, CA] B: 9/8/1961, Redlands, CA *Drafted:* 1984 Round 5 LARd
1984 LARd: 9 G. **1985** LARd: 16 G. **1986** LARd: 13 G; Rec 2-8 4.0 1 TD; 6 Pt. **1987** LARd: 12 G. **1988** LARd: 16 G; Rec 4-33 8.3. **1989** SD: 10 G; Rec 2-5 2.5 1 TD; 6 Pt. **1990** LARd: 5 G. **Total:** 81 G; Rec 8-46 5.8 2 TD; 12 Pt.

ARTIMUS PARKER Parker, Artimus L 6'3", 208 DB
Col: USC *HS:* Sacramento [CA] B: 6/25/1950, Winston-Salem, NC
Drafted: 1974 Round 12 Phi
1974 Phi: 14 G. **1975** Phi: 14 G; Int 4-15. **1976** Phi: 14 G. **1977** NYJ: 11 G; Int 1-45. **Total:** 53 G; Int 5-60.

CARL PARKER Parker, Carl Wayne 6'2", 201 WR
Col: Vanderbilt *HS:* Lowndes [Valdosta, GA] B: 2/5/1965, Columbus, GA *Drafted:* 1988 Round 12 Cin
1988 Cin: 3 G. **1989** Cin: 3 G; Rec 1-45 45.0. **Total:** 6 G; Rec 1-45 45.0.

CHARLIE PARKER Parker, Charles Ruffing 6'1", 245 OG
Col: Southern Mississippi *HS:* Mattie T. Blount [Prichard, AL]
B: 6/19/1941, Greenville, MS *Drafted:* 1964 Round 13 Den
1965 Den: 14 G.

CHRIS PARKER Parker, Christopher Lee 5'11", 213 RB
Col: Marshall *HS:* Heritage [Lynchburg, VA] B: 12/31/1972, Lynchburg, VA
1997 Jac: 1 G; KR 1-9 9.0.

ACE PARKER Parker, Clarence McKay 6'0", 178 TB-DB-QB
Col: Duke *HS:* Woodrow Wilson [Portsmouth, VA] B: 5/17/1912, Portsmouth, VA *Drafted:* 1937 Round 2 Bkn *HOF:* 1972
AAFC **1946** NY-A: PR 8-85 10.6; KR 2-27 13.5; Punt 27-911 33.7.

		Passing							
Year Team	**G**	**Att**	**Comp**	**Comp%**	**Yds**	**YPA**	**TD**	**Int**	**Rating**
1946 NY-A	12	115	62	53.9	763	6.63	8	3	87.0

	Rushing				Tot
Year Team	**Att**	**Yds**	**Avg**	**TD**	**TD**
1946 NY-A	75	184	2.5	3	4

NFL **1937** Bkn: PR **1** TD; Scor 13, 1 XK. **1938** Bkn: Rec 1-19 19.0 1 TD; Int **1** TD; Scor 29, 5-7 71.4% XK. **1939** Bkn: Rec 1-5 5.0; Scor 33, 1-5 20.0% FG, 0-1 XK. **1940** Bkn: Rec 3-139 46.3 2 TD; Int **6-146 1** TD; Scor 49, **19-22** 86.4% XK. **1941** Bkn: Rec 3-66 22.0; PR 16-153 9.6; KR 3-71 23.7; Int 1-5. **Total:** Rec 8-229 28.6 3 TD; PR 16-153 9.6 1 TD; KR 3-71 23.7; Int 7-151 2 TD; Scor 124, 1-5 20.0% FG, 25-30 80.0% XK.

		Passing							
Year Team	**G**	**Att**	**Comp**	**Comp%**	**Yds**	**YPA**	**TD**	**Int**	**Rating**
1937 Bkn	4	61	28	45.9	514	8.43	1	7	41.3
1938 Bkn	11	**148**	63	42.6	**865**	5.84	5	7	53.5
1939 Bkn	11	157	72	45.9	977	6.22	4	13	40.2
1940 Bkn	11	111	49	44.1	817	7.36	10	7	73.3
1941 Bkn	11	102	51	50.0	639	6.26	2	8	43.7
1945 Bos	8	24	10	41.7	123	5.13	0	5	18.6
NFL Total	56	603	273	45.3	3935	6.53	22	47	46.7

	Rushing				Punting				Tot
Year Team	**Att**	**Yds**	**Avg**	**TD**	**Punts**	**Yds**	**Avg**	**Fum**	**TD**
1937 Bkn	34	26	0.8	1	—	—	—	0	2
1938 Bkn	93	253	2.7	2	—	—	—	0	4
1939 Bkn	104	271	2.6	5	40	1678	42.0	0	5
1940 Bkn	89	306	3.4	2	49	1875	38.3	0	5
1941 Bkn	85	301	3.5	0	27	1079	40.0	0	0
1945 Bos	18	-49	-2.7	0	7	224	32.0	2	0
NFL Total	423	1108	2.6	10	123	4856	39.5	2	16

DAREN PARKER Parker, Daren Roger 6'0", 185 P
Col: South Carolina *HS:* Mount Pleasant [NC] B: 4/10/1968
1992 Den: 3 G; Punt 12-491 40.9.

DAVE PARKER Parker, David A 6'3", 200 OE-DE
Col: Hardin-Simmons *HS:* Ozona [TX] B: 1/30/1918, Novice, TX
D: 12/1991 *Drafted:* 1941 Round 17 Bkn
1941 Bkn: 7 G; Rec 1-10 10.0.

DON PARKER Parker, Donald Martin 6'3", 258 OG
Col: Virginia *HS:* Punahou School [Honolulu, HI] B: 8/9/1944, Honolulu, HI *Drafted:* 1966 Round 4 SF
1967 SF: 12 G.

ERVIN PARKER Parker, Ervin 6'4", 236 LB
Col: South Carolina State *HS:* Choppee [Georgetown, SC]
B: 8/19/1958, Georgetown, SC *Drafted:* 1980 Round 4 Buf
1980 Buf: 16 G. **1981** Buf: 16 G. **1982** Buf: 9 G. **1983** Buf: 16 G; 4 Sac.
Total: 57 G; 4 Sac.

FREDDIE PARKER Parker, Freddie R 5'10", 215 RB
Col: Mississippi Valley State *HS:* Heidelberg [MS] B: 7/6/1962, Heidelberg, MS
1987 GB: 1 G; Rush 8-33 4.1; Rec 3-22 7.3.

GLENN PARKER Parker, Glenn Andrew 6'5", 305 OT-OG
Col: Arizona *HS:* Edison [Huntington Beach, CA] B: 4/22/1966, Westminster, CA *Drafted:* 1990 Round 3 Buf
1990 Buf: 16 G. **1991** Buf: 16 G. **1992** Buf: 13 G. **1993** Buf: 16 G.
1994 Buf: 16 G. **1995** Buf: 13 G. **1996** Buf: 14 G. **1997** KC: 15 G.
1998 KC: 15 G. **Total:** 134 G.

HOWIE PARKER Parker, Howard Ingram 6'2", 220 BB-LB
Col: Southern Methodist *HS:* John Tyler [Tyler, TX] B: 8/23/1926, Greenville, TX
AAFC **1948** NY-A: 3 G; Rec 1-17 17.0.

JIM PARKER Parker, James Thomas 6'3", 273 OT-OG
Col: Ohio State *HS:* HS in [Macon, GA]; V. W. Scott [Toledo, OH]
B: 4/3/1934, Macon, GA *Drafted:* 1957 Round 1 Bal *HOF:* 1973
1957 Bal: 12 G. **1958** Bal: 12 G. **1959** Bal: 12 G. **1960** Bal: 12 G.
1961 Bal: 14 G. **1962** Bal: 14 G. **1963** Bal: 14 G; KR 1-15 15.0. **1964** Bal: 14 G. **1965** Bal: 14 G. **1966** Bal: 14 G. **1967** Bal: 3 G. **Total:** 135 G; KR 1-15 15.0.

JEFF PARKER Parker, Jeffrey 5'10", 185 WR
Col: Bethune-Cookman *HS:* Seabreeze [Daytona Beach, FL]
B: 7/16/1969, Daytona Beach, FL
1992 TB: 3 G; Rec 1-12 12.0.

JERRY PARKER Parker, Jerry Lynn 6'0", 227 LB
Col: Central State (Ohio) B: 9/13/1964
1987 Cle: 2 G.

JOE PARKER Parker, Joseph Jackson 6'1", 220 DE-OE
Col: Texas *HS:* Wichita Falls [TX] B: 7/11/1923, Wichita Falls, TX
Drafted: 1944 Round 3 Phi
1946 ChiC: 8 G; Rec 2-17 8.5; KR 1-0. **1947** ChiC: 12 G. **Total:** 20 G; Rec 2-17 8.5; KR 1-0.

JOEL PARKER Parker, Joseph Lee 6'5", 212 WR
Col: Florida *HS:* Clearwater [FL] B: 4/23/1952, Louisville, KY
Drafted: 1974 Round 5 NO
1974 NO: Pass 1-0; Rush 2-2 1.0. **Total:** Pass 1-0; Rush 2-2 1.0.

		Receiving			
Year Team	**G**	**Rec**	**Yds**	**Avg**	**TD**
1974 NO	14	41	455	11.1	4
1975 NO	7	9	123	13.7	2
1977 NO	1	1	7	7.0	0
NFL Total	22	51	585	11.5	6

KENNY PARKER Parker, Kenneth 6'1", 190 DB
Col: Fordham *HS:* Eastside [Paterson, NJ] B: 7/22/1946, Paterson, NJ
Drafted: 1968 Round 16 NYG
1970 NYG: 14 G.

KERRY PARKER Parker, Kerry Anthony 6'1", 192 DB
Col: Grambling State *HS:* George Washington Carver [New Orleans, LA]
B: 10/3/1955, New Orleans, LA
1984 KC: 15 G. **1987** Buf: 2 G. **Total:** 17 G.

ORLANDO PARKER Parker, Orlando Lateef 5'11", 190 WR
Col: Troy State *HS:* Jefferson Davis [Montgomery, AL] B: 3/7/1972, Montgomery, AL *Drafted:* 1994 Round 4 NYJ
1994 NYJ: 2 G; Rec 1-7 7.0.

BUDDY PARKER Parker, Raymond Klein 6'0", 193 BB-LB-FB-DB
Col: North Texas; Centenary *HS:* Kemp [TX] B: 12/16/1913, Slaton, TX
D: 3/22/1982, Kaufman, TX
1935 Det: Pass 1-0, 1 Int. **1937** ChiC: Pass 1-0; Scor 7, 1 XK. **1938** ChiC: Pass 2-2 100.0%, 21 10.50. **1939** ChiC: Pass 1-0. **1940** ChiC: Int 2-20; Scor 9, 0-1 FG, 3-3 100.0% XK. **1941** ChiC: Int 2-8; Scor 0-1 XK.
Total: Pass 5-2 40.0%, 21 4.20 1 Int; Int 4-28; Scor 28, 0-1 FG, 4-4 75.0% XK.

		Rushing				Receiving			
Year Team	**G**	**Att**	**Yds**	**Avg**	**TD**	**Rec**	**Yds**	**Avg**	**TD**
1935 Det	11	59	156	2.6	0	1	12	12.0	0
1936 Det	10	6	21	3.5	0	1	15	15.0	0
1937 ChiC	11	50	115	2.3	1	2	14	7.0	0
1938 ChiC	10	45	144	3.2	2	16	142	8.9	0
1939 ChiC	9	12	37	3.1	0	5	33	6.6	0
1940 ChiC	10	6	8	1.3	1	6	45	7.5	0
1941 ChiC	11	1	-1	-1.0	0	7	122	17.4	0
1942 ChiC	11	1	9	9.0	0	2	7	3.5	0
1943 ChiC	4	0	0	—	0	0	0	—	0
NFL Total	87	180	489	2.7	4	40	390	9.8	0

RICKY PARKER Parker, Ricky Duwayne 6'0", 194 DB
Col: San Diego State *HS:* Hiram Johnson [Sacramento, CA]
B: 12/4/1974, Burlington, VT *Drafted:* 1997 Round 6 ChiB
1997 Jac: 12 G.

RIDDICK PARKER Parker, Riddick Thurston Jr. 6'3", 274 DT
Col: North Carolina *HS:* Southampton [Courtland, VA] B: 11/20/1972, Emporia, VA
1997 Sea: 12 G. **1998** Sea: 8 G; 1 Sac. **Total:** 20 G; 1 Sac.

ROBERT PARKER Parker, Robert Lewis 6'1", 201 RB
Col: Northeastern Oklahoma A&M (J.C.); Brigham Young *HS:* Benjamin Russell [Alexander City, AL] B: 1/7/1963, Alexander City, AL
1987 KC: Rec 7-44 6.3; KR 3-49 16.3.

Year Team	G	Rushing Att	Yds	Avg	TD	Fum
1987 KC	3	47	150	3.2	1	1

ROD PARKER Parker, Rodney 6'1", 190 **WR**
Col: Tennessee State *HS:* Francis T. Nicholls [New Orleans, LA]
B: 7/18/1953, Mobile, AL *Drafted:* 1978 Round 6 Atl
1980 Phi: 8 G; Rec 9-148 16.4 1 TD; 6 Pt. **1981** Phi: 11 G; Rec 8-168 21.0 2 TD; 12 Pt. **Total:** 19 G; Rec 17-316 18.6 3 TD; 18 Pt.

STEVE PARKER Parker, Steven Franklin 6'6", 265 **DE**
Col: North Idaho Coll. (J.C.); Washington; Idaho *HS:* Couer d'Alene [ID]
B: 12/8/1956, Spokane, WA
1980 NO: 4 G.

STEVE PARKER Parker, Steven Royce 6'4", 256 **DE**
Col: East Tennessee State *HS:* Evanston Twp. [Evanston, IL]
B: 9/21/1959, Evanston, IL
1983 Bal: 16 G; 1.5 Sac. **1984** Ind: 9 G; 1 Sac. **Total:** 25 G; 2.5 Sac.

VAUGHN PARKER Parker, Vaughn Antoine 6'3", 296 **OT-OG**
Col: UCLA *HS:* St. Joseph's [Kenmore, NY] B: 6/5/1971, Buffalo, NY
Drafted: 1994 Round 2 SD
1994 SD: 6 G; KR 1-1 1.0. **1995** SD: 15 G. **1996** SD: 16 G. **1997** SD: 16 G. **1998** SD: 6 G. **Total:** 59 G; KR 1-1 1.0.

ANTHONY PARKER Parker, Will Anthony 5'10", 181 **DB**
Col: Arizona State *HS:* McClintock [Tempe, AZ] B: 2/11/1966, Sylacauga, AL
1992 Min: KR 2-30 15.0; 1 Fum TD. **1994** Min: 1 Fum TD. **1995** StL: 1 Fum TD. **1997** TB: 1 Sac. **1998** TB: 1 Sac. **Total:** KR 2-30 15.0; 3 Fum TD; 2 Sac.

Year Team	G	Punt Returns Ret	Yds	Avg	TD	Interceptions Int	Yds	TD	Fum	Tot TD
1989 Ind	1	0	0	—	0	0	0	0	0	0
1991 KC	2	0	0	—	0	0	0	0	0	0
1992 Min	16	33	336	10.2	0	3	23	0	2	1
1993 Min	14	9	64	7.1	0	1	1	0	0	0
1994 Min	15	4	31	7.8	0	4	99	2	1	3
1995 StL	16	0	0	—	0	2	-5	0	0	1
1996 StL	14	0	0	—	0	4	128	**2**	0	2
1997 TB	15	0	0	—	0	1	5	0	1	0
1998 TB	11	0	0	—	0	0	0	0	0	0
NFL Total	104	46	431	9.4	0	15	251	4	4	7

FRANK PARKER Parker, William Frank 6'5", 270 **DT**
Col: Oklahoma State *HS:* Broken Bow [OK] B: 10/16/1939, Broken Bow, OK *Drafted:* 1961 Round 6 Cle
1962 Cle: 14 G. **1963** Cle: 14 G. **1964** Cle: 8 G. **1966** Cle: 12 G. **1967** Cle: 12 G. **1968** Pit: 10 G. **1969** NYG: 8 G. **Total:** 78 G.

WILLIE PARKER Parker, William Nolen 6'3", 245 **C-OG**
Col: Wharton Co. JC TX; North Texas *HS:* Wharton [TX]
B: 12/28/1948, Baytown, TX *Drafted:* 1971 Round 3 SF
1973 Buf: 14 G; KR 1-16 16.0. **1974** Buf: 14 G. **1975** Buf: 14 G. **1976** Buf: 2 G. **1977** Buf: 14 G. **1978** Buf: 16 G; 1 Fum. **1979** Buf: 16 G. **1980** Det: 4 G. **Total:** 94 G; KR 1-16 16.0; 1 Fum.

WILLIE PARKER Parker, Willie David 6'3", 275 **DT**
Col: Arkansas-Pine Bluff *HS:* Morehouse [Bastrop, LA] B: 3/12/1945, Bastrop, LA *Drafted:* 1967 Round 5 Hou
1967 Hou: 14 G. **1968** Hou: 14 G. **1969** Hou: 12 G. **1970** Hou: 14 G. **Total:** 54 G.

DAVE PARKIN Parkin, David Rodney 6'0", 191 **DB**
Col: Utah State *HS:* Highland [Salt Lake City, UT] B: 1/7/1956, Salt Lake City, UT *Drafted:* 1979 Round 9 Atl
1979 Det: 9 G.

DOC PARKINSON Parkinson, Thomas H 6'1", 205 **FB-HB**
(Pug) *Col:* Pittsburgh *HS:* California [Coal Center, PA] B: 3/16/1907, Fayette City, PA D: 12/28/1976, Pittsburgh, PA
1931 SI: 11 G.

DAVE PARKS Parks, David Wayne 6'2", 220 **WR**
Col: Texas Tech *HS:* Abilene [TX] B: 12/25/1941, Muenster, TX
Drafted: 1964 Round 1 SF
1966 SF: Rush 1-(-1) -1.0. **1968** NO: Pass 1-0. **1971** NO: Rush 2-(-2) -1.0. **1972** NO: Rush 1-(-7) -7.0. **Total:** Pass 1-0; Rush 4-(-10) -2.5.

Year Team	G	Receiving Rec	Yds	Avg	TD	Fum
1964 SF	14	36	703	19.5	8	2
1965 SF	14	**80**	**1344**	16.8	**12**	1
1966 SF	13	66	974	14.8	5	0
1967 SF	9	26	313	12.0	2	1
1968 NO	10	25	258	10.3	0	0
1969 NO	14	31	439	14.2	3	0
1970 NO	13	26	447	17.2	2	0
1971 NO	14	35	568	16.2	5	0
1972 NO	12	32	542	16.9	6	0
1973 Hou	5	3	31	10.3	1	0
NFL Total	118	360	5619	15.6	44	4

MICKEY PARKS Parks, Edward Harry 6'0", 225 **C-LB**
Col: Oklahoma *HS:* Shawnee [OK] B: 12/4/1915, Shawnee, OK
D: 9/27/1976, Yountville, CA *Drafted:* 1938 Round 7 Was
AAFC **1946** ChiA: 13 G.

NFL **1938** Was: 8 G. **1939** Was: 10 G; Scor 0-1 XK. **1940** Was: 6 G. **Total:** 24 G; Scor 0-1 XK.

JEFF PARKS Parks, Jeffrey Dupree 6'4", 238 **TE**
Col: Auburn *HS:* Gardendale [AL] B: 9/14/1964, Columbia, SC
Drafted: 1986 Round 5 Hou
1986 Hou: 5 G. **1987** Hou: 7 G. **1988** TB: 3 G; Rec 1-22 22.0. **Total:** 15 G; Rec 1-22 22.0.

LIMBO PARKS Parks, Lemuel Tyrone 6'3", 265 **OG**
Col: Coffeyville CC KS; Arkansas *HS:* South [Raytown, MO]
B: 3/21/1965, Kansas City, MO
1987 SF: 3 G.

RICKEY PARKS Parks, Richard 6'1", 179 **WR**
Col: Arkansas-Pine Bluff B: 2/19/1964
1987 Min: 2 G; Rec 3-46 15.3.

BILLY PARKS Parks, William James 6'1", 185 **WR**
Col: Santa Monica Coll. CA (J.C.); Long Beach State *HS:* Culver City [CA] B: 1/1/1948, Santa Monica, CA *Drafted:* 1970 Round 6 SD
1971 SD: Rush 5-77 15.4. **Total:** Rush 5-77 15.4.

Year Team	G	Receiving Rec	Yds	Avg	TD	Fum
1971 SD	10	41	609	14.9	4	2
1972 Dal	12	18	298	16.6	1	0
1973 Hou	14	43	581	13.5	1	1
1974 Hou	14	20	330	16.5	1	0
1975 Hou	10	1	8	8.0	0	0
NFL Total	60	123	1826	14.8	7	3

CHET PARLAVECCHIO Parlavecchio, Chester Louis 6'2", 225 **LB**
Col: Penn State *HS:* Seton Hall Prep [South Orange, NJ] B: 2/14/1960, Newark, NJ *Drafted:* 1982 Round 6 GB
1983 GB-StL: 12 G. GB: 3 G. StL: 9 G. **Total:** 12 G.

BERNIE PARMALEE Parmalee, Bernard 5'11", 201 **RB**
Col: Ball State *HS:* Lincoln [Jersey City, NJ] B: 9/16/1967, Jersey City, NJ
1992 Mia: KR 14-289 20.6. **1994** Mia: KR 2-0; Scor 1 2XP.
Total: KR 16-289 18.1; Scor 1 2XP.

Year Team	G	Rushing Att	Yds	Avg	TD	Receiving Rec	Yds	Avg	TD	Fum	Tot TD
1992 Mia	10	6	38	6.3	0	0	0	—	0	3	0
1993 Mia	16	4	16	4.0	0	1	1	1.0	0	0	0
1994 Mia	15	216	868	4.0	6	34	249	7.3	1	5	7
1995 Mia	16	236	878	3.7	9	39	345	8.8	1	5	10
1996 Mia	16	25	80	3.2	0	21	189	9.0	0	1	0
1997 Mia	16	18	59	3.3	0	28	301	10.8	1	1	1
1998 Mia	15	8	20	2.5	0	21	221	10.5	0	2	0
NFL Total	104	513	1959	3.8	15	144	1306	9.1	3	17	18

JIM PARMER Parmer, James Richard 6'0", 193 **HB-FB-DB**
Col: Texas A&M; Oklahoma State *HS:* Mangum [OK] B: 4/25/1926, Dallas, TX *Drafted:* 1948 Round 23 Phi
1948 Phi: KR 1-14 14.0; Int 1-6. **1949** Phi: Int 2-12. **1952** Phi: KR 2-33 16.5. **1953** Phi: KR 1-18 18.0. **Total:** KR 4-65 16.3; Int 3-18.

Year Team	G	Rushing Att	Yds	Avg	TD	Receiving Rec	Yds	Avg	TD	Fum	Tot TD
1948 Phi	11	30	167	5.6	3	0	0	—	0	2	3
1949 Phi	12	66	234	3.5	5	5	33	6.6	0	3	5
1950 Phi	10	60	203	3.4	7	6	103	17.2	1	2	8
1951 Phi	11	92	316	3.4	2	13	80	6.2	0	2	2
1952 Phi	6	12	23	1.9	0	2	10	5.0	0	2	0
1953 Phi	12	38	158	4.2	2	14	89	6.4	0	0	2
1954 Phi	10	119	408	3.4	0	12	40	3.3	0	6	0
1955 Phi	12	34	129	3.8	1	1	-4	-4.0	0	0	1
1956 Phi	4	1	-2	-2.0	0	0	0	—	0	0	0
NFL Total	88	452	1636	3.6	20	53	351	6.6	1	17	21

BABE PARNELL Parnell, Frederick Anthony 6'3", 205 **T-G**
Col: Colgate; Allegheny *HS:* Ashtabula [OH] B: 1/9/1901, Ashtabula, OH D: 5/29/1982, Kingsville, OH
1925 NYG: 11 G. **1926** NYG: 4 G. **1927** NYG: 2 G. **1928** NYG: 1 G. **Total:** 18 G.

JOHN PARRELLA Parrella, John Lorin 6′3″, 290 **DE-DT**
Col: Nebraska *HS:* Central Catholic [Grand Island, NE] B: 11/22/1969, Topeka, KS *Drafted:* 1993 Round 2 Buf
1993 Buf: 10 G; 1 Sac. **1994** SD: 13 G; 1 Sac. **1995** SD: 16 G; 2 Sac. **1996** SD: 16 G; 2 Sac. **1997** SD: 16 G; 3.5 Sac. **1998** SD: 16 G; 1.5 Sac. **Total:** 87 G; 11 Sac.

BILL PARRIOTT Parriott, William Wright 5′10″, 165 **FB-LB**
Col: West Virginia *HS:* Morgantown [WV] B: 4/11/1911, Newburgh, WV D: 1/24/1984, Morgantown, WV
1934 Cin: 1 G.

GARY PARRIS Parris, Gary Thomas 6′2″, 226 **TE**
Col: Florida State *HS:* Vero Beach [FL] B: 6/13/1950, East St. Louis, IL *Drafted:* 1973 Round 15 SD
1974 SD: KR 3-29 9.7. **1979** StL: Scor **1** 1XP. **Total:** KR 3-29 9.7; Scor 1 1XP.

		Receiving				
Year Team	G	Rec	Yds	Avg	TD	Fum
1973 SD	9	0	0	—	0	0
1974 SD	14	3	36	12.0	0	0
1975 Cle	14	1	12	12.0	0	0
1976 Cle	14	5	73	14.6	0	0
1977 Cle	14	21	213	10.1	5	1
1978 Cle	16	1	4	4.0	0	0
1979 StL	9	14	174	12.4	0	0
1980 StL	1	0	0	—	0	0
NFL Total	91	45	512	11.4	5	1

BERNIE PARRISH Parrish, Bernard Paul 5′11″, 194 **DB**
Col: Florida *HS:* P.K. Yonge Lab [Gainesville, FL] B: 4/29/1936, Long Beach, CA *Drafted:* 1958 Round 9 Cle
1960 Cle: KR 2-0. **1961** Cle: **1** Fum TD. **1963** Cle: PR 3-31 10.3. **Total:** PR 3-31 10.3; KR 2-0; 1 Fum TD.

		Interceptions			Tot
Year Team	G	Int	Yds	TD	TD
1959 Cle	12	5	83	**1**	1
1960 Cle	12	6	**238**	1	1
1961 Cle	14	7	40	0	1
1962 Cle	13	2	37	0	0
1963 Cle	14	0	0	0	0
1964 Cle	14	4	98	1	1
1965 Cle	14	4	45	0	0
1966 Cle-Hou	12	3	16	0	0
1966 Cle	1	1	16	0	0
1966 Hou	11	2	0	0	0
NFL Total	105	31	557	3	4

DON PARRISH Parrish, Donald 6′2″, 255 **NT-DE**
Col: Pittsburgh *HS:* Amos P. Godby [Tallahassee, FL] B: 4/6/1955, Tallahassee, FL *Drafted:* 1977 Round 12 Atl
1978 KC: 15 G. **1979** KC: 16 G. **1980** KC: 16 G. **1981** KC: 16 G. **1982** KC: 8 G; 1 Sac. **Total:** 71 G; 1 Sac.

JAMES PARRISH Parrish, James Herbert Jr. 6′6″, 320 **OT**
Col: Temple *HS:* Dundalk [MD] B: 5/19/1968, Baltimore, MD
1993 SF: 1 G. **1995** Pit: 16 G. **1996** NYJ: 1 G. **Total:** 18 G.

LEMAR PARRISH Parrish, Lemar 5′11″, 185 **DB**
Col: Lincoln (Mo.) *HS:* John F. Kennedy [Riviera Beach, FL] B: 12/13/1947, West Palm Beach, FL *Drafted:* 1970 Round 7 Cin
1971 Cin: **1** Fum TD. **1973** Cin: **1** Fum TD. **1974** Cin: 1 Fum TD. **Total:** 3 Fum TD.

		Punt Returns				Kickoff Returns			
Year Team	G	Ret	Yds	Avg	TD	Ret	Yds	Avg	TD
1970 Cin	14	23	194	8.4	**1**	16	482	30.1	1
1971 Cin	14	12	93	7.8	0	13	296	22.8	0
1972 Cin	14	15	141	9.4	**1**	15	348	23.2	0
1973 Cin	14	25	200	8.0	0	7	143	20.4	0
1974 Cin	13	18	338	**18.8**	**2**	2	36	18.0	0
1975 Cin	11	13	83	6.4	0	4	114	28.5	0
1976 Cin	14	20	122	6.1	0	3	62	20.7	0
1977 Cin	11	4	30	7.5	0	1	23	23.0	0
1978 Was	11	1	4	4.0	0	0	0	—	0
1979 Was	16	0	0	—	0	0	0	—	0
1980 Was	15	0	0	—	0	0	0	—	0
1981 Was	12	0	0	—	0	0	0	—	0
1982 Buf	7	0	0	—	0	0	0	—	0
NFL Total	166	131	1205	9.2	4	61	1504	24.7	1

	Interceptions				Tot
Year Team	Int	Yds	TD	Fum	TD
1970 Cin	5	28	0	2	3
1971 Cin	7	105	1	1	2
1972 Cin	5	90	2	4	3
1973 Cin	2	10	0	1	1
1974 Cin	0	0	0	0	3
1975 Cin	1	26	0	3	0
1976 Cin	2	0	0	3	0
1977 Cin	3	95	**1**	1	1
1978 Was	4	21	0	0	0
1979 Was	9	65	0	0	0
1980 Was	7	13	0	1	0
1981 Was	1	1	0	0	0
1982 Buf	1	8	0	0	0
NFL Total	47	462	4	16	13

TONY PARRISH Parrish, Tony 5′10″, 205 **DB**
Col: Washington *HS:* Marina [Huntington Beach, CA] B: 11/23/1975, Los Angeles, CA *Drafted:* 1998 Round 2 ChiB
1998 ChiB: 16 G; Int 1-8; 1 Fum; 1 Sac.

RICK PARROS Parros, Rick U 5′11″, 200 **RB**
Col: Utah State *HS:* Granite [Salt Lake City, UT] B: 6/14/1958, Brooklyn, NY *Drafted:* 1980 Round 4 Den

		Rushing				Receiving					Tot
Year Team	G	Att	Yds	Avg	TD	Rec	Yds	Avg	TD	Fum	TD
1981 Den	16	176	749	4.3	2	25	216	8.6	1	6	3
1982 Den	9	77	277	3.6	1	37	259	7.0	2	3	3
1983 Den	6	30	96	3.2	1	12	126	10.5	2	3	3
1984 Den	15	46	208	4.5	2	6	25	4.2	0	0	2
1985 Sea	4	8	19	2.4	0	1	27	27.0	0	1	0
1987 Sea	1	13	32	2.5	1	1	7	7.0	0	0	1
NFL Total	51	350	1381	3.9	7	82	660	8.0	5	13	12

OX PARRY Parry, Owen Lloyd 6′4″, 230 **T**
Col: Baylor *HS:* Woodrow Wilson [Dallas, TX] B: 11/17/1914, San Antonio, TX D: 3/2/1976, Henrietta, TX
1937 NYG: 11 G. **1938** NYG: 10 G. **1939** NYG: 11 G. **Total:** 32 G.

ARA PARSEGHIAN Parseghian, Ara Raoul 5′10″, 194 **HB-DB**
Col: Akron; Miami (Ohio) *HS:* South [Akron, OH] B: 5/21/1923, Akron, OH
AAFC **1948** CleA: Rec 2-31 15.5 1 TD; KR 2-41 20.5; Int 1-56. **1949** CleA: Rec 1-2 2.0. **Total:** Rec 3-33 11.0 1 TD; KR 2-41 20.5; Int 1-56.

		Rushing				Tot
Year Team	G	Att	Yds	Avg	TD	TD
1948 CleA	12	32	135	4.2	1	2
1949 CleA	2	12	31	2.6	0	0
AAFC Total	14	44	166	3.8	1	2

CLIFF PARSLEY Parsley, Clifford Donald 6′1″, 211 **P**
Col: Oklahoma State *HS:* Grandview [MO] B: 12/26/1954, Kansas City, MO *Drafted:* 1977 Round 6 NO
1981 Hou: Pass 2-2 100.0%, 43 21.50. **Total:** Pass 2-2 100.0%, 43 21.50.

		Punting		
Year Team	G	Punts	Yds	Avg
1977 Hou	14	77	3030	39.4
1978 Hou	16	91	3539	38.9
1979 Hou	16	93	3777	40.6
1980 Hou	16	67	2727	40.7
1981 Hou	16	79	3137	39.7
1982 Hou	4	24	926	38.6
NFL Total	82	431	17136	39.8

RAY PARSON Parson, Ray A 6′4″, 245 **OT**
Col: McCook CC NE; Minnesota *HS:* Uniontown [PA] B: 5/30/1947, Uniontown, PA *Drafted:* 1970 Round 2 Det
1971 Det: 14 G; KR 2-26 13.0.

EARLE PARSONS Parsons, Earle 0 6′0″, 180 **HB-DB**
Col: Rancho Santiago Coll. CA (J.C.); USC *HS:* Helena [MT] B: 1920
AAFC **1946** SF-A: Rec 8-52 6.5; KR 4-94 23.5. **1947** SF-A: Rec 9-163 18.1 2 TD; KR 4-99 24.8. **Total:** Rec 17-215 12.6 2 TD; KR 8-193 24.1.

		Rushing				Punt Returns				Tot
Year Team	G	Att	Yds	Avg	TD	Ret	Yds	Avg	TD	TD
1946 SF-A	10	74	362	4.9	2	15	198	13.2	0	2
1947 SF-A	11	33	125	3.8	0	10	106	10.6	0	2
AAFC Total	21	107	487	4.6	2	25	304	12.2	0	4

LLOYD PARSONS Parsons, Lloyd Marion 5′11″, 197 **FB-LB**
Col: Minnesota; Gustavus Adolphus *HS:* Roosevelt [Minneapolis, MN] B: 6/10/1918, Minneapolis, MN D: 11/1986, Minneapolis, MN
1941 Det: 7 G; Rush 5-9 1.8; Rec 1-3 3.0.

BOB PARSONS Parsons, Robert Herber 6′4″, 234 **P-TE**
Col: Penn State *HS:* Pen Argyl [PA] B: 6/29/1950, Bethlehem, PA *Drafted:* 1972 Round 5 ChiB
1972 ChiB: Rush 1-0; Rec 1-6 6.0 1 TD. **1973** ChiB: Rush 2-2 1.0; Rec 2-23 11.5 1 TD; KR 2-15 7.5. **1974** ChiB: Pass 1-0; Rec 2-9 4.5 1 TD. **1975** ChiB: Pass 1-0; Rec 13-184 14.2 1 TD. **1976** ChiB: Pass 2-2 100.0%, 48 24.00; Rush 1-2 2.0; Rec 1-9 9.0. **1977** ChiB: Pass 4-4 100.0%, 61 15.25. **1978** ChiB: Pass 1-0; Rush 1-0. **1979** ChiB: Pass 2-1

50.0%, 22 11.00. **1980** ChiB: Pass 1-0; Rush 2-4 2.0. **1981** ChiB: Pass 1-0; Rush 1-(-6) -6.0. **1983** ChiB: Rush 1-27 27.0. **Total:** Pass 13-7 53.8%, 131 10.08; Rush 9-29 3.2; Rec 19-231 12.2 4 TD; KR 2-15 7.5.

		Punting			
Year Team	G	Punts	Yds	Avg	Fum
1972 ChiB	13	0	0	—	1
1973 ChiB	14	4	106	26.5	0
1974 ChiB	14	90	3408	37.9	0
1975 ChiB	14	**93**	3625	39.0	2
1976 ChiB	14	99	3726	37.6	0
1977 ChiB	14	80	3232	40.4	0
1978 ChiB	16	96	3549	37.0	2
1979 ChiB	16	92	3486	37.9	0
1980 ChiB	16	79	3207	40.6	2
1981 ChiB	16	**114**	**4531**	39.7	0
1982 ChiB	9	**58**	**2394**	41.3	0
1983 ChiB	14	79	2916	36.9	0
NFL Total	170	884	34180	38.7	7

DENNIS PARTEE Partee, Dennis Franklin 6′1″, 229 **K**
Col: Southern Methodist *HS:* Richfield [Waco, TX]; Irvin HS [El Paso, TX] B: 9/1/1946, Cameron, TX *Drafted:* 1968 Round 11 SD
1971 SD: Rush 1-7 7.0. **Total:** Rush 1-7 7.0.

		Punting		
Year Team	G	Punts	Yds	Avg
1968 SD	14	56	2281	40.7
1969 SD	14	71	3169	**44.6**
1970 SD	13	65	2852	43.9
1971 SD	14	55	2392	43.5
1972 SD	14	45	1813	40.3
1973 SD	14	72	2958	41.1
1974 SD	14	76	3042	40.0
1975 SD	14	79	2910	36.8
NFL Total	111	519	21417	41.3

	Scoring							
Year Team	Pts	FG	FGA	FG%	XK	XKA	XK%	Fum
1968 SD	106	22	32	68.8	40	43	93.0	0
1969 SD	78	15	28	53.6	33	33	100.0	0
1971 SD	87	17	29	58.6	36	37	97.3	0
1972 SD	71	15	25	60.0	26	28	92.9	0
1973 SD	9	1	2	50.0	6	6	100.0	0
1974 SD	29	1	5	20.0	26	28	92.9	0
1975 SD	0	0	0	—	0	0	—	1
NFL Total	380	71	121	58.7	167	175	95.4	1

TY PARTEN Parten, Ty Daniel 6′5″, 278 **DT-DE**
Col: Arizona *HS:* Horizon [Scottsdale, AZ] B: 10/13/1969, Washington, DC *Drafted:* 1993 Round 3 Cin
1993 Cin: 11 G. **1994** Cin: 14 G. **1995** Cin: 1 G. **1997** KC: 2 G. **1998** KC: 16 G; KR 2-22 11.0. **Total:** 44 G; KR 2-22 11.0.

LOU PARTLOW Partlow, Louis J 6′1″, 185 **FB-TB-WB-BB**
Col: No College *HS:* Miamisburg [OH] B: 10/9/1892, Miamisburg, OH D: 4/14/1981, Burbank, CA
1920 Day: 9 G. **1921** Day: 6 G; Pass 1 TD; Rush 1 TD; 6 Pt. **1922** Day: 6 G; Rush 1 TD; 6 Pt. **1923** Day-Cle: 9 G. Day: 8 G. Cle: 1 G. **1924** Day: 8 G; Rush 1 TD; Int **1** TD; Tot TD 2; 12 Pt. **1925** Day: 3 G. **1926** Day: 4 G. **1927** Day: 5 G. **1929** Day: 1 G. **Total:** 51 G; Pass 1 TD; Rush 3 TD; Int 1 TD; Tot TD 4; 24 Pt.

RICK PARTRIDGE Partridge, Richard Blake 6′1″, 175 **P**
Col: Golden West Coll. CA (J.C.); Utah *HS:* Tustin [CA] B: 8/26/1957, Orange, CA *Drafted:* 1979 Round 8 GB
1980 SD: Rush 3-0. **1987** Buf: Rush 1-13 13.0. **Total:** Rush 4-13 3.3.

		Punting		
Year Team	G	Punts	Yds	Avg
1979 NO	13	57	2330	40.9
1980 SD	16	60	2347	39.1
1987 Buf	3	18	678	37.7
NFL Total	32	135	5355	39.7

DOUG PASCHAL Paschal, Douglas Clyde 6′2″, 217 **RB**
Col: North Carolina *HS:* J.H. Rose [Greenville, NC] B: 3/5/1958, Greenville, NC *Drafted:* 1980 Round 5 Min
1980 Min: 16 G; Rush 15-53 3.5 1 TD; Rec 2-18 9.0; KR 4-66 16.5; 6 Pt.

BILL PASCHAL Paschal, William Avner Jr. 6′0″, 201 **FB-DB-LB**
Col: Georgia Tech *HS:* Atlanta Tech [GA] B: 5/28/1921, Atlanta, GA
1943 NYG: Punt 12-418 34.8. **1944** NYG: Pass 8-2 25.0%, 31 3.88 2 Int; Punt 1-6 6.0. **1945** NYG: Pass 1-0. **1946** NYG: Punt 1-47 47.0. **1947** NYG-Bos: Pass 1-0. NYG: Pass 1-0. **1948** Bos: Punt 2-80 40.0. **Total:** Pass 10-2 20.0%, 31 3.10 2 Int; Punt 16-551 34.4.

		Rushing				Receiving			
Year Team	G	Att	Yds	Avg	TD	Rec	Yds	Avg	TD
1943 NYG	9	**147**	**572**	3.9	**10**	9	74	8.2	2
1944 NYG	10	**196**	**737**	3.8	**9**	0	0	—	0
1945 NYG	4	59	247	4.2	2	2	11	5.5	0
1946 NYG	10	117	362	3.1	4	9	78	8.7	2
1947 NYG-Bos	12	78	263	3.4	2	4	70	17.5	0
1947 NYG	4	41	139	3.4	1	1	3	3.0	0
1947 Bos	8	37	124	3.4	1	3	67	22.3	0
1948 Bos	12	80	249	3.1	1	8	93	11.6	4
NFL Total	57	677	2430	3.6	28	32	326	10.2	8

	Punt Returns				Kickoff Returns					Tot
Year Team	Ret	Yds	Avg	TD	Ret	Yds	Avg	TD	Fum	TD
1943 NYG	9	92	10.2	0	7	183	26.1	0	0	**12**
1944 NYG	7	102	14.6	0	9	260	28.9	0	0	**9**
1945 NYG	0	0	—	0	2	43	21.5	0	2	2
1946 NYG	8	85	10.6	0	6	158	26.3	0	6	6
1947 NYG-Bos	1	11	11.0	0	5	103	20.6	0	3	2
1947 NYG	1	11	11.0	0	0	0	—	0	1	1
1947 Bos	0	0	—	0	5	103	20.6	0	2	1
1948 Bos	3	79	26.3	0	24	498	20.8	0	9	5
NFL Total	28	369	13.2	0	53	1245	23.5	0	20	36

GORDON PASCHKA Paschka, Gordon F 6′0″, 220 **FB-LB-G**
Col: Minnesota *HS:* Watertown [MN] B: 3/6/1920, Chaska, MN D: 6/9/1964, Rainy Lake, CA *Drafted:* 1942 Round 4 Phi
1943 PhPt: Scor 2, 2-2 100.0% XK. **1947** NYG: Rec 1-(-6) -6.0; KR 1-20 20.0. **Total:** Rec 1-(-6) -6.0; KR 1-20 20.0; Scor 14, 2-2 100.0% XK.

		Rushing				
Year Team	G	Att	Yds	Avg	TD	Fum
1943 PhPt	10	0	0	—	0	0
1947 NYG	6	48	143	3.0	2	3
NFL Total	16	48	143	3.0	2	3

BILL PASHE Pashe, William Thomas 5′11″, 185 **DB**
Col: George Washington *HS:* Teaneck [NJ] B: 8/5/1940, New York, NY *Drafted:* 1963 Round 18 NYG
1964 NYJ: 4 G; PR 4-28 7.0.

KEITH PASKETT Paskett, Keith Paxton 5′11″, 180 **WR**
Col: Western Kentucky *HS:* Glencliff [Nashville, TN] B: 12/7/1964, Nashville, TN
1987 GB: 12 G; Rec 12-188 15.7 1 TD; 6 Pt.

GEORGE PASKVAN Paskvan, George Oscar 6′0″, 190 **FB-DB**
Col: Wisconsin *HS:* Lyons Twp. [La Grange, IL] B: 4/28/1918, McCook, IL *Drafted:* 1941 Round 1 GB
1941 GB: Int 2-6.

		Rushing			
Year Team	G	Att	Yds	Avg	TD
1941 GB	7	38	116	3.1	0

JOE PASQUA Pasqua, Joseph Bernard 6′1″, 226 **T**
Col: Southern Methodist B: 7/31/1917, Dallas, TX
1942 Cle: 11 G; Scor 1, 1-1 100.0% XK. **1943** Was: 9 G; Scor 1, 1-1 100.0% XK. **1946** LARm: 4 G. **Total:** 24 G; Scor 2, 2-2 100.0% XK.

RON PASQUALE Pasquale, Ronald R 6′2″, 266 **OG**
Col: Akron *HS:* Chaney [Youngstown, OH] B: 2/28/1964, Youngstown, OH
1987 StL: 1 G.

RALPH PASQUARIELLO Pasquariello, Ralph Angelo 6′2″, 237 **FB**
(Pasky) *Col:* Villanova *HS:* Everett [MA] B: 5/30/1926, Brighton, MA *Drafted:* 1950 Round 1 LARm
1950 LARm: Rec 1-2 2.0; KR 1-14 14.0. **1951** ChiC: Rec 2-(-9) -4.5. **1952** ChiC: Rec 7-46 6.6; KR 1-13 13.0. **Total:** Rec 10-39 3.9; KR 2-27 13.5.

		Rushing				
Year Team	G	Att	Yds	Avg	TD	Fum
1950 LARm	9	7	31	4.4	1	0
1951 ChiC	10	53	251	4.7	1	0
1952 ChiC	10	48	129	2.7	0	1
NFL Total	29	108	411	3.8	2	1

TONY PASQUESI Pasquesi, Anthony Leonard 6′4″, 250 **DT-LB**
Col: Notre Dame *HS:* St.Phillip [Chicago, IL] B: 6/13/1933, Chicago, IL *Drafted:* 1955 Round 3 ChiC
1955 ChiC: 7 G. **1956** ChiC: 11 G. **1957** ChiC: 11 G. **Total:** 29 G.

BILL PASSUELO Passuelo, William 6′2″, 230 **G-T**
Col: No College B: 12/23/1897 D: 1/1965, MI
1923 Col: 3 G.

FRANK PASTIN Pastin, Frank Andrew 5′10″, 197 **G-LB**
Col: Waynesburg *HS:* Sto-Rox [McKees Rocks, PA] B: 12/16/1920, Pittsburgh, PA
1942 Pit: 1 G.

DAN PASTORINI Pastorini, Dante Anthony Jr. 6'2", 208 **QB**
Col: Santa Clara *HS:* Bellarmine Prep [San Jose, CA] B: 5/26/1949, Sonora, CA *Drafted:* 1971 Round 1 Hou
1977 Hou: Scor 12, 0-1 XK. **Total:** Scor 48, 0-1 XK.

		Passing							
Year Team	G	Att	Comp	Comp%	Yds	YPA	TD	Int	Rating
1971 Hou	14	270	127	47.0	1702	6.30	7	21	43.8
1972 Hou	14	299	144	48.2	1711	5.72	7	12	57.1
1973 Hou	14	290	154	53.1	1482	5.11	5	17	49.0
1974 Hou	11	247	140	56.7	1571	6.36	10	10	72.4
1975 Hou	14	342	163	47.7	2053	6.00	14	16	61.0
1976 Hou	13	309	167	54.0	1795	5.81	10	10	68.6
1977 Hou	14	319	169	53.0	1987	6.23	13	18	62.3
1978 Hou	16	368	199	54.1	2473	6.72	16	17	70.4
1979 Hou	15	324	163	50.3	2090	6.45	14	18	62.1
1980 Oak	5	130	66	50.8	932	7.17	5	8	61.4
1981 LARm	7	152	64	42.1	719	4.73	2	14	22.9
1983 Phi	3	5	0	0.0	0	0.00	0	0	39.6
NFL Total	140	3055	1556	50.9	18515	6.06	103	161	59.1

	Rushing				Punting			
Year Team	Att	Yds	Avg	TD	Punts	Yds	Avg	Fum
1971 Hou	26	140	5.4	3	75	3044	40.6	3
1972 Hou	38	205	5.4	2	**82**	3381	41.2	6
1973 Hou	31	102	3.3	0	27	1087	40.3	**17**
1974 Hou	24	-6	-0.3	0	0	0	—	8
1975 Hou	23	97	4.2	1	62	2447	39.5	3
1976 Hou	11	45	4.1	0	70	2571	36.7	6
1977 Hou	18	39	2.2	2	0	0	—	7
1978 Hou	18	11	0.6	0	0	0	—	5
1979 Hou	15	23	1.5	0	0	0	—	6
1980 Oak	4	24	6.0	0	0	0	—	3
1981 LARm	7	5	0.7	0	0	0	—	4
1983 Phi	1	0	0.0	0	0	0	—	1
NFL Total	216	685	3.2	8	316	12530	39.7	69

CHUCK PASTRANA Pastrana, Charles Alan 6'1", 190 **QB**
Col: Maryland *HS:* Annapolis [MD] B: 11/20/1944, Annapolis, MD
Drafted: 1969 Round 11 Den
1969 Den: Rec 1-15 15.0. **1970** Den: Rush 14-89 6.4 1 TD.
Total: Rush 14-89 6.4 1 TD; Rec 1-15 15.0.

		Passing								
Year Team	G	Att	Comp	Comp%	Yds	YPA	TD	Int	Rating	Fum
1969 Den	2	0	0	—	0	—	0	0	—	0
1970 Den	5	75	29	38.7	420	5.60	1	9	22.5	1
NFL Total	7	75	29	38.7	420	5.60	1	9	22.5	1

MIKE PATANELLI Patanelli, Michael Joseph 6'2", 218 **DE**
(Superman; Animal) *Col:* Manchester; Bowling Green State; Ball State
HS: Elkhart Central [IN] B: 8/12/1922, Elkhart, IN
AAFC **1947** BknA: 2 G.

LLOYD PATE Pate, Lloyd Robert 6'1", 205 **RB**
Col: Cincinnati *HS:* South [Columbus, OH] B: 3/11/1946, Columbus, OH *Drafted:* 1969 Round 12 Buf
1970 Buf: Rec 19-103 5.4; KR 1-21 21.0.

		Rushing				
Year Team	G	Att	Yds	Avg	TD	Fum
1970 Buf	9	46	162	3.5	1	3

RUPERT PATE Pate, Rupert George 6'1", 205 **G**
(Pete) *Col:* Wake Forest *HS:* Goldsboro [NC] B: 9/6/1917, Goldsboro, NC *Drafted:* 1940 Round 20 ChiC
1940 ChiC: 1 G. **1941** Phi: 1 G. **1942** Phi: 7 G; **1** Fum TD; 6 Pt. **Total:** 9 G; 1 Fum TD; 6 Pt.

DENNIS PATERA Patera, Dennis Allen 6'0", 214 **K**
Col: Columbia Basin Coll. WA (J.C.); Brigham Young *HS:* Cleveland [Portland, OR] B: 10/17/1945, Portland, OR *Drafted:* 1968 Round 17 SF
1968 SF: 5 G; Scor 16, 2-8 25.0% FG, 10-13 76.9% XK.

JACK PATERA Patera, John Arlen 6'1", 234 **LB**
Col: Oregon *HS:* Washington [Portland, OR] B: 8/1/1933, Bismarck, ND *Drafted:* 1955 Round 4 Bal
1955 Bal: 12 G; PR 1-2 2.0; Int 1-8. **1956** Bal: 12 G; Int 2-10. **1957** Bal: 12 G; Int 1-16. **1958** ChiC: 9 G. **1959** ChiC: 12 G; KR 1-0; Int 1-21. **1960** Dal: 3 G; Int 1-21. **1961** Dal: 1 G. **Total:** 61 G; PR 1-2 2.0; KR 1-0; Int 6-76.

GREG PATERRA Paterra, Greg Richard 5'11", 211 **RB**
Col: Harford CC MD; Slippery Rock *HS:* Elizabeth Forward [Elizabeth, PA] B: 5/12/1967, McKeesport, PA *Drafted:* 1989 Round 11 Atl
1989 Atl: 10 G; Rush 9-32 3.6; Rec 5-42 8.4; KR 8-129 16.1; 2 Fum.

HERB PATERRA Paterra, Herbert E 6'1", 232 **LB**
Col: Michigan State *HS:* Glassport [PA] B: 11/8/1940, Glassport, PA
Drafted: 1963 Round 18 Buf
1963 Buf: 10 G; KR 1-0.

JEROME PATHON Pathon, Jerome 6'0", 187 **WR**
Col: Acadia (Canada); Washington *HS:* Carson Graham Secondary School [North Vancouver, Canada] B: 12/16/1975, Capetown, South Africa *Drafted:* 1998 Round 2 Ind
1998 Ind: Rush 3-(-2) -0.7.

		Receiving			
Year Team	G	Rec	Yds	Avg	TD
1998 Ind	16	50	511	10.2	1

MIKE PATRICK Patrick, Charles Michael 6'0", 209 **P**
Col: Mississippi State *HS:* Biloxi [MS] B: 9/6/1952, Austin, TX
1976 NE: Rush 1-(-16) -16.0. **Total:** Rush 1-(-16) -16.0.

		Punting		
Year Team	G	Punts	Yds	Avg
1975 NE	14	83	3223	38.8
1976 NE	14	67	2688	40.1
1977 NE	14	65	2354	36.2
1978 NE	1	7	216	30.9
NFL Total	43	222	8481	38.2

FRANK PATRICK Patrick, Frank Andrew 6'7", 225 **QB**
Col: Nebraska *HS:* Derry [PA] B: 3/11/1947, Derry, PA *Drafted:* 1970 Round 10 GB
1970 GB: 1 G; Pass 14-6 42.9%, 59 4.21 1 Int; Rush 2-5 2.5. **1971** GB: 1 G; Pass 5-1 20.0%, 39 7.80 1 Int. **1972** GB: 2 G; Pass 4-1 25.0%, 9 2.25. **Total:** 4 G; Pass 23-8 34.8%, 107 4.65 2 Int; Rush 2-5 2.5.

FRANK PATRICK Patrick, Frank W 5'11", 190 **TB-DB-BB-LB**
Col: Pittsburgh *HS:* Theodore Roosevelt [East Chicago, IL]
B: 1/16/1916, East Chicago, IN *Drafted:* 1938 Round 2 ChiC
1938 ChiC: Rec 1-21 21.0 1 TD; Scor 17, 1-4 25.0% FG, 8-8 100.0% XK.
1939 ChiC: Punt 16-637 39.8; Scor 7, 1-1 100.0% XK. **Total:** Rec 1-21 21.0 1 TD; Punt 16-637 39.8; Scor 24, 1-4 25.0% FG, 9-9 100.0% XK.

		Passing							
Year Team	G	Att	Comp	Comp%	Yds	YPA	TD	Int	Rating
1938 ChiC	7	1	0	0.0	0	0.00	0	0	39.6
1939 ChiC	8	79	22	27.8	291	3.68	1	13	7.1
NFL Total	15	80	22	27.5	291	3.64	1	13	6.8

	Rushing				Tot
Year Team	Att	Yds	Avg	TD	TD
1938 ChiC	1	1	1.0	0	1
1939 ChiC	30	84	2.8	1	1
NFL Total	31	85	2.7	1	2

GARIN PATRICK Patrick, Garin James 6'3", 269 **OG**
Col: Louisville *HS:* St. Thomas Aquinas [Canton, OH] B: 8/31/1971, Canton, OH
1995 Ind: 5 G.

JOHN PATRICK Patrick, John Raymond 6'0", 202 **BB-LB-FB**
(Honey) *Col:* Penn State *HS:* Shade Twp. [Central City, PA]; Schenley HS [Pittsburgh, PA] B: 1/16/1918, Central City, PA *Drafted:* 1941 Round 10 Phi
1941 Pit: 11 G; Rec 1-12 12.0; KR 1-12 12.0; Int 1-25. **1945** Pit: 3 G.
1946 Pit: 4 G. **Total:** 18 G; Rec 1-12 12.0; KR 1-12 12.0; Int 1-25.

WAYNE PATRICK Patrick, Wayne Allen 6'2", 254 **RB**
Col: Louisville *HS:* Lincoln [Gainesville, FL] B: 9/1/1946, Gainesville, FL *Drafted:* 1968 Round 10 Cin
1970 Buf: KR 3-38 12.7. **Total:** KR 3-38 12.7.

		Rushing				Receiving					Tot
Year Team	G	Att	Yds	Avg	TD	Rec	Yds	Avg	TD	Fum	TD
1968 Buf	3	1	2	2.0	0	1	5	5.0	0	0	0
1969 Buf	14	83	361	4.3	3	35	229	6.5	0	6	3
1970 Buf	9	66	259	3.9	1	16	142	8.9	0	4	1
1971 Buf	14	79	332	4.2	1	36	327	9.1	0	5	1
1972 Buf	13	35	130	3.7	0	8	42	5.3	1	3	1
NFL Total	53	264	1084	4.1	5	96	745	7.8	1	18	6

MAURY PATT Patt, Maurice Howard 6'2", 205 **OE-DE**
(Babe) *Col:* Carnegie Mellon *HS:* Altoona [PA] B: 1/31/1915, Altoona, PA D: 4/2/1961, Altoona, PA *Drafted:* 1937 Round 5 Det
1938 Det: Rush 3-30 10.0. **1939** Cle: Rush 6-20 3.3. **1940** Cle: Rush 1-0.
1941 Cle: Rush 5-16 3.2. **Total:** Rush 15-66 4.4.

		Receiving			
Year Team	G	Rec	Yds	Avg	TD
1938 Det	10	7	80	11.4	0
1939 Cle	10	15	165	11.0	0
1940 Cle	10	2	52	26.0	1

1941 Cle	11	17	163	9.6	1
1942 Cle	7	0	0	—	0
NFL Total	48	41	460	11.2	2

DAVID PATTEN Patten, David 5′9″, 180 **WR**
Col: Western Carolina *HS:* Lower Richland [Hopkins, SC]
B: 8/19/1974, Hopkins, SC
1997 NYG: Rush 1-2 2.0; Rec 13-226 17.4 2 TD. **1998** NYG: Rec 11-119 10.8 1 TD. **Total:** Rush 1-2 2.0; Rec 24-345 14.4 3 TD.

		Kickoff Returns					Tot
Year Team	**G**	**Ret**	**Yds**	**Avg**	**TD**	**Fum**	**TD**
1997 NYG	16	8	123	15.4	0	2	2
1998 NYG	12	43	928	21.6	1	0	2
NFL Total	28	51	1051	20.6	1	2	4

JOEL PATTEN Patten, John Lawrence II 6′7″, 310 **OT**
Col: Duke *HS:* Robinson Secondary School [Fairfax, VA] B: 2/7/1958, Augsburg, Germany
1980 Cle: 6 G. **1987** Ind: 12 G. **1988** Ind: 15 G. **1989** SD: 14 G. **1990** SD: 8 G. **1991** LARd: 1 G. **Total:** 56 G.

PATTERSON Patterson 1 **BB-G**
Col: No College Deceased
1921 Cle: 2 G.

CLETE PATTERSON Patterson, Clitus Henry 5′10″, 205 **G**
Col: Ohio U. *HS:* Wellsville [OH] B: 3/18/1902, Wellsville, OH Deceased
1924 Ken: 3 G.

CRAIG PATTERSON Patterson, Craig Allan 6′4″, 314 **NT**
Col: Brigham Young *HS:* Emery Co. [Castle Dale, UT] B: 7/18/1964, Santa Cruz, CA
1991 Pho: 16 G; Int 1-0.

DON PATTERSON Patterson, Donald Ray 5′11″, 175 **DB**
Col: Georgia Tech *HS:* Jones Co. [Gray, GA] B: 10/31/1957, Gray, GA
1979 Det: 2 G. **1980** NYG: 3 G. **Total:** 5 G.

ELVIS PATTERSON Patterson, Elvis Vernell 5′11″, 193 **DB**
(Toast) *Col:* Kansas *HS:* Jack Yates [Houston, TX] B: 10/21/1960, Bryan, TX
1985 NYG: 0.5 Sac. **1988** SD: 1 Sac. **1991** LARd: Rec 1-34 34.0; 1 Fum TD. **Total:** Rec 1-34 34.0; 1 Fum TD; 1.5 Sac.

		Interceptions			Tot
Year Team	**G**	**Int**	**Yds**	**TD**	**TD**
1984 NYG	15	0	0	0	0
1985 NYG	16	6	88	**1**	1
1986 NYG	15	2	26	0	0
1987 NYG-SD	14	1	75	1	1
1987 NYG	1	0	0	0	0
1987 SD	13	1	75	1	1
1988 SD	14	1	0	0	0
1989 SD	16	2	44	0	0
1990 LARd	16	0	0	0	0
1991 LARd	16	0	0	0	1
1992 LARd	15	0	0	0	1
1993 LARd-Dal	14	0	0	0	0
1993 LARd	3	0	0	0	0
1993 Dal	11	0	0	0	0
NFL Total	151	12	233	2	4

GORDON PATTERSON Patterson, Gordon 165 **OE**
Col: No College B: 3/1900, St. Johnsbury, VT Deceased
1921 Was: 3 G.

BILLY PATTERSON Patterson, Joseph William Jr. 5′10″, 167 **TB-DB-QB-HB**
Col: Baylor *HS:* Hillsboro [TX] B: 8/28/1918, Hillsboro, TX
D: 7/8/1998, McAllen, TX *Drafted:* 1939 Round 3 Pit
1939 ChiB: Scor 1, 1-1 100.0% XK. **Total:** Scor 1, 1-1 100.0% XK.

		Passing							
Year Team	**G**	**Att**	**Comp**	**Comp%**	**Yds**	**YPA**	**TD**	**Int**	**Rating**
1939 ChiB	8	38	14	36.8	227	5.97	3	4	44.4
1940 Pit	11	117	34	29.1	529	4.52	3	15	14.9
NFL Total	19	155	48	31.0	756	4.88	6	19	21.5

	Rushing				Punting		
Year Team	**Att**	**Yds**	**Avg**	**TD**	**Punts**	**Yds**	**Avg**
1939 ChiB	14	34	2.4	0	8	300	37.5
1940 Pit	87	171	2.0	0	43	1693	39.4
NFL Total	101	205	2.0	0	51	1993	39.1

SHAWN PATTERSON Patterson, Kenneth Shawn 6′5″, 267 **DE-NT**
Col: Arizona State *HS:* McClintock [Tempe, AZ] B: 6/13/1964, Tempe, AZ *Drafted:* 1988 Round 2 GB
1988 GB: 15 G; 4 Sac. **1989** GB: 6 G; 0.5 Sac. **1990** GB: 11 G; Int 1-9 1 TD; 6 Pt; 4 Sac. **1991** GB: 11 G; 1.5 Sac. **1993** GB: 5 G; 1 Sac.
Total: 48 G; Int 1-9 1 TD; 6 Pt; 11 Sac.

PAUL PATTERSON Patterson, Paul L 5′9″, 185 **WB-DB**
Col: Illinois *HS:* Aurora East [IL] B: 2/16/1927, Aurora, IL
D: 6/11/1982, Chicago, IL
AAFC **1949** ChiA: 12 G; Rush 2-0; Rec 16-304 19.0 4 TD; PR 4-33 8.3; Int 3-104; 24 Pt.

RENO PATTERSON Patterson, Reno 6′3″, 275 **NT**
Col: Bethune-Cookman *HS:* Martin Luther King [Chicago, IL]
B: 4/22/1961, Chicago, IL
1987 SF: 1 G.

DARRELL PATTILLO Pattillo, Darrell Lester 5′10″, 194 **DB**
Col: Los Angeles Valley Coll. CA (J.C.); Long Beach State *HS:* Daniel Murphy [Los Angeles, CA] B: 9/28/1960, Los Angeles, CA
1983 SD: 1 G.

MARK PATTISON Pattison, Mark Lester 6′2″, 190 **WR**
Col: Washington *HS:* Roosevelt [Seattle, WA] B: 12/13/1961, Seattle, WA *Drafted:* 1985 Round 7 LARd
1986 LARm-LARd: 3 G; Rec 2-12 6.0. LARm: 1 G. LARd: 2 G; Rec 2-12 6.0. **1987** NO: 9 G; Rec 9-132 14.7. **1988** NO: 6 G; Rec 1-8 8.0.
Total: 18 G; Rec 12-152 12.7.

JAMES PATTON Patton, James Gregory 6′3″, 287 **NT-DE**
Col: Texas *HS:* Clear Creek [League City, TX] B: 1/5/1970, Houston, TX *Drafted:* 1992 Round 2 Buf
1993 Buf: 2 G. **1994** Buf: 11 G; KR 1-1 1.0. **Total:** 13 G; KR 1-1 1.0.

JIMMY PATTON Patton, James Russell Jr. 5′10″, 183 **DB**
Col: Mississippi *HS:* E.E. Bass [Greenville, MS] B: 9/29/1933, Greenville, MS D: 12/22/1972, Villa Rica, GA *Drafted:* 1955 Round 8 NYG
1956 NYG: Rush 2-(-1) -0.5. **Total:** Rush 2-(-1) -0.5.

		Punt Returns				Kickoff Returns			
Year Team	**G**	**Ret**	**Yds**	**Avg**	**TD**	**Ret**	**Yds**	**Avg**	**TD**
1955 NYG	11	3	69	23.0	1	5	229	45.8	**1**
1956 NYG	12	12	17	1.4	0	13	283	21.8	0
1957 NYG	12	11	29	2.6	0	10	223	22.3	0
1958 NYG	12	1	5	5.0	0	0	0	—	0
1959 NYG	11	8	23	2.9	0	0	0	—	0
1960 NYG	12	1	0	0.0	0	0	0	—	0
1961 NYG	14	0	0	—	0	0	0	—	0
1962 NYG	14	1	0	0.0	0	0	0	—	0
1963 NYG	14	0	0	—	0	0	0	—	0
1964 NYG	14	0	0	—	0	0	0	—	0
1965 NYG	14	0	0	—	0	0	0	—	0
1966 NYG	13	0	0	—	0	0	0	—	0
NFL Total	153	37	143	3.9	1	28	735	26.3	1

	Interceptions				Tot
Year Team	**Int**	**Yds**	**TD**	**Fum**	**TD**
1955 NYG	1	0	0	0	2
1956 NYG	1	2	0	2	0
1957 NYG	3	50	1	2	1
1958 NYG	**11**	183	0	0	0
1959 NYG	5	13	0	0	0
1960 NYG	6	100	0	1	0
1961 NYG	8	163	1	0	1
1962 NYG	7	125	0	1	0
1963 NYG	6	46	0	0	0
1964 NYG	2	0	0	0	0
1965 NYG	1	27	0	1	0
1966 NYG	1	3	0	0	0
NFL Total	52	712	2	7	4

JERRY PATTON Patton, Jerry Armstead 6′3″, 265 **DT**
Col: Nebraska *HS:* Saginaw [MI] B: 3/27/1946, Saginaw, MI
D: 5/20/1983, Shreveport, LA
1971 Min: 3 G. **1972** Buf: 14 G. **1973** Buf: 14 G. **1974** Phi: 14 G; Int 1-4.
1975 NE: 3 G. **Total:** 48 G; Int 1-4.

CLIFF PATTON Patton, John Clifton 6′2″, 243 **OG-DG-LB**
Col: Texas Christian *HS:* Big Spring [TX] B: 7/29/1923, Clyde, TX
1951 ChiC: Int 3-31. **Total:** Int 3-31.

		Scoring						
Year Team	**G**	**Pts**	**FG**	**FGA**	**FG%**	**XK**	**XKA**	**XK%**
1946 Phi	4	0	0	0	—	0	0	—
1947 Phi	12	45	3	14	21.4	36	40	90.0
1948 Phi	12	74	**8**	12	**66.7**	50	50	**100.0**
1949 Phi	12	69	**9**	18	50.0	42	43	97.7
1950 Phi	12	56	8	17	47.1	32	33	97.0
1951 ChiC	12	34	5	8	62.5	19	19	100.0
NFL Total	64	278	33	69	47.8	179	185	96.8

JOE PATTON Patton, Joseph Cephus IV 6′5″, 306 **OT-OG**
Col: Alabama A&M *HS:* Jones Valley [Birmingham, AL] B: 1/5/1972, Birmingham, AL *Drafted:* 1994 Round 3 Was
1994 Was: 2 G. **1995** Was: 16 G. **1996** Was: 16 G. **1997** Was: 16 G.
1998 Was: 11 G. **Total:** 61 G.

MARVCUS PATTON Patton, Marvcus Raymond 6'2", 236 **LB**
Col: UCLA *HS:* Leuzinger [Lawndale, CA] B: 5/1/1967, Los Angeles, CA *Drafted:* 1990 Round 8 Buf
1990 Buf: 0.5 Sac. **1992** Buf: 2 Sac. **1993** Buf: 1 Sac. **1995** Was: 2 Sac. **1996** Was: 2 Sac. **1997** Was: KR 1-10 10.0; 4.5 Sac. **1998** Was: 3 Sac. **Total:** KR 1-10 10.0; 15 Sac.

		Interceptions			
Year Team	G	Int	Yds	TD	Fum
1990 Buf	16	0	0	0	0
1991 Buf	16	0	0	0	0
1992 Buf	16	0	0	0	0
1993 Buf	16	2	0	0	0
1994 Buf	16	2	8	0	1
1995 Was	16	2	7	0	0
1996 Was	16	2	26	0	0
1997 Was	16	2	5	0	0
1998 Was	16	0	0	0	0
NFL Total	144	10	46	0	1

RICKY PATTON Patton, Ricky Riccardo 5'11", 190 **RB**
Col: Ferris State; Michigan; Jackson State *HS:* Southwestern [Flint, MI] B: 4/6/1954, Flint, MI *Drafted:* 1978 Round 10 Atl
1980 SF: KR 4-43 10.8. **1981** SF: KR 1-0. **Total:** KR 5-43 8.6.

		Rushing				Receiving					Tot
Year Team	G	Att	Yds	Avg	TD	Rec	Yds	Avg	TD	Fum	TD
1978 Atl	16	68	206	3.0	1	10	90	9.0	1	6	2
1979 Atl-GB	10	40	135	3.4	0	6	41	6.8	0	1	0
1979 Atl	4	3	1	0.3	0	0	0	—	0	0	0
1979 GB	6	37	134	3.6	0	6	41	6.8	0	1	0
1980 SF	9	1	1	1.0	0	0	0	—	0	1	0
1981 SF	16	152	543	3.6	4	27	195	7.2	1	3	5
1982 SF	1	0	0	—	0	0	0	—	0	0	0
NFL Total	52	261	885	3.4	5	43	326	7.6	2	11	7

ROBERT PATTON Patton, Robert Harold 6'0", 226 **OG**
Col: Clemson *HS:* Gray Court-Owings [Gray Court, SC] B: 8/25/1927, Oakland, CA Deceased *Drafted:* 1952 Round 5 NYG
1952 NYG: 12 G.

BOB PATTON Patton, Robert Thomas 6'1", 245 **C**
Col: Delaware *HS:* Central Catholic [Kingston, PA] B: 10/21/1954, Camp Lejeune, NC
1976 Buf: 12 G.

WALT PATULSKI Patulski, Walter George 6'6", 259 **DE**
Col: Notre Dame *HS:* Christian Brothers Acad. [Syracuse, NY] B: 2/3/1950, Fulton, NY *Drafted:* 1972 Round 1 Buf
1972 Buf: 14 G. **1973** Buf: 14 G. **1974** Buf: 14 G. **1975** Buf: 14 G. **1977** StL: 14 G. **Total:** 70 G.

DON PAUL Paul, Don 6'1", 228 **LB-C**
Col: UCLA *HS:* Los Angeles [CA] B: 3/18/1925, Fresno, CA *Drafted:* 1946 Round 3 LARm
1949 LARm: KR 2-32 16.0. **Total:** KR 2-32 16.0.

		Interceptions		
Year Team	G	Int	Yds	TD
1948 LARm	11	0	0	0
1949 LARm	12	2	23	0
1950 LARm	10	3	44	0
1951 LARm	12	1	16	0
1952 LARm	12	2	40	0
1953 LARm	10	3	50	0
1954 LARm	12	0	0	0
1955 LARm	8	0	0	0
NFL Total	87	11	173	0

DON PAUL Paul, Donald Ray 6'0", 187 **DB-HB**
Col: Washington State *HS:* Fife [WA] B: 7/23/1926, Tacoma, WA *Drafted:* 1950 Round 4 ChiC
1953 ChiC: Pass 2-1 50.0%, 13 6.50. **1957** Cle: 1 Fum TD. **Total:** Pass 2-1 50.0%, 13 6.50; 1 Fum TD.

		Rushing				Receiving			
Year Team	G	Att	Yds	Avg	TD	Rec	Yds	Avg	TD
1950 ChiC	12	14	80	5.7	0	5	93	18.6	1
1951 ChiC	12	37	247	6.7	3	23	398	17.3	3
1952 ChiC	5	6	28	4.7	0	4	32	8.0	1
1953 ChiC	12	16	114	7.1	0	16	167	10.4	2
1954 Cle	12	0	0	—	0	0	0	—	0
1955 Cle	11	0	0	—	0	0	0	—	0
1956 Cle	12	0	0	—	0	0	0	—	0
1957 Cle	12	0	0	—	0	0	0	—	0
1958 Cle	12	0	0	—	0	0	0	—	0
NFL Total	100	73	469	6.4	3	48	690	14.4	7

	Punt Returns				Kickoff Returns			
Year Team	Ret	Yds	Avg	TD	Ret	Yds	Avg	TD
1950 ChiC	18	194	10.8	1	**28**	693	24.8	0
1951 ChiC	19	143	7.5	0	15	424	28.3	0
1952 ChiC	10	97	9.7	0	3	54	18.0	0
1953 ChiC	18	85	4.7	0	4	106	26.5	0
1954 Cle	1	57	57.0	0	1	31	31.0	0
1955 Cle	19	148	7.8	1	5	109	21.8	0
1956 Cle	17	103	6.1	0	0	0	—	0
1957 Cle	9	75	8.3	0	0	0	—	0
1958 Cle	2	0	0.0	0	1	0	0.0	0
NFL Total	113	902	8.0	2	57	1417	24.9	0

	Interceptions				Tot
Year Team	Int	Yds	TD	Fum	TD
1950 ChiC	4	90	0	2	2
1951 ChiC	3	52	0	4	6
1952 ChiC	0	0	0	0	1
1953 ChiC	5	62	0	3	2
1954 Cle	3	42	0	0	0
1955 Cle	4	49	0	0	1
1956 Cle	7	190	1	2	1
1957 Cle	4	28	0	0	1
1958 Cle	4	80	0	0	0
NFL Total	34	593	1	11	14

HAROLD PAUL Paul, Harold Jr. 6'5", 245 **OT**
Col: Texas Southern; Oklahoma *HS:* Ball [Galveston, TX] B: 11/8/1949, Galveston, TX
1974 SD: 1 G.

MARKUS PAUL Paul, Markus Dwayne 6'2", 200 **DB**
Col: Syracuse *HS:* Osceola [Kissimmee, FL] B: 4/1/1966, Orlando, FL *Drafted:* 1989 Round 4 ChiB
1989 ChiB: 16 G; Int 1-20. **1990** ChiB: 16 G; Int 2-49; 1 Fum. **1991** ChiB: 14 G; Int 3-21. **1992** ChiB: 16 G; Int 1-10. **1993** ChiB-TB: 9 G. ChiB: 8 G. TB: 1 G. **Total:** 71 G; Int 7-100; 1 Fum.

TITO PAUL Paul, Tito Jermaine 6'0", 195 **DB**
Col: Ohio State *HS:* Osceola [Kissimmee, FL] B: 12/7/1972, Kissimmee, FL *Drafted:* 1995 Round 5 Ariz
1995 Ariz: 14 G; Int 1-4. **1996** Ariz: 16 G. **1997** Ariz-Cin: 15 G. Ariz: 1 G. Cin: 14 G. **1998** Den: 16 G; PR 1-0; 1 Fum. **Total:** 61 G; PR 1-0; Int 1-4; 1 Fum.

WHITNEY PAUL Paul, Whitney 6'3", 220 **LB-DE**
Col: Colorado *HS:* Ball [Galveston, TX] B: 10/8/1953, Galveston, TX *Drafted:* 1976 Round 10 KC
1978 KC: KR 1-0. **1980** KC: **1** Fum TD. **1981** KC: 1 Fum TD. **1982** NO: 3 Sac. **1983** NO: 5.5 Sac. **1984** NO: 9.5 Sac. **1985** NO: 5 Sac. **1986** KC: 1.5 Sac. **Total:** KR 1-0; 2 Fum TD; 24.5 Sac.

		Interceptions			
Year Team	G	Int	Yds	TD	Fum
1976 KC	14	0	0	0	0
1977 KC	14	1	6	0	0
1978 KC	16	3	21	0	1
1979 KC	15	1	28	0	0
1980 KC	12	1	0	0	0
1981 KC	16	2	30	0	0
1982 NO	9	1	14	0	0
1983 NO	16	2	3	0	0
1984 NO	16	0	0	0	0
1985 NO	14	0	0	0	0
1986 KC	13	0	0	0	0
NFL Total	155	11	102	0	1

TONY PAULEKAS Paulekas, Anthony J Jr. 5'10", 210 **G-C-LB**
Col: Washington & Jefferson *HS:* Farrell [PA] B: 8/11/1912, Cherry Hill, PA D: 9/18/1995, Farrell, PA
1936 GB: 10 G.

DAINARD PAULSON Paulson, Dainard Alexander 6'0", 190 **DB**
Col: Oregon State *HS:* Morningside [Inglewood, CA] B: 5/15/1937, Los Angeles, CA
1962 NYT: Punt 3-113 37.7. **1964** NYJ: PR 8-34 4.3. **1965** NYJ: KR 1-0. **Total:** PR 8-34 4.3; KR 1-0; Punt 3-113 37.7.

		Interceptions			
Year Team	G	Int	Yds	TD	Fum
1961 NYT	14	1	0	0	0
1962 NYT	14	3	0	0	0
1963 NYJ	14	6	114	0	0
1964 NYJ	14	**12**	157	**1**	3
1965 NYJ	14	7	72	0	2
1966 NYJ	14	0	0	0	0
NFL Total	84	29	343	1	5

FRANK PAULY Pauly, Frank George 6′1″, 270 **T**
(Heavy) *Col:* Washington & Jefferson *HS:* Morrison R. Waite [Toledo, OH] B: 1/24/1904 D: 6/10/1968
1930 ChiB: 6 G.

BRYCE PAUP Paup, Bryce Eric 6′5″, 247 **LB**
Col: Northern Iowa *HS:* Scranton [IA] B: 2/29/1968, Jefferson, IA
Drafted: 1990 Round 6 GB
1990 GB: 5 G. **1991** GB: 12 G; Scor 1 Saf; 2 Pt; 7.5 Sac. **1992** GB: 16 G; 6.5 Sac. **1993** GB: 15 G; Int 1-8; 11 Sac. **1994** GB: 16 G; Int 3-47 1 TD; 6 Pt; 7.5 Sac. **1995** Buf: 15 G; Int 2-0; **17.5** Sac. **1996** Buf: 12 G; 6 Sac. **1997** Buf: 16 G; 9.5 Sac. **1998** Jac: 16 G; 6.5 Sac. **Total:** 123 G; Int 6-55 1 TD; Scor 1 Saf; 8 Pt; 72 Sac.

TED PAVELEC Pavelec, Theodore Charles 6′0″, 218 **T-G**
Col: Detroit Mercy *HS:* St. Augustine [Kalamazoo, MI] B: 11/4/1918, Kalamazoo, MI *Drafted:* 1941 Round 10 Det
1941 Det: 10 G. **1942** Det: 10 G; Scor 3, 1-2 50.0% FG. **1943** Det: 5 G. **Total:** 25 G; Scor 3, 1-2 50.0% FG.

STAN PAVKOV Pavkov, Stonko 6′0″, 212 **G**
Col: Idaho *HS:* Gooding [ID] B: 10/23/1916, Gooding, ID
1939 Pit: 2 G. **1940** Pit: 9 G. **Total:** 11 G.

CHARLIE PAVLICH Pavlich, Charles J 6′2″, 210 **G**
Col: No College *HS:* Muskegon [MI] B: 1921
AAFC **1946** SF-A: 10 G.

CHARLIE PAYNE Payne, Charles Martin 5′11″, 186 **WB-DB**
Col: Detroit Mercy *HS:* Calumet [Chicago, IL] B: 10/27/1914
1937 Det: 1 G.

KEN PAYNE Payne, Kenneth Eugene Jr. 6′1″, 185 **WR**
Col: Langston *HS:* Dunjee [Spencer, OK] B: 10/6/1950, Oklahoma City, OK *Drafted:* 1974 Round 6 GB
1975 GB: Rush 1-(-2) -2.0. **1978** Phi: Rush 1-17 17.0. **Total:** Rush 2-15 7.5.

		Receiving				
Year Team	G	Rec	Yds	Avg	TD	Fum
1974 GB	12	5	63	12.6	0	0
1975 GB	14	58	766	13.2	0	1
1976 GB	14	33	467	14.2	4	1
1977 GB	4	7	99	14.1	1	0
1978 Phi	16	13	238	18.3	1	0
NFL Total	60	116	1633	14.1	6	2

ROD PAYNE Payne, Reginald Gerald 6′4″, 305 **C**
Col: Michigan *HS:* Miami Killian [FL] B: 6/14/1974, Miami, FL
Drafted: 1997 Round 3 Cin
1998 Cin: 6 G.

SETH PAYNE Payne, Seth Copeland 6′4″, 291 **DT**
Col: Cornell *HS:* Victor Central [NY] B: 2/12/1975, Clifton Springs, NY
Drafted: 1997 Round 4 Jac
1997 Jac: 12 G. **1998** Jac: 6 G. **Total:** 18 G.

RUSSELL PAYNE Payne, William Russell 6′1″, 240 **TE**
Col: Appalachian State *HS:* First Colonial [Virginia Beach, VA]
B: 3/21/1965, Virginia Beach, VA
1987 Den: 1 G; Rec 1-8 8.0.

EDDIE PAYTON Payton, Edward 5′8″, 175 **RB**
(Sweet P) *Col:* Jackson State *HS:* Columbia [MS] B: 8/3/1951, Columbia, MS
1977 Cle-Det: Pass 1-0; Rush 4-13 3.3; Rec 2-10 5.0. Det: Pass 1-0; Rush 4-13 3.3; Rec 2-10 5.0. **1980** Min: Rush 2-15 7.5. **Total:** Pass 1-0; Rush 6-28 4.7; Rec 2-10 5.0.

		Punt Returns				Kickoff Returns					Tot
Year Team	G	Ret	Yds	Avg	TD	Ret	Yds	Avg	TD	Fum	TD
1977 Cle-Det	10	30	290	9.7	1	22	548	24.9	1	4	2
1977 Cle	2	3	17	5.7	0	4	91	22.8	0	1	0
1977 Det	8	27	273	10.1	1	18	457	25.4	1	3	2
1978 KC	14	32	364	11.4	0	30	775	25.8	0	6	0
1980 Min	16	34	251	7.4	0	**53**	**1184**	22.3	0	3	0
1981 Min	16	38	303	8.0	0	39	898	23.0	**1**	5	1
1982 Min	9	22	179	8.1	0	12	271	22.6	0	3	0
NFL Total	65	156	1387	8.9	1	156	3676	23.6	2	21	3

SEAN PAYTON Payton, Patrick Sean 5′11″, 200 **QB**
Col: Eastern Illinois *HS:* Naperville [IL] B: 12/29/1963, Naperville, IL
1987 ChiB: 3 G; Pass 23-8 34.8%, 79 3.43 1 Int; Rush 1-28 28.0; 1 Fum.

WALTER PAYTON Payton, Walter Jerry 5′10″, 200 **RB**
(Sweetness) *Col:* Jackson State *HS:* Columbia [MS] B: 7/25/1954, Columbia, MS *Drafted:* 1975 Round 1 ChiB *HOF:* 1993
1975 ChiB: Pass 1-0, 1 Int; KR 14-444 **31.7**; Punt 1-39 39.0. **1976** ChiB: KR 1-0. **1977** ChiB: KR 2-95 47.5. **1979** ChiB: Pass 1-1 100.0%, 54 54.00 1 TD. **1980** ChiB: Pass 3-0. **1981** ChiB: Pass 2-0. **1982** ChiB: Pass 3-1 33.3%, 39 13.00 1 TD. **1983** ChiB: Pass 6-3 50.0%, 95 15.83 3 TD 2 Int. **1984** ChiB: Pass 8-3 37.5%, 47 5.88 2 TD 1 Int. **1985** ChiB: Pass 5-3 60.0%, 96 19.20 1 TD. **1986** ChiB: Pass 4-0, 1 Int. **1987** ChiB: Pass 1-0, 1 Int. **Total:** Pass 34-11 32.4%, 331 9.74 8 TD 6 Int; KR 17-539 31.7; Punt 1-39 39.0.

		Rushing				Receiving					Tot
Year Team	G	Att	Yds	Avg	TD	Rec	Yds	Avg	TD	Fum	TD
1975 ChiB	13	196	679	3.5	7	33	213	6.5	0	9	7
1976 ChiB	14	**311**	1390	4.5	13	15	149	9.9	0	10	13
1977 ChiB	14	**339**	**1852**	**5.5**	**14**	27	269	10.0	2	11	**16**
1978 ChiB	16	**333**	1395	4.2	11	50	480	9.6	0	5	11
1979 ChiB	16	**369**	1610	4.4	14	31	313	10.1	2	7	16
1980 ChiB	16	317	1460	4.6	6	46	367	8.0	1	5	7
1981 ChiB	16	339	1222	3.6	6	41	379	9.2	2	9	8
1982 ChiB	9	148	596	4.0	1	32	311	9.7	0	3	1
1983 ChiB	16	314	1421	4.5	6	53	607	11.5	2	5	8
1984 ChiB	16	381	1684	4.4	11	45	368	8.2	0	5	11
1985 ChiB	16	324	1551	4.8	9	49	483	9.9	2	6	11
1986 ChiB	16	321	1333	4.2	8	37	382	10.3	3	6	11
1987 ChiB	12	146	533	3.7	4	33	217	6.6	1	5	5
NFL Total	190	**3838**	**16726**	4.4	110	492	4538	9.2	15	86	125

DWIGHT PEABODY Peabody, Dwight Van Dorn 5′11″, 170 **OE-BB**
Col: Ohio State *HS:* Oberlin [OH] B: 1/26/1894, Oberlin, OH
D: 1/3/1972, Venice, FL
1920 Col: 1 G. **1922** Tol: 7 G. **Total:** 8 G.

LARRY PEACE Peace, Lawrence 5′11″, 185 **HB-DB**
Col: Pittsburgh *HS:* Bradford [PA] B: 2/13/1917, Bradford, PA
1941 Bkn: 7 G; Rush 4-2 0.5; Scor 1, 1-1 100.0% XK.

ELVIS PEACOCK Peacock, Elvis Zaring 6′1″, 212 **RB**
Col: Oklahoma *HS:* Miami Central [FL] B: 11/7/1956, Miami, FL
Drafted: 1978 Round 1 LARm
1979 LARm: KR 3-46 15.3. **Total:** KR 3-46 15.3.

		Rushing				Receiving					Tot
Year Team	G	Att	Yds	Avg	TD	Rec	Yds	Avg	TD	Fum	TD
1979 LARm	11	52	224	4.3	0	21	261	12.4	0	1	0
1980 LARm	13	164	777	4.7	7	25	213	8.5	2	1	9
1981 Cin	3	0	0	—	0	0	0	—	0	0	0
NFL Total	27	216	1001	4.6	7	46	474	10.3	2	2	9

JOHNNY PEACOCK Peacock, John Byron 6′1″, 200 **DB**
(Cocky) *Col:* Houston *HS:* Goliad [TX] B: 3/2/1947, Austin, TX
Drafted: 1969 Round 5 Hou
1969 Hou: 14 G; Int 2-56; **1** Fum TD; 6 Pt. **1970** Hou: 14 G; Int 3-24; 1 Fum TD; 6 Pt. **Total:** 28 G; Int 5-80; 2 Fum TD; 12 Pt.

CLARENCE PEAKS Peaks, Clarence Earl 6′1″, 218 **FB**
(High) *Col:* Michigan State *HS:* Central [Flint, MI] B: 9/23/1935, Greenville, MS *Drafted:* 1957 Round 1 Phi
1957 Phi: Pass 3-2 66.7%, 56 18.67 1 Int. **1961** Phi: Pass 1-0. **Total:** Pass 4-2 50.0%, 56 14.00 1 Int.

		Rushing				Receiving			
Year Team	G	Att	Yds	Avg	TD	Rec	Yds	Avg	TD
1957 Phi	12	125	495	4.0	1	11	99	9.0	0
1958 Phi	11	115	386	3.4	3	29	248	8.6	2
1959 Phi	12	124	451	3.6	3	28	209	7.5	0
1960 Phi	7	86	465	5.4	3	14	116	8.3	0
1961 Phi	13	135	471	3.5	5	32	472	14.8	0
1962 Phi	14	137	447	3.3	3	39	347	8.9	0
1963 Phi	14	64	212	3.3	1	22	167	7.6	1
1964 Pit	12	118	503	4.3	2	12	113	9.4	0
1965 Pit	10	47	230	4.9	0	3	22	7.3	0
NFL Total	105	951	3660	3.8	21	190	1793	9.4	3

	Kickoff Returns					Tot
Year Team	Ret	Yds	Avg	TD	Fum	TD
1957 Phi	5	98	19.6	0	5	1
1958 Phi	0	0	—	0	9	5
1959 Phi	0	0	—	0	7	3
1960 Phi	0	0	—	0	2	3
1961 Phi	2	29	14.5	0	2	5
1962 Phi	0	0	—	0	9	3
1963 Phi	0	0	—	0	5	2
1964 Pit	12	326	27.2	0	4	2
1965 Pit	20	429	21.5	0	3	0
NFL Total	39	882	22.6	0	46	24

DAVE PEAR Pear, David Louis 6′2″, 250 **NT-DT**
Col: Washington *HS:* Benson Polytechnic [Portland, OR] B: 6/1/1953, Vancouver, WA *Drafted:* 1975 Round 3 Bal
1975 Bal: 13 G. **1976** TB: 13 G. **1977** TB: 14 G. **1978** TB: 16 G. **1979** Oak: 16 G. **1980** Oak: 7 G. **Total:** 79 G.

HARLEY PEARCE Pearce, Harley Charles 5′10″, 180 **E-TB-BB-WB**
Col: Ohio Wesleyan *HS:* Hillsboro [OH]; Lake Forest Acad. [IL]
B: 3/24/1901, Hillsboro, OH D: 5/13/1979, Columbus, OH
1926 Col: 7 G; Rush 1 TD; 6 Pt.

PARD PEARCE Pearce, Walter Irving 5′5″, 150 **QB-BB**
Col: Pennsylvania *HS:* Classical [Providence, RI]; Morris Heights Prep Sch. [NJ] B: 10/23/1896, Providence, RI D: 5/24/1974, Newport, RI
1920 Sta: 13 G. **1921** Sta: 11 G; Rush 1 TD; 1 Fum TD; Tot TD 2; 12 Pt. **1922** ChiB: 8 G; Pass 1 TD; Rush 1 TD; 6 Pt. **1924** Ken: 2 G. **1925** Prov: 8 G. **Total:** 42 G; Pass 1 TD; Rush 2 TD; 1 Fum TD; Tot TD 3; 18 Pt.

JIM PEARCY Pearcy, James Wheeler 5′11″, 210 **G**
Col: Marshall *HS:* Clarksville [WV] B: 7/26/1920, Harrisville, WV
AAFC **1946** ChiA: 13 G. **1947** ChiA: 14 G. **1948** ChiA: 14 G. **1949** ChiA: 8 G. **Total:** 49 G.

NFL **1948** ChiA: 14 G.

RED PEARLMAN Pearlman, Isador Ralph 6′0″, 195 **G-T**
Col: Pittsburgh *HS:* Fifth Avenue [Pittsburgh, PA] B: 7/29/1898, Pittsburgh, PA D: 11/1985, Hollywood, FL
1920 Cle: 8 G. **1921** Cle: 8 G. **1924** Roch: 2 G. **Total:** 18 G.

AARON PEARSON Pearson, Aaron Dantianto 6′0″, 239 **LB**
Col: Itawamba CC MS; Mississippi State *HS:* Gadsden [AL] B: 8/22/1964, Gadsden, AL *Drafted:* 1986 Round 11 KC
1986 KC: 15 G; KR 1-0. **1987** KC: 12 G; KR 2-4 2.0; 2 Fum. **1988** KC: 16 G. **Total:** 43 G; KR 3-4 1.3; 2 Fum.

BARRY PEARSON Pearson, Barry Lynn 5′11″, 185 **WR**
Col: Northwestern *HS:* J.D. Darnall [Geneseo, IL] B: 2/4/1950, Geneseo, IL
1972 Pit: Postseason only. **1974** KC: Rush 1-1 1.0. **1975** KC: PR 2-31 15.5. **Total:** Rush 1-1 1.0; PR 2-31 15.5.

		Receiving				
Year Team	G	Rec	Yds	Avg	TD	Fum
1973 Pit	13	23	317	13.8	3	1
1974 KC	14	27	387	14.3	1	0
1975 KC	14	36	608	16.9	3	1
1976 KC	8	0	0	—	0	0
NFL Total	49	86	1312	15.3	7	2

DENNIS PEARSON Pearson, Dennis Mack 5′11″, 177 **WR**
Col: Washington; San Diego State *HS:* Monterey [CA] B: 2/9/1955, Gordo, AL *Drafted:* 1978 Round 5 Atl
1978 Atl: Rush 1-1 1.0; Rec 5-71 14.2. **1979** Atl: Rec 7-119 17.0; PR 12-115 9.6. **Total:** Rush 1-1 1.0; Rec 12-190 15.8; PR 12-115 9.6.

		Kickoff Returns				
Year Team	G	Ret	Yds	Avg	TD	Fum
1978 Atl	13	25	662	26.5	**1**	0
1979 Atl	16	30	570	19.0	0	4
NFL Total	29	55	1232	22.4	1	4

DREW PEARSON Pearson, Drew 6′0″, 184 **WR**
Col: Tulsa *HS:* South River [NJ] B: 1/12/1951, South River, NJ
1973 Dal: PR 2-13 6.5; KR 7-155 22.1. **1974** Dal: Pass 1-1 100.0%, 46 46.00 1 TD; Rush 3-6 2.0; 1 Fum TD. **1975** Dal: Rush 1-11 11.0. **1976** Dal: Pass 1-1 100.0%, 39 39.00 1 TD; Rush 2-20 10.0; **1** Fum TD. **1977** Dal: Rush 2-22 11.0. **1978** Dal: Rush 3-29 9.7. **1979** Dal: Rush 3-27 9.0. **1980** Dal: Rush 2-30 15.0. **1981** Dal: Pass 2-2 100.0%, 81 40.50 1 TD; Rush 3-31 10.3. **1982** Dal: Pass 2-1 50.0%, 26 13.00 1 Int. **1983** Dal: Pass 1-0, 1 Int; Rush 2-13 6.5. **Total:** Pass 7-5 71.4%, 192 27.43 3 TD 2 Int; Rush 21-189 9.0; PR 2-13 6.5; KR 7-155 22.1; 2 Fum TD.

		Receiving					Tot
Year Team	G	Rec	Yds	Avg	TD	Fum	TD
1973 Dal	14	22	388	17.6	2	1	2
1974 Dal	14	62	1087	17.5	2	1	3
1975 Dal	14	46	822	17.9	8	1	8
1976 Dal	14	58	806	13.9	6	1	7
1977 Dal	14	48	**870**	18.1	2	0	2
1978 Dal	16	44	714	16.2	3	0	3
1979 Dal	15	55	1026	18.7	8	0	8
1980 Dal	16	43	568	13.2	6	0	6
1981 Dal	16	38	614	16.2	3	4	3
1982 Dal	9	26	382	14.7	3	0	3
1983 Dal	14	47	545	11.6	5	1	5
NFL Total	156	489	7822	16.0	48	9	50

DUD PEARSON Pearson, Dudley Lester 5′9″, 165 **BB**
Col: Notre Dame *HS:* Chippewa Falls [WI] B: 2/8/1896, Outagamie Co., WI D: 9/3/1982, Milwaukee, WI
1922 Rac: 4 G.

J.C. PEARSON Pearson, Jayice 5′11″, 187 **DB**
Col: Fullerton Coll. CA (J.C.); Cal Poly-Pomona; Washington *HS:* El Camino [Oceanside, CA] B: 8/17/1963, Japan
1986 KC: 8 G; 1 Sac. **1987** KC: 12 G. **1988** KC: 16 G; Int 2-8. **1989** KC: 16 G; 6 Pt; 1 Sac. **1990** KC: 16 G; Int 1-10. **1991** KC: 15 G; Int 3-43; 1 Sac. **1992** KC: 7 G; 1 Sac. **1993** Min: 13 G; Int 1-0. **Total:** 103 G; Int 7-61; 6 Pt; 4 Sac.

LINDY PEARSON Pearson, Lindell Eugene 6′0″, 198 **HB**
Col: Oklahoma *HS:* Capitol Hill [Oklahoma City, OK] B: 3/6/1929, Oklahoma City, OK
1950 Det: Pass 3-0, 3 Int; Rec 1-4 4.0; PR 1-6 6.0; KR 7-120 17.1. **1951** Det: Rec 5-43 8.6. **1952** Det-GB: Rec 1-16 16.0. GB: Rec 1-16 16.0. **Total:** Pass 3-0, 3 Int; Rec 7-63 9.0; PR 1-6 6.0; KR 7-120 17.1.

		Rushing				
Year Team	G	Att	Yds	Avg	TD	Fum
1950 Det	11	31	82	2.6	2	2
1951 Det	12	22	88	4.0	0	1
1952 Det-GB	5	5	2	0.4	0	1
1952 Det	3	3	0	0.0	0	1
1952 GB	2	2	2	1.0	0	0
NFL Total	28	58	172	3.0	2	4

BERT PEARSON Pearson, Madison B 6′0″, 206 **C-LB-G-T**
Col: Kansas State *HS:* Manhattan [KS] B: 3/22/1905, Manhattan, KS Deceased
1929 ChiB: 12 G. **1930** ChiB: 14 G. **1931** ChiB: 13 G. **1932** ChiB: 9 G. **1933** ChiB: 5 G. **1934** ChiB: 4 G. **1935** ChiC: 10 G. **1936** ChiC: 10 G. **Total:** 77 G.

PRESTON PEARSON Pearson, Preston James 6′1″, 205 **RB-DB**
Col: Illinois *HS:* Freeport [IL] B: 1/17/1945, Freeport, IL *Drafted:* 1967 Round 12 Bal
1969 Bal: PR 6-37 6.2. **1971** Pit: **1** Fum TD. **1972** Pit: PR 1-3 3.0. **Total:** PR 7-40 5.7; 1 Fum TD.

		Rushing				Receiving			
Year Team	G	Att	Yds	Avg	TD	Rec	Yds	Avg	TD
1967 Bal	7	0	0	—	0	0	0	—	0
1968 Bal	14	19	78	4.1	0	2	70	35.0	2
1969 Bal	14	24	81	3.4	0	4	64	16.0	0
1970 Pit	14	173	503	2.9	2	6	71	11.8	0
1971 Pit	14	131	605	4.6	0	20	246	12.3	2
1972 Pit	11	67	264	3.9	0	11	79	7.2	0
1973 Pit	14	132	554	4.2	2	11	173	15.7	2
1974 Pit	9	70	317	4.5	4	11	118	10.7	0
1975 Dal	14	133	509	3.8	2	27	351	13.0	2
1976 Dal	10	68	233	3.4	1	23	316	13.7	2
1977 Dal	14	89	341	3.8	1	46	535	11.6	4
1978 Dal	16	25	104	4.2	0	47	526	11.2	0
1979 Dal	14	7	14	2.0	1	26	333	12.8	1
1980 Dal	11	3	6	2.0	0	20	213	10.7	2
NFL Total	176	941	3609	3.8	13	254	3095	12.2	17

	Kickoff Returns					Tot
Year Team	Ret	Yds	Avg	TD	Fum	TD
1968 Bal	15	527	**35.1**	**2**	2	4
1969 Bal	**31**	706	22.8	0	2	0
1970 Pit	4	114	28.5	0	6	2
1971 Pit	7	205	29.3	0	7	3
1972 Pit	13	292	22.5	0	4	0
1973 Pit	16	308	19.3	0	2	4
1974 Pit	12	258	21.5	0	0	4
1975 Dal	16	391	24.4	0	1	4
1976 Dal	0	0	—	0	1	3
1977 Dal	0	0	—	0	1	5
1979 Dal	0	0	—	0	0	2
1980 Dal	0	0	—	0	0	2
NFL Total	114	2801	24.6	2	26	33

WILLIE PEARSON Pearson, Willie Jr. 6′0″, 190 **DB**
Col: North Carolina A&T *HS:* Carver [Winston-Salem, NC] B: 5/9/1947, Bennettsville, SC *Drafted:* 1969 Round 5 Mia
1969 Mia: 5 G.

BRENT PEASE Pease, Brent Richard 6′2″, 201 **QB**
Col: Walla Walla CC WA; Montana *HS:* Mountain Home [ID] B: 10/8/1964, Moscow, ID *Drafted:* 1987 Round 11 Min
1987 Hou: Rush 15-33 2.2 1 TD. **1988** Hou: Rush 8-(-2) -0.3 1 TD. **Total:** Rush 23-31 1.3 2 TD.

		Passing								
Year Team	G	Att	Comp	Comp%	Yds	YPA	TD	Int	Rating	Fum
1987 Hou	7	113	56	49.6	728	6.44	3	5	60.6	2
1988 Hou	13	22	6	27.3	64	2.91	0	4	0.0	0
NFL Total	20	135	62	45.9	792	5.87	3	9	44.4	2

GEORGE PEASE Pease, George Gregory 5′8″, 185 **BB-TB**
Col: Columbia *HS:* Manual Training [Brooklyn, NY] B: 6/18/1903, Brooklyn, NY D: 10/26/1984, Dallas, TX
1929 Ora: 10 G; Pass 2 TD; Rec 1 TD; 6 Pt.

TODD PEAT Peat, Marion Todd 6'2", 300 **OG**
Col: Northern Illinois *HS:* Central [Champaign, IL] B: 5/20/1964, Champaign, IL *Drafted:* 1987 Round 11 StL
1987 StL: 12 G. **1988** Pho: 15 G. **1989** Pho: 4 G. **1990** LARd: 16 G. **1992** LARd: 16 G. **1993** LARd: 16 G; KR 2-18 9.0. **Total:** 79 G; KR 2-18 9.0.

JACK PEAVEY Peavey, John A 6'2", 260 **C**
Col: Springfield; Troy State *HS:* Foxboro [MA] B: 6/6/1963, Attleboro, MA
1987 Den: 3 G; 1 Fum.

FRANCIS PEAY Peay, Francis G 6'5", 250 **OT**
Col: Arizona; Cameron; Missouri *HS:* Schenley [Pittsburgh, PA] B: 5/23/1944, Pittsburgh, PA *Drafted:* 1966 Round 1 NYG
1966 NYG: 9 G. **1967** NYG: 13 G. **1968** GB: 14 G. **1969** GB: 14 G. **1970** GB: 14 G. **1971** GB: 14 G. **1972** GB: 6 G. **1973** KC: 9 G. **1974** KC: 10 G. **Total:** 103 G.

WIN PEDERSEN Pedersen, Windinge Christian 6'3", 223 **T**
Col: Minnesota *HS:* West [Minneapolis, MN] B: 6/8/1915, Chicago, IL D: 1/16/1983, Hopkins, MN *Drafted:* 1940 Round 6 NYG
1941 NYG: 9 G; Int 1-3; Scor 3, 1-1 100.0% FG. **1945** NYG: 4 G. **1946** Bos: 10 G. **Total:** 23 G; Int 1-3; Scor 3, 1-1 100.0% FG.

DOUG PEDERSON Pederson, Douglas Irvin 6'3", 212 **QB**
Col: Northeast Louisiana *HS:* Ferndale [WA] B: 1/31/1968, Bellingham, WA
1993 Mia: 7 G; Pass 8-4 50.0%, 41 5.13; Rush 2-(-1) -0.5; 2 Fum. **1996** GB: 1 G. **1997** GB: 1 G; Rush 3-(-4) -1.3. **1998** GB: 12 G; Pass 24-14 58.3%, 128 5.33 2 TD; Rush 8-(-4) -0.5; 1 Fum. **Total:** 21 G; Pass 32-18 56.3%, 169 5.28 2 TD; Rush 13-(-9) -0.7; 3 Fum.

JIM PEDERSON Pederson, James Palmer 5'9", 189 **WB-BB-HB**
Col: Augsburg *HS:* Willmar [MN] B: 10/19/1907, Harvey, ND D: 8/14/1978, Pawtucket, RI
1930 Min-Fra: 11 G. Min: 7 G. Fra: 4 G. **1931** Fra: 8 G. **1932** ChiB: 1 G; Rush 1-2 2.0. **Total:** 20 G; Rush 1-2 2.0.

DANNY PEEBLES Peebles, Daniel Percy III 5'11", 180 **WR**
Col: North Carolina State *HS:* Needham B. Broughton [Raleigh, NC] B: 5/30/1966, Raleigh, NC *Drafted:* 1989 Round 2 TB
1989 TB: Rush 2-(-6) -3.0; Rec 11-180 16.4. **1990** TB: Rec 6-50 8.3 1 TD. **Total:** Rush 2-(-6) -3.0; Rec 17-230 13.5 1 TD.

		Kickoff Returns				
Year Team	G	Ret	Yds	Avg	TD	Fum
1989 TB	13	0	0	—	0	1
1990 TB	10	18	369	20.5	0	1
1991 Cle	7	8	149	18.6	0	0
NFL Total	30	26	518	19.9	0	2

JIM PEEBLES Peebles, James McAden 6'4", 231 **DE-OE-OT**
(Mac) *Col:* Vanderbilt *HS:* Columbia Mil. Acad. [TN] B: 8/27/1920, Culleoka, TN D: 7/19/1997, Nashville, TN
1946 Was: 11 G; Rec 9-164 18.2 1 TD; Scor 6, 0-2 FG; 6 Pt; 2 Fum. **1947** Was: 12 G; Rec 4-26 6.5; KR 1-13 13.0; Scor 0-1 FG. **1948** Was: 11 G; Scor 1, 1-2 50.0% XK. **1949** Was: 11 G; Rush 1-(-3) -3.0; 1 Fum. **1951** Was: 12 G. **Total:** 57 G; Rush 1-(-3) -3.0; Rec 13-190 14.6 1 TD; KR 1-13 13.0; Scor 7, 0-3 FG, 1-2 50.0% XK; 3 Fum.

GORDON PEERY Peery, Gordon George 5'10", 155 **BB**
(Skeet) *Col:* Oklahoma State *HS:* Stillwater [OK] B: 1/12/1904, Stillwater, OK D: 5/21/1994, El Reno, OK
1927 Cle: 4 G.

RODNEY PEETE Peete, Rodney 6'0", 210 **QB**
Col: USC *HS:* Sahuaro [Tucson, AZ]; South HS [Shawnee Mission, KS] B: 3/16/1966, Mesa, AZ *Drafted:* 1989 Round 6 Det

		Passing							
Year Team	G	Att	Comp	Comp%	Yds	YPA	TD	Int	Rating
1989 Det	8	195	103	52.8	1479	7.58	5	9	67.0
1990 Det	11	271	142	52.4	1974	7.28	13	8	79.8
1991 Det	8	194	116	59.8	1339	6.90	5	9	69.9
1992 Det	10	213	123	57.7	1702	7.99	9	9	80.0
1993 Det	10	252	157	62.3	1670	6.63	6	14	66.4
1994 Dal	7	56	33	58.9	470	8.39	4	1	102.5
1995 Phi	15	375	215	57.3	2326	6.20	8	14	67.3
1996 Phi	5	134	80	59.7	992	7.40	3	5	74.6
1997 Phi	5	118	68	57.6	869	7.36	4	4	78.0
1998 Phi	5	129	71	55.0	758	5.88	2	4	64.7
NFL Total	84	1937	1108	57.2	13579	7.01	59	77	72.6

	Rushing				
Year Team	Att	Yds	Avg	TD	Fum
1989 Det	33	148	4.5	4	9
1990 Det	47	363	7.7	6	9
1991 Det	25	125	5.0	2	2
1992 Det	21	83	4.0	0	6
1993 Det	45	165	3.7	1	11
1994 Dal	9	-2	-0.2	0	3
1995 Phi	32	147	4.6	1	13
1996 Phi	20	31	1.6	1	2
1997 Phi	8	37	4.6	0	5
1998 Phi	5	30	6.0	1	1
NFL Total	245	1127	4.6	16	61

BRIAN PEETS Peets, Brian Canvin 6'4", 225 **TE**
Col: U. of Pacific *HS:* Linden [CA] B: 7/15/1956, Stockton, CA

		Receiving			
Year Team	G	Rec	Yds	Avg	TD
1978 Sea	8	1	14	14.0	0
1979 Sea	16	25	293	11.7	1
1981 SF	5	1	5	5.0	0
NFL Total	29	27	312	11.6	1

ERRIC PEGRAM Pegram, Erric Demont 5'10", 195 **RB**
Col: North Texas *HS:* Hillcrest [Dallas, TX] B: 1/7/1969, Dallas, TX *Drafted:* 1991 Round 6 Atl
1995 Pit: Scor 1 2XP. **Total:** Scor 1 2XP.

		Rushing				Receiving			
Year Team	G	Att	Yds	Avg	TD	Rec	Yds	Avg	TD
1991 Atl	16	101	349	3.5	1	1	-1	-1.0	0
1992 Atl	16	21	89	4.2	0	2	25	12.5	0
1993 Atl	16	292	1185	4.1	3	33	302	9.2	0
1994 Atl	13	103	358	3.5	1	16	99	6.2	0
1995 Pit	15	213	813	3.8	5	26	206	7.9	1
1996 Pit	12	97	509	5.2	1	17	112	6.6	0
1997 SD-NYG	15	28	95	3.4	2	21	90	4.3	0
1997 SD	4	9	23	2.6	1	2	7	3.5	0
1997 NYG	11	19	72	3.8	1	19	83	4.4	0
NFL Total	103	855	3398	4.0	13	116	833	7.2	1

	Kickoff Returns					Tot
Year Team	Ret	Yds	Avg	TD	Fum	TD
1991 Atl	16	260	16.3	0	1	1
1992 Atl	9	161	17.9	0	0	0
1993 Atl	4	63	15.8	0	6	3
1994 Atl	9	145	16.1	0	2	1
1995 Pit	4	85	21.3	0	9	6
1996 Pit	17	419	24.6	1	1	2
1997 SD-NYG	22	382	17.4	0	1	2
1997 SD	0	0	—	0	0	1
1997 NYG	22	382	17.4	0	1	1
NFL Total	81	1515	18.7	1	20	15

WILLIS PEGUESE Peguese, Willis 6'4", 273 **DE**
Col: Miami (Fla.) *HS:* Miami Southridge [FL] B: 12/18/1966, Miami, FL *Drafted:* 1990 Round 3 Hou
1990 Hou: 2 G. **1991** Hou: 7 G. **1992** Hou-Ind: 13 G. Hou: 1 G. Ind: 12 G. **1993** Ind: 13 G; 2 Sac. **Total:** 35 G; 2 Sac.

DAN PEIFFER Peiffer, Daniel William 6'3", 252 **C**
Col: Ellsworth CC IA; Southeast Missouri State *HS:* Keota [IA] B: 3/29/1951, Sigourney, IA *Drafted:* 1973 Round 14 StL
1975 ChiB: 11 G. **1976** ChiB: 4 G. **1977** ChiB: 14 G. **1980** Was: 8 G. **Total:** 37 G.

RAY PELFREY Pelfrey, Raymond Harrison 6'0", 190 **OE-HB**
Col: Eastern Kentucky *HS:* Portsmouth [OH] B: 1/11/1928, Sardinia, OH *Drafted:* 1951 Round 17 GB
1951 GB: Rush 3-44 14.7; Punt 5-220 44.0. **1952** GB-ChiC-Dal: KR 2-34 17.0. GB: KR 1-26 26.0. ChiC: KR 1-8 8.0. **Total:** Rush 3-44 14.7; KR 2-34 17.0; Punt 5-220 44.0.

		Receiving				
Year Team	G	Rec	Yds	Avg	TD	Fum
1951 GB	12	38	462	12.2	5	0
1952 GB-ChiC-Dal	8	20	264	13.2	2	1
1952 GB	1	1	10	10.0	0	1
1952 ChiC	1	1	11	11.0	0	0
1952 Dal	6	18	243	13.5	2	0
1953 NYG	12	17	233	13.7	3	1
NFL Total	32	75	959	12.8	10	2

DOUG PELFREY Pelfrey, William Douglas 5'11", 185 **K**
Col: Kentucky *HS:* Scott [Covington, KY] B: 9/25/1970, Fort Thomas, KY *Drafted:* 1993 Round 8 Cin
1995 Cin: Punt 2-52 26.0. **1996** Cin: Punt 1-4 4.0. **1998** Cin: Pass 1-0. **Total:** Pass 1-0; Punt 3-56 18.7.

		Scoring						
Year Team	G	Pts	FG	FGA	FG%	XK	XKA	XK%
1993 Cin	15	85	24	31	77.4	13	16	81.3
1994 Cin	16	108	28	33	84.8	24	25	96.0
1995 Cin	16	121	29	36	80.6	34	34	100.0
1996 Cin	16	110	23	28	82.1	41	41	100.0
1997 Cin	16	77	12	16	75.0	41	43	95.3

1998 Cin	16	78	19	27	70.4	21	21	100.0
NFL Total	95	579	135	171	78.9	174	180	96.7

JOSEPH PELLEGRINI Pellegrini, Joseph A 6′4″, 258 **OG-C**
Col: Harvard *HS:* Archbishop Williams [Braintree, MA] B: 4/8/1957, Boston, MA
1982 NYJ: 9 G. **1983** NYJ: 16 G. **1984** Atl: 15 G. **1985** Atl: 5 G. **1986** Atl: 8 G. **Total:** 53 G.

JOE PELLEGRINI Pellegrini, Joseph Jr. 6′2″, 270 **DT-NT**
Col: Idaho *HS:* Hoquiam [WA] B: 8/9/1956, Aberdeen, WA
1978 NYJ: 9 G. **1979** NYJ: 4 G. **Total:** 13 G.

BOB PELLEGRINI Pellegrini, Robert Francis 6′2″, 233 **LB-OG**
Col: Maryland *HS:* Shannock Valley [Rural Valley, PA] B: 11/13/1934, Williamsport, PA *Drafted:* 1956 Round 1 Phi
1956 Phi: KR 2-47 23.5. **1964** Was: KR 1-0. **1965** Was: PR 1-0; **1** Fum TD. **Total:** PR 1-0; KR 3-47 15.7; 1 Fum TD.

		Interceptions			
Year Team	G	Int	Yds	TD	Fum
1956 Phi	12	0	0	0	0
1958 Phi	12	4	90	0	0
1959 Phi	12	3	42	0	0
1960 Phi	9	0	0	0	0
1961 Phi	14	0	0	0	0
1962 Was	9	4	43	0	0
1963 Was	14	2	37	0	1
1964 Was	12	0	0	0	0
1965 Was	13	0	0	0	1
NFL Total	107	13	212	0	2

BILL PELLINGTON Pellington, William Alvin Jr. 6′2″, 234 **LB-OG**
Col: Rutgers *HS:* Ramsey [NJ] B: 9/25/1927, Ramsey, NJ
D: 4/25/1994, Baltimore, MD
1954 Bal: KR 2-26 13.0. **1955** Bal: Rec 1-10 10.0; PR 1-6 6.0; KR 2-36 18.0. **1956** Bal: KR 1-0. **1958** Bal: Rec 1-(-1) -1.0. **1960** Bal: KR 2-11 5.5. **Total:** Rec 2-9 4.5; PR 1-6 6.0; KR 7-73 10.4.

		Interceptions			
Year Team	G	Int	Yds	TD	Fum
1953 Bal	12	2	22	0	0
1954 Bal	12	0	0	0	0
1955 Bal	12	2	17	0	0
1956 Bal	12	1	4	0	0
1957 Bal	1	0	0	0	0
1958 Bal	12	4	44	0	0
1959 Bal	12	4	99	**1**	0
1960 Bal	12	1	4	0	1
1961 Bal	14	3	9	0	0
1962 Bal	14	2	29	0	0
1963 Bal	14	0	0	0	0
1964 Bal	14	2	20	0	0
NFL Total	141	21	248	1	1

SCOTT PELLUER Pelluer, Scott John 6′2″, 219 **LB**
Col: Washington State *HS:* Interlake [Bellevue, WA] B: 4/28/1959, Yakima, WA *Drafted:* 1981 Round 4 Dal
1981 NO: 16 G. **1982** NO: 6 G. **1983** NO: 16 G. **1984** NO: 16 G. **1985** NO: 11 G. **Total:** 65 G.

STEVE PELLUER Pelluer, Steven Carl 6′4″, 209 **QB**
Col: Washington *HS:* Interlake [Bellevue, WA] B: 7/29/1962, Yakima, WA *Drafted:* 1984 Round 5 Dal

		Passing							
Year Team	G	Att	Comp	Comp%	Yds	YPA	TD	Int	Rating
1984 Dal	1	0	0	—	0	—	0	0	—
1985 Dal	2	8	5	62.5	47	5.88	0	0	78.6
1986 Dal	16	378	215	56.9	2727	7.21	8	17	67.9
1987 Dal	12	101	55	54.5	642	6.36	3	2	75.6
1988 Dal	16	435	245	56.3	3139	7.22	17	19	73.9
1989 KC	5	47	26	55.3	301	6.40	1	0	82.0
1990 KC	13	5	2	40.0	14	2.80	0	1	8.3
NFL Total	65	974	548	56.3	6870	7.05	29	39	71.6

	Rushing				
Year Team	Att	Yds	Avg	TD	Fum
1985 Dal	3	-2	-0.7	0	0
1986 Dal	41	255	6.2	1	9
1987 Dal	25	142	5.7	1	0
1988 Dal	51	314	6.2	2	6
1989 KC	17	143	8.4	2	2
1990 KC	5	6	1.2	0	0
NFL Total	142	858	6.0	6	17

BUBBA PENA Pena, Robert B 6′2″, 250 **OG**
Col: Dean Coll. MA (J.C.); Massachusetts *HS:* Lawrence [Falmouth, MA] B: 8/8/1949, Wareham, MA *Drafted:* 1971 Round 4 Cle
1972 Cle: 7 G.

JAIRO PENARANDA Penaranda, Jairo Alonso 5′11″, 217 **RB**
Col: Los Angeles Valley Coll. CA (J.C.); UCLA *HS:* John Burroughs [Burbank, CA] B: 6/15/1958, Barranquilla, Colombia *Drafted:* 1981 Round 12 LARm
1981 LARm: 16 G; KR 1-1 1.0. **1985** Phi: 4 G. **Total:** 20 G; KR 1-1 1.0.

BOB PENCHION Penchion, Robert Earl 6′5″, 265 **OG-C**
Col: Alcorn State *HS:* Courtland [AL] B: 8/11/1949, Town Creek, AL
Drafted: 1972 Round 5 Buf
1972 Buf: 12 G. **1973** Buf: 5 G. **1974** SF: 8 G. **1975** SF: 9 G. **1976** Sea: 14 G. **Total:** 48 G.

CHRIS PENN Penn, Christopher Anthony 6′0″, 198 **WR**
Col: Northeastern Oklahoma A&M (J.C.); Tulsa *HS:* Oklahoma Union [Lenapah, OK] B: 4/20/1971, Nowata, OK *Drafted:* 1994 Round 3 KC
1994 KC: KR 9-194 21.6. **1995** KC: PR 4-12 3.0; KR 2-26 13.0. **1996** KC: PR 14-148 10.6. **1997** ChiB: Rush 1-(-1) -1.0. **1998** ChiB: Scor 1 2XP. **Total:** Rush 1-(-1) -1.0; PR 18-160 8.9; KR 11-220 20.0; Scor 1 2XP.

		Receiving				
Year Team	G	Rec	Yds	Avg	TD	Fum
1994 KC	8	3	24	8.0	0	0
1995 KC	2	1	12	12.0	0	0
1996 KC	16	49	628	12.8	5	3
1997 ChiB	14	47	576	12.3	3	1
1998 ChiB	14	31	448	14.5	3	1
NFL Total	54	131	1688	12.9	11	5

JESSE PENN Penn, Jesse Andrew II 6′3″, 220 **LB**
Col: Virginia Tech *HS:* Martinsville [VA] B: 9/6/1962, Martinsville, VA
Drafted: 1985 Round 2 Dal
1985 Dal: 16 G; 6 Pt. **1986** Dal: 15 G; 2.5 Sac. **1987** Dal: 11 G; Int 1-21. **Total:** 42 G; Int 1-21; 6 Pt; 2.5 Sac.

LEON PENNINGTON Pennington, Leon Tyrone 6′1″, 225 **LB**
Col: Florida *HS:* Oakland Park [Fort Lauderdale, FL] B: 12/25/1963
1987 TB: 3 G.

TOM PENNINGTON Pennington, Thomas Durward Jr. 6′2″, 210 **K**
Col: Georgia *HS:* Albany [GA] B: 11/26/1939, Albany, GA
Drafted: 1962 Round 11 Buf
1962 DalT: 3 G; Scor 19, 2-5 40.0% FG, 13-15 86.7% XK.

JAY PENNISON Pennison, Jay Leslie 6′1″, 276 **C**
Col: Nicholls State *HS:* Terrebonne [Houma, LA] B: 9/9/1961, Houma, LA
1986 Hou: 16 G; 1 Fum. **1987** Hou: 12 G; 1 Fum. **1988** Hou: 16 G; 1 Fum. **1989** Hou: 12 G; 2 Fum. **1990** Hou: 15 G. **Total:** 71 G; 5 Fum.

CARLOS PENNYWELL Pennywell, Carlos Jerome 6′2″, 180 **WR**
(Chilly) *Col:* Grambling State *HS:* Captain Shreve [Shreveport, LA]
B: 3/18/1956, Crowley, LA *Drafted:* 1978 Round 3 NE
1978 NE: 16 G; Rec 1-28 28.0. **1979** NE: 6 G; Rec 4-35 8.8 1 TD; 6 Pt. **1980** NE: 11 G; Rec 4-31 7.8 1 TD; KR 1-0; 6 Pt. **1981** NE: 5 G; Rush 1-3 3.0; Rec 3-49 16.3 1 TD; 6 Pt. **Total:** 38 G; Rush 1-3 3.0; Rec 12-143 11.9 3 TD; KR 1-0; 18 Pt.

ROBERT PENNYWELL Pennywell, Robert 6′1″, 222 **LB**
Col: Grambling State *HS:* Woodlawn [Shreveport, LA]; Captain Shreve HS [Shreveport, LA] B: 11/6/1954, Crowley, LA *Drafted:* 1976 Round 6 SF
1977 Atl: 14 G; Int 2-30 **1** TD; 6 Pt. **1978** Atl: 15 G. **1979** Atl: 16 G; Int 1-39 1 TD; 6 Pt. **1980** Atl: 16 G. **Total:** 61 G; Int 3-69 2 TD; 12 Pt.

CRAIG PENROSE Penrose, Craig R 6′3″, 211 **QB**
Col: Colorado; San Diego State *HS:* Woodland [CA] B: 7/25/1953, Woodland, CA *Drafted:* 1976 Round 4 Den
1976 Den: Rush 2-(-3) -1.5. **1977** Den: Rush 4-24 6.0. **1978** Den: Rush 1-0. **Total:** Rush 7-21 3.0.

		Passing								
Year Team	G	Att	Comp	Comp%	Yds	YPA	TD	Int	Rating	Fum
1976 Den	4	36	16	44.4	265	7.36	3	3	62.8	0
1977 Den	8	39	21	53.8	217	5.56	0	4	30.6	0
1978 Den	4	37	16	43.2	185	5.00	2	4	37.4	1
1979 Den	2	5	2	40.0	44	8.80	0	1	32.5	0
NFL Total	18	117	55	47.0	711	6.08	5	12	41.2	1

LEON PENSE Pense, James Leon 6′0″, 170 **BB-DB**
Col: Arkansas *HS:* Bartlesville [OK] B: 2/5/1922, Chewey, OK
Drafted: 1945 Round 9 Pit
1945 Pit: 10 G; Rush 6-1 0.2; Rec 1-32 32.0; KR 1-21 21.0; Int 3-39; 1 Fum.

JOHN PENTECOST Pentecost, John Mathew 6′2″, 251 **OG**
Col: UCLA *HS:* Orange [CA] B: 12/23/1943, Lawndale, CA
1967 Min: 4 G.

GEORGE PEOPLES Peoples, George Evans 6′0″, 214 **RB**
Col: Auburn *HS:* C. Leon King [Tampa, FL] B: 8/25/1960, Tampa, FL
Drafted: 1982 Round 8 Dal
1982 Dal: 8 G; Rush 7-22 3.1. **1983** NE: 16 G. **1984** TB: 6 G; Rush 1-2 2.0. **1985** TB: 2 G. **Total:** 32 G; Rush 8-24 3.0.

WOODY PEOPLES Peoples, Woodrow 6′2″, 252 **OG**
Col: Grambling State *HS:* Ullman [Birmingham, AL] B: 8/16/1943, Birmingham, AL
1968 SF: 13 G; KR 1-0. **1969** SF: 14 G. **1970** SF: 14 G. **1971** SF: 14 G. **1972** SF: 14 G. **1973** SF: 14 G. **1974** SF: 10 G. **1975** SF: 14 G. **1977** SF: 14 G. **1978** Phi: 15 G. **1979** Phi: 16 G. **1980** Phi: 16 G. **Total:** 168 G; KR 1-0.

PEPPER Pepper **G**
Col: No College Deceased
1920 Roch: 1 G.

GENE PEPPER Pepper, Eugene Francis 6′2″, 239 **OG-OT-DT-LB**
Col: Missouri *HS:* McBride [St. Louis, MO] B: 9/22/1927, Overland, MO *Drafted:* 1950 Round 6 Was
1950 Was: 12 G. **1951** Was: 11 G. **1952** Was: 12 G. **1953** Was: 6 G. **1954** Bal: 3 G. **Total:** 44 G.

FRANK PERANTONI Perantoni, Joseph Francis 6′0″, 220 **C**
Col: Princeton *HS:* Blair Acad. [Blairstown, NJ] B: 9/13/1923, Raritan, NJ D: 9/11/1991, Somerville, NJ
AAFC **1948** NY-A: 14 G. **1949** NY-A: 12 G. **Total:** 26 G.

MAC PERCIVAL Percival, Mac 6′4″, 220 **K**
Col: Texas Tech *HS:* Vernon [TX] B: 2/26/1940, Lubbock, TX
1970 ChiB: Rec 1-19 19.0. **Total:** Rec 1-19 19.0.

		Scoring						
Year Team	**G**	**Pts**	**FG**	**FGA**	**FG%**	**XK**	**XKA**	**XK%**
1967 ChiB	14	65	13	26	50.0	26	29	89.7
1968 ChiB	14	100	**25**	36	69.4	25	25	100.0
1969 ChiB	14	50	8	21	38.1	26	26	100.0
1970 ChiB	14	88	20	34	58.8	28	28	100.0
1971 ChiB	14	63	15	33	45.5	18	18	100.0
1972 ChiB	14	62	12	24	50.0	26	26	100.0
1973 ChiB	4	28	6	8	75.0	10	10	100.0
1974 Dal	3	10	2	8	25.0	4	5	80.0
NFL Total	91	466	101	190	53.2	163	167	97.6

BOLO PERDUE Perdue, Charles Willard 5′10″, 170 **DE-OE**
Col: Duke *HS:* Thomasville [NC] B: 5/10/1916, Thomasville, NC D: 3/31/1988 *Drafted:* 1940 Round 14 Was
AAFC **1946** BknA: 10 G.

NFL **1940** NYG: 10 G; Rec 2-28 14.0.

PETE PEREZ Perez, Peter J 5′9″, 220 **G**
Col: Illinois *HS:* Marmion Mil. Acad. [Aurora, IL] B: 4/23/1924, Aurora, IL
1945 ChiB: 3 G.

JOHN PERGINE Pergine, John Samuel 6′1″, 225 **LB**
Col: Notre Dame *HS:* Plymouth-Whitemarsh [Plymouth Meeting, PA] B: 9/13/1946, Norristown, PA *Drafted:* 1968 Round 11 LARm
1969 LARm: 14 G; PR 1-0; 1 Fum. **1970** LARm: 12 G. **1971** LARm: 12 G. **1972** LARm: 12 G; KR 3-46 15.3. **1973** Was: 14 G. **1974** Was: 12 G. **1975** Was: 14 G; Rec 2-41 20.5 1 TD; 6 Pt. **Total:** 90 G; Rec 2-41 20.5 1 TD; PR 1-0; KR 3-46 15.3; 6 Pt; 1 Fum.

BOB PERINA Perina, Robert Ian 6′1″, 205 **DB-TB-HB**
Col: Princeton *HS:* Newark Acad. [NJ] B: 1/16/1921, Irvington, NJ D: 8/2/1991, Madison, WI
AAFC **1946** NY-A: PR 15-205 13.7; KR 4-81 20.3; Punt 11-413 37.5. **1947** BknA: Rec 9-67 7.4 1 TD; PR 4-27 6.8; KR 3-67 22.3; Punt 7-209 29.9. **1948** ChiA: Rec 2-13 6.5; PR 2-14 7.0; KR 3-52 17.3. **Total:** Rec 11-80 7.3 1 TD; PR 21-246 11.7; KR 10-200 20.0; Punt 18-622 34.6.

		Passing							
Year Team	**G**	**Att**	**Comp**	**Comp%**	**Yds**	**YPA**	**TD**	**Int**	**Rating**
1946 NY-A	13	48	21	43.8	279	5.81	1	4	35.0
1947 BknA	14	24	11	45.8	91	3.79	0	2	21.4
1948 ChiA	13	0	0	—	0	—	0	0	—
AAFC Total	40	72	32	44.4	370	5.14	1	6	30.4

	Rushing				Interceptions			Tot
Year Team	**Att**	**Yds**	**Avg**	**TD**	**Int**	**Yds**	**TD**	**TD**
1946 NY-A	45	135	3.0	1	2	24	0	1
1947 BknA	67	116	1.7	3	4	40	0	4
1948 ChiA	6	1	0.2	0	6	87	0	0
AAFC Total	118	252	2.1	4	12	151	0	5

NFL **1949** ChiB: 12 G; Rush 4-4 1.0; Rec 3-33 11.0; KR 1-10 10.0; Int 6-23. **1950** Bal: 1 G. **Total:** 13 G; Rush 4-4 1.0; Rec 3-33 11.0; KR 1-10 10.0; Int 6-23.

PETE PERINI Perini, Evo Peter 6′0″, 225 **FB-LB**
Col: Ohio State *HS:* Warren Hills [Washington, NJ] B: 2/10/1928, New Village, NJ
1954 ChiB: 12 G; Rush 4-11 2.8; Rec 5-56 11.2; KR 3-44 14.7; Scor 1, 1-1 100.0% XK; 1 Fum. **1955** ChiB-Cle: 8 G; Rush 2-0; Rec 1-3 3.0. ChiB: 2 G; Rush 2-0; Rec 1-3 3.0. Cle: 6 G. **Total:** 20 G; Rush 6-11 1.8; Rec 6-59 9.8; KR 3-44 14.7; Scor 1, 1-1 100.0% XK; 1 Fum.

ART PERKINS Perkins, Arthur Ray 6′0″, 225 **FB**
Col: North Texas B: 5/1/1940, Fort Worth, TX *Drafted:* 1962 Round 4 LARm
1962 LARm: Rec 14-83 5.9. **1963** LARm: Rec 8-61 7.6; KR 1-15 15.0. **Total:** Rec 22-144 6.5; KR 1-15 15.0.

		Rushing				
Year Team	**G**	**Att**	**Yds**	**Avg**	**TD**	**Fum**
1962 LARm	13	48	181	3.8	2	5
1963 LARm	13	37	70	1.9	4	0
NFL Total	26	85	251	3.0	6	5

BRUCE PERKINS Perkins, Bruce Kerry 6′2″, 230 **RB**
Col: Butler County CC KS; Arizona State *HS:* Waterloo Central [IA] B: 8/14/1967, Waterloo, IA
1990 TB: 16 G; Rush 13-36 2.8; Rec 8-85 10.6 2 TD; 12 Pt. **1991** Ind: 14 G; Rush 4-11 2.8; Rec 3-(-2) -0.7. **Total:** 30 G; Rush 17-47 2.8; Rec 11-83 7.5 2 TD; 12 Pt.

DON PERKINS Perkins, Donald Anthony 5′10″, 204 **FB**
Col: New Mexico *HS:* West [Waterloo, IA] B: 3/4/1938, Waterloo, IA *Drafted:* 1960 Round 9 Bal
1961 Dal: PR 1-8 8.0; KR 22-443 20.1. **Total:** PR 1-8 8.0; KR 22-443 20.1.

		Rushing				Receiving					Tot
Year Team	**G**	**Att**	**Yds**	**Avg**	**TD**	**Rec**	**Yds**	**Avg**	**TD**	**Fum**	**TD**
1961 Dal	14	200	815	4.1	4	32	298	9.3	1	5	5
1962 Dal	14	222	945	4.3	7	13	104	8.0	0	2	7
1963 Dal	11	149	614	4.1	7	14	84	6.0	0	0	7
1964 Dal	13	174	768	4.4	6	15	155	10.3	0	4	6
1965 Dal	13	177	690	3.9	0	14	142	10.1	0	2	0
1966 Dal	14	186	726	3.9	8	23	231	10.0	0	1	8
1967 Dal	14	201	823	4.1	6	18	116	6.4	0	1	6
1968 Dal	14	191	836	4.4	4	17	180	10.6	2	3	6
NFL Total	107	1500	6217	4.1	42	146	1310	9.0	3	18	45

DON PERKINS Perkins, Donald E 6′0″, 196 **FB**
(Butch) *Col:* Wis.-Platteville *HS:* Dodgeville [WI] B: 9/18/1917, Dodgeville, WI
1944 GB: Rec 1-1 1.0; KR 2-34 17.0; Int 2-123 **2** TD; Punt 1-31 31.0. **1945** GB-ChiB: Rec 2-11 5.5; Punt 1-13 13.0. GB: Rec 2-11 5.5; Punt 1-13 13.0. **1946** ChiB: Rec 2-41 20.5; PR 1-14 14.0; KR 1-25 25.0. **Total:** Rec 5-53 10.6; PR 1-14 14.0; KR 3-59 19.7; Int 2-123 2 TD; Punt 2-44 22.0.

		Rushing					Tot
Year Team	**G**	**Att**	**Yds**	**Avg**	**TD**	**Fum**	**TD**
1944 GB	10	58	207	3.6	0	0	2
1945 GB-ChiB	9	46	273	5.9	2	0	2
1945 GB	7	35	175	5.0	1	0	1
1945 ChiB	2	11	98	8.9	1	0	1
1946 ChiB	8	34	105	3.1	0	1	0
NFL Total	27	138	585	4.2	2	1	4

HORACE PERKINS Perkins, Horace Alonzo Jr. 5′11″, 180 **DB**
Col: Colorado *HS:* El Campo [TX] B: 3/15/1954, El Campo, TX *Drafted:* 1977 Round 8 Mia
1979 KC: 16 G.

JIM PERKINS Perkins, James William 6′2″, 250 **OT**
Col: Colorado *HS:* Loyalton [CA] B: 6/16/1939, Loyalton, CA D: 7/24/1992 *Drafted:* 1962 Round 21 Den
1962 Den: 14 G. **1963** Den: 14 G. **1964** Den: 14 G. **Total:** 42 G.

JOHNNY PERKINS Perkins, John Eugene 6′2″, 205 **WR**
Col: Ranger Coll. TX (J.C.); Abilene Christian *HS:* Granbury [TX] B: 4/21/1953, Franklin, TX *Drafted:* 1977 Round 2 NYG
1978 NYG: Rush 1-3 3.0. **1981** NYG: Rush 2-(-1) -0.5. **Total:** Rush 3-2 0.7.

		Receiving				
Year Team	**G**	**Rec**	**Yds**	**Avg**	**TD**	**Fum**
1977 NYG	13	20	279	14.0	0	0
1978 NYG	14	32	514	16.1	3	0
1979 NYG	13	20	337	16.9	4	1
1980 NYG	6	14	193	13.8	3	1
1981 NYG	16	51	858	16.8	6	2
1982 NYG	8	26	430	16.5	2	2
1983 NYG	1	0	0	—	0	0
NFL Total	71	163	2611	16.0	18	6

RAY PERKINS Perkins, Rayotis 6′5″, 242 **DE**
Col: Virginia *HS:* Marshall-Walker [Richmond, VA] B: 9/25/1964, Richmond, VA
1987 Dal: 2 G; 2 Sac.

RAY PERKINS Perkins, Walter Ray 6′3″, 183 **WR**
Col: Alabama *HS:* Petal [MS] B: 12/6/1941, Mount Olive, MS
Drafted: 1966 Round 7 Bal
1969 Bal: Rush 3-36 12.0. **1970** Bal: Rush 2-6 3.0. **1971** Bal: Rush 5-35 7.0. **Total:** Rush 10-77 7.7.

		Receiving			
Year Team	**G**	**Rec**	**Yds**	**Avg**	**TD**
1967 Bal	8	16	302	18.9	2
1968 Bal	14	15	227	15.1	1
1969 Bal	11	28	391	14.0	3
1970 Bal	11	10	194	19.4	1
1971 Bal	14	24	424	17.7	4
NFL Total	58	93	1538	16.5	11

BILL PERKINS Perkins, William Osborne 6′2″, 225 **HB**
Col: Iowa *HS:* Henry Snyder [Jersey City, NJ] B: 1/12/1941, Jersey City, NJ *Drafted:* 1963 Round 12 Dal
1963 NYJ: 4 G; Rush 3-8 2.7; KR 4-55 13.8; 1 Fum.

WILLIS PERKINS Perkins, Willis LaFran 6′0″, 260 **DE-OG**
Col: Texas Southern B: 2/14/1934, Columbus, TX
1961 Bos-Hou: 2 G. Bos: 1 G. Hou: 1 G. **1963** Hou: 3 G. **Total:** 5 G.

JOHN PERKO Perko, John Francis 6′1″, 225 **G**
Col: Minnesota; Notre Dame *HS:* Ely [MN] B: 4/8/1918, Ely, MN
D: 6/7/1984, Hibbing, MN
AAFC **1946** BufA: 14 G.

JOHN PERKO Perko, John Joseph 6′1″, 207 **G-LB**
Col: Duquesne *HS:* Chisholm [MN] B: 2/20/1915, Hibbing, MN
D: 5/9/1973, Hibbing, MN
1937 Pit: 10 G; Rush 1-5 5.0. **1938** Pit: 10 G. **1939** Pit: 8 G. **1940** Pit: 11 G. **1944** ChPt: 10 G; KR 1-3 3.0; Int 1-10. **1945** Pit: 10 G; 1 Fum. **1946** Pit: 9 G. **1947** Pit: 7 G. **Total:** 75 G; Rush 1-5 5.0; KR 1-3 3.0; Int 1-10; 1 Fum.

MIKE PERKO Perko, Michael John 6′4″, 235 **NT**
Col: Foothill Coll. CA (J.C.); Gonzaga; Utah State *HS:* Campolindo [Moraga, CA] B: 3/30/1957, Seattle, WA *Drafted:* 1982 Round 6 Pit
1982 Atl: 9 G; 1 Sac.

TOM PERKO Perko, Thomas Patrick 6′3″, 233 **LB**
Col: Pittsburgh *HS:* Central Catholic [Steubenville, OH] B: 6/17/1954, Steubenville, OH D: 2/2/1980, Ambridge, PA *Drafted:* 1976 Round 4 GB
1976 GB: 14 G.

PHIL PERLO Perlo, Philip Donald 6′0″, 220 **LB**
Col: Maryland *HS:* Roosevelt [Washington, DC] B: 12/6/1935, Washington, DC D: 12/11/1993, Houston, TX
1960 Hou: 7 G.

PETEY PEROT Perot, Edward Joseph 6′2″, 261 **OG**
Col: Northwestern State-Louisiana *HS:* St. Mary's [Natchitoches, LA]
B: 4/28/1957, Natchitoches, LA *Drafted:* 1979 Round 2 Phi
1979 Phi: 14 G. **1980** Phi: 16 G. **1981** Phi: 16 G. **1982** Phi: 9 G. **1984** Phi: 12 G. **1985** NO: 7 G. **Total:** 74 G.

GEORGE PERPICH Perpich, George Rudolph 6′2″, 223 **T**
Col: Georgetown *HS:* Hibbing [MN] B: 6/22/1920, Croatia
D: 5/26/1993, Hibbing, MN
AAFC **1946** BknA: 13 G; PR 1-16 16.0. **1947** BalA: 14 G. **Total:** 27 G; PR 1-16 16.0.

PETE PERREAULT Perreault, Peter Wayne 6′3″, 248 **OG-OT**
Col: Boston U. *HS:* Shrewsbury [MA] B: 3/1/1939, Shrewsbury, MA
1963 NYJ: 3 G. **1964** NYJ: 14 G; KR 1-0. **1965** NYJ: 3 G. **1966** NYJ: 6 G. **1967** NYJ: 9 G. **1968** Cin: 14 G. **1969** NYJ: 14 G. **1970** NYJ: 13 G. **1971** Min: 10 G. **Total:** 86 G; KR 1-0.

RALPH PERRETTA Perretta, Ralph Joseph 6′2″, 252 **C-OG**
Col: Purdue *HS:* Holy Trinity [Hicksville, NY] B: 1/30/1953, Rockville Centre, NY *Drafted:* 1975 Round 8 SD
1975 SD: 5 G. **1976** SD: 13 G; KR 2-24 12.0; 1 Fum. **1977** SD: 14 G. **1978** SD: 15 G. **1979** SD: 16 G; KR 1-9 9.0. **1980** NYG-SD: 10 G; 1 Fum. NYG: 5 G. SD: 5 G; 1 Fum. **Total:** 73 G; KR 3-33 11.0; 2 Fum.

MIKE PERRIE Perrie, Michael 5′11″, 197 **QB**
(Iron Mike) *Col:* St. Mary's (Cal.) B: 10/1916, Spokane, WA
Drafted: 1939 Round 17 Cle
1939 Cle: 2 G.

BRETT PERRIMAN Perriman, Brett 5′9″, 180 **WR**
Col: Miami (Fla.) *HS:* Miami Northwestern [FL] B: 10/10/1965, Miami, FL *Drafted:* 1988 Round 2 NO
1989 NO: PR 1-10 10.0. **1992** Det: KR 4-59 14.8. **1994** Det: Pass 1-0; Scor 2 2XP. **1995** Det: PR 5-50 10.0; KR 5-65 13.0; Scor 1 2XP. **Total:** Pass 1-0; PR 6-60 10.0; KR 9-124 13.8; Scor 3 2XP.

		Rushing				Receiving				
Year Team	**G**	**Att**	**Yds**	**Avg**	**TD**	**Rec**	**Yds**	**Avg**	**TD**	**Fum**
1988 NO	16	3	17	5.7	0	16	215	13.4	2	1
1989 NO	14	1	-10	-10.0	0	20	356	17.8	0	0
1990 NO	16	0	0	—	0	36	382	10.6	2	2
1991 Det	15	4	10	2.5	0	52	668	12.8	1	0
1992 Det	16	0	0	—	0	69	810	11.7	4	1
1993 Det	15	4	16	4.0	0	49	496	10.1	2	1
1994 Det	16	9	86	9.6	0	56	761	13.6	4	1
1995 Det	16	5	48	9.6	0	108	1488	13.8	9	1
1996 Det	16	1	13	13.0	0	94	1021	10.9	5	0
1997 KC-Mia	13	0	0	—	0	25	392	15.7	1	0
1997 KC	5	0	0	—	0	6	83	13.8	0	0
1997 Mia	8	0	0	—	0	19	309	16.3	1	0
NFL Total	153	27	180	6.7	0	525	6589	12.6	30	7

DEAN PERRIMAN Perriman, Dean 6′3″, 260 **OG-OT**
Col: Washington B: 11/19/1959
1987 Sea: 1 G.

BENNY PERRIN Perrin, Jesse Bennett 6′2″, 178 **DB**
Col: Alabama *HS:* Decatur [AL] B: 10/20/1959, Orange Co., CA
Drafted: 1982 Round 3 StL
1982 StL: 9 G; Int 1-35. **1983** StL: 16 G; Pass 1-1 100.0%, 4 4.00; Rush 1-0; Int 4-50; 1 Fum TD; 6 Pt; 1 Sac. **1984** StL: 16 G; Pass 1-1 100.0%; Int 4-22. **1985** StL: 7 G. **Total:** 48 G; Pass 2-2 100.0%, 4 2.00; Rush 1-0; Int 9-107; 1 Fum TD; 6 Pt; 1 Sac.

JACK PERRIN Perrin, John Stephenson 5′9″, 160 **BB**
Col: Michigan *HS:* Escanaba [MI] B: 2/4/1898, Escanaba, MI
D: 6/24/1969, Detroit, MI
1926 Har: 6 G; Scor 6, 1 FG, 3 XK.

LONNIE PERRIN Perrin, William D 6′1″, 222 **RB**
Col: Illinois *HS:* McKinley [Washington, DC] B: 2/3/1952, Norfolk, VA
Drafted: 1976 Round 5 Den
1976 Den: Rec 4-35 8.8. **1977** Den: Rec 6-106 17.7 1 TD. **1978** Den: Rec 10-54 5.4 1 TD. **1979** Was-ChiB: Rec 1-27 27.0. ChiB: Rec 1-27 27.0. **Total:** Rec 21-222 10.6 2 TD.

		Rushing				Kickoff Returns					Tot
Year Team	**G**	**Ret**	**Yds**	**Avg**	**TD**	**Ret**	**Yds**	**Avg**	**TD**	**Fum**	**TD**
1976 Den	14	37	118	3.2	2	14	391	27.9	0	1	2
1977 Den	14	110	456	4.1	3	3	72	24.0	0	2	4
1978 Den	16	108	455	4.2	4	12	256	21.3	0	2	5
1979 Was-ChiB	14	7	18	2.6	0	4	86	21.5	0	0	0
1979 Was	5	2	4	2.0	0	3	73	24.3	0	0	0
1979 ChiB	9	5	14	2.8	0	1	13	13.0	0	0	0
NFL Total	58	262	1047	4.0	9	33	805	24.4	0	5	11

MIKE PERRINO Perrino, Michael Nicholas 6′5″, 285 **OT**
Col: Notre Dame *HS:* York [Elmhurst, IL] B: 3/2/1964, Chicago, IL
1987 Phi: 3 G.

MIKE PERROTTI Perrotti, Michael Anthony 6′3″, 243 **T**
Col: Ohio State; Cincinnati *HS:* Collinwood [Cleveland, OH]
B: 6/12/1923, Cleveland, OH D: 11/1974
AAFC **1948** LA-A: 14 G; Rec 0-7. **1949** LA-A: 12 G. **Total:** 26 G; Rec 0-7.

CLAUDE PERRY Perry, Claude 6′1″, 210 **T-G-DE-OE**
(Cupid) *Col:* Alabama *HS:* Walker [Jasper, AL] B: 10/31/1901, Jasper, AL D: 7/1975, Goodsprings, AL
1927 GB: 9 G. **1928** GB: 13 G. **1929** GB: 12 G. **1930** GB: 9 G. **1931** GB-Bkn: 9 G. GB: 5 G. Bkn: 4 G. **1932** GB: 13 G. **1933** GB: 11 G. **1934** GB: 12 G; Rush 1-2 2.0. **1935** GB: 5 G. **Total:** 93 G; Rush 1-2 2.0.

DARREN PERRY Perry, Darren 5′11″, 196 **DB**
Col: Penn State *HS:* Deep Creek [Chesapeake, VA] B: 12/29/1968, Chesapeake, VA *Drafted:* 1992 Round 8 Pit
1996 Pit: KR 1-8 8.0; 1 Sac. **1997** Pit: 1 Sac. **1998** Pit: 0.5 Sac.
Total: KR 1-8 8.0; 2.5 Sac.

		Interceptions			
Year Team	**G**	**Int**	**Yds**	**TD**	**Fum**
1992 Pit	16	6	69	0	0
1993 Pit	16	4	61	0	0
1994 Pit	16	7	112	0	0
1995 Pit	16	4	71	0	1
1996 Pit	16	5	115	1	1
1997 Pit	16	4	77	0	0
1998 Pit	14	2	69	0	1
NFL Total	110	32	574	1	3

ED PERRY Perry, Edwin Lewis 6′4″, 255 **TE**
Col: James Madison *HS:* Highland Springs [VA] B: 9/1/1974, Richmond, VA *Drafted:* 1997 Round 6 Mia
1997 Mia: KR 1-7 7.0. **Total:** KR 1-7 7.0.

		Receiving			
Year Team	**G**	**Rec**	**Yds**	**Avg**	**TD**
1997 Mia	16	11	45	4.1	1
1998 Mia	14	25	255	10.2	0
NFL Total	30	36	300	8.3	1

JOE PERRY Perry, Fletcher Joseph 6'0", 200 **FB-DB**
(The Jet) *Col:* Compton CC CA *HS:* David Starr Jordan [Los Angeles, CA] B: 1/27/1927, Stevens, AR *HOF:* 1969
AAFC **1948** SF-A: Rec 8-79 9.9 1 TD; KR 4-145 36.3 1 TD; Int 1-24. **1949** SF-A: Pass 2-0; Rec 11-146 13.3 3 TD; KR 14-337 24.1. **Total:** Pass 2-0; Rec 19-225 11.8 4 TD; KR 18-482 26.8 1 TD; Int 1-24.

		Rushing				Tot
Year Team	G	Att	Yds	Avg	TD	TD
1948 SF-A	14	77	562	7.3	10	12
1949 SF-A	11	115	783	6.8	8	11
AAFC Total	25	192	1345	7.0	18	23

NFL **1950** SF: KR 12-223 18.6. **1951** SF: Pass 1-1 100.0%, 31 31.00 1 TD; KR 1-32 32.0. **1952** SF: Pass 2-0. **1953** SF: Pass 1-1 100.0%, 14 14.00; KR 2-21 10.5; Scor 78, 0-3 FG. **1954** SF: Pass 1-1 100.0%, 34 34.00; Scor 57, 1-3 33.3% FG, 6-7 85.7% XK. **1955** SF: Pass 2-0. **1957** SF: Pass 1-0. **1963** SF: Pass 1-0. **Total:** Pass 9-3 33.3%, 79 8.78 1 TD; KR 15-276 18.4; Scor 375, 1-6 16.7% FG, 6-7 85.7% XK.

		Rushing				Receiving					Tot
Year Team	G	Att	Yds	Avg	TD	Rec	Yds	Avg	TD	Fum	TD
1950 SF	12	124	647	5.2	5	13	69	5.3	1	11	6
1951 SF	11	136	677	5.0	3	18	167	9.3	1	5	4
1952 SF	12	158	725	4.6	8	15	81	5.4	0	6	8
1953 SF	12	**192**	**1018**	5.3	**10**	19	191	10.1	3	8	**13**
1954 SF	12	**173**	**1049**	6.1	8	26	203	7.8	0	6	8
1955 SF	11	156	701	4.5	2	19	55	2.9	1	6	3
1956 SF	11	115	520	4.5	3	18	104	5.8	0	3	3
1957 SF	8	97	454	4.7	3	15	130	8.7	0	3	3
1958 SF	12	125	758	6.1	4	23	218	9.5	1	3	5
1959 SF	11	139	602	4.3	3	12	53	4.4	0	6	3
1960 SF	10	36	95	2.6	1	3	-3	-1.0	0	2	1
1961 Bal	13	168	675	4.0	3	34	322	9.5	1	3	4
1962 Bal	12	94	359	3.8	0	22	194	8.8	0	3	0
1963 SF	9	24	98	4.1	0	4	12	3.0	0	1	0
NFL Total	156	1737	8378	4.8	53	241	1796	7.5	8	66	61

GERALD PERRY Perry, Gerald 6'6", 300 **OG**
Col: Southern University *HS:* Dreher [Columbia, SC] B: 11/12/1964, Columbia, SC *Drafted:* 1988 Round 2 Den
1988 Den: 16 G. **1989** Den: 16 G. **1990** Den: 8 G. **1991** LARm: 11 G. **1992** LARm: 16 G. **1993** LARd: 15 G. **1994** LARd: 12 G. **1995** Oak: 3 G. **Total:** 97 G.

GERRY PERRY Perry, Gerald Edward 6'4", 237 **DT-DE-OT-OG**
Col: Compton CC CA; Pepperdine; California *HS:* John C. Fremont [Los Angeles, CA] B: 7/17/1930, Ballston Spa, NY *Drafted:* 1952 Round 29 LARm
1957 Det: KR 1-18 18.0. **Total:** KR 1-18 18.0.

		Scoring						
Year Team	G	Pts	FG	FGA	FG%	XK	XKA	XK%
1954 Det	11	0	0	0	—	0	0	—
1956 Det	12	0	0	0	—	0	0	—
1957 Det	12	0	0	0	—	0	0	—
1958 Det	12	13	4	4	100.0	1	1	100.0
1959 Det	10	27	3	6	50.0	18	18	100.0
1960 StL	12	44	13	20	65.0	5	5	100.0
1961 StL	13	51	7	16	43.8	30	33	90.9
1962 StL	14	53	5	12	41.7	38	39	97.4
NFL Total	96	188	32	58	55.2	92	96	95.8

LEON PERRY Perry, Leon Jr. 5'11", 224 **RB**
Col: Mississippi *HS:* Amite Co. [Gloster, MS] B: 8/14/1957, Gloster, MS
1980 NYG: Rec 8-84 10.5 1 TD. **1981** NYG: Rec 13-140 10.8 1 TD. **1982** NYG: Rec 1-(-1) -1.0. **Total:** Rec 22-223 10.1 2 TD.

		Rushing					Tot
Year Team	G	Att	Yds	Avg	TD	Fum	TD
1980 NYG	10	59	272	4.6	1	3	2
1981 NYG	16	72	257	3.6	0	4	1
1982 NYG	2	3	14	4.7	0	1	0
NFL Total	28	134	543	4.1	1	8	3

LOWELL PERRY Perry, Lowell Wesley 6'0", 195 **OE-HB**
Col: Michigan *HS:* Ypsilanti [MI] B: 12/5/1931, Ypsilanti, MI
1956 Pit: 6 G; Rush 2-37 18.5; Rec 14-334 23.9 2 TD; PR 11-127 11.5; KR 9-219 24.3; 12 Pt.

MARLO PERRY Perry, Malcolm Marlo 6'4", 250 **LB**
Col: Jackson State *HS:* Scott Central [Forest, MS] B: 8/25/1972, Forest, MS *Drafted:* 1994 Round 3 Buf
1994 Buf: 2 G. **1995** Buf: 16 G. **1996** Buf: 13 G; Int 1-6. **1997** Buf: 13 G; Int 1-4. **1998** Buf: 16 G. **Total:** 60 G; Int 2-10.

MICHAEL DEAN PERRY Perry, Michael Dean 6'1", 285 **DT-DE**
Col: Clemson *HS:* South Aiken [Aiken, SC] B: 8/27/1965, Aiken, SC *Drafted:* 1988 Round 2 Cle
1988 Cle: 16 G; KR 1-13 13.0; **1** Fum TD; 6 Pt; 6 Sac. **1989** Cle: 16 G; 7 Sac. **1990** Cle: 16 G; 11.5 Sac. **1991** Cle: 16 G; 8.5 Sac. **1992** Cle: 14 G; 8.5 Sac. **1993** Cle: 16 G; 6 Sac. **1994** Cle: 15 G; 4 Sac. **1995** Den: 14 G; 6 Sac. **1996** Den: 15 G; 3.5 Sac. **1997** Den-KC: 10 G. Den: 9 G. KC: 1 G. **Total:** 148 G; KR 1-13 13.0; 1 Fum TD; 6 Pt; 61.0 Sac.

ROD PERRY Perry, Rodney Cornell 5'9", 178 **DB**
Col: Fresno City Coll. CA (J.C.); Colorado *HS:* Herbert Hoover [Fresno, CA] B: 9/11/1953, Fresno, CA *Drafted:* 1975 Round 4 LARm

		Interceptions		
Year Team	G	Int	Yds	TD
1975 LARm	9	0	0	0
1976 LARm	14	8	79	0
1977 LARm	5	1	0	0
1978 LARm	16	8	117	**3**
1979 LARm	9	0	0	0
1980 LARm	16	5	115	1
1981 LARm	16	3	18	0
1982 LARm	9	3	57	0
1983 Cle	16	1	21	0
1984 Cle	8	1	17	0
NFL Total	118	30	424	4

MARIO PERRY Perry, Romauro Ron 6'6", 240 **TE**
Col: Mississippi *HS:* Hillcrest [Memphis, TN] B: 12/20/1963, Chicago, IL *Drafted:* 1987 Round 11 LARd
1987 LARd: 3 G; Rec 1-3 3.0 1 TD; 6 Pt.

SCOTT PERRY Perry, Scott Endecott 6'0", 180 **DB**
Col: Williams *HS:* Kent School [CT] B: 3/11/1954, Pleasanton, CA *Drafted:* 1976 Round 5 Cin
1976 Cin: 12 G. **1977** Cin: 9 G. **1978** Cin: 13 G; Int 3-59 2 TD; Tot TD 3; 18 Pt. **1979** Cin: 14 G; Int 1-11. **1980** SF-SD: 15 G. SF: 11 G. SD: 4 G. **Total:** 63 G; Int 4-70 2 TD; Tot TD 3; 18 Pt.

TODD PERRY Perry, Todd Joseph 6'5", 308 **OG**
Col: Kentucky *HS:* Elizabethtown [KY] B: 11/28/1970, Elizabethtown, KY *Drafted:* 1993 Round 4 ChiB
1993 ChiB: 13 G. **1994** ChiB: 15 G. **1995** ChiB: 15 G. **1996** ChiB: 16 G. **1997** ChiB: 11 G. **1998** ChiB: 16 G. **Total:** 86 G.

VERNON PERRY Perry, Vernon Jr. 6'2", 211 **DB**
Col: Jackson State *HS:* Wingfield [Jackson, MS] B: 9/22/1953, Jackson, MS

		Interceptions		
Year Team	G	Int	Yds	TD
1979 Hou	16	3	33	0
1980 Hou	16	5	85	0
1981 Hou	16	2	46	0
1982 Hou	7	1	8	0
1983 NO	12	0	0	0
NFL Total	67	11	172	0

VICTOR PERRY Perry, Victor Antonio 6'5", 278 **OT**
Col: Georgia *HS:* Fitzgerald [GA] B: 2/26/1964, Fitzgerald, GA
1987 StL: 1 G.

WILLIAM PERRY Perry, William Anthony 6'2", 335 **DT-DE-FB**
(Refrigerator) *Col:* Clemson *HS:* Aiken [SC] B: 12/16/1962, Aiken, SC *Drafted:* 1985 Round 1 ChiB
1985 ChiB: 16 G; Rush 5-7 1.4 2 TD; Rec 1-4 4.0 1 TD; Tot TD 3; 18 Pt; 5 Sac. **1986** ChiB: 16 G; Rush 1-(-1) -1.0; 1 Fum; 5 Sac. **1987** ChiB: 12 G; Rush 1-0; 1 Fum; 3 Sac. **1988** ChiB: 3 G. **1989** ChiB: 13 G; 4 Sac. **1990** ChiB: 16 G; Rush 1-(-1) -1.0; 4 Sac. **1991** ChiB: 16 G; 5.5 Sac. **1992** ChiB: 15 G; 2 Sac. **1993** ChiB-Phi: 15 G; 1 Sac. ChiB: 7 G. Phi: 8 G; 1 Sac. **1994** Phi: 16 G. **Total:** 138 G; Rush 8-5 0.6 2 TD; Rec 1-4 4.0 1 TD; Tot TD 3; 18 Pt; 2 Fum; 29.5 Sac.

WILMONT PERRY Perry, Wilmont Darnell 6'1", 230 **RB**
Col: Livingstone *HS:* Garner [NC] B: 2/24/1975, Franklinton, NC *Drafted:* 1998 Round 5 NO
1998 NO: Rec 1-2 2.0.

		Rushing				
Year Team	G	Att	Yds	Avg	TD	Fum
1998 NO	6	30	122	4.1	0	1

JIM PERRYMAN Perryman, James T Jr. 6'0", 180 **DB**
Col: Millikin *HS:* South Hills Catholic [Pittsburgh, PA] B: 12/23/1960, Oakland, CA
1985 Buf: 11 G; 2 Sac. **1987** Ind: 14 G; KR 1-4 4.0; Int 1-0; 1 Sac. **Total:** 25 G; KR 1-4 4.0; Int 1-0; 3 Sac.

BOB PERRYMAN Perryman, Robert Lewis Jr. 6'1", 233 **RB**
Col: Michigan *HS:* Bourne [MA] B: 10/16/1964, Raleigh, NC *Drafted:* 1987 Round 3 NE
1987 NE: KR 3-43 14.3. **Total:** KR 3-43 14.3.

		Rushing				Receiving				
Year Team	G	Att	Yds	Avg	TD	Rec	Yds	Avg	TD	Fum
1987 NE	9	41	187	4.6	0	3	13	4.3	0	1
1988 NE	16	146	448	3.1	6	17	134	7.9	0	4
1989 NE	16	150	562	3.7	2	29	195	6.7	0	2
1990 NE	8	32	97	3.0	1	15	88	5.9	0	2
1991 Den	15	21	45	2.1	0	17	171	10.1	0	1
1992 Den	4	3	-1	-0.3	0	2	15	7.5	0	0
NFL Total	68	393	1338	3.4	9	83	616	7.4	0	10

ARA PERSON Person, Ara Jr. 6′4″, 225 **TE**
Col: Morgan State *HS:* Baltimore City College [MD] B: 9/23/1948, Baltimore, MD *Drafted:* 1970 Round 3 Bal
1972 StL: 4 G.

DICK PESONEN Pesonen, Richard Martin 6′0″, 190 **DB**
Col: Minnesota; Minnesota-Duluth *HS:* Proctor [MN] B: 6/10/1938, Grand Rapids, MN
1960 GB: 12 G. **1961** Min: 11 G; KR 6-136 22.7; Int 1-28; 1 Fum. **1962** NYG: 13 G; Int 2-24. **1963** NYG: 14 G; PR 7-47 6.7; KR 8-197 24.6; Int 1-1. **1964** NYG: 5 G. **Total:** 55 G; PR 7-47 6.7; KR 14-333 23.8; Int 4-53; 1 Fum.

LOUIE PESSOLANO Pessolano, Louis Carl 6′0″, 215 **T-G-OE**
(Bon Gi; Pess) *Col:* Villanova *HS:* New Kensington [PA] B: 2/23/1907, New Kensington, PA D: 2/8/1983, Augusta, GA
1929 SI: 3 G.

WALLY PESUIT Pesuit, Walter George 6′4″, 252 **OG-C-OT-DE**
Col: Kentucky *HS:* Wintersville [OH] B: 3/4/1954, Steubenville, OH
Drafted: 1976 Round 5 Dal
1976 Atl: 1 G. **1977** Mia: 14 G. **1978** Mia: 16 G. **1979** Det: 16 G; PR 1-5 5.0. **1980** Det: 1 G. **Total:** 48 G; PR 1-5 5.0.

JOHN PETCHEL Petchel, John 5′11″, 185 **BB-DB-LB**
Col: Duquesne *HS:* Freeland [PA] B: 5/27/1919, Freeland, PA
D: 1/25/1988, Beaver, PA
1942 Cle: 7 G; Rush 1-(-2) -2.0; Rec 1-16 16.0; KR 2-26 13.0. **1944** Cle: 10 G; Pass 3-2 66.7%, 27 9.00; Rush 5-11 2.2; Rec 1-43 43.0 1 TD; KR 1-17 17.0; Int 1-25; 6 Pt. **1945** Pit: 9 G; Pass 1-1 100.0%, 8 8.00; Rush 2-2 1.0; Rec 2-25 12.5; Int 1-4. **Total:** 26 G; Pass 4-3 75.0%, 35 8.75; Rush 8-11 1.4; Rec 4-84 21.0 1 TD; KR 3-43 14.3; Int 2-29; 6 Pt.

BONI PETCOFF Petcoff, Boni Eli 5′10″, 223 **T**
Col: Ohio State *HS:* Morrison R. Waite [Toledo, OH] B: 2/1/1900
D: 8/5/1965, Todedo, OH
1924 Col: 8 G. **1925** Col: 9 G. **1926** Col: 4 G. **Total:** 21 G.

LAWRENCE PETE Pete, Lawrence 6′0″, 286 **DT**
Col: Nebraska *HS:* South [Wichita, KS] B: 1/18/1966, Wichita, KS
Drafted: 1989 Round 5 Det
1989 Det: 16 G; 1 Sac. **1990** Det: 6 G. **1991** Det: 14 G; 1.5 Sac. **1992** Det: 13 G; 1 Sac. **1993** Det: 12 G. **Total:** 61 G; 3.5 Sac.

CHRISTIAN PETER Peter, Christian 6′3″, 300 **DT**
Col: Nebraska *HS:* Middletown-South [NJ]; Milford Acad. [CT]
B: 10/5/1972, Locust, NJ *Drafted:* 1996 Round 5 NE
1997 NYG: 7 G; 0.5 Sac. **1998** NYG: 16 G; 1 Sac. **Total:** 23 G; 1.5 Sac.

JASON PETER Peter, Jason Michael 6′4″, 295 **DE**
Col: Nebraska *HS:* Middletown-South [NJ]; Milford Acad. [CT]
B: 9/13/1974, Locust, NJ *Drafted:* 1998 Round 1 Car
1998 Car: 14 G; 1 Sac.

TONY PETERS Peters, Anthony Lemont 6′1″, 187 **DB**
Col: Northeastern Oklahoma A&M (J.C.); Oklahoma *HS:* Pauls Valley [OK] B: 4/28/1953, Oklahoma City, OK *Drafted:* 1975 Round 4 Cle
1979 Was: PR 1-0. **1981** Was: KR 1-5 5.0. **Total:** PR 1-0; KR 1-5 5.0.

		Interceptions			
Year Team	G	Int	Yds	TD	Fum
1975 Cle	14	1	0	0	0
1976 Cle	14	0	0	0	0
1977 Cle	14	2	29	0	0
1978 Cle	16	2	7	0	0
1979 Was	16	1	-4	0	1
1980 Was	16	4	59	0	1
1981 Was	16	3	0	0	0
1982 Was	9	1	14	0	0
1984 Was	8	0	0	0	0
1985 Was	10	2	21	0	0
NFL Total	133	16	126	0	2

ANTON PETERS Peters, Anton Berdette Jr. 6′4″, 245 **DT**
Col: Florida *HS:* Hillsborough [Tampa, FL] B: 2/3/1941, Fort Myers, FL
Drafted: 1963 Round 6 Den
1963 Den: 10 G.

FLOYD PETERS Peters, Floyd Charles 6′4″, 254 **DT**
(Pete) *Col:* San Francisco State *HS:* John Swett [Crockett, CA]
B: 5/21/1936, Council Bluffs, IA *Drafted:* 1958 Round 8 Bal
1959 Cle: 12 G. **1960** Cle: 12 G. **1961** Cle: 13 G. **1962** Cle: 14 G; Int 1-9. **1963** Det: 14 G. **1964** Phi: 14 G. **1965** Phi: 9 G. **1966** Phi: 14 G. **1967** Phi: 14 G; Int 1-3. **1968** Phi: 5 G; Int 1-0. **1969** Phi: 14 G. **1970** Was: 10 G. **Total:** 145 G; Int 3-12.

FROSTY PETERS Peters, Forrest Ingman 5′10″, 183 **TB-BB-WB**
Col: Montana; Illinois *HS:* Billings [MT] B: 4/22/1904, Creston, IA
D: 4/17/1980, Decatur, IL
1930 Prov-Port: 15 G; Pass 2 TD; Rush 1 TD; Int 1 TD; Scor 25, **2** FG, 7 XK; Tot TD 2. Prov: 12 G; Pass 2 TD; Rush 1 TD; Int 1 TD; Scor 25, 2 FG, 7 XK; Tot TD 2. Port: 3 G. **1931** Bkn: 9 G; Pass 1 TD; Scor 2, 2 XK. **1932** ChiC: 1 G. **Total:** 25 G; Pass 3 TD; Rush 1 TD; Int 1 TD; Scor 27, 2 FG, 9 XK; Tot TD 2.

FRANK PETERS Peters, Frank D 6′4″, 250 **OT**
Col: Ohio U. *HS:* Hamilton Twp. [Lockborne, OH] B: 7/17/1947
Drafted: 1969 Round 9 NYJ
1969 Cin: 3 G.

TYRELL PETERS Peters, Tyrell 6′0″, 230 **LB**
Col: Oklahoma *HS:* Norman [OK] B: 8/4/1974, Oklahoma City, OK
1997 Bal: 4 G. **1998** Bal: 10 G. **Total:** 14 G.

VOLNEY PETERS Peters, Volney Monroe 6′4″, 237 **DT-OT-DE**
Col: Compton CC CA; USC *HS:* Herbert Hoover [San Diego, CA]
B: 1/1/1928, Minneapolis, MN *Drafted:* 1951 Round 13 ChiC
1952 ChiC: 12 G; Rush 1-(-7) -7.0; PR 1-0; KR 1-4 4.0; 1 Fum TD; 6 Pt; 1 Fum. **1953** ChiC: 12 G. **1954** Was: 8 G. **1955** Was: 12 G. **1956** Was: 12 G. **1957** Was: 12 G. **1958** Phi: 10 G. **1960** LAC: 14 G. **1961** Oak: 12 G. **Total:** 104 G; Rush 1-(-7) -7.0; PR 1-0; KR 1-4 4.0; 1 Fum TD; 6 Pt; 1 Fum.

KURT PETERSEN Petersen, Kurt David 6′4″, 264 **OG**
Col: Missouri *HS:* Lutheran North [St. Louis, MO] B: 6/17/1957, St. Louis, MO *Drafted:* 1980 Round 4 Dal
1980 Dal: 16 G. **1981** Dal: 16 G. **1982** Dal: 9 G. **1983** Dal: 14 G. **1984** Dal: 13 G. **1985** Dal: 16 G. **Total:** 84 G.

TED PETERSEN Petersen, Theodore Hans III 6′5″, 244 **OT-C-OG**
Col: Eastern Illinois *HS:* Momence [IL] B: 2/7/1955, Kankakee, IL
Drafted: 1977 Round 4 Pit
1977 Pit: 14 G. **1978** Pit: 15 G. **1979** Pit: 16 G. **1980** Pit: 16 G. **1981** Pit: 2 G. **1982** Pit: 7 G. **1983** Pit: 13 G. **1984** Cle-Ind: 9 G. Cle: 4 G. Ind: 5 G. **1987** Pit: 2 G. **Total:** 94 G.

KEN PETERSEN Petersen, Thornton Kenneth 6′2″, 235 **OG**
Col: Utah *HS:* South [Salt Lake City, UT] B: 3/26/1939, Logan, UT
Drafted: 1961 Round 14 Min
1961 Min: 12 G.

BRETT PETERSMARK Petersmark, Robert Brett 6′3″, 280 **C**
Col: Eastern Michigan *HS:* Catholic Central [Redford, MI] B: 3/5/1964
1987 Hou: 3 G.

ANDREW PETERSON Peterson, Andrew Scott 6′5″, 308 **OG-OT**
Col: Washington *HS:* South Kitsap [Port Orchard, WA] B: 6/11/1972, Greenock, Scotland *Drafted:* 1995 Round 5 Car
1995 Car: 4 G.

TONY PETERSON Peterson, Anthony Wayne 6′1″, 223 **LB**
Col: Notre Dame *HS:* Ringgold [Monongahela, PA] B: 1/23/1972, Cleveland, OH *Drafted:* 1994 Round 5 SF
1994 SF: 15 G. **1995** SF: 15 G. **1996** SF: 13 G. **1997** ChiB: 16 G. **1998** SF: 16 G; 1 Sac. **Total:** 75 G; 1 Sac.

CAL PETERSON Peterson, Calvin Elston 6′3″, 220 **LB**
Col: UCLA *HS:* Los Angeles [CA] B: 10/16/1952, Los Angeles, CA
Drafted: 1974 Round 3 Dal
1974 Dal: 14 G. **1975** Dal: 14 G; KR 1-10 10.0; Int 1-19. **1976** TB: 5 G; Int 1-15. **1979** KC: 16 G; KR 1-0. **1980** KC: 16 G. **1981** KC: 11 G. **1982** LARd: 4 G. **Total:** 80 G; KR 2-10 5.0; Int 2-34.

CARL PETERSON Peterson, Carl John 5′11″, 175 **E**
Col: Nebraska *HS:* Bethany Acad. [Lindsborg, KS] B: 3/26/1897, Salt Lake City, UT D: 7/1964, KS
1924 KC: 9 G.

JERRY PETERSON Peterson, Gerald Ray 6′3″, 290 **DT**
(The Heap) *Col:* Wharton Co. JC TX; Texas B: 10/8/1934, El Campo, TX *Drafted:* 1955 Round 15 Bal
1956 Bal: 1 G.

JIM PETERSON Peterson, James A 6′5″, 235 **LB**
Col: San Diego Mesa Coll. CA (J.C.); San Diego State *HS:* Crawford [San Diego, CA] B: 1/20/1950, San Diego, CA *Drafted:* 1973 Round 6 LARm
1974 LARm: 14 G. **1975** LARm: 14 G; **1** Fum TD; 6 Pt. **1976** TB: 3 G. **Total:** 31 G; 1 Fum TD; 6 Pt.

JOE PETERSON Peterson, Joseph 5′10″, 185 **DB**
Col: Nevada-Reno *HS:* Sacred Heart [San Francisco, CA]
B: 8/15/1964, San Francisco, CA
1987 NE: 3 G; Int 1-0.

TODD PETERSON Peterson, Joseph Todd 5′10″, 173 **K**
Col: Navy; Georgia *HS:* Valwood [Valdosta, GA] B: 2/4/1970, Washington, DC *Drafted:* 1993 Round 7 NYG

Year Team	G	Scoring Pts	FG	FGA	FG%	XK	XKA	XK%
1994 Ariz	2	10	2	4	50.0	4	4	100.0
1995 Sea	16	109	23	28	82.1	40	40	100.0
1996 Sea	16	111	28	34	82.4	27	27	100.0
1997 Sea	16	103	22	28	78.6	37	37	100.0
1998 Sea	16	98	19	24	79.2	41	41	100.0
NFL Total	66	431	94	118	79.7	149	149	100.0

IKE PETERSON Peterson, Kenneth 5′9″, 185 **TB-DB-WB**
Col: Gonzaga B: 7/8/1909, Berill, ID
1935 ChiC: Pass 17-5 29.4%, 92 5.41 1 TD 3 Int; Rec 2-37 18.5.
1936 Det: Pass 6-0, 1 Int; Rec 8-38 4.8. **Total:** Pass 23-5 21.7%, 92 4.00 1 TD 4 Int; Rec 10-75 7.5.

Year Team	G	Rushing Att	Yds	Avg	TD
1935 ChiC	11	95	297	3.1	0
1936 Det	11	41	278	6.8	3
NFL Total	22	136	575	4.2	3

LES PETERSON Peterson, Lester Carl 6′3″, 206 **OE-T**
(Tex) *Col:* Texas *HS:* Taylor [TX] B: 11/27/1909 D: 1/25/1993, Big Spring, TX
1931 Port: 10 G. **1932** GB-SI: 14 G; Rec 2-49 24.5. GB: 9 G; Rec 1-23 23.0. SI: 5 G; Rec 1-26 26.0. **1933** Bkn: 9 G; Rec 13-170 13.1. **1934** GB: 11 G; Rush 1-0; Rec 6-139 23.2. **Total:** 44 G; Rush 1-0; Rec 21-358 17.0.

NELS PETERSON Peterson, Nelson Lane 5′8″, 179 **WB-DB-TB**
(Banty) *Col:* West Virginia Wesleyan B: 9/22/1913, Weston, WV D: 12/4/1990
1937 Was: 2 G; Rush 2-8 4.0. **1938** Cle: 7 G; Pass 6-0, 2 Int; Rush 21-70 3.3 1 TD; Rec 4-43 10.8 1 TD; Scor 20, 2-2 100.0% FG, 2-2 100.0% XK; Tot TD 2. **Total:** 9 G; Pass 6-0, 2 Int; Rush 23-78 3.4 1 TD; Rec 4-43 10.8 1 TD; Scor 20, 2-2 100.0% FG, 2-2 100.0% XK; Tot TD 2.

PHIL PETERSON Peterson, Philip 5′11″, 195 **OE-DE**
Col: Wisconsin B: 3/29/1906 D: 3/1981, St.Croix Falls, WI
1934 Bkn: 3 G.

RAY PETERSON Peterson, Raymond 6′0″, 190 **TB-DB**
Col: San Francisco *HS:* Fort Bragg [CA] B: 1/8/1916 D: 7/1977, Seattle, WA
1937 GB: 2 G; Pass 6-3 50.0%, 47 7.83.

RUSS PETERSON Peterson, Russell Harold 6′3″, 216 **T**
Col: Montana *HS:* Custer Co. [Miles City, MT] B: 8/25/1905, Midale, Canada D: 10/1971
1932 Bos: 3 G.

BILL PETERSON Peterson, William Wallace 6′3″, 230 **LB-TE**
Col: San Jose State *HS:* Clairemont [San Diego, CA] B: 6/6/1945, San Jose, CA
1968 Cin: 7 G; Rec 1-10 10.0; KR 3-80 26.7. **1969** Cin: 14 G; Int 4-23. **1970** Cin: 14 G. **1971** Cin: 14 G; Int 1-16. **1972** Cin: 14 G. **1975** KC: 14 G; KR 1-8 8.0. **Total:** 77 G; Rec 1-10 10.0; KR 4-88 22.0; Int 5-39.

JOHNNY PETITBON Petitbon, John Ellis 5′11″, 186 **DB-HB**
Col: Notre Dame *HS:* Jesuit [New Orleans, LA] B: 6/4/1931, New Orleans, LA *Drafted:* 1952 Round 7 Dal
1952 Dal: 11 G; Rec 1-11 11.0; KR 1-11 11.0; Int 5-42; 1 Fum. **1955** Cle: 12 G; Rush 3-10 3.3; Int 2-11. **1956** Cle: 12 G. **1957** GB: 12 G; Int 1-0. **Total:** 47 G; Rush 3-10 3.3; Rec 1-11 11.0; KR 1-11 11.0; Int 8-53; 1 Fum.

RICHIE PETITBON Petitbon, Richard Alvin 6′3″, 206 **DB**
Col: Tulane *HS:* Jesuit [New Orleans, LA] B: 4/18/1938, New Orleans, LA *Drafted:* 1959 Round 2 ChiB
1959 ChiB: PR 11-72 6.5; KR 4-68 17.0. **1960** ChiB: PR 2-22 11.0.
1961 ChiB: PR 2-9 4.5. **1970** LARm: Rush 1-3 3.0. **1971** Was: Rush 1-(-2) -2.0. **Total:** Rush 2-1 0.5; PR 15-103 6.9; KR 4-68 17.0.

Year Team	G	Interceptions Int	Yds	TD	Fum
1959 ChiB	12	3	52	**1**	1
1960 ChiB	12	2	0	0	0
1961 ChiB	14	5	71	0	0
1962 ChiB	14	6	**212**	**1**	1
1963 ChiB	14	8	161	1	0
1964 ChiB	14	0	0	0	0
1965 ChiB	14	2	22	0	0
1966 ChiB	14	4	34	0	0
1967 ChiB	14	5	73	0	0
1968 ChiB	14	2	18	0	0
1969 LARm	12	5	46	0	0
1970 LARm	14	1	10	0	0
1971 Was	14	5	102	0	2
1972 Was	3	0	0	0	0
NFL Total	179	48	801	3	4

LEO PETREE Petree, Leo Harley 200 **HB**
Col: Northeast Missouri State *HS:* Kirksville [MO] B: 1/1893, Union Star, MO D: 1971, Toledo, OH
1920 Cle: 2 G. **1922** Tol: 5 G; Rush 1 TD; 6 Pt. **Total:** 7 G; Rush 1 TD; 6 Pt.

PEPPER PETRELLA Petrella, John Anton 5′7″, 160 **HB-DB**
Col: Penn State *HS:* Downingtown [PA] B: 5/7/1920, Downingtown, PA D: 12/21/1991, Azusa, CA
1945 Pit: 3 G; Rush 15-33 2.2; PR 6-52 8.7; KR 3-85 28.3; Int 1-8; 2 Fum.

BOB PETRELLA Petrella, Robert Francis 5′11″, 190 **DB**
(Pete) *Col:* Tennessee *HS:* South Philadelphia [Philadelphia, PA] B: 11/7/1944, Philadelphia, PA *Drafted:* 1966 Round 8 Mia
1966 Mia: 3 G. **1967** Mia: 9 G; Int 3-67. **1968** Mia: 9 G; Int 1-4. **1969** Mia: 14 G; Int 1-33. **1970** Mia: 14 G. **1971** Mia: 12 G. **Total:** 61 G; Int 5-104.

BOB PETRICH Petrich, Robert Mark 6′4″, 252 **DE**
Col: West Texas A&M *HS:* San Pedro [CA] B: 3/15/1941, Long Beach, CA *Drafted:* 1963 Round 11 SD
1963 SD: 14 G. **1964** SD: 14 G; Int 1-11. **1965** SD: 14 G. **1966** SD: 14 G. **1967** Buf: 6 G. **Total:** 62 G; Int 1-11.

BILL PETRILAS Petrilas, William A 6′1″, 195 **DB-WB**
Col: No College B: 9/28/1915, New Haven, CT D: 11/4/1976, Middletown, CT
1944 NYG: 9 G; Rush 12-29 2.4; PR 4-58 14.5; Int 5-144 **2** TD; 12 Pt.
1945 NYG: 5 G; Int 2-1. **Total:** 14 G; Rush 12-29 2.4; PR 4-58 14.5; Int 7-145 2 TD; 12 Pt.

STEVE PETRO Petro, Stephen Lawrence 5′10″, 195 **G-LB**
(Rock) *Col:* Pittsburgh *HS:* Johnstown [PA] B: 10/21/1914, Johnstown, PA D: 8/15/1994, Pittsburgh, PA *Drafted:* 1939 Round 9 Pit
1940 Bkn: 11 G. **1941** Bkn: 6 G. **Total:** 17 G.

GEORGE PETROVICH Petrovich, George John Jr. 6′2″, 225 **OG-OT-DT**
Col: Texas *HS:* Palestine [TX] B: 3/22/1926, Palestine, TX *Drafted:* 1948 Round 13 ChiC
1949 ChiC: 12 G. **1950** ChiC: 10 G. **Total:** 22 G.

STAN PETRY Petry, Stanley Edward 5′11″, 174 **DB**
Col: Texas Christian *HS:* Willowridge [Sugar Land, TX] B: 8/14/1966, Alvin, TX *Drafted:* 1989 Round 4 KC
1989 KC: 16 G; 0.5 Sac. **1990** KC: 16 G; Int 3-33 1 TD; 6 Pt.
1991 KC-NO: 4 G; Int 1-4. KC: 2 G. NO: 2 G; Int 1-4. **Total:** 36 G; Int 4-37 1 TD; 6 Pt; 0.5 Sac.

PHIL PETTEY Pettey, Philip Edward 6′4″, 274 **OG**
Col: Missouri *HS:* Mary Bradford [Kenosha, WI] B: 4/17/1961, Kenosha, WI
1987 Was: 3 G.

NEAL PETTIES Petties, Neal 6′2″, 198 **WR**
Col: San Diego State *HS:* San Diego [CA] B: 9/16/1940, San Diego, CA *Drafted:* 1963 Round 14 Bal
1964 Bal: 14 G; Rec 2-20 10.0 1 TD; KR 1-9 9.0; 6 Pt. **1965** Bal: 9 G.
1966 Bal: 10 G. **Total:** 33 G; Rec 2-20 10.0 1 TD; KR 1-9 9.0; 6 Pt.

GARY PETTIGREW Pettigrew, Gary Louis 6′5″, 255 **DT-DE**
Col: Stanford *HS:* Gonzaga Prep [Spokane, WA] B: 10/10/1944, Vancouver, Canada *Drafted:* 1966 Round 2 Phi
1966 Phi: 14 G. **1967** Phi: 13 G. **1968** Phi: 14 G. **1969** Phi: 7 G. **1970** Phi: 14 G; KR 1-11 11.0. **1971** Phi: 13 G; KR 2-37 18.5. **1972** Phi: 13 G; KR 1-17 17.0. **1973** Phi: 14 G. **1974** Phi-NYG: 9 G. Phi: 4 G. NYG: 5 G. **Total:** 111 G; KR 4-65 16.3.

DUANE PETTITT Pettitt, Duane Edward 6′4″, 265 **DE**
Col: San Diego State *HS:* Tehachapi [CA] B: 11/2/1964, Long Beach, CA
1987 SD: 3 G.

JOHN PETTY Petty, John 6′1″, 225 **FB**
Col: Purdue *HS:* Lebanon [PA] B: 10/3/1919, Lebanon, PA D: 4/6/1979, Wilmington, OH *Drafted:* 1942 Round 7 ChiB
1942 ChiB: Rec 4-53 13.3; Int 1-7; Punt 2-109 54.5.

Year Team	G	Rushing Att	Yds	Avg	TD
1942 ChiB	10	41	149	3.6	2

ROSS PETTY Petty, Manley Ross 6′1″, 180 **G**
Col: Illinois *HS:* Lawrenceville [IL] B: 9/11/1892, Sumner, IL D: 3/13/1966, Milwaukee, WI
1920 Sta: 10 G.

LARRY PETTY Petty, Otis Lawrence **G**
Col: Illinois State; Illinois *HS:* Lawrenceville [IL] B: 11/1893, Sumner, IL Deceased
1920 Can: 2 G.

BARRY PETTYJOHN Pettyjohn, Barry Glen 6′5″, 285 **C-OT**
Col: Pittsburgh *HS:* Deer Park [Cincinnati, OH] B: 3/29/1964, Cincinnati, OH
1987 Hou: 2 G.

DAVID PETWAY Petway, David Lawrence 6′1″, 207 **DB**
Col: Northern Illinois *HS:* Lakeview [Chicago, IL] B: 10/17/1955, Chicago, IL
1981 GB: 6 G.

BOB PEVIANI Peviani, Robert Angelo 6′1″, 210 **LB**
(Gene) *Col:* USC *HS:* James A. Garfield [Los Angeles, CA] B: 9/15/1931, Los Angeles, CA *Drafted:* 1953 Round 6 NYG
1953 NYG: 12 G.

LEO PEYTON Peyton, Leo 5′11″, 190 **BB-FB**
Col: No College *HS:* Canton [NY] Deceased
1923 Roch: 2 G. **1924** Roch: 4 G. **Total:** 6 G.

BOB PFOHL Pfohl, Robert Stormont 6′0″, 200 **HB-DB**
(Stormy) *Col:* Kings Point; Purdue *HS:* Goshen [IN] B: 5/21/1926, Vincennes, IN D: 5/11/1996, West Lafayette, IN
AAFC **1948** BalA: Rec 13-134 10.3 1 TD; PR 2-102 51.0 1 TD; KR 17-366 21.5. **1949** BalA: Rec 7-62 8.9; KR 4-98 24.5. **Total:** Rec 20-196 9.8 1 TD; PR 2-102 51.0 1 TD; KR 21-464 22.1.

		Rushing				Tot
Year Team	**G**	**Att**	**Yds**	**Avg**	**TD**	**TD**
1948 BalA	14	107	455	4.3	4	6
1949 BalA	12	67	205	3.1	2	2
AAFC Total	26	174	660	3.8	6	8

ART PHARMER Pharmer, Charles Arthur 5′10″, 186 **TB-FB-BB**
Col: Minnesota *HS:* Pasco [WA] B: 7/21/1908 D: 2/1970
1930 Min-Fra: 13 G; Pass 1 TD; Rush 1 TD; Scor 12, 6 XK. Min: 8 G; Rush 1 TD; Scor 8, 2 XK. Fra: 5 G; Pass 1 TD; Scor 4, 4 XK. **1931** Fra: 2 G. **Total:** 15 G; Pass 1 TD; Rush 1 TD.

TOMMY PHARR Pharr, Tommy Lee 5′10″, 187 **DB**
Col: Gordon Coll. GA (J.C.); Mississippi State *HS:* Cherokee [Canton, GA] B: 7/31/1947, Canton, GA
1970 Buf: 10 G; PR 23-184 8.0; KR 1-6 6.0; 2 Fum.

BOB PHELAN Phelan, Robert Richard 5′11″, 185 **FB-WB-BB-TB**
Col: Notre Dame *HS:* Fort Madison [IA] B: 6/20/1898, Charleston, IA D: 8/1973, Fort Madison, IA
1922 Tol: 8 G; Rush 2 TD; 12 Pt. **1923** RI: 7 G. **1924** RI: 6 G. **Total:** 21 G; Rush 2 TD; 12 Pt.

DON PHELPS Phelps, Donald Cooper 5′11″, 185 **HB-DB**
(Dopey) *Col:* Kentucky *HS:* Danville [KY] B: 1/7/1924, Richmond, KY D: 6/11/1982, Frankfort, KY *Drafted:* 1950 Round 5 Cle
1950 Cle: Rec 1-28 28.0; PR 13-174 13.4 1 TD; KR 12-325 27.1; Int 1-9. **1951** Cle: PR 1-3 3.0; KR 3-66 22.0. **1952** Cle: PR 5-15 3.0. **Total:** Rec 1-28 28.0; PR 19-192 10.1 1 TD; KR 15-391 26.1; Int 1-9.

		Rushing					Tot
Year Team	**G**	**Att**	**Yds**	**Avg**	**TD**	**Fum**	**TD**
1950 Cle	12	39	198	5.1	2	2	3
1951 Cle	4	16	65	4.1	1	1	1
1952 Cle	1	0	0	—	0	0	0
NFL Total	17	55	263	4.8	3	3	4

PERRY PHENIX Phenix, Perry 5′11″, 210 **DB**
Col: Trinity Valley CC TX; Southern Mississippi *HS:* Hillcrest [Dallas, TX] B: 11/14/1974, Dallas, TX
1998 Ten: 15 G.

ROMAN PHIFER Phifer, Roman Zubinski 6′2″, 240 **LB**
Col: UCLA *HS:* South Mecklenburg [Charlotte, NC] B: 3/5/1968, Plattsburgh, NY *Drafted:* 1991 Round 2 LARm
1991 LARm: 12 G; 2 Sac. **1992** LARm: 16 G; Int 1-3. **1993** LARm: 16 G. **1994** LARm: 16 G; Int 2-7; 1.5 Sac. **1995** StL: 16 G; Int 3-52; 1 Fum; 3 Sac. **1996** StL: 15 G; 1.5 Sac. **1997** StL: 16 G; 2 Sac. **1998** StL: 13 G; Int 1-41; 1 Fum; 6.5 Sac. **Total:** 120 G; Int 7-103; 2 Fum; 16.5 Sac.

GERRY PHILBIN Philbin, Gerald John 6′2″, 245 **DE**
Col: Buffalo *HS:* William E. Tolman [Pawtucket, RI] B: 7/31/1941, Pawtucket, RI *Drafted:* 1964 Round 3 NYJ
1964 NYJ: 6 G. **1965** NYJ: 14 G. **1966** NYJ: 14 G. **1967** NYJ: 14 G. **1968** NYJ: 14 G; PR 1-2 2.0. **1969** NYJ: 13 G; Int 1-18. **1970** NYJ: 11 G. **1971** NYJ: 10 G. **1972** NYJ: 14 G. **1973** Phi: 13 G. **Total:** 123 G; PR 1-2 2.0; Int 1-18.

TODD PHILCOX Philcox, Todd Stuart 6′4″, 218 **QB**
Col: Syracuse *HS:* Norwalk [CT] B: 9/25/1966, Norwalk, CT
1991 Cle: Rush 1-(-1) -1.0. **1993** Cle: Rush 2-3 1.5 1 TD. **1997** SD: Rush 1-3 3.0. **Total:** Rush 4-5 1.3 1 TD.

		Passing								
Year Team	**G**	**Att**	**Comp**	**Comp%**	**Yds**	**YPA**	**TD**	**Int**	**Rating**	**Fum**
1990 Cin	2	2	0	0.0	0	0.00	0	1	0.0	0
1991 Cle	4	8	4	50.0	49	6.13	0	1	29.7	0
1992 Cle	2	27	13	48.1	217	8.04	3	1	97.3	0
1993 Cle	5	108	52	48.1	699	6.47	4	7	54.5	2
1997 SD	2	28	16	57.1	173	6.18	0	1	60.6	2
NFL Total	15	173	85	49.1	1138	6.58	7	11	57.4	4

ED PHILION Philion, Edmond Paul 6′2″, 277 **DT**
Col: Ferris State *HS:* Essex [Canada] B: 3/27/1970, Windsor, Canada
1994 Buf: 4 G. **1995** Buf: 2 G. **Total:** 6 G.

ANTHONY PHILLIPS Phillips, Anthony Dwayne 6′2″, 209 **DB**
Col: Texas A&M–Kingsville *HS:* Ball [Galveston, TX] B: 10/5/1970, Galveston, TX *Drafted:* 1994 Round 3 Atl
1994 Atl: 5 G; Int 1-0. **1995** Atl: 6 G; Int 1-43. **1996** Atl: 7 G. **1998** Min: 2 G. **Total:** 20 G; Int 2-43.

BOBBY PHILLIPS Phillips, Bobby Eugene II 5′9″, 194 **RB**
Col: Virginia Union *HS:* John Marshall [Richmond, VA] B: 12/8/1969, Richmond, VA
1995 Min: 8 G; Rush 14-26 1.9; KR 4-60 15.0; 1 Fum.

CHARLIE PHILLIPS Phillips, Charles W 6′2″, 215 **DB**
Col: USC *HS:* Blair [Pasadena, CA] B: 12/22/1952, Greenville, MS *Drafted:* 1975 Round 2 Oak
1975 Oak: PR 2-0. **1976** Oak: PR 2-7 3.5. **1978** Oak: **2** Fum TD. **Total:** PR 4-7 1.8; 2 Fum TD.

		Interceptions				Tot
Year Team	**G**	**Int**	**Yds**	**TD**	**Fum**	**TD**
1975 Oak	14	6	45	0	2	0
1976 Oak	14	1	11	0	0	0
1977 Oak	7	2	35	0	0	0
1978 Oak	16	6	121	1	0	3
1979 Oak	16	4	92	0	0	0
NFL Total	67	19	304	1	2	3

EWELL PHILLIPS Phillips, Ewell Ivan 5′11″, 210 **G**
(Cap) *Col:* Oklahoma Baptist *HS:* Walters [OK] B: 4/20/1909, Comanche, OK D: 12/31/1990, Lancaster, NC
1936 NYG: 12 G; Rec 1-5 5.0.

GEORGE PHILLIPS Phillips, George Cannady 6′3″, 215 **LB**
Col: UCLA *HS:* John C. Fremont [Los Angeles, CA] B: 1921 *Drafted:* 1944 Round 6 Phi
1945 Cle: 1 G.

IRVIN PHILLIPS Phillips, Irvin Jerome 6′1″, 192 **DB**
Col: Arkansas Tech *HS:* Sarasota [FL] B: 1/23/1960, Leesburg, FL *Drafted:* 1981 Round 3 SD
1981 SD: 15 G; PR 1-0; 1 Fum. **1983** LARd: 5 G. **Total:** 20 G; PR 1-0; 1 Fum.

JIM PHILLIPS Phillips, James Jackson 6′1″, 197 **OE-FL**
(Red) *Col:* Auburn *HS:* Benjamin Russell [Alexander City, AL] B: 2/5/1936, Alexander City, AL *Drafted:* 1958 Round 1 LARm

		Receiving				
Year Team	**G**	**Rec**	**Yds**	**Avg**	**TD**	**Fum**
1958 LARm	12	35	524	15.0	2	0
1959 LARm	9	37	541	14.6	4	0
1960 LARm	12	52	883	17.0	8	0
1961 LARm	14	**78**	1092	14.0	5	1
1962 LARm	14	60	875	14.6	5	1
1963 LARm	14	54	793	14.7	1	0
1964 LARm	7	17	245	14.4	2	0
1965 Min	12	15	185	12.3	1	0
1966 Min	12	32	554	17.3	3	0
1967 Min	13	21	352	16.8	3	0
NFL Total	119	401	6044	15.1	34	2

JASON PHILLIPS Phillips, Jason Howell 5′7″, 166 **WR**
Col: Taft Coll. CA (J.C.); Houston *HS:* Ross C. Sterling [Houston, TX] B: 10/11/1966, Crowley, LA *Drafted:* 1989 Round 10 Det
1990 Det: KR 2-43 21.5. **1993** Atl: KR 2-38 19.0. **Total:** KR 4-81 20.3.

		Receiving				
Year Team	**G**	**Rec**	**Yds**	**Avg**	**TD**	**Fum**
1989 Det	16	30	352	11.7	1	1
1990 Det	13	8	112	14.0	0	0
1991 Atl	11	6	73	12.2	0	0
1992 Atl	12	4	26	6.5	1	0
1993 Atl	6	1	15	15.0	0	0
NFL Total	58	49	578	11.8	2	1

JESS PHILLIPS Phillips, Jess Willard Jr. 6′1″, 210 **RB-DB**
Col: Michigan State *HS:* Pollard [Beaumont, TX] B: 2/28/1947, Beaumont, TX *Drafted:* 1968 Round 4 Cin
1968 Cin: PR 2-16 8.0; Int 3-26. **Total:** PR 2-16 8.0; Int 3-26.

		Rushing				Receiving			
Year Team	**G**	**Att**	**Yds**	**Avg**	**TD**	**Rec**	**Yds**	**Avg**	**TD**
1968 Cin	14	1	7	7.0	0	0	0	—	0
1969 Cin	14	118	578	4.9	3	13	128	9.8	0

1970 Cin	14	163	648	4.0	4	31	124	4.0	1
1971 Cin	14	94	420	4.5	0	22	125	5.7	1
1972 Cin	13	48	207	4.3	1	10	50	5.0	0
1973 NO	14	198	663	3.3	0	22	169	7.7	0
1974 NO	14	174	556	3.2	2	11	55	5.0	0
1975 Oak	14	63	298	4.7	1	4	25	6.3	0
1976 NE	13	24	164	6.8	1	1	18	18.0	0
1977 NE	14	5	27	5.4	1	0	0	—	0
NFL Total	138	888	3568	4.0	13	114	694	6.1	2

	Kickoff Returns					Tot
Year Team	**Ret**	**Yds**	**Avg**	**TD**	**Fum**	**TD**
1968 Cin	1	23	23.0	0	0	0
1969 Cin	3	52	17.3	0	4	3
1970 Cin	0	0	—	0	5	5
1971 Cin	2	49	24.5	0	3	1
1972 Cin	0	0	—	0	1	1
1973 NO	0	0	—	0	3	0
1974 NO	7	124	17.7	0	3	2
1975 Oak	12	310	25.8	0	2	1
1976 NE	14	397	28.4	0	1	1
1977 NE	6	93	15.5	0	0	1
NFL Total	45	1048	23.3	0	22	15

JOE PHILLIPS Phillips, Joseph Gordon 6′5″, 298 **NT-DT-DE**
Col: Chemeketa CC OR; Oregon State; Southern Methodist
HS: Columbia River [Vancouver, WA] B: 7/15/1963, Portland, OR
Drafted: 1986 Round 4 Min
1986 Min: 16 G. **1987** SD: 13 G; 5 Sac. **1988** SD: 16 G; 2 Sac. **1989** SD: 16 G; 1 Sac. **1990** SD: 3 G; 0.5 Sac. **1991** SD: 16 G; 1 Sac. **1992** KC: 12 G; 2.5 Sac. **1993** KC: 16 G; 1.5 Sac. **1994** KC: 16 G; 3 Sac. **1995** KC: 16 G; Int 1-2; 4.5 Sac. **1996** KC: 16 G; 2 Sac. **1997** KC: 15 G; Scor **1** Saf; 2 Pt; 0.5 Sac. **1998** StL: 13 G. **Total:** 184 G; Int 1-2; Scor 1 Saf; 2 Pt; 23.5 Sac.

JOE PHILLIPS Phillips, Joseph Jr. 5′9″, 188 **WR**
Col: Kentucky *HS:* Simpson [Franklin, KY] B: 5/12/1963, Franklin, KY
1985 Was: 4 G. **1987** Was: 2 G. **Total:** 6 G.

KIM PHILLIPS Phillips, Kim Darnell 5′9″, 188 **DB**
Col: North Texas *HS:* New Boston [TX] B: 10/28/1966, New Boston, TX *Drafted:* 1989 Round 3 NO
1989 NO: 5 G; KR 1-24 24.0. **1990** Buf: 1 G. **Total:** 6 G; KR 1-24 24.0.

KIRK PHILLIPS Phillips, Kirk Douglas 6′1″, 202 **WR**
Col: Tulsa *HS:* Spiro [OK] B: 7/31/1960, Poteau, OK
1984 Dal: 8 G; Rec 1-6 6.0.

LAWRENCE PHILLIPS Phillips, Lawrence Lamond 6′0″, 223 **RB**
Col: Nebraska *HS:* Baldwin Park [CA] B: 5/12/1975, Little Rock, AR
Drafted: 1996 Round 1 StL
1996 StL: Rec 8-28 3.5 1 TD; KR 4-74 18.5. **1997** StL-Mia: Rec 11-39 3.5. StL: Rec 10-33 3.3. Mia: Rec 1-6 6.0. **Total:** Rec 19-67 3.5 1 TD; KR 4-74 18.5.

		Rushing					Tot
Year Team	**G**	**Att**	**Yds**	**Avg**	**TD**	**Fum**	**TD**
1996 StL	15	193	632	3.3	4	2	5
1997 StL-Mia	12	201	677	3.4	8	3	8
1997 StL	10	183	633	3.5	8	3	8
1997 Mia	2	18	44	2.4	0	0	0
NFL Total	27	394	1309	3.3	12	5	13

LOYD PHILLIPS Phillips, Loyd Wade 6′3″, 240 **DE**
Col: Arkansas *HS:* Longview [TX] B: 5/2/1945, Fort Worth, TX
Drafted: 1967 Round 1 ChiB
1967 ChiB: 7 G. **1968** ChiB: 13 G; Int 2-23. **1969** ChiB: 12 G. **Total:** 32 G; Int 2-23.

MEL PHILLIPS Phillips, Melvin Jr. 6′2″, 198 **DB**
Col: North Carolina A&T *HS:* Cleveland [Shelby, NC] B: 1/6/1942, Shelby, NC *Drafted:* 1966 Round 5 SF
1966 SF: KR 1-20 20.0. **Total:** KR 1-20 20.0.

		Interceptions			
Year Team	**G**	**Int**	**Yds**	**TD**	**Fum**
1966 SF	11	0	0	0	0
1967 SF	14	1	0	0	0
1968 SF	13	0	0	0	0
1969 SF	11	0	0	0	0
1970 SF	14	3	49	1	0
1971 SF	13	0	0	0	0
1972 SF	14	1	0	0	0
1973 SF	14	1	13	0	1
1974 SF	6	1	27	0	0
1975 SF	9	1	3	0	0
1976 SF	14	2	14	0	0
1977 SF	14	2	23	0	0
NFL Total	147	12	129	1	1

MIKE PHILLIPS Phillips, Michael 6′0″, 208 **C-LB**
Col: Western Maryland *HS:* Clifton Heights [PA] B: 11/22/1921, Clifton Heights, PA D: 4/17/1994, Midlothian, VA
AAFC **1947** BalA: 12 G.

RAY PHILLIPS Phillips, Ray Charles 6′4″, 224 **LB**
Col: Marshalltown CC IA; Nebraska *HS:* West Division [Milwaukee, WI] B: 3/18/1954, Fordyce, AR *Drafted:* 1977 Round 5 Cin
1977 Cin: 14 G. **1978** Cin-Phi: 12 G. Cin: 2 G. Phi: 10 G. **1979** Phi: 11 G. **1980** Phi: 16 G. **1981** Phi: 16 G; Int 1-0. **Total:** 69 G; Int 1-0.

RAY PHILLIPS Phillips, Raymond Thomas Jr. 6′3″, 243 **LB-DE**
Col: North Carolina State *HS:* North Mecklenburg [Huntersville, NC] B: 7/24/1964, Mooresville, NC *Drafted:* 1986 Round 7 Den
1986 Atl: 1 G. **1987** Phi: 3 G; 2 Sac. **Total:** 4 G; 2 Sac.

REGGIE PHILLIPS Phillips, Reginald Keith 5′10″, 170 **DB**
Col: Southern Methodist *HS:* Jack Yates [Houston, TX] B: 12/12/1960, Houston, TX *Drafted:* 1985 Round 2 ChiB
1985 ChiB: 16 G. **1986** ChiB: 16 G; Int 1-6. **1987** ChiB: 12 G; Int 2-1. **1988** Pho: 16 G; KR 1-4 4.0. **Total:** 60 G; KR 1-4 4.0; Int 3-7.

RYAN PHILLIPS Phillips, Richard Ryan 6′4″, 252 **LB**
Col: Idaho *HS:* Auburn [WA] B: 2/7/1974, Renton, WA *Drafted:* 1997 Round 3 NYG
1997 NYG: 10 G; 1 Sac. **1998** NYG: 16 G. **Total:** 26 G; 1 Sac.

ROD PHILLIPS Phillips, Rodney Augustus 6′0″, 220 **RB**
Col: Cincinnati; Jackson State *HS:* Harper [Mendenhall, MS]
B: 12/23/1952, Meridian, MS
1975 LARm: Rec 2-10 5.0. **1976** LARm: Rec 4-23 5.8. **1977** LARm: Rec 1-5 5.0; KR 1-10 10.0. **1978** LARm: Rec 7-48 6.9; KR 3-52 17.3. **1980** StL: KR 2-28 14.0. **Total:** Rec 14-86 6.1; KR 6-90 15.0.

		Rushing				
Year Team	**G**	**Att**	**Yds**	**Avg**	**TD**	**Fum**
1975 LARm	14	17	69	4.1	0	0
1976 LARm	14	34	206	6.1	1	2
1977 LARm	14	37	183	4.9	1	0
1978 LARm	15	28	81	2.9	0	0
1979 StL	11	3	50	16.7	1	0
1980 StL	16	2	6	3.0	0	0
NFL Total	84	121	595	4.9	3	2

WES PHILLIPS Phillips, Wesley Alan 6′5″, 275 **OT**
Col: Lenoir-Rhyne *HS:* Cross Keys [Atlanta, GA] B: 8/1/1953, Atlanta, GA
1979 Hou: 8 G.

DEAN PHILPOTT Philpott, Dean Earnest 6′0″, 200 **FB**
Col: Fresno State *HS:* Anaheim [CA] B: 11/11/1935, Mesa, AR
Drafted: 1958 Round 11 ChiC
1958 ChiC: 9 G; Rush 12-44 3.7; Rec 4-30 7.5; KR 3-18 6.0.

ED PHILPOTT Philpott, Edward Leigh 6′3″, 240 **LB**
Col: Miami (Ohio) *HS:* Brookside [Sheffield, OH] B: 9/14/1945, Wichita, KS *Drafted:* 1967 Round 4 Bos
1967 Bos: 13 G. **1968** Bos: 14 G; Int 4-31; **1** Fum TD; 6 Pt; 1 Fum. **1969** Bos: 14 G; Int 4-37. **1970** Bos: 14 G; Int 1-23. **1971** NE: 13 G. **Total:** 68 G; Int 9-91; 1 Fum TD; 6 Pt; 1 Fum.

CHARLES PHILYAW Philyaw, Charles Henry 6′9″, 276 **DE**
(King Kong) *Col:* Texas Southern *HS:* Bethune [Shreveport, LA]
B: 2/25/1954, Shreveport, LA *Drafted:* 1976 Round 2 Oak
1976 Oak: 14 G. **1977** Oak: 3 G. **1978** Oak: 15 G. **1979** Oak: 12 G. **Total:** 44 G.

DINO PHILYAW Philyaw, Delvic Dyvon 5′10″, 199 **RB**
Col: Taft Coll. CA (J.C.); Oregon *HS:* Southern Wayne [Dudley, NC]
B: 10/30/1970, Kenansville, NC *Drafted:* 1995 Round 6 NE
1995 Car: 1 G; KR 1-23 23.0. **1996** Car: 9 G; Rush 12-38 3.2 1 TD; 6 Pt. **Total:** 10 G; Rush 12-38 3.2 1 TD; KR 1-23 23.0; 6 Pt.

MIKE PHIPPS Phipps, Michael Elston 6′3″, 208 **QB**
Col: Purdue *HS:* Columbus [IN] B: 11/19/1947, Shelbyville, IN
Drafted: 1970 Round 1 Cle

		Passing							
Year Team	**G**	**Att**	**Comp**	**Comp%**	**Yds**	**YPA**	**TD**	**Int**	**Rating**
1970 Cle	14	60	29	48.3	529	8.82	1	5	49.9
1971 Cle	14	47	13	27.7	179	3.81	1	4	14.6
1972 Cle	14	305	144	47.2	1994	6.54	13	16	61.0
1973 Cle	14	299	148	49.5	1719	5.75	9	20	49.4
1974 Cle	14	256	117	45.7	1384	5.41	9	17	46.7
1975 Cle	14	313	162	51.8	1749	5.59	4	19	47.5
1976 Cle	4	37	20	54.1	146	3.95	3	0	90.6
1977 ChiB	3	5	3	60.0	5	1.00	0	0	64.6
1978 ChiB	6	83	44	53.0	465	5.60	2	10	38.1
1979 ChiB	12	255	134	52.5	1535	6.02	9	**8**	69.6
1980 ChiB	7	122	61	50.0	630	5.16	2	9	40.0
1981 ChiB	3	17	11	64.7	171	10.06	2	0	137.1
NFL Total	119	1799	886	49.2	10506	5.84	55	108	52.6

	Rushing				
Year Team	Att	Yds	Avg	TD	Fum
1970 Cle	11	94	8.5	0	1
1971 Cle	6	35	5.8	0	1
1972 Cle	60	256	4.3	5	8
1973 Cle	60	395	6.6	5	8
1974 Cle	39	279	7.2	1	4
1975 Cle	18	70	3.9	0	7
1976 Cle	4	26	6.5	0	2
1978 ChiB	13	34	2.6	0	0
1979 ChiB	27	51	1.9	0	2
1980 ChiB	15	38	2.5	2	6
1981 ChiB	1	0	0.0	0	0
NFL Total	254	1278	5.0	13	39

ALEX PIASECKY Piasecky, Alex 6'2", 197 **OE-DE**
Col: Duke; Georgia *HS:* Jeannette [PA] B: 2/1/1917, Greensburg, PA D: 9/16/1992, Orange City, FL
1943 Was: 9 G; Rec 3-17 5.7 1 TD; KR 1-17 17.0; Int 1-0; 6 Pt. **1944** Was: 10 G; Rec 8-77 9.6. **1945** Was: 9 G; Rec 1-18 18.0. **Total:** 28 G; Rec 12-112 9.3 1 TD; KR 1-17 17.0; Int 1-0; 6 Pt.

BOB PICARD Picard, Robert 6'1", 195 **WR**
Col: Eastern Washington *HS:* Omak [WA] B: 11/24/1949, Omak, WA
Drafted: 1973 Round 6 Phi
1973 Phi: 14 G. **1974** Phi: 14 G. **1975** Phi: 14 G. **1976** Phi-Det: 12 G. Phi: 4 G. Det: 8 G. **Total:** 54 G.

BRIAN PICCOLO Piccolo, Louis Brian 6'0", 205 **RB**
Col: Wake Forest *HS:* St. Thomas Aquinas [Fort Lauderdale, FL]
B: 10/31/1943, Pittsfield, MA D: 6/16/1970, New York, NY
1969 ChiB: PR 9-43 4.8. **Total:** PR 9-43 4.8.

		Rushing				Receiving					Tot
Year Team	G	Att	Yds	Avg	TD	Rec	Yds	Avg	TD	Fum	TD
1966 ChiB	14	3	12	4.0	0	0	0	—	0	0	0
1967 ChiB	14	87	317	3.6	0	13	103	7.9	0	2	0
1968 ChiB	14	123	450	3.7	2	28	291	10.4	0	0	2
1969 ChiB	9	45	148	3.3	2	17	143	8.4	1	2	3
NFL Total	51	258	927	3.6	4	58	537	9.3	1	4	5

BILL PICCOLO Piccolo, William James 5'11", 185 **C-LB**
Col: Canisius *HS:* East [Buffalo, NY] B: 5/1/1920, Buffalo, NY
Drafted: 1943 Round 8 NYG
1943 NYG: 10 G. **1944** NYG: 4 G; Int 2-5. **1945** NYG: 4 G; **1** Fum TD; 6 Pt. **Total:** 18 G; Int 2-5; 1 Fum TD; 6 Pt.

LOU PICCONE Piccone, Louis James 5'9", 175 **WR**
Col: West Liberty State *HS:* Vineland [NJ] B: 7/17/1949, Vineland, NJ
1976 NYJ: Rush 1-11 11.0. **1977** Buf: Rush 1-6 6.0. **1978** Buf: Scor **1** Saf. **Total:** Rush 2-17 8.5; Scor 1 Saf.

		Receiving				Punt Returns			
Year Team	G	Rec	Yds	Avg	TD	Ret	Yds	Avg	TD
1974 NYJ	14	0	0	—	0	9	75	8.3	0
1975 NYJ	13	7	79	11.3	0	18	74	4.1	0
1976 NYJ	14	12	147	12.3	0	21	173	8.2	1
1977 Buf	14	17	240	14.1	2	0	0	—	0
1978 Buf	16	7	71	10.1	2	14	88	6.3	0
1979 Buf	16	33	556	16.8	2	0	0	—	0
1980 Buf	9	7	82	11.7	0	2	15	7.5	0
1981 Buf	14	5	65	13.0	0	9	57	6.3	0
1982 Buf	8	12	140	11.7	0	0	0	—	0
NFL Total	118	100	1380	13.8	6	73	482	6.6	1

	Kickoff Returns					Tot
Year Team	Ret	Yds	Avg	TD	Fum	TD
1974 NYJ	**39**	**961**	24.6	0	2	0
1975 NYJ	26	637	24.5	0	3	0
1976 NYJ	**31**	699	22.5	0	5	1
1977 Buf	4	89	22.3	0	0	2
1978 Buf	3	51	17.0	0	1	2
1979 Buf	3	41	13.7	0	1	2
1980 Buf	0	0	—	0	1	0
1981 Buf	2	31	15.5	0	0	0
1982 Buf	3	50	16.7	0	0	0
NFL Total	111	2559	23.1	0	13	7

BOB PICKARD Pickard, Robert Harry 6'0", 190 **WR**
Col: Xavier (Ohio) *HS:* Central Catholic [Canton, OH] B: 9/3/1952, Canton, OH
1974 Det: 14 G; Rush 1-5 5.0; Rec 8-88 11.0 1 TD; 6 Pt.

BILL PICKEL Pickel, William George 6'5", 265 **DT-NT-DE**
Col: Rutgers *HS:* Milford Acad. [CT]; St. Francis Prep [Brooklyn, NY]
B: 11/5/1959, Queens, NY *Drafted:* 1983 Round 2 LARd
1983 LARd: 16 G; 6 Sac. **1984** LARd: 16 G; 12.5 Sac. **1985** LARd: 16 G; 12.5 Sac. **1986** LARd: 15 G; 11.5 Sac. **1987** LARd: 12 G; 1 Sac. **1988** LARd: 16 G; 5 Sac. **1989** LARd: 16 G; 3 Sac. **1990** LARd: 14 G; 1.5 Sac. **1991** NYJ: 15 G; 2 Sac. **1992** NYJ: 11 G; 1 Sac. **1993** NYJ: 16 G. **1994** NYJ: 11 G. **Total:** 174 G; 56.0 Sac.

BRUCE PICKENS Pickens, Bruce Evon 5'11", 190 **DB**
Col: Coffeyville CC KS; Nebraska *HS:* Westport [Kansas City, MO]
B: 5/9/1968, Kansas City, MO *Drafted:* 1991 Round 1 Atl
1991 Atl: 7 G. **1992** Atl: 16 G; Int 2-16; 1 Sac. **1993** Atl-GB-KC: 9 G. Atl: 4 G. GB: 2 G. KC: 3 G. **1995** Oak: 16 G. **Total:** 48 G; Int 2-16; 1 Sac.

CARL PICKENS Pickens, Carl McNally 6'2", 206 **WR**
Col: Tennessee *HS:* Murphy [NC] B: 3/23/1970, Murphy, NC
Drafted: 1992 Round 2 Cin
1993 Cin: Pass 1-0. **1995** Cin: Rush 1-6 6.0. **1996** Cin: Pass 1-1 100.0%, 12 12.00; Rush 2-2 1.0; Scor 1 2XP. **1997** Cin: Rush 1-(-6) -6.0. **1998** Cin: Rush 2-4 2.0; Scor 1 2XP. **Total:** Pass 2-1 50.0%, 12 6.00; Rush 6-6 1.0; Scor 2 2XP.

		Receiving				Punt Returns					Tot
Year Team	G	Rec	Yds	Avg	TD	Ret	Yds	Avg	TD	Fum	TD
1992 Cin	16	26	326	12.5	1	18	229	12.7	1	3	2
1993 Cin	13	43	565	13.1	6	4	16	4.0	0	1	6
1994 Cin	15	71	1127	15.9	11	9	62	6.9	0	1	11
1995 Cin	16	99	1234	12.5	**17**	5	-2	-0.4	0	1	17
1996 Cin	16	100	1180	11.8	12	1	2	2.0	0	0	12
1997 Cin	12	52	695	13.4	5	0	0	—	0	1	5
1998 Cin	16	82	1023	12.5	5	0	0	—	0	2	5
NFL Total	104	473	6150	13.0	57	37	307	8.3	1	9	58

LYLE PICKENS Pickens, Lyle Edward 5'10", 175 **DB**
Col: Los Angeles Valley Coll. CA (J.C.); Colorado *HS:* Birmingham [Van Nuys, CA] B: 9/5/1964, New Orleans, LA
1987 Den: 1 G.

BOB PICKENS Pickens, Robert James 6'4", 258 **OT**
Col: Wisconsin; Nebraska *HS:* Evanston Twp. [Evanston, IL]
B: 2/2/1943, Chicago, IL *Drafted:* 1966 Round 3 ChiB
1967 ChiB: 12 G. **1968** ChiB: 5 G. **1969** ChiB: 3 G. **Total:** 20 G.

CLAY PICKERING Pickering, Clay Floyd 6'5", 215 **WR**
Col: Maine *HS:* Archbishop Hoban [Akron, OH] B: 6/2/1961, Jacksonville, FL
1984 Cin: 3 G. **1985** Cin: 1 G. **1986** ChiB: 4 G. **1987** NE: 1 G; Rec 1-10 10.0. **Total:** 9 G; Rec 1-10 10.0.

TIM PIDGEON Pidgeon, Timothy Charles 6'0", 233 **LB**
Col: Syracuse *HS:* Oneonta [NY] B: 9/20/1964, Oneonta, NY
Drafted: 1987 Round 9 Mia
1987 Mia: 3 G.

MIKE PIEL Piel, Michael Lloyd 6'4", 268 **NT**
Col: Saddleback Coll. CA (J.C.); Illinois *HS:* El Toro [CA] B: 9/21/1965, Carmel, CA *Drafted:* 1988 Round 3 LARm
1989 LARm: 13 G; 4 Sac. **1990** LARm: 16 G; 5 Sac. **1991** LARm: 6 G; 1 Sac. **1992** LARm: 15 G; 3 Sac. **Total:** 50 G; 13 Sac.

MILT PIEPUL Piepul, Milton John 6'1", 215 **FB-LB**
Col: Notre Dame *HS:* Cathedral [Springfield, MA]; Enfield HS [CT]
B: 9/14/1918, Springfield, MA D: 3/19/1994, Northampton, MA
Drafted: 1941 Round 11 Det
1941 Det: 11 G; Pass 1-1 100.0%, 23 23.00; Rush 20-56 2.8; Punt 1-35 35.0.

AARON PIERCE Pierce, Aaron R 6'5", 252 **TE**
Col: Washington *HS:* Franklin [Seattle, WA] B: 9/6/1969, Seattle, WA
Drafted: 1992 Round 3 NYG
1995 NYG: Rush 1-6 6.0. **1996** NYG: Rush 1-1 1.0 1 TD. **1997** NYG: KR 1-10 10.0. **Total:** Rush 2-7 3.5 1 TD; KR 1-10 10.0.

		Receiving					Tot
Year Team	G	Rec	Yds	Avg	TD	Fum	TD
1992 NYG	1	0	0	—	0	0	0
1993 NYG	13	12	212	17.7	0	2	0
1994 NYG	16	20	214	10.7	4	0	4
1995 NYG	16	33	310	9.4	0	0	0
1996 NYG	10	11	144	13.1	1	0	2
1997 NYG	16	10	47	4.7	0	0	0
NFL Total	72	86	927	10.8	5	2	6

DON PIERCE Pierce, Donald Hite 6'1", 186 **C**
Col: Kansas *HS:* Topeka [KS] B: 2/7/1919, Topeka, KS D: 1/2/1965, Kansas City, KS
1942 Bkn: 2 G. **1943** ChiC: 1 G. **Total:** 3 G.

DANNY PIERCE Pierce, John Daniel 6'3", 216 **RB**
Col: Pearl River CC MS; Mississippi State; Memphis *HS:* Lumberton [MS] B: 1/17/1948, Laurel, MS *Drafted:* 1970 Round 5 Was
1970 Was: 2 G; Rush 5-6 1.2; Rec 1-6 6.0; 3 Fum.

DICK PIERCE Pierce, Richard 5'11", 185 **G**
Col: Michigan B: 3/1/1896 D: 9/1966, Detroit, MI
1920 ChiT: 4 G.

STEVE PIERCE Pierce, Stephen Nathan 5'10", 190 **WR**
Col: Southwestern Coll. CA (J.C.); Illinois *HS:* Abraham Lincoln [San Diego, CA] B: 12/12/1963
1987 Cle: 2 G; Rec 2-21 10.5.

DAMON PIERI Pieri, Mark Damon 6′0″, 186 **DB**
Col: Phoenix Coll. AZ (J.C.); San Diego State *HS:* St. Mary's [Phoenix, AZ] B: 9/25/1970, Phoenix, AZ
1993 NYJ: 5 G. **1996** Car: 16 G; Int 1-0. **1997** Car: 16 G. **Total:** 37 G; Int 1-0.

AL PIEROTTI Pierotti, Albert Felix 5′10″, 204 **C-G-T-BB**
Col: Washington & Lee *HS:* Everett [MA] B: 10/24/1895, Boston, MA D: 2/12/1964, Revere, MA
1920 Akr-Cle: 6 G. Akr: 1 G. Cle: 5 G. **1921** NYG: 2 G. **1922** Mil: 9 G. **1923** Rac-Mil: 5 G. Rac: 1 G. Mil: 4 G. **1924** Mil: 4 G. **1927** Prov: 14 G. **1929** Bost: 7 G. **Total:** 47 G.

JOE PIERRE Pierre, Joseph Nick 6′0″, 185 **OE-DE**
Col: Pittsburgh *HS:* Windber [PA] B: 1921
1945 Pit: 10 G; KR 1-10 10.0.

PETE PIERSON Pierson, Peter Samuel 6′5″, 295 **OT**
Col: Washington *HS:* David Douglas [Portland, OR] B: 2/4/1971, Portland, OR *Drafted:* 1994 Round 5 TB
1995 TB: 12 G. **1996** TB: 11 G. **1997** TB: 15 G. **1998** TB: 16 G. **Total:** 54 G.

REGGIE PIERSON Pierson, Reginald Lee 5′11″, 185 **DB**
Col: Arizona Western Coll. (J.C.); Oklahoma State *HS:* Centennial [Compton, CA] B: 12/13/1952, Los Angeles, CA
1976 Det-TB: 9 G. Det: 4 G. TB: 5 G. **Total:** 9 G.

NICK PIETROSANTE Pietrosante, Nicholas Vincent 6′2″, 225 **FB**
Col: Notre Dame *HS:* Notre Dame [West Haven, CT] B: 9/10/1937, Ansonia, CT D: 2/6/1988, Royal Oak, MI *Drafted:* 1959 Round 1 Det
1959 Det: KR 5-98 19.6. **1960** Det: KR 2-58 29.0. **1963** Det: Pass 1-1 100.0%, 37 37.00. **1964** Det: Pass 1-0, 1 Int. **1966** Cle: KR 2-9 4.5. **Total:** Pass 2-1 50.0%, 37 18.50 1 Int; KR 9-165 18.3.

		Rushing				Receiving					Tot
Year Team	G	Att	Yds	Avg	TD	Rec	Yds	Avg	TD	Fum	TD
1959 Det	10	76	447	5.9	3	16	140	8.8	0	4	3
1960 Det	12	161	872	5.4	8	13	129	9.9	0	4	8
1961 Det	14	201	841	4.2	5	26	315	12.1	0	7	5
1962 Det	13	134	445	3.3	2	26	251	9.7	2	3	4
1963 Det	12	112	418	3.7	5	16	173	10.8	0	4	5
1964 Det	14	147	536	3.6	4	19	152	8.0	0	4	4
1965 Det	14	107	374	3.5	1	18	163	9.1	0	3	1
1966 Cle	13	7	20	2.9	0	1	12	12.0	0	0	0
1967 Cle	14	10	73	7.3	0	6	56	9.3	0	0	0
NFL Total	116	955	4026	4.2	28	141	1391	9.9	2	29	30

JIM PIETRZAK Pietrzak, James Michael 6′5″, 260 **C-DT-OT**
Col: Eastern Michigan *HS:* University of Detroit [MI] B: 2/21/1953, Detroit, MI *Drafted:* 1974 Round 6 NYG
1974 NYG: 14 G. **1975** NYG: 14 G. **1977** NYG: 14 G. **1978** NYG: 16 G; 1 Fum. **1979** NYG-NO: 14 G. NYG: 3 G. NO: 11 G. **1980** NO: 15 G. **1981** NO: 16 G. **1982** NO: 9 G. **1983** NO: 16 G. **1984** NO: 10 G. **1987** KC: 2 G. **Total:** 140 G; 1 Fum.

BOB PIFFERINI Pifferini, Robert Marico Jr. 6′2″, 226 **LB**
Col: UCLA *HS:* Homestead [PA] B: 6/27/1950, San Jose, CA *Drafted:* 1972 Round 6 ChiB
1972 ChiB: 14 G. **1973** ChiB: 12 G. **1974** ChiB: 12 G. **1975** ChiB: 14 G. **1977** LARm: 5 G. **Total:** 57 G.

BOB PIFFERINI Pifferini, Robert Marico Sr. 6′0″, 210 **LB-C**
(Piff) *Col:* Modesto JC CA; San Jose State *HS:* Modesto [CA] B: 10/1/1922, Oakdale, CA *Drafted:* 1949 Round 15 Det
1949 Det: 12 G; Int 3-3.

BERT PIGGOTT Piggott, Bert Coley 6′2″, 195 **RB-DB**
Col: Illinois *HS:* Hinsdale Central [IL] B: 3/5/1921, Hinsdale, IL
AAFC **1947** LA-A: Rec 7-63 9.0 1 TD; PR 1-7 7.0; KR 5-120 24.0; Int 1-9.

		Rushing			
Year Team	G	Att	Yds	Avg	TD
1947 LA-A	13	46	161	3.5	0

CARL PIGNATELLI Pignatelli, Carlo Arthur 6′0″, 210 **HB-BB**
Col: Iowa *HS:* Rock Falls Twp. [Rock Falls, IL] B: 11/26/1907, Rock Falls, IL D: 6/14/1964, IL
1931 Cle: 7 G.

PETE PIHOS Pihos, Peter Louis 6′1″, 210 **OE-DE**
Col: Indiana *HS:* Austin [Chicago, IL] B: 10/22/1923, Orlando, FL *Drafted:* 1945 Round 3 Phi *HOF:* 1970
1947 Phi: PR 1-26 26.0 1 TD; KR 1-17 17.0. **1948** Phi: Rush 8-(-3) -0.4; KR 1-9 9.0. **1949** Phi: KR 1-0. **1951** Phi: KR 3-40 13.3; Int 2-30. **1952** Phi: 1 Fum TD. **1954** Phi: Rush 1-(-1) -1.0. **Total:** Rush 9-(-4) -0.4; PR 1-26 26.0 1 TD; KR 6-66 11.0; Int 2-30; 1 Fum TD.

		Receiving					Tot
Year Team	G	Rec	Yds	Avg	TD	Fum	TD
1947 Phi	12	23	382	16.6	7	1	8
1948 Phi	12	46	766	16.7	11	2	11
1949 Phi	11	34	484	14.2	4	0	4
1950 Phi	12	38	447	11.8	6	3	6
1951 Phi	12	35	536	15.3	5	1	5
1952 Phi	12	12	219	18.3	1	0	2
1953 Phi	12	**63**	**1049**	16.7	**10**	0	10
1954 Phi	12	**60**	872	14.5	10	1	10
1955 Phi	12	**62**	**864**	13.9	7	0	7
NFL Total	107	373	5619	15.1	61	8	63

CHRIS PIKE Pike, Christopher Holtz 6′8″, 290 **DT**
Col: North Carolina; Tulsa *HS:* Calvin Coolidge [Washington, DC] B: 1/13/1964, Washington, DC *Drafted:* 1987 Round 6 Phi
1989 Cle: 12 G; 1 Sac. **1990** Cle: 12 G. **1991** LARm: 8 G. **Total:** 32 G; 1 Sac.

MARK PIKE Pike, Mark Harold 6′4″, 272 **DE-LB**
Col: Georgia Tech *HS:* Dixie Heights [Edgewood, KY] B: 12/27/1963, Elizabethtown, KY *Drafted:* 1986 Round 7 Buf
1987 Buf: 3 G. **1988** Buf: 16 G; KR 1-5 5.0. **1989** Buf: 16 G. **1990** Buf: 16 G. **1991** Buf: 16 G. **1992** Buf: 16 G; 1 Sac. **1993** Buf: 14 G. **1994** Buf: 16 G; KR 2-9 4.5. **1995** Buf: 16 G; KR 1-20 20.0. **1996** Buf: 16 G. **1997** Buf: 15 G; KR 1-11 11.0. **1998** Buf: 13 G. **Total:** 173 G; KR 5-45 9.0; 1 Sac.

JOE PILCONIS Pilconis, Joseph George 6′1″, 189 **OE-DE**
Col: Temple *HS:* Shenandoah Valley [Shenandoah, PA] B: 10/9/1911, Shenandoah, PA D: 6/29/1993, New Ringgold, PA
1934 Phi: 9 G; Rush 1-5 5.0; Rec 1-3 3.0. **1936** Phi: 12 G; Rec 4-51 12.8 1 TD; 6 Pt. **1937** Phi: 11 G; Rush 2-21 10.5; Rec 6-59 9.8; 1 Fum TD; 6 Pt. **Total:** 32 G; Rush 3-26 8.7; Rec 11-113 10.3 1 TD; 1 Fum TD; Tot TD 2; 12 Pt.

EVAN PILGRIM Pilgrim, Evan Boyd 6′4″, 304 **OG**
Col: Brigham Young *HS:* Antioch [CA] B: 8/14/1972, Pittsburg, CA *Drafted:* 1995 Round 3 ChiB
1996 ChiB: 6 G. **1997** ChiB: 13 G. **1998** Ten: 3 G. **Total:** 22 G.

ROGER PILLATH Pillath, Roger Allen 6′4″, 242 **OT**
Col: Wisconsin *HS:* Coleman [WI] B: 12/21/1941, Marinette, WI *Drafted:* 1964 Round 3 LARm
1965 LARm: 14 G. **1966** Pit: 6 G. **Total:** 20 G.

LAWRENCE PILLERS Pillers, Lawrence Dwight 6′4″, 255 **DE-DT-NT**
Col: Alcorn State *HS:* Hazelhurst [MS] B: 11/4/1952, Hazelhurst, MS *Drafted:* 1976 Round 11 NYJ
1976 NYJ: 14 G. **1977** NYJ: 13 G. **1978** NYJ: 16 G. **1979** NYJ: 16 G. **1980** NYJ-SF: 16 G. NYJ: 3 G. SF: 13 G. **1981** SF: 14 G. **1982** SF: 9 G; 3 Sac. **1983** SF: 16 G; Int 1-16; 4 Sac. **1984** SF: 16 G; 2 Sac. **1985** Atl: 9 G; 2 Sac. **Total:** 139 G; Int 1-16; 11 Sac.

BRIAN PILLMAN Pillman, Brian William 5′10″, 228 **LB**
(The Loose Cannon) *Col:* Miami (Ohio) *HS:* Norwood [OH] B: 5/22/1962, Cincinnati, OH D: 10/5/1997, Bloomington, MN
1984 Cin: 6 G.

FRANK PILLOW Pillow, William Frank Jr. 5′10″, 170 **WR**
Col: Tennessee State *HS:* Whites Creek [TN] B: 3/11/1965, Nashville, TN *Drafted:* 1988 Round 11 TB
1988 TB: 15 G; Rec 15-206 13.7 1 TD; KR 3-38 12.7; 6 Pt. **1989** TB: 3 G; KR 1-17 17.0. **1990** TB: 16 G; Rec 8-118 14.8. **Total:** 34 G; Rec 23-324 14.1 1 TD; KR 4-55 13.8; 6 Pt.

ERNIE PINCKERT Pinckert, Erny 6′0″, 197 **WB-DB-BB-LB**
Col: USC *HS:* San Bernardino [CA] B: 5/1/1907, Medford, WI D: 8/30/1977, Los Angeles, CA
1933 Bos: Pass 2-0; Int **1** TD. **1940** Was: Int 2-26. **Total:** Pass 2-0; Int 2-26 1 TD.

		Rushing				Receiving				Tot
Year Team	G	Att	Yds	Avg	TD	Rec	Yds	Avg	TD	TD
1932 Bos	9	16	72	4.5	0	3	42	14.0	0	0
1933 Bos	12	53	216	4.1	0	4	71	17.8	0	1
1934 Bos	12	34	102	3.0	1	1	9	9.0	0	1
1935 Bos	11	16	32	2.0	0	5	60	12.0	0	0
1936 Bos	12	18	80	4.4	0	1	17	17.0	0	0
1937 Was	11	2	10	5.0	0	10	145	14.5	1	1
1938 Was	9	3	7	2.3	0	3	20	6.7	0	0
1939 Was	10	5	17	3.4	0	0	0	—	0	0
1940 Was	11	0	0	—	0	2	27	13.5	0	0
NFL Total	97	147	536	3.6	1	29	391	13.5	1	3

STAN PINCURA Pincura, Stanley 5′11″, 175 **BB-DB**
(China) *Col:* Ohio State *HS:* Lorain [OH] B: 5/2/1913, Lorain, OH D: 2/13/1979, Lorain, OH
1937 Cle: Rush 5-(-22) -4.4; Rec 12-139 11.6. **1938** Cle: Rush 2-(-6) -3.0; Rec 6-72 12.0 1 TD. **Total:** Rush 7-(-28) -4.0; Rec 18-211 11.7 1 TD.

		Passing							
Year Team	G	Att	Comp	Comp%	Yds	YPA	TD	Int	Rating
1937 Cle	11	27	9	33.3	92	3.41	0	3	4.5
1938 Cle	11	33	13	39.4	240	7.27	1	7	35.7
NFL Total	22	60	22	36.7	332	5.53	1	10	21.7

CYRIL PINDER Pinder, Cyril Calvin 6′2″, 210 **RB**
(Cy) *Col:* Illinois *HS:* Crispus Attucks [Hollywood, FL] B: 11/13/1946, Fort Lauderdale, FL *Drafted:* 1968 Round 2 Phi
1969 Phi: KR 4-56 14.0. **1972** ChiB: KR 1-14 14.0. **Total:** KR 5-70 14.0.

		Rushing				Receiving				
Year Team	G	Att	Yds	Avg	TD	Rec	Yds	Avg	TD	Fum
1968 Phi	14	40	117	2.9	0	16	166	10.4	0	2
1969 Phi	14	60	309	5.2	1	12	77	6.4	0	1
1970 Phi	14	166	657	4.0	2	28	249	8.9	0	5
1971 ChiB	12	63	311	4.9	1	10	51	5.1	0	0
1972 ChiB	13	87	300	3.4	3	1	13	13.0	0	4
1973 Dal	5	12	15	1.3	0	0	0	—	0	0
NFL Total	72	428	1709	4.0	7	67	556	8.3	0	12

ED PINE Pine, Edward Harry Jr. 6′4″, 235 **LB**
Col: Utah *HS:* Reno [NV] B: 7/13/1940, Reno, NV *Drafted:* 1962 Round 2 SF
1962 SF: 14 G; Int 2-16. **1963** SF: 14 G; Int 1-1. **1964** SF: 14 G; KR 1-0. **1965** Pit: 8 G. **Total:** 50 G; KR 1-0; Int 3-17.

JOHNNY PINGEL Pingel, John Spencer 6′0″, 180 **TB-DB**
Col: Michigan State *HS:* Mount Clemens [MI] B: 11/6/1916, Mount Clemens, MI *Drafted:* 1939 Round 1 Det
1939 Det: Pass 48-27 56.3%, 343 7.15 3 TD 4 Int; Punt 32-1368 42.8.

		Rushing			
Year Team	G	Att	Yds	Avg	TD
1939 Det	9	74	301	4.1	1

ALLEN PINKETT Pinkett, Allen Jerome 5′9″, 190 **RB**
Col: Notre Dame *HS:* Park View [Sterling, VA] B: 1/25/1964, Washington, DC *Drafted:* 1986 Round 3 Hou
1986 Hou: PR 1-(-1) -1.0. **Total:** PR 1-(-1) -1.0.

		Rushing				Receiving			
Year Team	G	Att	Yds	Avg	TD	Rec	Yds	Avg	TD
1986 Hou	16	77	225	2.9	2	35	248	7.1	1
1987 Hou	8	31	149	4.8	2	1	7	7.0	0
1988 Hou	16	122	513	4.2	7	12	114	9.5	2
1989 Hou	16	94	449	4.8	1	31	239	7.7	1
1990 Hou	15	66	268	4.1	0	11	85	7.7	0
1991 Hou	16	171	720	4.2	9	29	228	7.9	1
NFL Total	87	561	2324	4.1	21	119	921	7.7	5

	Kickoff Returns					Tot
Year Team	Ret	Yds	Avg	TD	Fum	TD
1986 Hou	26	519	20.0	0	2	3
1987 Hou	17	322	18.9	0	1	2
1988 Hou	7	137	19.6	0	2	9
1989 Hou	0	0	—	0	1	2
1990 Hou	4	91	22.8	0	0	0
1991 Hou	26	508	19.5	0	2	10
NFL Total	80	1577	19.7	0	8	26

LOVELL PINKNEY Pinkney, Lovell 6′4″, 248 **TE**
Col: Texas *HS:* Anacostia [Washington, DC] B: 8/18/1972, Washington, DC *Drafted:* 1995 Round 4 StL
1995 StL: 8 G; Rec 1-13 13.0; KR 1-26 26.0.

REGGIE PINKNEY Pinkney, Vernon Reginald 5′11″, 190 **DB**
Col: East Carolina *HS:* Reid Ross [Fort Bragg, NC] B: 5/27/1955, St. Louis, MO *Drafted:* 1977 Round 6 Det
1977 Det: 11 G; Int 2-61 **1** TD; 6 Pt. **1978** Det: 13 G; Int 1-22. **1979** Bal: 16 G. **1980** Bal: 16 G. **1981** Bal: 16 G; Int 1-0. **Total:** 72 G; Int 4-83 1 TD; 6 Pt.

RAY PINNEY Pinney, Raymond Earl Jr. 6′4″, 251 **OT-C-OG**
Col: Washington *HS:* Shorecrest [Seattle, WA] B: 6/29/1954, Seattle, WA *Drafted:* 1976 Round 2 Pit
1976 Pit: 14 G. **1977** Pit: 14 G. **1978** Pit: 13 G. **1980** Pit: 16 G. **1981** Pit: 16 G; Rec 1-1 1.0 1 TD; 6 Pt. **1982** Pit: 9 G; Rec 1-3 3.0 1 TD; 6 Pt. **1985** Pit: 15 G. **1986** Pit: 16 G. **1987** Pit: 12 G. **Total:** 125 G; Rec 2-4 2.0 2 TD; 12 Pt.

SCOTT PIPER Piper, Scott Cameron 6′1″, 180 **WR**
Col: Arizona *HS:* Lakewood [CO] B: 6/18/1954, Phildelphia, PA *Drafted:* 1976 Round 6 Buf
1976 Atl: 13 G.

JOYCE PIPKIN Pipkin, Joyce Clarence 6′1″, 204 **OE-DE-BB**
(Pip) *Col:* Arkansas *HS:* Hot Springs [AR] B: 1/9/1924, Lono, AR
AAFC **1949** LA-A: 8 G.

NFL **1948** NYG: 11 G; Rec 2-28 14.0.

WOODIE PIPPENS Pippens, A. Woodrow 5′11″, 225 **RB**
Col: Thiel *HS:* James Ford Rhodes [Cleveland, OH] B: 2/7/1963, CLeveland, OH
1987 KC: 2 G; Rush 3-16 5.3; Rec 2-12 6.0.

HANK PIRO Piro, Henry William 6′0″, 186 **OE-DB**
(Whitey) *Col:* Syracuse *HS:* Sewanhaka [Floral Park, NY] B: 12/20/1917, Northotz, Germany
1941 Phi: 10 G; Rec 10-141 14.1 1 TD; KR 1-33 33.0; Int 1-0; 6 Pt.

ROCCO PIRRO Pirro, Rocco Albert 6′0″, 226 **G-BB-LB-DB**
(Rocky) *Col:* Catholic *HS:* Solvay [NY] B: 6/30/1916, Syracuse, NY D: 1/26/1995, Solvay, NY *Drafted:* 1940 Round 12 Pit
AAFC **1946** BufA: 13 G. **1947** BufA: 13 G. **1948** BufA: 14 G. **1949** BufA: 11 G. **Total:** 51 G.

NFL **1940** Pit: 9 G. **1941** Pit: 11 G; Rush 1-1 1.0; Rec 2-31 15.5; Int 1-2. **Total:** 20 G; Rush 1-1 1.0; Rec 2-31 15.5; Int 1-2.

JOE PISARCIK Pisarcik, Joseph Anthony 6′4″, 220 **QB**
Col: New Mexico State *HS:* Central Catholic [Kingston, PA] B: 7/2/1952, Kingston, PA

		Passing							
Year Team	G	Att	Comp	Comp%	Yds	YPA	TD	Int	Rating
1977 NYG	13	241	103	42.7	1346	5.59	4	14	42.3
1978 NYG	15	301	143	47.5	2096	6.96	12	23	52.1
1979 NYG	4	108	43	39.8	537	4.97	2	6	39.0
1980 Phi	9	22	15	68.2	187	8.50	0	0	94.3
1981 Phi	7	15	8	53.3	154	10.27	2	2	89.3
1982 Phi	1	1	1	100.0	24	24.00	0	0	118.8
1983 Phi	5	34	16	47.1	172	5.06	1	0	72.2
1984 Phi	7	176	96	54.5	1036	5.89	3	3	70.6
NFL Total	61	898	425	47.3	5552	6.18	24	48	53.9

	Rushing				
Year Team	Att	Yds	Avg	TD	Fum
1977 NYG	27	57	2.1	2	6
1978 NYG	17	68	4.0	1	2
1979 NYG	1	6	6.0	0	1
1980 Phi	3	-3	-1.0	0	1
1981 Phi	7	1	0.1	0	0
1983 Phi	3	-1	-0.3	0	1
1984 Phi	7	19	2.7	2	4
NFL Total	65	147	2.3	5	15

STEVE PISARKIEWICZ Pisarkiewicz, Stephen John 6′2″, 205 **QB**
Col: Missouri *HS:* McCluer North [Florissant, MO] B: 11/10/1953, Florissant, MO *Drafted:* 1977 Round 1 StL
1978 StL: Rush 5-(-1) -0.2. **1979** StL: Rush 11-20 1.8. **Total:** Rush 16-19 1.2.

		Passing								
Year Team	G	Att	Comp	Comp%	Yds	YPA	TD	Int	Rating	Fum
1978 StL	3	29	10	34.5	164	5.66	0	3	14.8	2
1979 StL	6	109	52	47.7	621	5.70	3	4	59.5	5
1980 GB	1	5	2	40.0	19	3.80	0	0	51.3	0
NFL Total	10	143	64	44.8	804	5.62	3	7	49.4	7

ROMAN PISKOR Piskor, Roman John 6′0″, 245 **T**
(Ray) *Col:* Niagara *HS:* North Tonawanda [NY] B: 8/9/1917, North Tonawanda, NY D: 8/1981, North Tonawanda, NY
AAFC **1946** NY-A: 12 G. **1947** CleA: 10 G. **1948** ChiA: 12 G. **Total:** 34 G.

NFL **1948** ChiA: 12 G.

CHUCK PITCOCK Pitcock, Charles Clayton 6′4″, 272 **C**
Col: Tulane *HS:* Gulf [New Port Richey, FL] B: 2/20/1958, Homestead, FL
1987 TB: 2 G.

CHARLIE PITTMAN Pittman, Charles Vernon 6′1″, 200 **RB**
Col: Penn State *HS:* Edmondson [Baltimore, MD] B: 1/22/1948, Baltimore, MD *Drafted:* 1970 Round 3 StL
1970 StL: 8 G; Rush 2-4 2.0; KR 10-237 23.7. **1971** Bal: 10 G; Rush 2-3 1.5; KR 14-330 23.6; 2 Fum. **Total:** 18 G; Rush 4-7 1.8; KR 24-567 23.6; 2 Fum.

DANNY PITTMAN Pittman, Danny Ray 6′2″, 205 **WR**
Col: Pasadena City Coll. CA (J.C.); Wyoming *HS:* John Muir [Pasadena, CA] B: 4/3/1958, Memphis, TN *Drafted:* 1980 Round 4 NYG
1980 NYG: Rush 1-(-7) -7.0. **1981** NYG: PR 1-13 13.0. **1982** NYG: PR 6-40 6.7. **1984** StL: PR 4-10 2.5. **Total:** Rush 1-(-7) -7.0; PR 11-63 5.7.

		Receiving				Kickoff Returns				
Year Team	G	Rec	Yds	Avg	TD	Ret	Yds	Avg	TD	Fum
1980 NYG	11	25	308	12.3	0	2	41	20.5	0	1
1981 NYG	8	1	8	8.0	0	10	194	19.4	0	2
1982 NYG	8	1	21	21.0	0	5	117	23.4	0	0
1983 NYG-StL	12	9	175	19.4	1	6	107	17.8	0	0
1983 NYG	8	7	154	22.0	1	6	107	17.8	0	0
1983 StL	4	2	21	10.5	0	0	0	—	0	0
1984 StL	10	10	145	14.5	0	14	319	22.8	0	1
NFL Total	49	46	657	14.3	1	37	778	21.0	0	4

JULIAN PITTMAN Pittman, Julian 6′4″, 286 **DE**
Col: Florida State *HS:* Niceville [FL] B: 4/22/1975, Niceville, FL
Drafted: 1998 Round 4 NO
1998 NO: 2 G.

KAVIKA PITTMAN Pittman, Kavika Charles 6′6″, 267 **DE**
Col: McNeese State *HS:* Leesville [LA] B: 2/9/1974, Frankfurt, Germany *Drafted:* 1996 Round 2 Dal
1996 Dal: 15 G. **1997** Dal: 15 G; PR 1-0; 1 Sac. **1998** Dal: 15 G; 6 Sac. **Total:** 45 G; PR 1-0; 7 Sac.

SWEDE PITTMAN Pittman, Melvin Osroe 6′0″, 215 **C-LB**
(Blair) *Col:* Hardin-Simmons *HS:* Big Spring [TX] B: 2/23/1906, Abilene, TX D: 12/24/1975, Ennis, TX
1935 Pit: 2 G.

MICHAEL PITTMAN Pittman, Michael 5′11″, 214 **RB**
Col: Fresno State *HS:* Mira Mesa [San Diego, CA] B: 8/14/1975, New Orleans, LA *Drafted:* 1998 Round 4 Ariz
1998 Ariz: KR 4-84 21.0.

		Rushing				
Year Team	**G**	**Att**	**Yds**	**Avg**	**TD**	**Fum**
1998 Ariz	15	29	91	3.1	0	1

RALPH PITTMAN Pittman, Ralph Dale 5′10″, 200 **BB-WB**
(Bullet AKA Paxton) *Col:* Baylor B: 12/23/1901, DeLeon, TX D: 7/5/1977, DeLeon, TX
1926 Buf: 5 G.

ALABAMA PITTS Pitts, Edwin Collins 5′10″, 185 **HB-DB**
Col: No College B: 1908, Opelika, AL D: 6/7/1941, Valdese, NC
1935 Phi: 3 G; Rec 2-21 10.5.

ELIJAH PITTS Pitts, Elijah Eugene 6′1″, 210 **RB**
(Eli) *Col:* Philander Smith *HS:* Pine Street [Conway, AR] B: 2/3/1938, Mayflower, AR D: 7/10/1998, Buffalo, NY *Drafted:* 1961 Round 13 GB
1962 GB: Pass 2-0. **1963** GB: Pass 2-2 100.0%, 41 20.50 1 TD. **1965** GB: Pass 2-1 50.0%, 51 25.50. **1966** GB: Pass 2-0. **1967** GB: Pass 1-1 100.0%, 21 21.00. **Total:** Pass 9-4 44.4%, 113 12.56 1 TD.

		Rushing				Receiving			
Year Team	**G**	**Att**	**Yds**	**Avg**	**TD**	**Rec**	**Yds**	**Avg**	**TD**
1961 GB	14	23	75	3.3	1	1	5	5.0	0
1962 GB	14	22	110	5.0	2	3	44	14.7	0
1963 GB	14	54	212	3.9	5	9	54	6.0	1
1964 GB	14	27	127	4.7	1	6	38	6.3	0
1965 GB	14	54	122	2.3	4	11	182	16.5	1
1966 GB	14	115	393	3.4	7	26	460	17.7	3
1967 GB	8	77	247	3.2	6	15	210	14.0	0
1968 GB	14	72	264	3.7	2	17	142	8.4	0
1969 GB	14	35	134	3.8	0	9	47	5.2	1
1970 LARm-NO	8	35	104	3.0	0	7	63	9.0	0
1970 LARm	2	3	8	2.7	0	0	0	—	0
1970 NO	6	32	96	3.0	0	7	63	9.0	0
1971 GB	6	0	0	—	0	0	0	—	0
NFL Total	134	514	1788	3.5	28	104	1245	12.0	6

	Punt Returns				Kickoff Returns					Tot
Year Team	**Ret**	**Yds**	**Avg**	**TD**	**Ret**	**Yds**	**Avg**	**TD**	**Fum**	**TD**
1961 GB	0	0	—	0	1	14	14.0	0	0	1
1962 GB	7	17	2.4	0	0	0	—	0	2	2
1963 GB	7	60	8.6	0	0	0	—	0	2	6
1964 GB	15	191	12.7	1	0	0	—	0	1	2
1965 GB	8	27	3.4	0	20	396	19.8	0	2	5
1966 GB	7	9	1.3	0	1	0	0.0	0	4	10
1967 GB	9	16	1.8	0	0	0	—	0	1	6
1968 GB	1	1	1.0	0	2	40	20.0	0	0	2
1969 GB	16	60	3.8	0	1	22	22.0	0	2	1
1970 LARm-NO	0	0	—	0	1	22	22.0	0	3	0
1970 NO	0	0	—	0	1	22	22.0	0	3	0
1971 GB	5	13	2.6	0	2	41	20.5	0	0	0
NFL Total	75	394	5.3	1	28	535	19.1	0	17	35

FRANK PITTS Pitts, Frank H 6′3″, 199 **WR**
(Riddler) *Col:* Southern University *HS:* Archer [Atlanta, GA] B: 11/12/1943, Atlanta, GA *Drafted:* 1965 Round 4 KC
1965 KC: PR 1-4 4.0; KR 5-100 20.0. **1966** KC: KR 0-38. **1967** KC: KR 0-9. **1971** Cle: KR 9-238 26.4. **Total:** PR 1-4 4.0; KR 14-385 27.5.

		Rushing				Receiving					Tot
Year Team	**G**	**Att**	**Yds**	**Avg**	**TD**	**Rec**	**Yds**	**Avg**	**TD**	**Fum**	**TD**
1965 KC	7	0	0	—	0	1	11	11.0	0	1	0
1966 KC	14	0	0	—	0	1	11	11.0	0	0	1
1967 KC	14	3	19	6.3	1	4	131	32.8	1	1	2
1968 KC	13	11	107	9.7	0	30	655	21.8	6	1	6
1969 KC	14	5	28	5.6	0	31	470	15.2	2	0	2
1970 KC	12	5	84	16.8	0	11	172	15.6	2	0	2
1971 Cle	13	0	0	—	0	27	487	18.0	4	0	4
1972 Cle	14	3	29	9.7	0	36	620	17.2	8	0	8
1973 Cle	13	0	0	—	0	31	317	10.2	4	1	4
1974 Oak	13	1	-10	-10.0	0	3	23	7.7	0	0	0
NFL Total	127	28	257	9.2	1	175	2897	16.6	27	4	29

HUGH PITTS Pitts, Hugh Lynn 6′2″, 223 **LB**
Col: Texas Christian *HS:* Woodville [TX] B: 4/8/1934, Woodville, TX
Drafted: 1956 Round 2 LARm
1956 LARm: 9 G; Int 3-22. **1960** Hou: 12 G. **Total:** 21 G; Int 3-22.

JOHN PITTS Pitts, John Martin 6′4″, 218 **DB**
Col: Rancho Santiago Coll. CA (J.C.); Arizona State *HS:* Laguna Beach [CA] B: 2/28/1945, Birmingham, AL *Drafted:* 1967 Round 1 Buf

		Interceptions			
Year Team	**G**	**Int**	**Yds**	**TD**	**Fum**
1967 Buf	14	0	0	0	0
1968 Buf	14	2	21	0	0
1969 Buf	14	2	40	0	0
1970 Buf	14	1	11	0	1
1971 Buf	14	2	12	0	0
1972 Buf	14	1	10	0	0
1973 Buf-Den	10	0	0	0	0
1973 Buf	3	0	0	0	0
1973 Den	7	0	0	0	0
1974 Den	14	1	2	0	0
1975 Den-Cle	7	1	0	0	0
1975 Den	1	0	0	0	0
1975 Cle	6	1	0	0	0
NFL Total	115	10	96	0	1

MIKE PITTS Pitts, Michael Anthony 6′5″, 277 **DT-DE**
Col: Alabama *HS:* Baltimore Polytechnic Inst. [MD] B: 9/25/1960, Baltimore, MD *Drafted:* 1983 Round 1 Atl
1983 Atl: 16 G; 7 Sac. **1984** Atl: 14 G; 5.5 Sac. **1985** Atl: 16 G; Int 1-1; 1 Fum; 7 Sac. **1986** Atl: 16 G; **1** Fum TD; 6 Pt; 5.5 Sac. **1987** Phi: 12 G; 2 Sac. **1988** Phi: 16 G; 1.5 Sac. **1989** Phi: 16 G; 7 Sac. **1990** Phi: 4 G; 3 Sac. **1991** Phi: 16 G; 2 Sac. **1992** Phi: 11 G; 4 Sac. **1993** NE: 16 G; 3 Sac. **1994** NE: 16 G; 1 Sac. **Total:** 169 G; Int 1-1; 1 Fum TD; 6 Pt; 1 Fum; 48.5 Sac.

RON PITTS Pitts, Ronald Dwayne 5′10″, 175 **DB**
Col: UCLA *HS:* Orchard Park [NY] B: 10/14/1962, Detroit, MI
Drafted: 1985 Round 7 Buf
1986 Buf: KR 1-7 7.0. **1987** Buf: Int 3-19. **1988** GB: KR 1-17 17.0; Int 2-56. **1989** GB: Int 1-37. **1990** GB: Int 1-0. **Total:** KR 2-24 12.0; Int 7-112.

		Punt Returns				
Year Team	**G**	**Ret**	**Yds**	**Avg**	**TD**	**Fum**
1986 Buf	10	18	194	10.8	1	2
1987 Buf	12	23	149	6.5	0	3
1988 GB	14	9	93	10.3	1	1
1989 GB	14	0	0	—	0	0
1990 GB	16	0	0	—	0	0
NFL Total	66	50	436	8.7	2	6

JOE PIVARNIK Pivarnik, Joseph John 5′9″, 217 **G**
(Butch) *Col:* Notre Dame *HS:* Warren G. Harding [Bridgeport, CT] B: 2/18/1912, Bridgeport, CT D: 1/22/1976, Middletown, CT
1936 Phi: 6 G.

DAVE PIVEC Pivec, David John 6′3″, 230 **TE**
Col: Notre Dame *HS:* Patterson [Baltimore, MD] B: 9/25/1943, Baltimore, MD *Drafted:* 1965 Round 14 ChiB
1966 LARm: 3 G. **1967** LARm: 14 G; Rec 2-2 1.0 1 TD; 6 Pt. **1968** LARm: 14 G; Rec 3-27 9.0; KR 2-0; Scor **1** Saf; 2 Pt. **1969** Den: 14 G; Rec 9-117 13.0. **Total:** 45 G; Rec 14-146 10.4 1 TD; KR 2-0; Scor 1 Saf; 8 Pt.

JOE PLANANSKY Planansky, Joe 6′4″, 250 **TE**
Col: Chadron State *HS:* Hemingford [NE] B: 10/21/1971, Hemingford, NE
1995 Mia: 2 G.

DOUG PLANK Plank, Douglas Michael 6′0″, 200 **DB**
Col: Ohio State *HS:* Norwin [Irwin, PA] B: 3/4/1953, Greensburg, PA
Drafted: 1975 Round 12 ChiB
1975 ChiB: PR 3-23 7.7. **1977** ChiB: PR 1-21 21.0. **1980** ChiB: PR 1-0. **1981** ChiB: PR 1-3 3.0; Scor **1** Saf. **Total:** PR 6-47 7.8; Scor 1 Saf.

		Interceptions		
Year Team	**G**	**Int**	**Yds**	**TD**
1975 ChiB	14	2	50	0
1976 ChiB	14	4	31	0
1977 ChiB	11	4	32	0
1978 ChiB	14	1	0	0
1979 ChiB	16	3	33	0
1980 ChiB	15	1	20	0
1981 ChiB	16	0	0	0
1982 ChiB	1	0	0	0
NFL Total	101	15	166	0

EARL PLANK Plank, Earl A 174 **OE**
Col: No College B: 7/28/1905, Columbus, OH D: 9/30/1952, Bellefontaine, OH
1926 Col: 1 G. **1929** Buf: 2 G. **1930** Bkn: 7 G. **Total:** 10 G.

TONY PLANSKY Plansky, Anthony Joseph 6′2″, 215 **FB-BB-WB**
Col: Georgetown *HS:* South Boston [MA] B: 6/20/1900, South Boston, MA D: 2/10/1979, North Adams, MA
1928 NYG: 6 G; Rush 1 TD; 6 Pt. **1929** NYG: 11 G; Pass 2 TD; Rush 8 TD; Rec 1 TD; Scor 62, 2 FG, 2 XK; Tot TD 9. **1932** Bos: 1 G. **Total:** 18 G; Pass 2 TD; Rush 9 TD; Rec 1 TD; Scor 68, 2 FG, 2 XK; Tot TD 10.

RON PLANTZ Plantz, Ronald Anthony 6′4″, 272 **C**
Col: Notre Dame *HS:* Gordon Tech [Chicago, IL] B: 7/27/1964, Chicago, IL
1987 Ind: 3 G.

JERRY PLANUTIS Planutis, Gerald Robert 5′9″, 175 **HB**
Col: Michigan State *HS:* West Hazleton [PA] B: 5/18/1930, Detroit, MI
Drafted: 1956 Round 12 Was
1956 Was: 3 G; Rush 2-6 3.0; Rec 1-5 5.0.

DICK PLASMAN Plasman, Herbert G 6′3″, 218 **DE-OE-T**
Col: Vanderbilt *HS:* Miami Senior [FL] B: 4/6/1914, Metcalf, AZ D: 6/20/1981, Naples, FL *Drafted:* 1937 Round 3 ChiB
1937 ChiB: Scor 8, 2 XK. **1939** ChiB: Pass 1-0; Scor 21, 0-1 FG, 3-3 100.0% XK. **1940** ChiB: Scor 15, 3-3 100.0% XK. **1941** ChiB: Rush 1-1 1.0; Scor 6, 6-9 66.7% XK. **1944** ChiB: KR 1-(-1) -1.0. **Total:** Pass 1-0; Rush 1-1 1.0; KR 1-(-1) -1.0; Scor 56, 0-1 FG, 14-15 80.0% XK.

		Receiving			
Year Team	**G**	**Rec**	**Yds**	**Avg**	**TD**
1937 ChiB	9	3	18	6.0	1
1938 ChiB	8	8	117	14.6	1
1939 ChiB	11	19	403	21.2	3
1940 ChiB	11	11	245	22.3	2
1941 ChiB	10	14	283	20.2	0
1944 ChiB	3	1	17	17.0	0
1946 ChiC	3	0	0	—	0
1947 ChiC	4	0	0	—	0
NFL Total	59	56	1083	19.3	7

GEORGE PLATUKIS Platukis, George Paul 6′0″, 196 **OE-DE**
Col: Duquesne *HS:* West Hazelton [PA] B: 3/15/1915, West Hazleton, PA D: 5/17/1973, Benton, PA *Drafted:* 1938 Round 4 Pit
1938 Pit: Rush 3-6 2.0. **1942** Cle: Int 1-12; **1** Fum TD. **Total:** Rush 3-6 2.0; Int 1-12; 1 Fum TD.

		Receiving				Tot
Year Team	**G**	**Rec**	**Yds**	**Avg**	**TD**	**TD**
1938 Pit	5	4	82	20.5	0	0
1939 Pit	11	7	170	24.3	3	3
1940 Pit	11	15	290	19.3	2	2
1941 Pit	11	2	15	7.5	0	0
1942 Cle	9	5	64	12.8	1	2
NFL Total	47	33	621	18.8	6	7

SCOTT PLAYER Player, Scott Darwin 6′0″, 220 **P**
Col: Florida CC at Jacksonville; Flagler; Florida State *HS:* St. Augustine [FL] B: 12/17/1969, St. Augustine, FL

		Punting		
Year Team	**G**	**Punts**	**Yds**	**Avg**
1998 Ariz	16	81	3378	41.7

ANTHONY PLEASANT Pleasant, Anthony Devon 6′5″, 280 **DE**
Col: Tennessee State *HS:* Century [FL] B: 1/27/1968, Century, FL
Drafted: 1990 Round 3 Cle
1990 Cle: 16 G; 3.5 Sac. **1991** Cle: 16 G; 2.5 Sac. **1992** Cle: 16 G; 4 Sac. **1993** Cle: 16 G; Scor 1 Saf; 2 Pt; 11 Sac. **1994** Cle: 14 G; 4.5 Sac. **1995** Cle: 16 G; 8 Sac. **1996** Bal: 12 G; 4 Sac. **1997** Atl: 11 G; 0.5 Sac. **1998** NYJ: 16 G; 6 Sac. **Total:** 133 G; Scor 1 Saf; 2 Pt; 44 Sac.

MARQUIS PLEASANT Pleasant, Marquis Anthony 6′2″, 172 **WR**
Col: Southern Methodist *HS:* Justin F. Kimball [Dallas, TX]
B: 6/28/1965, Dallas, TX
1987 Cin: 3 G; Rec 2-45 22.5.

MIKE PLEASANT Pleasant, Michael Ricardo 6′2″, 193 **WR**
Col: Oklahoma *HS:* Muskogee [OK] B: 8/16/1955, Muskogee, OK
1984 LARm: 5 G; KR 2-48 24.0.

REGGIE PLEASANT Pleasant, Reginald Lecarno 5′9″, 175 **DB**
Col: Clemson *HS:* Furman [Sumter, SC] B: 5/2/1962, Sumter, SC
Drafted: 1985 Round 6 Atl
1985 Atl: 3 G.

JOE PLISKA Pliska, Joseph Stanley 5′10″, 185 **BB**
Col: Notre Dame *HS:* Englewood [Chicago, IL] B: 10/17/1890, Chicago, IL D: 8/25/1940, Chicago, IL
1920 Ham: 4 G. **1921** Ham: 1 G. **Total:** 5 G.

KURT PLOEGER Ploeger, Kurt Alan 6′5″, 259 **DE-DT**
Col: Gustavus Adolphus *HS:* Le Sueur [MN] B: 12/1/1962, Iowa Falls, IA *Drafted:* 1985 Round 6 Dal
1986 Dal-GB-Buf: 4 G. Dal: 3 G. GB: 1 G. **1987** Min: 1 G. **Total:** 5 G.

MILT PLUM Plum, Milton Ross 6′1″, 205 **QB**
Col: Penn State *HS:* Woodbury [NJ] B: 1/20/1935, Westville, NJ
Drafted: 1957 Round 2 Cle
1958 Cle: Scor 26, 2-2 100.0% XK. **1959** Cle: Rec 1-20 20.0. **1962** Det: Scor 21, 5-12 41.7% FG. **1963** Det: Scor 16, 1-4 25.0% FG, 13-13 100.0% XK. **1966** Det: Scor 1, 1-1 100.0% XK. **Total:** Rec 1-20 20.0; Scor 112, 6-16 37.5% FG, 16-16 100.0% XK.

		Passing							
Year Team	**G**	**Att**	**Comp**	**Comp%**	**Yds**	**YPA**	**TD**	**Int**	**Rating**
1957 Cle	9	76	41	53.9	590	7.76	2	5	60.7
1958 Cle	12	189	102	54.0	1619	8.57	11	11	77.9
1959 Cle	12	266	156	**58.6**	1992	7.49	14	8	87.2
1960 Cle	12	250	151	**60.4**	2297	**9.19**	21	5	110.4
1961 Cle	14	302	177	**58.6**	2416	8.00	18	10	90.3
1962 Det	14	325	179	55.1	2378	7.32	15	20	68.2
1963 Det	10	77	27	35.1	339	4.40	2	12	18.7
1964 Det	12	287	154	53.7	2241	7.81	18	15	78.5
1965 Det	14	308	143	46.4	1710	5.55	12	19	51.2
1966 Det	6	146	82	56.2	943	6.46	4	13	47.8
1967 Det	9	172	86	50.0	925	5.38	4	**8**	54.5
1968 LARm	4	12	5	41.7	49	4.08	1	1	46.9
1969 NYG	1	9	3	33.3	37	4.11	0	0	47.0
NFL Total	129	2419	1306	54.0	17536	7.25	122	127	72.2

	Rushing				
Year Team	**Att**	**Yds**	**Avg**	**TD**	**Fum**
1957 Cle	26	118	4.5	0	1
1958 Cle	37	107	2.9	4	2
1959 Cle	21	20	1.0	1	2
1960 Cle	17	-24	-1.4	2	2
1961 Cle	24	-17	-0.7	1	9
1962 Det	29	170	5.9	1	2
1963 Det	9	26	2.9	0	0
1964 Det	12	28	2.3	1	4
1965 Det	21	37	1.8	3	5
1966 Det	12	59	4.9	0	2
1967 Det	6	5	0.8	0	4
1968 LARm	2	3	1.5	0	0
1969 NYG	1	-1	-1.0	0	1
NFL Total	217	531	2.4	13	34

BRUCE PLUMMER Plummer, Bruce Elliot 6′0″, 197 **DB**
Col: Mississippi State *HS:* Bogalusa [LA] B: 9/1/1964, Bogalusa, LA
Drafted: 1987 Round 9 Den
1987 Den: 11 G. **1988** Den-Mia: 11 G. Den: 8 G. Mia: 3 G. **1989** Ind: 16 G; Int 1-18; 1 Sac. **1990** Den-SF: 8 G; Int 1-16. Den: 7 G; Int 1-16. SF: 1 G. **1991** Phi: 6 G. **Total:** 52 G; Int 2-34; 1 Sac.

GARY PLUMMER Plummer, Gary Lee 6′2″, 244 **LB**
Col: California *HS:* Mission San Jose [Fremont, CA] B: 1/26/1960, Fremont, CA
1986 SD: 15 G; KR 1-0; 2.5 Sac. **1987** SD: 8 G; Int 1-2. **1988** SD: 16 G. **1989** SD: 16 G; Rush 1-6 6.0. **1990** SD: 16 G; Rush 2-3 1.5 1 TD; Rec 1-2 2.0 1 TD; Tot TD 2; 12 Pt. **1991** SD: 16 G; 1 Sac. **1992** SD: 16 G; Int 2-40. **1993** SD: 16 G; Int 2-7. **1994** SF: 16 G; Int 1-1. **1995** SF: 16 G; 1 Sac. **1996** SF: 13 G. **1997** SF: 16 G. **Total:** 180 G; Rush 3-9 3.0 1 TD; Rec 1-2 2.0 1 TD; KR 1-0; Int 6-50; Tot TD 2; 12 Pt; 4.5 Sac.

JAKE PLUMMER Plummer, Jason Steven 6′2″, 197 **QB**
(The Snake) *Col:* Arizona State *HS:* Capital [Boise, ID]
B: 12/19/1974, Boise, ID *Drafted:* 1997 Round 2 Ariz
1997 Ariz: Rec 1-2 2.0; Scor 1 2XP. **Total:** Rec 1-2 2.0; Scor 1 2XP.

		Passing							
Year Team	**G**	**Att**	**Comp**	**Comp%**	**Yds**	**YPA**	**TD**	**Int**	**Rating**
1997 Ariz	10	296	157	53.0	2203	7.44	15	15	73.1
1998 Ariz	16	547	324	59.2	3737	6.83	17	20	75.0
NFL Total	26	843	481	57.1	5940	7.05	32	35	74.3

	Rushing				
Year Team	**Att**	**Yds**	**Avg**	**TD**	**Fum**
1997 Ariz	39	216	5.5	2	6
1998 Ariz	51	217	4.3	4	12
NFL Total	90	433	4.8	6	18

TONY PLUMMER Plummer, Tony Lamont 5′11″, 188 **DB**
Col: Coll. of San Mateo CA (J.C.); U. of Pacific *HS:* Redwood City [CA]
B: 1/21/1947, Dallas, TX *Drafted:* 1970 Round 10 StL
1970 StL: 1 G. **1971** Atl: 7 G. **1972** Atl: 14 G; KR 1-21 21.0. **1973** Atl: 14 G; KR 5-115 23.0; Int 1-39; Scor 1 Saf; 2 Pt. **1974** LARm: 5 G. **Total:** 41 G; KR 6-136 22.7; Int 1-39; Scor 1 Saf; 2 Pt.

DAVE PLUMP Plump, David 6′1″, 200 **DB**
Col: Vallejo JC CA; Fresno State *HS:* Vallejo [CA] B: 12/13/1942, Vicksburg, MS *Drafted:* 1965 Redshirt Round 10 SD
1966 SD: 14 G; PR 1-4 4.0; KR 15-345 23.0; 1 Fum.

TED PLUMRIDGE Plumridge, Theodore Earle Jr. 6′2″, 205 **C**
Col: Colgate; St. John's (N.Y.) *HS:* Manual Training [Brooklyn, NY]; Marquand Prep [Brooklyn, NY] B: 9/1/1901, Brooklyn, NY D: 10/6/1962, Brooklyn, NY
1926 Bkn: 2 G.

PLUNKETT Plunkett 5′7″, 160 **WB**
Col: No College Deceased
1920 ChiC: 1 G.

ART PLUNKETT Plunkett, Arthur Scott 6′7″, 269 **OT**
Col: Nevada-Las Vegas *HS:* Arlington [Arlington Heights, IL]; Skyline HS [Salt Lake City, UT] B: 3/8/1959, Chicago, IL *Drafted:* 1981 Round 8 LARm
1981 StL: 8 G. **1982** StL: 9 G. **1983** StL: 16 G. **1984** StL: 16 G. **1985** NE: 15 G. **1987** NE: 7 G. **Total:** 71 G.

JIM PLUNKETT Plunkett, James William Jr. 6′3″, 220 **QB**
Col: Stanford *HS:* Overfeldt [San Jose, CA]; James Lick HS [San Jose, CA] B: 12/5/1947, San Jose, CA *Drafted:* 1971 Round 1 NE

		Passing							
Year Team	**G**	**Att**	**Comp**	**Comp%**	**Yds**	**YPA**	**TD**	**Int**	**Rating**
1971 NE	14	328	158	48.2	2158	6.58	19	16	68.6
1972 NE	14	355	169	47.6	2196	6.19	8	25	45.7
1973 NE	14	376	193	51.3	2550	6.78	13	17	65.8
1974 NE	14	352	173	49.1	2457	6.98	19	22	64.1
1975 NE	5	92	36	39.1	571	6.21	3	7	39.7
1976 SF	12	243	126	51.9	1592	6.55	13	16	63.0
1977 SF	14	248	128	51.6	1693	6.83	9	14	62.1
1979 Oak	4	15	7	46.7	89	5.93	1	1	60.1
1980 Oak	13	320	165	51.6	2299	7.18	18	16	72.9
1981 Oak	9	179	94	52.5	1045	5.84	4	9	56.7
1982 LARd	9	261	152	58.2	2035	7.80	14	15	77.0
1983 LARd	14	379	230	60.7	2935	7.74	20	18	82.7
1984 LARd	8	198	108	54.5	1473	7.44	6	10	67.6
1985 LARd	3	103	71	68.9	803	7.80	3	3	89.6
1986 LARd	10	252	133	52.8	1986	7.88	14	9	82.5
NFL Total	157	3701	1943	52.5	25882	6.99	164	198	67.5

	Rushing				
Year Team	**Att**	**Yds**	**Avg**	**TD**	**Fum**
1971 NE	45	210	4.7	0	6
1972 NE	36	230	6.4	1	6
1973 NE	44	209	4.8	5	6
1974 NE	30	161	5.4	2	4
1975 NE	4	7	1.8	1	2
1976 SF	19	95	5.0	0	1
1977 SF	28	71	2.5	1	2
1979 Oak	3	18	6.0	0	0
1980 Oak	28	141	5.0	2	9
1981 Oak	12	38	3.2	1	3
1982 LARd	15	6	0.4	0	4
1983 LARd	26	78	3.0	0	7
1984 LARd	16	14	0.9	1	2
1985 LARd	5	12	2.4	0	6
1986 LARd	12	47	3.9	0	4
NFL Total	323	1337	4.1	14	62

SHERMAN PLUNKETT Plunkett, Sherman Eugene 6′4″, 290 **OT**
(Tank) *Col:* Maryland East. Shore *HS:* Frederick Douglass [Oklahoma City, OK] B: 4/17/1933, Oklahoma City, OK D: 11/18/1989, Baltimore, MD *Drafted:* 1956 Round 6 Cle
1958 Bal: 12 G. **1959** Bal: 12 G; KR 1-12 12.0. **1960** Bal: 12 G. **1961** SD: 12 G. **1962** SD: 14 G. **1963** NYJ: 14 G. **1964** NYJ: 14 G. **1965** NYJ: 14 G. **1966** NYJ: 14 G. **1967** NYJ: 14 G. **Total:** 132 G; KR 1-12 12.0.

WARREN PLUNKETT Plunkett, Warren Francis 6′0″, 200 **BB-LB**
Col: Minnesota *HS:* Austin [MN] B: 8/4/1920, St.Paul, MN
1942 Cle: 10 G; Rec 2-16 8.0; KR 1-4 4.0.

BOBBY PLY Ply, Robert Vernon 6′1″, 190 **DB**
Col: Baylor *HS:* Mission [TX] B: 8/13/1940, Mission, TX
Drafted: 1962 Round 5 DalT
1962 DalT: 14 G; Int 7-144. **1963** KC: 14 G. **1964** KC: 14 G; Int 1-12. **1965** KC: 14 G. **1966** KC: 14 G; PR 1-0; Int 1-0. **1967** KC-Buf-Den: 7 G. KC: 3 G. Buf: 3 G. Den: 1 G. **Total:** 77 G; PR 1-0; Int 9-156.

RAY POAGE Poage, Raymond Coy Jr. 6′3″, 215 **TE**
Col: Texas *HS:* Lamar [Houston, TX]; Happy HS [TX] B: 11/14/1940, Plainview, TX *Drafted:* 1963 Round 3 Min
1965 Phi: Pass 1-0. **1968** NO: Rush 1-22 22.0. **1969** NO: Rush 1-(-3) -3.0. **1970** NO: Rush 1-13 13.0; KR 1-6 6.0. **Total:** Pass 1-0; Rush 3-32 10.7; KR 1-6 6.0.

		Receiving				
Year Team	**G**	**Rec**	**Yds**	**Avg**	**TD**	**Fum**
1963 Min	7	15	354	23.6	2	0
1964 Phi	14	37	479	12.9	1	1
1965 Phi	13	31	612	19.7	5	0
1967 NO	12	24	380	15.8	0	1
1968 NO	10	1	11	11.0	0	0
1969 NO	14	18	236	13.1	4	1
1970 NO	12	15	166	11.1	1	0
1971 Atl	4	4	71	17.8	0	0
NFL Total	86	145	2309	15.9	13	3

PAUL PODMAJERSKY Podmajersky, Paul Jr. 5′11″, 220 **G**
Col: Michigan State; Wyoming; Iowa; Illinois *HS:* Albert G. Lane Tech [Chicago, IL] B: 11/17/1916, Chicago, IL D: 10/12/1993, Roseburg, OR
1944 ChiB: 1 G.

ED PODOLAK Podolak, Edward Joseph 6′1″, 204 **RB**
Col: Iowa *HS:* Atlantic [IA] B: 9/1/1947, Atlantic, IA *Drafted:* 1969 Round 2 KC
1970 KC: Pass 2-2 100.0%, 40 20.00. **1971** KC: Pass 2-2 100.0%, 42 21.00. **1973** KC: Pass 1-0. **1975** KC: Pass 1-0, 1 Int. **Total:** Pass 6-4 66.7%, 82 13.67 1 Int.

		Rushing				Receiving			
Year Team	**G**	**Att**	**Yds**	**Avg**	**TD**	**Rec**	**Yds**	**Avg**	**TD**
1969 KC	4	0	0	—	0	0	0	—	0
1970 KC	14	168	749	4.5	3	26	307	11.8	1
1971 KC	13	184	708	3.8	9	36	252	7.0	0
1972 KC	13	171	615	3.6	4	46	345	7.5	2
1973 KC	14	210	721	3.4	3	55	445	8.1	0
1974 KC	9	101	386	3.8	2	43	306	7.1	1
1975 KC	14	102	351	3.4	3	37	332	9.0	2
1976 KC	10	88	371	4.2	5	13	156	12.0	0
1977 KC	13	133	550	4.1	5	32	313	9.8	0
NFL Total	104	1157	4451	3.8	34	288	2456	8.5	6

	Punt Returns				Kickoff Returns					Tot
Year Team	**Ret**	**Yds**	**Avg**	**TD**	**Ret**	**Yds**	**Avg**	**TD**	**Fum**	**TD**
1969 KC	0	0	—	0	7	165	23.6	0	3	0
1970 KC	23	311	**13.5**	0	17	348	20.5	0	6	4
1971 KC	14	84	6.0	0	3	65	21.7	0	5	9
1972 KC	8	11	1.4	0	7	119	17.0	0	**10**	6
1973 KC	11	90	8.2	0	0	0	—	0	7	3
1974 KC	15	134	8.9	0	0	0	—	0	4	3
1975 KC	13	96	7.4	0	0	0	—	0	3	5
1976 KC	0	0	—	0	0	0	—	0	2	5
1977 KC	2	13	6.5	0	0	0	—	0	2	5
NFL Total	86	739	8.6	0	34	697	20.5	0	42	40

JIM PODOLEY Podoley, James 6′2″, 200 **HB-OE**
(Poodles) *Col:* Central Michigan *HS:* Otisville [MI] B: 9/16/1933, Mount Morris, MI *Drafted:* 1957 Round 4 Was
1957 Was: KR 3-56 18.7. **1959** Was: Pass 1-0; KR 5-126 25.2. **1960** Was: PR 3-3 1.0; KR 4-87 21.8. **Total:** Pass 1-0; PR 3-3 1.0; KR 12-269 22.4.

		Rushing				Receiving					Tot
Year Team	**G**	**Att**	**Yds**	**Avg**	**TD**	**Rec**	**Yds**	**Avg**	**TD**	**Fum**	**TD**
1957 Was	12	114	442	3.9	2	27	554	**20.5**	4	5	6
1958 Was	10	48	169	3.5	0	16	381	23.8	4	1	4
1959 Was	11	18	83	4.6	0	18	282	15.7	2	1	2
1960 Was	10	29	52	1.8	0	17	244	14.4	1	4	1
NFL Total	43	209	746	3.6	2	78	1461	18.7	11	11	13

BILLY POE Poe, Billy Gene 6′3″, 280 **OG**
Col: Morehead State *HS:* Rock Hill [Ironton, OH] B: 4/26/1964, Ironton, OH
1987 Cin: 3 G.

JOHNNIE POE Poe, Johnnie Edward 6′1″, 190 **DB**
Col: Missouri *HS:* Lincoln [East St. Louis, IL] B: 8/29/1959, St. Louis, MO *Drafted:* 1981 Round 6 NO
1981 NO: PR 1-2 2.0. **1986** NO: PR 8-71 8.9; 1 Sac. **Total:** PR 9-73 8.1; 1 Sac.

		Interceptions				Tot
Year Team	**G**	**Int**	**Yds**	**TD**	**Fum**	**TD**
1981 NO	15	1	0	0	0	0
1982 NO	9	0	0	0	0	0
1983 NO	16	7	146	1	0	1
1984 NO	16	1	16	0	0	0
1985 NO	16	3	63	**1**	1	1
1986 NO	16	4	42	0	0	0
1987 NO	12	1	0	0	0	1
NFL Total	100	17	267	2	1	3

JOHN POHLMAN Pohlman, John Theodore 5'9", 178 FB
Col: Brown *HS:* New Haven [CT] B: 9/18/1902, New Haven, CT
D: 5/8/1957, Milford, CT
1925 Prov: 2 G.

DICK POILLON Poillon, Richard Charles 6'0", 197 HB-DB-TB
(Whitey) *Col:* Canisius *HS:* Valley Stream [NY] B: 8/13/1920, Queens, NY D: 11/14/1994, West Palm Beach, FL
1942 Was: Pass 15-2 13.3%, 52 3.47 3 Int; PR 1-0; KR 3-65 21.7; Scor 5, 1-2 50.0% FG, 2-2 100.0% XK. **1946** Was: PR 1-13 13.0; KR 5-86 17.2; Scor 45, 6-16 37.5% FG, 21-21 100.0% XK. **1947** Was: PR 3-37 12.3; KR 4-23 5.8; Int 2-28; Scor 85, 4-6 66.7% FG, 37-41 90.2% XK. **1948** Was: Scor 66, 5-7 71.4% FG, 33-38 86.8% XK; 1 Fum TD. **1949** Was: Scor 46, 4-7 57.1% FG, 34-37 91.9% XK. **Total:** Pass 15-2 13.3%, 52 3.47 3 Int; PR 5-50 10.0; KR 12-174 14.5; Int 2-28; Scor 247, 20-38 52.6% FG, 127-139 91.4% XK; 1 Fum TD.

		Rushing				Receiving			
Year Team	G	Att	Yds	Avg	TD	Rec	Yds	Avg	TD
1942 Was	7	55	148	2.7	0	0	0	—	0
1946 Was	11	25	45	1.8	1	7	114	16.3	0
1947 Was	12	28	104	3.7	2	20	250	12.5	4
1948 Was	12	71	233	3.3	1	9	105	11.7	1
1949 Was	12	7	5	0.7	0	1	8	8.0	0
NFL Total	54	186	535	2.9	4	37	477	12.9	5

	Punting				Tot
Year Team	Punts	Yds	Avg	Fum	TD
1942 Was	11	424	38.5	0	0
1946 Was	0	0	—	3	1
1947 Was	15	533	35.5	1	6
1948 Was	51	2150	42.2	1	3
1949 Was	67	**2697**	40.3	1	0
NFL Total	144	5804	40.3	6	10

LANCE POIMBEOUF Poimbeouf, Lance Joseph 6'3", 225 OG
Col: Southwestern Louisiana *HS:* Franklin [LA] B: 11/10/1940
1963 Dal: 1 G.

JOHN POINTER Pointer, John Leslie 6'2", 225 LB
Col: Vanderbilt *HS:* Columbia Central [TN] B: 1/16/1958, Columbia, TN
1987 GB: 3 G.

FRANK POKORNY Pokorny, Frank Edward 6'0", 198 WR
Col: Youngstown State *HS:* Center [Monaca, PA] B: 5/13/1963, Uniontown, PA
1985 Pit: 4 G.

JOHN POLANSKI Polanski, John B 6'2", 211 FB-LB
Col: Wake Forest B: 9/6/1918, Buffalo, NY Deceased *Drafted:* 1942 Round 11 Det
AAFC **1946** LA-A: Rec 2-15 7.5 1 TD; Int 1-50.

		Rushing				Tot
Year Team	G	Att	Yds	Avg	TD	TD
1946 LA-A	13	28	77	2.8	1	2

NFL **1942** Det: 3 G; Rush 17-67 3.9; KR 2-49 24.5; Int 1-20.

BULL POLISKY Polisky, John 6'0", 225 G-T
Col: St. Edward's; Notre Dame *HS:* Bellaire [OH] B: 1/15/1901, Pittsburgh, PA D: 4/1978, Wellsville, OH
1929 ChiB: 9 G.

FRANK POLLACK Pollack, Frank Steven 6'5", 285 OT-OG
Col: Northern Arizona *HS:* Greenway [Phoenix, AZ] B: 11/5/1967, Camp Springs, MD *Drafted:* 1990 Round 6 SF
1990 SF: 16 G. **1991** SF: 15 G. **1994** SF: 12 G. **1995** SF: 15 G. **1996** SF: 16 G. **1997** SF: 16 G. **Total:** 90 G.

AL POLLARD Pollard, Alfred Lee 6'0", 196 HB-FB-DB
Col: Loyola Marymount; Army *HS:* Loyola [Los Angeles, CA]
B: 9/7/1928, Los Angeles, CA *Drafted:* 1951 Round 21 NYY
1951 NYY-Phi: Rec 3-35 11.7. NYY: Rec 0-18. Phi: Rec 3-17 5.7. **1952** Phi: Rec 8-59 7.4. **1953** Phi: Rec 7-33 4.7; Scor 1, 0-2 FG, 1-1 100.0% XK. **Total:** Rec 18-127 7.1; Scor 7, 0-2 FG, 1-1 100.0% XK.

		Rushing				Punt Returns			
Year Team	G	Att	Yds	Avg	TD	Ret	Yds	Avg	TD
1951 NYY-Phi	12	26	121	4.7	0	18	148	8.2	0
1951 NYY	6	2	2	1.0	0	3	34	11.3	0
1951 Phi	6	24	119	5.0	0	15	114	7.6	0
1952 Phi	12	55	186	3.4	1	0	0	—	0
1953 Phi	12	23	44	1.9	0	20	106	5.3	0
NFL Total	36	104	351	3.4	1	38	254	6.7	0

	Kickoff Returns				
Year Team	Ret	Yds	Avg	TD	Fum
1951 NYY-Phi	19	464	24.4	0	2
1951 NYY	5	138	27.6	0	0
1951 Phi	14	326	23.3	0	2
1952 Phi	21	528	25.1	0	3
1953 Phi	13	301	23.2	0	3
NFL Total	53	1293	24.4	0	8

DARRYL POLLARD Pollard, Cedric Darryl 5'11", 187 DB
Col: Weber State *HS:* General William Mitchell [Colorado Springs, CO]
B: 5/11/1964, Ellsworth, ME
1987 SF: 3 G; PR 1-0. **1988** SF: 14 G. **1989** SF: 16 G; Int 1-12. **1990** SF: 16 G; Int 1-0. **1992** TB: 16 G; Int 2-99. **Total:** 65 G; PR 1-0; Int 4-111.

FRANK POLLARD Pollard, Frank D Jr. 5'10", 218 RB
Col: Baylor *HS:* Meridian [TX] B: 6/15/1957, Clifton, TX
Drafted: 1980 Round 11 Pit
1980 Pit: PR 1-5 5.0; KR 22-494 22.5. **Total:** PR 1-5 5.0; KR 22-494 22.5.

		Rushing				Receiving				
Year Team	G	Att	Yds	Avg	TD	Rec	Yds	Avg	TD	Fum
1980 Pit	16	4	16	4.0	0	0	0	—	0	1
1981 Pit	14	123	570	4.6	2	19	156	8.2	0	5
1982 Pit	9	62	238	3.8	2	6	39	6.5	0	3
1983 Pit	16	135	608	4.5	4	16	127	7.9	0	5
1984 Pit	15	213	851	4.0	6	21	186	8.9	0	9
1985 Pit	16	233	991	4.3	3	24	250	10.4	0	2
1986 Pit	3	24	86	3.6	0	2	15	7.5	0	1
1987 Pit	12	128	536	4.2	3	14	77	5.5	0	3
1988 Pit	10	31	93	3.0	0	2	22	11.0	0	1
NFL Total	111	953	3989	4.2	20	104	872	8.4	0	30

FRITZ POLLARD Pollard, Frederick Douglass 5'9", 165 WB-TB-BB
Col: Bates; Brown *HS:* Albert G. Lane Tech [Chicago, IL] B: 1/27/1894, Chicago, IL D: 5/11/1986, Silver Spring, MD
1920 Akr: 11 G. **1921** Akr: 12 G; Pass 1 TD; Rush **6** TD; Rec 1 TD; Tot TD **7**; 42 Pt. **1922** Mil: 7 G; Rush 3 TD; Scor 20, 2 XK. **1923** Ham: 2 G; Scor 1, 1 XK. **1925** Ham-Akr-Prov: 13 G; Pass 3 TD; Rush 2 TD; 12 Pt. Ham: 1 G. Akr: 8 G; Pass 3 TD; Rush 2 TD; 12 Pt. Prov: 4 G. **1926** Akr: 4 G; Pass 1 TD. **Total:** 49 G; Pass 5 TD; Rush 11 TD; Rec 1 TD; Tot TD 12.

MARCUS POLLARD Pollard, Marcus LaJuan 6'4", 257 TE
Col: Seward Co. CC KS; Bradley *HS:* Valley [AL] B: 2/8/1972, Lanett, AL
1997 Ind: Scor 1 2XP. **1998** Ind: KR 1-4 4.0; Scor **2** 2XP. **Total:** KR 1-4 4.0; Scor 3 2XP.

		Receiving			
Year Team	G	Rec	Yds	Avg	TD
1995 Ind	8	0	0	—	0
1996 Ind	16	6	86	14.3	1
1997 Ind	16	10	116	11.6	0
1998 Ind	16	24	309	12.9	4
NFL Total	56	40	511	12.8	5

BOB POLLARD Pollard, Robert Lee 6'3", 250 DT-DE
Col: Texas Southern; Weber State *HS:* Hebert [Beaumont, TX]
B: 12/30/1948, Beaumont, TX *Drafted:* 1971 Round 11 NO
1971 NO: 14 G. **1972** NO: 14 G. **1973** NO: 14 G. **1974** NO: 14 G. **1975** NO: 14 G. **1976** NO: 8 G. **1977** NO: 14 G; 1 Fum TD; 6 Pt. **1978** StL: 15 G. **1979** StL: 16 G. **1980** StL: 16 G. **1981** StL: 15 G. **Total:** 154 G; 1 Fum TD; 6 Pt.

TRENT POLLARD Pollard, Trent Deshawn 6'4", 304 OT
Col: Eastern Washington *HS:* Rainier [WA] B: 11/20/1972, Seattle, WA
Drafted: 1994 Round 5 Cin
1994 Cin: 8 G. **1995** Cin: 9 G. **Total:** 17 G.

TOM POLLEY Polley, Thomas Craig 6'3", 246 LB
Col: Normandale CC MN; Nevada-Las Vegas *HS:* St. Louis Park [MN]
B: 2/17/1962, Minneapolis, MN *Drafted:* 1985 Round 8 Phi
1985 Phi: 2 G. **1987** Cle: 2 G. **Total:** 4 G.

RED POLLOCK Pollock, William Henry 6'2", 194 HB-LB-OE-DE
Col: Widener *HS:* Northeast [Philadelphia, PA] B: 12/5/1911, Philadelphia, PA D: 8/7/1993, Freeport, NY
1935 ChiB: Pass 12-1 8.3%, 18 1.50 2 Int; Rec 7-135 19.3 1 TD.
1936 ChiB: Rec 1-15 15.0. **Total:** Pass 12-1 8.3%, 18 1.50 2 Int; Rec 8-150 18.8 1 TD.

		Rushing				Tot
Year Team	G	Att	Yds	Avg	TD	TD
1935 ChiB	11	45	254	5.6	3	4
1936 ChiB	7	0	0	—	0	0
NFL Total	18	45	254	5.6	3	4

GORDON POLOFSKY Polofsky, Gordon Zelig 6'1", 219 OG-LB
Col: Tennessee *HS:* Cranston [RI] B: 1/10/1931, Providence, RI
Drafted: 1952 Round 5 LARm
1952 ChiC: 10 G. **1953** ChiC: 4 G. **1954** ChiC: 12 G. **Total:** 26 G.

LARRY POLOWSKI Polowski, Larry Robert 6'3", 235 LB
Col: Boise State *HS:* Yucca Valley [Twentynine Palms, CA]
B: 9/15/1957, Three Rivers, MI *Drafted:* 1979 Round 7 Sea
1979 Sea: 14 G.

FRAN POLSFOOT Polsfoot, Francis Charles 6′3″, 203 **OE**
Col: Washington State *HS:* Montesanto [WA] B: 4/19/1927, Montesano, WA D: 4/5/1985, Denver, CO *Drafted:* 1950 Round 3 ChiC

		Receiving				Punting		
Year Team	G	Rec	Yds	Avg	TD	Punts	Yds	Avg
1950 ChiC	12	38	653	17.2	6	0	0	—
1951 ChiC	12	57	796	14.0	4	47	1914	40.7
1952 ChiC	3	0	0	—	0	0	0	—
1953 Was	10	11	164	14.9	0	0	0	—
NFL Total	37	106	1613	15.2	10	47	1914	40.7

RANDY POLTL Poltl, Randall Patrick 6′3″, 190 **DB**
Col: Stanford *HS:* Bishop Alemany [Mission Hills, CA] B: 3/26/1952, Long Beach, CA *Drafted:* 1974 Round 12 Min
1974 Min: 5 G. **1975** Den: 13 G. **1976** Den: 12 G; Int 1-0; **1** Fum TD; 6 Pt. **1977** Den: 14 G. **Total:** 44 G; Int 1-0; 1 Fum TD; 6 Pt.

DAVE PONDER Ponder, David Earl 6′3″, 248 **DT**
Col: Florida State *HS:* Cairo [GA] B: 6/27/1962, Dade City, FL
1985 Dal: 4 G; 0.5 Sac.

ANTWAUNE PONDS Ponds, Antwaune 6′2″, 252 **LB**
Col: Syracuse *HS:* Paxon [Jacksonville, FL] B: 6/29/1975, Harrisburg, PA *Drafted:* 1998 Round 7 Was
1998 Was: 3 G.

DAVID POOL Pool, David Allen 5′9″, 188 **DB**
Col: Tennessee State; Carson-Newman *HS:* Cincinnati Academy of Physical Education [Cincinnati, OH] B: 12/20/1966, Cincinnati, OH *Drafted:* 1990 Round 6 SD
1990 Buf: 9 G; Int 1-0. **1991** NE: 15 G; PR 1-0; 1 Fum. **1992** NE: 16 G; Int 2-54 1 TD; 6 Pt. **1993** Buf: 2 G. **1994** Mia: 1 G. **Total:** 43 G; PR 1-0; Int 3-54 1 TD; 6 Pt; 1 Fum.

HAMP POOL Pool, Hampton John 6′3″, 221 **OE-DE**
Col: California; Army; Stanford *HS:* Paso Robles [CA] B: 3/11/1915, San Miguel, CA *Drafted:* 1940 Round 7 ChiB
AAFC **1946** MiaA: 4 G; Rec 3-63 21.0.

NFL Statistics

		Receiving			
Year Team	G	Rec	Yds	Avg	TD
1940 ChiB	5	2	55	27.5	0
1941 ChiB	7	5	101	20.2	1
1942 ChiB	11	10	321	**32.1**	5
1943 ChiB	10	18	363	20.2	5
NFL Total	33	35	840	24.0	11

BARNEY POOLE Poole, George Barney 6′2″, 231 **DE-OE**
Col: North Carolina; Army; Mississippi *HS:* Crosby [MS] B: 10/29/1923, Gloster, MS
AAFC **1949** NY-A: 11 G; Rec 6-83 13.8; PR 1-6 6.0; Int 1-0.

NFL **1950** NYY: 12 G; Rec 4-82 20.5 1 TD; KR 2-8 4.0; 6 Pt. **1951** NYY: 11 G. **1952** Dal: 12 G; Rec 2-23 11.5. **1953** Bal: 12 G; KR 2-24 12.0. **1954** NYG: 11 G. **Total:** 58 G; Rec 6-105 17.5 1 TD; KR 4-32 8.0; 6 Pt.

JIM POOLE Poole, James Eugene 6′3″, 218 **OE-DE**
Col: Mississippi *HS:* Crosby [MS] B: 9/9/1915, Gloster, MS D: 11/16/1994, Oxford, MS *Drafted:* 1937 Round 7 NYG
1941 NYG: Int 1-16. **1945** ChiC-NYG: Int 1-28. ChiC: Int 1-28. **Total:** Int 2-44.

		Receiving					Tot
Year Team	G	Rec	Yds	Avg	TD	Fum	TD
1937 NYG	11	5	79	15.8	2	0	2
1938 NYG	11	7	98	14.0	1	0	1
1939 NYG	11	7	99	14.1	0	0	0
1940 NYG	11	10	156	15.6	3	0	3
1941 NYG	11	6	74	12.3	2	0	3
1945 ChiC-NYG	12	6	82	13.7	2	0	2
1945 ChiC	9	6	82	13.7	2	0	2
1945 NYG	3	0	0	—	0	0	0
1946 NYG	11	24	307	12.8	3	1	3
NFL Total	78	65	895	13.8	13	1	14

KEITH POOLE Poole, Keith Robert Strohmaier 6′0″, 188 **WR**
Col: Arizona State *HS:* Clovis [CA] B: 6/18/1974, San Jose, CA *Drafted:* 1997 Round 4 NO

		Receiving			
Year Team	G	Rec	Yds	Avg	TD
1997 NO	3	4	98	24.5	2
1998 NO	15	24	509	21.2	2
NFL Total	18	28	607	21.7	4

KEN POOLE Poole, Kenneth Dawayne 6′3″, 251 **DE**
Col: Northeast Louisiana *HS:* Hermitage [AR] B: 10/20/1958, Hermitage, AR *Drafted:* 1981 Round 5 Mia
1981 Mia: 16 G.

LARRY POOLE Poole, Larry Eugene 6′1″, 195 **RB**
Col: Kent State *HS:* Garfield [Akron, OH] B: 7/31/1952, Akron, OH *Drafted:* 1975 Round 9 Cle
1975 Cle: PR 6-35 5.8; KR 2-65 32.5. **1976** Cle: KR 3-62 20.7. **1978** Hou: KR 4-107 26.8. **Total:** PR 6-35 5.8; KR 9-234 26.0.

		Rushing				Receiving					Tot
Year Team	G	Att	Yds	Avg	TD	Rec	Yds	Avg	TD	Fum	TD
1975 Cle	3	17	114	6.7	0	1	5	5.0	0	0	0
1976 Cle	13	78	356	4.6	1	14	70	5.0	0	2	1
1977 Cle	13	38	118	3.1	1	17	137	8.1	3	1	4
1978 Hou	9	0	0	—	0	0	0	—	0	0	0
NFL Total	38	133	588	4.4	2	32	212	6.6	3	3	5

NATHAN POOLE Poole, Nathan Lewis 5′9″, 210 **RB**
Col: Louisville *HS:* Benjamin Russell [Alexander City, AL] B: 12/17/1956, Alexander City, AL *Drafted:* 1979 Round 10 Cin
1979 Cin: Rec 1-(-10) -10.0; KR 7-128 18.3. **1980** Cin: Rec 2-(-4) -2.0; KR 1-8 8.0. **1982** Den: KR 1-0. **1983** Den: Rec 20-184 9.2. **1987** Den: Rec 1-9 9.0. **Total:** Rec 24-179 7.5; KR 9-136 15.1.

		Rushing				
Year Team	G	Att	Yds	Avg	TD	Fum
1979 Cin	16	1	-3	-3.0	0	2
1980 Cin	16	5	6	1.2	0	1
1982 Den	9	7	36	5.1	0	0
1983 Den	16	81	246	3.0	4	1
1985 Den	3	4	12	3.0	0	0
1987 Den	2	28	126	4.5	1	0
NFL Total	62	126	423	3.4	5	4

OLLIE POOLE Poole, Oliver Lamar 6′3″, 220 **DE-OE**
Col: North Carolina; Mississippi *HS:* Crosby [MS] B: 4/18/1922, Gloster, MS *Drafted:* 1944 Round 15 NYG
AAFC **1947** NY-A: 5 G; Rec 1-19 19.0; PR 1-5 5.0. **1948** BalA: 9 G; Rec 1-2 2.0. **Total:** 14 G; Rec 2-21 10.5; PR 1-5 5.0.

NFL **1949** Det: 8 G.

RAY POOLE Poole, Ray Smith 6′2″, 215 **DE-OE**
Col: North Carolina; Mississippi *HS:* Crosby [MS] B: 4/15/1921, Gloster, MS *Drafted:* 1944 Round 13 NYG
1947 NYG: Int 1-0. **1948** NYG: Scor **1** Saf; 1 Fum TD. **1949** NYG: KR 1-3 3.0. **1950** NYG: KR 1-12 12.0; Int 1-8. **1952** NYG: Int 1-6. **Total:** KR 2-15 7.5; Int 3-14; Scor 1 Saf; 1 Fum TD.

		Receiving			
Year Team	G	Rec	Yds	Avg	TD
1947 NYG	12	23	395	17.2	4
1948 NYG	12	35	492	14.1	3
1949 NYG	12	25	277	11.1	1
1950 NYG	12	0	0	—	0
1951 NYG	11	0	0	—	0
1952 NYG	12	0	0	—	0
NFL Total	71	83	1164	14.0	8

	Scoring								Tot
Year Team	Pts	FG	FGA	FG%	XK	XKA	XK%	Fum	TD
1947 NYG	0	0	0	—	0	0	—	0	4
1948 NYG	0	0	0	—	0	0	—	1	4
1949 NYG	0	0	0	—	0	0	—	1	1
1950 NYG	45	5	11	45.5	30	34	88.2	0	0
1951 NYG	66	12	16	75.0	30	31	96.8	0	0
1952 NYG	56	10	17	58.8	26	27	96.3	0	0
NFL Total	223	27	44	61.4	86	92	93.5	2	9

BOB POOLE Poole, Robert Edward 6′4″, 225 **TE**
Col: Clemson *HS:* Decatur [MS]; Coffee HS [Florence, AL] B: 10/5/1941, Paducah, KY *Drafted:* 1964 Round 8 SF
1964 SF: 13 G; Rec 1-8 8.0. **1965** SF: 9 G; Rec 2-29 14.5. **1966** Hou: 14 G; Rec 12-131 10.9. **1967** Hou: 14 G; Rec 4-55 13.8. **Total:** 50 G; Rec 19-223 11.7.

SHELLEY POOLE Poole, Shelley O'Neal 5′7″, 219 **RB**
Col: Temple *HS:* Norcross [GA] B: 12/3/1964, Button Gwinnett, GA
1987 Atl: 1 G.

STEVE POOLE Poole, Steven Albert 6′1″, 232 **LB**
Col: Tennessee *HS:* Fort Oglethorpe [GA] B: 8/25/1952, Fort Oglethorpe, GA
1976 NYJ: 9 G; 6 Pt.

TYRONE POOLE Poole, Tyrone 5′8″, 188 **DB**
Col: Fort Valley State *HS:* La Grange [GA] B: 2/3/1972, La Grange, GA
Drafted: 1995 Round 1 Car
1995 Car: Int 2-8; 2 Sac. **1996** Car: Int 1-35. **1997** Car: KR 1-5 5.0; Int 2-0; 1 Sac. **1998** Ind: Int 1-0. **Total:** KR 1-5 5.0; Int 6-43; 3 Sac.

		Punt Returns				
Year Team	**G**	**Ret**	**Yds**	**Avg**	**TD**	**Fum**
1995 Car	16	0	0	—	0	0
1996 Car	15	3	26	8.7	0	0
1997 Car	16	26	191	7.3	0	3
1998 Ind	15	12	107	8.9	0	0
NFL Total	62	41	324	7.9	0	3

ELI POPA Popa, Eli Charles 5′10″, 202 **LB**
Col: Illinois *HS:* McKinley [Canton, OH] B: 11/4/1930, Massillon, OH
1952 ChiC: 4 G.

BUCKY POPE Pope, Frank Buckley III 6′5″, 195 **WR**
(The Catawba Claw) *Col:* Duke; Catawba *HS:* Crafton [Pittsburgh, PA] B: 3/23/1941, Pittsburgh, PA *Drafted:* 1964 Round 8 LARm
1964 LARm: Rush 2-11 5.5. **Total:** Rush 2-11 5.5.

		Receiving			
Year Team	**G**	**Rec**	**Yds**	**Avg**	**TD**
1964 LARm	14	25	786	31.4	**10**
1966 LARm	3	1	14	14.0	1
1967 LARm	13	8	152	19.0	2
1968 GB	3	0	0	—	0
NFL Total	33	34	952	28.0	13

SPENCER POPE Pope, Gordon Spencer 5′10″, 170 **OE**
Col: Indiana *HS:* Linton [IN] B: 3/9/1893, Linton, IN D: 9/9/1976, Pottsville, PA
1920 Mun: 1 G.

KEN POPE Pope, Kenith Van 5′11″, 200 **DB**
Col: Oklahoma *HS:* Ball [Galveston, TX] B: 12/28/1951, Galveston, TX
Drafted: 1974 Round 9 Oak
1974 NE: 4 G.

LEW POPE Pope, Lewis Lawrence 6′0″, 196 **DB-TB-WB-BB**
(Chicken) *Col:* Purdue *HS:* Frederick [OK] B: 2/18/1908, West Lafayette, IN D: 2/5/1964
1933 Cin: Rec 1-20 20.0. **1934** Cin: Rec 1-17 17.0. **Total:** Rec 2-37 18.5.

		Passing							
Year Team	**G**	**Att**	**Comp**	**Comp%**	**Yds**	**YPA**	**TD**	**Int**	**Rating**
1931 Prov	8	—	—	—	—	—	0	—	—
1933 Cin	10	21	5	23.8	115	5.48	0	2	10.3
1934 Cin	8	42	10	23.8	115	2.74	0	10	0.0
NFL Total	26	63	15	23.8	230	3.65	0	12	2.7

	Rushing			
Year Team	**Att**	**Yds**	**Avg**	**TD**
1933 Cin	56	179	3.2	1
1934 Cin	40	163	4.1	0
NFL Total	96	342	3.6	1

MARQUEZ POPE Pope, Marquez Phillips 5′11″, 193 **DB**
Col: Fresno State *HS:* Long Beach Polytechnic [CA] B: 10/29/1970, Nashville, TN *Drafted:* 1992 Round 2 SD
1993 SD: 0.5 Sac. **Total:** 0.5 Sac.

		Interceptions		
Year Team	**G**	**Int**	**Yds**	**TD**
1992 SD	7	0	0	0
1993 SD	16	2	14	0
1994 LARm	16	3	66	0
1995 SF	16	1	-7	0
1996 SF	16	6	98	1
1997 SF	5	1	7	0
1998 SF	6	1	0	0
NFL Total	82	14	178	1

JOHN POPOVICH Popovich, John 5′8″, 160 **HB-DB**
Col: St. Vincent *HS:* Monessen [PA] B: 3/6/1918, Monessen, PA
1944 ChPt: 6 G; Rush 8-29 3.6; Rec 3-(-1) -0.3; KR 3-75 25.0. **1945** Pit: 1 G; Rush 4-(-8) -2.0; KR 1-39 39.0. **Total:** 7 G; Rush 12-21 1.8; Rec 3-(-1) -0.3; KR 4-114 28.5.

MILT POPOVICH Popovich, Milton John 5′11″, 196 **FB-DB-WB-LB**
(Popo) *Col:* Montana *HS:* Butte [MT] B: 12/25/1915, Butte, MT
Drafted: 1938 Round 1 ChiC
1938 ChiC: Rec 1-8 8.0. **1939** ChiC: Pass 6-5 83.3%, 52 8.67; Rec 2-10 5.0; Punt 27-1000 37.0; **1** Fum TD. **1940** ChiC: Rec 5-32 6.4; Punt 5-209 41.8. **1942** ChiC: Rec 2-21 10.5; Int 1-6; Punt 3-109 36.3. **Total:** Pass 6-5 83.3%, 52 8.67; Rec 10-71 7.1; Int 1-6; Punt 35-1318 37.7; 1 Fum TD.

		Rushing			
Year Team	**G**	**Att**	**Yds**	**Avg**	**TD**
1938 ChiC	7	6	13	2.2	0
1939 ChiC	10	26	78	3.0	0
1940 ChiC	10	41	138	3.4	0
1941 ChiC	6	5	4	0.8	0
1942 ChiC	10	0	0	—	0
NFL Total	43	78	233	3.0	0

TED POPSON Popson, Theodore Paul 6′4″, 250 **TE**
Col: Coll. of Marin CA (J.C.); Portland State *HS:* Tahoe Truckee [Truckee, CA] B: 9/10/1966, Granada Hills, CA *Drafted:* 1991 Round 11 NYG

		Receiving				
Year Team	**G**	**Rec**	**Yds**	**Avg**	**TD**	**Fum**
1994 SF	16	13	141	10.8	0	0
1995 SF	12	16	128	8.0	0	1
1996 SF	15	26	301	11.6	6	0
1997 KC	13	35	320	9.1	2	0
1998 KC	12	13	90	6.9	0	0
NFL Total	68	103	980	9.5	8	1

ROBERT PORCHER Porcher, Robert III 6′3″, 277 **DE**
Col: Tennessee State; South Carolina State *HS:* Cainhoy [Huger, SC] B: 7/30/1969, Wando, SC *Drafted:* 1992 Round 1 Det
1992 Det: 16 G; 1 Sac. **1993** Det: 16 G; 8.5 Sac. **1994** Det: 15 G; 3 Sac. **1995** Det: 16 G; 5 Sac. **1996** Det: 16 G; 10 Sac. **1997** Det: 16 G; Int 1-5; 12.5 Sac. **1998** Det: 16 G; 11.5 Sac. **Total:** 111 G; Int 1-5; 51.5 Sac.

TOM PORELL Porell, Thomas Reardon 6′3″, 275 **NT**
Col: Boston College *HS:* Winchester [MA] B: 9/23/1964, Cambridge, MA
1987 NE: 1 G.

CHRIS PORT Port, Christopher Charles 6′5″, 295 **OG-OT**
Col: Duke *HS:* Don Bosco Prep [Ramsey, NJ] B: 11/2/1967, Wanaque, NJ *Drafted:* 1990 Round 12 NO
1991 NO: 14 G. **1992** NO: 16 G. **1993** NO: 15 G. **1994** NO: 16 G. **1995** NO: 8 G. **Total:** 69 G.

DARYL PORTER Porter, Daryl Maurice 5′9″, 188 **DB**
(D.P.) *Col:* Boston College *HS:* St. Thomas Aquinas [Fort Lauderdale, FL] B: 1/16/1974, Fort Lauderdale, FL *Drafted:* 1997 Round 6 Pit
1997 Det: 7 G. **1998** Buf: 2 G. **Total:** 9 G.

JACK PORTER Porter, Jack David 6′3″, 255 **C**
Col: Oklahoma *HS:* Rush Springs [OK] B: 7/27/1948, Kingfisher, OK
Drafted: 1970 Round 8 NYJ
1971 SD: 1 G.

KERRY PORTER Porter, Kerry 6′1″, 215 **RB**
Col: Washington State *HS:* Great Falls [MT] B: 9/23/1964, Vicenza, Italy *Drafted:* 1987 Round 7 Buf
1987 Buf: 6 G; Rush 2-0. **1989** LARd: 16 G; Rush 13-54 4.2. **1990** Den: 13 G; Rush 1-3 3.0; Rec 4-44 11.0. **Total:** 35 G; Rush 16-57 3.6; Rec 4-44 11.0.

KEVIN PORTER Porter, Kevin James 5′10″, 215 **DB**
Col: Auburn *HS:* Warner Robins [GA] B: 4/11/1966, Bronx, NY
Drafted: 1988 Round 3 KC
1988 KC: 15 G; KR 1-16 16.0; 1 Fum; 0.5 Sac. **1989** KC: 16 G. **1990** KC: 16 G; Int 1-13; 1 Fum. **1991** KC: 16 G; 1 Sac. **1992** KC-NYJ: 15 G. KC: 13 G. NYJ: 2 G. **Total:** 78 G; KR 1-16 16.0; Int 1-13; 2 Fum; 1.5 Sac.

LEW PORTER Porter, Lewis 5′11″, 178 **WR**
Col: Southern University *HS:* Clarksville [MS] B: 3/7/1947, Clarksville, MS *Drafted:* 1970 Round 8 Den
1970 KC: 5 G; Rush 2-21 10.5; Rec 1-29 29.0; PR 1-(-3) -3.0; KR 1-22 22.0.

RICKY PORTER Porter, Richard Anthony 5′10″, 198 **RB**
Col: Slippery Rock *HS:* Milford Mill [Baltimore, MD] B: 1/14/1960, Sylacauga, AL *Drafted:* 1982 Round 12 Det
1983 Bal: PR 14-104 7.4. **1987** Buf: Rec 9-70 7.8. **Total:** Rec 9-70 7.8; PR 14-104 7.4.

		Rushing				Kickoff Returns				
Year Team	**G**	**Att**	**Yds**	**Avg**	**TD**	**Ret**	**Yds**	**Avg**	**TD**	**Fum**
1982 Det	1	0	0	—	0	0	0	—	0	0
1983 Bal	14	0	0	—	0	18	340	18.9	0	6
1987 Buf	9	47	177	3.8	0	8	219	27.4	0	0
NFL Total	24	47	177	3.8	0	26	559	21.5	0	6

ROB PORTER Porter, Robert Bryant 6′2″, 210 **DB**
Col: Holy Cross *HS:* Mahwah [NJ] B: 5/9/1962, Suffern, NY
1987 NYG: 3 G.

RON PORTER Porter, Ronald Dean 6′3″, 232 LB
Col: Idaho *HS:* Yuba City [CA] B: 7/27/1945, Columbus, GA
Drafted: 1967 Round 5 Bal
1967 Bal: 14 G; Int 1-0. **1968** Bal: 14 G; KR 1-19 19.0. **1969** Bal-Phi: 12 G. Bal: 2 G. Phi: 10 G. **1970** Phi: 14 G. **1971** Phi: 12 G. **1972** Phi: 14 G; Int 2-10; 1 Fum. **1973** Min: 13 G. **Total:** 93 G; KR 1-19 19.0; Int 3-10; 1 Fum.

RUFUS PORTER Porter, Rufus 6′1″, 228 LB-DE
Col: Southern University *HS:* Capitol [Baton Rouge, LA] B: 5/18/1965, Amite, LA
1988 Sea: 16 G. **1989** Sea: 16 G; 10.5 Sac. **1990** Sea: 12 G; 5 Sac. **1991** Sea: 15 G; Int 1-0; 10 Sac. **1992** Sea: 16 G; 9.5 Sac. **1993** Sea: 7 G; Int 1-4; 1 Sac. **1994** Sea: 16 G; Int 1-33; 1.5 Sac. **1995** NO: 13 G; 3 Sac. **1996** NO: 13 G. **1997** TB: 11 G; 0.5 Sac. **Total:** 135 G; Int 3-37; 41 Sac.

TRACY PORTER Porter, Tracy Randolph 6′2″, 196 WR
Col: Louisiana State *HS:* Southern U. Lab [Baton Rouge, LA]
B: 6/1/1959, Baton Rouge, LA *Drafted:* 1981 Round 4 Det
1982 Det: Pass 1-0. **Total:** Pass 1-0.

		Receiving				
Year Team	G	Rec	Yds	Avg	TD	Fum
1981 Det	12	3	63	21.0	1	0
1982 Det	8	9	124	13.8	0	0
1983 Bal	16	28	384	13.7	0	0
1984 Ind	16	39	590	15.1	2	2
NFL Total	52	79	1161	14.7	3	2

WILLIE PORTER Porter, Willie Church 5′11″, 190 DB
(Bubba) *Col:* Texas Southern *HS:* F.W. Gross [Victoria, TX]
B: 3/25/1946, Victoria, TX
1968 Bos: PR 22-135 6.1.

		Kickoff Returns				
Year Team	G	Ret	Yds	Avg	TD	Fum
1968 Bos	13	36	812	22.6	0	3

GARRY PORTERFIELD Porterfield, Garry Mark 6′3″, 231 DE
Col: Tulsa *HS:* Bixby [OK] B: 8/4/1943, Pawnee, OK *Drafted:* 1965 Round 14 Dal
1965 Dal: 2 G.

JOSE PORTILLA Portilla, Jose Casiano 6′6″, 320 OT
Col: Ricks Coll. ID (J.C.); Arizona *HS:* MacArthur [Houston, TX]
B: 9/11/1972, Houston, TX
1998 Atl: 16 G.

DAVID POSEY Posey, David Ellsworth 5′11″, 167 K
Col: Florida *HS:* St. Andrews [Boca Raton, FL] B: 4/1/1956, Painesville, OH *Drafted:* 1977 Round 9 SF
1978 NE: 11 G; Scor 62, 11-22 50.0% FG, 29-31 93.5% XK.

JEFF POSEY Posey, Jeff 6′4″, 240 DE
Col: Pearl River CC MS; Southern Mississippi *HS:* Bassfield [MS]
B: 8/14/1975, Bassfield, MS
1998 SF: 16 G; 0.5 Sac.

DICKIE POST Post, Richard Marvin 5′9″, 190 RB
Col: Houston *HS:* Pauls Valley [OK] B: 9/27/1945, San Pedro, CA
Drafted: 1967 Round 4 SD
1967 SD: Pass 6-1 16.7%, 9 1.50. **1968** SD: Pass 4-1 25.0%, 23 5.75. **1969** SD: Pass 2-1 50.0%, 4 2.00. **Total:** Pass 12-3 25.0%, 36 3.00.

		Rushing				Receiving			
Year Team	G	Att	Yds	Avg	TD	Rec	Yds	Avg	TD
1967 SD	13	161	663	4.1	7	32	278	8.7	1
1968 SD	13	151	758	**5.0**	3	18	165	9.2	0
1969 SD	14	182	**873**	4.8	6	24	235	9.8	0
1970 SD	9	74	225	3.0	1	13	113	8.7	0
1971 Den-Hou	13	40	86	2.2	0	9	112	12.4	1
1971 Den	6	18	44	2.4	0	4	46	11.5	1
1971 Hou	7	22	42	1.9	0	5	66	13.2	0
NFL Total	62	608	2605	4.3	17	96	903	9.4	2

	Kickoff Returns					Tot
Year Team	Ret	Yds	Avg	TD	Fum	TD
1967 SD	15	371	24.7	0	2	8
1968 SD	10	199	19.9	0	0	3
1969 SD	4	74	18.5	0	3	6
1970 SD	0	0	—	0	1	1
1971 Den-Hou	5	116	23.2	0	0	1
1971 Den	5	116	23.2	0	0	1
NFL Total	34	760	22.4	0	6	19

BOBBY POST Post, Robert Kent 6′1″, 195 DB
Col: Kings Point *HS:* Tracy [CA] B: 1/12/1944, Twin Falls, ID
1967 NYG: 5 G; KR 1-0.

AL POSTUS Postus, Albert Michael 5′10″, 180 TB-DB
Col: Villanova *HS:* St. Thomas More [Philadelphia, PA] B: 9/21/1920, Philadelphia, PA *Drafted:* 1944 Round 20 Phi
1945 Pit: 2 G; Pass 5-2 40.0%, 73 14.60 1 Int; Rush 2-4 2.0; KR 1-14 14.0.

PHIL POTH Poth, Philip J 5′11″, 195 G
Col: Gonzaga B: 5/2/1911, Seattle, WA D: 9/24/1998, Seattle, WA
1934 Phi: 1 G.

JOHN POTO Poto, John P 5′10″, 194 HB-DB
Col: No College *HS:* East Boston [MA] B: 4/10/1926, Boston, MA
D: 11/1965
1947 Bos: 6 G; Rush 6-27 4.5 1 TD; PR 1-12 12.0; KR 4-99 24.8; 6 Pt; 2 Fum. **1948** Bos: 12 G; Rush 13-32 2.5; Rec 10-101 10.1; PR 1-3 3.0; KR 1-16 16.0. **Total:** 18 G; Rush 19-59 3.1 1 TD; Rec 10-101 10.1; PR 2-15 7.5; KR 5-115 23.0; 6 Pt; 2 Fum.

EARL POTTEIGER Potteiger, William Earl 5′7″, 170 WB-BB-OE-FB
Col: Ursinus *HS:* Perkiomen Sem. [Pennsburg, PA] B: 1/11/1891, PA
D: 8/1962, PA
1920 Buf: 2 G. **1921** ChiC: 1 G. **1922** Mil: 3 G. **1924** Ken: 3 G. **1925** NYG: 2 G. **1926** NYG: 1 G. **1927** NYG: 2 G. **1928** NYG: 7 G. **Total:** 21 G.

KEVIN POTTER Potter, Kevin Craig 5′10″, 188 DB
Col: Missouri *HS:* DeSmet [St. Louis, MO]; Soldan HS [St. Louis, MO]
B: 12/19/1959, St. Louis, MO *Drafted:* 1983 Round 9 Hou
1983 ChiB: 8 G. **1984** ChiB: 1 G. **Total:** 9 G.

STEVE POTTER Potter, Stephen John 6′3″, 235 LB
Col: Virginia *HS:* Fairview [PA] B: 11/6/1957, Bradford, PA
1981 Mia: 16 G. **1982** Mia: 9 G. **1983** KC: 16 G; Int 1-0. **1984** Buf: 10 G. **Total:** 51 G; Int 1-0.

MYRON POTTIOS Pottios, Myron Joseph 6′2″, 232 LB
Col: Notre Dame *HS:* Charleroi [PA] B: 1/18/1939, Van Voorhis, PA
Drafted: 1961 Round 2 Pit

		Interceptions		
Year Team	G	Int	Yds	TD
1961 Pit	14	2	40	0
1963 Pit	14	4	78	0
1964 Pit	7	1	8	0
1965 Pit	6	0	0	0
1966 LARm	12	0	0	0
1967 LARm	11	1	24	0
1968 LARm	14	0	0	0
1969 LARm	5	1	16	0
1970 LARm	14	2	27	0
1971 Was	14	1	31	0
1972 Was	12	0	0	0
1973 Was	6	0	0	0
NFL Total	129	12	224	0

CHARLIE POTTS Potts, Charles 6′3″, 210 DB
Col: Purdue *HS:* Dunbar [Chicago, IL] B: 4/29/1949, Chicago, IL
Drafted: 1972 Round 6 Det
1972 Det: 10 G.

DADDY POTTS Potts, Robert Crockett 6′1″, 235 T
Col: Clemson *HS:* Fort Mill [SC] B: 8/16/1898, York Co., SC
D: 8/11/1981, Columbia, SC
1926 Fra: 16 G.

ROOSEVELT POTTS Potts, Roosevelt Bernard 6′0″, 250 RB
Col: Northeast Louisiana *HS:* Rayville [LA] B: 1/8/1971, Rayville, LA
Drafted: 1993 Round 2 Ind
1997 Ind-Mia: KR 1-16 16.0. Mia: KR 1-16 16.0. **1998** Bal: KR 1-3 3.0. **Total:** KR 2-19 9.5.

		Rushing				Receiving					Tot
Year Team	G	Att	Yds	Avg	TD	Rec	Yds	Avg	TD	Fum	TD
1993 Ind	16	179	711	4.0	0	26	189	7.3	0	8	0
1994 Ind	16	77	336	4.4	1	26	251	9.7	1	5	2
1995 Ind	15	65	309	4.8	0	21	228	10.9	1	0	1
1997 Ind-Mia	8	2	4	2.0	0	3	27	9.0	0	0	0
1997 Ind	2	1	1	1.0	0	0	0	—	0	0	0
1997 Mia	6	1	3	3.0	0	3	27	9.0	0	0	0
1998 Bal	16	36	115	3.2	0	30	168	5.6	2	4	2
NFL Total	71	359	1475	4.1	1	106	863	8.1	4	17	5

BILL POTTS Potts, William 200 HB
Col: Villanova
1934 Pit: 1 G.

ERNEST POUGH Pough, Ernest Leon 6′1″, 174 WR
Col: Texas Southern *HS:* New Stanton [Jacksonville, FL] B: 5/17/1952, Jacksonville, FL *Drafted:* 1976 Round 3 Pit
1976 Pit: Rush 2-8 4.0; Rec 8-161 20.1 1 TD. **1977** Pit: Rec 1-3 3.0. **1978** NYG: Rush 3-33 11.0; Rec 1-2 2.0. **Total:** Rush 5-41 8.2; Rec 10-166 16.6 1 TD.

Year Team	G	Kickoff Returns Ret	Yds	Avg	TD	Fum
1976 Pit	14	18	369	20.5	0	1
1977 Pit	14	7	111	15.9	0	0
1978 NYG	12	15	313	20.9	0	2
NFL Total	40	40	793	19.8	0	3

DARRYL POUNDS Pounds, Darryl Lamont 5′10″, 185 **DB**
Col: Nicholls State *HS:* South Pike [Magnolia, MS] B: 7/21/1972, Ft. Worth, TX *Drafted:* 1995 Round 3 Was
1995 Was: 9 G; Int 1-26; 1 Fum. **1996** Was: 12 G; Int 2-11. **1997** Was: 16 G; Int 3-42 1 TD; 1 Fum TD; Tot TD 2; 12 Pt; 2 Sac. **1998** Was: 16 G; 0.5 Sac. **Total:** 53 G; Int 6-79 1 TD; 1 Fum TD; Tot TD 2; 12 Pt; 1 Fum; 2.5 Sac.

SHAR POURDANESH Pourdanesh, Shahriar 6′6″, 312 **OT**
Col: Nevada-Las Vegas *HS:* University [Irvine, CA] B: 7/19/1970, Teheran, Iran
1996 Was: 16 G. **1997** Was: 16 G. **1998** Was: 16 G; 1 Fum. **Total:** 48 G; 1 Fum.

KARL POWE Powe, Karl Alonzo 6′2″, 175 **WR**
Col: Alabama State *HS:* Mattie T. Blount [Prichard, AL] B: 1/17/1962, Mobile, AL *Drafted:* 1985 Round 7 Dal
1985 Dal: 15 G; Rec 14-237 16.9; KR 1-17 17.0; 1 Fum. **1986** Dal: 1 G. **Total:** 16 G; Rec 14-237 16.9; KR 1-17 17.0; 1 Fum.

KEITH POWE Powe, Keith 6′3″, 265 **DE**
Col: Lamar; Texas-El Paso *HS:* Jersey Village [Houston, TX] B: 6/5/1969, Biloxi, MS
1994 TB: 5 G. **1995** TB: 3 G; 1 Sac. **Total:** 8 G; 1 Sac.

ALVIN POWELL Powell, Alvin Robert II 6′5″, 294 **OG**
Col: Winston-Salem State *HS:* Pine Forest [Fayetteville, NC] B: 11/19/1959, Panama *Drafted:* 1984 Supplemental Round 2 Sea
1987 Sea: 12 G; KR 3-23 7.7; 1 Fum. **1988** Sea: 6 G. **1989** Mia: 2 G. **Total:** 20 G; KR 3-23 7.7; 1 Fum.

ANDRE POWELL Powell, Andre Maurice 6′1″, 226 **LB**
Col: Penn State *HS:* William Penn [York, PA] B: 6/5/1969, York, PA *Drafted:* 1992 Round 8 Mia
1993 NYG: 15 G. **1994** NYG: 1 G. **Total:** 16 G.

ART POWELL Powell, Arthur Louis 6′3″, 211 **OE-DB-WR**
(King Pin) *Col:* San Diego City Coll. CA (J.C.); San Jose State *HS:* San Diego [CA] B: 2/25/1937, Dallas, TX *Drafted:* 1959 Round 11 Phi
1959 Phi: PR 15-124 8.3 1 TD; KR 14-379 27.1; Int 3-17. **1960** NYT: KR 2-63 31.5. **Total:** PR 15-124 8.3 1 TD; KR 16-442 27.6; Int 3-17.

Year Team	G	Receiving Rec	Yds	Avg	TD	Fum	Tot TD
1959 Phi	12	0	0	—	0	2	1
1960 NYT	14	69	1167	16.9	**14**	0	**14**
1961 NYT	14	71	881	12.4	5	1	5
1962 NYT	14	64	**1130**	17.7	8	1	8
1963 Oak	14	73	**1304**	17.9	**16**	0	**16**
1964 Oak	14	76	1361	17.9	11	0	11
1965 Oak	14	52	800	15.4	12	0	12
1966 Oak	14	53	1026	19.4	11	0	11
1967 Buf	6	20	346	17.3	4	0	4
1968 Min	1	1	31	31.0	0	0	0
NFL Total	117	479	8046	16.8	81	4	82

CARL POWELL Powell, Carl Demetris 6′3″, 265 **DE**
Col: Grand Rapids CC MI; Louisville *HS:* Northern [Detroit, MI] B: 1/4/1974, Detroit, MI *Drafted:* 1997 Round 5 Ind
1997 Ind: 11 G.

CHARLEY POWELL Powell, Charles Elvin 6′3″, 226 **DE-LB-OE**
Col: No College *HS:* San Diego [CA] B: 4/4/1932, TX
1952 SF: 7 G; Scor 1 Saf; 2 Pt. **1953** SF: 12 G; 1 Fum. **1955** SF: 12 G; KR 1-2 2.0; Int 0-7. **1956** SF: 12 G. **1957** SF: 12 G; Rec 1-27 27.0. **1960** Oak: 14 G. **1961** Oak: 14 G. **Total:** 83 G; Rec 1-27 27.0; KR 1-2 2.0; Int 0-7; Scor 1 Saf; 2 Pt; 1 Fum.

CRAIG POWELL Powell, Craig Steven 6′4″, 230 **LB**
Col: Ohio State *HS:* Rayen [Youngstown, OH] B: 11/13/1971, Youngstown, OH *Drafted:* 1995 Round 1 Cle
1995 Cle: 3 G. **1996** Bal: 9 G. **1998** NYJ: 2 G. **Total:** 14 G.

DARNELL POWELL Powell, Darnell 6′0″, 197 **RB**
Col: Tennessee-Chattanooga *HS:* Carrollton [GA] B: 5/31/1954, Atlanta, GA *Drafted:* 1976 Round 6 Buf
1976 Buf: Rec 1-6 6.0; KR 4-101 25.3. **1978** NYJ: KR 3-50 16.7. **Total:** Rec 1-6 6.0; KR 7-151 21.6.

Year Team	G	Rushing Att	Yds	Avg	TD
1976 Buf	11	11	40	3.6	0
1978 NYJ	14	20	77	3.9	1
NFL Total	25	31	117	3.8	1

JEFF POWELL Powell, Jeffrey O'Neal 5′10″, 185 **RB**
Col: William & Mary; Tennessee *HS:* Whites Creek [TN] B: 5/27/1963, Nashville, TN *Drafted:* 1986 Round 6 ChiB
1987 SD: 1 G.

JESSE POWELL Powell, Jesse Loy 6′2″, 220 **LB**
Col: West Texas A&M *HS:* Spur [TX] B: 4/14/1947, Matador, TX *Drafted:* 1969 Round 9 Mia
1969 Mia: 14 G. **1970** Mia: 11 G. **1971** Mia: 14 G. **1972** Mia: 14 G. **1973** Mia: 3 G. **Total:** 56 G.

MARVIN POWELL Powell, Marvin 6′5″, 268 **OT**
Col: USC *HS:* 71st [Fayetteville, NC] B: 8/30/1955, Fort Bragg, NC *Drafted:* 1977 Round 1 NYJ
1977 NYJ: 11 G. **1978** NYJ: 14 G. **1979** NYJ: 16 G. **1980** NYJ: 15 G. **1981** NYJ: 14 G. **1982** NYJ: 8 G. **1983** NYJ: 16 G. **1984** NYJ: 16 G. **1985** NYJ: 14 G. **1986** TB: 3 G. **1987** TB: 6 G. **Total:** 133 G.

PRESTON POWELL Powell, Preston 6′2″, 225 **FB**
Col: Grambling State *HS:* Pine Crest [Winnfield, LA] B: 9/23/1936, Winnfield, LA *Drafted:* 1961 Round 7 Cle
1961 Cle: 12 G; Rush 1-5 5.0; KR 16-321 20.1.

DICK POWELL Powell, Richard Lee 6′2″, 215 **OE-DE**
(Tiny) *Col:* Davis & Elkins *HS:* Glenville Normal [WV] B: 5/21/1904, Glenville Dist., Gilmer Co., WV D: 4/29/1986, Martinsville, VA
1932 NYG: 2 G. **1933** Cin: 3 G. **Total:** 5 G.

ROGER POWELL Powell, Roger Mills 6′0″, 180 **WB**
Col: Texas A&M *HS:* Austin Acad. [TX] B: 8/17/1894, Austin, TX D: 1/28/1988, Waco, TX
1926 Buf: 1 G.

STAN POWELL Powell, Stancil 5′11″, 185 **G**
(Possum AKA Wrinkle Meat) *Col:* Carlisle; Haskell Indian B: 1890 Deceased
1923 Oor: 8 G.

STEVE POWELL Powell, Steven Orville 5′11″, 186 **RB**
Col: Northeast Missouri State *HS:* Kirkwood [MO] B: 1/2/1956, St. Louis, MO *Drafted:* 1978 Round 7 Buf
1978 Buf: 10 G; KR 3-53 17.7; 1 Fum. **1979** Buf: 15 G; Rush 10-29 2.9; KR 6-97 16.2. **Total:** 25 G; Rush 10-29 2.9; KR 9-150 16.7; 1 Fum.

TIM POWELL Powell, Tim Arden 6′4″, 248 **DE**
Col: Northwestern *HS:* Hoover [North Canton, OH] B: 9/2/1942, North Canton, OH
1965 LARm: 8 G. **1966** Pit: 4 G. **Total:** 12 G.

CLYDE POWERS Powers, Clyde Joseph 6′1″, 195 **DB**
Col: Oklahoma *HS:* Lawton [OK] B: 8/19/1951, Pascagoula, MS *Drafted:* 1974 Round 5 NYG
1974 NYG: 14 G; KR 1-0. **1975** NYG: 14 G; Int 3-0. **1976** NYG: 14 G; Int 1-11. **1977** NYG: 14 G; Int 1-1; 1 Fum. **1978** KC: 1 G. **Total:** 57 G; KR 1-0; Int 5-12; 1 Fum.

JIM POWERS Powers, James W 6′0″, 185 **DB-QB-LB**
(Mystic) *Col:* USC *HS:* Beverly Hills [CA] B: 2/29/1928 *Drafted:* 1950 Round 26 SF
1950 SF: Rush 3-4 1.3. **1953** SF: Rush 3-(-10) -3.3. **Total:** Rush 6-(-6) -1.0.

Year Team	G	Passing Att	Comp	Comp%	Yds	YPA	TD	Int	Rating
1950 SF	10	20	9	45.0	108	5.40	0	2	22.5
1951 SF	12	0	0	—	0	—	0	0	—
1952 SF	12	1	0	0.0	0	0.00	0	0	39.6
1953 SF	12	49	22	44.9	259	5.29	1	2	51.3
NFL Total	46	70	31	44.3	367	5.24	1	4	41.8

Year Team	Interceptions Int	Yds	TD	Punting Punts	Yds	Avg	Fum
1950 SF	5	42	0	0	0	—	1
1951 SF	4	73	0	0	0	—	0
1952 SF	2	37	0	0	0	—	0
1953 SF	0	0	0	42	1706	40.6	0
NFL Total	11	152	0	42	1706	40.6	1

JOHN POWERS Powers, John Paul 6′2″, 215 **TE**
Col: Notre Dame *HS:* Campion Prep [Prairie du Chien, WI] B: 6/15/1940, Harvard, IL *Drafted:* 1962 Round 9 Pit
1962 Pit: 14 G; Rec 1-16 16.0. **1963** Pit: 14 G. **1964** Pit: 14 G; Rush 2-10 5.0; Rec 8-193 24.1. **1965** Pit: 2 G. **1966** Min: 5 G. **Total:** 49 G; Rush 2-10 5.0; Rec 9-209 23.2.

RICKY POWERS Powers, Richard A 6′0″, 213 **RB**
Col: Michigan *HS:* John R. Buchtel [Akron, OH] B: 11/30/1970, Akron, OH
1995 Cle: 3 G; Rush 14-51 3.6; Rec 1-6 6.0; KR 3-54 18.0.

SAMMY POWERS Powers, Sam 5′10″, 170 **G-T**
Col: No College *HS:* Marinette [WI] B: 1901 Deceased
1921 GB: 4 G.

WARREN POWERS Powers, Warren 6′6″, 287 **DE**
Col: Maryland *HS:* Edmondson [Baltimore, MD] B: 2/4/1965, Baltimore, MD *Drafted:* 1989 Round 2 Den
1989 Den: 15 G; 3 Sac. **1990** Den: 16 G; 4 Sac. **1991** Den: 13 G; 1 Fum TD; 6 Pt; 2 Sac. **1992** LARm: 7 G. **Total:** 51 G; 1 Fum TD; 6 Pt; 9 Sac.

WARREN POWERS Powers, Warren Anthony 6′0″, 185 **DB**
Col: Nebraska *HS:* Lillis [Kansas City, MO] B: 2/19/1941, Kansas City, MO
1966 Oak: KR 1-0. **1967** Oak: PR 2-19 9.5. **Total:** PR 2-19 9.5; KR 1-0.

		Interceptions			
Year Team	G	Int	Yds	TD	Fum
1963 Oak	5	0	0	0	0
1964 Oak	10	5	65	0	0
1965 Oak	12	5	56	0	0
1966 Oak	14	5	88	0	0
1967 Oak	14	6	154	2	1
1968 Oak	8	1	3	0	0
NFL Total	63	22	366	2	1

PHIL POZDERAC Pozderac, Philip Maurice 6′9″, 277 **OT**
Col: Notre Dame *HS:* Garfield Heights [OH] B: 12/19/1959, Cleveland, OH *Drafted:* 1982 Round 5 Dal
1982 Dal: 7 G. **1983** Dal: 16 G. **1984** Dal: 15 G; Rec 1-1 1.0. **1985** Dal: 14 G. **1986** Dal: 16 G. **1987** Dal: 2 G. **Total:** 70 G; Rec 1-1 1.0.

DEAN PRATER Prater, Troy Dean 6′4″, 255 **DE**
Col: Oklahoma State *HS:* S.H. Rider [Wichita Falls, TX] B: 9/29/1958, Altus, OK D: 3/14/1996, Horseheads, NY *Drafted:* 1981 Round 10 Cle
1982 KC: 2 G. **1983** KC: 16 G. **1984** Buf: 13 G. **1985** Buf: 16 G. **1986** Buf: 16 G; 1 Sac. **1987** Buf: 10 G. **1988** Buf: 4 G. **Total:** 77 G; 1 Sac.

DALE PRATHER Prather, Dale Lambert 6′2″, 190 **OE-DE-T**
Col: George Washington *HS:* Eureka [KS] B: 9/19/1910 D: 9/1973
1938 Cle: 6 G.

GUY PRATHER Prather, Guy Tyrone 6′2″, 230 **LB**
Col: Grambling State *HS:* Gaithersburg [MD] B: 3/28/1958, Gaithersburg, MD
1981 GB: 16 G. **1982** GB: 9 G. **1983** GB: 16 G. **1984** GB: 16 G; KR 1-7 7.0. **1985** GB: 16 G; Rush 1-0; 1 Fum; 2 Sac. **Total:** 73 G; Rush 1-0; KR 1-7 7.0; 1 Fum; 2 Sac.

BOB PRATT Pratt, Robert Henry Jr. 6′3″, 255 **OG**
Col: North Carolina *HS:* St. Christopher's [Richmond, VA] B: 5/25/1951, Richmond, VA *Drafted:* 1974 Round 3 Bal
1974 Bal: 13 G. **1975** Bal: 14 G; KR 4-64 16.0. **1976** Bal: 14 G; KR 1-21 21.0. **1977** Bal: 14 G; 1 Fum TD; 6 Pt. **1978** Bal: 16 G. **1979** Bal: 16 G. **1980** Bal: 16 G. **1981** Bal: 15 G; 1 Fum. **1982** Sea: 9 G. **1983** Sea: 15 G. **1984** Sea: 16 G; Rec 1-30 30.0. **1985** Sea: 12 G. **Total:** 170 G; Rec 1-30 30.0; KR 5-85 17.0; 1 Fum TD; 6 Pt; 1 Fum.

JOHN PRCHLIK Prchlik, John George 6′4″, 234 **DT-OT**
(Perch) *Col:* Yale *HS:* West Tech [Cleveland, OH] B: 7/20/1925, Cleveland, OH *Drafted:* 1947 Round 30 Bos
1949 Det: 12 G. **1950** Det: 12 G. **1951** Det: 12 G; KR 1-12 12.0; Scor **1** Saf; 2 Pt. **1952** Det: 12 G. **1953** Det: 11 G. **Total:** 59 G; KR 1-12 12.0; Scor 1 Saf; 2 Pt.

GEORGE PREAS Preas, George Robert 6′2″, 244 **OT-OG-LB**
Col: Virginia Tech *HS:* Jefferson [Roanoke, VA] B: 6/25/1933, Roanoke, VA *Drafted:* 1955 Round 5 Bal
1955 Bal: 12 G. **1956** Bal: 12 G. **1957** Bal: 10 G. **1958** Bal: 12 G. **1959** Bal: 12 G. **1960** Bal: 12 G. **1961** Bal: 14 G. **1962** Bal: 14 G. **1963** Bal: 14 G. **1964** Bal: 14 G. **1965** Bal: 14 G. **Total:** 140 G.

GENE PREBOLA Prebola, Eugene Nicholas 6′3″, 225 **TE**
Col: Boston U. *HS:* Memorial [West New York, NJ] B: 6/30/1938, Bronx, NY *Drafted:* 1960 Round 1 Hou
1961 Den: KR 1-8 8.0; Scor 1 2XP. **1962** Den: Scor **1** 2XP. **1963** Den: Scor **1** 2XP. **Total:** KR 1-8 8.0; Scor 3 2XP.

		Receiving				
Year Team	G	Rec	Yds	Avg	TD	Fum
1960 Oak	14	33	404	12.2	2	0
1961 Den	14	29	349	12.0	1	0
1962 Den	14	41	599	14.6	1	1
1963 Den	14	30	471	15.7	2	0
NFL Total	56	133	1823	13.7	6	1

STEVE PREECE Preece, Steven Packer 6′1″, 195 **DB**
Col: Oregon State *HS:* Borah [Boise, ID] B: 2/15/1947, Idaho Falls, ID
1969 NO: KR 1-0. **1970** Phi: 1 Fum TD. **1972** Phi-Den: KR 1-0. Den: KR 1-0. **1973** LARm: Rush 1-11 11.0 1 TD. **1974** LARm: Rush 1-(-4) -4.0. **1976** LARm: Rush 1-0. **1977** Sea: Pass 1-0. **Total:** Pass 1-0; Rush 3-7 2.3 1 TD; KR 2-0; 1 Fum TD.

		Interceptions				Tot
Year Team	G	Int	Yds	TD	Fum	TD
1969 NO	14	1	6	0	0	1
1970 Phi	14	2	19	0	0	1
1971 Phi	7	0	0	0	0	0
1972 Phi-Den	14	1	30	0	0	0
1972 Phi	1	0	0	0	0	0
1972 Den	13	1	30	0	0	0
1973 LARm	14	2	25	0	2	1
1974 LARm	14	3	38	0	1	0
1975 LARm	14	0	0	0	0	0
1976 LARm	14	1	6	0	0	0
1977 Sea	14	4	55	0	0	0
NFL Total	119	14	179	0	3	3

MERV PREGULMAN Pregulman, Mervin 6′3″, 215 **C-LB**
Col: Michigan *HS:* Central [Lansing, MI] B: 10/10/1922, Lansing, MI *Drafted:* 1944 Round 1 GB
1946 GB: 11 G. **1947** Det: 12 G; PR 1-9 9.0; Int 2-9. **1948** Det: 12 G; Int 1-6; Scor 32, 2-6 33.3% FG, 26-27 96.3% XK. **1949** NYB: 12 G. **Total:** 47 G; PR 1-9 9.0; Int 3-15; Scor 32, 2-6 33.3% FG, 26-27 96.3% XK.

HAL PRESCOTT Prescott, Harold Dougald 6′2″, 199 **OE-DB**
(Ace) *Col:* Hardin-Simmons *HS:* Phoenix Union [AZ] B: 10/18/1920, Abilene, TX *Drafted:* 1943 Round 17 GB
1946 GB: 2 G; Rec 1-8 8.0. **1947** Phi: 11 G; Rec 1-15 15.0; Int 3-5. **1948** Phi: 11 G. **1949** Phi-Det-NYB: 9 G; Rec 10-162 16.2 1 TD; 6 Pt. Phi: 3 G. Det: 1 G. NYB: 5 G; Rec 10-162 16.2 1 TD; 6 Pt. **Total:** 33 G; Rec 12-185 15.4 1 TD; Int 3-5; 6 Pt.

ANDRE PRESIDENT President, Andre N 6′3″, 255 **TE**
Col: Lamar CC CO; Angelo State *HS:* Everman [TX] B: 6/16/1971, Temple, TX
1995 NE-ChiB: 3 G. NE: 1 G. ChiB: 2 G. **Total:** 3 G.

LEE PRESLEY Presley, Leo Grady 6′2″, 230 **C**
Col: Oklahoma *HS:* Elk City [OK] B: 3/16/1922, El Campo, TX D: 9/1975
1945 Was: 8 G; Rush 1-1 1.0; 1 Fum.

GLENN PRESNELL Presnell, Glenn Emery 5′10″, 195 **TB-DB-WB-FB**
Col: Nebraska *HS:* DeWitt [NE] B: 7/28/1905, Gilead, NE
1931 Port: PR **1** TD; Scor 35, 1 FG, 7 XK, **1** 1XP. **1932** Port: Rec 4-54 13.5 1 TD; Scor 13, 1 XK. **1933** Port: Rec 3-23 7.7; Scor **64**, 5 FG, **13** XK. **1934** Det: Rec 3-42 14.0; Scor 63, 4 FG, 9 XK. **1935** Det: Rec 3-73 24.3 1 TD; PR 1 TD; Scor 28, 4 FG, 4 XK. **1936** Det: Scor 15, 1 FG, 6 XK. **Total:** Rec 13-192 14.8 2 TD; PR 2 TD; Scor 218, 15 FG, 40 XK, 1 1XP.

		Passing							
Year Team	G	Att	Comp	Comp%	Yds	YPA	TD	Int	Rating
1931 Port	14	—	—	—	—	—	5	—	—
1932 Port	12	46	17	37.0	259	5.63	2	4	34.6
1933 Port	11	125	50	40.0	774	6.19	6	12	37.6
1934 Det	13	57	13	22.8	223	3.91	2	8	15.5
1935 Det	12	45	15	33.3	193	4.29	0	6	8.1
1936 Det	12	36	15	41.7	221	6.14	2	7	41.3
NFL Total	74	309	110	35.6	1670	5.40	17	37	33.0

	Rushing				Tot
Year Team	Att	Yds	Avg	TD	TD
1931 Port	—	—	—	3	4
1932 Port	68	232	3.4	1	2
1933 Port	118	522	4.4	**6**	6
1934 Det	108	413	3.8	7	7
1935 Det	71	225	3.2	0	2
1936 Det	48	201	4.2	1	1
NFL Total	413	1593	3.9	18	22

JIM PRESTEL Prestel, James Francis 6′5″, 275 **DT**
Col: Idaho *HS:* Sacred Heart [Indianapolis, IN] B: 6/28/1937, Indianapolis, IN *Drafted:* 1959 Round 6 Cle
1960 Cle: 6 G. **1961** Min: 14 G. **1962** Min: 14 G; KR 2-29 14.5; 1 Fum. **1963** Min: 14 G. **1964** Min: 14 G; Int 1-26 1 TD; 6 Pt. **1965** Min: 13 G; Scor **1** Saf; 2 Pt. **1966** NYG: 13 G. **1967** Was: 8 G. **Total:** 96 G; KR 2-29 14.5; Int 1-26 1 TD; Scor 1 Saf; 8 Pt; 1 Fum.

JOHN PRESTON Preston, John Stanley 6′0″, 207 **DB**
Col: Texas Christian; Central Oklahoma *HS:* South Oak Cliff [Dallas, TX] B: 8/28/1962, Dallas, TX
1987 StL: 5 G.

PAT PRESTON Preston, Paddison Wade 6′2″, 216 **G-LB**
Col: Duke; Wake Forest *HS:* Mills Home [Thomaston, NC] B: 6/15/1921, Kernersville, NC *Drafted:* 1943 Round 15 ChiB
1946 ChiB: 11 G. **1947** ChiB: 3 G. **1948** ChiB: 12 G. **1949** ChiB: 12 G. **Total:** 38 G.

RAY PRESTON Preston, Raymond Newton Jr. 6′0″, 218 **LB**
Col: Syracuse *HS:* Lawrence [Falmouth, MA] B: 1/25/1954, Lawrence, MA *Drafted:* 1976 Round 11 SD
1976 SD: 14 G; KR 1-16 16.0. **1977** SD: 11 G. **1978** SD: 16 G; KR 1-15 15.0. **1979** SD: 16 G; Int 5-121. **1980** SD: 14 G. **1981** SD: 16 G. **1982** SD: 9 G. **1983** SD: 16 G; Int 1-13. **1984** SD: 10 G. **Total:** 122 G; KR 2-31 15.5; Int 6-134.

DAVE PRESTON Preston, Richard David 5′10″, 195 **RB**
Col: Bowling Green State *HS:* Defiance [OH] B: 5/29/1955, Dayton, OH *Drafted:* 1977 Round 12 NE
1978 Den: PR 10-68 6.8. **1979** Den: Pass 1-0; PR 7-78 11.1. **1980** Den: PR 1-7 7.0. **Total:** Pass 1-0; PR 18-153 8.5.

		Rushing				Receiving			
Year Team	**G**	**Att**	**Yds**	**Avg**	**TD**	**Rec**	**Yds**	**Avg**	**TD**
1978 Den	16	66	296	4.5	1	24	199	8.3	1
1979 Den	10	43	169	3.9	1	19	137	7.2	1
1980 Den	12	111	385	3.5	4	35	309	8.8	0
1981 Den	16	183	640	3.5	3	52	507	9.8	0
1982 Den	8	19	81	4.3	0	14	134	9.6	0
1983 Den	14	57	222	3.9	1	17	137	8.1	1
NFL Total	76	479	1793	3.7	10	161	1423	8.8	3

	Kickoff Returns					Tot
Year Team	**Ret**	**Yds**	**Avg**	**TD**	**Fum**	**TD**
1978 Den	7	154	22.0	0	4	2
1979 Den	13	336	25.8	0	1	2
1980 Den	5	106	21.2	0	3	4
1981 Den	1	1	1.0	0	4	3
1982 Den	0	0	—	0	3	0
1983 Den	0	0	—	0	0	2
NFL Total	26	597	23.0	0	15	13

ROELL PRESTON Preston, Roell 5′10″, 187 **WR**
Col: Northwest Mississippi CC; Mississippi *HS:* Hialeah [FL] B: 6/23/1972, Miami, FL *Drafted:* 1995 Round 5 Atl

		Receiving				Punt Returns			
Year Team	**G**	**Rec**	**Yds**	**Avg**	**TD**	**Ret**	**Yds**	**Avg**	**TD**
1995 Atl	14	7	129	18.4	1	0	0	—	0
1996 Atl	15	21	208	9.9	1	0	0	—	0
1997 GB	1	0	0	—	0	1	0	0.0	0
1998 GB	16	2	23	11.5	0	44	398	9.0	1
NFL Total	46	30	360	12.0	2	45	398	8.8	1

	Kickoff Returns					Tot
Year Team	**Ret**	**Yds**	**Avg**	**TD**	**Fum**	**TD**
1995 Atl	30	627	20.9	0	1	1
1996 Atl	32	681	21.3	0	0	1
1997 GB	7	211	30.1	0	0	0
1998 GB	57	1497	26.3	**2**	7	3
NFL Total	126	3016	23.9	2	8	5

BILL PRESTON Preston, William **T**
Col: No College Deceased
1920 Akr: 1 G.

LUKE PRESTRIDGE Prestridge, Luke Earl 6′4″, 235 **P**
Col: Baylor *HS:* Sharpstown [Houston, TX] B: 9/17/1956, Houston, TX *Drafted:* 1979 Round 7 Den
1979 Den: Pass 1-0; Rush 1-29 29.0. **1983** Den: Rush 1-7 7.0. **Total:** Pass 1-0; Rush 2-36 18.0.

		Punting			
Year Team	**G**	**Punts**	**Yds**	**Avg**	**Fum**
1979 Den	16	89	3555	39.9	0
1980 Den	16	70	3075	43.9	0
1981 Den	16	86	3478	40.4	1
1982 Den	9	45	2026	**45.0**	0
1983 Den	16	87	3620	41.6	0
1984 NE	9	44	1884	42.8	0
NFL Total	82	421	17638	41.9	1

FELTO PREWITT Prewitt, Felton Winters 5′11″, 207 **LB-C**
(Pluto) *Col:* Tulsa *HS:* Corsicana [TX] B: 5/17/1924, Corsicana, TX
AAFC **1946** BufA: 14 G; Int 4-89. **1947** BufA: 13 G; Int 2-20. **1948** BufA: 7 G. **1949** BalA: 12 G. **Total:** 46 G; Int 6-109.

BILL PRIATKO Priatko, William Daniel 6′2″, 220 **LB**
Col: Pittsburgh *HS:* Scott Twp. [North Braddock, PA] B: 10/16/1931, North Braddock, PA
1957 Pit: 2 G.

ART PRICE Price, Arthur Brennan 6′3″, 227 **LB**
Col: Wisconsin *HS:* Menchville [Newport News, VA] B: 5/17/1962, Hampton, VA
1987 Atl: 3 G.

COTTON PRICE Price, Charles Walemon 6′1″, 180 **TB-DB-QB**
Col: Texas A&M *HS:* Newcastle [TX] B: 5/31/1918, Bridgeport, TX
AAFC **1946** MiaA: Rush 15-(-55) -3.7; Rec 2-17 8.5; KR 2-32 16.0; Punt 4-105 26.3.

		Passing							
Year Team	**G**	**Att**	**Comp**	**Comp%**	**Yds**	**YPA**	**TD**	**Int**	**Rating**
1946 MiaA	7	74	36	48.6	484	6.54	2	5	50.7

NFL **1940** Det: Punt 9-374 41.6; Scor 16, 4-4 100.0% XK. **1941** Det: Rec 1-6 6.0; PR 3-48 16.0; KR 2-51 25.5; Punt 5-191 38.2. **1945** Det: PR 3-32 10.7; KR 4-79 19.8; Int 1-16; Punt 4-148 37.0. **Total:** Rec 1-6 6.0; PR 6-80 13.3; KR 6-130 21.7; Int 1-16; Punt 18-713 39.6; Scor 16, 4-4 100.0% XK.

		Passing							
Year Team	**G**	**Att**	**Comp**	**Comp%**	**Yds**	**YPA**	**TD**	**Int**	**Rating**
1940 Det	9	66	33	50.0	456	6.91	3	7	48.1
1941 Det	11	33	9	27.3	118	3.58	0	4	2.4
1945 Det	8	52	16	30.8	256	4.92	3	8	27.9
NFL Total	28	151	58	38.4	830	5.50	6	19	30.7

	Rushing				
Year Team	**Att**	**Yds**	**Avg**	**TD**	**Fum**
1940 Det	42	122	2.9	2	0
1941 Det	16	36	2.3	0	0
1945 Det	24	71	3.0	0	3
NFL Total	82	229	2.8	2	3

DARYL PRICE Price, Daryl 6′3″, 274 **DE**
Col: Colorado *HS:* Central [Beaumont, TX] B: 10/23/1972, Galveston, TX *Drafted:* 1996 Round 4 SF
1996 SF: 14 G. **1997** SF: 5 G. **Total:** 19 G.

DENNIS PRICE Price, Dennis Sean 6′1″, 175 **DB**
Col: UCLA *HS:* Long Beach Polytechnic [CA] B: 6/14/1965, Los Angeles, CA *Drafted:* 1988 Round 5 LARd
1988 LARd: 12 G; Int 2-18. **1989** LARd: 5 G. **1991** NYJ: Postseason only. **1992** NYJ: 14 G; Int 1-0. **Total:** 31 G; Int 3-18.

DEREK PRICE Price, Derek Christopher 6′3″, 240 **TE**
Col: Mesa CC AZ; Iowa *HS:* Marcos de Niza [Tempe, AZ] B: 8/17/1972, Dayton, OH
1996 Det: 13 G; Rec 1-14 14.0.

EDDIE PRICE Price, Edward Joseph Jr. 5′11″, 190 **FB**
Col: Tulane *HS:* Warren Easton [New Orleans, LA] B: 9/2/1925, New Orleans, LA D: 7/21/1979, New Orleans, LA *Drafted:* 1950 Round 2 NYG
1952 NYG: KR 1-21 21.0. **Total:** KR 1-21 21.0.

		Rushing				Receiving					Tot
Year Team	**G**	**Att**	**Yds**	**Avg**	**TD**	**Rec**	**Yds**	**Avg**	**TD**	**Fum**	**TD**
1950 NYG	10	126	703	5.6	4	4	30	7.5	0	5	4
1951 NYG	12	**271**	**971**	3.6	7	5	19	3.8	0	7	7
1952 NYG	11	**183**	748	4.1	5	11	36	3.3	0	3	5
1953 NYG	12	101	206	2.0	2	26	233	9.0	1	4	3
1954 NYG	12	135	555	4.1	2	28	352	12.6	3	2	5
1955 NYG	6	30	109	3.6	0	1	2	2.0	0	1	0
NFL Total	63	846	3292	3.9	20	75	672	9.0	4	22	24

ELEX PRICE Price, Elex Drummond 6′3″, 260 **DT**
Col: Alcorn State *HS:* N.D. Taylor [Yazoo City, MS] B: 8/11/1950, Yazoo City, MS
1973 NO: 14 G. **1974** NO: 14 G. **1975** NO: 14 G. **1976** NO: 14 G; Int 1-23 1 TD; 6 Pt. **1977** NO: 11 G. **1978** NO: 16 G. **1979** NO: 6 G. **1980** NO: 14 G; 6 Pt. **Total:** 103 G; Int 1-23 1 TD; Tot TD 2; 12 Pt.

ERNIE PRICE Price, Ernest R 6′4″, 255 **DE-DT**
Col: Texas A&M–Kingsville *HS:* Roy Miller [Corpus Christi, TX] B: 9/20/1950, Corpus Christi, TX *Drafted:* 1973 Round 1 Det
1973 Det: 12 G. **1974** Det: 11 G. **1975** Det: 13 G; Scor **1** Saf; 2 Pt. **1976** Det: 14 G. **1977** Det: 12 G. **1978** Det-Sea: 15 G. Det: 3 G. Sea: 12 G. **1979** Sea: 4 G. **Total:** 81 G; Scor 1 Saf; 2 Pt.

JIM PRICE Price, James Bluford 6′2″, 225 **LB**
Col: Auburn *HS:* Ysleta [El Paso, TX] B: 9/17/1940, Nettleton, MS *Drafted:* 1963 Round 6 NYJ
1963 NYJ: 14 G; Int 1-15. **1964** Den: 6 G. **Total:** 20 G; Int 1-15.

JIM PRICE Price, James Gregory 6′4″, 247 **TE**
Col: Stanford *HS:* Montville [NJ] B: 10/2/1966, Englewood, NJ

		Receiving				
Year Team	**G**	**Rec**	**Yds**	**Avg**	**TD**	**Fum**
1991 LARm	12	35	410	11.7	2	2
1992 LARm	15	34	324	9.5	2	2
1993 Dal	3	1	4	4.0	0	0
1995 StL	13	4	29	7.3	0	0
NFL Total	43	74	767	10.4	4	4

KENNY PRICE Price, Kenneth James 6′2″, 225 **LB**
Col: Iowa *HS:* Kashmere [Houston, TX] B: 4/7/1949, Houston, TX
1971 NE: 1 G.

MARCUS PRICE Price, Marcus Raymond 6′6″, 321 **OT**
Col: Louisiana State *HS:* Lincoln [Port Arthur, TX] B: 3/3/1972, Port Arthur, TX *Drafted:* 1995 Round 6 Jac
1997 SD: 2 G. **1998** SD: 10 G. **Total:** 12 G.

MITCHELL PRICE Price, Mitchell LaBraie 5'9", 181 DB
Col: Southern Methodist; Tulane *HS:* James Madison [San Antonio, TX] B: 5/10/1967, Jacksonville, TX *Drafted:* 1990 Round 9 Cin
1990 Cin: Int 1-0. **1991** Cin: Int 1-0. **Total:** Int 2-0.

		Punt Returns				Kickoff Returns				
Year Team	G	Ret	Yds	Avg	TD	Ret	Yds	Avg	TD	Fum
1990 Cin	16	29	251	8.7	**1**	10	191	19.1	0	2
1991 Cin	13	14	203	14.5	1	5	91	18.2	0	0
1992 Pho-Cin	6	6	56	9.3	0	2	20	10.0	0	0
1992 Pho	2	0	0	—	0	0	0	—	0	0
1992 Cin	4	6	56	9.3	0	2	20	10.0	0	0
1993 Cin-LARm	6	1	3	3.0	0	8	144	18.0	0	0
1993 Cin	1	0	0	—	0	0	0	—	0	0
1993 LARm	5	1	3	3.0	0	8	144	18.0	0	0
NFL Total	41	50	513	10.3	2	25	446	17.8	0	2

SAMMY PRICE Price, Samuel Lee 5'11", 215 RB
Col: Illinois *HS:* V. W. Scott [Toledo, OH] B: 10/1/1943, Margaret, AL *Drafted:* 1966 Round 11 Mia
1966 Mia: Rec 2-14 7.0. **1967** Mia: Rec 8-56 7.0 1 TD. **1968** Mia: KR 1-22 22.0. **Total:** Rec 10-70 7.0 1 TD; KR 1-22 22.0.

		Rushing					Tot
Year Team	G	Att	Yds	Avg	TD	Fum	TD
1966 Mia	14	31	107	3.5	0	0	0
1967 Mia	9	46	179	3.9	1	1	2
1968 Mia	13	5	27	5.4	0	1	0
NFL Total	36	82	313	3.8	1	2	2

SHAWN PRICE Price, Shawn Sterling 6'5", 268 DE
Col: Sierra Coll. CA (J.C.); U. of Pacific *HS:* North Tahoe [NV] B: 3/28/1970, Jacksonville, FL
1993 TB: 9 G; 3 Sac. **1994** TB: 6 G. **1995** Car: 16 G; 1 Sac. **1996** Buf: 15 G. **1997** Buf: 10 G. **1998** Buf: 14 G; 5 Sac. **Total:** 70 G; 9 Sac.

STACY PRICE Price, Stacy 6'2", 194 LB
Col: Arkansas State *HS:* Arkansas [Texarkana, AR] B: 3/24/1962
1987 SD: 3 G.

TERRY PRICE Price, Terrence Todd 6'4", 272 DE
Col: Texas A&M *HS:* Plano [TX] B: 4/5/1968, Atlanta, GA *Drafted:* 1990 Round 10 ChiB
1990 ChiB: 2 G.

BILLY PRICER Pricer, Billy Carol 5'10", 208 FB
(Stumpy) *Col:* Oklahoma *HS:* Perry [OK] B: 9/3/1934, Perry, OK *Drafted:* 1957 Round 6 Bal
1957 Bal: KR 2-40 20.0. **1958** Bal: Rec 3-14 4.7; KR 9-168 18.7. **1959** Bal: Rec 2-3 1.5; KR 6-66 11.0. **1960** Bal: Rec 8-77 9.6 1 TD; KR 6-88 14.7. **1961** DalT: Rec 2-21 10.5; KR 1-19 19.0. **Total:** Rec 15-115 7.7 1 TD; KR 24-381 15.9.

		Rushing					Tot
Year Team	G	Att	Yds	Avg	TD	Fum	TD
1957 Bal	12	2	18	9.0	0	1	0
1958 Bal	12	10	26	2.6	1	0	1
1959 Bal	12	34	128	3.8	0	1	0
1960 Bal	12	46	131	2.8	1	2	2
1961 DalT	6	5	13	2.6	0	0	0
NFL Total	54	97	316	3.3	2	4	3

DAN PRIDE Pride, Daniel M 6'3", 225 LB
Col: Tennessee State; Jackson State *HS:* Ironton [OH] B: 6/7/1942, Ironton, OH
1968 ChiB: 3 G. **1969** ChiB: 3 G; Int 1-1. **Total:** 6 G; Int 1-1.

TOM PRIDEMORE Pridemore, Lawrence Thomas Jr. 5'10", 186 DB
Col: West Virginia *HS:* Ansted [WV] B: 4/29/1956, Oak Hill, WV *Drafted:* 1978 Round 9 Atl
1978 Atl: KR 4-71 17.8. **1979** Atl: KR 9-111 12.3. **1980** Atl: KR 3-39 13.0. **1981** Atl: PR 1-0. **1984** Atl: Rush 1-7 7.0. **1985** Atl: Rush 1-48 48.0. **Total:** Rush 2-55 27.5; PR 1-0; KR 16-221 13.8.

		Interceptions		
Year Team	G	Int	Yds	TD
1978 Atl	16	1	0	0
1979 Atl	16	2	20	0
1980 Atl	16	2	2	0
1981 Atl	16	7	221	1
1982 Atl	9	1	28	0
1983 Atl	16	4	56	0
1984 Atl	16	2	0	0
1985 Atl	16	2	45	0
NFL Total	121	21	372	1

BOB PRIESTLEY Priestley, Robert Bagley 5'11", 192 OE-DE
Col: Brown *HS:* Melrose [MA] B: 1/5/1920, Everett, MA
1942 Phi: 9 G; Rec 4-47 11.8.

FRANK PRIMEAU Primeau, Francis E 5'11", 170 BB
Col: No College *HS:* North Tonawanda [NY] B: 2/1895, North Tonawanda, NY Deceased
1921 Ton: 1 G.

GREG PRIMUS Primus, Gregory Lamar 5'11", 188 WR
Col: Colorado State *HS:* George Washington [Denver, CO] B: 10/20/1970, Denver, CO
1994 ChiB: 3 G; Rec 3-25 8.3. **1995** ChiB: 4 G; KR 2-39 19.5. **Total:** 7 G; Rec 3-25 8.3; KR 2-39 19.5.

JAMES PRIMUS Primus, James Dewitt 5'11", 196 RB
Col: UCLA *HS:* Sweetwater [National City, CA] B: 5/18/1964, Yuma, AZ *Drafted:* 1988 Round 9 Atl
1988 Atl: Rec 8-42 5.3; KR 1-13 13.0. **1989** Atl: KR 1-16 16.0. **Total:** Rec 8-42 5.3; KR 2-29 14.5.

		Rushing			
Year Team	G	Att	Yds	Avg	TD
1988 Atl	16	35	95	2.7	1
1989 Atl	5	0	0	—	0
NFL Total	21	35	95	2.7	1

DOM PRINCIPE Principe, Dominic Alfred 6'0", 205 LB-BB-FB-DB
Col: Fordham *HS:* Brockton [MA] B: 2/9/1917, Brockton, MA *Drafted:* 1940 Round 7 NYG
AAFC **1946** BknA: Rec 3-25 8.3; KR 6-117 19.5.

		Rushing			
Year Team	G	Att	Yds	Avg	TD
1946 BknA	10	39	139	3.6	2

NFL **1940** NYG: 6 G; Rush 11-8 0.7; Int 1-12. **1941** NYG: 8 G; Rush 1-5 5.0; Rec 4-54 13.5. **1942** NYG: 11 G; Rec 2-33 16.5; Punt 1-32 32.0. **Total:** 25 G; Rush 12-13 1.1; Rec 6-87 14.5; Int 1-12; Punt 1-32 32.0.

MIKE PRINDLE Prindle, Michael John 5'9", 160 K
Col: Western Michigan *HS:* Grand Rapids Union [MI] B: 11/12/1963, Grand Rapids, MI
1987 Det: 3 G; Scor 24, 6-7 85.7% FG, 6-6 100.0% XK.

ALAN PRINGLE Pringle, Alan Keith 6'0", 195 K
Col: Rice *HS:* [England] B: 1/20/1952, Los Taques, Venezuela *Drafted:* 1975 Round 10 Hou
1975 Det: 1 G.

MIKE PRINGLE Pringle, Michael A 5'8", 186 RB
Col: Washington State; Cal State-Fullerton *HS:* John F. Kennedy [Los Angeles, CA] B: 10/1/1967, Los Angeles, CA *Drafted:* 1990 Round 6 Atl
1990 Atl: 3 G; Rush 2-9 4.5; KR 1-14 14.0.

BOB PRINT Print, Robert Thomas 6'0", 230 LB
Col: Dayton *HS:* St. Joseph [OH] B: 1/16/1944, Cleveland, OH
1967 SD: 7 G. **1968** SD: 8 G. **Total:** 15 G.

ANTHONY PRIOR Prior, Anthony Eugene 5'11", 185 DB
Col: Washington State *HS:* Rubidoux [Riverside, CA] B: 3/27/1970, Lowell, MA *Drafted:* 1992 Round 9 NYG
1998 Oak: PR 1-0. **Total:** PR 1-0.

		Kickoff Returns				
Year Team	G	Ret	Yds	Avg	TD	Fum
1993 NYJ	16	9	126	14.0	0	0
1994 NYJ	13	16	316	19.8	0	0
1995 NYJ	11	0	0	—	0	0
1996 Min	3	0	0	—	0	0
1997 Min	12	0	0	—	0	0
1998 Oak	4	0	0	—	0	1
NFL Total	59	25	442	17.7	0	1

MIKE PRIOR Prior, Michael Robert 6'0", 208 DB
Col: Illinois State *HS:* Marian Catholic [Chicago Heights, IL] B: 11/14/1963, Chicago Heights, IL *Drafted:* 1985 Round 7 TB
1985 TB: KR 10-131 13.1. **1987** Ind: KR 3-47 15.7; 1 Sac. **1988** Ind: 1 Sac. **1990** Ind: Rec 1-40 40.0. **1992** Ind: Rec 1-17 17.0. **1995** GB: 1.5 Sac. **Total:** Rec 2-57 28.5; KR 13-178 13.7; 3.5 Sac.

		Punt Returns				Interceptions			
Year Team	G	Ret	Yds	Avg	TD	Int	Yds	TD	Fum
1985 TB	16	13	105	8.1	0	0	0	0	4
1987 Ind	13	0	0	—	0	6	57	0	0
1988 Ind	16	1	0	0.0	0	3	46	0	1
1989 Ind	16	0	0	—	0	6	88	1	0
1990 Ind	16	2	0	0.0	0	3	66	0	1
1991 Ind	9	0	0	—	0	3	50	0	0
1992 Ind	16	1	7	7.0	0	6	44	0	0
1993 GB	16	17	194	11.4	0	1	1	0	3
1994 GB	16	8	62	7.8	0	0	0	0	3
1995 GB	16	1	10	10.0	0	1	9	0	0
1996 GB	16	0	0	—	0	1	7	0	0

1997 GB	16	1	0	0.0	0	4	72	0	1
1998 GB	16	1	0	0.0	0	1	0	0	1
NFL Total	198	45	378	8.4	0	35	440	1	14

ERROL PRISBY Prisby, Errol Dwain 5′10″, 184 **DB**
Col: Cincinnati *HS:* Theodore Roosevelt [Kent, OH] B: 1/24/1943, Ravenna, OH
1967 Den: 5 G.

NICK PRISCO Prisco, Nicholas Anthony 5′8″, 193 **TB-DB**
(AKA Nicholas Anthony Priscoe) *Col:* Rutgers *HS:* Leonia [NJ] B: 1/12/1909, Edgewater, NJ D: 6/13/1981, Tarpon Springs, FL
1933 Phi: 2 G; Pass 2-0; Rush 7-6 0.9; Rec 2-7 3.5.

BOSH PRITCHARD Pritchard, Abisha Collins 5′11″, 164 **HB-DB**
Col: Virginia Military *HS:* Hopewell [VA] B: 9/10/1919, Windsor, NC D: 11/7/1996, Fort Meyers, FL
1942 Cle-Phi: Int 3-23; Punt 18-629 34.9. Cle: Punt 1-34 34.0. Phi: Int 3-23; Punt 17-595 35.0. **1946** Phi: Pass 1-0; Int 3-7; Punt 7-242 34.6. **1947** Phi: Int 1-12; Punt 2-64 32.0. **1948** Phi: 1 Fum TD. **1949** Phi: Pass 1-0, 1 Int. **Total:** Pass 2-0, 1 Int; Int 7-42; Punt 27-935 34.6; 1 Fum TD.

		Rushing				Receiving			
Year Team	**G**	**Att**	**Yds**	**Avg**	**TD**	**Rec**	**Yds**	**Avg**	**TD**
1942 Cle-Phi	7	38	166	4.4	0	2	4	2.0	0
1942 Cle	1	3	-27	-9.0	0	0	0	—	0
1942 Phi	6	35	193	5.5	0	2	4	2.0	0
1946 Phi	11	42	218	5.2	3	14	309	22.1	3
1947 Phi	11	69	294	4.3	1	16	315	19.7	3
1948 Phi	12	117	517	4.4	4	27	252	9.3	2
1949 Phi	8	84	506	**6.0**	3	8	185	23.1	2
1951 Phi-NYG	11	42	29	0.7	0	8	103	12.9	0
1951 Phi	6	31	6	0.2	0	8	103	12.9	0
1951 NYG	5	11	23	2.1	0	0	0	—	0
NFL Total	60	392	1730	4.4	11	75	1168	15.6	10

	Punt Returns				Kickoff Returns					
Year Team	**Ret**	**Yds**	**Avg**	**TD**	**Ret**	**Yds**	**Avg**	**TD**	**Fum**	**Tot TD**
1942 Cle-Phi	11	107	9.7	0	4	158	39.5	**1**	0	1
1942 Cle	0	0	—	0	1	24	24.0	0	0	0
1942 Phi	11	107	9.7	0	3	134	44.7	1	0	1
1946 Phi	12	166	13.8	0	8	164	20.5	0	5	6
1947 Phi	24	271	11.3	0	8	148	18.5	0	1	4
1948 Phi	24	282	11.8	1	9	249	27.7	0	9	8
1949 Phi	13	99	7.6	0	5	99	19.8	0	2	5
1951 Phi-NYG	11	147	13.4	1	7	120	17.1	0	2	1
1951 Phi	7	50	7.1	0	5	81	16.2	0	2	0
1951 NYG	4	97	24.3	1	2	39	19.5	0	0	1
NFL Total	95	1072	11.3	2	41	938	22.9	1	19	25

MIKE PRITCHARD Pritchard, Michael Robert 5′10″, 188 **WR**
Col: Colorado *HS:* Rancho [North Las Vegas, NV] B: 10/25/1969, Shaw AFB, SC *Drafted:* 1991 Round 1 Atl
1991 Atl: KR 1-18 18.0. **1992** Atl: Rush 5-37 7.4. **1993** Atl: Rush 2-4 2.0. **1995** Den: Rush 6-17 2.8. **1996** Sea: Rush 2-13 6.5. **1997** Sea: Rush 1-14 14.0. **1998** Sea: Rush 1-17 17.0; Scor 1 2XP. **Total:** Rush 17-102 6.0; KR 1-18 18.0; Scor 1 2XP.

		Receiving				
Year Team	**G**	**Rec**	**Yds**	**Avg**	**TD**	**Fum**
1991 Atl	16	50	624	12.5	2	2
1992 Atl	16	77	827	10.7	5	3
1993 Atl	15	74	736	9.9	7	1
1994 Den	3	19	271	14.3	1	1
1995 Den	15	33	441	13.4	3	1
1996 Sea	16	21	328	15.6	1	0
1997 Sea	16	64	843	13.2	2	2
1998 Sea	16	58	742	12.8	3	1
NFL Total	113	396	4812	12.2	24	11

RON PRITCHARD Pritchard, Ronald David 6′1″, 235 **LB**
Col: Arizona State *HS:* Antioch [CA] B: 4/9/1947, Chicago, IL *Drafted:* 1969 Round 1 Hou
1969 Hou: 14 G. **1970** Hou: 14 G; Int 2-28; Scor **1** Saf; 2 Pt. **1971** Hou: 14 G. **1972** Hou-Cin: 13 G. Hou: 6 G. Cin: 7 G. **1973** Cin: 10 G. **1974** Cin: 14 G. **1975** Cin: 14 G. **1976** Cin: 6 G; Int 1-0. **1977** Cin: 6 G. **Total:** 105 G; Int 3-28; Scor 1 Saf; 2 Pt.

BILL PRITCHARD Pritchard, William England 5′10″, 185 **FB-WB-BB**
Col: Penn State *HS:* South Park [Buffalo, NY] B: 12/23/1901, Frostburg, MD D: 4/10/1978, Buffalo, NY
1927 Prov: 12 G; Rush 1 TD; Scor 9, 3 XK. **1928** NYY: 13 G; Rec 1 TD; Scor 7, 1 XK. **Total:** 25 G; Rush 1 TD; Rec 1 TD; Tot TD 2.

BILLY PRITCHETT Pritchett, Billy Ray 6′3″, 230 **RB**
Col: West Texas A&M *HS:* Van Vleck [TX] B: 2/22/1951, Mart, TX *Drafted:* 1974 Round 6 Cle
1975 Cle: Rec 16-109 6.8. **1976** Atl: Rec 1-1 1.0. **Total:** Rec 17-110 6.5.

		Rushing				
Year Team	**G**	**Att**	**Yds**	**Avg**	**TD**	**Fum**
1975 Cle	14	75	199	2.7	0	4
1976 Atl	6	14	74	5.3	1	0
1977 Atl	9	3	7	2.3	0	0
NFL Total	29	92	280	3.0	1	4

KELVIN PRITCHETT Pritchett, Kelvin Bratodd 6′3″, 289 **DE**
Col: Mississippi *HS:* D.M. Therrell [Atlanta, GA] B: 10/24/1969, Atlanta, GA *Drafted:* 1991 Round 1 Dal
1991 Det: 16 G; 1.5 Sac. **1992** Det: 16 G; 6.5 Sac. **1993** Det: 16 G; 4 Sac. **1994** Det: 16 G; 5.5 Sac. **1995** Jac: 16 G; 1.5 Sac. **1996** Jac: 13 G; 2 Sac. **1997** Jac: 8 G; 3 Sac. **1998** Jac: 15 G; 3 Sac. **Total:** 116 G; 27.0 Sac.

STANLEY PRITCHETT Pritchett, Stanley Jerome 6′1″, 242 **RB**
Col: South Carolina *HS:* Frederick Douglass [Atlanta, GA] B: 12/12/1973, Atlanta, GA *Drafted:* 1996 Round 4 Mia
1996 Mia: Rush 7-27 3.9. **1997** Mia: Rush 3-7 2.3. **1998** Mia: Rush 6-19 3.2 1 TD. **Total:** Rush 16-53 3.3 1 TD.

		Receiving					
Year Team	**G**	**Rec**	**Yds**	**Avg**	**TD**	**Fum**	**Tot TD**
1996 Mia	16	33	354	10.7	2	3	2
1997 Mia	6	5	35	7.0	0	0	0
1998 Mia	16	17	97	5.7	0	0	1
NFL Total	38	55	486	8.8	2	3	3

WES PRITCHETT Pritchett, Wesley Andrew 6′2″, 234 **LB**
Col: Notre Dame *HS:* Westminster [Atlanta, GA] B: 7/7/1966, Atlanta, GA *Drafted:* 1989 Round 6 Mia
1991 Atl: 3 G.

STEVE PRITKO Pritko, Stephen 6′2″, 209 **OE-DE**
Col: Villanova *HS:* Northampton [PA]; Admiral Farragut Acad. [St. Petersburg, FL] B: 12/21/1920, Northampton, PA *Drafted:* 1943 Round 28 Cle
1944 Cle: Int 1-3. **1948** Bos: KR 2-23 11.5; 1 Fum TD. **Total:** KR 2-23 11.5; Int 1-3; 1 Fum TD.

		Receiving					
Year Team	**G**	**Rec**	**Yds**	**Avg**	**TD**	**Fum**	**Tot TD**
1943 NYG	10	1	12	12.0	0	0	1
1944 Cle	10	18	296	16.4	3	0	3
1945 Cle	10	19	255	13.4	4	0	4
1946 LARm	11	18	185	10.3	2	0	2
1947 LARm	11	10	101	10.1	0	0	0
1948 Bos	12	3	42	14.0	0	0	1
1949 NYB-GB	10	7	98	14.0	2	0	2
1949 NYB	2	1	4	4.0	0	0	0
1949 GB	8	6	94	15.7	2	0	2
1950 GB	12	17	125	7.4	2	1	2
NFL Total	86	93	1114	12.0	13	1	15

BRYAN PROBY Proby, Bryan Craig 6′5″, 285 **DE**
Col: Los Angeles Southwest Coll. CA (J.C.); Arizona State *HS:* Phineas Banning [Los Angeles, CA] B: 11/30/1971, Compton, CA *Drafted:* 1995 Round 6 KC
1995 KC: 3 G.

RAY PROCHASKA Prochaska, Raymond Edward 6′3″, 205 **OE-DE**
Col: Nebraska *HS:* Ulysses [NE] B: 8/9/1919, Ulysses, NE *Drafted:* 1941 Round 7 Cle
1941 Cle: 8 G; Rec 4-29 7.3.

DEWEY PROCTOR Proctor, Dewey Michael 5′11″, 215 **FB-LB**
Col: Furman *HS:* Lake View [SC] B: 7/1/1921, Lake View, SC
AAFC **1946** NY-A: Rec 3-32 10.7 1 TD. **1947** NY-A: Pass 1-0; Rec 1-4 4.0; KR 1-15 15.0; Int 1-32. **1948** ChiA: Rec 2-18 9.0. **Total:** Pass 1-0; Rec 6-54 9.0 1 TD; KR 1-15 15.0; Int 1-32.

		Rushing				
Year Team	**G**	**Att**	**Yds**	**Avg**	**TD**	**Tot TD**
1946 NY-A	4	23	76	3.3	1	2
1947 NY-A	11	15	15	1.0	1	1
1948 ChiA	9	47	190	4.0	1	1
1949 NY-A	1	1	-1	-1.0	0	0
AAFC Total	25	86	280	3.3	3	4

REX PROCTOR Proctor, Rex Gardner 5′10″, 180 **DB**
Col: Rice B: 12/1/1929, Sour Lake, TX D: 11/28/1980, Fort Worth, TX
1953 ChiB: 3 G; Int 1-4.

RICKY PROEHL Proehl, Richard Scott 6′0″, 190 **WR**
Col: Wake Forest *HS:* Hillsborough [NJ] B: 3/7/1968, Belle Mead, NJ *Drafted:* 1990 Round 3 Pho
1990 Pho: Rush 1-4 4.0; PR 1-2 2.0; KR 4-53 13.3. **1991** Pho: Rush 3-21 7.0; PR 4-26 6.5. **1992** Pho: Pass 1-0, 1 Int; Rush 3-23 7.7. **1993** Pho: Rush 8-47 5.9. **1997** ChiB: PR 8-59 7.4; Scor 1 2XP. **1998** StL: Rush 1-14 14.0; Scor 1 2XP. **Total:** Pass 1-0, 1 Int; Rush 16-109 6.8; PR 13-87 6.7; KR 4-53 13.3; Scor 2 2XP.

Year Team	G	Receiving Rec	Yds	Avg	TD	Fum
1990 Pho	16	56	802	14.3	4	0
1991 Pho	16	55	766	13.9	2	0
1992 Pho	16	60	744	12.4	3	5
1993 Pho	16	65	877	13.5	7	1
1994 Ariz	16	51	651	12.8	5	2
1995 Sea	8	5	29	5.8	0	0
1996 Sea	16	23	309	13.4	2	0
1997 ChiB	15	58	753	13.0	7	2
1998 StL	16	60	771	12.9	3	0
NFL Total	135	433	5702	13.2	33	10

GENE PROFIT Profit, Eugene Anthony 5′10″, 168 **DB**
Col: Yale *HS:* Junipero Serra [Gardena, CA] B: 11/11/1964, Baton Rouge, LA
1986 NE: 4 G. **1987** NE: 7 G. **1988** NE: 1 G. **Total:** 12 G.

JOE PROFIT Profit, Joseph 6′0″, 213 **RB**
Col: Northeast Louisiana *HS:* Richwood [Monroe, LA] B: 8/13/1949, Lake Providence, LA *Drafted:* 1971 Round 1 Atl
1971 Atl: KR 10-247 24.7. **1972** Atl: Rec 3-22 7.3. **1973** Atl-NO: Rec 11-108 9.8; KR 8-144 18.0. Atl: KR 1-0. NO: Rec 11-108 9.8; KR 7-144 20.6. **Total:** Rec 14-130 9.3; KR 18-391 21.7.

Year Team	G	Rushing Att	Yds	Avg	TD	Fum
1971 Atl	4	3	10	3.3	1	2
1972 Atl	8	40	132	3.3	0	2
1973 Atl-NO	11	90	329	3.7	2	6
1973 Atl	3	18	55	3.1	2	3
1973 NO	8	72	274	3.8	0	3
NFL Total	23	133	471	3.5	3	10

EDDIE PROKOP Prokop, Edward Stanley 5′11″, 200 **FB-DB-HB-LB**
Col: Georgia Tech *HS:* Cathedral Latin [Cleveland, OH]; Baylor Prep [Chattanooga, TN] B: 2/11/1922, Cleveland, OH D: 5/30/1955, Cleveland, OH
AAFC **1946** NY-A: Pass 11-4 36.4%, 72 6.55; Rec 5-52 10.4 1 TD; PR 4-116 29.0 1 TD; Int 1-14. **1947** NY-A: Pass 8-4 50.0%, 137 17.13 2 TD 1 Int; Rec 3-79 26.3 1 TD; PR 7-78 11.1; Int 3-57. **1948** ChiA: Pass 1-0; Rec 7-223 31.9 3 TD; PR 6-80 13.3. **1949** NY-A: Rec 1-7 7.0. **Total:** Pass 20-8 40.0%, 209 10.45 2 TD 1 Int; Rec 16-361 22.6 5 TD; PR 17-274 16.1 1 TD; Int 4-71.

Year Team	G	Rushing Att	Yds	Avg	TD	Kickoff Returns Ret	Yds	Avg	TD	Tot TD
1946 NY-A	12	65	236	3.6	1	2	47	23.5	0	3
1947 NY-A	13	76	324	4.3	4	7	188	26.9	0	5
1948 ChiA	9	54	266	4.9	1	15	323	21.5	0	4
1949 NY-A	6	31	109	3.5	2	3	62	20.7	0	2
AAFC Total	40	226	935	4.1	8	27	620	23.0	0	14

JOE PROKOP Prokop, Joseph Michael 6′2″, 230 **P**
Col: Cal Poly-Pomona *HS:* White Bear Lake [MN] B: 7/7/1960, St. Paul, MN
1989 NYJ: Rush 1-17 17.0 1 TD. **1990** NYJ: Rush 3-2 0.7. **1991** SF: Rush 1-(-10) -10.0. **Total:** Rush 5-9 1.8 1 TD.

Year Team	G	Punting Punts	Yds	Avg	Fum
1985 GB	9	56	2210	39.5	0
1987 SD	3	17	654	38.5	0
1988 NYJ	16	85	3310	38.9	0
1989 NYJ	16	87	3426	39.4	0
1990 NYJ	16	59	2363	40.1	1
1991 SF	11	40	1541	38.5	1
1992 Mia-NYG	8	32	1184	37.0	0
1992 Mia	7	24	891	37.1	0
1992 NYG	1	8	293	36.6	0
NFL Total	79	376	14688	39.1	2

JOE PROKOP Prokop, Joseph Michael 6′2″, 170 **HB-DB**
Col: Notre Dame; Bradley *HS:* Cathedral Latin [Cleveland, OH] B: 1/9/1921, Cleveland, OH D: 4/29/1995, Warren, OH
AAFC **1948** ChiA: 2 G.

VINCE PROMUTO Promuto, Vincent Louis 6′1″, 245 **OG**
Col: Holy Cross *HS:* Mount St. Michael's [Bronx, NY] B: 6/8/1938, New York, NY *Drafted:* 1960 Round 4 Was
1960 Was: 12 G. **1961** Was: 14 G. **1962** Was: 14 G. **1963** Was: 14 G. **1964** Was: 13 G. **1965** Was: 14 G. **1966** Was: 14 G. **1967** Was: 14 G. **1968** Was: 4 G. **1969** Was: 14 G. **1970** Was: 3 G. **Total:** 130 G.

JACK PROTZ Protz, John Michael 6′1″, 218 **LB**
Col: North Carolina; Syracuse *HS:* Woodbridge [NJ] B: 4/14/1948, Jersey City, NJ *Drafted:* 1970 Round 11 SD
1970 SD: 14 G.

BOB PROUT Prout, Robert Alan 6′1″, 190 **DB**
Col: Knox *HS:* Fenger [Chicago, IL] B: 5/11/1951, Chicago, IL
1974 Oak: 2 G. **1975** NYJ: 7 G; Int 1-10. **Total:** 9 G; Int 1-10.

ANDREW PROVENCE Provence, Andrew Clark 6′3″, 265 **DT-DE**
Col: South Carolina *HS:* Benedictine Mil. School [Savannah, GA] B: 3/8/1961, Savannah, GA *Drafted:* 1983 Round 3 Atl
1983 Atl: 16 G; 1.5 Sac. **1984** Atl: 16 G; 2.5 Sac. **1985** Atl: 16 G; 1 Sac. **1986** Atl: 16 G. **1987** Atl: 5 G. **Total:** 69 G; 5 Sac.

KEN PROVENCIAL Provencial, Joseph Kenneth 6′2″, 190 **OE**
Col: Georgetown *HS:* Massena [NY] B: 1908, NY Deceased
1930 Fra: 1 G.

FRED PROVO Provo, Frederick Lewis 5′9″, 185 **HB-DB**
(Fleet Freddie) *Col:* Washington *HS:* Vancouver [WA] B: 4/17/1922, Seattle, WA *Drafted:* 1948 Round 12 GB
1948 GB: Pass 1-1 100.0%, 20 20.00 1 TD; Rec 4-(-9) -2.3; PR 18-208 11.6; KR 10-205 20.5.

Year Team	G	Rushing Att	Yds	Avg	TD	Fum
1948 GB	9	29	90	3.1	0	1

TED PROVOST Provost, Ted R 6′2″, 195 **DB**
Col: Ohio State *HS:* Fairless [Navarre, OH] B: 7/26/1948, Navarre, OH *Drafted:* 1970 Round 7 LARm
1970 Min: 7 G. **1971** StL: 2 G. **Total:** 9 G.

REMI PRUDHOMME Prudhomme, Joseph Remi 6′4″, 250 **OG-C-DE-DT**
Col: Louisiana State *HS:* Opelousas [LA] B: 4/24/1942, Opelousas, LA D: 12/6/1990, New Orleans, LA *Drafted:* 1964 Round 14 Buf
1966 Buf: 10 G; KR 1-16 16.0. **1967** Buf: 10 G. **1968** KC: 14 G; KR 1-0. **1969** KC: 14 G. **1971** NO: 14 G. **1972** NO-Buf: 13 G; KR 1-0; 2 Fum. NO: 5 G; KR 1-0; 1 Fum. Buf: 8 G; 1 Fum. **Total:** 79 G; KR 3-16 5.3; 2 Fum.

PERRY PRUETT Pruett, Perry W 6′0″, 185 **DB**
Col: North Texas *HS:* Dalworth [Grand Prairie, TX] B: 3/7/1949, Dallas, TX
1971 NE: 11 G.

GREG PRUITT Pruitt, Gregory Donald 5′10″, 190 **RB**
Col: Oklahoma *HS:* Elmore [Houston, TX] B: 8/18/1951, Houston, TX *Drafted:* 1973 Round 2 Cle
1973 Cle: Pass 1-0. **1974** Cle: Pass 2-2 100.0%, 115 57.50 2 TD. **1976** Cle: Pass 3-2 66.7%, 39 13.00 1 TD. **1977** Cle: Pass 9-4 44.4%, 28 3.11 3 TD. **1978** Cle: Pass 3-0, 2 Int. **1983** LARd: Pass 1-0. **Total:** Pass 19-8 42.1%, 182 9.58 6 TD 2 Int.

Year Team	G	Rushing Att	Yds	Avg	TD	Receiving Rec	Yds	Avg	TD
1973 Cle	13	61	369	6.0	4	9	110	12.2	1
1974 Cle	14	126	540	4.3	3	21	274	13.0	1
1975 Cle	14	217	1067	4.9	8	44	299	6.8	1
1976 Cle	14	209	1000	4.8	4	45	341	7.6	1
1977 Cle	14	236	1086	4.6	3	37	471	12.7	1
1978 Cle	12	176	960	5.5	3	38	292	7.7	2
1979 Cle	6	62	233	3.8	0	14	155	11.1	1
1980 Cle	16	40	117	2.9	0	50	444	8.9	5
1981 Cle	15	31	124	4.0	0	65	636	9.8	4
1982 LARd	9	4	22	5.5	0	2	29	14.5	1
1983 LARd	16	26	154	5.9	2	1	6	6.0	0
1984 LARd	15	8	0	0.0	0	2	12	6.0	0
NFL Total	158	1196	5672	4.7	27	328	3069	9.4	18

Year Team	Punt Returns Ret	Yds	Avg	TD	Kickoff Returns Ret	Yds	Avg	TD	Fum	Tot TD
1973 Cle	16	180	11.3	0	16	453	28.3	0	7	5
1974 Cle	27	349	12.9	0	22	606	27.5	**1**	10	5
1975 Cle	13	130	10.0	0	14	302	21.6	0	10	9
1976 Cle	0	0	—	0	1	27	27.0	0	7	5
1977 Cle	0	0	—	0	0	0	—	0	8	4
1978 Cle	0	0	—	0	1	31	31.0	0	**12**	5
1979 Cle	0	0	—	0	1	22	22.0	0	1	1
1980 Cle	0	0	—	0	0	0	—	0	1	5
1981 Cle	0	0	—	0	3	82	27.3	0	3	4
1982 LARd	27	209	7.7	0	14	371	26.5	0	5	1
1983 LARd	**58**	**666**	11.5	**1**	31	604	19.5	0	10	3
1984 LARd	53	473	8.9	0	3	16	5.3	0	9	0
NFL Total	194	2007	10.3	1	106	2514	23.7	1	83	47

JAMES PRUITT Pruitt, James Bouvias 6′3″, 199 **WR**
Col: Cal State-Fullerton *HS:* Thomas Jefferson [Los Angeles, CA] B: 1/29/1964, Los Angeles, CA *Drafted:* 1986 Round 4 Mia
1986 Mia: PR 11-150 13.6 1 TD. **1989** Ind: KR 12-257 21.4.
Total: PR 11-150 13.6 1 TD; KR 12-257 21.4.

Year Team	G	Receiving Rec	Yds	Avg	TD	Fum	Tot TD
1986 Mia	16	15	235	15.7	2	4	3

1987 Mia	12	26	404	15.5	3	1	3
1988 Mia-Ind	12	2	38	19.0	0	1	0
1988 Mia	11	2	38	19.0	0	1	0
1988 Ind	1	0	0	—	0	0	0
1989 Ind	16	5	71	14.2	1	2	1
1990 Mia	6	13	235	18.1	3	0	3
1991 Mia	5	2	30	15.0	0	0	0
NFL Total	67	63	1013	16.1	9	8	10

MIKE PRUITT Pruitt, Michael 6′0″, 222 **RB**
Col: Purdue *HS:* Wendell Phillips [Chicago, IL] B: 4/3/1954, Chicago, IL *Drafted:* 1976 Round 1 Cle
1976 Cle: KR 6-106 17.7. **1977** Cle: KR 6-131 21.8. **Total:** KR 12-237 19.8.

		Rushing				Receiving					Tot
Year Team	**G**	**Att**	**Yds**	**Avg**	**TD**	**Rec**	**Yds**	**Avg**	**TD**	**Fum**	**TD**
1976 Cle	13	52	138	2.7	0	8	26	3.3	0	4	0
1977 Cle	13	47	205	4.4	1	3	12	4.0	0	1	1
1978 Cle	16	135	560	4.1	5	20	112	5.6	0	3	5
1979 Cle	16	264	1294	4.9	9	41	372	9.1	2	6	11
1980 Cle	16	249	1034	4.2	6	63	471	7.5	0	9	6
1981 Cle	16	247	1103	4.5	7	63	442	7.0	1	5	8
1982 Cle	9	143	516	3.6	3	22	140	6.4	0	4	3
1983 Cle	15	293	1184	4.0	10	30	157	5.2	2	4	12
1984 Cle	10	163	506	3.1	6	5	29	5.8	0	1	6
1985 Buf-KC	13	112	390	3.5	2	7	43	6.1	0	0	2
1985 Buf	4	7	24	3.4	0	0	0	—	0	0	0
1985 KC	9	105	366	3.5	2	7	43	6.1	0	0	2
1986 KC	15	139	448	3.2	2	8	56	7.0	0	0	2
NFL Total	152	1844	7378	4.0	51	270	1860	6.9	5	37	56

MICKEY PRUITT Pruitt, Mickey Aaron 6′1″, 206 **LB-DB**
Col: Colorado *HS:* Paul Robeson [Chicago, IL] B: 1/10/1965, Bamberg, SC
1988 ChiB: 14 G. **1989** ChiB: 14 G; KR 2-17 8.5. **1990** ChiB: 16 G; 1 Sac. **1991** Dal: 12 G. **1992** Dal: 6 G. **Total:** 62 G; KR 2-17 8.5; 1 Sac.

TREVOR PRYCE Pryce, Trevor 6′5″, 295 **DT**
Col: Michigan; Clemson *HS:* Lake Howell [Winter Park, FL] B: 8/3/1975, Brooklyn, NY *Drafted:* 1997 Round 1 Den
1997 Den: 8 G; 2 Sac. **1998** Den: 16 G; Int 1-1; 8.5 Sac. **Total:** 24 G; Int 1-1; 10.5 Sac.

BARRY PRYOR Pryor, Barry L 6′0″, 215 **RB**
Col: Boston U. *HS:* South Hills [Pittsburgh, PA] B: 3/4/1946, Pittsburgh, PA
1969 Mia: 14 G; Rec 2-(-3) -1.5. **1970** Mia: 2 G; Rush 2-0. **Total:** 16 G; Rush 2-0; Rec 2-(-3) -1.5.

JIM PSALTIS Psaltis, David James 6′1″, 190 **DB**
Col: San Jose State; USC *HS:* Alameda [CA] B: 12/14/1927, Chicago, IL *Drafted:* 1953 Round 2 ChiC
1953 ChiC: 12 G; Int 2-43; 1 Fum. **1954** GB: 11 G; PR 1-0. **1955** ChiC: 12 G; Int 4-42 1 TD; 6 Pt. **Total:** 35 G; PR 1-0; Int 6-85 1 TD; 6 Pt; 1 Fum.

BOB PTACEK Ptacek, Robert J 6′1″, 205 **QB**
Col: Michigan *HS:* Holy Name [Cleveland, OH] B: 4/23/1937, Cleveland, OH *Drafted:* 1959 Round 8 Cle
1959 Cle: 12 G; Rush 3-13 4.3.

BEN PUCCI Pucci, Benito Modesto 6′4″, 255 **T**
Col: No College *HS:* Southwest [St. Louis, MO] B: 1/26/1925, St. Louis, MO
AAFC **1946** BufA: 12 G. **1947** ChiA: 13 G. **1948** CleA: 12 G. **Total:** 37 G.

HAL PUDDY Puddy, Marvin Harold 6′3″, 220 **T**
Col: Oregon State *HS:* Hood River [OR] B: 8/18/1924, Hood River, OR D: 1/31/1975, Port Angeles, WA
AAFC **1948** SF-A: 4 G.

CHET PUDLOSKI Pudloski, Chester E 6′1″, 210 **T**
Col: Villanova *HS:* Coughlin [Wilkes-Barre, PA] B: 8/3/1915, Wilkes-Barre, PA D: 8/1990
1944 Cle: 10 G.

GARRY PUETZ Puetz, Garry Spencer 6′3″, 263 **OG-OT**
Col: Valparaiso *HS:* Luther North [Chicago, IL] B: 3/14/1952, Elmhurst, IL *Drafted:* 1973 Round 12 NYJ
1973 NYJ: 7 G. **1974** NYJ: 14 G. **1975** NYJ: 14 G. **1976** NYJ: 14 G. **1977** NYJ: 14 G. **1978** NYJ-TB: 16 G. NYJ: 6 G. TB: 10 G. **1979** Phi-NE: 7 G. Phi: 2 G. NE: 5 G. **1980** NE: 16 G. **1981** NE: 15 G. **1982** Was: 2 G. **Total:** 119 G.

JETHRO PUGH Pugh, Jethro Jr. 6′6″, 260 **DT-DE**
Col: Elizabeth City State *HS:* W.F. Etheridge [Windsor, NC] B: 7/3/1944, Windsor, NC *Drafted:* 1965 Round 11 Dal
1965 Dal: 12 G. **1966** Dal: 14 G. **1967** Dal: 14 G; Scor **1** Saf; 2 Pt; 1 Fum. **1968** Dal: 13 G; Scor **1** Saf; 2 Pt. **1969** Dal: 12 G. **1970** Dal: 14 G; Int 1-0. **1971** Dal: 12 G. **1972** Dal: 14 G. **1973** Dal: 13 G. **1974** Dal: 14 G. **1975** Dal: 13 G. **1976** Dal: 13 G. **1977** Dal: 12 G. **1978** Dal: 13 G. **Total:** 183 G; Int 1-0; Scor 2 Saf; 4 Pt; 1 Fum.

MARION PUGH Pugh, Marion C 6′1″, 187 **QB-DB**
Col: Texas A&M *HS:* North Side [Fort Worth, TX] B: 9/6/1919, Fort Worth, TX D: 11/20/1976, College Station, TX *Drafted:* 1941 Round 2 Phi
AAFC **1946** MiaA: Rec 4-43 10.8; KR 1-24 24.0.

		Passing							
Year Team	**G**	**Att**	**Comp**	**Comp%**	**Yds**	**YPA**	**TD**	**Int**	**Rating**
1946 MiaA	14	118	55	46.6	608	5.15	5	12	36.9

	Rushing			
Year Team	**Att**	**Yds**	**Avg**	**TD**
1946 MiaA	29	-125	-4.3	2

NFL **1941** NYG: PR 1-5 5.0; Scor 0-1 XK. **Total:** PR 1-5 5.0; Scor 0-1 XK.

		Passing							
Year Team	**G**	**Att**	**Comp**	**Comp%**	**Yds**	**YPA**	**TD**	**Int**	**Rating**
1941 NYG	5	24	12	50.0	161	6.71	1	0	85.6
1945 NYG	5	58	27	46.6	390	6.72	3	3	64.6
NFL Total	10	82	39	47.6	551	6.72	4	3	70.7

	Rushing			
Year Team	**Att**	**Yds**	**Avg**	**TD**
1941 NYG	24	50	2.1	0
1945 NYG	24	-52	-2.2	0
NFL Total	48	-2	0.0	0

CRAIG PUKI Puki, Craig Alan 6′1″, 231 **LB**
Col: Tennessee *HS:* Glacier [Seattle, WA] B: 1/18/1957, Deadwood, SD *Drafted:* 1980 Round 3 SF
1980 SF: 16 G; Int 1-0. **1981** SF: 16 G. **1982** StL: 7 G. **Total:** 39 G; Int 1-0.

DON PUMPHREY Pumphrey, Donald Anson 6′4″, 275 **OG**
Col: Northeastern Oklahoma A&M (J.C.); Valdosta State *HS:* Lincoln [Tallahassee, FL] B: 11/22/1963, Tallahassee, FL
1987 TB: 3 G.

ANDY PUPLIS Puplis, Andrew Joseph 5′9″, 180 **WB-DB**
Col: Notre Dame *HS:* Harrison [Chicago, IL] B: 2/1/1915, Chicago, IL D: 1/25/1990, Maywood, IL
1943 ChiC: 8 G; KR 1-9 9.0; Int 1-19.

ALFRED PUPUNU Pupunu, Alfred Sione 6′2″, 260 **TE**
Col: Dixie Coll. UT (J.C.); Weber State *HS:* South [Salt Lake City, UT] B: 10/17/1969, Tonga
1996 SD: KR 1-15 15.0. **Total:** KR 1-15 15.0.

		Receiving				
Year Team	**G**	**Rec**	**Yds**	**Avg**	**TD**	**Fum**
1992 SD	15	0	0	—	0	0
1993 SD	16	13	142	10.9	0	0
1994 SD	13	21	214	10.2	2	0
1995 SD	15	35	315	9.0	0	1
1996 SD	9	24	271	11.3	1	1
1997 SD-KC-NYG	9	1	7	7.0	0	0
1997 SD	8	1	7	7.0	0	0
1997 KC	1	0	0	—	0	0
1998 NYG	9	1	2	2.0	0	0
NFL Total	86	95	951	10.0	3	2

CAL PURDIN Purdin, Calvin O'Neale 6′2″, 188 **WB-DB-HB**
Col: Tulsa *HS:* Augusta [KS] B: 2/22/1921, Jefferson, OK D: 12/1982, Augusta, KS *Drafted:* 1943 Round 25 ChiC
AAFC **1946** BknA-MiaA: 8 G; Pass 1-1 100.0%, -2 -2.00; Rush 10-12 1.2; Rec 12-108 9.0; PR 4-52 13.0; KR 4-77 19.3.

NFL **1943** ChiC: 4 G; Pass 2-1 50.0%, 7 3.50; Rush 9-20 2.2; Rec 3-36 12.0; PR 1-6 6.0; KR 1-24 24.0; Punt 8-341 42.6.

MIKE PURDY Purdy, Clair Joseph Jr. 5′10″, 179 **WB-BB**
Col: Brown *HS:* Dean Acad. [Franklin, MA] B: 1895, Auburn, NY D: 1/10/1950, Auburn, NY
1920 Roch: 3 G. **1921** NYG: 1 G. **1922** Mil: 9 G; Rush 1 TD; 6 Pt. **Total:** 13 G; Rush 1 TD; 6 Pt.

PID PURDY Purdy, Everett Virgil 5′6″, 145 **BB**
Col: Beloit *HS:* Beatrice [NE] B: 6/15/1904, Beatrice, NE D: 1/16/1951, Ingleside, NE
1926 GB: 11 G; Pass 1 TD; Scor 20, 2 FG, 14 XK. **1927** GB: 6 G; Rush 1 TD; Scor 10, 1 FG, 1 XK. **Total:** 17 G; Pass 1 TD; Rush 1 TD; Scor 30, 3 FG, 15 XK.

DAVE PUREIFORY Pureifory, David Lee 6′1″, 260 **DE-DT**
Col: Eastern Michigan *HS:* Ecorse [MI] B: 7/12/1949, Pensacola, FL *Drafted:* 1972 Round 6 GB
1972 GB: 14 G. **1973** GB: 13 G. **1974** GB: 13 G. **1975** GB: 14 G; Scor 4, 2-4 50.0% XK, **1** Saf. **1976** GB: 12 G. **1977** GB: 12 G. **1978** Cin-Det: 15 G. Cin: 7 G. Det: 8 G. **1979** Det: 15 G. **1980** Det: 16 G. **1981** Det: 15 G.

1982 Det: 9 G; 1 Fum; 7 Sac. **Total:** 148 G; Scor 4, 2-4 50.0% XK, 1 Saf; 1 Fum; 7 Sac.

DAVE PURLING Purling, David Alan 6′5″, 240 **DT**
Col: USC *HS:* San Marcos [Santa Barbara, CA] B: 6/26/1962, Long Beach, CA
1987 LARm: 1 G.

FRANK PURNELL Purnell, Frank 5′11″, 230 **FB**
Col: Alcorn State *HS:* Spring Hill [Sweatman, MS] B: 4/5/1933, Sweatman, MS
1957 GB: 9 G; Rush 5-22 4.4; Rec 2-16 8.0; 1 Fum.

JIM PURNELL Purnell, James Fred 6′3″, 238 **LB**
Col: Wisconsin *HS:* Evanston Twp. [Evanston, IL] B: 12/12/1941, La Porte, IN
1964 ChiB: 6 G; KR 1-8 8.0. **1965** ChiB: 12 G. **1966** ChiB: 14 G. **1967** ChiB: 14 G. **1968** ChiB: 14 G. **1969** LARm: 14 G. **1970** LARm: 14 G. **1971** LARm: 14 G; Int 2-32. **1972** LARm: 13 G; Int 1-2. **Total:** 115 G; KR 1-8 8.0; Int 3-34.

LOVETT PURNELL Purnell, Lovett Shaizer 6′3″, 245 **TE**
Col: West Virginia *HS:* Seaford [DE] B: 4/7/1972, Seaford, DE
Drafted: 1996 Round 7 NE
1996 NE: 2 G. **1997** NE: 16 G; Rec 5-57 11.4 3 TD; 18 Pt. **1998** NE: 16 G; Rec 12-92 7.7 2 TD; 12 Pt. **Total:** 34 G; Rec 17-149 8.8 5 TD; 30 Pt.

ANDRE PURVIS Purvis, Andre Lamont 6′4″, 310 **DT**
Col: North Carolina *HS:* White Oak [Jacksonville, NC]; Swansboro HS [NC] B: 7/14/1973, Jacksonville, NC *Drafted:* 1997 Round 5 Cin
1997 Cin: 7 G. **1998** Cin: 9 G; 1 Sac. **Total:** 16 G; 1 Sac.

VIC PURVIS Purvis, James Victor 5′11″, 190 **DB**
Col: Southern Mississippi *HS:* Puckett [MS] B: 11/17/1943, Brandon, MS
1966 Bos: 14 G; PR 5-43 8.6; KR 8-185 23.1; 1 Fum. **1967** Bos: 2 G. **Total:** 16 G; PR 5-43 8.6; KR 8-185 23.1; 1 Fum.

EARL PUTMAN Putman, Earl Robert 6′6″, 308 **C**
(Tiny) *Col:* Arizona State *HS:* Hughes [Cincinnati, OH] B: 1/10/1932, Cincinnati, OH *Drafted:* 1954 Round 5 NYG
1957 ChiC: 11 G.

DUANE PUTNAM Putnam, Duane Clifford 6′0″, 228 **OG-LB**
Col: U. of Pacific *HS:* Antioch [CA] B: 9/5/1928, Pollack, SD
1952 LARm: 6 G. **1953** LARm: 9 G. **1954** LARm: 11 G; KR 1-13 13.0. **1955** LARm: 12 G. **1956** LARm: 12 G; KR 1-0. **1957** LARm: 12 G; KR 2-11 5.5. **1958** LARm: 12 G. **1959** LARm: 10 G. **1960** Dal: 12 G; KR 1-13 13.0. **1961** Cle: 14 G. **1962** LARm: 11 G. **Total:** 121 G; KR 5-37 7.4.

FRED PUTZIER Putzier, Frederick Jerome 5′9″, 174 **E-WB**
Col: St. Olaf *HS:* Bird Island [MN] B: 6/11/1899, Bird Island, MN D: 9/17/1986, Prescott, WI
1924 Min: 3 G.

ROLLIN PUTZIER Putzier, Rollin William 6′4″, 279 **DT-NT**
Col: Oregon *HS:* Post Falls [ID] B: 12/10/1965, Coeur d'Alene, ID
Drafted: 1988 Round 4 GB
1988 Pit: 5 G. **1989** SF: 11 G. **Total:** 16 G.

DAVE PUZZUOLI Puzzuoli, Phillip David 6′3″, 260 **NT**
Col: Pittsburgh *HS:* Stamford Catholic [CT] B: 1/12/1961, Greenwich, CT *Drafted:* 1983 Round 6 Cle
1983 Cle: 16 G; 2 Sac. **1984** Cle: 16 G; 2 Sac. **1985** Cle: 16 G; KR 2-8 4.0. **1986** Cle: 16 G; KR 1-32 32.0; 6 Sac. **1987** Cle: 12 G; 5.5 Sac. **Total:** 76 G; KR 3-40 13.3; 15.5 Sac.

JACK PYBURN Pyburn, Jack Harris 6′6″, 250 **OT**
Col: Texas A&M *HS:* C.E. Byrd [Shreveport, LA] B: 12/28/1944, Shreveport, LA *Drafted:* 1967 Round 11 Mia
1967 Mia: 10 G. **1968** Mia: 13 G. **Total:** 23 G.

JOHNNY PYEATT Pyeatt, John Joseph 6′3″, 204 **DB**
Col: No College *HS:* Florence [AZ] B: 9/16/1933, Florence, AZ
1960 Den: 14 G; Int 4-60 1 TD; 6 Pt. **1961** Den: 3 G. **Total:** 17 G; Int 4-60 1 TD; 6 Pt.

MIKE PYLE Pyle, Michael Johnson 6′3″, 250 **C**
Col: Yale *HS:* New Trier Twp. [Winnetka, IL] B: 7/18/1939, Keokuk, IA
Drafted: 1961 Round 7 ChiB
1961 ChiB: 14 G. **1962** ChiB: 14 G. **1963** ChiB: 14 G; KR 1-0. **1964** ChiB: 11 G. **1965** ChiB: 13 G. **1966** ChiB: 13 G. **1967** ChiB: 14 G. **1968** ChiB: 14 G. **1969** ChiB: 14 G; 2 Fum. **Total:** 121 G; KR 1-0; 2 Fum.

PALMER PYLE Pyle, William Palmer 6′3″, 247 **OG**
Col: Michigan State *HS:* New Trier Twp. [Winnetka, IL] B: 6/12/1937, Keokuk, IA *Drafted:* 1959 Round 6 Bal
1960 Bal: 11 G. **1961** Bal: 14 G. **1962** Bal: 6 G. **1963** Bal: 7 G. **1964** Min: 10 G. **1966** Oak: 13 G. **Total:** 61 G.

DAVID PYLES Pyles, Robert David 6′5″, 275 **OT**
Col: Miami (Ohio) *HS:* Wheelersburg [OH] B: 9/3/1960, Portsmouth, OH
1987 LARd: 2 G.

BOB PYLMAN Pylman, Robert William 6′4″, 214 **T**
Col: South Dakota State *HS:* Gettysburg [SD] B: 10/30/1913, Ellendale, ND D: 4/9/1971
1938 Phi: 11 G; Rec 1-1 1.0; **1** Fum TD; 6 Pt. **1939** Phi: 10 G. **Total:** 21 G; Rec 1-1 1.0; 1 Fum TD; 6 Pt.

GEORGE PYNE Pyne, George Francis II 5′11″, 218 **T**
Col: Holy Cross *HS:* Milford [MA] B: 10/17/1909, Marlboro, MA D: 6/3/1974, Milford, MA
1931 Prov: 2 G.

GEORGE PYNE Pyne, George Francis III 6′4″, 285 **DT**
Col: Olivet *HS:* Milford [MA] B: 7/12/1941, Milford, MA *Drafted:* 1965 Round 16 Bos
1965 Bos: 14 G; KR 1-0; 1 Fum.

JIM PYNE Pyne, James George 6′2″, 290 **OG**
Col: Virginia Tech *HS:* Milford [MA]; Choate School [Wallingford, CT] B: 11/23/1971, Milford, MA *Drafted:* 1994 Round 7 TB
1995 TB: 15 G. **1996** TB: 12 G. **1997** TB: 15 G; 1 Fum. **1998** Det: 16 G. **Total:** 58 G; 1 Fum.

JERRY QUAERNA Quaerna, Jerold Oscar 6′6″, 275 **OT**
Col: Michigan *HS:* Fort Atkinson [WI] B: 10/9/1963, Janesville, WI
1987 Det: 3 G.

RED QUAM Quam, Arthur Charles 165 **BB**
Col: No College B: 7/10/1896, Minneapolis, MN D: 5/1/1973, Hibbing, MN
1926 Dul: 1 G.

BERNARD QUARLES Quarles, Bernard Durwin 6′2″, 215 **QB**
Col: UCLA; Hawaii *HS:* Thomas Jefferson [Los Angeles, CA] B: 1/4/1960, Los Angeles, CA
1987 LARm: 1 G; Pass 3-1 33.3%, 40 13.33 1 TD 1 Int; Rush 1-8 8.0.

SHELTON QUARLES Quarles, Shelton Eugene 6′1″, 236 **LB**
Col: Vanderbilt *HS:* White Creek [TN] B: 9/11/1971, Nashville, TN
1997 TB: 16 G. **1998** TB: 16 G; 1 Sac. **Total:** 32 G; 1 Sac.

JOHN QUAST Quast, John Henry 5′10″, 165 **OE**
Col: Purdue *HS:* Male [Louisville, KY] B: 4/4/1900, Louisville, KY D: 8/9/1966, Louisville, KY
1923 Lou: 1 G.

JESS QUATSE Quatse, Jesse 5′11″, 226 **T**
Col: Pittsburgh *HS:* Greensburg [PA] B: 4/4/1908, Rillton, PA D: 12/27/1977, Lakeland, FL
1933 GB-Pit: 10 G. GB: 9 G. Pit: 1 G. **1934** Pit: 12 G; Pass 1-0. **1935** NYG: 10 G. **Total:** 32 G; Pass 1-0.

FRANK QUAYLE Quayle, Frank Joseph III 5′10″, 195 **RB**
Col: Virginia *HS:* Garden City [NY] B: 1/15/1947, Brooklyn, NY
Drafted: 1969 Round 5 Den
1969 Den: Rec 11-167 15.2.

		Rushing				
Year Team	G	Att	Yds	Avg	TD	Fum
1969 Den	11	57	183	3.2	0	1

JEFF QUEEN Queen, Jeffrey Richard 6′1″, 217 **RB-TE**
(Fox) *Col:* Morgan State *HS:* Roosevelt [Washington, DC]
B: 8/15/1946, Boston, MA *Drafted:* 1968 Round 12 SD
1970 SD: KR 1-12 12.0. **Total:** KR 1-12 12.0.

		Rushing				Receiving					Tot
Year Team	G	Att	Yds	Avg	TD	Rec	Yds	Avg	TD	Fum	TD
1969 SD	14	0	0	—	0	10	148	14.8	0	0	0
1970 SD	14	77	261	3.4	1	20	236	11.8	1	4	2
1971 SD	14	95	318	3.3	4	23	270	11.7	3	4	7
1972 Oak	14	4	10	2.5	0	0	0	—	0	1	0
1973 Oak	9	0	0	—	0	0	0	—	0	0	0
1974 Hou	11	2	7	3.5	0	1	4	4.0	1	0	1
NFL Total	76	178	596	3.3	5	54	658	12.2	5	9	10

JEFF QUERY Query, Jeffrey Lee 6′0″, 165 **WR**
Col: Millikin *HS:* Maroa-Forsyth [Maroa, IL] B: 3/7/1967, Decatur, IL
Drafted: 1989 Round 5 GB
1989 GB: KR 6-125 20.8. **1990** GB: Rush 3-39 13.0; 1 Fum TD. **1992** Cin: Rush 1-1 1.0; KR 1-13 13.0. **1993** Cin: Rush 2-13 6.5. **Total:** Rush 6-53 8.8; KR 7-138 19.7; 1 Fum TD.

		Receiving				Punt Returns					Tot
Year Team	G	Rec	Yds	Avg	TD	Ret	Yds	Avg	TD	Fum	TD
1989 GB	16	23	350	15.2	2	30	247	8.2	0	1	2
1990 GB	16	34	458	13.5	2	32	308	9.6	0	3	3
1991 GB	16	7	94	13.4	0	14	157	11.2	0	1	0
1992 Cin	10	16	265	16.6	3	0	0	—	0	0	3
1993 Cin	16	56	654	11.7	4	0	0	—	0	1	4
1994 Cin	10	5	44	8.8	0	0	0	—	0	0	0
1995 Cin-Was	2	0	0	—	0	0	0	—	0	0	0
1995 Cin	1	0	0	—	0	0	0	—	0	0	0

1995 Was	1	0	0	—	0	0	0	—	0	0	0
NFL Total	86	141	1865	13.2	11	76	712	9.4	0	6	12

GREG QUICK Quick, Gregory 6'4", 280 **OT**
Col: Catawba *HS:* Scotland [Laurinburg, NC] B: 4/26/1964
1987 Atl: 1 G.

JERRY QUICK Quick, Jerry Dean 6'5", 279 **OT**
Col: Butler County CC KS; Kansas; Wichita State *HS:* Chaparral [Anthony, KS] B: 12/30/1963, Anthony, KS
1987 Pit: 1 G.

MIKE QUICK Quick, Michael Anthony 6'2", 190 **WR**
Col: North Carolina State *HS:* Richmond [Rockingham, NC]; Fork Union Mil. Acad. [VA] B: 5/14/1959, Hamlet, NC *Drafted:* 1982 Round 1 Phi
1984 Phi: Rush 1-(-5) -5.0. **1986** Phi: KR 2-6 3.0. **Total:** Rush 1-(-5) -5.0; KR 2-6 3.0.

		Receiving				
Year Team	**G**	**Rec**	**Yds**	**Avg**	**TD**	**Fum**
1982 Phi	9	10	156	15.6	1	0
1983 Phi	16	69	**1409**	20.4	13	1
1984 Phi	14	61	1052	17.2	9	0
1985 Phi	16	73	1247	17.1	11	1
1986 Phi	16	60	939	15.7	9	1
1987 Phi	12	46	790	17.2	11	3
1988 Phi	8	22	508	23.1	4	0
1989 Phi	6	13	228	17.5	2	0
1990 Phi	4	9	135	15.0	1	0
NFL Total	101	363	6464	17.8	61	6

RED QUIGLEY Quigley, Gerald 5'9", 155 **BB**
Col: No College *HS:* Cathedral [Rochester, NY] B: 12/18/1895, Rochester, NY D: 9/21/1966, Rochester, NY
1920 Roch: 9 G.

FRED QUILLAN Quillan, Frederick David 6'5", 261 **C**
Col: Oregon *HS:* Central Catholic [Portland, OR] B: 1/27/1956, West Palm Beach, FL *Drafted:* 1978 Round 7 SF
1978 SF: 14 G; KR 1-8 8.0. **1979** SF: 16 G; 2 Fum. **1980** SF: 16 G; 1 Fum. **1981** SF: 16 G; 1 Fum. **1982** SF: 9 G. **1983** SF: 14 G. **1984** SF: 16 G. **1985** SF: 15 G. **1986** SF: 16 G. **1987** SF: 11 G. **Total:** 143 G; KR 1-8 8.0; 4 Fum.

FRANK QUILLEN Quillen, Frank Harris 6'5", 225 **OE-DE**
Col: Pennsylvania *HS:* Ridley Park [PA]; Franklin and Marshall Acad. [Lancaster, PA] B: 12/18/1920, Ridley Park, PA D: 9/21/1990, Hockessin, DE
AAFC **1946** ChiA: 14 G; Rec 13-143 11.0 2 TD; KR 1-13 13.0; Int 1-9; 12 Pt. **1947** ChiA: 6 G; Rec 7-113 16.1 1 TD; 6 Pt. **Total:** 20 G; Rec 20-256 12.8 3 TD; KR 1-13 13.0; Int 1-9; 18 Pt.

CHARLEY QUILTER Quilter, Charles Rew 6'1", 240 **OT-DT**
(Chuck) *Col:* Tyler JC TX *HS:* Texas City [TX] B: 5/8/1926, Shreveport, LA
AAFC **1949** SF-A: 12 G.

NFL **1950** SF: 8 G.

SKEETS QUINLAN Quinlan, Volney Ralph Jr. 5'11", 173 **HB**
Col: Texas Christian; San Diego State *HS:* Grand Prairie [TX] B: 6/22/1928, San Angelo, TX *Drafted:* 1952 Round 4 LARm
1952 LARm: Pass 4-0. **1953** LARm: Pass 4-2 50.0%, 60 15.00 1 Int. **1954** LARm: Pass 2-1 50.0%, 34 17.00 1 Int. **Total:** Pass 10-3 30.0%, 94 9.40 2 Int.

		Rushing				Receiving			
Year Team	**G**	**Att**	**Yds**	**Avg**	**TD**	**Rec**	**Yds**	**Avg**	**TD**
1952 LARm	12	52	224	4.3	1	14	265	18.9	2
1953 LARm	12	97	705	**7.3**	4	17	260	15.3	2
1954 LARm	11	82	490	6.0	4	18	324	18.0	2
1955 LARm	6	15	70	4.7	0	19	245	12.9	0
1956 LARm-Cle	8	12	25	2.1	0	7	87	12.4	0
1956 LARm	2	10	21	2.1	0	3	24	8.0	0
1956 Cle	6	2	4	2.0	0	4	63	15.8	0
NFL Total	49	258	1514	5.9	9	75	1181	15.7	6

	Punt Returns				Kickoff Returns					Tot
Year Team	**Ret**	**Yds**	**Avg**	**TD**	**Ret**	**Yds**	**Avg**	**TD**	**Fum**	**TD**
1952 LARm	14	167	11.9	0	18	455	25.3	0	8	3
1953 LARm	0	0	—	0	2	38	19.0	0	3	6
1954 LARm	1	4	4.0	0	4	69	17.3	0	4	6
1955 LARm	1	55	55.0	1	0	0	—	0	2	1
1956 LARm-Cle	14	50	3.6	0	12	256	21.3	0	5	0
1956 LARm	4	41	10.3	0	3	37	12.3	0	3	0
1956 Cle	10	9	0.9	0	9	219	24.3	0	2	0
NFL Total	30	276	9.2	1	36	818	22.7	0	22	16

BILL QUINLAN Quinlan, William David 6'3", 248 **DE**
Col: Michigan State *HS:* Lawrence [MA] B: 6/19/1932, Lawrence, MA *Drafted:* 1956 Round 3 Cle
1957 Cle: 12 G. **1958** Cle: 10 G. **1959** GB: 12 G; Int 1-5. **1960** GB: 12 G. **1961** GB: 14 G. **1962** GB: 14 G; Int 1-4; 1 Fum. **1963** Phi: 11 G. **1964** Det: 12 G; Int 1-0. **1965** Was: 14 G. **Total:** 111 G; Int 3-9; 1 Fum.

IVAN QUINN Quinn, Ivan W 1 **G**
Col: Carroll (Wis.) *HS:* Waukesha [WI] B: 5/26/1899, NE D: 8/7/1969, San Diego, CA
1924 KC: 1 G.

JONATHAN QUINN Quinn, Jonathan Ryan 6'5", 244 **QB**
Col: Tulane; Middle Tennessee State *HS:* McGavock [Nashville, TN] B: 2/27/1975, Turlock, CA *Drafted:* 1998 Round 3 Jac
1998 Jac: Rush 11-77 7.0 1 TD.

		Passing								
Year Team	**G**	**Att**	**Comp**	**Comp%**	**Yds**	**YPA**	**TD**	**Int**	**Rating**	**Fum**
1998 Jac	4	64	34	53.1	387	6.05	2	3	62.4	3

KELLY QUINN Quinn, Kelly B 6'1", 220 **LB**
Col: Michigan State *HS:* Stone Mountain [GA] B: 8/20/1963, Thomaston, GA
1987 Min: 3 G.

MARCUS QUINN Quinn, Marcus 6'1", 205 **DB**
Col: Louisiana State *HS:* St. Augustine [New Orleans, LA] B: 6/27/1959, Tylertown, MS
1987 TB: 3 G.

MIKE QUINN Quinn, Michael Patrick 6'3", 220 **QB**
Col: Stephen F. Austin St. *HS:* Robert E. Lee [Houston, TX] B: 4/15/1974, Houston, TX
1997 Pit: 1 G; Pass 2-1 50.0%, 10 5.00. **1998** Dal: 3 G; Pass 1-1 100.0%, 10 10.00; Rush 5-(-6) -1.2. **Total:** 4 G; Pass 3-2 66.7%, 20 6.67; Rush 5-(-6) -1.2.

PADDY QUINN Quinn, Patrick George 5'7", 170 **HB**
Col: No College *HS:* Rock Island [IL] B: 2/5/1890, IA D: 2/1963, IL
1920 RI: 3 G. **1921** RI: 1 G. **Total:** 4 G.

STEVE QUINN Quinn, Stephen Timothy 6'1", 225 **C**
Col: Notre Dame *HS:* Loyola Acad. [Wilmette, IL] B: 2/11/1946, Pittsburg, KS
1968 Hou: 9 G.

ED QUIRK Quirk, Edward George 6'1", 231 **FB-LB-C**
Col: Missouri *HS:* St. Louis University [MO] B: 2/27/1925, St.Louis, MO Deceased *Drafted:* 1948 Round 13 Was
1948 Was: Rec 9-40 4.4. **1949** Was: Rec 5-33 6.6; KR 1-19 19.0. **1950** Was: Int 2-5. **Total:** Rec 14-73 5.2; KR 1-19 19.0; Int 2-5.

		Rushing				
Year Team	**G**	**Att**	**Yds**	**Avg**	**TD**	**Fum**
1948 Was	12	77	328	4.3	4	1
1949 Was	8	40	139	3.5	1	1
1950 Was	12	0	0	—	0	0
1951 Was	6	0	0	—	0	0
NFL Total	38	117	467	4.0	5	2

MARC RAAB Raab, Marc 6'3", 265 **C**
Col: USC *HS:* Helix [La Mesa, CA] B: 1/26/1969, San Diego, CA
1993 Was: 2 G. **1998** SD: 1 G. **Total:** 3 G.

BOB RABA Raba, Robert William 6'1", 222 **TE**
Col: Maryland *HS:* Walt Whitman [Bethesda, MD] B: 4/23/1955, Washington, DC
1977 NYJ: 14 G; KR 4-64 16.0; 1 Fum. **1978** NYJ: 4 G. **1979** NYJ: 8 G; Rec 2-9 4.5; KR 1-18 18.0. **1980** Bal: 3 G. **1981** Was: 8 G. **Total:** 37 G; Rec 2-9 4.5; KR 5-82 16.4; 1 Fum.

WARREN RABB Rabb, Samuel Warren 6'3", 204 **QB**
Col: Louisiana State *HS:* Baton Rouge [LA] B: 12/12/1937, Baton Rouge, LA *Drafted:* 1960 Round 2 Det
1961 Buf: Scor 1 2XP. **1962** Buf: Scor **1** 2XP. **Total:** Scor 2 2XP.

		Passing							
Year Team	**G**	**Att**	**Comp**	**Comp%**	**Yds**	**YPA**	**TD**	**Int**	**Rating**
1960 Det	7	0	0	—	0	—	0	0	—
1961 Buf	9	74	34	45.9	586	7.92	5	2	84.6
1962 Buf	14	177	67	37.9	1196	6.76	10	14	47.7
NFL Total	30	251	101	40.2	1782	7.10	15	16	58.6

	Rushing				
Year Team	**Att**	**Yds**	**Avg**	**TD**	**Fum**
1961 Buf	13	47	3.6	0	5
1962 Buf	37	77	2.1	3	6
NFL Total	50	124	2.5	3	11

MIKE RABOLD Rabold, Michael John 6'2", 239 **OG**
Col: Indiana *HS:* Fenwick [Chicago, IL] B: 3/12/1937, Chicago, IL
D: 10/13/1970, Greenwood, IN *Drafted:* 1959 Round 2 Det
1959 Det: 12 G; KR 1-0. **1960** StL: 12 G. **1961** Min: 14 G. **1962** Min: 14 G. **1964** ChiB: 14 G. **1965** ChiB: 14 G. **1966** ChiB: 14 G. **1967** ChiB: 11 G. **Total:** 105 G; KR 1-0.

BUSTER RABORN Raborn, Carroll M 6'0", 198 **C-LB**
Col: Southern Methodist B: 3/28/1913 D: 12/21/1991, Fortuna, CA
1936 Pit: 10 G. **1937** Pit: 11 G. **Total:** 21 G.

LATARIO RACHAL Rachal, Latario Deshawn 5'11", 183 **WR**
Col: El Camino Coll. CA (J.C.); Fresno State *HS:* Carson [CA]
B: 1/31/1973, Lynwood, CA

		Punt Returns				Kickoff Returns				
Year Team	G	Ret	Yds	Avg	TD	Ret	Yds	Avg	TD	Fum
1997 SD	14	0	0	—	0	15	336	22.4	0	1
1998 SD	11	32	387	12.1	0	11	192	17.5	0	4
NFL Total	25	32	387	12.1	0	26	528	20.3	0	5

FRANK RACIS Racis, Frank J 6'0", 200 **G-T-OE**
(Hercules; Champ) *Col:* No College *HS:* Shenandoah [PA]
B: 11/9/1899, Shenandoah, PA D: 8/19/1982, Shenandoah, PA
1925 Pott: 12 G. **1926** Pott: 14 G; 1 Fum TD; 6 Pt. **1927** Pott: 13 G; 6 Pt. **1928** Pott-NYY: 11 G. Pott: 10 G. NYY: 1 G. **1929** Bost: 7 G. **1930** Prov: 11 G; Int 1 TD; 6 Pt. **1931** Fra: 8 G. **Total:** 76 G; Int 1 TD; 1 Fum TD; Tot TD 3; 18 Pt.

DAVID RACKLEY Rackley, David Henry 5'9", 172 **WR**
Col: Miami-Dade CC North FL; Texas Southern *HS:* Miami Jackson [FL]
B: 2/2/1961, Miami, FL
1985 NO: 7 G; KR 1-63 63.0.

GEORGE RADACHOWSKY Radachowsky, George Joseph Jr. 5'11", 186 **DB**
Col: Boston College *HS:* Danbury [CT] B: 9/7/1962, Danbury, CT
Drafted: 1984 Round 7 LARm
1984 Ind: 16 G; KR 1-0; 1 Fum. **1985** Ind: 3 G. **1987** NYJ: 8 G; Int 2-45. **1988** NYJ: 9 G; 1.5 Sac. **1989** NYJ: 16 G; 6 Pt. **Total:** 52 G; KR 1-0; Int 2-45; 6 Pt; 1 Fum; 1.5 Sac.

JOHN RADE Rade, John Anthony 6'1", 232 **LB**
Col: Modesto JC CA; Boise State *HS:* Buena [Sierra Vista, AZ]
B: 8/31/1960, Ceres, CA *Drafted:* 1983 Round 8 Atl
1983 Atl: 16 G; 1 Fum TD; 6 Pt; 1.5 Sac. **1984** Atl: 7 G. **1985** Atl: 16 G; Int 2-42 **1** TD; 6 Pt; 5 Sac. **1986** Atl: 15 G; Int 1-6; 1 Sac. **1987** Atl: 11 G; 1 Sac. **1988** Atl: 15 G; 2 Sac. **1989** Atl: 15 G; 1 Fum. **1990** Atl: 16 G. **1991** Atl: 11 G. **Total:** 122 G; Int 3-48 1 TD; 1 Fum TD; Tot TD 2; 12 Pt; 1 Fum; 10.5 Sac.

KEITH RADECIC Radecic, J. Keith 6'1", 260 **C**
Col: Penn State *HS:* Brentwood [Pittsburgh, PA] B: 12/24/1963, Pittsburgh, PA
1987 StL: 3 G.

SCOTT RADECIC Radecic, J. Scott 6'3", 243 **LB**
Col: Penn State *HS:* Brentwood [Pittsburgh, PA] B: 6/14/1962, Pittsburgh, PA *Drafted:* 1984 Round 2 KC
1984 KC: 16 G; Int 2-54 1 TD; 6 Pt. **1985** KC: 16 G; Int 1-21; 3 Sac. **1986** KC: 16 G; Int 1-20; 1 Sac. **1987** Buf: 12 G; KR 1-14 14.0; Int 2-4. **1988** Buf: 16 G; 1.5 Sac. **1989** Buf: 16 G; 1.5 Sac. **1990** Ind: 15 G. **1991** Ind: 14 G; Int 1-26. **1992** Ind: 16 G; Int 1-0. **1993** Ind: 16 G; KR 1-10 10.0. **1994** Ind: 16 G; KR 1-17 17.0. **1995** Ind: 13 G; KR 1-(-5) -5.0. **Total:** 182 G; KR 4-36 9.0; Int 8-125 1 TD; 6 Pt; 7 Sac.

BILL RADEMACHER Rademacher, William Stiles 6'1", 190 **WR-DB**
Col: Northern Michigan *HS:* Menominee [MI] B: 5/13/1942, Menominee, MI
1964 NYJ: 6 G; PR 1-3 3.0; Int 1-16; 1 Fum. **1965** NYJ: 4 G. **1966** NYJ: 4 G; Rec 1-3 3.0. **1967** NYJ: 3 G. **1968** NYJ: 14 G; Rush 1-(-13) -13.0; Rec 2-11 5.5; KR 1-0. **1969** Bos: 13 G; Rec 17-217 12.8 3 TD; 18 Pt. **1970** Bos: 14 G; Rec 4-51 12.8. **Total:** 58 G; Rush 1-(-13) -13.0; Rec 24-282 11.8 3 TD; PR 1-3 3.0; KR 1-0; Int 1-16; 18 Pt; 1 Fum.

BRUCE RADFORD Radford, Bruce E 6'5", 257 **NT-DE**
Col: Grambling State *HS:* Tioga [LA] B: 10/5/1955, Pineville, LA
Drafted: 1979 Round 3 Den
1979 Den: 16 G. **1980** TB: 12 G. **1981** StL: 9 G. **Total:** 37 G.

KEN RADICK Radick, Kenneth Milton 5'10", 210 **OE-G-T**
(Fat) *Col:* Indiana; Marquette *HS:* Green Bay West [WI] B: 6/17/1907, Green Bay, WI D: 8/25/1987, Oshkosh, WI
1930 GB: 4 G. **1931** GB-Bkn: 3 G. GB: 1 G. Bkn: 2 G. **Total:** 7 G.

WAYNE RADLOFF Radloff, Wayne Richard 6'5", 274 **C-OG**
Col: Georgia *HS:* Winter Park [FL] B: 5/17/1961, London, England
1985 Atl: 16 G. **1986** Atl: 16 G. **1987** Atl: 12 G. **1988** Atl: 10 G. **1989** Atl: 11 G. **Total:** 65 G.

ALEX RADO Rado, Alexander 6'1", 200 **HB-DB**
(Pug; Moose) *Col:* West Virginia Tech *HS:* Roosevelt [Dayton, OH]
B: 7/19/1911, Dayton, OH D: 8/30/1995, Dayton, OH
1934 Pit: Pass 24-8 33.3%, 179 7.46 2 Int; Rec 5-93 18.6.

		Rushing			
Year Team	G	Att	Yds	Avg	TD
1934 Pit	8	38	210	5.5	0

GEORGE RADO Rado, George 5'9", 194 **G-DE**
(Mousie) *Col:* Duquesne *HS:* Brookfield [OH] B: 10/24/1912, Youngstown, OH D: 4/30/1992, New Cumberland, WV
1935 Pit: 11 G. **1936** Pit: 12 G. **1937** Pit-Phi: 10 G. Pit: 1 G. Phi: 9 G. **1938** Phi: 10 G. **Total:** 43 G.

GEORGE RADOSEVICH Radosevich, George 6'2", 228 **C-OT**
Col: Pittsburgh *HS:* Brentwood [Pittsburgh, PA] B: 1/25/1928, Brentwood, PA
1954 Bal: 10 G; KR 1-0. **1955** Bal: 12 G. **1956** Bal: 8 G. **Total:** 30 G; KR 1-0.

BILL RADOVICH Radovich, William Alex 5'10", 238 **G**
Col: USC *HS:* Hollywood [Los Angeles, CA] B: 6/24/1915, Chicago, IL
AAFC **1946** LA-A: 14 G. **1947** LA-A: 14 G. **Total:** 28 G.

NFL **1938** Det: 10 G. **1939** Det: 11 G. **1940** Det: 10 G. **1941** Det: 11 G. **1945** Det: 9 G. **Total:** 51 G.

VIC RADZIEVITCH Radzievitch, Victor John 5'10", 165 **BB-G-FB**
Col: Connecticut *HS:* Torrington [CT] B: 6/8/1903 D: 6/1974, Torrington, CT
1926 Har: 8 G; Pass 1 TD; Scor 5, 1 FG, 2 XK.

MIKE RAE Rae, Michael John 6'0", 193 **QB**
Col: USC *HS:* Lakewood [CA] B: 7/26/1951, Long Beach, CA
Drafted: 1973 Round 8 Oak

		Passing							
Year Team	G	Att	Comp	Comp%	Yds	YPA	TD	Int	Rating
1976 Oak	7	65	35	53.8	417	6.42	6	1	98.0
1977 Oak	10	30	15	50.0	162	5.40	1	4	37.8
1978 TB	6	118	57	48.3	705	5.97	4	7	53.8
1979 TB	5	36	17	47.2	252	7.00	1	2	56.7
NFL Total	28	249	124	49.8	1536	6.17	12	14	61.9

	Rushing				
Year Team	Att	Yds	Avg	TD	Fum
1976 Oak	10	37	3.7	1	0
1977 Oak	13	75	5.8	1	3
1978 TB	20	186	9.3	0	4
1979 TB	1	2	2.0	0	0
NFL Total	44	300	6.8	2	7

NORBERT RAEMER Raemer, Norbert LaVerne 5'11", 210 **G**
Col: Kansas State *HS:* Marysville [KS] B: 7/3/1920, Herkimer, KS
1942 Bkn: 1 G.

BILL RAFFEL Raffel, William 5'11", 195 **E**
Col: Pennsylvania *HS:* Ashland [KY] B: 8/26/1907, Ashland, KY
D: 7/24/1982, Wynnewood, PA
1932 Bkn: 4 G; Rec 1-15 15.0.

TOM RAFFERTY Rafferty, Thomas Michael 6'3", 256 **C-OG**
Col: Penn State *HS:* Manlius [NY] B: 8/2/1954, Syracuse, NY
Drafted: 1976 Round 4 Dal
1976 Dal: 13 G. **1977** Dal: 14 G; 1 Fum. **1978** Dal: 16 G. **1979** Dal: 16 G. **1980** Dal: 16 G. **1981** Dal: 16 G; 2 Fum. **1982** Dal: 9 G. **1983** Dal: 16 G; Rec 1-8 8.0. **1984** Dal: 16 G. **1985** Dal: 16 G. **1986** Dal: 16 G. **1987** Dal: 12 G. **1988** Dal: 15 G. **1989** Dal: 12 G. **Total:** 203 G; Rec 1-8 8.0; 3 Fum.

VINCE RAFFERTY Rafferty, Vincent Edward 6'4", 285 **C-OG**
Col: Colorado *HS:* Longmont [KS] B: 8/6/1961, Manhattan, KS
1987 GB: 3 G.

BILLY RAFTER Rafter, William John 5'6", 155 **BB-WB-FB**
Col: Syracuse *HS:* Lansingburg [Troy, NY]; St. Augustine's Acad. [Troy, NY] B: 10/7/1895, Troy, NY D: 6/28/1966, Syracuse, NY
1921 Roch: 1 G. **1924** Roch: 2 G. **Total:** 3 G.

PHIL RAGAZZO Ragazzo, Philip John 6'0", 216 **T-G**
Col: Case Western Reserve *HS:* McKinley [Niles, OH] B: 6/24/1915, Niles, OH D: 10/3/1994, Niles, OH *Drafted:* 1938 Round 6 GB
1938 Cle: 10 G. **1939** Cle: 11 G. **1940** Cle-Phi: 7 G. Cle: 1 G. Phi: 6 G. **1941** Phi: 10 G. **1945** NYG: 5 G; Int 1-7. **1946** NYG: 11 G. **1947** NYG: 9 G. **Total:** 63 G; Int 1-7.

FLOYD RAGLIN Raglin, Floyd C Jr. 5'9", 180 **WR**
Col: Nevada-Las Vegas; Southern University *HS:* Alton [IL]
B: 2/10/1961, Alton, IL
1987 Mia: 2 G.

GEORGE RAGSDALE Ragsdale, George Ellis 5'11", 185 **RB-WR**
Col: North Carolina A&T *HS:* Baltimore City College [MD]
B: 12/4/1952, Dinwiddie, VA *Drafted:* 1976 Round 12 TB
1977 TB: Rec 2-17 8.5. **1978** TB: Rec 3-41 13.7 1 TD. **1979** TB: Rec 3-28 9.3. **Total:** Rec 8-86 10.8 1 TD.

		Rushing				Kickoff Returns					Tot
Year Team	G	Ret	Yds	Avg	TD	Ret	Yds	Avg	TD	Fum	TD
1977 TB	9	3	21	7.0	0	3	68	22.7	0	0	0
1978 TB	15	25	121	4.8	1	24	555	23.1	0	2	2
1979 TB	15	6	5	0.8	0	34	675	19.9	0	2	0
NFL Total	39	34	147	4.3	1	61	1298	21.3	0	4	2

VINCE RAGUNAS Ragunas, Vincent Joseph 5′11″, 190 **BB-LB-FB**
Col: Virginia Military *HS:* Davenport [Plymouth, PA] B: 7/12/1924, Plymouth, PA
1949 Pit: 3 G.

PAT RAGUSA Ragusa, Patrick A 5′8″, 180 **K**
Col: St. John's (N.Y.) *HS:* East Rockaway [NY] B: 3/17/1963, Caracas, Venezuela
1987 NYJ: 3 G; Scor 13, 2-4 50.0% FG, 7-7 100.0% XK.

STEVE RAIBLE Raible, Steven Carl 6′2″, 195 **WR**
Col: Georgia Tech *HS:* Trinity [Louisville, KY] B: 6/2/1954, Louisville, KY *Drafted:* 1976 Round 2 Sea
1976 Sea: Rush 1-2 2.0. **1977** Sea: KR 2-19 9.5. **1978** Sea: Rush 2-13 6.5; Scor **1** Saf. **Total:** Rush 3-15 5.0; KR 2-19 9.5; Scor 1 Saf.

		Receiving					Tot
Year Team	G	Rec	Yds	Avg	TD	Fum	TD
1976 Sea	13	4	126	31.5	1	1	2
1977 Sea	14	5	79	15.8	0	0	0
1978 Sea	16	22	316	14.4	1	1	1
1979 Sea	16	20	252	12.6	1	0	1
1980 Sea	16	16	232	14.5	0	0	0
1981 Sea	9	1	12	12.0	0	0	0
NFL Total	84	68	1017	15.0	3	2	4

JIM RAIFF Raiff, James Herman 5′10″, 235 **OT**
Col: Dayton B: 12/21/1930 D: 9/17/1994, Dayton, OH
1954 Bal: 3 G.

DAVE RAIMEY Raimey, David E 5′10″, 195 **DB**
Col: Michigan *HS:* Roosevelt [Dayton, OH]; Woodrow Wilson HS [Xenia, OH] B: 11/18/1940, Dayton, OH *Drafted:* 1963 Round 9 Cle
1964 Cle: 5 G.

BEN RAIMONDI Raimondi, Benjamin Louis 5′10″, 175 **TB**
Col: William & Mary; Indiana *HS:* Erasmus Hall [Brooklyn, NY]
B: 1/23/1925, Brooklyn, NY
AAFC **1947** NY-A: 7 G; Pass 15-3 20.0%, 54 3.60; Rush 6-11 1.8.

MIKE RAINES Raines, Vaughn Michael 6′5″, 255 **DT-DE**
Col: Alabama *HS:* Sidney Lanier [Montgomery, AL] B: 2/14/1953, Montgomery, AL *Drafted:* 1974 Round 6 SF
1974 SF: 2 G.

DAN RAINS Rains, Daniel Paul 6′1″, 224 **LB**
Col: Cincinnati *HS:* Hopewell [Aliquippa, PA] B: 4/26/1956, Rochester, PA
1982 ChiB: 2 G. **1983** ChiB: 15 G; KR 2-11 5.5. **1984** ChiB: 16 G. **1986** ChiB: 9 G. **Total:** 42 G; KR 2-11 5.5.

PETER RAJKOVICH Rajkovich, Peter Joseph 5′10″, 190 **FB-LB**
Col: Detroit Mercy *HS:* Caro [MI] B: 1/17/1911, Austria
D: 11/13/1979, Caro, MI

		Rushing			
Year Team	G	Att	Yds	Avg	TD
1934 Pit	3	39	140	3.6	0

LARRY RAKESTRAW Rakestraw, Lawrence Clyde 6′2″, 195 **QB**
Col: Georgia *HS:* West Fulton [Atlanta, GA] B: 4/22/1942, Mableton, GA *Drafted:* 1964 Round 8 ChiB
1966 ChiB: Rush 1-(-5) -5.0. **1967** ChiB: Rush 11-42 3.8 2 TD. **1968** ChiB: Rush 9-12 1.3. **Total:** Rush 21-49 2.3 2 TD.

		Passing								
Year Team	G	Att	Comp	Comp%	Yds	YPA	TD	Int	Rating	Fum
1966 ChiB	1	0	0	—	0	—	0	0	—	1
1967 ChiB	5	44	21	47.7	228	5.18	3	2	67.2	2
1968 ChiB	7	67	30	44.8	361	5.39	1	7	27.2	3
NFL Total	13	111	51	45.9	589	5.31	4	9	40.7	6

GREGG RAKOCZY Rakoczy, Gregg Adam 6′6″, 290 **C-OG-OT**
Col: Miami (Fla.) *HS:* Shawnee [Medford, NJ] B: 5/18/1965, Medford Lakes, NJ *Drafted:* 1987 Round 2 Cle
1987 Cle: 12 G. **1988** Cle: 16 G; 2 Fum. **1989** Cle: 16 G. **1990** Cle: 16 G. **1991** NE: 5 G; KR 1-9 9.0; 1 Fum. **1992** NE: 16 G; 1 Fum. **Total:** 81 G; KR 1-9 9.0; 4 Fum.

DAN RALPH Ralph, Daniel Ray 6′4″, 260 **DT**
Col: Colorado; Oregon *HS:* Northglenn [CO] B: 3/9/1961, Denver, CO
Drafted: 1984 Round 6 Atl
1984 StL: 6 G.

JIM RAMEY Ramey, James Edward Jr. 6′4″, 261 **DE**
Col: Kentucky *HS:* Belfry [KY] B: 3/9/1957, Louisville, KY
Drafted: 1979 Round 3 Cle
1979 StL: 7 G. **1987** TB: 3 G. **Total:** 10 G.

TONY RAMIREZ Ramirez, Tony 6′6″, 296 **OT**
Col: Northern Colorado *HS:* Northglenn [CO] B: 1/26/1973, Lincoln, NE *Drafted:* 1997 Round 6 Det
1997 Det: 2 G. **1998** Det: 16 G. **Total:** 18 G.

JOE RAMONA Ramona, Joe Louis 6′1″, 210 **OG-DG**
Col: Santa Clara *HS:* Abraham Lincoln [San Jose, CA] B: 7/11/1931, San Jose, CA *Drafted:* 1953 Round 28 NYG
1953 NYG: 8 G.

DERRICK RAMSEY Ramsey, Derrick Kent 6′4″, 230 **TE**
Col: Kentucky *HS:* Hastings [FL]; Camden HS [NJ] B: 12/23/1956, Hastings, FL *Drafted:* 1978 Round 5 Oak
1978 Oak: KR 7-125 17.9. **1980** Oak: KR 1-10 10.0. **Total:** KR 8-135 16.9.

		Receiving				
Year Team	G	Rec	Yds	Avg	TD	Fum
1978 Oak	16	0	0	—	0	0
1979 Oak	16	13	161	12.4	3	0
1980 Oak	16	5	117	23.4	0	0
1981 Oak	16	52	674	13.0	4	2
1982 LARd	9	0	0	—	0	0
1983 LARd-NE	16	24	335	14.0	6	0
1983 LARd	2	0	0	—	0	0
1983 NE	14	24	335	14.0	6	0
1984 NE	16	66	792	12.0	7	0
1985 NE	16	28	285	10.2	1	1
1987 Det	1	0	0	—	0	0
NFL Total	122	188	2364	12.6	21	3

BUSTER RAMSEY Ramsey, Garrard Sliger 6′1″, 219 **OG-LB**
Col: William & Mary *HS:* Knoxville [TN] B: 3/16/1920, Townsend, TN
Drafted: 1943 Round 14 ChiC
1946 ChiC: 11 G; Rush 1-5 5.0; Int 1-6. **1947** ChiC: 8 G; Int 4-29. **1948** ChiC: 12 G; Int 1-13. **1949** ChiC: 12 G; KR 1-0; Int 1-0; Scor **1** Saf; 2 Pt. **1950** ChiC: 12 G. **1951** ChiC: 2 G. **Total:** 57 G; Rush 1-5 5.0; KR 1-0; Int 7-48; Scor 1 Saf; 2 Pt.

GREG RAMSEY Ramsey, Gregory Scott 6′3″, 244 **DE**
Col: Fresno State *HS:* Coalinga [CA] B: 12/19/1963, San Francisco, CA
1987 Sea: 2 G.

FRANK RAMSEY Ramsey, Harold Frank 6′1″, 240 **T**
Col: Oregon State *HS:* J.M. Weatherwax [Aberdeen, WA]
B: 5/16/1916, Corvallis, OR D: 1/1985, Corvallis, OR *Drafted:* 1938 Round 5 ChiB
1945 ChiB: 9 G.

RED RAMSEY Ramsey, Herschel Randolph 6′0″, 196 **OE-DE**
Col: Texas Tech *HS:* Chillicothe [TX] B: 4/9/1911, Chillicothe, TX
D: 4/1984, Kemp, TX *Drafted:* 1938 Round 4 Phi
1940 Phi: Int 1-5. **Total:** Int 1-5.

		Receiving			
Year Team	G	Rec	Yds	Avg	TD
1938 Phi	11	5	122	24.4	1
1939 Phi	11	31	359	11.6	1
1940 Phi	11	17	143	8.4	0
1945 Phi	2	0	0	—	0
NFL Total	35	53	624	11.8	2

KNOX RAMSEY Ramsey, Knox Wagner 6′1″, 216 **OG-LB-DG**
Col: William & Mary *HS:* Maryville [TN] B: 2/13/1926, Speed, IN
Drafted: 1948 Round 3 ChiB
AAFC **1948** LA-A: 13 G. **1949** LA-A: 12 G. **Total:** 25 G.

NFL **1950** ChiC: 12 G. **1951** ChiC: 10 G; KR 1-0. **1952** Phi-Was: 11 G. Phi: 3 G. Was: 8 G. **1953** Was: 11 G. **Total:** 44 G; KR 1-0.

CHUCK RAMSEY Ramsey, Lowell Wallace Jr. 6′2″, 191 **P**
Col: Wake Forest *HS:* West [Knoxville, TN] B: 2/24/1952, Rock Hill, SC
Drafted: 1974 Round 6 NE
1979 NYJ: Rush 2-0. **1980** NYJ: Pass 2-1 50.0%, 6 3.00; Rush 1-(-15) -15.0. **1981** NYJ: Rush 3-0. **Total:** Pass 2-1 50.0%, 6 3.00; Rush 6-(-15) -2.5.

		Punting			
Year Team	G	Punts	Yds	Avg	Fum
1977 NYJ	12	62	2298	37.1	0
1978 NYJ	16	74	2964	40.1	0
1979 NYJ	16	73	2979	40.8	2
1980 NYJ	16	73	3096	42.4	0
1981 NYJ	16	81	3290	40.6	2
1982 NYJ	9	35	1348	38.5	0
1983 NYJ	16	81	3218	39.7	0

1984 NYJ	16	74	2935	39.7	0
NFL Total	117	553	22128	40.0	4

NATE RAMSEY Ramsey, Nathan Lee 6′1″, 200 **DB**
Col: Indiana State *HS:* Neptune [NJ] B: 7/12/1941, Neptune, NJ
Drafted: 1963 Round 14 Phi
1967 Phi: KR 1-0. **Total:** KR 1-0.

		Interceptions			
Year Team	**G**	**Int**	**Yds**	**TD**	**Fum**
1963 Phi	14	1	0	0	0
1964 Phi	13	5	31	0	0
1965 Phi	14	6	74	0	0
1966 Phi	12	1	0	0	0
1967 Phi	14	0	0	0	0
1968 Phi	14	2	0	0	1
1969 Phi	14	2	26	1	0
1970 Phi	11	1	0	0	0
1971 Phi	14	0	0	0	0
1972 Phi	14	3	14	0	0
1973 NO	4	0	0	0	0
NFL Total	138	21	145	1	1

RAY RAMSEY Ramsey, Raymond Leroy 6′2″, 166 **DB-OE-WB-HB**
Col: Bradley *HS:* Lanphier [Springfield, IL] B: 7/18/1921, Springfield, IL *Drafted:* 1947 Round 8 ChiC
AAFC **1947** ChiA: PR 11-131 11.9. **1948** BknA: Pass 1-0; PR 5-82 16.4 1 TD. **1949** ChiA: PR 8-64 8.0. **Total:** Pass 1-0; PR 24-277 11.5 1 TD.

		Rushing				Receiving			
Year Team	**G**	**Att**	**Yds**	**Avg**	**TD**	**Rec**	**Yds**	**Avg**	**TD**
1947 ChiA	14	70	433	6.2	2	35	768	21.9	8
1948 BknA	11	22	48	2.2	0	13	315	24.2	2
1949 ChiA	12	32	43	1.3	0	17	366	21.5	4
AAFC Total	37	124	524	4.2	2	65	1449	22.3	14

	Kickoff Returns				Interceptions			Tot
Year Team	**Ret**	**Yds**	**Avg**	**TD**	**Int**	**Yds**	**TD**	**TD**
1947 ChiA	16	406	25.4	0	5	66	0	10
1948 BknA	10	233	23.3	0	7	124	0	3
1949 ChiA	14	407	29.1	0	2	79	0	4
AAFC Total	40	1046	26.2	0	14	269	0	17

NFL **1951** ChiC: Rec 8-135 16.9. **1952** ChiC: Rec 3-27 9.0. **1953** ChiC: Rec 12-118 9.8. **Total:** Rec 23-280 12.2.

		Interceptions			
Year Team	**G**	**Int**	**Yds**	**TD**	**Fum**
1950 ChiC	6	1	0	0	0
1951 ChiC	10	5	90	0	1
1952 ChiC	9	5	67	0	1
1953 ChiC	12	10	237	**1**	1
NFL Total	37	21	394	1	3

STEVE RAMSEY Ramsey, Stephen Wayne 6′2″, 210 **QB**
Col: North Texas *HS:* W.W. Samuell [Dallas, TX] B: 4/22/1947, Dallas, TX *Drafted:* 1970 Round 5 NO

		Passing							
Year Team	**G**	**Att**	**Comp**	**Comp%**	**Yds**	**YPA**	**TD**	**Int**	**Rating**
1970 NO	1	2	0	0.0	0	0.00	0	0	39.6
1971 Den	9	178	84	47.2	1120	6.29	5	13	46.6
1972 Den	9	137	65	47.4	1050	7.66	3	9	53.5
1973 Den	5	27	10	37.0	194	7.19	2	2	56.7
1974 Den	7	74	41	55.4	580	7.84	5	7	64.0
1975 Den	11	233	128	54.9	1562	6.70	9	14	63.6
1976 Den	12	270	128	47.4	1931	7.15	11	13	64.9
NFL Total	54	921	456	49.5	6437	6.99	35	58	58.9

	Rushing				
Year Team	**Att**	**Yds**	**Avg**	**TD**	**Fum**
1971 Den	3	6	2.0	0	2
1972 Den	6	15	2.5	2	5
1974 Den	5	-2	-0.4	0	3
1975 Den	6	38	6.3	0	2
1976 Den	13	51	3.9	0	5
NFL Total	33	108	3.3	2	17

TOM RAMSEY Ramsey, Thomas Lloyd 6′1″, 189 **QB**
Col: UCLA *HS:* John F. Kennedy [Los Angeles, CA] B: 7/9/1961, Encino, CA *Drafted:* 1983 Round 10 NE
1986 NE: Rush 1-(-6) -6.0. **1987** NE: Rush 13-75 5.8 1 TD. **1988** NE: Rush 3-8 2.7. **1989** Ind: Rush 4-5 1.3. **Total:** Rush 21-82 3.9 1 TD.

		Passing								
Year Team	**G**	**Att**	**Comp**	**Comp%**	**Yds**	**YPA**	**TD**	**Int**	**Rating**	**Fum**
1986 NE	5	3	1	33.3	7	2.33	0	0	42.4	0
1987 NE	9	134	71	53.0	898	6.70	6	6	70.4	4
1988 NE	7	27	12	44.4	100	3.70	0	3	15.0	0
1989 Ind	7	50	24	48.0	280	5.60	1	1	63.8	1
NFL Total	28	214	108	50.5	1285	6.00	7	10	60.6	5

EASON RAMSON Ramson, Eason Lloyd 6′2″, 232 **TE**
Col: Washington State *HS:* Christian Brothers [Sacramento, CA]
B: 4/30/1956, Sacramento, CA *Drafted:* 1978 Round 12 GB
1978 StL: Rush 2-8 4.0. **1980** SF: Rush 2-(-2) -1.0; KR 1-18 18.0. **1981** SF: KR 1-12 12.0. **1982** SF: KR 2-20 10.0. **1983** SF: Rush 1-3 3.0. **Total:** Rush 5-9 1.8; KR 4-50 12.5.

		Receiving				
Year Team	**G**	**Rec**	**Yds**	**Avg**	**TD**	**Fum**
1978 StL	15	23	238	10.3	1	0
1979 SF	2	0	0	—	0	0
1980 SF	16	21	179	8.5	2	0
1981 SF	11	4	45	11.3	0	0
1982 SF	9	2	27	13.5	0	0
1983 SF	16	17	125	7.4	1	2
1985 Buf	16	37	369	10.0	1	1
NFL Total	85	104	983	9.5	5	3

DENNIS RANDALL Randall, Dennis Allen 6′7″, 250 **DE-DT**
(Stretch) *Col:* Oklahoma State *HS:* McLain [Tulsa, OK] B: 7/7/1945, Tulsa, OK *Drafted:* 1967 Round 3 NYJ
1967 NYJ: 7 G. **1968** Cin: 13 G; KR 1-11 11.0. **Total:** 20 G; KR 1-11 11.0.

TOM RANDALL Randall, Thomas Gene 6′5″, 245 **OG**
Col: Iowa State *HS:* Mason City [IA] B: 8/3/1956, Mason City, IA
Drafted: 1978 Round 7 Dal
1978 Dal: 11 G. **1979** Hou: 13 G. **Total:** 24 G.

PROC RANDELS Randels, Horace 6′0″, 180 **E**
Col: Kansas State *HS:* Chaparral [Anthony, KS] B: 8/5/1900 Deceased
1926 KC: 11 G. **1927** Cle: 5 G; Rec 1 TD; Tot TD 2; 12 Pt. **1928** Det: 10 G; Rec 1 TD; 6 Pt. **Total:** 26 G; Rec 2 TD; Tot TD 3; 18 Pt.

TATE RANDLE Randle, Ernest Tate 6′0″, 202 **DB**
Col: Texas Tech *HS:* Fort Stockton [TX] B: 8/15/1959, Fredricksburg, TX *Drafted:* 1982 Round 8 Mia
1982 Hou: 7 G. **1983** Hou-Bal: 12 G; Int 1-41. Hou: 2 G. Bal: 10 G; Int 1-41. **1984** Ind: 16 G; Int 3-66. **1985** Ind: 16 G; Int 1-0; Scor 1 Saf; 2 Pt. **1986** Ind: 15 G. **1987** Mia: 3 G; Int 2-16. **Total:** 69 G; Int 7-123; Scor 1 Saf; 2 Pt.

ERVIN RANDLE Randle, Ervin 6′1″, 250 **LB**
Col: Baylor *HS:* Hearne [TX] B: 10/12/1962, Hearne, TX
Drafted: 1985 Round 3 TB
1985 TB: 16 G; Int 1-0; 1 Sac. **1986** TB: 16 G; KR 1-0; 0.5 Sac. **1987** TB: 12 G. **1988** TB: 9 G. **1989** TB: 16 G; 1 Sac. **1990** TB: 16 G; 5.5 Sac. **1991** KC: 12 G. **1992** KC: 8 G. **Total:** 105 G; KR 1-0; Int 1-0; 8 Sac.

JOHN RANDLE Randle, John Anthony 6′1″, 278 **DT-DE**
Col: Trinity Valley CC TX; Texas A&M–Kingsville *HS:* Hearne [TX]
B: 12/12/1967, Hearne, TX
1990 Min: 16 G; 1 Sac. **1991** Min: 16 G; 9.5 Sac. **1992** Min: 16 G; 11.5 Sac. **1993** Min: 16 G; 12.5 Sac. **1994** Min: 16 G; 13.5 Sac. **1995** Min: 16 G; 10.5 Sac. **1996** Min: 16 G; 11.5 Sac. **1997** Min: 16 G; **15.5** Sac. **1998** Min: 16 G; 10.5 Sac. **Total:** 144 G; 96.0 Sac.

SONNY RANDLE Randle, Ulmo Shannon Jr. 6′2″, 189 **OE-WR**
Col: Virginia *HS:* Fork Union Mil. Acad. [VA] B: 1/6/1936, Cohasset, VA
Drafted: 1958 Round 19 ChiC
1959 ChiC: KR 2-33 16.5. **Total:** KR 2-33 16.5.

		Receiving					Tot
Year Team	**G**	**Rec**	**Yds**	**Avg**	**TD**	**Fum**	**TD**
1959 ChiC	8	15	202	13.5	1	0	1
1960 StL	12	62	893	14.4	**15**	1	**15**
1961 StL	14	44	591	13.4	9	0	9
1962 StL	14	63	1158	18.4	7	1	7
1963 StL	14	51	1014	19.9	12	1	12
1964 StL	7	25	517	20.7	5	0	5
1965 StL	14	51	845	16.6	9	0	9
1966 StL	14	17	218	12.8	2	0	2
1967 SF	14	33	502	15.2	4	0	4
1968 SF-Dal	9	4	56	14.0	1	0	1
1968 SF	3	3	44	14.7	1	0	1
1968 Dal	6	1	12	12.0	0	0	0
NFL Total	120	365	5996	16.4	65	3	65

AL RANDOLPH Randolph, Alvin Chester 6′2″, 205 **DB**
Col: Iowa *HS:* East St. Louis [IL] B: 7/8/1944, East St. Louis, IL
Drafted: 1966 Round 3 SF
1970 SF: Scor **1** Saf. **1971** GB: PR 1-0. **Total:** PR 1-0; Scor 1 Saf.

		Interceptions			
Year Team	**G**	**Int**	**Yds**	**TD**	**Fum**
1966 SF	13	3	138	1	0
1967 SF	14	0	0	0	0
1968 SF	14	4	60	0	0
1969 SF	14	2	10	0	0
1970 SF	14	1	0	0	0

1971 GB	14	1	34	0	1
1972 Cin-Det	8	0	0	0	0
1972 Cin	2	0	0	0	0
1972 Det	6	0	0	0	0
1973 Min	11	0	0	0	0
1974 SF-Buf	9	0	0	0	0
1974 SF	6	0	0	0	0
1974 Buf	3	0	0	0	0
NFL Total	111	11	242	1	1

CLARE RANDOLPH Randolph, Clare Loring 6'2", 204 **C-LB-G-OE**
(Dutch) *Col:* Indiana *HS:* Elkhart Central [IN] B: 5/2/1907, Chicago, IL D: 12/24/1972, Glendale, CA
1930 ChiC: 9 G. **1931** Port: 14 G. **1932** Port: 10 G. **1933** Port: 10 G. **1934** Det: 12 G. **1935** Det: 12 G. **1936** Det: 11 G. **Total:** 78 G.

HARRY RANDOLPH Randolph, Harry F 5'11", 195 **BB**
Col: Bethany (W.V.) *HS:* Connellsville [PA] B: 1900, OH
D: 12/3/1957, Harrison, NJ
1923 Col: 2 G.

TERRY RANDOLPH Randolph, Terry Allen 6'0", 184 **DB**
Col: American International *HS:* Samuel J. Tilden [Brooklyn, NY]
B: 7/17/1955, Brooklyn, NY *Drafted:* 1977 Round 11 GB
1977 GB: 14 G.

THOMAS RANDOLPH Randolph, Thomas Carl II 5'9", 180 **DB**
Col: Kansas State *HS:* Manhattan [KS] B: 10/5/1970, Norfolk, VA
Drafted: 1994 Round 2 NYG
1994 NYG: 16 G; Int 1-0. **1995** NYG: 16 G; Int 2-15. **1996** NYG: 16 G. **1997** NYG: 16 G; Int 1-1. **1998** Cin: 16 G; Int 1-0. **Total:** 80 G; Int 5-16.

WALT RANKIN Rankin, Walter Velpo 5'11", 197 **LB-FB-DB**
(Bull) *Col:* Texas Tech *HS:* Colorado [Colorado City, TX]
B: 1/28/1919, Laverty, OK D: 12/7/1993, Lubbock, TX
1941 ChiC: 1 G. **1943** ChiC: 10 G; Rush 2-1 0.5; Rec 10-44 4.4; KR 4-57 14.3; Int 3-30. **1944** ChPt: 10 G; Rush 4-13 3.3; Rec 4-18 4.5; Int 2-9. **1945** ChiC: 6 G; Rush 8-11 1.4; Rec 3-25 8.3; KR 1-14 14.0; Int 1-0; 1 Fum. **1946** ChiC: 11 G; Rush 5-1 0.2; KR 1-11 11.0; Int 2-14. **1947** ChiC: 12 G; Rush 3-4 1.3. **Total:** 50 G; Rush 22-30 1.4; Rec 17-87 5.1; KR 6-82 13.7; Int 8-53; 1 Fum.

DERRICK RANSOM Ransom, Derrick Wayne Jr. 6'3", 291 **DT**
Col: Cincinnati *HS:* Lawrence Central [Indianapolis, IN] B: 9/13/1976, Indianapolis, IN *Drafted:* 1998 Round 6 KC
1998 KC: 7 G; KR 1-0.

KEITH RANSPOT Ranspot, Edgar Keith 6'3", 205 **OE-DE-DB**
Col: Southern Methodist B: 12/11/1913, Weatherford, TX
D: 10/11/1991, Dallas, TX
1944 Bos: KR 3-37 12.3; Scor 18, 0-1 FG. **Total:** KR 3-37 12.3; Scor 24, 0-1 FG.

		Receiving			
Year Team	**G**	**Rec**	**Yds**	**Avg**	**TD**
1940 ChiC	1	0	0	—	0
1942 Det-GB	6	1	25	25.0	1
1942 Det	1	0	0	—	0
1942 GB	5	1	25	25.0	1
1943 Bkn	9	7	80	11.4	0
1944 Bos	10	19	269	14.2	3
1945 Bos	9	8	117	14.6	0
NFL Total	35	35	491	14.0	4

JOHNNY RAPACZ Rapacz, John Joseph 6'4", 252 **C-LB**
Col: Western Michigan; Oklahoma *HS:* Kalamazoo Central [MI]
B: 4/25/1924, Rosedale, OH D: 1/2/1991, Midwest City, OK
Drafted: 1947 Round 3 Bos
AAFC **1948** ChiA: 10 G. **1949** ChiA: 12 G. **Total:** 22 G.

NFL **1950** NYG: 10 G. **1951** NYG: 12 G. **1952** NYG: 8 G. **1953** NYG: 12 G. **1954** NYG: 12 G. **Total:** 54 G.

HERB RAPP Rapp, Herbert Leo 6'0", 195 **C**
(Hub) *Col:* Xavier (Ohio) *HS:* Hamilton [OH] B: 7/21/1905, Hamilton, OH D: 7/21/1983, Los Altos Hills, CA
1930 SI: 8 G. **1931** SI: 11 G. **Total:** 19 G.

BOB RAPP Rapp, Joseph Robert 5'8", 159 **WB-BB-TB**
(Goldie) *Col:* No College B: 2/18/1898, Columbus, OH D: Columbus, OH
1922 Col: 7 G; Rush 1 TD; 6 Pt. **1923** Col: 10 G; Rush 2 TD; Rec **3** TD; Tot TD 5; 30 Pt. **1924** Col: 8 G; Rec **5** TD; 30 Pt. **1925** Col: 9 G; Rush 1 TD; Rec 1 TD; Tot TD 2; 12 Pt. **1926** Col: 6 G; Pass 1 TD. **1929** Buf: 3 G. **Total:** 43 G; Pass 1 TD; Rush 4 TD; Rec 9 TD; Tot TD 13; 78 Pt.

MANNY RAPP Rapp, Manuel Warren 6'0", 215 **TB-DB-FB-LB**
(Fat) *Col:* St. Louis *HS:* Herculaneum [MO] B: 9/17/1908, Pevely, MO
D: 5/17/1965, St. Louis, MO
1934 StL: 3 G; Pass 16-6 37.5%, 175 10.94 1 TD 6 Int; Rush 15-67 4.5. **1942** Cle: 1 G. **Total:** 4 G; Pass 16-6 37.5%, 175 10.94 1 TD 6 Int; Rush 15-67 4.5.

WALTER RASBY Rasby, Walter Herbert 6'3", 247 **TE**
Col: Wake Forest *HS:* Washington [NC] B: 9/7/1972, Washington, NC
1994 Pit: 2 G. **1995** Car: 9 G; Rec 5-47 9.4; Scor 1 2XP; 2 Pt. **1996** Car: 16 G. **1997** Car: 14 G; Rec 1-1 1.0; KR 3-32 10.7. **1998** Det: 16 G; Rec 15-119 7.9 1 TD; 6 Pt. **Total:** 57 G; Rec 21-167 8.0 1 TD; KR 3-32 10.7; Scor 1 2XP; 8 Pt.

AM RASCHER Rascher, Ambrose Henry 6'2", 210 **T-G**
Col: St. Viator; Indiana *HS:* Cedar Lake [IN] B: 11/3/1908, Cedar Lake, IN D: 3/6/1988
1932 Port: 7 G.

LOU RASH Rash, Louis Clyde 5'9", 180 **DB**
Col: Mississippi Valley State *HS:* East Side [Cleveland, MS]
B: 6/5/1960, Cleveland, MS
1984 Phi: 4 G. **1987** GB: 3 G. **Total:** 7 G.

AHMAD RASHAD Rashad, Ahmad 6'2", 205 **WR**
(AKA Bobby Moore) *Col:* Oregon *HS:* Mount Tahoma [Tacoma, WA]
B: 11/19/1949, Portland, OR *Drafted:* 1972 Round 1 StL
1972 StL: Rush 9-44 4.9; KR 20-437 21.9. **1974** Buf: KR 1-0; **2** Fum TD. **1980** Min: Rush 1-8 8.0. **Total:** Rush 10-52 5.2; KR 21-437 20.8; 2 Fum TD.

		Receiving					Tot
Year Team	**G**	**Rec**	**Yds**	**Avg**	**TD**	**Fum**	**TD**
1972 StL	14	29	500	17.2	3	5	3
1973 StL	13	30	409	13.6	3	0	3
1974 Buf	14	36	433	12.0	4	0	6
1976 Min	13	53	671	12.7	3	1	3
1977 Min	14	51	681	13.4	2	2	2
1978 Min	16	66	769	11.7	8	2	8
1979 Min	16	80	1156	14.5	9	2	9
1980 Min	16	69	1095	15.9	5	0	5
1981 Min	16	58	884	15.2	7	1	7
1982 Min	7	23	233	10.1	0	0	0
NFL Total	139	495	6831	13.8	44	13	46

KENYON RASHEED Rasheed, Kenyon A 5'10", 245 **RB**
Col: Oklahoma *HS:* Rockhurst [Kansas City, MO] B: 8/23/1970, Kansas City, MO
1993 NYG: Rec 1-3 3.0. **1994** NYG: Rec 10-97 9.7. **1995** NYJ: Rec 2-15 7.5. **Total:** Rec 13-115 8.8.

		Rushing				
Year Team	**G**	**Att**	**Yds**	**Avg**	**TD**	**Fum**
1993 NYG	5	9	42	4.7	1	0
1994 NYG	16	17	44	2.6	0	1
1995 NYJ	3	1	3	3.0	0	0
NFL Total	24	27	89	3.3	1	1

LEO RASKOWSKI Raskowski, Leo Thomas 6'3", 219 **T**
(Fat) *Col:* Ohio State *HS:* East [Cleveland, OH] B: 3/28/1906, Cleveland, OH Deceased
1932 SI: 11 G. **1933** Bkn-Pit: 6 G. Bkn: 3 G. Pit: 3 G. **1935** Phi: 2 G. **Total:** 19 G.

ROCKY RASLEY Rasley, Rocky 6'3", 250 **OG**
Col: Bakersfield Coll. CA (J.C.); Oregon State *HS:* South [Bakersfield, CA] B: 4/27/1947, Bakersfield, CA *Drafted:* 1969 Round 9 Det
1969 Det: 12 G. **1970** Det: 8 G. **1972** Det: 14 G. **1973** Det: 14 G. **1974** NO: 14 G. **1975** KC: 11 G. **1976** SF: 1 G. **Total:** 74 G.

RANDY RASMUSSEN Rasmussen, Randall Lee 6'2", 255 **OG**
Col: Nebraska-Kearney *HS:* Elba [NE] B: 5/10/1945, St. Paul, NE
Drafted: 1967 Round 12 NYJ
1967 NYJ: 14 G. **1968** NYJ: 14 G. **1969** NYJ: 13 G. **1970** NYJ: 13 G. **1971** NYJ: 14 G. **1972** NYJ: 14 G; **1** Fum TD; 6 Pt. **1973** NYJ: 14 G. **1974** NYJ: 14 G. **1975** NYJ: 14 G. **1976** NYJ: 14 G. **1977** NYJ: 14 G. **1978** NYJ: 16 G. **1979** NYJ: 16 G. **1980** NYJ: 8 G. **1981** NYJ: 15 G. **Total:** 207 G; 1 Fum TD; 6 Pt.

RANDY RASMUSSEN Rasmussen, Randy Robert 6'2", 253 **C-OG**
Col: Minnesota *HS:* Irondale [New Brighton, MN] B: 9/27/1960, Minneapolis, MN *Drafted:* 1984 Round 8 Pit
1984 Pit: 16 G. **1985** Pit: 11 G. **1986** Pit: 4 G. **1987** Min: 5 G. **1988** Min: 7 G. **Total:** 43 G.

WAYNE RASMUSSEN Rasmussen, Wayne Floyd 6'2", 175 **DB**
Col: South Dakota State *HS:* Howard [SD] B: 6/7/1942, Chicago, IL
Drafted: 1964 Round 9 Det
1964 Det: KR 1-20 20.0. **1971** Det: KR 1-0. **Total:** KR 2-20 10.0.

		Interceptions			
Year Team	**G**	**Int**	**Yds**	**TD**	**Fum**
1964 Det	11	0	0	0	0
1965 Det	14	5	122	2	0
1966 Det	14	3	14	0	0
1967 Det	10	0	0	0	1
1968 Det	14	0	0	0	0
1969 Det	14	0	0	0	0
1970 Det	14	2	21	0	0

1971 Det	14	4	31	0	0
1972 Det	7	2	1	0	0
NFL Total	112	16	189	2	1

NICK RASSAS Rassas, Nicholas Charles 6′0″, 190 **DB**
Col: Notre Dame *HS:* Loyola Acad. [Wilmette, IL] B: 1/13/1944, Baltimore, MD *Drafted:* 1966 Round 2 Atl
1966 Atl: 8 G; PR 4-10 2.5; KR 8-203 25.4; 1 Fum. **1967** Atl: 5 G; KR 2-51 25.5. **1968** Atl: 14 G; PR 4-10 2.5; KR 10-180 18.0; Int 1-18; 3 Fum. **Total:** 27 G; PR 8-20 2.5; KR 20-434 21.7; Int 1-18; 4 Fum.

ED RATE Rate, Edwin Schellhase 5′9″, 170 **BB**
(Speedy; Pete) *Col:* Purdue *HS:* McKinley [Canton, OH] B: 5/27/1899, Canton, OH D: 3/31/1990
1923 Mil: 1 G.

ROY RATEKIN Ratekin, Ralph Roy 5′10″, 180 **OE**
Col: Colorado State *HS:* Delta [CO] B: 9/24/1898, Surface Creek, CO D: 10/1984, Red Oak, IA
1921 Akr: 4 G.

BO RATHER Rather, David Elmer 6′1″, 184 **WR**
Col: Michigan *HS:* Sandusky [OH] B: 10/7/1950, Sandusky, OH *Drafted:* 1973 Round 4 Mia
1974 ChiB: Pass 1-0; Rush 2-10 5.0. **1975** ChiB: Rush 4-24 6.0; KR 1-6 6.0. **1976** ChiB: Rush 1-4 4.0. **1977** ChiB: Rush 2-8 4.0. **Total:** Pass 1-0; Rush 9-46 5.1; KR 1-6 6.0.

		Receiving				
Year Team	G	Rec	Yds	Avg	TD	Fum
1973 Mia	6	0	0	—	0	0
1974 ChiB	13	29	400	13.8	3	0
1975 ChiB	14	39	685	17.6	2	2
1976 ChiB	9	5	33	6.6	0	0
1977 ChiB	13	17	294	17.3	2	1
1978 ChiB-Mia	9	2	55	27.5	0	0
1978 ChiB	6	1	16	16.0	0	0
1978 Mia	3	1	39	39.0	0	0
NFL Total	64	92	1467	15.9	7	3

TOM RATHMAN Rathman, Thomas Dean 6′1″, 230 **RB**
Col: Nebraska *HS:* Grand Island [NE] B: 10/7/1962, Grand Island, NE *Drafted:* 1986 Round 3 SF
1986 SF: KR 3-66 22.0. **1987** SF: KR 2-37 18.5. **Total:** KR 5-103 20.6.

		Rushing				Receiving					Tot
Year Team	G	Att	Yds	Avg	TD	Rec	Yds	Avg	TD	Fum	TD
1986 SF	16	33	138	4.2	1	13	121	9.3	0	0	1
1987 SF	12	62	257	4.1	1	30	329	11.0	3	1	4
1988 SF	16	102	427	4.2	2	42	382	9.1	0	0	2
1989 SF	16	79	305	3.9	1	73	616	8.4	1	1	2
1990 SF	16	101	318	3.1	7	48	327	6.8	0	2	7
1991 SF	16	63	183	2.9	6	34	286	8.4	0	2	6
1992 SF	15	57	194	3.4	5	44	343	7.8	4	1	9
1993 SF	8	19	80	4.2	3	10	86	8.6	0	0	3
1994 LARd	16	28	118	4.2	0	26	194	7.5	0	0	0
NFL Total	131	544	2020	3.7	26	320	2684	8.4	8	7	34

JOE RATICA Ratica, Joseph H 6′0″, 205 **C-LB**
Col: St. Vincent *HS:* Centerville [PA] B: 8/4/1914, Dembo, PA D: 10/21/1942
1939 Bkn: 7 G.

BRIAN RATIGAN Ratigan, Brian Lee 6′4″, 241 **LB**
Col: Notre Dame *HS:* St. Albert [Council Bluffs, IA] B: 12/27/1970, Council Bluffs, IA
1994 Ind: 14 G.

RAY RATKOWSKI Ratkowski, Raymond James 6′0″, 195 **HB**
Col: Notre Dame *HS:* St. Francis Prep [Brooklyn, NY] B: 11/10/1939, New York, NY *Drafted:* 1961 Round 17 Bos
1961 Bos: 1 G; KR 1-17 17.0; 1 Fum.

DON RATLIFF Ratliff, Donald Eugene 6′5″, 250 **DE**
Col: Maryland *HS:* John Handley [Winchester, VA] B: 7/18/1950, Baltimore, MD
1975 Phi: 6 G.

GEORGE RATTERMAN Ratterman, George William 6′1″, 185 **QB**
(The Kid) *Col:* Notre Dame *HS:* Xavier [Cincinnati, OH] B: 11/12/1926, Cincinnati, OH
AAFC **1947** BufA: Scor 6, 0-1 XK. **Total:** Scor 48, 0-1 XK.

		Passing							
Year Team	G	Att	Comp	Comp%	Yds	YPA	TD	Int	Rating
1947 BufA	14	244	124	50.8	1840	7.54	22	20	71.8
1948 BufA	14	335	168	50.1	2577	7.69	16	22	64.5
1949 BufA	11	252	146	57.9	1777	7.05	14	13	76.8
AAFC Total	39	831	438	52.7	6194	7.45	52	55	70.3

	Rushing			
Year Team	Att	Yds	Avg	TD
1947 BufA	17	-49	-2.9	1
1948 BufA	12	-18	-1.5	3
1949 BufA	36	85	2.4	4
AAFC Total	65	18	0.3	8

NFL Statistics

		Passing							
Year Team	G	Att	Comp	Comp%	Yds	YPA	TD	Int	Rating
1950 NYY	12	294	140	47.6	2251	7.66	**22**	24	64.6
1951 NYY	6	67	31	46.3	340	5.07	2	6	34.4
1952 Cle	6	6	2	33.3	20	3.33	1	2	43.8
1953 Cle	9	41	23	56.1	301	7.34	4	0	111.9
1954 Cle	6	53	32	60.4	465	8.77	3	3	84.2
1955 Cle	10	47	32	68.1	504	10.72	6	3	116.5
1956 Cle	4	57	39	68.4	398	6.98	1	3	72.1
NFL Total	53	565	299	52.9	4279	7.57	39	41	70.5

	Rushing				
Year Team	Att	Yds	Avg	TD	Fum
1950 NYY	11	0	0.0	3	4
1951 NYY	3	9	3.0	0	1
1952 Cle	1	2	2.0	0	0
1953 Cle	2	6	3.0	0	0
1954 Cle	8	-13	-1.6	1	1
1955 Cle	6	8	1.3	1	2
1956 Cle	10	19	1.9	1	1
NFL Total	41	31	0.8	6	9

FRED RATTERMAN Ratterman, Lawrence Frederick 160 **HB**
Col: Michigan *HS:* St. Mary's [Cincinnati, OH]; Withrow HS [Cincinnati, OH] B: 8/9/1912, Cincinnati, OH D: 3/6/1988, Cincinnati, OH
1934 Cin: 1 G; Pass 3-0; Rush 2-1 0.5.

JOHNNY RAUCH Rauch, John 6′1″, 195 **QB-DB**
Col: Georgia *HS:* Yeadon [PA] B: 8/20/1927, Philadelphia, PA
1949 NYB: Rush 3-46 15.3 1 TD; Int 2-4. **1950** NYY: Rush 2-12 6.0. **1951** NYY-Phi: Rush 7-26 3.7. NYY: Rush 1-5 5.0. Phi: Rush 6-21 3.5. **Total:** Rush 12-84 7.0 1 TD; Int 2-4.

		Passing								
Year Team	G	Att	Comp	Comp%	Yds	YPA	TD	Int	Rating	Fum
1949 NYB	9	25	11	44.0	169	6.76	1	3	40.7	1
1950 NYY	8	51	29	56.9	502	9.84	6	2	113.4	0
1951 NYY-Phi	10	94	30	31.9	288	3.06	1	4	27.3	2
1951 NYY	6	82	25	30.5	237	2.89	1	3	28.8	0
1951 Phi	4	12	5	41.7	51	4.25	0	1	19.8	2
NFL Total	27	170	70	41.2	959	5.64	8	9	53.5	3

DICK RAUCH Rauch, Richard Harvie 5′9″, 178 **G-C**
Col: Penn State *HS:* Harrisburg Tech [PA]; Bethleham Prep [PA] B: 7/15/1895 D: 10/9/1970, Harrisburg, PA
1925 Pott: 6 G. **1928** NYY: 2 G. **1929** Bost: 1 G. **Total:** 9 G.

BOB RAVENSBERG Ravensberg, Robert Alexander 6′0″, 190 **OE-DB**
Col: Indiana *HS:* Bellevue [KY] B: 10/20/1925, Bellevue, KY *Drafted:* 1947 Round 15 ChiC
1948 ChiC: 11 G; Int 1-0. **1949** ChiC: 12 G; Rush 2-8 4.0; Rec 10-203 20.3 3 TD; 18 Pt; 1 Fum. **Total:** 23 G; Rush 2-8 4.0; Rec 10-203 20.3 3 TD; Int 1-0; 18 Pt; 1 Fum.

ERIC RAVOTTI Ravotti, Eric Allen 6′2″, 250 **LB**
Col: Penn State *HS:* Freeport [PA] B: 3/16/1971, Freeport, PA *Drafted:* 1994 Round 6 Pit
1994 Pit: 2 G. **1995** Pit: 6 G. **1996** Pit: 15 G; 2 Sac. **Total:** 23 G; 2 Sac.

BOB RAWLINGS Rawlings, Robert 1 **FB-TB-WB**
Col: No College Deceased
1922 Buf: 6 G.

BABY RAY Ray, Buford Garfield 6′6″, 249 **T**
Col: Vanderbilt *HS:* Nashville Central [TN] B: 9/30/1914, Una, TN D: 1/21/1986, Nashville, TN
1938 GB: 11 G. **1939** GB: 11 G. **1940** GB: 11 G. **1941** GB: 11 G. **1942** GB: 11 G. **1943** GB: 8 G. **1944** GB: 9 G. **1945** GB: 10 G. **1946** GB: 11 G; Int 1-2. **1947** GB: 11 G. **1948** GB: 12 G. **Total:** 116 G; Int 1-2.

DARROL RAY Ray, Darrol Anthony 6′1″, 200 **DB**
Col: Oklahoma *HS:* C.E. Ellison [Killeen, TX] B: 6/25/1958, San Francisco, CA *Drafted:* 1980 Round 2 NYJ
1980 NYJ: **1** Fum TD. **Total:** 1 Fum TD.

		Interceptions				Tot
Year Team	G	Int	Yds	TD	Fum	TD
1980 NYJ	16	6	132	1	1	2
1981 NYJ	16	7	227	2	1	2
1982 NYJ	9	3	91	0	1	0
1983 NYJ	16	3	77	0	0	0

1984 NYJ	15	2	54	0	0	0
NFL Total	72	21	581	3	3	4

DAVID RAY Ray, David Eugene Jr. 6'0", 195 **K**
Col: Alabama *HS:* Central [Phenix City, AL] B: 9/19/1944, Phenix City, AL *Drafted:* 1966 Round 16 Cle
1970 LARm: Rec 1-11 11.0. **Total:** Rec 1-11 11.0.

		Scoring						
Year Team	**G**	**Pts**	**FG**	**FGA**	**FG%**	**XK**	**XKA**	**XK%**
1969 LARm	1	0	0	0	—	0	0	—
1970 LARm	14	121	29	45	64.4	34	34	100.0
1971 LARm	14	91	18	29	62.1	37	37	100.0
1972 LARm	14	103	24	41	58.5	31	31	100.0
1973 LARm	14	**130**	**30**	**47**	63.8	40	42	95.2
1974 LARm	13	52	9	16	56.3	25	31	80.6
NFL Total	70	497	110	178	61.8	167	175	95.4

EDDIE RAY Ray, Edward Brown 6'2", 240 **RB-TE**
Col: Louisiana State *HS:* St. Aloysius [Vicksburg, MS] B: 4/5/1947, Vicksburg, MS *Drafted:* 1970 Round 4 Bos

		Rushing				Receiving					Tot
Year Team	**G**	**Att**	**Yds**	**Avg**	**TD**	**Rec**	**Yds**	**Avg**	**TD**	**Fum**	**TD**
1970 Bos	5	5	13	2.6	0	0	0	—	0	0	0
1971 SD	4	2	15	7.5	0	0	0	—	0	0	0
1972 Atl	7	8	34	4.3	0	1	14	14.0	0	1	0
1973 Atl	14	96	434	4.5	9	19	192	10.1	2	8	11
1974 Atl	11	46	139	3.0	0	10	43	4.3	0	7	0
1976 Buf	7	24	56	2.3	0	3	26	8.7	0	5	0
NFL Total	48	181	691	3.8	9	33	275	8.3	2	21	11

JOHN RAY Ray, John William 6'8", 350 **OT**
Col: West Virginia *HS:* George Washington [Charleston, WV] B: 4/26/1969, Charleston, WV
1993 Ind: 2 G.

RICKY RAY Ray, Ricky Lee 5'11", 180 **DB**
Col: Norfolk State *HS:* Waynesboro [VA] B: 5/30/1957, Waynesboro, VA *Drafted:* 1979 Round 6 NO
1979 NO: 6 G. **1980** NO: 13 G. **1981** NO-Mia: 12 G; Int 1-33. NO: 4 G; Int 1-33. Mia: 8 G. **Total:** 31 G; Int 1-33.

TERRY RAY Ray, Terry 6'1", 200 **DB**
Col: Oklahoma *HS:* C.E. Ellison [Killeen, TX] B: 10/12/1969, Belgium *Drafted:* 1992 Round 6 Atl
1992 Atl: 10 G. **1993** NE: 15 G; Int 1-0. **1994** NE: 16 G; Int 1-2. **1995** NE: 16 G; Int 1-21. **1996** NE: 16 G; Int 1-43; 1 Sac. **Total:** 73 G; Int 4-66; 1 Sac.

THOMAS RAYAM Rayam, Thomas Leon 6'6", 297 **DT**
Col: Alabama *HS:* Jones [Orlando, FL] B: 1/3/1968, Orlando, FL *Drafted:* 1990 Round 10 Was
1992 Cin: 10 G. **1993** Cin: 10 G. **Total:** 20 G.

ISRAEL RAYBON Raybon, Israel Deshon 6'6", 300 **DE**
Col: North Alabama *HS:* Robert E. Lee [Huntsville, AL] B: 2/5/1973, Huntsville, AL *Drafted:* 1996 Round 5 Pit
1996 Pit: 3 G; 1 Sac. **1997** Car: 9 G; 0.5 Sac. **Total:** 12 G; 1.5 Sac.

VAN RAYBURN Rayburn, Virgil Homer 6'1", 180 **OE-DE**
Col: Tennessee *HS:* Dyersburg [TN] B: 8/4/1910, Pulaski, TN D: 6/15/1991, Osceola, AR
1933 Bkn: 9 G; Rec 2-15 7.5.

JIMMY RAYE Raye, James Arthur 5'9", 165 **WR**
Col: San Diego State *HS:* Irvine [CA] B: 11/24/1968, Fayetteville, NC
1991 LARm: 2 G; Rec 1-19 19.0; KR 2-57 28.5.

JIMMY RAYE Raye, James Arthur 6'0", 185 **DB**
Col: Michigan State *HS:* E.E. Smith [Fayetteville, NC] B: 3/26/1946, Fayetteville, NC *Drafted:* 1968 Round 16 LARm
1969 Phi: 2 G.

FRED RAYHLE Rayhle, Frederick 6'5", 217 **TE**
Col: Tennessee-Chattanooga *HS:* Oak Hills [Cincinnati, OH] B: 4/9/1954, Covington, KY
1977 Sea: 2 G.

CORY RAYMER Raymer, Cory Gene 6'2", 289 **C**
Col: Wisconsin *HS:* Goodrich [Fond du Lac, WI] B: 3/3/1973, Fond du Lac, WI *Drafted:* 1995 Round 2 Was
1995 Was: 3 G. **1996** Was: 6 G. **1997** Was: 6 G. **1998** Was: 16 G. **Total:** 31 G.

COREY RAYMOND Raymond, Corey 5'11", 185 **DB**
Col: Louisiana State *HS:* New Iberia [LA] B: 7/28/1969, New Iberia, LA
1992 NYG: 1 Sac. **1995** Det: 2 Sac. **Total:** 3 Sac.

		Interceptions		
Year Team	**G**	**Int**	**Yds**	**TD**
1992 NYG	16	0	0	0
1993 NYG	16	2	11	0
1994 NYG	16	1	0	0
1995 Det	16	6	44	0
1996 Det	13	1	24	1
1997 Det	13	1	17	0
NFL Total	90	11	96	1

RICK RAZZANO Razzano, Richard Anthony 5'11", 227 **LB**
Col: Virginia Tech *HS:* New Castle [PA] B: 11/15/1955, New Castle, PA
1980 Cin: 14 G. **1981** Cin: 16 G; Int 1-11. **1982** Cin: 9 G. **1983** Cin: 16 G. **1984** Cin: 10 G. **Total:** 65 G; Int 1-11.

KEVIN REACH Reach, Kevin Thaddeus 6'3", 270 **OG-C**
Col: Utah *HS:* Stockbridge [GA] B: 10/24/1963, Atlanta, GA
1987 SF: 3 G.

JACK READ Read, Jack 1 **G-T**
Col: No College Deceased
1921 Akr: 3 G.

RUSS READER Reader, Russell Burton Jr. 6'0", 185 **DB**
Col: Michigan; Michigan State *HS:* Dearborn [MI] B: 6/26/1923, Ypsilanti, MI D: 8/11/1995, Lansing, MI *Drafted:* 1947 Round 19 ChiB
1947 ChiB: 2 G.

IKE READON Readon, Isaac 6'0", 273 **NT**
Col: Hampton *HS:* South Miami [Miami, FL] B: 5/16/1963, Miami, FL *Drafted:* 1986 Round 10 KC
1987 Mia: 3 G; 2 Sac.

FRANK REAGAN Reagan, Francis Xavier 5'11", 182 **DB-FB-QB-HB**
Col: Pennsylvania *HS:* Northeast Catholic [Philadelphia, PA] B: 7/28/1919, Philadelphia, PA D: 11/20/1972, Philadelphia, PA *Drafted:* 1941 Round 2 NYG
1941 NYG: Pass 6-1 16.7%, 16 2.67; KR 2-50 25.0. **1946** NYG: Pass 6-3 50.0%, 32 5.33; Rec 4-71 17.8; KR 2-77 38.5. **1947** NYG: Pass 25-12 48.0%, 191 7.64 1 TD 2 Int; KR 2-34 17.0. **Total:** Pass 37-16 43.2%, 239 6.46 1 TD 2 Int; Rec 4-71 17.8; KR 6-161 26.8.

		Rushing				Punt Returns			
Year Team	**G**	**Att**	**Yds**	**Avg**	**TD**	**Ret**	**Yds**	**Avg**	**TD**
1941 NYG	5	35	146	4.2	4	6	113	18.8	0
1946 NYG	6	62	246	4.0	2	5	48	9.6	0
1947 NYG	10	14	22	1.6	0	27	182	6.7	0
1948 NYG	11	0	0	—	0	0	0	—	0
1949 Phi	12	0	0	—	0	21	266	12.7	1
1950 Phi	12	3	55	18.3	0	6	38	6.3	0
1951 Phi	12	0	0	—	0	0	0	—	0
NFL Total	68	114	469	4.1	6	65	647	10.0	1

	Interceptions			Punting				Tot
Year Team	**Int**	**Yds**	**TD**	**Punts**	**Yds**	**Avg**	**Fum**	**TD**
1941 NYG	1	28	0	13	488	37.5	0	4
1946 NYG	0	0	0	20	857	42.9	5	2
1947 NYG	**10**	**203**	0	61	2613	42.8	6	0
1948 NYG	9	145	0	61	2331	38.2	0	0
1949 Phi	7	146	0	8	362	45.3	1	1
1950 Phi	4	132	1	54	2270	42.0	1	1
1951 Phi	4	60	0	10	367	36.7	0	0
NFL Total	35	714	1	227	9288	40.9	13	8

ED REAGEN Reagen, Edward J Jr. 1 **T**
Col: No College *HS:* Phillipsburg [NJ] B: 4/7/1900, Bethayres, PA D: 10/15/1983, Paoli, PA
1926 Bkn: 1 G.

CHUCK REAM Ream, Charles Daniel 6'2", 225 **T**
(Flash) *Col:* Ohio State *HS:* Navarre [OH] B: 12/12/1913, Youngstown, OH *Drafted:* 1938 Round 7 Cle
1938 Cle: 10 G.

TOMMY REAMON Reamon, Thomas Waverly 5'10", 192 **RB**
Col: Fort Scott CC KS; Missouri *HS:* George Washington Carver [Newport News, VA] B: 3/12/1952, Virgilinia, VA *Drafted:* 1974 Round 9 Pit
1976 KC: Rec 10-136 13.6 1 TD; PR 1-0; KR 19-424 22.3.

		Rushing					Tot
Year Team	**G**	**Att**	**Yds**	**Avg**	**TD**	**Fum**	**TD**
1976 KC	11	103	314	3.0	4	7	5

KERRY REARDON Reardon, Kerry Edward 5'11", 180 **DB**
Col: Iowa *HS:* Rockhurst [Kansas City, MO] B: 5/6/1949, Kansas City, MO *Drafted:* 1971 Round 6 KC
1971 KC: PR 3-5 1.7; KR 12-308 25.7. **1972** KC: PR 1-3 3.0; KR 2-35 17.5. **1973** KC: PR 2-9 4.5; KR 2-45 22.5. **1974** KC: PR 4-30 7.5. **1975** KC: PR 5-41 8.2. **1976** KC: PR 1-4 4.0. **Total:** PR 16-92 5.8; KR 16-388 24.3.

		Interceptions			
Year Team	**G**	**Int**	**Yds**	**TD**	**Fum**
1971 KC	6	0	0	0	0
1972 KC	7	0	0	0	0

1973 KC	12	2	17	0	0
1974 KC	11	4	0	0	1
1975 KC	8	3	40	0	0
1976 KC	14	5	26	0	0
NFL Total	58	14	83	0	1

GARY REASONS Reasons, Gary Phillip 6'4", 235 **LB**
Col: Northwestern State-Louisiana *HS:* Crowley [TX] B: 2/18/1962, Crowley, TX *Drafted:* 1984 Round 4 NYG
1984 NYG: 1 Sac. **1985** NYG: 0.5 Sac. **1987** NYG: 1 Sac. **1989** NYG: Rush 1-2 2.0; Scor **1** Saf; 1 Sac. **Total:** Rush 1-2 2.0; Scor 1 Saf; 3.5 Sac.

		Interceptions		
Year Team	**G**	**Int**	**Yds**	**TD**
1984 NYG	16	2	26	0
1985 NYG	16	1	10	0
1986 NYG	16	2	28	0
1987 NYG	10	0	0	0
1988 NYG	16	1	20	0
1989 NYG	16	1	40	0
1990 NYG	16	3	13	0
1991 NYG	16	0	0	0
1992 Cin	12	0	0	0
NFL Total	134	10	137	0

KEN REAVES Reaves, Kenneth Milton 6'3", 210 **DB**
Col: Norfolk State *HS:* Braddock [PA] B: 10/29/1944, Braddock, PA *Drafted:* 1966 Round 4 Atl
1966 Atl: PR 1-2 2.0; KR 4-85 21.3. **1974** NO-StL: KR 1-22 22.0. StL: KR 1-22 22.0. **1975** StL: KR 1-9 9.0. **Total:** PR 1-2 2.0; KR 6-116 19.3.

		Interceptions			
Year Team	**G**	**Int**	**Yds**	**TD**	**Fum**
1966 Atl	14	1	16	0	1
1967 Atl	14	7	153	0	0
1968 Atl	14	1	90	1	0
1969 Atl	14	3	14	0	0
1970 Atl	14	6	44	0	0
1971 Atl	14	6	43	0	0
1972 Atl	14	3	59	0	0
1973 Atl	14	2	20	0	1
1974 NO-StL	10	1	54	0	0
1974 NO	4	0	0	0	0
1974 StL	6	1	54	0	0
1975 StL	14	3	7	0	0
1976 StL	14	2	41	0	0
1977 StL	14	2	17	0	1
NFL Total	164	37	558	1	3

JOHN REAVES Reaves, Thomas Johnson 6'3", 210 **QB**
Col: Florida *HS:* T.R. Robinson [Tampa, FL] B: 3/2/1950, Anniston, AL *Drafted:* 1972 Round 1 Phi

		Passing							
Year Team	**G**	**Att**	**Comp**	**Comp%**	**Yds**	**YPA**	**TD**	**Int**	**Rating**
1972 Phi	11	224	108	48.2	1508	6.73	7	12	58.4
1973 Phi	1	19	5	26.3	17	0.89	0	1	17.7
1974 Phi	4	20	5	25.0	84	4.20	0	2	5.0
1975 Cin	7	51	25	49.0	297	5.82	2	3	55.8
1976 Cin	3	22	8	36.4	76	3.45	2	1	58.1
1977 Cin	9	59	24	40.7	383	6.49	0	5	27.7
1978 Cin	9	144	74	51.4	790	5.49	3	8	51.6
1981 Hou	5	61	31	50.8	379	6.21	2	2	67.6
1987 TB	2	16	6	37.5	83	5.19	1	0	75.8
NFL Total	51	616	286	46.4	3617	5.87	17	34	51.4

	Rushing				
Year Team	**Att**	**Yds**	**Avg**	**TD**	**Fum**
1972 Phi	18	109	6.1	1	5
1973 Phi	2	2	1.0	0	1
1974 Phi	1	8	8.0	0	0
1975 Cin	6	13	2.2	2	0
1977 Cin	5	0	0.0	0	5
1978 Cin	6	50	8.3	0	2
1981 Hou	6	13	2.2	0	2
1987 TB	0	0	—	0	1
NFL Total	44	195	4.4	3	16

WILLARD REAVES Reaves, Willard Sheldon 5'11", 200 **RB**
Col: Northern Arizona *HS:* Coconino [Flagstaff, AZ] B: 8/17/1959, Flagstaff, AZ
1989 Was-Mia: 3 G; Rush 1-(-1) -1.0; KR 6-84 14.0. Was: 1 G; Rush 1-(-1) -1.0. Mia: 2 G; KR 6-84 14.0. **Total:** 3 G; Rush 1-(-1) -1.0; KR 6-84 14.0.

DAVE REAVIS Reavis, David Craig 6'5", 257 **OT-OG**
Col: Arkansas *HS:* Hewitt [Trussville, AL]; Duncan HS [OK] B: 6/19/1950, Nashville, TN
1974 Pit: 14 G. **1975** Pit: 10 G. **1976** TB: 1 G. **1977** TB: 14 G. **1978** TB: 16 G. **1979** TB: 16 G. **1980** TB: 16 G. **1981** TB: 12 G. **1982** TB: 7 G. **1983** TB: 15 G. **Total:** 121 G.

RUSTY REBOWE Rebowe, Rusty 5'10", 213 **LB**
Col: Nicholls State *HS:* Destrehan [LA] B: 1/17/1956, Destrehan, LA
1978 NO: 1 G.

PAUL REBSAMEN Rebsamen, Paul Meyer 6'0", 188 **C**
Col: Centenary *HS:* Fort Smith [AR] B: 1905, Fort Smith, AR D: 3/13/1947, Hot Springs, AR
1927 Pott: 4 G.

DAVE RECHER Recher, David Eugene 6'1", 245 **C**
Col: Iowa *HS:* Niles Twp. [Skokie, IL] B: 12/30/1942, Chicago, IL
1965 Phi: 14 G. **1966** Phi: 10 G. **1967** Phi: 14 G. **1968** Phi: 8 G. **Total:** 46 G.

BERT RECHICHAR Rechichar, Albert Daniel 6'1", 209 **DB-LB-HB-OE**
Col: Tennessee *HS:* Rostraver [PA] B: 7/16/1930, Belle Vernon, PA *Drafted:* 1952 Round 1 Cle
1952 Cle: KR 4-70 17.5. **1953** Bal: Rec 3-151 50.3 2 TD; KR 1-28 28.0. **1954** Bal: KR 3-26 8.7. **1955** Bal: KR 9-235 26.1. **1956** Bal: Rush 1-(-1) -1.0; Punt 33-1276 38.7. **1957** Bal: KR 1-0; Punt 5-157 31.4. **1958** Bal: Rec 4-34 8.5 1 TD; KR 3-50 16.7. **1959** Bal: KR 2-39 19.5. **Total:** Rush 1-(-1) -1.0; Rec 7-185 26.4 3 TD; KR 23-448 19.5; Punt 38-1433 37.7.

		Punt Returns				Interceptions		
Year Team	**G**	**Ret**	**Yds**	**Avg**	**TD**	**Int**	**Yds**	**TD**
1952 Cle	12	14	58	4.1	0	6	79	0
1953 Bal	11	1	0	0.0	0	7	64	**1**
1954 Bal	12	6	22	3.7	0	2	27	0
1955 Bal	12	**30**	121	4.0	0	6	109	0
1956 Bal	10	5	10	2.0	0	4	63	0
1957 Bal	12	22	71	3.2	0	5	33	0
1958 Bal	12	7	29	4.1	0	0	0	0
1959 Bal	10	0	0	—	0	0	0	0
1960 Pit	6	0	0	—	0	1	10	0
1961 NYT	2	0	0	—	0	0	0	0
NFL Total	99	85	311	3.7	0	31	385	1

	Scoring								Tot
Year Team	**Pts**	**FG**	**FGA**	**FG%**	**XK**	**XKA**	**XK%**	**Fum**	**TD**
1953 Bal	33	5	13	38.5	0	0	—	0	3
1954 Bal	19	6	13	46.2	1	1	100.0	0	0
1955 Bal	55	10	**24**	41.7	25	26	96.2	0	0
1956 Bal	17	3	13	23.1	8	10	80.0	1	0
1957 Bal	31	3	13	23.1	22	25	88.0	1	0
1958 Bal	9	1	4	25.0	0	0	—	1	1
1959 Bal	0	0	1	0.0	0	0	—	0	0
1960 Pit	15	3	7	42.9	6	6	100.0	0	0
NFL Total	179	31	88	35.2	62	68	91.2	3	4

RAY RECKMACK Reckmack, Raymond V 6'0", 200 **BB-DB**
Col: Syracuse *HS:* Roxbury [Boston, MA]; Cheshire Acad. [CT] B: 8/26/1914 D: 5/1/1982, Emmaus, PA
1937 Bkn-Det: 2 G. Bkn: 1 G. Det: 1 G. **Total:** 2 G.

RON RECTOR Rector, Ronny S 6'0", 200 **RB**
Col: Northwestern *HS:* Barberton [OH] B: 5/29/1944, Akron, OH D: 12/4/1980, Barberton, OH *Drafted:* 1966 Round 9 GB
1966 Was-Atl: Rec 2-9 4.5; KR 3-65 21.7. Was: Rec 2-9 4.5; KR 3-65 21.7. **1967** Atl: Rec 4-13 3.3. **Total:** Rec 6-22 3.7; KR 3-65 21.7.

		Rushing				
Year Team	**G**	**Att**	**Yds**	**Avg**	**TD**	**Fum**
1966 Was-Atl	10	9	40	4.4	0	0
1966 Was	6	5	8	1.6	0	0
1966 Atl	4	4	32	8.0	0	0
1967 Atl	10	24	127	5.3	0	1
NFL Total	20	33	167	5.1	0	1

GLEN REDD Redd, Glen Herrscher 6'1", 229 **LB**
Col: Brigham Young *HS:* Ogden [UT] B: 6/17/1958, Ogden, UT *Drafted:* 1981 Round 6 NO
1981 NO: 16 G; Int 1-7. **1983** NO: 16 G. **1984** NO: 16 G. **1985** NO: 16 G; Int 1-25; 1 Sac. **1986** NO-Ind: 12 G. NO: 4 G. Ind: 8 G. **Total:** 76 G; Int 2-32; 1 Sac.

BARRY REDDEN Redden, Barry Dwayne 5'10", 210 **RB**
Col: Richmond *HS:* Sarasota [FL] B: 7/21/1960, Sarasota, FL *Drafted:* 1982 Round 1 LARm

		Rushing				Receiving			
Year Team	**G**	**Att**	**Yds**	**Avg**	**TD**	**Rec**	**Yds**	**Avg**	**TD**
1982 LARm	9	8	24	3.0	0	4	16	4.0	0
1983 LARm	15	75	372	5.0	2	4	30	7.5	0
1984 LARm	14	45	247	5.5	0	4	39	9.8	0
1985 LARm	14	87	380	4.4	0	16	162	10.1	0
1986 LARm	15	110	467	4.2	4	28	217	7.8	1
1987 SD	12	11	36	3.3	0	7	46	6.6	0
1988 SD	8	19	30	1.6	3	1	11	11.0	0
1989 Cle	16	40	180	4.5	1	6	34	5.7	0

1990 Cle	5	1	-1	-1.0	0	0	0	—	0
NFL Total	108	396	1735	4.4	10	70	555	7.9	1

	Kickoff Returns					Tot
Year Team	**Ret**	**Yds**	**Avg**	**TD**	**Fum**	**TD**
1982 LARm	22	502	22.8	0	2	0
1983 LARm	19	358	18.8	0	2	2
1984 LARm	23	530	23.0	0	0	0
1985 LARm	0	0	—	0	1	0
1986 LARm	0	0	—	0	1	5
1988 SD	0	0	—	0	0	3
1989 Cle	2	2	1.0	0	2	1
NFL Total	66	1392	21.1	0	8	11

REGGIE REDDING Redding, Reginald J 6'3", 298 **OT-OG**
Col: Laney Coll. CA (J.C.); Cal State-Fullerton *HS:* Forest Park [OH]
B: 9/22/1968, Cincinnati, OH *Drafted:* 1990 Round 5 Atl
1991 Atl: 13 G; 1 Fum. **1992** NE: 14 G. **Total:** 27 G; 1 Fum.

SHEEPY REDEEN Redeen, Clarence Elmer 185 **OE**
Col: No College *HS:* None B: 10/7/1891, Minneapolis, MN
D: 9/2/1971, Minneapolis, MN
1921 Min: 4 G.

CORN REDICK Redick, Cornelius 5'11", 185 **WR**
Col: Cal State-Fullerton *HS:* Pius X [Downey, CA] B: 1/7/1964, Los Angeles, CA *Drafted:* 1986 Round 7 Phi
1987 GB: 1 G; Rec 1-18 18.0.

RUEL REDINGER Redinger, Otis Ruel 5'10", 185 **WB-TB-BB**
(Pete) *Col:* Colgate; Penn State *HS:* Washington [PA] B: 12/31/1898
D: 9/26/1969, Valley City, OH
1925 Can: 7 G.

GUS REDMAN Redman, Augustus A 5'11", 170 **TB-WB-BB-FB**
Col: Norwich; Purdue *HS:* Lawrence [MA]; Hebron Acad. [ME]
B: 12/1896, Methuen, MA D: 7/19/1949, Lowell, MA
1921 Mun-Day: 7 G. Mun: 2 G. Day: 5 G. **1922** Day: 3 G; Rush 1 TD; 6 Pt.
1924 Day: 6 G; Pass 1 TD. **Total:** 16 G; Pass 1 TD; Rush 1 TD; 6 Pt.

RICK REDMAN Redman, Richard Clark 6'1", 220 **LB-P**
Col: Washington *HS:* Blanchett [Seattle, WA] B: 3/7/1943, Portland, OR *Drafted:* 1965 Round 5 SD
1965 SD: Int 1-11. **1966** SD: Rush 2-14 7.0; Int 2-7; **1** Fum TD. **1967** SD: Rush 1-(-13) -13.0; Int 2-26. **1969** SD: Int 1-3. **1971** SD: Int 1-0. **1972** SD: Int 1-14. **1973** SD: Int 1-1. **Total:** Rush 3-1 0.3; Int 9-62; 1 Fum TD.

		Punting			
Year Team	**G**	**Punts**	**Yds**	**Avg**	**Fum**
1965 SD	10	29	1145	39.5	0
1966 SD	14	66	2442	37.0	0
1967 SD	14	58	2147	37.0	1
1968 SD	1	0	0	—	0
1969 SD	14	0	0	—	0
1970 SD	14	0	0	—	0
1971 SD	12	0	0	—	0
1972 SD	10	0	0	—	0
1973 SD	11	0	0	—	0
NFL Total	100	153	5734	37.5	1

ANTHONY REDMON Redmon, Kendrick Anthony 6'5", 308 **OG**
Col: Auburn *HS:* T.R. Miller [Brewton, AL] B: 4/9/1971, Brewton, AL
Drafted: 1994 Round 5 Ariz
1994 Ariz: 6 G. **1995** Ariz: 12 G. **1996** Ariz: 16 G. **1997** Ariz: 16 G.
1998 Car: 10 G. **Total:** 60 G.

RUDY REDMOND Redmond, Rudolph Cruzette 6'1", 196 **DB**
Col: Riverside CC CA; U. of Pacific *HS:* Victor Valley [Victorville, CA]
B: 8/25/1947, Spokane, WA *Drafted:* 1969 Round 4 ChiB
1969 Atl: 14 G; Int 5-50. **1970** Atl: 14 G; Int 1-12. **1971** Atl: 8 G. **1972** Det: 14 G; Int 2-91 1 TD; 6 Pt. **Total:** 50 G; Int 8-153 1 TD; 6 Pt.

TOM REDMOND Redmond, Thomas Benjamin 6'5", 250 **DE-OG-OT**
Col: Vanderbilt *HS:* Russell [East Point, GA] B: 9/21/1937, Atlanta, GA
Drafted: 1959 Round 6 ChiC
1960 StL: 12 G. **1961** StL: 10 G. **1962** StL: 14 G. **1963** StL: 9 G; KR 1-0.
1964 StL: 14 G. **1965** StL: 1 G. **Total:** 60 G; KR 1-0.

JARVIS REDWINE Redwine, Jarvis John 5'10", 203 **RB**
Col: Oregon State; Nebraska *HS:* Inglewood [CA] B: 5/16/1957, Los Angeles, CA *Drafted:* 1981 Round 2 Min
1981 Min: Rush 5-20 4.0. **1982** Min: Rush 2-2 1.0. **1983** Min: Rush 10-48 4.8; Rec 1-4 4.0. **Total:** Rush 17-70 4.1; Rec 1-4 4.0.

		Kickoff Returns				
Year Team	**G**	**Ret**	**Yds**	**Avg**	**TD**	**Fum**
1981 Min	3	0	0	—	0	1
1982 Min	7	12	286	23.8	0	1
1983 Min	16	38	838	22.1	0	1
NFL Total	26	50	1124	22.5	0	3

LUCIEN REEBERG Reeberg, Lucien Henry 6'4", 285 **OT**
Col: Hampton B: 2/21/1942, Bronx, NY D: 1/31/1964, Detroit, MI
Drafted: 1963 Round 19 Det
1963 Det: 14 G.

BEASLEY REECE Reece, Beasley Young Jr. 6'1", 193 **DB**
Col: North Texas *HS:* Waco [TX] B: 3/18/1954, Waco, TX
Drafted: 1976 Round 9 Dal
1976 Dal: Rec 1-6 6.0. **1977** NYG: PR 1-(-5) -5.0. **1979** NYG: PR 1-8 8.0. **1980** NYG: PR 2-15 7.5. **1981** NYG: PR 1-0; 1 Fum TD. **1982** NYG: PR 1-8 8.0. **1983** NYG-TB: PR 9-26 2.9. NYG: PR 9-26 2.9.
Total: Rec 1-6 6.0; PR 15-52 3.5; 1 Fum TD.

		Kickoff Returns				Interceptions			
Year Team	**G**	**Ret**	**Yds**	**Avg**	**TD**	**Int**	**Yds**	**TD**	**Fum**
1976 Dal	10	0	0	—	0	0	0	0	1
1977 NYG	10	7	159	22.7	0	0	0	0	0
1978 NYG	8	2	40	20.0	0	0	0	0	0
1979 NYG	16	6	81	13.5	0	1	3	0	0
1980 NYG	16	24	471	19.6	0	3	24	0	1
1981 NYG	16	1	24	24.0	0	4	84	0	1
1982 NYG	9	0	0	—	0	1	0	0	0
1983 NYG-TB	16	0	0	—	0	8	103	0	1
1983 NYG	7	0	0	—	0	2	33	0	1
1983 TB	9	0	0	—	0	6	70	0	0
1984 TB	16	0	0	—	0	1	12	0	0
NFL Total	117	40	775	19.4	0	18	226	0	4

DANNY REECE Reece, Daniel Louis 5'11", 190 **DB**
Col: USC *HS:* Phineas Banning [Los Angeles, CA] B: 1/28/1955, Los Angeles, CA *Drafted:* 1976 Round 3 Cin
1976 TB: KR 1-30 30.0; **1** Fum TD. **1977** TB: Rec 2-59 29.5; KR 3-72 24.0. **1978** TB: Rec 1-25 25.0; KR 11-240 21.8; Int 1-13. **1979** TB: KR 1-13 13.0. **1980** TB: KR 7-128 18.3. **Total:** Rec 3-84 28.0; KR 23-483 21.0; Int 1-13; 1 Fum TD.

		Punt Returns				
Year Team	**G**	**Ret**	**Yds**	**Avg**	**TD**	**Fum**
1976 TB	11	20	143	7.2	0	2
1977 TB	14	31	274	8.8	0	0
1978 TB	15	44	393	8.9	0	2
1979 TB	16	**70**	431	6.2	0	2
1980 TB	16	**57**	313	5.5	0	2
NFL Total	72	222	1554	7.0	0	8

DON REECE Reece, Donald Miles 6'1", 230 **FB-LB-T**
Col: Missouri *HS:* Maysville [MO] B: 12/1/1919, Maysville, OH
D: 8/26/1992, Maysville, OH
AAFC **1946** MiaA: Rec 1-5 5.0; Int 1-17.

		Rushing			
Year Team	**G**	**Att**	**Yds**	**Avg**	**TD**
1946 MiaA	13	30	109	3.6	2

GEOFF REECE Reece, Geoffrey Robert 6'4", 247 **C**
Col: Washington State *HS:* Cascade [Everett, WA] B: 5/16/1952, Everett, WA *Drafted:* 1975 Round 3 LARm
1976 LARm: 14 G. **1977** Sea: 3 G. **Total:** 17 G.

JOHN REECE Reece, John L III 6'0", 203 **DB**
Col: Nebraska *HS:* Jersey Village [Houston, TX] B: 1/24/1971, Crowell, TX *Drafted:* 1994 Round 4 Ariz
1995 StL: 5 G.

TRAVIS REECE Reece, Travis 6'3", 252 **RB**
Col: Michigan State *HS:* Denby [Detroit, MI] B: 4/3/1975, Detroit, MI
1998 Det: 3 G.

ALVIN REED Reed, Alvin D 6'5", 235 **TE**
Col: Prairie View A&M *HS:* C. B. Dansby [Kilgore, TX] B: 8/1/1944, Kilgore, TX
1967 Hou: KR 1-0. **1969** Hou: KR 3-0. **1970** Hou: KR 1-0. **Total:** KR 5-0.

		Receiving				
Year Team	**G**	**Rec**	**Yds**	**Avg**	**TD**	**Fum**
1967 Hou	14	11	144	13.1	1	0
1968 Hou	14	46	747	16.2	5	2
1969 Hou	14	51	664	13.0	2	2
1970 Hou	13	47	604	12.9	2	1
1971 Hou	14	25	408	16.3	1	1
1972 Hou	14	19	251	13.2	0	2
1973 Was	5	9	124	13.8	0	0
1974 Was	14	4	36	9.0	1	0
1975 Was	14	2	5	2.5	2	0
NFL Total	116	214	2983	13.9	14	8

ANDRE REED Reed, Andre Darnell 6'2", 190 **WR**
Col: Kutztown *HS:* Louis E. Dieruff [Allentown, PA] B: 1/29/1964, Allentown, PA *Drafted:* 1985 Round 4 Buf
1985 Buf: PR 5-12 2.4. **1994** Buf: Pass 1-1 100.0%, 32 32.00.
Total: Pass 1-1 100.0%, 32 32.00; PR 5-12 2.4.

Year Team	G	Rushing Att	Yds	Avg	TD	Receiving Rec	Yds	Avg	TD	Fum	Tot TD
1985 Buf	16	3	-1	-0.3	1	48	637	13.3	4	2	5
1986 Buf	15	3	-8	-2.7	0	53	739	13.9	7	2	7
1987 Buf	12	1	1	1.0	0	57	752	13.2	5	0	5
1988 Buf	15	6	64	10.7	0	71	968	13.6	6	1	6
1989 Buf	16	2	31	15.5	0	88	1312	14.9	9	4	9
1990 Buf	16	3	23	7.7	0	71	945	13.3	8	1	8
1991 Buf	16	12	136	11.3	0	81	1113	13.7	10	1	10
1992 Buf	16	8	65	8.1	0	65	913	14.0	3	4	3
1993 Buf	15	9	21	2.3	0	52	854	16.4	6	3	6
1994 Buf	16	10	87	8.7	0	90	1303	14.5	8	3	8
1995 Buf	6	7	48	6.9	0	24	312	13.0	3	2	3
1996 Buf	16	8	22	2.8	0	66	1036	15.7	6	1	6
1997 Buf	15	3	11	3.7	0	60	880	14.7	5	1	5
1998 Buf	15	0	0	—	0	63	795	12.6	5	0	5
NFL Total	205	75	500	6.7	1	889	12559	14.1	85	25	86

TONY REED Reed, Anthony Wayne 5'11", 197 **RB**
Col: Antelope Valley Coll. CA (J.C.); Colorado *HS:* Chofu [Tokyo, Japan] B: 3/30/1955, San Francisco, CA *Drafted:* 1977 Round 2 KC
1977 KC: KR 11-239 21.7. **1981** Den: Pass 1-0, 1 Int. **Total:** Pass 1-0, 1 Int; KR 11-239 21.7.

Year Team	G	Rushing Att	Yds	Avg	TD	Receiving Rec	Yds	Avg	TD	Fum	Tot TD
1977 KC	14	126	505	4.0	2	12	125	10.4	0	7	2
1978 KC	16	206	1053	5.1	5	48	483	10.1	1	6	6
1979 KC	11	113	446	3.9	1	34	352	10.4	0	4	1
1980 KC	15	68	180	2.6	0	44	422	9.6	1	1	1
1981 Den	15	68	156	2.3	0	34	317	9.3	0	1	0
NFL Total	71	581	2340	4.0	8	172	1699	9.9	2	19	10

DOUG REED Reed, Douglass Nathaniel 6'3", 254 **DE-DT**
Col: San Diego Mesa Coll. CA (J.C.); San Diego State *HS:* Abraham Lincoln [San Diego, CA] B: 7/16/1960, San Diego, CA *Drafted:* 1983 Round 4 LARm
1984 LARm: 9 G; 1 Sac. **1985** LARm: 16 G; 7 Sac. **1986** LARm: 16 G; 6.5 Sac. **1987** LARm: 12 G; 2 Sac. **1988** LARm: 16 G; 1 Sac. **1989** LARm: 11 G; 3 Sac. **1990** LARm: 16 G; 2 Sac. **Total:** 96 G; 22.5 Sac.

FRANK REED Reed, Frank Rodney 5'11", 193 **DB**
Col: Washington *HS:* Oliver M. Hazen [Renton, WA] B: 5/13/1954, Seattle, WA *Drafted:* 1976 Round 8 Atl
1976 Atl: 14 G; Int 3-48. **1977** Atl: 14 G. **1978** Atl: 16 G; Int 1-38; Scor 1 Saf; 2 Pt. **1979** Atl: 11 G; Int 2-0. **1980** Atl: 16 G; 6 Pt. **Total:** 71 G; Int 6-86; Scor 1 Saf; 8 Pt.

BEN REED Reed, Henry Benton 6'5", 265 **DE**
Col: Mississippi *HS:* Woodlawn [Baton Rouge, LA] B: 5/7/1963, Baton Rouge, LA
1987 NE: 3 G.

HENRY REED Reed, Henry Elax Jr. 6'3", 230 **LB-DE**
Col: Iowa Central CC; Weber State *HS:* Northwestern [Detroit, MI] B: 1/15/1948, Detroit, MI *Drafted:* 1971 Round 10 NYG
1971 NYG: 14 G; Int 1-11. **1972** NYG: 14 G. **1973** NYG: 10 G; Int 1-36. **1974** NYG: 13 G. **Total:** 51 G; Int 2-47.

JAMES REED Reed, James Curtis 6'2", 230 **LB**
Col: California *HS:* Woodrow Wilson [San Francisco, CA] B: 10/10/1955, Corpus Christi, TX
1977 Phi: 4 G.

MAX REED Reed, John Maxwell 5'8", 185 **C**
Col: Bucknell *HS:* Lewisburg [PA] B: 5/15/1902, Lewisburg, PA D: 6/27/1973, Lewisburg, PA
1925 Buf: 9 G. **1926** Fra: 13 G; 6 Pt. **1927** Fra: 10 G. **1928** NYG: 3 G. **Total:** 35 G; 6 Pt.

JOE REED Reed, Joseph Butler 6'1", 195 **QB**
Col: Baylor; Mississippi State *HS:* Lorenzo [TX] B: 1/8/1948, Newport, RI *Drafted:* 1971 Round 11 SF

Year Team	G	Passing Att	Comp	Comp%	Yds	YPA	TD	Int	Rating
1972 SF	9	0	0	—	0	—	0	0	—
1973 SF	6	114	51	44.7	589	5.17	2	6	44.8
1974 SF	6	74	29	39.2	316	4.27	2	7	22.1
1975 Det	10	191	86	45.0	1181	6.18	9	10	59.3
1976 Det	13	62	32	51.6	425	6.85	3	3	69.6
1977 Det	3	40	13	32.5	150	3.75	0	4	5.2
1978 Det	1	0	0	—	0	—	0	0	—
1979 Det	2	32	14	43.8	164	5.13	2	1	67.7
NFL Total	50	513	225	43.9	2825	5.51	18	31	48.1

Year Team	Rushing Att	Yds	Avg	TD	Fum
1972 SF	4	22	5.5	0	1
1973 SF	15	85	5.7	0	3
1974 SF	16	107	6.7	0	2
1975 Det	34	193	5.7	1	3
1976 Det	11	63	5.7	1	1
1977 Det	1	3	3.0	0	1
1978 Det	1	0	0.0	0	1
1979 Det	2	11	5.5	0	0
NFL Total	84	484	5.8	2	12

ROCK REED Reed, Joseph T 5'8", 173 **HB**
Col: Louisiana State *HS:* Haynesville [LA] B: 8/7/1914, Bald Knob, AR
1937 ChiC: 8 G; Pass 1-0; Rush 10-33 3.3; Rec 2-26 13.0; 6 Pt.
1939 ChiC: 4 G; Pass 1-1 100.0%, 2 2.00; Rush 5-(-6) -1.2; Rec 3-67 22.3. **Total:** 12 G; Pass 2-1 50.0%, 2 1.00; Rush 15-27 1.8; Rec 5-93 18.6; 6 Pt.

LEO REED Reed, Leo Tautua 6'4", 240 **OT-OG**
Col: Colorado State *HS:* Kahuku [HI] B: 1/3/1940, Kahuku, HI
Drafted: 1961 Round 20 StL
1961 Hou-Den: 9 G. Hou: 5 G. Den: 4 G. **Total:** 9 G.

MARK REED Reed, Mark 6'3", 201 **QB**
Col: Morehead State *HS:* Moorhead [MN] B: 2/21/1959, Moorhead, MN *Drafted:* 1981 Round 8 NYG
1983 Bal: 1 G; Pass 10-6 60.0%, 34 3.40 1 Int; Rush 2-27 13.5.

MIKE REED Reed, Michael G Jr. 6'0", 215 **RB**
Col: Washington *HS:* American [Woodbridge, England]; Clover Park HS [Tacoma, WA] B: 1/6/1975, Woodbridge, England
1998 Phi: 4 G.

MICHAEL REED Reed, Michael Jerome 5'9", 180 **DB**
Col: Boston College *HS:* Salesianum [Wilmington, DE] B: 8/16/1972, Wilmington, DE *Drafted:* 1995 Round 7 Car
1995 Car: 1 G. **1996** Car: 2 G. **Total:** 3 G.

OSCAR REED Reed, Oscar Lee 6'0", 222 **RB**
Col: Colorado State *HS:* Booker T. Washington [Memphis, TN] B: 3/24/1944, Jonestown, MS *Drafted:* 1968 Round 7 Min
1969 Min: KR 1-38 38.0. **1970** Min: KR 5-71 14.2. **1973** Min: KR 2-29 14.5. **1975** Atl: KR 2-17 8.5. **Total:** KR 10-155 15.5.

Year Team	G	Rushing Att	Yds	Avg	TD	Receiving Rec	Yds	Avg	TD	Fum	Tot TD
1968 Min	7	2	6	3.0	0	0	0	—	0	0	0
1969 Min	14	83	393	4.7	1	7	59	8.4	2	1	3
1970 Min	12	42	132	3.1	1	6	53	8.8	0	2	1
1971 Min	13	50	182	3.6	1	15	138	9.2	0	1	1
1972 Min	14	151	639	4.2	2	30	205	6.8	0	7	2
1973 Min	12	100	401	4.0	3	19	122	6.4	0	2	3
1974 Min	7	62	215	3.5	0	15	99	6.6	1	0	1
1975 Atl	7	14	40	2.9	0	2	1	0.5	0	0	0
NFL Total	86	504	2008	4.0	8	94	677	7.2	3	13	11

BOBBY REED Reed, Robert 5'11", 187 **HB**
Col: Vallejo JC CA; U. of Pacific *HS:* Vallejo [CA] B: 11/14/1939, New Orleans, LA
1962 Min: Rec 4-37 9.3 1 TD; PR 9-82 9.1. **1963** Min: Rec 13-137 10.5; PR 9-91 10.1. **Total:** Rec 17-174 10.2 1 TD; PR 18-173 9.6.

Year Team	G	Rushing Att	Yds	Avg	TD	Kickoff Returns Ret	Yds	Avg	TD	Fum
1962 Min	6	6	22	3.7	0	13	337	25.9	0	3
1963 Min	10	21	88	4.2	0	13	367	28.2	0	1
NFL Total	16	27	110	4.1	0	26	704	27.1	0	4

ROBERT REED Reed, Robert Jr. 6'3", 250 **OG**
Col: Tennessee State *HS:* Marshall [TX] B: 2/23/1943, Longview, TX
Drafted: 1965 Round 16 Was
1965 Was: 8 G.

SMITH REED Reed, Smith Wayne 6'0", 215 **HB**
Col: Alcorn State *HS:* Temple [Vicksburg, MS] B: 6/25/1942, Vicksburg, MS *Drafted:* 1965 Round 19 NYG
1965 NYG: 10 G; Rush 19-70 3.7; Rec 6-42 7.0. **1966** NYG: 1 G. **Total:** 11 G; Rush 19-70 3.7; Rec 6-42 7.0.

TAFT REED Reed, Taft 6'2", 200 **DB**
Col: Jackson State *HS:* Rowan [Hattiesburg, MS] B: 6/12/1942, Hattiesburg, MS *Drafted:* 1966 Round 19 Phi
1967 Phi: 6 G; PR 1-0; KR 5-111 22.2; 2 Fum.

JAKE REED Reed, Willie 6'3", 216 **WR**
Col: Grambling State *HS:* Newton Co. [Covington, GA] B: 9/28/1967, Covington, GA *Drafted:* 1991 Round 3 Min
1992 Min: KR 1-1 1.0. **Total:** KR 1-1 1.0.

Year Team	G	Receiving Rec	Yds	Avg	TD	Fum
1991 Min	1	0	0	—	0	0
1992 Min	16	6	142	23.7	0	0
1993 Min	10	5	65	13.0	0	0
1994 Min	16	85	1175	13.8	4	3
1995 Min	16	72	1167	16.2	9	1

1996 Min	16	72	1320	18.3	7	0
1997 Min	16	68	1138	16.7	6	0
1998 Min	11	34	474	13.9	4	0
NFL Total	102	342	5481	16.0	30	4

DAN REEDER Reeder, Daniel Robert 5′11″, 235 **RB**
Col: Boston College; Delaware *HS:* Christiana [Newark, DE]
B: 3/18/1961, Shamokin, PA *Drafted:* 1985 Round 5 LARd
1986 Pit: 11 G; Rush 6-20 3.3; Rec 2-4 2.0; KR 4-52 13.0. **1987** Pit: 2 G; Rush 2-8 4.0. **Total:** 13 G; Rush 8-28 3.5; Rec 2-4 2.0; KR 4-52 13.0.

ALBERT REESE Reese, Albert 6′6″, 275 **DT**
Col: Grambling State *HS:* C.F. Vigor [Prichard, AL] B: 4/29/1973, Mobile, AL
1997 SF: 5 G.

ARCHIE REESE Reese, Archie Ronald Bernard 6′3″, 267 **DT**
Col: Clemson *HS:* Mayesville [SC] B: 2/4/1956, Mayesville, SC
Drafted: 1978 Round 5 SF
1978 SF: 16 G. **1979** SF: 16 G. **1980** SF: 16 G. **1981** SF: 16 G. **1982** LARd: 9 G; 1 Fum TD; 6 Pt; 1 Sac. **1983** LARd: 10 G; 4 Sac. **Total:** 83 G; 1 Fum TD; 6 Pt; 5 Sac.

BOOKER REESE Reese, Booker Ted 6′6″, 260 **DE**
Col: Bethune-Cookman *HS:* Jean Ribault [Jacksonville, FL]
B: 9/20/1959, Jacksonville, FL *Drafted:* 1982 Round 2 TB
1982 TB: 7 G; 1 Sac. **1983** TB: 16 G; Int 2-11; 1 Sac. **1984** TB-LARm: 10 G. TB: 1 G. LARm: 9 G. **1985** LARm: 2 G. **Total:** 35 G; Int 2-11; 2 Sac.

DAVE REESE Reese, David E 6′0″, 176 **OE**
(Doc) *Col:* Denison *HS:* Washington [Massillon, OH] B: 11/19/1892, Massillon, OH D: 6/26/1978, Dayton, OH
1920 Day: 9 G. **1921** Day: 9 G; Rec 1 TD; 6 Pt. **1922** Day: 8 G. **1923** Day: 8 G. **Total:** 34 G; Rec 1 TD; 6 Pt.

DON REESE Reese, Donald Francis 6′6″, 255 **DE-DT**
Col: Jackson State *HS:* C.F. Vigor [Prichard, AL] B: 9/4/1951, Mobile, AL *Drafted:* 1974 Round 1 Mia
1974 Mia: 13 G. **1975** Mia: 14 G; Scor **1** Saf; 2 Pt. **1976** Mia: 14 G. **1978** NO: 14 G. **1979** NO: 16 G. **1980** NO: 12 G; **1** Fum TD; 6 Pt. **1981** SD: 5 G. **Total:** 88 G; Scor 1 Saf; 1 Fum TD; 8 Pt.

GUY REESE Reese, Guy Price 6′5″, 258 **DT**
Col: Southern Methodist *HS:* South Oak Cliff [Dallas, TX]
B: 9/22/1939, Dallas, TX *Drafted:* 1962 Round 15 Dal
1962 Dal: 14 G. **1963** Dal: 14 G. **1964** Bal: 14 G. **1965** Bal: 13 G. **1966** Atl: 2 G. **Total:** 57 G.

HANK REESE Reese, Henry L 5′11″, 214 **C-LB-G**
Col: Temple B: 10/24/1909, Scranton, PA D: 8/3/1975, Ocean City, NJ
1933 NYG: 11 G. **1934** NYG: 13 G. **1935** Phi: 11 G; Scor 7, 1 FG, 4 XK. **1936** Phi: 10 G; Scor 9, 2 FG, 3 XK. **1937** Phi: 11 G; Scor 3, 3 XK. **1938** Phi: 11 G; Scor 13, 1-6 16.7% FG, 10-13 76.9% XK. **1939** Phi: 5 G; Scor 7, 2-4 50.0% FG, 1-1 100.0% XK. **Total:** 72 G; Scor 39, 6-10 30.0% FG, 21-14 78.6% XK.

IKE REESE Reese, Isaiah 6′2″, 222 **LB**
Col: Michigan State *HS:* Woodward [Cincinnati, OH]; Aiken HS [Cincinnati, OH] B: 10/16/1973, Jacksonville, NC *Drafted:* 1998 Round 5 Phi
1998 Phi: 16 G.

IZELL REESE Reese, Izell 6′2″, 196 **DB**
Col: Alabama-Birmingham *HS:* Northview [Dothan, AL] B: 5/7/1974, Dothan, AL *Drafted:* 1998 Round 6 Dal
1998 Dal: 16 G; Int 1-6.

JERRY REESE Reese, Jerry 6′2″, 267 **DE**
Col: Kentucky *HS:* Christian Co. [Hopkinsville, KY] B: 7/11/1964, Hopkinsville, KY *Drafted:* 1988 Round 5 Pit
1988 Pit: 15 G; 1 Sac.

JERRY REESE Reese, Jerry Louis 6′3″, 192 **DB**
Col: Oklahoma *HS:* St. Augustine [New Orleans, LA] B: 1/7/1955, New Orleans, LA
1979 KC: 7 G. **1980** KC: 14 G. **Total:** 21 G.

JERRY REESE Reese, Jerry Maurice 5′11″, 190 **WR**
Col: San Jose State *HS:* Mount Diablo [Concord, CA] B: 3/18/1973, Berkeley, CA
1997 Buf: 5 G; Rec 1-13 13.0.

KEN REESE Reese, Kenneth Earl 5′11″, 175 **HB-QB**
Col: Alabama *HS:* El Dorado [AR] B: 4/30/1921, El Dorado, AR
D: 3/1978, Tuscaloosa, AL *Drafted:* 1945 Round 29 Phi
1947 Det: 4 G; Rush 3-1 0.3; KR 2-40 20.0.

LLOYD REESE Reese, Lloyd George 6′2″, 240 **FB-LB**
(Bronco) *Col:* Tennessee *HS:* New Philadelphia [OH] B: 6/17/1920, New Philadelphia, OH D: 10/1981, New Philadelphia, OH
1946 ChiB: 3 G; Rush 18-84 4.7 2 TD; 12 Pt.

STEVE REESE Reese, Stephen 6′2″, 229 **LB**
Col: Louisville *HS:* William H. Spencer [Columbus, GA] B: 1/7/1952, Columbus, GA
1974 NYJ: 11 G. **1975** NYJ: 12 G. **1976** TB: 12 G. **Total:** 35 G.

LEW REEVE Reeve, Lew Parks 5′10″, 193 **T**
Col: Iowa State *HS:* Hampton [IA] B: 10/16/1890, Hampton, IA
D: 5/11/1960, Austin, MN
1920 ChiT: 3 G.

BRYAN REEVES Reeves, Bryan Keith 5′11″, 195 **WR**
Col: El Camino Coll. CA (J.C.); Arizona State; Nevada-Reno *HS:* Carson [CA] B: 7/10/1970, Los Angeles, CA
1994 Ariz: 14 G; Rush 1-(-1) -1.0; Rec 14-202 14.4 1 TD; PR 1-1 1.0; KR 3-83 27.7; 6 Pt; 1 Fum. **1995** Ariz: 5 G; Rec 6-62 10.3; PR 4-41 10.3. **Total:** 19 G; Rush 1-(-1) -1.0; Rec 20-264 13.2 1 TD; PR 5-42 8.4; KR 3-83 27.7; 6 Pt; 1 Fum.

CARL REEVES Reeves, Carl Don Mark 6′4″, 270 **DE**
Col: North Carolina State *HS:* Northern [Durham, NC] B: 12/17/1971, Durham, NC *Drafted:* 1995 Round 6 ChiB
1996 ChiB: 5 G. **1997** ChiB: 15 G; 0.5 Sac. **1998** ChiB: 11 G; 1 Sac. **Total:** 31 G; 1.5 Sac.

DAN REEVES Reeves, Daniel Edward 6′1″, 200 **RB**
Col: South Carolina *HS:* Americus [GA] B: 1/19/1944, Rome, GA
1965 Dal: Pass 2-1 50.0%, 11 5.50; KR 2-45 22.5. **1966** Dal: Pass 6-3 50.0%, 48 8.00; PR 2-(-1) -0.5; KR 3-56 18.7. **1967** Dal: Pass 7-4 57.1%, 195 27.86 2 TD 1 Int. **1968** Dal: Pass 4-2 50.0%, 43 10.75. **1969** Dal: Pass 3-1 33.3%, 35 11.67 1 Int. **1970** Dal: Pass 3-1 33.3%, 14 4.67 1 Int. **1971** Dal: Pass 5-2 40.0%, 24 4.80 1 Int; Scor 1, 1-1 100.0% XK. **1972** Dal: Pass 2-0. **Total:** Pass 32-14 43.8%, 370 11.56 2 TD 4 Int; PR 2-(-1) -0.5; KR 5-101 20.2; Scor 253, 1-1 100.0% XK.

		Rushing				Receiving					Tot
Year Team	**G**	**Att**	**Yds**	**Avg**	**TD**	**Rec**	**Yds**	**Avg**	**TD**	**Fum**	**TD**
1965 Dal	13	33	102	3.1	2	9	210	23.3	1	0	3
1966 Dal	14	175	757	4.3	8	41	557	13.6	8	6	**16**
1967 Dal	14	173	603	3.5	5	39	490	12.6	6	7	11
1968 Dal	4	40	178	4.5	4	7	84	12.0	1	0	5
1969 Dal	13	59	173	2.9	4	18	187	10.4	1	2	5
1970 Dal	14	35	84	2.4	2	12	140	11.7	0	4	2
1971 Dal	14	17	79	4.6	0	3	25	8.3	0	1	0
1972 Dal	14	3	14	4.7	0	0	0	—	0	0	0
NFL Total	100	535	1990	3.7	25	129	1693	13.1	17	20	42

KEN REEVES Reeves, Kenneth Wayne 6′5″, 270 **OT-OG**
Col: Texas A&M *HS:* Pittsburg [TX] B: 10/4/1961, Pittsburg, TX
Drafted: 1985 Round 6 Phi
1985 Phi: 15 G. **1986** Phi: 15 G. **1987** Phi: 10 G; KR 0-1. **1988** Phi: 15 G. **1989** Phi: 14 G. **1990** Cle: 16 G. **Total:** 85 G; KR 0-1.

MARION REEVES Reeves, Marion Francis 6′1″, 195 **DB**
Col: Clemson *HS:* Irmo [Columbia, SC] B: 2/23/1952, Lexington, SC
1974 Phi: 14 G; PR 3-12 4.0; 1 Fum.

ROY REEVES Reeves, Roy Don 6′0″, 182 **WR**
Col: South Carolina *HS:* Americus [GA] B: 2/8/1946, Americus, GA
Drafted: 1969 Round 14 Hou
1969 Buf: 2 G; PR 2-3 1.5.

WALTER REEVES Reeves, Walter James 6′4″, 264 **TE**
Col: Auburn *HS:* Eufaula [AL] B: 12/16/1965, Eufaula, AL
Drafted: 1989 Round 2 Pho
1989 Pho: KR 1-5 5.0. **Total:** KR 1-5 5.0.

		Receiving				
Year Team	**G**	**Rec**	**Yds**	**Avg**	**TD**	**Fum**
1989 Pho	16	1	5	5.0	0	0
1990 Pho	16	18	126	7.0	0	1
1991 Pho	15	8	45	5.6	0	1
1992 Pho	16	6	28	4.7	0	0
1993 Pho	16	9	67	7.4	1	0
1994 Cle	5	6	61	10.2	1	0
1995 Cle	5	6	12	2.0	1	0
1996 SD	9	1	3	3.0	0	0
NFL Total	98	55	347	6.3	3	2

JIM REGAN Regan, James 172 **BB**
Col: Still
1925 Col: 3 G.

SHAWN REGENT Regent, Shawn Michael 6′5″, 280 **C**
Col: Boston College *HS:* Cheektowaga [NY] B: 4/14/1963, Buffalo, NY
1987 LARd: 3 G.

JOHN REGER Reger, John George 6′0″, 225 **LB-OG**
Col: Pittsburgh *HS:* Linsly Mil. Inst. [Wheeling, WV] B: 9/11/1931, Wheeling, WV
1956 Pit: KR 1-13 13.0. **1957** Pit: 1 Fum TD. **Total:** KR 1-13 13.0; 1 Fum TD.

Year Team	G	Interceptions Int	Yds	TD	Fum	Tot TD
1955 Pit	12	2	11	0	0	0
1956 Pit	12	2	33	0	0	0
1957 Pit	12	0	0	0	0	1
1958 Pit	12	1	3	0	0	0
1959 Pit	12	0	0	0	0	0
1960 Pit	12	1	18	0	0	0
1961 Pit	14	1	17	0	1	0
1962 Pit	9	1	0	0	0	0
1963 Pit	9	1	16	0	0	0
1964 Was	14	3	37	1	0	1
1965 Was	12	0	0	0	0	0
1966 Was	14	3	27	0	0	1
NFL Total	144	15	162	1	1	3

TOM REGNER Regner, Thomas Eugene 6'1", 255 **OG**
Col: Notre Dame *HS:* St. Joseph's [Kenosha, WI] B: 4/19/1944, Kenosha, WI *Drafted:* 1967 Round 1 Hou
1967 Hou: 14 G. **1968** Hou: 14 G. **1969** Hou: 14 G. **1970** Hou: 3 G. **1971** Hou: 8 G. **1972** Hou: 14 G. **Total:** 67 G.

PETE REGNIER Regnier, Pierre Norman 170 **HB**
(Doc) *Col:* Minnesota *HS:* Marshall [Minneapolis, MN] B: 9/1896, Marshall, MN Deceased
1921 Min: 4 G. **1922** GB: 5 G. **Total:** 9 G.

MOSES REGULAR Regular, Moses Jr. 6'3", 255 **LB**
Col: Missouri Valley *HS:* Gateway [Kissimmee, FL] B: 10/30/1971, Miami, FL
1996 NYG: 3 G.

STEVE REHAGE Rehage, Stephen Michael 6'1", 190 **DB**
Col: Louisiana State *HS:* Alfred Bonnabel [Metairie, LA] B: 11/6/1963, New Orleans, LA
1987 NYG: 3 G; Int 1-14.

SCOTT REHBERG Rehberg, Scott Joseph 6'8", 330 **OT**
Col: Central Michigan *HS:* Kalamazoo Central [MI] B: 11/17/1973, Kalamazoo, MI *Drafted:* 1997 Round 7 NE
1997 NE: 6 G. **1998** NE: 2 G. **Total:** 8 G.

TOM REHDER Rehder, Thomas Bernard II 6'7", 280 **OT-OG**
Col: Notre Dame *HS:* St. Joseph [Santa Maria, CA] B: 1/27/1965, Sacramento, CA *Drafted:* 1988 Round 3 NE
1988 NE: 16 G. **1989** NE: 16 G; KR 1-14 14.0. **1990** NYG: 8 G. **Total:** 40 G; KR 1-14 14.0.

MILT REHNQUIST Rehnquist, Milton 6'0", 229 **G-C-T**
(Swede) *Col:* Bethany (KS) *HS:* Smoky Valley [Lindsborg, KS] B: 1897 Deceased
1924 KC: 3 G. **1925** KC-Cle: 11 G. KC: 7 G. Cle: 4 G. **1926** KC: 10 G. **1927** Cle: 13 G. **1928** Prov: 11 G. **1929** Prov: 8 G. **1930** Prov: 10 G. **1931** Prov-NYG: 10 G. Prov: 2 G. NYG: 8 G. **1932** Bos: 1 G. **Total:** 77 G.

FRANK REICH Reich, Frank Michael 6'4", 210 **QB**
Col: Maryland *HS:* Cedar Crest [Lebanon, PA] B: 12/4/1961, Freeport, NY *Drafted:* 1985 Round 3 Buf

Year Team	G	Passing Att	Comp	Comp%	Yds	YPA	TD	Int	Rating
1985 Buf	1	1	1	100.0	19	19.00	0	0	118.8
1986 Buf	3	19	9	47.4	104	5.47	0	2	24.8
1988 Buf	3	0	0	—	0	—	0	0	—
1989 Buf	7	87	53	60.9	701	8.06	7	2	103.7
1990 Buf	16	63	36	57.1	469	7.44	2	0	91.3
1991 Buf	16	41	27	65.9	305	7.44	6	2	107.2
1992 Buf	16	47	24	51.1	221	4.70	0	2	46.5
1993 Buf	15	26	16	61.5	153	5.88	2	0	103.5
1994 Buf	16	93	56	60.2	568	6.11	1	4	63.4
1995 Car	3	84	37	44.0	441	5.25	2	2	58.7
1996 NYJ	10	331	175	52.9	2205	6.66	15	16	68.9
1997 Det	6	30	11	36.7	121	4.03	0	2	21.7
1998 Det	6	110	63	57.3	768	6.98	5	4	78.9
NFL Total	118	932	508	54.5	6075	6.52	40	36	72.9

Year Team	Rushing Att	Yds	Avg	TD	Fum
1986 Buf	1	0	0.0	0	1
1988 Buf	3	-3	-1.0	0	0
1989 Buf	9	30	3.3	0	2
1990 Buf	15	24	1.6	0	1
1991 Buf	13	6	0.5	0	0
1992 Buf	9	-9	-1.0	0	3
1993 Buf	6	-6	-1.0	0	0
1994 Buf	6	3	0.5	0	1
1995 Car	1	3	3.0	0	3
1996 NYJ	18	31	1.7	0	9
1997 Det	4	-4	-1.0	0	0
1998 Det	6	3	0.5	0	2
NFL Total	91	78	0.9	0	22

BILL REICHARDT Reichardt, William John 5'11", 210 **FB**
(The Bull) *Col:* Iowa *HS:* Iowa City [IA] B: 6/24/1930, Iowa City, IA *Drafted:* 1952 Round 7 GB
1952 GB: Rec 5-18 3.6; KR 1-19 19.0; Scor 26, 5-20 25.0% FG, 5-5 100.0% XK.

Year Team	G	Rushing Att	Yds	Avg	TD	Fum
1952 GB	12	39	121	3.1	1	1

LOU REICHEL Reichel, Louis John 5'11", 180 **C**
Col: Butler *HS:* Emmerich Manual Training [Indianapolis, IN] B: 1902
1926 Col: 7 G; Scor 2, 2 XK.

MIKE REICHENBACH Reichenbach, Jon Michael 6'2", 235 **LB**
Col: East Stroudsburg *HS:* Liberty [Bethlehem, PA] B: 9/14/1961, Fort Meade, MD
1984 Phi: 12 G. **1985** Phi: 16 G; Int 1-10. **1986** Phi: 16 G. **1987** Phi: 11 G; 1 Sac. **1988** Phi: 16 G; 1 Sac. **1989** Phi: 16 G; Rush 1-30 30.0. **1990** Mia: 16 G. **1991** Mia: 16 G; Int 1-2. **Total:** 119 G; Rush 1-30 30.0; Int 2-12; 2 Sac.

DICK REICHLE Reichle, Richard Wendell 6'0", 190 **OE**
Col: Illinois *HS:* Lincoln [IL] B: 11/23/1896, Lincoln, IL D: 6/13/1967, Richmond Heights, MO
1923 Mil: 6 G.

CHUCK REICHOW Reichow, Charles J 5'9", 183 **FB-TB-BB**
Col: St. Thomas *HS:* Farmington [MN] B: 3/19/1901, St. Paul, MN D: 3/29/1993, Peoria, AZ
1925 Mil: 2 G. **1926** Rac: 5 G. **Total:** 7 G.

JERRY REICHOW Reichow, Garet Neal 6'2", 217 **OE-QB**
Col: Iowa *HS:* Decorah [IA] B: 5/19/1934, Decorah, IA *Drafted:* 1956 Round 4 Det
1956 Det: Pass 6-3 50.0%, 19 3.17 1 Int; Rush 1-1 1.0; KR 1-9 9.0. **1957** Det: Pass 2-0; Rush 2-9 4.5. **1959** Det: Pass 27-9 33.3%, 168 6.22 2 Int; Rush 13-98 7.5. **1960** Phi: KR 4-28 7.0. **1961** Min: Pass 3-0, 1 Int; Rush 3-9 3.0. **1963** Min: Rush 1-(-12) -12.0. **Total:** Pass 38-12 31.6%, 187 4.92 4 Int; Rush 20-105 5.3; KR 5-37 7.4.

Year Team	G	Receiving Rec	Yds	Avg	TD	Fum
1956 Det	8	4	63	15.8	1	0
1957 Det	12	17	215	12.6	3	0
1959 Det	9	7	118	16.9	1	0
1960 Phi	12	0	0	—	0	0
1961 Min	14	50	859	17.2	11	0
1962 Min	12	39	561	14.4	3	1
1963 Min	14	35	479	13.7	3	0
1964 Min	14	20	284	14.2	2	1
NFL Total	95	172	2579	15.0	24	2

ALAN REID Reid, Alan DeWitt 5'8", 190 **RB**
Col: Pierce Coll. CA (J.C.); Texas Christian; Minnesota *HS:* El Paso [TX] B: 9/6/1960, Wurzburg, Germany
1987 Phi: 1 G; KR 4-58 14.5.

ANDY REID Reid, Andrew Barton 6'0", 194 **RB**
Col: Georgia *HS:* Robert A. Taft [Cincinnati, OH] B: 2/26/1954, Hamilton, OH *Drafted:* 1976 Round 13 Sea
1976 Buf: 1 G.

BREEZY REID Reid, Floyd Jr. 5'10", 187 **HB**
Col: Georgia *HS:* Hamilton [OH] B: 9/14/1927, Bridgeton, NJ D: 3/15/1994, Cincinnati, OH *Drafted:* 1950 Round 9 ChiB
1951 GB: Pass 1-0. **1953** GB: KR 4-82 20.5. **1955** GB: KR 2-21 10.5. **1956** GB: PR 1-0. **Total:** Pass 1-0; PR 1-0; KR 6-103 17.2.

Year Team	G	Rushing Att	Yds	Avg	TD	Receiving Rec	Yds	Avg	TD	Fum	Tot TD
1950 GB	11	87	394	4.5	1	11	120	10.9	2	3	3
1951 GB	12	23	73	3.2	0	9	115	12.8	0	1	0
1952 GB	12	58	156	2.7	2	12	250	20.8	2	1	4
1953 GB	12	95	492	5.2	3	10	100	10.0	0	5	3
1954 GB	12	99	507	5.1	5	14	129	9.2	0	0	5
1955 GB	12	83	303	3.7	2	13	138	10.6	1	4	3
1956 GB	7	14	39	2.8	0	3	16	5.3	0	1	0
NFL Total	78	459	1964	4.3	13	72	868	12.1	5	15	18

JIM REID Reid, James Varrett 6'6", 306 **OT-OG**
Col: Virginia *HS:* Hampton Road Acad. [Newport News, VA] B: 2/13/1971, Newport News, VA *Drafted:* 1994 Round 5 Hou
1995 Hou: 6 G.

JOE REID Reid, Joseph Edmondson 6'3", 225 **LB-C-DG**
(Hollywood) *Col:* Louisiana State *HS:* Meridian [MS] B: 3/18/1929, Meridian, MS *Drafted:* 1951 Round 13 LARm
1951 LARm: 11 G. **1952** Dal: 11 G; KR 1-17 17.0; Int 1-0. **Total:** 22 G; KR 1-17 17.0; Int 1-0.

MIKE REID Reid, Michael Barry 6'3", 255 **DT**
Col: Penn State *HS:* Altoona [PA] B: 5/24/1947, Altoona, PA
Drafted: 1970 Round 1 Cin
1970 Cin: 9 G. **1971** Cin: 14 G. **1972** Cin: 14 G. **1973** Cin: 13 G. **1974** Cin: 14 G. **Total:** 64 G.

MICHAEL REID Reid, Michael Edward 6'2", 226 **LB**
Col: Wisconsin *HS:* Dougherty [Albany, GA] B: 6/25/1964, Albany, GA
Drafted: 1987 Round 7 Atl
1987 Atl: 11 G. **1988** Atl: 16 G. **1989** Atl: 16 G; 1 Sac. **1990** Atl: 6 G; PR 1-0; 1 Fum; 3 Sac. **1991** Atl: 2 G. **1992** Atl: 16 G. **Total:** 67 G; PR 1-0; 1 Fum; 4 Sac.

MIKE REID Reid, Michael Fitzgerald 6'1", 218 **DB**
Col: North Carolina State *HS:* Gettys D. Broome [Spartanburg, SC]
B: 11/24/1970, Spartanburg, SC *Drafted:* 1993 Round 3 Phi
1993 Phi: 9 G. **1994** Phi: 3 G. **Total:** 12 G.

SPENCER REID Reid, Spencer Eldon Kare 6'1", 247 **LB**
Col: Brigham Young *HS:* Leone [American Samoa] B: 2/8/1976, Pago Pago, American Samoa
1998 Car: 16 G.

BILL REID Reid, William John 6'1", 242 **C**
Col: Long Beach City Coll. CA (J.C.); Stanford *HS:* St. John Bosco [Bellflower, CA] B: 5/2/1952, Long Beach, CA
1975 SF: 13 G.

BOB REIFSNYDER Reifsnyder, Robert Harland 6'2", 250 **DE**
Col: Navy *HS:* Baldwin [NY] B: 6/18/1937, Brooklyn, NY
Drafted: 1959 Round 4 LARm
1960 NYT: 14 G; KR 1-16 16.0. **1961** NYT: 2 G. **Total:** 16 G; KR 1-16 16.0.

GEORGE REIHNER Reihner, George Arthur 6'4", 263 **OG**
Col: Penn State *HS:* Washington [PA] B: 4/27/1955, Pittsburgh, PA
Drafted: 1977 Round 2 Hou
1977 Hou: 13 G. **1978** Hou: 9 G. **1979** Hou: 2 G. **1982** Hou: 3 G. **Total:** 27 G.

MIKE REILLY Reilly, Charles Michael 6'3", 235 **LB**
Col: Iowa *HS:* Dubuque [IA] B: 3/27/1942, Dubuque, IA
Drafted: 1964 Round 4 ChiB
1964 ChiB: 8 G. **1965** ChiB: 14 G. **1966** ChiB: 14 G. **1967** ChiB: 14 G. **1968** ChiB: 14 G. **1969** Min: 10 G; 6 Pt. **Total:** 74 G; 6 Pt.

DAMEON REILLY Reilly, Dameon Elliott 5'11", 180 **WR**
Col: Nassau CC NY; Rhode Island *HS:* Aviation [Queens, NY]
B: 5/10/1963, Bronx, NY
1987 Mia: 3 G; Rec 5-70 14.0.

JIM REILLY Reilly, James Christopher 6'2", 260 **OG**
Col: Notre Dame *HS:* Hackley School [Tarrytown, NY] B: 2/8/1948, Yonkers, NY D: 8/10/1994, Greenburgh, NY *Drafted:* 1970 Round 3 Buf
1970 Buf: 13 G. **1971** Buf: 14 G. **Total:** 27 G.

KEVIN REILLY Reilly, Kevin Patrick 6'2", 220 **LB**
Col: Villanova *HS:* Salesianum [Wilmington, DE] B: 4/10/1951, Wilmington, DE *Drafted:* 1973 Round 7 Mia
1973 Phi: 7 G. **1974** Phi: 14 G. **1975** NE: 4 G; Int 1-54. **Total:** 25 G; Int 1-54.

MIKE REILLY Reilly, Michael Dennis 6'4", 217 **LB**
Col: Oklahoma *HS:* Christopher Columbus [Miami, FL] B: 2/14/1959, Miami, FL *Drafted:* 1982 Round 8 LARm
1982 LARm: 9 G.

BRUCE REIMERS Reimers, Bruce Michael 6'7", 285 **OT-OG**
Col: Iowa State *HS:* Humboldt [IA] B: 9/28/1960, Algona, IA
Drafted: 1984 Round 8 Cin
1984 Cin: 15 G. **1985** Cin: 14 G. **1986** Cin: 16 G. **1987** Cin: 10 G. **1988** Cin: 16 G. **1989** Cin: 15 G. **1990** Cin: 12 G. **1991** Cin: 10 G. **1992** TB: 16 G. **1993** TB: 11 G. **Total:** 135 G.

MIKE REINFELDT Reinfeldt, Michael Ray 6'2", 192 **DB**
Col: Wis.-Milwaukee *HS:* Baraboo [WI] B: 5/6/1953, Baraboo, WI
1982 Hou: 1 Fum TD. **Total:** 1 Fum TD.

		Interceptions		
Year Team	**G**	**Int**	**Yds**	**TD**
1976 Oak-Hou	13	1	19	0
1976 Oak	2	0	0	0
1976 Hou	11	1	19	0
1977 Hou	14	5	78	0
1978 Hou	16	1	0	0
1979 Hou	16	**12**	**205**	0
1980 Hou	16	4	36	0
1981 Hou	16	2	18	0
1982 Hou	9	0	0	0
1983 Hou	4	1	19	0
NFL Total	104	26	375	0

BOB REINHARD Reinhard, Robert Richard 6'4", 234 **DT-FB-OT**
Col: California *HS:* Glendale [CA] B: 10/17/1920, Los Angeles, CA
D: 8/2/1996, Salem, OR *Drafted:* 1942 Round 5 ChiC
AAFC **1946** LA-A: Pass 1-1 100.0%, 7 7.00. **1947** LA-A: Pass 4-2 50.0%, 21 5.25; Rec 3-34 11.3 1 TD; KR 3-42 14.0; Int 1-0. **1948** LA-A: Rec 4-54 13.5; PR 1-23 23.0; KR 3-51 17.0. **1949** LA-A: Rec 1-2 2.0.
Total: Pass 5-3 60.0%, 28 5.60; Rec 8-90 11.3 1 TD; PR 1-23 23.0; KR 6-93 15.5; Int 1-0.

		Rushing				Punting			Tot
Year Team	**G**	**Att**	**Yds**	**Avg**	**TD**	**Punts**	**Yds**	**Avg**	**TD**
1946 LA-A	14	1	-30	-30.0	0	44	1996	45.4	1
1947 LA-A	14	41	150	3.7	0	28	1279	45.7	1
1948 LA-A	14	1	21	21.0	0	6	204	34.0	0
1949 LA-A	12	0	0	—	0	0	0	—	0
AAFC Total	54	43	141	3.3	0	78	3479	44.6	2

NFL **1950** LARm: 12 G; Rec 1-11 11.0 1 TD; 6 Pt.

BILL REINHARD Reinhard, William Carl 5'10", 168 **DB-TB-HB-QB**
Col: California *HS:* Glendale [CA] B: 5/17/1922, Los Angeles, CA
AAFC **1947** LA-A: 8 G; Pass 2-0; Rush 1-2 2.0 1 TD; PR 2-22 11.0; Int 1-7; 6 Pt. **1948** LA-A: 14 G; Pass 5-0; Rush 6-31 5.2; Rec 5-48 9.6; PR 16-276 17.3 1 TD; KR 2-41 20.5; Int 4-52 1 TD; Tot TD 2; 12 Pt.
Total: 22 G; Pass 7-0; Rush 7-33 4.7 1 TD; Rec 5-48 9.6; PR 18-298 16.6 1 TD; KR 2-41 20.5; Int 5-59 1 TD; Tot TD 3; 18 Pt.

JEFF REINKE Reinke, Jeffrey Jay 6'4", 262 **DE**
Col: Mankato State *HS:* Sacred Heart [MN] B: 9/12/1962, Granite Falls, MN *Drafted:* 1986 Round 10 LARd
1987 Cin: 1 G.

EARL REISER Reiser, Earl 160 **WB**
Col: No College *HS:* Male [Louisville, KY] B: 1899 Deceased
1923 Lou: 2 G.

BILL REISSIG Reissig, William George 6'0", 195 **BB-LB-DE**
Col: Fort Hays State *HS:* Bunker Hill [KS] B: 11/2/1915, Bunker Hill, KS D: 7/8/1996, St. John, KS
1938 Bkn: 11 G; Scor 6, 2-2 100.0% FG. **1939** Bkn: 11 G; Scor 3, 1-1 100.0% FG, 0-1 XK. **Total:** 22 G; Scor 9, 3-3 100.0% FG, 0-1 XK.

ALBIE REISZ Reisz, Albert Harry 5'10", 174 **TB-DB-QB**
Col: Southeastern Louisiana *HS:* Lorain [OH] B: 11/29/1917, Lorain, OH D: 5/1/1985, New Orleans, LA
AAFC **1947** BufA: Rush 2-32 16.0.

		Punting		
Year Team	**G**	**Punts**	**Yds**	**Avg**
1947 BufA	13	57	2111	37.0

NFL **1944** Cle: PR 5-68 13.6; KR 12-285 23.8; Int 3-72; Punt 24-959 40.0. **1945** Cle: Rec 1-11 11.0; PR 8-78 9.8; Int 2-55; Punt 7-258 36.9. **Total:** Rec 1-11 11.0; PR 13-146 11.2; KR 12-285 23.8; Int 5-127; Punt 31-1217 39.3.

		Passing							
Year Team	**G**	**Att**	**Comp**	**Comp%**	**Yds**	**YPA**	**TD**	**Int**	**Rating**
1944 Cle	10	113	49	43.4	777	6.88	8	10	53.6
1945 Cle	10	21	8	38.1	146	6.95	2	3	55.0
1946 LARm	2	0	0	—	0	—	0	0	—
NFL Total	22	134	57	42.5	923	6.89	10	13	51.5

	Rushing				
Year Team	**Att**	**Yds**	**Avg**	**TD**	**Fum**
1944 Cle	69	134	1.9	2	0
1945 Cle	12	-2	-0.2	0	3
NFL Total	81	132	1.6	2	3

PECK REITER Reiter, Herbert Gustave 5'9", 185 **G-E**
Col: Miami (Ohio); Marietta *HS:* Steele [Dayton, OH] B: 2/15/1899, Dayton, OH D: 5/15/1968, Los Angeles, CA
1926 Day: 6 G. **1927** Day: 2 G. **Total:** 8 G.

JOHNNY REMBERT Rembert, John Lee 6'3", 234 **LB**
Col: Cowley Co. CC KS; Clemson *HS:* DeSoto [Arcadia, FL]
B: 1/19/1961, Hollandale, MS *Drafted:* 1983 Round 4 NE
1983 NE: 15 G; 2 Sac. **1984** NE: 7 G; 0.5 Sac. **1985** NE: 16 G; **1** Fum TD; 6 Pt. **1986** NE: 16 G; KR 3-27 9.0; Int 1-37; **1** Fum TD; 6 Pt; 4 Sac. **1987** NE: 11 G; Int 1-1; 2 Sac. **1988** NE: 16 G; Int 2-10; 3 Sac. **1989** NE: 16 G; Int 1-0; 2.5 Sac. **1990** NE: 5 G; Int 2-22; 1 Sac. **1991** NE: 12 G. **1992** NE: 12 G; 1 Sac. **Total:** 126 G; KR 3-27 9.0; Int 7-70; 2 Fum TD; 12 Pt; 16 Sac.

REGGIE REMBERT Rembert, Reginald Bernard 6'5", 200 **WR**
Col: Independence CC KS; West Virginia *HS:* Okeechobee [FL]
B: 12/25/1966, Okeechobee, FL *Drafted:* 1990 Round 2 NYJ

		Receiving			
Year Team	**G**	**Rec**	**Yds**	**Avg**	**TD**
1991 Cin	16	9	117	13.0	1

1992 Cin	9	19	219	11.5	0
1993 Cin	3	8	101	12.6	0
NFL Total	28	36	437	12.1	1

BILL REMINGTON Remington, Joseph William 6'1", 185 **C-LB**
Col: Washington State *HS:* South Bend [WA] B: 11/2/1920
AAFC **1946** SF-A: 9 G.

DENNIS REMMERT Remmert, Dennis 6'3", 215 **LB**
Col: Northern Iowa *HS:* Mason City [IA] B: 1939, Traer, IA
1960 Buf: 2 G.

ROGER REMO Remo, Roger M 6'3", 237 **LB**
Col: Syracuse *HS:* Mahwah [NJ] B: 8/7/1964
1987 Ind: 3 G.

DAN REMSBERG Remsberg, Daniel Lloyd 6'6", 275 **OT**
Col: Abilene Christian *HS:* Temple [TX] B: 4/7/1962, Temple, TX
Drafted: 1985 Round 9 SD
1986 Den: 16 G. **1987** Den: 5 G. **Total:** 21 G.

DICK RENFRO Renfro, Golie Richard 5'10", 200 **FB-LB**
Col: Washington State *HS:* Glendale [CA] B: 1/25/1919, Fort Worth, TX
AAFC **1946** SF-A: 3 G; Rush 18-85 4.7 3 TD; KR 1-20 20.0; 18 Pt.

LEONARD RENFRO Renfro, Leonard Andrew 6'2", 291 **DT**
Col: Colorado *HS:* St. Mary's Prep [Orchard Lake, MI] B: 6/29/1970, Detroit, MI *Drafted:* 1993 Round 1 Phi
1993 Phi: 14 G. **1994** Phi: 9 G. **Total:** 23 G.

MEL RENFRO Renfro, Melvin Lacy 6'0", 190 **DB-RB**
Col: Oregon *HS:* Jefferson [Portland, OR] B: 12/30/1941, Houston, TX
Drafted: 1964 Round 2 Dal *HOF:* 1996
1966 Dal: Rush 8-52 6.5; Rec 4-65 16.3. **Total:** Rush 8-52 6.5; Rec 4-65 16.3.

		Punt Returns				Kickoff Returns			
Year Team	**G**	**Ret**	**Yds**	**Avg**	**TD**	**Ret**	**Yds**	**Avg**	**TD**
1964 Dal	14	**32**	**418**	13.1	1	**40**	**1017**	25.4	0
1965 Dal	14	24	145	6.0	0	21	630	30.0	**1**
1966 Dal	11	21	123	5.9	0	19	487	25.6	1
1967 Dal	9	3	-1	-0.3	0	5	112	22.4	0
1968 Dal	14	0	0	—	0	0	0	—	0
1969 Dal	14	15	80	5.3	0	0	0	—	0
1970 Dal	14	13	77	5.9	0	0	0	—	0
1971 Dal	14	0	0	—	0	0	0	—	0
1972 Dal	14	0	0	—	0	0	0	—	0
1973 Dal	14	0	0	—	0	0	0	—	0
1974 Dal	11	1	0	0.0	0	0	0	—	0
1975 Dal	11	0	0	—	0	0	0	—	0
1976 Dal	9	0	0	—	0	0	0	—	0
1977 Dal	11	0	0	—	0	0	0	—	0
NFL Total	174	109	842	7.7	1	85	2246	26.4	2

	Interceptions				Tot
Year Team	**Int**	**Yds**	**TD**	**Fum**	**TD**
1964 Dal	7	110	1	4	2
1965 Dal	2	92	1	3	2
1966 Dal	2	57	0	2	1
1967 Dal	7	38	0	0	0
1968 Dal	3	5	0	0	0
1969 Dal	**10**	118	0	2	0
1970 Dal	4	3	0	1	0
1971 Dal	4	11	0	0	0
1972 Dal	1	0	0	0	0
1973 Dal	2	65	1	0	1
1974 Dal	1	6	0	0	0
1975 Dal	4	70	0	0	0
1976 Dal	3	23	0	0	0
1977 Dal	2	28	0	0	0
NFL Total	52	626	3	12	6

MIKE RENFRO Renfro, Michael Ray 6'0", 184 **WR**
Col: Texas Christian *HS:* Arlington Heights [Fort Worth, TX]
B: 6/19/1955, Fort Worth, TX *Drafted:* 1978 Round 4 Hou
1978 Hou: Rush 1-9 9.0. **1980** Hou: Rush 1-12 12.0. **1983** Hou: Rush 1-3 3.0. **1984** Dal: Pass 2-1 50.0%, 49 24.50 1 TD. **1986** Dal: Pass 1-1 100.0%, 23 23.00. **Total:** Pass 3-2 66.7%, 72 24.00 1 TD; Rush 3-24 8.0.

		Receiving				
Year Team	**G**	**Rec**	**Yds**	**Avg**	**TD**	**Fum**
1978 Hou	14	26	339	13.0	2	1
1979 Hou	15	16	323	20.2	2	1
1980 Hou	16	35	459	13.1	1	0
1981 Hou	12	39	451	11.6	1	2
1982 Hou	9	21	295	14.0	3	0
1983 Hou	9	23	316	13.7	2	1
1984 Dal	16	35	583	16.7	2	0
1985 Dal	16	60	955	15.9	8	3
1986 Dal	12	22	325	14.8	3	0
1987 Dal	14	46	662	14.4	4	1
NFL Total	133	323	4708	14.6	28	9

RAY RENFRO Renfro, Ray Austin 6'1", 190 **WR**
(Rabbit) *Col:* North Texas *HS:* Leonard [TX] B: 11/7/1929, Whitesboro, TX D: 8/4/1997, Fort Worth, TX *Drafted:* 1952 Round 4 Cle
1952 Cle: KR 8-130 16.3. **1953** Cle: Pass 3-1 33.3%, 36 12.00 1 TD. **1954** Cle: Pass 1-0, 1 Int; KR 1-24 24.0. **1955** Cle: Pass 2-0. **Total:** Pass 6-1 16.7%, 36 6.00 1 TD 1 Int; KR 9-154 17.1.

		Rushing				Receiving			
Year Team	**G**	**Att**	**Yds**	**Avg**	**TD**	**Rec**	**Yds**	**Avg**	**TD**
1952 Cle	11	10	26	2.6	0	1	8	8.0	0
1953 Cle	12	60	352	5.9	4	39	722	18.5	4
1954 Cle	7	29	151	5.2	0	13	228	17.5	1
1955 Cle	12	29	90	3.1	0	29	603	**20.8**	8
1956 Cle	12	4	24	6.0	0	17	325	19.1	4
1957 Cle	12	2	22	11.0	0	21	589	28.0	6
1958 Cle	12	3	17	5.7	0	24	573	23.9	6
1959 Cle	12	0	0	—	0	30	528	17.6	6
1960 Cle	12	0	0	—	0	24	378	15.8	4
1961 Cle	14	0	0	—	0	48	834	17.4	6
1962 Cle	14	0	0	—	0	31	638	20.6	4
1963 Cle	12	0	0	—	0	4	82	20.5	1
NFL Total	142	137	682	5.0	4	281	5508	19.6	50

	Punt Returns					Tot
Year Team	**Ret**	**Yds**	**Avg**	**TD**	**Fum**	**TD**
1952 Cle	22	169	7.7	0	4	0
1953 Cle	17	53	3.1	0	4	9
1954 Cle	0	0	—	0	0	1
1955 Cle	1	3	3.0	0	1	8
1956 Cle	0	0	—	0	0	4
1957 Cle	0	0	—	0	0	6
1958 Cle	0	0	—	0	0	6
1959 Cle	0	0	—	0	0	6
1960 Cle	0	0	—	0	0	4
1961 Cle	0	0	—	0	1	6
1962 Cle	0	0	—	0	0	4
1963 Cle	0	0	—	0	0	1
NFL Total	40	225	5.6	0	10	55

DEAN RENFRO Renfro, Weldon Eugene 5'11", 180 **HB**
Col: North Texas *HS:* Leonard [TX] B: 6/15/1932, Whitesboro, TX
1955 Bal: 7 G; Rush 4-13 3.3; KR 1-20 20.0.

WILL RENFRO Renfro, William Ellis 6'5", 233 **DT-DE-OT**
Col: Memphis *HS:* Batesville [MS] B: 3/15/1932, Crowder, MS
Drafted: 1954 Round 24 Was
1957 Was: 11 G. **1958** Was: 12 G; KR 1-12 12.0. **1959** Was: 11 G; KR 1-0. **1960** Pit: 12 G. **1961** Phi: 14 G. **Total:** 60 G; KR 2-12 6.0.

MIKE RENGEL Rengel, Michael James 6'5", 260 **DT**
Col: Air Force; Minnesota; Hawaii *HS:* De La Salle [Minneapolis, MN]
B: 12/1/1946, Minneapolis, MN
1969 NO: 5 G.

NEIL RENGEL Rengel, Neil Albert 5'9", 205 **FB**
Col: Minnesota; St. Cloud State; Davis & Elkins *HS:* St. Cloud Technical [MN] B: 4/9/1906, St. Cloud, MN D: 1/14/1995, Sauk Rapids, MN
1930 Fra: 11 G; Pass 1 TD.

BOB RENN Renn, Robert Clifton 6'0", 180 **HB**
Col: Florida State *HS:* Hendersonville [NC] B: 5/25/1934, Henderson, NC D: 10/21/1971 *Drafted:* 1958 Round 22 Cle
1961 NYT: 12 G; Rush 1-14 14.0; Rec 18-268 14.9 1 TD; KR 10-201 20.1; 6 Pt; 1 Fum.

TERRY RENNAKER Rennaker, Terry Lewis 6'6", 225 **LB**
Col: Stanford *HS:* Inglemoor [Seattle, WA] B: 5/1/1958, Newport, RI
1980 Sea: 15 G.

BILL RENNER Renner, William Arthur Jr. 6'0", 198 **P**
Col: Virginia Tech *HS:* Robert E. Lee [Springfield, VA] B: 5/23/1959, Quantico, VA
1986 GB: 3 G; Rush 1-0; Punt 15-622 41.5. **1987** GB: 3 G; Punt 20-712 35.6. **Total:** 6 G; Rush 1-0; Punt 35-1334 38.1.

JESS RENO Reno, Jessie Harry 5'9", 165 **OE**
Col: No College *HS:* Wabash [IN] B: 1890 Deceased
1920 Mun: 1 G. **1922** Eva: 2 G. **Total:** 3 G.

CAESAR RENTIE Rentie, Caesar Harris 6'3", 293 **OT**
Col: Oklahoma *HS:* Hartshorne [OK] B: 11/10/1964, Hartshorne, OK
Drafted: 1988 Round 7 ChiB
1988 ChiB: 5 G.

PUG RENTNER Rentner, Ernest John 6'1", 187 **DB-WB-FB-HB**
Col: Northwestern *HS:* Farragut [Joliet, IL] B: 9/18/1910, Joliet, IL
D: 8/24/1978, Glencoe, IL
1934 Bos: Rec 1-35 35.0 1 TD. **1935** Bos: Rec 1-9 9.0; Scor 13, 1 XK. **1936** Bos: Rec 4-33 8.3; Int **2** TD. **1937** ChiB: Rec 6-101 16.8 1 TD. **Total:** Rec 12-178 14.8 2 TD; Int 2 TD.

		Passing							
Year Team	**G**	**Att**	**Comp**	**Comp%**	**Yds**	**YPA**	**TD**	**Int**	**Rating**
1934 Bos	10	11	2	18.2	13	1.18	0	3	0.0
1935 Bos	11	50	9	18.0	148	2.96	1	15	6.7
1936 Bos	12	39	15	38.5	198	5.08	0	6	15.7
1937 ChiB	10	0	0	—	0	—	0	0	—
NFL Total	43	100	26	26.0	359	3.59	1	24	5.8

	Rushing				Tot
Year Team	**Att**	**Yds**	**Avg**	**TD**	**TD**
1934 Bos	23	96	4.2	0	1
1935 Bos	81	243	3.0	1	2
1936 Bos	95	404	4.3	1	3
1937 ChiB	21	70	3.3	0	1
NFL Total	220	813	3.7	2	7

LARRY RENTZ Rentz, Ralph Lawrence 6'1", 170 **DB**
Col: Florida *HS:* Coral Gables [FL] B: 8/1/1947, Miami, FL
Drafted: 1969 Round 17 SD
1969 SD: 2 G.

LANCE RENTZEL Rentzel, Thomas Lance 6'2", 202 **WR**
Col: Oklahoma *HS:* Casady [Oklahoma City, OK] B: 10/14/1943, Queens, NY *Drafted:* 1965 Round 2 Min
1969 Dal: **1** Fum TD. **1970** Dal: Pass 1-1 100.0%, 58 58.00 1 TD. **Total:** Pass 1-1 100.0%, 58 58.00 1 TD; 1 Fum TD.

		Rushing				Receiving			
Year Team	**G**	**Att**	**Yds**	**Avg**	**TD**	**Rec**	**Yds**	**Avg**	**TD**
1965 Min	11	1	-1	-1.0	0	0	0	—	0
1966 Min	9	0	0	—	0	2	10	5.0	0
1967 Dal	14	0	0	—	0	58	996	17.2	8
1968 Dal	14	0	0	—	0	54	1009	18.7	6
1969 Dal	14	2	11	5.5	0	43	960	**22.3**	**12**
1970 Dal	11	1	11	11.0	0	28	556	19.9	5
1971 LARm	14	14	113	8.1	1	38	534	14.1	5
1972 LARm	14	7	71	10.1	1	27	365	13.5	1
1974 LARm	14	1	-9	-9.0	0	18	396	22.0	1
NFL Total	115	26	196	7.5	2	268	4826	18.0	38

	Punt Returns				Kickoff Returns					Tot
Year Team	**Ret**	**Yds**	**Avg**	**TD**	**Ret**	**Yds**	**Avg**	**TD**	**Fum**	**TD**
1965 Min	4	9	2.3	0	23	602	26.2	**1**	4	1
1966 Min	11	16	1.5	0	9	181	20.1	0	1	0
1967 Dal	6	45	7.5	0	0	0	—	0	1	8
1968 Dal	14	93	6.6	0	0	0	—	0	2	6
1969 Dal	4	14	3.5	0	0	0	—	0	0	**13**
1970 Dal	0	0	—	0	0	0	—	0	1	5
1971 LARm	9	40	4.4	0	0	0	—	0	2	6
1972 LARm	0	0	—	0	0	0	—	0	1	2
1974 LARm	0	0	—	0	0	0	—	0	0	1
NFL Total	48	217	4.5	0	32	783	24.5	1	12	42

JAY REPKO Repko, Jay Kevin 6'3", 240 **TE**
Col: Ursinus; Pennsylvania *HS:* Boyertown [PA] B: 6/12/1958, Pottstown, PA
1987 Phi: 3 G; Rec 5-46 9.2.

JOE REPKO Repko, Joseph Stephen 6'0", 236 **T**
Col: Boston College *HS:* Seton Hall [Lansford, PA] B: 3/15/1920, Lansford, PA *Drafted:* 1943 Round 10 Pit
1946 Pit: 9 G. **1947** Pit: 8 G; 1 Fum TD; 6 Pt. **1948** LARm: 12 G. **1949** LARm: 8 G. **Total:** 37 G; 1 Fum TD; 6 Pt.

MIKE REPPOND Reppond, Michael Gene 5'11", 179 **WR**
Col: Arkansas *HS:* Parkwood [Joplin, MO] B: 11/24/1951, San Diego, CA *Drafted:* 1973 Round 9 Buf
1973 ChiB: 2 G.

GLENN RESSLER Ressler, Glenn Emanuel 6'3", 250 **OG-C-OT-DT**
Col: Penn State *HS:* Mahanoy City [PA] B: 5/21/1943, Dornsife, PA
Drafted: 1965 Round 3 Bal
1965 Bal: 12 G. **1966** Bal: 13 G. **1967** Bal: 14 G. **1968** Bal: 14 G. **1969** Bal: 8 G. **1970** Bal: 13 G. **1971** Bal: 14 G. **1972** Bal: 9 G. **1973** Bal: 14 G. **1974** Bal: 14 G. **Total:** 125 G.

JOE RESTIC Restic, Joseph 6'2", 180 **DB**
Col: St. Francis (Pa.); Villanova *HS:* Hastings [PA] B: 7/21/1927, Hastings, PA
1952 Phi: 3 G.

PETE RETZLAFF Retzlaff, Palmer Edward 6'1", 211 **OE-TE-FL**
Col: Ellendale State ND (J.C.); South Dakota State *HS:* Ellendale [ND]
B: 8/21/1931, Ellendale, ND *Drafted:* 1953 Round 22 Det
1958 Phi: Rush 1-(-4) -4.0. **1959** Phi: Rush 2-(-11) -5.5. **1960** Phi: Rush 2-3 1.5. **1961** Phi: Rush 1-8 8.0. **Total:** Rush 6-(-4) -0.7.

		Receiving				
Year Team	**G**	**Rec**	**Yds**	**Avg**	**TD**	**Fum**
1956 Phi	10	12	159	13.3	0	0
1957 Phi	12	10	120	12.0	0	0
1958 Phi	12	**56**	766	13.7	2	0
1959 Phi	10	34	595	17.5	1	1
1960 Phi	12	46	826	18.0	5	1
1961 Phi	14	50	769	15.4	8	0
1962 Phi	8	30	584	19.5	3	0
1963 Phi	14	57	895	15.7	4	2
1964 Phi	12	51	855	16.8	8	0
1965 Phi	14	66	1190	18.0	10	0
1966 Phi	14	40	653	16.3	6	0
NFL Total	132	452	7412	16.4	47	4

VIC REUTER Reuter, Victor John 6'0", 215 **C**
Col: Lafayette *HS:* Battin [PA] B: 12/1/1909, Elizabeth, NJ
1932 SI: 2 G.

RANDY REUTERSHAN Reutershan, Randy 5'10", 182 **WR**
Col: Pittsburgh *HS:* Mahwah [NJ] B: 6/30/1955, New York, NY
Drafted: 1978 Round 6 Pit
1978 Pit: 11 G; PR 20-148 7.4.

RAY REUTT Reutt, Raymond Francis 6'0", 195 **DE**
Col: Virginia Military *HS:* Woodrow Wilson [Portsmouth, VA]
B: 3/4/1917, Norfolk, VA
1943 PhPt: 2 G.

FUAD REVEIZ Reveiz, Fuad 5'11", 224 **K**
Col: Tennessee *HS:* Miami Sunset [FL] B: 2/24/1963, Bogota, Colombia *Drafted:* 1985 Round 7 Mia

		Scoring						
Year Team	**G**	**Pts**	**FG**	**FGA**	**FG%**	**XK**	**XKA**	**XK%**
1985 Mia	16	116	22	27	81.5	50	52	96.2
1986 Mia	16	94	14	22	63.6	**52**	**55**	94.5
1987 Mia	11	55	9	11	81.8	28	30	93.3
1988 Mia	11	55	8	12	66.7	31	32	96.9
1990 SD-Min	13	65	13	19	68.4	26	27	96.3
1990 SD	4	13	2	7	28.6	7	8	87.5
1990 Min	9	52	11	12	91.7	19	19	100.0
1991 Min	16	85	17	24	70.8	34	35	97.1
1992 Min	16	102	19	25	76.0	45	45	100.0
1993 Min	16	105	26	35	74.3	27	28	96.4
1994 Min	16	132	**34**	**39**	87.2	30	30	100.0
1995 Min	16	122	26	36	72.2	44	44	100.0
NFL Total	147	931	188	250	75.2	367	378	97.1

FREEMAN REXER Rexer, Freeman Riley 6'1", 211 **DE-OE**
Col: Tulane B: 6/18/1918, Houston, TX
1943 ChiC: 10 G; Rec 1-14 14.0. **1944** Bos-Det: 8 G. Bos: 2 G. Det: 6 G. **1945** ChiC: 1 G. **Total:** 19 G; Rec 1-14 14.0.

AL REYNOLDS Reynolds, Allan F 6'3", 250 **OG**
Col: Tarkio *HS:* Winchester [KS] B: 2/15/1938, Winchester, KS
1960 DalT: 6 G. **1961** DalT: 14 G. **1962** DalT: 14 G. **1963** KC: 9 G. **1964** KC: 13 G. **1965** KC: 14 G. **1966** KC: 14 G; 1 Fum. **1967** KC: 14 G. **Total:** 98 G; 1 Fum.

CHUCK REYNOLDS Reynolds, Charles Robert 6'2", 240 **C-OG**
Col: Texas Christian; Tulsa *HS:* Arlington Heights [Fort Worth, TX]
B: 10/5/1946, Fort Worth, TX *Drafted:* 1969 Round 8 Cle
1969 Cle: 11 G. **1970** Cle: 14 G; Scor **1** Saf; 2 Pt. **Total:** 25 G; Scor 1 Saf; 2 Pt.

RICKY REYNOLDS Reynolds, Derrick Scott 5'11", 190 **DB**
Col: Washington State *HS:* Luther Burbank [Sacramento, CA]
B: 1/19/1965, Sacramento, CA *Drafted:* 1987 Round 2 TB
1991 TB: 1 Sac. **1992** TB: 1 Fum TD; 1 Sac. **1993** TB: 1 Sac. **1994** NE: 1 Fum TD; 2 Sac. **1995** NE: 2.5 Sac. **Total:** 2 Fum TD; 7.5 Sac.

		Interceptions			Tot
Year Team	**G**	**Int**	**Yds**	**TD**	**TD**
1987 TB	12	0	0	0	0
1988 TB	16	4	7	0	0
1989 TB	16	5	87	1	2
1990 TB	15	3	70	0	0
1991 TB	16	2	7	0	0
1992 TB	16	2	0	0	1
1993 TB	14	1	3	0	0
1994 NE	15	1	11	1	2
1995 NE	16	3	6	0	0
1996 NE	11	2	7	0	0
NFL Total	147	23	198	2	5

ED REYNOLDS Reynolds, Edward Rannell 6′5″, 238 **LB**
Col: Virginia *HS:* Drewry Mason [Ridgeway, VA] B: 9/23/1961, Stuttgart, Germany
1983 NE: 12 G. **1984** NE: 16 G. **1985** NE: 12 G. **1986** NE: 16 G; 1 Sac. **1987** NE: 12 G; 2 Sac. **1988** NE: 14 G. **1989** NE: 16 G. **1990** NE: 12 G; 1 Sac. **1991** NE: 9 G. **1992** NYG: 16 G. **Total:** 135 G; 4 Sac.

HOMER REYNOLDS Reynolds, Homer 5′10″, 190 **G**
Col: Tulsa B: 10/31/1913 D: 2/7/1988, Woodstock, VA
1934 StL: 2 G.

JIM REYNOLDS Reynolds, James Albert 6′1″, 190 **FB-LB**
Col: Auburn *HS:* La Grange [GA] B: 1/8/1920, La Grange, GA
AAFC **1946** MiaA: Rec 1-32 32.0; KR 1-13 13.0; Int 2-33; Punt 1-39 39.0.

		Rushing			
Year Team	**G**	**Att**	**Yds**	**Avg**	**TD**
1946 MiaA	7	32	96	3.0	0

JIM REYNOLDS Reynolds, James Stephen 6′0″, 193 **DB**
Col: Oklahoma State *HS:* Capitol Hill [Oklahoma City, OK]
B: 8/21/1921, Bethany, OK Deceased
1946 Pit: 2 G.

JERRY REYNOLDS Reynolds, Jerry Bradford 6′6″, 320 **OT-C**
Col: Nevada-Las Vegas *HS:* Highlands [Fort Thomas, KY] B: 4/2/1970, Fort Thomas, KY *Drafted:* 1994 Round 6 Cin
1996 NYG: 8 G. **1997** NYG: 5 G. **1998** NYG: 12 G. **Total:** 25 G.

JOHN REYNOLDS Reynolds, John Duke 5′10″, 185 **C-LB**
(Tex) *Col:* Baylor *HS:* Waco [TX] B: 4/20/1914, Tyler, TX
D: 6/11/1979, Dallas, TX *Drafted:* 1937 Round 8 ChiC
1937 ChiC: 5 G.

JACK REYNOLDS Reynolds, John Sumner 6′1″, 232 **LB**
(Hacksaw) *Col:* Tennessee *HS:* Western Hills [Cincinnati, OH]
B: 11/22/1947, Cincinnati, OH *Drafted:* 1970 Round 1 LARm
1970 LARm: 14 G. **1971** LARm: 4 G. **1972** LARm: 14 G. **1973** LARm: 14 G; Int 2-52. **1974** LARm: 14 G. **1975** LARm: 14 G; Int 1-15. **1976** LARm: 14 G. **1977** LARm: 9 G. **1978** LARm: 16 G. **1979** LARm: 16 G; **1** Fum TD; 6 Pt. **1980** LARm: 16 G; Int 1-20. **1981** SF: 16 G; Int 1-0. **1982** SF: 9 G; Int 1-0. **1983** SF: 13 G; 1 Sac. **1984** SF: 15 G. **Total:** 198 G; Int 6-87; 1 Fum TD; 6 Pt; 1 Sac.

M.C. REYNOLDS Reynolds, Mack Charles 6′0″, 193 **QB**
(Chief) *Col:* Louisiana State *HS:* Mansfield [LA] B: 2/11/1935, Mansfield, LA D: 9/8/1991, Shreveport, LA

		Passing							
Year Team	**G**	**Att**	**Comp**	**Comp%**	**Yds**	**YPA**	**TD**	**Int**	**Rating**
1958 ChiC	11	195	105	53.8	1422	7.29	11	11	72.6
1959 ChiC	7	39	19	48.7	329	8.44	4	1	101.3
1960 Was	8	30	13	43.3	154	5.13	0	3	20.0
1961 Buf	12	181	83	45.9	1004	5.55	2	13	37.2
1962 Oak	1	5	2	40.0	23	4.60	0	0	54.6
NFL Total	39	450	222	49.3	2932	6.52	17	28	57.0

	Rushing				
Year Team	**Att**	**Yds**	**Avg**	**TD**	**Fum**
1958 ChiC	48	252	5.3	0	6
1959 ChiC	5	-4	-0.8	0	3
1960 Was	4	20	5.0	0	0
1961 Buf	30	142	4.7	4	1
1962 Oak	1	9	9.0	0	0
NFL Total	88	419	4.8	4	10

OWEN REYNOLDS Reynolds, Owen Gaston 6′3″, 212 **E-FB**
Col: Georgia *HS:* Douglas Acad. [Douglasville, GA] B: 1/12/1900, Douglasville, GA D: 3/10/1993, Spring Lake, MI
1925 NYG: 9 G. **1926** Bkn: 9 G. **Total:** 18 G.

QUENTIN REYNOLDS Reynolds, Quentin James 6′1″, 205 **G-T**
(Red) *Col:* Brown *HS:* Manual Training [Brooklyn, NY] B: 4/11/1902, Bronx, NY D: 3/17/1965, Travis AFB, CA
1926 Bkn: 6 G.

TOM REYNOLDS Reynolds, Raoul Thomas Jr. 6′3″, 200 **WR**
Col: El Camino Coll. CA (J.C.); San Diego State *HS:* John Muir [Pasadena, CA]; Morningside HS [Inglewood,CA] B: 4/11/1949, Pasadena, CA *Drafted:* 1972 Round 2 NE
1972 NE: 12 G; Rec 8-152 19.0 2 TD; 12 Pt. **1973** ChiB: 9 G; Rec 7-127 18.1. **Total:** 21 G; Rec 15-279 18.6 2 TD; 12 Pt.

BOB REYNOLDS Reynolds, Robert Louis 6′5″, 265 **OT**
Col: Bowling Green State *HS:* John Adams [Cleveland, OH]
B: 1/22/1939, Nashville, TN D: 10/10/1996, Naperville, IL
Drafted: 1963 Round 2 StL
1963 StL: 14 G. **1964** StL: 10 G. **1965** StL: 14 G. **1966** StL: 14 G. **1967** StL: 13 G. **1968** StL: 14 G. **1969** StL: 14 G. **1970** StL: 14 G. **1971** StL: 14 G; Rec 1-(-4) -4.0. **1972** NE: 12 G. **1973** NE-StL: 5 G. NE: 4 G. StL: 1 G. **Total:** 138 G; Rec 1-(-4) -4.0.

BOB REYNOLDS Reynolds, Robert O'Dell 6′4″, 221 **T**
(Horse) *Col:* Stanford *HS:* Okmulgee [OK] B: 3/30/1914, Norris, OK
D: 2/8/1994, San Rafael, CA *Drafted:* 1936 Round 6 GB
1937 Det: 9 G. **1938** Det: 11 G. **Total:** 20 G.

BILL REYNOLDS Reynolds, William 5′8″, 183 **HB-DB**
Col: Mississippi B: 10/10/1918, Chicago, IL
1944 Bkn: 5 G; Rush 11-71 6.5 1 TD; PR 1-12 12.0; KR 1-18 18.0; 6 Pt. **1945** ChiC: 9 G; Rush 7-10 1.4; Punt 38-1384 36.4; 1 Fum. **Total:** 14 G; Rush 18-81 4.5 1 TD; PR 1-12 12.0; KR 1-18 18.0; Punt 38-1384 36.4; 6 Pt; 1 Fum.

BILLY REYNOLDS Reynolds, William Dean 5′10″, 188 **HB**
(Rock) *Col:* Pittsburgh *HS:* St. Marys [WV] B: 7/20/1931, St. Mary's, WV *Drafted:* 1953 Round 2 Cle
1953 Cle: Rec 9-120 13.3. **1954** Cle: Rec 10-76 7.6. **1957** Cle: Rec 1-12 12.0. **1958** Pit: Rec 1-1 1.0. **1960** Oak: Rec 3-43 14.3. **Total:** Rec 24-252 10.5.

		Rushing				Punt Returns			
Year Team	**G**	**Att**	**Yds**	**Avg**	**TD**	**Ret**	**Yds**	**Avg**	**TD**
1953 Cle	12	72	313	4.3	3	18	111	6.2	0
1954 Cle	12	64	180	2.8	2	25	138	5.5	0
1957 Cle	12	29	57	2.0	1	24	114	4.8	0
1958 Pit	12	10	29	2.9	1	25	143	5.7	0
1960 Oak	6	1	6	6.0	0	7	24	3.4	0
NFL Total	54	176	585	3.3	7	99	530	5.4	0

	Kickoff Returns				
Year Team	**Ret**	**Yds**	**Avg**	**TD**	**Fum**
1953 Cle	4	74	18.5	0	4
1954 Cle	14	413	**29.5**	0	4
1957 Cle	7	152	21.7	0	2
1958 Pit	15	346	23.1	0	2
1960 Oak	0	0	—	0	2
NFL Total	40	985	24.6	0	14

FLOYD RHEA Rhea, Floyd Mack 6′0″, 218 **G-LB**
(Scrappy) *Col:* Fullerton Coll. CA (J.C.); Oregon *HS:* Fullerton [CA]
B: 9/21/1920, Rhea's Mills, AR *Drafted:* 1943 Round 15 Bkn
1943 ChiC: 1 G; KR 1-10 10.0. **1944** Bkn: 8 G; Int 1-0. **1945** Bos: 8 G. **1947** Det: 2 G. **Total:** 19 G; KR 1-10 10.0; Int 1-0.

HUGHIE RHEA Rhea, Hugh McCall 6′3″, 225 **G**
Col: Nebraska *HS:* Arlington [NE] B: 9/9/1909, Arlington, NE
D: 10/18/1973
1933 Bkn: 2 G.

LEONTA RHEAMS Rheams, Leonta DeMarkel 6′2″, 303 **DT**
Col: Houston *HS:* Robert E. Lee [Tyler, TX] B: 8/1/1976, Tyler, TX
Drafted: 1998 Round 4 NE
1998 NE: 6 G.

STEVE RHEM Rhem, Steve Lamar 6′2″, 212 **WR**
Col: Minnesota; Northeast Louisiana; Arkansas-Monticello; Rowan
HS: Vanguard [Ocala, FL] B: 11/9/1971, Ocala, FL
1994 NO: 7 G. **1995** NO: 8 G; Rec 4-50 12.5. **Total:** 15 G; Rec 4-50 12.5.

ELMER RHENSTROM Rhenstrom, Elmer Gustaf 5′10″, 185 **OE**
(Swede) *Col:* Beloit *HS:* Kenosha [WI] B: 8/18/1895, Beaver Dam, WI
D: 12/27/1967, Ontario, CA
1922 Rac: 6 G.

ERRICT RHETT Rhett, Errict Undra 5′11″, 210 **RB**
Col: Florida *HS:* McArthur [Hollywood, FL] B: 12/11/1970, Pembroke Pines, FL *Drafted:* 1994 Round 2 TB
1994 TB: Scor 1 2XP. **1997** TB: KR 1-16 16.0. **Total:** KR 1-16 16.0; Scor 1 2XP.

		Rushing				Receiving					Tot
Year Team	**G**	**Att**	**Yds**	**Avg**	**TD**	**Rec**	**Yds**	**Avg**	**TD**	**Fum**	**TD**
1994 TB	16	284	1011	3.6	7	22	119	5.4	0	2	7
1995 TB	16	332	1207	3.6	11	14	110	7.9	0	2	11
1996 TB	9	176	539	3.1	3	4	11	2.8	1	3	4
1997 TB	11	31	96	3.1	3	0	0	—	0	0	3
1998 Bal	13	44	180	4.1	0	11	65	5.9	0	0	0
NFL Total	65	867	3033	3.5	24	51	305	6.0	1	7	25

JAY RHODEMYRE Rhodemyre, Jay E 6′1″, 210 **C-LB**
Col: Kentucky *HS:* Ashland [KY] B: 12/16/1922, Ashland, KY
D: 6/7/1968, Lexington, KY *Drafted:* 1948 Round 5 GB
1948 GB: 9 G; Int 1-24. **1949** GB: 12 G; Int 4-12. **1951** GB: 12 G. **1952** GB: 12 G. **Total:** 45 G; Int 5-36.

BRUCE RHODES Rhodes, Bruce 6′0″, 187 **DB**
Col: San Francisco State *HS:* Woodrow Wilson [San Francisco, CA]
B: 4/17/1952, San Francisco, CA D: 2/23/1981, San Francisco, CA
1976 SF: 14 G; PR 16-142 8.9; Int 3-42; 3 Fum. **1978** Det: 15 G; Int 1-24. **Total:** 29 G; PR 16-142 8.9; Int 4-66; 3 Fum.

DANNY RHODES Rhodes, Danny Boyiet 6′2″, 220 **LB**
Col: Arkansas *HS:* Brazosport [Freeport, TX] B: 3/18/1951, Lake Jackson, TX *Drafted:* 1974 Round 6 Bal
1974 Bal: 14 G.

DON RHODES Rhodes, Donald Nelson 6′2″, 225 **T**
Col: Washington & Jefferson *HS:* Allentown Prep [PA] B: 7/9/1909 D: 1/1968
1933 Pit: 7 G.

RAY RHODES Rhodes, Raymond Earl 5′11″, 185 **DB-WR**
Col: Texas Christian; Tulsa *HS:* Dunbar [Mejia, TX]; Mexia HS [TX] B: 10/20/1950, Mexia, TX *Drafted:* 1974 Round 10 NYG
1974 NYG: Rush 1-(-6) -6.0; PR 10-124 12.4; KR 1-27 27.0. **1975** NYG: Rush 3-(-4) -1.3. **1976** NYG: Rush 2-10 5.0. **1977** NYG: Int 2-59. **1978** NYG: Int 3-74. **1979** NYG: Int 2-0. **1980** SF: Int 1-25. **Total:** Rush 6-0; PR 10-124 12.4; KR 1-27 27.0; Int 8-158.

		Receiving				
Year Team	G	Rec	Yds	Avg	TD	Fum
1974 NYG	14	9	138	15.3	0	1
1975 NYG	14	26	537	20.7	6	3
1976 NYG	13	16	305	19.1	1	1
1977 NYG	14	0	0	—	0	0
1978 NYG	13	0	0	—	0	0
1979 NYG	15	0	0	—	0	0
1980 SF	14	0	0	—	0	0
NFL Total	97	51	980	19.2	7	5

JERRY RHOME Rhome, Gerald Byron 6′0″, 190 **QB**
Col: Southern Methodist; Tulsa *HS:* Sunset [Dallas, TX] B: 3/6/1942, Dallas, TX *Drafted:* 1964 Round 13 Dal

		Passing							
Year Team	G	Att	Comp	Comp%	Yds	YPA	TD	Int	Rating
1965 Dal	11	21	9	42.9	157	7.48	1	1	65.0
1966 Dal	7	36	21	58.3	253	7.03	0	1	68.4
1967 Dal	14	18	9	50.0	86	4.78	0	1	40.5
1968 Dal	1	0	0	—	0	—	0	0	—
1969 Cle	11	19	7	36.8	35	1.84	0	2	5.7
1970 Hou	13	168	88	52.4	1031	6.14	5	8	61.4
1971 LARm	14	18	5	27.8	66	3.67	1	1	37.7
NFL Total	71	280	139	49.6	1628	5.81	7	14	55.2

	Rushing				
Year Team	Att	Yds	Avg	TD	Fum
1965 Dal	4	11	2.8	0	1
1966 Dal	7	37	5.3	0	1
1967 Dal	2	-11	-5.5	0	1
1969 Cle	1	0	0.0	0	1
1970 Hou	9	54	6.0	1	5
1971 LARm	3	0	0.0	0	0
NFL Total	26	91	3.5	1	9

EARNEST RHONE Rhone, Earnest Calvin 6′2″, 220 **LB**
Col: Henderson State *HS:* Rankin Street [Ashdown, AR] B: 8/20/1953, Ogden, AR
1982 Mia: 1 Sac. **1983** Mia: 3 Sac. **1984** Mia: 1 Sac. **Total:** 5 Sac.

		Interceptions		
Year Team	G	Int	Yds	TD
1975 Mia	14	2	2	0
1977 Mia	4	0	0	0
1978 Mia	16	2	4	0
1979 Mia	16	2	17	0
1980 Mia	14	3	33	0
1981 Mia	16	3	35	0
1982 Mia	9	1	4	0
1983 Mia	12	1	15	0
1984 Mia	15	0	0	0
NFL Total	116	14	110	0

BUSTER RHYMES Rhymes, George 6′2″, 217 **WR**
Col: Oklahoma *HS:* Miami Northwestern [FL] B: 1/27/1962, Miami, FL *Drafted:* 1985 Round 4 Min
1985 Min: Rec 5-124 24.8. **1986** Min: Rec 3-25 8.3. **Total:** Rec 8-149 18.6.

		Kickoff Returns				
Year Team	G	Ret	Yds	Avg	TD	Fum
1985 Min	15	**53**	**1345**	25.4	0	2
1986 Min	5	9	213	23.7	0	0
NFL Total	20	62	1558	25.1	0	2

FRANK RIBAR Ribar, Frank Andrew Jr. 6′1″, 190 **G-LB**
Col: Duke *HS:* Aliquippa [PA] B: 1/15/1915, Wickhaven, PA D: 10/1976 *Drafted:* 1940 Round 16 Det
1943 Was: 2 G.

DAVE RIBBLE Ribble, Loran Thomas 6′1″, 225 **G-T**
(Tex; Babe) *Col:* Hardin-Simmons *HS:* Anson [TX] B: 3/28/1907, Brownwood, TX D: 1944
1932 Port: 1 G. **1933** ChiC: 1 G. **1934** Pit: 10 G. **1935** Pit: 3 G. **Total:** 15 G.

PAUL RIBLETT Riblett, Paul Gerald 5′10″, 184 **OE-DE**
Col: Pennsylvania *HS:* Greensburg [PA]; Kiski School [Saltsburg, PA] B: 5/23/1908, Youngwood, PA D: 3/1/1976, Cherry Hill, NJ
1932 Bkn: Rush 2-4 2.0. **1934** Bkn: Rush 1-19 19.0. **1935** Bkn: Rush 2-16 8.0. **1936** Bkn: Rush 2-4 2.0. **Total:** Rush 7-43 6.1.

		Receiving			
Year Team	G	Rec	Yds	Avg	TD
1932 Bkn	11	10	110	11.0	1
1933 Bkn	10	12	173	14.4	1
1934 Bkn	11	8	154	19.3	1
1935 Bkn	12	6	86	14.3	0
1936 Bkn	12	4	49	12.3	0
NFL Total	56	40	572	14.3	3

BENNY RICARDO Ricardo, Benito Concepcion 5′10″, 175 **K**
Col: Orange Coast Coll. CA (J.C.); San Diego State *HS:* Costa Mesa [CA] B: 1/4/1954, Asuncion, Paraguay
1976 Buf-Det: Punt 1-16 16.0. Det: Punt 1-16 16.0. **Total:** Punt 1-16 16.0.

		Scoring						
Year Team	G	Pts	FG	FGA	FG%	XK	XKA	XK%
1976 Buf-Det	10	54	11	18	61.1	21	23	91.3
1976 Buf	2	5	1	4	25.0	2	2	100.0
1976 Det	8	49	10	14	71.4	19	21	90.5
1978 Det	16	92	20	28	71.4	32	33	97.0
1979 Det	16	55	10	18	55.6	25	26	96.2
1980 NO	14	61	10	17	58.8	31	34	91.2
1981 NO	16	63	13	25	52.0	24	24	100.0
1983 Min	16	108	25	33	75.8	33	34	97.1
1984 SD	2	14	3	3	100.0	5	6	83.3
NFL Total	90	447	92	142	64.8	171	180	95.0

JIM RICCA Ricca, James Emanuel 6′4″, 270 **OT-DG-DT**
(Big Jim) *Col:* Georgetown *HS:* Boys [Brooklyn, NY] B: 10/8/1927, Rockville Centre, NY
1951 Was: 11 G. **1952** Was: 12 G. **1953** Was: 12 G. **1954** Was: 12 G; KR 1-9 9.0; Scor **1** Saf; **1** Fum TD; 8 Pt. **1955** Det-Phi: 12 G; Int 1-33. Det: 6 G; Int 1-33. Phi: 6 G. **1956** Phi: 1 G. **Total:** 60 G; KR 1-9 9.0; Int 1-33; Scor 1 Saf; 1 Fum TD; 8 Pt.

RICE Rice **WB**
Col: No College Deceased
1921 Ham: 1 G.

ALLEN RICE Rice, Allen Troy 5′10″, 203 **RB**
Col: Wharton Co. JC TX; Ranger Coll. TX (J.C.); Baylor *HS:* Klein [TX] B: 4/5/1962, Houston, TX *Drafted:* 1984 Round 5 Min
1986 Min: Pass 1-0; PR 1-0. **Total:** Pass 1-0; PR 1-0.

		Rushing				Receiving			
Year Team	G	Att	Yds	Avg	TD	Rec	Yds	Avg	TD
1984 Min	14	14	58	4.1	1	4	59	14.8	1
1985 Min	14	31	104	3.4	3	9	61	6.8	1
1986 Min	14	73	220	3.0	2	30	391	13.0	3
1987 Min	12	51	131	2.6	1	19	201	10.6	1
1988 Min	16	110	322	2.9	6	30	279	9.3	0
1989 Min	4	6	25	4.2	0	4	29	7.3	0
1990 Min	15	22	74	3.4	0	4	46	11.5	0
1991 GB	6	30	100	3.3	0	2	10	5.0	0
NFL Total	95	337	1034	3.1	13	102	1076	10.5	6

	Kickoff Returns					Tot
Year Team	Ret	Yds	Avg	TD	Fum	TD
1984 Min	3	34	11.3	0	1	2
1985 Min	4	70	17.5	0	0	4
1986 Min	5	88	17.6	0	5	5
1987 Min	2	29	14.5	0	1	2
1988 Min	1	0	0.0	0	1	6
1989 Min	1	13	13.0	0	0	0
1990 Min	12	176	14.7	0	1	0
1991 GB	3	36	12.0	0	2	0
NFL Total	31	446	14.4	0	11	19

ANDY RICE Rice, Andrew 6′2″, 268 **DT**
(Hank) *Col:* Texas Southern *HS:* Steven Mays [Hallettsville, TX] B: 9/6/1940, Hallettsville, TX
1966 KC: 14 G. **1967** KC-Hou: 11 G. KC: 4 G. Hou: 7 G. **1968** Cin: 14 G. **1969** Cin: 14 G. **1970** SD: 9 G. **1971** SD: 12 G. **1972** ChiB: 14 G. **1973** ChiB: 14 G. **Total:** 102 G.

DAN RICE Rice, Daniel Jerome 6′1″, 241 **RB**
Col: Michigan *HS:* West Roxbury [Boston, MA] B: 11/9/1963, Boston, MA
1987 Cin: 3 G; Rush 18-59 3.3.

FLOYD RICE Rice, Floyd Elliott 6′3″, 223 **LB-TE**
Col: Alcorn State *HS:* Sadie V. Thompson [Natchez, MS]
B: 8/31/1949, Natchez, MS *Drafted:* 1971 Round 9 Hou
1971 Hou: 14 G; PR 2-0; KR 1-0. **1972** Hou: 14 G. **1973** Hou-SD: 10 G; KR 2-17 8.5; Int 1-8; **1** Fum TD; 6 Pt; 1 Fum. Hou: 5 G; KR 2-17 8.5. SD: 5 G; Int 1-8; 1 Fum TD; 6 Pt; 1 Fum. **1974** SD: 12 G; Int 3-44. **1975** SD: 14 G; Int 1-0. **1976** Oak: 10 G. **1977** Oak: 13 G; Int 2-5. **1978** NO: 15 G; KR 1-15 15.0. **Total:** 102 G; PR 2-0; KR 4-32 8.0; Int 7-57; 1 Fum TD; 6 Pt; 1 Fum.

GEORGE RICE Rice, George Gaylen 6′3″, 260 **DT**
Col: Louisiana State *HS:* Istrouma [Baton Rouge, LA] B: 6/10/1944, Liberty, MO *Drafted:* 1966 Round 3 Hou
1966 Hou: 5 G. **1967** Hou: 14 G. **1968** Hou: 11 G. **1969** Hou: 7 G. **Total:** 37 G.

HAROLD RICE Rice, Harold Thurston 6′2″, 235 **DE**
Col: Tennessee State *HS:* Cameron [Nashville, TN] B: 6/23/1945, Nashville, TN *Drafted:* 1969 Round 11 Oak
1971 Oak: 12 G.

JERRY RICE Rice, Jerry Lee 6′2″, 200 **WR**
Col: Mississippi Valley State *HS:* B.L. Moor [Crawford, MS]
B: 10/13/1962, Starkville, MS *Drafted:* 1985 Round 1 SF
1985 SF: KR 1-6 6.0. **1986** SF: Pass 2-1 50.0%, 16 8.00. **1988** SF: Pass 3-1 33.3%, 14 4.67 1 Int. **1994** SF: Scor 1 2XP. **1995** SF: Pass 1-1 100.0%, 41 41.00 1 TD; Scor 1 2XP; **1** Fum TD. **1996** SF: Pass 1-0. **1998** SF: Scor **2** 2XP. **Total:** Pass 7-3 42.9%, 71 10.14 1 TD 1 Int; KR 1-6 6.0; Scor 4 2XP; 1 Fum TD.

		Rushing				Receiving					Tot
Year Team	G	Att	Yds	Avg	TD	Rec	Yds	Avg	TD	Fum	TD
1985 SF	16	6	26	4.3	1	49	927	18.9	3	1	4
1986 SF	16	10	72	7.2	1	86	**1570**	18.3	**15**	2	16
1987 SF	12	8	51	6.4	1	65	1078	16.6	**22**	2	**23**
1988 SF	16	13	107	8.2	1	64	1306	20.4	9	2	10
1989 SF	16	5	33	6.6	0	82	**1483**	18.1	**17**	0	17
1990 SF	16	2	0	0.0	0	**100**	**1502**	15.0	**13**	1	13
1991 SF	16	1	2	2.0	0	80	1206	15.1	**14**	1	14
1992 SF	16	9	58	6.4	1	84	1201	14.3	10	2	11
1993 SF	16	3	69	23.0	1	98	**1503**	15.3	**15**	3	**16**
1994 SF	16	7	93	13.3	2	112	**1499**	13.4	13	1	15
1995 SF	16	5	36	7.2	1	122	**1848**	15.1	15	3	17
1996 SF	16	11	77	7.0	1	**108**	1254	11.6	8	0	9
1997 SF	2	1	-10	-10.0	0	7	78	11.1	1	0	1
1998 SF	16	0	0	—	0	82	1157	14.1	9	2	9
NFL Total	206	81	614	7.6	10	**1139**	**17612**	15.5	**164**	20	**175**

KEN RICE Rice, Kenneth Earl 6′2″, 240 **OT-OG**
Col: Auburn *HS:* Bainbridge [GA] B: 9/14/1939, Bainbridge, GA
Drafted: 1961 Round 1 Buf
1961 Buf: 14 G; KR 2-13 6.5. **1963** Buf: 14 G. **1964** Oak: 14 G. **1965** Oak: 14 G; 1 Fum. **1966** Mia: 14 G. **1967** Mia: 9 G. **Total:** 79 G; KR 2-13 6.5; 1 Fum.

ORIAN RICE Rice, Orian Earl 6′0″, 165 **BB-C**
(Bill) *Col:* Syracuse; Muhlenberg *HS:* Binghamton [NY] B: 3/21/1900, Binghamton, NY D: 5/1968, Roselle, NJ
1929 NYG: 2 G.

RODNEY RICE Rice, Rodney Donadrain 5′8″, 180 **DB**
Col: Merced Coll. CA (J.C.); Brigham Young *HS:* Atwater [CA]
B: 6/18/1966, Albany, GA *Drafted:* 1989 Round 8 NE
1989 NE: 10 G; KR 11-242 22.0. **1990** TB: 16 G; Int 2-7. **Total:** 26 G; KR 11-242 22.0; Int 2-7.

RON RICE Rice, Ronald Wilson 6′1″, 206 **DB**
Col: Eastern Michigan *HS:* University of Detroit [MI] B: 11/9/1972, Detroit, MI
1996 Det: 13 G. **1997** Det: 12 G; Int 1-18; 1 Sac. **1998** Det: 16 G; Int 3-25; 3.5 Sac. **Total:** 41 G; Int 4-43; 4.5 Sac.

SIMEON RICE Rice, Simeon James 6′5″, 259 **DE**
Col: Illinois *HS:* Mount Carmel [Chicago, IL] B: 2/24/1974, Chicago, IL
Drafted: 1996 Round 1 Ariz
1996 Ariz: 16 G; 12.5 Sac. **1997** Ariz: 16 G; Int 1-0; 5 Sac. **1998** Ariz: 16 G; 10 Sac. **Total:** 48 G; Int 1-0; 27.5 Sac.

RANDY RICH Rich, Randall Wayne 5′10″, 178 **DB**
Col: New Mexico *HS:* North [Bakersfield, CA] B: 12/28/1953, Bakersfield, CA
1977 Det: 2 G; PR 2-18 9.0; KR 5-73 14.6; 1 Fum. **1978** Oak-Cle: 11 G; KR 2-43 21.5. Oak: 2 G. Cle: 9 G; KR 2-43 21.5. **1979** Cle: 16 G; KR 2-10 5.0. **Total:** 29 G; PR 2-18 9.0; KR 9-126 14.0; 1 Fum.

HERB RICH Rich, Richard Herbert 5′11″, 181 **DB**
Col: Vanderbilt *HS:* Miami Beach [FL] B: 10/7/1928, Newark, NJ
Drafted: 1950 Round 6 Bal
1950 Bal: Rush 2-6 3.0; PR 12-276 **23.0** 1 TD; KR 17-434 25.5. **1952** LARm: PR 1-0. **1954** NYG: PR 1-5 5.0. **Total:** Rush 2-6 3.0; PR 14-281 20.1 1 TD; KR 17-434 25.5.

		Interceptions				Tot
Year Team	G	Int	Yds	TD	Fum	TD
1950 Bal	12	3	45	1	4	2
1951 LARm	7	3	11	0	0	0
1952 LARm	11	8	201	1	0	1
1953 LARm	7	3	95	**1**	1	1
1954 NYG	11	5	56	0	0	0
1955 NYG	11	6	61	0	0	0
1956 NYG	5	1	0	0	0	0
NFL Total	64	29	469	3	5	4

GARY RICHARD Richard, Gary Ross 5′9″, 171 **DB**
Col: Bakersfield Coll. CA (J.C.); Pittsburgh *HS:* East [Denver, CO]
B: 10/9/1965, Denver, CO *Drafted:* 1988 Round 7 GB
1988 GB: 10 G.

STANLEY RICHARD Richard, Stanley Palmer 6′2″, 198 **DB**
Col: Texas *HS:* La Porte [TX] *HS:* Hawkins [TX] B: 10/21/1967, Miniola, TX
Drafted: 1991 Round 1 SD
1993 SD: 2 Sac. **Total:** 2 Sac.

		Interceptions		
Year Team	G	Int	Yds	TD
1991 SD	15	2	5	0
1992 SD	14	3	26	0
1993 SD	16	1	-2	0
1994 SD	16	4	224	2
1995 Was	16	3	24	0
1996 Was	16	3	47	0
1997 Was	16	4	28	0
1998 Was	15	1	0	0
NFL Total	124	21	352	2

CURVIN RICHARDS Richards, Curvin Stephen 5′9″, 195 **RB**
Col: Pittsburgh *HS:* La Porte [TX] B: 12/26/1968, Port of Spain, Trinidad *Drafted:* 1991 Round 4 Dal
1992 Dal: Rec 3-8 2.7. **Total:** Rec 3-8 2.7.

		Rushing				
Year Team	G	Att	Yds	Avg	TD	Fum
1991 Dal	2	2	4	2.0	0	0
1992 Dal	9	49	176	3.6	1	3
1993 Det	1	4	1	0.3	0	0
NFL Total	12	55	181	3.3	1	3

DAVID RICHARDS Richards, David Reed 6′5″, 315 **OG-OT**
Col: Southern Methodist; UCLA *HS:* Highland Park [Dallas, TX]
B: 4/11/1966, Staten Island, TX *Drafted:* 1988 Round 4 SD
1988 SD: 16 G. **1989** SD: 16 G. **1990** SD: 16 G. **1991** SD: 16 G. **1992** SD: 16 G. **1993** Det: 15 G. **1994** Atl: 15 G. **1995** Atl: 14 G. **1996** Atl-NE: 11 G. Atl: 6 G. NE: 5 G. **Total:** 135 G.

TED RICHARDS Richards, Edward John 5′9″, 174 **OE**
Col: Illinois *HS:* New Trier Twp. [Winnetka, IL] B: 11/7/1901, Oshkosh, WI D: 12/1/1978, Stanwood, WA
1929 ChiB: 1 G.

KINK RICHARDS Richards, Elvin C 5′11″, 195 **FB-DB-TB**
Col: Des Moines CC IA; Simpson *HS:* Garden Grove [IA]
B: 12/27/1910, Garden Grove, IA D: 7/21/1976, Oakland, CA
1933 NYG: Scor 43, 1 XK. **1934** NYG: Pass 1-1 100.0%, 9 9.00; Scor 13, 1 XK. **1935** NYG: Scor 28, 1 FG, 1 XK. **1938** NYG: Pass 1-0, 1 Int; Scor 2, 2-2 100.0% XK. **1939** NYG: Punt 1-39 39.0. **Total:** Pass 2-1 50.0%, 9 4.50 1 Int; Punt 1-39 39.0; Scor 122, 1 FG, 5-2 100.0% XK.

		Rushing				Receiving				Tot
Year Team	G	Att	Yds	Avg	TD	Rec	Yds	Avg	TD	TD
1933 NYG	8	41	277	6.8	4	7	127	18.1	**3**	**7**
1934 NYG	13	48	173	3.6	1	6	56	9.3	1	2
1935 NYG	12	**153**	449	2.9	4	8	41	5.1	0	4
1936 NYG	11	114	421	3.7	1	7	146	20.9	1	2
1937 NYG	11	87	329	3.8	1	10	149	14.9	2	3
1938 NYG	9	25	111	4.4	0	1	8	8.0	0	0
1939 NYG	9	40	117	2.9	1	2	8	4.0	0	1
NFL Total	73	508	1877	3.7	12	41	535	13.0	7	19

HOWARD RICHARDS Richards, Howard Glen Jr. 6′6″, 263 **OT-OG**
Col: Missouri *HS:* Southwest [St. Louis, MO] B: 8/7/1959, St. Louis, MO *Drafted:* 1981 Round 1 Dal
1981 Dal: 16 G. **1982** Dal: 8 G. **1983** Dal: 16 G. **1984** Dal: 11 G. **1985** Dal: 7 G. **1986** Dal: 9 G. **1987** Sea: 2 G. **Total:** 69 G.

PETE RICHARDS Richards, J. Peter 5′10″, 190 **C**
Col: Swarthmore *HS:* Lansdowne [PA]; Tech HS [Philadelphia, PA]
B: 1905
1927 Fra: 3 G.

JIM RICHARDS Richards, James Buis Jr. 6′1″, 180 **DB**
Col: Virginia Tech *HS:* Garinger [Charlotte, NC] B: 10/28/1946, Charlotte, NC *Drafted:* 1968 Round 8 NYJ
1968 NYJ: 12 G; PR 4-57 14.3; 1 Fum. **1969** NYJ: 14 G; KR 2-36 18.0; Int 3-48. **Total:** 26 G; PR 4-57 14.3; KR 2-36 18.0; Int 3-48; 1 Fum.

GOLDEN RICHARDS Richards, John Golden 6′1″, 181 **WR**
Col: Hawaii; Brigham Young *HS:* Granite [Salt Lake City, UT] B: 12/31/1950, Salt Lake City, UT *Drafted:* 1973 Round 2 Dal
1973 Dal: Rush 1-2 2.0; KR 3-44 14.7. **1974** Dal: Rush 1-(-5) -5.0. **1975** Dal: Rush 3-18 6.0. **Total:** Rush 5-15 3.0; KR 3-44 14.7.

		Receiving				Punt Returns					Tot
Year Team	G	Rec	Yds	Avg	TD	Ret	Yds	Avg	TD	Fum	TD
1973 Dal	12	6	91	15.2	1	21	139	6.6	0	1	1
1974 Dal	14	26	467	18.0	5	13	74	5.7	0	1	5
1975 Dal	14	21	451	21.5	4	28	288	10.3	1	3	5
1976 Dal	11	19	414	21.8	3	0	0	—	0	0	3
1977 Dal	14	17	225	13.2	3	0	0	—	0	0	3
1978 Dal-ChiB	16	28	381	13.6	0	0	0	—	0	1	0
1978 Dal	1	1	2	2.0	0	0	0	—	0	0	0
1978 ChiB	15	27	379	14.0	0	0	0	—	0	1	0
1979 ChiB	5	5	107	21.4	1	0	0	—	0	0	1
NFL Total	86	122	2136	17.5	17	62	501	8.1	1	6	18

PERRY RICHARDS Richards, Perry Walter 6′2″, 205 **OE**
Col: Detroit Mercy *HS:* St. Rita [Detroit, MI] B: 1/14/1934, Detroit, MI *Drafted:* 1957 Round 5 Pit
1959 ChiC: PR 3-22 7.3. **1961** Buf: KR 1-10 10.0. **Total:** PR 3-22 7.3; KR 1-10 10.0.

		Receiving				
Year Team	G	Rec	Yds	Avg	TD	Fum
1957 Pit	7	1	15	15.0	0	1
1958 Det	3	7	90	12.9	0	0
1959 ChiC	4	5	89	17.8	1	1
1960 StL	8	1	10	10.0	0	0
1961 Buf	11	19	285	15.0	3	0
1962 NYT	14	6	69	11.5	0	1
NFL Total	47	39	558	14.3	4	3

RAY RICHARDS Richards, Ray William 6′1″, 230 **G-T-E**
Col: Nebraska *HS:* Pawnee City [NE] B: 7/16/1906, Lincoln, NE D: 9/18/1974, La Habra, CA
1930 Fra: 13 G. **1933** ChiB: 12 G. **1934** Det: 6 G. **1935** ChiB: 12 G. **1936** ChiB: 1 G. **Total:** 44 G.

DICK RICHARDS Richards, Richard 6′0″, 194 **WB-DB**
Col: Kentucky B: 11/17/1907 D: 11/12/1996, Riverside, CA
1933 Bkn: 9 G; Rush 14-40 2.9; Rec 2-22 11.0.

BOBBY RICHARDS Richards, Robert Griffin 6′2″, 245 **DE**
Col: Louisiana State *HS:* Oak Ridge [TN] B: 10/2/1938, Columbus, MS *Drafted:* 1961 Round 15 Phi
1962 Phi: 14 G. **1963** Phi: 14 G. **1964** Phi: 14 G. **1965** Phi: 14 G. **1966** Atl: 14 G. **1967** Atl: 14 G. **Total:** 84 G.

AL RICHARDSON Richardson, Alpette 6′2″, 211 **LB**
Col: Georgia Tech *HS:* Miami Central [FL] B: 9/23/1957, Abbeville, AL *Drafted:* 1980 Round 8 Atl
1980 Atl: 16 G; Int 7-139; **1** Fum TD; 6 Pt. **1981** Atl: 16 G; Int 1-9. **1982** Atl: 8 G; 2 Sac. **1983** Atl: 5 G; Int 1-38. **1984** Atl: 16 G; 3.5 Sac. **1985** Atl: 16 G; 3.5 Sac. **Total:** 77 G; Int 9-186; 1 Fum TD; 6 Pt; 9 Sac.

AL RICHARDSON Richardson, Alvin 6′3″, 250 **DE**
Col: Grambling State *HS:* Joseph S. Clark [New Orleans, LA] B: 2/1/1935, New Orleans, LA *Drafted:* 1957 Round 26 Phi
1960 Bos: 3 G.

TONY RICHARDSON Richardson, Antonio 6′1″, 230 **RB**
Col: Auburn *HS:* Daleville [AL] B: 12/17/1971, Frankfurt, Germany
1996 KC: Rec 2-18 9.0 1 TD. **1997** KC: Rec 3-6 2.0 3 TD. **1998** KC: Rec 2-13 6.5; PR 1-0. **Total:** Rec 7-37 5.3 4 TD; PR 1-0.

		Rushing				Tot
Year Team	G	Att	Yds	Avg	TD	TD
1995 KC	14	8	18	2.3	0	0
1996 KC	13	4	10	2.5	0	1
1997 KC	14	2	11	5.5	0	3
1998 KC	14	20	45	2.3	2	2
NFL Total	55	34	84	2.5	2	6

C.J. RICHARDSON Richardson, Carl Ray Jr. 5′10″, 209 **DB**
Col: Miami (Fla.) *HS:* H. Grady Spruce [Dallas, TX] B: 6/10/1972, Dallas, TX *Drafted:* 1995 Round 7 Hou
1995 Ariz: 1 G. **1997** Sea: 14 G. **Total:** 15 G.

CHARLIE RICHARDSON Richardson, Charles A 143 **BB**
Col: No College *HS:* Englewood [Chicago, IL] B: 12/23/1907, IL D: 3/1977, Chicago, IL
1925 Mil: 1 G.

DAMIEN RICHARDSON Richardson, Damien Arnold 6′1″, 210 **DB**
Col: Arizona State *HS:* Clovis West [Fresno, CA] B: 4/3/1976, Los Angeles, CA *Drafted:* 1998 Round 6 Car
1998 Car: 14 G.

PETE RICHARDSON Richardson, E C 6′0″, 193 **DB**
Col: Dayton *HS:* South [Youngstown, OH] B: 10/17/1946, Youngstown, OH *Drafted:* 1968 Round 7 Buf
1969 Buf: 14 G; PR 1-0; Int 2-17; 1 Fum. **1970** Buf: 12 G; Int 5-46. **1971** Buf: 13 G; Int 1-0. **Total:** 39 G; PR 1-0; Int 8-63; 1 Fum.

ERIC RICHARDSON Richardson, Eric 6′1″, 183 **WR**
Col: Monterey Peninsula Coll. CA (J.C.); San Jose State *HS:* Novato [CA] B: 4/18/1962, San Francisco, CA *Drafted:* 1984 Round 2 Buf
1985 Buf: 16 G; Rec 12-201 16.8; KR 3-69 23.0. **1986** Buf: 14 G; Rec 3-49 16.3; PR 1-0; KR 6-123 20.5; 4 Fum. **Total:** 30 G; Rec 15-250 16.7; PR 1-0; KR 9-192 21.3; 4 Fum.

ERNIE RICHARDSON Richardson, Ernest 6′5″, 225 **TE**
Col: Jackson State *HS:* Coleman [Greenville, MS] B: 7/17/1950, Greenville, MS
1974 Cle: 2 G.

GLOSTER RICHARDSON Richardson, Gloster Van 6′2″, 200 **WR**
Col: Jackson State *HS:* Coleman [Greenville, MS] B: 7/18/1942, Greenville, MS *Drafted:* 1965 Round 7 KC
1968 KC: Rush 1-(-3) -3.0. **1970** KC: Rush 1-4 4.0. **1973** Cle: Rush 3-(-10) -3.3. **Total:** Rush 5-(-9) -1.8.

		Receiving				
Year Team	G	Rec	Yds	Avg	TD	Fum
1967 KC	13	12	312	26.0	2	0
1968 KC	13	22	494	22.5	6	0
1969 KC	13	23	381	16.6	2	0
1970 KC	12	5	171	34.2	2	0
1971 Dal	11	8	170	21.3	3	0
1972 Cle	7	1	7	7.0	0	0
1973 Cle	14	12	175	14.6	1	1
1974 Cle	9	9	266	29.6	2	0
NFL Total	92	92	1976	21.5	18	1

GRADY RICHARDSON Richardson, Grady Gene 6′4″, 225 **TE**
Col: Pasadena City Coll. CA (J.C.); Cal State-Fullerton *HS:* Phillis Wheatley [Houston, TX] B: 4/2/1952, Houston, TX
1979 Was: 3 G. **1980** Was: 1 G. **Total:** 4 G.

GREG RICHARDSON Richardson, Gregory Lamar 5′7″, 171 **WR**
Col: Alabama *HS:* Lillie B. Williamson [Mobile, AL] B: 10/6/1964, Mobile, AL *Drafted:* 1987 Round 6 Min
1987 Min: 2 G; PR 4-19 4.8; KR 4-76 19.0; 1 Fum. **1988** TB: 2 G. **Total:** 4 G; PR 4-19 4.8; KR 4-76 19.0; 1 Fum.

HUEY RICHARDSON Richardson, Huey L Jr. 6′5″, 238 **LB-DE**
Col: Florida *HS:* Lakeside [Atlanta, GA] B: 2/2/1968, Atlanta, GA *Drafted:* 1991 Round 1 Pit
1991 Pit: 5 G. **1992** Was-NYJ: 11 G. Was: 4 G. NYJ: 7 G. **Total:** 16 G.

JEFF RICHARDSON Richardson, Jeffrey 6′3″, 250 **OT-OG-C**
Col: Michigan State *HS:* Johnstown [PA] B: 9/1/1944, Johnstown, PA *Drafted:* 1967 Round 6 NYJ
1967 NYJ: 11 G. **1968** NYJ: 14 G. **1969** Mia: 3 G. **Total:** 28 G.

JERRY RICHARDSON Richardson, Jerome J 6′3″, 190 **DB**
(Sticks) *Col:* West Texas A&M *HS:* Canyon [TX] B: 11/13/1941, Los Angeles, LA *Drafted:* 1964 Round 3 LARm

		Interceptions		
Year Team	G	Int	Yds	TD
1964 LARm	14	5	146	0
1965 LARm	14	1	33	0
1966 Atl	14	5	68	0
1967 Atl	13	0	0	0
NFL Total	55	11	247	0

JERRY RICHARDSON Richardson, Jerome Johnson 6′3″, 185 **FL-OE-HB**
(The Razor) *Col:* Wofford *HS:* Fayetteville [NC] B: 7/11/1936, Spring Hope, NC *Drafted:* 1958 Round 13 Bal
1959 Bal: 11 G; Rec 7-81 11.6 3 TD; 18 Pt; 1 Fum. **1960** Bal: 11 G; Rec 8-90 11.3 1 TD; 6 Pt; 1 Fum. **Total:** 22 G; Rec 15-171 11.4 4 TD; 24 Pt; 2 Fum.

JESS RICHARDSON Richardson, Jesse William 6′2″, 261 **DT**
Col: Alabama *HS:* Roxborough [Philadelphia, PA] B: 8/18/1930, Philadelphia, PA D: 6/17/1975, Philadelphia, PA *Drafted:* 1953 Round 8 Phi
1953 Phi: 12 G. **1954** Phi: 12 G; Int 1-10. **1955** Phi: 12 G. **1956** Phi: 11 G. **1958** Phi: 12 G. **1959** Phi: 12 G. **1960** Phi: 12 G. **1961** Phi: 14 G. **1962** Bos: 14 G. **1963** Bos: 14 G. **1964** Bos: 14 G. **Total:** 139 G; Int 1-10.

JOHN RICHARDSON Richardson, John Edward 6'3", 245 **DT**
Col: UCLA *HS:* Kearny [San Diego, CA] B: 5/25/1945, Minneapolis, MN *Drafted:* 1967 Round 9 Mia
1967 Mia: 14 G. **1968** Mia: 11 G; KR 1-1 1.0; 1 Fum. **1969** Mia: 14 G. **1970** Mia: 14 G. **1971** Mia: 10 G. **1972** StL: 11 G. **1973** StL: 14 G. **Total:** 88 G; KR 1-1 1.0; 1 Fum.

BUCKY RICHARDSON Richardson, John Powell 6'1", 228 **QB**
Col: Texas A&M *HS:* Broadmoor [Baton Rouge, LA] B: 2/7/1969, Baton Rouge, LA *Drafted:* 1992 Round 8 Hou

		Passing							
Year Team	G	Att	Comp	Comp%	Yds	YPA	TD	Int	Rating
1992 Hou	7	0	0	—	0	—	0	0	—
1993 Hou	2	4	3	75.0	55	13.75	0	0	116.7
1994 Hou	7	181	94	51.9	1202	6.64	6	6	70.3
NFL Total	16	185	97	52.4	1257	6.79	6	6	71.4

	Rushing				
Year Team	Att	Yds	Avg	TD	Fum
1992 Hou	1	-1	-1.0	0	0
1993 Hou	2	9	4.5	0	0
1994 Hou	30	217	7.2	1	7
NFL Total	33	225	6.8	1	7

KYLE RICHARDSON Richardson, Kyle Davis 6'2", 190 **P**
Col: Arkansas State *HS:* Farmington [MO] B: 3/2/1973, Farmington, MO
1997 Mia-Sea: Rush 1-0. Sea: Rush 1-0. **1998** Bal: Rush 1-0. **Total:** Rush 2-0.

		Punting			
Year Team	G	Punts	Yds	Avg	Fum
1997 Mia-Sea	5	19	804	42.3	1
1997 Mia	3	11	480	43.6	0
1997 Sea	2	8	324	40.5	1
1998 Bal	16	90	3948	43.9	0
NFL Total	21	109	4752	43.6	1

MIKE RICHARDSON Richardson, Michael Calvin 6'0", 187 **DB**
Col: Arizona State *HS:* Compton [CA] B: 5/23/1961, Compton, CA *Drafted:* 1983 Round 2 ChiB
1983 ChiB: KR 1-17 17.0. **Total:** KR 1-17 17.0.

		Interceptions			
Year Team	G	Int	Yds	TD	Fum
1983 ChiB	16	5	9	0	0
1984 ChiB	15	2	7	0	0
1985 ChiB	14	4	174	**1**	1
1986 ChiB	16	7	69	0	3
1987 ChiB	11	0	0	0	0
1988 ChiB	16	2	15	0	0
1989 SF	3	0	0	0	0
NFL Total	91	20	274	1	4

MIKE RICHARDSON Richardson, Michael Wayne 5'11", 196 **RB**
Col: Southern Methodist *HS:* Castleberry [Fort Worth, TX] B: 12/8/1946, Fort Worth, TX *Drafted:* 1969 Round 7 Hou
1969 Hou: PR 7-93 13.3; Scor **1** 2XP. **1970** Hou: PR 10-30 3.0. **1971** Hou: KR 1-26 26.0. **Total:** PR 17-123 7.2; KR 1-26 26.0; Scor 1 2XP.

		Rushing				Receiving					Tot
Year Team	G	Att	Yds	Avg	TD	Rec	Yds	Avg	TD	Fum	TD
1969 Hou	14	5	51	10.2	0	0	0	—	0	1	0
1970 Hou	14	103	368	3.6	2	34	381	11.2	1	2	3
1971 Hou	7	17	33	1.9	0	4	17	4.3	0	0	0
NFL Total	35	125	452	3.6	2	38	398	10.5	1	3	3

PAUL RICHARDSON Richardson, Paul P 6'3", 204 **WR**
Col: UCLA *HS:* University [Los Angeles, CA] B: 2/25/1969, Chicago, IL
1993 Phi: 1 G.

REGGIE RICHARDSON Richardson, Reginald Eugene 6'0", 180 **DB**
Col: Utah *HS:* Gardena [CA] B: 4/13/1963, Houston, TX
1987 LARm: 3 G.

BOB RICHARDSON Richardson, Robert George 6'1", 180 **DB**
(Red) *Col:* UCLA *HS:* Kearny [San Diego, CA] B: 2/24/1944, Minneapolis, MN
1966 Den: 9 G.

TERRY RICHARDSON Richardson, Terry J 6'1", 205 **RB**
Col: Syracuse *HS:* Northeast [Fort Lauderdale, FL] B: 10/8/1971, Fort Lauderdale, FL
1996 Pit: 1 G; Rush 5-17 3.4.

TOM RICHARDSON Richardson, Thomas Edward 6'2", 195 **WR**
Col: Jackson State *HS:* Coleman [Greenville, MS] B: 10/15/1944, Greenville, MS
1969 Bos: 14 G; Rec 1-5 5.0. **1970** Bos: 1 G. **Total:** 15 G; Rec 1-5 5.0.

WALLY RICHARDSON Richardson, Wallace Herman 6'4", 225 **QB**
Col: Penn State *HS:* Sumter [SC] B: 2/11/1974, Orangeburg, SC *Drafted:* 1997 Round 7 Bal
1998 Bal: 1 G; Pass 2-1 50.0%, 1 0.50; Rush 1-0; 1 Fum.

WILLIE RICHARDSON Richardson, Willie Louis 6'1", 198 **WR**
Col: Jackson State *HS:* Coleman [Greenville, MS] B: 11/17/1939, Clarksdale, MS *Drafted:* 1963 Round 7 Bal
1963 Bal: PR 5-43 8.6; KR 1-16 16.0. **1971** Bal: Rush 2-27 13.5. **Total:** Rush 2-27 13.5; PR 5-43 8.6; KR 1-16 16.0.

		Receiving				
Year Team	G	Rec	Yds	Avg	TD	Fum
1963 Bal	13	17	204	12.0	0	1
1964 Bal	10	3	42	14.0	0	0
1965 Bal	9	1	14	14.0	1	0
1966 Bal	13	14	246	17.6	2	0
1967 Bal	14	63	860	13.7	8	1
1968 Bal	14	37	698	18.9	8	0
1969 Bal	14	43	646	15.0	3	2
1970 Mia	10	7	67	9.6	1	0
1971 Bal	12	10	173	17.3	2	0
NFL Total	109	195	2950	15.1	25	4

RAY RICHESON Richeson, Thomas Raymond 6'0", 235 **G**
Col: Alabama *HS:* Russellville [AL] B: 9/27/1923, Russellville, AL
AAFC **1949** ChiA: 12 G; KR 1-0.

MIKE RICHEY Richey, James Michael 6'4", 263 **OT**
Col: North Carolina *HS:* Myers Park [Charlotte, NC] B: 1/30/1947, Washington, DC *Drafted:* 1969 Round 4 Buf
1969 Buf: 14 G. **1970** NO: 5 G. **Total:** 19 G.

TOM RICHEY Richey, Thomas John 6'4", 274 **OT**
Col: Kentucky *HS:* Mentor [OH] B: 6/13/1961, Euclid, OH
1987 Cin: 3 G.

WADE RICHEY Richey, Wade Edward 6'4", 200 **K**
Col: Louisiana State *HS:* Carencro [Lafayette, LA] B: 5/19/1976, Lafayette, LA
1998 SF: 16 G; Scor 103, 18-27 66.7% FG, 49-51 96.1% XK.

DAVID RICHIE Richie, David James 6'4", 280 **NT**
Col: Washington *HS:* Kelso [WA] B: 9/26/1973, Orange, CA
1997 Den: 2 G; 0.5 Sac. **1998** SF: 8 G; KR 1-11 11.0. **Total:** 10 G; KR 1-11 11.0; 0.5 Sac.

ALDO RICHINS Richins, Aldo 5'9", 188 **WB-DB**
Col: Utah *HS:* West [Salt Lake City, UT] B: 11/2/1910, Colonia Diaz, Mexico D: 4/19/1995, Midvale, UT
1935 Det: 1 G.

HARRY RICHMAN Richman, Harry Eugene 5'11", 186 **G**
Col: Illinois *HS:* Central [Champaign, IL] B: 1/9/1907, Chicago, IL D: 5/1967, Champaign, IL
1929 ChiB: 1 G.

ROCK RICHMOND Richmond, Rodney 5'10", 180 **DB**
Col: Los Angeles Valley Coll. CA (J.C.); Oregon *HS:* Manual Arts [Los Angeles, CA] B: 1/7/1958, Los Angeles, CA
1987 Pit: 2 G.

FRANK RICHTER Richter, Frank Ashton IV 6'3", 235 **LB**
Col: Georgia *HS:* Cairo [GA] B: 12/24/1944, Tocca, GA *Drafted:* 1967 Round 7 Den
1967 Den: 9 G; Int 2-6. **1968** Den: 11 G. **1969** Den: 14 G. **Total:** 34 G; Int 2-6.

PAT RICHTER Richter, Hugh Vernon 6'5", 229 **TE-P**
Col: Wisconsin *HS:* East [Madison, WI] B: 9/9/1941, Madison, WI *Drafted:* 1963 Round 1 Was
1964 Was: Rush 1-(-9) -9.0. **1969** Was: KR 1-0. **1970** Was: KR 2-0. **Total:** Rush 1-(-9) -9.0; KR 3-0.

		Receiving				Punting			
Year Team	G	Rec	Yds	Avg	TD	Punts	Yds	Avg	Fum
1963 Was	14	27	383	14.2	3	53	2210	41.7	2
1964 Was	14	4	49	12.3	0	**91**	**3749**	41.2	1
1965 Was	11	16	189	11.8	2	54	2364	43.8	1
1966 Was	14	7	100	14.3	0	68	2884	42.4	0
1967 Was	14	1	31	31.0	0	72	2976	41.3	0
1968 Was	14	42	533	12.7	9	0	0	—	0
1969 Was	11	0	0	—	0	0	0	—	0
1970 Was	11	2	30	15.0	0	0	0	—	0
NFL Total	103	99	1315	13.3	14	338	14183	42.0	4

LES RICHTER Richter, Leslie Alan 6'3", 238 **LB**
Col: California *HS:* Fresno [CA] B: 10/6/1930, Fresno, CA *Drafted:* 1952 Round 1 Dal
1956 LARm: KR 1-4 4.0. **1962** LARm: Rush 0-8. **Total:** Rush 0-8; KR 1-4 4.0.

Year Team	G	Interceptions Int	Yds	TD
1954 LARm	12	1	24	0
1955 LARm	12	2	23	0
1956 LARm	12	0	0	0
1957 LARm	12	4	60	0
1958 LARm	12	3	26	0
1959 LARm	12	0	0	0
1960 LARm	12	2	29	0
1961 LARm	14	4	44	0
1962 LARm	14	0	0	0
NFL Total	112	16	206	0

Year Team	Scoring						
	Pts	FG	FGA	FG%	XK	XKA	XK%
1954 LARm	62	8	15	53.3	38	38	100.0
1955 LARm	69	13	**24**	54.2	30	31	96.8
1956 LARm	60	8	15	53.3	36	38	94.7
1959 LARm	0	0	1	0.0	0	0	—
1960 LARm	2	0	0	—	2	2	100.0
NFL Total	193	29	55	52.7	106	109	97.2

PAUL RICKARDS Rickards, Paul E 6'1", 190 **QB**
Col: Pittsburgh *HS:* Wheeling [WV] B: 6/30/1926, Wheeling, WV
1948 LARm: 3 G; Pass 2-2 100.0%, 4 2.00; Rush 2-21 10.5.

TOM RICKETTS Ricketts, Thomas Gordon Jr. 6'5", 296 **OG-OT**
Col: Pittsburgh *HS:* Franklin Regional [Murrysville, PA] B: 11/21/1965, Pittsburgh, PA *Drafted:* 1989 Round 1 Pit
1989 Pit: 12 G. **1990** Pit: 16 G. **1991** Pit: 14 G. **1992** Ind: 8 G. **1993** KC: 3 G. **Total:** 53 G.

HAROLD RICKS Ricks, Harold 5'10", 200 **RB**
Col: Tennessee-Chattanooga B: 12/26/1962
1987 TB: 3 G; Rush 24-76 3.2 1 TD; Rec 1-12 12.0; KR 1-26 26.0; 6 Pt; 3 Fum.

LAWRENCE RICKS Ricks, Lawrence Tallmadge 5'9", 194 **RB**
Col: Michigan *HS:* Barberton [OH] B: 6/4/1961, Barberton, OH
Drafted: 1983 Round 8 Dal
1983 KC: 12 G; Rush 21-28 1.3; Rec 3-5 1.7; 1 Fum. **1984** KC: 5 G; Rush 2-1 0.5; KR 5-83 16.6. **Total:** 17 G; Rush 23-29 1.3; Rec 3-5 1.7; KR 5-83 16.6; 1 Fum.

MIKHAEL RICKS Ricks, Mikhael Roy 6'5", 237 **WR**
Col: Stephen F. Austin St. *HS:* Anahuac [TX] B: 11/14/1974, Galveston, TX *Drafted:* 1998 Round 2 SD

Year Team	G	Receiving Rec	Yds	Avg	TD	Fum
1998 SD	16	30	450	15.0	2	1

SPEED RIDDELL Riddell, Ted Eugene 5'10", 185 **E**
Col: Nebraska *HS:* Beatrice [NE] B: 6/17/1896, Beatrice, NE
D: 12/8/1968, Scottsbluff, NE
1920 RI: 1 G.

LOUIS RIDDICK Riddick, Louis Angelo 6'2", 215 **DB**
Col: Pittsburgh *HS:* Pennridge [Perkasie, PA] B: 3/15/1969, Quakertown, PA *Drafted:* 1991 Round 9 SF
1992 Atl: 16 G; 1 Sac. **1993** Cle: 15 G; Scor 1 Saf; 2 Pt. **1994** Cle: 16 G. **1995** Cle: 16 G; Rec 1-25 25.0. **1996** Atl: 16 G; 1 Sac. **1998** Oak: 15 G. **Total:** 94 G; Rec 1-25 25.0; Scor 1 Saf; 2 Pt; 2 Sac.

RAY RIDDICK Riddick, Raymond Ernest 6'1", 211 **OE-DE**
Col: Fordham *HS:* Lowell [MA] B: 10/17/1917, Lowell, MA
D: 7/14/1976, Hampton, NH
1940 GB: 10 G; Rec 11-148 13.5. **1941** GB: 11 G; Rec 3-33 11.0; KR 1-14 14.0. **1942** GB: 3 G; Rec 6-104 17.3 1 TD; 6 Pt. **1946** GB: 2 G. **Total:** 26 G; Rec 20-285 14.3 1 TD; KR 1-14 14.0; 6 Pt.

ROBB RIDDICK Riddick, Robbert Lee 6'0", 195 **RB**
Col: Millersville *HS:* Pennridge [Perkasie, PA] B: 4/26/1957, Quakertown, PA *Drafted:* 1981 Round 9 Buf
1987 Buf: Pass 1-1 100.0%, 35 35.00; Scor 1 Saf. **1988** Buf: Pass 2-2 100.0%, 31 15.50. **Total:** Pass 3-3 100.0%, 66 22.00; Scor 1 Saf.

Year Team	G	Rushing Att	Yds	Avg	TD	Receiving Rec	Yds	Avg	TD
1981 Buf	10	3	29	9.7	0	0	0	—	0
1983 Buf	16	4	18	4.5	0	3	43	14.3	0
1984 Buf	16	3	3	1.0	0	23	276	12.0	0
1986 Buf	15	150	632	4.2	4	49	468	9.6	1
1987 Buf	6	59	221	3.7	5	15	96	6.4	3
1988 Buf	15	111	438	3.9	12	30	282	9.4	1
NFL Total	78	330	1341	4.1	21	120	1165	9.7	5

Year Team	Punt Returns Ret	Yds	Avg	TD	Kickoff Returns Ret	Yds	Avg	TD	Fum	Tot TD
1981 Buf	4	48	12.0	0	14	257	18.4	0	1	0
1983 Buf	42	241	5.7	0	28	568	20.3	0	7	0
1984 Buf	0	0	—	0	0	0	—	0	1	0
1986 Buf	0	0	—	0	8	200	25.0	0	8	5
1987 Buf	0	0	—	0	7	151	21.6	0	2	8
1988 Buf	0	0	—	0	6	100	16.7	0	3	14
NFL Total	46	289	6.3	0	63	1276	20.3	0	22	27

HOUSTON RIDGE Ridge, Houston Robert Jr. 6'4", 270 **DE-DT**
Col: Kings River CC CA; San Diego State *HS:* Madera [CA]
B: 7/18/1944, Madera, CA *Drafted:* 1966 Round 13 SD
1966 SD: 11 G. **1967** SD: 14 G. **1968** SD: 14 G. **1969** SD: 5 G. **Total:** 44 G.

ELSTON RIDGLE Ridgle, Elston Albert 6'6", 265 **DE**
Col: Northern Arizona; Nevada-Reno *HS:* El Camino Real [Woodland Hills, CA] B: 8/24/1963, Los Angeles, CA
1987 SF: 3 G. **1989** Buf-Sea: 3 G. Buf: 1 G. Sea: 2 G. **1990** Pho: 10 G. **1992** Cin: 7 G; 3 Sac. **Total:** 23 G; 3 Sac.

COLIN RIDGWAY Ridgway, Colin 6'5", 211 **P**
Col: Lamar B: 2/19/1937, Melbourne, Australia D: 5/13/1993, University Park, TX
1965 Dal: 3 G; Punt 13-510 39.2.

PRESTON RIDLEHUBER Ridlehuber, Howard Preston 6'2", 217 **RB**
Col: Georgia *HS:* Gainesville [GA] B: 11/2/1943, Greenwood, SC
Drafted: 1966 Round 11 SF
1966 Atl: 3 G; Rush 4-23 5.8; Rec 4-84 21.0 2 TD; 12 Pt. **1968** Oak: 10 G; Rush 4-7 1.8; **1** Fum TD; 6 Pt; 1 Fum. **1969** Buf: 9 G; Pass 1-1 100.0%, 45 45.00 1 TD; Rush 4-25 6.3; PR 1-3 3.0. **Total:** 22 G; Pass 1-1 100.0%, 45 45.00 1 TD; Rush 12-55 4.6; Rec 4-84 21.0 2 TD; PR 1-3 3.0; 1 Fum TD; Tot TD 3; 18 Pt; 1 Fum.

DON RIDLER Ridler, Donald George 6'0", 210 **T**
Col: Michigan State B: 1907, Detroit, MI D: 1963
1931 Cle: 1 G.

JIMMY RIDLON Ridlon, James Arthur 6'1", 181 **DB**
Col: Syracuse *HS:* Nyack [Upper Nyack, NY] B: 7/11/1934, Nanuet, NY *Drafted:* 1957 Round 4 SF
1957 SF: 12 G. **1958** SF: 12 G; Int 4-10. **1959** SF: 12 G. **1960** SF: 12 G. **1961** SF: 11 G. **1962** SF: 9 G; Int 1-8. **1963** Dal: 7 G. **1964** Dal: 14 G; Int 4-121 1 TD; 1 Fum TD; Tot TD 2; 12 Pt. **Total:** 89 G; Int 9-139 1 TD; 1 Fum TD; Tot TD 2; 12 Pt.

CHRIS RIEHM Riehm, Christopher Alan 6'6", 275 **OG-OT**
Col: Ohio State *HS:* Highland [Medina, OH] B: 4/14/1961, Columbus, OH
1986 LARd: 12 G. **1987** LARd: 1 G. **1988** LARd: 8 G. **Total:** 21 G.

JAY RIEMERSMA Riemersma, Allen Jay 6'5", 254 **TE**
Col: Michigan *HS:* Zeeland [MI] B: 5/17/1973, Evansville, IN
Drafted: 1996 Round 7 Buf
1997 Buf: Scor 1 2XP. **1998** Buf: KR 1-9 9.0. **Total:** KR 1-9 9.0; Scor 1 2XP.

Year Team	G	Receiving Rec	Yds	Avg	TD	Fum
1997 Buf	16	26	208	8.0	2	1
1998 Buf	16	25	288	11.5	6	0
NFL Total	32	51	496	9.7	8	1

JOHN RIENSTRA Rienstra, John William 6'5", 273 **OG**
Col: Temple *HS:* Acad. of the New Church [Bryn Athen, PA]
B: 3/22/1963, Grand Rapids, MI *Drafted:* 1986 Round 1 Pit
1986 Pit: 4 G. **1987** Pit: 12 G. **1988** Pit: 5 G. **1989** Pit: 15 G. **1990** Pit: 6 G. **1991** Cle: 16 G. **1992** Cle: 7 G. **Total:** 65 G.

DOUG RIESENBERG Riesenberg, Douglas John 6'5", 280 **OT**
Col: California *HS:* Moscow [ID] B: 7/22/1965, Moscow, ID
Drafted: 1987 Round 6 NYG
1987 NYG: 8 G. **1988** NYG: 16 G. **1989** NYG: 16 G. **1990** NYG: 16 G. **1991** NYG: 15 G. **1992** NYG: 16 G. **1993** NYG: 16 G. **1994** NYG: 16 G. **1995** NYG: 16 G. **1996** TB: 10 G. **Total:** 145 G.

BILL RIETH Rieth, William John Jr. 5'11", 203 **C-LB-G**
Col: Western Maryland; Carnegie Mellon *HS:* Lorain [OH]
B: 6/20/1916, Cleveland, OH
1941 Cle: 6 G. **1942** Cle: 10 G. **1944** Cle: 9 G; Int 1-12. **1945** Cle: 1 G. **Total:** 26 G; Int 1-12.

CHARLIE RIEVES Rieves, Charles Ernest 6'1", 218 **LB**
Col: Alabama; Houston *HS:* Anguilla [MS] B: 1/6/1939, Stuttgart, AR
1962 Oak: 14 G. **1963** Oak: 9 G. **1964** Hou: 8 G; Int 1-3. **1965** Hou: 7 G. **Total:** 38 G; Int 1-3.

DICK RIFENBURG Rifenburg, Richard Gale 6'3", 195 **OE**
Col: Michigan *HS:* Arthur Hill [Saginaw, MI] B: 8/21/1926, Petoskey, MI D: 12/5/1994, Cheektowaga, NY *Drafted:* 1948 Round 13 Phi
1950 Det: 12 G; Rec 10-96 9.6 1 TD; 6 Pt.

CHARLEY RIFFLE Riffle, Charles Francis 6'0", 212 **G-LB**
(Chuck) *Col:* Notre Dame *HS:* Warren G. Harding [Warren, OH]
B: 1/6/1918, Dillonvale, OH
AAFC **1946** NY-A: 14 G. **1947** NY-A: 14 G. **1948** NY-A: 14 G; Int 1-11.
Total: 42 G; Int 1-11.

NFL **1944** Cle: 8 G.

DICK RIFFLE Riffle, Fred Richard 6'1", 200 **DB-FB-TB-HB**
Col: Albright *HS:* Northside [Corning, NY] B: 2/2/1915, Wellsboro, PA
D: 4/29/1981, Corning, NY *Drafted:* 1938 Round 1 Phi
1939 Phi: Rec 6-57 9.5; Punt 17-683 40.2. **1940** Phi: Rec 8-58 7.3 1 TD; Punt 14-479 34.2. **1941** Pit: Rec 2-24 12.0 1 TD; PR 3-38 12.7; KR 9-237 26.3; Punt 7-246 35.1. **1942** Pit: Rec 3-50 16.7; PR 1-8 8.0; KR 7-137 19.6; Punt 1-40 40.0; Scor 25, 1-1 100.0% XK. **Total:** Rec 19-189 9.9 2 TD; PR 4-46 11.5; KR 16-374 23.4; Punt 39-1448 37.1; Scor 73, 1-1 100.0% XK.

		Passing							
Year Team	**G**	**Att**	**Comp**	**Comp%**	**Yds**	**YPA**	**TD**	**Int**	**Rating**
1938 Phi	11	31	9	29.0	178	5.74	2	4	32.9
1939 Phi	10	4	1	25.0	2	0.50	0	1	0.0
1940 Phi	11	0	0	—	0	—	0	0	—
1941 Pit	10	39	8	20.5	88	2.26	1	9	8.5
1942 Pit	11	8	3	37.5	64	8.00	0	1	27.1
NFL Total	53	82	21	25.6	332	4.05	3	15	16.6

	Rushing				Interceptions			Tot
Year Team	**Att**	**Yds**	**Avg**	**TD**	**Int**	**Yds**	**TD**	**TD**
1938 Phi	65	227	3.5	1	—	—	0	1
1939 Phi	18	61	3.4	0	—	—	0	0
1940 Phi	81	238	2.9	4	0	0	0	5
1941 Pit	109	388	3.6	1	6	93	0	2
1942 Pit	115	467	4.1	4	4	59	0	4
NFL Total	388	1381	3.6	10	10	152	0	12

CHARLES RIGGINS Riggins, Charles LaCarda 6'5", 295 **DE**
Col: Bethune-Cookman *HS:* Seminole [Sanford, FL] B: 11/9/1959, Sanford, FL
1987 TB: 3 G; 2 Sac.

JOHN RIGGINS Riggins, Robert John 6'2", 230 **RB**
Col: Kansas *HS:* Centralla [KS] B: 8/4/1949, Centralla, KS
Drafted: 1971 Round 1 NYJ *HOF:* 1992
1983 Was: Pass 1-0. **1985** Was: Pass 1-0. **Total:** Pass 2-0.

		Rushing				Receiving					Tot
Year Team	**G**	**Att**	**Yds**	**Avg**	**TD**	**Rec**	**Yds**	**Avg**	**TD**	**Fum**	**TD**
1971 NYJ	14	180	769	4.3	1	36	231	6.4	2	6	3
1972 NYJ	12	207	944	4.6	7	21	230	11.0	1	2	8
1973 NYJ	11	134	482	3.6	4	23	158	6.9	0	6	4
1974 NYJ	10	169	680	4.0	5	19	180	9.5	2	3	7
1975 NYJ	14	238	1005	4.2	8	30	363	12.1	1	5	9
1976 Was	14	162	572	3.5	3	21	172	8.2	1	6	4
1977 Was	5	68	203	3.0	0	7	95	13.6	2	0	2
1978 Was	15	248	1014	4.1	5	31	299	9.6	0	7	5
1979 Was	16	260	1153	4.4	9	28	163	5.8	3	5	12
1981 Was	15	195	714	3.7	13	6	59	9.8	0	1	13
1982 Was	8	**177**	553	3.1	3	10	50	5.0	0	2	3
1983 Was	15	375	1347	3.6	**24**	5	29	5.8	0	5	**24**
1984 Was	14	327	1239	3.8	**14**	7	43	6.1	0	7	14
1985 Was	12	176	677	3.8	8	6	18	3.0	0	3	8
NFL Total	175	2916	11352	3.9	104	250	2090	8.4	12	58	116

BOB RIGGLE Riggle, Robert Dunbar 6'1", 200 **DB**
Col: Penn State *HS:* Washington [PA] B: 2/5/1944, Washington, PA
Drafted: 1966 Round 20 Atl
1966 Atl: 14 G; Int 3-71 1 TD; 6 Pt. **1967** Atl: 11 G. **Total:** 25 G; Int 3-71 1 TD; 6 Pt.

GERALD RIGGS Riggs, Gerald Antonio 6'1", 230 **RB**
Col: Arizona State *HS:* Bonanza [Las Vegas, NV] B: 11/6/1960, Tullos, LA *Drafted:* 1982 Round 1 Atl
1983 Atl: KR 17-330 19.4. **1986** Atl: Pass 1-0. **Total:** Pass 1-0; KR 17-330 19.4.

		Rushing				Receiving				
Year Team	**G**	**Att**	**Yds**	**Avg**	**TD**	**Rec**	**Yds**	**Avg**	**TD**	**Fum**
1982 Atl	9	78	299	3.8	5	23	185	8.0	0	1
1983 Atl	14	100	437	4.4	8	17	149	8.8	0	7
1984 Atl	15	353	1486	4.2	13	42	277	6.6	0	11
1985 Atl	16	**397**	1719	4.3	10	33	267	8.1	0	0
1986 Atl	16	343	1327	3.9	9	24	136	5.7	0	6
1987 Atl	12	203	875	4.3	2	25	199	8.0	0	4
1988 Atl	9	113	488	4.3	1	22	171	7.8	0	3
1989 Was	12	201	834	4.1	4	7	67	9.6	0	3
1990 Was	10	123	475	3.9	6	7	60	8.6	0	2
1991 Was	16	78	248	3.2	11	1	5	5.0	0	1
NFL Total	129	1989	8188	4.1	69	201	1516	7.5	0	38

JIM RIGGS Riggs, James Thomas Jr. 6'5", 245 **TE**
Col: Clemson *HS:* Scotland [Laurinburg, NC] B: 9/23/1963, Fort Knox, KY *Drafted:* 1987 Round 4 Cin
1990 Cin: KR 1-7 7.0. **1991** Cin: KR 2-28 14.0. **Total:** KR 3-35 11.7.

		Receiving				
Year Team	**G**	**Rec**	**Yds**	**Avg**	**TD**	**Fum**
1987 Cin	9	0	0	—	0	0
1988 Cin	16	9	82	9.1	0	2
1989 Cin	10	5	29	5.8	0	0
1990 Cin	16	8	79	9.9	0	0
1991 Cin	16	4	14	3.5	0	0
1992 Cin	12	11	70	6.4	0	0
1993 Was	3	0	0	—	0	0
NFL Total	82	37	274	7.4	0	2

THRON RIGGS Riggs, Thron 6'1", 225 **T**
(Chris) *Col:* Washington *HS:* Buckley [WV] B: 4/25/1921, Buckley, WA
1944 Bos: 10 G.

JOE RIGHETTI Righetti, Joseph William 6'2", 253 **DT**
Col: Waynesburg *HS:* Bethlehem Center [Fredericktown, PA]
B: 12/31/1947, Fredericktown, PA *Drafted:* 1969 Round 6 Cle
1969 Cle: 14 G. **1970** Cle: 9 G; KR 1-17 17.0. **Total:** 23 G; KR 1-17 17.0.

RILEY Riley 5'11", 195 **G**
Col: No College *HS:* DePaul Acad. [Chicago, IL] B: 1902
1924 Rac: 1 G.

AVON RILEY Riley, Avon Gabrielle 6'3", 230 **LB**
Col: Coll. of the Canyons CA (J.C.); UCLA *HS:* Savannah [GA]
B: 2/10/1958, Savannah, GA *Drafted:* 1981 Round 9 Hou
1981 Hou: 16 G; KR 1-51 51.0. **1982** Hou: 9 G; KR 1-27 27.0; 1.5 Sac. **1983** Hou: 16 G; KR 0-26; Int 1-0; 0.5 Sac. **1984** Hou: 16 G; 2.5 Sac. **1985** Hou: 15 G; Int 1-14; 2 Sac. **1986** Hou: 16 G; KR 2-17 8.5. **1987** Pit: 3 G; KR 1-0; Int 1-4; 1 Fum. **Total:** 91 G; KR 5-121 24.2; Int 3-18; 1 Fum; 6.5 Sac.

CAMERON RILEY Riley, Cameron 6'1", 195 **DB**
(Cam) *Col:* Missouri *HS:* Metropolis [IL] B: 5/13/1964, Metropolis, IL
1987 Pit: 2 G.

ERIC RILEY Riley, Eric 6'3", 230 **TE**
Col: Eastern Washington *HS:* Mount Si [Snoqualmie, WA]
B: 10/10/1964, Snoqualmie, WA
1987 NYJ: 2 G; Rec 4-42 10.5.

JIM RILEY Riley, James Glen 6'4", 250 **DE**
Col: Oklahoma *HS:* Enid [OK] B: 7/6/1945, Galveston, TX
Drafted: 1967 Round 2 Mia
1967 Mia: 14 G. **1968** Mia: 13 G. **1969** Mia: 14 G. **1970** Mia: 14 G. **1971** Mia: 13 G. **Total:** 68 G.

JACK RILEY Riley, John Horn 6'3", 220 **T-G**
Col: Northwestern *HS:* New Trier Twp. [Winnetka, IL]; St. John's Mil. Acad. [Delafield, WI] B: 6/13/1909, Chicago, IL D: 3/22/1993, Kenilworth, IL
1933 Bos: 12 G.

KEN RILEY Riley, Kenneth Jerome 5'11", 181 **DB**
(Scooter) *Col:* Florida A&M *HS:* Union Acad. [Bartow, FL]
B: 8/6/1947, Bartow, FL *Drafted:* 1969 Round 6 Cin
1969 Cin: Rec 2-15 7.5; KR 14-334 23.9. **Total:** Rec 2-15 7.5; KR 14-334 23.9.

		Interceptions			
Year Team	**G**	**Int**	**Yds**	**TD**	**Fum**
1969 Cin	14	4	66	0	1
1970 Cin	14	4	17	0	0
1971 Cin	13	5	22	0	0
1972 Cin	12	3	0	0	0
1973 Cin	14	2	2	0	0
1974 Cin	14	5	33	0	1
1975 Cin	14	6	76	1	0
1976 Cin	14	9	141	1	1
1977 Cin	14	2	14	0	0
1978 Cin	16	3	33	0	0
1979 Cin	13	1	0	0	0
1980 Cin	16	3	9	0	0
1981 Cin	16	5	6	0	0
1982 Cin	9	5	88	**1**	0
1983 Cin	14	8	89	**2**	0
NFL Total	207	65	596	5	3

LARRY RILEY Riley, Lawrence 5'10", 192 **DB**
Col: Salem (NC) *HS:* Arlington [Lagrangeville, NY] B: 11/21/1954, Eustis, FL
1977 Den: 5 G. **1978** NYJ: 4 G. **Total:** 9 G.

LEE RILEY Riley, Leon Francis 6′1″, 192 **DB**
Col: Detroit Mercy *HS:* St. Aloysius Acad. [Schenectady, NY]
B: 8/24/1932, Omaha, NE *Drafted:* 1955 Round 4 Det
1956 Phi: Rec 1-10 10.0. **Total:** Rec 1-10 10.0.

		Punt Returns				Kickoff Returns			
Year Team	**G**	**Ret**	**Yds**	**Avg**	**TD**	**Ret**	**Yds**	**Avg**	**TD**
1955 Det	12	14	107	7.6	0	5	111	22.2	0
1956 Phi	9	17	73	4.3	0	15	381	25.4	0
1958 Phi	12	7	27	3.9	0	9	205	22.8	0
1959 Phi	12	0	0	—	0	0	0	—	0
1960 NYG	12	10	42	4.2	0	3	67	22.3	0
1961 NYT	12	0	0	—	0	0	0	—	0
1962 NYT	14	0	0	—	0	0	0	—	0
NFL Total	83	48	249	5.2	0	32	764	23.9	0

	Interceptions			
Year Team	**Int**	**Yds**	**TD**	**Fum**
1955 Det	2	38	0	1
1956 Phi	3	57	0	2
1958 Phi	1	8	0	0
1959 Phi	1	0	0	0
1960 NYG	1	2	0	2
1961 NYT	4	59	0	0
1962 NYT	**11**	122	0	0
NFL Total	23	286	0	5

EUGENE RILEY Riley, Milton Eugene 6′2″, 236 **TE**
Col: Ball State *HS:* Mount Healthy [Cincinnati, OH] B: 10/9/1966, Cincinnati, OH
1990 Ind: 1 G. **1991** Det: 5 G; Rec 1-3 3.0. **Total:** 6 G; Rec 1-3 3.0.

PAT RILEY Riley, Patrick Joseph 6′5″, 286 **DE**
Col: Miami (Fla.) *HS:* Archbishop Shaw [Marrero, LA] B: 3/8/1972, Marrero, LA *Drafted:* 1995 Round 2 ChiB
1995 ChiB: 1 G.

PHILLIP RILEY Riley, Phillip Shayon 5′11″, 189 **WR**
Col: Garden City CC KS; Florida State *HS:* Jones [Orlando, FL]
B: 9/24/1972, Orlando, FL *Drafted:* 1996 Round 6 Phi
1996 NYJ: 1 G.

PRESTON RILEY Riley, Preston Troy 6′0″, 180 **WR**
Col: Memphis *HS:* Culkin Acad. [Warren County, MS] B: 10/30/1947, Vicksburg, MS *Drafted:* 1970 Round 9 SF
1970 SF: 14 G; Rec 7-136 19.4; PR 1-5 5.0; KR 1-0; 1 Fum. **1971** SF: 14 G; Rec 3-39 13.0; PR 1-2 2.0. **1972** SF: 14 G; Rec 11-156 14.2 1 TD; 6 Pt; 1 Fum. **1973** NO: 1 G. **Total:** 43 G; Rec 21-331 15.8 1 TD; PR 2-7 3.5; KR 1-0; 6 Pt; 2 Fum.

BOBBY RILEY Riley, Robert 5′8″, 168 **WR**
Col: Oklahoma State *HS:* Casa Grande Union [AZ] B: 10/17/1964
1987 NYJ: 1 G.

BOB RILEY Riley, Robert Henry III 6′5″, 276 **OT**
Col: Indiana *HS:* North Allegheny [Wexford, PA] B: 6/23/1964, Pittsburgh, PA *Drafted:* 1987 Round 10 Min
1987 Cin: 3 G.

STEVE RILEY Riley, Steven Bruce 6′5″, 258 **OT**
Col: USC *HS:* Castle Park [Chula Vista, CA] B: 11/23/1952, Chula Vista, CA *Drafted:* 1974 Round 1 Min
1974 Min: 2 G. **1975** Min: 14 G. **1976** Min: 14 G. **1977** Min: 14 G. **1978** Min: 5 G. **1979** Min: 16 G. **1980** Min: 16 G. **1981** Min: 16 G. **1982** Min: 9 G. **1983** Min: 16 G. **1984** Min: 16 G. **Total:** 138 G.

BUTCH RILEY Riley, Thomas Mitchem 6′2″, 220 **LB**
Col: Texas A&M–Kingsville *HS:* Ingleside [TX] B: 3/13/1947, Ingleside, TX *Drafted:* 1969 Round 12 Bal
1969 Bal: 11 G.

VICTOR RILEY Riley, Victor Allan 6′5″, 321 **OT**
Col: Auburn *HS:* Swansea [SC] B: 11/4/1974, Swansea, SC
Drafted: 1998 Round 1 KC
1998 KC: 16 G.

DAVE RIMINGTON Rimington, David Brian 6′3″, 288 **C**
Col: Nebraska *HS:* Omaha South [NE] B: 5/22/1960, Omaha, NE
Drafted: 1983 Round 1 Cin
1983 Cin: 12 G; 1 Fum. **1984** Cin: 16 G. **1985** Cin: 16 G. **1986** Cin: 12 G; 2 Fum. **1987** Cin: 8 G; 2 Fum. **1988** Phi: 16 G. **1989** Phi: 6 G. **Total:** 86 G; 5 Fum.

STUART RINDY Rindy, Stuart 6′5″, 266 **OT**
Col: Wis.-Whitewater B: 5/22/1964, Milwaukee, WI
1987 ChiB: 2 G.

BILL RING Ring, William Thomas 5′10″, 208 **RB**
Col: Coll. of San Mateo CA (J.C.); Brigham Young *HS:* Carlmont [Belmont, CA] B: 12/13/1956, Des Moines, IA
1981 SF: KR 10-217 21.7. **1982** SF: KR 6-145 24.2. **1983** SF: KR 4-68 17.0. **1984** SF: KR 1-27 27.0. **1986** SF: KR 1-15 15.0. **Total:** KR 22-472 21.5.

		Rushing				Receiving					Tot
Year Team	**G**	**Att**	**Yds**	**Avg**	**TD**	**Rec**	**Yds**	**Avg**	**TD**	**Fum**	**TD**
1981 SF	12	22	106	4.8	0	3	28	9.3	1	1	1
1982 SF	8	48	183	3.8	1	13	94	7.2	0	1	1
1983 SF	16	64	254	4.0	2	23	182	7.9	0	1	2
1984 SF	16	38	162	4.3	3	3	10	3.3	0	0	3
1985 SF	10	8	23	2.9	1	2	14	7.0	0	0	1
1986 SF	7	3	4	1.3	0	1	8	8.0	0	0	0
NFL Total	69	183	732	4.0	7	45	336	7.5	1	3	8

JIM RINGO Ringo, James Stephen 6′1″, 232 **C**
Col: Syracuse *HS:* Phillipsburg [NJ] B: 11/21/1931, Orange, NJ
Drafted: 1953 Round 7 GB *HOF:* 1981
1953 GB: 5 G. **1954** GB: 12 G. **1955** GB: 12 G. **1956** GB: 12 G. **1957** GB: 12 G. **1958** GB: 12 G; Rush 0-13. **1959** GB: 12 G. **1960** GB: 12 G. **1961** GB: 14 G. **1962** GB: 14 G. **1963** GB: 14 G. **1964** Phi: 14 G. **1965** Phi: 14 G. **1966** Phi: 14 G. **1967** Phi: 14 G. **Total:** 187 G; Rush 0-13.

CARROLL RINGWALT Ringwalt, Carroll Walter 6′0″, 210 **C-G**
Col: Indiana B: 12/15/1907, Bedford, IN D: 6/26/1990, Indianapolis, IN
1930 Port: 3 G. **1931** Fra: 7 G. **Total:** 10 G.

HOP RIOPEL Riopel, Albert Didace 5′8″, 165 **TB**
Col: Holy Cross *HS:* Worcester Tech [MA] B: 10/11/1900, Worcester, MA D: 9/4/1966, Worcester, MA
1925 Prov: 4 G.

MIKE RIORDAN Riordan, Charles J 5′11″, 195 **BB-OE**
(Iron Mike) *Col:* New York U. *HS:* Bristol Central [CT] Deceased
1929 SI: 9 G.

TIM RIORDAN Riordan, Timothy P 6′1″, 185 **QB**
Col: Temple *HS:* New London [CT] B: 7/15/1960, New London, CT
Drafted: 1984 Supplemental Round 3 StL
1987 NO: 1 G; Pass 1-0; Rush 1-3 3.0.

ALAN RISHER Risher, Alan David 6′2″, 190 **QB**
Col: Louisiana State *HS:* Salmen [Slidell, LA] B: 5/6/1961, New Orleans, LA
1985 TB: Rush 1-10 10.0. **1987** GB: Rush 11-64 5.8 1 TD.
Total: Rush 12-74 6.2 1 TD.

		Passing								
Year Team	**G**	**Att**	**Comp**	**Comp%**	**Yds**	**YPA**	**TD**	**Int**	**Rating**	**Fum**
1985 TB	16	0	0	—	0	—	0	0	—	0
1987 GB	3	74	44	59.5	564	7.62	3	3	80.0	4
NFL Total	19	74	44	59.5	564	7.62	3	3	80.0	4

CODY RISIEN Risien, Cody Lewis 6′7″, 269 **OT-OG**
Col: Texas A&M *HS:* Cy-Fair [Houston, TX] B: 3/22/1957, Bryan, TX
Drafted: 1979 Round 7 Cle
1979 Cle: 16 G. **1980** Cle: 16 G. **1981** Cle: 16 G. **1982** Cle: 9 G. **1983** Cle: 16 G. **1985** Cle: 12 G. **1986** Cle: 16 G. **1987** Cle: 13 G. **1988** Cle: 16 G. **1989** Cle: 16 G. **Total:** 146 G.

ED RISK Risk, Edward Jr. 5′11″, 180 **FB**
Col: Purdue *HS:* Gerstmeyer [Terre Haute, IN] B: 4/5/1908, Terre Haute, IN D: 1/22/1969, Jacksonville, FL
1932 ChiC: 2 G.

ELLIOT RISLEY Risley, Elliot Clarence 6′0″, 207 **T**
Col: Indiana *HS:* Aurora East [IL] B: 1/24/1896, Compton, IL
D: 8/23/1942, Dixon, IL
1921 Ham: 5 G; Scor 2, 2 XK. **1922** Ham: 2 G. **1923** Ham: 2 G. **Total:** 9 G.

ANDRE RISON Rison, Andre Previn 6′1″, 188 **WR**
(Spider Man) *Col:* Michigan State *HS:* Northwestern [Flint, MI]
B: 3/18/1967, Flint, MI *Drafted:* 1989 Round 1 Ind
1989 Ind: Rush 3-18 6.0; PR 2-20 10.0; KR 8-150 18.8. **1990** Atl: PR 2-10 5.0. **1991** Atl: Rush 1-(-9) -9.0. **1994** Atl: Scor 1 2XP. **1995** Cle: Rush 2-0. **1997** KC: Rush 1-2 2.0. **1998** KC: Rush 2-12 6.0. **Total:** Rush 9-23 2.6; PR 4-30 7.5; KR 8-150 18.8; Scor 1 2XP.

		Receiving				
Year Team	**G**	**Rec**	**Yds**	**Avg**	**TD**	**Fum**
1989 Ind	16	52	820	15.8	4	1
1990 Atl	16	82	1208	14.7	10	2
1991 Atl	16	81	976	12.0	12	1
1992 Atl	15	93	1119	12.0	11	2
1993 Atl	16	86	1242	14.4	**15**	2
1994 Atl	15	81	1088	13.4	8	1
1995 Cle	16	47	701	14.9	3	1
1996 Jac-GB	15	47	593	12.6	3	1
1996 Jac	10	34	458	13.5	2	0
1996 GB	5	13	135	10.4	1	1
1997 KC	16	72	1092	15.2	7	0
1998 KC	14	40	542	13.6	5	1
NFL Total	155	681	9381	13.8	78	12

RAY RISSMILLER Rissmiller, Raymond Harold 6′4″, 250 **OT**
Col: Georgia *HS:* Easton [PA] B: 7/22/1942, Easton, PA
Drafted: 1965 Round 2 Phi
1966 Phi: 1 G. **1967** NO: 11 G. **1968** Buf: 4 G. **Total:** 16 G.

RAY RISVOLD Risvold, Raymond T 170 **WB-BB-FB-TB**
Col: No College *HS:* Woodstock [IL] B: 3/27/1902, WI D: 10/2/1984, Quincy, FL
1927 ChiC: 7 G. **1928** ChiC: 3 G. **Total:** 10 G.

JIM RITCHER Ritcher, James Alexander 6′3″, 265 **OG-C**
Col: North Carolina State *HS:* Highland [Medina, OH] B: 5/21/1958, Berea, OH *Drafted:* 1980 Round 1 Buf
1980 Buf: 14 G. **1981** Buf: 14 G. **1982** Buf: 9 G. **1983** Buf: 16 G. **1984** Buf: 14 G. **1985** Buf: 16 G. **1986** Buf: 16 G. **1987** Buf: 12 G. **1988** Buf: 16 G. **1989** Buf: 16 G. **1990** Buf: 16 G. **1991** Buf: 16 G. **1992** Buf: 16 G. **1993** Buf: 12 G. **1994** Atl: 2 G. **1995** Atl: 13 G. **Total:** 218 G.

JAMES RITCHEY Ritchey, James Alan 6′2″, 220 **QB**
Col: Stephen F. Austin St. *HS:* Copperas Cove [TX] B: 7/10/1973, Honolulu, HI
1997 Ten: 1 G; Pass 2-2 100.0%, 15 7.50; Rush 1-6 6.0.

DEL RITCHHART Ritchhart, Delbert Bush 6′0″, 195 **C-LB**
Col: Colorado *HS:* La Junta [CO] B: 11/2/1910 D: 3/1981, Denver, CO
1936 Det: 11 G; Int 1 TD; 6 Pt. **1937** Det: 10 G. **Total:** 21 G; Int 1 TD; 6 Pt.

JON RITCHIE Ritchie, Jon David 6′1″, 250 **RB**
Col: Michigan; Stanford *HS:* Cumberland Valley [Mechanicsburg, PA] B: 9/4/1974, Harrisburg, PA *Drafted:* 1998 Round 3 Oak
1998 Oak: Rush 9-23 2.6.

		Receiving				
Year Team	**G**	**Rec**	**Yds**	**Avg**	**TD**	**Fum**
1998 Oak	15	29	225	7.8	0	2

GABE RIVERA Rivera, Adrian Gabriel 6′2″, 293 **NT**
Col: Texas Tech *HS:* Thomas Jefferson [San Antonio, TX] B: 4/7/1961, Crystal City, TX *Drafted:* 1983 Round 1 Pit
1983 Pit: 6 G; 2 Sac.

HANK RIVERA Rivera, Henry Charles 5′11″, 180 **DB**
Col: Los Angeles City Coll. CA (J.C.); Oregon State *HS:* Belmont [Los Angeles, CA] B: 12/25/1938, Los Angeles, CA *Drafted:* 1962 Round 10 Oak
1962 Oak: 9 G. **1963** Buf: 3 G; KR 1-20 20.0. **Total:** 12 G; KR 1-20 20.0.

MARCO RIVERA Rivera, Marco Anthony 6′4″, 305 **OG**
Col: Penn State *HS:* Memorial [Elmont, NY] B: 4/26/1972, Brooklyn, NY *Drafted:* 1996 Round 6 GB
1997 GB: 14 G. **1998** GB: 15 G. **Total:** 29 G.

RON RIVERA Rivera, Ronald Eugene 6′3″, 239 **LB**
Col: California *HS:* Seaside [CA] B: 1/7/1962, Fort Ord, CA
Drafted: 1984 Round 2 ChiB
1984 ChiB: 15 G. **1985** ChiB: 16 G; Int 1-4; **1** Fum TD; 6 Pt; 0.5 Sac. **1986** ChiB: 16 G; 1 Sac. **1987** ChiB: 12 G; Int 2-19; 1 Sac. **1988** ChiB: 16 G; Int 2-0; 1 Fum; 2 Sac. **1989** ChiB: 16 G; Int 2-1; 2 Sac. **1990** ChiB: 14 G; Int 2-13. **1991** ChiB: 16 G. **1992** ChiB: 16 G; KR 1-0; 1 Sac. **Total:** 137 G; KR 1-0; Int 9-37; 1 Fum TD; 6 Pt; 1 Fum; 7.5 Sac.

STEVE RIVERA Rivera, Steven Jose 5′11″, 184 **WR**
Col: California *HS:* Phineas Banning [Los Angeles, CA] B: 8/5/1954, Pensacola, FL *Drafted:* 1976 Round 4 SF
1976 SF: 11 G; Rec 1-7 7.0; PR 1-3 3.0; 1 Fum. **1977** SF-ChiB: 4 G; Rec 1-7 7.0; PR 3-7 2.3. SF: 1 G; PR 3-7 2.3. ChiB: 3 G; Rec 1-7 7.0. **Total:** 15 G; Rec 2-14 7.0; PR 4-10 2.5; 1 Fum.

GARLAND RIVERS Rivers, Garland A 6′1″, 181 **DB**
Col: Michigan *HS:* McKinley [Canton, OH] B: 11/3/1964
Drafted: 1987 Round 4 Det
1987 ChiB: 2 G.

JAMIE RIVERS Rivers, James Albert 6′2″, 245 **LB**
Col: Bowling Green State *HS:* South [Youngstown, OH] B: 9/22/1945, Youngstown, OH *Drafted:* 1967 Round 5 StL
1968 StL: 9 G; Int 2-22. **1969** StL: 10 G. **1970** StL: 14 G. **1971** StL: 12 G. **1972** StL: 2 G. **1973** StL: 10 G; Int 1-11. **1974** NYJ: 13 G; Int 1-0. **1975** NYJ: 6 G. **Total:** 76 G; Int 4-33.

NATE RIVERS Rivers, Nathan 6′3″, 215 **RB**
Col: South Carolina State *HS:* St. John's [John's Island, SC] B: 8/31/1955, Wadmalaw Island, SC *Drafted:* 1980 Round 5 Phi
1980 NYG: 3 G.

REGGIE RIVERS Rivers, Reginald C 6′1″, 215 **RB**
Col: Southwest Texas State *HS:* Randolph [Universal City, TX] B: 2/22/1968, Dayton, OH
1993 Den: Scor 1 Saf. **1994** Den: Pass 1-0. **Total:** Pass 1-0; Scor 1 Saf.

		Rushing				Receiving					Tot
Year Team	**G**	**Att**	**Yds**	**Avg**	**TD**	**Rec**	**Yds**	**Avg**	**TD**	**Fum**	**TD**
1991 Den	16	2	5	2.5	0	0	0	—	0	0	0
1992 Den	16	74	282	3.8	3	45	449	10.0	1	2	4
1993 Den	16	15	50	3.3	1	6	59	9.8	1	0	2
1994 Den	16	43	83	1.9	2	20	136	6.8	0	1	2
1995 Den	16	2	2	1.0	0	3	32	10.7	0	0	0
1996 Den	16	2	6	3.0	0	1	-1	-1.0	0	0	0
NFL Total	96	138	428	3.1	6	75	675	9.0	2	3	8

RON RIVERS Rivers, Ronald Leroy 5′8″, 205 **RB**
Col: Fresno State *HS:* San Gorgonio [San Bernardino, CA]
B: 11/13/1971, Elizabeth, NJ
1995 Det: Rec 1-5 5.0; KR 19-420 22.1. **1996** Det: Rec 2-28 14.0; KR 1-8 8.0. **1997** Det: KR 2-34 17.0. **1998** Det: Rec 3-58 19.3; KR 2-15 7.5.
Total: Rec 6-91 15.2; KR 24-477 19.9.

		Rushing				
Year Team	**G**	**Att**	**Yds**	**Avg**	**TD**	**Fum**
1995 Det	16	18	73	4.1	1	2
1996 Det	15	19	86	4.5	0	0
1997 Det	16	29	166	5.7	1	0
1998 Det	15	19	102	5.4	1	0
NFL Total	62	85	427	5.0	3	2

DON RIVES Rives, Donald Earl 6′2″, 225 **LB**
Col: Texas Tech *HS:* Wheeler [TX] B: 8/30/1951, Wheeler, TX
Drafted: 1973 Round 15 ChiB
1973 ChiB: 14 G. **1974** ChiB: 14 G; Rush 1-2 2.0. **1975** ChiB: 2 G. **1976** ChiB: 14 G. **1977** ChiB: 14 G. **1978** ChiB: 16 G; Int 2-8. **Total:** 74 G; Rush 1-2 2.0; Int 2-8.

JACK RIZZO Rizzo, John Ralph 5′10″, 195 **RB**
Col: Lehigh *HS:* Weston [MA]; Kimball Union HS [Meriden, NH]
B: 6/15/1949, Boston, MA
1973 NYG: 6 G; Rush 1-3 3.0; Rec 1-11 11.0; KR 4-86 21.5.

JOE RIZZO Rizzo, Joseph Vincent 6′1″, 220 **LB**
Col: Kings Point *HS:* Glen Cove [NY] B: 12/17/1950, New York, NY
Drafted: 1973 Round 15 Buf
1974 Den: 11 G. **1975** Den: 14 G. **1976** Den: 12 G; Int 1-8. **1977** Den: 13 G; Int 3-49. **1978** Den: 14 G; Int 3-10. **1979** Den: 13 G; Int 2-25. **1980** Den: 4 G. **Total:** 81 G; Int 9-92.

JOHN ROACH Roach, John Gipson 6′4″, 197 **QB-DB**
Col: Southern Methodist *HS:* Highland Park [Dallas, TX] B: 3/26/1933, Dallas, TX *Drafted:* 1956 Round 3 ChiC
1956 ChiC: Punt 11-449 40.8. **Total:** Punt 11-449 40.8.

		Passing							
Year Team	**G**	**Att**	**Comp**	**Comp%**	**Yds**	**YPA**	**TD**	**Int**	**Rating**
1956 ChiC	8	0	0	—	0	—	0	0	—
1959 ChiC	12	57	22	38.6	340	5.96	2	4	41.6
1960 StL	12	188	87	46.3	1423	7.57	17	19	62.7
1961 GB	7	4	0	0.0	0	0.00	0	0	39.6
1962 GB	8	12	3	25.0	33	2.75	0	0	39.6
1963 GB	8	84	38	45.2	620	7.38	4	8	46.8
1964 Dal	9	68	32	47.1	349	5.13	1	6	30.8
NFL Total	64	413	182	44.1	2765	6.69	24	37	48.7

	Rushing				
Year Team	**Att**	**Yds**	**Avg**	**TD**	**Fum**
1959 ChiC	9	20	2.2	0	2
1960 StL	19	39	2.1	1	8
1961 GB	2	-5	-2.5	1	1
1962 GB	1	5	5.0	0	1
1963 GB	3	31	10.3	0	2
1964 Dal	8	9	1.1	0	5
NFL Total	42	99	2.4	2	19

ROLLIN ROACH Roach, Rollin 5′6″, 145 **FB-WB**
Col: Texas Christian B: 12/20/1902
1927 ChiC: 1 G; Rush 1 TD; 6 Pt.

TRAVIS ROACH Roach, Travis Morgan Jr. 6′2″, 260 **OG**
Col: Texas *HS:* Marlin [TX] B: 3/18/1950, Hamilton, TX D: 5/30/1988, Austin, TX *Drafted:* 1973 Round 6 NYJ
1974 NYJ: 14 G.

CARL ROACHES Roaches, Carl Edward 5′8″, 168 **WR**
Col: Texas A&M *HS:* M.B. Smiley [Houston, TX] B: 10/2/1953, Houston, TX *Drafted:* 1976 Round 14 TB
1984 Hou: Rec 4-69 17.3. **Total:** Rec 4-69 17.3.

		Punt Returns				Kickoff Returns				
Year Team	**G**	**Ret**	**Yds**	**Avg**	**TD**	**Ret**	**Yds**	**Avg**	**TD**	**Fum**
1980 Hou	16	47	384	8.2	0	37	746	20.2	0	6
1981 Hou	16	39	296	7.6	0	28	769	27.5	**1**	0
1982 Hou	9	19	104	5.5	0	21	441	21.0	0	1
1983 Hou	16	20	159	8.0	0	34	641	18.9	**1**	3

1984 Hou	16	26	152	5.8	0	30	679	22.6	0	1
1985 NO	3	4	21	5.3	0	4	76	19.0	0	1
NFL Total	76	155	1116	7.2	0	154	3352	21.8	2	12

WILLIE ROAF Roaf, William Layton 6′5″, 300 **OT**
Col: Louisiana Tech *HS:* Pine Bluff [AR] B: 4/18/1970, Pine Bluff, AR
Drafted: 1993 Round 1 NO
1993 NO: 16 G. **1994** NO: 16 G. **1995** NO: 16 G. **1996** NO: 13 G. **1997** NO: 16 G. **1998** NO: 15 G. **Total:** 92 G.

MICHAEL ROAN Roan, Michael Phillip 6′3″, 251 **TE**
Col: Wisconsin *HS:* Iowa City [IA] B: 8/29/1972, Iowa City, IA
Drafted: 1995 Round 4 Hou
1996 Hou: KR 1-13 13.0. **1997** Ten: KR 2-20 10.0. **1998** Ten: KR 1-4 4.0; 1 Fum TD. **Total:** KR 4-37 9.3; 1 Fum TD.

		Receiving				
Year Team	**G**	**Rec**	**Yds**	**Avg**	**TD**	**Fum**
1995 Hou	5	8	46	5.8	0	1
1996 Hou	15	0	0	—	0	0
1997 Ten	14	12	159	13.3	0	0
1998 Ten	16	13	93	7.2	0	1
NFL Total	50	33	298	9.0	0	2

OSCAR ROAN Roan, Oscar Bennie III 6′6″, 215 **TE**
Col: UCLA; Southern Methodist *HS:* South Oak Cliff [Dallas, TX]
B: 10/17/1951, Dallas, TX *Drafted:* 1975 Round 3 Cle

		Receiving				
Year Team	**G**	**Rec**	**Yds**	**Avg**	**TD**	**Fum**
1975 Cle	14	41	463	11.3	3	2
1976 Cle	11	15	174	11.6	4	0
1977 Cle	10	13	136	10.5	2	0
1978 Cle	14	0	0	—	0	0
NFL Total	49	69	773	11.2	9	2

JOE ROBB Robb, Alvis Joe 6′3″, 238 **DE-LB**
Col: Texas Christian *HS:* Lufkin [TX] B: 3/15/1937, Lufkin, TX
D: 4/18/1987, Houston, TX *Drafted:* 1959 Round 14 ChiB
1959 Phi: 12 G. **1960** Phi: 12 G; KR 4-44 11.0; 1 Fum. **1961** StL: 12 G; Int 1-3. **1962** StL: 14 G. **1963** StL: 14 G. **1964** StL: 13 G. **1965** StL: 14 G. **1966** StL: 14 G. **1967** StL: 11 G. **1968** Det: 9 G. **1969** Det: 14 G. **1970** Det: 6 G. **1971** Det: 14 G. **Total:** 159 G; KR 4-44 11.0; Int 1-3; 1 Fum.

HARRY ROBB Robb, Harry Duplein 5′10″, 186 **BB-WB-TB**
Col: Penn State; Columbia *HS:* Peabody [Pittsburgh, PA] B: 5/11/1897
D: 12/1971, Greenville, PA
1921 Can: 5 G; Rec 1 TD; 6 Pt. **1922** Can: 9 G; Rush 3 TD; 18 Pt. **1923** Can: 11 G; Rush 1 TD; 6 Pt. **1925** Can: 8 G; Rec 3 TD; 18 Pt. **1926** Can: 13 G; Rush 2 TD; Scor 13, 1 XK. **Total:** 46 G; Rush 6 TD; Rec 4 TD; Tot TD 10.

LOYAL ROBB Robb, Loyal Vestus 5′9″, 184 **T**
Col: No College *HS:* Rock Island [IL] B: 7/11/1890, Fillmore Co., NE
D: 6/7/1966, Kansas City, MO
1920 RI: 1 G.

STAN ROBB Robb, Stanley 6′0″, 185 **E**
Col: Centre *HS:* Peabody [Pittsburgh, PA]; Mercersburg Acad. [PA]
B: 1901
1926 Can: 3 G; Rec 1 TD; 6 Pt.

AUSTIN ROBBINS Robbins, Austin Dion 6′6″, 290 **DT**
Col: North Carolina *HS:* Howard D. Woodson [Washington, DC]
B: 3/1/1971, Washington, DC *Drafted:* 1994 Round 4 LARd
1994 LARd: 2 G. **1995** Oak: 16 G; **1** Fum TD; 6 Pt; 2 Sac. **1996** NO: 15 G; 1 Sac. **1997** NO: 12 G. **1998** NO: 16 G; 1 Fum TD; 6 Pt; 1 Sac.
Total: 61 G; 2 Fum TD; 12 Pt; 4 Sac.

BARRET ROBBINS Robbins, Barret G 6′3″, 310 **C**
Col: Texas Christian *HS:* Sharpstown [Houston, TX] B: 8/26/1973, Houston, TX *Drafted:* 1995 Round 2 Oak
1995 Oak: 16 G. **1996** Oak: 14 G. **1997** Oak: 16 G. **1998** Oak: 16 G.
Total: 62 G.

JACK ROBBINS Robbins, Jack William 6′2″, 183 **TB-DB**
Col: Arkansas *HS:* Little Rock Central [AR] B: 1/23/1916, Little Rock, AR D: 1/1983, Lafayette, LA *Drafted:* 1938 Round 1 ChiC
1939 ChiC: Rec 2-12 6.0; Punt 2-83 41.5. **Total:** Rec 2-12 6.0; Punt 2-83 41.5.

		Passing							
Year Team	**G**	**Att**	**Comp**	**Comp%**	**Yds**	**YPA**	**TD**	**Int**	**Rating**
1938 ChiC	9	97	52	53.6	577	5.95	2	9	39.8
1939 ChiC	8	85	36	42.4	499	5.87	4	10	37.9
NFL Total	17	182	88	48.4	1076	5.91	6	19	38.4

	Rushing			
Year Team	**Att**	**Yds**	**Avg**	**TD**
1938 ChiC	63	213	3.4	0
1939 ChiC	38	97	2.6	0
NFL Total	101	310	3.1	0

TOOTIE ROBBINS Robbins, James Elbert 6′5″, 303 **OT**
Col: East Carolina *HS:* Bertie County [Windsor, NC] B: 6/2/1958, Windsor, NC *Drafted:* 1982 Round 4 StL
1982 StL: 9 G. **1983** StL: 13 G. **1984** StL: 16 G. **1985** StL: 12 G. **1986** StL: 12 G. **1987** StL: 14 G. **1988** Pho: 15 G. **1989** Pho: 9 G. **1990** Pho: 16 G. **1991** Pho: 16 G. **1992** GB: 15 G. **1993** GB: 12 G. **Total:** 159 G.

KEVIN ROBBINS Robbins, Kevin Avery 6′5″, 286 **OT-OG**
Col: Wichita State; Michigan State *HS:* Howard D. Woodson [Washington, DC] B: 12/12/1966, Washington, DC *Drafted:* 1989 Round 3 LARm
1989 Cle: 1 G. **1990** Cle: 6 G. **1993** LARm: 1 G. **Total:** 8 G.

RANDY ROBBINS Robbins, Randy 6′2″, 189 **DB**
Col: Arizona *HS:* Casa Grande Union [AZ] B: 9/14/1962, Casa Grande, AZ *Drafted:* 1984 Round 4 Den
1984 Den: 1 Sac. **1986** Den: 4 Sac. **1987** Den: 1 Sac. **1988** Den: 2 Sac.
Total: 8 Sac.

		Interceptions			
Year Team	**G**	**Int**	**Yds**	**TD**	**Fum**
1984 Den	16	2	62	1	0
1985 Den	10	1	3	0	0
1986 Den	16	0	0	0	0
1987 Den	10	3	9	0	0
1988 Den	16	2	66	0	1
1989 Den	16	2	18	1	0
1990 Den	16	0	0	0	0
1991 Den	16	1	35	0	0
1992 NE	15	2	27	0	0
NFL Total	131	13	220	2	1

BO ROBERSON Roberson, Irvin 6′1″, 195 **WR-HB**
Col: Cornell *HS:* Bartram [Philadelphia, PA]; Wyoming Seminary [Kingston, PA] B: 7/23/1935, Blakely, GA
1962 Oak: Pass 6-0; Scor **1** 2XP. **1963** Oak: PR 2-34 17.0. **1964** Oak: PR 1-20 20.0. **Total:** Pass 6-0; PR 3-54 18.0; Scor 1 2XP.

		Rushing				Receiving			
Year Team	**G**	**Att**	**Yds**	**Avg**	**TD**	**Rec**	**Yds**	**Avg**	**TD**
1961 SD	14	58	275	4.7	3	6	81	13.5	0
1962 Oak	14	89	270	3.0	3	29	583	20.1	3
1963 Oak	14	19	47	2.5	0	25	407	16.3	3
1964 Oak	14	1	-4	-4.0	0	44	624	14.2	1
1965 Oak-Buf	14	1	-4	-4.0	0	46	703	15.3	3
1965 Oak	6	1	-4	-4.0	0	15	220	14.7	0
1965 Buf	8	0	0	—	0	31	483	15.6	3
1966 Mia	11	0	0	—	0	26	519	20.0	2
NFL Total	81	168	584	3.5	6	176	2917	16.6	12

	Kickoff Returns					Tot
Year Team	**Ret**	**Yds**	**Avg**	**TD**	**Fum**	**TD**
1961 SD	13	207	15.9	0	3	3
1962 Oak	27	748	27.7	**1**	4	7
1963 Oak	38	809	21.3	0	3	3
1964 Oak	36	975	**27.1**	0	0	1
1965 Oak-Buf	16	318	19.9	0	0	3
1965 Oak	12	259	21.6	0	0	0
1965 Buf	4	59	14.8	0	0	3
1966 Mia	0	0	—	0	0	2
NFL Total	130	3057	23.5	1	10	19

JAMES ROBERSON Roberson, James Earl 6′3″, 275 **DE**
Col: Florida State *HS:* Lake Wales [FL] B: 5/3/1971, Bartow, FL
1996 Hou: 15 G; 3 Sac. **1997** Ten: 15 G; 2 Sac. **1998** Ten: 10 G.
Total: 40 G; 5 Sac.

LAKE ROBERSON Roberson, James Lake Jr. 6′1″, 210 **DE**
Col: Mississippi *HS:* Clarksdale [MS] B: 8/5/1918, Clarksdale, MS
D: 12/11/1984, Lyon, MS
1945 Det: 4 G.

VERN ROBERSON Roberson, Vernon Lee 6′1″, 195 **DB**
Col: Grambling State *HS:* Natchitoches Central [LA] B: 8/3/1952, Natchitoches, LA
1977 Mia: 14 G; Int 1-0; 1 Fum. **1978** SF: 16 G; PR 1-7 7.0; Int 1-31.
Total: 30 G; PR 1-7 7.0; Int 2-31; 1 Fum.

ALFREDO ROBERTS Roberts, Alfredo 6′3″, 250 **TE**
Col: Miami (Fla.) *HS:* South Plantation [Plantation, FL] B: 3/1/1965, Fort Lauderdale, FL *Drafted:* 1988 Round 8 KC
1990 KC: KR 1-0. **Total:** KR 1-0.

		Receiving			
Year Team	**G**	**Rec**	**Yds**	**Avg**	**TD**
1988 KC	16	10	104	10.4	0
1989 KC	16	8	55	6.9	1
1990 KC	16	11	119	10.8	0
1991 Dal	16	16	136	8.5	1
1992 Dal	16	3	36	12.0	0
NFL Total	80	48	450	9.4	2

ARCHIE ROBERTS Roberts, Arthur James Jr. 6'0", 190 **QB**
Col: Columbia *HS:* Holyoke [MA] B: 11/4/1942, Holyoke, MA
Drafted: 1965 Round 7 NYJ
1967 Mia: 1 G; Pass 10-5 50.0%, 11 1.10 1 Int.

CLIFF ROBERTS Roberts, Clifford Jr. 6'3", 260 **OT**
Col: Illinois *HS:* Murrell Dobbins Area Vo-Tech [Philadelphia, PA]
B: 1938 *Drafted:* 1961 Round 6 SD
1961 Oak: 10 G.

C.R. ROBERTS Roberts, Cornelius R 6'3", 202 **FB**
Col: USC *HS:* Oceanside [CA] B: 2/29/1936, Los Angeles, CA
Drafted: 1958 Round 14 NYG
1960 SF: Rec 9-49 5.4; KR 3-60 20.0. **1961** SF: Rec 10-83 8.3. **1962** SF: Rec 2-0. **Total:** Rec 21-132 6.3; KR 3-60 20.0.

		Rushing				
Year Team	**G**	**Att**	**Yds**	**Avg**	**TD**	**Fum**
1959 SF	1	10	67	6.7	1	1
1960 SF	12	73	213	2.9	2	2
1961 SF	12	63	338	5.4	1	2
1962 SF	2	9	19	2.1	0	0
NFL Total	27	155	637	4.1	4	5

CHOO-CHOO ROBERTS Roberts, Eugene 0 5'11", 188 **HB-FB-DB**
Col: Tennessee-Chattanooga *HS:* East [Kansas City, MO]
B: 1/20/1923 *Drafted:* 1946 Round 8 NYG
1947 NYG: KR 8-141 17.6. **1948** NYG: PR 1-10 10.0; KR 7-160 22.9. **1949** NYG: Pass 1-0, 1 Int; KR 1-16 16.0. **1950** NYG: KR 1-13 13.0; Scor **1** Saf. **Total:** Pass 1-0, 1 Int; PR 1-10 10.0; KR 17-330 19.4; Scor 1 Saf.

		Rushing				Receiving					Tot
Year Team	**G**	**Att**	**Yds**	**Avg**	**TD**	**Rec**	**Yds**	**Avg**	**TD**	**Fum**	**TD**
1947 NYG	9	86	296	3.4	1	4	58	14.5	0	1	1
1948 NYG	11	145	491	3.4	0	14	222	15.9	3	9	3
1949 NYG	12	152	634	4.2	9	35	711	20.3	8	3	**17**
1950 NYG	12	116	483	4.2	4	11	144	13.1	1	6	5
NFL Total	44	499	1904	3.8	14	64	1135	17.7	12	19	26

FRED ROBERTS Roberts, Fred Everett 6'1", 200 **G**
Col: Iowa *HS:* Knoxville [IA] B: 3/18/1907, Knoxville, IA
D: 1/17/1982, Kansas City, KS
1930 Port: 12 G. **1931** Port: 13 G. **1932** Port: 1 G. **Total:** 26 G.

GARY ROBERTS Roberts, Gary Lee 6'2", 242 **OG**
Col: Purdue *HS:* Theodore Roosevelt [Kent, OH] B: 11/30/1946, Parkersburg, WV *Drafted:* 1969 Round 11 NYJ
1970 Atl: 11 G.

GEORGE ROBERTS Roberts, George William 6'0", 181 **P**
Col: Virginia Tech *HS:* E.C. Glass [Lynchburg, VA] B: 6/10/1955, Lynchburg, VA
1978 Mia: Rush 1-(-7) -7.0. **1981** SD: Rush 1-2 2.0. **Total:** Rush 2-(-5) -2.5.

		Punting		
Year Team	**G**	**Punts**	**Yds**	**Avg**
1978 Mia	16	81	3263	40.3
1979 Mia	16	69	2772	40.2
1980 Mia	16	77	3279	42.6
1981 SD	16	62	2540	41.0
1982 Atl	3	17	690	40.6
NFL Total	67	306	12544	41.0

GREG ROBERTS Roberts, Gregory Lafayette 6'3", 260 **OG**
Col: Oklahoma *HS:* Nacogdoches [TX] B: 11/19/1956, Nacogdoches, TX *Drafted:* 1979 Round 2 TB
1979 TB: 16 G. **1980** TB: 6 G. **1981** TB: 16 G. **1982** TB: 7 G. **Total:** 45 G.

GUY ROBERTS Roberts, Guy Michael 6'1", 218 **LB**
Col: Maryland *HS:* North Babylon [NY] B: 6/12/1950, North Babylon, NY *Drafted:* 1972 Round 8 Hou
1972 Hou: 7 G. **1973** Hou: 14 G; Int 4-55. **1974** Hou: 14 G. **1975** Hou: 14 G. **1976** Atl: 14 G; PR 1-0; KR 1-0; Int 1-7. **1977** Mia: 4 G. **Total:** 67 G; PR 1-0; KR 1-0; Int 5-62.

GUY ROBERTS Roberts, Guy Thomas 5'8", 175 **WB-FB-TB-BB**
(Zeke) *Col:* Iowa State *HS:* Storm Lake [IA] B: 5/10/1900, Schaler, IA
D: 6/8/1993, Los Altos, CA
1926 Can: 3 G. **1927** Pott: 8 G. **Total:** 11 G.

HAL ROBERTS Roberts, Hal Lynn 6'1", 180 **P**
Col: Houston *HS:* W.T. White [Dallas, TX] B: 8/25/1952, Dallas, TX

		Punting		
Year Team	**G**	**Punts**	**Yds**	**Avg**
1974 StL	14	81	3131	38.7

RED ROBERTS Roberts, James Madison 6'1", 235 **T-OE-TB-G**
Col: Centre *HS:* Somerset [KY] B: 8/23/1900, Somerset, KY
D: 6/27/1945, Middlesboro, KY
1922 Tol: 2 G. **1923** Akr: 1 G. **Total:** 3 G.

JACK ROBERTS Roberts, James Thomas 6'0", 210 **HB-DB-FB-LB**
(The Ripper) *Col:* Georgia *HS:* Albany [GA] B: 9/27/1910, Pine Log, GA D: 10/29/1981, St. Matthews, KY
1933 Phi: Pass 10-4 40.0%, 97 9.70 1 TD 3 Int; Rec 1-6 6.0.
Total: Pass 10-4 40.0%, 97 9.70 1 TD 3 Int; Rec 1-6 6.0.

		Rushing			
Year Team	**G**	**Att**	**Yds**	**Avg**	**TD**
1932 Bos-SI	8	20	80	4.0	0
1932 Bos	5	6	21	3.5	0
1932 SI	3	14	59	4.2	0
1933 Phi	9	91	261	2.9	1
1934 Phi-Pit	7	34	83	2.4	0
1934 Phi	1	10	28	2.8	0
1934 Pit	6	24	55	2.3	0
NFL Total	24	145	424	2.9	1

LARRY ROBERTS Roberts, Larry P 6'3", 270 **DE**
Col: Alabama *HS:* Northview [Dothan, AL] B: 6/2/1963, Dothan, AL
Drafted: 1986 Round 2 SF
1986 SF: 16 G; 5.5 Sac. **1987** SF: 11 G; 2.5 Sac. **1988** SF: 16 G; 6 Sac. **1989** SF: 15 G; 3.5 Sac. **1990** SF: 6 G; 1 Sac. **1991** SF: 16 G; 7 Sac. **1992** SF: 3 G; Int 1-19; 1 Sac. **1993** SF: 6 G; 1.5 Sac. **Total:** 89 G; Int 1-19; 28.0 Sac.

MACE ROBERTS Roberts, Mason W 6'0", 185 **OE-G-T**
Col: No College B: 6/25/1896, IL D: 1/7/1971, Hammond, IN
1920 Ham: 5 G. **1921** Ham: 1 G. **1922** Ham: 2 G. **1924** Ham: 4 G. **Total:** 12 G.

RAY ROBERTS Roberts, Richard Ray Jr. 6'6", 308 **OT**
Col: Virginia *HS:* Asheville [NC] B: 6/3/1969, Asheville, NC
Drafted: 1992 Round 1 Sea
1992 Sea: 16 G. **1993** Sea: 16 G; Rec 1-4 4.0. **1994** Sea: 14 G. **1995** Sea: 11 G. **1996** Det: 16 G; Rec 0-5. **1997** Det: 14 G. **1998** Det: 16 G. **Total:** 103 G; Rec 1-9 9.0.

TOM ROBERTS Roberts, Thomas Albert 6'1", 215 **T-G**
Col: DePaul *HS:* Fenger [Chicago, IL] B: 4/1/1916, New Troy, MI
Deceased *Drafted:* 1939 Round 8 NYG
1943 NYG: 9 G. **1944** ChiB: 7 G. **1945** ChiB: 9 G. **Total:** 25 G.

TIM ROBERTS Roberts, Timothy 6'6", 310 **DT**
Col: Southern Mississippi *HS:* D.M. Therrell [Atlanta, GA]
B: 4/14/1969, Atlanta, GA *Drafted:* 1992 Round 5 Hou
1992 Hou: 6 G. **1993** Hou: 6 G. **1994** Hou: 12 G. **1995** NE: 13 G; 1 Sac. **Total:** 37 G; 1 Sac.

WALTER ROBERTS Roberts, Walter 5'9", 163 **WR**
(The Flea) *Col:* San Jose State *HS:* Compton [CA] B: 2/15/1942, Texarkana, TX
1965 Cle: Rush 3-30 10.0. **1967** NO: **1** Fum TD. **1970** Was: Rush 2-15 7.5. **Total:** Rush 5-45 9.0; 1 Fum TD.

		Receiving				Punt Returns			
Year Team	**G**	**Rec**	**Yds**	**Avg**	**TD**	**Ret**	**Yds**	**Avg**	**TD**
1964 Cle	14	1	24	24.0	1	10	132	13.2	0
1965 Cle	14	16	314	19.6	4	18	162	9.0	0
1966 Cle	14	2	19	9.5	0	11	42	3.8	0
1967 NO	13	17	384	22.6	3	11	50	4.5	0
1969 Was	14	4	66	16.5	0	12	32	2.7	0
1970 Was	14	27	411	15.2	1	10	28	2.8	0
NFL Total	83	67	1218	18.2	9	72	446	6.2	0

	Kickoff Returns					Tot
Year Team	**Ret**	**Yds**	**Avg**	**TD**	**Fum**	**TD**
1964 Cle	24	661	27.5	0	1	1
1965 Cle	18	493	27.4	0	1	4
1966 Cle	20	454	22.7	0	3	0
1967 NO	28	737	26.3	1	0	5
1969 Was	17	383	22.5	0	6	0
1970 Was	0	0	—	0	3	1
NFL Total	107	2728	25.5	1	14	11

WES ROBERTS Roberts, Wesley Lee 6'6", 253 **DE**
Col: Texas Christian *HS:* Palo Duro [Amarillo, TX] B: 8/1/1957, Dodge City, KS *Drafted:* 1980 Round 7 Bal
1980 NYJ: 6 G.

BILL ROBERTS Roberts, William 6'0", 200 **HB**
Col: Dartmouth *HS:* Dubuque [IA] B: 9/11/1929, Dubuque, IA
1956 GB: 4 G; Rec 1-14 14.0.

WILLIAM ROBERTS Roberts, William Harold 6'5", 291 **OG-OT**
Col: Ohio State *HS:* Miami Carol City [Miami, FL] B: 8/5/1962, Miami, FL *Drafted:* 1984 Round 1 NYG
1984 NYG: 11 G. **1986** NYG: 16 G. **1987** NYG: 12 G. **1988** NYG: 16 G. **1989** NYG: 16 G. **1990** NYG: 16 G. **1991** NYG: 16 G. **1992** NYG: 16 G. **1993** NYG: 16 G. **1994** NYG: 16 G. **1995** NE: 16 G. **1996** NE: 16 G. **1997** NYJ: 12 G. **Total:** 195 G.

WILLIE ROBERTS Roberts, Willie Lee 6'1", 190 **DB**
Col: Houston *HS:* Monroe [Rochester, NY]; Deerfield Academy [MA] B: 6/28/1948, Colquitt, GA
1973 ChiB: 4 G.

WOOKY ROBERTS Roberts, Wolcott 5'7", 160 **BB-TB**
Col: Colgate; Navy *HS:* Peoria [IL] B: 9/1/1897, Elmwood, IL D: 8/27/1951, Drexel Hill, PA
1922 Can: 11 G; Pass 1 TD; Rush 1 TD; 6 Pt. **1923** Can: 8 G; Rush 1 TD; 6 Pt. **1924** Cle: 9 G; Pass 2 TD; Rush 1 TD; Rec 3 TD; Scor 25, 1 XK; Tot TD 4. **1925** Cle: 2 G. **1926** Fra: 6 G; Rec 1 TD; 6 Pt. **Total:** 36 G; Pass 3 TD; Rush 3 TD; Rec 4 TD; Tot TD 7.

HARRY ROBERTSON Robertson, Harold J 5'10", 185 **T**
Col: Syracuse *HS:* Somerville [MA]; Worcester HS [MA] B: 3/4/1896, Chambly, Canada Deceased
1922 Roch: 1 G.

ISIAH ROBERTSON Robertson, Isiah B 6'3", 225 **LB**
Col: Southern University *HS:* Pine View [Covington, LA] B: 8/17/1949, New Orleans, LA *Drafted:* 1971 Round 1 LARm
1978 LARm: 1 Fum TD. **Total:** 1 Fum TD.

		Interceptions				Tot
Year Team	**G**	**Int**	**Yds**	**TD**	**Fum**	**TD**
1971 LARm	14	4	32	0	0	0
1972 LARm	14	0	0	0	0	0
1973 LARm	14	3	57	1	1	1
1974 LARm	14	2	11	0	0	0
1975 LARm	14	4	118	1	0	1
1976 LARm	14	4	28	0	1	0
1977 LARm	14	1	20	0	0	0
1978 LARm	13	0	0	0	0	1
1979 Buf	16	2	29	1	0	1
1980 Buf	16	2	39	0	0	0
1981 Buf	16	2	15	0	0	0
1982 Buf	9	1	0	0	0	0
NFL Total	168	25	349	3	2	4

JAMES ROBERTSON Robertson, James A 5'8", 160 **BB-WB-TB**
Col: Carnegie Mellon *HS:* Allegheny Prep [Pittsburgh, PA] B: 3/8/1901 D: 12/1974, Cuyahoga Falls, OH
1924 Akr: 8 G. **1925** Akr: 8 G; Rush 1 TD; Rec 1 TD; Tot TD 2; 12 Pt. **Total:** 16 G; Rush 1 TD; Rec 1 TD; Tot TD 2; 12 Pt.

BOB ROBERTSON Robertson, John Robert 6'4", 246 **OT**
Col: Illinois *HS:* Pleasant Hill [IL] B: 12/24/1946, Pittsfield, IL *Drafted:* 1968 Round 9 Hou
1968 Hou: 14 G; KR 2-9 4.5.

MARCUS ROBERTSON Robertson, Marcus Aaron 5'11", 198 **DB**
Col: Iowa State *HS:* John Muir [Pasadena, CA] B: 10/2/1969, Pasadena, CA *Drafted:* 1991 Round 4 Hou
1991 Hou: PR 1-0; 1 Sac. **1993** Hou: 1 Fum TD. **1994** Hou: PR 1-0. **1997** Ten: PR 1-0; 2 Fum TD. **Total:** PR 3-0; 3 Fum TD; 1 Sac.

		Interceptions			
Year Team	**G**	**Int**	**Yds**	**TD**	**Fum**
1991 Hou	16	0	0	0	1
1992 Hou	16	1	27	0	0
1993 Hou	13	7	137	0	0
1994 Hou	16	3	90	0	1
1995 Hou	2	0	0	0	0
1996 Hou	16	4	44	0	0
1997 Ten	14	5	127	0	0
1998 Ten	12	1	0	0	0
NFL Total	105	21	425	0	2

BOBBY ROBERTSON Robertson, Robert James 5'11", 185 **HB-DB**
Col: USC; St. Mary's (Cal.) *HS:* Central [Omaha, NE] B: 6/18/1917, Pine Ridge, SD *Drafted:* 1942 Round 1 Bkn
1942 Bkn: Pass 3-1 33.3%, 1 0.33 1 Int; Rec 5-61 12.2; PR 1-4 4.0; Int 2-30; Punt 1-32 32.0.

		Rushing			
Year Team	**G**	**Att**	**Yds**	**Avg**	**TD**
1942 Bkn	11	46	132	2.9	0

TOM ROBERTSON Robertson, Thomas Blane 6'0", 199 **C-LB**
Col: Kansas; Louisiana State; Tulsa *HS:* Duncan [OK] B: 7/25/1917, Lawton, OK
AAFC **1946** NY-A: 14 G.
NFL **1941** Bkn: 11 G. **1942** Bkn: 9 G; KR 1-9 9.0; Int 1-2. **Total:** 20 G; KR 1-9 9.0; Int 1-2.

PAUL ROBESON Robeson, Paul Leroy 6'3", 219 **E-T**
Col: Rutgers *HS:* Somerville [NJ] B: 4/9/1898, Princeton, NJ D: 1/23/1976, Philadelphia, PA
1921 Akr: 8 G. **1922** Mil: 7 G; Rec 1 TD; 1 Fum TD; Tot TD 2; 12 Pt. **Total:** 15 G; Rec 1 TD; 1 Fum TD; Tot TD 2; 12 Pt.

BRYAN ROBINSON Robinson, Bryan Keith 6'4", 295 **DE**
Col: Coll. of the Desert CA (J.C.); Fresno State *HS:* Woodward [Toledo, OH] B: 6/22/1974, Toledo, OH
1997 StL: 11 G; 1 Sac. **1998** ChiB: 11 G; 0.5 Sac. **Total:** 22 G; 1.5 Sac.

CHARLEY ROBINSON Robinson, Charles Rogers 5'11", 240 **OG-LB**
Col: Morgan State *HS:* Maggie L. Walker [Richmond, VA] B: 5/30/1927, Lester Manor, VA
1951 GB: 2 G. **1954** Bal: 6 G; KR 1-19 19.0; **1** Fum TD; 6 Pt. **Total:** 8 G; KR 1-19 19.0; 1 Fum TD; 6 Pt.

DAMIEN ROBINSON Robinson, Damien Arnold 6'2", 210 **DB**
Col: Iowa *HS:* Hillcrest [Dallas, TX] B: 12/22/1973, Dallas, TX *Drafted:* 1997 Round 4 Phi
1998 TB: 7 G.

JUNIOR ROBINSON Robinson, David Lee Jr. 5'9", 181 **DB**
Col: East Carolina *HS:* T. Wingate Andrews [High Point, NC] B: 2/3/1968, High Point, NC D: 9/30/1995, Winston-Salem, NC *Drafted:* 1990 Round 5 NE
1990 NE: 16 G; KR 11-211 19.2; 2 Fum. **1992** Det: 10 G. **Total:** 26 G; KR 11-211 19.2; 2 Fum.

DEJUAN ROBINSON Robinson, DeJuan Fitzgerald 5'10", 185 **DB**
Col: Northern Arizona *HS:* Serra [San Diego, CA] B: 6/3/1965, Selma, AL
1987 Cle: 3 G; Int 1-0.

DON ROBINSON Robinson, Don Kanary 6'5", 280 **OT**
Col: Baylor *HS:* North Dallas [Dallas, TX] B: 2/5/1965, Dallas, TX
1987 Atl: 2 G.

EDDIE ROBINSON Robinson, Eddie Joseph Jr. 6'1", 240 **LB**
Col: Alabama State *HS:* Brother Martin [New Orleans, LA] B: 4/13/1970, New Orleans, LA *Drafted:* 1992 Round 2 Hou
1992 Hou: 16 G; 1 Sac. **1993** Hou: 16 G; 1 Sac. **1994** Hou: 15 G. **1995** Hou: 16 G; Int 1-49 1 TD; 6 Pt; 3.5 Sac. **1996** Jac: 16 G; 1 Sac. **1997** Jac: 16 G; Int 1-0; 2 Sac. **1998** Ten: 16 G; Int 1-11; 3.5 Sac. **Total:** 111 G; Int 3-60 1 TD; 6 Pt; 12 Sac.

ED ROBINSON Robinson, Edward III 6'0", 228 **LB**
Col: Florida *HS:* Walton [De Funiak Springs, FL] B: 12/7/1970, DeFuniak Springs, FL
1994 Pit: 16 G.

ED ROBINSON Robinson, Eldred 5'8", 155 **BB-WB-WB-TB**
Col: No College *HS:* Oak Park [IL] Deceased
1923 Ham: 3 G; PR **1** TD; Scor 7, 1 XK. **1924** Ham: 4 G. **1925** Ham: 5 G; Rec 1 TD; 6 Pt. **1926** Ham-Lou: 5 G. Ham: 1 G. Lou: 4 G. **Total:** 17 G; Rec 1 TD; PR 1 TD; Tot TD 2.

EUGENE ROBINSON Robinson, Eugene Keefe 6'1", 190 **DB**
(The Prophet) *Col:* Colgate *HS:* Weaver [Hartford, CT] B: 5/28/1963, Hartford, CT
1985 Sea: KR 1-10 10.0. **1988** Sea: 1 Sac. **1990** Sea: 1 Fum TD. **1991** Sea: 1 Sac. **1993** Sea: 2 Sac. **1994** Sea: 1 Sac. **1995** Sea: PR 1-1 1.0. **1997** GB: 2.5 Sac. **Total:** PR 1-1 1.0; KR 1-10 10.0; 1 Fum TD; 7.5 Sac.

		Interceptions				Tot
Year Team	**G**	**Int**	**Yds**	**TD**	**Fum**	**TD**
1985 Sea	16	2	47	0	0	0
1986 Sea	16	3	39	0	0	0
1987 Sea	12	3	75	0	0	1
1988 Sea	16	1	0	0	0	0
1989 Sea	16	5	24	0	1	0
1990 Sea	16	3	89	0	0	1
1991 Sea	16	5	56	0	0	0
1992 Sea	16	7	126	0	0	0
1993 Sea	16	**9**	80	0	0	0
1994 Sea	14	3	18	0	0	0
1995 Sea	16	1	32	0	0	0
1996 GB	16	6	107	0	0	0
1997 GB	16	1	26	0	1	0
1998 Atl	16	4	36	1	0	1
NFL Total	218	53	755	1	2	3

RAFAEL ROBINSON Robinson, Eugene Rafael 5'11", 200 **DB**
Col: Wisconsin *HS:* Thomas Jefferson [San Antonio, TX] B: 6/19/1969, Marshall, TX
1992 Sea: 6 G. **1993** Sea: 16 G; 1.5 Sac. **1994** Sea: 16 G; Int 1-0. **1995** Sea: 13 G. **1996** Hou: 16 G; Int 1-2. **1997** Ten: 3 G. **Total:** 70 G; Int 2-2; 1.5 Sac.

FRANK ROBINSON Robinson, Frank Lawson 5′11″, 175 **DB**
Col: Boise State *HS:* Novato [CA] B: 1/11/1969, Newark, NJ
Drafted: 1992 Round 5 Den
1992 Cin-Den: 15 G; KR 4-89 22.3. Cin: 3 G. Den: 12 G; KR 4-89 22.3.
1993 Den: 16 G; Int 1-13. **Total:** 31 G; KR 4-89 22.3; Int 1-13.

FRED ROBINSON Robinson, Fred Lee 6′4″, 240 **DE-LB**
Col: Navarro Coll. TX (J.C.); Miami (Fla.) *HS:* Miami Jackson [FL]
B: 10/22/1961, Miami, FL *Drafted:* 1984 Round 8 TB
1984 SD: 16 G; 4.5 Sac. **1985** SD: 16 G; 7 Sac. **1986** SD-Mia: 14 G;
3 Sac. SD: 10 G; 1 Sac. Mia: 4 G; 2 Sac. **Total:** 46 G; 14.5 Sac.

FRED ROBINSON Robinson, Frederick Leroy Jr. 6′1″, 242 **OG**
Col: Washington *HS:* West Haven [CT] B: 9/2/1930, West Haven, CT
Drafted: 1955 Round 14 Cle
1957 Cle: 12 G; PR 1-0.

FREDDIE ROBINSON Robinson, Frederick O'Neal 6′1″, 191 **DB**
Col: Alabama *HS:* W.P. Davidson [Mobile, AL] B: 2/1/1964, Mobile, AL
Drafted: 1987 Round 6 Ind
1987 Ind: 9 G; Int 2-86. **1988** Ind: 13 G. **Total:** 22 G; Int 2-86.

JERRY ROBINSON Robinson, Gerald 5′11″, 190 **WR**
(Smiley) *Col:* Grambling State *HS:* Jackson [Jonesboro, LA]
B: 3/9/1939, Jonesboro, LA *Drafted:* 1962 Round 8 SD
1962 SD: Rush 2-10 5.0. **1964** SD: Rush 1-10 10.0; PR 7-41 5.9.
1965 NYJ: PR 3-36 12.0. **Total:** Rush 3-20 6.7; PR 10-77 7.7.

		Receiving				Kickoff Returns				
Year Team	**G**	**Rec**	**Yds**	**Avg**	**TD**	**Ret**	**Yds**	**Avg**	**TD**	**Fum**
1962 SD	14	21	391	18.6	3	32	748	23.4	0	1
1963 SD	14	18	315	17.5	2	2	27	13.5	0	0
1964 SD	14	10	93	9.3	0	3	70	23.3	0	3
1965 NYJ	4	0	0	—	0	7	164	23.4	0	1
NFL Total	46	49	799	16.3	5	44	1009	22.9	0	5

GERALD ROBINSON Robinson, Gerald 6′3″, 262 **DE-DT**
Col: Auburn *HS:* Notasulga [AL] B: 5/4/1963, Tuskegee, AL
Drafted: 1986 Round 1 Min
1986 Min: 12 G; 3.5 Sac. **1987** Min: 4 G. **1989** SD: 2 G. **1990** SD: 11 G;
2 Sac. **1991** LARm: 15 G; 3 Sac. **1992** LARm: 16 G; 5 Sac. **1993** LARm:
16 G; 3 Sac. **1994** LARm: 13 G; 2.5 Sac. **Total:** 89 G; 19 Sac.

GIL ROBINSON Robinson, Gilmer George 6′0″, 180 **E**
Col: Catawba *HS:* Spencer [NC] B: 4/18/1910, Spencer, NC
D: 7/11/1985, Hemet, CA
1933 Pit: 1 G.

GLENN ROBINSON Robinson, Glenn William 6′6″, 242 **DE-LB**
Col: Navarro Coll. TX (J.C.); Oklahoma State *HS:* Thomas Jefferson
[Dallas, TX] B: 10/20/1951, Killeen, TX *Drafted:* 1974 Round 3 Bal
1975 Bal: 11 G. **1976** TB: 14 G. **1977** TB: 14 G. **Total:** 39 G.

GREG ROBINSON Robinson, Greg 5′10″, 205 **RB**
Col: Holmes CC MS; Northeast Louisiana *HS:* Grenada [MS]
B: 8/7/1969, Grenada, MS *Drafted:* 1993 Round 8 LARd
1993 LARd: Rec 15-142 9.5; KR 4-57 14.3. **1995** StL: Rec 2-12 6.0.
1996 StL: Rec 1-6 6.0. **Total:** Rec 18-160 8.9; KR 4-57 14.3.

		Rushing				
Year Team	**G**	**Att**	**Yds**	**Avg**	**TD**	**Fum**
1993 LARd	12	156	591	3.8	1	3
1995 StL	5	40	165	4.1	0	0
1996 StL	11	32	134	4.2	1	1
NFL Total	28	228	890	3.9	2	4

GREGG ROBINSON Robinson, Gregg Alan 6′6″, 255 **DE-NT**
Col: Dartmouth *HS:* Minnechaug Regional [Wilbraham, MA]
B: 8/16/1956, Palmer, MA *Drafted:* 1978 Round 6 NYJ
1978 NYJ: 16 G.

GREG ROBINSON Robinson, Gregory Louis 6′5″, 280 **OT**
Col: Nevada-Reno; Sacramento State *HS:* Elk Grove [CA]
B: 12/25/1962, Sacramento, CA *Drafted:* 1986 Round 5 NE
1986 TB: 3 G. **1987** NE: 3 G. **Total:** 6 G.

JACK ROBINSON Robinson, Jack 6′3″, 220 **T-G**
Col: Northeast Missouri State B: 6/1/1911, Miami, NM
1935 Bkn: 8 G. **1936** Bkn-ChiC: 11 G. Bkn: 3 G. ChiC: 8 G. **1937** ChiC:
11 G. **1938** Pit-Cle: 8 G. Pit: 2 G. Cle: 6 G. **Total:** 38 G.

JACQUE ROBINSON Robinson, Jacque Cornelius 5′11″, 215 **RB**
Col: Washington *HS:* San Jose [CA] B: 3/5/1963, Oakland, CA
1987 Phi: 3 G; Rush 24-114 4.8; Rec 2-9 4.5; 1 Fum.

JIM ROBINSON Robinson, James Peter 5′9″, 170 **WR**
Col: Georgia Tech *HS:* Columbia [South Orange, NJ]; Ridgeview HS
[Atlanta, GA] B: 1/3/1953, New York, NY *Drafted:* 1975 Round 15 Atl

		Receiving				Punt Returns				
Year Team	**G**	**Rec**	**Yds**	**Avg**	**TD**	**Ret**	**Yds**	**Avg**	**TD**	**Fum**
1976 NYG	12	18	249	13.8	1	24	106	4.4	0	
1977 NYG	14	22	422	19.2	3	7	87	12.4	0	
1978 NYG	16	32	620	19.4	2	19	106	5.6	0	
1979 NYG	11	13	146	11.2	0	6	29	4.8	0	
1980 SF	5	0	0	—	0	3	36	12.0	0	
NFL Total	58	85	1437	16.9	6	59	364	6.2	0	

	Kickoff Returns				
Year Team	**Ret**	**Yds**	**Avg**	**TD**	**Fum**
1976 NYG	20	444	22.2	0	3
1978 NYG	0	0	—	0	1
1979 NYG	7	140	20.0	0	2
NFL Total	27	584	21.6	0	6

JEFF ROBINSON Robinson, Jeffrey William 6′4″, 269 **DE**
Col: Idaho *HS:* Joel E. Ferris [Spokane, WA] B: 2/20/1970, Kennewick,
WA *Drafted:* 1993 Round 4 Den
1993 Den: 16 G; 1 Fum; 3.5 Sac. **1994** Den: 16 G; 1 Sac. **1995** Den: 16 G;
KR 1-14 14.0; 1 Sac. **1996** Den: 16 G; 0.5 Sac. **1997** StL: 16 G; 0.5 Sac.
1998 StL: 16 G; Rec 1-4 4.0 1 TD; 6 Pt. **Total:** 96 G; Rec 1-4 4.0 1 TD;
KR 1-14 14.0; 6 Pt; 1 Fum; 6.5 Sac.

JEROY ROBINSON Robinson, Jeroy 6′1″, 241 **LB**
Col: Texas A&M *HS:* Bryan [TX] B: 6/14/1968, Houston, TX
Drafted: 1990 Round 4 Den
1990 Den-Pho: 6 G. Den: 3 G. Pho: 3 G. **Total:** 6 G.

JERRY ROBINSON Robinson, Jerry Dewayne 6′2″, 223 **LB**
Col: UCLA *HS:* Cardinal Newman [Santa Rosa, CA] B: 12/18/1956,
San Francisco, CA *Drafted:* 1979 Round 1 Phi
1980 Phi: **1** Fum TD. **1982** Phi: 1 Sac. **1983** Phi: 1 Sac. **1984** Phi: 1 Sac.
1986 LARd: 2 Sac. **1987** LARd: 4.5 Sac. **1988** LARd: 2 Sac. **1989** LARd:
0.5 Sac. **1990** LARd: 2 Sac. **Total:** 1 Fum TD; 14 Sac.

		Interceptions				Tot
Year Team	**G**	**Int**	**Yds**	**TD**	**Fum**	**TD**
1979 Phi	16	0	0	0	0	0
1980 Phi	16	2	13	0	1	1
1981 Phi	15	1	3	0	0	0
1982 Phi	9	3	19	0	0	0
1983 Phi	16	0	0	0	0	0
1984 Phi	15	0	0	0	0	0
1985 LARd	11	0	0	0	0	0
1986 LARd	16	4	42	1	0	2
1987 LARd	12	0	0	0	0	0
1988 LARd	15	0	0	0	0	0
1989 LARd	11	1	25	0	1	0
1990 LARd	16	1	5	1	0	1
1991 LARd	16	0	0	0	0	0
NFL Total	184	12	107	2	2	4

CRAIG ROBINSON Robinson, Joe Craig 6′4″, 250 **OT**
Col: Houston *HS:* Lanier [Austin, TX] B: 12/23/1948, Austin, TX
Drafted: 1971 Round 16 NO
1972 NO: 8 G. **1973** NO: 11 G. **Total:** 19 G.

JOHNNIE ROBINSON Robinson, John 6′3″, 205 **DB**
Col: Tennessee State *HS:* St. Elmo [AL] B: 11/6/1944, Mobile, AL
Drafted: 1966 Round 7 Det
1966 Det: 14 G; PR 13-185 14.2 **1** TD; KR 6-127 21.2; 6 Pt; 4 Fum.

BILLY ROBINSON Robinson, John William 6′1″, 200 **DB**
Col: Arizona State *HS:* Victor Valley [Victorville, CA] B: 2/13/1963,
Wichita, KS
1987 Cle: 3 G.

JOHNNY ROBINSON Robinson, Johnny Dean 6′2″, 260 **NT**
Col: Louisiana Tech *HS:* Ruston [LA] B: 2/14/1959, Jonesboro, LA
Drafted: 1981 Round 4 Oak
1981 Oak: 16 G; Scor **1** Saf; 2 Pt. **1982** LARd: 7 G. **1983** LARd: 4 G.
Total: 27 G; Scor 1 Saf; 2 Pt.

JOHNNY ROBINSON Robinson, Johnny Nolan 6′1″, 205 **DB-HB**
Col: Louisiana State *HS:* University [Baton Rouge, LA] B: 9/9/1938,
Delhi, LA *Drafted:* 1960 Round 1 DalT
1960 DalT: Pass 1-0, 1 Int; PR 14-207 14.8 **1** TD; KR 3-54 18.0.
1961 DalT: PR 2-4 2.0. **1963** KC: PR 1-16 16.0. **1964** KC: PR 1-16 16.0.
1967 KC: PR 1-3 3.0. **1968** KC: PR 2-26 13.0. **1970** KC: 1 Fum TD.
Total: Pass 1-0, 1 Int; PR 21-272 13.0 1 TD; KR 3-54 18.0; 1 Fum TD.

		Rushing				Receiving			
Year Team	**G**	**Att**	**Yds**	**Avg**	**TD**	**Rec**	**Yds**	**Avg**	**TD**
1960 DalT	14	98	458	4.7	4	41	611	14.9	4
1961 DalT	14	52	200	3.8	2	35	601	17.2	5
1962 DalT	14	0	0	—	0	1	16	16.0	0
1963 KC	14	0	0	—	0	0	0	—	0
1964 KC	10	0	0	—	0	0	0	—	0
1965 KC	14	0	0	—	0	0	0	—	0
1966 KC	14	0	0	—	0	0	0	—	0
1967 KC	14	0	0	—	0	0	0	—	0
1968 KC	14	0	0	—	0	0	0	—	0
1969 KC	14	0	0	—	0	0	0	—	0
1970 KC	14	0	0	—	0	0	0	—	0

1971 KC	14	0	0	—	0	0	0	—	0
NFL Total	164	150	658	4.4	6	77	1228	15.9	9

	Interceptions				Tot
Year Team	Int	Yds	TD	Fum	TD
1960 DalT	0	0	0	8	9
1961 DalT	0	0	0	1	7
1962 DalT	4	25	0	0	0
1963 KC	3	41	0	0	0
1964 KC	2	17	0	0	0
1965 KC	5	99	0	0	0
1966 KC	**10**	136	1	0	1
1967 KC	5	17	0	1	0
1968 KC	6	40	0	0	0
1969 KC	8	**158**	0	0	0
1970 KC	**10**	155	0	0	1
1971 KC	4	53	0	0	0
NFL Total	57	741	1	10	18

TONY ROBINSON Robinson, Kevin Altona 6′3″, 200 **QB**
Col: Tennessee *HS:* Leon [Tallahassee, FL] B: 1/22/1964, Monticello, FL
1987 Was: 1 G; Pass 18-11 61.1%, 152 8.44 2 Int; Rush 2-0.

LARRY ROBINSON Robinson, Lawrence Cordell 6′4″, 210 **RB**
Col: Ferrum; Tennessee *HS:* Carver-Price [Appomattox, VA]
B: 4/6/1951, Appomattox, VA
1973 Dal: 4 G; Rush 2-17 8.5; KR 4-86 21.5; 1 Fum.

LARRY ROBINSON Robinson, Lawrence Wayne 5′9″, 194 **DB**
Col: Northwestern State-Louisiana *HS:* Natchitoches Central [LA]
B: 4/30/1962, Shreveport, LA
1987 NYJ: 3 G; Int 1-38.

LYBRANT ROBINSON Robinson, Lybrant 6′4″, 250 **DE**
Col: Delaware State *HS:* James M. Bennett [Salisbury, MD]
B: 8/31/1964, Salisbury, MD *Drafted:* 1989 Round 5 Was
1989 Was: 5 G.

MARCUS ROBINSON Robinson, Marcus Antonio 6′3″, 213 **WR**
Col: South Carolina *HS:* Peach Co. [Fort Valley, GA] B: 2/27/1975, Fort Valley, GA *Drafted:* 1997 Round 4 ChiB
1998 ChiB: 3 G; Rec 4-44 11.0 1 TD; 6 Pt.

MARK ROBINSON Robinson, Mark Leon 5′11″, 206 **DB**
Col: Penn State *HS:* John F. Kennedy [Silver Spring, MD]
B: 9/13/1962, Washington, DC *Drafted:* 1984 Round 4 KC
1985 KC: 2 Sac. **1987** KC: KR 5-97 19.4. **1989** TB: 2.5 Sac.
Total: KR 5-97 19.4; 4.5 Sac.

		Interceptions		
Year Team	G	Int	Yds	TD
1984 KC	16	0	0	0
1985 KC	11	1	20	0
1986 KC	9	0	0	0
1987 KC	12	2	42	0
1988 TB	9	2	28	0
1989 TB	15	6	44	0
1990 TB	16	4	81	0
NFL Total	88	15	215	0

MATT ROBINSON Robinson, Matthew Gillette 6′2″, 196 **QB**
Col: Georgia *HS:* North Springs [Atlanta, GA] B: 6/28/1955, Farmington, MI *Drafted:* 1977 Round 9 NYJ

		Passing							
Year Team	G	Att	Comp	Comp%	Yds	YPA	TD	Int	Rating
1977 NYJ	4	54	20	37.0	310	5.74	2	8	29.6
1978 NYJ	16	266	124	46.6	2002	7.53	13	16	63.5
1979 NYJ	15	31	17	54.8	191	6.16	0	2	46.6
1980 Den	14	162	78	48.1	942	5.81	2	12	39.7
1981 Buf	15	2	0	0.0	0	0.00	0	0	39.6
1982 Buf	5	8	5	62.5	74	9.25	1	0	132.3
NFL Total	69	523	244	46.7	3519	6.73	18	38	50.2

	Rushing				
Year Team	Att	Yds	Avg	TD	Fum
1977 NYJ	5	45	9.0	0	1
1978 NYJ	28	23	0.8	0	6
1979 NYJ	3	4	1.3	1	0
1980 Den	21	47	2.2	3	6
1981 Buf	1	-2	-2.0	0	1
NFL Total	58	117	2.0	4	14

BO ROBINSON Robinson, Melvin Dell 6′2″, 228 **RB-TE**
Col: West Texas A&M *HS:* Lamesa [TX] B: 5/27/1956, La Mesa, TX
Drafted: 1979 Round 3 Det
1979 Det: KR 1-8 8.0. **1984** NE: KR 3-38 12.7. **Total:** KR 4-46 11.5.

		Rushing				Receiving					Tot
Year Team	G	Att	Yds	Avg	TD	Rec	Yds	Avg	TD	Fum	TD
1979 Det	14	87	302	3.5	2	14	118	8.4	0	3	2
1980 Det	14	3	2	0.7	0	0	0	—	0	0	0
1981 Atl	15	9	24	2.7	0	0	0	—	0	0	0
1982 Atl	9	19	108	5.7	0	7	55	7.9	2	0	2
1983 Atl	12	3	9	3.0	0	12	100	8.3	0	1	0
1984 NE	16	0	0	—	0	4	32	8.0	1	0	1
NFL Total	80	121	445	3.7	2	37	305	8.2	3	4	5

MIKE ROBINSON Robinson, Michael Bruce 6′4″, 265 **DE**
Col: Oklahoma State; Arizona *HS:* Glenville [Cleveland, OH]
B: 8/19/1956, Cleveland, OH *Drafted:* 1981 Round 4 Cle
1981 Cle: 10 G. **1982** Cle: 8 G; 3 Sac. **Total:** 18 G; 3 Sac.

MIKE ROBINSON Robinson, Michael F 6′1″, 192 **DB**
Col: Hampton *HS:* Cenrtal [King and Queen, VA] B: 6/24/1973, Richmond, VA
1996 GB: 6 G.

REX ROBINSON Robinson, Noble Rexford 5′11″, 205 **K**
Col: Georgia *HS:* Marietta [GA] B: 3/17/1959, Marietta, GA
Drafted: 1981 Round 6 Cin
1982 NE: 3 G; Scor 8, 1-2 50.0% FG, 5-5 100.0% XK.

PATRICK ROBINSON Robinson, Patrick Lavel 5′8″, 176 **WR**
Col: Tennessee State *HS:* Northside [Memphis, TN] B: 10/3/1969, Memphis, TN *Drafted:* 1993 Round 7 Hou
1993 Cin: Rush 1-6 6.0; Rec 8-72 9.0. **1994** Ariz: Rec 1-5 5.0.
Total: Rush 1-6 6.0; Rec 9-77 8.6.

		Punt Returns				Kickoff Returns				
Year Team	G	Ret	Yds	Avg	TD	Ret	Yds	Avg	TD	Fum
1993 Cin	15	**43**	305	7.1	0	30	567	18.9	0	2
1994 Ariz	15	41	285	7.0	0	12	231	19.3	0	1
NFL Total	30	84	590	7.0	0	42	798	19.0	0	3

PAUL ROBINSON Robinson, Paul Harvey 6′0″, 198 **RB**
(Straight Runner) *Col:* Eastern Arizona Coll. (J.C.); Arizona *HS:* Marana [Tuscon, AZ] B: 12/19/1944, Tucson, AZ *Drafted:* 1968 Round 3 Cin
1968 Cin: PR 1-1 1.0. **1970** Cin: PR 1-0. **Total:** PR 2-1 0.5.

		Rushing				Receiving			
Year Team	G	Att	Yds	Avg	TD	Rec	Yds	Avg	TD
1968 Cin	14	**238**	**1023**	4.3	**8**	24	128	5.3	1
1969 Cin	14	160	489	3.1	4	20	104	5.2	0
1970 Cin	14	149	622	4.2	6	17	175	10.3	1
1971 Cin	14	49	213	4.3	1	8	47	5.9	0
1972 Cin-Hou	12	107	449	4.2	3	14	112	8.0	0
1972 Cin	4	21	94	4.5	0	0	0	—	0
1972 Hou	8	86	355	4.1	3	14	112	8.0	0
1973 Hou	11	34	151	4.4	2	7	46	6.6	0
NFL Total	79	737	2947	4.0	24	90	612	6.8	2

	Kickoff Returns					Tot
Year Team	Ret	Yds	Avg	TD	Fum	TD
1968 Cin	3	58	19.3	0	4	9
1969 Cin	5	168	33.6	0	4	4
1970 Cin	14	363	25.9	0	0	7
1971 Cin	18	335	18.6	0	1	1
1972 Cin-Hou	0	0	—	0	0	3
1972 Hou	0	0	—	0	0	3
1973 Hou	0	0	—	0	0	2
NFL Total	40	924	23.1	0	9	26

DAVE ROBINSON Robinson, Richard David 6′3″, 245 **LB**
Col: Penn State *HS:* Moorestown [NJ] B: 5/3/1941, Mount Holly, NJ
Drafted: 1963 Round 1 GB
1967 GB: KR 1-0. **1968** GB: KR 2-29 14.5. **1969** GB: KR 3-31 10.3.
1972 GB: KR 1-20 20.0. **Total:** KR 7-80 11.4.

		Interceptions			
Year Team	G	Int	Yds	TD	Fum
1963 GB	14	0	0	0	0
1964 GB	11	0	0	0	0
1965 GB	14	3	141	0	0
1966 GB	14	5	60	0	0
1967 GB	14	4	16	0	0
1968 GB	14	2	18	0	1
1969 GB	14	0	0	0	0
1970 GB	4	2	33	0	0
1971 GB	14	3	44	0	0
1972 GB	14	2	10	0	0
1973 Was	14	4	98	1	0
1974 Was	14	2	29	0	0
NFL Total	155	27	449	1	1

SHELTON ROBINSON Robinson, Shelton Derrick 6′2″, 233 **LB**
Col: North Carolina *HS:* Charles B. Aycock [Pikeville, NC]
B: 9/14/1960, Goldsboro, NC
1982 Sea: 9 G. **1983** Sea: 16 G; Int 1-18; **2** Fum TD; 12 Pt; 1.5 Sac. **1984** Sea: 16 G; 0.5 Sac. **1985** Sea: 15 G. **1986** Det: 16 G; 0.5 Sac. **1987** Det: 12 G. **1988** Det: 12 G. **Total:** 96 G; Int 1-18; 2 Fum TD; 12 Pt; 2.5 Sac.

STACY ROBINSON Robinson, Stacy Laddell 5′11″, 186 **WR**
Col: Prairie View A&M; North Dakota State *HS:* Central [St. Paul, MN]
B: 2/19/1962, St. Paul, MN *Drafted:* 1985 Round 2 NYG

		Receiving				
Year Team	**G**	**Rec**	**Yds**	**Avg**	**TD**	**Fum**
1985 NYG	4	0	0	—	0	0
1986 NYG	12	29	494	17.0	2	1
1987 NYG	5	6	58	9.7	2	0
1988 NYG	11	7	143	20.4	3	0
1989 NYG	6	4	41	10.3	0	0
1990 NYG	5	2	13	6.5	0	0
NFL Total	43	48	749	15.6	7	1

VIRGIL ROBINSON Robinson, Virgil Jr. 5′11″, 195 **RB**
(Chick) *Col:* Grambling State *HS:* L.B. Landry [New Orleans, LA]
B: 11/2/1947, Inverence, MS *Drafted:* 1971 Round 2 GB
1971 NO: Rec 12-53 4.4 1 TD; KR 19-443 23.3. **Total:** Rec 12-53 4.4 1 TD; KR 19-443 23.3.

		Rushing					Tot
Year Team	**G**	**Att**	**Yds**	**Avg**	**TD**	**Fum**	**TD**
1971 NO	11	29	96	3.3	1	2	2
1972 NO	3	5	1	0.2	0	0	0
NFL Total	14	34	97	2.9	1	2	2

WAYNE ROBINSON Robinson, Wayne Lavern 6′2″, 225 **LB-C**
Col: Minnesota *HS:* North [Minneapolis, MN] B: 1/14/1930, Minneapolis, MN *Drafted:* 1952 Round 8 Phi
1952 Phi: 12 G. **1953** Phi: 11 G. **1954** Phi: 12 G; Int 4-41. **1955** Phi: 12 G; Int 1-20. **1956** Phi: 11 G. **Total:** 58 G; Int 5-61.

BILL ROBINSON Robinson, William Andrew 6′0″, 195 **HB**
Col: Lincoln (Mo.) *HS:* State College [Dover, DE] B: 9/29/1929
Drafted: 1952 Round 25 Pit
1952 GB: 2 G; Rush 3-4 1.3; KR 2-49 24.5. **1960** NYT: 1 G. **Total:** 3 G; Rush 3-4 1.3; KR 2-49 24.5.

TERRY ROBISKIE Robiskie, Terry Joseph 6′1″, 210 **RB**
Col: Louisiana State *HS:* Second Ward [Edgard, LA] B: 11/12/1954, New Orleans, LA *Drafted:* 1977 Round 8 Oak
1977 Oak: KR 6-83 13.8. **1978** Oak: Rec 5-51 10.2; KR 3-58 19.3. **1979** Oak: Rec 5-36 7.2; KR 1-6 6.0. **1980** Mia: Rec 13-60 4.6. **Total:** Rec 23-147 6.4; KR 10-147 14.7.

		Rushing				
Year Team	**G**	**Att**	**Yds**	**Avg**	**TD**	**Fum**
1977 Oak	14	22	100	4.5	1	2
1978 Oak	7	49	189	3.9	2	0
1979 Oak	3	10	14	1.4	0	2
1980 Mia	8	78	250	3.2	2	2
1981 Mia	1	0	0	—	0	0
NFL Total	33	159	553	3.5	5	6

BURLE ROBISON Robison, Burle Hoover 6′4″, 197 **OE-DE-C-LB**
Col: Brigham Young *HS:* Provo [UT] B: 2/17/1910, Provo, UT
D: 12/8/1962, Reno, NV
1935 Phi: 7 G; Rec 1-18 18.0.

GEORGE ROBISON Robison, George Alfred 6′2″, 215 **OG**
Col: Virginia Military *HS:* Piedmont [CA] B: 2/14/1931, Jackson Co., MO
1952 Dal: 4 G.

TOMMY ROBISON Robison, Tommy L Jr. 6′4″, 290 **OT-OG**
Col: Texas A&M *HS:* Gregory-Portland [Portland, TX] B: 11/17/1961, Merkel, TX *Drafted:* 1984 Supplemental Round 2 Cle
1987 GB: 3 G. **1989** Atl: 9 G. **Total:** 12 G.

HAL ROBL Robl, Harold 6′0″, 227 **LB**
Col: Wis.-Oshkosh B: 1918, Oshkosh, WI
1945 ChiC: 2 G.

MARSHALL ROBNETT Robnett, Marshall Foch 6′0″, 205 **LB-C-G**
(Mule; Foxey) *Col:* Texas A&M-Commerce; Texas A&M *HS:* Cooper [TX] B: 3/8/1918, Klondike, TX D: 11/28/1967, Lisbon, TX
Drafted: 1941 Round 6 ChiC
1943 ChiC: 9 G; KR 1-12 12.0. **1944** ChPt: 8 G; Int 1-48; Punt 1-14 14.0; Scor 1, 0-2 FG, 1-1 100.0% XK. **1945** ChiC: 5 G. **Total:** 22 G; KR 1-12 12.0; Int 1-48; Punt 1-14 14.0; Scor 1, 0-2 FG, 1-1 100.0% XK.

ED ROBNETT Robnett, William Edward 5′8″, 205 **FB-LB**
Col: Texas A&M; Texas Tech *HS:* Cooper [TX] B: 3/7/1920, Klondike, TX D: 9/20/1990, Lubbock, TX
AAFC **1947** SF-A: 4 G; Rush 7-18 2.6.

FRANK ROBOTTI Robotti, Frank P 6′0″, 220 **LB**
Col: Boston College *HS:* Fairfield Prep [CT] B: 1939
1961 Bos: 12 G; Int 2-18.

ANDY ROBUSTELLI Robustelli, Andrew Richard 6′1″, 230 **DE**
Col: Arnold *HS:* Stamford [CT]; La Salle Mil. Acad. [Oakdale, NY]
B: 12/6/1925, Stamford, CT *Drafted:* 1951 Round 19 LARm
HOF: 1971
1951 LARm: 11 G. **1952** LARm: 12 G; Int 1-14 1 TD; 1 Fum TD; Tot TD 2; 12 Pt. **1953** LARm: 12 G. **1954** LARm: 12 G; Rec 1-49 49.0 1 TD; KR 1-0; 6 Pt. **1955** LARm: 12 G; Int 1-10 1 TD; **1** Fum TD; Tot TD 2; 12 Pt. **1956** NYG: 12 G; Scor **1** Saf; 2 Pt. **1957** NYG: 12 G. **1958** NYG: 12 G. **1959** NYG: 12 G. **1960** NYG: 12 G. **1961** NYG: 14 G. **1962** NYG: 14 G; Rec 1-26 26.0. **1963** NYG: 14 G. **1964** NYG: 14 G. **Total:** 175 G; Rec 2-75 37.5 1 TD; KR 1-0; Int 2-24 2 TD; Scor 1 Saf; 2 Fum TD; Tot TD 5; 32 Pt.

DOUG ROBY Roby, Douglas Fergusson 5′10″, 190 **TB**
Col: Phillips; Michigan *HS:* Holland [MI] B: 3/24/1898, Port Tobacco, MD D: 3/31/1992, Ann Arbor, MI
1923 Cle: 7 G; Pass 3 TD; Rec 1 TD; Scor 7, 1 XK.

REGGIE ROBY Roby, Reginald Henry 6′3″, 249 **P**
Col: Iowa *HS:* East [Waterloo, IA] B: 7/30/1961, Waterloo, IA
Drafted: 1983 Round 6 Mia
1986 Mia: Rush 2-(-8) -4.0. **1987** Mia: Rush 1-0. **1989** Mia: Rush 2-0. **1993** Was: Rush 1-0. **1995** TB: Pass 1-1 100.0%, 48 48.00; Rush 1-0. **1997** Ten: Rush 1-12 12.0. **1998** SF: Rush 1-0. **Total:** Pass 1-1 100.0%, 48 48.00; Rush 9-4 0.4.

		Punting			
Year Team	**G**	**Punts**	**Yds**	**Avg**	**Fum**
1983 Mia	16	74	3189	43.1	0
1984 Mia	16	51	2281	44.7	0
1985 Mia	16	59	2576	43.7	0
1986 Mia	15	56	2476	44.2	2
1987 Mia	10	32	1371	42.8	0
1988 Mia	15	64	2754	43.0	0
1989 Mia	16	58	2458	42.4	0
1990 Mia	16	72	3022	42.0	0
1991 Mia	16	54	2466	**45.7**	0
1992 Mia	9	35	1443	41.2	0
1993 Was	15	78	3447	44.2	0
1994 Was	16	82	3639	44.4	1
1995 TB	16	77	3296	42.8	0
1996 Hou	16	67	2973	44.4	0
1997 Ten	16	73	3049	41.8	0
1998 SF	14	60	2511	41.9	0
NFL Total	238	992	42951	43.3	3

ALDEN ROCHE Roche, Alden Stephen Jr. 6′4″, 255 **DE**
Col: Southern University *HS:* Xavier Prep [New Orleans, LA]
B: 4/9/1945, New Orleans, LA *Drafted:* 1970 Round 2 Den
1970 Den: 14 G. **1971** GB: 14 G. **1972** GB: 14 G. **1973** GB: 13 G. **1974** GB: 14 G. **1975** GB: 14 G. **1976** GB: 14 G. **1977** Sea: 13 G. **1978** Sea: 10 G. **Total:** 120 G.

BRIAN ROCHE Roche, Brian Matthew 6′4″, 255 **TE**
Col: Cal Poly-S.L.O.; San Jose State *HS:* Damien [La Verne, CA]
B: 5/5/1973, Downey, CA *Drafted:* 1996 Round 3 SD
1996 SD: 13 G; Rec 13-111 8.5. **1997** SD: 5 G. **1998** KC: 4 G. **Total:** 22 G; Rec 13-111 8.5.

PAUL ROCHESTER Rochester, Paul Gordon 6′2″, 255 **DT**
(Rocky) *Col:* Michigan State *HS:* Sewanhaka [Floral Park, NY]
B: 7/15/1938, Lansing, MI
1960 DalT: 12 G; PR 1-0. **1961** DalT: 14 G. **1962** DalT: 13 G. **1963** KC-NYJ: 13 G. KC: 9 G. NYJ: 4 G. **1964** NYJ: 14 G. **1965** NYJ: 13 G. **1966** NYJ: 12 G. **1967** NYJ: 14 G. **1968** NYJ: 14 G. **1969** NYJ: 13 G. **Total:** 132 G; PR 1-0.

WALT ROCK Rock, Walter Warfield 6′5″, 255 **OT-DT**
Col: Maryland *HS:* Elyria [OH] B: 11/4/1941, Cleveland, OH
Drafted: 1963 Round 2 SF
1963 SF: 7 G. **1964** SF: 14 G. **1965** SF: 14 G. **1966** SF: 14 G. **1967** SF: 14 G. **1968** Was: 14 G; KR 2-10 5.0; 1 Fum. **1969** Was: 12 G. **1970** Was: 13 G. **1971** Was: 14 G. **1972** Was: 14 G. **1973** Was: 7 G. **Total:** 137 G; KR 2-10 5.0; 1 Fum.

LYLE ROCKENBACH Rockenbach, Lyle James 5′9″, 192 **G**
(Rock) *Col:* Michigan State *HS:* Crystal Lake Central [IL] B: 3/1/1915, Prairie View, IL
1943 Det: 9 G.

DAVID ROCKER Rocker, David Deaundra 6′4″, 267 **DT**
Col: Auburn *HS:* Fulton [Atlanta, GA] B: 3/12/1969, Atlanta, GA
Drafted: 1991 Round 4 Hou
1991 LARm: 6 G. **1992** LARm: 3 G. **1993** LARm: 14 G; 1 Sac. **1994** LARm: 11 G; 0.5 Sac. **Total:** 34 G; 1.5 Sac.

TRACY ROCKER Rocker, Tracy Quinton 6'3", 288 **DT**
Col: Auburn *HS:* Fulton [Atlanta, GA] B: 4/9/1966, Atlanta, GA
Drafted: 1989 Round 3 Was
1989 Was: 16 G. **1990** Was: 8 G; 3 Sac. **Total:** 24 G; 3 Sac.

JIM ROCKFORD Rockford, James Kyle 5'10", 180 **DB**
Col: Oklahoma *HS:* Griffin [Springfield, IL] B: 9/5/1961, Bloomington, IL *Drafted:* 1985 Round 12 TB
1985 SD: 1 G.

CHRIS ROCKINS Rockins, Christopher Alexander 6'0", 195 **DB**
Col: Oklahoma State *HS:* Sherman [TX] B: 5/18/1962, Sherman, TX
Drafted: 1984 Round 2 Cle
1984 Cle: 16 G; Int 1-0. **1985** Cle: 16 G; Int 1-8; 0.5 Sac. **1986** Cle: 16 G; Int 2-41; 1 Fum. **1987** Cle: 12 G; Int 2-25. **Total:** 60 G; Int 6-74; 1 Fum; 0.5 Sac.

HANK ROCKWELL Rockwell, Henry Albert 6'4", 231 **C-G-LB-DE**
Col: Fullerton Coll. CA (J.C.); Arizona State *HS:* Puente Union [CA]
B: 2/10/1917, Whittier, CA
AAFC **1946** LA-A: 13 G. **1948** LA-A: 13 G; Rec 0-6. **Total:** 26 G; Rec 0-6.

NFL **1940** Cle: 11 G; Rush 1-5 5.0; Rec 1-5 5.0 1 TD; Int 3-7; 6 Pt.
1941 Cle: 10 G; Int 1-9. **1942** Cle: 8 G; Int 1-58. **Total:** 29 G; Rush 1-5 5.0; Rec 1-5 5.0 1 TD; Int 5-74; 6 Pt.

MIKE RODAK Rodak, Michael 5'10", 194 **BB-LB-DE-G**
Col: Case Western Reserve *HS:* Weir [Weirton, WV] B: 2/11/1917, Orient, PA D: 12/1980, Weirton, WV
1939 Cle: 6 G; Pass 1-0, 1 Int; Rush 1-(-1) -1.0; Rec 4-54 13.5. **1940** Cle: 1 G; Rush 1-4 4.0. **1942** Pit: 5 G. **Total:** 12 G; Pass 1-0, 1 Int; Rush 2-3 1.5; Rec 4-54 13.5.

JEFF RODENBERGER Rodenberger, Jeffrey Lee 6'3", 235 **RB**
Col: Maryland *HS:* Quakertown [PA] B: 11/3/1959, Quakertown, PA
1987 NO: 3 G; Rush 17-35 2.1; Rec 2-17 8.5.

MARK RODENHAUSER Rodenhauser, Mark Todd 6'5", 270 **C**
Col: Illinois State *HS:* Addison Trail [Addison, IL] B: 6/1/1961, Elmhurst, IL
1987 ChiB: 9 G. **1989** Min: 16 G. **1990** SD: 16 G. **1991** SD: 10 G.
1992 ChiB: 13 G. **1993** Det: 16 G. **1994** Det: 16 G. **1995** Car: 16 G.
1996 Car: 16 G. **1997** Car: 16 G. **1998** Pit: 16 G. **Total:** 160 G.

MIRRO RODER Roder, Mirro Victor 6'1", 218 **K**
Col: No College *HS:* Olomouc [Czech Republic] B: 1/22/1944, Olomouc, Czech Republic
1973 ChiB: 13 G; Scor 35, 8-16 50.0% FG, 11-12 91.7% XK. **1974** ChiB: 14 G; Scor 44, 9-13 69.2% FG, 17-17 100.0% XK. **1976** TB: 2 G; Scor 0-3 FG. **Total:** 29 G; Scor 79, 17-32 53.1% FG, 28-29 96.6% XK.

BEN RODERICK Roderick, Benjamin Aaron 5'9", 175 **WB-TB-FB**
Col: Wooster; Boston College; Columbia *HS:* Washington [Massillon, OH] B: 5/11/1899, Navarre, OH D: 11/30/1974, Canton, OH
1923 Can-Buf: 8 G. Can: 4 G. Buf: 4 G. **1926** Can: 11 G. **1927** Buf: 3 G. **Total:** 22 G.

JOHN RODERICK Roderick, John William 6'0", 180 **WR**
Col: Southern Methodist *HS:* Highland Park [Dallas, TX] B: 8/21/1944, Fort Worth, TX *Drafted:* 1966 Redshirt Round 1 Mia
1966 Mia: 6 G; Rec 11-156 14.2 1 TD; KR 1-17 17.0; 6 Pt. **1967** Mia: 1 G; KR 4-63 15.8. **1968** Oak: 11 G. **Total:** 18 G; Rec 11-156 14.2 1 TD; KR 5-80 16.0; 6 Pt.

DERRICK RODGERS Rodgers, Derrick Andre 6'1", 225 **LB**
Col: Riverside CC CA; Arizona State *HS:* St. Augustine [New Orleans, LA] B: 10/14/1971, Cordova, TN *Drafted:* 1997 Round 3 Mia
1997 Mia: 15 G; 5 Sac. **1998** Mia: 16 G; 2.5 Sac. **Total:** 31 G; 7.5 Sac.

HOSEA RODGERS Rodgers, Hosea Weaver 6'1", 192 **FB**
Col: Alabama; North Carolina *HS:* Brewton [AL] B: 12/25/1921, Brewton, AL
AAFC **1949** LA-A: Pass 1-0; Rec 7-97 13.9.

		Rushing			
Year Team	G	Att	Yds	Avg	TD
1949 LA-A	12	131	494	3.8	5

JOHN RODGERS Rodgers, John Darren 6'2", 226 **TE**
Col: Louisiana Tech *HS:* Daingerfield [TX] B: 2/7/1960, Omaha, TX
1982 Pit: 7 G; 6 Pt. **1983** Pit: 15 G; Rec 2-36 18.0. **1984** Pit: 6 G. **Total:** 28 G; Rec 2-36 18.0; 6 Pt.

JOHNNY RODGERS Rodgers, John Steven 5'10", 180 **WR**
Col: Nebraska *HS:* Omaha Tech [NE] B: 7/5/1951, Omaha, NE
Drafted: 1973 Round 1 SD
1977 SD: Rush 3-44 14.7; Rec 12-187 15.6; KR 4-66 16.5. **1978** SD: Rush 1-5 5.0; Rec 5-47 9.4; KR 11-287 26.1. **Total:** Rush 4-49 12.3; Rec 17-234 13.8; KR 15-353 23.5.

		Punt Returns				
Year Team	G	Ret	Yds	Avg	TD	Fum
1977 SD	11	15	158	10.5	0	2
1978 SD	6	11	88	8.0	0	1
NFL Total	17	26	246	9.5	0	3

DEL RODGERS Rodgers, Roderick Del 5'10", 201 **RB**
Col: Utah *HS:* North Salinas [Salinas, CA] B: 6/22/1960, Tacoma, WA
Drafted: 1982 Round 3 GB
1982 GB: Rec 3-23 7.7; **2** Fum TD. **1984** GB: Rec 5-56 11.2. **1987** SF: Rec 2-45 22.5. **Total:** Rec 10-124 12.4; 2 Fum TD.

		Rushing				Kickoff Returns					Tot
Year Team	G	Ret	Yds	Avg	TD	Ret	Yds	Avg	TD	Fum	TD
1982 GB	9	46	175	3.8	1	20	436	21.8	0	2	3
1984 GB	14	25	94	3.8	0	39	843	21.6	**1**	1	1
1987 SF	7	11	46	4.2	1	17	358	21.1	0	1	1
1988 SF	1	0	0	—	0	6	98	16.3	0	0	0
NFL Total	31	82	315	3.8	2	82	1735	21.2	1	4	5

TOM RODGERS Rodgers, Thomas Edward 6'0", 248 **T**
Col: Bucknell *HS:* New Kensington [PA] B: 1/20/1923, New Kensington, PA D: 9/9/1992, Las Vegas, NV *Drafted:* 1947 Round 29 Bos
1947 Bos: 9 G.

TYRONE RODGERS Rodgers, Tyrone Dworin 6'3", 271 **DT**
Col: Oklahoma; Washington *HS:* Phineas Banning [Los Angeles, CA]
B: 4/27/1969, Longview, TX
1992 Sea: 16 G. **1993** Sea: 16 G; 1 Sac. **1994** Sea: 5 G. **Total:** 37 G; 1 Sac.

WILLIE RODGERS Rodgers, Willie Daniel Jr. 6'0", 215 **RB**
Col: Kentucky State *HS:* John F. Kennedy [Suffolk, VA] B: 2/8/1949, Suffolk, VA *Drafted:* 1972 Round 12 Hou
1972 Hou: KR 17-335 19.7. **1975** Hou: KR 1-13 13.0; Scor **1** Saf.
Total: KR 18-348 19.3; Scor 1 Saf.

		Rushing				Receiving				
Year Team	G	Att	Yds	Avg	TD	Rec	Yds	Avg	TD	Fum
1972 Hou	14	71	204	2.9	2	6	61	10.2	0	5
1974 Hou	14	122	413	3.4	5	24	153	6.4	0	5
1975 Hou	14	18	55	3.1	1	0	0	—	0	0
NFL Total	42	211	672	3.2	8	30	214	7.1	0	10

JESS RODRIGUEZ Rodriguez, Jess 5'7", 160 **TB**
Col: Salem (NC) *HS:* Victory [Clarksburg, WV] B: 8/7/1901, Salem, WV
D: 10/12/1983, Clarksburg, WV
1929 Buf: 5 G.

KELLY RODRIGUEZ Rodriguez, Kelly 5'10", 180 **WB-HB-TB-BB**
(Rod) *Col:* West Virginia Wesleyan *HS:* Victory [Clarksburg, WV]
B: 8/9/1907, Aviles, Spain
1930 Fra-Min: 15 G. Fra: 13 G; Pass 1 TD; Rec 1 TD; 6 Pt. Min: 2 G.
Total: 15 G; Pass 1 TD; Rec 1 TD; 6 Pt.

MIKE RODRIGUEZ Rodriguez, Miguel Eduardo 6'1", 275 **LB**
Col: Alabama *HS:* Eau Gallie [FL] B: 12/5/1961, Melbourne, FL
1987 LARd: 1 G.

RUBEN RODRIGUEZ Rodriguez, Ruben Angel 6'2", 210 **P**
Col: Coll. of the Sequoias CA (J.C.); Arizona *HS:* Woodlake [CA]
B: 3/3/1965, Visalia, CA *Drafted:* 1987 Round 5 Sea
1987 Sea: Rush 1-0. **1988** Sea: Rush 1-0. **1989** Sea: Pass 1-1 100.0%, 4 4.00; Rush 1-0. **Total:** Pass 1-1 100.0%, 4 4.00; Rush 3-0.

		Punting			
Year Team	G	Punts	Yds	Avg	Fum
1987 Sea	12	47	1880	40.0	0
1988 Sea	16	70	2858	40.8	1
1989 Sea	16	75	2995	39.9	0
1992 Den-NYG	9	46	1907	41.5	0
1992 Den	5	25	1066	42.6	0
1992 NYG	4	21	841	40.0	0
NFL Total	53	238	9640	40.5	1

JAMES ROE Roe, James Edward III 6'1", 187 **WR**
Col: Norfolk State *HS:* Henrico [Richmond, VA] B: 8/23/1973, Richmond, VA *Drafted:* 1996 Round 6 Bal
1996 Bal: 1 G. **1997** Bal: 12 G; Rec 7-124 17.7; PR 8-72 9.0; KR 9-189 21.0; 1 Fum. **1998** Bal: 10 G; Rec 8-115 14.4 1 TD; PR 9-87 9.7; KR 2-40 20.0; 6 Pt. **Total:** 23 G; Rec 15-239 15.9 1 TD; PR 17-159 9.4; KR 11-229 20.8; 6 Pt; 1 Fum.

BILL ROE Roe, William Oliver II 6'3", 233 **LB**
Col: Colorado *HS:* Thornwood [South Holland, IL] B: 2/6/1958, South Bend, IN *Drafted:* 1980 Round 3 Dal
1980 Dal: 16 G. **1987** NO: 3 G. **Total:** 19 G.

HERB ROEDEL Roedel, Herbert Thomas 6'3", 230 **OG**
Col: Marquette *HS:* St. Mary's [Menasha, WI] B: 3/30/1939, Appleton, WI
1961 Oak: 14 G.

JON ROEHLK Roehlk, Jon Michael 6'2", 257 **OG**
Col: Iowa *HS:* Durant [IA] B: 6/25/1961, Davenport, IA
1987 ChiB: 3 G.

BILL ROEHNELT Roehnelt, William Edward 6'1", 227 **LB**
Col: Bradley *HS:* Chillicothe [IL] B: 6/4/1936, Peoria, IL D: 7/19/1968
Drafted: 1958 Round 19 ChiB
1958 ChiB: 12 G. **1959** ChiB: 12 G; KR 1-0. **1960** Was: 12 G. **1961** Den: 4 G. **1962** Den: 14 G. **Total:** 54 G; KR 1-0.

JOHNNY ROEPKE Roepke, John Peter 5'11", 175 **TB-WB**
Col: Penn State *HS:* William L. Dickinson [Jersey City, NJ]
B: 12/28/1905 D: 2/26/1962, Passaic, NJ
1928 Fra: 10 G; Pass 1 TD; Rush 1 TD; Scor 10, 1 FG, 1 XK.

FRITZ ROESELER Roeseler, Fred C 6'1", 189 **OE**
Col: North Central; Marquette *HS:* North Division [Milwaukee, WI]
B: 10/1/1897, Milwaukee, WI D: 7/18/1985, Milwaukee, WI
1922 Rac: 11 G; Rec 1 TD; 6 Pt. **1923** Rac: 6 G. **1924** Rac: 3 G. **1925** Mil: 6 G. **Total:** 26 G; Rec 1 TD; 6 Pt.

BILL ROFFLER Roffler, William Hartman 6'1", 200 **DB**
(Bud) *Col:* Washington State *HS:* Lewis and Clark [Spokane, WA]
B: 9/16/1930, Spokane, WA *Drafted:* 1952 Round 10 GB
1954 Phi: 3 G; KR 1-19 19.0.

JOHN ROGALLA Rogalla, John Francis 6'0", 215 **FB-LB**
Col: Scranton *HS:* Duryea [PA] B: 5/31/1917, Duryea, PA
Drafted: 1940 Round 15 NYG
1945 Phi: 8 G; Rush 2-2 1.0; Rec 2-22 11.0; Scor 1 1XP; 1 Pt.

DAN ROGAS Rogas, Daniel William 6'1", 230 **OG-DT-OT**
Col: Tulane *HS:* Thomas Jefferson [Port Arthur, TX] B: 8/9/1926, Port Arthur, TX *Drafted:* 1951 Round 6 Cle
1951 Det: 12 G. **1952** Phi: 10 G. **Total:** 22 G.

FRAN ROGEL Rogel, Francis Stephen 5'11", 203 **FB**
Col: California (Pa.); Penn State *HS:* Scott Twp. [North Braddock, PA]
B: 12/12/1927, North Braddock, PA *Drafted:* 1950 Round 8 Pit
1950 Pit: Pass 4-3 75.0%, 30 7.50; KR 1-20 20.0. **1951** Pit: Pass 1-0; KR 2-9 4.5. **1953** Pit: Pass 1-0. **1955** Pit: KR 1-81 81.0. **1957** Pit: KR 1-4 4.0. **Total:** Pass 6-3 50.0%, 30 5.00; KR 5-114 22.8.

		Rushing				Receiving					Tot
Year Team	**G**	**Att**	**Yds**	**Avg**	**TD**	**Rec**	**Yds**	**Avg**	**TD**	**Fum**	**TD**
1950 Pit	12	92	418	4.5	3	24	304	12.7	1	7	4
1951 Pit	12	109	385	3.5	3	10	59	5.9	0	4	3
1952 Pit	12	84	230	2.7	3	12	140	11.7	0	1	3
1953 Pit	12	137	527	3.8	2	19	95	5.0	0	2	2
1954 Pit	12	111	415	3.7	1	18	51	2.8	1	4	2
1955 Pit	12	168	588	3.5	2	24	222	9.3	0	5	2
1956 Pit	12	131	476	3.6	2	23	88	3.8	0	4	2
1957 Pit	12	68	232	3.4	1	20	128	6.4	0	1	1
NFL Total	96	900	3271	3.6	17	150	1087	7.2	2	28	19

CHARLEY ROGERS Rogers, Charles Stagg 5'10", 167 **TB-WB-BB**
(The Camden Comet) *Col:* Pennsylvania *HS:* Camden [NJ] B: 1903
D: 6/26/1986
1927 Fra: 18 G; Rush 2 TD; Rec 1 TD; Tot TD 3; 18 Pt. **1928** Fra: 13 G; Rush 1 TD; Rec 2 TD; Tot TD 3; 18 Pt. **1929** Fra: 7 G. **Total:** 38 G; Rush 3 TD; Rec 3 TD; Tot TD 6; 36 Pt.

CULLEN ROGERS Rogers, Cullen James 5'10", 178 **HB-DB**
(Slick) *Col:* Texas A&M *HS:* Mart [TX] B: 5/29/1921, Mart, TX
Drafted: 1943 Round 16 Cle
1946 Pit: 5 G; Pass 1-0; Rush 6-(-8) -1.3; 3 Fum.

DON ROGERS Rogers, Donald Clinton 6'2", 240 **C**
Col: South Carolina *HS:* Columbia [Maplewood, NJ] B: 12/4/1936, South Orange, NJ *Drafted:* 1959 Round 7 SF
1960 LAC: 14 G. **1961** SD: 14 G. **1962** SD: 12 G. **1963** SD: 14 G. **1964** SD: 14 G. **Total:** 68 G.

DON ROGERS Rogers, Donald Lavert 6'1", 206 **DB**
Col: UCLA *HS:* Norte del Rio [Sacramento, CA] B: 9/17/1962, Texarkana, TX D: 6/27/1986, Sacramento, CA *Drafted:* 1984 Round 1 Cle
1984 Cle: 15 G; Int 1-39. **1985** Cle: 16 G; Int 1-3. **Total:** 31 G; Int 2-42.

DOUG ROGERS Rogers, Douglas Keith 6'5", 266 **DE**
Col: Stanford *HS:* Highland [Bakersfield, CA] B: 6/23/1960, Chico, CA
Drafted: 1982 Round 2 Atl
1982 Atl: 9 G; 2 Sac. **1983** Atl-NE: 12 G; 0.5 Sac. Atl: 2 G. NE: 10 G; 0.5 Sac. **1984** NE: 12 G; 2 Sac. **1986** SF: 8 G. **Total:** 41 G; 4.5 Sac.

GEORGE ROGERS Rogers, George Washington Jr. 6'2", 228 **RB**
Col: South Carolina *HS:* Duluth [GA] B: 12/8/1958, Duluth, GA
Drafted: 1981 Round 1 NO

		Rushing				Receiving					Tot
Year Team	**G**	**Att**	**Yds**	**Avg**	**TD**	**Rec**	**Yds**	**Avg**	**TD**	**Fum**	**TD**
1981 NO	16	**378**	**1674**	4.4	13	16	126	7.9	0	13	13
1982 NO	6	122	535	4.4	3	4	21	5.3	0	4	3
1983 NO	13	256	1144	4.5	5	12	69	5.8	0	8	5
1984 NO	16	239	914	3.8	2	12	76	6.3	0	2	2
1985 Was	15	231	1093	4.7	7	4	29	7.3	0	9	7
1986 Was	15	303	1203	4.0	**18**	3	24	8.0	0	7	**18**
1987 Was	11	163	613	3.8	6	4	23	5.8	0	2	6
NFL Total	92	1692	7176	4.2	54	55	368	6.7	0	45	54

GLENN ROGERS Rogers, Glenn Edward Jr. 6'0", 185 **DB**
Col: Memphis *HS:* South Side [Memphis, TN] B: 6/8/1969, Memphis, TN
1991 TB: 5 G.

GLYNN ROGERS Rogers, Glynn Odell 5'10", 220 **G**
Col: Texas Christian *HS:* Mart [TX] B: 3/31/1914, Big Hill, TX
1939 ChiC: 1 G.

JIMMY ROGERS Rogers, James Lee 5'10", 190 **RB**
Col: Oklahoma *HS:* Forrest City [AR] B: 6/29/1955, Forrest City, AR

		Rushing				Receiving			
Year Team	**G**	**Att**	**Yds**	**Avg**	**TD**	**Rec**	**Yds**	**Avg**	**TD**
1980 NO	16	80	366	4.6	1	27	267	9.9	2
1981 NO	15	9	37	4.1	0	2	12	6.0	0
1982 NO	9	60	178	3.0	2	4	17	4.3	0
1983 NO	16	26	80	3.1	0	0	0	—	0
1984 NO	16	0	0	—	0	0	0	—	0
NFL Total	72	175	661	3.8	3	33	296	9.0	2

	Kickoff Returns					Tot
Year Team	**Ret**	**Yds**	**Avg**	**TD**	**Fum**	**TD**
1980 NO	41	930	22.7	0	6	3
1981 NO	28	621	22.2	0	3	0
1982 NO	1	24	24.0	0	0	2
1983 NO	7	103	14.7	0	2	0
NFL Total	77	1678	21.8	0	11	5

JOHN ROGERS Rogers, John Bert 5'8", 208 **C-LB**
(Bee) *Col:* Notre Dame *HS:* Alexis [IL] B: 1/18/1910 D: 10/1968
1933 Cin: 9 G. **1934** Cin: 5 G. **Total:** 14 G.

LAMAR ROGERS Rogers, Lamar 6'4", 290 **DE**
Col: Auburn *HS:* Opp [AL] B: 11/5/1967, Opp, AL *Drafted:* 1991 Round 2 Cin
1991 Cin: 11 G. **1992** Cin: 15 G; 4 Sac. **Total:** 26 G; 4 Sac.

MEL ROGERS Rogers, Melvin Nathaniel 6'2", 231 **LB**
Col: Florida A&M *HS:* Gibbs [St. Petersburg, FL] B: 4/23/1947, St. Petersburg, FL
1971 SD: 13 G; KR 1-20 20.0. **1973** SD: 10 G; KR 1-4 4.0; Int 1-3. **1974** SD: 3 G. **1976** LARm: 11 G. **1977** ChiB: 5 G. **Total:** 42 G; KR 2-24 12.0; Int 1-3.

REGGIE ROGERS Rogers, Reginald O'Keith 6'6", 278 **DE**
Col: Washington *HS:* Norte del Rio [Sacramento, CA] B: 1/21/1964, Sacramento, CA *Drafted:* 1987 Round 1 Det
1987 Det: 6 G. **1988** Det: 5 G; 1 Sac. **1991** Buf: 2 G; 1 Sac. **1992** TB: 2 G. **Total:** 15 G; 2 Sac.

SAM ROGERS Rogers, Sammy Lee 6'3", 245 **LB**
Col: West Hills CC CA (J.C.); West Los Angeles Coll. CA (J.C.); Colorado
HS: St. Mary's Prep [Orchard Lake, MI] B: 5/30/1970, Pontiac, MI
Drafted: 1994 Round 2 Buf
1994 Buf: 14 G. **1995** Buf: 16 G; 2 Sac. **1996** Buf: 14 G; 3.5 Sac. **1997** Buf: 15 G; 3.5 Sac. **1998** Buf: 15 G; 4.5 Sac. **Total:** 74 G; 13.5 Sac.

STAN ROGERS Rogers, Stanley Gerald 6'4", 256 **OT**
Col: Maryland *HS:* St. Pius X [Pottstown, PA] B: 3/10/1952, Peckville, PA *Drafted:* 1975 Round 5 Den
1975 Den: 14 G.

STEVE ROGERS Rogers, Steven C 6'4", 260 **OT**
Col: Palomar Coll. CA (J.C.); Oregon State; Brigham Young *HS:* Orange Glen [Escondido, CA] B: 1/9/1959, Escondido, CA
1987 KC: 3 G.

STEVEN ROGERS Rogers, Steven Jerel 6'2", 203 **RB**
Col: Louisiana State *HS:* Ruston [LA] B: 8/26/1953, Jonesboro, LA
Drafted: 1975 Round 7 NO
1975 NO: 13 G; Rush 17-62 3.6; Rec 1-2 2.0; KR 6-98 16.3. **1976** NYJ: 1 G. **Total:** 14 G; Rush 17-62 3.6; Rec 1-2 2.0; KR 6-98 16.3.

TRACY ROGERS Rogers, Tracy Darin 6'2", 240 **LB**
Col: Taft Coll. CA (J.C.); Fresno State *HS:* Taft Union [CA]
B: 8/13/1967, Taft, CA *Drafted:* 1989 Round 7 Hou
1990 KC: 10 G. **1991** KC: 10 G. **1992** KC: 8 G; 6 Pt. **1993** KC: 14 G. **1994** KC: 14 G. **1995** KC: 16 G. **1996** KC: 3 G. **Total:** 75 G; 6 Pt.

WALT ROGERS Rogers, Walter Charles 5'9", 215 **FB-LB**
Col: Christian Brothers (Mo.); Ohio U. B: 4/18/1893 D: 9/15/1964, Dallas, TX
1921 Col: 1 G. **1922** Col: 3 G. **Total:** 4 G.

BILL ROGERS Rogers, William Curtis 5′11″, 243 **T**
Col: Villanova *HS:* Westborough [MA]; Bridgton Acad. [North Bridgton, ME] B: 6/24/1913, Westborough, MA D: 4/30/1977, Northborough, MA
1938 Det: 7 G. **1939** Det: 9 G. **1940** Det: 7 G. **1944** Det: 2 G. **Total:** 25 G.

GEORGE ROGGE Rogge, George Ross 6′0″, 186 **OE-DE**
Col: Iowa *HS:* Ida Grove [IA] B: 9/3/1907, Odebolt, IA
1931 ChiC: 6 G; Rec 1 TD; 6 Pt. **1932** ChiC: 10 G; Rec 6-96 16.0. **1933** ChiC: 6 G. **1934** StL: 2 G; Rec 1-4 4.0. **Total:** 24 G; Rec 7-100 14.3 1 TD; 6 Pt.

TOM ROGGEMAN Roggeman, Thomas John 6′0″, 235 **OG**
Col: Purdue *HS:* Mishawaka [IN] B: 9/5/1931, Mishawaka, IN
1956 ChiB: 12 G. **1957** ChiB: 12 G. **Total:** 24 G.

LEN ROHDE Rohde, Leonard Emil 6′4″, 247 **OT**
Col: Utah State *HS:* Palatine [IL] B: 4/16/1938, Palatine, IL
Drafted: 1960 Round 5 SF
1960 SF: 12 G. **1961** SF: 14 G. **1962** SF: 14 G. **1963** SF: 14 G. **1964** SF: 14 G. **1965** SF: 14 G. **1966** SF: 14 G. **1967** SF: 14 G. **1968** SF: 14 G. **1969** SF: 14 G. **1970** SF: 14 G. **1971** SF: 14 G. **1972** SF: 14 G. **1973** SF: 14 G. **1974** SF: 14 G. **Total:** 208 G.

GEORGE ROHLEDER Rohleder, George J 5′11″, 213 **G-T-FB**
Col: Wittenberg *HS:* Bryan [OH] B: 3/10/1898, Bryan, OH D: 2/17/1958
1925 Col: 9 G; Scor 10, 3 FG, 1 XK. **1926** Akr: 6 G; Scor 5, 1 FG, 2 XK. **Total:** 15 G; Scor 15, 4 FG, 3 XK.

JEFF ROHRER Rohrer, Jeffrey Charles 6′3″, 228 **LB**
Col: Yale *HS:* Mira Costa [Manhattan Beach, CA] B: 12/25/1958, Inglewood, CA *Drafted:* 1982 Round 2 Dal
1982 Dal: 8 G. **1983** Dal: 16 G. **1984** Dal: 16 G; 1 Fum. **1985** Dal: 15 G; 1.5 Sac. **1986** Dal: 16 G; 2 Sac. **1987** Dal: 12 G; 4 Sac. **Total:** 83 G; 1 Fum; 7.5 Sac.

HERM ROHRIG Rohrig, Herman Francis 5′8″, 190 **DB-HB-TB**
(Stumpy) *Col:* Nebraska *HS:* Lincoln [NE] B: 3/19/1918, Mason City, IA *Drafted:* 1941 Round 4 GB
1941 GB: Pass 1-1 100.0%, 3 3.00; Rec 11-58 5.3; KR 3-60 20.0; Punt 5-214 42.8; Scor 4, 1-1 100.0% FG, 1-1 100.0% XK. **1946** GB: Pass 8-2 25.0%, 97 12.13 1 TD 1 Int; Rec 2-36 18.0; KR 5-106 21.2. **Total:** Pass 9-3 33.3%, 100 11.11 1 TD 1 Int; Rec 13-94 7.2; KR 8-166 20.8; Punt 5-214 42.8; Scor 4, 1-1 100.0% FG, 1-1 100.0% XK.

		Rushing				Punt Returns			
Year Team	**G**	**Att**	**Yds**	**Avg**	**TD**	**Ret**	**Yds**	**Avg**	**TD**
1941 GB	10	21	2	0.1	0	4	46	11.5	0
1946 GB	8	14	-23	-1.6	0	8	98	12.3	0
1947 GB	7	7	22	3.1	0	18	213	11.8	0
NFL Total	25	42	1	0.0	0	30	357	11.9	0

	Interceptions			
Year Team	**Int**	**Yds**	**TD**	**Fum**
1941 GB	1	17	0	0
1946 GB	5	134	0	2
1947 GB	5	80	0	2
NFL Total	11	231	0	4

TUBBY ROHSENBERGER Rohsenberger, Otto Lee 1 **T**
Col: Wisconsin *HS:* Central [Evansville, IN] B: 11/6/1896, Evansville, IN D: 1/15/1954
1921 Eva: 2 G.

JOHN ROKISKY Rokisky, John Joseph 6′2″, 202 **DE-OE**
Col: Duquesne *HS:* Clarksburg [WV] B: 7/24/1915, Mount Clare, WV D: 11/28/1993, Wintersville, OH
AAFC **1946** CleA: 5 G; Rec 1-13 13.0; Scor 1, 1-1 100.0% XK. **1947** ChiA: 14 G; Rec 1-8 8.0; Scor 45, 4-8 50.0% FG, 33-35 94.3% XK. **1948** NY-A: 6 G. **Total:** 25 G; Rec 2-21 10.5; Scor 46, 4-8 50.0% FG, 34-36 94.4% XK.

JOHNNY ROLAND Roland, John Earl 6′2″, 220 **RB**
Col: Missouri *HS:* Roy Miller [Corpus Christi, TX] B: 5/21/1943, Corpus Christi, TX *Drafted:* 1965 Round 4 StL
1966 StL: Pass 8-5 62.5%, 130 16.25 1 TD; KR 15-347 23.1. **1967** StL: Pass 4-0, 1 Int; KR 2-33 16.5. **1968** StL: Pass 1-0, 1 Int. **1970** StL: KR 3-40 13.3. **1971** StL: KR 2-24 12.0. **Total:** Pass 13-5 38.5%, 130 10.00 1 TD 2 Int; KR 22-444 20.2.

		Rushing				Receiving			
Year Team	**G**	**Att**	**Yds**	**Avg**	**TD**	**Rec**	**Yds**	**Avg**	**TD**
1966 StL	14	192	695	3.6	5	21	213	10.1	0
1967 StL	13	234	876	3.7	10	20	269	13.5	1
1968 StL	14	121	455	3.8	2	8	97	12.1	0
1969 StL	14	138	498	3.6	5	12	136	11.3	1
1970 StL	14	94	392	4.2	3	17	96	5.6	1
1971 StL	13	78	278	3.6	0	15	108	7.2	0
1972 StL	14	105	414	3.9	2	38	321	8.4	2
1973 NYG	7	53	142	2.7	1	22	190	8.6	1
NFL Total	103	1015	3750	3.7	28	153	1430	9.3	6

	Punt Returns					Tot
Year Team	**Ret**	**Yds**	**Avg**	**TD**	**Fum**	**TD**
1966 StL	20	221	**11.1**	**1**	4	6
1967 StL	3	17	5.7	0	5	11
1968 StL	3	11	3.7	0	6	2
1969 StL	10	53	5.3	0	4	6
1970 StL	10	140	14.0	**1**	2	5
1971 StL	3	10	3.3	0	4	0
1972 StL	0	0	—	0	7	4
1973 NYG	0	0	—	0	2	2
NFL Total	49	452	9.2	2	34	36

BENJI ROLAND Roland, Mitchell Benjamin 6′3″, 260 **DE**
Col: Auburn *HS:* Dodge Co. [Eastman, GA] B: 4/4/1967, Eastman, GA
Drafted: 1989 Round 7 Min
1990 TB: 3 G.

DAVE ROLLE Rolle, David S 6′0″, 215 **FB**
Col: Oklahoma *HS:* Poteau [OK] B: 3/22/1937, Poteau, OK
1960 Den: Rec 21-122 5.8 1 TD.

		Rushing					Tot
Year Team	**G**	**Att**	**Yds**	**Avg**	**TD**	**Fum**	**TD**
1960 Den	14	130	501	3.9	2	9	3

BUTCH ROLLE Rolle, Donald Demetrius 6′3″, 242 **TE**
Col: Michigan State *HS:* Hallandale [FL] B: 8/19/1964, Miami, FL
Drafted: 1986 Round 7 Buf
1987 Buf: KR 1-6 6.0. **1988** Buf: KR 1-12 12.0. **1989** Buf: KR 2-20 10.0. **1990** Buf: KR 2-22 11.0. **1992** Pho: KR 1-10 10.0. **Total:** KR 7-70 10.0.

		Receiving			
Year Team	**G**	**Rec**	**Yds**	**Avg**	**TD**
1986 Buf	16	4	56	14.0	0
1987 Buf	12	2	6	3.0	2
1988 Buf	16	2	3	1.5	2
1989 Buf	16	1	1	1.0	1
1990 Buf	16	3	6	2.0	3
1991 Buf	16	3	10	3.3	2
1992 Pho	16	13	64	4.9	0
1993 Pho	16	10	67	6.7	1
NFL Total	124	38	213	5.6	11

SAMARI ROLLE Rolle, Samari 6′0″, 175 **DB**
Col: Florida State *HS:* Miami Beach [FL] B: 8/10/1976, Miami, FL
Drafted: 1998 Round 2 Ten
1998 Ten: 15 G; 2 Sac.

DAVE ROLLER Roller, David Euell 6′2″, 270 **DT**
Col: Kentucky *HS:* Rhea Co. [Evensville, TN] B: 10/28/1949, Dayton, TN *Drafted:* 1971 Round 13 NYG
1971 NYG: 14 G. **1975** GB: 6 G. **1976** GB: 13 G. **1977** GB: 13 G. **1978** GB: 16 G. **1979** Min: 15 G. **1980** Min: 15 G. **Total:** 92 G.

HENRY ROLLING Rolling, Henry Lee 6′2″, 232 **LB**
Col: Nevada-Reno *HS:* Basic [Henderson, NV] B: 9/8/1965, Fort Eustis, VA *Drafted:* 1987 Round 5 TB
1988 TB: 15 G; 1 Sac. **1989** TB: 6 G. **1990** SD: 16 G; Int 1-67; 3.5 Sac. **1991** SD: 15 G; Int 2-54; 1 Fum; 1 Sac. **1992** SD: 15 G; 1 Sac. **1993** LARm: 12 G; Int 2-21. **1994** LARm: 9 G. **Total:** 88 G; Int 5-142; 1 Fum; 6.5 Sac.

GEORGE ROMAN Roman, George Jr. 6′4″, 242 **DT-OT**
Col: Case Western Reserve *HS:* Penn [Pittsburgh, PA] B: 2/20/1925, Rankin, PA *Drafted:* 1948 Round 9 Bos
1948 Bos: 12 G. **1949** NYB: 8 G. **1950** NYG: 6 G. **Total:** 26 G.

JOHN ROMAN Roman, John George 6′4″, 255 **OT-OG**
Col: Idaho State *HS:* Holy Spirit [Absecon, NJ] B: 8/31/1952, Ventnor City, NJ *Drafted:* 1975 Round 13 Bal
1976 NYJ: 11 G. **1977** NYJ: 9 G. **1978** NYJ: 16 G; Rec 1-(-2) -2.0. **1979** NYJ: 16 G. **1980** NYJ: 16 G. **1981** NYJ: 16 G. **1982** NYJ: 9 G. **Total:** 93 G; Rec 1-(-2) -2.0.

NICK ROMAN Roman, Nicholas George 6′3″, 244 **DE**
Col: Ohio State *HS:* McKinley [Canton, OH] B: 9/23/1947, Canton, OH
Drafted: 1970 Round 10 Cin
1970 Cin: 4 G. **1971** Cin: 12 G. **1972** Cle: 10 G; Int 1-36 1 TD; 6 Pt. **1973** Cle: 14 G. **1974** Cle: 12 G. **Total:** 52 G; Int 1-36 1 TD; 6 Pt.

STEVE ROMANIK Romanik, Stephen 6′1″, 190 **QB**
Col: Villanova *HS:* Millville [NJ] B: 5/27/1924, Millville, NJ
Drafted: 1950 Round 3 ChiB

		Passing							
Year Team	**G**	**Att**	**Comp**	**Comp%**	**Yds**	**YPA**	**TD**	**Int**	**Rating**
1950 ChiB	1	2	0	0.0	0	0.00	0	0	39.6
1951 ChiB	12	101	43	42.6	791	7.83	3	9	43.0
1952 ChiB	10	126	49	38.9	772	6.13	4	11	34.2
1953 ChiB-ChiC	7	125	51	40.8	650	5.20	4	11	31.8
1953 ChiB	1	8	1	12.5	9	1.13	0	2	0.0

1953 ChiC	6	117	50	42.7	641	5.48	4	9	39.9
1954 ChiC	8	79	36	45.6	343	4.34	2	5	40.2
NFL Total	38	433	179	41.3	2556	5.90	13	36	36.5

	Rushing				
Year Team	Att	Yds	Avg	TD	Fum
1951 ChiB	12	23	1.9	1	2
1952 ChiB	6	9	1.5	0	2
1953 ChiB-ChiC	2	1	0.5	1	0
1953 ChiB	1	0	0.0	0	0
1953 ChiC	1	1	1.0	1	0
1954 ChiC	7	2	0.3	1	3
NFL Total	27	35	1.3	3	7

JIM ROMANISZYN Romaniszyn, James Christopher 6'2", 224 **LB**
Col: Edinboro *HS:* Titusville [PA] B: 9/17/1951, Titusville, PA
Drafted: 1973 Round 13 Cle
1973 Cle: 14 G; KR 2-21 10.5. **1974** Cle: 14 G; KR 5-48 9.6; 1 Fum. **1976** NE: 11 G. **Total:** 39 G; KR 7-69 9.9; 1 Fum.

JIM ROMANO Romano, James John 6'3", 260 **C**
Col: Penn State *HS:* North Shore [Glen Cove, NY] B: 9/7/1959, Glen Cove, NY *Drafted:* 1982 Round 2 LARd
1982 LARd: 5 G. **1983** LARd: 1 G. **1984** LARd-Hou: 14 G; 1 Fum. LARd: 6 G. Hou: 8 G; 1 Fum. **1985** Hou: 16 G. **1986** Hou: 9 G. **Total:** 45 G; 1 Fum.

BILL ROMANOWSKI Romanowski, William Thomas 6'4", 241 **LB**
(Romo) *Col:* Boston College *HS:* Rockville [Vernon, CT] B: 4/2/1966, Vernon, CT *Drafted:* 1988 Round 3 SF
1989 SF: PR 1-0; 1 Sac. **1990** SF: 1 Sac. **1991** SF: 1 Sac. **1992** SF: 1 Sac. **1993** SF: 3 Sac. **1994** Phi: 2.5 Sac. **1995** Phi: 1 Sac. **1996** Den: 3 Sac. **1997** Den: 2 Sac. **1998** Den: 7.5 Sac. **Total:** PR 1-0; 23.0 Sac.

		Interceptions			
Year Team	G	Int	Yds	TD	Fum
1988 SF	16	0	0	0	0
1989 SF	16	1	13	0	1
1990 SF	16	0	0	0	0
1991 SF	16	1	7	0	0
1992 SF	16	0	0	0	0
1993 SF	16	0	0	0	0
1994 Phi	16	2	8	0	0
1995 Phi	16	2	5	0	0
1996 Den	16	3	1	0	0
1997 Den	16	1	7	0	0
1998 Den	16	2	22	0	0
NFL Total	176	12	63	0	1

DAVE ROMASKO Romasko, David Sherman 6'3", 241 **RB**
Col: Carroll (Mont.) *HS:* Pocatello [ID] B: 11/3/1963, Pocatello, ID
1987 Cin: 3 G.

RUDY ROMBOLI Romboli, Rudolph Louis 5'10", 213 **FB-LB**
Col: No College *HS:* Everett [MA] B: 5/21/1923, Stoneham, MA
D: 1/3/1980, Boston, MA
1946 Bos: Int 1-12. **1947** Bos: Rec 4-30 7.5; KR 3-64 21.3; Int 1-14. **1948** Bos: Rec 8-77 9.6; KR 1-22 22.0. **Total:** Rec 12-107 8.9; KR 4-86 21.5; Int 2-26.

		Rushing				
Year Team	G	Att	Yds	Avg	TD	Fum
1946 Bos	3	1	-3	-3.0	0	0
1947 Bos	12	23	50	2.2	0	1
1948 Bos	12	25	90	3.6	1	2
NFL Total	27	49	137	2.8	1	3

TAG ROME Rome, Anthony Nicholas 5'9", 175 **WR**
Col: Northeast Louisiana *HS:* Cedar Creek [Ruston, LA] B: 8/13/1961, Donalsonville, LA
1987 SD: 3 G; Rec 6-49 8.2; PR 3-12 4.0; KR 2-28 14.0.

STAN ROME Rome, Stanford Bernard 6'5", 212 **WR**
Col: Clemson *HS:* Valdosta [GA] B: 6/4/1956, Valdosta, GA
Drafted: 1979 Round 11 KC
1979 KC: 9 G; Rush 1-(-5) -5.0. **1980** KC: 10 G; Rec 3-58 19.3. **1981** KC: 16 G; Rec 17-203 11.9 1 TD; 6 Pt. **1982** KC: 7 G; Rec 2-25 12.5. **Total:** 42 G; Rush 1-(-5) -5.0; Rec 22-286 13.0 1 TD; 6 Pt.

TONY ROMEO Romeo, Anthony Lamar 6'2", 230 **TE**
Col: Florida State *HS:* Hillsborough [Tampa, FL] B: 3/7/1938, St. Petersburg, FL D: 5/2/1996, Matthews, NC *Drafted:* 1961 Round 19 Was
1964 Bos: KR 1-5 5.0. **1966** Bos: Scor **1** 2XP. **Total:** KR 1-5 5.0; Scor 1 2XP.

		Receiving				
Year Team	G	Rec	Yds	Avg	TD	Fum
1961 DalT	14	7	89	12.7	0	0
1962 Bos	14	34	608	17.9	1	1
1963 Bos	14	32	418	13.1	3	0
1964 Bos	14	26	445	17.1	4	0
1965 Bos	14	15	203	13.5	2	0
1966 Bos	14	2	46	23.0	0	0
1967 Bos	5	1	4	4.0	0	0
NFL Total	89	117	1813	15.5	10	1

RICH ROMER Romer, Richard H 6'3", 222 **LB**
Col: Union (N.Y.) *HS:* Columbia [East Greenbush, NY] B: 2/27/1966, East Greenbush, NY *Drafted:* 1988 Round 7 Cin
1988 Cin: 4 G. **1989** Cin: 5 G. **Total:** 9 G.

RAY ROMERO Romero, Ray Rene 5'11", 213 **OG**
Col: Kansas State *HS:* North [Wichita, KS] B: 12/31/1927, Wichita, KS
1951 Phi: 7 G.

CHARLES ROMES Romes, Charles Michael 6'1", 191 **DB**
Col: Lake City CC FL; North Carolina Central *HS:* Hillside [Durham, NC] B: 12/16/1954, Verdun, France *Drafted:* 1977 Round 12 Buf
1977 Buf: KR 1-18 18.0. **Total:** KR 1-18 18.0.

		Interceptions				Tot
Year Team	G	Int	Yds	TD	Fum	TD
1977 Buf	14	0	0	0	1	0
1978 Buf	16	2	95	1	1	1
1979 Buf	16	1	0	0	0	1
1980 Buf	16	2	41	0	0	0
1981 Buf	16	4	113	0	1	0
1982 Buf	9	1	8	0	0	0
1983 Buf	16	2	27	0	0	0
1984 Buf	16	5	130	0	0	0
1985 Buf	16	7	56	0	0	0
1986 Buf	16	4	23	0	0	0
1987 SD	5	0	0	0	0	0
NFL Total	156	28	493	1	3	2

AL ROMINE Romine, Alton Rollon 6'2", 191 **DB-HB**
Col: Florida; North Alabama *HS:* Florence [AL] B: 3/10/1932, Florence, AL
1955 ChiB-GB: 5 G; PR 1-0. ChiB: 1 G; PR 1-0. GB: 4 G. **1958** GB: 12 G; Rush 1-0; PR 2-7 3.5; Int 1-0. **1960** Den: 14 G; Int 3-69. **1961** Bos: 1 G. **Total:** 32 G; Rush 1-0; PR 3-7 2.3; Int 4-69.

MILT ROMNEY Romney, Milton Addas 5'8", 166 **QB-HB-BB-TB**
Col: Utah; Chicago *HS:* East [Salt Lake City, UT] B: 6/20/1899, Salt Lake City, UT D: 11/10/1975, North Little Rock, AR
1923 Rac: 8 G; Rec 1 TD; 6 Pt. **1924** Rac: 10 G; Rec 1 TD; 6 Pt. **1925** ChiB: 14 G. **1926** ChiB: 16 G; Rush 3 TD; Rec 1 TD; Scor **1** 1XP; Tot TD 4; 25 Pt. **1927** ChiB: 14 G; Rush 1 TD; 6 Pt. **1928** ChiB: 11 G; Pass 1 TD; Rush 1 TD; Rec 1 TD; Scor **1** 1XP; Tot TD 2; 13 Pt. **Total:** 73 G; Pass 1 TD; Rush 5 TD; Rec 4 TD; Scor 2 1XP; Tot TD 9; 56 Pt.

GENE RONZANI Ronzani, Eugene 5'9", 200 **QB-HB-DB-LB**
(Tuffy) *Col:* Marquette *HS:* Iron Mountain [MI] B: 3/28/1909, Iron Mountain, MI D: 9/12/1975, Lardo Flambeau, WI
1933 ChiB: Rec 3-62 20.7 1 TD. **1934** ChiB: Rec 5-114 22.8 3 TD. **1935** ChiB: Rec 8-122 15.3 1 TD; Scor 15, 3 XK. **1936** ChiB: Rec 4-58 14.5 2 TD. **1937** ChiB: Rec 2-40 20.0 1 TD. **1944** ChiB: Int 3-19. **1945** ChiB: PR 1-6 6.0; KR 1-0. **Total:** Rec 22-396 18.0 8 TD; PR 1-6 6.0; KR 1-0; Int 3-19.

		Passing							
Year Team	G	Att	Comp	Comp%	Yds	YPA	TD	Int	Rating
1933 ChiB	11	9	0	0.0	0	0.00	0	0	39.6
1934 ChiB	12	36	9	25.0	150	4.17	3	6	32.6
1935 ChiB	11	41	16	39.0	230	5.61	2	5	34.7
1936 ChiB	10	12	8	66.7	170	14.17	1	2	97.9
1937 ChiB	11	13	4	30.8	84	6.46	0	1	22.6
1938 ChiB	8	1	0	0.0	0	0.00	0	0	39.6
1944 ChiB	8	56	26	46.4	448	**8.00**	9	5	76.5
1945 ChiB	7	24	10	41.7	119	4.96	0	2	22.7
NFL Total	78	192	73	38.0	1201	6.26	15	21	46.3

	Rushing				Tot
Year Team	Att	Yds	Avg	TD	TD
1933 ChiB	26	91	3.5	0	1
1934 ChiB	84	485	5.8	0	3
1935 ChiB	79	356	4.5	1	2
1936 ChiB	37	186	5.0	0	2
1937 ChiB	12	17	1.4	0	1
1938 ChiB	7	12	1.7	0	0
1944 ChiB	12	26	2.2	0	0
1945 ChiB	3	-20	-6.7	0	0
NFL Total	260	1153	4.4	1	9

COBB ROONEY Rooney, Harry Cobb 6'0", 185 **BB-WB-TB**
Col: No College *HS:* Roosevelt [Virginia, MN] B: 3/23/1900, Virginia, MN D: 5/14/1973, Bremerton, WA
1924 Dul: 6 G; Pass 2 TD. **1925** Dul: 2 G. **1926** Dul: 14 G; Rec 1 TD; 6 Pt. **1927** Dul: 8 G; Rush 1 TD; 6 Pt. **1928** NYY: 3 G. **1929** ChiC: 11 G;

Rush 1 TD; Rec 2 TD; Tot TD 3; 18 Pt. **1930** ChiC: 10 G; Rec 1 TD; 6 Pt. **Total:** 54 G; Pass 2 TD; Rush 2 TD; Rec 4 TD; Tot TD 6; 36 Pt.

JOE ROONEY Rooney, Joseph P 6'0", 177 **OE-T**
Col: No College *HS:* Roosevelt [Virginia, MN] B: 8/28/1898, Canada D: 3/1979, Franklin, MN
1923 Dul: 7 G; Rec 1 TD; 6 Pt. **1924** Dul: 6 G; Int **1** TD; 6 Pt. **1925** RI: 10 G; Rec 1 TD; 6 Pt. **1926** Dul: 13 G; Rec 1 TD; 6 Pt. **1927** Dul: 9 G; Rec 3 TD; 18 Pt. **1928** Pott: 10 G; Rec 1 TD; 6 Pt. **Total:** 55 G; Rec 7 TD; Int 1 TD; Tot TD 8; 48 Pt.

BILL ROONEY Rooney, William 6'2", 194 **FB-WB-C-BB**
Col: No College *HS:* Roosevelt [Virginia, MN] B: 7/16/1896, Canada D: 3/17/1966, Bronx, NY
1923 Dul: 5 G. **1924** Dul: 6 G; Rec 2 TD; 12 Pt. **1925** Dul-NYG: 11 G. Dul: 2 G. NYG: 9 G; Rush 1 TD; 6 Pt. **1926** Bkn: 7 G. **1927** Dul: 9 G. **1929** ChiC: 9 G. **Total:** 47 G; Rush 1 TD; Rec 2 TD; Tot TD 3; 18 Pt.

MARK ROOPENIAN Roopenian, Mark Christopher 6'5", 254 **NT**
Col: Boston College *HS:* Watertown [MA] B: 7/10/1958, Medford, MA
1982 Buf: 9 G; KR 1-0. **1983** Buf: 3 G. **Total:** 12 G; KR 1-0.

JIM ROOT Root, James Frederick 6'1", 185 **QB**
Col: Miami (Ohio) *HS:* Edward D. Libbey [Toledo, OH] B: 8/17/1931, Toledo, OH *Drafted:* 1953 Round 23 ChiC

		Passing							
Year Team	**G**	**Att**	**Comp**	**Comp%**	**Yds**	**YPA**	**TD**	**Int**	**Rating**
1953 ChiC	11	192	80	41.7	1149	5.98	8	11	51.8
1956 ChiC	9	57	28	49.1	333	5.84	3	5	48.4
NFL Total	20	249	108	43.4	1482	5.95	11	16	51.0

	Rushing				
Year Team	**Att**	**Yds**	**Avg**	**TD**	**Fum**
1953 ChiC	26	12	0.5	1	7
1956 ChiC	17	45	2.6	2	2
NFL Total	43	57	1.3	3	9

JOHN ROPER Roper, John Alfred 6'1", 232 **LB**
Col: Texas A&M *HS:* Jack Yates [Houston, TX] B: 10/4/1965, Houston, TX *Drafted:* 1989 Round 2 ChiB
1989 ChiB: 16 G; Int 2-46; 1 Fum; 4.5 Sac. **1990** ChiB: 14 G; KR 1-0; 1 Sac. **1991** ChiB: 16 G; 8 Sac. **1992** ChiB: 16 G; 2.5 Sac. **1993** Dal-Phi: 6 G; 2 Sac. Dal: 3 G; 2 Sac. Phi: 3 G. **Total:** 68 G; KR 1-0; Int 2-46; 1 Fum; 18 Sac.

JUAN ROQUE Roque, Juan Armando 6'8", 333 **OT**
Col: Arizona State *HS:* Ontario [CA] B: 2/6/1974, San Diego, CA *Drafted:* 1997 Round 2 Det
1997 Det: 13 G.

DURWOOD ROQUEMORE Roquemore, Durwood Clinton 6'1", 183 **DB**
Col: Texas A&M–Kingsville *HS:* South Oak Cliff [Dallas, TX] B: 1/19/1960, Dallas, TX *Drafted:* 1982 Round 6 KC
1982 KC: 9 G; KR 2-25 12.5; Int 1-17. **1983** KC: 15 G; KR 3-36 12.0; Int 4-117 1 TD; 6 Pt. **1987** Buf: 5 G. **Total:** 29 G; KR 5-61 12.2; Int 5-134 1 TD; 6 Pt.

JIM RORISON Rorison, James 6'3", 250 **T**
(Red) *Col:* USC *HS:* Manual Arts [Los Angeles, CA] B: 7/23/1916 D: 10/1980
1938 Pit: 6 G.

SPENCER RORK Rork, Joseph Spencer 5'9", 160 **BB-WB**
Col: Kentucky *HS:* Paducah [KY] B: 8/18/1896, Paducah, KY D: 4/1982, Key Largo, FL
1922 Eva: 2 G.

DAN ROSADO Rosado, Daniel Peter 6'3", 280 **OG-C**
Col: Northern Illinois *HS:* Cherokee [Canton, GA] B: 7/6/1959, Lawton, OK
1987 SD: 4 G. **1988** SD: 12 G; 1 Fum. **Total:** 16 G; 1 Fum.

SAL ROSATO Rosato, Salvatore 6'1", 228 **FB-LB**
(The Tank) *Col:* Villanova *HS:* Williamsport [PA] B: 6/6/1918, Williamsport, PA D: 1/12/1959, Alhambra, CA
1945 Was: Rec 1-7 7.0; KR 1-17 17.0. **1946** Was: Rec 1-17 17.0; PR 1-12 12.0. **1947** Was: Rec 7-107 15.3 1 TD; KR 2-36 18.0. **Total:** Rec 9-131 14.6 1 TD; PR 1-12 12.0; KR 3-53 17.7.

		Rushing					Tot
Year Team	**G**	**Att**	**Yds**	**Avg**	**TD**	**Fum**	**TD**
1945 Was	7	23	85	3.7	2	2	2
1946 Was	5	62	238	3.8	2	1	2
1947 Was	11	74	297	4.0	0	1	1
NFL Total	23	159	620	3.9	4	4	5

RUDY ROSATTI Rosatti, Rudolph F 6'0", 211 **T**
(Rosey) *Col:* Western Michigan; North Dakota State; Michigan *HS:* Norway [MI] B: 9/12/1895, Norway, MI D: 7/8/1975, Norway, MI
1923 Cle: 7 G. **1924** GB: 11 G. **1926** GB: 10 G. **1927** GB: 6 G. **1928** NYG: 11 G. **Total:** 45 G.

HATCH ROSDAHL Rosdahl, Harrison Lynn 6'4", 250 **DT-OG**
Col: Penn State *HS:* Ridgefield [NJ] B: 8/24/1941, Hackensack, NJ *Drafted:* 1963 Round 14 SD
1964 Buf-KC: 11 G; KR 1-0; 1 Fum. Buf: 4 G. KC: 7 G; KR 1-0; 1 Fum. **1965** KC: 14 G. **1966** KC: 7 G. **Total:** 32 G; KR 1-0; 1 Fum.

AL ROSE Rose, Alfred Grady 6'3", 205 **OE-DE**
(Big Un) *Col:* Texas *HS:* Highland Park [Dallas, TX] B: 1/26/1907, Temple, TX D: 1988
1930 Prov: 11 G. **1931** Prov: 11 G; Pass 1 TD; Rec 2 TD; Tot TD 3; 18 Pt. **1932** GB: 13 G; Rec 1-20 20.0; **1** Fum TD; Tot TD 2; 12 Pt. **1933** GB: 12 G; Rec 6-89 14.8 1 TD; 6 Pt. **1934** GB: 9 G; Rec 6-117 19.5 2 TD; 12 Pt. **1935** GB: 12 G; Rec 8-91 11.4. **1936** GB: 2 G. **Total:** 70 G; Pass 1 TD; Rec 21-317 15.1 5 TD; 1 Fum TD; Tot TD 8; 48 Pt.

BARRY ROSE Rose, Barry Allan 6'0", 185 **WR**
Col: Wis.-Stevens Point *HS:* Baldwin-Woodville [Baldwin, WI] B: 7/28/1968, Hudson, WI *Drafted:* 1992 Round 10 Buf
1993 Den: 3 G.

CARLTON ROSE Rose, Carlton 6'2", 220 **LB**
Col: Michigan *HS:* Stranahan [Fort Lauderdale, FL] B: 2/8/1962, Pompano Beach, FL
1987 Was: 2 G; 1 Sac.

DONOVAN ROSE Rose, Donovan James 6'1", 187 **DB**
Col: Hampton *HS:* Norview [Norfolk, VA] B: 3/9/1957, Norfolk, VA
1980 KC: 7 G. **1986** Mia: 12 G; Int 2-63. **1987** Mia: 12 G. **Total:** 31 G; Int 2-63.

GENE ROSE Rose, Eugene Harry 5'8", 172 **WB-FB-BB**
Col: Wisconsin *HS:* Racine [WI] B: 7/11/1904, Racine, WI D: 2/1/1979, Torrance, CA
1929 ChiC: 13 G; Rush 1 TD; 6 Pt. **1930** ChiC: 12 G; Rush 3 TD; Rec 1 TD; Scor 25, 1 XK; Tot TD 4. **1931** ChiC: 8 G; Rush 1 TD; 6 Pt. **1932** ChiC: 1 G; Pass 5-2 40.0%, 40 8.00; Rush 1-0. **Total:** 34 G; Pass 5-2 40.0%, 40 8.00; Rush 1-0 5 TD; Rec 1 TD; Tot TD 6.

GEORGE ROSE Rose, George Lee 5'11", 200 **DB**
Col: Auburn *HS:* Glynn Acad. [Brunswick, GA] B: 1/1/1942, Brunswick, GA *Drafted:* 1964 Round 3 Min
1964 Min: 14 G; KR 8-180 22.5; Int 6-48 1 TD; 6 Pt; 1 Fum. **1965** Min: 10 G; Int 1-6. **1966** Min: 10 G; KR 1-20 20.0; Int 1-17; 1 Fum. **1967** NO: 13 G; KR 1-21 21.0; Int 1-15; 1 Fum. **Total:** 47 G; KR 10-221 22.1; Int 9-86 1 TD; 6 Pt; 3 Fum.

JOE ROSE Rose, Joseph Harold 6'3", 228 **TE**
Col: California *HS:* Marysville [CA] B: 6/24/1957, Marysville, CA *Drafted:* 1980 Round 7 Mia
1981 Mia: KR 1-5 5.0. **Total:** KR 1-5 5.0.

		Receiving			
Year Team	**G**	**Rec**	**Yds**	**Avg**	**TD**
1980 Mia	16	13	149	11.5	0
1981 Mia	16	23	316	13.7	2
1982 Mia	9	16	182	11.4	2
1983 Mia	16	29	345	11.9	3
1984 Mia	9	12	195	16.3	2
1985 Mia	16	19	306	16.1	4
1987 LARm	1	0	0	—	0
NFL Total	83	112	1493	13.3	13

KEN ROSE Rose, Kenny Frank 6'1", 215 **LB**
Col: Nevada-Las Vegas *HS:* Christian Brothers [Sacramento, CA] B: 6/9/1962, Sacramento, CA
1987 NYJ: 10 G; Int 1-1; 1.5 Sac. **1988** NYJ: 12 G; KR 1-0; 5 Sac. **1989** NYJ: 15 G. **1990** Cle-Phi: 15 G. Cle: 7 G. Phi: 8 G. **1991** Phi: 16 G. **1992** Phi: 16 G; 6 Pt. **1993** Phi: 5 G. **1994** Phi: 16 G. **Total:** 105 G; KR 1-0; Int 1-1; 6 Pt; 6.5 Sac.

GENE ROSE Rose, Roy Eugene 6'1", 185 **OE-DE**
Col: Tennessee *HS:* Lockland [OH] B: 8/15/1913, Cincinnati, OH D: 1/16/1986, Memphis, TN *Drafted:* 1936 Round 4 NYG
1936 NYG: 7 G; Rush 2-13 6.5; Rec 6-73 12.2.

TAM ROSE Rose, Walter Sumner 5'11", 170 **TB**
Col: Syracuse *HS:* Tonawanda [NY] B: 6/20/1889 D: 12/1965, NY
1921 Ton: 1 G.

JAMES ROSECRANS Rosecrans, James Edward 6'1", 230 **LB**
Col: Penn State *HS:* West Genesee [Camillus, NY] B: 1/13/1953, Asheville, NC
1976 NYJ: 1 G.

ROCKY ROSEMA Rosema, Roger William 6'2", 230 **LB**
Col: Michigan *HS:* Central [Grand Rapids, MI] B: 2/5/1946, Grand Rapids, MI *Drafted:* 1968 Round 5 StL
1968 StL: 12 G. **1969** StL: 14 G; Int 1-3. **1970** StL: 4 G. **1971** StL: 2 G. **Total:** 32 G; Int 1-3.

STAN ROSEN Rosen, Stanley 5'6", 155 **BB-TB**
(Tex) *Col:* Rutgers *HS:* New Utrecht [Brooklyn, NY] B: 3/28/1906, New York, NY D: 7/23/1984, Claremont, NH
1929 Buf: 8 G.

TIMM ROSENBACH Rosenbach, Timm Lane 6′2″, 215 **QB**
Col: Washington State *HS:* Hellgate [Missoula, MT]; Pullman HS [WA]
B: 10/27/1966, Everett, WA *Drafted:* 1989 Supplemental Round 1 Pho

		Passing							
Year Team	**G**	**Att**	**Comp**	**Comp%**	**Yds**	**YPA**	**TD**	**Int**	**Rating**
1989 Pho	2	22	9	40.9	95	4.32	0	1	35.2
1990 Pho	16	437	237	54.2	3098	7.09	16	17	72.8
1992 Pho	8	92	49	53.3	483	5.25	0	6	41.2
NFL Total	26	551	295	53.5	3676	6.67	16	24	66.0

	Rushing				
Year Team	**Att**	**Yds**	**Avg**	**TD**	**Fum**
1989 Pho	6	26	4.3	0	2
1990 Pho	86	470	5.5	3	10
1992 Pho	9	11	1.2	0	4
NFL Total	101	507	5.0	3	16

ERIK ROSENMEIER Rosenmeier, Erik Michael 6′4″, 240 **C**
Col: Colgate *HS:* Arthur L. Johnson Regional [Clark, NJ] B: 5/26/1965, Plainfield, NJ
1987 Buf: 1 G.

BOB ROSENSTIEL Rosenstiel, Robert 6′3″, 240 **TE**
Col: Shasta Coll. CA (J.C.); Coll. of the Sequoias CA (J.C.); Eastern Illinois *HS:* Junction City [OR] B: 2/7/1974, Prineville, OR
1997 Oak: 4 G.

TED ROSEQUIST Rosequist, Theodore Anthony 6′4″, 222 **T**
Col: John Carroll; Ohio State *HS:* Central [Cleveland, OH]
B: 4/17/1908, Emlenton, PA D: 11/29/1988, West Palm Beach, FL
1934 ChiB: 11 G; Rec 2-20 10.0. **1935** ChiB: 11 G. **1936** ChiB: 4 G; Rec 1-15 15.0. **1937** Cle: 7 G. **Total:** 33 G; Rec 3-35 11.7.

KEN ROSKIE Roskie, Kenneth 6′1″, 225 **FB-LB**
Col: Gordon Coll. GA (J.C.); South Carolina *HS:* Rockford Central [IL]
B: 11/29/1920, Rockford, IL D: 8/1986, Redmond, WA *Drafted:* 1943 Round 30 GB
AAFC **1946** SF-A: 8 G; Rush 9-16 1.8; Rec 0-7.

NFL **1948** GB-Det: 13 G; Rush 6-29 4.8 1 TD; KR 1-30 30.0; Int 1-12; 6 Pt; 1 Fum. GB: 6 G; Rush 5-28 5.6 1 TD; Int 1-12; 6 Pt. Det: 7 G; Rush 1-1 1.0; KR 1-30 30.0; 1 Fum. **Total:** 13 G; Rush 6-29 4.8 1 TD; KR 1-30 30.0; Int 1-12; 6 Pt; 1 Fum.

TED ROSNAGLE Rosnagle, Theodore 6′3″, 205 **DB**
Col: Fullerton Coll. CA (J.C.); Portland State *HS:* Tustin [CA]
B: 9/29/1961, Pasadena, CA
1985 Min: 6 G. **1987** Min: 3 G. **Total:** 9 G.

ADRIAN ROSS Ross, Adrian Lamont 6′2″, 244 **LB**
Col: Colorado State *HS:* Elk Grove [CA] B: 2/19/1975, Santa Clara, CA
1998 Cin: 14 G; Int 1-11.

ALVIN ROSS Ross, Alvin 5′11″, 235 **RB**
Col: Oklahoma; Central Oklahoma *HS:* Aurora West [IL] B: 5/3/1963, Chicago, IL
1987 Phi: 2 G; Rush 14-54 3.9 1 TD; Rec 5-41 8.2; 6 Pt.

DAN ROSS Ross, Daniel Richard 6′4″, 238 **TE**
Col: Northeastern *HS:* Everett [MA] B: 2/9/1957, Malden, MA
Drafted: 1979 Round 2 Cin

		Receiving				
Year Team	**G**	**Rec**	**Yds**	**Avg**	**TD**	**Fum**
1979 Cin	16	41	516	12.6	1	0
1980 Cin	16	56	724	12.9	4	1
1981 Cin	16	71	910	12.8	5	3
1982 Cin	9	47	508	10.8	3	1
1983 Cin	16	42	483	11.5	3	0
1985 Cin-Sea	16	16	135	8.4	2	1
1985 Cin	6	6	63	10.5	0	1
1985 Sea	10	10	72	7.2	2	0
1986 GB	15	17	143	8.4	1	0
NFL Total	104	290	3419	11.8	19	6

DAVE ROSS Ross, David 6′3″, 210 **OE**
Col: Cerritos Coll. CA (J.C.); Los Angeles State *HS:* California [Whittier, CA] B: 2/1/1938 *Drafted:* 1960 Round 1 NYT
1960 NYT: 12 G; Rec 10-122 12.2 1 TD; 6 Pt.

DOMINIQUE ROSS Ross, Dominique 6′0″, 203 **RB**
Col: Valdosta State *HS:* William M. Raines [Jacksonville, FL]
B: 1/12/1972, Jacksonville, FL
1995 Dal: 1 G. **1996** Dal: 2 G. **Total:** 3 G.

JERMAINE ROSS Ross, Jermaine Lewis 6′0″, 192 **WR**
Col: Purdue *HS:* Jeffersonville [IN] B: 4/27/1971, Jeffersonville, IN
1994 LARm: 4 G; Rec 1-36 36.0 1 TD; 6 Pt. **1996** StL: 15 G; Rush 1-3 3.0 1 TD; Rec 15-160 10.7; 6 Pt. **1997** StL: 4 G; Rec 3-37 12.3; PR 2-12 6.0; KR 6-130 21.7. **Total:** 23 G; Rush 1-3 3.0 1 TD; Rec 19-233 12.3 1 TD; PR 2-12 6.0; KR 6-130 21.7; Tot TD 2; 12 Pt.

KEVIN ROSS Ross, Kevin Lesley 5′9″, 185 **DB**
Col: Temple *HS:* Paulsboro [NJ] B: 1/16/1962, Camden, NJ
Drafted: 1984 Round 7 KC
1986 KC: **1** Fum TD; 2 Sac. **1987** KC: 1 Sac. **1989** KC: PR 2-0. **1992** KC: 0.5 Sac. **1993** KC: 0.5 Sac. **1994** Atl: 1 Sac. **Total:** PR 2-0; 1 Fum TD; 5 Sac.

		Interceptions				Tot
Year Team	**G**	**Int**	**Yds**	**TD**	**Fum**	**TD**
1984 KC	16	6	124	1	0	1
1985 KC	16	3	47	0	0	0
1986 KC	16	4	66	0	0	1
1987 KC	12	3	40	0	0	1
1988 KC	15	1	0	0	0	0
1989 KC	15	4	29	0	1	0
1990 KC	16	5	97	0	0	1
1991 KC	14	1	0	0	0	0
1992 KC	16	1	99	1	0	1
1993 KC	15	2	49	0	0	0
1994 Atl	16	3	26	0	0	0
1995 Atl	16	3	70	0	0	1
1996 SD	16	2	7	0	0	0
1997 KC	5	0	0	0	0	0
NFL Total	204	38	654	2	1	6

LOUIS ROSS Ross, Louis Edward 6′6″, 248 **DE**
Col: South Carolina State *HS:* Jones [Orlando, FL] B: 8/31/1947, Orlando, FL *Drafted:* 1971 Round 8 Buf
1971 Buf: 5 G. **1972** Buf: 14 G. **1975** KC: 1 G. **Total:** 20 G.

OLIVER ROSS Ross, Oliver 6′4″, 300 **OT**
Col: Southwestern Coll. CA (J.C.); Iowa State *HS:* George Washington [Los Angeles, CA] B: 9/27/1974, Culver City, CA *Drafted:* 1998 Round 5 Dal
1998 Dal: 2 G.

OLIVER ROSS Ross, Oliver Stevenson 6′0″, 210 **RB**
Col: Alabama A&M *HS:* Gainesville [FL] B: 9/18/1949, Gainesville, FL
Drafted: 1973 Round 16 Den
1974 Den: Rec 1-13 13.0. **1975** Den: Rec 7-69 9.9. **1976** Sea: Rec 2-22 11.0. **Total:** Rec 10-104 10.4.

		Rushing				Kickoff Returns				
Year Team	**G**	**Att**	**Yds**	**Avg**	**TD**	**Ret**	**Yds**	**Avg**	**TD**	**Fum**
1973 Den	4	5	21	4.2	0	0	0	—	0	0
1974 Den	7	3	8	2.7	0	7	117	16.7	0	1
1975 Den	14	42	121	2.9	0	1	20	20.0	0	5
1976 Sea	10	13	23	1.8	0	30	655	21.8	0	1
NFL Total	35	63	173	2.7	0	38	792	20.8	0	7

SCOTT ROSS Ross, Scott 6′1″, 235 **LB**
Col: USC *HS:* El Toro [CA] B: 12/7/1968, El Toro, CA *Drafted:* 1991 Round 11 NO
1991 NO: 4 G.

TIM ROSS Ross, Timothy Leon 6′5″, 225 **LB**
Col: Bowling Green State *HS:* Woodward [Toledo, OH] B: 12/27/1958, Toledo, OH
1987 Det: 3 G; 1 Sac.

WILLIE ROSS Ross, William James 5′10″, 200 **FB**
(Twister) *Col:* Nebraska *HS:* Elize Meller [Helena, AR] B: 6/6/1941, Helena, AR *Drafted:* 1964 Round 12 Buf
1964 Buf: 12 G; Rush 4-14 3.5 1 TD; 6 Pt.

GEORGE ROSSO Rosso, George Anthony 5′11″, 177 **DB**
Col: Ohio State *HS:* Langley [Pittsburgh, PA] B: 1/15/1930, Pittsburgh, PA D: 1/29/1994, Columbus, OH *Drafted:* 1954 Round 25 Was
1954 Was: 12 G; PR 4-15 3.8; Int 4-9.

TIM ROSSOVICH Rossovich, Timothy John 6′4″, 240 **LB-DE**
Col: USC *HS:* St. Francis [Mountain View, CA] B: 3/14/1946, Palo Alto, CA *Drafted:* 1968 Round 1 Phi
1968 Phi: 14 G; KR 2-20 10.0. **1969** Phi: 14 G. **1970** Phi: 14 G; KR 1-22 22.0. **1971** Phi: 13 G; Int 1-24. **1972** SD: 6 G; Int 1-0. **1973** SD: 13 G; Int 1-9. **1976** Hou: 14 G. **Total:** 88 G; KR 3-42 14.0; Int 3-33.

ALLEN ROSSUM Rossum, Allen 5′8″, 178 **DB**
Col: Notre Dame *HS:* Skyline [Dallas, TX] B: 10/22/1975, Dallas, TX
Drafted: 1998 Round 3 Phi
1998 Phi: PR 22-187 8.5; 1 Sac.

		Kickoff Returns				
Year Team	**G**	**Ret**	**Yds**	**Avg**	**TD**	**Fum**
1998 Phi	15	44	1080	24.5	0	4

ERNIE ROSTECK Rosteck, Ernest W 6′1″, 218 **C-LB**
Col: No College *HS:* Southeastern [Detroit, MI] B: 5/12/1922, Detroit, MI D: 3/1986, Waterloo, IA
1943 Det: 1 G. **1944** Det: 9 G. **Total:** 10 G.

PETE ROSTOSKY Rostosky, Peter Joseph 6'4", 259 **OT**
Col: Connecticut *HS:* Elizabeth Forward [Elizabeth, PA] B: 7/29/1961, Monongahela, PA
1984 Pit: 8 G. **1985** Pit: 16 G. **1986** Pit: 11 G; KR 1-3 3.0. **Total:** 35 G; KR 1-3 3.0.

TOBIN ROTE Rote, Tobin Cornelius Jr. 6'2", 211 **QB**
Col: Rice *HS:* Harlandale [San Antonio, TX] B: 1/18/1928, San Antonio, TX *Drafted:* 1950 Round 2 GB
1951 GB: Rec 0-11; Punt 1-55 55.0. **1952** GB: Rec 1-28 28.0 1 TD. **1953** GB: Punt 1-57 57.0. **1964** SD: Rec 1-(-11) -11.0. **Total:** Rec 2-28 14.0 1 TD; Punt 2-112 56.0.

		Passing							
Year Team	**G**	**Att**	**Comp**	**Comp%**	**Yds**	**YPA**	**TD**	**Int**	**Rating**
1950 GB	12	224	83	37.1	1231	5.50	7	24	26.7
1951 GB	12	256	106	41.4	1540	6.02	15	20	48.6
1952 GB	12	157	82	52.2	1268	8.08	13	**8**	85.6
1953 GB	12	185	72	38.9	1005	5.43	5	15	32.4
1954 GB	12	**382**	**180**	47.1	2311	6.05	14	18	59.1
1955 GB	12	342	157	45.9	1977	5.78	**17**	19	57.8
1956 GB	12	**308**	**146**	47.4	**2203**	7.15	**18**	15	70.6
1957 Det	12	177	76	42.9	1070	6.05	11	10	60.2
1958 Det	12	257	118	45.9	1678	6.53	14	10	69.5
1959 Det	10	162	62	38.3	861	5.31	5	19	26.8
1963 SD	14	286	170	**59.4**	2510	**8.78**	20	17	86.7
1964 SD	14	163	74	45.4	1156	7.09	9	15	49.5
1966 Den	3	8	3	37.5	40	5.00	0	1	14.6
NFL Total	149	2907	1329	45.7	18850	6.48	148	191	56.8

	Rushing					Tot
Year Team	**Att**	**Yds**	**Avg**	**TD**	**Fum**	**TD**
1950 GB	27	158	5.9	0	9	0
1951 GB	76	523	**6.9**	3	4	3
1952 GB	58	313	5.4	2	**10**	3
1953 GB	33	180	5.5	0	2	0
1954 GB	67	301	4.5	8	4	8
1955 GB	74	332	4.5	5	**10**	5
1956 GB	84	398	4.7	11	5	11
1957 Det	70	366	5.2	1	6	1
1958 Det	77	351	4.6	3	7	3
1959 Det	35	156	4.5	2	2	2
1963 SD	24	62	2.6	2	2	2
1964 SD	10	-12	-1.2	0	6	0
NFL Total	635	3128	4.9	37	67	38

KYLE ROTE Rote, William Kyle 6'0", 199 **OE**
(The Mighty Mustang) *Col:* Southern Methodist *HS:* Thomas Jefferson [San Antonio, TX] B: 10/27/1927, Bellevue, TX *Drafted:* 1951 Round 1 NYG
1951 NYG: KR 6-185 30.8. **1952** NYG: Pass 4-2 50.0%, 113 28.25 1 TD; KR 6-110 18.3. **1953** NYG: Pass 8-2 25.0%, 45 5.63 1 Int. **1954** NYG: Pass 6-2 33.3%, 36 6.00 1 TD 1 Int. **1955** NYG: Pass 1-0. **1956** NYG: Pass 1-0. **Total:** Pass 20-6 30.0%, 194 9.70 2 TD 2 Int; KR 12-295 24.6.

		Rushing				Receiving					Tot
Year Team	**G**	**Att**	**Yds**	**Avg**	**TD**	**Rec**	**Yds**	**Avg**	**TD**	**Fum**	**TD**
1951 NYG	5	21	114	5.4	1	8	62	7.8	0	1	1
1952 NYG	12	103	421	4.1	2	21	240	11.4	2	3	4
1953 NYG	9	63	213	3.4	1	26	440	16.9	5	0	6
1954 NYG	11	30	59	2.0	0	29	551	19.0	2	0	2
1955 NYG	12	10	46	4.6	0	31	580	18.7	8	1	8
1956 NYG	12	3	5	1.7	0	28	405	14.5	4	0	4
1957 NYG	12	1	13	13.0	0	25	358	14.3	3	0	3
1958 NYG	12	0	0	—	0	12	244	20.3	3	1	3
1959 NYG	10	0	0	—	0	25	362	14.5	4	0	4
1960 NYG	11	0	0	—	0	42	750	17.9	10	0	10
1961 NYG	14	0	0	—	0	53	805	15.2	7	2	7
NFL Total	120	231	871	3.8	4	300	4797	16.0	48	8	52

PETE ROTH Roth, Peter William 5'11", 210 **RB**
Col: Northern Illinois *HS:* Princeton [IL] B: 1/12/1962, Worthington, MN
1987 Mia: 3 G; Rush 3-10 3.3; KR 2-49 24.5.

TIM ROTHER Rother, Timothy Jay 6'7", 285 **DT**
Col: Nebraska *HS:* Bellevue [NE] B: 9/28/1965, St. Paul, NE *Drafted:* 1988 Round 4 LARd
1989 LARd: 16 G. **1990** LARd: 4 G. **Total:** 20 G.

CLIFF ROTHROCK Rothrock, Clifford Crossley 5'10", 198 **C-LB**
(Bony) *Col:* North Dakota State *HS:* Fargo [ND] B: 1/10/1922, Fargo, ND
AAFC **1947** ChiA: 2 G.

DOUG ROTHSCHILD Rothschild, Douglas Robert 6'2", 231 **LB**
Col: Wheaton *HS:* Fremont [Oakland, CA] B: 4/27/1965, Sunnyvale, CA
1987 ChiB: 3 G.

FRED ROTHWELL Rothwell, Donald Fred 6'3", 240 **C**
Col: Kansas State *HS:* P.K. Yonge Lab [Gainesville, FL] B: 10/8/1952, Lafayette, IN *Drafted:* 1974 Round 13 Det
1974 Det: 14 G.

HERB ROTON Roton, Herbert Carl 6'2", 210 **OE-DE**
(Bummie) *Col:* Auburn *HS:* Sidney Lanier [Montgomery, AL] B: 8/28/1913, Montgomery, AL
1937 Phi: 9 G.

GEORGE ROUDEBUSH Roudebush, George Milton 5'11", 180 **TB-FB**
(Rowdy) *Col:* Denison *HS:* Milford [OH] B: 1/25/1894, Newtonville, OH D: 3/1/1992, Chardon, OH
1920 Day: 9 G. **1921** Day: 9 G; Pass 2 TD; Rush 1 TD; 6 Pt. **Total:** 18 G; Pass 2 TD; Rush 1 TD; 6 Pt.

TOM ROUEN Rouen, Thomas Francis 6'3", 218 **P**
Col: Colorado State; Colorado *HS:* Heritage [Littleton, CO] B: 6/9/1968, Hinsdale, IL
1993 Den: Rush 1-0. **1998** Den: Rush 1-0; Scor 0-1 XK. **Total:** Rush 2-0; Scor 0-1 XK.

		Punting			
Year Team	**G**	**Punts**	**Yds**	**Avg**	**Fum**
1993 Den	16	67	3017	45.0	0
1994 Den	16	76	3258	42.9	0
1995 Den	16	52	2192	42.2	0
1996 Den	16	65	2714	41.8	0
1997 Den	16	60	2598	43.3	0
1998 Den	16	66	3097	46.9	1
NFL Total	96	386	16876	43.7	1

RALEIGH ROUNDTREE Roundtree, Raleigh Cito 6'4", 295 **OT**
Col: South Carolina State *HS:* Josey [Augusta, GA] B: 8/31/1975, Augusta, GA *Drafted:* 1997 Round 4 SD
1998 SD: 15 G.

RAY ROUNDTREE Roundtree, Raymond Anthony 6'0", 180 **WR**
Col: Penn State *HS:* South Aiken [Aiken, SC] B: 4/19/1966, Aiken, SC *Drafted:* 1988 Round 3 Det
1988 Det: 4 G.

JIM ROURKE Rourke, James Peter 6'5", 264 **OT-OG-C**
Col: Boston College *HS:* Boston College [MA] B: 2/10/1957, Weymouth, MA *Drafted:* 1979 Round 9 Oak
1980 KC: 15 G. **1981** KC: 12 G; KR 2-0. **1982** KC: 9 G. **1983** KC: 11 G. **1984** KC: 13 G. **1985** NO: 13 G. **1986** KC: 4 G. **1988** Cin: Postseason only. **Total:** 77 G; KR 2-0.

TUBBY ROUSCH Rousch, Frank 5'7", 170 **WB-G**
Col: Toledo *HS:* Morrison R. Waite [Toledo, OH] B: 1898 Deceased
1922 Tol: 5 G; Rush 1 TD; 6 Pt.

CURTIS ROUSE Rouse, Curtis Lamar 6'3", 316 **OG-OT**
Col: Tennessee-Chattanooga *HS:* Lucy Craft Laney [Augusta, GA] B: 7/13/1960, Augusta, GA *Drafted:* 1982 Round 11 Min
1982 Min: 5 G. **1983** Min: 16 G. **1984** Min: 16 G; KR 2-22 11.0. **1985** Min: 16 G. **1986** Min: 5 G. **1987** SD: 10 G. **Total:** 68 G; KR 2-22 11.0.

JAMES ROUSE Rouse, James David 6'0", 220 **RB**
Col: Arkansas *HS:* Parkview [Little Rock, AR] B: 12/18/1966, Little Rock, AR *Drafted:* 1990 Round 8 ChiB
1990 ChiB: KR 3-17 5.7. **1991** ChiB: Rec 15-93 6.2; KR 2-10 5.0. **Total:** Rec 15-93 6.2; KR 5-27 5.4.

		Rushing				
Year Team	**G**	**Att**	**Yds**	**Avg**	**TD**	**Fum**
1990 ChiB	16	16	56	3.5	0	0
1991 ChiB	14	27	74	2.7	0	1
NFL Total	30	43	130	3.0	0	1

STILLMAN ROUSE Rouse, Stillman Ivan 6'2", 205 **OE-DE**
Col: Missouri *HS:* McKinley [St. Louis, MO] B: 9/22/1917, St. Louis, MO *Drafted:* 1940 Round 13 Det
1940 Det: 10 G; Rush 2-0; Rec 2-17 8.5.

WARDELL ROUSE Rouse, Wardell Jr. 6'2", 235 **LB**
Col: Itawamba CC MS; Clemson *HS:* Clewiston [FL] B: 6/9/1972, Clewiston, FL *Drafted:* 1995 Round 6 TB
1995 TB: 16 G; 0.5 Sac.

LEE ROUSON Rouson, Cecil Lee 6'1", 220 **RB**
Col: Colorado *HS:* Walter H. Page [Greensboro, NC] B: 10/18/1962, Elizabeth City, NC *Drafted:* 1985 Round 8 NYG

		Rushing				Receiving			
Year Team	**G**	**Att**	**Yds**	**Avg**	**TD**	**Rec**	**Yds**	**Avg**	**TD**
1985 NYG	2	1	1	1.0	0	0	0	—	0
1986 NYG	14	54	179	3.3	2	8	121	15.1	1
1987 NYG	12	41	155	3.8	0	11	129	11.7	1
1988 NYG	16	1	1	1.0	0	4	61	15.3	0
1989 NYG	16	11	51	4.6	0	7	121	17.3	0
1990 NYG	16	3	14	4.7	0	1	12	12.0	0

1991 Cle	16	3	14	4.7	0	2	9	4.5	0
NFL Total	92	114	415	3.6	2	33	453	13.7	2

	Kickoff Returns					
Year Team	**Ret**	**Yds**	**Avg**	**TD**	**Fum**	**Tot TD**
1985 NYG	2	35	17.5	0	0	0
1986 NYG	2	21	10.5	0	0	3
1987 NYG	22	497	22.6	0	3	1
1988 NYG	8	130	16.3	0	2	0
1989 NYG	1	17	17.0	0	0	0
1991 Cle	1	16	16.0	0	0	0
NFL Total	36	716	19.9	0	5	4

TOM ROUSSEL Roussel, Thomas James 6′3″, 235 **LB**
Col: Southern Mississippi *HS:* Thibodaux [LA] B: 1/20/1945, Thibodaux, LA *Drafted:* 1968 Round 2 Was
1968 Was: 14 G. **1969** Was: 14 G. **1970** Was: 14 G. **1971** NO: 7 G. **1972** NO: 14 G; Int 2-15. **1973** Phi: 3 G. **Total:** 66 G; Int 2-15.

MIKE ROUSSOS Roussos, Michael Christ 6′3″, 238 **T**
Col: Pittsburgh *HS:* New Castle [PA] B: 2/8/1926, New Castle, PA D: 4/6/1987, New Castle, PA
1948 Was: 12 G. **1949** Was-Det: 12 G. Was: 6 G. Det: 6 G. **Total:** 24 G.

JOHN ROVETO Roveto, John Charles 6′0″, 180 **K**
Col: Southwestern Louisiana *HS:* Spring [TX] B: 2/20/1958, Fort Lauderdale, FL
1981 ChiB: 11 G; Scor 49, 10-18 55.6% FG, 19-20 95.0% XK. **1982** ChiB: 7 G; Scor 22, 4-13 30.8% FG, 10-10 100.0% XK. **Total:** 18 G; Scor 71, 14-31 45.2% FG, 29-30 96.7% XK.

TONY ROVINSKI Rovinski, Anthony Charles 5′9″, 195 **OE-DE**
Col: Holy Cross *HS:* Kingston [PA]; St. John's Prep [Danvers, PA] B: 9/11/1908, Nanticoke, PA D: 4/16/1973, Wilkes-Barre, PA
1933 NYG: 1 G.

EV ROWAN Rowan, Everett Lawrence 6′1″, 187 **OE-DE-DB-FB**
(Deb) *Col:* Ohio State *HS:* Chillicothe [OH] B: 1903 D: 11/1956
1930 Bkn: 2 G. **1932** Bkn: 11 G; Rec 2-40 20.0. **1933** Phi: 2 G; Rec 1-12 12.0. **Total:** 15 G; Rec 3-52 17.3.

JOHN ROWAN Rowan, John 5′8″, 165 **TB-BB**
Col: Tennessee B: 6/3/1896, Decatur Twp., Washington Co., OH D: 4/1967, Belpre, OH
1923 Lou: 3 G.

LARRY ROWDEN Rowden, Larry David 6′2″, 220 **LB**
Col: Houston *HS:* Pampa [TX] B: 3/17/1949, Pampa, TX
Drafted: 1971 Round 10 ChiB
1971 ChiB: 14 G. **1972** ChiB: 2 G. **Total:** 16 G.

DAVE ROWE Rowe, David Homeyer 6′7″, 280 **DT**
Col: Penn State *HS:* Deptford [NJ] B: 6/20/1945, Neptune, NJ
Drafted: 1967 Round 2 NO
1967 NO: 14 G. **1968** NO: 14 G. **1969** NO: 14 G. **1970** NO: 14 G. **1971** NE: 14 G. **1972** NE: 14 G. **1973** NE: 14 G. **1974** SD: 14 G. **1975** SD-Oak: 11 G. SD: 1 G. Oak: 10 G. **1976** Oak: 14 G. **1977** Oak: 14 G. **1978** Oak-Bal: 14 G. Oak: 1 G. Bal: 13 G. **Total:** 165 G.

HARMON ROWE Rowe, Harmon Beasley 6′0″, 182 **DB-HB-WB**
Col: Baylor; San Francisco *HS:* Livingston [TX] B: 8/22/1923, Livingston, TX *Drafted:* 1946 Round 3 Pit
AAFC **1947** NY-A: 10 G; Rush 2-(-3) -1.5; KR 1-18 18.0; Int 2-20. **1948** NY-A: 11 G; PR 1-12 12.0. **1949** NY-A: 9 G; Rush 6-21 3.5; Int 3-53. **Total:** 30 G; Rush 8-18 2.3; PR 1-12 12.0; KR 1-18 18.0; Int 5-73.

NFL **1950** NYG: 7 G; Int 3-48; 1 Fum. **1951** NYG: 8 G; Int 2-19; Scor **1** Saf; 2 Pt. **1952** NYG: 12 G; Int 1-22. **Total:** 27 G; Int 6-89; Scor 1 Saf; 2 Pt; 1 Fum.

JOE ROWE Rowe, Joeseph III 6′0″, 195 **DB**
Col: Virginia *HS:* Greensville Co. [Emporia, VA] B: 12/8/1973, East Elmhurst, NY
1997 StL: 2 G.

PATRICK ROWE Rowe, Patrick Donald Edward 6′1″, 195 **WR**
Col: San Diego State *HS:* Abraham Lincoln [San Diego, CA] B: 2/17/1969, San Diego, CA *Drafted:* 1992 Round 2 Cle
1993 Cle: 5 G; Rec 3-37 12.3; 1 Fum.

RAY ROWE Rowe, Raymond Henry 6′2″, 256 **TE**
Col: San Diego State *HS:* Mira Mesa [San Diego, CA] B: 7/28/1969, Rota, Spain *Drafted:* 1992 Round 6 Was
1992 Was: 3 G. **1993** Was: 1 G. **Total:** 4 G.

BOB ROWE Rowe, Robert Buell 6′4″, 270 **DT-DE**
Col: Western Michigan *HS:* Flushing [MI] B: 5/23/1945, Flint, MI
Drafted: 1967 Round 2 StL
1967 StL: 11 G. **1968** StL: 14 G. **1969** StL: 13 G; Int 2-19 1 TD; 6 Pt. **1970** StL: 14 G. **1971** StL: 14 G. **1972** StL: 14 G. **1973** StL: 14 G. **1974** StL: 14 G. **1975** StL: 14 G. **Total:** 122 G; Int 2-19 1 TD; 6 Pt.

BOB ROWE Rowe, Robert Casper 6′0″, 198 **HB**
Col: Colgate *HS:* Hillsdale [MI] B: 5/28/1911, Jackson, MI D: 12/23/1992, Slingerlands, NY
1934 Det: 11 G; Pass 2-0; Rush 16-44 2.8; Rec 1-4 4.0. **1935** Phi: 4 G; Pass 11-1 9.1%, 6 0.55 2 Int; Rush 7-21 3.0. **Total:** 15 G; Pass 13-1 7.7%, 6 0.46 2 Int; Rush 23-65 2.8; Rec 1-4 4.0.

EUGENE ROWELL Rowell, Eugene Anthony 6′1″, 180 **WR**
Col: Southern Mississippi *HS:* Auburn [AL] B: 6/12/1968, Amityville, NY *Drafted:* 1990 Round 9 Cle
1990 Cle: 3 G.

EUGENE ROWELL Rowell, Eugene Blair 6′3″, 265 **DT**
Col: Dubuque B: 2/15/1958, San Diego, CA
1987 ChiB: 1 G.

BRAD ROWLAND Rowland, Andrew Bradford 6′1″, 190 **HB**
(Ramblin') *Col:* McMurry *HS:* Hamlin [TX] B: 7/14/1928, Hamlin, TX
Drafted: 1951 Round 5 ChiB
1951 ChiB: 12 G; Rush 10-50 5.0; Rec 1-(-2) -2.0; KR 15-350 23.3; Punt 1-18 18.0; 1 Fum.

JUSTIN ROWLAND Rowland, Justin David 6′2″, 188 **DB**
Col: Texas Christian *HS:* Hamlin [TX] B: 5/10/1937, Hamlin, TX
Drafted: 1959 Round 12 ChiB
1960 ChiB: 6 G. **1961** Min: 5 G; KR 8-175 21.9; Int 1-4. **1962** Den: 10 G. **Total:** 21 G; KR 8-175 21.9; Int 1-4.

BOB ROWLEY Rowley, Eldwood Robert 6′2″, 235 **LB**
Col: Virginia *HS:* Fort Hill [Cumberland, MD] B: 9/16/1941, Somerset, PA
1963 Pit: 3 G. **1964** NYJ: 6 G; PR 0-10. **Total:** 9 G; PR 0-10.

JOHN ROWSER Rowser, John Felix 6′1″, 190 **DB**
Col: Michigan *HS:* East Detroit [Eastpointe, MI] B: 4/24/1944, Birmingham, AL *Drafted:* 1967 Round 3 GB

		Interceptions		
Year Team	**G**	**Int**	**Yds**	**TD**
1967 GB	14	0	0	0
1968 GB	14	0	0	0
1969 GB	14	0	0	0
1970 Pit	7	3	27	0
1971 Pit	12	4	94	1
1972 Pit	14	4	30	0
1973 Pit	14	6	131	1
1974 Den	11	4	56	0
1975 Den	13	1	2	0
1976 Den	14	4	104	2
NFL Total	127	26	444	4

SPIN ROY Roy, Elmer T 6′0″, 175 **OE**
Col: No College *HS:* North Tonawanda [NY] B: 10/19/1897 D: 8/1987, Loveland, OH
1921 Roch: 2 G. **1922** Roch: 4 G; Rec 1 TD; 6 Pt. **1923** Roch: 4 G. **1924** Roch: 7 G. **1925** Roch: 2 G. **1927** Buf: 3 G. **Total:** 22 G; Rec 1 TD; 6 Pt.

FRANK ROY Roy, Frank Edward 6′2″, 230 **OG**
Col: Long Beach City Coll. CA (J.C.); Utah *HS:* St. Albans [WV] B: 6/19/1942, Montgomery, WV *Drafted:* 1965 Round 7 StL
1966 StL: 11 G; KR 2-10 5.0.

ANDRE ROYAL Royal, Andre Tierre 6′2″, 232 **LB**
Col: Alabama *HS:* Tuscaloosa Co. [Northport, AL] B: 12/1/1972, Northport, AL
1995 Car: 12 G. **1996** Car: 16 G. **1997** Car: 16 G; 5 Sac. **1998** Ind: 13 G. **Total:** 57 G; 5 Sac.

RICKY ROYAL Royal, Ricky Bernard 5′9″, 187 **DB**
Col: Sam Houston State *HS:* Gainesville [TX] B: 7/26/1966, Gainesville, TX *Drafted:* 1989 Round 7 Pho
1990 Atl: 1 G.

MARK ROYALS Royals, Mark Alan 6′5″, 215 **P**
Col: Chowan Coll. NC; Appalachian State *HS:* Mathews [VA] B: 6/22/1964, Hampton, VA
1992 Pit: Pass 1-1 100.0%, 44 44.00. **1994** Pit: Rush 1-(-13) -13.0. **1995** Det: Rush 1-(-7) -7.0. **1996** Det: Pass 1-1 100.0%, -8 -8.00. **Total:** Pass 2-2 100.0%, 36 18.00; Rush 2-(-20) -10.0.

		Punting		
Year Team	**G**	**Punts**	**Yds**	**Avg**
1987 StL-Phi	2	11	431	39.2
1987 StL	1	6	222	37.0
1987 Phi	1	5	209	41.8
1990 TB	16	72	2902	40.3
1991 TB	16	84	3389	40.3
1992 Pit	16	73	3119	42.7
1993 Pit	16	89	3781	42.5
1994 Pit	16	97	3849	39.7
1995 Det	16	57	2393	42.0
1996 Det	16	69	3020	43.8

1997 NO	16	88	4038	**45.9**
1998 NO	16	88	4017	45.6
NFL Total	146	728	30939	42.5

ORPHEUS ROYE Roye, Orpheus Michael 6′4″, 290 **DE**
Col: Jones Co. JC MS; Florida State *HS:* Miami Springs [FL]
B: 1/21/1974, Miami, FL *Drafted:* 1996 Round 6 Pit
1996 Pit: 13 G. **1997** Pit: 16 G; 1 Sac. **1998** Pit: 16 G; KR 1-0; 3.5 Sac. **Total:** 45 G; KR 1-0; 4.5 Sac.

MAZIO ROYSTER Royster, Mazio Denmar Vesey 6′1″, 205 **RB**
Col: USC *HS:* Bishop Amat [La Puente, CA] B: 8/3/1970, Pomona, CA
Drafted: 1992 Round 11 TB
1992 TB: Rec 1-8 8.0. **1993** TB: Rec 5-18 3.6; KR 8-102 12.8. **1994** TB: Rec 7-36 5.1. **Total:** Rec 13-62 4.8; KR 8-102 12.8.

		Rushing				
Year Team	**G**	**Att**	**Yds**	**Avg**	**TD**	**Fum**
1992 TB	5	0	0	—	0	0
1993 TB	14	33	115	3.5	1	0
1994 TB	14	9	7	0.8	0	1
NFL Total	33	42	122	2.9	1	1

ED ROYSTON Royston, Edwin F 6′1″, 220 **G**
(Bud) *Col:* Wake Forest *HS:* Patterson [Baltimore, MD] B: 9/19/1923, Baltimore, MD *Drafted:* 1948 Round 7 NYG
1948 NYG: 10 G; KR 1-5 5.0. **1949** NYG: 11 G. **Total:** 21 G; KR 1-5 5.0.

MIKE ROZIER Rozier, Michael Thomas 5′10″, 209 **RB**
Col: Coffeyville CC KS; Nebraska *HS:* Woodrow Wilson [Camden, NJ]
B: 3/1/1961, Camden, NJ *Drafted:* 1984 Supplemental Round 1 Hou
1986 Hou: Pass 1-1 100.0%, 13 13.00. **Total:** Pass 1-1 100.0%, 13 13.00.

		Rushing				Receiving					Tot
Year Team	**G**	**Att**	**Yds**	**Avg**	**TD**	**Rec**	**Yds**	**Avg**	**TD**	**Fum**	**TD**
1985 Hou	14	133	462	3.5	8	9	96	10.7	0	3	8
1986 Hou	13	199	662	3.3	4	24	180	7.5	0	6	4
1987 Hou	11	229	957	4.2	3	27	192	7.1	0	5	3
1988 Hou	15	251	1002	4.0	10	11	99	9.0	1	7	11
1989 Hou	12	88	301	3.4	2	4	28	7.0	0	4	2
1990 Hou-Atl	16	163	717	4.4	3	13	105	8.1	0	6	3
1990 Hou	3	10	42	4.2	0	5	46	9.2	0	0	0
1990 Atl	13	153	675	4.4	3	8	59	7.4	0	6	3
1991 Atl	11	96	361	3.8	0	2	15	7.5	0	2	0
NFL Total	92	1159	4462	3.8	30	90	715	7.9	1	33	31

BOB ROZIER Rozier, Robert Earnest 6′3″, 240 **DE**
Col: Grays Harbor Coll. WA (J.C.); California *HS:* Cordova [Sacramento, CA] B: 7/28/1955, Anchorage, AK *Drafted:* 1979 Round 9 StL
1979 StL: 6 G.

DAVE ROZUMEK Rozumek, David John 6′1″, 215 **LB**
Col: New Hampshire *HS:* Lawrence [Falmouth, MA] B: 4/25/1954, Lawrence, MA *Drafted:* 1976 Round 15 KC
1976 KC: 8 G. **1977** KC: 14 G. **1978** KC: 16 G; Int 2-5. **1979** KC: 7 G. **Total:** 45 G; Int 2-5.

AUBREY ROZZELL Rozzell, Aubrey Dale 6′2″, 215 **LB**
Col: Delta State *HS:* Clarksdale [MS] B: 11/2/1932, Rome, MS
1957 Pit: 7 G; PR 1-0; Int 1-4.

ED RUBBERT Rubbert, Edward 6′5″, 225 **QB**
Col: Louisville *HS:* Clarkstown North [NY] B: 5/28/1964, Suffern, NY
1987 Was: 3 G; Pass 49-26 53.1%, 532 10.86 4 TD 1 Int; Rush 9-31 3.4; 1 Fum.

LARRY RUBENS Rubens, Larry Duane 6′1″, 253 **C**
Col: Montana State *HS:* Mead [Spokane, WA] B: 1/25/1959, Spokane, WA
1982 GB: 9 G; 1 Fum. **1983** GB: 16 G. **1986** ChiB: 16 G. **Total:** 41 G; 1 Fum.

ROB RUBICK Rubick, Robin James 6′3″, 232 **TE**
Col: Grand Valley State *HS:* Newberry [MI] B: 9/27/1960, Newberry, MI *Drafted:* 1982 Round 12 Det
1982 Det: Rush 1-1 1.0 1 TD. **Total:** Rush 1-1 1.0 1 TD.

		Receiving				Tot
Year Team	**G**	**Rec**	**Yds**	**Avg**	**TD**	**TD**
1982 Det	7	0	0	—	0	1
1983 Det	16	10	81	8.1	1	1
1984 Det	16	14	188	13.4	1	1
1985 Det	9	2	33	16.5	0	0
1986 Det	16	5	62	12.4	0	0
1987 Det	9	13	147	11.3	1	1
1988 Det	15	0	0	—	0	0
NFL Total	88	44	511	11.6	3	4

TONY RUBINO Rubino, Anthony Eugene 5′10″, 208 **G**
Col: Wake Forest *HS:* Elizabeth [PA] B: 6/20/1921, Elizabeth, PA
D: 11/30/1983, Elizabeth, PA
1943 Det: 10 G. **1946** Det: 11 G. **Total:** 21 G.

KARL RUBKE Rubke, Karl John 6′4″, 240 **LB-DE-C-DT**
Col: Santa Rosa JC CA; USC *HS:* Mount Carmel [Los Angeles, CA]
B: 12/6/1935, Los Angeles, CA *Drafted:* 1957 Round 5 SF
1957 SF: 12 G; Int 1-16. **1958** SF: 12 G. **1959** SF: 12 G. **1960** SF: 12 G. **1961** Min: 13 G; Int 1-12. **1962** SF: 14 G. **1963** SF: 14 G. **1964** SF: 14 G. **1965** SF: 14 G; KR 1-0. **1966** Atl: 14 G. **1967** Atl: 8 G. **1968** Oak: 4 G. **Total:** 143 G; KR 1-0; Int 2-28.

T.J. RUBLEY Rubley, Theron Joseph 6′3″, 205 **QB**
Col: Tulsa *HS:* West [Davenport, IA] B: 11/29/1968, Davenport, IA
Drafted: 1992 Round 9 LARm

		Passing							
Year Team	**G**	**Att**	**Comp**	**Comp%**	**Yds**	**YPA**	**TD**	**Int**	**Rating**
1993 LARm	9	189	108	57.1	1338	7.08	8	6	80.1
1995 GB	1	6	4	66.7	39	6.50	0	1	45.1
NFL Total	10	195	112	57.4	1377	7.06	8	7	78.1

	Rushing				
Year Team	**Att**	**Yds**	**Avg**	**TD**	**Fum**
1993 LARm	29	102	3.5	0	4
1995 GB	2	6	3.0	0	1
NFL Total	31	108	3.5	0	5

MARTIN RUBY Ruby, Martin Owen 6′4″, 249 **DT-OT**
Col: Texas A&M *HS:* Waco [TX] B: 6/9/1922, Lubbock, TX
AAFC **1946** BknA: 14 G; Rec 1-3 3.0. **1947** BknA: 14 G. **1948** BknA: 14 G. **1949** NY-A: 11 G; Int 1-19 1 TD; 6 Pt. **Total:** 53 G; Rec 1-3 3.0; Int 1-19 1 TD; 6 Pt.

NFL **1950** NYY: 12 G; Scor **1** Saf; 2 Pt.

TODD RUCCI Rucci, Todd Louis 6′5″, 296 **OT**
Col: Penn State *HS:* Upper Darby [PA] B: 7/14/1970, Upper Darby, PA
Drafted: 1993 Round 2 NE
1993 NE: 2 G. **1994** NE: 13 G. **1995** NE: 6 G. **1996** NE: 16 G. **1997** NE: 16 G. **1998** NE: 16 G. **Total:** 69 G.

EDDIE RUCINSKI Rucinski, Edward Anthony 6′3″, 197 **OE-DE-DB**
Col: Indiana *HS:* Theodore Roosevelt [East Chicago, IL] B: 7/12/1916, East Chicago, IN D: 4/22/1995, Indian Rocks Beach, FL *Drafted:* 1941 Round 4 Bkn
1941 Bkn: Rush 2-13 6.5. **1944** ChPt: Rush 16-72 4.5; KR 3-67 22.3; Int 4-35. **Total:** Rush 18-85 4.7; KR 3-67 22.3; Int 4-35.

		Receiving			
Year Team	**G**	**Rec**	**Yds**	**Avg**	**TD**
1941 Bkn	11	17	204	12.0	1
1942 Bkn	11	9	99	11.0	1
1943 ChiC	10	26	398	15.3	3
1944 ChPt	10	22	284	12.9	1
1945 ChiC	8	23	400	17.4	2
1946 ChiC	10	2	23	11.5	0
NFL Total	60	99	1408	14.2	8

LEO RUCKA Rucka, Leo Victor 6′3″, 212 **LB**
Col: Rice *HS:* Crosby [TX] B: 8/18/1931, Baytown, TX *Drafted:* 1954 Round 2 SF
1956 SF: 5 G.

CONRAD RUCKER Rucker, Conrad Robert 6′3″, 255 **TE**
Col: Southern University *HS:* Withrow [Cincinnati, OH] B: 11/15/1954, Cincinnati, OH *Drafted:* 1978 Round 6 Hou
1978 Hou: 13 G; Rec 2-38 19.0. **1979** Hou: 16 G; Rec 4-40 10.0. **1980** TB-LARm: 4 G. TB: 2 G. LARm: 2 G. **Total:** 33 G; Rec 6-78 13.0.

KEITH RUCKER Rucker, Keith V 6′4″, 332 **DT-NT**
Col: Eastern Michigan; Ohio Wesleyan *HS:* Shaker Heights [OH]
B: 11/20/1968, University Park, IL
1992 Pho: 14 G; 2 Sac. **1993** Pho: 16 G. **1994** Cin: 16 G; 2 Sac. **1995** Cin: 15 G; 2 Sac. **1997** Was: 2 G. **Total:** 63 G; 6 Sac.

REGGIE RUCKER Rucker, Reginald Joseph 6′2″, 195 **WR**
Col: Boston U. *HS:* Anacostia [Washington, DC] B: 9/21/1947, Washington, DC
1971 Dal-NYG-NE: Rush 1-14 14.0; KR 2-45 22.5. NYG: Rush 1-14 14.0. NE: KR 2-45 22.5. **1972** NE: Rush 3-5 1.7; KR 8-227 28.4. **1973** NE: Rush 2-(-1) -0.5; KR 5-103 20.6. **1976** Cle: Rush 2-30 15.0. **1977** Cle: Rush 2-6 3.0. **1978** Cle: Rush 2-14 7.0; KR 1-1 1.0. **Total:** Rush 12-68 5.7; KR 16-376 23.5.

		Receiving				
Year Team	**G**	**Rec**	**Yds**	**Avg**	**TD**	**Fum**
1970 Dal	7	9	200	22.2	1	0
1971 Dal-NYG-NE	11	4	52	13.0	1	0

1971 Dal	2	1	19	19.0	1	0
1971 NYG	4	1	9	9.0	0	0
1971 NE	5	2	24	12.0	0	0
1972 NE	14	44	681	15.5	3	2
1973 NE	14	53	743	14.0	3	2
1974 NE	10	27	436	16.1	4	1
1975 Cle	14	60	770	12.8	3	0
1976 Cle	14	49	676	13.8	8	1
1977 Cle	14	36	565	15.7	2	2
1978 Cle	15	43	893	20.8	8	3
1979 Cle	16	43	749	17.4	6	0
1980 Cle	16	52	768	14.8	4	0
1981 Cle	14	27	532	19.7	1	0
NFL Total	159	447	7065	15.8	44	11

DWAYNE RUDD Rudd, Dwayne Dupree 6'2", 248 **LB**
Col: Alabama *HS:* South Panola [Batesville, MS] B: 2/3/1976, Batesville, MS *Drafted:* 1997 Round 1 Min
1997 Min: 16 G; 5 Sac. **1998** Min: 15 G; 2 Fum TD; 12 Pt; 2 Sac. **Total:** 31 G; 2 Fum TD; 12 Pt; 7 Sac.

TIM RUDDY Ruddy, Timothy Daniel 6'3", 294 **C**
Col: Notre Dame *HS:* Dunmore [PA] B: 4/27/1972, Scranton, PA
Drafted: 1994 Round 2 Mia
1994 Mia: 16 G. **1995** Mia: 16 G; 1 Fum. **1996** Mia: 16 G; 1 Fum. **1997** Mia: 15 G. **1998** Mia: 16 G; 1 Fum. **Total:** 79 G; 3 Fum.

JACK RUDNAY Rudnay, John Carl 6'3", 240 **C**
Col: Northwestern *HS:* Kenston [Chagrin Falls, OH] B: 11/20/1947, Cleveland, OH *Drafted:* 1969 Round 4 KC
1970 KC: 14 G. **1971** KC: 13 G. **1972** KC: 14 G. **1973** KC: 14 G. **1974** KC: 14 G. **1975** KC: 14 G. **1976** KC: 14 G. **1977** KC: 14 G. **1978** KC: 16 G. **1979** KC: 16 G. **1980** KC: 12 G. **1981** KC: 16 G; 1 Fum. **1982** KC: 7 G. **Total:** 178 G; 1 Fum.

TIM RUDNICK Rudnick, Timothy John 5'10", 185 **DB**
Col: Notre Dame *HS:* Notre Dame [Niles, IL] B: 3/6/1952, Chicago, IL
Drafted: 1974 Round 11 Bal
1974 Bal: 14 G; PR 2-23 11.5; KR 1-5 5.0.

BEN RUDOLPH Rudolph, Benjamin 6'5", 271 **DT-DE**
Col: Long Beach State *HS:* Fairhope [AL] B: 8/29/1957, Evergreen, AL
Drafted: 1981 Round 3 NYJ
1981 NYJ: 15 G; KR 1-8 8.0. **1982** NYJ: 9 G; 2 Sac. **1983** NYJ: 16 G; 2 Sac. **1984** NYJ: 16 G; 1.5 Sac. **1985** NYJ: 16 G. **1986** NYJ: 16 G; KR 3-17 5.7; 1 Sac. **Total:** 88 G; KR 4-25 6.3; 6.5 Sac.

COLEMAN RUDOLPH Rudolph, Coleman Harris 6'4", 270 **DE-DT-LB**
Col: Georgia Tech *HS:* Valdosta [GA] B: 10/22/1970, Valdosta, GA
Drafted: 1993 Round 2 NYJ
1993 NYJ: 4 G. **1994** NYG: 12 G. **1995** NYG: 16 G; 4 Sac. **1996** NYG: 16 G; 1 Sac. **Total:** 48 G; 5 Sac.

COUNCIL RUDOLPH Rudolph, Council Jr. 6'4", 255 **DE**
Col: Kentucky State *HS:* Cobb [Anniston, AL] B: 1/18/1950, Anniston, AL *Drafted:* 1972 Round 7 StL
1972 Hou: 12 G. **1973** StL: 5 G. **1974** StL: 14 G. **1975** StL: 13 G; Int 1-18. **1976** TB: 14 G. **1977** TB: 14 G. **Total:** 72 G; Int 1-18.

JACK RUDOLPH Rudolph, John Lawrence 6'3", 225 **LB**
Col: Georgia Tech *HS:* Henry Grady [Atlanta, GA] B: 3/21/1938, St. Louis, MO *Drafted:* 1960 Round 2 Bos
1960 Bos: 8 G; Int 2-13; 1 Fum. **1962** Bos: 14 G. **1963** Bos: 14 G. **1964** Bos: 14 G; Scor 1 Saf; 2 Pt. **1965** Bos: 14 G; KR 1-4 4.0. **1966** Mia: 11 G; Int 1-3. **Total:** 75 G; KR 1-4 4.0; Int 3-16; Scor 1 Saf; 2 Pt; 1 Fum.

JOE RUDOLPH Rudolph, Joseph D 6'1", 285 **OG**
Col: Wisconsin *HS:* Belle Vernon [PA] B: 7/21/1972, Belle Vernon, PA
1995 Phi: 4 G. **1997** SF: 6 G. **Total:** 10 G.

MARTIN RUDOLPH Rudolph, Martin Jerome 5'10", 183 **DB**
Col: Arizona *HS:* Phineas Banning [Los Angeles, CA] B: 10/19/1964, San Pedro, CA
1987 Den: 3 G.

PAUL RUDZINSKI Rudzinski, Paul Gerard 6'1", 220 **LB**
Col: Michigan State *HS:* Catholic Central [Detroit, MI] B: 7/28/1956, Detroit, MI
1978 GB: 16 G. **1979** GB: 11 G. **1980** GB: 6 G; Int 1-14. **Total:** 33 G; Int 1-14.

MIKE RUETHER Ruether, Michael Alan 6'4", 279 **C-OG**
Col: Texas *HS:* Bishop Miege [Shawnee Mission, KS] B: 9/20/1962, Inglewood, CA *Drafted:* 1984 Supplemental Round 1 StL
1986 StL: 10 G. **1987** StL: 12 G. **1988** Den: 14 G. **1989** Den: 3 G. **1990** Atl: 16 G. **1991** Atl: 16 G; Rec 1-22 22.0. **1992** Atl: 16 G. **1993** Atl: 16 G; KR 1-7 7.0. **Total:** 103 G; Rec 1-22 22.0; KR 1-7 7.0.

KEN RUETTGERS Ruettgers, Kenneth Francis 6'6", 295 **OT**
(Rut) *Col:* USC *HS:* Garces Memorial [Bakersfield, CA] B: 8/20/1962, Bakersfield, CA *Drafted:* 1985 Round 1 GB
1985 GB: 15 G. **1986** GB: 16 G. **1987** GB: 12 G. **1988** GB: 15 G. **1989** GB: 16 G. **1990** GB: 11 G. **1991** GB: 4 G. **1992** GB: 16 G. **1993** GB: 16 G. **1994** GB: 16 G. **1995** GB: 15 G. **1996** GB: 4 G. **Total:** 156 G.

HOWIE RUETZ Ruetz, Howard Peter 6'3", 255 **DT**
Col: Loras *HS:* St. Catherine's [Racine, WI] B: 8/18/1927, Racine, WI
Drafted: 1951 Round 26 LARm
1951 GB: 12 G; Int 1-11. **1952** GB: 3 G. **1953** GB: 5 G. **Total:** 20 G; Int 1-11.

JOE RUETZ Ruetz, Joseph Hubert 6'0", 200 **G-LB**
Col: Notre Dame *HS:* South Bend Central [IN] B: 10/21/1916, Racine, WI
AAFC **1946** ChiA: 13 G; Int 2-13. **1948** ChiA: 13 G. **Total:** 26 G; Int 2-13.

GUY RUFF Ruff, Guy Moroney 6'1", 215 **LB**
Col: Syracuse *HS:* Windham [OH] B: 8/18/1960, Ravenna, OH
1982 Pit: 2 G.

EMMETT RUH Ruh, Emmett E 5'8", 168 **WB-OE**
Col: Davis & Elkins *HS:* South [Columbus, OH] B: 8/29/1893, Columbus, OH D: 9/23/1979, Fort Lauderdale, FL
1921 Col: 7 G; Rec 1 TD; Scor 13, 2 FG, 1 XK. **1922** Col: 7 G; Rush 1 TD; 6 Pt. **Total:** 14 G; Rush 1 TD; Rec 1 TD; Scor 19, 2 FG, 1 XK; Tot TD 2.

HOMER RUH Ruh, Homer 5'10", 178 **OE-WB-BB-FB**
Col: No College *HS:* South [Columbus, OH] B: 9/19/1895, Columbus, OH D: 10/4/1971, Madison, WI
1920 Col: 9 G. **1921** Col: 7 G; Rec 1 TD; 6 Pt. **1922** Col: 7 G. **1923** Col: 8 G. **1924** Col: 7 G. **1925** Col: 8 G. **Total:** 46 G; Rec 1 TD; 6 Pt.

CHRIS RUHMAN Ruhman, Christopher Aamon 6'5", 321 **OT**
Col: Texas A&M *HS:* Nimitz [Irving, TX] B: 12/19/1974, Houston, TX
Drafted: 1998 Round 3 SF
1998 SF: 6 G.

JUSTIN RUKAS Rukas, Justin Matthew 6'0", 205 **G**
(Ruke) *Col:* Louisiana State B: 2/24/1910, Gary, IN D: 9/28/1963, New Orleans, LA
1936 Bkn: 12 G.

GORDON RULE Rule, Gordon Alan 6'2", 180 **DB**
Col: Dartmouth *HS:* Chandler [AZ] B: 3/1/1946, Columbus, OH
Drafted: 1968 Round 11 GB
1968 GB: 1 G. **1969** GB: 14 G. **Total:** 15 G.

MAX RUNAGER Runager, Max Culp 6'1", 189 **P**
Col: South Carolina *HS:* Orangeburg-Wilkinson [Orangeburg, SC]
B: 3/24/1956, Greenwood, SC *Drafted:* 1979 Round 8 Phi
1983 Phi: Rush 1-6 6.0. **1984** SF: Rush 1-(-5) -5.0. **1988** SF-Cle: Rush 1-0. Cle: Rush 1-0. **1989** Phi: Rush 2-5 2.5. **Total:** Rush 5-6 1.2.

		Punting			
Year Team	**G**	**Punts**	**Yds**	**Avg**	**Fum**
1979 Phi	16	74	2927	39.6	1
1980 Phi	16	75	2947	39.3	0
1981 Phi	15	63	2567	40.7	0
1982 Phi	9	44	1784	40.5	0
1983 Phi	12	59	2459	41.7	0
1984 SF	14	56	2341	41.8	0
1985 SF	16	86	3422	39.8	0
1986 SF	16	83	3450	41.6	0
1987 SF	12	55	2157	39.2	0
1988 SF-Cle	14	49	1959	40.0	1
1988 SF	1	1	24	24.0	0
1988 Cle	13	48	1935	40.3	1
1989 Phi	4	17	568	33.4	0
NFL Total	144	661	26581	40.2	2

SWEDE RUNDQUIST Rundquist, Elmer Theodore 6'2", 210 **T**
Col: Illinois *HS:* Thornton Twp. [Harvey, IL] B: 11/22/1894, Harvey, IL
D: 2/7/1958, Lackland AFB, TX
1922 ChiC: 10 G.

PORKY RUNDQUIST Rundquist, Henning 5'10", 220 **T-G-C**
Col: Michigan Tech B: 11/24/1893, Sweden D: 12/1980, Ludington, MI
1925 Dul: 1 G. **1926** Dul: 4 G. **Total:** 5 G.

GIL RUNKEL Runkel, Gilbert A 210 **C-G**
Col: No College B: 6/2/1891, MI D: 10/26/1976, Trenton, MI
1920 Det: 7 G.

TOMMY RUNNELS Runnels, Melvin Thomas 5'10", 187 **HB**
Col: North Texas *HS:* North Side [Fort Worth, TX] B: 1/28/1934, Fort Worth, TX *Drafted:* 1956 Round 14 LARm
1956 Was: Pass 3-1 33.3%, 34 11.33; Rec 6-56 9.3 1 TD; PR 8-91 11.4; KR 17-375 22.1. **1957** Was: Pass 1-1 100.0%, 35 35.00; Rec 1-4 4.0; PR 10-76 7.6; KR 2-66 33.0. **Total:** Pass 4-2 50.0%, 69 17.25; Rec 7-60 8.6 1 TD; PR 18-167 9.3; KR 19-441 23.2.

		Rushing				
Year Team	**G**	**Att**	**Yds**	**Avg**	**TD**	**Fum**
1956 Was	11	96	334	3.5	0	4
1957 Was	10	20	52	2.6	0	3
NFL Total	21	116	386	3.3	0	7

JON RUNYAN Runyan, Jon Daniel 6′7″, 320 **OT**
Col: Michigan *HS:* Carman-Ainsworth [Flint, MI] B: 11/27/1973, Flint, MI *Drafted:* 1996 Round 4 Hou
1996 Hou: 10 G. **1997** Ten: 16 G. **1998** Ten: 16 G. **Total:** 42 G.

ERNIE RUPLE Ruple, Coy Ernest 6′4″, 256 **DE**
Col: Arkansas *HS:* Conway [AR] B: 10/27/1945, Conway, AR
Drafted: 1968 Round 2 Pit
1968 Pit: 14 G.

JOHN RUPP Rupp, John 1 **G**
Col: No College B: 12/1896, Buffalo, NY Deceased
1920 Buf: 1 G.

NELSON RUPP Rupp, Nelson Gadd 5′10″, 180 **WB-FB**
(Nocky) *Col:* Denison *HS:* Doane Acad. [Granville, OH] B: 6/15/1891, Cincinnati, OH D: 8/9/1948, South Norwalk, CT
1921 Day: 5 G.

CLIVE RUSH Rush, Clive Harold 6′2″, 197 **OE**
Col: Miami (Ohio) *HS:* Springfield [OH] B: 2/14/1931, De Graff, OH
D: 8/22/1980, London, OH
1953 GB: Rush 1-(-6) -6.0; Rec 14-190 13.6.

		Punting			
Year Team	**G**	**Punts**	**Yds**	**Avg**	**Fum**
1953 GB	11	60	2263	37.7	1

JERRY RUSH Rush, Gerald Mitchell 6′4″, 265 **DT**
Col: Michigan State *HS:* Pontiac Central [MI] B: 8/7/1942, Pontiac, MI
Drafted: 1965 Round 2 Det
1965 Det: 11 G. **1966** Det: 11 G. **1967** Det: 14 G. **1968** Det: 14 G.
1969 Det: 11 G. **1970** Det: 14 G. **1971** Det: 14 G. **Total:** 89 G.

BOB RUSH Rush, Robert Jeffrey 6′5″, 265 **C-OT**
Col: Memphis *HS:* Northwest [Clarksville, TN] B: 2/27/1955, Santa Monica, CA *Drafted:* 1977 Round 1 SD
1977 SD: 14 G. **1979** SD: 16 G. **1980** SD: 15 G; 2 Fum. **1981** SD: 16 G.
1982 SD: 9 G. **1983** KC: 15 G; 2 Fum. **1984** KC: 16 G. **1985** KC: 16 G.
Total: 117 G; 4 Fum.

TYRONE RUSH Rush, Tyrone Antonio 5′11″, 196 **RB**
Col: North Alabama *HS:* Neshoba Central [Philadelphia, MS]
B: 2/5/1971, Philadelphia, MS
1994 Was: 5 G; KR 3-45 15.0.

MARION RUSHING Rushing, Marion Glen 6′2″, 223 **LB**
Col: Southern Illinois *HS:* Pinckneyville [IL] B: 9/3/1936, Pinckneyville, IL
1959 ChiC: 12 G. **1962** StL: 13 G. **1963** StL: 14 G. **1964** StL: 12 G;
Scor **1** Saf; 2 Pt. **1965** StL: 14 G. **1966** Atl: 14 G; KR 2-52 26.0; Int 3-5.
1967 Atl: 14 G; Int 1-2. **1968** Atl-Hou: 12 G. Atl: 7 G. Hou: 5 G.
Total: 105 G; KR 2-52 26.0; Int 4-7; Scor 1 Saf; 2 Pt.

MIKE RUSINEK Rusinek, John Michael 6′3″, 250 **NT**
Col: Scottsdale CC AZ; California *HS:* Camelback [Phoenix, AZ]
B: 5/1/1963, Phoenix, AZ
1987 Cle: 3 G; 1 Sac.

REGGIE RUSK Rusk, Reggie Leon 5′10″, 190 **DB**
Col: San Francisco City Coll. CA (J.C.); Kentucky *HS:* Texas City [TX]
B: 10/19/1972, Galveston, TX *Drafted:* 1996 Round 7 TB
1996 TB: 1 G. **1997** TB-Sea: 6 G. TB: 4 G. Sea: 2 G. **Total:** 7 G.

ROY RUSKUSKY Ruskusky, Roy J 6′3″, 200 **DE**
Col: St. Mary's (Cal.) *HS:* Hall [Spring Valley, IL] B: 4/6/1921
AAFC **1947** NY-A: 11 G; Int 1-8.

BERNARD RUSS Russ, Bernard Dion 6′1″, 238 **LB**
Col: Arizona Western Coll. (J.C.); West Virginia *HS:* Collinwood [Utica, NY] B: 11/4/1973, Utica, NY
1997 NE: 2 G. **1998** NE: 1 G. **Total:** 3 G.

CARL RUSS Russ, James Carlton 6′2″, 227 **LB**
Col: Michigan *HS:* Muskegon Heights [MI] B: 2/16/1953, Muskegon, MI *Drafted:* 1975 Round 13 Atl
1975 Atl: 14 G. **1976** NYJ: 3 G. **1977** NYJ: 2 G. **Total:** 19 G.

PAT RUSS Russ, Patrick Joseph 6′3″, 255 **DT**
Col: Purdue *HS:* Roger Bacon [Cincinnati, OH] B: 1/8/1940, Cincinnati, OH D: 2/4/1984, Anderson Twp., Hamilton Co., OH
Drafted: 1962 Round 14 Min
1963 Min: 14 G.

STEVE RUSS Russ, Steve 6′4″, 245 **LB**
Col: Air Force *HS:* Medford [WI] B: 9/16/1972, Stetsonville, WI
Drafted: 1995 Round 7 Den
1997 Den: 14 G.

AL RUSSAS Russas, Alfred Victor 6′2″, 210 **T-DE**
Col: Tennessee *HS:* Hope [Providence, RI] B: 8/22/1923, Providence, RI D: 2/14/1995, Dearborn, MI *Drafted:* 1949 Round 13 Det
1949 Det: 9 G.

BENNY RUSSELL Russell, Bennett Coe 6′1″, 190 **QB**
Col: Pensacola JC FL; Louisville *HS:* Jay [FL] B: 5/12/1944, Brewton, AL *Drafted:* 1966 Redshirt Round 1 Buf
1968 Buf: 1 G; Pass 2-1 50.0%, 3 1.50.

BOOKER RUSSELL Russell, Booker Taylor 6′2″, 233 **RB**
Col: Southwest Texas State *HS:* Belton [TX] B: 2/28/1956, Belton, TX
1978 Oak: KR 2-(-3) -1.5. **1979** Oak: Rec 6-79 13.2; KR 3-21 7.0.
1980 SD: KR 1-19 19.0. **1981** Phi: Rec 1-(-5) -5.0; KR 2-28 14.0.
Total: Rec 7-74 10.6; KR 8-65 8.1.

		Rushing				
Year Team	**G**	**Att**	**Yds**	**Avg**	**TD**	**Fum**
1978 Oak	16	11	65	5.9	0	1
1979 Oak	16	33	190	5.8	4	1
1980 SD	15	8	41	5.1	0	1
1981 Phi	12	38	123	3.2	4	3
NFL Total	59	90	419	4.7	8	6

ANDY RUSSELL Russell, Charles Andrew 6′2″, 225 **LB**
Col: Missouri *HS:* Ladue [MO] B: 10/29/1941, Detroit, MI
Drafted: 1963 Round 16 Pit
1966 Pit: KR 2-12 6.0; Scor **1** 1XP. **1967** Pit: KR 6-97 16.2.
Total: KR 8-109 13.6; Scor 1 1XP.

		Interceptions				Tot
Year Team	**G**	**Int**	**Yds**	**TD**	**Fum**	**TD**
1963 Pit	14	3	20	0	1	0
1966 Pit	14	0	0	0	0	1
1967 Pit	14	3	50	0	0	0
1968 Pit	14	2	2	0	0	0
1969 Pit	14	2	48	0	0	0
1970 Pit	14	3	64	0	0	0
1971 Pit	14	0	0	0	0	0
1972 Pit	14	0	0	0	0	0
1973 Pit	14	3	54	1	0	1
1974 Pit	14	1	0	0	0	0
1975 Pit	14	0	0	0	0	0
1976 Pit	14	1	0	0	0	0
NFL Total	168	18	238	1	1	2

DAMIEN RUSSELL Russell, Damien Eduardo 6′1″, 204 **DB**
Col: Virginia Tech *HS:* Howard D. Woodson [Washington, DC]
B: 8/20/1970, New York, NY *Drafted:* 1992 Round 6 SF
1993 SF: 16 G.

DARRELL RUSSELL Russell, Darrell A 6′5″, 320 **DT**
Col: USC *HS:* St. Augustine [San Diego, CA] B: 5/27/1976, Pensacola, FL *Drafted:* 1997 Round 1 Oak
1997 Oak: 16 G; 3.5 Sac. **1998** Oak: 16 G; 10 Sac. **Total:** 32 G; 13.5 Sac.

DARRYL RUSSELL Russell, Darryl James 6′0″, 190 **DB**
Col: Appalachian State *HS:* Bloom [Chicago Heights, IL]
B: 12/14/1964, Chicago Heights, IL
1987 Den: 3 G.

DEREK RUSSELL Russell, Derek Dwayne 6′0″, 195 **WR**
Col: Arkansas *HS:* Little Rock Central [AR] B: 6/22/1969, Little Rock, AR *Drafted:* 1991 Round 4 Den
1993 Den: 1 Fum TD. **1994** Den: Rush 1-6 6.0. **Total:** Rush 1-6 6.0;
1 Fum TD.

		Receiving				Kickoff Returns					Tot
Year Team	**G**	**Rec**	**Yds**	**Avg**	**TD**	**Ret**	**Yds**	**Avg**	**TD**	**Fum**	**TD**
1991 Den	13	21	317	15.1	1	7	120	17.1	0	0	1
1992 Den	12	12	140	11.7	0	7	154	22.0	0	0	0
1993 Den	13	44	719	16.3	3	18	374	20.8	0	1	4
1994 Den	12	25	342	13.7	1	5	105	21.0	0	0	1
1995 Hou	11	24	321	13.4	0	0	0	—	0	0	0
1996 Hou	16	34	421	12.4	2	0	0	—	0	0	2
1997 Ten	11	12	141	11.8	1	0	0	—	0	0	1
NFL Total	88	172	2401	14.0	8	37	753	20.4	0	1	9

DOUG RUSSELL Russell, Dougal Jr. 6′0″, 187 **TB-WB-DB**
Col: Muskingum; Kansas State *HS:* McDonald [PA] B: 6/11/1911, Bulger, PA D: 10/10/1995, Lebanon, MO
1934 ChiC: KR **1** TD. **1937** ChiC: PR **1** TD. **1939** ChiC-Cle: Punt 8-329 41.1. Cle: Punt 8-329 41.1. **Total:** PR 1 TD; KR 1 TD; Punt 8-329 41.1.

		Passing							
Year Team	**G**	**Att**	**Comp**	**Comp%**	**Yds**	**YPA**	**TD**	**Int**	**Rating**
1934 ChiC	11	23	7	30.4	59	2.57	0	2	3.7
1935 ChiC	12	28	7	25.0	108	3.86	1	4	15.5
1936 ChiC	2	1	0	0.0	0	0.00	0	0	39.6
1937 ChiC	11	11	4	36.4	94	8.55	1	2	58.7
1938 ChiC	8	7	1	14.3	98	14.00	1	2	79.2
1939 ChiC-Cle	8	1	0	0.0	0	0.00	0	0	39.6
1939 ChiC	1	0	0	—	0	—	0	0	—
1939 Cle	7	1	0	0.0	0	0.00	0	0	39.6
NFL Total	52	71	19	26.8	359	5.06	3	10	22.7

Year Team	Rushing Att	Yds	Avg	TD	Receiving Rec	Yds	Avg	TD	Tot TD
1934 ChiC	75	407	5.4	1	1	2	2.0	0	2
1935 ChiC	140	**499**	3.6	0	3	33	11.0	0	0
1936 ChiC	3	11	3.7	0	0	0	—	0	0
1937 ChiC	23	76	3.3	0	12	263	21.9	1	2
1938 ChiC	31	60	1.9	1	6	36	6.0	0	1
1939 ChiC-Cle	9	21	2.3	0	5	67	13.4	1	1
1939 ChiC	4	-5	-1.3	0	0	0	—	0	0
1939 Cle	5	26	5.2	0	5	67	13.4	1	1
NFL Total	281	1074	3.8	2	27	401	14.9	2	6

JIM RUSSELL Russell, James L 5′11″, 210 **T**
(Casey) *Col:* Temple *HS:* Williamsport [PA] B: 8/18/1908, Sinnemahoning, PA D: 1/21/1990, Evans City, PA
1936 Phi: 11 G. **1937** Phi: 3 G. **Total:** 14 G.

JACK RUSSELL Russell, James Monroe 6′1″, 215 **OE-DE**
Col: Baylor *HS:* Cleburne [TX] B: 8/29/1919, Nemo, TX
AAFC **1947** NY-A: KR 4-66 16.5; Int 1-33. **1948** NY-A: Int 1-0. **1949** NY-A: Int 1-5. **Total:** KR 4-66 16.5; Int 3-38.

Year Team	G	Receiving Rec	Yds	Avg	TD	Tot TD
1946 NY-A	14	23	223	9.7	4	4
1947 NY-A	14	20	368	18.4	2	3
1948 NY-A	14	23	433	18.8	6	6
1949 NY-A	12	7	130	18.6	1	2
AAFC Total	54	73	1154	15.8	13	15

NFL **1950** NYY: 11 G; Rec 10-177 17.7 2 TD; KR 2-8 4.0; **1** Fum TD; Tot TD 3; 18 Pt.

KEN RUSSELL Russell, Kenneth E 6′3″, 252 **OT**
Col: Bowling Green State *HS:* Fostoria [OH] B: 11/2/1935, Fostoria, OH *Drafted:* 1957 Round 6 Det
1957 Det: 10 G. **1958** Det: 12 G. **1959** Det: 4 G; KR 1-0. **Total:** 26 G; KR 1-0.

REB RUSSELL Russell, Lafayette H 6′1″, 205 **DB-HB-LB-FB**
Col: Nebraska; Northwestern *HS:* Mexico Mil. Acad. [MO]
B: 5/31/1905, Osawatomie, KS D: 3/16/1978, Coffeyville, KS
1933 NYG-Phi: Pass 8-2 25.0%, 32 4.00 2 Int. Phi: Pass 8-2 25.0%, 32 4.00 2 Int. **Total:** Pass 8-2 25.0%, 32 4.00 2 Int.

Year Team	G	Rushing Att	Yds	Avg	TD
1933 NYG-Phi	10	48	164	3.4	0
1933 NYG	3	16	68	4.3	0
1933 Phi	7	32	96	3.0	0
NFL Total	10	48	164	3.4	0

LEONARD RUSSELL Russell, Leonard James 6′2″, 235 **RB**
Col: Mount San Antonio Coll. CA (J.C.); Arizona State *HS:* Long Beach Polytechnic [CA] B: 11/17/1969, Long Beach, CA *Drafted:* 1991 Round 1 NE
1996 SD: KR 1-10 10.0. **Total:** KR 1-10 10.0.

Year Team	G	Rushing Att	Yds	Avg	TD	Receiving Rec	Yds	Avg	TD	Fum
1991 NE	16	266	959	3.6	4	18	81	4.5	0	8
1992 NE	11	123	390	3.2	2	11	24	2.2	0	3
1993 NE	16	300	1088	3.6	7	26	245	9.4	0	4
1994 Den	14	190	620	3.3	9	38	227	6.0	0	4
1995 StL	13	66	203	3.1	0	16	89	5.6	0	2
1996 SD	15	219	713	3.3	7	13	180	13.8	0	6
NFL Total	85	1164	3973	3.4	29	122	846	6.9	0	27

MATT RUSSELL Russell, Matthew Jason 6′2″, 245 **LB**
Col: Colorado *HS:* Lake Braddock [Washington, DC]; Belleville East HS [IL] B: 7/5/1973, Tokyo, Japan *Drafted:* 1997 Round 4 Det
1997 Det: 14 G; KR 1-0.

REGGIE RUSSELL Russell, Reginald 190 **E**
Col: No College
1928 ChiB: 1 G.

BO RUSSELL Russell, Torance Albert Jr. 6′1″, 223 **T**
Col: Auburn *HS:* Woodlawn [Birmingham, AL] B: 1/23/1916, Birmingham, AL *Drafted:* 1939 Round 6 Was
1939 Was: 11 G; Scor 24, 1-6 16.7% FG, 15-16 93.8% XK. **1940** Was: 11 G; Scor 14, 1-1 100.0% FG, 11-12 91.7% XK. **Total:** 22 G; Scor 38, 2-7 28.6% FG, 26-28 92.9% XK.

TWAN RUSSELL Russell, Twan Sanchez 6′2″, 219 **LB**
Col: Miami (Fla.) *HS:* St. Thomas Aquinas [Fort Lauderdale, FL]
B: 4/25/1974, Fort Lauderdale, FL *Drafted:* 1997 Round 5 Was
1997 Was: 15 G. **1998** Was: 3 G. **Total:** 18 G.

WADE RUSSELL Russell, Wade O'Brien 6′4″, 250 **TE**
Col: Taylor *HS:* Oak Hill [Converse, IN] B: 8/16/1963, Marion, IN
1987 Cin: 3 G; Rec 2-27 13.5 1 TD; 6 Pt.

RUSTY RUSSELL Russell, William 6′5″, 295 **OT**
Col: South Carolina *HS:* Orangeburg-Wilkinson [Orangeburg, SC]
B: 8/16/1963, Orangeburg, SC *Drafted:* 1984 Round 3 Phi
1984 Phi: 1 G.

REGGIE RUST Rust, Reginald Porter 6′2″, 210 **TB-BB**
Col: Oregon State *HS:* Santa Ana [CA] B: 5/23/1909, Santa Barbara, CA D: 1/11/1984, Arroyo Grande, CA
1932 Bos: 5 G; Pass 5-2 40.0%, 25 5.00 1 Int; Rush 17-57 3.4; Rec 1-12 12.0.

JOE RUTGENS Rutgens, Joseph Casimere 6′2″, 255 **DT**
Col: Illinois *HS:* La Salle-Peru Twp. [La Salle, IL] B: 1/26/1939, Cedar Point, IL *Drafted:* 1961 Round 1 Was
1961 Was: 14 G. **1962** Was: 14 G. **1963** Was: 14 G. **1964** Was: 13 G. **1965** Was: 14 G. **1966** Was: 5 G. **1967** Was: 14 G. **1968** Was: 13 G. **1969** Was: 9 G. **Total:** 110 G.

MIKE RUTH Ruth, Michael Joseph 6′2″, 266 **NT**
Col: Boston College *HS:* Methacton [Fairview Village, PA]
B: 6/25/1964, Norristown, PA *Drafted:* 1986 Round 2 NE
1986 NE: 6 G; 1 Sac. **1987** NE: 2 G. **Total:** 8 G; 1 Sac.

RALPH RUTHSTROM Ruthstrom, Ralph David 6′5″, 212 **LB-FB**
(Ridge) *Col:* Sam Houston State; Southern Methodist *HS:* Milby [Houston, TX] B: 7/12/1921, Schenectady, NY D: 3/29/1962, Houston, TX
AAFC **1949** BalA: 4 G; Int 1-15.

NFL **1945** Cle: 6 G; Rush 10-74 7.4; PR 3-47 15.7; Int 1-46. **1946** LARm: 6 G; Rush 2-(-4) -2.0; Rec 1-9 9.0; PR 1-2 2.0; 2 Fum. **1947** Was: 2 G; Rush 2-5 2.5; KR 1-5 5.0. **Total:** 14 G; Rush 14-75 5.4; Rec 1-9 9.0; PR 4-49 12.3; KR 1-5 5.0; Int 1-46; 2 Fum.

CHARLIE RUTKOWSKI Rutkowski, Charles Robert 6′3″, 248 **DE**
Col: Ripon *HS:* St. Catherine's [Racine, WI] B: 1/17/1938, Racine, WI
1960 Buf: 2 G.

ED RUTKOWSKI Rutkowski, Edward John Anthony 6′1″, 198 **WR-QB**
Col: Notre Dame *HS:* Kingston [PA] B: 3/21/1941, Kingston, PA

Year Team	G	Passing Att	Comp	Comp%	Yds	YPA	TD	Int	Rating
1963 Buf	14	1	0	0.0	0	0.00	0	0	39.6
1964 Buf	14	0	0	—	0	—	0	0	—
1965 Buf	14	0	0	—	0	—	0	0	—
1966 Buf	14	0	0	—	0	—	0	0	—
1967 Buf	14	1	0	0.0	0	0.00	0	0	39.6
1968 Buf	13	100	41	41.0	380	3.80	0	6	27.1
NFL Total	83	102	41	40.2	380	3.73	0	6	26.6

Year Team	Rushing Att	Yds	Avg	TD	Receiving Rec	Yds	Avg	TD
1963 Buf	48	144	3.0	0	19	264	13.9	1
1964 Buf	0	0	—	0	13	234	18.0	1
1965 Buf	0	0	—	0	18	247	13.7	1
1966 Buf	1	10	10.0	0	6	150	25.0	1
1967 Buf	0	0	—	0	6	59	9.8	0
1968 Buf	20	96	4.8	1	1	27	27.0	0
NFL Total	69	250	3.6	1	63	981	15.6	4

Year Team	Punt Returns Ret	Yds	Avg	TD	Kickoff Returns Ret	Yds	Avg	TD	Fum	Tot TD
1963 Buf	8	67	8.4	0	13	396	30.5	0	1	1
1964 Buf	8	45	5.6	0	21	498	23.7	0	1	1
1965 Buf	11	127	11.5	0	5	97	19.4	0	0	1
1966 Buf	18	209	11.6	**1**	6	121	20.2	0	1	2
1967 Buf	15	43	2.9	0	3	71	23.7	0	0	0
1968 Buf	8	23	2.9	0	5	87	17.4	0	2	1
NFL Total	68	514	7.6	1	53	1270	24.0	0	5	6

CRAIG RUTLEDGE Rutledge, Craig Alan 6′0″, 190 **DB**
Col: UCLA *HS:* El Dorado [Placentia, CA] B: 1/30/1964, Upland, CA
1987 LARm: 3 G; PR 3-10 3.3; 1 Fum.

JEFF RUTLEDGE Rutledge, Jeffrey Ronald 6′1″, 195 **QB**
Col: Alabama *HS:* Banks [Birmingham, AL] B: 1/22/1957, Birmingham, AL *Drafted:* 1979 Round 9 LARm

Year Team	G	Passing Att	Comp	Comp%	Yds	YPA	TD	Int	Rating
1979 LARm	3	32	13	40.6	125	3.91	1	4	23.0
1980 LARm	1	4	1	25.0	26	6.50	0	0	54.2
1981 LARm	4	50	30	60.0	442	8.84	3	4	75.6
1983 NYG	4	174	87	50.0	1208	6.94	3	8	59.3
1984 NYG	16	1	1	100.0	9	9.00	0	0	104.2
1985 NYG	16	0	0	—	0	—	0	0	—

1986 NYG	16	3	1	33.3	13	4.33	1	0	87.5
1987 NYG	13	155	79	51.0	1048	6.76	5	11	53.9
1988 NYG	1	17	11	64.7	113	6.65	0	1	59.2
1989 NYG	1	0	0	—	0	—	0	0	—
1990 Was	10	68	40	58.8	455	6.69	2	1	82.7
1991 Was	16	22	11	50.0	189	8.59	1	0	94.7
1992 Was	16	0	0	—	0	—	0	0	—
NFL Total	117	526	274	52.1	3628	6.90	16	29	61.4

	Rushing				
Year Team	**Att**	**Yds**	**Avg**	**TD**	**Fum**
1979 LARm	5	27	5.4	0	0
1981 LARm	5	-3	-0.6	0	0
1983 NYG	7	27	3.9	0	6
1985 NYG	2	-6	-3.0	0	1
1986 NYG	3	19	6.3	0	0
1987 NYG	15	31	2.1	0	7
1988 NYG	3	-1	-0.3	0	2
1990 Was	4	12	3.0	1	1
1991 Was	8	-13	-1.6	0	0
NFL Total	52	93	1.8	1	17

ROD RUTLEDGE Rutledge, Rodrick Almar 6'5", 262 **TE**
Col: Alabama *HS:* Erwin [Birmingham, AL] B: 8/12/1975, Birmingham, AL *Drafted:* 1998 Round 2 NE
1998 NE: 16 G.

TOM RUUD Ruud, Thomas Robert 6'3", 223 **LB**
Col: Nebraska *HS:* Thomas Jefferson [Bloomington, MN]
B: 7/26/1953, Oliva, MN *Drafted:* 1975 Round 1 Buf
1975 Buf: 14 G; KR 1-4 4.0. **1976** Buf: 14 G; KR 6-68 11.3; 1 Fum. **1977** Buf: 8 G. **1978** Cin: 7 G. **1979** Cin: 16 G. **Total:** 59 G; KR 7-72 10.3; 1 Fum.

ROGER RUZEK Ruzek, Roger Brian 6'1", 195 **K**
Col: Weber State *HS:* El Camino [South San Francisco, CA]
B: 12/17/1960, San Francisco, CA
1989 Dal-Phi: Pass 1-1 100.0%, 22 22.00 1 TD; Rec 1-4 4.0; Punt 1-28 28.0. Dal: Rec 1-4 4.0; Punt 1-28 28.0. Phi: Pass 1-1 100.0%, 22 22.00 1 TD. **Total:** Pass 1-1 100.0%, 22 22.00 1 TD; Rec 1-4 4.0; Punt 1-28 28.0.

		Scoring						
Year Team	**G**	**Pts**	**FG**	**FGA**	**FG%**	**XK**	**XKA**	**XK%**
1987 Dal	12	92	22	25	88.0	26	26	100.0
1988 Dal	14	63	12	22	54.5	27	27	100.0
1989 Dal-Phi	14	67	13	22	59.1	28	29	96.6
1989 Dal	9	29	5	11	45.5	14	15	93.3
1989 Phi	5	38	8	11	72.7	14	14	100.0
1990 Phi	16	108	21	29	72.4	45	48	93.8
1991 Phi	16	111	28	33	84.8	27	29	93.1
1992 Phi	16	88	16	25	64.0	40	44	90.9
1993 Phi	5	37	8	10	80.0	13	16	81.3
NFL Total	93	566	120	166	72.3	206	219	94.1

STEVE RUZICH Ruzich, Stephen 6'2", 228 **OG-LB-OT-DT**
Col: Ohio State *HS:* Madison [OH] B: 12/24/1927, Cleveland, OH
D: 11/30/1991, Columbus, OH *Drafted:* 1952 Round 14 Cle
1952 GB: 12 G. **1953** GB: 12 G. **1954** GB: 12 G. **Total:** 36 G.

CASSY RYAN Ryan, Clarence Daniel 5'9", 160 **BB-WB**
Col: West Virginia *HS:* Mannington [WV] B: 5/10/1905, Mannington, WV D: 1/6/1981, Fairmont, WV
1929 Buf: 9 G; Rec 1 TD; KR **1** TD; Tot TD 2; 12 Pt.

DAVE RYAN Ryan, David Henry 5'10", 190 **TB-DB-HB**
Col: Hardin-Simmons *HS:* Kaufman [TX] B: 2/3/1923, Kaufman, TX
D: 12/5/1988, Kaufman, TX
1945 Det: Rec 2-67 33.5 1 TD; PR 15-220 14.7; KR 6-138 23.0; Int 3-90; Punt 17-669 39.4; Scor 15, 1-3 33.3% FG. **1946** Det: Rec 1-(-5) -5.0; PR 7-57 8.1; KR 16-332 20.8; Int 4-105; **1** Fum TD. **Total:** Rec 3-62 20.7 1 TD; PR 22-277 12.6; KR 22-470 21.4; Int 7-195; Punt 17-669 39.4; Scor 27, 1-3 33.3% FG; 1 Fum TD.

		Passing							
Year Team	**G**	**Att**	**Comp**	**Comp%**	**Yds**	**YPA**	**TD**	**Int**	**Rating**
1945 Det	10	44	13	29.5	331	7.52	3	10	41.6
1946 Det	11	154	73	47.4	965	6.27	6	17	41.1
1947 Det	1	0	0	—	0	—	0	0	—
1948 Bos	6	0	0	—	0	—	0	0	—
NFL Total	28	198	86	43.4	1296	6.55	9	27	41.1

	Rushing					Tot
Year Team	**Att**	**Yds**	**Avg**	**TD**	**Fum**	**TD**
1945 Det	36	93	2.6	1	4	2
1946 Det	71	65	0.9	1	7	2
1948 Bos	3	1	0.3	0	1	0
NFL Total	110	159	1.4	2	12	4

ED RYAN Ryan, Edward Denis 6'2", 215 **OE-DE**
Col: British Columbia (Canada); St. Mary's (Cal.) *HS:* Vancouver College School [Canada] B: 12/29/1925, Banff, Canada *Drafted:* 1948 Round 7 Pit
1948 Pit: 9 G.

FRANK RYAN Ryan, Frank Beall 6'3", 199 **QB**
Col: Rice *HS:* R.L. Paschal [Fort Worth, TX] B: 7/12/1936, Fort Worth, TX *Drafted:* 1958 Round 5 LARm
1960 LARm: Rec 0-32 1 TD. **Total:** Rec 0-31 1 TD.

		Passing							
Year Team	**G**	**Att**	**Comp**	**Comp%**	**Yds**	**YPA**	**TD**	**Int**	**Rating**
1958 LARm	5	14	5	35.7	34	2.43	1	3	28.6
1959 LARm	10	89	42	47.2	709	7.97	2	4	63.4
1960 LARm	11	128	62	48.4	816	6.38	7	9	57.9
1961 LARm	14	142	72	50.7	1115	7.85	5	**7**	68.3
1962 Cle	11	194	112	57.7	1541	7.94	10	**7**	85.4
1963 Cle	13	256	135	52.7	2026	7.91	25	13	90.4
1964 Cle	14	334	174	52.1	2404	7.20	**25**	19	76.7
1965 Cle	12	243	119	49.0	1751	7.21	18	13	75.3
1966 Cle	14	382	200	52.4	2974	7.79	**29**	14	88.2
1967 Cle	13	280	136	48.6	2026	7.24	20	16	72.7
1968 Cle	7	66	31	47.0	639	9.68	7	6	79.0
1969 Was	1	1	1	100.0	4	4.00	0	0	83.3
1970 Was	1	4	1	25.0	3	0.75	0	0	39.6
NFL Total	126	2133	1090	51.1	16042	7.52	149	111	77.6

	Rushing					Tot
Year Team	**Att**	**Yds**	**Avg**	**TD**	**Fum**	**TD**
1958 LARm	5	45	9.0	0	1	0
1959 LARm	19	57	3.0	1	5	1
1960 LARm	19	85	4.5	1	1	2
1961 LARm	38	139	3.7	0	3	0
1962 Cle	42	242	5.8	1	6	1
1963 Cle	62	224	3.6	2	6	2
1964 Cle	37	217	5.9	1	4	1
1965 Cle	19	72	3.8	0	5	0
1966 Cle	36	156	4.3	0	5	0
1967 Cle	22	57	2.6	0	4	0
1968 Cle	11	64	5.8	0	2	0
NFL Total	310	1358	4.4	6	42	7

JIM RYAN Ryan, James Joseph 6'1", 217 **LB**
Col: William & Mary *HS:* Bishop Eustace [Pennsauken, NJ]
B: 5/18/1957, Camden, NJ
1979 Den: 16 G. **1980** Den: 16 G; KR 1-0; Int 1-21. **1981** Den: 16 G; KR 1-2 2.0. **1982** Den: 9 G. **1983** Den: 15 G. **1984** Den: 16 G; Int 1-13; 3 Sac. **1985** Den: 16 G; 1 Sac. **1986** Den: 16 G; KR 1-0; 1 Sac. **1987** Den: 14 G; KR 2-9 4.5; Int 3-7; Scor **1** Saf; 2 Pt; 1 Fum; 1.5 Sac. **1988** Den: 16 G; 3.5 Sac. **Total:** 150 G; KR 5-11 2.2; Int 5-41; Scor 1 Saf; 2 Pt; 1 Fum; 10 Sac.

SOD RYAN Ryan, John Joseph 6'2", 205 **T**
Col: Detroit Mercy *HS:* St. Edward's Prep [Austin, TX] B: 1906, Kewanee, IL
1929 ChiB: 5 G. **1930** Port: 3 G. **Total:** 8 G.

ROCKY RYAN Ryan, John Raymond 6'1", 202 **OE-DB**
Col: Illinois *HS:* Unity [Tolono, IL] B: 7/5/1932, Tolono, IL
Drafted: 1954 Round 2 Phi
1956 Phi: 12 G; Rec 1-31 31.0; Int 1-17. **1957** Phi: 9 G; Rec 4-91 22.8 2 TD; 12 Pt. **1958** Phi-ChiB: 7 G; Rec 1-66 66.0; PR 1-0; Int 1-38; 1 Fum. Phi: 3 G; PR 1-0; Int 1-38; 1 Fum. ChiB: 4 G; Rec 1-66 66.0. **Total:** 28 G; Rec 6-188 31.3 2 TD; PR 1-0; Int 2-55; 12 Pt; 1 Fum.

JOE RYAN Ryan, Joseph James 6'2", 235 **DE**
Col: Villanova *HS:* New Dorp [Staten Island, NY] B: 7/15/1934, Staten Island, NY *Drafted:* 1957 Round 25 ChiB
1960 NYT: 4 G; KR 1-29 29.0.

RIP RYAN Ryan, Orson Kent 6'2", 193 **HB**
Col: Utah State *HS:* James Logan [Logan, UT] B: 2/2/1915, Midvale, UT
1938 Det: Pass 9-2 22.2%, 27 3.00; Rec 7-78 11.1. **1939** Det: Rec 7-46 6.6 1 TD; Punt 3-112 37.3. **1940** Det: Pass 2-0; Rec 9-96 10.7; Int **6**-65; Punt 9-350 38.9. **Total:** Pass 11-2 18.2%, 27 2.45; Rec 23-220 9.6 1 TD; Int 6-65; Punt 12-462 38.5.

		Rushing				Tot
Year Team	**G**	**Att**	**Yds**	**Avg**	**TD**	**TD**
1938 Det	9	24	180	7.5	0	0
1939 Det	6	8	41	5.1	1	2
1940 Det	10	22	42	1.9	0	0
NFL Total	25	54	263	4.9	1	2

PAT RYAN Ryan, Patrick Lee 6'3", 210 **QB**
Col: Tennessee *HS:* Putnam City [Oklahoma City, OK] B: 9/16/1955, Hutchinson, KS *Drafted:* 1978 Round 11 NYJ
1983 NYJ: Scor **1** 1XP. **1984** NYJ: Scor **1** 1XP. **Total:** Scor 2 1XP.

		Passing							
Year Team	G	Att	Comp	Comp%	Yds	YPA	TD	Int	Rating
1978 NYJ	2	14	9	64.3	106	7.57	0	2	47.6
1979 NYJ	1	4	2	50.0	13	3.25	0	1	17.7
1980 NYJ	14	0	0	—	0	—	0	0	—
1981 NYJ	15	10	4	40.0	48	4.80	1	1	49.2
1982 NYJ	9	18	12	66.7	146	8.11	2	1	105.3
1983 NYJ	16	40	21	52.5	259	6.48	2	2	68.6
1984 NYJ	16	285	156	54.7	1939	6.80	14	14	72.0
1985 NYJ	16	9	6	66.7	95	10.56	0	0	101.6
1986 NYJ	16	55	34	61.8	342	6.22	2	1	84.1
1987 NYJ	13	53	32	60.4	314	5.92	4	2	86.5
1988 NYJ	16	113	63	55.8	807	7.14	5	4	78.3
1989 NYJ	7	30	15	50.0	153	5.10	1	3	36.5
1991 Phi	4	26	10	38.5	98	3.77	0	4	10.3
NFL Total	145	657	364	55.4	4320	6.58	31	35	69.2

	Rushing				
Year Team	Att	Yds	Avg	TD	Fum
1979 NYJ	0	0	—	0	1
1981 NYJ	3	-5	-1.7	0	0
1982 NYJ	1	-1	-1.0	0	0
1983 NYJ	4	23	5.8	0	2
1984 NYJ	23	92	4.0	0	4
1985 NYJ	3	-5	-1.7	0	0
1986 NYJ	8	28	3.5	0	0
1987 NYJ	4	5	1.3	1	0
1988 NYJ	5	22	4.4	0	1
1989 NYJ	1	-1	-1.0	0	0
1991 Phi	1	-2	-2.0	0	2
NFL Total	53	156	2.9	1	10

TIM RYAN Ryan, Timothy Edward 6′4″, 268 **DE-DT**
Col: USC *HS:* Oak Grove [San Jose, CA] B: 9/8/1967, Memphis, TN
Drafted: 1990 Round 3 ChiB
1990 ChiB: 15 G; KR 1-(-1) -1.0. **1991** ChiB: 16 G; 1.5 Sac. **1992** ChiB: 16 G; 3 Sac. **1993** ChiB: 11 G; KR 1-5 5.0. **Total:** 58 G; KR 2-4 2.0; 4.5 Sac.

TIM RYAN Ryan, Timothy Thomas 6′2″, 280 **OG**
Col: Notre Dame *HS:* Rockhurst [Kansas City, MO] B: 9/2/1968, Kansas City, MO *Drafted:* 1991 Round 5 TB
1991 TB: 15 G; KR 1-4 4.0. **1992** TB: 16 G; KR 2-24 12.0. **1993** TB: 6 G. **Total:** 37 G; KR 3-28 9.3.

BILL RYAN Ryan, William 5′11″, 190 **T**
Col: Fordham *HS:* Englewood [Chicago, IL]
1924 Roch-ChiC: 2 G. Roch: 1 G. ChiC: 1 G. **1925** Mil: 1 G. **Total:** 3 G.

LARRY RYANS Ryans, Larry Bernard Jr. 5′11″, 182 **WR**
Col: Clemson *HS:* Greenwood [SC] B: 7/28/1971, Greenwood, SC
1996 TB: 3 G.

TOM RYCHLEC Rychlec, Thomas Richard 6′3″, 220 **OE**
(Rye) *Col:* American International *HS:* Meriden [CT] B: 9/11/1934, Meriden, CT *Drafted:* 1957 Round 10 Det
1958 Det: KR 1-0. **1960** Buf: KR 1-3 3.0. **1961** Buf: Rush 1-(-18) -18.0. **Total:** Rush 1-(-18) -18.0; KR 2-3 1.5.

		Receiving			
Year Team	G	Rec	Yds	Avg	TD
1958 Det	12	2	21	10.5	0
1960 Buf	14	45	590	13.1	0
1961 Buf	14	33	405	12.3	2
1962 Buf	6	6	66	11.0	1
1963 Den	3	1	7	7.0	0
NFL Total	49	87	1089	12.5	3

BILLY RYCKMAN Ryckman, William Thomas 5′11″, 172 **WR**
Col: Louisiana Tech *HS:* Lafayette [LA] B: 2/28/1955, Lafayette, LA
Drafted: 1977 Round 10 Atl
1977 Atl: KR 1-0. **Total:** KR 1-0.

		Receiving				Punt Returns				
Year Team	G	Rec	Yds	Avg	TD	Ret	Yds	Avg	TD	Fum
1977 Atl	14	1	5	5.0	1	7	40	5.7	0	0
1978 Atl	16	45	679	15.1	2	28	227	8.1	0	4
1979 Atl	14	4	59	14.8	2	12	72	6.0	0	0
NFL Total	44	50	743	14.9	5	47	339	7.2	0	4

DAN RYCZEK Ryczek, Daniel Stanley 6′3″, 249 **C**
Col: Virginia *HS:* Mentor [OH] B: 8/24/1949, Painesville, OH
Drafted: 1971 Round 13 Was
1973 Was: 14 G; 1 Fum. **1974** Was: 14 G; KR 1-11 11.0. **1975** Was: 14 G. **1976** TB: 14 G; Rec 1-6 6.0; 1 Fum. **1977** TB: 14 G; 1 Fum. **1978** LARm: 16 G. **1979** LARm: 16 G. **Total:** 102 G; Rec 1-6 6.0; KR 1-11 11.0; 3 Fum.

PAUL RYCZEK Ryczek, Paul Andrew 6′2″, 230 **C**
Col: Virginia *HS:* Mentor [OH] B: 6/25/1952, Painesville, OH
Drafted: 1974 Round 10 Atl
1974 Atl: 14 G; KR 1-0. **1975** Atl: 14 G. **1976** Atl: 14 G. **1977** Atl: 14 G. **1978** Atl: 16 G. **1979** Atl: 16 G; 2 Fum. **1981** NO: 8 G. **1987** Phi: 3 G. **Total:** 99 G; KR 1-0; 2 Fum.

RON RYDALCH Rydalch, Ronald James 6′4″, 260 **DT**
Col: Utah *HS:* Tooele [UT] B: 1/1/1952, Tooele, UT *Drafted:* 1974 Round 8 NYJ
1975 ChiB: 3 G. **1976** ChiB: 13 G. **1977** ChiB: 14 G. **1978** ChiB: 12 G. **1979** ChiB: 16 G. **1980** ChiB: 16 G. **Total:** 74 G.

NICK RYDER Ryder, Nicholas F 5′11″, 210 **FB**
Col: Miami (Fla.) *HS:* Haverstraw [NY] B: 10/31/1941, Nyack, NY
Drafted: 1963 Round 10 Det
1963 Det: 10 G; Rush 10-23 2.3 1 TD; KR 3-33 11.0; 6 Pt; 1 Fum. **1964** Det: 14 G; Rush 11-11 1.0; Rec 4-30 7.5 1 TD; KR 2-37 18.5; 6 Pt. **Total:** 24 G; Rush 21-34 1.6 1 TD; Rec 4-30 7.5 1 TD; KR 5-70 14.0; Tot TD 2; 12 Pt; 1 Fum.

FRANK RYDZEWSKI Rydzewski, Francis Xavier 6′1″, 220 **C-T-G**
Col: Notre Dame *HS:* St. Stanislaus [Chicago, IL] B: 11/16/1892, Chicago, IL D: 10/1979, Chicago, IL
1920 Cle-ChiT-Ham: 9 G. Cle: 3 G. ChiT: 4 G. Ham: 2 G. **1921** ChiC: 8 G. **1922** Ham: 6 G. **1923** ChiB-Ham: 6 G. ChiB: 1 G. Ham: 5 G. **1924** Ham: 5 G. **1925** Ham-Mil: 4 G. Ham: 1 G. Mil: 3 G. **1926** Ham: 4 G. **Total:** 42 G.

JULIE RYKOVICH Rykovich, Julius Alphonsus 6′2″, 204 **HB-DB**
Col: Notre Dame; Illinois *HS:* Lew Wallace [Gary, IN] B: 4/6/1923, Gary, IN D: 12/22/1974, Merrillville, IN *Drafted:* 1946 Round 2 ChiB
AAFC **1947** BufA: Rec 4-44 11.0; PR 7-93 13.3; KR 12-257 21.4; Int 2-61. **1948** BufA-ChiA: Pass 1-1 100.0%, 12 12.00; Rec 5-71 14.2; PR 1-23 23.0; KR 7-129 18.4; Int 3-65. **Total:** Pass 1-1 100.0%, 12 12.00; Rec 9-115 12.8; PR 8-116 14.5; KR 19-386 20.3; Int 5-126.

		Rushing			
Year Team	G	Att	Yds	Avg	TD
1947 BufA	13	92	414	4.5	4
1948 BufA-ChiA	12	96	425	4.4	6
AAFC Total	25	188	839	4.5	10

NFL **1950** ChiB: Punt 1-48 48.0. **1951** ChiB: Pass 3-0, 1 Int. **1952** Was: Scor 13, 1-1 100.0% XK. **1953** Was: KR 2-39 19.5. **Total:** Pass 3-0, 1 Int; KR 2-39 19.5; Punt 1-48 48.0; Scor 133, 1-1 100.0% XK.

		Rushing				Receiving					Tot
Year Team	G	Att	Yds	Avg	TD	Rec	Yds	Avg	TD	Fum	TD
1949 ChiB	11	88	340	3.9	6	16	210	13.1	2	2	8
1950 ChiB	12	122	394	3.2	7	21	344	16.4	0	2	7
1951 ChiB	12	83	399	4.8	4	6	133	22.2	0	3	4
1952 Was	11	94	361	3.8	1	16	283	17.7	1	2	2
1953 Was	12	73	251	3.4	0	7	73	10.4	1	2	1
NFL Total	58	460	1745	3.8	18	66	1043	15.8	4	11	22

LOU RYMKUS Rymkus, Louis Joseph 6′4″, 231 **OT-DT**
Col: Notre Dame *HS:* Tilden [Chicago, IL] B: 11/6/1919, Royalton, IL D: 10/31/1998, Houston, TX *Drafted:* 1943 Round 5 Was
AAFC **1946** CleA: 14 G. **1947** CleA: 13 G. **1948** CleA: 14 G. **1949** CleA: 12 G; KR 1-16 16.0. **Total:** 53 G; KR 1-16 16.0.

NFL **1943** Was: 10 G; Int 1-21 **1** TD; Tot TD 2; 12 Pt. **1950** Cle: 12 G; KR 1-0. **1951** Cle: 11 G. **Total:** 33 G; KR 1-0; Int 1-21 1 TD; Tot TD 2; 12 Pt.

MARK RYPIEN Rypien, Mark Robert 6′4″, 231 **QB**
Col: Washington State *HS:* Shadle Park [Spokane, WA] B: 10/2/1962, Calgary, Canada *Drafted:* 1986 Round 6 Was

		Passing							
Year Team	G	Att	Comp	Comp%	Yds	YPA	TD	Int	Rating
1988 Was	9	208	114	54.8	1730	8.32	18	13	85.2
1989 Was	14	476	280	58.8	3768	7.92	22	13	88.1
1990 Was	10	304	166	54.6	2070	6.81	16	11	78.4
1991 Was	16	421	249	59.1	3564	8.47	28	11	97.9
1992 Was	16	479	269	56.2	3282	6.85	13	17	71.7
1993 Was	12	319	166	52.0	1514	4.75	4	10	56.3
1994 Cle	6	128	59	46.1	694	5.42	4	3	63.7
1995 StL	11	217	129	59.4	1448	6.67	9	8	77.9
1996 Phi	1	13	10	76.9	76	5.85	1	0	116.2
1997 StL	5	39	19	48.7	270	6.92	0	2	50.2
NFL Total	100	2604	1461	56.1	18416	7.07	115	88	78.9

	Rushing				
Year Team	Att	Yds	Avg	TD	Fum
1988 Was	9	31	3.4	1	6
1989 Was	26	56	2.2	1	14
1990 Was	15	4	0.3	0	2
1991 Was	15	6	0.4	1	9
1992 Was	36	50	1.4	2	4

1993 Was	9	4	0.4	3	7
1994 Cle	7	4	0.6	0	2
1995 StL	9	10	1.1	0	1
1997 StL	1	1	1.0	0	0
NFL Total	127	166	1.3	8	45

TED RZEMPOLUCH Rzempoluch, Theodore Charles 6′1″, 195 **DB**
Col: Virginia *HS:* Cliffside Park [NJ] B: 5/31/1941, Jersey City, NJ
1963 Was: 6 G.

KELLY SAALFELD Saalfeld, Kelly Dean 6′3″, 246 **C**
Col: Nebraska *HS:* Lakeview [Columbus, NE] B: 2/15/1956, Columbus, NE *Drafted:* 1980 Round 9 GB
1980 NYG: 7 G.

BRAD SAAR Saar, Bradford Louis 6′1″, 220 **LB**
Col: Coll. of Lake Co. IL (J.C.); Penn State; Ball State *HS:* Adlai E. Stevenson [Lincolnshire, IL] B: 2/24/1963, Buffalo, NY
1987 Ind: 1 G.

ANDY SABADOS Sabados, Andrew Alex 5′11″, 209 **G**
Col: The Citadel *HS:* Aurora East [IL] B: 11/25/1916, Aurora, IL
Drafted: 1939 Round 11 ChiC
1939 ChiC: 8 G. **1940** ChiC: 10 G. **Total:** 18 G.

RON SABAL Sabal, Ronald Joseph 6′3″, 245 **OT-OG**
Col: Purdue *HS:* St. Rita [Chicago, IL] B: 7/23/1936, Chicago, IL
Drafted: 1958 Round 19 Phi
1960 Oak: 14 G. **1961** Oak: 14 G. **Total:** 28 G.

LOU SABAN Saban, Louis Henry 6′0″, 202 **LB-FB**
Col: Indiana *HS:* Lyons Twp. [La Grange, IL] B: 10/13/1921, Brookfield, IL
AAFC **1946** CleA: Pass 3-0, 1 Int; Rush 4-(-4) -1.0; Rec 1-45 45.0.
1947 CleA: Scor 10, 10-11 90.9% XK. **1949** CleA: Scor 17, 0-2 FG, 11-11 100.0% XK. **Total:** Pass 3-0, 1 Int; Rush 4-(-4) -1.0; Rec 1-45 45.0; Scor 27, 0-2 FG, 21-22 95.5% XK.

		Interceptions		
Year Team	**G**	**Int**	**Yds**	**TD**
1946 CleA	14	4	32	0
1947 CleA	14	2	2	0
1948 CleA	14	5	41	0
1949 CleA	12	2	35	1
AAFC Total	54	13	110	1

JOE SABASTEANSKI Sabasteanski, Joseph Edward 6′0″, 207 **G-LB-C**
Col: Fordham *HS:* Portland [ME] B: 2/24/1921, Portland, ME
D: 7/1/1972 *Drafted:* 1943 Round 11 Bkn
1947 Bos: 10 G; Int 1-0; 1 Fum. **1948** Bos: 12 G; Int 2-38. **1949** NYB: 12 G. **Total:** 34 G; Int 3-38; 1 Fum.

BILL SABATINO Sabatino, Louis William 6′3″, 245 **DT**
Col: Colorado *HS:* West Covina [CA] B: 8/9/1945, Alliance, OH
Drafted: 1967 Round 11 Cle
1968 Cle: 7 G. **1969** Atl: 6 G. **Total:** 13 G.

DWAYNE SABB Sabb, Dwayne Irving 6′4″, 248 **LB**
Col: New Hampshire *HS:* Hudson Catholic [Union City, NJ]
B: 10/9/1969, Jersey City, NJ *Drafted:* 1992 Round 5 NE
1992 NE: 16 G; 1 Sac. **1993** NE: 14 G; KR 2-0; 2 Sac. **1994** NE: 16 G; Int 2-6; 3.5 Sac. **1995** NE: 12 G. **1996** NE: 16 G; Int 1-0; 0.5 Sac.
Total: 74 G; KR 2-0; Int 3-6; 7 Sac.

TINO SABUCO Sabuco, Valentino 6′1″, 206 **C**
Col: Wayne State (Mich.); San Francisco *HS:* MacKenzie [Detroit, MI]
B: 12/20/1926, Detroit, MI
AAFC **1949** SF-A: 10 G.

TONY SACCA Sacca, Anthony John 6′5″, 230 **QB**
Col: Penn State *HS:* Delran [NJ] B: 4/17/1970, Delran, NJ
Drafted: 1992 Round 2 Pho
1992 Pho: 2 G; Pass 11-4 36.4%, 29 2.64 2 Int.

FRANK SACCO Sacco, Frank J 6′4″, 240 **LB**
Col: Fordham B: 4/8/1964
1987 NE: 2 G.

LENNY SACHS Sachs, Leonard David 5′8″, 176 **OE**
Col: American Coll. of Physical Education *HS:* Carl Schurz [Chicago, IL]
B: 8/7/1897, Chicago, IL D: 10/27/1942, Chicago, IL
1920 ChiC: 8 G. **1921** ChiC: 8 G; Rec 1 TD; 6 Pt. **1922** ChiC: 7 G.
1923 Mil: 13 G; Rec 1 TD; 6 Pt. **1924** Mil-Ham: 5 G. Mil: 2 G. Ham: 3 G.
1925 Ham-ChiC: 6 G. Ham: 4 G. ChiC: 2 G. **1926** Lou: 4 G. **Total:** 51 G; Rec 2 TD; 12 Pt.

FRANK SACHSE Sachse, Francis Marion 6′0″, 197 **DB-TB-QB-HB**
(Butch) *Col:* Texas Tech *HS:* Quitaque [TX] B: 7/24/1917, Brice, TX
D: 10/1/1989, Dallas, TX
1943 Bkn: Rush 8-14 1.8; Rec 3-26 8.7; PR 2-37 18.5. **1944** Bkn: Rush 9-13 1.4; PR 1-23 23.0; KR 1-25 25.0. **1945** Bos: Rush 5-9 1.8; Int 2-25. **Total:** Rush 22-36 1.6; Rec 3-26 8.7; PR 3-60 20.0; KR 1-25 25.0; Int 2-25.

		Passing								
Year Team	**G**	**Att**	**Comp**	**Comp%**	**Yds**	**YPA**	**TD**	**Int**	**Rating**	**Fum**
1943 Bkn	6	9	5	55.6	72	8.00	1	1	79.2	0
1944 Bkn	6	45	18	40.0	226	5.02	0	5	16.8	0
1945 Bos	8	21	9	42.9	203	9.67	2	0	109.8	1
NFL Total	20	75	32	42.7	501	6.68	3	6	45.5	1

JACK SACHSE Sachse, Jack Clarence 6′0″, 210 **C-LB**
Col: Southwestern (Tex.); Texas *HS:* Electra [TX] B: 1/14/1921, Wichita Falls, TX D: 7/1958, Velpen, IN *Drafted:* 1944 Round 8 Bkn
1945 Bos: 4 G.

JACK SACK Sack, Jacob Bernard 6′2″, 195 **G**
(AKA Sacklowsky) *Col:* Pittsburgh *HS:* Fifth Avenue [Pittsburgh, PA]
B: 2/22/1902, Pittsburgh, PA D: 3/7/1980, Pittsburgh, PA
1923 Col: 9 G. **1926** Can: 3 G. **Total:** 12 G.

NORB SACKSTEDER Sacksteder, Norbert N 5′9″, 173 **TB-WB-BB**
(Saxy) *Col:* Dayton; Christian Brothers (Mo.) *HS:* U. of Dayton Prep [OH] B: 9/25/1895 D: 6/19/1986, St. Petersburg, FL
1920 Day: 8 G. **1921** Det: 7 G. **1922** Can: 11 G; Pass 1 TD; Rush 2 TD; Rec 1 TD; PR **1** TD; Tot TD 4; 24 Pt. **1925** Can: 1 G. **Total:** 27 G; Pass 1 TD; Rush 2 TD; Rec 1 TD; PR 1 TD; Tot TD 4; 24 Pt.

NICK SACRINTY Sacrinty, Nicholas William 5′11″, 185 **QB-DB**
Col: Wake Forest *HS:* Reidsville [NC] B: 6/10/1924, Reidsville, NC
Drafted: 1945 Round 15 ChiB
1947 ChiB: 11 G; Pass 48-15 31.3%, 299 6.23 5 TD 3 Int; Rush 4-4 1.0; Int 1-7; 1 Fum.

ROD SADDLER Saddler, Roderick 6′5″, 276 **DT**
Col: Texas A&M *HS:* Columbus [Decatur, GA] B: 9/26/1965, Atlanta, GA *Drafted:* 1987 Round 4 StL
1987 StL: 12 G; Int 1-0; 3 Sac. **1988** Pho: 16 G; **1** Fum TD; 6 Pt; 2 Sac.
1989 Pho: 15 G; 3.5 Sac. **1990** Pho: 16 G; 4 Sac. **1991** Pho-Cin: 6 G; 1 Fum TD; 6 Pt. Pho: 4 G; 1 Fum TD; 6 Pt. Cin: 2 G. **Total:** 65 G; Int 1-0; 2 Fum TD; 12 Pt; 12.5 Sac.

STEVE SADER Sader, Steven 5′11″, 180 **FB-LB**
Col: No College *HS:* Southeast Catholic [Philadelphia, PA] B: 1921
1943 PhPt: 2 G; Rush 3-5 1.7.

TROY SADOWSKI Sadowski, Troy Robert 6′5″, 255 **TE**
Col: Georgia *HS:* Chamblee [GA] B: 12/8/1965, Atlanta, GA
Drafted: 1989 Round 6 Atl
1990 Atl: 13 G. **1991** KC: 14 G. **1992** NYJ: 6 G; Rec 1-20 20.0. **1993** NYJ: 13 G; Rec 2-14 7.0; KR 1-0. **1994** Cin: 15 G; Rec 11-54 4.9. **1995** Cin: 12 G; Rec 5-37 7.4. **1996** Cin: 16 G; Rec 3-15 5.0; KR 2-7 3.5. **1997** Pit: 6 G; Rec 1-12 12.0. **1998** Jac: 5 G; KR 1-0. **Total:** 100 G; Rec 23-152 6.6; KR 4-7 1.8.

EDDIE SAENZ Saenz, Edwin Matthew 5′11″, 169 **HB-DB**
(Tortilla) *Col:* Loyola Marymount; USC *HS:* Venice [Los Angeles, CA]
B: 9/21/1922, Santa Monica, CA D: 4/28/1971, Santa Monica, CA
Drafted: 1945 Round 13 Was
1946 Was: Int 1-0. **1950** Was: Int 1-0. **Total:** Int 2-0.

		Rushing				Receiving			
Year Team	**G**	**Att**	**Yds**	**Avg**	**TD**	**Rec**	**Yds**	**Avg**	**TD**
1946 Was	10	55	213	3.9	1	12	242	20.2	3
1947 Was	12	51	143	2.8	0	34	598	17.6	4
1948 Was	4	8	21	2.6	0	4	62	15.5	0
1949 Was	12	53	170	3.2	0	23	251	10.9	0
1950 Was	10	20	64	3.2	1	10	165	16.5	1
1951 Was	2	3	8	2.7	0	1	9	9.0	0
NFL Total	50	190	619	3.3	2	84	1327	15.8	8

	Punt Returns				Kickoff Returns					Tot
Year Team	**Ret**	**Yds**	**Avg**	**TD**	**Ret**	**Yds**	**Avg**	**TD**	**Fum**	**TD**
1946 Was	0	0	—	0	11	264	24.0	0	1	4
1947 Was	24	308	12.8	0	**29**	**797**	27.5	**2**	5	6
1948 Was	2	26	13.0	0	8	173	21.6	0	1	0
1949 Was	17	178	10.5	0	**24**	465	19.4	0	6	0
1950 Was	14	125	8.9	0	12	347	28.9	0	1	2
1951 Was	2	6	3.0	0	9	145	16.1	0	0	0
NFL Total	59	643	10.9	0	93	2191	23.6	2	14	12

SAINT SAFFOLD Saffold, Samuel T 6′4″, 202 **WR**
Col: San Jose State *HS:* Edison [Stockton, CA] B: 5/18/1944, Slater, MS *Drafted:* 1966 Redshirt Round 7 SD
1968 Cin: 14 G; Rush 1-21 21.0; Rec 16-172 10.8; KR 1-0; 1 Fum.

PIO SAGAPOLUTELE Sagapolutele, Pio Alika 6′6″, 297 **DE-DT**
Col: San Diego State *HS:* Maryknoll [Honolulu, HI] B: 11/28/1969, American Samoa *Drafted:* 1991 Round 4 Cle
1991 Cle: 15 G; 1.5 Sac. **1992** Cle: 14 G. **1993** Cle: 8 G. **1994** Cle: 11 G.
1995 Cle: 15 G; 0.5 Sac. **1996** NE: 15 G; 3 Sac. **1997** NO: 14 G; 2 Sac.
Total: 92 G; 7 Sac.

FLOYD SAGELY Sagely, Floyd Eugene 6′1″, 191 **DB-OE**
Col: Arkansas *HS:* Van Buren [AR] B: 3/26/1932, Rudy, AR
Drafted: 1954 Round 6 SF
1954 SF: 12 G. **1956** SF: 3 G. **1957** ChiC: 10 G; Int 1-7. **Total:** 25 G; Int 1-7.

KEN SAGER Sager, Kenneth A 6′4″, 228 **TE**
Col: Western Washington *HS:* Glendale [WA] B: 10/15/1963
1987 Sea: 3 G.

ANTHONY SAGNELLA Sagnella, Anthony 6′5″, 260 **DT**
Col: Rutgers *HS:* Hamden [CT] B: 2/28/1964, New Haven, CT
1987 Was: 3 G; 1 Sac.

TOM SAIDOCK Saidock, Thomas 6′5″, 261 **DT**
Col: Michigan State *HS:* Fordson [Dearborn, MI] B: 2/26/1930, Detroit, MI *Drafted:* 1957 Round 7 Phi
1957 Phi: 11 G. **1960** NYT: 14 G. **1961** NYT: 14 G; KR 2-26 13.0. **1962** Buf: 2 G. **Total:** 41 G; KR 2-26 13.0.

GEORGE SAIMES Saimes, George Thomas 5′11″, 186 **DB**
Col: Michigan State *HS:* Lincoln [Cleveland, OH] B: 9/1/1941, Canton, OH *Drafted:* 1963 Round 6 Buf
1963 Buf: Rush 12-41 3.4; Rec 6-23 3.8; KR 7-140 20.0. **1965** Buf: PR 0-1; **1** Fum TD. **Total:** Rush 12-41 3.4; Rec 6-23 3.8; PR 0-1; KR 7-140 20.0; 1 Fum TD.

		Interceptions		
Year Team	**G**	**Int**	**Yds**	**TD**
1963 Buf	14	4	29	0
1964 Buf	14	6	56	0
1965 Buf	14	4	24	0
1966 Buf	14	1	32	0
1967 Buf	14	2	14	0
1968 Buf	13	2	36	0
1969 Buf	8	3	47	0
1970 Den	8	0	0	0
1971 Den	13	0	0	0
1972 Den	9	0	0	0
NFL Total	121	22	238	0

PAT SAINDON Saindon, Patrick Arthur 6′3″, 273 **OG**
Col: Vanderbilt *HS:* Samuel W. Wolfson [Jacksonville, FL] B: 3/3/1961, Nice, France
1986 NO: 8 G. **1987** Atl: 3 G. **Total:** 11 G.

MIKE ST. CLAIR St. Clair, Richard Michael 6′5″, 249 **DE**
Col: Central Coll. (Iowa); Grambling State *HS:* East Tech [Cleveland, OH] B: 9/2/1953, Cleveland, OH *Drafted:* 1976 Round 4 Cle
1976 Cle: 14 G. **1977** Cle: 11 G. **1978** Cle: 16 G. **1979** Cle: 16 G. **1980** Cin: 10 G. **1981** Cin: 16 G; 1 Fum TD; 6 Pt. **1982** Cin: 8 G. **Total:** 91 G; 1 Fum TD; 6 Pt.

BOB ST. CLAIR St. Clair, Robert Bruce 6′9″, 263 **OT**
(The Geek) *Col:* San Francisco; Tulsa *HS:* San Francisco Polytechnic [CA] B: 2/18/1931, San Francisco, CA *Drafted:* 1953 Round 3 SF
HOF: 1990
1953 SF: 10 G. **1954** SF: 12 G. **1955** SF: 12 G. **1956** SF: 12 G. **1957** SF: 5 G. **1958** SF: 12 G. **1959** SF: 12 G. **1960** SF: 10 G. **1961** SF: 12 G. **1962** SF: 8 G. **1963** SF: 14 G; KR 2-3 1.5. **Total:** 119 G; KR 2-3 1.5.

TED ST. GERMAINE St. Germaine, Thomas Leo 6′2″, 250 **T-C-G**
Col: Carlisle; Howard *HS:* Haskell Indian School [Lawrence, KS] B: 1885, Lac du Flambeau, WI D: 10/4/1947, Lac du Flambeau, WI
1922 Oor: 5 G.

LEN ST. JEAN St. Jean, Leonard Wayne 5′11″, 250 **OG**
Col: Northern Michigan *HS:* Newberry [MI] B: 10/27/1941, Newberry, MI *Drafted:* 1964 Round 9 Bos
1964 Bos: 14 G. **1965** Bos: 14 G. **1966** Bos: 14 G. **1967** Bos: 14 G. **1968** Bos: 14 G. **1969** Bos: 14 G. **1970** Bos: 14 G. **1971** NE: 14 G. **1972** NE: 14 G. **1973** NE: 14 G. **Total:** 140 G.

HERB ST. JOHN St. John, Herbert LeGrande 5′10″, 215 **G**
Col: Georgia *HS:* Andrew Jackson [Jacksonville, FL] B: 1/17/1926, Perry, FL
AAFC **1948** BknA: 10 G. **1949** ChiA: 11 G. **Total:** 21 G.

ABDUL SALAAM Salaam, Abdul 6′3″, 262 **DT-DE**
(AKA Larry J. Faulk) *Col:* Kent State *HS:* Woodward [Cincinnati, OH] B: 2/12/1953, Cincinnati, OH *Drafted:* 1976 Round 7 NYJ
1976 NYJ: 14 G. **1977** NYJ: 14 G. **1978** NYJ: 15 G. **1979** NYJ: 12 G. **1980** NYJ: 16 G. **1981** NYJ: 16 G. **1982** NYJ: 9 G; 2.5 Sac. **1983** NYJ: 1 G. **Total:** 97 G; 2.5 Sac.

EPHRAIM SALAAM Salaam, Ephraim Mateen 6′6″, 290 **OT**
Col: San Diego State *HS:* Florin [Sacramento, CA] B: 6/19/1976, Chicago, IL *Drafted:* 1998 Round 7 Atl
1998 Atl: 16 G.

RASHAAN SALAAM Salaam, Rashaan Iman 6′1″, 224 **RB**
Col: Colorado *HS:* La Jolla Country Day School [La Jolla, CA] B: 10/8/1974, San Diego, CA *Drafted:* 1995 Round 1 ChiB
1995 ChiB: Rec 7-56 8.0. **1996** ChiB: Rec 7-44 6.3 1 TD. **1997** ChiB: Rec 2-20 10.0. **Total:** Rec 16-120 7.5 1 TD.

		Rushing					Tot
Year Team	**G**	**Att**	**Yds**	**Avg**	**TD**	**Fum**	**TD**
1995 ChiB	16	296	1074	3.6	10	9	10
1996 ChiB	12	143	496	3.5	3	3	4
1997 ChiB	3	31	112	3.6	0	2	0
NFL Total	31	470	1682	3.6	13	14	14

ANDY SALATA Salata, Andrew J 5′10″, 188 **G**
Col: Pittsburgh *HS:* Wyoming Seminary [Kingston, PA] B: 9/30/1905 D: 1/14/1978, Hancock, MI
1929 Ora: 10 G. **1930** Nwk: 10 G. **Total:** 20 G.

PAUL SALATA Salata, Paul Thomas 6′2″, 191 **OE**
(Slats) *Col:* USC *HS:* Benjamin Franklin [Los Angeles, CA] B: 10/17/1926, Los Angeles, CA
AAFC **1949** SF-A: 12 G; Rec 24-289 12.0 4 TD; 24 Pt.

NFL **1950** SF-Bal: KR 3-12 4.0. Bal: KR 3-12 4.0. **Total:** KR 3-12 4.0.

		Receiving				
Year Team	**G**	**Rec**	**Yds**	**Avg**	**TD**	**Fum**
1950 SF-Bal	11	50	618	12.4	4	1
1950 SF	4	5	46	9.2	2	0
1950 Bal	7	45	572	12.7	2	1
NFL Total	11	50	618	12.4	4	1

JOE SALAVE'A Salave'a, Joe Fagaone 6′3″, 290 **DT**
Col: Arizona *HS:* Oceanside [CA] B: 3/23/1975, Leone, American Samoa *Drafted:* 1998 Round 4 Ten
1998 Ten: 13 G; 1 Sac.

JAY SALDI Saldi, John Jay IV 6′3″, 225 **TE-WR**
Col: South Carolina *HS:* White Plains [NY] B: 10/8/1954, White Plains, NY
1976 Dal: Rush 1-19 19.0; KR 1-9 9.0. **1977** Dal: 1 Fum TD. **1978** Dal: KR 1-0. **1979** Dal: Rush 1-(-1) -1.0. **1980** Dal: KR 1-23 23.0. **Total:** Rush 2-18 9.0; KR 3-32 10.7; 1 Fum TD.

		Receiving					Tot
Year Team	**G**	**Rec**	**Yds**	**Avg**	**TD**	**Fum**	**TD**
1976 Dal	13	1	6	6.0	0	0	0
1977 Dal	14	11	108	9.8	2	0	3
1978 Dal	4	3	8	2.7	2	0	2
1979 Dal	16	14	181	12.9	1	0	1
1980 Dal	16	25	311	12.4	1	0	1
1981 Dal	16	8	82	10.3	1	0	1
1982 Dal	5	1	8	8.0	0	0	0
1983 ChiB	13	12	119	9.9	0	0	0
1984 ChiB	15	9	90	10.0	0	2	0
NFL Total	112	84	913	10.9	7	2	8

DAN SALEAUMUA Saleaumua, Raymond Daniel 6′0″, 305 **NT-DT-DE**
Col: Arizona State *HS:* Sweetwater [National City, CA] B: 11/25/1964, San Diego, CA *Drafted:* 1987 Round 7 Det
1987 Det: 9 G; KR 3-57 19.0; 2 Sac. **1988** Det: 16 G; KR 1-0; 1 Fum; 2 Sac. **1989** KC: 16 G; KR 1-8 8.0; Int 1-21; 2 Sac. **1990** KC: 16 G; 1 Fum TD; 6 Pt; 7 Sac. **1991** KC: 16 G; Scor 1 Saf; 2 Pt; 1.5 Sac. **1992** KC: 16 G; 6 Sac. **1993** KC: 16 G; Int 1-13; 1 Fum TD; 6 Pt; 3.5 Sac. **1994** KC: 14 G; 1 Sac. **1995** KC: 16 G; Int 1-0; 7 Sac. **1996** KC: 15 G; Scor 1 Saf; 2 Pt. **1997** Sea: 16 G; Scor **1** Saf; 2 Pt; 3.5 Sac. **1998** Sea: 11 G. **Total:** 177 G; KR 5-65 13.0; Int 3-34; Scor 3 Saf; 2 Fum TD; 18 Pt; 1 Fum; 35.5 Sac.

TAREK SALEH Saleh, Tarek Muhammad 6′1″, 240 **LB**
Col: Wisconsin *HS:* Notre Dame [West Haven, CT] B: 11/7/1974, New Haven, CT *Drafted:* 1997 Round 4 Car
1997 Car: 3 G; 1 Sac. **1998** Car: 11 G; KR 1-8 8.0. **Total:** 14 G; KR 1-8 8.0; 1 Sac.

ED SALEM Salem, Edward Joseph 5′11″, 193 **QB-DB**
Col: Alabama *HS:* Ramsey [Birmingham, AL] B: 8/28/1928, Birmingham, AL *Drafted:* 1951 Round 2 Was
1951 Was: 12 G; Pass 3-0, 2 Int; Int 5-26.

HARVEY SALEM Salem, Harvey Maynard 6′6″, 283 **OT-OG**
Col: California *HS:* El Cerrito [CA] B: 1/15/1961, Berkeley, CA
Drafted: 1983 Round 2 Hou
1983 Hou: 16 G. **1984** Hou: 16 G. **1985** Hou: 14 G. **1986** Hou-Det: 14 G. Hou: 1 G. Det: 13 G. **1987** Det: 11 G. **1988** Det: 16 G. **1989** Det: 10 G. **1990** Det: 15 G. **1991** Den: 10 G. **1992** GB: 4 G. **Total:** 126 G.

SAM SALEMI Salemi, Sam 5′9″, 180 **WB**
(Smoke AKA Salem) *Col:* Columbia; St. John's (N.Y.); Canisius
HS: New Utrecht [Brooklyn, NY] B: 6/4/1903, New York, NY
D: 7/7/1969, Brooklyn, NY
1928 NYY: 5 G; Rec 1 TD; 6 Pt.

SEAN SALISBURY Salisbury, Richard Sean 6′5″, 225 **QB**
Col: USC *HS:* Orange Glen [Escondido, CA] B: 3/9/1963, Escondido, CA

Year Team	G	Passing Att	Comp	Comp%	Yds	YPA	TD	Int	Rating
1987 Ind	2	12	8	66.7	68	5.67	0	2	41.7
1992 Min	10	175	97	55.4	1203	6.87	5	2	81.7
1993 Min	11	195	115	59.0	1413	7.25	9	6	84.0
1994 Min	1	34	16	47.1	156	4.59	0	1	48.2
1996 SD	16	161	82	50.9	984	6.11	5	8	59.6
NFL Total	40	577	318	55.1	3824	6.63	19	19	72.9

Year Team	Rushing Att	Yds	Avg	TD	Fum
1987 Ind	0	0	—	0	1
1992 Min	11	0	0.0	0	4
1993 Min	10	-1	-0.1	0	3
1994 Min	3	2	0.7	0	0
1996 SD	6	14	2.3	0	3
NFL Total	30	15	0.5	0	11

JEROME SALLY Sally, Jerome Eli 6′3″, 267 **NT**
Col: Missouri *HS:* Proviso East [Maywood, IL] B: 2/24/1959, Chicago, IL
1982 NYG: 4 G; 1 Sac. **1983** NYG: 16 G; 4.5 Sac. **1984** NYG: 16 G; 2 Sac. **1985** NYG: 16 G; KR 1-4 4.0; 7.5 Sac. **1986** NYG: 16 G; 3.5 Sac. **1987** Ind: 12 G; 1 Sac. **1988** KC: 3 G. **Total:** 83 G; KR 1-4 4.0; 19.5 Sac.

MIKE SALMON Salmon, Michael William 6′1″, 210 **DB**
Col: USC *HS:* Greenway [Phoenix, AZ] B: 12/27/1970, Long Beach, CA
1997 SF: 1 G.

BRIAN SALONEN Salonen, Brian Scott 6′3″, 229 **LB-TE**
Col: Montana *HS:* Great Falls [MT] B: 7/29/1961, Glasgow, MT
Drafted: 1984 Round 10 Dal
1984 Dal: 16 G; KR 2-30 15.0. **1985** Dal: 16 G. **Total:** 32 G; KR 2-30 15.0.

JIM SALSBURY Salsbury, James Woodrow 6′1″, 233 **OG-OT**
Col: UCLA *HS:* Alexander Hamilton [Los Angeles, CA] B: 8/8/1932, Los Angeles, CA *Drafted:* 1955 Round 2 Det
1955 Det: 12 G. **1956** Det: 11 G; KR 1-13 13.0. **1957** GB: 12 G. **1958** GB: 12 G; Rush 0-3. **Total:** 47 G; Rush 0-3; KR 1-13 13.0.

JACK SALSCHEIDER Salscheider, John Joseph 5′10″, 185 **HB**
Col: St. Thomas *HS:* St. Thomas Acad. [St. Paul, MN] B: 12/17/1924, St. Paul, MN D: 5/14/1998, St. Croix Falls, WI *Drafted:* 1949 Round 8 NYG
1949 NYG: Rec 4-9 2.3; KR 15-474 **31.6 1** TD; Punt 14-495 35.4.

Year Team	G	Rushing Att	Yds	Avg	TD	Fum
1949 NYG	11	26	105	4.0	0	3

BRYANT SALTER Salter, Bryant J 6′4″, 195 **DB**
Col: Pittsburgh *HS:* South Hills [Pittsburgh, PA] B: 1/22/1950, Pittsburgh, PA *Drafted:* 1971 Round 5 SD
1971 SD: KR 8-172 21.5. **Total:** KR 8-172 21.5.

Year Team	G	Interceptions Int	Yds	TD	Fum
1971 SD	14	6	48	0	1
1972 SD	14	7	111	0	0
1973 SD	13	1	20	0	0
1974 Was	3	1	0	0	0
1975 Was	14	1	17	0	0
1976 Mia-Sea-Bal	13	1	0	0	0
1976 Mia	12	1	0	0	0
1976 Bal	1	0	0	0	0
NFL Total	71	17	196	0	1

CHUCK SAMPLE Sample, Charles E 5′9″, 205 **FB-LB**
Col: Toledo *HS:* West [Appleton, WI] B: 1/5/1920, Green Bay, WI
1942 GB: Rec 6-35 5.8 1 TD; KR 3-91 30.3. **Total:** Rec 6-35 5.8 1 TD; KR 3-91 30.3.

Year Team	G	Rushing Att	Yds	Avg	TD	Tot TD
1942 GB	9	57	255	4.5	4	5
1945 GB	1	2	2	1.0	0	0
NFL Total	10	59	257	4.4	4	5

JOHNNY SAMPLE Sample, John B Jr. 6′1″, 203 **DB-HB**
Col: Maryland East. Shore *HS:* Overbrook [Philadelphia, PA] B: 6/15/1937, Cape Charles, VA *Drafted:* 1958 Round 7 Bal
1960 Bal: Rush 1-7 7.0. **Total:** Rush 1-7 7.0.

Year Team	G	Punt Returns Ret	Yds	Avg	TD	Kickoff Returns Ret	Yds	Avg	TD
1958 Bal	12	0	0	—	0	0	0	—	0
1959 Bal	12	22	129	5.9	0	17	457	26.9	0
1960 Bal	11	14	101	7.2	0	18	519	28.8	**1**
1961 Pit	14	**26**	**283**	10.9	1	23	532	23.1	0
1962 Pit	6	4	1	0.3	0	2	52	26.0	0
1963 Was	2	2	45	22.5	0	0	0	—	0
1964 Was	14	0	0	—	0	0	0	—	0
1965 Was	13	0	0	—	0	0	0	—	0
1966 NYJ	13	0	0	—	0	0	0	—	0
1967 NYJ	14	0	0	—	0	0	0	—	0
1968 NYJ	14	0	0	—	0	0	0	—	0
NFL Total	125	68	559	8.2	1	60	1560	26.0	1

Year Team	Interceptions Int	Yds	TD	Fum	Tot TD
1959 Bal	1	10	0	1	0
1960 Bal	4	27	0	3	1
1961 Pit	8	141	1	0	2
1962 Pit	0	21	0	0	0
1963 Was	1	0	0	0	0
1964 Was	4	31	1	0	1
1965 Was	6	57	0	0	0
1966 NYJ	6	32	0	0	0
1967 NYJ	4	53	1	0	1
1968 NYJ	7	88	1	0	1
NFL Total	41	460	4	4	6

LAWRENCE SAMPLETON Sampleton, Lawrence M Jr. 6′5″, 233 **TE**
Col: Texas *HS:* Seguin [TX] B: 9/25/1959, Waelder, TX *Drafted:* 1982 Round 2 Phi
1982 Phi: 9 G; Rec 1-24 24.0. **1983** Phi: 7 G; Rec 2-28 14.0. **1984** Phi: 16 G. **1987** Mia: 3 G; Rec 8-64 8.0; 1 Fum. **Total:** 35 G; Rec 11-116 10.5; 1 Fum.

ARCHIE SAMPSON Sampson, Archer M 6′1″, 206 **G**
Col: No College B: 10/29/1897, Muncie, IN D: 10/1965
1921 Day: 9 G.

CLINT SAMPSON Sampson, Clinton Bernard 5′11″, 183 **WR**
Col: Mount San Antonio Coll. CA (J.C.); San Diego State *HS:* Crenshaw [Los Angeles, CA] B: 1/4/1961, Los Angeles, CA *Drafted:* 1983 Round 3 Den

Year Team	G	Receiving Rec	Yds	Avg	TD	Fum
1983 Den	16	10	200	20.0	3	0
1984 Den	12	9	123	13.7	1	1
1985 Den	16	26	432	16.6	4	0
1986 Den	15	21	259	12.3	0	1
NFL Total	59	66	1014	15.4	8	2

EBER SAMPSON Sampson, Eber 6′0″, 197 **FB**
Col: No College *HS:* None B: 1895 Deceased
1921 Min: 4 G; Rush 2 TD; 12 Pt. **1922** Min: 3 G. **1923** Min: 7 G; Rush 1 TD; 6 Pt. **Total:** 14 G; Rush 3 TD; 18 Pt.

HOWARD SAMPSON Sampson, Howard Earl 5′10″, 185 **DB**
Col: Arkansas *HS:* Ross C. Sterling [Houston, TX] B: 7/7/1956, Baytown, TX
1978 GB: 15 G; PR 1-0; KR 1-23 23.0; 1 Fum. **1979** GB: 16 G; KR 3-45 15.0. **Total:** 31 G; PR 1-0; KR 4-68 17.0; 1 Fum.

GREG SAMPSON Sampson, Ralph Gregory 6′6″, 265 **OT-DT-DE**
Col: Stanford *HS:* R.A. Millikan [Long Beach, CA] B: 10/25/1950, Bellingham, WA *Drafted:* 1972 Round 1 Hou
1972 Hou: 14 G. **1973** Hou: 13 G. **1974** Hou: 14 G. **1975** Hou: 14 G. **1976** Hou: 8 G. **1977** Hou: 14 G. **1978** Hou: 16 G; Rec 1-(-4) -4.0. **Total:** 93 G; Rec 1-(-4) -4.0.

RON SAMS Sams, Ronald F Jr. 6′3″, 261 **OG**
Col: Pittsburgh *HS:* South Fayette [McDonald, PA] B: 4/12/1961, Bridgeville, PA *Drafted:* 1983 Round 6 GB
1983 GB: 3 G. **1984** Min: 12 G; 1 Fum. **Total:** 15 G; 1 Fum.

MICHAEL SAMSON Samson, Michael 6′3″, 294 **DT**
Col: Grambling State *HS:* Heidelberg [MS] B: 2/17/1973, Laurel, MS
1996 Phi: 2 G.

SENECA SAMSON Samson, Seneca Gadsden 5′8″, 160 **HB**
Col: Brown *HS:* Stuyvesant [New York, NY] B: 11/10/1899, New York, NY D: 4/2/1930, Wakefield, RI
1926 Prov: 2 G.

DON SAMUEL Samuel, Donald Allen 5′11″, 190 **DB-HB**
Col: Oregon State *HS:* Hood River [OR] B: 2/16/1924, Hood River, OR
Drafted: 1946 Round 2 LARm
1949 Pit: Pass 21-7 33.3%, 67 3.19 1 Int; Rec 1-2 2.0; PR 7-80 11.4; Int 1-4. **Total:** Pass 21-7 33.3%, 67 3.19 1 Int; Rec 1-2 2.0; PR 7-80 11.4; Int 1-4.

Year Team	G	Rushing Att	Yds	Avg	TD	Fum
1949 Pit	5	39	163	4.2	1	6
1950 Pit	1	0	0	—	0	0
NFL Total	6	39	163	4.2	1	6

TONY SAMUELS Samuels, Andre Antonio 6'4", 229 **TE**
Col: Bethune-Cookman *HS:* Northeast [St. Petersburg, FL]
B: 12/30/1954, Tampa, FL *Drafted:* 1977 Round 4 KC
1979 KC: **1** Fum TD. **1980** KC-TB: KR 1-10 10.0. TB: KR 1-10 10.0. **Total:** KR 1-10 10.0; 1 Fum TD.

Year Team	G	Receiving Rec	Yds	Avg	TD	Fum	Tot TD
1977 KC	14	5	65	13.0	0	1	0
1978 KC	16	6	97	16.2	0	0	0
1979 KC	16	14	147	10.5	0	1	1
1980 KC-TB	10	8	110	13.8	2	0	2
1980 KC	4	8	110	13.8	2	0	2
1980 TB	6	0	0	—	0	0	0
NFL Total	56	33	419	12.7	2	2	3

CHRIS SAMUELS Samuels, Christopher Auburn 5'10", 202 **RB**
Col: Texas *HS:* Judson [Converse, TX] B: 5/16/1969, Montego Bay, Jamaica *Drafted:* 1991 Round 12 SD
1991 SD: 3 G; Rush 2-10 5.0; Rec 2-33 16.5.

TERRY SAMUELS Samuels, Terrance Eugene 6'2", 254 **TE**
Col: Kentucky *HS:* Male [Louisville, KY] B: 9/27/1970, Louisville, KY
Drafted: 1994 Round 6 Ariz
1994 Ariz: 16 G; Rush 1-1 1.0; Rec 8-57 7.1; KR 1-6 6.0. **1995** Ariz: 4 G; Rec 2-19 9.5. **Total:** 20 G; Rush 1-1 1.0; Rec 10-76 7.6; KR 1-6 6.0.

CARL SAMUELSON Samuelson, Carl Clinton 6'4", 250 **DT-OT**
Col: Nebraska *HS:* Grand Island [ME] B: 4/11/1923, Grand Island, NE
D: 8/17/1995, Lincoln, NE *Drafted:* 1947 Round 8 LARm
1948 Pit: 11 G; Int 1-33. **1949** Pit: 12 G; Scor **1** Saf; **1** Fum TD; 8 Pt. **1950** Pit: 8 G. **1951** Pit: 12 G; 1 Fum. **Total:** 43 G; Int 1-33; Scor 1 Saf; 1 Fum TD; 8 Pt; 1 Fum.

WILLIAM SANBORN Sanborn, William **E**
Col: No College B: 1899 Deceased
1921 Ton: 1 G.

LUPE SANCHEZ Sanchez, Guadalupe Ledezma 5'10", 193 **DB**
Col: UCLA *HS:* Mount Whitney [Visalia, CA] B: 10/28/1961, Tulane, CA
Drafted: 1984 Supplemental Round 2 KC
1986 Pit: Int 3-71 1 TD. **1988** Pit: PR 2-11 5.5; Int 1-0. **Total:** PR 2-11 5.5; Int 4-71 1 TD.

Year Team	G	Kickoff Returns Ret	Yds	Avg	TD	Fum
1986 Pit	11	25	591	23.6	0	2
1987 Pit	12	6	116	19.3	0	1
1988 Pit	16	4	71	17.8	0	0
NFL Total	39	35	778	22.2	0	3

JOHN SANCHEZ Sanchez, John Claude 6'3", 239 **OT-DT**
Col: Los Angeles City Coll. CA (J.C.); Redlands; San Francisco *HS:* San Diego [CA] B: 10/12/1920, Los Angeles, CA D: 9/11/1992, Hayward, CA *Drafted:* 1944 Round 9 NYG

NFL **1947** ChiA-Det-Was: 7 G; Int 1-0. Det: 3 G. Was: 4 G; Int 1-0. **1948** Was: 12 G. **1949** Was-NYG: 10 G. Was: 2 G. NYG: 8 G. **1950** NYG: 12 G. **Total:** 41 G; Int 1-0.

ARTIE SANDBERG Sandberg, Arthur W 192 **BB-WB**
(Swede; Carl) *Col:* No College B: 9/13/1899, MN D: 7/2/1983, Elbow Lake, MN
1926 LA: 5 G. **1929** Min: 3 G. **Total:** 8 G.

SANDY SANDBERG Sandberg, Sigurd E 6'2", 228 **T**
Col: Iowa Wesleyan *HS:* Eddyville [IA] B: 6/14/1910, Eddyville, IA
D: 4/10/1989, St.Louis, MO
1934 StL: 3 G. **1935** Pit: 11 G. **1936** Pit: 12 G. **1937** Pit-Bkn: 10 G. Pit: 7 G. Bkn: 3 G. **Total:** 36 G.

DICK SANDEFUR Sandefur, Wayne Thomas 5'10", 195 **FB-LB-DB**
Col: Purdue *HS:* Memorial [Evansville, IN] B: 8/1/1912, Evansville, IN
Drafted: 1936 Round 5 Pit
1936 Pit: 8 G; Rush 7-13 1.9. **1937** Pit: 1 G. **Total:** 9 G; Rush 7-13 1.9.

BILL SANDEMAN Sandeman, William Stewart 6'6", 252 **OT-DT**
(Sandy) *Col:* San Joaquin Delta Coll. CA (J.C.); U. of Pacific
HS: Lincoln [Stockton, CA] B: 11/30/1942, Providence, RI
1966 Dal: 8 G. **1967** NO-Atl: 13 G; KR 1-0. NO: 2 G. Atl: 11 G; KR 1-0. **1968** Atl: 4 G. **1969** Atl: 13 G. **1970** Atl: 6 G. **1971** Atl: 14 G. **1972** Atl: 14 G. **1973** Atl: 12 G. **Total:** 84 G; KR 1-0.

MARK SANDER Sander, Mark Leonard 6'2", 232 **LB**
Col: Louisville *HS:* DeSales [Louisville, KY] B: 3/21/1968, Louisville, KY
1992 Mia: 12 G.

BARRY SANDERS Sanders, Barry David 5'8", 203 **RB**
Col: Oklahoma State *HS:* North [Wichita, KS] B: 7/16/1968, Wichita, KS *Drafted:* 1989 Round 1 Det
1989 Det: KR 5-118 23.6. **1992** Det: Pass 1-0. **1995** Det: Pass 2-1 50.0%, 11 5.50. **1996** Det: Pass 1-0, 1 Int. **Total:** Pass 4-1 25.0%, 11 2.75 1 Int; KR 5-118 23.6.

Year Team	G	Rushing Att	Yds	Avg	TD	Receiving Rec	Yds	Avg	TD	Fum	Tot TD
1989 Det	15	280	1470	5.3	14	24	282	11.8	0	10	14
1990 Det	16	255	**1304**	5.1	13	36	480	13.3	3	4	**16**
1991 Det	15	342	1548	4.5	**16**	41	307	7.5	1	5	**17**
1992 Det	16	312	1352	4.3	9	29	225	7.8	1	6	10
1993 Det	11	243	1115	4.6	3	36	205	5.7	0	3	3
1994 Det	16	331	**1883**	**5.7**	7	44	283	6.4	1	0	8
1995 Det	16	314	1500	4.8	11	48	398	8.3	1	3	12
1996 Det	16	307	**1553**	5.1	11	24	147	6.1	0	4	11
1997 Det	16	335	**2053**	6.1	11	33	305	9.2	3	3	14
1998 Det	16	343	1491	4.3	4	37	289	7.8	0	3	4
NFL Total	153	3062	15269	5.0	99	352	2921	8.3	10	41	109

BRANDON SANDERS Sanders, Brandon Christopher 5'9", 185 **DB**
Col: Arizona *HS:* Helix [La Mesa, CA] B: 6/10/1973, San Diego, CA
1997 NYG: 12 G. **1998** NYG: 13 G. **Total:** 25 G.

CHARLIE SANDERS Sanders, Charles Alvin 6'4", 225 **TE**
Col: Minnesota *HS:* James B. Dudley [Greensboro, NC] B: 8/25/1946, Richlands, NC *Drafted:* 1968 Round 3 Det
1968 Det: Rush 2-3 1.5. **1969** Det: Rush 1-(-8) -8.0. **1973** Det: Rush 1-(-1) -1.0. **Total:** Rush 4-(-6) -1.5.

Year Team	G	Receiving Rec	Yds	Avg	TD	Fum
1968 Det	14	40	533	13.3	1	2
1969 Det	14	42	656	15.6	3	0
1970 Det	14	40	544	13.6	6	0
1971 Det	13	31	502	16.2	5	0
1972 Det	9	27	416	15.4	2	1
1973 Det	14	28	433	15.5	2	1
1974 Det	14	42	532	12.7	3	1
1975 Det	13	37	486	13.1	3	1
1976 Det	13	35	545	15.6	5	0
1977 Det	10	14	170	12.1	1	0
NFL Total	128	336	4817	14.3	31	6

CHUCK SANDERS Sanders, Charles Samuel 6'1", 233 **RB**
Col: Slippery Rock *HS:* Penn Hills [Pittsburgh, PA] B: 4/24/1964, Pittsburgh, PA *Drafted:* 1986 Round 11 SD
1986 Pit: 14 G; Rush 4-12 3.0; Rec 2-19 9.5; KR 8-148 18.5. **1987** Pit: 5 G; Rush 11-65 5.9 1 TD; Rec 1-11 11.0; 6 Pt. **Total:** 19 G; Rush 15-77 5.1 1 TD; Rec 3-30 10.0; KR 8-148 18.5; 6 Pt.

CHRIS SANDERS Sanders, Christopher 6'2", 217 **WR**
(Aggie) *Col:* Texas A&M *HS:* Lyndon B. Johnson [Austin, TX]
B: 4/22/1973
1997 Was: 1 G.

CHRIS SANDERS Sanders, Christopher Dwayne 6'1", 188 **WR**
(Tippy Toes) *Col:* Ohio State *HS:* Montbello [Denver, CO]
B: 5/8/1972, Denver, CO *Drafted:* 1995 Round 3 Hou
1995 Hou: Rush 2-(-19) -9.5. **1997** Ten: Rush 1-(-8) -8.0. **1998** Ten: Rush 1-(-9) -9.0. **Total:** Rush 4-(-36) -9.0.

Year Team	G	Receiving Rec	Yds	Avg	TD	Fum
1995 Hou	16	35	823	**23.5**	9	0
1996 Hou	16	48	882	18.4	4	0
1997 Ten	15	31	498	16.1	3	1
1998 Ten	14	5	136	27.2	0	1
NFL Total	61	119	2339	19.7	16	2

CLARENCE SANDERS Sanders, Clarence 6'4", 228 **LB**
Col: Cincinnati *HS:* George Washington Carver [Montgomery, AL]
B: 12/28/1952, Montgomery, AL *Drafted:* 1976 Round 17 SD
1978 KC: 16 G; PR 1-5 5.0; KR 2-15 7.5. **1980** KC: 1 G. **Total:** 17 G; PR 1-5 5.0; KR 2-15 7.5.

DARYL SANDERS Sanders, Daryl Theodore 6'5", 250 **OT**
Col: Ohio State *HS:* Mayfield [OH] B: 4/24/1941, Canton, OH
Drafted: 1963 Round 1 Det
1963 Det: 14 G. **1964** Det: 14 G. **1965** Det: 14 G; Rush 1-2 2.0. **1966** Det: 14 G. **Total:** 56 G; Rush 1-2 2.0.

DEION SANDERS Sanders, Deion Luwynn 6′1″, 195 **DB-WR**
(Neon; Prime Time) *Col:* Florida State *HS:* North Fort Myers [FL]
B: 8/9/1967, Fort Myers, FL *Drafted:* 1989 Round 1 Atl
1991 Atl: 1 Sac. **1992** Atl: Rush 1-(-4) -4.0. **1993** Atl: Pass 1-0. **1995** Dal: Rush 2-9 4.5. **1996** Dal: Rush 3-2 0.7; **1** Fum TD. **1997** Dal: Rush 1-(-11) -11.0. **Total:** Pass 1-0; Rush 7-(-4) -0.6; 1 Fum TD; 1 Sac.

		Receiving				Punt Returns			
Year Team	G	Rec	Yds	Avg	TD	Ret	Yds	Avg	TD
1989 Atl	15	1	-8	-8.0	0	28	307	11.0	**1**
1990 Atl	16	0	0	—	0	29	250	8.6	**1**
1991 Atl	15	1	17	17.0	0	21	170	8.1	0
1992 Atl	13	3	45	15.0	1	13	41	3.2	0
1993 Atl	11	6	106	17.7	1	2	21	10.5	0
1994 SF	14	0	0	—	0	0	0	—	0
1995 Dal	9	2	25	12.5	0	1	54	54.0	0
1996 Dal	16	36	475	13.2	1	1	4	4.0	0
1997 Dal	13	0	0	—	0	33	407	12.3	1
1998 Dal	11	7	100	14.3	0	24	375	**15.6**	**2**
NFL Total	133	56	760	13.6	3	152	1629	10.7	5

	Kickoff Returns				Interceptions				Tot
Year Team	Ret	Yds	Avg	TD	Int	Yds	TD	Fum	TD
1989 Atl	35	725	20.7	0	5	52	0	2	1
1990 Atl	39	851	21.8	0	3	153	2	4	3
1991 Atl	26	576	22.2	**1**	6	119	1	1	2
1992 Atl	40	**1067**	26.7	**2**	3	105	0	3	3
1993 Atl	7	169	24.1	0	7	91	0	0	1
1994 SF	0	0	—	0	6	**303**	**3**	0	3
1995 Dal	1	15	15.0	0	2	34	0	0	0
1996 Dal	0	0	—	0	2	3	0	2	2
1997 Dal	1	18	18.0	0	2	81	1	1	2
1998 Dal	1	16	16.0	0	5	153	1	1	3
NFL Total	150	3437	22.9	3	41	1094	8	14	20

ERIC SANDERS Sanders, Eric Downer 6′6″, 277 **OT-OG-C**
Col: Nevada-Reno *HS:* Earl Wooster [Reno, NV] B: 10/22/1958, Reno, NV *Drafted:* 1981 Round 5 Atl
1981 Atl: 16 G. **1982** Atl: 9 G. **1983** Atl: 16 G. **1984** Atl: 10 G. **1985** Atl: 16 G; 1 Fum. **1986** Atl-Det: 11 G. Atl: 8 G. Det: 3 G. **1987** Det: 12 G. **1988** Det: 16 G; 1 Fum. **1989** Det: 16 G. **1990** Det: 16 G. **1991** Det: 14 G. **1992** Det: 6 G. **Total:** 158 G; 2 Fum.

GENE SANDERS Sanders, Eugene 6′3″, 273 **OT-OG-DE-NT**
Col: Washington; Texas A&M *HS:* West Jefferson [Harvey, LA]
B: 11/10/1956, New Orleans, LA *Drafted:* 1979 Round 8 TB
1979 TB: 16 G. **1980** TB: 11 G. **1981** TB: 16 G. **1982** TB: 4 G. **1983** TB: 12 G. **1984** TB: 16 G. **1985** TB: 2 G. **Total:** 77 G.

FRANK SANDERS Sanders, Frank Vondel 6′2″, 201 **WR**
Col: Auburn *HS:* Dillard [Fort Lauderdale, FL] B: 2/17/1973, Fort Lauderdale, FL *Drafted:* 1995 Round 2 Ariz
1995 Ariz: Rush 1-1 1.0; Scor 2 2XP. **1996** Ariz: Rush 2-(-4) -2.0. **1997** Ariz: Pass 1-1 100.0%, 26 26.00; Rush 1-5 5.0; Scor 1 2XP. **1998** Ariz: Rush 4-0. **Total:** Pass 1-1 100.0%, 26 26.00; Rush 8-2 0.3; Scor 3 2XP.

		Receiving				
Year Team	G	Rec	Yds	Avg	TD	Fum
1995 Ariz	16	52	883	17.0	2	0
1996 Ariz	16	69	813	11.8	4	1
1997 Ariz	16	75	1017	13.6	4	3
1998 Ariz	16	89	1145	12.9	3	3
NFL Total	64	285	3858	13.5	13	7

GLENELL SANDERS Sanders, Glenell 6′1″, 228 **LB**
Col: Louisiana Tech *HS:* Clinton [LA] B: 11/4/1966, New Orleans, LA
1990 ChiB: 2 G. **1991** LARm: 16 G; KR 1-2 2.0. **1994** Den: 1 G. **1995** Ind: 9 G. **Total:** 28 G; KR 1-2 2.0.

JACK SANDERS Sanders, Jack 6′0″, 219 **G-LB**
(Bull; Hoss) *Col:* Southern Methodist *HS:* Rockport [TX]
B: 3/11/1917, San Antonio, TX D: 10/26/1991, Aransas Pass, TX
Drafted: 1939 Round 15 NYG
1940 Pit: 10 G. **1941** Pit: 11 G; KR 1-8 8.0; Scor 5, 5-5 100.0% XK. **1942** Pit: 9 G; Int 1-8; Scor 7, 7-8 87.5% XK. **1945** Phi: 3 G. **Total:** 33 G; KR 1-8 8.0; Int 1-8; Scor 12, 12-13 92.3% XK.

DEAC SANDERS Sanders, John Maurice 6′1″, 175 **DB**
Col: South Dakota *HS:* Sunshine Bible Academy [Miller, SD]
B: 1/11/1950, Chicago, IL

		Interceptions			
Year Team	G	Int	Yds	TD	Fum
1974 NE	14	5	57	1	0
1975 NE	14	1	18	0	0
1976 NE	2	0	0	0	0
1977 Phi	14	6	122	0	0
1978 Phi	15	5	43	1	2
1979 Phi	1	0	0	0	0
NFL Total	60	17	240	2	2

JOE SANDERS Sanders, Joseph 5′10″, 250 **G-OE**
Col: No College *HS:* Central [Evansville, IN] B: 5/26/1901, Evansville, IN D: 4/1979, Smithfield, NC
1922 Eva: 2 G.

KEN SANDERS Sanders, Kenneth Roy 6′5″, 240 **DE**
Col: Howard Payne *HS:* Valley Mills [TX] B: 8/22/1950, Valley Mills, TX
Drafted: 1972 Round 3 Det
1972 Det: 6 G. **1973** Det: 14 G. **1974** Det: 14 G. **1975** Det: 14 G. **1976** Det: 14 G. **1977** Det: 11 G. **1978** Det: 7 G. **1979** Det: 5 G. **1980** Min: 6 G. **1981** Min: 9 G. **Total:** 100 G.

LONNIE SANDERS Sanders, Lonnie J Jr. 6′3″, 207 **DB**
Col: Michigan State *HS:* Pershing [Detroit, MI] B: 11/6/1941, Detroit, MI *Drafted:* 1963 Round 2 Was

		Interceptions		
Year Team	G	Int	Yds	TD
1963 Was	14	3	46	0
1964 Was	14	2	4	0
1965 Was	7	4	121	0
1966 Was	9	0	0	0
1967 Was	13	0	0	0
1968 StL	13	3	6	0
1969 StL	1	0	0	0
NFL Total	71	12	177	0

SPEC SANDERS Sanders, Orban Eugene 6′1″, 196 **TB-DB-WB-HB**
Col: Cameron; Texas *HS:* Temple [OK] B: 1/26/1919, Temple, OK
Drafted: 1942 Round 1 Was
AAFC **1946** NY-A: Rec 17-259 15.2 3 TD; Int 2-71 1 TD. **1947** NY-A: Rec 1-13 13.0; Int 3-63. **1948** NY-A: Int 1-24. **Total:** Rec 18-272 15.1 3 TD; Int 6-158 1 TD.

		Passing							
Year Team	G	Att	Comp	Comp%	Yds	YPA	TD	Int	Rating
1946 NY-A	13	79	33	41.8	411	5.20	4	9	35.9
1947 NY-A	14	171	93	54.4	1442	8.43	14	17	70.2
1948 NY-A	13	168	78	46.4	918	5.46	5	11	46.2
AAFC Total	40	418	204	48.8	2771	6.63	23	37	51.8

	Rushing				Punt Returns			
Year Team	Att	Yds	Avg	TD	Ret	Yds	Avg	TD
1946 NY-A	140	709	5.1	6	17	257	15.1	1
1947 NY-A	231	1432	6.2	18	6	164	27.3	0
1948 NY-A	169	759	4.5	9	13	128	9.8	0
AAFC Total	540	2900	5.4	33	36	549	15.3	1

	Kickoff Returns				Punting			Tot
Year Team	Ret	Yds	Avg	TD	Punts	Yds	Avg	TD
1946 NY-A	13	395	30.4	1	33	1208	36.6	12
1947 NY-A	22	593	27.0	1	46	1938	42.1	19
1948 NY-A	9	217	24.1	0	42	1707	40.6	9
AAFC Total	44	1205	27.4	2	121	4853	40.1	40

NFL **1950** NYY: Pass 3-2 66.7%, 58 19.33; PR 6-93 15.5.

		Interceptions			Punting			
Year Team	G	Int	Yds	TD	Punts	Yds	Avg	Fum
1950 NYY	12	**13**	199	0	71	3001	42.3	1

PAUL SANDERS Sanders, Paul E 5′11″, 192 **HB-DB**
Col: Utah State *HS:* Basin [WY] B: 12/15/1918, Otto, WY
1944 Bos: 6 G; Rush 6-4 0.7; Rec 4-5 1.3.

RICKY SANDERS Sanders, Ricky Wayne 5′11″, 180 **WR-RET**
Col: Southwest Texas State *HS:* Belton [TX] B: 8/30/1962, Temple, TX
1987 Was: Rush 1-(-4) -4.0. **1988** Was: Rush 2-14 7.0. **1989** Was: Pass 1-1 100.0%, 32 32.00; Rush 4-19 4.8; PR 2-12 6.0. **1990** Was: Rush 4-17 4.3. **1991** Was: Rush 7-47 6.7 1 TD. **1992** Was: Rush 4-(-6) -1.5. **1993** Was: Rush 1-7 7.0. **Total:** Pass 1-1 100.0%, 32 32.00; Rush 23-94 4.1 1 TD; PR 2-12 6.0.

		Receiving				Kickoff Returns					Tot
Year Team	G	Rec	Yds	Avg	TD	Ret	Yds	Avg	TD	Fum	TD
1986 Was	10	14	286	20.4	2	0	0	—	0	0	2
1987 Was	12	37	630	17.0	3	4	118	29.5	0	0	3
1988 Was	16	73	1148	15.7	12	19	362	19.1	0	0	12
1989 Was	16	80	1138	14.2	4	9	134	14.9	0	0	4
1990 Was	16	56	727	13.0	3	1	22	22.0	0	0	3
1991 Was	16	45	580	12.9	5	0	0	—	0	0	6
1992 Was	15	51	707	13.9	3	0	0	—	0	0	3
1993 Was	16	58	638	11.0	4	0	0	—	0	1	4
1994 Atl	14	67	599	8.9	1	0	0	—	0	0	1
1995 Atl	3	2	24	12.0	0	0	0	—	0	0	0
NFL Total	134	483	6477	13.4	37	33	636	19.3	0	1	38

BOB SANDERS Sanders, Robert Joe 6′3″, 235 **LB**
Col: North Texas *HS:* Van [TX] B: 6/9/1943, Dallas, TX *Drafted:* 1966 Round 9 Atl
1967 Atl: 9 G.

THOMAS SANDERS Sanders, Thomas Derrick 5′11″, 203 **RB**
Col: Texas A&M *HS:* Giddings [TX] B: 1/4/1962, Giddings, TX
Drafted: 1985 Round 9 ChiB

		Rushing				Receiving			
Year Team	G	Att	Yds	Avg	TD	Rec	Yds	Avg	TD
1985 ChiB	15	25	104	4.2	1	1	9	9.0	0
1986 ChiB	16	27	224	8.3	5	2	18	9.0	0
1987 ChiB	12	23	122	5.3	1	3	53	17.7	0
1988 ChiB	16	95	332	3.5	3	9	94	10.4	0
1989 ChiB	16	41	127	3.1	0	3	28	9.3	1
1990 Phi	10	56	208	3.7	1	2	20	10.0	0
1991 Phi	5	54	122	2.3	1	8	62	7.8	0
NFL Total	90	321	1239	3.9	12	28	284	10.1	1

	Kickoff Returns					Tot
Year Team	Ret	Yds	Avg	TD	Fum	TD
1985 ChiB	1	10	10.0	0	1	1
1986 ChiB	22	399	18.1	0	2	5
1987 ChiB	20	349	17.5	0	1	1
1988 ChiB	13	248	19.1	0	5	3
1989 ChiB	23	491	21.3	**1**	2	2
1990 Phi	15	299	19.9	0	0	1
1991 Phi	10	160	16.0	0	2	1
NFL Total	104	1956	18.8	1	13	14

REGGIE SANDERSON Sanderson, Reginald John 5′10″, 206 **RB**
Col: Stanford *HS:* St. Francis [La Canada, CA] B: 11/4/1950, Galveston, TX
1973 ChiB: 2 G; Rush 3-8 2.7; Rec 5-23 4.6; KR 2-44 22.0.

SCOTT SANDERSON Sanderson, Scott Michael 6′6″, 295 **OT**
Col: Washington State *HS:* Clayton Valley [Concord, CA]
B: 7/25/1974, Walnut Creek, CA *Drafted:* 1997 Round 3 Ten
1997 Ten: 10 G. **1998** Ten: 16 G. **Total:** 26 G.

TODD SANDHAM Sandham, Todd 6′3″, 255 **OG**
Col: Northeastern B: 12/3/1963
1987 NE: 2 G.

DAN SANDIFER Sandifer, Daniel Padgett 6′1″, 190 **DB-HB**
Col: Louisiana State *HS:* C.E. Byrd [Shreveport, LA] B: 3/1/1927, Shreveport, LA D: 8/15/1987, Shreveport, LA *Drafted:* 1948 Round 3 Was

		Rushing				Receiving			
Year Team	G	Att	Yds	Avg	TD	Rec	Yds	Avg	TD
1948 Was	12	18	67	3.7	0	9	181	20.1	1
1949 Was	12	20	64	3.2	0	19	293	15.4	3
1950 Det-SF-Phi	12	1	3	3.0	0	0	0	—	0
1950 Det	5	1	3	3.0	0	0	0	—	0
1950 SF	2	0	0	—	0	0	0	—	0
1950 Phi	5	0	0	—	0	0	0	—	0
1951 Phi	12	35	113	3.2	1	2	36	18.0	1
1952 GB	12	0	0	—	0	0	0	—	0
1953 ChiC-GB	4	0	0	—	0	0	0	—	0
1953 ChiC	3	0	0	—	0	0	0	—	0
1953 GB	1	0	0	—	0	0	0	—	0
NFL Total	64	74	247	3.3	1	30	510	17.0	5

	Punt Returns				Kickoff Returns			
Year Team	Ret	Yds	Avg	TD	Ret	Yds	Avg	TD
1948 Was	20	236	11.8	0	**26**	**594**	22.8	**1**
1949 Was	18	199	11.1	0	**24**	518	21.6	0
1950 Det-SF-Phi	15	155	10.3	0	5	108	21.6	0
1950 SF	0	0	—	0	1	19	19.0	0
1950 Phi	15	155	10.3	0	4	89	22.3	0
1951 Phi	14	137	9.8	0	8	147	18.4	0
1952 GB	2	5	2.5	0	0	0	—	0
1953 ChiC-GB	3	35	11.7	0	0	0	—	0
1953 GB	3	35	11.7	0	0	0	—	0
NFL Total	72	767	10.7	0	63	1367	21.7	1

	Interceptions				Tot
Year Team	Int	Yds	TD	Fum	TD
1948 Was	**13**	**258**	**2**	3	4
1949 Was	5	82	0	6	3
1950 Det-SF-Phi	2	27	0	2	0
1950 Det	2	27	0	0	0
1950 Phi	0	0	0	2	0
1951 Phi	1	28	0	3	2
1952 GB	2	25	0	0	0
NFL Total	23	420	2	14	9

BILL SANDIFER Sandifer, William Patrick 6′6″, 278 **DT-DE**
Col: Mira Costa Coll. CA (J.C.); UCLA *HS:* Oceanside [CA]
B: 1/5/1952, Quantico, VA *Drafted:* 1974 Round 1 SF
1974 SF: 4 G. **1975** SF: 13 G. **1976** SF: 13 G. **1977** Sea: 1 G. **1978** Sea: 15 G. **Total:** 46 G.

CURT SANDIG Sandig, Curtis Walter 5′10″, 170 **HB-DB**
(Two Tone) *Col:* St. Mary's (Tex.) *HS:* Mart [TX] B: 7/12/1918, Mart, TX *Drafted:* 1942 Round 5 Pit
AAFC **1946** BufA: 9 G; Rush 22-52 2.4 1 TD; Rec 2-15 7.5; PR 2-20 10.0; KR 2-43 21.5; Punt 4-155 38.8.

NFL **1942** Pit: Pass 4-2 50.0%, 10 2.50; Rec 6-103 17.2; PR 6-142 23.7 **1** TD; KR 7-168 24.0; Int 5-94; Punt 37-1437 38.8.

		Rushing				Tot
Year Team	G	Att	Yds	Avg	TD	TD
1942 Pit	11	50	116	2.3	3	4

ALEX SANDUSKY Sandusky, Alexander Vincent 6′1″, 235 **OG**
Col: Clarion *HS:* Sto-Rox [McKees Rocks, PA] B: 8/17/1932, McKees Rocks, PA *Drafted:* 1954 Round 16 Bal
1954 Bal: 12 G. **1955** Bal: 12 G. **1956** Bal: 11 G; KR 1-24 24.0. **1957** Bal: 12 G. **1958** Bal: 12 G. **1959** Bal: 12 G. **1960** Bal: 12 G. **1961** Bal: 14 G. **1962** Bal: 13 G. **1963** Bal: 14 G. **1964** Bal: 14 G. **1965** Bal: 14 G. **1966** Bal: 14 G. **Total:** 166 G; KR 1-24 24.0.

JOHN SANDUSKY Sandusky, John Thomas 6′1″, 251 **OT-DT**
Col: Villanova *HS:* South Philadelphia [Philadelphia, PA]
B: 12/28/1925, Philadelphia, PA *Drafted:* 1950 Round 2 Cle
1950 Cle: 12 G. **1951** Cle: 11 G. **1952** Cle: 11 G. **1953** Cle: 12 G. **1954** Cle: 12 G. **1955** Cle: 12 G. **1956** GB: 12 G. **Total:** 82 G.

MIKE SANDUSKY Sandusky, Michael George 6′0″, 231 **OG**
Col: Maryland *HS:* Bound Brook [NJ] B: 3/14/1935, NJ *Drafted:* 1957 Round 4 SF
1957 Pit: 12 G. **1958** Pit: 12 G. **1959** Pit: 11 G. **1960** Pit: 12 G. **1961** Pit: 12 G. **1962** Pit: 14 G; KR 1-0. **1963** Pit: 13 G. **1964** Pit: 6 G. **1965** Pit: 12 G. **Total:** 104 G; KR 1-0.

SANDY SANFORD Sanford, Hayward Allen 6′1″, 210 **OE-DE**
Col: Arkansas Tech; Alabama *HS:* Adona [AR] B: 6/15/1916, Plainview, AR *Drafted:* 1940 Round 13 Was
1940 Was: 7 G; Rec 1-13 13.0; Scor 3, 0-2 FG, 3-5 60.0% XK.

JIM SANFORD Sanford, James Leo 5′8″, 195 **T**
Col: Lehigh *HS:* Mercersburg Acad. [PA] B: 12/25/1898, Brooklyn, NY D: 4/7/1938, New Brunswick, NJ
1924 Dul: 1 G.

LUCIUS SANFORD Sanford, Lucius Martin Jr. 6′2″, 216 **LB**
Col: Georgia Tech *HS:* West Fulton [Atlanta, GA] B: 2/14/1956, Milledgeville, GA *Drafted:* 1978 Round 4 Buf
1978 Buf: 16 G; Int 1-41. **1979** Buf: 16 G; Int 2-44; 6 Pt. **1980** Buf: 16 G; 6 Pt. **1981** Buf: 16 G. **1982** Buf: 9 G. **1983** Buf: 16 G; Int 2-39. **1984** Buf: 8 G; **1** Fum TD; 6 Pt. **1985** Buf: 11 G; 2 Sac. **1986** Buf: 10 G; 1 Sac. **1987** Cle: 11 G. **Total:** 129 G; Int 5-124; 1 Fum TD; Tot TD 3; 18 Pt; 3 Sac.

LEO SANFORD Sanford, Ottis Leo 6′1″, 224 **LB**
Col: Louisiana Tech *HS:* Fair Park [Shreveport, LA] B: 10/4/1929, Dallas, TX *Drafted:* 1951 Round 8 ChiC
1956 ChiC: PR 1-6 6.0. **Total:** PR 1-6 6.0.

		Interceptions		
Year Team	G	Int	Yds	TD
1951 ChiC	12	1	20	0
1952 ChiC	12	2	5	0
1953 ChiC	12	2	56	**1**
1954 ChiC	12	2	2	0
1955 ChiC	12	3	97	1
1956 ChiC	12	5	24	0
1957 ChiC	12	1	2	0
1958 Bal	9	1	7	0
NFL Total	93	17	213	2

RICK SANFORD Sanford, Richard Francis 6′1″, 192 **DB**
Col: South Carolina *HS:* Northwestern [Rock Hill, SC] B: 1/9/1957, Rock Hill, SC *Drafted:* 1979 Round 1 NE
1979 NE: PR 1-1 1.0; KR 10-179 17.9. **1980** NE: **1** Fum TD. **1981** NE: KR 4-82 20.5. **1983** NE: PR 1-0. **Total:** PR 2-1 0.5; KR 14-261 18.6; 1 Fum TD.

		Interceptions				Tot
Year Team	G	Int	Yds	TD	Fum	TD
1979 NE	16	1	39	0	0	1
1980 NE	16	1	0	0	0	1
1981 NE	16	3	28	0	0	0
1982 NE	9	2	105	**1**	0	1
1983 NE	16	7	24	0	1	0

1984 NE	16	2	2	0	0	0
1985 Sea	5	0	0	0	0	0
NFL Total	94	16	198	1	1	3

OLLIE SANSEN Sansen, Oliver Marsten 6′1″, 193 **DB-WB-HB-FB**
Col: Iowa *HS:* Alta [IA] B: 3/6/1908, Alta, IA D: 3/21/1987, San Lorenzo, CA
1932 Bkn: Rec 2-45 22.5. **1934** Bkn: Rec 6-22 3.7. **1935** Bkn: Rec 1-3 3.0. **Total:** Rec 9-70 7.8.

		Rushing			
Year Team	**G**	**Att**	**Yds**	**Avg**	**TD**
1932 Bkn	10	44	148	3.4	1
1933 Bkn	10	12	29	2.4	1
1934 Bkn	11	17	79	4.6	0
1935 Bkn	10	3	3	1.0	0
NFL Total	41	76	259	3.4	2

O.J. SANTIAGO Santiago, Otis Jason 6′7″, 267 **TE**
Col: Kent State *HS:* St. Mitchael's [Toronto, Canada] B: 4/4/1974, Whitby, Canada *Drafted:* 1997 Round 3 Atl

		Receiving				
Year Team	**G**	**Rec**	**Yds**	**Avg**	**TD**	**Fum**
1997 Atl	11	17	217	12.8	2	1
1998 Atl	16	27	428	15.9	5	1
NFL Total	27	44	645	14.7	7	2

JOSEPH SANTONE Santone, Joseph 180 **G**
(AKA Scanlon) *Col:* No College B: 10/1/1893, Campobasso, Italy D: 10/27/1963, Hartford, CT
1926 Har: 2 G.

FRANK SANTORA Santora, Frank 5′10″, 166 **DB-QB**
Col: No College *HS:* Garfield [NJ] B: 5/22/1926, Garfield, NJ
1944 Bos: 1 G; KR 1-27 27.0.

MICKEY SANZOTTA Sanzotta, Dominic Franklin 5′9″, 188 **WB-DB-TB**
Col: Case Western Reserve *HS:* Geneva [OH] B: 4/28/1921, Geneva, OH D: 1/21/1999, Geneva, OH *Drafted:* 1942 Round 4 Det
1942 Det: Pass 15-4 26.7%, 45 3.00; Rec 5-16 3.2; PR 5-46 9.2; Int 2-16; Punt 1-42 42.0. **1946** Det: Pass 1-0; Rec 2-19 9.5; PR 2-41 20.5; KR 2-40 20.0. **Total:** Pass 16-4 25.0%, 45 2.81; Rec 7-35 5.0; PR 7-87 12.4; KR 2-40 20.0; Int 2-16; Punt 1-42 42.0.

		Rushing				
Year Team	**G**	**Att**	**Yds**	**Avg**	**TD**	**Fum**
1942 Det	10	71	268	3.8	0	0
1946 Det	10	6	72	12.0	0	1
NFL Total	20	77	340	4.4	0	1

RICK SAPIENZA Sapienza, Americo 5′11″, 185 **DB-HB**
Col: Villanova *HS:* Everett [MA] B: 2/8/1936, Boston, MA
1960 NYT: 2 G; Rec 1-4 4.0; Punt 8-299 37.4; 1 Fum.

JESSE SAPOLU Sapolu, Manase Jesse 6′4″, 271 **OG**
Col: Hawaii *HS:* Farrington [Honolulu, HI] B: 3/10/1961, Laie, Western Samoa *Drafted:* 1983 Round 11 SF
1983 SF: 16 G. **1984** SF: 1 G. **1987** SF: 12 G. **1988** SF: 16 G. **1989** SF: 16 G. **1990** SF: 16 G. **1991** SF: 16 G. **1992** SF: 16 G. **1993** SF: 16 G. **1994** SF: 13 G. **1995** SF: 16 G. **1996** SF: 16 G. **1997** SF: 12 G. **Total:** 182 G.

PATRICK SAPP Sapp, Patrick Zolley 6′4″, 258 **LB**
Col: Clemson *HS:* William M. Raines [Jacksonville, FL] B: 5/11/1973, Jacksonville, FL *Drafted:* 1996 Round 2 SD
1996 SD: 16 G. **1997** SD: 16 G. **1998** Ariz: 16 G; 1 Sac. **Total:** 48 G; 1 Sac.

BOB SAPP Sapp, Robert Malcom Jr. 6′4″, 319 **OG**
Col: Washington *HS:* General William Mitchell [Colorado Springs, CO] B: 9/22/1973, Colorado Springs, CO *Drafted:* 1997 Round 3 ChiB
1997 Min: 1 G.

THERON SAPP Sapp, Theron Coleman 6′1″, 203 **HB-FB**
Col: Georgia *HS:* Lanier [Macon, GA] B: 6/15/1935, Macon, GA *Drafted:* 1958 Round 10 Phi
1959 Phi: Rec 6-47 7.8. **1960** Phi: Rec 2-20 10.0. **1961** Phi: Rec 3-10 3.3. **1962** Phi: Rec 6-80 13.3. **1963** Phi-Pit: Rec 4-36 9.0; KR 5-58 11.6. Phi: Rec 1-(-5) -5.0; KR 3-40 13.3. Pit: Rec 3-41 13.7; KR 2-18 9.0. **1964** Pit: Rec 1-44 44.0; KR 4-43 10.8. **1965** Pit: Rec 1-10 10.0; KR 5-77 15.4. **Total:** Rec 23-247 10.7; KR 14-178 12.7.

		Rushing				
Year Team	**G**	**Att**	**Yds**	**Avg**	**TD**	**Fum**
1959 Phi	12	41	145	3.5	1	0
1960 Phi	5	9	20	2.2	0	0
1961 Phi	14	7	24	3.4	1	1
1962 Phi	12	23	53	2.3	2	1
1963 Phi-Pit	14	104	452	4.3	1	4
1963 Phi	4	8	21	2.6	0	1
1963 Pit	10	96	431	4.5	1	3
1964 Pit	11	4	15	3.8	0	1
1965 Pit	14	14	54	3.9	0	0
NFL Total	82	202	763	3.8	5	7

WARREN SAPP Sapp, Warren Carlos 6′2″, 281 **DT**
Col: Miami (Fla.) *HS:* Apopka [FL] B: 12/19/1972, Orlando, FL *Drafted:* 1995 Round 1 TB
1995 TB: 16 G; Int 1-5 1 TD; 6 Pt; 3 Sac. **1996** TB: 15 G; 9 Sac. **1997** TB: 15 G; 10.5 Sac. **1998** TB: 16 G; 7 Sac. **Total:** 62 G; Int 1-5 1 TD; 6 Pt; 29.5 Sac.

AL SARAFINY Sarafiny, Albert Joseph 5′11″, 235 **C-LB**
Col: St. Edward's *HS:* Stambaugh [MI] B: 9/2/1906, Caspian, MI D: 2/1981, Chicago, IL
1933 GB: 7 G.

TONY SARAUSKY Sarausky, Anthony Olgird 5′11″, 201 **TB-DB-QB-FB**
(Big T) *Col:* Fordham *HS:* Rindge Tech [Cambridge, MA] B: 4/7/1913, Cambridge, MA D: 6/21/1990, Littleton, NH
1935 NYG: Rec 1-17 17.0; Scor 7, 1 XK. **1936** NYG: Scor 10, 1 FG, 1 XK. **Total:** Rec 1-17 17.0; Scor 17, 1 FG, 2 XK.

		Passing							
Year Team	**G**	**Att**	**Comp**	**Comp%**	**Yds**	**YPA**	**TD**	**Int**	**Rating**
1935 NYG	8	9	3	33.3	21	2.33	0	2	2.8
1936 NYG	11	27	6	22.2	87	3.22	2	1	49.8
1937 NYG	4	10	3	30.0	31	3.10	0	0	40.0
1938 Bkn	4	8	2	25.0	10	1.25	0	0	39.6
NFL Total	27	54	14	25.9	149	2.76	2	3	28.8

	Rushing			
Year Team	**Att**	**Yds**	**Avg**	**TD**
1935 NYG	14	39	2.8	1
1936 NYG	32	150	4.7	1
1937 NYG	4	18	4.5	0
1938 Bkn	8	42	5.3	0
NFL Total	58	249	4.3	2

PHIL SARBOE Sarboe, Philip John 5′10″, 167 **DB-BB-TB**
(AKA Philip John Sorboe) *Col:* Washington State *HS:* Lincoln [Tacoma, WA] B: 8/22/1911, Fairbanks, AK D: 11/19/1985, Spokane, WA
1935 ChiC: Rec 2-22 11.0; PR **2** TD. **1936** ChiC-Bkn: Rec 1-18 18.0. Bkn: Rec 1-18 18.0. **Total:** Rec 3-40 13.3; PR 2 TD.

		Passing							
Year Team	**G**	**Att**	**Comp**	**Comp%**	**Yds**	**YPA**	**TD**	**Int**	**Rating**
1934 Bos-ChiC	9	20	7	35.0	85	4.25	1	3	26.0
1934 Bos	5	4	2	50.0	14	3.50	0	0	58.3
1934 ChiC	4	16	5	31.3	71	4.44	1	3	27.9
1935 ChiC	12	67	31	46.3	368	5.49	0	10	23.9
1936 ChiC-Bkn	11	114	47	41.2	680	5.96	3	13	30.5
1936 ChiC	6	62	25	40.3	398	6.42	1	8	28.2
1936 Bkn	5	52	22	42.3	282	5.42	2	5	33.2
NFL Total	32	201	85	42.3	1133	5.64	4	26	27.9

	Rushing			
Year Team	**Att**	**Yds**	**Avg**	**TD**
1934 Bos-ChiC	2	11	5.5	0
1934 Bos	2	11	5.5	0
1935 ChiC	38	129	3.4	0
1936 ChiC-Bkn	83	103	1.2	0
1936 ChiC	45	21	0.5	0
1936 Bkn	38	82	2.2	0
NFL Total	123	243	2.0	0

TONY SARDISCO Sardisco, Anthony Guy 6′2″, 226 **OG-LB**
Col: Tulane *HS:* St.John's [Shreveport, LA] B: 12/5/1932, Shreveport, LA *Drafted:* 1956 Round 6 SF
1956 SF-Was: 10 G; KR 1-15 15.0. SF: 3 G. Was: 7 G; KR 1-15 15.0. **1960** Bos: 13 G. **1961** Bos: 13 G. **1962** Bos: 14 G. **Total:** 50 G; KR 1-15 15.0.

BRODERICK SARGENT Sargent, Broderick Lawrence 5′10″, 215 **RB**
Col: Baylor *HS:* Waxahachie [TX] B: 9/16/1962, Waxahachie, TX
1986 StL: Rec 1-8 8.0; KR 2-27 13.5. **1987** StL: Rec 2-19 9.5; KR 3-37 12.3. **1989** Dal: Rec 6-50 8.3; KR 1-0. **Total:** Rec 9-77 8.6; KR 6-64 10.7.

		Rushing				
Year Team	**G**	**Att**	**Yds**	**Avg**	**TD**	**Fum**
1986 StL	16	0	0	—	0	0
1987 StL	15	18	90	5.0	0	1
1989 Dal	14	20	87	4.4	1	1
NFL Total	45	38	177	4.7	1	2

KEVIN SARGENT Sargent, Kevin L 6′6″, 289 **OT**
Col: Eastern Washington *HS:* Bremerton [WA] B: 3/31/1969, Bremerton, WA
1992 Cin: 16 G. **1993** Cin: 1 G. **1994** Cin: 15 G. **1995** Cin: 15 G. **1997** Cin: 10 G. **1998** Cin: 16 G. **Total:** 73 G.

HARVEY SARK Sark, Harvey George 5′10″, 210 **G**
Col: Phillips *HS:* Bartlesville [OK]; Enid HS [OK] B: 1/30/1907, Lawrence, IN Deceased
1931 NYG: 4 G. **1934** Cin: 1 G. **Total:** 5 G.

CHARLEY SARRATT Sarratt, Charles Franklin 6′1″, 185 **QB-DB**
(Chuck) *Col:* Clemson; Oklahoma *HS:* Belton [SC] B: 10/22/1922, Greenville, SC *Drafted:* 1947 Round 10 ChiC
1948 Det: 8 G; Pass 1-1 100.0%, 48 48.00; Rush 3-3 1.0; Rec 1-3 3.0; PR 1-2 2.0; Punt 5-166 33.2.

PAUL SARRINGHAUS Sarringhaus, Paul Richard 6′0″, 185 **HB-DB**
Col: Ohio State *HS:* Hamilton [OH] B: 8/13/1920, Hamilton, OH *Drafted:* 1944 Round 7 Phi
1946 ChiC: 2 G; Rush 2-1 0.5. **1948** Det: 5 G; Rush 19-38 2.0; Rec 1-(-1) -1.0; KR 5-95 19.0. **Total:** 7 G; Rush 21-39 1.9; Rec 1-(-1) -1.0; KR 5-95 19.0.

DAN SARTIN Sartin, Daniel Mathias 6′1″, 250 **DT**
Col: Mississippi *HS:* Lumberton [MS] B: 6/23/1946, Gulfport, MS *Drafted:* 1968 Round 4 NO
1969 SD: 13 G.

MARTIN SARTIN Sartin, Martin 5′10″, 202 **RB**
Col: Coll. of the Sequoias CA (J.C.); Long Beach State *HS:* Camden [NJ] B: 3/9/1963, Philadelphia, PA
1987 SD: 3 G; Rush 19-52 2.7 1 TD; Rec 6-19 3.2; KR 5-117 23.4; 6 Pt; 2 Fum.

LARRY SARTORI Sartori, Lawrence Matthews 6′0″, 208 **G**
Col: Fordham *HS:* Sheppton [PA] B: 8/20/1917, Sheppton, PA D: 11/6/1980, Paramus, NJ
1942 Det: 10 G; Punt 1-42 42.0. **1945** Det: 1 G. **Total:** 11 G; Punt 1-42 42.0.

DON SASA Sasa, Don 6′3″, 290 **DT**
Col: Long Beach City Coll. CA (J.C.); Washington State *HS:* Long Beach Polytechnic [CA] B: 9/16/1972, American Samoa *Drafted:* 1995 Round 3 SD
1995 SD: 5 G. **1996** SD: 4 G. **1997** Was: 1 G. **1998** Car-Det: 4 G. Car: 2 G. Det: 2 G. **Total:** 14 G.

DOUG SATCHER Satcher, Douglas Kenneth 6′0″, 220 **LB**
Col: Southern Mississippi *HS:* Sandersville [MS] B: 5/28/1945, Sandersville, MS *Drafted:* 1966 Round 9 Bos
1966 Bos: 14 G. **1967** Bos: 14 G. **1968** Bos: 14 G; Int 1-1; Scor **1** Saf; 2 Pt. **Total:** 42 G; Int 1-1; Scor 1 Saf; 2 Pt.

OLLIE SATENSTEIN Satenstein, Bernard Oliver 6′0″, 213 **G-OE-DE-T**
Col: New York U. *HS:* Cushing Acad. [Ashburnham, MA] B: 1906 D: 4/30/1959, Yonkers, NY
1929 SI: 6 G. **1930** SI: 11 G. **1931** SI: 11 G. **1932** SI: 12 G. **1933** NYG: 9 G. **Total:** 49 G.

AL SATTERFIELD Satterfield, Alfred Neal 6′3″, 225 **T**
Col: Vanderbilt *HS:* Russellville [AR] B: 11/28/1921, Belleville, AR D: 10/28/1989, Little Rock, AR
AAFC **1947** SF-A: 12 G.

BRIAN SATTERFIELD Satterfield, Brian Sydney 6′0″, 225 **FB**
(Sat) *Col:* North Alabama *HS:* Fannin Co. [Blue Ridge, GA] B: 12/22/1969, Ducktown, TN
1996 GB: 1 G.

HOWARD SATTERWHITE Satterwhite, Howard Eugene 5′11″, 185 **WR**
Col: Sam Houston State *HS:* Flatonia [TX] B: 5/24/1953, Monthalia, TX
1976 NYJ: 12 G; Rec 7-110 15.7; 1 Fum. **1977** Bal: 1 G. **Total:** 13 G; Rec 7-110 15.7; 1 Fum.

CRAIG SAUER Sauer, Craig Curtis 6′1″, 240 **LB**
Col: Minnesota *HS:* Sartell [MN] B: 12/13/1972, Sartell, MN *Drafted:* 1996 Round 6 Atl
1996 Atl: 16 G. **1997** Atl: 16 G. **1998** Atl: 16 G; Int 1-0. **Total:** 48 G; Int 1-0.

ED SAUER Sauer, Edward Adam 5′10″, 246 **T-G**
(Tubby) *Col:* Miami (Ohio) *HS:* Steele [Dayton, OH] B: 11/27/1898, Van Buren Twp., OH D: 2/1980, Dayton, OH
1920 Day: 9 G. **1921** Can-Day: 10 G. Can: 1 G. Day: 9 G. **1922** Akr-Day: 10 G. Akr: 2 G. Day: 8 G. **1923** Day: 8 G. **1924** Day: 8 G. **1925** Pott-Day: 9 G. Pott: 1 G. Day: 8 G. **1926** Day: 5 G. **Total:** 59 G.

GEORGE SAUER Sauer, George Henry Jr. 6′2″, 195 **WR**
Col: Texas *HS:* Waco [TX] B: 11/10/1943, Sheboygan, WI *Drafted:* 1965 Redshirt Round 5 NYJ
1965 NYJ: KR 1-20 20.0. **1966** NYJ: Scor **1** 2XP. **1967** NYJ: Rush 1-(-3) -3.0; Scor 1 2XP. **1968** NYJ: Rush 2-21 10.5. **1969** NYJ: Rush 1-5 5.0; KR 1-0. **Total:** Rush 4-23 5.8; KR 2-20 10.0; Scor 2 2XP.

		Receiving				
Year Team	**G**	**Rec**	**Yds**	**Avg**	**TD**	**Fum**
1965 NYJ	14	29	301	10.4	2	0
1966 NYJ	14	63	1079	17.1	5	1
1967 NYJ	14	**75**	1189	15.9	6	1
1968 NYJ	14	66	1141	17.3	3	1
1969 NYJ	14	45	745	16.6	8	0
1970 NYJ	14	31	510	16.5	4	0
NFL Total	84	309	4965	16.1	28	3

GEORGE SAUER Sauer, George Henry Sr. 6′2″, 208 **HB-FB-DB-LB**
Col: Nebraska *HS:* Stratton [NE]; Lincoln HS [NE] B: 12/11/1910, Stratton, NE D: 2/5/1994, Waco, TX
1935 GB: Pass 21-9 42.9%, 177 8.43 1 TD 5 Int; Rec 3-32 10.7; Int **1** TD. **1936** GB: Pass 4-2 50.0%, 26 6.50 1 Int; Rec 6-110 18.3. **Total:** Pass 25-11 44.0%, 203 8.12 1 TD 6 Int; Rec 9-142 15.8; Int 1 TD.

		Rushing				Tot
Year Team	**G**	**Att**	**Yds**	**Avg**	**TD**	**TD**
1935 GB	9	89	334	3.8	3	4
1936 GB	9	94	305	3.2	3	3
1937 GB	2	7	17	2.4	0	0
NFL Total	20	190	656	3.5	6	7

TODD SAUERBRUN Sauerbrun, Todd Scott 5′10″, 209 **P**
Col: West Virginia *HS:* Ward Melville [Setauket, NY] B: 1/4/1973, Setauket, NY *Drafted:* 1995 Round 2 ChiB
1996 ChiB: Pass 2-2 100.0%, 63 31.50; Rush 1-3 3.0. **1997** ChiB: Rush 2-8 4.0. **Total:** Pass 2-2 100.0%, 63 31.50; Rush 3-11 3.7.

		Punting			
Year Team	**G**	**Punts**	**Yds**	**Avg**	**Fum**
1995 ChiB	15	55	2080	37.8	0
1996 ChiB	16	78	3491	44.8	0
1997 ChiB	16	95	4059	42.7	1
1998 ChiB	3	15	741	49.4	0
NFL Total	50	243	10371	42.7	1

RICH SAUL Saul, Richard Robert 6′3″, 241 **C-OG-OT-LB**
Col: Michigan State *HS:* Butler [PA] B: 2/5/1948, Butler, PA *Drafted:* 1970 Round 8 LARm
1970 LARm: 14 G. **1971** LARm: 14 G; KR 1-0. **1972** LARm: 14 G. **1973** LARm: 14 G; 1 Fum. **1974** LARm: 14 G. **1975** LARm: 14 G. **1976** LARm: 14 G. **1977** LARm: 14 G. **1978** LARm: 16 G. **1979** LARm: 16 G. **1980** LARm: 16 G; 1 Fum. **1981** LARm: 16 G. **Total:** 176 G; KR 1-0; 2 Fum.

RON SAUL Saul, Ronald Reed 6′2″, 255 **OG**
Col: Michigan State *HS:* Butler [PA] B: 2/5/1948, Butler, PA *Drafted:* 1970 Round 5 Hou
1970 Hou: 14 G. **1971** Hou: 3 G. **1972** Hou: 13 G. **1973** Hou: 3 G. **1974** Hou: 14 G; KR 1-10 10.0. **1975** Hou: 14 G. **1976** Was: 11 G. **1977** Was: 14 G. **1978** Was: 15 G. **1979** Was: 15 G. **1980** Was: 16 G. **1981** Was: 10 G. **Total:** 142 G; KR 1-10 10.0.

BILL SAUL Saul, William Neal 6′4″, 224 **LB**
Col: Penn State *HS:* Butler [PA] B: 11/19/1940, Unionville, PA *Drafted:* 1962 Round 2 Bal
1962 Bal: 14 G; Scor 1 Saf; 2 Pt. **1963** Bal: 14 G. **1964** Pit: 13 G; Int 1-13. **1966** Pit: 14 G; KR 2-35 17.5; Int 2-21. **1967** Pit: 14 G; Int 1-0; 1 Fum. **1968** Pit: 3 G. **1969** NO: 3 G. **1970** Det: 13 G. **Total:** 88 G; KR 2-35 17.5; Int 4-34; Scor 1 Saf; 2 Pt; 1 Fum.

MACK SAULS Sauls, Kirby McGee 6′0″, 185 **DB**
Col: Southwest Texas State *HS:* San Antonio [TX] B: 8/15/1945, Long Beach, CA *Drafted:* 1968 Round 13 StL
1968 StL: 6 G. **1969** StL: 4 G. **Total:** 10 G.

PETE SAUMER Saumer, Sylvan Leon 6′1″, 195 **TB-DB-FB-LB**
Col: St. Olaf *HS:* Canby [MN] B: 4/30/1910, St.Paul, MN D: 1/1/1983, Reno, NV
1934 Cin-Pit: Pass 7-1 14.3%, 9 1.29 1 Int; Rec 1-6 6.0. Cin: Pass 4-1 25.0%, 9 2.25; Rec 1-6 6.0. Pit: Pass 3-0, 1 Int. **Total:** Pass 7-1 14.3%, 9 1.29 1 Int; Rec 1-6 6.0.

		Rushing			
Year Team	**G**	**Att**	**Yds**	**Avg**	**TD**
1934 Cin-Pit	6	55	204	3.7	1
1934 Cin	3	48	183	3.8	1
1934 Pit	3	7	21	3.0	0
NFL Total	6	55	204	3.7	1

CEDRIC SAUNDERS Saunders, Cedric Randall 6′3″, 240 **TE**
Col: Ohio State *HS:* Sarasota [FL] B: 9/30/1972, Tallahassee, FL
1995 TB: 3 G.

JOHN SAUNDERS Saunders, John Wesley III 6′3″, 198 **DB**
Col: Toledo *HS:* Macomber [Toledo, OH] B: 4/29/1950, Toledo, OH *Drafted:* 1972 Round 4 LARm
1972 Buf: 2 G. **1974** SF: 4 G. **1975** SF: 3 G. **Total:** 9 G.

RUSS SAUNDERS Saunders, Russell S 5′9″, 190 **FB**
(Racehorse) *Col:* USC *HS:* Green Bay East [WI]; San Diego HS [CA] B: 1/26/1906 D: 4/28/1987, Burbank, CA
1931 GB: 9 G; Pass 1 TD; Rush 1 TD; 6 Pt.

BUCK SAUNDERS Saunders, Ward Bishop 6′1″, 190 **BB**
Col: California *HS:* Gilroy [CA] B: 1892 Deceased
1922 Tol: 1 G.

STILLWELL SAUNOOKE Saunooke, Stillwell 5′8″, 175 **OE-WB**
Col: Carlisle *HS:* Carlisle Indian School [PA] B: 9/1891, Whittier, NC Deceased
1922 Oor: 9 G.

TONY SAVAGE Savage, Anthony John 6′3″, 300 **NT**
Col: Washington State *HS:* Archbishop Riordan [San Francisco, CA] B: 7/7/1967, San Francisco, CA *Drafted:* 1990 Round 5 NYJ
1990 SD: 2 G. **1992** SD-Cin: 3 G. SD: 2 G. Cin: 1 G. **Total:** 5 G.

SEBASTIAN SAVAGE Savage, Sebastian Eugene 5′10″, 187 **DB**
Col: North Carolina State *HS:* Union [SC] B: 12/12/1969, Carlisle, SC *Drafted:* 1993 Round 5 Buf
1994 Was: 1 G. **1995** Was: 2 G. **Total:** 3 G.

OLLIE SAVATSKY Savatsky, Oliver John 6′2″, 215 **OE-DE**
Col: Miami (Ohio) *HS:* Cathedral Latin [Cleveland, OH]; Lincoln HS [Cleveland, OH] B: 5/13/1912, Cleveland, OH
1937 Cle: 1 G.

GEORGE SAVITSKY Savitsky, George Michael 6′2″, 244 **T**
Col: Pennsylvania *HS:* Camden [NJ] B: 7/30/1924, New York, NY *Drafted:* 1947 Round 3 Phi
1948 Phi: 12 G. **1949** Phi: 12 G. **Total:** 24 G.

NICKY SAVOIE Savoie, Nicky John 6′5″, 253 **TE**
Col: Gulf Coast CC FL; Louisiana State *HS:* South Lafourche [Galliano, LA] B: 9/21/1973, Cut Off, LA *Drafted:* 1997 Round 6 NO
1997 NO: 1 G; Rec 1-14 14.0.

JOE SAVOLDI Savoldi, Joseph A 5′11″, 194 **FB**
(Jumpin' Joe) *Col:* Notre Dame *HS:* Three Oaks [MI] B: 3/5/1908, Milan, Italy D: 1/25/1974, Cadiz, KY
1930 ChiB: 3 G; Rush 1 TD; 6 Pt.

COREY SAWYER Sawyer, Corey Franklyn 5′11″, 177 **DB**
Col: Florida State *HS:* Key West [FL] B: 10/4/1971, Key West, FL *Drafted:* 1994 Round 4 Cin
1994 Cin: KR 1-14 14.0. **1995** Cin: KR 2-50 25.0; 2 Sac. **1996** Cin: KR 12-241 20.1; 1.5 Sac. **Total:** KR 15-305 20.3; 3.5 Sac.

		Punt Returns				Interceptions				Tot
Year Team	G	Ret	Yds	Avg	TD	Int	Yds	TD	Fum	TD
1994 Cin	15	26	307	11.8	1	2	0	0	2	1
1995 Cin	12	9	58	6.4	0	2	61	0	1	0
1996 Cin	15	15	117	7.8	0	2	0	0	2	0
1997 Cin	15	0	0	—	0	4	44	0	0	0
1998 Cin	3	0	0	—	0	1	58	1	0	1
NFL Total	60	50	482	9.6	1	11	163	1	5	2

HERM SAWYER Sawyer, Herman W 5′8″, 170 **WB-BB**
Col: Syracuse *HS:* Missoula [MT] B: 10/18/1898 D: 9/1968, New York, NY
1922 Roch: 3 G.

JOHN SAWYER Sawyer, John Wesley 6′2″, 230 **TE**
Col: Southern Mississippi *HS:* Baker [LA] B: 7/26/1953, Brookhaven, MS *Drafted:* 1975 Round 11 Hou
1976 Hou: Punt 1-32 32.0. **1981** Sea: KR 1-8 8.0. **1983** Was-Den: KR 1-15 15.0. Was: KR 1-15 15.0. **Total:** KR 2-23 11.5; Punt 1-32 32.0.

		Receiving				
Year Team	G	Rec	Yds	Avg	TD	Fum
1975 Hou	8	7	144	20.6	1	1
1976 Hou	14	18	208	11.6	1	0
1977 Sea	14	10	105	10.5	0	1
1978 Sea	11	9	101	11.2	0	1
1980 Sea	16	36	410	11.4	0	1
1981 Sea	16	21	272	13.0	0	0
1982 Sea	7	8	92	11.5	0	0
1983 Was-Den	14	3	42	14.0	0	1
1983 Was	7	0	0	—	0	0
1983 Den	7	3	42	14.0	0	1
1984 Den	10	17	122	7.2	0	0
NFL Total	110	129	1496	11.6	2	5

JON SAWYER Sawyer, Jonathan LaJuan 5′9″, 175 **DB**
Col: Merced Coll. CA (J.C.); Cincinnati *HS:* Hialeah [FL] B: 4/6/1964
1987 NE: 2 G.

KEN SAWYER Sawyer, Kenneth Lee 6′0″, 192 **DB**
Col: Syracuse *HS:* Arlington [Lagrangeville, NY] B: 7/22/1952, Clearfield, PA *Drafted:* 1974 Round 7 Cin
1974 Cin: 12 G.

BUZZ SAWYER Sawyer, Robert Meade 6′1″, 201 **P**
Col: Texas A&M; Baylor *HS:* Waxahachie [TX] B: 11/18/1962, Waxahachie, TX
1987 Dal: 3 G; Punt 16-639 39.9.

JAMES SAXON Saxon, James Elijah 5′11″, 230 **RB**
Col: American River Coll. CA (J.C.); San Jose State *HS:* Battery Creek [Burton, SC] B: 3/23/1966, Buford, SC *Drafted:* 1988 Round 6 KC
1988 KC: KR 2-40 20.0. **1989** KC: Pass 1-0, 1 Int; KR 3-16 5.3. **1990** KC: KR 5-81 16.2. **1991** KC: KR 4-56 14.0. **1993** Mia: KR 1-7 7.0. **1994** Mia: KR 1-12 12.0. **1995** Phi: KR 1-3 3.0. **Total:** Pass 1-0, 1 Int; KR 17-215 12.6.

		Rushing				Receiving				
Year Team	G	Att	Yds	Avg	TD	Rec	Yds	Avg	TD	Fum
1988 KC	16	60	236	3.9	2	19	177	9.3	0	0
1989 KC	16	58	233	4.0	3	11	86	7.8	0	2
1990 KC	6	3	15	5.0	0	1	5	5.0	0	1
1991 KC	16	6	13	2.2	0	6	55	9.2	0	1
1992 Mia	16	4	7	1.8	0	5	41	8.2	0	0
1993 Mia	16	5	13	2.6	0	0	0	—	0	0
1994 Mia	16	8	16	2.0	0	27	151	5.6	0	0
1995 Phi	9	1	0	0.0	0	0	0	—	0	0
NFL Total	111	145	533	3.7	5	69	515	7.5	0	4

MIKE SAXON Saxon, Michael Eric 6′3″, 197 **P**
Col: Pasadena City Coll. CA (J.C.); San Diego State *HS:* Arcadia [CA] B: 7/10/1962, Whittier, CA *Drafted:* 1984 Round 11 Det
1989 Dal: Pass 1-1 100.0%, 4 4.00; Rush 1-1 1.0. **1990** Dal: Rush 1-20 20.0. **1993** NE: Rush 2-2 1.0. **1994** Min: Pass 1-0; Rush 1-0. **Total:** Pass 2-1 50.0%, 4 2.00; Rush 5-23 4.6.

		Punting			
Year Team	G	Punts	Yds	Avg	Fum
1985 Dal	16	81	3396	41.9	0
1986 Dal	16	86	3498	40.7	0
1987 Dal	12	68	2685	39.5	0
1988 Dal	16	80	3271	40.9	0
1989 Dal	16	79	3233	40.9	0
1990 Dal	16	79	3413	43.2	0
1991 Dal	16	57	2426	42.6	0
1992 Dal	16	61	2620	43.0	0
1993 NE	16	73	3096	42.4	1
1994 Min	16	77	3301	42.9	1
1995 Min	16	72	2948	40.9	0
NFL Total	172	813	33887	41.7	2

JIMMY SAXTON Saxton, James Everett Jr. 5′11″, 173 **HB**
Col: Texas *HS:* Palestine [TX] B: 5/21/1940, Bryan, TX *Drafted:* 1962 Round 10 DalT
1962 DalT: 13 G; Rush 3-1 0.3; Rec 5-64 12.8; KR 4-77 19.3; Punt 3-139 46.3.

BRIAN SAXTON Saxton, Paul Brian 6′6″, 256 **TE**
Col: Boston College *HS:* Whippany Park [Whippany, NJ] B: 3/13/1972, Whippany, NJ
1996 NYG: 16 G; Rec 4-31 7.8; KR 3-31 10.3. **1997** Atl: 3 G. **Total:** 19 G; Rec 4-31 7.8; KR 3-31 10.3.

GALE SAYERS Sayers, Gale Eugene 6′0″, 198 **RB**
Col: Kansas *HS:* Central [Omaha, NE] B: 5/30/1943, Wichita, KS *Drafted:* 1965 Round 1 ChiB *HOF:* 1977
1965 ChiB: Pass 3-2 66.7%, 53 17.67 1 TD 1 Int. **1966** ChiB: Pass 6-2 33.3%, 58 9.67 1 Int. **1967** ChiB: Pass 5-0. **1968** ChiB: Pass 2-0. **1969** ChiB: Pass 2-0. **Total:** Pass 18-4 22.2%, 111 6.17 1 TD 2 Int.

		Rushing				Receiving			
Year Team	G	Att	Yds	Avg	TD	Rec	Yds	Avg	TD
1965 ChiB	14	166	867	5.2	14	29	507	17.5	6
1966 ChiB	14	229	**1231**	5.4	8	34	447	13.1	2
1967 ChiB	13	186	880	4.7	7	16	126	7.9	1
1968 ChiB	9	138	856	**6.2**	2	15	117	7.8	0
1969 ChiB	14	**236**	**1032**	4.4	8	17	116	6.8	0
1970 ChiB	2	23	52	2.3	0	1	-6	-6.0	0
1971 ChiB	2	13	38	2.9	0	0	0	—	0
NFL Total	68	991	4956	5.0	39	112	1307	11.7	9

	Punt Returns				Kickoff Returns					Tot
Year Team	Ret	Yds	Avg	TD	Ret	Yds	Avg	TD	Fum	TD
1965 ChiB	16	238	14.9	1	21	660	31.4	**1**	9	**22**
1966 ChiB	6	44	7.3	0	23	718	**31.2**	**2**	2	12
1967 ChiB	3	80	26.7	**1**	16	603	37.7	3	**8**	12
1968 ChiB	2	29	14.5	0	17	461	27.1	0	7	2
1969 ChiB	0	0	—	0	14	339	24.2	0	7	8
1970 ChiB	0	0	—	0	0	0	—	0	1	0
NFL Total	27	391	14.5	2	91	2781	**30.6**	**6**	34	56

RON SAYERS Sayers, Ronald 6′1″, 209 **RB**
Col: Nebraska-Omaha *HS:* Omaha [NE] B: 8/29/1947, Wichita, KS *Drafted:* 1969 Round 2 SD
1969 SD: 8 G; Rush 14-53 3.8; KR 2-42 21.0; 1 Fum.

RALPH SAZIO Sazio, Ralph Joseph 6'1", 220 T
(Saz) *Col:* William & Mary *HS:* Columbia [South Orange, NJ]
B: 7/22/1922, Avellino, Italy
AAFC **1948** BknA: 13 G; Rush 0-5.

RONALD SBRANTI Sbranti, Albert Ronald 6'2", 230 LB
Col: Utah State *HS:* Antioch [CA] B: 10/24/1944, Antioch, CA
Drafted: 1966 Round 9 Den
1966 Den: 14 G.

JOHN SCAFIDE Scafide, John Andrew 6'0", 210 T
(Baby Grand) *Col:* Tulane *HS:* St. Stanislaus [Bay St. Louis, MS]
B: 6/21/1911, Bay St. Louis, MS D: 10/24/1979, Bay St.Louis, MS
1933 Bos: 2 G.

CHARLIE SCALES Scales, Charles Anderson 5'11", 210 FB
(Chuck) *Col:* Indiana *HS:* Homestead [PA] B: 1/11/1938, Pittsburgh, PA
1960 Pit: Rec 1-(-2) -2.0. **1961** Pit: Rec 7-43 6.1. **1962** Cle: Pass 1-0, 1 Int; Rec 8-67 8.4. **1963** Cle: Rec 1-13 13.0. **1964** Cle: 1 Fum TD. **1965** Cle: Rec 1-7 7.0; PR 1-0. **1966** Atl: Rec 3-16 5.3. **Total:** Pass 1-0, 1 Int; Rec 21-144 6.9; PR 1-0; 1 Fum TD.

		Rushing				Kickoff Returns					Tot
Year Team	G	Ret	Yds	Avg	TD	Ret	Yds	Avg	TD	Fum	TD
1960 Pit	12	26	81	3.1	0	5	100	20.0	0	2	0
1961 Pit	14	50	184	3.7	0	3	41	13.7	0	4	0
1962 Cle	14	56	239	4.3	3	9	154	17.1	0	1	3
1963 Cle	14	2	-3	-1.5	1	16	432	27.0	0	3	1
1964 Cle	14	2	5	2.5	0	5	75	15.0	0	1	1
1965 Cle	14	11	59	5.4	0	4	88	22.0	0	1	0
1966 Atl	5	10	38	3.8	0	5	101	20.2	0	0	0
NFL Total	87	157	603	3.8	4	47	991	21.1	0	12	5

DWIGHT SCALES Scales, Dwight Austin 6'2", 178 WR
Col: Grambling State *HS:* Robert E. Lee [Huntsville, AL] B: 5/30/1953, Little Rock, AR *Drafted:* 1976 Round 5 LARm
1976 LARm: PR 4-46 11.5; KR 7-136 19.4. **1979** NYG: PR 2-3 1.5. **1983** SD: PR 2-34 17.0; KR 1-16 16.0. **Total:** PR 8-83 10.4; KR 8-152 19.0.

		Receiving					Tot
Year Team	G	Rec	Yds	Avg	TD	Fum	TD
1976 LARm	14	3	105	35.0	1	1	1
1977 LARm	12	5	104	20.8	1	0	1
1978 LARm	13	5	105	21.0	0	0	1
1979 NYG	15	14	222	15.9	0	0	0
1981 SD	16	19	429	22.6	1	1	1
1982 SD	9	6	105	17.5	1	0	1
1983 SD	7	2	28	14.0	0	0	0
1984 Sea	4	2	22	11.0	0	0	0
NFL Total	90	56	1120	20.0	4	2	5

GREG SCALES Scales, Gregory Denard 6'4", 253 TE
Col: Wake Forest *HS:* East Forsyth [Kernerville, NC] B: 5/9/1966, Winston-Salem, NC *Drafted:* 1988 Round 5 NO
1988 NO: 12 G; Rec 2-20 10.0 1 TD; 6 Pt. **1989** NO: 14 G; Rec 8-89 11.1; KR 1-0. **1990** NO: 16 G; Rec 8-64 8.0 1 TD; 6 Pt. **1991** NO: 2 G; Rec 3-23 7.7. **Total:** 44 G; Rec 21-196 9.3 2 TD; KR 1-0; 12 Pt.

HURLES SCALES Scales, Hurles Eulis Jr. 6'1", 200 DB
Col: Cisco JC TX; North Texas *HS:* Amarillo [TX] B: 12/1/1950, Amarillo, TX *Drafted:* 1973 Round 14 Cin
1974 ChiB-StL: 8 G. ChiB: 1 G. StL: 7 G. **1975** GB: 7 G. **Total:** 15 G.

TED SCALISSI Scalissi, Theodore Glenn 5'8", 173 HB-DB
Col: Ripon *HS:* Central [Madison, WI] B: 10/26/1921, Madison, WI
D: 1/6/1987, Janesville, WI
AAFC **1947** ChiA: Rec 5-67 13.4 2 TD; PR 2-26 13.0; KR 8-171 21.4.

		Rushing			
Year Team	G	Att	Yds	Avg	TD
1947 ChiA	10	35	37	1.1	0

JOHNNY SCALZI Scalzi, John Anthony 5'7", 168 BB-TB-WB
Col: Georgetown *HS:* Stamford [CT] B: 3/22/1907, Stamford, CT
D: 9/27/1962, Port Chester, NY
1931 Bkn: 7 G; Pass 1 TD.

JERRY SCANLAN Scanlan, Jerry Lafaele 6'5", 270 OT-OG
Col: Hawaii *HS:* Iolani [Honolulu, HI] B: 1/4/1957, Honolulu, HI
1980 Was: 3 G. **1981** Was: 3 G. **Total:** 6 G.

DEWEY SCANLON Scanlon, Dewey D 5'9", 192 WB
Col: Valparaiso *HS:* Denfeld [Duluth, MN] B: 8/16/1899, West Duluth, MN Deceased
1926 Dul: 1 G.

JOHN SCANLON Scanlon, John 185 TB-WB
Col: DePaul *HS:* Loyola Acad. [Chicago, IL] B: 1900, IL Deceased
1921 ChiC: 4 G; Rush 1 TD; 6 Pt. **1926** Lou: 2 G. **Total:** 6 G; Rush 1 TD; 6 Pt.

JACK SCARBATH Scarbath, John Carl 6'2", 206 QB
Col: Maryland *HS:* Baltimore Polytechnic Inst. [MD] B: 8/12/1930, Baltimore, MD *Drafted:* 1953 Round 1 Was

		Passing							
Year Team	G	Att	Comp	Comp%	Yds	YPA	TD	Int	Rating
1953 Was	12	129	45	34.9	862	6.68	9	12	43.5
1954 Was	10	109	44	40.4	798	7.32	7	13	48.1
1956 Pit	7	41	12	29.3	208	5.07	2	5	24.9
NFL Total	29	279	101	36.2	1868	6.70	18	30	42.1

	Rushing				
Year Team	Att	Yds	Avg	TD	Fum
1953 Was	22	98	4.5	0	7
1954 Was	17	36	2.1	0	4
1956 Pit	4	19	4.8	0	1
NFL Total	43	153	3.6	0	12

SAM SCARBER Scarber, Sam Willis 6'3", 230 RB
Col: Northeastern JC CO; New Mexico *HS:* O'Fallon Tech [St. Louis, MO] B: 6/24/1949, St. Louis, MO *Drafted:* 1971 Round 3 Dal

		Rushing				Receiving					Tot
Year Team	G	Att	Yds	Avg	TD	Rec	Yds	Avg	TD	Fum	TD
1975 SD	11	15	68	4.5	1	12	68	5.7	1	2	2
1976 SD	14	61	236	3.9	1	14	96	6.9	1	3	2
NFL Total	25	76	304	4.0	2	26	164	6.3	2	5	4

JOHN SCARDINA Scardina, John 6'4", 265 OT
Col: Concordia (Wis.); Lincoln (Mo.) B: 7/26/1958, Milwaukee, WI
1987 Min: 3 G.

CARMEN SCARDINE Scardine, Carmen 1 WB
Col: No College B: 3/9/1911, Chicago, IL
1932 ChiC: 1 G; Rush 1-10 10.0; Rec 1-3 3.0.

JOE SCARPATI Scarpati, Joseph Henry Jr. 5'10", 185 DB
Col: North Carolina State *HS:* Fanwood [NJ] B: 3/5/1943, Brooklyn, NY *Drafted:* 1964 Round 13 Bos
1964 Phi: PR 1-6 6.0. **1965** Phi: Rush 1-6 6.0. **1966** Phi: PR 2-(-8) -4.0. **1967** Phi: PR 1-2 2.0. **1968** Phi: Pass 2-1 50.0%, 3 1.50; PR 5-17 3.4. **1969** Phi: PR 4-6 1.5. **Total:** Pass 2-1 50.0%, 3 1.50; Rush 1-6 6.0; PR 13-23 1.8.

		Interceptions			
Year Team	G	Int	Yds	TD	Fum
1964 Phi	12	3	41	1	0
1965 Phi	14	3	4	0	0
1966 Phi	14	8	**182**	0	1
1967 Phi	14	4	99	1	0
1968 Phi	14	2	22	0	1
1969 Phi	14	4	54	1	0
1970 NO	14	1	4	0	0
NFL Total	96	25	406	3	2

BOB SCARPITTO Scarpitto, Robert Frank 5'11", 192 WR-P
Col: Notre Dame *HS:* Rahway [NJ] B: 1/7/1939, Rahway, NJ
Drafted: 1961 Round 9 SD
1961 SD: PR 4-47 11.8; KR 3-50 16.7. **1963** Den: KR 1-8 8.0. **1964** Den: Rush 1-5 5.0. **1965** Den: Rush 4-94 23.5. **1966** Den: Rush 4-110 27.5 1 TD; Scor **1** 2XP. **1967** Den: Rush 1-5 5.0. **Total:** Rush 10-214 21.4 1 TD; PR 4-47 11.8; KR 4-58 14.5; Scor 1 2XP.

		Receiving				Punting				Tot
Year Team	G	Rec	Yds	Avg	TD	Punts	Yds	Avg	Fum	TD
1961 SD	7	9	163	18.1	2	0	0	—	0	2
1962 Den	14	35	667	19.1	6	0	0	—	0	6
1963 Den	11	21	463	22.0	5	0	0	—	0	5
1964 Den	14	35	375	10.7	4	0	0	—	0	4
1965 Den	14	32	585	18.3	5	67	2833	42.3	1	5
1966 Den	14	21	335	16.0	4	**77**	**3480**	**45.2**	1	5
1967 Den	14	1	14	14.0	0	**105**	**4713**	**44.9**	0	0
1968 Bos	14	2	49	24.5	1	34	1382	40.6	0	1
NFL Total	102	156	2651	17.0	27	283	12408	43.8	2	28

MIKE SCARRY Scarry, Michael Joseph 6'0", 214 C-LB-T
(Mo) *Col:* Waynesburg *HS:* Duquesne [PA] B: 2/1/1920, Duquesne, PA
AAFC **1946** CleA: 14 G; Int 2-0. **1947** CleA: 11 G. **Total:** 25 G; Int 2-0.

NFL **1944** Cle: 10 G; Int 1-5. **1945** Cle: 10 G; Int 4-32. **Total:** 20 G; Int 5-37.

ELMER SCHAAKE Schaake, Elmer Earl 5'11", 207 FB-LB-WB-TB
(Dutch) *Col:* Kansas *HS:* Messick [Memphis, TN] B: 2/7/1911, Lawrence, KS D: 1/24/1966
1933 Port: Pass 3-2 66.7%, 8 2.67 1 Int; Rec 4-23 5.8 1 TD.

Year Team	G	Rushing Att	Yds	Avg	TD
1933 Port	10	125	412	3.3	0

PETE SCHABARUM Schabarum, Peter Frank 5′11″, 185 **HB-DB**
(Pistol; Kodak) *Col:* California *HS:* Covina [CA] B: 1/9/1929, Los Angeles, CA *Drafted:* 1951 Round 2 SF
1951 SF: Rec 10-162 16.2. **1953** SF: Rec 10-96 9.6; PR 2-0; KR 2-50 25.0. **1954** SF: Pass 1-0; Rec 4-70 17.5; PR 2-10 5.0; KR 1-34 34.0; Int 1-9. **Total:** Pass 1-0; Rec 24-328 13.7; PR 4-10 2.5; KR 3-84 28.0; Int 1-9.

Year Team	G	Rushing Att	Yds	Avg	TD	Fum
1951 SF	12	76	311	4.1	2	4
1953 SF	10	18	104	5.8	0	1
1954 SF	12	21	79	3.8	1	0
NFL Total	34	115	494	4.3	3	5

MIKE SCHAD Schad, Michael 6′5″, 290 **OG**
Col: Queens (Canada) *HS:* Moira Secondary School [Bellville, Canada] B: 10/2/1963, Trenton, Canada *Drafted:* 1986 Round 1 LARm
1987 LARm: 1 G. **1988** LARm: 6 G. **1989** Phi: 16 G. **1990** Phi: 12 G. **1992** Phi: 14 G. **1993** Phi: 13 G. **Total:** 62 G.

DON SCHAEFER Schaefer, Donald Thomas 6′0″, 210 **FB**
Col: Notre Dame *HS:* Central Catholic [Pittsburgh, PA] B: 2/13/1934, Pittsburgh, PA *Drafted:* 1956 Round 3 Phi
1956 Phi: Pass 3-1 33.3%, 11 3.67 1 TD; Rec 13-117 9.0.

Year Team	G	Rushing Att	Yds	Avg	TD	Fum
1956 Phi	12	102	320	3.1	2	3

JOE SCHAFFER Schaffer, Joseph Leonard 6′0″, 210 **LB**
Col: Tennessee *HS:* Elder [Cincinnati, OH] B: 10/14/1937, Cincinnati, OH *Drafted:* 1960 Round 1 Buf
1960 Buf: 14 G; Int 1-19.

PETE SCHAFFNIT Schaffnit, Peter Cornelius 5′11″, 180 **E-BB-WB-FB**
Col: California *HS:* Bakersfield [CA] B: 1902
1926 LA: 9 G.

DICK SCHAFRATH Schafrath, Richard Phillip 6′3″, 253 **OT-OG-DE**
Col: Ohio State *HS:* Wooster [OH] B: 3/21/1937, Canton, OH
Drafted: 1959 Round 2 Cle
1959 Cle: 12 G. **1960** Cle: 12 G. **1961** Cle: 13 G. **1962** Cle: 14 G. **1963** Cle: 14 G. **1964** Cle: 14 G. **1965** Cle: 14 G. **1966** Cle: 13 G. **1967** Cle: 14 G. **1968** Cle: 14 G. **1969** Cle: 14 G. **1970** Cle: 14 G. **1971** Cle: 14 G. **Total:** 176 G.

DUKE SCHAMEL Schamel, Duke Wayne 6′3″, 235 **LB**
Col: Coll. of the Siskiyous CA (J.C.); South Dakota *HS:* Tulelake [CA] B: 11/3/1963, Glendale, CA
1987 Mia: 3 G.

ZUD SCHAMMEL Schammel, Francis William 6′2″, 235 **G-DE**
Col: Iowa *HS:* Lincoln [IA] B: 8/26/1910, Waterloo, IA D: 1/1973
1937 GB: 8 G; 6 Pt.

SCOTT SCHANKWEILER Schankweiler, Scott Brian 6′0″, 225 **LB**
Col: Maryland *HS:* Cedar Cliff [Camp Hill, PA] B: 10/15/1963, Sunbury, PA
1987 Buf: 3 G; Int 1-7.

EDDIE SCHARER Scharer, Edward 5′6″, 165 **TB-BB-WB**
Col: Detroit Mercy; Notre Dame *HS:* V. W. Scott [Toledo, OH] B: 1/26/1902, Toledo, OH D: 5/5/1989, Long Beach, CA
1926 Det: 12 G; Pass **6** TD; Rush 1 TD; 6 Pt. **1927** Pott: 11 G. **1928** Det: 7 G; Scor 1, 1 XK. **Total:** 30 G; Pass 6 TD; Rush 1 TD.

CARL SCHAUKOWITCH Schaukowitch, Carl 6′3″, 235 **OG**
Col: Penn State *HS:* Sto-Rox [McKees Rocks, PA] B: 2/14/1951, Pittsburgh, PA *Drafted:* 1973 Round 15 NYG
1975 Den: 11 G.

GREG SCHAUM Schaum, Gregory James 6′4″, 246 **DE**
Col: Michigan State *HS:* Baltimore Polytechnic Inst. [MD] B: 1/1/1954, Baltimore, MD *Drafted:* 1976 Round 7 Dal
1976 Dal: 12 G. **1978** NE: 14 G. **Total:** 26 G.

SKIPPY SCHEIB Scheib, Lee Raymond 6′2″, 210 **C**
Col: West Virginia Wesleyan; Washington-St. Louis *HS:* Arthur Hill [Saginaw, MI] B: 7/28/1903, Saginaw, MI D: 2/27/1989, Saginaw, MI
1930 Bkn: 6 G.

JOE SCHEIN Schein, Joseph 5′10″, 212 **T**
Col: Brown *HS:* South Side [Newark, NJ] B: 11/11/1910, Brooklyn, NY D: 5/27/1969, Providence, RI
1931 Prov: 11 G.

HERB SCHELL Schell, Herbert Phillip 5′9″, 175 **WB-FB-TB**
Col: Ohio State *HS:* Commerce [Columbus, OH] B: 1/5/1902, Boyertown, PA D: 8/26/1985, Columbus, OH
1924 Col: 5 G; Rush 1 TD; Scor 9, 1 FG.

ED SCHENK Schenk, Edward 6′4″, 230 **TE**
Col: Baldwin-Wallace; Central Florida B: 12/20/1960
1987 Min: 3 G; Rec 1-10 10.0.

NATE SCHENKER Schenker, Nathan 6′2″, 220 **T**
Col: Samford *HS:* East Tech [Cleveland, OH] B: 1/27/1918, Cleveland, OH
1939 Cle: 4 G.

BERNIE SCHERER Scherer, Bernard Joseph 6′1″, 190 **OE-DE**
Col: Nebraska *HS:* Dallas [SD] B: 1/28/1913, Spencer, NE
Drafted: 1936 Round 3 GB
1936 GB: 8 G; Rec 2-13 6.5; Int 1 TD; 6 Pt. **1937** GB: 9 G; Rec 7-149 21.3 2 TD; 12 Pt. **1938** GB: 9 G; Rec 2-31 15.5 1 TD; 6 Pt. **1939** Pit: 9 G; Rec 2-49 24.5. **Total:** 35 G; Rec 13-242 18.6 3 TD; Int 1 TD; Tot TD 4; 24 Pt.

BABE SCHEUER Scheuer, Abraham 6′3″, 240 **T**
Col: New York U. *HS:* James Madison [Brooklyn, NY] B: 1912
1934 NYG: 1 G.

ALEX SCHIBANOFF Schibanoff, Alexander 6′1″, 218 **T**
Col: Franklin & Marshall *HS:* Freehold Twp. [Freehold, NJ] B: 10/17/1919, Freehold, NJ D: 11/27/1995, Wingdale, NY
Drafted: 1941 Round 14 Det
1941 Det: 2 G. **1942** Det: 6 G. **Total:** 8 G.

HENRY SCHICHTLE Schichtle, Henry Ernest 6′2″, 190 **QB**
(Hank) *Col:* Coffeyville CC KS; Hawaii; Wichita State *HS:* Coffeyville [KS] B: 10/13/1941, Tulsa, OK *Drafted:* 1964 Round 6 NYG
1964 NYG: 1 G.

DOYLE SCHICK Schick, Doyle Dean 6′1″, 210 **LB**
Col: Kansas *HS:* Lawrence [KS] B: 2/23/1939, Lawrence, KS
Drafted: 1961 Round 14 Was
1961 Was: 5 G.

ART SCHIEBEL Schiebel, Arthur Charles 6′0″, 220 **T**
Col: Colgate *HS:* Roxbury Prep [Cheshire, CT] B: 11/2/1907, New York, NY D: 7/1/1985, Stroudsburg, PA
1932 SI: 1 G.

JOHN SCHIECHL Schiechl, John George 6′2″, 244 **C-LB**
Col: Santa Clara *HS:* Balboa [San Francisco, CA] B: 8/22/1917, San Francisco, CA D: 2/1964 *Drafted:* 1940 Round 2 Phi
AAFC **1947** SF-A: 14 G; Int 2-45.

NFL **1941** Pit: 4 G; Int 1-0. **1942** Pit-Det: 11 G. Pit: 2 G. Det: 9 G. **1945** ChiB: 9 G. **1946** ChiB: 11 G; Int 3-26. **Total:** 35 G; Int 4-26.

RALPH SCHILLING Schilling, Ralph Franklin Jr. 6′3″, 218 **DE-OE**
Col: Oklahoma City B: 7/5/1921, Morris, OK D: 5/9/1994, McAllen, TX

NFL **1946** Was: 5 G; Rec 1-14 14.0.

ANDY SCHILLINGER Schillinger, Andrew Clemens 5′11″, 179 **WR**
Col: Miami (Ohio) *HS:* Avon Lake [OH] B: 11/22/1964, Lakewood, OH
Drafted: 1988 Round 10 Pho
1988 Pho: 3 G; KR 1-10 10.0.

STEVE SCHINDLER Schindler, Steven Wayne 6′3″, 256 **OG**
Col: Boston College *HS:* Conestoga [Berwyn, PA] B: 7/24/1954, Caldwell, NJ *Drafted:* 1977 Round 1 Den
1977 Den: 14 G. **1978** Den: 14 G. **Total:** 28 G.

VIC SCHLEICH Schleich, Victor 6′3″, 240 **T**
Col: Nebraska *HS:* Lincoln [NE] B: 4/26/1920, Montrose, CO
AAFC **1947** NY-A: 11 G.

MAURY SCHLEICHER Schleicher, Maurice Gene 6′3″, 238 **LB-DE**
Col: Penn State *HS:* Slatington [PA] B: 7/17/1937, Walnutport, PA
Drafted: 1959 Round 5 ChiC
1959 ChiC: 10 G. **1960** LAC: 12 G; Int 1-5. **1961** SD: 14 G. **1962** SD: 4 G. **Total:** 40 G; Int 1-5.

MARK SCHLERETH Schlereth, Mark Frederick 6′3″, 282 **OG-C**
Col: Idaho *HS:* Robert Service [Anchorage, AK] B: 1/25/1966, Anchorage, AK *Drafted:* 1989 Round 10 Was
1989 Was: 6 G. **1990** Was: 12 G. **1991** Was: 16 G. **1992** Was: 16 G. **1993** Was: 9 G. **1994** Was: 16 G. **1995** Den: 16 G. **1996** Den: 14 G. **1997** Den: 11 G. **1998** Den: 16 G. **Total:** 132 G.

CORY SCHLESINGER Schlesinger, Cory Michael 6′0″, 230 **RB**
Col: Nebraska *HS:* Columbus [NE] B: 6/23/1972, Columbus, NE
Drafted: 1995 Round 6 Det
1995 Det: 16 G; Rush 1-1 1.0; Rec 1-2 2.0. **1996** Det: 16 G. **1997** Det: 16 G; Rush 7-11 1.6; Rec 5-69 13.8 1 TD; 6 Pt. **1998** Det: 15 G; Rush 5-17 3.4; Rec 3-16 5.3 1 TD; 6 Pt. **Total:** 63 G; Rush 13-29 2.2; Rec 9-87 9.7 2 TD; 12 Pt.

VIN SCHLEUSNER Schleusner, Vincent Louis 6'3", 225 **T**
Col: Iowa *HS:* Garner-Hayfield [Garner, IA] B: 3/3/1908, Garner, IA
D: 6/5/1979, Rock Rapids, IA
1930 Port: 14 G; 1 Fum TD; 6 Pt. **1931** Port: 11 G. **Total:** 25 G; 1 Fum TD; 6 Pt.

ART SCHLICHTER Schlichter, Arthur Ernest 6'3", 210 **QB**
Col: Ohio State *HS:* Miami Trace [Washington Court House, OH]
B: 4/25/1960, Washington Court House, OH *Drafted:* 1982 Round 1 Bal
1982 Bal: Rush 1-3 3.0. **1984** Ind: Rush 19-145 7.6 1 TD. **1985** Ind: Rush 2-13 6.5. **Total:** Rush 22-161 7.3 1 TD.

		Passing								
Year Team	**G**	**Att**	**Comp**	**Comp%**	**Yds**	**YPA**	**TD**	**Int**	**Rating**	**Fum**
1982 Bal	3	37	17	45.9	197	5.32	0	2	40.0	3
1984 Ind	9	140	62	44.3	702	5.01	3	7	46.2	4
1985 Ind	1	25	12	48.0	107	4.28	0	2	26.6	1
NFL Total	13	202	91	45.0	1006	4.98	3	11	42.6	8

WALT SCHLINKMAN Schlinkman, Walter Gaye 5'9", 205 **FB**
Col: Texas Tech *HS:* Dumas [TX] B: 5/2/1922, Channing, TX
D: 10/5/1994, Weimar, TX *Drafted:* 1945 Round 1 GB
1946 GB: Rec 1-5 5.0; KR 2-43 21.5. **1947** GB: Rec 2-(-6) -3.0. **1948** GB: KR 4-89 22.3. **1949** GB: KR 1-23 23.0. **Total:** Rec 3-(-1) -0.3; KR 7-155 22.1.

		Rushing				
Year Team	**G**	**Att**	**Yds**	**Avg**	**TD**	**Fum**
1946 GB	11	97	379	3.9	2	2
1947 GB	12	115	439	3.8	2	8
1948 GB	11	106	441	4.2	4	4
1949 GB	12	47	196	4.2	0	6
NFL Total	46	365	1455	4.0	8	20

TODD SCHLOPY Schlopy, Ross Todd 5'10", 165 **K**
Col: Michigan *HS:* Orchard Park [NY] B: 6/17/1961, Bradford, PA
1987 Buf: 3 G; Scor 7, 2-5 40.0% FG, 1-2 50.0% XK.

ART SCHMAEHL Schmaehl, Arthur 5'8", 170 **FB**
Col: No College B: 2/5/1894 D: 12/1967, Chicago, IL
1921 GB: 6 G; Rush 2 TD; 12 Pt.

HERM SCHMARR Schmarr, Herman Raymond 6'2", 210 **DE**
Col: Catholic *HS:* New Britain [CT]; Vermont Acad. [Saxtons River, VT]
B: 10/1/1912, New Britain, CT D: 3/13/1989, Bradenton, FL
Drafted: 1937 Round 8 Cle
1943 Bkn: 5 G.

RAY SCHMAUTZ Schmautz, Raymond Ludwig 6'1", 225 **LB**
Col: San Diego State *HS:* Chula Vista [CA] B: 1/26/1943, Chula Vista, CA *Drafted:* 1966 Redshirt Round 8 Oak
1966 Oak: 10 G.

JIM SCHMEDDING Schmedding, James Edward 6'2", 250 **OG**
Col: Coll. of San Mateo CA (J.C.); Weber State *HS:* Granada Hills [Los Angeles, CA] B: 2/10/1946, San Diego, CA *Drafted:* 1968 Round 6 ChiB
1968 SD: 1 G. **1969** SD: 14 G. **1970** SD: 9 G. **Total:** 24 G.

GEORGE SCHMIDT Schmidt, George 6'2", 230 **DE-C-LB**
Col: Illinois Tech *HS:* Carl Schurz [Chicago, IL] B: 10/28/1927, Chicago, IL D: 8/29/1995, Schaumburg, IL
1952 GB: 7 G; KR 1-14 14.0. **1953** ChiC: 6 G; Scor **1** Saf; 2 Pt.
Total: 13 G; KR 1-14 14.0; Scor 1 Saf; 2 Pt.

HENRY SCHMIDT Schmidt, Henry Joseph 6'4", 254 **DT-OE**
(Hank) *Col:* East Los Angeles Coll. CA (J.C.); USC; Trinity (Tex.)
HS: John C. Fremont [Los Angeles, CA] B: 9/28/1935, South Gate, CA
Drafted: 1958 Round 6 SF
1959 SF: 12 G. **1960** SF: 12 G. **1961** SD: 14 G; KR 1-22 22.0; 1 Fum.
1962 SD: 14 G. **1963** SD: 14 G. **1964** SD: 14 G; Int 1-58 **1** TD; 6 Pt.
1965 Buf: 8 G. **1966** NYJ: 11 G. **Total:** 99 G; KR 1-22 22.0; Int 1-58 1 TD; 6 Pt; 1 Fum.

JOHN SCHMIDT Schmidt, John Peter 6'3", 210 **C-LB**
Col: Carnegie Mellon *HS:* St. Joseph [Pittsburgh, PA] B: 8/12/1918, Detroit, MI
1940 Pit: 1 G.

JOE SCHMIDT Schmidt, Joseph Paul 6'1", 220 **LB**
Col: Pittsburgh *HS:* Brentwood [Pittsburgh, PA] B: 1/19/1932, Pittsburgh, PA *Drafted:* 1953 Round 7 Det *HOF:* 1973
1953 Det: PR 1-0. **1954** Det: PR 1-0. **1955** Det: PR 1-0; KR 1-6 6.0.
1960 Det: **1** Fum TD. **Total:** PR 3-0; KR 1-6 6.0; 1 Fum TD.

		Interceptions				Tot
Year Team	**G**	**Int**	**Yds**	**TD**	**Fum**	**TD**
1953 Det	12	2	51	0	0	0
1954 Det	12	2	13	0	0	0
1955 Det	12	0	0	0	0	0
1956 Det	12	1	7	0	0	0
1957 Det	12	1	8	0	0	0
1958 Det	12	6	69	0	2	0
1959 Det	12	1	17	0	1	0
1960 Det	10	2	46	1	0	2
1961 Det	14	4	38	1	0	1
1962 Det	14	1	3	0	0	0
1963 Det	10	0	0	0	0	0
1964 Det	9	0	0	0	0	0
1965 Det	14	4	42	0	0	0
NFL Total	155	24	294	2	3	3

KERMIT SCHMIDT Schmidt, Kermit Roosevelt 6'0", 200 **OE-DE-WB-DB**
(Dutch) *Col:* California-Davis *HS:* Manual Arts [Los Angeles, CA]
B: 7/3/1910 D: 4/1980, Tulsa, OK
1932 Bos: 1 G. **1933** Cin: 5 G; Rec 2-36 18.0. **Total:** 6 G; Rec 2-36 18.0.

BOB SCHMIDT Schmidt, Robert Malcolm 6'4", 248 **C-OT-OG**
Col: Minnesota *HS:* Rochester [MN] B: 7/9/1936, Rochester, MN
Drafted: 1958 Round 14 ChiC
1959 NYG: 12 G. **1960** NYG: 11 G. **1961** Hou: 12 G. **1962** Hou: 14 G.
1963 Hou: 14 G. **1964** Bos: 14 G. **1966** Buf: 14 G; KR 1-2 2.0; 1 Fum.
1967 Buf: 7 G. **Total:** 98 G; KR 1-2 2.0; 1 Fum.

ROY SCHMIDT Schmidt, Roy Lee 6'3", 248 **OG-OT**
Col: Long Beach State *HS:* Oxnard [CA] B: 5/3/1942, Colorado Springs, CO *Drafted:* 1965 Round 13 GB
1967 NO: 10 G. **1968** NO: 9 G. **1969** Atl: 9 G. **1970** Was: 11 G. **1971** Min: 4 G. **Total:** 43 G.

TERRY SCHMIDT Schmidt, Terrence Richard 6'0", 177 **DB**
Col: Ball State *HS:* North [Columbus, IN] B: 5/28/1952, Columbus, IN
Drafted: 1974 Round 5 NO
1974 NO: KR 1-23 23.0. **1975** NO: PR 11-76 6.9; KR 2-54 27.0.
Total: PR 11-76 6.9; KR 3-77 25.7.

		Interceptions			
Year Team	**G**	**Int**	**Yds**	**TD**	**Fum**
1974 NO	9	4	27	1	0
1975 NO	13	1	37	0	3
1976 ChiB	9	0	0	0	0
1977 ChiB	10	0	0	0	0
1978 ChiB	16	2	23	0	0
1979 ChiB	16	6	44	1	0
1980 ChiB	16	1	0	0	0
1981 ChiB	16	2	4	0	0
1982 ChiB	9	4	39	0	0
1983 ChiB	13	5	31	1	0
1984 ChiB	16	1	0	0	0
NFL Total	143	26	205	3	3

JOE SCHMIESING Schmiesing, Joseph Frank 6'4", 245 **DT-DE**
Col: North Dakota State Coll. of Science (JC); Minnesota; New Mexico State *HS:* Sauk Centre [MN] B: 4/1/1945, Melrose, MN
Drafted: 1968 Round 4 StL
1968 StL: 14 G. **1969** StL: 11 G. **1970** StL: 14 G. **1971** StL: 9 G. **1972** Det: 5 G. **1973** Bal: 14 G. **1974** NYJ: 13 G. **Total:** 80 G.

BOB SCHMIT Schmit, Robert Steven 6'1", 220 **LB**
Col: Nebraska *HS:* Boys Town [NE] B: 6/28/1950, Queens, NY
1975 NYG: 13 G. **1976** NYG: 2 G. **Total:** 15 G.

GEORGE SCHMITT Schmitt, George Paul 5'11", 193 **DB**
Col: Delaware *HS:* Marple Newtown [Newtown Square, PA]
B: 3/6/1961, Bryn Mawr, PA *Drafted:* 1983 Round 6 StL
1983 StL: 16 G; KR 4-41 10.3; 1 Fum.

JOHN SCHMITT Schmitt, John Charles 6'4", 250 **C**
Col: Hofstra *HS:* Seton Hall Prep [South Orange, NJ] B: 11/12/1942, Brooklyn, NY
1964 NYJ: 2 G. **1965** NYJ: 2 G. **1966** NYJ: 14 G. **1967** NYJ: 14 G.
1968 NYJ: 14 G. **1969** NYJ: 14 G. **1970** NYJ: 14 G. **1971** NYJ: 14 G.
1972 NYJ: 14 G. **1973** NYJ: 14 G. **1974** GB: 14 G. **Total:** 130 G.

THEODORE SCHMITT Schmitt, Theodore Alfred 5'11", 216 **G-C-LB**
Col: Pittsburgh *HS:* Carrick [Pittsburgh, PA] B: 10/2/1916, Pittsburgh, PA
1938 Phi: 11 G. **1939** Phi: 11 G; **1** Fum TD; 6 Pt. **1940** Phi: 11 G; Rush 1-6 6.0; Rec 1-8 8.0. **Total:** 33 G; Rush 1-6 6.0; Rec 1-8 8.0; 1 Fum TD; 6 Pt.

BOB SCHMITZ Schmitz, Robert Joseph 6'1", 240 **LB**
Col: Wisconsin; Montana State *HS:* New Holstein [WI] B: 9/10/1938, Marytown, WI *Drafted:* 1961 Round 14 Pit
1961 Pit: 14 G; KR 1-0. **1962** Pit: 9 G; Int 3-65 **1** TD; 6 Pt. **1963** Pit: 11 G; Scor **1** Saf; 2 Pt. **1964** Pit: 6 G. **1965** Pit: 1 G. **1966** Pit-Min: 10 G. Pit: 8 G. Min: 2 G. **Total:** 51 G; KR 1-0; Int 3-65 1 TD; Scor 1 Saf; 8 Pt.

STEVE SCHNARR Schnarr, Steven Donald 6'2", 216 **RB**
Col: Otterbein *HS:* Grove City [OH] B: 7/30/1952, Philadelphia, PA
1975 Buf: 12 G; KR 4-80 20.0.

DON SCHNEIDER Schneider, Donald Paul 5'9", 170 **HB**
Col: Pennsylvania *HS:* Lancaster [PA] B: 4/4/1924, Crafton, PA
AAFC **1948** BufA: 9 G; Rush 15-70 4.7; Rec 1-14 14.0; PR 1-4 4.0; KR 4-77 19.3.

JOHN SCHNEIDER Schneider, John J 5'10", 180 **WB**
(Pop) *Col:* No College B: 2/15/1894, Columbus, OH D: 7/19/1963, Cleveland, OH
1920 Col: 8 G.

LEROY SCHNEIDER Schneider, Leroy 5'11", 237 **T**
Col: Tulane *HS:* Baltimore Polytechnic Inst. [MD] B: 7/16/1923, Baltimore, MD
AAFC **1947** BknA: 1 G.

HERM SCHNEIDMAN Schneidman, Herman 5'11", 201 **BB-DB-LB-OE**
(Biff) *Col:* Iowa *HS:* Quincy [IL] B: 11/22/1912, Rock Island, IL
1935 GB: 11 G; Rush 4-12 3.0; Rec 2-16 8.0. **1936** GB: 7 G; Rec 3-68 22.7 1 TD; 6 Pt. **1937** GB: 11 G; Rush 5-17 3.4; Rec 2-35 17.5 1 TD; 6 Pt. **1938** GB: 10 G; Rush 4-8 2.0. **1939** GB: 1 G. **1940** ChiC: 6 G; Int 1-48. **Total:** 46 G; Rush 13-37 2.8; Rec 7-119 17.0 2 TD; Int 1-48; 12 Pt.

BOB SCHNELKER Schnelker, Robert Bernard 6'3", 214 **OE**
Col: Bowling Green State *HS:* Upper Sandusky [OH] B: 10/17/1928, Galion, OH *Drafted:* 1950 Round 29 Cle
1955 NYG: **1** Fum TD. **Total:** 1 Fum TD.

Year Team	G	Receiving Rec	Yds	Avg	TD	Fum	Tot TD
1953 Phi	8	4	34	8.5	0	0	0
1954 NYG	12	30	550	18.3	8	0	8
1955 NYG	12	25	326	13.0	2	1	3
1956 NYG	12	9	122	13.6	1	0	1
1957 NYG	12	20	450	22.5	5	0	5
1958 NYG	12	24	460	19.2	5	0	5
1959 NYG	11	37	714	19.3	6	0	6
1960 NYG	12	38	610	16.1	2	0	2
1961 Min-Pit	14	24	401	16.7	4	0	4
1961 Min	6	6	70	11.7	1	0	1
1961 Pit	8	18	331	18.4	3	0	3
NFL Total	105	211	3667	17.4	33	1	34

OTTO SCHNELLBACHER Schnellbacher, Otto Ole 6'4", 188 **DB-OE**
(The Claw) *Col:* Kansas *HS:* Sublette [KS] B: 4/15/1923, Sublette, KS *Drafted:* 1947 Round 23 ChiC
AAFC **1948** NY-A: Rec 5-72 14.4; PR 5-45 9.0. **1949** NY-A: Rec 1-11 11.0; PR 4-31 7.8. **Total:** Rec 6-83 13.8; PR 9-76 8.4.

Year Team	G	Interceptions Int	Yds	TD
1948 NY-A	14	11	239	1
1949 NY-A	12	4	26	0
AAFC Total	26	15	265	1

NFL **1950** NYG: PR 3-22 7.3. **1951** NYG: PR 7-32 4.6. **Total:** PR 10-54 5.4.

Year Team	G	Interceptions Int	Yds	TD	Fum
1950 NYG	12	8	99	0	1
1951 NYG	12	**11**	**194**	**2**	0
NFL Total	24	19	293	2	1

JOHN SCHNELLER Schneller, John Benjamin 6'2", 204 **OE-DE**
Col: Wisconsin *HS:* Neenah [WI] B: 11/1/1911, Neenah, WI D: 11/1978, Denver, CO
1933 Port: 9 G; Rush 5-12 2.4; Rec 3-45 15.0. **1934** Det: 13 G; Rec 4-58 14.5. **1935** Det: 12 G; Rec 7-149 21.3 2 TD; 12 Pt. **1936** Det: 12 G; Rec 7-124 17.7 1 TD; 6 Pt. **Total:** 46 G; Rush 5-12 2.4; Rec 21-376 17.9 3 TD; 18 Pt.

MIKE SCHNITKER Schnitker, James Michael 6'3", 245 **OG**
(Corky) *Col:* Colorado *HS:* Lakewood [CO] B: 12/30/1946, Atcheson Co., MO *Drafted:* 1969 Round 4 Den
1969 Den: 7 G. **1970** Den: 14 G. **1971** Den: 13 G; Rec 1-(-11) -11.0. **1972** Den: 14 G. **1973** Den: 14 G. **1974** Den: 12 G. **Total:** 74 G; Rec 1-(-11) -11.0.

ROY SCHOEMANN Schoemann, Leroy Herbert 6'1", 192 **C-LB**
(Bunny) *Col:* Marquette *HS:* South Division [Milwaukee, WI] B: 8/30/1914 D: 5/1972
1938 GB: 3 G.

TOM SCHOEN Schoen, Thomas Ralph 5'11", 185 **DB**
Col: Notre Dame *HS:* St. Joseph [Cleveland, OH] B: 1/30/1946, Cleveland, OH *Drafted:* 1968 Round 8 Cle
1970 Cle: 4 G; PR 8-18 2.3; KR 1-27 27.0; 1 Fum.

RAY SCHOENKE Schoenke, Raymond Frederick Jr. 6'4", 250 **OG-OT**
Col: Southern Methodist *HS:* Punahou School [Honolulu, HI]; Weatherford [TX] B: 9/10/1941, Wahiawa, HI *Drafted:* 1963 Round 11 Dal
1963 Dal: 9 G. **1964** Dal: 14 G. **1966** Was: 11 G. **1967** Was: 14 G. **1968** Was: 11 G. **1969** Was: 13 G. **1970** Was: 14 G. **1971** Was: 14 G. **1972** Was: 12 G. **1973** Was: 7 G. **1974** Was: 14 G. **1975** Was: 12 G. **Total:** 145 G.

ROY SCHOLL Scholl, Roy Franklin 5'8", 205 **G**
Col: Lehigh *HS:* Liberty [Bethlehem, PA] B: 9/15/1904 D: 10/8/1993, Topton, PA
1929 Bost: 1 G.

BRUCE SCHOLTZ Scholtz, Bruce Daniel 6'6", 240 **LB**
Col: Texas *HS:* David Crockett [Austin, TX] B: 9/26/1958, La Grange, TX *Drafted:* 1982 Round 2 Sea
1982 Sea: 9 G; Int 1-31 1 TD; 6 Pt; 1 Sac. **1983** Sea: 16 G; Int 1-8; 1.5 Sac. **1984** Sea: 16 G; Int 1-15. **1985** Sea: 16 G; 2.5 Sac. **1986** Sea: 16 G; KR 3-39 13.0; Int 2-10; 3 Sac. **1987** Sea: 8 G; KR 1-11 11.0; 0.5 Sac. **1988** Sea: 15 G; 1 Sac. **1989** NE: 8 G. **Total:** 104 G; KR 4-50 12.5; Int 5-64 1 TD; 6 Pt; 9.5 Sac.

BOB SCHOLTZ Scholtz, Robert Joseph 6'4", 250 **C-OT**
Col: Notre Dame *HS:* Marquette [Tulsa, OK] B: 12/25/1937, Watertown, SD *Drafted:* 1960 Round 3 Det
1960 Det: 12 G. **1961** Det: 14 G. **1962** Det: 14 G. **1963** Det: 9 G. **1964** Det: 11 G. **1965** NYG: 14 G. **1966** NYG: 7 G. **Total:** 81 G.

TURK SCHONERT Schonert, Turk Leroy 6'1", 191 **QB**
Col: Stanford *HS:* Servite [Anaheim, CA] B: 1/15/1957, Torrance, CA *Drafted:* 1980 Round 9 ChiB

Year Team	G	Passing Att	Comp	Comp%	Yds	YPA	TD	Int	Rating
1981 Cin	4	19	10	52.6	166	8.74	0	0	82.3
1982 Cin	2	1	1	100.0	6	6.00	0	0	91.7
1983 Cin	9	156	92	59.0	1159	7.43	2	5	73.1
1984 Cin	8	117	78	66.7	945	8.08	4	7	77.8
1985 Cin	7	51	33	64.7	460	9.02	1	0	100.1
1986 Atl	8	154	95	61.7	1032	6.70	4	8	68.4
1987 Cin	11	0	0	—	0	—	0	0	—
1988 Cin	16	4	2	50.0	20	5.00	0	0	64.6
1989 Cin	7	2	0	0.0	0	0.00	0	0	39.6
NFL Total	72	504	311	61.7	3788	7.52	11	20	75.6

Year Team	Rushing Att	Yds	Avg	TD	Fum
1981 Cin	7	41	5.9	0	1
1982 Cin	3	-8	-2.7	0	1
1983 Cin	29	117	4.0	2	6
1984 Cin	13	77	5.9	1	2
1985 Cin	8	39	4.9	0	3
1986 Atl	11	12	1.1	1	5
1988 Cin	2	10	5.0	0	0
NFL Total	73	288	3.9	4	18

IVAN SCHOTTEL Schottel, Ivan Estil 6'2", 204 **BB-DB-DE**
Col: Northwest Missouri State *HS:* King City [MO] B: 10/11/1921, Cosby, MO
1946 Det: 10 G; Rush 4-12 3.0; Rec 4-147 36.8 1 TD; KR 1-20 20.0; Punt 5-208 41.6; 6 Pt. **1948** Det: 6 G. **Total:** 16 G; Rush 4-12 3.0; Rec 4-147 36.8 1 TD; KR 1-20 20.0; Punt 5-208 41.6; 6 Pt.

MARTY SCHOTTENHEIMER Schottenheimer, Martin Edward 6'3", 224 **LB**
Col: Pittsburgh *HS:* Fort Cherry [McDonald, PA] B: 9/23/1943, Canonsburg, PA *Drafted:* 1965 Round 7 Buf
1965 Buf: 14 G. **1966** Buf: 14 G; Int 1-20. **1967** Buf: 14 G; Int 3-88 1 TD; 6 Pt. **1968** Buf: 14 G; Int 1-22. **1969** Bos: 11 G; KR 1-13 13.0; Int 1-3. **1970** Bos: 12 G; KR 1-8 8.0. **Total:** 79 G; KR 2-21 10.5; Int 6-133 1 TD; 6 Pt.

JIM SCHRADER Schrader, James Lee 6'2", 244 **C-OT**
Col: Notre Dame *HS:* Scott Twp. [North Braddock, PA] B: 6/27/1932, Weston, WV D: 1/16/1972, Norristown, PA *Drafted:* 1954 Round 2 Was
1954 Was: 10 G. **1956** Was: 4 G. **1957** Was: 12 G. **1958** Was: 12 G. **1959** Was: 12 G. **1960** Was: 12 G. **1961** Was: 14 G. **1962** Phi: 13 G. **1963** Phi: 13 G. **1964** Phi: 14 G. **Total:** 116 G.

ADAM SCHREIBER Schreiber, Adam Blayne 6'4", 290 **OG-C**
Col: Texas *HS:* S.R. Butler [Huntsville, AL] B: 2/20/1962, Galveston, TX *Drafted:* 1984 Round 9 Sea
1984 Sea: 6 G. **1985** NO: 1 G. **1986** Phi: 9 G. **1987** Phi: 12 G. **1988** Phi-NYJ: 13 G. Phi: 6 G. NYJ: 7 G. **1989** NYJ: 16 G. **1990** Min: 16 G; KR 1-5 5.0. **1991** Min: 15 G. **1992** Min: 16 G. **1993** Min: 16 G. **1994** NYG: 16 G. **1995** NYG: 16 G. **1996** NYG: 15 G. **1997** Atl: 16 G. **1998** Atl: 16 G. **Total:** 199 G; KR 1-5 5.0.

LARRY SCHREIBER Schreiber, Lawrence Anthony 6'0", 210 **RB**
Col: Tennessee Tech *HS:* Dixie Heights [Edgewood, KY] B: 8/11/1947, Covington, KY *Drafted:* 1970 Round 10 SF
1971 SF: Scor **1** 1XP. **1972** SF: KR 2-41 20.5. **Total:** KR 2-41 20.5; Scor 1 1XP.

		Rushing				Receiving					Tot
Year Team	G	Att	Yds	Avg	TD	Rec	Yds	Avg	TD	Fum	TD
1971 SF	14	34	180	5.3	0	3	79	26.3	1	0	1
1972 SF	14	118	420	3.6	2	31	283	9.1	1	4	3
1973 SF	4	42	163	3.9	0	12	98	8.2	0	1	0
1974 SF	14	174	634	3.6	3	30	217	7.2	1	2	4
1975 SF	14	134	337	2.5	5	40	289	7.2	1	6	6
1976 ChiB	14	4	15	3.8	0	1	16	16.0	0	1	0
NFL Total	74	506	1749	3.5	10	117	982	8.4	4	14	14

GENE SCHROEDER Schroeder, Eugene Willard 6'3", 192 **OE-DB**
Col: Virginia *HS:* Anacostia [Washington, DC] B: 3/3/1929, Washington, DC *Drafted:* 1951 Round 1 ChiB
1951 ChiB: Rush 1-4 4.0; KR 1-18 18.0; Int 5-62. **Total:** Rush 1-4 4.0; KR 1-18 18.0; Int 5-62.

		Receiving				
Year Team	G	Rec	Yds	Avg	TD	Fum
1951 ChiB	12	24	461	19.2	3	0
1952 ChiB	12	39	660	16.9	6	3
1954 ChiB	5	1	71	71.0	1	0
1955 ChiB	12	17	315	18.5	2	0
1956 ChiB	11	20	315	15.8	1	1
1957 ChiB	12	3	48	16.0	0	0
NFL Total	64	104	1870	18.0	13	4

JAY SCHROEDER Schroeder, Jay Brian 6'4", 215 **QB**
Col: UCLA *HS:* Pacific Palisades [CA] B: 6/28/1961, Milwaukee, WI *Drafted:* 1984 Round 3 Was
1985 Was: Punt 4-132 33.0. **Total:** Punt 4-132 33.0.

		Passing							
Year Team	G	Att	Comp	Comp%	Yds	YPA	TD	Int	Rating
1985 Was	9	209	112	53.6	1458	6.98	5	5	73.8
1986 Was	16	541	276	51.0	4109	7.60	22	22	72.9
1987 Was	11	267	129	48.3	1878	7.03	12	10	71.0
1988 LARd	9	256	113	44.1	1839	7.18	13	13	64.6
1989 LARd	11	194	91	46.9	1550	7.99	8	13	60.3
1990 LARd	16	334	182	54.5	2849	**8.53**	19	9	90.8
1991 LARd	15	357	189	52.9	2562	7.18	15	16	71.4
1992 LARd	13	253	123	48.6	1476	5.83	11	11	63.3
1993 Cin	9	159	78	49.1	832	5.23	5	2	70.0
1994 Ariz	9	238	133	55.9	1510	6.34	4	**7**	68.4
NFL Total	118	2808	1426	50.8	20063	7.14	114	108	71.7

	Rushing				
Year Team	Att	Yds	Avg	TD	Fum
1985 Was	17	30	1.8	0	5
1986 Was	36	47	1.3	1	9
1987 Was	26	120	4.6	3	5
1988 LARd	29	109	3.8	1	6
1989 LARd	15	38	2.5	0	6
1990 LARd	37	81	2.2	0	11
1991 LARd	28	76	2.7	0	7
1992 LARd	28	160	5.7	0	5
1993 Cin	10	41	4.1	0	5
1994 Ariz	16	59	3.7	0	5
NFL Total	242	761	3.1	5	64

BILL SCHROEDER Schroeder, William Fredrich 6'3", 200 **WR**
Col: Wis.-La Crosse *HS:* South [Sheboygan, WI] B: 1/9/1971, Eau Claire, WI *Drafted:* 1994 Round 6 GB
1994 GB: Postseason only. **1997** GB: KR 24-562 23.4. **Total:** KR 24-562 23.4.

		Receiving				Punt Returns				
Year Team	G	Rec	Yds	Avg	TD	Ret	Yds	Avg	TD	Fum
1997 GB	15	2	15	7.5	1	33	342	10.4	0	4
1998 GB	13	31	452	14.6	1	2	5	2.5	0	1
NFL Total	28	33	467	14.2	2	35	347	9.9	0	5

BILL SCHROEDER Schroeder, William Henry 6'0", 190 **DB-HB-TB**
Col: Wisconsin *HS:* Sheboygan Central [WI] B: 4/11/1923, Sheboygan, WI D: 2/18/1994, Litchfield, MN
AAFC **1946** ChiA: 14 G; Pass 2-1 50.0%, 10 5.00; Rush 12-42 3.5; Rec 1-9 9.0; PR 0-7; KR 1-19 19.0; Int 1-4. **1947** ChiA: 12 G; Rush 11-45 4.1; Rec 2-19 9.5 1 TD; KR 5-92 18.4; Int 4-148 2 TD; Tot TD 3; 18 Pt. **Total:** 26 G; Pass 2-1 50.0%, 10 5.00; Rush 23-87 3.8; Rec 3-28 9.3 1 TD; PR 0-7; KR 6-111 18.5; Int 5-152 2 TD; Tot TD 3; 18 Pt.

BILL SCHROLL Schroll, Charles William 6'0", 214 **LB-FB**
(Bonk) *Col:* Louisiana State *HS:* Jesuit [Alexandria, LA] B: 1/24/1926, Alexandria, LA
AAFC **1949** BufA: 12 G; Int 1-4.

NFL **1950** Det: 12 G; Rush 1-1 1.0; Int 2-8. **1951** GB: 12 G. **Total:** 24 G; Rush 1-1 1.0; Int 2-8.

KEN SCHROY Schroy, Kenneth Michael 6'2", 198 **DB**
Col: Maryland *HS:* Quakertown [PA] B: 9/22/1952, Valley Forge, PA *Drafted:* 1975 Round 10 Phi
1977 NYJ: PR 3-38 12.7. **1978** NYJ: PR 3-35 11.7; KR 0-26. **1979** NYJ: PR 2-24 12.0; KR 6-179 29.8. **1980** NYJ: PR 4-27 6.8; KR 1-17 17.0. **1981** NYJ: PR 1-5 5.0. **1983** NYJ: PR 1-11 11.0; 2 Sac. **Total:** PR 14-140 10.0; KR 7-222 31.7; 2 Sac.

		Interceptions			
Year Team	G	Int	Yds	TD	Fum
1977 NYJ	14	0	0	0	0
1978 NYJ	16	0	0	0	1
1979 NYJ	16	1	4	0	0
1980 NYJ	14	8	91	1	0
1981 NYJ	16	2	58	0	0
1982 NYJ	9	1	34	0	0
1983 NYJ	16	2	6	0	0
1984 NYJ	12	2	13	0	0
NFL Total	113	16	206	1	1

JIM SCHUBER Schuber, James Buchanon Jr. 5'8", 160 **HB**
Col: Navy *HS:* Balboa [Panama Canal Zone] B: 6/23/1904, Ancon, Panama Canal Zone D: 5/26/1982, Naples, FL
1930 Bkn: 1 G.

ERIC SCHUBERT Schubert, Eric Jon 5'8", 185 **K**
Col: Pittsburgh *HS:* Lakeland Regional [Wanaque, NJ] B: 5/28/1962, Abington, PA
1985 NYG: 8 G; Scor 56, 10-13 76.9% FG, 26-27 96.3% XK. **1986** StL: 5 G; Scor 18, 3-11 27.3% FG, 9-9 100.0% XK. **1987** NE: 1 G; Scor 4, 1-2 50.0% FG, 1-1 100.0% XK. **Total:** 14 G; Scor 78, 14-26 53.8% FG, 36-37 97.3% XK.

STEVE SCHUBERT Schubert, Steven William 5'10", 185 **WR**
Col: Massachusetts *HS:* Manchester Central [NH] B: 3/15/1951, Brooklyn, NY
1974 NE: Rec 1-21 21.0 1 TD; KR 5-112 22.4. **1975** ChiB: Rec 5-68 13.6; KR 9-146 16.2. **1976** ChiB: Rec 4-74 18.5; KR 1-3 3.0. **1977** ChiB: Rec 8-119 14.9. **1978** ChiB: Rec 4-51 12.8; KR 4-80 20.0. **1979** ChiB: Rec 2-29 14.5; KR 2-45 22.5. **Total:** Rec 24-362 15.1 1 TD; KR 21-386 18.4.

		Punt Returns					Tot
Year Team	G	Ret	Yds	Avg	TD	Fum	TD
1974 NE	8	3	15	5.0	0	0	1
1975 ChiB	12	6	33	5.5	0	1	0
1976 ChiB	14	11	60	5.5	0	1	0
1977 ChiB	13	31	291	9.4	1	4	1
1978 ChiB	13	27	229	8.5	**1**	0	1
1979 ChiB	14	25	238	9.5	1	0	1
NFL Total	74	103	866	8.4	3	6	4

JAKE SCHUEHLE Schuehle, Charles John 6'0", 196 **LB**
Col: Rice *HS:* Hondo [TX] B: 9/28/1917, Hondo, TX *Drafted:* 1939 Round 6 Phi
1939 Phi: 2 G.

KARL SCHUELKE Schuelke, Karl Herman Jr. 5'10", 200 **FB-DB**
Col: Wisconsin *HS:* McKinley [Marshfield, WI] B: 9/5/1914, Marshfield, WI D: 2/18/1992, Wausau, WI
1939 Pit: 1 G; Rush 2-2 1.0.

CARL SCHUETTE Schuette, Charles William 6'1", 206 **LB-C-DB**
Col: Marquette *HS:* Sheboygan Central [WI] B: 4/4/1922, Sheboygan, WI D: 12/1975 *Drafted:* 1947 Round 22 Det
AAFC **1948** BufA: 14 G; Int 4-97 1 TD; 6 Pt. **1949** BufA: 10 G. **Total:** 24 G; Int 4-97 1 TD; 6 Pt.

NFL **1950** GB: 12 G; Int 1-0. **1951** GB: 12 G. **Total:** 24 G; Int 1-0.

PAUL SCHUETTE Schuette, Paul August Jr. 6'0", 220 **G**
Col: Wisconsin *HS:* Manitowoc [WI]; Lake Forest Acad., [IL] B: 3/10/1906, South Bend, IN D: 10/20/1960
1928 NYG: 4 G. **1930** ChiB: 11 G. **1931** ChiB: 11 G. **1932** ChiB-Bos: 5 G. ChiB: 1 G. Bos: 4 G. **Total:** 31 G.

HARRY SCHUH Schuh, Harry Frederick 6'3", 260 **OT**
(Horse) *Col:* Memphis *HS:* Neshaminy [Langhorne, PA] B: 9/25/1942, Philadelphia, PA *Drafted:* 1965 Round 1 Oak
1965 Oak: 14 G. **1966** Oak: 14 G. **1967** Oak: 14 G. **1968** Oak: 14 G. **1969** Oak: 14 G. **1970** Oak: 14 G. **1971** LARm: 14 G. **1972** LARm: 14 G. **1973** LARm: 14 G. **1974** GB: 14 G. **Total:** 140 G.

JEFF SCHUH Schuh, Jeffrey John 6′2″, 228 **LB**
Col: North Hennepin CC MN; Minnesota *HS:* Armstrong [Plymouth, MN]
B: 5/22/1958, Crystal, MN *Drafted:* 1981 Round 7 Cin
1981 Cin: 16 G. **1982** Cin: 9 G. **1983** Cin: 16 G. **1984** Cin: 16 G; Int 1-0; 2 Sac. **1985** Cin: 16 G; 4 Sac. **1986** GB-Min: 14 G. GB: 12 G. Min: 2 G. **Total:** 87 G; Int 1-0; 6 Sac.

JOHN SCHUHMACHER Schuhmacher, John 6′3″, 271 **OG-OT**
Col: USC *HS:* Arcadia [CA] B: 9/23/1955, Salem, OR *Drafted:* 1978 Round 12 Hou
1978 Hou: 11 G. **1981** Hou: 16 G. **1982** Hou: 9 G. **1983** Hou: 1 G. **1984** Hou: 16 G. **1985** Hou: 16 G. **Total:** 69 G.

BILL SCHULER Schuler, William Moughon 6′0″, 215 **T**
Col: Auburn; Yale *HS:* Phillips [Birmingham, AL] B: 10/18/1922, Birmingham, AL
1947 NYG: 11 G. **1948** NYG: 12 G. **Total:** 23 G.

RICK SCHULTE Schulte, Richard J 6′2″, 270 **OG-OT**
Col: Illinois *HS:* Maine West [Des Plaines, IL] B: 11/24/1963, Chicago, IL
1987 Buf: 3 G.

LANCE SCHULTERS Schulters, Lance 6′2″, 195 **DB**
Col: Nassau CC NY; Hofstra *HS:* Canarsie [Brooklyn, NY]
B: 5/27/1975, Brooklyn, NY *Drafted:* 1998 Round 4 SF
1998 SF: 15 G.

HEINIE SCHULTZ Schultz, ? 5′10″, 182 **OE**
Col: No College Deceased
1920 Det: 1 G.

CHARLIE SCHULTZ Schultz, Charles William 6′3″, 231 **T**
Col: Minnesota *HS:* Johnson [St. Paul, MN] B: 10/8/1915, St.Paul, MN
D: 3/15/1989, Pebble Beach, CA *Drafted:* 1939 Round 18 GB
1939 GB: 9 G. **1940** GB: 2 G. **1941** GB: 10 G. **Total:** 21 G.

CHRIS SCHULTZ Schultz, Christopher 6′8″, 277 **OT**
Col: Arizona *HS:* Aldershot [Burlington, Canada] B: 2/16/1960, Hamilton, Canada *Drafted:* 1983 Round 7 Dal
1983 Dal: 5 G. **1985** Dal: 16 G. **Total:** 21 G.

ELBIE SCHULTZ Schultz, Eberle Hynson 6′4″, 252 **T-G**
Col: Oregon State *HS:* Oregon City [OR] B: 12/23/1917, Eugene, OR
Drafted: 1940 Round 4 Phi
1940 Phi: 11 G. **1941** Pit: 11 G. **1942** Pit: 11 G. **1943** PhPt: 10 G. **1944** ChPt: 10 G; 6 Pt. **1945** Cle: 10 G. **1946** LARm: 11 G. **1947** LARm: 12 G. **Total:** 86 G; 6 Pt.

JOHN SCHULTZ Schultz, John Andreas 5′10″, 182 **WR**
Col: Maryland *HS:* Vestal [NY] B: 6/10/1953, Binghamton, NY
1976 Den: 14 G; Rec 2-29 14.5; PR 1-2 2.0; KR 3-82 27.3; 1 Fum.
1977 Den: 14 G; PR 1-11 11.0; KR 6-135 22.5. **1978** Den: 4 G; KR 1-20 20.0. **Total:** 32 G; Rec 2-29 14.5; PR 2-13 6.5; KR 10-237 23.7; 1 Fum.

PETE SCHULTZ Schultz, Peter 187 **FB**
Col: No College Deceased
1920 ChiC: 1 G. **1922** Col: 1 G. **Total:** 2 G.

RANDY SCHULTZ Schultz, Randolph B 6′0″, 210 **RB**
Col: Northern Iowa *HS:* Alden [IA] B: 11/17/1943, Iowa Falls, IA
D: 10/4/1996, Cedar Falls, IA *Drafted:* 1966 Round 5 Cle
1966 Cle: KR 3-52 17.3. **Total:** KR 3-52 17.3.

		Rushing				Receiving				
Year Team	G	Att	Yds	Avg	TD	Rec	Yds	Avg	TD	Fum
1966 Cle	14	7	32	4.6	0	0	0	—	0	0
1967 NO	8	32	117	3.7	2	14	186	13.3	0	0
1968 NO	9	43	152	3.5	0	12	34	2.8	0	1
NFL Total	31	82	301	3.7	2	26	220	8.5	0	1

BILL SCHULTZ Schultz, William 6′5″, 305 **OG-OT**
Col: Glendale CC CA; USC *HS:* John F. Kennedy [Los Angeles, CA]
B: 5/1/1967, Granada Hills, CA *Drafted:* 1990 Round 4 Ind
1990 Ind: 12 G. **1991** Ind: 10 G. **1992** Ind: 10 G; Rec 1-3 3.0 1 TD; 6 Pt. **1993** Ind: 14 G. **1995** Den: 2 G. **1997** ChiB: 8 G. **Total:** 56 G; Rec 1-3 3.0 1 TD; 6 Pt.

JODY SCHULZ Schulz, Jody John 6′3″, 235 **LB**
Col: Chowan Coll. NC; East Carolina *HS:* Queen Annes Co. [Centerville, MD] B: 8/17/1960, Chester, MD *Drafted:* 1983 Round 2 Phi
1983 Phi: 6 G. **1984** Phi: 15 G; 1.5 Sac. **1986** Phi: 16 G; KR 1-9 9.0; Int 1-11. **1987** Phi: 7 G. **Total:** 44 G; KR 1-9 9.0; Int 1-11; 1.5 Sac.

KURT SCHULZ Schulz, Kurt Erich 6′1″, 208 **DB**
Col: Eastern Washington *HS:* Eisenhower [Yakima, WA]
B: 12/12/1968, Wenatchee, WA *Drafted:* 1992 Round 7 Buf

		Interceptions		
Year Team	G	Int	Yds	TD
1992 Buf	8	0	0	0
1993 Buf	12	0	0	0
1994 Buf	16	0	0	0
1995 Buf	13	6	48	1
1996 Buf	15	4	24	0
1997 Buf	15	2	23	0
1998 Buf	12	6	48	0
NFL Total	91	18	143	1

GREGG SCHUMACHER Schumacher, Gregg Harold 6′2″, 240 **DE**
(Shoe) *Col:* Illinois *HS:* Taft [Chicago, IL] B: 6/30/1942, Chicago, IL
1967 LARm: 11 G. **1968** LARm: 14 G. **Total:** 25 G.

KURT SCHUMACHER Schumacher, Kurt 6′3″, 252 **OG-OT**
Col: Ohio State *HS:* Lorain [OH] B: 12/26/1952, Cleveland, OH
Drafted: 1975 Round 1 NO
1975 NO: 13 G. **1976** NO: 14 G; KR 2-17 8.5. **1977** NO: 14 G. **1978** TB: 4 G. **Total:** 45 G; KR 2-17 8.5.

WALT SCHUPP Schupp, Walter Lee 6′0″, 185 **T-G**
Col: Miami (Ohio) *HS:* Bucyrus [OH] B: 9/1895 Deceased
1921 Cin: 4 G.

DICK SCHUSTER Schuster, Richard Louis 6′1″, 185 **G**
Col: Dayton; Penn State *HS:* Williamsport [PA] B: 3/2/1900
D: 2/8/1980, Binghamton, NY
1925 Can: 4 G.

SCOTT SCHUTT Schutt, Scott Joseph 6′4″, 218 **LB**
Col: North Dakota State *HS:* Sauk Prairie [Prairie du Sac, WI]
B: 8/31/1963, Prairie du Sac, WI
1987 Cin: 3 G; Scor 1 Saf; 2 Pt; 1 Sac.

RAY SCHWAB Schwab, Raymond 205 **BB-OE**
Col: Oklahoma City *HS:* Carnegie [OK] B: 2/28/1908, MO
1931 NYG: 1 G. **1932** SI: 1 G. **Total:** 2 G.

VIC SCHWALL Schwall, Victor Henry 5′8″, 188 **HB**
(Stumpy) *Col:* Northwestern *HS:* Carl Schurz [Chicago, IL]
B: 1/21/1925, Oak Park, IL *Drafted:* 1947 Round 1 NYG
1947 ChiC: KR 1-20 20.0. **1948** ChiC: Pass 1-0; Rec 2-13 6.5. **1949** ChiC: Pass 2-0; Rec 3-8 2.7 2 TD; KR 4-63 15.8. **1950** ChiC: Rec 1-7 7.0; KR 1-21 21.0. **Total:** Pass 3-0; Rec 6-28 4.7 2 TD; KR 6-104 17.3.

		Rushing					Tot
Year Team	G	Att	Yds	Avg	TD	Fum	TD
1947 ChiC	11	12	33	2.8	0	2	0
1948 ChiC	7	15	107	7.1	1	0	1
1949 ChiC	11	12	47	3.9	0	2	2
1950 ChiC	12	17	114	6.7	0	1	0
NFL Total	41	56	301	5.4	1	5	3

ADE SCHWAMMEL Schwammel, Adolphe John 6′2″, 225 **T**
(Tar) *Col:* Oregon State *HS:* Fremont [Oakland, CA] B: 10/14/1908, Los Angeles, CA D: 11/18/1979, Hololulu, HI
1934 GB: 13 G; Scor 3, 1 FG. **1935** GB: 11 G; Scor 15, 4 FG, 3 XK. **1936** GB: 12 G; Scor 8, 1 FG, 5 XK. **1943** GB: 2 G. **1944** GB: 8 G; Scor 0-1 FG. **Total:** 46 G; Scor 26, 6-1 FG, 8 XK.

JIM SCHWANTZ Schwantz, James William 6′2″, 240 **LB**
Col: Purdue *HS:* William Fremd [Palatine, IL] B: 1/23/1970, Arlington Heights, IL
1992 ChiB: 1 G. **1994** Dal: 7 G. **1995** Dal: 16 G; KR 1-9 9.0. **1996** Dal: 16 G. **1997** SF: 16 G. **1998** ChiB: 16 G. **Total:** 72 G; KR 1-9 9.0.

BRYAN SCHWARTZ Schwartz, Bryan Lee 6′4″, 253 **LB**
Col: Augustana (S.D.) *HS:* Miller [SD] B: 12/5/1971, St. Lawrence, SD
Drafted: 1995 Round 2 Jac
1995 Jac: 14 G. **1996** Jac: 4 G. **1997** Jac: 16 G; 0.5 Sac. **1998** Jac: 13 G. **Total:** 47 G; 0.5 Sac.

DONALD SCHWARTZ Schwartz, Donald Jeffrey 6′1″, 191 **DB**
Col: Washington State *HS:* Archbishop Mitty [San Jose, CA]
B: 2/24/1956, Billings, MT *Drafted:* 1978 Round 4 NO
1978 NO: 16 G; PR 1-4 4.0; KR 3-51 17.0. **1979** NO: 14 G; Int 2-31. **1980** NO: 16 G. **1981** StL: 5 G. **Total:** 51 G; PR 1-4 4.0; KR 3-51 17.0; Int 2-31.

ELMER SCHWARTZ Schwartz, Elmer George 6′0″, 212 **FB-LB-HB-DB**
(Elmer the Great) *Col:* Washington State *HS:* South Kitsap [Port Orchard, WA] B: 1907 Deceased
1931 Port: Int 1 TD. **1933** Pit: Pass 22-5 22.7%, 103 4.68 3 Int; Rec 2-20 10.0. **Total:** Pass 22-5 22.7%, 103 4.68 3 Int; Rec 2-20 10.0; Int 1 TD.

		Rushing				Tot
Year Team	G	Att	Yds	Avg	TD	TD
1931 Port	12	—	—	—	2	3
1932 ChiC	3	2	9	4.5	0	0
1933 Pit	10	38	94	2.5	0	0
NFL Total	25	40	103	2.6	2	3

PERRY SCHWARTZ Schwartz, Perry 6′2″, 199 **OE-DE**
Col: Sacramento City Coll. CA (J.C.); California *HS:* Tamalpais [Mill Valley, CA] B: 4/27/1915, Chicago, IL *Drafted:* 1938 Round 4 Bkn
AAFC **1946** NY-A: 14 G; Rec 5-82 16.4; KR 2-23 11.5.

NFL **1938** Bkn: Rush 2-(-3) -1.5. **1941** Bkn: Rush 1-7 7.0; KR 1-6 6.0. **1942** Bkn: Rush 2-20 10.0; KR 2-25 12.5. **Total:** Rush 5-24 4.8; KR 3-31 10.3.

		Receiving			
Year Team	G	Rec	Yds	Avg	TD
1938 Bkn	10	8	132	16.5	1
1939 Bkn	11	33	550	16.7	3
1940 Bkn	11	21	370	17.6	3
1941 Bkn	11	25	362	14.5	2
1942 Bkn	11	13	200	15.4	1
NFL Total	54	100	1614	16.1	10

TED SCHWARZER Schwarzer, Theodore 5′11″, 190 **G-C**
Col: Centenary *HS:* Wesley [LA] B: 1902 Deceased
1926 Buf: 6 G.

BRIAN SCHWEDA Schweda, Brian Christopher 6′3″, 250 **DE**
Col: Kansas *HS:* Lawrence [KS] B: 4/30/1943, Kansas City, KS
Drafted: 1965 Round 8 ChiB
1966 ChiB: 14 G. **1967** NO: 14 G. **1968** NO: 10 G. **Total:** 38 G.

JOHN SCHWEDER Schweder, John Anthony 6′1″, 224 **OG-LB**
(Bull) *Col:* Pennsylvania *HS:* Bethlehem [PA] B: 12/23/1927, Bethlehem, PA *Drafted:* 1949 Round 25 Phi
1950 Bal: 11 G. **1951** Pit: 12 G; Int 1-20. **1952** Pit: 12 G. **1953** Pit: 12 G. **1954** Pit: 12 G. **1955** Pit: 12 G. **Total:** 71 G; Int 1-20.

GERHARD SCHWEDES Schwedes, Gerhard 6′1″, 205 **HB**
(Ger) *Col:* Syracuse *HS:* Hunterdon Central [Flemington, NJ]
B: 4/23/1938, Freiburg, Germany *Drafted:* 1960 Round 1 Bos
1960 NYT-Bos: 5 G. NYT: 3 G. Bos: 2 G. **1961** Bos: 5 G; Rush 10-14 1.4; Rec 1-21 21.0; KR 1-0; 2 Fum. **Total:** 10 G; Rush 10-14 1.4; Rec 1-21 21.0; KR 1-0; 2 Fum.

SCOTT SCHWEDES Schwedes, Scott Andrew 6′0″, 182 **WR**
Col: Syracuse *HS:* Jamesville-DeWitt [DeWitt, NY] B: 6/30/1965, Syracuse, NY *Drafted:* 1987 Round 2 Mia
1987 Mia: KR 9-177 19.7. **1988** Mia: Rec 6-130 21.7; KR 3-49 16.3. **1989** Mia: Rec 7-174 24.9 1 TD; KR 3-24 8.0. **1990** Mia-SD: Rec 6-66 11.0 1 TD; KR 2-52 26.0. Mia: Rec 6-66 11.0 1 TD; KR 2-52 26.0. **Total:** Rec 19-370 19.5 2 TD; KR 17-302 17.8.

		Punt Returns					Tot
Year Team	G	Ret	Yds	Avg	TD	Fum	TD
1987 Mia	12	24	203	8.5	0	7	0
1988 Mia	16	24	230	9.6	0	1	0
1989 Mia	9	18	210	11.7	**1**	3	2
1990 Mia-SD	9	14	122	8.7	0	0	1
1990 Mia	4	9	89	9.9	0	0	1
1990 SD	5	5	33	6.6	0	0	0
NFL Total	46	80	765	9.6	1	11	3

BOB SCHWEICKERT Schweickert, Robert Lynn 6′1″, 190 **QB**
Col: Virginia Tech *HS:* Midlothian [VA] B: 9/17/1942, Richmond, VA
Drafted: 1965 Round 4 NYJ
1965 NYJ: 3 G. **1967** NYJ: 3 G; Rush 1-1 1.0. **Total:** 6 G; Rush 1-1 1.0.

DICK SCHWEIDLER Schweidler, Richard M 6′0″, 182 **HB-DB**
Col: St. Louis *HS:* Lyons Twp. [La Grange, IL] B: 8/18/1915, Culver, IN
1938 ChiB: Pass 1-0; Rec 1-21 21.0. **1939** ChiB: Rec 2-43 21.5. **1946** ChiB: Rec 1-11 11.0; PR 1-13 13.0; KR 3-63 21.0; Int 1-31. **Total:** Pass 1-0; Rec 4-75 18.8; PR 1-13 13.0; KR 3-63 21.0; Int 1-31.

		Rushing				
Year Team	G	Att	Yds	Avg	TD	Fum
1938 ChiB	10	16	57	3.6	0	0
1939 ChiB	4	5	15	3.0	0	0
1946 ChiB	5	20	94	4.7	3	1
NFL Total	19	41	166	4.0	3	1

BUD SCHWENK Schwenk, Wilson Rutherford 6′2″, 200 **QB**
Col: Illinois; Washington-St. Louis *HS:* Beaumont [St. Louis, MO]
B: 8/26/1917, St.Louis, MO D: 10/1/1980, St. Louis, MO
Drafted: 1942 Round 3 ChiC
AAFC.

		Passing							
Year Team	G	Att	Comp	Comp%	Yds	YPA	TD	Int	Rating
1946 CleA	4	23	15	65.2	276	12.00	4	0	146.0
1947 BalA	14	327	168	51.4	2236	6.84	13	20	61.2
1948 NY-A	8	17	6	35.3	52	3.06	0	3	4.7
AAFC Total	26	367	189	51.5	2564	6.99	17	23	63.4

	Rushing			
Year Team	Att	Yds	Avg	TD
1946 CleA	6	-1	-0.2	1
1947 BalA	25	58	2.3	1
1948 NY-A	3	6	2.0	0
AAFC Total	34	63	1.9	2

NFL **1942** ChiC: KR 2-24 12.0; Int 1-21; Punt 3-114 38.0.

		Passing							
Year Team	G	Att	Comp	Comp%	Yds	YPA	TD	Int	Rating
1942 ChiC	11	**295**	126	42.7	1360	4.61	6	27	25.5

	Rushing			
Year Team	Att	Yds	Avg	TD
1942 ChiC	111	313	2.8	2

JOHN SCIARRA Sciarra, John Michael 5′11″, 185 **DB-QB**
Col: UCLA *HS:* Bishop Amat [La Puente, CA] B: 3/2/1954, Los Angeles, CA *Drafted:* 1976 Round 4 ChiB
1978 Phi: Pass 1-0; Rush 8-11 1.4 2 TD; Int 1-21. **1979** Phi: Int 2-47. **1980** Phi: Rush 3-11 3.7. **1981** Phi: Rush 1-0; Int 1-0. **Total:** Pass 1-0; Rush 12-22 1.8 2 TD; Int 4-68.

		Punt Returns				
Year Team	G	Ret	Yds	Avg	TD	Fum
1978 Phi	16	37	251	6.8	0	2
1979 Phi	16	16	182	**11.4**	0	0
1980 Phi	16	36	330	9.2	0	1
1981 Phi	10	4	26	6.5	0	3
1982 Phi	8	2	5	2.5	0	0
1983 Phi	10	22	115	5.2	0	2
NFL Total	76	117	909	7.8	0	8

JOE SCIBELLI Scibelli, Joseph Albert 6′0″, 255 **OG**
Col: Notre Dame; American International *HS:* Cathedral [Springfield, MA] B: 4/19/1939, Springfield, MA D: 12/11/1991, Boston, MA
Drafted: 1961 Round 10 LARm
1961 LARm: 14 G; Rec 1-1 1.0. **1962** LARm: 14 G. **1963** LARm: 14 G. **1964** LARm: 14 G. **1965** LARm: 14 G. **1966** LARm: 14 G. **1967** LARm: 14 G. **1968** LARm: 14 G. **1969** LARm: 7 G. **1970** LARm: 14 G. **1971** LARm: 14 G. **1972** LARm: 13 G. **1973** LARm: 14 G. **1974** LARm: 14 G. **1975** LARm: 14 G. **Total:** 202 G; Rec 1-1 1.0.

STEVE SCIFRES Scifres, Steve William 6′4″, 300 **OG**
Col: Wyoming *HS:* Gen. William Mitchell [Colorado, CO];Air Force Acad. Prep [Col. Springs, CO] B: 1/22/1972, Colorado Springs, CO
Drafted: 1997 Round 3 Dal
1997 Dal: 6 G. **1998** Car: 1 G. **Total:** 7 G.

WILLARD SCISSUM Scissum, Willard Sebastian 6′3″, 275 **OT-OG**
Col: Alabama *HS:* Robert E. Lee [Huntsville, AL] B: 10/28/1962, Guntersville, AL
1987 Was: 3 G.

ERIC SCOGGINS Scoggins, Eric Thomas 6′2″, 235 **LB**
Col: USC *HS:* Inglewood [CA] B: 1/23/1959, Inglewood, CA
1982 SF: 3 G.

RON SCOGGINS Scoggins, Ronald Alonzo 6′6″, 305 **OT**
Col: Los Angeles Southwest Coll. CA (J.C.); Nevada-Las Vegas
HS: Inglewood [CA] B: 8/3/1961, Inglewood, CA
1987 Sea: 3 G.

NICK SCOLLARD Scollard, Nicholas M 6′4″, 217 **DE-OE**
Col: St. Joseph's (Ind.) *HS:* Catholic [Indianapolis, IN] B: 4/3/1920
D: 1/1985, Indianapolis, IN *Drafted:* 1946 Round 2 Bos
1946 Bos: 11 G; Rec 7-78 11.1 1 TD; KR 1-12 12.0; Scor 33, 0-1 FG, 21-24 87.5% XK; **1** Fum TD; Tot TD 2. **1947** Bos: 12 G; Rec 3-19 6.3; Scor 5, 1-4 25.0% FG, 2-2 100.0% XK. **1948** Bos: 12 G; Rec 2-23 11.5; Scor 14, 2-3 66.7% FG, 8-8 100.0% XK. **1949** NYB: 12 G; Rec 3-81 27.0 2 TD; PR 1-6 6.0; KR 2-16 8.0; Int 1-5; Scor 39, 3-10 30.0% FG, 18-21 85.7% XK. **Total:** 47 G; Rec 15-201 13.4 3 TD; PR 1-6 6.0; KR 3-28 9.3; Int 1-5; Scor 91, 6-18 33.3% FG, 49-55 89.1% XK; 1 Fum TD; Tot TD 4.

GLENN SCOLNIK Scolnik, Glenn 6′3″, 204 **WR**
Col: Indiana *HS:* Munster [IN] B: 6/16/1951, Hammond, IN
Drafted: 1973 Round 6 Pit
1973 Pit: 1 G.

DAVE SCOTT Scott, Arthur David 6′4″, 276 **OG-OT**
Col: Kansas *HS:* Paterson [NJ] B: 12/26/1953, Hackensack, NJ
1976 Atl: 13 G. **1977** Atl: 14 G. **1978** Atl: 16 G. **1979** Atl: 16 G. **1980** Atl: 16 G. **1981** Atl: 14 G. **1982** Atl: 9 G. **Total:** 98 G.

RONALD SCOTT Scott, Arthur Ronald 5′11″, 200 **RB**
Col: Southern University *HS:* Thibodaux [LA] B: 3/3/1963, Thibodaux, LA
1987 Mia: Rec 2-7 3.5; KR 1-22 22.0.

		Rushing				
Year Team	G	Att	Yds	Avg	TD	Fum
1987 Mia	3	47	199	4.2	3	1

CARLOS SCOTT Scott, Carlos B Jr. 6′4″, 295 **C-OT**
Col: Texas-El Paso *HS:* Waller [TX] B: 7/2/1960, Hempstead, TX
Drafted: 1983 Round 7 StL
1983 StL: 13 G. **1984** StL: 16 G. **1985** StL: 16 G; 1 Fum. **Total:** 45 G; 1 Fum.

CHAD SCOTT Scott, Chad Oliver 6′1″, 203 **DB**
Col: Towson State; Maryland *HS:* Suitland [District Heights, MD]
B: 9/6/1974, Washington, DC *Drafted:* 1997 Round 1 Pit
1997 Pit: 13 G; Int 2-(-4).

CHUCK SCOTT Scott, Charles John Miller 6′2″, 198 **WR**
Col: Vanderbilt *HS:* Lake Howell [Winter Park, FL] B: 5/24/1963, Jacksonville, FL *Drafted:* 1985 Round 2 LARm
1986 LARm: 9 G; Rec 5-76 15.2. **1987** Dal: 2 G; Rec 1-11 11.0.
Total: 11 G; Rec 6-87 14.5.

CHRIS SCOTT Scott, Christopher Sterling 6′5″, 260 **DE**
Col: Purdue *HS:* Berea [OH] B: 12/11/1961, Berea, OH *Drafted:* 1984 Round 3 Ind
1984 Ind: 14 G. **1985** Ind: 16 G; 5 Sac. **1987** Ind: 3 G. **Total:** 33 G; 5 Sac.

CLARENCE SCOTT Scott, Clarence 6′1″, 186 **DB**
Col: Morgan State *HS:* Upper Merion [King of Prussia, PA]
B: 5/5/1944, Norristown, PA
1969 Bos: 14 G; KR 6-43 7.2; 1 Fum. **1970** Bos: 14 G; Int 1-18; 1 Fum.
1971 NE: 5 G. **1972** NE: 10 G. **Total:** 43 G; KR 6-43 7.2; Int 1-18; 2 Fum.

CLARENCE SCOTT Scott, Clarence Raymond Jr. 6′0″, 190 **DB**
Col: Kansas State *HS:* Trinity [Decatur, GA] B: 4/9/1949, Atlanta, GA
Drafted: 1971 Round 1 Cle

		Interceptions				Tot
Year Team	**G**	**Int**	**Yds**	**TD**	**Fum**	**TD**
1971 Cle	13	4	47	0	0	0
1972 Cle	14	0	0	0	0	1
1973 Cle	14	5	71	1	0	1
1974 Cle	14	4	42	0	0	0
1975 Cle	14	2	4	0	0	0
1976 Cle	14	4	11	0	1	0
1977 Cle	14	3	72	**1**	0	1
1978 Cle	16	3	15	0	0	0
1979 Cle	16	3	56	0	0	0
1980 Cle	16	2	14	0	0	0
1981 Cle	16	4	46	0	0	0
1982 Cle	9	3	29	0	0	0
1983 Cle	16	2	0	0	0	0
NFL Total	186	39	407	2	1	3

CLYDE SCOTT Scott, Clyde Luther 6′0″, 174 **HB-DB**
(Smackover) *Col:* Navy; Arkansas *HS:* Smackover [AR]; The Bullis School [Potomac, MD] B: 8/29/1924, Dixie, LA *Drafted:* 1948 Round 1 Phi
1949 Phi: Rec 8-148 18.5 1 TD; PR 5-114 22.8 1 TD; KR 1-54 54.0.
1951 Phi: Rec 10-212 21.2 3 TD; PR 4-72 18.0; KR 8-171 21.4.
1952 Phi-Det: Rec 1-21 21.0; PR 3-14 4.7; KR 3-68 22.7; Int 1-0. Phi: Int 1-0. Det: Rec 1-21 21.0; PR 3-14 4.7; KR 3-68 22.7. **Total:** Rec 19-381 20.1 4 TD; PR 12-200 16.7 1 TD; KR 12-293 24.4; Int 1-0.

		Rushing					Tot
Year Team	**G**	**Att**	**Yds**	**Avg**	**TD**	**Fum**	**TD**
1949 Phi	8	40	195	4.9	1	4	3
1950 Phi	1	13	46	3.5	0	1	0
1951 Phi	12	45	161	3.6	1	6	4
1952 Phi-Det	7	2	-2	-1.0	0	0	0
1952 Phi	2	0	0	—	0	0	0
1952 Det	5	2	-2	-1.0	0	0	0
NFL Total	28	100	400	4.0	2	11	7

DARNAY SCOTT Scott, Darnay 6′1″, 187 **WR**
Col: San Diego State *HS:* Kearny [San Diego, CA] B: 7/7/1972, St. Louis, MO *Drafted:* 1994 Round 2 Cin
1994 Cin: Pass 1-1 100.0%, 53 53.00; Rush 10-106 10.6; KR 15-342 22.8. **1995** Cin: Rush 5-11 2.2. **1996** Cin: Rush 3-4 1.3. **1997** Cin: Rush 1-6 6.0. **1998** Cin: Rush 2-10 5.0. **Total:** Pass 1-1 100.0%, 53 53.00; Rush 21-137 6.5; KR 15-342 22.8.

		Receiving			
Year Team	**G**	**Rec**	**Yds**	**Avg**	**TD**
1994 Cin	16	46	866	18.8	5
1995 Cin	16	52	821	15.8	5
1996 Cin	16	58	833	14.4	5
1997 Cin	16	54	797	14.8	5
1998 Cin	13	51	817	16.0	7
NFL Total	77	261	4134	15.8	27

ED SCOTT Scott, Edward 5′10″, 182 **DB**
Col: Grambling State *HS:* George Washington Carver [New Orleans, LA]
B: 2/15/1961, New Orleans, LA
1987 StL: 3 G.

NED SCOTT Scott, Edward 6′0″, 200 **T**
Col: Monmouth (N.J.) *HS:* Monmouth [IL] B: 6/8/1901, IL Deceased
1924 RI: 9 G.

FREDDIE SCOTT Scott, Fred Lee 6′2″, 180 **WR**
Col: Amherst *HS:* Southeast [Pine Bluff, AR] B: 8/5/1952, Grady, AR
Drafted: 1974 Round 7 Bal
1974 Bal: PR 3-31 10.3; KR 3-61 20.3. **1976** Bal: KR 1-20 20.0. **1978** Det: PR 8-55 6.9; KR 3-72 24.0. **1981** Det: Pass 1-0. **Total:** Pass 1-0; PR 11-86 7.8; KR 7-153 21.9.

		Rushing				Receiving					Tot
Year Team	**G**	**Att**	**Yds**	**Avg**	**TD**	**Rec**	**Yds**	**Avg**	**TD**	**Fum**	**TD**
1974 Bal	14	2	12	6.0	0	18	317	17.6	0	0	0
1975 Bal	8	0	0	—	0	0	0	—	0	0	0
1976 Bal	10	0	0	—	0	3	35	11.7	0	0	0
1977 Bal	14	0	0	—	0	18	267	14.8	2	0	2
1978 Det	16	4	53	13.3	0	37	564	15.2	2	1	2
1979 Det	14	6	21	3.5	0	62	929	15.0	5	2	5
1980 Det	16	5	86	17.2	1	53	834	15.7	4	2	5
1981 Det	16	7	25	3.6	0	53	1022	19.3	5	0	5
1982 Det	9	1	-6	-6.0	0	13	231	17.8	1	1	1
1983 Det	15	0	0	—	0	5	71	14.2	1	1	1
NFL Total	132	25	191	7.6	1	262	4270	16.3	20	7	21

FREDDIE SCOTT Scott, Freddie Lee 5′10″, 188 **WR**
Col: Penn State *HS:* Southfield [MI] B: 8/26/1974, Miami Beach, FL
1996 Atl: 10 G; Rec 7-80 11.4. **1997** Atl: 2 G. **1998** Ind: 1 G. **Total:** 13 G; Rec 7-80 11.4.

GEORGE SCOTT Scott, George Wendell Jr. 6′1″, 180 **HB**
Col: Miami (Ohio) *HS:* Urbana [OH] B: 7/14/1937, Bainbridge, OH
Deceased *Drafted:* 1959 Round 19 NYG
1959 NYG: 7 G; Rush 2-10 5.0; Rec 1-12 12.0; PR 12-17 1.4; KR 10-253 25.3; 4 Fum.

HERBERT SCOTT Scott, Herbert Carnell Jr. 6′2″, 254 **OG**
Col: Virginia Union *HS:* Floyd E. Kellam [Virginia Beach, VA]
B: 1/18/1953, Virginia Beach, VA *Drafted:* 1975 Round 13 Dal
1975 Dal: 14 G. **1976** Dal: 14 G. **1977** Dal: 11 G. **1978** Dal: 16 G.
1979 Dal: 16 G. **1980** Dal: 16 G. **1981** Dal: 16 G. **1982** Dal: 6 G. **1983** Dal: 16 G. **1984** Dal: 15 G. **Total:** 140 G.

JOHNNY SCOTT Scott, Ian Grant 5′10″, 176 **BB-TB-WB-FB**
Col: Lafayette B: 5/3/1897, Trenton, NJ D: 11/17/1964, Cape May, NJ
1920 Buf: 2 G. **1921** Buf: 7 G; Pass 1 TD; Rush 2 TD; Rec 2 TD; Int **1** TD; Tot TD 5; 30 Pt. **1922** Buf: 1 G. **1923** Buf: 2 G. **Total:** 12 G; Pass 1 TD; Rush 2 TD; Rec 2 TD; Int 1 TD; Tot TD 5; 30 Pt.

JAKE SCOTT Scott, Jacob E III 6′0″, 188 **DB**
Col: Georgia *HS:* Washington & Lee [Arlington, VA]; Bullis Prep [Silver Spring, MD] B: 7/20/1945, Greenwood, SC *Drafted:* 1970 Round 7 Mia
1970 Mia: KR 4-117 29.3. **1973** Mia: KR 2-20 10.0. **Total:** KR 6-137 22.8.

		Punt Returns				Interceptions			
Year Team	**G**	**Ret**	**Yds**	**Avg**	**TD**	**Int**	**Yds**	**TD**	**Fum**
1970 Mia	14	27	290	10.7	**1**	5	112	0	1
1971 Mia	14	33	**318**	9.6	0	7	34	0	3
1972 Mia	14	13	100	7.7	0	5	73	0	1
1973 Mia	14	22	266	12.1	0	4	71	0	1
1974 Mia	14	31	346	11.2	0	8	75	0	2
1975 Mia	14	1	10	10.0	0	6	60	0	0
1976 Was	12	3	27	9.0	0	4	12	0	1
1977 Was	14	0	0	—	0	3	42	0	0
1978 Was	16	0	0	—	0	7	72	0	0
NFL Total	126	130	1357	10.4	1	49	551	0	9

JAMES SCOTT Scott, James 6′1″, 190 **WR**
Col: Trinity Valley CC TX *HS:* Gladewater [TX] B: 3/28/1952, Longview, TX *Drafted:* 1975 Round 8 NYJ
1976 ChiB: Rush 2-(-4) -2.0. **Total:** Rush 2-(-4) -2.0.

		Receiving				
Year Team	**G**	**Rec**	**Yds**	**Avg**	**TD**	**Fum**
1976 ChiB	11	26	512	19.7	6	0
1977 ChiB	14	50	809	16.2	3	1
1978 ChiB	15	42	759	18.1	5	1
1979 ChiB	10	21	382	18.2	3	0
1980 ChiB	15	36	696	19.3	3	0
1982 ChiB	5	2	44	22.0	0	0
1983 ChiB	1	0	0	—	0	0
NFL Total	71	177	3202	18.1	20	2

JACK SCOTT Scott, John Edward 6′4″, 260 **DT**
Col: Ohio State *HS:* Rock Hill [Ironton, OH] B: 4/12/1936, Ashland, KY
Drafted: 1959 Round 26 Pit
1960 Buf: 14 G. **1961** Buf: 7 G. **Total:** 21 G.

JOE SCOTT Scott, Joseph Oscar Jr. 6′1″, 198 **HB-DB-OE**
Col: San Francisco *HS:* Athens [TX] B: 3/17/1926, Athens, TX
Drafted: 1948 Round 2 NYG
1948 NYG: PR 3-25 8.3; Int 5-10. **1949** NYG: Int 1-16. **1950** NYG: PR 1-23 23.0. **Total:** PR 4-48 12.0; Int 6-26.

		Rushing				Receiving			
Year Team	G	Att	Yds	Avg	TD	Rec	Yds	Avg	TD
1948 NYG	10	48	198	4.1	2	17	235	13.8	2
1949 NYG	8	70	224	3.2	6	15	111	7.4	1
1950 NYG	10	72	322	4.5	2	9	240	26.7	1
1951 NYG	12	94	367	3.9	1	23	356	15.5	2
1952 NYG	8	38	107	2.8	3	14	251	17.9	1
1953 NYG	3	0	0	—	0	1	10	10.0	0
NFL Total	51	322	1218	3.8	14	79	1203	15.2	7

	Kickoff Returns					Tot
Year Team	Ret	Yds	Avg	TD	Fum	TD
1948 NYG	20	569	28.5	**1**	6	5
1949 NYG	7	203	29.0	0	2	7
1950 NYG	14	351	25.1	0	5	3
1951 NYG	6	154	25.7	0	1	3
1952 NYG	7	190	27.1	0	4	4
NFL Total	54	1467	27.2	1	18	22

KEVIN SCOTT Scott, Kevin Bernard 5′9″, 181 **RB**
Col: Stanford *HS:* Gov. John R. Rogers [Puyallup, WA] B: 10/24/1963, Fort Bragg, NC
1988 SD: 1 G. **1989** Dal: 3 G; Rush 2-(-4) -2.0; Rec 9-63 7.0. **Total:** 4 G; Rush 2-(-4) -2.0; Rec 9-63 7.0.

KEVIN SCOTT Scott, Kevin Tommorse 5′9″, 175 **DB**
Col: Stanford *HS:* St. Mary's [Phoenix, AZ] B: 5/19/1969, Phoenix, AZ
Drafted: 1991 Round 4 Det
1991 Det: 16 G; KR 1-16 16.0. **1992** Det: 16 G; KR 3-5 1.7; Int 4-35. **1993** Det: 12 G. **Total:** 44 G; KR 4-21 5.3; Int 4-35.

LANCE SCOTT Scott, Lance Robert 6′3″, 300 **C**
Col: Utah *HS:* Taylorsville [Salt Lake City, UT] B: 2/15/1972, Salt Lake City, UT *Drafted:* 1995 Round 5 Ariz
1997 NYG: 16 G. **1998** NYG: 16 G; 1 Fum. **Total:** 32 G; 1 Fum.

PERRY SCOTT Scott, Leonard Perry Jr. 6′2″, 210 **E**
Col: Muhlenberg *HS:* Bernards [Bernardsville, NJ] B: 8/27/1917, East Orange, NJ D: 4/4/1988, Allentown, PA *Drafted:* 1941 Round 15 Det
1942 Det: 7 G; Rec 1-7 7.0.

LES SCOTT Scott, Leslie Henry 5′10″, 205 **T-G-OE**
Col: Hamline *HS:* Albert Lea Central [MN] B: 12/20/1899, Albert Lea, MN D: 5/23/1993, Yuma, CO
1923 Akr: 6 G. **1924** Min: 6 G. **Total:** 12 G.

LEW SCOTT Scott, Lewis Simon 5′11″, 170 **DB**
Col: Oregon State *HS:* West Conshohocken [PA] B: 6/6/1943, Bryn Mawr, PA
1966 Den: 13 G; PR 7-56 8.0; KR 9-282 31.3.

LINDSAY SCOTT Scott, Lindsay Eugene 6′1″, 195 **WR**
Col: Georgia *HS:* Wayne Co. [Jesup, GA] B: 12/6/1960, Jesup, GA
Drafted: 1982 Round 1 NO
1982 NO: Rush 1-(-4) -4.0. **Total:** Rush 1-(-4) -4.0.

		Receiving				
Year Team	G	Rec	Yds	Avg	TD	Fum
1982 NO	8	17	251	14.8	0	0
1983 NO	16	24	274	11.4	0	1
1984 NO	16	21	278	13.2	1	1
1985 NO	9	7	61	8.7	0	0
NFL Total	49	69	864	12.5	1	2

MALCOLM SCOTT Scott, Malcolm Matthew 6′4″, 243 **TE**
Col: Louisiana State *HS:* St. Augustine [New Orleans, LA]
B: 7/10/1961, New Orleans, LA *Drafted:* 1983 Round 5 NYG
1983 NYG: 16 G; Rec 17-206 12.1. **1987** NO: 3 G; Rec 6-35 5.8. **Total:** 19 G; Rec 23-241 10.5.

PATRICK SCOTT Scott, Patrick Sterling 5′10″, 170 **WR**
Col: Grambling State *HS:* Ringgold [LA] B: 9/13/1964, Shreveport, LA
Drafted: 1987 Round 11 GB
1987 GB: Rush 1-2 2.0; PR 6-71 11.8; KR 2-32 16.0. **1988** GB: KR 12-207 17.3. **Total:** Rush 1-2 2.0; PR 6-71 11.8; KR 14-239 17.1.

		Receiving				
Year Team	G	Rec	Yds	Avg	TD	Fum
1987 GB	8	8	79	9.9	0	2
1988 GB	16	20	275	13.8	1	0
NFL Total	24	28	354	12.6	1	2

PHIL SCOTT Scott, Phillip 1 **OE**
Col: No College B: 4/11/1906 D: 1/1/1975, Montclair, NJ
1929 Ora: 8 G.

PRINCE SCOTT Scott, Prince Arthur 6′1″, 190 **OE-DB**
(Scotty) *Col:* Texas Tech *HS:* Grapevine [TX] B: 6/30/1917, Grapevine, TX
AAFC **1946** MiaA: 14 G; Rec 13-180 13.8 2 TD; PR 1-6 6.0; KR 2-28 14.0; Int 1-0; 12 Pt.

RALPH SCOTT Scott, Ralph Vernon 6′2″, 235 **T-G**
Col: Wisconsin *HS:* La Crosse [WI]; Hardin HS [MT] B: 9/26/1894, Dewey Twp., WI D: 8/15/1936, Hardin, MT
1921 Sta: 11 G; 6 Pt. **1922** ChiB: 12 G. **1923** ChiB: 12 G; Scor 1, 1 XK. **1924** ChiB: 10 G. **1925** ChiB: 13 G. **1927** NYY: 10 G. **Total:** 68 G.

RANDY SCOTT Scott, Randolph Charles 6′1″, 223 **LB**
Col: Alabama *HS:* Columbia [Decatur, GA] B: 1/31/1959, Decatur, GA
1981 GB: 16 G. **1982** GB: 9 G. **1983** GB: 6 G; Int 1-12. **1984** GB: 16 G; 3 Sac. **1985** GB: 16 G; Int 2-50; 3 Sac. **1986** GB: 15 G; 1 Sac. **1987** Min: 2 G. **Total:** 80 G; Int 3-62; 7 Sac.

BOB SCOTT Scott, Robert 195 **C-G-T**
Col: No College *HS:* Phil Campbell [AL] B: 8/8/1895, Phil Campbell, AL D: Phil Campbell, AL
1926 Prov: 6 G.

BOBBY SCOTT Scott, Robert Benson 6′1″, 201 **QB**
Col: Tennessee *HS:* Rossville [GA] B: 4/2/1949, Chattanooga, TN
Drafted: 1971 Round 14 NO
1977 NO: Punt 3-95 31.7. **Total:** Punt 3-95 31.7.

		Passing							
Year Team	G	Att	Comp	Comp%	Yds	YPA	TD	Int	Rating
1973 NO	6	54	18	33.3	245	4.54	1	3	31.8
1974 NO	5	71	31	43.7	366	5.15	4	4	55.3
1975 NO	1	17	8	47.1	96	5.65	0	1	40.3
1976 NO	11	190	103	54.2	1065	5.61	4	6	64.5
1977 NO	5	82	36	43.9	516	6.29	3	8	37.5
1978 NO	1	5	3	60.0	36	7.20	0	0	82.1
1979 NO	3	2	2	100.0	12	6.00	0	0	91.7
1980 NO	5	33	16	48.5	200	6.06	2	1	75.3
1981 NO	4	46	20	43.5	245	5.33	1	5	28.2
NFL Total	41	500	237	47.4	2781	5.56	15	28	51.4

	Rushing				
Year Team	Att	Yds	Avg	TD	Fum
1973 NO	9	18	2.0	0	0
1974 NO	1	1	1.0	0	0
1976 NO	12	48	4.0	1	3
1977 NO	4	11	2.8	0	0
1978 NO	1	0	0.0	0	0
1980 NO	0	0	—	0	1
1981 NO	3	-4	-1.3	0	1
NFL Total	30	74	2.5	1	5

BO SCOTT Scott, Robert Marilla 6′3″, 215 **RB**
Col: Ohio State *HS:* Connellsville [PA] B: 3/30/1943, Connellsville, PA
Drafted: 1965 Round 3 Cle

		Rushing				Receiving			
Year Team	G	Att	Yds	Avg	TD	Rec	Yds	Avg	TD
1969 Cle	13	44	157	3.6	0	6	25	4.2	0
1970 Cle	13	151	625	4.1	7	40	351	8.8	4
1971 Cle	14	179	606	3.4	9	30	233	7.8	1
1972 Cle	12	123	571	4.6	2	23	172	7.5	0
1973 Cle	7	34	79	2.3	0	6	23	3.8	1
1974 Cle	14	23	86	3.7	0	7	22	3.1	0
NFL Total	73	554	2124	3.8	18	112	826	7.4	6

	Kickoff Returns					Tot
Year Team	Ret	Yds	Avg	TD	Fum	TD
1969 Cle	25	**722**	28.9	0	1	0
1970 Cle	0	0	—	0	4	11
1971 Cle	0	0	—	0	4	10
1972 Cle	0	0	—	0	2	2
1973 Cle	0	0	—	0	0	1
NFL Total	25	722	28.9	0	11	24

SEAN SCOTT Scott, Sean Vaughn 6′1″, 226 **LB**
Col: Maryland *HS:* Archbishop Riordan [San Francisco, CA]
B: 4/10/1966, Washington, DC
1988 Dal: 5 G.

STANLEY SCOTT Scott, Stanley 6′3″, 255 **DE**
Col: Florida State *HS:* Brandon [FL] B: 1/30/1964, Tampa, FL
1987 Mia: 3 G; 1 Sac.

TOM SCOTT Scott, Thomas Coster Jr. 6′2″, 218 **LB-DE**
Col: Virginia *HS:* Calvert Hall [Baltimore, MD] B: 9/3/1930, Baltimore, MD *Drafted:* 1953 Round 5 LARm
1953 Phi: 12 G; KR 1-0; **1** Fum TD; 6 Pt. **1954** Phi: 12 G. **1955** Phi: 12 G. **1956** Phi: 12 G; Int 1-12. **1957** Phi: 12 G. **1958** Phi: 12 G; Int 2-15. **1959** NYG: 11 G. **1960** NYG: 12 G; Int 1-14 1 TD; 6 Pt. **1961** NYG: 13 G; Int 1-65 1 TD; 6 Pt. **1962** NYG: 14 G; Int 1-0. **1963** NYG: 14 G; KR 0-9.

1964 NYG: 14 G; Int 2-31. **Total:** 150 G; KR 1-9 9.0; Int 8-137 2 TD; 1 Fum TD; Tot TD 3; 18 Pt.

TODD SCOTT Scott, Todd Carlton 5′11″, 200 **DB**
Col: Southwestern Louisiana *HS:* Ball [Galveston, TX] B: 1/23/1968, Galveston, TX *Drafted:* 1991 Round 6 Min
1991 Min: 16 G. **1992** Min: 16 G; Int 5-79 1 TD; 6 Pt; 1 Sac. **1993** Min: 13 G; Int 2-26. **1994** Min: 15 G. **1995** NYJ-TB: 11 G. NYJ: 10 G. TB: 1 G. **1996** TB: 2 G. **1997** KC: 10 G. **Total:** 83 G; Int 7-105 1 TD; 6 Pt; 1 Sac.

TOM SCOTT Scott, Tom 6′6″, 330 **OT**
Col: East Carolina *HS:* Union [Clinton, NC] B: 6/25/1970, Burke Co., NC *Drafted:* 1993 Round 6 Cin
1993 Cin: 13 G.

VICTOR SCOTT Scott, Victor Ramone 6′0″, 200 **DB**
Col: Colorado *HS:* East St. Louis [IL] B: 6/1/1962, East St. Louis, IL *Drafted:* 1984 Round 2 Dal
1984 Dal: 16 G; Int 1-5. **1985** Dal: 16 G; Int 2-26 **1** TD; 6 Pt; 1 Fum; 3 Sac. **1986** Dal: 5 G; Int 1-31. **1987** Dal: 6 G; Int 1-1. **1988** Dal: 2 G. **Total:** 45 G; Int 5-63 1 TD; 6 Pt; 1 Fum; 3 Sac.

VIN SCOTT Scott, Vincent Joseph 5′8″, 215 **G**
(Boomer) *Col:* Notre Dame *HS:* Le Roy [NY] B: 7/10/1925, Le Roy, NY D: 7/13/1992, Hamilton, Canada
AAFC **1947** BufA: 14 G. **1948** BufA: 14 G. **Total:** 28 G.

WALTER SCOTT Scott, Walter Bernard 6′3″, 285 **DE**
(Wally) *Col:* East Carolina *HS:* Strom Thurmond [Edgefield, SC] B: 5/18/1973, Augusta, GA
1996 NE: 1 G.

WILBERT SCOTT Scott, Wilbert James 6′0″, 215 **LB**
Col: Indiana *HS:* Connellsville [PA] B: 3/13/1939, Conellsville, PA *Drafted:* 1961 Round 16 Pit
1961 Pit: 4 G.

BILL SCOTT Scott, William James 6′0″, 188 **DB**
Col: Idaho *HS:* Laurel [MD] B: 5/18/1944, Washington, DC
1968 Cin: 14 G.

WILLIE SCOTT Scott, Willie Louis Jr. 6′4″, 245 **TE**
Col: South Carolina *HS:* Newberry [SC] B: 2/13/1959, Newberry, SC *Drafted:* 1981 Round 1 KC
1983 KC: Rush 1-1 1.0. **1984** KC: KR 1-9 9.0. **Total:** Rush 1-1 1.0; KR 1-9 9.0.

		Receiving				Tot
Year Team	G	Rec	Yds	Avg	TD	TD
1981 KC	16	5	72	14.4	1	1
1982 KC	9	8	49	6.1	1	1
1983 KC	16	29	247	8.5	6	6
1984 KC	15	28	253	9.0	3	3
1985 KC	16	5	61	12.2	0	0
1986 NE	14	8	41	5.1	3	3
1987 NE	9	5	35	7.0	1	2
1988 NE	3	1	8	8.0	0	0
NFL Total	98	89	766	8.6	15	16

BEN SCOTTI Scotti, Benjamin Joseph 6′1″, 185 **DB**
Col: Maryland *HS:* St. Benedict's Prep [Newark, NJ] B: 6/9/1937, Newark, NJ
1959 Was: KR 1-0. **Total:** KR 1-0.

		Interceptions			
Year Team	G	Int	Yds	TD	Fum
1959 Was	11	0	0	0	1
1960 Was	11	4	76	0	0
1961 Was	14	1	10	0	0
1962 Phi	14	4	72	0	0
1963 Phi	9	1	17	0	0
1964 SF	12	0	0	0	0
NFL Total	71	10	175	0	1

COLIN SCOTTS Scotts, Colin Roberts 6′5″, 263 **DT**
Col: Hawaii *HS:* Scots Coll. [Sydney, Australia] B: 4/26/1963, Sydney, Australia *Drafted:* 1987 Round 3 StL
1987 StL: 7 G; 2 Sac.

BOB SCRABIS Scrabis, Robert Dennis 6′3″, 225 **QB**
Col: Penn State *HS:* Baldwin [Pittsburgh, PA] B: 3/26/1936, Pittsburgh, PA
1960 NYT: 7 G; Pass 3-0. **1961** NYT: 11 G; Pass 21-7 33.3%, 82 3.90 1 TD 2 Int; Rush 1-1 1.0 1 TD; 6 Pt; 1 Fum. **1962** NYT: 6 G; Pass 2-0, 1 Int; 1 Fum. **Total:** 24 G; Pass 26-7 26.9%, 82 3.15 1 TD 3 Int; Rush 1-1 1.0 1 TD; 6 Pt; 2 Fum.

KIRK SCRAFFORD Scrafford, Kirk Tippet 6′6″, 270 **OT-OG**
Col: Montana *HS:* Billings West [MT] B: 3/16/1967, Billings, MT
1990 Cin: 2 G. **1991** Cin: 9 G. **1992** Cin: 8 G. **1993** Den: 16 G. **1994** Den: 16 G. **1995** SF: 16 G. **1996** SF: 7 G. **1997** SF: 16 G. **1998** SF: 9 G. **Total:** 99 G.

ROB SCRIBNER Scribner, Robert Bruce 6′0″, 200 **RB**
Col: UCLA *HS:* Van Nuys [CA] B: 4/9/1951, Dallas, TX
1973 LARm: Rec 2-19 9.5; KR 11-314 28.5. **1974** LARm: Rec 2-28 14.0 1 TD; KR 1-0. **1975** LARm: Rec 2-28 14.0; KR 1-24 24.0. **1976** LARm: KR 3-54 18.0. **Total:** Rec 6-75 12.5 1 TD; KR 16-392 24.5.

		Rushing				Punt Returns					Tot
Year Team	G	Att	Yds	Avg	TD	Ret	Yds	Avg	TD	Fum	TD
1973 LARm	10	20	109	5.5	0	3	32	10.7	0	1	0
1974 LARm	11	9	24	2.7	0	8	70	8.8	0	1	1
1975 LARm	14	42	216	5.1	2	26	205	7.9	0	2	2
1976 LARm	14	2	12	6.0	1	8	54	6.8	0	0	1
NFL Total	49	73	361	4.9	3	45	361	8.0	0	4	4

BUCKY SCRIBNER Scribner, William Charles 6′0″, 207 **P**
Col: Pratt CC KS; Kansas *HS:* Lawrence [KS] B: 7/11/1960, Lawrence, KS *Drafted:* 1983 Round 11 GB
1984 GB: Pass 1-0. **1987** Min: Rush 1-(-7) -7.0. **1988** Min: Rush 1-0. **Total:** Pass 1-0; Rush 2-(-7) -3.5.

		Punting			
Year Team	G	Punts	Yds	Avg	Fum
1983 GB	16	69	2869	41.6	0
1984 GB	16	85	3596	42.3	0
1987 Min	4	20	827	41.4	1
1988 Min	16	84	3387	40.3	1
1989 Min	16	72	2864	39.8	0
NFL Total	68	330	13543	41.0	2

TRACY SCROGGINS Scroggins, Tracy 6′2″, 255 **DE**
Col: Coffeyville CC KS; Tulsa *HS:* Checotah [OK] B: 9/11/1969, Checotah, OK *Drafted:* 1992 Round 2 Det
1992 Det: 16 G; 7.5 Sac. **1993** Det: 16 G; Int 1-0; 8 Sac. **1994** Det: 16 G; 2.5 Sac. **1995** Det: 16 G; **1** Fum TD; 6 Pt; 9.5 Sac. **1996** Det: 6 G; 2 Sac. **1997** Det: 15 G; Scor **1** Saf; 1 Fum TD; 8 Pt; 7.5 Sac. **1998** Det: 11 G; 6.5 Sac. **Total:** 96 G; Int 1-0; Scor 1 Saf; 2 Fum TD; 14 Pt; 43.5 Sac.

TED SCRUGGS Scruggs, Edwin Theodore Jr. 6′1″, 195 **OE-DE**
Col: Rice *HS:* Stephen F. Austin [Houston, TX] B: 4/18/1923, Houston, TX
AAFC **1947** BknA: 12 G; Rec 2-9 4.5. **1948** BknA: 14 G; Rec 1-8 8.0. **Total:** 26 G; Rec 3-17 5.7.

ED SCRUTCHINS Scrutchins, Edward Sean 6′3″, 260 **DE**
Col: Toledo *HS:* Aliquippa [PA] B: 7/28/1941, Americus, GA *Drafted:* 1963 Round 15 StL
1966 Hou: 4 G.

JOE SCUDERO Scudero, Joseph Andrew 5′10″, 173 **DB-HB**
(Scooter) *Col:* San Francisco *HS:* Mission [San Francisco, CA] B: 7/2/1930, San Francisco, CA
1954 Was: Rec 4-32 8.0 1 TD. **1957** Was: Rec 2-30 15.0. **Total:** Rec 6-62 10.3 1 TD.

		Rushing				Punt Returns			
Year Team	G	Att	Yds	Avg	TD	Ret	Yds	Avg	TD
1954 Was	12	21	19	0.9	0	14	53	3.8	0
1955 Was	12	6	27	4.5	0	25	241	9.6	1
1956 Was	11	2	3	1.5	0	10	50	5.0	0
1957 Was	10	9	60	6.7	0	9	84	9.3	0
1958 Was	8	5	30	6.0	0	8	27	3.4	0
1960 Pit	4	0	0	—	0	2	3	1.5	0
NFL Total	57	43	139	3.2	0	68	458	6.7	1

	Kickoff Returns				Interceptions				Tot
Year Team	Ret	Yds	Avg	TD	Int	Yds	TD	Fum	TD
1954 Was	3	70	23.3	0	1	26	0	2	1
1955 Was	25	699	28.0	**1**	5	60	0	2	2
1956 Was	9	157	17.4	0	2	26	0	3	0
1957 Was	3	95	31.7	0	0	0	0	0	0
1958 Was	4	122	30.5	0	2	25	0	3	0
1960 Pit	0	0	—	0	0	0	0	1	0
NFL Total	44	1143	26.0	1	10	137	0	11	3

JOHN SCULLY Scully, John Francis Jr. 6′6″, 262 **C**
Col: Notre Dame *HS:* Holy Family [Huntington, NY] B: 8/2/1958, Huntington, NY *Drafted:* 1981 Round 4 Atl
1981 Atl: 16 G. **1982** Atl: 9 G; KR 1-0. **1983** Atl: 16 G. **1984** Atl: 16 G. **1985** Atl: 8 G. **1986** Atl: 14 G. **1987** Atl: 12 G. **1988** Atl: 11 G. **1990** Atl: 10 G. **Total:** 112 G; KR 1-0.

MIKE SCULLY Scully, Michael John 6′5″, 280 **C-OG**
Col: Illinois *HS:* Buffalo Grove [IL] B: 11/1/1965, Chicago, IL
1988 Was: 1 G.

MIKE SCURLOCK Scurlock, Michael Lee 5′10″, 200 **DB**
Col: Arizona *HS:* Sunnyside [Tuscon, AZ]; Cholla HS [Tuscon, AZ] B: 2/26/1972, Casa Grande, AZ *Drafted:* 1995 Round 5 StL
1995 StL: 14 G; Int 1-13. **1996** StL: 16 G. **1997** StL: 5 G. **1998** StL: 16 G. **Total:** 51 G; Int 1-13.

STAN SCZUREK Sczurek, Stanley Rudolph 5′11″, 230 **LB**
Col: Purdue *HS:* Benedictine [Cleveland, OH] B: 3/7/1937, Cleveland, OH *Drafted:* 1962 Round 4 Cle
1963 Cle: 9 G. **1964** Cle: 14 G. **1965** Cle: 11 G; Int 1-10. **1966** NYG: 11 G. **Total:** 45 G; Int 1-10.

TODD SEABAUGH Seabaugh, Raymond Todd 6′4″, 225 **LB**
Col: Ventura Coll. CA (J.C.); San Diego State *HS:* Santa Paula Union [CA] B: 3/16/1961, Encino, CA *Drafted:* 1983 Round 3 Pit
1984 Pit: 16 G.

CHARLIE SEABRIGHT Seabright, Charles Edward 6′2″, 204 **BB-LB**
(Lefty) *Col:* West Virginia *HS:* Benwood Union [WV] B: 2/13/1918, McMechen, WV D: 3/18/1981, Bridgeport, OH
1941 Cle: Pass 1-0, 1 Int. **1946** Pit: Int 1-3. **1947** Pit: Rush 1-4 4.0; KR 3-23 7.7; Int 3-80 1 TD. **1948** Pit: Pass 1-0; KR 1-4 4.0; Int 1-16. **1949** Pit: Pass 1-1 100.0%, 17 17.00 1 TD; KR 1-24 24.0. **1950** Pit: Pass 3-1 33.3%, 3 1.00. **Total:** Pass 6-2 33.3%, 20 3.33 1 TD 1 Int; Rush 1-4 4.0; KR 5-51 10.2; Int 5-99 1 TD.

		Receiving					Tot
Year Team	G	Rec	Yds	Avg	TD	Fum	TD
1941 Cle	7	5	44	8.8	0	0	0
1946 Pit	10	4	77	19.3	1	1	1
1947 Pit	12	7	16	2.3	0	2	1
1948 Pit	12	8	63	7.9	1	1	1
1949 Pit	12	4	4	1.0	0	0	0
1950 Pit	10	3	37	12.3	1	0	1
NFL Total	63	31	241	7.8	3	4	4

THOMAS SEABRON Seabron, Thomas Hall Jr. 6′3″, 215 **LB**
Col: Michigan *HS:* Cass Tech [Detroit, MI] B: 5/24/1957, Baltimore, MD *Drafted:* 1979 Round 5 SF
1979 SF: 16 G. **1980** SF-StL: 8 G. SF: 6 G. StL: 2 G. **Total:** 24 G.

PAUL SEAL Seal, Paul Nathan 6′4″, 222 **TE**
Col: Michigan *HS:* Pershing [Detroit, MI] B: 2/27/1952, Detroit, MI *Drafted:* 1974 Round 2 NO
1974 NO: Rush 2-7 3.5 1 TD. **1975** NO: Rush 1-10 10.0. **1976** NO: Rush 2-(-7) -3.5. **Total:** Rush 5-10 2.0 1 TD.

		Receiving					Tot
Year Team	G	Rec	Yds	Avg	TD	Fum	TD
1974 NO	14	32	466	14.6	3	0	4
1975 NO	14	28	414	14.8	1	0	1
1976 NO	14	9	72	8.0	0	1	0
1977 SF	14	13	230	17.7	1	0	1
1978 SF	14	21	370	17.6	2	0	2
1979 SF	15	3	34	11.3	0	0	0
NFL Total	85	106	1586	15.0	7	1	8

RANDY SEALBY Sealby, Randall Lee 6′2″, 230 **LB**
Col: Missouri *HS:* California [MO] B: 5/16/1960, Ann Arbor, MI
1987 NE: 2 G.

EUGENE SEALE Seale, Eugene Jr. 5′10″, 250 **LB**
Col: Lamar *HS:* Jasper [TX] B: 6/3/1964, Jasper, TX
1987 Hou: 9 G; Int 1-73 1 TD; 6 Pt; 1 Sac. **1988** Hou: 16 G; Int 1-46; Scor 1 Saf; 2 Pt; 1 Sac. **1989** Hou: 15 G; 6 Pt. **1990** Hou: 15 G. **1991** Hou: 15 G. **1992** Hou: 9 G. **Total:** 79 G; Int 2-119 1 TD; Scor 1 Saf; Tot TD 2; 14 Pt; 2 Sac.

SAM SEALE Seale, Samuel Ricardo 5′9″, 182 **DB**
Col: Western State (Colo.) *HS:* Orange [NJ] B: 10/6/1962, Barbados *Drafted:* 1984 Round 8 LARd
1985 LARd: KR 23-482 21.0. **1988** SD: **1** Fum TD. **Total:** KR 23-482 21.0; 1 Fum TD.

		Interceptions			Tot
Year Team	G	Int	Yds	TD	TD
1984 LARd	12	0	0	0	0
1985 LARd	16	1	38	**1**	1
1986 LARd	16	4	2	0	0
1987 LARd	12	0	0	0	0
1988 SD	14	0	0	0	1
1989 SD	13	4	47	0	0
1990 SD	16	2	14	0	0
1991 SD	16	0	0	0	0
1992 LARd	5	0	0	0	0
1993 LARm	1	0	0	0	0
NFL Total	121	11	101	1	2

GEORGE SEALS Seals, George Edward 6′3″, 260 **DT-OG**
Col: Missouri *HS:* Lafayette Co. [Higginsville, MO] B: 10/2/1942, Higginsville, MO *Drafted:* 1964 Round 4 NYG
1964 Was: 12 G. **1965** ChiB: 14 G. **1966** ChiB: 14 G. **1967** ChiB: 14 G. **1968** ChiB: 14 G. **1969** ChiB: 14 G; KR 2-20 10.0. **1970** ChiB: 14 G; Int 1-0. **1971** ChiB: 14 G; **1** Fum TD; 6 Pt. **1972** KC: 11 G. **1973** KC: 13 G. **Total:** 134 G; KR 2-20 10.0; Int 1-0; 1 Fum TD; 6 Pt.

LEON SEALS Seals, Leon Jr. 6′5″, 265 **DE**
Col: Jackson State *HS:* Scotlandville [Baton Rouge, LA] B: 1/30/1964, New Orleans, LA *Drafted:* 1987 Round 4 Buf
1987 Buf: 13 G; 3.5 Sac. **1988** Buf: 16 G; **1** Fum TD; 6 Pt; 2 Sac. **1989** Buf: 16 G; 4 Sac. **1990** Buf: 16 G; Int 1-0; 4 Sac. **1991** Buf: 16 G; 1 Sac. **1992** Phi: 5 G. **Total:** 82 G; Int 1-0; 1 Fum TD; 6 Pt; 14.5 Sac.

RAY SEALS Seals, Raymond Bernard 6′3″, 296 **DE-NT**
Col: No College *HS:* Henninger [Syracuse, NY] B: 6/17/1965, Syracuse, NY
1989 TB: 2 G; 1 Sac. **1990** TB: 8 G. **1991** TB: 10 G; 1 Sac. **1992** TB: 11 G; 5 Sac. **1993** TB: 16 G; Int 1-0 1 TD; 6 Pt; 8.5 Sac. **1994** Pit: 13 G; 7 Sac. **1995** Pit: 16 G; Int 1-0; 8.5 Sac. **1997** Car: 14 G; 1 Sac. **Total:** 90 G; Int 2-0 1 TD; 6 Pt; 32 Sac.

BILL SEARCEY Searcey, William Alexander 6′1″, 281 **OG**
Col: Alabama *HS:* Benedictine [Savannah, GA] B: 3/3/1958, Savannah, GA
1985 SD: 1 G.

LEON SEARCY Searcy, Leon Jr. 6′4″, 313 **OT**
Col: Miami (Fla.) *HS:* Maynard Evans [Orlando, FL] B: 12/21/1969, Washington, DC *Drafted:* 1992 Round 1 Pit
1992 Pit: 15 G. **1993** Pit: 16 G. **1994** Pit: 16 G. **1995** Pit: 16 G. **1996** Jac: 16 G. **1997** Jac: 16 G. **1998** Jac: 15 G. **Total:** 110 G.

COREY SEARS Sears, Corey Alexander 6′3″, 300 **DT**
Col: Navarro Coll. TX (J.C.); Mississippi State *HS:* Judson [Converse, TX] B: 4/15/1973, San Antonio, TX
1998 StL: 4 G.

JIMMY SEARS Sears, James Herbert 5′11″, 183 **HB-DB**
Col: El Camino Coll. CA (J.C.); USC *HS:* Inglewood [CA] B: 3/20/1931, Los Angeles, CA *Drafted:* 1953 Round 6 Bal
1957 ChiC: Pass 3-0; Rec 5-66 13.2; PR 1-0. **1958** ChiC: Pass 1-0; Rec 13-187 14.4 2 TD; PR 14-94 6.7. **1960** LAC: PR 9-101 11.2; Int 2-73. **Total:** Pass 4-0; Rec 18-253 14.1 2 TD; PR 24-195 8.1; Int 2-73.

		Rushing				Kickoff Returns					Tot
Year Team	G	Ret	Yds	Avg	TD	Ret	Yds	Avg	TD	Fum	TD
1954 ChiC	1	0	0	—	0	2	38	19.0	0	0	0
1957 ChiC	12	17	68	4.0	1	8	220	27.5	0	2	1
1958 ChiC	12	17	51	3.0	0	**32**	**756**	23.6	0	4	2
1960 LAC	10	0	0	—	0	8	155	19.4	0	1	0
1961 Den	2	0	0	—	0	0	0	—	0	0	0
NFL Total	37	34	119	3.5	1	50	1169	23.4	0	7	3

DICK SEARS Sears, Richard Maurice 5′10″, 185 **T**
Col: Kansas State *HS:* Eureka [KS] B: 6/6/1899, Eureka, KS D: 1/15/1972, Topeka, KS
1924 KC: 1 G.

VIC SEARS Sears, Victor Wilson 6′3″, 223 **DT-OT**
Col: Oregon State *HS:* Eugene [OR] B: 3/4/1918, Ashwood, OR *Drafted:* 1941 Round 4 Pit
1941 Phi: 11 G. **1942** Phi: 11 G; **1** Fum TD; 6 Pt. **1943** PhPt: 10 G; KR 1-15 15.0. **1945** Phi: 10 G. **1946** Phi: 11 G. **1947** Phi: 7 G; PR 1-6 6.0. **1948** Phi: 12 G. **1949** Phi: 11 G. **1950** Phi: 12 G. **1951** Phi: 12 G. **1952** Phi: 12 G; KR 1-45 45.0; Int 1-9 1 TD; 6 Pt. **1953** Phi: 12 G. **Total:** 131 G; PR 1-6 6.0; KR 2-60 30.0; Int 1-9 1 TD; 1 Fum TD; Tot TD 2; 12 Pt.

GEORGE SEASHOLTZ Seasholtz, George Donald 5′8″, 185 **FB-TB-WB**
(Dutch) *Col:* Lafayette *HS:* Mercersburg Acad. [PA] B: 11/14/1900, Pottstown, PA D: 4/11/1945, Pottstown, PA
1922 Mil: 4 G. **1924** Ken: 5 G; Rush 1 TD; Rec 1 TD; Tot TD 2; 12 Pt. **Total:** 9 G; Rush 1 TD; Rec 1 TD; Tot TD 2; 12 Pt.

JUNIOR SEAU Seau, Tiaina Jr. 6′3″, 250 **LB**
Col: USC *HS:* Oceanside [CA] B: 1/19/1969, San Diego, CA *Drafted:* 1990 Round 1 SD
1990 SD: 1 Sac. **1991** SD: 7 Sac. **1992** SD: 4.5 Sac. **1994** SD: 5.5 Sac. **1995** SD: **1** Fum TD; 2 Sac. **1996** SD: 7 Sac. **1997** SD: 7 Sac. **1998** SD: 3.5 Sac. **Total:** 1 Fum TD; 37.5 Sac.

		Interceptions			
Year Team	G	Int	Yds	TD	Fum
1990 SD	16	0	0	0	0
1991 SD	16	0	0	0	0
1992 SD	15	2	51	0	0
1993 SD	16	2	58	0	0
1994 SD	16	0	0	0	0
1995 SD	16	2	5	0	0
1996 SD	15	2	18	0	0
1997 SD	15	2	33	0	1
1998 SD	16	0	0	0	0
NFL Total	141	10	165	0	1

MARK SEAY Seay, Mark Edward 6'0", 175 **WR**
Col: Long Beach State *HS:* San Bernardino [CA] B: 4/11/1967, Los Angeles, CA
1995 SD: Scor 1 2XP. **1996** Phi: KR 4-51 12.8. **Total:** KR 4-51 12.8; Scor 1 2XP.

		Receiving				Punt Returns				
Year Team	G	Rec	Yds	Avg	TD	Ret	Yds	Avg	TD	Fum
1993 SD	1	0	0	—	0	0	0	—	0	0
1994 SD	16	58	645	11.1	6	0	0	—	0	0
1995 SD	16	45	537	11.9	3	0	0	—	0	0
1996 Phi	16	19	260	13.7	0	35	305	8.7	0	2
1997 Phi	12	13	187	14.4	1	16	172	10.8	0	3
NFL Total	61	135	1629	12.1	10	51	477	9.4	0	5

VIRGIL SEAY Seay, Virgil LeVan 5'8", 175 **WR**
Col: East Mississippi CC; Troy State *HS:* Moultrie [GA] B: 1/1/1958, Moultrie, GA *Drafted:* 1980 Round 10 Den
1981 Was: KR 2-36 18.0. **1983** Was: PR 5-57 11.4; KR 9-218 24.2. **1984** Was-Atl: PR 8-10 1.3; KR 5-108 21.6. Was: PR 1-(-2) -2.0; KR 3-53 17.7. Atl: PR 7-12 1.7; KR 2-55 27.5. **Total:** PR 13-67 5.2; KR 16-362 22.6.

		Receiving			
Year Team	G	Rec	Yds	Avg	TD
1981 Was	16	26	472	18.2	3
1982 Was	8	6	154	25.7	0
1983 Was	14	2	55	27.5	1
1984 Was-Atl	14	9	111	12.3	1
1984 Was	11	9	111	12.3	1
1984 Atl	3	0	0	—	0
NFL Total	52	43	792	18.4	5

MIKE SEBASTIAN Sebastian, Michael John 5'11", 185 **DB-HB-WB**
(The Sharon Express) *Col:* Pittsburgh *HS:* Sharon [PA] B: 6/7/1910, Greensburg, PA D: 6/28/1989, Hemet, CA
1935 Bos-Phi-Pit: Pass 6-1 16.7%, 12 2.00 1 Int; Rec 1-19 19.0. Bos: Pass 1-1 100.0%, 12 12.00. Phi: Pass 4-0, 1 Int; Rec 1-19 19.0. Pit: Pass 1-0. **Total:** Pass 6-1 16.7%, 12 2.00 1 Int; Rec 1-19 19.0.

		Rushing			
Year Team	G	Att	Yds	Avg	TD
1935 Bos-Phi-Pit	7	22	79	3.6	0
1935 Bos	1	1	0	0.0	0
1935 Phi	4	17	76	4.5	0
1935 Pit	2	4	3	0.8	0
1937 Cle	1	6	4	0.7	0
NFL Total	8	28	83	3.0	0

NICK SEBEK Sebek, Nicholas 6'1", 194 **QB**
Col: Indiana *HS:* North Tonawanda [NY] B: 10/11/1927, Niagara Falls, NY *Drafted:* 1949 Round 25 Was
1950 Was: 2 G; Pass 3-0, 2 Int.

SAM SEBO Sebo, Samuel E 5'7", 165 **FB-WB**
Col: Syracuse *HS:* Garfield [NJ] B: 1906 D: 9/10/1933
1930 Nwk: 2 G.

HERMAN SEBORG Seborg, Herman W 5'11", 195 **G-BB-WB**
(Porky) *Col:* Western Michigan *HS:* Grand Rapids Union [MI] B: 1/9/1907, Grand Rapids, MI D: 9/1985, Marcellus, NY
1930 Min-Fra: 13 G. Min: 9 G. Fra: 4 G. **1931** Fra: 7 G. **Total:** 20 G.

WALT SECHRIST Sechrist, Walter F 6'0", 258 **G-T**
(Covered Wagon) *Col:* No College B: 9/16/1896, Warsaw, IN D: 12/19/1977, Bradenton, FL
1920 Ham: 1 G. **1924** Akr: 1 G; Scor 1, 1 XK. **1925** Fra-Cle: 11 G. Fra: 9 G. Cle: 2 G. **1926** Lou-Ham: 5 G; Scor 3, 1 FG. Lou: 1 G. Ham: 4 G; Scor 3, 1 FG. **Total:** 18 G; Scor 4, 1 FG, 1 XK.

JOE SECORD Secord, Joseph L 190 **C**
Col: No College *HS:* Green Bay West [WI] B: 8/22/1897, Green Bay, WI D: 8/21/1970, Green Bay, WI
1922 GB: 2 G.

SCOTT SECULES Secules, Thomas Wescott 6'3", 220 **QB**
Col: Virginia *HS:* Chantilly [VA] B: 11/8/1964, Newport News, VA *Drafted:* 1988 Round 6 Dal
1989 Mia: Rush 4-39 9.8. **1990** Mia: Rush 8-34 4.3. **1991** Mia: Rush 4-30 7.5 1 TD. **1993** NE: Rush 8-33 4.1. **Total:** Rush 24-136 5.7 1 TD.

		Passing								
Year Team	G	Att	Comp	Comp%	Yds	YPA	TD	Int	Rating	Fum
1989 Mia	15	50	22	44.0	286	5.72	1	3	44.3	0
1990 Mia	16	7	3	42.9	17	2.43	0	1	10.7	0
1991 Mia	14	13	8	61.5	90	6.92	1	1	75.8	0
1993 NE	12	134	75	56.0	918	6.85	2	9	54.3	4
NFL Total	57	204	108	52.9	1311	6.43	4	14	50.9	4

LEN SEDBROOK Sedbrook, Leonard Roy 5'10", 174 **WB-FB-TB-BB**
(Twinkle) *Col:* Phillips *HS:* Goltry [OK] B: 1/13/1905, Goltry, OK D: 4/22/1986, Oklahoma City, OK
1928 Det: 9 G; Rush 1 TD; Rec 2 TD; Int **1** TD; Tot TD 4; 24 Pt. **1929** NYG: 15 G; Rush 4 TD; Rec 6 TD; Int **1** TD; Tot TD 11; 66 Pt. **1930** NYG: 16 G; Rush 5 TD; Rec 2 TD; Int 1 TD; Tot TD 8; 48 Pt. **1931** NYG: 11 G; Rush 2 TD; 12 Pt. **Total:** 51 G; Rush 12 TD; Rec 10 TD; Int 3 TD; Tot TD 25; 150 Pt.

BOB SEDLOCK Sedlock, Robert John 6'4", 295 **OT**
Col: Georgia *HS:* McKinley [Canton, OH] B: 2/7/1937, Canton, OH
1960 Buf: 14 G.

CHRIS SEDORIS Sedoris, Christopher Jude 6'3", 295 **C**
Col: Purdue *HS:* St. Xavier [Louisville, KY] B: 4/25/1973, Columbus, IN
1996 Was: 9 G.

JOHN SEEDBORG Seedborg, John Sherwood 6'0", 227 **P**
Col: Arizona State *HS:* Woodrow Wilson [Long Beach, CA] B: 1/23/1943, Paso Robles, CA *Drafted:* 1964 Round 19 Was
1965 Was: 1 G; Punt 7-247 35.3.

FRANK SEEDS Seeds, Frank 170 **WB**
(Slippery) *Col:* No College B: 3/26/1897 D: 10/1963, PA
1926 Can: 1 G.

GEORGE SEEMAN Seeman, George McHenry Jr. 6'1", 195 **OE-DE**
(Dirty George) *Col:* Nebraska *HS:* Central [Omaha, NE] B: 4/3/1916, Lincoln, NE D: 8/31/1998, Glen, NH *Drafted:* 1940 Round 6 GB
1940 GB: 1 G.

MAURY SEGAL Segal, Maurice 1 **E**
Col: No College *HS:* Alliance [OH] B: 1902, England Deceased
1925 Cle: 5 G.

ROCKY SEGRETTA Segretta, Rocco 1 **E**
(AKA Segrito) *Col:* No College B: 1899, Italy Deceased
1926 Har: 1 G.

JASON SEHORN Sehorn, Jason Heath 6'2", 210 **DB**
Col: Shasta Coll. CA (J.C.); USC *HS:* Mount Shasta [CA] B: 4/15/1971, Sacramento, CA *Drafted:* 1994 Round 2 NYG
1996 NYG: PR 1-0; 3 Sac. **1997** NYG: 1.5 Sac. **Total:** PR 1-0; 4.5 Sac.

		Interceptions			
Year Team	G	Int	Yds	TD	Fum
1994 NYG	8	0	0	0	0
1995 NYG	14	0	0	0	0
1996 NYG	16	5	61	1	1
1997 NYG	16	6	74	1	0
NFL Total	54	11	135	2	1

ED SEIBERT Seibert, Edward 5'10", 195 **G-E**
Col: West Virginia
1923 Ham: 2 G.

ED SEIBERT Seibert, Edward White 5'10", 190 **T-G**
Col: Otterbein *HS:* Steele [Dayton, OH] B: 1/7/1904, Fremont, OH D: 2/8/1983, Dayton, OH
1927 Day: 3 G. **1928** Day: 1 G. **Total:** 4 G.

CHAMP SEIBOLD Seibold, Champ Clark 6'4", 237 **T-G**
Col: Ripon; Wisconsin *HS:* Oshkosh [WI] B: 12/5/1911, Oshkosh, WI D: 11/2/1971, Oshkosh, WI
1934 GB: 1 G. **1935** GB: 6 G. **1936** GB: 10 G. **1937** GB: 10 G. **1938** GB: 11 G. **1940** GB: 10 G. **1942** ChiC: 11 G; Int 1-3 **1** TD; 6 Pt. **Total:** 59 G; Int 1-3 1 TD; 6 Pt.

RED SEICK Seick, Frederick Earl 6'0", 195 **G-LB**
Col: Buffalo; Manhattan *HS:* Lafayette [Buffalo, NY]; Cook Acad. [Montour Falls, NY] B: 4/28/1911, Lewiston, NY D: 10/31/1989
1942 NYG: 6 G.

RED SEIDELSON Seidelson, Harry 6'1", 202 **G-T**
Col: Pittsburgh *HS:* Fifth Avenue [Pittsburgh, PA]; Schenley HS [Pittsburgh, PA] B: 8/13/1901, Romania D: 7/6/1986, Pittsburgh, PA
1925 Fra: 10 G. **1926** Akr: 7 G. **Total:** 17 G.

MIKE SEIFERT Seifert, Michael Patrick 6'3", 245 **DE**
Col: Wisconsin *HS:* Kiel [WI] B: 3/30/1951, Port Washington, WI *Drafted:* 1974 Round 13 Cle
1974 Cle: 12 G.

DEXTER SEIGLER Seigler, Dexter 5'9", 178 **DB**
Col: Miami (Fla.) *HS:* Avon Park [FL] B: 1/11/1972, Miami, FL
1996 Sea: 12 G. **1997** Sea: 2 G. **Total:** 14 G.

PAUL SEILER Seiler, Paul Herman 6'4", 260 **OT-C**
Col: Notre Dame *HS:* Bishop Garrigan [Algona, IA] B: 11/1/1945, Algona, IA *Drafted:* 1967 Round 1 NYJ
1967 NYJ: 2 G. **1969** NYJ: 11 G. **1971** Oak: 8 G; KR 1-0. **1972** Oak: 14 G; KR 1-0. **1973** Oak: 4 G. **Total:** 39 G; KR 2-0.

LARRY SEIPLE Seiple, Lawrence Robert 6'0", 214 **TE-HB-P**
Col: Kentucky *HS:* William Allen [Allentown, PA] B: 2/14/1945, Allentown, PA *Drafted:* 1967 Round 7 Mia
1967 Mia: Pass 2-2 100.0%, 61 30.50; Rush 3-58 19.3. **1968** Mia: Rush 5-42 8.4. **1969** Mia: Pass 1-1 100.0%, 8 8.00; Rush 1-6 6.0. **1970** Mia: Rush 2-21 10.5; KR 2-5 2.5. **1971** Mia: Rush 1-14 14.0. **1973** Mia: KR 1-0. **1975** Mia: Rush 1-4 4.0. **1976** Mia: Rush 3-14 4.7. **Total:** Pass 3-3 100.0%, 69 23.00; Rush 16-159 9.9; KR 3-5 1.7.

		Receiving				Punting			
Year Team	**G**	**Rec**	**Yds**	**Avg**	**TD**	**Punts**	**Yds**	**Avg**	**Fum**
1967 Mia	14	1	21	21.0	0	70	2909	41.6	0
1968 Mia	14	7	69	9.9	1	75	3044	40.6	0
1969 Mia	14	41	577	14.1	5	**80**	3263	40.8	1
1970 Mia	14	2	14	7.0	0	58	2392	41.2	0
1971 Mia	14	1	32	32.0	0	52	2087	40.1	0
1972 Mia	11	0	0	—	0	36	1437	39.9	0
1973 Mia	14	0	0	—	0	48	2031	42.3	0
1974 Mia	14	0	0	—	0	65	2511	38.6	0
1975 Mia	14	10	84	8.4	0	65	2506	38.6	0
1976 Mia	14	10	138	13.8	1	62	2366	38.2	0
1977 Mia	13	1	-1	-1.0	0	22	801	36.4	0
NFL Total	150	73	934	12.8	7	633	25347	40.0	1

WARREN SEITZ Seitz, Warren Troy 6'4", 217 **TE-WR**
Col: Missouri *HS:* Topeka West [KS] B: 9/29/1962, Kansas City, MO
Drafted: 1986 Round 10 Pit
1986 Pit: 16 G; Rush 3-2 0.7; KR 2-25 12.5. **1987** NYG: 2 G. **Total:** 18 G; Rush 3-2 0.7; KR 2-25 12.5.

GENE SELAWSKI Selawski, Eugene Frank 6'4", 252 **OT-OG**
Col: Purdue *HS:* John Adams [Cleveland, OH] B: 11/28/1935, Cleveland, OH D: 5/11/1993, Duluth, GA
1959 LARm: 12 G. **1960** Cle: 12 G. **1961** SD: 8 G; KR 1-1 1.0. **Total:** 32 G; KR 1-1 1.0.

ROB SELBY Selby, Robert Seth Jr. 6'4", 290 **OG-OT**
Col: Auburn *HS:* W.A. Berry [Birmingham, AL] B: 10/11/1967, Birmingham, AL *Drafted:* 1991 Round 3 Phi
1991 Phi: 13 G. **1992** Phi: 16 G. **1993** Phi: 1 G. **1994** Phi: 2 G. **1995** Ariz: 7 G. **1996** Ariz: 13 G. **1997** Ariz: 10 G. **Total:** 62 G.

RON SELESKY Selesky, Ronald 6'1", 266 **C**
Col: North Central B: 9/4/1965, New Brunswick, NJ
1987 Min: 2 G.

CLARENCE SELF Self, Clarence Elbert 5'8", 181 **DB-HB**
Col: Wisconsin *HS:* J. Sterling Morton [Cicero, IL] B: 10/10/1925, Birmingham, AL *Drafted:* 1948 Round 10 ChiC
1949 ChiC: 12 G; Rush 4-16 4.0; PR 2-20 10.0; Int 1-0. **1950** Det: 12 G; Rush 3-9 3.0; Rec 1-12 12.0; PR 12-129 10.8; KR 6-155 25.8; Int 3-84 1 TD; 6 Pt; 1 Fum. **1951** Det: 12 G. **1952** GB: 12 G; Rush 0-21; KR 3-85 28.3; Int 1-0. **1954** GB: 12 G; Int 2-23. **1955** GB: 2 G. **Total:** 62 G; Rush 7-46 6.6; Rec 1-12 12.0; PR 14-149 10.6; KR 9-240 26.7; Int 7-107 1 TD; 6 Pt; 1 Fum.

ANDY SELFRIDGE Selfridge, Andrew Paul 6'3", 218 **LB**
Col: Virginia *HS:* Gilmour Acad. [Great Mills, OH] B: 1/12/1949, Cleveland, OH *Drafted:* 1972 Round 13 SD
1972 Buf: 13 G; KR 3-36 12.0. **1974** NYG: 14 G; Int 1-12. **1975** NYG: 14 G; KR 1-0. **1976** Mia: 1 G. **1977** NYG: 11 G; KR 1-9 9.0. **Total:** 53 G; KR 5-45 9.0; Int 1-12.

FRANK SELIGER Seliger, Frank H 200 **G-T**
HS: Hammond [IN] B: 8/31/1891, Chicago, IL D: 8/28/1975, Hammond, IN
1920 Ham: 4 G. **1921** Ham: 1 G. **Total:** 5 G.

GOLDIE SELLERS Sellers, Goldie 6'2", 198 **DB**
Col: Grambling State *HS:* Richwood [Monroe, LA] B: 1/9/1942, Winnsboro, LA *Drafted:* 1966 Round 8 Den
1966 Den: PR 6-49 8.2. **1967** Den: PR 4-24 6.0. **1968** KC: PR 7-129 18.4 1 TD. **1969** KC: PR 2-15 7.5; **1** Fum TD. **Total:** PR 19-217 11.4 1 TD; 1 Fum TD.

		Kickoff Returns				Interceptions				Tot
Year Team	**G**	**Ret**	**Yds**	**Avg**	**TD**	**Int**	**Yds**	**TD**	**Fum**	**TD**
1966 Den	14	19	541	**28.5**	**2**	3	24	0	4	2
1967 Den	13	6	120	20.0	0	7	78	1	2	1
1968 KC	14	2	40	20.0	0	3	19	0	0	1
1969 KC	14	0	0	—	0	0	0	0	1	1
NFL Total	55	27	701	26.0	2	13	121	1	7	5

LANCE SELLERS Sellers, Lance Kevin 6'1", 230 **LB**
Col: Boise State *HS:* Twin Falls [ID] B: 2/24/1963, Seattle, WA
1987 Cin: 3 G.

MIKE SELLERS Sellers, Mike 6'3", 260 **TE**
Col: Walla Walla CC WA *HS:* North Thurston [Lacey, WA]
B: 7/21/1975, Frankfurt, Germany
1998 Was: 14 G; Rec 3-18 6.0; KR 2-33 16.5.

RON SELLERS Sellers, Ronald Franklin 6'4", 205 **WR**
Col: Florida State *HS:* Paxon [Jacksonville, FL] B: 2/5/1947, Jacksonville, FL *Drafted:* 1969 Round 1 Bos

		Receiving				
Year Team	**G**	**Rec**	**Yds**	**Avg**	**TD**	**Fum**
1969 Bos	12	27	705	26.1	6	0
1970 Bos	13	38	550	14.5	4	0
1971 NE	10	14	222	15.9	3	0
1972 Dal	14	31	653	21.1	5	1
1973 Mia	3	2	54	27.0	0	1
NFL Total	52	112	2184	19.5	18	2

DEWEY SELMON Selmon, Dewey Willis 6'1", 246 **LB-DT**
Col: Oklahoma *HS:* Eufaula [OK] B: 11/19/1953, Eufaula, OK
Drafted: 1976 Round 2 TB
1976 TB: 12 G. **1977** TB: 14 G; Int 2-29. **1978** TB: 16 G; Int 1-0. **1979** TB: 15 G. **1980** TB: 15 G. **1982** SD: 8 G. **Total:** 80 G; Int 3-29.

LEE ROY SELMON Selmon, Lee Roy 6'3", 256 **DE**
Col: Oklahoma *HS:* Eufaula [OK] B: 10/20/1954, Eufaula, OK
Drafted: 1976 Round 1 TB *HOF:* 1995
1976 TB: 8 G. **1977** TB: 14 G. **1978** TB: 14 G. **1979** TB: 16 G; **1** Fum TD; 6 Pt. **1980** TB: 16 G. **1981** TB: 14 G. **1982** TB: 9 G; 4 Sac. **1983** TB: 14 G; 11 Sac. **1984** TB: 16 G; 8 Sac. **Total:** 121 G; 1 Fum TD; 6 Pt; 23.0 Sac.

HARRY SELTZER Seltzer, Harry 5'9", 195 **FB-LB**
Col: Charleston (WV) B: 3/26/1919, Philadelphia, PA D: 7/13/1990
1942 Det: 6 G; Rush 14-44 3.1; Rec 2-23 11.5.

BERNIE SEMES Semes, Bernard Claude 5'7", 188 **HB-DB**
Col: Duquesne *HS:* Braddock [PA] B: 1/29/1919, Braddock, PA
1944 ChPt: 8 G; Rush 17-38 2.2; Rec 3-22 7.3; Int 1-0.

TONY SEMPLE Semple, Anthony Lee 6'5", 286 **OG**
Col: Memphis *HS:* Lincoln [East St. Louis, IL] B: 12/20/1970, Lincoln, IL *Drafted:* 1994 Round 5 Det
1995 Det: 16 G. **1996** Det: 15 G. **1997** Det: 16 G. **1998** Det: 16 G. **Total:** 63 G.

ROBIN SENDLEIN Sendlein, Robin Bruno 6'3", 225 **LB**
Col: Texas *HS:* Western [Las Vegas, NV] B: 12/1/1958, Las Vegas, NV
Drafted: 1981 Round 2 Min
1981 Min: 16 G. **1982** Min: 9 G. **1983** Min: 16 G. **1984** Min: 15 G; 1 Sac. **1985** Mia: 16 G. **Total:** 72 G; 1 Sac.

BILL SENN Senn, William Franklin 6'0", 177 **HB-DB-TB-WB**
Col: Knox *HS:* Macomb [IL] B: 7/14/1905, Macomb, IL D: 9/5/1973, Macomb, IL
1926 ChiB: 15 G; Rush 7 TD; Scor 45, 3 XK. **1927** ChiB: 13 G; Rush 5 TD; Rec 1 TD; Tot TD **6**; 36 Pt. **1928** ChiB: 12 G; Pass 3 TD; Rush 1 TD; Rec 4 TD; PR **1** TD; Scor 37, 1 XK; Tot TD 6. **1929** ChiB: 15 G; Rush 1 TD; Rec 2 TD; 1 Fum TD; Tot TD 4; 24 Pt. **1930** ChiB: 11 G; Rush 1 TD; 6 Pt. **1931** ChiB-Bkn: 10 G; Rush 1 TD; Scor 7, 1 XK. ChiB: 1 G; Rush 1 TD; Scor 7, 1 XK. Bkn: 9 G. **1933** Cin: 1 G; Rush 4-4 1.0. **1934** StL: 2 G; Pass 3-0, 1 Int; Rush 3-8 2.7; Rec 5-65 13.0; Scor 3, 1 FG. **Total:** 79 G; Pass 3-0, 3 TD 1 Int; Rush 7-12 1.7 16 TD; Rec 5-65 13.0 7 TD; PR 1 TD; Scor 158, 1 FG, 5 XK; 1 Fum TD; Tot TD 25.

FRANK SENO Seno, Frank 6'0", 191 **DB-HB-WB**
Col: George Washington *HS:* Mendota Twp. [Mendota, IL]
B: 2/15/1921, Mendota, IL D: 3/1974
1945 ChiC: Pass 1-0. **1946** ChiC: Pass 1-0. **Total:** Pass 2-0.

		Rushing				Receiving			
Year Team	**G**	**Att**	**Yds**	**Avg**	**TD**	**Rec**	**Yds**	**Avg**	**TD**
1943 Was	10	26	152	5.8	0	12	195	16.3	0
1944 Was	10	43	140	3.3	0	17	146	8.6	0
1945 ChiC	9	93	355	3.8	2	7	129	18.4	0
1946 ChiC	11	62	191	3.1	0	12	124	10.3	1
1947 Bos	11	69	212	3.1	0	12	118	9.8	1
1948 Bos	12	71	242	3.4	0	13	322	24.8	3
1949 Was	4	0	0	—	0	0	0	—	0
NFL Total	67	364	1292	3.5	2	73	1034	14.2	5

	Punt Returns				Kickoff Returns			
Year Team	**Ret**	**Yds**	**Avg**	**TD**	**Ret**	**Yds**	**Avg**	**TD**
1943 Was	2	27	13.5	0	3	61	20.3	0
1944 Was	10	129	12.9	0	8	193	24.1	0
1945 ChiC	10	103	10.3	0	**19**	**408**	21.5	0
1946 ChiC	17	176	10.4	0	13	408	**31.4**	**1**
1947 Bos	12	213	**17.8**	**1**	27	636	23.6	0
1948 Bos	13	99	7.6	0	8	171	21.4	0
1949 Was	0	0	—	0	2	39	19.5	0
NFL Total	64	747	11.7	1	80	1916	24.0	1

	Interceptions				Tot
Year Team	**Int**	**Yds**	**TD**	**Fum**	**TD**
1943 Was	1	0	0	0	0
1944 Was	2	27	0	0	0
1945 ChiC	1	0	0	3	2

1946 ChiC	4	33	0	7	2
1947 Bos	**10**	100	0	3	2
1948 Bos	1	0	0	2	3
NFL Total	19	160	0	15	9

DEAN SENSANBAUGHER Sensanbaugher, Dean Sparks 5'9", 190 **HB-DB**
Col: Army; Ohio State *HS:* Uhrichsville [OH] B: 8/12/1925, Midvale, OH
AAFC **1948** CleA: 11 G; Rush 18-59 3.3 1 TD; 6 Pt.

NFL **1949** NYB: 4 G; Rush 20-36 1.8 1 TD; PR 1-9 9.0; KR 3-81 27.0; 6 Pt; 3 Fum.

JOE SENSER Senser, Joseph Spence 6'4", 235 **TE**
Col: West Chester *HS:* Milton S. Hershey [Hershey, PA] B: 8/18/1956, Philadelphia, PA *Drafted:* 1979 Round 6 Min
1980 Min: Pass 1-0; Rush 1-(-1) -1.0. **1981** Min: Rush 1-2 2.0. **Total:** Pass 1-0; Rush 2-1 0.5.

		Receiving				
Year Team	G	Rec	Yds	Avg	TD	Fum
1980 Min	16	42	447	10.6	7	0
1981 Min	16	79	1004	12.7	8	3
1982 Min	9	29	261	9.0	1	0
1984 Min	8	15	110	7.3	0	0
NFL Total	49	165	1822	11.0	16	3

MIKE SENSIBAUGH Sensibaugh, James Michael 5'11", 192 **DB**
Col: Ohio State *HS:* Lockland [OH] B: 1/3/1949, Cincinnati, OH *Drafted:* 1971 Round 8 KC
1971 KC: PR 5-(-2) -0.4; KR 4-71 17.8. **Total:** PR 5-(-2) -0.4; KR 4-71 17.8.

		Interceptions			
Year Team	G	Int	Yds	TD	Fum
1971 KC	7	0	0	0	2
1972 KC	14	8	65	0	0
1973 KC	14	3	58	0	0
1974 KC	14	4	85	0	0
1975 KC	14	5	123	0	0
1976 StL	14	4	60	1	0
1977 StL	10	3	110	**1**	0
1978 StL	5	0	0	0	0
NFL Total	92	27	501	2	2

RAFAEL SEPTIEN Septien, Jose Rafael [Michel] 5'10", 176 **K**
Col: Southwestern Louisiana *HS:* Colegio Vista Hernosa [Mexico City, Mexico] B: 12/12/1953, Mexico City, Mexico *Drafted:* 1977 Round 10 NO
1981 Dal: Punt 2-62 31.0. **Total:** Punt 2-62 31.0.

		Scoring						
Year Team	G	Pts	FG	FGA	FG%	XK	XKA	XK%
1977 LARm	14	86	18	30	60.0	32	35	91.4
1978 Dal	16	94	16	26	61.5	**46**	**47**	97.9
1979 Dal	16	97	19	29	65.5	40	44	90.9
1980 Dal	16	92	11	17	64.7	**59**	**60**	98.3
1981 Dal	16	**121**	**27**	35	77.1	40	40	100.0
1982 Dal	9	58	10	14	71.4	28	28	100.0
1983 Dal	16	123	22	27	81.5	57	59	96.6
1984 Dal	16	102	23	29	79.3	33	34	97.1
1985 Dal	16	99	19	28	67.9	42	43	97.7
1986 Dal	16	88	15	21	71.4	43	43	100.0
NFL Total	151	960	180	256	70.3	420	433	97.0

GEORGE SERGIENKO Sergienko, George Jr. 6'1", 248 **T**
(Sarge) *Col:* American International *HS:* Chicopee [MA]
B: 5/22/1918, Chicopee Falls, MA D: 12/4/1993, Chicopee, MA
AAFC **1946** BknA: 7 G.

NFL **1943** Bkn: 10 G. **1944** Bkn: 10 G. **1945** Bos: 10 G. **Total:** 30 G.

WASH SERINI Serini, William Washington 6'2", 236 **OG-DG-OT**
Col: Kentucky *HS:* Eastchester [NY] B: 3/11/1922, Tuckahoe, NY D: 6/21/1994, Highland, NY
1948 ChiB: 12 G. **1949** ChiB: 12 G. **1950** ChiB: 12 G; Scor **1** Saf; 2 Pt. **1951** ChiB: 12 G; KR 1-2 2.0. **1952** GB: 11 G. **Total:** 59 G; KR 1-2 2.0; Scor 1 Saf; 2 Pt.

TOM SESTAK Sestak, Thomas Joseph 6'4", 260 **DT**
Col: Texas A&M; Baylor; McNeese State *HS:* Gonzales [TX]
B: 3/9/1936, Gonzales, TX D: 4/3/1987, Buffalo, NY *Drafted:* 1962 Round 17 Buf
1962 Buf: 14 G; Int 1-6 **1** TD; 6 Pt. **1963** Buf: 14 G. **1964** Buf: 14 G; Int 1-15 **1** TD; 6 Pt. **1965** Buf: 14 G. **1966** Buf: 14 G. **1967** Buf: 14 G; **1** Fum TD; 6 Pt. **1968** Buf: 12 G. **Total:** 96 G; Int 2-21 2 TD; 1 Fum TD; Tot TD 3; 18 Pt.

JOE SETCAVAGE Setcavage, Joseph W 5'11", 190 **BB-DB**
Col: Duquesne *HS:* Mahanoy City [PA] B: 11/12/1918, Mahanoy City, PA D: 6/20/1996, North East, PA
1943 Bkn: 10 G; Pass 1-0; Rush 1-3 3.0; Rec 5-26 5.2; PR 1-2 2.0; KR 1-5 5.0; Int 1-10.

JOE SETRON Setron, Joseph Louis 5'9", 195 **G**
Col: West Virginia *HS:* Parkersburg [WV] B: 8/10/1900, Buffalo, NY D: 9/25/1958, Cleveland, OH
1923 Cle: 1 G.

JOHN SETTLE Settle, John R 5'9", 207 **RB**
Col: Appalachian State *HS:* Rockingham Co. [Wentworth, NC]
B: 6/2/1965, Reidsville, NC
1987 Atl: KR 10-158 15.8. **Total:** KR 10-158 15.8.

		Rushing				Receiving					Tot
Year Team	G	Att	Yds	Avg	TD	Rec	Yds	Avg	TD	Fum	TD
1987 Atl	9	19	72	3.8	0	11	153	13.9	0	2	0
1988 Atl	16	232	1024	4.4	7	68	570	8.4	1	3	8
1989 Atl	15	179	689	3.8	3	39	316	8.1	2	1	5
1990 Atl	6	9	16	1.8	0	0	0	—	0	0	0
NFL Total	46	439	1801	4.1	10	118	1039	8.8	3	6	13

TONY SETTLES Settles, Anthony 6'3", 210 **LB**
Col: Elon *HS:* Scotland [Laurinburg, NC] B: 8/29/1964
1987 Was: 3 G.

TAWAMBI SETTLES Settles, Tawambi Jahmon 6'2", 194 **DB**
Col: Duke *HS:* McCallie School [Chattanooga, TN] B: 1/19/1976, Chattanooga, TN
1998 Jac: 7 G.

FRANK SEURER Seurer, Frank Anthony 6'1", 195 **QB**
Col: Kansas *HS:* Edison [Huntington Beach, CA] B: 8/16/1962, Huntington Beach, CA *Drafted:* 1984 Supplemental Round 3 Sea
1987 KC: Rush 9-33 3.7. **Total:** Rush 9-33 3.7.

		Passing								
Year Team	G	Att	Comp	Comp%	Yds	YPA	TD	Int	Rating	Fum
1986 KC	1	0	0	—	0	—	0	0	—	0
1987 KC	8	55	26	47.3	340	6.18	0	4	36.9	2
NFL Total	9	55	26	47.3	340	6.18	0	4	36.9	2

JEFF SEVERSON Severson, Jeffrey Kent 6'1", 183 **DB**
Col: Long Beach City Coll. CA (J.C.); Long Beach State *HS:* Woodrow Wilson [Long Beach, CA] B: 9/16/1949, Fargo, ND *Drafted:* 1971 Round 12 Was
1973 Hou: KR 1-17 17.0; Int 4-24. **1974** Hou: KR 6-108 18.0; Int 1-0. **1975** Den: KR 1-20 20.0. **1976** StL: KR 1-3 3.0. **1977** StL: Int 1-0. **Total:** KR 9-148 16.4; Int 6-24.

		Punt Returns				
Year Team	G	Ret	Yds	Avg	TD	Fum
1972 Was	12	0	0	—	0	0
1973 Hou	14	16	126	7.9	0	0
1974 Hou	14	11	86	7.8	0	0
1975 Den	14	0	0	—	0	1
1976 StL	14	0	0	—	0	0
1977 StL	14	1	0	0.0	0	0
1979 LARm	1	0	0	—	0	0
NFL Total	83	28	212	7.6	0	1

JEFF SEVY Sevy, Jeffrey Evan 6'5", 260 **OT-OG-DT-DE**
Col: De Anza Coll. CA (J.C.); California *HS:* Homestead [Cupertino, CA]
B: 10/24/1951, Palo Alto, CA *Drafted:* 1974 Round 12 ChiB
1975 ChiB: 14 G; Rec 1-6 6.0. **1976** ChiB: 14 G. **1977** ChiB: 12 G. **1978** ChiB: 14 G. **1979** Sea: 4 G. **1980** Sea: 15 G. **Total:** 73 G; Rec 1-6 6.0.

HARLEY SEWELL Sewell, Harley Edward 6'1", 230 **OG-LB**
Col: Texas *HS:* St. Jo [TX] B: 4/18/1931, St. Jo, TX *Drafted:* 1953 Round 1 Det
1953 Det: 12 G; Int 1-4. **1954** Det: 12 G; KR 1-0; **1** Fum TD; 6 Pt. **1955** Det: 12 G. **1956** Det: 12 G. **1957** Det: 10 G. **1958** Det: 12 G. **1959** Det: 11 G. **1960** Det: 12 G. **1961** Det: 14 G. **1962** Det: 13 G. **1963** LARm: 2 G. **Total:** 122 G; KR 1-0; Int 1-4; 1 Fum TD; 6 Pt.

STEVEN SEWELL Sewell, Steven Edward 6'3", 210 **RB-WR**
Col: Oklahoma *HS:* Archbishop Riordan [San Francisco, CA]
B: 4/2/1963, San Francisco, CA *Drafted:* 1985 Round 1 Den
1985 Den: Pass 1-0; KR 1-29 29.0. **1986** Den: Pass 1-1 100.0%, 23 23.00 1 TD. **1988** Den: Pass 1-0. **1990** Den: Pass 1-0. **1991** Den: Pass 3-1 33.3%, 24 8.00; KR 1-14 14.0. **Total:** Pass 7-2 28.6%, 47 6.71 1 TD; KR 2-43 21.5.

		Rushing				Receiving					Tot
Year Team	G	Att	Yds	Avg	TD	Rec	Yds	Avg	TD	Fum	TD
1985 Den	16	81	275	3.4	4	24	224	9.3	1	1	5
1986 Den	11	23	123	5.3	1	23	294	12.8	1	0	2
1987 Den	7	19	83	4.4	2	13	209	16.1	1	1	3

1988 Den	16	32	135	4.2	1	38	507	13.3	5	2	6
1989 Den	16	7	44	6.3	0	25	416	16.6	3	0	3
1990 Den	12	17	46	2.7	3	26	268	10.3	0	0	3
1991 Den	16	50	211	4.2	2	38	436	11.5	2	1	4
NFL Total	94	229	917	4.0	13	187	2354	12.6	13	5	26

LIN SEXTON Sexton, Linwood Bookard 6′0″, 180 **HB-DB**
Col: Wichita State *HS:* East [Wichita, KS] B: 4/16/1926, Wichita, KS
AAFC **1948** LA-A: 11 G; Rush 7-39 5.6; PR 3-47 15.7; KR 3-49 16.3; Int 1-30.

BRENT SEXTON Sexton, Russell Brent 6′1″, 190 **DB**
Col: Elon *HS:* Terry Sanford [Fayetteville, NC] B: 7/23/1953, Fayetteville, NC *Drafted:* 1975 Round 5 Pit
1977 Pit: 11 G.

FRANK SEYBOTH Seyboth, Frank C 5′9″, 180 **WB**
Col: Vermont *HS:* Attleboro [MA] B: 4/5/1904, Attleboro, MA
D: 4/30/1979, Attleboro, MA
1926 Prov: 1 G.

SI SEYFRIT Seyfrit, Michael Franklin 5′10″, 170 **OE**
Col: Notre Dame *HS:* Carlinville [IL] B: 1/31/1898, Carlinville, IL
D: 9/1/1955, Bloomington, IL
1923 Tol: 8 G; Rec 1 TD; 6 Pt. **1924** Ham: 5 G. **Total:** 13 G; Rec 1 TD; 6 Pt.

SEYMOUR Seymour **E**
Col: No College
1941 ChiC: 1 G; Rec 1-3 3.0.

JIM SEYMOUR Seymour, James Patrick 6′4″, 210 **WR**
Col: Notre Dame *HS:* Shrine [Royal Oak, MI] B: 11/24/1946, Detroit, MI *Drafted:* 1969 Round 1 LARm
1970 ChiB: 7 G; Rec 6-145 24.2 4 TD; 24 Pt. **1971** ChiB: 10 G; Rec 5-75 15.0. **1972** ChiB: 14 G; Rush 1-(-9) -9.0; Rec 10-165 16.5 1 TD; 6 Pt.
Total: 31 G; Rush 1-(-9) -9.0; Rec 21-385 18.3 5 TD; 30 Pt.

PAUL SEYMOUR Seymour, Paul Christopher 6′5″, 252 **TE**
Col: Michigan *HS:* Shrine [Royal Oak, MI] B: 2/6/1950, Detroit, MI
Drafted: 1973 Round 1 Buf

		Receiving				
Year Team	G	Rec	Yds	Avg	TD	Fum
1973 Buf	14	10	114	11.4	0	0
1974 Buf	14	15	246	16.4	2	0
1975 Buf	14	19	268	14.1	1	0
1976 Buf	13	16	169	10.6	0	1
1977 Buf	14	2	21	10.5	0	0
NFL Total	69	62	818	13.2	3	1

BOB SEYMOUR Seymour, Robert Arnold 6′2″, 205 **DB-FB-HB-WB**
Col: Oklahoma *HS:* Commerce [OK] B: 6/13/1916, Wyandotte, OK
D: 5/1977, Golden, CO *Drafted:* 1940 Round 8 Was
AAFC **1946** LA-A: Rec 17-188 11.1 3 TD; PR 18-211 11.7; KR 4-87 21.8; Int 4-34.

		Rushing			
Year Team	G	Att	Yds	Avg	TD
1946 LA-A	13	37	165	4.5	0

NFL **1940** Was: Scor 24, 0-1 XK. **1941** Was: KR 3-96 32.0. **1943** Was: KR 2-34 17.0. **1944** Was: Punt 10-355 35.5. **Total:** KR 5-130 26.0; Punt 10-355 35.5; Scor 120, 0-1 XK.

		Rushing				Receiving			
Year Team	G	Att	Yds	Avg	TD	Rec	Yds	Avg	TD
1940 Was	9	57	170	3.0	4	2	3	1.5	0
1941 Was	10	62	137	2.2	2	6	85	14.2	2
1942 Was	11	54	190	3.5	1	3	20	6.7	0
1943 Was	10	65	232	3.6	0	17	167	9.8	2
1944 Was	10	92	315	3.4	3	19	263	13.8	3
1945 Was	10	30	102	3.4	2	8	91	11.4	1
NFL Total	60	360	1146	3.2	12	55	629	11.4	8

	Punt Returns				Interceptions				Tot
Year Team	Ret	Yds	Avg	TD	Int	Yds	TD	Fum	TD
1940 Was	—	—	—	0	1	13	0	0	4
1941 Was	10	128	12.8	0	2	36	0	0	4
1942 Was	4	79	19.8	0	3	39	0	0	1
1943 Was	13	173	13.3	0	2	5	0	0	2
1944 Was	1	6	6.0	0	2	20	0	0	6
1945 Was	0	0	—	0	4	28	0	2	3
NFL Total	28	386	13.8	0	14	141	0	2	20

DON SHACKELFORD Shackelford, Donald Vernon 6′4″, 255 **OG**
Col: U. of Pacific *HS:* Tulare [CA] B: 2/18/1943, Wichita Falls, TX
Drafted: 1964 Round 6 Den
1964 Den: 8 G; KR 1-13 13.0.

SAM SHADE Shade, Samuel Richard 6′1″, 196 **DB**
Col: Alabama *HS:* Wenonah [Birmingham, AL] B: 6/14/1973, Birmingham, AL *Drafted:* 1995 Round 4 Cin
1995 Cin: 16 G. **1996** Cin: 12 G. **1997** Cin: 16 G; Int 1-21; 1 Fum; 4 Sac.
1998 Cin: 16 G; Int 3-33; 1 Fum TD; 6 Pt; 1 Sac. **Total:** 60 G; Int 4-54; 1 Fum TD; 6 Pt; 1 Fum; 5 Sac.

CRAIG SHAFFER Shaffer, Craig Alan 6′0″, 230 **LB**
Col: Indiana State *HS:* Schulte [Terre Haute, IN] B: 3/31/1959, Terre Haute, IN *Drafted:* 1982 Round 6 StL
1982 StL: 5 G. **1983** StL: 9 G. **1984** StL: 4 G. **Total:** 18 G.

GEORGE SHAFFER Shaffer, George Adam 6′0″, 190 **BB-DB**
Col: Washington & Jefferson *HS:* Greensburg [PA] B: 6/20/1910
Deceased
1933 Pit: 5 G; Rush 5-6 1.2; Rec 1-11 11.0.

LEE SHAFFER Shaffer, Leland Knoy 6′2″, 205 **BB-DB-LB-WB**
Col: Kansas State B: 5/9/1912, Minneola, KS D: 1/24/1993, Hillsboro Beach, FL
1936 NYG: Rush 3-10 3.3. **1937** NYG: Rush 8-35 4.4. **1938** NYG: Rush 1-4 4.0. **1939** NYG: Rush 3-6 2.0. **1940** NYG: Rush 7-20 2.9 1 TD; Int 4-14. **1941** NYG: Int 1-4. **1942** NYG: Rush 1-3 3.0; KR 2-40 20.0.
1943 NYG: Rush 1-3 3.0; Int 1-18. **1945** NYG: KR 2-42 21.0.
Total: Rush 24-81 3.4 1 TD; KR 4-82 20.5; Int 6-36.

		Receiving				Tot
Year Team	G	Rec	Yds	Avg	TD	TD
1935 NYG	12	7	123	17.6	0	0
1936 NYG	10	2	30	15.0	1	1
1937 NYG	9	7	72	10.3	0	0
1938 NYG	11	12	86	7.2	2	2
1939 NYG	9	2	8	4.0	0	0
1940 NYG	11	15	121	8.1	2	3
1941 NYG	10	1	5	5.0	0	0
1942 NYG	10	3	20	6.7	0	0
1943 NYG	10	3	66	22.0	0	0
1945 NYG	6	0	0	—	0	0
NFL Total	98	52	531	10.2	5	6

STANLEY SHAKESPEARE Shakespeare, Stanley C 6′0″, 190 **WR**
Col: Miami (Fla.) *HS:* Lake Worth [FL] B: 2/5/1963, Auburn, NY
1987 TB: 1 G.

HENRY SHANK Shank, Henry A 5′8″, 160 **HB**
Col: Maryland *HS:* Hyde Park [Chicago, IL] B: 5/29/1896, Sumner, IL
D: 11/1977, Mount Erie, IL
1920 Sta: 5 G.

RON SHANKLIN Shanklin, Ronnie Eugene 6′1″, 190 **WR**
Col: Cooke Co. Coll. TX (J.C.); North Texas *HS:* George Washington Carver [Amarillo, TX] B: 1/21/1948, Hubbard, TX *Drafted:* 1970 Round 2 Pit
1971 Pit: Rush 2-1 0.5. **1973** Pit: Rush 3-1 0.3. **Total:** Rush 5-2 0.4.

		Receiving				
Year Team	G	Rec	Yds	Avg	TD	Fum
1970 Pit	14	30	691	23.0	4	1
1971 Pit	14	49	652	13.3	6	1
1972 Pit	14	38	669	17.6	3	0
1973 Pit	13	30	711	23.7	10	1
1974 Pit	12	19	324	17.1	1	0
1976 ChiB	5	2	32	16.0	0	0
NFL Total	72	168	3079	18.3	24	3

SIMON SHANKS Shanks, Simon 6′1″, 215 **LB**
Col: Coahoma CC MS; Tennessee State *HS:* R.H. Watkins [Laurel, MS]
B: 10/16/1971, Laurel, MS
1995 Ariz: 15 G.

SHANLEY Shanley 214 **T**
Col: No College
1927 Dul: 1 G.

JIM SHANLEY Shanley, James Donald 5′9″, 174 **HB**
Col: Oregon *HS:* North Bend [OR] B: 7/27/1936, Shelton, NE
1958 GB: 12 G; Rush 23-30 1.3; Rec 3-13 4.3; PR 14-105 7.5; 1 Fum.

BOB SHANN Shann, Robert Allen 6′1″, 189 **DB**
Col: Boston College *HS:* St. George's School [Newport, RI]
B: 3/27/1943, Andover, MA *Drafted:* 1965 Round 20 Phi
1965 Phi: 4 G; PR 1-63 63.0 1 TD; 6 Pt. **1967** Phi: 6 G; PR 3-17 5.7; KR 6-133 22.2; Int 1-8. **Total:** 10 G; PR 4-80 20.0 1 TD; KR 6-133 22.2; Int 1-8; 6 Pt.

CARVER SHANNON Shannon, Carver Beauregard 6′1″, 198 **DB-HB**
Col: Southern Illinois *HS:* Corinth [MS] B: 4/28/1938, Corinth, MS
Drafted: 1959 Round 19 LARm
1962 LARm: Int 4-33. **1963** LARm: Rec 2-7 3.5. **1964** LARm: Rush 17-35 2.1; Rec 2-4 2.0. **Total:** Rush 17-35 2.1; Rec 4-11 2.8; Int 4-33.

Year Team	G	Punt Returns Ret	Yds	Avg	TD	Kickoff Returns Ret	Yds	Avg	TD	Fum
1962 LARm	12	0	0	—	0	0	0	—	0	0
1963 LARm	14	15	132	8.8	0	28	823	29.4	1	4
1964 LARm	12	15	81	5.4	0	18	442	24.6	0	3
NFL Total	38	30	213	7.1	0	46	1265	27.5	1	7

JOHN SHANNON Shannon, John Byron 6′3″, 269 **DT-DE**
Col: Kentucky *HS:* Boone Co. [Florence, KY] B: 1/18/1965, Lexington, KY
1988 ChiB: 13 G. **1989** ChiB: 12 G. **Total:** 25 G.

RANDY SHANNON Shannon, Randy Leonard 6′0″, 221 **LB**
Col: Miami (Fla.) *HS:* Miami Norland [FL] B: 2/24/1966, Miami, FL
Drafted: 1989 Round 11 Dal
1989 Dal: 16 G. **1990** Dal: 1 G. **Total:** 17 G.

JACK SHAPIRO Shapiro, Jack Emanuel 5′1″, 119 **BB**
(Soapy) *Col:* New York U. *HS:* Evander Childs [Bronx, NY]
B: 3/22/1907, New York, NY
1929 SI: 1 G.

NATE SHARE Share, Nathan Louis 6′1″, 210 **G-T**
Col: Tufts *HS:* Boston English [MA] B: NY Deceased
1925 Prov: 10 G.

ED SHARKEY Sharkey, Edward Joseph 6′3″, 229 **OG-LB-OT-DG**
Col: Duke; Nevada-Reno *HS:* DeSoto [Arcadia, FL] B: 7/6/1927, Brooklyn, NY
AAFC **1947** NY-A: 9 G. **1948** NY-A: 10 G. **1949** NY-A: 12 G; Int 1-0.
Total: 31 G; Int 1-0.

NFL **1950** NYY: 12 G; Int 1-7. **1952** Cle: 12 G; KR 2-24 12.0. **1953** Bal: 12 G. **1954** Phi: 12 G; PR 1-5 5.0; Int 1-4. **1955** Phi-SF: 12 G; KR 1-11 11.0. Phi: 7 G; KR 1-11 11.0. SF: 5 G. **1956** SF: 7 G; Int 1-4. **Total:** 67 G; PR 1-5 5.0; KR 3-35 11.7; Int 3-15.

ED SHAROCKMAN Sharockman, Edward Charles 6′0″, 200 **DB**
Col: Pittsburgh *HS:* St. Clair [PA] B: 11/4/1939, St. Clair, PA
Drafted: 1961 Round 5 Min
1962 Min: PR 1-16 16.0; KR 3-71 23.7; **1** Fum TD. **1963** Min: KR 7-139 19.9. **1966** Min: PR 9-95 10.6. **1967** Min: PR 4-0; KR 1-22 22.0. **1968** Min: KR 1-14 14.0. **Total:** PR 14-111 7.9; KR 12-246 20.5; 1 Fum TD.

Year Team	G	Interceptions Int	Yds	TD	Fum	Tot TD
1961 Min	1	0	0	0	0	0
1962 Min	14	6	92	0	2	1
1963 Min	14	5	93	1	1	1
1964 Min	14	1	22	0	1	0
1965 Min	14	6	118	1	0	1
1966 Min	11	1	38	0	2	0
1967 Min	14	3	94	0	0	0
1968 Min	14	4	70	0	0	0
1969 Min	11	1	36	0	0	0
1970 Min	14	7	132	1	0	3
1971 Min	14	6	109	0	0	0
1972 Min	7	0	0	0	0	0
NFL Total	142	40	804	3	6	6

DAN SHARP Sharp, Daniel Ira 6′2″, 235 **TE**
Col: Ranger Coll. TX (J.C.); Texas Christian *HS:* Boerne [TX]
B: 2/5/1962, Dallas, TX
1987 Atl: 9 G; Rec 2-6 3.0; KR 1-11 11.0.

EV SHARP Sharp, Everett 6′1″, 223 **T**
Col: Cal Poly-Pomona *HS:* Corinth [MS] B: 6/25/1918, Corinth, MS
D: 2/1996, North Beach, MD
1944 Was: 5 G. **1945** Was: 9 G. **Total:** 14 G.

RICK SHARP Sharp, Vaughan Richard 6′3″, 265 **OT**
Col: Washington *HS:* Queen Anne [Seattle, WA] B: 6/1/1948, London, England *Drafted:* 1970 Round 12 Pit
1970 Pit: 14 G; KR 1-9 9.0. **1971** Pit: 3 G. **1972** Den: 12 G. **Total:** 29 G; KR 1-9 9.0.

LUIS SHARPE Sharpe, Luis Ernesto Jr. 6′5″, 275 **OT**
Col: UCLA *HS:* Southwestern [Detroit, MI] B: 6/16/1960, Havana, Cuba *Drafted:* 1982 Round 1 StL
1982 StL: 9 G. **1983** StL: 16 G; Rush 1-11 11.0. **1984** StL: 16 G. **1985** StL: 16 G. **1986** StL: 16 G. **1987** StL: 12 G. **1988** Pho: 16 G. **1989** Pho: 14 G. **1990** Pho: 16 G; Rec 1-1 1.0 1 TD; 6 Pt. **1991** Pho: 16 G. **1992** Pho: 15 G. **1993** Pho: 16 G. **1994** Ariz: 11 G. **Total:** 189 G; Rush 1-11 11.0; Rec 1-1 1.0 1 TD; 6 Pt.

SHANNON SHARPE Sharpe, Shannon 6′2″, 230 **TE-WR**
Col: Savannah State *HS:* Glennville [GA] B: 6/26/1968, Chicago, IL
Drafted: 1990 Round 7 Den
1991 Den: Rush 1-15 15.0. **1992** Den: Rush 2-(-6) -3.0. **1993** Den: KR 1-0. **1994** Den: Scor 2 2XP. **1997** Den: Scor 1 2XP. **Total:** Rush 3-9 3.0; KR 1-0; Scor 3 2XP.

Year Team	G	Receiving Rec	Yds	Avg	TD	Fum
1990 Den	16	7	99	14.1	1	1
1991 Den	16	22	322	14.6	1	0
1992 Den	16	53	640	12.1	2	1
1993 Den	16	81	995	12.3	9	1
1994 Den	15	87	1010	11.6	4	1
1995 Den	13	63	756	12.0	4	1
1996 Den	15	80	1062	13.3	10	1
1997 Den	16	72	1107	15.4	3	1
1998 Den	16	64	768	12.0	10	0
NFL Total	139	529	6759	12.8	44	7

STERLING SHARPE Sharpe, Sterling 6′0″, 207 **WR**
Col: South Carolina *HS:* Glennville [GA] B: 4/6/1965, Chicago, IL
Drafted: 1988 Round 1 GB
1988 GB: Rush 4-(-2) -0.5; PR 9-48 5.3; KR 1-17 17.0. **1989** GB: Rush 2-25 12.5; 1 Fum TD. **1990** GB: Rush 2-14 7.0. **1991** GB: Rush 4-4 1.0. **1992** GB: Rush 4-8 2.0. **1993** GB: Pass 1-1 100.0%, 1 1.00; Rush 4-8 2.0. **1994** GB: Rush 3-15 5.0. **Total:** Pass 1-1 100.0%, 1 1.00; Rush 23-72 3.1; PR 9-48 5.3; KR 1-17 17.0; 1 Fum TD.

Year Team	G	Receiving Rec	Yds	Avg	TD	Fum	Tot TD
1988 GB	16	55	791	14.4	1	3	1
1989 GB	16	**90**	1423	15.8	12	1	13
1990 GB	16	67	1105	16.5	6	0	6
1991 GB	16	69	961	13.9	4	1	4
1992 GB	16	**108**	**1461**	13.5	**13**	2	13
1993 GB	16	**112**	1274	11.4	11	1	11
1994 GB	16	94	1119	11.9	**18**	1	18
NFL Total	112	595	8134	13.7	65	9	66

DARREN SHARPER Sharper, Darren Mallory 6′2″, 210 **DB**
Col: William & Mary *HS:* Hermitage [Richmond, VA] B: 11/3/1975, Richmond, VA *Drafted:* 1997 Round 2 GB
1997 GB: 14 G; PR 7-32 4.6; KR 1-3 3.0; Int 2-70 2 TD; 1 Fum TD; Tot TD 3; 18 Pt; 1 Fum. **1998** GB: 16 G. **Total:** 30 G; PR 7-32 4.6; KR 1-3 3.0; Int 2-70 2 TD; 1 Fum TD; Tot TD 3; 18 Pt; 1 Fum.

JAMIE SHARPER Sharper, Harry James Jr. 6′3″, 240 **LB**
Col: Virginia *HS:* Hermitage [Richmond, VA] B: 11/23/1974, Richmond, VA *Drafted:* 1997 Round 2 Bal
1997 Bal: 16 G; Int 1-4; 1 Fum; 3 Sac. **1998** Bal: 16 G; 1 Sac. **Total:** 32 G; Int 1-4; 1 Fum; 4 Sac.

HARRY SHAUB Shaub, Harry 5′7″, 215 **G**
Col: Cornell B: 7/15/1911 D: 4/22/1988, Fort Lauderdale, FL
1935 Phi: 1 G.

TYRONE SHAVERS Shavers, Tyrone Pernell 6′3″, 210 **WR**
Col: Tyler JC TX; Lamar *HS:* Liberty-Eylau [Texarkana, TX]
B: 7/14/1967, Texarkana, TX *Drafted:* 1990 Round 6 Pho
1991 Cle: 1 G.

BEN SHAW Shaw, Benjamin 5′10″, 190 **G**
Col: No College B: 1894, OH Deceased
1923 Can: 1 G.

CHARLIE SHAW Shaw, Charles Edward 6′2″, 220 **OG**
Col: Oklahoma State *HS:* Classen [Oklahoma City, OK] B: 3/6/1927, Durant, OK D: 6/17/1994, Kingston, OK *Drafted:* 1950 Round 16 SF
1950 SF: 6 G.

DENNIS SHAW Shaw, Dennis Wendell 6′3″, 217 **QB**
Col: Mount San Antonio Coll. CA (J.C.); USC; San Diego State
HS: Damien [La Verne, CA] B: 3/3/1947, Los Angeles, CA
Drafted: 1970 Round 2 Buf

Year Team	G	Passing Att	Comp	Comp%	Yds	YPA	TD	Int	Rating
1970 Buf	14	321	178	55.5	2507	7.81	10	20	65.3
1971 Buf	13	291	149	51.2	1813	6.23	11	26	46.1
1972 Buf	14	258	136	52.7	1666	6.46	14	17	63.5
1973 Buf	4	46	22	47.8	300	6.52	0	4	32.9
1974 StL	2	0	0	—	0	—	0	0	—
1975 StL	3	8	4	50.0	61	7.63	0	1	35.9
NFL Total	50	924	489	52.9	6347	6.87	35	68	56.8

Year Team	Rushing Att	Yds	Avg	TD	Fum
1970 Buf	39	210	5.4	0	**10**
1971 Buf	14	82	5.9	0	4
1972 Buf	35	138	3.9	0	6
1973 Buf	4	2	0.5	0	2
1975 StL	3	-12	-4.0	0	2
NFL Total	95	420	4.4	0	24

ED SHAW Shaw, Edson Walter 6'1", 203 **FB-T-WB-G**
Col: Nebraska *HS:* Tecumseh [NE] B: 8/7/1895, Tecumseh, NE
D: 10/30/1964, Omaha, NE
1920 RI: 7 G. **1922** Can: 12 G; Rush 4 TD; Scor 38, 2 FG, **8** XK. **1923** Akr: 2 G. **Total:** 21 G; Rush 4 TD; Scor 38, 2 FG, 8 XK.

ERIC SHAW Shaw, Eric Wendell 6'3", 248 **LB**
Col: Florida State; Louisiana Tech *HS:* Pensacola [FL] B: 9/17/1971, Pensacola, FL *Drafted:* 1992 Round 12 Cin
1992 Cin: 11 G. **1993** Cin: 14 G. **1994** Cin: 3 G; KR 1-1 1.0. **Total:** 28 G; KR 1-1 1.0.

GEORGE SHAW Shaw, George Howard 6'1", 183 **QB**
Col: Oregon *HS:* U.S. Grant [Portland, OR] B: 7/25/1933, Portland, OR
D: 1/3/1998, Portland, OR *Drafted:* 1955 Round 1 Bal
1958 Bal: Scor 6, 0-1 XK. **Total:** Scor 36, 0-1 XK.

		Passing							
Year Team	**G**	**Att**	**Comp**	**Comp%**	**Yds**	**YPA**	**TD**	**Int**	**Rating**
1955 Bal	12	237	119	50.2	1586	6.69	10	19	52.5
1956 Bal	5	75	45	60.0	645	8.60	3	7	62.4
1957 Bal	7	9	5	55.6	58	6.44	1	1	72.7
1958 Bal	12	89	41	46.1	531	5.97	7	4	72.8
1959 NYG	5	36	24	66.7	433	12.03	1	1	105.4
1960 NYG	9	155	76	49.0	1263	8.15	11	13	65.6
1961 Min	8	91	46	50.5	530	5.82	4	4	64.8
1962 Den	13	110	49	44.5	783	7.12	4	14	41.4
NFL Total	71	802	405	50.5	5829	7.27	41	63	58.8

	Rushing				
Year Team	**Att**	**Yds**	**Avg**	**TD**	**Fum**
1955 Bal	68	301	4.4	3	6
1956 Bal	20	63	3.2	0	0
1957 Bal	5	30	6.0	1	0
1958 Bal	5	-3	-0.6	1	0
1959 NYG	3	3	1.0	0	0
1960 NYG	15	-12	-0.8	0	4
1961 Min	10	39	3.9	0	1
1962 Den	4	10	2.5	1	0
NFL Total	130	431	3.3	6	11

GLENN SHAW Shaw, Glenn Edd 6'2", 220 **FB**
Col: Kentucky *HS:* Paducah [KY] B: 7/11/1938, Paducah, KY
Drafted: 1960 Round 11 ChiB
1962 LARm: Rec 3-51 17.0. **1963** Oak: Rec 2-64 32.0 1 TD; KR 2-19 9.5. **1964** Oak: Rec 3-31 10.3. **Total:** Rec 8-146 18.3 1 TD; KR 2-19 9.5.

		Rushing				Tot
Year Team	**G**	**Att**	**Yds**	**Avg**	**TD**	**TD**
1960 ChiB	12	0	0	—	0	0
1962 LARm	3	18	76	4.2	0	0
1963 Oak	12	20	46	2.3	1	2
1964 Oak	2	9	26	2.9	2	2
NFL Total	29	47	148	3.1	3	4

HAROLD SHAW Shaw, Harold Lamar 6'0", 228 **RB**
Col: Southern Mississippi *HS:* Magee [MS] B: 9/3/1974, Magee, MS
Drafted: 1998 Round 6 NE
1998 NE: 11 G.

JESSE SHAW Shaw, Jesse M 6'1", 210 **G**
Col: USC *HS:* Selma [CA] B: 6/11/1907 D: 10/25/1965, Woodland Hills, CA
1931 ChiC: 5 G.

PETE SHAW Shaw, Kenneth Edward 5'10", 183 **DB**
Col: Northwestern *HS:* Barringer [Newark, NJ] B: 8/25/1954, Newark, NJ *Drafted:* 1977 Round 6 SD
1981 SD: KR 6-103 17.2. **1982** NYG: KR 1-0. **1983** NYG: 1 Sac.
Total: KR 7-103 14.7; 1 Sac.

		Punt Returns				Interceptions			
Year Team	**G**	**Ret**	**Yds**	**Avg**	**TD**	**Int**	**Yds**	**TD**	**Fum**
1977 SD	14	0	0	—	0	0	0	0	0
1978 SD	16	4	46	11.5	0	2	0	0	0
1979 SD	16	2	21	10.5	0	3	54	0	0
1980 SD	12	5	20	4.0	0	4	50	0	0
1981 SD	16	1	1	1.0	0	3	50	0	0
1982 NYG	9	0	0	—	0	0	0	0	1
1983 NYG	15	29	234	8.1	0	0	0	0	4
1984 NYG	16	0	0	—	0	0	0	0	0
NFL Total	114	41	322	7.9	0	12	154	0	5

NATE SHAW Shaw, Nathaniel 6'2", 205 **DB**
Col: USC *HS:* Abraham Lincoln [San Diego, CA] B: 5/20/1945, San Diego, CA *Drafted:* 1967 Round 5 LARm
1969 LARm: 7 G. **1970** LARm: 8 G. **Total:** 15 G.

RICKY SHAW Shaw, Ricky Andrew 6'4", 240 **LB**
Col: Oklahoma State *HS:* Douglas Byrd [Fayetteville, NC]
B: 7/28/1965, Mount Vernon, NY *Drafted:* 1988 Round 4 NYG
1988 NYG: 14 G. **1989** NYG-Phi: 15 G. NYG: 7 G. Phi: 8 G. **1990** Phi: 8 G. **Total:** 37 G.

BOB SHAW Shaw, Robert 6'4", 226 **OE-DE**
Col: Ohio State *HS:* Ross [Fremont, OH] B: 5/22/1921, Richwood, OH
Drafted: 1944 Round 8 Cle
1945 Cle: KR 1-1 1.0. **1946** LARm: KR 1-52 52.0 **1** TD. **Total:** KR 2-53 26.5 1 TD.

		Receiving					Tot
Year Team	**G**	**Rec**	**Yds**	**Avg**	**TD**	**Fum**	**TD**
1945 Cle	5	0	0	—	0	0	0
1946 LARm	10	4	63	15.8	2	0	3
1949 LARm	11	29	535	18.4	6	1	6
1950 ChiC	12	48	971	20.2	**12**	1	**12**
NFL Total	38	81	1569	19.4	20	2	21

BOB SHAW Shaw, Robert K 6'0", 194 **WR**
Col: Winston-Salem State B: 3/16/1947, Wilson, NC
1970 NO: 4 G; Rec 1-49 49.0.

ROBERT SHAW Shaw, Robert Leslie 6'4", 245 **C-OG**
Col: Tennessee *HS:* Joseph Wheeler [Marietta, GA] B: 10/15/1956, Tuscaloosa, AL *Drafted:* 1979 Round 1 Dal
1979 Dal: 16 G; 1 Fum. **1980** Dal: 14 G. **1981** Dal: 3 G. **Total:** 33 G; 1 Fum.

SCOTT SHAW Shaw, Scott Harold 6'3", 303 **OG**
Col: Michigan State *HS:* Henry Ford II [Sterling Heights, MI]
B: 6/2/1974, Detroit, MI *Drafted:* 1998 Round 5 Mia
1998 Cin: 2 G.

SEDRICK SHAW Shaw, Sedrick Anton 6'0", 214 **RB**
Col: Iowa *HS:* Lyndon B. Johnson [Austin, TX] B: 11/16/1973, Austin, TX *Drafted:* 1997 Round 3 NE
1998 NE: Rec 6-30 5.0; KR 1-16 16.0. **Total:** Rec 6-30 5.0; KR 1-16 16.0.

		Rushing				
Year Team	**G**	**Att**	**Yds**	**Avg**	**TD**	**Fum**
1997 NE	1	0	0	—	0	0
1998 NE	13	48	236	4.9	0	2
NFL Total	14	48	236	4.9	0	2

TERRANCE SHAW Shaw, Terrance Bernard 5'11", 190 **DB**
Col: Stephen F. Austin St. *HS:* Marshall [TX] B: 11/11/1973, Marshall, TX *Drafted:* 1995 Round 2 SD
1995 SD: 16 G; Int 1-31. **1996** SD: 16 G; Int 3-78. **1997** SD: 16 G; Int 1-11. **1998** SD: 13 G; Int 2-0. **Total:** 61 G; Int 7-120.

BILLY SHAW Shaw, William Lewis 6'2", 258 **OG**
Col: Georgia Tech *HS:* Carr Central [Vicksburg, MS] B: 12/15/1938, Natchez, MS *Drafted:* 1961 Round 2 Buf *HOF:* 1999
1961 Buf: 14 G. **1962** Buf: 14 G. **1963** Buf: 14 G. **1964** Buf: 14 G. **1965** Buf: 14 G. **1966** Buf: 14 G. **1967** Buf: 9 G. **1968** Buf: 13 G. **1969** Buf: 13 G. **Total:** 119 G.

JERRY SHAY Shay, Jerome Paul 6'3", 250 **DT**
(AKA Jerome Paul Dzedzeji) *Col:* Purdue *HS:* Lew Wallace [Gary, IN]
B: 7/10/1944, Gary, IN *Drafted:* 1966 Round 1 Min
1966 Min: 14 G. **1967** Min: 1 G. **1968** Atl: 14 G. **1969** Atl: 14 G. **1970** NYG: 14 G. **1971** NYG: 6 G. **Total:** 63 G.

PAT SHEA Shea, Patrick Beardsley 6'1", 250 **OG**
Col: USC *HS:* Mission Bay [San Diego, CA] B: 6/28/1939, La Jolla, CA
1962 SD: 5 G. **1963** SD: 14 G. **1964** SD: 14 G. **1965** SD: 8 G; Rush 1-(-5) -5.0. **Total:** 41 G; Rush 1-(-5) -5.0.

SHAG SHEARD Sheard, Alfred Scotchard 5'11", 177 **TB-WB**
Col: St. Lawrence *HS:* Canton [NY] B: 11/17/1898, Canton, NY
D: 11/11/1980, Canton, NY
1923 Roch: 4 G; Pass 1 TD. **1924** Roch: 7 G; Scor **1** 1XP; 1 Pt. **1925** Roch: 7 G; Rec 2 TD; 12 Pt. **Total:** 18 G; Pass 1 TD; Rec 2 TD; Scor 1 1XP; 13 Pt.

RON SHEARER Shearer, Ronald Elmer 6'0", 195 **T**
Col: Drake *HS:* West [Des Moines, IA] B: 9/12/1905, Creston, IA
1930 Port: 1 G.

BRAD SHEARER Shearer, Sterling Bradford 6'3", 250 **DT**
Col: Texas *HS:* Westlake [Austin, TX] B: 8/10/1955, Houston, TX
Drafted: 1978 Round 3 ChiB
1978 ChiB: 15 G. **1980** ChiB: 13 G. **1981** ChiB: 6 G. **Total:** 34 G.

JOE SHEARIN Shearin, Joseph Leslie 6'4", 254 **OG-C**
Col: Texas *HS:* Woodrow Wilson [Dallas, TX] B: 4/16/1960, Dallas, TX
Drafted: 1982 Round 7 LARm
1983 LARm: 16 G. **1984** LARm: 15 G. **1985** TB: 10 G. **1987** Dal: 1 G. **Total:** 42 G.

LARRY SHEARS Shears, Larry 5'10", 185 DB
Col: Lincoln (Mo.) *HS:* Mobile Co. Training School [Plateau, AL]
B: 8/1/1949, Mobile, AL *Drafted:* 1971 Round 11 Atl
1971 Atl: 9 G. **1972** Atl: 1 G. **Total:** 10 G.

KENNY SHEDD Shedd, Kendrick Dwayne 5'10", 168 WR
Col: Northern Iowa *HS:* West [Davenport, IA] B: 2/14/1971, Davenport, IA *Drafted:* 1993 Round 5 NYJ
1996 Oak: 16 G; Rec 3-87 29.0 1 TD; KR 3-51 17.0; Scor 1 Saf; 8 Pt.
1997 Oak: 16 G; Rec 10-115 11.5; KR 2-38 19.0; 1 Fum TD; 6 Pt.
1998 Oak: 15 G; Rec 3-50 16.7; KR 2-32 16.0. **Total:** 47 G; Rec 16-252 15.8 1 TD; KR 7-121 17.3; Scor 1 Saf; 1 Fum TD; Tot TD 2; 14 Pt.

ED SHEDLOSKY Shedlosky, Edmond Francis 6'0", 185 WB-DB
Col: Tulsa; Fordham *HS:* Nanticoke [PA] B: 8/2/1920, Nanticoke, PA Deceased
1945 NYG: 3 G; Rush 9-11 1.2; Rec 2-15 7.5; PR 1-19 19.0; KR 2-40 20.0.

FRED SHEEHAN Sheehan, Fredric William 6'2", 210 G
Col: Georgetown *HS:* Abington [MA]; St. John's Prep [Danvers, MA]
B: 12/21/1902, Abington, MA D: 9/2/1984, Boston, MA
1925 Prov: 1 G.

PAUL SHEEKS Sheeks, Paul Preston 5'8", 173 BB
(Pepper) *Col:* Dakota Wesleyan; South Dakota *HS:* Mitchell [SD]
B: 10/18/1889, Grand Rapids, ND D: 9/17/1968, Akron, OH
1921 Akr: 12 G; Rec 1 TD; Scor 13, 2 FG, 1 XK. **1922** Akr: 9 G; Scor 17, 3 FG, **8** XK. **Total:** 21 G; Rec 1 TD; Scor 30, 5 FG, 9 XK.

CHRIS SHEFFIELD Sheffield, Christopher Jonathan 6'1", 193 DB
Col: Albany State (Ga.) *HS:* Cairo [GA] B: 1/9/1963, Cairo, GA
1986 Pit: 10 G. **1987** Pit-Det: 11 G; Int 1-2. Pit: 5 G; Int 1-2. Det: 6 G.
Total: 21 G; Int 1-2.

RON SHEGOG Shegog, Ronald 5'11", 190 DB
Col: Northwest Mississippi CC; Austin Peay State *HS:* South Panola [Batesville, MS] B: 3/2/1963, Batesville, MS
1987 NE: 3 G; Int 1-7.

RASHAAN SHEHEE Shehee, Rashaan 5'10", 205 RB
Col: Washington *HS:* Foothill [Bakersfield, CA] B: 6/20/1975, Bakersfield, CA *Drafted:* 1998 Round 3 KC
1998 KC: 16 G; Rush 22-57 2.6; Rec 10-73 7.3; KR 4-72 18.0; 2 Fum.

VIN SHEKLETON Shekleton, Vincent S 5'8", 165 C
Col: Colgate; Marquette *HS:* Dubuque [IA] B: 11/16/1896, Lawler, IA Deceased
1922 Rac: 3 G.

JOHN SHELBURNE Shelburne, John Andrew 5'11", 200 FB
(Jack) *Col:* Dartmouth *HS:* Boston English [MA]; Colby Acad. [NH]
B: 9/26/1894, Boston, MA D: 1/29/1978, Boston, MA
1922 Ham: 6 G.

WILLIE SHELBY Shelby, Willie Earl 5'11", 195 RB
Col: Alabama *HS:* Purvis [MS] B: 7/24/1953, Hattiesburg, MS
Drafted: 1976 Round 5 Cin
1976 Cin: Rush 5-9 1.8; Rec 1-3 3.0. **1978** StL: Rush 2-5 2.5; Rec 1-11 11.0. **Total:** Rush 7-14 2.0; Rec 2-14 7.0.

		Punt Returns				Kickoff Returns					Tot
Year Team	G	Ret	Yds	Avg	TD	Ret	Yds	Avg	TD	Fum	TD
1976 Cin	13	21	162	7.7	0	30	**761**	25.4	**1**	8	1
1977 Cin	14	11	54	4.9	0	19	403	21.2	0	2	1
1978 StL	3	10	88	8.8	0	9	211	23.4	0	0	0
NFL Total	30	42	304	7.2	0	58	1375	23.7	1	10	2

JIM SHELDON Sheldon, James Hurlon 5'11", 180 E
Col: Brown *HS:* Auburn [NY]; Williston Acad. [Easthampton, MA]
B: 1/9/1901, Oneonta, NY D: 2/26/1980, Round Hill, VA
1926 Bkn: 1 G.

MIKE SHELDON Sheldon, Michael Joseph 6'4", 305 OT
Col: Grand Valley State *HS:* Willowbrook [Villa Park, IL] B: 6/8/1973, Hinsdale, IL
1997 Mia: 11 G. **1998** Mia: 9 G. **Total:** 20 G.

ART SHELL Shell, Arthur 6'5", 265 OT
Col: Maryland East. Shore *HS:* Bonds-Wilson [North Charleston, SC]
B: 11/26/1946, Charleston, SC *Drafted:* 1968 Round 3 Oak
HOF: 1989
1968 Oak: 14 G; PR 1-0; 1 Fum. **1969** Oak: 14 G. **1970** Oak: 14 G.
1971 Oak: 14 G. **1972** Oak: 14 G. **1973** Oak: 14 G. **1974** Oak: 14 G.
1975 Oak: 14 G. **1976** Oak: 14 G. **1977** Oak: 14 G. **1978** Oak: 16 G.
1979 Oak: 11 G. **1980** Oak: 16 G. **1981** Oak: 16 G. **1982** LARd: 8 G.
Total: 207 G; PR 1-0; 1 Fum.

DONNIE SHELL Shell, Donnie 5'11", 190 DB
Col: South Carolina State *HS:* Whitmire [SC] B: 8/26/1952, Whitmire, SC
1975 Pit: Rec 2-39 19.5. **1978** Pit: PR 1-6 6.0; 1 Fum TD. **1982** Pit: 1 Sac.
1987 Pit: **1** Fum TD. **Total:** Rec 2-39 19.5; PR 1-6 6.0; 2 Fum TD; 1 Sac.

		Interceptions			Tot
Year Team	G	Int	Yds	TD	TD
1974 Pit	14	1	0	0	0
1975 Pit	14	1	29	0	0
1976 Pit	14	1	4	0	0
1977 Pit	12	3	14	0	0
1978 Pit	16	3	21	0	1
1979 Pit	16	5	10	0	0
1980 Pit	16	7	135	0	0
1981 Pit	14	5	52	0	0
1982 Pit	9	5	27	0	0
1983 Pit	16	5	18	0	0
1984 Pit	16	7	61	1	1
1985 Pit	16	4	40	0	0
1986 Pit	15	3	29	0	0
1987 Pit	13	1	50	1	2
NFL Total	201	51	490	2	4

TODD SHELL Shell, Todd Andrew 6'4", 225 LB
Col: Brigham Young *HS:* Mountain View [Mesa, AZ] B: 6/24/1962, Mesa, AZ *Drafted:* 1984 Round 1 SF
1984 SF: 16 G; Int 3-81 1 TD; 6 Pt; 2 Sac. **1985** SF: 15 G; Int 1-33; 4 Sac.
1986 SF: 1 G. **1987** SF: 6 G; Int 1-1; 1 Sac. **Total:** 38 G; Int 5-115 1 TD; 6 Pt; 7 Sac.

DECK SHELLEY Shelley, Dexter 5'11", 191 TB-WB-HB
(AKA Robert P. Shelley) *Col:* Texas *HS:* I.M. Terrell [Dallas, TX]
B: 6/4/1906, San Antonio, TX D: 12/17/1968, Temple, TX
1931 Prov-Port: 10 G; Pass 3 TD; Scor 4, 4 XK. Prov: 8 G; Pass 3 TD; Scor 4, 4 XK. Port: 10 G. **1932** GB-ChiC: 4 G; Pass 1-1 100.0%, 3 3.00; Rush 10-14 1.4. GB: 2 G; Rush 5-3 0.6. ChiC: 2 G; Pass 1-1 100.0%, 3 3.00; Rush 5-11 2.2. **Total:** 22 G; Pass 1-1 100.0%, 3 3.00 3 TD; Rush 10-14 1.4.

ELBERT SHELLEY Shelley, Elbert Vernell 5'11", 185 DB
Col: Arkansas State *HS:* Trumann [AR] B: 12/24/1964, Tyronza, AR
Drafted: 1987 Round 11 Atl
1987 Atl: 4 G. **1988** Atl: 12 G; KR 2-5 2.5; 1 Fum. **1989** Atl: 10 G; Int 1-31.
1990 Atl: 12 G. **1991** Atl: 11 G; 2 Sac. **1992** Atl: 13 G. **1993** Atl: 16 G.
1994 Atl: 16 G. **1995** Atl: 13 G. **1996** Atl: 12 G. **Total:** 119 G; KR 2-5 2.5; Int 1-31; 1 Fum; 2 Sac.

JONATHAN SHELLEY Shelley, Jonathan 6'0", 176 DB
Col: Mississippi *HS:* Warren Central [Vicksburg, MS] B: 8/6/1964, Vicksburg, MS
1987 SF: 1 G.

CHRIS SHELLING Shelling, Christopher A 5'10", 180 DB
Col: Auburn *HS:* Baker [Columbus, GA] B: 11/3/1972, Columbus, GA
1995 Cin: 13 G. **1996** Cin: 1 G. **1997** Atl: 2 G. **Total:** 16 G.

KENDEL SHELLO Shello, Kendel Ray 6'3", 301 DE
Col: Southern University *HS:* New Iberia [LA] B: 11/24/1973, New Iberia, LA
1996 Ind: 1 G. **1997** Ind: 6 G; 1 Sac. **1998** Ind: 6 G; 1 Sac. **Total:** 13 G; 2 Sac.

ALEC SHELLOGG Shellogg, Alec Regis 6'0", 215 T
Col: Notre Dame *HS:* New Castle [PA] B: 2/7/1914, New Castle, PA
D: 7/12/1968
1939 ChiB-Bkn: 3 G. ChiB: 1 G. Bkn: 2 G. **Total:** 3 G.

ANTHONY SHELTON Shelton, Anthony Levala 6'1", 195 DB
Col: Tennessee State *HS:* Lincoln Co. [Fayetteville, TN] B: 9/4/1967, Fayetteville, TN *Drafted:* 1990 Round 11 SF
1990 SD: 14 G. **1991** SD: 11 G; Int 1-19; 1 Sac. **Total:** 25 G; Int 1-19; 1 Sac.

DAIMON SHELTON Shelton, Daimon 6'0", 247 RB
Col: Fresno City Coll. CA (J.C.); Sacramento State *HS:* Duarte [CA]
B: 9/15/1972, Duarte, CA *Drafted:* 1997 Round 6 Jac
1998 Jac: Rec 10-79 7.9. **Total:** Rec 10-79 7.9.

		Rushing				
Year Team	G	Att	Yds	Avg	TD	Fum
1997 Jac	13	6	4	0.7	0	1
1998 Jac	14	30	95	3.2	1	0
NFL Total	27	36	99	2.8	1	1

MURRAY SHELTON Shelton, Murray Norcross 6'1", 175 E
Col: Cornell *HS:* Dunkirk [NY]; Phillips Andover Acad. [Andover, MA]
B: 4/20/1893, Dunkirk, NY D: 8/14/1985, Columbia, MO
1920 Buf: 11 G.

RICHARD SHELTON Shelton, Richard Eddie 5'10", 180 DB
Col: Liberty *HS:* Marietta [GA] B: 1/2/1966, Marietta, GA
Drafted: 1989 Round 11 Den
1989 Den: 3 G. **1990** Pit: 2 G. **1991** Pit: 14 G; Int 3-57 1 TD; 6 Pt. **1992** Pit: 16 G; Int 0-15. **1993** Pit: 9 G. **Total:** 44 G; Int 3-72 1 TD; 6 Pt.

PAUL SHENEFELT Shenefelt, Paul Jesse 6'0", 195 **T**
Col: Manchester *HS:* Polo [IL] B: 3/4/1911, Ames, IA D: 10/30/1988, Palm Beach Gardens, FL
1934 ChiC: 2 G.

CHARLIE SHEPARD Shepard, Charles Lafayette 6'2", 215 **HB-DB**
(Choo Choo) *Col:* North Texas *HS:* Crozier Tech [Dallas, TX] B: 7/11/1933, Dallas, TX *Drafted:* 1955 Round 18 Bal
1956 Pit: Rec 1-31 31.0; Punt 26-951 36.6.

Year Team	G	Rushing Att	Yds	Avg	TD	Fum
1956 Pit	12	30	91	3.0	0	1

DERRICK SHEPARD Shepard, Derrick Lathell 5'10", 183 **WR**
Col: Oklahoma *HS:* Odessa [TX] B: 1/22/1964, Odessa, TX
1989 NO-Dal: Rush 3-12 4.0; Rec 20-304 15.2 1 TD. NO: Rec 2-36 18.0. Dal: Rush 3-12 4.0; Rec 18-268 14.9 1 TD. **Total:** Rush 3-12 4.0; Rec 20-304 15.2 1 TD.

Year Team	G	Punt Returns Ret	Yds	Avg	TD	Kickoff Returns Ret	Yds	Avg	TD	Fum	Tot TD
1987 Was	2	6	146	24.3	0	1	20	20.0	0	0	0
1988 Was	5	12	104	8.7	0	16	329	20.6	0	3	0
1989 NO-Dal	15	31	251	8.1	**1**	27	529	19.6	0	2	2
1989 NO	4	7	91	13.0	1	8	135	16.9	0	1	1
1989 Dal	11	24	160	6.7	0	19	394	20.7	0	1	1
1990 Dal	8	20	121	6.1	0	4	75	18.8	0	1	0
1991 Dal	6	6	57	9.5	0	3	54	18.0	0	0	0
NFL Total	36	75	679	9.1	1	51	1007	19.7	0	6	2

JOHNNY SHEPHERD Shepherd, Johnny Ray 5'10", 185 **RB**
Col: West Alabama *HS:* Petersburg [NC] B: 4/24/1957, La Grange, NC
1987 Buf: 2 G; Rush 12-42 3.5; Rec 1-2 2.0.

LESLIE SHEPHERD Shepherd, Leslie Glenard 5'11", 186 **WR**
Col: Temple *HS:* Forestville [Oxon Hill, MD] B: 11/3/1969, Washington, DC
1995 Was: Rush 7-63 9.0 1 TD; KR 3-85 28.3. **1996** Was: Rush 6-96 16.0 2 TD. **1997** Was: Rush 4-27 6.8. **1998** Was: Rush 6-91 15.2 1 TD; Scor 1 2XP. **Total:** Rush 23-277 12.0 4 TD; KR 3-85 28.3; Scor 1 2XP.

Year Team	G	Receiving Rec	Yds	Avg	TD	Tot TD
1994 Was	3	1	8	8.0	0	0
1995 Was	14	29	486	16.8	2	3
1996 Was	12	23	344	15.0	3	5
1997 Was	11	29	562	19.4	5	5
1998 Was	16	43	712	16.6	8	9
NFL Total	56	125	2112	16.9	18	22

BILL SHEPHERD Shepherd, William Leroy 5'9", 198 **FB-LB-TB-DB**
Col: Western Maryland *HS:* Clearfield [PA]; Keystone Acad. [Wyoming, PA] B: 12/4/1911, Clearfield, PA D: 3/8/1967, Detroit, MI
1935 Bos-Det: Rec 4-33 8.3; Scor 25, 1 XK. Bos: Rec 2-20 10.0; Scor 7, 1 XK. Det: Rec 2-13 6.5. **1936** Det: Scor 13, 1 XK; **1** Fum TD. **1937** Det: Int **1** TD; Scor 31, 2 FG, 7 XK. **1938** Det: Scor 23, 1-2 50.0% FG, 2-2 100.0% XK. **1939** Det: Rec 14-143 10.2 1 TD; Punt 23-850 37.0. **1940** Det: Rec 2-12 6.0; Punt 1-40 40.0. **Total:** Rec 20-188 9.4 1 TD; Int 1 TD; Punt 24-890 37.1; Scor 110, 3-2 50.0% FG, 11-2 100.0% XK; 1 Fum TD.

Year Team	G	Passing Att	Comp	Comp%	Yds	YPA	TD	Int	Rating
1935 Bos-Det	12	64	28	43.8	417	6.52	2	14	36.5
1935 Bos	7	55	21	38.2	318	5.78	1	14	24.5
1935 Det	5	9	7	77.8	99	11.00	1	0	149.5
1936 Det	12	9	3	33.3	57	6.33	0	1	16.7
1937 Det	11	46	19	41.3	297	6.46	2	7	38.3
1938 Det	9	32	8	25.0	167	5.22	0	6	9.2
1939 Det	11	1	0	0.0	0	0.00	0	0	39.6
1940 Det	3	0	0	—	0	—	0	0	—
NFL Total	58	152	58	38.2	938	6.17	4	28	28.8

Year Team	Rushing Att	Yds	Avg	TD	Tot TD
1935 Bos-Det	143	425	3.0	4	4
1935 Bos	89	285	3.2	1	1
1935 Det	54	140	2.6	3	3
1936 Det	74	292	3.9	1	2
1937 Det	93	325	3.5	2	3
1938 Det	100	455	4.6	3	3
1939 Det	105	420	4.0	2	3
1940 Det	24	67	2.8	0	0
NFL Total	539	1984	3.7	12	15

ASHLEY SHEPPARD Sheppard, Ashley Guy 6'3", 240 **LB**
Col: Clemson *HS:* North Pitt [Bethel, NC]; Fork Union Mil. Acad. [VA] B: 1/21/1969, Greenville, NC *Drafted:* 1993 Round 4 Min
1993 Min: 10 G; 1 Sac. **1994** Min: 7 G; 0.5 Sac. **1995** Jac-Min-StL: 4 G. Jac: 2 G. StL: 2 G. **Total:** 21 G; 1.5 Sac.

HENRY SHEPPARD Sheppard, Henry Fossett 6'6", 255 **OG-OT**
Col: Southern Methodist *HS:* Cuero [TX] B: 11/12/1952, Cuero, TX *Drafted:* 1976 Round 5 Cle
1976 Cle: 14 G. **1977** Cle: 13 G. **1978** Cle: 14 G. **1979** Cle: 16 G. **1980** Cle: 16 G. **1981** Cle: 9 G. **Total:** 82 G.

DAVE SHERER Sherer, David McDonald Jr. 6'3", 210 **OE**
Col: New Mexico Mil. Inst. (J.C.); Southern Methodist *HS:* Carlsbad [NM] B: 2/14/1937, Galion, OH *Drafted:* 1959 Round 2 Bal
1959 Bal: Rec 1-9 9.0. **1960** Dal: KR 1-0. **Total:** Rec 1-9 9.0; KR 1-0.

Year Team	G	Punting Punts	Yds	Avg	Fum
1959 Bal	12	51	2132	41.8	1
1960 Dal	11	57	2420	42.5	0
NFL Total	23	108	4552	42.1	1

STAN SHERIFF Sheriff, Bruce Stanley 6'1", 224 **LB-OG-C**
Col: Cal Poly-S.L.O. *HS:* George Washington [San Francisco, CA] B: 4/24/1932, Honolulu, HI D: 1/16/1993, Honolulu, HI
1954 Pit: 12 G; Int 1-18. **1956** SF: 7 G. **1957** SF-Cle: 5 G. SF: 2 G. Cle: 3 G. **Total:** 24 G; Int 1-18.

JERRY SHERK Sherk, Jerry Martin 6'4", 258 **DT-DE-NT**
Col: Grays Harbor Coll. WA (J.C.); Oklahoma State *HS:* Grants Pass [OR] B: 7/7/1948, Grants Pass, OR *Drafted:* 1970 Round 2 Cle
1970 Cle: 14 G. **1971** Cle: 14 G; Int 2-3. **1972** Cle: 14 G. **1973** Cle: 14 G. **1974** Cle: 14 G. **1975** Cle: 14 G. **1976** Cle: 14 G; Int 1-0. **1977** Cle: 7 G; Scor 1 Saf; 2 Pt. **1978** Cle: 16 G. **1979** Cle: 10 G. **1980** Cle: 1 G. **1981** Cle: 15 G. **Total:** 147 G; Int 3-3; Scor 1 Saf; 2 Pt.

BOB SHERLAG Sherlag, Robert Joseph 6'0", 195 **WR**
(Jimmy) *Col:* Memphis *HS:* Carl Schurz [Chicago, IL] B: 4/19/1943, Chicago, IL *Drafted:* 1966 Round 6 Phi
1966 Atl: 9 G; Rec 4-53 13.3 1 TD; PR 2-8 4.0; KR 1-0; 6 Pt.

ALLIE SHERMAN Sherman, Alexander 5'11", 170 **QB-DB**
Col: Brooklyn College *HS:* Boys [Brooklyn, NY] B: 2/10/1923, Brooklyn, NY
1944 Phi: Int 2-34; Punt 1-27 27.0. **Total:** Int 2-34; Punt 1-27 27.0.

Year Team	G	Passing Att	Comp	Comp%	Yds	YPA	TD	Int	Rating
1943 PhPt	9	37	16	43.2	208	5.62	2	**1**	68.3
1944 Phi	10	31	16	51.6	156	5.03	1	2	49.9
1945 Phi	10	29	15	51.7	172	5.93	2	3	53.3
1946 Phi	11	33	17	51.5	264	**8.00**	4	3	80.1
1947 Phi	11	5	2	40.0	23	4.60	0	1	15.0
NFL Total	51	135	66	48.9	823	6.10	9	10	59.6

Year Team	Rushing Att	Yds	Avg	TD	Fum
1943 PhPt	17	-20	-1.2	1	0
1944 Phi	22	-42	-1.9	1	0
1945 Phi	16	-7	-0.4	1	2
1946 Phi	21	8	0.4	0	6
1947 Phi	17	17	1.0	1	2
NFL Total	93	-44	-0.5	4	10

HEATH SHERMAN Sherman, Heath 6'0", 195 **RB**
Col: Texas A&M–Kingsville *HS:* El Campo [TX] B: 3/27/1967, Wharton, TX *Drafted:* 1989 Round 6 Phi
1989 Phi: KR 13-222 17.1. **1991** Phi: KR 4-61 15.3. **Total:** KR 17-283 16.6.

Year Team	G	Rushing Att	Yds	Avg	TD	Receiving Rec	Yds	Avg	TD	Fum	Tot TD
1989 Phi	15	40	177	4.4	2	8	85	10.6	0	4	2
1990 Phi	14	164	685	4.2	1	23	167	7.3	3	4	4
1991 Phi	16	106	279	2.6	0	14	59	4.2	0	3	0
1992 Phi	16	112	583	**5.2**	5	18	219	12.2	1	3	6
1993 Phi	15	115	406	3.5	2	12	78	6.5	0	3	2
NFL Total	76	537	2130	4.0	10	75	608	8.1	4	17	14

BOB SHERMAN Sherman, Robert David 6'2", 195 **DB**
Col: Iowa *HS:* Durand [MI] B: 7/4/1942, Owosso, MI *Drafted:* 1964 Round 12 Pit
1964 Pit: 14 G. **1965** Pit: 11 G; Int 1-35. **Total:** 25 G; Int 1-35.

ROD SHERMAN Sherman, Rodney Jarvis 6'0", 190 **WR**
Col: USC *HS:* John Muir [Pasadena, CA] B: 12/25/1944, Pasadena, CA *Drafted:* 1966 Redshirt Round 1 Oak
1967 Oak: Rush 1-13 13.0 1 TD. **1968** Cin: Rush 1-3 3.0; Scor 10, 0-1 FG, 4-4 100.0% XK. **1970** Oak: Rush 1-2 2.0. **1972** Den: Rush 1-2 2.0. **Total:** Rush 4-20 5.0 1 TD; Scor 40, 0-1 FG, 4-4 100.0% XK.

Year Team	G	Receiving Rec	Yds	Avg	TD	Punt Returns Ret	Yds	Avg	TD
1967 Oak	13	5	61	12.2	0	0	0	—	0
1968 Cin	13	31	374	12.1	1	0	0	—	0
1969 Oak	14	0	0	—	0	9	46	5.1	0
1970 Oak	14	18	285	15.8	0	8	65	8.1	0
1971 Oak	12	12	187	15.6	1	2	2	1.0	0
1972 Den	14	38	661	17.4	3	10	89	8.9	0
1973 LARm	3	1	8	8.0	0	0	0	—	0
NFL Total	83	105	1576	15.0	5	29	202	7.0	0

Year Team	Kickoff Returns Ret	Yds	Avg	TD	Fum	Tot TD
1967 Oak	12	279	23.3	0	1	1
1968 Cin	0	0	—	0	0	1
1969 Oak	12	300	25.0	0	1	0
1970 Oak	2	39	19.5	0	1	0
1971 Oak	0	0	—	0	2	1
1972 Den	0	0	—	0	1	3
NFL Total	26	618	23.8	0	6	6

SOLLY SHERMAN Sherman, Saul S 6′1″, 190 **QB-DB**
Col: Chicago *HS:* John Marshall [Chicago, IL] B: 9/25/1917, Chicago, IL *Drafted:* 1939 Round 16 ChiB
1939 ChiB: 7 G; Pass 4-2 50.0%, 43 10.75; Rush 3-(-5) -1.7; Rec 1-42 42.0; Int **1** TD; 6 Pt. **1940** ChiB: 7 G; Pass 4-1 25.0%, 15 3.75 1 TD; Rush 8-10 1.3; Int 2-0. **Total:** 14 G; Pass 8-3 37.5%, 58 7.25 1 TD; Rush 11-5 0.5; Rec 1-42 42.0; Int 2-0 1 TD; 6 Pt.

TOM SHERMAN Sherman, Thomas Joseph 6′0″, 190 **QB**
Col: Penn State *HS:* Union Joint [Rimersburg, PA] B: 12/5/1945, Bellevue, PA

Year Team	G	Passing Att	Comp	Comp%	Yds	YPA	TD	Int	Rating
1968 Bos	14	226	90	39.8	1199	5.31	12	16	45.6
1969 Bos-Buf	5	2	2	100.0	20	10.00	1	0	147.9
1969 Bos	4	0	0	—	0	—	0	0	—
1969 Buf	1	2	2	100.0	20	10.00	1	0	147.9
NFL Total	19	228	92	40.4	1219	5.35	13	16	47.8

Year Team	Rushing Att	Yds	Avg	TD	Fum
1968 Bos	25	80	3.2	0	**8**
1969 Bos-Buf	2	14	7.0	0	0
1969 Buf	2	14	7.0	0	0
NFL Total	27	94	3.5	0	8

WILL SHERMAN Sherman, Willard Arthur 6′2″, 190 **DB-HB**
Col: USC; St. Mary's (Cal.) *HS:* Yreka [CA] B: 10/20/1927, Weed, CA *Drafted:* 1951 Round 26 NYY
1954 LARm: PR 6-89 14.8; KR 6-130 21.7. **1956** LARm: PR 12-100 8.3 **1** TD. **1957** LARm: PR 1-0. **1958** LARm: PR 1-0. **1960** LARm: PR 1-1 1.0. **1961** Min: Rec 2-40 20.0. **Total:** Rec 2-40 20.0; PR 21-190 9.0 1 TD; KR 6-130 21.7.

Year Team	G	Interceptions Int	Yds	TD	Fum	Tot TD
1952 Dal	2	1	23	0	0	0
1954 LARm	12	6	70	0	1	0
1955 LARm	12	**11**	101	0	0	0
1956 LARm	12	4	122	1	0	2
1957 LARm	10	1	51	0	0	0
1958 LARm	11	5	171	**2**	0	2
1959 LARm	10	0	0	0	0	0
1960 LARm	10	1	0	0	0	0
1961 Min	8	0	0	0	0	0
NFL Total	87	29	538	3	1	4

MIKE SHERRARD Sherrard, Michael Watson 6′1″, 185 **WR**
Col: UCLA *HS:* Chino [CA] B: 6/21/1963, Oakland, CA *Drafted:* 1986 Round 1 Dal
1986 Dal: Rush 2-11 5.5. **1989** SF: Postseason only. **1992** SF: 1 Fum TD. **1994** NYG: Rush 1-(-10) -10.0. **Total:** Rush 3-1 0.3; 1 Fum TD.

Year Team	G	Receiving Rec	Yds	Avg	TD	Fum	Tot TD
1986 Dal	16	41	744	18.1	5	0	5
1990 SF	7	17	264	15.5	2	0	2
1991 SF	16	24	296	12.3	2	0	2
1992 SF	16	38	607	16.0	0	1	1
1993 NYG	6	24	433	18.0	2	0	2
1994 NYG	16	53	825	15.6	6	0	6
1995 NYG	13	44	577	13.1	4	2	4
1996 Den	15	16	185	11.6	1	0	1
NFL Total	105	257	3931	15.3	22	3	23

BUD SHERROD Sherrod, Horace Monroe Jr. 6′0″, 190 **OE-DE**
Col: Tennessee *HS:* Central [Knoxville, TN] B: 12/2/1927, Knoxville, TN D: 8/31/1980, Dallas, TX
1952 NYG: 11 G; KR 2-33 16.5; 6 Pt.

GERRY SHERRY Sherry, Gerald **FB**
1926 Lou: 1 G.

TIM SHERWIN Sherwin, Timothy Thomas 6′6″, 243 **TE**
Col: Boston College *HS:* Watervliet [NY] B: 5/4/1958, Troy, NY *Drafted:* 1981 Round 4 Bal
1982 Bal: 1 Fum TD. **1984** Ind: KR 1-2 2.0. **Total:** KR 1-2 2.0; 1 Fum TD.

Year Team	G	Receiving Rec	Yds	Avg	TD	Fum	Tot TD
1981 Bal	16	2	19	9.5	0	0	0
1982 Bal	9	21	280	13.3	0	0	1
1983 Bal	15	25	358	14.3	0	0	0
1984 Ind	16	11	169	15.4	0	0	0
1985 Ind	8	5	64	12.8	0	1	0
1986 Ind	7	3	26	8.7	1	0	1
1987 Ind	8	9	86	9.6	1	0	1
1988 NYG	3	0	0	—	0	0	0
NFL Total	82	76	1002	13.2	2	1	3

RHOTEN SHETLEY Shetley, Rhoten Nathan 5′11″, 208 **BB-LB-FB**
Col: Furman *HS:* Union [SC] B: 2/7/1918, Wolf Creek, TN D: 1/7/1993, Greenville, SC *Drafted:* 1940 Round 3 Bkn
AAFC **1946** BknA: 13 G; Rush 9-21 2.3; Rec 1-10 10.0.

NFL **1940** Bkn: 11 G; Pass 4-1 25.0%, 2 0.50 1 Int; Rush 7-30 4.3; Rec 8-126 15.8 1 TD; Int 1-37; 6 Pt. **1941** Bkn: 11 G; Pass 1-0; Rush 1-7 7.0; Rec 4-41 10.3; KR 4-80 20.0; Int 1-22; 6 Pt. **1942** Bkn: 3 G; Rec 3-19 6.3 1 TD; Int 1-7; 6 Pt. **Total:** 25 G; Pass 5-1 20.0%, 2 0.40 1 Int; Rush 8-37 4.6; Rec 15-186 12.4 2 TD; KR 4-80 20.0; Int 3-66; Tot TD 3; 18 Pt.

JAMES SHIBEST Shibest, James John 5′10″, 187 **WR**
Col: Arkansas *HS:* MacArthur [Houston, TX] B: 10/31/1964, Fort Riley, KS
1987 Atl: 1 G.

JOE SHIELD Shield, Joseph Michael 6′1″, 185 **QB**
Col: Trinity (Conn.) *HS:* Worcester Acad. [MA] B: 6/26/1962, Brattleboro, VT *Drafted:* 1985 Round 11 GB
1986 GB: 3 G.

BURRELL SHIELDS Shields, Burrell A 6′2″, 203 **HB-DB**
Col: John Carroll *HS:* East Tech [Cleveland, OH] B: 9/6/1929, Cleveland, OH *Drafted:* 1952 Round 6 Cle
1954 Pit: 6 G; Rush 7-28 4.0; Rec 1-22 22.0; PR 3-0; KR 9-183 20.3; Int 1-8; 1 Fum. **1955** Bal: 8 G; Rush 10-34 3.4; Rec 3-27 9.0. **Total:** 14 G; Rush 17-62 3.6; Rec 4-49 12.3; PR 3-0; KR 9-183 20.3; Int 1-8; 1 Fum.

JON SHIELDS Shields, Jon Rayborn 6′5″, 293 **OG**
Col: Walla Walla CC WA; Portland State *HS:* Fort Vancouver [Vancouver, WA] B: 4/30/1964
1987 Dal: 1 G.

LEBRON SHIELDS Shields, Lebron 6′4″, 250 **DE-OT**
Col: Tennessee *HS:* La Fayette [GA] B: 7/23/1937, Walker Co., GA *Drafted:* 1960 Round 1 Den
1960 Bal: 12 G; Scor **1** Saf; 2 Pt. **1961** Min: 6 G. **Total:** 18 G; Scor 1 Saf; 2 Pt.

WILL SHIELDS Shields, Will Herthie 6′3″, 306 **OG**
Col: Nebraska *HS:* Lawton [OK] B: 9/15/1971, Fort Riley, KS *Drafted:* 1993 Round 3 KC
1993 KC: 16 G. **1994** KC: 16 G. **1995** KC: 16 G. **1996** KC: 16 G. **1997** KC: 16 G. **1998** KC: 16 G; Rec 1-4 4.0. **Total:** 96 G; Rec 1-4 4.0.

BILLY SHIELDS Shields, William Dean 6′8″, 272 **OT**
Col: Georgia Tech *HS:* Banks [Birmingham, AL] B: 8/23/1953, Vicksburg, MS *Drafted:* 1975 Round 6 SD
1975 SD: 11 G. **1976** SD: 14 G. **1977** SD: 13 G. **1978** SD: 16 G. **1979** SD: 16 G. **1980** SD: 16 G. **1981** SD: 16 G. **1982** SD: 9 G. **1983** SD: 16 G. **1984** SF: 10 G. **1985** NYJ-KC: 5 G. NYJ: 3 G. KC: 2 G. **Total:** 142 G.

DICK SHINER Shiner, Richard Earl Jr. 6′0″, 201 **QB**
Col: Maryland *HS:* Lebanon [PA] B: 7/18/1942, Lebanon, PA *Drafted:* 1964 Round 7 Was

Year Team	G	Passing Att	Comp	Comp%	Yds	YPA	TD	Int	Rating
1964 Was	1	1	0	0.0	0	0.00	0	0	39.6
1965 Was	14	65	28	43.1	470	7.23	3	4	57.9
1966 Was	14	5	0	0.0	0	0.00	0	1	0.0
1967 Cle	13	9	3	33.3	34	3.78	0	1	6.0
1968 Pit	13	304	148	48.7	1856	6.11	18	17	64.5
1969 Pit	12	209	97	46.4	1422	6.80	7	10	60.3
1970 NYG	14	12	9	75.0	87	7.25	0	0	94.8
1971 Atl	10	57	30	52.6	463	8.12	5	5	72.5
1973 Atl-NE	7	68	36	52.9	432	6.35	3	4	62.9

1973 Atl	4	64	34	53.1	401	6.27	3	4	62.0
1973 NE	3	4	2	50.0	31	7.75	0	0	76.0
1974 NE	1	6	3	50.0	37	6.17	0	1	29.9
NFL Total	99	736	354	48.1	4801	6.52	36	43	61.3

	Rushing				
Year Team	**Att**	**Yds**	**Avg**	**TD**	**Fum**
1964 Was	2	8	4.0	0	0
1965 Was	12	35	2.9	0	5
1966 Was	1	10	10.0	0	1
1967 Cle	2	-7	-3.5	0	0
1968 Pit	14	53	3.8	0	7
1969 Pit	14	55	3.9	1	3
1971 Atl	10	9	0.9	1	3
1973 Atl-NE	3	-2	-0.7	0	4
1973 Atl	3	-2	-0.7	0	4
NFL Total	58	161	2.8	2	23

JOHN SHINNERS Shinners, John Joseph T. 6'3", 255 **OG**
Col: Xavier (Ohio) *HS:* Campion Prep [Prairie du Chien, WI]
B: 3/1/1947, Hartford, WI *Drafted:* 1969 Round 1 NO
1969 NO: 2 G. **1970** NO: 9 G. **1971** NO: 14 G. **1972** Bal: 6 G. **1973** Cin: 14 G. **1974** Cin: 13 G. **1975** Cin: 14 G. **1976** Cin: 13 G. **1977** Cin: 12 G. **Total:** 97 G.

DON SHINNICK Shinnick, Donald Dee 6'0", 232 **LB**
Col: UCLA *HS:* San Pedro [CA] B: 5/15/1935, Kansas City, MO
Drafted: 1957 Round 2 Bal
1957 Bal: PR 1-2 2.0. **1959** Bal: PR 1-0. **1962** Bal: PR 0-29. **Total:** PR 2-31 15.5.

		Interceptions		
Year Team	**G**	**Int**	**Yds**	**TD**
1957 Bal	12	2	31	0
1958 Bal	12	3	23	0
1959 Bal	12	**7**	70	0
1960 Bal	12	5	40	0
1961 Bal	14	2	15	0
1962 Bal	14	5	16	0
1963 Bal	14	2	20	0
1964 Bal	14	3	10	0
1965 Bal	10	1	4	0
1966 Bal	14	3	4	0
1967 Bal	14	3	20	0
1968 Bal	11	1	2	0
1969 Bal	6	0	0	0
NFL Total	159	37	255	0

JERRY SHIPKEY Shipkey, Gerald Wade 6'1", 213 **FB-DB-LB**
Col: USC; UCLA *HS:* Anaheim [CA] B: 10/31/1925, Fullerton, CA
Drafted: 1947 Round 6 Pit
1948 Pit: Rec 10-106 10.6; KR 2-34 17.0. **1949** Pit: Rec 2-32 16.0. **Total:** Rec 12-138 11.5; KR 2-34 17.0.

		Rushing				Interceptions				Tot
Year Team	**G**	**Att**	**Yds**	**Avg**	**TD**	**Int**	**Yds**	**TD**	**Fum**	**TD**
1948 Pit	12	64	199	3.1	8	0	0	0	4	8
1949 Pit	12	26	93	3.6	5	3	76	0	2	5
1950 Pit	12	18	17	0.9	3	2	34	0	2	3
1951 Pit	10	0	0	—	0	6	113	1	0	1
1952 Pit	12	1	1	1.0	0	2	15	0	0	0
1953 ChiB	8	0	0	—	0	0	0	0	0	0
NFL Total	66	109	310	2.8	16	13	238	1	8	17

JACKIE SHIPP Shipp, Jackie Renardo 6'2", 235 **LB**
Col: Oklahoma *HS:* C.E. Donart [Stillwater, OK] B: 3/17/1962, Muskogee, OK *Drafted:* 1984 Round 1 Mia
1984 Mia: 16 G. **1985** Mia: 16 G; Int 1-7. **1986** Mia: 16 G; 1 Sac. **1987** Mia: 12 G. **1988** Mia: 11 G. **1989** LARd: 3 G. **Total:** 74 G; Int 1-7; 1 Sac.

JOSEPH SHIPP Shipp, Joseph Delano 6'4", 225 **TE**
Col: USC *HS:* Carson [CA] B: 7/25/1955, Long Beach, CA
1979 Buf: 16 G; Rec 3-43 14.3 1 TD; 6 Pt.

BILLY SHIPP Shipp, William Leonard 6'5", 275 **OT**
Col: Alabama B: 10/16/1929, Mobile, AL *Drafted:* 1952 Round 8 NYG
1954 NYG: 11 G.

ABE SHIRES Shires, Marshall Abraham 6'2", 220 **T**
Col: Tennessee *HS:* Alderson [WV] B: 2/12/1917, Alderson, WV
D: 7/23/1993, Sacramento, CA *Drafted:* 1941 Round 2 Cle
1945 Phi: 7 G.

FRED SHIREY Shirey, Charles Frederick 6'2", 223 **T**
Col: Washington & Jefferson; Nebraska *HS:* Latrobe [PA]
B: 1/12/1916, Latrobe, PA D: 11/1/1961
1940 GB-Cle: 9 G. GB: 3 G. Cle: 6 G. **1941** Cle: 3 G. **Total:** 12 G.

GARY SHIRK Shirk, Gary Lee 6'1", 220 **TE**
Col: Morehead State *HS:* Marysville [OH] B: 2/23/1950, Marysville, OH
1976 NYG: KR 6-109 18.2. **1977** NYG: KR 3-38 12.7. **1978** NYG: KR 5-63 12.6. **Total:** KR 14-210 15.0.

		Receiving				
Year Team	**G**	**Rec**	**Yds**	**Avg**	**TD**	**Fum**
1976 NYG	14	4	52	13.0	1	0
1977 NYG	14	16	280	17.5	2	4
1978 NYG	16	10	127	12.7	2	0
1979 NYG	16	31	471	15.2	2	2
1980 NYG	16	21	211	10.0	1	2
1981 NYG	16	42	445	10.6	3	1
1982 NYG	9	6	54	9.0	0	0
NFL Total	101	130	1640	12.6	11	9

JOHN SHIRK Shirk, John F 6'4", 200 **OE-DE**
Col: Oklahoma *HS:* Central [Oklahoma City, OK] B: 6/24/1917, Oklahoma City, OK D: 11/8/1993, Glendora, CA *Drafted:* 1940 Round 4 ChiC
1940 ChiC: 11 G; Rec 11-91 8.3; Int 1-8.

GEORGE SHIRKEY Shirkey, George Rogers 6'4", 260 **DT**
Col: Stephen F. Austin St. *HS:* Fort Stockton [TX] B: 8/20/1936, Fort Stockton, TX *Drafted:* 1958 Round 16 SF
1960 Hou: 14 G. **1961** Hou: 7 G. **1962** Oak: 14 G. **Total:** 35 G.

MARION SHIRLEY Shirley, Marion Vaughn 6'4", 260 **T**
(Bus) *Col:* Oklahoma State; Oklahoma City *HS:* Classen [Oklahoma City, OK] B: 4/17/1922, Denver, CO D: 9/13/1996, Stafford, TX
AAFC **1948** NY-A: 13 G. **1949** NY-A: 7 G. **Total:** 20 G.

REX SHIVER Shiver, Raymond Orville 6'0", 190 **DB**
Col: Miami (Fla.) *HS:* Miami Jackson [Miami, FL] B: 1/1/1932, Miami, FL
1956 LARm: 8 G; Int 1-0.

SANDERS SHIVER Shiver, Sanders Thomas 6'2", 227 **LB**
Col: Carson-Newman *HS:* Lower Richland [Hopkins, SC]
B: 2/14/1954, Gadsden, SC *Drafted:* 1976 Round 5 Bal
1976 Bal: 14 G. **1977** Bal: 14 G; KR 1-7 7.0. **1978** Bal: 16 G. **1979** Bal: 16 G; Int 4-85. **1980** Bal: 14 G; Int 1-34 1 TD; 6 Pt. **1981** Bal: 14 G. **1982** Bal: 8 G. **1983** Bal: 16 G; 1 Sac. **1984** Mia: 14 G. **1985** Mia: 6 G; 1 Sac. **Total:** 132 G; KR 1-7 7.0; Int 5-119 1 TD; 6 Pt; 2 Sac.

CLAY SHIVER Shiver, Spencer Clay 6'2", 283 **C**
Col: Florida State *HS:* Tift Co. [Tifton, GA] B: 12/7/1972, Tifton, GA
Drafted: 1996 Round 3 Dal
1996 Dal: 14 G. **1997** Dal: 16 G; 2 Fum. **1998** Dal: 14 G. **Total:** 44 G; 2 Fum.

ROY SHIVERS Shivers, Roy Lee 5'11", 200 **RB**
Col: Merritt Coll. CA (J.C.); Utah State *HS:* McClymonds [Oakland, CA]
B: 7/5/1941, Holly, AR *Drafted:* 1965 Round 19 StL
1971 StL: Pass 1-0. **Total:** Pass 1-0.

		Rushing				Receiving			
Year Team	**G**	**Att**	**Yds**	**Avg**	**TD**	**Rec**	**Yds**	**Avg**	**TD**
1966 StL	13	1	5	5.0	0	5	81	16.2	0
1967 StL	9	20	64	3.2	1	3	15	5.0	0
1968 StL	14	44	184	4.2	4	9	103	11.4	3
1969 StL	12	27	115	4.3	2	7	61	8.7	1
1970 StL	12	24	98	4.1	2	3	44	14.7	0
1971 StL	11	55	202	3.7	1	10	76	7.6	0
1972 StL	2	5	12	2.4	0	1	20	20.0	0
NFL Total	73	176	680	3.9	10	38	400	10.5	4

	Punt Returns				Kickoff Returns					Tot
Year Team	**Ret**	**Yds**	**Avg**	**TD**	**Ret**	**Yds**	**Avg**	**TD**	**Fum**	**TD**
1966 StL	16	49	3.1	0	27	762	28.2	1	3	1
1967 StL	9	36	4.0	0	9	160	17.8	0	3	1
1968 StL	0	0	—	0	3	63	21.0	0	1	7
1969 StL	9	44	4.9	0	10	205	20.5	0	2	3
1970 StL	0	0	—	0	2	35	17.5	0	0	2
1971 StL	0	0	—	0	0	0	—	0	3	1
NFL Total	34	129	3.8	0	51	1225	24.0	1	12	15

BORIS SHLAPAK Shlapak, Boris Vladimir 6'0", 175 **K**
Col: Drake; Michigan State *HS:* Maine South [Park Ridge, IL]
B: 5/18/1950, Chicago, IL
1972 Bal: 8 G; Scor 4, 0-8 FG, 4-4 100.0% XK.

ROGER SHOALS Shoals, Roger Richard 6'4", 260 **OT**
Col: Maryland *HS:* Norwalk [CT]; Greenbrier Mil. Acad. [Lewisburg, WV]
B: 12/13/1938, Baltimore, MD *Drafted:* 1961 Round 16 Cle
1963 Cle: 2 G. **1964** Cle: 14 G; 1 Fum TD; 6 Pt. **1965** Det: 14 G. **1966** Det: 14 G. **1967** Det: 4 G. **1968** Det: 14 G. **1969** Det: 14 G. **1970** Det: 14 G. **1971** Den: 14 G. **Total:** 104 G; 1 Fum TD; 6 Pt.

ROD SHOATE Shoate, Roderick 6′1″, 214 **LB**
Col: Oklahoma *HS:* Spiro [OK] B: 4/26/1953, Spiro, OK
Drafted: 1975 Round 2 NE
1975 NE: 4 G. **1977** NE: 14 G. **1978** NE: 15 G. **1979** NE: 14 G; Int 1-0.
1980 NE: 16 G; Int 3-50 1 TD; 6 Pt. **1981** NE: 16 G; Int 1-0; 1 Fum.
Total: 79 G; Int 5-50 1 TD; 6 Pt; 1 Fum.

ARNIE SHOCKLEY Shockley, Arnold 6′2″, 220 **T**
(AKA J. Parnel Jackson) *Col:* Southwestern Oklahoma State
B: 11/27/1904, TX D: 8/1974, Melbourne, FL
1929 Bost: 6 G.

BILL SHOCKLEY Shockley, William Albert Jr. 6′0″, 185 **HB-K**
Col: West Chester *HS:* Conestoga [Berwyn, PA] B: 3/13/1937, West Chester, PA D: 12/7/1992, New York, NY
1960 NYT: Rec 8-69 8.6 2 TD; PR 3-12 4.0. **1961** NYT-Buf: Rec 3-27 9.0; PR 2-6 3.0. NYT: Rec 3-27 9.0; PR 2-6 3.0. **Total:** Rec 11-96 8.7 2 TD; PR 5-18 3.6.

		Rushing				Kickoff Returns			
Year Team	**G**	**Att**	**Yds**	**Avg**	**TD**	**Ret**	**Yds**	**Avg**	**TD**
1960 NYT	14	37	156	4.2	0	17	411	24.2	0
1961 NYT-Buf	8	5	9	1.8	0	12	261	21.8	0
1961 NYT	6	5	9	1.8	0	10	223	22.3	0
1961 Buf	2	0	0	—	0	2	38	19.0	0
1962 NYT	14	0	0	—	0	3	73	24.3	0
1968 Pit	1	0	0	—	0	0	0	—	0
NFL Total	37	42	165	3.9	0	32	745	23.3	0

	Scoring							
Year Team	**Pts**	**FG**	**FGA**	**FG%**	**XK**	**XKA**	**XK%**	**Fum**
1960 NYT	86	9	21	42.9	**47**	**50**	94.0	3
1961 NYT-Buf	25	4	9	44.4	13	13	100.0	0
1961 NYT	22	3	7	42.9	13	13	100.0	0
1961 Buf	3	1	2	50.0	0	0	—	0
1962 NYT	68	13	26	50.0	29	30	96.7	1
1968 Pit	2	0	1	0.0	2	3	66.7	0
NFL Total	181	26	57	45.6	91	96	94.8	4

HUB SHOEMAKE Shoemake, Charles Hubbard 6′0″, 186 **G**
Col: Lake Forest; Illinois; Bethany (W.V.) *HS:* Oskaloosa [IA]
B: 9/29/1899, Oskaloosa, IA D: 3/10/1984, Washington, DC
1920 Sta: 6 G.

HAL SHOENER Shoener, Harold Phillip 6′3″, 200 **OE-DE**
Col: Iowa *HS:* Charleston [WV] B: 1/2/1923, Reedsville, WV
D: 12/13/1983, Oakland, CA
AAFC **1948** SF-A: 14 G; Rec 15-76 5.1 3 TD; 18 Pt. **1949** SF-A: 12 G; Rec 7-84 12.0; PR 1-8 8.0; KR 1-17 17.0. **Total:** 26 G; Rec 22-160 7.3 3 TD; PR 1-8 8.0; KR 1-17 17.0; 18 Pt.

NFL **1950** SF: 12 G; Rush 1-1 1.0; KR 4-53 13.3; Int 1-14.

HERBERT SHOENER Shoener, Herbert George 6′3″, 205 **DE**
Col: Lehigh; Iowa *HS:* Charleston [WV] B: 1/2/1923, Reedsville, WV
D: 12/24/1985, Anaheim, CA
1948 Was: 7 G. **1949** Was: 11 G; **1** Fum TD; 6 Pt. **Total:** 18 G; 1 Fum TD; 6 Pt.

DEL SHOFNER Shofner, Delbert Martin 6′3″, 186 **OE-DB**
(T-Bone) *Col:* Baylor *HS:* Center [TX] B: 12/11/1934, Center, TX
Drafted: 1957 Round 1 LARm
1957 LARm: Int 2-27. **1958** LARm: Pass 1-0. **1959** LARm: Rush 1-6 6.0.
1960 LARm: Rush 1-(-15) -15.0; Int 1-19. **1961** NYG: Rush 1-6 6.0.
1962 NYG: Rush 1-4 4.0. **Total:** Pass 1-0; Rush 4-1 0.3; Int 3-46.

		Receiving				Punting			
Year Team	**G**	**Rec**	**Yds**	**Avg**	**TD**	**Punts**	**Yds**	**Avg**	**Fum**
1957 LARm	12	0	0	—	0	2	97	48.5	0
1958 LARm	12	51	**1097**	21.5	8	49	2018	41.2	1
1959 LARm	12	47	936	19.9	7	48	2004	41.8	0
1960 LARm	11	12	122	10.2	1	54	2301	42.6	0
1961 NYG	14	68	1125	16.5	11	0	0	—	1
1962 NYG	13	53	1133	21.4	12	0	0	—	0
1963 NYG	14	64	1181	18.5	9	0	0	—	0
1964 NYG	6	22	323	14.7	0	0	0	—	0
1965 NYG	12	22	388	17.6	2	0	0	—	0
1966 NYG	9	3	19	6.3	0	0	0	—	0
1967 NYG	10	7	146	20.9	1	0	0	—	0
NFL Total	125	349	6470	18.5	51	153	6420	42.0	2

JIM SHOFNER Shofner, James Bernard 6′2″, 191 **DB**
Col: Texas Christian *HS:* North Side [Fort Worth, TX] B: 12/18/1935, Grapevine, TX *Drafted:* 1958 Round 1 Cle
1959 Cle: Punt 23-860 37.4. **1963** Cle: KR 1-0. **Total:** KR 1-0; Punt 23-860 37.4.

		Punt Returns				Interceptions			
Year Team	**G**	**Ret**	**Yds**	**Avg**	**TD**	**Int**	**Yds**	**TD**	**Fum**
1958 Cle	12	4	10	2.5	0	1	0	0	1
1959 Cle	12	0	0	—	0	2	50	0	0
1960 Cle	12	11	105	9.5	0	8	75	0	0
1961 Cle	14	14	119	8.5	0	5	8	0	0
1962 Cle	14	8	33	4.1	0	4	86	0	1
1963 Cle	12	9	41	4.6	0	0	0	0	2
NFL Total	76	46	308	6.7	0	20	219	0	4

JOHN SHONK Shonk, John J III 6′1″, 190 **OE-DB**
Col: West Virginia *HS:* Charleston [WV] B: 4/30/1918, Charleston, WV
D: 4/26/1984, Christiansburg, VA *Drafted:* 1941 Round 17 Phi
1941 Phi: 10 G; Rec 5-52 10.4; KR 1-16 16.0; Int 1-1.

CHUCK SHONTA Shonta, Charles Joseph Jr. 6′0″, 200 **DB**
Col: Eastern Michigan *HS:* Pershing [Detroit, MI] B: 8/29/1937, Detroit, MI
1960 Bos: **1** Fum TD. **1961** Bos: Rec 1-9 9.0. **Total:** Rec 1-9 9.0; 1 Fum TD.

		Interceptions		
Year Team	**G**	**Int**	**Yds**	**TD**
1960 Bos	14	2	101	0
1961 Bos	8	1	12	0
1962 Bos	14	2	0	0
1963 Bos	13	3	15	0
1964 Bos	14	1	21	0
1965 Bos	14	2	46	0
1966 Bos	14	1	9	0
1967 Bos	14	3	57	0
NFL Total	105	15	261	0

AL SHOOK Shook, Albert **G**
Col: No College B: 1/15/1898, Pierce City, MO D: 4/14/1984, Atchison, KS
1921 Col: 2 G.

FRED SHOOK Shook, Fredric Warden 6′0″, 218 **C-LB**
Col: Texas Christian B: 3/30/1919, Fort Worth, TX D: 4/16/1992
1941 ChiC: 4 G.

LAVAL SHORT Short, Laval Howard Jr. 6′3″, 250 **NT**
Col: Colorado *HS:* East [Denver, CO]; Columbine HS [Littleton, CO]
B: 9/29/1958, Nashville, TN *Drafted:* 1980 Round 5 Den
1980 Den: 15 G. **1981** TB: 4 G. **Total:** 19 G.

JIM SHORTER Shorter, James 5′11″, 185 **DB**
Col: Detroit Mercy *HS:* Pontiac Central [MI] B: 6/8/1939, Montgomery, AL *Drafted:* 1962 Round 14 Cle
1963 Cle: PR 7-134 19.1; KR 9-219 24.3. **1964** Was: PR 6-19 3.2; KR 5-81 16.2. **1965** Was: **1** Fum TD. **Total:** PR 13-153 11.8; KR 14-300 21.4; 1 Fum TD.

		Interceptions			
Year Team	**G**	**Int**	**Yds**	**TD**	**Fum**
1962 Cle	9	0	0	0	0
1963 Cle	11	0	0	0	1
1964 Was	14	1	2	0	0
1965 Was	13	2	20	0	0
1966 Was	13	5	123	0	0
1967 Was	13	4	32	0	0
1969 Pit	14	3	47	0	0
NFL Total	87	15	224	0	1

GEORGE SHORTHOSE Shorthose, George Edward 6′0″, 198 **WR**
Col: Missouri *HS:* Jefferson City [MO] B: 12/22/1961, Stanton, CA
Drafted: 1985 Round 6 Mia
1985 KC: 3 G; KR 1-11 11.0.

PETER SHORTS Shorts, John Peter 6′8″, 278 **DT**
Col: Illinois State *HS:* Clinton [WI] B: 7/12/1966, Janesville, WI
1989 NE: 1 G.

DARIN SHOULDERS Shoulders, Darin 6′3″, 288 **OT**
Col: Tulane *HS:* Forest Hill [Jackson, MS] B: 5/23/1968, Jackson, MS
1991 Ind: 1 G.

PAUL SHOULTS Shoults, Paul Arthur 5′11″, 178 **HB**
Col: Miami (Ohio) *HS:* Washington Court House [OH] B: 10/9/1925, Washington Court House, OH *Drafted:* 1948 Round 23 ChiC
1949 NYB: Rec 10-124 12.4; PR 8-27 3.4; KR 14-271 19.4.

		Rushing				
Year Team	**G**	**Att**	**Yds**	**Avg**	**TD**	**Fum**
1949 NYB	12	46	124	2.7	0	8

PETE SHUFELT Shufelt, Peter Julian 6′3″, 241 **LB**
Col: Texas-El Paso *HS:* Canyon del Oro [Tucson, AZ] B: 10/28/1969, Chicago, IL
1994 NYG: 5 G.

CLYDE SHUGART Shugart, Clyde Earl 6′1″, 221 **G-LB-T**
Col: Iowa State *HS:* Ames [IA] B: 12/7/1916, Elberon, IA
Drafted: 1939 Round 15 Was
1939 Was: 11 G. **1940** Was: 9 G. **1941** Was: 11 G; KR 1-0. **1942** Was: 11 G. **1943** Was: 10 G; Int 1-8. **1944** Was: 4 G. **Total:** 56 G; KR 1-0; Int 1-8.

BRET SHUGARTS Shugarts, J. Bret 6′2″, 250 **DE**
Col: Lock Haven; Clarion; Indiana (Pa.) *HS:* Du Bois [PA] B: 2/17/1960, Du Bois, PA
1987 Pit: 2 G.

DAVID SHULA Shula, David Donald 5′11″, 182 **WR**
Col: Dartmouth *HS:* Chaminade [Hollywood, FL] B: 5/28/1959, Lexington, KY
1981 Bal: 16 G; PR 10-50 5.0; KR 5-65 13.0; 2 Fum.

DON SHULA Shula, Donald Francis 5′11″, 190 **DB-HB**
Col: John Carroll *HS:* Harvey [Painesville, OH] B: 1/4/1930, Grand River, OH *Drafted:* 1951 Round 9 Cle
1951 Cle: KR 1-6 6.0. **1953** Bal: Rec 1-6 6.0. **1954** Bal: Rush 2-3 1.5. **1956** Bal: KR 1-0. **Total:** Rush 2-3 1.5; Rec 1-6 6.0; KR 2-6 3.0.

		Interceptions		
Year Team	**G**	**Int**	**Yds**	**TD**
1951 Cle	12	4	23	0
1952 Cle	5	0	0	0
1953 Bal	12	3	46	0
1954 Bal	12	5	84	0
1955 Bal	9	5	64	0
1956 Bal	12	1	2	0
1957 Was	11	3	48	0
NFL Total	73	21	267	0

HEATH SHULER Shuler, Joseph Heath 6′2″, 216 **QB**
Col: Tennessee *HS:* Swain Co. [Bryson City, NC] B: 12/31/1971, Bryson City, NC *Drafted:* 1994 Round 1 Was

		Passing							
Year Team	**G**	**Att**	**Comp**	**Comp%**	**Yds**	**YPA**	**TD**	**Int**	**Rating**
1994 Was	11	265	120	45.3	1658	6.26	10	12	59.6
1995 Was	7	125	66	52.8	745	5.96	3	7	55.6
1996 Was	1	0	0	—	0	—	0	0	—
1997 NO	10	203	106	52.2	1288	6.34	2	14	46.6
NFL Total	29	593	292	49.2	3691	6.22	15	33	54.3

	Rushing				
Year Team	**Att**	**Yds**	**Avg**	**TD**	**Fum**
1994 Was	26	103	4.0	0	3
1995 Was	18	57	3.2	0	1
1996 Was	1	0	0.0	0	1
1997 NO	22	38	1.7	1	8
NFL Total	67	198	3.0	1	13

MICKEY SHULER Shuler, Mickey Charles 6′3″, 232 **TE**
Col: Penn State *HS:* East Pennsboro [Enola, PA] B: 8/21/1956, Harrisburg, PA *Drafted:* 1978 Round 3 NYJ
1978 NYJ: KR 1-12 12.0. **1979** NYJ: KR 1-15 15.0. **1980** NYJ: KR 2-25 12.5. **1983** NYJ: KR 1-3 3.0. **1984** NYJ: KR 1-0. **1986** NYJ: KR 2-(-3) -1.5. **Total:** KR 8-52 6.5.

		Receiving				
Year Team	**G**	**Rec**	**Yds**	**Avg**	**TD**	**Fum**
1978 NYJ	16	11	67	6.1	3	1
1979 NYJ	16	16	225	14.1	3	1
1980 NYJ	16	22	226	10.3	2	1
1981 NYJ	6	0	0	—	0	0
1982 NYJ	9	8	132	16.5	3	0
1983 NYJ	16	26	272	10.5	1	0
1984 NYJ	16	68	782	11.5	6	1
1985 NYJ	16	76	879	11.6	7	1
1986 NYJ	16	69	675	9.8	4	0
1987 NYJ	11	43	434	10.1	3	2
1988 NYJ	15	70	805	11.5	5	1
1989 NYJ	7	29	322	11.1	0	0
1990 Phi	16	18	190	10.6	0	1
1991 Phi	4	6	91	15.2	0	0
NFL Total	180	462	5100	11.0	37	9

STEVE SHULL Shull, Steven Mark 6′1″, 220 **LB**
Col: William & Mary *HS:* Neshaminy [Langhorne, PA] B: 3/27/1958, Philadelphia, PA
1980 Mia: 16 G. **1981** Mia: 16 G. **1982** Mia: 9 G. **Total:** 41 G.

JOHNNY SHULTZ Shultz, John H 6′1″, 189 **WB-FB**
(Shebo) *Col:* Temple *HS:* Pen Argyl [PA] D: 11/26/1932, Ashland, PA
1930 Fra: 6 G; Pass 1 TD.

MIKE SHUMANN Shumann, Michael William 6′1″, 178 **WR**
Col: Florida State *HS:* Leon [Tallahassee, FL] B: 10/13/1955, Louisville, KY
1978 SF: PR 8-40 5.0. **1979** SF: Rush 1-19 19.0. **Total:** Rush 1-19 19.0; PR 8-40 5.0.

		Receiving				
Year Team	**G**	**Rec**	**Yds**	**Avg**	**TD**	**Fum**
1978 SF	6	0	0	—	0	2
1979 SF	16	39	452	11.6	4	0
1980 TB	6	4	75	18.8	1	0
1981 SF	13	3	21	7.0	0	1
1982 StL	6	5	58	11.6	0	0
1983 StL	16	11	154	14.0	0	0
NFL Total	63	62	760	12.3	5	3

MARK SHUMATE Shumate, Mark Anthony 6′5″, 265 **NT**
Col: Wisconsin *HS:* Poynette [WI] B: 3/30/1960, Poynette, WI
Drafted: 1983 Round 10 KC
1985 NYJ-GB: 8 G. NYJ: 4 G. GB: 4 G. **Total:** 8 G.

RON SHUMON Shumon, Ronnie 6′1″, 230 **LB**
Col: Wichita State *HS:* Haverford [Havertown, PA] B: 12/11/1955, Flint, MI *Drafted:* 1978 Round 9 Cin
1978 Cin: 13 G; Int 1-48. **1979** SF: 8 G. **Total:** 21 G; Int 1-48.

MARK SHUPE Shupe, Mark Andrew 6′5″, 285 **C**
Col: Arizona State *HS:* Ben Davis [Indianapolis, IN] B: 4/25/1961, Lafayette, IN
1987 Buf: 2 G.

MARSHALL SHURNAS Shurnas, Marshall Kenneth 6′1″, 205 **OE-DE**
(Iggie) *Col:* Missouri *HS:* Central [St. Louis, MO] B: 4/1/1922, St. Louis, MO
AAFC **1947** CleA: 11 G; Rec 2-30 15.0.

BERT SHURTLEFF Shurtleff, Bertrand Leslie 5′11″, 190 **C-G**
(Scrappy) *Col:* Brown *HS:* East Greenwich Acad. [RI] B: 8/3/1897, Adamsville, RI D: 2/15/1967, Anaheim, CA
1925 Prov: 11 G. **1929** Bost: 4 G. **Total:** 15 G.

RED SHURTLIFFE Shurtliffe, Charles West 5′9″, 160 **WB-TB**
Col: Marietta *HS:* Sistersville [WV] B: 4/12/1907 D: 9/1986, Lincolnville, SC
1929 Buf: 4 G.

HUBERT SHURTZ Shurtz, Hubert D 6′3″, 235 **T**
Col: Louisiana State *HS:* Pinckneyville [IL] B: 7/1/1923, Pinckneyville, IL *Drafted:* 1947 Round 15 Phi
1948 Pit: 12 G.

DON SHY Shy, Donald Frederic 6′1″, 210 **RB**
Col: Mount San Antonio Coll. CA (J.C.); San Diego State *HS:* Ganesha [Pomona, CA] B: 11/15/1945, Cleveland, OH *Drafted:* 1967 Round 2 Pit
1967 Pit: PR 1-(-5) -5.0. **1971** ChiB: Pass 1-1 100.0%, 23 23.00 1 TD. **Total:** Pass 1-1 100.0%, 23 23.00 1 TD; PR 1-(-5) -5.0.

		Rushing				Receiving			
Year Team	**G**	**Att**	**Yds**	**Avg**	**TD**	**Rec**	**Yds**	**Avg**	**TD**
1967 Pit	14	99	341	3.4	4	12	152	12.7	1
1968 Pit	13	35	106	3.0	1	13	106	8.2	0
1969 NO	14	21	75	3.6	1	9	141	15.7	1
1970 ChiB	8	79	227	2.9	1	10	149	14.9	0
1971 ChiB	11	116	420	3.6	2	19	163	8.6	0
1972 ChiB	13	91	342	3.8	1	10	109	10.9	0
1973 StL	11	16	66	4.1	0	3	15	5.0	1
NFL Total	84	457	1577	3.5	10	76	835	11.0	3

	Kickoff Returns					Tot
Year Team	**Ret**	**Yds**	**Avg**	**TD**	**Fum**	**TD**
1967 Pit	21	473	22.5	0	5	5
1968 Pit	28	682	24.4	0	1	1
1969 NO	16	447	27.9	0	2	2
1970 ChiB	0	0	—	0	3	1
1971 ChiB	0	0	—	0	3	2
1972 ChiB	0	0	—	0	5	1
1973 StL	16	445	27.8	1	1	2
NFL Total	81	2047	25.3	1	20	14

LES SHY Shy, Leslie Freeman 6′1″, 206 **RB**
Col: Long Beach State *HS:* Ganesha [Pomona, CA] B: 4/5/1944, Cleveland, OH *Drafted:* 1966 Round 12 Dal
1967 Dal: Rec 3-36 12.0. **1968** Dal: Rec 10-105 10.5. **1969** Dal: Rec 8-124 15.5 1 TD. **1970** NYG: Rec 2-8 4.0. **Total:** Rec 23-273 11.9 1 TD.

		Rushing				Kickoff Returns					Tot
Year Team	**G**	**Ret**	**Yds**	**Avg**	**TD**	**Ret**	**Yds**	**Avg**	**TD**	**Fum**	**TD**
1966 Dal	11	17	118	6.9	1	0	0	—	0	1	1
1967 Dal	13	17	59	3.5	0	5	96	19.2	0	0	0

1968 Dal	14	64	179	2.8	1	0	0	—	0	0	1
1969 Dal	14	42	154	3.7	1	3	47	15.7	0	1	2
1970 NYG	13	4	13	3.3	0	21	544	25.9	0	3	0
NFL Total	65	144	523	3.6	3	29	687	23.7	0	5	4

MIKE SIANI Siani, Michael Joseph 6′2″, 195 **WR**
Col: Villanova *HS:* New Dorp [Staten Island, NY] B: 5/27/1950, Staten Island, NY *Drafted:* 1972 Round 1 Oak

		Receiving				
Year Team	**G**	**Rec**	**Yds**	**Avg**	**TD**	**Fum**
1972 Oak	14	28	496	17.7	5	1
1973 Oak	14	45	742	16.5	3	1
1974 Oak	6	3	30	10.0	1	0
1975 Oak	14	17	294	17.3	0	0
1976 Oak	14	11	173	15.7	2	0
1977 Oak	12	24	344	14.3	2	0
1978 Bal	7	6	151	25.2	1	0
1979 Bal	10	15	214	14.3	2	0
1980 Bal	10	9	174	19.3	1	0
NFL Total	101	158	2618	16.6	17	2

MIKE SIANO Siano, Michael P 6′4″, 220 **WR**
Col: Syracuse *HS:* Springfield [PA]; Haverford HS [Havertown, PA] B: 11/29/1963, Yeadon, PA
1987 Phi: 3 G; Rec 9-137 15.2 1 TD; KR 1-13 13.0; 6 Pt.

TONY SIANO Siano, Thomas Anthony 5′8″, 172 **C**
Col: Fordham *HS:* Waltham [MA] B: 1/10/1907 D: 4/1986, Rochelle Park, NJ
1932 Bos: 9 G. **1934** Bkn: 11 G. **Total:** 20 G.

JIMMY SIDLE Sidle, James Corbin 6′2″, 215 **FB**
Col: Auburn *HS:* Banks [Birmingham, AL] B: 2/7/1943, Birmingham, AL *Drafted:* 1965 Round 4 Dal
1966 Atl: 6 G; Rush 1-12 12.0; Rec 1-16 16.0; KR 6-117 19.5; 1 Fum.

DAINON SIDNEY Sidney, Dainon Tarquinius 6′0″, 188 **DB**
Col: East Tennessee State; Alabama-Birmingham *HS:* Riverdale [GA] B: 5/30/1975, Atlanta, GA *Drafted:* 1998 Round 3 Ten
1998 Ten: 16 G.

ALEX SIDORIK Sidorik, Alexander Theodore 6′0″, 248 **T**
Col: East Central CC MS; Mississippi State *HS:* Weaver [Hartford, CT] B: 12/19/1919, Hartford, CT D: 4/1980, Middletown, CT
Drafted: 1947 Round 11 Bos
AAFC **1948** BalA: 9 G. **1949** BalA: 12 G. **Total:** 21 G.

NFL **1947** Bos: 12 G.

WALLY SIEB Sieb, Walter J 5′10″, 175 **WB**
Col: Ripon *HS:* Racine [WI] B: 5/6/1899, Racine, WI D: 1/18/1974, Racine, WI
1922 Rac: 2 G; Rush 2 TD; Scor **1** 1XP; 13 Pt.

JOHN SIEGAL Siegal, John Walter 6′1″, 203 **OE-DE**
Col: Columbia *HS:* Larksville [PA] B: 5/15/1918, Larksville, PA
Drafted: 1939 Round 17 Bkn
1940 ChiB: Int 1-20; **1** Fum TD. **Total:** Int 1-20; 1 Fum TD.

		Receiving				Tot
Year Team	**G**	**Rec**	**Yds**	**Avg**	**TD**	**TD**
1939 ChiB	10	3	71	23.7	1	1
1940 ChiB	8	4	53	13.3	0	1
1941 ChiB	11	9	220	24.4	3	3
1942 ChiB	11	13	264	20.3	2	2
1943 ChiB	3	2	29	14.5	0	0
NFL Total	43	31	637	20.5	6	7

HERB SIEGERT Siegert, Herbert Frank 6′3″, 216 **OG-LB**
Col: Illinois *HS:* Pana [IL] B: 1/10/1924, Pana, IL *Drafted:* 1949 Round 18 Was
1949 Was: 12 G; Int 2-16. **1950** Was: 12 G; KR 1-0. **1951** Was: 12 G; KR 1-0. **Total:** 36 G; KR 2-0; Int 2-16.

WAYNE SIEGERT Siegert, Wayne Ewald 6′3″, 225 **OT-LB-OG**
Col: Illinois *HS:* Pana [IL] B: 3/24/1929, Pana, IL *Drafted:* 1951 Round 13 Det
1951 NYY: 4 G; KR 1-2 2.0.

ORVILLE SIEGFRIED Siegfried, Orville Maynard 5′10″, 160 **HB**
Col: Washington & Jefferson *HS:* Lee's Summit [MO] B: 2/19/1903 D: 5/28/1965
1923 StL: 7 G.

JULES SIEGLE Siegle, Julius Joseph 6′0″, 210 **FB-LB**
Col: Northwestern *HS:* Washington [East Chicago, IN] B: 2/16/1923, East Chicago, IN
1948 NYG: 3 G; Rush 2-6 3.0; KR 1-12 12.0.

LARRY SIEMERING Siemering, Lawrence E 6′3″, 206 **C-LB**
Col: San Francisco *HS:* Lodi [CA] B: 11/24/1910, Lodi, CA
1935 Bos: 11 G. **1936** Bos: 11 G; 6 Pt. **Total:** 22 G; 6 Pt.

CHUCK SIEMINSKI Sieminski, Charles Lee 6′5″, 270 **DT**
Col: Penn State *HS:* Swoyersville [PA] B: 7/3/1940, Swoyersville, PA
Drafted: 1962 Round 4 SF
1963 SF: 14 G. **1964** SF: 14 G. **1965** SF: 14 G. **1966** Atl: 14 G. **1967** Atl: 14 G. **1968** Det: 8 G. **Total:** 78 G.

JEFF SIEMON Siemon, Jeffrey Glenn 6′2″, 235 **LB**
Col: Stanford *HS:* Bakersfield [CA] B: 6/2/1950, Rochester, MN
Drafted: 1972 Round 1 Min
1981 Min: Rush 1-0. **Total:** Rush 1-0.

		Interceptions			
Year Team	**G**	**Int**	**Yds**	**TD**	**Fum**
1972 Min	13	2	23	0	0
1973 Min	14	2	24	0	0
1974 Min	14	2	24	0	0
1975 Min	14	3	24	0	0
1976 Min	14	1	0	0	0
1977 Min	14	1	9	0	0
1978 Min	16	0	0	0	0
1979 Min	16	0	0	0	0
1980 Min	16	0	0	0	0
1981 Min	16	0	0	0	1
1982 Min	9	0	0	0	0
NFL Total	156	11	104	0	1

TROY SIENKIEWICZ Sienkiewicz, Troy Allen 6′5″, 313 **OG-OT**
Col: New Mexico State *HS:* Alamogordo [NM] B: 5/27/1972, Charleston, SC *Drafted:* 1995 Round 6 SD
1996 SD: 7 G. **1997** SD: 14 G. **1998** SD: 7 G. **Total:** 28 G.

STAN SIERACKI Sieracki, Stanley Joseph 6′1″, 192 **T**
Col: Pennsylvania *HS:* Meriden [CT] B: 4/29/1904, Meriden, CT D: 12/1986, McKeesport, PA
1926 Har: 1 G.

STEVE SIERADZKI Sieradzki, Stephen Henry 6′0″, 194 **DB**
Col: Michigan State *HS:* Muskegon [MI] B: 4/7/1924 D: 5/1968
AAFC **1948** NY-A: 2 G.

STEVE SIEROCINSKI Sierocinski, Stephen Peter 6′3″, 245 **T**
Col: No College B: 1922
1946 Bos: 3 G.

HERB SIES Sies, Dale Hubert 6′1″, 203 **G-T-BB**
Col: Pittsburgh *HS:* Cedar Rapids [IA] B: 1/2/1893, Ames, IA Deceased
1920 Cle: 1 G. **1921** Day: 9 G. **1922** Day: 8 G. **1923** RI: 8 G; Scor 17, 3 FG, 8 XK. **1924** Day: 3 G; Scor 3, 1 FG. **Total:** 29 G; Scor 20, 4 FG, 8 XK.

ERIC SIEVERS Sievers, Eric Scott 6′4″, 236 **TE**
Col: Maryland *HS:* Washington Lee [Arlington, VA] B: 11/9/1957, Urbana, IL *Drafted:* 1981 Round 4 SD
1981 SD: KR 2-4 2.0. **1982** SD: KR 1-17 17.0. **1983** SD: Rush 1-(-7) -7.0; KR 1-6 6.0. **1985** SD: KR 1-3 3.0. **Total:** Rush 1-(-7) -7.0; KR 5-30 6.0.

		Receiving				
Year Team	**G**	**Rec**	**Yds**	**Avg**	**TD**	**Fum**
1981 SD	16	22	276	12.5	3	1
1982 SD	9	12	173	14.4	1	0
1983 SD	16	33	452	13.7	3	0
1984 SD	14	41	438	10.7	3	1
1985 SD	16	41	438	10.7	6	0
1986 SD	9	2	14	7.0	0	0
1987 SD	12	0	0	—	0	0
1988 SD-LARm	6	1	2	2.0	0	0
1988 SD	5	1	2	2.0	0	0
1988 LARm	1	0	0	—	0	0
1989 NE	16	54	615	11.4	0	1
1990 NE	8	8	77	9.6	0	1
NFL Total	122	214	2485	11.6	16	4

DOM SIGILLO Sigillo, Dominic Frederick 6′0″, 230 **T**
Col: Xavier (Ohio) *HS:* Central [Columbus, OH] B: 3/7/1913, Storrs, CT Deceased
1943 ChiB: 6 G. **1944** ChiB: 9 G. **1945** Det: 8 G. **Total:** 23 G.

RICKY SIGLAR Siglar, Ricky Allan 6′7″, 308 **OT-OG**
Col: Arizona Western Coll. (J.C.); San Jose State *HS:* Manzano [Albuquerque, NM] B: 6/14/1966, Albuquerque, NM
1990 SF: 16 G. **1993** KC: 14 G. **1994** KC: 16 G. **1995** KC: 16 G. **1996** KC: 16 G. **1997** NO: 16 G. **1998** Car-NO-KC: 6 G. Car: 1 G. NO: 1 G. KC: 4 G. **Total:** 100 G.

JOE SIGNAIGO Signaigo, Joseph Salvatore 6′1″, 220 **OG-DG**
Col: Notre Dame *HS:* Memphis Catholic [TN] B: 2/9/1923, Memphis, TN
AAFC **1948** NY-A: 14 G. **1949** NY-A: 12 G. **Total:** 26 G.

NFL **1950** NYY: 12 G.

SIG SIGURDSON Sigurdson, Sigurd Frederick 6'2", 206 **OE-DE**
Col: Pacific Lutheran *HS:* Ballard [Seattle, WA] B: 11/27/1918, Seattle, WA
AAFC **1947** BalA: 8 G; Rec 8-104 13.0.

VAI SIKAHEMA Sikahema, Vai 5'9", 191 **RB**
Col: Brigham Young *HS:* Mesa [AZ] B: 8/29/1962, Nuku'Alofa, Tonga
Drafted: 1986 Round 10 StL
1989 Pho: Pass 1-0. **Total:** Pass 1-0.

		Rushing				Receiving			
Year Team	G	Att	Yds	Avg	TD	Rec	Yds	Avg	TD
1986 StL	16	16	62	3.9	0	10	99	9.9	1
1987 StL	15	0	0	—	0	0	0	—	0
1988 Pho	12	0	0	—	0	0	0	—	0
1989 Pho	16	38	145	3.8	0	23	245	10.7	0
1990 Pho	16	3	8	2.7	0	7	51	7.3	0
1991 GB	11	0	0	—	0	0	0	—	0
1992 Phi	16	2	2	1.0	0	13	142	10.9	0
1993 Phi	16	0	0	—	0	0	0	—	0
NFL Total	118	59	217	3.7	0	53	537	10.1	1

	Punt Returns				Kickoff Returns					Tot
Year Team	Ret	Yds	Avg	TD	Ret	Yds	Avg	TD	Fum	TD
1986 StL	43	**522**	12.1	**2**	37	847	22.9	0	2	3
1987 StL	**44**	**550**	12.5	1	34	761	22.4	0	0	1
1988 Pho	33	341	10.3	0	23	475	20.7	0	2	0
1989 Pho	37	433	11.7	0	43	874	20.3	0	2	0
1990 Pho	36	306	8.5	0	27	544	20.1	0	2	0
1991 GB	26	239	9.2	0	15	325	21.7	0	3	0
1992 Phi	40	503	12.6	1	26	528	20.3	0	0	1
1993 Phi	33	275	8.3	0	30	579	19.3	0	4	0
NFL Total	292	3169	10.9	4	235	4933	21.0	0	15	5

MIKE SIKICH Sikich, Michael P 6'2", 243 **OG**
Col: Northwestern *HS:* Lyons Twp. [La Grange, IL] B: 3/3/1949, Chicago, IL *Drafted:* 1971 Round 11 Cle
1971 Cle: 3 G.

RUDY SIKICH Sikich, Rudolph 6'1", 220 **T**
Col: Minnesota *HS:* Hibbing [MN] B: 1923, Hibbing, MN
Drafted: 1944 Round 4 Bkn
1945 Cle: 6 G.

MIKE SIKORA Sikora, Michael Wasyl 6'2", 230 **OG**
Col: Indiana; Oregon *HS:* Hammond [IN] B: 11/29/1926, Hammond, IN
1952 ChiC: 12 G.

SAM SILAS Silas, Samuel Louis 6'4", 255 **DT**
Col: Southern Illinois *HS:* Union Acad. [Bartow, FL] B: 9/25/1940, Homeland, FL *Drafted:* 1963 Round 6 Bos
1963 StL: 14 G. **1964** StL: 14 G. **1965** StL: 14 G. **1966** StL: 14 G. **1967** StL: 14 G. **1968** NYG: 14 G. **1969** SF: 4 G. **1970** SF: 12 G. **Total:** 100 G.

DAN SILEO Sileo, Daniel William 6'2", 282 **NT**
Col: Maryland; Cincinnati; Miami (Fla.) *HS:* Stamford Catholic [CT] B: 1/3/1964, Stamford, CT *Drafted:* 1987 Supplemental Round 3 TB
1987 TB: 10 G.

RICH SILER Siler, Richard Anthony 6'4", 240 **TE**
Col: Illinois; Texas A&M *HS:* Father Lopez [Daytona Beach, FL] B: 11/1/1963, Miami, FL
1987 Mia: 1 G.

JOE SILIPO Silipo, Joseph Martin 6'3", 295 **OT**
Col: Tulane *HS:* Ward Melville [Setauket, NY] B: 12/31/1957, Glen Cove, NY
1987 Buf: 1 G.

FRANK SILLIN Sillin, Franklin Paul 5'11", 179 **WB-TB-BB-FB**
Col: Western Maryland *HS:* Stivers [Dayton, OH] B: 1904, Wapakoneta, OH D: 12/30/1932
1921 Day: 1 G. **1927** Day: 7 G. **1928** Day: 4 G; Rush 1 TD; 6 Pt. **1929** Day: 5 G. **Total:** 17 G; Rush 1 TD; 6 Pt.

NILO SILVAN Silvan, Nilo Kyle 5'9", 175 **WR**
Col: Tennessee *HS:* St. Paul [Covington, LA] B: 10/2/1973, Covington, LA *Drafted:* 1996 Round 6 TB
1996 TB: PR 14-113 8.1.

		Kickoff Returns			
Year Team	G	Ret	Yds	Avg	TD
1996 TB	7	28	626	22.4	0

CARL SILVESTRI Silvestri, Carl Anthony 5'11", 190 **DB**
Col: Wisconsin *HS:* Shorewood [WI] B: 3/27/1943, Milwaukee, WI
Drafted: 1965 Round 16 StL
1965 StL: 14 G; PR 3-21 7.0; KR 4-96 24.0; 1 Fum. **1966** Atl: 3 G. **Total:** 17 G; PR 3-21 7.0; KR 4-96 24.0; 1 Fum.

DON SILVESTRI Silvestri, Donald Gerard 6'4", 220 **K**
Col: Pittsburgh *HS:* Pennridge [Perkasie, PA] B: 12/25/1968, Pittsburgh, PA
1995 NYJ: 16 G; Punt 5-238 47.6. **1996** NYJ: 12 G. **Total:** 28 G; Punt 5-238 47.6.

BUTCH SIMAS Simas, William T 6'0", 185 **BB-DB**
Col: St. Mary's (Cal.) *HS:* Hanford [CA] B: 8/31/1908 D: 5/24/1989, Hermosa Beach, CA
1932 ChiC: 7 G; Rush 2-0; Rec 1-23 23.0. **1933** ChiC: 3 G; Rec 1-9 9.0. **Total:** 10 G; Rush 2-0; Rec 2-32 16.0.

KEN SIMENDINGER Simendinger, Kenneth Alphonse 5'10", 175 **WB**
(Cy) *Col:* Lehigh; Holy Cross *HS:* La Salle Prep [Philadelphia, PA] B: 10/23/1899, Philadelphia, PA D: 5/26/1972, Philadelphia, PA
1926 Har: 2 G.

DON SIMENSEN Simensen, Donald Roy 6'2", 220 **OT**
(Si) *Col:* St. Thomas *HS:* Central [St. Paul, MN] B: 9/11/1926, Minot, ND D: 4/22/1994, Fridley, MN
1951 LARm: 12 G; KR 1-13 13.0. **1952** LARm: 12 G. **Total:** 24 G; KR 1-13 13.0.

JOHN SIMERSON Simerson, John Cooke Jr. 6'3", 257 **C-OT**
(Bunny) *Col:* Purdue *HS:* Roosevelt [Honolulu, HI] B: 4/20/1935, Honolulu, HI D: 8/2/1992, Los Angeles, CA *Drafted:* 1957 Round 22 Phi
1957 Phi: 12 G. **1958** Phi-Pit: 7 G. Phi: 4 G. Pit: 3 G. **1960** Hou: 14 G. **1961** Bos: 10 G. **Total:** 43 G.

TRACY SIMIEN Simien, Tracy Anthony 6'1", 252 **LB**
Col: Texas Christian *HS:* Sweeny [TX] B: 5/21/1967, Bay City, TX
1989 Pit: Postseason only. **1991** KC: 15 G; 2 Sac. **1992** KC: 15 G; Int 3-18; 1 Sac. **1993** KC: 16 G. **1994** KC: 15 G. **1995** KC: 16 G; 1 Sac. **1996** KC: 16 G; Int 1-2. **1997** KC: 16 G. **Total:** 109 G; Int 4-20; 4 Sac.

MILT SIMINGTON Simington, Milton R 6'2", 217 **G**
Col: Arkansas *HS:* Ida Bell [OK]; Dierks HS [AR] B: 8/26/1918, Wright City, OK D: 1/17/1943, Shreveport, LA *Drafted:* 1941 Round 9 Cle
1941 Cle: 7 G. **1942** Pit: 11 G; Scor 5, 1-1 100.0% FG, 2-3 66.7% XK. **Total:** 18 G; Scor 5, 1-1 100.0% FG, 2-3 66.7% XK.

ARNIE SIMKUS Simkus, Arnold 6'4", 240 **DE-DT**
Col: Michigan *HS:* Cass Tech [Detroit, MI] B: 3/25/1943, Schlava, Germany *Drafted:* 1965 Round 6 Cle
1965 NYJ: 1 G. **1967** Min: 11 G. **Total:** 12 G.

MIKE SIMMONDS Simmonds, Michael Todd 6'4", 285 **OG**
Col: Indiana State *HS:* West [Belleville, IL] B: 8/12/1964, Belleville, IL
Drafted: 1987 Round 10 TB
1989 TB: 5 G.

TONY SIMMONS Simmons, Anthony Earl 6'4", 270 **DE**
Col: Tennessee *HS:* McClymonds [Oakland, CA] B: 12/18/1962, Oakland, CA *Drafted:* 1985 Round 12 SD
1985 SD: 13 G. **1987** SD: 3 G; 1 Sac. **Total:** 16 G; 1 Sac.

ANTHONY SIMMONS Simmons, Anthony Lamont 6'0", 231 **LB**
Col: Clemson *HS:* Spartanburg [SC] B: 6/20/1976, Spartanburg, SC
Drafted: 1998 Round 1 Sea
1998 Sea: 12 G; Int 1-36 1 TD; 6 Pt.

BRIAN SIMMONS Simmons, Brian Eugene 6'3", 233 **LB**
Col: North Carolina *HS:* New Bern [NC] B: 6/21/1975, New Bern, NC
Drafted: 1998 Round 1 Cin
1998 Cin: 14 G; Int 1-18; 3 Sac.

CLEO SIMMONS Simmons, Cleo 6'2", 225 **TE**
Col: Jackson State *HS:* S.S. Murphy [Mobile, AL] B: 10/21/1960, Mobile, AL
1983 Dal: 11 G.

CLYDE SIMMONS Simmons, Clyde Jr. 6'5", 279 **DE-DT**
Col: Western Carolina *HS:* New Hanover [Wilmington, NC] B: 8/4/1964, Lanes, SC *Drafted:* 1986 Round 9 Phi
1986 Phi: 16 G; KR 1-0; 2 Sac. **1987** Phi: 12 G; 6 Sac. **1988** Phi: 16 G; Scor 1 Saf; 8 Pt; 8 Sac. **1989** Phi: 16 G; Int 1-60 1 TD; 6 Pt; 15.5 Sac. **1990** Phi: 16 G; 1 Fum TD; 6 Pt; 7.5 Sac. **1991** Phi: 16 G; 1 Fum TD; 6 Pt; 13 Sac. **1992** Phi: 16 G; **19** Sac. **1993** Phi: 16 G; Int 1-0; 5 Sac. **1994** Ariz: 16 G; 6 Sac. **1995** Ariz: 16 G; Int 1-25 1 TD; 6 Pt; 11 Sac. **1996** Jac: 16 G; 7.5 Sac. **1997** Jac: 16 G; 8.5 Sac. **1998** Cin: 16 G; 5 Sac. **Total:** 204 G; KR 1-0; Int 3-85 2 TD; Scor 1 Saf; 2 Fum TD; Tot TD 5; 32 Pt; 114.0 Sac.

DAVE SIMMONS Simmons, David Alan 6'4", 245 **LB**
Col: Georgia Tech *HS:* Stephen F. Austin [El Paso, TX] B: 8/3/1943, Elizabethtown, KY *Drafted:* 1965 Round 2 StL
1965 StL: 14 G. **1966** StL: 6 G. **1967** NO: 11 G; Int 1-12. **1968** Dal: 13 G; Int 1-8. **Total:** 44 G; Int 2-20.

DAVE SIMMONS Simmons, David Devone 6'4", 221 **LB**
Col: North Carolina *HS:* Rosewood [Goldsboro, NC] B: 1/19/1957, Goldsboro, NC *Drafted:* 1979 Round 6 GB
1979 GB: 16 G. **1980** Det: 1 G. **1982** Bal: 6 G. **1983** ChiB: 13 G. **Total:** 36 G.

ED SIMMONS Simmons, Edward Lamar 6'5", 315 **OT-OG**
Col: Eastern Washington *HS:* Nathan Hale [Seattle, WA]
B: 12/31/1963, Seattle, WA *Drafted:* 1987 Round 6 Was
1987 Was: 5 G. **1988** Was: 16 G. **1989** Was: 16 G. **1990** Was: 13 G. **1991** Was: 6 G. **1992** Was: 16 G. **1993** Was: 13 G. **1994** Was: 16 G. **1995** Was: 16 G. **1996** Was: 11 G. **1997** Was: 14 G. **Total:** 142 G.

FLOYD SIMMONS Simmons, Floyd Weston 6'1", 200 **HB-DB**
Col: Notre Dame *HS:* Jefferson [Portland, OR] B: 2/19/1925, Portland, OR D: 8/6/1996, Portland, OR
AAFC **1948** ChiA: Rec 2-60 30.0 1 TD; KR 3-77 25.7.

		Rushing				Tot
Year Team	**G**	**Att**	**Yds**	**Avg**	**TD**	**TD**
1948 ChiA	11	36	121	3.4	1	2

JIM SIMMONS Simmons, James A 6'0", 186 **WB-FB-TB**
(Jinks) *Col:* Southwestern Oklahoma State *HS:* Sentinel [OK]
B: 4/17/1902, TX D: 2/1984, Elmore City, OK
1927 Cle: 12 G; Rush 5 TD; 30 Pt. **1928** Prov: 8 G. **Total:** 20 G; Rush 5 TD; 30 Pt.

JASON SIMMONS Simmons, Jason Lawrence 5'8", 188 **DB**
Col: Arizona State *HS:* Leuzinger [Lawndale, CA] B: 3/30/1976, Inglewood, CA *Drafted:* 1998 Round 5 Pit
1998 Pit: 6 G.

JEFF SIMMONS Simmons, Jeffery Thomas 6'3", 195 **WR**
Col: USC *HS:* Edison [Stockton, CA] B: 7/6/1960, Stockton, CA
Drafted: 1983 Round 7 LARm
1983 LARm: 3 G; KR 1-0.

JERRY SIMMONS Simmons, Jerry Bernard 6'0", 190 **WR**
Col: Bethune-Cookman *HS:* Union Acad. [Bartow, FL] B: 11/14/1942, Nichols, FL
1965 Pit: KR 1-28 28.0. **1966** Pit: PR 2-0; KR 10-196 19.6. **1967** NO-Atl: PR 3-0; KR 2-38 19.0. Atl: PR 3-0; KR 2-38 19.0. **1968** Atl: Rush 1-(-6) -6.0. **1971** Den: Rush 1-7 7.0. **1973** Den: Rush 1-(-4) -4.0.
Total: Rush 3-(-3) -1.0; PR 5-0; KR 13-262 20.2.

		Receiving				
Year Team	**G**	**Rec**	**Yds**	**Avg**	**TD**	**Fum**
1965 Pit	4	2	16	8.0	0	0
1966 Pit	13	6	68	11.3	1	1
1967 NO-Atl	14	23	312	13.6	2	1
1967 NO	2	2	25	12.5	0	0
1967 Atl	12	21	287	13.7	2	1
1968 Atl	14	28	479	17.1	0	0
1969 Atl-ChiB	10	14	182	13.0	0	0
1969 Atl	2	1	4	4.0	0	0
1969 ChiB	8	13	178	13.7	0	0
1971 Den	14	25	403	16.1	1	0
1972 Den	9	17	235	13.8	2	0
1973 Den	14	13	249	19.2	1	0
1974 Den	14	10	161	16.1	2	0
NFL Total	106	138	2105	15.3	9	2

JACK SIMMONS Simmons, John Charles 6'4", 236 **C-G-T**
(Moose) *Col:* Maryland; Detroit Mercy *HS:* St. Ambrose [Detroit, MI]
B: 10/8/1924, Grosse Pointe, MI D: 9/17/1978, Royal Oak, MI
Drafted: 1946 Round 20 Det
AAFC **1948** BalA: 10 G.

NFL **1949** Det: 12 G. **1950** Det: 12 G. **1951** ChiC: 12 G. **1952** ChiC: 12 G. **1953** ChiC: 12 G; Punt 22-845 38.4. **1954** ChiC: 12 G. **1955** ChiC: 12 G; KR 1-7 7.0. **1956** ChiC: 12 G. **Total:** 96 G; KR 1-7 7.0; Punt 22-845 38.4.

JOHN SIMMONS Simmons, John Christopher 5'11", 192 **DB**
Col: Southern Methodist *HS:* Parkview [Little Rock, AR] B: 12/1/1958, Little Rock, AR *Drafted:* 1981 Round 3 Cin
1981 Cin: KR 1-10 10.0. **1983** Cin: KR 14-317 22.6. **1984** Cin: KR 1-15 15.0; Int 2-43 1 TD. **1986** Cin-GB: KR 1-0; 1 Sac. Cin: KR 1-0; 1 Sac.
Total: KR 17-342 20.1; Int 2-43 1 TD; 1 Sac.

		Punt Returns					Tot
Year Team	**G**	**Ret**	**Yds**	**Avg**	**TD**	**Fum**	**TD**
1981 Cin	11	5	24	4.8	0	1	0
1982 Cin	2	0	0	—	0	0	0
1983 Cin	16	25	173	6.9	0	4	0
1984 Cin	16	12	98	8.2	0	0	1
1985 Cin	9	0	0	—	0	0	0
1986 Cin-GB	16	2	7	3.5	0	1	1
1986 Cin	10	2	7	3.5	0	1	0
1986 GB	6	0	0	—	0	0	1
1987 Ind	2	2	5	2.5	0	0	0
NFL Total	72	46	307	6.7	0	6	2

KING SIMMONS Simmons, King David 6'2", 200 **DB**
Col: Texas Tech *HS:* Killeen [TX] B: 2/12/1963, Atlanta, GA
1987 SD: 3 G; 1.5 Sac.

LEON SIMMONS Simmons, Leon 6'0", 225 **LB**
Col: Grambling State *HS:* Lincoln [Dallas, TX] B: 9/27/1938, Dallas, TX
1963 Den: 2 G.

MARCELLO SIMMONS Simmons, Marcello Muhammad 6'1", 180 **DB**
Col: Southern Methodist *HS:* Tomball [TX] B: 8/8/1971, Tomball, TX
Drafted: 1993 Round 4 Cin
1993 Cin: 16 G; PR 1-0.

MICHAEL SIMMONS Simmons, Michael Glenn 6'4", 269 **DE**
Col: Mississippi State *HS:* Eupora [MS] B: 11/14/1965, Eupora, MS
1989 NO: 1 G. **1990** NO: 16 G; 1 Sac. **Total:** 17 G; 1 Sac.

BOB SIMMONS Simmons, Robert Gatling 6'4", 260 **OG-OT**
Col: Texas *HS:* Temple [TX] B: 7/7/1954, Temple, TX *Drafted:* 1976 Round 3 NO
1977 KC: 14 G. **1978** KC: 16 G. **1979** KC: 16 G. **1980** KC: 15 G. **1981** KC: 4 G. **1982** KC: 8 G. **1983** KC: 15 G. **Total:** 88 G.

ROY SIMMONS Simmons, Roy Franklin 6'3", 264 **OG**
Col: Georgia Tech *HS:* Alfred E. Beach [Savannah, GA] B: 11/8/1956, Savannah, GA *Drafted:* 1979 Round 8 NYG
1979 NYG: 16 G. **1980** NYG: 16 G. **1981** NYG: 16 G. **1983** Was: 10 G.
Total: 58 G.

STACEY SIMMONS Simmons, Stacey Andrew 5'9", 183 **WR**
Col: Florida *HS:* Dunedin [FL] B: 8/5/1968, Clearwater, FL
Drafted: 1990 Round 4 Ind
1990 Ind: 14 G; Rec 4-33 8.3; KR 19-348 18.3; 1 Fum.

TONY SIMMONS Simmons, Tony De'Angelo 6'1", 205 **WR**
(Touchdown Tony) *Col:* Wisconsin *HS:* St. Rita [Chicago, IL]
B: 12/8/1974, Chicago, IL *Drafted:* 1998 Round 2 NE
1998 NE: 11 G; Rec 23-474 20.6 3 TD; 18 Pt.

VICTOR SIMMONS Simmons, Victor T 6'2", 230 **LB**
Col: Central State (Ohio) *HS:* Austin [Chicago, IL] B: 5/9/1964, Chicago, IL
1987 Dal: 3 G.

WAYNE SIMMONS Simmons, Wayne General 6'2", 245 **LB**
(Big Money) *Col:* Clemson *HS:* Hilton Head [SC] B: 12/15/1969, Beauford, SC *Drafted:* 1993 Round 1 GB
1993 GB: 14 G; Int 2-21; 1 Sac. **1994** GB: 12 G. **1995** GB: 16 G; 4 Sac. **1996** GB: 16 G; Int 1-0; 2.5 Sac. **1997** GB-KC: 16 G; 3.5 Sac. GB: 6 G. KC: 10 G; 3.5 Sac. **1998** KC-Buf: 16 G; 0.5 Sac. KC: 10 G. Buf: 6 G; 0.5 Sac. **Total:** 90 G; Int 3-21; 11.5 Sac.

PHIL SIMMS Simms, Phillip Martin 6'3", 216 **QB**
Col: Morehead State *HS:* Southern [Louisville, KY] B: 11/3/1954, Lebanon, KY *Drafted:* 1979 Round 1 NYG
1984 NYG: Rec 1-13 13.0. **1993** NYG: Rec 1-(-6) -6.0. **Total:** Rec 2-7 3.5.

		Passing							
Year Team	**G**	**Att**	**Comp**	**Comp%**	**Yds**	**YPA**	**TD**	**Int**	**Rating**
1979 NYG	12	265	134	50.6	1743	6.58	13	14	66.0
1980 NYG	13	402	193	48.0	2321	5.77	15	19	58.9
1981 NYG	10	316	172	54.4	2031	6.43	11	**9**	74.0
1983 NYG	2	13	7	53.8	130	10.00	0	1	56.6
1984 NYG	16	533	286	53.7	4044	7.59	22	18	78.1
1985 NYG	16	495	275	55.6	3829	7.74	22	20	78.6
1986 NYG	16	468	259	55.3	3487	7.45	21	22	74.6
1987 NYG	9	282	163	57.8	2230	7.91	17	9	90.0
1988 NYG	15	479	263	54.9	3359	7.01	21	11	82.1
1989 NYG	15	405	228	56.3	3061	7.56	14	14	77.6
1990 NYG	14	311	184	59.2	2284	7.34	15	**4**	92.7
1991 NYG	6	141	82	58.2	993	7.04	8	4	87.0
1992 NYG	4	137	83	60.6	912	6.66	5	3	83.3
1993 NYG	16	400	247	61.8	3038	7.60	15	9	88.3
NFL Total	164	4647	2576	55.4	33462	7.20	199	157	78.5

	Rushing				
Year Team	**Att**	**Yds**	**Avg**	**TD**	**Fum**
1979 NYG	29	166	5.7	1	9
1980 NYG	36	190	5.3	1	6
1981 NYG	19	42	2.2	0	7
1984 NYG	42	162	3.9	0	8
1985 NYG	37	132	3.6	0	**16**
1986 NYG	43	72	1.7	1	9
1987 NYG	14	44	3.1	0	4
1988 NYG	33	152	4.6	0	7
1989 NYG	32	141	4.4	1	9
1990 NYG	21	61	2.9	1	7
1991 NYG	9	42	4.7	1	4
1992 NYG	6	17	2.8	0	0
1993 NYG	28	31	1.1	0	7
NFL Total	349	1252	3.6	6	93

BOB SIMMS Simms, Robert Alderson 6′1″, 230 **LB-OE**
Col: Rutgers *HS:* Charleston [WV] B: 9/3/1938, Clendenin, WV
Drafted: 1960 Round 10 NYG
1960 NYG: 9 G; Rec 1-58 58.0. **1961** NYG: 14 G; KR 1-14 14.0.
1962 NYG-Pit: 8 G. NYG: 3 G. Pit: 5 G. **Total:** 31 G; Rec 1-58 58.0; KR 1-14 14.0.

JIM SIMON Simon, James E 6′4″, 240 **OG-OT**
Col: Miami (Fla.) *HS:* Scott Twp. [North Braddock, PA] B: 3/22/1940, Pittsburgh, PA *Drafted:* 1963 Round 15 Det
1963 Det: 13 G. **1964** Det: 14 G; KR 1-0. **1965** Det: 14 G. **1966** Atl: 14 G. **1967** Atl: 14 G. **1968** Atl: 13 G. **Total:** 82 G; KR 1-0.

MIKE SIMONE Simone, Michael Anthony 6′0″, 210 **LB**
Col: Stanford *HS:* Ravenna [OH] B: 5/20/1950, Ravenna, OH
1972 Den: 14 G; PR 1-5 5.0; KR 1-(-6) -6.0. **1973** Den: 14 G; KR 1-3 3.0.
1974 Den: 14 G. **Total:** 42 G; PR 1-5 5.0; KR 2-(-3) -1.5.

LEN SIMONETTI Simonetti, Leonard Patrick 5′11″, 225 **T**
(Meatball; Diz) *Col:* Tennessee *HS:* New Philadelphia [OH]
B: 11/20/1919, Roswell, OH D: 8/14/1973, Dennison, OH
AAFC **1947** CleA: 14 G; Int 1-22. **1948** CleA: 14 G. **Total:** 28 G; Int 1-22.

ED SIMONINI Simonini, Edward Charles 6′0″, 210 **LB**
Col: Texas A&M *HS:* Valley [Las Vegas, NV] B: 2/2/1954, Portsmouth, VA *Drafted:* 1976 Round 3 Bal
1976 Bal: 14 G. **1977** Bal: 14 G; Int 1-0. **1978** Bal: 16 G; Int 2-4. **1979** Bal: 13 G. **1980** Bal: 16 G. **1981** Bal: 1 G. **1982** NO: 9 G. **Total:** 83 G; Int 3-4.

JOHN SIMONS Simons, John Brimhall 5′11″, 200 **FB-OE**
(Jack) *Col:* Hamline *HS:* Bemidji [MN] B: 1/22/1901, St. Paul, MN
D: 1/22/1978, Las Vegas, NV
1924 Min: 6 G; Scor 1, 1 XK.

KEITH SIMONS Simons, Keith Michael 6′3″, 254 **NT-DT**
Col: Minnesota *HS:* Belleville [MI] B: 4/26/1954, Ypsilanti, MI
Drafted: 1976 Round 3 KC
1976 KC: 6 G. **1977** KC: 14 G. **1978** StL: 13 G. **1979** StL: 16 G.
Total: 49 G.

KEVIN SIMONS Simons, Kevin Bradley 6′3″, 315 **OT**
Col: Tennessee *HS:* Miami Carol City [Miami, FL] B: 4/25/1967, Miami, FL
1989 Cle: 1 G.

DAVE SIMONSON Simonson, David Arnold 6′6″, 246 **OT**
Col: Minnesota *HS:* Austin [MN] B: 5/2/1952, Austin, MN
Drafted: 1974 Round 12 Bal
1974 Bal: 13 G. **1975** NYG: 2 G. **1976** Hou-Sea: 7 G. Hou: 2 G. Sea: 5 G.
1977 Det: 7 G. **Total:** 29 G.

RON SIMPKINS Simpkins, Ronald Bernard 6′1″, 235 **LB**
Col: Michigan *HS:* Western [Detroit, MI] B: 4/2/1958, Detroit, MI
Drafted: 1980 Round 7 Cin
1980 Cin: 16 G; KR 3-8 2.7; 1 Fum. **1982** Cin: 5 G. **1983** Cin: 15 G.
1984 Cin: 16 G. **1985** Cin: 16 G; 3.5 Sac. **1986** Cin: 16 G; KR 2-24 12.0.
1988 GB: 7 G. **Total:** 91 G; KR 5-32 6.4; 1 Fum; 3.5 Sac.

AL SIMPSON Simpson, Allen Ralph Jr. 6′5″, 255 **OT-OG**
Col: McCook CC NE; Colorado State *HS:* Wilkinsburg [PA]; Westinghouse HS [Pittsburgh, PA] B: 7/27/1951, Pittsburgh, PA
Drafted: 1975 Round 2 NYG
1975 NYG: 13 G. **1976** NYG: 10 G. **Total:** 23 G.

CARL SIMPSON Simpson, Carl Wilhelm 6′2″, 292 **DT**
Col: Florida State *HS:* Appling Co. [Baxley, GA] B: 4/18/1970, Baxley, GA *Drafted:* 1993 Round 2 ChiB
1993 ChiB: 11 G; 0.5 Sac. **1994** ChiB: 15 G. **1995** ChiB: 16 G; 1 Sac.
1996 ChiB: 16 G; 1.5 Sac. **1997** ChiB: 16 G; 4.5 Sac. **1998** Ariz: 13 G.
Total: 87 G; 7.5 Sac.

EBER SIMPSON Simpson, Eber Edward Jr. 5′8″, 170 **QB**
Col: Wis.-Oshkosh; Wisconsin *HS:* Oshkosh [WI] B: 7/24/1895, Oshkosh, WI Deceased
1923 StL: 7 G; Pass 1 TD.

HOWARD SIMPSON Simpson, Howard Jesse 6′5″, 230 **DE**
Col: Auburn *HS:* Marietta [GA] B: 12/14/1942, Lancaster, SC
1964 Min: 3 G.

JACKIE SIMPSON Simpson, Jack Maylon 6′0″, 225 **LB-K**
Col: Mississippi *HS:* Corinth [MS] B: 8/20/1936, Corinth, MS
D: 6/2/1983, Pontiac, MI *Drafted:* 1958 Round 21 Was
1961 Den: 6 G. **1962** Oak: 14 G; Int 3-20; Scor 15, 3-10 30.0% FG, 6-7 85.7% XK. **1963** Oak: 14 G; KR 1-11 11.0; Int 2-19. **1964** Oak: 2 G.
Total: 36 G; KR 1-11 11.0; Int 5-39; Scor 15, 3-10 30.0% FG, 6-7 85.7% XK.

JIMMY SIMPSON Simpson, James Felix 5′10″, 160 **BB-TB**
Col: Detroit Mercy *HS:* Morrison R. Waite [Toledo, OH] B: 10/6/1897
D: 8/1979, Toledo, OH
1922 Tol: 3 G. **1924** Ken: 4 G. **Total:** 7 G.

JACKIE SIMPSON Simpson, John Maylen 5′10″, 183 **DB**
Col: Florida *HS:* Miami Edison [FL] B: 4/2/1934, Miami, FL
D: 6/2/1983, Pontiac, MI
1958 Bal: 2 G; PR 1-1 1.0; KR 3-59 19.7; 1 Fum. **1959** Bal: 10 G.
1960 Bal: 12 G. **1961** Pit: 8 G; Int 2-46. **1962** Pit: 13 G. **Total:** 45 G; PR 1-1 1.0; KR 3-59 19.7; Int 2-46; 1 Fum.

KEITH SIMPSON Simpson, Keith Edward 6′1″, 195 **DB**
Col: Memphis *HS:* Hamilton [Memphis, TN] B: 3/9/1956, Memphis, TN
Drafted: 1978 Round 1 Sea
1983 Sea: 1 Sac. **1984** Sea: 2 Sac. **1985** Sea: 3 Sac. **Total:** 6 Sac.

		Interceptions			
Year Team	**G**	**Int**	**Yds**	**TD**	**Fum**
1978 Sea	13	2	40	1	0
1979 Sea	15	4	72	0	0
1980 Sea	16	3	15	0	0
1981 Sea	12	2	34	0	0
1982 Sea	8	0	0	0	0
1983 Sea	14	4	39	0	1
1984 Sea	15	4	138	**2**	0
1985 Sea	15	0	0	0	0
NFL Total	108	19	338	3	1

MIKE SIMPSON Simpson, Michael Harry 5′9″, 170 **DB**
Col: Houston *HS:* Port Neches [TX] B: 3/13/1947, Mena, AR
Drafted: 1969 Round 13 SD
1970 SF: 7 G. **1971** SF: 8 G; Int 1-15. **1972** SF: 13 G; Int 2-32 1 TD; 6 Pt.
1973 SF: 13 G; KR 1-0. **Total:** 41 G; KR 1-0; Int 3-47 1 TD; 6 Pt.

NATE SIMPSON Simpson, Nathan Joseph 5′11″, 189 **RB**
Col: Tennessee State *HS:* East [Nashville, TN] B: 11/30/1954, Nashville, TN *Drafted:* 1977 Round 5 GB
1977 GB: Rec 5-19 3.8; KR 1-0. **1978** GB: Rec 1-4 4.0. **1979** GB: Rec 11-46 4.2. **Total:** Rec 17-69 4.1; KR 1-0.

		Rushing				
Year Team	**G**	**Att**	**Yds**	**Avg**	**TD**	**Fum**
1977 GB	12	60	204	3.4	0	4
1978 GB	16	27	58	2.1	0	1
1979 GB	15	66	235	3.6	1	2
NFL Total	43	153	497	3.2	1	7

O.J. SIMPSON Simpson, Orenthal James 6′1″, 212 **RB**
(The Juice) *Col:* San Francisco City Coll. CA (J.C.); USC *HS:* Galileo [San Francisco, CA] B: 7/9/1947, San Francisco, CA *Drafted:* 1969 Round 1 Buf *HOF:* 1985
1970 Buf: Pass 2-0. **1971** Buf: Pass 2-0. **1972** Buf: Pass 8-5 62.5%, 113 14.13 1 TD. **1973** Buf: Pass 2-1 50.0%, -3 -1.50. **1974** Buf: Pass 1-0.
1977 Buf: Pass 1-0. **Total:** Pass 16-6 37.5%, 110 6.88 1 TD.

		Rushing				Receiving			
Year Team	**G**	**Att**	**Yds**	**Avg**	**TD**	**Rec**	**Yds**	**Avg**	**TD**
1969 Buf	13	181	697	3.9	2	30	343	11.4	3
1970 Buf	8	120	488	4.1	5	10	139	13.9	0
1971 Buf	14	183	742	4.1	5	21	162	7.7	0
1972 Buf	14	292	**1251**	4.3	6	27	198	7.3	0
1973 Buf	14	**332**	**2003**	6.0	**12**	6	70	11.7	0
1974 Buf	14	**270**	1125	4.2	3	15	189	12.6	1
1975 Buf	14	**329**	**1817**	**5.5**	**16**	28	426	15.2	7
1976 Buf	14	290	**1503**	5.2	8	22	259	11.8	1
1977 Buf	7	126	557	4.4	0	16	138	8.6	0
1978 SF	10	161	593	3.7	1	21	172	8.2	2
1979 SF	13	120	460	3.8	3	7	46	6.6	0
NFL Total	135	2404	11236	4.7	61	203	2142	10.6	14

	Kickoff Returns					Tot
Year Team	**Ret**	**Yds**	**Avg**	**TD**	**Fum**	**TD**
1969 Buf	21	529	25.2	0	6	5
1970 Buf	7	333	47.6	1	6	6
1971 Buf	4	107	26.8	0	5	5
1972 Buf	1	21	21.0	0	8	6
1973 Buf	0	0	—	0	7	12
1974 Buf	0	0	—	0	7	4
1975 Buf	0	0	—	0	7	**23**
1976 Buf	0	0	—	0	6	9
1977 Buf	0	0	—	0	2	0
1978 SF	0	0	—	0	5	3
1979 SF	0	0	—	0	3	3
NFL Total	33	990	30.0	1	62	76

BOB SIMPSON Simpson, Robert Morris 6′5″, 235 **DE**
Col: Colorado *HS:* Arapahoe [Littleton, CO] B: 3/29/1954, Bloomington, IL *Drafted:* 1976 Round 8 Mia
1978 Mia: 5 G.

TIM SIMPSON Simpson, Timothy James 6′2″, 284 **OG-C**
Col: Illinois *HS:* East Peoria [IL] B: 3/5/1969, Peoria, IL *Drafted:* 1992 Round 12 Cle
1994 Pit: 4 G.

TRAVIS SIMPSON Simpson, Travis Theron 6'3", 272 **C**
Col: Oklahoma *HS:* Norman [OK] B: 11/19/1963, Norman, OK
1987 GB: 3 G.

WILLIE SIMPSON Simpson, William 6'0", 218 **FB**
Col: San Francisco State *HS:* Edison [Stockton, CA] B: 3/11/1938
1962 Oak: 10 G; Rush 10-32 3.2; KR 1-7 7.0; 1 Fum.

BILL SIMPSON Simpson, William Thomas 6'1", 184 **DB**
Col: Michigan State *HS:* Shrine [Royal Oak, MI] B: 12/5/1951, Detroit, MI *Drafted:* 1974 Round 2 LARm
1975 LARm: PR 1-(-3) -3.0. **1980** Buf: Scor **1** Saf. **1982** Buf: PR 1-0; 1 Sac. **Total:** PR 2-(-3) -1.5; Scor 1 Saf; 1 Sac.

		Interceptions			
Year Team	**G**	**Int**	**Yds**	**TD**	**Fum**
1974 LARm	14	1	0	0	1
1975 LARm	14	6	90	0	0
1976 LARm	14	4	62	0	0
1977 LARm	14	6	157	0	0
1978 LARm	16	5	82	0	0
1980 Buf	11	4	36	0	0
1981 Buf	16	4	42	0	0
1982 Buf	9	4	45	0	0
NFL Total	108	34	514	0	1

BILLY SIMS Sims, Billy Ray 6'0", 212 **RB**
Col: Oklahoma *HS:* Hooks [TX] B: 9/18/1955, St. Louis, MO
Drafted: 1980 Round 1 Det

		Rushing				Receiving					Tot
Year Team	**G**	**Att**	**Yds**	**Avg**	**TD**	**Rec**	**Yds**	**Avg**	**TD**	**Fum**	**TD**
1980 Det	16	313	1303	4.2	**13**	51	621	12.2	3	12	**16**
1981 Det	14	296	1437	4.9	13	28	451	16.1	2	9	15
1982 Det	9	172	639	3.7	4	34	342	10.1	0	7	4
1983 Det	13	220	1040	4.7	7	42	419	10.0	0	6	7
1984 Det	8	130	687	5.3	5	31	239	7.7	0	6	5
NFL Total	60	1131	5106	4.5	42	186	2072	11.1	5	40	47

DARRYL SIMS Sims, Darryl Leon 6'3", 278 **DE-NT**
Col: Wisconsin *HS:* Bassick [Bridgeport, CT] B: 7/23/1961, Winston-Salem, NC *Drafted:* 1985 Round 1 Pit
1985 Pit: 16 G; 2 Sac. **1986** Pit: 16 G; 1 Sac. **1987** Cle: 10 G. **1988** Cle: 16 G. **Total:** 58 G; 3 Sac.

DAVID SIMS Sims, David Bernard 6'3", 216 **RB**
Col: Georgia Tech *HS:* Decatur [GA] B: 10/26/1955, Atlanta, GA
Drafted: 1977 Round 7 Sea
1977 Sea: Pass 4-1 25.0%, 43 10.75 1 TD 1 Int; KR 4-52 13.0. **1978** Sea: Pass 1-1 100.0%, 15 15.00. **1979** Sea: Pass 2-1 50.0%, 18 9.00. **Total:** Pass 7-3 42.9%, 76 10.86 1 TD 1 Int; KR 4-52 13.0.

		Rushing				Receiving					Tot
Year Team	**G**	**Att**	**Yds**	**Avg**	**TD**	**Rec**	**Yds**	**Avg**	**TD**	**Fum**	**TD**
1977 Sea	14	99	369	3.7	5	12	176	14.7	3	6	8
1978 Sea	12	174	752	4.3	**14**	30	195	6.5	1	4	**15**
1979 Sea	3	20	53	2.7	0	4	28	7.0	0	2	0
NFL Total	29	293	1174	4.0	19	46	399	8.7	4	12	23

GEORGE SIMS Sims, George P 5'11", 170 **DB**
(Gabby) *Col:* Baylor *HS:* Seymour [TX] B: 10/23/1927, Afton, TX
Drafted: 1949 Round 2 LARm

		Interceptions			
Year Team	**G**	**Int**	**Yds**	**TD**	**Fum**
1949 LARm	12	9	78	1	1
1950 LARm	9	1	5	0	0
NFL Total	21	10	83	1	1

JACK SIMS Sims, Jack Willard 6'3", 260 **OG**
Col: Santa Rosa JC CA; Hawaii *HS:* Radford [Honolulu, HI]
B: 4/21/1962, San Mateo, CA
1987 Sea: 3 G.

JIMMY SIMS Sims, James 6'0", 195 **LB**
Col: Los Angeles Harbor Coll. CA (J.C.); USC *HS:* Alain Leroy Locke [Los Angeles, CA] B: 12/28/1953, Galveston, TX
1976 TB: 2 G.

JOE SIMS Sims, Joseph Anthony 6'3", 302 **OT-OG**
Col: Nebraska *HS:* Lincoln-Sudbury Regional [Sudbury, MA]
B: 3/1/1969, Sudbury, MA *Drafted:* 1991 Round 11 Atl
1991 Atl: 6 G. **1992** GB: 15 G; KR 1-11 11.0. **1993** GB: 13 G. **1994** GB: 15 G. **1995** GB: 4 G. **Total:** 53 G; KR 1-11 11.0.

KEITH SIMS Sims, Keith Alexander 6'3", 309 **OG**
Col: Iowa State *HS:* Watchung Hills Regional [Warren, NJ]
B: 6/17/1967, Baltimore, MD *Drafted:* 1990 Round 2 Mia
1990 Mia: 14 G; KR 1-9 9.0. **1991** Mia: 12 G; Rec 1-9 9.0. **1992** Mia: 16 G. **1993** Mia: 16 G. **1994** Mia: 16 G. **1995** Mia: 16 G. **1996** Mia: 15 G. **1997** Mia: 8 G. **1998** Was: 4 G. **Total:** 117 G; Rec 1-9 9.0; KR 1-9 9.0.

KEN SIMS Sims, Kenneth L 5'9", 177 **DB**
Col: Iowa *HS:* Lincoln [East St. Louis, IL] B: 11/9/1963, East St. Louis, IL
1987 StL: 3 G.

KENNETH SIMS Sims, Kenneth Wayne 6'5", 272 **DE**
Col: Texas *HS:* Groesbeck [TX] B: 10/31/1959, Kosse, TX
Drafted: 1982 Round 1 NE
1982 NE: 9 G; 3 Sac. **1983** NE: 5 G. **1984** NE: 16 G; 3.5 Sac. **1985** NE: 13 G; 5.5 Sac. **1986** NE: 3 G; 0.5 Sac. **1987** NE: 12 G; 1.5 Sac. **1988** NE: 1 G. **1989** NE: 15 G; 3 Sac. **Total:** 74 G; 17 Sac.

MARVIN SIMS Sims, Marvin 6'4", 234 **FB**
Col: Clemson *HS:* Pacelli [Columbus, GA] B: 6/8/1957, Columbus, GA
Drafted: 1980 Round 12 Bal
1980 Bal: Rec 9-64 7.1; KR 1-10 10.0. **1981** Bal: KR 1-22 22.0.
Total: Rec 9-64 7.1; KR 2-32 16.0.

		Rushing			
Year Team	**G**	**Att**	**Yds**	**Avg**	**TD**
1980 Bal	16	54	186	3.4	2
1981 Bal	16	0	0	—	0
NFL Total	32	54	186	3.4	2

REGGIE SIMS Sims, Reginald Kenneth 6'4", 253 **TE**
Col: Northern Illinois *HS:* Rockford West [IL] B: 7/30/1962, Waynesboro, GA
1987 Cin: 1 G.

MICKEY SIMS Sims, Robert Anderson 6'5", 278 **DT**
Col: South Carolina State *HS:* Lockhart [SC] B: 3/5/1955, Union, SC
Drafted: 1977 Round 4 Cle
1977 Cle: 12 G. **1978** Cle: 15 G. **1979** Cle: 16 G. **Total:** 43 G.

TOMMY SIMS Sims, Thomas Edward 6'0", 190 **DB**
Col: Tennessee *HS:* Americus [GA] B: 9/29/1964, Americus, GA
Drafted: 1986 Round 7 Ind
1986 Ind: 1 G.

TOM SIMS Sims, Thomas Sidney 6'2", 291 **DT-NT**
Col: Western Michigan; Pittsburgh *HS:* Cass Tech [Detroit, MI]
B: 4/18/1967, Detroit, MI *Drafted:* 1990 Round 6 KC
1991 KC: 14 G. **1992** KC: 12 G; 3 Sac. **1993** Ind: 5 G; 1 Sac. **1994** Ind: 16 G. **Total:** 47 G; 4 Sac.

WILLIAM SIMS Sims, William Alfred 6'3", 258 **LB**
Col: Southwestern Louisiana *HS:* Brooks Co. [Quitman, GA]
B: 12/30/1970, Frankfurt, Germany
1994 Min: 8 G.

KASEEM SINCENO Sinceno, Kaseem T 6'4", 259 **TE**
Col: Syracuse *HS:* Liberty [NY] B: 3/26/1976, Bronx, NY
1998 Phi: 10 G; Rec 3-42 14.0 1 TD; 6 Pt; 1 Fum.

MICHAEL SINCLAIR Sinclair, Michael Glenn 6'4", 267 **DE**
Col: Eastern New Mexico *HS:* Charlton-Pollard [Beaumont, TX]
B: 1/31/1968, Galveston, TX *Drafted:* 1991 Round 6 Sea
1992 Sea: 12 G; 1 Sac. **1993** Sea: 9 G; 8 Sac. **1994** Sea: 12 G; 4.5 Sac. **1995** Sea: 16 G; 5.5 Sac. **1996** Sea: 16 G; 13 Sac. **1997** Sea: 16 G; 1 Fum TD; 6 Pt; 12 Sac. **1998** Sea: 16 G; **16.5** Sac. **Total:** 97 G; 1 Fum TD; 6 Pt; 60.5 Sac.

CURT SINGER Singer, Curt Edward 6'5", 278 **OT**
Col: Tennessee *HS:* Hopewell [Aliquippa, PA] B: 11/4/1961, Aliquippa, PA *Drafted:* 1984 Round 6 Was
1986 Sea: 11 G. **1988** Det: 3 G. **1989** NYJ: 6 G. **1991** Sea: 13 G.
Total: 33 G.

KARL SINGER Singer, Karl Kenneth 6'3", 250 **OT**
Col: Purdue *HS:* McKinley [Niles, OH] B: 10/12/1943, Warren, OH
Drafted: 1966 Round 1 Bos
1966 Bos: 14 G; KR 1-27 27.0. **1967** Bos: 14 G; KR 2-29 14.5; 1 Fum.
1968 Bos: 11 G. **Total:** 39 G; KR 3-56 18.7; 1 Fum.

WALT SINGER Singer, Walter Wallace 6'0", 198 **OE-DE**
Col: Syracuse *HS:* William L. Dickinson [Jersey City, NJ] B: 12/6/1911, Jersey City, NJ D: 2/5/1992, New York, NY
1935 NYG: 10 G; Rec 2-22 11.0 1 TD; 6 Pt. **1936** NYG: 12 G; Rec 6-38 6.3; **1** Fum TD; 6 Pt. **Total:** 22 G; Rec 8-60 7.5 1 TD; 1 Fum TD; Tot TD 2; 12 Pt.

MIKE SINGLETARY Singletary, Michael 6'0", 230 **LB**
Col: Baylor *HS:* Evan E. Worthing [Houston, TX] B: 10/9/1958, Houston, TX *Drafted:* 1981 Round 2 ChiB *HOF:* 1998
1981 ChiB: 16 G; Int 1-(-3). **1982** ChiB: 9 G; 1 Sac. **1983** ChiB: 16 G; Int 1-0; 3.5 Sac. **1984** ChiB: 16 G; Int 1-4; 3.5 Sac. **1985** ChiB: 16 G; Int 1-23; 3 Sac. **1986** ChiB: 14 G; Int 1-3; 2 Sac. **1987** ChiB: 12 G; 2 Sac. **1988** ChiB: 16 G; Int 1-13; 1 Sac. **1989** ChiB: 16 G; 1 Sac. **1990** ChiB: 16 G; 1 Sac. **1991** ChiB: 16 G. **1992** ChiB: 16 G; Int 1-4; 1 Sac.
Total: 179 G; Int 7-44; 19 Sac.

REGGIE SINGLETARY Singletary, Reggie Leslie 6'3", 279 **OG-OT-DT**
Col: North Carolina State *HS:* West Columbus [Cerro Gordo, NC]
B: 1/17/1964, Whiteville, NC *Drafted:* 1986 Round 12 Phi
1986 Phi: 16 G; 1 Sac. **1987** Phi: 12 G; Rec 1-(-11) -11.0. **1988** Phi: 16 G. **1989** Phi: 1 G. **1990** Phi: 16 G. **Total:** 61 G; Rec 1-(-11) -11.0; 1 Sac.

BILL SINGLETARY Singletary, William James 6'2", 233 **LB**
Col: Temple *HS:* Woodrow Wilson [Camden, NJ] B: 3/18/1951, Camden, NJ *Drafted:* 1973 Round 4 SD
1974 NYG: 3 G.

ALSHERMOND SINGLETON Singleton, Alshermond Glendale 6'2", 227 **LB**
Col: Temple *HS:* Frank H. Morrell [Irvington, NJ] B: 8/7/1975, Newark, NJ *Drafted:* 1997 Round 4 TB
1997 TB: 12 G; 6 Pt. **1998** TB: 15 G. **Total:** 27 G; 6 Pt.

CHRIS SINGLETON Singleton, Chris 6'2", 246 **LB**
Col: Arizona *HS:* Parsippany Hills [Morris Plains, NJ] B: 2/20/1967, Parsippany, NJ *Drafted:* 1990 Round 1 NE
1990 NE: 13 G; 3 Sac. **1991** NE: 12 G; 1 Sac. **1992** NE: 8 G; Int 1-82 1 TD; 6 Pt. **1993** NE-Mia: 17 G. NE: 8 G. Mia: 9 G. **1994** Mia: 11 G; 2 Sac. **1995** Mia: 15 G; Int 1-3; 1 Sac. **1996** Mia: 14 G. **Total:** 90 G; Int 2-85 1 TD; 6 Pt; 7 Sac.

JOHN SINGLETON Singleton, John Edward 5'11", 175 **TB-WB**
(Sheriff; Jack) *Col:* No College B: 11/27/1896, Gallipolis, OH
D: 10/23/1937, Dayton, OH
1929 Day: 5 G.

NATE SINGLETON Singleton, Nathaniel III 5'11", 190 **WR**
Col: Grambling State *HS:* L.W. Higgins [Marrero, LA] B: 7/5/1968, New Orleans, LA *Drafted:* 1992 Round 11 NYG
1994 SF: PR 2-13 6.5; KR 2-23 11.5. **1995** SF: PR 5-27 5.4. **1996** SF: PR 2-32 16.0; KR 1-10 10.0. **1997** Bal: KR 4-64 16.0. **Total:** PR 9-72 8.0; KR 7-97 13.9.

		Receiving				
Year Team	**G**	**Rec**	**Yds**	**Avg**	**TD**	**Fum**
1993 SF	16	8	126	15.8	1	0
1994 SF	16	21	294	14.0	2	0
1995 SF	6	8	108	13.5	1	1
1996 SF	2	1	11	11.0	0	0
1997 Bal	4	0	0	—	0	0
NFL Total	44	38	539	14.2	4	1

RON SINGLETON Singleton, Ronald Lee 6'7", 260 **OT**
Col: Grambling State *HS:* West Jefferson [Harvey, LA] B: 4/15/1952, New Orleans, LA *Drafted:* 1976 Round 4 SD
1976 SD: 13 G. **1977** SF: 1 G. **1978** SF: 14 G. **1979** SF: 16 G. **1980** SF: 15 G. **Total:** 59 G.

BILL SINGLETON Singleton, William 5'9", 190 **G**
Col: Washington-St. Louis B: 2/7/1897 D: 10/1971, Sycamore, IL
1922 Ham: 1 G.

STEVE SINKO Sinko, Stephen Patrick 6'3", 232 **T-G**
Col: Duquesne *HS:* Chisholm [MN] B: 9/15/1910, Chisholm, MN
1934 Bos: 10 G. **1935** Bos: 9 G. **1936** Bos: 11 G. **Total:** 30 G.

FRANK SINKOVITZ Sinkovitz, Frank Bernard 6'1", 218 **LB-C**
Col: Duke *HS:* John Harris [Harrisburg, PA] B: 5/20/1923, Steelton, PA
D: 8/6/1989, Baltimore, MD

		Interceptions		
Year Team	**G**	**Int**	**Yds**	**TD**
1947 Pit	9	3	57	1
1948 Pit	9	1	65	0
1949 Pit	12	1	54	0
1950 Pit	11	2	24	0
1951 Pit	12	2	6	0
1952 Pit	11	1	5	0
NFL Total	64	10	211	1

FRANKIE SINKWICH Sinkwich, Francis Frank 5'11", 190 **TB-DB-HB**
(Fireball) *Col:* Georgia *HS:* Chaney [Youngstown, OH] B: 10/10/1920, McKees Rocks, PA D: 10/22/1990, Athens, GA *Drafted:* 1943 Round 1 Det
AAFC **1946** NY-A: Pass 12-5 41.7%, 61 5.08 2 Int. **1947** NY-A-BalA: Pass 15-8 53.3%, 93 6.20; Rec 1-3 3.0; PR 1-15 15.0; KR 5-118 23.6; Punt 7-260 37.1. **Total:** Pass 27-13 48.1%, 154 5.70 2 Int; Rec 1-3 3.0; PR 1-15 15.0; KR 5-118 23.6; Punt 7-260 37.1.

		Rushing			
Year Team	**G**	**Att**	**Yds**	**Avg**	**TD**
1946 NY-A	4	7	20	2.9	0
1947 NY-A-BalA	11	71	241	3.4	0
AAFC Total	15	78	261	3.3	0

NFL **1943** Det: Rec 1-8 8.0; PR 11-**228 20.7**; KR 5-128 25.6; Int 1-39 **1** TD; Scor 12, 0-1 FG. **1944** Det: PR 11-148 13.5; KR 6-144 24.0; Int 3-28; Scor 66, 2-8 25.0% FG, 24-30 80.0% XK. **Total:** Rec 1-8 8.0; PR 22-376 17.1; KR 11-272 24.7; Int 4-67 1 TD; Scor 78, 2-9 22.2% FG, 24-30 80.0% XK.

		Passing							
Year Team	**G**	**Att**	**Comp**	**Comp%**	**Yds**	**YPA**	**TD**	**Int**	**Rating**
1943 Det	10	126	50	39.7	699	5.55	7	20	37.2
1944 Det	10	148	58	39.2	1060	7.16	12	20	52.0
NFL Total	20	274	108	39.4	1759	6.42	19	40	45.2

	Rushing				Punting			Tot
Year Team	**Att**	**Yds**	**Avg**	**TD**	**Punts**	**Yds**	**Avg**	**TD**
1943 Det	93	266	2.9	1	12	551	**45.9**	2
1944 Det	150	563	3.8	6	45	1845	41.0	6
NFL Total	243	829	3.4	7	57	2396	42.0	8

GREG SINNOTT Sinnott, Edward Greg 6'7", 280 **OT**
Col: Utah State *HS:* Marello Prep [Felton, CA] B: 8/29/1964, Santa Cruz, CA
1987 LARm: 1 G.

JOHN SINNOTT Sinnott, John Desmond 6'4", 275 **OT**
Col: Brown *HS:* Dedham [MA] B: 4/18/1958, Wexford, Ireland
Drafted: 1980 Round 3 StL
1982 Bal: 9 G.

BRIAN SIPE Sipe, Brian Winfield 6'1", 195 **QB**
Col: Grossmont Coll. CA (J.C.); San Diego State *HS:* Grossmont [La Mesa, CA] B: 8/8/1949, San Diego, CA *Drafted:* 1972 Round 13 Cle
1976 Cle: Scor **1** 1XP. **Total:** Scor 1 1XP.

		Passing							
Year Team	**G**	**Att**	**Comp**	**Comp%**	**Yds**	**YPA**	**TD**	**Int**	**Rating**
1974 Cle	10	108	59	54.6	603	5.58	1	7	47.0
1975 Cle	7	88	45	51.1	427	4.85	1	3	54.5
1976 Cle	14	312	178	57.1	2113	6.77	17	14	77.3
1977 Cle	9	195	112	57.4	1233	6.32	9	14	61.8
1978 Cle	16	399	222	55.6	2906	7.28	21	15	80.7
1979 Cle	16	535	286	53.5	3793	7.09	**28**	26	73.4
1980 Cle	16	554	337	60.8	4132	7.46	30	14	**91.4**
1981 Cle	16	567	313	55.2	3876	6.84	17	25	68.2
1982 Cle	6	185	101	54.6	1064	5.75	4	8	60.7
1983 Cle	15	496	291	58.7	3566	7.19	26	23	79.1
NFL Total	125	3439	1944	56.5	23713	6.90	154	149	74.8

	Rushing				
Year Team	**Att**	**Yds**	**Avg**	**TD**	**Fum**
1974 Cle	16	44	2.8	4	8
1975 Cle	9	60	6.7	0	1
1976 Cle	18	71	3.9	0	7
1977 Cle	10	14	1.4	0	4
1978 Cle	28	87	3.1	3	**12**
1979 Cle	45	178	4.0	2	10
1980 Cle	20	55	2.8	1	3
1981 Cle	38	153	4.0	1	10
1982 Cle	13	44	3.4	0	1
1983 Cle	26	56	2.2	0	6
NFL Total	223	762	3.4	11	62

TONY SIRAGUSA Siragusa, Anthony 6'3", 330 **NT-DT**
(The Goose) *Col:* Pittsburgh *HS:* David Brearly Regional [Kenilworth, NJ] B: 5/14/1967, Kenilworth, NJ
1990 Ind: 13 G; 1 Sac. **1991** Ind: 13 G; 2 Sac. **1992** Ind: 16 G; 3 Sac. **1993** Ind: 14 G; 1.5 Sac. **1994** Ind: 16 G; 5 Sac. **1995** Ind: 14 G; 2 Sac. **1996** Ind: 10 G; 2 Sac. **1997** Bal: 14 G. **1998** Bal: 15 G. **Total:** 125 G; 16.5 Sac.

GEORGE SIROCHMAN Sirochman, George Jr. 6'2", 215 **G**
Col: Duquesne *HS:* Centerville [OH] B: 3/23/1918, Maxwell, PA
D: 1/2/1996, Washington, PA
1942 Pit: 2 G. **1944** Det: 9 G. **Total:** 11 G.

JERRY SISEMORE Sisemore, Jerald Grant 6'4", 265 **OT-OG**
Col: Texas *HS:* Plainview [TX] B: 7/16/1951, Olton, TX *Drafted:* 1973 Round 1 Phi
1973 Phi: 13 G. **1974** Phi: 14 G. **1975** Phi: 14 G; KR 1-15 15.0. **1976** Phi: 14 G. **1977** Phi: 14 G. **1978** Phi: 16 G. **1979** Phi: 16 G. **1980** Phi: 16 G. **1981** Phi: 16 G. **1982** Phi: 7 G. **1983** Phi: 14 G. **1984** Phi: 2 G. **Total:** 156 G; KR 1-15 15.0.

JOHN SISK Sisk, John Martin Jr. 6'3", 195 **DB**
Col: Marquette; Miami (Fla.) *HS:* Marquette [Wauwatosa, WI]
B: 7/15/1941, Milwaukee, WI *Drafted:* 1963 Round 17 ChiB
1964 ChiB: 3 G.

JOHNNY SISK Sisk, John Martin Sr. 6'2", 197 **HB**
(Big Train) *Col:* Marquette *HS:* St. Viator's Acad. [Kankakee, IL]
B: 12/11/1905, New Haven, CT D: 5/27/1986, Wauwatosa, WI
1932 ChiB: Pass 3-1 33.3%, 8 2.67; Rec 3-32 10.7. **1933** ChiB: Pass 1-0; Rec 5-93 18.6. **1934** ChiB: Pass 9-2 22.2%, 13 1.44 2 Int; Rec 2-44 22.0.

1935 ChiB: Pass 1-1 100.0%, -1 -1.00; Rec 1-44 44.0. **1936** ChiB: Rec 1-39 39.0. **Total:** Pass 14-4 28.6%, 20 1.43 2 Int; Rec 12-252 21.0.

		Rushing			
Year Team	G	Att	Yds	Avg	TD
1932 ChiB	13	28	124	4.4	0
1933 ChiB	13	52	219	4.2	1
1934 ChiB	8	41	166	4.0	1
1935 ChiB	12	38	222	5.8	1
1936 ChiB	10	41	163	4.0	0
NFL Total	56	200	894	4.5	3

BRIAN SISLEY Sisley, Brian 6'4", 235 **DE**
Col: South Dakota State *HS:* Edgemont [SD] B: 1/18/1964, Hot Springs, AR
1987 NYG: 3 G.

SCOTT SISSON Sisson, Scott O'Neal 6'0", 197 **K**
Col: Georgia Tech *HS:* Marietta [GA] B: 7/21/1971, Marietta, GA
Drafted: 1993 Round 5 NE

		Scoring						
Year Team	G	Pts	FG	FGA	FG%	XK	XKA	XK%
1993 NE	13	57	14	26	53.8	15	15	100.0
1996 Min	16	96	22	29	75.9	30	30	100.0
NFL Total	29	153	36	55	65.5	45	45	100.0

MANNY SISTRUNK Sistrunk, Manuel 6'5", 269 **DT-DE**
Col: Arkansas-Pine Bluff *HS:* Booker T. Washington [Montgomery, AL] B: 6/16/1947, Montgomery, AL *Drafted:* 1970 Round 5 Was
1970 Was: 10 G. **1971** Was: 14 G. **1972** Was: 12 G. **1973** Was: 12 G. **1974** Was: 2 G. **1975** Was: 13 G. **1976** Phi: 14 G. **1977** Phi: 14 G. **1978** Phi: 16 G. **1979** Phi: 16 G. **Total:** 123 G.

OTIS SISTRUNK Sistrunk, Otis 6'4", 265 **DT-DE-NT**
Col: No College *HS:* William H. Spencer [Columbus, GA] B: 9/18/1946, Columbus, GA
1972 Oak: 14 G; Int 1-0. **1973** Oak: 14 G. **1974** Oak: 14 G; Int 1-2; Scor **1** Saf; 2 Pt. **1975** Oak: 14 G. **1976** Oak: 14 G. **1977** Oak: 12 G; Int 1-0. **1978** Oak: 16 G. **Total:** 98 G; Int 3-2; Scor 1 Saf; 2 Pt.

VINNIE SITES Sites, Vincent J 6'2", 215 **OE-DE**
Col: Pittsburgh *HS:* St.John's [Pittston, PA]; Wyoming Seminary [Kingston, PA] B: 7/9/1912, Pittston, PA D: 9/12/1983, San Diego, CA
1936 Pit: 12 G; Rec 2-22 11.0. **1937** Pit: 7 G; Rec 2-10 5.0. **Total:** 19 G; Rec 4-32 8.0.

EMIL SITKO Sitko, Emil Martin 5'8", 183 **HB**
(Red; 6-Yard) *Col:* Notre Dame *HS:* Central [Fort Wayne, IN] B: 9/7/1923, Fort Wayne, IN D: 12/15/1973, Fort Wayne, IN
Drafted: 1946 Round 1 LARm
1950 SF: Rec 3-43 14.3 1 TD. **1951** ChiC: Rec 4-28 7.0; KR 17-429 25.2. **1952** ChiC: Rec 2-16 8.0; KR 1-19 19.0. **Total:** Rec 9-87 9.7 1 TD; KR 18-448 24.9.

		Rushing					Tot
Year Team	G	Att	Yds	Avg	TD	Fum	TD
1950 SF	8	23	105	4.6	1	1	2
1951 ChiC	11	52	183	3.5	0	3	0
1952 ChiC	11	88	348	4.0	1	3	1
NFL Total	30	163	636	3.9	2	7	3

JIM SIVELL Sivell, Ralph James 5'9", 205 **G**
(Happy) *Col:* Auburn *HS:* Monroe Acad. [Forsyth, GA] B: 3/12/1914, Pine Mountain, GA *Drafted:* 1938 Round 8 Bkn
AAFC **1946** MiaA: 10 G.

NFL **1938** Bkn: 11 G. **1939** Bkn: 10 G. **1940** Bkn: 11 G. **1941** Bkn: 11 G. **1942** Bkn: 8 G. **1944** Bkn-NYG: 10 G. Bkn: 5 G. NYG: 5 G. **1945** NYG: 9 G. **Total:** 70 G.

MIKE SIWEK Siwek, Michael Joseph 6'3", 265 **DT**
Col: Western Michigan *HS:* St. Joseph's [South Bend, IN] B: 4/12/1948, Mishawaka, IN *Drafted:* 1970 Round 11 StL
1970 StL: 2 G.

JIM SKAGGS Skaggs, James Lee 6'3", 250 **OG-OT**
Col: Washington *HS:* Arroyo Grande [CA] B: 1/3/1940, Wetumka, OK
Drafted: 1962 Round 10 Phi
1963 Phi: 3 G. **1964** Phi: 14 G. **1965** Phi: 14 G. **1966** Phi: 14 G. **1967** Phi: 14 G. **1969** Phi: 7 G. **1970** Phi: 14 G. **1971** Phi: 10 G. **1972** Phi: 10 G. **Total:** 100 G.

PAUL SKANSI Skansi, Paul Anthony 5'11", 186 **WR**
Col: Washington *HS:* Peninsula [Gig Harbor, WA] B: 1/11/1960, Tacoma, WA *Drafted:* 1983 Round 5 Pit
1985 Sea: KR 19-358 18.8. **1986** Sea: KR 1-21 21.0. **Total:** KR 20-379 19.0.

		Receiving				Punt Returns				
Year Team	G	Rec	Yds	Avg	TD	Ret	Yds	Avg	TD	Fum
1983 Pit	15	3	39	13.0	0	43	363	8.4	0	5
1984 Sea	7	7	85	12.1	0	16	145	9.1	0	0
1985 Sea	12	21	269	12.8	1	31	312	10.1	0	1
1986 Sea	16	22	271	12.3	0	5	38	7.6	0	1
1987 Sea	12	19	207	10.9	1	0	0	—	0	1
1988 Sea	16	24	238	9.9	1	0	0	—	0	0
1989 Sea	16	39	488	12.5	5	0	0	—	0	0
1990 Sea	16	22	257	11.7	2	0	0	—	0	0
1991 Sea	5	9	96	10.7	0	1	5	5.0	0	1
NFL Total	115	166	1950	11.7	10	96	863	9.0	0	9

DARYLE SKAUGSTAD Skaugstad, Daryle Eugene 6'5", 254 **NT**
Col: California *HS:* Mount Rainier [Des Moines, WA] B: 4/8/1957, Seattle, WA *Drafted:* 1980 Round 2 Hou
1981 Hou: 16 G. **1982** Hou: 9 G; 3 Sac. **1983** SF-GB: 12 G. SF: 3 G. GB: 9 G. **Total:** 37 G; 3 Sac.

GIL SKEATE Skeate, Gilbert 5'10", 190 **FB**
Col: Gonzaga *HS:* J.M. Weatherwax [Aberdeen, WA] B: 5/19/1901 D: 1/1952
1927 GB: 2 G.

DOUG SKENE Skene, Douglas C 6'6", 295 **OG**
Col: Michigan *HS:* Allen Fairview [Fairview, TX] B: 6/17/1970, Fairview, TX *Drafted:* 1993 Round 8 Phi
1994 NE: 6 G.

JOHN SKIBINSKI Skibinski, John Joseph 6'0", 222 **RB**
Col: Purdue *HS:* La Salle-Peru Twp. [La Salle, IL] B: 4/27/1955, Chicago, IL *Drafted:* 1978 Round 6 ChiB
1978 ChiB: 16 G; KR 3-36 12.0. **1979** ChiB: 1 G; Rush 3-10 3.3; Rec 1-4 4.0. **1980** ChiB: 16 G; Rush 13-54 4.2; Rec 5-18 3.6. **1981** ChiB: 11 G. **Total:** 44 G; Rush 16-64 4.0; Rec 6-22 3.7; KR 3-36 12.0.

JOE SKIBINSKI Skibinski, Joseph John 5'11", 245 **OG**
(Skiba-Joe) *Col:* Purdue *HS:* Chicago Vocational [IL] B: 12/23/1928, Chicago, IL *Drafted:* 1951 Round 15 Cle
1952 Cle: 12 G; PR 0-5; KR 1-8 8.0. **1955** GB: 12 G. **1956** GB: 12 G. **Total:** 36 G; PR 0-5; KR 1-8 8.0.

GERALD SKINNER Skinner, Gerald Lynn 6'4", 260 **OT**
Col: Arkansas *HS:* Malvern [AR] B: 9/12/1954, Malvern, AR
Drafted: 1977 Round 4 NE
1978 GB: 15 G.

LEW SKINNER Skinner, Lewis B **G-C**
Col: Purdue B: 11/1898, Indianapolis, IN Deceased
1920 Ham: 1 G. **1922** Eva: 1 G. **Total:** 2 G.

JOE SKLADANY Skladany, Joseph Peter 5'10", 210 **OE-DE**
(Muggsy) *Col:* Pittsburgh *HS:* Larksville [PA] B: 5/25/1911, Larksville, PA
1934 Pit: 12 G; Rec 9-222 24.7 2 TD; 12 Pt.

LEO SKLADANY Skladany, Leo Bernard 6'2", 210 **DE**
(Scoop) *Col:* Pittsburgh *HS:* Larksville [PA]; Plymouth HS [PA] B: 8/9/1927, Larksville, PA *Drafted:* 1949 Round 17 Phi
1949 Phi: 3 G. **1950** NYG: 4 G. **Total:** 7 G.

TOM SKLADANY Skladany, Thomas Edward 6'0", 192 **P**
Col: Ohio State *HS:* Bethel Park [PA] B: 6/29/1955, Bethel Park, PA
Drafted: 1977 Round 2 Cle
1978 Det: Pass 1-0. **1979** Det: Pass 1-0. **1980** Det: Pass 2-2 100.0%, 38 19.00. **1981** Det: Pass 3-3 100.0%, 43 14.33. **1982** Det: Pass 1-0. **Total:** Pass 8-5 62.5%, 81 10.13.

		Punting		
Year Team	G	Punts	Yds	Avg
1978 Det	16	86	3654	42.5
1979 Det	2	10	406	40.6
1980 Det	16	72	3036	42.2
1981 Det	16	64	2784	43.5
1982 Det	7	36	1483	41.2
1983 Phi	4	27	1062	39.3
NFL Total	61	295	12425	42.1

JOHN SKLOPAN Sklopan, John Joseph 5'10", 200 **DB**
Col: Southern Mississippi B: 9/12/1940, Pittsburgh, PA *Drafted:* 1963 Round 8 KC
1963 Den: 3 G.

STAN SKOCZEN Skoczen, Stanley Edward 5'11", 187 **HB-DB**
(Skoz) *Col:* Case Western Reserve *HS:* Independence [OH] B: 10/12/1920, Independence, OH
1944 Cle: 1 G; Rush 1-0.

BOB SKOGLUND Skoglund, Robert Walter 6'1", 198 **DE**
Col: Notre Dame *HS:* Loyola Acad. [Chicago, IL] B: 7/29/1925, Chicago, IL D: 1/1/1949, Chicago, IL *Drafted:* 1947 Round 11 GB
1947 GB: 9 G.

NICK SKORICH Skorich, Nicholas Leonard 5'9", 197 **G-LB**
Col: Cincinnati *HS:* Bellaire [OH] B: 6/26/1921, Bellaire, OH
Drafted: 1943 Round 15 Pit
1946 Pit: 8 G. **1947** Pit: 12 G. **1948** Pit: 12 G. **Total:** 32 G.

ED SKORONSKI Skoronski, Edmund John 6'2", 213 **E-DE-C-LB**
(Rabbit) *Col:* Georgetown; Purdue *HS:* Bowen [Chicago, IL]
B: 10/15/1910, Chicago, IL
1935 Pit: 3 G. **1936** Pit: 12 G; Rec 8-95 11.9 1 TD; 6 Pt. **1937** Cle-Bkn: 8 G. Cle: 3 G. Bkn: 5 G. **Total:** 23 G; Rec 8-95 11.9 1 TD; 6 Pt.

BOB SKORONSKI Skoronski, Robert Francis 6'3", 249 **OT-C**
Col: Indiana *HS:* Derby [CT]; Fairfield Prep [CT]; Admiral Billard Acad. [New London, CT] B: 3/5/1934, Ansonia, CT *Drafted:* 1956 Round 5 GB
1956 GB: 12 G. **1959** GB: 12 G. **1960** GB: 12 G. **1961** GB: 13 G. **1962** GB: 13 G. **1963** GB: 14 G. **1964** GB: 14 G. **1965** GB: 14 G. **1966** GB: 14 G. **1967** GB: 14 G. **1968** GB: 14 G. **Total:** 146 G.

JOHN SKORUPAN Skorupan, John Paul 6'2", 222 **LB**
Col: Penn State *HS:* Beaver [PA] B: 5/17/1951, Beaver, PA
Drafted: 1973 Round 6 Buf
1973 Buf: 14 G. **1974** Buf: 6 G. **1975** Buf: 14 G; Int 1-0. **1976** Buf: 14 G; Int 1-13; 1 Fum. **1977** Buf: 2 G. **1978** NYG: 16 G; KR 4-52 13.0. **1979** NYG: 14 G; Scor 1 Saf; 2 Pt. **1980** NYG: 12 G. **Total:** 92 G; KR 4-52 13.0; Int 2-13; Scor 1 Saf; 2 Pt; 1 Fum.

JIM SKOW Skow, James Jeffrey 6'3", 253 **DE**
Col: Nebraska *HS:* Roncalli [Omaha, NE] B: 6/29/1963, Omaha, NE
Drafted: 1986 Round 3 Cin
1986 Cin: 16 G; 3 Sac. **1987** Cin: 12 G; 4.5 Sac. **1988** Cin: 16 G; 9.5 Sac. **1989** Cin: 11 G; 4.5 Sac. **1990** TB: 12 G; 2 Sac. **1991** Sea: 11 G; 0.5 Sac. **1992** SD-LARm: 5 G. SD: 1 G. LARm: 4 G. **Total:** 83 G; 24.0 Sac.

GREG SKREPENAK Skrepenak, Gregory Andrew 6'7", 316 **OT-OG**
Col: Michigan *HS:* G.A.R. Memorial [Wilkes-Barre, PA] B: 1/31/1970, Wilkes-Barre, PA *Drafted:* 1992 Round 2 LARd
1992 LARd: 10 G. **1994** LARd: 12 G. **1995** Oak: 14 G. **1996** Car: 16 G. **1997** Car: 16 G. **Total:** 68 G.

DAVE SKUDIN Skudin, Harry David 5'11", 195 **G-E**
Col: New York U. *HS:* Erasmus Hall [Brooklyn, NY] B: 1/21/1905, Brooklyn, NY D: 4/13/1972, New York, NY
1929 SI: 6 G.

LOU SLABY Slaby, Louis Richard 6'3", 235 **LB**
Col: Pittsburgh *HS:* Salem [OH] B: 12/13/1941, Cleveland, OH
Drafted: 1963 Round 5 NYG
1964 NYG: 14 G; Int 2-32. **1965** NYG: 12 G. **1966** Det: 13 G; KR 1-14 14.0. **Total:** 39 G; KR 1-14 14.0; Int 2-32.

FRITZ SLACKFORD Slackford, Frederick William 6'0", 180 **FB-WB-OE**
Col: Denison; Notre Dame *HS:* Sandusky [OH] B: 3/1894, Sandusky, OH Deceased
1920 Day: 6 G. **1921** Can: 10 G; Rush 2 TD; 12 Pt. **Total:** 16 G; Rush 2 TD; 12 Pt.

CHRIS SLADE Slade, Christopher Carroll 6'5", 245 **LB**
Col: Virginia *HS:* Tabb [Yorktown, VA] B: 1/30/1971, Newport News, VA *Drafted:* 1993 Round 2 NE
1993 NE: 16 G; 9 Sac. **1994** NE: 16 G; 9.5 Sac. **1995** NE: 16 G; **1** Fum TD; 6 Pt; 4 Sac. **1996** NE: 16 G; Int 1-2; 1 Fum; 7 Sac. **1997** NE: 16 G; Int 1-1 1 TD; 6 Pt; 9 Sac. **1998** NE: 15 G; 4 Sac. **Total:** 95 G; Int 2-3 1 TD; 1 Fum TD; Tot TD 2; 12 Pt; 1 Fum; 42.5 Sac.

GEORGE SLAGLE Slagle, George **G**
Col: No College B: 1899, SD Deceased
1926 Lou: 1 G.

DUKE SLATER Slater, Frederick Wayman 6'1", 215 **T**
Col: Iowa *HS:* Clinton [IA] B: 12/9/1898, Normal, IL D: 8/14/1966, Chicago, IL
1922 RI-Mil: 9 G. RI: 7 G. Mil: 2 G. **1923** RI: 8 G; Scor 1, 1 XK. **1924** RI: 8 G. **1925** RI: 11 G. **1926** ChiC: 2 G. **1927** ChiC: 11 G. **1928** ChiC: 6 G. **1929** ChiC: 13 G; Int **1** TD; 6 Pt. **1930** ChiC: 13 G. **1931** ChiC: 9 G. **Total:** 90 G; Int 1 TD.

HOWIE SLATER Slater, Howard Whitman 5'10", 186 **FB**
Col: Washington State *HS:* Deer Park [WA] B: 3/9/1903, Deer Park, WA Deceased
1926 Mil: 9 G; Int **1** TD; 6 Pt.

JACKIE SLATER Slater, Jackie Ray 6'4", 277 **OT-OG**
Col: Jackson State *HS:* Wingfield [Jackson, MS] B: 5/27/1954, Jackson, MS *Drafted:* 1976 Round 3 LARm
1976 LARm: 14 G. **1977** LARm: 14 G. **1978** LARm: 16 G. **1979** LARm: 16 G. **1980** LARm: 15 G. **1981** LARm: 11 G. **1982** LARm: 9 G. **1983** LARm: 16 G. **1984** LARm: 7 G. **1985** LARm: 16 G. **1986** LARm: 16 G. **1987** LARm: 12 G. **1988** LARm: 16 G. **1989** LARm: 16 G. **1990** LARm: 15 G. **1991** LARm: 13 G. **1992** LARm: 16 G. **1993** LARm: 8 G. **1994** LARm: 12 G. **1995** StL: 1 G. **Total:** 259 G.

MARK SLATER Slater, Mark William 6'2", 257 **C**
Col: Minnesota *HS:* Ryan [Minot, ND] B: 2/1/1955, Crosby, ND
Drafted: 1978 Round 12 Phi
1978 SD: 9 G; KR 1-3 3.0. **1979** Phi: 16 G. **1980** Phi: 16 G. **1981** Phi: 16 G. **1982** Phi: 9 G; KR 2-30 15.0. **1983** Phi: 16 G. **Total:** 82 G; KR 3-33 11.0.

WALT SLATER Slater, Walter Edward 5'11", 187 **TB-DB**
Col: Tennessee *HS:* Massanutten Mil. Acad. [Woodstock, VA]
B: 1/31/1920, Providence, RI *Drafted:* 1946 Round 3 Phi
1947 Pit: Pass 39-18 46.2%, 215 5.51 1 TD 5 Int; KR 22-480 21.8; Int 4-38.

		Rushing				Punt Returns				
Year Team	**G**	**Att**	**Yds**	**Avg**	**TD**	**Ret**	**Yds**	**Avg**	**TD**	**Fum**
1947 Pit	11	46	167	3.6	0	**28**	**435**	15.5	0	2

MIKE SLATON Slaton, Michael Lee 6'2", 194 **DB**
Col: South Dakota *HS:* West [Bellevue, NE] B: 9/25/1964, Sacramento, CA
1987 Min: 1 G.

TONY SLATON Slaton, Tony Tyrone 6'3", 265 **C-OG**
Col: USC *HS:* Merced [CA] B: 4/12/1961, Merced, CA *Drafted:* 1984 Round 6 Buf
1985 LARm: 13 G; KR 1-18 18.0. **1986** LARm: 14 G. **1987** LARm: 11 G. **1988** LARm: 15 G. **1989** LARm: 15 G. **1990** Dal: 6 G. **Total:** 74 G; KR 1-18 18.0.

CHUCK SLAUGHTER Slaughter, Charles Gary 6'5", 260 **OT**
Col: South Carolina *HS:* Fort Johnson [Charleston, SC] B: 11/21/1958, Conway, SC *Drafted:* 1982 Round 8 NO
1982 NO: 1 G.

MICKEY SLAUGHTER Slaughter, Milton Eugene 6'2", 204 **QB**
Col: Louisiana Tech *HS:* Bolton [Alexandria, LA] B: 8/22/1941, Monroe, LA *Drafted:* 1963 Round 7 Den
1964 Den: Scor 1 2XP. **Total:** Scor 1 2XP.

		Passing							
Year Team	**G**	**Att**	**Comp**	**Comp%**	**Yds**	**YPA**	**TD**	**Int**	**Rating**
1963 Den	13	223	112	50.2	1689	7.57	13	15	66.9
1964 Den	14	189	97	51.3	930	4.92	3	**11**	46.4
1965 Den	10	147	75	51.0	864	5.88	6	12	48.7
1966 Den	3	25	7	28.0	124	4.96	1	0	61.1
NFL Total	40	584	291	49.8	3607	6.18	23	38	55.4

	Rushing				
Year Team	**Att**	**Yds**	**Avg**	**TD**	**Fum**
1963 Den	29	127	4.4	1	7
1964 Den	20	54	2.7	0	7
1965 Den	20	75	3.8	0	5
1966 Den	1	10	10.0	0	1
NFL Total	70	266	3.8	1	20

WEBSTER SLAUGHTER Slaughter, Webster Melvin 6'1", 175 **WR**
Col: San Joaquin Delta Coll. CA (J.C.); San Diego State *HS:* Franklin [Stockton, CA] B: 10/19/1964, Stockton, CA *Drafted:* 1986 Round 2 Cle
1986 Cle: Rush 1-1 1.0; **1** Fum TD. **1990** Cle: Rush 5-29 5.8. **1992** Hou: Rush 3-20 6.7; KR 1-21 21.0. **Total:** Rush 9-50 5.6; KR 1-21 21.0; 1 Fum TD.

		Receiving				Punt Returns					Tot
Year Team	**G**	**Rec**	**Yds**	**Avg**	**TD**	**Ret**	**Yds**	**Avg**	**TD**	**Fum**	**TD**
1986 Cle	16	40	577	14.4	4	1	2	2.0	0	1	5
1987 Cle	12	47	806	17.1	7	0	0	—	0	1	7
1988 Cle	8	30	462	15.4	3	0	0	—	0	1	3
1989 Cle	16	65	1236	19.0	6	0	0	—	0	2	6
1990 Cle	16	59	847	14.4	4	0	0	—	0	2	4
1991 Cle	16	64	906	14.2	3	17	112	6.6	0	1	3
1992 Hou	12	39	486	12.5	4	20	142	7.1	0	3	4
1993 Hou	14	77	904	11.7	5	0	0	—	0	4	5
1994 Hou	16	68	846	12.4	2	0	0	—	0	2	2
1995 KC	16	34	514	15.1	4	0	0	—	0	0	4
1996 NYJ	10	32	434	13.6	2	0	0	—	0	0	2
1998 SD	10	8	93	11.6	0	0	0	—	0	0	0
NFL Total	162	563	8111	14.4	44	38	256	6.7	0	17	45

HENRY SLAY Slay, Henry 6'2", 290 **DT**
Col: West Virginia *HS:* West [Elyria, OH] B: 4/28/1975, Cleveland, OH
Drafted: 1998 Round 7 Atl
1998 Phi: 3 G.

LEROY SLEDGE Sledge, Leroy James Jr. 6'2", 230 **RB**
Col: Bakersfield Coll. CA (J.C.) *HS:* Maggie L. Walker [Richmond, VA]
B: 10/11/1946, Richmond, VA
1971 Hou: 6 G; Rush 24-74 3.1; Rec 6-32 5.3 1 TD; 6 Pt; 1 Fum.

RED SLEIGHT Sleight, Elmer Noble 6'2", 226 **T**
Col: Purdue *HS:* Morris [IL] B: 7/8/1907, Morris, IL D: 8/9/1978, Naples, FL
1930 GB: 13 G. **1931** GB: 13 G. **Total:** 26 G.

RICHARD SLIGH Sligh, Richard Ellis 7'0", 300 **DT**
Col: North Carolina Central *HS:* Gallman [Newberry, SC] B: 8/18/1944, Newberry, SC *Drafted:* 1967 Round 10 Oak
1967 Oak: 8 G.

STEVE SLIVINSKI Slivinski, Stephen Paul 5′10″, 214 **G-LB**
Col: Washington *HS:* Tilden [Chicago, IL] B: 8/23/1917, Cicero, IL
Drafted: 1939 Round 11 Was
1939 Was: 11 G. **1940** Was: 10 G. **1941** Was: 11 G; Int 1-20. **1942** Was: 11 G. **1943** Was: 10 G; Int 1-2. **Total:** 53 G; Int 2-22.

BONNIE SLOAN Sloan, Bonnie Ryan 6′5″, 260 **DT**
Col: Austin Peay State *HS:* Isaac Litton [Nashville, TN] B: 6/1/1948, Lebanon, TN *Drafted:* 1973 Round 10 StL
1973 StL: 4 G.

DAVID SLOAN Sloan, David Lyle 6′6″, 254 **TE**
Col: Fresno City Coll. CA (J.C.); New Mexico *HS:* Sierra [Tollhouse, CA]
B: 6/8/1972, Fresno, CA *Drafted:* 1995 Round 3 Det
1995 Det: KR 1-14 14.0. **Total:** KR 1-14 14.0.

		Receiving			
Year Team	**G**	**Rec**	**Yds**	**Avg**	**TD**
1995 Det	16	17	184	10.8	1
1996 Det	4	7	51	7.3	0
1997 Det	14	29	264	9.1	0
1998 Det	10	11	146	13.3	1
NFL Total	44	64	645	10.1	2

DWIGHT SLOAN Sloan, Dwight Henry 5′10″, 180 **TB-DB**
(Paddlefoot) *Col:* Arkansas *HS:* Alma [AR]; Van Buren HS [AR]
B: 4/7/1914, Rudy, AR *Drafted:* 1938 Round 8 ChiC
1938 ChiC: Rec 1-10 10.0. **1939** Det: Punt 1-43 43.0. **1940** Det: Int 1-4; Punt 2-54 27.0. **Total:** Rec 1-10 10.0; Int 1-4; Punt 3-97 32.3.

		Passing							
Year Team	**G**	**Att**	**Comp**	**Comp%**	**Yds**	**YPA**	**TD**	**Int**	**Rating**
1938 ChiC	10	79	37	46.8	333	4.22	1	7	26.0
1939 Det	10	102	45	44.1	658	6.45	2	3	60.0
1940 Det	11	46	18	39.1	260	5.65	0	8	18.7
NFL Total	31	227	100	44.1	1251	5.51	3	18	33.1

	Rushing			
Year Team	**Att**	**Yds**	**Avg**	**TD**
1938 ChiC	56	126	2.3	0
1939 Det	79	225	2.8	4
1940 Det	58	225	3.9	0
NFL Total	193	576	3.0	4

STEVE SLOAN Sloan, Stephen Charles 6′0″, 185 **QB**
Col: Alabama *HS:* Bradley [Cleveland, TN] B: 8/19/1944, Austin, TN
Drafted: 1966 Round 11 Atl
1966 Atl: 3 G; Pass 13-6 46.2%, 96 7.38 2 Int. **1967** Atl: 5 G; Pass 18-4 22.2%, 38 2.11 2 Int; Rush 1-2 2.0. **Total:** 8 G; Pass 31-10 32.3%, 134 4.32 4 Int; Rush 1-2 2.0.

PETE SLONE Slone, Peter J 5′8″, 160 **OE**
Col: No College B: 12/23/1896, Braddock, PA D: 8/1962
1921 Mun: 1 G.

PHIL SLOSBURG Slosburg, Philip Jay 5′10″, 170 **DB-HB-TB**
(Sonny) *Col:* Temple *HS:* Central Philadelphia [Philadelphia, PA]
B: 10/30/1926, Philadelphia, PA *Drafted:* 1948 Round 4 Bos
1948 Bos: Pass 20-8 40.0%, 119 5.95 1 TD 3 Int; Rec 2-29 14.5; PR 10-141 14.1; KR 1-37 37.0. **1949** NYB: Rec 4-11 2.8; PR 4-32 8.0; KR 4-98 24.5; Int 1-0. **Total:** Pass 20-8 40.0%, 119 5.95 1 TD 3 Int; Rec 6-40 6.7; PR 14-173 12.4; KR 5-135 27.0; Int 1-0.

		Rushing				
Year Team	**G**	**Att**	**Yds**	**Avg**	**TD**	**Fum**
1948 Bos	12	32	89	2.8	0	2
1949 NYB	3	37	121	3.3	1	2
NFL Total	15	69	210	3.0	1	4

ELMER SLOUGH Slough, Elmer Cumming 5′8″, 160 **BB-WB**
(Ben; Peanuts) *Col:* Oklahoma *HS:* Ardmore [OK] B: 7/19/1903, Madill, OK Deceased
1926 Buf: 8 G; Rec 2 TD; 12 Pt.

GREG SLOUGH Slough, Gregory C 6′3″, 230 **LB**
Col: San Diego City Coll. CA (J.C.); USC *HS:* Point Loma [San Diego, CA] B: 2/26/1948, Detroit, MI *Drafted:* 1971 Round 6 Oak
1971 Oak: 13 G. **1972** Oak: 9 G; KR 1-0. **Total:** 22 G; KR 1-0.

EMIL SLOVACEK Slovacek, Emil Raymond Jr. 6′3″, 300 **OT**
Col: Navarro Coll. TX (J.C.); Stephen F. Austin St. *HS:* St. John [Ennis, TX] B: 2/26/1963, Dallas, TX
1987 SD: 2 G.

MARTY SLOVAK Slovak, Martin 5′9″, 179 **TB-DB**
(Elliston Eel) *Col:* Toledo B: 12/25/1916, Newport, MI D: 3/22/1950, Toledo, OH
1939 Cle: Punt 1-15 15.0. **1940** Cle: Int 2-20. **1941** Cle: PR 4-30 7.5; KR 6-126 21.0. **Total:** PR 4-30 7.5; KR 6-126 21.0; Int 2-20; Punt 1-15 15.0.

		Passing							
Year Team	**G**	**Att**	**Comp**	**Comp%**	**Yds**	**YPA**	**TD**	**Int**	**Rating**
1939 Cle	10	27	13	48.1	97	3.59	2	5	42.3
1940 Cle	9	28	17	60.7	234	8.36	0	4	47.9
1941 Cle	8	54	27	50.0	307	5.69	2	9	40.2
NFL Total	27	109	57	52.3	638	5.85	4	18	42.7

	Rushing			
Year Team	**Att**	**Yds**	**Avg**	**TD**
1939 Cle	42	135	3.2	0
1940 Cle	53	129	2.4	1
1941 Cle	46	132	2.9	0
NFL Total	141	396	2.8	1

SCOTT SLUTZKER Slutzker, Scott Lawrence 6′4″, 250 **TE**
Col: Iowa *HS:* Hasbrouck Heights [NJ] B: 12/20/1972, Hasbrouck Heights, NJ *Drafted:* 1996 Round 3 Ind
1996 Ind: 15 G. **1997** Ind: 12 G; Rec 3-22 7.3. **1998** NO: 3 G; Rec 1-10 10.0. **Total:** 30 G; Rec 4-32 8.0.

BILL SLYKER Slyker, William Valentine 6′1″, 180 **E**
Col: Ohio State *HS:* Huron [OH] B: 2/14/1899, Huron, OH
D: 9/1/1949, Evansville, IN
1922 Eva: 1 G; Rec 1 TD; 6 Pt.

STAN SMAGALA Smagala, Stanley Adam 5′10″, 184 **DB**
Col: Notre Dame *HS:* St. Laurence [Burbank, IL] B: 4/6/1968, Chicago, IL *Drafted:* 1990 Round 5 LARd
1990 Dal: 3 G. **1991** Dal: 8 G. **Total:** 11 G.

ALEX SMAIL Smail, Alex 5′8″, 235 **LB**
Col: Detroit Mercy B: 5/31/1926
1952 Pit: 1 G.

DONOVAN SMALL Small, Donovan Oliver 5′11″, 190 **DB**
Col: Minnesota *HS:* Wheeling [IL] B: 7/10/1964, Kingston, Jamaica
1987 Hou: 1 G; Int 1-3.

ELDRIDGE SMALL Small, Eldridge 6′1″, 190 **DB**
Col: Texas A&M–Kingsville *HS:* Phillis Wheatley [Houston, TX]
B: 8/2/1949, Houston, TX *Drafted:* 1972 Round 1 NYG
1972 NYG: 14 G; KR 1-100 100.0. **1973** NYG: 8 G; KR 11-207 18.8. **1974** NYG: 12 G; KR 2-46 23.0; Int 1-0. **Total:** 34 G; KR 14-353 25.2; Int 1-0.

GEORGE SMALL Small, George Michael 6′2″, 260 **NT**
Col: Allegany CC MD; North Carolina A&T *HS:* Hoke Co. [Raeford, NC]
B: 11/18/1956, Shreveport, LA
1980 NYG: 7 G.

GERALD SMALL Small, Gerald David 5′11″, 192 **DB**
Col: San Jose State *HS:* Edwards AFB [Desert, CA] B: 8/10/1956, Washington, NC *Drafted:* 1978 Round 4 Mia

		Interceptions		
Year Team	**G**	**Int**	**Yds**	**TD**
1978 Mia	16	4	157	1
1979 Mia	16	5	74	0
1980 Mia	16	7	46	0
1981 Mia	16	0	0	0
1982 Mia	9	2	41	0
1983 Mia	15	5	60	0
1984 Atl	16	1	2	0
NFL Total	104	24	380	1

JESSIE SMALL Small, Jessie Lee 6′3″, 239 **LB**
Col: Eastern Kentucky *HS:* Central [Thomasville, GA] B: 11/30/1966, Boston, GA *Drafted:* 1989 Round 2 Phi
1989 Phi: 16 G. **1990** Phi: 15 G; 3.5 Sac. **1991** Phi: 16 G. **1992** Pho: 6 G. **Total:** 53 G; 3.5 Sac.

FRED SMALL Small, John Frederick 5′11″, 232 **LB**
Col: Washington *HS:* John C. Fremont [Los Angeles, CA]
B: 7/15/1963, Los Angeles, CA *Drafted:* 1985 Round 9 Pit
1985 Pit: 16 G.

JOHN SMALL Small, John Kenneth 6′4″, 269 **DT-LB**
Col: The Citadel *HS:* Richmond Acad. [Atlanta, GA] B: 11/20/1946, Lumberton, NC *Drafted:* 1970 Round 1 Atl
1970 Atl: 10 G. **1971** Atl: 14 G; KR 1-12 12.0. **1972** Atl: 9 G; PR 1-0. **1973** Det: 1 G. **1974** Det: 13 G. **Total:** 47 G; PR 1-0; KR 1-12 12.0.

TORRANCE SMALL Small, Torrance Ramon 6′3″, 209 **WR**
Col: Alcorn State *HS:* Thomas Jefferson [Tampa, FL] B: 9/6/1970, Tampa, FL *Drafted:* 1992 Round 5 NO
1994 NO: Scor 1 2XP. **1995** NO: Rush 6-75 12.5 1 TD. **1996** NO: Rush 4-51 12.8 1 TD. **1998** Ind: Pass 1-0; Rush 1-2 2.0. **Total:** Pass 1-0; Rush 11-128 11.6 2 TD; Scor 1 2XP.

		Receiving					Tot
Year Team	**G**	**Rec**	**Yds**	**Avg**	**TD**	**Fum**	**TD**
1992 NO	13	23	278	12.1	3	0	3

1993 NO	11	16	164	10.3	1	0	1
1994 NO	16	49	719	14.7	5	0	5
1995 NO	16	38	461	12.1	5	0	6
1996 NO	16	50	558	11.2	2	1	3
1997 StL	13	32	488	15.3	1	0	1
1998 Ind	16	45	681	15.1	7	0	7
NFL Total	101	253	3349	13.2	24	1	26

FRED SMALLS Smalls, Frederick 6′3″, 225 **LB**
(Boom Boom) *Col:* West Virginia *HS:* Battery Creek School [Beaufort, SC] B: 1/7/1963, Beaufort, SC
1987 Phi: 3 G; 2.5 Sac.

METZ SMEACH Smeach, Metzger Franklin 6′3″, 195 **T**
Col: Georgetown *HS:* Connellsville [PA] B: 6/1/1895, Connellsville, PA D: 5/26/1985, Garrettsville, OH
1921 Was: 3 G.

ERIC SMEDLEY Smedley, Eric Alan 5′11″, 199 **DB**
Col: Indiana *HS:* Capitol [Charleston, WV] B: 7/23/1973, Charleston, WV *Drafted:* 1996 Round 7 Buf
1996 Buf: 6 G. **1997** Buf: 13 G. **1998** Buf: 16 G; 2 Sac. **Total:** 35 G; 2 Sac.

JOEL SMEENGE Smeenge, Joel Andrew 6′6″, 262 **LB-DE**
Col: Western Michigan *HS:* Hudsonville [MI] B: 4/1/1968, Holland, MI *Drafted:* 1990 Round 3 NO
1990 NO: 15 G. **1991** NO: 14 G. **1992** NO: 11 G; 0.5 Sac. **1993** NO: 16 G; 1 Sac. **1994** NO: 16 G. **1995** Jac: 15 G; Int 1-12; 1 Fum; 4 Sac. **1996** Jac: 10 G; 5 Sac. **1997** Jac: 16 G; 6.5 Sac. **1998** Jac: 16 G; 7.5 Sac.
Total: 129 G; Int 1-12; 1 Fum; 24.5 Sac.

RUDY SMEJA Smeja, Rudolph M 6′2″, 195 **OE-DE**
Col: Michigan *HS:* Lindblom [Chicago, IL] B: 12/1/1920, Chicago, IL D: 10/1982 *Drafted:* 1944 Round 2 ChiB
1944 ChiB: 10 G; Rec 7-110 15.7 1 TD; KR 1-7 7.0; 6 Pt. **1945** ChiB: 8 G; Rec 1-11 11.0. **1946** Phi: 11 G; Rec 3-45 15.0; KR 1-12 12.0. **Total:** 29 G; Rec 11-166 15.1 1 TD; KR 2-19 9.5; 6 Pt.

DON SMEREK Smerek, Donald Frederick 6′7″, 255 **DT-DE**
Col: Nevada-Reno *HS:* Basic [Henderson, NV] B: 12/20/1957, Waterford, MI
1981 Dal: 2 G. **1982** Dal: 7 G; 1 Sac. **1983** Dal: 15 G; 6 Sac. **1984** Dal: 16 G; 1 Sac. **1985** Dal: 10 G; 2 Sac. **1986** Dal: 11 G; 4.5 Sac. **1987** Dal: 8 G. **Total:** 69 G; 14.5 Sac.

FRED SMERLAS Smerlas, Frederic Charles 6′3″, 277 **NT-DT**
Col: Boston College *HS:* Waltham [MA] B: 4/8/1957, Waltham, MA *Drafted:* 1979 Round 2 Buf
1979 Buf: 13 G; **1** Fum TD; 6 Pt. **1980** Buf: 16 G. **1981** Buf: 16 G. **1982** Buf: 9 G; 2 Sac. **1983** Buf: 16 G; 6 Sac. **1984** Buf: 16 G; Int 1-25; 2 Sac. **1985** Buf: 16 G; 0.5 Sac. **1986** Buf: 16 G; Int 1-3; 2 Sac. **1987** Buf: 12 G; 1 Sac. **1988** Buf: 16 G; 4 Sac. **1989** Buf: 16 G; 1 Sac. **1990** SF: 6 G. **1991** NE: 16 G. **1992** NE: 16 G. **Total:** 200 G; Int 2-28; 1 Fum TD; 6 Pt; 18.5 Sac.

DAVE SMIGELSKY Smigelsky, David William 5′11″, 180 **P**
Col: Virginia Tech *HS:* North Hunterdon [Annandale, NJ] B: 7/3/1959, Perth Amboy, NJ
1982 Atl: 6 G; Punt 26-1000 38.5.

BRANKO SMILANICH Smilanich, Branko Michael 5′11″, 180 **TB-DB**
Col: Arizona *HS:* Chisholm [MN] B: 10/7/1915, Chisholm, MN
1939 Cle: 2 G; Pass 2-1 50.0%, 11 5.50; Rush 1-(-3) -3.0.

TOMMIE SMILEY Smiley, Tommie Belton Jr. 6′1″, 235 **RB**
Col: Arizona; Lamar *HS:* Port Arthur [TX] B: 2/18/1944, Port Arthur, TX *Drafted:* 1968 Round 2 Cin
1968 Cin: Rec 19-86 4.5. **1969** Den: Rec 5-23 4.6 1 TD.
Total: Rec 24-109 4.5 1 TD.

		Rushing					Tot
Year Team	G	Att	Yds	Avg	TD	Fum	TD
1968 Cin	8	63	146	2.3	1	3	1
1969 Den	14	56	166	3.0	3	3	4
1970 Hou	7	1	0	0.0	0	0	0
NFL Total	29	120	312	2.6	4	6	5

AARON SMITH Smith, Aaron Clayton 6′2″, 223 **LB**
Col: Utah State *HS:* St. Bernard [Los Angeles, CA] B: 8/10/1962, Los Angeles, CA *Drafted:* 1984 Round 6 Den
1984 Den: 10 G; KR 1-2 2.0; 1 Fum.

AL SMITH Smith, Al Fredrick 6′1″, 244 **LB**
Col: Cal Poly-Pomona; Utah State *HS:* St. Bernard [Los Angeles, CA] B: 11/26/1964, Los Angeles, CA *Drafted:* 1987 Round 6 Hou
1987 Hou: 12 G. **1988** Hou: 16 G. **1989** Hou: 15 G. **1990** Hou: 15 G; 1 Sac. **1991** Hou: 16 G; Int 1-16; 1 Fum TD; 6 Pt; 1 Sac. **1992** Hou: 16 G; Int 1-26; 1 Fum; 1 Sac. **1993** Hou: 16 G. **1994** Hou: 16 G; 2.5 Sac. **1995** Hou: 2 G. **1996** Hou: 1 G. **Total:** 125 G; Int 2-42; 1 Fum TD; 6 Pt; 1 Fum; 5.5 Sac.

ALLEN SMITH Smith, Allen Duncan 5′11″, 202 **RB**
Col: Fort Valley State *HS:* Turner [Atlanta, GA] B: 11/20/1942, Fort Valley, GA *Drafted:* 1966 Round 15 Buf
1966 Buf: Rec 1-1 1.0. **1967** Buf: KR 16-346 21.6. **Total:** Rec 1-1 1.0; KR 16-346 21.6.

		Rushing				
Year Team	G	Att	Yds	Avg	TD	Fum
1966 Buf	14	31	148	4.8	0	0
1967 Buf	5	0	0	—	0	1
NFL Total	19	31	148	4.8	0	1

ALLEN SMITH Smith, Allen Tyrone 5′11″, 195 **HB**
Col: Findlay B: 10/7/1942, Chattanooga, TN *Drafted:* 1966 Redshirt Round 6 NYJ
1966 NYJ: 1 G.

ANTHONY SMITH Smith, Anthony Wayne 6′3″, 265 **DE**
Col: Alabama; Arizona *HS:* Northeastern [Elizabeth City, NC] B: 6/28/1967, Elizabeth City, NC *Drafted:* 1990 Round 1 LARd
1991 LARd: 16 G; 10.5 Sac. **1992** LARd: 15 G; 13 Sac. **1993** LARd: 16 G; 12.5 Sac. **1994** LARd: 16 G; 1 Fum TD; 6 Pt; 6 Sac. **1995** Oak: 16 G; 7 Sac. **1996** Oak: 6 G; 2 Sac. **1997** Oak: 13 G; Scor **1** Saf; 2 Pt; 6.5 Sac. **Total:** 98 G; Scor 1 Saf; 1 Fum TD; 8 Pt; 57.5 Sac.

ANTOWAIN SMITH Smith, Antowain 6′2″, 224 **RB**
(Pokey) *Col:* East Mississippi CC; Houston *HS:* Elmore Co. [Electric, AL] B: 3/14/1972, Montgomery, AL *Drafted:* 1997 Round 1 Buf

		Rushing				Receiving				
Year Team	G	Att	Yds	Avg	TD	Rec	Yds	Avg	TD	Fum
1997 Buf	16	194	840	4.3	8	28	177	6.3	0	4
1998 Buf	16	300	1124	3.7	8	5	11	2.2	0	5
NFL Total	32	494	1964	4.0	16	33	188	5.7	0	9

DOUG SMITH Smith, Arthur Douglas 6′4″, 294 **NT-DT**
Col: Auburn *HS:* Pamlico Co. [Bayboro, NC] B: 6/13/1959, Mesic, NC *Drafted:* 1984 Round 2 Hou
1985 Hou: 11 G; 2 Sac. **1986** Hou: 13 G; 2 Sac. **1987** Hou: 15 G; 3.5 Sac. **1988** Hou: 12 G; Int 1-20; 3 Sac. **1989** Hou: 15 G; 1 Sac. **1990** Hou: 14 G; 2 Sac. **1991** Hou: 15 G; 0.5 Sac. **1992** Hou: 6 G. **Total:** 101 G; Int 1-20; 14 Sac.

ART SMITH Smith, Arthur Henry Thompson 6′1″, 222 **LB**
Col: Hawaii *HS:* Radford [Honolulu, HI] B: 4/20/1956, Honolulu, HI
1980 Den: 2 G.

ARTIE SMITH Smith, Artie Enlow 6′5″, 296 **DE**
Col: Louisiana Tech *HS:* Stillwater [OK] B: 5/15/1970, Stillwater, OK *Drafted:* 1993 Round 5 SF
1993 SF: 16 G; 1.5 Sac. **1994** SF-Cin: 9 G. SF: 2 G. Cin: 7 G. **1995** Cin: 16 G; 2 Sac. **1996** Cin: 16 G; 1 Sac. **1998** Dal: 16 G. **Total:** 73 G; 4.5 Sac.

BARRY SMITH Smith, Barrett Benjamin 6′1″, 190 **WR**
Col: Florida State *HS:* Miami Coral Park [Miami, FL] B: 1/15/1951, West Palm Beach, FL *Drafted:* 1973 Round 1 GB
1973 GB: Rush 1-5 5.0. **Total:** Rush 1-5 5.0.

		Receiving			
Year Team	G	Rec	Yds	Avg	TD
1973 GB	14	15	233	15.5	2
1974 GB	14	20	294	14.7	1
1975 GB	13	6	77	12.8	1
1976 TB	13	4	88	22.0	0
NFL Total	54	45	692	15.4	4

BARTY SMITH Smith, Barton Elliott 6′3″, 240 **RB**
Col: Richmond *HS:* Douglas Freeman [Richmond, VA] B: 4/23/1952, Richmond, VA *Drafted:* 1974 Round 1 GB
1975 GB: KR 4-53 13.3. **1978** GB: KR 1-0. **Total:** KR 5-53 10.6.

		Rushing				Receiving					Tot
Year Team	G	Att	Yds	Avg	TD	Rec	Yds	Avg	TD	Fum	TD
1974 GB	8	9	19	2.1	0	0	0	—	0	0	0
1975 GB	14	60	243	4.1	4	16	140	8.8	1	2	5
1976 GB	8	97	355	3.7	5	11	88	8.0	0	4	5
1977 GB	14	166	554	3.3	2	37	340	9.2	1	1	3
1978 GB	16	154	567	3.7	4	37	256	6.9	0	5	4
1979 GB	6	57	201	3.5	3	19	155	8.2	1	1	4
1980 GB	1	1	3	3.0	0	0	0	—	0	0	0
NFL Total	67	544	1942	3.6	18	120	979	8.2	3	13	21

BEN SMITH Smith, Ben H Jr. 6′3″, 208 **OE-DE**
(Big Ben) *Col:* Alabama *HS:* Haleyville [AL] B: 6/16/1911, Haleyville, AL Deceased

		Receiving			
Year Team	G	Rec	Yds	Avg	TD
1933 GB	9	2	23	11.5	0
1934 Pit	11	14	218	15.6	0
1935 Pit	11	9	166	18.4	0

1937 Was	11	2	37	18.5	0
NFL Total	42	27	444	16.4	0

BEN SMITH Smith, Benjamin Joseph 5′11″, 185 **DB**
Col: Georgia *HS:* Warner Robins [GA] B: 5/14/1967, Warner Robins, GA *Drafted:* 1990 Round 1 Phi
1990 Phi: 16 G; Int 3-1. **1991** Phi: 10 G; Int 2-6. **1993** Phi: 13 G. **1994** Den: 14 G; Int 1-0. **1995** Ariz: 2 G. **1996** Ariz: 2 G; 1 Sac. **Total:** 57 G; Int 6-7; 1 Sac.

BILLY RAY SMITH Smith, Billy Ray Jr. 6′3″, 235 **LB**
Col: Arkansas *HS:* Plano [TX] B: 8/10/1961, Fayetteville, AR *Drafted:* 1983 Round 1 SD
1983 SD: KR 1-10 10.0; 3 Sac. **1984** SD: 3 Sac. **1985** SD: 2 Sac. **1986** SD: 11 Sac. **1987** SD: Pass 1-0, 1 Int; 3 Sac. **1988** SD: 1 Sac. **1989** SD: 1 Fum TD; 2.5 Sac. **1990** SD: 1 Sac. **Total:** Pass 1-0, 1 Int; KR 1-10 10.0; 1 Fum TD; 26.5 Sac.

		Interceptions		
Year Team	**G**	**Int**	**Yds**	**TD**
1983 SD	16	0	0	0
1984 SD	16	3	41	0
1985 SD	15	1	0	0
1986 SD	16	0	0	0
1987 SD	12	5	28	0
1988 SD	9	1	9	0
1989 SD	16	1	9	0
1990 SD	11	2	12	0
1991 SD	14	2	0	0
1992 SD	1	0	0	0
NFL Total	126	15	99	0

BILLY RAY SMITH Smith, Billy Ray Sr. 6′4″, 240 **DT-DE**
Col: Auburn; Arkansas *HS:* Conner [Augusta, AR] B: 1/27/1935, Augusta, AR *Drafted:* 1957 Round 1 LARm
1957 LARm: 12 G. **1958** Pit: 12 G; 1 Fum. **1959** Pit: 6 G. **1960** Pit: 12 G. **1961** Bal: 14 G. **1962** Bal: 13 G. **1964** Bal: 13 G. **1965** Bal: 14 G; Int 1-5. **1966** Bal: 14 G. **1967** Bal: 14 G. **1968** Bal: 14 G. **1969** Bal: 14 G. **1970** Bal: 14 G. **Total:** 166 G; Int 1-5; 1 Fum.

BLANE SMITH Smith, Blane 6′3″, 238 **LB**
Col: Purdue *HS:* Theodore Roosevelt [Gary, IN] B: 7/13/1954, Gary, IN *Drafted:* 1977 Round 7 Cle
1977 GB: 1 G.

ERIC SMITH Smith, Blane Eric 5′10″, 190 **DB**
Col: Southern Methodist *HS:* Jack Yates [Houston, TX] B: 12/22/1959, Houston, TX
1987 KC: 3 G; KR 1-10 10.0; 1 Fum.

BRAD SMITH Smith, Bradley James 6′2″, 228 **LB**
Col: Texas Christian *HS:* St. Thomas [Houston, TX] B: 9/5/1969, Houston, TX
1993 Cin: 7 G.

BRADY SMITH Smith, Brady McKay 6′5″, 260 **DE**
Col: Colorado State *HS:* Barrington [IL] B: 6/5/1973, Royal Oak, MI *Drafted:* 1996 Round 3 NO
1996 NO: 16 G; KR 2-14 7.0; 2 Sac. **1997** NO: 16 G; 5 Sac. **1998** NO: 14 G. **Total:** 46 G; KR 2-14 7.0; 7 Sac.

BRIAN SMITH Smith, Brian Mark 6′6″, 242 **LB-DT**
Col: Auburn *HS:* Opelika [AL] B: 4/23/1966, Brooklyn, NY *Drafted:* 1989 Round 2 LARm
1989 LARm: 3 G; 2 Sac. **1990** LARm: 16 G; 1 Sac. **Total:** 19 G; 3 Sac.

BRUCE SMITH Smith, Bruce Bernard 6′4″, 280 **DE**
Col: Virginia Tech *HS:* Booker T. Washington [Norfolk, VA] B: 6/18/1963, Norfolk, VA *Drafted:* 1985 Round 1 Buf
1985 Buf: 16 G; Rush 1-0; 6.5 Sac. **1986** Buf: 16 G; 15 Sac. **1987** Buf: 12 G; **1** Fum TD; 6 Pt; 12 Sac. **1988** Buf: 12 G; Scor 1 Saf; 2 Pt; 11 Sac. **1989** Buf: 16 G; 13 Sac. **1990** Buf: 16 G; 19 Sac. **1991** Buf: 5 G; 1.5 Sac. **1992** Buf: 15 G; 14 Sac. **1993** Buf: 16 G; Int 1-0; 14 Sac. **1994** Buf: 15 G; Int 1-0; 10 Sac. **1995** Buf: 15 G; 10.5 Sac. **1996** Buf: 16 G; 13.5 Sac. **1997** Buf: 16 G; 14 Sac. **1998** Buf: 15 G; 10 Sac. **Total:** 201 G; Rush 1-0; Int 2-0; Scor 1 Saf; 1 Fum TD; 8 Pt; 164 Sac.

BRUCE SMITH Smith, Bruce Philip 6′0″, 197 **HB-DB-TB**
(Boo) *Col:* Minnesota *HS:* Faribault [MN] B: 2/8/1920, Faribault, MN D: 8/28/1967, Alexandria, MN *Drafted:* 1942 Round 11 GB
1945 GB: PR 6-67 11.2; KR 2-46 23.0. **1946** GB: PR 2-12 6.0; KR 1-21 21.0. **1947** GB: Rec 4-50 12.5 1 TD; PR 1-22 22.0; KR 3-61 20.3; Scor **1** Saf. **1948** GB-LARm: Pass 1-0; Rec 4-29 7.3; PR 1-10 10.0. GB: Pass 1-0. LARm: Rec 4-29 7.3; PR 1-10 10.0. **Total:** Pass 1-0; Rec 8-79 9.9 1 TD; PR 10-111 11.1; KR 6-128 21.3; Scor 1 Saf.

		Rushing					Tot
Year Team	**G**	**Att**	**Yds**	**Avg**	**TD**	**Fum**	**TD**
1945 GB	3	21	94	4.5	0	2	0
1946 GB	6	22	119	5.4	0	1	0
1947 GB	10	47	288	6.1	1	0	2
1948 GB-LARm	12	18	59	3.3	0	2	0
1948 GB	4	6	21	3.5	0	1	0
1948 LARm	8	12	38	3.2	0	1	0
NFL Total	31	108	560	5.2	1	5	2

BYRON SMITH Smith, Byron Keith 6′5″, 278 **DT**
Col: California *HS:* Canoga Park [CA] B: 12/21/1962, Los Angeles, CA
1984 Ind: 3 G. **1985** Ind: 16 G; 3 Sac. **Total:** 19 G; 3 Sac.

DOUG SMITH Smith, Carl Douglas 6′3″, 259 **C-OG-OT**
Col: Bowling Green State *HS:* Northland [Columbus, OH] B: 11/25/1956, Columbus, OH
1978 LARm: 16 G; KR 1-8 8.0. **1979** LARm: 4 G. **1980** LARm: 8 G. **1981** LARm: 16 G; 1 Fum. **1982** LARm: 9 G. **1983** LARm: 14 G; 1 Fum. **1984** LARm: 16 G. **1985** LARm: 13 G. **1986** LARm: 16 G. **1987** LARm: 12 G. **1988** LARm: 16 G. **1989** LARm: 16 G. **1990** LARm: 16 G. **1991** LARm: 15 G. **Total:** 187 G; KR 1-8 8.0; 2 Fum.

CARL SMITH Smith, Carl Eddie 6′0″, 200 **FB**
Col: Tennessee *HS:* Washington Court House [OH] B: 11/22/1932, Washington Court House, OH *Drafted:* 1959 Round 9 Det
1960 Buf: 14 G; Rush 19-61 3.2; Rec 7-127 18.1 1 TD; KR 2-72 36.0; 6 Pt.

PAT SMITH Smith, Cedric Crawford 6′0″, 198 **FB**
Col: Michigan *HS:* Central [Bay City, MI] B: 3/12/1895, Minneapolis, MN D: 4/23/1969, Detroit, MI
1920 Buf: 7 G. **1921** Buf: 11 G; Rush 3 TD; 18 Pt. **1923** Buf: 1 G. **Total:** 19 G; Rush 3 TD; 18 Pt.

CEDRIC SMITH Smith, Cedric Delon 5′11″, 238 **FB**
Col: Florida *HS:* Enterprise [AL] B: 5/27/1968, Enterprise, AL *Drafted:* 1990 Round 5 Min
1990 Min: KR 1-16 16.0. **1994** Was: Rec 15-118 7.9 1 TD. **1996** Ariz: Rec 3-3 1.0 1 TD; KR 1-14 14.0. **1997** Ariz: Rec 2-20 10.0; KR 3-50 16.7. **Total:** Rec 20-141 7.1 2 TD; KR 5-80 16.0.

		Rushing					Tot
Year Team	**G**	**Att**	**Yds**	**Avg**	**TD**	**Fum**	**TD**
1990 Min	15	9	19	2.1	0	0	0
1991 NO	6	0	0	—	0	0	0
1994 Was	14	10	48	4.8	0	1	1
1995 Was	6	3	13	4.3	0	0	0
1996 Ariz	15	14	15	1.1	1	0	2
1997 Ariz	16	4	5	1.3	1	0	1
NFL Total	72	40	100	2.5	2	1	4

BUBBA SMITH Smith, Charles Aaron 6′7″, 265 **DE-DT**
Col: Michigan State *HS:* Pollard [Beaumont, TX] B: 2/28/1945, Beaumont, TX *Drafted:* 1967 Round 1 Bal
1967 Bal: 13 G. **1968** Bal: 14 G. **1969** Bal: 14 G. **1970** Bal: 14 G. **1971** Bal: 14 G. **1973** Oak: 12 G. **1974** Oak: 14 G. **1975** Hou: 12 G. **1976** Hou: 4 G. **Total:** 111 G.

CHARLIE SMITH Smith, Charles Albert 6′1″, 185 **WR**
Col: Grambling State *HS:* Richwood [Monroe, LA] B: 7/26/1950, Monroe, LA
1974 Phi: PR 4-7 1.8. **1976** Phi: KR 1-(-3) -3.0. **1979** Phi: KR 1-1 1.0. **Total:** PR 4-7 1.8; KR 2-(-2) -1.0.

		Rushing				Receiving					Tot
Year Team	**G**	**Att**	**Yds**	**Avg**	**TD**	**Rec**	**Yds**	**Avg**	**TD**	**Fum**	**TD**
1974 Phi	14	0	0	—	0	1	28	28.0	0	1	0
1975 Phi	14	9	85	9.4	0	37	515	13.9	6	0	6
1976 Phi	14	9	25	2.8	1	27	412	15.3	4	0	5
1977 Phi	14	2	13	6.5	0	33	464	14.1	4	1	4
1978 Phi	14	0	0	—	0	11	142	12.9	2	0	2
1979 Phi	16	0	0	—	0	24	399	16.6	1	0	1
1980 Phi	16	5	33	6.6	0	47	825	17.6	3	0	3
1981 Phi	16	2	5	2.5	0	38	564	14.8	4	2	4
NFL Total	118	27	161	6.0	1	218	3349	15.4	24	4	25

CHARLES SMITH Smith, Charles Harlin 5′11″, 170 **HB-DB**
(Rabbit) *Col:* Georgia *HS:* Palatka [FL] B: 3/13/1924, Aldrich, MO *Drafted:* 1947 Round 14 ChiC
1947 ChiC: 7 G; Rush 9-23 2.6; Rec 1-(-6) -6.0; KR 1-14 14.0; Int 1-5.

CHARLIE SMITH Smith, Charles Henry 6′0″, 205 **RB**
Col: Bakersfield Coll. CA (J.C.); Utah *HS:* Castlemont [Oakland, CA] B: 1/18/1946, Natchez, MS *Drafted:* 1968 Round 4 Oak

		Rushing				Receiving			
Year Team	**G**	**Att**	**Yds**	**Avg**	**TD**	**Rec**	**Yds**	**Avg**	**TD**
1968 Oak	14	95	504	5.3	5	22	321	14.6	2
1969 Oak	14	177	600	3.4	2	30	322	10.7	2
1970 Oak	14	168	681	4.1	3	23	173	7.5	2
1971 Oak	8	11	4	0.4	1	2	67	33.5	0
1972 Oak	14	170	686	4.0	8	28	353	12.6	2
1973 Oak	14	173	682	3.9	4	28	260	9.3	1
1974 Oak	13	64	194	3.0	1	8	100	12.5	1
1975 SD	4	0	0	—	0	0	0	—	0
NFL Total	95	858	3351	3.9	24	141	1596	11.3	10

Year Team	Kickoff Returns Ret	Yds	Avg	TD	Fum	Tot TD
1968 Oak	8	167	20.9	0	5	7
1969 Oak	10	247	24.7	0	3	4
1970 Oak	0	0	—	0	4	5
1971 Oak	1	0	0.0	0	0	1
1972 Oak	1	0	0.0	0	2	10
1973 Oak	2	23	11.5	0	4	5
1974 Oak	0	0	—	0	0	2
1975 SD	8	222	27.8	0	0	0
NFL Total	30	659	22.0	0	18	34

CHUCK SMITH Smith, Charles Henry III 6'2", 257 **DE-LB**
Col: Northeastern Oklahoma A&M (J.C.); Tennessee *HS:* Clarke Central [Athens, GA] B: 12/21/1969, Athens, GA *Drafted:* 1992 Round 2 Atl
1992 Atl: 16 G; 2 Sac. **1993** Atl: 15 G; 3.5 Sac. **1994** Atl: 15 G; Int 1-36 1 TD; 6 Pt; 11 Sac. **1995** Atl: 14 G; 5.5 Sac. **1996** Atl: 15 G; Int 1-21; 6 Sac. **1997** Atl: 16 G; Int 1-4; 12 Sac. **1998** Atl: 16 G; 1 Fum TD; 6 Pt; 8.5 Sac. **Total:** 107 G; Int 3-61 1 TD; 1 Fum TD; Tot TD 2; 12 Pt; 48.5 Sac.

CHARLIE SMITH Smith, Charles W 6'2", 205 **DE**
Col: Abilene Christian B: 4/6/1933, Sweetwater, TX *Drafted:* 1956 Round 8 SF
1956 SF: 12 G; Rec 1-13 13.0; KR 1-14 14.0.

CHRIS SMITH Smith, Christopher Montane 6'1", 232 **RB**
Col: Notre Dame *HS:* La Salle [Cincinnati, OH] B: 6/1/1963, Cincinnati, OH
1987 KC: Rec 2-21 10.5. **Total:** Rec 2-21 10.5.

Year Team	G	Rushing Att	Yds	Avg	TD	Fum
1986 KC	1	0	0	—	0	0
1987 KC	3	26	114	4.4	0	2
NFL Total	4	26	114	4.4	0	2

CLYDE SMITH Smith, Clyde Wise 5'10", 184 **C**
Col: Missouri *HS:* Sapulpa [OK] B: 7/17/1904, Steelville, MO D: 12/30/1982, Lawrenceville, IL
1926 KC: 9 G. **1927** Cle: 12 G. **1928** Prov: 11 G. **Total:** 32 G.

DALLIS SMITH Smith, Dallis Kelvin 5'11", 170 **DB**
Col: Valdosta State *HS:* Westover [Albany, GA] B: 7/31/1965
1987 Sea: 3 G.

DAN SMITH Smith, Daniel Eugene 5'10", 180 **DB**
Col: Northeastern State (Okla.) *HS:* Sulphur [OK] B: 1/29/1935, Matoy, OK
1961 Den: 4 G.

DARRIN SMITH Smith, Darrin Andrew 6'1", 230 **LB**
Col: Miami (Fla.) *HS:* Miami Norland [FL] B: 4/15/1970, Miami, FL *Drafted:* 1993 Round 2 Dal
1993 Dal: 16 G; 1 Sac. **1994** Dal: 16 G; Int 2-13 1 TD; 6 Pt; 4 Sac. **1995** Dal: 9 G; 3 Sac. **1996** Dal: 16 G; 1 Sac. **1997** Phi: 7 G; 1 Sac. **1998** Sea: 13 G; Int 3-56 2 TD; 12 Pt; 5 Sac. **Total:** 77 G; Int 5-69 3 TD; 18 Pt; 15 Sac.

DARYL SMITH Smith, Daryl Dimitri 5'9", 185 **DB**
Col: North Alabama *HS:* Opelika [AL] B: 5/8/1963, Opelika, AL
1987 Cin: 3 G; Int 2-0. **1988** Cin: 7 G. **1989** Min: 5 G. **Total:** 15 G; Int 2-0.

DARYLE SMITH Smith, Daryle Ray 6'5", 277 **OT**
Col: Tennessee *HS:* Powell [TN] B: 1/18/1964, Knoxville, TN
1987 Dal: 9 G. **1988** Dal: 14 G; KR 2-24 12.0. **1989** Cle: 4 G. **1990** Phi: 3 G. **1991** Phi: 14 G. **1992** Phi: 16 G. **Total:** 60 G; KR 2-24 12.0.

DAVE SMITH Smith, David 6'1", 210 **RB**
Col: Utah *HS:* Davis [Kaysville, UT] B: 12/9/1947, Salt Lake City, UT *Drafted:* 1970 Round 13 GB
1970 SD: 7 G; Rush 14-42 3.0; Rec 4-65 16.3.

DAVE SMITH Smith, David Allan 6'6", 290 **OT**
Col: Southern Illinois *HS:* Thornton Fractional South [Lansing, IL] B: 12/12/1964, Hammond, IN
1988 Cin: 14 G.

DAVE SMITH Smith, David Lewis 6'2", 205 **WR**
Col: Waynesburg; Indiana (Pa.) B: 5/18/1947, New York, NY *Drafted:* 1970 Round 8 Pit
1970 Pit: Rush 1-6 6.0. **1971** Pit: Rush 1-(-10) -10.0. **Total:** Rush 2-(-4) -2.0.

Year Team	G	Receiving Rec	Yds	Avg	TD	Fum
1970 Pit	14	30	458	15.3	2	1
1971 Pit	14	47	663	14.1	5	1
1972 Pit-Hou	14	30	316	10.5	0	0
1972 Pit	6	10	98	9.8	0	0
1972 Hou	8	20	218	10.9	0	0
1973 KC	2	2	20	10.0	0	0
NFL Total	44	109	1457	13.4	7	2

DAVE SMITH Smith, David William 6'1", 210 **FB**
Col: Ripon *HS:* Greendale [WI] B: 3/23/1937, Milwaukee, WI *Drafted:* 1959 Round 21 GB
1960 Hou: Pass 5-3 60.0%, 70 14.00 1 TD. **1961** Hou: Pass 2-1 50.0%, 33 16.50; PR 1-15 15.0; KR 1-5 5.0. **1962** Hou: Pass 3-2 66.7%, 34 11.33; KR 2-37 18.5. **1963** Hou: Pass 2-0. **Total:** Pass 12-6 50.0%, 137 11.42 1 TD; PR 1-15 15.0; KR 3-42 14.0.

Year Team	G	Rushing Att	Yds	Avg	TD	Receiving Rec	Yds	Avg	TD	Fum	Tot TD
1960 Hou	14	154	643	4.2	5	22	216	9.8	2	4	7
1961 Hou	14	60	258	4.3	2	10	131	13.1	1	3	3
1962 Hou	14	56	249	4.4	1	17	117	6.9	2	0	3
1963 Hou	14	50	202	4.0	3	24	270	11.3	2	2	5
1964 Hou	9	8	16	2.0	0	7	38	5.4	0	1	0
NFL Total	65	328	1368	4.2	11	80	772	9.7	7	10	18

DENNIS SMITH Smith, Dennis 6'3", 200 **DB**
Col: USC *HS:* Santa Monica [CA] B: 2/3/1959, Santa Monica, CA *Drafted:* 1981 Round 1 Den
1982 Den: 2 Sac. **1983** Den: 5 Sac. **1984** Den: **1** Fum TD; 1 Sac. **1985** Den: 4 Sac. **1986** Den: 1 Sac. **1988** Den: 1 Sac. **1994** Den: 1 Sac. **Total:** 1 Fum TD; 15 Sac.

Year Team	G	Interceptions Int	Yds	TD
1981 Den	16	1	65	0
1982 Den	8	1	29	0
1983 Den	14	4	39	0
1984 Den	15	3	13	0
1985 Den	13	3	46	0
1986 Den	14	1	0	0
1987 Den	6	2	21	0
1988 Den	11	0	0	0
1989 Den	14	2	78	0
1990 Den	15	1	13	0
1991 Den	16	5	60	0
1992 Den	16	4	10	0
1993 Den	14	3	57	0
1994 Den	12	0	0	0
NFL Total	184	30	431	0

DENNIS SMITH Smith, Dennis Preston 6'0", 230 **RB**
Col: Utah *HS:* Hemet [CA] B: 2/14/1967, Hemet, CA
1990 Pho: 4 G.

DEREK SMITH Smith, Derek Mecham 6'2", 239 **LB**
Col: Snow Coll. UT (J.C.); Arizona State *HS:* American Fork [UT] B: 1/18/1975, American Fork, UT *Drafted:* 1997 Round 3 Was
1997 Was: 16 G; 2 Sac. **1998** Was: 16 G; 0.5 Sac. **Total:** 32 G; 2.5 Sac.

DETRON SMITH Smith, Detron Negil 5'9", 231 **RB**
Col: Texas A&M *HS:* Lake Highlands [Dallas, TX] B: 2/25/1974, Dallas, TX *Drafted:* 1996 Round 3 Den
1996 Den: 13 G. **1997** Den: 16 G; Rush 4-10 2.5; Rec 4-41 10.3 1 TD; KR 1-0; 6 Pt. **1998** Den: 15 G; Rec 3-24 8.0; KR 3-51 17.0. **Total:** 44 G; Rush 4-10 2.5; Rec 7-65 9.3 1 TD; KR 4-51 12.8; 6 Pt.

DON SMITH Smith, Donald **G**
Col: No College
1930 Nwk: 2 G.

DON SMITH Smith, Donald L 6'4", 240 **OG**
Col: Florida A&M *HS:* Union Acad. [Bartow, FL] B: 2/8/1943 *Drafted:* 1967 Round 15 Den
1967 Den: 2 G.

DON SMITH Smith, Donald Loren 6'5", 256 **NT-DE-DT**
Col: Miami (Fla.) *HS:* Tarpon Springs [FL] B: 5/9/1957, Oakland, CA *Drafted:* 1979 Round 1 Atl
1979 Atl: 16 G. **1980** Atl: 16 G. **1981** Atl: 16 G. **1982** Atl: 9 G; 3.5 Sac. **1983** Atl: 14 G; 6 Sac. **1984** Atl: 16 G; 6 Sac. **1985** Buf: 16 G; 3 Sac. **1986** Buf: 5 G. **1987** NYJ: 3 G. **Total:** 111 G; 18.5 Sac.

DON SMITH Smith, Donald Michael 5'11", 200 **RB-WR**
Col: Mississippi State *HS:* Hamilton [MS] B: 10/30/1963, Hamilton, MS *Drafted:* 1987 Round 2 TB
1990 Buf: Pass 1-0. **Total:** Pass 1-0.

Year Team	G	Rushing Att	Yds	Avg	TD	Receiving Rec	Yds	Avg	TD
1988 TB	10	13	46	3.5	1	12	138	11.5	0
1989 TB	11	7	37	5.3	0	7	110	15.7	0
1990 Buf	16	20	82	4.1	2	21	225	10.7	0
NFL Total	37	40	165	4.1	3	40	473	11.8	0

Year Team	Kickoff Returns Ret	Yds	Avg	TD	Fum
1988 TB	9	188	20.9	0	0
1989 TB	0	0	—	0	1

1990 Buf	32	643	20.1	0	1
NFL Total	41	831	20.3	0	2

DONALD SMITH Smith, Donald Ray 5′11″, 189 **DB**
Col: Liberty *HS:* George Washington [Danville, VA] B: 2/21/1968, Danville, VA *Drafted:* 1990 Round 10 Min
1991 Dal: 3 G.

DONNELL SMITH Smith, Donnell 6′4″, 245 **DE**
Col: Southern University *HS:* Kathleen [Lakeland, FL] B: 5/25/1949, Lakeland, FL *Drafted:* 1971 Round 5 GB
1971 GB: 4 G. **1973** NE: 12 G. **1974** NE: 9 G; KR 1-0. **Total:** 25 G; KR 1-0.

DOUG SMITH Smith, Douglas Batrone 6′0″, 192 **DB**
Col: Ohio State *HS:* Fulton [Atlanta, GA] B: 2/4/1963, Atlanta, GA
1987 NYG: 3 G.

PERRY SMITH Smith, Ealthon Perry 6′1″, 195 **DB**
Col: Mesa; Colorado State *HS:* Lincoln [Greer, SC] B: 3/29/1951, Spartanburg, SC *Drafted:* 1973 Round 4 Oak
1977 StL: KR 1-10 10.0. **1978** StL: PR 1-0. **Total:** PR 1-0; KR 1-10 10.0.

		Interceptions		
Year Team	**G**	**Int**	**Yds**	**TD**
1973 GB	8	0	0	0
1974 GB	12	0	0	0
1975 GB	14	6	97	0
1976 GB	13	1	0	0
1977 StL	3	0	0	0
1978 StL	16	3	6	0
1979 StL	16	1	22	0
1980 Den	14	2	3	0
1981 Den	12	0	0	0
NFL Total	108	13	128	0

ED SMITH Smith, Edward 6′2″, 207 **FB-TB-DB**
Col: New York U. *HS:* George Washington [New York, NY] B: 6/17/1913, New York, NY *Drafted:* 1936 Round 3 Bos
1936 Bos: 8 G; Pass 40-11 27.5%, 120 3.00 1 TD **2** Int; Rush 7-39 5.6; Scor 3, 1 FG. **1937** GB: 2 G; Pass 2-0, 1 Int. **Total:** 10 G; Pass 42-11 26.2%, 120 2.86 1 TD 3 Int; Rush 7-39 5.6; Scor 3, 1 FG.

ED SMITH Smith, Edward Martin 6′4″, 253 **TE**
Col: No College *HS:* Pemberton Twp. [Pemberton, NJ] B: 6/5/1969, Trenton, NJ
1997 Atl: 5 G; Rec 1-2 2.0. **1998** Atl: 15 G. **Total:** 20 G; Rec 1-2 2.0.

ED SMITH Smith, Edwin Alexander 6′5″, 241 **DE**
Col: Colorado College *HS:* [Nassau, Bahamas] B: 10/23/1950, Nassau, Bahamas *Drafted:* 1973 Round 13 Den
1973 Den: 5 G. **1974** Den: 11 G; Int 1-2; 1 Fum. **Total:** 16 G; Int 1-2; 1 Fum.

ELLIOT SMITH Smith, Elliot 6′2″, 192 **DB**
Col: Alcorn State *HS:* Callaway [Jackson, MS] B: 8/14/1967, Jackson, MS *Drafted:* 1989 Round 5 SD
1989 SD: 2 G. **1990** Den: 9 G. **Total:** 11 G.

EMMITT SMITH Smith, Emmitt James III 5′9″, 207 **RB**
Col: Florida *HS:* Escambia [Pensacola, FL] B: 5/15/1969, Pensacola, FL *Drafted:* 1990 Round 1 Dal
1997 Dal: Scor 1 2XP. **Total:** Scor 1 2XP.

		Rushing				Receiving					Tot
Year Team	**G**	**Att**	**Yds**	**Avg**	**TD**	**Rec**	**Yds**	**Avg**	**TD**	**Fum**	**TD**
1990 Dal	16	241	937	3.9	11	24	228	9.5	0	7	11
1991 Dal	16	**365**	**1563**	4.3	12	49	258	5.3	1	8	13
1992 Dal	16	373	**1713**	4.6	**18**	59	335	5.7	1	4	**19**
1993 Dal	14	283	**1486**	**5.3**	9	57	414	7.3	1	4	10
1994 Dal	15	**368**	1484	4.0	**21**	50	341	6.8	1	1	**22**
1995 Dal	16	**377**	**1773**	4.7	**25**	62	375	6.0	0	7	**25**
1996 Dal	15	327	1204	3.7	12	47	249	5.3	3	5	15
1997 Dal	16	261	1074	4.1	4	40	234	5.9	0	1	4
1998 Dal	16	319	1332	4.2	13	27	175	6.5	2	3	15
NFL Total	140	2914	12566	4.3	**125**	415	2609	6.3	9	40	134

ERIC SMITH Smith, Eric Lamonte 5′11″, 183 **WR**
Col: Northwest Mississippi CC; Louisiana State *HS:* Vero Beach [FL] B: 1/5/1971, Vero Beach, FL
1997 ChiB: 7 G; Rush 1-12 12.0; Rec 2-22 11.0; KR 10-196 19.6.

ERNIE SMITH Smith, Ernest Frederick 6′2″, 224 **T**
Col: USC *HS:* Spearfish [SD]; Gardena HS [CA] B: 11/26/1909, Spearfish, SD D: 4/25/1985, Los Angeles, CA
1935 GB: 12 G; Scor 14, 1 FG, 11 XK. **1936** GB: 12 G; Scor 29, 4 FG, 17 XK. **1937** GB: 10 G; Scor 14, 1 FG, 11 XK. **1939** GB: 6 G; Scor 3, 3-4 75.0% XK. **Total:** 40 G; Scor 60, 6 FG, 42-4 75.0% XK.

ERNIE SMITH Smith, Ernest W 6′3″, 190 **DB-HB**
Col: Compton CC CA; San Diego City Coll. CA (J.C.) *HS:* San Diego [CA] B: 7/6/1930
1955 SF: 1 G. **1956** SF: 3 G; Int 1-0. **Total:** 4 G; Int 1-0.

RUSS SMITH Smith, Eugene Russell 5′10″, 220 **G-C**
Col: Navy; Southern Illinois; Illinois *HS:* Carbondale [IL] B: 11/11/1895, Carbondale, IL D: 7/7/1958, Johnson City, IL
1921 Sta: 11 G. **1922** ChiB: 10 G. **1923** Can-Mil: 9 G. Can: 1 G. Mil: 8 G. **1924** Mil-Cle: 7 G. Mil: 1 G. Cle: 6 G. **1925** Det-ChiB: 10 G. Det: 9 G. ChiB: 1 G. **1926** Ham: 3 G. **Total:** 50 G.

FERNANDO SMITH Smith, Fernando Dewitt 6′6″, 277 **DE**
Col: Jackson State *HS:* Northwestern [Flint, MI] B: 8/2/1971, Flint, MI *Drafted:* 1994 Round 2 Min
1994 Min: 7 G. **1995** Min: 12 G; 2.5 Sac. **1996** Min: 16 G; 9.5 Sac. **1997** Min: 12 G; 4 Sac. **1998** Jac: 15 G; 2 Sac. **Total:** 62 G; 18 Sac.

FLETCHER SMITH Smith, Fletcher Leon 6′0″, 178 **DB-K**
(Duck) *Col:* Tennessee State *HS:* Booker T. Washington [Dallas, TX] B: 10/13/1943, Hearne, TX *Drafted:* 1966 Round 8 KC
1966 KC: Scor 2, 2-4 50.0% XK. **1968** Cin: Punt 8-230 28.8. **1970** Cin: PR 1-0. **Total:** PR 1-0; Punt 8-230 28.8; Scor 2, 2-4 50.0% XK.

		Interceptions		
Year Team	**G**	**Int**	**Yds**	**TD**
1966 KC	11	0	0	0
1967 KC	13	6	150	0
1968 Cin	14	1	16	0
1969 Cin	14	4	67	0
1970 Cin	14	3	17	0
1971 Cin	14	1	0	0
NFL Total	80	15	250	0

FRANKY SMITH Smith, Frank Lee 6′6″, 279 **OT**
Col: Alabama A&M *HS:* Jackson-Olin [Birmingham, AL] B: 1/16/1956, Birmingham, AL
1980 KC: 4 G.

FRANKIE SMITH Smith, Frankie Lee 5′9″, 186 **DB**
Col: Baylor *HS:* Groesbeck [TX] B: 10/8/1968, Fort Worth, TX *Drafted:* 1992 Round 4 Atl
1993 Mia: 5 G. **1994** Mia: 13 G; 1 Sac. **1995** Mia: 11 G. **1996** SF: 14 G. **1997** SF: 16 G. **1998** ChiB: 15 G. **Total:** 74 G; 1 Sac.

BRENT SMITH Smith, Gary Brent 6′5″, 315 **OT**
Col: Mississippi State *HS:* Pontotoc [MS] B: 11/21/1973, Dallas, TX *Drafted:* 1997 Round 3 Mia
1998 Mia: 8 G.

GARY SMITH Smith, Gary Lovell 6′2″, 265 **OG**
Col: Virginia Tech *HS:* Kecoughtan [Hampton, VA] B: 1/27/1960, Bitburg AFB, Germany
1984 Cin: 8 G.

GAYLON SMITH Smith, Gaylon Wesley 5′11″, 202 **FB-DB-LB-WB**
Col: Rhodes *HS:* Lonoke [AR]; Beebe HS [AR] B: 7/15/1916, Lonoke, AR *Drafted:* 1939 Round 2 Cle
AAFC **1946** CleA: Rec 7-73 10.4; Int 1-0.

		Rushing			
Year Team	**G**	**Att**	**Yds**	**Avg**	**TD**
1946 CleA	14	62	240	3.9	5

NFL **1939** Cle: Pass 5-4 80.0%, 3 0.60; Rec 3-57 19.0. **1940** Cle: Pass 18-10 55.6%, 150 8.33 2 TD 2 Int; Rec 2-65 32.5; Int 3-48; Punt 11-391 35.5. **1941** Cle: Pass 2-0, 1 Int; PR 1-33 33.0; Int 1-16; Punt 1-23 23.0. **1942** Cle: Pass 12-2 16.7%, 49 4.08 1 Int; Rec 3-61 20.3; PR 6-62 10.3; KR 6-109 18.2; Int 4-20. **Total:** Pass 37-16 43.2%, 202 5.46 2 TD 4 Int; Rec 8-183 22.9; PR 7-95 13.6; KR 6-109 18.2; Int 8-84; Punt 12-414 34.5.

		Rushing			
Year Team	**G**	**Att**	**Yds**	**Avg**	**TD**
1939 Cle	11	58	98	1.7	2
1940 Cle	11	19	18	0.9	0
1941 Cle	4	11	22	2.0	0
1942 Cle	11	83	332	4.0	2
NFL Total	37	171	470	2.7	4

GEORGE SMITH Smith, George James 6′1″, 200 **FB-DB**
Col: Villanova *HS:* McKeesport [PA] B: 3/26/1921 D: 6/27/1994, McKeesport, PA *Drafted:* 1943 Round 21 ChiC
1943 ChiC: 3 G; Rush 4-12 3.0; Rec 1-18 18.0.

GEORGE SMITH Smith, George William 6′2″, 220 **C**
Col: Glendale CC CA; California *HS:* Abraham Lincoln [Los Angeles, CA] B: 6/3/1914, Los Angeles, CA D: 3/5/1986, Walnut Creek, CA
AAFC **1947** SF-A: 10 G; Int 1-10.

NFL **1937** Was: 7 G. **1941** Was: 9 G. **1942** Was: 4 G; Scor 0-1 FG. **1943** Was: 9 G; PR 1-3 3.0; Int 2-40. **1944** Bkn: 10 G; Int 1-8; Punt 6-223 37.2. **1945** Bos: 10 G; KR 1-0; Int 2-23; Punt 9-355 39.4; 1 Fum. **Total:** 49 G; PR 1-3 3.0; KR 1-0; Int 5-71; Punt 15-578 38.5; Scor 0-1 FG; 1 Fum.

JERRY SMITH Smith, Gerald Thomas 6′3″, 208 **TE**
Col: Eastern Arizona Coll. (J.C.); Arizona State *HS:* San Lorenzo [CA]
B: 7/19/1943, Eugene, OR D: 10/15/1986, Silver Spring, MD
Drafted: 1965 Round 9 Was
1969 Was: Rush 3-8 2.7. **1970** Was: Rush 2-29 14.5. **1971** Was: Rush 1-5 5.0. **1972** Was: Rush 1-9 9.0. **1973** Was: PR 1-0. **1974** Was: Rush 1-5 5.0. **Total:** Rush 8-56 7.0; PR 1-0.

		Receiving				
Year Team	**G**	**Rec**	**Yds**	**Avg**	**TD**	**Fum**
1965 Was	14	19	257	13.5	2	0
1966 Was	14	54	686	12.7	6	0
1967 Was	14	67	849	12.7	12	2
1968 Was	13	45	626	13.9	6	0
1969 Was	14	54	682	12.6	9	0
1970 Was	14	43	575	13.4	9	0
1971 Was	8	16	227	14.2	1	1
1972 Was	14	21	353	16.8	7	0
1973 Was	13	19	215	11.3	0	1
1974 Was	14	44	554	12.6	3	1
1975 Was	14	31	391	12.6	3	0
1976 Was	13	7	75	10.7	2	0
1977 Was	9	1	6	6.0	0	0
NFL Total	168	421	5496	13.1	60	5

GORDON SMITH Smith, Gordon Chilton 6′2″, 220 **TE**
(Gordie) *Col:* Arizona State; Missouri *HS:* West [Phoenix, AZ]
B: 4/9/1939, Douglas, AZ
1963 Min: KR 2-24 12.0. **1964** Min: Rush 1-2 2.0. **Total:** Rush 1-2 2.0; KR 2-24 12.0.

		Receiving				
Year Team	**G**	**Rec**	**Yds**	**Avg**	**TD**	**Fum**
1961 Min	9	12	320	26.7	4	1
1962 Min	5	7	138	19.7	1	0
1963 Min	14	6	177	29.5	2	0
1964 Min	12	10	211	21.1	1	0
1965 Min	14	22	431	19.6	5	1
NFL Total	54	57	1277	22.4	13	2

GREG SMITH Smith, Gregory 6′3″, 270 **NT**
Col: Kansas *HS:* Mendel [Chicago, IL] B: 10/22/1959, Chicago, IL
1984 Min: 16 G; KR 2-26 13.0.

HAL SMITH Smith, Harold Wallace Jr. 6′5″, 250 **DT**
Col: UCLA *HS:* Canoga Park [CA] B: 10/3/1935, Santa Monica, CA
1960 Bos-Den: 13 G; KR 1-13 13.0. Bos: 10 G; KR 1-13 13.0. Den: 3 G.
1961 Oak: 8 G; PR 1-2 2.0. **Total:** 21 G; PR 1-2 2.0; KR 1-13 13.0.

HARRY SMITH Smith, Harry Elliott 5′11″, 215 **T**
(Blackjack) *Col:* USC *HS:* Chaffey [Ontario, CA] B: 8/26/1918, Russellville, MO *Drafted:* 1940 Round 3 Det
1940 Det: 10 G.

STRUGGY SMITH Smith, Henri F 6′2″, 190 **DB**
Col: Appalachian State *HS:* West Charlotte [Charlotte, NC]
B: 2/13/1964, Charlotte, NC
1987 Atl: 2 G.

HANK SMITH Smith, Henry A 6′1″, 189 **C-G-T**
Col: No College *HS:* None B: 7/23/1893, Lancaster, NY D: 2/3/1985, Buffalo, NY
1920 Roch: 10 G. **1921** Roch: 5 G. **1922** Roch: 5 G. **1923** Roch: 2 G. **1924** Roch: 7 G. **1925** Roch: 5 G. **Total:** 34 G.

ED SMITH Smith, Henry Edward IV 6′2″, 216 **LB**
Col: Vanderbilt *HS:* McCallie School [Chattanooga, TN] B: 5/18/1957, Knoxville, TN *Drafted:* 1979 Round 12 Pit
1980 Bal: 16 G. **1981** Bal: 16 G; Int 2-11. **Total:** 32 G; Int 2-11.

GENE SMITH Smith, Henry Eugene 5′9″, 190 **G**
Col: Georgia *HS:* Columbus [GA] B: 9/25/1905, Montgomery, AL
D: 12/10/1979, Atlanta, GA
1930 Fra-Port: 5 G. Fra: 1 G. Port: 4 G. **Total:** 5 G.

HERMAN SMITH Smith, Herman III 6′5″, 261 **DE**
Col: Merced Coll. CA (J.C.); Portland State *HS:* Dillard [Fort Lauderdale, FL] B: 1/25/1971, Mound Bayou, MS
1995 TB: 3 G. **1996** TB: 5 G. **Total:** 8 G.

HOLDEN SMITH Smith, Holden Eugene 6′1″, 191 **WR**
Col: California *HS:* Los Gatos [CA] B: 11/5/1958, San Jose, CA
Drafted: 1981 Round 11 Bal
1982 Bal: 3 G; Rec 2-36 18.0.

ALLEN SMITH Smith, Houston Allen Jr. 6′2″, 218 **DE-OE**
Col: Copiah-Lincoln CC MS; Mississippi *HS:* Hazelhurst [MS]
B: 3/29/1922, Hazlehurst, MS D: 10/18/1970, Hattiesburg, MS
Drafted: 1947 Round 6 ChiB
1947 ChiB: 12 G; KR 2-18 9.0. **1948** ChiB: 10 G; Rec 3-29 9.7.
Total: 22 G; Rec 3-29 9.7; KR 2-18 9.0.

HUGH SMITH Smith, Hugh Ben 6′4″, 217 **WR**
Col: Kansas *HS:* Guymon [OK] B: 8/27/1936, Henryetta, OK
1962 Was: 2 G.

IRV SMITH Smith, Irvin Martin 6′3″, 249 **TE**
Col: Notre Dame *HS:* Pemberton Twp. [Pemberton, NJ]
B: 10/13/1971, Trenton, NJ *Drafted:* 1993 Round 1 NO
1994 NO: KR 2-10 5.0. **1995** NO: KR 1-6 6.0; Scor 1 2XP. **1998** SF: KR 2-35 17.5. **Total:** KR 5-51 10.2; Scor 1 2XP.

		Receiving				
Year Team	**G**	**Rec**	**Yds**	**Avg**	**TD**	**Fum**
1993 NO	16	16	180	11.3	2	1
1994 NO	16	41	330	8.0	3	0
1995 NO	16	45	466	10.4	3	1
1996 NO	7	15	144	9.6	0	0
1997 NO	11	17	180	10.6	1	1
1998 SF	16	25	266	10.6	5	0
NFL Total	82	159	1566	9.8	14	3

J.D. SMITH Smith, J. D Jr. 6′1″, 205 **FB-HB-DB**
Col: North Carolina A&T *HS:* Sterling [Greenville, SC] B: 7/19/1932, Plainville, SC *Drafted:* 1955 Round 15 ChiB
1957 SF: Int 2-17. **1961** SF: Pass 1-0, 1 Int. **Total:** Pass 1-0, 1 Int; Int 2-17.

		Rushing				Receiving			
Year Team	**G**	**Att**	**Yds**	**Avg**	**TD**	**Rec**	**Yds**	**Avg**	**TD**
1956 ChiB-SF	11	0	0	—	0	0	0	—	0
1956 ChiB	6	0	0	—	0	0	0	—	0
1956 SF	5	0	0	—	0	0	0	—	0
1957 SF	12	0	0	—	0	0	0	—	0
1958 SF	12	26	209	8.0	3	6	59	9.8	0
1959 SF	12	207	1036	5.0	10	13	133	10.2	1
1960 SF	12	174	780	4.5	5	36	181	5.0	1
1961 SF	14	167	823	4.9	8	28	343	12.3	1
1962 SF	14	258	907	3.5	6	21	197	9.4	1
1963 SF	14	162	560	3.5	5	17	196	11.5	1
1964 SF	2	13	55	4.2	0	0	0	—	0
1965 Dal	14	86	295	3.4	2	5	10	2.0	1
1966 Dal	14	7	7	1.0	1	1	3	3.0	0
NFL Total	131	1100	4672	4.2	40	127	1122	8.8	6

	Kickoff Returns					
Year Team	**Ret**	**Yds**	**Avg**	**TD**	**Fum**	**Tot TD**
1957 SF	14	368	26.3	0	0	0
1958 SF	15	356	23.7	0	3	3
1959 SF	0	0	—	0	3	11
1960 SF	0	0	—	0	1	6
1961 SF	7	158	22.6	0	3	9
1962 SF	0	0	—	0	1	7
1963 SF	0	0	—	0	4	6
1965 Dal	0	0	—	0	2	3
1966 Dal	0	0	—	0	0	1
NFL Total	36	882	24.5	0	17	46

JACK SMITH Smith, Jack 6′4″, 204 **DB**
Col: Memphis; Troy State *HS:* Irwin Co. [Ocilla, GA] B: 12/4/1947, Ocilla, GA *Drafted:* 1971 Round 6 Phi
1971 Phi: 5 G.

JACK SMITH Smith, Jack Bullas 6′1″, 200 **DE-OE**
Col: Stanford *HS:* Glendale [CA] B: 8/11/1917, Los Angeles, CA
1942 Phi: 6 G; KR 1-13 13.0. **1943** Was: 3 G. **Total:** 9 G; KR 1-13 13.0.

JACKIE SMITH Smith, Jackie Larue 6′4″, 235 **TE**
Col: Northwestern State-Louisiana *HS:* Kentwood [LA] B: 2/23/1940, Columbia, MS *Drafted:* 1963 Round 10 StL *HOF:* 1994
1967 StL: Pass 1-0, 1 Int. **1972** StL: Pass 2-0. **1975** StL: KR 1-25 25.0.
1976 StL: KR 3-63 21.0. **1977** StL: KR 1-15 15.0. **Total:** Pass 3-0, 1 Int; KR 5-103 20.6.

		Rushing				Receiving			
Year Team	**G**	**Att**	**Yds**	**Avg**	**TD**	**Rec**	**Yds**	**Avg**	**TD**
1963 StL	14	0	0	—	0	28	445	15.9	2
1964 StL	14	0	0	—	0	47	657	14.0	4
1965 StL	14	0	0	—	0	41	648	15.8	2
1966 StL	14	1	8	8.0	0	45	810	18.0	3
1967 StL	14	9	86	9.6	0	56	1205	21.5	9
1968 StL	14	12	163	13.6	3	49	789	16.1	2
1969 StL	14	4	0	0.0	0	43	561	13.0	1
1970 StL	14	5	43	8.6	0	37	687	18.6	4
1971 StL	9	1	10	10.0	0	21	379	18.0	4
1972 StL	14	5	31	6.2	0	26	407	15.7	2
1973 StL	14	1	-14	-14.0	0	41	600	14.6	1
1974 StL	14	0	0	—	0	25	413	16.5	3
1975 StL	9	0	0	—	0	13	246	18.9	2
1976 StL	12	0	0	—	0	3	22	7.3	0
1977 StL	14	0	0	—	0	5	49	9.8	1

Year Team									
1978 Dal	12	0	0	—	0	0	0	—	0
NFL Total	210	38	327	8.6	3	480	7918	16.5	40

	Punting				Tot
Year Team	**Punts**	**Yds**	**Avg**	**Fum**	**TD**
1963 StL	0	0	—	2	2
1964 StL	41	1658	40.4	2	4
1965 StL	39	1532	39.3	0	2
1966 StL	47	1781	37.9	1	3
1967 StL	0	0	—	3	9
1968 StL	0	0	—	0	5
1969 StL	0	0	—	1	1
1970 StL	0	0	—	0	4
1971 StL	0	0	—	0	4
1972 StL	0	0	—	0	2
1973 StL	0	0	—	1	1
1974 StL	0	0	—	1	3
1975 StL	0	0	—	0	2
1977 StL	0	0	—	1	1
NFL Total	127	4971	39.1	12	43

JIM SMITH Smith, James Arthur 6′2″, 205 **WR**
Col: Michigan *HS:* Dwight D. Eisenhower [Blue Island, IL]
B: 7/20/1955, Harvey, IL *Drafted:* 1977 Round 3 Pit
1977 Pit: KR 16-381 23.8. **1978** Pit: KR 1-16 16.0. **1979** Pit: Rush 1-12 12.0. **1980** Pit: Rush 1-(-1) -1.0. **1981** Pit: Rush 1-15 15.0.
Total: Rush 3-26 8.7; KR 17-397 23.4.

		Receiving				Punt Returns				
Year Team	**G**	**Rec**	**Yds**	**Avg**	**TD**	**Ret**	**Yds**	**Avg**	**TD**	**Fum**
1977 Pit	14	4	80	20.0	0	36	294	8.2	0	3
1978 Pit	9	6	83	13.8	2	9	65	7.2	0	1
1979 Pit	15	17	243	14.3	2	16	146	9.1	0	1
1980 Pit	12	37	711	19.2	9	7	28	4.0	0	1
1981 Pit	15	29	571	19.7	7	30	204	6.8	0	1
1982 Pit	8	17	387	22.8	4	0	0	—	0	1
1985 LARd	6	3	28	9.3	1	0	0	—	0	0
NFL Total	79	113	2103	18.6	25	98	737	7.5	0	8

J.D. SMITH Smith, James D 6′1″, 210 **FB-HB**
(Jetstream) *Col:* Compton CC CA *HS:* Thomas Jefferson [Los Angeles, CA] B: 1936
1960 Oak: Rec 17-194 11.4 1 TD; KR 14-373 26.6 1 TD; Scor 1 2XP.
1961 ChiB: KR 1-18 18.0. **Total:** Rec 17-194 11.4 1 TD; KR 15-391 26.1 1 TD; Scor 1 2XP.

		Rushing					Tot
Year Team	**G**	**Att**	**Yds**	**Avg**	**TD**	**Fum**	**TD**
1960 Oak	14	63	214	3.4	6	4	8
1961 ChiB	3	3	6	2.0	0	0	0
NFL Total	17	66	220	3.3	6	4	8

JIM SMITH Smith, James Dale 6′4″, 270 **T**
Col: Colorado *HS:* Centennial [Pueblo, CO] B: 9/8/1922, Alto, TX
AAFC **1947** LA-A: 7 G.

JIMMY SMITH Smith, James Earl 6′3″, 190 **DB**
Col: San Joaquin Delta Coll. CA (J.C.); Utah State *HS:* Edison [Stockton, CA] B: 7/12/1945, Stockton, CA *Drafted:* 1969 Round 10 Den
1969 Den: 2 G.

JIMMY SMITH Smith, James Kevin 6′0″, 205 **RB**
Col: Purdue; Elon *HS:* Westview [Kankakee, IL] B: 9/25/1960, Kankakee, IL
1984 Was-LARd-GB: 8 G; KR 2-38 19.0. Was: 1 G; KR 2-38 19.0. LARd: 7 G. **1987** Min: 1 G; Rush 7-13 1.9; KR 2-42 21.0. **Total:** 9 G; Rush 7-13 1.9; KR 4-80 20.0.

JIM SMITH Smith, James McCoy 6′3″, 195 **DB**
(Yazoo) *Col:* Oregon *HS:* Kearny [San Diego, CA] B: 11/4/1946, Yazoo City, MS *Drafted:* 1968 Round 1 Was
1968 Was: 14 G; PR 6-38 6.3; KR 3-61 20.3; **1** Fum TD; 6 Pt; 1 Fum.

JIM RAY SMITH Smith, James Ray 6′3″, 241 **OG-OT-DE**
Col: Baylor *HS:* West Columbia [TX] B: 2/27/1932, West Columbia, TX
Drafted: 1954 Round 6 Cle
1956 Cle: 6 G. **1957** Cle: 12 G. **1958** Cle: 12 G. **1959** Cle: 12 G. **1960** Cle: 12 G. **1961** Cle: 14 G. **1962** Cle: 13 G. **1963** Dal: 8 G. **1964** Dal: 4 G.
Total: 93 G.

BOB SMITH Smith, James Robert 6′1″, 191 **DB-HB-WB**
Col: Tulsa; Iowa *HS:* Will Rogers [Tulsa, OK] B: 8/20/1925, Ranger, TX
Drafted: 1947 Round 22 Was
AAFC **1948** BufA-BknA: 13 G; Rush 1-7 7.0; PR 1-1 1.0; Int 4-29; Punt 14-538 38.4. **1949** ChiA: 3 G; Rec 1-31 31.0. **Total:** 16 G; Rush 1-7 7.0; Rec 1-31 31.0; PR 1-1 1.0; Int 4-29; Punt 14-538 38.4.

NFL **1949** Det: Rec 2-16 8.0; PR 2-25 12.5; KR 7-172 24.6. **1952** Det: Rec 1-18 18.0. **Total:** Rec 3-34 11.3; PR 2-25 12.5; KR 7-172 24.6.

		Rushing				Interceptions		
Year Team	**G**	**Att**	**Yds**	**Avg**	**TD**	**Int**	**Yds**	**TD**
1949 Det	12	33	162	4.9	0	9	218	1
1950 Det	12	0	0	—	0	5	128	1
1951 Det	12	0	0	—	0	3	70	0
1952 Det	12	3	12	4.0	0	9	184	1
1953 Det	12	0	0	—	0	3	119	0
1954 Det	2	0	0	—	0	0	0	0
NFL Total	62	36	174	4.8	0	29	719	3

	Punting			
Year Team	**Punts**	**Yds**	**Avg**	**Fum**
1949 Det	0	0	—	4
1950 Det	32	1310	40.9	0
1951 Det	49	2082	42.5	0
1952 Det	61	2729	44.7	1
1953 Det	40	1647	41.2	0
NFL Total	182	7768	42.7	5

WADDELL SMITH Smith, James Waddell 6′2″, 180 **WR**
Col: Los Angeles Southwest Coll. CA (J.C.); Kansas *HS:* Manual Arts [Los Angeles, CA] B: 8/24/1955, New Orleans, LA
1984 Dal: 2 G; Rush 1-(-5) -5.0; Rec 1-7 7.0.

JEFF SMITH Smith, Jeff Keith 5′9″, 201 **RB**
Col: Nebraska *HS:* Southeast [Wichita, KS] B: 3/22/1962, Wichita, KS
Drafted: 1985 Round 10 KC

		Rushing				Receiving			
Year Team	**G**	**Att**	**Yds**	**Avg**	**TD**	**Rec**	**Yds**	**Avg**	**TD**
1985 KC	13	30	118	3.9	0	18	157	8.7	2
1986 KC	15	54	238	4.4	3	33	230	7.0	3
1987 TB	12	100	309	3.1	2	20	197	9.9	2
1988 TB	16	20	87	4.4	0	16	134	8.4	0
NFL Total	56	204	752	3.7	5	87	718	8.3	7

	Punt Returns				Kickoff Returns					Tot
Year Team	**Ret**	**Yds**	**Avg**	**TD**	**Ret**	**Yds**	**Avg**	**TD**	**Fum**	**TD**
1985 KC	0	0	—	0	33	654	19.8	0	1	2
1986 KC	29	245	8.4	0	29	557	19.2	0	4	6
1987 TB	0	0	—	0	5	84	16.8	0	2	4
1988 TB	8	45	5.6	0	10	180	18.0	0	0	0
NFL Total	37	290	7.8	0	77	1475	19.2	0	7	12

JEFF SMITH Smith, Jeffery Lee 6′3″, 322 **C**
Col: Tennessee *HS:* Meigs Co. [Decatur, TN] B: 5/25/1973, Decatur, TN *Drafted:* 1996 Round 7 KC
1997 KC: 3 G. **1998** KC: 11 G. **Total:** 14 G.

JEFF SMITH Smith, Jeffrey 6′0″, 237 **LB**
Col: USC *HS:* Long Beach Polytechnic [CA] B: 11/12/1943, Freeport, LA *Drafted:* 1966 Round 10 NYG
1966 NYG: 14 G; Int 1-0.

JEFF SMITH Smith, Jeffrey A 6′4″, 248 **DE**
Col: Air Force; Earlham *HS:* Tiskilwa [IL] B: 5/4/1962, Spring Valley, TN
1987 Cin: 3 G.

JEFF SMITH Smith, Jeffrey Allen 6′3″, 240 **TE**
Col: Tennessee *HS:* Milan [TN] B: 12/28/1962, Milan, TN
1987 NYG: 3 G; Rec 6-72 12.0.

JERRY SMITH Smith, Jerome Anthony 6′1″, 230 **OG-LB**
Col: Wisconsin *HS:* Chaminade [Dayton, OH] B: 9/9/1930, Dayton, OH
1952 SF: 12 G. **1953** SF: 12 G. **1956** SF-GB: 5 G. SF: 2 G. GB: 3 G.
Total: 29 G.

J.D. SMITH Smith, Jesse Daley 6′5″, 250 **OT**
Col: Rice *HS:* Richland Springs [TX] B: 5/27/1936, Richland Springs, TX
1959 Phi: 11 G. **1960** Phi: 12 G; **1** Fum TD; 6 Pt. **1961** Phi: 14 G. **1962** Phi: 14 G. **1963** Phi: 14 G. **1964** Det: 7 G. **1966** Det: 14 G. **Total:** 86 G; 1 Fum TD; 6 Pt.

JIMMY SMITH Smith, Jimmy Lee Jr. 6′1″, 206 **WR**
Col: Jackson State *HS:* Callaway [Jackson, MS] B: 2/9/1969, Detroit, MI *Drafted:* 1992 Round 2 Dal

		Receiving				Kickoff Returns					Tot
Year Team	**G**	**Rec**	**Yds**	**Avg**	**TD**	**Ret**	**Yds**	**Avg**	**TD**	**Fum**	**TD**
1992 Dal	7	0	0	—	0	0	0	—	0	0	0
1995 Jac	16	22	288	13.1	3	24	540	22.5	1	2	5
1996 Jac	16	83	1244	15.0	7	2	49	24.5	0	1	7
1997 Jac	16	82	1324	16.1	4	0	0	—	0	1	4
1998 Jac	16	78	1182	15.2	8	0	0	—	0	2	8
NFL Total	71	265	4038	15.2	22	26	589	22.7	1	6	24

JOE SMITH Smith, Joe H 6′1″, 183 **OE-DB**
Col: Schreiner Coll.; Texas Tech *HS:* Electra [TX] B: 7/23/1922, Electra, TX D: 4/8/1978, Odessa, TX
AAFC **1948** BalA: 12 G; Rush 1-1 1.0; Rec 8-131 16.4 1 TD; Int 1-0; 6 Pt.

JOEY SMITH Smith, Joey Leon 5′10″, 177 **WR**
Col: Louisville *HS:* Austin-East [Knoxville, TN] B: 5/30/1969, Knoxville, TN
1992 NYG: Rec 3-45 15.0. **Total:** Rec 3-45 15.0.

		Kickoff Returns				
Year Team	**G**	**Ret**	**Yds**	**Avg**	**TD**	**Fum**
1991 NYG	1	3	34	11.3	0	0
1992 NYG	16	30	564	18.8	0	1
NFL Total	17	33	598	18.1	0	1

JOHN SMITH Smith, John G Jr. 6′2″, 200 **T**
Col: Florida B: 1919
1945 Phi: 1 G.

JOHN SMITH Smith, John Henry 6′0″, 175 **WR**
Col: Tennessee State *HS:* Tuskegee [AL] B: 1/27/1956, Tuskegee, AL
Drafted: 1979 Round 10 Cle
1979 Cle: 6 G.

JOHN SMITH Smith, John Michael 6′0″, 186 **K**
Col: King Alfred's (England); Southampton (England) *HS:* Burford School [England] B: 12/30/1949, Leafield, England

		Scoring						
Year Team	**G**	**Pts**	**FG**	**FGA**	**FG%**	**XK**	**XKA**	**XK%**
1974 NE	14	90	16	22	72.7	42	43	97.7
1975 NE	14	60	9	17	52.9	33	33	100.0
1976 NE	14	87	15	25	60.0	42	46	91.3
1977 NE	14	78	15	21	71.4	33	33	100.0
1978 NE	3	9	1	1	100.0	6	7	85.7
1979 NE	16	**115**	23	**33**	69.7	46	49	93.9
1980 NE	16	**129**	26	34	76.5	51	51	100.0
1981 NE	16	82	15	24	62.5	37	39	94.9
1982 NE	4	21	5	8	62.5	6	7	85.7
1983 NE	5	21	3	6	50.0	12	15	80.0
NFL Total	116	692	128	191	67.0	308	323	95.4

J.T. SMITH Smith, John Thomas 6′2″, 185 **WR**
Col: North Texas *HS:* Big Spring [TX] B: 10/29/1955, Leonard, TX
1985 StL: Rush 3-36 12.0. **1988** Pho: Rush 1-15 15.0. **1989** Pho: Rush 2-21 10.5. **1990** Pho: Rush 1-4 4.0. **Total:** Rush 7-76 10.9.

		Receiving				Punt Returns			
Year Team	**G**	**Rec**	**Yds**	**Avg**	**TD**	**Ret**	**Yds**	**Avg**	**TD**
1978 Was-KC	9	0	0	—	0	4	33	8.3	0
1978 Was	3	0	0	—	0	4	33	8.3	0
1978 KC	6	0	0	—	0	0	0	—	0
1979 KC	16	33	444	13.5	3	58	**612**	10.6	**2**
1980 KC	16	46	655	14.2	2	40	**581**	**14.5**	**2**
1981 KC	16	63	852	13.5	2	50	528	10.6	0
1982 KC	5	10	168	16.8	1	3	26	8.7	0
1983 KC	9	7	85	12.1	0	26	210	8.1	0
1984 KC	15	8	69	8.6	0	39	332	8.5	0
1985 StL	14	43	581	13.5	1	26	283	10.9	0
1986 StL	16	80	1014	12.7	6	1	6	6.0	0
1987 StL	15	**91**	**1117**	12.3	8	0	0	—	0
1988 Pho	16	83	986	11.9	5	17	119	7.0	0
1989 Pho	9	62	778	12.5	5	0	0	—	0
1990 Pho	13	18	225	12.5	2	3	34	11.3	0
NFL Total	169	544	6974	12.8	35	267	2764	10.4	4

	Kickoff Returns					Tot
Year Team	**Ret**	**Yds**	**Avg**	**TD**	**Fum**	**TD**
1978 Was-KC	1	18	18.0	0	0	0
1978 Was	1	18	18.0	0	0	0
1979 KC	0	0	—	0	3	5
1980 KC	0	0	—	0	1	4
1981 KC	0	0	—	0	2	2
1982 KC	0	0	—	0	0	1
1983 KC	1	5	5.0	0	0	0
1984 KC	19	391	20.6	0	1	0
1985 StL	4	59	14.8	0	3	1
1986 StL	0	0	—	0	1	6
1987 StL	0	0	—	0	2	8
1988 Pho	0	0	—	0	4	5
1989 Pho	0	0	—	0	0	5
1990 Pho	0	0	—	0	0	2
NFL Total	25	473	18.9	0	17	39

JOHNNY RAY SMITH Smith, Johnny Ray 5′9″, 183 **DB**
Col: Lamar *HS:* Cleveland [TX] B: 9/7/1957, Crockett, TX
Drafted: 1981 Round 11 TB
1982 TB: 9 G; KR 3-47 15.7; 2 Fum. **1983** TB: 16 G; KR 8-136 17.0; 2 Fum. **1984** SD: 1 G. **Total:** 26 G; KR 11-183 16.6; 4 Fum.

KENDAL SMITH Smith, Kendal Carson 5′10″, 189 **WR**
Col: Utah State *HS:* Mountain View [CA] B: 11/23/1965, San Mateo, CA *Drafted:* 1989 Round 7 Cin
1989 Cin: 11 G; Rec 10-140 14.0 1 TD; PR 12-54 4.5; KR 5-65 13.0; 6 Pt; 1 Fum. **1990** Cin: 9 G; Rec 7-45 6.4; PR 1-4 4.0; KR 2-35 17.5.
Total: 20 G; Rec 17-185 10.9 1 TD; PR 13-58 4.5; KR 7-100 14.3; 6 Pt; 1 Fum.

KEN SMITH Smith, Kenneth James 6′2″, 285 **OG**
Col: Evansville; Miami (Ohio) *HS:* North Central [Indianapolis, IN]
B: 10/16/1960, Indianapolis, IN
1987 Cin: 3 G.

KEN SMITH Smith, Kenneth Leslie 6′4″, 225 **TE**
Col: Navarro Coll. TX (J.C.); New Mexico *HS:* Malakoff [TX]
B: 7/27/1951, Houston, TX
1973 Cle: 13 G.

KEVIN SMITH Smith, Kevin Anthony 5′11″, 204 **DB**
Col: Rhode Island *HS:* Rogers [Newport, RI] B: 4/2/1967, Newport, RI
1991 Pit: 16 G.

KEVIN SMITH Smith, Kevin Linn 6′4″, 255 **TE**
Col: UCLA *HS:* Skyline [Oakland, CA] B: 7/25/1969, Bakersfield, CA
Drafted: 1992 Round 7 LARd
1992 LARd: 1 G. **1993** LARd: 10 G; KR 2-15 7.5. **1994** LARd: 3 G; Rush 1-2 2.0; Rec 1-8 8.0. **1996** GB: 1 G. **Total:** 15 G; Rush 1-2 2.0; Rec 1-8 8.0; KR 2-15 7.5.

KEVIN SMITH Smith, Kevin Rey 5′11″, 183 **DB**
Col: Texas A&M *HS:* West Orange-Stark [Orange, TX] B: 4/7/1970, Orange, TX *Drafted:* 1992 Round 1 Dal
1992 Dal: PR 1-17 17.0; KR 1-9 9.0. **1993** Dal: KR 1-33 33.0. **1998** Dal: PR 1-11 11.0. **Total:** PR 2-28 14.0; KR 2-42 21.0.

		Interceptions		
Year Team	**G**	**Int**	**Yds**	**TD**
1992 Dal	16	2	10	0
1993 Dal	16	6	56	1
1994 Dal	16	2	11	0
1995 Dal	1	0	0	0
1996 Dal	16	5	45	0
1997 Dal	16	1	21	0
1998 Dal	14	2	31	0
NFL Total	95	18	174	1

LAMAR SMITH Smith, Lamar 5′11″, 222 **RB**
Col: Houston *HS:* South Side [Fort Wayne, IN] B: 11/29/1970, Fort Wayne, IN *Drafted:* 1994 Round 3 Sea
1995 Sea: KR 1-20 20.0. **1996** Sea: Scor **3** 2XP. **1997** Sea: KR 1-14 14.0; Scor 1 2XP. **1998** NO: Pass 2-1 50.0%, 20 10.00 1 TD. **Total:** Pass 2-1 50.0%, 20 10.00 1 TD; KR 2-34 17.0; Scor 4 2XP.

		Rushing				Receiving					Tot
Year Team	**G**	**Att**	**Yds**	**Avg**	**TD**	**Rec**	**Yds**	**Avg**	**TD**	**Fum**	**TD**
1994 Sea	2	2	-1	-0.5	0	0	0	—	0	0	0
1995 Sea	12	36	215	6.0	0	1	10	10.0	0	1	0
1996 Sea	16	153	680	4.4	8	9	58	6.4	0	4	8
1997 Sea	12	91	392	4.3	2	23	183	8.0	0	0	2
1998 NO	14	138	457	3.3	1	24	249	10.4	2	4	3
NFL Total	56	420	1743	4.2	11	57	500	8.8	2	9	13

LANCE SMITH Smith, Lance 6′3″, 283 **OG-OT**
Col: Louisiana State *HS:* A.L. Brown [Kannapolis, NC] B: 1/1/1963, New York, NY *Drafted:* 1985 Round 3 StL
1985 StL: 14 G. **1986** StL: 15 G. **1987** StL: 15 G. **1988** Pho: 16 G. **1989** Pho: 16 G. **1990** Pho: 16 G. **1991** Pho: 16 G. **1992** Pho: 16 G; KR 2-16 8.0. **1993** Pho: 16 G; KR 1-11 11.0. **1994** NYG: 13 G. **1995** NYG: 13 G. **1996** NYG: 16 G. **Total:** 182 G; KR 3-27 9.0.

LAVERNE SMITH Smith, Laverne 5′10″, 193 **RB**
Col: Kansas *HS:* Southeast [Wichita, KS] B: 9/12/1954, Greenwood, MS *Drafted:* 1977 Round 4 Pit
1977 Pit: 7 G; Rush 14-55 3.9; KR 16-365 22.8; 1 Fum.

LARRY SMITH Smith, Lawrence Abell 6′1″, 210 **LB**
Col: Kentucky *HS:* Washington Co. [Springfield, KY] B: 2/7/1965
1987 Hou: 3 G.

TODY SMITH Smith, Lawrence Edward 6′5″, 250 **DE**
Col: Michigan State; USC *HS:* Charlton-Pollard [Beaumont, TX]
B: 12/24/1948, Orange, TX *Drafted:* 1971 Round 1 Dal
1971 Dal: 7 G. **1972** Dal: 10 G. **1973** Hou: 14 G. **1974** Hou: 14 G; Int 1-34. **1975** Hou: 13 G. **1976** Hou-Buf: 11 G. Hou: 9 G. Buf: 2 G. **Total:** 69 G; Int 1-34.

LEN SMITH Smith, Leonard Marshall 5′11″, 195 **T**
(Fat) *Col:* Wis.-Oshkosh; Wisconsin *HS:* Oshkosh [WI] B: 12/14/1896 Deceased
1923 Rac: 10 G. **1924** Rac: 10 G. **Total:** 20 G.

LEONARD SMITH Smith, Leonard Phillip 5′11″, 200 **DB**
Col: McNeese State *HS:* Robert E. Lee [Baton Rouge, LA]
B: 9/2/1960, New Orleans, LA *Drafted:* 1983 Round 1 StL
1983 StL: KR 1-19 19.0. **1984** StL: 1 Sac. **1985** StL: KR 5-68 13.6; 3 Sac. **1986** StL: 5 Sac. **1987** StL: **1** Fum TD; 2 Sac. **1988** Pho-Buf: 1 Sac. Buf: 1 Sac. **1991** Buf: 2 Sac. **Total:** KR 6-87 14.5; 1 Fum TD; 14 Sac.

		Interceptions				Tot
Year Team	**G**	**Int**	**Yds**	**TD**	**Fum**	**TD**
1983 StL	16	0	0	0	0	0
1984 StL	12	2	31	1	0	1
1985 StL	16	2	73	0	1	0
1986 StL	16	1	13	0	0	0
1987 StL	15	0	0	0	0	1
1988 Pho-Buf	16	2	29	0	0	0
1988 Pho	3	1	15	0	0	0
1988 Buf	13	1	14	0	0	0
1989 Buf	15	2	46	0	0	0
1990 Buf	16	2	39	1	0	1
1991 Buf	16	3	22	0	0	0
NFL Total	138	14	253	2	1	3

LUCIOUS SMITH Smith, Lucious Irvin 5′10″, 190 **DB**
Col: San Diego State; Cal State-Fullerton *HS:* Kearny [San Diego, CA]
B: 1/17/1957, Columbus, GA
1980 LARm: 16 G. **1981** LARm: 16 G. **1982** LARm: 8 G. **1983** KC: 16 G; Int 3-99 1 TD; 6 Pt. **1984** Buf-SD: 13 G; PR 1-0; Int 1-7; 1 Fum. Buf: 4 G; Int 1-7. SD: 9 G; PR 1-0; 1 Fum. **1985** SD: 5 G. **Total:** 74 G; PR 1-0; Int 4-106 1 TD; 6 Pt; 1 Fum.

LYMAN SMITH Smith, Lyman Scott-William 6′5″, 250 **DT**
Col: Duke *HS:* North Shore [Glen Cove, NY] B: 9/24/1956, Portland, OR *Drafted:* 1978 Round 3 Mia
1978 Min: 11 G.

MARK SMITH Smith, Mark Anthony 6′4″, 290 **DE**
Col: Navarro Coll. TX (J.C.); Hinds CC MS; Auburn *HS:* Vicksburg [MS]
B: 8/28/1974, Vicksburg, MS *Drafted:* 1997 Round 7 Ariz
1997 Ariz: 16 G; 6 Sac. **1998** Ariz: 14 G; 9 Sac. **Total:** 30 G; 15 Sac.

MARTY SMITH Smith, Martin Joseph 6′3″, 250 **DE**
Col: Louisville *HS:* East [Cleveland, OH] B: 10/20/1953, Pattison, MS
Drafted: 1975 Round 15 Pit
1976 Buf: 14 G.

MARV SMITH Smith, Marvin McCammon 5′11″, 185 **TB**
Col: Purdue *HS:* McKinley [Canton, OH] B: 4/15/1898, Canton, OH
D: 4/24/1986, Muncie, IN
1921 Can: 1 G.

JERMAINE SMITH Smith, Matt Jermaine 6′2″, 289 **DT**
Col: Georgia Mil. Coll. (J.C.); Georgia *HS:* Lucy Craft Laney [Augusta, GA] B: 2/3/1972, Augusta, GA *Drafted:* 1997 Round 4 GB
1997 GB: 9 G; 1 Sac.

REX SMITH Smith, Matthew Everett 6′0″, 195 **E**
Col: Wis.-La Crosse; Beloit *HS:* Rushford [MN] B: 3/8/1896, Rushford, MN D: 1/16/1972, Wolfeboro, NH
1922 GB: 2 G.

MATT SMITH Smith, Matthew Morgan 6′2″, 234 **LB**
Col: West Virginia *HS:* Gahanna [OH] B: 9/1/1965, Columbus, OH
1987 Den: 3 G.

MICHAEL SMITH Smith, Michael Charles Jr. 5′8″, 160 **WR**
Col: Kansas State *HS:* Jesuit [New Orleans, LA] B: 11/21/1970, New Orleans, LA
1992 KC: 2 G.

MIKE SMITH Smith, Michael T 5′10″, 194 **WR**
Col: Grambling State *HS:* Bastrop [LA] B: 4/28/1958, Bastrop, LA
Drafted: 1980 Round 7 Atl
1980 Atl: 5 G; KR 3-58 19.3.

MIKE SMITH Smith, Michael Wayne 6′0″, 171 **DB**
Col: Texas-El Paso *HS:* Booker T. Washington [Houston, TX]
B: 10/24/1962, Houston, TX *Drafted:* 1985 Round 4 Mia
1985 Mia: 7 G. **1986** Mia: 14 G; 1 Sac. **1987** Mia: 8 G. **Total:** 29 G; 1 Sac.

MILT SMITH Smith, Milton Bradley 6′3″, 185 **DB-QB**
(Snuffy) *Col:* UCLA *HS:* Santa Ana [CA] B: 7/7/1919 D: 10/1/1988, Landrum, SC *Drafted:* 1944 Round 21 Phi
1945 Phi: 5 G.

MONTE SMITH Smith, Monte Gene 6′5″, 270 **OG**
Col: North Dakota *HS:* Oregon [WI] B: 4/24/1967, Madison, WI
Drafted: 1989 Round 9 Den
1989 Den: 14 G.

NEIL SMITH Smith, Neil 6′4″, 270 **DE**
Col: Nebraska *HS:* McDonogh 35 [New Orleans, LA] B: 4/10/1966, New Orleans, LA *Drafted:* 1988 Round 1 KC
1988 KC: 13 G; 2.5 Sac. **1989** KC: 15 G; 1 Fum TD; 6 Pt; 6.5 Sac. **1990** KC: 16 G; 9.5 Sac. **1991** KC: 16 G; 8 Sac. **1992** KC: 16 G; Int 1-22 1 TD; 6 Pt; 14.5 Sac. **1993** KC: 16 G; Int 1-3; **15** Sac. **1994** KC: 14 G; Int 1-41; 11.5 Sac. **1995** KC: 16 G; 12 Sac. **1996** KC: 16 G; 6 Sac. **1997** Den: 14 G; 8.5 Sac. **1998** Den: 14 G; Int 1-2; 4 Sac. **Total:** 166 G; Int 4-68 1 TD; 1 Fum TD; Tot TD 2; 12 Pt; 98.0 Sac.

NOLAND SMITH Smith, Noland 5′5″, 154 **WR-HB**
(Super Gnat) *Col:* Tennessee State *HS:* Brinkley [Jackson, MS]
B: 10/20/1943, Jackson, MS *Drafted:* 1967 Round 6 KC
1967 KC: Rush 1-8 8.0; Rec 1-42 42.0. **1968** KC: Rush 2-(-2) -1.0; Rec 1-15 15.0. **Total:** Rush 3-6 2.0; Rec 2-57 28.5.

		Punt Returns				Kickoff Returns					Tot
Year Team	**G**	**Ret**	**Yds**	**Avg**	**TD**	**Ret**	**Yds**	**Avg**	**TD**	**Fum**	**TD**
1967 KC	14	26	212	8.2	0	**41**	**1148**	28.0	**1**	6	1
1968 KC	12	18	270	**15.0**	1	23	549	23.9	0	1	1
1969 KC-SF	13	19	153	8.1	0	18	440	24.4	0	6	0
1969 KC	6	9	107	11.9	0	4	125	31.3	0	2	0
1969 SF	7	10	46	4.6	0	14	315	22.5	0	4	0
NFL Total	39	63	635	10.1	1	82	2137	26.1	1	13	2

OAK SMITH Smith, Okla Eugene 6′2″, 185 **OE-FB-WB**
Col: Drake *HS:* Centerville [IA] B: 2/27/1894, Downing, MO
D: 5/2/1974, Long Beach, CA
1920 RI: 9 G. **1921** RI: 7 G. **Total:** 16 G.

OLIN SMITH Smith, Olin Bashford 6′1″, 230 **T-G**
Col: Ohio Wesleyan *HS:* Perry [Cridersville, OH] B: 3/25/1900
D: 5/4/1966, Columbus, OH
1924 Cle: 8 G; Scor 8, 2 XK.

OLLIE SMITH Smith, Ollie P 6′3″, 203 **WR**
Col: Tennessee State *HS:* Brinkley [Jackson, MS] B: 3/8/1949, Jackson, MS *Drafted:* 1973 Round 4 Bal
1973 Bal: Rush 1-(-3) -3.0. **1976** GB: KR 1-12 12.0. **Total:** Rush 1-(-3) -3.0; KR 1-12 12.0.

		Receiving				
Year Team	**G**	**Rec**	**Yds**	**Avg**	**TD**	**Fum**
1973 Bal	7	1	37	37.0	0	1
1974 Bal	1	1	14	14.0	0	1
1976 GB	13	20	364	18.2	1	2
1977 GB	12	22	357	16.2	0	1
NFL Total	33	44	772	17.5	1	5

ORLAND SMITH Smith, Orland Francis 5′11″, 215 **T-G**
Col: Brown *HS:* Brockton [MA] B: 11/5/1905, Gorham, ME
D: 8/14/1977, Providence, RI
1927 Prov: 13 G. **1928** Prov: 9 G. **1929** Prov: 10 G. **Total:** 32 G.

OSCAR SMITH Smith, Oscar E 5′9″, 203 **RB**
Col: Nicholls State *HS:* Thomas Jefferson [Tampa, FL] B: 4/5/1963, Tampa, FL *Drafted:* 1986 Round 5 Det
1986 Det: 2 G; KR 5-81 16.2.

ED SMITH Smith, Oscar Edwin 6′3″, 185 **HB-DB**
Col: Texas-El Paso *HS:* San Pedro [CA] B: 7/20/1923, Fort Monroe, VA
Drafted: 1948 Round 2 GB
1948 GB: Rec 12-121 10.1; PR 8-71 8.9; KR 12-287 23.9. **1949** GB-NYB: PR 5-31 6.2; KR 2-36 18.0; Int 2-21. GB: PR 2-9 4.5; KR 2-36 18.0. NYB: PR 3-22 7.3; Int 2-21. **Total:** Rec 12-121 10.1; PR 13-102 7.8; KR 14-323 23.1; Int 2-21.

		Rushing				
Year Team	**G**	**Att**	**Yds**	**Avg**	**TD**	**Fum**
1948 GB	12	27	85	3.1	0	2
1949 GB-NYB	11	16	24	1.5	0	1
1949 GB	3	9	15	1.7	0	0
1949 NYB	8	7	9	1.3	0	1
NFL Total	23	43	109	2.5	0	3

OTIS SMITH Smith, Otis III 5′11″, 188 **DB**
(My Man) *Col:* Taft Coll. CA (J.C.); Missouri *HS:* East Jefferson [Metairie, LA] B: 10/22/1965, New Orleans, LA
1993 Phi: PR 0-9; KR 0-24. **1994** Phi: KR 1-14 14.0; 1 Sac. **1995** NYJ: KR 1-6 6.0. **1996** NYJ-NE: 1 Sac. NE: 1 Sac. **Total:** PR 0-9; KR 2-44 22.0; 2 Sac.

		Interceptions		
Year Team	**G**	**Int**	**Yds**	**TD**
1991 Phi	15	2	74	1
1992 Phi	16	1	0	0
1993 Phi	15	1	0	0
1994 Phi	16	0	0	0
1995 NYJ	11	6	101	1
1996 NYJ-NE	13	2	20	0
1996 NYJ	2	0	0	0
1996 NE	11	2	20	0
1997 NYJ	16	6	158	**3**
1998 NYJ	16	2	34	0
NFL Total	118	20	387	5

PAUL SMITH Smith, Paul Edward 6′3″, 256 **DT-DE**
Col: New Mexico *HS:* Roswell [NM] B: 8/13/1945, Ada, OK
Drafted: 1968 Round 9 Den
1968 Den: 12 G. **1969** Den: 14 G. **1970** Den: 14 G. **1971** Den: 14 G. **1972** Den: 14 G. **1973** Den: 14 G. **1974** Den: 4 G. **1975** Den: 13 G; **1** Fum TD; 6 Pt. **1976** Den: 11 G. **1977** Den: 12 G; Int 1-6. **1978** Den: 11 G. **1979** Was: 15 G. **1980** Was: 16 G; Int 1-8. **Total:** 164 G; Int 2-14; 1 Fum TD; 6 Pt.

PHIL SMITH Smith, Phillip Keith 6′3″, 190 **WR**
Col: San Diego State *HS:* Junipero Serra [Gardena, CA] B: 4/28/1960, Los Angeles, CA *Drafted:* 1983 Round 4 Bal
1984 Ind: Rush 2-(-10) -5.0. **1986** Phi: Rec 6-94 15.7; PR 4-18 4.5. **1987** LARm: Rec 3-95 31.7; PR 2-5 2.5. **Total:** Rush 2-(-10) -5.0; Rec 9-189 21.0; PR 6-23 3.8.

		Kickoff Returns				
Year Team	**G**	**Ret**	**Yds**	**Avg**	**TD**	**Fum**
1983 Bal	1	0	0	—	0	0
1984 Ind	16	32	651	20.3	**1**	1
1986 Phi	3	0	0	—	0	1
1987 LARm	2	0	0	—	0	1
NFL Total	22	32	651	20.3	1	3

QUINTIN SMITH Smith, Quintin Anton 5′10″, 172 **WR**
Col: Kansas *HS:* Jack Yates [Houston, TX] B: 8/17/1968, Houston, TX
1990 ChiB: 4 G; Rec 2-20 10.0.

RALPH SMITH Smith, Ralph Allon 6′2″, 215 **TE**
(Catfish) *Col:* Mississippi *HS:* Brookhaven [MS] B: 12/1/1938, Brookhaven, MS *Drafted:* 1962 Round 8 Phi
1962 Phi: Rush 1-13 13.0; PR 1-2 2.0. **1963** Phi: KR 2-18 9.0. **1966** Cle: KR 1-0. **1967** Cle: **1** Fum TD. **1968** Cle: Rush 1-13 13.0; KR 1-3 3.0. **Total:** Rush 2-26 13.0; PR 1-2 2.0; KR 4-21 5.3; 1 Fum TD.

		Receiving				Tot
Year Team	**G**	**Rec**	**Yds**	**Avg**	**TD**	**TD**
1962 Phi	13	1	29	29.0	0	0
1963 Phi	14	5	63	12.6	1	1
1964 Phi	11	4	35	8.8	0	0
1965 Cle	14	0	0	—	0	0
1966 Cle	14	13	183	14.1	3	3
1967 Cle	14	14	211	15.1	1	2
1968 Cle	14	2	11	5.5	0	0
1969 Atl	14	2	17	8.5	0	0
NFL Total	108	41	549	13.4	5	6

RAY GENE SMITH Smith, Ray Gene 5′10″, 187 **DB-HB**
Col: Midwestern State *HS:* Lawton [OK] B: 11/27/1928, Andarko, OK
1954 ChiB: KR 2-38 19.0; Int 2-0. **1955** ChiB: Rec 1-13 13.0; KR 1-24 24.0; Int 2-12. **1956** ChiB: KR 1-16 16.0; Int 4-90. **1957** ChiB: Rush 1-8 8.0; Rec 3-37 12.3; Int 1-22. **Total:** Rush 1-8 8.0; Rec 4-50 12.5; KR 4-78 19.5; Int 9-124.

		Punt Returns				
Year Team	**G**	**Ret**	**Yds**	**Avg**	**TD**	**Fum**
1954 ChiB	7	7	43	6.1	0	1
1955 ChiB	12	12	47	3.9	0	1
1956 ChiB	12	6	65	10.8	0	0
1957 ChiB	5	2	1	0.5	0	1
NFL Total	36	27	156	5.8	0	3

RAY SMITH Smith, Raymond Henry 5′10″, 195 **C**
Col: Tulsa; Missouri *HS:* Sapulpa [OK] B: 1908
1930 Prov: 10 G. **1931** Prov: 10 G. **1933** Phi: 1 G. **Total:** 21 G.

REGGIE SMITH Smith, Reginald Lernard 6′5″, 295 **OT**
Col: Kansas *HS:* Chicago Vocational [IL] B: 8/29/1961, Chicago, IL
Drafted: 1984 Supplemental Round 3 Den
1987 TB: 3 G.

REGGIE SMITH Smith, Reginald R 5′4″, 168 **WR**
Col: North Carolina Central *HS:* Wilson [NC] B: 7/15/1956, Kinston, NC

		Punt Returns				Kickoff Returns				
Year Team	**G**	**Ret**	**Yds**	**Avg**	**TD**	**Ret**	**Yds**	**Avg**	**TD**	**Fum**
1980 Atl	8	27	262	9.7	0	25	512	20.5	0	3
1981 Atl	15	12	99	8.3	0	47	1143	24.3	0	4
1987 NYJ	1	2	9	4.5	0	4	60	15.0	0	1
NFL Total	24	41	370	9.0	0	76	1715	22.6	0	8

DICK SMITH Smith, Richard Henry 6′0″, 205 **DB-HB**
Col: Northwestern *HS:* Garfield [Hamilton, OH] B: 6/19/1944, Hamilton, OH D: 1/16/1972
1967 Was: 10 G; KR 4-120 30.0; Int 3-0. **1968** Was: 10 G; Rush 3-5 1.7; Rec 1-15 15.0; KR 10-228 22.8; Int 1-0. **Total:** 20 G; Rush 3-5 1.7; Rec 1-15 15.0; KR 14-348 24.9; Int 4-0.

RED SMITH Smith, Richard Paul 5′10″, 192 **BB-G-TB-FB**
Col: Lawrence; Notre Dame *HS:* Kaukauna [WI] B: 5/18/1904, Combined Locks, WI D: 3/8/1978, Toledo, OH
1927 GB: 5 G. **1928** NYG-NYY: 11 G; Rush 3 TD; Scor 20, 2 XK. NYG: 1 G. NYY: 10 G; Rush 3 TD; Scor 20, 2 XK. **1929** GB: 5 G. **1930** Nwk: 7 G; Scor 1, 1 XK. **1931** NYG: 9 G; Pass 1 TD; Scor 2, 2 XK. **Total:** 37 G; Pass 1 TD; Rush 3 TD.

DICK SMITH Smith, Richard Scott 6′2″, 225 **C**
Col: Ohio State *HS:* Washington [East Chicago, IN] B: 1/24/1912, East Chicago, IN D: 4/15/1980, New Canaan, CT
1933 Bos-ChiB-Phi: 5 G. Bos: 1 G. ChiB: 1 G. Phi: 3 G. **Total:** 5 G.

RICKY SMITH Smith, Ricky DeCarlo 6′0″, 182 **DB-WR**
(Rick) *Col:* Alabama State *HS:* James A. Shanks [Quincy, FL] B: 7/20/1960, Quincy, FL *Drafted:* 1982 Round 6 NE
1984 NE-Was: Int 1-37. Was: Int 1-37. **1987** Det: Int 1-34 1 TD. **Total:** Int 2-71 1 TD.

		Punt Returns				Kickoff Returns					Tot
Year Team	**G**	**Ret**	**Yds**	**Avg**	**TD**	**Ret**	**Yds**	**Avg**	**TD**	**Fum**	**TD**
1982 NE	9	16	139	8.7	0	24	567	23.6	**1**	3	1
1983 NE	16	38	398	10.5	0	42	916	21.8	0	11	0
1984 NE-Was	12	0	0	—	0	1	22	22.0	0	0	0
1984 NE	1	0	0	—	0	1	22	22.0	0	0	0
1984 Was	11	0	0	—	0	0	0	—	0	0	0
1987 Det	12	0	0	—	0	0	0	—	0	0	1
NFL Total	49	54	537	9.9	0	67	1505	22.5	1	14	2

RICO SMITH Smith, Rico Louis Jr. 6′0″, 185 **WR**
Col: Cerritos Coll. CA (J.C.); Colorado *HS:* Paramount [CA]
B: 1/14/1969, Compton, CA *Drafted:* 1992 Round 6 Cle
1992 Cle: 10 G; Rec 5-64 12.8. **1993** Cle: 10 G; Rec 4-55 13.8; KR 1-13 13.0. **1994** Cle: 5 G; Rec 2-61 30.5. **1995** Cle: 4 G; Rec 13-173 13.3 1 TD; 6 Pt; 1 Fum. **Total:** 29 G; Rec 24-353 14.7 1 TD; KR 1-13 13.0; 6 Pt; 1 Fum.

RILEY SMITH Smith, Riley Henry 6′2″, 200 **BB-LB**
(General) *Col:* Alabama *HS:* Greenwood [MS]; Columbus HS [MS]
B: 7/14/1911, Carrollton, MS *Drafted:* 1936 Round 1 Bos
1936 Bos: Pass 33-14 42.4%, 239 **7.24** 3 Int; Rec 3-76 25.3 2 TD; Scor 38, 4 FG, 14 XK. **1937** Was: Pass 9-4 44.4%, 33 3.67 3 TD; Rec 11-93 8.5; Int **1** TD; Scor 55, 5 FG, **22** XK. **1938** Was: Pass 4-1 25.0%, 18 4.50; Rec 4-131 32.8 1 TD; Scor 15, 2-5 40.0% FG, 3-6 50.0% XK. **Total:** Pass 46-19 41.3%, 290 6.30 3 TD 3 Int; Rec 18-300 16.7 3 TD; Int 1 TD; Scor 108, 11-5 40.0% FG, 39-6 50.0% XK.

		Rushing				Tot
Year Team	**G**	**Att**	**Yds**	**Avg**	**TD**	**TD**
1936 Bos	12	30	26	0.9	0	2
1937 Was	11	12	39	3.3	2	3
1938 Was	7	3	-7	-2.3	0	1
NFL Total	30	45	58	1.3	2	6

ROBERT SMITH Smith, Robert Benjamin 6′5″, 255 **DE**
Col: Grambling State *HS:* Bogalusa [LA] B: 12/3/1962, Bogalusa, LA
Drafted: 1984 Supplemental Round 2 Min
1985 Min: 16 G.

BOB SMITH Smith, Robert Bert 6′0″, 181 **DB**
Col: Miami (Ohio) *HS:* Hughes [Cincinnati, OH] B: 12/28/1945, Williamson, WV *Drafted:* 1968 Round 16 Hou
1968 Hou: 6 G.

BOB SMITH Smith, Robert Gerald 5′10″, 195 **HB**
Col: Nebraska *HS:* Grand Island [NE] B: 2/23/1933, Council Bluffs, IA
Drafted: 1955 Round 15 Cle
1955 Cle: Rec 2-12 6.0; PR 1-5 5.0; KR 13-320 24.6. **1956** Cle-Phi: KR 1-14 14.0. Cle: KR 1-14 14.0. **Total:** Rec 2-12 6.0; PR 1-5 5.0; KR 14-334 23.9.

		Rushing				
Year Team	**G**	**Att**	**Yds**	**Avg**	**TD**	**Fum**
1955 Cle	10	37	142	3.8	1	1
1956 Cle-Phi	6	11	18	1.6	0	0
1956 Cle	2	2	10	5.0	0	0
1956 Phi	4	9	8	0.9	0	0
NFL Total	16	48	160	3.3	1	1

BOBBY SMITH Smith, Robert Lee 6′0″, 203 **HB**
Col: North Texas *HS:* Roy Miller [Corpus Christi, TX] B: 5/18/1942, Corpus Christi, TX *Drafted:* 1964 Round 11 Buf
1964 Buf: Rec 6-72 12.0; KR 3-68 22.7. **1965** Buf: Rec 12-116 9.7. **1966** Pit: Rec 3-26 8.7. **Total:** Rec 21-214 10.2; KR 3-68 22.7.

		Rushing				
Year Team	**G**	**Att**	**Yds**	**Avg**	**TD**	**Fum**
1964 Buf	14	62	306	4.9	4	2
1965 Buf	14	43	137	3.2	1	2
1966 Pit	8	24	93	3.9	0	2
NFL Total	36	129	536	4.2	5	6

BOB SMITH Smith, Robert Lee 6′0″, 205 **FB**
Col: Texas A&M *HS:* Mirabeau B. Lamar [Houston, TX] B: 2/28/1929, Houston, TX *Drafted:* 1951 Round 4 Cle
1953 Det: 3 G; Rush 6-51 8.5; Rec 1-11 11.0; 1 Fum. **1954** Det: 12 G; Rush 3-1 0.3. **Total:** 15 G; Rush 9-52 5.8; Rec 1-11 11.0; 1 Fum.

BOBBY SMITH Smith, Robert Lee 5′11″, 197 **DB**
Col: Compton CC CA; UCLA *HS:* Compton [CA] B: 7/5/1938, Plain Dealing, LA *Drafted:* 1961 Round 7 LARm
1962 LARm: Int 1-47. **1963** LARm: Int 2-11. **1964** LARm: Int 2-97 1 TD. **Total:** Int 5-155 1 TD.

		Punt Returns				Kickoff Returns					Tot
Year Team	G	Ret	Yds	Avg	TD	Ret	Yds	Avg	TD	Fum	TD
1962 LARm	14	1	7	7.0	0	2	60	30.0	0	0	0
1963 LARm	14	2	20	10.0	0	0	0	—	0	1	0
1964 LARm	14	12	68	5.7	0	20	489	24.5	0	2	2
1965 LARm-Det	13	10	56	5.6	0	18	475	26.4	0	4	0
1965 LARm	7	9	56	6.2	0	17	457	26.9	0	2	0
1965 Det	6	1	0	0.0	0	1	18	18.0	0	2	0
1966 Det	14	0	0	—	0	0	0	—	0	0	0
NFL Total	69	25	151	6.0	0	40	1024	25.6	0	7	2

ROBERT SMITH Smith, Robert Scott 6′2″, 212 **RB**
Col: Ohio State *HS:* Euclid [OH] B: 3/4/1972, Euclid, OH *Drafted:* 1993 Round 1 Min
1993 Min: PR 1-4 4.0; KR 3-41 13.7. **1994** Min: KR 16-419 26.2. **1995** Min: Scor 1 2XP. **Total:** PR 1-4 4.0; KR 19-460 24.2; Scor 1 2XP.

		Rushing				Receiving					Tot
Year Team	G	Att	Yds	Avg	TD	Rec	Yds	Avg	TD	Fum	TD
1993 Min	10	82	399	4.9	2	24	111	4.6	0	0	2
1994 Min	14	31	106	3.4	1	15	105	7.0	0	0	1
1995 Min	9	139	632	4.5	5	7	35	5.0	0	1	5
1996 Min	8	162	692	4.3	3	7	39	5.6	0	2	3
1997 Min	14	232	1266	5.5	6	37	197	5.3	1	0	7
1998 Min	14	249	1187	4.8	6	28	291	10.4	2	1	8
NFL Total	69	895	4282	4.8	23	118	778	6.6	3	4	26

ROD SMITH Smith, Rod 6′0″, 191 **WR**
Col: Missouri Southern State *HS:* Arkansas [Texarkana, AR] B: 5/15/1970, Texarkana, AR
1995 Den: KR 4-54 13.5. **1996** Den: Rush 1-1 1.0; PR 23-283 12.3; KR 1-29 29.0. **1997** Den: Rush 5-16 3.2; PR 1-12 12.0. **1998** Den: Pass 1-1 100.0%, 14 14.00; Rush 6-63 10.5; 1 Fum TD. **Total:** Pass 1-1 100.0%, 14 14.00; Rush 12-80 6.7; PR 24-295 12.3; KR 5-83 16.6; 1 Fum TD.

		Receiving					Tot
Year Team	G	Rec	Yds	Avg	TD	Fum	TD
1995 Den	16	6	152	25.3	1	0	1
1996 Den	10	16	237	14.8	2	1	2
1997 Den	16	70	1180	16.9	12	3	12
1998 Den	16	86	1222	14.2	6	0	7
NFL Total	58	178	2791	15.7	21	4	22

ROD SMITH Smith, Rodney Marc 5′11″, 187 **DB**
Col: Notre Dame *HS:* Roseville [MN] B: 3/12/1970, St. Paul, MN *Drafted:* 1992 Round 2 NE
1992 NE: 16 G; Int 1-0. **1993** NE: 16 G; PR 1-0. **1994** NE: 16 G; Int 2-10; 0.5 Sac. **1995** Car: 16 G. **1996** Car: 8 G; 1 Sac. **1997** Car: 16 G. **1998** Car-GB: 14 G; Int 2-43. Car: 6 G; Int 1-43. GB: 8 G; Int 1-0. **Total:** 102 G; PR 1-0; Int 5-53; 1.5 Sac.

ZEKE SMITH Smith, Roger Duane 6′2″, 235 **LB-OG-DE**
Col: Auburn *HS:* Uniontown [AL] B: 9/29/1936, Walker Springs, AL *Drafted:* 1960 Round 1 NYT
1960 Bal: 12 G. **1961** NYG: 12 G. **Total:** 24 G.

RON SMITH Smith, Ronald 6′1″, 195 **DB-WR**
(Pinto) *Col:* Wisconsin *HS:* Washington [East Chicago, IN] B: 5/3/1943, Chicago, IL
1967 Atl: Rush 8-42 5.3; Rec 11-227 20.6. **Total:** Rush 8-42 5.3; Rec 11-227 20.6.

		Punt Returns				Kickoff Returns				Interceptions				Tot
Year Team	G	Ret	Yds	Avg	TD	Ret	Yds	Avg	TD	Int	Yds	TD	Fum	TD
1965 ChiB	14	1	2	2.0	0	1	17	17.0	0	0	0	0	1	0
1966 Atl	14	11	80	7.3	0	**43**	**1013**	23.6	0	2	6	0	2	0
1967 Atl	13	20	92	4.6	0	**39**	**976**	25.0	1	0	0	0	6	1
1968 LARm	14	27	171	6.3	0	26	718	27.6	1	3	28	0	2	1
1969 LARm	14	23	122	5.3	0	27	585	21.7	0	3	70	1	3	1
1970 ChiB	14	33	126	3.8	0	28	651	23.3	0	0	0	0	4	0
1971 ChiB	14	26	194	7.5	0	26	671	25.8	0	3	48	0	6	0
1972 ChiB	14	26	163	6.3	0	30	924	**30.8**	**1**	1	2	0	3	1
1973 SD	14	27	352	13.0	**2**	36	947	26.3	0	1	4	0	10	2
1974 Oak	14	41	486	11.9	0	19	420	22.1	0	0	0	0	2	0
NFL Total	139	235	1788	7.6	2	275	6922	25.2	3	13	158	1	39	6

RON SMITH Smith, Ronald Christopher 6′5″, 220 **QB**
Col: Wake Forest; Richmond *HS:* Varina [Richmond, VA] B: 6/27/1942, Richmond, VA *Drafted:* 1964 Round 10 LARm
1966 Pit: Rush 4-(-9) -2.3. **Total:** Rush 4-(-9) -2.3.

		Passing								
Year Team	G	Att	Comp	Comp%	Yds	YPA	TD	Int	Rating	Fum
1965 LARm	1	0	0	—	0	—	0	0	—	0
1966 Pit	9	181	79	43.6	1249	6.90	8	12	54.3	2
NFL Total	10	181	79	43.6	1249	6.90	8	12	54.3	2

RON SMITH Smith, Ronnie Bernard 6′0″, 185 **WR**
Col: Fullerton Coll. CA (J.C.); San Diego State *HS:* Kathleen [Lakeland, FL] B: 11/20/1956, Lakeland, FL *Drafted:* 1978 Round 2 LARm
1980 SD: KR 10-186 18.6. **1981** SD-Phi: Rush 1-7 7.0; KR 2-32 16.0. SD: KR 2-32 16.0. Phi: Rush 1-7 7.0. **Total:** Rush 1-7 7.0; KR 12-218 18.2.

		Receiving				
Year Team	G	Rec	Yds	Avg	TD	Fum
1978 LARm	16	1	15	15.0	0	0
1979 LARm	12	16	300	18.8	1	2
1980 SD	15	4	48	12.0	0	0
1981 SD-Phi	12	7	168	24.0	2	0
1981 SD	9	3	84	28.0	2	0
1981 Phi	3	4	84	21.0	0	0
1982 Phi	9	34	475	14.0	1	1
1983 Phi	2	1	8	8.0	0	0
NFL Total	66	63	1014	16.1	4	3

ROYCE SMITH Smith, Royce Lionel 6′3″, 250 **OG**
Col: Georgia *HS:* Robert W. Groves [Savannah, GA] B: 6/17/1949, Savannah, GA *Drafted:* 1972 Round 1 NO
1972 NO: 10 G. **1973** NO: 14 G. **1974** Atl: 14 G. **1975** Atl: 14 G. **1976** Atl: 10 G. **Total:** 62 G.

RUSS SMITH Smith, Russell Conway 6′0″, 212 **RB**
Col: Miami (Fla.) *HS:* Stranahan [Fort Lauderdale, FL] B: 8/4/1944, Bronxville, NY *Drafted:* 1966 Round 5 SD
1967 SD: Rec 1-6 6.0; KR 3-51 17.0. **1968** SD: Pass 3-0; Rec 7-71 10.1; PR 8-25 3.1; KR 1-20 20.0. **1969** SD: Rec 10-144 14.4; PR 1-5 5.0; KR 6-138 23.0. **1970** SD: Rec 5-44 8.8; PR 9-31 3.4; KR 1-9 9.0. **Total:** Pass 3-0; Rec 23-265 11.5; PR 18-61 3.4; KR 11-218 19.8.

		Rushing				
Year Team	G	Att	Yds	Avg	TD	Fum
1967 SD	12	22	115	5.2	1	0
1968 SD	14	88	426	4.8	4	4
1969 SD	14	51	211	4.1	2	0
1970 SD	12	52	163	3.1	3	1
NFL Total	52	213	915	4.3	10	5

SAMMIE SMITH Smith, Sammie Lee 6′2″, 226 **RB**
Col: Florida State *HS:* Apopka [FL] B: 5/16/1967, Orlando, FL *Drafted:* 1989 Round 1 Mia
1992 Den: KR 2-31 15.5. **Total:** KR 2-31 15.5.

		Rushing				Receiving					Tot
Year Team	G	Att	Yds	Avg	TD	Rec	Yds	Avg	TD	Fum	TD
1989 Mia	13	200	659	3.3	6	7	81	11.6	0	6	6
1990 Mia	16	226	831	3.7	8	11	134	12.2	1	8	9
1991 Mia	12	83	297	3.6	1	14	95	6.8	0	3	1
1992 Den	3	23	94	4.1	0	0	0	—	0	0	0
NFL Total	44	532	1881	3.5	15	32	310	9.7	1	17	16

SEAN SMITH Smith, Sean Lamar 6′4″, 280 **DE-DT**
Col: Grambling State *HS:* Bogalusa [LA] B: 3/27/1965, Bogalusa, LA *Drafted:* 1987 Round 4 ChiB
1987 ChiB: 10 G. **1988** ChiB: 9 G; 1 Sac. **1989** Dal-TB-LARm: 7 G; Scor **1** Saf; 2 Pt; 1 Sac. Dal: 2 G. TB: 3 G; Scor 1 Saf; 2 Pt; 1 Sac. LARm: 2 G. **Total:** 26 G; Scor 1 Saf; 2 Pt; 2 Sac.

SEAN SMITH Smith, Sean Warfield 6′7″, 280 **DE**
Col: Georgia Tech *HS:* Wyoming [OH] B: 5/29/1967, Cincinnati, OH *Drafted:* 1990 Round 11 NE
1990 NE: 15 G; 1.5 Sac. **1991** NE: 2 G. **Total:** 17 G; 1.5 Sac.

SHERMAN SMITH Smith, Sherman Lennell 6′4″, 225 **RB**
Col: Miami (Ohio) *HS:* North [Youngstown, OH] B: 11/1/1954, Youngstown, OH *Drafted:* 1976 Round 2 Sea
1976 Sea: Pass 2-0; KR 5-78 15.6. **1977** Sea: Pass 1-0; KR 3-56 18.7. **1979** Sea: Pass 1-1 100.0%, 11 11.00. **1982** Sea: Pass 1-0. **1983** SD: Pass 1-0; KR 2-32 16.0. **Total:** Pass 6-1 16.7%, 11 1.83; KR 10-166 16.6.

		Rushing				Receiving					Tot
Year Team	G	Att	Yds	Avg	TD	Rec	Yds	Avg	TD	Fum	TD
1976 Sea	12	119	537	4.5	4	36	384	10.7	1	8	5
1977 Sea	14	163	763	4.7	4	30	419	14.0	2	6	6
1978 Sea	12	165	805	4.9	6	28	366	13.1	1	3	7
1979 Sea	16	194	775	4.0	11	48	499	10.4	4	1	15
1980 Sea	3	23	94	4.1	0	6	72	12.0	1	0	1
1981 Sea	16	83	253	3.0	3	44	406	9.2	1	3	4
1982 Sea	9	63	202	3.2	0	19	196	10.3	0	1	0
1983 SD	13	24	91	3.8	0	6	51	8.5	0	2	0
NFL Total	95	834	3520	4.2	28	217	2393	11.0	10	24	38

SHEVIN SMITH Smith, Shevin Jamar 5′11″, 191 **DB**
Col: Florida State *HS:* Miami Southridge [FL] B: 6/17/1975, Miami, FL *Drafted:* 1998 Round 6 TB
1998 TB: 3 G.

SID SMITH Smith, Sidney Ercil 6′4″, 260 **OT-C**
Col: USC *HS:* Woodrow Wilson [Long Beach, CA] B: 7/6/1948, Wichita, KS *Drafted:* 1970 Round 1 KC
1970 KC: 14 G; KR 1-12 12.0. **1971** KC: 14 G; Rec 1-12 12.0. **1972** KC: 14 G. **1974** Hou: 11 G. **Total:** 53 G; Rec 1-12 12.0; KR 1-12 12.0.

STEVE SMITH Smith, Stephen Conant 6′5″, 250 **OT-DE**
Col: Michigan *HS:* Maine East [Park Ridge, IL] B: 5/29/1944, St. Louis, MO *Drafted:* 1966 Round 5 SF
1966 Pit: 3 G. **1968** Min: 14 G. **1969** Min: 14 G; KR 1-3 3.0. **1970** Min: 14 G; KR 1-0; 1 Fum. **1971** Phi: 14 G; **1** Fum TD; 6 Pt. **1972** Phi: 14 G; 2 Fum. **1973** Phi: 14 G. **1974** Phi: 13 G. **Total:** 100 G; KR 2-3 1.5; 1 Fum TD; 6 Pt; 3 Fum.

STEVE SMITH Smith, Steven Anthony 6′1″, 236 **RB**
Col: Penn State *HS:* DeMatha [Hyattsville, MD] B: 8/30/1964, Washington, DC *Drafted:* 1987 Round 3 LARd
1988 LARd: KR 3-46 15.3. **1989** LARd: KR 2-19 9.5. **1991** LARd: KR 1-0. **1995** Sea: KR 1-11 11.0. **Total:** KR 7-76 10.9.

		Rushing				Receiving					Tot
Year Team	G	Att	Yds	Avg	TD	Rec	Yds	Avg	TD	Fum	TD
1987 LARd	7	5	18	3.6	0	3	46	15.3	0	0	0
1988 LARd	16	38	162	4.3	3	26	299	11.5	6	1	9
1989 LARd	16	117	471	4.0	1	19	140	7.4	0	2	1
1990 LARd	16	81	327	4.0	2	4	30	7.5	3	3	5
1991 LARd	16	62	265	4.3	1	15	130	8.7	1	4	2
1992 LARd	16	44	129	2.9	0	28	217	7.8	1	0	1
1993 LARd	16	47	156	3.3	0	18	187	10.4	0	1	0
1994 Sea	16	26	80	3.1	2	11	142	12.9	1	0	3
1995 Sea	9	9	19	2.1	0	7	59	8.4	1	0	1
NFL Total	128	429	1627	3.8	9	131	1250	9.5	13	11	22

STU SMITH Smith, Stuart Moore 6′0″, 195 **FB-LB-TB-DB**
Col: Bucknell *HS:* Cook Acad. [Montour Falls, NY] B: 2/3/1915, Montour Falls, NY D: 11/7/1969, Baltimore, MD
1937 Pit: Pass 2-0, 1 Int. **1938** Pit: Rec 3-30 10.0. **Total:** Pass 2-0, 1 Int; Rec 3-30 10.0.

		Rushing			
Year Team	G	Att	Yds	Avg	TD
1937 Pit	10	66	211	3.2	0
1938 Pit	11	80	241	3.0	0
NFL Total	21	146	452	3.1	0

TOM SMITH Smith, Thomas Eric 6′1″, 216 **RB**
Col: Iowa; Miami (Fla.) *HS:* East [Waterloo, IA] B: 10/4/1949, Waterloo, IA *Drafted:* 1973 Round 7 Mia
1973 Mia: 2 G.

THOMAS SMITH Smith, Thomas Lee Jr. 5′11″, 188 **DB**
Col: North Carolina *HS:* Gates Co. [Gatesville, NC] B: 12/5/1970, Gates, NC *Drafted:* 1993 Round 1 Buf
1993 Buf: 16 G. **1994** Buf: 16 G; Int 1-4. **1995** Buf: 16 G; Int 2-23. **1996** Buf: 16 G; Int 1-0. **1997** Buf: 16 G; 1 Fum. **1998** Buf: 14 G; Int 1-0. **Total:** 94 G; Int 5-27; 1 Fum.

TIM SMITH Smith, Timothy Francis 6′2″, 201 **WR**
Col: Nebraska *HS:* St. Augustine [San Diego, CA] B: 3/20/1957, Tucson, AZ *Drafted:* 1980 Round 3 Hou
1980 Hou: KR 1-0. **1982** Hou: KR 0-7. **1983** Hou: Rush 2-16 8.0. **1985** Hou: Punt 1-26 26.0. **Total:** Rush 2-16 8.0; KR 1-7 7.0; Punt 1-26 26.0.

		Receiving				
Year Team	G	Rec	Yds	Avg	TD	Fum
1980 Hou	16	2	21	10.5	0	1
1981 Hou	4	2	37	18.5	0	0
1982 Hou	9	0	0	—	0	0
1983 Hou	16	83	1176	14.2	6	1
1984 Hou	16	69	1141	16.5	4	0
1985 Hou	16	46	660	14.3	2	1
1986 Hou	13	4	72	18.0	0	0
NFL Total	90	206	3107	15.1	12	3

TIMMY SMITH Smith, Timothy LaRay 5′11″, 216 **RB**
Col: Texas Tech *HS:* Hobbs [NM] B: 1/24/1964, Hobbs, NM *Drafted:* 1987 Round 5 Was
1987 Was: Rec 1-(-2) -2.0. **1988** Was: Rec 8-53 6.6. **Total:** Rec 9-51 5.7.

		Rushing				
Year Team	G	Att	Yds	Avg	TD	Fum
1987 Was	7	29	126	4.3	0	0
1988 Was	14	155	470	3.0	3	4
1990 Dal	1	6	6	1.0	0	0
NFL Total	22	190	602	3.2	3	4

TOMMIE SMITH Smith, Tommie 6′3″, 190 **WR**
Col: San Jose State *HS:* Lemoore [CA] B: 6/6/1944, Clarksville, TN
1969 Cin: 2 G; Rec 1-41 41.0.

TONY SMITH Smith, Tony Derrell 6′1″, 212 **RB**
Col: Southern Mississippi *HS:* Warren Central [Vicksburg, MS] B: 6/29/1970, Chicago, IL *Drafted:* 1992 Round 1 Atl
1992 Atl: Rec 2-14 7.0. **Total:** Rec 2-14 7.0.

		Rushing				Punt Returns			
Year Team	G	Att	Yds	Avg	TD	Ret	Yds	Avg	TD
1992 Atl	14	87	329	3.8	2	16	155	9.7	0
1993 Atl	15	0	0	—	0	32	255	8.0	0
1994 Atl	4	0	0	—	0	8	75	9.4	0
NFL Total	33	87	329	3.8	2	56	485	8.7	0

	Kickoff Returns					Tot
Year Team	Ret	Yds	Avg	TD	Fum	TD
1992 Atl	7	172	24.6	0	4	2
1993 Atl	38	948	24.9	**1**	4	1
1994 Atl	16	333	20.8	0	1	0
NFL Total	61	1453	23.8	1	9	3

TORIN SMITH Smith, Torin Nathaniel 6′4″, 320 **DE**
Col: Hampton B: 9/30/1961
1987 NYG: 1 G.

TRAVIAN SMITH Smith, Travian 6′4″, 238 **LB**
(Machine) *Col:* Oklahoma *HS:* Tatum [TX] B: 8/26/1975, Good Shepard, TX *Drafted:* 1998 Round 5 Oak
1998 Oak: 2 G.

TRUETT SMITH Smith, Truett Henry 6′2″, 208 **BB**
Col: Wyoming; Mississippi State *HS:* Hazelhurst [MS] B: 3/17/1924, New Orleans, LA *Drafted:* 1950 Round 7 Pit
1950 Pit: 9 G. **1951** Pit: 11 G; Rush 1-1 1.0; Rec 4-71 17.8. **Total:** 20 G; Rush 1-1 1.0; Rec 4-71 17.8.

VITAMIN SMITH Smith, Verda Thomas Jr. 5′8″, 179 **HB**
(V.T.) *Col:* Abilene Christian *HS:* Sweetwater [TX]; Ventura HS [CA] B: 10/30/1923, Sweetwater, TX
1950 LARm: Pass 1-1 100.0%, 11 11.00. **1952** LARm: Pass 1-0. **1953** LARm: Pass 2-1 50.0%, 50 25.00. **Total:** Pass 4-2 50.0%, 61 15.25.

		Rushing				Receiving			
Year Team	G	Att	Yds	Avg	TD	Rec	Yds	Avg	TD
1949 LARm	12	40	117	2.9	2	5	63	12.6	1
1950 LARm	12	51	250	4.9	1	16	279	17.4	4
1951 LARm	12	52	143	2.8	1	16	278	17.4	1
1952 LARm	12	57	133	2.3	3	16	254	15.9	3
1953 LARm	11	8	26	3.3	0	6	151	25.2	3
NFL Total	59	208	669	3.2	7	59	1025	17.4	12

	Punt Returns				Kickoff Returns					Tot
Year Team	Ret	Yds	Avg	TD	Ret	Yds	Avg	TD	Fum	TD
1949 LARm	**27**	**427**	15.8	1	13	235	18.1	0	3	4
1950 LARm	22	218	9.9	0	22	**742**	**33.7**	**3**	4	8
1951 LARm	12	139	11.6	0	15	274	18.3	0	2	2
1952 LARm	2	0	0.0	0	5	158	31.6	0	3	6
1953 LARm	12	30	2.5	0	2	44	22.0	0	1	3
NFL Total	75	814	10.9	1	57	1453	25.5	3	13	23

VERNICE SMITH Smith, Vernice Carlton 6′3″, 300 **OG-OT**
Col: Florida A&M *HS:* Oak Ridge [Orlando, FL] B: 10/24/1965, Orlando, FL
1990 Pho: 11 G. **1991** Pho: 14 G. **1992** Pho: 12 G. **1993** ChiB-Was: 14 G. ChiB: 6 G. Was: 8 G. **1994** Was: 4 G. **1995** Was: 9 G. **1997** StL: 10 G. **Total:** 74 G.

VINSON SMITH Smith, Vinson Robert 6′2″, 243 **LB**
Col: East Carolina *HS:* Statesville [NC] B: 7/3/1965, Statesville, NC
1988 Atl: 3 G. **1990** Dal: 16 G. **1991** Dal: 13 G. **1992** Dal: 16 G; 1 Sac. **1993** ChiB: 16 G. **1994** ChiB: 12 G; 1 Sac. **1995** ChiB: 16 G; 1 Fum; 4 Sac. **1996** ChiB: 15 G; 1 Sac. **1997** Dal: 14 G; 1 Sac. **1998** NO: 15 G. **Total:** 136 G; 1 Fum; 8 Sac.

WARREN SMITH Smith, Warren 175 **G**
Col: Western Michigan *HS:* Carlton [MN] B: 1895, MN Deceased
1921 GB: 2 G.

WAYNE SMITH Smith, Wayne Lester 6′0″, 171 **DB**
Col: Harold Washington Coll. IL (J.C.); Wis.-La Crosse; Purdue *HS:* Harper [Chicago, IL] B: 5/9/1957, Chicago, IL *Drafted:* 1980 Round 11 Det
1982 Det-StL: 1 Sac. Det: 1 Sac. **Total:** 1 Sac.

		Interceptions		
Year Team	**G**	**Int**	**Yds**	**TD**
1980 Det	16	1	23	0
1981 Det	16	0	0	0
1982 Det-StL	6	1	10	0
1982 Det	5	1	10	0
1982 StL	1	0	0	0
1983 StL	16	2	3	0
1984 StL	16	4	35	0
1985 StL	16	0	0	0
1986 StL	16	1	35	0
1987 Min	6	1	24	0
NFL Total	108	10	130	0

WES SMITH Smith, Wes 5′11″, 194 **WR**
Col: Texas A&M-Commerce B: 6/24/1963
1987 GB: 1 G.

WILFRID SMITH Smith, Wilfrid Russell 6′4″, 204 **T-G-OE-C**
Col: DePauw *HS:* Huntington [IN] B: 4/7/1899, Milroy, IN D: 8/3/1976, Chicago, IL
1920 Mun: 1 G. **1921** Mun: 2 G. **1922** Lou: 1 G. **1923** ChiC-Ham: 8 G. ChiC: 3 G. Ham: 5 G. **1924** ChiC: 6 G. **1925** ChiC: 13 G. **Total:** 31 G.

BILL SMITH Smith, William Arley 6′1″, 198 **OE-DE**
Col: Washington *HS:* Portage [WA] B: 1/13/1912, Seattle, WA
1934 ChiC: Pass 1-1 100.0%, 9 9.00; Rush 13-56 4.3 2 TD; Scor 25, 1 FG, 4 XK. **1935** ChiC: Rush 8-33 4.1; Scor 35, **6** FG, 5 XK. **1936** ChiC: Pass 1-0, 1 Int; Rush 2-13 6.5; Scor 11, 1 FG, 2 XK. **1937** ChiC: Scor 9, 3 XK; 1 Fum TD. **1938** ChiC: Scor 16, 2-2 100.0% FG, 4-5 80.0% XK. **1939** ChiC: Rush 1-3 3.0; Punt 1-36 36.0; Scor 36, 2-8 25.0% FG, 6-8 75.0% XK. **Total:** Pass 2-1 50.0%, 9 4.50 1 Int; Rush 24-105 4.4 2 TD; Punt 1-36 36.0; Scor 132, 12-10 40.0% FG, 24-13 76.9% XK; 1 Fum TD.

		Receiving				Tot
Year Team	**G**	**Rec**	**Yds**	**Avg**	**TD**	**TD**
1934 ChiC	11	6	103	17.2	1	3
1935 ChiC	11	24	318	13.3	2	2
1936 ChiC	11	20	414	20.7	1	1
1937 ChiC	9	3	52	17.3	0	1
1938 ChiC	11	18	338	18.8	1	1
1939 ChiC	11	21	387	18.4	4	4
NFL Total	64	92	1612	17.5	9	12

BILL SMITH Smith, William Gerald 6′2″, 250 **T**
(Earthquake) *Col:* North Carolina *HS:* Lexington [NC] B: 10/23/1926, Lexington, NC
AAFC **1948** ChiA-LA-A: 12 G.

LARRY SMITH Smith, William Lawrence 6′3″, 220 **RB**
Col: Florida *HS:* T.R. Robinson [Tampa, FL] B: 9/2/1947, Tampa, FL
1969 LARm: Pass 1-0. **1970** LARm: Pass 2-0. **1973** LARm: Pass 2-2 100.0%, 31 15.50; KR 1-16 16.0. **1974** Was: KR 2-57 28.5. **Total:** Pass 5-2 40.0%, 31 6.20; KR 3-73 24.3.

		Rushing				Receiving					Tot
Year Team	**G**	**Att**	**Yds**	**Avg**	**TD**	**Rec**	**Yds**	**Avg**	**TD**	**Fum**	**TD**
1969 LARm	14	166	599	3.6	1	46	300	6.5	2	1	3
1970 LARm	11	77	338	4.4	1	24	164	6.8	1	4	2
1971 LARm	14	91	404	4.4	5	31	324	10.5	0	2	5
1972 LARm	12	60	276	4.6	2	15	186	12.4	1	1	3
1973 LARm	14	79	291	3.7	2	10	65	6.5	0	0	2
1974 Was	7	55	149	2.7	0	23	137	6.0	1	1	1
NFL Total	72	528	2057	3.9	11	149	1176	7.9	5	9	16

WILLIE SMITH Smith, Willie 6′2″, 235 **TE**
Col: Miami (Fla.) *HS:* Englewood [Jacksonville, FL] B: 8/6/1964, Jacksonville, FL
1987 Mia: 3 G; Rec 2-13 6.5 1 TD; 6 Pt.

WILLIE SMITH Smith, Willie 6′3″, 255 **OT-OG**
Col: Michigan *HS:* Dunbar [Little Rock, AR] B: 11/1/1937 *Drafted:* 1959 Round 8 ChiB
1960 Den: 14 G. **1961** Oak: 14 G. **Total:** 28 G.

WEE WILLIE SMITH Smith, Willis Merton 5′6″, 148 **DB-TB-FB**
(Little Giant) *Col:* Idaho *HS:* Lexington [NE]; Sheridan HS [WY]; Boise HS [ID] B: 7/2/1910, Lexington, NE D: 9/4/1996, Albuquerque, NM
1934 NYG: Pass 5-2 40.0%, 37 7.40 1 TD 1 Int; Rec 2-32 16.0.

		Rushing			
Year Team	**G**	**Att**	**Yds**	**Avg**	**TD**
1934 NYG	9	80	323	4.0	2

MARK SMOLINSKI Smolinski, Mark Wayne 6′1″, 215 **FB-TE**
Col: Wyoming *HS:* Rogers City [MI] B: 5/9/1939, Alpena, MI
1961 Bal: PR 1-2 2.0; KR 3-27 9.0. **1962** Bal: KR 2-20 10.0. **1963** NYJ: KR 1-10 10.0. **1964** NYJ: KR 2-19 9.5. **1965** NYJ: KR 6-98 16.3. **1966** NYJ: KR 6-59 9.8. **1967** NYJ: KR 1-3 3.0. **1968** NYJ: KR 1-17 17.0. **Total:** PR 1-2 2.0; KR 22-253 11.5.

		Rushing				Receiving					Tot
Year Team	**G**	**Att**	**Yds**	**Avg**	**TD**	**Rec**	**Yds**	**Avg**	**TD**	**Fum**	**TD**
1961 Bal	14	31	98	3.2	0	9	100	11.1	1	3	1
1962 Bal	14	85	265	3.1	1	13	128	9.8	1	0	2
1963 NYJ	14	150	561	3.7	4	34	278	8.2	1	2	5
1964 NYJ	14	34	117	3.4	1	3	19	6.3	0	2	1
1965 NYJ	12	24	59	2.5	0	6	25	4.2	0	1	0
1966 NYJ	14	21	69	3.3	2	11	74	6.7	1	0	3
1967 NYJ	13	64	139	2.2	1	21	177	8.4	3	1	4
1968 NYJ	14	12	15	1.3	0	6	40	6.7	0	0	1
NFL Total	109	421	1323	3.1	9	103	841	8.2	7	9	17

RAYMOND SMOOT Smoot, Raymond Eugene 6′4″, 305 **OG-OT**
Col: Louisiana State *HS:* Leesville [LA] B: 7/24/1970, Leesville, LA
1993 SD: 2 G.

DAVE SMUKLER Smukler, David 6′1″, 226 **FB-LB**
(Dynamite) *Col:* Missouri; Temple *HS:* Gloversville [NY] B: 5/28/1914, Newark, NJ D: 2/22/1971, Los Angeles, CA
1936 Phi: Scor 5, 1 FG, 2 XK. **1937** Phi: Rec 1-(-4) -4.0; Scor 17, 1 FG, 8 XK. **1938** Phi: KR **1** TD; Scor 18, 0-2 FG, 6-6 100.0% XK. **1939** Phi: Punt 10-483 48.3. **1944** Bos: Punt 2-49 24.5. **Total:** Rec 1-(-4) -4.0; KR 1 TD; Punt 12-532 44.3; Scor 40, 2-2 FG, 16-6 100.0% XK.

		Passing							
Year Team	**G**	**Att**	**Comp**	**Comp%**	**Yds**	**YPA**	**TD**	**Int**	**Rating**
1936 Phi	10	68	21	30.9	345	5.07	3	6	26.9
1937 Phi	11	118	42	35.6	432	3.66	5	14	21.5
1938 Phi	11	102	42	41.2	524	5.14	7	8	48.0
1939 Phi	4	20	7	35.0	56	2.80	0	4	4.2
1944 Bos	2	0	0	—	0	—	0	0	—
NFL Total	38	308	112	36.4	1357	4.41	15	32	27.4

	Rushing				Tot
Year Team	**Att**	**Yds**	**Avg**	**TD**	**TD**
1936 Phi	99	321	3.2	0	0
1937 Phi	92	247	2.7	1	1
1938 Phi	96	313	3.3	1	2
1939 Phi	45	218	4.8	0	0
1944 Bos	2	7	3.5	0	0
NFL Total	334	1106	3.3	2	3

LOU SMYTH Smyth, Louis Lehman 6′1″, 200 **TB-FB-WB**
(Hammer) *Col:* Texas; Centre *HS:* Sherman [TX] B: 3/19/1898, Cleburne, TX D: 9/11/1964, Long Beach, CA
1920 Can: 9 G. **1921** Can: 6 G; Pass 1 TD; Rush 2 TD; 12 Pt. **1922** Can: 5 G; Pass 1 TD; Rush 1 TD; 6 Pt. **1923** Can: 12 G; Pass **6** TD; Rush **7** TD; Tot TD **7**; 42 Pt. **1924** Roch: 1 G. **1925** Roch-Fra: 10 G; Pass 3 TD; Rush 2 TD; 12 Pt. Roch: 7 G; Pass 3 TD. Fra: 3 G; Rush 2 TD; 12 Pt. **1926** Fra-Har-Prov: 12 G; Pass 1 TD; Rush 1 TD; 6 Pt. Fra: 4 G. Har: 5 G; Pass 1 TD; Rush 1 TD; 6 Pt. Prov: 3 G. **Total:** 55 G; Pass 12 TD; Rush 13 TD; 78 Pt.

BILL SMYTH Smyth, William Krantz 6′3″, 243 **DE-OE-T**
Col: Notre Dame; Cincinnati; Penn State *HS:* Roger Bacon [Cincinnati, OH] B: 4/8/1922, Batavia, OH D: 11/6/1966 *Drafted:* 1947 Round 5 LARm
1947 LARm: 12 G; Rec 3-26 8.7. **1948** LARm: 11 G; Rec 6-66 11.0 1 TD; 6 Pt. **1949** LARm: 12 G; Rec 2-21 10.5. **1950** LARm: 11 G; Rec 2-10 5.0. **Total:** 46 G; Rec 13-123 9.5 1 TD; 6 Pt.

NORM SNEAD Snead, Norman Bailey 6′4″, 215 **QB**
Col: Wake Forest *HS:* Warwick [Newport News, VA] B: 7/31/1939, Halifax Co., VA *Drafted:* 1961 Round 1 Was

		Passing							
Year Team	**G**	**Att**	**Comp**	**Comp%**	**Yds**	**YPA**	**TD**	**Int**	**Rating**
1961 Was	14	375	172	45.9	2337	6.23	11	22	51.6
1962 Was	14	354	184	52.0	2926	8.27	22	22	74.7
1963 Was	14	363	175	48.2	3043	8.38	13	27	58.1
1964 Phi	12	283	138	48.8	1906	6.73	14	12	69.6
1965 Phi	11	288	150	52.1	2346	8.15	15	13	78.0
1966 Phi	10	226	103	45.6	1275	5.64	8	11	55.1
1967 Phi	14	434	240	55.3	3399	7.83	29	24	80.0

1968 Phi	11	291	152	52.2	1655	5.69	11	21	51.8
1969 Phi	13	379	190	50.1	2768	7.30	19	23	65.7
1970 Phi	14	335	181	54.0	2323	6.93	15	20	66.1
1971 Min	7	75	37	49.3	470	6.27	1	6	40.4
1972 NYG	14	325	196	**60.3**	2307	7.10	17	12	84.0
1973 NYG	10	235	131	55.7	1483	6.31	7	22	45.8
1974 NYG-SF	8	159	97	61.0	983	6.18	5	8	68.2
1974 NYG	5	111	67	60.4	615	5.54	3	7	58.2
1974 SF	3	48	30	62.5	368	7.67	2	1	91.3
1975 SF	9	189	108	57.1	1337	7.07	9	10	73.0
1976 NYG	3	42	22	52.4	239	5.69	0	4	29.9
NFL Total	178	4353	2276	52.3	30797	7.07	196	257	65.5

	Rushing				
Year Team	Att	Yds	Avg	TD	Fum
1961 Was	34	47	1.4	3	6
1962 Was	20	10	0.5	3	5
1963 Was	23	100	4.3	2	6
1964 Phi	16	59	3.7	2	3
1965 Phi	24	81	3.4	3	5
1966 Phi	15	32	2.1	1	7
1967 Phi	9	30	3.3	2	5
1968 Phi	9	27	3.0	0	2
1969 Phi	8	2	0.3	2	4
1970 Phi	18	35	1.9	3	3
1971 Min	6	6	1.0	1	2
1972 NYG	10	21	2.1	0	4
1973 NYG	4	13	3.3	0	2
1974 NYG-SF	4	29	7.3	0	0
1974 NYG	3	4	1.3	0	0
1974 SF	1	25	25.0	0	0
1975 SF	9	30	3.3	1	5
1976 NYG	3	-1	-0.3	0	1
NFL Total	212	521	2.5	23	60

BOB SNEDDON Sneddon, Robert Lee 5′10″, 180 **DB-HB-WB**
Col: Weber State; St. Mary's (Cal.) *HS:* Ogden [UT] B: 7/9/1921, Ogden, UT *Drafted:* 1944 Round 8 Was
AAFC **1946** LA-A: 11 G; Rush 3-6 2.0; Rec 2-11 5.5; Int 1-15.

NFL **1944** Was: 10 G; Rush 14-30 2.1; Rec 3-42 14.0; Int 1-20. **1945** Det: 1 G. **Total:** 11 G; Rush 14-30 2.1; Rec 3-42 14.0; Int 1-20.

DONALD SNELL Snell, Donald Wayne 6′2″, 177 **WR**
Col: Virginia Tech *HS:* Radford [VA] B: 3/13/1965
1987 Sea: 1 G.

GEORGE SNELL Snell, George Albert 5′10″, 185 **FB-BB-WB**
Col: Penn State *HS:* Reading [PA] B: 7/9/1897 Deceased
1926 Bkn: 11 G; Rush 1 TD; 6 Pt. **1927** Buf: 3 G. **Total:** 14 G; Rush 1 TD; 6 Pt.

MATT SNELL Snell, Matthews 6′2″, 219 **RB**
Col: Ohio State *HS:* Carle Place [NY] B: 8/18/1941, Garfield, GA
Drafted: 1964 Round 1 NYJ
1964 NYJ: Pass 1-0, 1 Int; KR 7-158 22.6. **1966** NYJ: Pass 1-0. **1968** NYJ: Pass 1-1 100.0%, 26 26.00; KR 3-28 9.3. **1972** NYJ: KR 1-14 14.0. **Total:** Pass 3-1 33.3%, 26 8.67 1 Int; KR 11-200 18.2.

		Rushing				Receiving					Tot
Year Team	G	Att	Yds	Avg	TD	Rec	Yds	Avg	TD	Fum	TD
1964 NYJ	14	215	948	4.4	5	56	393	7.0	1	0	6
1965 NYJ	14	169	763	4.5	4	38	264	6.9	0	3	4
1966 NYJ	12	178	644	3.6	4	48	346	7.2	4	3	8
1967 NYJ	7	61	207	3.4	0	11	54	4.9	0	2	0
1968 NYJ	14	179	747	4.2	6	16	105	6.6	1	2	7
1969 NYJ	14	191	695	3.6	4	22	187	8.5	1	5	5
1970 NYJ	3	64	281	4.4	1	2	26	13.0	0	2	1
1971 NYJ	5	0	0	—	0	0	0	—	0	0	0
1972 NYJ	4	0	0	—	0	0	0	—	0	0	0
NFL Total	87	1057	4285	4.1	24	193	1375	7.1	7	17	31

RAY SNELL Snell, Ray Michael 6′4″, 262 **OG-OT**
Col: Wisconsin *HS:* Northwestern [Hyattsville, MD] B: 2/24/1958, Baltimore, MD *Drafted:* 1980 Round 1 TB
1980 TB: 13 G. **1981** TB: 16 G. **1982** TB: 7 G. **1983** TB: 9 G. **1984** Pit: 13 G. **1985** Pit-Det: 7 G. Pit: 5 G. Det: 2 G. **Total:** 65 G.

KEN SNELLING Snelling, Kenneth Edward 6′0″, 210 **FB-LB**
(Rhino) *Col:* UCLA *HS:* Bell [CA] B: 12/11/1918, Musselshell, MT D: 9/17/1994, Ruch, OR *Drafted:* 1943 Round 5 GB
1945 GB: 2 G; Rush 3-10 3.3; 1 Fum.

JIM SNIADECKI Sniadecki, James Bert 6′2″, 230 **LB**
Col: Indiana *HS:* St. Joseph's [South Bend, IN] B: 3/23/1947, South Bend, IN *Drafted:* 1969 Round 4 SF
1969 SF: 14 G; KR 1-0. **1970** SF: 14 G. **1971** SF: 14 G. **1972** SF: 2 G. **1973** SF: 14 G; KR 1-0; Int 1-11; 1 Fum. **Total:** 58 G; KR 2-0; Int 1-11; 1 Fum.

MAL SNIDER Snider, Malcolm Pratt 6′4″, 251 **OT-OG**
Col: Stanford *HS:* Salem [OR] B: 4/5/1947, Battle Creek, MI
Drafted: 1969 Round 3 Atl
1969 Atl: 14 G; KR 1-48 48.0 **1** TD; 6 Pt. **1970** Atl: 14 G. **1971** Atl: 13 G. **1972** GB: 14 G. **1973** GB: 14 G. **1974** GB: 14 G. **Total:** 83 G; KR 1-48 48.0 1 TD; 6 Pt.

RON SNIDOW Snidow, Ronald Wayne 6′3″, 250 **DE-DT**
Col: Oregon *HS:* San Rafael [CA] B: 12/30/1941, Newport News, VA
Drafted: 1963 Round 3 Was
1963 Was: 13 G; KR 1-0; 1 Fum. **1964** Was: 14 G; KR 1-16 16.0. **1965** Was: 14 G; Int 1-3; Punt 9-336 37.3. **1966** Was: 14 G. **1967** Was: 14 G. **1968** Cle: 13 G. **1969** Cle: 14 G. **1970** Cle: 14 G; Scor **1** Saf; 2 Pt. **1971** Cle: 13 G; Int 0-3. **1972** Cle: 3 G. **Total:** 126 G; KR 2-16 8.0; Int 1-6; Punt 9-336 37.3; Scor 1 Saf; 2 Pt; 1 Fum.

ANGELO SNIPES Snipes, Angelo Bernard 6′0″, 222 **LB**
Col: West Georgia *HS:* Walker [Atlanta, GA] B: 1/11/1963, Atlanta, GA
1986 Was-SD: 16 G; 2 Sac. Was: 10 G; 2 Sac. SD: 6 G. **1987** SD-KC: 6 G; 2 Sac. SD: 2 G; 1 Sac. KC: 4 G; 1 Sac. **1988** KC: 15 G; 2 Sac. **1989** KC: 2 G; Int 1-16. **Total:** 39 G; Int 1-16; 6 Sac.

LEE SNOOTS Snoots, John Lee 5′9″, 185 **TB-BB-WB-FB**
(Bullet) *Col:* No College B: 8/12/1892 D: 11/29/1968, Columbus, OH
1920 Col: 7 G. **1922** Col: 7 G; Pass 1 TD; Rush 1 TD; 6 Pt. **1923** Col: 10 G; Rush 1 TD; 6 Pt. **1925** Col: 1 G. **Total:** 25 G; Pass 1 TD; Rush 2 TD; 12 Pt.

MATT SNORTON Snorton, Hickman Matthew 6′5″, 250 **TE**
Col: Michigan State *HS:* Northwestern [Detroit, MI] B: 9/26/1942, Crofton, KY *Drafted:* 1964 Round 3 Den
1964 Den: 5 G.

JACK SNOW Snow, Jack Thomas 6′2″, 190 **WR**
Col: Notre Dame *HS:* St. Anthony's [Long Beach, CA] B: 1/25/1943, Rock Springs, WY *Drafted:* 1965 Round 1 Min
1971 LARm: Rush 1-(-10) -10.0. **1974** LARm: Rush 1-13 13.0.
Total: Rush 2-3 1.5.

		Receiving				
Year Team	G	Rec	Yds	Avg	TD	Fum
1965 LARm	14	38	559	14.7	3	0
1966 LARm	14	34	634	18.6	3	0
1967 LARm	14	28	735	26.3	8	0
1968 LARm	14	29	500	17.2	3	1
1969 LARm	14	49	734	15.0	6	3
1970 LARm	14	51	859	16.8	7	0
1971 LARm	14	37	666	18.0	5	0
1972 LARm	14	30	590	19.7	4	0
1973 LARm	14	16	252	15.8	2	0
1974 LARm	14	24	397	16.5	3	0
1975 LARm	10	4	86	21.5	1	0
NFL Total	150	340	6012	17.7	45	4

PERCY SNOW Snow, Percy Lee 6′2″, 248 **LB**
Col: Michigan State *HS:* McKinley [Canton, OH] B: 11/5/1967, Canton, OH *Drafted:* 1990 Round 1 KC
1990 KC: 15 G; Int 1-0; 2 Sac. **1992** KC: 15 G. **1993** ChiB: 10 G.
Total: 40 G; Int 1-0; 2 Sac.

CAL SNOWDEN Snowden, Calvin Reginald 6′4″, 253 **DE**
Col: Indiana *HS:* Roosevelt [Washington, DC] B: 11/29/1946, Washington, DC *Drafted:* 1969 Round 9 StL
1969 StL: 7 G. **1970** StL: 14 G. **1971** Buf: 14 G. **1972** SD: 8 G. **1973** SD: 4 G. **Total:** 47 G.

JIM SNOWDEN Snowden, James John 6′3″, 255 **OT-DE**
Col: Notre Dame *HS:* East [Youngstown, OH] B: 1/12/1942, Youngstown, OH *Drafted:* 1964 Round 5 Was
1965 Was: 14 G. **1966** Was: 14 G. **1967** Was: 14 G. **1968** Was: 14 G. **1969** Was: 14 G; KR 1-2 2.0. **1970** Was: 14 G. **1971** Was: 14 G.
Total: 98 G; KR 1-2 2.0.

AL SNYDER Snyder, Albert Russell 6′1″, 196 **WR**
(Spike) *Col:* Holy Cross *HS:* Loyola [Baltimore, MD] B: 6/20/1941, Baltimore, MD *Drafted:* 1963 Round 23 Bos
1964 Bos: 2 G; Rec 1-12 12.0. **1966** Bal: 5 G. **Total:** 7 G; Rec 1-12 12.0.

SNITZ SNYDER Snyder, Gerald Theodore 5′8″, 190 **BB-FB-WB-HB**
Col: Maryland *HS:* Windber [PA]; Bellefonte Acad. [PA] B: 8/6/1905, Windber, PA D: 6/1983, Brooklyn Heights, OH
1929 NYG: 12 G; Rush 2 TD; Rec 1 TD; Tot TD 3; 18 Pt. **1930** SI: 11 G.
Total: 23 G; Rush 2 TD; Rec 1 TD; Tot TD 3; 18 Pt.

JIM SNYDER Snyder, James 162 **TB**
Col: No College *HS:* Englewood [Chicago, IL] B: 1/1909 Deceased
1925 Mil: 1 G.

TODD SNYDER Snyder, James Todd 6′1″, 187 **WR**
Col: Ohio U. *HS:* Athens [OH] B: 10/22/1948, Athens, OH
Drafted: 1970 Round 3 Atl
1970 Atl: 12 G; Rec 23-311 13.5 2 TD; 12 Pt. **1971** Atl: 4 G. **1972** Atl: 14 G; Rec 1-19 19.0. **Total:** 30 G; Rec 24-330 13.8 2 TD; 12 Pt.

LUM SNYDER Snyder, Kenneth David 6'5", 228 **OT**
Col: Georgia Tech *HS:* Bradley [Cleveland, TN] B: 8/12/1930, Cleveland, TN D: 10/11/1985, Winter Haven, FL *Drafted:* 1952 Round 3 Phi
1952 Phi: 11 G. **1953** Phi: 12 G. **1954** Phi: 12 G; KR 2-18 9.0. **1955** Phi: 12 G; KR 3-34 11.3. **1958** Phi: 12 G. **Total:** 59 G; KR 5-52 10.4.

LOREN SNYDER Snyder, Loren Howard 6'4", 207 **QB**
Col: Northern Colorado *HS:* Thornton [CO] B: 11/28/1963
1987 Dal: 2 G; Pass 9-4 44.4%, 44 4.89; Rush 2-0; 1 Fum.

PAT SNYDER Snyder, Patrick A 6'1", 225 **LB**
Col: Purdue *HS:* New Haven [IN] B: 11/23/1963
1987 Ind: 2 G. **1991** Ind: 1 G. **Total:** 3 G.

BOB SNYDER Snyder, Robert A 6'0", 200 **QB-DB-TB**
Col: Ohio U. *HS:* Edward D. Libbey [Toledo, OH] B: 2/6/1913, Fremont, OH
1937 Cle: Rec 3-20 6.7; Scor 16, 1 FG, 7 XK. **1938** Cle: Rec 1-16 16.0; Scor 10, 1-2 50.0% FG, 7-10 70.0% XK. **1939** ChiB: Punt 7-291 41.6; Scor 4, 1-1 100.0% FG, 1-2 50.0% XK. **1940** ChiB: Punt 5-176 35.2; Scor 7, 1-4 25.0% FG, 4-5 80.0% XK. **1941** ChiB: Int 1-24; Punt 2-76 38.0; Scor 26, 2-2 100.0% FG, **20-24** 83.3% XK. **1943** ChiB: Int 1-8; Punt 10-378 37.8; Scor 45, 2-7 28.6% FG, **39-42** 92.9% XK.
Total: Rec 4-36 9.0; Int 2-32; Punt 24-921 38.4; Scor 108, 8-16 43.8% FG, 78-83 85.5% XK.

		Passing							
Year Team	**G**	**Att**	**Comp**	**Comp%**	**Yds**	**YPA**	**TD**	**Int**	**Rating**
1937 Cle	10	66	25	37.9	378	5.73	2	6	29.7
1938 Cle	10	87	36	41.4	631	7.25	7	9	54.0
1939 ChiB	8	12	5	41.7	135	11.25	0	2	44.1
1940 ChiB	11	22	5	22.7	145	6.59	1	1	50.8
1941 ChiB	11	28	13	46.4	353	12.61	3	2	98.8
1943 ChiB	10	26	7	26.9	116	4.46	0	4	6.1
NFL Total	60	241	91	37.8	1758	7.29	13	24	42.3

	Rushing			
Year Team	**Att**	**Yds**	**Avg**	**TD**
1937 Cle	82	232	2.8	1
1938 Cle	44	78	1.8	0
1939 ChiB	15	56	3.7	0
1940 ChiB	7	12	1.7	0
1941 ChiB	7	-10	-1.4	0
1943 ChiB	6	-20	-3.3	0
NFL Total	161	348	2.2	1

BULL SNYDER Snyder, William Howard 6'2", 230 **G-T**
Col: Ohio U. *HS:* London [OH] B: 10/29/1911, London, OH D: 10/1973
1934 Pit: 5 G. **1935** Pit: 7 G. **Total:** 12 G.

HANK SOAR Soar, Albert Henry 6'2", 205 **DB-FB-WB-QB**
Col: Providence *HS:* Pawtucket [RI] B: 8/17/1914, Alton, RI
1937 NYG: Scor 17, 1 FG, 2 XK. **1938** NYG: Scor 13, 1-1 100.0% XK. **1939** NYG: Scor 20, 0-1 FG, 2-2 100.0% XK. **1940** NYG: Scor 12, 0-1 FG. **1941** NYG: PR 4-54 13.5; Scor 3, 3-3 100.0% XK. **1942** NYG: PR 3-29 9.7; KR 5-134 26.8; Punt 3-126 42.0; Scor 8, 0-2 FG, 2-3 66.7% XK. **1943** NYG: PR 2-15 7.5. **1944** NYG: PR 6-52 8.7. **1946** NYG: PR 4-83 20.8. **Total:** PR 19-233 12.3; KR 5-134 26.8; Punt 3-126 42.0; Scor 73, 1-4 FG, 10-9 88.9% XK.

		Passing							
Year Team	**G**	**Att**	**Comp**	**Comp%**	**Yds**	**YPA**	**TD**	**Int**	**Rating**
1937 NYG	9	21	5	23.8	83	3.95	1	2	19.8
1938 NYG	11	7	1	14.3	0	0.00	0	3	0.0
1939 NYG	11	0	0	—	0	—	0	0	—
1940 NYG	11	0	0	—	0	—	0	0	—
1941 NYG	11	5	3	60.0	75	15.00	1	0	143.8
1942 NYG	11	10	3	30.0	34	3.40	0	1	1.7
1943 NYG	4	0	0	—	0	—	0	0	—
1944 NYG	3	10	4	40.0	113	11.30	2	1	82.5
1946 NYG	11	0	0	—	0	—	0	0	—
NFL Total	82	53	16	30.2	305	5.75	4	7	36.8

	Rushing				Receiving			
Year Team	**Att**	**Yds**	**Avg**	**TD**	**Rec**	**Yds**	**Avg**	**TD**
1937 NYG	120	442	3.7	0	6	77	12.8	1
1938 NYG	122	401	3.3	2	13	164	12.6	0
1939 NYG	66	158	2.4	2	12	134	11.2	0
1940 NYG	80	246	3.1	1	4	36	9.0	1
1941 NYG	29	90	3.1	0	0	0	—	0
1942 NYG	49	187	3.8	1	0	0	—	0
1943 NYG	2	8	4.0	0	0	0	—	0
1944 NYG	9	10	1.1	0	0	0	—	0
1946 NYG	1	3	3.0	0	0	0	—	0
NFL Total	478	1545	3.2	6	35	411	11.7	2

	Interceptions			Tot
Year Team	**Int**	**Yds**	**TD**	**TD**
1937 NYG	—	—	**1**	2
1938 NYG	—	—	0	2
1939 NYG	—	—	**1**	3
1940 NYG	2	27	0	2
1941 NYG	2	31	0	0
1942 NYG	3	31	0	1
1943 NYG	3	43	0	0
1944 NYG	1	18	0	0
1946 NYG	3	35	0	0
NFL Total	14	185	2	10

PHILIP SOBOCINSKI Sobocinski, Philip Lee 6'3", 235 **C**
Col: Wisconsin *HS:* South Milwaukee [WI] B: 12/6/1945, South Milwaukee, WI
1968 Atl: 7 G.

JOE SOBOLESKI Soboleski, Joseph Robert 6'0", 213 **OG-OT-DT-DG**
Col: Michigan *HS:* Catholic Central [Grand Rapids, MI] B: 8/22/1926
Drafted: 1949 Round 9 NYG
AAFC **1949** ChiA: 5 G.

NFL **1949** Was: 7 G. **1950** Det: 12 G. **1951** NYY: 2 G. **1952** Dal: 1 G. **Total:** 22 G.

BRIAN SOCHIA Sochia, Brian John 6'3", 270 **NT-DE**
Col: Northwestern Okla. State *HS:* St. Lawrence [Brasher Falls, NY] B: 7/2/1961, Massena, NY
1983 Hou: 12 G; 2.5 Sac. **1984** Hou: 16 G; 3.5 Sac. **1985** Hou: 16 G; 2 Sac. **1986** Mia: 6 G; 1 Sac. **1987** Mia: 12 G; 3.5 Sac. **1988** Mia: 16 G; 4.5 Sac. **1989** Mia: 16 G; 5 Sac. **1990** Mia: 5 G; 1 Fum TD; 6 Pt; 1 Sac. **1991** Mia-Den: 13 G; 1 Sac. Mia: 3 G. Den: 10 G; 1 Sac. **1992** Den: 16 G; 1.5 Sac. **Total:** 128 G; 1 Fum TD; 6 Pt; 25.5 Sac.

JOHN SODASKI Sodaski, John Joseph Jr. 6'2", 222 **LB-DB**
Col: Villanova *HS:* St. Pius X [Pottstown, PA] B: 1/14/1948, Phoenixville, PA *Drafted:* 1969 Round 9 Pit
1970 Pit: 3 G. **1972** Phi: 4 G. **1973** Phi: 14 G; Int 1-0; 1 Fum. **Total:** 21 G; Int 1-0; 1 Fum.

ALEC SOFISH Sofish, Alexander N 6'2", 200 **G**
Col: Grove City *HS:* Uniontown [PA] D: 3/1959
1931 Prov: 11 G.

BENNY SOHN Sohn, Ben 5'8", 170 **WB-DB-FB-LB**
Col: Washington *HS:* Austin [Chicago, IL] B: 11/18/1911 D: 11/1969
1934 Cin: 2 G; Rush 1-7 7.0.

BEN SOHN Sohn, Benjamin Forester 6'2", 220 **G**
Col: USC *HS:* San Diego [CA] B: 9/16/1918, San Diego, CA
Drafted: 1941 Round 7 NYG
1941 NYG: 11 G.

KURT SOHN Sohn, Kurt Frederick 5'11", 180 **WR**
Col: Nassau CC NY; North Carolina State; Fordham *HS:* Huntington [NY] B: 6/26/1957, Ithaca, NY
1985 NYJ: Rush 1-12 12.0. **1986** NYJ: Rush 2-(-11) -5.5. **Total:** Rush 3-1 0.3.

		Receiving				Punt Returns			
Year Team	**G**	**Rec**	**Yds**	**Avg**	**TD**	**Ret**	**Yds**	**Avg**	**TD**
1981 NYJ	16	0	0	—	0	13	66	5.1	0
1982 NYJ	9	0	0	—	0	0	0	—	0
1984 NYJ	5	2	28	14.0	0	0	0	—	0
1985 NYJ	15	39	534	13.7	4	16	149	9.3	0
1986 NYJ	15	8	129	16.1	2	35	289	8.3	0
1987 NYJ	12	23	261	11.3	2	1	6	6.0	0
1988 NYJ	15	7	66	9.4	2	3	9	3.0	0
NFL Total	87	79	1018	12.9	10	68	519	7.6	0

	Kickoff Returns				
Year Team	**Ret**	**Yds**	**Avg**	**TD**	**Fum**
1981 NYJ	26	528	20.3	0	5
1982 NYJ	15	299	19.9	0	0
1985 NYJ	3	7	2.3	0	0
1986 NYJ	7	124	17.7	0	3
1987 NYJ	3	47	15.7	0	0
1988 NYJ	9	159	17.7	0	0
NFL Total	63	1164	18.5	0	8

JOHN SOKOLOSKY Sokolosky, John Joseph 6'2", 240 **C**
Col: Wayne State (Mich.) *HS:* De La Salle [Detroit, MI] B: 4/2/1956, Detroit, MI
1978 Det: 11 G.

ROBERT SOLEAU Soleau, Robert Heyde Jr. 6'2", 230 **LB**
Col: William & Mary *HS:* North Hills [Pittsburgh, PA] B: 4/2/1941, Amherst, MA *Drafted:* 1964 Round 11 Pit
1964 Pit: 14 G.

ARIEL SOLOMON Solomon, Ariel Mace 6′5″, 285 **C-OT-OG**
Col: Colorado *HS:* Boulder [CO] B: 7/16/1968, Brooklyn, NY
Drafted: 1991 Round 10 Pit
1991 Pit: 5 G. **1992** Pit: 4 G. **1993** Pit: 16 G. **1994** Pit: 16 G. **1995** Pit: 4 G. **1996** Min: 16 G. **Total:** 61 G.

FREDDIE SOLOMON Solomon, Fred 5′11″, 185 **WR-QB-RB**
Col: Tampa *HS:* Sumter [SC] B: 1/11/1953, Sumter, SC
Drafted: 1975 Round 2 Mia
1976 Mia: Pass 1-0. **1978** SF: Pass 10-5 50.0%, 85 8.50 1 Int. **1979** SF: Pass 1-1 100.0%, 12 12.00. **1980** SF: Pass 1-0. **1981** SF: Pass 1-1 100.0%, 25 25.00. **1985** SF: Pass 1-0. **Total:** Pass 15-7 46.7%, 122 8.13 1 Int.

		Rushing				Receiving			
Year Team	**G**	**Att**	**Yds**	**Avg**	**TD**	**Rec**	**Yds**	**Avg**	**TD**
1975 Mia	14	4	87	21.8	0	22	339	15.4	2
1976 Mia	10	4	60	15.0	1	27	453	16.8	2
1977 Mia	13	6	43	7.2	0	12	181	15.1	1
1978 SF	16	14	70	5.0	1	31	458	14.8	2
1979 SF	15	6	85	14.2	1	57	807	14.2	7
1980 SF	16	8	56	7.0	0	48	658	13.7	8
1981 SF	15	9	43	4.8	0	59	969	16.4	8
1982 SF	9	1	-4	-4.0	0	19	323	17.0	3
1983 SF	13	1	3	3.0	0	31	662	21.4	4
1984 SF	14	6	72	12.0	1	40	737	18.4	10
1985 SF	16	2	4	2.0	0	25	259	10.4	1
NFL Total	151	61	519	8.5	4	371	5846	15.8	48

	Punt Returns				Kickoff Returns					Tot
Year Team	**Ret**	**Yds**	**Avg**	**TD**	**Ret**	**Yds**	**Avg**	**TD**	**Fum**	**TD**
1975 Mia	26	320	12.3	1	17	348	20.5	0	2	3
1976 Mia	13	205	15.8	1	1	12	12.0	0	0	4
1977 Mia	32	285	8.9	0	10	273	27.3	1	2	2
1978 SF	9	35	3.9	0	0	0	—	0	5	3
1979 SF	23	142	6.2	0	0	0	—	0	3	8
1980 SF	27	298	11.0	**2**	4	61	15.3	0	5	10
1981 SF	29	173	6.0	0	0	0	—	0	3	8
1982 SF	13	122	9.4	0	0	0	—	0	2	3
1983 SF	5	34	6.8	0	0	0	—	0	1	4
1984 SF	0	0	—	0	0	0	—	0	0	11
1985 SF	0	0	—	0	0	0	—	0	1	1
NFL Total	177	1614	9.1	4	32	694	21.7	1	24	57

FREDDIE SOLOMON Solomon, Freddie Lee Jr. 5′10″, 180 **WR**
Col: South Carolina State *HS:* Santa Fe [Alachua, FL] B: 8/15/1972, Gainesville, FL
1997 Phi: Scor 1 2XP. **Total:** Scor 1 2XP.

		Receiving				Punt Returns				
Year Team	**G**	**Rec**	**Yds**	**Avg**	**TD**	**Ret**	**Yds**	**Avg**	**TD**	**Fum**
1996 Phi	12	8	125	15.6	0	5	27	5.4	0	0
1997 Phi	15	29	455	15.7	3	10	55	5.5	0	3
1998 Phi	16	21	193	9.2	1	11	100	9.1	0	0
NFL Total	43	58	773	13.3	4	26	182	7.0	0	3

JESSE SOLOMON Solomon, Jesse William 6′0″, 240 **LB**
(Early Man) *Col:* North Florida CC FL; Florida State *HS:* Madison Co. [Madison, FL] B: 11/4/1963, Madison, FL *Drafted:* 1986 Round 12 Min
1986 Min: 13 G; Int 2-34. **1987** Min: 12 G; Int 1-30; 2 Sac. **1988** Min: 16 G; Int 4-84 1 TD; 6 Pt; 2.5 Sac. **1989** Min-Dal: 15 G. Min: 4 G. Dal: 11 G. **1990** Dal: 9 G; 1 Sac. **1991** TB: 13 G. **1992** Atl: 16 G; Rush 2-12 6.0; Int 1-13; 4.5 Sac. **1993** Atl: 16 G. **1994** Mia: 6 G. **Total:** 116 G; Rush 2-12 6.0; Int 8-161 1 TD; 6 Pt; 10 Sac.

ROLAND SOLOMON Solomon, Roland Howard 6′0″, 193 **DB**
Col: Utah *HS:* Cabrillo [Lompoc, CA] B: 2/6/1956, Fort Worth, TX
1980 Dal-Buf: 11 G; PR 1-8 8.0. Dal: 10 G; PR 1-8 8.0. Buf: 1 G. **1981** Den: 4 G. **Total:** 15 G; PR 1-8 8.0.

RON SOLT Solt, Ronald Matthew 6′3″, 279 **OG**
Col: Maryland *HS:* James M. Coughlin [Wilkes-Barre, PA]
B: 5/19/1962, Bainbridge, MD *Drafted:* 1984 Round 1 Ind
1984 Ind: 16 G. **1985** Ind: 15 G. **1986** Ind: 16 G. **1987** Ind: 12 G. **1988** Ind-Phi: 2 G. Ind: 1 G. Phi: 1 G. **1989** Phi: 13 G. **1990** Phi: 15 G. **1991** Phi: 15 G. **1992** Ind: 12 G. **Total:** 116 G.

GORDIE SOLTAU Soltau, Gordon Leroy 6′2″, 195 **OE**
Col: Minnesota *HS:* Central [Duluth, MN] B: 1/25/1925, Duluth, MN
Drafted: 1950 Round 3 GB
1951 SF: Rush 1-(-4) -4.0. **Total:** Rush 1-(-4) -4.0.

		Receiving			
Year Team	**G**	**Rec**	**Yds**	**Avg**	**TD**
1950 SF	12	14	170	12.1	1
1951 SF	12	59	826	14.0	7
1952 SF	12	55	774	14.1	7
1953 SF	12	43	620	14.4	6
1954 SF	11	22	316	14.4	2
1955 SF	12	26	358	13.8	1
1956 SF	12	18	299	16.6	1
1957 SF	12	5	47	9.4	0
1958 SF	12	7	77	11.0	0
NFL Total	107	249	3487	14.0	25

	Scoring							
Year Team	**Pts**	**FG**	**FGA**	**FG%**	**XK**	**XKA**	**XK%**	**Fum**
1950 SF	44	4	8	50.0	26	28	92.9	0
1951 SF	90	6	18	33.3	30	32	93.8	3
1952 SF	**94**	6	12	50.0	34	36	94.4	1
1953 SF	**114**	10	15	66.7	**48**	**49**	98.0	1
1954 SF	76	11	18	61.1	31	33	93.9	2
1955 SF	42	3	12	25.0	27	30	90.0	0
1956 SF	71	13	20	65.0	26	28	92.9	0
1957 SF	60	9	15	60.0	33	33	100.0	1
1958 SF	53	8	21	38.1	29	34	85.3	0
NFL Total	644	70	139	50.4	284	303	93.7	8

ROBERT SOLTIS Soltis, Robert Lawrence 6′2″, 205 **DB**
Col: Minnesota *HS:* North [Minneapolis, MN] B: 4/1/1936
Drafted: 1959 Round 16 NYG
1960 Bos: 14 G; Int 2-33. **1961** Bos: 3 G. **Total:** 17 G; Int 2-33.

GEORGE SOMERS Somers, George Anthony 6′2″, 253 **T**
Col: La Salle *HS:* St. Clair [PA] B: 10/5/1915, Fountain Springs, PA
Drafted: 1939 Round 8 Phi
1939 Phi: 9 G. **1940** Phi: 10 G; Scor 7, 2-9 22.2% FG, 1-1 100.0% XK. **1941** Pit: 10 G; Scor 0-2 FG. **1942** Pit: 11 G; Scor 1, 0-1 FG, 1-1 100.0% XK. **Total:** 40 G; Scor 8, 2-12 16.7% FG, 2-2 100.0% XK.

DON SOMMER Sommer, Donald Martin 6′4″, 290 **OT**
Col: Texas-El Paso *HS:* Bellaire [TX] B: 2/1/1964, Corsicanna, TX
1987 Buf: 3 G.

MIKE SOMMER Sommer, Michael Sandor 5′11″, 190 **HB-DB**
Col: George Washington *HS:* Woodrow Wilson [Washington, DC]
B: 10/9/1934, Washington, DC *Drafted:* 1958 Round 2 Was
1958 Was: PR 3-3 1.0; KR 4-77 19.3. **1959** Was-Bal: Rec 7-111 15.9; KR 9-185 20.6. Was: KR 1-19 19.0. Bal: Rec 7-111 15.9; KR 8-166 20.8. **1960** Bal: KR 1-10 10.0. **1961** Bal-Was: Rec 1-31 31.0; PR 2-26 13.0; KR 4-98 24.5. Bal: Rec 1-31 31.0. Was: PR 2-26 13.0; KR 4-98 24.5. **1963** Oak: Rec 1-24 24.0; PR 4-44 11.0; KR 5-102 20.4. **Total:** Rec 9-166 18.4; PR 9-73 8.1; KR 23-472 20.5.

		Rushing				
Year Team	**G**	**Att**	**Yds**	**Avg**	**TD**	**Fum**
1958 Was	2	0	0	—	0	0
1959 Was-Bal	9	62	231	3.7	2	1
1959 Was	1	1	4	4.0	0	0
1959 Bal	8	61	227	3.7	2	1
1960 Bal	1	0	0	—	0	1
1961 Bal-Was	6	11	1	0.1	0	0
1961 Bal	4	6	10	1.7	0	0
1961 Was	2	5	-9	-1.8	0	0
1963 Oak	4	5	21	4.2	0	0
NFL Total	22	78	253	3.2	2	2

JACK SOMMERS Sommers, Jack William 6′3″, 232 **C-LB**
Col: UCLA *HS:* Norristown [PA]; Mercersburg Acad. [PA] B: 2/9/1919
1947 Was: 8 G; Scor 0-1 FG.

BUTCH SONGIN Songin, Edward Frank 6′2″, 190 **QB**
Col: Boston College *HS:* Walpole [MA]; Newman Prep [Boston, MA]
B: 5/11/1924, Walpole, MA D: 5/26/1976, Wrentham, MA
1960 Bos: Rush 11-40 3.6 2 TD. **1961** Bos: Rush 8-39 4.9. **1962** NYT: Rush 4-11 2.8. **Total:** Rush 23-90 3.9 2 TD.

		Passing								
Year Team	**G**	**Att**	**Comp**	**Comp%**	**Yds**	**YPA**	**TD**	**Int**	**Rating**	**Fum**
1960 Bos	14	392	187	47.7	2476	6.32	22	15	70.9	3
1961 Bos	14	212	98	46.2	1429	6.74	14	**9**	73.0	4
1962 NYT	7	90	42	46.7	442	4.91	2	7	36.4	0
NFL Total	35	694	327	47.1	4347	6.26	38	31	67.1	7

TREG SONGY Songy, Treg Joseph 6′2″, 200 **DB**
Col: Tulane *HS:* St. Augustine [New Orleans, LA] B: 6/15/1962, New Orleans, LA
1987 NYJ: 2 G.

GUSTAVE SONNENBERG Sonnenberg, Gustave Adolph 5′6″, 196 **T-FB-TB**
(Dynamite; The Iron Duke) *Col:* Dartmouth; Detroit Mercy
HS: Marquette [MI] B: 3/6/1898, Ewen, MI D: 9/13/1944, Bethesda, MD
1923 Buf-Col: 11 G; Rush 1 TD; 6 Pt. Buf: 1 G. Col: 10 G; Rush 1 TD; 6 Pt. **1925** Det: 12 G; Scor 27, 5 FG, 12 XK. **1926** Det: 12 G; Scor 34, 9 FG, 7 XK. **1927** Prov: 14 G; Scor 16, 3 FG, 7 XK. **1928** Prov: 11 G; Pass 1 TD; Scor 10, 1 FG, 6 XK, **1** 1XP. **1930** Prov: 1 G. **Total:** 61 G; Pass 1 TD; Rush 1 TD; Scor 93, 18 FG, 32 XK, 1 1XP.

ROSS SORCE Sorce, Ross Paul Jr. 6′4″, 255 **T**
Col: Georgetown *HS:* Central Catholic [Pittsburgh, PA] B: 1920, Pittsburgh, PA D: 12/28/1959, Bethel, PA
1945 Pit: 1 G.

GLEN SORENSON Sorenson, Glen 6′0″, 217 **G-LB**
(Lefty; Goof) *Col:* Utah State *HS:* West [Salt Lake City, UT] B: 2/29/1920, Salt Lake City, UT D: 2/26/1972, Salt Lake City, UT
1943 GB: 7 G; Scor 0-2 FG. **1944** GB: 10 G; Scor 1, 0-1 FG, 1-1 100.0% XK. **1945** GB: 10 G; Scor 0-1 FG. **Total:** 27 G; Scor 1, 0-4 FG, 1-1 100.0% XK.

JIM SOREY Sorey, James 6′4″, 285 **DT**
(Bull) *Col:* Texas Southern B: 9/5/1936, Marianna, FL *Drafted:* 1960 Round 2 Buf
1960 Buf: 14 G. **1961** Buf: 14 G. **1962** Buf: 14 G. **Total:** 42 G.

REVIE SOREY Sorey, Revie Cee Jr. 6′2″, 260 **OG**
Col: Illinois *HS:* Boys [Brooklyn, NY] B: 9/10/1953, Brooklyn, NY *Drafted:* 1975 Round 5 ChiB
1975 ChiB: 14 G. **1976** ChiB: 14 G. **1977** ChiB: 14 G. **1978** ChiB: 16 G. **1979** ChiB: 16 G. **1980** ChiB: 16 G. **1981** ChiB: 16 G. **1983** ChiB: 3 G. **Total:** 109 G.

HENRY SORRELL Sorrell, Henry Thomas 6′1″, 215 **LB**
Col: Tennessee-Chattanooga *HS:* Talladega [AL] B: 6/10/1943, Talladega, AL
1967 Den: 10 G.

BILL SORTET Sortet, Wilbur John 6′1″, 187 **OE-DE**
Col: West Virginia *HS:* Huntington [WV] B: 6/25/1912, Vincennes, IN D: 1/22/1998, Charleston, WV
1936 Pit: Rush 1-47 47.0. **1938** Pit: Rush 1-(-5) -5.0. **Total:** Rush 2-42 21.0.

		Receiving			
Year Team	**G**	**Rec**	**Yds**	**Avg**	**TD**
1933 Pit	9	1	28	28.0	0
1934 Pit	12	7	93	13.3	1
1935 Pit	12	7	178	25.4	0
1936 Pit	12	14	197	14.1	1
1937 Pit	9	9	121	13.4	1
1938 Pit	8	11	166	15.1	4
1939 Pit	11	16	196	12.3	1
1940 Pit	11	7	112	16.0	0
NFL Total	84	72	1091	15.2	8

RICK SORTUN Sortun, Henrik Martin 6′2″, 235 **OG**
Col: Washington *HS:* Kent-Meridian [Kent, WA] B: 9/26/1942, Tacoma, WA *Drafted:* 1964 Round 12 StL
1964 StL: 14 G. **1965** StL: 13 G. **1966** StL: 14 G; Rec 1-7 7.0. **1967** StL: 13 G; KR 1-0. **1968** StL: 14 G. **1969** StL: 14 G. **Total:** 82 G; Rec 1-7 7.0; KR 1-0.

LOU SOSSAMON Sossamon, Louis Cody 6′1″, 207 **C-LB**
Col: South Carolina *HS:* Gaffney [SC] B: 6/2/1921, Gaffney, SC
AAFC **1946** NY-A: 14 G. **1947** NY-A: 14 G; 6 Pt. **1948** NY-A: 14 G. **Total:** 42 G; 6 Pt.

FRANK SOUCHAK Souchak, Frank S 6′0″, 205 **OE-DE**
Col: Pittsburgh *HS:* Berwick [PA] B: 1916, Berwick, PA *Drafted:* 1938 Round 4 NYG
1939 Pit: 4 G; Rec 1-12 12.0.

CECIL SOUDERS Souders, Cecil B 6′1″, 210 **DE-OE-T**
(Cy) *Col:* Ohio State *HS:* Bucyrus [OH] B: 1/3/1921, Bucyrus, OH *Drafted:* 1945 Round 23 Was
1947 Det: 11 G; Rec 15-184 12.3 1 TD; 6 Pt. **1948** Det: 12 G; Rec 2-19 9.5. **1949** Det: 12 G; KR 1-7 7.0. **Total:** 35 G; Rec 17-203 11.9 1 TD; KR 1-7 7.0; 6 Pt.

RONNIE LEE SOUTH South, Ronnie Lee 6′1″, 195 **QB-P**
Col: Arkansas *HS:* Russellville [AR] B: 5/8/1945, Wynne, AR *Drafted:* 1968 Round 5 NO
1968 NO: 4 G; Pass 38-14 36.8%, 129 3.39 1 TD 3 Int; Rush 4-5 1.3; Punt 14-387 27.6.

TOMMY SOUTHARD Southard, Thomas 6′0″, 185 **WR**
Col: Furman *HS:* Druid Hills [Atlanta, GA] B: 6/29/1955
1978 StL: 2 G; PR 2-(-2) -1.0; KR 2-47 23.5.

JERALD SOWELL Sowell, Jerald Monye 6′0″, 248 **RB**
Col: Tulane *HS:* Baker [LA] B: 1/21/1974, Elyria, OH *Drafted:* 1997 Round 7 GB
1997 NYJ: Rec 1-8 8.0. **1998** NYJ: Rec 10-59 5.9. **Total:** Rec 11-67 6.1.

		Rushing				
Year Team	**G**	**Att**	**Yds**	**Avg**	**TD**	**Fum**
1997 NYJ	9	7	35	5.0	0	0
1998 NYJ	16	40	164	4.1	0	2
NFL Total	25	47	199	4.2	0	2

ROBERT SOWELL Sowell, Robert Donnell Jr. 5′11″, 175 **DB**
Col: Howard *HS:* Mifflin [Columbus, OH] B: 6/23/1961, Columbus, OH
1983 Mia: 16 G; PR 1-0. **1984** Mia: 16 G; Int 1-7. **1985** Mia: 10 G; 1 Sac. **1987** Mia: 3 G; Int 1-29. **Total:** 45 G; PR 1-0; Int 2-36; 1 Sac.

RICH SOWELLS Sowells, Richard Allen 6′0″, 179 **DB**
Col: Alcorn State *HS:* Sam Houston [Huntsville, TX] B: 10/27/1948, Prarie View, TX *Drafted:* 1971 Round 12 NYJ
1975 NYJ: PR 1-0. **Total:** PR 1-0.

		Interceptions			
Year Team	**G**	**Int**	**Yds**	**TD**	**Fum**
1971 NYJ	8	0	0	0	0
1972 NYJ	11	2	14	0	0
1973 NYJ	12	3	55	1	0
1974 NYJ	14	2	0	0	0
1975 NYJ	14	1	0	0	1
1976 NYJ	10	2	46	0	1
1977 Hou	9	0	0	0	0
NFL Total	78	10	115	1	2

VIC SPADACCINI Spadaccini, Victor Michael 6′0″, 222 **BB-DB-WB**
Col: Minnesota *HS:* Keewatin [MN] B: 3/2/1916, Keewatin, MN D: 4/28/1981, West St. Paul, MN *Drafted:* 1938 Round 10 Cle
1938 Cle: Rush 9-46 5.1. **1939** Cle: Scor 18, 12-16 75.0% XK. **1940** Cle: Pass 1-0; Int 3-83 **1** TD; Scor 23, 5-7 71.4% XK. **Total:** Pass 1-0; Rush 9-46 5.1; Int 3-83 1 TD; Scor 41, 17-23 73.9% XK.

		Receiving				Tot
Year Team	**G**	**Rec**	**Yds**	**Avg**	**TD**	**TD**
1938 Cle	10	8	101	12.6	0	0
1939 Cle	11	32	292	9.1	1	1
1940 Cle	9	22	276	12.5	2	3
NFL Total	30	62	669	10.8	3	4

BUTCH SPAGNA Spagna, Joseph 6′0″, 215 **G-T**
(Stonewall) *Col:* Brown; Lehigh *HS:* Avon [MA] B: 5/15/1897, Mew York, NY D: 12/11/1948, Philadelphia, PA
1920 Cle-Buf: 7 G. Cle: 4 G. Buf: 3 G. **1921** Buf: 4 G. **1924** Fra: 14 G; 1 Fum TD; 6 Pt. **1925** Fra: 7 G. **Total:** 32 G; 1 Fum TD; 6 Pt.

JOHN SPAGNOLA Spagnola, John Stephen 6′4″, 240 **TE**
Col: Yale *HS:* Bethlehem Catholic [Fredericktown, PA] B: 8/1/1957, Bethlehem, PA *Drafted:* 1979 Round 9 NE
1980 Phi: KR 1-0. **Total:** KR 1-0.

		Receiving				
Year Team	**G**	**Rec**	**Yds**	**Avg**	**TD**	**Fum**
1979 Phi	16	2	24	12.0	0	0
1980 Phi	16	18	193	10.7	3	2
1981 Phi	11	6	83	13.8	0	0
1982 Phi	9	26	313	12.0	2	0
1984 Phi	16	65	701	10.8	1	2
1985 Phi	16	64	772	12.1	5	1
1986 Phi	15	39	397	10.2	1	2
1987 Phi	12	36	350	9.7	2	2
1988 Sea	16	5	40	8.0	1	0
1989 GB	6	2	13	6.5	0	0
NFL Total	133	263	2886	11.0	15	9

DICK SPAIN Spain, Richard R 5′8″, 180 **C-T**
Col: No College *HS:* Central [Evansville, IN] B: 5/1893, Evansville, IN D: 10/3/1948
1921 Eva: 1 G. **1922** Eva: 3 G. **Total:** 4 G.

GENE SPANGLER Spangler, Eugene Douglas 5′10″, 196 **WB-DB**
Col: Tulsa *HS:* Coffeyville [KS] B: 12/17/1922, Huntington, AR
1946 Det: 6 G; Rush 1-1 1.0; KR 4-63 15.8.

GARY SPANI Spani, Gary Leland 6′2″, 229 **LB**
Col: Kansas State *HS:* Manhattan [KS] B: 1/9/1956, Satanta, KS *Drafted:* 1978 Round 3 KC
1978 KC: 14 G. **1979** KC: 16 G. **1980** KC: 16 G; Int 1-47 1 TD; **1** Fum TD; Tot TD 2; 12 Pt. **1981** KC: 16 G; 1 Fum TD; 6 Pt. **1982** KC: 8 G. **1983** KC: 10 G; 3 Sac. **1984** KC: 14 G; 1 Sac. **1985** KC: 14 G; 1 Sac. **1986** KC: 16 G; Int 1-24. **Total:** 124 G; Int 2-71 1 TD; 2 Fum TD; Tot TD 3; 18 Pt; 5 Sac.

FRANK SPANIEL Spaniel, Francis James 5′10″, 185 **HB**
Col: Notre Dame *HS:* Vandergrift [PA] B: 5/21/1928, Vandergrift, PA D: 10/27/1994, North Fort Myers, FL *Drafted:* 1950 Round 5 Was
1950 Was-Bal: 12 G; Rush 15-22 1.5 1 TD; Rec 5-84 16.8; PR 2-11 5.5; KR 14-316 22.6; Int 1-29 1 TD; Tot TD 2; 12 Pt. Was: 6 G; Rush 1-1 1.0; PR 2-11 5.5; KR 8-175 21.9. Bal: 6 G; Rush 14-21 1.5 1 TD; Rec 5-84 16.8; KR 6-141 23.5; Int 1-29 1 TD; Tot TD 2; 12 Pt. **Total:** 12 G; Rush 15-22 1.5 1 TD; Rec 5-84 16.8; PR 2-11 5.5; KR 14-316 22.6; Int 1-29 1 TD; Tot TD 2; 12 Pt.

GARY SPANN Spann, Gary Lynn 6′1″, 218 **LB**
Col: Texas Christian *HS:* South Oak Cliff [Dallas, TX] B: 2/3/1963, Dallas, TX
1987 KC: 2 G.

DAVE SPARENBERG Sparenberg, David 6′3″, 267 **OG**
Col: Western Ontario (Canada) B: 5/28/1959, Chatham, Canada
1987 Cle: 1 G.

AL SPARKMAN Sparkman, Temple Alan 6′6″, 253 **T**
Col: Texas A&M *HS:* Thomas Jefferson [San Antonio, TX]
B: 2/17/1926, Baltimore, MD
1948 LARm: 12 G; KR 1-0; 1 Fum. **1949** LARm: 4 G. **Total:** 16 G; KR 1-0; 1 Fum.

DAVE SPARKS Sparks, David Walter 6′1″, 229 **OG-OT**
Col: South Carolina *HS:* Lorain [OH] B: 4/28/1928 D: 12/5/1954, Arlington, VA *Drafted:* 1951 Round 15 SF
1951 SF: 8 G. **1954** Was: 10 G. **Total:** 18 G.

PHILLIPPI SPARKS Sparks, Phillippi Dwaine 5′11″, 195 **DB**
Col: Glendale CC AZ; Arizona State *HS:* Maryvale [Phoenix, AZ]
B: 4/15/1969, Oklahoma City, OK *Drafted:* 1992 Round 2 NYG
1992 NYG: KR 2-23 11.5. **1997** NYG: KR 1-8 8.0; 1 Sac. **Total:** KR 3-31 10.3; 1 Sac.

		Interceptions		
Year Team	G	Int	Yds	TD
1992 NYG	16	1	0	0
1993 NYG	5	0	0	0
1994 NYG	11	3	4	0
1995 NYG	16	5	11	0
1996 NYG	14	3	23	0
1997 NYG	13	5	72	0
1998 NYG	13	4	25	0
NFL Total	88	21	135	0

AL SPARLIS Sparlis, Albert Alexander 5′11″, 185 **G-LB**
(Gunga) *Col:* UCLA *HS:* Los Angeles Polytechnic [CA] B: 5/20/1920, Los Angeles, CA *Drafted:* 1946 Round 28 GB
1946 GB: 3 G.

ED SPARR Sparr, Edwin A 6′0″, 210 **T**
Col: Carroll (Wis.) *HS:* Wausau [WI] B: 7/29/1898, Hazelhurst, WI
D: 5/19/1974, Detroit, MI
1926 Rac: 2 G.

JIM SPAVITAL Spavital, James J 6′1″, 210 **FB-LB**
Col: Oklahoma State *HS:* Central [Edmond, OK] B: 9/15/1926, Oklahoma City, OK D: 3/7/1993, Stillwater, OK *Drafted:* 1948 Round 1 ChiC
AAFC **1949** LA-A: 12 G; Rush 15-44 2.9; Rec 1-(-1) -1.0; PR 6-58 9.7; KR 1-32 32.0; Int 4-58.

NFL **1950** Bal: Rec 21-238 11.3 1 TD.

		Rushing					Tot
Year Team	G	Att	Yds	Avg	TD	Fum	TD
1950 Bal	11	58	246	4.2	2	3	3

GLEN SPEAR Spear, Glen Owen 5′10″, 185 **FB-WB-E**
(Farmer) *Col:* Drake *HS:* Fairfield [NE] B: 1/18/1900, Fairfield, NE
D: 12/19/1971, Sutton, NE
1926 KC: 10 G; 1 Fum TD; 6 Pt.

ERNEST SPEARS Spears, Ernest Phillip 5′11″, 192 **DB**
Col: USC *HS:* El Camino [Oceanside, CA] B: 11/6/1967, Oceanside, CA *Drafted:* 1990 Round 10 NO
1990 NO: 16 G.

MARCUS SPEARS Spears, Marcus Dewayne 6′4″, 310 **OT**
Col: Northwestern State-Louisiana *HS:* Belaire [Scotlandville, LA]
B: 9/28/1971, Baton Rouge, LA *Drafted:* 1994 Round 2 ChiB
1996 ChiB: 9 G; Rec 1-1 1.0 1 TD; 6 Pt. **1997** KC: 3 G. **1998** KC: 12 G. **Total:** 24 G; Rec 1-1 1.0 1 TD; 6 Pt.

RON SPEARS Spears, Ronald Darnell 6′6″, 255 **DE**
Col: East Los Angeles Coll. CA (J.C.); San Diego State *HS:* John Marshall [Los Angeles, CA] B: 11/23/1959, Los Angeles, CA
1982 NE: 7 G. **1983** NE-GB: 14 G; 0.5 Sac. NE: 1 G. GB: 13 G; 0.5 Sac. **Total:** 21 G; 0.5 Sac.

ANTHONY SPEARS Spears, William Anthony 6′5″, 260 **DE**
Col: Diablo Valley Coll. CA (J.C.); Portland State *HS:* Pittsburg [CA]
B: 11/4/1965, Martinez, CA
1989 Hou: Postseason only.

ROBERT SPECHT Specht, Robert 5′9″, 170 **TB**
Col: No College *HS:* Albert G. Lane Tech [Chicago, IL] Deceased
1920 Ham: 7 G.

DUTCH SPECK Speck, Norman J 5′10″, 220 **G-C-T**
Col: No College *HS:* McKinley [Canton, OH] B: 1886, Canton, OH
D: 11/18/1952, Canton, OH
1920 Can: 9 G. **1921** Can: 7 G. **1922** Can: 11 G. **1923** Can: 6 G. **1924** Akr: 1 G. **1925** Can: 5 G. **1926** Can: 7 G. **Total:** 46 G.

MAC SPEEDIE Speedie, Mac Curtis 6′3″, 203 **OE-DE**
Col: Utah *HS:* South [Salt Lake City, UT] B: 1/12/1920, Odell, IL
D: 3/12/1993, Laguna Hills, CA *Drafted:* 1942 Round 15 Det
AAFC **1946** CleA: KR 1-1 1.0; Punt 3-84 28.0; Scor 43, 1-1 100.0% XK. **1947** CleA: Rush 1-(-7) -7.0. **1948** CleA: Rush 1-7 7.0; KR 1-13 13.0. **Total:** Rush 2-0; KR 2-14 7.0; Punt 3-84 28.0; Scor 151, 1-1 100.0% XK.

		Receiving				Tot
Year Team	G	Rec	Yds	Avg	TD	TD
1946 CleA	14	24	564	23.5	7	7
1947 CleA	14	67	1146	17.1	6	7
1948 CleA	12	58	816	14.1	4	4
1949 CleA	12	62	1028	16.6	7	7
AAFC Total	52	211	3554	16.8	24	25

NFL Statistics

		Receiving				
Year Team	G	Rec	Yds	Avg	TD	Fum
1950 Cle	12	42	548	13.0	1	0
1951 Cle	10	34	589	17.3	3	1
1952 Cle	12	**62**	911	14.7	5	0
NFL Total	34	138	2048	14.8	9	1

CLIFF SPEEGLE Speegle, Clifton M 6′1″, 195 **C-LB**
Col: Oklahoma *HS:* Capitol Hill [Oklahoma City, OK] B: 11/5/1917, Roosevelt, OK D: 9/5/1994, Dallas, TX
1945 ChiC: 8 G; Int 2-13.

HARRY SPEELMAN Speelman, Harry E 5′11″, 220 **G**
Col: Michigan State *HS:* Central [Lansing, MI] B: 10/4/1916
D: 4/1/1983, Pigeon, MI
1940 Det: 4 G.

DEL SPEER Speer, Delfoncio Arnese 6′0″, 196 **DB**
Col: Florida *HS:* Miami Carol City [Miami, FL] B: 2/1/1970, Miami, FL
1993 Cle: 16 G; Int 1-22; 1 Fum. **1994** Cle-Sea: 9 G. Cle: 8 G. Sea: 1 G. **Total:** 25 G; Int 1-22; 1 Fum.

DICK SPEIGHTS Speights, Richard Blan 5′11″, 175 **DB**
Col: Wyoming *HS:* Battle Creek Central [MI] B: 6/30/1946, Battle Creek, MI
1968 SD: 2 G; KR 1-21 21.0.

JEFF SPEK Spek, Jeffrey Martin 6′3″, 238 **TE**
Col: Nevada-Las Vegas; San Diego State *HS:* El Modena [Orange, CA]
B: 10/1/1960, Calgary, Canada *Drafted:* 1984 Supplemental Round 3 Dal
1986 TB: 2 G.

FRANK SPELLACY Spellacy, Francis **E**
Col: No College B: 1901, NY Deceased
1922 Buf: 1 G.

ALONZO SPELLMAN Spellman, Alonzo Robert 6′4″, 287 **DE-DT**
Col: Ohio State *HS:* Rancocas Valley Regional [Mount Holly, NJ]
B: 9/27/1971, Mount Holly, NJ *Drafted:* 1992 Round 1 ChiB
1992 ChiB: 15 G; 4 Sac. **1993** ChiB: 16 G; 2.5 Sac. **1994** ChiB: 16 G; Int 1-31; 7 Sac. **1995** ChiB: 16 G; 8.5 Sac. **1996** ChiB: 16 G; 8 Sac. **1997** ChiB: 7 G; 2 Sac. **Total:** 86 G; Int 1-31; 32 Sac.

JACK SPELLMAN Spellman, John Franklin 5′10″, 201 **E-T-FB-WB**
Col: Brown *HS:* Enfield [CT] B: 6/14/1899, Middletown, CT
D: 8/1/1966, Mangula, Zimbabwe
1925 Prov: 10 G; 6 Pt. **1926** Prov: 12 G. **1927** Prov: 14 G. **1928** Prov: 11 G. **1929** Prov: 12 G. **1930** Prov: 11 G. **1931** Prov: 11 G. **1932** Bos: 7 G. **Total:** 88 G; 6 Pt.

BLAKE SPENCE Spence, Blake Andrew 6′4″, 249 **TE**
Col: Oregon *HS:* Capistrano Valley [Mission Viejo, CA] B: 6/20/1975, Garden Grove, CA *Drafted:* 1998 Round 5 NYJ
1998 NYJ: 5 G; Rec 1-5 5.0.

JULIAN SPENCE Spence, Julian Carroll 5′11″, 170 **DB-FL**
(Sus) *Col:* Sam Houston State *HS:* L. C. Anderson [Austin, TX]
B: 5/5/1929, Austin, TX D: 3/6/1990, Houston, TX
1956 ChiC: 8 G; Int 1-7. **1957** SF: 3 G. **1960** Hou: 14 G; Int 4-5; 1 Fum. **1961** Hou: 10 G; Rec 1-14 14.0; Int 1-23. **Total:** 35 G; Rec 1-14 14.0; Int 6-35; 1 Fum.

DARRYL SPENCER Spencer, Darryl Eugene 5′8″, 172 **WR**
Col: Miami (Fla.) *HS:* Merritt Island [FL] B: 3/21/1970, Merritt Island, FL
1994 Atl: 8 G; Rec 2-51 25.5. **1995** Atl: 5 G; Rec 5-60 12.0. **Total:** 13 G; Rec 7-111 15.9.

HERB SPENCER Spencer, Herbert Seabrook 6′3″, 230 **LB**
Col: Newberry *HS:* Hanahan [SC] B: 9/23/1959, Charleston, SC
1987 Atl: 3 G.

JIMMY SPENCER Spencer, James Arthur Jr. 5′10″, 181 **DB**
Col: Florida *HS:* Glades Central [Belle Glade, FL] B: 3/29/1969, Manning, SC *Drafted:* 1991 Round 8 Was
1996 Cin: 1 Fum TD. **Total:** 1 Fum TD.

		Interceptions		
Year Team	G	Int	Yds	TD
1992 NO	16	0	0	0
1993 NO	16	0	0	0
1994 NO	16	5	24	0
1995 NO	16	4	11	0
1996 Cin	15	5	48	0
1997 Cin	16	1	-2	0
1998 SD	15	1	0	0
NFL Total	110	16	81	0

JIM SPENCER Spencer, James M 6′0″, 205 **G**
Col: Dayton *HS:* St. Louis [Honolulu, HI] B: 11/1/1901 D: 2/28/1972, Cleveland, OH
1928 Day: 5 G. **1929** Day: 6 G. **Total:** 11 G.

JOE SPENCER Spencer, Joseph Emerson 6′3″, 239 **DT-OT**
Col: Oklahoma State *HS:* Capitol Hill [Oklahoma City, OK]
B: 8/15/1923, Elk City, OK D: 10/24/1996, Houston, TX *Drafted:* 1945 Round 17 Phi
AAFC **1948** BknA: 3 G. **1949** CleA: 11 G. **Total:** 14 G.

NFL **1950** GB: 12 G; Int 1-0. **1951** GB: 12 G. **Total:** 24 G; Int 1-0.

OLLIE SPENCER Spencer, Oliver Lee 6′2″, 245 **OT-OG-C**
Col: Kansas *HS:* Ulysses [KS] B: 4/17/1931, Hopewell, KS
D: 4/28/1991, Ukiah, CA *Drafted:* 1953 Round 6 Det
1953 Det: 12 G. **1956** Det: 12 G. **1957** GB: 12 G. **1958** GB: 12 G. **1959** Det: 12 G. **1960** Det: 12 G. **1961** Det: 13 G. **1963** Oak: 14 G. **Total:** 99 G.

MO SPENCER Spencer, Thurmon Maurice 6′0″, 175 **DB**
Col: North Carolina Central *HS:* Walter H. Page [Greensboro, NC]
B: 6/15/1952, Winston-Salem, NC *Drafted:* 1974 Round 3 Atl
1974 StL-LARm-NO: 12 G; KR 1-(-2) -2.0; 1 Fum. StL: 7 G. NO: 5 G; KR 1-(-2) -2.0; 1 Fum. **1975** NO: 14 G; PR 1-0; KR 5-68 13.6; Int 0-11. **1976** NO: 14 G; Int 1-0. **1978** NO: 16 G; Int 4-83. **Total:** 56 G; PR 1-0; KR 6-66 11.0; Int 5-94; 1 Fum.

TIM SPENCER Spencer, Timothy Arnold 6′1″, 224 **RB**
Col: Ohio State *HS:* Richland [St. Clairsville, OH] B: 12/10/1960, Martins Ferry, OH *Drafted:* 1983 Round 11 SD
1986 SD: KR 5-81 16.2. **1988** SD: KR 1-16 16.0. **Total:** KR 6-97 16.2.

		Rushing				Receiving				
Year Team	G	Att	Yds	Avg	TD	Rec	Yds	Avg	TD	Fum
1985 SD	16	124	478	3.9	10	11	135	12.3	0	1
1986 SD	14	99	350	3.5	6	6	48	8.0	0	2
1987 SD	12	73	228	3.1	0	17	123	7.2	0	1
1988 SD	16	44	215	4.9	0	1	14	14.0	0	0
1989 SD	16	134	521	3.9	3	18	112	6.2	0	3
1990 SD	4	0	0	—	0	0	0	—	0	0
NFL Total	78	474	1792	3.8	19	53	432	8.2	0	7

TODD SPENCER Spencer, Todd Lamont 6′0″, 203 **RB**
Col: USC *HS:* El Cerrito [CA] B: 7/26/1962, Portland, OR
1985 Pit: Rec 3-25 8.3. **1987** SD: Rec 2-47 23.5. **Total:** Rec 5-72 14.4.

		Rushing				Kickoff Returns				
Year Team	G	Att	Yds	Avg	TD	Ret	Yds	Avg	TD	Fum
1984 Pit	7	1	0	0.0	0	18	373	20.7	0	5
1985 Pit	16	13	56	4.3	0	27	617	22.9	0	3
1987 SD	3	14	24	1.7	0	0	0	—	0	2
NFL Total	26	28	80	2.9	0	45	990	22.0	0	10

WILLIE SPENCER Spencer, Willie Thomas 6′3″, 235 **RB**
Col: No College *HS:* Washington [Massillon, OH] B: 1/28/1953, Massillon, OH
1977 NYG: Rec 4-20 5.0; KR 3-44 14.7. **1978** NYG: Rec 2-25 12.5; KR 1-14 14.0. **Total:** Rec 6-45 7.5; KR 4-58 14.5.

		Rushing				
Year Team	G	Att	Yds	Avg	TD	Fum
1976 Min	3	4	2	0.5	0	1
1977 NYG	13	62	184	3.0	3	4
1978 NYG	15	38	61	1.6	2	2
NFL Total	31	104	247	2.4	5	7

GEORGE SPETH Speth, George Carl 6′2″, 220 **T**
Col: Murray State *HS:* Seneca Vocational [Buffalo, NY] B: 7/25/1918, Buffalo, NY *Drafted:* 1942 Round 18 Det
1942 Det: 10 G.

COTTON SPEYRER Speyrer, Charles Wayne 6′0″, 175 **WR**
Col: Texas *HS:* Thomas Jefferson [Port Arthur, TX] B: 4/29/1949, Port Arthur, TX *Drafted:* 1971 Round 2 Was
1973 Bal: Pass 1-1 100.0%, 54 54.00 1 TD; Rush 1-1 1.0. **1974** Bal: PR 8-54 6.8. **Total:** Pass 1-1 100.0%, 54 54.00 1 TD; Rush 1-1 1.0; PR 8-54 6.8.

		Receiving				Kickoff Returns					Tot
Year Team	G	Rec	Yds	Avg	TD	Ret	Yds	Avg	TD	Fum	TD
1972 Bal	5	8	114	14.3	0	0	0	—	0	0	0
1973 Bal	14	17	311	18.3	4	17	496	29.2	1	0	5
1974 Bal	13	9	110	12.2	1	22	539	24.5	0	2	1
1975 Mia	4	0	0	—	0	0	0	—	0	0	0
NFL Total	36	34	535	15.7	5	39	1035	26.5	1	2	6

ROB SPICER Spicer, Robin Edward 6′4″, 238 **LB**
Col: Indiana *HS:* Lee M. Thurston [Reford, MI] B: 7/20/1951, Detroit, MI *Drafted:* 1973 Round 9 NYJ
1973 NYJ: 13 G; Int 1-12.

ADOLPH SPIEGEL Spiegel, Clarence Adolph 5′11″, 190 **T-G**
(Rip) *Col:* Campion *HS:* Central [Evansville, IN] B: 7/12/1898, Evansville, IN D: 5/28/1970, Evansville, IN
1921 Eva: 5 G. **1922** Eva: 1 G. **Total:** 6 G.

CHRIS SPIELMAN Spielman, Charles Christopher 6′0″, 247 **LB**
Col: Ohio State *HS:* Washington [Massillon, OH] B: 10/11/1965, Canton, OH *Drafted:* 1988 Round 2 Det
1988 Det: 16 G. **1989** Det: 16 G; 5 Sac. **1990** Det: 12 G; Int 1-12; 2 Sac. **1991** Det: 16 G; 1 Sac. **1992** Det: 16 G; 1 Sac. **1993** Det: 16 G; Int 2-(-2); 0.5 Sac. **1994** Det: 16 G; 1 Fum TD; 6 Pt. **1995** Det: 16 G; Int 1-4; 1 Sac. **1996** Buf: 16 G; Int 1-14. **1997** Buf: 8 G; Int 1-8. **Total:** 148 G; Int 6-36; 1 Fum TD; 6 Pt; 10.5 Sac.

BOB SPIERS Spiers, Robert Hugh 5′11″, 193 **T-G**
Col: Hiram; Ohio State *HS:* Freedom Station [OH] B: 1/4/1895, OH
D: 7/8/1984, Naples, FL
1922 Akr: 10 G. **1925** Cle: 3 G. **Total:** 13 G.

IRVING SPIKES Spikes, Irving E 5′8″, 212 **RB**
Col: Alabama; Northeast Louisiana *HS:* Ocean Springs [MS]
B: 12/21/1970, Ocean Springs, MS
1994 Mia: Rec 4-16 4.0. **1995** Mia: Rec 5-18 3.6 1 TD. **1996** Mia: Rec 8-81 10.1 1 TD. **1997** Mia: Rec 7-70 10.0. **Total:** Rec 24-185 7.7 2 TD.

		Rushing				Kickoff Returns					Tot
Year Team	G	Ret	Yds	Avg	TD	Ret	Yds	Avg	TD	Fum	TD
1994 Mia	12	70	312	4.5	2	19	434	22.8	0	1	2
1995 Mia	9	32	126	3.9	1	18	378	21.0	0	0	2
1996 Mia	15	87	316	3.6	3	28	681	24.3	0	1	4
1997 Mia	12	63	180	2.9	2	24	565	23.5	0	3	2
NFL Total	48	252	934	3.7	8	89	2058	23.1	0	5	10

JACK SPIKES Spikes, Jack Erwin 6′2″, 210 **FB-K**
Col: Texas Christian *HS:* Snyder [TX] B: 2/5/1937, Big Spring, TX
Drafted: 1960 Round 1 Den
1960 DalT: Scor 104, 13-31 41.9% FG, 35-37 94.6% XK. **1961** DalT: Scor 54, 4-13 30.8% FG, 10-14 71.4% XK, 1 2XP. **1962** DalT: KR 2-30 15.0; Scor 7, 1-1 100.0% XK. **1963** KC: Pass 1-0, 1 Int; KR 2-12 6.0; Scor 47, 2-13 15.4% FG, 23-24 95.8% XK. **1964** KC: Pass 1-0. **1965** Hou: KR 4-41 10.3; Scor 27, 1-2 50.0% FG, 6-6 100.0% XK. **Total:** Pass 2-0, 1 Int; KR 8-83 10.4; Scor 263, 20-59 33.9% FG, 75-82 91.5% XK, 1 2XP.

		Rushing				Receiving					Tot
Year Team	G	Att	Yds	Avg	TD	Rec	Yds	Avg	TD	Fum	TD
1960 DalT	14	115	457	4.0	5	11	158	14.4	0	2	5
1961 DalT	6	39	334	8.6	5	8	136	17.0	0	1	5
1962 DalT	10	57	232	4.1	0	10	132	13.2	1	1	1
1963 KC	14	84	257	3.1	2	11	125	11.4	1	4	3
1964 KC	7	34	112	3.3	0	5	17	3.4	0	0	0
1965 Hou	14	47	173	3.7	3	8	57	7.1	0	3	3
1966 Buf	14	28	119	4.3	3	2	45	22.5	1	1	4
1967 Buf	7	4	9	2.3	0	1	9	9.0	0	0	0
NFL Total	86	408	1693	4.1	18	56	679	12.1	3	12	21

TAKEO SPIKES Spikes, Takeo Gerard 6′2″, 230 **LB**
Col: Auburn *HS:* Washington Co. [Sandersville, GA] B: 12/17/1976, Sandersville, GA *Drafted:* 1998 Round 1 Cin
1998 Cin: 16 G; 2 Sac.

JOHN SPILIS Spilis, John Arthur 6′3″, 205 **WR**
Col: Northern Illinois *HS:* Thornridge [Dolton, IL] B: 10/14/1947, Chicago, IL *Drafted:* 1969 Round 3 GB

		Receiving				
Year Team	G	Rec	Yds	Avg	TD	Fum
1969 GB	12	7	89	12.7	0	0
1970 GB	14	6	76	12.7	0	0
1971 GB	14	14	281	20.1	1	1
NFL Total	40	27	446	16.5	1	1

PHILIP SPILLER Spiller, Philip A 6′0″, 195 **DB**
Col: Orange Coast Coll. CA (J.C.); Los Angeles State *HS:* Newport Harbor [Newport Beach, CA] B: 4/2/1945, Santa Monica, CA
Drafted: 1967 Round 16 StL
1967 StL: 14 G; PR 15-124 8.3; KR 10-219 21.9; Int 2-13. **1968** Atl-Cin: 11 G; PR 3-51 17.0; KR 6-109 18.2; 1 Fum. Atl: 7 G; PR 1-0; KR 1-18 18.0. Cin: 4 G; PR 2-51 25.5; KR 5-91 18.2; 1 Fum. **Total:** 25 G; PR 18-175 9.7; KR 16-328 20.5; Int 2-13; 1 Fum.

RAY SPILLERS Spillers, Raymond Carl 6′3″, 218 **T**
(Brush) *Col:* Arkansas *HS:* Van Buren [AR] B: 10/23/1912, North Little Rock, AR
1937 Phi: 10 G.

MARC SPINDLER Spindler, Marc Rudolph 6′5″, 290 **DE-NT**
Col: Pittsburgh *HS:* West Scranton [Scranton, PA] B: 11/28/1969, Scranton, PA *Drafted:* 1990 Round 3 Det
1990 Det: 3 G; 1 Sac. **1991** Det: 16 G; 3.5 Sac. **1992** Det: 13 G; 2.5 Sac. **1993** Det: 16 G; 2 Sac. **1994** Det: 9 G. **1995** NYJ: 10 G. **1996** NYJ: 15 G; Int 1-(-1); 0.5 Sac. **1997** Det: 10 G. **1998** Det: 15 G. **Total:** 107 G; Int 1-(-1); 9.5 Sac.

JACK SPINKS Spinks, John Robert 6′0″, 236 **OG-FB-DT**
Col: Alcorn State *HS:* Stevenson [Toomsuba, MS] B: 8/15/1930, Toomsuba, MS D: 9/29/1994, Jackson, MS *Drafted:* 1952 Round 11 Pit
1952 Pit: Rec 2-22 11.0. **1953** ChiC: Rec 1-6 6.0. **Total:** Rec 3-28 9.3.

		Rushing			
Year Team	**G**	**Att**	**Yds**	**Avg**	**TD**
1952 Pit	10	22	94	4.3	0
1953 ChiC	3	6	0	0.0	0
1955 GB	6	0	0	—	0
1956 GB-NYG	4	0	0	—	0
1956 GB	1	0	0	—	0
1956 NYG	3	0	0	—	0
1957 NYG	7	0	0	—	0
NFL Total	30	28	94	3.4	0

ART SPINNEY Spinney, Arthur F Jr. 6′0″, 230 **OG-DE-OE**
Col: Boston College *HS:* Saugus [MA]; Manlius Military Academy [NY] B: 11/8/1927, Saugus, MA D: 5/27/1994, Lynn, MA *Drafted:* 1950 Round 15 Bal
1950 Bal: 2 G; Rec 2-19 9.5. **1953** Bal: 12 G. **1954** Bal: 12 G. **1955** Bal: 12 G. **1956** Bal: 11 G; KR 1-10 10.0. **1957** Bal: 11 G. **1958** Bal: 12 G. **1959** Bal: 12 G. **1960** Bal: 10 G. **Total:** 94 G; Rec 2-19 9.5; KR 1-10 10.0.

GREG SPIRES Spires, Greg Tyrone 6′1″, 260 **DE**
Col: Florida State *HS:* Mariner [North Cape Coral, FL] B: 8/12/1974, Marianna, FL *Drafted:* 1998 Round 3 NE
1998 NE: 15 G; 3 Sac.

JOHNNY SPIRIDA Spirida, John Martin 6′0″, 195 **BB-DE-OE**
Col: St. Anselm B: 11/4/1914 D: 4/1966
1939 Was: 9 G; Rush 2-5 2.5; Rec 2-95 47.5; Punt 10-385 38.5.

BOB SPITULSKI Spitulski, Bob 6′3″, 240 **LB**
Col: Central Florida *HS:* Bishop Moore [Orlando, FL] B: 9/10/1969, Toledo, OH *Drafted:* 1992 Round 3 Sea
1992 Sea: 4 G. **1993** Sea: 6 G. **1994** Sea: 16 G; Int 1-7; 3 Sac. **Total:** 26 G; Int 1-7; 3 Sac.

ANDY SPIVA Spiva, Howard Andrew 6′2″, 220 **LB**
Col: Tennessee *HS:* Chamblee [GA] B: 2/6/1955, Chattanooga, TN D: 4/3/1979, Atlanta, GA *Drafted:* 1977 Round 5 StL
1977 Atl: 13 G.

MIKE SPIVEY Spivey, Michael James 6′0″, 197 **DB**
Col: Colorado *HS:* Aldine [Houston, TX] B: 3/10/1954, Houston, TX
Drafted: 1977 Round 2 ChiB
1977 ChiB: 14 G. **1978** ChiB: 16 G; KR 2-34 17.0; 6 Pt. **1979** ChiB: 16 G. **1980** Oak-NO: 11 G. Oak: 9 G. NO: 2 G. **1981** NO: 12 G; Int 1-0. **1982** Atl: 8 G. **Total:** 77 G; KR 2-34 17.0; Int 1-0; 6 Pt.

SEBRON SPIVEY Spivey, Sebron Ervin 5′11″, 180 **WR**
Col: Southern Illinois *HS:* Rayen [Youngstown, OH] B: 8/2/1964
1987 Dal: 2 G; Rec 2-34 17.0; KR 2-49 24.5.

BOB SPONAUGLE Sponaugle, Robert Ralph Jr. 6′1″, 203 **OE-DE**
Col: Pennsylvania *HS:* Milton S. Hershey [Hershey, PA] B: 1/31/1928, Harrisburg, PA D: 11/19/1986, Hershey, PA
1949 NYB: 4 G; Rec 2-26 13.0.

DANNY SPRADLIN Spradlin, Daniel Ray 6′1″, 235 **LB**
Col: Tennessee *HS:* Maryville [TN] B: 3/3/1959, Detroit, MI
Drafted: 1981 Round 5 Dal
1981 Dal: 16 G. **1982** Dal: 9 G. **1983** TB: 16 G; KR 3-35 11.7; 1 Sac. **1984** TB: 15 G; KR 1-5 5.0. **1985** StL: 7 G. **Total:** 63 G; KR 4-40 10.0; 1 Sac.

MARCUS SPRIGGS Spriggs, Thomas Marcus 6′3″, 295 **OT**
Col: Hinds CC MS; Houston *HS:* Byram [Jackson, MS] B: 5/17/1974, Hattiesburg, MS *Drafted:* 1997 Round 6 Buf
1997 Buf: 2 G. **1998** Buf: 1 G. **Total:** 3 G.

HAL SPRINGER Springer, Harold Clayton 6′4″, 212 **OE-DE**
Col: Central Oklahoma *HS:* Elk City [OK] B: 5/10/1922, Albuquerque, NM D: 5/17/1981, Staten Island, NY
1945 NYG: 7 G; Rec 4-63 15.8; 2 Fum.

KIRK SPRINGS Springs, Kirk Edward 6′0″, 192 **DB**
Col: Miami (Ohio) *HS:* Woodward [Cincinnati, OH] B: 8/16/1958, Cincinnati, OH
1981 NYJ: Int 2-5. **1982** NYJ: Int 1-0. **1984** NYJ: Int 1-13. **1985** NYJ: 0.5 Sac. **Total:** Int 4-18; 0.5 Sac.

		Punt Returns				Kickoff Returns				
Year Team	**G**	**Ret**	**Yds**	**Avg**	**TD**	**Ret**	**Yds**	**Avg**	**TD**	**Fum**
1981 NYJ	10	0	0	—	0	0	0	—	0	1
1982 NYJ	9	0	0	—	0	0	0	—	0	0
1983 NYJ	16	23	287	12.5	**1**	16	364	22.8	0	2
1984 NYJ	16	28	247	8.8	0	23	521	22.7	0	3
1985 NYJ	16	14	147	10.5	0	10	227	22.7	0	1
NFL Total	67	65	681	10.5	1	49	1112	22.7	0	7

RON SPRINGS Springs, Ronald Edward 6′0″, 213 **RB**
Col: Coffeyville CC KS; Ohio State *HS:* Lafayette [Williamsburg, VA] B: 11/4/1956, Williamsburg, VA *Drafted:* 1979 Round 5 Dal
1979 Dal: Pass 3-1 33.3%, 30 10.00 1 TD. **1981** Dal: Pass 1-0, 1 Int. **1983** Dal: Pass 2-1 50.0%, 15 7.50 1 TD. **1984** Dal: Pass 1-0. **1986** TB: Punt 1-43 43.0. **Total:** Pass 7-2 28.6%, 45 6.43 2 TD 1 Int; Punt 1-43 43.0.

		Rushing				Receiving			
Year Team	**G**	**Att**	**Yds**	**Avg**	**TD**	**Rec**	**Yds**	**Avg**	**TD**
1979 Dal	16	67	248	3.7	2	25	251	10.0	1
1980 Dal	15	89	326	3.7	6	15	212	14.1	1
1981 Dal	16	172	625	3.6	10	46	359	7.8	2
1982 Dal	9	59	243	4.1	2	17	163	9.6	2
1983 Dal	16	149	541	3.6	7	73	589	8.1	1
1984 Dal	16	68	197	2.9	1	46	454	9.9	3
1985 TB	12	16	54	3.4	0	3	44	14.7	0
1986 TB	12	74	285	3.9	0	24	187	7.8	0
NFL Total	112	694	2519	3.6	28	249	2259	9.1	10

	Kickoff Returns					Tot
Year Team	**Ret**	**Yds**	**Avg**	**TD**	**Fum**	**TD**
1979 Dal	38	780	20.5	0	2	3
1980 Dal	0	0	—	0	1	7
1981 Dal	0	0	—	0	3	12
1982 Dal	0	0	—	0	3	4
1983 Dal	1	13	13.0	0	3	8
1984 Dal	0	0	—	0	1	4
1985 TB	5	112	22.4	0	0	0
1986 TB	0	0	—	0	2	0
NFL Total	44	905	20.6	0	15	38

SHAWN SPRINGS Springs, Shawn 6′0″, 195 **DB**
Col: Ohio State *HS:* Springbrook [Silver Springs, MD] B: 3/11/1975, Williamsburg, VA *Drafted:* 1997 Round 1 Sea
1997 Sea: 10 G; Int 1-0. **1998** Sea: 16 G; Int 7-142 2 TD; 1 Fum TD; Tot TD 3; 18 Pt. **Total:** 26 G; Int 8-142 2 TD; 1 Fum TD; Tot TD 3; 18 Pt.

BILL SPRINGSTEEN Springsteen, William Watson 6′0″, 200 **C-OE**
(Kid) *Col:* Lehigh *HS:* Northwestern [Detroit, MI] B: 10/27/1899, New York, NY D: 10/1/1985, Lakeville, CT
1925 Fra: 18 G. **1926** Fra: 17 G. **1927** ChiC: 11 G. **1928** ChiC: 4 G. **Total:** 50 G.

ED SPRINKLE Sprinkle, Edward Alexander 6′1″, 206 **DE-OE-OG-LB**
(The Claw) *Col:* Hardin-Simmons; Navy *HS:* Tuscola [TX]
B: 9/3/1923, Bradshaw, TX
1944 ChiB: Int 1-15. **1946** ChiB: KR 2-11 5.5; Int 1-34; **1** Fum TD. **1948** ChiB: Rush 1-(-2) -2.0. **1949** ChiB: Pass 1-0; Rush 1-5 5.0; Scor **1** Saf. **1950** ChiB: Rush 1-(-1) -1.0; KR 1-5 5.0. **1951** ChiB: Int 1-0; 1 Fum TD. **1952** ChiB: KR 4-39 9.8. **1953** ChiB: KR 1-0. **1954** ChiB: KR 3-8 2.7; Int 1-6. **Total:** Pass 1-0; Rush 3-2 0.7; KR 11-63 5.7; Int 4-55; Scor 1 Saf; 2 Fum TD.

		Receiving					Tot
Year Team	**G**	**Rec**	**Yds**	**Avg**	**TD**	**Fum**	**TD**
1944 ChiB	9	0	0	—	0	0	0
1945 ChiB	6	0	0	—	0	0	0
1946 ChiB	11	7	124	17.7	2	0	3
1947 ChiB	12	4	43	10.8	0	0	0
1948 ChiB	10	10	132	13.2	3	0	3
1949 ChiB	12	4	69	17.3	0	0	0
1950 ChiB	12	4	70	17.5	0	0	0
1951 ChiB	12	2	11	5.5	1	0	2
1952 ChiB	12	1	2	2.0	1	0	1
1953 ChiB	12	0	0	—	0	1	1
1954 ChiB	12	0	0	—	0	0	0
1955 ChiB	12	0	0	—	0	0	0
NFL Total	132	32	451	14.1	7	1	10

HUGH SPRINKLE Sprinkle, Hubert Owen 6'2", 220 **T-G**
Col: Missouri; Carnegie Mellon *HS:* Webb City [MO] B: 1897 D: 12/11/1961
1923 Akr: 2 G. **1924** Akr: 5 G. **1925** Cle: 7 G. **Total:** 14 G.

JIMMY SPROTTE Sprotte, John Wild 6'3", 237 **LB**
Col: Arizona *HS:* Blue Ridge [Lakeside, AZ] B: 10/2/1974, Olathe, KS
Drafted: 1998 Round 7 Ten
1998 Cin: 5 G.

DENNIS SPROUL Sproul, Dennis Eugene 6'2", 210 **QB**
Col: Arizona State *HS:* Los Altos [Hacienda Heights, CA]
B: 7/17/1956, Downey, CA *Drafted:* 1978 Round 8 GB
1978 GB: 6 G; Pass 13-5 38.5%, 87 6.69; Rush 2-0; 2 Fum.

JIM SPRUILL Spruill, James Winfred 6'3", 225 **T**
Col: Rice *HS:* Dublin [TX] B: 2/26/1923, Dublin, TX
AAFC **1948** BalA: 14 G. **1949** BalA: 12 G. **Total:** 26 G.

STEVE SPURRIER Spurrier, Steven Orr 6'2", 204 **QB-P**
Col: Florida *HS:* Science Hill [Johnson City, TN] B: 4/20/1945, Miami Beach, FL *Drafted:* 1967 Round 1 SF

		Passing							
Year Team	**G**	**Att**	**Comp**	**Comp%**	**Yds**	**YPA**	**TD**	**Int**	**Rating**
1967 SF	14	50	23	46.0	211	4.22	0	7	18.4
1968 SF	14	0	0	—	0	—	0	0	—
1969 SF	6	146	81	55.5	926	6.34	5	11	54.8
1970 SF	14	4	3	75.0	49	12.25	1	0	155.2
1971 SF	6	4	1	25.0	46	11.50	0	0	75.0
1972 SF	13	269	147	54.6	1983	7.37	18	16	75.9
1973 SF	11	157	83	52.9	882	5.62	4	7	59.5
1974 SF	3	3	1	33.3	2	0.67	0	0	42.4
1975 SF	11	207	102	49.3	1151	5.56	5	7	60.3
1976 TB	14	311	156	50.2	1628	5.23	7	12	57.1
NFL Total	106	1151	597	51.9	6878	5.98	40	60	60.1

	Rushing				Punting			
Year Team	**Att**	**Yds**	**Avg**	**TD**	**Punts**	**Yds**	**Avg**	**Fum**
1967 SF	5	18	3.6	0	73	2745	37.6	1
1968 SF	1	-15	-15.0	0	68	2651	39.0	1
1969 SF	5	49	9.8	0	12	468	39.0	2
1970 SF	2	-18	-9.0	0	75	2877	38.4	1
1971 SF	1	2	2.0	0	2	77	38.5	0
1972 SF	11	51	4.6	0	0	0	—	2
1973 SF	9	32	3.6	2	0	0	—	3
1974 SF	0	0	—	0	0	0	—	1
1975 SF	15	91	6.1	0	0	0	—	4
1976 TB	12	48	4.0	0	0	0	—	5
NFL Total	61	258	4.2	2	230	8818	38.3	20

JACK SQUIREK Squirek, Jack Steven 6'4", 230 **LB**
Col: Illinois *HS:* Cuyahoga Heights [OH] B: 2/16/1959, Cleveland, OH
Drafted: 1982 Round 2 LARd
1982 LARd: 9 G. **1983** LARd: 16 G; 1 Sac. **1984** LARd: 12 G; 2 Sac. **1985** LARd: 16 G; Int 1-3. **1986** Mia: 2 G. **Total:** 55 G; Int 1-3; 3 Sac.

SEAMAN SQUYRES Squyres, Charles Seaman 6'3", 200 **TB-DB**
(Cob) *Col:* Rice *HS:* Cleburne [TX] B: 3/2/1910 D: 11/1979, Houston, TX
1933 Cin: 4 G; Pass 9-2 22.2%, 15 1.67 1 Int; Rush 11-22 2.0.

JEREMY STAAT Staat, Jeremy Ray 6'5", 299 **DE**
Col: Bakersfield Coll. CA (J.C.); Arizona State *HS:* Bakersfield [CA]
B: 10/10/1976, Bakersfield, CA *Drafted:* 1998 Round 2 Pit
1998 Pit: 6 G.

BRIAN STABLEIN Stablein, Brian Patrick 6'1", 193 **WR**
Col: Ohio State *HS:* McDowell [Erie, PA] B: 4/14/1970, Erie, PA
Drafted: 1993 Round 8 Den
1996 Ind: PR 6-56 9.3. **1997** Ind: PR 17-133 7.8; Scor 1 2XP.
Total: PR 23-189 8.2; Scor 1 2XP.

		Receiving			
Year Team	**G**	**Rec**	**Yds**	**Avg**	**TD**
1995 Ind	15	8	95	11.9	0
1996 Ind	16	18	192	10.7	1
1997 Ind	16	25	253	10.1	1
1998 Det	10	7	80	11.4	0
NFL Total	57	58	620	10.7	2

KEN STABLER Stabler, Kenneth Michael 6'3", 215 **QB**
(Snake) *Col:* Alabama *HS:* Foley [AL] B: 12/25/1945, Foley, AL
Drafted: 1968 Round 2 Oak

		Passing							
Year Team	**G**	**Att**	**Comp**	**Comp%**	**Yds**	**YPA**	**TD**	**Int**	**Rating**
1970 Oak	3	7	2	28.6	52	7.43	0	1	18.5
1971 Oak	14	48	24	50.0	268	5.58	1	4	39.2
1972 Oak	14	74	44	59.5	524	7.08	4	3	82.3
1973 Oak	14	260	163	**62.7**	1997	7.68	14	10	88.3
1974 Oak	14	310	178	57.4	2469	7.96	**26**	12	94.9
1975 Oak	14	293	171	58.4	2296	7.84	16	24	67.4
1976 Oak	12	291	194	**66.7**	2737	**9.41**	**27**	17	**103.4**
1977 Oak	13	294	169	57.5	2176	7.40	20	20	75.2
1978 Oak	16	406	237	58.4	2944	7.25	16	30	63.3
1979 Oak	16	498	304	61.0	3615	7.26	26	22	82.2
1980 Hou	16	457	293	64.1	3202	7.01	13	28	68.7
1981 Hou	13	285	165	57.9	1988	6.98	14	18	69.5
1982 NO	8	189	117	61.9	1343	7.11	6	10	71.8
1983 NO	14	311	176	56.6	1988	6.39	9	18	61.4
1984 NO	3	70	33	47.1	339	4.84	2	5	41.3
NFL Total	184	3793	2270	59.8	27938	7.37	194	222	75.3

	Rushing				
Year Team	**Att**	**Yds**	**Avg**	**TD**	**Fum**
1970 Oak	1	-4	-4.0	0	1
1971 Oak	4	29	7.3	2	1
1972 Oak	6	27	4.5	0	2
1973 Oak	21	101	4.8	0	5
1974 Oak	12	-2	-0.2	1	3
1975 Oak	6	-5	-0.8	0	4
1976 Oak	7	-2	-0.3	1	5
1977 Oak	3	-3	-1.0	0	3
1978 Oak	4	0	0.0	0	9
1979 Oak	16	-4	-0.3	0	10
1980 Hou	15	-22	-1.5	0	7
1981 Hou	10	-3	-0.3	0	7
1982 NO	3	-4	-1.3	0	4
1983 NO	9	-14	-1.6	0	4
1984 NO	1	-1	-1.0	0	1
NFL Total	118	93	0.8	4	66

ED STACCO Stacco, Edward Adam 6'2", 261 **T**
Col: Colgate *HS:* Carbondale [PA] B: 4/16/1925, Carbondale, PA
Drafted: 1946 Round 23 Det
1947 Det: 10 G. **1948** Was: 4 G. **Total:** 14 G.

RAY STACHOWICZ Stachowicz, Raymond Mark 5'11", 185 **P**
Col: Michigan State *HS:* Brecksville [Broadview Heights, OH]
B: 3/6/1959, Cleveland, OH *Drafted:* 1981 Round 3 GB
1982 GB: Rush 2-0. **Total:** Rush 2-0.

		Punting			
Year Team	**G**	**Punts**	**Yds**	**Avg**	**Fum**
1981 GB	16	82	3330	40.6	0
1982 GB	9	42	1687	40.2	1
1983 ChiB	2	12	447	37.3	0
NFL Total	27	136	5464	40.2	1

RICH STACHOWSKI Stachowski, Richard Charles 6'4", 245 **NT**
Col: California *HS:* Burbank [CA] B: 3/29/1961, Los Angeles, CA
1983 Den: 14 G.

JACK STACKPOOL Stackpool, John Lawrence 6'1", 207 **FB-LB**
Col: Washington *HS:* Proviso East [Maywood, IL] B: 9/6/1917, Chicago, IL D: 8/20/1976, Lincoln City, OR *Drafted:* 1942 Round 10 Phi
1942 Phi: 8 G; Rush 15-47 3.1; Rec 2-59 29.5; KR 1-13 13.0.

BILLY STACY Stacy, Billy McGovern 6'1", 191 **DB**
Col: Mississippi State *HS:* Winona [MS] B: 7/30/1936, Drew, MS
Drafted: 1959 Round 1 ChiC
1960 StL: **1** Fum TD. **1961** StL: Rec 12-241 20.1 1 TD; **1** Fum TD.
Total: Rec 12-241 20.1 1 TD; 2 Fum TD.

		Punt Returns				Kickoff Returns			
Year Team	**G**	**Ret**	**Yds**	**Avg**	**TD**	**Ret**	**Yds**	**Avg**	**TD**
1959 ChiC	12	**29**	**281**	9.7	**2**	12	280	23.3	0
1960 StL	11	14	62	4.4	0	6	146	24.3	0
1961 StL	13	5	9	1.8	0	3	60	20.0	0
1962 StL	13	5	35	7.0	0	5	121	24.2	0
1963 StL	9	1	6	6.0	0	0	0	—	0
NFL Total	58	54	393	7.3	2	26	607	23.3	0

	Interceptions				
Year Team	**Int**	**Yds**	**TD**	**Fum**	**Tot TD**
1959 ChiC	5	114	0	2	2
1960 StL	4	42	0	1	1
1961 StL	4	95	**2**	0	4
1962 StL	6	72	0	1	0
1963 StL	1	0	0	0	0
NFL Total	20	323	2	4	7

RED STACY Stacy, James William 6'2", 210 **T-G**
Col: Oklahoma *HS:* Altus [OK] B: 3/4/1912, Hollis, OK
1935 Det: 12 G. **1936** Det: 10 G. **1937** Det: 9 G. **Total:** 31 G.

SIRAN STACY Stacy, Siran 5'11", 203 **RB**
Col: Coffeyville CC KS; Alabama *HS:* Geneva Co. [Hartford, AL]
B: 8/6/1968, Geneva, AL *Drafted:* 1992 Round 2 Phi
1992 Phi: 16 G.

JOHN STADNIK Stadnik, John Steven 6'4", 273 **C**
Col: Western Illinois *HS:* Dwight D. Eisenhower [Blue Island, IL]
B: 2/18/1959, Chicago, IL
1987 SD: 3 G.

SPIKE STAFF Staff, Edgar Jonathan 6'0", 210 **G**
Col: Brown *HS:* Brockton [MA] B: 3/13/1892, Brockton, MA
D: 2/14/1970, Providence, RI
1925 Prov: 1 G.

HARRY STAFFORD Stafford, Albert Harrison 5'11", 205 **WB-DB**
Col: Texas; Army *HS:* Wharton [TX] B: 6/18/1912, Austin, TX
1934 NYG: 6 G; Rush 4-4 1.0; Rec 4-70 17.5.

DICK STAFFORD Stafford, Richard Wade 6'4", 255 **DE**
Col: Texas Tech *HS:* Matador [TX] B: 8/21/1940, Matador, TX
1962 Phi: 7 G. **1963** Phi: 4 G. **Total:** 11 G.

JON STAGGERS Staggers, Jonathan Leroy 5'10", 185 **WR**
Col: Missouri *HS:* Helias [Jefferson City, MO] B: 12/14/1948, Richmond, VA *Drafted:* 1970 Round 5 Pit
1971 Pit: Rush 1-5 5.0. **1972** GB: Pass 1-0; Rush 1-(-8) -8.0. **1973** GB: Rush 4-33 8.3 1 TD. **1975** Det: Rush 2-26 13.0. **Total:** Pass 1-0; Rush 8-56 7.0 1 TD.

		Receiving				Punt Returns			
Year Team	**G**	**Rec**	**Yds**	**Avg**	**TD**	**Ret**	**Yds**	**Avg**	**TD**
1970 Pit	12	6	118	19.7	1	13	70	5.4	0
1971 Pit	14	8	103	12.9	0	31	262	8.5	**1**
1972 GB	11	8	123	15.4	1	9	148	16.4	**1**
1973 GB	14	25	412	16.5	3	19	90	4.7	0
1974 GB	14	32	450	14.1	0	22	222	10.1	1
1975 Det	5	14	174	12.4	2	0	0	—	0
NFL Total	70	93	1380	14.8	7	94	792	8.4	3

	Kickoff Returns					Tot
Year Team	**Ret**	**Yds**	**Avg**	**TD**	**Fum**	**TD**
1970 Pit	14	333	23.8	0	2	1
1971 Pit	10	261	26.1	0	3	1
1972 GB	11	260	23.6	0	2	2
1973 GB	0	0	—	0	1	4
1974 GB	0	0	—	0	0	1
1975 Det	0	0	—	0	0	2
NFL Total	35	854	24.4	0	8	11

JEFF STAGGS Staggs, Jeffery Hugh 6'1", 240 **LB-DE**
Col: San Diego City Coll. CA (J.C.); Brigham Young; San Diego State
HS: Point Loma [San Diego, CA] B: 5/14/1944, Elgin, IL
1967 SD: 14 G. **1968** SD: 12 G; Int 2-2. **1969** SD: 13 G. **1970** SD: 14 G. **1971** SD: 5 G. **1972** StL: 8 G; Int 1-7; 1 Fum. **1973** StL: 13 G. **1974** SD: 3 G. **Total:** 82 G; Int 3-9; 1 Fum.

JAKE STAHL Stahl, Edward Adam 5'11", 185 **G-T**
Col: Pittsburgh *HS:* Greensburg [PA]; Bellfonte Acad. [PA]
B: 1/16/1891, Scranton, PA D: 10/8/1966, Pittsburgh, PA
1920 Cle: 3 G. **1921** Day-Cle: 2 G. Day: 1 G. Cle: 1 G. **Total:** 5 G.

DICK STAHLMAN Stahlman, Richard Frederick 6'2", 219 **T-G-OE-DE**
Col: DePaul; Northwestern B: 10/20/1902, Chicago, IL D: 5/11/1970, Chicago, IL
1924 KC-Ham-Ken-Akr: 9 G. KC: 1 G. Ham: 1 G. Ken: 5 G. Akr: 2 G. **1925** Akr: 8 G. **1927** NYG: 10 G. **1930** NYG: 7 G. **1931** GB: 14 G. **1932** GB: 13 G. **1933** ChiB: 8 G. **Total:** 69 G.

BRENDEN STAI Stai, Brenden Michael 6'4", 305 **OG**
Col: Nebraska *HS:* Esperanza [Anaheim, CA] B: 3/30/1972, Phoenix, AZ *Drafted:* 1995 Round 3 Pit
1995 Pit: 16 G. **1996** Pit: 9 G. **1997** Pit: 11 G. **1998** Pit: 16 G. **Total:** 52 G.

JERRY STALCUP Stalcup, Gerald Newell 6'1", 240 **LB**
Col: Wisconsin *HS:* Rockford East [IL] B: 11/19/1938, Rockford, IL
Drafted: 1960 Round 6 LARm
1960 LARm: 12 G; Int 1-12. **1961** Den: 8 G. **1962** Den: 14 G. **Total:** 34 G; Int 1-12.

DUCE STALEY Staley, Duce 5'11", 220 **RB**
Col: Itawamba CC MS; South Carolina *HS:* Airport [West Columbia, SC]
B: 2/27/1975, Columbia, SC *Drafted:* 1997 Round 3 Phi

		Rushing				Receiving			
Year Team	**G**	**Att**	**Yds**	**Avg**	**TD**	**Rec**	**Yds**	**Avg**	**TD**
1997 Phi	16	7	29	4.1	0	2	22	11.0	0
1998 Phi	16	258	1065	4.1	5	57	432	7.6	1
NFL Total	32	265	1094	4.1	5	59	454	7.7	1

	Kickoff Returns					Tot
Year Team	**Ret**	**Yds**	**Avg**	**TD**	**Fum**	**TD**
1997 Phi	47	1139	24.2	0	0	0
1998 Phi	1	19	19.0	0	2	6
NFL Total	48	1158	24.1	0	2	6

BILL STALEY Staley, William Patrick 6'3", 250 **DT**
Col: Utah State *HS:* Los Lomas [Walnut Creek, CA] B: 9/9/1946, Walnut Creek, CA *Drafted:* 1968 Round 2 Cin
1968 Cin: 12 G. **1969** Cin: 11 G. **1970** ChiB: 11 G. **1971** ChiB: 11 G. **1972** ChiB: 4 G. **Total:** 49 G.

DON STALLINGS Stallings, Alva Donald 6'4", 250 **DT-DE-OT**
(Bucket) *Col:* North Carolina *HS:* Rocky Mount [NC] B: 11/18/1938, Rocky Mount, NC
1960 Was: 9 G; KR 1-19 19.0.

DENNIS STALLINGS Stallings, Dennis Dawon 6'0", 240 **LB**
(D-Stall) *Col:* Illinois *HS:* East St. Louis [IL] B: 5/25/1974, East St. Louis, IL *Drafted:* 1997 Round 6 Ten
1997 Ten: 13 G. **1998** Ten: 15 G. **Total:** 28 G.

LARRY STALLINGS Stallings, Lawrence Joseph 6'1", 230 **LB**
Col: Georgia Tech *HS:* Memorial [Evansville, IN] B: 12/11/1941, Evansville, IN *Drafted:* 1963 Round 18 StL
1963 StL: 14 G. **1964** StL: 8 G; Int 2-31. **1965** StL: 7 G; **1** Fum TD; 6 Pt. **1966** StL: 14 G; Int 1-0. **1967** StL: 14 G; KR 2-39 19.5. **1968** StL: 14 G. **1969** StL: 14 G; **1** Fum TD; 6 Pt. **1970** StL: 14 G; Int 1-9. **1971** StL: 14 G; PR 1-8 8.0; Int 1-26 1 TD; 6 Pt. **1972** StL: 13 G. **1973** StL: 14 G; Int 1-0. **1974** StL: 14 G; Int 2-13. **1975** StL: 13 G; Int 1-(-3); 1 Fum. **1976** StL: 14 G. **Total:** 181 G; PR 1-8 8.0; KR 2-39 19.5; Int 9-76 1 TD; 2 Fum TD; Tot TD 3; 18 Pt; 1 Fum.

RAMONDO STALLINGS Stallings, Ramondo Antonio 6'7", 286 **DE**
Col: San Diego State *HS:* Ansonia [CT] B: 11/21/1971, Winston-Salem, NC *Drafted:* 1994 Round 7 Cin
1994 Cin: 6 G. **1995** Cin: 13 G; 1 Fum; 1 Sac. **1996** Cin: 13 G; 2 Sac. **1997** Cin: 6 G. **Total:** 38 G; 1 Fum; 3 Sac.

ROBERT STALLINGS Stallings, Robert Raymond 6'6", 250 **TE**
Col: Southern Mississippi *HS:* South Pike [Magnolia, MS]
B: 1/23/1964, McComb, MS
1986 StL: 3 G.

DAVE STALLS Stalls, David Milton DeForest 6'5", 250 **DE-DT-NT**
Col: Northern Colorado *HS:* Taft [Hamilton, OH] B: 9/19/1955, Madison, WI *Drafted:* 1977 Round 7 Dal
1977 Dal: 11 G. **1978** Dal: 16 G. **1979** Dal: 16 G. **1980** TB: 15 G. **1981** TB: 16 G. **1982** TB: 9 G; 6.5 Sac. **1983** TB-LARd: 12 G; 1 Sac. TB: 6 G; 0.5 Sac. LARd: 6 G; 0.5 Sac. **1985** LARd: 4 G. **Total:** 99 G; 7.5 Sac.

JOHN STALLWORTH Stallworth, Johnny Lee 6'2", 191 **WR**
Col: Alabama A&M *HS:* Tuscaloosa [AL] B: 7/15/1952, Tuscaloosa, AL
Drafted: 1974 Round 4 Pit
1974 Pit: Rush 1-(-9) -9.0. **1976** Pit: Rush 0-47 1 TD. **1977** Pit: Rush 6-47 7.8. **1981** Pit: Rush 1-17 17.0. **1982** Pit: Rush 1-9 9.0. **Total:** Rush 9-111 12.3 1 TD.

		Receiving					Tot
Year Team	**G**	**Rec**	**Yds**	**Avg**	**TD**	**Fum**	**TD**
1974 Pit	13	16	269	16.8	1	0	1
1975 Pit	11	20	423	21.2	4	0	4
1976 Pit	8	9	111	12.3	2	0	3
1977 Pit	14	44	784	17.8	7	1	7
1978 Pit	16	41	798	19.5	9	2	9
1979 Pit	16	70	1183	16.9	8	4	8
1980 Pit	3	9	197	21.9	1	0	1
1981 Pit	16	63	1098	17.4	5	4	5
1982 Pit	9	27	441	16.3	7	2	7
1983 Pit	4	8	100	12.5	0	0	0
1984 Pit	16	80	1395	17.4	11	1	11
1985 Pit	16	75	937	12.5	5	0	5
1986 Pit	11	34	466	13.7	1	0	1
1987 Pit	12	41	521	12.7	2	1	2
NFL Total	165	537	8723	16.2	63	15	64

RON STALLWORTH Stallworth, Ronald Tobias 6'5", 262 **DE**
Col: Auburn *HS:* W.J. Woodham [Pensacola, FL] B: 2/25/1966, Pensacola, FL *Drafted:* 1989 Round 4 NYJ
1989 NYJ: 16 G; 2 Sac. **1990** NYJ: 16 G; 1 Sac. **Total:** 32 G; 3 Sac.

TIM STALLWORTH Stallworth, Timothy James 5'10", 185 **WR**
Col: Washington State *HS:* Montclair Prep [Van Nuys, CA]
B: 8/26/1966, Pacoima, CA *Drafted:* 1990 Round 6 LARm
1990 Den: 1 G.

SYLVESTER STAMPS Stamps, Sylvester 5'7", 172 **RB-WR**
Col: Jackson State *HS:* Vicksburg [MS] B: 2/24/1961, Vicksburg, MS
1986 Atl: PR 1-8 8.0. **Total:** PR 1-8 8.0.

		Rushing				Receiving			
Year Team	**G**	**Att**	**Yds**	**Avg**	**TD**	**Rec**	**Yds**	**Avg**	**TD**
1984 Atl	10	3	15	5.0	0	4	48	12.0	0
1985 Atl	2	0	0	—	0	0	0	—	0
1986 Atl	14	30	220	7.3	0	20	221	11.1	1
1987 Atl	7	1	6	6.0	0	4	40	10.0	0
1988 Atl	4	3	0	0.0	0	5	22	4.4	0

1989 TB	10	29	141	4.9	1	15	82	5.5	0
NFL Total	47	66	382	5.8	1	48	413	8.6	1

	Kickoff Returns					Tot
Year Team	Ret	Yds	Avg	TD	Fum	TD
1984 Atl	19	452	23.8	0	2	0
1985 Atl	4	89	22.3	0	0	0
1986 Atl	24	514	21.4	0	4	1
1987 Atl	24	660	**27.5**	1	1	1
1988 Atl	12	219	18.3	0	1	0
1989 TB	9	145	16.1	0	2	1
NFL Total	92	2079	22.6	1	10	3

FRANK STAMS Stams, Frank Michael Jr. 6′2″, 240 **LB**
Col: Notre Dame *HS:* St. Vincent-St. Mary [Akron, OH] B: 7/17/1965, Akron, OH *Drafted:* 1989 Round 2 LARm
1989 LARm: 16 G; Int 1-20. **1990** LARm: 14 G. **1991** LARm: 5 G. **1992** Cle: 12 G. **1993** Cle: 14 G. **1994** Cle: 16 G; Int 1-7; 2 Sac. **1995** KC-Cle: 5 G. KC: 1 G. Cle: 4 G. **Total:** 82 G; Int 2-27; 2 Sac.

HARRY STANBACK Stanback, Harry David 6′5″, 255 **DE**
Col: North Carolina *HS:* Richmond [Rockingham, NC] B: 8/17/1958, Rockingham, NC *Drafted:* 1981 Round 6 Atl
1982 Bal: 2 G.

HASKEL STANBACK Stanback, Haskel LaVon 6′0″, 210 **RB**
Col: Tennessee *HS:* A.L. Brown [Kannapolis, NC] B: 3/19/1952, Kannapolis, NC *Drafted:* 1974 Round 5 Cin
1975 Atl: Pass 1-1 100.0%, 41 41.00 1 TD. **1976** Atl: KR 1-18 18.0. **1979** Atl: KR 6-109 18.2. **Total:** Pass 1-1 100.0%, 41 41.00 1 TD; KR 7-127 18.1.

		Rushing				Receiving					Tot
Year Team	G	Att	Yds	Avg	TD	Rec	Yds	Avg	TD	Fum	TD
1974 Atl	13	57	235	4.1	1	8	39	4.9	0	5	1
1975 Atl	14	105	440	4.2	5	14	115	8.2	0	2	5
1976 Atl	14	95	324	3.4	3	21	174	8.3	1	2	4
1977 Atl	14	247	873	3.5	6	30	261	8.7	0	8	6
1978 Atl	15	188	588	3.1	5	12	108	9.0	0	5	5
1979 Atl	13	36	202	5.6	5	13	89	6.8	0	2	5
NFL Total	83	728	2662	3.7	25	98	786	8.0	1	24	26

JEFF STANCIEL Stanciel, Jeffrey Richard 6′0″, 192 **RB**
Col: Mississippi Valley State *HS:* Amanda Elzy [Greenwood, MS] B: 5/4/1947, Moorhead, MS *Drafted:* 1969 Round 10 Atl
1969 Atl: 2 G; Rush 4-(-1) -0.3; KR 1-10 10.0; 1 Fum.

NORM STANDLEE Standlee, Norman Stevenson 6′2″, 238 **FB-LB**
Col: Stanford *HS:* Woodrow Wilson [Long Beach, CA] B: 7/19/1919, Downey, CA D: 1/4/1981, Mountain View, CA *Drafted:* 1941 Round 2 ChiB
AAFC **1946** SF-A: Rec 2-(-5) -2.5; KR 1-33 33.0; Punt 1-34 34.0. **1947** SF-A: Rec 2-22 11.0; KR 3-24 8.0. **1948** SF-A: Rec 1-1 1.0; KR 1-31 31.0. **1949** SF-A: Punt 8-276 34.5. **Total:** Rec 5-18 3.6; KR 5-88 17.6; Punt 9-310 34.4.

		Rushing			
Year Team	G	Att	Yds	Avg	TD
1946 SF-A	13	134	651	4.9	2
1947 SF-A	14	145	585	4.0	8
1948 SF-A	14	52	261	5.0	3
1949 SF-A	12	44	237	5.4	4
AAFC Total	53	375	1734	4.6	17

NFL **1941** ChiB: Rec 2-(-3) -1.5; KR 2-32 16.0; Int 2-31; Punt 2-126 63.0. **1950** SF: KR 1-17 17.0. **Total:** Rec 2-(-3) -1.5; KR 3-49 16.3; Int 2-31; Punt 2-126 63.0.

		Rushing				
Year Team	G	Att	Yds	Avg	TD	Fum
1941 ChiB	10	81	414	5.1	5	0
1950 SF	11	12	23	1.9	1	1
1951 SF	11	16	65	4.1	0	1
1952 SF	1	2	8	4.0	0	0
NFL Total	33	111	510	4.6	6	2

DICK STANFEL Stanfel, Richard Anthony 6′3″, 236 **OG**
Col: San Francisco *HS:* Commerce [San Francisco, CA] B: 7/20/1927, San Francisco, CA *Drafted:* 1951 Round 2 Det
1952 Det: 12 G. **1953** Det: 12 G; KR 1-4 4.0. **1954** Det: 6 G. **1955** Det: 9 G. **1956** Was: 11 G. **1957** Was: 12 G. **1958** Was: 11 G. **Total:** 73 G; KR 1-4 4.0.

BILL STANFILL Stanfill, William Thomas 6′5″, 250 **DE**
Col: Georgia *HS:* Cairo [GA] B: 1/13/1947, Cairo, GA *Drafted:* 1969 Round 1 Mia
1969 Mia: 13 G; Int 2-32 **2** TD; 12 Pt. **1970** Mia: 14 G. **1971** Mia: 13 G. **1972** Mia: 14 G. **1973** Mia: 14 G. **1974** Mia: 14 G. **1975** Mia: 13 G. **1976** Mia: 14 G. **Total:** 109 G; Int 2-32 2 TD; 12 Pt.

SCOTT STANKAVAGE Stankavage, Leo Scott 6′1″, 194 **QB**
Col: North Carolina *HS:* Central Bucks East [Buckingham, PA] B: 7/5/1962, Philadelpia, PA
1984 Den: 1 G; Pass 18-4 22.2%, 58 3.22 1 Int. **1987** Mia: 3 G; Pass 7-4 57.1%, 8 1.14 1 Int. **Total:** 4 G; Pass 25-8 32.0%, 66 2.64 2 Int.

BASIL STANLEY Stanley, Basil Laron 5′9″, 195 **G**
(B.L.) *Col:* Wabash; Notre Dame; Illinois; St. Mary's (Cal.) *HS:* South Bend Central [IN] B: 2/8/1896, OH D: 7/17/1975, San Francisco, CA
1924 RI: 1 G.

C.B. STANLEY Stanley, Clair B 6′4″, 225 **T**
Col: Tulsa *HS:* Holdenville [OK] B: 1/25/1919, Holdenville, OK D: 4/1977, Tulsa, OK
AAFC **1946** BufA: 13 G.

ISRAEL STANLEY Stanley, Israel Damon 6′3″, 260 **LB**
Col: Arizona State *HS:* Point Loma [San Diego, CA] B: 4/21/1970, San Diego, CA
1995 NO: 14 G; 2 Sac.

SYLVESTER STANLEY Stanley, Sylvester Walter 6′2″, 286 **NT**
(Buster) *Col:* Michigan *HS:* East [Youngstown, OH] B: 5/14/1970, Youngstown, OH
1994 NE: 7 G.

WALTER STANLEY Stanley, Walter 5′9″, 180 **WR**
Col: Colorado; Mesa *HS:* South Shore [Chicago, IL] B: 11/5/1962, Chicago, IL *Drafted:* 1985 Round 4 GB
1986 GB: Rush 1-19 19.0. **1987** GB: Rush 4-38 9.5. **1988** GB: Rush 1-1 1.0. **Total:** Rush 6-58 9.7.

		Receiving				Punt Returns			
Year Team	G	Rec	Yds	Avg	TD	Ret	Yds	Avg	TD
1985 GB	13	0	0	—	0	14	179	12.8	0
1986 GB	16	35	723	20.7	2	33	316	9.6	1
1987 GB	12	38	672	17.7	3	28	173	6.2	0
1988 GB	7	28	436	15.6	0	12	52	4.3	0
1989 Det	14	24	304	12.7	0	36	496	**13.8**	0
1990 Was	9	2	15	7.5	0	24	176	7.3	0
1992 SD-NE	14	3	63	21.0	0	28	227	8.1	0
1992 SD	1	0	0	—	0	0	0	—	0
1992 NE	13	3	63	21.0	0	28	227	8.1	0
NFL Total	85	130	2213	17.0	5	175	1619	9.3	1

	Kickoff Returns					Tot
Year Team	Ret	Yds	Avg	TD	Fum	TD
1985 GB	9	212	23.6	0	2	0
1986 GB	28	559	20.0	0	1	3
1987 GB	3	47	15.7	0	5	3
1988 GB	2	39	19.5	0	3	0
1989 Det	9	95	10.6	0	5	0
1990 Was	9	177	19.7	0	3	0
1992 SD-NE	29	529	18.2	0	5	0
1992 NE	29	529	18.2	0	5	0
NFL Total	89	1658	18.6	0	24	6

DON STANSAUK Stansauk, Donald J 6′1″, 255 **DT**
Col: Pasadena City Coll. CA (J.C.); Denver *HS:* Benjamin Franklin [Los Angeles, CA] B: 4/2/1925, Los Angeles, CA *Drafted:* 1950 Round 18 Det
1950 GB: 11 G. **1951** GB: 4 G. **Total:** 15 G.

HENRY STANTON Stanton, Henry R 6′2″, 200 **DE-OE**
(Hank) *Col:* Arizona *HS:* Clifton [AZ] B: 8/24/1920 D: 3/11/1975, Phoenix, AZ
AAFC **1946** NY-A: 6 G; Rec 2-25 12.5. **1947** NY-A: 9 G. **Total:** 15 G; Rec 2-25 12.5.

JACK STANTON Stanton, John Edward 6′1″, 190 **HB**
Col: North Carolina State *HS:* Scott Twp. [North Braddock, PA] B: 6/7/1938, Bridgeville, PA
1961 Pit: 2 G.

BILL STANTON Stanton, William McKimmon 6′2″, 210 **DE**
Col: North Carolina State *HS:* South Robeson [Rowland, NC] B: 4/21/1924, Dillon, SC
AAFC **1949** BufA: 10 G.

KEN STARCH Starch, Kenneth Earl 5′11″, 219 **RB**
Col: Wisconsin *HS:* East [Madison, WI] B: 3/5/1954, Madison, WI
1976 GB: 6 G.

TONY STARGELL Stargell, Tony L 5′11″, 190 **DB**
Col: Tennessee State *HS:* La Grange [GA] B: 8/7/1966, La Grange, GA *Drafted:* 1990 Round 3 NYJ
1990 NYJ: 16 G; Int 2-(-3). **1991** NYJ: 16 G. **1992** Ind: 13 G; Int 2-26. **1993** Ind: 16 G; 1 Sac. **1994** TB: 10 G; Int 1-0. **1995** TB: 14 G. **1996** KC: 8 G; Int 1-9. **1997** ChiB: 1 G. **Total:** 94 G; Int 6-32; 1 Sac.

CHAD STARK Stark, Chad William 6′1″, 220 **RB**
Col: North Dakota State *HS:* Brookings [SD] B: 4/4/1965, Decorah, IA
1987 Sea: 2 G.

HOWIE STARK Stark, Howard Bailey 6′0″, 210 **T**
Col: Wisconsin *HS:* West Division [Milwaukee, WI] B: 12/20/1896 D: 3/13/1981, Nashotah, WI
1923 Rac: 3 G.

ROHN STARK Stark, Rohn Taylor 6′3″, 203 **P**
Col: Florida State *HS:* Pine River [MN]; Air Force Academy Prep [Colorado Springs, CO] B: 5/4/1959, Minneapolis, MN *Drafted:* 1982 Round 2 Bal
1982 Bal: Pass 1-0; Rush 1-8 8.0. **1983** Bal: Pass 1-0; Rush 1-8 8.0. **1984** Ind: Pass 1-0, 1 Int; Rush 2-0. **1985** Ind: Pass 1-0. **1989** Ind: Rush 1-(-11) -11.0. **1990** Ind: Pass 1-1 100.0%, 40 40.00. **1991** Ind: Rush 1-(-13) -13.0. **1992** Ind: Pass 1-1 100.0%, 17 17.00. **1993** Ind: Rush 1-11 11.0. **Total:** Pass 6-2 33.3%, 57 9.50 1 Int; Rush 7-3 0.4.

		Punting			
Year Team	**G**	**Punts**	**Yds**	**Avg**	**Fum**
1982 Bal	9	46	2044	44.4	1
1983 Bal	16	91	**4124**	**45.3**	0
1984 Ind	16	**98**	4383	44.7	0
1985 Ind	16	78	3584	**45.9**	0
1986 Ind	16	76	3432	**45.2**	1
1987 Ind	12	61	2440	40.0	0
1988 Ind	16	64	2784	43.5	0
1989 Ind	16	79	3392	42.9	0
1990 Ind	16	71	3084	43.4	0
1991 Ind	16	82	3492	42.6	1
1992 Ind	16	83	3716	44.8	0
1993 Ind	16	83	3595	43.3	0
1994 Ind	16	73	3092	42.4	0
1995 Pit	16	59	2368	40.1	0
1996 Car	16	77	3128	40.6	0
1997 Sea	4	20	813	40.7	0
NFL Total	233	1141	**49471**	43.4	3

GEORGE STARKE Starke, George Lawrence 6′5″, 260 **OT**
Col: Columbia *HS:* New Rochelle [NY] B: 7/18/1948, New York, NY *Drafted:* 1971 Round 11 Was
1973 Was: 14 G. **1974** Was: 14 G. **1975** Was: 14 G. **1976** Was: 14 G. **1977** Was: 14 G. **1978** Was: 9 G. **1979** Was: 16 G. **1980** Was: 13 G. **1981** Was: 14 G. **1982** Was: 9 G. **1983** Was: 16 G. **1984** Was: 9 G. **Total:** 156 G.

DUANE STARKS Starks, Duane Lonell 5′10″, 170 **DB**
Col: Holmes CC MS; Miami (Fla.) *HS:* Miami Beach [FL] B: 5/23/1974, Miami, FL *Drafted:* 1998 Round 1 Bal
1998 Bal: 16 G; Int 5-3.

MARSHALL STARKS Starks, Marshall L 6′0″, 195 **DB**
Col: Illinois *HS:* Rockford West [IL] B: 3/6/1939 *Drafted:* 1961 Round 8 StL
1963 NYJ: PR 3-7 2.3; Int 0-19. **1964** NYJ: PR 5-36 7.2; Int 1-20. **Total:** PR 8-43 5.4; Int 1-39.

		Kickoff Returns				
Year Team	**G**	**Ret**	**Yds**	**Avg**	**TD**	**Fum**
1963 NYJ	14	19	336	17.7	0	1
1964 NYJ	4	7	183	26.1	0	0
NFL Total	18	26	519	20.0	0	1

TIMOTHY STARKS Starks, Timothy Jerome 5′9″, 175 **DB**
Col: Kent State *HS:* Cleveland Heights [OH] B: 12/30/1963, Mobile, AL
1987 Min: 1 G.

JOHN STARNES Starnes, John Greg 6′3″, 185 **P**
Col: North Texas *HS:* Flour Bluff [Corpus Christi, TX] B: 12/25/1962, Corpus Christi, TX
1987 Atl: 1 G; Punt 6-203 33.8.

PAUL STAROBA Staroba, Paul Louis 6′3″, 204 **WR**
Col: Michigan *HS:* St. Matthew [Flint, MI] B: 1/20/1949, Flint, MI *Drafted:* 1971 Round 3 Cle
1972 Cle: 8 G; Rec 1-19 19.0 1 TD; 6 Pt. **1973** GB: 2 G; Rush 1-11 11.0; Rec 1-23 23.0; Punt 12-373 31.1. **Total:** 10 G; Rush 1-11 11.0; Rec 2-42 21.0 1 TD; Punt 12-373 31.1; 6 Pt.

BART STARR Starr, Bryan Bartlett 6′1″, 197 **QB**
Col: Alabama *HS:* Sidney Lanier [Montgomery, AL] B: 1/9/1934, Montgomery, AL *Drafted:* 1956 Round 17 GB *HOF:* 1977

		Passing							
Year Team	**G**	**Att**	**Comp**	**Comp%**	**Yds**	**YPA**	**TD**	**Int**	**Rating**
1956 GB	9	44	24	54.5	325	7.39	2	3	65.1
1957 GB	12	215	117	54.4	1489	6.93	8	10	69.3
1958 GB	12	157	78	49.7	875	5.57	3	12	41.2
1959 GB	12	134	70	52.2	972	7.25	6	7	69.0
1960 GB	12	172	98	57.0	1358	7.90	4	8	70.8
1961 GB	14	295	172	58.3	2418	8.20	16	16	80.3
1962 GB	14	285	178	**62.5**	2438	8.55	12	9	90.7
1963 GB	13	244	132	54.1	1855	7.60	15	**10**	82.3
1964 GB	14	272	163	59.9	2144	7.88	15	4	97.1
1965 GB	14	251	140	55.8	2055	8.19	16	9	89.0
1966 GB	14	251	156	**62.2**	2257	**8.99**	14	**3**	105.0
1967 GB	14	210	115	54.8	1823	**8.68**	9	17	64.4
1968 GB	12	171	109	**63.7**	1617	**9.46**	15	**8**	104.3
1969 GB	12	148	92	**62.2**	1161	7.84	9	**6**	89.9
1970 GB	14	255	140	54.9	1645	6.45	8	13	63.9
1971 GB	4	45	24	53.3	286	6.36	0	3	45.2
NFL Total	196	3149	1808	57.4	24718	7.85	152	138	80.5

	Rushing				
Year Team	**Att**	**Yds**	**Avg**	**TD**	**Fum**
1956 GB	5	35	7.0	0	0
1957 GB	31	98	3.2	3	4
1958 GB	25	113	4.5	1	2
1959 GB	16	83	5.2	0	2
1960 GB	7	12	1.7	0	3
1961 GB	12	56	4.7	1	8
1962 GB	21	72	3.4	1	8
1963 GB	13	116	8.9	0	5
1964 GB	24	165	6.9	3	7
1965 GB	18	169	9.4	1	2
1966 GB	21	104	5.0	2	7
1967 GB	21	90	4.3	0	3
1968 GB	11	62	5.6	1	2
1969 GB	7	60	8.6	0	4
1970 GB	12	62	5.2	1	6
1971 GB	3	11	3.7	1	1
NFL Total	247	1308	5.3	15	64

BEN STARRET Starret, Benjamin L 5′11″, 213 **BB-DE-LB-TB**
Col: St. Mary's (Cal.) *HS:* Santa Rosa [CA] B: 11/19/1917, Santa Rosa, CA D: 1/1982, Burnt Ranch, CA
1941 Pit: 4 G; Pass 2-0, 1 Int; Rush 7-9 1.3; KR 2-42 21.0. **1942** GB: 5 G; Punt 1-43 43.0. **1943** GB: 7 G; Rush 1-1 1.0; Int 1-4. **1944** GB: 7 G; Rush 10-21 2.1 2 TD; Rec 1-6 6.0; KR 1-13 13.0; Punt 2-66 33.0; 12 Pt. **1945** GB: 8 G; Rush 5-26 5.2; KR 1-3 3.0; Int 1-27; 1 Fum. **Total:** 31 G; Pass 2-0, 1 Int; Rush 23-57 2.5 2 TD; Rec 1-6 6.0; KR 4-58 14.5; Int 2-31; Punt 3-109 36.3; 12 Pt; 1 Fum.

STEPHEN STARRING Starring, Stephen Dale 5′10″, 172 **WR**
Col: McNeese State *HS:* Vinton [LA] B: 7/30/1961, Baton Rouge, LA *Drafted:* 1983 Round 3 NE
1984 NE: Rush 2-(-16) -8.0; PR 10-73 7.3. **1985** NE: PR 2-0. **1986** NE: Rush 1-0; PR 6-18 3.0. **1987** NE: Rush 2-13 6.5; PR 1-17 17.0. **Total:** Rush 5-(-3) -0.6; PR 19-108 5.7.

		Receiving				Kickoff Returns				
Year Team	**G**	**Rec**	**Yds**	**Avg**	**TD**	**Ret**	**Yds**	**Avg**	**TD**	**Fum**
1983 NE	15	17	389	22.9	2	0	0	—	0	1
1984 NE	16	46	657	14.3	4	0	0	—	0	1
1985 NE	16	16	235	14.7	0	48	1012	21.1	0	4
1986 NE	14	16	295	18.4	2	36	802	22.3	0	4
1987 NE	11	17	289	17.0	3	23	445	19.3	0	2
1988 Det-TB	12	8	164	20.5	0	8	130	16.3	0	0
1988 Det	6	5	89	17.8	0	8	130	16.3	0	0
1988 TB	6	3	75	25.0	0	0	0	—	0	0
NFL Total	84	120	2029	16.9	11	115	2389	20.8	0	12

LEO STASICA Stasica, Leo Walter 5′11″, 185 **DB-QB-TB**
(Stas) *Col:* Colorado *HS:* Rockford Central [IL] B: 6/15/1916, Rockford, IL D: 9/1982, Denver, CO *Drafted:* 1941 Round 2 Bkn
1941 Bkn: PR 2-14 7.0; KR 1-43 43.0. **1943** Was: PR 1-11 11.0; Int 1-0; Punt 1-38 38.0. **1944** Bos: PR 3-30 10.0; KR 3-75 25.0; Int 1-15; Punt 2-96 48.0. **Total:** PR 6-55 9.2; KR 4-118 29.5; Int 2-15; Punt 3-134 44.7.

		Passing							
Year Team	**G**	**Att**	**Comp**	**Comp%**	**Yds**	**YPA**	**TD**	**Int**	**Rating**
1941 Bkn	5	2	1	50.0	14	7.00	0	0	72.9
1943 Was	6	6	1	16.7	34	5.67	0	1	11.1
1944 Bos	7	47	21	44.7	225	4.79	1	7	26.8
NFL Total	18	55	23	41.8	273	4.96	1	8	24.1

	Rushing			
Year Team	**Att**	**Yds**	**Avg**	**TD**
1941 Bkn	3	17	5.7	0
1943 Was	9	-10	-1.1	0
1944 Bos	22	-16	-0.7	0
NFL Total	34	-9	-0.3	0

STAN STASICA Stasica, Stanley Joseph 5′10″, 175 **HB-DB**
Col: Gordon Coll. GA (J.C.); South Carolina; Illinois *HS:* Rockford Central [IL] B: 6/24/1919, Rockford, IL
AAFC **1946** MiaA: 1 G.

RALPH STATEN Staten, Ralph Lahquan 6'3", 205 **DB**
Col: Alabama *HS:* Mary Montgomery [Mobile, HS] B: 12/3/1974, Mobile, AL *Drafted:* 1997 Round 7 Bal
1997 Bal: 10 G; Int 2-12. **1998** Bal: 15 G; Int 3-25; 1 Fum; 1 Sac.
Total: 25 G; Int 5-37; 1 Fum; 1 Sac.

RANDY STATEN Staten, Randolph Wilbert 6'1", 225 **DE**
(Thunder) *Col:* Minnesota *HS:* Second Ward [Charlotte, NC]
B: 1/24/1944, Charlotte, NC
1967 NYG: 14 G.

ROBERT STATEN Staten, Robert 5'11", 235 **RB**
Col: Jackson State *HS:* Quitman [MS] B: 1/23/1969, Shubata, MS
1996 TB: 6 G.

LARRY STATION Station, Lawrence Wilson Jr. 5'11", 227 **LB**
Col: Iowa *HS:* Central [Omaha, NE] B: 12/5/1963, Omaha, NE
Drafted: 1986 Round 11 Pit
1986 Pit: 6 G.

JIM STATON Staton, James Brooks Jr. 6'4", 246 **DT**
Col: Wake Forest *HS:* Greensboro [NC] B: 5/23/1927, Ansonville, NC
D: 9/16/1993, Greensboro, NC *Drafted:* 1951 Round 2 Was
1951 Was: 8 G.

ART STATUTO Statuto, Arthur John 6'2", 221 **C**
Col: Notre Dame *HS:* Saugus [MA] B: 7/17/1925, Saugus, MA
Drafted: 1948 Round 29 Phi
AAFC **1948** BufA: 14 G; Rec 0-2. **1949** BufA: 12 G. **Total:** 26 G; Rec 0-2.

NFL **1950** LARm: 12 G.

ROGER STAUBACH Staubach, Roger Thomas 6'3", 197 **QB**
(The Dodger) *Col:* New Mexico Mil. Inst. (J.C.); Navy *HS:* Purcell [Cincinnati, OH] B: 2/5/1942, Cincinnati, OH *Drafted:* 1964 Round 10 Dal *HOF:* 1985
1974 Dal: Rec 1-(-13) -13.0. **Total:** Rec 1-(-13) -13.0.

		Passing							
Year Team	**G**	**Att**	**Comp**	**Comp%**	**Yds**	**YPA**	**TD**	**Int**	**Rating**
1969 Dal	6	47	23	48.9	421	8.96	1	2	69.5
1970 Dal	8	82	44	53.7	542	6.61	2	8	42.9
1971 Dal	13	211	126	59.7	1882	**8.92**	15	**4**	104.8
1972 Dal	4	20	9	45.0	98	4.90	0	2	20.4
1973 Dal	14	286	179	62.6	2428	**8.49**	**23**	15	**94.6**
1974 Dal	14	360	190	52.8	2552	7.09	11	15	68.4
1975 Dal	13	348	198	56.9	2666	7.66	17	16	78.5
1976 Dal	14	369	208	56.4	2715	7.36	14	11	79.9
1977 Dal	14	361	210	58.2	2620	7.26	18	9	87.0
1978 Dal	15	413	231	55.9	3190	7.72	25	16	**84.9**
1979 Dal	16	461	267	57.9	3586	7.78	27	11	**92.3**
NFL Total	131	2958	1685	57.0	22700	7.67	153	109	83.4

	Rushing				
Year Team	**Att**	**Yds**	**Avg**	**TD**	**Fum**
1969 Dal	15	60	4.0	1	2
1970 Dal	27	221	8.2	0	4
1971 Dal	41	343	8.4	2	6
1972 Dal	6	45	7.5	0	1
1973 Dal	46	250	5.4	3	5
1974 Dal	47	320	6.8	3	7
1975 Dal	55	316	5.7	4	5
1976 Dal	43	184	4.3	3	4
1977 Dal	51	171	3.4	3	8
1978 Dal	42	182	4.3	1	5
1979 Dal	37	172	4.6	0	8
NFL Total	410	2264	5.5	20	55

SCOTT STAUCH Stauch, Scott Roy 5'11", 204 **RB**
Col: UCLA *HS:* Grants Pass [OR] B: 1/3/1959, Seattle, WA
1981 NO: 10 G; Rush 2-6 3.0; Rec 1-7 7.0; KR 3-65 21.7; 1 Fum.

JASON STAUROVSKY Staurovsky, Jason Charles 5'9", 167 **K**
Col: Tulsa *HS:* Bishop Kelley [Tulsa, OK] B: 3/23/1963, Tulsa, OK

		Scoring						
Year Team	**G**	**Pts**	**FG**	**FGA**	**FG%**	**XK**	**XKA**	**XK%**
1987 StL	2	9	1	3	33.3	6	6	100.0
1988 NE	8	35	7	11	63.6	14	15	93.3
1989 NE	7	56	14	17	82.4	14	14	100.0
1990 NE	16	67	16	22	72.7	19	19	100.0
1991 NE	9	49	13	19	68.4	10	11	90.9
1992 NYJ	4	15	3	8	37.5	6	6	100.0
NFL Total	46	231	54	80	67.5	69	71	97.2

JERRY STAUTBERG Stautberg, Gerald James 6'2", 228 **OG-LB**
Col: Cincinnati *HS:* Purcell [Cincinnati, OH] B: 4/6/1929, Cincinnati, OH
1951 ChiB: 3 G.

ERNIE STAUTNER Stautner, Ernest Alfred 6'1", 230 **DT-DE-OG**
Col: Boston College *HS:* Columbia [East Greenbush, NY]; Vincentian Inst. [Albany, NY] B: 4/20/1925, Prinzing-by-Cham, Germany
Drafted: 1950 Round 2 Pit *HOF:* 1969
1950 Pit: 12 G; Scor **1** Saf; 2 Pt. **1951** Pit: 12 G. **1952** Pit: 12 G. **1953** Pit: 11 G. **1954** Pit: 12 G; Int 1-3. **1955** Pit: 12 G. **1956** Pit: 12 G. **1957** Pit: 12 G. **1958** Pit: 12 G; Scor **1** Saf; 2 Pt. **1959** Pit: 12 G. **1960** Pit: 12 G. **1961** Pit: 14 G. **1962** Pit: 14 G; Int 1-2; Scor 1 Saf; 2 Pt. **1963** Pit: 14 G.
Total: 173 G; Int 2-5; Scor 3 Saf; 6 Pt.

ODELL STAUTZENBERGER Stautzenberger, Weldon Odell 6'0", 218 **G**
Col: Texas A&M *HS:* Thomas Jefferson [San Antonio, TX]
B: 10/23/1924, San Antonio, TX
AAFC **1949** BufA: 9 G.

JOE STAYSNIAK Staysniak, Joseph Andrew 6'5", 297 **OG-OT**
Col: Ohio State *HS:* Midview [Grafton, OH] B: 12/8/1966, Elyria, OH
Drafted: 1990 Round 7 SD
1991 Buf: 2 G. **1992** KC: 6 G. **1993** Ind: 14 G. **1994** Ind: 16 G; 1 Fum.
1995 Ind: 16 G. **1996** Ariz: 9 G. **Total:** 63 G; 1 Fum.

JOHN STEBER Steber, John Warren III 6'0", 225 **OG-DG**
Col: Georgia Tech; Vanderbilt *HS:* S.S. Murphy [Mobile, AL]
B: 9/12/1923, Mobile, AL D: 10/1975 *Drafted:* 1945 Round 5 Was
1946 Was: 10 G. **1947** Was: 12 G; KR 1-0. **1948** Was: 12 G. **1949** Was: 9 G. **1950** Was: 12 G. **Total:** 55 G; KR 1-0.

TROY STEDMAN Stedman, Troy M 6'3", 243 **LB**
Col: Kirkwood CC IA; Central Coll. (Iowa); Washburn *HS:* Cedar Falls [IA] B: 5/19/1965, Cedar Falls, IA *Drafted:* 1988 Round 7 KC
1988 KC: 5 G.

JOEL STEED Steed, Joel Edward 6'2", 300 **NT**
Col: Colorado *HS:* W.C. Hinkley [Aurora, CO] B: 2/17/1969, Frankfurt, Germany *Drafted:* 1992 Round 3 Pit
1992 Pit: 11 G. **1993** Pit: 14 G; 1.5 Sac. **1994** Pit: 16 G; 2 Sac. **1995** Pit: 12 G; 1 Sac. **1996** Pit: 16 G. **1997** Pit: 16 G; 1 Sac. **1998** Pit: 16 G; 1 Sac.
Total: 101 G; 6.5 Sac.

CHUCK STEELE Steele, Charles Anson 6'1", 255 **C**
Col: Saddleback Coll. CA (J.C.); California *HS:* El Modena [Orange, CA]
B: 6/22/1964, Los Angeles, CA
1987 Det: 3 G.

CLIFF STEELE Steele, Clifford 5'8", 150 **BB-WB**
Col: Syracuse; Fordham *HS:* Mechanic Arts [St. Paul, MN] B: 1898
Deceased
1922 Roch-Akr: 5 G; Scor 1, 1 XK. Roch: 1 G; Scor 1, 1 XK. Akr: 4 G.
Total: 5 G.

ERNIE STEELE Steele, Ernest Raymond 6'0", 187 **HB-DB**
Col: Washington *HS:* Highline [Seattle, WA] B: 11/2/1917, Bothell, WA
Drafted: 1942 Round 10 Pit
1942 Phi: Punt 2-61 30.5; Scor 13, 1-1 100.0% XK. **1943** PhPt: Pass 1-0, 1 Int. **1945** Phi: Pass 2-1 50.0%, 12 6.00 1 Int. **1948** Phi: Pass 1-0, 1 Int.
Total: Pass 4-1 25.0%, 12 3.00 3 Int; Punt 2-61 30.5; Scor 115, 1-1 100.0% XK.

		Rushing				Receiving			
Year Team	**G**	**Att**	**Yds**	**Avg**	**TD**	**Rec**	**Yds**	**Avg**	**TD**
1942 Phi	10	24	124	5.2	0	7	114	16.3	1
1943 PhPt	10	85	409	4.8	4	9	168	18.7	2
1944 Phi	9	59	247	4.2	5	1	22	22.0	0
1945 Phi	7	20	212	10.6	1	3	42	14.0	0
1946 Phi	9	31	108	3.5	1	5	69	13.8	0
1947 Phi	12	26	138	5.3	1	4	62	15.5	0
1948 Phi	12	13	99	7.6	1	2	43	21.5	1
NFL Total	69	258	1337	5.2	13	31	520	16.8	4

	Punt Returns				Kickoff Returns			
Year Team	**Ret**	**Yds**	**Avg**	**TD**	**Ret**	**Yds**	**Avg**	**TD**
1942 Phi	9	184	20.4	0	6	140	23.3	0
1943 PhPt	12	152	12.7	0	11	236	21.5	0
1944 Phi	11	181	16.5	0	5	128	25.6	0
1945 Phi	2	22	11.0	0	3	72	24.0	0
1946 Phi	9	82	9.1	0	8	120	15.0	0
1947 Phi	11	183	16.6	0	2	17	8.5	0
1948 Phi	1	5	5.0	0	2	30	15.0	0
NFL Total	55	809	14.7	0	37	743	20.1	0

	Interceptions				
Year Team	**Int**	**Yds**	**TD**	**Fum**	**Tot TD**
1942 Phi	2	49	0	0	2
1943 PhPt	0	0	0	0	6
1944 Phi	6	113	0	0	5
1945 Phi	1	15	0	2	2
1946 Phi	3	69	0	4	1
1947 Phi	6	103	0	3	1
1948 Phi	6	55	0	3	2
NFL Total	24	404	0	12	19

GLEN STEELE Steele, James Lendale Jr. 6'4", 295 **DT**
Col: Michigan *HS:* West Noble [Ligonier, IN] B: 10/4/1974, Ligonier, IN
Drafted: 1998 Round 4 Cin
1998 Cin: 10 G.

LARRY STEELE Steele, Lawrence Clinton 5'10", 182 **P**
Col: Santa Rosa JC CA B: 1/5/1950, Santa Rosa, CA
1974 Den: 1 G.

RED STEELE Steele, Percy Davis 6'0", 176 **E**
Col: Miami (Ohio); Harvard *HS:* McArthur [OH] B: 8/9/1897, McArthur, OH D: 3/28/1974, Ojai, CA
1921 Can: 8 G.

ROBERT STEELE Steele, Robert Hugh 6'4", 196 **WR**
Col: North Alabama *HS:* Hardaway [Columbus, GA] B: 8/2/1956, Columbus, GA
1978 Dal: 14 G. **1979** Min: 16 G; Rec 1-10 10.0; KR 1-0. **Total:** 30 G; Rec 1-10 10.0; KR 1-0.

ANTHONY STEELS Steels, William Anthony 5'9", 200 **RB**
Col: Nebraska *HS:* John W. North [Riverside, CA]; Jacksonville HS [AR];American School [Zaragoz] B: 1/8/1959, Sacramento, CA
1985 SD-Buf: Rush 10-38 3.8; Rec 2-9 4.5. SD: Rush 6-12 2.0. Buf: Rush 4-26 6.5; Rec 2-9 4.5. **1987** SD: Rush 1-3 3.0; Rec 1-4 4.0. **Total:** Rush 11-41 3.7; Rec 3-13 4.3.

		Kickoff Returns				
Year Team	**G**	**Ret**	**Yds**	**Avg**	**TD**	**Fum**
1985 SD-Buf	15	30	561	18.7	0	2
1985 SD	6	10	223	22.3	0	0
1985 Buf	9	20	338	16.9	0	2
1987 SD	2	0	0	—	0	0
NFL Total	17	30	561	18.7	0	2

FRANK STEEN Steen, Frank William 6'1", 190 **OE-DE**
Col: Rice *HS:* Forest Avenue [Dallas, TX] B: 10/5/1913, Longview, TX D: 4/2/1998, Houston, TX
1939 GB: 3 G.

JIM STEEN Steen, James 6'2", 205 **T**
Col: Syracuse *HS:* New Rochelle [NY] B: 3/28/1913, Brooklyn, NY D: 11/23/1983, Detroit, MI
1935 Det: 9 G. **1936** Det: 11 G. **Total:** 20 G.

DICK STEERE Steere, Edward Richard 6'4", 240 **OG**
Col: Drake *HS:* Thornton Twp. [Harvey, IL] B: 3/2/1927, Chicago, IL
Drafted: 1951 Round 5 SF
1951 Phi: 5 G.

JIM STEFFEN Steffen, James William 6'0", 195 **DB**
Col: Rancho Santiago Coll. CA (J.C.); Occidental; UCLA *HS:* Tustin [CA] B: 5/1/1936, Orange, CA *Drafted:* 1959 Round 13 Det
1962 Was: **1** Fum TD. **Total:** 1 Fum TD.

		Punt Returns				Kickoff Returns			
Year Team	**G**	**Ret**	**Yds**	**Avg**	**TD**	**Ret**	**Yds**	**Avg**	**TD**
1959 Det	8	3	0	0.0	0	0	0	—	0
1960 Det	12	14	83	5.9	0	8	225	28.1	0
1961 Det-Was	14	19	153	8.1	0	**29**	691	23.8	0
1961 Det	8	11	95	8.6	0	19	435	22.9	0
1961 Was	6	8	58	7.3	0	10	256	25.6	0
1962 Was	14	6	30	5.0	0	4	107	26.8	0
1963 Was	13	5	83	16.6	0	3	84	28.0	0
1964 Was	13	0	0	—	0	0	0	—	0
1965 Was	14	0	0	—	0	0	0	—	0
NFL Total	88	47	349	7.4	0	44	1107	25.2	0

	Interceptions				Tot
Year Team	**Int**	**Yds**	**TD**	**Fum**	**TD**
1961 Det-Was	1	11	0	0	0
1961 Was	1	11	0	0	0
1962 Was	4	37	0	1	1
1963 Was	5	140	1	0	1
1964 Was	4	20	0	0	0
1965 Was	3	56	0	0	0
NFL Total	17	264	1	1	2

BOB STEFIK Stefik, Robert Mathias 5'11", 180 **OE**
Col: Niagara *HS:* St. Mary's [Niagara Falls, NY] B: 10/8/1923, Madison, WI
AAFC **1948** BufA: 1 G; Scor 0-1 XK.

MILT STEGALL Stegall, Milt Eugene 6'0", 184 **WR**
Col: Miami (Ohio) *HS:* Roger Bacon [Cincinnati, OH] B: 1/25/1970, Cincinnati, OH
1992 Cin: Rec 3-35 11.7 1 TD. **1993** Cin: Rec 1-8 8.0. **Total:** Rec 4-43 10.8 1 TD.

		Kickoff Returns				
Year Team	**G**	**Ret**	**Yds**	**Avg**	**TD**	**Fum**
1992 Cin	16	25	430	17.2	0	1
1993 Cin	4	0	0	—	0	0
1994 Cin	1	1	16	16.0	0	0
NFL Total	21	26	446	17.2	0	1

LARRY STEGENT Stegent, Larry Raymond 6'1", 200 **RB**
Col: Texas A&M *HS:* St. Thomas [Houston, TX] B: 12/1/1947, Houston, TX *Drafted:* 1970 Round 1 StL
1971 StL: 7 G; Rec 1-12 12.0; KR 1-0; 1 Fum.

PETE STEGER Steger, Peter 1 **WB-BB**
Col: No College *HS:* Oak Park [IL] B: 11/1896, Chicago, IL Deceased
1921 ChiC: 6 G.

RON STEHOUWER Stehouwer, Ronald Dwayne 6'2", 230 **OG**
Col: Colorado State *HS:* Wayland [MI] B: 2/4/1937, Hopkins, MI
Drafted: 1960 Round 1 LAC
1960 Pit: 12 G. **1961** Pit: 14 G. **1962** Pit: 14 G. **1963** Pit: 14 G. **1964** Pit: 14 G. **Total:** 68 G.

HERB STEIN Stein, Herbert Alfred 6'1", 186 **C-G**
Col: Pittsburgh *HS:* McKinley [Niles, OH]; Kiski School [Saltsburg, PA] B: 3/27/1898, Warren, OH D: 10/25/1980, Rocky River, OH
1921 Buf: 1 G. **1922** Tol: 8 G. **1924** Fra: 13 G. **1925** Pott: 12 G. **1926** Pott: 10 G. **1928** Pott: 10 G. **Total:** 54 G.

BOB STEIN Stein, Robert Allen 6'3", 235 **LB**
Col: Minnesota *HS:* St. Louis Park [MN] B: 1/22/1948, Minneapolis, MN *Drafted:* 1969 Round 5 KC
1969 KC: 14 G. **1970** KC: 14 G; KR 3-23 7.7; 1 Fum. **1971** KC: 14 G; Int 1-5; Scor 0-1 FG. **1972** KC: 8 G. **1973** LARm: 13 G; Int 1-6. **1974** LARm: 14 G. **1975** SD-Min: 12 G. SD: 3 G. Min: 9 G. **Total:** 89 G; KR 3-23 7.7; Int 2-11; Scor 0-1 FG; 1 Fum.

RUSS STEIN Stein, Russell Frederick 6'1", 210 **T-OE-C**
Col: Washington & Jefferson *HS:* McKinley [Niles, OH]; Kiski School [Saltsburg, PA] B: 4/21/1896, Warren, OH D: 6/1/1970, Niles, OH
1922 Tol: 7 G; Scor 5, 1 FG, 2 XK. **1924** Fra: 12 G; Scor 15, 1 FG, 12 XK. **1925** Pott: 10 G. **1926** Can: 8 G. **Total:** 37 G; Scor 20, 2 FG, 14 XK.

SAMMY STEIN Stein, Samuel 6'0", 195 **OE-T**
Col: No College B: 4/1/1905, New York, NY D: 3/30/1966, Las Vegas, NV
1929 SI: 9 G; Rec 1 TD; 6 Pt. **1930** SI: 12 G; Rec 1 TD; 6 Pt. **1931** NYG: 8 G. **1932** Bkn: 2 G. **Total:** 31 G; Rec 2 TD; 12 Pt.

BILL STEIN Stein, William Earl 6'0", 190 **G-C-T**
(Red) *Col:* Macalester; Fordham *HS:* Two Harbors [MN] B: 5/28/1899, Two Harbors, MN D: 8/27/1983, Two Harbors, MN
1923 Dul: 6 G. **1924** Dul: 6 G. **1925** Dul: 3 G. **1926** Dul: 14 G. **1927** Dul: 3 G. ChiC: 3 G. **1928** ChiC: 2 G. **1929** ChiC: 5 G. **Total:** 42 G.

LARRY STEINBACH Steinbach, Lawrence Joseph 6'0", 214 **T-G**
Col: St. Thomas *HS:* New Rockford [ND]; St. Thomas Acad. [St. Paul, MN] B: 12/23/1900, New Rockford, ND D: 1/29/1967, Carrington, ND
1930 ChiB: 11 G. **1931** ChiB-ChiC: 7 G. ChiB: 4 G. ChiC: 3 G. **1932** ChiC: 7 G. **1933** ChiC-Phi: 4 G; Rec 1-5 5.0. ChiC: 1 G. Phi: 3 G; Rec 1-5 5.0. **Total:** 29 G; Rec 1-5 5.0.

DON STEINBRUNNER Steinbrunner, Donald Thomas 6'3", 220 **OT**
Col: Washington State *HS:* Wickersham [WA] B: 4/5/1932, Bellingham, WA D: 7/20/1967, Vietnam *Drafted:* 1953 Round 6 Cle
1953 Cle: 8 G; KR 1-23 23.0.

REBEL STEINER Steiner, Rebel Roy 6'0", 185 **DB**
Col: Alabama *HS:* Ensley [Birmingham, AL] B: 8/27/1927, Birmingham, AL *Drafted:* 1948 Round 23 Det

		Interceptions		
Year Team	**G**	**Int**	**Yds**	**TD**
1950 GB	12	7	190	1
1951 GB	12	3	4	0
NFL Total	24	10	194	1

AL STEINFELD Steinfeld, Alan A 6'5", 256 **OG-C-OT**
Col: C.W. Post *HS:* South Shore [Brooklyn, NY] B: 10/28/1958, Brooklyn, NY
1982 KC: 7 G. **1983** Hou-NYG: 13 G. Hou: 8 G. NYG: 5 G. **Total:** 20 G.

FRED STEINFORT Steinfort, Frederick W 5'11", 180 **K**
Col: Boston College *HS:* Brighton [MA] B: 11/3/1952, Wetter, Germany *Drafted:* 1976 Round 5 Oak

		Scoring						
Year Team	**G**	**Pts**	**FG**	**FGA**	**FG%**	**XK**	**XKA**	**XK%**
1976 Oak	7	28	4	8	50.0	16	19	84.2
1977 Atl	7	31	6	11	54.5	13	13	100.0
1978 Atl	6	17	3	10	30.0	8	9	88.9
1979 Den	1	0	0	0	—	0	0	—
1980 Den	16	110	26	34	76.5	32	33	97.0
1981 Den	16	87	17	30	56.7	36	37	97.3
1983 Buf-NE	11	38	7	21	33.3	17	18	94.4
1983 Buf	2	4	1	6	16.7	1	1	100.0

1983 NE	9	34	6	15	40.0	16	17	94.1
NFL Total	64	311	63	114	55.3	122	129	94.6

GIL STEINKE Steinke, Gilbert Ervin 6'0", 175 **HB-DB**
Col: Texas A&M *HS:* Ganado [TX] B: 5/3/1919, Brenham, TX
D: 5/10/1995, Austin, TX
1945 Phi: Rec 2-12 6.0; PR 2-27 13.5; KR 1-18 18.0. **1946** Phi: Rec 5-107 21.4 2 TD; PR 8-116 **14.5**; KR 3-92 30.7; Int 6-72 **1** TD. **1947** Phi: Rec 4-90 22.5 1 TD; PR 6-69 11.5; KR 1-2 2.0; Int 1-17. **1948** Phi: KR 1-17 17.0. **Total:** Rec 11-209 19.0 3 TD; PR 16-212 13.3; KR 6-129 21.5; Int 7-89 1 TD.

		Rushing					Tot
Year Team	G	Att	Yds	Avg	TD	Fum	TD
1945 Phi	7	7	46	6.6	1	1	1
1946 Phi	10	38	154	4.1	1	5	4
1947 Phi	6	16	50	3.1	0	3	1
1948 Phi	2	5	17	3.4	0	0	0
NFL Total	25	66	267	4.0	2	9	6

BILL STEINKEMPER Steinkemper, William Jacob 6'2", 220 **T**
Col: Notre Dame *HS:* DePaul Acad. [Chicago, IL] B: 12/27/1913, Anna, OK D: 11/26/1973, Franklin Park, IL
1943 ChiB: 10 G.

DEAN STEINKUHLER Steinkuhler, Dean Elmer 6'3", 283 **OT**
Col: Nebraska *HS:* Sterling [NE] B: 1/27/1961, Burr, NE
Drafted: 1984 Round 1 Hou
1984 Hou: 10 G. **1986** Hou: 16 G. **1987** Hou: 11 G. **1988** Hou: 16 G. **1989** Hou: 16 G. **1990** Hou: 15 G. **1991** Hou: 16 G. **Total:** 100 G.

KEN STEINMETZ Steinmetz, Kenneth Clifton 6'0", 188 **FB-LB**
Col: No College *HS:* Aldrich [Warwick, RI] B: 8/7/1924, Providence, RI
D: 10/13/1995, Las Vegas, NV
1944 Bos: 8 G; Pass 1-0; Rush 11-24 2.2; Punt 1-17 17.0. **1945** Bos: 10 G; Rush 4-12 3.0; Int 1-0; Punt 8-239 29.9. **Total:** 18 G; Pass 1-0; Rush 15-36 2.4; Int 1-0; Punt 9-256 28.4.

GREG STEMRICK Stemrick, Gregory Earl 5'11", 185 **DB**
Col: Colorado State *HS:* Lincoln Heights [OH] B: 10/25/1951, Cincinnati, OH
1976 Hou: Rec 1-10 10.0. **1977** Hou: PR 1-0; 1 Fum TD. **1979** Hou: KR 1-0. **Total:** Rec 1-10 10.0; PR 1-0; KR 1-0; 1 Fum TD.

		Interceptions			
Year Team	G	Int	Yds	TD	Fum
1975 Hou	11	0	0	0	0
1976 Hou	14	1	0	0	0
1977 Hou	9	1	18	0	1
1978 Hou	16	3	65	0	0
1979 Hou	16	2	50	0	0
1980 Hou	16	4	25	0	0
1981 Hou	16	3	94	0	0
1982 Hou	8	0	0	0	0
1983 NO	11	1	26	0	0
NFL Total	117	15	278	0	1

JAN STENERUD Stenerud, Jan 6'2", 187 **K**
Col: Montana State *HS:* Lillestrom [Norway] B: 11/26/1942, Fetsund, Norway *Drafted:* 1966 Redshirt Round 3 KC *HOF:* 1991
1976 KC: Rush 1-0; Punt 1-28 28.0. **Total:** Rush 1-0; Punt 1-28 28.0.

		Scoring							
Year Team	G	Pts	FG	FGA	FG%	XK	XKA	XK%	Fum
1967 KC	14	108	**21**	**36**	58.3	45	45	100.0	0
1968 KC	14	129	30	40	**75.0**	39	40	**97.5**	0
1969 KC	14	119	27	35	**77.1**	38	38	**100.0**	0
1970 KC	14	116	**30**	42	71.4	26	26	100.0	0
1971 KC	14	110	26	44	59.1	32	32	100.0	0
1972 KC	14	95	21	36	58.3	32	32	100.0	0
1973 KC	14	93	24	38	63.2	21	23	91.3	0
1974 KC	14	75	17	24	70.8	24	26	92.3	0
1975 KC	14	96	**22**	32	68.8	30	31	96.8	0
1976 KC	14	90	21	**38**	55.3	27	33	81.8	1
1977 KC	14	51	8	18	44.4	27	28	96.4	0
1978 KC	16	85	20	30	66.7	25	26	96.2	0
1979 KC	16	64	12	23	52.2	28	29	96.6	0
1980 GB	4	12	3	5	60.0	3	3	100.0	0
1981 GB	16	101	22	24	**91.7**	35	36	**97.2**	0
1982 GB	9	64	13	18	72.2	25	27	92.6	0
1983 GB	16	115	21	26	80.8	52	52	100.0	0
1984 Min	16	90	20	23	**87.0**	30	31	**96.8**	0
1985 Min	16	86	15	26	57.7	41	43	95.3	0
NFL Total	263	1699	373	558	66.8	580	601	96.5	1

BRIAN STENGER Stenger, Brian Francis 6'4", 241 **LB**
Col: Notre Dame *HS:* St. Joseph [Cleveland, OH] B: 1/16/1947, Euclid, OH
1969 Pit: 14 G; Int 3-36. **1970** Pit: 7 G. **1971** Pit: 14 G. **1972** Pit: 14 G. **1973** NE: 10 G. **Total:** 59 G; Int 3-36.

PAUL STENN Stenn, Paul James Jr. 6'2", 242 **OT-DT**
(AKA Paul James Stenko Jr.) *Col:* Villanova *HS:* Berwick [PA]
B: 7/12/1918, Berwick, PA
1942 NYG: 11 G. **1946** Was: 11 G. **1947** Pit: 11 G. **1948** ChiB: 12 G. **1949** ChiB: 11 G; Rec 2-11 5.5. **1950** ChiB: 12 G; KR 1-16 16.0. **1951** ChiB: 12 G. **Total:** 80 G; Rec 2-11 5.5; KR 1-16 16.0.

STUD STENNETT Stennett, Fredrick F 6'0", 194 **TB-WB-FB-BB**
Col: St. Mary's (Cal.) B: 2/8/1907, LeRoy, KS D: 8/23/1989, Ventura, CA
1931 Port: 10 G. **1932** ChiC: 2 G; Pass 3-1 33.3%, 11 3.67; Rush 7-(-3) -0.4. **Total:** 12 G; Pass 3-1 33.3%, 11 3.67; Rush 7-(-3) -0.4.

MIKE STENSRUD Stensrud, Michael Iver 6'5", 280 **NT-DT-DE**
Col: Iowa State *HS:* Lake Mills [IA] B: 2/19/1956, Forest City, IA
Drafted: 1979 Round 2 Hou
1979 Hou: 6 G. **1980** Hou: 16 G. **1981** Hou: 16 G. **1982** Hou: 9 G; 1.5 Sac. **1983** Hou: 16 G; 2 Sac. **1984** Hou: 16 G; 4.5 Sac. **1985** Hou: 16 G; Int 1-0; 5 Sac. **1986** Min: 11 G; 1 Sac. **1987** TB: 12 G. **1988** KC: 13 G; Int 1-5; 2.5 Sac. **1989** Was: 8 G. **Total:** 139 G; Int 2-5; 16.5 Sac.

STEVE STENSTROM Stenstrom, Stephan Ryan 6'2", 206 **QB**
Col: Stanford *HS:* El Toro [CA] B: 12/23/1971, El Toro, CA
Drafted: 1995 Round 4 KC
1997 ChiB: Rush 1-6 6.0. **1998** ChiB: Rush 18-79 4.4 2 TD.
Total: Rush 19-85 4.5 2 TD.

		Passing								
Year Team	G	Att	Comp	Comp%	Yds	YPA	TD	Int	Rating	Fum
1996 ChiB	1	4	3	75.0	37	9.25	0	0	103.1	0
1997 ChiB	3	14	8	57.1	70	5.00	0	2	31.0	1
1998 ChiB	7	196	112	57.1	1252	6.39	4	6	70.4	6
NFL Total	11	214	123	57.5	1359	6.35	4	8	67.1	7

JOE STEPANEK Stepanek, Joseph Paul 6'5", 268 **DT**
Col: Waldorf Coll. IA (J.C.); Minnesota *HS:* St. Regis [Cedar Rapids, IA]
B: 11/6/1963, Tama, IA
1987 Min: 1 G; Scor **1** Saf; 2 Pt.

SCOTT STEPHEN Stephen, Scott Dewitt 6'2", 237 **LB**
Col: Arizona State *HS:* Manual Arts [Los Angeles, CA] B: 6/18/1964, Los Angeles, CA *Drafted:* 1987 Round 3 GB
1987 GB: 8 G. **1988** GB: 16 G; 1 Sac. **1989** GB: 16 G; Int 2-16; 1 Sac. **1990** GB: 16 G; Int 2-26; 1 Fum; 1 Sac. **1991** GB: 16 G; Int 1-23; 1.5 Sac. **1992** LARm: 16 G; KR 2-12 6.0. **Total:** 88 G; KR 2-12 6.0; Int 5-65; 1 Fum; 4.5 Sac.

BRUCE STEPHENS Stephens, Bruce Anthony 5'9", 170 **WR**
Col: Columbia *HS:* Central [Phenix City, AL] B: 10/31/1956, Columbus, GA
1978 NYJ: 6 G; KR 3-42 14.0.

CALVIN STEPHENS Stephens, Calvin Herbert 6'2", 285 **OG**
Col: South Carolina *HS:* Kings Mountain [NC] B: 10/25/1967, Kings Mountain, NC *Drafted:* 1991 Round 3 NE
1992 NE: 13 G.

DARNELL STEPHENS Stephens, Darnell Jermain 5'11", 243 **LB**
Col: Clemson *HS:* Judson [Converse, TX] B: 1/29/1973, San Antonio, TX
1995 TB: 13 G. **1996** TB: 1 G. **Total:** 14 G.

HAROLD STEPHENS Stephens, Ernest Harold 5'11", 175 **QB**
Col: Hardin-Simmons *HS:* Abilene [TX] B: 10/30/1938, Caps, TX
Drafted: 1962 Round 1 NYT
1962 NYT: 6 G; Pass 22-15 68.2%, 123 5.59; Rush 6-33 5.5; 3 Fum.

HAL STEPHENS Stephens, Hal Franklin 6'4", 252 **DE**
Col: East Carolina *HS:* Whiteville [NC] B: 4/14/1961, Whiteville, NC
Drafted: 1984 Round 5 LARm
1985 Det-KC: 2 G. Det: 1 G. KC: 1 G. **Total:** 2 G.

JAMAIN STEPHENS Stephens, Jamain 6'6", 336 **OT**
Col: North Carolina A&T *HS:* Lumberton [NC] B: 1/9/1974, Lumberton, NC *Drafted:* 1996 Round 1 Pit
1997 Pit: 8 G. **1998** Pit: 11 G. **Total:** 19 G.

JOHNNY STEPHENS Stephens, John Bailey 6'1", 190 **OE-DE**
Col: Marshall B: 1/15/1914, Parkersburg, WV D: 9/10/1996, Bellaire, TX
1938 Cle: 11 G; Rec 6-75 12.5.

JOHN STEPHENS Stephens, John Milton 6'1", 220 **RB**
Col: Northwestern State-Louisiana *HS:* Springhill [LA] B: 2/23/1966, Shreveport, LA *Drafted:* 1988 Round 1 NE
1988 NE: **1** Fum TD. **1990** NE: Pass 1-0, 1 Int. **1993** GB-Atl-KC: KR 5-88 17.6. KC: KR 5-88 17.6. **Total:** Pass 1-0, 1 Int; KR 5-88 17.6; 1 Fum TD.

		Rushing				Receiving					Tot
Year Team	G	Att	Yds	Avg	TD	Rec	Yds	Avg	TD	Fum	TD
1988 NE	16	297	1168	3.9	4	14	98	7.0	0	3	5
1989 NE	14	244	833	3.4	7	21	207	9.9	0	3	7
1990 NE	16	212	808	3.8	2	28	196	7.0	1	5	3

1991 NE	14	63	163	2.6	2	16	119	7.4	0	0	2
1992 NE	16	75	277	3.7	2	21	161	7.7	0	0	2
1993 GB-Atl-KC	12	54	191	3.5	1	5	31	6.2	0	1	1
1993 GB	5	48	173	3.6	1	5	31	6.2	0	0	1
1993 KC	7	6	18	3.0	0	0	0	—	0	1	0
NFL Total	88	945	3440	3.6	18	105	812	7.7	1	12	20

LARRY STEPHENS Stephens, Lawrence Clifton 6'3", 250 **DE-DT**
(Huey) *Col:* Texas *HS:* Angleton [TX] B: 9/24/1938, Buda, TX
Drafted: 1960 Round 2 Cle
1960 Cle: 12 G; KR 1-0; Int 1-34 1 TD; 6 Pt. **1961** Cle: 14 G; KR 1-15 15.0. **1962** LARm: 14 G. **1963** Dal: 14 G. **1964** Dal: 13 G. **1965** Dal: 13 G. **1966** Dal: 14 G. **1967** Dal: 9 G. **Total:** 103 G; KR 2-15 7.5; Int 1-34 1 TD; 6 Pt.

RAY STEPHENS Stephens, Leslie Ray 5'11", 190 **C-G**
Col: Idaho *HS:* Blackfoot [ID] D: 1944
1927 NYY: 10 G.

RED STEPHENS Stephens, Louis Edward 6'0", 230 **OG**
Col: San Francisco *HS:* St.Joseph's [Oakland, CA] B: 5/10/1930, Denver, CO *Drafted:* 1952 Round 23 ChiC
1955 Was: 11 G. **1956** Was: 11 G. **1957** Was: 12 G. **1958** Was: 12 G. **1959** Was: 12 G. **1960** Was: 12 G. **Total:** 70 G.

MAC STEPHENS Stephens, Mac Arthur 6'3", 220 **LB**
Col: Minnesota *HS:* Firestone [Akron, OH] B: 1/21/1968, Akron, OH
1990 NYJ: 4 G. **1991** Min: 3 G. **Total:** 7 G.

RICHARD STEPHENS Stephens, Michard Scott 6'7", 300 **OG-OT**
Col: Tulsa *HS:* Northwest [House Springs, MO] B: 1/1/1965, St. Louis, MO
1993 LARd: 16 G. **1995** Oak: 13 G. **Total:** 29 G.

ROD STEPHENS Stephens, Rodrequis La'vant 6'1", 236 **LB**
Col: Georgia Tech *HS:* North Fulton [Atlanta, GA] B: 6/14/1966, Atlanta, GA
1989 Sea: 10 G. **1990** Sea: 4 G. **1991** Sea: 16 G. **1992** Sea: 16 G. **1993** Sea: 13 G; Scor **2** Saf; 1 Fum TD; 10 Pt; 2.5 Sac. **1994** Sea: 16 G; 2.5 Sac. **1995** Was: 16 G. **1996** Was: 16 G; Int 1-0; 1 Sac. **Total:** 107 G; Int 1-0; Scor 2 Saf; 1 Fum TD; 10 Pt; 6 Sac.

SANTO STEPHENS Stephens, Santo Sean 6'4", 232 **LB**
Col: Temple *HS:* Forestville [Oxon Hill, MD] B: 6/16/1969, Washington, DC
1993 KC: 16 G. **1994** Cin: 14 G. **1995** Jac: 13 G. **Total:** 43 G.

STEVE STEPHENS Stephens, Stephen B 6'3", 227 **TE**
Col: Oklahoma State *HS:* Thomas Jefferson [Tampa, FL] B: 3/4/1957, Tampa, FL *Drafted:* 1979 Round 10 Bal
1981 NYJ: 16 G; KR 2-21 10.5.

THOMAS STEPHENS Stephens, Thomas Glenn 6'2", 215 **TE-DB**
Col: Syracuse *HS:* Washington [Mohawk, NY] B: 8/29/1935, Galveston, TX *Drafted:* 1959 Round 11 Bal
1961 Bos: KR 1-6 6.0; 1 Fum TD. **1962** Bos: KR 2-46 23.0. **1963** Bos: PR 14-117 8.4; Int 1-22. **1964** Bos: PR 5-34 6.8; KR 2-5 2.5.
Total: PR 19-151 7.9; KR 5-57 11.4; Int 1-22; 1 Fum TD.

		Receiving					Tot
Year Team	**G**	**Rec**	**Yds**	**Avg**	**TD**	**Fum**	**TD**
1960 Bos	9	22	320	14.5	3	0	3
1961 Bos	9	19	186	9.8	2	0	3
1962 Bos	3	0	0	—	0	1	0
1963 Bos	14	0	0	—	0	1	0
1964 Bos	14	0	0	—	0	0	0
NFL Total	49	41	506	12.3	5	2	6

TREMAYNE STEPHENS Stephens, Tremayne Raphael 5'11", 206 **RB**
Col: North Carolina State *HS:* Riverside [Greer, SC] B: 4/16/1976, Greenville, SC
1998 SD: Rec 2-9 4.5; KR 16-349 21.8.

		Rushing				
Year Team	**G**	**Att**	**Yds**	**Avg**	**TD**	**Fum**
1998 SD	13	35	122	3.5	1	1

BILL STEPHENS Stephens, William Alexander 5'8", 185 **C**
Col: Brown *HS:* Manual Training [Brooklyn, NY] B: 7/28/1904, New York, NY D: 7/25/1993, Claremont, CA
1926 Bkn: 5 G.

DWIGHT STEPHENSON Stephenson, Dwight Eugene 6'2", 255 **C-OT**
Col: Alabama *HS:* Hampton [VA] B: 11/20/1957, Murfreesboro, NC
Drafted: 1980 Round 2 Mia *HOF:* 1998
1980 Mia: 16 G. **1981** Mia: 16 G. **1982** Mia: 9 G. **1983** Mia: 16 G. **1984** Mia: 16 G. **1985** Mia: 16 G. **1986** Mia: 16 G. **1987** Mia: 9 G; 1 Fum. **Total:** 114 G; 1 Fum.

KAY STEPHENSON Stephenson, George Kay 6'1", 210 **QB**
Col: Florida *HS:* Pensacola [FL] B: 12/17/1944, DeFuniak Springs, FL
1967 SD: Rush 2-11 5.5. **1968** Buf: Rush 4-30 7.5. **Total:** Rush 6-41 6.8.

		Passing							
Year Team	**G**	**Att**	**Comp**	**Comp%**	**Yds**	**YPA**	**TD**	**Int**	**Rating**
1967 SD	7	26	11	42.3	117	4.50	2	2	49.7
1968 Buf	10	79	29	36.7	364	4.61	4	7	31.8
NFL Total	17	105	40	38.1	481	4.58	6	9	36.3

DAVE STEPHENSON Stephenson, James David 6'2", 232 **OG-C-DG**
(Trapper) *Col:* Tennessee; West Virginia *HS:* Charleston [WV]
B: 10/22/1925, Clendenin, WV D: 7/19/1975, Charleston, WV
1950 LARm: 12 G; KR 1-5 5.0. **1951** GB: 12 G. **1952** GB: 11 G. **1953** GB: 12 G. **1954** GB: 12 G. **1955** GB: 2 G. **Total:** 61 G; KR 1-5 5.0.

MARK STEPNOSKI Stepnoski, Mark Matthew 6'2", 269 **C-OG**
Col: Pittsburgh *HS:* Cathedral Prep [Erie, PA] B: 1/20/1967, Erie, PA
Drafted: 1989 Round 3 Dal
1989 Dal: 16 G. **1990** Dal: 16 G; KR 1-15 15.0. **1991** Dal: 16 G. **1992** Dal: 14 G. **1993** Dal: 13 G; 1 Fum. **1994** Dal: 16 G; 4 Fum. **1995** Hou: 16 G. **1996** Hou: 16 G. **1997** Ten: 16 G; 2 Fum. **1998** Ten: 13 G; Rush 1-0; 2 Fum. **Total:** 152 G; Rush 1-0; KR 1-15 15.0; 9 Fum.

TONY STEPONOVICH Steponovich, Anthony Andrew 5'10", 185 **E-G**
Col: USC *HS:* Inglewood [CA] B: 1/15/1907, Globe, AZ
1930 Min-Fra: 12 G. Min: 9 G. Fra: 3 G. **Total:** 12 G.

MIKE STEPONOVICH Steponovich, Michael M 5'9", 205 **G**
Col: St. Mary's (Cal.) *HS:* Inglewood [CA] B: 11/22/1908, Lead, SD
D: 5/24/1974, Inglewood, CA
1933 Bos: 1 G.

JACK STEPTOE Steptoe, Jack Eugene 6'1", 173 **WR**
Col: Los Angeles Valley Coll. CA (J.C.); Utah *HS:* Alain Leroy Locke [Los Angeles, CA] B: 1/21/1956, Los Angeles, CA
1978 SF: 6 G; Rec 2-46 23.0 1 TD; PR 11-129 11.7; 6 Pt; 3 Fum.

JOHN STERLING Sterling, John Fitzgerald 6'2", 203 **RB**
Col: Central Oklahoma *HS:* Altus [OK] B: 9/15/1964, Altus, OK
1987 GB: 2 G; Rush 5-20 4.0; KR 1-0; 1 Fum.

DUTCH STERNAMAN Sternaman, Edward Carl 5'8", 176 **HB-FB-QB**
Col: Illinois *HS:* Springfield [IL] B: 2/9/1895, Chicago, IL D: 2/1/1973, Chicago, IL
1920 Sta: 13 G. **1921** Sta: 11 G; Pass 1 TD; Rush 2 TD; Scor 36, **5** FG, 9 XK. **1922** ChiB: 11 G; Rush 3 TD; Scor 41, 6 FG, 5 XK. **1923** ChiB: 12 G; Rush 4 TD; Rec 1 TD; Scor 52, 5 FG, 7 XK; Tot TD 5. **1924** ChiB: 11 G; Rush 3 TD; Scor 23, 1 FG, 2 XK. **1925** ChiB: 17 G; Rush 1 TD; 6 Pt. **1926** ChiB: 14 G; Rush 1 TD; Scor 11, 1 FG, 2 XK. **1927** ChiB: 5 G. **Total:** 94 G; Pass 1 TD; Rush 14 TD; Rec 1 TD; Scor 169, 18 FG, 25 XK; Tot TD 15.

JOEY STERNAMAN Sternaman, Joseph Theodore 5'6", 152 **QB-BB**
Col: Illinois *HS:* Springfield [IL] B: 2/1/1900, Springfield, IL
D: 3/10/1988, Oak Park, IL
1922 ChiB: 12 G; Rush 4 TD; Rec 1 TD; Scor 32, 2 XK; Tot TD 5. **1923** Dul-ChiB: 11 G; Rush 2 TD; Scor 34, 6 FG, 4 XK. Dul: 7 G; Scor 17, 5 FG, 2 XK. ChiB: 4 G; Rush 2 TD; Scor 17, 1 FG, 2 XK. **1924** ChiB: 11 G; Pass 1 TD; Rush 4 TD; Rec 1 TD; PR **1** TD; Scor **75**, **9** FG, 12 XK; Tot TD 6. **1925** ChiB: 17 G; Pass 3 TD; Rush 5 TD; Rec 1 TD; Scor 62, 3 FG, 17 XK; Tot TD 6. **1927** ChiB: 14 G; Pass 1 TD; Rush 1 TD; Rec 1 TD; Scor 16, 4 XK; Tot TD 2. **1928** ChiB: 13 G; Pass 3 TD; Rush 4 TD; Scor 30, 6 XK. **1929** ChiB: 15 G; Scor 8, 8 XK. **1930** ChiB: 9 G; Pass 2 TD; Rush 1 TD; Scor 11, 5 XK. **Total:** 102 G; Pass 10 TD; Rush 21 TD; Rec 4 TD; PR 1 TD; Scor 268, 18 FG, 58 XK; Tot TD 26.

GIL STERR Sterr, Gilbert N 5'6", 150 **BB**
(Pee Wee) *Col:* Carroll (Wis.) *HS:* Beaver Dam [WI] B: 7/3/1900, Beaver Dam, WI D: 3/12/1974, Beaver Dam, WI
1926 Rac: 3 G.

BILL STETZ Stetz, William Alan 6'3", 250 **OG**
Col: Boston College *HS:* Catholic Memorial [Waukesha, WI]
B: 9/28/1945, Milwaukee, WI *Drafted:* 1967 Round 13 NO
1967 Phi: 2 G.

BOB STEUBER Steuber, Robert James 6'2", 200 **FB-HB-LB-DB**
Col: Missouri; DePauw *HS:* Christian Brothers Acad. [St. Louis, MO]
B: 10/25/1921, Wenonah, NJ D: 11/29/1996, St. Louis, MO
Drafted: 1943 Round 1 ChiB
AAFC **1946** CleA: Rec 1-9 9.0; KR 2-53 26.5; Int 1-52. **1948** BufA: Pass 2-1 50.0%, -4 -2.00; Rec 2-14 7.0; KR 6-123 20.5; Punt 1-40 40.0; Scor 41, 1-2 50.0% FG, 20-23 87.0% XK. **Total:** Pass 2-1 50.0%, -4 -2.00; Rec 3-23 7.7; KR 8-176 22.0; Int 1-52; Punt 1-40 40.0; Scor 41, 1-2 50.0% FG, 20-23 87.0% XK.

		Rushing			
Year Team	**G**	**Att**	**Yds**	**Avg**	**TD**
1946 CleA	6	8	19	2.4	0
1947 LA-A	3	1	2	2.0	0
1948 BufA	9	69	437	6.3	3
AAFC Total	18	78	458	5.9	3

NFL **1943** ChiB: 1 G; Rush 1-3 3.0.

TODD STEUSSIE Steussie, Todd Edward 6'6", 313 **OT**
Col: California *HS:* Agoura [CA] B: 12/1/1970, Canoga Park, CA
Drafted: 1994 Round 1 Min
1994 Min: 16 G. **1995** Min: 16 G. **1996** Min: 16 G. **1997** Min: 16 G. **1998** Min: 15 G. **Total:** 79 G.

DON STEVENS Stevens, Donald James 5'9", 176 **HB-DB**
Col: Illinois *HS:* South [Youngstown, OH] B: 5/25/1928, Massillon, OH
Drafted: 1952 Round 30 Phi
1952 Phi: Rec 13-174 13.4; PR 16-172 10.8 1 TD; KR 16-433 27.1.
1954 Phi: KR 1-6 6.0. **Total:** Rec 13-174 13.4; PR 16-172 10.8 1 TD; KR 17-439 25.8.

		Rushing				
Year Team	**G**	**Att**	**Yds**	**Avg**	**TD**	**Fum**
1952 Phi	11	33	95	2.9	0	7
1954 Phi	4	0	0	—	0	0
NFL Total	15	33	95	2.9	0	7

HOWARD STEVENS Stevens, Howard Melvin Jr. 5'5", 165 **RB**
Col: Randolph-Macon; Louisville *HS:* Harrisonburg [WV] B: 2/9/1950, Harrisonburg, WV *Drafted:* 1973 Round 16 NO
1973 NO: Rec 4-39 9.8. **1974** NO: Rec 13-81 6.2. **Total:** Rec 17-120 7.1.

		Rushing				Punt Returns			
Year Team	**G**	**Att**	**Yds**	**Avg**	**TD**	**Ret**	**Yds**	**Avg**	**TD**
1973 NO	14	45	183	4.1	2	17	171	10.1	0
1974 NO	14	43	190	4.4	1	37	376	10.2	0
1975 Bal	12	0	0	—	0	36	396	11.0	0
1976 Bal	14	1	3	3.0	1	39	315	8.1	0
1977 Bal	12	0	0	—	0	34	301	8.9	0
NFL Total	66	89	376	4.2	4	163	1559	9.6	0

	Kickoff Returns				
Year Team	**Ret**	**Yds**	**Avg**	**TD**	**Fum**
1973 NO	26	590	22.7	0	9
1974 NO	33	749	22.7	0	7
1975 Bal	3	71	23.7	0	3
1976 Bal	30	710	23.7	0	6
1977 Bal	11	216	19.6	0	5
NFL Total	103	2336	22.7	0	30

MARK STEVENS Stevens, Mark 6'1", 190 **QB**
Col: Coll. of Eastern Utah (J.C.); Purdue; Utah *HS:* Passaic [NJ]
B: 2/19/1962, Passaic, NJ
1987 SF: 2 G; Pass 4-2 50.0%, 52 13.00 1 TD; Rush 10-45 4.5 1 TD; 6 Pt.

MATT STEVENS Stevens, Matt Brian 6'0", 206 **DB**
Col: Appalachian State *HS:* Chapel Hill [NC] B: 6/15/1973, Chapel Hill, NC *Drafted:* 1996 Round 3 Buf
1996 Buf: 13 G; Int 2-0. **1997** Phi: 11 G; Int 1-0. **1998** Phi-Was: 10 G. Phi: 7 G. Was: 3 G. **Total:** 34 G; Int 3-0.

MATT STEVENS Stevens, Matthew Anthony 6'0", 190 **QB**
Col: UCLA *HS:* Fountain Valley [CA] B: 7/30/1964, Sulphur, LA
1987 KC: Rush 3-7 2.3.

		Passing							
Year Team	**G**	**Att**	**Comp**	**Comp%**	**Yds**	**YPA**	**TD**	**Int**	**Rating**
1987 KC	3	57	32	56.1	315	5.53	1	1	70.4

PETE STEVENS Stevens, Peter Paul 6'0", 215 **C-LB**
Col: Temple *HS:* Pitman [PA] B: 6/18/1909, Wilkes-Barre, PA
D: 5/5/1989, Melbourne, FL
1936 Phi: 4 G.

DICK STEVENS Stevens, Richard Glenn 6'4", 240 **OT**
Col: Baylor *HS:* Dublin [TX] B: 2/23/1948, Dublin, TX *Drafted:* 1970 Round 13 Phi
1970 Phi: 14 G. **1971** Phi: 14 G. **1972** Phi: 7 G. **1973** Phi: 11 G. **1974** Phi: 14 G. **Total:** 60 G.

BILLY STEVENS Stevens, William S 6'2", 195 **QB**
Col: Texas-El Paso *HS:* Ball [Galveston, TX] B: 8/27/1945, Galveston, TX *Drafted:* 1968 Round 3 GB
1968 GB: 2 G; Pass 2-0. **1969** GB: 1 G; Pass 3-1 33.3%, 12 4.00.
Total: 3 G; Pass 5-1 20.0%, 12 2.40.

ART STEVENSON Stevenson, Arthur 6'0", 190 **C**
Col: Fordham B: 12/27/1897 D: 6/1986, Brooklyn, NY
1926 NYG-Bkn: 4 G. NYG: 2 G. Bkn: 2 G. **1928** NYY: 1 G. **Total:** 5 G.

MARK STEVENSON Stevenson, Mark Oliver 6'3", 285 **OG-C**
Col: Missouri; Western Illinois *HS:* Rock Island [IL] B: 2/24/1956, Waukegan, IL
1985 Det: 2 G.

MARK STEVENSON Stevenson, Martin Lindsey 196 **G-C**
Col: Notre Dame *HS:* East [Columbus, OH] B: 3/1893 D: 3/30/1961, Columbus, OH
1922 Col: 8 G.

RALPH STEVENSON Stevenson, Ralph Lee 5'10", 196 **G-LB**
Col: Oklahoma *HS:* Ponca City [OK] B: 4/11/1917, Ponca City, OK
D: 7/7/1987, Norman, OK *Drafted:* 1940 Round 18 Cle
1940 Cle: 3 G.

RICKY STEVENSON Stevenson, Ricky Anthony 5'11", 188 **DB**
Col: Indian Hills CC IA; Arizona *HS:* McKinley [St. Louis, MO]
B: 6/27/1948, St. Louis, MO *Drafted:* 1970 Round 4 Cle
1970 Cle: 1 G.

NORRIS STEVERSON Steverson, Norris Joseph 5'10", 185 **TB-DB**
(Steve) *Col:* Arizona State *HS:* Mesa [AZ] B: 7/20/1910, Mesa, AZ
1934 Cin: 5 G; Pass 3-1 33.3%, 14 4.67; Rush 8-22 2.8.

DEAN STEWARD Steward, Harold Dean Jr. 6'0", 210 **HB**
Col: Ursinus *HS:* Parsippany [NJ] B: 7/12/1923, Elizabeth, NJ
D: 7/8/1979, Budd Lake, NJ
1943 PhPt: 6 G; Rush 1-(-6) -6.0; Punt 2-84 42.0.

ANDREW STEWART Stewart, Andrew 6'5", 265 **DE**
Col: Fresno City Coll. CA (J.C.); Cincinnati *HS:* West Hempstead [NY]
B: 11/20/1965, Queens, NY *Drafted:* 1989 Round 4 Cle
1989 Cle: 16 G; 3 Sac.

CHARLIE STEWART Stewart, Charles Edward 5'9", 160 **G**
Col: Cornell; Colgate *HS:* Williston Northampton School [Easthampson, MA] B: 7/8/1890, Pittsfield, MA D: 12/18/1965, North Grafton, MA
1920 Roch: 2 G. **1923** Akr: 2 G. **Total:** 4 G.

CURTIS STEWART Stewart, Curtis James 5'11", 208 **RB**
Col: Auburn *HS:* Jefferson Davis [Montgomery, AL] B: 6/4/1963, Montgomery, AL
1989 Dal: 2 G.

JAMES STEWART Stewart, James 6'2", 238 **RB**
Col: Miami (Fla.) *HS:* Vero Beach [FL] B: 12/8/1971, Vero Beach, FL
Drafted: 1995 Round 5 Min
1995 Min: Rec 1-3 3.0.

		Rushing				
Year Team	**G**	**Att**	**Yds**	**Avg**	**TD**	**Fum**
1995 Min	4	31	144	4.6	0	2

JIMMY STEWART Stewart, James 5'11", 190 **DB**
Col: Tulsa *HS:* Normandy [St. Louis, MO] B: 10/15/1954, St. Louis, MO *Drafted:* 1977 Round 8 NO
1977 NO: 9 G; KR 1-33 33.0. **1979** Det: 5 G. **Total:** 14 G; KR 1-33 33.0.

JAMES STEWART Stewart, James Ottis 6'1", 233 **RB**
(Little Man) *Col:* Tennessee *HS:* Hamblen West [Morristown, TN]
B: 12/27/1971, Morristown, TN *Drafted:* 1995 Round 1 Jac

		Rushing				Receiving					Tot
Year Team	**G**	**Att**	**Yds**	**Avg**	**TD**	**Rec**	**Yds**	**Avg**	**TD**	**Fum**	**TD**
1995 Jac	14	137	525	3.8	2	21	190	9.0	1	1	3
1996 Jac	13	190	723	3.8	8	30	177	5.9	2	2	10
1997 Jac	16	136	555	4.1	8	41	336	8.2	1	0	9
1998 Jac	3	53	217	4.1	2	6	42	7.0	1	2	3
NFL Total	46	516	2020	3.9	20	98	745	7.6	5	5	25

JOE STEWART Stewart, Joseph Lawrence 5'11", 180 **WR**
Col: Missouri *HS:* Evanston Twp. [Evanston, IL] B: 11/18/1955, Evanston, IL *Drafted:* 1978 Round 4 Oak
1978 Oak: 16 G; KR 4-120 30.0. **1979** Oak: 3 G; Rec 1-3 3.0; KR 2-63 31.5. **Total:** 19 G; Rec 1-3 3.0; KR 6-183 30.5.

KORDELL STEWART Stewart, Kordell 6'1", 212 **QB-WR-RB**
(Slash) *Col:* Colorado *HS:* John Ehret [Marrero, LA] B: 10/16/1972, New Orleans, LA *Drafted:* 1995 Round 2 Pit
1998 Pit: Punt 1-35 35.0. **Total:** Punt 1-35 35.0.

		Passing							
Year Team	**G**	**Att**	**Comp**	**Comp%**	**Yds**	**YPA**	**TD**	**Int**	**Rating**
1995 Pit	10	7	5	71.4	60	8.57	1	0	136.9
1996 Pit	16	30	11	36.7	100	3.33	0	2	18.8
1997 Pit	16	440	236	53.6	3020	6.86	21	17	75.2
1998 Pit	16	458	252	55.0	2560	5.59	11	18	62.9
NFL Total	58	935	504	53.9	5740	6.14	33	37	67.9

	Rushing				Receiving					Tot
Year Team	**Att**	**Yds**	**Avg**	**TD**	**Rec**	**Yds**	**Avg**	**TD**	**Fum**	**TD**
1995 Pit	15	86	5.7	1	14	235	16.8	1	0	2
1996 Pit	39	171	4.4	5	17	293	17.2	3	1	8
1997 Pit	88	476	5.4	11	0	0	—	0	6	11
1998 Pit	81	406	5.0	2	1	17	17.0	0	3	2
NFL Total	223	1139	5.1	19	32	545	17.0	4	10	23

MARK STEWART Stewart, Mark Anthony 6′2″, 230 **LB**
Col: Washington *HS:* Camden [San Jose, CA] B: 10/13/1959, Palo Alto, CA
1984 Min: 4 G.

MICHAEL STEWART Stewart, Michael Anthony 5′11″, 197 **DB**
Col: Bakersfield Coll. CA (J.C.); Fresno State *HS:* Bakersfield [CA] B: 7/12/1965, Atascadero, CA *Drafted:* 1987 Round 8 LARm
1987 LARm: Scor **1** Saf. **1988** LARm: KR 1-0; 1 Sac. **1991** LARm: 1 Sac. **1992** LARm: 2 Sac. **1993** LARm: 1 Sac. **Total:** KR 1-0; Scor 1 Saf; 5 Sac.

		Interceptions			
Year Team	G	Int	Yds	TD	Fum
1987 LARm	12	0	0	0	0
1988 LARm	16	2	61	0	0
1989 LARm	16	2	76	1	1
1990 LARm	16	0	0	0	0
1991 LARm	16	2	8	0	0
1992 LARm	11	0	0	0	0
1993 LARm	16	1	30	0	0
1994 Mia	16	3	11	0	0
1995 Mia	16	1	0	0	0
1996 Mia	9	0	0	0	0
NFL Total	144	11	186	1	1

RALPH STEWART Stewart, Ralph Edward 6′0″, 205 **C-LB**
Col: Notre Dame; Missouri *HS:* McKinley [St. Louis, MO] B: 12/10/1925, St. Louis, MO
AAFC **1947** NY-A: 9 G. **1948** NY-A-BalA: 15 G. **Total:** 24 G.

RAYNA STEWART Stewart, Rayna Cottrell II 5′10″, 198 **DB**
Col: Northern Arizona *HS:* Chatsworth [CA] B: 6/18/1973, Oklahoma City, OK *Drafted:* 1996 Round 5 Hou
1996 Hou: 15 G. **1997** Ten: 16 G; 0.5 Sac. **1998** Mia: 14 G. **Total:** 45 G; 0.5 Sac.

RYAN STEWART Stewart, Ryan Evan 6′1″, 207 **DB**
Col: Georgia Tech *HS:* Berkeley [Moncks Corner, SC] B: 9/30/1973, Moncks Corner, SC *Drafted:* 1996 Round 3 Det
1996 Det: 14 G; Int 1-14. **1997** Det: 8 G. **1998** Det: 16 G. **Total:** 38 G; Int 1-14.

STEVE STEWART Stewart, Steven Andrew 6′2″, 217 **LB**
Col: Minnesota *HS:* Richfield [MN] B: 5/1/1956, Minneapolis, MN *Drafted:* 1978 Round 2 Atl
1978 Atl: 12 G. **1979** GB: 3 G. **Total:** 15 G.

VAUGHN STEWART Stewart, Vaughn Morton 6′1″, 190 **C-LB**
Col: Alabama *HS:* Anniston [AL] B: 1/16/1919, Anniston, AL D: 12/18/1992, Huntsville, AL
1943 Bkn-ChiC: 10 G. Bkn: 1 G. ChiC: 9 G. **1944** Bkn: 9 G. **Total:** 19 G.

WAYNE STEWART Stewart, Wayne Murray 6′7″, 219 **TE**
Col: California *HS:* Earl Warren [Downey, CA] B: 8/18/1947, Cochrane, Canada *Drafted:* 1969 Round 15 NYJ
1974 SD: KR 1-1 1.0. **Total:** KR 1-1 1.0.

		Receiving				
Year Team	G	Rec	Yds	Avg	TD	Fum
1969 NYJ	14	5	39	7.8	0	0
1970 NYJ	7	1	7	7.0	0	0
1971 NYJ	3	0	0	—	0	0
1972 NYJ	14	2	26	13.0	1	0
1974 SD	14	19	283	14.9	1	1
NFL Total	52	27	355	13.1	2	1

WALT STICKEL Stickel, Walter Eugene 6′3″, 247 **DT-OT**
Col: Tulsa; Pennsylvania *HS:* Northeast [Philadelphia, PA] B: 3/31/1922, Philadelphia, PA D: 12/6/1987, Tequesta, FL *Drafted:* 1945 Round 19 ChiB
1946 ChiB: 11 G. **1947** ChiB: 12 G. **1948** ChiB: 10 G. **1949** ChiB: 12 G. **1950** Phi: 12 G. **1951** Phi: 11 G; Scor **1** Saf; 2 Pt. **Total:** 68 G; Scor 1 Saf; 2 Pt.

MONTY STICKLES Stickles, Montford Anthony 6′4″, 235 **TE**
(Iron Jaw) *Col:* Notre Dame *HS:* Poughkeepsie [NY] B: 8/16/1938, Kingston, NY *Drafted:* 1960 Round 1 SF
1963 SF: KR 1-0. **Total:** KR 1-0.

		Receiving				
Year Team	G	Rec	Yds	Avg	TD	Fum
1960 SF	12	22	252	11.5	0	0
1961 SF	14	43	794	18.5	5	0
1962 SF	14	22	366	16.6	3	0
1963 SF	12	11	152	13.8	0	1
1964 SF	14	40	685	17.1	3	1
1965 SF	14	35	343	9.8	1	0
1966 SF	14	27	315	11.7	2	0
1967 SF	8	7	86	12.3	0	0
1968 NO	13	15	206	13.7	2	0
NFL Total	115	222	3199	14.4	16	2

HOWARD STIDHAM Stidham, Howard 6′2″, 215 **LB**
Col: Tennessee Tech *HS:* North Hardin [Radcliff, KY] B: 12/17/1954, Radcliff, KY *Drafted:* 1976 Round 15 SF
1977 SF: 4 G.

DAVE STIEF Stief, David P 6′3″, 195 **WR-DB**
Col: Portland State *HS:* John Marshall [Portland, OR] B: 1/29/1956, Portland, OR *Drafted:* 1978 Round 7 StL
1978 StL: Pass 1-1 100.0%, 43 43.00; Rush 1-(-8) -8.0. **1981** StL: Rush 1-8 8.0. **Total:** Pass 1-1 100.0%, 43 43.00; Rush 2-0.

		Receiving				
Year Team	G	Rec	Yds	Avg	TD	Fum
1978 StL	15	24	477	19.9	4	0
1979 StL	16	22	324	14.7	0	2
1980 StL	16	16	165	10.3	0	0
1981 StL	12	5	77	15.4	1	0
1982 StL	9	0	0	—	0	0
1983 Was	3	0	0	—	0	0
NFL Total	71	67	1043	15.6	5	2

JIM STIENKE Stienke, James Lee 5′11″, 182 **DB**
Col: Southwest Texas State *HS:* Lyndon B. Johnson [Johnson City, TX] B: 11/7/1950, Houston, TX *Drafted:* 1973 Round 2 Cle
1973 Cle: 7 G. **1974** NYG: 13 G. **1975** NYG: 14 G; Int 2-41. **1976** NYG: 13 G; PR 3-18 6.0; Int 2-0; 6 Pt. **1977** NYG: 14 G; PR 5-30 6.0; 1 Fum. **1978** Atl: 5 G. **Total:** 66 G; PR 8-48 6.0; Int 4-41; 6 Pt; 1 Fum.

TERRY STIEVE Stieve, Terrence Allan 6′2″, 256 **OG**
Col: Wisconsin *HS:* Baraboo [WI] B: 3/10/1954, Baraboo, WI *Drafted:* 1976 Round 6 NO
1976 NO: 14 G. **1977** NO: 14 G. **1978** StL: 16 G. **1979** StL: 14 G. **1981** StL: 16 G. **1982** StL: 9 G. **1983** StL: 16 G. **1984** StL: 14 G. **Total:** 113 G.

JIM STIFLER Stifler, James Madison 5′10″, 175 **E-WB**
Col: Brown *HS:* Peddie School [Highstown, NJ] B: 8/25/1901, Swarthmore, PA D: 7/17/1954, Boston, MA
1926 Prov: 7 G. **1927** Prov: 2 G. **Total:** 9 G.

JIM STIGER Stiger, James Edward 5′10″, 214 **FB**
Col: Bakersfield Coll. CA (J.C.); Washington *HS:* Corcoran [CA] B: 1/7/1941, Carthio, TX D: 12/12/1981, Lompoc, CA *Drafted:* 1963 Round 19 Dal
1964 Dal: Pass 1-0. **Total:** Pass 1-0.

		Rushing				Receiving			
Year Team	G	Att	Yds	Avg	TD	Rec	Yds	Avg	TD
1963 Dal	14	31	140	4.5	1	13	131	10.1	0
1964 Dal	14	68	280	4.1	1	9	85	9.4	1
1965 Dal-LARm	11	14	62	4.4	0	1	9	9.0	0
1965 Dal	5	11	50	4.5	0	1	9	9.0	0
1965 LARm	6	3	12	4.0	0	0	0	—	0
1966 LARm	14	24	95	4.0	0	8	72	9.0	1
1967 LARm	5	3	6	2.0	0	0	0	—	0
NFL Total	58	140	583	4.2	2	31	297	9.6	2

	Punt Returns				Kickoff Returns					Tot
Year Team	Ret	Yds	Avg	TD	Ret	Yds	Avg	TD	Fum	TD
1963 Dal	14	141	10.1	0	18	432	24.0	0	4	1
1964 Dal	1	0	0.0	0	0	0	—	0	0	2
1965 Dal-LARm	16	120	7.5	0	2	28	14.0	0	2	0
1965 Dal	3	14	4.7	0	2	28	14.0	0	1	0
1965 LARm	13	106	8.2	0	0	0	—	0	1	0
1966 LARm	33	259	7.8	0	7	150	21.4	0	2	1
1967 LARm	4	9	2.3	0	0	0	—	0	0	0
NFL Total	68	529	7.8	0	27	610	22.6	0	8	4

ART STILL Still, Arthur Barry 6′7″, 253 **DE**
Col: Kentucky *HS:* Camden [NJ] B: 12/5/1955, Camden, NJ *Drafted:* 1978 Round 1 KC
1978 KC: 16 G. **1979** KC: 16 G. **1980** KC: 16 G. **1981** KC: 11 G. **1982** KC: 9 G; 4 Sac. **1983** KC: 15 G; 4 Sac. **1984** KC: 16 G; 14.5 Sac. **1985** KC: 9 G; 4 Sac. **1986** KC: 16 G; 10.5 Sac. **1987** KC: 12 G; 5.5 Sac. **1988** Buf: 15 G; 6 Sac. **1989** Buf: 16 G; Int 1-10. **Total:** 167 G; Int 1-10; 48.5 Sac.

BRYAN STILL Still, Bryan Andrei 5′11″, 174 **WR**
Col: Virginia Tech *HS:* Huguenot [Richmond, VA] B: 6/3/1974, Newport News, VA *Drafted:* 1996 Round 2 SD
1996 SD: PR 1-1 1.0; KR 4-113 28.3. **Total:** PR 1-1 1.0; KR 4-113 28.3.

		Receiving				
Year Team	G	Rec	Yds	Avg	TD	Fum
1996 SD	16	6	142	23.7	0	2
1997 SD	15	24	324	13.5	0	0
1998 SD	14	43	605	14.1	2	0
NFL Total	45	73	1071	14.7	2	2

JIM STILL Still, James Edward Jr. 6'3", 193 **QB-DB**
Col: Mississippi Gulf Coast CC; Georgia Tech *HS:* Panama City [FL]
B: 3/5/1924, Columbia, SC
AAFC **1948** BufA: Pass 14-5 35.7%, 89 6.36 1 TD 3 Int; Rush 5-(-26) -5.2; Int 1-37. **1949** BufA: Pass 12-6 50.0%, 86 7.17 1 TD 1 Int; Rush 2-6 3.0. **Total:** Pass 26-11 42.3%, 175 6.73 2 TD 4 Int; Rush 7-(-20) -2.9; Int 1-37.

		Punting		
Year Team	G	Punts	Yds	Avg
1948 BufA	12	47	1825	38.8
1949 BufA	9	16	614	38.4
AAFC Total	21	63	2439	38.7

KEN STILLS Stills, Kenneth Lee 5'10", 185 **DB**
Col: El Camino Coll. CA (J.C.); Wisconsin *HS:* El Camino [Oceanside, CA] B: 9/6/1963, Oceanside, CA *Drafted:* 1985 Round 8 GB
1985 GB: 8 G; KR 1-14 14.0. **1986** GB: 16 G; KR 10-209 20.9; Int 1-58 1 TD; 6 Pt; 1 Fum. **1987** GB: 11 G. **1988** GB: 14 G; KR 1-4 4.0; Int 3-29; 1 Sac. **1989** GB: 16 G; Int 3-20. **1990** Min: 12 G. **Total:** 77 G; KR 12-227 18.9; Int 7-107 1 TD; 6 Pt; 1 Fum; 1 Sac.

ROGER STILLWELL Stillwell, Roger Howard 6'5", 260 **DT-DE**
Col: Coll. of Marin CA (J.C.); Stanford *HS:* J.E.B. Stuart [Falls Church, VA] B: 11/17/1951, Santa Monica, CA *Drafted:* 1975 Round 9 ChiB
1975 ChiB: 13 G. **1976** ChiB: 13 G. **1977** ChiB: 5 G. **Total:** 31 G.

PETE STINCHCOMB Stinchcomb, Gaylord Roscoe 5'8", 157 **HB-WB-TB-QB**
Col: Ohio State *HS:* Fostoria [OH] B: 6/24/1895, Sycamore, OH
D: 8/24/1973, Findlay, OH
1921 Sta: 11 G; Rush 4 TD; 24 Pt. **1922** ChiB: 12 G; Rush 3 TD; 18 Pt. **1923** Col-Cle: 8 G. Col: 7 G. Cle: 1 G. **1926** Lou: 3 G. **Total:** 34 G; Rush 7 TD; 42 Pt.

THOMAS STINCIC Stincic, Thomas Dorn 6'4", 230 **LB**
Col: Michigan *HS:* John Marshall [Cleveland, OH] B: 11/24/1946, Cleveland, OH *Drafted:* 1969 Round 3 Dal
1969 Dal: 14 G. **1970** Dal: 14 G; Int 1-11. **1971** Dal: 7 G. **1972** NO: 7 G. **Total:** 42 G; Int 1-11.

DARRYL STINGLEY Stingley, Darryl Floyd 6'0", 194 **WR**
Col: Purdue *HS:* John Marshall [Chicago, IL] B: 9/18/1951, Chicago, IL *Drafted:* 1973 Round 1 NE
1973 NE: PR 3-21 7.0; KR 6-143 23.8. **1975** NE: PR 15-113 7.5; KR 2-44 22.0. **1976** NE: PR 1-2 2.0. **Total:** PR 19-136 7.2; KR 8-187 23.4.

		Rushing				Receiving					Tot
Year Team	G	Att	Yds	Avg	TD	Rec	Yds	Avg	TD	Fum	TD
1973 NE	14	6	64	10.7	0	23	339	14.7	2	1	2
1974 NE	5	5	63	12.6	1	10	139	13.9	1	0	2
1975 NE	14	6	39	6.5	0	21	378	18.0	2	2	2
1976 NE	13	8	45	5.6	0	17	370	21.8	4	1	4
1977 NE	14	3	33	11.0	1	39	657	16.8	5	0	6
NFL Total	60	28	244	8.7	2	110	1883	17.1	14	4	16

JAMES STINNETTE Stinnette, James Edward 6'1", 230 **FB-LB**
Col: Oregon State *HS:* Corvallis [OR] B: 12/3/1938, Corvallis, OR
Drafted: 1960 Round 1 NYT
1961 Den: Rec 11-58 5.3 1 TD; KR 1-6 6.0; Int 1-40. **1962** Den: Rec 13-109 8.4; KR 2-27 13.5. **Total:** Rec 24-167 7.0 1 TD; KR 3-33 11.0; Int 1-40.

		Rushing					Tot
Year Team	G	Att	Yds	Avg	TD	Fum	TD
1961 Den	14	18	8	0.4	0	1	1
1962 Den	10	21	87	4.1	1	1	1
NFL Total	24	39	95	2.4	1	2	2

LEMUEL STINSON Stinson, Lemuel Dale 5'9", 166 **DB**
Col: Texas Tech *HS:* Evan E. Worthing [Houston, TX] B: 5/10/1966, Houston, TX *Drafted:* 1988 Round 6 ChiB

		Interceptions		
Year Team	G	Int	Yds	TD
1988 ChiB	15	0	0	0
1989 ChiB	12	4	59	1
1990 ChiB	10	6	66	0
1991 ChiB	16	4	69	1
1992 ChiB	16	2	46	0
NFL Total	69	16	240	2

CAREL STITH Stith, Carel Lewis 6'5", 270 **DT-DE**
Col: Nebraska *HS:* Southeast [Lincoln, NE] B: 5/24/1945, Lincoln, NE
Drafted: 1967 Round 4 Hou
1967 Hou: 14 G. **1968** Hou: 3 G. **1969** Hou: 14 G. **Total:** 31 G.

HOWARD STITH Stith, Howard Seymour 1 **G**
Col: No College D: 4/6/1951, Louisville, KY
1921 Lou: 1 G.

BILL STITS Stits, William David 6'0", 194 **DB-HB**
Col: UCLA *HS:* Nathaniel Narbonne [Los Angeles, CA] B: 7/26/1931, Lomita, CA *Drafted:* 1954 Round 4 Det
1955 Det: Pass 2-2 100.0%, 62 31.00 1 TD; Rec 5-17 3.4. **1956** Det: Pass 1-0, 1 Int; Rec 3-52 17.3. **Total:** Pass 3-2 66.7%, 62 20.67 1 TD 1 Int; Rec 8-69 8.6.

		Rushing				Punt Returns			
Year Team	G	Att	Yds	Avg	TD	Ret	Yds	Avg	TD
1954 Det	12	0	0	—	0	0	0	—	0
1955 Det	12	46	165	3.6	0	1	0	0.0	0
1956 Det	12	3	0	0.0	0	0	0	—	0
1957 SF	12	0	0	—	0	0	0	—	0
1958 SF	12	0	0	—	0	0	0	—	0
1959 Was-NYG	10	0	0	—	0	4	7	1.8	0
1959 Was	5	0	0	—	0	0	0	—	0
1959 NYG	5	0	0	—	0	4	7	1.8	0
1960 NYG	12	0	0	—	0	**18**	166	9.2	0
1961 NYG	10	0	0	—	0	17	132	7.8	0
NFL Total	92	49	165	3.4	0	40	305	7.6	0

	Kickoff Returns				Interceptions			
Year Team	Ret	Yds	Avg	TD	Int	Yds	TD	Fum
1954 Det	0	0	—	0	6	73	0	0
1955 Det	0	0	—	0	3	7	1	4
1956 Det	3	48	16.0	0	1	11	0	0
1957 SF	0	0	—	0	2	28	0	0
1958 SF	0	0	—	0	3	3	0	0
1959 Was-NYG	0	0	—	0	0	0	0	2
1959 NYG	0	0	—	0	0	0	0	2
1960 NYG	20	486	24.3	0	0	0	0	3
1961 NYG	4	87	21.8	0	0	0	0	1
NFL Total	27	621	23.0	0	15	122	1	10

BILL STOBBS Stobbs, Thomas William Jr. 5'7", 165 **BB**
Col: Washington & Jefferson *HS:* Wheeling [WV] B: 5/28/1896, Wheeling, WV D: 11/14/1968, Richmond, VA
1921 Det: 7 G.

HERB STOCK Stock, Herbert Louis 6'0", 180 **BB-FB**
Col: Kenyon *HS:* Commerce [Columbus, OH] B: 9/3/1899
1924 Col: 7 G.

JOHN STOCK Stock, John H 6'2", 210 **OE**
Col: Pittsburgh *HS:* Scott Twp. [North Braddock, PA] B: 1934
1956 Pit: 2 G.

MARK STOCK Stock, Mark Anthony 5'11", 180 **WR**
Col: Virginia Military *HS:* Marist [Atlanta, GA] B: 4/27/1966, Canton, OH *Drafted:* 1989 Round 6 Pit
1989 Pit: 8 G; Rec 4-74 18.5. **1993** Was: 3 G. **1996** Ind: 14 G; Rec 2-24 12.0; PR 5-13 2.6; KR 12-254 21.2. **Total:** 25 G; Rec 6-98 16.3; PR 5-13 2.6; KR 12-254 21.2.

RALPH STOCKEMER Stockemer, Ralph William 6'1", 212 **RB**
Col: Baylor *HS:* Alma [AR] B: 12/20/1962, Shreveport, LA
1987 KC: 2 G; Rush 1-2 2.0; Rec 1-4 4.0.

HUST STOCKTON Stockton, John Houston 5'11", 193 **FB-TB**
(Bud) *Col:* Gonzaga *HS:* Parma [ID] B: 9/23/1901 D: 4/1967, Bremerton, WA
1925 Fra: 14 G; Pass 7 TD. **1926** Fra: 17 G; Pass 5 TD; Rush 2 TD; 12 Pt. **1928** Fra: 13 G; Rush 3 TD; Int **1** TD; Tot TD 4; 24 Pt. **1929** Prov-Bost: 9 G; Pass 3 TD; Rush 1 TD; 6 Pt. Prov: 1 G; Pass 1 TD. Bost: 8 G; Pass 2 TD; Rush 1 TD; 6 Pt. **Total:** 53 G; Pass 15 TD; Rush 6 TD; Int 1 TD; Tot TD 7; 42 Pt.

MULE STOCKTON Stockton, Willis Herschel 6'1", 214 **G**
Col: McMurry *HS:* Crosbyton [TX] B: 12/29/1913, Abilene, TX
D: 11/12/1965, Odessa, TX
1937 Phi: 11 G. **1938** Phi: 11 G. **Total:** 22 G.

ERIC STOCZ Stocz, Eric Richard 6'4", 258 **TE**
Col: Westminster (Pa.) *HS:* Lakeview [Cortland, OH] B: 5/25/1974, Warren, OH
1996 Det: 1 G. **1997** Det: 6 G. **Total:** 7 G.

EARL STOECKLEIN Stoecklein, Earl E 6'2", 205 **G**
(Stecks) *Col:* No College *HS:* None B: 10/1/1896, Dayton, OH
D: 1/6/1975, Bridgeport, CT
1920 Day: 2 G.

TERRY STOEPEL Stoepel, Terry K 6'4", 235 **TE-OT**
Col: Tulsa *HS:* Richardson [TX] B: 2/8/1945, Cincinnati, OH
1967 ChiB: 6 G; Rec 1-6 6.0; KR 1-0. **1970** Hou: 14 G. **Total:** 20 G; Rec 1-6 6.0; KR 1-0.

JOHN STOFA Stofa, John Carl 6'3", 210 **QB**
Col: Buffalo *HS:* Bishop McCort [Johnstown, PA] B: 6/29/1942, Johnstown, PA
1966 Mia: Rush 3-17 5.7. **1967** Mia: Rush 2-2 1.0 1 TD. **1968** Cin: Rush 10-1 0.1. **1970** Mia: Rush 2-5 2.5. **Total:** Rush 17-25 1.5 1 TD.

Year Team	G	Passing Att	Comp	Comp%	Yds	YPA	TD	Int	Rating	Fum
1966 Mia	7	57	29	50.9	425	7.46	4	2	84.3	1
1967 Mia	1	2	2	100.0	51	25.50	0	0	118.8	1
1968 Cin	10	177	85	48.0	896	5.06	5	**5**	60.8	5
1969 Mia	1	23	14	60.9	146	6.35	0	2	43.0	0
1970 Mia	8	53	16	30.2	240	4.53	3	2	49.3	0
NFL Total	27	312	146	46.8	1758	5.63	12	11	62.7	7

KEN STOFER Stofer, Kenneth Lamont 5′9″, 188 **QB-DB**
Col: Cornell *HS:* Olmstead Falls [OH]; Dickinson Seminary [Williamsport, PA] B: 8/10/1919, Lakewood, OH
AAFC **1946** BufA: 11 G; Pass 26-9 34.6%, 86 3.31 1 TD 1 Int; Rush 16-36 2.3; Rec 1-14 14.0; PR 5-53 10.6; KR 2-81 40.5; Punt 3-108 36.0.

ED STOFKO Stofko, Albert Edward 6′1″, 192 **TB-DB**
Col: St. Francis (Pa.) *HS:* Johnstown [PA] B: 5/17/1920, Johnstown, PA D: 12/19/1988, Johnstown, PA *Drafted:* 1944 Round 9 Pit
1945 Pit: 2 G; Pass 17-7 41.2%, 94 5.53 4 Int; Rush 13-(-16) -1.2; Punt 3-109 36.3; 1 Fum.

FRANK STOJACK Stojack, Frank Nicholas 5′10″, 194 **G**
(Toughie) *Col:* Washington State *HS:* Lincoln [Tacoma, WA] B: 2/11/1912, Wycliff, Canada D: 8/30/1987, Tacoma, WA
1935 Bkn: 12 G. **1936** Bkn: 11 G. **Total:** 23 G.

BARRY STOKES Stokes, Barry Wade 6′4″, 288 **OG**
Col: Eastern Michigan *HS:* Davison [MI] B: 12/20/1973, Davison, MI
1998 Mia: 3 G.

ERIC STOKES Stokes, Eric 5′11″, 200 **DB**
Col: Nebraska *HS:* Lincoln East [NE] B: 12/18/1973, Hebron, NE *Drafted:* 1997 Round 5 Sea
1997 Sea: 7 G. **1998** Sea: 4 G. **Total:** 11 G.

ERIC STOKES Stokes, Eric R 6′4″, 255 **C-OG**
Col: Northeastern *HS:* Ansonia [CT] B: 1/13/1962, Derby, CT
1987 NE: 1 G.

J.J. STOKES Stokes, Jerel Jamal 6′4″, 219 **WR**
Col: UCLA *HS:* Point Loma [San Diego, CA] B: 10/6/1972, San Diego, CA *Drafted:* 1995 Round 1 SF

Year Team	G	Receiving Rec	Yds	Avg	TD	Fum
1995 SF	12	38	517	13.6	4	0
1996 SF	6	18	249	13.8	0	0
1997 SF	16	58	733	12.6	4	1
1998 SF	16	63	770	12.2	8	0
NFL Total	50	177	2269	12.8	16	1

JESSE STOKES Stokes, Jesse Van 6′0″, 190 **DB**
Col: Corpus Christi *HS:* Doyle [TX] B: 8/27/1944, Kerrville, TX
1968 Den: 2 G; KR 5-106 21.2.

DIXIE STOKES Stokes, Lee James Jr. 6′0″, 205 **C-LB**
Col: Centenary *HS:* C.E. Byrd [Shreveport, LA] B: 8/24/1913, Shreveport, LA D: 12/1967
1937 Det: 11 G. **1938** Det: 10 G. **1939** Det: 1 G. **1943** ChiC: 6 G; Scor 8, 1-3 33.3% FG, 5-6 83.3% XK. **Total:** 28 G; Scor 8, 1-3 33.3% FG, 5-6 83.3% XK.

FRED STOKES Stokes, Louis Fred 6′3″, 274 **DE**
Col: Georgia Southern *HS:* Vidalia [GA] B: 3/14/1964, Vidalia, GA *Drafted:* 1987 Round 12 LARm
1987 LARm: 8 G; 0.5 Sac. **1988** LARm: 5 G; 1 Sac. **1989** Was: 16 G; Scor **1** Saf; 2 Pt; 3 Sac. **1990** Was: 16 G; 7.5 Sac. **1991** Was: 16 G; Int 1-0; 6.5 Sac. **1992** Was: 16 G; 3.5 Sac. **1993** LARm: 15 G; 9.5 Sac. **1994** LARm: 16 G; 2 Sac. **1995** StL: 14 G; 3.5 Sac. **1996** NO: 9 G; 1 Sac. **Total:** 131 G; Int 1-0; Scor 1 Saf; 2 Pt; 38 Sac.

SIMS STOKES Stokes, Sims Edward III 6′1″, 197 **WR**
Col: Kansas; Northern Arizona *HS:* Mattie T. Blount [Prichard, AL] B: 4/18/1944, Mobile, AL *Drafted:* 1967 Round 6 Dal
1967 Dal: 3 G; KR 4-92 23.0.

TIMOTHY STOKES Stokes, Timothy Paul 6′5″, 252 **OT**
Col: Oregon *HS:* San Leandro [CA] B: 3/16/1950, Oakland, CA *Drafted:* 1973 Round 3 LARm
1974 LARm: 6 G. **1975** Was: 5 G. **1976** Was: 14 G. **1977** Was: 14 G. **1978** GB: 16 G. **1979** GB: 16 G. **1980** GB: 15 G. **1981** NYG-GB: 11 G. NYG: 3 G. GB: 8 G. **1982** GB: 8 G. **Total:** 105 G.

ANTON STOLFA Stolfa, Anton James 6′0″, 195 **QB-DB**
(Butch) *Col:* Luther *HS:* Riverside-Brookfield Twp. [Riverside, IL] B: 9/6/1917, Cicero, IL D: 5/8/1976, Iowa City, IA *Drafted:* 1939 Round 12 ChiB
1939 ChiB: 1 G.

TOM STOLHANDSKE Stolhandske, Carl Thomas 6′2″, 210 **LB-DE**
Col: Texas *HS:* Baytown [TX] B: 6/28/1931, Baytown, TX *Drafted:* 1953 Round 1 SF
1955 SF: 12 G; Int 1-6.

BRYAN STOLTENBERG Stoltenberg, Bryan Douglas 6′1″, 300 **C**
Col: Colorado *HS:* Clements [Sugar Land, TX] B: 8/25/1972, Kearney, NE *Drafted:* 1996 Round 6 SD
1996 SD: 9 G. **1997** NYG: 3 G; 1 Fum. **1998** Car: 14 G. **Total:** 26 G; 1 Fum.

AVATUS STONE Stone, Avatus Harry 6′1″, 195 **HB**
Col: Syracuse *HS:* Armstrong [Washington, DC] B: 4/21/1931, Washington, DC *Drafted:* 1953 Round 9 ChiC
1958 Bal: 1 G; Punt 1-28 28.0.

DWIGHT STONE Stone, Dwight 6′0″, 191 **RB-WR**
Col: Middle Tennessee State *HS:* Florala [AL], Marion Mil. Inst. [AL] B: 1/28/1964, Florala, AL
1994 Pit: Scor 1 2XP. **1997** Car: Scor **1** Saf. **Total:** Scor 1 Saf, 1 2XP.

Year Team	G	Rushing Att	Yds	Avg	TD	Receiving Rec	Yds	Avg	TD
1987 Pit	14	17	135	7.9	0	1	22	22.0	0
1988 Pit	16	40	127	3.2	0	11	196	17.8	1
1989 Pit	16	10	53	5.3	0	7	92	13.1	0
1990 Pit	16	2	-6	-3.0	0	19	332	17.5	1
1991 Pit	16	1	2	2.0	0	32	649	20.3	5
1992 Pit	15	12	118	9.8	0	34	501	14.7	3
1993 Pit	16	12	121	10.1	1	41	587	14.3	2
1994 Pit	15	2	7	3.5	0	7	81	11.6	0
1995 Car	16	1	3	3.0	0	0	0	—	0
1996 Car	16	1	6	6.0	0	1	11	11.0	0
1997 Car	16	0	0	—	0	0	0	—	0
1998 Car	16	0	0	—	0	1	7	7.0	0
NFL Total	188	98	566	5.8	1	154	2478	16.1	12

Year Team	Kickoff Returns Ret	Yds	Avg	TD	Fum	Tot TD
1987 Pit	28	568	20.3	0	0	0
1988 Pit	29	610	21.0	**1**	5	2
1989 Pit	7	173	24.7	0	2	0
1990 Pit	5	91	18.2	0	1	1
1991 Pit	6	75	12.5	0	0	5
1992 Pit	12	219	18.3	0	0	3
1993 Pit	11	168	15.3	0	2	3
1994 Pit	11	182	16.5	0	0	0
1995 Car	12	269	22.4	0	0	0
1997 Car	3	76	25.3	0	0	0
1998 Car	9	252	28.0	0	0	1
NFL Total	133	2683	20.2	1	10	15

DONNIE STONE Stone, Edward Donald 6′1″, 205 **FB-HB**
Col: Arkansas *HS:* Fayetteville [AR] B: 1/5/1937, Sioux City, IA
1961 Den: Pass 2-1 50.0%, 18 9.00 1 TD; KR 9-215 23.9. **1962** Den: Pass 3-1 33.3%, 13 4.33. **1963** Den: Pass 3-0. **Total:** Pass 8-2 25.0%, 31 3.88 1 TD; KR 9-215 23.9.

Year Team	G	Rushing Att	Yds	Avg	TD	Receiving Rec	Yds	Avg	TD	Fum	Tot TD
1961 Den	14	127	505	4.0	4	38	344	9.1	4	3	8
1962 Den	11	94	360	3.8	3	20	223	11.2	2	2	5
1963 Den	14	96	382	4.0	2	22	208	9.5	2	5	4
1964 Den	9	12	26	2.2	0	4	38	9.5	0	0	0
1965 Buf	14	19	61	3.2	0	6	29	4.8	0	1	0
1966 Hou	5	6	18	3.0	0	1	17	17.0	0	1	0
NFL Total	67	354	1352	3.8	9	91	859	9.4	8	12	17

JACK STONE Stone, Jack Richard 6′2″, 245 **OT**
Col: Oregon *HS:* Gresham [OR] B: 7/28/1936, Ellensburg, WA *Drafted:* 1960 Round 1 DalT
1960 DalT: 14 G. **1961** Oak: 14 G. **1962** Oak: 14 G. **Total:** 42 G.

KEN STONE Stone, Kenneth Bernard Jr. 6′1″, 179 **DB-WR**
Col: Vanderbilt *HS:* Forest Hill [West Palm Beach, FL] B: 9/14/1950, Cincinnati, OH *Drafted:* 1973 Round 10 Was
1974 Was: PR 1-2 2.0. **1976** TB: PR 1-11 11.0. **1977** StL: Rec 1-40 40.0. **1978** StL: KR 1-3 3.0. **1980** StL: KR 3-34 11.3. **Total:** Rec 1-40 40.0; PR 2-13 6.5; KR 4-37 9.3.

Year Team	G	Interceptions Int	Yds	TD
1973 Buf-Was	10	0	31	0
1973 Buf	6	0	31	0
1973 Was	4	0	0	0
1974 Was	14	5	95	0
1975 Was	3	0	0	0
1976 TB	14	2	47	0
1977 StL	14	0	0	0
1978 StL	14	9	139	0
1979 StL	16	6	70	0
1980 StL	16	5	63	0
NFL Total	101	27	445	0

RON STONE Stone, Ronald Christopher 6'5", 319 **OT-OG**
Col: Boston College *HS:* West Roxbury [Boston, MA] B: 7/20/1971, Boston, MA *Drafted:* 1993 Round 4 Dal
1994 Dal: 16 G. **1995** Dal: 16 G. **1996** NYG: 16 G. **1997** NYG: 16 G. **1998** NYG: 14 G. **Total:** 78 G.

BILLY STONE Stone, William John 6'0", 191 **HB-DB**
Col: Bradley *HS:* Lanphier [Springfield, IL] B: 10/25/1925, Peoria, IL *Drafted:* 1949 Round 12 ChiC
AAFC **1949** BalA: KR 1-25 25.0.

		Rushing				Receiving				Tot
Year Team	G	Att	Yds	Avg	TD	Rec	Yds	Avg	TD	TD
1949 BalA	12	51	205	4.0	2	31	621	20.0	6	8

NFL **1950** Bal: KR 2-35 17.5. **1951** ChiB: KR 5-108 21.6. **1952** ChiB: KR 2-40 20.0. **1954** ChiB: KR 8-215 26.9. **Total:** KR 17-398 23.4.

		Rushing				Receiving			
Year Team	G	Att	Yds	Avg	TD	Rec	Yds	Avg	TD
1950 Bal	8	14	113	8.1	1	12	324	27.0	4
1951 ChiB	12	30	123	4.1	1	18	320	17.8	1
1952 ChiB	10	50	196	3.9	2	13	283	21.8	2
1953 ChiB	12	72	169	2.3	2	34	376	11.1	4
1954 ChiB	12	79	306	3.9	3	35	395	11.3	3
NFL Total	54	245	907	3.7	9	112	1698	15.2	14

	Punt Returns				Interceptions				Tot
Year Team	Ret	Yds	Avg	TD	Int	Yds	TD	Fum	TD
1950 Bal	2	7	3.5	0	6	56	0	2	5
1951 ChiB	14	120	8.6	0	4	20	0	1	2
1952 ChiB	0	0	—	0	1	13	0	3	4
1953 ChiB	4	12	3.0	0	0	0	0	7	6
1954 ChiB	14	40	2.9	0	0	0	0	3	6
NFL Total	34	179	5.3	0	11	89	0	16	23

JOHN STONEBRAKER Stonebraker, John S 6'3", 200 **OE-DE**
Col: USC *HS:* Fairfax [Los Angeles, CA]; Black-Foxe Acad. [Los Angeles, CA] B: 4/25/1918, Frankfort, IN
1942 GB: 8 G.

MIKE STONEBREAKER Stonebreaker, Michael David 6'0", 226 **LB**
Col: Notre Dame *HS:* John Curtis Christian [River Ridge, LA] B: 1/14/1967, Baltimore, MD *Drafted:* 1991 Round 9 ChiB
1991 ChiB: 16 G. **1994** NO: 2 G. **Total:** 18 G.

STEVE STONEBREAKER Stonebreaker, Thornton Steven 6'3", 235 **LB-OE**
Col: Detroit Mercy *HS:* Utica [MI] B: 10/28/1937, Moline, IL D: 3/28/1995, River Ridge, LA *Drafted:* 1961 Round 12 Min
1962 Min: 14 G; Rec 12-227 18.9 1 TD; KR 1-12 12.0; 6 Pt. **1963** Min: 14 G. **1964** Bal: 14 G; 1 Fum TD; 6 Pt. **1965** Bal: 14 G; Int 1-0. **1966** Bal: 4 G; Int 1-8. **1967** NO: 10 G. **1968** NO: 14 G; KR 1-22 22.0. **Total:** 84 G; Rec 12-227 18.9 1 TD; KR 2-34 17.0; Int 2-8; 1 Fum TD; Tot TD 2; 12 Pt.

DON STONESIFER Stonesifer, Donald Humphrey 6'0", 200 **OE**
Col: Northwestern *HS:* Carl Schurz [Chicago, IL] B: 1/29/1927, Chicago, IL *Drafted:* 1951 Round 3 ChiC
1952 ChiC: KR 2-27 13.5. **Total:** KR 2-27 13.5.

		Receiving				
Year Team	G	Rec	Yds	Avg	TD	Fum
1951 ChiC	12	27	343	12.7	2	2
1952 ChiC	12	54	617	11.4	0	0
1953 ChiC	12	56	684	12.2	2	1
1954 ChiC	12	44	607	13.8	3	0
1955 ChiC	12	28	330	11.8	5	0
1956 ChiC	12	22	320	14.5	2	0
NFL Total	72	231	2901	12.6	14	3

MIKE STOOPS Stoops, Michael J 6'1", 182 **DB**
Col: Iowa *HS:* Cardinal Mooney [Youngstown, OH] B: 12/13/1961, Youngstown, OH
1987 ChiB: 3 G.

JACK STORER Storer, John Waddell Jr. 5'10", 180 **TB**
Col: Lehigh *HS:* Mercersburg Acad. [PA] B: 11/11/1900, Wheeling, WV D: 1/16/1927, Wheeling, WV
1924 Fra: 14 G; Pass 1 TD; Rush 7 TD; Rec 1 TD; Tot TD 8; 48 Pt.

ED STORM Storm, Edward Charles 6'1", 195 **TB-DB-FB-LB**
Col: Santa Clara *HS:* Salinas [CA] B: 10/2/1907, Salinas, CA D: 1980, Castroville, CA
1934 Phi: Rec 5-34 6.8. **1935** Phi: Rec 3-44 14.7. **Total:** Rec 8-78 9.8.

		Passing							
Year Team	G	Att	Comp	Comp%	Yds	YPA	TD	Int	Rating
1934 Phi	10	30	8	26.7	97	3.23	0	6	1.0
1935 Phi	11	44	15	34.1	372	8.45	3	10	48.9
NFL Total	21	74	23	31.1	469	6.34	3	16	28.3

	Rushing			
Year Team	Att	Yds	Avg	TD
1934 Phi	81	281	3.5	2
1935 Phi	84	164	2.0	0
NFL Total	165	445	2.7	2

GREG STORR Storr, Gregory Scott 6'2", 225 **LB**
Col: Boston College *HS:* Wilson [West Lawn, PA] B: 10/16/1960, Reading, PA
1987 Mia: 3 G.

BILL STORY Story, William Frank 6'3", 245 **OT**
Col: Southern Illinois *HS:* Melrose [Memphis, TN] B: 11/21/1951, Memphis, TN *Drafted:* 1973 Round 9 KC
1975 KC: 14 G.

ERIK STORZ Storz, Erik Erwin 6'2", 234 **LB**
Col: Boston College *HS:* Morris Catholic [Denville, NJ]; Milford Acad. [CT] B: 6/24/1975, Rockaway, NJ
1998 Jac: 1 G.

HAL STOTSBERY Stotsbery, Herald 5'11", 235 **T**
Col: Xavier (Ohio) *HS:* Aquinas [Columbus, OH] B: 1907, Belmont Co., OH Deceased
1930 Bkn: 2 G.

RICHARD STOTTER Stotter, Richard Lee 6'0", 225 **LB**
Col: Houston *HS:* Shaker Heights [OH] B: 4/5/1945, Cleveland, OH *Drafted:* 1968 Round 14 Hou
1968 Hou: 3 G.

CLIFF STOUDT Stoudt, Clifford Lewis 6'4", 215 **QB**
Col: Youngstown State *HS:* Oberlin [OH] B: 3/27/1955, Oberlin, OH *Drafted:* 1977 Round 5 Pit

		Passing							
Year Team	G	Att	Comp	Comp%	Yds	YPA	TD	Int	Rating
1980 Pit	6	60	32	53.3	493	8.22	2	2	78.0
1981 Pit	2	3	1	33.3	17	5.67	0	0	53.5
1982 Pit	6	35	14	40.0	154	4.40	0	5	14.2
1983 Pit	16	381	197	51.7	2553	6.70	12	21	60.6
1986 StL	5	91	52	57.1	542	5.96	3	7	53.5
1987 StL	12	1	0	0.0	0	0.00	0	0	39.6
1988 Pho	16	113	63	55.8	747	6.61	6	8	64.3
1989 Mia	3	0	0	—	0	—	0	0	—
NFL Total	66	684	359	52.5	4506	6.59	23	43	58.3

	Rushing				
Year Team	Att	Yds	Avg	TD	Fum
1980 Pit	9	35	3.9	0	1
1981 Pit	3	11	3.7	0	0
1982 Pit	11	28	2.5	0	1
1983 Pit	77	479	6.2	4	10
1986 StL	7	53	7.6	0	1
1987 StL	1	-2	-2.0	0	0
1988 Pho	14	57	4.1	0	4
NFL Total	122	661	5.4	4	17

KELLY STOUFFER Stouffer, Kelly Wayne 6'3", 210 **QB**
Col: Garden City CC KS; Colorado State *HS:* Rushville [NE] B: 7/6/1964, Scottsbluff, NC *Drafted:* 1987 Round 1 StL

		Passing							
Year Team	G	Att	Comp	Comp%	Yds	YPA	TD	Int	Rating
1988 Sea	8	173	98	56.6	1106	6.39	4	6	69.2
1989 Sea	3	59	29	49.2	270	4.58	0	3	40.9
1991 Sea	2	15	6	40.0	57	3.80	0	1	23.5
1992 Sea	9	190	92	48.4	900	4.74	3	9	47.7
NFL Total	22	437	225	51.5	2333	5.34	7	19	54.5

	Rushing				
Year Team	Att	Yds	Avg	TD	Fum
1988 Sea	19	27	1.4	0	5
1989 Sea	2	11	5.5	0	3
1992 Sea	9	37	4.1	0	12
NFL Total	30	75	2.5	0	20

GLEN STOUGH Stough, Glen Kintigh 6'5", 240 **T**
Col: Duke *HS:* Norwin [Irwin, PA] B: 9/7/1921, Irwin, PA D: 10/17/1984, Greensburg, PA *Drafted:* 1945 Round 27 Pit
1945 Pit: 10 G; KR 1-6 6.0.

PETE STOUT Stout, J. Peter 6'0", 201 **FB-LB**
Col: Texas-Arlington; Texas Christian *HS:* Throckmorton [TX] B: 6/1/1924, Throckmorton, TX *Drafted:* 1946 Round 5 NYG
1949 Was: Rec 8-102 12.8 2 TD; Int 1-8. **1950** Was: Rec 2-15 7.5; Int 1-9. **Total:** Rec 10-117 11.7 2 TD; Int 2-17.

Year Team	G	Rushing Att	Yds	Avg	TD	Fum	Tot TD
1949 Was	8	62	245	4.0	4	3	6
1950 Was	8	9	53	5.9	0	0	0
NFL Total	16	71	298	4.2	4	3	6

OMAR STOUTMIRE Stoutmire, Omar Array 5′11″, 201 **DB**
Col: Fresno State *HS:* Long Beach Polytechnic [CA] B: 7/9/1974, Pensacola, FL *Drafted:* 1997 Round 7 Dal
1997 Dal: 16 G; Int 2-8; 2 Sac. **1998** Dal: 16 G; 1 Sac. **Total:** 32 G; Int 2-8; 3 Sac.

JERRY STOVALL Stovall, Jerry Lane 6′2″, 205 **DB-P**
Col: Louisiana State *HS:* West Monroe [LA] B: 4/30/1941, West Monroe, LA *Drafted:* 1963 Round 1 StL
1963 StL: Rush 1-32 32.0. **1966** StL: Rush 1-17 17.0. **Total:** Rush 2-49 24.5.

Year Team	G	Kickoff Returns Ret	Yds	Avg	TD	Interceptions Int	Yds	TD
1963 StL	14	15	419	27.9	0	1	0	0
1964 StL	14	24	566	23.6	0	3	71	1
1965 StL	10	7	198	28.3	0	2	30	0
1966 StL	14	0	0	—	0	3	43	1
1967 StL	14	0	0	—	0	4	6	0
1968 StL	4	0	0	—	0	0	0	0
1969 StL	10	0	0	—	0	1	28	0
1970 StL	11	0	0	—	0	2	45	0
1971 StL	6	0	0	—	0	2	20	0
NFL Total	97	46	1183	25.7	0	18	243	2

Year Team	Punting Punts	Yds	Avg
1963 StL	65	2647	40.7
1964 StL	15	632	42.1
1965 StL	2	80	40.0
1966 StL	5	139	27.8
NFL Total	87	3498	40.2

DICK STOVALL Stovall, Richard Southerton 6′0″, 202 **LB-G-C**
(Moose) *Col:* Abilene Christian *HS:* Abilene [TX] B: 5/4/1922, Albany, TX
1947 Det: 11 G; Int 1-0. **1948** Det: 10 G. **1949** Was: 10 G. **Total:** 31 G; Int 1-0.

JEFF STOVER Stover, Jeffrey Owen 6′5″, 275 **DT**
Col: Oregon *HS:* Corning [CA] B: 5/22/1958, Corning, CA
1982 SF: 9 G; 2 Sac. **1983** SF: 16 G; 2.5 Sac. **1984** SF: 6 G; 1.5 Sac. **1985** SF: 16 G; 10 Sac. **1986** SF: 15 G; 11 Sac. **1987** SF: 12 G; 3.5 Sac. **1988** SF: 7 G. **Total:** 81 G; 30.5 Sac.

MATT STOVER Stover, John Matthew 5′11″, 178 **K**
Col: Louisiana Tech *HS:* Lake Highlands [Dallas, TX] B: 1/27/1968, Dallas, TX *Drafted:* 1990 Round 12 NYG
1992 Cle: Pass 1-0, 1 Int. **Total:** Pass 1-0, 1 Int.

Year Team	G	Scoring Pts	FG	FGA	FG%	XK	XKA	XK%
1991 Cle	16	81	16	22	72.7	33	34	97.1
1992 Cle	16	92	21	29	72.4	29	30	96.7
1993 Cle	16	84	16	22	72.7	36	36	100.0
1994 Cle	16	110	26	28	**92.9**	32	32	**100.0**
1995 Cle	16	113	29	33	87.9	26	26	100.0
1996 Bal	16	91	19	25	76.0	34	35	97.1
1997 Bal	16	110	26	34	76.5	32	32	100.0
1998 Bal	16	87	21	28	75.0	24	24	100.0
NFL Total	128	768	174	221	78.7	246	249	98.8

SMOKEY STOVER Stover, Stewart Lynn 6′0″, 227 **LB**
Col: Northeast Louisiana *HS:* Seminole [OK] B: 8/24/1938, McPherson, KS
1960 DalT: 14 G; Int 1-10. **1961** DalT: 14 G; KR 1-15 15.0; Int 3-45. **1962** DalT: 14 G. **1963** KC: 14 G; KR 2-18 9.0. **1964** KC: 14 G; KR 1-0; Int 2-11. **1965** KC: 14 G; KR 3-7 2.3. **1966** KC: 14 G; KR 3-0; Int 1-6. **Total:** 98 G; KR 10-40 4.0; Int 7-72.

OTTO STOWE Stowe, Otto William 6′2″, 188 **WR**
Col: Iowa State *HS:* Feitshans [Springfield, IL] B: 2/25/1949, Chicago, IL *Drafted:* 1971 Round 2 Mia
1973 Dal: Rush 3-28 9.3. **1974** Den: Rush 1-1 1.0. **Total:** Rush 4-29 7.3.

Year Team	G	Receiving Rec	Yds	Avg	TD
1971 Mia	12	5	68	13.6	1
1972 Mia	9	13	276	21.2	2
1973 Dal	7	23	389	16.9	6
1974 Den	8	2	9	4.5	1
NFL Total	36	43	742	17.3	10

TYRONNE STOWE Stowe, Tyronne Kevin 6′1″, 244 **LB**
Col: Rutgers *HS:* Passaic [NJ] B: 5/30/1965, Passaic, NJ
1987 Pit: 13 G. **1988** Pit: 10 G. **1989** Pit: 16 G. **1990** Pit: 16 G; Scor **1** Saf; 2 Pt. **1991** Pho: 13 G. **1992** Pho: 15 G. **1993** Pho: 15 G; 1.5 Sac. **1994** Was: 16 G; Int 1-2; 1 Fum. **1995** Sea: 6 G. **Total:** 120 G; Int 1-2; Scor 1 Saf; 2 Pt; 1 Fum; 1.5 Sac.

TOMMIE STOWERS Stowers, Tommie D Jr. 6′3″, 240 **TE**
Col: Missouri *HS:* Hickman Mills [Kansas City, MO] B: 11/18/1966, Kansas City, MO *Drafted:* 1990 Round 11 SD
1992 NO: 12 G; Rec 4-23 5.8. **1993** NO: 4 G; Scor 1 Saf; 2 Pt. **1994** KC: 1 G. **Total:** 17 G; Rec 4-23 5.8; Scor 1 Saf; 2 Pt.

PETE STOYANOVICH Stoyanovich, Peter 5′11″, 187 **K**
Col: Indiana *HS:* Crestwood [Dearborn Heights, MI] B: 4/28/1967, Dearborn, MI *Drafted:* 1989 Round 8 Mia
1991 Mia: Punt 2-85 42.5. **1992** Mia: Punt 2-90 45.0. **1997** KC: Punt 1-24 24.0. **1998** KC: Punt 1-29 29.0. **Total:** Punt 6-228 38.0.

Year Team	G	Scoring Pts	FG	FGA	FG%	XK	XKA	XK%
1989 Mia	16	95	19	26	73.1	38	39	97.4
1990 Mia	16	100	21	25	84.0	37	37	100.0
1991 Mia	14	121	**31**	37	83.8	28	29	96.6
1992 Mia	16	**124**	**30**	37	81.1	34	36	94.4
1993 Mia	16	109	24	32	75.0	37	37	100.0
1994 Mia	16	107	24	31	77.4	35	35	100.0
1995 Mia	16	118	27	34	79.4	37	37	100.0
1996 KC	16	85	17	24	70.8	34	34	100.0
1997 KC	16	113	26	27	**96.3**	35	36	**97.2**
1998 KC	16	115	27	32	84.4	34	34	100.0
NFL Total	158	1087	246	305	80.7	349	354	98.6

MICHAEL STRACHAN Strachan, Michael David 6′0″, 199 **RB**
Col: Iowa State *HS:* Miami Jackson [FL] B: 5/24/1953, Miami, FL *Drafted:* 1975 Round 9 NO
1975 NO: KR 5-91 18.2. **1978** NO: Pass 1-0. **Total:** Pass 1-0; KR 5-91 18.2.

Year Team	G	Rushing Att	Yds	Avg	TD	Receiving Rec	Yds	Avg	TD	Fum
1975 NO	11	161	668	4.1	2	30	224	7.5	0	4
1976 NO	10	66	258	3.9	2	6	22	3.7	0	3
1977 NO	13	55	271	4.9	0	3	26	8.7	0	4
1978 NO	15	108	388	3.6	4	10	51	5.1	0	3
1979 NO	10	62	276	4.5	6	3	9	3.0	0	1
1980 NO	3	20	41	2.1	0	5	60	12.0	0	2
NFL Total	62	472	1902	4.0	14	57	392	6.9	0	17

STEVE STRACHAN Strachan, Stephen Michael 6′1″, 221 **RB**
Col: Boston College *HS:* Burlington [MA] B: 3/22/1963, Everrett, MA *Drafted:* 1985 Round 11 LARd
1987 LARd: Rec 4-42 10.5. **1988** LARd: Rec 3-19 6.3 1 TD. **Total:** Rec 7-61 8.7 1 TD.

Year Team	G	Rushing Att	Yds	Avg	TD	Fum
1985 LARd	4	2	1	0.5	0	0
1986 LARd	16	18	53	2.9	0	0
1987 LARd	11	28	108	3.9	0	1
1988 LARd	16	4	12	3.0	0	2
1989 LARd	16	0	0	—	0	0
NFL Total	63	52	174	3.3	0	3

CHARLIE STRACK Strack, Charles William 6′0″, 215 **G**
Col: Colgate; Oklahoma State *HS:* Spring Valley [NY] B: 7/15/1899, Nyack, NY D: 5/1967, Spring Valley, NY
1928 ChiC: 3 G.

TIM STRACKA Stracka, Timothy Terrill 6′3″, 225 **TE**
Col: Wisconsin *HS:* West [Madison, WI] B: 9/27/1959, Madison, WI *Drafted:* 1983 Round 6 Cle
1983 Cle: 13 G; Rec 1-12 12.0. **1984** Cle: 6 G; Rec 1-15 15.0. **Total:** 19 G; Rec 2-27 13.5.

JOHN STRADA Strada, John Frank 6′3″, 230 **TE**
Col: William Jewell *HS:* De La Salle [Kansas City, MO] B: 11/13/1952, Kansas City, MO
1974 NYG-KC: 12 G; Rec 1-16 16.0; 1 Fum. NYG: 1 G. KC: 11 G; Rec 1-16 16.0; 1 Fum. **Total:** 12 G; Rec 1-16 16.0; 1 Fum.

RED STRADER Strader, Norman Parker 5′9″, 200 **TB-FB-WB**
Col: St. Mary's (Cal.) *HS:* Modesto [CA] B: 12/21/1902, Newton, NJ D: 5/26/1956, Berkeley, CA
1927 ChiC: 6 G; Rush 1 TD; 6 Pt.

TROY STRADFORD Stradford, Troy Edwin 5′9″, 191 **RB-WR**
Col: Boston College *HS:* Linden [NJ] B: 9/11/1964, Elizabeth, NJ *Drafted:* 1987 Round 4 Mia
1987 Mia: Pass 1-1 100.0%, 6 6.00. **1988** Mia: Pass 1-0. **Total:** Pass 2-1 50.0%, 6 3.00.

Year Team	G	Rushing Att	Yds	Avg	TD	Receiving Rec	Yds	Avg	TD
1987 Mia	12	145	619	4.3	6	48	457	9.5	1
1988 Mia	15	95	335	3.5	2	56	426	7.6	1
1989 Mia	7	66	240	3.6	1	25	233	9.3	0
1990 Mia	14	37	138	3.7	1	30	257	8.6	0
1991 KC	10	1	7	7.0	0	9	91	10.1	0
1992 LARm-Det	8	12	41	3.4	0	2	15	7.5	0
1992 LARm	2	3	12	4.0	0	0	0	—	0
1992 Det	6	9	29	3.2	0	2	15	7.5	0
NFL Total	66	356	1380	3.9	10	170	1479	8.7	2

Year Team	Punt Returns Ret	Yds	Avg	TD	Kickoff Returns Ret	Yds	Avg	TD	Fum	Tot TD
1987 Mia	0	0	—	0	14	258	18.4	0	6	7
1988 Mia	0	0	—	0	0	0	—	0	2	3
1989 Mia	14	129	9.2	0	0	0	—	0	4	1
1990 Mia	3	4	1.3	0	3	56	18.7	0	5	1
1991 KC	22	150	6.8	0	14	292	20.9	0	0	0
1992 LARm-Det	1	1	1.0	0	7	94	13.4	0	0	0
1992 LARm	1	1	1.0	0	3	59	19.7	0	0	0
1992 Det	0	0	—	0	4	35	8.8	0	0	0
NFL Total	40	284	7.1	0	38	700	18.4	0	17	12

ART STRAHAN Strahan, Arthur Ray 6′5″, 250 **DT-DE**
Col: Texas Southern *HS:* Booker T. Washington [Newton, TX] B: 7/17/1943, Newton, TX
1965 Hou: 4 G. **1968** Atl: 5 G. **Total:** 9 G.

MICHAEL STRAHAN Strahan, Michael Anthony 6′4″, 280 **DE**
Col: Texas Southern *HS:* Westbury [Houston, TX]; American School [Mannheim, Germany] B: 11/21/1971, Houston, TX *Drafted:* 1993 Round 2 NYG
1993 NYG: 9 G; 1 Sac. **1994** NYG: 15 G; 4.5 Sac. **1995** NYG: 15 G; Int 2-56; Scor **1** Saf; 2 Pt; 7.5 Sac. **1996** NYG: 16 G; 5 Sac. **1997** NYG: 16 G; 14 Sac. **1998** NYG: 16 G; Int 1-24 1 TD; 6 Pt; 15 Sac. **Total:** 87 G; Int 3-80 1 TD; Scor 1 Saf; 8 Pt; 47.0 Sac.

CLEM STRALKA Stralka, Clement Frank 5′10″, 215 **G**
(Little Bull) *Col:* Georgetown *HS:* Pennington Prep [NJ] B: 5/19/1913, Glen Lyon, PA D: 1/10/1994, Denver, CO
1938 Was: 9 G. **1939** Was: 10 G. **1940** Was: 10 G. **1941** Was: 11 G. **1942** Was: 11 G. **1945** Was: 3 G. **1946** Was: 8 G. **Total:** 62 G.

MIKE STRAMIELLO Stramiello, Michael Jr. 6′1″, 199 **OE-DE**
Col: Colgate *HS:* Poly Prep [Brooklyn, NY] B: 2/2/1907, New York, NY
1930 Bkn: 12 G; Rec 1 TD; Scor 12, 6 XK. **1931** Bkn: 13 G; Int **1** TD; 6 Pt. **1932** Bkn-SI: 8 G. Bkn: 3 G. SI: 5 G. **1934** Bkn: 2 G. **Total:** 35 G; Rec 1 TD; Int 1 TD; Tot TD 2.

ELI STRAND Strand, Eli S Jr. 6′2″, 250 **OG**
Col: Iowa State *HS:* Tuckahoe [NY] B: 2/11/1943, Mount Vernon, NY
1966 Pit: 8 G. **1967** NO: 14 G. **Total:** 22 G.

LEIF STRAND Strand, Leif Richard 6′0″, 210 **C**
Col: Fordham; Minnesota *HS:* Two Harbors [MN] B: 1/6/1899, Two Harbors, MN D: 4/26/1968, Orlando, FL
1924 Dul: 6 G.

BOB STRANSKY Stransky, Robert Joseph 6′1″, 180 **HB**
Col: Colorado *HS:* Yankton [SD] B: 6/30/1936, Yankton, SD
1960 Den: Rec 3-11 3.7; KR 7-153 21.9.

Year Team	G	Rushing Att	Yds	Avg	TD	Fum
1960 Den	14	28	78	2.8	0	2

DUTCH STRASSNER Strassner, Clarence 1 **E**
(Clyde) *Col:* Findlay *HS:* McKinley [Canton, OH] B: 3/31/1904, Canton, OH D: 6/1978, Burghill, OH
1925 Can: 3 G.

MIKE STRATTON Stratton, David Michael 6′3″, 224 **LB**
Col: Tennessee *HS:* Tellico Plains [TN] B: 4/10/1941, Vonore, TN *Drafted:* 1962 Round 13 Buf
1963 Buf: Rec 1-19 19.0. **1964** Buf: Scor 1 Saf. **1966** Buf: PR 0-4; **1** Fum TD. **Total:** Rec 1-19 19.0; PR 0-4; Scor 1 Saf; 1 Fum TD.

Year Team	G	Interceptions Int	Yds	TD	Tot TD
1962 Buf	12	6	99	0	0
1963 Buf	14	3	31	1	1
1964 Buf	14	1	0	0	0
1965 Buf	14	2	19	0	0
1966 Buf	14	3	37	0	1
1967 Buf	14	1	3	0	0
1968 Buf	14	1	15	0	0
1969 Buf	14	0	0	0	0
1970 Buf	9	0	0	0	0
1971 Buf	13	0	0	0	0
1972 Buf	10	1	0	0	0
1973 SD	14	3	46	0	0
NFL Total	156	21	250	1	2

JIMMY STRAUSBAUGH Strausbaugh, James Edwin 5′9″, 190 **HB-DB**
Col: Ohio State *HS:* Chillicothe [OH] B: 2/25/1918, Chillicothe, OH D: 11/25/1991, Chillicothe, OH *Drafted:* 1941 Round 18 GB
1946 ChiC: Pass 1-1 100.0%, 35 35.00; Rec 5-56 11.2; PR 2-34 17.0; KR 6-104 17.3.

Year Team	G	Rushing Att	Yds	Avg	TD	Fum
1946 ChiC	11	37	183	4.9	3	4

DUTCH STRAUSS Strauss, J. Arthur 5′10″, 205 **FB-WB**
Col: Phillips *HS:* Bluff City [KS]; Enid HS [OK] B: 1/7/1897, Hennessey, OK D: 8/10/1969, Enid, OK
1923 Tol: 6 G. **1924** KC: 7 G; Rush 1 TD; 6 Pt. **Total:** 13 G; Rush 1 TD; 6 Pt.

THOMAS STRAUTHERS Strauthers, Thomas Bryan 6′4″, 262 **DE-DT**
Col: Jackson State *HS:* Brookhaven [MS] B: 4/6/1961, Wesson, MS *Drafted:* 1983 Round 10 Phi
1983 Phi: 4 G. **1984** Phi: 16 G; KR 1-12 12.0; 2 Sac. **1985** Phi: 16 G; 5.5 Sac. **1986** Phi: 11 G. **1988** Det: 10 G; 2 Sac. **1989** Min: 12 G; 1 Sac. **1990** Min: 13 G; 4 Sac. **1991** Min: 15 G; 2.5 Sac. **Total:** 97 G; KR 1-12 12.0; 17 Sac.

DON STRAW Straw, Donald McAlpine 5′11″, 210 **G-T**
Col: Washington & Jefferson *HS:* Central [Detroit, MI] B: 11/22/1896 D: 7/31/1961
1920 Det: 1 G. **1921** Det: 1 G. **Total:** 2 G.

LES STRAYHORN Strayhorn, Leslie Dewey 5′10″, 205 **RB**
Col: East Carolina *HS:* Jones [Trenton, NC] B: 9/1/1951, Trenton, NC *Drafted:* 1973 Round 17 Dal
1973 Dal: 11 G; Rush 11-62 5.6 1 TD; KR 2-44 22.0; 6 Pt; 2 Fum. **1974** Dal: 13 G; Rush 11-66 6.0; Rec 2-12 6.0; KR 2-19 9.5; 2 Fum. **Total:** 24 G; Rush 22-128 5.8 1 TD; Rec 2-12 6.0; KR 4-63 15.8; 6 Pt; 4 Fum.

ERIC STREATER Streater, Eric Maurice 5′11″, 165 **WR**
Col: North Carolina *HS:* Sylva-Webster [Sylva, NC] B: 3/21/1964, Sylva, NC
1987 TB: 3 G; Rush 1-5 5.0; Rec 5-117 23.4 2 TD; 12 Pt.

GEORGE STREETER Streeter, George Leon 6′2″, 212 **DB**
Col: Notre Dame *HS:* Percy L. Julian [Chicago, IL] B: 8/28/1967, Chicago, IL *Drafted:* 1989 Round 11 ChiB
1989 ChiB: 4 G. **1990** Ind: 4 G. **Total:** 8 G.

RICH STRENGER Strenger, Richard Gene 6′7″, 280 **OT**
Col: Michigan *HS:* Grafton [WI] B: 3/10/1960, Port Washington, WI *Drafted:* 1983 Round 2 Det
1983 Det: 16 G. **1984** Det: 1 G. **1985** Det: 13 G. **1986** Det: 16 G. **1987** Det: 3 G. **Total:** 49 G.

BILL STRIBLING Stribling, Majure Blanks 6′1″, 206 **OE**
Col: Mississippi *HS:* Philadelphia [MS] B: 11/5/1927, Edinburg, MS *Drafted:* 1950 Round 21 NYG
1952 NYG: KR 1-11 11.0. **Total:** KR 1-11 11.0.

Year Team	G	Receiving Rec	Yds	Avg	TD	Fum
1951 NYG	6	18	226	12.6	2	1
1952 NYG	12	26	399	15.3	5	1
1953 NYG	12	16	175	10.9	0	0
1955 Phi	12	38	568	14.9	6	0
1956 Phi	2	2	11	5.5	0	0
1957 Phi	12	14	194	13.9	1	1
NFL Total	56	114	1573	13.8	14	3

TONY STRICKER Stricker, Antony Elling 6′0″, 185 **DB**
Col: Cameron; Colorado *HS:* Midwest City [OK] B: 9/2/1940, Lawton, OK
1963 NYJ: 12 G; KR 4-90 22.5; Int 1-6; 1 Fum.

DAVE STRICKLAND Strickland, David G 6′0″, 220 **OG**
Col: Northeast Mississippi CC; Memphis *HS:* Holly Springs [MS] B: 6/13/1931, Holly Springs, MS
1960 Den: 14 G; KR 1-9 9.0.

BISHOP STRICKLAND Strickland, Frank Bishop 5′10″, 195 **FB**
Col: South Carolina *HS:* Mullins [SC] B: 1/4/1927, Mullins, SC *Drafted:* 1951 Round 6 SF
1951 SF: KR 1-14 14.0.

Year Team	G	Rushing Att	Yds	Avg	TD	Fum
1951 SF	9	34	165	4.9	0	2

FRED STRICKLAND Strickland, Fredrick William Jr. 6'2", 246 LB
Col: Purdue *HS:* Lakeland Regional [Wanaque, NJ] B: 8/15/1966, Buffalo, NY *Drafted:* 1988 Round 2 LARm
1988 LARm: 16 G; 4 Sac. **1989** LARm: 12 G; Int 2-56; 2 Sac. **1990** LARm: 5 G. **1991** LARm: 14 G; 1 Sac. **1992** LARm: 16 G. **1993** Min: 16 G. **1994** GB: 16 G; Int 1-7. **1995** GB: 14 G. **1996** Dal: 16 G; Int 1-0; 1 Sac. **1997** Dal: 15 G; 0.5 Sac. **1998** Dal: 16 G. **Total:** 156 G; Int 4-63; 8.5 Sac.

LARRY STRICKLAND Strickland, Lawrence Wayne 6'4", 248 C
Col: North Texas *HS:* John Tyler [Tyler, TX] B: 9/3/1931, Tyler, TX D: 8/29/1979, Tyler, TX *Drafted:* 1953 Round 13 ChiB
1954 ChiB: 12 G. **1955** ChiB: 12 G. **1956** ChiB: 12 G. **1957** ChiB: 11 G. **1958** ChiB: 12 G. **1959** ChiB: 3 G. **Total:** 62 G.

BILL STRICKLAND Strickland, William 5'9", 220 G
Col: Western Illinois; Lombard *HS:* Macomb [IL] B: 9/14/1898, Youngstown, IL D: 1/31/1976, Quincy, IL
1923 Mil: 3 G.

BILL STRIEGEL Striegel, William Joseph 6'2", 235 OG-OT-LB
Col: U. of Pacific *HS:* Chico [CA] B: 5/28/1936, Easton, KS *Drafted:* 1958 Round 8 Phi
1959 Phi: 12 G. **1960** Oak-Bos: 6 G. Oak: 1 G. Bos: 5 G. **Total:** 18 G.

ART STRINGER Stringer, Arthur 6'1", 223 LB
Col: Ball State *HS:* Northwestern [Detroit, MI] B: 1/30/1954, Troy, AL *Drafted:* 1976 Round 9 Hou
1977 Hou: 13 G; KR 1-15 15.0; Int 1-20. **1978** Hou: 7 G; Int 1-20. **1979** Hou: 8 G; Int 2-21. **1980** Hou: 8 G. **1981** Hou: 5 G. **Total:** 41 G; KR 1-15 15.0; Int 4-61.

GENE STRINGER Stringer, Eugene Charles 6'0", 200 FB-TB-BB-WB
Col: John Carroll B: 5/29/1903, Cleveland, OH D: 6/1/1985, Pueblo, CO
1925 Cle: 10 G.

KOREY STRINGER Stringer, Korey D 6'4", 350 OT
Col: Ohio State *HS:* Warren G. Harding [Warren, OH] B: 5/8/1974, Warren, OH *Drafted:* 1995 Round 1 Min
1995 Min: 16 G; Rec 1-(-1) -1.0. **1996** Min: 16 G. **1997** Min: 15 G. **1998** Min: 14 G. **Total:** 61 G; Rec 1-(-1) -1.0.

BOB STRINGER Stringer, Robert Jean 6'1", 197 LB-FB
Col: Tulsa *HS:* Shawnee [OK] B: 10/8/1929, Shawnee, OK *Drafted:* 1952 Round 14 Phi
1952 Phi: 12 G; Rush 2-5 2.5; Rec 1-4 4.0; KR 1-22 22.0; Int 1-9. **1953** Phi: 12 G; Rush 1-5 5.0; KR 1-11 11.0; Int 1-7. **Total:** 24 G; Rush 3-10 3.3; Rec 1-4 4.0; KR 2-33 16.5; Int 2-16.

SCOTT STRINGER Stringer, Scott Lee 5'11", 180 DB
Col: San Joaquin Delta Coll. CA (J.C.); California *HS:* Joint Union [Tracy, CA] B: 8/5/1951, Tracy, CA
1974 StL: 5 G.

HAL STRINGERT Stringert, Harold Lloyd 5'11", 185 DB
Col: Hawaii; Willamette *HS:* St. Louis [Honolulu, HI] B: 1/2/1952, Honolulu, HI
1975 SD: 6 G. **1976** SD: 11 G; Int 1-24. **1977** SD: 14 G; Int 4-64. **1978** SD: 13 G; KR 1-0; Int 2-4. **1979** SD: 15 G. **1980** SD: 10 G; Int 1-0. **Total:** 69 G; KR 1-0; Int 8-92.

JOE STRINGFELLOW Stringfellow, Joseph Elbert 6'0", 185 TB-DB-DE
Col: Southern Mississippi B: 3/10/1918, Meridian, MS D: 9/16/1992, Savannah, GA *Drafted:* 1942 Round 12 Det
1942 Det: 9 G; Pass 13-5 38.5%, 67 5.15 2 Int; Rush 16-41 2.6; Rec 8-89 11.1; KR 2-54 27.0; Punt 9-363 40.3.

DON STROCK Strock, Donald Joseph 6'5", 220 QB
Col: Virginia Tech *HS:* Owen J. Roberts [Pottstown, PA] B: 11/27/1950, Pottstown, PA *Drafted:* 1973 Round 5 Mia
1987 Mia: Punt 9-277 30.8. **Total:** Punt 9-277 30.8.

		Passing							
Year Team	**G**	**Att**	**Comp**	**Comp%**	**Yds**	**YPA**	**TD**	**Int**	**Rating**
1974 Mia	1	0	0	—	0	—	0	0	—
1975 Mia	6	45	26	57.8	230	5.11	2	2	67.8
1976 Mia	4	47	21	44.7	359	7.64	3	2	74.7
1977 Mia	4	4	2	50.0	12	3.00	0	1	16.7
1978 Mia	16	135	72	53.3	825	6.11	12	6	83.1
1979 Mia	16	100	56	56.0	830	8.30	6	6	78.3
1980 Mia	16	62	30	48.4	313	5.05	1	5	35.2
1981 Mia	16	130	79	60.8	901	6.93	6	8	71.3
1982 Mia	9	55	30	54.5	306	5.56	2	5	45.0
1983 Mia	15	52	34	65.4	403	7.75	4	1	106.5
1984 Mia	16	6	4	66.7	27	4.50	0	0	76.4
1985 Mia	16	9	7	77.8	141	15.67	1	0	155.8
1986 Mia	16	20	14	70.0	152	7.60	2	0	125.4
1987 Mia	12	23	13	56.5	114	4.96	0	1	51.7
1988 Cle	4	91	55	60.4	736	8.09	6	5	85.2
NFL Total	167	779	443	56.9	5349	6.87	45	42	74.9

	Rushing				
Year Team	**Att**	**Yds**	**Avg**	**TD**	**Fum**
1974 Mia	1	-7	-7.0	0	0
1975 Mia	6	38	6.3	1	1
1976 Mia	2	13	6.5	1	1
1978 Mia	10	23	2.3	0	4
1979 Mia	3	18	6.0	0	3
1980 Mia	1	-3	-3.0	0	1
1981 Mia	14	-26	-1.9	0	0
1982 Mia	3	-9	-3.0	0	1
1983 Mia	6	-16	-2.7	0	0
1984 Mia	2	-5	-2.5	0	1
1985 Mia	2	-6	-3.0	0	0
1986 Mia	1	0	0.0	0	1
1988 Cle	6	-2	-0.3	0	4
NFL Total	57	18	0.3	2	17

WOODY STRODE Strode, Woodrow Wilson Woolwine 6'3", 205 OE-DE
Col: UCLA *HS:* Thomas Jefferson [Los Angeles, CA] B: 7/25/1914, Los Angelees, CA D: 12/31/1994, Glendora, CA
1946 LARm: 10 G; Rec 4-37 9.3; KR 1-6 6.0.

MIKE STROFOLINO Strofolino, Michael James 6'2", 230 LB
Col: Villanova *HS:* St. Francis Prep [Brooklyn, NY] B: 2/6/1944, Brooklyn, NY *Drafted:* 1965 Round 4 LARm
1965 LARm-Bal: 12 G. LARm: 9 G. Bal: 3 G. **1966** StL: 8 G. **1967** StL: 1 G. **1968** StL: 14 G. **Total:** 35 G.

GEORGE STROHMEYER Strohmeyer, George Ferdinand Jr. 5'10", 205 C-LB
Col: Texas A&M; Notre Dame *HS:* McAllen [TX] B: 1/27/1924, Kansas City, MO D: 1/12/1992, Murphys, CA
AAFC **1948** BknA: 14 G; PR 1-5 5.0; Int 4-79. **1949** ChiA: 12 G; Int 3-9. **Total:** 26 G; PR 1-5 5.0; Int 7-88.

FRANK STROM Strom, Frank E 6'2", 252 T
Col: Rogers State Coll. OK (J.C.) B: 8/29/1916, Ballinger, TX D: 6/8/1992, Clinton, OK
1944 Bkn: 7 G.

RICK STROM Strom, Richard James 6'2", 210 QB
Col: Georgia Tech *HS:* Fox Chapel [PA] B: 3/11/1965, Pittsburgh, PA
1989 Pit: 3 G; Pass 1-0; Rush 4-(-3) -0.8; 1 Fum. **1990** Pit: 6 G; Pass 21-14 66.7%, 162 7.71 1 Int; Rush 4-10 2.5; 1 Fum. **1991** Pit: 1 G. **Total:** 10 G; Pass 22-14 63.6%, 162 7.36 1 Int; Rush 8-7 0.9; 2 Fum.

MIKE STROMBERG Stromberg, Michael David 6'2", 235 LB
Col: Temple *HS:* Samuel J. Tilden [Brooklyn, NY] B: 5/25/1945, Brooklyn, NY *Drafted:* 1967 Round 14 NYJ
1968 NYJ: 2 G.

KEN STRONG Strong, Elmer Kenneth Jr. 6'0", 206 FB-DB-TB-K
Col: New York U. *HS:* West Haven [CT] B: 3/21/1906, West Haven, CT D: 10/5/1979, New York, NY *HOF:* 1967
1929 SI: PR **1** TD. **1930** SI: Rec **5** TD. **1931** SI: PR **1** TD. **1932** SI: Rec 5-56 11.2. **1933** NYG: Rec 10-146 14.6 2 TD; Int **1** TD. **1934** NYG: Rec 7-52 7.4. **1939** NYG: Punt 5-277 55.4. **1944** NYG: Punt 1-44 44.0. **1945** NYG: Punt 3-134 44.7. **Total:** Rec 22-254 11.5 7 TD; PR 2 TD; Int 1 TD; Punt 9-455 50.6.

		Passing							
Year Team	**G**	**Att**	**Comp**	**Comp%**	**Yds**	**YPA**	**TD**	**Int**	**Rating**
1929 SI	10	—	—	—	—	—	0	—	—
1930 SI	12	—	—	—	—	—	2	—	—
1931 SI	11	—	—	—	—	—	1	—	—
1932 SI	11	23	4	17.4	94	4.09	1	3	19.0
1933 NYG	14	11	8	72.7	194	17.64	2	0	154.4
1934 NYG	13	15	8	53.3	92	6.13	0	1	44.3
1935 NYG	11	3	0	0.0	0	0.00	0	1	0.0
1939 NYG	9	0	0	—	0	—	0	0	—
1944 NYG	10	0	0	—	0	—	0	0	—
1945 NYG	9	0	0	—	0	—	0	0	—
1946 NYG	11	0	0	—	0	—	0	0	—
1947 NYG	10	0	0	—	0	—	0	0	—
NFL Total	131	52	20	38.5	380	7.31	6	5	63.5

	Rushing			
Year Team	**Att**	**Yds**	**Avg**	**TD**
1929 SI	—	—	—	4
1930 SI	—	—	—	2
1931 SI	—	—	—	6
1932 SI	96	375	3.9	2
1933 NYG	96	272	2.8	3
1934 NYG	138	431	3.1	6
1935 NYG	46	151	3.3	1
1939 NYG	1	1	1.0	0
1944 NYG	2	-2	-1.0	0
NFL Total	379	1228	3.2	24

Year Team	Scoring Pts	FG	FGA	FG%	XK	XKA	XK%	Tot TD
1929 SI	39	0	—	—	9	—	—	5
1930 SI	53	1	—	—	8	—	—	7
1931 SI	53	**2**	—	—	5	—	—	7
1932 SI	15	0	—	—	3	—	—	2
1933 NYG	**64**	5	—	—	**13**	—	—	6
1934 NYG	56	4	—	—	8	—	—	6
1935 NYG	29	4	—	—	11	—	—	1
1939 NYG	19	4	8	50.0	7	7	100.0	0
1944 NYG	41	**6**	**12**	**50.0**	23	24	**95.8**	0
1945 NYG	41	6	**13**	46.2	23	23	100.0	0
1946 NYG	44	4	9	44.4	32	32	100.0	0
1947 NYG	30	2	5	40.0	24	25	96.0	0
NFL Total	484	38	47	46.8	166	111	98.2	34

JIM STRONG Strong, James Harold Jr. 6'1", 215 **RB**
Col: Houston *HS:* Sam Houston [San Antonio, TX] B: 12/12/1946, San Antonio, TX *Drafted:* 1970 Round 7 SF
1971 NO: KR 9-134 14.9. **1972** NO: KR 4-53 13.3. **Total:** KR 13-187 14.4.

Year Team	G	Rushing Att	Yds	Avg	TD	Receiving Rec	Yds	Avg	TD	Fum
1970 SF	3	2	3	1.5	0	0	0	—	0	0
1971 NO	14	95	404	4.3	3	16	78	4.9	0	5
1972 NO	14	37	120	3.2	0	14	123	8.8	0	1
NFL Total	31	134	527	3.9	3	30	201	6.7	0	6

MACK STRONG Strong, Mack Carlington 6'0", 229 **RB**
Col: Georgia *HS:* Brookstone [Columbus, GA] B: 9/11/1971, Fort Benning, GA
1995 Sea: KR 4-65 16.3. **1997** Sea: KR 1-16 16.0. **Total:** KR 5-81 16.2.

Year Team	G	Rushing Att	Yds	Avg	TD	Receiving Rec	Yds	Avg	TD	Fum	Tot TD
1994 Sea	8	27	114	4.2	2	3	3	1.0	0	1	2
1995 Sea	16	8	23	2.9	1	12	117	9.8	3	2	4
1996 Sea	14	5	8	1.6	0	9	78	8.7	0	0	0
1997 Sea	16	4	8	2.0	0	13	91	7.0	2	0	2
1998 Sea	16	15	47	3.1	0	8	48	6.0	2	2	2
NFL Total	70	59	200	3.4	3	45	337	7.5	7	5	10

RAY STRONG Strong, Raymond 5'9", 184 **RB**
Col: Contra Costa Coll. CA (J.C.); Nevada-Las Vegas *HS:* St. Mary's Prep [Berkeley, CA] B: 5/7/1956, Berkeley, CA *Drafted:* 1978 Round 10 Atl
1978 Atl: Rec 7-56 8.0. **1979** Atl: Rec 1-6 6.0. **1981** Atl: Rec 1-9 9.0. **Total:** Rec 9-71 7.9.

Year Team	G	Rushing Att	Yds	Avg	TD	Kickoff Returns Ret	Yds	Avg	TD	Fum
1978 Atl	14	30	99	3.3	2	3	50	16.7	0	1
1979 Atl	6	2	7	3.5	0	15	343	22.9	0	2
1980 Atl	16	6	42	7.0	1	10	168	16.8	0	4
1981 Atl	16	3	6	2.0	0	0	0	—	0	1
1982 Atl	9	4	9	2.3	0	0	0	—	0	0
NFL Total	61	45	163	3.6	3	28	561	20.0	0	8

WILLIAM STRONG Strong, William Blake 5'10", 191 **DB**
Col: North Carolina State *HS:* Lewisville [Richburg, SC] B: 11/3/1971, Chester, SC *Drafted:* 1995 Round 5 NO
1996 NO: 9 G.

JAMES STROSCHEIN Stroschein, James Breckenridge 6'1", 205 **DE**
Col: UCLA *HS:* Alhambra [CA] B: 4/3/1929, Santa Ana, CA
D: 8/7/1983, Covina, CA *Drafted:* 1951 Round 24 NYY
1951 NYY: 11 G.

AUBREY STROSNIDER Strosnider, Aubrey J 6'1", 205 **T**
(Ab) *Col:* Dayton *HS:* U. of Dayton Prep [OH] B: 5/9/1904
D: 10/27/1964, Cleveland, OH
1928 Day: 1 G.

VINCE STROTH Stroth, Vincent Martin 6'4", 267 **OT-OG-TE**
Col: Brigham Young *HS:* Bellarmine Prep [San Jose, CA]
B: 11/25/1960, San Jose, CA
1985 SF: 1 G. **1987** Hou: 9 G. **1988** Hou: 6 G. **Total:** 16 G.

DEON STROTHER Strother, Deon 5'11", 213 **RB**
Col: USC *HS:* Skyline [Oakland, CA] B: 4/12/1972, Saginaw, MI
1994 Den: 2 G.

JACK STROUD Stroud, Jack Chester 6'1", 235 **OG-OT**
Col: Tennessee *HS:* Lowell [San Francisco, CA] B: 1/29/1928, Fresno, CA D: 6/1/1994, Flemington, NJ *Drafted:* 1951 Round 5 NYG
1953 NYG: 12 G. **1954** NYG: 6 G. **1955** NYG: 12 G. **1956** NYG: 11 G. **1957** NYG: 11 G. **1958** NYG: 7 G. **1959** NYG: 12 G. **1960** NYG: 12 G. **1961** NYG: 12 G. **1962** NYG: 14 G. **1963** NYG: 14 G. **1964** NYG: 9 G. **Total:** 132 G.

MORRIS STROUD Stroud, Morris Jr. 6'10", 255 **TE**
Col: Clark Atlanta *HS:* Fairmont [Griffin, GA] B: 5/17/1946, Miami, FL
Drafted: 1969 Round 3 KC

Year Team	G	Receiving Rec	Yds	Avg	TD	Fum
1970 KC	13	4	86	21.5	1	0
1971 KC	14	22	454	20.6	1	0
1972 KC	14	4	80	20.0	1	0
1973 KC	14	12	216	18.0	2	1
1974 KC	14	12	141	11.8	2	0
NFL Total	69	54	977	18.1	7	1

ART STROZIER Strozier, Arthur A 6'2", 220 **TE**
Col: Kansas State *HS:* Manual [Kansas City, MO] B: 5/23/1946, Kansas City, MO
1970 SD: 14 G; Rec 2-40 20.0. **1971** SD: 6 G; Rec 1-6 6.0. **Total:** 20 G; Rec 3-46 15.3.

WILBUR STROZIER Strozier, Wilbur Lamar 6'4", 255 **TE**
Col: Georgia *HS:* La Grange [GA] B: 11/12/1964, La Grange, GA
Drafted: 1987 Round 7 Den
1987 Sea: 12 G. **1988** SD: 6 G. **Total:** 18 G.

GEORGE STRUGAR Strugar, George Ralph 6'5", 259 **DT**
Col: Washington *HS:* Renton [WA] B: 4/2/1934, Cle Elum, WA
D: 6/13/1997, Anza, CA *Drafted:* 1957 Round 3 LARm
1957 LARm: 9 G. **1958** LARm: 12 G. **1959** LARm: 11 G. **1960** LARm: 11 G. **1961** LARm: 14 G; Int 1-4. **1962** Pit-NYT: 13 G. Pit: 1 G. NYT: 12 G. **1963** NYJ: 8 G. **Total:** 78 G; Int 1-4.

ART STRUTT Strutt, Arthur Eugene 6'0", 202 **HB-DB**
(Jake) *Col:* Duquesne *HS:* Mingo Junction [OH] B: 12/4/1912, Mingo Junction, OH
1935 Pit: Pass 2-0; Rec 7-112 16.0; Int **1** TD. **1936** Pit: Pass 1-1 100.0%, 15 15.00; Rec 11-166 15.1. **Total:** Pass 3-1 33.3%, 15 5.00; Rec 18-278 15.4; Int 1 TD.

Year Team	G	Rushing Att	Yds	Avg	TD	Tot TD
1935 Pit	9	46	111	2.4	0	1
1936 Pit	10	84	180	2.1	1	1
NFL Total	19	130	291	2.2	1	2

DAN STRYZINSKI Stryzinski, Daniel Thomas 6'2", 196 **P**
Col: Indiana *HS:* Lincoln [Vincennes, IN] B: 5/15/1965, Indianapolis, IN
1990 Pit: Rush 3-17 5.7. **1991** Pit: Rush 4-(-11) -2.8. **1992** TB: Pass 2-2 100.0%, 14 7.00; Rush 1-7 7.0. **1994** TB: Pass 1-1 100.0%, 21 21.00. **1995** Atl: Rush 1-0. **Total:** Pass 3-3 100.0%, 35 11.67; Rush 9-13 1.4.

Year Team	G	Punting Punts	Yds	Avg	Fum
1990 Pit	16	65	2454	37.8	0
1991 Pit	16	74	2996	40.5	1
1992 TB	16	74	3015	40.7	0
1993 TB	16	**93**	3772	40.6	0
1994 TB	16	72	2800	38.9	0
1995 Atl	16	67	2759	41.2	0
1996 Atl	16	75	3152	42.0	0
1997 Atl	16	89	3498	39.3	0
1998 Atl	16	74	2963	40.0	0
NFL Total	144	683	27409	40.1	1

JUSTIN STRZELCZYK Strzelczyk, Justin Conrad 6'6", 301 **OT-OG**
Col: Maine *HS:* West Seneca West [NY] B: 8/18/1968, Seneca, NY
Drafted: 1990 Round 11 Pit
1990 Pit: 16 G. **1991** Pit: 16 G. **1992** Pit: 16 G. **1993** Pit: 16 G. **1994** Pit: 16 G. **1995** Pit: 16 G. **1996** Pit: 16 G. **1997** Pit: 14 G. **1998** Pit: 7 G. **Total:** 133 G.

JOHNNY STRZYKALSKI Strzykalski, John Raymond 5'9", 190 **HB-DB**
(Strike) *Col:* Marquette *HS:* South Division [Milwaukee, WI]
B: 12/14/1921, Milwaukee, WI *Drafted:* 1946 Round 1 GB
AAFC **1946** SF-A: KR 7-142 20.3; Int 3-55. **1947** SF-A: Pass 4-1 25.0%, 38 9.50; KR 6-124 20.7; Int 2-25. **1948** SF-A: Pass 1-0; KR 9-185 20.6; Int 3-21. **1949** SF-A: KR 2-57 28.5. **Total:** Pass 5-1 20.0%, 38 7.60; KR 24-508 21.2; Int 8-101.

Year Team	G	Rushing Att	Yds	Avg	TD	Receiving Rec	Yds	Avg	TD
1946 SF-A	13	79	346	4.4	2	9	80	8.9	0
1947 SF-A	14	143	906	6.3	5	15	258	17.2	3
1948 SF-A	14	141	915	6.5	4	26	485	18.7	7
1949 SF-A	7	66	287	4.3	3	6	99	16.5	1
AAFC Total	48	429	2454	5.7	14	56	922	16.5	11

Year Team	Punt Returns Ret	Yds	Avg	TD	Tot TD
1946 SF-A	3	26	8.7	0	2

1947 SF-A	8	70	8.8	0	8
1948 SF-A	13	201	15.5	0	11
1949 SF-A	2	19	9.5	0	4
AAFC Total	26	316	12.2	0	25

NFL Statistics

		Rushing				Receiving					Tot
Year Team	**G**	**Att**	**Yds**	**Avg**	**TD**	**Rec**	**Yds**	**Avg**	**TD**	**Fum**	**TD**
1950 SF	12	136	612	4.5	2	24	187	7.8	1	2	3
1951 SF	11	81	296	3.7	3	12	105	8.8	0	0	3
1952 SF	10	16	53	3.3	0	1	4	4.0	0	0	0
NFL Total	33	233	961	4.1	5	37	296	8.0	1	2	6

JIM STUART Stuart, James Robert 6'0", 212 **T**
(Bob) *Col:* Oregon *HS:* Hermiston [OR] B: 7/2/1919, Enterprise, OR D: 12/15/1985, Hermiston, OR *Drafted:* 1941 Round 3 Was
1941 Was: 5 G.

ROY STUART Stuart, Roy J Jr. 5'8", 188 **G-LB**
Col: Tulsa *HS:* Shawnee [OK] B: 7/25/1920, Shawnee, OK
AAFC **1946** BufA: 9 G.

NFL **1942** Cle: 10 G; Int 1-25. **1943** Det: 6 G. **Total:** 16 G; Int 1-25.

DANA STUBBLEFIELD Stubblefield, Dana William 6'2", 302 **DT**
Col: Kansas *HS:* Taylor [North Bend, OH] B: 11/14/1970, Cleves, OH *Drafted:* 1993 Round 1 SF
1993 SF: 16 G; 10.5 Sac. **1994** SF: 14 G; 8.5 Sac. **1995** SF: 16 G; Int 1-12; 4.5 Sac. **1996** SF: 15 G; Int 1-15; 1 Sac. **1997** SF: 16 G; 15 Sac. **1998** Was: 7 G; 1.5 Sac. **Total:** 84 G; Int 2-27; 41 Sac.

DANNY STUBBS Stubbs, Daniel II 6'4", 265 **DE-LB**
Col: Miami (Fla.) *HS:* Red Bank Regional [Little Silver, NJ] B: 1/3/1965, Long Branch, NJ *Drafted:* 1988 Round 2 SF
1988 SF: 16 G; 6 Sac. **1989** SF: 16 G; 4.5 Sac. **1990** Dal: 16 G; 7.5 Sac. **1991** Dal-Cin: 16 G; 4 Sac. Dal: 9 G; 1 Sac. Cin: 7 G; 3 Sac. **1992** Cin: 16 G; 9 Sac. **1993** Cin: 16 G; 5 Sac. **1995** Phi: 16 G; 5.5 Sac. **1996** Mia: 16 G; 9 Sac. **1997** Mia: 1 G; 1 Sac. **1998** Mia: 5 G. **Total:** 134 G; 51.5 Sac.

HENRY STUCKEY Stuckey, Henry L 6'1", 180 **DB**
Col: Merritt Coll. CA (J.C.); Missouri *HS:* Oakland College Prep [CA] B: 8/24/1950, Oakland, CA *Drafted:* 1972 Round 8 Det
1972 Mia: Postseason only. **1973** Mia: 6 G; Int 1-4. **1974** Mia: 14 G; PR 1-0; Int 1-21. **1975** NYG: 4 G. **1976** NYG: 3 G. **Total:** 27 G; PR 1-0; Int 2-25.

JIM STUCKEY Stuckey, James Davis 6'4", 251 **DE**
Col: Clemson *HS:* Airport [West Columbia, SC] B: 6/21/1958, Cayce, SC *Drafted:* 1980 Round 1 SF
1980 SF: 16 G; Scor **1** Saf; 2 Pt. **1981** SF: 15 G. **1982** SF: 9 G. **1983** SF: 16 G; 2.5 Sac. **1984** SF: 16 G; 3 Sac. **1985** SF: 15 G; 2 Sac. **1986** SF-NYJ: 6 G. SF: 1 G. NYJ: 5 G. **Total:** 93 G; Scor 1 Saf; 2 Pt; 7.5 Sac.

SHAWN STUCKEY Stuckey, Shawn 6'0", 230 **LB**
Col: Troy State B: 10/22/1975, Daleville, AL
1998 NE: 6 G.

MARK STUDAWAY Studaway, Mark Wayne 6'3", 273 **DE**
Col: Tennessee *HS:* South Side [Memphis, TN] B: 9/20/1960, Memphis, TN *Drafted:* 1984 Round 4 Hou
1984 Hou: 6 G. **1985** TB: 6 G. **1987** Atl: 2 G; 0.5 Sac. **Total:** 14 G; 0.5 Sac.

DAVE STUDDARD Studdard, David Derald 6'4", 260 **OT-OG-TE**
Col: Texas *HS:* Pearsall [TX] B: 11/22/1955, San Antonio, TX *Drafted:* 1978 Round 9 Bal
1979 Den: 16 G; Rec 1-2 2.0 1 TD; 6 Pt. **1980** Den: 16 G. **1981** Den: 16 G; Rec 1-10 10.0. **1982** Den: 9 G. **1983** Den: 16 G; KR 2-8 4.0. **1984** Den: 16 G; Rec 1-(-4) -4.0. **1985** Den: 16 G. **1986** Den: 15 G; Rec 1-2 2.0 1 TD; 6 Pt. **1987** Den: 14 G. **1988** Den: 11 G. **Total:** 145 G; Rec 4-10 2.5 2 TD; KR 2-8 4.0; 12 Pt.

LES STUDDARD Studdard, Leslie Elvin 6'4", 260 **C**
Col: Texas *HS:* Pearsall [TX] B: 12/14/1958, El Paso, TX *Drafted:* 1981 Round 10 KC
1982 KC: 9 G; Rush 1-0; 1 Fum. **1983** Hou: 6 G. **Total:** 15 G; Rush 1-0; 1 Fum.

VERN STUDDARD Studdard, Vernon Aaron Jr. 5'11", 175 **WR**
Col: Mississippi *HS:* Stephen D. Lee [Columbus, MS] B: 4/30/1948, Columbus, MS *Drafted:* 1971 Round 11 NYJ
1971 NYJ: 8 G; PR 4-3 0.8; KR 15-329 21.9.

DARREN STUDSTILL Studstill, Darren Henry 6'1", 193 **DB**
Col: West Virginia *HS:* Palm Beach Gardens [FL] B: 8/9/1970, Palm Beach Gardens, FL *Drafted:* 1994 Round 6 Dal
1994 Dal: 1 G. **1995** Jac: 8 G. **1996** Jac: 7 G. **Total:** 16 G.

PAT STUDSTILL Studstill, Patrick Lewis Jr. 6'0", 180 **WR-P**
Col: Houston *HS:* C.E. Byrd [Shreveport, LA] B: 6/4/1938, Shreveport, LA
1962 Det: Rush 1-(-11) -11.0. **1965** Det: Rush 1-(-4) -4.0. **1966** Det: Rush 2-20 10.0. **1968** LARm: Pass 1-0. **1970** LARm: Pass 1-0; Rush 1-23 23.0. **1972** NE: Pass 1-0; Rush 1-11 11.0. **Total:** Pass 3-0; Rush 6-39 6.5.

		Receiving				Punt Returns			
Year Team	**G**	**Rec**	**Yds**	**Avg**	**TD**	**Ret**	**Yds**	**Avg**	**TD**
1961 Det	14	5	54	10.8	0	8	75	9.4	0
1962 Det	14	36	479	13.3	4	**29**	**457**	**15.8**	0
1964 Det	14	7	102	14.6	1	17	137	8.1	0
1965 Det	14	28	389	13.9	3	5	47	9.4	0
1966 Det	14	67	**1266**	18.9	5	0	0	—	0
1967 Det	7	10	162	16.2	2	0	0	—	0
1968 LARm	14	7	108	15.4	1	0	0	—	0
1969 LARm	14	3	28	9.3	0	0	0	—	0
1970 LARm	14	18	252	14.0	2	0	0	—	0
1971 LARm	14	0	0	—	0	0	0	—	0
1972 NE	14	0	0	—	0	0	0	—	0
NFL Total	147	181	2840	15.7	18	59	716	12.1	0

	Kickoff Returns				Punting				Tot
Year Team	**Ret**	**Yds**	**Avg**	**TD**	**Punts**	**Yds**	**Avg**	**Fum**	**TD**
1961 Det	16	448	28.0	**1**	1	32	32.0	0	1
1962 Det	20	511	25.6	0	0	0	—	2	4
1964 Det	29	708	24.4	0	0	0	—	3	1
1965 Det	10	257	25.7	0	**78**	3335	42.8	0	3
1966 Det	0	0	—	0	72	2956	41.1	3	5
1967 Det	0	0	—	0	36	1602	44.5	0	2
1968 LARm	0	0	—	0	**81**	3207	39.6	0	1
1969 LARm	0	0	—	0	**80**	**3259**	40.7	0	0
1970 LARm	0	0	—	0	67	2618	39.1	0	2
1971 LARm	0	0	—	0	70	2896	41.4	0	0
1972 NE	0	0	—	0	75	2859	38.1	0	0
NFL Total	75	1924	25.7	1	560	22764	40.7	8	19

SCOTT STUDWELL Studwell, John Scott 6'2", 228 **LB**
Col: Illinois *HS:* William Henry Harrison [Evansville, IN] B: 8/27/1954, Evansville, IN *Drafted:* 1977 Round 9 Min
1979 Min: KR 1-0. **1982** Min: 3 Sac. **1983** Min: 2 Sac. **1986** Min: 1 Sac. **1987** Min: 1 Sac. **1988** Min: 1 Sac. **1989** Min: 1 Sac. **Total:** KR 1-0; 9 Sac.

		Interceptions		
Year Team	**G**	**Int**	**Yds**	**TD**
1977 Min	14	1	4	0
1978 Min	13	0	0	0
1979 Min	14	1	18	0
1980 Min	16	1	4	0
1981 Min	16	0	0	0
1982 Min	8	1	3	0
1983 Min	16	0	0	0
1984 Min	16	1	20	0
1985 Min	14	2	20	0
1986 Min	15	1	2	0
1987 Min	12	2	26	0
1988 Min	16	0	0	0
1989 Min	16	1	0	0
1990 Min	15	0	0	0
NFL Total	201	11	97	0

MEL STUESSY Stuessy, Melvin Matthias 5'9", 180 **T**
Col: St. Edward's B: 8/8/1901 D: 10/1980, Woodstock, IL
1926 ChiC: 1 G.

HARRY STUHLDREHER Stuhldreher, Harry Augustus 5'7", 165 **TB**
Col: Notre Dame *HS:* Washington [Massillon, OH]; Kiski School [Saltsburg, PA] B: 10/14/1901, Massillon, OH D: 1/25/1965, Pittsburgh, PA
1926 Bkn: 1 G.

CHARLES STUKES Stukes, Charles 6'3", 212 **DB**
(The Chesapeake Comet) *Col:* Maryland East. Shore *HS:* Crestwood [Chesapeake, VA] B: 9/13/1943, Chesapeake, VA *Drafted:* 1967 Round 4 Bal
1967 Bal: KR 1-19 19.0. **1970** Bal: KR 1-0. **1971** Bal: KR 1-8 8.0. **Total:** KR 3-27 9.0.

		Interceptions			
Year Team	**G**	**Int**	**Yds**	**TD**	**Fum**
1967 Bal	14	2	13	0	0
1968 Bal	14	1	60	1	0
1969 Bal	14	1	6	0	0
1970 Bal	11	3	52	0	0
1971 Bal	14	8	95	0	1
1972 Bal	12	5	23	0	0
1973 LARm	14	5	104	0	0
1974 LARm	14	7	90	0	1
NFL Total	107	32	443	1	2

CECIL STURGEON Sturgeon, Cecil Owen 6'2", 254 **T**
Col: North Dakota State *HS:* Moorhead [ND] B: 6/27/1919, Carenduff, Canada D: 2/1972
1941 Phi: 6 G.

LYLE STURGEON Sturgeon, Lyle Robert 6'3", 250 **T**
Col: North Dakota State *HS:* Moorhead [MN] B: 1/18/1914, Carenduff, Canada D: 11/30/1958, Green Bay, WI
1937 GB: 7 G.

OSCAR STURGIS Sturgis, Oscar Lee 6'5", 278 **DE**
Col: North Carolina *HS:* Richmond Co. [Hamlet, NC]; Fork Union Mil. Acad. [VA] B: 1/12/1971, Hamlet, NC *Drafted:* 1995 Round 7 Dal
1995 Dal: 1 G.

JERRY STURM Sturm, Jerry Gordon 6'3", 260 **OT-OG-C**
Col: Illinois *HS:* Gerstmeyer [Terre Haute, IN] B: 12/31/1936, English, IN
1961 Den: 14 G; Rush 8-31 3.9; Rec 2-(-1) -0.5; 1 Fum. **1962** Den: 14 G. **1963** Den: 14 G. **1964** Den: 14 G; KR 1-0. **1965** Den: 14 G. **1966** Den: 14 G; KR 1-2 2.0; 1 Fum. **1967** NO: 7 G; KR 1-0; 1 Fum. **1968** NO: 14 G. **1969** NO: 14 G; 1 Fum. **1970** NO: 10 G. **1971** Hou: 14 G. **1972** Phi: 1 G. **Total:** 144 G; Rush 8-31 3.9; Rec 2-(-1) -0.5; KR 3-2 0.7; 4 Fum.

FRED STURT Sturt, Frederick Neil 6'4", 255 **OG**
Col: Bowling Green State *HS:* Swanton [OH] B: 1/6/1951, Toledo, OH *Drafted:* 1973 Round 3 StL
1974 Was: 7 G. **1976** NE: 14 G. **1977** NE: 14 G. **1978** NE-NO: 13 G. NE: 1 G. NO: 12 G. **1979** NO: 16 G. **1980** NO: 15 G. **1981** NO: 16 G. **Total:** 95 G.

DICK STURTRIDGE Sturtridge, Richard Nelson 6'1", 171 **HB**
Col: DePauw *HS:* Emerson [Gary, IN] B: 3/8/1904, Vandergrift, PA D: 12/4/1978, Los Angeles, CA
1928 ChiB: 10 G; Pass 1 TD; Rec 2 TD; PR **1** TD; Scor **1** 1XP; Tot TD 3; 19 Pt. **1929** ChiB: 2 G. **Total:** 12 G; Pass 1 TD; Rec 2 TD; PR 1 TD; Scor 1 1XP; Tot TD 3; 19 Pt.

JOE STYDAHAR Stydahar, Joseph Lee 6'4", 233 **T**
(Jumbo Joe) *Col:* Pittsburgh; West Virginia *HS:* Shinnston [WV] B: 3/17/1912, Kaylor, PA D: 3/23/1977, Beckley, WV *Drafted:* 1936 Round 1 ChiB *HOF:* 1967
1936 ChiB: 12 G; Scor 3, 3 XK. **1937** ChiB: 10 G. **1938** ChiB: 11 G. **1939** ChiB: 11 G; Rec 1-9 9.0; Scor 4, 4-6 66.7% XK. **1940** ChiB: 10 G. **1941** ChiB: 8 G; Int 1-55; Scor 4, 4-4 100.0% XK. **1942** ChiB: 9 G; KR 1-0; Scor 5, 5-8 62.5% XK. **1945** ChiB: 3 G. **1946** ChiB: 10 G; Scor 12, 0-2 FG, 12-13 92.3% XK. **Total:** 84 G; Rec 1-9 9.0; KR 1-0; Int 1-55; Scor 28, 0-2 FG, 28-31 80.6% XK.

LORENZO STYLES Styles, Lorenzo Cavelle 6'1", 245 **LB**
Col: Ohio State *HS:* Independence [Columbus, OH]; Farrell HS [PA] B: 1/31/1974, Columbus, OH *Drafted:* 1995 Round 3 Atl
1995 Atl: 12 G. **1996** Atl: 16 G; KR 1-12 12.0. **1997** StL: 3 G. **1998** StL: 7 G. **Total:** 38 G; KR 1-12 12.0.

ANDY STYNCHULA Stynchula, Andrew Ralph 6'3", 250 **DE-DT-C**
Col: Penn State *HS:* Latrobe [PA] B: 1/7/1939, Latrobe, PA D: 8/1/1985, Great Harbour Cay, Bahamas *Drafted:* 1960 Round 3 Was
1960 Was: 12 G. **1961** Was: 14 G; KR 2-73 36.5; 1 Fum. **1962** Was: 13 G. **1963** Was: 14 G. **1964** NYG: 14 G; Scor 1, 1-1 100.0% XK. **1965** NYG: 11 G; Scor 21, 3-7 42.9% FG, 12-13 92.3% XK. **1966** Bal: 8 G. **1967** Bal: 13 G. **1968** Dal: 5 G. **Total:** 104 G; KR 2-73 36.5; Scor 22, 3-7 42.9% FG, 13-14 92.9% XK; 1 Fum.

NICKY SUALUA Sualua, Nicky 5'11", 260 **RB**
Col: Ohio State *HS:* Mater Dei [Santa Ana, CA] B: 4/16/1975, Santa Ana, CA *Drafted:* 1997 Round 4 Dal
1997 Dal: 10 G. **1998** Dal: 16 G. **Total:** 26 G.

NICK SUBIS Subis, Nicholas Alexander 6'4", 278 **OT-C**
Col: San Diego State *HS:* West [Torrance, CA] B: 12/24/1967, Inglewood, CA *Drafted:* 1991 Round 6 Den
1991 Den: 16 G.

LARRY SUCHY Suchy, Larry Wayne 5'10", 180 **DB**
Col: Jones Co. JC MS; Mississippi College *HS:* Heidelberg [MS] B: 7/12/1946, Heidelberg, MS D: 4/30/1972, Leland, MS
1968 Atl: 1 G.

PAUL SUCHY Suchy, Paul 188 **E**
Col: No College B: 3/28/1904 D: 11/1986, Inverness, IL
1925 Cle: 2 G.

BOB SUCI Suci, Robert Leslie 5'10", 185 **DB**
Col: Michigan State *HS:* Grand Blanc [MI] B: 4/7/1939, Flint, MI
1962 Hou: Int 1-22. **1963** Bos: KR 17-360 21.2; Int 7-**277** **2** TD. **Total:** KR 17-360 21.2; Int 8-299 2 TD.

		Punt Returns				
Year Team	**G**	**Ret**	**Yds**	**Avg**	**TD**	**Fum**
1962 Hou	6	0	0	—	0	0
1963 Bos	14	25	233	9.3	0	2
NFL Total	20	25	233	9.3	0	2

STEVE SUCIC Sucic, Stephen 6'0", 207 **FB-LB**
Col: Illinois *HS:* Lake View [Chicago, IL] B: 4/21/1921, Chicago, IL
1946 LARm: 4 G; Rush 7-18 2.6; Rec 1-1 1.0; KR 1-20 20.0; 1 Fum. **1947** Bos-Det: 8 G; Rush 3-3 1.0; Rec 1-20 20.0; KR 1-18 18.0. Bos: 3 G; Rush 3-3 1.0. Det: 5 G; Rec 1-20 20.0; KR 1-18 18.0. **1948** Det: 3 G; Rush 6-20 3.3. **Total:** 15 G; Rush 16-41 2.6; Rec 2-21 10.5; KR 2-38 19.0; 1 Fum.

RAY SUESS Suess, Raymond R Jr. 204 **T-G-OE**
Col: No College B: 8/8/1903 D: 8/11/1970, Santa Ana, CA
1926 Dul: 7 G. **1927** Dul: 9 G. **Total:** 16 G.

BOB SUFFRIDGE Suffridge, Robert Lee 6'0", 205 **G**
Col: Tennessee *HS:* Central [Knoxville, TN] B: 3/17/1916, Fountain City, TN D: 2/3/1974, Knoxville, TN *Drafted:* 1941 Round 5 Pit
1941 Phi: 10 G. **1945** Phi: 10 G. **Total:** 20 G.

LEO SUGAR Sugar, Leo Tateusz 6'1", 214 **DE**
Col: Purdue *HS:* Northern [Flint, MI] B: 4/6/1929, Flint, MI *Drafted:* 1952 Round 11 ChiC
1954 ChiC: 12 G; KR 1-7 7.0; **1** Fum TD; 6 Pt. **1955** ChiC: 12 G; Int 1-29. **1956** ChiC: 12 G; 1 Fum. **1957** ChiC: 12 G; Rec 1-14 14.0; **2** Fum TD; 12 Pt. **1958** ChiC: 12 G. **1959** ChiC: 12 G; PR 1-0. **1960** StL: 12 G. **1961** Phi: 14 G. **1962** Det: 6 G. **Total:** 104 G; Rec 1-14 14.0; PR 1-0; KR 1-7 7.0; Int 1-29; 3 Fum TD; 18 Pt; 1 Fum.

SHAFER SUGGS Suggs, Shafer L 6'1", 200 **DB**
Col: Ball State *HS:* Elkhart Central [IN] B: 4/28/1953, Elkhart, IN *Drafted:* 1976 Round 2 NYJ
1976 NYJ: 11 G; Int 1-12. **1977** NYJ: 9 G. **1978** NYJ: 16 G; Int 3-61. **1979** NYJ: 16 G; Int 3-41 1 TD; 6 Pt. **1980** NYJ-Cin: 8 G. NYJ: 4 G. Cin: 4 G. **Total:** 60 G; Int 7-114 1 TD; 6 Pt.

WALT SUGGS Suggs, William Walter Jr. 6'5", 260 **OT**
Col: Mississippi State *HS:* Forrest Co. [Brooklyn, MS] B: 5/15/1939, Hattiesburg, MS *Drafted:* 1961 Round 3 Hou
1962 Hou: 14 G. **1963** Hou: 14 G. **1964** Hou: 14 G. **1965** Hou: 14 G. **1966** Hou: 14 G. **1967** Hou: 14 G. **1968** Hou: 14 G. **1969** Hou: 14 G. **1970** Hou: 14 G. **1971** Hou: 11 G. **Total:** 137 G.

MATT SUHEY Suhey, Matthew Jerome 5'11", 217 **RB**
Col: Penn State *HS:* State College [PA] B: 7/7/1958, Bellefonte, PA *Drafted:* 1980 Round 2 ChiB
1980 ChiB: PR 1-4 4.0. **1983** ChiB: Pass 1-1 100.0%, 74 74.00 1 TD. **1984** ChiB: Pass 1-0. **Total:** Pass 2-1 50.0%, 74 37.00 1 TD; PR 1-4 4.0.

		Rushing				Receiving			
Year Team	**G**	**Att**	**Yds**	**Avg**	**TD**	**Rec**	**Yds**	**Avg**	**TD**
1980 ChiB	16	22	45	2.0	0	7	60	8.6	0
1981 ChiB	15	150	521	3.5	3	33	168	5.1	0
1982 ChiB	9	70	206	2.9	3	36	333	9.3	0
1983 ChiB	16	149	681	4.6	4	49	429	8.8	1
1984 ChiB	16	124	424	3.4	4	42	312	7.4	2
1985 ChiB	16	115	471	4.1	1	33	295	8.9	1
1986 ChiB	16	84	270	3.2	2	24	235	9.8	0
1987 ChiB	12	7	24	3.4	0	7	54	7.7	0
1988 ChiB	16	87	253	2.9	2	20	154	7.7	0
1989 ChiB	16	20	51	2.6	1	9	73	8.1	1
NFL Total	148	828	2946	3.6	20	260	2113	8.1	5

	Kickoff Returns					Tot
Year Team	**Ret**	**Yds**	**Avg**	**TD**	**Fum**	**TD**
1980 ChiB	19	406	21.4	0	1	0
1981 ChiB	0	0	—	0	3	3
1982 ChiB	0	0	—	0	2	3
1983 ChiB	0	0	—	0	5	5
1984 ChiB	0	0	—	0	6	6
1985 ChiB	0	0	—	0	2	2
1986 ChiB	0	0	—	0	1	2
1987 ChiB	1	9	9.0	0	0	0
1988 ChiB	0	0	—	0	1	2
1989 ChiB	6	93	15.5	0	1	2
NFL Total	26	508	19.5	0	22	25

STEVE SUHEY Suhey, Steven Joseph 5'11", 215 **G**
Col: Penn State *HS:* Cazenovia [NY] B: 1/8/1922, Janesville, NY D: 1/8/1977, State College, PA
1948 Pit: 12 G; KR 1-11 11.0; 1 Fum. **1949** Pit: 12 G. **Total:** 24 G; KR 1-11 11.0; 1 Fum.

JOE SULAITIS Sulaitis, Joseph 6'2", 212 **BB-DE-LB-OG**
HS: William L. Dickinson [Jersey City, NJ] B: 6/20/1921, Hoboken, NJ D: 2/8/1980, Point Pleasant, NJ
1944 NYG: Pass 17-4 23.5%, 53 3.12 1 TD 4 Int. **1945** NYG: Pass 13-7 53.8%, 126 9.69; KR 3-50 16.7. **1947** NYG: KR 2-23 11.5; Int 1-18. **1948** NYG: Pass 1-0; KR 4-66 16.5. **1949** NYG: KR 1-27 27.0. **1950** NYG: KR 4-112 28.0. **1951** NYG: KR 1-37 37.0. **1952** NYG: KR 4-91 22.8. **1953** NYG: KR 1-15 15.0; Int 1-6. **Total:** Pass 31-11 35.5%, 179 5.77 1 TD 4 Int; KR 20-421 21.1; Int 2-24.

Year Team	G	Rushing Att	Yds	Avg	TD	Receiving Rec	Yds	Avg	TD	Fum	Tot TD
1943 NYG	7	1	6	6.0	0	1	12	12.0	0	0	0
1944 NYG	6	9	38	4.2	0	0	0	—	0	0	0
1945 NYG	8	10	37	3.7	0	2	12	6.0	0	2	0
1946 Bos	3	0	0	—	0	0	0	—	0	0	0
1947 NYG	11	0	0	—	0	7	53	7.6	0	0	0
1948 NYG	12	5	18	3.6	1	26	298	11.5	1	2	2
1949 NYG	12	14	42	3.0	0	3	35	11.7	0	0	0
1950 NYG	12	0	0	—	0	1	3	3.0	0	0	0
1951 NYG	12	0	0	—	0	4	25	6.3	0	0	0
1952 NYG	12	0	0	—	0	4	31	7.8	0	0	0
1953 NYG	12	0	0	—	0	0	0	—	0	0	0
NFL Total	107	39	141	3.6	1	48	469	9.8	1	4	2

GEORGE SULIMA Sulima, George E 6'2", 200 **DE**
Col: Boston U. *HS:* New Britain [CT] B: 2/27/1928, New Britain, CT
D: 10/31/1987, Colchester, VT

Year Team	G	Receiving Rec	Yds	Avg	TD	Fum
1952 Pit	9	9	176	19.6	1	1
1953 Pit	10	10	131	13.1	0	1
1954 Pit	12	30	439	14.6	1	0
NFL Total	31	49	746	15.2	2	2

JOHN SULLINS Sullins, John Robertson 6'1", 225 **LB**
Col: Alabama *HS:* Lafayette [Oxford, MS] B: 9/7/1969, Oxford, MS
1992 Den: 6 G.

SULLIVAN Sullivan **FB**
Col: No College Deceased
1920 RI: 1 G.

CARL SULLIVAN Sullivan, Carl Jeffery 6'4", 248 **DE**
Col: San Francisco City Coll. CA (J.C.); San Jose State *HS:* Abraham Lincoln [San Francisco, CA] B: 4/30/1962, San Jose, CA
1987 GB: 3 G; 0.5 Sac.

CHRIS SULLIVAN Sullivan, Christopher Patrick 6'4", 279 **DE**
Col: Boston College *HS:* North Attleboro [MA] B: 3/14/1973, North Attleboro, MA *Drafted:* 1996 Round 4 NE
1996 NE: 16 G. **1997** NE: 16 G. **1998** NE: 15 G; KR 2-14 7.0; 2 Sac.
Total: 47 G; KR 2-14 7.0; 2 Sac.

DAN SULLIVAN Sullivan, Daniel Joseph 6'3", 250 **OG-OT**
Col: Boston College *HS:* Boston Technical [MA] B: 9/1/1939, Boston, MA *Drafted:* 1962 Round 3 Bal
1962 Bal: 14 G. **1963** Bal: 7 G. **1964** Bal: 14 G. **1965** Bal: 14 G. **1966** Bal: 13 G. **1967** Bal: 14 G. **1968** Bal: 14 G. **1969** Bal: 10 G. **1970** Bal: 14 G. **1971** Bal: 12 G. **1972** Bal: 14 G. **Total:** 140 G.

DAVE SULLIVAN Sullivan, David Allan 5'11", 185 **WR**
(Silky) *Col:* Virginia *HS:* Highspire [Steelton, PA] B: 1/31/1951, Steelton, PA *Drafted:* 1973 Round 15 Cle
1973 Cle: 1 G. **1974** Cle: 6 G; Rec 5-92 18.4; 1 Fum. **Total:** 7 G; Rec 5-92 18.4; 1 Fum.

FRANK SULLIVAN Sullivan, Frank Joseph 6'3", 206 **C-LB**
Col: Loyola (N.O.) *HS:* Father Ryan [Nashville, TN] B: 8/16/1912, Nashville, TN D: 6/1956
1935 ChiB: 11 G. **1936** ChiB: 3 G. **1937** ChiB: 7 G. **1938** ChiB: 10 G. **1939** ChiB: 9 G. **1940** Pit: 9 G; Int 1-0. **Total:** 49 G; Int 1-0.

GEORGE SULLIVAN Sullivan, George Albert 6'2", 205 **DE-OE**
Col: Notre Dame *HS:* Walpole [MA] B: 3/3/1926, Norwood, MA
Drafted: 1947 Round 6 Bos
1948 Bos: 1 G.

GEORGE SULLIVAN Sullivan, George Henry 5'9", 170 **TB-WB-BB**
Col: Pennsylvania B: 3/15/1897 D: 7/5/1989, Woodbury, NJ
1924 Fra: 6 G; Rush 5 TD; 30 Pt. **1925** Fra: 16 G; Rush 2 TD; Rec 1 TD; Tot TD 3; 18 Pt. **Total:** 22 G; Rush 7 TD; Rec 1 TD; Tot TD 8; 48 Pt.

GERRY SULLIVAN Sullivan, Gerald B 6'4", 250 **C-OT-OG**
Col: Illinois *HS:* Oak Park [IL] B: 1/15/1952, Oak Park, IL
Drafted: 1974 Round 7 Cle
1974 Cle: 13 G. **1975** Cle: 14 G. **1976** Cle: 14 G. **1977** Cle: 14 G. **1978** Cle: 16 G; 2 Fum. **1979** Cle: 16 G. **1980** Cle: 16 G; 1 Fum. **1981** Cle: 16 G. **Total:** 119 G; 3 Fum.

HEW SULLIVAN Sullivan, Harold C 195 **G**
(Red) *Col:* No College *HS:* Chisholm [MN] B: 3/2/1898, MN
D: 10/1975, Minneapolis, MN
1926 Dul: 1 G.

JIM SULLIVAN Sullivan, James Edmund 6'4", 240 **DT-DE**
Col: Lincoln (Mo.) *HS:* Yerger [Hope, AR] B: 8/20/1944, Detroit, MI
1970 Atl: 7 G.

JACK SULLIVAN Sullivan, John Henry 170 **FB**
Col: No College *HS:* Holyoke [MA] Deceased
1921 Buf: 3 G.

JACK SULLIVAN Sullivan, John Henry 170 **FB**
Col: North Carolina State *HS:* Holyoke [MA] B: 11/12/1891, Holyoke, MA Deceased
1921 Was: 1 G.

JOHN SULLIVAN Sullivan, John Lloyd 6'1", 190 **DB**
Col: California *HS:* Abraham Lincoln [San Francisco, CA]
B: 11/15/1961, Hartford, CT *Drafted:* 1984 Supplemental Round 3 ChiB
1986 GB-SD: 15 G. GB: 6 G. SD: 9 G. **1987** SF: 1 G. **Total:** 16 G.

JOHN SULLIVAN Sullivan, John Patrick 6'1", 221 **LB**
Col: Illinois *HS:* John the Baptist [Massapequa, NY] B: 10/1/1956, Massapequa Park, NY *Drafted:* 1979 Round 6 ChiB
1979 NYJ: 12 G. **1980** NYJ: 16 G. **Total:** 28 G.

KENT SULLIVAN Sullivan, Kent Allen 5'11", 197 **P**
Col: California Lutheran *HS:* Northridge [Middlebury, IN] B: 5/15/1964, Plymouth, IN
1991 Hou: 1 G; Punt 3-106 35.3. **1992** KC: 1 G; Punt 6-247 41.2.
1993 Hou-SD: 3 G; Punt 15-614 40.9. Hou: 1 G; Punt 2-73 36.5. SD: 2 G; Punt 13-541 41.6. **Total:** 5 G; Punt 24-967 40.3.

MIKE SULLIVAN Sullivan, Michael Gerard 6'3", 292 **OG-OT**
Col: Miami (Fla.) *HS:* St. Francis de Sales [Chicago, IL] B: 12/22/1967, Chicago, IL *Drafted:* 1991 Round 6 Dal
1992 TB: 9 G. **1993** TB: 11 G. **1994** TB: 16 G. **1995** TB: 12 G. **Total:** 48 G.

PAT SULLIVAN Sullivan, Patrick Joseph 6'0", 198 **QB**
Col: Auburn *HS:* John Carroll [Birmingham, AL] B: 1/18/1950, Birmingham, AL *Drafted:* 1972 Round 2 Atl
1972 Atl: Rush 2-8 4.0. **1973** Atl: Rush 3-19 6.3. **1974** Atl: Rush 3-19 6.3.
1975 Atl: Rush 6-9 1.5. **Total:** Rush 14-55 3.9.

Year Team	G	Passing Att	Comp	Comp%	Yds	YPA	TD	Int	Rating	Fum
1972 Atl	14	19	3	15.8	44	2.32	0	3	0.0	2
1973 Atl	4	26	14	53.8	175	6.73	1	0	87.8	1
1974 Atl	6	105	48	45.7	556	5.30	1	8	33.7	1
1975 Atl	6	70	28	40.0	380	5.43	3	5	42.6	4
NFL Total	30	220	93	42.3	1155	5.25	5	16	36.5	8

BOB SULLIVAN Sullivan, Robert Gerard 5'9", 191 **HB-TB-DB-LB**
Col: Iowa *HS:* Cathedral [Springfield, MA] B: 12/24/1924, Attleboro, MA D: 11/12/1992, Carmichael, CA *Drafted:* 1947 Round 13 Bos
AAFC **1948** BknA: 2 G; Rush 2-(-1) -0.5; KR 1-22 22.0.

NFL **1947** Pit: 3 G; Pass 9-3 33.3%, 52 5.78 1 Int; Rush 21-61 2.9; Rec 4-72 18.0 1 TD; PR 1-10 10.0; KR 4-86 21.5; 6 Pt; 2 Fum.

BOB SULLIVAN Sullivan, Robert Joseph 5'10", 190 **HB-DB**
Col: Holy Cross *HS:* North Andover [MA] B: 8/15/1923, Lowell, MA
D: 6/19/1981, North Andover, MA
AAFC **1948** SF-A: Rec 4-58 14.5 1 TD; KR 2-40 20.0; Int 1-6.

Year Team	G	Rushing Att	Yds	Avg	TD
1948 SF-A	13	33	121	3.7	0

STEVE SULLIVAN Sullivan, Stephen Patrick 5'9", 180 **TB-WB-OE**
(Paddy) *Col:* Montana *HS:* Butte [MT] B: 7/1/1898, Butte, MT
D: 8/17/1969, Concord, CA
1922 Mil-Eva-Ham: 5 G. Mil: 2 G. Eva: 1 G. Ham: 2 G. **1923** Ham: 4 G.
1924 KC-Ham: 2 G. KC: 1 G. Ham: 1 G. **Total:** 11 G.

TOM SULLIVAN Sullivan, Thomas Ashley 6'0", 190 **RB**
(Silky) *Col:* Miami (Fla.) *HS:* Fletcher [Jacksonville, FL]; Neptune Beach HS [FL] B: 3/5/1950, Jacksonville, FL *Drafted:* 1972 Round 15 Phi

Year Team	G	Rushing Att	Yds	Avg	TD	Receiving Rec	Yds	Avg	TD
1972 Phi	12	13	13	1.0	0	4	17	4.3	0
1973 Phi	13	217	968	4.5	4	50	322	6.4	1
1974 Phi	14	244	760	3.1	**11**	39	312	8.0	1
1975 Phi	14	173	632	3.7	0	28	276	9.9	0
1976 Phi	13	99	399	4.0	2	14	116	8.3	1
1977 Phi	14	125	363	2.9	0	26	223	8.6	2
1978 Cle	4	5	7	1.4	0	1	20	20.0	0
NFL Total	84	876	3142	3.6	17	162	1286	7.9	5

Year Team	Kickoff Returns Ret	Yds	Avg	TD	Fum	Tot TD
1972 Phi	3	72	24.0	0	1	0
1973 Phi	12	280	23.3	0	6	5
1974 Phi	0	0	—	0	6	12
1975 Phi	3	42	14.0	0	4	0
1976 Phi	5	108	21.6	0	1	3
1977 Phi	0	0	—	0	2	2
1978 Cle	4	90	22.5	0	1	0
NFL Total	27	592	21.9	0	21	22

IVORY SULLY Sully, Ivory Ulyysses 6'0", 198 **DB**
Col: Delaware *HS:* Leonia [NJ] B: 6/20/1957, Salisbury, MD
1979 LARm: 8 G. **1980** LARm: 16 G; KR 4-36 9.0; 1 Fum. **1981** LARm: 16 G; KR 3-31 10.3; 1 Fum. **1982** LARm: 9 G; KR 5-84 16.8. **1983** LARm: 16 G; 1 Sac. **1984** LARm: 16 G; KR 1-3 3.0; Scor **1** Saf; 2 Pt. **1985** TB: 16 G; Int 1-20. **1986** TB: 16 G. **1987** Det: 11 G. **Total:** 124 G; KR 13-154 11.8; Int 1-20; Scor 1 Saf; 2 Pt; 2 Fum; 1 Sac.

DAVE SUMINSKI Suminski, David Mitchell 5'11", 230 **OG**
Col: Wisconsin *HS:* Ashland [WI] B: 6/18/1931, Ashland, WI
Drafted: 1953 Round 15 Was
1953 Was-ChiC: 8 G. Was: 2 G. ChiC: 6 G. **Total:** 8 G.

TONY SUMLER Sumler, Tony Bernard 5'10", 185 **DB**
Col: Wichita State *HS:* Chadsey [Detroit, MI] B: 4/10/1956, Detroit, MI
1978 Det: 1 G.

PAT SUMMERALL Summerall, George Allen 6'4", 228 **DE-OE-K**
Col: Arkansas *HS:* Columbia [Lake City, FL] B: 5/10/1930, Lake City, FL *Drafted:* 1952 Round 4 Det
1955 ChiC: Int 1-26 1 TD. **1957** ChiC: KR 1-3 3.0. **1959** NYG: Rec 2-32 16.0; KR 1-3 3.0. **1960** NYG: Pass 1-0; Rec 1-15 15.0. **Total:** Pass 1-0; Rec 3-47 15.7; KR 2-6 3.0; Int 1-26 1 TD.

		Scoring							
Year Team	**G**	**Pts**	**FG**	**FGA**	**FG%**	**XK**	**XKA**	**XK%**	**Fum**
1952 Det	2	0	0	0	—	0	0	—	0
1953 ChiC	12	50	9	24	37.5	23	23	100.0	0
1954 ChiC	12	45	8	18	44.4	21	23	91.3	0
1955 ChiC	11	53	8	19	42.1	23	25	92.0	0
1956 ChiC	12	60	10	22	45.5	30	30	100.0	0
1957 ChiC	12	42	6	17	35.3	24	26	92.3	0
1958 NYG	10	64	12	23	52.2	28	30	93.3	0
1959 NYG	12	90	**20**	**29**	**69.0**	30	30	**100.0**	0
1960 NYG	12	71	13	26	50.0	32	32	100.0	1
1961 NYG	14	88	14	34	41.2	**46**	**46**	100.0	0
NFL Total	109	563	100	212	47.2	257	265	97.0	1

CARL SUMMERELL Summerell, Carl Leigh 6'4", 208 **QB**
Col: East Carolina *HS:* Floyd E. Kellam [Virginia Beach, VA]
B: 12/6/1951, Virginia Beach, VA *Drafted:* 1974 Round 4 NYG
1974 NYG: 7 G; Pass 13-6 46.2%, 59 4.54 3 Int; Rush 2-8 4.0. **1975** NYG: 3 G; Pass 16-7 43.8%, 98 6.13 2 Int; Rush 3-4 1.3; 2 Fum. **Total:** 10 G; Pass 29-13 44.8%, 157 5.41 5 Int; Rush 5-12 2.4; 2 Fum.

BOB SUMMERHAYS Summerhays, Robert William 6'1", 210 **LB-FB**
Col: Utah *HS:* East [Salt Lake City, UT] B: 3/19/1927, Salt Lake City, UT *Drafted:* 1949 Round 4 GB
1949 GB: Rec 1-34 34.0. **1950** GB: Int 1-0. **1951** GB: KR 1-21 21.0; Int 2-112 1 TD. **Total:** Rec 1-34 34.0; KR 1-21 21.0; Int 3-112 1 TD.

		Rushing				
Year Team	**G**	**Att**	**Yds**	**Avg**	**TD**	**Fum**
1949 GB	12	29	101	3.5	0	1
1950 GB	11	0	0	—	0	0
1951 GB	12	0	0	—	0	0
NFL Total	35	29	101	3.5	0	1

DON SUMMERS Summers, Donald 0 6'4", 230 **TE**
Col: Oregon Tech; Boise State *HS:* Eagle Point [OR]; Medford HS [OR]
B: 2/22/1961, Grants Pass, OR
1984 Den: 16 G; Rec 3-32 10.7. **1985** Den: 2 G. **1987** GB: 3 G; Rec 7-83 11.9 1 TD; 6 Pt. **Total:** 21 G; Rec 10-115 11.5 1 TD; 6 Pt.

FREDDIE SUMMERS Summers, Freddie S 6'1", 180 **DB**
Col: McCook CC NE; Washington (Md) *HS:* Dorchester [Boston, MA]
B: 2/16/1947, Columbia, SC *Drafted:* 1969 Round 4 Cle
1969 Cle: 8 G. **1970** Cle: 12 G. **1971** Cle: 3 G. **Total:** 23 G.

JIM SUMMERS Summers, James III 5'10", 180 **DB**
Col: Michigan State *HS:* Orangeburg-Wilkinson [Orangeburg, SC]
B: 12/23/1945, Orangeburg, SC *Drafted:* 1967 Round 9 Den
1967 Den: 11 G.

WILBUR SUMMERS Summers, Wilbur Thomas 6'4", 220 **P**
Col: Louisville *HS:* Miami Norland [FL] B: 8/6/1954, Irvington, NJ
Drafted: 1976 Round 15 Den
1977 Det: Pass 1-1 100.0%, 5 5.00; Rush 1-0.

		Punting		
Year Team	**G**	**Punts**	**Yds**	**Avg**
1977 Det	13	93	3420	36.8

CHARLIE SUMNER Sumner, Charles Edward 6'1", 194 **DB**
Col: William & Mary *HS:* Dublin [VA] B: 10/19/1930, Radford, VA
Drafted: 1954 Round 22 ChiB
1955 ChiB: PR 1-0; KR 10-288 28.8. **1958** ChiB: PR 9-25 2.8; KR 1-19 19.0; **1** Fum TD. **Total:** PR 10-25 2.5; KR 11-307 27.9; 1 Fum TD.

		Interceptions			
Year Team	**G**	**Int**	**Yds**	**TD**	**Fum**
1955 ChiB	10	7	162	0	1
1958 ChiB	12	6	67	0	0
1959 ChiB	12	3	22	0	1
1960 ChiB	12	0	0	0	0
1961 Min	13	2	6	0	0
1962 Min	14	3	46	0	0
NFL Total	73	21	303	0	2

WALT SUMNER Sumner, Walter Herman 6'1", 195 **DB**
Col: Florida State *HS:* Irwin Co. [Ocilla, GA] B: 2/2/1947, Ocilla, GA
Drafted: 1969 Round 7 Cle
1969 Cle: PR 9-88 9.8. **1970** Cle: PR 8-70 8.8. **1972** Cle: PR 1-14 14.0.
Total: PR 18-172 9.6.

		Interceptions			
Year Team	**G**	**Int**	**Yds**	**TD**	**Fum**
1969 Cle	14	4	82	1	3
1970 Cle	12	4	85	0	2
1971 Cle	14	5	35	0	0
1972 Cle	13	0	0	0	0
1973 Cle	13	2	4	0	0
1974 Cle	10	0	0	0	0
NFL Total	76	15	206	1	5

TONY SUMPTER Sumpter, Anthony B 6'1", 215 **G**
Col: Cameron *HS:* Lawton [OK] B: 9/13/1923, Fletcher, OK
AAFC **1946** ChiA: 12 G. **1947** ChiA: 1 G. **Total:** 13 G.

MILT SUNDE Sunde, Milton John 6'2", 250 **OG**
Col: Minnesota *HS:* Bloomington [MN] B: 2/1/1942, Minneapolis, MN
Drafted: 1964 Round 20 Min
1964 Min: 14 G. **1965** Min: 14 G. **1966** Min: 14 G; KR 1-0. **1967** Min: 10 G. **1968** Min: 14 G. **1969** Min: 14 G; KR 1-0. **1970** Min: 14 G. **1971** Min: 14 G. **1972** Min: 14 G. **1973** Min: 14 G. **1974** Min: 11 G. **Total:** 147 G; KR 2-0.

IAN SUNTER Sunter, Ian James 6'1", 215 **K**
Col: No College *HS:* Burlington Central Sec. School [Canada]
B: 12/21/1952, Dundee, Scotland
1976 Det: 3 G. **1980** Cin: 10 G; Scor 48, 11-20 55.0% FG, 15-15 100.0% XK. **Total:** 13 G; Scor 48, 11-20 55.0% FG, 15-15 100.0% XK.

STEVE SUPERICK Superick, Stephen Wayne 5'11", 204 **P**
Col: West Virginia *HS:* North Brunswick [NJ] B: 8/9/1963, Memphis, TN
1987 Hou: 2 G; Punt 8-269 33.6.

KYWIN SUPERNAW Supernaw, Kywin 6'1", 206 **DB**
Col: Northeastern Oklahoma A&M (J.C.); Indiana *HS:* Skiatook [OK]
B: 6/2/1975, Claremore, OK
1998 Det: 2 G.

LEN SUPULSKI Supulski, Leonard P 6'0", 175 **OE-DB**
Col: Dickinson B: 12/15/1920, Kingston, PA D: 9/1/1943, NE
1942 Phi: 9 G; Rush 1-1 1.0; Rec 8-149 18.6 1 TD; Int 1-5; 6 Pt.

PATRICK SURTAIN Surtain, Patrick Frank 5'11", 196 **DB**
Col: Southern Mississippi *HS:* Edna Karr [New Orleans, LA]
B: 6/19/1976, New Orleans, LA *Drafted:* 1998 Round 2 Mia
1998 Mia: 16 G; Int 2-1.

NICK SUSOEFF Susoeff, Nicholas 6'1", 211 **OE-DE**
Col: Washington State *HS:* Theodore Roosevelt [Los Angeles, CA]
B: 4/15/1921, Umapine, OR D: 1/31/1967, Palo Alto, CA
AAFC **1946** SF-A: KR 1-10 10.0. **1948** SF-A: KR 1-12 12.0.
Total: KR 2-22 11.0.

		Receiving			
Year Team	**G**	**Rec**	**Yds**	**Avg**	**TD**
1946 SF-A	6	5	98	19.6	0
1947 SF-A	14	24	223	9.3	2
1948 SF-A	13	27	237	8.8	1
1949 SF-A	11	5	52	10.4	1
AAFC Total	44	61	610	10.0	4

ED SUSTERSIC Sustersic, Edward J 6'0", 205 **FB-LB**
Col: Findlay *HS:* John Marshall [Cleveland, OH] B: 1/7/1922, Cleveland, OH D: 1/18/1967, Brecksville, OH
AAFC **1949** CleA: 11 G; Rush 23-114 5.0 1 TD; Rec 1-7 7.0; KR 2-39 19.5; 6 Pt.

GEORGE SUTCH Sutch, George Russell Jr. 6'1", 205 **HB-DB**
Col: Rochester; Temple B: 8/28/1921, Jeffersonville, PA *Drafted:* 1943 Round 22 ChiC
1946 ChiC: 3 G; Rush 5-4 0.8; KR 1-4 4.0; 3 Fum.

DON SUTHERIN Sutherin, Donald Paul 5'10", 193 **DB**
(Suds) *Col:* Ohio State *HS:* Toronto [OH] B: 2/29/1936, Empire, OH
Drafted: 1958 Round 8 NYG
1959 NYG-Pit: 8 G; PR 12-68 5.7; KR 11-225 20.5; Scor 0-1 FG; 1 Fum. NYG: 2 G. Pit: 6 G; PR 12-68 5.7; KR 11-225 20.5; Scor 0-1 FG; 1 Fum. **1960** Pit: 4 G; Int 1-0. **Total:** 12 G; PR 12-68 5.7; KR 11-225 20.5; Int 1-0; Scor 0-1 FG; 1 Fum.

DOUG SUTHERLAND Sutherland, Douglas A 6'3", 250 **DT-OG-DE**
Col: Wis.-Superior *HS:* Superior [WI] B: 8/1/1948, Superior, WI
Drafted: 1970 Round 14 NO
1970 NO: 10 G. **1971** Min: 11 G. **1972** Min: 14 G. **1973** Min: 9 G. **1974** Min: 14 G. **1975** Min: 14 G. **1976** Min: 14 G. **1977** Min: 14 G. **1978** Min: 16 G. **1979** Min: 16 G. **1980** Min: 16 G. **1981** Sea: 16 G. **Total:** 164 G.

JOHN SUTRO Sutro, John Robert 6'4", 245 **OT**
Col: San Jose State *HS:* Harry Ellis [Richmond, CA] B: 5/8/1940
Drafted: 1962 Round 6 GB
1962 SF: 5 G.

EDDIE SUTTER Sutter, Edward Lee 6'3", 240 **LB**
Col: Northwestern *HS:* Richwoods [Peoria, IL] B: 10/3/1969, Peoria, IL
1993 Cle: 15 G. **1994** Cle: 16 G. **1995** Cle: 16 G. **1996** Bal: 16 G. **1997** Atl: 16 G. **Total:** 79 G.

RYAN SUTTER Sutter, Ryan Allen 6'1", 203 **DB**
Col: Colorado *HS:* Fort Collins [CO] B: 9/14/1974, Fort Collins, CO
Drafted: 1998 Round 5 Bal
1998 Car: 1 G.

ARCHIE SUTTON Sutton, Archie Michael 6'4", 262 **OT**
Col: Illinois *HS:* Xavier Prep [New Orleans, LA] B: 11/2/1941, New Orleans, LA *Drafted:* 1965 Round 2 Min
1965 Min: 14 G. **1966** Min: 3 G. **1967** Min: 2 G. **Total:** 19 G.

ED SUTTON Sutton, Edward Wike 6'1", 205 **HB-DB**
(The Cullowhee Comet) *Col:* North Carolina *HS:* Cullowhee [NC]
B: 3/16/1935, Sylva, NC *Drafted:* 1957 Round 3 Was
1957 Was: Pass 5-3 60.0%, 95 19.00; Rec 2-32 16.0 1 TD; KR 1-19 19.0; Int 1-11. **1958** Was: Pass 3-0; Rec 6-112 18.7. **1959** Was: Pass 7-2 28.6%, 51 7.29 1 TD; Rec 4-63 15.8. **1960** NYG: Rec 2-30 15.0; KR 12-223 18.6. **Total:** Pass 15-5 33.3%, 146 9.73 1 TD; Rec 14-237 16.9 1 TD; KR 13-242 18.6; Int 1-11.

		Rushing					Tot
Year Team	G	Att	Yds	Avg	TD	Fum	TD
1957 Was	12	108	407	3.8	5	6	6
1958 Was	10	93	335	3.6	3	1	3
1959 Was	11	61	232	3.8	1	0	1
1960 NYG	12	20	135	6.8	0	6	0
NFL Total	45	282	1109	3.9	9	13	10

ERIC SUTTON Sutton, Eric Dontay 5'10", 170 **DB**
Col: San Diego State *HS:* Inglewood [CA] B: 10/24/1972, Los Angeles, CA
1996 Was: 4 G.

FRANK SUTTON Sutton, Frank LaRose 6'3", 280 **OT**
Col: Jackson State *HS:* Forest Hill [Jackson, MS] B: 3/29/1963
1987 NYG: 2 G.

RICKY SUTTON Sutton, Frederick DeWayne 6'2", 281 **DE-DT**
Col: Auburn *HS:* Tucker [GA] B: 4/27/1971, Atlanta, GA
1993 Pit: 7 G.

JON SUTTON Sutton, Jonathan E 6'1", 195 **DB**
Col: New Mexico *HS:* Morningside [Inglewood, CA] B: 7/2/1957, New Orleans, LA
1987 NO: 2 G.

JOE SUTTON Sutton, Joseph Boyle 5'11", 180 **DB-HB**
(Bud) *Col:* Temple *HS:* Northeast [Philadelphia, PA] B: 4/26/1924, Philadelphia, PA
AAFC **1949** BufA: 9 G; Rush 9-63 7.0; Rec 5-63 12.6 1 TD; PR 6-62 10.3; KR 4-82 20.5; 6 Pt.

NFL **1950** Phi: Rush 1-1 1.0; PR 9-75 8.3; KR 1-21 21.0. **Total:** Rush 1-1 1.0; PR 9-75 8.3; KR 1-21 21.0.

		Interceptions			
Year Team	G	Int	Yds	TD	Fum
1950 Phi	9	8	67	0	2
1951 Phi	11	2	8	0	0
1952 Phi	10	3	54	0	0
NFL Total	30	13	129	0	2

MICKEY SUTTON Sutton, Michael Thomas 6'0", 190 **DB**
Col: Auburn *HS:* S.S. Murphy [Mobile, AL] B: 7/17/1943, Mobile, AL
1966 Hou: 5 G.

MIKE SUTTON Sutton, Mike 6'4", 272 **DE**
Col: Louisiana Coll. *HS:* Salmen [Slidell, LA] B: 4/21/1975, Jacksonville, NC
1998 Ten: 1 G.

MITCH SUTTON Sutton, Mitchell Andrew 6'4", 260 **DE**
Col: Fort Scott CC KS; Kansas *HS:* Stone Mountain [GA]
B: 5/10/1951, Stone Mountain, GA *Drafted:* 1974 Round 3 Phi
1974 Phi: 14 G. **1975** Phi: 4 G. **Total:** 18 G.

REGGIE SUTTON Sutton, Reginald Eugene 5'10", 180 **DB**
Col: Miami (Fla.) *HS:* Miami Killian [FL] B: 2/15/1965, Miami, FL
Drafted: 1986 Round 5 NO
1987 NO: 11 G; Int 5-68; 6 Pt. **1988** NO: 15 G; Int 3-32; 1 Fum.
Total: 26 G; Int 8-100; 6 Pt; 1 Fum.

MICKEY SUTTON Sutton, William Earl 5'8", 165 **DB**
Col: Montana *HS:* James Logan [Logan, UT] B: 8/28/1960, Greenville, MS
1986 LARm: KR 5-91 18.2; Int 2-25. **1987** LARm: KR 2-37 18.5; Int 1-4. **1988** LARm: KR 2-41 20.5; Int 1-1. **1989** GB-Buf: Int 1-3. Buf: Int 1-3.
Total: KR 9-169 18.8; Int 5-33.

		Punt Returns				
Year Team	G	Ret	Yds	Avg	TD	Fum
1986 LARm	16	28	234	8.4	0	0
1987 LARm	12	0	0	—	0	0
1988 LARm	15	3	52	17.3	0	0
1989 GB-Buf	15	31	273	8.8	0	2
1989 GB	3	5	42	8.4	0	1
1989 Buf	12	26	231	8.9	0	1
1990 LARm	7	14	136	9.7	0	0
NFL Total	65	76	695	9.1	0	2

HARLAND SVARE Svare, Harland James 6'0", 214 **LB-TB**
(Swede) *Col:* Washington State *HS:* North Kitsap [Poulsbo, WA]
B: 11/15/1930, Clarkfield, MN *Drafted:* 1953 Round 17 LARm
1953 LARm: 10 G; Int 1-9. **1954** LARm: 10 G. **1955** NYG: 12 G; Int 2-19. **1956** NYG: 11 G. **1957** NYG: 12 G; Int 1-21. **1958** NYG: 10 G; Int 1-25. **1959** NYG: 12 G; Int 3-118 1 TD; 6 Pt. **1960** NYG: 12 G; Int 1-37.
Total: 89 G; Int 9-229 1 TD; 6 Pt.

BUD SVENDSEN Svendsen, Earl Gilbert 6'1", 190 **C-LB-G**
Col: Minnesota *HS:* Marshall [Minneapolis, MN] B: 2/7/1915, Minneapolis, MN D: 8/6/1996, Edina, MN
1937 GB: 11 G. **1939** GB: 10 G; **1** Fum TD; 6 Pt. **1940** Bkn: 11 G; Int 2-13. **1941** Bkn: 11 G; PR 1-2 2.0; Int 1-1. **1942** Bkn: 4 G; Int 1-18. **1943** Bkn: 10 G; Int 1-20. **Total:** 57 G; PR 1-2 2.0; Int 5-52; 1 Fum TD; 6 Pt.

GEORGE SVENDSEN Svendsen, George Peter Jr. 6'4", 230 **C-LB**
Col: Oregon State; Minnesota *HS:* Marshall [Minneapolis, MN]
B: 3/22/1913, Minneapolis, MN D: 8/6/1995, Minneapolis, MN
1935 GB: 9 G. **1936** GB: 11 G. **1937** GB: 11 G; Rec 1-11 11.0. **1940** GB: 10 G; Int 1-6. **1941** GB: 11 G; Int 1-42. **Total:** 52 G; Rec 1-11 11.0; Int 2-48.

PAUL SVERCHEK Sverchek, Paul Anthony 6'3", 252 **NT**
Col: Cal Poly-S.L.O. *HS:* San Luis Obispo [CA] B: 5/9/1961, San Luis Obispo, CA
1984 Min: 3 G.

BOB SVIHUS Svihus, Robert Craig 6'4", 245 **OT**
(Condor) *Col:* USC *HS:* Sequoia [Redwood City, CA] B: 6/21/1943, Los Angeles, CA *Drafted:* 1965 Round 4 Dal
1965 Oak: 14 G. **1966** Oak: 14 G. **1967** Oak: 14 G. **1968** Oak: 14 G. **1969** Oak: 13 G. **1970** Oak: 13 G. **1971** NYJ: 14 G. **1972** NYJ: 14 G. **1973** NYJ: 12 G. **Total:** 122 G.

BILL SVOBODA Svoboda, William Ray 6'0", 210 **LB-FB**
Col: Tulane *HS:* Bonham [TX] B: 7/12/1928, Wichita Falls, TX
D: 6/20/1980, Houma, LA *Drafted:* 1950 Round 3 ChiC
1950 ChiC: 12 G. **1951** ChiC: 12 G; Rush 5-15 3.0; Rec 6-(-9) -1.5; KR 1-29 29.0. **1952** ChiC: 9 G; Int 2-2. **1953** ChiC: 12 G; KR 1-15 15.0; Int 1-0. **1954** NYG: 11 G; KR 1-21 21.0; Int 1-30. **1955** NYG: 12 G; Int 1-24. **1956** NYG: 11 G; Int 2-3. **1957** NYG: 11 G; Int 2-43. **1958** NYG: 10 G. **Total:** 100 G; Rush 5-15 3.0; Rec 6-(-9) -1.5; KR 3-65 21.7; Int 9-102.

AL SWAIN Swain, Arthur Alton 6'1", 190 **OE**
(Judge) *Col:* Trinity (Tex.) *HS:* Alvord [TX] B: 9/5/1904, Alvord, TX Deceased
1926 Buf: 3 G; Rec 1 TD; 6 Pt.

JOHN SWAIN Swain, John Wesley 6'1", 195 **DB**
Col: Miami (Fla.) *HS:* Miami Carol City [Miami, FL] B: 9/4/1959, Miami, FL *Drafted:* 1981 Round 4 Min

		Interceptions		
Year Team	G	Int	Yds	TD
1981 Min	12	2	18	0
1982 Min	9	2	20	0
1983 Min	14	6	12	0
1984 Min	15	2	20	0
1985 Mia-Pit	15	2	4	0
1985 Mia	6	0	0	0
1985 Pit	9	2	4	0
1986 Pit	11	0	9	0
1987 Mia	1	0	0	0
NFL Total	77	14	83	0

BILL SWAIN Swain, William Steven 6′2″, 230 **LB**
Col: Clark Coll. WA (J.C.); Oregon *HS:* North Bend [OR] B: 2/22/1941, Dickinson, ND
1963 LARm: 14 G. **1964** Min: 14 G. **1965** NYG: 14 G. **1967** NYG: 14 G; Int 1-0. **1968** Det: 12 G; Int 1-50 1 TD; 6 Pt. **1969** Det: 14 G. **Total:** 82 G; Int 2-50 1 TD; 6 Pt.

RUSS SWAN Swan, Russell Scott 6′4″, 223 **LB**
Col: Virginia *HS:* Yorktown [Yorktown Heights, NY] B: 3/30/1963, Fairview Park, OH
1987 Dal: 5 G.

KARL SWANKE Swanke, Karl Vance 6′6″, 257 **OT-C-OG**
Col: Boston College *HS:* Newington [CT] B: 12/29/1957, Elmhurst, IL *Drafted:* 1980 Round 6 GB
1980 GB: 16 G. **1981** GB: 4 G; Rec 1-2 2.0 1 TD; 6 Pt. **1982** GB: 8 G. **1983** GB: 16 G. **1984** GB: 15 G. **1985** GB: 15 G. **1986** GB: 10 G; Rush 1-0; 3 Fum. **Total:** 84 G; Rush 1-0; Rec 1-2 2.0 1 TD; 6 Pt; 3 Fum.

CHARLES SWANN Swann, Charles Derek 6′1″, 188 **WR**
Col: Indiana State *HS:* La Salle [South Bend, IN] B: 10/29/1970, Memphis, TN *Drafted:* 1992 Round 12 NYG
1994 Den: 13 G; KR 1-16 16.0.

ERIC SWANN Swann, Eric Jerrod 6′5″, 307 **DE-DT**
Col: No College *HS:* Western Harnett [Lillington, NC] B: 8/16/1970, Swann Station, NC *Drafted:* 1991 Round 1 Pho
1991 Pho: 12 G; 4 Sac. **1992** Pho: 16 G; Scor 1 Saf; 2 Pt; 2 Sac. **1993** Pho: 9 G; Scor 1 Saf; 2 Pt; 3.5 Sac. **1994** Ariz: 16 G; Int 1-0; Scor **1** Saf; 2 Pt; 7 Sac. **1995** Ariz: 12 G; 8.5 Sac. **1996** Ariz: 16 G; 5 Sac. **1997** Ariz: 13 G; Rush 1-0; 1 Fum; 7.5 Sac. **1998** Ariz: 7 G; 4 Sac. **Total:** 101 G; Rush 1-0; Int 1-0; Scor 3 Saf; 6 Pt; 1 Fum; 41.5 Sac.

LYNN SWANN Swann, Lynn Curtis 5′11″, 180 **WR**
Col: USC *HS:* Serra [Foster City, CA] B: 3/7/1952, Alcoa, TN *Drafted:* 1974 Round 1 Pit
1974 Pit: Rush 1-14 14.0; KR 2-11 5.5. **1975** Pit: Rush 3-13 4.3. **1976** Pit: Rush 1-2 2.0. **1977** Pit: Rush 2-6 3.0. **1978** Pit: Rush 1-7 7.0. **1979** Pit: Rush 1-9 9.0 1 TD. **1980** Pit: Rush 1-(-4) -4.0. **1982** Pit: Rush 1-25 25.0; KR 1-0. **Total:** Rush 11-72 6.5 1 TD; KR 3-11 3.7.

		Receiving				Punt Returns					Tot
Year Team	**G**	**Rec**	**Yds**	**Avg**	**TD**	**Ret**	**Yds**	**Avg**	**TD**	**Fum**	**TD**
1974 Pit	11	11	208	18.9	2	41	**577**	14.1	1	5	3
1975 Pit	14	49	781	15.9	**11**	7	64	9.1	0	4	11
1976 Pit	12	28	516	18.4	3	3	11	3.7	0	0	3
1977 Pit	14	50	789	15.8	7	9	88	9.8	0	1	7
1978 Pit	16	61	880	14.4	11	0	0	—	0	0	11
1979 Pit	13	41	808	19.7	5	1	-1	-1.0	0	0	6
1980 Pit	13	44	710	16.1	7	0	0	—	0	0	7
1981 Pit	13	34	505	14.9	5	0	0	—	0	1	5
1982 Pit	9	18	265	14.7	0	0	0	—	0	0	0
NFL Total	115	336	5462	16.3	51	61	739	12.1	1	11	53

ERIC SWANSON Swanson, Eric Charles 5′11″, 186 **WR**
Col: San Bernardino Valley Coll. CA (J.C.); Tennessee *HS:* Pacific [San Bernardino, CA] B: 8/25/1963, San Bernardino, CA *Drafted:* 1986 Round 7 StL
1986 StL: 9 G; KR 10-206 20.6.

EVAR SWANSON Swanson, Ernest Evar 5′9″, 171 **OE-WB-BB**
Col: Lombard *HS:* De Kalb [IL] B: 10/15/1902, DeKalb, IL D: 7/17/1973, Galesburg, IL
1924 Mil: 9 G; Rec 3 TD; 18 Pt. **1925** RI-ChiC: 4 G. RI: 2 G. ChiC: 2 G. **1926** ChiC: 7 G; Scor 1, 1 XK. **1927** ChiC: 7 G; Scor 5, 1 FG, 2 XK. **Total:** 27 G; Rec 3 TD; Scor 24, 1 FG, 3 XK.

SHANE SWANSON Swanson, Shane Dru 5′9″, 200 **WR**
Col: Nebraska *HS:* Hershey [NE] B: 10/4/1962, Tracy, CA *Drafted:* 1985 Round 12 Cle
1987 Den: 3 G; Rec 6-87 14.5 1 TD; PR 9-132 14.7; KR 9-234 26.0; 6 Pt; 1 Fum.

TERRY SWANSON Swanson, Terry G 6′0″, 210 **P**
Col: Massachusetts *HS:* Belmont [MA] B: 1/8/1944, Cambridge, MA

		Punting			
Year Team	**G**	**Punts**	**Yds**	**Avg**	**Fum**
1967 Bos	14	65	2632	40.5	1
1968 Bos	10	62	2449	39.5	0
1969 Cin	2	12	459	38.3	0
NFL Total	26	139	5540	39.9	1

GEORGE SWARN Swarn, George W 5′10″, 205 **RB**
Col: Miami (Ohio) *HS:* Malabar [Mansfield, OH] B: 2/15/1964, Cincinnati, OH *Drafted:* 1987 Round 5 StL
1987 Cle: 1 G.

GREGG SWARTWOUDT Swartwoudt, Gregg Henry 6′3″, 275 **OT**
Col: North Dakota *HS:* Northfield [MN] B: 3/21/1964
1987 NYG: 1 G.

RICHARD SWATLAND Swatland, Richard Thomas 6′3″, 245 **OG**
(Swat) *Col:* Notre Dame *HS:* Stamford Catholic [CT] B: 10/8/1945, Stamford, CT *Drafted:* 1968 Round 8 NO
1968 Hou: 4 G.

SHAWN SWAYDA Swayda, Shawn Gerald 6′5″, 290 **DE**
Col: Arizona State *HS:* Brophy Prep [Phoenix, AZ] B: 9/4/1974, Phoenix, AZ *Drafted:* 1997 Round 6 ChiB
1998 Atl: 5 G.

HARRY SWAYNE Swayne, Harry Vonray 6′5″, 290 **OT-DE**
Col: Rutgers *HS:* Cardinal Dougherty [Philadelphia, PA] B: 2/2/1965, Philadelphia, PA *Drafted:* 1987 Round 7 TB
1987 TB: 8 G. **1988** TB: 10 G. **1989** TB: 16 G. **1990** TB: 10 G. **1991** SD: 12 G. **1992** SD: 16 G. **1993** SD: 11 G. **1994** SD: 16 G. **1995** SD: 16 G. **1996** SD: 16 G. **1997** Den: 7 G. **1998** Den: 16 G. **Total:** 154 G.

CALVIN SWEENEY Sweeney, Calvin Eugene 6′2″, 190 **WR**
Col: Riverside CC CA; California-Riverside; USC *HS:* Perris [CA] B: 1/12/1955, Riverside, CA *Drafted:* 1979 Round 4 Pit
1980 Pit: KR 3-42 14.0. **1983** Pit: Rush 1-(-2) -2.0. **1986** Pit: KR 1-0. **Total:** Rush 1-(-2) -2.0; KR 4-42 10.5.

		Receiving				
Year Team	**G**	**Rec**	**Yds**	**Avg**	**TD**	**Fum**
1980 Pit	15	12	282	23.5	1	1
1981 Pit	14	2	53	26.5	0	1
1982 Pit	7	5	50	10.0	0	0
1983 Pit	16	39	577	14.8	5	0
1984 Pit	9	2	25	12.5	0	0
1985 Pit	16	16	234	14.6	0	0
1986 Pit	16	21	337	16.0	1	0
1987 Pit	9	16	217	13.6	0	0
NFL Total	102	113	1775	15.7	7	2

JAKE SWEENEY Sweeney, Jacob Baum 6′3″, 240 **T**
Col: Cincinnati *HS:* Roger Bacon [Cincinnati, OH] B: 5/25/1922, Cincinnati, OH D: 7/28/1996, Glendale, OH
1944 ChiB: 8 G.

JIM SWEENEY Sweeney, James Joseph 6′4″, 287 **C-OG-OT**
Col: Pittsburgh *HS:* Seton-La Salle [Pittsburgh, PA] B: 8/8/1962, Pittsburgh, PA *Drafted:* 1984 Round 2 NYJ
1984 NYJ: 10 G. **1985** NYJ: 16 G. **1986** NYJ: 16 G. **1987** NYJ: 12 G. **1988** NYJ: 16 G. **1989** NYJ: 16 G. **1990** NYJ: 16 G. **1991** NYJ: 16 G. **1992** NYJ: 16 G. **1993** NYJ: 16 G. **1994** NYJ: 16 G. **1995** Sea: 16 G. **1996** Pit: 16 G. **1997** Pit: 16 G. **1998** Pit: 8 G. **Total:** 222 G.

KEVIN SWEENEY Sweeney, Kevin Joseph 6′0″, 191 **QB**
Col: Fresno State *HS:* Bullard [Fresno, CA] B: 11/16/1963, Bozeman, MT *Drafted:* 1987 Round 7 Dal
1987 Dal: Rush 5-8 1.6. **1988** Dal: Rush 6-34 5.7. **Total:** Rush 11-42 3.8.

		Passing								
Year Team	**G**	**Att**	**Comp**	**Comp%**	**Yds**	**YPA**	**TD**	**Int**	**Rating**	**Fum**
1987 Dal	3	28	14	50.0	291	10.39	4	1	111.8	0
1988 Dal	3	78	33	42.3	314	4.03	3	5	40.2	3
NFL Total	6	106	47	44.3	605	5.71	7	6	61.2	3

NEAL SWEENEY Sweeney, Neal 6′2″, 170 **WR**
Col: Pierce Coll. CA (J.C.); Tulsa *HS:* Birmingham [Van Nuys, CA] B: 6/13/1945, Van Nuys, CA *Drafted:* 1967 Round 6 Den
1967 Den: 10 G; Rec 6-136 22.7.

STEVE SWEENEY Sweeney, Steven Hollis 6′3″, 205 **WR**
Col: Yakima Valley CC WA; California *HS:* Davis [CA] B: 9/6/1950, Bozeman, MT
1973 Oak: 14 G; Rec 2-52 26.0 1 TD; 6 Pt.

WALT SWEENEY Sweeney, Walter Francis 6′4″, 256 **OG**
Col: Syracuse *HS:* Cohasset [MA] B: 4/18/1941, Cohasset, MA
1963 SD: 14 G; KR 1-18 18.0. **1964** SD: 14 G. **1965** SD: 14 G; Rush 0-8. **1966** SD: 14 G. **1967** SD: 14 G. **1968** SD: 14 G. **1969** SD: 14 G. **1970** SD: 14 G. **1971** SD: 14 G; KR 1-13 13.0. **1972** SD: 14 G. **1973** SD: 14 G. **1974** Was: 14 G. **1975** Was: 13 G. **Total:** 181 G; Rush 0-8; KR 2-31 15.5.

TONY SWEET Sweet, Anthony 6′4″, 230 **TE**
Col: Montclair State B: 12/13/1963
1987 NYJ: 3 G; Rec 3-45 15.0.

FRED SWEET Sweet, Frederick 5′10″, 165 **WB-FB-TB-DB**
Col: Brown *HS:* West Philadelphia [Philadelphia, PA] B: 8/17/1901, Philadelphia, PA D: 10/31/1976, Cape May, NJ
1925 Prov: 8 G; Scor 7, 2 FG, 1 XK. **1926** Prov: 9 G. **Total:** 17 G; Scor 7, 2 FG, 1 XK.

JOE SWEET Sweet, Joseph Lamar 6′2″, 196 **WR**
Col: Tennessee State *HS:* Rochelle [Lakeland, FL] B: 7/5/1948, Lakeland, FL *Drafted:* 1971 Round 17 LARm
1972 LARm: 11 G; Rush 1-1 1.0; Rec 2-26 13.0 1 TD; Scor **1** Saf; 8 Pt. **1973** LARm: 8 G. **1974** NE: 4 G. **1975** SD: 11 G; Rec 8-147 18.4. **Total:** 34 G; Rush 1-1 1.0; Rec 10-173 17.3 1 TD; Scor 1 Saf; 8 Pt.

KARL SWEETAN Sweetan, Karl Robert 6'2", 200 **QB**
Col: Navarro Coll. TX (J.C.); Texas A&M; Wake Forest *HS:* South Oak Cliff [Dallas, TX] B: 10/2/1942, Dallas, TX *Drafted:* 1965 Round 18 Det

		Passing							
Year Team	G	Att	Comp	Comp%	Yds	YPA	TD	Int	Rating
1966 Det	10	309	157	50.8	1809	5.85	4	14	54.3
1967 Det	10	177	74	41.8	901	5.09	10	11	51.1
1968 NO	5	78	27	34.6	318	4.08	1	9	12.6
1969 LARm	5	13	5	38.5	101	7.77	1	0	92.1
1970 LARm	6	13	6	46.2	81	6.23	1	0	92.1
NFL Total	36	590	269	45.6	3210	5.44	17	34	48.3

	Rushing				
Year Team	Att	Yds	Avg	TD	Fum
1966 Det	34	219	6.4	1	6
1967 Det	17	93	5.5	1	4
1968 NO	4	-5	-1.3	0	1
1969 LARm	1	-1	-1.0	0	0
NFL Total	56	306	5.5	2	11

FRED SWEETLAND Sweetland, Frederick Greenhalge 5'10", 175 **WB-FB**
(Buck) *Col:* Washington & Lee; Fordham *HS:* Everett [MA] B: 11/1893, Everett, MA Deceased
1920 Akr: 4 G. **1921** NYG: 1 G. **Total:** 5 G.

BOB SWEIGER Sweiger, Robert Michael 6'0", 209 **BB-LB-DB-WB**
Col: Minnesota *HS:* Central [Minneapolis, MN] B: 9/20/1919, Minneapolis, MN D: 11/1975
AAFC **1946** NY-A: Rush 7-22 3.1; PR 1-14 14.0; KR 5-103 20.6; Int 4-82; Punt 1-52 52.0. **1947** NY-A: Rush 9-44 4.9; KR 1-12 12.0; Int 2-51 1 TD. **1948** NY-A: Rush 3-4 1.3; KR 1-3 3.0. **1949** ChiA: Rush 3-17 5.7; KR 3-59 19.7; Int 1-21. **Total:** Rush 22-87 4.0; PR 1-14 14.0; KR 10-177 17.7; Int 7-154 1 TD; Punt 1-52 52.0.

		Receiving				
Year Team	G	Rec	Yds	Avg	TD	Tot TD
1946 NY-A	13	8	55	6.9	1	1
1947 NY-A	14	11	108	9.8	1	2
1948 NY-A	14	12	129	10.8	0	0
1949 ChiA	12	11	126	11.5	0	0
AAFC Total	53	42	418	10.0	2	3

BOB SWENSON Swenson, Robert Charles 6'3", 225 **LB**
Col: California *HS:* Tracy [CA] B: 7/1/1953, Stockton, CA
1979 Den: **1** Fum TD. **Total:** 1 Fum TD.

		Interceptions			
Year Team	G	Int	Yds	TD	Fum
1975 Den	14	1	4	0	0
1976 Den	14	2	26	0	0
1977 Den	14	1	0	0	0
1978 Den	16	1	0	0	0
1979 Den	16	3	0	0	1
1981 Den	16	3	53	0	0
1982 Den	4	0	0	0	0
1983 Den	2	0	0	0	0
NFL Total	96	11	83	0	1

BILL SWIACKI Swiacki, William Adam 6'2", 195 **OE**
Col: Holy Cross; Columbia *HS:* Southbridge [MA] B: 10/2/1922, Southbridge, MA D: 7/7/1976, Sturbridge, MA *Drafted:* 1946 Round 16 Bos
1948 NYG: KR 1-0. **1950** NYG: KR 1-11 11.0. **Total:** KR 2-11 5.5.

		Receiving				
Year Team	G	Rec	Yds	Avg	TD	Fum
1948 NYG	12	39	550	14.1	10	1
1949 NYG	12	47	652	13.9	4	0
1950 NYG	12	20	280	14.0	3	1
1951 Det	12	16	188	11.8	0	0
1952 Det	11	17	213	12.5	1	1
NFL Total	59	139	1883	13.5	18	3

PHIL SWIADON Swiadon, Philip Edward 6'0", 220 **G**
Col: New York U. *HS:* Erasmus Hall [Brooklyn, NY] B: 12/5/1914, Brooklyn, NY
1943 Bkn: 3 G.

LARRY SWIDER Swider, Lawrence John 6'2", 195 **P**
Col: Pittsburgh *HS:* Du Bois [PA] B: 2/1/1955, Limestone, ME *Drafted:* 1977 Round 7 Den
1979 Det: Pass 1-1 100.0%, 36 36.00; Rush 1-0. **1981** TB: Rush 1-(-9) -9.0. **Total:** Pass 1-1 100.0%, 36 36.00; Rush 2-(-9) -4.5.

		Punting			
Year Team	G	Punts	Yds	Avg	Fum
1979 Det	14	88	3523	40.0	1
1980 StL	16	**99**	4111	41.5	0
1981 TB	13	58	2476	42.7	0
1982 TB	9	39	1620	41.5	0
NFL Total	52	284	11730	41.3	1

DOUG SWIFT Swift, Douglas A 6'3", 226 **LB**
Col: Amherst *HS:* Nottingham [Syracuse, NY] B: 10/24/1948, Syracuse, NY
1970 Mia: 14 G. **1971** Mia: 14 G; Int 1-12. **1972** Mia: 14 G; Int 3-5. **1973** Mia: 14 G; Int 1-0. **1974** Mia: 8 G. **1975** Mia: 14 G. **Total:** 78 G; Int 5-17.

MICHAEL SWIFT Swift, Michael Aaron 5'10", 165 **DB**
Col: Austin Peay State *HS:* Lake Co. [Tiptonville, TN] B: 2/28/1974, Dyersburg, TN
1997 SD: 12 G.

DENNIS SWILLEY Swilley, Dennis Neal 6'3", 253 **C-OG-OT**
Col: Texas A&M; North Texas *HS:* Pine Bluff [AR] B: 6/28/1955, Bossier City, LA *Drafted:* 1977 Round 2 Min
1977 Min: 14 G; KR 1-0; 1 Fum. **1978** Min: 14 G. **1979** Min: 16 G. **1980** Min: 16 G. **1981** Min: 16 G. **1982** Min: 9 G. **1983** Min: 16 G. **1985** Min: 16 G. **1986** Min: 16 G; 1 Fum. **1987** Min: 6 G. **Total:** 139 G; KR 1-0; 2 Fum.

PAT SWILLING Swilling, Patrick Travis 6'3", 245 **DE**
Col: Georgia Tech *HS:* Stephens Co. [Toccoa, GA] B: 10/25/1964, Toccoa, GA *Drafted:* 1986 Round 3 NO
1986 NO: 16 G; 4 Sac. **1987** NO: 12 G; Int 1-10; 10.5 Sac. **1988** NO: 15 G; 7 Sac. **1989** NO: 16 G; Int 1-14; 16.5 Sac. **1990** NO: 16 G; 11 Sac. **1991** NO: 16 G; Int 1-39 1 TD; 6 Pt; **17** Sac. **1992** NO: 16 G; 10.5 Sac. **1993** Det: 14 G; Int 3-16; 6.5 Sac. **1994** Det: 16 G; 3.5 Sac. **1995** Oak: 16 G; 13 Sac. **1996** Oak: 16 G; 6 Sac. **1998** Oak: 16 G; 2 Sac. **Total:** 185 G; Int 6-79 1 TD; 6 Pt; 107.5 Sac.

WAYNE SWINFORD Swinford, Lenis Wayne 6'0", 192 **DB-WR**
Col: Georgia *HS:* Munford [AL] B: 5/3/1943, Anniston, AL *Drafted:* 1965 Round 9 SF
1965 SF: 14 G; PR 2-18 9.0; KR 4-61 15.3; 1 Fum. **1966** SF: 7 G; PR 8-12 1.5; KR 4-73 18.3; 1 Fum. **1967** SF: 5 G; KR 2-51 25.5. **Total:** 26 G; PR 10-30 3.0; KR 10-185 18.5; 2 Fum.

RASHOD SWINGER Swinger, Rashod Alexander 6'2", 286 **DT-DE**
Col: Rutgers *HS:* Manalapan [Englishtown, NJ] B: 11/27/1974, Paterson, NJ
1997 Ariz: 1 G. **1998** Ariz: 16 G. **Total:** 17 G.

JIM SWINK Swink, James Edward 6'1", 185 **HB**
Col: Texas Christian *HS:* Rusk [TX] B: 3/14/1936, Sacul, TX *Drafted:* 1957 Round 2 ChiB
1960 DalT: 5 G; Rush 10-15 1.5; Rec 4-37 9.3; KR 1-36 36.0.

CLOVIS SWINNEY Swinney, Clovis G 6'3", 249 **DT**
Col: Arkansas; Arkansas State *HS:* Jonesboro [AR] B: 8/17/1945, Mexico, MO *Drafted:* 1970 Round 3 NO
1970 NO: 14 G. **1971** NYJ: 4 G. **Total:** 18 G.

BOB SWISHER Swisher, Robert Emerson 5'11", 163 **HB-DB**
Col: Northwestern *HS:* Peoria [IL] B: 7/14/1914, Victoria, IL D: 9/27/1979, Memphis, TN
1938 ChiB: Pass 4-1 25.0%, 8 2.00 1 TD 1 Int; Rec 5-65 13.0. **1939** ChiB: Rec 7-228 32.6 1 TD; Punt 3-93 31.0. **1940** ChiB: Pass 1-0; Rec 2-106 53.0. **1941** ChiB: Rec 6-179 29.8 2 TD; PR 7-101 14.4; KR 2-70 35.0; Int 1-60 **1** TD. **1945** ChiB: Rec 2-4 2.0; Int 1-0. **Total:** Pass 5-1 20.0%, 8 1.60 1 TD 1 Int; Rec 22-582 26.5 3 TD; PR 7-101 14.4; KR 2-70 35.0; Int 2-60 1 TD; Punt 3-93 31.0.

		Rushing					
Year Team	G	Att	Yds	Avg	TD	Fum	Tot TD
1938 ChiB	9	22	133	6.0	0	0	0
1939 ChiB	9	30	192	6.4	2	0	3
1940 ChiB	9	15	70	4.7	0	0	0
1941 ChiB	11	37	149	4.0	0	0	3
1945 ChiB	3	0	0	—	0	1	0
NFL Total	41	104	544	5.2	2	1	6

MIKE SWISTOWICZ Swistowicz, Michael Paul 5'10", 185 **DB**
Col: Notre Dame *HS:* Tilden [Chicago, IL] B: 4/22/1927, Chicago, IL
1950 NYY-ChiC: 9 G; PR 4-59 14.8; 1 Fum. NYY: 1 G. ChiC: 8 G; PR 4-59 14.8; 1 Fum. **Total:** 9 G; PR 4-59 14.8; 1 Fum.

MARVIN SWITZER Switzer, Marvin Duane 6'0", 192 **DB**
Col: Kansas State *HS:* Bogue [KS] B: 10/28/1954, Bogue, KS
1978 Buf: 10 G.

VERYL SWITZER Switzer, Veryl Allen 5'11", 190 **HB-DB**
Col: Kansas State *HS:* Bogue [KS] B: 8/6/1932, Nicodemus, KS *Drafted:* 1954 Round 1 GB
1954 GB: **1** Fum TD. **Total:** 1 Fum TD.

		Rushing				Receiving			
Year Team	G	Att	Yds	Avg	TD	Rec	Yds	Avg	TD
1954 GB	12	15	59	3.9	0	17	166	9.8	2

1955 GB	12	16	101	6.3	0	14	103	7.4	1
NFL Total	24	31	160	5.2	0	31	269	8.7	3

	Punt Returns				Kickoff Returns					Tot
Year Team	**Ret**	**Yds**	**Avg**	**TD**	**Ret**	**Yds**	**Avg**	**TD**	**Fum**	**TD**
1954 GB	24	**306**	**12.8**	**1**	20	500	25.0	0	3	4
1955 GB	24	158	6.6	0	17	445	26.2	0	6	1
NFL Total	48	464	9.7	1	37	945	25.5	0	9	5

CRAIG SWOOPE Swoope, Craig Avery 6'1", 205 **DB**
Col: Illinois *HS:* Fort Pierce Westwood [FL] B: 2/3/1964, Fort Pierce, FL *Drafted:* 1986 Round 4 TB
1986 TB: 15 G; Int 1-23; 1 Sac. **1987** TB-Ind: 4 G. TB: 1 G. Ind: 3 G. **1988** Ind: 11 G; 1 Sac. **Total:** 30 G; Int 1-23; 2 Sac.

PATRICK SWOOPES Swoopes, Patrick Roaman 6'4", 280 **NT**
Col: Mississippi State *HS:* Bradshaw [Florence, AL] B: 3/4/1964, Florence, AL *Drafted:* 1986 Round 11 NO
1987 NO: 9 G; 1 Sac. **1989** NO: 15 G. **1991** KC-Mia: 7 G. KC: 4 G. Mia: 3 G. **Total:** 31 G; 1 Sac.

JEFF SYDNER Sydner, Jeffrey Lynn 5'6", 170 **WR**
Col: Hawaii *HS:* East [Columbus, OH] B: 11/11/1969, Columbus, OH *Drafted:* 1992 Round 6 Phi
1993 Phi: Rec 2-42 21.0. **1994** Phi: Rec 1-10 10.0. **Total:** Rec 3-52 17.3.

		Punt Returns				Kickoff Returns				
Year Team	**G**	**Ret**	**Yds**	**Avg**	**TD**	**Ret**	**Yds**	**Avg**	**TD**	**Fum**
1992 Phi	15	7	52	7.4	0	17	368	21.6	0	1
1993 Phi	4	0	0	—	0	9	158	17.6	0	3
1994 Phi	16	40	381	9.5	0	20	392	19.6	0	2
1995 NYJ	6	17	178	10.5	0	4	80	20.0	0	0
NFL Total	41	64	611	9.5	0	50	998	20.0	0	6

HARRY SYDNEY Sydney, Harry Flanroy III 6'0", 217 **RB**
Col: Kansas *HS:* 71st [Fayetteville, NC] B: 6/26/1959, Petersburg, VA
1987 SF: Pass 1-1 100.0%, 50 50.00 1 TD; KR 12-243 20.3. **1988** SF: Pass 1-0; KR 1-8 8.0. **1989** SF: KR 3-16 5.3. **1990** SF: KR 2-33 16.5. **1991** SF: Pass 1-0; KR 1-13 13.0. **Total:** Pass 3-1 33.3%, 50 16.67 1 TD; KR 19-313 16.5.

		Rushing				Receiving					Tot
Year Team	**G**	**Att**	**Yds**	**Avg**	**TD**	**Rec**	**Yds**	**Avg**	**TD**	**Fum**	**TD**
1987 SF	14	29	125	4.3	0	1	3	3.0	0	2	0
1988 SF	16	9	50	5.6	0	2	18	9.0	0	0	0
1989 SF	7	9	56	6.2	0	9	71	7.9	0	1	0
1990 SF	16	35	166	4.7	2	10	116	11.6	1	1	3
1991 SF	16	57	245	4.3	5	13	90	6.9	2	3	7
1992 GB	16	51	163	3.2	2	49	384	7.8	1	2	3
NFL Total	85	190	805	4.2	9	84	682	8.1	4	9	13

WILLIE SYDNOR Sydnor, George Ross 5'11", 170 **WR**
Col: Northwestern; Villanova; Syracuse *HS:* Radnor [PA] B: 3/21/1959, Bryn Mawr, PA
1982 Pit: 8 G; PR 22-172 7.8; KR 2-37 18.5.

AL SYKES Sykes, Alfred J 6'2", 170 **WR**
Col: Florida A&M B: 12/20/1947, Tallahassee, FL *Drafted:* 1971 Round 14 NE
1971 NE: 4 G; Rec 1-15 15.0.

EUGENE SYKES Sykes, Eugene Charles 6'1", 201 **DB**
Col: Louisiana State *HS:* Covington [LA] B: 9/26/1941, New Orleans, LA *Drafted:* 1963 Round 19 Buf
1963 Buf: 9 G. **1964** Buf: 10 G; Int 2-36. **1965** Buf: 4 G. **1967** Den: 4 G; Int 2-29. **Total:** 27 G; Int 4-65.

JOHN SYKES Sykes, John 5'11", 195 **WR**
Col: Morgan State *HS:* Baltimore City College [MD] B: 5/13/1949, Baltimore, MD *Drafted:* 1972 Round 7 Bal
1972 SD: 2 G; KR 2-44 22.0.

BOB SYKES Sykes, Robert Eugene 6'1", 218 **FB**
Col: San Jose State *HS:* St. Aloysius [New Orleans, LA] B: 3/15/1927, Oakland, CA
1952 Was: 4 G; Rush 4-10 2.5; Rec 1-5 5.0.

JOHN SYLVESTER Sylvester, John J 6'0", 183 **DB-HB**
Col: Temple *HS:* Norristown [PA] B: 1/14/1923, Norristown, PA
AAFC **1947** NY-A: 7 G; Pass 1-0; Rush 17-101 5.9; Rec 1-5 5.0; PR 3-37 12.3; KR 1-25 25.0; Punt 1-42 42.0. **1948** BalA: 12 G; PR 2-16 8.0; Int 1-0. **Total:** 19 G; Pass 1-0; Rush 17-101 5.9; Rec 1-5 5.0; PR 5-53 10.6; KR 1-25 25.0; Int 1-0; Punt 1-42 42.0.

STEVE SYLVESTER Sylvester, Steven Phillip 6'4", 260 **C-OG-OT**
Col: Notre Dame *HS:* Moeller [Cincinnati, OH] B: 3/4/1953, Cincinnati, OH *Drafted:* 1975 Round 10 Oak
1975 Oak: 11 G. **1976** Oak: 14 G. **1977** Oak: 14 G. **1978** Oak: 16 G. **1979** Oak: 16 G; 1 Fum. **1980** Oak: 7 G. **1981** Oak: 15 G. **1982** LARd: 4 G. **1983** LARd: 9 G. **Total:** 106 G; 1 Fum.

JOHN SYMANK Symank, John Richard 5'11", 180 **DB**
Col: Texas-Arlington; Florida *HS:* Caldwell [TX] B: 8/31/1935, La Grange, TX *Drafted:* 1957 Round 23 GB
1957 GB: PR 3-0. **1958** GB: PR 1-0. **1959** GB: PR 1-0; KR 14-338 24.1. **1960** GB: KR 4-103 25.8. **1961** GB: KR 4-121 30.3. **Total:** PR 5-0; KR 22-562 25.5.

		Interceptions			
Year Team	**G**	**Int**	**Yds**	**TD**	**Fum**
1957 GB	12	9	198	0	1
1958 GB	12	1	23	0	1
1959 GB	12	2	46	0	4
1960 GB	12	1	0	0	0
1961 GB	14	5	99	0	1
1962 GB	14	0	0	0	0
1963 StL	13	1	21	1	0
NFL Total	89	19	387	1	7

JOHN SYNHORST Synhorst, John Benjamin 1 **T**
Col: Iowa *HS:* Pella [IA] B: 11/13/1895, Leighton, IA D: 3/19/1982, Des Moines, IA
1920 RI: 2 G.

STAN SYTSMA Sytsma, Stanley Allan 6'2", 220 **LB**
Col: Minnesota *HS:* Hutchinson [MN] B: 5/3/1956, Glendale, AZ
1980 Atl: 2 G.

LEN SZAFARYN Szafaryn, Leonard Adolph 6'2", 226 **OT-OG-LB-DT**
Col: North Carolina *HS:* Ambridge [PA] B: 1/19/1928, Ambridge, PA D: 9/23/1990, Baden, PA *Drafted:* 1949 Round 3 Was
1949 Was: 12 G. **1950** GB: 12 G. **1953** GB: 7 G. **1954** GB: 12 G. **1955** GB: 12 G; PR 1-28 28.0 1 TD; 6 Pt. **1956** GB: 12 G. **1957** Phi: 1 G. **1958** Phi: 7 G. **Total:** 75 G; PR 1-28 28.0 1 TD; 6 Pt.

PAUL SZAKASH Szakash, Paul Michael 6'0", 213 **BB-DB-FB-LB**
(Socko) *Col:* Montana *HS:* Fenger [Chicago, IL] B: 5/5/1913, Chicago, IL D: 10/24/1984, Missoula, MT *Drafted:* 1938 Round 5 Det
1938 Det: 7 G; Rush 20-55 2.8; Rec 1-0. **1939** Det: 11 G; Rush 3-11 3.7; Scor 0-1 XK. **1941** Det: 10 G; Rec 3-77 25.7; KR 1-17 17.0. **1942** Det: 10 G; Rec 5-53 10.6. **Total:** 38 G; Rush 23-66 2.9; Rec 9-130 14.4; KR 1-17 17.0; Scor 0-1 XK.

RICHIE SZARO Szaro, Richard Julian 5'11", 205 **K**
Col: Harvard *HS:* St. Francis Prep [Brooklyn, NY] B: 3/7/1948, Rzeszow, Poland

		Scoring						
Year Team	**G**	**Pts**	**FG**	**FGA**	**FG%**	**XK**	**XKA**	**XK%**
1975 NO	11	47	10	16	62.5	17	17	100.0
1976 NO	14	79	18	23	**78.3**	25	29	**86.2**
1977 NO	14	44	5	12	41.7	29	31	93.5
1978 NO	4	21	4	6	66.7	9	9	100.0
1979 NYJ	1	2	0	2	0.0	2	2	100.0
NFL Total	44	193	37	59	62.7	82	88	93.2

JOE SZCZECKO Szczecko, Joseph 6'0", 245 **DT**
Col: Northwestern *HS:* Gordon Tech [Chicago, IL] B: 8/25/1942, Lahr, Germany
1966 Atl: 12 G. **1967** Atl: 12 G. **1968** Atl: 10 G; KR 3-18 6.0; 1 Fum. **1969** NYG: 14 G. **Total:** 48 G; KR 3-18 6.0; 1 Fum.

WALT SZOT Szot, Walter Stanley 6'1", 222 **DT-OT**
Col: Bucknell *HS:* Henry P. Becton [East Rutherford, NJ] B: 3/30/1920, Clifton, NJ D: 11/3/1981, Passaic, NJ *Drafted:* 1944 Round 18 ChiC
1946 ChiC: 9 G. **1947** ChiC: 12 G. **1948** ChiC: 12 G. **1949** Pit: 12 G. **1950** Pit: 11 G. **Total:** 56 G.

DAVID SZOTT Szott, David Andrew 6'4", 293 **OG**
Col: Penn State *HS:* Clifton [NJ] B: 12/12/1967, Passaic, NJ *Drafted:* 1990 Round 7 KC
1990 KC: 16 G. **1991** KC: 16 G. **1992** KC: 16 G. **1993** KC: 14 G. **1994** KC: 16 G. **1995** KC: 16 G. **1996** KC: 16 G. **1997** KC: 16 G. **1998** KC: 1 G. **Total:** 127 G.

DAVE SZYMAKOWSKI Szymakowski, David John 6'2", 198 **WR**
Col: West Texas A&M *HS:* Liberty [Bethlehem, PA] B: 3/15/1946, Bethlehem, PA *Drafted:* 1968 Round 3 NO
1968 NO: 3 G.

FRANK SZYMANSKI Szymanski, Frank Stanislaus 6'0", 220 **C-LB**
Col: St. Mary's (Cal.); Notre Dame *HS:* Northeastern [Detroit, MI] B: 7/6/1923, Detroit, MI D: 4/26/1987, Detroit, MI *Drafted:* 1945 Round 1 Det
1945 Det: 4 G; Int 1-11. **1946** Det: 11 G. **1947** Det: 12 G; KR 1-0. **1948** Phi: 9 G. **1949** ChiB: 11 G. **Total:** 47 G; KR 1-0; Int 1-11.

JIM SZYMANSKI Szymanski, James Paul 6'5", 268 **DE**
Col: Michigan State *HS:* Stevenson [Sterling Heights, MI] B: 9/7/1967, Sterling Heights, MI *Drafted:* 1990 Round 10 Den
1990 Den: 6 G. **1991** Den: 1 G. **Total:** 7 G.

DICK SZYMANSKI Szymanski, Richard Frank 6′3″, 233 **C-LB**
Col: Notre Dame *HS:* Edward D. Libbey [Toledo, OH] B: 10/7/1932, Toledo, OH *Drafted:* 1955 Round 2 Bal
1955 Bal: 12 G. **1957** Bal: 5 G. **1958** Bal: 8 G. **1959** Bal: 12 G; Int 5-24 **1** TD; 6 Pt. **1960** Bal: 12 G; Int 1-15. **1961** Bal: 14 G; Rec 1-5 5.0. **1962** Bal: 14 G. **1963** Bal: 14 G. **1964** Bal: 14 G. **1965** Bal: 10 G. **1966** Bal: 14 G. **1967** Bal: 14 G. **1968** Bal: 14 G. **Total:** 157 G; Rec 1-5 5.0; Int 6-39 1 TD; 6 Pt.

PAUL TABOR Tabor, Paul Carrol 6′4″, 241 **C-OG**
Col: Oklahoma *HS:* Spring Branch [Houston, TX] B: 11/30/1956, Little Rock, AR *Drafted:* 1980 Round 5 ChiB
1980 ChiB: 16 G.

PHILIP TABOR Tabor, Philip Martin 6′4″, 255 **DE-NT-DT**
Col: Oklahoma *HS:* Spring Branch [Houston, TX] B: 11/30/1956, Little Rock, AR *Drafted:* 1979 Round 4 NYG
1979 NYG: 15 G. **1980** NYG: 16 G. **1981** NYG: 16 G. **1982** NYG: 9 G; 3.5 Sac. **Total:** 56 G; 3.5 Sac.

DOYLE TACKETT Tackett, Doyle Lee 6′0″, 205 **BB-DB-WB**
Col: No College *HS:* Atkins [AR] B: 8/22/1924, Hector, AR
AAFC **1946** BknA: 14 G; Rush 11-(-6) -0.5; Rec 10-191 19.1 2 TD; PR 1-3 3.0; KR 5-76 15.2; Int 1-16; 12 Pt. **1947** BknA: 12 G; Rec 0-25; Int 1-17. **1948** BknA: 1 G; PR 1-10 10.0. **Total:** 27 G; Rush 11-(-6) -0.5; Rec 10-216 21.6 2 TD; PR 2-13 6.5; KR 5-76 15.2; Int 2-33; 12 Pt.

COOKIE TACKWELL Tackwell, Charles 0 6′2″, 215 **OE-T-G**
(Ben) *Col:* Kansas State Deceased
1930 Fra-Min: 18 G; Rec 1 TD; Scor 7, 1 XK. Fra: 17 G; Rec 1 TD; Scor 7, 1 XK. Min: 1 G. **1931** Fra-ChiB: 12 G; Scor 3, 3 XK. Fra: 8 G; Scor 1, 1 XK. ChiB: 4 G; Scor 2, 2 XK. **1932** ChiB: 11 G; Scor 3, 3 XK. **1933** ChiB-Cin: 8 G; Rec 1-20 20.0. ChiB: 3 G; Rec 1-20 20.0. Cin: 5 G. **1934** Cin: 8 G; Rush 1-6 6.0; Rec 5-58 11.6. **Total:** 57 G; Rush 1-6 6.0; Rec 6-78 13.0 1 TD.

JOE TAFFONI Taffoni, Joseph Albert 6′3″, 255 **OT-OG**
Col: West Virginia; Tennessee-Martin *HS:* Carmichaels [PA] B: 3/27/1945, Brownsville, PA *Drafted:* 1967 Round 4 Cle
1967 Cle: 14 G. **1968** Cle: 13 G. **1969** Cle: 14 G. **1970** Cle: 14 G. **1972** NYG: 14 G. **1973** NYG: 9 G. **Total:** 78 G.

JERRY TAGGE Tagge, Jerry Lee 6′2″, 220 **QB**
Col: Nebraska *HS:* Green Bay West [WI] B: 4/12/1950, Omaha, NE
Drafted: 1972 Round 1 GB

		Passing							
Year Team	G	Att	Comp	Comp%	Yds	YPA	TD	Int	Rating
1972 GB	4	29	10	34.5	154	5.31	0	0	52.9
1973 GB	7	106	56	52.8	720	6.79	2	7	53.2
1974 GB	7	146	70	47.9	709	4.86	1	10	36.0
NFL Total	18	281	136	48.4	1583	5.63	3	17	44.2

	Rushing				
Year Team	Att	Yds	Avg	TD	Fum
1972 GB	8	-3	-0.4	1	0
1973 GB	15	62	4.1	2	1
1974 GB	18	58	3.2	0	5
NFL Total	41	117	2.9	3	6

JOHN TAGLIAFERRI Tagliaferri, John Stanton 5′11″, 195 **RB**
Col: Cornell *HS:* West Windsor-Plainsboro [Princeton Junction, NJ] B: 4/13/1964, Orange, NJ
1987 Mia: 3 G; Rush 13-45 3.5 1 TD; Rec 12-117 9.8; 6 Pt.

JOE TAIBI Taibi, Joseph Paul 6′5″, 265 **DE**
Col: Southern Colorado; Idaho *HS:* East [Pueblo, CO] B: 2/22/1963
1987 NYG: 3 G.

ART TAIT Tait, Arthur William 5′11″, 205 **DE**
Col: Mississippi State *HS:* Central [Memphis, TN] B: 2/8/1929, Memphis, TN
1951 NYY: 12 G; **2** Fum TD; 12 Pt. **1952** Dal: 8 G; KR 1-0. **Total:** 20 G; KR 1-0; 2 Fum TD; 12 Pt.

BOB TALAMINI Talamini, Robert Guy 6′1″, 255 **OG**
Col: Kentucky *HS:* St. Xavier [Louisville, KY] B: 1/8/1939, Louisville, KY *Drafted:* 1960 Round 2 Hou
1960 Hou: 14 G; Rush 0-14. **1961** Hou: 14 G. **1962** Hou: 14 G. **1963** Hou: 14 G. **1964** Hou: 14 G. **1965** Hou: 14 G. **1966** Hou: 14 G. **1967** Hou: 14 G. **1968** NYJ: 14 G. **Total:** 126 G; Rush 0-14.

DIRON TALBERT Talbert, Diron Vester 6′5″, 255 **DT-DE**
Col: Texas *HS:* Texas City [TX] B: 7/1/1944, Pascagoula, MS
Drafted: 1966 Round 5 LARm
1967 LARm: 2 G. **1968** LARm: 14 G. **1969** LARm: 14 G. **1970** LARm: 14 G. **1971** Was: 14 G. **1972** Was: 14 G. **1973** Was: 14 G. **1974** Was: 14 G. **1975** Was: 14 G. **1976** Was: 14 G. **1977** Was: 14 G. **1978** Was: 12 G. **1979** Was: 16 G. **1980** Was: 16 G. **Total:** 186 G.

DON TALBERT Talbert, Don Larry 6′5″, 255 **OT-LB**
Col: Texas *HS:* Texas City [TX] B: 3/1/1939, Louisville, MS
Drafted: 1961 Round 8 Dal
1962 Dal: 14 G; KR 1-0. **1965** Dal: 14 G. **1966** Atl: 12 G. **1967** Atl: 12 G; KR 1-2 2.0. **1968** Atl: 14 G; KR 3-30 10.0. **1969** NO: 14 G. **1970** NO: 14 G. **1971** Dal: 9 G. **Total:** 103 G; KR 5-32 6.4.

JOHN TALBOT Talbot, John Orechia 6′2″, 182 **E**
Col: Brown *HS:* Mercersburg Acad. [PA] B: 4/27/1900, South Weymouth, MA D: 12/5/1981, Keene, NH
1926 Prov: 2 G.

JIM TALBOTT Talbott, James Stropes **BB**
Col: North Dakota *HS:* Linton [IN] B: 7/26/1893, Marco, IN
D: 11/9/1972, Miami, FL
1920 Ham: 1 G.

DAN TALCOTT Talcott, Daniel 6′2″, 235 **T**
Col: Nevada-Reno *HS:* Reno [NV] B: 5/21/1921, Grass Valley, CA
Deceased *Drafted:* 1945 Round 24 Phi
1947 Phi: 8 G.

GEORGE TALIAFERRO Taliaferro, George 5′11″, 196 **HB-QB-TB-DB**
(Scoop) *Col:* Indiana *HS:* Theodore Roosevelt [Gary, IN] B: 1/8/1927, Gates, TN
AAFC **1949** LA-A: Rec 0-42 1 TD; PR 2-53 26.5 1 TD; KR 13-313 24.1; Punt 27-982 36.4.

		Passing							
Year Team	G	Att	Comp	Comp%	Yds	YPA	TD	Int	Rating
1949 LA-A	11	124	45	36.3	790	6.37	4	14	30.0

	Rushing				Tot
Year Team	Att	Yds	Avg	TD	TD
1949 LA-A	95	472	5.0	5	7

NFL **1951** NYY: Int 4-74. **Total:** Int 4-74.

		Passing							
Year Team	G	Att	Comp	Comp%	Yds	YPA	TD	Int	Rating
1950 NYY	12	7	3	42.9	83	11.86	1	0	126.8
1951 NYY	12	33	13	39.4	251	7.61	1	3	38.8
1952 Dal	12	63	16	25.4	298	4.73	2	6	17.8
1953 Bal	11	55	15	27.3	211	3.84	2	5	17.3
1954 Bal	11	2	0	0.0	0	0.00	0	1	0.0
1955 Phi	3	0	0	—	0	—	0	0	—
NFL Total	61	160	47	29.4	843	5.27	6	15	22.5

	Rushing				Receiving			
Year Team	Att	Yds	Avg	TD	Rec	Yds	Avg	TD
1950 NYY	88	411	4.7	4	21	299	14.2	5
1951 NYY	62	330	5.3	3	16	230	14.4	2
1952 Dal	100	419	4.2	1	21	244	11.6	1
1953 Bal	102	479	4.7	2	20	346	17.3	2
1954 Bal	48	157	3.3	0	14	122	8.7	1
1955 Phi	3	-2	-0.7	0	3	17	5.7	0
NFL Total	403	1794	4.5	10	95	1258	13.2	11

	Punt Returns				Kickoff Returns			
Year Team	Ret	Yds	Avg	TD	Ret	Yds	Avg	TD
1950 NYY	9	129	14.3	0	25	473	18.9	0
1951 NYY	9	68	7.6	0	**27**	**622**	23.0	0
1952 Dal	1	4	4.0	0	6	146	24.3	0
1953 Bal	10	31	3.1	0	16	331	20.7	0
1954 Bal	5	34	6.8	0	7	134	19.1	0
1955 Phi	0	0	—	0	1	16	16.0	0
NFL Total	34	266	7.8	0	82	1722	21.0	0

	Punting				Tot
Year Team	Punts	Yds	Avg	Fum	TD
1950 NYY	1	39	39.0	11	9
1951 NYY	**76**	2881	37.9	5	5
1952 Dal	0	0	—	6	2
1953 Bal	65	2437	37.5	**10**	4
1954 Bal	0	0	—	1	1
1955 Phi	0	0	—	2	0
NFL Total	142	5357	37.7	35	21

MIKE TALIAFERRO Taliaferro, Myron Eugene 6′2″, 202 **QB**
Col: Illinois *HS:* Wheaton [IL] B: 7/26/1941, Houston, TX
Drafted: 1963 Round 28 NYJ
1966 NYJ: Scor **1** 2XP. **Total:** Scor 1 2XP.

		Passing							
Year Team	G	Att	Comp	Comp%	Yds	YPA	TD	Int	Rating
1964 NYJ	14	73	23	31.5	341	4.67	2	5	28.4
1965 NYJ	14	119	45	37.8	531	4.46	3	7	36.1
1966 NYJ	14	41	19	46.3	177	4.32	2	2	54.6

1967 NYJ	3	20	11	55.0	96	4.80	1	1	63.8
1968 Bos	7	176	67	38.1	889	5.05	4	15	26.9
1969 Bos	14	331	160	48.3	2160	6.53	19	18	66.0
1970 Bos	11	173	78	45.1	871	5.03	4	11	41.8
1972 Buf	5	33	16	48.5	176	5.33	1	4	35.2
NFL Total	82	966	419	43.4	5241	5.43	36	63	46.1

	Rushing				
Year Team	**Att**	**Yds**	**Avg**	**TD**	**Fum**
1964 NYJ	9	45	5.0	0	2
1965 NYJ	7	4	0.6	0	2
1967 NYJ	2	20	10.0	0	0
1968 Bos	8	51	6.4	0	4
1969 Bos	12	-16	-1.3	0	3
1970 Bos	3	11	3.7	0	5
1972 Buf	5	19	3.8	0	1
NFL Total	46	134	2.9	0	17

DAVE TALLANT Tallant, David 6′1″, 205 **T**
Col: Muskingum; Grove City *HS:* Wilkinsburg [PA] B: 8/1896, Murrysville, PA Deceased
1921 Ham: 4 G. **1922** Ham: 5 G. **1923** Ham: 7 G. **1924** Ham: 1 G. **1925** Ham: 3 G. **Total:** 20 G.

BEN TALLEY Talley, Benjamin Jermaine 6′3″, 248 **LB**
Col: Tennessee *HS:* Griffin [GA] B: 7/14/1972, Griffin, GA
Drafted: 1995 Round 4 NYG
1995 NYG: 4 G. **1998** Atl: 8 G. **Total:** 12 G.

DARRYL TALLEY Talley, Darryl Victor 6′4″, 235 **LB**
Col: West Virginia *HS:* Shaw [East Cleveland, OH] B: 7/10/1960, Cleveland, OH *Drafted:* 1983 Round 2 Buf
1983 Buf: KR 2-9 4.5; 5 Sac. **1984** Buf: 5 Sac. **1985** Buf: 2 Sac. **1986** Buf: 3 Sac. **1987** Buf: 1 Sac. **1988** Buf: 2.5 Sac. **1989** Buf: 6 Sac. **1990** Buf: 4 Sac. **1991** Buf: 4 Sac. **1992** Buf: 4 Sac. **1993** Buf: 2 Sac. **Total:** KR 2-9 4.5; 38.5 Sac.

		Interceptions		
Year Team	**G**	**Int**	**Yds**	**TD**
1983 Buf	16	0	0	0
1984 Buf	16	1	0	0
1985 Buf	16	0	0	0
1986 Buf	16	0	0	0
1987 Buf	12	0	0	0
1988 Buf	16	0	0	0
1989 Buf	16	0	0	0
1990 Buf	16	2	60	1
1991 Buf	16	5	45	0
1992 Buf	16	0	0	0
1993 Buf	16	3	74	1
1994 Buf	16	0	0	0
1995 Atl	16	0	0	0
1996 Min	12	1	10	0
NFL Total	216	12	189	2

JOHN TALLEY Talley, John Thomas Eugene Jr. 6′5″, 245 **WR**
Col: West Virginia *HS:* Shaw [East Cleveland, OH] B: 12/19/1964, Cleveland, OH
1990 Cle: 14 G; Rec 2-28 14.0; KR 1-6 6.0. **1991** Cle: 3 G; Rec 1-13 13.0. **Total:** 17 G; Rec 3-41 13.7; KR 1-6 6.0.

STAN TALLEY Talley, Robert Stanley 6′5″, 220 **P**
Col: El Camino Coll. CA (J.C.); Texas Christian *HS:* West [Torrance, CA] B: 9/5/1958, Dallas, TX

		Punting		
Year Team	**G**	**Punts**	**Yds**	**Avg**
1987 LARd	12	56	2277	40.7

CHARLES TALLMAN Tallman, Charles W **T**
Col: No College B: 1/9/1896, NY D: 4/1970, Franklin, NJ
1921 Ton: 1 G.

KEN TALTON Talton, Kenneth B 6′0″, 208 **RB**
Col: Cornell *HS:* Shadyside Acad. [Homestead, PA] B: 6/25/1956, Mansfield, OH
1980 KC: 2 G.

BEN TAMBURELLO Tamburello, Ben Allen Jr. 6′3″, 278 **OG-C**
Col: Auburn *HS:* Shades Valley [Birmingham, AL]; Tennessee Acad. [Sweetwater, TN] B: 9/9/1964, Birmingham, AL *Drafted:* 1987 Round 3 Phi
1987 Phi: 2 G. **1988** Phi: 16 G. **1989** Phi: 16 G. **1990** Phi: 16 G. **Total:** 50 G.

SAM TAMBURO Tamburo, Samuel Joseph Jr. 6′2″, 200 **DE**
Col: Penn State *HS:* New Kensington [PA] B: 7/1/1926, New Kensington, PA *Drafted:* 1949 Round 6 NYB
1949 NYB: 12 G.

RALPH TAMM Tamm, Ralph Earl 6′4″, 280 **OG-C**
Col: West Chester *HS:* Bensalem [PA] B: 3/11/1966, Philadelphia, PA
Drafted: 1988 Round 9 NYJ
1990 Cle: 16 G. **1991** Cle-Was-Cin: 4 G. Cle: 1 G. Was: 2 G. Cin: 1 G. **1992** SF: 14 G. **1993** SF: 16 G; 1 Fum TD; 6 Pt. **1994** SF: 1 G. **1995** Den: 13 G. **1996** Den: 9 G. **1997** KC: 16 G. **1998** KC: 16 G. **Total:** 105 G; 1 Fum TD; 6 Pt.

GEORGE TANDY Tandy, George Wendell 6′1″, 210 **C-OE**
(Yank) *Col:* North Carolina B: 11/27/1893, Jacksonville, IL
D: 5/11/1969, Springfield, IL
1920 Roch: 1 G. **1921** Cle: 5 G. **Total:** 6 G.

BILL TANGUAY Tanguay, James 6′0″, 190 **TB-DB**
Col: New York U. *HS:* Central [Washington, DC] B: 5/24/1909
D: 3/1971
1933 Pit: 3 G; Pass 17-5 29.4%, 101 5.94 1 TD 5 Int.

STEVE TANNEN Tannen, Steven Olson 6′1″, 194 **DB**
Col: Florida *HS:* Southwest Miami [Miami, FL] B: 7/23/1948, Miami, FL
Drafted: 1970 Round 1 NYJ
1970 NYJ: KR 1-(-1) -1.0. **1973** NYJ: PR 2-0. **Total:** PR 2-0; KR 1-(-1) -1.0.

		Interceptions			
Year Team	**G**	**Int**	**Yds**	**TD**	**Fum**
1970 NYJ	14	2	16	0	0
1971 NYJ	11	0	0	0	0
1972 NYJ	13	7	125	0	0
1973 NYJ	9	1	30	0	1
1974 NYJ	14	2	33	0	0
NFL Total	61	12	204	0	1

BARRON TANNER Tanner, Barron Keith 6′3″, 312 **DT**
(Beep) *Col:* Oklahoma *HS:* Athens [TX] B: 9/14/1973, Athens, TX
Drafted: 1997 Round 5 Mia
1997 Mia: 16 G. **1998** Mia: 13 G. **Total:** 29 G.

HAMP TANNER Tanner, Elijah Hampton 6′2″, 280 **OT-DT**
Col: Georgia *HS:* Lanier [Macon, GA] B: 6/30/1927, Nichols, GA
D: 1/1988, Sandersville, GA
1951 SF: 12 G; Scor **1** Saf; 2 Pt. **1952** Dal: 10 G; KR 1-19 19.0. **Total:** 22 G; KR 1-19 19.0; Scor 1 Saf; 2 Pt.

JOHN TANNER Tanner, John Porter 5′5″, 165 **WB-FB-BB-TB**
(Shorty; Hump) *Col:* Centre *HS:* Owensboro [KY] B: 12/3/1897, Owensboro, KY D: 12/23/1976, Owensboro, KY
1922 Tol: 2 G. **1923** Cle: 6 G; Rec 1 TD; Scor 8, 2 XK. **1924** Cle: 2 G; Rush 2 TD; 12 Pt. **Total:** 10 G; Rush 2 TD; Rec 1 TD; Tot TD 3.

JOHN TANNER Tanner, John Vance 6′4″, 231 **LB**
Col: Brevard CC FL; Tennessee Tech *HS:* Cocoa [FL] B: 3/8/1945, Orlando, FL *Drafted:* 1971 Round 9 SD
1971 SD: 14 G; Rec 1-6 6.0. **1973** NE: 13 G. **1974** NE: 13 G; Rec 2-23 11.5 1 TD; KR 2-17 8.5; 6 Pt; 1 Fum. **Total:** 40 G; Rec 3-29 9.7 1 TD; KR 2-17 8.5; 6 Pt; 1 Fum.

BOB TANNER Tanner, Robert Erwin 6′0″, 190 **OE-T**
Col: Minnesota *HS:* East [Minneapolis, MN]; Marshall HS [Minneapolis, MN] B: 9/27/1907, Fairmont, MN D: 12/9/1997, Homosassa, FL
1930 Fra: 12 G; Rec 1 TD; Int 1 TD; Tot TD 2; 12 Pt.

MAA TANUVASA Tanuvasa, Maa Junior 6′2″, 270 **DT**
Col: Hawaii *HS:* Mililani [HI] B: 11/6/1970, Nu'uli, American Samoa
Drafted: 1993 Round 8 LARm
1995 Den: 1 G. **1996** Den: 16 G; 5 Sac. **1997** Den: 15 G; 8.5 Sac. **1998** Den: 16 G; KR 1-13 13.0; 8.5 Sac. **Total:** 48 G; KR 1-13 13.0; 22 Sac.

GEORGE TARASOVIC Tarasovic, George Kenneth 6′4″, 245 **DE-LB-C**
Col: Boston College; Louisiana State *HS:* Warren G. Harding [Bridgeport, CT] B: 5/6/1930, Granville, NY *Drafted:* 1952 Round 2 Pit
1959 Pit: **1** Fum TD. **1965** Phi: **1** Fum TD. **Total:** 2 Fum TD.

		Interceptions				Tot
Year Team	**G**	**Int**	**Yds**	**TD**	**Fum**	**TD**
1952 Pit	12	0	0	0	1	0
1953 Pit	12	0	0	0	0	0
1956 Pit	12	3	60	0	0	0
1957 Pit	12	2	21	0	0	0
1958 Pit	12	0	0	0	0	0
1959 Pit	12	0	0	0	1	1
1960 Pit	12	1	8	0	0	0
1961 Pit	12	1	16	0	0	0
1962 Pit	14	4	55	0	0	0
1963 Pit-Phi	14	0	0	0	0	0
1963 Pit	8	0	0	0	0	0
1963 Phi	6	0	0	0	0	0
1964 Phi	11	0	0	0	0	0
1965 Phi	14	1	40	1	0	2
1966 Den	6	0	0	0	0	0
NFL Total	155	12	200	1	2	3

BRUCE TARBOX Tarbox, Bruce P 6'2", 230 **OG**
Col: Syracuse *HS:* Kent Prep [CT] B: 5/10/1939, Nyack, NY
D: 3/6/1979, Pittsburgh, PA *Drafted:* 1961 Round 2 NYG
1961 LARm: 7 G.

RICHARD TARDITS Tardits, Richard 6'2", 228 **LB**
Col: Georgia *HS:* Lycee Rene-Cassin [Biarritz, France] B: 7/30/1965, Biarritz, France *Drafted:* 1989 Round 5 Pho
1990 NE: 2 G. **1991** NE: 16 G. **1992** NE: 9 G. **Total:** 27 G.

FRAN TARKENTON Tarkenton, Francis Asbury 6'0", 190 **QB**
Col: Georgia *HS:* Athens [GA] B: 2/3/1940, Richmond, VA
Drafted: 1961 Round 3 Min *HOF:* 1986

		Passing							
Year Team	G	Att	Comp	Comp%	Yds	YPA	TD	Int	Rating
1961 Min	14	280	157	56.1	1997	7.13	18	17	74.7
1962 Min	14	329	163	49.5	2595	7.89	22	25	66.9
1963 Min	14	297	170	57.2	2311	7.78	15	15	78.0
1964 Min	14	306	171	55.9	2506	8.19	22	11	91.8
1965 Min	14	329	171	52.0	2609	7.93	19	11	83.8
1966 Min	14	358	192	53.6	2561	7.15	17	16	73.8
1967 NYG	14	377	204	54.1	3088	8.19	29	19	85.9
1968 NYG	14	337	182	54.0	2555	7.58	21	12	84.6
1969 NYG	14	409	220	53.8	2918	7.13	23	8	87.2
1970 NYG	14	389	219	56.3	2777	7.14	19	12	82.2
1971 NYG	13	386	226	58.5	2567	6.65	11	21	65.4
1972 Min	14	378	215	56.9	2651	7.01	18	13	80.2
1973 Min	14	274	169	61.7	2113	7.71	15	7	93.2
1974 Min	13	351	199	56.7	2598	7.40	17	12	82.1
1975 Min	14	**425**	**273**	64.2	2994	7.04	**25**	13	91.8
1976 Min	13	412	**255**	61.9	2961	7.19	17	8	89.3
1977 Min	9	258	155	**60.1**	1734	6.72	9	14	69.2
1978 Min	16	**572**	**345**	60.3	**3468**	6.06	25	32	68.9
NFL Total	246	6467	3686	57.0	47003	7.27	342	266	80.4

	Rushing				
Year Team	Att	Yds	Avg	TD	Fum
1961 Min	56	308	5.5	5	8
1962 Min	41	361	8.8	2	5
1963 Min	28	162	5.8	1	7
1964 Min	50	330	6.6	2	6
1965 Min	56	356	6.4	1	5
1966 Min	62	376	6.1	4	8
1967 NYG	44	306	7.0	2	4
1968 NYG	57	301	5.3	3	2
1969 NYG	37	172	4.6	0	7
1970 NYG	43	236	5.5	2	3
1971 NYG	30	111	3.7	3	4
1972 Min	27	180	6.7	0	3
1973 Min	41	202	4.9	1	5
1974 Min	21	120	5.7	2	2
1975 Min	16	108	6.8	2	1
1976 Min	27	45	1.7	1	4
1977 Min	15	6	0.4	0	3
1978 Min	24	-6	-0.3	1	7
NFL Total	675	3674	5.4	32	84

JERRY TARR Tarr, Gerald LaVern 6'0", 190 **WR**
Col: Bakersfield Coll. CA (J.C.); Oregon *HS:* Bakersfield [CA]
B: 8/27/1939, Bakersfield, CA *Drafted:* 1962 Round 17 Den
1962 Den: 14 G; Rec 8-211 26.4 2 TD; KR 8-217 27.1; 12 Pt; 2 Fum.

JIM TARR Tarr, James Lloyd 6'2", 190 **OE**
Col: Missouri *HS:* Nevada [MO]; Kemper Mil. School [Boonville, MO]
B: 9/26/1906, Nevada, MO D: 5/6/1995, Eugene, OR
1931 Cle: 1 G.

JIMMY TARRANT Tarrant, James Robert Jr. 5'9", 160 **QB**
Col: Samford; Tennessee *HS:* Woodlawn [Birmingham, AL]
B: 2/18/1921, Birmingham, AL
AAFC **1946** MiaA: 4 G; Pass 12-5 41.7%, 95 7.92 1 TD; Rush 5-(-46) -9.2.

BOB TARRANT Tarrant, Robert Everett 6'0", 180 **OE-DE**
Col: Pittsburg State *HS:* El Dorado [KS] B: 4/4/1914, Hamilton, KS
D: 12/16/1991, Danbury, CT
1936 NYG: 1 G.

JOHN TARVER Tarver, John William 6'3", 227 **RB**
Col: Bakersfield Coll. CA (J.C.); Colorado *HS:* Arvin [OH] B: 1/1/1949, Bakersfield, CA *Drafted:* 1972 Round 7 NE
1973 NE: KR 1-17 17.0. **Total:** KR 1-17 17.0.

		Rushing				Receiving					Tot
Year Team	G	Att	Yds	Avg	TD	Rec	Yds	Avg	TD	Fum	TD
1972 NE	8	42	132	3.1	1	11	112	10.2	1	0	2
1973 NE	9	72	321	4.5	4	9	51	5.7	0	8	4
1974 NE	14	41	101	2.5	2	9	37	4.1	0	2	2
1975 Phi	8	7	20	2.9	0	5	14	2.8	0	0	0
NFL Total	39	162	574	3.5	7	34	214	6.3	1	10	8

CARL TASEFF Taseff, Carl N 5'11", 192 **DB-HB**
Col: John Carroll *HS:* East [Cleveland, OH] B: 9/28/1928, Parma, OH
Drafted: 1951 Round 22 Cle
1951 Cle: Rec 1-18 18.0. **1954** Bal: Rec 16-159 9.9 1 TD. **1955** Bal: Rec 1-3 3.0. **1960** Bal: Rec 1-13 13.0. **1962** Buf: Pass 1-0.
Total: Pass 1-0; Rec 19-193 10.2 1 TD.

		Rushing				Punt Returns			
Year Team	G	Att	Yds	Avg	TD	Ret	Yds	Avg	TD
1951 Cle	9	13	49	3.8	2	1	6	6.0	0
1953 Bal	9	1	1	1.0	1	1	71	71.0	**1**
1954 Bal	12	41	228	5.6	0	8	52	6.5	0
1955 Bal	11	0	0	—	0	14	46	3.3	0
1956 Bal	12	1	2	2.0	0	**27**	**233**	8.6	**1**
1957 Bal	4	0	0	—	0	7	60	8.6	0
1958 Bal	12	0	0	—	0	**29**	196	6.8	0
1959 Bal	12	0	0	—	0	15	104	6.9	0
1960 Bal	12	4	3	0.8	0	6	25	4.2	0
1961 Bal-Phi	12	0	0	—	0	5	39	7.8	0
1961 Bal	7	0	0	—	0	5	39	7.8	0
1961 Phi	5	0	0	—	0	0	0	—	0
1962 Buf	11	0	0	—	0	4	18	4.5	0
NFL Total	116	60	283	4.7	3	117	850	7.3	2

	Kickoff Returns				Interceptions				Tot
Year Team	Ret	Yds	Avg	TD	Int	Yds	TD	Fum	TD
1951 Cle	3	56	18.7	0	0	0	0	3	2
1953 Bal	4	87	21.8	0	3	36	0	0	2
1954 Bal	7	167	23.9	0	2	15	0	0	1
1955 Bal	7	162	23.1	0	1	0	0	0	0
1956 Bal	9	206	22.9	0	2	13	0	0	2
1957 Bal	0	0	—	0	1	7	0	1	0
1958 Bal	1	50	50.0	0	7	52	0	3	0
1959 Bal	0	0	—	0	2	60	0	1	1
1960 Bal	14	291	20.8	0	0	0	0	0	0
1961 Bal-Phi	0	0	—	0	1	15	0	1	0
1961 Bal	0	0	—	0	1	15	0	1	0
1962 Buf	0	0	—	0	2	21	0	0	0
NFL Total	45	1019	22.6	0	21	219	0	9	8

STEVE TASKER Tasker, Steven Jay 5'9", 185 **WR**
Col: Dodge City CC KS; Northwestern *HS:* Wichita Co. [Leoti, KS]
B: 4/10/1962, Smith Center, KS *Drafted:* 1985 Round 9 Hou
1985 Hou: Rush 2-16 8.0. **1987** Buf: Scor **1** Saf. **1992** Buf: Rush 1-9 9.0. **1995** Buf: Rush 8-74 9.3. **1996** Buf: Rush 9-31 3.4. **Total:** Rush 20-130 6.5; Scor 1 Saf.

		Receiving				Punt Returns			
Year Team	G	Rec	Yds	Avg	TD	Ret	Yds	Avg	TD
1985 Hou	7	2	19	9.5	0	0	0	—	0
1986 Hou-Buf	9	0	0	—	0	0	0	—	0
1986 Hou	2	0	0	—	0	0	0	—	0
1986 Buf	7	0	0	—	0	0	0	—	0
1987 Buf	12	0	0	—	0	0	0	—	0
1988 Buf	14	0	0	—	0	0	0	—	0
1989 Buf	16	0	0	—	0	0	0	—	0
1990 Buf	16	2	44	22.0	2	0	0	—	0
1991 Buf	16	2	39	19.5	1	0	0	—	0
1992 Buf	15	2	24	12.0	0	0	0	—	0
1993 Buf	15	2	26	13.0	0	1	0	0.0	0
1994 Buf	14	0	0	—	0	0	0	—	0
1995 Buf	13	20	255	12.8	3	17	204	12.0	0
1996 Buf	8	21	372	17.7	3	2	18	9.0	0
1997 Buf	14	0	0	—	0	12	113	9.4	0
NFL Total	169	51	779	15.3	9	32	335	10.5	0

	Kickoff Returns				
Year Team	Ret	Yds	Avg	TD	Fum
1985 Hou	17	447	26.3	0	0
1986 Hou-Buf	12	213	17.8	0	0
1986 Hou	3	65	21.7	0	0
1986 Buf	9	148	16.4	0	0
1987 Buf	11	197	17.9	0	2
1989 Buf	2	39	19.5	0	0
1993 Buf	0	0	—	0	1
1994 Buf	1	2	2.0	0	0
1996 Buf	0	0	—	0	3
1997 Buf	1	12	12.0	0	1
NFL Total	44	910	20.7	0	7

DAMON TASSOS Tassos, Damon Gus 6'1", 224 **G-LB**
(Greek) *Col:* Texas A&M *HS:* Thomas Jefferson [San Antonio, TX]
B: 12/5/1923, San Antonio, TX *Drafted:* 1945 Round 3 Bos
1945 Det: 9 G; Int 3-49. **1946** Det: 11 G; Int 1-30; Scor 3, 0-1 FG, 3-3 100.0% XK. **1947** GB: 3 G. **1948** GB: 11 G. **1949** GB: 12 G; Int 1-10.
Total: 46 G; Int 5-89; Scor 3, 0-1 FG, 3-3 100.0% XK.

BOB TATAREK Tatarek, Robert Francis 6′4″, 270 DT
Col: Miami (Fla.) *HS:* Jeannette [PA] B: 7/3/1946, Greensburg, PA
Drafted: 1968 Round 2 Buf
1968 Buf: 14 G. **1969** Buf: 14 G. **1970** Buf: 4 G. **1971** Buf: 14 G.
1972 Buf-Det: 3 G. Buf: 1 G. Det: 2 G. **Total:** 49 G.

DAVID TATE Tate, David Fitzgerald 6′1″, 197 DB
Col: Colorado *HS:* J.K. Mullen [Denver, CO] B: 11/22/1964, Denver, CO *Drafted:* 1988 Round 8 ChiB
1989 ChiB: KR 1-12 12.0. **1996** Ind: 1 Sac. **Total:** KR 1-12 12.0; 1 Sac.

		Interceptions			
Year Team	**G**	**Int**	**Yds**	**TD**	**Fum**
1988 ChiB	16	4	35	0	0
1989 ChiB	14	1	0	0	0
1990 ChiB	16	0	0	0	0
1991 ChiB	16	2	35	0	0
1992 ChiB	16	0	0	0	0
1993 NYG	14	1	12	0	1
1994 Ind	16	3	51	0	0
1995 Ind	16	0	0	0	0
1996 Ind	10	0	0	0	0
1997 Ind	8	0	0	0	0
NFL Total	142	11	133	0	1

FRANKLIN TATE Tate, Franklin Eugene 6′3″, 225 LB
Col: North Carolina Central *HS:* Ashbrook [Gastonia, NC]
B: 11/14/1952, Gastonia, NC
1975 SD: 4 G.

JOHN TATE Tate, John 6′2″, 230 LB
Col: Jackson State *HS:* Mobile [AL] B: 5/1/1953, Mobile, AL
1976 NYG: 2 G.

LARS TATE Tate, Lars Jamel 6′2″, 215 RB
Col: Georgia *HS:* North Central [Indianapolis, IN] B: 2/2/1966, Indianapolis, IN *Drafted:* 1988 Round 2 TB
1988 TB: Rec 5-23 4.6 1 TD. **1989** TB: Rec 11-75 6.8 1 TD. **1990** ChiB: KR 1-0. **Total:** Rec 16-98 6.1 2 TD; KR 1-0.

		Rushing					Tot
Year Team	**G**	**Att**	**Yds**	**Avg**	**TD**	**Fum**	**TD**
1988 TB	15	122	467	3.8	7	2	8
1989 TB	15	167	589	3.5	8	2	9
1990 ChiB	3	3	5	1.7	0	0	0
NFL Total	33	292	1061	3.6	15	4	17

ROBERT TATE Tate, Robert 5′10″, 188 WR
Col: Cincinnati *HS:* John Harris [Harrisburg, PA]; Milford Acad. [CT]
B: 10/19/1973, Crowley, LA *Drafted:* 1997 Round 6 Min
1997 Min: 4 G; KR 10-196 19.6. **1998** Min: 15 G; Rec 1-17 17.0; KR 2-43 21.5. **Total:** 19 G; Rec 1-17 17.0; KR 12-239 19.9.

RODNEY TATE Tate, Rodney Dane 5′11″, 190 RB
Col: Texas *HS:* Beggs [OK] B: 2/14/1959, Okmulgee, OK
Drafted: 1982 Round 4 Cin
1983 Cin: Rec 18-142 7.9. **Total:** Rec 18-142 7.9.

		Rushing				Kickoff Returns				
Year Team	**G**	**Att**	**Yds**	**Avg**	**TD**	**Ret**	**Yds**	**Avg**	**TD**	**Fum**
1982 Cin	9	2	2	1.0	0	14	314	22.4	0	2
1983 Cin	12	25	77	3.1	0	13	218	16.8	0	3
1984 Atl	7	0	0	—	0	9	148	16.4	0	1
NFL Total	28	27	79	2.9	0	36	680	18.9	0	6

WILLY TATE Tate, William Russell 6′3″, 251 TE
Col: Oregon *HS:* Elk Grove [CA] B: 9/7/1972, Fontana, CA
1996 TB: 13 G. **1998** KC: 1 G. **Total:** 14 G.

PETE TATMAN Tatman, Allen Kent 6′1″, 220 RB
Col: Nebraska *HS:* North Platte [NE] B: 4/27/1945, Sutherland, NE
Drafted: 1967 Round 10 Min
1967 Min: 5 G; KR 1-14 14.0.

JESS TATUM Tatum, Jess Bolt 6′1″, 215 OE-DE
Col: North Carolina State *HS:* McColl [SC] B: 10/8/1914, McColl, SC
D: 2/4/1992, Lancaster, NC
1938 Pit: 5 G; Rec 1-16 16.0.

JACK TATUM Tatum, John David 5′10″, 200 DB
(The Assassin) *Col:* Ohio State *HS:* Passaic [NJ] B: 11/18/1948, Cherryville, NC *Drafted:* 1971 Round 1 Oak
1972 Oak: **1** Fum TD. **Total:** 1 Fum TD.

		Interceptions			
Year Team	**G**	**Int**	**Yds**	**TD**	**Fum**
1971 Oak	14	4	136	0	1
1972 Oak	14	4	91	0	1
1973 Oak	13	1	26	0	0
1974 Oak	10	4	84	0	0
1975 Oak	13	4	67	0	1
1976 Oak	14	2	0	0	0
1977 Oak	11	6	146	0	0
1978 Oak	15	3	60	0	0
1979 Oak	16	2	26	0	0
1980 Hou	16	7	100	0	0
NFL Total	136	37	736	0	3

KINNON TATUM Tatum, Kinnon Ray II 6′0″, 222 LB
Col: Notre Dame *HS:* Douglas Byrd [Fayetteville, NC] B: 7/19/1975, Fayetteville, NC *Drafted:* 1997 Round 3 Car
1997 Car: 16 G. **1998** Car: 15 G. **Total:** 31 G.

MOSI TATUPU Tatupu, Mosiula Faasuka 6′0″, 227 RB
Col: USC *HS:* Punahou School [Honolulu, HI] B: 4/26/1955, Pago Pago, American Samoa *Drafted:* 1978 Round 8 NE
1978 NE: KR 1-17 17.0. **1979** NE: KR 3-15 5.0. **1984** NE: KR 1-9 9.0. **1987** NE: Pass 1-1 100.0%, 15 15.00 1 TD. **1988** NE: KR 1-13 13.0. **1989** NE: Pass 1-1 100.0%, 15 15.00; KR 1-2 2.0. **Total:** Pass 2-2 100.0%, 30 15.00 1 TD; KR 7-56 8.0.

		Rushing				Receiving					Tot
Year Team	**G**	**Att**	**Yds**	**Avg**	**TD**	**Rec**	**Yds**	**Avg**	**TD**	**Fum**	**TD**
1978 NE	16	3	6	2.0	0	0	0	—	0	0	0
1979 NE	16	23	71	3.1	0	2	9	4.5	0	0	0
1980 NE	16	33	97	2.9	3	4	27	6.8	0	0	3
1981 NE	16	38	201	5.3	2	12	132	11.0	1	2	3
1982 NE	9	30	168	5.6	0	0	0	—	0	0	0
1983 NE	16	106	578	**5.5**	4	10	97	9.7	1	1	5
1984 NE	16	133	553	4.2	4	16	159	9.9	0	4	4
1985 NE	16	47	152	3.2	2	2	16	8.0	0	1	2
1986 NE	16	71	172	2.4	1	15	145	9.7	0	1	2
1987 NE	12	79	248	3.1	0	15	136	9.1	0	1	0
1988 NE	16	22	75	3.4	2	8	58	7.3	0	0	2
1989 NE	14	11	38	3.5	0	10	54	5.4	0	0	0
1990 NE	15	16	56	3.5	0	2	10	5.0	0	0	0
1991 LARm	5	0	0	—	0	0	0	—	0	0	0
NFL Total	199	612	2415	3.9	18	96	843	8.8	2	10	21

BIFF TAUGHER Taugher, Claude B 5′10″, 185 FB
(Doc) *Col:* Carroll (Wis.); Marquette *HS:* Wausau [WI] B: 3/2/1895, Marathon, WI Deceased
1922 GB: 2 G; Rush 1 TD; 6 Pt.

TERRY TAUSCH Tausch, Terry Wayne 6′5″, 275 OT-OG
Col: Texas *HS:* New Braunfels [TX] B: 2/5/1959, New Braunfels, TX
Drafted: 1982 Round 2 Min
1982 Min: 2 G. **1983** Min: 10 G. **1984** Min: 16 G. **1985** Min: 16 G. **1986** Min: 16 G. **1987** Min: 5 G. **1988** Min: 16 G. **1989** SF: 9 G. **Total:** 90 G.

JUNIOR TAUTALATASI Tautalatasi, Taivale Jr. 5′10″, 207 RB
Col: Chabot Coll. CA (J.C.); Washington State *HS:* Encinal [Alameda, CA] B: 3/24/1963, Oakland, CA *Drafted:* 1986 Round 10 Phi
1986 Phi: KR 18-344 19.1. **1987** Phi: KR 3-53 17.7. **1989** Dal: KR 1-9 9.0. **Total:** KR 22-406 18.5.

		Rushing				Receiving				
Year Team	**G**	**Att**	**Yds**	**Avg**	**TD**	**Rec**	**Yds**	**Avg**	**TD**	**Fum**
1986 Phi	16	51	163	3.2	0	41	325	7.9	2	6
1987 Phi	12	26	69	2.7	0	25	176	7.0	0	1
1988 Phi	10	14	28	2.0	0	5	48	9.6	0	0
1989 Dal	13	6	15	2.5	0	17	157	9.2	0	3
NFL Total	51	97	275	2.8	0	88	706	8.0	2	10

JOHN TAUTOLO Tautolo, John William 6′3″, 267 OG
Col: UCLA *HS:* R.A. Millikan [Long Beach, CA] B: 5/29/1959, Long Beach, CA
1982 NYG: 1 G. **1983** NYG: 6 G. **1987** LARd: 3 G. **Total:** 10 G.

TERRY TAUTOLO Tautolo, Terry Lynn 6′2″, 232 LB
Col: Long Beach City Coll. CA (J.C.); UCLA *HS:* R.A. Millikan [Long Beach, CA] B: 8/30/1954, Corona, CA *Drafted:* 1976 Round 13 Phi
1976 Phi: 13 G. **1977** Phi: 14 G. **1978** Phi: 16 G; KR 3-45 15.0. **1979** Phi: 16 G. **1980** SF: 14 G; KR 1-16 16.0; Int 1-0. **1981** SF-Det: 16 G. SF: 5 G. Det: 11 G. **1982** Det: 2 G. **1983** Mia: 9 G. **1984** Det: 4 G. **Total:** 104 G; KR 4-61 15.3; Int 1-0.

JOHN TAVENER Tavener, John Harold 6′0″, 225 C-LB
Col: Indiana *HS:* Johnstown [OH] B: 1/10/1921, Newark, OH
D: 9/19/1993, Johnstown, OH
AAFC **1946** MiaA: 3 G.

AARON TAYLOR Taylor, Aaron Matthew 6′4″, 305 OG
(A.T.) *Col:* Notre Dame *HS:* De La Salle [Concord, CA]
B: 11/14/1972, San Francisco, CA *Drafted:* 1994 Round 1 GB
1995 GB: 16 G. **1996** GB: 16 G. **1997** GB: 14 G. **1998** SD: 15 G. **Total:** 61 G.

ALPHONSO TAYLOR Taylor, Alphonso 6′3″, 350 DT
Col: Temple *HS:* Central [Trenton, NJ] B: 9/7/1969, Trenton, NJ
1993 Den: 3 G.

ALTIE TAYLOR Taylor, Altie 5'10", 200 **RB**
Col: Diablo Valley Coll. CA (J.C.); Utah State *HS:* Pittsburg [CA]
B: 9/29/1947, Pittsburg, CA *Drafted:* 1969 Round 2 Det

		Rushing				Receiving			
Year Team	**G**	**Att**	**Yds**	**Avg**	**TD**	**Rec**	**Yds**	**Avg**	**TD**
1969 Det	10	118	348	2.9	0	13	86	6.6	0
1970 Det	14	198	666	3.4	2	27	261	9.7	2
1971 Det	14	174	736	4.2	4	26	270	10.4	1
1972 Det	13	154	658	4.3	4	29	250	8.6	2
1973 Det	13	176	719	4.1	5	27	252	9.3	0
1974 Det	13	150	532	3.5	5	30	293	9.8	1
1975 Det	14	195	638	3.3	4	21	111	5.3	0
1976 Hou	11	5	11	2.2	0	2	15	7.5	0
NFL Total	102	1170	4308	3.7	24	175	1538	8.8	6

	Kickoff Returns					Tot
Year Team	**Ret**	**Yds**	**Avg**	**TD**	**Fum**	**TD**
1969 Det	0	0	—	0	4	0
1970 Det	0	0	—	0	6	4
1971 Det	0	0	—	0	**11**	5
1972 Det	0	0	—	0	2	6
1973 Det	12	295	24.6	0	5	5
1974 Det	0	0	—	0	2	6
1975 Det	0	0	—	0	3	4
1976 Hou	15	302	20.1	0	0	0
NFL Total	27	597	22.1	0	33	30

BRIAN TAYLOR Taylor, Brian Teon 5'10", 185 **DB-RB**
Col: Laney Coll. CA (J.C.); Oregon State *HS:* St. Augustine [New Orleans, LA] B: 10/1/1967, New Orleans, LA
1989 ChiB: 5 G; Rush 2-7 3.5. **1991** Buf: 3 G; KR 1-18 18.0. **Total:** 8 G; Rush 2-7 3.5; KR 1-18 18.0.

BRUCE TAYLOR Taylor, Bruce Lawrence 6'0", 193 **DB**
Col: Boston U. *HS:* Perth Amboy [NJ] B: 5/28/1948, Perth Amboy, NJ
Drafted: 1970 Round 1 SF
1970 SF: KR 12-190 15.8. **Total:** KR 12-190 15.8.

		Punt Returns				Interceptions				Tot
Year Team	**G**	**Ret**	**Yds**	**Avg**	**TD**	**Int**	**Yds**	**TD**	**Fum**	**TD**
1970 SF	14	43	**516**	12.0	0	3	70	0	3	1
1971 SF	14	**34**	235	6.9	0	3	68	0	5	1
1972 SF	14	21	145	6.9	0	2	4	0	3	0
1973 SF	14	15	207	**13.8**	0	6	30	0	1	0
1974 SF	14	10	38	3.8	0	1	0	0	0	0
1975 SF	12	16	166	10.4	0	3	29	0	2	0
1976 SF	13	3	16	5.3	0	0	0	0	1	0
1977 SF	14	0	0	—	0	0	0	0	0	0
NFL Total	109	142	1323	9.3	0	18	201	0	15	2

CORKY TAYLOR Taylor, Cecil Reign Jr. 5'10", 189 **DB-HB**
Col: Kansas State *HS:* Southeast [Kansas City, MO] B: 10/31/1933, Kansas City, MO *Drafted:* 1955 Round 2 LARm
1955 LARm: Rec 7-47 6.7 1 TD; Int 2-55 1 TD. **1957** LARm: PR 3-41 13.7; KR 1-35 35.0. **Total:** Rec 7-47 6.7 1 TD; PR 3-41 13.7; KR 1-35 35.0; Int 2-55 1 TD.

		Rushing					Tot
Year Team	**G**	**Att**	**Yds**	**Avg**	**TD**	**Fum**	**TD**
1955 LARm	10	26	95	3.7	0	1	2
1957 LARm	2	0	0	—	0	0	0
NFL Total	12	26	95	3.7	0	1	2

CHUCK TAYLOR Taylor, Charles Albert 5'11", 205 **G**
Col: Stanford *HS:* San Jose [CA] B: 1/24/1920, Portland, OR
D: 5/7/1994, Stanford, CA
AAFC **1946** MiaA: 14 G.

CHUCK TAYLOR Taylor, Charles G 5'10", 210 **BB-LB**
Col: Arkansas Tech; Ouachita Baptist B: 1/12/1920, Tupelo, AR
D: 6/3/1977, CO
1944 Bkn: 10 G; Rush 7-19 2.7; Rec 2-22 11.0; PR 2-25 12.5; KR 1-12 12.0.

CHARLEY TAYLOR Taylor, Charles Robert 6'3", 210 **WR-RB**
Col: Arizona State *HS:* Dalworth [Grand Prairie, TX] B: 9/28/1941, Grand Prairie, TX *Drafted:* 1964 Round 1 Was *HOF:* 1984
1964 Was: Pass 10-2 20.0%, 54 5.40 1 Int; KR 1-20 20.0. **1965** Was: Pass 4-1 25.0%, 45 11.25 1 TD; KR 1-15 15.0. **1966** Was: PR 5-63 12.6; KR 3-98 32.7. **Total:** Pass 14-3 21.4%, 99 7.07 1 TD 1 Int; PR 5-63 12.6; KR 5-133 26.6.

		Rushing				Receiving					Tot
Year Team	**G**	**Att**	**Yds**	**Avg**	**TD**	**Rec**	**Yds**	**Avg**	**TD**	**Fum**	**TD**
1964 Was	14	199	755	3.8	5	53	814	15.4	5	7	10
1965 Was	13	145	402	2.8	3	40	577	14.4	3	10	6
1966 Was	14	87	262	3.0	3	**72**	1119	15.5	12	6	15
1967 Was	12	0	0	—	0	**70**	990	14.1	9	3	9
1968 Was	14	2	-3	-1.5	0	48	650	13.5	5	1	5
1969 Was	14	3	24	8.0	0	71	883	12.4	8	1	8
1970 Was	10	1	17	17.0	0	42	593	14.1	8	1	8
1971 Was	6	0	0	—	0	24	370	15.4	4	0	4
1972 Was	14	3	39	13.0	0	49	673	13.7	7	1	7
1973 Was	14	1	-7	-7.0	0	59	801	13.6	7	1	7
1974 Was	14	1	-1	-1.0	0	54	738	13.7	5	0	5
1975 Was	14	0	0	—	0	53	744	14.0	6	0	6
1977 Was	12	0	0	—	0	14	158	11.3	0	0	0
NFL Total	165	442	1488	3.4	11	649	9110	14.0	79	31	90

CLIFF TAYLOR Taylor, Clifton Durett 5'11", 198 **RB**
Col: Memphis *HS:* South Side [Memphis, TN] B: 5/10/1952, Memphis, TN *Drafted:* 1974 Round 3 ChiB
1974 ChiB: Rush 9-18 2.0 1 TD; Rec 3-23 7.7. **1976** GB: Rush 14-47 3.4 1 TD; Rec 2-21 10.5. **Total:** Rush 23-65 2.8 2 TD; Rec 5-44 8.8.

		Kickoff Returns				
Year Team	**G**	**Ret**	**Yds**	**Avg**	**TD**	**Fum**
1974 ChiB	14	27	567	21.0	0	1
1976 GB	7	3	59	19.7	0	0
NFL Total	21	30	626	20.9	0	1

CORDELL TAYLOR Taylor, Cordell Jerome 5'11", 190 **DB**
Col: Hampton *HS:* Booker T. Washington [Norfolk, VA] B: 12/22/1973, Norfolk, VA *Drafted:* 1998 Round 2 Jac
1998 Jac: 11 G.

CRAIG TAYLOR Taylor, Craig Garrett 5'11", 224 **RB**
Col: West Virginia *HS:* Linden [NJ] B: 1/3/1966, Elizabeth, NJ
Drafted: 1989 Round 6 Cin
1989 Cin: KR 1-5 5.0. **1990** Cin: KR 1-16 16.0. **Total:** KR 2-21 10.5.

		Rushing				Receiving					Tot
Year Team	**G**	**Att**	**Yds**	**Avg**	**TD**	**Rec**	**Yds**	**Avg**	**TD**	**Fum**	**TD**
1989 Cin	12	30	111	3.7	3	4	44	11.0	2	0	5
1990 Cin	12	51	216	4.2	2	3	22	7.3	1	0	3
1991 Cin	12	33	153	4.6	2	21	122	5.8	0	1	2
NFL Total	36	114	480	4.2	7	28	188	6.7	3	1	10

DAVID TAYLOR Taylor, David Merritt 6'4", 260 **OT**
Col: Catawba *HS:* Chapel Hill [NC] B: 10/17/1949, Statesville, NC
Drafted: 1973 Round 5 Bal
1973 Bal: 13 G. **1974** Bal: 14 G. **1975** Bal: 14 G. **1976** Bal: 14 G. **1977** Bal: 14 G. **1979** Bal: 3 G. **Total:** 72 G.

DERRICK TAYLOR Taylor, Derrick Howard 5'11", 186 **DB**
Col: Davidson; North Carolina State *HS:* Charlotte Catholic [NC]
B: 3/15/1964, St. Louis, MO
1987 NO: 3 G; 0.5 Sac.

JAY TAYLOR Taylor, Emanuel Jay 5'10", 170 **DB**
Col: Grossmont Coll. CA (J.C.); San Jose State *HS:* St. Augustine [San Diego, CA] B: 11/8/1967, San Diego, CA *Drafted:* 1989 Round 6 Pho
1989 Pho: 16 G. **1990** Pho: 16 G; Int 3-50. **1991** Pho: 16 G. **1993** KC: 15 G; Int 1-0. **1994** KC: 16 G; Int 1-0. **Total:** 79 G; Int 5-50.

ERK TAYLOR Taylor, Erquiet 6'2", 210 **G-T**
(Babe) *Col:* Auburn *HS:* Jefferson Co. [AL] B: 10/7/1907
D: 11/2/1959
1931 SI: 11 G.

GENE TAYLOR Taylor, Eugene Yarman 6'2", 189 **WR**
Col: Contra Costa Coll. CA (J.C.); Fresno State *HS:* Salesian [Richmond, CA] B: 11/12/1962, Oakland, CA *Drafted:* 1987 Round 6 NE
1987 TB: 8 G; Rec 2-21 10.5. **1988** TB: 4 G; Rec 5-53 10.6. **1991** NE: 1 G. **Total:** 13 G; Rec 7-74 10.6.

ED TAYLOR Taylor, Everett Earl 6'0", 174 **DB**
Col: Memphis *HS:* South Side [Memphis, TN] B: 5/13/1953, Memphis, TN
1975 NYJ: 14 G; KR 7-151 21.6. **1976** NYJ: 11 G; Int 2-22. **1977** NYJ: 14 G; Int 1-0. **1978** NYJ: 16 G; Int 2-0. **1979** NYJ-Mia: 9 G. NYJ: 4 G. Mia: 5 G. **1980** Mia: 16 G; Int 3-55. **1981** Mia: 6 G. **Total:** 86 G; KR 7-151 21.6; Int 8-77.

FRED TAYLOR Taylor, Frederick Antwon 6'0", 231 **RB**
Col: Florida *HS:* Glades Central [Belle Glade, FL] B: 6/27/1976, Pahokee, FL *Drafted:* 1998 Round 1 Jac

		Rushing				Receiving					Tot
Year Team	**G**	**Att**	**Yds**	**Avg**	**TD**	**Rec**	**Yds**	**Avg**	**TD**	**Fum**	**TD**
1998 Jac	15	264	1223	4.6	14	44	421	9.6	3	3	17

GREG TAYLOR Taylor, Gregory O'Neil 5'8", 175 **RB**
Col: Virginia *HS:* Highland Springs [VA] B: 10/23/1958, Richmond, VA
1982 NE: 1 G; KR 2-46 23.0.

HENRY TAYLOR Taylor, Henry 6'2", 295 **DT**
Col: South Carolina *HS:* Barnwell [SC] B: 11/29/1975, Broward Co., FL
1998 Det: 1 G.

HOSEA TAYLOR Taylor, Hosea Jr. 6′5″, 255 **DE**
Col: Houston *HS:* Longview [TX] B: 12/3/1958, Jefferson, TX
Drafted: 1981 Round 8 Bal
1981 Bal: 16 G; Scor **1** Saf; 2 Pt. **1983** Bal: 4 G. **Total:** 20 G; Scor 1 Saf; 2 Pt.

HUGH TAYLOR Taylor, Hugh Wilson 6′4″, 194 **OE**
(Bones) *Col:* Northeast Louisiana; Tulane; Oklahoma City *HS:* Wynne [AR] B: 7/6/1923, Wynne, AR D: 11/1/1992, Wynne, AR
1947 Was: Rush 1-7 7.0. **1948** Was: Pass 1-0. **Total:** Pass 1-0; Rush 1-7 7.0.

		Receiving				
Year Team	**G**	**Rec**	**Yds**	**Avg**	**TD**	**Fum**
1947 Was	10	26	511	19.7	6	2
1948 Was	12	20	341	17.1	3	1
1949 Was	12	45	781	17.4	**9**	0
1950 Was	12	39	833	**21.4**	9	0
1951 Was	12	29	444	15.3	3	0
1952 Was	12	41	961	23.4	12	0
1953 Was	12	35	703	20.1	8	0
1954 Was	12	37	659	17.8	8	1
NFL Total	94	272	5233	19.2	58	4

JIM TAYLOR Taylor, James Charles 6′0″, 214 **FB**
Col: Hinds CC MS; Louisiana State *HS:* Baton Rouge [LA]
B: 9/20/1935, Baton Rouge, LA *Drafted:* 1958 Round 2 GB *HOF:* 1976
1958 GB: KR 7-185 26.4. **Total:** KR 7-185 26.4.

		Rushing				Receiving					Tot
Year Team	**G**	**Att**	**Yds**	**Avg**	**TD**	**Rec**	**Yds**	**Avg**	**TD**	**Fum**	**TD**
1958 GB	12	52	247	4.8	1	4	72	18.0	1	1	2
1959 GB	12	120	452	3.8	6	9	71	7.9	2	2	8
1960 GB	12	**230**	1101	4.8	11	15	121	8.1	0	5	11
1961 GB	14	243	1307	5.4	**15**	25	175	7.0	1	2	**16**
1962 GB	14	**272**	**1474**	5.4	**19**	22	106	4.8	0	5	**19**
1963 GB	14	248	1018	4.1	9	13	68	5.2	1	5	10
1964 GB	13	235	1169	5.0	12	38	354	9.3	3	6	15
1965 GB	13	207	734	3.5	4	20	207	10.4	0	3	4
1966 GB	14	204	705	3.5	4	41	331	8.1	2	4	6
1967 NO	14	130	390	3.0	2	38	251	6.6	0	1	2
NFL Total	132	1941	8597	4.4	83	225	1756	7.8	10	34	93

JIM TAYLOR Taylor, James Glen 6′2″, 232 **LB-C**
Col: Baylor *HS:* Clyde [TX] B: 6/27/1934, Rowden, TX *Drafted:* 1956 Round 3 Pit
1956 Pit: 12 G. **1957** ChiC: 5 G. **1958** ChiC: 12 G; Int 1-5. **Total:** 29 G; Int 1-5.

J.T. TAYLOR Taylor, James Michael 6′4″, 265 **OT**
Col: Missouri *HS:* Woodruff [Peoria, IL] B: 8/12/1956, Peoria, IL
Drafted: 1978 Round 2 NO
1978 NO: 16 G. **1979** NO: 16 G. **1980** NO: 13 G. **1981** NO: 12 G. **Total:** 57 G.

JIM BOB TAYLOR Taylor, James Robert 6′2″, 205 **QB**
Col: Southern Methodist; Georgia Tech *HS:* Somerset [TX]
B: 9/9/1959, San Antonio, TX *Drafted:* 1983 Round 11 Bal
1983 Bal: 8 G; Pass 2-1 50.0%, 20 10.00 1 Int.

JASON TAYLOR Taylor, Jason Paul 6′6″, 260 **DE**
Col: Akron *HS:* Woodland Hills [Pittsburgh, PA] B: 9/1/1974, Pittsburgh, PA *Drafted:* 1997 Round 3 Mia
1997 Mia: 13 G; 5 Sac. **1998** Mia: 16 G; 9 Sac. **Total:** 29 G; 14 Sac.

JESSE TAYLOR Taylor, Jesse C Jr. 6′0″, 200 **RB**
Col: Cincinnati *HS:* Kiski Area [Vandergrift, PA] B: 5/26/1948, Pittsburgh, PA *Drafted:* 1971 Round 10 Was
1972 SD: Rush 13-58 4.5; PR 1-0.

		Kickoff Returns				
Year Team	**G**	**Ret**	**Yds**	**Avg**	**TD**	**Fum**
1972 SD	14	31	676	21.8	0	3

JOHN TAYLOR Taylor, John Gregory 6′1″, 185 **WR**
Col: Delaware State *HS:* Pennsauken [NJ] B: 3/31/1962, Pennsauken, NJ *Drafted:* 1986 Round 3 SF
1987 SF: **1** Fum TD. **1988** SF: KR 12-225 18.8. **1989** SF: Rush 1-6 6.0; KR 2-51 25.5. **1992** SF: Rush 1-10 10.0. **1993** SF: Pass 1-1 100.0%, 41 41.00; Rush 2-17 8.5. **1994** SF: Rush 2-(-2) -1.0. **1995** SF: Pass 1-1 100.0%, 21 21.00. **Total:** Pass 2-2 100.0%, 62 31.00; Rush 6-31 5.2; KR 14-276 19.7; 1 Fum TD.

		Receiving				Punt Returns					Tot
Year Team	**G**	**Rec**	**Yds**	**Avg**	**TD**	**Ret**	**Yds**	**Avg**	**TD**	**Fum**	**TD**
1987 SF	12	9	151	16.8	0	1	9	9.0	0	0	1
1988 SF	12	14	325	23.2	2	44	**556**	**12.6**	**2**	6	4
1989 SF	15	60	1077	18.0	10	36	417	11.6	0	3	10
1990 SF	14	49	748	15.3	7	26	212	8.2	0	2	7
1991 SF	16	64	1011	15.8	9	31	267	8.6	0	1	9
1992 SF	9	25	428	17.1	3	0	0	—	0	0	3
1993 SF	16	56	940	16.8	5	0	0	—	0	1	5
1994 SF	15	41	531	13.0	5	0	0	—	0	1	5
1995 SF	12	29	387	13.3	2	11	56	5.1	0	2	2
NFL Total	121	347	5598	16.1	43	149	1517	10.2	2	16	46

JOHNNY TAYLOR Taylor, John Herbert 6′4″, 237 **LB**
Col: Wenatchee Valley Coll. WA (J.C.); Hawaii *HS:* James A. Garfield [Seattle, WA] B: 6/21/1961, Seattle, WA
1984 Atl: 2 G. **1985** Atl: 15 G; 1 Sac. **1986** Atl-Mia: 6 G. Atl: 5 G. Mia: 1 G. **1987** SD: 7 G. **Total:** 30 G; 1 Sac.

TARZAN TAYLOR Taylor, John Lachlan 5′11″, 178 **G-T**
Col: Ohio State *HS:* Duluth Central [MN]; Martins Ferry HS [OH]
B: 1/10/1895, Superior, WI D: 5/1/1971, Green Bay, WI
1921 Sta: 11 G. **1922** Can: 11 G. **1926** Bkn: 2 G. **Total:** 24 G.

JOE TAYLOR Taylor, Joseph Lee 6′1″, 200 **DB**
Col: North Carolina A&T *HS:* George Washington Carver [Orlando, FL]
B: 8/27/1939, Miami, FL
1967 ChiB: KR 1-8 8.0. **Total:** KR 1-8 8.0.

		Interceptions		
Year Team	**G**	**Int**	**Yds**	**TD**
1967 ChiB	14	1	27	0
1968 ChiB	14	1	0	0
1969 ChiB	14	3	37	0
1970 ChiB	11	2	18	0
1971 ChiB	13	3	69	0
1972 ChiB	14	4	0	0
1973 ChiB	14	0	0	0
1974 ChiB	14	1	27	0
NFL Total	108	15	178	0

KEITH TAYLOR Taylor, Keith Gerard 5′11″, 200 **DB**
Col: Illinois *HS:* Pennsauken [NJ] B: 12/21/1964, Pennsauken, NJ
Drafted: 1988 Round 5 NO
1995 Was: 1 Sac. **Total:** 1 Sac.

		Interceptions		
Year Team	**G**	**Int**	**Yds**	**TD**
1988 Ind	3	0	0	0
1989 Ind	16	7	225	1
1990 Ind	16	2	51	0
1991 Ind	16	0	0	0
1992 NO	16	2	20	0
1993 NO	16	2	32	0
1994 Was	1	0	0	0
1995 Was	16	0	0	0
1996 Was	3	0	0	0
NFL Total	103	13	326	1

KEN TAYLOR Taylor, Kenneth Daniel 6′1″, 185 **DB**
Col: Oregon State *HS:* Yerba Buena [San Jose, CA] B: 9/2/1963, San Jose, CA
1985 ChiB: KR 1-18 18.0; Int 3-28. **1986** SD: Int 1-0. **Total:** KR 1-18 18.0; Int 4-28.

		Punt Returns				
Year Team	**G**	**Ret**	**Yds**	**Avg**	**TD**	**Fum**
1985 ChiB	16	25	198	7.9	0	3
1986 SD	14	0	0	—	0	0
NFL Total	30	25	198	7.9	0	3

KITRICK TAYLOR Taylor, Kitrick Lavell 5′11″, 194 **WR**
Col: Washington State *HS:* Pomona [CA] B: 7/22/1964, Los Angeles, CA *Drafted:* 1987 Round 5 KC
1988 KC: Rush 1-2 2.0; KR 5-80 16.0. **1989** NE: KR 3-52 17.3.
Total: Rush 1-2 2.0; KR 8-132 16.5.

		Receiving				Punt Returns					Tot
Year Team	**G**	**Rec**	**Yds**	**Avg**	**TD**	**Ret**	**Yds**	**Avg**	**TD**	**Fum**	**TD**
1988 KC	16	9	105	11.7	0	29	187	6.4	0	1	0
1989 NE	4	0	0	—	0	0	0	—	0	0	0
1990 SD	3	0	0	—	0	6	112	18.7	**1**	0	1
1991 SD	12	24	218	9.1	0	28	269	9.6	0	2	0
1992 GB	10	2	63	31.5	1	0	0	—	0	0	1
1993 Den	2	1	28	28.0	0	0	0	—	0	0	0
NFL Total	47	36	414	11.5	1	63	568	9.0	1	3	2

LAWRENCE TAYLOR Taylor, Lawrence Julius 6′3″, 237 **LB**
(L.T.) *Col:* North Carolina *HS:* Lafayette [Williamsburg, VA]
B: 2/4/1959, Williamsburg, VA *Drafted:* 1981 Round 1 NYG *HOF:* 1999
1981 NYG: 16 G; Int 1-1; 1 Fum. **1982** NYG: 9 G; Int 1-97 **1** TD; 6 Pt; 7.5 Sac. **1983** NYG: 16 G; Int 2-10; 1 Fum; 9 Sac. **1984** NYG: 16 G; Int 1-(-1); 11.5 Sac. **1985** NYG: 16 G; 13 Sac. **1986** NYG: 16 G; **20.5** Sac. **1987** NYG: 12 G; Int 3-16; 12 Sac. **1988** NYG: 12 G; 15.5 Sac. **1989** NYG: 16 G; 15 Sac. **1990** NYG: 16 G; Int 1-11 1 TD; 6 Pt; 10.5 Sac. **1991** NYG: 14 G; 7 Sac. **1992** NYG: 9 G; 5 Sac. **1993** NYG: 16 G; 6 Sac.
Total: 184 G; Int 9-134 2 TD; 12 Pt; 2 Fum; 132.5 Sac.

LELAND TAYLOR Taylor, Leland Morrisclay 6'3", 305 **DT**
Col: Louisville *HS:* Fairdale [Louisville, KY] B: 10/25/1972, Louisville, KY *Drafted:* 1997 Round 7 Bal
1997 Bal: 1 G.

LENNY TAYLOR Taylor, Leonard Moore 5'10", 173 **WR**
Col: Tennessee *HS:* Miami Southridge [FL] B: 2/15/1961, Miami, FL *Drafted:* 1984 Round 12 GB
1984 GB: 2 G; Rec 1-8 8.0. **1987** Atl: 3 G; Rush 1-(-13) -13.0; Rec 12-171 14.3 1 TD; 6 Pt. **Total:** 5 G; Rush 1-(-13) -13.0; Rec 13-179 13.8 1 TD; 6 Pt.

LIONEL TAYLOR Taylor, Lionel Thomas 6'2", 215 **OE-WR-FL**
Col: New Mexico Highlands *HS:* Buffalo [WV] B: 8/15/1935, Kansas City, MO
1960 Den: Rush 2-(-6) -3.0. **1961** Den: Pass 2-0, 1 Int. **1962** Den: Pass 2-0; Rush 2-26 13.0. **1963** Den: Pass 1-0. **1964** Den: Pass 1-0, 1 Int. **Total:** Pass 6-0, 2 Int; Rush 4-20 5.0.

		Receiving				
Year Team	**G**	**Rec**	**Yds**	**Avg**	**TD**	**Fum**
1959 ChiB	8	0	0	—	0	0
1960 Den	12	**92**	1235	13.4	12	2
1961 Den	14	**100**	1176	11.8	4	0
1962 Den	14	**77**	908	11.8	4	3
1963 Den	14	**78**	1101	14.1	10	0
1964 Den	14	76	873	11.5	7	2
1965 Den	14	**85**	1131	13.3	6	0
1966 Den	14	35	448	12.8	1	0
1967 Hou	8	18	233	12.9	1	0
1968 Hou	9	6	90	15.0	0	0
NFL Total	121	567	7195	12.7	45	7

MALCOLM TAYLOR Taylor, Malcolm 6'6", 288 **DE**
Col: Tennessee State *HS:* Crystal Springs [MS] B: 6/20/1960, Crystal Springs, MS *Drafted:* 1982 Round 5 Hou
1982 Hou: 9 G. **1983** Hou: 16 G; 4.5 Sac. **1986** Hou: 3 G; 1 Sac. **1987** LARd: 12 G; 3 Sac. **1988** LARd: 15 G; 1 Sac. **1989** Atl: 13 G; 1 Sac. **Total:** 68 G; 10.5 Sac.

MICHAEL TAYLOR Taylor, Michael 6'1", 230 **LB**
Col: Michigan *HS:* Martin Luther King [Detroit, MI] B: 9/21/1949, Detroit, MI *Drafted:* 1972 Round 1 NYJ
1972 NYJ: 14 G; Int 1-2. **1973** NYJ: 8 G. **Total:** 22 G; Int 1-2.

MIKE TAYLOR Taylor, Michael Ray 6'4", 255 **OT**
(Big Mike) *Col:* San Francisco City Coll. CA (J.C.); USC *HS:* Manual [Louisville, KY]; Mission HS [San Francisco, CA] B: 5/5/1945, San Francisco, CA *Drafted:* 1968 Round 1 Pit
1968 Pit: 14 G; KR 1-9 9.0. **1969** Pit-NO: 10 G. Pit: 9 G. NO: 1 G. **1970** NO: 11 G. **1971** Was: 5 G. **1973** StL: 6 G. **Total:** 46 G; KR 1-9 9.0.

OTIS TAYLOR Taylor, Otis Jr. 6'3", 215 **WR**
Col: Prairie View A&M *HS:* Evan E. Worthing [Houston, TX] B: 8/11/1942, Houston, TX *Drafted:* 1965 Round 4 KC
1966 KC: Pass 1-0, 1 Int; KR 2-0. **Total:** Pass 1-0, 1 Int; KR 2-0.

		Rushing				Receiving					Tot
Year Team	**G**	**Att**	**Yds**	**Avg**	**TD**	**Rec**	**Yds**	**Avg**	**TD**	**Fum**	**TD**
1965 KC	14	2	17	8.5	0	26	446	17.2	5	1	5
1966 KC	14	2	33	16.5	0	58	1297	**22.4**	8	0	8
1967 KC	14	5	29	5.8	1	59	958	16.2	**11**	1	12
1968 KC	11	5	41	8.2	1	20	420	21.0	4	0	5
1969 KC	11	2	-2	-1.0	0	41	696	17.0	7	1	7
1970 KC	13	3	13	4.3	0	34	618	18.2	3	1	3
1971 KC	14	1	25	25.0	1	57	**1110**	19.5	7	0	8
1972 KC	14	5	13	2.6	0	57	821	14.4	6	2	6
1973 KC	14	4	-14	-3.5	0	34	565	16.6	4	2	4
1974 KC	10	1	6	6.0	0	24	375	15.6	2	0	2
1975 KC	1	0	0	—	0	0	0	—	0	0	0
NFL Total	130	30	161	5.4	3	410	7306	17.8	57	8	60

ROB TAYLOR Taylor, Robert Earl 6'6", 293 **OT**
Col: Northwestern *HS:* Fairmont East [Kettering, OH] B: 11/14/1960, St. Charles, IL *Drafted:* 1982 Round 12 Phi
1986 TB: 16 G. **1987** TB: 5 G. **1988** TB: 16 G. **1989** TB: 16 G. **1990** TB: 16 G. **1991** TB: 16 G. **1992** TB: 9 G. **1993** TB: 16 G. **Total:** 110 G.

BOB TAYLOR Taylor, Robert F 6'3", 240 **DE-DT**
Col: Maryland East. Shore *HS:* Lucy Craft Laney [Augusta, GA] B: 2/5/1940, Columbia, SC *Drafted:* 1963 Round 9 NYG
1963 NYG: 14 G. **1964** NYG: 14 G. **Total:** 28 G.

BOBBY TAYLOR Taylor, Robert III 6'3", 216 **DB**
Col: Notre Dame *HS:* Longview [TX] B: 12/28/1973, Houston, TX *Drafted:* 1995 Round 2 Phi
1995 Phi: 16 G; Int 2-52. **1996** Phi: 16 G; Int 3-(-1); 1 Fum; 1 Sac. **1997** Phi: 6 G; 2 Sac. **1998** Phi: 11 G. **Total:** 49 G; Int 5-51; 1 Fum; 3 Sac.

ROGER TAYLOR Taylor, Roger Wayne 6'6", 271 **OT**
Col: Oklahoma State *HS:* Star Spencer [Spencer, OK] B: 1/5/1958, Shawnee, OK *Drafted:* 1981 Round 3 KC
1981 KC: 13 G.

ROSEY TAYLOR Taylor, Roosevelt 5'11", 186 **DB**
Col: Grambling State *HS:* Joseph S. Clark [New Orleans, LA] B: 7/4/1937, New Orleans, LA
1961 ChiB: PR 1-4 4.0. **1962** ChiB: PR 2-11 5.5 **1** TD. **1963** ChiB: PR 12-51 4.3. **1967** ChiB: **1** Fum TD. **Total:** PR 15-66 4.4 1 TD; 1 Fum TD.

		Kickoff Returns				Interceptions				Tot
Year Team	**G**	**Ret**	**Yds**	**Avg**	**TD**	**Int**	**Yds**	**TD**	**Fum**	**TD**
1961 ChiB	14	14	379	27.1	0	0	0	0	1	0
1962 ChiB	14	4	98	24.5	0	2	64	**1**	1	2
1963 ChiB	14	6	118	19.7	0	**9**	172	1	0	1
1964 ChiB	14	0	0	—	0	2	45	0	0	0
1965 ChiB	14	0	0	—	0	1	3	0	0	1
1966 ChiB	14	1	3	3.0	0	1	15	0	0	0
1967 ChiB	14	0	0	—	0	5	19	0	0	1
1968 ChiB	14	0	0	—	0	3	96	1	0	1
1969 ChiB-SF	14	1	16	16.0	0	2	15	0	0	0
1969 ChiB	6	0	0	—	0	0	0	0	0	0
1969 SF	8	1	16	16.0	0	2	15	0	0	0
1970 SF	14	0	0	—	0	3	27	0	0	0
1971 SF	12	0	0	—	0	3	13	0	0	0
1972 Was	14	0	0	—	0	1	17	0	0	0
NFL Total	166	26	614	23.6	0	32	486	3	2	6

SAMMIE TAYLOR Taylor, Samuel 6'0", 194 **WR**
Col: Grambling State *HS:* Jack Yates [Houston, TX] B: 4/23/1940, Houston, TX
1965 SD: 12 G; Rec 1-13 13.0.

STEVE TAYLOR Taylor, Steven Lawrence 6'3", 204 **CB**
Col: Kansas *HS:* Dunbar [Fort Worth, TX] B: 12/27/1953, Fort Worth, TX *Drafted:* 1976 Round 6 KC
1976 KC: 14 G.

TERRY TAYLOR Taylor, Terry Lee 5'10", 188 **DB**
Col: Southern Illinois *HS:* Rayen [Youngstown, OH] B: 7/18/1961, Warren, OH *Drafted:* 1984 Round 1 Sea

		Interceptions			Tot
Year Team	**G**	**Int**	**Yds**	**TD**	**TD**
1984 Sea	16	3	63	0	0
1985 Sea	16	4	75	**1**	2
1986 Sea	16	2	0	0	0
1987 Sea	12	1	11	0	0
1988 Sea	14	5	53	1	1
1989 Det	15	1	0	0	0
1990 Det	2	0	0	0	0
1991 Det	11	4	26	0	0
1992 Cle	16	1	0	0	0
1993 Cle	10	0	0	0	0
1994 Sea	5	1	0	0	0
1995 Atl	16	3	31	0	0
NFL Total	149	25	259	2	3

TOM TAYLOR Taylor, Thomas Joseph 6'3", 267 **OG**
Col: Pierce Coll. CA (J.C.); Georgia Tech *HS:* Palmdale [CA] B: 9/14/1962, Lancaster, CA
1987 LARm: 3 G.

TROY TAYLOR Taylor, Troy Scott 6'4", 200 **QB**
Col: California *HS:* Cordova [Rancho Cordova, CA] B: 4/5/1968, Downey, CA *Drafted:* 1990 Round 4 NYJ
1990 NYJ: 2 G; Pass 10-7 70.0%, 49 4.90 1 TD; Rush 2-20 10.0 1 TD; 6 Pt. **1991** NYJ: 5 G; Pass 10-5 50.0%, 76 7.60 1 TD 1 Int; Rush 7-23 3.3. **Total:** 7 G; Pass 20-12 60.0%, 125 6.25 2 TD 1 Int; Rush 9-43 4.8 1 TD; 6 Pt.

BILLY TAYLOR Taylor, William Turner 6'0", 215 **RB**
(B.T. Express) *Col:* Texas Tech *HS:* John Jay [San Antonio, TX] B: 7/6/1956, San Antonio, TX *Drafted:* 1978 Round 4 NYG
1978 NYG: KR 11-192 17.5. **1979** NYG: KR 6-131 21.8. **Total:** KR 17-323 19.0.

		Rushing				Receiving					Tot
Year Team	**G**	**Att**	**Yds**	**Avg**	**TD**	**Rec**	**Yds**	**Avg**	**TD**	**Fum**	**TD**
1978 NYG	13	73	250	3.4	0	9	70	7.8	0	3	0
1979 NYG	16	198	700	3.5	7	28	253	9.0	4	4	11
1980 NYG	11	147	580	3.9	4	33	253	7.7	0	4	4
1981 NYG-NYJ	8	38	111	2.9	2	8	71	8.9	0	2	2
1981 NYG	5	36	110	3.1	2	8	71	8.9	0	2	2
1981 NYJ	3	2	1	0.5	0	0	0	—	0	0	0
1982 LARd	1	4	3	0.8	0	0	0	—	0	0	0
NFL Total	49	460	1644	3.6	13	78	647	8.3	4	13	17

WILLIE TAYLOR Taylor, Willis T 6′1″, 179 **WR**
Col: Pittsburgh *HS:* Verona [NJ] B: 12/9/1955, Montclair, NJ
Drafted: 1978 Round 9 TB
1978 GB: 1 G.

JIMMY TAYS Tays, James Elmer 5′8″, 174 **WB-FB-BB-HB**
(Bing) *Col:* Penn State; Chicago *HS:* Tolono [IL] B: 3/10/1899, Chicago, IL D: 6/21/1986, Champaign, IL
1925 ChiC: 9 G; 1 Fum TD; 6 Pt. **1927** Day: 7 G. **1930** Nwk-SI: 4 G. Nwk: 1 G. SI: 3 G. **Total:** 20 G; 1 Fum TD; 6 Pt.

GUY TEAFATILLER Teafatiller, Guy Robert 6′2″, 260 **DT**
Col: Cerritos Coll. CA (J.C.); Illinois *HS:* Earl Warren [Downey, CA]
B: 5/10/1964, Concord, CA
1987 ChiB: 3 G; 1.5 Sac.

GEORGE TEAGUE Teague, George Theo 6′1″, 198 **DB**
(Mr. Glue) *Col:* Alabama *HS:* Jefferson Davis [Montgomery, AL]
B: 2/18/1971, Lansing, MI *Drafted:* 1993 Round 1 GB
1993 GB: PR 1-(-1) -1.0. **1998** Dal: 2 Sac. **Total:** PR 1-(-1) -1.0; 2 Sac.

		Interceptions		
Year Team	**G**	**Int**	**Yds**	**TD**
1993 GB	16	1	22	0
1994 GB	16	3	33	0
1995 GB	15	2	100	0
1996 Dal	16	4	47	0
1997 Mia	15	2	25	0
1998 Dal	16	0	0	0
NFL Total	94	12	227	0

MATTHEW TEAGUE Teague, Matthew Nathaniel 6′5″, 240 **DE**
Col: Prairie View A&M *HS:* Alcee Fortier [New Orleans, LA]
B: 10/22/1958, Cincinnati, OH *Drafted:* 1980 Supplemental Round 7 Atl
1981 Atl: 11 G.

PAT TEAGUE Teague, Patrick Ethan 6′1″, 225 **LB**
Col: North Carolina State *HS:* Sanderson [Raleigh, NC] B: 10/22/1963, Asheville, NC
1987 TB: 1 G.

JIM TEAL Teal, James Franklin 6′3″, 225 **LB**
Col: Purdue *HS:* Boyden [Salisbury, NC] B: 5/14/1950, Baltimore, MD
Drafted: 1972 Round 10 Det
1973 Det: 14 G; PR 1-0; 1 Fum.

JIMMY TEAL Teal, Jimmy Dewayne 5′10″, 170 **WR**
Col: Texas A&M *HS:* Diboll [TX] B: 8/18/1962, Lufkin, TX
Drafted: 1985 Round 5 Buf
1985 Buf: 3 G; Rec 1-24 24.0; KR 1-20 20.0. **1986** Buf: 5 G; Rec 6-60 10.0 1 TD; 6 Pt. **1987** Sea: 4 G; Rec 14-198 14.1 2 TD; PR 6-38 6.3; KR 6-95 15.8; 12 Pt; 1 Fum. **1988** Sea: 2 G. **Total:** 14 G; Rec 21-282 13.4 3 TD; PR 6-38 6.3; KR 7-115 16.4; 18 Pt; 1 Fum.

WILLIE TEAL Teal, Willie Jr. 5′10″, 195 **DB**
Col: Louisiana State *HS:* Liberty-Eylau [Texarkana, TX] B: 12/20/1957, Texarkana, TX *Drafted:* 1980 Round 2 Min
1980 Min: Postseason only. **1984** Min: PR 1-0. **1985** Min: **1** Fum TD.
Total: PR 1-0; 1 Fum TD.

		Interceptions				Tot
Year Team	**G**	**Int**	**Yds**	**TD**	**Fum**	**TD**
1981 Min	16	4	23	0	0	0
1982 Min	9	4	15	0	0	0
1983 Min	16	3	26	0	0	0
1984 Min	11	1	53	1	1	1
1985 Min	16	3	6	0	0	1
1986 Min	11	0	0	0	0	0
1987 LARd	1	0	0	0	0	0
NFL Total	80	15	123	1	1	2

LARRY TEARRY Tearry, Larry Wayne 6′3″, 260 **C**
Col: Wake Forest *HS:* E.E. Smith [Fayetteville, NC] B: 4/24/1956, Erwin, NC *Drafted:* 1978 Round 5 Det
1978 Det: 14 G. **1979** Det: 11 G. **Total:** 25 G.

GUS TEBELL Tebell, Gustave Kenneth 5′10″, 178 **OE**
Col: Wisconsin *HS:* Aurora West [IL] B: 9/6/1897, St. Charles, IL
D: 5/28/1969, Richmond, VA
1923 Col: 10 G; Rec 2 TD; Scor 37, 4 FG, 7 XK; 1 Fum TD; Tot TD 3.
1924 Col: 1 G; Scor 6, 1 FG, 3 XK. **Total:** 11 G; Rec 2 TD; Scor 43, 5 FG, 10 XK; 1 Fum TD; Tot TD 3.

JOHN TEERLINCK Teerlinck, John Edward 6′5″, 248 **DT**
Col: Ellsworth CC IA; Western Illinois *HS:* Fenwick [Chicago, IL]
B: 4/9/1951, Rochester, NY *Drafted:* 1974 Round 5 SD
1974 SD: 14 G. **1975** SD: 6 G. **Total:** 20 G.

AL TEETER Teeter, Allen M 6′1″, 202 **OE**
(Tuck) *Col:* Minnesota *HS:* Gladstone [Minneapolis, MN]
B: 6/24/1908, Austin, MN D: 4/14/1994, Holiday, FL
1932 SI: 5 G; Rec 1-11 11.0.

MIKE TEETER Teeter, Michael Lee 6′2″, 267 **DE-DT**
Col: Michigan *HS:* Fruitport [MI] B: 10/4/1967, Grand Haven, MI
1991 Min: 1 G. **1993** Hou: 14 G; 1 Sac. **1994** Hou: 14 G; KR 2-9 4.5; 1 Fum. **Total:** 29 G; KR 2-9 4.5; 1 Fum; 1 Sac.

LEN TEEUWS Teeuws, Leonard 6′5″, 242 **DT-OT**
Col: Tulane *HS:* Oak Park [IL] B: 4/19/1927, Oak Park, IL
Drafted: 1952 Round 25 LARm
1952 LARm: 12 G. **1953** LARm: 12 G. **1954** ChiC: 12 G. **1955** ChiC: 12 G. **1956** ChiC: 12 G. **1957** ChiC: 12 G. **Total:** 72 G.

LANCE TEICHELMAN Teichelman, Lance Theodore 6′4″, 274 **DE-DT**
Col: Texas A&M *HS:* Westwood [Palestine, TX] B: 10/21/1970, San Antonio, TX *Drafted:* 1994 Round 7 Ind
1994 Ind: 1 G.

MIKE TEIFKE Teifke, Michael Edward 6′4″, 255 **C**
Col: Akron *HS:* St. John's [Toledo, OH] B: 12/29/1963
1987 Cle: 3 G.

JOHN TELTSCHIK Teltschik, John Robert 6′2″, 212 **P**
Col: Texas *HS:* Tivy [Kerrville, TX] B: 3/8/1964, Floresville, TX
Drafted: 1986 Round 9 ChiB
1986 Phi: Rush 1-0. **1987** Phi: Rush 3-32 10.7. **1988** Phi: Pass 3-1 33.3%, 18 6.00; Rush 2-36 18.0. **1989** Phi: Rush 1-23 23.0.
Total: Pass 3-1 33.3%, 18 6.00; Rush 7-91 13.0.

		Punting			
Year Team	**G**	**Punts**	**Yds**	**Avg**	**Fum**
1986 Phi	16	**108**	**4493**	41.6	0
1987 Phi	12	**82**	3131	38.2	0
1988 Phi	16	**98**	3958	40.4	1
1989 Phi	10	57	2246	39.4	0
NFL Total	54	345	13828	40.1	1

JIM TEMP Temp, James Arthur 6′4″, 245 **DE**
Col: Wisconsin *HS:* Aquinas [La Crosse, WI] B: 10/10/1933, La Crosse, WI *Drafted:* 1955 Round 2 GB
1957 GB: 12 G. **1958** GB: 12 G; KR 1-0. **1959** GB: 12 G; Int 1-13.
1960 GB: 7 G; KR 1-16 16.0. **Total:** 43 G; KR 2-16 8.0; Int 1-13.

MARK TEMPLE Temple, Mark Vernon 5′10″, 175 **TB-DB**
Col: Oregon *HS:* Pendleton [OR] B: 3/28/1911, Pendleton, OR
D: 12/20/1990
1936 Bkn-Bos: 9 G; Pass 7-0, 5 Int; Rush 5-4 0.8 1 TD; Rec 1-10 10.0; 6 Pt. Bkn: 7 G; Pass 7-0, 5 Int; Rush 5-4 0.8 1 TD; Rec 1-10 10.0; 6 Pt. Bos: 2 G. **Total:** 9 G; Pass 7-0, 5 Int; Rush 5-4 0.8 1 TD; Rec 1-10 10.0; 6 Pt.

GARTH TEN NAPEL Ten Napel, Garth 6′1″, 213 **LB**
Col: Texas A&M *HS:* Trinity [Euless, TX] B: 3/27/1954, Los Angeles, CA *Drafted:* 1976 Round 7 Det
1976 Det: 14 G; PR 1-0; 1 Fum. **1977** Det: 14 G. **1978** Atl: 1 G.
Total: 29 G; PR 1-0; 1 Fum.

DEREK TENNELL Tennell, Derek Wayne 6′5″, 245 **TE**
Col: UCLA *HS:* West Covina [CA] B: 2/12/1964, Los Angeles, CA
Drafted: 1987 Round 7 Sea
1988 Cle: KR 1-11 11.0. **Total:** KR 1-11 11.0.

		Receiving			
Year Team	**G**	**Rec**	**Yds**	**Avg**	**TD**
1987 Cle	11	9	102	11.3	3
1988 Cle	16	9	88	9.8	1
1989 Cle	14	1	4	4.0	1
1991 Det	15	4	43	10.8	0
1992 Min	3	2	12	6.0	0
1993 Min	16	15	122	8.1	0
NFL Total	75	40	371	9.3	5

BOB TENNER Tenner, Robert Johnson 6′0″, 212 **OE-DE**
Col: Minnesota *HS:* West [Minneapolis, MN] B: 6/1/1913, Minneapolis, MN D: 11/17/1984, Minneapolis, MN
1935 GB: 11 G; Rec 3-38 12.7.

STEVE TENSI Tensi, Stephen Michael 6′5″, 215 **QB**
(Stretch) *Col:* Florida State *HS:* Elder [Cincinnati, OH] B: 12/8/1942, Cincinnati, OH *Drafted:* 1965 Round 4 SD

		Passing							
Year Team	**G**	**Att**	**Comp**	**Comp%**	**Yds**	**YPA**	**TD**	**Int**	**Rating**
1965 SD	1	0	0	—	0	—	0	0	—
1966 SD	14	52	21	40.4	405	7.79	5	1	92.2
1967 Den	14	325	131	40.3	1915	5.89	16	17	54.8
1968 Den	7	119	48	40.3	709	5.96	5	8	46.5
1969 Den	13	286	131	45.8	1990	6.96	14	12	68.1
1970 Den	7	80	38	47.5	539	6.74	3	8	42.7
NFL Total	56	862	369	42.8	5558	6.45	43	46	59.0

	Rushing				
Year Team	**Att**	**Yds**	**Avg**	**TD**	**Fum**
1966 SD	1	-1	-1.0	0	1

1967 Den	24	4	0.2	0	11
1968 Den	6	2	0.3	0	0
1969 Den	12	63	5.3	0	1
1970 Den	4	14	3.5	0	1
NFL Total	47	82	1.7	0	14

LOU TEPE Tepe, Louis Charles 6′2″, 208 **C-LB**
Col: Duke *HS:* Dwight Morrow [Englewood, NJ] B: 6/18/1930, North Bergen, NJ *Drafted:* 1953 Round 30 Pit
1953 Pit: 10 G; KR 3-47 15.7; 1 Fum. **1954** Pit: 12 G; Int 3-67; 1 Fum. **1955** Pit: 12 G. **Total:** 34 G; KR 3-47 15.7; Int 3-67; 2 Fum.

TONY TERESA Teresa, Anthony Michael 5′9″, 188 **HB**
Col: San Jose State *HS:* Salinas [CA] B: 12/8/1933, Pittsburg, CA D: 10/16/1984, Salinas, CA
1960 Oak: Pass 18-9 50.0%, 111 6.17 1 TD 3 Int; PR 5-12 2.4; KR 4-61 15.3. **Total:** Pass 18-9 50.0%, 111 6.17 1 TD 3 Int; PR 5-12 2.4; KR 4-61 15.3.

		Rushing				Receiving					Tot
Year Team	G	Att	Yds	Avg	TD	Rec	Yds	Avg	TD	Fum	TD
1958 SF	1	0	0	—	0	0	0	—	0	0	0
1960 Oak	14	139	608	4.4	6	35	393	11.2	4	**13**	10
NFL Total	15	139	608	4.4	6	35	393	11.2	4	13	10

JOE TERESHINSKI Tereshinski, Joseph Peter 6′2″, 215 **DE-OE-LB**
Col: Georgia *HS:* Newport [PA] B: 12/7/1923, Glen Lyon, PA *Drafted:* 1946 Round 11 Was
1952 Was: Int 1-31. **Total:** Int 1-31.

		Receiving			
Year Team	G	Rec	Yds	Avg	TD
1947 Was	11	10	76	7.6	1
1948 Was	11	4	98	24.5	1
1949 Was	9	4	36	9.0	0
1950 Was	12	17	148	8.7	0
1951 Was	12	6	74	12.3	2
1952 Was	12	2	19	9.5	0
1953 Was	12	0	0	—	0
1954 Was	7	0	0	—	0
NFL Total	86	43	451	10.5	4

GEORGE TERLEP Terlep, George Rudolph 5′10″, 180 **QB-DB**
(Duke) *Col:* Notre Dame *HS:* Elkhart Central [IN] B: 4/12/1923, Elkhart, IN
AAFC **1946** BufA: KR 1-23 23.0; Punt 1-31 31.0. **1947** BufA: PR 1-17 17.0; Int 1-0. **Total:** PR 1-17 17.0; KR 1-23 23.0; Int 1-0; Punt 1-31 31.0.

		Passing							
Year Team	G	Att	Comp	Comp%	Yds	YPA	TD	Int	Rating
1946 BufA	12	123	48	39.0	574	4.67	7	14	33.4
1947 BufA	11	23	5	21.7	51	2.22	2	3	29.0
1948 BufA-CleA	12	4	1	25.0	27	6.75	0	2	15.6
AAFC Total	35	150	54	36.0	652	4.35	9	19	30.6

	Rushing			
Year Team	Att	Yds	Avg	TD
1946 BufA	36	29	0.8	1
1947 BufA	4	11	2.8	0
1948 BufA-CleA	1	4	4.0	0
AAFC Total	41	44	1.1	1

MARVIN TERRELL Terrell, Marvin Jr. 6′1″, 235 **OG**
Col: Mississippi *HS:* Indianola [MS] B: 6/10/1938, West Memphis, AR *Drafted:* 1960 Round 1 DalT
1960 DalT: 9 G. **1961** DalT: 3 G. **1962** DalT: 12 G. **1963** KC: 14 G. **Total:** 38 G.

PAT TERRELL Terrell, Patrick Christopher 6′1″, 204 **DB**
Col: Notre Dame *HS:* Lakewood [St. Petersburg, FL] B: 3/18/1968, Memphis, TN *Drafted:* 1990 Round 2 LARm
1998 GB: 1 Sac. **Total:** 1 Sac.

		Interceptions		
Year Team	G	Int	Yds	TD
1990 LARm	15	1	6	0
1991 LARm	16	1	4	0
1992 LARm	15	0	0	0
1993 LARm	13	2	1	0
1994 NYJ	16	0	0	0
1995 Car	16	3	33	0
1996 Car	16	3	6	0
1997 Car	16	0	0	0
1998 GB	16	1	9	0
NFL Total	139	11	59	0

RAY TERRELL Terrell, Raymond Willard 6′0″, 185 **HB-DB**
(Spud) *Col:* Mississippi *HS:* Water Valley [MS] B: 6/29/1919, Water Valley, MS D: 2/11/1997, Gulfport, MS
AAFC **1946** CleA: Pass 2-0; Rec 4-21 5.3; KR 3-80 26.7; Int 3-101 1 TD. **1947** BalA-CleA: Rec 6-21 3.5; PR 1-18 18.0; KR 9-204 22.7; Int 1-12. **Total:** Pass 2-0; Rec 10-42 4.2; PR 1-18 18.0; KR 12-284 23.7; Int 4-113 1 TD.

		Rushing			
Year Team	G	Att	Yds	Avg	TD
1946 CleA	9	39	117	3.0	0
1947 BalA-CleA	13	26	48	1.8	0
AAFC Total	22	65	165	2.5	0

DOUG TERRY Terry, Douglas Maurice 5′11″, 200 **DB**
Col: Kansas *HS:* Liberal [KS] B: 12/12/1969, Dumas, AR
1992 KC: 16 G; Int 1-9. **1993** KC: 15 G; Int 1-21; 1 Sac. **1994** KC: 10 G. **1995** KC: 16 G. **Total:** 57 G; Int 2-30; 1 Sac.

JOE TERRY Terry, Joseph Thomas 6′2″, 230 **LB**
Col: Cal State-Hayward *HS:* Amador Valley [Pleasanton, CA] B: 5/7/1965
1987 Sea: 2 G.

NAT TERRY Terry, Nathaniel 5′11″, 167 **DB**
Col: Florida State *HS:* T.R. Robinson [Tampa, FL] B: 7/20/1956, Tampa, FL *Drafted:* 1978 Round 11 Pit
1978 Pit-Det: 10 G; PR 7-80 11.4; KR 7-145 20.7. Pit: 6 G; PR 7-80 11.4. Det: 4 G; KR 7-145 20.7. **Total:** 10 G; PR 7-80 11.4; KR 7-145 20.7.

RICK TERRY Terry, Richard Ross Jr. 6′4″, 302 **DT**
Col: North Carolina *HS:* Lexington [NC] B: 4/5/1974, Lexington, NC *Drafted:* 1997 Round 2 NYJ
1997 NYJ: 14 G; 2 Sac. **1998** Car: 7 G; 2 Sac. **Total:** 21 G; 4 Sac.

RYAN TERRY Terry, Ryan L 6′0″, 206 **RB**
Col: Tennessee State; Iowa *HS:* Steubenville [OH] B: 9/20/1971, Fort Bragg, NC
1996 Ariz: Rec 1-0. **Total:** Rec 1-0.

		Kickoff Returns				
Year Team	G	Ret	Yds	Avg	TD	Fum
1995 Ariz	15	37	808	21.8	0	1
1996 Ariz	5	4	84	21.0	0	1
NFL Total	20	41	892	21.8	0	2

TIM TERRY Terry, Tim 6′3″, 235 **LB**
Col: Temple *HS:* Hempstead [NY] B: 7/26/1974, Hempstead, NY
1997 Cin: 5 G.

RUDY TERSCH Tersch, Fred 195 **T-G**
Col: No College B: 4/1/1895 D: 10/1964, MN
1921 Min: 3 G. **1922** Min: 4 G. **1923** Min: 8 G; 1 Fum TD; 6 Pt. **Total:** 15 G; 1 Fum TD; 6 Pt.

RAY TESSER Tesser, Raymond Charles 6′2″, 204 **OE-DE**
Col: Carnegie Mellon *HS:* Titusville [PA] B: 6/2/1912, Titusville, PA D: 11/2/1982, Corry, PA
1933 Pit: 11 G; Pass 1-0; Rec 14-282 20.1. **1934** Pit: 12 G; Pass 1-0; Rec 5-67 13.4. **Total:** 23 G; Pass 2-0; Rec 19-349 18.4.

VINNY TESTAVERDE Testaverde, Vincent Frank 6′5″, 222 **QB**
Col: Miami (Fla.) *HS:* Sewanhaka [Floral Park, NY]; Fork Union Mil. Acad. [VA] B: 11/13/1963, Brooklyn, NY *Drafted:* 1987 Round 1 TB
1990 TB: Rec 1-3 3.0. **1995** Cle: Rec 1-7 7.0. **1996** Bal: Scor 1 2XP. **1997** Bal: Rec 1-(-4) -4.0. **Total:** Rec 3-6 2.0; Scor 1 2XP.

		Passing							
Year Team	G	Att	Comp	Comp%	Yds	YPA	TD	Int	Rating
1987 TB	6	165	71	43.0	1081	6.55	5	6	60.2
1988 TB	15	466	222	47.6	3240	6.95	13	35	48.8
1989 TB	14	480	258	53.8	3133	6.53	20	22	68.9
1990 TB	14	365	203	55.6	2818	7.72	17	18	75.6
1991 TB	13	326	166	50.9	1994	6.12	8	15	59.0
1992 TB	14	358	206	57.5	2554	7.13	14	16	74.2
1993 Cle	10	230	130	56.5	1797	7.81	14	9	85.7
1994 Cle	14	376	207	55.1	2575	6.85	16	18	70.7
1995 Cle	13	392	241	61.5	2883	7.35	17	10	87.8
1996 Bal	16	549	325	59.2	4177	7.61	33	19	88.7
1997 Bal	13	470	271	57.7	2971	6.32	18	15	75.9
1998 NYJ	14	421	259	61.5	3256	7.73	29	7	101.6
NFL Total	156	4598	2559	55.7	32479	7.06	204	190	75.5

	Rushing				
Year Team	Att	Yds	Avg	TD	Fum
1987 TB	13	50	3.8	1	7
1988 TB	28	138	4.9	1	8
1989 TB	25	139	5.6	0	4
1990 TB	38	280	7.4	1	10
1991 TB	32	101	3.2	0	5
1992 TB	36	197	5.5	2	4

1993 Cle	18	74	4.1	0	4
1994 Cle	21	37	1.8	2	3
1995 Cle	18	62	3.4	2	4
1996 Bal	34	188	5.5	2	9
1997 Bal	34	138	4.1	0	11
1998 NYJ	24	104	4.3	1	7
NFL Total	321	1508	4.7	12	76

DON TESTERMAN Testerman, Donald Ray 6′2″, 230 **RB**
Col: Ferrum; Virginia Tech; Lenoir-Rhyne; Clemson *HS:* Halifax Co. [South Boston, VA] B: 11/7/1952, Danville, VA *Drafted:* 1976 Round 10 Mia
1976 Sea: KR 2-29 14.5. **1977** Sea: KR 1-14 14.0. **1978** Sea: KR 1-19 19.0. **Total:** KR 4-62 15.5.

		Rushing				Receiving					Tot
Year Team	**G**	**Att**	**Yds**	**Avg**	**TD**	**Rec**	**Yds**	**Avg**	**TD**	**Fum**	**TD**
1976 Sea	14	67	246	3.7	1	25	232	9.3	1	2	2
1977 Sea	14	119	459	3.9	1	31	219	7.1	4	3	5
1978 Sea	16	43	155	3.6	0	17	143	8.4	0	3	0
1980 Mia	5	1	5	5.0	0	0	0	—	0	0	0
NFL Total	49	230	865	3.8	2	73	594	8.1	5	8	7

DERAL TETEAK Teteak, Deral Dean 5′10″, 210 **LB-OG**
(Little Bull) *Col:* Wisconsin *HS:* Oshkosh [WI] B: 12/11/1929, Oconto, WI *Drafted:* 1952 Round 9 GB
1952 GB: 12 G; Int 1-0. **1953** GB: 7 G; KR 2-62 31.0. **1954** GB: 6 G; Int 1-23. **1955** GB: 12 G; Int 2-41. **1956** GB: 12 G; Int 2-20. **Total:** 49 G; KR 2-62 31.0; Int 6-84.

LEE TEVIS Tevis, Lee Kessler 5′11″, 190 **FB-LB**
Col: George Washington; Miami (Ohio) B: 9/29/1921
AAFC **1947** BknA: 8 G; Pass 3-0; Rush 4-44 11.0; Int 2-9; Punt 5-246 49.2. **1948** BknA: 14 G; Pass 1-0; Rec 1-(-8) -8.0; PR 6-59 9.8; KR 2-40 20.0; Punt 5-214 42.8; Scor 10, 2-7 28.6% FG, 4-4 100.0% XK. **Total:** 22 G; Pass 4-0; Rush 4-44 11.0; Rec 1-(-8) -8.0; PR 6-59 9.8; KR 2-40 20.0; Int 2-9; Punt 10-460 46.0; Scor 10, 2-7 28.6% FG, 4-4 100.0% XK.

LOWELL TEW Tew, Lowell William 5′11″, 195 **FB**
Col: Alabama *HS:* Wayne Co. [Waynesboro, MS] B: 1/2/1927, Waynesboro, MS D: 3/16/1981, Laurel, MS
AAFC **1948** NY-A: Rec 7-97 13.9; KR 3-75 25.0. **1949** NY-A: KR 1-17 17.0. **Total:** Rec 7-97 13.9; KR 4-92 23.0.

		Rushing			
Year Team	**G**	**Att**	**Yds**	**Avg**	**TD**
1948 NY-A	14	24	95	4.0	5
1949 NY-A	1	14	65	4.6	1
AAFC Total	15	38	160	4.2	6

AL THACKER Thacker, Alvin Monroe 5′10″, 200 **DB**
(Tubby) *Col:* Charleston (WV) *HS:* East Bank [WV] B: 3/1/1919, Kayford, WV
1942 Phi: 3 G.

CORKY THARP Tharp, Thomas Allen 5′10″, 180 **DB**
Col: Alabama *HS:* Ramsey [Birmingham, AL] B: 4/19/1931, Birmingham, AL *Drafted:* 1955 Round 6 LARm
1960 NYT: 9 G; PR 1-0; Int 2-19; 1 Fum.

LARRY THARPE Tharpe, Larry James 6′4″, 300 **OT**
Col: Tennessee State *HS:* Southwest [Macon, GA] B: 11/19/1970, Macon, GA *Drafted:* 1992 Round 6 Det
1992 Det: 11 G. **1993** Det: 5 G. **1995** Ariz: 16 G. **1997** Det: 16 G. **1998** Det: 16 G. **Total:** 64 G.

RICHARD THARPE Tharpe, Richard Thomas 6′3″, 255 **DE-NT**
Col: Louisville *HS:* Central Islip [NY] B: 10/31/1960, New York, NY
1987 Buf: 3 G.

GALAND THAXTON Thaxton, Galand Walter 6′1″, 242 **LB**
Col: Wyoming *HS:* South [Denver, CO] B: 10/23/1964, Mildinhall, England
1989 Atl: 16 G. **1991** SD: 14 G. **Total:** 30 G.

JIM THAXTON Thaxton, James Ivory 6′2″, 240 **TE-WR**
Col: Tennessee State *HS:* George Washington Carver [Memphis, TN] B: 1/11/1949, Brownsville, TN *Drafted:* 1973 Round 4 SD
1974 SD-Cle: Rush 1-(-10) -10.0; Int 1-0. Cle: Rush 1-(-10) -10.0; Int 1-0. **1976** NO: KR 8-185 23.1. **1977** NO: Rush 1-(-3) -3.0; KR 0-8. **1978** StL: Scor 1 Saf. **Total:** Rush 2-(-13) -6.5; KR 8-193 24.1; Int 1-0; Scor 1 Saf.

		Receiving			
Year Team	**G**	**Rec**	**Yds**	**Avg**	**TD**
1973 SD	10	7	119	17.0	2
1974 SD-Cle	14	4	71	17.8	0
1974 SD	2	0	0	—	0
1974 Cle	12	4	71	17.8	0
1976 NO	11	7	112	16.0	1
1977 NO	14	14	211	15.1	1
1978 StL	5	3	31	10.3	1
NFL Total	54	35	544	15.5	5

HARRY THAYER Thayer, Harry James 6′1″, 215 **T-G**
(Hobo) *Col:* Tennessee *HS:* Knoxville [TN] B: 3/21/1907, Charleston, WV D: 5/8/1961, Knoxville, TN
1933 Port: 9 G.

TOM THAYER Thayer, Thomas Allen 6′4″, 271 **OG-C**
Col: Notre Dame *HS:* Joliet Catholic [IL] B: 8/16/1961, Joliet, IL *Drafted:* 1983 Round 4 ChiB
1985 ChiB: 16 G. **1986** ChiB: 16 G. **1987** ChiB: 11 G. **1988** ChiB: 16 G. **1989** ChiB: 16 G. **1990** ChiB: 16 G. **1991** ChiB: 16 G. **1992** ChiB: 16 G. **1993** Mia: 3 G. **Total:** 126 G.

JOE THEISMANN Theismann, Joseph Robert 6′0″, 192 **QB**
Col: Notre Dame *HS:* South River [NJ] B: 9/9/1949, New Brunswick, NJ *Drafted:* 1971 Round 4 Mia
1974 Was: PR 15-157 10.5. **1975** Was: PR 2-5 2.5. **1985** Was: Punt 1-1 1.0. **Total:** PR 17-162 9.5; Punt 1-1 1.0.

		Passing							
Year Team	**G**	**Att**	**Comp**	**Comp%**	**Yds**	**YPA**	**TD**	**Int**	**Rating**
1974 Was	9	11	9	81.8	145	13.18	1	0	149.1
1975 Was	14	22	10	45.5	96	4.36	1	3	33.7
1976 Was	14	163	79	48.5	1036	6.36	8	10	59.8
1977 Was	14	182	84	46.2	1097	6.03	7	9	57.9
1978 Was	16	390	187	47.9	2593	6.65	13	18	61.6
1979 Was	16	395	233	59.0	2797	7.08	20	13	83.9
1980 Was	16	454	262	57.7	2962	6.52	17	16	75.2
1981 Was	16	496	293	59.1	3568	7.19	19	20	77.3
1982 Was	9	252	161	63.9	2033	8.07	13	9	91.3
1983 Was	16	459	276	60.1	3714	8.09	29	11	97.0
1984 Was	16	477	283	59.3	3391	7.11	24	13	86.6
1985 Was	11	301	167	55.5	1774	5.89	8	16	59.6
NFL Total	167	3602	2044	56.7	25206	7.00	160	138	77.4

	Rushing				
Year Team	**Att**	**Yds**	**Avg**	**TD**	**Fum**
1974 Was	3	12	4.0	1	0
1975 Was	3	34	11.3	0	0
1976 Was	17	97	5.7	1	2
1977 Was	29	149	5.1	1	0
1978 Was	37	177	4.8	1	8
1979 Was	46	181	3.9	4	3
1980 Was	29	175	6.0	3	6
1981 Was	36	177	4.9	2	7
1982 Was	31	150	4.8	0	4
1983 Was	37	234	6.3	1	1
1984 Was	62	314	5.1	1	7
1985 Was	25	115	4.6	2	4
NFL Total	355	1815	5.1	17	42

RYAN THELWELL Thelwell, Ryan 6′2″, 192 **WR**
Col: Minnesota *HS:* Central Catholic [London, Canada] B: 4/6/1973, London, Canada *Drafted:* 1998 Round 7 SF
1998 SD: 6 G; Rec 16-268 16.8 1 TD; 6 Pt.

HARRY THEOFILEDES Theofiledes, Aris Harry 5′10″, 180 **QB**
Col: Waynesburg *HS:* Homestead [PA] B: 4/19/1944, Homestead, PA
1968 Was: 5 G; Pass 20-11 55.0%, 211 10.55 2 TD 1 Int; Rush 3-0; 1 Fum.

JIM THIBAUT Thibaut, James Pierre 5′11″, 205 **FB-LB**
Col: Tulane B: 8/31/1919, New Orleans, LA
AAFC **1946** BufA: 3 G; Rush 10-48 4.8 1 TD; 6 Pt.

JIM THIBERT Thibert, James Gerald 6′3″, 230 **LB**
Col: Toledo *HS:* Central Catholic [Toledo, OH] B: 6/14/1940, Toledo, OH *Drafted:* 1962 Round 22 SD
1965 Den: 13 G.

KEITH THIBODEAUX Thibodeaux, Keith Trevis 5′11″, 189 **DB**
Col: Northwestern State-Louisiana *HS:* Beau Chene [Arnaudville, LA] B: 5/16/1974, Opelousas, LA *Drafted:* 1997 Round 5 Was
1997 Was: 15 G.

DUTCH THIELE Thiele, Carl Louis Jr. 6′1″, 195 **E**
Col: Denison *HS:* Stivers [Dayton, OH] B: 11/14/1892, Dayton, OH D: 7/11/1986, Dayton, OH
1920 Day: 9 G. **1921** Day: 7 G; Rec 1 TD; 6 Pt. **1922** Day: 7 G; Rec 1 TD; 6 Pt. **1923** Day: 8 G. **Total:** 31 G; Rec 2 TD; 12 Pt.

R.C. THIELEMANN Thielemann, Ray Charles 6′4″, 255 **OG-C**
Col: Arkansas *HS:* Spring Woods [Houston, TX] B: 8/12/1955, Houston, TX *Drafted:* 1977 Round 2 Atl
1977 Atl: 14 G. **1978** Atl: 16 G. **1979** Atl: 11 G. **1980** Atl: 16 G. **1981** Atl: 16 G. **1982** Atl: 9 G. **1983** Atl: 16 G. **1984** Atl: 16 G. **1985** Was: 3 G. **1986** Was: 14 G. **1987** Was: 12 G. **1988** Was: 14 G. **Total:** 157 G.

KARL THIELSCHER Thielscher, Karl Leavitt 5'11", 180 **FB**
Col: Dartmouth *HS:* Brookline [MA] B: 4/24/1895, Brookline, MA
D: 5/5/1990, Palm Beach, FL
1920 Buf: 1 G.

JOHN THIERRY Thierry, John Fitzgerald 6'4", 265 **DE**
Col: Alcorn State *HS:* Plaisance [Opelousas, LA] B: 9/4/1971, Opelousas, LA *Drafted:* 1994 Round 1 ChiB
1994 ChiB: 16 G; KR 1-0. **1995** ChiB: 16 G; 4 Sac. **1996** ChiB: 16 G; 2 Sac. **1997** ChiB: 9 G; 3 Sac. **1998** ChiB: 16 G; Int 1-14; Scor **1** Saf; 2 Pt; 3.5 Sac. **Total:** 73 G; KR 1-0; Int 1-14; Scor 1 Saf; 2 Pt; 12.5 Sac.

YANCEY THIGPEN Thigpen, Yancey Dirk 6'1", 208 **WR**
Col: Winston-Salem State *HS:* Southwest Edgecombe [Pinetops, NC]
B: 8/15/1969, Tarboro, NC *Drafted:* 1991 Round 4 SD
1992 Pit: KR 2-44 22.0. **1993** Pit: KR 1-23 23.0. **1994** Pit: KR 5-121 24.2. **1995** Pit: Rush 1-1 1.0. **1997** Pit: Rush 1-3 3.0; Scor 1 2XP.
Total: Rush 2-4 2.0; KR 8-188 23.5; Scor 1 2XP.

		Receiving				
Year Team	**G**	**Rec**	**Yds**	**Avg**	**TD**	**Fum**
1991 SD	4	0	0	—	0	0
1992 Pit	12	1	2	2.0	0	0
1993 Pit	12	9	154	17.1	3	0
1994 Pit	15	36	546	15.2	4	0
1995 Pit	16	85	1307	15.4	5	1
1996 Pit	6	12	244	20.3	2	0
1997 Pit	16	79	1398	17.7	7	1
1998 Ten	9	38	493	13.0	3	0
NFL Total	90	260	4144	15.9	24	2

AARON THOMAS Thomas, Aaron Norman 6'3", 210 **TE**
Col: Oregon State *HS:* Weed [CA] B: 11/7/1937, Dierks, AR
Drafted: 1961 Round 4 SF
1961 SF: Rush 1-(-15) -15.0. **1962** SF-NYG: Rush 1-(-9) -9.0. SF: Rush 1-(-9) -9.0. **1968** NYG: Rush 2-14 7.0. **Total:** Rush 4-(-10) -2.5.

		Receiving				
Year Team	**G**	**Rec**	**Yds**	**Avg**	**TD**	**Fum**
1961 SF	14	15	301	20.1	2	1
1962 SF-NYG	14	4	80	20.0	0	0
1962 SF	2	0	0	—	0	0
1962 NYG	12	4	80	20.0	0	0
1963 NYG	14	22	469	21.3	3	0
1964 NYG	14	43	624	14.5	6	1
1965 NYG	13	27	631	23.4	5	1
1966 NYG	14	43	683	15.9	4	0
1967 NYG	14	51	877	17.2	9	0
1968 NYG	12	29	449	15.5	4	0
1969 NYG	10	22	348	15.8	3	0
1970 NYG	14	6	92	15.3	1	0
NFL Total	133	262	4554	17.4	37	3

SKIP THOMAS Thomas, Alonzo 6'1", 205 **DB**
(Dr. Death) *Col:* Arizona Western Coll. (J.C.); USC *HS:* Wyandotte [Kansas City, KS] B: 2/7/1950, Higginsville, MO *Drafted:* 1972 Round 7 Oak

		Interceptions			
Year Team	**G**	**Int**	**Yds**	**TD**	**Fum**
1972 Oak	14	0	0	0	0
1973 Oak	14	2	24	0	0
1974 Oak	14	6	70	1	0
1975 Oak	14	6	86	0	1
1976 Oak	14	2	26	0	0
1977 Oak	12	1	16	0	0
NFL Total	82	17	222	1	1

ANDRE THOMAS Thomas, Andre 6'0", 205 **RB**
Col: Mississippi *HS:* Tupelo [MS] B: 11/28/1960, Tupelo, MS
1987 Min: 1 G; Rush 6-4 0.7; Rec 2-13 6.5.

BEN THOMAS Thomas, Benjamin Jr. 6'4", 280 **DE-NT**
Col: Auburn *HS:* Turner Co. [Ashburn, GA] B: 7/2/1961, Ashburn, GA
Drafted: 1985 Round 2 NE
1985 NE: 15 G. **1986** NE-GB: 13 G; 2 Sac. NE: 4 G; 1 Sac. GB: 9 G; 1 Sac. **1988** Pit: 8 G; 0.5 Sac. **1989** Atl: 16 G; 1 Sac. **1991** LARm: 2 G.
Total: 54 G; 3.5 Sac.

BLAIR THOMAS Thomas, Blair Lamar 5'10", 198 **RB**
Col: Penn State *HS:* Frankford [Philadelphia, PA] B: 10/7/1967, Philadelphia, PA *Drafted:* 1990 Round 1 NYJ
1991 NYJ: Pass 1-1 100.0%, 16 16.00 1 TD. **1993** NYJ: KR 2-39 19.5.
1994 NE-Dal: KR 3-40 13.3. NE: KR 3-40 13.3. **Total:** Pass 1-1 100.0%, 16 16.00 1 TD; KR 5-79 15.8.

		Rushing				Receiving					Tot
Year Team	**G**	**Att**	**Yds**	**Avg**	**TD**	**Rec**	**Yds**	**Avg**	**TD**	**Fum**	**TD**
1990 NYJ	15	123	620	5.0	1	20	204	10.2	1	3	2
1991 NYJ	16	189	728	3.9	3	30	195	6.5	1	3	4
1992 NYJ	9	97	440	4.5	0	7	49	7.0	0	2	0
1993 NYJ	11	59	221	3.7	1	7	25	3.6	0	0	1
1994 NE-Dal	6	43	137	3.2	2	4	16	4.0	0	0	2
1994 NE	4	19	67	3.5	1	2	15	7.5	0	0	1
1994 Dal	2	24	70	2.9	1	2	1	0.5	0	0	1
1995 Car	7	22	90	4.1	0	3	24	8.0	0	0	0
NFL Total	64	533	2236	4.2	7	71	513	7.2	2	8	9

CLENDON THOMAS Thomas, Bobby Clendon 6'2", 196 **DB-OE-FL-HB**
Col: Oklahoma *HS:* Southeast [Oklahoma City, OK] B: 12/28/1935, Oklahoma City, OK *Drafted:* 1958 Round 2 LARm
1958 LARm: Punt 2-66 33.0. **1959** LARm: PR 3-6 2.0; KR 3-95 31.7.
1960 LARm: Rush 16-63 3.9. **1963** Pit: PR 6-24 4.0; KR 12-286 23.8.
1964 Pit: Rush 2-7 3.5; KR 7-171 24.4. **1965** Pit: PR 5-9 1.8. **1966** Pit: **1** Fum TD. **1967** Pit: PR 9-34 3.8. **Total:** Rush 18-70 3.9; PR 23-73 3.2; KR 22-552 25.1; Punt 2-66 33.0; 1 Fum TD.

		Receiving				Interceptions				Tot
Year Team	**G**	**Rec**	**Yds**	**Avg**	**TD**	**Int**	**Yds**	**TD**	**Fum**	**TD**
1958 LARm	6	0	0	—	0	0	0	0	0	0
1959 LARm	10	1	6	6.0	0	0	0	0	1	0
1960 LARm	12	17	275	16.2	2	1	0	0	3	2
1961 LARm	13	0	0	—	0	3	11	0	0	0
1962 Pit	14	0	0	—	0	7	48	0	0	0
1963 Pit	13	0	0	—	0	8	122	0	0	0
1964 Pit	14	17	334	19.6	1	1	0	0	0	1
1965 Pit	14	25	431	17.2	1	0	0	0	2	1
1966 Pit	14	0	0	—	0	2	24	0	0	1
1967 Pit	13	0	0	—	0	2	39	0	0	0
1968 Pit	14	0	0	—	0	3	0	0	0	0
NFL Total	137	60	1046	17.4	4	27	244	0	6	5

BRODERICK THOMAS Thomas, Broderick 6'4", 250 **LB-DE**
Col: Nebraska *HS:* James Madison [Houston, TX] B: 2/20/1967, Houston, TX *Drafted:* 1989 Round 1 TB
1989 TB: 16 G; 2 Sac. **1990** TB: 16 G; 7.5 Sac. **1991** TB: 16 G; 11 Sac.
1992 TB: 16 G; Int 2-81 1 TD; 6 Pt; 5 Sac. **1993** TB: 16 G; 1 Sac.
1994 Det: 16 G; 7 Sac. **1995** Min: 16 G; 6 Sac. **1996** Dal: 16 G; 4.5 Sac.
1997 Dal: 16 G; 3.5 Sac. **Total:** 144 G; Int 2-81 1 TD; 6 Pt; 47.5 Sac.

CALVIN THOMAS Thomas, Calvin Lewis 5'11", 239 **RB**
Col: Illinois *HS:* McKinley [St. Louis, MO] B: 1/7/1960, St. Louis, MO
1983 ChiB: Rec 2-13 6.5. **1984** ChiB: Rec 9-39 4.3. **1985** ChiB: Rec 5-45 9.0. **1986** ChiB: Rec 4-18 4.5. **Total:** Rec 20-115 5.8.

		Rushing				
Year Team	**G**	**Att**	**Yds**	**Avg**	**TD**	**Fum**
1982 ChiB	6	5	4	0.8	0	1
1983 ChiB	13	8	25	3.1	0	0
1984 ChiB	16	40	186	4.7	1	1
1985 ChiB	14	31	125	4.0	4	0
1986 ChiB	16	56	224	4.0	0	3
1987 ChiB	12	25	88	3.5	0	0
1988 ChiB-Den	3	6	20	3.3	0	0
1988 ChiB	1	5	20	4.0	0	0
1988 Den	2	1	0	0.0	0	0
NFL Total	80	171	672	3.9	5	5

CAL THOMAS Thomas, Calvin O 6'2", 210 **G**
Col: Tulsa *HS:* Pawhuska [OK] B: 7/1/1915 D: 4/14/1982, Harper Woods, MI
1939 Det: 5 G. **1940** Det: 8 G. **Total:** 13 G.

CARL THOMAS Thomas, Carl Herbert 5'10", 195 **T-OE-BB-FB**
(Whitey) *Col:* Pennsylvania *HS:* Frankford [PA]; Philadelphia Central HS [PA] B: 3/2/1897, Philadelphia, PA D: 10/30/1961
1920 Roch: 1 G. **1921** Roch: 5 G. **1922** Buf: 9 G; Int 1 TD; 6 Pt. **1923** Buf: 10 G. **Total:** 25 G; Int 1 TD; 6 Pt.

CARLTON THOMAS Thomas, Carlton Fitzgerald 6'0", 200 **DB**
Col: Elizabeth City State *HS:* Woodrow Wilson [Portsmouth, VA]
B: 11/25/1963, Portsmouth, VA
1987 KC: 4 G.

CHUCK THOMAS Thomas, Charles Gene 6'3", 277 **C**
Col: Oklahoma *HS:* Stratford [Houston, TX] B: 12/24/1960, Houston, TX *Drafted:* 1985 Round 8 Hou
1985 Atl: 4 G. **1987** SF: 7 G. **1988** SF: 16 G; KR 1-5 5.0; 1 Fum. **1989** SF: 16 G. **1990** SF: 16 G. **1991** SF: 12 G. **1992** SF: 2 G. **Total:** 73 G; KR 1-5 5.0; 1 Fum.

CHARLIE THOMAS Thomas, Charles Ray 5'9", 180 **RB**
Col: Tennessee State *HS:* Phillis Wheatley [Houston, TX]
B: 11/27/1948, Houston, TX
1975 KC: 7 G; PR 12-112 9.3; KR 22-516 23.5; 2 Fum.

CHRIS THOMAS Thomas, Chris Eric 6'2", 185 **WR**
Col: Cal Poly-S.L.O. *HS:* Ventura [CA] B: 7/16/1971, Ventura, CA
1995 SF: PR 1-25 25.0; KR 3-49 16.3. **Total:** PR 1-25 25.0; KR 3-49 16.3.

Year Team	G	Receiving Rec	Yds	Avg	TD
1995 SF	15	6	73	12.2	0
1997 Was	13	11	93	8.5	0
1998 Was	14	14	173	12.4	0
NFL Total	42	31	339	10.9	0

COREY THOMAS Thomas, Corey 6'0", 174 **WR**
Col: Duke *HS:* Beddingfield [Wilson, NC] B: 6/6/1975, Wilson, NC
1998 Det: 1 G.

CORNELL THOMAS Thomas, Cornell 6'3", 250 **DE**
Col: West Georgia *HS:* Meadowcreek [Norcross, GA] B: 11/11/1972, Livingston, NJ
1994 SD: Postseason only.

CURTLAND THOMAS Thomas, Curtland Parrish 6'0", 185 **WR**
Col: Missouri *HS:* Sumner [St. Louis, MO] B: 2/19/1962, St. Louis, MO
Drafted: 1984 Round 12 Was
1987 NO: 2 G; Rec 1-14 14.0; KR 1-11 11.0.

DAMON THOMAS Thomas, Damon Andrew 6'2", 215 **WR**
Col: Fresno City Coll. CA (J.C.); Wayne State (Neb.) *HS:* Clovis [CA]
B: 12/15/1970, Clovis, CA
1994 Buf: 3 G; Rec 2-31 15.5. **1995** Buf: 14 G; Rec 1-18 18.0; PR 1-0; 1 Fum. **Total:** 17 G; Rec 3-49 16.3; PR 1-0; 1 Fum.

DAVE THOMAS Thomas, Dave Garfield 6'3", 213 **DB**
Col: Butler County CC KS; Tennessee *HS:* Miami Beach [FL]
B: 8/25/1968, Miami, FL *Drafted:* 1993 Round 8 Dal
1993 Dal: 12 G. **1994** Dal: 16 G. **1995** Jac: 16 G. **1996** Jac: 9 G; PR 1-1 1.0; Int 2-7; 1 Fum. **1997** Jac: 16 G; Int 2-34. **1998** Jac: 14 G; Int 1-0.
Total: 83 G; PR 1-1 1.0; Int 5-41; 1 Fum.

DERRICK THOMAS Thomas, Derrick LeRoy 6'0", 232 **RB**
Col: Arkansas *HS:* Tilghman [Paducah, KY] B: 3/8/1965, Paducah, KY
1987 TB: 1 G; Rush 1-2 2.0.

DERRICK THOMAS Thomas, Derrick Vincent 6'3", 243 **LB-DE**
Col: Alabama *HS:* South Miami [Miami, FL] B: 1/1/1967, Miami, FL
Drafted: 1989 Round 1 KC
1989 KC: 16 G; 10 Sac. **1990** KC: 15 G; **20** Sac. **1991** KC: 16 G; 1 Fum TD; 6 Pt; 13.5 Sac. **1992** KC: 16 G; 1 Fum TD; 6 Pt; 14.5 Sac. **1993** KC: 16 G; 1 Fum TD; 6 Pt; 8 Sac. **1994** KC: 16 G; Scor **1** Saf; 2 Pt; 11 Sac. **1995** KC: 15 G; 8 Sac. **1996** KC: 16 G; 13 Sac. **1997** KC: 12 G; Scor **1** Saf; 2 Pt; 9.5 Sac. **1998** KC: 15 G; Scor **1** Saf; 1 Fum TD; 8 Pt; 12 Sac. **Total:** 153 G; Scor 3 Saf; 4 Fum TD; 30 Pt; 119.5 Sac.

DEE THOMAS Thomas, Derward Heith 5'10", 176 **DB**
Col: Nicholls State *HS:* Central Catholic [Morgan City, LA]
B: 11/7/1967, Morgan City, LA *Drafted:* 1990 Round 10 Hou
1990 Hou: 6 G.

DONNIE THOMAS Thomas, Donnie Murrice 6'2", 245 **LB**
Col: Indiana *HS:* Isaac C. Elston [Michigan City, IN] B: 3/12/1953, Michigan City, IN
1976 NE: 3 G.

DOUG THOMAS Thomas, Douglas Sandy 5'10", 178 **WR**
Col: Clemson *HS:* Richmond [Rockingham, NC] B: 9/18/1969, Rockingham, NC *Drafted:* 1991 Round 2 Sea
1991 Sea: 11 G; Rec 3-27 9.0. **1992** Sea: 12 G; Rush 3-7 2.3; Rec 8-85 10.6; KR 1-19 19.0; 1 Fum. **1993** Sea: 16 G; Rush 1-4 4.0; Rec 11-95 8.6.
Total: 39 G; Rush 4-11 2.8; Rec 22-207 9.4; KR 1-19 19.0; 1 Fum.

DUANE THOMAS Thomas, Duane Julius 6'1", 220 **RB**
Col: West Texas A&M *HS:* Lincoln [Dallas, TX] B: 6/21/1947, Dallas, TX
Drafted: 1970 Round 1 Dal
1970 Dal: KR 19-416 21.9. **1971** Dal: Pass 1-0; KR 2-64 32.0.
Total: Pass 1-0; KR 21-480 22.9.

Year Team	G	Rushing Att	Yds	Avg	TD	Receiving Rec	Yds	Avg	TD	Fum	Tot TD
1970 Dal	14	151	803	**5.3**	5	10	73	7.3	0	6	5
1971 Dal	11	175	793	4.5	**11**	13	153	11.8	2	3	**13**
1973 Was	13	32	95	3.0	0	5	40	8.0	0	1	0
1974 Was	11	95	347	3.7	5	10	31	3.1	1	1	6
NFL Total	49	453	2038	4.5	21	38	297	7.8	3	11	24

EARL THOMAS Thomas, Earl Lewis 6'3", 224 **WR-TE**
Col: Houston *HS:* Greenville [TX] B: 10/4/1948, Greenville, TX
Drafted: 1971 Round 6 ChiB
1972 ChiB: Rush 5-13 2.6; KR 0-82 **1** TD. **1973** ChiB: Pass 1-0, 1 Int; Rush 1-5 5.0; KR 0-12. **Total:** Pass 1-0, 1 Int; Rush 6-18 3.0; KR 0-94 1 TD.

Year Team	G	Receiving Rec	Yds	Avg	TD	Fum	Tot TD
1971 ChiB	11	3	40	13.3	0	0	0
1972 ChiB	14	20	365	18.3	3	1	4
1973 ChiB	14	24	343	14.3	4	1	4
1974 StL	14	34	513	15.1	5	0	5
1975 StL	11	21	375	17.9	2	0	2
1976 Hou	7	4	15	3.8	0	0	0
NFL Total	71	106	1651	15.6	14	2	15

EARLIE THOMAS Thomas, Early Bee 6'1", 190 **DB**
Col: Colorado State *HS:* Annunciation [Denver, CO] B: 12/11/1945, Denton, TX *Drafted:* 1970 Round 11 NYJ
1970 NYJ: 14 G; Int 2-46 1 TD; 6 Pt. **1971** NYJ: 13 G. **1972** NYJ: 14 G; Int 1-14. **1973** NYJ: 12 G; Int 2-25. **1974** NYJ: 8 G. **1975** Den: 10 G; Int 2-66. **Total:** 71 G; Int 7-151 1 TD; 6 Pt.

ED THOMAS Thomas, Edward Lee 6'3", 240 **TE**
Col: Houston *HS:* Booker T. Washington [New Orleans, LA]
B: 5/4/1966, New Orleans, LA
1990 TB: 7 G. **1991** TB: 6 G; Rec 4-55 13.8. **Total:** 13 G; Rec 4-55 13.8.

EMMITT THOMAS Thomas, Emmitt Earl 6'2", 192 **DB**
Col: Bishop *HS:* Marshall [Angleton, TX] B: 6/3/1943, Angleton, TX
1966 KC: PR 9-56 6.2. **1967** KC: PR 2-8 4.0. **Total:** PR 11-64 5.8.

Year Team	G	Kickoff Returns Ret	Yds	Avg	TD	Interceptions Int	Yds	TD	Fum
1966 KC	14	29	673	23.2	0	0	0	0	0
1967 KC	11	0	0	—	0	4	60	1	0
1968 KC	14	0	0	—	0	4	25	0	0
1969 KC	14	0	0	—	0	**9**	146	1	0
1970 KC	14	0	0	—	0	5	87	0	0
1971 KC	14	0	0	—	0	8	145	1	0
1972 KC	14	0	0	—	0	2	46	0	0
1973 KC	14	0	0	—	0	3	65	0	1
1974 KC	14	0	0	—	0	**12**	**214**	**2**	0
1975 KC	14	0	0	—	0	6	119	0	0
1976 KC	14	0	0	—	0	2	30	0	0
1977 KC	14	0	0	—	0	1	0	0	0
1978 KC	16	0	0	—	0	2	0	0	0
NFL Total	181	29	673	23.2	0	58	937	5	1

ENID THOMAS Thomas, Enid Anthony 5'8", 170 **WB-BB-TB**
Col: Slippery Rock; Pennsylvania *HS:* No High School B: 1/28/1897, Clairton, PA D: 10/2/1968
1926 Har: 7 G.

ERIC THOMAS Thomas, Eric Jason 5'11", 184 **DB**
Col: Pasadena City Coll. CA (J.C.); Tulane *HS:* Norte del Rio [Sacramento, CA] B: 9/11/1964, Tucson, AZ *Drafted:* 1987 Round 2 Cin
1987 Cin: 1 Sac. **1989** Cin: 2 Sac. **1991** Cin: KR 1-(-1) -1.0.
Total: KR 1-(-1) -1.0; 3 Sac.

Year Team	G	Interceptions Int	Yds	TD
1987 Cin	12	1	3	0
1988 Cin	16	7	61	0
1989 Cin	16	4	18	1
1990 Cin	4	0	0	0
1991 Cin	16	3	0	0
1992 Cin	16	0	0	0
1993 NYJ	16	2	20	0
1994 NYJ	1	0	0	0
1995 Den	14	0	0	0
NFL Total	111	17	102	1

GENE THOMAS Thomas, Eugene Warren 6'1", 210 **RB**
Col: Florida A&M *HS:* North [Akron, OH] B: 9/1/1942, Barberton, OH
1966 KC: KR 3-62 20.7. **1967** KC: Rec 13-99 7.6 2 TD; KR 6-56 9.3.
1968 Bos: Rec 10-85 8.5; KR 1-22 22.0. **Total:** Rec 23-184 8.0 2 TD; KR 10-140 14.0.

Year Team	G	Rushing Att	Yds	Avg	TD	Fum	Tot TD
1966 KC	14	7	53	7.6	1	1	1
1967 KC	14	35	133	3.8	1	0	3
1968 Bos	9	88	215	2.4	2	2	2
NFL Total	37	130	401	3.1	4	3	6

FRED THOMAS Thomas, Fredrick L 5'9", 172 **DB**
Col: Northwest Mississippi CC; Mississippi Valley State; Mississippi; Tennessee-Marti *HS:* Bruce [MS] B: 9/11/1973, Grand Rapids, MI
Drafted: 1996 Round 2 Sea
1996 Sea: 15 G. **1997** Sea: 16 G. **1998** Sea: 15 G. **Total:** 46 G.

GARTH THOMAS Thomas, Garth C 6'3", 260 **OG**
Col: Washington *HS:* Redmond [WA] B: 11/26/1963, Bellevue, WA
1987 Sea: 1 G.

GEORGE THOMAS Thomas, George Carroll Jr. 6'1", 183 **HB-DB**
(Junior) *Col:* Oklahoma *HS:* Fairland [OK] B: 3/4/1928, Fairland, OK
D: 5/23/1989, Scottsdale, AL *Drafted:* 1950 Round 1 Was
1950 Was: Rec 2-7 3.5; PR 3-15 5.0; KR 8-169 21.1. **1951** Was: Rec 7-193 27.6 2 TD. **1952** NYG: Rec 1-8 8.0. **Total:** Rec 10-208 20.8 2 TD; PR 3-15 5.0; KR 8-169 21.1.

Year Team	G	Rushing Att	Yds	Avg	TD	Fum
1950 Was	12	20	41	2.1	0	0
1951 Was	12	42	130	3.1	0	3
1952 NYG	7	6	18	3.0	0	0
NFL Total	31	68	189	2.8	0	3

GEORGE THOMAS Thomas, George Ray Jr. 5′9″, 169 **WR**
Col: Nevada-Las Vegas *HS:* Indio [CA] B: 7/11/1964, Riverside, CA
Drafted: 1988 Round 6 Atl
1989 Atl: KR 7-142 20.3. **1992** Atl-TB: KR 3-72 24.0. TB: KR 3-72 24.0.
Total: KR 10-214 21.4.

Year Team	G	Receiving Rec	Yds	Avg	TD
1989 Atl	16	4	46	11.5	0
1990 Atl	13	18	383	21.3	1
1991 Atl	12	28	365	13.0	2
1992 Atl-TB	10	6	54	9.0	0
1992 Atl	5	6	54	9.0	0
1992 TB	5	0	0	—	0
NFL Total	51	56	848	15.1	3

HENRY THOMAS Thomas, Henry Lee Jr. 6′2″, 277 **DT**
(Hank) *Col:* Louisiana State *HS:* Eisenhower [Houston, TX]
B: 1/12/1965, Houston, TX *Drafted:* 1987 Round 3 Min
1987 Min: 12 G; Int 1-0; 2.5 Sac. **1988** Min: 15 G; Int 1-7; **1** Fum TD; 6 Pt; 6 Sac. **1989** Min: 14 G; 1 Fum TD; 6 Pt; 9 Sac. **1990** Min: 16 G; 8.5 Sac. **1991** Min: 16 G; 8 Sac. **1992** Min: 16 G; 6 Sac. **1993** Min: 13 G; Scor 1 Saf; 2 Pt; 9 Sac. **1994** Min: 16 G; 7 Sac. **1995** Det: 16 G; 10.5 Sac. **1996** Det: 15 G; 6 Sac. **1997** NE: 16 G; 7 Sac. **1998** NE: 16 G; Int 1-24 1 TD; 6 Pt; 6.5 Sac. **Total:** 181 G; Int 3-31 1 TD; Scor 1 Saf; 2 Fum TD; Tot TD 3; 20 Pt; 86 Sac.

HENRY THOMAS Thomas, Henry Louis 6′2″, 275 **OG**
Col: Southwest Texas State *HS:* Lamar [Rosenberg, TX] B: 2/12/1964, Richmond, TX
1987 NO: 3 G.

HOLLIS THOMAS Thomas, Hollis 6′0″, 305 **DT**
Col: Northern Illinois *HS:* Math & Science [St. Louis, MO], played for Sumner HS [St. Louis, MO] B: 1/10/1974, Abilene, TX
1996 Phi: 16 G; 1 Sac. **1997** Phi: 16 G; 2.5 Sac. **1998** Phi: 12 G; 5 Sac.
Total: 44 G; 8.5 Sac.

IKE THOMAS Thomas, Isaac 6′2″, 193 **DB-WR**
Col: Bishop *HS:* Langston [Hot Springs, AR] B: 11/4/1947, Newton, LA *Drafted:* 1971 Round 2 Dal
1975 Buf: Int 2-74. **Total:** Int 2-74.

Year Team	G	Kickoff Returns Ret	Yds	Avg	TD	Fum
1971 Dal	7	7	295	42.1	**2**	0
1972 GB	12	21	572	27.2	0	0
1973 GB	13	23	527	22.9	0	2
1975 Buf	5	0	0	—	0	0
NFL Total	37	51	1394	27.3	2	2

JIMMY THOMAS Thomas, James 6′2″, 214 **RB-WR**
Col: Texas-Arlington *HS:* George Washington Carver [Greenville, TX]
B: 8/17/1947, Greenville, TX *Drafted:* 1969 Round 6 SF
1970 SF: KR 6-177 29.5. **1973** SF: KR 5-81 16.2. **Total:** KR 11-258 23.5.

Year Team	G	Rushing Att	Yds	Avg	TD	Receiving Rec	Yds	Avg	TD	Fum	Tot TD
1969 SF	14	23	190	8.3	1	18	364	20.2	5	0	6
1970 SF	14	31	89	2.9	0	12	221	18.4	3	2	3
1971 SF	10	3	36	12.0	1	3	33	11.0	0	0	1
1972 SF	14	52	250	4.8	1	15	148	9.9	0	3	1
1973 SF	11	56	259	4.6	1	19	157	8.3	0	2	1
NFL Total	63	165	824	5.0	4	67	923	13.8	8	7	12

JIM THOMAS Thomas, James F 5′11″, 200 **G**
Col: Oklahoma *HS:* Oilton [OK] B: 5/6/1917 D: 6/1981, Florence, SC
1939 ChiC: 5 G. **1940** ChiC: 8 G; Int 1-0. **Total:** 13 G; Int 1-0.

J.T. THOMAS Thomas, James Jr. 6′2″, 196 **DB**
Col: Florida State *HS:* Lanier [Macon, GA] B: 4/22/1951, Macon, GA
Drafted: 1973 Round 1 Pit
1974 Pit: 1 Fum TD. **1975** Pit: **1** Fum TD. **Total:** 2 Fum TD.

Year Team	G	Interceptions Int	Yds	TD	Fum
1973 Pit	14	1	10	0	0
1974 Pit	14	5	22	0	1
1975 Pit	14	3	44	0	0
1976 Pit	14	2	43	0	1
1977 Pit	14	2	10	0	0
1979 Pit	14	0	0	0	0
1980 Pit	16	2	0	0	0
1981 Pit	16	4	18	0	0
1982 Den	9	1	0	0	0
NFL Total	125	20	147	0	2

JESSE THOMAS Thomas, Jesse LeRoy 5′10″, 180 **DB**
Col: Michigan State *HS:* Central [Flint, MI] B: 5/23/1928, Guthrie, OK
Drafted: 1951 Round 10 NYY
1955 Bal: 12 G; Int 1-23. **1956** Bal: 11 G; Int 2-36; **1** Fum TD; 6 Pt.
1957 Bal: 10 G; Int 1-0. **1960** LAC: 3 G. **Total:** 36 G; Int 4-59; 1 Fum TD; 6 Pt.

JEWERL THOMAS Thomas, Jewerl Jr. 5′10″, 230 **RB**
Col: UCLA; San Jose State *HS:* Hanford [CA] B: 9/10/1957, Hanford, CA *Drafted:* 1980 Round 3 LARm
1980 LARm: KR 2-21 10.5. **1981** LARm: KR 1-15 15.0. **1983** KC: Pass 2-1 50.0%, 18 9.00 1 TD 1 Int. **Total:** Pass 2-1 50.0%, 18 9.00 1 TD 1 Int; KR 3-36 12.0.

Year Team	G	Rushing Att	Yds	Avg	TD	Receiving Rec	Yds	Avg	TD	Fum	Tot TD
1980 LARm	16	65	427	6.6	2	5	30	6.0	0	1	3
1981 LARm	15	34	118	3.5	0	5	37	7.4	0	1	0
1982 LARm	8	16	80	5.0	0	8	49	6.1	0	0	0
1983 KC	10	44	115	2.6	0	10	51	5.1	0	4	0
1984 SD	7	14	43	3.1	2	0	0	—	0	1	2
NFL Total	56	173	783	4.5	4	28	167	6.0	0	7	5

JOHN THOMAS Thomas, John Henry Jr. 6′4″, 280 **OT**
Col: Toledo *HS:* Woodward [Cincinnati, OH] B: 3/6/1964, Cincinnati, OH
1987 NYJ: 3 G.

JOHN THOMAS Thomas, John Louis 6′4″, 246 **OG-OT-LB**
Col: U. of Pacific *HS:* El Cerrito [CA] B: 1/25/1935, Tyler, TX
Drafted: 1957 Round 23 SF
1958 SF: 12 G. **1959** SF: 12 G. **1960** SF: 9 G. **1961** SF: 14 G. **1962** SF: 14 G. **1963** SF: 14 G. **1964** SF: 14 G; KR 1-0. **1965** SF: 14 G. **1966** SF: 14 G. **1967** SF: 5 G. **Total:** 122 G; KR 1-0.

RUSS THOMAS Thomas, John Russell 6′3″, 237 **T**
Col: Ohio State *HS:* Charleston [WV] B: 7/24/1924, Griffithsville, WV
D: 3/19/1991, Naples, FL *Drafted:* 1946 Round 2 Det
1946 Det: 11 G; Int 1-1. **1947** Det: 12 G. **1948** Det: 12 G. **1949** Det: 9 G.
Total: 44 G; Int 1-1.

JOHN THOMAS Thomas, John Webster 6′1″, 188 **FB**
(AKA John Webster) *Col:* Jamestown; Chicago *HS:* Jamestown [ND]
B: 2/13/1900, Ocheyedan, IA D: 8/19/1977, Woodstock, IL
1924 Rac: 2 G. **1925** Prov: 1 G. **Total:** 3 G.

JOHNNY THOMAS Thomas, Johnny Jr. 5′9″, 188 **DB**
Col: Baylor *HS:* Ross C. Sterling [Houston, TX] B: 8/3/1964, Houston, TX *Drafted:* 1987 Round 7 Was
1988 Was: 4 G. **1989** SD: 13 G. **1990** Was: 4 G; PR 1-0; 1 Fum.
1992 Was: 16 G; PR 1-0; 1 Fum. **1993** Was: 16 G. **1994** Was: 16 G.
1995 Cle: 16 G. **1996** Phi: 9 G. **Total:** 94 G; PR 2-0; 2 Fum.

J.T. THOMAS Thomas, Johnny le'Mon 5′10″, 180 **WR**
Col: San Bernardino Valley Coll. CA (J.C.); Arizona State *HS:* San Bernardino [CA] B: 7/11/1971, San Bernardino, CA *Drafted:* 1995 Round 7 StL
1995 StL: PR 0-61. **1996** StL: Rush 1-(-1) -1.0. **Total:** Rush 1-(-1) -1.0; PR 0-61.

Year Team	G	Receiving Rec	Yds	Avg	TD	Kickoff Returns Ret	Yds	Avg	TD	Fum
1995 StL	15	5	42	8.4	0	32	752	23.5	0	1
1996 StL	16	7	46	6.6	0	30	643	21.4	0	1
1997 StL	4	2	25	12.5	0	5	97	19.4	0	0
1998 StL	16	20	287	14.4	0	4	79	19.8	0	0
NFL Total	51	34	400	11.8	0	71	1571	22.1	0	2

JOE THOMAS Thomas, Joseph Earl 5′11″, 175 **WR**
Col: Mississippi Valley State *HS:* Franklin [LA] B: 3/25/1963, Lafayette, LA
1987 NO: 1 G.

KELLY THOMAS Thomas, Kelly Scott 6′6″, 270 **OT**
Col: USC *HS:* La Mirada [CA] B: 9/9/1960, Lynwood, CA
Drafted: 1983 Round 4 TB
1983 TB: 14 G. **1984** TB: 10 G. **1987** LARm: 3 G. **Total:** 27 G.

KEN THOMAS Thomas, Kenneth Ray 5′9″, 211 **RB**
Col: San Jose State *HS:* Hanford [CA] B: 2/11/1960, Hanford, CA
Drafted: 1983 Round 7 KC
1983 KC: Rush 15-55 3.7; KR 1-6 6.0.

Year Team	G	Receiving Rec	Yds	Avg	TD	Fum
1983 KC	14	28	236	8.4	1	2

KEVIN THOMAS Thomas, Kevin Alan 6′2″, 268 **C**
Col: Arizona State *HS:* Canyon del Oro [Tucson, AZ] B: 7/27/1964, Tucson, AZ
1988 TB: 10 G.

LAMAR THOMAS Thomas, Lamar Nathaniel 6′1″, 175 **WR**
Col: Miami (Fla.) *HS:* F.W. Buchholz [Gainesville, FL] B: 2/12/1970, Ocala, FL *Drafted:* 1993 Round 3 TB
1995 TB: Rush 1-5 5.0. **Total:** Rush 1-5 5.0.

		Receiving				
Year Team	G	Rec	Yds	Avg	TD	Fum
1993 TB	14	8	186	23.3	2	0
1994 TB	11	7	94	13.4	0	0
1995 TB	11	10	107	10.7	0	0
1996 Mia	9	10	166	16.6	1	0
1997 Mia	12	28	402	14.4	2	1
1998 Mia	16	43	603	14.0	5	0
NFL Total	73	106	1558	14.7	10	1

LAVALE THOMAS Thomas, Lavale Alvin 6′0″, 205 **RB**
Col: Fresno State *HS:* Tulare Western [CA] B: 12/12/1963, Los Angeles, CA
1987 GB: 1 G; Rush 5-19 3.8; Rec 2-52 26.0 1 TD; 6 Pt. **1988** GB: 1 G. **Total:** 2 G; Rush 5-19 3.8; Rec 2-52 26.0 1 TD; 6 Pt.

LEE THOMAS Thomas, Lee Edward 6′5″, 246 **DE**
Col: Wiley; Jackson State *HS:* George Washington [Karnack, TX] B: 3/12/1946, Karnack, TX
1971 SD: 9 G; KR 1-0. **1972** SD: 14 G. **1973** Cin: 9 G. **Total:** 32 G; KR 1-0.

SPEEDY THOMAS Thomas, Louis Timothy 6′1″, 170 **WR**
Col: Utah B: 4/13/1947, Houston, TX *Drafted:* 1969 Round 3 Cin
1969 Cin: Rush 4-16 4.0 1 TD; PR 4-15 3.8. **1970** Cin: Rush 2-7 3.5; PR 4-20 5.0. **1971** Cin: Rush 2-(-1) -0.5; PR 4-10 2.5. **Total:** Rush 8-22 2.8 1 TD; PR 12-45 3.8.

		Receiving					Tot
Year Team	G	Rec	Yds	Avg	TD	Fum	TD
1969 Cin	14	33	481	14.6	3	1	4
1970 Cin	14	21	257	12.2	2	1	2
1971 Cin	12	22	327	14.9	2	1	2
1972 Cin	11	17	171	10.1	1	1	1
1973 NO	6	0	0	—	0	0	0
1974 NO	1	1	3	3.0	0	0	0
NFL Total	58	94	1239	13.2	8	4	9

MIKE THOMAS Thomas, Malcolm 5′11″, 190 **RB**
Col: Oklahoma; Nevada-Las Vegas *HS:* Greenville [TX] B: 7/17/1953, Greenville, TX *Drafted:* 1975 Round 5 Was
1979 SD: Pass 1-1 100.0%, 18 18.00. **1980** SD: Pass 2-0, 1 Int. **Total:** Pass 3-1 33.3%, 18 6.00 1 Int.

		Rushing				Receiving					Tot
Year Team	G	Att	Yds	Avg	TD	Rec	Yds	Avg	TD	Fum	TD
1975 Was	14	235	919	3.9	4	40	483	12.1	3	9	7
1976 Was	13	254	1101	4.3	5	28	290	10.4	4	7	9
1977 Was	13	228	806	3.5	3	28	245	8.8	2	10	5
1978 Was	13	161	533	3.3	3	35	387	11.1	2	7	5
1979 SD	14	91	353	3.9	1	32	388	12.1	0	4	1
1980 SD	10	118	484	4.1	3	29	218	7.5	0	0	3
NFL Total	77	1087	4196	3.9	19	192	2011	10.5	11	37	30

MARK THOMAS Thomas, Mark Andrew 6′5″, 272 **DE**
Col: North Carolina State *HS:* Parkview [Lilburn, GA] B: 5/6/1969, Lilburn, GA *Drafted:* 1992 Round 4 SF
1993 SF: 11 G; 0.5 Sac. **1994** SF: 9 G; 1 Sac. **1995** Car: 10 G; 2 Sac. **1996** Car: 12 G; 4 Sac. **1997** ChiB: 16 G; 4.5 Sac. **1998** ChiB-Ind: 14 G; 5.5 Sac. ChiB: 10 G; 4.5 Sac. Ind: 4 G; 1 Sac. **Total:** 72 G; 17.5 Sac.

MARVIN THOMAS Thomas, Marvin 6′5″, 264 **DE**
Col: Memphis *HS:* Baldwin Co. [Bay Minette, AL] B: 10/19/1973, Bay Minette, AL *Drafted:* 1997 Round 7 ChiB
1998 Det: 4 G.

NORRIS THOMAS Thomas, Norris Lee 6′0″, 180 **DB**
Col: Southern Mississippi *HS:* Pascagoula [MS] B: 5/3/1954, Inverness, MS *Drafted:* 1976 Round 9 Mia
1977 Mia: 14 G; Int 3-23. **1978** Mia: 16 G; Int 2-63 1 TD; 6 Pt. **1979** Mia: 16 G; Int 2-29. **1980** TB: 16 G; Int 1-0. **1981** TB: 16 G. **1982** TB: 9 G; Int 1-0. **1983** TB: 10 G. **1984** TB: 15 G. **Total:** 112 G; Int 9-115 1 TD; 6 Pt.

ORLANDO THOMAS Thomas, Orlando Paul 6′1″, 215 **DB**
Col: Southwestern Louisiana *HS:* Crowley [LA] B: 10/21/1972, Crowley, LA *Drafted:* 1995 Round 2 Min
1995 Min: **1** Fum TD. **1997** Min: 1 Fum TD. **1998** Min: 0.5 Sac. **Total:** 2 Fum TD; 0.5 Sac.

		Interceptions				Tot
Year Team	G	Int	Yds	TD	Fum	TD
1995 Min	16	**9**	108	1	1	2
1996 Min	16	5	57	0	0	0
1997 Min	15	2	1	0	1	1
1998 Min	16	2	27	0	0	0
NFL Total	63	18	193	1	2	3

PAT THOMAS Thomas, Patrick Shane 5′9″, 183 **DB**
Col: Texas A&M *HS:* Plano [TX] B: 9/1/1954, Plano, TX *Drafted:* 1976 Round 2 LARm
1976 LARm: KR 7-140 20.0. **1980** LARm: KR 1-12 12.0. **Total:** KR 8-152 19.0.

		Interceptions		
Year Team	G	Int	Yds	TD
1976 LARm	14	0	0	0
1977 LARm	14	5	97	0
1978 LARm	16	8	96	1
1979 LARm	8	3	5	0
1980 LARm	14	3	14	0
1981 LARm	12	4	80	0
1982 LARm	9	3	0	0
NFL Total	87	26	292	1

RALPH THOMAS Thomas, Ralph Werner 5′11″, 190 **OE-DE**
Col: San Francisco *HS:* St. Catherine [Racine, WI] B: 12/6/1927, Kenosha, WI
1952 ChiC: 11 G. **1955** Was: 12 G; Rec 9-105 11.7 2 TD; Tot TD 3; 18 Pt. **1956** Was: 12 G; KR 1-0. **Total:** 35 G; Rec 9-105 11.7 2 TD; KR 1-0; Tot TD 3; 18 Pt.

RATCLIFF THOMAS Thomas, Ratcliff 6′1″, 238 **LB**
Col: Maryland *HS:* T.C. Williams [Woodbridge, VA]; Hargrave Mil. Acad. [Chatham, VA] B: 1/2/1974
1998 Ind: 5 G.

RICKY THOMAS Thomas, Ricky L 6′0″, 185 **DB**
Col: Alabama *HS:* Niceville [FL] B: 3/29/1965, Eglin AFB, FL
1987 Sea: 1 G.

ROBB THOMAS Thomas, Robb Douglas 5′11″, 175 **WR**
Col: Oregon State *HS:* Corvallis [OR] B: 3/29/1966, Portland, OR *Drafted:* 1989 Round 6 KC
1992 Sea: Rush 1-(-1) -1.0. **Total:** Rush 1-(-1) -1.0.

		Receiving				
Year Team	G	Rec	Yds	Avg	TD	Fum
1989 KC	8	8	58	7.3	2	1
1990 KC	16	41	545	13.3	4	0
1991 KC	15	43	495	11.5	1	0
1992 Sea	15	11	136	12.4	0	1
1993 Sea	16	7	67	9.6	0	0
1994 Sea	16	4	70	17.5	0	0
1995 Sea	15	12	239	19.9	1	0
1996 TB	12	33	427	12.9	2	0
1997 TB	16	13	129	9.9	0	0
1998 TB	7	2	63	31.5	1	0
NFL Total	136	174	2229	12.8	11	2

BOB THOMAS Thomas, Robert Lee 5′10″, 201 **RB**
Col: Mesa CC AZ; Arizona State *HS:* Centennial [Compton, CA] B: 8/23/1948, Pittsburgh, PA
1971 LARm: KR 1-12 12.0. **1972** LARm: Rec 11-95 8.6; KR 8-212 26.5. **1973** SD: Rec 7-51 7.3 1 TD. **1974** SD: Rec 1-9 9.0; KR 2-32 16.0. **Total:** Rec 19-155 8.2 1 TD; KR 11-256 23.3.

		Rushing					Tot
Year Team	G	Att	Yds	Avg	TD	Fum	TD
1971 LARm	6	0	0	—	0	0	0
1972 LARm	14	77	433	5.6	3	1	3
1973 SD	14	22	48	2.2	0	3	1
1974 SD	14	21	56	2.7	0	0	0
NFL Total	48	120	537	4.5	3	4	4

ROBERT THOMAS Thomas, Robert Lee IV 6′1″, 260 **LB**
Col: Henderson State *HS:* Jacksonville [AR] B: 12/1/1974, Little Rock, AR
1998 Dal: 16 G.

BOB THOMAS Thomas, Robert Randall 5′10″, 178 **K**
Col: Notre Dame *HS:* McQuaid [Rochester, NY] B: 8/7/1952, Rochester, NY *Drafted:* 1974 Round 15 LARm

		Scoring						
Year Team	G	Pts	FG	FGA	FG%	XK	XKA	XK%
1975 ChiB	14	57	13	23	56.5	18	22	81.8
1976 ChiB	14	63	12	25	48.0	27	30	90.0
1977 ChiB	14	69	14	27	51.9	27	30	90.0
1978 ChiB	16	77	17	22	77.3	26	28	92.9
1979 ChiB	16	82	16	27	59.3	34	37	91.9
1980 ChiB	16	74	13	18	72.2	35	37	94.6
1981 ChiB	2	8	2	3	66.7	2	3	66.7
1982 Det-ChiB	4	39	10	12	83.3	9	9	100.0

1982 Det	2	18	5	5	100.0	3	3	100.0
1982 ChiB	2	21	5	7	71.4	6	6	100.0
1983 ChiB	16	77	14	25	56.0	35	38	92.1
1984 ChiB	16	101	22	28	78.6	35	37	94.6
1985 SD	15	105	18	28	64.3	51	**55**	92.7
1986 NYG	1	4	0	1	0.0	4	4	100.0
NFL Total	144	756	151	239	63.2	303	330	91.8

RODELL THOMAS Thomas, Rodell 6′2″, 225 **LB**
Col: Alabama State *HS:* Quincy [FL] B: 8/2/1958, Quincy, FL
1981 Mia-Sea: 14 G; 1 Fum TD; 6 Pt. Mia: 3 G. Sea: 11 G; 1 Fum TD; 6 Pt. **1982** Sea: 8 G. **1983** Mia: 16 G. **1984** Mia: 14 G; 1 Sac. **Total:** 52 G; 1 Fum TD; 6 Pt; 1 Sac.

RODNEY THOMAS Thomas, Rodney Dejuane 5′10″, 210 **RB**
Col: Texas A&M *HS:* Groveton [TX] B: 3/30/1973, Trinity, TX
Drafted: 1995 Round 3 Hou
1995 Hou: Scor 1 2XP. **Total:** Scor 1 2XP.

		Rushing				Receiving			
Year Team	**G**	**Att**	**Yds**	**Avg**	**TD**	**Rec**	**Yds**	**Avg**	**TD**
1995 Hou	16	251	947	3.8	5	39	204	5.2	2
1996 Hou	16	49	151	3.1	1	13	128	9.8	0
1997 Ten	16	67	310	4.6	3	14	111	7.9	0
1998 Ten	11	24	100	4.2	2	6	55	9.2	0
NFL Total	59	391	1508	3.9	11	72	498	6.9	2

	Kickoff Returns					Tot
Year Team	**Ret**	**Yds**	**Avg**	**TD**	**Fum**	**TD**
1995 Hou	3	48	16.0	0	8	7
1996 Hou	5	80	16.0	0	0	1
1997 Ten	17	346	20.4	0	1	3
1998 Ten	3	64	21.3	0	0	2
NFL Total	28	538	19.2	0	9	13

RODNEY THOMAS Thomas, Rodney Lamar 5′10″, 190 **DB**
Col: Brigham Young *HS:* Chaffey [Ontario, CA] B: 12/21/1965, Los Angeles, CA *Drafted:* 1988 Round 5 Mia
1988 Mia: 12 G; Int 1-48. **1989** Mia: 16 G; Int 2-4; 1 Sac. **1990** Mia: 15 G. **1991** LARm: 3 G. **Total:** 46 G; Int 3-52; 1 Sac.

REX THOMAS Thomas, Rolla 5′9″, 174 **WB-FB-TB-HB**
Col: Tulsa; St. John's (N.Y.) *HS:* Sapulpa [OK] B: 1/14/1901, Weatherford, OK D: Hollywood, TX
1926 Bkn: 10 G; Pass 1 TD; Rush 3 TD; Rec 1 TD; Scor **1** 1XP; Tot TD 4; 25 Pt. **1927** Cle: 13 G; Rush 1 TD; Rec 2 TD; Tot TD 3; 18 Pt. **1928** Det: 10 G; Pass 2 TD; Rush 1 TD; Rec 1 TD; Tot TD 2; 12 Pt. **1930** Bkn: 6 G; Rec **5** TD; Scor 31, 1 XK. **1931** Bkn: 8 G; Rec 1 TD; 6 Pt. **Total:** 47 G; Pass 3 TD; Rush 5 TD; Rec 10 TD; Scor 1 1XP; Tot TD 15.

LYNN THOMAS Thomas, Ronald Lynn 5′11″, 181 **DB**
Col: Pittsburgh *HS:* Pascagoula [MS] B: 7/9/1959, Pascagoula, MS
1981 SF: 15 G. **1982** SF: 9 G. **Total:** 24 G.

SEAN THOMAS Thomas, Sean 5′11″, 190 **DB**
Col: Sacramento City Coll. CA (J.C.); Texas Christian *HS:* Luther Burbank [Sacramento, CA] B: 4/12/1962, Sacramento, CA
Drafted: 1985 Round 3 Cin
1985 Cin-Atl: 11 G. Cin: 5 G. Atl: 6 G. **Total:** 11 G.

SPENCER THOMAS Thomas, Spencer Lee 6′2″, 185 **DB**
Col: Washburn *HS:* Wyandotte [Kansas City, KS] B: 3/9/1951, Kansas City, KS
1975 Was: 14 G. **1976** Bal: 2 G. **Total:** 16 G.

STAN THOMAS Thomas, Stanley 6′5″, 295 **OT**
Col: Texas *HS:* Central [El Centro, CA] B: 10/28/1968, El Centro, CA
Drafted: 1991 Round 1 ChiB
1991 ChiB: 15 G. **1992** ChiB: 11 G. **1993** Hou: 14 G. **1994** Hou: 16 G. **Total:** 56 G.

THURMAN THOMAS Thomas, Thurman Lee 5′10″, 198 **RB**
Col: Oklahoma State *HS:* Willowridge [Sugar Land, TX] B: 5/16/1966, Houston, TX *Drafted:* 1988 Round 2 Buf
1993 Buf: Pass 1-0. **Total:** Pass 1-0.

		Rushing				Receiving					Tot
Year Team	**G**	**Att**	**Yds**	**Avg**	**TD**	**Rec**	**Yds**	**Avg**	**TD**	**Fum**	**TD**
1988 Buf	15	207	881	4.3	2	18	208	11.6	0	9	2
1989 Buf	16	298	1244	4.2	6	60	669	11.2	6	7	12
1990 Buf	16	271	1297	4.8	11	49	532	10.9	2	6	13
1991 Buf	15	288	1407	**4.9**	7	62	631	10.2	5	5	12
1992 Buf	16	312	1487	4.8	9	58	626	10.8	3	6	12
1993 Buf	16	**355**	1315	3.7	6	48	387	8.1	0	6	6
1994 Buf	15	287	1093	3.8	7	50	349	7.0	2	1	9
1995 Buf	14	267	1005	3.8	6	26	220	8.5	2	6	8
1996 Buf	15	281	1033	3.7	8	26	254	9.8	0	1	8
1997 Buf	16	154	643	4.2	1	30	208	6.9	0	2	1
1998 Buf	14	93	381	4.1	2	26	220	8.5	1	0	3
NFL Total	168	2813	11786	4.2	65	453	4304	9.5	21	49	86

TODD THOMAS Thomas, Todd Robin 6′5″, 262 **C**
Col: North Dakota *HS:* Cedarburg [WI] B: 12/2/1959, Mankato, MN
Drafted: 1981 Round 5 KC
1981 KC: 15 G.

VERN THOMAS Thomas, Vernon P 155 **OE**
Col: No College B: 2/2/1898, IL D: 4/1973, Richland, NY
1920 Roch: 10 G.

WHITEY THOMAS Thomas, William C 5′10″, 180 **OE**
Col: Penn State *HS:* Atlantic City [NJ] B: 8/17/1895 D: 8/1978, Lavallette, NJ
1924 Fra: 14 G.

WILLIAM THOMAS Thomas, William Harrison Jr. 6′2″, 223 **LB**
Col: Texas A&M *HS:* Palo Duro [Amarillo, TX] B: 8/13/1968, Amarillo, TX *Drafted:* 1991 Round 4 Phi
1991 Phi: 2 Sac. **1992** Phi: 1.5 Sac. **1993** Phi: 6.5 Sac. **1994** Phi: 6 Sac. **1995** Phi: 2 Sac. **1996** Phi: **1** Fum TD; 5.5 Sac. **1997** Phi: 1 Fum TD; 5 Sac. **1998** Phi: 2 Sac. **Total:** 2 Fum TD; 30.5 Sac.

		Interceptions			Tot
Year Team	**G**	**Int**	**Yds**	**TD**	**TD**
1991 Phi	16	0	0	0	0
1992 Phi	16	2	4	0	0
1993 Phi	16	2	39	0	0
1994 Phi	16	1	7	0	0
1995 Phi	16	7	104	1	1
1996 Phi	16	3	47	0	1
1997 Phi	14	2	11	0	1
1998 Phi	16	1	21	0	0
NFL Total	126	18	233	1	3

TRA THOMAS Thomas, William III 6′7″, 349 **OT**
Col: Florida State *HS:* Deland [FL] B: 11/20/1974, Deland, FL
Drafted: 1998 Round 1 Phi
1998 Phi: 16 G.

BILL THOMAS Thomas, William Jeffrey 6′2″, 225 **RB**
Col: Boston College *HS:* Peekskill [NY] B: 8/7/1949, Ossining, NY
Drafted: 1972 Round 1 Dal
1973 Hou: Rush 10-39 3.9; Rec 1-4 4.0. **1974** KC: Rush 3-(-3) -1.0. **Total:** Rush 13-36 2.8; Rec 1-4 4.0.

		Kickoff Returns				
Year Team	**G**	**Ret**	**Yds**	**Avg**	**TD**	**Fum**
1972 Dal	7	2	50	25.0	0	0
1973 Hou	6	0	0	—	0	0
1974 KC	14	25	571	22.8	0	1
NFL Total	27	27	621	23.0	0	1

ZACH THOMAS Thomas, Zachary Dwayne 6′0″, 182 **WR**
Col: South Carolina State *HS:* Cocoa [FL] B: 9/8/1960, Cocoa, FL
1983 Den: Rec 12-182 15.2. **Total:** Rec 12-182 15.2.

		Punt Returns				Kickoff Returns				
Year Team	**G**	**Ret**	**Yds**	**Avg**	**TD**	**Ret**	**Yds**	**Avg**	**TD**	**Fum**
1983 Den	16	33	368	11.2	**1**	28	573	20.5	0	4
1984 Den-TB	14	21	125	6.0	0	18	351	19.5	0	3
1984 Den	12	20	118	5.9	0	18	351	19.5	0	3
1984 TB	2	1	7	7.0	0	0	0	—	0	0
NFL Total	30	54	493	9.1	1	46	924	20.1	0	7

ZACH THOMAS Thomas, Zachary Michael 5′11″, 235 **LB**
Col: Texas Tech *HS:* White Deer [TX]; Pampa HS [TX] B: 9/1/1973, Lubbock, TX *Drafted:* 1996 Round 5 Mia
1996 Mia: 16 G; KR 1-17 17.0; Int 3-64 1 TD; 6 Pt; 2 Sac. **1997** Mia: 15 G; Int 1-10; 0.5 Sac. **1998** Mia: 16 G; Int 3-21 2 TD; 12 Pt; 2 Sac. **Total:** 47 G; KR 1-17 17.0; Int 7-95 3 TD; 18 Pt; 4.5 Sac.

RICH THOMASELLI Thomaselli, Richard J 6′1″, 199 **RB**
Col: West Virginia Wesleyan *HS:* Brooke [Wellsburg, WV]
B: 2/26/1957, Follansbee, WV
1981 Hou: 12 G. **1982** Hou: 9 G; Rec 1-8 8.0; KR 1-7 7.0. **Total:** 21 G; Rec 1-8 8.0; KR 1-7 7.0.

JIM THOMASON Thomason, James N 6′0″, 200 **WB-DB**
Col: Texas A&M *HS:* Brownwood [TX] B: 10/4/1919 D: 6/2/1989, Lyons, TX *Drafted:* 1941 Round 1 Det
1945 Det: 5 G; Rush 9-9 1.0; Rec 1-6 6.0; 3 Fum.

JEFF THOMASON Thomason, Jeffrey David 6′5″, 243 **TE**
Col: Oregon *HS:* Corona Del Mar [Newport Beach, CA] B: 12/30/1969, San Diego, CA
1995 GB: KR 1-16 16.0. **1996** GB: KR 1-20 20.0. **Total:** KR 2-36 18.0.

		Receiving				
Year Team	**G**	**Rec**	**Yds**	**Avg**	**TD**	**Fum**
1992 Cin	4	2	14	7.0	0	0
1993 Cin	3	2	8	4.0	0	0
1995 GB	16	3	32	10.7	0	0
1996 GB	16	3	45	15.0	0	0

1997 GB	13	9	115	12.8	1	1
1998 GB	16	9	89	9.9	0	0
NFL Total	68	28	303	10.8	1	1

STUMPY THOMASON Thomason, John Griffin 5'7", 189 **DB-FB-LB-BB**
Col: Georgia Tech *HS:* Tech [Atlanta, GA] B: 2/24/1906, Atlanta, GA
D: 4/20/1989, Thomasville, NC
1930 Bkn: Rec 1 TD. **1931** Bkn: Rec 1 TD. **1932** Bkn: Pass 10-1 10.0%, -4 -0.40 2 Int; Rec 1 TD. **1935** Bkn-Phi: Rec 1-16 16.0. Phi: Rec 1-16 16.0. **1936** Phi: Pass 10-1 10.0%, 11 1.10 3 Int; PR **1** TD; Scor 7, 1 XK. **Total:** Pass 20-2 10.0%, 7 0.35 5 Int; Rec 1-16 16.0 3 TD; PR 1 TD.

		Rushing				Tot
Year Team	**G**	**Att**	**Yds**	**Avg**	**TD**	**TD**
1930 Bkn	6	—	—	—	3	4
1931 Bkn	13	—	—	—	0	1
1932 Bkn	10	64	197	3.1	0	1
1933 Bkn	9	45	158	3.5	0	0
1934 Bkn	8	40	131	3.3	0	0
1935 Bkn-Phi	8	3	14	4.7	0	0
1935 Bkn	1	0	0	—	0	0
1935 Phi	7	3	14	4.7	0	0
1936 Phi	12	109	333	3.1	0	1
NFL Total	66	261	833	3.2	3	7

BOBBY THOMASON Thomason, Robert Lee 6'1", 196 **QB**
Col: Virginia Military *HS:* Leeds [AL] B: 3/26/1928, Birmingham, AL
Drafted: 1949 Round 1 LARm

		Passing							
Year Team	**G**	**Att**	**Comp**	**Comp%**	**Yds**	**YPA**	**TD**	**Int**	**Rating**
1949 LARm	6	12	6	50.0	50	4.17	0	1	26.4
1951 GB	11	221	125	**56.6**	1306	5.91	11	9	73.5
1952 Phi	12	212	95	44.8	1334	6.29	8	9	60.5
1953 Phi	12	304	162	53.3	2462	8.10	**21**	20	75.8
1954 Phi	10	170	83	48.8	1242	7.31	10	13	61.0
1955 Phi	10	171	88	51.5	1337	7.82	10	7	80.0
1956 Phi	12	164	82	50.0	1119	6.82	4	21	40.7
1957 Phi	12	92	46	50.0	630	6.85	4	10	47.2
NFL Total	85	1346	687	51.0	9480	7.04	68	90	62.9

	Rushing				
Year Team	**Att**	**Yds**	**Avg**	**TD**	**Fum**
1951 GB	5	-5	-1.0	0	2
1952 Phi	17	88	5.2	0	3
1953 Phi	9	23	2.6	1	4
1954 Phi	10	45	4.5	0	1
1955 Phi	17	29	1.7	0	4
1956 Phi	21	48	2.3	2	2
1957 Phi	15	62	4.1	3	1
NFL Total	94	290	3.1	6	17

LEON THOMASSON Thomasson, Leon S 5'11", 190 **DB**
Col: Texas Southern *HS:* Nettie Lee Roth [Dayton, OH] B: 6/20/1963, Dayton, OH
1987 Atl: 3 G.

CHRIS THOME Thome, Christopher John 6'4", 278 **C**
Col: Minnesota *HS:* St. Thomas Acad. [St. Paul, MN] B: 1/15/1969, St. Cloud, MN *Drafted:* 1991 Round 5 Min
1991 Cle: 8 G. **1992** Cle: 3 G. **Total:** 11 G.

PINKY THOMPSON Thompson, ? **WB**
Col: No College
1927 Buf: 2 G.

WOODY THOMPSON Thompson, Alexander Woodrow 6'1", 228 **RB**
Col: Miami (Fla.) *HS:* East [Erie, PA] B: 8/20/1952, Erie, PA
Drafted: 1975 Round 3 Atl
1975 Atl: KR 4-62 15.5. **Total:** KR 4-62 15.5.

		Rushing				Receiving				
Year Team	**G**	**Att**	**Yds**	**Avg**	**TD**	**Rec**	**Yds**	**Avg**	**TD**	**Fum**
1975 Atl	14	68	247	3.6	0	14	92	6.6	0	4
1976 Atl	7	42	152	3.6	0	16	111	6.9	0	2
1977 Atl	14	132	478	3.6	1	12	56	4.7	0	4
NFL Total	35	242	877	3.6	1	42	259	6.2	0	10

ALVIE THOMPSON Thompson, Alvie Gunder 6'3", 210 **T-G**
Col: Lombard; Nebraska *HS:* Cambridge [NE] B: 1/27/1901, Cambridge, NE D: 11/19/1985, Wenatchee, WA
1925 KC: 8 G. **1926** KC: 2 G. **Total:** 10 G.

ANTHONY THOMPSON Thompson, Anthony 6'1", 227 **LB**
Col: East Carolina *HS:* Ralph L. Fike [Wilson, NC] B: 6/19/1967, Stantonburg, NC *Drafted:* 1990 Round 10 Den
1990 Den: 10 G.

ANTHONY THOMPSON Thompson, Anthony Q 5'11", 207 **RB**
Col: Indiana *HS:* North Vigo [Terre Haute, IN] B: 4/8/1967, Terre Haute, IN *Drafted:* 1990 Round 2 Pho
1990 Pho: Rec 2-11 5.5. **1991** Pho: Pass 1-0; Rec 7-52 7.4.
1992 Pho-LARm: Rec 5-11 2.2; KR 4-34 8.5. LARm: Rec 5-11 2.2; KR 4-34 8.5. **Total:** Pass 1-0; Rec 14-74 5.3; KR 4-34 8.5.

		Rushing				
Year Team	**G**	**Att**	**Yds**	**Avg**	**TD**	**Fum**
1990 Pho	13	106	390	3.7	4	1
1991 Pho	16	126	376	3.0	1	3
1992 Pho-LARm	8	19	65	3.4	1	1
1992 Pho	1	8	8	1.0	1	0
1992 LARm	7	11	57	5.2	0	1
NFL Total	37	251	831	3.3	6	5

ARLAND THOMPSON Thompson, Arland Baron 6'4", 265 **OG**
Col: Baylor *HS:* Plainview [TX] B: 9/19/1957, Lockney, TX
Drafted: 1980 Round 4 ChiB
1980 Den: 2 G. **1981** GB: 9 G. **1982** Bal: 3 G. **1987** KC: 3 G. **Total:** 17 G.

AUNDRA THOMPSON Thompson, Aundra 6'1", 186 **WR-RB**
Col: Texas A&M-Commerce *HS:* L. V. Berkner [Richardson, TX]
B: 1/2/1953, Dallas, TX *Drafted:* 1976 Round 5 GB
1978 GB: Rush 4-25 6.3. **1979** GB: Rush 2-(-18) -9.0. **1980** GB: Rush 5-5 1.0. **1981** GB-SD-NO: Rush 1-2 2.0. GB: Rush 1-2 2.0. **1982** NO: Rush 1-2 2.0. **Total:** Rush 13-16 1.2.

		Receiving				Kickoff Returns					Tot
Year Team	**G**	**Rec**	**Yds**	**Avg**	**TD**	**Ret**	**Yds**	**Avg**	**TD**	**Fum**	**TD**
1977 GB	14	2	12	6.0	0	4	82	20.5	0	0	0
1978 GB	16	26	527	20.3	2	6	124	20.7	0	1	2
1979 GB	15	25	395	15.8	3	15	346	23.1	**1**	3	4
1980 GB	15	40	609	15.2	2	15	283	18.9	0	2	2
1981 GB-SD-NO	14	8	111	13.9	0	2	44	22.0	0	0	0
1981 GB	3	2	30	15.0	0	0	0	—	0	0	0
1981 SD	1	0	0	—	0	2	44	22.0	0	0	0
1981 NO	10	6	81	13.5	0	0	0	—	0	0	0
1982 NO	9	8	138	17.3	1	10	211	21.1	0	1	1
NFL Total	83	109	1792	16.4	8	52	1090	21.0	1	7	9

BENNIE THOMPSON Thompson, Bennie 6'0", 210 **DB**
Col: Grambling State *HS:* John McDonogh [New Orleans, LA]
B: 2/10/1963, New Orleans, LA
1989 NO: 2 G. **1990** NO: 16 G; Int 2-0. **1991** NO: 16 G; Int 1-14. **1992** KC: 16 G; Int 4-26; 1.5 Sac. **1993** KC: 16 G; 0.5 Sac. **1994** Cle: 16 G; 1 Sac. **1995** Cle: 13 G. **1996** Bal: 16 G; 3 Sac. **1997** Bal: 16 G. **1998** Bal: 16 G; PR 1-43 43.0. **Total:** 143 G; PR 1-43 43.0; Int 7-40; 6 Sac.

BOBBY THOMPSON Thompson, Bobby 5'11", 195 **RB**
Col: Arizona Western Coll. (J.C.); Oklahoma *HS:* Central [Providence, RI] B: 1/16/1947, Raleigh, NC

		Rushing				Receiving			
Year Team	**G**	**Att**	**Yds**	**Avg**	**TD**	**Rec**	**Yds**	**Avg**	**TD**
1975 Det	14	51	268	5.3	1	19	122	6.4	0
1976 Det	14	13	42	3.2	0	10	108	10.8	0
NFL Total	28	64	310	4.8	1	29	230	7.9	0

	Kickoff Returns				
Year Team	**Ret**	**Yds**	**Avg**	**TD**	**Fum**
1975 Det	22	565	25.7	0	0
1976 Det	22	431	19.6	0	1
NFL Total	44	996	22.6	0	1

BRODERICK THOMPSON Thompson, Broderick Lorenzo 6'5", 295 **OG-OT**
Col: Cerritos Coll. CA (J.C.); Kansas *HS:* Richard Gahr [Cerritos, CA]
B: 8/14/1960, Birmingham, AL
1985 Dal: 11 G. **1987** SD: 9 G. **1988** SD: 16 G. **1989** SD: 16 G. **1990** SD: 16 G. **1991** SD: 16 G. **1992** SD: 12 G. **1993** Phi: 10 G. **1994** Phi: 14 G. **1995** Den: 16 G. **1996** Den: 16 G. **Total:** 152 G.

TUFFY THOMPSON Thompson, Clarence Leonard 5'11", 172 **HB-DB-TB**
Col: North Dakota; Minnesota *HS:* Montevideo [MN] B: 9/28/1914, Montevideo, MN
1937 Pit: Pass 14-6 42.9%, 100 7.14 1 TD 4 Int; Rec 6-126 21.0 1 TD.
1938 Pit: Pass 7-0, 3 Int; Rec 9-55 6.1. **1939** GB: Rec 1-1 1.0.
Total: Pass 21-6 28.6%, 100 4.76 1 TD 7 Int; Rec 16-182 11.4 1 TD.

		Rushing				Tot
Year Team	**G**	**Att**	**Yds**	**Avg**	**TD**	**TD**
1937 Pit	7	43	80	1.9	0	1
1938 Pit	10	39	139	3.6	1	1
1939 GB	1	6	9	1.5	0	0
NFL Total	18	88	228	2.6	1	2

CRAIG THOMPSON Thompson, Craig Antonio 6'2", 244 **TE**
Col: North Carolina A&T *HS:* Hartsville [SC] B: 1/13/1969, Hartsville, SC *Drafted:* 1992 Round 5 Cin

Year Team	G	Receiving Rec	Yds	Avg	TD
1992 Cin	16	19	194	10.2	2
1993 Cin	13	17	87	5.1	1
NFL Total	29	36	281	7.8	3

DARRELL THOMPSON Thompson, Darrell Alexander 6'0", 215 **RB**
Col: Minnesota *HS:* John Marshall [Rochester, MN] B: 11/23/1967, Rochester, MN *Drafted:* 1990 Round 1 GB
1990 GB: KR 3-103 34.3 1 TD. **1991** GB: KR 7-127 18.1. **1993** GB: KR 9-171 19.0. **1994** GB: KR 4-67 16.8. **Total:** KR 23-468 20.3 1 TD.

Year Team	G	Rushing Att	Yds	Avg	TD	Receiving Rec	Yds	Avg	TD	Fum	Tot TD
1990 GB	16	76	264	3.5	1	3	1	0.3	0	1	2
1991 GB	13	141	471	3.3	1	7	71	10.1	0	1	1
1992 GB	7	76	254	3.3	2	13	129	9.9	1	2	3
1993 GB	16	169	654	3.9	3	18	129	7.2	0	2	3
1994 GB	8	2	-2	-1.0	0	0	0	—	0	0	0
NFL Total	60	464	1641	3.5	7	41	330	8.0	1	6	9

DAVE THOMPSON Thompson, David Dean 5'10", 215 **WB**
(Chubby) *Col:* Denison *HS:* Newark [OH] B: 11/17/1897 Deceased
1921 Cin: 1 G.

DAVID THOMPSON Thompson, David Farod 5'8", 196 **RB**
Col: Oklahoma State *HS:* Okmulgee [OK] B: 1/13/1975, Okmulgee, OK
1997 StL: Rush 16-30 1.9 1 TD. **Total:** Rush 16-30 1.9 1 TD.

Year Team	G	Kickoff Returns Ret	Yds	Avg	TD	Fum
1997 StL	11	49	1110	22.7	0	2
1998 StL	1	0	0	—	0	0
NFL Total	12	49	1110	22.7	0	2

DAVE THOMPSON Thompson, David Wayne 6'4", 270 **C-OT-OG**
Col: Clemson *HS:* Valley [Fairfax, AL] B: 2/1/1949, Langdale, AL *Drafted:* 1971 Round 2 Det
1971 Det: 14 G; PR 1-4 4.0. **1972** Det: 7 G; 1 Fum. **1973** Det: 14 G; 1 Fum. **1974** NO: 14 G. **1975** NO: 7 G; 1 Fum. **Total:** 56 G; PR 1-4 4.0; 3 Fum.

DEL THOMPSON Thompson, Delbert Ray 6'0", 203 **RB**
Col: Ranger Coll. TX (J.C.); Texas; Texas-El Paso *HS:* Hamlin [TX] B: 2/21/1958, Kermit, TX *Drafted:* 1982 Round 5 KC
1982 KC: 6 G; Rush 4-7 1.8; KR 2-41 20.5.

DON THOMPSON Thompson, Donald Wayne 6'4", 240 **DE**
Col: Ferrum; Richmond *HS:* Danville [VA] B: 10/7/1939, Danville, VA
1962 Bal: 10 G. **1963** Bal: 14 G. **1964** Phi: 3 G; KR 1-0. **Total:** 27 G; KR 1-0.

EMMUEL THOMPSON Thompson, Emmuel Lee 5'11", 180 **DB**
Col: Texas A&M–Kingsville *HS:* Booker T. Washington [Houston, TX] B: 11/15/1959, Houston, TX
1987 Hou: 3 G.

ERNIE THOMPSON Thompson, Ernie 5'11", 244 **RB**
Col: Indiana *HS:* North Vigo [Terre Haute, IN] B: 10/25/1969, Terre Haute, IN *Drafted:* 1991 Round 12 LARm
1991 LARm: 4 G; Rush 2-9 4.5; Rec 2-35 17.5 1 TD; 6 Pt. **1993** KC: 16 G; Rush 11-28 2.5; Rec 4-33 8.3. **Total:** 20 G; Rush 13-37 2.8; Rec 6-68 11.3 1 TD; 6 Pt.

GARY THOMPSON Thompson, Gary 6'0", 180 **DB**
Col: Coll of the Redwoods CA (J.C.); San Jose State *HS:* Eureka [CA] B: 2/23/1959, Castro Valley, CA
1983 Buf: 16 G. **1984** Buf: 8 G. **Total:** 24 G.

TINY THOMPSON Thompson, George Bryant 5'10", 233 **G**
Col: Syracuse *HS:* Luzerne [PA] B: 1899 Deceased
1922 Roch: 5 G.

GEORGE THOMPSON Thompson, George Delmar 6'1", 210 **G-T**
Col: Iowa *HS:* Fort Dodge [IA] B: 8/31/1899, Lehigh, IA D: 8/1965, IL
1923 RI: 7 G. **1924** RI: 9 G. **1925** RI: 11 G. **Total:** 27 G.

MARTY THOMPSON Thompson, Glenn Martin 6'3", 243 **TE**
Col: Fresno State *HS:* Mammoth Lakes [CA] B: 12/9/1969, Whittier, CA
1993 Det: 6 G; Rec 1-15 15.0.

HAL THOMPSON Thompson, Harold Charles 6'1", 205 **OE-DE**
Col: Delaware *HS:* Manasquan [NJ]; Franklin & Marshall Acad. [Lancaster, PA] B: 10/18/1922, Manasquan, NJ
AAFC **1947** BknA: 12 G; Rush 1-4 4.0; Rec 15-148 9.9. **1948** BknA: 9 G; Rec 4-37 9.3 1 TD; 6 Pt. **Total:** 21 G; Rush 1-4 4.0; Rec 19-185 9.7 1 TD; 6 Pt.

HARRY THOMPSON Thompson, Harry Julius 6'2", 226 **OG-DE-LB-DG**
(Sam) *Col:* Los Angeles City Coll. CA (J.C.); UCLA *HS:* Los Angeles [CA] B: 1/8/1926, Memphis, TN
1950 LARm: 12 G. **1951** LARm: 12 G. **1952** LARm: 12 G. **1953** LARm: 8 G; KR 1-0. **1954** LARm: 12 G. **1955** ChiC: 12 G. **Total:** 68 G; KR 1-0.

JACK THOMPSON Thompson, Jack Byron 6'3", 217 **QB**
(The Throwin' Samoan) *Col:* Washington State *HS:* Evergreen [Seattle, WA] B: 5/19/1956, Tutuwila, American Samoa *Drafted:* 1979 Round 1 Cin

Year Team	G	Passing Att	Comp	Comp%	Yds	YPA	TD	Int	Rating
1979 Cin	9	87	39	44.8	481	5.53	1	5	42.4
1980 Cin	14	234	115	49.1	1324	5.66	11	12	60.9
1981 Cin	8	49	21	42.9	267	5.45	1	2	50.3
1982 Cin	1	0	0	—	0	—	0	0	—
1983 TB	14	423	249	58.9	2906	6.87	18	21	73.3
1984 TB	5	52	25	48.1	337	6.48	2	5	42.4
NFL Total	51	845	449	53.1	5315	6.29	33	45	63.4

Year Team	Rushing Att	Yds	Avg	TD	Fum
1979 Cin	21	116	5.5	5	3
1980 Cin	18	84	4.7	1	5
1983 TB	26	27	1.0	0	10
1984 TB	5	35	7.0	0	1
NFL Total	70	262	3.7	6	19

JAMES THOMPSON Thompson, James III 6'0", 178 **WR**
Col: Memphis *HS:* Melrose [Memphis, TN] B: 1/9/1953, Memphis, TN
1978 NYG: 13 G; Rec 7-113 16.1; PR 2-4 2.0.

JIM THOMPSON Thompson, James L 6'3", 255 **DT**
Col: Southern Illinois *HS:* Peoria [IL] B: 12/4/1940, Peoria, IL
1965 Den: 4 G.

JESSE THOMPSON Thompson, Jesse III 6'1", 185 **WR**
Col: California *HS:* Merced [CA] B: 3/12/1956, Merced, CA *Drafted:* 1978 Round 6 Det
1978 Det: Rush 2-7 3.5; PR 16-161 10.1; KR 14-346 24.7. **1980** Det: Rush 1-(-4) -4.0. **Total:** Rush 3-3 1.0; PR 16-161 10.1; KR 14-346 24.7.

Year Team	G	Receiving Rec	Yds	Avg	TD	Fum
1978 Det	11	18	175	9.7	4	4
1980 Det	11	11	137	12.5	0	1
NFL Total	22	29	312	10.8	4	5

JOHNNY THOMPSON Thompson, John Henry Jr. 5'10", 215 **G**
Col: Lafayette *HS:* Kiski School [Saltsburg, PA] B: 10/24/1905, Lykens, PA D: 5/27/1958
1929 Fra: 4 G.

RUSS THOMPSON Thompson, John Russell 6'5", 249 **T**
Col: Nebraska *HS:* Chadron [NE] B: 5/10/1912, Edgar, NE
1936 ChiB: 9 G. **1937** ChiB: 11 G. **1938** ChiB: 11 G. **1939** ChiB: 11 G. **1940** Phi: 11 G. **Total:** 53 G.

JOHN THOMPSON Thompson, John Washington Jr. 6'3", 228 **TE**
Col: Weber State; Utah State *HS:* Skyline [Oakland, CA] B: 1/18/1957, Jackson, MS *Drafted:* 1979 Round 9 GB
1979 GB: 16 G. **1980** GB: 7 G. **1981** GB: 2 G. **1982** GB: 9 G; Rec 2-24 12.0 2 TD; 12 Pt. **Total:** 34 G; Rec 2-24 12.0 2 TD; 12 Pt.

KEN THOMPSON Thompson, Kenneth Wayne 6'1", 178 **WR**
Col: San Diego Mesa Coll. CA (J.C.); West Texas A&M; Utah State *HS:* Snyder [TX] B: 12/6/1958, Snyder, TX
1982 StL: 1 G; Rec 1-5 5.0. **1983** StL: 5 G; Rec 2-31 15.5. **Total:** 6 G; Rec 3-36 12.0.

DONNELL THOMPSON Thompson, Lawrence Donnell 6'4", 270 **DE**
Col: North Carolina *HS:* Lumberton [NC] B: 10/27/1958, Lumberton, NC *Drafted:* 1981 Round 1 Bal
1981 Bal: 13 G. **1982** Bal: 9 G; 1 Sac. **1983** Bal: 14 G; Scor 1 Saf; 2 Pt; 4 Sac. **1984** Ind: 10 G; 4 Sac. **1985** Ind: 15 G; 5 Sac. **1986** Ind: 16 G; 4 Sac. **1987** Ind: 12 G; **1** Fum TD; 6 Pt; 5.5 Sac. **1988** Ind: 16 G; 3 Sac. **1989** Ind: 16 G; 7 Sac. **1990** Ind: 12 G; 1.5 Sac. **1991** Ind: 14 G; 5 Sac. **Total:** 147 G; Scor 1 Saf; 1 Fum TD; 8 Pt; 40 Sac.

LEONARD THOMPSON Thompson, Leonard Irwin 5'11", 192 **WR-HB**
Col: Arizona Western Coll. (J.C.); Oklahoma State *HS:* Pueblo [Tucson, CA] B: 7/28/1952, Oklahoma City, OK *Drafted:* 1975 Round 8 Det
1977 Det: Pass 1-0. **1978** Det: PR 3-19 6.3. **1979** Det: PR 9-117 13.0. **Total:** Pass 1-0; PR 12-136 11.3.

Year Team	G	Rushing Att	Yds	Avg	TD	Receiving Rec	Yds	Avg	TD
1975 Det	14	1	-12	-12.0	0	0	0	—	0
1976 Det	14	1	0	0.0	0	3	52	17.3	0
1977 Det	14	31	91	2.9	1	7	42	6.0	0

1978 Det	16	1	7	7.0	0	10	167	16.7	4
1979 Det	15	5	24	4.8	0	24	451	18.8	2
1980 Det	16	6	61	10.2	0	19	511	26.9	3
1981 Det	16	10	75	7.5	1	30	550	18.3	3
1982 Det	9	2	16	8.0	0	17	328	19.3	4
1983 Det	13	4	72	18.0	1	41	752	18.3	3
1984 Det	16	3	-7	-2.3	0	50	773	15.5	6
1985 Det	16	0	0	—	0	51	736	14.4	5
1986 Det	16	0	0	—	0	25	320	12.8	5
NFL Total	175	64	327	5.1	3	277	4682	16.9	35

	Kickoff Returns					Tot
Year Team	**Ret**	**Yds**	**Avg**	**TD**	**Fum**	**TD**
1975 Det	12	271	22.6	0	2	0
1976 Det	5	86	17.2	0	0	0
1977 Det	5	84	16.8	0	0	2
1978 Det	8	207	25.9	0	2	4
1979 Det	6	151	25.2	0	3	2
1980 Det	0	0	—	0	1	3
1981 Det	0	0	—	0	1	4
1982 Det	0	0	—	0	0	4
1983 Det	0	0	—	0	2	4
1984 Det	0	0	—	0	1	6
1985 Det	0	0	—	0	0	5
1986 Det	0	0	—	0	0	5
NFL Total	36	799	22.2	0	12	39

MIKE THOMPSON Thompson, Michael John 6'4", 279 **DT**
Col: Wisconsin *HS:* Portage [WI] B: 12/22/1971, Portage, WI
Drafted: 1995 Round 4 Jac
1995 Jac: 2 G. **1998** Cin: 10 G; 0.5 Sac. **Total:** 12 G; 0.5 Sac.

NORM THOMPSON Thompson, Norman Jack 6'1", 180 **DB**
Col: Laney Coll. CA (J.C.); Utah *HS:* Galileo [San Francisco, CA]
B: 3/5/1945, San Francisco, CA *Drafted:* 1971 Round 1 StL
1971 StL: PR 5-27 5.4; KR 7-182 26.0. **1972** StL: **1** Fum TD. **1973** StL: PR 6-18 3.0. **1979** Bal: PR 1-40 40.0. **Total:** PR 12-85 7.1; KR 7-182 26.0; 1 Fum TD.

		Interceptions				Tot
Year Team	**G**	**Int**	**Yds**	**TD**	**Fum**	**TD**
1971 StL	14	4	45	0	4	0
1972 StL	12	1	5	0	0	2
1973 StL	11	0	0	0	0	0
1974 StL	12	6	190	1	1	1
1975 StL	14	7	141	1	0	1
1976 StL	13	4	83	0	0	0
1977 Bal	14	3	39	0	0	0
1978 Bal	13	6	52	0	0	0
1979 Bal	12	2	38	0	0	0
NFL Total	115	33	593	2	5	4

ROCKY THOMPSON Thompson, Ralph Gary 5'11", 200 **RB**
(AKA Ralph Gary Symonds-Thompson) *Col:* Hartnell Coll. CA (J.C.); West Texas A&M *HS:* American [Yokohama, Japan]; Marshall HS [Chicago, IL] B: 11/8/1947, Paget, Bermuda *Drafted:* 1971 Round 1 NYG
1971 NYG: Rec 16-85 5.3. **Total:** Rec 16-85 5.3.

		Rushing				Kickoff Returns					Tot
Year Team	**G**	**Ret**	**Yds**	**Avg**	**TD**	**Ret**	**Yds**	**Avg**	**TD**	**Fum**	**TD**
1971 NYG	14	54	177	3.3	1	36	947	26.3	1	5	2
1972 NYG	14	9	35	3.9	0	29	821	28.3	**1**	3	1
1973 NYG	1	5	5	1.0	0	0	0	—	0	0	0
NFL Total	29	68	217	3.2	1	65	1768	27.2	2	8	3

REYNA THOMPSON Thompson, Reyna Onald 6'0", 194 **DB**
Col: Baylor *HS:* Thomas Jefferson [Dallas, TX] B: 8/28/1963, Dallas, TX *Drafted:* 1986 Round 9 Mia
1986 Mia: 16 G; PR 1-0; 1 Fum. **1987** Mia: 9 G. **1988** Mia: 16 G.
1989 NYG: 16 G. **1990** NYG: 16 G; 1 Sac. **1991** NYG: 12 G. **1992** NYG: 16 G; Int 2-69 1 TD; 6 Pt. **1993** NE: 15 G; Int 1-4; 1 Sac. **Total:** 116 G; PR 1-0; Int 3-73 1 TD; 6 Pt; 1 Fum; 2 Sac.

RICKY THOMPSON Thompson, Ricky Don 6'0", 176 **WR**
Col: Baylor *HS:* Gatesville [TX] B: 5/15/1954, El Paso, TX
Drafted: 1976 Round 8 Bal
1980 Was: KR 1-0. **Total:** KR 1-0.

		Receiving			
Year Team	**G**	**Rec**	**Yds**	**Avg**	**TD**
1976 Bal	9	1	11	11.0	0
1977 Bal	5	1	15	15.0	0
1978 Was	16	23	350	15.2	1
1979 Was	15	22	368	16.7	4
1980 Was	16	22	313	14.2	5
1981 Was	16	28	423	15.1	4
1982 StL	3	0	0	—	0
NFL Total	80	97	1480	15.3	14

ROBERT THOMPSON Thompson, Robert Charles 6'3", 227 **LB**
Col: Michigan *HS:* Dwight D. Eisenhower [Blue Island, IL] B: 2/4/1960, Chicago, IL *Drafted:* 1983 Round 8 Hou
1983 TB: 10 G. **1984** TB: 9 G. **1987** Det: 3 G; 2 Sac. **Total:** 22 G; 2 Sac.

DON THOMPSON Thompson, Robert Donald 6'2", 205 **G**
(Tommy) *Col:* Redlands B: 12/29/1903 D: 8/1973, Los Angeles, CA
1926 LA: 10 G; Int **1** TD; 1 Fum TD; Tot TD 2; 12 Pt.

BOB THOMPSON Thompson, Robert Lee 5'9", 170 **WR**
Col: Youngstown State *HS:* Cooper City [FL] B: 9/9/1962, Hollywood, FL *Drafted:* 1986 Round 6 NO
1987 Den: 2 G.

BOBBY THOMPSON Thompson, Robert Lee 5'11", 188 **DB**
Col: Compton CC CA; Arizona *HS:* Centennial [Compton, CA]
B: 3/30/1939, Minden, LA *Drafted:* 1962 Round 3 Det
1964 Det: PR 1-27 27.0. **1967** Det: PR 9-20 2.2. **1969** NO: PR 4-25 6.3.
Total: PR 14-72 5.1.

		Kickoff Returns				Interceptions			
Year Team	**G**	**Ret**	**Yds**	**Avg**	**TD**	**Int**	**Yds**	**TD**	**Fum**
1964 Det	14	1	24	24.0	0	3	45	0	0
1965 Det	11	0	0	—	0	2	3	0	0
1966 Det	14	0	0	—	0	4	52	0	0
1967 Det	12	4	134	33.5	0	0	0	0	2
1968 Det	14	17	363	21.4	0	0	0	0	0
1969 NO	7	5	101	20.2	0	1	2	0	1
NFL Total	72	27	622	23.0	0	10	102	0	3

STEVE THOMPSON Thompson, Stephen Merall 6'5", 250 **DT-DE**
Col: Washington *HS:* Lake Stevens [WA] B: 2/12/1945, Seattle, WA
Drafted: 1968 Round 2 NYJ
1968 NYJ: 4 G. **1969** NYJ: 14 G. **1970** NYJ: 12 G. **1972** NYJ: 5 G.
1973 NYJ: 8 G. **Total:** 43 G.

STEVE THOMPSON Thompson, Steven Kenneth 6'2", 275 **DT**
Col: Minnesota *HS:* Aurora West [IL] B: 6/24/1965, Aurora, IL
1987 Was: 1 G; 1 Sac.

TED THOMPSON Thompson, Ted Clarence 6'1", 220 **LB**
Col: Southern Methodist *HS:* Atlanta [TX] B: 1/17/1953, Atlanta, TX
1975 Hou: 14 G; KR 1-(-5) -5.0; 1 Fum. **1976** Hou: 14 G. **1977** Hou: 14 G; KR 1-9 9.0. **1978** Hou: 16 G. **1979** Hou: 16 G. **1980** Hou: 15 G; Scor 4, 4-4 100.0% XK. **1981** Hou: 16 G. **1982** Hou: 9 G. **1983** Hou: 16 G; 1 Sac.
1984 Hou: 16 G; KR 1-16 16.0; Int 0-5. **Total:** 146 G; KR 3-20 6.7; Int 0-5; Scor 4, 4-4 100.0% XK; 1 Fum; 1 Sac.

TOMMY THOMPSON Thompson, Thomas Lee 6'1", 205 **RB**
Col: Northwest Mississippi CC; Southern Illinois *HS:* Central [Oxford, MS] B: 9/22/1951, Oxford, MS
1974 SD: 12 G; Rush 6-8 1.3; KR 12-242 20.2.

TOMMY THOMPSON Thompson, Thomas Pryor 6'1", 192 **QB**
Col: Tulsa *HS:* R.L. Paschal [Fort Worth, TX] B: 8/15/1916, Hutchinson, KS D: 4/21/1989, Calico Rock, AR
1940 Pit: Rec 4-55 13.8. **1941** Phi: Rec 4-30 7.5 1 TD; PR 5-27 5.4; KR 1-23 23.0; Punt 1-43 43.0. **1942** Phi: PR 8-60 7.5; KR 5-76 15.2.
Total: Rec 8-85 10.6 1 TD; PR 13-87 6.7; KR 6-99 16.5; Punt 1-43 43.0.

		Passing							
Year Team	**G**	**Att**	**Comp**	**Comp%**	**Yds**	**YPA**	**TD**	**Int**	**Rating**
1940 Pit	11	28	9	32.1	145	5.18	1	3	22.8
1941 Phi	11	162	86	53.1	959	5.92	8	14	51.4
1942 Phi	11	203	95	46.8	1410	6.95	8	16	50.3
1945 Phi	8	28	15	53.6	146	5.21	0	**2**	38.7
1946 Phi	10	103	57	**55.3**	745	7.23	6	9	61.3
1947 Phi	12	201	106	52.7	1680	8.36	16	15	76.3
1948 Phi	12	246	141	57.3	1965	7.99	**25**	11	98.4
1949 Phi	12	214	116	54.2	1727	8.07	16	11	84.4
1950 Phi	12	239	107	44.8	1608	6.73	11	22	44.4
NFL Total	99	1424	732	51.4	10385	7.29	91	103	66.5

	Rushing				Interceptions				Tot
Year Team	**Att**	**Yds**	**Avg**	**TD**	**Int**	**Yds**	**TD**	**Fum**	**TD**
1940 Pit	40	39	1.0	0	3	23	0	0	0
1941 Phi	54	-2	0.0	0	3	24	0	0	1
1942 Phi	92	-32	-0.3	1	4	28	0	0	1
1945 Phi	8	-13	-1.6	0	2	33	0	3	0
1946 Phi	34	-116	-3.4	0	0	0	0	8	0
1947 Phi	23	52	2.3	2	0	0	0	6	2
1948 Phi	12	46	3.8	1	0	0	0	0	1
1949 Phi	15	17	1.1	2	0	0	0	4	2
1950 Phi	15	34	2.3	0	0	0	0	3	0
NFL Total	293	25	0.1	6	12	108	0	24	7

TOMMY THOMPSON Thompson, Thomas Wright 6'1", 221 **LB-C**
Col: William & Mary *HS:* Woodbridge [NJ] B: 1/6/1927, Jersey City, NJ
D: 10/1/1990, Baltimore, MD *Drafted:* 1948 Round 2 Was
AAFC **1949** CleA: 9 G; Int 1-9.

NFL **1950** Cle: 12 G. **1951** Cle: 12 G; Int 2-23. **1952** Cle: 12 G; Int 1-21. **1953** Cle: 9 G; Int 2-13. **Total:** 45 G; Int 5-57.

TOMMY THOMPSON Thompson, Tommy Ralph 5′10″, 192 **P**
Col: Oregon *HS:* Lompoc [CA] B: 4/27/1972, Lompoc, CA

		Punting		
Year Team	**G**	**Punts**	**Yds**	**Avg**
1995 SF	16	57	2312	40.6
1996 SF	16	73	3217	44.1
1997 SF	16	78	3182	40.8
NFL Total	48	208	8711	41.9

LEROY THOMPSON Thompson, Ulys Leroy 5′10″, 217 **RB**
Col: Penn State *HS:* Austin-East [Knoxville, TN] B: 2/3/1968, Knoxville, TN *Drafted:* 1991 Round 6 Pit

		Rushing				Receiving			
Year Team	**G**	**Att**	**Yds**	**Avg**	**TD**	**Rec**	**Yds**	**Avg**	**TD**
1991 Pit	13	20	60	3.0	0	14	118	8.4	0
1992 Pit	15	35	157	4.5	1	22	278	12.6	0
1993 Pit	15	205	763	3.7	3	38	259	6.8	0
1994 NE	16	102	312	3.1	2	65	465	7.2	5
1995 KC	16	28	73	2.6	0	9	37	4.1	0
1996 TB	5	14	25	1.8	0	5	36	7.2	0
NFL Total	80	404	1390	3.4	6	153	1193	7.8	5

	Kickoff Returns					Tot
Year Team	**Ret**	**Yds**	**Avg**	**TD**	**Fum**	**TD**
1991 Pit	1	8	8.0	0	1	0
1992 Pit	2	51	25.5	0	2	1
1993 Pit	4	77	19.3	0	7	3
1994 NE	18	376	20.9	0	2	7
1995 KC	6	152	25.3	0	0	0
NFL Total	31	664	21.4	0	12	11

VINCE THOMPSON Thompson, Vincent 6′0″, 230 **RB**
Col: Villanova *HS:* Woodrow Wilson [Levittown, PA] B: 2/21/1957, Trenton, NJ
1981 Det: Rec 4-40 10.0. **1983** Det: Rec 4-16 4.0. **Total:** Rec 8-56 7.0.

		Rushing				
Year Team	**G**	**Att**	**Yds**	**Avg**	**TD**	**Fum**
1981 Det	13	35	211	6.0	1	1
1983 Det	10	40	138	3.5	1	1
NFL Total	23	75	349	4.7	2	2

WARREN THOMPSON Thompson, Warren Keith 6′3″, 241 **LB**
Col: Independence CC KS; Oklahoma State *HS:* Garfield [Dale City, VA] B: 4/13/1963, Birmingham, AL
1987 NYG: 3 G; 2 Sac.

BILL THOMPSON Thompson, William 182 **C**
Col: No College *HS:* Englewood [Chicago, IL] B: 1907 Deceased
1925 Mil: 1 G.

BILLY THOMPSON Thompson, William Allen 6′1″, 201 **DB**
Col: Maryland East. Shore *HS:* Sterling [Greenville, SC] B: 10/10/1946, Greenville, SC *Drafted:* 1969 Round 3 Den
1973 Den: **1** Fum TD. **1978** Den: 1 Fum TD. **1979** Den: **1** Fum TD. **1980** Den: **1** Fum TD. **Total:** 4 Fum TD.

		Punt Returns				Kickoff Returns			
Year Team	**G**	**Ret**	**Yds**	**Avg**	**TD**	**Ret**	**Yds**	**Avg**	**TD**
1969 Den	14	25	288	**11.5**	0	18	513	**28.5**	0
1970 Den	9	23	233	10.1	0	9	188	20.9	0
1971 Den	14	29	274	9.4	0	5	105	21.0	0
1972 Den	8	4	82	20.5	0	0	0	—	0
1973 Den	14	30	**366**	12.2	0	1	25	25.0	0
1974 Den	14	26	350	13.5	0	13	325	25.0	0
1975 Den	14	13	158	12.2	0	0	0	—	0
1976 Den	14	6	60	10.0	0	0	0	—	0
1977 Den	14	0	0	—	0	0	0	—	0
1978 Den	16	1	3	3.0	0	0	0	—	0
1979 Den	16	0	0	—	0	0	0	—	0
1980 Den	16	0	0	—	0	0	0	—	0
1981 Den	16	0	0	—	0	0	0	—	0
NFL Total	179	157	1814	11.6	0	46	1156	25.1	0

	Interceptions				Tot
Year Team	**Int**	**Yds**	**TD**	**Fum**	**TD**
1969 Den	3	92	1	4	1
1970 Den	2	65	0	1	0
1971 Den	5	83	0	5	0
1972 Den	1	4	0	0	0
1973 Den	3	96	1	2	2
1974 Den	5	105	1	1	1
1975 Den	2	97	0	1	0
1977 Den	5	122	0	0	0
1978 Den	4	0	0	0	1
1979 Den	4	57	0	0	1
1980 Den	2	49	0	0	1
1981 Den	4	14	0	0	0
NFL Total	40	784	3	14	7

WEEGIE THOMPSON Thompson, Willis Hope 6′6″, 212 **WR**
Col: Florida State *HS:* Midlothian [VA] B: 3/21/1961, Pensacola, FL
Drafted: 1984 Round 4 Pit
1989 Pit: KR 4-41 10.3. **Total:** KR 4-41 10.3.

		Receiving				
Year Team	**G**	**Rec**	**Yds**	**Avg**	**TD**	**Fum**
1984 Pit	16	17	291	17.1	3	1
1985 Pit	16	8	138	17.3	1	0
1986 Pit	16	17	191	11.2	5	0
1987 Pit	12	17	313	18.4	1	0
1988 Pit	16	16	370	23.1	1	0
1989 Pit	16	4	74	18.5	0	0
NFL Total	92	79	1377	17.4	11	1

ART THOMS Thoms, Arthur William Jr. 6′5″, 260 **DT**
Col: Syracuse *HS:* Brick Twp. [Brick Town, NJ] B: 10/20/1946, Teaneck, NJ *Drafted:* 1969 Round 1 Oak
1969 Oak: 12 G. **1970** Oak: 6 G; KR 2-30 15.0. **1971** Oak: 14 G. **1972** Oak: 14 G; Int 1-0. **1973** Oak: 13 G. **1974** Oak: 14 G; 1 Fum TD; 6 Pt. **1975** Oak: 13 G; Int 1-0. **1977** Phi: 12 G. **Total:** 98 G; KR 2-30 15.0; Int 2-0; 1 Fum TD; 6 Pt.

FRED THOMSEN Thomsen, Frederick Charles 5′11″, 180 **E**
Col: Nebraska *HS:* Minden [AR] B: 4/25/1897, Minden, AR
D: 1/7/1986, Springfield, MO
1924 RI: 9 G.

BOB THORNBLADH Thornbladh, Robert N.M. 6′1″, 220 **LB**
Col: Michigan *HS:* Plymouth [MI] B: 9/19/1952, Cleveland, OH
Drafted: 1974 Round 11 KC
1974 KC: 14 G.

TINY THORNHILL Thornhill, Claudis Earl 5′11″, 185 **T**
Col: Pittsburgh *HS:* Beaver [PA] B: 4/14/1893, Richmond, VA
D: 6/28/1956, Berkeley, CA
1920 Cle-Buf: 10 G. Cle: 8 G. Buf: 2 G. **Total:** 10 G.

BRUCE THORNTON Thornton, Bruce Edward 6′5″, 263 **DE-DT**
Col: Illinois *HS:* Chadsey [Detroit, MI] B: 2/14/1958, Detroit, MI
Drafted: 1979 Round 8 Dal
1979 Dal: 16 G; Int 1-3. **1980** Dal: 13 G. **1981** Dal: 12 G. **1982** StL: 6 G; 1 Sac. **Total:** 47 G; Int 1-3; 1 Sac.

BUBBA THORNTON Thornton, Charles Garland 6′0″, 174 **WR**
Col: Navarro Coll. TX (J.C.); Texas Christian *HS:* Keller [TX]
B: 3/9/1947, Fort Worth, TX *Drafted:* 1969 Round 14 Buf
1969 Buf: Rec 14-134 9.6.

		Kickoff Returns				
Year Team	**G**	**Ret**	**Yds**	**Avg**	**TD**	**Fum**
1969 Buf	14	30	749	25.0	0	2

GEORGE THORNTON Thornton, George Renardo 6′3″, 300 **DT-DE-NT**
Col: Alabama *HS:* Jefferson Davis [Montgomery, AL] B: 4/27/1968, Montgomery, AL *Drafted:* 1991 Round 2 SD
1991 SD: 16 G. **1992** SD: 16 G; 2 Sac. **1993** NYG: 5 G. **Total:** 37 G; 2 Sac.

DICK THORNTON Thornton, Harry Richard 5′6″, 165 **BB-DB**
Col: Michigan; Missouri-Rolla *HS:* Nicholas Senn [Chicago, IL]
B: 2/4/1908, Chicago, IL D: 1/15/1973, Chicago, IL
1933 Phi: 4 G; Pass 13-2 15.4%, 52 4.00 4 Int; Rush 5-14 2.8; Rec 2-14 7.0.

JIM THORNTON Thornton, James Michael 6′2″, 242 **TE**
(Robocop) *Col:* Cal State-Fullerton *HS:* Analy [Sebastopol, CA]
B: 2/8/1965, Santa Rosa, CA *Drafted:* 1988 Round 4 ChiB
1989 ChiB: Rush 1-4 4.0. **1994** NYJ: KR 1-0. **Total:** Rush 1-4 4.0; KR 1-0.

		Receiving				
Year Team	**G**	**Rec**	**Yds**	**Avg**	**TD**	**Fum**
1988 ChiB	16	15	135	9.0	0	1
1989 ChiB	16	24	392	16.3	3	2
1990 ChiB	16	19	254	13.4	1	1
1991 ChiB	16	17	278	16.4	1	1
1993 NYJ	13	12	108	9.0	2	0
1994 NYJ	15	20	171	8.6	0	0
1995 Hou	4	0	0	—	0	0
NFL Total	96	107	1338	12.5	7	5

JOHN THORNTON Thornton, John Earvin Jr. 6′3″, 303 **DT**
Col: Cincinnati *HS:* Beecher [Flint, MI] B: 6/28/1969, Flint, MI
1991 Cle: 5 G; 1 Sac.

JACK THORNTON Thornton, Lawrence Jackson 6'1", 230 **LB**
Col: Auburn *HS:* Washington [GA] B: 4/23/1944
1966 Mia: 6 G.

REGGIE THORNTON Thornton, Reginald Orlando 5'10", 170 **WR**
Col: Bowling Green State *HS:* MacKenzie [Detroit, MI] B: 9/26/1967, Detroit, MI *Drafted:* 1990 Round 5 Min
1991 Ind: 5 G; Rec 1-38 38.0. **1993** Cin: 1 G. **Total:** 6 G; Rec 1-38 38.0.

RUPE THORNTON Thornton, Rupert Vance 5'10", 205 **G-T**
Col: Santa Clara *HS:* Franklin [Portland, OR] B: 1/5/1920, Denver, CO
AAFC **1946** SF-A: 11 G. **1947** SF-A: 14 G; PR 1-32 32.0. **Total:** 25 G; PR 1-32 32.0.

SIDNEY THORNTON Thornton, Sidney 5'11", 230 **RB**
Col: Northwestern State-Louisiana *HS:* Capitol [Baton Rouge, LA]
B: 9/2/1954, New Orleans, LA *Drafted:* 1977 Round 2 Pit
1978 Pit: KR 1-37 37.0. **1980** Pit: KR 1-15 15.0. **1981** Pit: KR 1-1 1.0.
Total: KR 3-53 17.7.

		Rushing				Receiving					Tot
Year Team	**G**	**Att**	**Yds**	**Avg**	**TD**	**Rec**	**Yds**	**Avg**	**TD**	**Fum**	**TD**
1977 Pit	13	27	103	3.8	2	1	5	5.0	0	1	2
1978 Pit	16	71	264	3.7	2	5	66	13.2	1	3	3
1979 Pit	13	118	585	5.0	6	16	231	14.4	4	7	10
1980 Pit	12	78	325	4.2	3	15	131	8.7	1	5	4
1981 Pit	16	56	202	3.6	4	8	78	9.8	0	6	4
1982 Pit	4	6	33	5.5	1	1	4	4.0	0	0	1
NFL Total	74	356	1512	4.2	18	46	515	11.2	6	22	24

BILL THORNTON Thornton, William Albert 6'1", 215 **FB**
(Thunder) *Col:* Nebraska *HS:* Edward D. Libbey [Toledo, OH]
B: 9/20/1939, Toledo, OH *Drafted:* 1963 Round 5 StL
1963 StL: Rec 4-10 2.5; KR 4-70 17.5. **1964** StL: Rec 7-43 6.1; KR 1-5 5.0. **1965** StL: Rec 1-6 6.0. **1967** StL: Rec 1-9 9.0. **Total:** Rec 13-68 5.2; KR 5-75 15.0.

		Rushing				
Year Team	**G**	**Att**	**Yds**	**Avg**	**TD**	**Fum**
1963 StL	14	19	111	5.8	1	0
1964 StL	13	39	236	6.1	1	4
1965 StL	14	31	188	6.1	0	0
1967 StL	6	4	9	2.3	0	0
NFL Total	47	93	544	5.8	2	4

DON THORP Thorp, Donald Kevin 6'4", 260 **NT-DE**
Col: Illinois *HS:* Buffalo Grove [IL] B: 7/10/1962, Chicago, IL
Drafted: 1984 Round 6 NO
1984 NO: 5 G. **1987** Ind: 5 G; 3 Sac. **1988** Ind-KC: 4 G. Ind: 1 G. KC: 3 G.
Total: 14 G; 3 Sac.

JACK THORPE Thorpe, Jack 6'0", 210 **C-G-T-WB**
(AKA Deadeye) *Col:* No College B: 1899 Deceased
1923 Oor: 8 G.

JIM THORPE Thorpe, James Francis 6'1", 202 **TB-OE-FB**
(AKA Bright Path) *Col:* Carlisle *HS:* Carlisle Indian School [PA]
B: 5/28/1887, Prague, OK D: 3/28/1953, Lomita, CA *HOF:* 1963
1920 Can: 9 G. **1921** Cle: 5 G; Pass 1 TD; Rush 1 TD; Scor 11, 1 FG, 2 XK. **1922** Oor: 5 G; Pass 1 TD; Rush 3 TD; 18 Pt. **1923** Oor: 9 G; Pass 1 TD; Scor 3, 1 FG. **1924** RI: 9 G; Pass 1 TD; Scor 7, 2 FG, 1 XK.
1925 NYG-RI: 5 G. NYG: 3 G. RI: 2 G. **1926** Can: 9 G; Rush 2 TD; 12 Pt.
1928 ChiC: 1 G. **Total:** 52 G; Pass 4 TD; Rush 6 TD; Scor 51, 4 FG, 3 XK.

WILFRED THORPE Thorpe, Wilfred Egner 6'3", 205 **G-LB-DE**
Col: Arkansas *HS:* Little Rock Central [AR] B: 1/8/1917, Little Rock, AR D: 1/17/1998, Little Rock, AR *Drafted:* 1940 Round 9 Cle
1941 Cle: 5 G; Int 1-5. **1942** Cle: 11 G; Int 1-5. **Total:** 16 G; Int 2-10.

JAMES THRASH Thrash, James 6'0", 200 **WR**
Col: Missouri Southern State *HS:* Wewoka [OK] B: 4/28/1975, Denver, CO
1997 Was: 4 G; Rec 2-24 12.0. **1998** Was: 10 G; Rec 10-163 16.3 1 TD; KR 6-129 21.5; 6 Pt. **Total:** 14 G; Rec 12-187 15.6 1 TD; KR 6-129 21.5; 6 Pt.

BRUCE THREADGILL Threadgill, Bruce Craig 6'0", 190 **DB-QB**
Col: Mississippi State *HS:* New Iberia [LA] B: 5/7/1956, Nocona, TX
Drafted: 1978 Round 5 SF
1978 SF: 14 G; Pass 2-0, 2 Int.

JABBAR THREATS Threats, Anaphayus Jabbar 6'5", 268 **DE**
Col: Garden City CC KS; Michigan State *HS:* Springfield North [OH]
B: 4/26/1975, Springfield, OH
1997 Jac: 2 G. **1998** Jac: 2 G. **Total:** 4 G.

CLIFF THRIFT Thrift, Clifford Ray 6'1", 232 **LB**
Col: East Central (OK) *HS:* Purcell [OK] B: 5/3/1956, Dallas, TX
Drafted: 1979 Round 3 SD
1979 SD: 16 G; KR 1-11 11.0. **1980** SD: 15 G; Int 1-0. **1981** SD: 7 G.
1982 SD: 9 G; Int 2-16. **1983** SD: 6 G. **1984** SD: 16 G. **1985** ChiB: 16 G.
1986 LARm: 12 G. **Total:** 97 G; KR 1-11 11.0; Int 3-16.

JIM THROWER Thrower, James Fredrick 6'2", 195 **DB**
Col: Texas A&M-Commerce *HS:* Lincoln [Camden, AR] B: 11/6/1947, Camden, AR
1970 Phi: 5 G. **1971** Phi: 14 G; KR 12-299 24.9; 1 Fum. **1972** Phi: 5 G.
1973 Det: 10 G; KR 3-54 18.0. **1974** Det: 12 G. **Total:** 46 G; KR 15-353 23.5; 1 Fum.

WILLIE THROWER Thrower, Willie Lee 5'11", 182 **QB**
Col: Michigan State *HS:* New Kensington [PA] B: 3/22/1930, New Kensington, PA
1953 ChiB: 1 G; Pass 8-3 37.5%, 27 3.38 1 Int.

OWEN THUERK Thuerk, Owen 6'2", 192 **E**
Col: No College B: 2/5/1918
1941 Det: 3 G.

BAPTISTE THUNDER Thunder, Baptiste 5'10", 215 **T**
Col: No College B: MN Deceased
1922 Oor: 1 G.

BOB THURBON Thurbon, Robert William 5'10", 176 **HB-DB**
Col: Pittsburgh *HS:* Erie Acad. [PA] B: 2/22/1918, Erie, PA
AAFC **1946** BufA: 2 G; Rush 3-2 0.7; Rec 1-(-3) -3.0; KR 1-15 15.0.

NFL **1943** PhPt: Rec 6-100 16.7 1 TD; PR 2-19 9.5; KR 6-150 25.0; Int 1-3. **1944** ChPt: Rec 7-134 19.1 1 TD; PR 1-2 2.0; KR 12-291 24.3; Int 2-14; Punt 15-450 30.0. **Total:** Rec 13-234 18.0 2 TD; PR 3-21 7.0; KR 18-441 24.5; Int 3-17; Punt 15-450 30.0.

		Rushing				Tot
Year Team	**G**	**Att**	**Yds**	**Avg**	**TD**	**TD**
1943 PhPt	10	71	291	4.1	5	6
1944 ChPt	10	69	185	2.7	4	5
NFL Total	20	140	476	3.4	9	11

BRIAN THURE Thure, Brian Douglas 6'5", 300 **OT**
Col: California *HS:* Salinas [CA] B: 9/3/1973, Downey, CA
Drafted: 1995 Round 6 Was
1995 Was: 4 G.

STEVE THURLOW Thurlow, Stephen Charles 6'3", 222 **RB**
Col: Stanford *HS:* Escondido [CA] B: 4/25/1942, Long Beach, CA
Drafted: 1964 Round 2 NYG
1964 NYG: Pass 5-3 60.0%, 65 13.00. **1965** NYG: Pass 1-1 100.0%, 49 49.00; KR 1-19 19.0. **Total:** Pass 6-4 66.7%, 114 19.00; KR 1-19 19.0.

		Rushing				Receiving					Tot
Year Team	**G**	**Att**	**Yds**	**Avg**	**TD**	**Rec**	**Yds**	**Avg**	**TD**	**Fum**	**TD**
1964 NYG	11	64	210	3.3	0	7	74	10.6	1	2	1
1965 NYG	14	106	440	4.2	4	9	54	6.0	1	4	5
1966 NYG-Was	13	80	260	3.3	0	23	165	7.2	0	2	0
1966 NYG	1	1	7	7.0	0	0	0	—	0	0	0
1966 Was	12	79	253	3.2	0	23	165	7.2	0	2	0
1967 Was	6	13	33	2.5	0	10	95	9.5	0	0	0
1968 Was	6	51	184	3.6	0	12	151	12.6	0	1	0
NFL Total	50	314	1127	3.6	4	61	539	8.8	2	9	6

DENNIS THURMAN Thurman, Dennis Lee 5'11", 176 **DB**
Col: USC *HS:* Santa Monica [CA] B: 4/13/1956, Los Angeles, CA
Drafted: 1978 Round 11 Dal
1978 Dal: PR 1-0; KR 3-42 14.0. **1982** Dal: KR 1-17 17.0. **1983** Dal: 1 Fum TD; 1 Sac. **1984** Dal: 1 Sac. **1985** Dal: 1 Sac. **Total:** PR 1-0; KR 4-59 14.8; 1 Fum TD; 3 Sac.

		Interceptions				Tot
Year Team	**G**	**Int**	**Yds**	**TD**	**Fum**	**TD**
1978 Dal	16	2	35	0	2	0
1979 Dal	16	1	0	0	0	0
1980 Dal	16	5	114	1	0	1
1981 Dal	16	9	187	0	0	0
1982 Dal	9	3	75	**1**	0	1
1983 Dal	16	6	49	0	0	1
1984 Dal	16	5	81	1	0	1
1985 Dal	16	5	21	**1**	0	1
1986 StL	16	0	0	0	0	0
NFL Total	137	36	562	4	2	5

JOHN THURMAN Thurman, John Cochran 6'1", 225 **T**
(Hackle) *Col:* Pennsylvania B: 2/9/1900 D: 3/5/1976, Pasadena, CA
1926 LA: 10 G.

JUNIOR THURMAN Thurman, Ulyses 6'0", 180 **DB**
Col: Santa Monica Coll. CA (J.C.); West Los Angeles Coll. CA (J.C.); USC
HS: Santa Monica [CA] B: 9/8/1964, Los Angeles, CA
1987 NO: 3 G.

FUZZY THURSTON Thurston, Frederick Charles 6'1", 247 OG
Col: Valparaiso *HS:* Altoona [WI] B: 12/29/1933, Altoona, WI
Drafted: 1956 Round 5 Phi
1958 Bal: 4 G. **1959** GB: 12 G. **1960** GB: 12 G. **1961** GB: 14 G. **1962** GB: 14 G. **1963** GB: 14 G. **1964** GB: 11 G. **1965** GB: 14 G. **1966** GB: 12 G. **1967** GB: 9 G. **Total:** 116 G.

JOHN TICE Tice, John 6'5", 242 TE
Col: Maryland *HS:* Central Islip [NY] B: 6/22/1960, Bayshore, NY
Drafted: 1983 Round 3 NO

		Receiving				
Year Team	G	Rec	Yds	Avg	TD	Fum
1983 NO	16	7	33	4.7	1	0
1984 NO	10	6	55	9.2	1	0
1985 NO	16	24	266	11.1	2	0
1986 NO	16	37	330	8.9	3	1
1987 NO	12	16	181	11.3	6	0
1988 NO	15	26	297	11.4	1	0
1989 NO	15	9	98	10.9	1	0
1990 NO	16	11	113	10.3	0	1
1991 NO	15	22	230	10.5	0	1
1992 NO	3	0	0	—	0	0
NFL Total	134	158	1603	10.1	15	3

MIKE TICE Tice, Michael Peter 6'7", 246 TE
Col: Maryland *HS:* Central Islip [NY] B: 2/2/1959, Bayshore, NY
1983 Sea: KR 2-28 14.0. **1985** Sea: KR 1-17 17.0. **1986** Sea: KR 1-17 17.0. **1988** Sea: KR 1-17 17.0. **1991** Sea: KR 3-46 15.3. **Total:** KR 8-125 15.6.

		Receiving				
Year Team	G	Rec	Yds	Avg	TD	Fum
1981 Sea	16	5	47	9.4	0	0
1982 Sea	9	9	46	5.1	0	0
1983 Sea	15	0	0	—	0	0
1984 Sea	16	8	90	11.3	3	0
1985 Sea	9	2	13	6.5	0	0
1986 Sea	16	15	150	10.0	0	0
1987 Sea	12	14	106	7.6	2	0
1988 Sea	16	29	244	8.4	0	1
1989 Was	16	1	2	2.0	0	0
1990 Sea	5	0	0	—	0	0
1991 Sea	16	10	70	7.0	4	0
1992 Min	12	5	65	13.0	1	0
1993 Min	16	6	39	6.5	1	1
1995 Min	3	3	22	7.3	0	0
NFL Total	177	107	894	8.4	11	2

GLENN TIDD Tidd, Glenn E 5'11", 202 C-G-T-WB
Col: No College *HS:* Springfield [OH] B: 4/23/1894, Silvercreek Twp., Greene Co., OH D: 10/3/1970, Dayton, OH
1920 Day: 8 G. **1921** Day: 5 G. **1922** Day: 4 G; 1 Fum TD; 6 Pt. **1923** Day: 6 G. **1924** Day: 8 G; Int **1** TD; 6 Pt. **Total:** 31 G; Int 1 TD; 1 Fum TD; Tot TD 2; 12 Pt.

SAM TIDMORE Tidmore, Samuel Edward 6'1", 230 LB
Col: Ohio State *HS:* John Adams [Cleveland, OH] B: 10/28/1938, Decatur, IL *Drafted:* 1962 Round 6 Cle
1962 Cle: 13 G; KR 2-39 19.5. **1963** Cle: 5 G; KR 1-5 5.0. **Total:** 18 G; KR 3-44 14.7.

BILLY TIDWELL Tidwell, Billy Reyhne 5'9", 178 HB-DB
Col: Texas A&M *HS:* Hearne [TX] B: 8/3/1930, Hearne, TX
D: 12/19/1990, Trinity, TX *Drafted:* 1952 Round 3 SF
1954 SF: 10 G; Pass 1-0; Rush 1-1 1.0; PR 3-0; KR 10-287 28.7; 1 Fum.

TRAVIS TIDWELL Tidwell, Travis Vaughn 5'10", 190 QB
(Travelin' Trav) *Col:* Auburn *HS:* Woodlawn [Birmingham, AL]
B: 2/5/1925, Florence, AL *Drafted:* 1950 Round 1 NYG

		Passing							
Year Team	G	Att	Comp	Comp%	Yds	YPA	TD	Int	Rating
1950 NYG	8	55	25	45.5	338	6.15	4	3	67.1
1951 NYG	6	21	8	38.1	155	7.38	1	4	40.9
NFL Total	14	76	33	43.4	493	6.49	5	7	48.8

	Rushing				
Year Team	Att	Yds	Avg	TD	Fum
1950 NYG	29	133	4.6	2	3
1951 NYG	11	14	1.3	0	0
NFL Total	40	147	3.7	2	3

LEO TIERNEY Tierney, Clarence Leo III 6'3", 248 C
Col: Georgia Tech *HS:* Bishop David [Louisville, KY] B: 1/28/1954, San Antonio, TX *Drafted:* 1977 Round 12 Cle
1978 Cle-NYG: 7 G. Cle: 2 G. NYG: 5 G. **Total:** 7 G.

FESTUS TIERNEY Tierney, Festus Patrick 6'1", 198 G-T
Col: Minnesota *HS:* North [Minneapolis, MN] B: 7/1/1899, St. Paul, MN D: 8/14/1973, Minneapolis, MN
1922 Ham-Tol: 8 G. Ham: 6 G. Tol: 2 G. **1923** Min: 8 G. **1924** Min: 6 G. **1925** Mil: 3 G. **Total:** 25 G.

VAN TIFFIN Tiffin, Van Leigh 5'9", 155 K
Col: Alabama *HS:* Red Bay [AL] B: 9/6/1965, Tupelo, MS
1987 TB-Mia: 4 G; Scor 26, 5-7 71.4% FG, 11-11 100.0% XK. TB: 3 G; Scor 22, 5-6 83.3% FG, 7-7 100.0% XK. Mia: 1 G; Scor 4, 0-1 FG, 4-4 100.0% XK. **Total:** 4 G; Scor 26, 5-7 71.4% FG, 11-11 100.0% XK.

MARK TIGGES Tigges, Mark John 6'3", 290 OT
Col: North Iowa Area CC; Western Illinois *HS:* Central [Fenton, IA]
B: 2/5/1964, Algona, IA
1987 Cin: 3 G.

CALVIN TIGGLE Tiggle, Calvin Bernard 6'1", 235 LB
Col: Lees-McRae JC NC; Georgia Tech *HS:* Friendly [Fort Washington, MD] B: 11/10/1968, Fort Washington, MD *Drafted:* 1991 Round 7 TB
1991 TB: 16 G; 1 Sac. **1992** TB: 8 G. **Total:** 24 G; 1 Sac.

MIKE TILLEMAN Tilleman, Michael John 6'7", 272 DT
Col: Montana *HS:* Chinook [MT] B: 3/30/1944, Chinook, MT
Drafted: 1965 Round 12 Min
1966 Min: 12 G. **1967** NO: 14 G. **1968** NO: 14 G. **1969** NO: 14 G. **1970** NO: 14 G. **1971** Hou: 14 G. **1972** Hou: 14 G. **1973** Atl: 13 G. **1974** Atl: 12 G. **1975** Atl: 14 G. **1976** Atl: 14 G. **Total:** 149 G.

JIM TILLER Tiller, James Thomas 5'9", 165 HB
Col: Purdue *HS:* Fremont [OH] B: 12/21/1935, Fremont, OH
1962 NYT: Rec 13-108 8.3; PR 9-47 5.2; KR 22-462 21.0.

		Rushing				
Year Team	G	Att	Yds	Avg	TD	Fum
1962 NYT	11	31	43	1.4	0	6

MORGAN TILLER Tiller, Morgan John 6'1", 195 OE-DE
Col: Denver *HS:* Trinidad [CO] B: 10/13/1918, Trinidad, CO
D: 12/6/1983, Oakton, VA
1944 Bos: 4 G; KR 1-12 12.0. **1945** Pit: 10 G; Rec 10-146 14.6; KR 3-47 15.7. **Total:** 14 G; Rec 10-146 14.6; KR 4-59 14.8.

EMMETT TILLEY Tilley, Emmett 5'11", 240 LB
Col: Duke *HS:* Hillside [Durham, NC] B: 2/13/1961, Durham, NC
1983 Mia: 6 G.

PAT TILLEY Tilley, Patrick Lee 5'10", 178 WR
Col: Louisiana Tech *HS:* Fair Park [Shreveport, LA] B: 2/15/1953, Shreveport, LA *Drafted:* 1976 Round 4 StL
1978 StL: Rush 1-32 32.0. **Total:** Rush 1-32 32.0.

		Receiving				Punt Returns				
Year Team	G	Rec	Yds	Avg	TD	Ret	Yds	Avg	TD	Fum
1976 StL	13	26	407	15.7	1	15	146	9.7	0	2
1977 StL	14	5	64	12.8	0	13	111	8.5	0	1
1978 StL	16	62	900	14.5	3	2	8	4.0	0	1
1979 StL	16	57	938	16.5	6	0	0	—	0	0
1980 StL	14	68	966	14.2	6	0	0	—	0	0
1981 StL	16	66	1040	15.8	3	0	0	—	0	1
1982 StL	9	36	465	12.9	2	0	0	—	0	0
1983 StL	16	44	690	15.7	5	0	0	—	0	1
1984 StL	16	52	758	14.6	5	0	0	—	0	1
1985 StL	16	49	726	14.8	6	1	-1	-1.0	0	0
1986 StL	1	3	51	17.0	0	0	0	—	0	0
NFL Total	147	468	7005	15.0	37	31	264	8.5	0	7

ED TILLISON Tillison, Edward L 6'0", 225 FB
Col: Northwest Missouri State *HS:* Pearl River [LA] B: 2/12/1969, Pearl River, LA *Drafted:* 1992 Round 11 Det
1992 Det: 6 G; Rush 4-22 5.5; KR 1-27 27.0.

PETE TILLMAN Tillman, Alonzo Monroe 6'0", 210 C-LB
Col: Southwestern Oklahoma State; Oklahoma *HS:* Mangum [OK]
B: 5/9/1922, Mangum, OK
AAFC **1949** BalA: 11 G.

ANDRE TILLMAN Tillman, Andre 6'4", 230 TE
Col: Texas Tech *HS:* Hamilton Park [Dallas, TX] B: 11/1/1952, Dallas, TX *Drafted:* 1974 Round 2 Mia
1976 Mia: KR 1-0. **Total:** KR 1-0.

		Receiving				
Year Team	G	Rec	Yds	Avg	TD	Fum
1975 Mia	14	5	60	12.0	0	0
1976 Mia	14	13	130	10.0	1	0
1977 Mia	14	17	169	9.9	2	1
1978 Mia	16	31	398	12.8	3	0
NFL Total	58	66	757	11.5	6	1

CEDRIC TILLMAN Tillman, Cedric Carnel 6′2″, 204 **WR**
Col: Alcorn State *HS:* Gulfport [MS] B: 7/22/1970, Natchez, MS
Drafted: 1992 Round 11 Den
1995 Jac: PR 2-6 3.0. **Total:** PR 2-6 3.0.

Year Team	G	Receiving Rec	Yds	Avg	TD	Fum
1992 Den	9	12	211	17.6	1	0
1993 Den	14	17	193	11.4	2	1
1994 Den	16	28	455	16.3	1	1
1995 Jac	13	30	368	12.3	3	1
NFL Total	52	87	1227	14.1	7	3

FADDIE TILLMAN Tillman, Faddie Charles 6′5″, 235 **DT-DE**
Col: Arizona Western Coll. (J.C.); Boise State *HS:* Hamilton Park [Dallas, TX] B: 10/7/1948, Dallas, TX
1972 NO: 1 G.

LAWYER TILLMAN Tillman, Lawyer James Jr. 6′5″, 230 **WR**
Col: Auburn *HS:* John L. LeFlore [Mobile, AL] B: 5/20/1966, Mobile, AL *Drafted:* 1989 Round 2 Cle
1992 Cle: Rush 2-15 7.5. **Total:** Rush 2-15 7.5.

Year Team	G	Receiving Rec	Yds	Avg	TD	Fum	Tot TD
1989 Cle	14	6	70	11.7	2	0	3
1992 Cle	11	25	498	19.9	0	1	0
1993 Cle	7	5	68	13.6	1	0	1
1995 Car	5	2	22	11.0	0	0	0
NFL Total	37	38	658	17.3	3	1	4

LEWIS TILLMAN Tillman, Lewis Darnell 6′0″, 204 **RB**
Col: Jackson State *HS:* Hazelhurst [MS] B: 4/16/1966, Oklahoma City, OK *Drafted:* 1989 Round 4 NYG
1991 NYG: KR 2-29 14.5. **1995** ChiB: KR 1-20 20.0. **Total:** KR 3-49 16.3.

Year Team	G	Rushing Att	Yds	Avg	TD	Receiving Rec	Yds	Avg	TD	Fum
1989 NYG	16	79	290	3.7	0	1	9	9.0	0	1
1990 NYG	16	84	231	2.8	1	8	18	2.3	0	0
1991 NYG	16	65	287	4.4	1	5	30	6.0	0	2
1992 NYG	16	6	13	2.2	0	1	15	15.0	0	0
1993 NYG	16	121	585	4.8	3	1	21	21.0	0	1
1994 ChiB	16	275	899	3.3	7	27	222	8.2	0	1
1995 ChiB	13	29	78	2.7	0	0	0	—	0	0
NFL Total	109	659	2383	3.6	12	43	315	7.3	0	5

PAT TILLMAN Tillman, Patrick Daniel 5′11″, 204 **DB**
Col: Arizona State *HS:* Leland [San Jose, CA] B: 11/6/1976, Fremont, CA *Drafted:* 1998 Round 7 Ariz
1998 Ariz: 16 G; 1 Sac.

RUSTY TILLMAN Tillman, Russell Arthur 6′2″, 230 **LB**
Col: Arizona; Northern Arizona *HS:* Beloit [WI] B: 2/27/1946, Beloit, WI
1970 Was: 14 G; KR 1-10 10.0. **1971** Was: 9 G; KR 1-4 4.0; 1 Fum. **1972** Was: 14 G; KR 2-6 3.0. **1973** Was: 14 G; KR 3-42 14.0; 1 Fum. **1974** Was: 14 G; KR 1-10 10.0. **1975** Was: 14 G; KR 1-4 4.0. **1976** Was: 14 G; KR 1-14 14.0. **1977** Was: 14 G; KR 3-39 13.0. **Total:** 107 G; KR 13-129 9.9; 2 Fum.

SPENCER TILLMAN Tillman, Spencer Allen 5′11″, 206 **RB**
Col: Oklahoma *HS:* Thomas Edison [Tulsa, OK] B: 4/21/1964, Tulsa, OK *Drafted:* 1987 Round 5 Hou
1991 SF: Rec 2-3 1.5. **1993** Hou: Rec 1-4 4.0 1 TD. **Total:** Rec 3-7 2.3 1 TD.

Year Team	G	Rushing Ret	Yds	Avg	TD	Kickoff Returns Ret	Yds	Avg	TD	Fum	Tot TD
1987 Hou	5	12	29	2.4	1	1	0	0.0	0	1	1
1988 Hou	16	3	5	1.7	0	1	13	13.0	0	0	0
1989 SF	15	0	0	—	0	10	206	20.6	0	0	0
1990 SF	16	0	0	—	0	6	111	18.5	0	0	0
1991 SF	16	13	40	3.1	0	9	132	14.7	0	2	0
1992 Hou	16	1	1	1.0	0	10	157	15.7	0	2	0
1993 Hou	15	9	94	10.4	0	0	0	—	0	0	1
1994 Hou	16	2	12	6.0	0	4	51	12.8	0	1	0
NFL Total	115	40	181	4.5	1	41	670	16.3	0	6	2

TONY TILLMON Tillmon, Anthony Vinzell 5′10″, 170 **DB**
Col: Texas *HS:* Borger [TX] B: 9/12/1963, Borger, TX
1987 LARd: 3 G.

RON TILTON Tilton, Ronald John 6′4″, 250 **OG**
Col: Florida; Tulane *HS:* H.B. Plant [Tampa, FL] B: 8/9/1963, Homestead, FL
1986 Was: 7 G.

GEORGE TIMBERLAKE Timberlake, George Robert 6′1″, 220 **LB-OG**
Col: Long Beach City Coll. CA (J.C.); USC *HS:* Jordan [Long Beach, CA] B: 11/3/1932, Long Beach, CA *Drafted:* 1954 Round 3 GB
1955 GB: 6 G.

BOB TIMBERLAKE Timberlake, Robert W 6′4″, 220 **K**
Col: Michigan *HS:* Franklin [OH] B: 10/18/1943, Middletown, OH
Drafted: 1965 Round 3 NYG
1965 NYG: 13 G; Scor 24, 1-15 6.7% FG, 21-22 95.5% XK.

KEN TIMES Times, Kenneth 6′2″, 246 **NT-DT**
Col: Southern University *HS:* Deerfield Beach [FL] B: 1/1/1956, Deerfield Beach, FL *Drafted:* 1980 Round 5 SF
1980 SF: 3 G. **1981** StL: 2 G. **Total:** 5 G.

KIRK TIMMER Timmer, Kirk Richard 6′3″, 242 **LB**
Col: Montana State *HS:* Jefferson [Boulder, MT] B: 12/18/1963, Butte, MT
1987 Dal: 1 G.

ADAM TIMMERMAN Timmerman, Adam Larry 6′4″, 295 **OG**
Col: South Dakota State *HS:* Washington [Cherokee, IA] B: 8/14/1971, Cherokee, IA *Drafted:* 1995 Round 7 GB
1995 GB: 13 G. **1996** GB: 16 G. **1997** GB: 16 G. **1998** GB: 16 G. **Total:** 61 G.

CHARLIE TIMMONS Timmons, Charles Truman 5′10″, 210 **FB-LB**
(Cotton; Tuffy) *Col:* Clemson; Georgia *HS:* Abbeville [SC]
B: 2/8/1917, Piedmont, SC D: 3/27/1996, Greenville, SC
AAFC **1946** BknA: 13 G; Rush 23-65 2.8; Rec 1-4 4.0.

MICHAEL TIMPSON Timpson, Michael Dwain 5′10″, 178 **WR**
Col: Penn State *HS:* Hialeah-Miami Lakes [Hialeah, FL] B: 6/6/1967, Baxley, GA *Drafted:* 1989 Round 4 NE
1991 NE: Rush 1-(-4) -4.0. **1992** NE: PR 8-47 5.9. **1994** NE: Rush 2-14 7.0. **1995** ChiB: Rush 3-28 9.3 1 TD. **1996** ChiB: Rush 3-21 7.0. **Total:** Rush 9-59 6.6 1 TD; PR 8-47 5.9.

Year Team	G	Receiving Rec	Yds	Avg	TD	Kickoff Returns Ret	Yds	Avg	TD	Fum	Tot TD
1989 NE	2	0	0	—	0	2	13	6.5	0	1	0
1990 NE	5	5	91	18.2	0	3	62	20.7	0	0	0
1991 NE	16	25	471	18.8	2	2	37	18.5	0	2	2
1992 NE	16	26	315	12.1	1	2	28	14.0	0	0	1
1993 NE	16	42	654	15.6	2	0	0	—	0	1	2
1994 NE	15	74	941	12.7	3	1	28	28.0	0	0	3
1995 ChiB	16	24	289	12.0	2	18	420	23.3	0	1	3
1996 ChiB	15	62	802	12.9	0	0	0	—	0	2	0
1997 Phi	15	42	484	11.5	2	0	0	—	0	1	2
NFL Total	116	300	4047	13.5	12	28	588	21.0	0	8	13

TIM TINDALE Tindale, Timothy Scott 5′10″, 220 **FB**
Col: Western Ontario (Canada) *HS:* Saunders Secondary School [London, Canada] B: 4/15/1971, London, Canada
1995 Buf: 16 G; Rush 5-16 3.2; KR 6-62 10.3. **1996** Buf: 14 G; Rush 14-49 3.5; Rec 1-(-1) -1.0; 1 Fum. **1997** Buf: 7 G; Rec 4-105 26.3. **Total:** 37 G; Rush 19-65 3.4; Rec 5-104 20.8; KR 6-62 10.3; 1 Fum.

MICK TINGELHOFF Tingelhoff, Henry Michael 6′2″, 237 **C**
Col: Nebraska *HS:* Lexington [NE] B: 5/22/1940, Lexington, NE
1962 Min: 14 G. **1963** Min: 14 G. **1964** Min: 14 G. **1965** Min: 14 G. **1966** Min: 14 G; 1 Fum. **1967** Min: 14 G. **1968** Min: 14 G. **1969** Min: 14 G. **1970** Min: 14 G. **1971** Min: 14 G; 1 Fum. **1972** Min: 14 G. **1973** Min: 14 G. **1974** Min: 14 G; 1 Fum. **1975** Min: 14 G. **1976** Min: 14 G; 1 Fum. **1977** Min: 14 G. **1978** Min: 16 G. **Total:** 240 G; 4 Fum.

GERALD TINKER Tinker, Gerald Alexander 5′9″, 173 **WR**
Col: Memphis; Kent State *HS:* Coral Gables [FL] B: 1/19/1951, Miami, FL *Drafted:* 1974 Round 2 Atl
1974 Atl: Rush 2-5 2.5; Rec 1-12 12.0; PR 14-195 13.9 1 TD. **1975** Atl-GB: Rush 1-5 5.0; Rec 7-121 17.3 2 TD; PR 6-23 3.8. Atl: Rec 3-37 12.3 1 TD; PR 6-23 3.8. GB: Rush 1-5 5.0; Rec 4-84 21.0 1 TD. **Total:** Rush 3-10 3.3; Rec 8-133 16.6 2 TD; PR 20-218 10.9 1 TD.

Year Team	G	Kickoff Returns Ret	Yds	Avg	TD	Fum	Tot TD
1974 Atl	12	29	704	24.3	0	3	1
1975 Atl-GB	14	13	307	23.6	0	1	2
1975 Atl	8	13	307	23.6	0	1	1
1975 GB	6	0	0	—	0	0	1
NFL Total	26	42	1011	24.1	0	4	3

PETE TINSLEY Tinsley, Elijah Pope Jr. 5′8″, 205 **G-LB**
Col: Georgia *HS:* Spartanburg [GA] B: 3/16/1913, Sumter, SC
1938 GB: Postseason only. **1939** GB: Postseason only. **1941** GB: 9 G; Int 1-24. **1942** GB: 11 G; Int 1-3. **1943** GB: 10 G; Int 1-8. **1944** GB: 10 G. **1945** GB: 10 G; Int 1-6. **Total:** 50 G; Int 4-41.

GUS TINSLEY Tinsley, Gaynell Charles 6′1″, 198 **OE-DE**
Col: Louisiana State *HS:* Homer [LA] B: 2/1/1915, Ruple, LA
Drafted: 1937 Round 2 ChiC
1937 ChiC: Rush 1-2 2.0; 1 Fum TD. **1938** ChiC: Rush 4-26 6.5. **1940** ChiC: Rush 1-17 17.0; Int 2-10. **Total:** Rush 6-45 7.5; Int 2-10; 1 Fum TD.

Year Team	G	Receiving Rec	Yds	Avg	TD	Tot TD
1937 ChiC	11	36	**675**	18.8	5	6
1938 ChiC	11	**41**	516	12.6	1	1
1940 ChiC	7	16	165	10.3	1	1
NFL Total	29	93	1356	14.6	7	8

JESS TINSLEY Tinsley, Jess D 6'0", 201 **T-OE-DE**
Col: Louisiana State *HS:* Homer [LA] B: 10/18/1908
1929 ChiC: 12 G. **1930** ChiC: 10 G. **1931** ChiC: 6 G. **1932** ChiC: 10 G. **1933** ChiC: 11 G. **Total:** 49 G.

KEITH TINSLEY Tinsley, Keith Anthony 5'9", 184 **WR**
Col: Pittsburgh *HS:* Cooley [Detroit, MI] B: 3/31/1965, Detroit, MI
1987 Cle: 3 G; Rec 1-17 17.0; KR 2-31 15.5.

BUDDY TINSLEY Tinsley, Robert Porter Jr. 6'4", 245 **T**
Col: Baylor *HS:* Barbers Hill [Mont Belvieu, TX] B: 8/16/1924, Damon, TX
AAFC **1949** LA-A: 10 G.

SCOTT TINSLEY Tinsley, Scott 6'2", 195 **QB**
Col: USC *HS:* Putnam City West [Oklahoma City, OK] B: 11/14/1959, Oklahoma City, OK
1987 Phi: Rush 4-2 0.5.

Year Team	G	Passing Att	Comp	Comp%	Yds	YPA	TD	Int	Rating	Fum
1987 Phi	3	86	48	55.8	637	7.41	3	4	71.7	3

SID TINSLEY Tinsley, Sidney Wallace 5'9", 168 **HB-DB**
Col: Clemson *HS:* Spartanburg [SC] B: 1/14/1920, Spartanburg, SC
1945 Pit: Rush 5-3 0.6; Int 1-(-2).

Year Team	G	Punting Punts	Yds	Avg	Fum
1945 Pit	9	**57**	**2308**	40.5	1

ANDRE TIPPETT Tippett, Andre Bernard 6'3", 240 **LB**
Col: Iowa *HS:* Barringer [Newark, NJ] B: 12/27/1959, Birmingham, AL
Drafted: 1982 Round 2 NE
1982 NE: 9 G. **1983** NE: 15 G; 8.5 Sac. **1984** NE: 16 G; 18.5 Sac. **1985** NE: 16 G; **1** Fum TD; 6 Pt; 16.5 Sac. **1986** NE: 11 G; Int 0-32; 9.5 Sac. **1987** NE: 13 G; **1** Fum TD; 6 Pt; 12.5 Sac. **1988** NE: 12 G; 7 Sac. **1990** NE: 13 G; 3.5 Sac. **1991** NE: 16 G; Int 1-10; 8.5 Sac. **1992** NE: 14 G; 7 Sac. **1993** NE: 16 G; 8.5 Sac. **Total:** 151 G; Int 1-42; 2 Fum TD; 12 Pt; 100.0 Sac.

KEN TIPPINS Tippins, Kenneth 6'1", 235 **LB**
Col: Middle Tennessee State *HS:* Cook [Adel, GA] B: 7/22/1966, Adel, GA
1989 Dal: 6 G. **1990** Atl: 16 G. **1991** Atl: 16 G; Int 1-35; 1 Fum TD; 6 Pt; 1 Sac. **1992** Atl: 16 G; 3 Sac. **1993** Atl: 14 G. **1994** Atl: 16 G. **1995** Atl: 16 G; KR 1-15 15.0; Int 1-0. **Total:** 100 G; KR 1-15 15.0; Int 2-35; 1 Fum TD; 6 Pt; 4 Sac.

DAVE TIPTON Tipton, David Joseph 6'1", 255 **NT-DT**
Col: Western Illinois *HS:* Hobart [IN] B: 12/10/1953, Superior, WI
1975 NE: 4 G. **1976** NE: 8 G. **Total:** 12 G.

DAVE TIPTON Tipton, David Lance 6'6", 245 **DE-DT**
Col: Gavilan Coll. CA (J.C.); Stanford *HS:* San Benito [Hollister, CA]
B: 4/23/1949, Hollister, CA *Drafted:* 1971 Round 4 NYG
1971 NYG: 5 G. **1972** NYG: 14 G. **1973** NYG: 6 G. **1974** SD: 11 G. **1975** SD: 14 G. **1976** Sea: 12 G. **Total:** 62 G.

RICO TIPTON Tipton, Enrico A 6'2", 240 **LB**
Col: Washington State *HS:* Pittsburg [CA]; San Juan HS [Sacramento, CA] B: 7/31/1961, Pittsburg, CA
1987 Sea: 3 G.

HOWIE TIPTON Tipton, Howard Durward 5'11", 186 **G-OE-LB-DB**
Col: USC *HS:* Belmont [Los Angeles, CA] B: 4/19/1911, Los Angeles, CA D: 3/19/1966, San Bernardino Co., CA
1933 ChiC: Rec 5-106 21.2 1 TD. **1936** ChiC: Rec 1-15 15.0. **1937** ChiC: Rec 1-2 2.0. **Total:** Rec 7-123 17.6 1 TD.

Year Team	G	Rushing Att	Yds	Avg	TD
1933 ChiC	11	16	46	2.9	0
1934 ChiC	10	1	10	10.0	0
1935 ChiC	7	0	0	—	0
1936 ChiC	12	0	0	—	0
1937 ChiC	11	9	23	2.6	0
NFL Total	51	26	79	3.0	0

BOB TITCHENAL Titchenal, Robert Alden 6'2", 194 **LB-OE-C-DE**
Col: Glendale CC CA; San Jose State *HS:* Herbert Hoover [Glendale, CA]; Cumnock Prep [CA] B: 10/17/1917, Ventura, CA
AAFC **1946** SF-A: 14 G; Rush 1-2 2.0; Rec 7-160 22.9 2 TD; 12 Pt. **1947** LA-A: 14 G; Rush 1-0; Rec 7-97 13.9. **Total:** 28 G; Rush 2-2 1.0; Rec 14-257 18.4 2 TD; 12 Pt.

NFL **1940** Was: 11 G. **1941** Was: 11 G; Int 2-3. **1942** Was: 10 G; Rec 1-7 7.0; Int 1-19. **Total:** 32 G; Rec 1-7 7.0; Int 3-22.

GLEN TITENSOR Titensor, Glen Weston 6'4", 263 **OG-C**
Col: UCLA; Brigham Young *HS:* Bolsa Grande [Garden Grove, CA]
B: 2/21/1958, Bellflower, GA *Drafted:* 1981 Round 3 Dal
1981 Dal: 16 G. **1982** Dal: 4 G. **1983** Dal: 15 G. **1984** Dal: 15 G. **1985** Dal: 16 G. **1986** Dal: 16 G. **1988** Dal: 10 G. **Total:** 92 G.

HERB TITMAS Titmas, Herbert James 5'8", 185 **BB**
Col: Syracuse *HS:* Manlius Mil. Acad. [NY]; St.John's School [Manlius, NY] B: 12/14/1905 D: 8/16/1976, Cleveland, OH
1931 Prov: 11 G; Rec 1 TD; 6 Pt.

Y.A. TITTLE Tittle, Yelberton Abraham 6'0", 192 **QB**
(The Bald Eagle) *Col:* Louisiana State *HS:* Marshall [TX]
B: 10/24/1926, Marshall, TX *Drafted:* 1948 Round 1 Det *HOF:* 1971
AAFC.

Year Team	G	Passing Att	Comp	Comp%	Yds	YPA	TD	Int	Rating
1948 BalA	14	289	161	55.7	2522	8.73	16	9	90.3
1949 BalA	11	289	148	51.2	2209	7.64	14	18	66.8
AAFC Total	25	578	309	53.5	4731	8.19	30	27	78.6

Year Team	Rushing Att	Yds	Avg	TD
1948 BalA	52	157	3.0	4
1949 BalA	29	89	3.1	2
AAFC Total	81	246	3.0	6

NFL **1959** SF: Rec 1-4 4.0. **Total:** Rec 1-4 4.0.

Year Team	G	Passing Att	Comp	Comp%	Yds	YPA	TD	Int	Rating
1950 Bal	12	315	**161**	51.1	1884	5.98	8	19	52.9
1951 SF	12	114	63	55.3	808	7.09	8	9	68.2
1952 SF	12	208	106	51.0	1407	6.76	11	12	66.3
1953 SF	11	259	149	57.5	2121	8.19	20	16	84.1
1954 SF	12	295	170	57.6	2205	7.47	9	9	78.7
1955 SF	12	287	147	51.2	2185	7.61	**17**	28	56.6
1956 SF	10	218	124	56.9	1641	7.53	7	12	68.6
1957 SF	12	279	**176**	**63.1**	2157	7.73	13	15	80.0
1958 SF	11	208	120	57.7	1467	7.05	9	15	63.9
1959 SF	11	199	102	51.3	1331	6.69	10	15	58.0
1960 SF	9	127	69	54.3	694	5.46	4	**3**	70.8
1961 NYG	13	285	163	57.2	2272	7.97	17	12	85.3
1962 NYG	14	375	200	53.3	3224	8.60	**33**	20	89.5
1963 NYG	13	367	221	**60.2**	3145	**8.57**	**36**	14	104.8
1964 NYG	14	281	147	52.3	1798	6.40	10	22	51.6
NFL Total	178	3817	2118	55.5	28339	7.42	212	221	73.6

Year Team	Rushing Att	Yds	Avg	TD	Fum
1950 Bal	20	77	3.9	2	2
1951 SF	13	18	1.4	1	3
1952 SF	11	-11	-1.0	0	3
1953 SF	14	41	2.9	6	3
1954 SF	28	68	2.4	4	4
1955 SF	23	114	5.0	0	2
1956 SF	24	67	2.8	4	3
1957 SF	40	220	5.5	6	0
1958 SF	22	35	1.6	2	5
1959 SF	11	24	2.2	0	7
1960 SF	10	61	6.1	0	2
1961 NYG	25	85	3.4	3	0
1962 NYG	17	108	6.4	2	6
1963 NYG	18	99	5.5	2	5
1964 NYG	15	-7	-0.5	1	11
NFL Total	291	999	3.4	33	56

GEORGE TITUS Titus, George Timms 5'10", 185 **C-LB**
Col: Holy Cross *HS:* Brooklyn Prep [NY] B: 1/7/1922, Brooklyn, NY
Drafted: 1944 Round 8 Pit
1946 Pit: 11 G.

SI TITUS Titus, Silas John 6'0", 195 **C-LB-DE**
Col: Holy Cross *HS:* Brooklyn Prep [NY] B: 9/23/1918, Brooklyn, NY
D: 2/17/1989, Pittsburgh, PA
1940 Bkn: 4 G. **1941** Bkn: 6 G; Int 2-5. **1942** Bkn: 9 G. **1945** Pit: 9 G. **Total:** 28 G; Int 2-5.

CASEY TIUMALU Tiumalu, Casey James 5'8", 206 **RB**
Col: Grossmont Coll. CA (J.C.); Brigham Young *HS:* Helix [La Mesa, CA]
B: 6/19/1961, San Diego, CA
1987 LARm: 3 G; KR 8-158 19.8.

ROBBIE TOBECK Tobeck, Robert Lee 6′4″, 300 **C**
Col: Kilgore Coll. TX (J.C.); Washington State *HS:* New Port Richey [FL]
B: 3/6/1970, Tarpon Springs, FL
1994 Atl: 5 G. **1995** Atl: 16 G. **1996** Atl: 16 G; Rec 2-15 7.5 1 TD; 6 Pt.
1997 Atl: 16 G. **1998** Atl: 16 G. **Total:** 69 G; Rec 2-15 7.5 1 TD; 6 Pt.

DAVE TOBEY Tobey, David Morgan 6′3″, 231 **LB**
Col: Oregon *HS:* South Eugene [OR] B: 3/17/1943, Portland, OR
Drafted: 1965 Round 10 Pit
1966 Min: 14 G. **1967** Min: 2 G. **1968** Den: 7 G. **Total:** 23 G.

ELGIE TOBIN Tobin, Elza W 5′9″, 160 **BB**
(Yegg; Pat) *Col:* West Virginia; Penn State *HS:* California [Coal Center, PA] B: 5/1885 Deceased
1920 Akr: 1 G. **1921** Akr: 8 G. **Total:** 9 G.

REX TOBIN Tobin, Ernest V 1 **OE**
Col: No College *HS:* Cathedral [Duluth, MN] B: 2/1900, Duluth, MN
Deceased
1925 Dul: 1 G.

GEORGE TOBIN Tobin, George Edward 5′10″, 205 **G-LB**
Col: Notre Dame *HS:* Marianapolis Acad. [Thompson, CT]
B: 7/9/1921, Belmont, PA D: 1/2/1999, Farmington Hills, MI
1947 NYG: 11 G.

LEO TOBIN Tobin, Leaman 5′9″, 220 **G**
Col: Grove City *HS:* California [Coal Center, PA] B: 3/1890 Deceased
1921 Akr: 12 G; Scor 1, 1 XK.

STEVEN TOBIN Tobin, Steven Arthur 6′4″, 258 **C**
Col: Minnesota *HS:* Moorhead [MN] B: 3/29/1957, Breckenridge, MN
1980 NYG: 4 G.

BILL TOBIN Tobin, William Hugh 5′11″, 210 **HB**
Col: Missouri *HS:* Maryville [MO] B: 2/16/1941, Burlington Junction, MO *Drafted:* 1963 Round 14 SF
1963 Hou: Rec 13-173 13.3 1 TD; KR 1-10 10.0.

		Rushing					Tot
Year Team	G	Att	Yds	Avg	TD	Fum	TD
1963 Hou	10	75	271	3.6	4	3	5

NELSON TOBUREN Toburen, Nelson Edward 6′3″, 235 **LB**
Col: Wichita State *HS:* Colby [KS] B: 11/24/1938, Boulder, CO
Drafted: 1961 Round 14 GB
1961 GB: 14 G. **1962** GB: 10 G. **Total:** 24 G.

RICHARD TODD Todd, Carl Richard 6′2″, 207 **QB**
Col: Alabama *HS:* W.P. Davidson [Mobile, AL] B: 11/19/1953, Birmingham, AL *Drafted:* 1976 Round 1 NYJ
1981 NYJ: Rec 1-1 1.0. **Total:** Rec 1-1 1.0.

		Passing							
Year Team	G	Att	Comp	Comp%	Yds	YPA	TD	Int	Rating
1976 NYJ	13	162	65	40.1	870	5.37	3	12	33.2
1977 NYJ	12	265	133	50.2	1863	7.03	11	17	60.3
1978 NYJ	5	107	60	56.1	849	7.93	6	10	61.6
1979 NYJ	15	334	171	51.2	2660	**7.96**	16	22	66.5
1980 NYJ	16	479	264	55.1	3329	6.95	17	30	62.7
1981 NYJ	16	497	279	56.1	3231	6.50	25	13	81.8
1982 NYJ	9	261	153	58.6	1961	7.51	14	8	87.3
1983 NYJ	16	518	308	59.5	3478	6.71	18	26	70.3
1984 NO	15	312	161	51.6	2178	6.98	11	19	60.6
1985 NO	2	32	16	50.0	191	5.97	3	4	60.3
NFL Total	119	2967	1610	54.3	20610	6.95	124	161	67.6

	Rushing				
Year Team	Att	Yds	Avg	TD	Fum
1976 NYJ	28	107	3.8	1	5
1977 NYJ	24	46	1.9	2	4
1978 NYJ	14	18	1.3	0	1
1979 NYJ	36	93	2.6	5	7
1980 NYJ	49	330	6.7	5	10
1981 NYJ	32	131	4.1	0	5
1982 NYJ	13	-5	-0.4	1	4
1983 NYJ	35	101	2.9	0	5
1984 NO	28	111	4.0	0	9
NFL Total	259	932	3.6	14	50

DICK TODD Todd, D S 5′11″, 172 **HB-K**
Col: Texas A&M *HS:* Crowell [TX] B: 10/2/1914, Thrall, TX
Drafted: 1939 Round 3 Was
1939 Was: Pass 4-3 75.0%, 86 21.50; Punt 5-159 31.8; Scor 38, 2-3 66.7% XK. **1940** Was: Pass 1-1 100.0%, 7 7.00; Punt 12-436 36.3. **1941** Was: KR 3-58 19.3; Punt 10-435 43.5. **1942** Was: Pass 6-1 16.7%, 11 1.83 1 Int; KR 2-92 46.0; Punt 11-442 40.2; Scor 26, 2-3 66.7% XK. **1946** Was: KR 3-47 15.7. **1947** Was: KR 9-189 21.0. **1948** Was: KR 3-50 16.7. **Total:** Pass 11-5 45.5%, 104 9.45 1 Int; KR 20-436 21.8; Punt 38-1472 38.7; Scor 208, 4-6 66.7% XK.

		Rushing				Receiving			
Year Team	G	Att	Yds	Avg	TD	Rec	Yds	Avg	TD
1939 Was	10	57	266	4.7	2	19	230	12.1	3
1940 Was	11	76	408	**5.4**	4	20	402	20.1	4
1941 Was	7	55	138	2.5	1	8	125	15.6	1
1942 Was	11	65	195	3.0	0	23	328	14.3	5
1945 Was	6	7	54	7.7	0	0	0	—	0
1946 Was	11	41	266	6.5	3	8	107	13.4	2
1947 Was	11	10	45	4.5	0	4	84	21.0	0
1948 Was	12	57	201	3.5	1	37	550	14.9	6
NFL Total	79	368	1573	4.3	11	119	1826	15.3	21

	Punt Returns				Interceptions				Tot
Year Team	Ret	Yds	Avg	TD	Int	Yds	TD	Fum	TD
1939 Was	—	—	—	**1**	—	—	0	0	6
1940 Was	—	—	—	**1**	2	3	0	0	**9**
1941 Was	14	238	17.0	**1**	0	0	0	0	3
1942 Was	13	143	11.0	0	2	39	0	0	4
1945 Was	5	67	13.4	0	4	35	0	1	0
1946 Was	5	64	12.8	0	4	26	0	2	5
1947 Was	4	48	12.0	0	4	59	0	1	0
1948 Was	3	21	7.0	0	0	0	0	1	7
NFL Total	44	581	13.2	3	16	162	0	5	34

JIM TODD Todd, James Ulysses 5′11″, 195 **HB**
Col: Ball State B: 3/2/1943, Greenville, MS *Drafted:* 1966 Round 9 Phi
1966 Det: 10 G; Rush 2-6 3.0; PR 5-12 2.4; KR 3-105 35.0; 2 Fum.

LARRY TODD Todd, Lawrence 6′1″, 185 **RB**
Col: Arizona State *HS:* Centennial [Compton, CA] B: 10/7/1942, Memphis, TN D: 1/17/1990, Oakland, CA *Drafted:* 1965 Redshirt Round 1 Oak
1965 Oak: Pass 1-0. **Total:** Pass 1-0.

		Rushing				Receiving			
Year Team	G	Att	Yds	Avg	TD	Rec	Yds	Avg	TD
1965 Oak	14	32	183	5.7	0	8	106	13.3	0
1966 Oak	14	0	0	—	0	14	134	9.6	1
1967 Oak	5	29	116	4.0	2	4	42	10.5	0
1968 Oak	3	13	89	6.8	2	4	40	10.0	0
1969 Oak	11	47	198	4.2	1	16	149	9.3	1
1970 Oak	10	17	39	2.3	0	5	51	10.2	0
NFL Total	57	138	625	4.5	5	51	522	10.2	2

	Kickoff Returns					Tot
Year Team	Ret	Yds	Avg	TD	Fum	TD
1965 Oak	20	461	23.1	0	2	0
1966 Oak	0	0	—	0	1	1
1967 Oak	5	123	24.6	0	0	2
1968 Oak	0	0	—	0	0	2
1969 Oak	0	0	—	0	1	2
NFL Total	25	584	23.4	0	4	7

JEFF TOEWS Toews, Jeffrey Mark 6′3″, 255 **OG**
Col: Washington *HS:* Del Mar [San Jose, CA] B: 11/4/1957, San Jose, CA *Drafted:* 1979 Round 2 Mia
1979 Mia: 11 G. **1980** Mia: 7 G. **1981** Mia: 9 G. **1982** Mia: 9 G. **1983** Mia: 8 G. **1984** Mia: 16 G. **1985** Mia: 11 G. **Total:** 71 G.

LOREN TOEWS Toews, Loren James 6′3″, 220 **LB**
Col: California *HS:* Del Mar [San Jose, CA] B: 11/3/1951, Dinuba, CA
Drafted: 1973 Round 8 Pit
1973 Pit: 14 G; Int 2-13. **1974** Pit: 14 G. **1975** Pit: 14 G. **1976** Pit: 14 G; Scor 1 Saf; 2 Pt. **1977** Pit: 14 G. **1978** Pit: 11 G; Int 1-12. **1979** Pit: 11 G. **1980** Pit: 16 G; Scor **1** Saf; 2 Pt. **1981** Pit: 16 G. **1982** Pit: 9 G; Int 1-20; 2.5 Sac. **1983** Pit: 16 G. **Total:** 149 G; Int 4-45; Scor 2 Saf; 4 Pt; 2.5 Sac.

JOE TOFFLEMIRE Tofflemire, Joseph Salvatore 6′3″, 273 **C**
Col: Arizona *HS:* Post Falls [ID] B: 7/7/1965, Los Angeles, CA
Drafted: 1989 Round 2 Sea
1990 Sea: 16 G. **1992** Sea: 16 G; 1 Fum. **1994** Sea: 1 G. **Total:** 33 G; 1 Fum.

JOE TOFIL Tofil, Joe John 6′1″, 205 **OE-DB**
Col: Indiana *HS:* Memorial [Campbell, OH] B: 3/15/1918, Campbell, OH D: 5/1973
1942 Bkn: 11 G; Rec 3-33 11.0.

BRENDAN TOIBIN Toibin, Brendan Patrick 6′0″, 205 **K**
Col: Richmond *HS:* Monacan [Richmond, VA] B: 2/2/1964, Columbia, SC
1987 Was: 1 G; Scor 4, 0-2 FG, 4-4 100.0% XK.

CHARLEY TOLAR Tolar, Charles Guy 5′5″, 200 **FB**
(The Human Bowling Ball) *Col:* Louisiana State; Northwestern State-Louisiana *HS:* Natchitoches Central [LA] B: 9/5/1937, Natchitoches, LA *Drafted:* 1959 Round 27 Pit
1960 Hou: PR 5-40 8.0; KR 13-249 19.2. **1961** Hou: Pass 1-0; KR 2-42 21.0. **1962** Hou: Pass 1-0, 1 Int; KR 2-18 9.0. **1963** Hou: KR 1-4 4.0. **1965** Hou: Pass 1-0. **1966** Hou: Pass 1-0. **Total:** Pass 4-0, 1 Int; PR 5-40 8.0; KR 18-313 17.4.

Year Team	G	Rushing Att	Yds	Avg	TD	Receiving Rec	Yds	Avg	TD	Fum	Tot TD
1960 Hou	14	54	179	3.3	3	7	71	10.1	0	6	3
1961 Hou	14	157	577	3.7	4	24	219	9.1	1	3	5
1962 Hou	14	**244**	1012	4.1	7	30	251	8.4	1	7	8
1963 Hou	14	194	659	3.4	3	41	275	6.7	0	8	3
1964 Hou	14	139	515	3.7	4	35	244	7.0	0	2	4
1965 Hou	11	73	230	3.2	0	25	138	5.5	0	0	0
1966 Hou	14	46	105	2.3	0	13	68	5.2	0	3	0
NFL Total	95	907	3277	3.6	21	175	1266	7.2	2	29	23

JIM TOLBERT Tolbert, Love James 6′4″, 200 **DB**
(Rabbit) *Col:* Lincoln (Mo.) *HS:* Fairfield [AL] B: 3/12/1944, Fairfield, AL *Drafted:* 1966 Round 7 SD
1967 SD: KR 18-441 24.5. **1974** StL: PR 1-0. **Total:** PR 1-0; KR 18-441 24.5.

Year Team	G	Interceptions Int	Yds	TD	Fum
1966 SD	1	1	0	0	0
1967 SD	14	1	9	0	3
1968 SD	12	2	42	0	0
1969 SD	4	0	0	0	0
1970 SD	14	2	19	0	0
1971 SD	12	0	0	0	0
1972 Hou	3	0	0	0	0
1973 StL	13	2	34	0	1
1974 StL	14	2	22	0	0
1975 StL	14	0	0	0	0
1976 SD	4	0	0	0	0
NFL Total	105	10	126	0	4

TONY TOLBERT Tolbert, Tony Lewis 6′6″, 268 **DE**
Col: Texas-El Paso *HS:* Dwight Morrow [Englewood, NJ] B: 12/29/1967, Tuskegee, AL *Drafted:* 1989 Round 4 Dal
1989 Dal: 16 G; 2 Sac. **1990** Dal: 16 G; 6 Sac. **1991** Dal: 16 G; 7 Sac. **1992** Dal: 16 G; 8.5 Sac. **1993** Dal: 16 G; 7.5 Sac. **1994** Dal: 16 G; Int 1-54 1 TD; 6 Pt; 5.5 Sac. **1995** Dal: 16 G; 5.5 Sac. **1996** Dal: 16 G; 12 Sac. **1997** Dal: 16 G; 5 Sac. **Total:** 144 G; Int 1-54 1 TD; 6 Pt; 59.0 Sac.

KENNETH TOLER Toler, Kenneth Pack 6′2″, 195 **WR**
(Ken) *Col:* Mississippi *HS:* Jackson Prep [MS] B: 4/9/1959, Greenville, MS *Drafted:* 1981 Round 7 NE
1981 NE: 16 G; Rec 5-70 14.0; KR 9-148 16.4. **1982** NE: 9 G; Rush 1-4 4.0; Rec 2-63 31.5 2 TD; 12 Pt. **Total:** 25 G; Rush 1-4 4.0; Rec 7-133 19.0 2 TD; KR 9-148 16.4; 12 Pt.

ALVIN TOLES Toles, Alvin 6′1″, 211 **LB**
Col: Tennessee *HS:* Mary Persons [Forsyth, GA] B: 3/23/1963, Barnesville, GA *Drafted:* 1985 Round 1 NO
1985 NO: 16 G. **1986** NO: 16 G. **1987** NO: 12 G; 6 Pt. **1988** NO: 11 G. **Total:** 55 G; 6 Pt.

STUART TOLLE Tolle, Stuart Alexander 6′3″, 265 **NT**
Col: Bowling Green State *HS:* Alliance [OH] B: 2/7/1962, Columbus, OH
1987 Det: 1 G.

CHUCK TOLLEFSON Tollefson, Charles William 6′0″, 215 **G**
Col: Iowa *HS:* Elk Point [SD] B: 2/28/1917, Elk Point, SD D: 8/20/1989, Green Bay, WI
1944 GB: 7 G. **1945** GB: 9 G. **1946** GB: 2 G. **Total:** 18 G.

TOMMY TOLLESON Tolleson, Thomas Anthony 6′1″, 195 **WR**
Col: Alabama B: 1/30/1943, Birmingham, AL *Drafted:* 1966 Round 15 Atl
1966 Atl: 8 G.

ED TOLLEY Tolley, Edgar A 5′8″, 175 **G**
Col: No College *HS:* Steele [Dayton, OH] B: 1900, OH Deceased
1929 Day: 1 G.

BILLY JOE TOLLIVER Tolliver, Billy Joe 6′1″, 217 **QB**
Col: Texas Tech *HS:* Boyd [TX] B: 2/7/1966, Dallas, TX *Drafted:* 1989 Round 2 SD

Year Team	G	Passing Att	Comp	Comp%	Yds	YPA	TD	Int	Rating
1989 SD	5	185	89	48.1	1097	5.93	5	8	57.9
1990 SD	15	410	216	52.7	2574	6.28	16	16	68.9
1991 Atl	7	82	40	48.8	531	6.48	4	2	75.8
1992 Atl	9	131	73	55.7	787	6.01	5	5	70.4
1993 Atl	7	76	39	51.3	464	6.11	3	5	56.0
1994 Hou	10	240	121	50.4	1287	5.36	6	**7**	62.6
1997 Atl-KC	9	116	64	55.2	677	5.84	5	1	83.2
1997 Atl	6	115	63	54.8	685	5.96	5	1	83.4
1997 KC	3	1	1	100.0	-8	-8.00	0	0	79.2
1998 NO	7	199	110	55.3	1427	7.17	8	4	83.1
NFL Total	69	1439	752	52.3	8844	6.15	52	48	69.4

Year Team	Rushing Att	Yds	Avg	TD	Fum
1989 SD	7	0	0.0	0	4
1990 SD	14	22	1.6	0	6
1991 Atl	9	6	0.7	0	3
1992 Atl	4	15	3.8	0	5
1993 Atl	7	48	6.9	0	0
1994 Hou	12	37	3.1	2	7
1997 Atl-KC	9	7	0.8	0	7
1997 Atl	7	8	1.1	0	6
1997 KC	2	-1	-0.5	0	1
1998 NO	11	43	3.9	0	3
NFL Total	73	178	2.4	2	35

MEL TOM Tom, Melvyn Maile 6′4″, 249 **DE**
Col: San Francisco City Coll. CA (J.C.); Hawaii; San Jose State *HS:* Maryknoll [Honolulu, HI] B: 8/4/1941, Honolulu, HI *Drafted:* 1966 Round 6 Phi
1967 Phi: 14 G. **1968** Phi: 14 G. **1969** Phi: 14 G; Scor **1** Saf; 2 Pt. **1970** Phi: 14 G. **1971** Phi: 14 G. **1972** Phi: 14 G. **1973** Phi-ChiB: 13 G. Phi: 4 G. ChiB: 9 G. **1974** ChiB: 14 G. **1975** ChiB: 6 G. **Total:** 117 G; Scor 1 Saf; 2 Pt.

ARMY TOMAINI Tomaini, Amadeo Frederick 6′0″, 245 **T**
Col: Catawba *HS:* Long Branch [NJ] B: 2/5/1918, Long Branch, NJ
1945 NYG: 8 G.

JOHNNY TOMAINI Tomaini, John P 6′0″, 192 **OE-T**
(Biff) *Col:* Georgetown *HS:* Long Branch [NJ]; Asbury Park HS [NJ]; Swarthmore Prep [PA]; Lawrence HS [NY] B: 7/19/1902, Long Branch, NJ D: 7/21/1985, Spring Lake Heights, NJ
1929 Ora: 11 G; Scor **1** 1XP; 1 Pt. **1930** Nwk: 12 G; Rec 1 TD; 6 Pt. Bkn: 2 G. **1931** Bkn: 10 G. **Total:** 35 G; Rec 1 TD; Scor 1 1XP; 7 Pt.

CARL TOMASELLO Tomasello, Carl Antonio 6′0″, 210 **DE**
Col: Scranton B: 1/26/1917, Dunmore, PA D: 10/29/1991, Rutherford, NJ
1940 NYG: 1 G.

LOU TOMASETTI Tomasetti, Louis Vincent 6′0″, 198 **HB-DB-TB-WB**
(Babe) *Col:* Bucknell *HS:* Old Forge [PA] B: 1/8/1916, Old Forge, PA *Drafted:* 1939 Round 11 Pit
AAFC **1946** BufA: PR 7-138 19.7; KR 2-85 42.5; Int 1-0. **1947** BufA: KR 4-74 18.5; Int 1-44 1 TD. **1948** BufA: KR 2-14 7.0. **1949** BufA: PR 2-13 6.5; KR 1-19 19.0. **Total:** PR 9-151 16.8; KR 9-192 21.3; Int 2-44 1 TD.

Year Team	G	Rushing Att	Yds	Avg	TD	Receiving Rec	Yds	Avg	TD	Tot TD
1946 BufA	14	43	139	3.2	1	6	81	13.5	1	2
1947 BufA	13	92	326	3.5	2	13	125	9.6	0	3
1948 BufA	14	134	716	5.3	7	22	213	9.7	1	8
1949 BufA	12	54	249	4.6	2	9	56	6.2	1	3
AAFC Total	53	323	1430	4.4	12	50	475	9.5	3	16

NFL **1939** Pit: Rec 4-22 5.5; Punt 3-111 37.0. **1940** Pit: Rec 6-129 21.5 1 TD. **1941** Phi-Det: Rec 5-54 10.8 1 TD; PR 3-48 16.0; KR 1-18 18.0; Int 1-13. Phi: Rec 5-54 10.8 1 TD; PR 2-30 15.0. Det: PR 1-18 18.0; KR 1-18 18.0; Int 1-13. **1942** Phi: Rec 4-22 5.5; PR 3-37 12.3; KR 4-90 22.5; Int 1-23. **Total:** Rec 19-227 11.9 2 TD; PR 6-85 14.2; KR 5-108 21.6; Int 2-36; Punt 3-111 37.0.

Year Team	G	Passing Att	Comp	Comp%	Yds	YPA	TD	Int	Rating
1939 Pit	11	47	13	27.7	140	2.98	1	7	7.1
1940 Pit	10	6	3	50.0	30	5.00	0	2	25.0
1941 Phi-Det	10	0	0	—	0	—	0	0	—
1941 Phi	6	0	0	—	0	—	0	0	—
1941 Det	4	0	0	—	0	—	0	0	—
1942 Phi	10	0	0	—	0	—	0	0	—
NFL Total	41	53	16	30.2	170	3.21	1	9	7.3

Year Team	Rushing Att	Yds	Avg	TD	Tot TD
1939 Pit	49	86	1.8	1	1
1940 Pit	68	246	3.6	1	2
1941 Phi-Det	16	41	2.6	0	1
1941 Phi	10	37	3.7	0	1
1941 Det	6	4	0.7	0	0
1942 Phi	45	102	2.3	0	0
NFL Total	178	475	2.7	2	4

ANDY TOMASIC Tomasic, Andrew John 6′0″, 175 **TB-DB**
Col: Temple *HS:* Whitehall [PA] B: 12/10/1919, Hokendauqua, PA *Drafted:* 1942 Round 16 Pit
1942 Pit: Rec 1-27 27.0; PR 12-199 16.6 **1** TD; KR 4-94 23.5; Int 2-75; Punt 17-604 35.5; Scor 6, 0-1 XK. **1946** Pit: PR 1-20 20.0; Punt 1-56 56.0. **Total:** Rec 1-27 27.0; PR 13-219 16.8 1 TD; KR 4-94 23.5; Int 2-75; Punt 18-660 36.7; Scor 6, 0-1 XK.

Year Team	G	Passing Att	Comp	Comp%	Yds	YPA	TD	Int	Rating
1942 Pit	11	54	11	20.4	174	3.22	0	5	1.9
1946 Pit	4	12	4	33.3	53	4.42	0	1	13.5
NFL Total	15	66	15	22.7	227	3.44	0	6	3.5

Year Team	Rushing Att	Yds	Avg	TD
1942 Pit	60	214	3.6	0
NFL Total	60	214	3.6	0

PAT TOMBERLIN Tomberlin, Howard Patrick 6′2″, 312 **OG-OT**
Col: Florida State *HS:* Middleburg [FL] B: 1/29/1966, Jacksonville, FL
Drafted: 1989 Round 4 Ind
1990 Ind: 16 G. **1993** TB: 2 G. **Total:** 18 G.

MIKE TOMCZAK Tomczak, Michael John 6′1″, 202 **QB**
Col: Ohio State *HS:* Thornton Fractional North [Calumet City, IL]
B: 10/23/1962, Chicago, IL
1990 ChiB: Rec 1-5 5.0. **Total:** Rec 1-5 5.0.

Year Team	G	Passing Att	Comp	Comp%	Yds	YPA	TD	Int	Rating
1985 ChiB	6	6	2	33.3	33	5.50	0	0	52.8
1986 ChiB	13	151	74	49.0	1105	7.32	2	10	50.2
1987 ChiB	12	178	97	54.5	1220	6.85	5	10	62.0
1988 ChiB	14	170	86	50.6	1310	7.71	7	6	75.4
1989 ChiB	16	306	156	51.0	2058	6.73	16	16	68.2
1990 ChiB	16	104	39	37.5	521	5.01	3	5	43.8
1991 GB	12	238	128	53.8	1490	6.26	11	9	72.6
1992 Cle	12	211	120	56.9	1693	8.02	7	7	80.1
1993 Pit	7	54	29	53.7	398	7.37	2	5	51.3
1994 Pit	6	93	54	58.1	804	8.65	4	0	100.8
1995 Pit	7	113	65	57.5	666	5.89	1	9	44.3
1996 Pit	16	401	222	55.4	2767	6.90	15	17	71.8
1997 Pit	16	24	16	66.7	185	7.71	1	2	68.9
1998 Pit	16	30	21	70.0	204	6.80	2	2	83.2
NFL Total	169	2079	1109	53.3	14454	6.95	76	98	68.0

Year Team	Rushing Att	Yds	Avg	TD	Fum
1985 ChiB	2	3	1.5	0	1
1986 ChiB	23	117	5.1	3	2
1987 ChiB	18	54	3.0	1	6
1988 ChiB	13	40	3.1	1	1
1989 ChiB	24	71	3.0	1	2
1990 ChiB	12	41	3.4	2	2
1991 GB	17	93	5.5	1	5
1992 Cle	24	39	1.6	0	5
1993 Pit	5	-4	-0.8	0	2
1994 Pit	4	22	5.5	0	2
1995 Pit	11	25	2.3	0	2
1996 Pit	22	-7	-0.3	0	7
1997 Pit	7	13	1.9	0	0
1998 Pit	0	0	—	0	2
NFL Total	182	507	2.8	9	39

JARED TOMICH Tomich, Jared James 6′2″, 258 **DE**
Col: Nebraska *HS:* Lake Central [St. John, IN] B: 4/24/1974, St. John, IN *Drafted:* 1997 Round 2 NO
1997 NO: 16 G; KR 1-0; 1 Fum; 1 Sac. **1998** NO: 16 G; KR 1-0; 6 Sac.
Total: 32 G; KR 2-0; 1 Fum; 7 Sac.

TOMMY TOMLIN Tomlin, John Thomas 5′10″, 197 **G-T**
(Dowie; J.T.) *Col:* Syracuse B: 9/1893, S. Miller Dstrct, Albemarle Co, VA D: 5/11/1953, Woodstock, NY
1920 Akr: 11 G. **1921** Ham-Akr: 7 G. Ham: 2 G. Akr: 5 G. **1922** Mil: 4 G.
1925 NYG: 9 G. **1926** NYG: 4 G. **Total:** 35 G.

DICK TOMLINSON Tomlinson, Richard Kent 6′1″, 205 **OG**
Col: Kansas *HS:* Dodge City [KS] B: 8/5/1928, Chicago, IL
Drafted: 1950 Round 21 Pit
1950 Pit: 11 G. **1951** Pit: 12 G. **Total:** 23 G.

CLARENCE TOMMERSON Tommerson, Clarence Leonard 6′2″, 196 **DB-HB**
(Tommy) *Col:* Wisconsin *HS:* Logan [La Crosse, WI] B: 4/8/1915, La Crosse, WI
1938 Pit: 3 G. **1939** Pit: 1 G. **Total:** 4 G.

BOB TONEFF Toneff, Robert 6′2″, 260 **DT-DG-DE-OT**
Col: Notre Dame *HS:* Barberton [OH] B: 6/23/1930, Detroit, MI
Drafted: 1952 Round 2 SF
1952 SF: 12 G. **1954** SF: 10 G; KR 1-10 10.0; Int 1-15. **1955** SF: 11 G; KR 1-13 13.0. **1956** SF: 12 G. **1957** SF: 12 G. **1958** SF: 12 G; Int 1-5.
1959 Was: 12 G. **1960** Was: 12 G. **1961** Was: 14 G. **1962** Was: 14 G.
1963 Was: 14 G. **1964** Was: 14 G. **Total:** 149 G; KR 2-23 11.5; Int 2-20.

TONY TONELLI Tonelli, Amerigo S 6′0″, 210 **C-LB-G**
Col: USC *HS:* Thomas [WV] B: 9/1/1917, Wheeling, WV
D: 1/30/1987, Newport Beach, CA *Drafted:* 1939 Round 17 Det
1939 Det: 9 G.

MARIO TONELLI Tonelli, Mario George 5′11″, 200 **FB-DB**
(Motts) *Col:* Notre Dame *HS:* DePaul Acad. [Chicago, IL]
B: 3/28/1916, Lemont, IL *Drafted:* 1939 Round 19 NYG
1940 ChiC: Rec 5-53 10.6; Punt 1-15 15.0.

Year Team	G	Rushing Att	Yds	Avg	TD
1940 ChiC	9	51	148	2.9	1

ED TONER Toner, Edward William 6′2″, 250 **DT**
Col: Massachusetts *HS:* Lynn English [MA] B: 9/11/1944, Reading, MA *Drafted:* 1966 Redshirt Round 3 Bos
1967 Bos: 14 G. **1968** Bos: 5 G. **1969** Bos: 7 G. **Total:** 26 G.

ED TONER Toner, Edward William 6′0″, 240 **RB**
Col: Boston College *HS:* Swampscott [MA] B: 3/22/1968, Lynn, MA
1992 Ind: 8 G. **1993** Ind: 16 G; Rush 2-6 3.0; Rec 1-5 5.0. **1994** Ind: 9 G; Rush 1-11 11.0; KR 1-8 8.0. **Total:** 33 G; Rush 3-17 5.7; Rec 1-5 5.0; KR 1-8 8.0.

TOM TONER Toner, Thomas Edward 6′3″, 235 **LB**
Col: Idaho State *HS:* Swampscott [MA] B: 1/25/1950, Woburn, MA
D: 8/26/1990, Solana Beach, CA *Drafted:* 1973 Round 6 GB
1973 GB: 14 G; Int 1-1. **1975** GB: 14 G; Int 1-0; Scor **1** Saf; 2 Pt.
1976 GB: 11 G; Int 1-28. **1977** GB: 14 G; Int 1-10. **Total:** 53 G; Int 4-39; Scor 1 Saf; 2 Pt.

ANTHONY TONEY Toney, Anthony 6′0″, 227 **RB**
Col: Hartnell Coll. CA (J.C.); Texas A&M *HS:* North Salinas [Salinas, CA]
B: 9/23/1962, Salinas, CA *Drafted:* 1986 Round 2 Phi
1987 Phi: Pass 1-0. **Total:** Pass 1-0.

Year Team	G	Rushing Att	Yds	Avg	TD	Receiving Rec	Yds	Avg	TD	Fum	Tot TD
1986 Phi	12	69	285	4.1	1	13	177	13.6	0	0	1
1987 Phi	11	127	473	3.7	5	39	341	8.7	1	5	6
1988 Phi	15	139	502	3.6	4	34	256	7.5	1	2	5
1989 Phi	14	172	582	3.4	3	19	124	6.5	0	4	3
1990 Phi	15	132	452	3.4	1	17	133	7.8	3	3	4
NFL Total	67	639	2294	3.6	14	122	1031	8.5	5	14	19

MARCO TONGUE Tongue, Marco Charles 5′9″, 177 **DB**
Col: Bowie State *HS:* Annapolis [MD] B: 4/6/1960, Annapolis, MD
1983 Bal: 7 G. **1984** Buf: 1 G. **Total:** 8 G.

REGGIE TONGUE Tongue, Reginald Clinton 6′1″, 205 **DB**
Col: Oregon State *HS:* Lathrop [Fairbanks, AK] B: 4/11/1973, Baltimore, MD *Drafted:* 1996 Round 2 KC
1996 KC: 16 G. **1997** KC: 16 G; Int 1-0; 2.5 Sac. **1998** KC: 15 G; 2 Sac.
Total: 47 G; Int 1-0; 4.5 Sac.

CLAYTON TONNEMAKER Tonnemaker, Frank Clayton 6′2″, 237 **LB-C**
Col: Minnesota *HS:* Edison [Minneapolis, MN] B: 6/8/1928, Ogilvie, MN D: 12/25/1996, St. Paul, MN *Drafted:* 1950 Round 1 GB
1950 GB: 12 G; Int 1-1; Scor 1, 1-1 100.0% XK. **1953** GB: 12 G. **1954** GB: 12 G; Int 1-1. **Total:** 36 G; Int 2-2; Scor 1, 1-1 100.0% XK.

CHARLIE TOOGOOD Toogood, Charles Wayne 6′0″, 232 **DT-OT-OG**
Col: Nebraska *HS:* North Platte [NE] B: 7/16/1927, North Platte, NE
D: 2/24/1997, Auburn, CA *Drafted:* 1951 Round 3 LARm
1951 LARm: 8 G; Int 1-0. **1952** LARm: 10 G. **1953** LARm: 12 G; KR 1-19 19.0; Int 1-0; 1 Fum. **1954** LARm: 12 G; KR 1-11 11.0; Int 1-3.
1955 LARm: 12 G; KR 1-11 11.0. **1956** LARm: 7 G; KR 1-13 13.0.
1957 ChiC: 6 G. **Total:** 67 G; KR 4-54 13.5; Int 3-3; 1 Fum.

PAT TOOMAY Toomay, Patrick Jay 6′5″, 247 **DE**
Col: Vanderbilt *HS:* Thomas Edison [Alexandria, VA] B: 5/17/1945, Pomona, CA *Drafted:* 1970 Round 6 Dal
1970 Dal: 14 G. **1971** Dal: 14 G. **1972** Dal: 14 G. **1973** Dal: 14 G; Int 1-35.
1974 Dal: 14 G. **1975** Buf: 14 G; Int 1-44 1 TD; 6 Pt. **1976** TB: 14 G.
1977 Oak: 14 G. **1978** Oak: 16 G. **1979** Oak: 14 G. **Total:** 142 G; Int 2-79 1 TD; 6 Pt.

AMANI TOOMER Toomer, Amani 6′3″, 202 **WR**
Col: Michigan *HS:* De La Salle [Concord, CA] B: 9/8/1974, Berkeley, CA *Drafted:* 1996 Round 2 NYG
1996 NYG: KR 11-191 17.4. **1998** NYG: Pass 1-0; KR 4-66 16.5.
Total: Pass 1-0; KR 15-257 17.1.

Year Team	G	Receiving Rec	Yds	Avg	TD	Punt Returns Ret	Yds	Avg	TD	Fum	Tot TD
1996 NYG	7	1	12	12.0	0	18	298	16.6	2	1	2
1997 NYG	16	16	263	16.4	1	47	455	9.7	1	0	2
1998 NYG	16	27	360	13.3	5	35	252	7.2	0	0	5
NFL Total	39	44	635	14.4	6	100	1005	10.1	3	1	9

AL TOON Toon, Albert Lee Jr. 6′4″, 205 **WR**
Col: Wisconsin *HS:* Menchville [Newport News, VA] B: 4/30/1963, Newport News, VA *Drafted:* 1985 Round 1 NYJ
1985 NYJ: Rush 1-5 5.0. **1986** NYJ: Rush 2-(-3) -1.5. **1988** NYJ: Rush 1-5 5.0. **1990** NYJ: Pass 2-0. **1991** NYJ: Pass 1-1 100.0%, 27 27.00. **Total:** Pass 3-1 33.3%, 27 9.00; Rush 4-7 1.8.

		Receiving				
Year Team	**G**	**Rec**	**Yds**	**Avg**	**TD**	**Fum**
1985 NYJ	15	46	662	14.4	3	0
1986 NYJ	16	85	1176	13.8	8	3
1987 NYJ	12	68	976	14.4	5	0
1988 NYJ	15	**93**	1067	11.5	5	2
1989 NYJ	11	63	693	11.0	2	0
1990 NYJ	14	57	757	13.3	6	0
1991 NYJ	15	74	963	13.0	0	0
1992 NYJ	9	31	311	10.0	2	0
NFL Total	107	517	6605	12.8	31	5

CHIEF TOOROCK Toorock, Meyer 5′9″, 180 **WB**
Col: New York U. B: 1902
1926 Bkn: 2 G.

JEFF TOOTLE Tootle, Jeffrey Edward 6′2″, 240 **LB**
Col: Mesa B: 8/29/1962
1987 NYG: 3 G.

TED TOPOR Topor, Ted Peter 6′1″, 210 **LB**
Col: Michigan *HS:* Theodore Roosevelt [East Chicago, IN] B: 5/1/1930, East Chicago, IN *Drafted:* 1953 Round 15 Det
1955 Det: 6 G; KR 1-13 13.0.

BOB TOPP Topp, Eugene Robert 6′2″, 180 **OE**
Col: Michigan *HS:* Kalamazoo Central [MI] B: 4/22/1932, Kalamazoo, MI *Drafted:* 1954 Round 13 NYG
1954 NYG: 6 G; Rec 6-90 15.0 3 TD; KR 1-10 10.0; 18 Pt.

STACEY TORAN Toran, Stacey Jeffery 6′2″, 200 **DB**
Col: Notre Dame *HS:* Broad Ripple [Indianapolis, IN] B: 11/10/1961, Indianapolis, IN D: 8/5/1989, Marina del Rey, CA *Drafted:* 1984 Round 6 LARd
1984 LARd: 16 G. **1985** LARd: 16 G; Int 1-76 **1** TD; 6 Pt; 1 Sac. **1986** LARd: 16 G; Int 2-28; 6 Sac. **1987** LARd: 12 G; Int 3-48 1 TD; 6 Pt. **1988** LARd: 12 G; KR 2-0; 2 Sac. **Total:** 72 G; KR 2-0; Int 6-152 2 TD; 12 Pt; 9 Sac.

LAVERNE TORCZON Torczon, LaVerne Joseph 6′3″, 250 **DE**
Col: Nebraska B: 1/1/1936, Columbus, NE *Drafted:* 1957 Round 18 Cle
1960 Buf: 14 G. **1961** Buf: 14 G. **1962** Buf-NYT: 14 G. Buf: 4 G. NYT: 10 G. **1963** NYJ: 14 G; Int 1-2. **1964** NYJ: 14 G; Int 1-40 **1** TD; 6 Pt. **1965** NYJ: 14 G. **1966** Mia: 14 G. **Total:** 98 G; Int 2-42 1 TD; 6 Pt.

LAVERN TORGESON Torgeson, LaVern Earl 6′0″, 215 **LB-C**
(Torgy) *Col:* Washington State *HS:* Lacrosse [WA] B: 2/28/1929, Lacrosse, WA *Drafted:* 1951 Round 5 Det

		Interceptions		
Year Team	**G**	**Int**	**Yds**	**TD**
1951 Det	12	1	0	0
1952 Det	12	5	100	1
1953 Det	11	5	27	0
1954 Det	12	2	33	0
1955 Was	11	3	45	0
1956 Was	12	1	0	0
1957 Was	12	1	6	0
NFL Total	82	18	211	1

ERIC TORKELSON Torkelson, Eric Grove 6′2″, 194 **RB**
Col: Connecticut *HS:* Burnt Hills [NY] B: 3/23/1952, Troy, NY *Drafted:* 1974 Round 11 GB
1974 GB: PR 1-0; KR 1-20 20.0; 1 Fum TD. **1975** GB: KR 5-89 17.8. **1976** GB: KR 6-123 20.5. **1977** GB: KR 2-36 18.0. **Total:** PR 1-0; KR 14-268 19.1; 1 Fum TD.

		Rushing				Receiving					Tot
Year Team	**G**	**Att**	**Yds**	**Avg**	**TD**	**Rec**	**Yds**	**Avg**	**TD**	**Fum**	**TD**
1974 GB	14	13	60	4.6	0	2	10	5.0	0	0	1
1975 GB	14	42	226	5.4	2	6	37	6.2	0	0	2
1976 GB	14	88	289	3.3	2	19	140	7.4	0	3	2
1977 GB	14	103	309	3.0	1	11	107	9.7	0	4	1
1978 GB	14	6	18	3.0	0	2	36	18.0	0	0	0
1979 GB	14	98	401	4.1	3	19	139	7.3	0	3	3
1981 GB	9	1	4	4.0	0	0	0	—	0	0	0
NFL Total	93	351	1307	3.7	8	59	469	7.9	0	10	9

JACK TORRANCE Torrance, Jack 6′5″, 285 **T**
(Black Jack) *Col:* Louisiana State *HS:* Oak Grove [LA] B: 6/20/1912, Oak Grove, LA D: 11/10/1969, Baton Rouge, LA
1939 ChiB: 8 G. **1940** ChiB: 7 G. **Total:** 15 G.

GINO TORRETTA Torretta, Gino Louis 6′3″, 215 **QB**
Col: Miami (Fla.) *HS:* Pinole Valley [Pinole, CA] B: 8/10/1970, Pinole Valley, CA *Drafted:* 1993 Round 7 Min
1993 Min: 1 G. **1996** Sea: 1 G; Pass 16-5 31.3%, 41 2.56 1 TD 1 Int; Rush 2-12 6.0. **Total:** 2 G; Pass 16-5 31.3%, 41 2.56 1 TD 1 Int; Rush 2-12 6.0.

BOB TORREY Torrey, Robert Douglas 6′4″, 231 **RB**
Col: Penn State *HS:* Bolivar [NY] B: 1/30/1957, Ceres, NY *Drafted:* 1979 Round 6 NYG
1979 NYG-Mia: 13 G; Rush 13-61 4.7 1 TD; Rec 2-3 1.5; 6 Pt. NYG: 6 G. Mia: 7 G; Rush 13-61 4.7 1 TD; Rec 2-3 1.5; 6 Pt. **1980** Phi: 1 G. **Total:** 14 G; Rush 13-61 4.7 1 TD; Rec 2-3 1.5; 6 Pt.

BUD TOSCANI Toscani, Francis 5′8″, 168 **WB-HB**
Col: St. Mary's (Cal.) *HS:* Santa Rosa [CA] B: 4/19/1909 D: 6/1966
1932 Bkn-ChiC: 8 G; Rush 24-80 3.3; Rec 1-12 12.0. Bkn: 5 G; Rush 9-37 4.1. ChiC: 3 G; Rush 15-43 2.9; Rec 1-12 12.0. **Total:** 8 G; Rush 24-80 3.3; Rec 1-12 12.0.

FLAVIO TOSI Tosi, Flavio Joseph 6′1″, 191 **OE-DE**
(Bull) *Col:* Boston College *HS:* Beverly [MA] B: 4/30/1912, Beverly, MA D: 12/18/1994, Beverly, MA
1934 Bos: 9 G; Rec 3-26 8.7. **1935** Bos: 11 G; Rec 10-169 16.9 1 TD; 6 Pt. **1936** Bos: 7 G; Rec 4-70 17.5; **1** Fum TD; 6 Pt. **Total:** 27 G; Rec 17-265 15.6 1 TD; 1 Fum TD; Tot TD 2; 12 Pt.

JOHN TOSI Tosi, John Joseph 5′10″, 225 **C-LB-T-G**
Col: Niagara B: 12/3/1914 *Drafted:* 1939 Round 15 Pit
1939 Pit-Bkn: 4 G. Pit: 3 G. Bkn: 1 G. **Total:** 4 G.

TOM TOTH Toth, Thomas Jeffrey 6′5″, 279 **OG-OT**
Col: Western Michigan *HS:* Carl Sandburg [Orland Park, IL] B: 5/23/1962, Chicago, IL *Drafted:* 1985 Round 4 NE
1986 Mia: 13 G; KR 1-0; 1 Fum. **1987** Mia: 12 G. **1988** Mia: 9 G. **1989** Mia: 16 G. **1990** SD: 1 G. **Total:** 51 G; KR 1-0; 1 Fum.

ZOLLIE TOTH Toth, Zollie Anthony 6′2″, 219 **FB**
(Tugboat) *Col:* Louisiana State *HS:* Pocohontas [VA] B: 1/26/1924, McKeesport, PA
1952 Dal: KR 1-18 18.0. **1954** Bal: Pass 1-0, 1 Int; KR 1-13 13.0. **Total:** Pass 1-0, 1 Int; KR 2-31 15.5.

		Rushing				Receiving					Tot
Year Team	**G**	**Att**	**Yds**	**Avg**	**TD**	**Rec**	**Yds**	**Avg**	**TD**	**Fum**	**TD**
1950 NYY	11	131	636	4.9	5	15	189	12.6	3	5	8
1951 NYY	10	119	384	3.2	4	10	100	10.0	0	2	4
1952 Dal	12	82	266	3.2	4	13	54	4.2	0	2	4
1954 Bal	12	86	303	3.5	1	11	51	4.6	0	2	1
NFL Total	45	418	1589	3.8	14	49	394	8.0	3	11	17

WILLIE TOTTEN Totten, Willie Horace 6′2″, 195 **QB**
Col: Mississippi Valley State *HS:* J.Z. George [North Carrollton, MS] B: 7/4/1962, Leflore, MS
1987 Buf: 2 G; Pass 33-13 39.4%, 155 4.70 2 TD 2 Int; Rush 12-11 0.9; 9 Fum.

DARREL TOUSSAINT Toussaint, Darrel Lee 6′0″, 175 **DB**
Col: Northwestern State-Louisiana *HS:* Opelousas [LA] B: 10/3/1958, Chicago, IL
1987 NO: 2 G.

STEVE TOVAR Tovar, Steven Eric 6′3″, 246 **LB**
Col: Ohio State *HS:* West [Elyria, OH] B: 4/25/1970, Elyria, OH *Drafted:* 1993 Round 3 Cin
1993 Cin: 16 G; Int 1-0. **1994** Cin: 16 G; KR 1-8 8.0; Int 1-14; 3 Sac. **1995** Cin: 14 G; Int 1-13; 1 Sac. **1996** Cin: 13 G; Int 4-42; 1 Fum; 3 Sac. **1997** Cin: 14 G. **1998** SD: 16 G; 1 Sac. **Total:** 89 G; KR 1-8 8.0; Int 7-69; 1 Fum; 8 Sac.

THURSTON TOWLE Towle, Edward Thurston 5′10″, 172 **E**
Col: Brown *HS:* Moses Brown School [Providence, RI] B: 1/1/1905, Pawtucket, RI D: 10/19/1960, Providence, RI
1929 Bost: 1 G.

STEVE TOWLE Towle, Stephen Richards 6′2″, 233 **LB**
Col: Kansas *HS:* Shawnee Mission West [KS] B: 10/23/1953, Kansas City, KS *Drafted:* 1975 Round 6 Mia
1975 Mia: 14 G; Int 1-16. **1976** Mia: 14 G. **1977** Mia: 12 G. **1978** Mia: 13 G; Int 1-14. **1979** Mia: 16 G; Int 1-0. **1980** Mia: 9 G. **Total:** 78 G; Int 3-30.

DAN TOWLER Towler, Daniel Lee 6′2″, 225 **FB**
(Deacon Dan) *Col:* Washington & Jefferson *HS:* Donora [PA] B: 3/6/1928, Donora, PA *Drafted:* 1950 Round 25 LARm
1950 LARm: KR 5-47 9.4. **1951** LARm: KR 1-10 10.0. **1952** LARm: PR 1-0; KR 1-9 9.0. **Total:** PR 1-0; KR 7-66 9.4.

		Rushing				Receiving					Tot
Year Team	**G**	**Att**	**Yds**	**Avg**	**TD**	**Rec**	**Yds**	**Avg**	**TD**	**Fum**	**TD**
1950 LARm	12	46	130	2.8	6	8	63	7.9	0	3	6
1951 LARm	12	126	854	6.8	6	16	257	16.1	0	7	6
1952 LARm	12	156	**894**	5.7	**10**	11	68	6.2	0	4	10

1953 LARm	12	152	879	5.8	7	11	125	11.4	1	6	8
1954 LARm	12	149	599	4.0	**11**	10	127	12.7	0	5	11
1955 LARm	7	43	137	3.2	3	6	25	4.2	0	2	3
NFL Total	67	672	3493	5.2	43	62	665	10.7	1	27	44

WILLIE TOWNES Townes, Willie Carroll 6′4″, 260 **DE-DT**
Col: Tulsa *HS:* Rowan [Hattiesburg, MS] B: 7/21/1943, Hattiesburg, MS *Drafted:* 1966 Round 2 Dal
1966 Dal: 13 G; Scor **1** Saf; 2 Pt. **1967** Dal: 14 G. **1968** Dal: 5 G; **1** Fum TD; 6 Pt. **1970** NO: 6 G. **Total:** 38 G; Scor 1 Saf; 1 Fum TD; 8 Pt.

MORRIS TOWNS Towns, Morris M 6′4″, 270 **OT**
Col: Missouri *HS:* Vashon [St. Louis, MO] B: 1/10/1954, St. Louis, MO *Drafted:* 1977 Round 1 Hou
1977 Hou: 1 G. **1978** Hou: 16 G. **1979** Hou: 16 G. **1980** Hou: 16 G. **1981** Hou: 16 G. **1982** Hou: 9 G. **1983** Hou: 14 G. **1984** Was: 4 G. **Total:** 92 G.

BOBBY TOWNS Towns, Robert Forrest 6′1″, 180 **DB**
Col: Georgia *HS:* Athens [GA] B: 3/17/1938, Elberton, GA *Drafted:* 1960 Round 11 StL
1960 StL: 4 G. **1961** Bos: 2 G. **Total:** 6 G.

JO-JO TOWNSELL Townsell, Joseph Ray 5′9″, 180 **WR**
Col: UCLA *HS:* Hug [Reno, NV] B: 11/4/1960, Reno, NV *Drafted:* 1983 Round 3 NYJ
1986 NYJ: Rush 1-2 2.0. **1987** NYJ: Rush 1-(-2) -2.0. **Total:** Rush 2-0.

		Receiving				Punt Returns			
Year Team	**G**	**Rec**	**Yds**	**Avg**	**TD**	**Ret**	**Yds**	**Avg**	**TD**
1985 NYJ	16	12	187	15.6	0	6	65	10.8	0
1986 NYJ	14	1	11	11.0	0	4	52	13.0	0
1987 NYJ	12	4	37	9.3	0	32	381	11.9	1
1988 NYJ	16	4	40	10.0	0	35	409	11.7	1
1989 NYJ	16	45	787	17.5	5	33	299	9.1	0
1990 NYJ	9	4	57	14.3	0	17	154	9.1	0
NFL Total	83	70	1119	16.0	5	127	1360	10.7	2

	Kickoff Returns					Tot
Year Team	**Ret**	**Yds**	**Avg**	**TD**	**Fum**	**TD**
1985 NYJ	2	42	21.0	0	1	0
1986 NYJ	13	322	24.8	**1**	0	1
1987 NYJ	11	272	24.7	0	3	1
1988 NYJ	31	601	19.4	0	3	1
1989 NYJ	34	653	19.2	0	4	5
1990 NYJ	7	158	22.6	0	2	0
NFL Total	98	2048	20.9	1	13	8

ANDRE TOWNSEND Townsend, Andre 6′3″, 265 **DE-NT**
Col: Mississippi *HS:* Aberdeen [MS] B: 10/8/1962, Chicago, IL *Drafted:* 1984 Round 2 Den
1984 Den: 16 G; 5 Sac. **1985** Den: 16 G; 5 Sac. **1986** Den: 16 G; **1** Fum TD; 6 Pt; 2.5 Sac. **1987** Den: 12 G; 1 Sac. **1988** Den: 16 G; 5.5 Sac. **1989** Den: 13 G; 2 Sac. **1990** Den: 15 G; 1 Sac. **Total:** 104 G; 1 Fum TD; 6 Pt; 22 Sac.

BRIAN TOWNSEND Townsend, Brian Lewis 6′3″, 242 **LB**
Col: Michigan *HS:* Northwest [Cincinnati, OH] B: 11/7/1968, Cincinnati, OH *Drafted:* 1992 Round 11 LARm
1992 Cin: 3 G.

CURTIS TOWNSEND Townsend, Curtis 6′1″, 229 **LB**
Col: Hutchinson CC KS; Arkansas *HS:* Robert E. Lee [Montgomery, AL] B: 1/20/1955, Birmingham, AL *Drafted:* 1977 Round 10 SD
1978 StL: 9 G; KR 1-13 13.0.

GREG TOWNSEND Townsend, Gregory 6′3″, 264 **DE-NT-LB**
Col: Long Beach City Coll. CA (J.C.); Texas Christian *HS:* Dominguez [Compton, CA] B: 11/3/1961, Los Angeles, CA *Drafted:* 1983 Round 4 LARd
1983 LARd: 16 G; Scor 1 Saf; 1 Fum TD; 8 Pt; 10.5 Sac. **1984** LARd: 16 G; 7 Sac. **1985** LARd: 16 G; 10 Sac. **1986** LARd: 15 G; Scor **1** Saf; 2 Pt; 11.5 Sac. **1987** LARd: 13 G; 8.5 Sac. **1988** LARd: 16 G; Int 1-86 1 TD; **1** Fum TD; Tot TD 2; 12 Pt; 11.5 Sac. **1989** LARd: 16 G; 10.5 Sac. **1990** LARd: 16 G; Int 1-0; 1 Fum TD; 6 Pt; 12.5 Sac. **1991** LARd: 16 G; Int 1-31; 13 Sac. **1992** LARd: 14 G; 5 Sac. **1993** LARd: 16 G; 7.5 Sac. **1994** Phi: 16 G; 2 Sac. **1997** Oak: 4 G. **Total:** 190 G; Int 3-117 1 TD; Scor 2 Saf; 3 Fum TD; Tot TD 4; 28 Pt; 109.5 Sac.

OTTO TOWNSEND Townsend, Otto 190 **G-T**
Col: No College Deceased
1922 Min: 2 G.

DESHEA TOWNSEND Townsend, Trevor Deshea 5′9″, 174 **DB**
Col: Alabama *HS:* South Panola [Batesville, MS] B: 9/8/1975, Batesville, MS *Drafted:* 1998 Round 4 Pit
1998 Pit: 12 G.

JACK TRACEY Tracey, John Joseph 6′3″, 225 **LB-OE-TE**
Col: Texas A&M *HS:* Northeast [Philadelphia, PA] B: 6/27/1933, Philadelphia, PA D: 9/18/1978, Medford Lakes, NJ *Drafted:* 1959 Round 4 LARm
1959 ChiC: Rec 17-258 15.2; KR 1-14 14.0. **1960** StL: Scor **1** Saf. **1962** Buf: Rec 1-28 28.0. **1963** Buf: KR 1-21 21.0; Scor **1** 2XP. **1965** Buf: Rec 1-2 2.0. **1967** Buf: Rec 1-15 15.0. **Total:** Rec 20-303 15.2; KR 2-35 17.5; Scor 1 Saf, 1 2XP.

		Interceptions		
Year Team	**G**	**Int**	**Yds**	**TD**
1959 ChiC	8	0	0	0
1960 StL	12	1	14	0
1961 Phi	9	0	0	0
1962 Buf	12	0	0	0
1963 Buf	14	5	22	0
1964 Buf	14	3	12	0
1965 Buf	14	1	8	0
1966 Buf	14	1	0	0
1967 Buf	13	1	3	0
NFL Total	110	12	59	0

TOM TRACY Tracy, John Thomas 5′9″, 205 **HB-FB**
(The Bomb) *Col:* Tennessee *HS:* Birmingham [MI] B: 9/7/1934, Birmingham, MI D: 1/24/1996, Madison Heights, MI *Drafted:* 1956 Round 5 Det
1959 Pit: PR 4-5 1.3; KR 7-145 20.7. **1960** Pit: KR 1-30 30.0; Scor 63, 3-6 50.0% FG. **1961** Pit: Scor 20, 0-1 FG, 2-2 100.0% XK. **1963** Pit-Was: Scor 8, 2-2 100.0% XK. Pit: Scor 2, 2-2 100.0% XK. **Total:** PR 4-5 1.3; KR 8-175 21.9; Scor 199, 3-7 42.9% FG, 4-4 100.0% XK.

		Passing							
Year Team	**G**	**Att**	**Comp**	**Comp%**	**Yds**	**YPA**	**TD**	**Int**	**Rating**
1956 Det	4	0	0	—	0	—	0	0	—
1957 Det	9	0	0	—	0	—	0	0	—
1958 Pit	12	16	6	37.5	270	16.88	2	2	85.4
1959 Pit	12	12	3	25.0	159	13.25	0	2	39.6
1960 Pit	12	22	9	40.9	322	14.64	4	1	108.9
1961 Pit	14	12	4	33.3	73	6.08	0	0	55.2
1962 Pit	4	1	1	100.0	7	7.00	0	0	95.8
1963 Pit-Was	8	4	1	25.0	23	5.75	0	0	51.0
1963 Pit	6	1	0	0.0	0	0.00	0	0	39.6
1963 Was	2	3	1	33.3	23	7.67	0	0	61.8
1964 Was	14	0	0	—	0	—	0	0	—
NFL Total	89	67	24	35.8	854	12.75	6	5	82.8

	Rushing				Receiving					Tot
Year Team	**Att**	**Yds**	**Avg**	**TD**	**Rec**	**Yds**	**Avg**	**TD**	**Fum**	**TD**
1956 Det	12	32	2.7	0	3	6	2.0	0	1	0
1957 Det	16	46	2.9	0	6	24	4.0	0	1	0
1958 Pit	169	714	4.2	5	32	535	16.7	4	10	9
1959 Pit	199	794	4.0	3	23	273	11.9	5	7	8
1960 Pit	192	680	3.5	5	24	349	14.5	4	6	9
1961 Pit	147	402	2.7	2	14	133	9.5	1	1	3
1962 Pit	20	116	5.8	0	2	11	5.5	0	0	0
1963 Pit-Was	29	61	2.1	1	7	112	16.0	0	1	1
1963 Pit	10	11	1.1	0	1	21	21.0	0	0	0
1963 Was	19	50	2.6	1	6	91	15.2	0	1	1
1964 Was	24	67	2.8	1	2	25	12.5	0	2	1
NFL Total	808	2912	3.6	17	113	1468	13.0	14	29	31

GEORGE TRAFTON Trafton, George Edward 6′2″, 230 **C**
(Cyclone; The Beast) *Col:* Notre Dame *HS:* Oak Park [IL] B: 12/6/1896, Chicago, IL D: 9/5/1971, Los Angeles, CA *HOF:* 1964
1920 Sta: 13 G. **1921** Sta: 10 G. **1923** ChiB: 13 G. **1924** ChiB: 11 G. **1925** ChiB: 17 G. **1926** ChiB: 14 G. **1927** ChiB: 14 G. **1928** ChiB: 9 G. **1929** ChiB: 12 G. **1930** ChiB: 14 G. **1931** ChiB: 11 G. **1932** ChiB: 11 G. **Total:** 149 G.

JOHN TRAHAN Trahan, John 5′9″, 160 **WR**
Col: Southern Colorado *HS:* Thomas Jefferson [Denver, CO] B: 4/19/1961, Grand Forks, ND
1987 KC: 3 G; Rec 4-40 10.0.

MIKE TRAINOR Trainor, Michael J 5′9″, 165 **WB-BB-TB**
Col: Canisius B: 12/18/1899, New York, NY D: 4/1980, Lake Success, NY
1923 Buf: 12 G; Rush 1 TD; Rec 1 TD; Tot TD 2; 12 Pt. **1924** Buf: 11 G; Rec 1 TD; 6 Pt. **Total:** 23 G; Rush 1 TD; Rec 2 TD; Tot TD 3; 18 Pt.

ALLEN TRAMMEL Trammel, Allen Raymond Jr. 6′0″, 190 **DB**
Col: Florida *HS:* Eufaula [AL]; Baylor Prep [Chattanooga, TN] B: 7/19/1942, Montgomery, AL
1966 Hou: 3 G; PR 5-19 3.8; KR 3-63 21.0.

STEVE TRAPILO Trapilo, Stephen Paul 6′5″, 290 **OG**
Col: Boston College *HS:* Boston College [MA] B: 9/20/1964, Boston, MA *Drafted:* 1987 Round 4 NO
1987 NO: 11 G. **1988** NO: 9 G. **1989** NO: 16 G. **1990** NO: 16 G. **1992** NO: 5 G. **Total:** 57 G.

JAMES TRAPP Trapp, James Harold 6'0", 190 **DB**
Col: Clemson *HS:* Lawton [OK] B: 12/28/1969, Greenville, SC
Drafted: 1993 Round 1 LARd
1993 LARd: 14 G; Int 1-7. **1994** LARd: 16 G; 1 Sac. **1995** Oak: 14 G. **1996** Oak: 12 G; Int 1-23. **1997** Oak: 16 G; Int 2-24. **1998** Oak: 16 G. **Total:** 88 G; Int 4-54; 1 Sac.

RICHARD TRAPP Trapp, Richard Earl 6'1", 175 **WR**
Col: Florida *HS:* Manatee [Bradenton, FL] B: 9/21/1946, Lynwood, CA
Drafted: 1968 Round 3 Buf
1968 Buf: PR 5-26 5.2. **Total:** PR 5-26 5.2.

		Receiving				
Year Team	**G**	**Rec**	**Yds**	**Avg**	**TD**	**Fum**
1968 Buf	14	24	235	9.8	0	1
1969 SD	8	2	39	19.5	0	0
NFL Total	22	26	274	10.5	0	1

ORVILLE TRASK Trask, Orville Luther 6'4", 260 **DT**
Col: San Jacinto Coll. TX (J.C.); Rice *HS:* San Jacinto [Houston, TX] B: 12/3/1934, Pueblo, CO *Drafted:* 1956 Round 24 ChiC
1960 Hou: 14 G. **1961** Hou: 14 G; Int 1-17. **1962** Oak: 7 G. **Total:** 35 G; Int 1-17.

HERB TRAVENIO Travenio, Herbert Charles 6'0", 218 **K**
Col: No College B: 2/28/1933
1964 SD: 3 G; Scor 16, 2-5 40.0% FG, 10-12 83.3% XK. **1965** SD: 14 G; Scor 94, 18-30 60.0% FG, **40-40** 100.0% XK. **Total:** 17 G; Scor 110, 20-35 57.1% FG, 50-52 96.2% XK.

BRICK TRAVIS Travis, James Edward 6'1", 205 **T**
Col: Tarkio; Missouri *HS:* Tarkio [MO] B: 9/17/1897, Tarkio, MO D: 9/18/1982, Chesterfield, MO
1921 RI: 5 G. **1923** StL: 7 G. **Total:** 12 G.

JOHN TRAVIS Travis, John Reginald 6'1", 216 **FB**
Col: Foothill Coll. CA (J.C.); San Jose State *HS:* Fremont [Sunnyvale, CA] B: 8/23/1943, San Jose, CA *Drafted:* 1966 Round 18 SD
1966 SD: 6 G.

MACK TRAVIS Travis, Mack Henry Jr. 6'1", 280 **NT**
Col: California *HS:* Valley [Las Vegas, NV] B: 7/3/1970, Las Vegas, NV
1993 Det: 4 G.

KEITH TRAYLOR Traylor, Byron Keith 6'2", 285 **DT**
Col: Coffeyville CC KS; Oklahoma; Central Oklahoma *HS:* Malvern [AR] B: 9/3/1969, Little Rock, AR *Drafted:* 1991 Round 3 Den
1991 Den: 16 G. **1992** Den: 16 G; KR 1-13 13.0; 1 Sac. **1993** GB: 5 G. **1995** KC: 16 G; 1.5 Sac. **1996** KC: 15 G; 1 Sac. **1997** Den: 16 G; Int 1-62 1 TD; 6 Pt; 2 Sac. **1998** Den: 15 G; 2 Sac. **Total:** 99 G; KR 1-13 13.0; Int 1-62 1 TD; 6 Pt; 7.5 Sac.

JERRY TRAYNHAM Traynham, Gerald Francis 5'10", 190 **HB**
Col: USC *HS:* Woodland [CA] B: 1/23/1939, Sacramento, CA
1961 Den: 2 G; Rush 6-12 2.0; Rec 1-(-1) -1.0.

WADE TRAYNHAM Traynham, Wade Lanier 6'2", 218 **K**
Col: Frederick CC MD *HS:* Hampton [VA] B: 2/3/1942, Hampton, VA
1966 Atl: 2 G; Scor 2, 0-1 FG, 2-2 100.0% XK. **1967** Atl: 14 G; Scor 43, 7-18 38.9% FG, 22-22 100.0% XK. **Total:** 16 G; Scor 45, 7-19 36.8% FG, 24-24 100.0% XK.

BARNEY TRAYNOR Traynor, Bernard Philip 6'1", 190 **C**
Col: Colgate *HS:* South Division [Milwaukee, WI] B: 11/24/1896, Beaver Dam, WI D: 8/26/1980, Austin, TX
1925 Mil: 5 G.

MARK TRAYNOWICZ Traynowicz, Mark Joseph 6'5", 277 **OG-C**
Col: Nebraska *HS:* West [Bellevue, NE] B: 11/20/1962, Omaha, NE
Drafted: 1985 Round 2 Buf
1985 Buf: 14 G. **1986** Buf: 16 G. **1987** Buf: 11 G. **1988** Buf-Pho: 9 G. Buf: 4 G. Pho: 5 G. **1989** Pho: 2 G. **Total:** 52 G.

JOHN TREADAWAY Treadaway, John Charles 6'5", 258 **T**
(Long John) *Col:* Lon Morris Coll. TX (J.C.); Hardin-Simmons *HS:* Nacogdoches [TX] B: 8/21/1917, Moscow, TX
1948 NYG: 12 G. **1949** Det: 7 G; 1 Fum. **Total:** 19 G; 1 Fum.

DAVID TREADWELL Treadwell, David Mark 6'1", 180 **K**
Col: Clemson *HS:* The Bolles [Jacksonville, FL] B: 2/27/1965, Columbia, SC

		Scoring						
Year Team	**G**	**Pts**	**FG**	**FGA**	**FG%**	**XK**	**XKA**	**XK%**
1989 Den	16	120	27	33	81.8	39	40	97.5
1990 Den	16	109	25	34	73.5	34	36	94.4
1991 Den	16	112	27	36	75.0	31	32	96.9
1992 Den	16	88	20	24	83.3	28	28	100.0
1993 NYG	16	103	25	31	80.6	28	29	96.6
1994 NYG	13	55	11	17	64.7	22	23	95.7
NFL Total	93	587	135	175	77.1	182	188	96.8

BUZZ TREBOTICH Trebotich, Ivan Peter 5'10", 208 **BB-DB-LB-FB**
Col: St. Mary's (Cal.) *HS:* St. Mary's Prep [Berkeley, CA] B: 12/30/1920, Oakland, CA D: 8/4/1992, Napa, CA
AAFC **1947** BalA: 2 G; Rush 3-(-4) -1.3; KR 1-17 17.0.

NFL **1944** Det: 10 G; Rush 1-2 2.0. **1945** Det: 9 G; Pass 1-1 100.0%, 8 8.00; Rush 3-3 1.0; Int 3-46; 1 Fum. **Total:** 19 G; Pass 1-1 100.0%, 8 8.00; Rush 4-5 1.3; Int 3-46; 1 Fum.

BRIAN TREGGS Treggs, Brian Allan 5'9", 161 **WR**
Col: California *HS:* Carson [CA] B: 6/11/1970, Los Angeles, CA
1992 Sea: 2 G; PR 4-31 7.8.

GREG TREMBLE Tremble, Gregory Deshawn 5'11", 188 **DB**
Col: Northeastern Oklahoma A&M (J.C.); Georgia *HS:* Warner Robins [GA] B: 4/16/1972, Warner Robins, GA
1995 Dal-Phi: 11 G. Dal: 7 G. Phi: 4 G. **Total:** 11 G.

ADAM TREU Treu, Adam 6'5", 300 **OT**
Col: Nebraska *HS:* Pius X [Lincoln, NE] B: 6/24/1974, Lincoln, NE
Drafted: 1997 Round 3 Oak
1997 Oak: 16 G. **1998** Oak: 16 G. **Total:** 32 G.

JACK TRIGGS Triggs, John Stephen 6'0", 200 **FB**
Col: Providence *HS:* Brockton [MA]; Little Rock Central HS [AR] B: 1/11/1903, Brockton, MA D: 2/16/1951, Brockton, MA
1926 Prov: 3 G.

FRANK TRIGILIO Trigilio, Frank J 5'11", 200 **RB-LB**
Col: Vermont; Alfred *HS:* Oakfield [NY] B: 1919
AAFC.

		Rushing			
Year Team	**G**	**Att**	**Yds**	**Avg**	**TD**
1946 LA-A-MiaA	8	41	126	3.1	1

STEVE TRIMBLE Trimble, Steven Garfield 5'10", 181 **DB**
Col: Maryland *HS:* Fort Hill [Cumberland, MD] B: 5/11/1958, Cumberland, MD
1981 Den: 3 G. **1982** Den: 6 G. **1983** Den: 5 G. **1987** ChiB: 3 G. **Total:** 17 G.

WAYNE TRIMBLE Trimble, Wayne Allen 6'3", 203 **DB**
Col: Alabama *HS:* Cullman [AL] B: 12/10/1944, Cullman, AL
Drafted: 1967 Round 4 SF
1967 SF: 1 G.

MEL TRIPLETT Triplett, Melvin C 6'1", 215 **FB**
Col: Toledo *HS:* Girard [OH] B: 12/24/1931, Indianola, MS
Drafted: 1955 Round 5 NYG
1955 NYG: KR 3-47 15.7. **1956** NYG: KR 1-2 2.0. **1958** NYG: KR 4-59 14.8. **1960** NYG: KR 2-38 19.0. **1961** Min: KR 3-41 13.7. **Total:** KR 13-187 14.4.

		Rushing				Receiving					Tot
Year Team	**G**	**Att**	**Yds**	**Avg**	**TD**	**Rec**	**Yds**	**Avg**	**TD**	**Fum**	**TD**
1955 NYG	12	34	138	4.1	0	3	9	3.0	0	3	0
1956 NYG	12	125	515	4.1	5	6	48	8.0	1	10	6
1957 NYG	10	61	216	3.5	0	4	75	18.8	0	1	0
1958 NYG	12	118	466	3.9	1	7	110	15.7	0	7	1
1959 NYG	11	91	381	4.2	1	6	78	13.0	0	5	1
1960 NYG	12	124	573	4.6	4	5	48	9.6	2	7	6
1961 Min	14	80	407	5.1	1	10	41	4.1	0	4	1
1962 Min	14	52	160	3.1	2	2	30	15.0	1	2	3
NFL Total	97	685	2856	4.2	14	43	439	10.2	4	39	18

WALLY TRIPLETT Triplett, Wallace III 5'10", 170 **HB-DB**
Col: Penn State *HS:* Cheltenham [Wyncote, PA] B: 4/18/1926, La Mott, PA *Drafted:* 1949 Round 19 Det
1949 Det: Rec 8-90 11.3. **1950** Det: Rec 6-70 11.7; KR 8-411 51.4 1 TD; 1 Fum TD. **1953** ChiC: Rec 3-15 5.0; KR 10-253 25.3. **Total:** Rec 17-175 10.3; KR 18-664 36.9 1 TD; 1 Fum TD.

		Rushing				Punt Returns					Tot
Year Team	**G**	**Att**	**Yds**	**Avg**	**TD**	**Ret**	**Yds**	**Avg**	**TD**	**Fum**	**TD**
1949 Det	11	53	221	4.2	1	21	281	13.4	1	3	2
1950 Det	7	14	92	6.6	0	11	94	8.5	0	1	2
1952 ChiC	2	0	0	—	0	2	26	13.0	0	0	0
1953 ChiC	4	3	8	2.7	0	0	0	—	0	1	0
NFL Total	24	70	321	4.6	1	34	401	11.8	1	5	4

BILL TRIPLETT Triplett, William Clarence 6'2", 215 **RB-DB**
Col: Miami (Ohio) *HS:* Girard [OH] B: 5/9/1940, Indianola, MS
Drafted: 1962 Round 6 NYG
1962 StL: Int 1-24. **Total:** Int 1-24.

		Rushing				Receiving			
Year Team	**G**	**Att**	**Yds**	**Avg**	**TD**	**Rec**	**Yds**	**Avg**	**TD**
1962 StL	14	2	12	6.0	0	0	0	—	0
1963 StL	13	134	652	4.9	5	31	396	12.8	3
1965 StL	14	174	617	3.5	6	26	256	9.8	1

Year Team									
1966 StL	8	13	25	1.9	0	2	6	3.0	0
1967 NYG	11	58	171	2.9	2	7	69	9.9	0
1968 Det	12	120	384	3.2	0	28	135	4.8	0
1969 Det	14	111	377	3.4	3	13	141	10.8	1
1970 Det	14	48	156	3.3	1	6	52	8.7	0
1971 Det	14	4	4	1.0	0	0	0	—	0
1972 Det	14	17	48	2.8	0	0	0	—	0
NFL Total	128	681	2446	3.6	17	113	1055	9.3	5

	Kickoff Returns					Tot
Year Team	Ret	Yds	Avg	TD	Fum	TD
1962 StL	24	608	25.3	0	1	0
1963 StL	14	229	16.4	0	4	8
1965 StL	0	0	—	0	1	7
1967 NYG	7	139	19.9	0	2	2
1968 Det	0	0	—	0	3	0
1969 Det	0	0	—	0	1	4
1970 Det	0	0	—	0	2	1
1971 Det	3	70	23.3	0	1	0
1972 Det	1	12	12.0	0	0	0
NFL Total	49	1058	21.6	0	15	22

PAUL TRIPOLI Tripoli, Paul Randall 6′0″, 197 **DB**
Col: Alabama *HS:* Liverpool [NY] B: 12/14/1961, Utica, NY
1987 TB: 13 G; Int 3-17 1 TD; 6 Pt.

CHARLIE TRIPPI Trippi, Charles Louis 6′0″, 186 **HB-DB-QB**
Col: Georgia *HS:* Pittston [PA]; La Salle Acad. [New York, NY]
B: 12/14/1922, Pittston, PA *Drafted:* 1945 Round 1 ChiC *HOF:* 1968
1947 ChiC: Int 1-59 1 TD. **1954** ChiC: Int 3-34. **Total:** Int 4-93 1 TD.

		Passing							
Year Team	G	Att	Comp	Comp%	Yds	YPA	TD	Int	Rating
1947 ChiC	11	2	1	50.0	49	24.50	0	1	56.3
1948 ChiC	12	8	4	50.0	118	14.75	1	0	135.4
1949 ChiC	12	2	0	0.0	0	0.00	0	0	39.6
1950 ChiC	12	3	1	33.3	19	6.33	0	0	56.2
1951 ChiC	12	191	88	46.1	1191	6.24	8	13	52.1
1952 ChiC	11	181	84	46.4	890	4.92	5	13	40.5
1953 ChiC	12	34	20	58.8	195	5.74	2	1	82.4
1954 ChiC	12	13	7	53.8	85	6.54	0	3	34.6
1955 ChiC	5	0	0	—	0	—	0	0	—
NFL Total	99	434	205	47.2	2547	5.87	16	31	48.4

	Rushing				Receiving			
Year Team	Att	Yds	Avg	TD	Rec	Yds	Avg	TD
1947 ChiC	83	401	4.8	2	23	240	10.4	0
1948 ChiC	128	690	5.4	6	22	228	10.4	2
1949 ChiC	112	553	4.9	3	34	412	12.1	6
1950 ChiC	99	426	4.3	3	32	270	8.4	1
1951 ChiC	78	501	6.4	4	0	0	—	0
1952 ChiC	72	350	4.9	4	5	66	13.2	0
1953 ChiC	97	433	4.5	0	11	87	7.9	2
1954 ChiC	18	152	8.4	1	3	18	6.0	0
NFL Total	687	3506	5.1	23	130	1321	10.2	11

	Punt Returns				Kickoff Returns			
Year Team	Ret	Yds	Avg	TD	Ret	Yds	Avg	TD
1947 ChiC	8	141	17.6	0	15	321	21.4	0
1948 ChiC	11	213	19.4	**2**	16	354	22.1	0
1949 ChiC	10	160	16.0	0	18	427	23.7	0
1950 ChiC	7	54	7.7	0	8	139	17.4	0
1953 ChiC	21	239	**11.4**	0	8	199	24.9	0
1954 ChiC	6	57	9.5	0	1	17	17.0	0
NFL Total	63	864	13.7	2	66	1457	22.1	0

	Punting				Tot
Year Team	Punts	Yds	Avg	Fum	TD
1947 ChiC	0	0	—	4	3
1948 ChiC	13	564	43.4	5	10
1949 ChiC	8	292	36.5	3	9
1950 ChiC	2	94	47.0	5	4
1951 ChiC	12	446	37.2	4	4
1952 ChiC	16	588	36.8	3	4
1953 ChiC	54	2314	42.9	5	2
1954 ChiC	59	2308	39.1	1	1
1955 ChiC	32	1301	40.7	0	0
NFL Total	196	7907	40.3	30	37

JOHN TRIPSON Tripson, John Robert 6′3″, 210 **T**
Col: Mississippi State *HS:* Mission [TX] B: 9/17/1919, Madero, TX
Drafted: 1941 Round 6 Det
1941 Det: 11 G.

FRANK TRIPUCKA Tripucka, Francis Joseph 6′2″, 192 **QB**
(Trip) *Col:* Notre Dame *HS:* Bloomfield [IN] B: 12/8/1927, Bloomfield, NJ *Drafted:* 1949 Round 1 Phi

		Passing							
Year Team	G	Att	Comp	Comp%	Yds	YPA	TD	Int	Rating
1949 Det	6	145	62	42.8	833	5.74	9	14	42.8
1950 ChiC	10	108	47	43.5	720	6.67	4	**7**	51.5
1951 ChiC	3	29	17	58.6	244	8.41	2	1	94.6
1952 ChiC-Dal	12	186	91	48.9	809	4.35	3	17	28.3
1952 ChiC	6	12	5	41.7	40	3.33	0	0	50.7
1952 Dal	6	174	86	49.4	769	4.42	3	17	27.8
1960 Den	14	**478**	**248**	51.9	**3038**	6.36	24	34	58.9
1961 Den	14	344	167	48.5	1690	4.91	10	21	47.3
1962 Den	14	**440**	**240**	54.5	**2917**	6.63	17	25	64.4
1963 Den	2	15	7	46.7	31	2.07	0	5	13.9
NFL Total	75	1745	879	50.4	10282	5.89	69	124	52.2

	Rushing				Punting			
Year Team	Att	Yds	Avg	TD	Punts	Yds	Avg	Fum
1949 Det	12	36	3.0	1	27	1074	39.8	1
1950 ChiC	4	35	8.8	1	18	787	43.7	2
1951 ChiC	1	14	14.0	0	10	429	42.9	0
1952 ChiC-Dal	10	25	2.5	3	34	1322	38.9	6
1952 ChiC	1	-3	-3.0	0	30	1155	38.5	2
1952 Dal	9	28	3.1	3	4	167	41.8	4
1960 Den	10	0	0.0	0	0	0	—	7
1961 Den	4	-8	-2.0	0	0	0	—	3
1962 Den	2	-1	-0.5	1	0	0	—	2
NFL Total	43	101	2.3	6	89	3612	40.6	21

RICK TROCANO Trocano, Richard Charles 6′0″, 188 **QB-DB**
Col: Pittsburgh *HS:* Brooklyn [OH] B: 4/4/1959, Cleveland, OH
Drafted: 1981 Round 11 Pit
1981 Cle: 6 G. **1982** Cle: 2 G. **Total:** 8 G.

BOB TROCOLOR Trocolor, Robert G 6′2″, 207 **QB-DB-HB**
Col: Long Island University; Alabama *HS:* Hackensack [NJ]
B: 3/31/1917, Oak Hill, TX D: 7/27/1984, Franklin Lakes, NJ
1942 NYG: Pass 5-3 60.0%, 52 10.40 1 TD 1 Int; PR 2-24 12.0; KR 1-35 35.0; Punt 16-661 41.3. **1943** NYG: Pass 7-2 28.6%, 4 0.57 1 Int; PR 1-17 17.0; KR 2-64 32.0; Punt 5-155 31.0. **1944** Bkn: Punt 1-10 10.0. **Total:** Pass 12-5 41.7%, 56 4.67 1 TD 2 Int; PR 3-41 13.7; KR 3-99 33.0; Punt 22-826 37.5.

		Rushing			
Year Team	G	Att	Yds	Avg	TD
1942 NYG	7	26	0	0.0	0
1943 NYG	5	6	-4	-0.7	0
1944 Bkn	2	3	8	2.7	0
NFL Total	14	35	4	0.1	0

GENE TROSCH Trosch, Eugene Lloyd 6′7″, 277 **DE**
Col: Miami (Fla.) *HS:* Madonna [Weirton, WV] B: 6/7/1945, Steubenville, OH *Drafted:* 1967 Round 1 KC
1967 KC: 14 G. **1969** KC: 13 G. **Total:** 27 G.

MILT TROST Trost, Milton Frank 6′1″, 206 **T-DE-OE**
(Bud) *Col:* Marquette *HS:* Washington [Milwaukee, WI] B: 3/4/1913, Detroit, MI D: 4/2/1986, Zephyrhills, FL
1935 ChiB: 5 G. **1936** ChiB: 11 G. **1937** ChiB: 10 G. **1938** ChiB: 10 G. **1939** ChiB: 10 G. **1940** Phi: 7 G. **Total:** 53 G.

JEREMIAH TROTTER Trotter, Jeremiah 6′0″, 261 **LB**
Col: Stephen F. Austin St. *HS:* Hooks [TX] B: 1/20/1977, Hooks, TX
Drafted: 1998 Round 3 Phi
1998 Phi: 8 G.

BILL TROUP Troup, Paul William III 6′5″, 220 **QB**
Col: Virginia; South Carolina *HS:* Bethel Park [PA] B: 4/2/1951, Pittsburgh, PA

		Passing							
Year Team	G	Att	Comp	Comp%	Yds	YPA	TD	Int	Rating
1974 Bal	1	0	0	—	0	—	0	0	—
1976 Bal	14	18	8	44.4	117	6.50	0	1	43.1
1977 Bal	14	2	0	0.0	0	0.00	0	1	0.0
1978 Bal	12	296	154	52.0	1882	6.36	10	21	53.6
1980 GB	2	12	4	33.3	48	4.00	0	3	6.9
NFL Total	43	328	166	50.6	2047	6.24	10	26	47.4

	Rushing				
Year Team	Att	Yds	Avg	TD	Fum
1976 Bal	5	-1	-0.2	1	2
1977 Bal	7	-8	-1.1	0	0
1978 Bal	18	25	1.4	1	7
NFL Total	30	16	0.5	2	9

DAVID TROUT Trout, David Marshall 5′6″, 165 **K**
Col: Pittsburgh *HS:* Southmoreland [Alverton, PA] B: 11/12/1957, Mount Pleasant, PA
1981 Pit: 16 G; Scor 74, 12-17 70.6% FG, 38-46 82.6% XK. **1987** Pit: 3 G; Scor 10, 0-2 FG, 10-10 100.0% XK. **Total:** 19 G; Scor 84, 12-19 63.2% FG, 48-56 85.7% XK.

RAY TROWBRIDGE Trowbridge, Raymond Newton 6'0", 170 **OE**
Col: Boston College; Purdue *HS:* Everett [MA] B: 7/19/1898, South Bend, IN D: 1/17/1975, Atlanta, GA
1920 Cle: 3 G. **1921** NYG: 2 G. **Total:** 5 G.

DALTON TRUAX Truax, Dalton Lloyd 6'2", 235 **OT**
Col: Tulane *HS:* Holy Cross [New Orleans, LA] B: 1/17/1935, New Orleans, LA
1960 Oak: 14 G.

BILLY TRUAX Truax, William Frederick 6'5", 240 **TE**
Col: Louisiana State *HS:* Holy Cross [New Orleans, LA] B: 7/15/1943, Gulfport, MS *Drafted:* 1964 Round 2 Cle
1966 LARm: **1** Fum TD. **Total:** 1 Fum TD.

		Receiving					Tot
Year Team	G	Rec	Yds	Avg	TD	Fum	TD
1964 LARm	10	0	0	—	0	0	0
1965 LARm	14	6	108	18.0	1	0	1
1966 LARm	14	29	314	10.8	0	0	1
1967 LARm	14	37	487	13.2	4	1	4
1968 LARm	14	35	417	11.9	3	0	3
1969 LARm	14	37	431	11.6	5	1	5
1970 LARm	14	36	420	11.7	3	0	3
1971 Dal	12	15	232	15.5	1	0	1
1972 Dal	6	4	49	12.3	0	0	0
1973 Dal	2	0	0	—	0	0	0
NFL Total	114	199	2458	12.4	17	2	18

JACK TRUDEAU Trudeau, Jack Francis 6'3", 220 **QB**
Col: Illinois *HS:* Granada [Livermore, CA] B: 9/9/1962, Forest Lake, MN *Drafted:* 1986 Round 2 Ind

		Passing							
Year Team	G	Att	Comp	Comp%	Yds	YPA	TD	Int	Rating
1986 Ind	12	417	204	48.9	2225	5.34	8	18	53.5
1987 Ind	10	229	128	55.9	1587	6.93	6	**6**	75.4
1988 Ind	2	34	14	41.2	158	4.65	0	3	19.0
1989 Ind	13	362	190	52.5	2317	6.40	15	13	71.3
1990 Ind	6	144	84	58.3	1078	7.49	6	6	78.4
1991 Ind	2	7	2	28.6	19	2.71	0	1	0.0
1992 Ind	11	181	105	58.0	1271	7.02	4	8	68.6
1993 Ind	5	162	85	52.5	992	6.12	2	7	57.4
1994 NYJ	5	91	50	54.9	496	5.45	1	4	55.9
1995 Car	1	17	11	64.7	100	5.88	0	3	40.9
NFL Total	67	1644	873	53.1	10243	6.23	42	69	63.3

	Rushing				
Year Team	Att	Yds	Avg	TD	Fum
1986 Ind	13	21	1.6	1	**13**
1987 Ind	15	7	0.5	0	10
1989 Ind	35	91	2.6	2	10
1990 Ind	10	28	2.8	0	11
1992 Ind	13	6	0.5	0	3
1993 Ind	5	3	0.6	0	2
1994 NYJ	6	30	5.0	0	2
1995 Car	0	0	—	0	1
NFL Total	97	186	1.9	3	52

HAL TRUESDELL Truesdell, Harold Palmer 6'0", 200 **T**
Col: Hamline *HS:* Pine City [MN] D: 1932
1930 Min: 1 G.

DAVE TRUITT Truitt, David Moreland 6'4", 232 **TE**
Col: North Carolina *HS:* Gaithersburg [MD] B: 2/18/1964
1987 Was: 1 G.

GREG TRUITT Truitt, Gregory Hoyt 6'0", 235 **C**
Col: Penn State *HS:* Riverview [Sarasota, FL] B: 12/8/1965, Sarasota, FL
1994 Cin: 16 G. **1995** Cin: 16 G. **1996** Cin: 16 G. **1997** Cin: 16 G; 2 Fum. **1998** Cin: 11 G; 1 Fum. **Total:** 75 G; 3 Fum.

OLANDA TRUITT Truitt, Olanda Raynard 6'0", 187 **WR**
Col: Pittsburgh; Mississippi State *HS:* A.H. Parker [Birmingham, AL] B: 1/4/1971, Bessemer, AL *Drafted:* 1993 Round 5 LARd
1993 Min: 8 G; Rec 4-40 10.0. **1994** Was: 9 G; Rec 2-89 44.5 1 TD; 6 Pt. **1995** Was: 5 G; Rec 9-154 17.1 1 TD; 6 Pt; 1 Fum. **1996** Oak: 10 G. **1997** Oak: 14 G; Rec 7-91 13.0 1 TD; KR 2-51 25.5; 6 Pt; 1 Fum. **Total:** 46 G; Rec 22-374 17.0 3 TD; KR 2-51 25.5; 18 Pt; 2 Fum.

DON TRULL Trull, Donald Dean 6'1", 195 **QB**
Col: Baylor *HS:* Southeast [Oklahoma City, OK] B: 10/20/1941, Oklahoma City, OK *Drafted:* 1963 Round 14 Hou

		Passing							
Year Team	G	Att	Comp	Comp%	Yds	YPA	TD	Int	Rating
1964 Hou	14	86	36	41.9	439	5.10	1	2	52.4
1965 Hou	14	107	38	35.5	528	4.93	5	5	48.3
1966 Hou	14	172	84	48.8	1200	6.98	10	**5**	79.1
1967 Hou-Bos	10	92	31	33.7	480	5.22	1	7	23.8
1967 Hou	3	11	4	36.4	38	3.45	0	0	46.8
1967 Bos	7	81	27	33.3	442	5.46	1	7	20.7
1968 Hou	11	105	53	50.5	864	8.23	10	3	98.3
1969 Hou	14	75	34	45.3	469	6.25	3	6	45.9
NFL Total	77	637	276	43.3	3980	6.25	30	28	61.6

	Rushing				
Year Team	Att	Yds	Avg	TD	Fum
1964 Hou	12	42	3.5	0	2
1965 Hou	29	145	5.0	2	3
1966 Hou	38	139	3.7	7	3
1967 Hou-Bos	22	30	1.4	3	4
1967 Hou	3	-5	-1.7	0	0
1967 Bos	19	35	1.8	3	4
1968 Hou	14	47	3.4	0	4
1969 Hou	8	25	3.1	2	1
NFL Total	123	428	3.5	14	17

BOB TRUMPY Trumpy, Robert Theodore Jr. 6'6", 228 **TE**
Col: Illinois; Utah *HS:* Springfield [IL] B: 3/6/1945, Springfield, IL *Drafted:* 1968 Round 12 Cin
1968 Cin: Rush 1-(-1) -1.0. **Total:** Rush 1-(-1) -1.0.

		Receiving				
Year Team	G	Rec	Yds	Avg	TD	Fum
1968 Cin	14	37	639	17.3	3	1
1969 Cin	14	37	835	22.6	9	2
1970 Cin	11	29	480	16.6	2	1
1971 Cin	14	40	531	13.3	3	0
1972 Cin	12	44	500	11.4	2	0
1973 Cin	14	29	435	15.0	5	0
1974 Cin	13	21	330	15.7	2	0
1975 Cin	11	22	276	12.5	1	1
1976 Cin	13	21	323	15.4	7	1
1977 Cin	12	18	251	13.9	1	1
NFL Total	128	298	4600	15.4	35	7

ERIC TRUVILLION Truvillion, Eric Brian 6'4", 205 **WR**
Col: Florida A&M *HS:* Springfield Gardens [Queens, NY] B: 6/18/1959, New York, NY
1987 Det: 3 G; Rec 12-207 17.3 1 TD; 6 Pt; 1 Fum.

EDDIE TRYON Tryon, Joseph Edward 5'8", 180 **WB-TB**
(Cannonball) *Col:* Colgate *HS:* Medford [MA]; Suffield Prep [CT] B: 7/25/1900, Medford, MA D: 5/1/1982, St. Petersburg, FL
1927 NYY: 14 G; Rush 2 TD; Rec 2 TD; Int **2** TD; Scor 44, 8 XK; Tot TD **6**.

CHALMERS TSCHAPPAT Tschappat, John Chalmers Jr. 5'11", 180 **T**
Col: West Virginia Wesleyan *HS:* Bellaire [OH] B: 6/1896, Bellaire, OH Deceased
1921 Day: 2 G.

SAM TSOUTSOUVAS Tsoutsouvas, John Samuel 6'0", 205 **C-LB**
Col: Ventura Coll. CA (J.C.); Oregon State *HS:* Santa Barbara [CA] B: 10/8/1917, Madera, CA D: 3/27/1989, Santa Barbara, CA
1940 Det: 3 G.

LOU TSOUTSOUVAS Tsoutsouvas, Louis Samuel 5'11", 210 **C-LB**
(Chooch) *Col:* Stanford *HS:* Santa Barbara [CA] B: 7/4/1915, Fresno, CA
1938 Pit: 5 G.

ESERA TUAOLO Tuaolo, Esera Tavai 6'2", 277 **NT**
Col: Oregon State *HS:* Don Antonio Lugo [Chino, CA] B: 7/11/1968, Honolulu, HI *Drafted:* 1991 Round 2 GB
1991 GB: 16 G; Int 1-23; 3.5 Sac. **1992** GB-Min: 7 G; 1 Sac. GB: 4 G; 1 Sac. Min: 3 G. **1993** Min: 11 G. **1994** Min: 16 G. **1995** Min: 16 G; 3 Sac. **1996** Min: 14 G; 2.5 Sac. **1997** Jac: 6 G; 1 Sac. **1998** Atl: 13 G. **Total:** 99 G; Int 1-23; 11 Sac.

NATU TUATAGALOA Tuatagaloa, Gerardus Mauritius Natuitasina 6'4", 273 **DE**
Col: California *HS:* San Rafael [CA] B: 5/25/1966, San Francisco, CA *Drafted:* 1989 Round 5 Cin
1989 Cin: 14 G; 2.5 Sac. **1990** Cin: 16 G; 4.5 Sac. **1991** Cin: 16 G; 2 Sac. **1992** Sea: 13 G; Int 1-0; 3 Sac. **1993** Sea: 16 G; KR 1-10 10.0; 3.5 Sac. **1995** Hou: 1 G. **Total:** 76 G; KR 1-10 10.0; Int 1-0; 15.5 Sac.

JERRY TUBBS Tubbs, Gerald J 6'2", 221 **LB-C**
Col: Oklahoma *HS:* Breckenridge [TX] B: 1/23/1935, Throckmorton, TX *Drafted:* 1957 Round 1 ChiC
1958 ChiC-SF: KR 1-11 11.0. ChiC: KR 1-11 11.0. **Total:** KR 1-11 11.0.

		Interceptions		
Year Team	G	Int	Yds	TD
1957 ChiC	11	0	0	0
1958 ChiC-SF	11	0	0	0
1958 ChiC	7	0	0	0
1958 SF	4	0	0	0
1959 SF	12	2	32	0
1960 Dal	12	1	5	0
1961 Dal	14	3	33	0

1962 Dal	14	4	35	0
1963 Dal	14	2	61	0
1964 Dal	13	2	27	0
1965 Dal	14	2	9	0
1966 Dal	4	1	6	0
NFL Total	119	17	208	0

WINFRED TUBBS Tubbs, Winfred O'Neal 6'4", 250 **LB**
Col: Texas *HS:* Fairfield [TX] B: 9/24/1970, Hollywood, FL
Drafted: 1994 Round 3 NO
1994 NO: 13 G; Int 1-0; 1 Sac. **1995** NO: 7 G; Int 1-6; 1 Sac. **1996** NO: 16 G; Int 1-11; 1 Sac. **1997** NO: 16 G; Int 2-21; 2.5 Sac. **1998** SF: 16 G; Int 1-7; 1 Sac. **Total:** 68 G; Int 6-45; 6.5 Sac.

ERROLL TUCKER Tucker, Erroll R 5'8", 169 **DB**
Col: Long Beach City Coll. CA (J.C.); Utah *HS:* Lynwood [CA]
B: 7/6/1964, Pittsburgh, PA *Drafted:* 1986 Round 5 Pit

		Punt Returns				Kickoff Returns				
Year Team	**G**	**Ret**	**Yds**	**Avg**	**TD**	**Ret**	**Yds**	**Avg**	**TD**	**Fum**
1988 Buf	9	10	80	8.0	0	15	310	20.7	0	1
1989 Buf-NE	9	19	165	8.7	0	23	436	19.0	0	2
1989 Buf	4	6	63	10.5	0	10	166	16.6	0	0
1989 NE	5	13	102	7.8	0	13	270	20.8	0	2
NFL Total	18	29	245	8.4	0	38	746	19.6	0	3

GARY TUCKER Tucker, Gary 5'11", 205 **RB**
Col: Vanderbilt; Tennessee-Chattanooga *HS:* Brainerd [Chattanooga, TN] B: 2/19/1945, Shelbyville, TN *Drafted:* 1967 Round 5 Mia
1968 Mia: 14 G; Rush 4-13 3.3; PR 5-40 8.0; KR 3-54 18.0; 1 Fum.

MARK TUCKER Tucker, Mark Frederick 6'3", 290 **OG**
Col: USC *HS:* Phineas Banning [Los Angeles, CA] B: 4/29/1968, Spokane, WA *Drafted:* 1991 Round 7 Atl
1994 Ariz: 16 G.

BOB TUCKER Tucker, Robert Louis 6'3", 230 **TE**
Col: Bloomsburg *HS:* Hazleton [PA] B: 6/8/1945, Hazleton, PA
1971 NYG: Rush 1-1 1.0. **1972** NYG: Rush 3-6 2.0 1 TD. **1973** NYG: Rush 1-4 4.0. **1975** NYG: Rush 1-(-5) -5.0. **Total:** Rush 6-6 1.0 1 TD.

		Receiving					Tot
Year Team	**G**	**Rec**	**Yds**	**Avg**	**TD**	**Fum**	**TD**
1970 NYG	14	40	571	14.3	5	0	5
1971 NYG	12	59	791	13.4	4	3	4
1972 NYG	14	55	764	13.9	4	4	5
1973 NYG	14	50	681	13.6	5	2	5
1974 NYG	13	41	496	12.1	2	1	2
1975 NYG	14	34	484	14.2	1	1	1
1976 NYG	14	42	498	11.9	1	1	1
1977 NYG-Min	13	15	200	13.3	2	1	2
1977 NYG	5	6	91	15.2	0	1	0
1977 Min	8	9	109	12.1	2	0	2
1978 Min	16	47	540	11.5	0	2	0
1979 Min	16	24	223	9.3	2	1	2
1980 Min	16	15	173	11.5	1	1	1
NFL Total	156	422	5421	12.8	27	17	28

RYAN TUCKER Tucker, Ryan Huey 6'5", 305 **C**
Col: Texas Christian *HS:* Robert E. Lee [Midland, TX] B: 6/12/1975, Lubbock, TX *Drafted:* 1997 Round 4 StL
1997 StL: 7 G. **1998** StL: 5 G. **Total:** 12 G.

TRAVIS TUCKER Tucker, Travis Tyrone 6'3", 234 **TE**
Col: Southern Connecticut State *HS:* South Shore [Brooklyn, NY]
B: 9/19/1963, Brooklyn, NY *Drafted:* 1985 Round 11 Cle
1985 Cle: 16 G; Rec 2-20 10.0. **1986** Cle: 16 G; Rec 2-29 14.5. **1987** Cle: 4 G. **Total:** 36 G; Rec 4-49 12.3.

WENDELL TUCKER Tucker, Wendell Edward 5'10", 185 **WR**
Col: South Carolina State *HS:* Benjamin Franklin [Philadelphia, PA]
B: 9/4/1943, Philadelphia, PA
1967 LARm: PR 6-40 6.7; KR 11-242 22.0. **Total:** PR 6-40 6.7; KR 11-242 22.0.

		Receiving				
Year Team	**G**	**Rec**	**Yds**	**Avg**	**TD**	**Fum**
1967 LARm	7	0	0	—	0	3
1968 LARm	10	7	124	17.7	4	0
1969 LARm	14	38	629	16.6	7	0
1970 LARm	12	12	230	19.2	0	0
NFL Total	43	57	983	17.2	11	3

BILL TUCKER Tucker, William 6'2", 219 **RB**
Col: Tennessee State *HS:* Weir [Weirton, WV] B: 9/14/1943, Union, SC
Drafted: 1967 Round 3 SF
1967 SF: PR 1-1 1.0. **Total:** PR 1-1 1.0.

		Rushing				Receiving			
Year Team	**G**	**Att**	**Yds**	**Avg**	**TD**	**Rec**	**Yds**	**Avg**	**TD**
1967 SF	14	3	5	1.7	0	2	22	11.0	0
1968 SF	14	30	135	4.5	3	15	197	13.1	4
1969 SF	13	20	72	3.6	2	14	104	7.4	2
1970 SF	14	42	137	3.3	1	17	108	6.4	1
1971 ChiB	14	32	82	2.6	0	11	65	5.9	0
NFL Total	69	127	431	3.4	6	59	496	8.4	7

	Kickoff Returns					Tot
Year Team	**Ret**	**Yds**	**Avg**	**TD**	**Fum**	**TD**
1967 SF	9	199	22.1	0	0	0
1968 SF	5	103	20.6	0	2	7
1969 SF	1	0	0.0	0	0	4
1970 SF	25	577	23.1	0	6	2
1971 ChiB	0	0	—	0	1	0
NFL Total	40	879	22.0	0	9	13

PHIL TUCKETT Tuckett, Phillip Evans 6'0", 185 **WR**
Col: Weber State *HS:* Olympus [Salt Lake City, UT] B: 4/27/1946, Eugene, OR
1968 SD: 1 G.

DICK TUCKEY Tuckey, Richard James Kenneth Jr. 6'2", 205 **TB-DB**
Col: Manhattan *HS:* Naugatuck [CT]; Dean Acad. [Franklin, MA]
B: 9/29/1913, Naugatuck, CT D: 12/25/1974, West Haven, CT
1938 Was-Cle: 7 G; Pass 32-8 25.0%, 140 4.38 1 TD 3 Int; Rush 23-76 3.3; Rec 1-10 10.0; Scor 2, 2-3 66.7% XK. Was: 3 G; Pass 6-1 16.7%, 30 5.00 1 Int; Rush 9-39 4.3; Scor 0-1 XK. Cle: 4 G; Pass 26-7 26.9%, 110 4.23 1 TD 2 Int; Rush 14-37 2.6; Rec 1-10 10.0; Scor 2, 2-2 100.0% XK. **Total:** 7 G; Pass 32-8 25.0%, 140 4.38 1 TD 3 Int; Rush 23-76 3.3; Rec 1-10 10.0; Scor 2, 2-3 66.7% XK.

ANTHONY TUGGLE Tuggle, Anthony Ivan 6'1", 211 **DB**
Col: Southern University; Nicholls State *HS:* Baker [LA] B: 9/13/1963, Baton Rouge, LA *Drafted:* 1985 Round 4 Cin
1985 Pit: 2 G; KR 1-8 8.0. **1987** Pit: 2 G. **Total:** 4 G; KR 1-8 8.0.

JESSIE TUGGLE Tuggle, Jessie Floyd Jr. 5'11", 230 **LB**
Col: Valdosta State *HS:* Griffin [GA] B: 4/4/1965, Spalding Co., GA
1987 Atl: 12 G; 1 Sac. **1988** Atl: 16 G; **1** Fum TD; 6 Pt. **1989** Atl: 16 G; 1 Sac. **1990** Atl: 16 G; 1 Fum TD; 6 Pt; 5 Sac. **1991** Atl: 16 G; Int 1-21; 1 Fum TD; 6 Pt; 1 Sac. **1992** Atl: 15 G; Int 1-1; 1 Fum TD; 6 Pt; 1 Sac. **1993** Atl: 16 G; 2 Sac. **1994** Atl: 16 G; Int 1-0; 1 Fum. **1995** Atl: 16 G; Int 3-84 1 TD; 6 Pt; 1 Sac. **1996** Atl: 16 G; 1 Sac. **1997** Atl: 16 G; 1.5 Sac. **1998** Atl: 16 G; 1 Fum TD; 6 Pt; 3 Sac. **Total:** 187 G; Int 6-106 1 TD; 5 Fum TD; Tot TD 6; 36 Pt; 1 Fum; 17.5 Sac.

JOHN TUGGLE Tuggle, John Davis 6'1", 210 **RB**
Col: California *HS:* Independence [San Jose, CA] B: 1/13/1961, Honolulu, HI D: 8/30/1986, Tijuana, Mexico *Drafted:* 1983 Round 12 NYG
1983 NYG: 16 G; Rush 17-49 2.9 1 TD; Rec 3-50 16.7; KR 9-156 17.3; 6 Pt.

MANU TUIASOSOPO Tuiasosopo, Manu'ula Asovalu 6'3", 255 **DE**
Col: UCLA *HS:* St. Anthony's [Long Beach, CA] B: 8/30/1957, Los Angeles, CA *Drafted:* 1979 Round 1 Sea
1979 Sea: 16 G. **1980** Sea: 16 G. **1981** Sea: 16 G. **1982** Sea: 9 G; 2 Sac. **1983** Sea: 16 G; 0.5 Sac. **1984** SF: 16 G; 4 Sac. **1985** SF: 15 G; 3 Sac. **1986** SF: 15 G; Int 1-22. **Total:** 119 G; Int 1-22; 9.5 Sac.

NAVY TUIASOSOPO Tuiasosopo, Navy Asoaoga 6'2", 285 **C**
Col: Utah State *HS:* Phineas Banning [Los Angeles, CA] B: 5/24/1965, American Samoa
1987 LARm: 3 G.

MARK TUINEI Tuinei, Mark Pulemau 6'5", 302 **OT-C-DT**
Col: UCLA; Hawaii *HS:* Punahou School [Honolulu, HI] B: 3/31/1960, Oceanside, CA
1983 Dal: 10 G. **1984** Dal: 16 G; 1 Sac. **1985** Dal: 16 G. **1986** Dal: 16 G; KR 1-0; 1 Fum. **1987** Dal: 8 G. **1988** Dal: 5 G. **1989** Dal: 16 G. **1990** Dal: 13 G. **1991** Dal: 12 G. **1992** Dal: 15 G. **1993** Dal: 16 G. **1994** Dal: 15 G. **1995** Dal: 16 G. **1996** Dal: 15 G. **1997** Dal: 6 G. **Total:** 195 G; KR 1-0; 1 Fum; 1 Sac.

TOM TUINEI Tuinei, Tumua 6'4", 250 **DT**
Col: Hawaii *HS:* Waianae [HI] B: 2/21/1958, Oceanside, CA
Drafted: 1980 Round 9 Det
1980 Det: 12 G.

VAN TUINEI Tuinei, Vaega Van 6'3", 266 **DE**
Col: Golden West Coll. CA (J.C.); Arizona *HS:* Westminster [CA]
B: 2/16/1971, Garden Grove, CA
1997 SD: 3 G. **1998** Ind: 12 G; 2 Sac. **Total:** 15 G; 2 Sac.

PETER TUIPULOTU Tuipulotu, Peter Henry 5'11", 210 **RB**
Col: Brigham Young *HS:* San Mateo [CA] B: 2/20/1969, Nu'ukalofa, Tonga
1992 SD: 6 G.

WALTER TULLIS Tullis, Walter Henry 6'0", 170 **WR**
Col: Delaware State *HS:* Weaver [Hartford, CT] B: 4/12/1953, Americus, GA *Drafted:* 1976 Round 12 Was
1978 GB: 16 G; PR 1-0. **1979** GB: 16 G; Rec 10-173 17.3 1 TD; 6 Pt. **Total:** 32 G; Rec 10-173 17.3 1 TD; PR 1-0; 6 Pt.

WILLIE TULLIS Tullis, Willie James 6'0", 193 **DB**
Col: Southern Mississippi; Troy State *HS:* Headland [AL] B: 4/5/1958, Newville, AL *Drafted:* 1981 Round 8 Hou
1988 Ind: 1 Sac. **Total:** 1 Sac.

Year Team	G	Punt Returns Ret	Yds	Avg	TD	Kickoff Returns Ret	Yds	Avg	TD
1981 Hou	16	2	29	14.5	0	32	779	24.3	**1**
1982 Hou	9	0	0	—	0	5	91	18.2	0
1983 Hou	16	0	0	—	0	1	16	16.0	0
1984 Hou	16	0	0	—	0	0	0	—	0
1985 NO	14	17	141	8.3	0	23	470	20.4	0
1986 NO	7	2	10	5.0	0	2	28	14.0	0
1987 Ind	12	4	27	6.8	0	0	0	—	0
1988 Ind	16	0	0	—	0	0	0	—	0
NFL Total	106	25	207	8.3	0	63	1384	22.0	1

Year Team	Interceptions Int	Yds	TD	Fum
1983 Hou	5	65	0	0
1984 Hou	4	48	0	1
1985 NO	2	22	0	1
1987 Ind	3	0	0	0
1988 Ind	4	36	0	0
NFL Total	18	171	0	2

DARRELL TULLY Tully, Darrell Dean 6'1", 200 **TB-DB**
Col: Texas A&M-Commerce; Georgia *HS:* Eastland [TX]
B: 12/14/1917, Henryetta, OK

Year Team	G	Passing Att	Comp	Comp%	Yds	YPA	TD	Int	Rating
1939 Det	9	75	20	26.7	356	4.75	2	13	16.2

Year Team	Rushing Att	Yds	Avg	TD
1939 Det	31	50	1.6	1

GEORGE TULLY Tully, George Chandler 5'10", 180 **E**
Col: Dartmouth *HS:* East Orange [NJ] B: 3/12/1904, Orange, NJ
D: 5/1/1980, Worcester, MA
1927 Fra: 1 G.

TOM TUMULTY Tumulty, Thomas Patrick 6'3", 247 **LB**
Col: Pittsburgh *HS:* Penn Hills [Pittsburgh, PA] B: 2/11/1973, Penn Hills, PA *Drafted:* 1996 Round 6 Cin
1996 Cin: 16 G. **1997** Cin: 11 G; 1 Sac. **1998** Cin: 4 G; 0.5 Sac.
Total: 31 G; 1.5 Sac.

EMLEN TUNNELL Tunnell, Emlen Lewis 6'1", 187 **DB-HB**
(The Gremlin) *Col:* Toledo; Iowa *HS:* Radnor [PA] B: 3/29/1922, Bryn Mawr, PA D: 7/23/1975, Pleasantville, NY *HOF:* 1967
1948 NYG: Pass 2-1 50.0%, 23 11.50; Rush 17-43 2.5; Rec 4-32 8.0.
1949 NYG: Rec 1-7 7.0. **Total:** Pass 2-1 50.0%, 23 11.50; Rush 17-43 2.5; Rec 5-39 7.8.

Year Team	G	Punt Returns Ret	Yds	Avg	TD	Kickoff Returns Ret	Yds	Avg	TD
1948 NYG	10	12	115	9.6	0	1	21	21.0	0
1949 NYG	12	26	315	12.1	1	2	26	13.0	0
1950 NYG	12	31	305	9.8	0	0	0	—	0
1951 NYG	12	**34**	**489**	14.4	3	6	227	37.8	**1**
1952 NYG	12	30	**411**	13.7	0	15	364	24.3	0
1953 NYG	12	**38**	223	5.9	0	17	479	28.2	0
1954 NYG	12	25	78	3.1	0	5	98	19.6	0
1955 NYG	12	25	98	3.9	1	0	0	—	0
1956 NYG	12	22	120	5.5	0	0	0	—	0
1957 NYG	12	12	60	5.0	0	0	0	—	0
1958 NYG	12	6	0	0.0	0	0	0	—	0
1959 GB	12	1	3	3.0	0	0	0	—	0
1960 GB	12	0	0	—	0	0	0	—	0
1961 GB	13	0	0	—	0	0	0	—	0
NFL Total	167	262	2217	8.5	5	46	1215	26.4	1

Year Team	Interceptions Int	Yds	TD	Fum	Tot TD
1948 NYG	7	116	1	3	1
1949 NYG	10	251	**2**	0	3
1950 NYG	7	167	0	1	0
1951 NYG	9	74	0	2	4
1952 NYG	7	149	0	4	0
1953 NYG	6	117	0	0	0
1954 NYG	8	108	0	1	0
1955 NYG	7	76	0	1	1
1956 NYG	6	87	0	0	0
1957 NYG	6	87	1	0	1
1958 NYG	1	8	0	0	0
1959 GB	2	20	0	0	0
1960 GB	3	22	0	0	0
NFL Total	79	**1282**	4	12	10

TOM TUPA Tupa, Joseph Thomas 6'4", 220 **QB-P**
Col: Ohio State *HS:* Brecksville [Broadview Heights, OH] B: 2/6/1966, Cleveland, OH *Drafted:* 1988 Round 3 Pho
1994 Cle: Scor **3** 2XP. **Total:** Scor 3 2XP.

Year Team	G	Passing Att	Comp	Comp%	Yds	YPA	TD	Int	Rating
1988 Pho	2	6	4	66.7	49	8.17	0	0	91.7
1989 Pho	14	134	65	48.5	973	7.26	3	9	52.2
1990 Pho	15	0	0	—	0	—	0	0	—
1991 Pho	11	315	165	52.4	2053	6.52	6	13	62.0
1992 Ind	3	33	17	51.5	156	4.73	1	2	49.6
1994 Cle	16	0	0	—	0	—	0	0	—
1995 Cle	16	1	1	100.0	25	25.00	0	0	118.8
1996 NE	16	2	0	0.0	0	0.00	0	0	39.6
1997 NE	16	0	0	—	0	—	0	0	—
1998 NE	16	0	0	—	0	—	0	0	—
NFL Total	125	491	252	51.3	3256	6.63	10	24	58.9

Year Team	Rushing Att	Yds	Avg	TD	Punting Punts	Yds	Avg	Fum
1989 Pho	15	75	5.0	0	6	280	46.7	2
1990 Pho	1	0	0.0	0	0	0	—	1
1991 Pho	28	97	3.5	1	0	0	—	8
1992 Ind	3	9	3.0	0	0	0	—	1
1994 Cle	0	0	—	0	80	3211	40.1	0
1995 Cle	1	9	9.0	0	65	2831	43.6	0
1996 NE	0	0	—	0	63	2739	43.5	0
1997 NE	0	0	—	0	78	3569	45.8	0
1998 NE	2	-2	-1.0	0	74	3294	44.5	0
NFL Total	50	188	3.8	1	366	15924	43.5	12

JEFF TUPPER Tupper, Jeffrey Culver 6'5", 269 **DE**
Col: Oklahoma *HS:* Parkwood [Joplin, MO] B: 12/26/1962, Joplin, MO
Drafted: 1986 Round 5 StL
1986 Phi: 3 G. **1987** Den: 4 G; 1.5 Sac. **Total:** 7 G; 1.5 Sac.

FRANK TURBERT Turbert, Francis J 5'11", 200 **QB-DB**
Col: Charleston (WV) B: 9/7/1917, New Haven, CT D: 8/1/1987, Pembroke Pines, FL
1944 Bos: 5 G; Pass 15-5 33.3%, 37 2.47; Rush 14-(-16) -1.1; Rec 1-16 16.0; PR 1-7 7.0.

DAN TURK Turk, Daniel Anthony 6'4", 290 **C-OG**
Col: Drake; Wisconsin *HS:* James Madison [Milwaukee, WI]
B: 6/25/1962, Milwaukee, WI *Drafted:* 1985 Round 4 Pit
1985 Pit: 1 G. **1986** Pit: 16 G. **1987** TB: 13 G. **1988** TB: 12 G; 1 Fum.
1989 LARd: 16 G; KR 1-2 2.0; 1 Fum. **1990** LARd: 16 G; KR 1-7 7.0.
1991 LARd: 16 G; KR 1-0. **1992** LARd: 16 G; KR 1-3 3.0. **1993** LARd: 16 G; KR 1-0. **1994** LARd: 16 G. **1995** Oak: 16 G. **1996** Oak: 16 G; 1 Fum.
1997 Was: 16 G. **1998** Was: 16 G; 1 Fum. **Total:** 202 G; KR 5-12 2.4; 4 Fum.

GODWIN TURK Turk, Godwin Lee 6'3", 230 **LB**
Col: California; Southern University *HS:* Phillis Wheatley [Houston, TX]
B: 10/15/1950, Houston, TX *Drafted:* 1974 Round 3 NYJ
1975 NYJ: 14 G; Int 2-20. **1976** Den: 13 G. **1977** Den: 13 G. **1978** Den: 16 G; KR 1-14 14.0; Int 2-36. **Total:** 56 G; KR 1-14 14.0; Int 4-56.

MATT TURK Turk, Matt Edward 6'5", 237 **P**
Col: Wis.-Whitewater *HS:* Greenfield [WI] B: 6/16/1968, Milwaukee, WI
1996 Was: Rush 1-0. **1997** Was: Rush 1-0. **1998** Was: Rush 2-(-12) -6.0.
Total: Rush 4-(-12) -3.0.

Year Team	G	Punting Punts	Yds	Avg	Fum
1995 Was	16	74	3140	42.4	0
1996 Was	16	75	3386	45.1	1
1997 Was	16	84	3788	45.1	1
1998 Was	16	93	4103	44.1	1
NFL Total	64	326	14417	44.2	3

DOUG TURLEY Turley, Douglas Pershing 6'2", 215 **DE-OE**
Col: Scranton *HS:* John S. Fine [Nanticoke, PA] B: 11/25/1918, Nanticoke, PA D: 11/1/1992, Oak Hill, DE
1944 Was: KR 1-12 12.0. **1947** Was: KR 1-10 10.0. **1948** Was: 1 Fum TD.
Total: KR 2-22 11.0; 1 Fum TD.

Year Team	G	Receiving Rec	Yds	Avg	TD	Tot TD
1944 Was	7	8	112	14.0	1	1
1945 Was	10	17	185	10.9	1	1
1946 Was	9	6	105	17.5	0	0
1947 Was	12	6	95	15.8	1	1
1948 Was	12	8	111	13.9	0	1
NFL Total	50	45	608	13.5	3	4

JOHN TURLEY Turley, John 0 5′10″, 183 **BB-DB**
Col: Ohio Wesleyan *HS:* Delaware [OH] B: 11/20/1912, Delaware, OH D: 7/21/1977, Dayton, OH
1935 Pit: 10 G; Pass 27-12 44.4%, 144 5.33 1 TD 6 Int; Rush 4-(-3) -0.8. **1936** Pit: 4 G. **Total:** 14 G; Pass 27-12 44.4%, 144 5.33 1 TD 6 Int; Rush 4-(-3) -0.8.

KYLE TURLEY Turley, Kyle John 6′5″, 307 **OT**
Col: San Diego State *HS:* Valley View [Moreno Valley, CA] B: 9/24/1975, Provo, UT *Drafted:* 1998 Round 1 NO
1998 NO: 15 G.

GUY TURNBOW Turnbow, Guy Nicholson 6′2″, 217 **T-OE-DB**
Col: Mississippi *HS:* Brookhaven [MS] B: 3/28/1908, Brookhaven, MS D: 10/4/1975, Oxford, MS
1933 Phi: 9 G; Scor 3, 1 FG. **1934** Phi: 2 G. **Total:** 11 G; Scor 3, 1 FG.

JESSE TURNBOW Turnbow, Jesse James 6′7″, 272 **DT**
Col: Tennessee *HS:* Princeton [Cincinnati, OH] B: 10/8/1956, Cincinnati, OH *Drafted:* 1978 Round 8 Cle
1978 Cle: 16 G.

RENALDO TURNBULL Turnbull, Renaldo Antonio 6′4″, 250 **DE-LB**
Col: West Virginia *HS:* Charlotte Amalie [St. Thomas, Virgin Islands] B: 1/5/1966, St. Thomas, Virgin Islands *Drafted:* 1990 Round 1 NO
1990 NO: 16 G; 9 Sac. **1991** NO: 16 G; 1 Sac. **1992** NO: 14 G; 1.5 Sac. **1993** NO: 15 G; Int 1-2; 13 Sac. **1994** NO: 16 G; 6.5 Sac. **1995** NO: 15 G; 7 Sac. **1996** NO: 12 G; 6.5 Sac. **1997** Car: 16 G; 1 Sac. **Total:** 120 G; Int 1-2; 45.5 Sac.

CALVIN TURNER Turner, Calvin Eugene 6′4″, 270 **DE**
Col: West Virginia *HS:* West [Fairmont, WV] B: 4/10/1960, Fairmont, WV
1987 TB: 3 G; 3.5 Sac.

CECIL TURNER Turner, Cecil Angelo 5′10″, 176 **WR-CB**
Col: Cal Poly-S.L.O. *HS:* Spingarn [Washington, DC] B: 4/2/1944, Washington, DC *Drafted:* 1968 Round 5 ChiB
1968 ChiB: Rush 2-16 8.0; Rec 14-208 14.9 2 TD. **1969** ChiB: Rec 1-19 19.0. **1970** ChiB: Rush 3-(-3) -1.0; Rec 2-53 26.5. **1971** ChiB: Rec 1-13 13.0. **1972** ChiB: Rush 3-0; Rec 3-71 23.7. **Total:** Rush 8-13 1.6; Rec 21-364 17.3 2 TD.

		Punt Returns				Kickoff Returns					Tot
Year Team	**G**	**Ret**	**Yds**	**Avg**	**TD**	**Ret**	**Yds**	**Avg**	**TD**	**Fum**	**TD**
1968 ChiB	14	9	19	2.1	0	20	363	18.2	0	3	2
1969 ChiB	9	8	32	4.0	0	10	326	32.6	0	2	0
1970 ChiB	14	1	0	0.0	0	23	752	32.7	**4**	1	4
1971 ChiB	14	9	63	7.0	0	31	639	20.6	0	1	0
1972 ChiB	14	0	0	—	0	16	409	25.6	0	2	0
1973 ChiB	11	0	0	—	0	8	127	15.9	0	1	0
NFL Total	76	27	114	4.2	0	108	2616	24.2	4	10	6

CLEM TURNER Turner, Clement 6′1″, 236 **RB**
Col: Cincinnati *HS:* Woodward [Cincinnati, OH] B: 5/28/1945, Cincinnati, OH *Drafted:* 1969 Round 4 Cin
1969 Cin: Rec 5-14 2.8; KR 3-15 5.0. **1970** Den: Rec 8-23 2.9; KR 1-31 31.0. **1971** Den: Rec 7-65 9.3 1 TD; KR 5-100 20.0. **1972** Den: Rec 1-10 10.0; KR 1-25 25.0. **Total:** Rec 21-112 5.3 1 TD; KR 10-171 17.1.

		Rushing					Tot
Year Team	**G**	**Att**	**Yds**	**Avg**	**TD**	**Fum**	**TD**
1969 Cin	14	23	105	4.6	0	2	0
1970 Den	11	29	106	3.7	2	0	2
1971 Den	14	17	43	2.5	0	1	1
1972 Den	12	5	16	3.2	0	0	0
NFL Total	51	74	270	3.6	2	3	3

BULLDOG TURNER Turner, Clyde Douglas 6′1″, 237 **C-LB-OG-OT**
Col: Hardin-Simmons *HS:* Newman [Sweetwater, TX] B: 3/10/1919, Plains, TX D: 10/30/1998, Gatesville, TX *Drafted:* 1940 Round 1 ChiB *HOF:* 1966
1941 ChiB: KR 1-4 4.0. **1942** ChiB: KR 1-6 6.0; **1** Fum TD. **1944** ChiB: Rush 1-48 48.0 1 TD; PR 1-9 9.0. **1946** ChiB: KR 1-2 2.0. **1952** ChiB: Rec 1-2 2.0; KR 1-29 29.0. **Total:** Rush 1-48 48.0 1 TD; Rec 1-2 2.0; PR 1-9 9.0; KR 4-41 10.3; 1 Fum TD.

		Interceptions			Tot
Year Team	**G**	**Int**	**Yds**	**TD**	**TD**
1940 ChiB	11	1	9	0	0
1941 ChiB	11	1	12	0	0
1942 ChiB	11	**8**	96	**1**	2
1943 ChiB	10	0	0	0	0
1944 ChiB	10	2	44	0	1
1945 ChiB	2	0	0	0	0
1946 ChiB	11	1	15	0	0
1947 ChiB	12	2	103	1	1
1948 ChiB	12	2	19	0	0
1949 ChiB	12	0	0	0	0
1950 ChiB	12	0	0	0	0
1951 ChiB	12	0	0	0	0
1952 ChiB	12	0	0	0	0
NFL Total	138	17	298	2	4

DARYL TURNER Turner, Daryl 6′3″, 194 **WR**
Col: Michigan State *HS:* Southwestern [Flint, MI] B: 12/15/1961, Wadley, GA *Drafted:* 1984 Round 2 Sea

		Receiving			
Year Team	**G**	**Rec**	**Yds**	**Avg**	**TD**
1984 Sea	16	35	715	20.4	10
1985 Sea	16	34	670	19.7	**13**
1986 Sea	15	18	334	18.6	7
1987 Sea	12	14	153	10.9	6
NFL Total	59	101	1872	18.5	36

DEACON TURNER Turner, David L 5′11″, 212 **RB**
Col: Bakersfield Coll. CA (J.C.); San Diego State *HS:* Shafter [CA] B: 1/2/1955, Jackson, MS *Drafted:* 1978 Round 2 Cin

		Rushing				Receiving			
Year Team	**G**	**Att**	**Yds**	**Avg**	**TD**	**Rec**	**Yds**	**Avg**	**TD**
1978 Cin	16	84	333	4.0	0	11	50	4.5	0
1979 Cin	16	28	86	3.1	1	2	18	9.0	0
1980 Cin	12	30	130	4.3	0	12	73	6.1	1
NFL Total	44	142	549	3.9	1	25	141	5.6	1

	Kickoff Returns					Tot
Year Team	**Ret**	**Yds**	**Avg**	**TD**	**Fum**	**TD**
1978 Cin	1	24	24.0	0	4	0
1979 Cin	**55**	1149	20.9	0	3	1
1980 Cin	9	173	19.2	0	1	1
NFL Total	65	1346	20.7	0	8	2

DWAIN TURNER Turner, Dwain Fitzgerald 6′0″, 290 **NT**
Col: Rice *HS:* Westbury [Houston, TX] B: 10/7/1964, Houston, TX
1987 Hou: 1 G.

ERIC TURNER Turner, Eric Ray 6′1″, 208 **DB**
Col: UCLA *HS:* Ventura [CA] B: 9/20/1968, Ventura, CA *Drafted:* 1991 Round 1 Cle
1992 Cle: 1 Sac. **1993** Cle: PR 0-7. **1994** Cle: PR 1-0; 1 Sac. **1997** Oak: 1 Fum TD. **1998** Oak: 1 Sac. **Total:** PR 1-7 7.0; 1 Fum TD; 3 Sac.

		Interceptions				Tot
Year Team	**G**	**Int**	**Yds**	**TD**	**Fum**	**TD**
1991 Cle	8	2	42	1	0	1
1992 Cle	15	1	6	0	0	0
1993 Cle	16	5	25	0	0	0
1994 Cle	16	**9**	199	1	0	1
1995 Cle	8	0	0	0	0	0
1996 Bal	14	5	1	0	0	0
1997 Oak	16	2	45	0	1	1
1998 Oak	6	3	108	1	0	1
NFL Total	99	27	426	3	1	4

SCOTT TURNER Turner, Eric Scott 5′10″, 180 **DB**
Col: Illinois *HS:* J.J. Pearce [Richardson, TX] B: 2/26/1972, Richardson, TX *Drafted:* 1995 Round 7 Was
1995 Was: 16 G; PR 1-0; Int 1-0; 1 Fum; 1 Sac. **1996** Was: 16 G; Int 2-16; **1** Fum TD; 6 Pt. **1997** Was: 9 G. **1998** SD: 16 G; Int 1-0; 1 Sac. **Total:** 57 G; PR 1-0; Int 4-16; 1 Fum TD; 6 Pt; 1 Fum; 2 Sac.

FLOYD TURNER Turner, Floyd Jr. 5′11″, 192 **WR**
Col: Northwestern State-Louisiana *HS:* Mansfield [LA] B: 5/29/1966, Shreveport, LA *Drafted:* 1989 Round 6 NO
1989 NO: Rush 2-8 4.0; PR 1-7 7.0. **1992** NO: PR 3-10 3.3. **1994** Ind: Rush 3-(-3) -1.0. **1995** Ind: Scor 2 2XP. **1996** Bal: Rush 2-12 6.0. **1998** Bal: Scor **2** 2XP. **Total:** Rush 7-17 2.4; PR 4-17 4.3; Scor 4 2XP.

		Receiving				
Year Team	**G**	**Rec**	**Yds**	**Avg**	**TD**	**Fum**
1989 NO	13	22	279	12.7	1	1
1990 NO	16	21	396	18.9	4	0
1991 NO	16	64	927	14.5	8	1
1992 NO	2	5	43	8.6	0	2
1993 NO	10	12	163	13.6	1	0
1994 Ind	16	52	593	11.4	6	1
1995 Ind	14	35	431	12.3	4	0
1996 Bal	11	38	461	12.1	2	0
1998 Bal	16	32	512	16.0	5	0
NFL Total	114	281	3805	13.5	31	5

ROCKY TURNER Turner, Harley 6′0″, 190 **DB-WR**
Col: Tennessee-Chattanooga *HS:* Augusta [GA] B: 8/6/1950, Augusta, GA *Drafted:* 1972 Round 10 NYJ
1972 NYJ: 8 G; PR 5-38 7.6; KR 3-57 19.0; 1 Fum. **1973** NYJ: 14 G; PR 11-54 4.9; 2 Fum. **Total:** 22 G; PR 16-92 5.8; KR 3-57 19.0; 3 Fum.

HAL TURNER Turner, Harold 6′2″, 235 **DE**
Col: Tennessee State *HS:* Booker T. Washington [Tulsa, OK]
B: 12/5/1929 D: 6/1981, Doddsville, MS *Drafted:* 1952 Round 28 Det
1954 Det: 3 G.

HERSCHEL TURNER Turner, Herschel 6′3″, 230 **OG-OT**
Col: Kentucky *HS:* Campbell Co. [Alexandria, KY] B: 6/17/1942, Houston, TX *Drafted:* 1964 Round 2 StL
1964 StL: 14 G. **1965** StL: 13 G. **Total:** 27 G.

TINY TURNER Turner, Irwin L 6′0″, 195 **G**
Col: Ohio State B: 1895 Deceased
1920 Day: 1 G.

JIMMIE TURNER Turner, James 6′2″, 220 **LB**
Col: Presbyterian *HS:* Vienna [GA] B: 2/16/1962, Vienna, GA
1984 Dal: 5 G.

JIM TURNER Turner, James Alfonso 5′8″, 165 **WB**
(Buddy) *Col:* Northwestern *HS:* Evanston Twp. [Evanston, IL]
B: 4/18/1899, Abbeville, SC D: 3/28/1932, Chicago, IL
1923 Mil: 3 G; 6 Pt.

JIM TURNER Turner, James Bayard 6′2″, 205 **K**
Col: Utah State *HS:* John Swett [Crockett, CA] B: 3/28/1941, Martinez, CA *Drafted:* 1963 Round 19 Was
1964 NYJ: Rush 1-3 3.0. **1967** NYJ: Pass 4-2 50.0%, 25 6.25. **1970** NYJ: Rush 1-1 1.0. **1973** Den: Pass 1-0, 1 Int. **1977** Den: Rec 1-25 25.0 1 TD. **1978** Den: Rec 1-(-4) -4.0. **1979** Den: Rec 1-6 6.0. **Total:** Pass 5-2 40.0%, 25 5.00 1 Int; Rush 2-4 2.0; Rec 3-27 9.0 1 TD.

		Scoring						
Year Team	**G**	**Pts**	**FG**	**FGA**	**FG%**	**XK**	**XKA**	**XK%**
1964 NYJ	14	72	13	27	48.1	33	33	100.0
1965 NYJ	14	91	20	34	58.8	31	31	100.0
1966 NYJ	14	88	18	35	51.4	34	35	97.1
1967 NYJ	14	87	17	32	53.1	36	39	92.3
1968 NYJ	14	**145**	**34**	**46**	73.9	43	43	100.0
1969 NYJ	14	**129**	**32**	**47**	68.1	33	33	100.0
1970 NYJ	14	85	19	35	54.3	28	28	100.0
1971 Den	14	93	25	38	65.8	18	18	100.0
1972 Den	14	97	20	29	69.0	37	37	100.0
1973 Den	14	106	22	33	66.7	40	40	100.0
1974 Den	14	68	11	21	52.4	35	38	92.1
1975 Den	14	86	21	28	75.0	23	26	88.5
1976 Den	14	81	15	21	71.4	36	39	92.3
1977 Den	14	76	13	19	68.4	31	34	91.2
1978 Den	16	64	11	22	50.0	31	35	88.6
1979 Den	16	71	13	21	61.9	32	34	94.1
NFL Total	228	1439	304	488	62.3	521	543	95.9

J.T. TURNER Turner, James Denis 6′3″, 253 **OG**
Col: Duke *HS:* Benjamin Franklin [Philadelphia, PA] B: 4/17/1953, Moultrie, GA
1977 NYG: 13 G. **1978** NYG: 16 G. **1979** NYG: 16 G. **1980** NYG: 16 G. **1981** NYG: 16 G. **1982** NYG: 9 G. **1983** NYG: 16 G. **1984** Was: 1 G. **Total:** 103 G.

JIM TURNER Turner, James Kay 6′2″, 210 **C**
Col: Oklahoma State *HS:* Wichita Falls [TX] B: 1/14/1912, Roff, OK
1937 Cle: 7 G.

JIMMY TURNER Turner, James Lee 6′0″, 187 **DB**
Col: UCLA *HS:* Sherman [TX] B: 6/15/1959, Sherman, TX
Drafted: 1983 Round 3 Cin
1983 Cin: 16 G. **1984** Cin: 16 G; Int 1-4. **1985** Cin: 16 G; Int 1-40. **1986** Cin-Atl: 14 G. Cin: 8 G. Atl: 6 G. **1987** Atl: 2 G. **Total:** 64 G; Int 2-44.

JAY TURNER Turner, Jay Lewis 5′10″, 202 **BB-LB**
Col: George Washington *HS:* Oklahoma Mil. Acad. [Claremore, OK]
B: 7/11/1914, Springfield, MO D: 11/1960
1938 Was: 8 G; Rush 5-25 5.0; Rec 2-10 5.0. **1939** Was: 8 G; Rush 2-1 0.5; Rec 2-15 7.5; Punt 1-33 33.0. **Total:** 16 G; Rush 7-26 3.7; Rec 4-25 6.3; Punt 1-33 33.0.

MIKE TURNER Turner, Jerry Michael 6′3″, 255 **OG**
Col: Louisiana State *HS:* C.E. Byrd [Shreveport, LA] B: 9/10/1960, Oceanside, CA
1987 Min: 1 G.

JOHN TURNER Turner, John Jr. 6′0″, 197 **DB**
Col: Miami (Fla.) *HS:* Miami Norland [FL] B: 2/22/1956, Miami, FL
Drafted: 1978 Round 2 Min
1979 Min: PR 1-0. **1983** Min: 1 Sac. **Total:** PR 1-0; 1 Sac.

		Interceptions			
Year Team	**G**	**Int**	**Yds**	**TD**	**Fum**
1978 Min	14	1	15	0	0
1979 Min	16	2	48	0	1
1980 Min	16	6	22	0	0
1981 Min	13	0	0	0	0
1982 Min	9	2	43	**1**	0
1983 Min	16	6	37	0	0
1984 SD	15	2	43	0	0
1985 Min	15	5	62	0	0
1987 Min	2	0	0	0	0
NFL Total	116	24	270	1	1

KEENA TURNER Turner, Keena 6′2″, 219 **LB**
Col: Purdue *HS:* Chicago Vocational [IL] B: 10/22/1958, Chicago, IL
Drafted: 1980 Round 2 SF
1982 SF: 1 Sac. **1983** SF: 3.5 Sac. **1984** SF: 2 Sac. **1985** SF: **1** Fum TD; 6 Sac. **1986** SF: 3 Sac. **1987** SF: 3 Sac. **1990** SF: Scor **1** Saf; 1 Sac.
Total: Scor 1 Saf; 1 Fum TD; 19.5 Sac.

		Interceptions		
Year Team	**G**	**Int**	**Yds**	**TD**
1980 SF	16	2	15	0
1981 SF	16	1	0	0
1982 SF	9	0	0	0
1983 SF	15	0	0	0
1984 SF	16	4	51	0
1985 SF	15	0	0	0
1986 SF	16	1	9	0
1987 SF	10	1	15	0
1988 SF	11	1	2	0
1989 SF	13	1	42	0
1990 SF	16	0	0	0
NFL Total	153	11	134	0

KEVIN TURNER Turner, Kevin Ray 6′2″, 223 **LB**
Col: U. of Pacific *HS:* Mission [San Jose, CA] B: 2/5/1958, Fremont, CA
1980 NYG: 3 G. **1981** Was-Sea: 12 G. Was: 4 G. Sea: 8 G. **1982** Cle: 8 G.
Total: 23 G.

MARCUS TURNER Turner, Marcus Jared 6′0″, 190 **DB**
Col: UCLA *HS:* Jordan [Long Beach, CA] B: 1/13/1966, Harbor City, CA *Drafted:* 1989 Round 11 KC
1989 Pho: 13 G. **1990** Pho: 16 G; Int 1-70 2 TD; 12 Pt. **1991** Pho: 3 G. **1992** NYJ: 16 G; Int 2-15. **1993** NYJ: 16 G; 1 Sac. **1994** NYJ: 16 G; Int 5-155 1 TD; 6 Pt. **1995** NYJ: 6 G. **Total:** 86 G; Int 8-240 3 TD; 18 Pt; 1 Sac.

MAURICE TURNER Turner, Maurice Antoine 5′11″, 200 **RB**
Col: Utah State *HS:* Layton [UT] B: 9/10/1960, Salt Lake City, UT
Drafted: 1983 Round 12 Min
1984 Min: 13 G; KR 2-21 10.5. **1985** Min-GB: 13 G; KR 4-61 15.3. Min: 10 G; KR 4-61 15.3. GB: 3 G. **1987** NYJ: 1 G. **Total:** 27 G; KR 6-82 13.7.

BUFF TURNER Turner, Milton 188 **T-G**
Col: No College B: 1/1891, MD Deceased
1921 Was: 3 G.

NATE TURNER Turner, Nathaniel Adam 6′1″, 255 **TE**
Col: Nebraska *HS:* Mount Carmel [Chicago, IL] B: 5/28/1969, Chicago, IL *Drafted:* 1992 Round 6 Buf
1993 Buf: 13 G; Rush 11-36 3.3; KR 1-10 10.0. **1994** Buf: 13 G; Rush 2-4 2.0; Rec 1-26 26.0 1 TD; KR 6-102 17.0; 6 Pt. **1995** Car: 2 G. **Total:** 28 G; Rush 13-40 3.1; Rec 1-26 26.0 1 TD; KR 7-112 16.0; 6 Pt.

ODESSA TURNER Turner, Odessa 6′3″, 205 **WR**
Col: Northwestern State-Louisiana *HS:* Wossman [Monroe, LA]
B: 10/12/1964, Monroe, LA *Drafted:* 1987 Round 4 NYG
1989 NYG: Rush 2-11 5.5. **1992** SF: KR 1-0. **Total:** Rush 2-11 5.5; KR 1-0.

		Receiving				
Year Team	**G**	**Rec**	**Yds**	**Avg**	**TD**	**Fum**
1987 NYG	7	10	195	19.5	1	0
1988 NYG	4	10	128	12.8	1	0
1989 NYG	13	38	467	12.3	4	1
1990 NYG	4	6	69	11.5	0	0
1991 NYG	16	21	356	17.0	0	0
1992 SF	16	9	200	22.2	2	1
1993 SF	7	3	64	21.3	0	1
NFL Total	67	97	1479	15.2	8	3

KEVIN TURNER Turner, Paul Kevin 6′1″, 231 **RB**
Col: Alabama *HS:* Prattville [AL] B: 6/12/1969, Prattville, AL
Drafted: 1992 Round 3 NE
1992 NE: KR 1-11 11.0. **1993** NE: Pass 1-0. **1997** Phi: KR 3-48 16.0. **1998** Phi: KR 1-15 15.0. **Total:** Pass 1-0; KR 5-74 14.8.

		Rushing				Receiving					Tot
Year Team	**G**	**Att**	**Yds**	**Avg**	**TD**	**Rec**	**Yds**	**Avg**	**TD**	**Fum**	**TD**
1992 NE	16	10	40	4.0	0	7	52	7.4	2	2	2
1993 NE	16	50	231	4.6	0	39	333	8.5	2	1	2
1994 NE	16	36	111	3.1	1	52	471	9.1	2	4	3
1995 Phi	2	2	9	4.5	0	4	29	7.3	0	0	0
1996 Phi	16	18	39	2.2	0	43	409	9.5	1	1	1
1997 Phi	16	18	96	5.3	0	48	443	9.2	3	1	3
1998 Phi	16	20	94	4.7	0	34	232	6.8	0	1	0
NFL Total	98	154	620	4.0	1	227	1969	8.7	10	10	11

RICHARD TURNER Turner, Richard Junior 6'2", 260 **NT**
Col: Oklahoma *HS:* Edmond Memorial [OK] B: 2/14/1959, Hugo, OK
Drafted: 1981 Round 4 GB
1981 GB: 15 G. **1982** GB: 9 G. **1983** GB: 6 G; 1 Sac. **Total:** 30 G; 1 Sac.

RICKY TURNER Turner, Ricky 6'0", 190 **QB**
Col: Washington State *HS:* Compton [CA] B: 5/14/1962, Los Angeles, CA
1988 Ind: 4 G; Pass 4-3 75.0%, 92 23.00; Rush 16-42 2.6 2 TD; 12 Pt.

ROBERT TURNER Turner, Robert Dean 5'11", 200 **RB**
Col: Oklahoma State *HS:* Wynnewood [OK] B: 3/6/1954, Wynnewood, OK *Drafted:* 1977 Round 9 Mia
1978 Hou: 4 G; KR 4-69 17.3.

BAKE TURNER Turner, Robert Hardy 6'1", 179 **WR**
Col: Texas Tech *HS:* Alpine [TX] B: 7/22/1940, Alpine, TX
Drafted: 1962 Round 12 Bal
1962 Bal: Rush 1-17 17.0; PR 10-95 9.5. **1965** NYJ: PR 1-1 1.0.
1966 NYJ: PR 10-60 6.0. **1969** NYJ: Rush 1-(-4) -4.0; Punt 2-89 44.5.
Total: Rush 2-13 6.5; PR 21-156 7.4; Punt 2-89 44.5.

		Receiving				Kickoff Returns				
Year Team	**G**	**Rec**	**Yds**	**Avg**	**TD**	**Ret**	**Yds**	**Avg**	**TD**	**Fum**
1962 Bal	14	1	111	111.0	1	20	504	25.2	0	1
1963 NYJ	14	71	1009	14.2	6	14	299	21.4	0	1
1964 NYJ	14	58	974	16.8	9	0	0	—	0	0
1965 NYJ	13	31	402	13.0	2	18	402	22.3	0	1
1966 NYJ	14	7	115	16.4	0	2	50	25.0	0	2
1967 NYJ	8	3	40	13.3	0	4	40	10.0	0	0
1968 NYJ	13	10	241	24.1	2	14	319	22.8	0	0
1969 NYJ	14	11	221	20.1	3	3	74	24.7	0	1
1970 Bos	14	28	428	15.3	2	0	0	—	0	0
NFL Total	118	220	3541	16.1	25	75	1688	22.5	0	6

SAM TURNER Turner, Samuel Washington Jr. 195 **G**
Col: No College *HS:* Western [Washington, DC] B: 4/16/1902, Southampton Co., VA D: 8/5/1976, Franklin, VA
1921 Was: 2 G.

T.J. TURNER Turner, Thomas James 6'4", 279 **DE-NT**
Col: Houston *HS:* Lufkin [TX] B: 5/16/1963, Lufkin, TX *Drafted:* 1986 Round 3 Mia
1986 Mia: 16 G; 2 Sac. **1987** Mia: 12 G; 4 Sac. **1988** Mia: 16 G; 5 Sac. **1989** Mia: 14 G. **1990** Mia: 14 G; 1 Sac. **1991** Mia: 13 G; 4 Sac. **1992** Mia: 16 G. **Total:** 101 G; 16 Sac.

VERNON TURNER Turner, Vernon Maurice 5'8", 185 **WR-RB**
Col: Carson-Newman *HS:* Curtis [Staten Island, NY] B: 1/6/1967, Brooklyn, NY
1991 LARm: Rush 7-44 6.3; Rec 3-41 13.7 1 TD. **1992** LARm: Rush 2-14 7.0; Rec 5-42 8.4. **1993** Det-TB: Rec 1-7 7.0. Det: Rec 1-7 7.0. **1994** TB: Rush 4-13 3.3. **Total:** Rush 13-71 5.5; Rec 9-90 10.0 1 TD.

		Punt Returns				Kickoff Returns					Tot
Year Team	**G**	**Ret**	**Yds**	**Avg**	**TD**	**Ret**	**Yds**	**Avg**	**TD**	**Fum**	**TD**
1990 Buf	1	0	0	—	0	0	0	—	0	0	0
1991 LARm	15	23	201	8.7	0	24	457	19.0	0	4	1
1992 LARm	12	28	207	7.4	0	29	569	19.6	0	3	0
1993 Det-TB	8	17	152	8.9	0	21	391	18.6	0	1	0
1993 Det	7	17	152	8.9	0	15	330	22.0	0	1	0
1993 TB	1	0	0	—	0	6	61	10.2	0	0	0
1994 TB	12	21	218	10.4	1	43	886	20.6	0	1	1
1995 Det	6	6	39	6.5	0	17	323	19.0	0	1	0
NFL Total	54	95	817	8.6	1	134	2626	19.6	0	10	2

VINCE TURNER Turner, Vincent Kerby 5'11", 190 **DB**
Col: Missouri *HS:* Chillicothe [MO] B: 12/31/1942 *Drafted:* 1964 Round 9 Bal
1964 NYJ: 6 G; PR 2-2 1.0; KR 1-25 25.0; Int 1-0.

BILL TURNER Turner, William James 6'4", 245 **OG**
Col: Boston College B: 3/5/1960
1987 NE: 2 G.

WYLIE TURNER Turner, Wylie Dewayen 5'10", 182 **DB**
Col: Angelo State *HS:* W.T. White [Dallas, TX] B: 4/19/1957, Dallas, TX
1979 GB: 12 G. **1980** GB: 16 G; Int 2-13. **Total:** 28 G; Int 2-13.

TOM TURNURE Turnure, Thomas William 6'4", 250 **C-OG**
Col: Washington *HS:* Roosevelt [Seattle, WA] B: 7/9/1957, Seattle, WA
Drafted: 1980 Round 3 Det
1980 Det: 3 G. **1981** Det: 16 G. **1982** Det: 9 G. **1983** Det: 16 G. **1985** Det: 6 G. **1986** Det: 13 G. **Total:** 63 G.

MILES TURPIN Turpin, Miles John 6'4", 230 **LB**
Col: California *HS:* American [Fremont, CA] B: 5/15/1964, Minneapolis, MN
1986 GB: 1 G. **1987** TB: 3 G; 2 Sac. **Total:** 4 G; 2 Sac.

WILLIE TURRAL Turral, Willie James 5'10", 190 **RB**
Col: New Mexico *HS:* Amos P. Godby [Tallahassee, FL] B: 2/1/1964, Tallahassee, FL
1987 Phi: 1 G; KR 1-21 21.0.

MELVIN TUTEN Tuten, Melvin Eugene Jr. 6'6", 305 **OT**
Col: Syracuse *HS:* Woodrow Wilson [Washington, DC] B: 11/11/1971, Washington, DC *Drafted:* 1995 Round 3 Cin
1995 Cin: 16 G; Rec 2-12 6.0 1 TD; 6 Pt. **1996** Cin: 16 G. **Total:** 32 G; Rec 2-12 6.0 1 TD; 6 Pt.

RICK TUTEN Tuten, Richard Lamar 6'2", 221 **P**
(Bootin') *Col:* Miami (Fla.); Florida State *HS:* Forest [Ocala, FL]
B: 1/5/1965, Perry, FL
1992 Sea: Pass 1-0; Rush 1-0. **1993** Sea: Pass 1-0. **1994** Sea: Pass 1-0; Scor 1 2XP. **1998** StL: Pass 1-0. **Total:** Pass 4-0; Rush 1-0; Scor 1 2XP.

		Punting			
Year Team	**G**	**Punts**	**Yds**	**Avg**	**Fum**
1989 Phi	2	7	256	36.6	0
1990 Buf	14	53	2107	39.8	0
1991 Sea	10	49	2106	43.0	0
1992 Sea	16	**108**	**4760**	44.1	2
1993 Sea	16	90	**4007**	44.5	0
1994 Sea	16	91	3905	42.9	0
1995 Sea	16	83	3735	**45.0**	0
1996 Sea	16	85	3746	44.1	0
1997 Sea	11	48	2007	41.8	0
1998 StL	16	95	4202	44.2	0
NFL Total	133	709	30831	43.5	2

TOM TUTSON Tutson, Thomas 6'1", 180 **DB**
Col: South Carolina State *HS:* Jean Ribault [Jacksonville, FL]
B: 5/20/1958, Jacksonville, FL *Drafted:* 1982 Round 6 Mia
1983 Atl: 10 G.

GEORGE TUTTLE Tuttle, George Karl 5'11", 180 **OE**
Col: Minnesota *HS:* South [Minneapolis, MN] B: 1/14/1905, Minneapolis, MN D: 10/20/1986, Minneapolis, MN
1927 GB: 1 G.

ORVILLE TUTTLE Tuttle, James Orville 5'9", 210 **G**
Col: Phillips; Oklahoma City *HS:* Bartlesville [OK] B: 9/18/1912, Licking, MO D: 4/1978, Guymon, OK
1937 NYG: 11 G. **1938** NYG: 11 G; Rec 1-(-2) -2.0. **1939** NYG: 11 G. **1940** NYG: 11 G. **1941** NYG: 11 G. **1946** NYG: 5 G. **Total:** 60 G; Rec 1-(-2) -2.0.

PERRY TUTTLE Tuttle, Perry Warren 6'0", 178 **WR**
Col: Clemson *HS:* North Davidson [Lexington, NC] B: 8/2/1959, Lexington, NC *Drafted:* 1982 Round 1 Buf

		Receiving				
Year Team	**G**	**Rec**	**Yds**	**Avg**	**TD**	**Fum**
1982 Buf	7	7	107	15.3	0	0
1983 Buf	9	17	261	15.4	3	1
1984 TB-Atl	8	1	7	7.0	0	0
1984 TB	3	0	0	—	0	0
1984 Atl	5	1	7	7.0	0	0
NFL Total	24	25	375	15.0	3	1

FRANK TWEDELL Twedell, Francis A 5'11", 220 **G**
Col: Minnesota *HS:* Austin [MN] B: 5/29/1917, Austin, MN D: 5/1969
Drafted: 1939 Round 5 GB
1939 GB: 4 G.

RODNEY TWEET Tweet, Rodney Lee 6'1", 195 **WR**
Col: South Dakota *HS:* Austin [MN] B: 2/20/1964, Madison, SD
1987 Cin: 2 G.

HOWARD TWILLEY Twilley, Howard James Jr. 5'10", 185 **WR**
Col: Tulsa *HS:* Galena Park [TX] B: 12/25/1943, Houston, TX
Drafted: 1966 Round 14 Min
1969 Mia: PR 1-0. **Total:** PR 1-0.

		Receiving				
Year Team	**G**	**Rec**	**Yds**	**Avg**	**TD**	**Fum**
1966 Mia	6	10	128	12.8	0	0
1967 Mia	14	24	314	13.1	2	0
1968 Mia	14	39	604	15.5	1	0
1969 Mia	4	10	158	15.8	1	1
1970 Mia	14	22	281	12.8	5	0
1971 Mia	14	23	349	15.2	4	0
1972 Mia	13	20	364	18.2	3	0
1973 Mia	6	2	30	15.0	0	0
1974 Mia	13	24	256	10.7	2	0
1975 Mia	14	24	366	15.3	4	0
1976 Mia	8	14	214	15.3	1	0
NFL Total	120	212	3064	14.5	23	1

DARREN TWOMBLY Twombly, Darren William 6'4", 270 **C**
Col: Boston College *HS:* Manchester [MA] B: 5/14/1965
1987 NE: 1 G.

GUNNARD TWYNER Twyner, Gunnard 5'10", 165 **WR**
Col: Western Illinois *HS:* Pleasant Valley [IA] B: 7/14/1973, Bettendorf, IA
1997 Cin-NO: 4 G; Rec 4-45 11.3; KR 4-72 18.0. Cin: 2 G; Rec 4-45 11.3; KR 4-72 18.0. NO: 2 G. **Total:** 4 G; Rec 4-45 11.3; KR 4-72 18.0.

ANDRE TYLER Tyler, Andre Miguel 6'0", 180 **WR**
Col: Stanford *HS:* Long Beach Polytechnic [CA] B: 7/17/1959, Tucson, AZ *Drafted:* 1982 Round 6 TB
1983 TB: Rec 6-77 12.8.

		Punt Returns				
Year Team	G	Ret	Yds	Avg	TD	Fum
1983 TB	14	27	208	7.7	0	1

PETE TYLER Tyler, Glenn Pete 5'11", 190 **BB-LB**
Col: Hardin-Simmons *HS:* Clyde [TX] B: 6/18/1914 D: 6/8/1986, San Angelo, TX
1937 ChiC: 6 G; Pass 1-0; Rush 5-(-5) -1.0; Rec 7-60 8.6 1 TD; 6 Pt.
1938 ChiC: 10 G; Rush 1-1 1.0; Rec 2-24 12.0 1 TD; 6 Pt. **Total:** 16 G; Pass 1-0; Rush 6-(-4) -0.7; Rec 9-84 9.3 2 TD; 12 Pt.

MAURICE TYLER Tyler, Maurice Michael 6'0", 188 **DB**
Col: Baltimore City CC MD; Morgan State *HS:* Mergenthaler Tech [Baltimore, MD] B: 7/19/1950, Karnack, TX *Drafted:* 1972 Round 10 Buf
1972 Buf: 14 G; Int 4-61. **1973** Den: 14 G; PR 4-20 5.0; KR 1-23 23.0.
1974 Den: 14 G; Int 1-0. **1975** SD: 13 G. **1976** Det: 9 G. **1977** NYJ: 14 G.
1978 NYG: 8 G; PR 1-6 6.0; KR 1-2 2.0; 6 Pt. **Total:** 86 G; PR 5-26 5.2; KR 2-25 12.5; Int 5-61; 6 Pt.

ROBERT TYLER Tyler, Robert 6'5", 259 **TE**
Col: South Carolina State *HS:* Wagener-Salley [Wagener, SC] B: 10/12/1965, Savannah, GA *Drafted:* 1988 Round 8 Sea
1989 Sea: 9 G; Rec 14-148 10.6.

TOUSSAINT TYLER Tyler, Toussaint L'Overture 6'2", 220 **RB**
Col: Washington *HS:* El Camino [Oceanside, CA] B: 3/19/1959, Los Angeles, CA *Drafted:* 1981 Round 9 NO

		Rushing				Receiving				
Year Team	G	Att	Yds	Avg	TD	Rec	Yds	Avg	TD	Fum
1981 NO	16	36	183	5.1	0	23	135	5.9	0	4
1982 NO	2	10	21	2.1	0	4	31	7.8	0	0
NFL Total	18	46	204	4.4	0	27	166	6.1	0	4

WENDELL TYLER Tyler, Wendell Avery 5'10", 198 **RB**
Col: UCLA *HS:* Crenshaw [Los Angeles, CA] B: 5/20/1955, Shreveport, LA *Drafted:* 1977 Round 3 LARm

		Rushing				Receiving			
Year Team	G	Att	Yds	Avg	TD	Rec	Yds	Avg	TD
1977 LARm	14	61	317	5.2	3	1	3	3.0	0
1978 LARm	2	14	45	3.2	0	2	17	8.5	0
1979 LARm	16	218	1109	**5.1**	9	32	308	9.6	1
1980 LARm	4	30	157	5.2	0	2	8	4.0	0
1981 LARm	15	260	1074	4.1	12	45	436	9.7	5
1982 LARm	9	137	564	4.1	9	38	375	9.9	4
1983 SF	14	176	856	4.9	4	34	285	8.4	2
1984 SF	16	246	1262	5.1	7	28	230	8.2	2
1985 SF	13	171	867	5.1	6	20	154	7.7	2
1986 SF	5	31	127	4.1	0	0	0	—	0
NFL Total	108	1344	6378	4.7	50	202	1816	9.0	16

	Kickoff Returns					Tot
Year Team	Ret	Yds	Avg	TD	Fum	TD
1977 LARm	24	523	21.8	0	4	3
1978 LARm	2	31	15.5	0	2	0
1979 LARm	1	16	16.0	0	9	10
1980 LARm	0	0	—	0	1	0
1981 LARm	0	0	—	0	11	17
1982 LARm	0	0	—	0	**10**	13
1983 SF	0	0	—	0	7	6
1984 SF	0	0	—	0	13	9
1985 SF	0	0	—	0	6	8
1986 SF	0	0	—	0	1	0
NFL Total	27	570	21.1	0	64	66

RICH TYLSKI Tylski, Richard Lee 6'5", 309 **OG**
Col: Utah State *HS:* Madison [San Diego, CA] B: 2/27/1971, San Diego, CA
1996 Jac: 16 G. **1997** Jac: 13 G. **1998** Jac: 12 G. **Total:** 41 G.

SCOTT TYNER Tyner, Scott Dalton 6'1", 189 **P**
Col: Trinity Valley CC TX; Oklahoma State *HS:* Edgewood [TX] B: 4/11/1972, Houston, TX
1994 Atl: 6 G; Punt 8-285 35.6.

BUDDY TYNES Tynes, David Lane 6'0", 185 **FB-TB-BB-WB**
(Cowboy) *Col:* Texas *HS:* Cooper [Abilene, TX] B: 2/26/1902, Cooper, TX D: 11/28/1984, Anchorage, KY
1924 Col: 8 G; Rush 1 TD; Rec 1 TD; Tot TD 2; 12 Pt. **1925** Col: 9 G; Rush 1 TD; 6 Pt. **Total:** 17 G; Rush 2 TD; Rec 1 TD; Tot TD 3; 18 Pt.

JIM TYREE Tyree, James Edward 6'3", 204 **OE-DE**
Col: Oklahoma *HS:* Capitol Hill [Oklahoma City, OK] B: 5/30/1922, Sperry, OK *Drafted:* 1944 Round 12 Bkn
1948 Bos: 12 G; Rec 13-106 8.2; KR 1-17 17.0; 1 Fum TD; 6 Pt; 1 Fum.

JIM TYRER Tyrer, James Efflo 6'6", 280 **OT**
Col: Ohio State *HS:* Newark [OH] B: 2/25/1939, Newark, OH D: 9/15/1980, Kansas City, MO *Drafted:* 1961 Round 3 DalT
1961 DalT: 14 G. **1962** DalT: 14 G. **1963** KC: 14 G. **1964** KC: 14 G. **1965** KC: 14 G. **1966** KC: 14 G. **1967** KC: 14 G. **1968** KC: 14 G. **1969** KC: 14 G. **1970** KC: 14 G. **1971** KC: 14 G. **1972** KC: 14 G. **1973** KC: 12 G. **1974** Was: 14 G. **Total:** 194 G.

JOE TYRRELL Tyrrell, Joseph Paul 5'11", 216 **OG**
Col: Temple *HS:* Roman Catholic [Philadelphia, PA] B: 4/6/1929, Philadelphia, PA D: 6/10/1994, Philadelphia, PA *Drafted:* 1952 Round 24 Phi
1952 Phi: 2 G.

TIM TYRRELL Tyrrell, Timothy Gordan 6'1", 204 **RB**
Col: William Rainey Harper Coll. IL (J.C.); Northern Illinois *HS:* James B. Conant [Hoffman Estates, IL] B: 2/19/1961, Chicago, IL
1984 Atl: 11 G; KR 1-0. **1985** Atl: 16 G; KR 1-13 13.0; 1 Fum.
1986 Atl-LARm: 9 G; Rec 1-9 9.0; 1 Fum. Atl: 3 G. LARm: 6 G; Rec 1-9 9.0; 1 Fum. **1987** LARm: 11 G; Rush 11-44 4.0; Rec 6-59 9.8; KR 6-116 19.3. **1988** LARm: 12 G. **1989** Pit: 7 G; Rush 1-3 3.0. **Total:** 66 G; Rush 12-47 3.9; Rec 7-68 9.7; KR 8-129 16.1; 2 Fum.

DICK TYSON Tyson, Richard Hal 6'2", 245 **OG**
Col: Independence CC KS; Tulsa *HS:* Sumner [Kansas City, KS] B: 1/5/1943, Kansas City, KS *Drafted:* 1966 Round 4 Oak
1966 Oak: 3 G. **1967** Den: 7 G. **Total:** 10 G.

MITCH UCOVICH Ucovich, Mitchell A 5'11", 208 **T**
Col: San Jose State B: 9/27/1915, San Jose, CA D: 12/1/1989, San Jose, CA
1944 Was: 8 G. **1945** ChiC: 1 G. **Total:** 9 G.

KEITH UECKER Uecker, Richard Keith 6'5", 278 **OT-OG**
Col: Auburn *HS:* Hollywood Hills [Hollywood, FL] B: 6/20/1960, Hollywood, FL *Drafted:* 1982 Round 9 Den
1982 Den: 5 G; KR 1-12 12.0; 1 Fum. **1983** Den: 16 G. **1984** GB: 6 G. **1985** GB: 7 G. **1987** GB: 8 G. **1988** GB: 16 G. **1990** GB: 13 G. **1991** GB: 14 G. **Total:** 85 G; KR 1-12 12.0; 1 Fum.

ROCKY UGUCCIONI Uguccioni, Enrico R 6'0", 195 **OE-DE**
Col: Murray State B: 4/19/1918, New London, CT
1944 Bkn: 10 G; Rec 7-94 13.4; PR 1-12 12.0 **1** TD; 6 Pt.

JEFF UHLENHAKE Uhlenhake, Jeffrey Alan 6'3", 285 **C**
Col: Ohio State *HS:* Newark Catholic [OH] B: 1/28/1966, Indianapolis, IN *Drafted:* 1989 Round 5 Mia
1989 Mia: 16 G; 1 Fum. **1990** Mia: 16 G. **1991** Mia: 13 G. **1992** Mia: 13 G; 1 Fum. **1993** Mia: 5 G. **1994** NO: 16 G. **1995** NO: 14 G. **1996** Was: 12 G. **1997** Was: 14 G. **Total:** 119 G; 2 Fum.

STEVE UHRINYAK Uhrinyak, Steven James 6'2", 218 **G**
Col: Franklin & Marshall *HS:* Shadyside Acad. [Homestead, PA] B: 11/23/1914
1939 Was: 1 G.

ED ULINSKI Ulinski, Edward Franklin 5'11", 203 **G**
(U-Lee) *Col:* Marshall *HS:* Ambridge [PA] B: 12/7/1919, Pittsburgh, PA
AAFC **1946** CleA: 14 G; Rush 1-2 2.0. **1947** CleA: 14 G. **1948** CleA: 14 G. **1949** CleA: 12 G. **Total:** 54 G; Rush 1-2 2.0.

HARRY ULINSKI Ulinski, Harry John 6'4", 229 **C**
(Hoss; Ulee) *Col:* Kentucky *HS:* Ambridge [PA] B: 4/4/1925, Pittsburgh, PA *Drafted:* 1950 Round 4 Was
1950 Was: 12 G. **1951** Was: 12 G. **1953** Was: 12 G. **1954** Was: 12 G. **1955** Was: 12 G. **1956** Was: 12 G. **Total:** 72 G.

JIGGS ULLERY Ullery, William Warner 6'0", 200 **WB-FB**
Col: Penn State *HS:* Bradford [PA] B: 5/2/1897 D: 12/23/1989, Centerville, PA
1922 Day: 7 G.

MIKE ULMER Ulmer, Michael Walter 6'0", 196 **DB**
Col: Doane *HS:* Clay Center [NE] B: 12/28/1954, York, NE
1980 ChiB: 3 G; KR 1-(-2) -2.0. **1987** Phi: 1 G; PR 2-10 5.0; KR 1-8 8.0. **Total:** 4 G; PR 2-10 5.0; KR 2-6 3.0.

CHUCK ULRICH Ulrich, Charles Jr. 6'4", 250 **DT**
Col: Illinois *HS:* Fenger [Chicago, IL] B: 12/14/1929, Chicago, IL *Drafted:* 1952 Round 4 Phi
1954 ChiC: 11 G. **1955** ChiC: 12 G. **1956** ChiC: 5 G. **1957** ChiC: 11 G. **1958** ChiC: 12 G. **Total:** 51 G.

HUB ULRICH Ulrich, Hubert Jr. 6′0″, 205 **OE-DE**
Col: Kansas *HS:* Quinter [KS] B: 12/12/1920, Jennigs, OK
D: 3/10/1974, Topeka, KS
AAFC **1946** MiaA: 14 G; Rec 4-75 18.8 1 TD; 6 Pt.

MIKE ULUFALE Ulufale, Mike Fuimaono 6′4″, 284 **DT**
Col: San Bernardino Valley Coll. CA (J.C.); Brigham Young *HS:* James Campbell [Ewa Beach, HI] B: 2/1/1972, Honolulu, HI *Drafted:* 1996 Round 3 Dal
1996 Dal: 3 G.

FRANK UMONT Umont, Frank William 5′11″, 218 **G-T**
Col: No College B: 11/21/1917, Staten Island, NY D: 6/20/1991, Fort Lauderdale, FL
1944 NYG: 8 G. **1945** NYG: 8 G. **Total:** 16 G.

RICH UMPHREY Umphrey, Richard Vernon III 6′3″, 263 **C-OG**
Col: Utah; Colorado *HS:* Tustin [CA] B: 12/13/1958, Garden Grove, CA *Drafted:* 1982 Round 5 NYG
1982 NYG: 9 G; 1 Fum. **1983** NYG: 10 G. **1984** NYG: 15 G. **1985** SD: 11 G. **Total:** 45 G; 1 Fum.

WAYNE UNDERWOOD Underwood, Forrest Wayne 6′1″, 190 **T**
Col: Davis & Elkins; Marshall *HS:* Doddridge Co. [West Union, WV]
B: 12/8/1913, West Union, WV D: 10/26/1967, Grantsville, WV
1937 Cle: 3 G.

JACK UNDERWOOD Underwood, John 6′0″, 196 **OE-G-C**
Col: No College B: 8/1897, Duluth, MN D: 1938, Duluth, MN
1924 Dul: 6 G; Rec 2 TD; 12 Pt. **1925** Dul: 2 G. **1926** Dul: 12 G; 1 Fum TD; 6 Pt. **1927** Dul-Pott-Buf: 4 G. Pott: 1 G. Buf: 3 G. **1929** ChiC: 9 G. **Total:** 33 G; Rec 2 TD; 1 Fum TD; Tot TD 3; 18 Pt.

JOHN UNDERWOOD Underwood, John Arthur Jr. 6′3″, 265 **G**
(Big Heavy) *Col:* Rice *HS:* Honey Grove [TX] B: 1900
D: 12/15/1932, Bonham, TX
1923 Mil: 13 G.

OLEN UNDERWOOD Underwood, Olen Ulesus 6′1″, 220 **LB**
Col: Texas *HS:* Channelview [TX] B: 5/25/1942, Holly Grove, TX *Drafted:* 1965 Round 14 NYG
1965 NYG: 10 G; Int 1-20. **1966** Hou: 11 G. **1967** Hou: 14 G; Int 1-8. **1968** Hou: 14 G; Int 1-0; Scor **1** Saf; 2 Pt. **1969** Hou: 14 G; Int 1-2. **1970** Hou: 12 G. **1971** Den: 14 G; Int 1-5. **Total:** 89 G; Int 5-35; Scor 1 Saf; 2 Pt.

JOE UNGERER Ungerer, Joseph C 6′0″, 243 **T**
Col: Fordham *HS:* Bethlehem [PA] B: 12/10/1916, Bethlehem, PA
D: 7/15/1990, Absecon, NJ *Drafted:* 1941 Round 18 Bkn
1944 Was: 5 G. **1945** Was: 10 G. **Total:** 15 G.

JOHNNY UNITAS Unitas, John Constantine 6′1″, 194 **QB**
Col: Louisville *HS:* St. Justin's [Pittsburgh, PA] B: 5/7/1933, Pittsburgh, PA *Drafted:* 1955 Round 9 Pit *HOF:* 1979
1956 Bal: Rec 1-1 1.0. **Total:** Rec 1-1 1.0.

		Passing							
Year Team	**G**	**Att**	**Comp**	**Comp%**	**Yds**	**YPA**	**TD**	**Int**	**Rating**
1956 Bal	12	198	110	55.6	1498	7.57	9	10	74.0
1957 Bal	12	**301**	172	57.1	**2550**	8.47	**24**	17	88.0
1958 Bal	10	263	136	51.7	2007	7.63	**19**	**7**	90.0
1959 Bal	12	**367**	**193**	52.6	**2899**	7.90	**32**	14	92.0
1960 Bal	12	**378**	**190**	50.3	**3099**	8.20	**25**	24	73.7
1961 Bal	14	**420**	229	54.5	2990	7.12	16	24	66.1
1962 Bal	14	389	222	57.1	2967	7.63	23	23	76.5
1963 Bal	14	410	**237**	57.8	**3481**	8.49	20	12	89.7
1964 Bal	14	305	158	51.8	2824	**9.26**	19	6	96.4
1965 Bal	11	282	164	58.2	2530	**8.97**	23	12	97.4
1966 Bal	14	348	195	56.0	2748	7.90	22	24	74.0
1967 Bal	14	436	255	**58.5**	3428	7.86	20	16	83.6
1968 Bal	5	32	11	34.4	139	4.34	2	4	30.1
1969 Bal	13	327	178	54.4	2342	7.16	12	20	64.0
1970 Bal	14	321	166	51.7	2213	6.89	14	18	65.1
1971 Bal	13	176	92	52.3	942	5.35	3	9	52.3
1972 Bal	8	157	88	56.1	1111	7.08	4	**6**	70.8
1973 SD	5	76	34	44.7	471	6.20	3	7	40.0
NFL Total	211	5186	2830	54.6	40239	7.76	290	253	78.2

	Rushing				
Year Team	**Att**	**Yds**	**Avg**	**TD**	**Fum**
1956 Bal	28	155	5.5	1	4
1957 Bal	42	171	4.1	1	7
1958 Bal	33	139	4.2	3	5
1959 Bal	29	145	5.0	2	6
1960 Bal	36	195	5.4	0	8
1961 Bal	54	190	3.5	2	9
1962 Bal	50	137	2.7	0	5
1963 Bal	47	224	4.8	0	13
1964 Bal	37	162	4.4	2	6
1965 Bal	17	68	4.0	1	7
1966 Bal	20	44	2.2	1	5
1967 Bal	22	89	4.0	0	4
1968 Bal	3	-1	-0.3	0	3
1969 Bal	11	23	2.1	0	2
1970 Bal	9	16	1.8	0	2
1971 Bal	9	5	0.6	0	3
1972 Bal	3	15	5.0	0	3
1973 SD	0	0	—	0	3
NFL Total	450	1777	3.9	13	95

PONG UNITAS Unitas, Matthew J 180 **G**
(Pug) *Col:* No College B: 9/13/1895 D: 10/28/1972, Baltimore, MD
1921 Was: 2 G.

TERRY UNREIN Unrein, Terrance Lynn 6′5″, 281 **NT-DE**
Col: Colorado State *HS:* Fort Lupton [CO] B: 10/24/1962, Brighton, CO *Drafted:* 1986 Round 3 SD
1986 SD: 12 G; 0.5 Sac. **1987** SD: 9 G; 2.5 Sac. **Total:** 21 G; 3 Sac.

MORRIS UNUTOA Unutoa, Morris Taua 6′1″, 284 **C**
Col: Brigham Young *HS:* Carson [CA] B: 3/10/1971, Torrance, CA
1996 Phi: 16 G; 1 Fum. **1997** Phi: 16 G. **1998** Phi: 16 G. **Total:** 48 G; 1 Fum.

ERIC UNVERZAGT Unverzagt, Eric James 6′1″, 241 **LB**
Col: Wisconsin *HS:* Central Islip [NY] B: 12/18/1972, Central Islip, NY *Drafted:* 1996 Round 4 Sea
1996 Sea: 8 G. **1997** Sea: 1 G. **Total:** 9 G.

RICK UPCHURCH Upchurch, Richard 5′10″, 175 **WR**
Col: Indian Hills CC IA; Minnesota *HS:* Springfield [OH] B: 5/20/1952, Toledo, OH *Drafted:* 1975 Round 4 Den
1979 Den: Pass 1-0. **1983** Den: Pass 2-0. **Total:** Pass 3-0.

		Rushing				Receiving			
Year Team	**G**	**Att**	**Yds**	**Avg**	**TD**	**Rec**	**Yds**	**Avg**	**TD**
1975 Den	14	16	97	6.1	1	18	436	24.2	2
1976 Den	13	6	71	11.8	1	12	340	28.3	1
1977 Den	14	1	19	19.0	1	12	245	20.4	2
1978 Den	12	5	31	6.2	0	17	210	12.4	1
1979 Den	16	3	17	5.7	0	64	937	14.6	7
1980 Den	16	5	49	9.8	0	46	605	13.2	3
1981 Den	13	5	56	11.2	0	32	550	17.2	3
1982 Den	9	2	-10	-5.0	0	26	407	15.7	3
1983 Den	12	6	19	3.2	0	40	639	16.0	2
NFL Total	119	49	349	7.1	3	267	4369	16.4	24

	Punt Returns				Kickoff Returns					Tot
Year Team	**Ret**	**Yds**	**Avg**	**TD**	**Ret**	**Yds**	**Avg**	**TD**	**Fum**	**TD**
1975 Den	27	312	11.6	0	40	1084	27.1	0	3	3
1976 Den	39	536	**13.7**	**4**	22	514	23.4	0	5	6
1977 Den	51	**653**	12.8	1	20	456	22.8	0	6	4
1978 Den	36	493	**13.7**	**1**	8	222	27.8	0	2	2
1979 Den	30	304	10.1	0	5	79	15.8	0	5	7
1980 Den	37	353	9.5	0	0	0	—	0	2	3
1981 Den	9	63	7.0	0	0	0	—	0	0	3
1982 Den	15	242	**16.1**	**2**	0	0	—	0	4	5
1983 Den	4	52	13.0	0	0	0	—	0	0	2
NFL Total	248	3008	12.1	8	95	2355	24.8	0	27	35

TUUFULI UPERESA Uperesa, Tuufuli 6′3″, 254 **OG**
Col: Montana *HS:* Aiea [HI] B: 1/20/1948, American Samoa
1971 Phi: 2 G.

GENE UPSHAW Upshaw, Eugene Thurman Jr. 6′5″, 255 **OG**
Col: Texas A&M–Kingsville *HS:* Robstown [TX] B: 8/15/1945, Robstown, TX *Drafted:* 1967 Round 1 Oak *HOF:* 1987
1967 Oak: 14 G. **1968** Oak: 14 G. **1969** Oak: 14 G. **1970** Oak: 14 G. **1971** Oak: 14 G. **1972** Oak: 14 G. **1973** Oak: 14 G. **1974** Oak: 14 G. **1975** Oak: 14 G. **1976** Oak: 14 G. **1977** Oak: 14 G. **1978** Oak: 16 G. **1979** Oak: 16 G. **1980** Oak: 16 G. **1981** Oak: 15 G. **Total:** 217 G.

MARV UPSHAW Upshaw, Marvin Allen 6′4″, 260 **DE-DT**
Col: Trinity (Tex.) *HS:* Robstown [TX] B: 11/22/1946, Robstown, TX *Drafted:* 1968 Round 1 Cle
1968 Cle: 14 G. **1969** Cle: 14 G; Int 1-0. **1970** KC: 7 G. **1971** KC: 14 G. **1972** KC: 14 G; KR 1-4 4.0. **1973** KC: 14 G. **1974** KC: 14 G; Int 1-52 1 TD; 6 Pt. **1975** KC: 4 G. **1976** StL: 4 G. **Total:** 99 G; KR 1-4 4.0; Int 2-52 1 TD; 6 Pt.

REGAN UPSHAW Upshaw, Regan Charles 6′4″, 268 **DE**
Col: California *HS:* Pittsburg [CA] B: 8/12/1975, Berrien Springs, MI *Drafted:* 1996 Round 1 TB
1996 TB: 16 G; 4 Sac. **1997** TB: 15 G; 7.5 Sac. **1998** TB: 16 G; Int 1-26; 7 Sac. **Total:** 47 G; Int 1-26; 18.5 Sac.

ANDY URAM Uram, Andrew 5′10″, 188 **HB**
Col: Minnesota *HS:* Marshall [Minneapolis, MN] B: 3/21/1915, Minneapolis, MN D: 12/9/1984, Green Bay, WI *Drafted:* 1938 Round 4 GB
1939 GB: Pass 1-0. **1940** GB: Int 3-27; Scor 19, 1-1 100.0% XK. **1941** GB: PR 7-121 17.3 **1** TD; KR 2-27 13.5; Int 2-37. **1942** GB: PR 7-50 7.1; KR 8-208 26.0 **1** TD; Int 2-18; Scor 31, 1-1 100.0% XK. **1943** GB: Pass 6-2 33.3%, 60 10.00 1 TD 1 Int; PR 5-48 9.6; Int 2-40.

Total: Pass 7-2 28.6%, 60 8.57 1 TD 1 Int; PR 19-219 11.5 1 TD; KR 10-235 23.5 1 TD; Int 9-122; Scor 98, 2-2 100.0% XK.

Year Team	G	Rushing Att	Yds	Avg	TD	Receiving Rec	Yds	Avg	TD	Tot TD
1938 GB	11	28	145	5.2	2	4	46	11.5	0	2
1939 GB	10	52	272	5.2	1	7	93	13.3	2	3
1940 GB	11	71	270	3.8	1	10	188	18.8	2	3
1941 GB	11	49	258	5.3	0	6	124	20.7	0	1
1942 GB	11	24	75	3.1	0	21	420	20.0	4	5
1943 GB	8	15	53	3.5	0	10	212	21.2	2	2
NFL Total	62	239	1073	4.5	4	58	1083	18.7	10	16

ALEX URBAN Urban, Alexander William 6′3″, 207 **DE-OE**
(Jeep) *Col:* South Carolina B: 7/16/1917, Bessemer, PA
1941 GB: 7 G; Rec 2-26 13.0 1 TD; 6 Pt. **1944** GB: 3 G; Rush 1-2 2.0; Rec 1-10 10.0; KR 1-20 20.0. **1945** GB: 1 G; Rec 1-55 55.0. **Total:** 11 G; Rush 1-2 2.0; Rec 4-91 22.8 1 TD; KR 1-20 20.0; 6 Pt.

GASPER URBAN Urban, Gasper George 6′1″, 215 **G-LB**
Col: Notre Dame *HS:* Classical [Lynn, MA] B: 3/18/1923, Lynn, MA
AAFC **1948** ChiA: 14 G; Int 1-5.

LUKE URBAN Urban, Louis John 5′8″, 165 **OE-BB**
Col: Boston College *HS:* B.M.C. Durfee [Fall River, MA] B: 3/22/1897, Fall River, MA D: 12/7/1980, Somerset, MA
1921 Buf: 12 G; Rec 1 TD; 6 Pt. **1922** Buf: 9 G. **1923** Buf: 11 G; Int **1** TD; 6 Pt. **Total:** 32 G; Rec 1 TD; Int 1 TD; Tot TD 2; 12 Pt.

JIM URBANEK Urbanek, James Eugene 6′4″, 270 **DT**
Col: Mississippi *HS:* Oxford [MS] B: 4/8/1945, Oxford, MS
Drafted: 1968 Round 3 Mia
1968 Mia: 8 G; KR 2-15 7.5.

SCOTT URCH Urch, Scott Eric 6′2″, 270 **OT**
Col: Virginia *HS:* Plum [Pittsburgh, PA] B: 7/25/1965, Niagara Falls, NY
1987 NYG: 3 G; KR 1-13 13.0.

EMIL UREMOVICH Uremovich, Emil 6′2″, 233 **DE-OE-T**
(Moose) *Col:* Indiana *HS:* Hobart [IN] B: 9/29/1916, Gary, IN
D: 4/22/1994, Knox, IN *Drafted:* 1941 Round 9 Pit
AAFC **1948** ChiA: 8 G; Int 1-1.

NFL **1941** Det: 10 G. **1942** Det: 11 G. **1945** Det: 8 G. **1946** Det: 11 G. **Total:** 40 G.

HERM URENDA Urenda, Herman Joseph 6′0″, 182 **OE-DB**
(Squirmin' Herman) *Col:* U. of Pacific *HS:* Liberty [Brentwood, CA]
B: 4/24/1938, Brentwood, CA
1963 Oak: 2 G.

RUBE URSELLA Ursella, Reuben J 5′9″, 172 **BB-WB-TB-FB**
Col: No College *HS:* None B: 1/11/1890 D: 2/1/1980, Minneapolis, MN
1920 RI: 7 G. **1921** Min: 4 G; Scor 7, 1 FG, 4 XK. **1924** RI: 7 G; Rec 1 TD; Scor 13, 1 FG, 4 XK. **1925** RI: 11 G; Scor 11, 3 FG, 2 XK. **1926** Akr-Ham: 9 G. Akr: 8 G. Ham: 1 G. **1929** Min: 8 G. **Total:** 46 G; Rec 1 TD; Scor 31, 5 FG, 10 XK.

DARRYL USHER Usher, Darryl Craig 5′8″, 170 **WR**
Col: Illinois *HS:* San Mateo [CA] B: 1/3/1965, Los Angeles, CA
D: 2/24/1990, Phoenix, AZ
1989 SD-Pho: Rec 1-8 8.0; PR 4-25 6.3. SD: PR 3-15 5.0. Pho: Rec 1-8 8.0; PR 1-10 10.0. **Total:** Rec 1-8 8.0; PR 4-25 6.3.

Year Team	G	Kickoff Returns Ret	Yds	Avg	TD	Fum
1989 SD-Pho	13	27	506	18.7	0	1
1989 SD	6	10	159	15.9	0	1
1989 Pho	7	17	347	20.4	0	0
NFL Total	13	27	506	18.7	0	1

EDDIE USHER Usher, Edward T 5′11″, 192 **WB-HB-TB-FB**
Col: Michigan *HS:* V. W. Scott [Toledo, OH] B: 6/19/1898, Toledo, OH
D: 4/1973, Bradenton, FL
1921 Buf: 1 G. **1922** RI-GB: 10 G; Rush 2 TD; 12 Pt. RI: 5 G; Rush 1 TD; 6 Pt. GB: 5 G; Rush 1 TD; 6 Pt. **1924** GB-KC: 7 G. GB: 1 G. KC: 6 G. **Total:** 18 G; Rush 2 TD; 12 Pt.

LOU USHER Usher, Louis C 6′2″, 240 **T-G-C**
Col: Detroit Mercy; Syracuse *HS:* Hyde Park [Chicago, IL] B: 1898, Chicago, IL Deceased
1920 Roch: 4 G. **1921** Roch-Ham-Sta: 5 G. Roch: 1 G. Ham: 1 G. Sta: 3 G. **1923** Ham-ChiB: 11 G. Ham: 3 G. ChiB: 8 G. **1924** Ham-Ken-Mil: 11 G. Ham: 1 G. Ken: 5 G. Mil: 5 G. **1926** Ham: 4 G. **Total:** 35 G.

MIKE UTLEY Utley, Michael Gerald 6′6″, 288 **OG-OT**
Col: Washington State *HS:* John F. Kennedy Memorial [Seattle, WA]
B: 12/20/1965, Seattle, WA *Drafted:* 1989 Round 3 Det
1989 Det: 5 G. **1990** Det: 16 G. **1991** Det: 11 G. **Total:** 32 G.

BEN UTT Utt, Benjamin Michael 6′5″, 275 **OT**
Col: Georgia Tech *HS:* Vidalia [GA] B: 6/13/1959, Richmond, CA
1982 Bal: 9 G. **1983** Bal: 16 G. **1984** Ind: 16 G. **1985** Ind: 16 G. **1986** Ind: 9 G. **1987** Ind: 12 G; Rec 1-(-4) -4.0. **1988** Ind: 16 G. **1989** Ind: 16 G.
Total: 110 G; Rec 1-(-4) -4.0.

IHEANYI UWAEZUOKE Uwaezuoke, Iheanyi 6′2″, 198 **WR**
Col: California *HS:* Harvard [North Hollywood, CA] B: 7/24/1973, Lagos, Nigeria *Drafted:* 1996 Round 5 SF
1996 SF: Rec 7-91 13.0 1 TD; KR 1-21 21.0. **1997** SF: Rec 14-165 11.8; KR 6-131 21.8. **1998** SF-Mia: Rec 3-67 22.3. SF: Rec 3-67 22.3.
Total: Rec 24-323 13.5 1 TD; KR 7-152 21.7.

Year Team	G	Punt Returns Ret	Yds	Avg	TD	Fum
1996 SF	14	0	0	—	0	0
1997 SF	14	34	373	11.0	0	4
1998 SF-Mia	11	0	0	—	0	0
1998 SF	7	0	0	—	0	0
1998 Mia	4	0	0	—	0	0
NFL Total	39	34	373	11.0	0	4

WALT UZDAVINIS Uzdavinis, Walter Alfred 6′2″, 210 **DE-OE-T**
(Uzzie) *Col:* Fordham *HS:* Brockton [MA] B: 6/19/1911, Middleboro, MA D: 12/23/1988, Glastonbury, CT
1937 Cle: 7 G; Rec 1-15 15.0.

SAM VACANTI Vacanti, Samuel Filadelfo 5′11″, 203 **QB**
Col: Iowa; Purdue; Nebraska *HS:* Omaha Tech [NE] B: 3/20/1922, Omaha, NE D: 12/17/1981, Omaha, NE
AAFC **1949** BalA: KR 1-10 10.0; Scor 3, 0-2 FG, 3-3 100.0% XK.
Total: KR 1-10 10.0; Scor 21, 0-2 FG, 3-3 100.0% XK.

Year Team	G	Passing Att	Comp	Comp%	Yds	YPA	TD	Int	Rating
1947 ChiA	13	225	96	42.7	1571	6.98	16	16	60.8
1948 ChiA-BalA	14	116	47	40.5	633	5.46	2	15	24.7
1949 BalA	12	27	11	40.7	134	4.96	0	1	41.3
AAFC Total	39	368	154	41.8	2338	6.35	18	32	43.5

Year Team	Rushing Att	Yds	Avg	TD
1947 ChiA	11	-9	-0.8	1
1948 ChiA-BalA	7	7	1.0	2
1949 BalA	7	10	1.4	0
AAFC Total	25	8	0.3	3

TED VACTOR Vactor, Theodore Francis 6′0″, 185 **DB**
Col: Nebraska *HS:* Washington [PA] B: 5/27/1944, Washington, PA
1972 Was: Int 1-28. **1973** Was: Int 1-34 1 TD. **Total:** Int 2-62 1 TD.

Year Team	G	Punt Returns Ret	Yds	Avg	TD	Kickoff Returns Ret	Yds	Avg	TD	Fum
1969 Was	14	0	0	—	0	0	0	—	0	0
1970 Was	14	2	7	3.5	0	28	700	25.0	0	0
1971 Was	14	23	194	8.4	0	0	0	—	0	5
1972 Was	14	17	88	5.2	0	1	21	21.0	0	4
1973 Was	9	0	0	—	0	0	0	—	0	0
1975 ChiB	4	0	0	—	0	1	25	25.0	0	0
NFL Total	69	42	289	6.9	0	30	746	24.9	0	9

PETE VAINOWSKI Vainowski, Peter S 1 **G**
Col: No College B: 9/7/1902 D: 7/16/1957, Chicago, IL
1926 Lou: 1 G.

DOM VAIRO Vairo, Dominic Martin 6′2″, 203 **OE-DE**
Col: Notre Dame *HS:* Calumet [MI] B: 11/2/1913, Calumet, MI
1935 GB: 1 G.

VERN VALDEZ Valdez, Vernon 6′0″, 190 **DB**
Col: Antelope Valley Coll. CA (J.C.); Cal Poly-Pomona; San Diego
HS: Antelope Valley [Lancaster, CA] B: 8/12/1935
1960 LARm: 9 G; Int 1-0. **1961** Buf: 13 G; PR 1-30 30.0; Int 2-54.
1962 Oak: 10 G; PR 2-14 7.0; Int 4-47. **Total:** 32 G; PR 3-44 14.7; Int 7-101.

IRA VALENTINE Valentine, Ira Lynn 6′0″, 212 **RB**
Col: Texas A&M *HS:* Marshall [TX] B: 6/4/1963, Marshall, TX
Drafted: 1987 Round 12 Hou
1987 Hou: 7 G; Rush 5-10 2.0; Rec 2-10 5.0; KR 1-13 13.0.

ZACK VALENTINE Valentine, Zachary Bernard 6′2″, 220 **LB**
Col: East Carolina *HS:* John A. Holmes [Edenton, NC] B: 5/29/1957, Edenton, NC *Drafted:* 1979 Round 2 Pit
1979 Pit: 16 G. **1980** Pit: 16 G; KR 1-0. **1981** Pit: 16 G. **1982** Phi: 8 G.
Total: 56 G; KR 1-0.

JOE VALERIO Valerio, Joseph William 6′5″, 295 **OT-OG-C**
Col: Pennsylvania *HS:* Ridley [Folsom, PA] B: 2/11/1969, Swarthmore, PA *Drafted:* 1991 Round 2 KC
1992 KC: 16 G. **1993** KC: 13 G; Rec 1-1 1.0 1 TD; 6 Pt. **1994** KC: 16 G; Rec 2-5 2.5 2 TD; 12 Pt. **1995** KC: 16 G; Rec 1-1 1.0 1 TD; KR 2-15 7.5;

6 Pt. **1996** StL: 1 G; 1 Fum. **Total:** 62 G; Rec 4-7 1.8 4 TD; KR 2-15 7.5; 24 Pt; 1 Fum.

EMILIO VALLEZ Vallez, Emilio Fidel 6′2″, 210 **TE**
Col: New Mexico *HS:* Belen [NM] B: 4/30/1946, Vegvita, NM
Drafted: 1968 Round 12 ChiB
1968 ChiB: 6 G. **1969** ChiB: 3 G. **Total:** 9 G.

NORM VAN BROCKLIN Van Brocklin, Norman Mack 6′1″, 190 **QB**
(The Dutchman) *Col:* Oregon *HS:* Acalanes [Lafayette, CA]
B: 3/15/1926, Eagle Butte, SD D: 5/2/1983, Social Circle, GA
Drafted: 1949 Round 4 LARm *HOF:* 1971

		Passing							
Year Team	G	Att	Comp	Comp%	Yds	YPA	TD	Int	Rating
1949 LARm	8	58	32	55.2	601	**10.36**	6	**2**	111.4
1950 LARm	12	233	127	54.5	2061	**8.85**	18	14	85.1
1951 LARm	12	194	100	51.5	1725	8.89	13	11	80.8
1952 LARm	12	205	113	**55.1**	1736	**8.47**	14	17	71.5
1953 LARm	12	286	156	54.5	2393	8.37	19	14	84.1
1954 LARm	12	260	139	53.5	**2637**	**10.14**	13	21	71.9
1955 LARm	12	272	144	52.9	1890	6.95	8	15	62.0
1956 LARm	12	124	68	54.8	966	7.79	7	12	59.5
1957 LARm	12	265	132	49.8	2105	7.94	20	21	68.8
1958 Phi	12	**374**	**198**	52.9	2409	6.44	15	20	64.1
1959 Phi	12	340	191	56.2	2617	7.70	16	14	79.5
1960 Phi	12	284	153	53.9	2471	8.70	24	17	86.5
NFL Total	140	2895	1553	53.6	23611	8.16	173	178	75.1

	Rushing				Punting			
Year Team	Att	Yds	Avg	TD	Punts	Yds	Avg	Fum
1949 LARm	4	-1	-0.3	0	2	91	45.5	2
1950 LARm	15	22	1.5	1	11	466	42.4	6
1951 LARm	7	2	0.3	2	48	1992	41.5	3
1952 LARm	7	-10	-1.4	0	29	1250	43.1	5
1953 LARm	8	11	1.4	0	60	2529	42.2	3
1954 LARm	6	-10	-1.7	0	44	1874	42.6	3
1955 LARm	11	24	2.2	0	60	2676	**44.6**	3
1956 LARm	4	1	0.3	1	48	2070	**43.1**	2
1957 LARm	10	-4	-0.4	4	54	2392	44.3	4
1958 Phi	8	5	0.6	1	54	2225	41.2	3
1959 Phi	11	13	1.2	2	53	2263	42.7	4
1960 Phi	11	-13	-1.2	0	60	2585	43.1	7
NFL Total	102	40	0.4	11	523	22413	42.9	45

EBERT VAN BUREN Van Buren, Harry Ebert 6′2″, 210 **LB-FB-HB**
(Ebert the Red) *Col:* Louisiana State *HS:* Metarie [LA] B: 12/6/1924, Tela, Honduras *Drafted:* 1951 Round 1 Phi
1951 Phi: 12 G; Rush 16-60 3.8; Int 1-23; 2 Fum. **1952** Phi: 12 G; Rush 7-1 0.1; Rec 4-73 18.3; PR 1-0; KR 1-12 12.0; Scor **1** Saf; 1 Fum TD; 8 Pt; 2 Fum. **1953** Phi: 12 G; Int 1-13. **Total:** 36 G; Rush 23-61 2.7; Rec 4-73 18.3; PR 1-0; KR 1-12 12.0; Int 2-36; Scor 1 Saf; 1 Fum TD; 8 Pt; 4 Fum.

STEVE VAN BUREN Van Buren, Stephen W 6′0″, 200 **HB**
Col: Louisiana State *HS:* Warren Easton [New Orleans, LA]
B: 12/28/1920, La Ceiba, Honduras *Drafted:* 1944 Round 1 Phi
HOF: 1965
1944 Phi: Int 5-47; Punt 1-35 35.0. **1945** Phi: Pass 1-0; Int 1-2; Scor **110**, 2-2 100.0% XK. **1946** Phi: Pass 1-1 100.0%, 35 35.00; Punt 1-41 41.0. **1947** Phi: Int 1-0. **1948** Phi: Pass 1-0; Int 2-32. **Total:** Pass 3-1 33.3%, 35 11.67; Int 9-81; Punt 2-76 38.0; Scor 464, 2-2 100.0% XK.

		Rushing				Receiving			
Year Team	G	Att	Yds	Avg	TD	Rec	Yds	Avg	TD
1944 Phi	9	80	444	5.6	5	0	0	—	0
1945 Phi	10	143	**832**	5.8	**15**	10	123	12.3	2
1946 Phi	9	116	529	4.6	5	6	75	12.5	0
1947 Phi	12	**217**	**1008**	4.6	**13**	9	79	8.8	0
1948 Phi	11	**201**	**945**	4.7	**10**	10	96	9.6	0
1949 Phi	12	**263**	**1146**	4.4	**11**	4	88	22.0	1
1950 Phi	10	**188**	629	3.3	4	2	34	17.0	0
1951 Phi	10	112	327	2.9	6	4	28	7.0	0
NFL Total	83	1320	5860	4.4	69	45	523	11.6	3

	Punt Returns				Kickoff Returns					Tot
Year Team	Ret	Yds	Avg	TD	Ret	Yds	Avg	TD	Fum	TD
1944 Phi	15	230	15.3	**1**	8	266	**33.3**	**1**	0	7
1945 Phi	14	154	11.0	0	13	373	28.7	**1**	7	**18**
1946 Phi	5	89	17.8	**1**	11	319	29.0	0	8	6
1947 Phi	0	0	—	0	13	382	**29.4**	1	4	**14**
1948 Phi	0	0	—	0	14	292	20.9	0	6	10
1949 Phi	0	0	—	0	12	288	24.0	0	3	12
1950 Phi	0	0	—	0	5	110	22.0	0	3	4
1951 Phi	0	0	—	0	0	0	—	0	3	6
NFL Total	34	473	13.9	2	76	2030	26.7	3	34	77

ERIC VANCE Vance, Eric Devon 6′2″, 215 **DB**
Col: Vanderbilt *HS:* L.D. Bell [Hurst, TX] B: 7/14/1975, Tampa, FL
1998 TB: 3 G.

JOE VANCE Vance, Joseph Albert 6′1″, 180 **WB-FB**
(Sandy) *Col:* Southwest Texas State; Texas *HS:* Devine [TX]
B: 9/16/1905, Devine, TX D: 7/4/1978, San Antonio, TX
1931 Bkn: 11 G; Rush 2 TD; 12 Pt.

MATT VANDERBEEK Vanderbeek, Matthew James 6′3″, 252 **LB-DE**
Col: Michigan State *HS:* West Ottawa [Holland, MI] B: 8/16/1967, Saugatuck, MI
1990 Ind: 16 G. **1991** Ind: 5 G. **1992** Ind: 15 G; KR 1-6 6.0. **1993** Dal: 16 G. **1994** Dal: 12 G. **1995** Was: 16 G; KR 1-7 7.0. **1996** Was: 1 G. **Total:** 81 G; KR 2-13 6.5.

SKIP VANDERBUNDT Vanderbundt, William Gerard 6′3″, 225 **LB**
Col: Oregon State *HS:* El Dorado [Placentia, CA] B: 12/4/1946, Martinez, CA *Drafted:* 1968 Round 3 SF
1971 SF: PR 1-0. **1972** SF: **1** Fum TD. **Total:** PR 1-0; 1 Fum TD.

		Interceptions				Tot
Year Team	G	Int	Yds	TD	Fum	TD
1969 SF	14	0	0	0	0	0
1970 SF	12	3	18	0	0	0
1971 SF	14	1	10	0	0	0
1972 SF	14	2	58	2	0	3
1973 SF	9	1	7	0	0	0
1974 SF	14	2	22	0	1	0
1975 SF	14	2	36	0	0	0
1976 SF	14	2	8	0	1	0
1977 SF	14	1	6	0	0	0
1978 NO	15	0	0	0	0	0
NFL Total	134	14	165	2	2	3

MIKE VANDERJAGT Vanderjagt, Michael John 6′5″, 210 **P-K**
Col: Allan Hancock Coll. CA (J.C.); West Virginia *HS:* White Oaks Secondary School [Oakville, Canada] B: 3/24/1970, Oakville, Canada

		Scoring						
Year Team	G	Pts	FG	FGA	FG%	XK	XKA	XK%
1998 Ind	14	104	27	31	87.1	23	23	100.0

RON VANDER KELEN Vander Kelen, Ronald 6′1″, 185 **QB**
Col: Wisconsin *HS:* Preble [Green Bay, WI] B: 11/6/1939, Green Bay, WI *Drafted:* 1963 Round 21 NYJ

		Passing							
Year Team	G	Att	Comp	Comp%	Yds	YPA	TD	Int	Rating
1963 Min	6	58	27	46.6	376	6.48	1	2	59.3
1964 Min	5	19	7	36.8	78	4.11	0	1	28.0
1965 Min	4	40	18	45.0	252	6.30	2	0	82.5
1966 Min	3	20	10	50.0	147	7.35	0	1	53.5
1967 Min	11	115	45	39.1	522	4.54	3	7	36.9
NFL Total	29	252	107	42.5	1375	5.46	6	11	50.0

	Rushing				
Year Team	Att	Yds	Avg	TD	Fum
1963 Min	8	65	8.1	0	0
1964 Min	1	10	10.0	0	0
1965 Min	4	13	3.3	0	1
1966 Min	4	19	4.8	0	2
1967 Min	9	9	1.0	1	3
NFL Total	26	116	4.5	1	6

VIV VANDERLOO Vanderloo, Vivian Bernard 5′10″, 190 **FB**
Col: Iowa State *HS:* Coon Rapids [IA] B: 4/11/1897, Coon Rapids, IA
D: 6/18/1972, Mesa, AZ
1921 RI: 3 G.

MARK VANDER POEL Vander Poel, John Mark 6′7″, 303 **OT**
Col: Colorado *HS:* Chino [CA] B: 3/5/1968, Upland, CA
Drafted: 1991 Round 4 Ind
1991 Ind: 10 G. **1992** Ind: 13 G. **Total:** 23 G.

PHIL VANDERSEA Vandersea, Phillip John 6′3″, 245 **LB-DE**
Col: Massachusetts *HS:* Northbridge [Whitinsville, MA] B: 2/25/1943, Whitinsville, MA *Drafted:* 1965 Round 16 GB
1966 GB: 14 G; KR 3-50 16.7. **1967** NO: 8 G; KR 1-13 13.0. **1968** GB: 10 G; KR 1-8 8.0. **1969** GB: 14 G. **Total:** 46 G; KR 5-71 14.2.

AL VANDEWEGHE Vandeweghe, Alfred Bernard 5′11″, 200 **OE-DE**
Col: William & Mary *HS:* Hampton [VA] B: 10/25/1920, Wyckoff, NJ
AAFC **1946** BufA: 5 G; Rec 6-67 11.2 1 TD; KR 1-15 15.0; Tot TD 2; 12 Pt.

RANDY VAN DIVIER Van Divier, Randall Lee 6′5″, 274 **OT-OG**
Col: Washington *HS:* Anaheim [CA] B: 6/5/1958, Anaheim, CA
Drafted: 1981 Round 3 Bal
1981 Bal: 16 G.

BOB VAN DOREN Van Doren, Robert S 6′3″, 215 **DE**
Col: USC *HS:* San Diego [CA]; Farragut Mil. Acad. [NJ] B: 1929, Baltimore, MD *Drafted:* 1953 Round 5 Cle
1953 SF: 10 G.

BOB VAN DUYNE Van Duyne, Robert Scott 6′5″, 243 **OG-OT**
Col: Idaho *HS:* Highline [Seattle, WA] B: 5/15/1952, San Bernardino, CA *Drafted:* 1974 Round 10 Bal
1974 Bal: 14 G. **1975** Bal: 14 G. **1976** Bal: 14 G. **1977** Bal: 9 G. **1978** Bal: 14 G; KR 1-0; 1 Fum. **1979** Bal: 16 G; KR 1-12 12.0. **1980** Bal: 7 G. **Total:** 88 G; KR 2-12 6.0; 1 Fum.

BRUCE VAN DYKE Van Dyke, Bruce Robert 6′2″, 255 **OG**
Col: Missouri *HS:* Fort Osage [Independence, MO] B: 8/6/1944, Lancaster, CA *Drafted:* 1966 Round 12 Phi
1966 Phi: 4 G. **1967** Pit: 14 G. **1968** Pit: 14 G. **1969** Pit: 14 G. **1970** Pit: 14 G. **1971** Pit: 12 G. **1972** Pit: 13 G. **1973** Pit: 14 G. **1974** GB: 1 G. **1975** GB: 14 G. **1976** GB: 14 G. **Total:** 128 G.

ALEX VAN DYKE Van Dyke, Franklin Alexander 6′0″, 205 **WR**
Col: Sacramento City Coll. CA (J.C.); Nevada-Reno *HS:* Luther Burbank [Sacramento, CA] B: 7/24/1974, Sacramento, CA *Drafted:* 1996 Round 2 NYJ
1996 NYJ: KR 15-289 19.3. **1997** NYJ: KR 6-138 23.0. **Total:** KR 21-427 20.3.

		Receiving			
Year Team	**G**	**Rec**	**Yds**	**Avg**	**TD**
1996 NYJ	15	17	118	6.9	1
1997 NYJ	5	3	53	17.7	2
1998 NYJ	16	5	40	8.0	0
NFL Total	36	25	211	8.4	3

JIMMY VAN DYKE Van Dyke, James B 5′7″, 140 **TB-BB**
(Slim Jimmy) *Col:* No College *HS:* Male [Louisville, KY] B: 10/2/1898, Louisville, KY D: 8/30/1980, Louisville, KY
1921 Lou: 1 G. **1922** Lou: 3 G; Rush 1 TD; Scor 7, 1 XK. **1923** Lou: 1 G. **Total:** 5 G; Rush 1 TD.

RALPH VAN DYKE Van Dyke, Ralph Waldo III 6′6″, 273 **OT**
Col: Southern Illinois *HS:* Bloom [Chicago Heights, IL] B: 1/19/1964, Chicago Heights, IL
1987 Cle: 2 G.

CHASE VAN DYNE Van Dyne, Charles M 6′1″, 194 **T**
Col: Missouri *HS:* Smith Cotton [Sedalia, MO] B: 2/12/1901 D: 9/1962
1925 Buf: 8 G.

MARK VAN EEGHEN van Eeghen, Mark 6′2″, 223 **RB**
Col: Colgate *HS:* Cranston West [RI] B: 4/19/1952, Cambridge, MA *Drafted:* 1974 Round 3 Oak
1975 Oak: KR 7-112 16.0. **1978** Oak: 1 Fum TD. **Total:** KR 7-112 16.0; 1 Fum TD.

		Rushing				Receiving					Tot
Year Team	**G**	**Att**	**Yds**	**Avg**	**TD**	**Rec**	**Yds**	**Avg**	**TD**	**Fum**	**TD**
1974 Oak	14	28	139	5.0	0	4	33	8.3	0	0	0
1975 Oak	14	136	597	4.4	2	12	42	3.5	1	5	3
1976 Oak	14	233	1012	4.3	3	17	173	10.2	0	3	3
1977 Oak	14	324	1273	3.9	7	15	135	9.0	0	3	7
1978 Oak	16	270	1080	4.0	9	27	291	10.8	0	5	10
1979 Oak	16	223	818	3.7	7	51	474	9.3	2	3	9
1980 Oak	16	222	838	3.8	5	29	259	8.9	0	3	5
1981 Oak	8	39	150	3.8	2	7	60	8.6	0	0	2
1982 NE	9	82	386	4.7	0	2	14	7.0	1	2	1
1983 NE	15	95	358	3.8	2	10	102	10.2	0	1	2
NFL Total	136	1652	6651	4.0	37	174	1583	9.1	4	25	42

HAL VAN EVERY Van Every, Harold 6′0″, 195 **TB-DB-HB**
Col: Minnesota *HS:* Wayzata [MN] B: 2/10/1918, Minnetonka Beach, MN *Drafted:* 1940 Round 1 GB
1940 GB: Rec 4-41 10.3; Int 3-30; Punt 17-620 36.5. **1941** GB: Rec 1-3 3.0; PR 4-58 14.5; KR 4-99 24.8; Int 3-104 **1** TD; Punt 13-505 38.8. **Total:** Rec 5-44 8.8; PR 4-58 14.5; KR 4-99 24.8; Int 6-134 1 TD; Punt 30-1125 37.5.

		Passing							
Year Team	**G**	**Att**	**Comp**	**Comp%**	**Yds**	**YPA**	**TD**	**Int**	**Rating**
1940 GB	9	41	12	29.3	199	4.85	4	6	40.2
1941 GB	11	30	11	36.7	195	6.50	0	**2**	31.9
NFL Total	20	71	23	32.4	394	5.55	4	8	31.4

	Rushing				Tot
Year Team	**Att**	**Yds**	**Avg**	**TD**	**TD**
1940 GB	38	154	4.1	0	0
1941 GB	25	127	5.1	2	3
NFL Total	63	281	4.5	2	3

TIM VAN GALDER Van Galder, Thomas Scott 6′2″, 200 **QB**
Col: New Mexico Mil. Inst. (J.C.); Iowa State *HS:* West [Madison, WI] B: 5/26/1944, Racine, WI *Drafted:* 1966 Round 6 StL
1972 StL: Rush 9-28 3.1.

		Passing								
Year Team	**G**	**Att**	**Comp**	**Comp%**	**Yds**	**YPA**	**TD**	**Int**	**Rating**	**Fum**
1972 StL	5	79	40	50.6	434	5.49	1	7	34.5	3

BILLY VAN HEUSEN Van Heusen, William Proctor 6′1″, 200 **WR-P**
Col: Maryland *HS:* Mamaroneck [NY] B: 8/27/1946, New Rochelle, NY
1968 Den: Rush 1-6 6.0. **1970** Den: Pass 1-0. **1971** Den: Pass 1-0; Rush 1-10 10.0. **1972** Den: Rush 3-76 25.3 1 TD. **1973** Den: Pass 1-0; Rush 4-34 8.5. **1974** Den: Pass 1-1 100.0%, 41 41.00; Rush 1-(-1) -1.0. **1975** Den: Pass 1-1 100.0%, 30 30.00; Rush 2-26 13.0. **1976** Den: Rush 1-20 20.0. **Total:** Pass 5-2 40.0%, 71 14.20; Rush 13-171 13.2 1 TD.

		Receiving				Punting				Tot
Year Team	**G**	**Rec**	**Yds**	**Avg**	**TD**	**Punts**	**Yds**	**Avg**	**Fum**	**TD**
1968 Den	13	19	353	18.6	3	88	3853	43.8	0	3
1969 Den	5	3	64	21.3	0	25	1021	40.8	0	0
1970 Den	14	16	382	23.9	2	**87**	**3732**	42.9	1	2
1971 Den	14	1	10	10.0	0	76	3176	41.8	0	0
1972 Den	14	4	59	14.8	0	60	2408	40.1	0	1
1973 Den	14	8	149	18.6	1	69	3114	45.1	0	1
1974 Den	14	16	421	26.3	4	75	3024	40.3	1	4
1975 Den	14	15	246	16.4	1	63	2515	39.9	1	1
1976 Den	7	0	0	—	0	31	1093	35.3	0	0
NFL Total	109	82	1684	20.5	11	574	23936	41.7	3	12

CHARLIE VAN HORN Van Horn, Charles Edgar 6′2″, 185 **TB-FB-WB**
Col: Washington & Lee *HS:* Allegheny Prep [Pittsburgh, PA] B: 11/23/1901 D: 1/5/1994, Arlington, VA
1927 Buf: 4 G. **1929** Ora: 4 G. **Total:** 8 G.

DOUG VAN HORN Van Horn, Douglas Claydon 6′3″, 245 **OG-OT**
Col: Ohio State *HS:* Eastmoor [Columbus, OH] B: 6/24/1944, Sedalia, MO *Drafted:* 1966 Round 4 Det
1966 Det: 14 G. **1968** NYG: 3 G. **1969** NYG: 14 G. **1970** NYG: 14 G. **1971** NYG: 12 G. **1972** NYG: 14 G. **1973** NYG: 14 G. **1974** NYG: 14 G. **1975** NYG: 14 G. **1976** NYG: 14 G. **1977** NYG: 14 G. **1978** NYG: 16 G. **1979** NYG: 15 G. **Total:** 172 G.

KEITH VAN HORNE Van Horne, Keith 6′6″, 281 **OT**
Col: USC *HS:* Fullerton [CA] B: 11/6/1957, Mount Lebanon, PA *Drafted:* 1981 Round 1 ChiB
1981 ChiB: 14 G. **1982** ChiB: 9 G. **1983** ChiB: 14 G. **1984** ChiB: 14 G. **1985** ChiB: 16 G. **1986** ChiB: 16 G. **1987** ChiB: 12 G. **1988** ChiB: 15 G. **1989** ChiB: 15 G. **1990** ChiB: 16 G. **1991** ChiB: 16 G. **1992** ChiB: 16 G. **1993** ChiB: 13 G. **Total:** 186 G.

SEAN VANHORSE Vanhorse, Sean Joseph 5′10″, 180 **DB**
Col: Howard *HS:* Northwestern [Baltimore, MD] B: 7/22/1968, Baltimore, MD *Drafted:* 1990 Round 6 Mia
1992 SD: 16 G; Int 1-11. **1993** SD: 15 G; Int 2-0. **1994** SD: 16 G; Int 2-56 1 TD; 6 Pt. **1995** Det: 14 G; Int 1-0. **1996** Min: 9 G. **Total:** 70 G; Int 6-67 1 TD; 6 Pt.

ED VAN METER Van Meter, Edward 6′1″, 212 **G**
Col: No College *HS:* West [Columbus, OH] B: 1899 Deceased
1921 Was: 2 G.

NORWOOD VANN Vann, Norwood Jacob Jr. 6′1″, 228 **LB**
Col: East Carolina *HS:* James Kenan [Warsaw, NC] B: 2/18/1962, Philadelphia, PA *Drafted:* 1984 Round 10 LARm
1984 LARm: 16 G; Scor **1** Saf; 2 Pt. **1985** LARm: 8 G. **1986** LARm: 16 G. **1987** LARm: 11 G. **1988** LARd: 1 G. **Total:** 52 G; Scor 1 Saf; 2 Pt.

JEFF VAN NOTE Van Note, Jeffrey Aloysius 6′2″, 247 **C-OG-LB**
Col: Kentucky *HS:* St. Joseph Prep [Bardstown, KY] B: 2/7/1946, South Orange, NJ *Drafted:* 1969 Round 11 Atl
1969 Atl: 1 G. **1970** Atl: 14 G. **1971** Atl: 14 G; 1 Fum. **1972** Atl: 14 G. **1973** Atl: 14 G. **1974** Atl: 14 G. **1975** Atl: 14 G; 1 Fum. **1976** Atl: 10 G. **1977** Atl: 14 G. **1978** Atl: 16 G. **1979** Atl: 16 G. **1980** Atl: 16 G. **1981** Atl: 16 G; 1 Fum. **1982** Atl: 9 G. **1983** Atl: 16 G. **1984** Atl: 16 G. **1985** Atl: 16 G. **1986** Atl: 16 G. **Total:** 246 G; 3 Fum.

TAMARICK VANOVER Vanover, Tamarick 5′11″, 220 **WR**
Col: Florida State *HS:* Leon [Tallahassee, FL] B: 2/15/1970, Tallahassee, FL *Drafted:* 1995 Round 3 KC
1995 KC: Rush 6-31 5.2. **1996** KC: Rush 4-6 1.5. **1997** KC: Rush 5-50 10.0; Scor 1 2XP. **1998** KC: Rush 2-1 0.5. **Total:** Rush 17-88 5.2; Scor 1 2XP.

		Receiving				Punt Returns			
Year Team	**G**	**Rec**	**Yds**	**Avg**	**TD**	**Ret**	**Yds**	**Avg**	**TD**
1995 KC	15	11	231	21.0	2	51	**540**	10.6	**1**
1996 KC	13	21	241	11.5	1	17	116	6.8	0
1997 KC	16	7	92	13.1	0	35	383	10.9	1
1998 KC	12	0	0	—	0	27	264	9.8	0
NFL Total	56	39	564	14.5	3	130	1303	10.0	2

	Kickoff Returns					Tot
Year Team	**Ret**	**Yds**	**Avg**	**TD**	**Fum**	**TD**
1995 KC	43	1095	25.5	**2**	1	5

1996 KC	33	854	25.9	1	1	2
1997 KC	51	1308	25.6	1	6	2
1998 KC	41	956	23.3	0	2	0
NFL Total	168	4213	25.1	4	10	9

VERN VANOY Vanoy, Vernon Eugene 6′8″, 275 **DT**
Col: Kansas *HS:* Lincoln Prep [Kansas City, MO] B: 12/31/1946, Kansas City, MO *Drafted:* 1969 Round 3 NYG
1971 NYG: 6 G. **1972** GB: 13 G. **1973** Hou: 1 G. **Total:** 20 G.

BRAD VAN PELT Van Pelt, Bradley Alan 6′5″, 235 **LB**
Col: Michigan State *HS:* Owosso [MI] B: 4/5/1951, Owosso, MI
Drafted: 1973 Round 2 NYG
1979 NYG: Rec 1-20 20.0. **1982** NYG: 2 Sac. **1983** NYG: 3 Sac. **1985** LARd: 5 Sac. **Total:** Rec 1-20 20.0; 10 Sac.

		Interceptions		
Year Team	**G**	**Int**	**Yds**	**TD**
1973 NYG	5	0	0	0
1974 NYG	12	2	22	0
1975 NYG	14	3	8	0
1976 NYG	14	2	13	0
1977 NYG	14	2	9	0
1978 NYG	14	3	32	0
1979 NYG	16	0	0	0
1980 NYG	15	3	3	0
1981 NYG	14	1	10	0
1982 NYG	9	0	0	0
1983 NYG	16	2	7	0
1984 LARd	9	1	9	0
1985 LARd	16	1	22	0
1986 Cle	16	0	0	0
NFL Total	184	20	135	0

ALEX VAN PELT Van Pelt, Gregory Alexander 6′0″, 220 **QB**
Col: Pittsburgh *HS:* Winston Churchill [San Antonio, TX] B: 5/1/1970, Grafton, WV *Drafted:* 1993 Round 8 Pit
1996 Buf: Rush 3-(-5) -1.7. **1997** Buf: Rush 11-33 3.0 1 TD. **1998** Buf: Rush 1-(-1) -1.0. **Total:** Rush 15-27 1.8 1 TD.

		Passing								
Year Team	**G**	**Att**	**Comp**	**Comp%**	**Yds**	**YPA**	**TD**	**Int**	**Rating**	**Fum**
1995 Buf	1	18	10	55.6	106	5.89	2	0	110.0	0
1996 Buf	1	5	2	40.0	9	1.80	0	0	47.9	0
1997 Buf	6	124	60	48.4	684	5.52	2	10	37.2	3
1998 Buf	1	0	0	—	0	—	0	0	—	0
NFL Total	9	147	72	49.0	799	5.44	4	10	46.3	3

JEFF VAN RAAPHORST Van Raaphorst, Jeffrey Richard 6′1″, 210 **QB**
Col: Arizona State *HS:* Grossmont [La Mesa, CA] B: 12/7/1963, Columbus, OH
1987 Atl: 2 G; Pass 34-18 52.9%, 174 5.12 1 TD 2 Int; Rush 1-6 6.0; 1 Fum.

DICK VAN RAAPHORST Van Raaphorst, Richard William 6′0″, 218 **K**
Col: Ohio State *HS:* Charlevoix [MI] B: 12/10/1942, Port Huron, MI
Drafted: 1964 Round 10 Cle

		Scoring						
Year Team	**G**	**Pts**	**FG**	**FGA**	**FG%**	**XK**	**XKA**	**XK%**
1964 Dal	14	70	14	29	48.3	28	29	96.6
1966 SD	14	87	16	31	51.6	39	40	97.5
1967 SD	14	90	15	30	50.0	45	45	100.0
NFL Total	42	247	45	90	50.0	112	114	98.2

CLYDE VAN SICKLE Van Sickle, Clyde Huntus 6′1″, 220 **G**
Col: Arkansas *HS:* Morris [OK]; Okmulgee HS [OK] B: 5/26/1907, Pryor, OK D: 2/15/1995, Dallas, TX
1930 Fra: 11 G. **1932** GB: 1 G. **1933** GB: 8 G. **Total:** 20 G.

FRED VANT HULL Vant Hull, Frederick Nels 6′0″, 214 **G-LB**
Col: Minnesota *HS:* West [Minneapolis, MN] B: 8/21/1920, Winnepeg, Canada D: 4/10/1975, Minneapolis, MN
1942 GB: 8 G.

ART VAN TONE Van Tone, Arthur 5′10″, 185 **WB-DB**
Col: Southern Mississippi B: 9/30/1918, Ottawa, OH D: 8/9/1990, Conyers, GA
AAFC **1946** BknA: 9 G; Rush 4-10 2.5; Rec 7-152 21.7 3 TD; PR 1-5 5.0; KR 2-25 12.5; Int 1-5; 18 Pt.

NFL **1943** Det: Pass 3-1 33.3%, 7 2.33 1 Int; Rec 6-112 18.7 1 TD; PR 3-47 15.7; Int 2-29. **1944** Det: Pass 1-0; Rec 9-237 26.3 4 TD; PR 5-70 14.0; KR 9-227 25.2 **1** TD; Int 4-16; Punt 2-94 47.0. **1945** Det: Rec 3-67 22.3. **Total:** Pass 4-1 25.0%, 7 1.75 1 Int; Rec 18-416 23.1 5 TD; PR 8-117 14.6; KR 9-227 25.2 1 TD; Int 6-45; Punt 2-94 47.0.

		Rushing					Tot
Year Team	**G**	**Att**	**Yds**	**Avg**	**TD**	**Fum**	**TD**
1943 Det	10	2	1	0.5	0	0	1
1944 Det	10	25	30	1.2	1	0	6
1945 Det	2	3	14	4.7	0	1	0
NFL Total	22	30	45	1.5	1	1	7

PETE VAN VALKENBERG Van Valkenberg, Peter 6′2″, 192 **RB**
Col: Brigham Young *HS:* Hillcrest [Sandy, UT] B: 5/19/1950, Salt Lake City, UT *Drafted:* 1973 Round 3 NO
1973 Buf: 13 G; Rush 2-20 10.0; Rec 1-7 7.0; KR 1-0. **1974** GB-ChiB: 11 G; PR 4-22 5.5; KR 2-42 21.0; 1 Fum. GB: 5 G; KR 1-22 22.0. ChiB: 6 G; PR 4-22 5.5; KR 1-20 20.0; 1 Fum. **Total:** 24 G; Rush 2-20 10.0; Rec 1-7 7.0; PR 4-22 5.5; KR 3-42 14.0; 1 Fum.

JAMES VAN WAGNER Van Wagner, James Parker 6′0″, 202 **RB**
Col: Michigan Tech *HS:* Novi [MI] B: 5/3/1955, Ann Arbor, MI
Drafted: 1977 Round 7 SF
1978 NO: 5 G; Rec 1-(-1) -1.0.

FRED VANZO Vanzo, Fred Ferdinand 6′2″, 230 **BB-LB**
(Chopper) *Col:* Northwestern *HS:* Clinton [Michigantown, IN] B: 1/8/1916, Universal, IN D: 2/7/1976, Plymouth, MN *Drafted:* 1938 Round 2 NYG
1938 Det: 10 G; Rec 4-52 13.0. **1939** Det: 10 G; Rush 5-46 9.2; Rec 4-110 27.5. **1940** Det: 10 G; Rush 1-(-1) -1.0; Rec 7-75 10.7. **1941** Det-ChiC: 9 G; Rec 2-20 10.0. Det: 6 G; Rec 2-20 10.0. ChiC: 3 G. **Total:** 39 G; Rush 6-45 7.5; Rec 17-257 15.1.

MIKE VARAJON Varajon, Michael Joseph 6′1″, 232 **RB**
Col: Toledo *HS:* Catholic Central [Detroit, MI] B: 7/12/1964, Detroit, MI
1987 SF: 3 G; Rush 18-82 4.6; Rec 3-25 8.3; KR 1-13 13.0.

TOMMY VARDELL Vardell, Thomas Arthur 6′2″, 234 **RB**
(Touchdown Tommy) *Col:* Stanford *HS:* Granite Hills [El Cajon, CA] B: 2/20/1969, El Cajon, CA *Drafted:* 1992 Round 1 Cle
1992 Cle: KR 2-14 7.0. **1993** Cle: KR 4-58 14.5. **1997** Det: KR 1-15 15.0. **1998** Det: KR 1-23 23.0. **Total:** KR 8-110 13.8.

		Rushing				Receiving					Tot
Year Team	**G**	**Att**	**Yds**	**Avg**	**TD**	**Rec**	**Yds**	**Avg**	**TD**	**Fum**	**TD**
1992 Cle	14	99	369	3.7	0	13	128	9.8	0	0	0
1993 Cle	16	171	644	3.8	3	19	151	7.9	1	3	4
1994 Cle	5	15	48	3.2	0	16	137	8.6	1	0	1
1995 Cle	5	4	9	2.3	0	6	18	3.0	0	0	0
1996 SF	11	58	192	3.3	2	28	179	6.4	0	0	2
1997 Det	16	32	122	3.8	6	16	218	13.6	0	1	6
1998 Det	14	18	37	2.1	6	14	143	10.2	1	1	7
NFL Total	81	397	1421	3.6	17	112	974	8.7	3	5	20

JOHNNY VARDIAN Vardian, John Joseph 5′8″, 167 **HB-DB**
HS: Johnstown Catholic [PA] B: 9/25/1921, Johnstown, PA
D: 8/8/1989, Tampa, FL
AAFC **1946** MiaA: Pass 1-1 100.0%, -4 -4.00; KR 1-23 23.0. **1947** BalA: PR 5-66 13.2; KR 6-128 21.3; Int 3-48. **1948** BalA: PR 3-34 11.3; KR 3-66 22.0. **Total:** Pass 1-1 100.0%, -4 -4.00; PR 8-100 12.5; KR 10-217 21.7; Int 3-48.

		Rushing				Receiving			
Year Team	**G**	**Att**	**Yds**	**Avg**	**TD**	**Rec**	**Yds**	**Avg**	**TD**
1946 MiaA	6	5	-8	-1.6	0	7	108	15.4	0
1947 BalA	14	35	57	1.6	0	16	280	17.5	1
1948 BalA	12	6	13	2.2	0	3	26	8.7	0
AAFC Total	32	46	62	1.3	0	26	414	15.9	1

LARRY VARGO Vargo, Lawrence F Jr. 6′3″, 215 **DB-LB**
Col: Detroit Mercy *HS:* Servite [Detroit, MI] B: 4/5/1939, Iron Mountain, MI *Drafted:* 1961 Round 11 Det
1962 Det: 9 G. **1963** Det: 14 G; KR 1-8 8.0; Int 1-42 1 TD; 6 Pt. **1964** Min: 14 G; Rec 1-13 13.0; Int 1-0. **1965** Min: 13 G; Int 3-18. **1966** NYG: 7 G; Int 1-1. **Total:** 57 G; Rec 1-13 13.0; KR 1-8 8.0; Int 6-61 1 TD; 6 Pt.

FRANK VARRICHIONE Varrichione, Frank Joseph 6′1″, 234 **OT**
Col: Notre Dame *HS:* Natick [MA]; St. Thomas Aquinas Prep [Rochester, NY] B: 1/14/1932, Natick, MA *Drafted:* 1955 Round 1 Pit
1955 Pit: 12 G. **1956** Pit: 12 G; KR 1-8 8.0. **1957** Pit: 12 G. **1958** Pit: 12 G; KR 3-38 12.7. **1959** Pit: 12 G. **1960** Pit: 12 G; KR 1-0. **1961** LARm: 14 G; KR 3-23 7.7. **1962** LARm: 12 G. **1963** LARm: 14 G. **1964** LARm: 10 G. **1965** LARm: 11 G. **Total:** 133 G; KR 8-69 8.6.

MIKE VARTY Varty, Michael Scott Matthew 6′1″, 223 **LB**
Col: Northwestern *HS:* Austin [Grosse Pointe Park, MI] B: 2/10/1952, Detroit, MI *Drafted:* 1974 Round 7 Was
1974 Was: 2 G. **1975** Bal: 6 G. **Total:** 8 G.

VIC VASICEK Vasicek, Victor Frederick 5′11″, 223 **OG-LB-DG**
Col: USC; Texas *HS:* El Campo [TX] B: 5/5/1926, Austin, TX
Drafted: 1949 Round 10 Was
AAFC **1949** BufA: 12 G; Rec 0-5.

NFL **1950** LARm: 12 G; KR 2-30 15.0; Int 1-52.

ROY VASSAU Vassau, Roy E 6′0″, 220 **T**
(Tiny) *Col:* St. Thomas B: 12/1893, St. Paul, MN Deceased
1923 Mil: 1 G.

ARUNAS VASYS Vasys, Arunas Bruno 6′2″, 235 **LB**
Col: Notre Dame *HS:* St. Phillip [Chicago, IL] B: 8/18/1943, Lithuania
Drafted: 1966 Round 16 Phi
1966 Phi: 10 G. **1967** Phi: 9 G; KR 1-0. **1968** Phi: 3 G. **Total:** 22 G; KR 1-0.

RANDY VATAHA Vataha, Randel Edward 5′10″, 176 **WR**
Col: Golden West Coll. CA (J.C.); Stanford *HS:* Rancho Alamitos [Garden Grove, CA] B: 12/4/1948, Santa Maria, CA *Drafted:* 1971 Round 17 LARm
1973 NE: Rush 2-(-15) -7.5; **1** Fum TD. **1974** NE: Rush 3-21 7.0. **1975** NE: Rush 1-4 4.0. **Total:** Rush 6-10 1.7; 1 Fum TD.

		Receiving					Tot
Year Team	**G**	**Rec**	**Yds**	**Avg**	**TD**	**Fum**	**TD**
1971 NE	14	51	872	17.1	9	0	9
1972 NE	14	25	369	14.8	2	0	2
1973 NE	14	20	341	17.1	2	0	3
1974 NE	12	25	561	22.4	3	1	3
1975 NE	14	46	720	15.7	6	0	6
1976 NE	12	11	192	17.5	1	0	1
1977 GB	6	10	109	10.9	0	0	0
NFL Total	86	188	3164	16.8	23	1	24

CHARLES VATTEROTT Vatterott, Charles Francis 6′4″, 263 **OG-OT**
Col: Southwest Texas State *HS:* St. Thomas [Houston, TX]
B: 1/31/1964, St. Louis, MO
1987 StL: 2 G.

PUG VAUGHAN Vaughan, Charles Wesley 5′11″, 181 **TB-DB**
Col: Tennessee *HS:* Knoxville [TN] B: 3/18/1911, Knoxville, TN
D: 3/30/1964, Knoxville, TN
1935 Det: Rec 1-9 9.0. **Total:** Rec 1-9 9.0.

		Passing							
Year Team	**G**	**Att**	**Comp**	**Comp%**	**Yds**	**YPA**	**TD**	**Int**	**Rating**
1935 Det	7	15	7	46.7	104	6.93	2	2	69.9
1936 ChiC	12	79	30	38.0	546	6.91	2	10	31.4
NFL Total	19	94	37	39.4	650	6.91	4	12	38.3

	Rushing			
Year Team	**Att**	**Yds**	**Avg**	**TD**
1935 Det	13	51	3.9	0
1936 ChiC	67	79	1.2	0
NFL Total	80	130	1.6	0

HARP VAUGHAN Vaughan, John J 5′7″, 150 **DB-TB-BB-HB**
Col: No College *HS:* Bellefonte Acad. [PA] B: 11/19/1903, PA
D: 12/26/1978, Macclenny, FL
1933 Pit: Rec 6-101 16.8. **1934** Pit: Rec 2-56 28.0. **Total:** Rec 8-157 19.6.

		Passing							
Year Team	**G**	**Att**	**Comp**	**Comp%**	**Yds**	**YPA**	**TD**	**Int**	**Rating**
1933 Pit	8	8	2	25.0	2	0.25	0	3	0.0
1934 Pit	11	42	19	45.2	262	6.24	2	5	42.1
NFL Total	19	50	21	42.0	264	5.28	2	8	32.8

	Rushing			
Year Team	**Att**	**Yds**	**Avg**	**TD**
1933 Pit	26	74	2.8	1
1934 Pit	58	196	3.4	0
NFL Total	84	270	3.2	1

RUBEN VAUGHAN Vaughan, Ruben Charles Jr. 6′2″, 261 **DT-NT-DE**
Col: Colorado *HS:* David Starr Jordan [Los Angeles, CA] B: 8/5/1956, Los Angeles, CA *Drafted:* 1979 Round 6 SF
1979 SF: 13 G. **1982** LARd: 9 G; 4 Sac. **1984** Min: 5 G. **Total:** 27 G; 4 Sac.

CLARENCE VAUGHN Vaughn, Clarence 6′0″, 202 **DB**
Col: Northern Illinois *HS:* Gage Park [Chicago, IL] B: 7/17/1964, Chicago, IL *Drafted:* 1987 Round 8 Was
1987 Was: 5 G. **1988** Was: 14 G; 1 Sac. **1989** Was: 16 G. **1990** Was: 1 G. **1991** Was: 12 G. **Total:** 48 G; 1 Sac.

JON VAUGHN Vaughn, Jonathan Stewart 5′9″, 203 **RB**
Col: Michigan *HS:* McCluer North [Florissant, MO] B: 3/12/1970, Florissant, MO *Drafted:* 1991 Round 5 NE
1991 NE: Pass 2-1 50.0%, 13 6.50 1 TD; Rec 9-89 9.9. **1992** NE: Rec 13-84 6.5. **1994** Sea-KC: Rec 1-5 5.0 1 TD; Scor 1 2XP. Sea: Rec 1-5 5.0 1 TD; Scor 1 2XP. **Total:** Pass 2-1 50.0%, 13 6.50 1 TD; Rec 23-178 7.7 1 TD; Scor 1 2XP.

		Rushing				Kickoff Returns					Tot
Year Team	**G**	**Ret**	**Yds**	**Avg**	**TD**	**Ret**	**Yds**	**Avg**	**TD**	**Fum**	**TD**
1991 NE	16	31	146	4.7	2	34	717	21.1	**1**	1	3
1992 NE	16	113	451	4.0	1	20	564	**28.2**	1	6	2
1993 Sea	16	36	153	4.3	0	16	280	17.5	0	1	0
1994 Sea-KC	13	27	96	3.6	1	33	829	25.1	2	3	4
1994 Sea	9	27	96	3.6	1	18	443	24.6	1	3	3
1994 KC	3	0	0	—	0	15	386	25.7	1	0	1
NFL Total	60	207	846	4.1	4	103	2390	23.2	4	11	9

BOB VAUGHN Vaughn, Robert Curtis 6′4″, 240 **OG**
Col: Mississippi *HS:* East [Memphis, TN] B: 6/8/1945, Memphis, TN
Drafted: 1968 Round 3 Den
1968 Den: 1 G.

TOM VAUGHN Vaughn, Thomas Robert 5′11″, 190 **DB**
Col: Iowa State *HS:* Troy [OH] B: 2/28/1943, Troy, OH *Drafted:* 1965 Round 5 Det
1966 Det: Int 1-16. **1967** Det: Int 1-0. **1968** Det: Int 3-33. **1969** Det: Int 2-0. **1970** Det: Int 1-0. **1971** Det: Int 1-8. **Total:** Int 9-57.

		Punt Returns				Kickoff Returns				
Year Team	**G**	**Ret**	**Yds**	**Avg**	**TD**	**Ret**	**Yds**	**Avg**	**TD**	**Fum**
1965 Det	14	2	50	25.0	0	13	316	24.3	0	0
1966 Det	13	18	179	9.9	0	23	595	25.9	0	2
1967 Det	14	4	7	1.8	0	16	446	27.9	0	0
1968 Det	13	2	0	0.0	0	5	128	25.6	0	1
1969 Det	14	2	10	5.0	0	2	44	22.0	0	0
1970 Det	11	3	22	7.3	0	3	66	22.0	0	0
1971 Det	9	2	30	15.0	0	0	0	—	0	0
NFL Total	88	33	298	9.0	0	62	1595	25.7	0	3

BILL VAUGHN Vaughn, William Lee 5′10″, 192 **FB-WB-BB**
Col: Southern Methodist *HS:* I.M. Terrell [Dallas, TX] B: 1/10/1902, Van Zandt Co., TX D: 4/21/1971, Mesquite, TX
1926 Buf: 10 G.

TED VAUGHT Vaught, Teddy Gene 6′0″, 208 **DE-OE**
Col: Texas Christian *HS:* Lubbock [TX] B: 7/19/1932, Littlefield, TX
1955 SF: 2 G.

WALT VEACH Veach, William Walter 5′11″, 180 **HB**
Col: No College B: 9/29/1892 D: 2/1976, Vienna, IL
1920 Sta: 2 G.

ELTON VEALS Veals, Elton Alvin 5′11″, 230 **RB**
Col: Merritt Coll. CA (J.C.); Tulane *HS:* Istrouma [Baton Rouge, LA]
B: 3/26/1961, Baton Rouge, LA *Drafted:* 1984 Round 11 Pit
1984 Pit: KR 4-40 10.0.

		Rushing			
Year Team	**G**	**Att**	**Yds**	**Avg**	**TD**
1984 Pit	15	31	87	2.8	0

CRAIG VEASEY Veasey, Anthony Craig 6′2″, 285 **DT-NT-DE**
Col: Houston *HS:* Clear Lake [Houston, TX] B: 12/25/1965, Houston, TX *Drafted:* 1990 Round 3 Pit
1990 Pit: 10 G. **1991** Pit: 13 G; 2 Sac. **1992** Hou: 4 G. **1993** Hou-Mia: 15 G; 2 Sac. Hou: 1 G. Mia: 14 G; 2 Sac. **1994** Mia: 12 G; Int 1-7; 2.5 Sac. **1995** Hou: 15 G. **Total:** 69 G; Int 1-7; 6.5 Sac.

LOU VEDDER Vedder, Louis D 5′7″, 165 **FB**
Col: No College *HS:* Northwestern [Detroit, MI] B: 4/20/1897, Ypslanti, MI D: 3/1990, Avon Park, FL
1927 Buf: 2 G.

ALAN VEINGRAD Veingrad, Alan Stuart 6′5″, 277 **OT-OG**
Col: Texas A&M-Commerce *HS:* Miami Sunset [FL] B: 7/24/1963, Brooklyn, NY
1986 GB: 16 G. **1987** GB: 11 G. **1989** GB: 16 G. **1990** GB: 16 G. **1991** Dal: 16 G. **1992** Dal: 11 G. **Total:** 86 G.

TONY VELAND Veland, Tony Marceles 6′1″, 209 **DB**
Col: Nebraska *HS:* Benson [Omaha, NE] B: 3/11/1973, Omaha, NE
Drafted: 1996 Round 6 Den
1997 Den: 12 G. **1998** Car: 15 G; Int 1-24. **Total:** 27 G; Int 1-24.

JOHN VELLA Vella, John 6′4″, 258 **OT**
Col: USC *HS:* Notre Dame [Los Angeles, CA] B: 4/21/1950, Cleveland, OH *Drafted:* 1972 Round 2 Oak
1972 Oak: 14 G. **1973** Oak: 14 G. **1974** Oak: 13 G. **1975** Oak: 13 G. **1976** Oak: 14 G. **1977** Oak: 5 G. **1979** Oak: 11 G. **1980** Min: 8 G. **Total:** 92 G.

JIM VELLONE Vellone, James Carl 6′3″, 255 **OG**
Col: USC *HS:* California [Whittier, CA] B: 8/20/1944, Camp Lejeune, NC D: 8/21/1977, Huntington Beach, CA
1966 Min: 14 G. **1967** Min: 14 G. **1968** Min: 14 G. **1969** Min: 13 G. **1970** Min: 11 G. **Total:** 66 G.

FRED VENTURELLI Venturelli, Fred 5′11″, 235 **K**
Col: No College B: 8/22/1917, Farmington, IL D: 1/20/1990, Racine, WI
1948 ChiB: 1 G; Scor 7, 1-2 50.0% FG, 4-4 100.0% XK.

SAM VENUTO Venuto, Samuel Joseph 6′1″, 195 **HB**
Col: Guilford *HS:* Haverford [Havertown, PA] B: 11/2/1927, Havertown, PA
1952 Was: 3 G; Rush 4-16 4.0 1 TD; KR 2-28 14.0; 6 Pt.

ROSS VERBA Verba, Ross Robert 6′4″, 302 **OT**
Col: Iowa *HS:* Dowling [West Des Moines, IA] B: 10/31/1973, Des Moines, IA *Drafted:* 1997 Round 1 GB
1997 GB: 16 G. **1998** GB: 16 G. **Total:** 32 G.

CLARENCE VERDIN Verdin, Clarence 5′8″, 160 **WR**
Col: Southwestern Louisiana *HS:* South Terrebonne [Bourg, LA] B: 6/14/1963, New Orleans, LA *Drafted:* 1984 Supplemental Round 3 Was
1987 Was: Rush 1-14 14.0. **1988** Ind: Rush 8-77 9.6. **1989** Ind: Rush 4-39 9.8. **1991** Ind: Rush 1-4 4.0. **1993** Ind: Rush 3-33 11.0.
Total: Rush 17-167 9.8.

		Receiving				Punt Returns			
Year Team	G	Rec	Yds	Avg	TD	Ret	Yds	Avg	TD
1986 Was	8	0	0	—	0	0	0	—	0
1987 Was	3	2	62	31.0	0	0	0	—	0
1988 Ind	16	20	437	21.9	4	22	239	10.9	1
1989 Ind	16	20	381	19.1	1	23	296	12.9	**1**
1990 Ind	15	14	178	12.7	1	31	396	**12.8**	0
1991 Ind	16	21	214	10.2	0	25	165	6.6	0
1992 Ind	16	3	37	12.3	0	24	268	11.2	**2**
1993 Ind	16	2	20	10.0	1	30	173	5.8	0
1994 Atl	12	0	0	—	0	23	113	4.9	0
NFL Total	118	82	1329	16.2	7	178	1650	9.3	4

	Kickoff Returns					Tot
Year Team	Ret	Yds	Avg	TD	Fum	TD
1986 Was	12	240	20.0	0	0	0
1987 Was	12	244	20.3	0	0	0
1988 Ind	7	145	20.7	0	0	5
1989 Ind	19	371	19.5	0	1	2
1990 Ind	18	350	19.4	0	1	1
1991 Ind	36	689	19.1	**1**	2	1
1992 Ind	39	815	20.9	0	2	2
1993 Ind	**50**	**1050**	21.0	0	3	1
1994 Atl	44	1026	23.3	0	3	0
NFL Total	237	4930	20.8	1	12	12

ED VEREB Vereb, Edward John 6′0″, 190 **HB**
Col: Maryland *HS:* Central Catholic [Pittsburgh, PA] B: 5/21/1934, Pittsburgh, PA *Drafted:* 1956 Round 1 Was
1960 Was: 9 G; Pass 1-0; Rush 19-38 2.0; Rec 9-119 13.2; PR 1-0; KR 5-119 23.8; 3 Fum.

CARL VEREEN Vereen, Carl Harry 6′2″, 247 **OT**
Col: Georgia Tech *HS:* Miami Senior [FL] B: 1/27/1936, Miami, FL *Drafted:* 1957 Round 4 GB
1957 GB: 12 G.

GEORGE VERGARA Vergara, George Aloysius 6′1″, 190 **E**
(Zip) *Col:* Fordham; Notre Dame *HS:* Clason Point Mil. Acad. [Bronx, NY] B: 3/18/1901, New York, NY D: 8/13/1982, Montrose, NY
1925 GB: 12 G.

CHRIS VERHULST Verhulst, Christopher Sean 6′3″, 249 **TE**
Col: Cal State-Chico *HS:* California [San Ramon, CA] B: 5/16/1966, Sacramento, CA *Drafted:* 1988 Round 5 Hou
1988 Hou: 1 G. **1989** Hou: 16 G; Rec 4-48 12.0; KR 1-0. **1990** Den: 11 G; Rec 3-13 4.3. **Total:** 28 G; Rec 7-61 8.7; KR 1-0.

GARIN VERIS Veris, Garin Lee 6′4″, 255 **DE**
Col: Stanford *HS:* Chillicothe [OH] B: 2/27/1963, Chillicothe, OH *Drafted:* 1985 Round 2 NE
1985 NE: 16 G; 10 Sac. **1986** NE: 16 G; 11 Sac. **1987** NE: 12 G; 7 Sac. **1988** NE: 11 G; 2 Sac. **1990** NE: 7 G; 2 Sac. **1991** NE: 16 G; 4 Sac. **1992** SF: 10 G. **Total:** 88 G; 36 Sac.

NORM VERRY Verry, David Norman 6′1″, 240 **T**
Col: USC *HS:* Visalia [CA] B: 9/18/1922, Hanford, CA
AAFC **1946** ChiA: 10 G. **1947** ChiA: 1 G. **Total:** 11 G.

DAVID VERSER Verser, David 6′1″, 200 **WR**
Col: Kansas *HS:* Sumner [Kansas City, KS] B: 3/1/1958, Kansas City, KS *Drafted:* 1981 Round 1 Cin
1981 Cin: Rush 2-11 5.5; Rec 6-161 26.8 2 TD. **1982** Cin: Rush 1-1 1.0; Rec 4-98 24.5 1 TD. **1983** Cin: Rush 2-31 15.5; Rec 7-82 11.7. **1984** Cin: Rush 2-5 2.5; Rec 6-113 18.8. **1987** Cle: Rush 1-9 9.0. **Total:** Rush 8-57 7.1; Rec 23-454 19.7 3 TD.

		Kickoff Returns				
Year Team	G	Ret	Yds	Avg	TD	Fum
1981 Cin	16	29	691	23.8	0	2
1982 Cin	9	16	320	20.0	0	0
1983 Cin	13	13	253	19.5	0	0
1984 Cin	11	3	46	15.3	0	0
1985 TB	1	4	61	15.3	0	1
1987 Cle	2	0	0	—	0	0
NFL Total	52	65	1371	21.1	0	3

MIKE VERSTEGEN Verstegen, Michael Robert 6′6″, 311 **OG-OT**
Col: Wisconsin *HS:* Kimberly [WI] B: 10/24/1971, Appleton, WI *Drafted:* 1995 Round 3 NO
1996 NO: 8 G. **1997** NO: 14 G. **Total:** 22 G.

BRIAN VERTEFEUILLE Vertefeuille, Brian Lionel 6′3″, 252 **OT**
Col: Idaho State *HS:* Windham [Willimantic, CT] B: 4/4/1951, Willimantic, CT *Drafted:* 1974 Round 13 SD
1974 SD: 14 G.

BILLY VESSELS Vessels, Billy Dale 6′0″, 190 **HB**
Col: Oklahoma *HS:* Cleveland [OK] B: 3/22/1931, Cleveland, OK *Drafted:* 1953 Round 1 Bal
1956 Bal: Rec 11-177 16.1 1 TD; KR 16-379 23.7.

		Rushing				Tot
Year Team	G	Att	Yds	Avg	TD	TD
1956 Bal	12	44	215	4.9	2	3

JOHN VESSER Vesser, John Martin 6′0″, 186 **OE**
Col: Idaho *HS:* Coeur d'Alene [ID] B: 10/1/1900, Coeur d'Alene, ID D: 3/20/1996, Pocatello, ID
1927 ChiC: 11 G; Rec 1 TD; 6 Pt. **1930** ChiC: 9 G. **1931** ChiC: 1 G. **Total:** 21 G; Rec 1 TD; 6 Pt.

JOE VETRANO Vetrano, Joseph George 5′9″, 170 **HB-DB**
(Joe The Toe) *Col:* Southern Mississippi *HS:* Neptune [NJ] B: 10/15/1918, Neptune, NJ D: 5/10/1995, Berkeley, CA
AAFC **1946** SF-A: Rec 4-37 9.3; PR 7-84 12.0; KR 3-49 16.3; Int 3-32; Punt 6-236 39.3; Scor 49, 4-7 57.1% FG, 31-38 81.6% XK. **1947** SF-A: PR 12-137 11.4; KR 5-117 23.4; Scor 50, 4-12 33.3% FG, 38-43 88.4% XK. **1948** SF-A: Rec 1-34 34.0; KR 1-38 38.0; Punt 1-38 38.0; Scor 83, 5-8 62.5% FG, 62-66 93.9% XK. **1949** SF-A: PR 1-16 16.0; Scor 65, 3-7 42.9% FG, 56-56 100.0% XK. **Total:** Rec 5-71 14.2; PR 20-237 11.9; KR 9-204 22.7; Int 3-32; Punt 7-274 39.1; Scor 247, 16-34 47.1% FG, 187-203 92.1% XK.

		Rushing			
Year Team	G	Att	Yds	Avg	TD
1946 SF-A	13	23	69	3.0	1
1947 SF-A	14	10	11	1.1	0
1948 SF-A	14	12	71	5.9	1
1949 SF-A	12	11	50	4.5	0
AAFC Total	53	56	201	3.6	2

JACK VETTER Vetter, Jack Robbins 6′2″, 198 **HB-DB**
Col: McPherson *HS:* Paseo Acad. [Kansas City, MO] B: 10/30/1920, Kansas City, MO
1942 Bkn: 4 G; Rush 1-4 4.0.

ROY VEXALL Vexall, Roy 190 **FB**
Col: No College B: 6/6/1902 D: 5/1982, Blaine, MN
1924 Dul: 2 G. **1925** Dul: 1 G. **Total:** 3 G.

WALT VEZMAR Vezmar, Walter 5′11″, 235 **G**
Col: Michigan State *HS:* Northeastern [Detroit, MI] B: 1/1/1925, Detroit, MI D: 5/28/1981, Pollock, LA *Drafted:* 1947 Round 13 Det
1946 Det: 11 G. **1947** Det: 2 G. **Total:** 13 G.

DAVID VIAENE Viaene, David Ronald 6′5″, 300 **C-OT-OG**
Col: Wis.-Platteville; Minnesota-Duluth *HS:* Kaukauna [WI] B: 7/14/1965, Appleton, WI *Drafted:* 1988 Round 8 Hou
1989 NE: 16 G. **1990** NE: 4 G. **1992** GB: 1 G. **Total:** 21 G.

ERNIE VICK Vick, Henry Arthur 5′10″, 190 **C-G-T**
Col: Michigan *HS:* V. W. Scott [Toledo, OH] B: 7/2/1900, Toledo, OH D: 7/16/1980, Ann Arbor, MI
1925 Det: 10 G. **1927** ChiB: 10 G. **1928** ChiB-Det: 7 G. ChiB: 1 G. Det: 6 G. **Total:** 27 G.

DICK VICK Vick, Richard D 5′9″, 167 **TB-BB**
(Dutch) *Col:* Washington & Jefferson *HS:* Denfeld [Duluth, MN] B: 4/16/1892, Edwards Twp., Kandiyohi Co., MN D: 9/1980, Bozeman, MT
1924 Ken: 5 G; Pass 1 TD. **1925** Det: 11 G; Pass 7 TD. **1926** Det-Can: 13 G. Det: 6 G. Can: 7 G; Pass 1 TD. **Total:** 29 G; Pass 9 TD.

ROGER VICK Vick, Roger Hamilton 6′3″, 239 **RB**
Col: Texas A&M *HS:* Tomball [TX] B: 8/11/1964, Conroe, TX *Drafted:* 1987 Round 1 NYJ
1990 Phi: KR 2-22 11.0. **Total:** KR 2-22 11.0.

		Rushing				Receiving					Tot
Year Team	G	Att	Yds	Avg	TD	Rec	Yds	Avg	TD	Fum	TD
1987 NYJ	12	77	257	3.3	1	13	108	8.3	0	3	1
1988 NYJ	16	128	540	4.2	3	19	120	6.3	0	5	3
1989 NYJ	16	112	434	3.9	5	34	241	7.1	2	4	7
1990 Phi	14	16	58	3.6	1	0	0	—	0	0	1
NFL Total	58	333	1289	3.9	10	66	469	7.1	2	12	12

KIPP VICKERS Vickers, Kipp 6′2″, 300 **OG**
Col: Miami (Fla.) *HS:* Tarpon Springs [FL] B: 8/27/1969, Holiday, FL
1995 Ind: 9 G. **1996** Ind: 10 G. **1997** Ind: 9 G. **Total:** 28 G.

GENE VIDAL Vidal, Eugene Luther 5′10″, 170 **FB**
Col: Nebraska; South Dakota; Army *HS:* Madison [SD] B: 4/13/1895, Madison, SD D: 2/20/1969, Palos Verdes, CA
1921 Was: 1 G.

VIC VIDONI Vidoni, Victor Joseph 6′1″, 210 **OE-DE**
(Putt) *Col:* Duquesne *HS:* Fostoria [OH]; Bridgeville HS [PA] B: 12/8/1912, Fostoria, OH D: 10/17/1994, Black Horse, OH
1935 Pit: 11 G; Rec 11-111 10.1. **1936** Pit: 2 G; Rec 2-35 17.5. **Total:** 13 G; Rec 13-146 11.2.

TOMMY VIGORITO Vigorito, Thomas J 5′10″, 193 **RB-WR**
Col: Virginia *HS:* DePaul [Wayne, NJ] B: 10/23/1959, Passaic, NJ
Drafted: 1981 Round 5 Mia
1981 Mia: KR 4-84 21.0. **Total:** KR 4-84 21.0.

		Rushing				Receiving			
Year Team	**G**	**Att**	**Yds**	**Avg**	**TD**	**Rec**	**Yds**	**Avg**	**TD**
1981 Mia	16	35	116	3.3	1	33	237	7.2	2
1982 Mia	9	19	99	5.2	1	24	186	7.8	0
1983 Mia	1	0	0	—	0	1	7	7.0	0
1985 Mia	9	0	0	—	0	1	9	9.0	0
NFL Total	35	54	215	4.0	2	59	439	7.4	2

	Punt Returns					Tot
Year Team	**Ret**	**Yds**	**Avg**	**TD**	**Fum**	**TD**
1981 Mia	36	379	10.5	1	1	4
1982 Mia	20	192	9.6	1	2	2
1983 Mia	1	62	62.0	0	0	0
1985 Mia	22	197	9.0	0	3	0
NFL Total	79	830	10.5	2	6	6

DANNY VILLA Villa, Daniel 6′5″, 304 **OT-OG-C**
Col: Arizona State *HS:* Nogales [AZ] B: 9/21/1964, Nogales, AZ
Drafted: 1987 Round 5 NE
1987 NE: 11 G; 1 Fum. **1988** NE: 16 G; 1 Fum. **1989** NE: 15 G. **1990** NE: 16 G. **1991** NE: 10 G. **1992** Pho: 16 G. **1993** KC: 13 G. **1994** KC: 14 G. **1995** KC: 16 G. **1996** KC: 16 G. **1997** NE: 7 G. **1998** Car: 7 G. **Total:** 157 G; 2 Fum.

VINCE VILLANUCCI Villanucci, Vincent Anthony 6′2″, 265 **NT**
Col: Bowling Green State *HS:* Lorain [OH] B: 5/30/1964, Lorain, OH
1987 GB: 2 G.

DANNY VILLANUEVA Villanueva, Daniel Dario 5′11″, 200 **K**
Col: Kings River CC CA; New Mexico State *HS:* Calexico [CA]
B: 11/5/1937, Tucumcari, NM
1961 LARm: Pass 1-0. **1966** Dal: Rush 1-23 23.0. **1967** Dal: Rush 1-(-15) -15.0. **Total:** Pass 1-0; Rush 2-8 4.0.

		Punting		
Year Team	**G**	**Punts**	**Yds**	**Avg**
1960 LARm	12	0	0	—
1961 LARm	14	46	1845	40.1
1962 LARm	14	**87**	**3960**	45.5
1963 LARm	14	**81**	**3678**	45.4
1964 LARm	14	82	3616	44.1
1965 Dal	14	60	2505	41.8
1966 Dal	14	65	2551	39.2
1967 Dal	14	67	2707	40.4
NFL Total	110	488	20862	42.8

	Scoring						
Year Team	**Pts**	**FG**	**FGA**	**FG%**	**XK**	**XKA**	**XK%**
1960 LARm	64	12	19	63.2	28	28	100.0
1961 LARm	71	13	27	48.1	32	32	100.0
1962 LARm	56	10	20	50.0	26	27	96.3
1963 LARm	52	9	17	52.9	25	26	96.2
1965 Dal	85	16	27	59.3	37	38	97.4
1966 Dal	107	17	31	54.8	**56**	**56**	100.0
1967 Dal	56	8	19	42.1	32	34	94.1
NFL Total	491	85	160	53.1	236	241	97.9

PHIL VILLAPIANO Villapiano, Philip James 6′2″, 225 **LB**
Col: Bowling Green State *HS:* Ocean Twp. [Oakhurst, NJ]
B: 2/26/1949, Long Branch, NJ *Drafted:* 1971 Round 2 Oak
1978 Oak: Scor **1** Saf. **Total:** Scor 1 Saf.

		Interceptions		
Year Team	**G**	**Int**	**Yds**	**TD**
1971 Oak	14	2	25	0
1972 Oak	14	3	97	1
1973 Oak	14	1	6	0
1974 Oak	14	0	0	0
1975 Oak	14	2	32	0
1976 Oak	14	1	0	0
1977 Oak	2	0	0	0
1978 Oak	16	2	0	0
1979 Oak	16	0	0	0
1980 Buf	16	0	0	0
1981 Buf	16	0	0	0
1982 Buf	9	0	0	0
1983 Buf	4	0	0	0
NFL Total	163	11	160	1

CHRIS VILLARRIAL Villarrial, Chris 6′4″, 310 **C**
Col: Indiana (Pa.) *HS:* Milton S. Hershey [Hershey, PA] B: 6/9/1973, Hummelstown, PA *Drafted:* 1996 Round 5 ChiB
1996 ChiB: 14 G. **1997** ChiB: 11 G. **1998** ChiB: 16 G. **Total:** 41 G.

THEO VILTZ Viltz, Theophile Anthony Jr. 6′2″, 190 **DB**
Col: USC *HS:* Serra [Los Angeles, CA] B: 4/20/1943, Lafayette, LA
Drafted: 1964 Round 18 Dal
1966 Hou: 14 G.

ADAM VINATIERI Vinatieri, Adam Mathew 6′0″, 200 **K**
Col: South Dakota State *HS:* Central [Rapid City, SD] B: 12/28/1972, Yankton, SD
1996 NE: Punt 1-27 27.0. **1998** NE: Scor 1 2XP. **Total:** Punt 1-27 27.0; Scor 1 2XP.

		Scoring						
Year Team	**G**	**Pts**	**FG**	**FGA**	**FG%**	**XK**	**XKA**	**XK%**
1996 NE	16	120	27	35	77.1	39	42	92.9
1997 NE	16	115	25	29	86.2	40	40	100.0
1998 NE	16	127	31	39	79.5	32	32	100.0
NFL Total	48	362	83	103	80.6	111	114	97.4

RALPH VINCE Vince, Ralph D 5′8″, 175 **G**
Col: Washington & Jefferson *HS:* Martins Ferry [OH] B: 3/18/1900, Vinci, Italy D: 10/29/1996, Shaker Heights, OH
1923 Cle: 7 G. **1925** Cle: 6 G. **Total:** 13 G.

SHAWN VINCENT Vincent, Shawn David 5′10″, 180 **DB**
Col: Akron *HS:* St. Clairsville [OH] B: 6/2/1968, Bellaire, OH
1991 Pit: 10 G; PR 1-1 1.0; Int 2-52.

TED VINCENT Vincent, Theodore Michael 6′4″, 262 **DT**
Col: Wichita State *HS:* Fort Zumwalt [St. Peters, MO] B: 8/10/1956, O'Fallon, MO *Drafted:* 1978 Round 3 Cin
1978 Cin: 16 G; KR 1-2 2.0. **1979** SF: 16 G. **1980** SF: 12 G. **Total:** 44 G; KR 1-2 2.0.

TROY VINCENT Vincent, Troy Darnell 6′0″, 195 **DB**
Col: Wisconsin *HS:* Pennsbury [Fairless Hills, PA] B: 6/8/1970, Trenton, NJ *Drafted:* 1992 Round 1 Mia
1992 Mia: PR 5-16 3.2. **1993** Mia: PR 0-9; KR 0-2. **1997** Phi: PR 1-(-8) -8.0. **1998** Phi: 1 Sac. **Total:** PR 6-15 2.5; KR 0-2; 1 Sac.

		Interceptions			
Year Team	**G**	**Int**	**Yds**	**TD**	**Fum**
1992 Mia	15	2	47	0	2
1993 Mia	13	2	29	0	0
1994 Mia	13	5	113	1	0
1995 Mia	16	5	95	1	0
1996 Phi	16	3	144	1	0
1997 Phi	16	3	14	0	1
1998 Phi	13	2	29	0	0
NFL Total	102	22	471	3	3

PAUL VINNOLA Vinnola, Paul Peter 5′10″, 180 **HB-DB**
Col: Santa Clara *HS:* St. Joseph's [Denver, CO] B: 8/24/1922, Denver, CO D: 10/23/1994, Denver, CO
AAFC **1946** LA-A: 13 G; Rush 23-36 1.6; Rec 4-39 9.8; PR 2-24 12.0; KR 5-83 16.6; Int 1-4.

TONY VINSON Vinson, Anthony Cho 6′1″, 229 **RB**
Col: Purdue; Towson State *HS:* Denbigh [Newport News, VA]
B: 3/13/1971, Frankfurt, Germany *Drafted:* 1994 Round 5 SD
1997 Bal: 13 G.

FERNANDUS VINSON Vinson, Fernandus Lamar 5′10″, 197 **DB**
Col: North Carolina State *HS:* George Washington Carver [Montgomery, AL] B: 11/3/1968, Montgomery, AL *Drafted:* 1991 Round 7 Cin
1991 Cin: 13 G. **1992** Cin: 13 G; 1 Fum TD; 6 Pt; 1 Sac. **1993** Cin: 16 G. **1994** Cin: 16 G. **Total:** 58 G; 1 Fum TD; 6 Pt; 1 Sac.

KEN VINYARD Vinyard, Kenneth Raymond 5′10″, 190 **K**
Col: Texas Tech *HS:* Amarillo [TX] B: 6/18/1947, Amarillo, TX
Drafted: 1969 Round 6 GB
1970 Atl: 14 G; Scor 50, 9-25 36.0% FG, 23-26 88.5% XK.

SCOTT VIRKUS Virkus, Scott 6′5″, 260 **DE**
Col: San Francisco City Coll. CA (J.C.); Purdue *HS:* Olympia [Rochester, NY] B: 9/7/1959, Rochester, NY
1983 Buf: 15 G. **1984** Buf-NE-Ind: 8 G. Buf: 2 G. NE: 5 G. Ind: 1 G. **1985** Ind: 15 G; 4 Sac. **Total:** 38 G; 4 Sac.

GEORGE VISGER Visger, George Anthony 6′4″, 250 **DT**
Col: Colorado *HS:* Amos Alonzo Stagg [Stockton, CA] B: 9/26/1958, Stockton, CA *Drafted:* 1980 Round 6 NYJ
1980 SF: 3 G.

LARRY VISNIC Visnic, Lawrence 5′11″, 190 **LB-G-BB**
Col: Benedictine *HS:* St. John's [Shadyside, OH]; Belmont HS [NC]
B: 4/7/1919, Jacobsburg, OH *Drafted:* 1943 Round 6 NYG
1943 NYG: 7 G. **1944** NYG: 7 G; Int 2-56. **1945** NYG: 8 G; KR 1-0; Int 1-3. **Total:** 22 G; KR 1-0; Int 3-59.

LIONEL VITAL Vital, Lionel 5′9″, 195 **RB**
Col: Nicholls State *HS:* Loreauville [LA] B: 7/15/1963, New Iberia, LA
Drafted: 1985 Round 7 Was
1987 Was: Rec 1-13 13.0; KR 2-31 15.5.

Year Team	G	Rushing Att	Yds	Avg	TD	Fum
1987 Was	3	80	346	4.3	2	3

SANDRO VITIELLO Vitiello, Sandro 6′2″, 197 **K**
Col: Nassau CC NY; Massachusetts *HS:* East Meadow [NY]
B: 2/21/1958, Broccastella, Italy *Drafted:* 1980 Round 10 Cin
1980 Cin: 2 G; Scor 1, 0-2 FG, 1-1 100.0% XK.

MARK VLASIC Vlasic, Mark Richard 6′3″, 205 **QB**
Col: Iowa *HS:* Center [Monaca, PA] B: 10/25/1963, Rochester, PA
Drafted: 1987 Round 4 SD
1988 SD: Rush 2-0. **1990** SD: Rush 1-0. **1991** KC: Rush 1-(-1) -1.0. **Total:** Rush 4-(-1) -0.3.

Year Team	G	Passing Att	Comp	Comp%	Yds	YPA	TD	Int	Rating	Fum
1987 SD	1	6	3	50.0	8	1.33	0	1	16.7	1
1988 SD	2	52	25	48.1	270	5.19	1	2	54.2	1
1990 SD	6	40	19	47.5	168	4.20	1	2	46.7	1
1991 KC	6	44	28	63.6	316	7.18	2	0	100.2	1
NFL Total	15	142	75	52.8	762	5.37	4	5	63.2	4

JOE VODICKA Vodicka, Joseph J 5′10″, 189 **HB-DB**
Col: Illinois Tech *HS:* Albert G. Lane Tech [Chicago, IL] B: 3/4/1921, Chicago, IL D: 2/1985, Chicago, IL
1943 ChiB: 3 G. **1945** ChiB-ChiC: 8 G; Rush 3-(-1) -0.3; Rec 1-3 3.0; PR 4-9 2.3; KR 1-20 20.0. ChiB: 4 G. ChiC: 4 G; Rush 3-(-1) -0.3; Rec 1-3 3.0; PR 4-9 2.3; KR 1-20 20.0. **Total:** 11 G; Rush 3-(-1) -0.3; Rec 1-3 3.0; PR 4-9 2.3; KR 1-20 20.0.

EVAN VOGDS Vogds, Evan Edward 5′10″, 210 **G**
Col: Wisconsin *HS:* Fond Du Lac [WI] B: 2/10/1923, Johnsburg, WI
D: 8/6/1994, Fond Du Lac, WI
AAFC **1946** ChiA: 14 G. **1947** ChiA: 13 G. **Total:** 27 G.

NFL **1948** GB: 12 G. **1949** GB: 12 G; KR 1-0. **Total:** 24 G; KR 1-0.

PAUL VOGEL Vogel, Paul Richard 6′1″, 220 **LB**
Col: South Carolina *HS:* Eastside [Taylors, SC] B: 2/2/1961, New York, NY
1987 Hou: 1 G.

BOB VOGEL Vogel, Robert Louis 6′5″, 250 **OT**
Col: Ohio State *HS:* Washington [Massillon, OH]; Toronto HS [OH]; Brilliant HS [OH] B: 9/23/1941, Columbus, OH *Drafted:* 1963 Round 1 Bal
1963 Bal: 14 G. **1964** Bal: 14 G. **1965** Bal: 13 G. **1966** Bal: 14 G. **1967** Bal: 14 G. **1968** Bal: 14 G. **1969** Bal: 14 G. **1970** Bal: 14 G. **1971** Bal: 14 G. **1972** Bal: 14 G. **Total:** 139 G.

CARROLL VOGELAAR Vogelaar, Carroll Robert 6′3″, 253 **DT-OT**
Col: Loyola Marymount; San Francisco *HS:* Hemet [CA] B: 4/8/1920, Idyllwild, CA D: 12/7/1967, Palm Springs, CA
1947 Bos: 12 G. **1948** Bos: 12 G. **1949** NYB: 12 G. **1950** NYY: 10 G. **Total:** 46 G.

TIM VOGLER Vogler, Timothy Gene 6′3″, 259 **C-OG**
Col: Ohio State *HS:* Covington [OH] B: 10/2/1956, Troy, OH
1979 Buf: 10 G. **1980** Buf: 10 G; KR 1-0. **1981** Buf: 14 G. **1982** Buf: 6 G. **1983** Buf: 16 G. **1984** Buf: 16 G. **1985** Buf: 14 G. **1986** Buf: 9 G. **1987** Buf: 12 G. **1988** Buf: 10 G. **Total:** 117 G; KR 1-0.

MIKE VOIGHT Voight, Michael Ray 6′0″, 214 **RB**
Col: North Carolina *HS:* Indian River [Chesapeake, VA] B: 2/28/1954, Norfolk, VA *Drafted:* 1977 Round 3 Cin
1977 Hou: 14 G; Rush 7-20 2.9; KR 8-156 19.5.

BOB VOIGHT Voight, Robert 6′5″, 265 **DT**
Col: Mount San Antonio Coll. CA (J.C.); Los Angeles State *HS:* El Rancho [Pico Rivera, CA] B: 1938 *Drafted:* 1961 Round 18 Min
1961 Oak: 14 G.

WALTER VOIGHT Voight, Walter 5′8″, 200 **G-C-BB**
Col: No College *HS:* Oak Park [IL] B: 1895 Deceased
1920 ChiT: 7 G. **1921** Ham-ChiC: 4 G. Ham: 3 G. ChiC: 1 G. **Total:** 11 G.

STU VOIGT Voigt, Stuart Alan 6′1″, 223 **TE**
Col: Wisconsin *HS:* West [Madison, WI] B: 8/12/1948, Madison, WI
Drafted: 1970 Round 10 Min
1971 Min: KR 1-0. **1972** Min: Rush 1-1 1.0 1 TD; KR 1-2 2.0. **1973** Min: Rush 1-2 2.0. **1979** Min: KR 1-0. **Total:** Rush 2-3 1.5 1 TD; KR 3-2 0.7.

Year Team	G	Receiving Rec	Yds	Avg	TD	Fum	Tot TD
1970 Min	3	0	0	—	0	0	0
1971 Min	12	15	214	14.3	1	1	1
1972 Min	14	6	50	8.3	1	0	2
1973 Min	13	23	318	13.8	2	1	2
1974 Min	14	32	268	8.4	5	1	5
1975 Min	13	34	363	10.7	4	0	4
1976 Min	14	28	303	10.8	1	0	1
1977 Min	14	20	212	10.6	1	0	1
1978 Min	15	4	52	13.0	0	0	0
1979 Min	16	15	139	9.3	2	1	2
1980 Min	3	0	0	—	0	0	0
NFL Total	131	177	1919	10.8	17	4	18

OTTO VOKATY Vokaty, Otto 6′1″, 191 **FB-LB-BB-TB**
(Lefty; The Stud) *Col:* Heidelberg B: 1/17/1909
1932 NYG: Rec 1-20 20.0. **1934** Cin: Rec 1-22 22.0. **Total:** Rec 2-42 21.0.

Year Team	G	Rushing Att	Yds	Avg	TD
1931 Cle	8	—	—	—	4
1932 NYG	6	22	61	2.8	0
1933 ChiC	1	0	0	—	0
1934 Cin	3	8	39	4.9	0
NFL Total	18	30	100	3.3	4

ELMER VOLGENAU Volgenau, Elmer Porter 6′2″, 190 **G**
Col: Colgate *HS:* Masten Park [Buffalo, NY] B: 8/2/1900, New Haven, CT D: 12/6/1965, Clarence Compact, NY
1924 Roch: 1 G.

RICK VOLK Volk, Richard Robert 6′3″, 195 **DB**
Col: Michigan *HS:* Wauseon [OH] B: 3/15/1945, Toledo, OH
Drafted: 1967 Round 2 Bal
1973 Bal: KR 2-16 8.0. **Total:** KR 2-16 8.0.

Year Team	G	Punt Returns Ret	Yds	Avg	TD	Interceptions Int	Yds	TD	Fum
1967 Bal	14	11	88	8.0	0	6	145	1	0
1968 Bal	14	25	198	7.9	0	6	154	0	0
1969 Bal	14	10	58	5.8	0	4	36	0	0
1970 Bal	12	3	15	5.0	0	4	61	0	0
1971 Bal	14	22	118	5.4	0	4	36	0	1
1972 Bal	14	5	25	5.0	0	4	86	0	0
1973 Bal	14	7	45	6.4	0	1	0	0	0
1974 Bal	14	1	1	1.0	0	2	0	0	1
1975 Bal	13	0	0	—	0	0	0	0	0
1976 NYG	8	0	0	—	0	2	14	0	0
1977 Mia	3	0	0	—	0	1	0	0	0
1978 Mia	16	0	0	—	0	4	42	0	0
NFL Total	150	84	548	6.5	0	38	574	1	2

JIM VOLLENWEIDER Vollenweider, James Stephen 6′1″, 205 **HB**
Col: Miami (Fla.) *HS:* D.C. Everest [Schofield, WI] B: 9/2/1939, WI
D: 6/1/1998, Ewa Beach, HI *Drafted:* 1962 Round 8 SF
1962 SF: Rec 4-21 5.3; KR 6-113 18.8. **1963** SF: Pass 1-0, 1 Int; Rec 1-26 26.0; KR 4-75 18.8. **Total:** Pass 1-0, 1 Int; Rec 5-47 9.4; KR 10-188 18.8.

Year Team	G	Rushing Att	Yds	Avg	TD	Fum
1962 SF	14	11	37	3.4	0	0
1963 SF	13	47	124	2.6	2	1
NFL Total	27	58	161	2.8	2	1

BILL VOLOK Volok, William James 6′2″, 215 **G-T**
Col: Tulsa *HS:* Lucas [KS] B: 3/23/1910, Lucas, KS D: 8/6/1991, Drumright, OK
1934 ChiC: 9 G. **1935** ChiC: 12 G; **1** Fum TD; 6 Pt. **1936** ChiC: 12 G. **1937** ChiC: 11 G; Rec 1-9 9.0. **1938** ChiC: 11 G. **1939** ChiC: 1 G. **Total:** 56 G; Rec 1-9 9.0; 1 Fum TD; 6 Pt.

PETE VOLZ Volz, Peter 190 **E-G**
(The Caveman) *Col:* Northwestern B: 1/13/1897 D: 11/1957
1920 ChiT: 1 G. **1921** Cin: 4 G. **Total:** 5 G.

WILBUR VOLZ Volz, Wilbur Edward 6′0″, 192 **HB-DB**
Col: Missouri *HS:* Edwardsville [IL] B: 1/1/1924, Edwardsville, IL
AAFC **1949** BufA: 8 G; Rush 4-7 1.8 1 TD; Rec 1-6 6.0; KR 3-43 14.3; 6 Pt.

SCOTT VON DER AHE Von der Ahe, Scott Fraser 5′11″, 242 **LB**
Col: Saddleback Coll. CA (J.C.); Iowa; Arizona State *HS:* Mission Viejo [CA] B: 10/12/1975, Lancaster, CA *Drafted:* 1997 Round 6 Ind
1997 Ind: 9 G.

KIMO VON OELHOFFEN von Oelhoffen, Kimo Kukuiokalani 6′4″, 305 **DT**
Col: Walla Walla CC WA; Hawaii; Boise State *HS:* Molokai [Hoolehua, HI] B: 1/30/1971, Kaunakaki, HI *Drafted:* 1994 Round 6 Cin
1994 Cin: 7 G. **1995** Cin: 16 G; KR 1-10 10.0. **1996** Cin: 11 G; 1 Sac. **1997** Cin: 13 G. **1998** Cin: 16 G. **Total:** 63 G; KR 1-10 10.0; 1 Sac.

UWE VON SCHAMANN von Schamann, Uwe Detlef Walter 6′0″, 190 **K**
Col: Oklahoma *HS:* Eastern Hills [Fort Worth, TX] B: 4/23/1956, Berlin, Germany *Drafted:* 1979 Round 7 Mia
1979 Mia: Punt 1-31 31.0. **Total:** Punt 1-31 31.0.

		Scoring						
Year Team	**G**	**Pts**	**FG**	**FGA**	**FG%**	**XK**	**XKA**	**XK%**
1979 Mia	16	99	21	29	72.4	36	40	90.0
1980 Mia	16	74	14	23	60.9	32	32	100.0
1981 Mia	16	109	24	31	77.4	37	38	97.4
1982 Mia	9	66	15	20	75.0	21	22	95.5
1983 Mia	16	99	18	27	66.7	45	48	93.8
1984 Mia	16	93	9	19	47.4	**66**	**70**	94.3
NFL Total	89	540	101	149	67.8	237	250	94.8

ANDY VON SONN Von Sonn, Andrew Vsevolod 6′2″, 229 **LB**
Col: UCLA *HS:* Reseda [Los Angeles, CA] B: 11/5/1940, Los Angeles, CA *Drafted:* 1962 Round 14 ChiB
1964 LARm: 14 G.

DON VOSBERG Vosberg, Donald Theodore 6′3″, 196 **OE-DE**
(Huck) *Col:* Marquette *HS:* Dubuque [IA] B: 10/3/1919, Dubuque, IA D: 6/21/1997, Tucson, AZ *Drafted:* 1941 Round 5 NYG
1941 NYG: 7 G.

VOSS Voss **G-T**
Col: No College Deceased
1920 Buf: 4 G.

LLOYD VOSS Voss, Lloyd John 6′4″, 256 **DE-DT**
Col: Nebraska *HS:* Magnolia [NM] B: 2/13/1942, Adrian, NM
Drafted: 1964 Round 1 GB
1964 GB: 14 G. **1965** GB: 14 G. **1966** Pit: 14 G. **1967** Pit: 13 G; Int 1-4. **1968** Pit: 14 G. **1969** Pit: 14 G. **1970** Pit: 14 G. **1971** Pit: 13 G. **1972** Den: 13 G. **Total:** 123 G; Int 1-4.

TILLIE VOSS Voss, Walter Clarence 6′3″, 207 **OE-T**
Col: Detroit Mercy *HS:* Georgetown Prep [Washington, DC]; U. of Detroit [MI] B: 3/28/1897, Detroit, MI D: 12/14/1975, Stuart, FL
1921 Det-Buf: 11 G; Scor 8, 2 XK; 1 Fum TD. Det: 7 G; Scor 8, 2 XK; 1 Fum TD. Buf: 4 G. **1922** RI-Akr: 10 G; Rec 1 TD; Scor 18, 6 XK; 1 Fum TD; Tot TD 2. RI: 7 G; Rec 1 TD; Scor 18, 6 XK; 1 Fum TD; Tot TD 2. Akr: 3 G. **1923** Tol: 8 G; Rush 1 TD; Scor 7, 1 XK. **1924** GB: 11 G; Rec **5** TD; 30 Pt. **1925** Det: 10 G. **1926** NYG: 12 G. **1927** ChiB: 11 G. **1928** ChiB: 13 G; Rec 1 TD; 6 Pt. **1929** Day-Buf: 9 G. Day: 1 G. Buf: 8 G. **Total:** 95 G; Rush 1 TD; Rec 7 TD; 2 Fum TD; Tot TD 10.

ED VOYTEK Voytek, Edward Louis 6′2″, 235 **OG**
Col: Purdue *HS:* Cathedral Latin [Cleveland, OH] B: 4/4/1935, Cleveland, OH *Drafted:* 1957 Round 22 Was
1957 Was: 12 G. **1958** Was: 12 G. **Total:** 24 G.

MIKE VRABEL Vrabel, Michael George 6′4″, 245 **DE**
Col: Ohio State *HS:* Walsh Jesuit [Akron, OH] B: 8/14/1975, Akron, OH
Drafted: 1997 Round 3 Pit
1997 Pit: 15 G; KR 1-0; 1.5 Sac. **1998** Pit: 11 G; 2.5 Sac. **Total:** 26 G; KR 1-0; 4 Sac.

MILT VUCINICH Vucinich, Milton Christopher 6′0″, 215 **C-LB**
Col: Stanford *HS:* Lowell [San Francisco, CA] B: 11/1/1920, San Francisco, CA *Drafted:* 1943 Round 5 ChiB
1945 ChiB: 3 G.

TOM WADDLE Waddle, Gregory Thomas 6′0″, 185 **WR**
Col: Boston College *HS:* Moeller [Cincinnati, OH] B: 2/20/1967, Cincinnati, OH
1989 ChiB: PR 1-2 2.0. **1991** ChiB: PR 5-31 6.2. **1992** ChiB: PR 8-28 3.5. **1994** ChiB: PR 3-8 2.7. **Total:** PR 17-69 4.1.

		Receiving				
Year Team	**G**	**Rec**	**Yds**	**Avg**	**TD**	**Fum**
1989 ChiB	3	1	8	8.0	0	0
1990 ChiB	5	2	32	16.0	0	0
1991 ChiB	16	55	599	10.9	3	2
1992 ChiB	12	46	674	14.7	4	1
1993 ChiB	15	44	552	12.5	1	0
1994 ChiB	9	25	244	9.8	1	1
NFL Total	60	173	2109	12.2	9	4

JUDE WADDY Waddy, Jude Michael 6′2″, 220 **LB**
Col: William & Mary *HS:* Suitland [MD] B: 9/12/1975, Washington, DC
1998 GB: 13 G; 1 Sac.

RAY WADDY Waddy, Raymond Jr. 5′11″, 175 **DB**
Col: Wharton Co. JC TX; Texas A&M–Kingsville *HS:* Brazoswood [Freeport, TX] B: 8/21/1956, Freeport, TX
1979 Was: 16 G; Int 1-6. **1980** Was: 7 G. **Total:** 23 G; Int 1-6.

BILLY WADDY Waddy, William Dean 5′11″, 187 **WR**
Col: Colorado *HS:* Boling [TX] B: 2/19/1954, Wharton, TX
Drafted: 1977 Round 2 LARm
1977 LARm: Rush 2-34 17.0. **1978** LARm: Rush 5-31 6.2. **1980** LARm: Rush 1-(-1) -1.0. **1982** LARm: Rush 2-(-11) -5.5. **1984** Min: Rush 3-24 8.0; KR 3-64 21.3. **Total:** Rush 13-77 5.9; KR 3-64 21.3.

		Receiving				Punt Returns				
Year Team	**G**	**Rec**	**Yds**	**Avg**	**TD**	**Ret**	**Yds**	**Avg**	**TD**	**Fum**
1977 LARm	14	23	355	15.4	1	31	219	7.1	0	8
1978 LARm	11	14	258	18.4	1	10	45	4.5	0	3
1979 LARm	13	14	220	15.7	3	0	0	—	0	0
1980 LARm	15	38	670	17.6	5	2	10	5.0	0	1
1981 LARm	15	31	460	14.8	0	0	0	—	0	2
1982 LARm	3	0	0	—	0	0	0	—	0	1
1984 Min	4	0	0	—	0	1	-3	-3.0	0	1
NFL Total	75	120	1963	16.4	10	44	271	6.2	0	16

CHARLIE WADE Wade, Charles Garnell 5′10″, 164 **WR**
Col: Tennessee State *HS:* Meigs [Nashville, TN] B: 2/23/1950, Nashville, TN *Drafted:* 1973 Round 17 Mia
1974 ChiB: Rush 1-(-15) -15.0. **Total:** Rush 1-(-15) -15.0.

		Receiving				
Year Team	**G**	**Rec**	**Yds**	**Avg**	**TD**	**Fum**
1974 ChiB	14	39	683	17.5	1	1
1975 GB	2	0	0	—	0	0
1977 KC	5	0	0	—	0	0
NFL Total	21	39	683	17.5	1	1

JIM WADE Wade, James 5′11″, 175 **HB-DB**
Col: Oklahoma City *HS:* Talihina [OK] B: 2/14/1926, Talihina, OK
Drafted: 1948 Round 25 LARm
1949 NYB: 10 G; Rush 9-23 2.6; Rec 4-58 14.5; PR 7-32 4.6; KR 3-58 19.3; Int 1-12; 1 Fum.

JOHN WADE Wade, Robert John 6′5″, 300 **C**
Col: Marshall *HS:* Harrisonburg [VA] B: 1/25/1975, Port Republic, VA
Drafted: 1998 Round 5 Jac
1998 Jac: 5 G.

BOB WADE Wade, Robert Pernell 6′2″, 200 **DB**
Col: Morgan State *HS:* Paul Laurence Dunbar [Baltimore, MD]
B: 12/9/1944, Baltimore, MD *Drafted:* 1967 Round 15 Bal
1968 Pit: 14 G. **1969** Was: 13 G; Int 0-14. **1970** Den: 3 G; Int 1-10. **Total:** 30 G; Int 1-24.

TOMMY WADE Wade, Thomas Virgil 6′2″, 195 **QB**
Col: Texas *HS:* Henderson [TX] B: 3/23/1942, Henderson, TX
1965 Pit: Rush 8-43 5.4. **Total:** Rush 8-43 5.4.

		Passing								
Year Team	**G**	**Att**	**Comp**	**Comp%**	**Yds**	**YPA**	**TD**	**Int**	**Rating**	**Fum**
1964 Pit	1	3	1	33.3	7	2.33	0	0	42.4	0
1965 Pit	4	66	33	50.0	463	7.02	2	13	43.5	6
NFL Total	5	69	34	49.3	470	6.81	2	13	41.6	6

BILLY WADE Wade, William James Jr. 6′2″, 202 **QB**
Col: Vanderbilt *HS:* Montgomery Bell Acad. [Nashville, TN]
B: 10/4/1930, Nashville, TN *Drafted:* 1952 Round 1 LARm
1960 LARm: Rec 0-10. **Total:** Rec 0-10.

		Passing							
Year Team	**G**	**Att**	**Comp**	**Comp%**	**Yds**	**YPA**	**TD**	**Int**	**Rating**
1954 LARm	10	59	31	52.5	509	8.63	2	1	86.1
1955 LARm	7	71	31	43.7	316	4.45	1	3	44.1
1956 LARm	12	178	91	51.1	1461	8.21	10	13	67.2
1957 LARm	5	24	10	41.7	116	4.83	1	1	53.5
1958 LARm	12	341	181	53.1	**2875**	8.43	18	22	72.2
1959 LARm	12	261	153	58.6	2001	7.67	12	17	71.1
1960 LARm	11	182	106	58.2	1294	7.11	12	11	77.0
1961 ChiB	13	250	139	55.6	2258	9.03	22	13	93.7
1962 ChiB	14	**412**	**225**	54.6	3172	7.70	18	24	70.0
1963 ChiB	14	356	192	53.9	2301	6.46	15	12	74.0
1964 ChiB	11	327	182	55.7	1944	5.94	13	14	68.6
1965 ChiB	5	41	20	48.8	204	4.98	0	2	43.1
1966 ChiB	2	21	9	42.9	79	3.76	0	1	33.6
NFL Total	128	2523	1370	54.3	18530	7.34	124	134	72.2

	Rushing				
Year Team	**Att**	**Yds**	**Avg**	**TD**	**Fum**
1954 LARm	28	190	6.8	1	5
1955 LARm	11	43	3.9	0	4
1956 LARm	26	93	3.6	3	4
1957 LARm	1	5	5.0	0	0

1958 LARm	42	90	2.1	2	**14**
1959 LARm	25	95	3.8	2	6
1960 LARm	26	171	6.6	2	5
1961 ChiB	45	255	5.7	2	3
1962 ChiB	40	146	3.7	5	7
1963 ChiB	45	132	2.9	6	5
1964 ChiB	24	96	4.0	1	2
1965 ChiB	5	18	3.6	0	2
NFL Total	318	1334	4.2	24	57

ANDRE WADSWORTH Wadsworth, Andre 6'4", 278 **DE**
Col: Florida State *HS:* Florida Christian [Miami, FL] B: 10/19/1974, St. Croix, Virgin Islands *Drafted:* 1998 Round 1 Ariz
1998 Ariz: 16 G; 5 Sac.

HENRY WAECHTER Waechter, Henry Carl 6'5", 270 **DE-DT**
Col: Waldorf Coll. IA (J.C.); Nebraska *HS:* Western Dubuque [Epworth, IA] B: 2/13/1959, Epworth, IA *Drafted:* 1982 Round 7 ChiB
1982 ChiB: 9 G. **1983** Bal: 11 G; 1.5 Sac. **1984** Ind-ChiB: 3 G; 2 Sac. Ind: 1 G. ChiB: 2 G; 2 Sac. **1985** ChiB: 13 G; Scor 1 Saf; 2 Pt; 2.5 Sac. **1986** ChiB: 16 G. **1987** Was: 1 G; 1 Sac. **Total:** 53 G; Scor 1 Saf; 2 Pt; 7 Sac.

CARL WAFER Wafer, Carl 6'4", 250 **DE**
Col: Tennessee State B: 1/17/1951, Magnolia, AR *Drafted:* 1974 Round 2 Den
1974 GB-NYG: 3 G. GB: 2 G. NYG: 1 G. **Total:** 3 G.

CLINT WAGER Wager, Clinton B 6'6", 218 **OE-DE**
Col: St. Mary's (Minn.) *HS:* Winona [MN] B: 1/20/1920, Winona, MN D: 2/29/1996, Excelsior, MN
1942 ChiB: 7 G. **1943** ChiC: 5 G; Rec 1-11 11.0. **1944** ChPt: 8 G; Rec 5-73 14.6. **1945** ChiC: 3 G; Rec 1-32 32.0. **Total:** 23 G; Rec 7-116 16.6.

JOHN WAGER Wager, John Byron 5'11", 203 **C-LB-G-T**
(Popeye; Red) *Col:* Carthage *HS:* Mount Carmel [IL] B: 4/28/1905, Massillon, OH D: 1982
1931 Port: 11 G. **1932** Port: 9 G. **1933** Port: 10 G. **Total:** 30 G.

HARMON WAGES Wages, Harmon Leon 6'1", 215 **RB**
(Charmin) *Col:* Florida *HS:* Robert E. Lee [Jacksonville, FL] B: 5/18/1946, Jacksonville, FL
1968 Atl: Pass 2-1 50.0%, 21 10.50; KR 1-23 23.0. **1969** Atl: Pass 1-1 100.0%, 16 16.00 1 TD; KR 6-76 12.7. **1970** Atl: Pass 1-1 100.0%, 13 13.00; KR 1-22 22.0. **1971** Atl: KR 1-21 21.0. **1973** Atl: KR 1-0. **Total:** Pass 4-3 75.0%, 50 12.50 1 TD; KR 10-142 14.2.

		Rushing				Receiving					Tot
Year Team	**G**	**Att**	**Yds**	**Avg**	**TD**	**Rec**	**Yds**	**Avg**	**TD**	**Fum**	**TD**
1968 Atl	13	59	211	3.6	0	16	121	7.6	1	2	1
1969 Atl	14	72	375	5.2	2	22	228	10.4	1	3	3
1970 Atl	13	119	422	3.5	1	26	153	5.9	2	4	3
1971 Atl	14	64	266	4.2	1	19	249	13.1	1	2	2
1973 Atl	6	18	47	2.6	1	2	14	7.0	0	0	1
NFL Total	60	332	1321	4.0	5	85	765	9.0	5	11	10

BUFF WAGNER Wagner, Almore C 5'9", 165 **HB-FB-BB**
Col: Carroll (Wis.) *HS:* Marinette [WI] B: 2/21/1897, Marinette, WI D: 2/1962
1921 GB: 4 G.

BARRY WAGNER Wagner, Barry 6'3", 213 **WR**
Col: Alabama A&M *HS:* Greensboro [AL] B: 11/24/1967
1992 ChiB: 1 G; Rec 1-16 16.0.

BRYAN WAGNER Wagner, Bryan Jeffrey 6'2", 200 **P**
Col: California Lutheran; Cal State-Northridge *HS:* Hilltop [Chula Vista, CA] B: 3/28/1962, Escondido, CA
1988 ChiB: Pass 1-1 100.0%, 3 3.00; Rush 2-0. **Total:** Pass 1-1 100.0%, 3 3.00; Rush 2-0.

		Punting			
Year Team	**G**	**Punts**	**Yds**	**Avg**	**Fum**
1987 ChiB	10	36	1461	40.6	0
1988 ChiB	16	79	3282	41.5	1
1989 Cle	16	**97**	**3817**	39.4	0
1990 Cle	16	74	2879	38.9	0
1991 NE	3	14	548	39.1	0
1992 GB	7	30	1222	40.7	0
1993 GB	16	74	3174	42.9	0
1994 SD	14	65	2705	41.6	0
1995 NE	8	37	1557	42.1	0
NFL Total	106	506	20645	40.8	1

LOWELL WAGNER Wagner, Lowell R 6'0", 194 **DB-WB-HB**
Col: USC *HS:* Gardena [CA] B: 8/21/1923
AAFC **1946** NY-A: 13 G; Rush 15-29 1.9; Rec 9-126 14.0 1 TD; PR 2-55 27.5 1 TD; KR 4-119 29.8; Tot TD 2; 12 Pt. **1947** NY-A: 7 G; Rec 4-50 12.5 1 TD; 6 Pt. **1948** NY-A: 14 G; Rec 6-99 16.5 1 TD; Int 1-31; 6 Pt. **1949** SF-A: 10 G; Rush 3-17 5.7; PR 1-2 2.0; Int 6-121 1 TD; 6 Pt. **Total:** 44 G; Rush 18-46 2.6; Rec 19-275 14.5 3 TD; PR 3-57 19.0 1 TD; KR 4-119 29.8; Int 7-152 1 TD; Tot TD 5; 30 Pt.
NFL **1950** SF: Rush 2-5 2.5; PR 1-4 4.0. **1952** SF: Rec 1-6 6.0. **1953** SF: Rush 1-4 4.0. **Total:** Rush 3-9 3.0; Rec 1-6 6.0; PR 1-4 4.0.

		Interceptions			
Year Team	**G**	**Int**	**Yds**	**TD**	**Fum**
1950 SF	12	4	12	0	1
1951 SF	12	9	115	0	0
1952 SF	12	6	69	0	0
1953 SF	10	6	135	0	0
1955 SF	1	0	0	0	0
NFL Total	47	25	331	0	1

MIKE WAGNER Wagner, Michael Robert 6'1", 210 **DB**
Col: Western Illinois *HS:* Mount Carmel [Mundelein, IL] B: 6/22/1949, Waukegan, IL *Drafted:* 1971 Round 11 Pit
1971 Pit: PR 2-2 1.0. **Total:** PR 2-2 1.0.

		Interceptions			
Year Team	**G**	**Int**	**Yds**	**TD**	**Fum**
1971 Pit	12	2	53	0	1
1972 Pit	14	6	77	0	0
1973 Pit	14	**8**	134	0	2
1974 Pit	13	2	13	0	1
1975 Pit	12	4	122	0	1
1976 Pit	14	2	0	0	0
1977 Pit	3	0	0	0	0
1978 Pit	14	2	34	0	0
1979 Pit	8	4	31	0	0
1980 Pit	15	6	27	0	0
NFL Total	119	36	491	0	5

RAY WAGNER Wagner, Raymond John 5'10", 172 **OE**
Col: Columbia *HS:* Masten Park [Buffalo, NY] B: 2/25/1902, Buffalo, NY D: 12/3/1990, St. Petersburg, FL
1929 Ora: 1 G. **1930** Nwk: 5 G. **1931** Bkn: 6 G. **Total:** 12 G.

RAY WAGNER Wagner, Raymond L Jr. 6'3", 290 **OT**
Col: Kent State *HS:* Delaware Valley [Milford, PA] B: 11/15/1957, Altoona, PA
1982 Cin: 4 G.

SID WAGNER Wagner, Sidney P 5'11", 192 **G**
Col: Michigan State *HS:* Central [Lansing, MI] B: 10/29/1912, Lansing, MI D: 11/17/1972, Forest, MI *Drafted:* 1936 Round 1 Det
1936 Det: 5 G. **1937** Det: 11 G. **1938** Det: 11 G. **Total:** 27 G.

STEVE WAGNER Wagner, Steven John 6'2", 208 **DB**
Col: Wisconsin *HS:* Oconomowoc [WI] B: 4/18/1954, Milwaukee, WI *Drafted:* 1976 Round 5 Min
1976 GB: 11 G; KR 1-27 27.0. **1977** GB: 14 G; KR 6-62 10.3. **1978** GB: 16 G; KR 6-84 14.0. **1979** GB: 16 G; Rush 1-16 16.0; KR 1-8 8.0. **1980** Phi: 4 G. **Total:** 61 G; Rush 1-16 16.0; KR 14-181 12.9.

DAN WAGONER Wagoner, Daniel Wright 5'10", 180 **DB**
Col: Kansas *HS:* T. Wingate Andrews [High Point, NC] B: 12/12/1959, High Point, NC *Drafted:* 1982 Round 9 Det
1982 Det: 1 G. **1983** Det: 14 G. **1984** Det-Min: 5 G. Det: 1 G. Min: 4 G. **1985** Atl: 14 G; KR 13-262 20.2. **Total:** 34 G; KR 13-262 20.2.

JIM WAGSTAFF Wagstaff, James Burke 6'2", 192 **DB**
Col: Idaho State *HS:* American Falls [ID] B: 6/12/1936, American Falls, ID *Drafted:* 1958 Round 21 Det
1959 ChiC: 3 G. **1960** Buf: 14 G; Int 6-93 1 TD; 6 Pt. **1961** Buf: 14 G; PR 1-35 35.0; Int 3-25. **Total:** 31 G; PR 1-35 35.0; Int 9-118 1 TD; 6 Pt.

MIKE WAHLE Wahle, Michael James 6'6", 308 **OT**
Col: Navy *HS:* Rim of the World [Lake Arrowhead, CA] B: 3/29/1977, Portland, OR
1998 GB: 1 G.

JIM WAHLER Wahler, James Joseph 6'4", 275 **DT-NT**
Col: UCLA *HS:* Bellarmine Prep [San Jose, CA] B: 7/29/1966, San Jose, CA *Drafted:* 1989 Round 4 Pho
1989 Pho: 13 G; Int 1-5; 1 Sac. **1990** Pho: 16 G; 2.5 Sac. **1991** Pho: 15 G; 1 Sac. **1992** Pho-Was: 10 G. Pho: 5 G. Was: 5 G. **1993** Was: 8 G. **Total:** 62 G; Int 1-5; 4.5 Sac.

FRANK WAINRIGHT Wainright, Frank Wesley 6'3", 243 **TE**
Col: Northern Colorado *HS:* Pomona [Arvada, CO] B: 10/10/1967, Peoria, IL *Drafted:* 1991 Round 8 NO
1991 NO: 14 G; Rec 1-3 3.0. **1992** NO: 13 G; Rec 9-143 15.9. **1993** NO: 16 G. **1995** Phi-Mia: 13 G. Phi: 7 G. Mia: 6 G. **1996** Mia: 16 G; Rec 1-2 2.0 1 TD; KR 1-10 10.0; 6 Pt. **1997** Mia: 9 G. **1998** Mia: 16 G. **Total:** 97 G; Rec 11-148 13.5 1 TD; KR 1-10 10.0; 6 Pt.

LOYD WAINSCOTT Wainscott, Loyd Dale 6'2", 235 **LB**
Col: Texas *HS:* La Marque [TX] B: 10/26/1946, Texas City, TX *Drafted:* 1969 Round 16 Hou
1969 Hou: 14 G. **1970** Hou: 11 G. **Total:** 25 G.

CARL WAITE Waite, Carl Ebenezer 5'9", 205 **WB-E-BB-FB**
(Rusty) *Col:* Rutgers; Georgetown *HS:* White Plains [NY]
B: 2/27/1902, White Plains, NY D: 10/14/1961, Monticello, NY
1928 Fra: 8 G; Rec 1 TD; 6 Pt. **1929** Ora: 12 G; Rush 1 TD; 6 Pt. **1930** Nwk: 7 G; Rec 1 TD; 6 Pt. **Total:** 27 G; Rush 1 TD; Rec 2 TD; Tot TD 3; 18 Pt.

WILL WAITE Waite, Willard 6'2", 200 **G-C-T-WB**
Col: No College B: 1/4/1893 D: 1/1964, Cleveland, OH
1920 Col: 10 G. **1921** Col: 7 G. **Total:** 17 G.

VAN WAITERS Waiters, Van Allen 6'4", 240 **LB**
Col: Indiana *HS:* Coral Gables [FL] B: 2/27/1965, Coral Gables, FL
Drafted: 1988 Round 3 Cle
1988 Cle: 16 G. **1989** Cle: 16 G; Rec 1-14 14.0 1 TD; 6 Pt. **1990** Cle: 16 G; PR 1-0; Int 1-15; 0.5 Sac. **1991** Cle: 16 G; 1.5 Sac. **1992** Min: 16 G. **Total:** 80 G; Rec 1-14 14.0 1 TD; PR 1-0; Int 1-15; 6 Pt; 2 Sac.

ALEX WAITS Waits, Alexander John 6'2", 208 **P**
Col: Texas *HS:* East Plano [Plano, TX] B: 6/21/1968, Glasgow, Scotland
1991 Sea: 3 G; Punt 14-474 33.9.

LARRY WALBRIDGE Walbridge, Lyman Norman 5'7", 200 **C**
Col: Lafayette; Fordham *HS:* Indiana [PA] B: 9/11/1897, Wellsboro, PA
D: 1/11/1982, Woodland Hills, CA
1925 NYG: 2 G.

MARK WALCZAK Walczak, Mark Charles 6'6", 246 **TE**
Col: Arizona *HS:* Greece Athena [Rochester, NY] B: 4/26/1962, Rochester, NY
1987 Buf-Ind: 10 G; 1 Fum. Buf: 2 G; 1 Fum. Ind: 8 G. **1988** Pho: 16 G; 1 Fum. **1989** SD: 6 G. **1991** SD: 1 G. **Total:** 33 G; 2 Fum.

STAN WALDEMORE Waldemore, Stanley A 6'4", 263 **OG-C-OT**
Col: Nebraska *HS:* Essex Catholic [Newark, NJ] B: 2/20/1955, Newark, NJ *Drafted:* 1978 Round 3 Atl
1978 NYJ: 4 G. **1979** NYJ: 16 G. **1980** NYJ: 16 G; 1 Fum. **1981** NYJ: 16 G. **1982** NYJ: 9 G. **1983** NYJ: 4 G. **1984** NYJ: 14 G. **Total:** 79 G; 1 Fum.

BOBBY WALDEN Walden, Robert Earl 6'0", 190 **P**
Col: Georgia *HS:* Cairo [GA] B: 3/9/1938, Boston, GA *Drafted:* 1961 Round 4 Hou
1964 Min: Rush 1-18 18.0. **1966** Min: Rush 5-82 16.4. **1968** Pit: Pass 1-0; Rush 2-5 2.5. **1970** Pit: Pass 1-1 100.0%, 20 20.00. **1971** Pit: Pass 1-1 100.0%, 10 10.00; Rush 1-14 14.0. **1972** Pit: Pass 1-0. **1973** Pit: Rush 1-0. **1975** Pit: Pass 3-2 66.7%, 39 13.00. **1976** Pit: Rush 3-7 2.3. **1977** Pit: Rush 1-0. **Total:** Pass 7-4 57.1%, 69 9.86; Rush 14-126 9.0.

		Punting			
Year Team	**G**	**Punts**	**Yds**	**Avg**	**Fum**
1964 Min	14	72	3341	**46.4**	0
1965 Min	14	51	2146	42.1	0
1966 Min	14	60	2463	41.1	1
1967 Min	14	75	3117	41.6	0
1968 Pit	14	68	2745	40.4	1
1969 Pit	14	77	3254	42.3	0
1970 Pit	13	75	3393	45.2	0
1971 Pit	14	79	3455	43.7	1
1972 Pit	14	65	2846	43.8	0
1973 Pit	14	62	2548	41.1	1
1974 Pit	14	78	3040	39.0	0
1975 Pit	14	69	2717	39.4	0
1976 Pit	14	76	2982	39.2	1
1977 Pit	13	67	2482	37.0	2
NFL Total	194	974	40529	41.6	7

TIM WALDRON Waldron, Austin 195 **G-C**
(Pinky) *Col:* Gonzaga *HS:* Colorado Springs [CO] B: 1903
1927 ChiC: 4 G.

ROB WALDROP Waldrop, Robert F 6'1", 276 **DT**
Col: Arizona *HS:* Horizon [Scottsdale, AZ] B: 12/1/1971, Atlanta, GA
Drafted: 1994 Round 5 KC
1994 KC: 3 G.

KERWIN WALDROUP Waldroup, Kerwin 6'3", 260 **DE**
Col: Michigan; Central State (Ohio) *HS:* Rich Central [Olympia Fields, IL]
B: 8/1/1974, Chicago, IL *Drafted:* 1996 Round 5 Det
1996 Det: 16 G; 2.5 Sac. **1997** Det: 11 G; 1 Sac. **1998** Det: 13 G; 1.5 Sac. **Total:** 40 G; 5 Sac.

RALPH WALDSMITH Waldsmith, Ralph George 5'9", 225 **C-G**
(Fat) *Col:* Akron *HS:* South [Akron, OH] B: 8/7/1892, Akron, OH
D: 6/7/1925, Wilkes-Barre, PA
1921 Cle: 4 G. **1922** Can: 5 G. **Total:** 9 G.

MARK WALEN Walen, Mark Hartley 6'5", 265 **DT-DE**
Col: UCLA *HS:* Burlingame [CA] B: 3/10/1963, San Francisco, CA
Drafted: 1986 Round 3 Dal
1987 Dal: 9 G; 1 Sac. **1988** Dal: 15 G; 4 Sac. **Total:** 24 G; 5 Sac.

BILLY WALIK Walik, William S 5'11", 180 **WR-DB**
Col: Villanova *HS:* Hopkins School [New Haven, CT] B: 11/8/1947, New Haven, CT *Drafted:* 1970 Round 11 Phi
1970 Phi: Rec 1-0. **1972** Phi: Rec 1-15 15.0 1 TD. **Total:** Rec 2-15 7.5 1 TD.

		Punt Returns				Kickoff Returns				
Year Team	**G**	**Ret**	**Yds**	**Avg**	**TD**	**Ret**	**Yds**	**Avg**	**TD**	**Fum**
1970 Phi	14	20	78	3.9	0	32	805	25.2	0	3
1971 Phi	8	5	48	9.6	0	14	369	26.4	0	0
1972 Phi	10	3	4	1.3	0	21	466	22.2	0	0
NFL Total	32	28	130	4.6	0	67	1640	24.5	0	3

ADAM WALKER Walker, Adam 5'11", 220 **RB**
Col: Carthage B: 4/9/1963, New York, NY
1987 Min: 2 G; Rush 5-24 4.8; Rec 2-3 1.5.

ADAM WALKER Walker, Adam Clayton 6'1", 210 **RB**
Col: Pittsburgh *HS:* Steel Valley [Munhall, PA] B: 6/7/1968, Pittsburgh, PA
1993 SF: Rec 1-4 4.0; KR 3-51 17.0. **1994** SF: KR 6-82 13.7. **1995** SF: Rec 11-78 7.1; KR 1-17 17.0. **Total:** Rec 12-82 6.8; KR 10-150 15.0.

		Rushing				
Year Team	**G**	**Att**	**Yds**	**Avg**	**TD**	**Fum**
1992 SF	1	0	0	—	0	0
1993 SF	10	5	17	3.4	0	0
1994 SF	8	13	54	4.2	1	0
1995 SF	13	14	44	3.1	1	2
1996 Phi	13	0	0	—	0	0
NFL Total	45	32	115	3.6	2	2

BRACEY WALKER Walker, Bracey Wardell 6'0", 200 **DB**
Col: North Carolina *HS:* Pine Forest [Fayetteville, NC] B: 10/28/1970, Portsmouth, VA *Drafted:* 1994 Round 4 KC
1994 KC-Cin: 9 G. KC: 2 G. Cin: 7 G. **1995** Cin: 14 G; Int 4-56. **1996** Cin: 16 G; Int 2-35. **1997** Mia: 12 G. **1998** KC: 8 G. **Total:** 59 G; Int 6-91.

BRIAN WALKER Walker, Brian 6'1", 198 **DB**
Col: Snow Coll. UT (J.C.); Washington State *HS:* Widefield [Colorado Springs, CO] B: 5/31/1972, Colorado Springs, CO
1996 Was: 16 G; 1 Sac. **1997** Was: 5 G. **1998** Mia: 16 G; Int 4-12. **Total:** 37 G; Int 4-12; 1 Sac.

BRUCE WALKER Walker, Bruce Romell 6'4", 310 **NT**
Col: UCLA *HS:* Dominguez [Compton, CA] B: 7/18/1972, Compton, CA *Drafted:* 1994 Round 2 Phi
1995 NE: 11 G.

BYRON WALKER Walker, Byron Burneil 6'4", 190 **WR**
Col: The Citadel *HS:* Warner Robins [GA] B: 7/28/1960, Scott AFB, IL

		Receiving					Tot
Year Team	**G**	**Rec**	**Yds**	**Avg**	**TD**	**Fum**	**TD**
1982 Sea	9	10	156	15.6	2	0	2
1983 Sea	16	12	248	20.7	2	0	2
1984 Sea	16	13	236	18.2	1	0	1
1985 Sea	16	19	285	15.0	2	1	3
1986 Sea	1	0	0	—	0	0	0
NFL Total	58	54	925	17.1	7	1	8

CHUCK WALKER Walker, Charles David 6'3", 250 **DT-DE**
Col: Duke *HS:* North Catholic [Pittsburgh, PA] B: 8/10/1941, Uniontown, PA *Drafted:* 1963 Round 12 StL
1964 StL: 3 G. **1965** StL: 14 G. **1966** StL: 14 G. **1967** StL: 13 G. **1968** StL: 14 G. **1969** StL: 14 G. **1970** StL: 11 G. **1971** StL: 11 G. **1972** StL-Atl: 11 G. StL: 2 G. Atl: 9 G. **1973** Atl: 14 G; Int 1-0. **1974** Atl: 14 G. **1975** Atl: 10 G. **Total:** 143 G; Int 1-0.

CLARENCE WALKER Walker, Clarence 6'1", 205 **HB**
Col: Southern Illinois B: 9/23/1938, DeQuincy, LA
1963 Den: 1 G; Rush 2-14 7.0.

CLEO WALKER Walker, Cleo Franklin 6'3", 219 **LB-C**
Col: Louisville *HS:* William H. Spencer [Columbus, GA] B: 2/7/1948, Columbus, GA *Drafted:* 1970 Round 7 GB
1970 GB: 11 G. **1971** Atl: 11 G. **Total:** 22 G.

COREY WALKER Walker, Corey 5'10", 188 **RB**
Col: Arkansas State *HS:* Hillcrest [Memphis, TN] B: 6/4/1973, Memphis, TN
1998 Phi: 14 G; Rush 12-55 4.6; Rec 2-35 17.5; KR 8-150 18.8.

DARNELL WALKER Walker, Darnell Robert 5'8", 168 **DB**
Col: Oklahoma *HS:* Sumner [St. Louis, MO] B: 1/17/1970, St. Louis, MO *Drafted:* 1993 Round 7 Atl
1994 Atl: 1 Sac. **1997** SF: 1 Sac. **Total:** 2 Sac.

		Interceptions		
Year Team	**G**	**Int**	**Yds**	**TD**
1993 Atl	15	3	7	0
1994 Atl	16	3	105	1

Year Team				
1995 Atl	16	0	0	0
1996 Atl	15	1	0	0
1997 SF	16	3	49	0
1998 SF	16	4	78	0
NFL Total	94	14	239	1

DENARD WALKER Walker, Denard Antuan 6′1″, 190 **CB**
Col: Louisiana State *HS:* South Garland [Garland, TX]; Harlingen Mil. Inst. [TX] B: 8/9/1973, Dallas, TX *Drafted:* 1997 Round 3 Ten
1997 Ten: 15 G; Int 2-53 1 TD; 6 Pt. **1998** Ten: 16 G; Int 2-6. **Total:** 31 G; Int 4-59 1 TD; 6 Pt.

DERRICK WALKER Walker, Derrick Norval 6′0″, 246 **TE**
Col: Michigan *HS:* Bloom [Chicago Heights, IL] B: 6/23/1967, Glenwood, IL *Drafted:* 1990 Round 6 SD

		Receiving				
Year Team	G	Rec	Yds	Avg	TD	Fum
1990 SD	16	23	240	10.4	1	1
1991 SD	16	20	134	6.7	0	0
1992 SD	16	34	393	11.6	2	0
1993 SD	12	21	212	10.1	1	0
1994 KC	15	36	382	10.6	2	1
1995 KC	16	25	205	8.2	1	0
1996 KC	11	9	73	8.1	1	0
1997 KC	16	5	60	12.0	0	0
NFL Total	118	173	1699	9.8	8	2

DONNIE WALKER Walker, Donnie Mack 6′2″, 180 **DB**
Col: Central State (Ohio) *HS:* Lindenhurst [NY] B: 12/26/1950, Bronx, NY *Drafted:* 1973 Round 4 Buf
1973 Buf: Int 1-22. **1974** Buf: KR 1-20 20.0. **Total:** KR 1-20 20.0; Int 1-22.

		Punt Returns				
Year Team	G	Ret	Yds	Avg	TD	Fum
1973 Buf	11	25	210	8.4	0	0
1974 Buf	14	**43**	384	8.9	0	3
1975 NYJ	2	0	0	—	0	0
NFL Total	27	68	594	8.7	0	3

DWIGHT WALKER Walker, Dwight Gerard 5′10″, 185 **RB-WR**
Col: Nicholls State *HS:* East Jefferson [Metairie, LA] B: 1/10/1959, Metarie, LA *Drafted:* 1982 Round 4 Cle
1983 Cle: Pass 3-1 33.3%, 25 8.33 1 Int; Rush 19-100 5.3. **1984** Cle: Rush 1-(-8) -8.0. **Total:** Pass 3-1 33.3%, 25 8.33 1 Int; Rush 20-92 4.6.

		Receiving				Punt Returns			
Year Team	G	Rec	Yds	Avg	TD	Ret	Yds	Avg	TD
1982 Cle	9	8	136	17.0	0	19	101	5.3	0
1983 Cle	16	29	273	9.4	1	3	26	8.7	0
1984 Cle	11	10	122	12.2	0	6	50	8.3	0
1987 NO	2	2	15	7.5	0	0	0	—	0
NFL Total	38	49	546	11.1	1	28	177	6.3	0

	Kickoff Returns				
Year Team	Ret	Yds	Avg	TD	Fum
1982 Cle	13	295	22.7	0	2
1983 Cle	29	627	21.6	0	1
1984 Cle	0	0	—	0	1
NFL Total	42	922	22.0	0	4

ELLIOT WALKER Walker, Elliot 5′11″, 193 **RB**
Col: Pittsburgh *HS:* Miami Jackson [FL] B: 9/10/1956, Indianola, MS *Drafted:* 1978 Round 6 SF
1978 SF: 9 G; KR 2-25 12.5; 1 Fum.

DOAK WALKER Walker, Ewell Doak Jr. 5′11″, 173 **HB-DB**
Col: Southern Methodist *HS:* Highland Park [Dallas, TX] B: 1/1/1927, Dallas, TX D: 9/27/1998, Steamboat Springs, CO *Drafted:* 1949 Round 1 NYB *HOF:* 1986
1950 Det: Pass 7-1 14.3%, 6 0.86; PR 5-77 15.4; Int 1-40. **1951** Det: Pass 5-2 40.0%, 29 5.80 1 TD; PR 7-85 12.1. **1952** Det: Pass 2-1 50.0%, 9 4.50 1 Int. **1953** Det: Pass 7-3 42.9%, 31 4.43 1 TD. **1954** Det: Pass 4-0, 1 Int; PR 4-117 29.3 **1** TD. **1955** Det: Pass 3-0; PR 2-5 2.5; Int 1-20. **Total:** Pass 28-7 25.0%, 75 2.68 2 TD 2 Int; PR 18-284 15.8 1 TD; Int 2-60.

		Rushing				Receiving			
Year Team	G	Att	Yds	Avg	TD	Rec	Yds	Avg	TD
1950 Det	12	83	386	4.7	5	35	534	15.3	6
1951 Det	12	79	356	4.5	2	22	421	19.1	4
1952 Det	7	26	106	4.1	0	11	90	8.2	0
1953 Det	12	66	337	5.1	2	30	502	16.7	3
1954 Det	12	32	240	7.5	1	32	564	17.6	3
1955 Det	12	23	95	4.1	2	22	428	19.5	5
NFL Total	67	309	1520	4.9	12	152	2539	16.7	21

	Kickoff Returns				Punting		
Year Team	Ret	Yds	Avg	TD	Punts	Yds	Avg
1950 Det	10	225	22.5	0	32	1278	39.9
1951 Det	15	408	27.2	0	9	316	35.1
1953 Det	4	139	34.8	0	0	0	—
1954 Det	8	172	21.5	0	0	0	—
1955 Det	1	24	24.0	0	9	362	40.2
NFL Total	38	968	25.5	0	50	1956	39.1

	Scoring								Tot
Year Team	Pts	FG	FGA	FG%	XK	XKA	XK%	Fum	TD
1950 Det	**128**	8	18	44.4	38	41	92.7	3	11
1951 Det	97	6	12	50.0	**43**	**44**	97.7	1	6
1952 Det	14	3	5	60.0	5	5	100.0	1	0
1953 Det	93	12	19	63.2	27	29	93.1	2	5
1954 Det	106	11	17	64.7	**43**	**43**	100.0	1	5
1955 Det	**96**	9	16	56.3	27	29	93.1	1	7
NFL Total	534	49	87	56.3	183	191	95.8	9	34

FULTON WALKER Walker, Fulton Luther Jr. 5′10″, 193 **DB**
Col: West Virginia *HS:* Martinsburg [WV] B: 4/30/1958, Martinsburg, WV *Drafted:* 1981 Round 6 Mia
1981 Mia: Int 1-0. **1982** Mia: Int 3-54. **1983** Mia: Int 1-7. **Total:** Int 5-61.

		Punt Returns				Kickoff Returns					Tot
Year Team	G	Ret	Yds	Avg	TD	Ret	Yds	Avg	TD	Fum	TD
1981 Mia	16	5	50	10.0	0	38	932	24.5	**1**	4	1
1982 Mia	9	0	0	—	0	20	433	21.7	0	0	0
1983 Mia	15	8	86	10.8	0	36	962	**26.7**	0	1	0
1984 Mia	12	21	169	8.0	0	29	617	21.3	0	2	0
1985 Mia-LARd	15	**62**	**692**	11.2	0	21	467	22.2	0	5	0
1985 Mia	2	0	0	—	0	0	0	—	0	0	0
1985 LARd	13	62	692	11.2	0	21	467	22.2	0	5	0
1986 LARd	14	49	440	9.0	1	23	368	16.0	0	3	1
NFL Total	81	145	1437	9.9	1	167	3779	22.6	1	15	2

GARY WALKER Walker, Gary Lamar 6′2″, 287 **DE-DT**
Col: Hinds CC MS; Auburn *HS:* Franklin Co. [Carnesville, GA] B: 2/28/1973, Royston, GA *Drafted:* 1995 Round 5 Hou
1995 Hou: 15 G; 2.5 Sac. **1996** Hou: 16 G; 5.5 Sac. **1997** Ten: 15 G; 7 Sac. **1998** Ten: 16 G; 1 Sac. **Total:** 62 G; 16 Sac.

GARY WALKER Walker, Gary Wayne 6′3″, 283 **C**
Col: Boston U. *HS:* Portsmouth [NH] B: 12/15/1963, Hassfurt, Germany
1987 Dal: 1 G.

MICKEY WALKER Walker, George Mickey 6′0″, 235 **OG-LB-C**
Col: Michigan State *HS:* East Detroit [Eastpointe, MI] B: 10/14/1939, Petosky, MI *Drafted:* 1957 Round 3 Cle
1961 NYG: 14 G. **1962** NYG: 14 G; KR 1-0. **1963** NYG: 13 G. **1964** NYG: 7 G. **1965** NYG: 4 G. **Total:** 52 G; KR 1-0.

GLEN WALKER Walker, Glen Joe 6′1″, 210 **P**
Col: Los Angeles Harbor Coll. CA (J.C.); USC *HS:* Gardena [CA] B: 1/16/1952, Torrance, CA
1977 LARm: Pass 1-1 100.0%, 13 13.00. **1978** LARm: Pass 1-0, 1 Int. **Total:** Pass 2-1 50.0%, 13 6.50 1 Int.

		Punting		
Year Team	G	Punts	Yds	Avg
1977 LARm	14	73	2568	35.2
1978 LARm	16	83	3069	37.0
NFL Total	30	156	5637	36.1

HERSCHEL WALKER Walker, Herschel Junior 6′1″, 225 **RB**
Col: Georgia *HS:* Johnson Co. [Wrightsville, GA] B: 3/3/1962, Wrightsville, GA *Drafted:* 1985 Round 5 Dal
1990 Min: Pass 2-1 50.0%, 12 6.00. **1992** Phi: Pass 1-0. **Total:** Pass 3-1 33.3%, 12 4.00.

		Rushing				Receiving			
Year Team	G	Att	Yds	Avg	TD	Rec	Yds	Avg	TD
1986 Dal	16	151	737	4.9	12	76	837	11.0	2
1987 Dal	12	209	891	4.3	7	60	715	11.9	1
1988 Dal	16	361	1514	4.2	5	53	505	9.5	2
1989 Dal-Min	16	250	915	3.7	7	40	423	10.6	2
1989 Dal	5	81	246	3.0	2	22	261	11.9	1
1989 Min	11	169	669	4.0	5	18	162	9.0	1
1990 Min	16	184	770	4.2	5	35	315	9.0	4
1991 Min	15	198	825	4.2	10	33	204	6.2	0
1992 Phi	16	267	1070	4.0	8	38	278	7.3	2
1993 Phi	16	174	746	4.3	1	75	610	8.1	3
1994 Phi	16	113	528	4.7	5	50	500	10.0	2
1995 NYG	16	31	126	4.1	0	31	234	7.5	1
1996 Dal	16	10	83	8.3	1	7	89	12.7	0
1997 Dal	16	6	20	3.3	0	14	149	10.6	2
NFL Total	187	1954	8225	4.2	61	512	4859	9.5	21

	Kickoff Returns					Tot
Year Team	Ret	Yds	Avg	TD	Fum	TD
1986 Dal	0	0	—	0	5	14
1987 Dal	0	0	—	0	4	8

1988 Dal	0	0	—	0	6	7
1989 Dal-Min	13	374	28.8	**1**	7	10
1989 Dal	0	0	—	0	2	3
1989 Min	13	374	28.8	1	5	7
1990 Min	44	966	22.0	0	4	9
1991 Min	5	83	16.6	0	2	10
1992 Phi	3	69	23.0	0	6	10
1993 Phi	11	184	16.7	0	3	4
1994 Phi	21	581	27.7	1	4	8
1995 NYG	41	881	21.5	0	0	1
1996 Dal	27	779	28.9	0	0	1
1997 Dal	50	1167	23.3	0	0	2
NFL Total	215	5084	23.6	2	41	84

JACKIE WALKER Walker, Jackie A 6′5″, 245 **LB-TE**
Col: Jackson State *HS:* Carroll [Monroe, LA] B: 11/3/1962, Monroe, LA *Drafted:* 1986 Round 2 TB
1986 TB: 15 G. **1987** TB: 12 G. **1988** TB: 16 G. **1989** TB: 14 G. **Total:** 57 G.

JIMMY WALKER Walker, James 6′2″, 265 **DT**
Col: Arkansas *HS:* Little Rock Central [AR] B: 12/30/1957, Camden, AR
1987 Min: 2 G; 1 Sac.

JAMES WALKER Walker, James Charles 6′1″, 250 **LB**
Col: Kansas State *HS:* East [Wichita, KS] B: 12/9/1958, Muskogee, OK
1983 KC: 4 G.

JEFF WALKER Walker, Jeffrey Lynn 6′4″, 295 **OT-OG**
Col: Memphis *HS:* Olive Branch [MS] B: 1/22/1963, Jonesboro, AR *Drafted:* 1986 Round 3 SD
1986 SD: 16 G. **1988** NO: 1 G. **1989** NO: 13 G. **Total:** 30 G.

JAY WALKER Walker, Jewell Jay 6′3″, 229 **QB**
(Sky) *Col:* Pasadena City Coll. CA (J.C.); Long Beach State; Howard *HS:* University [Los Angeles, CA] B: 1/24/1972, Los Angeles, CA *Drafted:* 1994 Round 7 NE
1996 Min: 1 G; Pass 2-2 100.0%, 31 15.50. **1997** Min: Postseason only.

JOHN WALKER Walker, John Wayne 6′6″, 270 **NT-DT**
Col: Nebraska-Omaha *HS:* Benson [Omaha, NE] B: 9/12/1961, Omaha, NE
1987 KC: 3 G.

MIKE WALKER Walker, Joseph Michael 6′4″, 235 **DE**
Col: Tulane *HS:* Sulphur [LA] B: 11/7/1949, Texarkana, AR *Drafted:* 1971 Round 11 Min
1971 NO: 5 G.

KENNY WALKER Walker, Kenny Wayne 6′3″, 260 **DE**
Col: Nebraska *HS:* South [Denver, CO] B: 4/6/1967, Crane, TX *Drafted:* 1991 Round 8 Den
1991 Den: 16 G; 3 Sac. **1992** Den: 15 G; 1.5 Sac. **Total:** 31 G; 4.5 Sac.

KEVIN WALKER Walker, Kevin Cornelius 5′11″, 180 **DB**
Col: East Carolina *HS:* Ben L. Smith [Greensboro, NC] B: 10/20/1963, Greensboro, NC *Drafted:* 1986 Round 6 TB
1986 TB: 4 G; PR 9-27 3.0; KR 8-146 18.3; 1 Fum. **1987** TB: 3 G; KR 1-0; Int 2-30 1 TD; 6 Pt. **Total:** 7 G; PR 9-27 3.0; KR 9-146 16.2; Int 2-30 1 TD; 6 Pt; 1 Fum.

KEVIN WALKER Walker, Kevin P 6′2″, 238 **LB**
Col: Maryland *HS:* West Milford [NJ] B: 12/24/1965, Denville, NJ *Drafted:* 1988 Round 3 Cin
1988 Cin: 3 G. **1989** Cin: 16 G. **1990** Cin: 16 G; 1 Sac. **1991** Cin: 5 G; 1 Sac. **1992** Cin: 4 G. **Total:** 44 G; 2 Sac.

QUENTIN WALKER Walker, LaQuentin Antonio 6′1″, 205 **RB**
Col: Virginia *HS:* Teaneck [NJ] B: 8/27/1961, Teaneck, NJ *Drafted:* 1984 Round 7 StL
1984 StL: 3 G.

LOUIE WALKER Walker, Louis Jr. 6′1″, 216 **LB**
Col: Colorado State *HS:* George Washington [Los Angeles, CA] B: 7/23/1952, Los Angeles, CA
1974 Dal: 8 G.

MALCOLM WALKER Walker, Malcolm Ernest Jr. 6′4″, 250 **C-OT**
Col: Rice *HS:* South Oak Cliff [Dallas, TX] B: 5/24/1943, Dallas, TX *Drafted:* 1965 Round 2 Dal
1966 Dal: 5 G. **1967** Dal: 14 G. **1968** Dal: 14 G. **1969** Dal: 14 G. **1970** GB: 11 G. **Total:** 58 G.

MARQUIS WALKER Walker, Marquis Roche 5′10″, 175 **DB**
Col: Blinn Coll. TX (J.C.); Cisco JC TX; Southeast Missouri State *HS:* Berkeley [MO] B: 7/6/1972, St. Louis, MO
1996 Was-StL: 9 G; Int 1-0. Was: 1 G. StL: 8 G; Int 1-0. **1997** StL: 11 G. **1998** Oak: 16 G; Int 2-28. **Total:** 36 G; Int 3-28.

MIKE WALKER Walker, Michael R 6′0″, 190 **K**
Col: No College *HS:* in [Lancaster, England] B: 10/18/1949, Lancaster, England
1972 NE: 8 G; Scor 21, 2-8 25.0% FG, 15-15 100.0% XK.

PAUL WALKER Walker, Paul Frederick 6′3″, 210 **DB-OE**
Col: Yale *HS:* Oak Park [IL] B: 7/9/1925, Springfield, MO D: 10/20/1972, West Hartford, CT *Drafted:* 1945 Round 8 Det
1948 NYG: 12 G; Rec 1-11 11.0; Int 1-5.

RANDY WALKER Walker, Randell Paul 5′10″, 177 **P**
Col: Northwestern State-Louisiana *HS:* Bossier [Bossier City, LA] B: 8/29/1951, Shreveport, LA *Drafted:* 1974 Round 12 GB
1974 GB: Rush 1-18 18.0.

		Punting		
Year Team	**G**	**Punts**	**Yds**	**Avg**
1974 GB	14	69	2648	38.4

RICK WALKER Walker, Richard 6′4″, 235 **TE**
Col: Rancho Santiago Coll. CA (J.C.); UCLA *HS:* Valley [Santa Ana, CA] B: 5/28/1955, Santa Ana, CA *Drafted:* 1977 Round 4 Cin
1980 Was: Rush 1-(-8) -8.0. **1981** Was: Rush 1-5 5.0. **1982** Was: Rush 2-11 5.5. **1983** Was: Rush 2-10 5.0. **1984** Was: Rush 1-2 2.0. **1985** Was: Rush 3-16 5.3. **Total:** Rush 10-36 3.6.

		Receiving				
Year Team	**G**	**Rec**	**Yds**	**Avg**	**TD**	**Fum**
1977 Cin	6	1	13	13.0	0	0
1978 Cin	15	12	126	10.5	2	1
1979 Cin	10	1	14	14.0	1	0
1980 Was	15	10	88	8.8	1	1
1981 Was	16	11	112	10.2	1	0
1982 Was	9	12	92	7.7	1	0
1983 Was	16	17	168	9.9	2	0
1984 Was	16	5	52	10.4	1	0
1985 Was	16	1	8	8.0	0	0
NFL Total	119	70	673	9.6	9	2

ROBERT WALKER Walker, Robert 5′10″, 208 **RB**
Col: West Virginia *HS:* Huntington [WV] B: 6/26/1972, Huntington, WV
1996 NYG: 1 G.

WAYNE WALKER Walker, Ronald Wayne 5′8″, 162 **WR**
(Bug) *Col:* Texas Tech *HS:* Jefferson-Moore [Waco, TX] B: 12/27/1966, Waco, TX
1989 SD: 13 G; Rush 1-9 9.0; Rec 24-395 16.5 1 TD; PR 6-31 5.2; 6 Pt; 2 Fum.

SAMMY WALKER Walker, Sammy William 5′11″, 203 **DB**
Col: Texas Tech *HS:* McKinney [TX] B: 1/20/1969, McKinney, TX *Drafted:* 1991 Round 4 Pit
1991 Pit: 2 G. **1992** Pit: 16 G. **1993** GB: 8 G. **Total:** 26 G.

TIM WALKER Walker, Timothy Alan 6′1″, 230 **LB**
Col: Savannah State *HS:* Northside [Warner Robins, GA] B: 5/12/1958, Hartford, CT
1980 Sea: 16 G.

TONY WALKER Walker, Tony Maurice 6′3″, 235 **LB**
Col: Southeast Missouri State *HS:* Phillips [Birmingham, AL] B: 4/2/1968, Birmingham, AL *Drafted:* 1990 Round 6 Ind
1990 Ind: 14 G. **1991** Ind: 16 G. **1992** Ind: 13 G; 1 Sac. **Total:** 43 G; 1 Sac.

VAL JOE WALKER Walker, Val Joe 6′1″, 179 **DB**
Col: Southern Methodist *HS:* Seminole [TX] B: 1/7/1930, Tahoka, TX *Drafted:* 1952 Round 7 NYG

		Interceptions			
Year Team	**G**	**Int**	**Yds**	**TD**	**Fum**
1953 GB	12	4	74	**1**	0
1954 GB	10	4	83	0	0
1955 GB	12	6	77	0	1
1956 GB	12	1	0	0	0
1957 SF	12	2	20	0	0
NFL Total	58	17	254	1	1

WAYNE WALKER Walker, Wayne 6′3″, 230 **P**
Col: Northwestern State-Louisiana *HS:* Bossier [Bossier City, LA] B: 10/14/1944, Shreveport, LA *Drafted:* 1966 Round 13 KC
1967 KC: 4 G; Punt 19-736 38.7. **1968** Hou: 8 G; Scor 50, 8-16 50.0% FG, 26-26 100.0% XK. **Total:** 12 G; Punt 19-736 38.7; Scor 50, 8-16 50.0% FG, 26-26 100.0% XK.

WAYNE WALKER Walker, Wayne Harrison 6′2″, 225 **LB**
Col: Idaho *HS:* Boise [ID] B: 9/30/1936, Boise, ID *Drafted:* 1958 Round 4 Det
1958 Det: **1** Fum TD. **1960** Det: Scor **1** Saf. **Total:** Scor 1 Saf; 1 Fum TD.

		Interceptions		
Year Team	**G**	**Int**	**Yds**	**TD**
1958 Det	12	1	33	1
1959 Det	9	0	0	0
1960 Det	12	1	21	0
1961 Det	14	2	16	0
1962 Det	14	1	47	0
1963 Det	14	1	17	0

1964 Det	14	1	14	0
1965 Det	14	2	0	0
1966 Det	13	1	3	0
1967 Det	14	0	0	0
1968 Det	14	1	0	0
1969 Det	14	1	0	0
1970 Det	14	0	0	0
1971 Det	14	2	12	0
1972 Det	14	0	0	0
NFL Total	200	14	163	1

	Scoring								Tot
Year Team	Pts	FG	FGA	FG%	XK	XKA	XK%	Fum	TD
1958 Det	0	0	0	—	0	0	—	0	2
1959 Det	5	0	0	—	5	6	83.3	0	0
1961 Det	6	0	3	0.0	6	6	100.0	0	0
1962 Det	64	9	22	40.9	37	37	100.0	1	0
1963 Det	56	9	22	40.9	29	29	100.0	0	0
1964 Det	74	14	25	56.0	32	34	94.1	0	0
1965 Det	57	8	22	36.4	33	33	100.0	0	0
1966 Det	17	2	8	25.0	11	11	100.0	0	0
1967 Det	26	5	15	33.3	11	11	100.0	1	0
1968 Det	24	6	14	42.9	6	6	100.0	0	0
1971 Det	2	0	0	—	2	2	100.0	0	0
NFL Total	345	53	131	40.5	172	175	98.3	2	2

WESLEY WALKER Walker, Wesley Darcel 6′0″, 179 **WR**
Col: California *HS:* Carson [CA] B: 5/26/1955, San Bernardino, CA
Drafted: 1977 Round 2 NYJ
1977 NYJ: Rush 3-25 8.3. **1978** NYJ: Rush 1-(-3) -3.0. **1984** NYJ: Rush 1-1 1.0. **1985** NYJ: Scor 1 Saf. **1988** NYJ: Rush 1-12 12.0. **Total:** Rush 6-35 5.8; Scor 1 Saf.

		Receiving				
Year Team	G	Rec	Yds	Avg	TD	Fum
1977 NYJ	14	35	740	**21.1**	3	2
1978 NYJ	16	48	**1169**	**24.4**	8	2
1979 NYJ	9	23	569	24.7	5	0
1980 NYJ	10	18	376	20.9	1	0
1981 NYJ	13	47	770	16.4	9	0
1982 NYJ	9	39	620	15.9	6	0
1983 NYJ	16	61	868	14.2	7	0
1984 NYJ	12	41	623	15.2	7	0
1985 NYJ	12	34	725	21.3	5	1
1986 NYJ	16	49	1016	20.7	12	3
1987 NYJ	5	9	190	21.1	1	0
1988 NYJ	16	26	551	21.2	7	1
1989 NYJ	6	8	89	11.1	0	0
NFL Total	154	438	8306	19.0	71	9

BILL WALKER Walker, William Bradley 6′0″, 220 **G**
Col: Virginia Military B: 9/16/1920, Richmond, VA
1944 Bos: 10 G. **1945** Bos: 5 G; KR 1-3 3.0. **Total:** 15 G; KR 1-3 3.0.

WILLIE WALKER Walker, Willie 6′3″, 200 **WR**
Col: Coahoma CC MS; Tennessee State B: 9/15/1942, Anquilla, MS
Drafted: 1966 Round 20 SF
1966 Det: 9 G; Rush 1-4 4.0; Rec 1-21 21.0.

EDDIE WALL Wall, Edmund A 5′9″, 170 **BB**
(AKA Waleski) *Col:* Allegheny; Grove City *HS:* Turtle Creek [PA]
B: 4/21/1907, Braddock, PA D: 9/9/1986, York, PA
1930 Fra: 1 G.

AARON WALLACE Wallace, Aaron Jon 6′3″, 240 **LB**
Col: Texas A&M *HS:* Franklin D. Roosevelt [Dallas, TX] B: 4/17/1967, Paris, TX *Drafted:* 1990 Round 2 LARd
1990 LARd: 16 G; 9 Sac. **1991** LARd: 16 G; 2 Sac. **1992** LARd: 16 G; 4 Sac. **1993** LARd: 16 G; 2 Sac. **1994** LARd: 16 G; 2 Sac. **1995** Oak: 13 G; 2 Sac. **1997** Oak: 5 G. **1998** Oak: 4 G. **Total:** 102 G; 21 Sac.

AL WALLACE Wallace, Alonzo Dwight 6′5″, 258 **DE**
Col: Maryland *HS:* Spanish River [Boca Raton, FL] B: 3/25/1974, Delray Beach, FL
1997 Phi: 1 G. **1998** Phi: 15 G; 6 Sac. **Total:** 16 G; 6 Sac.

STEVE WALLACE Wallace, Barron Steven 6′4″, 285 **OT-OG**
Col: Auburn *HS:* Chamblee [GA] B: 12/27/1964, Atlanta, GA
Drafted: 1986 Round 4 SF
1986 SF: 16 G. **1987** SF: 11 G. **1988** SF: 16 G. **1989** SF: 16 G. **1990** SF: 16 G. **1991** SF: 16 G. **1992** SF: 16 G. **1993** SF: 15 G. **1994** SF: 15 G. **1995** SF: 13 G. **1996** SF: 16 G. **1997** KC: 10 G. **Total:** 176 G.

BEV WALLACE Wallace, Beverly William 6′2″, 180 **QB**
Col: Compton CC CA *HS:* Santa Paula [CA]; Compton HS [CA]
B: 3/7/1923 D: 6/17/1992, Newport Beach, CA
AAFC **1947** SF-A: Punt 2-78 39.0. **1948** SF-A: Rush 3-2 0.7; Punt 5-192 38.4. **1949** SF-A: Rush 2-2 1.0 1 TD; Punt 1-30 30.0. **Total:** Rush 5-4 0.8 1 TD; Punt 8-300 37.5.

		Passing							
Year Team	G	Att	Comp	Comp%	Yds	YPA	TD	Int	Rating
1947 SF-A	4	16	5	31.3	48	3.00	0	2	1.0
1948 SF-A	10	22	8	36.4	114	5.18	1	3	29.5
1949 SF-A	9	23	9	39.1	95	4.13	0	4	12.3
AAFC Total	23	61	22	36.1	257	4.21	1	9	15.6

NFL **1951** NYY: 1 G; Pass 8-1 12.5%, 9 1.13; Rush 1-(-8) -8.0; 1 Fum.

CALVIN WALLACE Wallace, Calvin Kerr 6′3″, 230 **DE**
Col: West Virginia Tech *HS:* Valley [Smithers, WV] B: 4/17/1965, Montgomery, WV
1987 GB: 1 G.

DUTCH WALLACE Wallace, Clarence 6′0″, 203 **G-C-T**
Col: No College *HS:* South [Akron, OH] B: 4/18/1900, Akron, OH
D: 2/1977, Akron, OH
1923 Akr: 5 G. **1924** Akr: 1 G; Scor 2, 2 XK. **1925** Cle: 10 G. **1926** Can-Akr: 8 G. Can: 7 G. Akr: 1 G. **Total:** 24 G.

GORDON WALLACE Wallace, Gordon Lewis 5′10″, 170 **FB-C**
Col: Rochester *HS:* East [Rochester, NY] B: 8/6/1899 D: 12/28/1992, Ticonderoga, NY
1923 Roch: 2 G. **1924** Roch: 1 G. **Total:** 3 G.

HENRY WALLACE Wallace, Henry Marshall 6′0″, 195 **DB**
(Pete) *Col:* U. of Pacific *HS:* Long Beach Polytechnic [CA]
B: 9/26/1938, Bakersfield, CA
1960 LAC: 2 G.

JACKIE WALLACE Wallace, Jackie 6′3″, 197 **DB**
Col: Arizona *HS:* St. Augustine [New Orleans, LA] B: 3/13/1951, New Orleans, LA *Drafted:* 1973 Round 2 Min
1974 Min: KR 2-31 15.5. **1975** Bal: KR 1-0. **1976** Bal: KR 3-61 20.3. **1977** LARm: Rec 1-13 13.0. **Total:** Rec 1-13 13.0; KR 6-92 15.3.

		Punt Returns				Interceptions			
Year Team	G	Ret	Yds	Avg	TD	Int	Yds	TD	Fum
1974 Min	14	25	191	7.6	0	1	3	0	2
1975 Bal	14	6	43	7.2	0	4	126	**2**	1
1976 Bal	14	0	0	—	0	5	105	0	1
1977 LARm	10	0	0	—	0	1	23	0	0
1978 LARm	14	**52**	**618**	11.9	0	0	0	0	6
1979 LARm	4	0	0	—	0	0	0	0	0
NFL Total	70	83	852	10.3	0	11	257	2	10

JOHN WALLACE Wallace, John James 6′0″, 180 **OE**
Col: Notre Dame *HS:* Emerson [Gary, IN] B: 9/2/1904, Coal City, IN
D: 7/1981, Mission Viejo, CA
1928 ChiB: 12 G; Rec 1 TD; 6 Pt. **1929** Day: 4 G. **Total:** 16 G; Rec 1 TD; 6 Pt.

RAY WALLACE Wallace, Raymond Duryea 6′0″, 224 **RB**
Col: Purdue *HS:* North Central [Indianapolis, IN] B: 12/3/1963, Indianapolis, IN *Drafted:* 1986 Round 6 Hou
1986 Hou: Rec 17-177 10.4 2 TD. **1987** Hou: Rec 7-34 4.9. **Total:** Rec 24-211 8.8 2 TD.

		Rushing					Tot
Year Team	G	Att	Yds	Avg	TD	Fum	TD
1986 Hou	8	52	218	4.2	3	1	5
1987 Hou	12	19	102	5.4	0	1	0
1989 Pit	9	5	10	2.0	1	0	1
NFL Total	29	76	330	4.3	4	2	6

BOB WALLACE Wallace, Robert Charles 6′3″, 211 **WR-TE**
Col: Texas-El Paso *HS:* South Mountain [Phoenix, AZ] B: 10/7/1945, Texarkana, AR *Drafted:* 1968 Round 2 ChiB
1968 ChiB: Rush 3-29 9.7; PR 6-27 4.5; KR 3-80 26.7. **1969** ChiB: Rush 4-16 4.0. **1971** ChiB: Pass 1-0; Rush 1-0. **Total:** Pass 1-0; Rush 8-45 5.6; PR 6-27 4.5; KR 3-80 26.7.

		Receiving				
Year Team	G	Rec	Yds	Avg	TD	Fum
1968 ChiB	12	19	281	14.8	2	1
1969 ChiB	14	47	553	11.8	5	1
1970 ChiB	5	15	160	10.7	0	0
1971 ChiB	14	27	400	14.8	2	0
1972 ChiB	14	1	9	9.0	0	0
NFL Total	59	109	1403	12.9	9	2

RODNEY WALLACE Wallace, Rodney Allan 6′5″, 255 **OT-OG**
Col: New Mexico *HS:* Central [Pueblo, CO] B: 2/10/1949, Pueblo, CO
Drafted: 1971 Round 10 Dal
1971 Dal: 11 G. **1972** Dal: 14 G. **1973** Dal: 12 G. **Total:** 37 G.

ROGER WALLACE Wallace, Roger Lee 5′11″, 180 **WR**
Col: Bowling Green State *HS:* Urbana [OH] B: 7/22/1952, Urbana, OH
Drafted: 1974 Round 12 StL
1976 NYG: 3 G.

STAN WALLACE Wallace, Stanley Howard 6′3″, 208 **DB**
Col: Illinois *HS:* Hillsboro [IL] B: 11/15/1931, Hillsboro, IL
Drafted: 1954 Round 1 ChiB
1956 ChiB: KR 1-13 13.0. **Total:** KR 1-13 13.0.

		Interceptions			
Year Team	**G**	**Int**	**Yds**	**TD**	**Fum**
1954 ChiB	7	4	63	0	0
1956 ChiB	6	1	7	0	0
1957 ChiB	12	2	23	0	0
1958 ChiB	12	3	16	0	1
NFL Total	37	10	109	0	1

RON WALLER Waller, Ronald Bowles 5′11″, 180 **HB**
Col: Maryland *HS:* Laurel [DE] B: 2/14/1933, Hastings, FL
Drafted: 1955 Round 2 LARm
1955 LARm: Pass 1-0. **1956** LARm: Pass 3-1 33.3%, 44 14.67.
1957 LARm: Pass 6-2 33.3%, 35 5.83. **1960** LAC: Pass 1-0, 1 Int.
Total: Pass 11-3 27.3%, 79 7.18 1 Int.

		Rushing				Receiving			
Year Team	**G**	**Att**	**Yds**	**Avg**	**TD**	**Rec**	**Yds**	**Avg**	**TD**
1955 LARm	12	151	716	4.7	7	24	228	9.5	1
1956 LARm	9	83	543	6.5	1	9	76	8.4	0
1957 LARm	11	48	292	6.1	0	5	40	8.0	0
1958 LARm	10	3	13	4.3	0	3	75	25.0	0
1960 LAC	2	9	5	0.6	0	3	24	8.0	0
NFL Total	44	294	1569	5.3	8	44	443	10.1	1

	Punt Returns				Kickoff Returns					Tot
Year Team	**Ret**	**Yds**	**Avg**	**TD**	**Ret**	**Yds**	**Avg**	**TD**	**Fum**	**TD**
1955 LARm	14	60	4.3	0	17	461	27.1	0	6	8
1956 LARm	14	65	4.6	0	11	276	25.1	0	3	1
1957 LARm	16	33	2.1	0	13	289	22.2	0	4	0
1958 LARm	13	7	0.5	0	7	120	17.1	0	2	0
1960 LAC	0	0	—	0	0	0	—	0	2	0
NFL Total	57	165	2.9	0	48	1146	23.9	0	17	9

BILL WALLER Waller, William Howell 6′1″, 190 **OE-DE**
(Blondy) *Col:* Illinois *HS:* Benton [IL] B: 12/16/1911, Thompsonville, IL
1938 Bkn: 10 G; Rec 3-15 5.0.

BRETT WALLERSTEDT Wallerstedt, Brett Robert 6′1″, 240 **LB**
Col: Arizona State *HS:* Manhattan [KS] B: 11/24/1970, Tacoma, WA
Drafted: 1993 Round 6 Pho
1993 Pho: 7 G. **1994** Cin: 10 G. **1995** Cin: 11 G. **1997** StL: 2 G.
Total: 30 G.

FRED WALLNER Wallner, Frederick William 6′2″, 231 **LB-OG**
Col: Notre Dame *HS:* Greenfield [MA] B: 4/12/1928, Greenfield, MA
Drafted: 1951 Round 20 ChiC
1951 ChiC: 12 G; Int 1-10. **1952** ChiC: 9 G. **1954** ChiC: 12 G. **1955** ChiC: 12 G; Int 2-4. **1960** Hou: 7 G. **Total:** 52 G; Int 3-14.

WESLEY WALLS Walls, Charles Wesley 6′5″, 250 **TE**
Col: Mississippi *HS:* Pontotoc [MS] B: 2/26/1966, Batesville, MS
Drafted: 1989 Round 2 SF
1990 SF: KR 1-16 16.0. **1994** NO: Scor 1 2XP. **1995** NO: KR 1-6 6.0; Scor 1 2XP. **Total:** KR 2-22 11.0; Scor 2 2XP.

		Receiving				
Year Team	**G**	**Rec**	**Yds**	**Avg**	**TD**	**Fum**
1989 SF	16	4	16	4.0	1	1
1990 SF	16	5	27	5.4	0	0
1991 SF	15	2	24	12.0	0	0
1993 SF	6	0	0	—	0	0
1994 NO	15	38	406	10.7	4	0
1995 NO	16	57	694	12.2	4	1
1996 Car	16	61	713	11.7	10	0
1997 Car	15	58	746	12.9	6	0
1998 Car	14	49	506	10.3	5	0
NFL Total	129	274	3132	11.4	30	2

CRAIG WALLS Walls, Craig Stevens 6′1″, 215 **LB**
Col: Indiana *HS:* Peabody [Pittsburgh, PA] B: 12/24/1958, Pittsburgh, PA
1987 Buf: 3 G.

EVERSON WALLS Walls, Everson Collins 6′1″, 194 **DB**
Col: Grambling State *HS:* L.V. Berkner [Richardson, TX]
B: 12/28/1959, Dallas, TX
1988 Dal: PR 1-0; 1 Sac. **1991** NYG: 0.5 Sac. **1992** NYG-Cle: 0.5 Sac. Cle: 0.5 Sac. **1993** Cle: 1 Sac. **Total:** PR 1-0; 3 Sac.

		Interceptions			
Year Team	**G**	**Int**	**Yds**	**TD**	**Fum**
1981 Dal	16	**11**	133	0	0
1982 Dal	9	**7**	61	0	1
1983 Dal	16	4	70	0	0
1984 Dal	16	3	12	0	0
1985 Dal	16	**9**	31	0	0
1986 Dal	16	3	46	0	0
1987 Dal	12	5	38	0	0
1988 Dal	16	2	0	0	1
1989 Dal	16	0	0	0	0
1990 NYG	16	6	80	1	0
1991 NYG	14	4	7	0	0
1992 NYG-Cle	16	3	26	0	0
1992 NYG	6	1	0	0	0
1992 Cle	10	2	26	0	0
1993 Cle	7	0	0	0	0
NFL Total	186	57	504	1	2

HENRY WALLS Walls, Henry Jerod 6′2″, 220 **LB**
Col: Clemson *HS:* Central Davidson [Lexington,NC] B: 2/13/1964, Lexington, NC
1987 NYJ: 3 G.

HERKIE WALLS Walls, McCurey Hercules 5′8″, 159 **WR**
Col: Texas *HS:* Garland [TX] B: 7/18/1961, Garland, TX
Drafted: 1983 Round 7 Hou
1983 Hou: Rush 5-44 8.8. **1984** Hou: Rush 4-20 5.0. **1987** TB: PR 4-12 3.0. **Total:** Rush 9-64 7.1; PR 4-12 3.0.

		Receiving				Kickoff Returns				
Year Team	**G**	**Rec**	**Yds**	**Avg**	**TD**	**Ret**	**Yds**	**Avg**	**TD**	**Fum**
1983 Hou	16	12	276	23.0	1	9	110	12.2	0	0
1984 Hou	14	18	291	16.2	1	15	289	19.3	0	0
1985 Hou	6	1	7	7.0	0	12	234	19.5	0	0
1987 TB	2	1	13	13.0	0	6	136	22.7	0	1
NFL Total	38	32	587	18.3	2	42	769	18.3	0	1

WILL WALLS Walls, William Thomas 6′4″, 214 **OE**
Col: Texas Christian *HS:* North Little Rock [AR] B: 12/8/1912, Lonoke, AR D: 1/2/1993, Dallas, TX
1941 NYG: KR 2-28 14.0. **1942** NYG: KR 2-26 13.0. **1943** NYG: KR 1-3 3.0. **Total:** KR 5-57 11.4.

		Receiving			
Year Team	**G**	**Rec**	**Yds**	**Avg**	**TD**
1937 NYG	11	7	55	7.9	0
1938 NYG	4	1	23	23.0	0
1939 NYG	10	2	19	9.5	0
1941 NYG	11	4	76	19.0	0
1942 NYG	11	7	192	27.4	2
1943 NYG	8	14	231	16.5	2
NFL Total	55	35	596	17.0	4

LAURIE WALQUIST Walquist, Lawrence Wilfred 5′8″, 167 **HB-QB-FB**
(Larry) *Col:* Illinois *HS:* Evanston Twp. [IL]; Rockford Central HS [IL]
B: 3/9/1898, Rockford, IL D: 9/28/1985, Deerfield Lake, IL
1922 ChiB: 12 G; Pass 1 TD. **1924** ChiB: 9 G; Pass 1 TD; Rush 1 TD; 6 Pt. **1925** ChiB: 16 G; Rush 2 TD; Rec 1 TD; Tot TD 3; 18 Pt. **1926** ChiB: 15 G; Pass 2 TD; Rush 1 TD; Rec 1 TD; Tot TD 2; 12 Pt. **1927** ChiB: 14 G; Pass 1 TD; Rec 1 TD; 6 Pt. **1928** ChiB: 12 G; Pass 1 TD; Rush 2 TD; 12 Pt. **1929** ChiB: 13 G; Rush 3 TD; 18 Pt. **1930** ChiB: 10 G; Pass 1 TD; Rush 1 TD; Scor 7, 1 XK. **1931** ChiB: 10 G. **Total:** 111 G; Pass 7 TD; Rush 10 TD; Rec 3 TD; Tot TD 13.

CHRIS WALSH Walsh, Christopher Lee 6′1″, 194 **WR**
Col: Stanford *HS:* Ygnacio Valley [Concord, CA] B: 12/12/1968, Cleveland, OH *Drafted:* 1992 Round 9 Buf
1992 Buf: 2 G. **1993** Buf: 3 G. **1994** Min: 10 G; KR 1-6 6.0. **1995** Min: 16 G; Rec 7-66 9.4; KR 3-42 14.0. **1996** Min: 15 G; Pass 1-0; Rec 4-39 9.8 1 TD; Scor 1 2XP; 8 Pt. **1997** Min: 14 G; Rec 11-114 10.4 1 TD; KR 1-10 10.0; 6 Pt. **1998** Min: 15 G; Rec 2-46 23.0. **Total:** 75 G; Pass 1-0; Rec 24-265 11.0 2 TD; KR 5-58 11.6; Scor 1 2XP; 14 Pt.

ED WALSH Walsh, Edward Henry 6′4″, 243 **OT**
Col: Widener *HS:* Eddystone [PA] B: 7/11/1935, Fort Meade, MD
1961 NYT: 6 G; KR 2-15 7.5.

JIM WALSH Walsh, James Kevin 5′11″, 220 **RB**
Col: San Jose State *HS:* Serra [San Mateo, CA] B: 12/17/1956, Burlingame, CA
1980 Sea: 4 G; Rush 2-4 2.0.

STEVE WALSH Walsh, Steven John 6′3″, 207 **QB**
Col: Miami (Fla.) *HS:* Cretin [St. Paul, MN] B: 12/1/1966, St. Paul, MN
Drafted: 1989 Supplemental Round 1 Dal

		Passing							
Year Team	**G**	**Att**	**Comp**	**Comp%**	**Yds**	**YPA**	**TD**	**Int**	**Rating**
1989 Dal	8	219	110	50.2	1371	6.26	5	9	60.5
1990 Dal-NO	13	336	179	53.3	2010	5.98	12	13	67.2
1990 Dal	1	9	4	44.4	40	4.44	0	0	57.6
1990 NO	12	327	175	53.5	1970	6.02	12	13	67.5
1991 NO	8	255	141	55.3	1638	6.42	11	6	79.5
1993 NO	2	38	20	52.6	271	7.13	2	3	60.3
1994 ChiB	12	343	208	60.6	2078	6.06	10	8	77.9
1995 ChiB	1	0	0	—	0	—	0	0	—

1996 StL	3	77	33	42.9	344	4.47	0	5	29.4
1997 TB	12	17	6	35.3	58	3.41	0	1	21.2
1998 TB	5	19	9	47.4	58	3.05	0	3	14.7
NFL Total	64	1304	706	54.1	7828	6.00	40	48	67.1

	Rushing				
Year Team	Att	Yds	Avg	TD	Fum
1989 Dal	6	16	2.7	0	3
1990 Dal-NO	20	25	1.3	0	6
1990 Dal	1	0	0.0	0	1
1990 NO	19	25	1.3	0	5
1991 NO	8	0	0.0	0	3
1993 NO	4	-4	-1.0	0	0
1994 ChiB	30	4	0.1	1	7
1996 StL	6	10	1.7	0	1
1997 TB	6	-4	-0.7	0	1
NFL Total	80	47	0.6	1	21

BILL WALSH Walsh, William Henry 6′2″, 230 **C**
Col: Notre Dame *HS:* Phillipsburg [NJ] B: 9/8/1927, Phillipsburg, NJ
Drafted: 1949 Round 3 Pit
1949 Pit: 12 G. **1950** Pit: 12 G. **1951** Pit: 12 G. **1952** Pit: 12 G. **1953** Pit: 12 G. **1954** Pit: 12 G. **Total:** 72 G.

WARD WALSH Walsh, William Ward 6′0″, 213 **RB**
Col: Colorado *HS:* Paradise [CA] B: 11/21/1947, Paradise, CA
1971 Hou: Rec 6-36 6.0 1 TD; KR 1-24 24.0. **1972** Hou-GB: Rec 4-22 5.5. Hou: Rec 4-22 5.5. **Total:** Rec 10-58 5.8 1 TD; KR 1-24 24.0.

		Rushing					Tot
Year Team	G	Att	Yds	Avg	TD	Fum	TD
1971 Hou	13	38	129	3.4	0	2	1
1972 Hou-GB	8	8	36	4.5	0	0	1
1972 Hou	6	8	36	4.5	0	0	1
1972 GB	2	0	0	—	0	0	0
NFL Total	21	46	165	3.6	0	2	2

BULLETS WALSON Walson, Charles 174 **BB**
Col: No College B: 1/6/1893 D: 12/1963, NJ
1921 Was: 2 G; Rec 1 TD; 6 Pt.

BOBBY WALSTON Walston, Robert Harold 6′0″, 190 **OE**
Col: Georgia *HS:* Linden-McKinley [Columbus, GA]; B: 10/17/1928, Columbus, OH D: 10/7/1987, Roselle, IL *Drafted:* 1951 Round 14 Phi
1951 Phi: KR 5-57 11.4. **1952** Phi: PR 2-13 6.5. **1955** Phi: Rush 1-(-3) -3.0. **1957** Phi: Rush 1-7 7.0. **1959** Phi: Rush 2-8 4.0. **Total:** Rush 4-12 3.0; PR 2-13 6.5; KR 5-57 11.4.

		Receiving			
Year Team	G	Rec	Yds	Avg	TD
1951 Phi	12	31	512	16.5	8
1952 Phi	12	26	469	18.0	3
1953 Phi	12	41	750	18.3	5
1954 Phi	12	31	581	18.7	11
1955 Phi	12	27	443	16.4	3
1956 Phi	12	39	590	15.1	3
1957 Phi	12	11	266	24.2	1
1958 Phi	12	21	298	14.2	3
1959 Phi	12	16	279	17.4	3
1960 Phi	12	30	563	18.8	4
1961 Phi	14	34	569	16.7	2
1962 Phi	14	4	43	10.8	0
NFL Total	148	311	5363	17.2	46

	Scoring							
Year Team	Pts	FG	FGA	FG%	XK	XKA	XK%	Fum
1951 Phi	94	6	11	54.5	28	31	90.3	1
1952 Phi	82	11	20	55.0	31	31	100.0	1
1953 Phi	87	4	13	30.8	45	48	93.8	0
1954 Phi	**114**	4	10	40.0	36	39	92.3	0
1955 Phi	30	2	3	66.7	6	7	85.7	0
1956 Phi	53	6	13	46.2	17	18	94.4	0
1957 Phi	53	9	12	**75.0**	20	21	**95.2**	1
1958 Phi	67	6	14	42.9	31	31	100.0	0
1959 Phi	51	0	1	0.0	33	34	97.1	1
1960 Phi	105	14	20	**70.0**	39	40	**97.5**	0
1961 Phi	97	14	25	56.0	43	**46**	93.5	0
1962 Phi	48	4	15	26.7	36	38	94.7	0
NFL Total	881	80	157	51.0	365	384	95.1	4

DAVE WALTER Walter, David Lee Russell 6′3″, 230 **QB**
Col: Michigan Tech *HS:* Meridian [Sanford, MI] B: 12/9/1964, West Branch, MI *Drafted:* 1987 Round 11 NYG
1987 Cin: 3 G; Pass 21-10 47.6%, 113 5.38; Rush 16-70 4.4; 6 Fum.

JOE WALTER Walter, Joseph Follmann Jr. 6′7″, 292 **OT-OG**
Col: Texas Tech *HS:* North Garland [Garland, TX] B: 6/18/1963, Dallas, TX *Drafted:* 1985 Round 7 Cin
1985 Cin: 14 G. **1986** Cin: 15 G. **1987** Cin: 12 G. **1988** Cin: 16 G. **1989** Cin: 10 G. **1990** Cin: 16 G. **1991** Cin: 15 G. **1992** Cin: 16 G. **1993** Cin: 16 G. **1995** Cin: 16 G. **1996** Cin: 15 G. **1997** Cin: 5 G. **Total:** 166 G.

KEN WALTER Walter, Kenneth Matthew Jr. 6′1″, 195 **P**
Col: Kent State *HS:* Euclid [OH] B: 8/15/1972, Cleveland, OH
1997 Car: Rush 1-(-5) -5.0. **1998** Car: Pass 1-0; Rush 3-0.
Total: Pass 1-0; Rush 4-(-5) -1.3.

		Punting			
Year Team	G	Punts	Yds	Avg	Fum
1997 Car	16	85	3604	42.4	0
1998 Car	16	77	3131	40.7	2
NFL Total	32	162	6735	41.6	2

MICHAEL WALTER Walter, Michael David 6′3″, 240 **LB**
Col: Oregon *HS:* Henry D. Sheldon [Eugene, OR] B: 11/30/1960, Salem, OR *Drafted:* 1983 Round 2 Dal
1983 Dal: 15 G. **1984** SF: 16 G; 1 Sac. **1985** SF: 14 G; Int 1-0; 3 Sac. **1986** SF: 16 G; 1 Sac. **1987** SF: 12 G; Int 1-16. **1988** SF: 16 G; 1 Sac. **1989** SF: 16 G; 1 Sac. **1990** SF: 3 G. **1991** SF: 11 G. **1992** SF: 15 G; 1 Sac. **1993** SF: 15 G. **Total:** 149 G; Int 2-16; 8 Sac.

DALE WALTERS Walters, Dale James 6′0″, 200 **P**
Col: Rice *HS:* Grand Prairie [TX] B: 6/21/1961, Dighton, KS
1987 Cle: 2 G; Punt 11-400 36.4.

DANNY WALTERS Walters, Daniel Eugene 6′1″, 189 **DB**
Col: Arkansas *HS:* Percy L. Julian [Chicago, IL] B: 11/4/1960, Prescott, AR *Drafted:* 1983 Round 4 SD

		Interceptions		
Year Team	G	Int	Yds	TD
1983 SD	16	7	55	0
1984 SD	8	0	0	0
1985 SD	16	5	71	0
1986 SD	2	0	0	0
1987 SD	12	0	0	0
NFL Total	54	12	126	0

JOEY WALTERS Walters, Joseph Laverne 6′0″, 175 **WR**
Col: Clemson *HS:* West Florence [Florence, SC] B: 10/29/1954, Florence, SC
1987 Hou: 5 G; Rec 5-99 19.8; PR 2-19 9.5; KR 1-18 18.0.

LES WALTERS Walters, Lester Kenneth Jr. 6′0″, 185 **DB**
Col: Penn State *HS:* Milton S. Hershey [Hershey, PA] B: 2/13/1937, Palmyra, PA *Drafted:* 1958 Round 4 Bal
1958 Was: 8 G; Int 1-19.

PETE WALTERS Walters, Peter 6′2″, 265 **OG**
Col: Western Kentucky *HS:* Webster Co. [Dixon, KY] B: 3/17/1959, Compton, CA
1987 Phi: 3 G.

STAN WALTERS Walters, Stanley Peter 6′6″, 275 **OT**
Col: Syracuse *HS:* St. Mary's [Rutherford, NJ]; Bordentown Mil. Inst. [NJ] B: 5/27/1948, Rutherford, NJ *Drafted:* 1972 Round 9 Cin
1972 Cin: 8 G. **1973** Cin: 4 G. **1974** Cin: 14 G. **1975** Phi: 14 G. **1976** Phi: 14 G. **1977** Phi: 14 G. **1978** Phi: 16 G. **1979** Phi: 16 G. **1980** Phi: 16 G. **1981** Phi: 16 G. **1982** Phi: 9 G. **1983** Phi: 12 G. **Total:** 153 G.

TOM WALTERS Walters, Thomas Herrin 6′2″, 195 **DB**
Col: Pearl River CC MS; Southern Mississippi *HS:* Petal [MS]
B: 6/11/1942, Petal, MS *Drafted:* 1964 Round 16 Was
1964 Was: 13 G; Int 2-36. **1965** Was: 14 G; KR 2-30 15.0; Int 1-63 1 TD; 6 Pt. **1966** Was: 12 G. **1967** Was: 10 G. **Total:** 49 G; KR 2-30 15.0; Int 3-99 1 TD; 6 Pt.

ROD WALTERS Walters, Wayne Roderick 6′3″, 258 **OG-OT**
Col: Iowa *HS:* Berkley [MI] B: 2/27/1954, Lansing, MI *Drafted:* 1976 Round 1 KC
1976 KC: 14 G. **1978** KC: 16 G. **1979** KC: 16 G. **1980** KC-Mia-Det: 9 G. KC: 6 G. Mia: 1 G. Det: 2 G. **Total:** 55 G.

LEN WALTERSCHEID Walterscheid, Leonard Raymond 5′11″, 190 **DB**
Col: Southern Utah *HS:* Grand [Moab, UT] B: 9/13/1954, Gainesville, TX
1978 ChiB: Int 1-0. **1979** ChiB: Int 1-15. **1980** ChiB: Int 4-84 1 TD.
1981 ChiB: Int 1-0. **Total:** Int 7-99 1 TD.

		Punt Returns				Kickoff Returns				
Year Team	G	Ret	Yds	Avg	TD	Ret	Yds	Avg	TD	Fum
1977 ChiB	14	6	59	9.8	0	3	59	19.7	0	2
1978 ChiB	14	3	24	8.0	0	11	335	30.5	0	0
1979 ChiB	15	14	96	6.9	0	19	427	22.5	0	2
1980 ChiB	15	33	239	7.2	0	1	12	12.0	0	0
1981 ChiB	6	1	6	6.0	0	0	0	—	0	0
1982 ChiB	9	0	0	—	0	0	0	—	0	0
1983 Buf	3	0	0	—	0	0	0	—	0	0
1984 Buf	3	0	0	—	0	0	0	—	0	0
NFL Total	79	57	424	7.4	0	34	833	24.5	0	4

ALVIN WALTON Walton, Alvin Earl 6'0", 180 **DB**
Col: Mount San Jacinto Coll. CA (J.C.); Kansas *HS:* Banning [CA]
B: 3/14/1964, Riverside, CA *Drafted:* 1986 Round 3 Was
1986 Was: 1 Sac. **1987** Was: 3 Sac. **1988** Was: 1 Sac. **Total:** 5 Sac.

		Interceptions			
Year Team	**G**	**Int**	**Yds**	**TD**	**Fum**
1986 Was	16	0	0	0	0
1987 Was	12	3	28	0	0
1988 Was	16	3	54	0	0
1989 Was	13	4	58	1	1
1990 Was	16	2	118	1	0
1991 Was	4	0	0	0	0
NFL Total	77	12	258	2	1

BRUCE WALTON Walton, Bruce Edward 6'6", 251 **OT-OG-C**
Col: UCLA *HS:* Helix [La Mesa, CA] B: 6/14/1951, San Diego, CA
Drafted: 1973 Round 5 Dal
1973 Dal: 7 G; KR 1-11 11.0. **1974** Dal: 13 G. **1975** Dal: 13 G. **Total:** 33 G; KR 1-11 11.0.

CHUCK WALTON Walton, Charles Richard 6'3", 255 **OG**
Col: Iowa State *HS:* Canon City [CO] B: 7/7/1941, Shattuck, OK
Drafted: 1963 Round 4 Det
1967 Det: 14 G; Rec 1-(-4) -4.0. **1968** Det: 14 G. **1969** Det: 14 G.
1970 Det: 14 G. **1971** Det: 14 G. **1972** Det: 10 G. **1973** Det: 4 G.
1974 Det: 14 G. **Total:** 98 G; Rec 1-(-4) -4.0.

FRANK WALTON Walton, Frank Joseph 5'11", 230 **G**
(Tiger) *Col:* Pittsburgh *HS:* Beaver Falls [PA] B: 12/25/1911, Beaver Falls, PA D: 9/22/1953, Beaver Falls, PA
1934 Bos: 12 G. **1944** Was: 10 G. **1945** Was: 3 G. **Total:** 25 G.

WAYNE WALTON Walton, Gerald Wayne 6'5", 255 **OT-OG**
Col: Abilene Christian *HS:* Azle [TX] B: 10/15/1948, Waco, TX
Drafted: 1971 Round 2 NYG
1971 NYG: 14 G; KR 1-0. **1973** KC: 14 G. **1974** KC: 9 G. **Total:** 37 G; KR 1-0.

JOHN WALTON Walton, John B 6'2", 210 **QB**
Col: Elizabeth City State *HS:* P.W. Moore [Elizabeth City, NC]
B: 10/4/1947, Elizabeth City, NC
1976 Phi: Rush 2-1 0.5. **1978** Phi: Rush 2-0. **1979** Phi: Rush 6-(-5) -0.8.
Total: Rush 10-(-4) -0.4.

		Passing								
Year Team	**G**	**Att**	**Comp**	**Comp%**	**Yds**	**YPA**	**TD**	**Int**	**Rating**	**Fum**
1976 Phi	3	28	12	42.9	125	4.46	0	2	26.6	0
1978 Phi	4	1	0	0.0	0	0.00	0	0	39.6	0
1979 Phi	8	36	19	52.8	213	5.92	3	1	86.9	1
NFL Total	15	65	31	47.7	338	5.20	3	3	59.6	1

JOE WALTON Walton, Joseph Frank 5'11", 202 **OE-DE**
Col: Pittsburgh *HS:* Beaver Falls [PA] B: 12/15/1935, Beaver Falls, PA
Drafted: 1957 Round 2 Was
1957 Was: Int 1-55. **Total:** Int 1-55.

		Receiving				
Year Team	**G**	**Rec**	**Yds**	**Avg**	**TD**	**Fum**
1957 Was	12	3	57	19.0	0	0
1958 Was	12	32	532	16.6	5	1
1959 Was	9	21	317	15.1	3	1
1960 Was	12	27	401	14.9	3	0
1961 NYG	12	36	544	15.1	2	1
1962 NYG	13	33	406	12.3	9	1
1963 NYG	12	26	371	14.3	6	0
NFL Total	82	178	2628	14.8	28	4

LARRY WALTON Walton, Larry James 6'0", 180 **WR**
Col: Trinidad State JC CO; Arizona State *HS:* Johnstown [PA]
B: 2/8/1947, Johnstown, PA *Drafted:* 1969 Round 3 Det
1969 Det: Pass 1-1 100.0%, 43 43.00 1 TD; Rush 2-6 3.0; PR 9-24 2.7; KR 12-230 19.2. **1970** Det: Rush 2-20 10.0; PR 2-0; KR 1-21 21.0.
1971 Det: Rush 1-(-7) -7.0; PR 6-38 6.3. **1972** Det: PR 3-(-8) -2.7; KR 0-96. **1973** Det: Rush 5-100 20.0 1 TD; PR 1-9 9.0. **1974** Det: Pass 2-1 50.0%, 29 14.50; Rush 2-3 1.5; KR 1-22 22.0. **1976** Det: Rush 1-5 5.0. **Total:** Pass 3-2 66.7%, 72 24.00 1 TD; Rush 13-127 9.8 1 TD; PR 21-63 3.0; KR 14-369 26.4.

		Receiving					Tot
Year Team	**G**	**Rec**	**Yds**	**Avg**	**TD**	**Fum**	**TD**
1969 Det	14	12	109	9.1	0	0	0
1970 Det	13	30	532	17.7	5	0	5
1971 Det	14	30	491	16.4	5	1	5
1972 Det	14	24	485	20.2	6	2	6
1973 Det	13	22	309	14.0	4	0	5
1974 Det	13	31	404	13.0	3	1	3
1976 Det	14	20	293	14.7	3	0	3
1978 Buf	12	4	66	16.5	1	0	1
NFL Total	107	173	2689	15.5	27	4	28

RILEY WALTON Walton, Riley Henry 6'4", 245 **TE**
Col: Tennessee State *HS:* Pearl [Nashville, TN] B: 8/6/1962, Nashville, TN
1987 KC: 2 G.

SAM WALTON Walton, Samuel Thaw 6'5", 270 **OT**
Col: Texas A&M-Commerce *HS:* Melrose [Memphis, TN] B: 1/3/1943, Memphis, TN *Drafted:* 1968 Round 3 NYJ
1968 NYJ: 14 G. **1969** NYJ: 6 G. **1971** Hou: 14 G. **Total:** 34 G.

WHIP WALTON Walton, Whip 6'2", 225 **LB**
Col: San Diego State *HS:* Bolsa Grande [Garden Grove, CA]
B: 7/16/1955, Westminster, CA *Drafted:* 1978 Round 3 Min
1980 NYG: 2 G.

ZACK WALZ Walz, Zachary Christian 6'4", 228 **LB**
Col: Dartmouth *HS:* Florida Christian [Miami, FL] B: 2/13/1976, Mountain View, CA *Drafted:* 1998 Round 6 Ariz
1998 Ariz: 16 G.

GEORGE WANLESS Wanless, George S 5'8", 160 **WB-OE-G**
Col: No College B: 7/1898, Louisville, KY Deceased
1922 Lou: 1 G. **1923** Lou: 2 G. **Total:** 3 G.

HAL WANTLAND Wantland, Howell Smith 6'0", 195 **DB**
Col: Tennessee *HS:* Columbia Central [TN] B: 7/9/1944, Columbia, TN
Drafted: 1966 Round 16 Was
1966 Mia: 2 G.

WARD Ward **WB**
Deceased
1920 Ham: 3 G.

CARL WARD Ward, Carl Davis 5'9", 180 **DB**
Col: Michigan *HS:* Robert A. Taft [Cincinnati, OH] B: 7/26/1944, Hartsond, AL *Drafted:* 1967 Round 4 Cle
1967 Cle: PR 6-62 10.3; Int 1-0. **1969** NO: PR 1-5 5.0. **Total:** PR 7-67 9.6; Int 1-0.

		Kickoff Returns				
Year Team	**G**	**Ret**	**Yds**	**Avg**	**TD**	**Fum**
1967 Cle	14	22	546	24.8	1	3
1968 Cle	14	13	236	18.2	0	2
1969 NO	2	3	58	19.3	0	1
NFL Total	30	38	840	22.1	1	6

CHRIS WARD Ward, Christopher Jamal 6'3", 271 **DE**
Col: Kentucky *HS:* Southwest DeKalb [Decatur, GA] B: 2/4/1974, Atlanta, GA *Drafted:* 1997 Round 7 Bal
1997 Bal: 5 G.

CHRIS WARD Ward, Christopher Lamar 6'3", 267 **OT**
Col: Ohio State *HS:* Patterson Cooperative [Dayton, OH]
B: 12/16/1955, Cleveland, OH *Drafted:* 1978 Round 1 NYJ
1978 NYJ: 16 G. **1979** NYJ: 16 G. **1980** NYJ: 14 G. **1981** NYJ: 16 G.
1982 NYJ: 9 G. **1983** NYJ: 16 G. **1984** NO: 13 G. **Total:** 100 G.

DAVID WARD Ward, David 5'10", 195 **OE-DE**
(Nubbin) *Col:* Haskell Indian; New Mexico B: 3/10/1907 D: 3/1982, Clouis, NM
1933 Bos: 1 G.

DAVID WARD Ward, David Fontaine 6'2", 230 **LB**
Col: Southern Arkansas *HS:* Central [West Helena, AR] B: 3/10/1964, Helena, AR
1987 Cin: 3 G; 1 Sac. **1989** NE: 16 G. **Total:** 19 G; 1 Sac.

DEDRIC WARD Ward, Dedric Lamar 5'9", 184 **WR**
Col: Northern Iowa *HS:* George Washington [Cedar Rapids, IA]
B: 9/29/1974, Cedar Rapids, IA *Drafted:* 1997 Round 3 NYJ
1997 NYJ: Rush 2-25 12.5; PR 8-55 6.9; KR 2-10 5.0. **1998** NYJ: Rush 2-7 3.5; PR 8-72 9.0; KR 3-60 20.0. **Total:** Rush 4-32 8.0; PR 16-127 7.9; KR 5-70 14.0.

		Receiving				
Year Team	**G**	**Rec**	**Yds**	**Avg**	**TD**	**Fum**
1997 NYJ	11	18	212	11.8	1	1
1998 NYJ	16	25	477	19.1	4	0
NFL Total	27	43	689	16.0	5	1

ELMER WARD Ward, Elmer Henry 6'2", 215 **C-LB**
(Bear) *Col:* Utah State *HS:* Bingham [Riverton, UT]; Box Elder HS [Brigham City, UT] B: 10/13/1912, Willard, UT D: 3/26/1996, Ogden, UT
1935 Det: 11 G.

HINES WARD Ward, Hines Jr. 6'0", 194 **WR**
Col: Georgia *HS:* Forest Park [GA] B: 3/8/1976, Rex, GA
Drafted: 1998 Round 3 Pit
1998 Pit: 16 G; Pass 1-1 100.0%, 17 17.00; Rush 1-13 13.0; Rec 15-246 16.4.

JIM WARD Ward, James Edgar Harold 6'2", 196 QB
Col: Gettysburg *HS:* Gaithersburg [MD] B: 7/16/1944, Frederick, MD
Drafted: 1966 Round 14 Bal
1967 Bal: 6 G; Pass 16-9 56.3%, 115 7.19 2 TD 1 Int; Rush 5-23 4.6.
1968 Bal: 5 G; Pass 9-3 33.3%, 46 5.11 1 Int; 1 Fum. **1971** Phi: 2 G; Pass 1-1 100.0%, 4 4.00. **Total:** 13 G; Pass 26-13 50.0%, 165 6.35 2 TD 2 Int; Rush 5-23 4.6; 1 Fum.

JOHNNY WARD Ward, John 6'2", 215 T
Col: Rancho Santiago Coll. CA (J.C.); USC *HS:* Garden Grove [CA]
B: 1907
1930 Fra-Min: 13 G. Fra: 4 G. Min: 9 G. **Total:** 13 G.

JOHN WARD Ward, John Henry 6'4", 258 OG-DE-C
Col: Oklahoma State *HS:* Will Rogers [Tulsa, OK] B: 5/27/1948, Enid, OK *Drafted:* 1970 Round 1 Min
1970 Min: 14 G. **1971** Min: 14 G. **1972** Min: 14 G. **1973** Min: 8 G; Rec 1-1 1.0. **1975** Min: 14 G. **1976** TB-ChiB: 14 G. TB: 4 G. ChiB: 10 G.
Total: 78 G; Rec 1-1 1.0.

PAUL WARD Ward, Paul Earl 6'3", 247 DT-OG
Col: Whitworth *HS:* Burbank [CA] B: 1/30/1937, Santa Fe, NM
1961 Det: 8 G. **1962** Det: 6 G. **Total:** 14 G.

PHILLIP WARD Ward, Phillip Eugene 6'2", 235 LB
Col: UCLA *HS:* Pius X [Downey, CA] B: 11/11/1974, Gardena, CA
1998 StL: 2 G.

RONNIE WARD Ward, Rodney Glen 6'0", 232 LB
Col: Kansas *HS:* Hazelwood East [St. Louis, MO] B: 2/11/1974, St. Louis, MO *Drafted:* 1997 Round 3 Mia
1997 Mia: 4 G.

BILL WARD Ward, William Clark 6'0", 230 G
(Smiley) *Col:* Washington State; Washington *HS:* Sequim [WA]
B: 2/19/1921, Sequim, WA D: 12/3/1992, Bellingham, WA
1946 Was: 10 G; KR 1-2 2.0. **1947** Was-Det: 10 G. Was: 6 G. Det: 4 G.
1948 Det: 12 G. **1949** Det: 12 G. **Total:** 44 G; KR 1-2 2.0.

BILL WARD Ward, William Hogan 6'0", 212 T
Col: Pennsylvania B: 1898 D: 5/21/1973
1921 Buf: 9 G; 6 Pt.

DUANE WARDLOW Wardlow, Clyde Duane 6'4", 215 DE
Col: Washington *HS:* Hoquiam [WA] B: 7/2/1932
1954 LARm: 12 G. **1956** LARm: 9 G. **Total:** 21 G.

ANDRE WARE Ware, Andre Trevor 6'2", 205 QB
Col: Alvin CC TX; Houston *HS:* Dickinson [TX] B: 7/31/1968, Galveston, TX *Drafted:* 1990 Round 1 Det

		Passing							
Year Team	**G**	**Att**	**Comp**	**Comp%**	**Yds**	**YPA**	**TD**	**Int**	**Rating**
1990 Det	4	30	13	43.3	164	5.47	1	2	44.3
1991 Det	1	0	0	—	0	—	0	0	—
1992 Det	4	86	50	58.1	677	7.87	3	4	75.6
1993 Det	5	45	20	44.4	271	6.02	1	2	53.1
NFL Total	14	161	83	51.6	1112	6.91	5	8	63.5

	Rushing				
Year Team	**Att**	**Yds**	**Avg**	**TD**	**Fum**
1990 Det	7	64	9.1	0	0
1991 Det	4	6	1.5	0	1
1992 Det	20	124	6.2	0	6
1993 Det	7	23	3.3	0	0
NFL Total	38	217	5.7	0	7

CHARLIE WARE Ware, Charles 6'3", 245 T
Col: Birmingham-Southern *HS:* Citronelle [AL] B: 3/2/1918, Atlanta, GA
1944 Bkn: 7 G.

DEREK WARE Ware, Derek Gene 6'2", 251 TE
Col: Sacramento City Coll. CA (J.C.); Texas A&M; Central Oklahoma
HS: Christian Brothers [Sacramento, CA] B: 9/17/1967, Sacramento, CA *Drafted:* 1992 Round 7 Pho
1992 Pho: 15 G; Rec 1-13 13.0. **1993** Pho: 16 G; Rec 3-45 15.0.
1994 Ariz: 15 G; Rec 17-171 10.1 1 TD; 6 Pt; 1 Fum. **1995** Cin: 7 G; Rec 2-36 18.0. **1996** Dal: 5 G; Rec 1-5 5.0. **Total:** 58 G; Rec 24-270 11.3 1 TD; 6 Pt; 1 Fum.

TIMMIE WARE Ware, Timothy Eugene 5'10", 171 WR
Col: USC *HS:* Centennial [Compton, CA] B: 4/2/1962, Los Angeles, CA
1986 SD: 9 G; Rec 1-11 11.0. **1987** SD: 12 G; Rec 2-38 19.0. **1989** LARd: 13 G; KR 4-86 21.5; 1 Fum. **Total:** 34 G; Rec 3-49 16.3; KR 4-86 21.5; 1 Fum.

WAR EAGLE War Eagle 5'9", 195 T-G
Col: No College Deceased
1922 Oor: 5 G.

ERIC WARFIELD Warfield, Eric Andrew 6'0", 192 DB
Col: Nebraska *HS:* Arkansas [Texarkana, AR] B: 3/3/1976, Vicksburg, MS *Drafted:* 1998 Round 7 KC
1998 KC: 12 G.

PAUL WARFIELD Warfield, Paul Dryden 6'0", 188 WR
Col: Ohio State *HS:* Warren G. Harding [Warren, OH] B: 11/28/1942, Warren, OH *Drafted:* 1964 Round 1 Cle *HOF:* 1983
1964 Cle: KR 1-4 4.0. **1966** Cle: **1** Fum TD. **1967** Cle: Rush 2-10 5.0.
1969 Cle: Rush 2-23 11.5. **1970** Mia: Rush 2-13 6.5. **1971** Mia: Rush 9-115 12.8. **1972** Mia: Rush 4-23 5.8. **1973** Mia: Rush 1-15 15.0.
1976 Cle: Rush 1-3 3.0. **1977** Cle: Rush 1-2 2.0. **Total:** Rush 22-204 9.3; KR 1-4 4.0; 1 Fum TD.

		Receiving					Tot
Year Team	**G**	**Rec**	**Yds**	**Avg**	**TD**	**Fum**	**TD**
1964 Cle	14	52	920	17.7	9	0	9
1965 Cle	1	3	30	10.0	0	0	0
1966 Cle	14	36	741	20.6	5	0	6
1967 Cle	14	32	702	21.9	8	0	8
1968 Cle	14	50	1067	21.3	**12**	0	12
1969 Cle	14	42	886	21.1	10	0	10
1970 Mia	11	28	703	25.1	6	0	6
1971 Mia	14	43	996	23.2	**11**	3	11
1972 Mia	12	29	606	20.9	3	1	3
1973 Mia	14	29	514	17.7	11	1	11
1974 Mia	9	27	536	19.9	2	0	2
1976 Cle	14	38	613	16.1	6	3	6
1977 Cle	12	18	251	13.9	2	0	2
NFL Total	157	427	8565	20.1	85	8	86

ERNIE WARLICK Warlick, Ernest 6'3", 235 TE
Col: North Carolina Central *HS:* Ridgeview [Hickory, NC]
B: 7/21/1932, Washington, DC

		Receiving				
Year Team	**G**	**Rec**	**Yds**	**Avg**	**TD**	**Fum**
1962 Buf	14	35	482	13.8	2	1
1963 Buf	14	24	479	20.0	1	0
1964 Buf	14	23	478	20.8	0	0
1965 Buf	14	8	112	14.0	1	0
NFL Total	56	90	1551	17.2	4	1

JIM WARNE Warne, James E Jr. 6'7", 315 OT
Col: Mesa CC AZ; Arizona State *HS:* Tempe [AZ] B: 11/27/1964, Phoenix, AZ
1987 Det: 3 G.

CHARLEY WARNER Warner, Charles Allen 6'0", 176 DB-HB
Col: Prairie View A&M *HS:* Booker T. Washington [Granger, TX]
B: 4/14/1940, Granger, TX
1963 KC: PR 4-25 6.3; Int 1-12. **1964** KC-Buf: PR 12-165 13.8; Int 1-30. KC: PR 9-110 12.2. Buf: PR 3-55 18.3; Int 1-30. **1965** Buf: Rush 1-2 2.0; Rec 1-11 11.0 1 TD; PR 1-16 16.0; Int 5-84 1 TD. **Total:** Rush 1-2 2.0; Rec 1-11 11.0 1 TD; PR 17-206 12.1; Int 7-126 1 TD.

		Kickoff Returns					Tot
Year Team	**G**	**Ret**	**Yds**	**Avg**	**TD**	**Fum**	**TD**
1963 KC	14	9	215	23.9	0	0	0
1964 KC-Buf	9	12	301	25.1	0	3	0
1964 KC	5	7	180	25.7	0	1	0
1964 Buf	4	5	121	24.2	0	2	0
1965 Buf	14	32	825	25.8	**2**	1	4
1966 Buf	14	33	846	25.6	1	1	1
NFL Total	51	86	2187	25.4	3	5	5

CURT WARNER Warner, Curtis Edward 5'11", 205 RB
Col: Penn State *HS:* Pineville [WV] B: 3/18/1961, Wyoming, WV
Drafted: 1983 Round 1 Sea

		Rushing				Receiving					Tot
Year Team	**G**	**Att**	**Yds**	**Avg**	**TD**	**Rec**	**Yds**	**Avg**	**TD**	**Fum**	**TD**
1983 Sea	16	335	1449	4.3	13	42	325	7.7	1	6	14
1984 Sea	1	10	40	4.0	0	1	19	19.0	0	0	0
1985 Sea	16	291	1094	3.8	8	47	307	6.5	1	8	9
1986 Sea	16	319	1481	4.6	13	41	342	8.3	0	6	13
1987 Sea	12	234	985	4.2	8	17	167	9.8	2	4	10
1988 Sea	16	266	1025	3.9	10	22	154	7.0	2	5	12
1989 Sea	16	194	631	3.3	3	23	153	6.7	1	7	4
1990 LARm	7	49	139	2.8	1	0	0	—	0	1	1
NFL Total	100	1698	6844	4.0	56	193	1467	7.6	7	37	63

KURT WARNER Warner, Kurtis Eugene 6'2", 220 QB
Col: Northern Iowa *HS:* Regis [Cedar Rapids, IA] B: 6/22/1971, Burlington, IA
1998 StL: 1 G; Pass 11-4 36.4%, 39 3.55.

RON WARNER Warner, Ron 6'2", 249 LB
Col: Independence CC KS; Kansas *HS:* Independence [KS]
B: 9/26/1975, Independence, KS *Drafted:* 1998 Round 7 NO
1998 NO: 1 G.

DAVID WARNKE Warnke, David 5′11″, 185 **K**
Col: Augsburg *HS:* Windsor [CO] B: 12/30/1960
1983 TB: 1 G; Scor 1, 0-1 FG, 1-2 50.0% XK.

WARREN Warren **WB**
Col: No College Deceased
1920 Ham: 2 G.

BUSS WARREN Warren, Buist Lamb 5′11″, 175 **TB-DB-HB**
Col: Tennessee *HS:* Miami Edison [FL] B: 8/13/1916, Provo, UT
D: 5/1986, Newhall, CA
1945 Phi-Pit: Rec 1-(-1) -1.0; PR 13-168 12.9; KR 5-135 27.0; Int 1-19. Pit: Rec 1-(-1) -1.0; PR 13-168 12.9; KR 5-135 27.0; Int 1-19. **Total:** Rec 1-(-1) -1.0; PR 13-168 12.9; KR 5-135 27.0; Int 1-19.

		Passing							
Year Team	**G**	**Att**	**Comp**	**Comp%**	**Yds**	**YPA**	**TD**	**Int**	**Rating**
1945 Phi-Pit	9	92	36	39.1	368	4.00	0	10	11.8
1945 Phi	1	0	0	—	0	—	0	0	—
1945 Pit	8	92	36	39.1	368	4.00	0	10	11.8
NFL Total	9	92	36	39.1	368	4.00	0	10	11.8

	Rushing				
Year Team	**Att**	**Yds**	**Avg**	**TD**	**Fum**
1945 Phi-Pit	96	285	3.0	2	5
1945 Phi	1	-7	-7.0	0	1
1945 Pit	95	292	3.1	2	4
NFL Total	96	285	3.0	2	5

CHRIS WARREN Warren, Christopher Collins Jr. 6′2″, 228 **RB**
Col: Virginia; Ferrum *HS:* Robinson Secondary School [Fairfax, VA]
B: 1/24/1968, Silver Spring, MD *Drafted:* 1990 Round 4 Sea
1994 Sea: Scor 1 2XP. **1996** Sea: Scor 1 2XP. **Total:** Scor 2 2XP.

		Rushing				Receiving			
Year Team	**G**	**Att**	**Yds**	**Avg**	**TD**	**Rec**	**Yds**	**Avg**	**TD**
1990 Sea	16	6	11	1.8	1	0	0	—	0
1991 Sea	16	11	13	1.2	0	2	9	4.5	0
1992 Sea	16	223	1017	4.6	3	16	134	8.4	0
1993 Sea	14	273	1072	3.9	7	15	99	6.6	0
1994 Sea	16	333	1545	4.6	9	41	323	7.9	2
1995 Sea	16	310	1346	4.3	15	35	247	7.1	1
1996 Sea	14	203	855	4.2	5	40	273	6.8	0
1997 Sea	15	200	847	4.2	4	45	257	5.7	0
1998 Dal	9	59	291	4.9	4	13	66	5.1	1
NFL Total	132	1618	6997	4.3	48	207	1408	6.8	4

	Punt Returns				Kickoff Returns					Tot
Year Team	**Ret**	**Yds**	**Avg**	**TD**	**Ret**	**Yds**	**Avg**	**TD**	**Fum**	**TD**
1990 Sea	28	269	9.6	0	23	478	20.8	0	3	1
1991 Sea	32	298	9.3	1	35	792	22.6	0	3	1
1992 Sea	34	252	7.4	0	28	524	18.7	0	2	3
1993 Sea	0	0	—	0	0	0	—	0	3	7
1994 Sea	0	0	—	0	0	0	—	0	5	11
1995 Sea	0	0	—	0	0	0	—	0	5	16
1996 Sea	0	0	—	0	0	0	—	0	3	5
1997 Sea	0	0	—	0	0	0	—	0	2	4
1998 Dal	2	11	5.5	0	5	90	18.0	0	0	5
NFL Total	96	830	8.6	1	91	1884	20.7	0	26	53

DON WARREN Warren, Donald James 6′4″, 242 **TE**
Col: Mount San Antonio Coll. CA (J.C.); San Diego State *HS:* Royal Oak [Covina, CA] B: 5/5/1956, Bellingham, WA *Drafted:* 1979 Round 4 Was
1985 Was: Rush 1-5 5.0. **Total:** Rush 1-5 5.0.

		Receiving				
Year Team	**G**	**Rec**	**Yds**	**Avg**	**TD**	**Fum**
1979 Was	16	26	303	11.7	0	0
1980 Was	13	31	323	10.4	0	1
1981 Was	16	29	335	11.6	1	0
1982 Was	9	27	310	11.5	0	0
1983 Was	13	20	225	11.3	2	0
1984 Was	16	18	192	10.7	0	0
1985 Was	16	15	163	10.9	1	0
1986 Was	16	20	164	8.2	1	1
1987 Was	12	7	43	6.1	0	0
1988 Was	14	12	112	9.3	0	1
1989 Was	15	15	167	11.1	1	0
1990 Was	16	15	123	8.2	1	0
1991 Was	10	5	51	10.2	0	0
1992 Was	11	4	25	6.3	0	0
NFL Total	193	244	2536	10.4	7	3

FRANK WARREN Warren, Frank William III 6′4″, 285 **DE-NT**
Col: Auburn *HS:* Phillips [Birmingham, AL] B: 9/14/1959, Birmingham, AL *Drafted:* 1981 Round 3 NO
1981 NO: 16 G. **1982** NO: 9 G; 1 Sac. **1983** NO: 16 G; Int 1-6; 2 Sac. **1984** NO: 16 G; 4 Sac. **1985** NO: 16 G; **1** Fum TD; Tot TD 2; 12 Pt; 5.5 Sac. **1986** NO: 16 G; 7.5 Sac. **1987** NO: 12 G; 6 Sac. **1988** NO: 16 G; 1 Sac. **1989** NO: 16 G; Scor **1** Saf; 2 Pt; 9.5 Sac. **1991** NO: 16 G; 6 Pt; 7 Sac. **1992** NO: 16 G; 4 Sac. **1993** NO: 8 G; 1 Fum TD; 6 Pt; 1 Sac. **1994** NO: 16 G; 4 Sac. **Total:** 189 G; Int 1-6; Scor 1 Saf; 2 Fum TD; Tot TD 4; 26 Pt; 52.5 Sac.

JIMMY WARREN Warren, James David 5′11″, 175 **DB**
(Country) *Col:* Illinois *HS:* Walter L. Cohen [New Orleans, LA]
B: 7/20/1939, Ferriday, LA
1964 SD: PR 1-0. **1967** Mia: **1** Fum TD. **1968** Mia: PR 2-(-1) -0.5. **1973** Oak: PR 1-0. **Total:** PR 4-(-1) -0.3; 1 Fum TD.

		Kickoff Returns				Interceptions				Tot
Year Team	**G**	**Ret**	**Yds**	**Avg**	**TD**	**Int**	**Yds**	**TD**	**Fum**	**TD**
1964 SD	14	13	353	27.2	0	2	28	0	1	0
1965 SD	14	0	0	—	0	5	43	0	0	0
1966 Mia	14	0	0	—	0	5	**198**	1	1	1
1967 Mia	14	0	0	—	0	4	22	0	0	1
1968 Mia	14	10	227	22.7	0	2	27	0	0	0
1969 Mia	13	1	0	0.0	0	0	0	0	0	0
1970 Oak	10	2	47	23.5	0	2	26	0	0	0
1971 Oak	14	0	0	—	0	2	114	2	0	2
1972 Oak	7	4	57	14.3	0	0	0	0	2	0
1973 Oak	10	0	0	—	0	1	0	0	0	0
1974 Oak	14	0	0	—	0	2	58	0	0	0
1977 Oak	2	0	0	—	0	0	0	0	0	0
NFL Total	140	30	684	22.8	0	25	516	3	4	4

JOHN WARREN Warren, John Sheppard 6′0″, 207 **P**
Col: Tennessee *HS:* Wayne Co. [Jesup, GA] B: 11/8/1960, Jesup, GA

		Punting		
Year Team	**G**	**Punts**	**Yds**	**Avg**
1983 Dal	9	39	1551	39.8
1984 Dal	3	21	799	38.0
NFL Total	12	60	2350	39.2

LAMONT WARREN Warren, Lamont Allen 5′11″, 202 **RB**
Col: Colorado *HS:* Susan Miller Dorsey [Los Angeles, CA] B: 1/4/1973, Indianapolis, IN *Drafted:* 1994 Round 6 Ind
1994 Ind: Pass 1-0. **1997** Ind: Pass 1-0. **Total:** Pass 2-0.

		Rushing				Receiving			
Year Team	**G**	**Att**	**Yds**	**Avg**	**TD**	**Rec**	**Yds**	**Avg**	**TD**
1994 Ind	11	18	80	4.4	0	3	47	15.7	0
1995 Ind	12	47	152	3.2	1	17	159	9.4	0
1996 Ind	13	67	230	3.4	1	22	174	7.9	0
1997 Ind	13	28	80	2.9	2	20	192	9.6	0
1998 Ind	12	25	61	2.4	1	11	44	4.0	1
NFL Total	61	185	603	3.3	5	73	616	8.4	1

	Kickoff Returns					Tot
Year Team	**Ret**	**Yds**	**Avg**	**TD**	**Fum**	**TD**
1994 Ind	2	56	28.0	0	0	0
1995 Ind	15	315	21.0	0	1	1
1996 Ind	3	54	18.0	0	3	1
1997 Ind	1	19	19.0	0	0	2
1998 Ind	8	152	19.0	0	0	2
NFL Total	29	596	20.6	0	4	6

DEWEY WARREN Warren, Madison Dewey 6′0″, 205 **QB**
(Swamp Rat) *Col:* Tennessee *HS:* Herschel V. Jenkins [Savannah, GA]
B: 5/7/1945, Savannah, GA *Drafted:* 1968 Round 6 Cin
1968 Cin: Rush 4-17 4.3.

		Passing								
Year Team	**G**	**Att**	**Comp**	**Comp%**	**Yds**	**YPA**	**TD**	**Int**	**Rating**	**Fum**
1968 Cin	7	80	47	58.8	506	6.33	1	4	60.7	2

MORRIE WARREN Warren, Morrison Fulbright 5′11″, 208 **FB-LB**
(Dit) *Col:* Phoenix Coll. AZ (J.C.); Arizona State *HS:* Carver [Phoenix, AZ] B: 12/6/1923, Marlin, TX
AAFC **1948** BknA: 2 G; Rush 1-1 1.0; KR 1-36 36.0.

TERRENCE WARREN Warren, Terrence Lamonte 6′1″, 205 **WR**
Col: Hampton *HS:* John F. Kennedy [Suffolk, VA] B: 8/2/1969, Suffolk, VA *Drafted:* 1993 Round 5 Sea
1993 Sea: 2 G. **1994** Sea: 14 G; Rush 3-15 5.0; KR 14-350 25.0. **1995** SF: 1 G; KR 4-67 16.8. **Total:** 17 G; Rush 3-15 5.0; KR 18-417 23.2.

VINCE WARREN Warren, Vincent Leo 6′0″, 180 **WR**
Col: San Diego State *HS:* Eldorado [Albuquerque, NM] B: 2/18/1963, Little Rock, AR *Drafted:* 1986 Round 5 NYG
1986 NYG: 4 G.

XAVIER WARREN Warren, Xavier Rogerlyn 6′1″, 250 **DE**
(X) *Col:* Tulsa *HS:* Cleburne [TX] B: 8/12/1964, Cleburne, TX
1987 Pit: 2 G; 1 Sac.

TEX WARRINGTON Warrington, Caleb Van Jr. 6'2", 210 C-G-LB
Col: William & Mary; Auburn *HS:* Dover [DE]; Bordentown Mil. Acad. [NJ] B: 3/21/1921, Dover, DE D: 9/20/1993, Gifford, FL
AAFC **1946** BknA: 12 G. **1947** BknA: 13 G; Rec 0-2. **1948** BknA: 14 G. **Total:** 39 G; Rec 0-2.

EARL WARWEG Warweg, Earl 0 5'6", 145 WB
Col: No College *HS:* Mater Dei [Evansville, IN] B: 1/11/1892, Indianapolis, IN D: 12/7/1979, Newburgh, IN
1921 Eva: 1 G.

LONNIE WARWICK Warwick, Lonnie Preston 6'3", 238 LB
Col: Tennessee Tech *HS:* Mount Hope [WV] B: 2/26/1942, Raleigh, WV
1965 Min: PR 1-10 10.0 1 TD. **Total:** PR 1-10 10.0 1 TD.

		Interceptions			
Year Team	**G**	**Int**	**Yds**	**TD**	**Fum**
1965 Min	14	0	0	0	0
1966 Min	12	2	27	0	0
1967 Min	14	2	36	0	1
1968 Min	14	0	0	0	0
1969 Min	14	4	46	0	0
1970 Min	14	3	30	0	0
1971 Min	4	0	0	0	0
1972 Min	6	1	6	0	0
1973 Atl	14	0	0	0	0
1974 Atl	14	0	0	0	0
NFL Total	120	12	145	0	1

RON WARZEKA Warzeka, Ronald Dwain 6'4", 250 DT
Col: Montana State *HS:* Great Falls [MT] B: 12/24/1935, Great Falls, MT *Drafted:* 1957 Round 14 SF
1960 Oak: 14 G.

AL WASHINGTON Washington, Alvin Kent 6'3", 235 LB
Col: Ohio State *HS:* Benedictine [Cleveland, OH] B: 9/25/1958, Erie, PA *Drafted:* 1981 Round 4 NYJ
1981 NYJ: 16 G.

ANTHONY WASHINGTON Washington, Anthony Wayne 6'1", 204 DB
Col: Fresno City Coll. CA (J.C.); California; Fresno State *HS:* Fresno [CA] B: 2/4/1958, San Francisco, CA *Drafted:* 1981 Round 2 Pit
1981 Pit: 16 G; Int 3-46. **1982** Pit: 9 G. **1983** Was: 16 G; Int 4-12; 1 Fum. **1984** Was: 16 G; Int 1-25. **Total:** 57 G; Int 8-83; 1 Fum.

BRIAN WASHINGTON Washington, Brian Wayne 6'1", 210 DB
Col: Nebraska *HS:* Highland Springs [VA] B: 9/10/1965, Richmond, VA *Drafted:* 1988 Round 10 Cle
1988 Cle: 0.5 Sac. **1990** NYJ: 1 Sac. **1991** NYJ: 2 Sac. **1992** NYJ: 1 Sac. **1996** KC: 0.5 Sac. **Total:** 5 Sac.

		Interceptions			
Year Team	**G**	**Int**	**Yds**	**TD**	**Fum**
1988 Cle	16	3	104	1	0
1990 NYJ	14	3	22	0	0
1991 NYJ	16	1	0	0	1
1992 NYJ	16	6	59	1	0
1993 NYJ	16	6	128	1	0
1994 NYJ	15	2	-3	0	0
1995 KC	15	3	100	1	0
1996 KC	16	3	39	0	0
NFL Total	124	27	449	4	1

CHUCK WASHINGTON Washington, Charles Edward 5'11", 186 DB
Col: Arkansas *HS:* Pine Bluff [AR] B: 1/9/1964, Topeka, KS
1987 GB: 3 G.

CHARLES WASHINGTON Washington, Charles Edwin 6'1", 212 DB
Col: Texas; Cameron *HS:* H. Grady Spruce [Dallas, TX] B: 10/8/1966, Shreveport, LA *Drafted:* 1989 Round 7 Ind
1989 Ind: 16 G; PR 1-6 6.0. **1990** KC: 6 G. **1991** KC: 16 G; Int 1-34. **1992** Atl: 14 G. **1993** Atl: 6 G. **1994** Atl: 16 G. **Total:** 74 G; PR 1-6 6.0; Int 1-34.

CHRIS WASHINGTON Washington, Christopher 6'4", 231 LB
Col: Iowa State *HS:* Percy L. Julian [Chicago, IL] B: 3/6/1962, Jackson, MS *Drafted:* 1984 Round 6 TB
1984 TB: 16 G; 5 Sac. **1985** TB: 16 G; 2 Sac. **1986** TB: 16 G; Int 1-12; 4 Sac. **1987** TB: 12 G; 6.5 Sac. **1988** TB: 16 G. **1990** Pho: 8 G. **Total:** 84 G; Int 1-12; 17.5 Sac.

CLARENCE WASHINGTON Washington, Clarence Cornelius Jr. 6'3", 264 DT
Col: Arkansas-Pine Bluff *HS:* Horace Mann [Little Rock, AR] B: 12/23/1946, Little Rock, AR *Drafted:* 1969 Round 11 Pit
1969 Pit: 13 G. **1970** Pit: 14 G; KR 1-0. **Total:** 27 G; KR 1-0.

CLYDE WASHINGTON Washington, Clyde George 6'1", 197 DB-P
Col: Purdue *HS:* Carlisle [PA] B: 3/21/1938, Carlisle, PA D: 12/29/1974, Carlisle, PA *Drafted:* 1960 Round 10 Cle
1960 Bos: 13 G; Rush 2-10 5.0; Int 3-13; Punt 17-539 31.7; 1 Fum. **1961** Bos: 14 G; Rush 1-3 3.0; Int 4-45; 1 Fum. **1963** NYJ: 14 G; Int 2-2. **1964** NYJ: 8 G. **1965** NYJ: 14 G. **Total:** 63 G; Rush 3-13 4.3; Int 9-60; Punt 17-539 31.7; 2 Fum.

DAVE WASHINGTON Washington, David Eugene 6'4", 228 TE
(Mac) *Col:* USC *HS:* Oroville [CA] B: 12/28/1940, Oroville, CA
1968 Den: 2 G; Rec 1-12 12.0.

DAVE WASHINGTON Washington, David Jr. 6'5", 223 LB-TE
Col: Alcorn State *HS:* Druid [Tuscaloosa, AL] B: 9/12/1948, Tuscaloosa, AL *Drafted:* 1970 Round 9 Den
1970 Den: 13 G; KR 1-20 20.0; Scor **1** Saf; 2 Pt. **1971** Den: 14 G; Rec 1-0; Int 1-8. **1972** Buf: 14 G; Rec 1-4 4.0; Int 1-4. **1973** Buf: 7 G. **1974** Buf: 14 G; Int 2-72 1 TD; 1 Fum TD; Tot TD 2; 12 Pt. **1975** SF: 14 G; 6 Pt. **1976** SF: 14 G. **1977** SF: 9 G; Int 2-68. **1978** Det: 16 G. **1979** Det: 7 G. **1980** NO: 16 G. **Total:** 138 G; Rec 2-4 2.0; KR 1-20 20.0; Int 6-152 1 TD; Scor 1 Saf; 1 Fum TD; Tot TD 3; 20 Pt.

DEWAYNE WASHINGTON Washington, Dewayne Neron 5'11", 192 DB
Col: North Carolina State *HS:* Northern [Durham, NC] B: 12/27/1972, Durham, NC *Drafted:* 1994 Round 1 Min
1994 Min: 1 Fum TD. **Total:** 1 Fum TD.

		Interceptions			Tot
Year Team	**G**	**Int**	**Yds**	**TD**	**TD**
1994 Min	16	3	135	2	3
1995 Min	15	1	25	0	0
1996 Min	16	2	27	1	1
1997 Min	16	4	71	0	0
1998 Pit	16	5	178	2	2
NFL Total	79	15	436	5	6

ERIC WASHINGTON Washington, Eric Christopher 6'2", 190 DB
Col: Texas-El Paso; Rice *HS:* McKinley [Washington, DC] B: 4/22/1950, Washington, DC D: 5/14/1984, St. Louis, MO *Drafted:* 1972 Round 10 StL
1972 StL: 6 G. **1973** StL: 9 G. **Total:** 15 G.

GENE WASHINGTON Washington, Eugene 6'3", 208 WR
Col: Michigan State *HS:* George Washington Carver [Baytown, TX] B: 1/25/1944, La Porte, TX *Drafted:* 1967 Round 1 Min

		Receiving				
Year Team	**G**	**Rec**	**Yds**	**Avg**	**TD**	**Fum**
1967 Min	14	13	384	29.5	2	0
1968 Min	14	46	756	16.4	6	1
1969 Min	14	39	821	21.1	9	1
1970 Min	14	44	702	16.0	4	1
1971 Min	13	12	165	13.8	0	1
1972 Min	12	18	259	14.4	2	0
1973 Den	14	10	150	15.0	3	0
NFL Total	95	182	3237	17.8	26	4

GENE WASHINGTON Washington, Eugene Henry 5'9", 172 WR
Col: Georgia *HS:* Lower Richland [Hopkins, SC] B: 6/6/1953, Gadsden, SC *Drafted:* 1977 Round 9 SD
1979 NYG: 2 G.

FRED WASHINGTON Washington, Fred Earl Jr. 6'2", 277 DT
Col: Texas Christian *HS:* Denison [TX] B: 7/11/1967, Denison, TX D: 12/21/1990, Lake Forest, IL *Drafted:* 1990 Round 2 ChiB
1990 ChiB: 11 G.

FRED WASHINGTON Washington, Fred Earl Sr. 6'5", 268 OT
Col: Cisco JC TX; North Texas *HS:* Booker T. Washington [Marlin, TX] B: 6/14/1944, Marlin, TX D: 8/1985, Beaumont, TX
1968 Was: 1 G.

GENE WASHINGTON Washington, Gene Alden 6'2", 185 WR
Col: Stanford *HS:* Long Beach Polytechnic [CA] B: 1/14/1947, Tuscaloosa, AL *Drafted:* 1969 Round 1 SF
1969 SF: Rush 1-(-4) -4.0. **1974** SF: Rush 2-4 2.0. **1975** SF: Pass 1-0; Rush 1-(-4) -4.0. **1976** SF: Rush 1-3 3.0. **1979** Det: Rush 1-24 24.0. **Total:** Pass 1-0; Rush 6-23 3.8.

		Receiving				
Year Team	**G**	**Rec**	**Yds**	**Avg**	**TD**	**Fum**
1969 SF	14	51	711	13.9	3	0
1970 SF	13	53	**1100**	20.8	12	0
1971 SF	14	46	884	19.2	4	0
1972 SF	14	46	918	20.0	**12**	0
1973 SF	13	37	606	16.4	2	1
1974 SF	14	29	615	**21.2**	6	0
1975 SF	14	44	735	16.7	9	1
1976 SF	14	33	457	13.8	6	0
1977 SF	14	32	638	19.9	5	0
1979 Det	16	14	192	13.7	1	0
NFL Total	140	385	6856	17.8	60	2

TEDDY WASHINGTON Washington, Harold L 5′11″, 210 **RB**
Col: Colorado; San Diego State *HS:* Scotlandville [Baton Rouge, LA]
B: 11/20/1945
1968 Cin: 1 G; Rush 1-4 4.0.

HARRY WASHINGTON Washington, Harry 6′0″, 180 **WR**
Col: Grays Harbor Coll. WA (J.C.); Colorado State *HS:* Stadium [Tacoma, WA]; Henry Foss HS [Tacoma, WA] B: 7/30/1956, Tacoma, WA
1978 Min: 10 G; Rec 1-24 24.0; KR 4-71 17.8. **1979** ChiB: 6 G.
Total: 16 G; Rec 1-24 24.0; KR 4-71 17.8.

JAMES WASHINGTON Washington, James McArthur 6′1″, 202 **DB**
Col: UCLA *HS:* David Starr Jordan [Los Angeles, CA] B: 1/10/1965, Los Angeles, CA *Drafted:* 1988 Round 5 LARm
1993 Dal: PR 1-0. **Total:** PR 1-0.

		Interceptions			
Year Team	**G**	**Int**	**Yds**	**TD**	**Fum**
1988 LARm	16	1	7	0	0
1989 LARm	9	0	0	0	0
1990 Dal	15	3	24	0	0
1991 Dal	16	2	9	0	0
1992 Dal	16	3	31	0	0
1993 Dal	14	1	38	0	1
1994 Dal	16	5	43	0	0
1995 Was	12	2	35	0	0
NFL Total	114	17	187	0	1

JOE WASHINGTON Washington, Joe Dan Jr. 5′10″, 179 **RB**
Col: Oklahoma *HS:* Lincoln [Port Arthur, TX] B: 9/24/1953, Crockett, TX *Drafted:* 1976 Round 1 SD
1977 SD: Pass 1-1 100.0%, 32 32.00 1 TD. **1978** Bal: Pass 4-2 50.0%, 80 20.00 2 TD; PR 7-37 5.3; KR 19-499 26.3 **1** TD. **1979** Bal: Pass 1-0, 1 Int; KR 1-1 1.0. **1981** Was: Pass 2-1 50.0%, 32 16.00. **1982** Was: Pass 1-1 100.0%, 35 35.00. **1983** Was: Pass 1-0; KR 1-16 16.0. **1984** Was: Pass 1-0. **Total:** Pass 11-5 45.5%, 179 16.27 3 TD 1 Int; PR 7-37 5.3; KR 21-516 24.6 1 TD.

		Rushing				Receiving					Tot
Year Team	**G**	**Att**	**Yds**	**Avg**	**TD**	**Rec**	**Yds**	**Avg**	**TD**	**Fum**	**TD**
1977 SD	13	62	217	3.5	0	31	244	7.9	0	1	0
1978 Bal	16	240	956	4.0	0	45	377	8.4	1	**12**	2
1979 Bal	15	242	884	3.7	4	**82**	750	9.1	3	8	7
1980 Bal	16	144	502	3.5	1	51	494	9.7	3	5	4
1981 Was	14	210	916	4.4	4	70	558	8.0	3	8	7
1982 Was	7	44	190	4.3	1	19	134	7.1	1	2	2
1983 Was	15	145	772	5.3	0	47	454	9.7	6	2	6
1984 Was	7	56	192	3.4	1	13	74	5.7	0	3	1
1985 Atl	16	52	210	4.0	1	37	328	8.9	1	1	2
NFL Total	119	1195	4839	4.0	12	395	3413	8.6	18	42	31

JOHN WASHINGTON Washington, John Earl 6′4″, 280 **DE-NT**
Col: Oklahoma State *HS:* Ross C. Sterling [Houston, TX]
B: 2/20/1963, Houston, TX *Drafted:* 1986 Round 3 NYG
1986 NYG: 16 G. **1987** NYG: 12 G; 1 Sac. **1988** NYG: 16 G. **1989** NYG: 16 G. **1990** NYG: 16 G. **1991** NYG: 12 G. **1992** NYG-Atl: 15 G. NYG: 12 G. Atl: 3 G. **1993** NE: 16 G. **Total:** 119 G; 1 Sac.

JOE WASHINGTON Washington, Joseph Willie 5′9″, 180 **RB**
Col: Illinois State *HS:* McKinley [Baton Rouge, LA] B: 7/10/1951, Baton Rouge, LA
1973 Atl: 9 G; Rush 4-36 9.0; KR 20-432 21.6.

KEITH WASHINGTON Washington, Keith LeMon 6′4″, 270 **DE**
Col: Nevada-Las Vegas *HS:* Wilmer-Hutchins [Hutchins, TX]
B: 12/18/1972, Dallas, TX
1996 Det: 12 G; KR 1-14 14.0. **1997** Bal: 10 G; 2 Sac. **1998** Bal: 16 G; 1 Sac. **Total:** 38 G; KR 1-14 14.0; 3 Sac.

KENNY WASHINGTON Washington, Kenneth Stanley 6′1″, 212 **HB-DB**
Col: UCLA *HS:* Abraham Lincoln [Los Angeles, CA] B: 8/31/1918, Los Angeles, CA D: 6/24/1971, Los Angeles, CA
1946 LARm: Pass 8-1 12.5%, 19 2.38; Rec 6-83 13.8; KR 2-39 19.5.
1947 LARm: Pass 5-2 40.0%, 14 2.80 1 Int; Rec 3-40 13.3; PR 3-44 14.7; KR 2-52 26.0. **1948** LARm: Pass 1-0; Rec 6-104 17.3 1 TD; PR 1-12 12.0; KR 2-54 27.0; Int 2-45. **Total:** Pass 14-3 21.4%, 33 2.36 1 Int; Rec 15-227 15.1 1 TD; PR 4-56 14.0; KR 6-145 24.2; Int 2-45.

		Rushing					Tot
Year Team	**G**	**Att**	**Yds**	**Avg**	**TD**	**Fum**	**TD**
1946 LARm	6	23	114	5.0	1	2	1
1947 LARm	11	60	444	**7.4**	5	4	5
1948 LARm	10	57	301	5.3	2	4	3
NFL Total	27	140	859	6.1	8	10	9

LIONEL WASHINGTON Washington, Lionel 6′0″, 185 **DB**
Col: Tulane *HS:* Lutcher [LA] B: 10/21/1960, New Orleans, LA
Drafted: 1983 Round 4 StL
1989 LARd: 1 Fum TD. **1993** LARd: 1 Sac. **Total:** 1 Fum TD; 1 Sac.

		Interceptions				Tot
Year Team	**G**	**Int**	**Yds**	**TD**	**Fum**	**TD**
1983 StL	16	8	92	0	0	0
1984 StL	15	5	42	0	0	0
1985 StL	5	1	48	**1**	0	1
1986 StL	16	2	19	0	0	0
1987 LARd	11	0	0	0	0	0
1988 LARd	12	1	0	0	0	0
1989 LARd	16	3	46	1	0	2
1990 LARd	15	1	2	0	0	0
1991 LARd	16	5	22	0	0	0
1992 LARd	16	2	21	0	0	0
1993 LARd	16	2	0	0	0	0
1994 LARd	11	3	65	1	0	1
1995 Den	16	0	0	0	1	0
1996 Den	14	2	17	0	0	0
1997 Oak	9	2	44	1	0	1
NFL Total	204	37	418	4	1	5

MARK WASHINGTON Washington, Mark Henry 5′10″, 188 **DB**
Col: Morgan State *HS:* John Marshall Harlan [Chicago, IL]
B: 12/28/1947, Chicago, IL *Drafted:* 1970 Round 13 Dal
1970 Dal: KR 5-242 48.4 1 TD. **1972** Dal: Scor **1** Saf. **1973** Dal: KR 1-0.
1979 NE: KR 1-18 18.0. **Total:** KR 7-260 37.1 1 TD; Scor 1 Saf.

		Interceptions		
Year Team	**G**	**Int**	**Yds**	**TD**
1970 Dal	14	1	0	0
1971 Dal	2	0	0	0
1972 Dal	10	0	0	0
1973 Dal	14	1	0	0
1974 Dal	13	1	0	0
1975 Dal	14	4	26	0
1976 Dal	13	4	49	0
1977 Dal	13	2	32	0
1978 Dal	13	0	0	0
1979 NE	12	0	0	0
NFL Total	118	13	107	0

MARVIN WASHINGTON Washington, Marvin Andrew 6′6″, 275 **DE-DT**
Col: Hinds CC MS; Texas-El Paso; Idaho *HS:* Justin F. Kimball [Dallas, TX] B: 10/22/1965, Denver, CO *Drafted:* 1989 Round 6 NYJ
1989 NYJ: 16 G; KR 1-11 11.0; 1.5 Sac. **1990** NYJ: 16 G; 4.5 Sac.
1991 NYJ: 15 G; 6 Sac. **1992** NYJ: 16 G; Scor 1 Saf; 2 Pt; 8.5 Sac.
1993 NYJ: 16 G; 5.5 Sac. **1994** NYJ: 15 G; Int 1-7; 1 Fum; 3 Sac.
1995 NYJ: 16 G; 6 Sac. **1996** NYJ: 14 G; 2.5 Sac. **1997** SF: 10 G; 1 Sac.
1998 Den: 16 G; 2 Sac. **Total:** 150 G; KR 1-11 11.0; Int 1-7; Scor 1 Saf; 2 Pt; 1 Fum; 40.5 Sac.

MIKE WASHINGTON Washington, Michael Lee 6′2″, 197 **DB**
Col: Alabama *HS:* Robert E. Lee [Montgomery, AL]; Booker T. Washington HS [Montgomery, AL] B: 7/1/1953, Montgomery, AL
Drafted: 1975 Round 3 Bal

		Interceptions			Tot
Year Team	**G**	**Int**	**Yds**	**TD**	**TD**
1976 TB	6	0	0	0	0
1977 TB	14	5	71	**1**	1
1978 TB	16	5	43	0	1
1979 TB	15	3	64	1	1
1980 TB	16	4	30	0	0
1981 TB	14	6	156	1	1
1982 TB	8	3	13	0	0
1983 TB	10	2	41	0	0
1984 TB	1	0	0	0	0
NFL Total	100	28	418	3	4

MICKEY WASHINGTON Washington, Mickey Lin 5′9″, 195 **DB**
Col: Texas A&M *HS:* West Brook [Beaumont, TX] B: 7/8/1968, Galveston, TX *Drafted:* 1990 Round 8 Pho
1993 Buf: 0.5 Sac. **1994** Buf: 0.5 Sac. **Total:** 1 Sac.

		Interceptions			Tot
Year Team	**G**	**Int**	**Yds**	**TD**	**TD**
1990 NE	9	0	0	0	0
1991 NE	16	2	0	0	0
1992 Was	3	0	0	0	0
1993 Buf	16	1	27	1	1
1994 Buf	16	3	63	0	0
1995 Jac	16	1	48	1	1
1996 Jac	16	1	1	0	1
1997 NO	16	2	30	0	0
NFL Total	108	10	169	2	3

DICK WASHINGTON Washington, Richard 6′1″, 205 **DB**
Col: Bethune-Cookman *HS:* Miami Northwestern [FL] B: 2/15/1945, Savannah, GA
1968 Mia: 4 G; PR 1-15 15.0.

ROBERT WASHINGTON Washington, Robert James 6′4″, 251 **OT**
Col: Alcorn State *HS:* Franklin [Meadville, MS] B: 4/2/1963
1987 Pit: 3 G.

RONNIE WASHINGTON Washington, Ronald Carroll 6′1″, 245 **LB**
Col: Northeast Louisiana *HS:* Richwood [Monroe, LA] B: 7/29/1963, Monroe, LA *Drafted:* 1985 Round 8 Atl
1985 Atl: 16 G; KR 1-0; 1 Fum; 0.5 Sac. **1987** LARd: 2 G; KR 1-0; 1 Sac. **1989** Ind: 2 G. **Total:** 20 G; KR 2-0; 1 Fum; 1.5 Sac.

RUSS WASHINGTON Washington, Russell Eugene 6′6″, 289 **OT-DT**
Col: Missouri *HS:* Southeast [Kansas City, MO] B: 12/17/1946, Kansas City, MO *Drafted:* 1968 Round 1 SD
1968 SD: 14 G. **1969** SD: 14 G. **1970** SD: 14 G. **1971** SD: 14 G. **1972** SD: 14 G. **1973** SD: 14 G. **1974** SD: 14 G. **1975** SD: 14 G. **1976** SD: 14 G. **1977** SD: 14 G. **1978** SD: 16 G. **1979** SD: 16 G. **1980** SD: 6 G. **1981** SD: 13 G. **1982** SD: 9 G. **Total:** 200 G.

SAM WASHINGTON Washington, Samuel Lee Jr. 5′8″, 180 **DB**
Col: Mississippi Valley State *HS:* Tampa Bay Tech [Tampa, FL] B: 3/7/1960, Tampa, FL
1982 Pit: 4 G. **1983** Pit: 16 G; Int 1-25. **1984** Pit: 14 G; Int 6-138 **2** TD; 12 Pt. **1985** Pit-Cin: 15 G; KR 3-34 11.3. Pit: 7 G; KR 3-34 11.3. Cin: 8 G. **Total:** 49 G; KR 3-34 11.3; Int 7-163 2 TD; 12 Pt.

TED WASHINGTON Washington, Theodore 6′4″, 316 **NT-DT-DE**
Col: Louisville *HS:* Tampa Bay Tech [Tampa, FL] B: 4/13/1968, Tampa, FL *Drafted:* 1991 Round 1 SF
1991 SF: 16 G; 1 Sac. **1992** SF: 16 G; 2 Sac. **1993** SF: 12 G; 3 Sac. **1994** Den: 15 G; Int 1-5; 2.5 Sac. **1995** Buf: 16 G; 2.5 Sac. **1996** Buf: 16 G; 3.5 Sac. **1997** Buf: 16 G; 4 Sac. **1998** Buf: 16 G; Int 1-0; Scor **1** Saf; 2 Pt; 4.5 Sac. **Total:** 123 G; Int 2-5; Scor 1 Saf; 2 Pt; 23.0 Sac.

TED WASHINGTON Washington, Theodore Bernard 6′1″, 244 **LB**
Col: Mississippi Valley State *HS:* Middleton [Tampa, FL]; Tuskegee HS [AL] B: 2/16/1948, Tampa, FL *Drafted:* 1972 Round 17 KC
1973 Hou: 1 G. **1974** Hou: 14 G. **1975** Hou: 14 G; Int 3-30. **1976** Hou: 13 G. **1977** Hou: 14 G; Int 3-26; 1 Fum. **1978** Hou: 16 G. **1979** Hou: 15 G. **1980** Hou: 16 G. **1981** Hou: 16 G; Int 1-19. **1982** Hou: 9 G; 1 Sac. **Total:** 128 G; Int 7-75; 1 Fum; 1 Sac.

TIM WASHINGTON Washington, Timothy Bernard 5′9″, 184 **DB**
Col: Fresno City Coll. CA (J.C.); California; Fresno State *HS:* Fresno [CA] B: 11/7/1959, Fresno, CA D: 1/4/1992, Fremont, CA *Drafted:* 1982 Round 12 SF
1982 SF-KC: 2 G. SF: 1 G. KC: 1 G. **Total:** 2 G.

TODD WASHINGTON Washington, Todd Page 6′3″, 312 **C**
Col: Virginia Tech *HS:* Nandua [Olney, VA] B: 7/19/1976, Nassawadox, VA *Drafted:* 1998 Round 4 TB
1998 TB: 4 G.

VIC WASHINGTON Washington, Victor Arnold 5′11″, 197 **RB-DB-WR**
Col: Wyoming *HS:* Plainfield [NJ] B: 3/23/1946, Plainfield, NJ *Drafted:* 1970 Round 4 SF

		Rushing				Receiving			
Year Team	**G**	**Att**	**Yds**	**Avg**	**TD**	**Rec**	**Yds**	**Avg**	**TD**
1971 SF	14	191	811	4.2	3	36	317	8.8	4
1972 SF	13	141	468	3.3	3	43	393	9.1	1
1973 SF	13	151	534	3.5	8	33	238	7.2	0
1974 Hou	12	74	281	3.8	2	13	92	7.1	0
1975 Buf	13	9	49	5.4	0	2	21	10.5	0
1976 Buf	2	22	65	3.0	0	3	29	9.7	0
NFL Total	67	588	2208	3.8	16	130	1090	8.4	5

	Kickoff Returns					Tot
Year Team	**Ret**	**Yds**	**Avg**	**TD**	**Fum**	**TD**
1971 SF	33	858	26.0	0	10	7
1972 SF	27	771	28.6	**1**	7	5
1973 SF	24	549	22.9	0	9	8
1974 Hou	7	177	25.3	0	4	2
1975 Buf	35	923	26.4	0	1	0
1976 Buf	3	63	21.0	0	0	0
NFL Total	129	3341	25.9	1	31	22

JIM WASKIEWICZ Waskiewicz, James Allan 6′4″, 240 **C-LB-OT**
Col: Wichita State *HS:* East [Wichita, KS] B: 2/10/1944, Milwaukee, WI *Drafted:* 1966 Round 4 NYJ
1966 NYJ: 14 G. **1967** NYJ: 13 G; KR 2-0. **1969** Atl: 12 G. **Total:** 39 G; KR 2-0.

LLOYD WASSERBACH Wasserbach, Lloyd George 5′11″, 205 **T**
Col: Wisconsin *HS:* Sturgeon Bay [WI] B: 1/30/1921, Baileys Harbor, WI
AAFC **1946** ChiA: 12 G; KR 1-13 13.0; Int 1-0. **1947** ChiA: 5 G. **Total:** 17 G; KR 1-13 13.0; Int 1-0.

BOB WATERFIELD Waterfield, Robert Stanton 6′1″, 200 **QB**
(Buckets) *Col:* UCLA *HS:* Van Nuys [CA] B: 7/26/1920, Elmira, NY D: 3/25/1983, Burbank, CA *Drafted:* 1944 Round 3 Cle *HOF:* 1965
1945 Cle: PR 2-34 17.0. **1946** LARm: PR 1-12 12.0. **1947** LARm: Rec 2-14 7.0; PR 1-2 2.0. **1952** LARm: Rec 1-5 5.0. **Total:** Rec 3-19 6.3; PR 4-48 12.0.

		Passing							
Year Team	**G**	**Att**	**Comp**	**Comp%**	**Yds**	**YPA**	**TD**	**Int**	**Rating**
1945 Cle	10	171	89	52.0	1609	**9.41**	**14**	17	72.4
1946 LARm	11	**251**	**127**	50.6	1747	6.96	**17**	17	67.6
1947 LARm	12	221	96	43.4	1210	5.48	8	18	39.2
1948 LARm	11	180	87	48.3	1354	7.52	14	18	60.0
1949 LARm	12	296	154	52.0	2168	7.32	17	24	61.3
1950 LARm	12	213	122	**57.3**	1540	7.23	11	13	71.7
1951 LARm	11	176	88	50.0	1566	**8.90**	13	10	81.8
1952 LARm	12	109	51	46.8	655	6.01	3	11	35.7
NFL Total	91	1617	814	50.3	11849	7.33	97	128	61.6

	Rushing				Interceptions		
Year Team	**Att**	**Yds**	**Avg**	**TD**	**Int**	**Yds**	**TD**
1945 Cle	18	18	1.0	5	6	92	0
1946 LARm	16	-60	-3.8	1	5	72	0
1947 LARm	3	6	2.0	1	5	56	0
1948 LARm	7	12	1.7	0	4	8	0
1949 LARm	5	-4	-0.8	1	0	0	0
1950 LARm	8	14	1.8	1	0	0	0
1951 LARm	9	49	5.4	3	0	0	0
1952 LARm	9	-14	-1.6	1	0	0	0
NFL Total	75	21	0.3	13	20	228	0

	Punting		
Year Team	**Punts**	**Yds**	**Avg**
1945 Cle	39	1585	40.6
1946 LARm	39	1743	44.7
1947 LARm	59	2500	42.4
1948 LARm	43	1833	42.6
1949 LARm	49	2177	44.4
1950 LARm	52	2087	40.1
1951 LARm	4	166	41.5
1952 LARm	30	1276	42.5
NFL Total	315	13367	42.4

	Scoring							
Year Team	**Pts**	**FG**	**FGA**	**FG%**	**XK**	**XKA**	**XK%**	**Fum**
1945 Cle	64	1	3	33.3	**31**	34	91.2	9
1946 LARm	61	6	9	**66.7**	**37**	**37**	**100.0**	6
1947 LARm	54	**7**	**16**	43.8	27	30	90.0	2
1948 LARm	56	6	11	54.5	38	44	86.4	5
1949 LARm	76	**9**	16	56.3	43	45	95.6	4
1950 LARm	81	7	14	50.0	**54**	**58**	93.1	4
1951 LARm	98	**13**	**23**	56.5	41	43	95.3	2
1952 LARm	83	11	18	**61.1**	**44**	**45**	**97.8**	4
NFL Total	573	60	110	54.5	315	336	93.8	36

ANDRE WATERS Waters, Andre 5′11″, 194 **DB**
Col: Cheyney *HS:* Pahokee [FL] B: 3/10/1962, Belle Glade, FL
1984 Phi: KR 13-319 24.5 **1** TD. **1985** Phi: PR 1-23 23.0; KR 4-74 18.5. **1986** Phi: 2 Sac. **1988** Phi: 0.5 Sac. **1989** Phi: 1 Fum TD; 1 Sac. **Total:** PR 1-23 23.0; KR 17-393 23.1 1 TD; 1 Fum TD; 3.5 Sac.

		Interceptions				Tot
Year Team	**G**	**Int**	**Yds**	**TD**	**Fum**	**TD**
1984 Phi	16	0	0	0	1	1
1985 Phi	16	0	0	0	1	0
1986 Phi	16	6	39	0	0	0
1987 Phi	12	3	63	0	0	0
1988 Phi	16	3	19	0	0	0
1989 Phi	16	1	20	0	0	1
1990 Phi	14	0	0	0	0	0
1991 Phi	16	1	0	0	0	0
1992 Phi	6	1	23	0	0	0
1993 Phi	9	0	0	0	0	0
1994 Ariz	12	0	0	0	0	0
1995 Ariz	7	0	0	0	0	0
NFL Total	156	15	164	0	2	2

CHARLIE WATERS Waters, Charlie Tutan 6′1″, 193 **DB**
Col: Clemson *HS:* North Augusta [SC] B: 9/10/1948, Miami, FL *Drafted:* 1970 Round 3 Dal
1970 Dal: KR 1-6 6.0. **1971** Dal: PR 9-109 12.1; KR 1-18 18.0. **1972** Dal: PR 9-56 6.2; KR 2-18 9.0. **1974** Dal: Rush 1-6 6.0; PR 1-8 8.0. **1975** Dal: KR 1-0. **1978** Dal: Scor **1** Saf. **1980** Dal: KR 1-0. **Total:** Rush 1-6 6.0; PR 19-173 9.1; KR 6-42 7.0; Scor 1 Saf.

		Interceptions				Tot
Year Team	**G**	**Int**	**Yds**	**TD**	**Fum**	**TD**
1970 Dal	14	5	45	0	0	0
1971 Dal	14	2	37	0	2	0

1972 Dal	14	6	132	1	0	1
1973 Dal	14	5	112	0	0	0
1974 Dal	14	2	26	0	1	0
1975 Dal	14	3	55	1	0	1
1976 Dal	14	3	6	0	1	0
1977 Dal	14	3	11	0	0	1
1978 Dal	16	4	61	0	0	0
1980 Dal	16	5	78	0	0	0
1981 Dal	16	3	21	0	0	0
NFL Total	160	41	584	2	4	3

DALE WATERS Waters, Dale Barnard 6′2″, 212 **T-OE-DE-G**
(Muddy) *Col:* Florida *HS:* New Castle [IN] B: 5/27/1909, Henry Co., IN
1931 Port-Cle: 7 G. Port: 1 G. Cle: 6 G. **1932** Bos: 9 G; Pass 1-0, 1 Int; Rush 1-15 15.0. **1933** Bos: 11 G. **Total:** 27 G; Pass 1-0, 1 Int; Rush 1-15 15.0.

BOB WATERS Waters, Robert Lee 6′2″, 184 **QB**
Col: Presbyterian *HS:* Screven Co. [Sylvania, GA] B: 6/22/1938, Millen, GA D: 5/29/1989, Cullowhee, NC *Drafted:* 1960 Round 7 SF

		Passing							
Year Team	**G**	**Att**	**Comp**	**Comp%**	**Yds**	**YPA**	**TD**	**Int**	**Rating**
1960 SF	8	2	2	100.0	61	30.50	1	0	158.3
1961 SF	8	28	13	46.4	183	6.54	1	2	50.1
1962 SF	7	6	2	33.3	28	4.67	0	0	49.3
1963 SF	7	88	42	47.7	435	4.94	1	6	37.8
NFL Total	30	124	59	47.6	707	5.70	3	8	46.7

	Rushing				
Year Team	**Att**	**Yds**	**Avg**	**TD**	**Fum**
1960 SF	1	8	8.0	0	0
1961 SF	47	233	5.0	3	3
1962 SF	12	42	3.5	0	1
1963 SF	5	-2	-0.4	0	3
NFL Total	65	281	4.3	3	7

MIKE WATERS Waters, Robert Michael 6′2″, 228 **TE-RB**
Col: Bakersfield Coll. CA (J.C.); San Diego State *HS:* Burroughs [Ridgecrest, CA] B: 3/15/1962, San Diego, CA *Drafted:* 1985 Round 9 NYJ
1986 Phi: 5 G; Rush 5-8 1.6; Rec 2-27 13.5; PR 7-30 4.3; 3 Fum. **1987** NO: 5 G; Rec 5-140 28.0 1 TD; 6 Pt. **Total:** 10 G; Rush 5-8 1.6; Rec 7-167 23.9 1 TD; PR 7-30 4.3; 6 Pt; 3 Fum.

JERRY WATFORD Watford, Jerry Ray 6′3″, 205 **OE-DE**
Col: Alabama *HS:* Gadsden [AL] B: 12/19/1930, Gadsden, AL D: 3/10/1993, Blountville, TN *Drafted:* 1953 Round 8 ChiC
1953 ChiC: 12 G. **1954** ChiC: 12 G. **Total:** 24 G.

PETE WATHEN Wathen, Chapeze 5′10″, 175 **BB**
Col: Kentucky *HS:* Owensboro [KY] B: 5/15/1903, Owensboro, KY D: 7/5/1949, Owensboro, KY
1922 Eva: 2 G.

BOBBY WATKINS Watkins, Bobby Lawrence 5′10″, 184 **DB**
Col: Southwest Texas State *HS:* Bishop Dunne [Dallas, TX] B: 5/31/1960, Cottonwood, ID *Drafted:* 1982 Round 2 Det

		Interceptions			
Year Team	**G**	**Int**	**Yds**	**TD**	**Fum**
1982 Det	9	5	22	0	0
1983 Det	16	4	48	0	1
1984 Det	16	6	0	0	0
1985 Det	16	5	15	0	0
1986 Det	5	0	0	0	0
1987 Det	5	0	0	0	0
1988 Det	16	0	0	0	0
NFL Total	83	20	85	0	1

FOSTER WATKINS Watkins, Foster Forrest 5′9″, 163 **QB-DB-HB**
(Flippin') *Col:* West Texas A&M *HS:* Dumas [TX] B: 11/17/1917, Memphis, TX *Drafted:* 1939 Round 15 Phi
1940 Phi: Punt 2-45 22.5; Scor 2, 2-2 100.0% XK. **1941** Phi: Rec 4-36 9.0; PR 3-17 5.7; KR 1-17 17.0. **Total:** Rec 4-36 9.0; PR 3-17 5.7; KR 1-17 17.0; Punt 2-45 22.5; Scor 2, 2-2 100.0% XK.

		Passing							
Year Team	**G**	**Att**	**Comp**	**Comp%**	**Yds**	**YPA**	**TD**	**Int**	**Rating**
1940 Phi	9	85	28	32.9	565	6.65	1	3	46.4
1941 Phi	11	10	6	60.0	62	6.20	1	0	111.3
NFL Total	20	95	34	35.8	627	6.60	2	3	53.3

	Rushing			
Year Team	**Att**	**Yds**	**Avg**	**TD**
1940 Phi	14	-76	-5.4	0
1941 Phi	15	11	0.7	0
NFL Total	29	-65	-2.2	0

GORDON WATKINS Watkins, Gordon Campbell 6′1″, 220 **T-G**
(Coot) *Col:* Georgia Tech *HS:* Tech [Atlanta, GA] B: 6/19/1907, Atlanta, GA D: 4/8/1974, Atlanta, GA
1930 Min-Fra: 10 G. Min: 2 G. Fra: 8 G. **1931** Bkn: 7 G. **Total:** 17 G.

KENDELL WATKINS Watkins, Kendell Mairo 6′1″, 282 **TE**
Col: Mississippi State *HS:* Provine [Jackson, MS] B: 3/8/1973, Jackson, MS *Drafted:* 1995 Round 2 Dal
1995 Dal: 16 G; Rec 1-8 8.0; KR 1-(-6) -6.0; 1 Fum.

LARRY WATKINS Watkins, Lawrence 6′2″, 230 **RB**
Col: Alcorn State *HS:* J.S. Abrams [Bessemer, AL] B: 10/5/1946, Bessemer, AL
1973 Buf: KR 1-18 18.0. **1976** NYG: KR 1-9 9.0. **Total:** KR 2-27 13.5.

		Rushing				Receiving					Tot
Year Team	**G**	**Att**	**Yds**	**Avg**	**TD**	**Rec**	**Yds**	**Avg**	**TD**	**Fum**	**TD**
1969 Det	14	62	201	3.2	1	13	87	6.7	0	0	1
1970 Phi	11	32	96	3.0	1	3	6	2.0	0	1	1
1971 Phi	12	35	98	2.8	1	6	40	6.7	0	0	1
1972 Phi	14	67	262	3.9	1	6	-2	-0.3	0	8	1
1973 Buf	14	98	414	4.2	2	12	86	7.2	1	3	3
1974 Buf	10	41	170	4.1	2	1	7	7.0	0	0	2
1975 NYG	14	68	303	4.5	3	7	43	6.1	0	1	3
1976 NYG	13	26	96	3.7	1	2	8	4.0	0	0	1
1977 NYG	9	19	71	3.7	0	1	9	9.0	0	0	0
NFL Total	111	448	1711	3.8	12	51	284	5.6	1	13	13

BOBBY WATKINS Watkins, Robert Archibald Jr. 5′10″, 198 **HB**
Col: Ohio State *HS:* New Bedford [MA] B: 3/30/1932, New Bedford, MA *Drafted:* 1955 Round 2 ChiB
1955 ChiB: Rec 6-79 13.2; KR 5-145 29.0. **1956** ChiB: Rec 2-3 1.5 1 TD. **1957** ChiB: Rec 3-90 30.0 1 TD. **1958** ChiC: Rec 4-62 15.5 1 TD; KR 1-24 24.0. **Total:** Rec 15-234 15.6 3 TD; KR 6-169 28.2.

		Rushing					Tot
Year Team	**G**	**Att**	**Yds**	**Avg**	**TD**	**Fum**	**TD**
1955 ChiB	12	110	553	5.0	8	5	8
1956 ChiB	9	68	276	4.1	2	1	3
1957 ChiB	12	57	212	3.7	1	2	2
1958 ChiC	5	3	17	5.7	0	0	1
NFL Total	38	238	1058	4.4	11	8	14

TOM WATKINS Watkins, Thomas 6′0″, 195 **HB**
Col: East Los Angeles Coll. CA (J.C.); Iowa State *HS:* West Memphis [AR] B: 10/23/1937, West Memphis, AR *Drafted:* 1960 Round 15 Cle
1964 Det: Pass 1-1 100.0%, 58 58.00 1 TD. **Total:** Pass 1-1 100.0%, 58 58.00 1 TD.

		Rushing				Receiving			
Year Team	**G**	**Att**	**Yds**	**Avg**	**TD**	**Rec**	**Yds**	**Avg**	**TD**
1961 Cle	10	43	209	4.9	0	4	66	16.5	1
1962 Det	13	113	485	4.3	3	12	85	7.1	0
1963 Det	13	97	423	4.4	2	16	168	10.5	1
1964 Det	14	80	218	2.7	1	10	125	12.5	1
1965 Det	11	29	95	3.3	0	5	53	10.6	0
1967 Det	13	106	361	3.4	4	8	93	11.6	1
1968 Pit	1	0	0	—	0	0	0	—	0
NFL Total	75	468	1791	3.8	10	55	590	10.7	4

	Punt Returns				Kickoff Returns					Tot
Year Team	**Ret**	**Yds**	**Avg**	**TD**	**Ret**	**Yds**	**Avg**	**TD**	**Fum**	**TD**
1961 Cle	0	0	—	0	9	226	25.1	0	2	1
1962 Det	8	42	5.3	0	17	452	26.6	0	5	3
1963 Det	**32**	**399**	12.5	**1**	21	447	21.3	0	4	4
1964 Det	16	238	**14.9**	**2**	16	368	23.0	0	4	4
1965 Det	23	234	10.2	0	17	584	**34.4**	0	3	0
1967 Det	15	57	3.8	0	20	411	20.6	0	5	5
1968 Pit	2	0	0.0	0	1	22	22.0	0	0	0
NFL Total	96	970	10.1	3	101	2510	24.9	0	23	17

ALLAN WATSON Watson, Allan 5′9″, 162 **K**
Col: Newport (Wales) *HS:* Blockwood [Wales] B: 11/5/1944, Blockwood, Wales
1970 Pit: 4 G; Scor 22, 5-10 50.0% FG, 7-8 87.5% XK.

DAVE WATSON Watson, Carl David 6′1″, 245 **OG**
Col: Georgia Tech *HS:* Eufaula [AL] B: 1941 *Drafted:* 1963 Round 11 Bos
1963 Bos: 14 G; KR 1-9 9.0; 1 Fum. **1964** Bos: 14 G; KR 1-0. **Total:** 28 G; KR 2-9 4.5; 1 Fum.

ED WATSON Watson, Edward Louis 6′4″, 220 **LB**
(Anteater) *Col:* Grambling State *HS:* Springville [Coushatta, LA] B: 5/8/1945, Coushatta, LA *Drafted:* 1969 Round 9 Hou
1969 Hou: 3 G.

ERNEST WATSON Watson, Ernest J **BB**
Col: Olivet *HS:* Pontiac Central [MI] B: 12/13/1895 D: 3/10/1995, Newberry, MI
1920 Det: 2 G.

RAT WATSON Watson, Grady 5′10″, 181 **BB-TB-WB-FB**
Col: Southwestern (Tex.); Texas *HS:* Orange [TX] B: 5/12/1899, Orange, TX D: 4/1985, Edmond, OK
1922 Tol: 7 G; Pass 2 TD; Rush 1 TD; Scor 9, 3 XK. **1923** Tol: 5 G; Scor 1, 1 XK. **1924** Ham-KC: 4 G. Ham: 3 G. KC: 1 G. **1925** Ham: 2 G. **1927** Buf: 2 G. **Total:** 20 G; Pass 2 TD; Rush 1 TD.

JIM WATSON Watson, James Robert 6′0″, 205 **C-LB**
(Jimbo) *Col:* Yuba Coll. CA (J.C.); U. of Pacific *HS:* Marysville [CA] B: 3/26/1921, Stockton, CA
1945 Was: 4 G.

TIM WATSON Watson, James Timothy Jr. 6′2″, 214 **DB**
Col: Howard *HS:* Peach Co. [Fort Valley, GA] B: 8/13/1970, Fort Valley, GA *Drafted:* 1993 Round 6 GB
1993 KC: 4 G. **1994** KC: 1 G. **1995** KC-NYG: 5 G. KC: 4 G. NYG: 1 G. **1997** Phi: 3 G. **Total:** 13 G.

JOHN WATSON Watson, John Ace 6′4″, 249 **OT-OG-C**
Col: Oklahoma *HS:* McLain [Tulsa, OK] B: 1/11/1949, Palo Alto, CA *Drafted:* 1971 Round 7 SF
1971 SF: 14 G. **1972** SF: 14 G. **1973** SF: 14 G; 1 Fum. **1974** SF: 13 G. **1975** SF: 14 G. **1976** SF: 11 G. **1977** NO: 5 G. **1978** NO: 5 G. **1979** NO: 5 G. **Total:** 95 G; 1 Fum.

JOE WATSON Watson, Joseph LaVerne 6′3″, 235 **C-LB**
Col: Rice B: 8/19/1925 *Drafted:* 1950 Round 1 Det
1950 Det: 8 G; Int 1-5.

LOUIS WATSON Watson, Louis Teddy 5′11″, 175 **WR**
Col: Mississippi Valley State *HS:* W.P. Davidson [Mobile, AL] B: 1/11/1963, Mobile, AL
1987 Cle: 2 G; Rec 1-9 9.0.

REMI WATSON Watson, Remi Fitzgerald 6′0″, 174 **WR**
Col: South Carolina State; Bethune-Cookman *HS:* Plant City [FL] B: 8/8/1964
1987 Cle: 1 G; Rec 1-13 13.0.

PETE WATSON Watson, Rodney Peter 6′1″, 210 **TE**
Col: Tufts B: 9/19/1950, New York, NY
1972 Cin: 2 G.

SID WATSON Watson, Sidney John 5′11″, 187 **HB**
Col: Northeastern *HS:* Andover [MA] B: 5/4/1932, Andover, MA
1956 Pit: Scor 37, 1-1 100.0% FG, 10-12 83.3% XK. **Total:** Scor 49, 1-1 100.0% FG, 10-12 83.3% XK.

		Rushing				Receiving			
Year Team	**G**	**Att**	**Yds**	**Avg**	**TD**	**Rec**	**Yds**	**Avg**	**TD**
1955 Pit	12	29	31	1.1	0	19	223	11.7	1
1956 Pit	12	112	298	2.7	4	12	138	11.5	0
1957 Pit	11	12	21	1.8	0	3	24	8.0	0
1958 Was	10	46	166	3.6	0	5	38	7.6	1
NFL Total	45	199	516	2.6	4	39	423	10.8	2

	Punt Returns				Kickoff Returns					Tot
Year Team	**Ret**	**Yds**	**Avg**	**TD**	**Ret**	**Yds**	**Avg**	**TD**	**Fum**	**TD**
1955 Pit	23	15	0.7	0	**27**	**716**	26.5	0	7	1
1956 Pit	1	2	2.0	0	4	110	27.5	0	4	4
1957 Pit	0	0	—	0	0	0	—	0	2	0
1958 Was	4	21	5.3	0	19	443	23.3	0	1	1
NFL Total	28	38	1.4	0	50	1269	25.4	0	14	6

STEVE WATSON Watson, Stephen Ross 6′4″, 195 **WR**
Col: Temple *HS:* St. Mark's [Wilmington, DE] B: 5/28/1957, Baltimore, MD
1980 Den: KR 1-5 5.0. **1981** Den: Rush 2-6 3.0. **1982** Den: Rush 1-(-4) -4.0. **1983** Den: Rush 3-17 5.7. **Total:** Rush 6-19 3.2; KR 1-5 5.0.

		Receiving				
Year Team	**G**	**Rec**	**Yds**	**Avg**	**TD**	**Fum**
1979 Den	16	6	83	13.8	0	0
1980 Den	16	6	146	24.3	0	0
1981 Den	16	60	1244	20.7	**13**	0
1982 Den	9	36	555	15.4	2	1
1983 Den	16	59	1133	19.2	5	1
1984 Den	16	69	1170	17.0	7	0
1985 Den	16	61	915	15.0	5	0
1986 Den	16	45	699	15.5	3	0
1987 Den	5	11	167	15.2	1	0
NFL Total	126	353	6112	17.3	36	2

JOE WATT Watt, Joseph Chester 5′11″, 184 **DB-HB**
Col: Syracuse *HS:* Erasmus Hall [Brooklyn, NY] B: 6/18/1919, Montreal, Canada D: 6/27/1983, Ithaca, NY *Drafted:* 1947 Round 7 Bos
1947 Bos-Det: Rec 4-104 26.0 2 TD; PR 10-143 14.3; KR 4-68 17.0; Int 2-32. Bos: PR 2-28 14.0. Det: Rec 4-104 26.0 2 TD; PR 8-115 14.4; KR 4-68 17.0; Int 2-32. **1948** Det: Rec 2-29 14.5; PR 8-87 10.9; KR 12-180 15.0; Int 4-39. **1949** NYB: Int 1-5. **Total:** Rec 6-133 22.2 2 TD; PR 18-230 12.8; KR 16-248 15.5; Int 7-76.

		Rushing				
Year Team	**G**	**Att**	**Yds**	**Avg**	**TD**	**Fum**
1947 Bos-Det	9	11	7	0.6	0	1
1947 Bos	1	0	0	—	0	0
1947 Det	8	11	7	0.6	0	1
1948 Det	12	20	54	2.7	0	1
1949 NYB	5	0	0	—	0	0
NFL Total	26	31	61	2.0	0	2

WALT WATT Watt, Walter Wilson 6′0″, 187 **HB-DB**
Col: Miami (Fla.) *HS:* Lash [Zanesville, OH] B: 6/16/1922, Dennison, OH D: 12/29/1994, Miami, FL *Drafted:* 1945 Round 3 ChiC
1945 ChiC: 4 G; Rush 6-9 1.5; Rec 1-22 22.0; KR 1-18 18.0.

FRANK WATTELET Wattelet, Frank Lee 6′0″, 185 **DB**
Col: Kansas *HS:* Abilene [KS] B: 10/25/1958, Paola, KS
1983 NO: KR 1-4 4.0. **1984** NO: **1** Fum TD. **1985** NO: Rush 2-42 21.0; 1 Sac. **1986** NO: Pass 1-1 100.0%, 13 13.00. **Total:** Pass 1-1 100.0%, 13 13.00; Rush 2-42 21.0; KR 1-4 4.0; 1 Fum TD; 1 Sac.

		Interceptions			Tot
Year Team	**G**	**Int**	**Yds**	**TD**	**TD**
1981 NO	16	3	16	0	0
1982 NO	9	0	0	0	0
1983 NO	16	2	33	0	0
1984 NO	16	2	52	1	2
1985 NO	16	2	0	0	0
1986 NO	16	3	34	0	0
1987 NO-LARm	7	0	0	0	0
1987 NO	2	0	0	0	0
1987 LARm	5	0	0	0	0
1988 LARm	2	0	0	0	0
NFL Total	98	12	135	1	2

LEN WATTERS Watters, Leonard Alvyn 5′10″, 185 **E**
(Cupid) *Col:* Springfield *HS:* South Bend Central [IN] B: 6/4/1898, Dubuque, IA D: 12/10/1986, Venice, FL
1924 Buf: 8 G; Rec 1 TD; 6 Pt.

ORLANDO WATTERS Watters, Orlando L 5′11″, 173 **DB**
Col: Arkansas *HS:* Anniston [AL] B: 10/26/1971, Anniston, AL
1994 Sea: 16 G; Int 3-39 1 TD; 6 Pt.

RICKY WATTERS Watters, Richard James 6′1″, 217 **RB**
Col: Notre Dame *HS:* Bishop McDevitt [Harrisburg, PA] B: 4/7/1969, Harrisburg, PA *Drafted:* 1991 Round 2 SF
1992 SF: Pass 1-0. **1998** Sea: Pass 1-1 100.0%, 1 1.00 1 TD; Scor 1 2XP. **Total:** Pass 2-1 50.0%, 1 0.50 1 TD; Scor 1 2XP.

		Rushing				Receiving					Tot
Year Team	**G**	**Att**	**Yds**	**Avg**	**TD**	**Rec**	**Yds**	**Avg**	**TD**	**Fum**	**TD**
1992 SF	14	206	1013	4.9	9	43	405	9.4	2	2	11
1993 SF	13	208	950	4.6	10	31	326	10.5	1	5	11
1994 SF	16	239	877	3.7	6	66	719	10.9	5	8	11
1995 Phi	16	337	1273	3.8	11	62	434	7.0	1	6	12
1996 Phi	16	**353**	1411	4.0	13	51	444	8.7	0	5	13
1997 Phi	16	285	1110	3.9	7	48	440	9.2	0	3	7
1998 Sea	16	319	1239	3.9	9	52	373	7.2	0	4	9
NFL Total	107	1947	7873	4.0	65	353	3141	8.9	9	33	74

BOB WATTERS Watters, Robert Lee 6′4″, 245 **DE**
Col: Lincoln (Mo.) B: 9/25/1935, Fort Worth, TX *Drafted:* 1958 Round 28 NYG
1962 NYT: 12 G. **1963** NYJ: 12 G. **1964** NYJ: 5 G. **Total:** 29 G.

SCOTT WATTERS Watters, Scott Henry 6′2″, 230 **LB**
Col: Wittenberg *HS:* Columbus Acad. [Gahanna, OH] B: 1/1/1965, Columbus, OH
1987 Buf: 3 G.

DAMON WATTS Watts, Damon Shanel 5′10″, 180 **DB**
Col: Indiana *HS:* Lawrence North [Indianapolis, IN] B: 4/8/1972, Indianapolis, IN
1994 Ind: 16 G; Int 1-0. **1995** Ind: 13 G; Int 1-9. **1996** Ind: 10 G; Int 1-21. **1997** Ind: 8 G. **Total:** 47 G; Int 3-30.

ELBERT WATTS Watts, Elbert T 6′1″, 205 **DB**
Col: East Los Angeles Coll. CA (J.C.); Santa Monica Coll. CA (J.C.); Oklahoma; USC *HS:* Venice [Los Angeles, CA] B: 3/20/1963, Carson, CA *Drafted:* 1986 Round 9 LARm
1986 GB: 9 G; KR 12-239 19.9; Int 1-6; 1 Sac.

GEORGE WATTS Watts, George 6′1″, 225 **T**
Col: Appalachian State B: 7/12/1918, McAdenville, NC D: 1991 *Drafted:* 1942 Round 15 Was
1942 Was: 8 G.

RANDY WATTS Watts, Randy 6′6″, 275 **DE-DT**
Col: East Carolina; Catawba *HS:* Washington Co. [Sandersville, GA] B: 6/22/1963, Sandersville, GA *Drafted:* 1987 Round 9 KC
1987 Dal: 5 G; 3 Sac.

RICKEY WATTS Watts, Rickey Ricardo 6'1", 203 **WR**
Col: Tulsa *HS:* Longview [TX] B: 5/16/1957, Longview, TX
Drafted: 1979 Round 2 ChiB
1979 ChiB: Rush 1-(-6) -6.0. **1980** ChiB: Rush 1-(-16) -16.0; PR 2-20 10.0. **1982** ChiB: Rush 1-(-1) -1.0. **Total:** Rush 3-(-23) -7.7; PR 2-20 10.0.

		Receiving				Kickoff Returns					Tot
Year Team	G	Rec	Yds	Avg	TD	Ret	Yds	Avg	TD	Fum	TD
1979 ChiB	16	24	421	17.5	3	14	289	20.6	**1**	1	4
1980 ChiB	15	22	444	20.2	2	1	12	12.0	0	1	2
1981 ChiB	12	27	465	17.2	3	0	0	—	0	3	3
1982 ChiB	9	8	217	27.1	0	14	330	23.6	0	1	0
1983 ChiB	4	0	0	—	0	5	79	15.8	0	0	0
NFL Total	56	81	1547	19.1	8	34	710	20.9	1	6	9

ROBERT WATTS Watts, Robert 6'3", 218 **LB**
Col: Boston College *HS:* Vermont Acad. [Saxtons River, VT]
B: 6/16/1954, New York, NY *Drafted:* 1977 Round 3 NO
1978 Oak: 2 G.

TED WATTS Watts, Ted W 6'0", 195 **DB**
Col: Coffeyville CC KS; Texas Tech *HS:* Tarpon Springs [FL]
B: 5/29/1952, Tarpon Springs, FL *Drafted:* 1981 Round 1 Oak
1981 Oak: Int 1-12. **1982** LARd: Int 1-0; 1 Sac. **1983** LARd: Int 1-13. **1984** LARd: Int 1-0. **1985** NYG: Int 1-0. **Total:** Int 5-25; 1 Sac.

		Punt Returns				
Year Team	G	Ret	Yds	Avg	TD	Fum
1981 Oak	16	35	284	8.1	1	3
1982 LARd	9	0	0	—	0	0
1983 LARd	16	0	0	—	0	0
1984 LARd	16	0	0	—	0	0
1985 NYG	16	0	0	—	0	0
1987 SD	1	0	0	—	0	0
NFL Total	74	35	284	8.1	1	3

CHARLIE WAY Way, Charles Ash 5'8", 144 **WB**
(Pie) *Col:* Penn State *HS:* Downingtown [PA] B: 12/29/1897, Embreeville, PA D: 1/31/1988, Honeybrook, PA
1921 Can: 6 G; Rec 1 TD; 6 Pt. **1924** Fra: 13 G; Rush 4 TD; 24 Pt. **Total:** 19 G; Rush 4 TD; Rec 1 TD; Tot TD 5; 30 Pt.

CHARLES WAY Way, Charles Christopher 6'0", 245 **RB**
Col: Virginia *HS:* Northeast [Philadelphia, PA] B: 12/27/1972, Philadelphia, PA *Drafted:* 1995 Round 6 NYG
1995 NYG: KR 1-8 8.0. **1996** NYG: KR 2-19 9.5. **1997** NYG: KR 2-46 23.0. **Total:** KR 5-73 14.6.

		Rushing				Receiving					Tot
Year Team	G	Att	Yds	Avg	TD	Rec	Yds	Avg	TD	Fum	TD
1995 NYG	16	2	6	3.0	0	7	76	10.9	1	0	1
1996 NYG	16	22	79	3.6	1	32	328	10.3	1	0	2
1997 NYG	16	151	698	4.6	4	37	304	8.2	1	3	5
1998 NYG	16	113	432	3.8	3	31	131	4.2	1	0	4
NFL Total	64	288	1215	4.2	8	107	839	7.8	4	3	12

DAVE WAYMER Waymer, David Benjamin Jr. 6'1", 195 **DB**
Col: Notre Dame *HS:* West Charlotte [Charlotte, NC] B: 7/1/1958, Brooklyn, NY D: 4/28/1993, Mooresville, NC *Drafted:* 1980 Round 2 NO
1980 NO: PR 3-29 9.7. **1986** NO: Rec 1-13 13.0. **1988** NO: KR 2-39 19.5. **1991** SF: 1 Sac. **Total:** Rec 1-13 13.0; PR 3-29 9.7; KR 2-39 19.5; 1 Sac.

		Interceptions			
Year Team	G	Int	Yds	TD	Fum
1980 NO	16	0	0	0	1
1981 NO	16	4	54	0	0
1982 NO	9	0	0	0	0
1983 NO	16	0	0	0	0
1984 NO	16	4	9	0	0
1985 NO	16	6	49	0	1
1986 NO	16	9	48	0	0
1987 NO	12	5	78	0	0
1988 NO	16	3	91	0	1
1989 NO	16	6	66	0	0
1990 SF	16	7	64	0	0
1991 SF	16	4	77	0	0
1992 LARd	16	0	0	0	0
NFL Total	197	48	536	0	3

NATE WAYNE Wayne, Nathaniel Jr. 6'0", 230 **LB**
Col: Mississippi *HS:* Noxubee Co. [Macon, MS] B: 1/12/1975, Chicago, IL *Drafted:* 1998 Round 7 Den
1998 Den: 1 G.

RUSSELL WAYT Wayt, Russell Gene 6'4", 235 **LB**
Col: Rice *HS:* White Oak [TX] B: 10/6/1942, Oklahoma City, OK
Drafted: 1965 Round 8 Dal
1965 Dal: 9 G.

BOB WEAR Wear, Robert Foster 5'11", 205 **C-LB**
Col: Sacramento State; Penn State *HS:* Huntingdon [PA] B: 1/5/1919, Yeagertown, PA D: 4/22/1992, Martinsburg, PA
1942 Phi: 3 G.

FRED WEARY Weary, Joseph Fredrick 5'10", 177 **DB**
Col: Florida *HS:* Mandarin [Jacksonville, FL] B: 4/12/1974, Jacksonville, FL *Drafted:* 1998 Round 4 NO
1998 NO: 14 G; Int 2-64 1 TD; 6 Pt.

JIM WEATHERALL Weatherall, James Preston 6'4", 245 **DT-OT**
Col: Oklahoma *HS:* White Deer [TX] B: 10/26/1929, Graham, OK
D: 8/2/1992, Oklahoma City, OK *Drafted:* 1952 Round 2 Phi
1955 Phi: 12 G. **1956** Phi: 12 G. **1957** Phi: 12 G. **1958** Was: 9 G. **1959** Det: 8 G. **1960** Det: 12 G. **Total:** 65 G.

JIM WEATHERFORD Weatherford, James Earl 5'11", 186 **DB**
Col: Tennessee *HS:* Dalton [GA] B: 8/16/1946, Athens, GA
Drafted: 1969 Round 15 Atl
1969 Atl: 14 G; Int 1-18; **1** Fum TD; 6 Pt.

BONES WEATHERLY Weatherly, Gerald Craft 6'5", 218 **LB**
Col: Rice *HS:* Cuero [TX] B: 12/26/1928, Houston, TX *Drafted:* 1949 Round 8 ChiB
1950 ChiB: 6 G; Int 2-58 **2** TD; 12 Pt. **1952** ChiB: 5 G; Int 3-13. **1953** ChiB: 12 G; Int 1-13. **1954** ChiB: 12 G; Int 2-56; 6 Pt. **Total:** 35 G; Int 8-140 2 TD; Tot TD 3; 18 Pt.

JIM WEATHERLY Weatherly, James E 6'3", 245 **C**
Col: Mount San Antonio Coll. CA (J.C.) B: 4/13/1952, Hazen, AR
1976 Atl: 3 G.

CARL WEATHERS Weathers, Carl 6'2", 220 **LB**
Col: San Diego State *HS:* Long Beach Polytechnic [CA] B: 1/14/1948, New Orleans, LA
1970 Oak: 7 G. **1971** Oak: 1 G. **Total:** 8 G.

CLARENCE WEATHERS Weathers, Clarence 5'9", 170 **WR**
Col: Delaware State *HS:* Fort Pierce Westwood [FL] B: 1/10/1962, Green Pond, SC
1983 NE: Rush 1-28 28.0; KR 3-58 19.3. **1985** Cle: Rush 1-18 18.0; KR 1-17 17.0. **Total:** Rush 2-46 23.0; KR 4-75 18.8.

		Receiving				Punt Returns				
Year Team	G	Rec	Yds	Avg	TD	Ret	Yds	Avg	TD	Fum
1983 NE	16	19	379	19.9	3	4	1	0.3	0	2
1984 NE	9	8	115	14.4	2	1	7	7.0	0	0
1985 Cle	13	16	449	28.1	3	28	218	7.8	0	3
1986 Cle	16	9	100	11.1	0	0	0	—	0	0
1987 Cle	12	11	153	13.9	2	0	0	—	0	0
1988 Cle	16	29	436	15.0	1	2	10	5.0	0	2
1989 Ind-KC	15	23	254	11.0	0	0	0	—	0	1
1989 Ind	4	6	62	10.3	0	0	0	—	0	1
1989 KC	11	17	192	11.3	0	0	0	—	0	0
1990 GB	14	33	390	11.8	1	0	0	—	0	0
1991 GB	14	12	150	12.5	0	0	0	—	0	1
NFL Total	125	160	2426	15.2	12	35	236	6.7	0	9

CURTIS WEATHERS Weathers, Curtis Lenard 6'5", 224 **LB-TE**
Col: Mississippi *HS:* Bishop Byrne [Memphis, TN] B: 9/16/1956, Memphis, TN *Drafted:* 1979 Round 9 Cle
1979 Cle: 16 G; Rec 1-14 14.0; KR 1-0; 1 Fum. **1980** Cle: 10 G. **1981** Cle: 13 G. **1982** Cle: 7 G; 1 Sac. **1983** Cle: 16 G. **1984** Cle: 16 G. **1985** Cle: 16 G; Int 1-9; 3 Sac. **Total:** 94 G; Rec 1-14 14.0; KR 1-0; Int 1-9; 1 Fum; 4 Sac.

COP WEATHERS Weathers, Guy Barton 5'9", 230 **G**
Col: Baylor *HS:* Waco [TX] B: 6/9/1898, Gatesville, TX D: 9/27/1964, Marlin, TX
1926 Buf: 5 G.

ROBERT WEATHERS Weathers, Robert James 6'2", 220 **RB**
Col: Arizona *HS:* Fort Pierce Westwood [FL] B: 9/13/1960, Westfield, NY *Drafted:* 1982 Round 2 NE
1983 NE: KR 3-68 22.7. **1985** NE: KR 1-18 18.0. **Total:** KR 4-86 21.5.

		Rushing				Receiving				
Year Team	G	Att	Yds	Avg	TD	Rec	Yds	Avg	TD	Fum
1982 NE	6	24	83	3.5	1	3	24	8.0	0	1
1983 NE	15	73	418	5.7	1	23	212	9.2	0	4
1984 NE	2	0	0	—	0	0	0	—	0	0
1985 NE	16	41	174	4.2	1	2	18	9.0	0	0
1986 NE	5	21	58	2.8	1	1	14	14.0	0	0
NFL Total	44	159	733	4.6	4	29	268	9.2	0	5

CEPHUS WEATHERSPOON Weatherspoon, Cephus Jr. 6'1", 182 **WR**
Col: Mesa CC AZ; Fort Lewis *HS:* Globe [AZ] B: 6/14/1948, Meridian, MS *Drafted:* 1972 Round 13 NO
1972 NO: 1 G.

CHUCK WEATHERSPOON Weatherspoon, Johnny Jr. 5'7", 229 **RB**
Col: Houston *HS:* La Habra [CA] B: 7/31/1968, Hinesville, GA
Drafted: 1991 Round 9 Phi
1991 TB: 4 G.

JIM WEATHERWAX Weatherwax, James Michael 6'7", 260 **DT**
(Jungle Jim) *Col:* West Texas A&M; Los Angeles State *HS:* Redlands [CA] B: 1/9/1943, Porterville, CA *Drafted:* 1965 Round 11 GB
1966 GB: 14 G. **1967** GB: 14 G. **1969** GB: 6 G. **Total:** 34 G.

BUCK WEAVER Weaver, Charles A 6'4", 235 **G**
Col: Chicago *HS:* Jonesboro [AR] B: 11/1/1905, Cushman, AR
D: 9/1967
1930 ChiC-Port: 10 G. ChiC: 6 G. Port: 4 G. **Total:** 10 G.

CHARLIE WEAVER Weaver, Charles Earl Jr. 6'2", 220 **LB**
Col: Arizona Western Coll. (J.C.); USC *HS:* Richmond [CA]
B: 7/12/1949, Greenwood, MS *Drafted:* 1971 Round 2 Det
1973 Det: KR 1-0. **Total:** KR 1-0.

		Interceptions			
Year Team	**G**	**Int**	**Yds**	**TD**	**Fum**
1971 Det	14	0	0	0	0
1972 Det	14	1	0	0	0
1973 Det	13	2	32	0	1
1974 Det	14	3	4	0	0
1975 Det	12	1	31	0	0
1976 Det	14	2	24	0	0
1977 Det	14	1	0	0	0
1978 Det	16	3	32	0	0
1979 Det	8	1	17	0	0
1980 Det	16	1	-3	0	0
1981 Det-Was	12	0	0	0	0
1981 Det	7	0	0	0	0
1981 Was	5	0	0	0	0
NFL Total	147	15	137	0	1

EMANUEL WEAVER Weaver, Emanuel III 6'4", 260 **NT**
Col: Arizona Western Coll. (J.C.); South Carolina State *HS:* John McDonogh [New Orleans, LA] B: 6/28/1960, New Orleans, LA
Drafted: 1982 Round 2 Cin
1982 Cin: 5 G. **1987** Atl: 2 G. **Total:** 7 G.

GARY WEAVER Weaver, Gary Lynn 6'1", 224 **LB**
Col: Trinidad State JC CO; Fresno State *HS:* Bradshaw [Florence, AL]
B: 3/13/1949, Florence, AL *Drafted:* 1973 Round 7 Oak
1973 Oak: 10 G. **1974** Oak: 14 G. **1975** GB: 14 G. **1976** GB: 14 G.
1977 GB: 5 G. **1978** GB: 16 G. **1979** GB: 14 G. **Total:** 87 G.

RED WEAVER Weaver, James Redwick 5'10", 185 **C**
Col: Centre *HS:* North Side [Fort Worth, TX]; Somerset HS [KY]
B: 7/19/1897, Garland, TX D: 11/23/1968, Mayfield, KY
1923 Col: 10 G; Scor 2, 2 XK.

JOHN WEAVER Weaver, John Dean 6'2", 215 **G**
(Big John) *Col:* Miami (Ohio) *HS:* Versailles [OH] B: 3/31/1926, Dayton, OH
1949 NYB: 12 G.

LARRYE WEAVER Weaver, Lawerence Bernard 5'11", 190 **HB-DB**
Col: Antelope Valley Coll. CA (J.C.); Fullerton Coll. CA (J.C.)
HS: Anaheim [CA] B: 11/17/1931, Monte Vista, CO
1955 NYG: 6 G; Rush 3-0.

HERMAN WEAVER Weaver, William Herman 6'4", 210 **P**
(Thunderfoot) *Col:* Tennessee *HS:* Villa Rica [GA] B: 11/17/1948, Villa Rica, GA *Drafted:* 1970 Round 9 Det
1973 Det: Rush 1-18 18.0. **1975** Det: Pass 1-0. **1976** Det: Pass 2-1 50.0%, 14 7.00; Rush 1-0. **1977** Sea: Rush 1-(-2) -2.0. **1978** Sea: Pass 1-1 100.0%, 9 9.00; Rush 2-(-5) -2.5. **1979** Sea: Pass 4-3 75.0%, 73 18.25; Rush 2-(-6) -3.0. **1980** Sea: Pass 2-0. **Total:** Pass 10-5 50.0%, 96 9.60; Rush 7-5 0.7.

		Punting			
Year Team	**G**	**Punts**	**Yds**	**Avg**	**Fum**
1970 Det	14	62	2483	40.0	0
1971 Det	13	42	1752	41.7	0
1972 Det	14	43	1734	40.3	0
1973 Det	14	54	2333	43.2	1
1974 Det	14	72	2772	38.5	0
1975 Det	14	80	3361	42.0	0
1976 Det	14	83	3280	39.5	1
1977 Sea	13	58	2293	39.5	0
1978 Sea	16	66	2440	37.0	0
1979 Sea	16	66	2651	40.2	1
1980 Sea	16	67	2798	41.8	0
NFL Total	158	693	27897	40.3	3

ALLAN WEBB Webb, Allan 5'11", 180 **DB-HB**
Col: Arnold *HS:* Ansonia [CT] B: 1/22/1933, Washington, DC
1961 NYG: 10 G; Rush 6-51 8.5; PR 5-61 12.2; KR 8-156 19.5; 1 Fum.
1962 NYG: 14 G; Int 3-24. **1963** NYG: 7 G; PR 3-45 15.0; KR 3-62 20.7; Int 3-34. **1964** NYG: 14 G; Int 1-0. **1965** NYG: 3 G; KR 2-48 24.0.
Total: 48 G; Rush 6-51 8.5; PR 8-106 13.3; KR 13-266 20.5; Int 7-58; 1 Fum.

ART WEBB Webb, Arthur E 5'10", 210 **T-G**
Col: No College *HS:* Genessee Wesleyan Seminary [Lima, NY]
B: 2/17/1893 D: 4/9/1973, Cleveland, OH
1920 Roch: 8 G. **1922** Mil: 8 G. **Total:** 16 G.

CHUCK WEBB Webb, Charles Eugene 5'9", 201 **FB**
Col: Tennessee *HS:* Macomber-Whitney [Toledo, OH] B: 11/17/1969, Toledo, OH *Drafted:* 1991 Round 3 GB
1991 GB: 2 G; KR 2-40 20.0.

DON WEBB Webb, Donald Wayne 5'10", 182 **DB**
Col: Iowa State *HS:* Jefferson City [MO] B: 5/22/1939, Jefferson City, MO *Drafted:* 1961 Round 24 Bos
1961 Bos: KR 1-21 21.0; 1 Fum TD. **1962** Bos: Rec 1-11 11.0. **1971** NE: KR 1-0. **Total:** Rec 1-11 11.0; KR 2-21 10.5; 1 Fum TD.

		Interceptions			Tot
Year Team	**G**	**Int**	**Yds**	**TD**	**TD**
1961 Bos	14	5	153	2	4
1962 Bos	14	0	0	0	0
1964 Bos	14	6	43	0	0
1965 Bos	14	2	45	0	0
1966 Bos	14	1	0	0	0
1967 Bos	14	4	91	0	0
1968 Bos	10	0	0	0	0
1969 Bos	14	2	32	0	0
1970 Bos	14	1	2	0	0
1971 NE	12	0	0	0	0
NFL Total	134	21	366	2	4

GEORGE WEBB Webb, George Louis 6'1", 180 **OE-DE**
(Country) *Col:* Texas Tech *HS:* Itasca [TX] B: 4/2/1916, Itasca, TX
D: 9/9/1993, Amarillo, TX
1943 Bkn: 9 G; Rec 7-60 8.6.

JIMMY WEBB Webb, James Rogers 6'5", 247 **DT-DE**
Col: Mississippi State *HS:* Florence [MS] B: 4/13/1952, Jackson, MS
Drafted: 1975 Round 1 SF
1975 SF: 14 G. **1976** SF: 14 G. **1977** SF: 14 G. **1978** SF: 16 G. **1979** SF: 16 G. **1980** SF: 16 G. **1981** SD: 16 G. **Total:** 106 G.

KEN WEBB Webb, Kenneth Lee 5'11", 207 **HB-DB**
Col: Presbyterian *HS:* Decatur [GA] B: 8/15/1935, Albany, GA
Drafted: 1958 Round 14 Det

		Rushing				Receiving			
Year Team	**G**	**Att**	**Yds**	**Avg**	**TD**	**Rec**	**Yds**	**Avg**	**TD**
1958 Det	12	56	172	3.1	2	11	85	7.7	1
1959 Det	12	60	222	3.7	2	12	201	16.8	0
1960 Det	12	59	166	2.8	2	10	68	6.8	0
1961 Det	11	7	6	0.9	1	1	7	7.0	0
1962 Det	14	70	267	3.8	1	10	120	12.0	0
1963 Cle	12	12	58	4.8	0	2	2	1.0	0
NFL Total	73	264	891	3.4	8	46	483	10.5	1

	Kickoff Returns					Tot
Year Team	**Ret**	**Yds**	**Avg**	**TD**	**Fum**	**TD**
1958 Det	7	154	22.0	0	3	3
1959 Det	16	352	22.0	0	5	2
1960 Det	3	38	12.7	0	2	2
1961 Det	0	5	—	0	1	1
1962 Det	0	0	—	0	3	1
1963 Cle	1	12	12.0	0	0	0
NFL Total	27	561	20.8	0	14	9

RICHMOND WEBB Webb, Richmond Jewel 6'6", 310 **OT**
Col: Texas A&M *HS:* Franklin D. Roosevelt [Dallas, TX] B: 1/11/1967, Dallas, TX *Drafted:* 1990 Round 1 Mia
1990 Mia: 16 G. **1991** Mia: 14 G. **1992** Mia: 16 G. **1993** Mia: 16 G.
1994 Mia: 16 G. **1995** Mia: 16 G. **1996** Mia: 16 G. **1997** Mia: 16 G.
1998 Mia: 9 G. **Total:** 135 G.

HARRY WEBBER Webber, Harry 173 **E-BB**
Col: Morningside B: 10/18/1892, SD D: 10/1970, Salinas, CA
1920 RI: 3 G. **1923** RI: 1 G. **Total:** 4 G.

DUTCH WEBBER Webber, Howard Gilbert 6'2", 190 **OE-BB-TB**
(Cowboy) *Col:* Kansas State B: 12/15/1901, Oxford, NE D: 6/1985, Ulysses, KS
1924 KC: 9 G. **1925** KC-Cle: 12 G. KC: 8 G. Cle: 4 G. **1926** Har-NYG-KC: 11 G. Har: 8 G. NYG: 2 G. KC: 1 G. **1927** Cle: 3 G. **1928** GB: 3 G.
1930 Prov-Nwk: 4 G. Prov: 1 G. Nwk: 3 G. **Total:** 42 G.

CHUCK WEBER Weber, Charles Fredrick Jr. 6'1", 229 **LB-DE-OG**
Col: West Chester *HS:* Abington [PA] B: 3/25/1930, Philadelphia, PA
1956 Cle-ChiC: KR 2-3 1.5. Cle: KR 1-3 3.0. ChiC: KR 1-0. **1958** ChiC: KR 1-2 2.0. **1959** Phi: **1** Fum TD. **Total:** KR 3-5 1.7; 1 Fum TD.

Year Team	G	Interceptions Int	Yds	TD
1955 Cle	11	0	0	0
1956 Cle-ChiC	9	1	19	0
1956 Cle	4	0	0	0
1956 ChiC	5	1	19	0
1957 ChiC	12	0	0	0
1958 ChiC	10	0	0	0
1959 Phi	12	2	8	0
1960 Phi	12	6	48	0
1961 Phi	14	1	15	0
NFL Total	80	10	90	0

CHARLIE WEBER Weber, Charles Louis Jr. 6′1″, 203 **G**
Col: Colgate *HS:* HS of Commerce [New York, NY] B: 9/3/1892, New York, NY D: 10/1964
1926 Bkn: 8 G.

DICK WEBER Weber, Richard Wilfred 5′11″, 195 **TB-DB**
Col: St. Louis *HS:* Lawrence [MA] B: 4/10/1919, Lawrence, MA D: 11/19/1991, Salem, NH
1945 Det: 3 G; Pass 22-6 27.3%, 70 3.18 5 Int; Rush 7-10 1.4; KR 1-24 24.0; Punt 1-42 42.0; 1 Fum.

ALEX WEBSTER Webster, Alexander 6′3″, 225 **HB-FB**
(Red) *Col:* North Carolina State *HS:* Kearny [NJ] B: 4/19/1931, Kearny, NJ *Drafted:* 1953 Round 11 Was
1959 NYG: Pass 1-0. **Total:** Pass 1-0.

Year Team	G	Rushing Att	Yds	Avg	TD	Receiving Rec	Yds	Avg	TD	Fum	Tot TD
1955 NYG	12	128	634	5.0	5	22	269	12.2	1	3	6
1956 NYG	12	178	694	3.9	7	21	197	9.4	3	4	10
1957 NYG	11	135	478	3.5	5	30	330	11.0	1	5	6
1958 NYG	9	100	398	4.0	3	25	279	11.2	3	5	6
1959 NYG	10	79	250	3.2	5	27	381	14.1	2	2	7
1960 NYG	8	22	48	2.2	0	8	106	13.3	0	1	0
1961 NYG	14	196	928	4.7	2	26	313	12.0	3	5	5
1962 NYG	14	207	743	3.6	5	47	477	10.1	4	4	9
1963 NYG	7	75	255	3.4	4	15	128	8.5	0	2	4
1964 NYG	12	76	210	2.8	3	19	199	10.5	0	3	3
NFL Total	109	1196	4638	3.9	39	240	2679	11.2	17	34	56

CORNELL WEBSTER Webster, Cornell Preston 6′0″, 180 **DB**
Col: Scottsdale CC AZ; UCLA; Tulsa *HS:* Garey [Pomona, CA] B: 11/2/1954, Greeneville, TN
1977 Sea: 14 G; Int 1-(-4). **1978** Sea: 15 G; Int 5-9. **1979** Sea: 15 G; Rec 1-39 39.0; Int 1-0; **1** Fum TD; 6 Pt. **1980** Sea: 8 G; KR 21-406 19.3; Int 1-0; 1 Fum. **Total:** 52 G; Rec 1-39 39.0; KR 21-406 19.3; Int 8-5; 1 Fum TD; 6 Pt; 1 Fum.

DAVE WEBSTER Webster, David 6′4″, 220 **DB**
Col: Prairie View A&M *HS:* Westside [Anderson, SC] B: 7/23/1937
1960 DalT: **1** Fum TD. **Total:** 1 Fum TD.

Year Team	G	Interceptions Int	Yds	TD	Tot TD
1960 DalT	14	6	**156**	**2**	3
1961 DalT	14	5	50	0	0
NFL Total	28	11	206	2	3

ELNARDO WEBSTER Webster, Elnardo Julian 6′2″, 243 **LB**
Col: Rutgers *HS:* St. Peter's Prep [Jersey City, NJ] B: 12/23/1969, Goritza, Italy *Drafted:* 1992 Round 9 Pit
1992 Pit: 3 G.

GEORGE WEBSTER Webster, George Delano 6′4″, 220 **LB**
Col: Michigan State *HS:* Westside [Anderson, SC] B: 11/25/1945, Anderson, SC *Drafted:* 1967 Round 1 Hou
1967 Hou: 14 G; Int 1-23. **1968** Hou: 14 G; Int 1-9. **1969** Hou: 14 G; Int 2-35. **1970** Hou: 7 G. **1971** Hou: 10 G. **1972** Hou-Pit: 11 G. Hou: 5 G. Pit: 6 G. **1973** Pit: 12 G; KR 1-9 9.0. **1974** NE: 14 G. **1975** NE: 10 G; Int 1-0. **1976** NE: 13 G. **Total:** 119 G; KR 1-9 9.0; Int 5-67.

KEVIN WEBSTER Webster, Kevin 6′2″, 260 **OG**
Col: Northern Iowa B: 3/6/1962, Berwyn, IL
1987 Min: 3 G.

LARRY WEBSTER Webster, Larry Melvin Jr. 6′5″, 290 **DT-DE**
Col: Maryland *HS:* Elkton [MD] B: 1/18/1969, Elkton, MD *Drafted:* 1992 Round 3 Mia
1992 Mia: 16 G; 1.5 Sac. **1993** Mia: 13 G. **1994** Mia: 16 G. **1995** Cle: 10 G. **1997** Bal: 16 G. **1998** Bal: 15 G. **Total:** 86 G; 1.5 Sac.

MIKE WEBSTER Webster, Michael Lewis 6′1″, 255 **C-OG**
Col: Wisconsin *HS:* Rhinelander [WI] B: 3/18/1952, Tomahawk, WI *Drafted:* 1974 Round 5 Pit *HOF:* 1997
1974 Pit: 14 G. **1975** Pit: 14 G. **1976** Pit: 14 G; 2 Fum. **1977** Pit: 14 G. **1978** Pit: 16 G; 1 Fum. **1979** Pit: 16 G. **1980** Pit: 16 G. **1981** Pit: 16 G. **1982** Pit: 9 G. **1983** Pit: 16 G. **1984** Pit: 16 G. **1985** Pit: 16 G. **1986** Pit: 12 G. **1987** Pit: 15 G. **1988** Pit: 16 G; 2 Fum. **1989** KC: 16 G. **1990** KC: 9 G. **Total:** 245 G; 5 Fum.

TIM WEBSTER Webster, Timothy Duane 6′0″, 195 **K**
Col: Arkansas *HS:* Grove [OK] B: 9/11/1949, Henryetta, OK
1971 GB: 4 G; Scor 26, 6-11 54.5% FG, 8-8 100.0% XK.

MIKE WEDDINGTON Weddington, Michael Wayne 6′4″, 245 **LB**
Col: Oklahoma *HS:* Temple [TX] B: 10/9/1960, Belton, TX
1986 GB: 3 G. **1987** GB: 12 G. **1988** GB: 16 G. **1989** GB: 15 G; 1 Sac. **1990** GB: 6 G. **Total:** 52 G; 1 Sac.

DICK WEDEL Wedel, Richard Wesley 5′11″, 205 **G**
(Bud) *Col:* Wake Forest *HS:* Fort Pierce Central [FL] B: 5/29/1923, Toledo, OH *Drafted:* 1948 Round 22 ChiC
1948 ChiC: 1 G.

HERMAN WEDEMEYER Wedemeyer, Herman John 5′10″, 178 **HB-TB**
(Squirmin' Herman) *Col:* St. Mary's (Cal.) *HS:* St. Louis [Honolulu, HI] B: 5/20/1924, Honolulu, HI D: 1/25/1999, Honolulu, HI
AAFC **1948** LA-A: Pass 30-9 30.0%, 79 2.63 3 Int; Punt 1-10 10.0. **1949** BalA: Pass 1-0, 1 Int; Punt 3-54 18.0. **Total:** Pass 31-9 29.0%, 79 2.55 4 Int; Punt 4-64 16.0.

Year Team	G	Rushing Att	Yds	Avg	TD	Receiving Rec	Yds	Avg	TD
1948 LA-A	14	79	249	3.2	0	36	330	9.2	2
1949 BalA	11	64	291	4.5	0	10	112	11.2	0
AAFC Total	25	143	540	3.8	0	46	442	9.6	2

Year Team	Punt Returns Ret	Yds	Avg	TD	Kickoff Returns Ret	Yds	Avg	TD
1948 LA-A	23	368	16.0	0	11	240	21.8	0
1949 BalA	16	221	13.8	0	30	602	20.1	0
AAFC Total	39	589	15.1	0	41	842	20.5	0

TAD WEED Weed, Thurlow 5′5″, 140 **K**
Col: Ohio State *HS:* Grandview Heights [OH] B: 1/18/1933, Columbus, OH
1955 Pit: 6 G; Scor 21, 3-6 50.0% FG, 12-12 100.0% XK.

DON WEEDON Weedon, John Donald 5′11″, 220 **G**
Col: Texas *HS:* Bryan [TX] B: 1/13/1919, Bryan, TX D: 11/19/1981, Austin, TX
1947 Phi: 12 G.

GEORGE WEEKS Weeks, George Ellison 6′2″, 195 **DE**
Col: Alabama *HS:* Dothan [AL] B: 12/16/1918, Dothan, AL D: 3/1980, Florence, AL *Drafted:* 1943 Round 14 Phi
1944 Bkn: 3 G.

NORRIS WEESE Weese, Norris Lee 6′1″, 195 **QB-P**
Col: Mississippi *HS:* Chalmette [LA] B: 8/12/1951, Baton Rouge, LA D: 1/19/1995, Denver, CO *Drafted:* 1974 Round 4 LARm

Year Team	G	Passing Att	Comp	Comp%	Yds	YPA	TD	Int	Rating
1976 Den	14	47	24	51.1	314	6.68	1	6	40.0
1977 Den	14	20	11	55.0	119	5.95	1	0	89.4
1978 Den	13	87	55	63.2	723	8.31	4	5	80.8
1979 Den	16	97	53	54.6	731	7.54	1	3	69.6
NFL Total	57	251	143	57.0	1887	7.52	7	14	66.9

Year Team	Rushing Att	Yds	Avg	TD	Punting Punts	Yds	Avg	Fum
1976 Den	23	142	6.2	0	52	1852	35.6	2
1977 Den	11	56	5.1	1	1	38	38.0	0
1978 Den	17	48	2.8	1	0	0	—	3
1979 Den	18	116	6.4	3	0	0	—	4
NFL Total	69	362	5.2	5	53	1890	35.7	9

BUCKY WEGENER Wegener, William Leslie 5′10″, 245 **OG**
Col: Missouri *HS:* Lafayette Co. [Higginsville, MO] B: 10/31/1939 *Drafted:* 1962 Round 16 StL
1962 Hou: 4 G. **1963** Hou: 14 G. **Total:** 18 G.

MIKE WEGER Weger, Michael Roy 6′2″, 200 **DB**
Col: Bowling Green State *HS:* Bowling Green [OH] B: 10/2/1945, Dallas, TX *Drafted:* 1967 Round 9 Det
1967 Det: PR 1-0; KR 2-27 13.5. **1971** Det: **1** Fum TD. **1975** Det: KR 3-42 14.0. **Total:** PR 1-0; KR 5-69 13.8; 1 Fum TD.

Year Team	G	Interceptions Int	Yds	TD	Fum	Tot TD
1967 Det	14	0	0	0	1	0
1968 Det	14	5	50	0	0	0
1969 Det	13	3	44	0	0	0
1970 Det	14	5	52	1	0	1
1971 Det	14	1	16	0	0	1
1972 Det	14	0	0	0	0	0
1973 Det	12	2	20	0	0	0
1975 Det	13	1	23	0	0	0
1976 Hou	4	0	0	0	0	0

1977 Hou	11	0	0	0	0	0
NFL Total	123	17	205	1	1	2

TED WEGERT Wegert, Theodore Addison 5′11″, 202 **HB**
Col: No College *HS:* Riverhead [NY] B: 4/17/1932, Riverhead, NY D: 2/18/1986, Port Charlotte, FL
1955 Phi: Rec 3-17 5.7; KR 4-87 21.8. **1956** Phi: Rec 6-46 7.7. **1960** NYT-Den-Buf: Rec 5-68 13.6 1 TD; PR 4-25 6.3; KR 10-252 25.2. NYT: Rec 5-68 13.6 1 TD. Den: KR 6-143 23.8. Buf: PR 4-25 6.3; KR 4-109 27.3. **Total:** Rec 14-131 9.4 1 TD; PR 4-25 6.3; KR 14-339 24.2.

		Rushing					Tot
Year Team	G	Att	Yds	Avg	TD	Fum	TD
1955 Phi	7	26	120	4.6	2	2	2
1956 Phi	7	47	127	2.7	1	3	1
1960 NYT-Den-Buf	12	36	161	4.5	1	1	2
1960 NYT	6	31	124	4.0	1	1	2
1960 Den	4	5	37	7.4	0	0	0
1960 Buf	2	0	0	—	0	0	0
NFL Total	26	109	408	3.7	4	6	5

RAY WEHBA Wehba, Raymond E 6′0″, 215 **OE-DE**
Col: USC *HS:* Central [Oklahoma City, OK] B: 8/16/1916, Sherman, TX
1943 Bkn: 10 G; Rec 4-43 10.8; KR 1-15 15.0. **1944** GB: 10 G; Rec 6-67 11.2; Int 1-7. **Total:** 20 G; Rec 10-110 11.0; KR 1-15 15.0; Int 1-7.

ROGER WEHRLI Wehrli, Roger Russel 6′0″, 190 **DB**
Col: Missouri *HS:* King City [MO] B: 11/26/1947, New Point, MO
Drafted: 1969 Round 1 StL
1969 StL: KR 1-18 18.0. **1972** StL: KR 1-10 10.0. **1973** StL: KR 2-0. **1975** StL: KR 1-10 10.0; Scor **1** 1XP. **1976** StL: Pass 1-0; Rush 2-8 4.0. **1977** StL: Rush 1-19 19.0. **1978** StL: Rush 1-0. **1982** StL: Rush 1-18 18.0 1 TD. **Total:** Pass 1-0; Rush 5-45 9.0 1 TD; KR 5-38 7.6; Scor 1 1XP.

		Punt Returns				Interceptions				Tot
Year Team	G	Ret	Yds	Avg	TD	Int	Yds	TD	Fum	TD
1969 StL	13	13	65	5.0	0	3	44	0	0	0
1970 StL	14	1	4	4.0	0	6	50	0	0	0
1971 StL	13	9	84	9.3	0	2	11	0	2	0
1972 StL	14	5	24	4.8	0	0	0	0	2	0
1973 StL	11	9	92	10.2	0	1	0	0	0	0
1974 StL	14	4	39	9.8	0	2	54	1	1	1
1975 StL	14	1	2	2.0	0	6	31	0	0	0
1976 StL	14	0	0	—	0	4	31	0	1	0
1977 StL	14	0	0	—	0	5	44	0	0	0
1978 StL	16	0	0	—	0	4	3	0	0	0
1979 StL	16	0	0	—	0	2	8	1	1	1
1980 StL	16	0	0	—	0	1	25	0	0	0
1981 StL	16	0	0	—	0	4	8	0	0	0
1982 StL	8	0	0	—	0	0	0	0	0	1
NFL Total	193	42	310	7.4	0	40	309	2	7	3

BERT WEIDNER Weidner, Bert James 6′3″, 288 **C-OG**
Col: Kent State *HS:* Eden [NY] B: 1/20/1966, Eden, NY
Drafted: 1989 Round 11 Mia
1990 Mia: 8 G. **1991** Mia: 15 G. **1992** Mia: 16 G. **1993** Mia: 16 G. **1994** Mia: 14 G. **1995** Mia: 12 G. **Total:** 81 G.

LEE WEIGEL Weigel, Lee Elmer 5′11″, 220 **RB**
Col: Wis.-Eau Claire B: 11/15/1963
1987 GB: 2 G; Rush 10-26 2.6; Rec 1-17 17.0.

JACK WEIL Weil, Jack Lee 5′11″, 175 **P**
Col: Wyoming *HS:* Northglenn [CO] B: 3/16/1962, Denver, CO

		Punting		
Year Team	G	Punts	Yds	Avg
1986 Den	6	34	1344	39.5
1987 Was	3	14	482	34.4
NFL Total	9	48	1826	38.0

CHUCK WEIMER Weimer, Howard Lee 5′9″, 178 **TB-HB-BB**
(Dutch) *Col:* Wilmington (Del.) *HS:* London [OH] B: 9/5/1904, London, OH D: 4/27/1990, Grove City, OH
1929 Buf: 9 G; Pass 3 TD; Rush 1 TD; Scor 18, **3** FG, 3 XK. **1930** Bkn: 11 G; Rec 2 TD; Scor 13, 1 XK. **1931** Cle: 7 G. **Total:** 27 G; Pass 3 TD; Rush 1 TD; Rec 2 TD; Scor 31, 3 FG, 4 XK; Tot TD 3.

HENRY WEINBERG Weinberg, Henry K 5′7″, 190 **G-T**
Col: Duquesne *HS:* Mount Pleasant [PA] B: 3/4/1910, Mount Pleasant, PA D: 10/31/1992, Baton Rouge, LA
1934 Pit: 8 G.

SOL WEINBERG Weinberg, Sol Edward 5′10″, 165 **TB**
(AKA Weinberger) *Col:* Case Western Reserve *HS:* Central [Cleveland, OH] B: 6/2/1894 D: 7/1962, NJ
1923 Cle: 2 G.

REDS WEINER Weiner, Albert 5′9″, 180 **FB-LB-BB-DB**
Col: Muhlenberg *HS:* Frank H. Morrell [Irvington, NJ] B: 1/24/1911, Woodbine, NJ D: 9/17/1988, Sea Isle City, NJ
1934 Phi: 5 G; Pass 6-3 50.0%, 40 6.67 2 TD; Rush 9-37 4.1; Scor 6, 1 FG, 3 XK.

ART WEINER Weiner, Arthur Edward 6′3″, 212 **OE-DE**
Col: North Carolina *HS:* West Side [Newark, NJ] B: 8/16/1924, Newark, NJ

		Receiving				
Year Team	G	Rec	Yds	Avg	TD	Fum
1950 NYY	12	35	722	20.6	6	1

BERNIE WEINER Weiner, Bernard Morris 5′11″, 222 **T-G**
Col: Kansas State B: 1/24/1918, Newark, NJ D: 4/1980, Passaic, NJ
Drafted: 1941 Round 9 Bkn
1942 Bkn: 10 G.

TODD WEINER Weiner, Todd Michael 6′4″, 300 **OT**
Col: Kansas State *HS:* J.P. Taravella [Coral Springs, FL] B: 9/16/1975, Bristol, PA *Drafted:* 1998 Round 2 Sea
1998 Sea: 6 G.

ARNIE WEINMEISTER Weinmeister, Arnold George 6′4″, 235 **DT-OT**
Col: Washington *HS:* Jefferson [Portland, OR] B: 3/23/1923, Rhein, Canada *Drafted:* 1945 Round 17 Bkn *HOF:* 1984
AAFC **1948** NY-A: 14 G. **1949** NY-A: 11 G. **Total:** 25 G.

NFL **1950** NYG: 10 G; Rec 1-16 16.0. **1951** NYG: 12 G. **1952** NYG: 12 G; Scor **1** Saf; 2 Pt. **1953** NYG: 12 G. **Total:** 46 G; Rec 1-16 16.0; Scor 1 Saf; 2 Pt.

IZZY WEINSTOCK Weinstock, Isadore 5′11″, 190 **LB-FB-BB**
Col: Pittsburgh *HS:* James M. Coughlin [Wilkes-Barre, PA] B: 6/27/1913, Wilkes-Barre, PA D: 9/26/1997, Fort Lauderdale, FL
1935 Phi: Pass 5-1 20.0%, 12 2.40 1 Int; Rec 8-107 13.4. **1937** Pit: Scor 4, 4 XK. **Total:** Pass 5-1 20.0%, 12 2.40 1 Int; Rec 8-107 13.4.

		Rushing			
Year Team	G	Att	Yds	Avg	TD
1935 Phi	11	58	176	3.0	0
1937 Pit	11	30	88	2.9	0
1938 Pit	2	1	0	0.0	0
NFL Total	24	89	264	3.0	0

JOE WEIR Weir, Joseph Erwin 5′11″, 185 **E**
Col: Nebraska *HS:* Superior [NE] B: 8/26/1905, Superior, NE D: 2/6/1986, Sioux City, IA
1927 Fra: 12 G.

ED WEIR Weir, Samuel Edwin 5′10″, 192 **T-E**
Col: Nebraska *HS:* Superior [NE] B: 3/14/1903, Superior, NE D: 5/15/1991, Lincoln, NE
1926 Fra: 4 G; Scor 5, 1 FG, 2 XK. **1927** Fra: 18 G; Scor 1, 1 XK. **1928** Fra: 14 G; Scor 7, 1 XK; 1 Fum TD. **Total:** 36 G; Scor 13, 1 FG, 4 XK; 1 Fum TD.

SAMMY WEIR Weir, Samuel Orville 5′9″, 170 **WR**
Col: Arkansas State *HS:* Walnut Ridge [AR] B: 3/18/1941, Moxie, AR
1965 Hou: 9 G; Rec 1-12 12.0; PR 1-0; KR 10-215 21.5; 1 Fum. **1966** NYJ: 11 G; Rec 1-4 4.0; PR 8-48 6.0; KR 6-121 20.2; 2 Fum. **Total:** 20 G; Rec 2-16 8.0; PR 9-48 5.3; KR 16-336 21.0; 3 Fum.

ED WEISACOSKY Weisacosky, Edward L 6′1″, 230 **LB**
Col: Miami (Fla.) *HS:* Pottsville [PA] B: 5/4/1944, Pottsville, PA
1967 NYG: 14 G. **1968** Mia: 8 G. **1969** Mia: 14 G; Int 3-10. **1970** Mia: 3 G. **1971** NE: 14 G. **1972** NE: 14 G. **Total:** 67 G; Int 3-10.

HEINIE WEISENBAUGH Weisenbaugh, Henry A 5′11″, 190 **BB-LB-HB-DB**
Col: Pittsburgh *HS:* Tarentum [PA]; Kiski School [Saltsburg, PA] B: 3/12/1914, Tarentum, PA D: 1965
1935 Bos-Pit: Pass 11-1 9.1%, 14 1.27 1 Int; Rec 7-73 10.4 2 TD. Bos: Rec 1-6 6.0. Pit: Pass 11-1 9.1%, 14 1.27 1 Int; Rec 6-67 11.2 2 TD. **1936** Bos: Rec 3-37 12.3. **Total:** Pass 11-1 9.1%, 14 1.27 1 Int; Rec 10-110 11.0 2 TD.

		Rushing			
Year Team	G	Att	Yds	Avg	TD
1935 Bos-Pit	9	36	50	1.4	0
1935 Bos	4	15	39	2.6	0
1935 Pit	5	21	11	0.5	0
1936 Bos	9	3	9	3.0	0
NFL Total	18	39	59	1.5	0

DICK WEISGERBER Weisgerber, Richard Arthur 5′10″, 200 **BB-DE-DB**
Col: Willamette *HS:* St. Benedict's Prep [Newark, NJ] B: 2/19/1913, Kearny, NJ D: 6/1/1984, Sturgeon Bay, WI
1938 GB: 1 G; Rush 6-13 2.2. **1939** GB: 4 G. **1940** GB: 10 G; Rec 1-37 37.0; Int 4-51. **1942** GB: 9 G; Rush 5-21 4.2; Scor 2, 2-2 100.0% XK.

Total: 24 G; Rush 11-34 3.1; Rec 1-37 37.0; Int 4-51; Scor 2, 2-2 100.0% XK.

CLAYTON WEISHUHN Weishuhn, Clayton Charles 6'2", 220 LB
Col: Angelo State *HS:* Wall [TX] B: 10/9/1959, San Angelo, TX
Drafted: 1982 Round 3 NE
1982 NE: 9 G; 2 Sac. **1983** NE: 16 G; Int 0-27 1 TD; 6 Pt; 2 Sac. **1984** NE: 1 G. **1986** NE: 4 G. **1987** GB: 9 G; KR 1-1 1.0. **Total:** 39 G; KR 1-1 1.0; Int 0-27 1 TD; 6 Pt; 4 Sac.

HOWIE WEISS Weiss, Howard William 6'0", 210 FB-LB
Col: Wisconsin *HS:* Fort Atkinson [WI] B: 10/12/1917, Fort Atkinson, WI D: 11/23/1997, Milwaukee, WI *Drafted:* 1939 Round 2 Det
1939 Det: Rec 4-25 6.3. **1940** Det: Rec 4-56 14.0; Int 2-14; **1** Fum TD.
Total: Rec 8-81 10.1; Int 2-14; 1 Fum TD.

		Rushing				Tot
Year Team	G	Att	Yds	Avg	TD	TD
1939 Det	9	37	150	4.1	0	0
1940 Det	11	79	298	3.8	3	4
NFL Total	20	116	448	3.9	3	4

JOHN WEISS Weiss, John 6'3", 198 OE-DB
Col: No College *HS:* Henry Snyder [Jersey City, NJ] B: 2/7/1922, Jersey City, NJ D: 8/1976
1944 NYG: 10 G; Rec 1-10 10.0. **1945** NYG: 10 G; Rec 4-82 20.5 1 TD; KR 2-36 18.0; 6 Pt. **1946** NYG: 7 G; Rec 4-70 17.5 1 TD; 6 Pt. **1947** NYG: 1 G. **Total:** 28 G; Rec 9-162 18.0 2 TD; KR 2-36 18.0; 12 Pt.

RON WEISSENHOFER Weissenhofer, Ronald Allen 6'3", 235 LB
Col: Notre Dame *HS:* St. Rita [Chicago, IL] B: 2/3/1964, Chicago, IL
1987 NO: 1 G.

TRIPP WELBORNE Welborne, Sullivan Anthony 6'0", 205 DB
Col: Michigan *HS:* Walter H. Page [Greensboro, NC] B: 11/20/1968, Reidsville, NC *Drafted:* 1991 Round 7 Min
1992 Min: 2 G.

CLAXTON WELCH Welch, Claxton Nathaniel 5'11", 203 RB
Col: Oregon *HS:* David Douglas [Portland, OR] B: 7/3/1947, Portland, OR *Drafted:* 1969 Round 9 Dal
1969 Dal: KR 5-112 22.4. **1971** Dal: Rec 1-(-1) -1.0; KR 4-105 26.3; Scor 1 Saf. **1973** NE: Rec 6-22 3.7. **Total:** Rec 7-21 3.0; KR 9-217 24.1; Scor 1 Saf.

		Rushing				
Year Team	G	Att	Yds	Avg	TD	Fum
1969 Dal	6	6	21	3.5	0	0
1970 NO-Dal	9	5	13	2.6	1	0
1970 NO	1	0	0	—	0	0
1970 Dal	8	5	13	2.6	1	0
1971 Dal	14	14	51	3.6	1	1
1973 NE	2	1	-2	-2.0	0	1
NFL Total	31	26	83	3.2	2	2

GIBBY WELCH Welch, Gilbert Laverne 5'11", 178 WB-BB-TB
Col: Pittsburgh *HS:* Parkersburg [WV]; Bellefonte Acad. [PA]
B: 12/24/1904, Parkersburg, WV D: 2/10/1984, Pittsburgh, PA
1928 NYY: 13 G; Pass 1 TD; Rush 1 TD; Rec **6** TD; Int **1** TD; Tot TD 8; 48 Pt. **1929** Prov: 12 G; Rush 2 TD; Rec 4 TD; Tot TD 6; 36 Pt.
Total: 25 G; Pass 1 TD; Rush 3 TD; Rec 10 TD; Int 1 TD; Tot TD 14; 84 Pt.

HERB WELCH Welch, Herbert Doyan Jr. 5'11", 180 DB
Col: UCLA *HS:* Earl Warren [Downey, CA] B: 1/12/1961, Los Angeles, CA *Drafted:* 1985 Round 12 NYG
1985 NYG: 16 G; Int 2-8. **1986** NYG: 16 G; Int 2-22. **1987** NYG: 12 G; Int 2-7. **1989** Was: 9 G. **1990** Det: 16 G; Int 1-16. **1991** Det: 10 G.
Total: 79 G; Int 7-53.

JIM WELCH Welch, James Evan 6'0", 196 DB
Col: Southern Methodist *HS:* Abilene [TX] B: 3/17/1938, Anson, TX
Drafted: 1960 Round 3 Bal
1960 Bal: 11 G; Rush 5-23 4.6; KR 4-80 20.0. **1961** Bal: 14 G; Rush 1-60 60.0 1 TD; KR 5-146 29.2; 6 Pt. **1962** Bal: 13 G; Int 1-30. **1963** Bal: 14 G; Int 4-49. **1964** Bal: 13 G. **1965** Bal: 14 G. **1966** Bal: 11 G. **1967** Bal: 10 G; Rush 2-6 3.0; 1 Fum. **1968** Det: 14 G; Rush 3-14 4.7. **Total:** 114 G; Rush 11-103 9.4 1 TD; KR 9-226 25.1; Int 5-79; 6 Pt; 1 Fum.

HAL WELDIN Weldin, Harold George 6'1", 198 C-LB
(Hank) *Col:* Northwestern *HS:* Manual [Peoria, IL] B: 5/25/1909
D: 12/15/1988, Hilton Head, SC
1934 StL: 1 G.

BODIE WELDON Weldon, John Ambrose 5'7", 165 WB-TB
Col: Lafayette *HS:* MacKenzie [Detroit, MI] B: 11/7/1895, Watertown, NY D: 5/24/1928, Columbus, OH
1920 Buf: 9 G.

LARRY WELDON Weldon, Lawrence Davis 6'0", 198 QB-DB-DE
Col: Presbyterian *HS:* Hillcrest [Dalzell, SC] B: 6/24/1915, Sumter, SC
D: 8/17/1990, Virginia Beach, VA
1944 Was: 8 G; Pass 6-4 66.7%, 33 5.50; Rush 8-8 1.0; KR 3-28 9.3; Scor 4, 4-4 100.0% XK. **1945** Was: 4 G; Scor 1, 1-1 100.0% XK.
Total: 12 G; Pass 6-4 66.7%, 33 5.50; Rush 8-8 1.0; KR 3-28 9.3; Scor 5, 5-5 100.0% XK.

CASEY WELDON Weldon, William Casey 6'1", 203 QB
Col: Florida State *HS:* North Florida Christian [Tallahassee, FL]
B: 2/3/1969, Americus, GA *Drafted:* 1992 Round 4 Phi
1995 TB: Rush 5-5 1.0 1 TD. **1996** TB: Rush 2-(-1) -0.5. **Total:** Rush 7-4 0.6 1 TD.

		Passing								
Year Team	G	Att	Comp	Comp%	Yds	YPA	TD	Int	Rating	Fum
1993 TB	3	11	6	54.5	55	5.00	0	1	30.5	0
1994 TB	2	9	7	77.8	63	7.00	0	0	95.8	0
1995 TB	16	91	42	46.2	519	5.70	1	2	58.8	4
1996 TB	3	9	5	55.6	76	8.44	0	1	44.0	1
NFL Total	24	120	60	50.0	713	5.94	1	4	57.4	5

JOE WELLBORN Wellborn, Joseph Holler 6'2", 230 C
Col: Texas A&M *HS:* St. Thomas [Houston, TX] B: 6/3/1944, Wellborn, MS
1966 NYG: 7 G.

RABBIT WELLER Weller, Louis 5'5", 150 WB-DB
(Bub) *Col:* Haskell Indian *HS:* Haskell Indian [Lawrence, KS]
B: 3/2/1904, Anadarko, OK D: 4/17/1979, Albuquerque, NM
1933 Bos: 7 G; Pass 2-0; Rush 12-112 9.3 2 TD; Rec 1-1 1.0; 12 Pt.

BUB WELLER Weller, Raymond Fred 6'4", 224 T-E
Col: Nebraska *HS:* Seward [NE] B: 8/7/1902, Seward, NE
D: 2/21/1986, Citrus Heights, CA
1923 StL: 7 G. **1924** Mil: 13 G. **1925** ChiC: 3 G. **1926** ChiC: 12 G.
1927 ChiC: 11 G; Rec 1 TD; Scor 8, 2 XK. **1928** Fra: 15 G. **Total:** 61 G; Rec 1 TD.

GARY WELLMAN Wellman, Gary James 5'9", 170 WR
Col: USC *HS:* Westlake [Westlake Village, CA] B: 8/9/1967, Syracuse, NY *Drafted:* 1991 Round 5 Hou
1993 Hou: Rush 2-6 3.0. **1994** Hou: Rush 1-(-3) -3.0. **Total:** Rush 3-3 1.0.

		Receiving				
Year Team	G	Rec	Yds	Avg	TD	Fum
1992 Hou	9	0	0	—	0	0
1993 Hou	11	31	430	13.9	1	1
1994 Hou	8	10	112	11.2	0	1
NFL Total	28	41	542	13.2	1	2

MIKE WELLMAN Wellman, Michael Jay 6'3", 253 C
Col: Kansas *HS:* Lawrence [KS] B: 7/15/1956, Newton, KS
Drafted: 1979 Round 3 LARm
1979 GB: 16 G; KR 1-10 10.0. **1980** GB: 4 G. **Total:** 20 G; KR 1-10 10.0.

ARTHUR WELLS Wells, Arthur Lee 6'4", 236 TE
Col: Grambling State *HS:* Mansfield [LA] B: 2/1/1963, Shreveport, LA
1987 TB: 2 G; **1** Fum TD; 6 Pt.

DANA WELLS Wells, Dana Clemmer Jr. 6'0", 272 NT
Col: Arizona *HS:* Brophy Prep [Phoenix, AZ] B: 8/5/1966, Phoenix, AZ
Drafted: 1989 Round 11 Cin
1989 Cin: 1 G.

DEAN WELLS Wells, Donald Dean 6'3", 248 LB
Col: Kentucky *HS:* Holy Cross [Louisville, KY] B: 7/20/1970, Louisville, KY *Drafted:* 1993 Round 4 Sea
1993 Sea: 14 G. **1994** Sea: 15 G. **1995** Sea: 14 G. **1996** Sea: 16 G; 1 Sac. **1997** Sea: 16 G; 1 Sac. **1998** Sea: 9 G; Int 1-25. **Total:** 84 G; Int 1-25; 2 Sac.

DON WELLS Wells, Donald Ray 6'2", 200 DE-OE
Col: Georgia *HS:* Fort Pierce Central [FL] B: 7/12/1922, Waycross, GA
D: 2/14/1989, Stuart, FL *Drafted:* 1945 Round 4 GB
1946 GB: 11 G; Rec 2-74 37.0. **1947** GB: 12 G. **1948** GB: 12 G. **1949** GB: 3 G. **Total:** 38 G; Rec 2-74 37.0.

HAROLD WELLS Wells, Harold 6'2", 220 LB
Col: Purdue *HS:* Sumner [St. Louis, MO] B: 11/26/1938, St. Louis, MO
1965 Phi: 14 G; KR 1-8 8.0. **1966** Phi: 14 G; Int 1-8; **1** Fum TD; 6 Pt.
1967 Phi: 14 G; Int 1-17. **1968** Phi: 14 G; Int 2-0. **Total:** 56 G; KR 1-8 8.0; Int 4-25; 1 Fum TD; 6 Pt.

JOEL WELLS Wells, Joel Whitlock 6'1", 200 HB
Col: Clemson *HS:* Dreher [Columbia, SC] B: 11/26/1935, Columbia, SC *Drafted:* 1957 Round 2 GB
1961 NYG: Rec 6-31 5.2 1 TD; PR 17-90 5.3; KR 12-273 22.8.

		Rushing					Tot
Year Team	G	Att	Yds	Avg	TD	Fum	TD
1961 NYG	14	65	216	3.3	1	6	2

KENT WELLS Wells, Kent Eugene 6'4", 295 DT
Col: Nebraska *HS:* Lincoln East [NE] B: 7/25/1967, Lincoln, NE
Drafted: 1990 Round 6 Was
1990 NYG: 6 G.

MIKE WELLS Wells, Michael 6′3″, 233 **TE**
Col: San Diego State *HS:* Quincy [CA] B: 1/22/1962, Quincy, CA
1987 SF: 1 G; 6 Pt.

MIKE WELLS Wells, Michael Allan 6′3″, 292 **DT**
Col: Iowa *HS:* Fox [Arnold, MO] B: 1/6/1971, Arnold, MO
Drafted: 1994 Round 4 Min
1994 Det: 4 G. **1995** Det: 15 G; 0.5 Sac. **1996** Det: 16 G; **1** Fum TD; 6 Pt. **1997** Det: 16 G; 1 Sac. **1998** ChiB: 16 G; 3 Sac. **Total:** 67 G; 1 Fum TD; 6 Pt; 4.5 Sac.

MIKE WELLS Wells, Michael Eugene 6′5″, 225 **QB**
Col: Illinois *HS:* Normal [IL] B: 6/18/1951, Normal, IL *Drafted:* 1973 Round 4 Min
1977 Cin: 7 G.

NORM WELLS Wells, Norman Edward 6′5″, 261 **DT**
Col: Northwestern *HS:* Warren Mott [Warren, MI] B: 9/8/1957, Detroit, MI *Drafted:* 1980 Round 12 Dal
1980 Dal: 3 G.

BOB WELLS Wells, Robert Leroy Jr. 6′4″, 280 **OT**
(Hoss) *Col:* Johnson C. Smith *HS:* Lucy Craft Laney [Augusta, GA] B: 8/4/1945, New York, NY D: 8/7/1994, Decatur, GA *Drafted:* 1968 Round 15 SD
1968 SD: 2 G. **1969** SD: 14 G. **1970** SD: 4 G. **Total:** 20 G.

TERRY WELLS Wells, Terrence Lorenzo 5′11″, 195 **RB**
Col: Southern Mississippi *HS:* East Central [Wade, MS] B: 4/20/1951, Wade, MS
1974 Hou: Rec 1-9 9.0. **1975** GB: Rec 6-11 1.8; KR 1-26 26.0. **Total:** Rec 7-20 2.9; KR 1-26 26.0.

		Rushing				
Year Team	**G**	**Att**	**Yds**	**Avg**	**TD**	**Fum**
1974 Hou	6	0	0	—	0	0
1975 GB	13	33	139	4.2	0	1
NFL Total	19	33	139	4.2	0	1

WARREN WELLS Wells, Warren 6′1″, 190 **WR**
Col: Texas Southern *HS:* Hebert [Beaumont, TX] B: 11/14/1942, Franklin, LA *Drafted:* 1964 Round 12 Det
1967 Oak: Rush 1-7 7.0. **1968** Oak: Rush 2-38 19.0 1 TD. **1969** Oak: Rush 3-24 8.0. **1970** Oak: Rush 3-34 11.3. **Total:** Rush 9-103 11.4 1 TD.

		Receiving					Tot
Year Team	**G**	**Rec**	**Yds**	**Avg**	**TD**	**Fum**	**TD**
1964 Det	9	2	21	10.5	0	0	0
1967 Oak	14	13	302	23.2	6	0	6
1968 Oak	14	53	1137	21.5	**11**	2	**12**
1969 Oak	14	47	**1260**	**26.8**	**14**	3	**14**
1970 Oak	14	43	935	21.7	11	0	11
NFL Total	65	158	3655	23.1	42	5	43

BILLY WELLS Wells, William Prescott 5′9″, 180 **HB**
Col: Michigan State *HS:* Menominee [MI]; Phillips Exeter Acad. [Exeter, NH] B: 12/7/1931, Menominee, MI *Drafted:* 1954 Round 5 Was
1956 Was: **1** Fum TD. **Total:** 1 Fum TD.

		Rushing				Receiving			
Year Team	**G**	**Att**	**Yds**	**Avg**	**TD**	**Rec**	**Yds**	**Avg**	**TD**
1954 Was	12	100	516	5.2	3	19	295	15.5	1
1956 Was	7	69	185	2.7	1	6	86	14.3	0
1957 Was-Pit	11	154	532	3.5	0	14	89	6.4	0
1957 Was	1	0	0	—	0	0	0	—	0
1957 Pit	10	154	532	3.5	0	14	89	6.4	0
1958 Phi	12	24	92	3.8	1	4	49	12.3	0
1960 Bos	12	14	59	4.2	0	14	206	14.7	1
NFL Total	54	361	1384	3.8	5	57	725	12.7	2

	Punt Returns				Kickoff Returns					Tot
Year Team	**Ret**	**Yds**	**Avg**	**TD**	**Ret**	**Yds**	**Avg**	**TD**	**Fum**	**TD**
1954 Was	3	24	8.0	0	17	319	18.8	0	4	4
1956 Was	2	36	18.0	0	1	12	12.0	0	2	2
1957 Was-Pit	21	143	6.8	0	12	325	27.1	**1**	8	1
1957 Was	0	0	—	0	1	19	19.0	0	1	0
1957 Pit	21	143	6.8	0	11	306	27.8	1	7	1
1958 Phi	19	158	8.3	0	14	336	24.0	0	7	1
1960 Bos	12	66	5.5	0	11	275	25.0	0	3	1
NFL Total	57	427	7.5	0	55	1267	23.0	1	24	9

DOUG WELLSANDT Wellsandt, Douglas D 6′3″, 248 **TE**
Col: Washington State *HS:* Ritzville [WA] B: 2/9/1967, Moses Lake, WA *Drafted:* 1990 Round 8 Cin
1990 NYJ: 16 G; Rush 1-(-3) -3.0; Rec 5-57 11.4.

WOODCHUCK WELMAS Welmas, Woodchuck 5′7″, 170 **E**
Col: Carlisle B: 1893 Deceased
1923 Oor: 4 G.

JIM WELSH Welsh, James Edward 5′11″, 250 **G-T-C**
(Tiny) *Col:* Colgate *HS:* Malden [MA] B: 9/17/1902 D: 2/12/1958
1923 Roch: 2 G. **1924** Fra: 10 G; Scor 38, 7 FG, **17** XK. **1925** Fra: 8 G. **1926** Pott: 13 G; Scor 30, 5 FG, **15** XK. **Total:** 33 G; Scor 68, 12 FG, 32 XK.

TOM WELTER Welter, Thomas Lawrence 6′5″, 280 **OT-OG**
Col: Nebraska *HS:* Yankton [SD] B: 2/24/1964, Yankton, SD
1987 StL: 3 G.

LARRY WELTMAN Weltman, Lawrence Abraham 5′11″, 175 **BB-TB**
Col: Syracuse *HS:* Pittsfield [MA] B: 6/1898, Pittsfield, MA D: 9/13/1959, Troy, NY
1922 Roch: 4 G; Pass 1 TD.

DON WEMPLE Wemple, Donald Lester 6′2″, 195 **OE-DE**
Col: Colgate *HS:* Gloversville [NY] B: 10/14/1917, Gloversville, NY D: 6/23/1943, India
1941 Bkn: 11 G; Rec 2-37 18.5 1 TD; 6 Pt.

MARTY WENDELL Wendell, Martin Peter 5′10″, 215 **G**
Col: Notre Dame *HS:* St. George [Evanston, IL] B: 11/22/1926, Chicago, IL
AAFC **1949** ChiA: 10 G.

JACK WENDER Wender, Jack 6′0″, 210 **RB**
Col: Fresno State B: 5/31/1954, San Francisco, CA
1977 TB: 2 G.

HAL WENDLER Wendler, Harold William 5′10″, 175 **BB**
(Windy) *Col:* Ohio State *HS:* Fremont [OH] B: 1/20/1902, Gibsonburg, OH D: 8/23/1984, Baton Rouge, LA
1926 Ham-Akr: 8 G. Ham: 1 G. Akr: 7 G. **Total:** 8 G.

JOE WENDLICK Wendlick, Joseph Peter 6′0″, 207 **OE-DE**
Col: Oregon State *HS:* Jefferson [Portland, OR] B: 12/14/1915, Portland, OR *Drafted:* 1939 Round 4 Det
1940 Phi: 9 G; Rec 8-67 8.4. **1941** Pit: 10 G; Rec 7-84 12.0. **Total:** 19 G; Rec 15-151 10.1.

JOE WENDRYHOSKI Wendryhoski, Joseph Stanley 6′2″, 245 **C**
(Windy) *Col:* Illinois *HS:* Frankfort [West Frankfort, IL] B: 3/1/1938, West Frankfort, IL *Drafted:* 1961 Round 13 NYT
1964 LARm: 13 G. **1965** LARm: 4 G. **1966** LARm: 14 G. **1967** NO: 14 G. **1968** NO: 14 G. **Total:** 59 G.

KEN WENDT Wendt, Kenneth Robert 6′0″, 195 **G**
Col: Marquette *HS:* DePaul Acad. [Chicago, IL] B: 1/29/1910, Chicago, IL D: 1/19/1982, Chicago, IL
1932 ChiC: 1 G.

AL WENGLIKOWSKI Wenglikowski, Alan Lee 6′1″, 215 **LB**
Col: Pittsburgh *HS:* Franklin [OH] B: 8/3/1960, Burlington, IA
Drafted: 1984 Round 10 KC
1984 Buf: 5 G. **1987** Buf: 1 G. **Total:** 6 G.

OBE WENIG Wenig, Obe 5′9″, 185 **E-BB**
Col: Morningside Deceased
1920 RI: 1 G. **1921** RI: 7 G; Rec 2 TD; Scor 26, 8 XK; Tot TD 3. **1922** RI: 6 G. **Total:** 14 G; Rec 2 TD; Tot TD 3.

AD WENKE Wenke, Adolph Eilert 6′4″, 220 **T**
Col: Nebraska *HS:* Pender [NE] B: 1/22/1898, Pender, NE D: 3/3/1961, Lincoln, NE
1923 Mil: 12 G.

CY WENTWORTH Wentworth, Shirley P 5′8″, 160 **TB-WB-BB-FB**
Col: New Hampshire *HS:* Salem [MA]; Thayer Acad. [South Braintree, MA] B: 1/2/1904, Salem, MA D: 1/19/1986, Salem, MA
1925 Prov: 12 G; Rush 2 TD; KR **1** TD; Tot TD 3; 18 Pt. **1926** Prov: 8 G; Pass 1 TD; Scor 6, 1 FG, 2 XK, **1** 1XP. **1929** Bost: 6 G; Rec 2 TD; PR **1** TD; Scor 24, 6 XK; Tot TD 3. **Total:** 26 G; Pass 1 TD; Rush 2 TD; Rec 2 TD; PR 1 TD; KR 1 TD; Scor 48, 1 FG, 8 XK, 1 1XP; Tot TD 6.

BARNEY WENTZ Wentz, Byron W 5′11″, 204 **FB**
(Shenandoah Councilman) *Col:* Penn State *HS:* Shenandoah Valley [Shenandoah, PA] B: 4/21/1901, Shenandoah, PA D: 5/1963, PA
1925 Pott: 12 G; Rush 5 TD; Scor 31, 1 XK. **1926** Pott: 14 G; Rush **10** TD; Tot TD **10**; 60 Pt. **1927** Pott: 12 G; Rush 2 TD; Scor 17, 1 FG, 2 XK. **1928** Pott: 2 G. **Total:** 40 G; Rush 17 TD; Scor 108, 1 FG, 3 XK.

JEFF WENZEL Wenzel, Jeffrey Gustave 6′7″, 270 **OT**
Col: Tulane *HS:* New Orleans Country Day School [LA] B: 10/21/1963, New Orleans, LA
1987 Phi: 3 G.

RALPH WENZEL Wenzel, Ralph Milton 6′0″, 205 **DE**
Col: Tulane B: 7/22/1918, Ferda, AR *Drafted:* 1940 Round 2 Pit
1942 Pit: 6 G.

RALPH WENZEL Wenzel, Ralph Richard 6'2", 250 **OG**
Col: Foothill Coll. CA (J.C.); San Jose State; San Diego State
HS: Cubberley [Palo Alto, CA] B: 3/13/1943, San Mateo, CA
Drafted: 1966 Round 11 GB
1966 Pit: 6 G. **1967** Pit: 13 G. **1968** Pit: 2 G. **1969** Pit: 8 G. **1970** Pit: 14 G; KR 1-6 6.0. **1972** SD: 14 G. **1973** SD: 14 G; KR 1-0. **Total:** 71 G; KR 2-6 3.0.

RED WERDER Werder, Gerard J 185 **C-T**
(Bus) *Col:* Dayton *HS:* U. of Dayton Prep [OH] B: Pittsburgh, PA Deceased
1920 Buf: 4 G. **1921** Ton: 1 G. **Total:** 5 G.

DICK WERDER Werder, Richard Irving 5'9", 210 **G**
(Bus) *Col:* Georgetown *HS:* Canisius Prep [Buffalo, NY]
B: 7/31/1922, Buffalo, NY
AAFC **1948** NY-A: 3 G.

BOB WERL Werl, Robert George 6'3", 240 **DE-OG**
Col: Miami (Fla.) *HS:* South Hills Catholic [Pittsburgh, PA] B: 1/7/1943, Pittsburgh, PA D: 3/27/1988, Pittsburgh, PA *Drafted:* 1965 Redshirt Round 4 NYJ
1966 NYJ: 8 G.

CLYDE WERNER Werner, Clyde Leroy 6'4", 225 **LB**
Col: Washington *HS:* Woodrow Wilson [Tacoma, WA] B: 12/10/1947, Munising, MI *Drafted:* 1970 Round 2 KC
1970 KC: 7 G. **1972** KC: 14 G; Int 1-11. **1973** KC: 14 G; KR 1-13 13.0. **1974** KC: 14 G; Int 1-7. **1976** KC: 14 G. **Total:** 63 G; KR 1-13 13.0; Int 2-18.

GREG WERNER Werner, Gregory Alan 6'4", 236 **TE**
Col: DePauw *HS:* Mount Vernon [Fortville, IN] B: 10/21/1966, Batesville, IN
1989 NYJ: 10 G; Rec 8-115 14.4.

RAY WERSCHING Wersching, Raimund 5'11", 213 **K**
Col: Cerritos Coll. CA (J.C.); California *HS:* Earl Warren [Downey, CA]
B: 8/21/1950, Mondsee, Austria

		Scoring						
Year Team	**G**	**Pts**	**FG**	**FGA**	**FG%**	**XK**	**XKA**	**XK%**
1973 SD	14	46	11	25	44.0	13	15	86.7
1974 SD	14	15	5	11	45.5	0	0	—
1975 SD	14	56	12	24	50.0	20	21	95.2
1976 SD	9	26	4	8	50.0	14	16	87.5
1977 SF	10	53	10	17	58.8	23	23	100.0
1978 SF	16	69	15	23	65.2	24	25	96.0
1979 SF	16	92	20	24	83.3	32	35	91.4
1980 SF	16	78	15	19	78.9	33	39	84.6
1981 SF	12	81	17	23	73.9	30	30	100.0
1982 SF	9	59	12	17	70.6	23	25	92.0
1983 SF	16	126	25	30	83.3	51	51	100.0
1984 SF	16	**131**	25	35	71.4	56	56	100.0
1985 SF	16	91	13	21	61.9	**52**	53	98.1
1986 SF	16	116	25	35	71.4	41	42	97.6
1987 SF	12	83	13	17	76.5	**44**	**46**	95.7
NFL Total	206	1122	222	329	67.5	456	477	95.6

MULE WERWAISS Werwaiss, Elbert 235 **T-G**
Col: No College *HS:* Dean Acad. [Franklin, MA] B: 1904, CT
1926 Har: 9 G.

AL WESBECHER Wesbecher, Aloysius Augustus 5'10", 190 **C-T**
Col: Washington & Jefferson *HS:* Greensburg [PA] B: 11/3/1892, Greensburg, PA D: 3/27/1966, Greensburg, PA
1920 Cle: 5 G.

BULL WESLEY Wesley, Lecil Olen 6'1", 190 **C-G-T-FB**
(Rat) *Col:* Alabama *HS:* Marion Co. [Guin, AL] B: 9/26/1901, Guin, AL D: 1/1980, Tuscaloosa, AL
1926 Prov: 7 G. **1927** Prov: 10 G. **1928** NYG: 5 G. **1930** Port: 13 G. **Total:** 35 G.

RICKY WESSON Wesson, Ricky Charles 5'9", 163 **DB**
Col: Southern Methodist *HS:* South Oak Cliff [Dallas, TX]
B: 6/29/1955, Dallas, TX
1977 KC: 14 G; KR 7-129 18.4; 2 Fum.

CHARLIE WEST West, Charles 6'1", 197 **DB**
Col: Angelo State; Texas-El Paso *HS:* Big Spring [TX] B: 8/31/1946, Terrell, TX *Drafted:* 1968 Round 2 Min

		Punt Returns				Kickoff Returns			
Year Team	**G**	**Ret**	**Yds**	**Avg**	**TD**	**Ret**	**Yds**	**Avg**	**TD**
1968 Min	14	20	201	10.1	1	22	576	26.2	0
1969 Min	14	**39**	245	6.3	0	9	240	26.7	0
1970 Min	14	29	169	5.8	0	11	319	29.0	0
1971 Min	14	18	94	5.2	0	24	556	23.2	0
1972 Min	14	16	111	6.9	0	9	196	21.8	0
1973 Min	5	1	0	0.0	0	3	104	34.7	0
1974 Det	13	6	32	5.3	0	4	71	17.8	0
1975 Det	14	22	219	10.0	0	2	41	20.5	0
1976 Det	14	3	9	3.0	0	0	0	—	0
1977 Det	13	0	0	—	0	0	0	—	0
1978 Den	16	3	20	6.7	0	1	24	24.0	0
1979 Den	16	1	-1	-1.0	0	0	0	—	0
NFL Total	161	158	1099	7.0	1	85	2127	25.0	0

	Interceptions			
Year Team	**Int**	**Yds**	**TD**	**Fum**
1968 Min	0	0	0	2
1969 Min	0	0	0	2
1970 Min	1	0	0	1
1971 Min	7	236	0	2
1972 Min	3	7	0	2
1974 Det	1	0	0	1
1976 Det	1	0	0	0
1977 Det	1	7	0	0
1979 Den	1	26	0	0
NFL Total	15	276	0	10

BELF WEST West, David Belford 6'2", 200 **T**
(Hi) *Col:* Colgate *HS:* Hamilton [NY];Colgate Acad.[Hamilton, NY];Phillips Andover Acad.[Andover, MA] B: 5/7/1896, Hamilton, NY D: 9/11/1973, Cooperstown, NY
1921 Can: 10 G; Scor 7, 1 FG, 4 XK.

DAVE WEST West, David Norman 6'3", 190 **DB**
Col: Central State (Ohio) *HS:* Xenia [OH] B: 6/5/1938, Selma, OH
1963 NYJ: 2 G.

DEREK WEST West, Derek Steven 6'8", 309 **OT**
Col: Colorado *HS:* Pomona [Arvada, CO] B: 3/28/1972, Denver, CO
Drafted: 1995 Round 5 Ind
1995 Ind: 3 G. **1996** Ind: 1 G. **1997** Ind: 1 G. **Total:** 5 G.

ED WEST West, Edward Lee III 6'1", 250 **TE**
Col: Auburn *HS:* Colbert Co. [Leighton, AL] B: 8/2/1961, Colbert Co., AL
1984 GB: Rush 1-2 2.0 1 TD. **1985** GB: Rush 1-0. **1990** GB: KR 1-0. **1992** GB: KR 1-0. **1994** GB: Scor 1 2XP. **Total:** Rush 2-2 1.0 1 TD; KR 2-0; Scor 1 2XP.

		Receiving					Tot
Year Team	**G**	**Rec**	**Yds**	**Avg**	**TD**	**Fum**	**TD**
1984 GB	16	6	54	9.0	4	0	5
1985 GB	16	8	95	11.9	1	1	1
1986 GB	16	15	199	13.3	1	0	1
1987 GB	12	19	261	13.7	1	0	1
1988 GB	16	30	276	9.2	3	1	3
1989 GB	13	22	269	12.2	5	0	5
1990 GB	16	27	356	13.2	5	3	5
1991 GB	16	15	151	10.1	3	0	3
1992 GB	16	4	30	7.5	0	0	0
1993 GB	16	25	253	10.1	0	0	0
1994 GB	14	31	377	12.2	2	1	2
1995 Phi	16	20	190	9.5	1	0	1
1996 Phi	16	8	91	11.4	0	0	0
1997 Atl	12	7	63	9.0	1	0	1
NFL Total	211	237	2665	11.2	27	6	28

JEFF WEST West, Jeffrey Harold 6'3", 212 **P-TE**
Col: Cincinnati *HS:* Ravenna [OH] B: 4/6/1953, Wheeling, WV
Drafted: 1975 Round 5 Cin
1976 SD: Rush 1-0. **1977** SD: Rec 1-3 3.0. **1978** SD: Rush 1-0. **1979** SD: Rush 1-(-2) -2.0. **1981** Sea: Pass 1-0; Rush 3-25 8.3. **Total:** Pass 1-0; Rush 6-23 3.8; Rec 1-3 3.0.

		Punting			
Year Team	**G**	**Punts**	**Yds**	**Avg**	**Fum**
1975 StL	14	64	2412	37.7	0
1976 SD	6	38	1548	40.7	0
1977 SD	13	72	2707	37.6	0
1978 SD	16	73	2720	37.3	1
1979 SD	16	75	2736	36.5	0
1981 Sea	15	66	2578	39.1	1
1982 Sea	9	48	1835	38.2	0
1983 Sea	16	79	3118	39.5	0
1984 Sea	16	95	3567	37.5	0
1985 Sea	2	11	420	38.2	0
NFL Total	123	621	23641	38.1	2

MEL WEST West, Melvin Gerald 5'9", 190 **HB**
Col: Missouri *HS:* Jefferson City [MO] B: 1/14/1939, Columbia, MO
Drafted: 1961 Round 11 Bos
1961 Bos-NYT: Rec 13-146 11.2; PR 2-51 25.5; KR 13-306 23.5. Bos: Rec 5-42 8.4; KR 7-191 27.3. NYT: Rec 8-104 13.0; PR 2-51 25.5; KR 6-115 19.2. **1962** NYT: Rec 1-1 1.0; PR 1-0; KR 3-131 43.7. **Total:** Rec 14-147 10.5; PR 3-51 17.0; KR 16-437 27.3.

		Rushing				
Year Team	**G**	**Att**	**Yds**	**Avg**	**TD**	**Fum**
1961 Bos-NYT	13	72	322	4.5	3	2

1961 Bos	4	26	90	3.5	0	1
1961 NYT	9	46	232	5.0	3	1
1962 NYT	3	9	16	1.8	0	3
NFL Total	16	81	338	4.2	3	5

PAT WEST West, Patrick Michael 6′0″, 201 **FB-LB**
Col: Pittsburgh; USC *HS:* Burgettstown [PA] B: 2/21/1923, Florence, PA D: 2/7/1996, Winston-Salem, NC *Drafted:* 1945 Round 28 Cle
1945 Cle: Rec 1-(-2) -2.0. **1946** LARm: KR 4-49 12.3. **1947** LARm: KR 1-21 21.0; Int 1-24. **1948** LARm-GB: Rec 3-37 12.3. LARm: Rec 3-37 12.3. **Total:** Rec 4-35 8.8; KR 5-70 14.0; Int 1-24.

		Rushing				
Year Team	**G**	**Att**	**Yds**	**Avg**	**TD**	**Fum**
1945 Cle	10	19	45	2.4	0	2
1946 LARm	10	40	226	5.7	1	4
1947 LARm	12	42	162	3.9	2	2
1948 LARm-GB	7	4	24	6.0	0	0
1948 LARm	4	4	24	6.0	0	0
1948 GB	3	0	0	—	0	0
NFL Total	39	105	457	4.4	3	8

BOB WEST West, Robert Harold 6′4″, 218 **WR**
Col: San Diego Mesa Coll. CA (J.C.); San Diego State *HS:* Abraham Lincoln [San Diego, CA] B: 10/3/1950, San Diego, CA *Drafted:* 1972 Round 4 Dal
1972 KC: 11 G; Rush 2-2 1.0; Rec 9-165 18.3 2 TD; **1** Fum TD; Tot TD 3; 18 Pt. **1973** KC: 8 G; Rec 4-65 16.3; KR 1-0. **1974** SF: 10 G; KR 1-0; 1 Fum. **Total:** 29 G; Rush 2-2 1.0; Rec 13-230 17.7 2 TD; KR 2-0; 1 Fum TD; Tot TD 3; 18 Pt; 1 Fum.

RONNIE WEST West, Ronnie Lee 6′1″, 215 **WR**
Col: Northeastern Oklahoma A&M (J.C.); Valdosta State; Pittsburg State *HS:* Wilcox Co. [Rochelle, GA] B: 6/23/1968, Pineview, GA *Drafted:* 1992 Round 9 Min
1992 Min: 12 G; KR 2-27 13.5; 1 Fum.

STAN WEST West, Stanley Byron 6′2″, 235 **DG-OG-C**
Col: Oklahoma *HS:* Enid [OK] B: 9/22/1926, Weatherford, OK *Drafted:* 1950 Round 1 LARm
1950 LARm: 12 G. **1951** LARm: 12 G. **1952** LARm: 12 G. **1953** LARm: 12 G; Int 1-10. **1954** LARm: 9 G; Int 1-0. **1955** NYG: 11 G; KR 1-6 6.0. **1956** ChiC: 11 G. **1957** ChiC: 5 G. **Total:** 84 G; KR 1-6 6.0; Int 2-10.

TROY WEST West, Troy H 6′1″, 205 **DB**
Col: Mount San Antonio Coll. CA (J.C.); USC *HS:* Covina [CA] B: 8/26/1961, Los Angeles, CA
1987 Phi: 3 G; Int 1-0; 1 Sac.

WALTER WEST West, Walter James 6′0″, 197 **FB-DB**
Col: Pittsburgh *HS:* Burgettstown [PA] B: 10/26/1917, Florence, PA D: 9/13/1984, Carlsbad, CA
1944 Cle: Rec 9-64 7.1; PR 1-0; KR 1-15 15.0; Int 2-5; Scor 12, 6-8 75.0% XK.

		Rushing			
Year Team	**G**	**Att**	**Yds**	**Avg**	**TD**
1944 Cle	9	66	220	3.3	1

BILL WEST West, William Henry III 5′10″, 185 **DB**
Col: Tennessee State *HS:* Steubenville [OH] B: 3/3/1947, Weirton, WV *Drafted:* 1971 Round 10 Oak
1972 Den: 8 G.

BURR WEST West, William Hodges 6′1″, 220 **T**
Col: Tennessee *HS:* Central [Knoxville, TN] B: 9/30/1918, Knoxville, TN
1941 Phi: 10 G.

WILLIE WEST West, Willie Tennyson 5′10″, 190 **DB**
Col: Oregon *HS:* San Diego [CA] B: 5/1/1938, Lexington, MS *Drafted:* 1960 Round 4 StL
1960 StL: Rush 7-45 6.4. **1961** StL: **1** Fum TD. **1968** Mia: **1** Fum TD. **Total:** Rush 7-45 6.4; 2 Fum TD.

		Punt Returns				Kickoff Returns			
Year Team	**G**	**Ret**	**Yds**	**Avg**	**TD**	**Ret**	**Yds**	**Avg**	**TD**
1960 StL	7	5	58	11.6	0	13	370	28.5	0
1961 StL	14	11	98	8.9	0	16	340	21.3	0
1962 Buf	12	15	124	8.3	0	0	0	—	0
1963 Buf	14	11	86	7.8	0	6	146	24.3	0
1964 Den-NYJ	10	0	0	—	0	5	142	28.4	0
1964 Den	7	0	0	—	0	0	0	—	0
1964 NYJ	3	0	0	—	0	5	142	28.4	0
1965 NYJ	14	10	34	3.4	0	0	0	—	0
1966 Mia	14	0	0	—	0	0	0	—	0
1967 Mia	7	0	0	—	0	0	0	—	0
1968 Mia	13	0	0	—	0	0	0	—	0
NFL Total	105	52	400	7.7	0	40	998	25.0	0

	Interceptions			
Year Team	**Int**	**Yds**	**TD**	**Fum**
1961 StL	1	14	0	2
1962 Buf	3	24	0	0
1963 Buf	5	57	0	1
1964 Den-NYJ	2	0	0	0
1964 Den	1	0	0	0
1964 NYJ	1	0	0	0
1965 NYJ	6	57	0	0
1966 Mia	8	62	0	0
1967 Mia	1	16	0	0
1968 Mia	4	102	0	0
NFL Total	30	332	0	3

BRYANT WESTBROOK Westbrook, Bryant Antoine 6′0″, 199 **DB**
Col: Texas *HS:* El Camino [Oceanside, CA] B: 12/19/1974, Charlotte, NC *Drafted:* 1997 Round 1 Det
1997 Det: 15 G; Int 2-64 1 TD; 6 Pt. **1998** Det: 16 G; Int 3-49 1 TD; 6 Pt. **Total:** 31 G; Int 5-113 2 TD; 12 Pt.

DONALD WESTBROOK Westbrook, Donald Joseph Jr. 5′10″, 185 **WR**
Col: Nebraska *HS:* Central [Cheyenne, WY] B: 11/1/1952, Cheyenne, WY *Drafted:* 1975 Round 6 Bal
1977 NE: 13 G; 1 Fum. **1978** NE: 16 G; Rush 1-(-2) -2.0; Rec 3-38 12.7; KR 7-125 17.9. **1979** NE: 16 G; Pass 2-2 100.0%, 52 26.00; Rush 2-8 4.0; Rec 9-173 19.2 1 TD; PR 2-5 2.5; KR 11-151 13.7; 6 Pt. **1980** NE: 14 G; Rec 4-60 15.0; KR 1-14 14.0. **1981** NE: 12 G; Rec 7-122 17.4 2 TD; 12 Pt. **Total:** 71 G; Pass 2-2 100.0%, 52 26.00; Rush 3-6 2.0; Rec 23-393 17.1 3 TD; PR 2-5 2.5; KR 19-290 15.3; 18 Pt; 1 Fum.

MICHAEL WESTBROOK Westbrook, Michael Deanailo 6′3″, 220 **WR**
Col: Colorado *HS:* Chadsey [Detroit, MI] B: 7/7/1972, Detroit, MI *Drafted:* 1995 Round 1 Was
1995 Was: Rush 6-114 19.0 1 TD. **1996** Was: Rush 2-2 1.0. **1997** Was: Rush 3-(-11) -3.7. **1998** Was: Rush 1-11 11.0. **Total:** Rush 12-116 9.7 1 TD.

		Receiving				Tot
Year Team	**G**	**Rec**	**Yds**	**Avg**	**TD**	**TD**
1995 Was	11	34	522	15.4	1	2
1996 Was	11	34	505	14.9	1	1
1997 Was	13	34	559	16.4	3	3
1998 Was	11	44	736	16.7	6	6
NFL Total	46	146	2322	15.9	11	12

GREG WESTBROOKS Westbrooks, Gregory Melvin 6′2″, 215 **LB**
Col: Mesa; Colorado *HS:* Lincoln Prep [Kansas City, MO] B: 2/24/1953, Chicago, IL *Drafted:* 1975 Round 17 NO
1975 NO: 14 G; Int 1-21. **1976** NO: 14 G. **1977** NO: 7 G. **1978** StL-Oak: 11 G; KR 1-12 12.0. StL: 10 G; KR 1-12 12.0. Oak: 1 G. **1979** Oak-LARm: 9 G. Oak: 4 G. LARm: 5 G. **1980** Oak-LARm: 7 G. Oak: 1 G. LARm: 6 G. **1981** Oak: 4 G. **Total:** 66 G; KR 1-12 12.0; Int 1-21.

CLEVE WESTER Wester, Cleveland F 5′8″, 188 **RB**
Col: Concordia (Minn.) *HS:* Lake Worth [FL] B: 6/14/1964

		Rushing			
Year Team	**G**	**Att**	**Yds**	**Avg**	**TD**
1987 Det	3	33	113	3.4	0

ED WESTFALL Westfall, Edgar Ralph 5′9″, 170 **TB-DB-BB**
Col: Ohio Wesleyan B: 11/8/1909 D: 3/1968, OH
1932 Bos: Pass 5-0. **1933** Bos-Pit: Pass 30-9 30.0%, 133 4.43 1 TD 6 Int; Rec 4-79 19.8 1 TD; Scor 16, 1 FG, 1 XK. Bos: Pass 4-1 25.0%, 33 8.25 1 TD 1 Int. Pit: Pass 26-8 30.8%, 100 3.85 5 Int; Rec 4-79 19.8 1 TD; Scor 16, 1 FG, 1 XK. **Total:** Pass 35-9 25.7%, 133 3.80 1 TD 6 Int; Rec 4-79 19.8 1 TD; Scor 16, 1 FG, 1 XK.

		Rushing				Tot
Year Team	**G**	**Att**	**Yds**	**Avg**	**TD**	**TD**
1932 Bos	2	5	16	3.2	0	0
1933 Bos-Pit	9	47	87	1.9	1	2
1933 Bos	3	3	26	8.7	0	0
1933 Pit	6	44	61	1.4	1	2
NFL Total	11	52	103	2.0	1	2

BOB WESTFALL Westfall, Robert Barton 5′8″, 190 **FB-LB-TB**
Col: Michigan *HS:* Ann Arbor [MI] B: 5/5/1919, Detroit, MI D: 10/23/1980, Adrian, MI *Drafted:* 1942 Round 1 Det
1944 Det: PR 3-38 12.7; KR 3-79 26.3; Int 1-30; Punt 1-11 11.0. **1945** Det: PR 1-16 16.0; KR 2-26 13.0. **1946** Det: KR 4-58 14.5. **1947** Det: KR 2-27 13.5. **Total:** PR 4-54 13.5; KR 11-190 17.3; Int 1-30; Punt 1-11 11.0.

		Passing							
Year Team	**G**	**Att**	**Comp**	**Comp%**	**Yds**	**YPA**	**TD**	**Int**	**Rating**
1944 Det	10	47	23	48.9	342	7.28	4	6	62.0
1945 Det	9	4	3	75.0	91	22.75	1	0	156.3
1946 Det	10	2	1	50.0	-5	-2.50	0	1	16.7

1947 Det	12	0	0	—	0	—	0	0	—
NFL Total	41	53	27	50.9	428	8.08	5	7	70.0

	Rushing				Receiving					Tot
Year Team	Att	Yds	Avg	TD	Rec	Yds	Avg	TD	Fum	TD
1944 Det	65	277	4.3	3	16	218	13.6	2	0	5
1945 Det	82	234	2.9	6	12	209	17.4	3	3	9
1946 Det	28	54	1.9	1	17	142	8.4	0	0	1
1947 Det	34	132	3.9	1	2	19	9.5	0	1	1
NFL Total	209	697	3.3	11	47	588	12.5	5	4	16

DICK WESTMORELAND Westmoreland, Richard Carl 6′1″, 190 **DB**
Col: North Carolina A&T *HS:* Second Ward [Charlotte, NC]
B: 2/17/1941, Charlotte, NC
1964 SD: PR 2-10 5.0. **Total:** PR 2-10 5.0.

		Kickoff Returns				Interceptions			
Year Team	G	Ret	Yds	Avg	TD	Int	Yds	TD	Fum
1963 SD	14	10	204	20.4	0	0	0	0	0
1964 SD	14	18	360	20.0	0	6	51	0	3
1965 SD	4	0	0	—	0	1	28	0	0
1966 Mia	14	0	0	—	0	4	104	1	0
1967 Mia	14	0	0	—	0	**10**	127	1	0
1968 Mia	11	0	0	—	0	1	0	0	0
1969 Mia	10	0	0	—	0	0	0	0	0
NFL Total	81	28	564	20.1	0	22	310	2	3

JEFF WESTON Weston, Jeffrey Graham 6′5″, 259 **OT-DT**
Col: Notre Dame *HS:* Cardinal Mooney [Rochester, NY] B: 4/10/1956, Jersey City, NJ *Drafted:* 1979 Round 9 Mia
1979 NYG: 16 G. **1980** NYG: 6 G. **1981** NYG: 14 G. **1982** NYG: 1 G. **Total:** 37 G.

RHONDY WESTON Weston, Rhondy 6′5″, 274 **DE**
Col: Florida *HS:* Glades Central [Belle Glade, FL] B: 6/7/1966, Belle Glade, FL *Drafted:* 1989 Round 3 Dal
1989 TB: 12 G; 2 Sac.

RYAN WETNIGHT Wetnight, Ryan Scott 6′2″, 235 **TE**
Col: Fresno City Coll. CA (J.C.); Stanford *HS:* Herbert Hoover [Fresno, CA] B: 11/5/1970, Fresno, CA
1997 ChiB: KR 1-9 9.0. **Total:** KR 1-9 9.0.

		Receiving				
Year Team	G	Rec	Yds	Avg	TD	Fum
1993 ChiB	10	9	93	10.3	1	0
1994 ChiB	11	11	104	9.5	1	0
1995 ChiB	12	24	193	8.0	2	0
1996 ChiB	11	21	223	10.6	1	0
1997 ChiB	16	46	464	10.1	1	1
1998 ChiB	15	23	168	7.3	2	1
NFL Total	75	134	1245	9.3	8	2

BOB WETOSKA Wetoska, Robert Stephen 6′3″, 240 **OT-OG-C**
Col: Notre Dame *HS:* De La Salle [Minneapolis, MN] B: 8/22/1937, Minneapolis, MN *Drafted:* 1959 Round 5 Was
1960 ChiB: 12 G. **1961** ChiB: 14 G. **1962** ChiB: 14 G. **1963** ChiB: 14 G. **1964** ChiB: 14 G. **1965** ChiB: 14 G. **1966** ChiB: 14 G. **1967** ChiB: 12 G. **1968** ChiB: 14 G. **1969** ChiB: 6 G. **Total:** 128 G.

CHET WETTERLUND Wetterlund, Chester Jerome 6′2″, 185 **TB-DB**
Col: Illinois Wesleyan *HS:* Morgan Park [Chicago, IL] B: 3/19/1918, Chicago, IL D: 9/5/1944, Atlantic Ocean, near NJ *Drafted:* 1942 Round 9 ChiC
1942 Det: 6 G; Pass 44-13 29.5%, 230 5.23 10 Int; Rush 23-6 0.3; PR 3-26 8.7; KR 5-89 17.8; Int 1-0; Punt 11-449 40.8.

MAX WETTSTEIN Wettstein, Max Elbert Jr. 6′3″, 225 **TE**
Col: Florida State B: 7/3/1944, Leesburg, FL
1966 Den: 2 G.

HARLAN WETZ Wetz, Harlan Henry 6′5″, 265 **T**
Col: Texas *HS:* New Braunfels [TX] B: 9/15/1925, New Braunfels, TX D: 11/14/1983, San Antonio, TX
AAFC **1947** BknA: 11 G.

BUZZ WETZEL Wetzel, Damon Henry 5′10″, 190 **FB-LB**
Col: Ohio State *HS:* North [Cleveland, OH] B: 11/7/1910, Roseville, OH D: 10/15/1985, El Paso, TX
1935 ChiB-Pit: 10 G; Pass 8-2 25.0%, 21 2.63 1 Int; Rush 22-41 1.9 1 TD; Rec 4-18 4.5; 6 Pt. ChiB: 1 G; Rush 3-0. Pit: 9 G; Pass 8-2 25.0%, 21 2.63 1 Int; Rush 19-41 2.2 1 TD; Rec 4-18 4.5; 6 Pt. **Total:** 10 G; Pass 8-2 25.0%, 21 2.63 1 Int; Rush 22-41 1.9 1 TD; Rec 4-18 4.5; 6 Pt.

RON WETZEL Wetzel, Ronald Joseph 6′5″, 242 **TE**
Col: Arizona State *HS:* South Hills [Pittsburgh, PA] B: 11/10/1960, Pittsburgh, PA *Drafted:* 1983 Round 4 KC
1983 KC: 16 G.

MARTY WETZEL Wetzel, William Martin 6′3″, 235 **LB**
Col: Tulane *HS:* East Jefferson [Metairie, LA] B: 1/29/1958, New Orleans, LA
1981 NYJ: 5 G.

BILL WEXLER Wexler, William W 5′9″, 170 **C**
Col: New York U. *HS:* New Utrecht [Brooklyn, NY] B: 12/25/1904 D: 12/1983, Loch Sheldrake, NY
1930 SI: 1 G.

JERRY WHALEN Whalen, Gerald Cornelius 6′1″, 235 **C-G**
Col: Canisius *HS:* Canisius Prep [Buffalo, NY] B: 4/23/1928, Buffalo, NY D: 11/1973, Buffalo, NY
AAFC **1948** BufA: 7 G.

JIM WHALEN Whalen, James Francis Jr. 6′2″, 210 **TE**
Col: Boston College *HS:* Cambridge Latin [MA] B: 5/20/1943, Cambridge, MA *Drafted:* 1965 Round 3 Bos
1968 Bos: Rush 1-0. **Total:** Rush 1-0.

		Receiving				
Year Team	G	Rec	Yds	Avg	TD	Fum
1965 Bos	14	22	381	17.3	0	0
1966 Bos	14	29	502	17.3	4	0
1967 Bos	14	39	651	16.7	5	1
1968 Bos	14	47	718	15.3	7	0
1969 Bos	14	16	235	14.7	1	0
1970 Den	14	36	503	14.0	3	1
1971 Den-Phi	5	8	165	20.6	0	0
1971 Den	3	7	124	17.7	0	0
1971 Phi	2	1	41	41.0	0	0
NFL Total	89	197	3155	16.0	20	2

BILL WHALEN Whalen, William 5′7″, 165 **C-T-G**
Col: No College B: 9/11/1900 D: 1/1975, Chicago, IL
1920 ChiC: 6 G. **1922** ChiC: 3 G. **1923** ChiC: 1 G. **1924** ChiC: 1 G. **Total:** 11 G.

BEN WHALEY Whaley, Benjamin Franklyn 5′11″, 210 **G**
(Cat) *Col:* Virginia State *HS:* Maggie L. Walker [Richmond, VA] B: 10/14/1926, Richmond, VA
AAFC **1949** LA-A: 3 G.

TOM WHAM Wham, Thomas Arthur 6′2″, 217 **OE-DE**
Col: Furman *HS:* Thornwell Orphanage [Greer, SC]; Clinton [SC] B: 11/22/1923, Greenville, SC *Drafted:* 1949 Round 5 ChiC
1949 ChiC: 12 G; Rec 1-11 11.0; Int 1-46 1 TD; 6 Pt. **1950** ChiC: 11 G; KR 3-25 8.3; **1** Fum TD; 6 Pt. **1951** ChiC: 12 G. **Total:** 35 G; Rec 1-11 11.0; KR 3-25 8.3; Int 1-46 1 TD; 1 Fum TD; Tot TD 2; 12 Pt.

HOGAN WHARTON Wharton, Robert Glen 6′2″, 250 **OG**
Col: Houston *HS:* Orange [TX] B: 12/13/1935, Hood Co., TX *Drafted:* 1958 Round 11 SF
1960 Hou: 14 G. **1961** Hou: 14 G; KR 1-8 8.0. **1962** Hou: 4 G. **1963** Hou: 14 G. **Total:** 46 G; KR 1-8 8.0.

JIM WHATLEY Whatley, James William 6′5″, 223 **T-DE-OE**
Col: Alabama *HS:* Benjamin Russell [Alexander City, AL] B: 3/11/1913, Tuscaloosa, AL
1936 Bkn: 11 G. **1937** Bkn: 11 G. **1938** Bkn: 11 G. **Total:** 33 G.

WARREN WHEAT Wheat, Warren 6′6″, 274 **OG**
Col: Brigham Young *HS:* Camelback [Phoenix, AZ] B: 5/13/1967, Phoenix, AZ *Drafted:* 1989 Round 8 LARm
1989 Sea: 2 G. **1991** Sea: 14 G. **Total:** 16 G.

TYRONE WHEATLEY Wheatley, Tyrone Anthony 6′0″, 230 **RB**
Col: Michigan *HS:* Robichaud [Dearborn Heights, MI] B: 1/19/1972, Inkster, MI *Drafted:* 1995 Round 1 NYG
1996 NYG: Pass 1-1 100.0%, 24 24.00 1 TD. **Total:** Pass 1-1 100.0%, 24 24.00 1 TD.

		Rushing				Receiving			
Year Team	G	Att	Yds	Avg	TD	Rec	Yds	Avg	TD
1995 NYG	13	78	245	3.1	3	5	27	5.4	0
1996 NYG	14	112	400	3.6	1	12	51	4.3	2
1997 NYG	14	152	583	3.8	4	16	140	8.8	0
1998 NYG	5	14	52	3.7	0	0	0	—	0
NFL Total	46	356	1280	3.6	8	33	218	6.6	2

	Kickoff Returns					Tot
Year Team	Ret	Yds	Avg	TD	Fum	TD
1995 NYG	10	186	18.6	0	2	3
1996 NYG	23	503	21.9	0	6	3
1997 NYG	0	0	—	0	3	4
1998 NYG	1	16	16.0	0	0	0
NFL Total	34	705	20.7	0	11	10

KENNY WHEATON Wheaton, Kenneth Tyron 5'10", 195 **DB**
Col: Oregon *HS:* McClintock [Tempe, AZ] B: 3/8/1975, Phoenix, AZ *Drafted:* 1997 Round 3 Dal
1997 Dal: 2 G. **1998** Dal: 15 G; Int 1-41; Scor **1** Saf; 1 Fum TD; 8 Pt. **Total:** 17 G; Int 1-41; Scor 1 Saf; 1 Fum TD; 8 Pt.

DWIGHT WHEELER Wheeler, Dwight 6'3", 269 **C-OT-OG**
Col: Tennessee State *HS:* Manassas [Memphis, TN] B: 1/13/1955, Memphis, TN *Drafted:* 1978 Round 4 NE
1978 NE: 2 G; KR 1-0. **1979** NE: 13 G; 1 Fum. **1980** NE: 16 G; 1 Fum. **1981** NE: 16 G. **1982** NE: 9 G. **1983** NE: 16 G. **1984** LARd: 4 G. **1987** SD-LARd: 7 G. SD: 3 G. LARd: 4 G. **1988** LARd: 8 G. **Total:** 91 G; KR 1-0; 2 Fum.

ERNIE WHEELER Wheeler, Ernest Martin 6'1", 190 **DB-TB**
Col: North Dakota State *HS:* Central [ND] B: 1/28/1915, Fargo, ND D: 6/18/1982, Detroit Lakes, MN *Drafted:* 1939 Round 5 Pit
1939 Pit-ChiC: 7 G; Pass 17-5 29.4%, 94 5.53 1 TD 7 Int; Rush 17-0; Punt 10-460 46.0. Pit: 5 G; Pass 13-3 23.1%, 59 4.54 1 TD 6 Int; Rush 15-8 0.5; Punt 10-460 46.0. ChiC: 2 G; Pass 4-2 50.0%, 35 8.75 1 Int; Rush 2-(-8) -4.0. **1942** ChiC: 3 G; Punt 1-40 40.0. **Total:** 10 G; Pass 17-5 29.4%, 94 5.53 1 TD 7 Int; Rush 17-0; Punt 11-500 45.5.

COWBOY WHEELER Wheeler, Kyle 5'9", 180 **OE**
Col: Ripon *HS:* Green Bay West [WI] B: 4/1898, Stiles Twp., Oconto Co., WI Deceased
1921 GB: 3 G. **1922** GB: 9 G. **1923** GB: 10 G; Rec 1 TD; 6 Pt. **Total:** 22 G; Rec 1 TD; 6 Pt.

LEONARD WHEELER Wheeler, Leonard Tyrone 6'0", 192 **DB**
Col: Lees-McRae JC NC; Northwest Mississippi CC; Mississippi; Troy State *HS:* Stephens Co. [Toccoa, GA] B: 1/15/1969, Taccoa, GA *Drafted:* 1992 Round 3 Cin
1992 Cin: 16 G; Int 1-12. **1993** Cin: 16 G; Int 0-24. **1995** Cin: 16 G. **1996** Cin: 13 G. **1997** Min: 15 G; 2 Sac. **1998** Car: 16 G. **Total:** 92 G; Int 1-36; 2 Sac.

MANCH WHEELER Wheeler, Manchester Haynes Jr. 6'1", 190 **QB**
Col: Maine *HS:* Phillips Andover Acad. [Andover, MA] B: 3/2/1939, Augusta, ME
1962 Buf: 4 G; Rush 3-7 2.3.

MARK WHEELER Wheeler, Mark Anthony 6'3", 285 **DT-NT**
Col: Navarro Coll. TX (J.C.); Texas A&M *HS:* San Marcos [TX] B: 4/1/1970, San Marcos, TX *Drafted:* 1992 Round 3 TB
1992 TB: 16 G; 5 Sac. **1993** TB: 10 G; 2 Sac. **1994** TB: 15 G; 3 Sac. **1995** TB: 14 G; 1 Sac. **1996** NE: 16 G; 1 Sac. **1997** NE: 14 G; 4 Sac. **1998** NE: 10 G. **Total:** 95 G; 16 Sac.

MARK WHEELER Wheeler, Mark William 6'2", 232 **TE**
Col: Kentucky *HS:* Bishop Dennis J. O'Connell [Arlington, VA] B: 6/15/1964, Indianapolis, IN
1987 Det: 3 G; Rec 2-17 8.5.

RON WHEELER Wheeler, Ronald Wayne 6'5", 235 **TE**
Col: Merritt Coll. CA (J.C.); Washington *HS:* Fremont [Oakland, CA] B: 9/5/1958, Oakland, CA
1987 LARd: 3 G; Rec 3-61 20.3; 1 Fum.

TED WHEELER Wheeler, Theodore I III 6'3", 245 **OG-TE**
Col: West Texas A&M *HS:* Pershing [Detroit, MI] B: 9/16/1945, Detroit, MI *Drafted:* 1967 Round 9 StL
1967 StL: 4 G. **1968** StL: 5 G. **1970** ChiB: 6 G. **Total:** 15 G.

WAYNE WHEELER Wheeler, Wayne B Jr. 6'2", 185 **WR**
Col: Alabama *HS:* William R. Boone [Orlando, FL] B: 3/28/1950, Orlando, FL *Drafted:* 1974 Round 3 ChiB
1974 ChiB: 12 G; Rec 5-59 11.8 1 TD; 6 Pt.

ERNIE WHEELWRIGHT Wheelwright, Ernest 6'3", 239 **RB**
(The Wheel) *Col:* Southern Illinois *HS:* Central [Columbus, OH] B: 11/28/1939, Columbus, OH

		Rushing				Receiving					Tot
Year Team	G	Att	Yds	Avg	TD	Rec	Yds	Avg	TD	Fum	TD
1964 NYG	11	100	402	4.0	0	14	204	14.6	3	2	3
1965 NYG	13	24	96	4.0	0	2	17	8.5	0	1	0
1966 Atl	14	121	458	3.8	3	15	137	9.1	3	2	6
1967 Atl-NO	12	80	241	3.0	1	13	107	8.2	0	4	1
1967 Atl	3	21	43	2.0	1	4	46	11.5	0	0	1
1967 NO	9	59	198	3.4	0	9	61	6.8	0	4	0
1968 NO	12	21	99	4.7	1	1	-9	-9.0	0	1	1
1969 NO	13	25	85	3.4	4	8	68	8.5	1	1	5
1970 NO	4	16	45	2.8	0	1	7	7.0	0	1	0
NFL Total	79	387	1426	3.7	9	54	531	9.8	7	12	16

TOMMY WHELAN Whelan, Thomas Joseph 5'8", 165 **TB-DB**
(Moose) *Col:* Catholic B: 3/4/1911, New York, NY D: 6/1974, Olney, MD
1933 Pit: 1 G.

TOM WHELAN Whelan, Thomas Joseph 5'10", 180 **OE-C-G**
Col: Notre Dame; Dartmouth; Georgetown *HS:* Lynn English [MA]; Worcester Acad. [MA] B: 1/3/1894, Lynn, MA D: 6/26/1957, Boston, MA
1920 Can: 12 G. **1921** Cle: 8 G; Rec 1 TD; 6 Pt. **Total:** 20 G; Rec 1 TD; 6 Pt.

CRAIG WHELIHAN Whelihan, Craig Dominic 6'5", 220 **QB**
Col: Oregon State; U. of Pacific *HS:* Santa Teresa [San Jose, CA] B: 4/15/1971, Santa Clara, CA *Drafted:* 1995 Round 6 SD
1998 SD: Scor 1 2XP. **Total:** Scor 1 2XP.

		Passing							
Year Team	G	Att	Comp	Comp%	Yds	YPA	TD	Int	Rating
1997 SD	9	237	118	49.8	1357	5.73	6	10	58.3
1998 SD	10	320	149	46.6	1803	5.63	8	19	48.0
NFL Total	19	557	267	47.9	3160	5.67	14	29	52.4

	Rushing				
Year Team	Att	Yds	Avg	TD	Fum
1997 SD	13	29	2.2	0	7
1998 SD	18	38	2.1	0	9
NFL Total	31	67	2.2	0	16

LARRY WHIGHAM Whigham, Larry Jerome 6'2", 205 **DB**
Col: Pearl River CC MS; Northeast Louisiana *HS:* Hattiesburg [MS] B: 6/23/1972, Hattiesburg, MS *Drafted:* 1994 Round 4 Sea
1994 NE: 12 G; Int 1-21; 1 Fum. **1995** NE: 16 G. **1996** NE: 16 G. **1997** NE: 16 G; Int 2-60 1 TD; 6 Pt; 2 Sac. **1998** NE: 16 G; KR 1-0; Int 1-0. **Total:** 76 G; KR 1-0; Int 4-81 1 TD; 6 Pt; 1 Fum; 2 Sac.

RAY WHIPPLE Whipple, Raymond Christopher 5'9", 170 **OE**
Col: Notre Dame *HS:* Elgin [IL] B: 11/14/1893 D: 12/1973, Crest Hill, IL
1920 Det: 5 G.

JODIE WHIRE Whire, John Joseph 6'1", 185 **FB-LB**
Col: Georgia *HS:* Albany [GA] B: 6/11/1910, Albany, GA D: 2/1983, Albany, GA
1933 Phi: 2 G; Pass 5-1 20.0%, 10 2.00 2 Int; Rush 8-14 1.8; Rec 1-15 15.0.

KEN WHISENHUNT Whisenhunt, Kenneth Moore 6'3", 237 **TE**
Col: Georgia Tech *HS:* Richmond [Augusta, GA] B: 2/28/1962, Atlanta, GA *Drafted:* 1985 Round 12 Atl
1985 Atl: Rush 1-3 3.0; KR 4-33 8.3. **1986** Atl: Rush 1-20 20.0. **Total:** Rush 2-23 11.5; KR 4-33 8.3.

		Receiving				
Year Team	G	Rec	Yds	Avg	TD	Fum
1985 Atl	16	3	48	16.0	0	0
1986 Atl	16	20	184	9.2	3	0
1987 Atl	7	17	145	8.5	1	1
1988 Atl	16	16	174	10.9	1	1
1990 Was	2	0	0	—	0	0
1991 NYJ	7	4	34	8.5	0	0
1992 NYJ	10	2	11	5.5	0	0
NFL Total	74	62	596	9.6	5	2

CRESTON WHITAKER Whitaker, Creston B 6'2", 187 **WR**
Col: North Texas *HS:* Jacksonville [IL] B: 8/12/1947, Quincy, IL
1972 NO: 2 G; Rec 1-6 6.0.

DANTA WHITAKER Whitaker, Danta Antonio 6'4", 252 **TE**
Col: Mississippi Valley State *HS:* Walter F. George [Atlanta, GA] B: 3/14/1964, Atlanta, GA *Drafted:* 1988 Round 7 NYG
1990 KC: 16 G; Rec 2-17 8.5 1 TD; PR 1-0; 6 Pt; 1 Fum. **1992** Min: 6 G; Rec 1-4 4.0. **1993** ChiB: 5 G; Rec 6-53 8.8. **Total:** 27 G; Rec 9-74 8.2 1 TD; PR 1-0; 6 Pt; 1 Fum.

BILL WHITAKER Whitaker, William Andrew 6'0", 182 **DB**
Col: Missouri *HS:* Rockhurst [Kansas City, MO] B: 11/18/1959, Kansas City, MO *Drafted:* 1981 Round 7 GB
1981 GB: 16 G; PR 2-1 0.5. **1982** GB: 9 G. **1983** StL: 7 G. **1984** StL: 7 G. **Total:** 39 G; PR 2-1 0.5.

FRANK WHITCOMB Whitcomb, Frank E 6'3", 217 **G-T-C**
Col: Syracuse *HS:* Mercersburg Acad. [PA] B: 12/7/1896 D: 8/23/1977, Fulton, NY
1920 Roch: 5 G. **1921** Roch: 3 G. **Total:** 8 G.

ADRIAN WHITE White, Adrian Darnell 6'0", 200 **DB**
Col: Southern Illinois; Florida *HS:* Orange Park [FL] B: 4/6/1964, Orange Park, FL *Drafted:* 1987 Round 2 NYG
1987 NYG: 6 G. **1988** NYG: 16 G; Int 1-29. **1989** NYG: 15 G; Int 2-8. **1991** NYG: 13 G; Int 1-30. **1992** GB: 15 G. **1993** NE: 5 G. **Total:** 70 G; Int 4-67.

ALBERTO WHITE White, Alberto Eduardo 6′3″, 245 **DE**
Col: Texas Southern *HS:* Miami Southridge [FL] B: 4/8/1971, Miami, FL *Drafted:* 1992 Round 10 LARd
1994 LARd: 8 G; 2 Sac. **1995** StL: 2 G; 1 Sac. **1996** StL: 3 G. **Total:** 13 G; 3 Sac.

ANDRE WHITE White, Andre Moses 6′3″, 225 **TE**
Col: Florida A&M *HS:* Middletown [Tampa, FL]; Lincoln HS [Tallahassee, FL] B: 10/7/1944, Winter Park, FL *Drafted:* 1966 Redshirt Round 10 Den
1967 Den: 14 G; Rec 5-87 17.4; Scor **1** Saf; 2 Pt. **1968** Cin-SD: 8 G; Rec 2-18 9.0. Cin: 3 G; Rec 2-18 9.0. SD: 5 G. **Total:** 22 G; Rec 7-105 15.0; Scor 1 Saf; 2 Pt.

TARZAN WHITE White, Arthur Pershing 5′9″, 217 **G**
Col: Alabama *HS:* Escambia Co. [Altmore, AL] B: 12/6/1915, Lockhart, AL D: 1/23/1996, Gaylesville, AL *Drafted:* 1937 Round 2 NYG
1937 NYG: 11 G. **1938** NYG: 10 G. **1939** NYG: 6 G. **1940** ChiC: 10 G. **1941** ChiC: 8 G. **1945** NYG: 5 G. **Total:** 50 G.

BRAD WHITE White, Bradley Dee 6′2″, 256 **NT-DT**
Col: Tennessee *HS:* Skyline [Idaho Falls, ID] B: 8/18/1958, Rexburg, ID *Drafted:* 1981 Round 12 TB
1981 TB: 16 G. **1982** TB: 9 G. **1983** TB: 16 G. **1984** Ind: 15 G; 2 Sac. **1985** Ind: 16 G; 1 Sac. **1987** Min: 1 G. **Total:** 73 G; 3 Sac.

WHIZZER WHITE White, Byron Raymond 6′1″, 187 **TB-DB-HB-FB**
Col: Colorado *HS:* Wellington [CO] B: 6/8/1917, Fort Collins, CO *Drafted:* 1938 Round 1 Pit
1938 Pit: Rec 7-88 12.6. **1940** Det: Rec 4-55 13.8; Int 4-37; Scor 32, 0-1 FG, 2-4 50.0% XK. **1941** Det: Rec 5-158 31.6 1 TD; PR **19-262** 13.8; KR 11-285 25.9; Int 1-82 **1** TD. **Total:** Rec 16-301 18.8 1 TD; PR 19-262 13.8; KR 11-285 25.9; Int 5-119 1 TD; Scor 80, 0-1 FG, 2-4 50.0% XK.

		Passing							
Year Team	G	Att	Comp	Comp%	Yds	YPA	TD	Int	Rating
1938 Pit	11	73	29	39.7	393	5.38	2	18	27.2
1940 Det	11	80	35	43.8	461	5.76	0	12	23.0
1941 Det	11	62	22	35.5	338	5.45	2	5	31.5
NFL Total	33	215	86	40.0	1192	5.54	4	35	25.1

	Rushing				Punting			Tot
Year Team	Att	Yds	Avg	TD	Punts	Yds	Avg	TD
1938 Pit	**152**	**567**	3.7	4	—	—	—	4
1940 Det	**146**	**514**	3.5	5	52	2132	41.0	5
1941 Det	89	240	2.7	2	48	**1997**	41.6	4
NFL Total	387	1321	3.4	11	100	4129	41.3	13

CHARLIE WHITE White, Charles Frankie 6′0″, 222 **RB**
Col: Iowa Central CC; Bethune-Cookman *HS:* Spring Valley [NY] B: 8/31/1953, Suffern, NY *Drafted:* 1977 Round 7 NYJ
1977 NYJ: Rec 2-5 2.5 1 TD. **1978** TB: Rec 2-31 15.5. **Total:** Rec 4-36 9.0 1 TD.

		Rushing					Tot
Year Team	G	Att	Yds	Avg	TD	Fum	TD
1977 NYJ	13	50	151	3.0	1	2	2
1978 TB	7	11	42	3.8	0	1	0
NFL Total	20	61	193	3.2	1	3	2

CHARLES WHITE White, Charles Raymond 5′10″, 190 **RB**
Col: USC *HS:* San Fernando [CA] B: 1/22/1958, Los Angeles, CA *Drafted:* 1980 Round 1 Cle
1985 LARm: PR 1-0. **Total:** PR 1-0.

		Rushing				Receiving			
Year Team	G	Att	Yds	Avg	TD	Rec	Yds	Avg	TD
1980 Cle	14	86	279	3.2	5	17	153	9.0	1
1981 Cle	16	97	342	3.5	1	27	219	8.1	0
1982 Cle	9	69	259	3.8	3	34	283	8.3	0
1984 Cle	10	24	62	2.6	0	5	29	5.8	0
1985 LARm	16	70	310	4.4	3	1	12	12.0	0
1986 LARm	16	22	126	5.7	0	1	7	7.0	0
1987 LARm	15	**324**	**1374**	4.2	**11**	23	121	5.3	0
1988 LARm	12	88	323	3.7	0	6	36	6.0	0
NFL Total	108	780	3075	3.9	23	114	860	7.5	1

	Kickoff Returns					Tot
Year Team	Ret	Yds	Avg	TD	Fum	TD
1980 Cle	1	20	20.0	0	1	6
1981 Cle	12	243	20.3	0	8	1
1982 Cle	0	0	—	0	2	3
1984 Cle	5	80	16.0	0	0	0
1985 LARm	17	300	17.6	0	3	3
1986 LARm	12	216	18.0	0	2	0
1987 LARm	3	73	24.3	0	8	11
1988 LARm	2	37	18.5	0	3	0
NFL Total	52	969	18.6	0	27	24

CRAIG WHITE White, Craig C 6′1″, 194 **WR**
Col: Missouri *HS:* Stephen Decatur [Decatur, IL]; Lawrence HS [KS] B: 10/8/1961, St. Joseph, MO *Drafted:* 1984 Round 11 Buf
1984 Buf: 14 G; Rec 4-28 7.0; KR 1-5 5.0.

DAVID WHITE White, David Maurice 6′2″, 235 **LB**
Col: Nebraska *HS:* St. Augustine [New Orleans, LA] B: 2/27/1970, Oak Ridge, TN
1993 NE: 6 G. **1995** Buf: 15 G; Int 1-9; 1 Sac. **1996** Buf: 16 G; **1** Fum TD; 6 Pt; 0.5 Sac. **Total:** 37 G; Int 1-9; 1 Fum TD; 6 Pt; 1.5 Sac.

DWAYNE WHITE White, Dwayne Allen 6′2″, 315 **OG**
Col: Alcorn State *HS:* South Philadelphia [Philadelphia, PA] B: 2/10/1967, Philadelphia, PA *Drafted:* 1990 Round 7 NYJ
1990 NYJ: 11 G. **1991** NYJ: 16 G. **1992** NYJ: 16 G. **1993** NYJ: 15 G. **1994** NYJ: 16 G. **1995** StL: 15 G. **1996** StL: 16 G. **Total:** 105 G.

DWIGHT WHITE White, Dwight Lynn 6′4″, 255 **DE**
Col: Texas A&M-Commerce *HS:* James Madison [Dallas, TX] B: 7/30/1949, Hampton, VA *Drafted:* 1971 Round 4 Pit
1971 Pit: 14 G. **1972** Pit: 14 G. **1973** Pit: 14 G; Int 2-10; Scor 1 Saf; 2 Pt. **1974** Pit: 14 G. **1975** Pit: 14 G; Scor **1** Saf; 2 Pt. **1976** Pit: 9 G. **1977** Pit: 14 G; Int 2-27. **1978** Pit: 15 G. **1979** Pit: 11 G. **1980** Pit: 7 G. **Total:** 126 G; Int 4-37; Scor 2 Saf; 4 Pt.

ED WHITE White, Edward Alvin 6′1″, 269 **OG**
Col: California *HS:* Helix [La Mesa, CA]; Indio HS [CA] B: 4/4/1947, San Diego, CA *Drafted:* 1969 Round 2 Min
1969 Min: 14 G. **1970** Min: 14 G. **1971** Min: 14 G. **1972** Min: 14 G; Rec 0-3. **1973** Min: 14 G. **1974** Min: 13 G. **1975** Min: 13 G. **1976** Min: 13 G. **1977** Min: 13 G. **1978** SD: 15 G. **1979** SD: 16 G. **1980** SD: 16 G. **1981** SD: 16 G. **1982** SD: 9 G. **1983** SD: 16 G. **1984** SD: 15 G. **1985** SD: 16 G. **Total:** 241 G; Rec 0-3.

ELLERY WHITE White, Ellery 175 **WB-FB**
Col: No College
1926 LA: 8 G.

GENE WHITE White, Eugene 6′1″, 197 **HB**
Col: Florida A&M B: 1940
1962 Oak: 7 G; Rec 6-101 16.8 1 TD; Scor **1** 2XP; 8 Pt.

GENE WHITE White, Eugene George 6′2″, 205 **G**
Col: Indiana *HS:* South Bend Central [IN] B: 8/3/1919, South Bend, IN D: 4/24/1989, South Bend, IN
AAFC **1946** BufA: 1 G.

FREEMAN WHITE White, Freeman III 6′5″, 225 **TE-LB-DB**
Col: Nebraska *HS:* Chadsey [Detroit, MI] B: 12/17/1943, Montgomery, AL *Drafted:* 1966 Round 9 NYG
1966 NYG: KR 2-14 7.0. **1967** NYG: Int 2-53. **Total:** KR 2-14 7.0; Int 2-53.

		Receiving			
Year Team	G	Rec	Yds	Avg	TD
1966 NYG	14	0	0	—	0
1967 NYG	14	0	0	—	0
1968 NYG	14	0	0	—	0
1969 NYG	13	29	315	10.9	1
NFL Total	55	29	315	10.9	1

GENE WHITE White, Gene Carlton 6′2″, 205 **DB**
Col: Georgia *HS:* Commerce [GA] B: 6/21/1932, Greensboro, NC
1954 GB: 9 G; Int 1-20.

GERALD WHITE White, Gerald Eugene 5′11″, 223 **RB**
Col: Michigan *HS:* Titusville [FL] B: 12/9/1964
1987 Dal: 3 G; Rush 1-(-4) -4.0; Rec 5-46 9.2.

HARVEY WHITE White, Harvey Talbert 6′1″, 191 **QB-OE**
Col: Clemson *HS:* Greenwood [SC] B: 3/3/1938 *Drafted:* 1960 Round 1 Bos
1960 Bos: 9 G; Pass 7-3 42.9%, 44 6.29; Rush 5-7 1.4; Rec 2-24 12.0.

JIM WHITE White, James Charles 6′4″, 256 **DE**
Col: Northeastern JC CO; Colorado State *HS:* Francis W. Parker [Chicago, IL] B: 9/5/1948, Chicago, IL *Drafted:* 1972 Round 3 NE
1972 NE: 13 G. **1974** Hou: 12 G. **1975** Hou: 14 G. **1976** Sea-Den: 9 G. Sea: 2 G. Den: 7 G. **Total:** 48 G.

JAMES WHITE White, James Curtis 6′3″, 265 **DT-NT**
(Duck) *Col:* Oklahoma State *HS:* Hot Springs [AR] B: 10/26/1953, Hot Springs, AR *Drafted:* 1976 Round 1 Min
1976 Min: 14 G. **1977** Min: 14 G. **1978** Min: 16 G. **1979** Min: 16 G. **1980** Min: 16 G. **1981** Min: 16 G. **1982** Min: 9 G; 3 Sac. **1983** Min: 16 G; Int 1-22; 1 Sac. **Total:** 117 G; Int 1-22; 4 Sac.

JIM WHITE White, James Joseph William 6′2″, 227 **OT-DT**
Col: Notre Dame *HS:* All Hallows [Bronx, NY] B: 2/8/1920, Edgewater, NJ D: 4/1987, Dumont, NJ
1946 NYG: 11 G; 6 Pt. **1947** NYG: 11 G; Int 1-16; 1 Fum TD; 6 Pt. **1948** NYG: 11 G; KR 1-6 6.0; 6 Pt. **1949** NYG: 11 G. **1950** NYG: 11 G. **Total:** 55 G; KR 1-6 6.0; Int 1-16; 1 Fum TD; Tot TD 3; 18 Pt.

MIKE WHITE White, James Michael 6′5″, 266 **DT-DE-NT**
Col: Albany State (Ga.) *HS:* Westside [Augusta, GA] B: 8/11/1957, Augusta, GA *Drafted:* 1979 Round 4 Cin
1979 Cin: 16 G. **1980** Cin: 15 G. **1981** Sea: 15 G. **1982** Sea: 5 G. **Total:** 51 G.

JAN WHITE White, Jan Andre 6′2″, 216 **TE**
Col: Ohio State *HS:* John Harris [Harrisburg, PA] B: 10/6/1948, Harrisburg, PA *Drafted:* 1971 Round 2 Buf

		Receiving			
Year Team	G	Rec	Yds	Avg	TD
1971 Buf	13	13	130	10.0	0
1972 Buf	14	12	148	12.3	2
NFL Total	27	25	278	11.1	2

JEFF WHITE White, Jeffrey Charles 5′10″, 170 **K-P**
Col: Texas-El Paso *HS:* Bronxville [NY] B: 6/10/1948, Bronxville, NY
1973 NE: 11 G; Punt 6-163 27.2; Scor 63, 14-25 56.0% FG, 21-25 84.0% XK; 1 Fum.

JERIS WHITE White, Jeris Jerome 5′9″, 188 **DB**
Col: Hawaii *HS:* Radford [Honolulu, HI] B: 9/3/1952, Fort Worth, TX *Drafted:* 1974 Round 2 Mia

		Interceptions		
Year Team	G	Int	Yds	TD
1974 Mia	14	0	0	0
1975 Mia	14	0	0	0
1976 Mia	14	2	4	0
1977 TB	14	4	61	0
1978 TB	16	5	56	0
1979 TB	16	3	39	0
1980 Was	16	2	1	0
1981 Was	16	0	0	0
1982 Was	9	3	4	0
NFL Total	129	19	165	0

JOHN WHITE White, John L 6′3″, 230 **TE**
Col: Texas Southern B: 10/9/1935
1960 Hou: 4 G; Rec 1-18 18.0; KR 0-11. **1961** Hou: 14 G; Rec 13-238 18.3 1 TD; 6 Pt. **Total:** 18 G; Rec 14-256 18.3 1 TD; KR 0-11; 6 Pt.

JOSE WHITE White, Jose Cornelius 6′3″, 290 **DT**
Col: Howard *HS:* Howard D. Woodson [Washington, DC] B: 3/2/1973, Washington, DC *Drafted:* 1995 Round 7 Min
1997 Jac: 3 G. **1998** Jac: 15 G; 3 Sac. **Total:** 18 G; 3 Sac.

LAWRENCE WHITE White, Lawrence 6′2″, 187 **WR**
Col: Dana B: 6/3/1963, Tuscaloosa, AL
1987 ChiB: 2 G; KR 1-17 17.0.

LEE WHITE White, Lee Andrew 6′2″, 232 **RB**
Col: Arizona Western Coll. (J.C.); Weber State *HS:* Las Vegas [NV] B: 5/9/1946, Las Vegas, NV *Drafted:* 1968 Round 1 NYJ
1969 NYJ: Rec 1-(-2) -2.0; KR 1-5 5.0. **1970** NYJ: Rec 12-125 10.4 1 TD. **1972** SD: Rec 3-20 6.7. **Total:** Rec 16-143 8.9 1 TD; KR 1-5 5.0.

		Rushing				
Year Team	G	Att	Yds	Avg	TD	Fum
1968 NYJ	1	0	0	—	0	0
1969 NYJ	14	28	88	3.1	0	0
1970 NYJ	14	70	215	3.1	0	3
1971 LARm	7	2	11	5.5	0	0
1972 SD	8	23	75	3.3	0	0
NFL Total	44	123	389	3.2	0	3

BOB WHITE White, Loren Robert 6′2″, 220 **FB**
Col: Ohio State *HS:* Covington [KY] B: 8/22/1938, Portsmouth, OH
1960 Hou: 6 G.

LORENZO WHITE White, Lorenzo Maurice 5′11″, 222 **RB**
Col: Michigan State *HS:* Dillard [Fort Lauderdale, FL] B: 4/12/1966, Hollywood, FL *Drafted:* 1988 Round 1 Hou

		Rushing				Receiving			
Year Team	G	Att	Yds	Avg	TD	Rec	Yds	Avg	TD
1988 Hou	11	31	115	3.7	0	0	0	—	0
1989 Hou	16	104	349	3.4	5	6	37	6.2	0
1990 Hou	16	168	702	4.2	8	39	368	9.4	4
1991 Hou	13	110	465	4.2	4	27	211	7.8	0
1992 Hou	16	265	1226	4.6	7	57	641	11.2	1
1993 Hou	8	131	465	3.5	2	34	229	6.7	0
1994 Hou	15	191	757	4.0	3	21	188	9.0	1
1995 Cle	12	62	163	2.6	1	8	64	8.0	0
NFL Total	107	1062	4242	4.0	30	192	1738	9.1	6

	Kickoff Returns					Tot
Year Team	Ret	Yds	Avg	TD	Fum	TD
1988 Hou	8	196	24.5	**1**	0	1
1989 Hou	17	303	17.8	0	2	5
1990 Hou	0	0	—	0	7	12
1991 Hou	0	0	—	0	3	4
1992 Hou	0	0	—	0	2	8
1993 Hou	0	0	—	0	1	2
1994 Hou	8	167	20.9	0	2	4
1995 Cle	0	0	—	0	0	1
NFL Total	33	666	20.2	1	17	37

LYMAN WHITE White, Lyman Dan Jr. 6′0″, 217 **LB**
Col: Louisiana State *HS:* Franklin [LA] B: 1/3/1959, Lafayette, LA *Drafted:* 1981 Round 2 Atl
1981 Atl: 16 G. **1982** Atl: 2 G. **Total:** 18 G.

MARSH WHITE White, Marsh Reginald 6′2″, 220 **RB**
Col: Arkansas *HS:* Bonham [TX] B: 4/1/1953, Bonham, TX *Drafted:* 1975 Round 12 NYG
1975 NYG: Rec 3-15 5.0. **1976** NYG: Rec 2-7 3.5. **Total:** Rec 5-22 4.4.

		Rushing				
Year Team	G	Att	Yds	Avg	TD	Fum
1975 NYG	14	17	90	5.3	1	1
1976 NYG	14	69	223	3.2	1	0
NFL Total	28	86	313	3.6	2	1

PAUL WHITE White, Paul Grover 6′1″, 183 **HB-DB**
Col: Michigan *HS:* River Rouge [MI] B: 11/13/1921 D: 6/3/1974, Duluth, GA *Drafted:* 1944 Round 11 Det
1947 Pit: 11 G; Pass 3-1 33.3%, 21 7.00; Rush 22-85 3.9 1 TD; Rec 2-55 27.5; PR 5-50 10.0; KR 3-50 16.7; Int 2-22; 6 Pt; 2 Fum.

PAUL WHITE White, Paul Nathaniel 6′0″, 200 **RB**
Col: Texas-El Paso *HS:* Thomas Jefferson [San Antonio, TX] B: 9/17/1948, San Antonio, TX *Drafted:* 1970 Round 9 StL
1970 StL: 5 G; KR 3-65 21.7. **1971** StL: 6 G; Rush 1-3 3.0. **Total:** 11 G; Rush 1-3 3.0; KR 3-65 21.7.

PHIL WHITE White, Phillip Elmer 6′2″, 210 **FB-BB-WB-TB**
(Doc; Tex) *Col:* Oklahoma *HS:* Andarko [OK]; Central HS [Oklahoma City, OK] B: 5/17/1900, Enid, OK D: 5/29/1982, Oklahoma City, OK
1925 KC-NYG: 11 G; Pass 2 TD; Rush 3 TD; Rec 1 TD; Int 1 TD; Scor 34, 1 FG, 1 XK; Tot TD 5. KC: 8 G; Pass 2 TD; Rec 1 TD; Int 1 TD; Scor 16, 1 FG, 1 XK; Tot TD 2. NYG: 3 G; Rush 3 TD; 18 Pt. **1927** NYG: 12 G; Rush 3 TD; Scor 19, 1 XK. **Total:** 23 G; Pass 2 TD; Rush 6 TD; Rec 1 TD; Int 1 TD; Scor 53, 1 FG, 2 XK; Tot TD 8.

RALPH WHITE White, Ralph S 5′9″, 175 **E**
Col: New York U. *HS:* East Side [Newark, NJ] B: 11/18/1902 D: 3/1982, Riverhead, NY
1927 Buf: 3 G.

RANDY WHITE White, Randy Lee 6′4″, 257 **DT-LB-DE**
(The Manster) *Col:* Maryland *HS:* Thomas McKean [Wilmington, DE] B: 1/15/1953, Wilmington, DE *Drafted:* 1975 Round 1 Dal *HOF:* 1994
1975 Dal: 14 G. **1976** Dal: 14 G. **1977** Dal: 14 G. **1978** Dal: 16 G; KR 1-15 15.0. **1979** Dal: 15 G. **1980** Dal: 16 G. **1981** Dal: 16 G. **1982** Dal: 9 G; 2.5 Sac. **1983** Dal: 16 G; 12.5 Sac. **1984** Dal: 16 G; 12.5 Sac. **1985** Dal: 16 G; 10.5 Sac. **1986** Dal: 16 G; 6.5 Sac. **1987** Dal: 15 G; Int 1-0; 6 Sac. **1988** Dal: 16 G; 1.5 Sac. **Total:** 209 G; KR 1-15 15.0; Int 1-0; 52.0 Sac.

RAY WHITE White, Raymond C 6′1″, 227 **LB**
Col: Syracuse *HS:* Weymouth [MA] B: 5/18/1949, Weymouth, MA *Drafted:* 1971 Round 5 SD
1971 SD: 14 G; Scor 1 Saf; 2 Pt. **1972** SD: 4 G. **1975** StL: 14 G. **1976** StL: 6 G; Int 2-20. **Total:** 38 G; Int 2-20; Scor 1 Saf; 2 Pt.

REGGIE WHITE White, Reginald Eugene 6′4″, 297 **DT**
Col: North Carolina A&T *HS:* Milford Mill [Baltimore, MD] B: 3/22/1970, Baltimore, MD *Drafted:* 1992 Round 6 SD
1992 SD: 3 G; 1 Sac. **1993** SD: 8 G. **1994** SD: 11 G; 2 Sac. **1995** NE: 16 G; 1.5 Sac. **Total:** 38 G; 4.5 Sac.

REGGIE WHITE White, Reginald Howard 6′5″, 291 **DE-DT**
(The Minister of Defense) *Col:* Tennessee *HS:* Howard [Chattanooga, TN] B: 12/19/1961, Chattanooga, TN *Drafted:* 1984 Supplemental Round 1 Phi
1985 Phi: 13 G; 13 Sac. **1986** Phi: 16 G; 18 Sac. **1987** Phi: 12 G; **1** Fum TD; 6 Pt; **21** Sac. **1988** Phi: 16 G; **18** Sac. **1989** Phi: 16 G; 11 Sac. **1990** Phi: 16 G; Int 1-33; 14 Sac. **1991** Phi: 16 G; Int 1-0; 15 Sac. **1992** Phi: 16 G; 1 Fum TD; 6 Pt; 14 Sac. **1993** GB: 16 G; 13 Sac. **1994** GB: 16 G; 8 Sac. **1995** GB: 15 G; 12 Sac. **1996** GB: 16 G; Int 1-46; 2 Fum; 8.5 Sac. **1997** GB: 16 G; 11 Sac. **1998** GB: 16 G; 16 Sac. **Total:** 216 G; Int 3-79; 2 Fum TD; 12 Pt; 2 Fum; **192.5** Sac.

ROBB WHITE White, Robb Steven 6′4″, 270 **DE-NT**
Col: South Dakota *HS:* Central [Aberdeen, SD] B: 5/26/1965, Aberdeen, SD
1988 NYG: 1 G. **1989** NYG: 15 G. **1990** TB: 7 G; 2.5 Sac. **Total:** 23 G; 2.5 Sac.

BUCKY WHITE White, Robert 6′2″, 180 **DB**
Col: Lamar B: 11/24/1962
1987 Hou: 3 G.

BOB WHITE White, Robert 150 **OE**
Col: No College *HS:* Manual [Louisville, KY] B: 1903 Deceased
1923 Lou: 2 G.

BOB WHITE White, Robert Arlen 6'5", 272 **C-OG**
Col: Rhode Island *HS:* Lunenburg [MA] B: 4/9/1963, Fitchburg, MA
Drafted: 1986 Round 7 NYJ
1987 Dal: 4 G; 2 Fum. **1988** Dal: 12 G; KR 1-7 7.0. **1989** Dal: 8 G; 1 Fum.
Total: 24 G; KR 1-7 7.0; 3 Fum.

CHRIS WHITE White, Robert Christopher 6'3", 200 **DB**
Col: Tennessee *HS:* Bradley [Cleveland, TN] B: 3/1/1962, Cleveland, TN
1987 Sea: 1 G.

DARYL WHITE White, Robert Daryl 6'3", 250 **OG**
Col: Nebraska *HS:* East Orange [NJ] B: 10/12/1951, Newark, NJ
Drafted: 1974 Round 4 Cin
1974 Det: 10 G.

BOB WHITE White, Robert William 5'11", 176 **HB**
Col: Glendale CC CA; Stanford *HS:* Herbert Hoover [Glendale, CA]
B: 5/25/1929, Los Angeles, CA *Drafted:* 1951 Round 16 SF
1951 SF: Rec 3-36 12.0; Int 1-11. **1952** SF: Rec 12-173 14.4 2 TD.
1955 Cle-Bal: PR 2-28 14.0; KR 14-400 28.6. Cle: PR 2-28 14.0;
KR 10-258 25.8. Bal: KR 4-142 35.5. **Total:** Rec 15-209 13.9 2 TD;
PR 2-28 14.0; KR 14-400 28.6; Int 1-11.

		Rushing					Tot
Year Team	G	Att	Yds	Avg	TD	Fum	TD
1951 SF	12	8	33	4.1	0	0	0
1952 SF	12	24	33	1.4	1	1	3
1955 Cle-Bal	11	0	0	—	0	1	0
1955 Cle	8	0	0	—	0	1	0
1955 Bal	3	0	0	—	0	0	0
NFL Total	35	32	66	2.1	1	2	3

BUCK WHITE White, Roy Eldon 6'0", 195 **FB**
Col: Howard Payne; Valparaiso *HS:* Brownwood [TX] B: 2/28/1900, Brownwood, TX D: 5/15/1993, San Antonio, TX
1925 ChiB: 10 G; Rush 3 TD; 18 Pt. **1927** ChiB: 13 G; Rush 2 TD; 12 Pt.
1928 ChiB: 13 G; Rush 3 TD; 18 Pt. **1929** ChiB: 10 G; Rush 2 TD; 12 Pt.
Total: 46 G; Rush 10 TD; 60 Pt.

RUSSELL WHITE White, Russell Lamar 5'11", 216 **RB**
Col: California *HS:* Crespi [Encino, CA] B: 12/15/1970, Pacoima, CA
Drafted: 1993 Round 3 LARm
1993 LARm: 5 G; Rush 2-10 5.0; KR 8-122 15.3.

SAMMY WHITE White, Samuel 5'11", 190 **WR**
Col: Grambling State *HS:* Richwood [Monroe, LA] B: 3/16/1954, Winnsboro, LA *Drafted:* 1976 Round 2 Min
1976 Min: Rush 5-(-10) -2.0; PR 3-45 15.0; KR 9-173 19.2. **1977** Min:
KR 7-113 16.1. **1978** Min: Rush 5-30 6.0; PR 1-0; KR 3-50 16.7.
1979 Min: Rush 1-6 6.0. **1980** Min: Rush 4-65 16.3. **1981** Min: Rush 2-(-1) -0.5; PR 1-0. **1983** Min: Rush 1-7 7.0. **Total:** Rush 18-97 5.4; PR 5-45 9.0; KR 19-336 17.7.

		Receiving				
Year Team	G	Rec	Yds	Avg	TD	Fum
1976 Min	14	51	906	17.8	10	3
1977 Min	14	41	760	18.5	9	2
1978 Min	16	53	741	14.0	9	1
1979 Min	15	42	715	17.0	4	1
1980 Min	16	53	887	16.7	5	0
1981 Min	16	66	1001	15.2	3	1
1982 Min	7	29	503	17.3	5	0
1983 Min	11	29	412	14.2	4	0
1984 Min	13	21	399	19.0	1	1
1985 Min	6	8	76	9.5	0	0
NFL Total	128	393	6400	16.3	50	9

SHELDON WHITE White, Sheldon Darnell 5'11", 188 **DB**
Col: Miami (Ohio) *HS:* Meadowdale [Dayton, OH] B: 3/1/1965, Dayton, OH *Drafted:* 1988 Round 3 NYG
1988 NYG: KR 3-62 20.7. **Total:** KR 3-62 20.7.

		Interceptions		
Year Team	G	Int	Yds	TD
1988 NYG	16	4	70	0
1989 NYG	16	2	18	0
1990 Det	3	0	0	0
1991 Det	16	1	18	1
1992 Det	13	2	26	0
1993 Cin	8	2	19	0
NFL Total	72	11	151	1

SHERMAN WHITE White, Sherman Eugene 6'5", 250 **DE**
Col: Laney Coll. CA (J.C.); California *HS:* Portsmouth [NH]
B: 10/6/1948, Manchester, NH *Drafted:* 1972 Round 1 Cin
1972 Cin: 13 G; Scor **1** Saf; 2 Pt. **1973** Cin: 13 G. **1974** Cin: 12 G.
1975 Cin: 14 G. **1976** Buf: 13 G; Int 1-5. **1977** Buf: 14 G. **1978** Buf: 16 G.
1979 Buf: 15 G. **1980** Buf: 15 G; Int 1-0. **1981** Buf: 16 G. **1982** Buf: 9 G;
4 Sac. **1983** Buf: 8 G; 3 Sac. **Total:** 158 G; Int 2-5; Scor 1 Saf; 2 Pt; 7 Sac.

STAN WHITE White, Stanley Ray 6'1", 225 **LB**
Col: Ohio State *HS:* Theodore Roosevelt [Kent, OH] B: 10/24/1949, Dover, OH *Drafted:* 1972 Round 17 Bal
1973 Bal: KR 1-17 17.0. **1979** Bal: Rush 1-3 3.0. **Total:** Rush 1-3 3.0;
KR 1-17 17.0.

		Interceptions		
Year Team	G	Int	Yds	TD
1972 Bal	14	0	0	0
1973 Bal	14	4	40	1
1974 Bal	14	1	40	0
1975 Bal	14	8	135	1
1976 Bal	14	3	26	0
1977 Bal	14	7	84	0
1978 Bal	12	1	12	0
1979 Bal	16	1	11	0
1980 Det	16	2	22	0
1981 Det	16	4	37	0
1982 Det	9	3	21	0
NFL Total	153	34	428	2

STEVE WHITE White, Stephen Gregory 6'2", 256 **DE**
Col: Tennessee *HS:* Westwood [Memphis, TN] B: 10/25/1973, Memphis, TN *Drafted:* 1996 Round 6 Phi
1996 TB: 4 G. **1997** TB: 15 G; KR 1-0. **1998** TB: 16 G; 2 Sac. **Total:** 35 G;
KR 1-0; 2 Sac.

ALLIE WHITE White, Thomas Allison 5'11", 212 **G-T**
Col: Texas Christian *HS:* Masonic Home School [Fort Worth, TX]
B: 3/23/1915, Crosby, TX D: 10/21/1996, Fort Worth, TX *Drafted:* 1939 Round 13 Phi
1939 Phi: 7 G.

LEON WHITE White, Thomas Leon 6'3", 240 **LB**
Col: Brigham Young *HS:* Helix [La Mesa, CA] B: 10/4/1963, San Diego, CA *Drafted:* 1986 Round 5 Cin
1986 Cin: 16 G; Scor **1** Saf; 2 Pt. **1987** Cin: 12 G. **1988** Cin: 16 G; 3 Sac.
1989 Cin: 16 G; Int 1-22; 1 Fum TD; 6 Pt; 2 Sac. **1990** Cin: 16 G; Int 1-21;
1 Sac. **1991** Cin: 16 G. **1992** LARm: 13 G; Int 2-49. **1993** LARm: 14 G.
Total: 119 G; Int 4-92; Scor 1 Saf; 1 Fum TD; 8 Pt; 6 Sac.

WALTER WHITE White, Walter Lee 6'3", 216 **TE**
Col: Mesa CC AZ; Maryland *HS:* Albemarle [Charlottesville, VA]
B: 7/19/1951, Charlottesville, VA *Drafted:* 1975 Round 3 Pit
1975 KC: Pass 1-0, 1 Int; Rush 3-(-10) -3.3. **1976** KC: Rush 2-15 7.5.
1977 KC: Rush 2-(-3) -1.5. **1978** KC: Pass 1-1 100.0%, 44 44.00.
Total: Pass 2-1 50.0%, 44 22.00 1 Int; Rush 7-2 0.3.

		Receiving				
Year Team	G	Rec	Yds	Avg	TD	Fum
1975 KC	14	23	559	24.3	3	0
1976 KC	14	47	808	17.2	7	0
1977 KC	13	48	674	14.0	5	1
1978 KC	16	42	340	8.1	1	0
1979 KC	6	3	15	5.0	0	1
NFL Total	63	163	2396	14.7	16	2

MAC WHITE White, Wilbur McKee 6'0", 178 **E-WB**
Col: Marietta *HS:* Hillsboro [OH] B: 2/22/1890, Hillsboro, OH
D: 12/1973, Hillsboro, OH
1922 Tol: 7 G. **1923** Tol: 8 G. **Total:** 15 G.

WILBUR WHITE White, Wilbur Walter 6'0", 167 **TB-DB-WB**
(Red) *Col:* Colorado State *HS:* Fort Collins [CO] B: 4/30/1912, Seibert, CO D: 4/1968
1935 Bkn: 8 G; Pass 32-10 31.3%, 73 2.28 2 TD 5 Int; Rush 16-41 2.6.
1936 Det: 3 G; Pass 1-0, 1 Int; Rush 8-21 2.6; Rec 2-21 10.5. **Total:** 11 G;
Pass 33-10 30.3%, 73 2.21 2 TD 6 Int; Rush 24-62 2.6; Rec 2-21 10.5.

DANNY WHITE White, Wilford Daniel 6'2", 193 **QB**
Col: Arizona State *HS:* Westwood [Mesa, AZ] B: 2/9/1952, Mesa, AZ
Drafted: 1974 Round 3 Dal
1980 Dal: Rec 1-(-9) -9.0. **1983** Dal: Rec 1-15 15.0 1 TD. **1985** Dal:
Rec 1-12 12.0 1 TD. **Total:** Rec 3-18 6.0 2 TD.

		Passing							
Year Team	G	Att	Comp	Comp%	Yds	YPA	TD	Int	Rating
1976 Dal	14	20	13	65.0	213	10.65	2	2	94.4
1977 Dal	14	10	4	40.0	35	3.50	0	1	10.4
1978 Dal	16	34	20	58.8	215	6.32	0	1	65.2
1979 Dal	16	39	19	48.7	267	6.85	1	2	58.4
1980 Dal	16	436	260	59.6	3287	7.54	28	25	80.7
1981 Dal	16	391	223	57.0	3098	7.92	22	13	87.5
1982 Dal	9	247	156	63.2	2079	8.42	16	12	91.1
1983 Dal	16	533	334	62.7	3980	7.47	29	23	85.6
1984 Dal	14	233	126	54.1	1580	6.78	11	11	71.5
1985 Dal	14	450	267	59.3	3157	7.02	21	17	80.6
1986 Dal	7	153	95	62.1	1157	7.56	12	5	97.9
1987 Dal	11	362	215	59.4	2617	7.23	12	17	73.2

1988 Dal	3	42	29	69.0	274	6.52	1	3	65.0
NFL Total	166	2950	1761	59.7	21959	7.44	155	132	81.7

	Rushing				Punting				Tot
Year Team	Att	Yds	Avg	TD	Punts	Yds	Avg	Fum	TD
1976 Dal	6	17	2.8	0	70	2690	38.4	0	0
1977 Dal	1	-2	-2.0	0	80	3171	39.6	0	0
1978 Dal	5	7	1.4	0	76	3076	40.5	2	0
1979 Dal	1	25	25.0	0	76	3168	41.7	1	0
1980 Dal	27	114	4.2	1	71	2903	40.9	8	1
1981 Dal	38	104	2.7	0	79	3222	40.8	**14**	0
1982 Dal	17	91	5.4	0	37	1542	41.7	**10**	0
1983 Dal	18	31	1.7	4	38	1543	40.6	10	5
1984 Dal	6	21	3.5	0	82	3151	38.4	2	0
1985 Dal	22	44	2.0	1	1	43	43.0	6	2
1986 Dal	8	16	2.0	1	0	0	—	6	1
1987 Dal	10	14	1.4	1	0	0	—	9	1
NFL Total	159	482	3.0	8	610	24509	40.2	68	10

WHIZZER WHITE White, Wilford Parley 5'9", 172 **HB**
Col: Arizona State *HS:* Mesa [AZ] B: 9/26/1928, Mesa, AZ
Drafted: 1951 Round 3 ChiB
1951 ChiB: Pass 1-0; Rec 4-45 11.3 1 TD; Scor 16, 1-2 50.0% FG, 1-1 100.0% XK. **1952** ChiB: Pass 2-0; Rec 8-152 19.0; KR 5-134 26.8; Scor 7, 2-3 66.7% FG, 1-1 100.0% XK. **Total:** Pass 3-0; Rec 12-197 16.4 1 TD; KR 5-134 26.8; Scor 23, 3-5 60.0% FG, 2-2 100.0% XK.

		Rushing				Punt Returns					Tot
Year Team	G	Att	Yds	Avg	TD	Ret	Yds	Avg	TD	Fum	TD
1951 ChiB	6	9	86	9.6	1	14	131	9.4	0	1	2
1952 ChiB	11	19	-19	-1.0	0	23	117	5.1	0	6	0
NFL Total	17	28	67	2.4	1	37	248	6.7	0	7	2

WILLIAM WHITE White, William Eugene 5'10", 199 **DB**
Col: Ohio State *HS:* Lima [OH] B: 2/19/1966, Lima, OH
Drafted: 1988 Round 4 Det
1989 Det: 1 Fum TD; 1 Sac. **1993** Det: 1.5 Sac. **1995** KC: 1 Sac. **1998** Atl: 1 Fum TD. **Total:** 2 Fum TD; 3.5 Sac.

		Interceptions				Tot
Year Team	G	Int	Yds	TD	Fum	TD
1988 Det	16	0	0	0	0	0
1989 Det	15	1	0	0	0	1
1990 Det	16	5	120	1	0	1
1991 Det	16	2	35	0	0	1
1992 Det	16	4	54	0	1	0
1993 Det	16	1	5	0	0	0
1994 KC	15	2	0	0	0	0
1995 KC	16	2	48	0	0	0
1996 KC	12	0	0	0	0	0
1997 Atl	16	1	11	0	0	0
1998 Atl	16	2	36	0	0	1
NFL Total	170	20	309	1	1	4

MARV WHITED Whited, Marvin Eugene Jr. 5'10", 208 **LB-BB-G**
Col: Oklahoma *HS:* Hollis [OK] B: 7/26/1918, Crowell, TX Deceased
Drafted: 1942 Round 13 Was
1942 Was: 5 G; Rush 1-3 3.0. **1945** Was: 10 G; Int 1-12. **Total:** 15 G; Rush 1-3 3.0; Int 1-12.

MIKE WHITED Whited, Michael Douglas 6'4", 250 **OT**
Col: U. of Pacific *HS:* Thomas Downey [Modesto, CA] B: 3/30/1958, Chico, CA
1980 Det: 16 G.

WALKER WHITEHEAD Whitehead, B. Walker 6'0", 180 **TB**
Col: No College *HS:* Central [Evansville, IN] B: 6/22/1902, IN
D: 1/3/1969, Evansville, IN
1922 Eva: 1 G.

BUD WHITEHEAD Whitehead, Ruben Angus 6'0", 185 **DB**
Col: Florida State *HS:* Marianna [FL] B: 1/1/1939, Marianna, FL
Drafted: 1961 Round 16 SD
1964 SD: Rec 1-(-4) -4.0; Punt 1-30 30.0. **1965** SD: Punt 1-40 40.0. **1967** SD: Pass 1-0. **1968** SD: KR 2-81 40.5. **Total:** Pass 1-0; Rec 1-(-4) -4.0; KR 2-81 40.5; Punt 2-70 35.0.

		Interceptions		
Year Team	G	Int	Yds	TD
1961 SD	9	1	0	0
1962 SD	14	1	18	0
1963 SD	14	1	0	0
1964 SD	12	3	43	0
1965 SD	14	7	127	1
1966 SD	14	2	89	0
1967 SD	14	0	0	0
1968 SD	3	0	0	0
NFL Total	94	15	277	1

DAVID WHITEHURST Whitehurst, Charles David 6'2", 204 **QB**
Col: Furman *HS:* Walker [Atlanta, GA] B: 4/27/1955, Baumhaulder, Germany *Drafted:* 1977 Round 8 GB

		Passing							
Year Team	G	Att	Comp	Comp%	Yds	YPA	TD	Int	Rating
1977 GB	7	105	50	47.6	634	6.04	1	7	42.3
1978 GB	16	328	168	51.2	2093	6.38	10	17	59.9
1979 GB	13	322	179	55.6	2247	6.98	10	18	64.5
1980 GB	2	15	5	33.3	55	3.67	0	1	17.4
1981 GB	9	128	66	51.6	792	6.19	7	5	72.8
1982 GB	3	47	18	38.3	235	5.00	0	1	46.0
1983 GB	4	35	18	51.4	149	4.26	0	2	38.9
NFL Total	54	980	504	51.4	6205	6.33	28	51	59.2

	Rushing				
Year Team	Att	Yds	Avg	TD	Fum
1977 GB	14	55	3.9	1	2
1978 GB	28	67	2.4	1	8
1979 GB	18	73	4.1	4	3
1980 GB	0	0	—	0	1
1981 GB	15	51	3.4	1	4
1983 GB	2	-4	-2.0	0	2
NFL Total	77	242	3.1	7	20

A.D. WHITFIELD Whitfield, A. D Jr. 5'10", 200 **RB**
Col: North Texas *HS:* Wilson White [Rosebud, TX] B: 9/2/1943, Rosebud, TX

		Rushing				Receiving					Tot
Year Team	G	Att	Yds	Avg	TD	Rec	Yds	Avg	TD	Fum	TD
1965 Dal	2	1	0	0.0	0	0	0	—	0	0	0
1966 Was	14	93	472	5.1	2	18	101	5.6	1	3	3
1967 Was	13	91	384	4.2	1	36	494	13.7	2	2	3
1968 Was	10	37	125	3.4	0	13	107	8.2	0	3	0
NFL Total	39	222	981	4.4	3	67	702	10.5	3	8	6

BOB WHITFIELD Whitfield, Robert Lectress Jr. 6'5", 303 **OT**
Col: Stanford *HS:* Phineas Banning [Los Angeles, CA] B: 10/18/1971, Carson, CA *Drafted:* 1992 Round 1 Atl
1992 Atl: 11 G. **1993** Atl: 16 G. **1994** Atl: 16 G. **1995** Atl: 16 G. **1996** Atl: 16 G. **1997** Atl: 16 G. **1998** Atl: 16 G. **Total:** 107 G.

BRANDON WHITING Whiting, Brandon Renee 6'3", 278 **DT**
Col: California *HS:* Long Beach Polytechnic [CA] B: 7/30/1976, Santa Rosa, CA *Drafted:* 1998 Round 4 Phi
1998 Phi: 16 G; 1.5 Sac.

BLAKE WHITLATCH Whitlatch, Blake 6'1", 233 **LB**
Col: Louisiana State *HS:* Broadmoor [Baton Rouge, LA]
B: 10/13/1955, Baton Rouge, LA *Drafted:* 1978 Round 9 SD
1978 NYJ: 4 G.

CURTIS WHITLEY Whitley, Curtis Wayne 6'1", 295 **C**
Col: Chowan Coll. NC; Clemson *HS:* Selma [Smithfield, NC]
B: 5/10/1969, Lowgrounds, NC *Drafted:* 1992 Round 5 SD
1992 SD: 3 G. **1993** SD: 15 G. **1994** SD: 12 G. **1995** Car: 16 G. **1996** Car: 11 G. **1997** Oak: 15 G. **Total:** 72 G.

HALL WHITLEY Whitley, Hall Wood III 6'2", 225 **LB**
Col: Texas A&M–Kingsville *HS:* Anahuac [TX] B: 7/18/1935
Drafted: 1957 Round 15 Bal
1960 NYT: 4 G.

WILSON WHITLEY Whitley, Wilson Carl Jr. 6'3", 265 **DT-NT**
Col: Houston *HS:* Brenham [TX] B: 4/28/1955, Brenham, TX
D: 10/25/1992, Marietta, GA *Drafted:* 1977 Round 1 Cin
1977 Cin: 13 G. **1978** Cin: 16 G. **1979** Cin: 14 G; Int 1-2. **1980** Cin: 16 G. **1981** Cin: 14 G. **1982** Cin: 9 G; 1 Sac. **Total:** 82 G; Int 1-2; 1 Sac.

KEN WHITLOW Whitlow, Kenneth Moody 6'1", 190 **C-LB**
Col: Rice *HS:* Wichita Falls [TX] B: 11/30/1917, Wichita Falls, TX
D: 11/12/1969, Houston, TX
AAFC **1946** MiaA: 13 G; Int 2-20.

BOB WHITLOW Whitlow, Robert Edward 6'2", 236 **C**
Col: Compton CC CA; Indiana; Arizona *HS:* Bloomington [IN]
B: 2/15/1936, Shelbyville, IN
1960 Was: 12 G. **1961** Was-Det: 14 G. Was: 8 G. Det: 6 G. **1962** Det: 14 G. **1963** Det: 14 G. **1964** Det: 12 G. **1965** Det: 9 G. **1966** Atl: 11 G. **1968** Cle: 14 G. **Total:** 100 G.

S.J. WHITMAN Whitman, Laverne Scott Jr. 5'11", 185 **DB**
(Lav) *Col:* Tulsa *HS:* Hollis [OK] B: 8/17/1926, Hollis, OK
Drafted: 1951 Round 22 ChiC

		Interceptions		
Year Team	G	Int	Yds	TD
1951 ChiC	12	7	102	0
1952 ChiC	7	3	27	0
1953 ChiC-ChiB	12	3	39	0
1953 ChiC	3	1	3	0

1953 ChiB	9	2	36	0
1954 ChiB	8	5	117	1
NFL Total	39	18	285	1

VIC WHITMARSH Whitmarsh, Victor L 5′11″, 190 **E**
Col: Syracuse *HS:* Central [Detroit, MI] B: 3/1896, Detroit, MI Deceased
1921 Det: 3 G.

DAVID WHITMORE Whitmore, David Lawrence 6′0″, 232 **DB**
Col: Stephen F. Austin St. *HS:* Daingerfield [TX] B: 7/6/1967, Daingerfield, TX *Drafted:* 1990 Round 4 NYG
1990 NYG: 16 G; KR 1-0; 1 Fum. **1991** SF: 11 G; KR 1-7 7.0; Int 1-5; 1 Sac. **1992** SF: 16 G; Int 1-0. **1993** KC: 6 G. **1994** KC: 12 G. **1995** Phi: 3 G. **Total:** 64 G; KR 2-7 3.5; Int 2-5; 1 Fum; 1 Sac.

NAT WHITMYER Whitmyer, Nathaniel 5′11″, 180 **DB**
Col: Allan Hancock Coll. CA (J.C.); Washington *HS:* Dunbar [Washington, DC] B: 8/31/1940, Washington, DC
1963 LARm: 7 G; KR 3-80 26.7; Int 1-27; 1 Fum. **1966** SD: 14 G; KR 1-10 10.0. **Total:** 21 G; KR 4-90 22.5; Int 1-27; 1 Fum.

DAVE WHITSELL Whitsell, David Andrew 6′0″, 189 **DB-HB**
Col: Indiana *HS:* Shelby [MI] B: 6/14/1936, Shelby, MI *Drafted:* 1958 Round 24 Det
1958 Det: KR 3-63 21.0. **1963** ChiB: Rush 1-(-8) -8.0. **1964** ChiB: Rush 1-14 14.0. **1968** NO: Rush 1-(-1) -1.0; KR 1-0. **Total:** Rush 3-5 1.7; KR 4-63 15.8.

		Interceptions				Tot
Year Team	**G**	**Int**	**Yds**	**TD**	**Fum**	**TD**
1958 Det	12	1	29	0	1	0
1959 Det	12	0	0	0	0	0
1960 Det	11	0	0	0	0	0
1961 ChiB	14	6	123	0	0	0
1962 ChiB	14	5	45	0	0	0
1963 ChiB	14	6	61	1	1	1
1964 ChiB	14	2	57	0	1	0
1965 ChiB	14	4	67	1	0	1
1966 ChiB	14	3	44	0	0	0
1967 NO	14	**10**	178	2	0	2
1968 NO	14	6	44	0	0	1
1969 NO	14	3	14	0	0	0
NFL Total	161	46	662	4	3	5

ALVIS WHITTED Whitted, Alvis James 5′11″, 184 **WR**
Col: North Carolina State *HS:* Orange [Hillsborough, NC] B: 9/4/1974, Durham, NC *Drafted:* 1998 Round 7 Jac
1998 Jac: 16 G; Rush 3-13 4.3; Rec 2-61 30.5; 6 Pt.

BOBBY WHITTEN Whitten, Bobby Gene 6′3″, 265 **OG**
Col: Kansas *HS:* Junction City [KS] B: 5/7/1959, Junction City, KS
1981 Cin: 1 G.

TODD WHITTEN Whitten, Phillip Todd 6′0″, 185 **QB**
Col: Stephen F. Austin St. *HS:* Justin F. Kimball [Dallas, TX] B: 2/16/1965, Dallas, TX
1987 NE: 1 G; Rush 2-(-6) -3.0.

JESSE WHITTENTON Whittenton, Urshell Jesse 6′0″, 193 **DB**
Col: Texas-El Paso *HS:* Ysleta [El Paso, TX] B: 5/9/1934, Big Spring, TX *Drafted:* 1956 Round 5 LARm
1956 LARm: PR 10-21 2.1; KR 4-85 21.3. **Total:** PR 10-21 2.1; KR 4-85 21.3.

		Interceptions		
Year Team	**G**	**Int**	**Yds**	**TD**
1956 LARm	12	3	83	1
1957 LARm	12	1	31	0
1958 GB	8	1	0	0
1959 GB	12	0	0	0
1960 GB	12	6	101	0
1961 GB	14	5	98	1
1962 GB	14	3	40	0
1963 GB	14	4	90	0
1964 GB	14	1	0	0
NFL Total	112	24	443	2

CARY WHITTINGHAM Whittingham, Cary L 6′2″, 230 **LB**
Col: Brigham Young *HS:* Provo [UT] B: 5/30/1963, San Luis Obispo, CA
1987 LARm: 3 G.

FRED WHITTINGHAM Whittingham, Fred George 6′2″, 235 **LB-OG**
Col: Brigham Young; Cal Poly-S.L.O. *HS:* Warwick [RI] B: 2/4/1939, Boston, MA
1964 LARm: 5 G. **1966** Phi: 14 G; KR 2-33 16.5; Int 1-0. **1967** NO: 7 G; Int 1-8. **1968** NO: 13 G; Int 1-16. **1969** Dal: 7 G. **1970** Bos: 13 G; KR 1-24 24.0. **1971** Phi: 4 G. **Total:** 63 G; KR 3-57 19.0; Int 3-24.

KYLE WHITTINGHAM Whittingham, Kyle David 6′0″, 232 **LB**
Col: Brigham Young *HS:* Provo [UT] B: 11/21/1959, San Luis Obispo, CA
1987 LARm: 3 G.

ART WHITTINGTON Whittington, Arthur Lee 5′11″, 185 **RB**
Col: Southern Methodist *HS:* Cuero [TX] B: 9/4/1955, Cuero, TX
Drafted: 1978 Round 7 Oak
1981 Oak: PR 2-4 2.0. **Total:** PR 2-4 2.0.

		Rushing				Receiving			
Year Team	**G**	**Att**	**Yds**	**Avg**	**TD**	**Rec**	**Yds**	**Avg**	**TD**
1978 Oak	16	172	661	3.8	7	23	106	4.6	0
1979 Oak	9	109	397	3.6	2	19	240	12.6	0
1980 Oak	15	91	299	3.3	3	19	205	10.8	0
1981 Oak	16	69	220	3.2	1	23	213	9.3	2
1982 Buf	2	7	15	2.1	0	0	0	—	0
NFL Total	58	448	1592	3.6	13	84	764	9.1	2

	Kickoff Returns					Tot
Year Team	**Ret**	**Yds**	**Avg**	**TD**	**Fum**	**TD**
1978 Oak	23	473	20.6	0	2	7
1979 Oak	5	46	9.2	0	3	2
1980 Oak	21	392	18.7	**1**	3	4
1981 Oak	25	563	22.5	0	4	3
1982 Buf	2	39	19.5	0	2	0
NFL Total	76	1513	19.9	1	14	16

BERNARD WHITTINGTON Whittington, Bernard 6′6″, 280 **DE**
Col: Indiana *HS:* Hazelwood East [St. Louis, MO] B: 8/20/1971, St. Louis, MO
1994 Ind: 13 G. **1995** Ind: 16 G; 2 Sac. **1996** Ind: 16 G; 3 Sac. **1997** Ind: 15 G. **1998** Ind: 15 G; 4 Sac. **Total:** 75 G; 9 Sac.

C.L. WHITTINGTON Whittington, Columbus Lorenzo 6′1″, 200 **DB**
Col: Prairie View A&M *HS:* Charlton-Pollard [Beaumont, TX] B: 8/1/1952, Beaumont, TX
1974 Hou: 14 G; KR 3-37 12.3. **1975** Hou: 14 G; KR 1-0; Int 1-5. **1976** Hou: 14 G; PR 3-10 3.3; Int 5-103; **1** Fum TD; 6 Pt; 1 Fum. **1978** Hou: 12 G; Int 1-6. **Total:** 54 G; PR 3-10 3.3; KR 4-37 9.3; Int 7-114; 1 Fum TD; 6 Pt; 1 Fum.

MIKE WHITTINGTON Whittington, Michael Scott 6′2″, 220 **LB**
Col: Notre Dame *HS:* Christopher Columbus [Miami, FL] B: 8/9/1958, Miami, FL
1980 NYG: 16 G. **1981** NYG: 6 G. **1982** NYG: 9 G. **1983** NYG: 8 G. **Total:** 39 G.

JASON WHITTLE Whittle, Jason 6′6″, 300 **OT**
Col: Southwest Missouri State B: 3/7/1975, Springfield, MO
1998 NYG: 1 G.

RICKY WHITTLE Whittle, Ricky Jerome 5′9″, 200 **RB**
Col: Oregon *HS:* Edison [Fresno, CA] B: 12/21/1971, Fresno, CA
Drafted: 1996 Round 4 NO
1996 NO: Rush 20-52 2.6.

		Receiving				
Year Team	**G**	**Rec**	**Yds**	**Avg**	**TD**	**Fum**
1996 NO	10	26	162	6.2	0	1

MIKE WHITWELL Whitwell, Michael Carroll 6′0″, 175 **DB-WR**
Col: Texas A&M *HS:* Cotulla [TX] B: 11/14/1958, Kenedy, TX
Drafted: 1982 Round 6 Cle
1982 Cle: 9 G. **1983** Cle: 16 G; Int 3-67; 1 Sac. **Total:** 25 G; Int 3-67; 1 Sac.

JOHNNY WIATRAK Wiatrak, John Philip 6′0″, 220 **C-LB**
Col: Washington *HS:* DePaul Acad. [Chicago, IL] B: 3/30/1913, Chicago, IL *Drafted:* 1937 Round 4 Cle
1939 Det: 1 G.

OSSIE WIBERG Wiberg, Oscar Malker Hilding 5′11″, 207 **BB-LB-DB-FB**
(Swede) *Col:* Nebraska Wesleyan *HS:* Edgar [NE] B: 10/11/1904, Edgar, NE D: 8/14/1989, Gering, NE
1927 Cle: 10 G; Rush 1 TD; Rec 2 TD; Int 1 TD; Scor **1** 1XP; Tot TD 4; 25 Pt. **1928** Det: 10 G; Rec 2 TD; Scor 13, 1 XK. **1930** NYG: 17 G; Rush 4 TD; Scor 30, 6 XK. **1932** Bkn: 6 G; Pass 3-1 33.3%, 20 6.67; Rush 17-59 3.5; Rec 1-29 29.0; Scor 1, 1 XK. **1933** Cin: 1 G. **Total:** 44 G; Pass 3-1 33.3%, 20 6.67; Rush 17-59 3.5 5 TD; Rec 1-29 29.0 4 TD; Int 1 TD; Scor 1 1XP; Tot TD 10.

MURRAY WICHARD Wichard, Murray 6′2″, 260 **NT-DE**
Col: Frostburg State B: 11/16/1963
1987 NE: 3 G; 1 Sac.

TOM WICKERT Wickert, Thomas Kirk 6′4″, 246 **OT-OG**
Col: Washington State *HS:* Redwood [Larkspur, CA] B: 4/5/1952, Astoria, OR *Drafted:* 1974 Round 9 Mia
1974 Mia: 13 G. **1975** NO: 1 G. **1976** NO: 7 G. **1977** Det-KC: 6 G. Det: 1 G. KC: 5 G. **Total:** 27 G.

LLOYD WICKETT Wickett, Lloyd Meldrum 6'1", 208 T
(Red) *Col:* Oregon State *HS:* J.M. Weatherwax [Aberdeen, WA]
B: 4/3/1920, Ontario, Canada *Drafted:* 1943 Round 5 Det
1943 Det: 4 G. **1946** Det: 10 G. **Total:** 14 G.

BOB WICKS Wicks, Robert Blaine 6'3", 200 WR
Col: Utah State *HS:* Royal Oak [Covina, CA] B: 7/24/1950, Pasadena, CA *Drafted:* 1972 Round 8 StL
1972 StL: 9 G; Rec 1-8 8.0. **1974** GB-NO: 6 G. GB: 1 G. NO: 5 G.
Total: 15 G; Rec 1-8 8.0.

RON WIDBY Widby, George Ronald 6'4", 210 P
Col: Tennessee *HS:* Fulton [Knoxville, TN] B: 3/9/1945, Knoxville, TN
Drafted: 1967 Round 4 NO
1972 GB: Pass 2-2 100.0%, 102 51.00 1 TD. **Total:** Pass 2-2 100.0%, 102 51.00 1 TD.

		Punting		
Year Team	**G**	**Punts**	**Yds**	**Avg**
1968 Dal	13	59	2415	40.9
1969 Dal	14	63	2729	43.3
1970 Dal	14	69	2847	41.3
1971 Dal	14	56	2329	41.6
1972 GB	14	65	2714	41.8
1973 GB	12	56	2414	43.1
NFL Total	81	368	15448	42.0

DAVE WIDELL Widell, David Harold Jr. 6'7", 303 OT-OG-C
Col: Boston College *HS:* South Catholic [Hartford, CT] B: 5/14/1965, Hartford, CT *Drafted:* 1988 Round 4 Dal
1988 Dal: 14 G. **1989** Dal: 15 G. **1990** Den: 16 G. **1991** Den: 16 G; 1 Fum. **1992** Den: 16 G. **1993** Den: 15 G. **1994** Den: 16 G; 1 Fum. **1995** Jac: 16 G. **1996** Jac: 15 G. **1997** Jac: 16 G. **1998** Atl: 1 G. **Total:** 156 G; 2 Fum.

DOUG WIDELL Widell, Douglas Joseph 6'4", 289 OG-OT
Col: Boston College *HS:* South Catholic [Hartford, CT] B: 9/23/1966, Hartford, CT *Drafted:* 1989 Round 2 Den
1989 Den: 16 G. **1990** Den: 16 G. **1991** Den: 16 G. **1992** Den: 16 G; Rec 1-(-7) -7.0. **1993** GB: 16 G. **1994** Det: 16 G. **1995** Det: 11 G. **1996** Ind: 16 G. **1997** Ind: 16 G. **Total:** 139 G; Rec 1-(-7) -7.0.

CHET WIDERQUIST Widerquist, Chester Carl 6'1", 219 T-G
Col: Northwestern; Washington & Jefferson *HS:* Moline [IL]
B: 9/23/1895, Moline, IL D: 7/14/1976, Knoxville, IA
1923 Mil: 2 G. **1924** Mil: 13 G. **1925** RI: 11 G. **1926** ChiC: 1 G. **1928** ChiC-Det: 10 G. ChiC: 6 G. Det: 4 G. **1929** Min: 9 G. **Total:** 46 G.

BUD WIDICK Widick, Ralph Hayden 6'1", 205 C-T
Col: Emporia State B: 11/7/1900, Belle Plaine, KS D: 2/3/1968, Atchison, KS
1924 KC: 2 G.

COREY WIDMER Widmer, Corey Edward 6'3", 256 LB-DT
Col: Montana State *HS:* Bozeman [MT] B: 12/25/1968, Alexandria, VA
Drafted: 1992 Round 7 NYG
1992 NYG: 8 G. **1993** NYG: 11 G. **1994** NYG: 16 G; 1 Sac. **1995** NYG: 16 G; KR 1-0. **1996** NYG: 16 G; Int 2-8; 1 Fum; 2 Sac. **1997** NYG: 16 G; Int 2-0; 1.5 Sac. **1998** NYG: 16 G. **Total:** 99 G; KR 1-0; Int 4-8; 1 Fum; 4.5 Sac.

ED WIDSETH Widseth, Edwin Clarence 6'1", 223 T
Col: Minnesota-Crookston; Minnesota *HS:* McIntosh [MN]
B: 1/5/1910, Gonvick, MN D: 12/3/1998, Minneapolis, MN
Drafted: 1937 Round 1 NYG
1937 NYG: 11 G. **1938** NYG: 11 G. **1939** NYG: 11 G. **1940** NYG: 11 G.
Total: 44 G.

ERIC WIEGAND Wiegand, Eric 6'2", 260 C
Col: Missouri-Rolla B: 3/13/1964
1987 Atl: 2 G.

ZACH WIEGERT Wiegert, Zachary Allen 6'4", 310 OT
Col: Nebraska *HS:* Bergan [Fremont, NE] B: 8/16/1972, Fremont, NE
Drafted: 1995 Round 2 StL
1995 StL: 5 G. **1996** StL: 16 G. **1997** StL: 15 G; Rec 1-1 1.0; 1 Fum TD; 6 Pt. **1998** StL: 13 G. **Total:** 49 G; Rec 1-1 1.0; 1 Fum TD; 6 Pt.

CASEY WIEGMANN Wiegmann, Casey Peter 6'3", 295 C
Col: Iowa *HS:* Applington-Parkersburg [IA] B: 7/20/1975, Parkersburg, IA
1997 NYJ-ChiB: 4 G. NYJ: 3 G. ChiB: 1 G. **1998** ChiB: 16 G; KR 1-8 8.0; 1 Fum. **Total:** 20 G; KR 1-8 8.0; 1 Fum.

JOE WIEHL Wiehl, Joseph John 5'11", 254 T
(Tiny) *Col:* Washington & Jefferson; Duquesne *HS:* Charleroi [PA]
B: 1/30/1910, Coal Center, PA D: 1/22/1996, Charleroi, PA
1935 Pit: 3 G.

BOB WIESE Wiese, Robert Lee 6'3", 198 DB-HB-LB
Col: Michigan *HS:* Jamestown [ND] B: 1/25/1923, Jamestown, ND
D: 11/1971 *Drafted:* 1945 Round 3 Det
1947 Det: 12 G; Rush 20-61 3.1; Rec 5-53 10.6; Int 5-54; Punt 1-61 61.0; 2 Fum. **1948** Det: 4 G. **Total:** 16 G; Rush 20-61 3.1; Rec 5-53 10.6; Int 5-54; Punt 1-61 61.0; 2 Fum.

RAY WIETECHA Wietecha, Raymond Walter 6'1", 225 C-LB
Col: Michigan State; Northwestern *HS:* Theodore Roosevelt [East Chicago, IL] B: 11/4/1928, East Chicago, IN *Drafted:* 1950 Round 12 NYG
1953 NYG: 12 G; Int 1-0. **1954** NYG: 12 G. **1955** NYG: 12 G. **1956** NYG: 12 G. **1957** NYG: 12 G. **1958** NYG: 12 G. **1959** NYG: 12 G. **1960** NYG: 12 G. **1961** NYG: 14 G. **1962** NYG: 14 G. **Total:** 124 G; Int 1-0.

SOCKO WIETHE Wiethe, John Albert 6'0", 198 G-LB
Col: Xavier (Ohio) *HS:* Roger Bacon [Cincinnati, OH]; Xavier HS [Cincinnati, OH] B: 10/17/1912, Cincinnati, OH D: 5/3/1989, Cincinnati, OH
1939 Det: 11 G; Rec 2-5 2.5. **1940** Det: 10 G; Int 1-8. **1941** Det: 8 G; Int 2-8. **1942** Det: 6 G. **Total:** 35 G; Rec 2-5 2.5; Int 3-16.

PAUL WIGGIN Wiggin, Paul David 6'3", 242 DE
Col: Modesto JC CA; Stanford *HS:* Manteca [CA] B: 11/18/1934, Modesto, CA *Drafted:* 1956 Round 6 Cle
1957 Cle: 12 G. **1958** Cle: 12 G. **1959** Cle: 12 G. **1960** Cle: 12 G; Int 1-20 1 TD; 6 Pt. **1961** Cle: 14 G. **1962** Cle: 14 G. **1963** Cle: 14 G; Int 1-2. **1964** Cle: 14 G; 1 Fum TD; 6 Pt. **1965** Cle: 14 G. **1966** Cle: 14 G; Int 1-0. **1967** Cle: 14 G. **Total:** 146 G; Int 3-22 1 TD; 1 Fum TD; Tot TD 2; 12 Pt.

PAUL WIGGINS Wiggins, Paul Anthony 6'3", 305 OT
Col: Oregon *HS:* Benson Polytechnic [Portland, OR] B: 8/17/1973, Portland, OR *Drafted:* 1997 Round 3 Pit
1997 Pit: 1 G. **1998** Was: 1 G. **Total:** 2 G.

GENE WIGGS Wiggs, Eugene G
Col: No College B: 1900, IN Deceased
1921 Lou: 2 G.

HUBERT WIGGS Wiggs, Hubert T 5'8", 183 FB-T
Col: Vanderbilt *HS:* Fitzgerald Clark [Tullahoma, TN] B: 1896 Deceased
1921 Lou: 1 G. **1922** Lou: 3 G. **1923** Lou: 3 G. **Total:** 7 G.

BILL WIGHTKIN Wightkin, William John 6'3", 235 OT-OE-DE
Col: Notre Dame *HS:* Catholic Central [Detroit, MI] B: 7/28/1927, Detroit, MI D: 1/25/1997, Westchester, IL *Drafted:* 1949 Round 8 ChiB
1950 ChiB: 12 G; Rec 3-24 8.0; 1 Fum. **1951** ChiB: 10 G; Rec 1-47 47.0; PR 1-3 3.0 1 TD; 6 Pt. **1952** ChiB: 11 G; Rec 7-120 17.1 2 TD; Int 0-9; 12 Pt. **1953** ChiB: 12 G; Rec 2-22 11.0; KR 1-0; **1** Fum TD; 6 Pt. **1954** ChiB: 12 G. **1955** ChiB: 12 G. **1956** ChiB: 12 G. **1957** ChiB: 11 G. **Total:** 92 G; Rec 13-213 16.4 2 TD; PR 1-3 3.0 1 TD; KR 1-0; Int 0-9; 1 Fum TD; Tot TD 4; 24 Pt; 1 Fum.

JOHN WILBUR Wilbur, John Leonard 6'3", 251 OG-DE
Col: Stanford *HS:* Alexander Hamilton [Los Angeles, CA]
B: 5/21/1943, San Diego, CA
1966 Dal: 8 G. **1967** Dal: 14 G. **1968** Dal: 14 G. **1969** Dal: 14 G. **1970** LARm: 8 G. **1971** Was: 14 G. **1972** Was: 14 G. **1973** Was: 14 G. **1974** Was: 1 G. **Total:** 101 G.

BARRY WILBURN Wilburn, Barry Todd 6'3", 186 DB
Col: Mississippi *HS:* Melrose [Memphis, TN] B: 12/9/1963, Memphis, TN *Drafted:* 1985 Round 8 Was

		Interceptions		
Year Team	**G**	**Int**	**Yds**	**TD**
1985 Was	16	1	10	0
1986 Was	16	2	14	0
1987 Was	12	**9**	135	1
1988 Was	10	4	24	0
1989 Was	8	3	13	0
1992 Cle	6	0	0	0
1995 Phi	16	1	0	0
1996 Phi	7	0	0	0
NFL Total	91	20	196	1

J.R. WILBURN Wilburn, Johnnie Richard Jr. 6'2", 190 WR
Col: South Carolina *HS:* Cradock [Portsmouth, VA] B: 4/27/1943, Portsmouth, VA *Drafted:* 1965 Round 13 Pit
1969 Pit: Rush 2-29 14.5. **1970** Pit: Rush 5-25 5.0. **Total:** Rush 7-54 7.7.

		Receiving				
Year Team	**G**	**Rec**	**Yds**	**Avg**	**TD**	**Fum**
1966 Pit	14	7	103	14.7	0	1
1967 Pit	14	51	767	15.0	5	1
1968 Pit	14	39	514	13.2	3	0
1969 Pit	10	20	373	18.7	0	0
1970 Pit	6	6	77	12.8	0	1
NFL Total	58	123	1834	14.9	8	3

STEVE WILBURN Wilburn, Steven T 6'4", 266 DE
Col: Illinois State *HS:* Mendel [Chicago, IL] B: 2/25/1961, Chicago, IL
1987 NE: 3 G; 1 Sac.

MIKE WILCHER Wilcher, Michael D 6'3", 238 LB
Col: North Carolina *HS:* Eastern [Washington, DC] B: 3/20/1960, Washington, DC *Drafted:* 1983 Round 2 LARm
1983 LARm: 15 G. **1984** LARm: 15 G; 2 Sac. **1985** LARm: 16 G; Int 1-0; 12.5 Sac. **1986** LARm: 16 G; Int 1-0; 5.5 Sac. **1987** LARm: 12 G; Int 1-11;

1 Fum TD; 6 Pt; 5 Sac. **1988** LARm: 16 G; 7.5 Sac. **1989** LARm: 16 G; Int 1-4; 1 Fum; 5 Sac. **1990** LARm: 16 G; 1 Sac. **1991** SD: 2 G. **Total:** 124 G; Int 4-15; 1 Fum TD; 6 Pt; 1 Fum; 38.5 Sac.

SOLOMON WILCOTS Wilcots, Solomon 5′11″, 189 **DB**
Col: Colorado *HS:* Rubidoux [Riverside, CA] B: 10/3/1964, Los Angeles, CA *Drafted:* 1987 Round 8 Cin
1987 Cin: 12 G; Int 1-37. **1988** Cin: 16 G; Int 1-6. **1989** Cin: 16 G; 1 Sac. **1990** Cin: 16 G. **1991** Min: 16 G. **1992** Pit: 16 G. **Total:** 92 G; Int 2-43; 1 Sac.

DAVE WILCOX Wilcox, David 6′3″, 241 **LB**
Col: Boise State; Oregon *HS:* Vale Union [OR] B: 9/29/1942, Ontario, OR *Drafted:* 1964 Round 3 SF
1965 SF: **1** Fum TD. **1969** SF: KR 1-10 10.0. **Total:** KR 1-10 10.0; 1 Fum TD.

		Interceptions				Tot
Year Team	**G**	**Int**	**Yds**	**TD**	**Fum**	**TD**
1964 SF	14	1	6	0	0	0
1965 SF	14	1	16	0	1	1
1966 SF	14	0	0	0	0	0
1967 SF	14	2	17	0	0	0
1968 SF	14	0	0	0	0	0
1969 SF	14	2	17	0	0	0
1970 SF	13	2	46	0	0	0
1971 SF	14	0	0	0	0	0
1972 SF	14	3	12	0	0	0
1973 SF	14	2	14	0	0	0
1974 SF	14	1	21	1	0	1
NFL Total	153	14	149	1	1	2

NED WILCOX Wilcox, Edmund Quincy 5′11″, 185 **FB-WB-TB**
Col: Swarthmore *HS:* Lansdowne [PA] B: 2/7/1904 D: 9/1968, NJ
1926 Fra: 12 G; Rush 2 TD; Int **1** TD; Tot TD 3; 18 Pt. **1927** Fra: 14 G; Rush 2 TD; 12 Pt. **Total:** 26 G; Rush 4 TD; Int 1 TD; Tot TD 5; 30 Pt.

JOHN WILCOX Wilcox, John Dale 6′5″, 230 **DT**
Col: Boise State; Oregon *HS:* Vale Union [OR] B: 3/15/1938, Vale, OR *Drafted:* 1960 Round 15 Phi
1960 Phi: 12 G.

FIRPO WILCOX Wilcox, John Harrison 6′0″, 220 **T**
Col: Oklahoma *HS:* Bixby [OK] B: 4/23/1903, Bixby, OK
1926 Buf: 6 G. **1930** SI: 2 G. **Total:** 8 G.

JOSH WILCOX Wilcox, Joshua David 6′2″, 253 **TE**
Col: Oregon *HS:* Junction City [OR] B: 6/5/1974, Eugene, OR
1998 NO: 3 G; Rec 1-10 10.0.

GEORGE WILDE Wilde, George Hall 6′1″, 193 **HB-DB**
Col: Texas A&M; Texas Christian *HS:* Graham [TX] B: 3/26/1923, Olney, TX D: 5/26/1975, Marshall, TX
1947 Was: 9 G; Rush 4-(-1) -0.3; Rec 6-45 7.5 1 TD; KR 1-19 19.0; 6 Pt.

BERT WILDER Wilder, Albert Green 6′3″, 245 **DE-DT**
Col: North Carolina State *HS:* Grimsley [Greensboro, NC] B: 4/14/1939, Greensboro, NC *Drafted:* 1962 Round 14 NYT
1964 NYJ: 14 G. **1965** NYJ: 14 G. **1966** NYJ: 14 G; KR 1-6 6.0. **1967** NYJ: 13 G; KR 1-0; 1 Fum. **Total:** 55 G; KR 2-6 3.0; 1 Fum.

HAL WILDER Wilder, Harold Fremont 5′10″, 190 **G**
Col: Nebraska Wesleyan; Nebraska *HS:* Central City [NE] B: 2/8/1893, Merrick, NE D: 2/5/1989, Lincoln, NE
1923 StL: 1 G.

JAMES WILDER Wilder, James Curtis 6′3″, 225 **RB**
Col: Northeastern Oklahoma A&M (J.C.); Missouri *HS:* Sikeston [MO] B: 5/12/1958, Sikeston, MO *Drafted:* 1981 Round 2 TB
1981 TB: KR 1-19 19.0. **1984** TB: Pass 1-1 100.0%, 16 16.00 1 TD. **1989** TB: KR 2-42 21.0. **Total:** Pass 1-1 100.0%, 16 16.00 1 TD; KR 3-61 20.3.

		Rushing				Receiving					Tot
Year Team	**G**	**Att**	**Yds**	**Avg**	**TD**	**Rec**	**Yds**	**Avg**	**TD**	**Fum**	**TD**
1981 TB	16	107	370	3.5	4	48	507	10.6	1	3	5
1982 TB	9	83	324	3.9	3	53	466	8.8	1	5	4
1983 TB	10	161	640	4.0	4	57	380	6.7	2	1	6
1984 TB	16	**407**	1544	3.8	13	85	685	8.1	0	10	13
1985 TB	16	365	1300	3.6	10	53	341	6.4	0	9	10
1986 TB	12	190	704	3.7	2	43	326	7.6	1	10	3
1987 TB	12	106	488	4.6	0	40	328	8.2	1	3	1
1988 TB	7	86	343	4.0	1	15	124	8.3	0	1	1
1989 TB	15	70	244	3.5	0	36	335	9.3	3	2	3
1990 Was-Det	16	11	51	4.6	0	1	8	8.0	1	0	1
1990 Was	1	0	0	—	0	0	0	—	0	0	0
1990 Det	15	11	51	4.6	0	1	8	8.0	1	0	1
NFL Total	129	1586	6008	3.8	37	431	3500	8.1	10	44	47

DICK WILDUNG Wildung, Richard Kay 6′0″, 221 **OT-DT-OG-DG**
Col: Minnesota *HS:* Luverne [MN] B: 8/16/1921, Anoka, MN *Drafted:* 1943 Round 1 GB
1946 GB: 11 G. **1947** GB: 3 G; Scor **1** Saf; 2 Pt. **1948** GB: 12 G. **1949** GB: 12 G. **1950** GB: 12 G. **1951** GB: 12 G. **1953** GB: 12 G; KR 1-6 6.0. **Total:** 74 G; KR 1-6 6.0; Scor 1 Saf; 2 Pt.

CHARLES WILEY Wiley, Charles Kennedy 6′2″, 268 **NT**
Col: Nevada-Las Vegas *HS:* Madison [San Diego, CA] B: 12/9/1964
1987 Sea: 1 G; 1 Sac.

JACK WILEY Wiley, John Franklin 5′11″, 208 **OT-DT**
Col: Waynesburg *HS:* Richill Twp. [PA] B: 4/18/1920, Wind Ridge, PA
1946 Pit: 11 G. **1947** Pit: 11 G. **1948** Pit: 12 G. **1949** Pit: 12 G; Rec 1-10 10.0. **1950** Pit: 11 G. **Total:** 57 G; Rec 1-10 10.0.

MARCELLUS WILEY Wiley, Marcellus Vernon 6′5″, 271 **DE**
Col: West Los Angeles Coll. CA (J.C.); Columbia *HS:* St. Monica's [Santa Monica, CA] B: 11/30/1974, Los Angeles, CA *Drafted:* 1997 Round 2 Buf
1997 Buf: 16 G; KR 1-12 12.0; 1 Fum. **1998** Buf: 16 G; 3.5 Sac. **Total:** 32 G; KR 1-12 12.0; 1 Fum; 3.5 Sac.

ERIK WILHELM Wilhelm, Erik Bradley 6′3″, 217 **QB**
Col: Oregon State *HS:* Gladstone [OR]; Lakeridge HS [Lake Oswego, OR] B: 11/19/1965, Dayton, OH *Drafted:* 1989 Round 3 Cin
1989 Cin: Rush 6-30 5.0. **1990** Cin: Rush 6-6 1.0. **1991** Cin: Rush 1-9 9.0. **1996** Cin: Rush 6-24 4.0. **Total:** Rush 19-69 3.6.

		Passing								
Year Team	**G**	**Att**	**Comp**	**Comp%**	**Yds**	**YPA**	**TD**	**Int**	**Rating**	**Fum**
1989 Cin	6	56	30	53.6	425	7.59	4	2	87.3	2
1990 Cin	7	19	12	63.2	117	6.16	0	0	80.4	1
1991 Cin	4	42	24	57.1	217	5.17	0	2	51.4	1
1993 Cin	1	6	4	66.7	63	10.50	0	0	101.4	0
1994 Cin	1	0	0	—	0	—	0	0	—	0
1996 Cin	3	13	7	53.8	90	6.92	1	2	61.9	0
NFL Total	22	136	77	56.6	912	6.71	5	6	71.1	4

ELMER WILKENS Wilkens, Elmer Sutter 5′9″, 175 **OE**
(Swede) *Col:* Indiana B: 6/25/1901, Fort Wayne, IN D: 3/18/1967, Fort Wayne, IN
1925 GB: 6 G.

BASIL WILKERSON Wilkerson, Basil 6′0″, 218 **OE-DE-T**
Col: Oklahoma City *HS:* Duncan [OK] B: 1/22/1907, Alex, OK D: 9/1967
1932 Bos-SI: 9 G. Bos: 6 G. SI: 3 G. **1934** Cin: 1 G. **Total:** 10 G.

BRUCE WILKERSON Wilkerson, Bruce Alan 6′5″, 295 **OT-OG**
Col: Tennessee *HS:* Loudon [TN] B: 7/28/1964, Loudon, TN *Drafted:* 1987 Round 2 LARd
1987 LARd: 11 G. **1988** LARd: 16 G. **1989** LARd: 16 G. **1990** LARd: 8 G. **1991** LARd: 16 G. **1992** LARd: 15 G. **1993** LARd: 14 G. **1994** LARd: 11 G. **1995** Jac: 10 G. **1996** GB: 14 G. **1997** GB: 16 G. **Total:** 147 G.

DARYL WILKERSON Wilkerson, Daryl Wayne 6′4″, 255 **DE**
Col: Houston *HS:* Aldine [Houston, TX] B: 9/25/1958, Houston, TX
1981 Bal: 5 G.

DOUG WILKERSON Wilkerson, Douglas 6′3″, 253 **OG**
Col: North Carolina Central *HS:* E.E. Smith [Fayetteville, NC] B: 3/27/1947, Fayetteville, NC *Drafted:* 1970 Round 1 Hou
1970 Hou: 9 G. **1971** SD: 14 G; KR 1-0. **1972** SD: 14 G. **1973** SD: 14 G. **1974** SD: 14 G. **1975** SD: 14 G. **1976** SD: 14 G. **1977** SD: 14 G. **1978** SD: 16 G. **1979** SD: 12 G. **1980** SD: 16 G. **1981** SD: 16 G. **1982** SD: 9 G. **1983** SD: 12 G. **1984** SD: 16 G. **Total:** 204 G; KR 1-0.

ERIC WILKERSON Wilkerson, Eric LaShawn 5′9″, 185 **RB-WR**
Col: Kent State *HS:* Cleveland [OH] B: 12/19/1966, Cleveland, OH
1989 Pit: 1 G.

REGGIE WILKES Wilkes, Reginald Wayman 6′4″, 235 **LB**
Col: Georgia Tech *HS:* Southwest [Atlanta, GA] B: 5/27/1956, Pine Bluff, AR *Drafted:* 1978 Round 3 Phi
1978 Phi: 16 G. **1979** Phi: 16 G; Int 2-0. **1980** Phi: 16 G; Int 1-0. **1981** Phi: 14 G; Int 2-18; Scor **1** 1XP; 1 Pt. **1982** Phi: 9 G; 1 Sac. **1983** Phi: 14 G. **1984** Phi: 14 G; Int 1-6; 2 Sac. **1985** Phi: 16 G; 2 Sac. **1986** Atl: 16 G; Int 2-11. **1987** Atl: 6 G. **Total:** 137 G; Int 8-35; Scor 1 1XP; 1 Pt; 5 Sac.

WILLIE WILKIN Wilkin, Wilbur B 6′4″, 261 **T**
(Wee Willie) *Col:* St. Mary's (Cal.) *HS:* Springville [UT] B: 4/21/1916, Bingham Canyon, UT D: 5/16/1973, Palo Alto, CA
AAFC **1946** ChiA: 10 G; Rec 0-3; Int 0-18.

NFL **1938** Was: 11 G. **1939** Was: 11 G; Scor 0-1 XK. **1940** Was: 11 G. **1941** Was: 11 G; KR 2-25 12.5. **1942** Was: 11 G; KR 1-15 15.0; Scor 2 Saf; 10 Pt. **1943** Was: 9 G. **Total:** 64 G; KR 3-40 13.3; Scor 10, 0-1 XK, 2 Saf; 10 Pt.

DAVID WILKINS Wilkins, David 6′4″, 240 **DE**
Col: Eastern Kentucky *HS:* Aiken [Cincinnati, OH] B: 2/24/1969, Cincinnati, OH
1992 SF: 13 G; 1.5 Sac.

GABE WILKINS Wilkins, Gabriel Nicholas 6′5″, 304 **DE**
(Big Willie) *Col:* Gardner-Webb *HS:* Gettys D. Broome [Spartanburg, SC] B: 9/1/1971, Cowpens, SC *Drafted:* 1994 Round 4 GB
1994 GB: 15 G; 1 Sac. **1995** GB: 13 G; 3 Sac. **1996** GB: 16 G; 3 Sac. **1997** GB: 16 G; Int 1-77 1 TD; 1 Fum TD; Tot TD 2; 12 Pt; 5.5 Sac. **1998** SF: 8 G. **Total:** 68 G; Int 1-77 1 TD; 1 Fum TD; Tot TD 2; 12 Pt; 12.5 Sac.

GARY WILKINS Wilkins, Gary Clifton 6′1″, 235 **RB-TE**
Col: Georgia Tech *HS:* Twin Lakes [West Palm Beach, FL]
B: 11/23/1963, West Palm Beach, FL
1986 Buf: Rush 3-18 6.0. **1990** Atl: KR 1-7 7.0. **Total:** Rush 3-18 6.0; KR 1-7 7.0.

		Receiving			
Year Team	**G**	**Rec**	**Yds**	**Avg**	**TD**
1986 Buf	16	8	74	9.3	0
1987 Buf	1	0	0	—	0
1988 Atl	14	11	134	12.2	0
1989 Atl	13	8	179	22.4	3
1990 Atl	16	12	175	14.6	2
1991 Atl	5	3	22	7.3	1
NFL Total	65	42	584	13.9	6

JEFF WILKINS Wilkins, Jeffrey Allen 6′2″, 195 **K**
Col: Youngstown State *HS:* Fitch [Austintown, OH] B: 4/19/1972, Youngstown, OH

		Scoring						
Year Team	**G**	**Pts**	**FG**	**FGA**	**FG%**	**XK**	**XKA**	**XK%**
1994 Phi	6	0	0	0	—	0	0	—
1995 SF	7	63	12	13	92.3	27	29	93.1
1996 SF	16	130	30	34	88.2	40	40	100.0
1997 StL	16	107	25	37	67.6	32	32	100.0
1998 StL	16	85	20	26	76.9	25	26	96.2
NFL Total	61	385	87	110	79.1	124	127	97.6

DICK WILKINS Wilkins, Richard Maurice 6′2″, 194 **OE**
Col: Oregon *HS:* Lincoln [Portland, OR] B: 9/28/1925, Portland, OR
Drafted: 1948 Round 25 NYG
AAFC **1949** LA-A: Pass 1-0; Rush 8-28 3.5.

		Receiving			
Year Team	**G**	**Rec**	**Yds**	**Avg**	**TD**
1949 LA-A	11	32	589	18.4	3

NFL Statistics

		Receiving				
Year Team	**G**	**Rec**	**Yds**	**Avg**	**TD**	**Fum**
1952 Dal	12	32	416	13.0	3	2
1954 NYG	6	4	45	11.3	1	0
NFL Total	18	36	461	12.8	4	2

ROY WILKINS Wilkins, Roy Lee 6′3″, 224 **LB-DE**
Col: Georgia *HS:* Dalton [GA]; Seneca HS [SC] B: 12/26/1933, Murray Co., GA *Drafted:* 1957 Round 6 LARm
1958 LARm: 12 G; PR 1-0. **1959** LARm: 12 G; KR 2-29 14.5. **1960** Was: 12 G; KR 2-24 12.0. **1961** Was: 14 G. **Total:** 50 G; PR 1-0; KR 4-53 13.3.

DAN WILKINSON Wilkinson, Daniel Raymon 6′5″, 313 **DT-DE**
(Big Daddy) *Col:* Ohio State *HS:* Paul L. Dunbar [Dayton, OH]
B: 3/13/1973, Dayton, OH *Drafted:* 1994 Round 1 Cin
1994 Cin: 16 G; 5.5 Sac. **1995** Cin: 14 G; 8 Sac. **1996** Cin: 16 G; Int 1-7; 1 Fum; 6.5 Sac. **1997** Cin: 15 G; 5 Sac. **1998** Was: 16 G; Int 1-4; 7.5 Sac. **Total:** 77 G; Int 2-11; 1 Fum; 32.5 Sac.

JERRY WILKINSON Wilkinson, Gerald Edward 6′9″, 248 **DE**
Col: Oregon State *HS:* San Mateo [CA] B: 2/27/1956, San Francisco, CA *Drafted:* 1979 Round 4 LARm
1979 LARm: 16 G. **1980** Cle-SF: 13 G. Cle: 7 G. SF: 6 G. **Total:** 29 G.

BOB WILKINSON Wilkinson, Robert Raymond 6′3″, 215 **OE-DB-HB**
(The Arrowhead Antelope) *Col:* Loyola Marymount; UCLA *HS:* Lake Arrowhead [CA]; Loyola HS [Los Angeles, CA] B: 10/8/1926
Drafted: 1950 Round 10 NYG
1951 NYG: Rec 11-182 16.5 1 TD; Int 1-12. **1952** NYG: Rec 6-148 24.7 2 TD. **Total:** Rec 17-330 19.4 3 TD; Int 1-12.

		Rushing				
Year Team	**G**	**Att**	**Yds**	**Avg**	**TD**	**Fum**
1951 NYG	12	0	0	—	0	1
1952 NYG	7	26	26	1.0	0	1
NFL Total	19	26	26	1.0	0	2

JIM WILKS Wilks, Jimmy Ray 6′5″, 266 **DE-NT**
Col: Pasadena City Coll. CA (J.C.); California; San Diego State
HS: Pasadena [CA] B: 3/12/1958, Los Angeles, CA *Drafted:* 1981 Round 12 NO
1981 NO: 16 G. **1982** NO: 8 G; 2 Sac. **1983** NO: 16 G; 8 Sac. **1984** NO: 16 G; 7.5 Sac. **1985** NO: 16 G; 2.5 Sac. **1986** NO: 16 G; 1 Sac. **1987** NO: 12 G; 5.5 Sac. **1988** NO: 16 G; 3.5 Sac. **1989** NO: 16 G; 4 Sac. **1990** NO: 15 G; 5.5 Sac. **1991** NO: 16 G; 2 Sac. **1992** NO: 12 G; 4 Sac. **1993** NO: 8 G. **Total:** 183 G; 45.5 Sac.

ERWIN WILL Will, Erwin Arthur Jr. 6′5″, 275 **DT**
Col: Dayton *HS:* Wickliffe [OH] B: 1/14/1943, Cleveland, OH
Drafted: 1965 Round 7 Phi
1965 Phi: 5 G.

JERROTT WILLARD Willard, Jerrott Michael 6′1″, 233 **LB**
Col: California *HS:* Corona Del Mar [Newport Beach, CA]
B: 7/11/1972, Fullerton, CA *Drafted:* 1995 Round 5 KC
1998 KC: 1 G.

KEN WILLARD Willard, Kenneth Henderson 6′1″, 219 **RB**
Col: North Carolina *HS:* Varina [Richmond, VA] B: 7/14/1943, Richmond, VA *Drafted:* 1965 Round 1 SF
1965 SF: Pass 1-0, 1 Int. **1973** SF: KR 1-0. **Total:** Pass 1-0, 1 Int; KR 1-0.

		Rushing				Receiving					Tot
Year Team	**G**	**Att**	**Yds**	**Avg**	**TD**	**Rec**	**Yds**	**Avg**	**TD**	**Fum**	**TD**
1965 SF	14	189	778	4.1	5	32	253	7.9	4	7	9
1966 SF	14	191	763	4.0	5	42	351	8.4	2	7	7
1967 SF	13	169	510	3.0	5	23	242	10.5	1	1	6
1968 SF	14	227	967	4.3	7	36	232	6.4	0	4	7
1969 SF	14	171	557	3.3	7	36	326	9.1	3	6	10
1970 SF	14	236	789	3.3	7	31	259	8.4	3	3	10
1971 SF	14	216	855	4.0	4	27	202	7.5	1	8	5
1972 SF	14	100	345	3.5	4	24	131	5.5	1	3	5
1973 SF	14	83	366	4.4	1	22	160	7.3	1	2	2
1974 StL	7	40	175	4.4	0	4	28	7.0	1	0	1
NFL Total	132	1622	6105	3.8	45	277	2184	7.9	17	41	62

HENRY WILLEGALE Willegale, Henry Minard 5′11″, 190 **BB-HB-FB**
Col: Carleton *HS:* Worthington [MN] B: 6/9/1901, Madison, WI
D: 6/26/1964, Minneapolis, MN
1929 Min: 9 G.

WILLERT Willert **C**
Col: No College Deceased
1922 Ham: 1 G.

NORM WILLEY Willey, Norman Earle 6′2″, 224 **DE-OG-OE**
(Wild Man) *Col:* Marshall *HS:* Pine Grove [WV] B: 8/22/1927, Hastings, WV *Drafted:* 1950 Round 13 Phi
1950 Phi: 12 G; Int 1-41 1 TD; 6 Pt. **1951** Phi: 11 G. **1952** Phi: 12 G; Int 1-0. **1953** Phi: 12 G. **1954** Phi: 12 G; Rec 2-50 25.0; **1** Fum TD; 6 Pt. **1955** Phi: 12 G. **1956** Phi: 9 G; KR 2-32 16.0. **1957** Phi: 12 G. **Total:** 92 G; Rec 2-50 25.0; KR 2-32 16.0; Int 2-41 1 TD; 1 Fum TD; Tot TD 2; 12 Pt.

COLE WILLGING Willging, Coleman G 6′3″, 205 **OE-DE**
Col: Xavier (Ohio) *HS:* Norwood [OH] B: 1911 D: 3/10/1973, Cincinnati, OH
1934 Cin: 4 G; Rec 2-14 7.0.

GERALD WILLHITE Willhite, Gerald William 5′10″, 200 **RB**
Col: American River Coll. CA (J.C.); San Jose State *HS:* Cordova [Rancho Cordova, CA] B: 5/30/1959, Sacramento, CA *Drafted:* 1982 Round 1 Den
1982 Den: Pass 2-0, 1 Int. **1983** Den: Pass 1-0. **1984** Den: Pass 2-1 50.0%, 20 10.00. **1985** Den: Pass 3-0. **1986** Den: Pass 4-1 25.0%, 11 2.75. **1987** Den: Pass 1-0. **Total:** Pass 13-2 15.4%, 31 2.38 1 Int.

		Rushing				Receiving			
Year Team	**G**	**Att**	**Yds**	**Avg**	**TD**	**Rec**	**Yds**	**Avg**	**TD**
1982 Den	9	70	347	5.0	2	26	227	8.7	0
1983 Den	8	43	188	4.4	3	14	153	10.9	1
1984 Den	16	77	371	4.8	2	27	298	11.0	0
1985 Den	15	66	237	3.6	3	35	297	8.5	1
1986 Den	16	85	365	4.3	5	64	529	8.3	3
1987 Den	3	26	141	5.4	0	9	25	2.8	0
1988 Den	11	13	39	3.0	2	32	238	7.4	0
NFL Total	78	380	1688	4.4	17	207	1767	8.5	5

	Punt Returns				Kickoff Returns					Tot
Year Team	**Ret**	**Yds**	**Avg**	**TD**	**Ret**	**Yds**	**Avg**	**TD**	**Fum**	**TD**
1982 Den	6	63	10.5	0	17	337	19.8	0	5	2
1983 Den	0	0	—	0	0	0	—	0	0	4
1984 Den	20	200	10.0	0	4	109	27.3	0	3	2
1985 Den	16	169	10.6	0	2	40	20.0	0	2	4
1986 Den	42	468	11.1	1	3	35	11.7	0	5	9
1987 Den	4	22	5.5	0	0	0	—	0	1	0
1988 Den	13	90	6.9	0	0	0	—	0	2	2
NFL Total	101	1012	10.0	1	26	521	20.0	0	18	23

KEVIN WILLHITE Willhite, Kevin Alfred 5′11″, 208 **RB**
Col: Oregon *HS:* Cordova [Rancho Cordova, CA] B: 5/11/1963, Sacramento, CA
1987 GB: Rec 6-37 6.2; KR 0-37.

Year Team	G	Rushing Att	Yds	Avg	TD	Fum
1987 GB	3	53	251	4.7	0	2

A.D. WILLIAMS Williams, A D 6'2", 210 **OE-FL**
Col: Santa Monica Coll. CA (J.C.); U. of Pacific *HS:* Santa Monica [CA] B: 11/21/1933, Little Rock, AR *Drafted:* 1956 Round 3 LARm
1959 GB: 12 G; Rec 1-11 11.0. **1960** Cle: 12 G; Rec 1-5 5.0. **1961** Min: 13 G; Rec 13-174 13.4 1 TD; 6 Pt. **Total:** 37 G; Rec 15-190 12.7 1 TD; 6 Pt.

AENEAS WILLIAMS Williams, Aeneas Demetrius 5'11", 194 **DB**
Col: Southern University *HS:* Alcee Fortier [New Orleans, LA] B: 1/29/1968, New Orleans, LA *Drafted:* 1991 Round 3 Pho
1993 Pho: 1 Fum TD. **1996** Ariz: 1 Sac. **1998** Ariz: 1 Sac. **Total:** 1 Fum TD; 2 Sac.

Year Team	G	Interceptions Int	Yds	TD	Fum	Tot TD
1991 Pho	16	6	60	0	1	0
1992 Pho	16	3	25	0	0	0
1993 Pho	16	2	87	1	0	2
1994 Ariz	16	**9**	89	0	0	0
1995 Ariz	16	6	86	**2**	1	3
1996 Ariz	16	6	89	1	0	1
1997 Ariz	16	6	95	2	0	2
1998 Ariz	16	1	15	0	0	0
NFL Total	128	39	546	6	2	8

ALBERT WILLIAMS Williams, Albert Donnell 6'3", 229 **LB**
Col: Texas-El Paso *HS:* Southside [San Antonio, TX] B: 9/7/1964, San Antonio, TX
1987 Pit: 3 G.

ALFRED WILLIAMS Williams, Alfred Hamilton 6'6", 260 **DE**
Col: Colorado *HS:* Jesse H. Jones [Houston, TX] B: 11/6/1968, Houston, TX *Drafted:* 1991 Round 1 Cin
1991 Cin: 16 G; 3 Sac. **1992** Cin: 15 G; 10 Sac. **1993** Cin: 16 G; Scor 1 Saf; 2 Pt; 4 Sac. **1994** Cin: 16 G; Scor **1** Saf; 2 Pt; 9.5 Sac. **1995** SF: 16 G; 4.5 Sac. **1996** Den: 16 G; 13 Sac. **1997** Den: 16 G; 1 Fum TD; 6 Pt; 8.5 Sac. **1998** Den: 10 G; 3 Sac. **Total:** 121 G; Scor 2 Saf; 1 Fum TD; 10 Pt; 55.5 Sac.

ALLEN WILLIAMS Williams, Allen 5'10", 205 **RB**
Col: Georgia Mil. Coll. (J.C.); Maryland *HS:* Thomasville [GA] B: 9/17/1972, Thomasville, GA
1995 Det: 5 G; KR 4-100 25.0; 1 Fum.

ALONZO WILLIAMS Williams, Alonzo Fitzgerald 5'9", 192 **RB**
Col: Santa Monica Coll. CA (J.C.); Los Angeles Southwest Coll. CA (J.C.); Mesa *HS:* Morningside [Inglewood, CA] B: 8/9/1963, Los Angeles, CA
1987 LARm: 3 G; Rush 2-9 4.5; KR 5-114 22.8.

AL WILLIAMS Williams, Alphonso 5'10", 180 **WR**
Col: Nevada-Reno *HS:* Long Beach Polytechnic [CA] B: 10/5/1961, Vidalia, GA *Drafted:* 1984 Supplemental Round 1 Det
1987 SD: 3 G; Rush 1-11 11.0; Rec 12-247 20.6 1 TD; PR 10-96 9.6; 6 Pt; 1 Fum.

ARMON WILLIAMS Williams, Armon Abdule 6'1", 221 **DB**
Col: Arizona *HS:* Valley Christian [Tempe, AZ] B: 8/13/1973, Chandler, AZ *Drafted:* 1997 Round 7 Ten
1997 Ten: 6 G.

POP WILLIAMS Williams, Arthur Vincent 6'0", 207 **WB-FB-TB-HB**
Col: Connecticut *HS:* Killingly [CT] B: 5/4/1906, Jewett City, CT D: 2/5/1979, Brooklyn, CT
1928 Prov: 7 G; Rush 3 TD; Rec 1 TD; Tot TD 4; 24 Pt. **1929** Prov: 12 G; Rush 6 TD; Rec 1 TD; Tot TD 7; 42 Pt. **1930** Prov: 11 G; Rush 2 TD; 12 Pt. **1931** Prov: 8 G. **1932** Bkn: 1 G. **Total:** 39 G; Rush 11 TD; Rec 2 TD; Tot TD 13; 78 Pt.

BERNARD WILLIAMS Williams, Bennie Bernard 6'8", 317 **OT**
Col: Georgia *HS:* Hamilton [Memphis, TN] B: 7/18/1972, Memphis, TN *Drafted:* 1994 Round 1 Phi
1994 Phi: 16 G.

BILLY WILLIAMS Williams, Billy Louis 5'11", 175 **WR**
Col: Northeastern Oklahoma A&M (J.C.); Tennessee *HS:* Alcoa [TN] B: 6/7/1971, Alcoa, TN *Drafted:* 1995 Round 7 Ariz
1996 StL: 1 G.

BOBBY WILLIAMS Williams, Bobby Ray 6'0", 205 **DB**
Col: Central Oklahoma *HS:* Lincoln [NE] B: 2/28/1942, Giger, AL *Drafted:* 1966 Round 11 StL
1967 StL: Int 2-21. **1970** Det: Int 1-0. **Total:** Int 3-21.

Year Team	G	Kickoff Returns Ret	Yds	Avg	TD	Fum
1966 StL	14	7	132	18.9	0	0
1967 StL	14	24	583	24.3	0	3
1969 Det	13	17	563	**33.1**	**1**	1
1970 Det	14	25	544	21.8	1	3
1971 Det	14	4	112	28.0	0	0
NFL Total	69	77	1934	25.1	2	7

BOYD WILLIAMS Williams, Boyd Horace 6'3", 218 **C-LB**
Col: Syracuse *HS:* Cresson [PA] B: 5/4/1922, Patton, PA
1947 Phi: 6 G.

BRENT WILLIAMS Williams, Brent Dione 6'4", 276 **DE-NT**
Col: Toledo *HS:* Northern [Flint, MI] B: 10/23/1964, Flint, MI *Drafted:* 1986 Round 7 NE
1986 NE: 16 G; **1** Fum TD; 6 Pt; 7 Sac. **1987** NE: 12 G; 5 Sac. **1988** NE: 16 G; 8 Sac. **1989** NE: 16 G; 8 Sac. **1990** NE: 16 G; 1 Fum TD; 6 Pt; 6 Sac. **1991** NE: 16 G; 3.5 Sac. **1992** NE: 16 G; 4 Sac. **1993** NE: 13 G; 2 Sac. **1994** Sea: 10 G; 1 Sac. **1995** Sea: 11 G; 1 Fum; 1 Sac. **1996** NYJ: 5 G. **Total:** 147 G; 2 Fum TD; 12 Pt; 1 Fum; 45.5 Sac.

BRIAN WILLIAMS Williams, Brian Keith 6'5", 240 **TE**
Col: Southern University *HS:* Hahnville [Boutte, LA] B: 10/14/1957, New Orleans, LA *Drafted:* 1981 Round 12 Min
1982 NE: 1 G.

BRIAN WILLIAMS Williams, Brian Marcee 6'1", 240 **LB**
Col: USC *HS:* Bishop Dunne [Dallas, TX] B: 12/17/1972, Dallas, TX *Drafted:* 1995 Round 3 GB
1995 GB: 13 G. **1996** GB: 16 G; 0.5 Sac. **1997** GB: 16 G; Int 2-30; 1 Sac. **1998** GB: 16 G; 2 Sac. **Total:** 61 G; Int 2-30; 3.5 Sac.

BRIAN WILLIAMS Williams, Brian Scott 6'5", 304 **OG-C**
Col: Minnesota *HS:* Mount Lebanon [PA] B: 6/8/1966, Mount Lebanon, PA *Drafted:* 1989 Round 1 NYG
1989 NYG: 14 G. **1990** NYG: 16 G. **1991** NYG: 14 G. **1992** NYG: 13 G. **1993** NYG: 16 G. **1994** NYG: 14 G; 2 Fum. **1995** NYG: 16 G. **1996** NYG: 14 G. **Total:** 117 G; 2 Fum.

CY WILLIAMS Williams, Burton Caswell 6'0", 200 **T**
Col: Florida *HS:* Tallahassee [FL] B: 10/10/1903, FL Deceased
1929 SI: 10 G. **1930** SI: 12 G. **1932** Bkn: 1 G. **Total:** 23 G.

BYRON WILLIAMS Williams, Byron Keith 6'2", 182 **WR**
Col: Texas-Arlington *HS:* Liberty-Eylau [Texarkana, TX] B: 10/31/1960, Texarkana, TX *Drafted:* 1983 Round 10 GB
1985 NYG: Rush 2-18 9.0. **Total:** Rush 2-18 9.0.

Year Team	G	Receiving Rec	Yds	Avg	TD	Fum
1983 NYG	5	20	346	17.3	1	1
1984 NYG	16	24	471	19.6	2	0
1985 NYG	16	15	280	18.7	0	0
NFL Total	37	59	1097	18.6	3	1

CALVIN WILLIAMS Williams, Calvin John Jr. 5'11", 187 **WR**
Col: Purdue *HS:* Paul Laurence Dunbar [Baltimore, MD] B: 3/3/1967, Baltimore, MD *Drafted:* 1990 Round 5 Phi
1990 Phi: Rush 2-20 10.0; PR 2-(-1) -0.5. **1994** Phi: Rush 2-11 5.5. **1995** Phi: Rush 1-(-2) -2.0; Scor 1 2XP. **Total:** Rush 5-29 5.8; PR 2-(-1) -0.5; Scor 1 2XP.

Year Team	G	Receiving Rec	Yds	Avg	TD	Fum
1990 Phi	16	37	602	16.3	9	2
1991 Phi	12	33	326	9.9	3	1
1992 Phi	16	42	598	14.2	7	0
1993 Phi	16	60	725	12.1	10	0
1994 Phi	16	58	813	14.0	3	0
1995 Phi	16	63	768	12.2	2	2
1996 Bal-Phi	8	15	93	6.2	1	0
1996 Bal	7	13	85	6.5	1	0
1996 Phi	1	2	8	4.0	0	0
NFL Total	100	308	3925	12.7	35	5

CHARLES WILLIAMS Williams, Charles 6'1", 180 **DB**
Col: Jackson State *HS:* Mendenhall [MS] B: 9/14/1953, Magee, MS *Drafted:* 1978 Round 9 Phi
1978 Phi: 7 G.

DONNIE WILLIAMS Williams, Charles Donell 6'3", 210 **WR**
Col: Prairie View A&M *HS:* L.G. Pinkston [Dallas, TX] B: 3/12/1948, Dallas, TX *Drafted:* 1970 Round 2 LARm
1970 LARm: 5 G; Rec 1-9 9.0.

MONK WILLIAMS Williams, Charles Lee 5'7", 155 **WR**
Col: Arkansas-Pine Bluff *HS:* Clark [Shreveport, LA] B: 2/15/1945, Shreveport, LA *Drafted:* 1968 Round 16 Cin
1968 Cin: 2 G; PR 2-14 7.0; KR 5-112 22.4.

CHARLIE WILLIAMS Williams, Charlie U 6'0", 193 **DB**
Col: Bowling Green State *HS:* Henry Ford [Detroit, MI] B: 2/2/1972, Detroit, MI *Drafted:* 1995 Round 3 Dal
1995 Dal: 16 G. **1996** Dal: 7 G; KR 2-21 10.5; 1 Fum. **1997** Dal: 16 G; 2 Sac. **1998** Dal: 15 G. **Total:** 54 G; KR 2-21 10.5; 1 Fum; 2 Sac.

CHRIS WILLIAMS Williams, Chris 6′3″, 304 **NT**
Col: American International *HS:* Southeastern Regional [South Easton, MA] B: 11/23/1968, Chelsea, MA
1991 Pho: 15 G.

CHRIS WILLIAMS Williams, Chris Albany 6′0″, 197 **DB**
Col: Louisiana State *HS:* Tioga [LA] B: 1/2/1959, Alexandria, LA
Drafted: 1981 Round 2 Buf
1981 Buf: Postseason only. **1982** Buf: 5 G. **1983** Buf: 16 G; Int 3-6.
Total: 21 G; Int 3-6.

CLARENCE WILLIAMS Williams, Clarence 6′1″, 265 **RB**
(Pooh Bear) *Col:* Florida State *HS:* Crescent City [FL] B: 1/20/1975, Crescent City, FL
1998 Buf: 3 G; Rush 2-5 2.5.

CLARENCE WILLIAMS Williams, Clarence 5′9″, 194 **RB**
Col: South Carolina *HS:* Berkeley [Moncks Corner, SC] B: 1/25/1955, Oakley, SC D: 9/17/1994, Columbia, SC *Drafted:* 1977 Round 5 SD
1977 SD: PR 1-0. **Total:** PR 1-0.

		Rushing				Receiving			
Year Team	**G**	**Att**	**Yds**	**Avg**	**TD**	**Rec**	**Yds**	**Avg**	**TD**
1977 SD	14	50	215	4.3	2	3	20	6.7	0
1978 SD	10	27	76	2.8	0	1	17	17.0	0
1979 SD	16	200	752	3.8	12	51	352	6.9	0
1980 SD	13	97	258	2.7	3	26	230	8.8	1
1981 SD	14	20	26	1.3	0	12	108	9.0	1
NFL Total	67	394	1327	3.4	17	93	727	7.8	2

	Kickoff Returns					Tot
Year Team	**Ret**	**Yds**	**Avg**	**TD**	**Fum**	**TD**
1977 SD	24	481	20.0	0	2	2
1978 SD	6	143	23.8	0	0	0
1979 SD	1	19	19.0	0	1	12
1980 SD	0	0	—	0	3	4
1981 SD	4	47	11.8	0	2	1
NFL Total	35	690	19.7	0	8	19

SWEENY WILLIAMS Williams, Clarence 6′5″, 255 **DE**
Col: Prairie View A&M *HS:* George Washington Carver [Sweeny, TX]
B: 9/3/1946, Brazoria, TX *Drafted:* 1969 Round 11 Dal
1970 GB: 14 G; PR 1-0; 1 Fum. **1971** GB: 14 G. **1972** GB: 14 G; **1** Fum TD; 6 Pt. **1973** GB: 14 G. **1974** GB: 14 G; Int 1-23. **1975** GB: 14 G. **1976** GB: 14 G. **1977** GB: 13 G. **Total:** 111 G; PR 1-0; Int 1-23; 1 Fum TD; 6 Pt; 1 Fum.

CLARENCE WILLIAMS Williams, Clarence III 6′2″, 240 **TE-RB**
Col: Washington State *HS:* Renton [WA] B: 8/7/1969, Los Angeles, CA
Drafted: 1993 Round 7 Den
1993 Cle: 7 G; Rec 1-14 14.0.

CLANCY WILLIAMS Williams, Clarence Jr. 6′3″, 194 **DB**
Col: Washington State *HS:* Renton [WA] B: 9/24/1942, Deweyville, TX
D: 9/21/1986, Seattle, WA *Drafted:* 1965 Round 1 LARm
1965 LARm: Rush 3-3 1.0. **Total:** Rush 3-3 1.0.

		Kickoff Returns				Interceptions		
Year Team	**G**	**Ret**	**Yds**	**Avg**	**TD**	**Int**	**Yds**	**TD**
1965 LARm	12	9	213	23.7	0	0	0	0
1966 LARm	14	15	420	28.0	0	8	97	1
1967 LARm	14	7	161	23.0	0	4	75	0
1968 LARm	14	1	16	16.0	0	7	51	0
1969 LARm	14	0	0	—	0	4	97	0
1970 LARm	14	0	0	—	0	5	108	1
1971 LARm	6	0	0	—	0	0	0	0
1972 LARm	9	0	0	—	0	0	0	0
NFL Total	97	32	810	25.3	0	28	428	2

CLYDE WILLIAMS Williams, Clyde A 6′3″, 250 **OT-OG**
Col: Southern University *HS:* Minden [LA] B: 7/27/1940, Shreveport, LA
1967 StL: 9 G; PR 1-0. **1968** StL: 10 G. **1969** StL: 13 G; KR 1-0. **1970** StL: 14 G. **1971** StL: 14 G. **Total:** 60 G; PR 1-0; KR 1-0.

CLYDE WILLIAMS Williams, Clyde Walter 6′2″, 210 **T**
(Weenie) *Col:* Georgia Tech *HS:* Little Rock Central [AR]
B: 9/17/1910
1935 Phi: 3 G.

WIN WILLIAMS Williams, Dale Windell 6′2″, 185 **OE**
Col: Rice; Southwestern Louisiana *HS:* Midland [TX] B: 3/10/1923, Fort Towson, OK D: 5/12/1992, Houston, TX
AAFC **1948** BalA: KR 1-20 20.0. **Total:** KR 1-20 20.0.

		Receiving			
Year Team	**G**	**Rec**	**Yds**	**Avg**	**TD**
1948 BalA	15	32	360	11.3	2
1949 BalA	12	20	266	13.3	1
AAFC Total	27	52	626	12.0	3

DOC WILLIAMS Williams, Dan Adauf 6′7″, 218 **G**
Col: St. Cloud State *HS:* Model School [St. Cloud, MN] B: 4/3/1899, St. Cloud, MN D: 4/11/1992, Arden Hills, MN
1923 Dul: 6 G. **1924** Dul: 6 G. **1925** Dul: 3 G. **1926** Dul: 13 G. **Total:** 28 G.

DAN WILLIAMS Williams, Daniel II 6′4″, 290 **DE**
Col: Tennessee State; Toledo *HS:* Ypsilanti [MI] B: 12/15/1969, Ypsilanti, MI *Drafted:* 1993 Round 1 Den
1993 Den: 13 G; 1 Sac. **1994** Den: 12 G; Int 1-(-3). **1995** Den: 6 G; 2 Sac. **1996** Den: 15 G; 1 Sac. **1997** KC: 15 G; 10.5 Sac. **Total:** 61 G; Int 1-(-3); 14.5 Sac.

DARRYL WILLIAMS Williams, Darryl Edwin 6′0″, 198 **DB**
Col: Miami (Fla.) *HS:* American Senior [Hialeah, FL] B: 1/7/1970, Miami, FL *Drafted:* 1992 Round 1 Cin
1992 Cin: 2 Sac. **1993** Cin: 2 Sac. **1994** Cin: PR 1-4 4.0; 1 Sac. **1995** Cin: Scor 1 Saf; 1 Sac. **Total:** PR 1-4 4.0; Scor 1 Saf; 6 Sac.

		Interceptions		
Year Team	**G**	**Int**	**Yds**	**TD**
1992 Cin	16	4	65	0
1993 Cin	16	2	126	1
1994 Cin	16	2	45	0
1995 Cin	16	1	1	0
1996 Sea	16	5	148	1
1997 Sea	16	8	172	1
1998 Sea	16	3	41	0
NFL Total	112	25	598	3

DOKIE WILLIAMS Williams, Darryl Eugene 5′11″, 180 **WR**
Col: UCLA *HS:* El Camino [Oceanside, CA] B: 8/25/1960, Oceanside, CA *Drafted:* 1983 Round 5 LARd
1986 LARd: Rush 3-27 9.0. **Total:** Rush 3-27 9.0.

		Receiving				Kickoff Returns				
Year Team	**G**	**Rec**	**Yds**	**Avg**	**TD**	**Ret**	**Yds**	**Avg**	**TD**	**Fum**
1983 LARd	16	14	259	18.5	3	5	88	17.6	0	2
1984 LARd	16	22	509	23.1	4	24	621	25.9	0	0
1985 LARd	16	48	925	19.3	5	1	19	19.0	0	0
1986 LARd	15	43	843	19.6	8	0	0	—	0	2
1987 LARd	11	21	330	15.7	5	14	221	15.8	0	0
NFL Total	74	148	2866	19.4	25	44	949	21.6	0	4

DAVID WILLIAMS Williams, David Lamar 6′3″, 190 **WR**
Col: Los Angeles Harbor Coll. CA (J.C.); Illinois *HS:* Junipero Serra [Gardena, CA] B: 6/10/1963, Los Angeles, CA *Drafted:* 1986 Round 3 ChiB
1986 TB: 15 G; Rec 6-91 15.2; KR 2-29 14.5. **1987** LARd: 3 G; Rec 4-104 26.0. **Total:** 18 G; Rec 10-195 19.5; KR 2-29 14.5.

DAVE WILLIAMS Williams, David Laverne 6′2″, 207 **WR**
Col: Washington *HS:* Lincoln [Tacoma, WA] B: 8/10/1945, Cedar Rapids, IA *Drafted:* 1967 Round 1 StL
1967 StL: Rush 1-7 7.0. **1968** StL: Rush 3-47 15.7. **1969** StL: Rush 1-1 1.0. **1972** SD: Rush 1-14 14.0; KR 0-9. **Total:** Rush 6-69 11.5; KR 0-9.

		Receiving				
Year Team	**G**	**Rec**	**Yds**	**Avg**	**TD**	**Fum**
1967 StL	14	28	405	14.5	5	0
1968 StL	12	43	682	15.9	6	1
1969 StL	14	56	702	12.5	7	1
1970 StL	14	23	364	15.8	3	0
1971 StL	13	12	182	15.2	1	0
1972 SD	12	14	315	22.5	3	0
1973 SD-Pit	7	7	118	16.9	0	0
1973 SD	6	7	118	16.9	0	0
1973 Pit	1	0	0	—	0	0
NFL Total	86	183	2768	15.1	25	2

DAVE WILLIAMS Williams, David Ray 6′2″, 210 **RB**
Col: Colorado *HS:* Homer [LA] B: 3/10/1954, Minden, LA
Drafted: 1976 Round 7 Dal
1977 SF: PR 1-60 60.0. **Total:** PR 1-60 60.0.

		Rushing				Receiving			
Year Team	**G**	**Att**	**Yds**	**Avg**	**TD**	**Rec**	**Yds**	**Avg**	**TD**
1977 SF	12	2	6	3.0	0	0	0	—	0
1978 SF	16	15	18	1.2	0	10	63	6.3	0
1979 ChiB	14	127	401	3.2	1	42	354	8.4	5
1980 ChiB	16	26	57	2.2	0	22	132	6.0	0
1981 ChiB	8	2	19	9.5	0	18	126	7.0	2
NFL Total	66	172	501	2.9	1	92	675	7.3	7

	Kickoff Returns					Tot
Year Team	**Ret**	**Yds**	**Avg**	**TD**	**Fum**	**TD**
1977 SF	4	122	30.5	1	0	1
1978 SF	34	745	21.9	**1**	6	1
1979 ChiB	0	0	—	0	4	6
1980 ChiB	27	666	24.7	**1**	2	1

1981 ChiB	23	486	21.1	0	0	2
NFL Total	88	2019	22.9	3	12	11

DAVID WILLIAMS Williams, David Wayne 6'5", 294 **OT**
Col: Florida *HS:* Lakeland [FL] B: 6/21/1966, Mulberry, FL
Drafted: 1989 Round 1 Hou
1989 Hou: 14 G; KR 2-8 4.0. **1990** Hou: 15 G. **1991** Hou: 16 G. **1992** Hou: 16 G. **1993** Hou: 15 G. **1994** Hou: 16 G. **1995** Hou: 10 G. **1996** NYJ: 14 G. **1997** NYJ: 12 G. **Total:** 128 G; KR 2-8 4.0.

DEL WILLIAMS Williams, Delano Roper 6'2", 240 **OG**
Col: Florida State *HS:* Suwannee [Live Oak, FL] B: 11/9/1945, Live Oak, FL D: 11/28/1984, New Orleans, LA *Drafted:* 1967 Round 3 NO
1967 NO: 14 G. **1968** NO: 14 G. **1969** NO: 14 G. **1970** NO: 14 G. **1971** NO: 14 G; 1 Fum. **1972** NO: 8 G. **1973** NO: 14 G. **Total:** 92 G; 1 Fum.

DELVIN WILLIAMS Williams, Delvin Jr. 6'0", 195 **RB**
Col: Kansas *HS:* Kashmere [Houston, TX] B: 4/17/1951, Houston, TX
Drafted: 1974 Round 2 SF
1975 SF: KR 1-24 24.0. **1976** SF: Pass 1-1 100.0%, 18 18.00. **1977** SF: Pass 1-0, 1 Int; KR 1-9 9.0. **1978** Mia: Pass 1-0. **1979** Mia: Pass 1-0. **1980** Mia: Pass 1-0. **Total:** Pass 5-1 20.0%, 18 3.60 1 Int; KR 2-33 16.5.

		Rushing				Receiving					Tot
Year Team	G	Att	Yds	Avg	TD	Rec	Yds	Avg	TD	Fum	TD
1974 SF	13	36	201	5.6	3	1	9	9.0	0	2	3
1975 SF	14	117	631	5.4	3	34	370	10.9	1	1	4
1976 SF	13	248	1203	4.9	7	27	283	10.5	2	6	9
1977 SF	14	268	931	3.5	7	20	179	9.0	2	3	9
1978 Mia	16	272	1258	4.6	8	18	192	10.7	0	4	8
1979 Mia	14	184	703	3.8	3	21	175	8.3	1	4	4
1980 Mia	15	187	671	3.6	2	31	207	6.7	0	5	2
1981 GB	1	0	0	—	0	0	0	—	0	0	0
NFL Total	100	1312	5598	4.3	33	152	1415	9.3	6	25	39

DEMISE WILLIAMS Williams, Demise Lamar 6'1", 225 **DB**
Col: Oklahoma State *HS:* Anacostia [Washington, DC] B: 7/9/1964, Greenville, SC
1987 LARd: 1 G.

DERWIN WILLIAMS Williams, Derwin Dawayne 6'0", 180 **WR**
Col: New Mexico *HS:* Brownwood [TX] B: 5/6/1961, Brownwood, TX
Drafted: 1984 Round 7 NE
1985 NE: 16 G; Rec 9-163 18.1. **1986** NE: 16 G; Rec 2-35 17.5. **1987** NE: 10 G; Rec 3-30 10.0. **Total:** 42 G; Rec 14-228 16.3.

DON WILLIAMS Williams, Don Donaho 5'8", 210 **G**
Col: Texas *HS:* Amarillo [TX] B: 5/23/1919, Claude, TX *Drafted:* 1941 Round 8 Phi
1941 Pit: 6 G.

DOUG WILLIAMS Williams, Douglas 6'5", 286 **OT-OG**
Col: Texas A&M *HS:* Moeller [Cincinnati, OH] B: 10/1/1962, Cincinnati, OH *Drafted:* 1986 Round 2 NYJ
1986 Hou: 15 G. **1987** Hou: 8 G. **Total:** 23 G.

LAWRENCE WILLIAMS Williams, Douglas Lawrence 5'10", 173 **WR**
Col: Texas Tech *HS:* Wichita Falls [TX] B: 9/3/1953, Wichita Falls, TX
Drafted: 1975 Round 7 NE
1976 KC: Rec 1-9 9.0. **1977** KC-Cle: Rush 2-30 15.0 1 TD; Rec 7-94 13.4. KC: Rush 2-30 15.0 1 TD; Rec 7-94 13.4. **Total:** Rush 2-30 15.0 1 TD; Rec 8-103 12.9.

		Kickoff Returns				
Year Team	G	Ret	Yds	Avg	TD	Fum
1976 KC	12	25	688	27.5	0	1
1977 KC-Cle	9	25	518	20.7	0	1
1977 KC	6	17	319	18.8	0	1
1977 Cle	3	8	199	24.9	0	0
NFL Total	21	50	1206	24.1	0	2

DOUG WILLIAMS Williams, Douglas Lee 6'4", 220 **QB**
Col: Grambling State *HS:* Chaneyville [Zachary, LA] B: 8/9/1955, Zachary, LA *Drafted:* 1978 Round 1 TB

		Passing							
Year Team	G	Att	Comp	Comp%	Yds	YPA	TD	Int	Rating
1978 TB	10	194	73	37.6	1170	6.03	7	**8**	53.4
1979 TB	16	397	166	41.8	2448	6.17	18	24	52.5
1980 TB	16	521	254	48.8	3396	6.52	20	16	69.9
1981 TB	16	471	238	50.5	3563	7.56	19	14	76.8
1982 TB	9	307	164	53.4	2071	6.75	9	11	69.6
1986 Was	1	1	0	0.0	0	0.00	0	0	39.6
1987 Was	5	143	81	56.6	1156	8.08	11	5	94.0
1988 Was	11	380	213	56.1	2609	6.87	15	12	77.4
1989 Was	4	93	51	54.8	585	6.29	1	3	64.1
NFL Total	88	2507	1240	49.5	16998	6.78	100	93	69.4

	Rushing				
Year Team	Att	Yds	Avg	TD	Fum
1978 TB	27	23	0.9	1	5
1979 TB	35	119	3.4	2	2
1980 TB	58	370	6.4	4	7
1981 TB	48	209	4.4	4	9
1982 TB	35	158	4.5	2	9
1987 Was	7	9	1.3	1	3
1988 Was	9	0	0.0	1	6
1989 Was	1	-4	-4.0	0	0
NFL Total	220	884	4.0	15	41

SCOTT WILLIAMS Williams, Edmund Scott 6'2", 234 **RB**
Col: Georgia *HS:* North Mecklenburg [Huntersville, NC] B: 7/21/1962, Charlotte, NC *Drafted:* 1985 Round 9 StL
1986 Det: Rec 2-9 4.5. **1987** Det: Rec 4-16 4.0 1 TD. **1988** Det: Rec 3-46 15.3. **Total:** Rec 9-71 7.9 1 TD.

		Rushing				Tot
Year Team	G	Att	Yds	Avg	TD	TD
1986 Det	16	13	22	1.7	2	2
1987 Det	5	8	29	3.6	0	1
1988 Det	11	9	22	2.4	1	1
NFL Total	32	30	73	2.4	3	4

ED WILLIAMS Williams, Edward Eugene 6'4", 244 **LB**
Col: Texas *HS:* Ector [TX] B: 9/8/1961, Odessa, TX *Drafted:* 1984 Round 2 NE
1984 NE: 14 G. **1985** NE: 13 G. **1986** NE: 8 G. **1987** NE: 12 G; Int 1-51. **1990** NE: 15 G; 2 Sac. **Total:** 62 G; Int 1-51; 2 Sac.

ED WILLIAMS Williams, Edward Lee 6'2", 245 **RB**
Col: Langston *HS:* Dunjee [Spencer, OK] B: 6/19/1950, Oklahoma City, OK
1974 Cin: KR 2-33 16.5. **Total:** KR 2-33 16.5.

		Rushing				Receiving					Tot
Year Team	G	Att	Yds	Avg	TD	Rec	Yds	Avg	TD	Fum	TD
1974 Cin	14	58	238	4.1	3	13	98	7.5	1	0	4
1975 Cin	14	35	136	3.9	2	10	96	9.6	1	4	3
1976 TB	12	87	324	3.7	2	23	166	7.2	0	2	2
1977 TB	14	63	198	3.1	0	10	67	6.7	0	6	0
NFL Total	54	243	896	3.7	7	56	427	7.6	2	12	9

ELIJAH WILLIAMS Williams, Elijah Elgebra 5'10", 181 **DB**
Col: Florida *HS:* Milton [FL] B: 8/20/1975, Milton, FL *Drafted:* 1998 Round 6 Atl
1998 Atl: 15 G; Rush 2-(-2) -1.0; KR 7-132 18.9.

ELLERY WILLIAMS Williams, Ellery Frederick 6'0", 185 **OE**
Col: Pasadena City Coll. CA (J.C.); Santa Clara *HS:* Ferguson [St.Louis, MO]; Pasadena HS [CA] B: 3/20/1926, St. Louis, MO *Drafted:* 1950 Round 8 SF
1950 NYG: 12 G; Rec 4-78 19.5.

ERIC WILLIAMS Williams, Eric D 6'2", 227 **LB**
Col: USC *HS:* Central [Kansas City, MO] B: 6/17/1955, Los Angeles, CA *Drafted:* 1977 Round 8 StL
1977 StL: 14 G. **1978** StL: 13 G; Int 1-24. **1979** StL: 16 G; Int 1-25. **1980** StL: 12 G; Int 2-31. **1981** StL: 15 G; Int 1-17. **1982** LARm: 3 G. **1983** LARm: 11 G. **1984** SD: 13 G. **Total:** 97 G; Int 5-97.

ERIC WILLIAMS Williams, Eric Michael 6'4", 282 **DT-DE-NT**
Col: Washington State *HS:* St. Mary's [Stockton, CA] B: 2/24/1962, Stockton, CA *Drafted:* 1984 Round 3 Det
1984 Det: 12 G. **1985** Det: 12 G; 6 Sac. **1986** Det: 16 G; Int 1-2; 4 Sac. **1987** Det: 11 G; 2 Sac. **1988** Det: 16 G; 6.5 Sac. **1989** Det: 16 G; 5.5 Sac. **1990** Was: 13 G; 3 Sac. **1991** Was: 15 G; 3 Sac. **1992** Was: 6 G. **1993** Was: 4 G. **Total:** 121 G; Int 1-2; 30.0 Sac.

ERIC WILLIAMS Williams, Eric Thomas 6'1", 188 **DB**
Col: North Carolina State *HS:* Garner [NC] B: 2/21/1960, Raleigh, NC
Drafted: 1983 Round 6 Pit
1984 Pit: 2 Sac. **Total:** 2 Sac.

		Interceptions		
Year Team	G	Int	Yds	TD
1983 Pit	3	0	0	0
1984 Pit	16	3	49	0
1985 Pit	14	4	47	0
1986 Pit	16	3	44	0
1987 Det	1	0	0	0
NFL Total	50	10	140	0

ERIK WILLIAMS Williams, Erik George 6'6", 324 **OT**
Col: Central State (Ohio) *HS:* John Bartram [Philadelphia, PA]
B: 9/7/1968, Philadelphia, PA *Drafted:* 1991 Round 3 Dal
1991 Dal: 11 G. **1992** Dal: 16 G. **1993** Dal: 16 G. **1994** Dal: 7 G. **1995** Dal: 15 G. **1996** Dal: 16 G. **1997** Dal: 15 G. **1998** Dal: 15 G. **Total:** 111 G.

ERWIN WILLIAMS Williams, Erwin B 6′5″, 214 **WR**
Col: Maryland East. Shore *HS:* Crestwood [Portsmouth, VA]
B: 6/21/1947, Portsmouth, VA
1969 Pit: 9 G; Rec 3-14 4.7 1 TD; 6 Pt.

EUGENE WILLIAMS Williams, Eugene III 6′1″, 220 **LB**
Col: Tulsa *HS:* Longview [TX] B: 6/15/1960, Longview, TX
Drafted: 1982 Round 7 Sea
1982 Sea: 9 G. **1983** Sea: 4 G; Int 1-0. **Total:** 13 G; Int 1-0.

GENE WILLIAMS Williams, Eugene III 6′2″, 310 **OT-OG**
Col: Iowa State *HS:* Creighton Prep [Omaha, NE] B: 10/14/1968, Blair, NE *Drafted:* 1991 Round 5 Mia
1991 Mia: 10 G. **1992** Mia: 5 G. **1993** Cle: 16 G. **1994** Cle: 15 G. **1995** Atl: 12 G. **1996** Atl: 10 G. **1997** Atl: 15 G. **1998** Atl: 16 G. **Total:** 99 G.

FRANK WILLIAMS Williams, Frank Gordon Jr. 6′2″, 215 **FB**
Col: Pepperdine *HS:* David Starr Jordan [Los Angeles, CA]
B: 5/9/1932, Bowie Co., TX
1961 LARm: 2 G.

FRANK WILLIAMS Williams, Frank Ralph 6′0″, 212 **FB-LB**
(Buss) *Col:* Utah State *HS:* Davis [Kaysville, UT] B: 2/27/1922, Bountiful, UT *Drafted:* 1948 Round 20 NYG
1948 NYG: 9 G; Rec 1-5 5.0; Scor 4, 0-1 FG, 4-5 80.0% XK; 1 Fum.

JEFF WILLIAMS Williams, Franklin Jeff 6′1″, 210 **HB**
Col: Oklahoma State *HS:* A.L. Melbane [Alachua, FL] B: 5/7/1943, High Springs, FL
1966 Min: 3 G; Rush 1-2 2.0; PR 4-(-2) -0.5; KR 3-61 20.3; 1 Fum.

FRED WILLIAMS Williams, Fred 6′4″, 249 **OT-OG**
(Fat Freddie) *Col:* Arkansas *HS:* Little Rock Central [AR] B: 2/8/1929, Little Rock, AR *Drafted:* 1952 Round 5 ChiB
1952 ChiB: 12 G; Int 1-54. **1953** ChiB: 12 G. **1954** ChiB: 12 G. **1955** ChiB: 12 G. **1956** ChiB: 12 G; Int 1-11. **1957** ChiB: 12 G; KR 1-6 6.0. **1958** ChiB: 12 G. **1959** ChiB: 11 G. **1960** ChiB: 12 G. **1961** ChiB: 14 G. **1962** ChiB: 14 G. **1963** ChiB: 5 G. **1964** Was: 14 G. **1965** Was: 14 G. **Total:** 168 G; KR 1-6 6.0; Int 2-65.

GARDNER WILLIAMS Williams, Gardner 6′2″, 199 **DB**
Col: St. Mary's (Cal.) *HS:* Bishop O'Dowd [Oakland, CA]
B: 12/11/1961, Washington, DC *Drafted:* 1984 Round 11 LARd
1984 Det: 3 G.

GARLAND WILLIAMS Williams, Garland Hare 6′3″, 220 **T**
(Bulldog) *Col:* Duke; Georgia *HS:* Forrest City [AR] B: 8/21/1921, Parkin, AR D: 4/7/1989, Alpharetta, GA
AAFC **1947** BknA: 14 G. **1948** BknA: 12 G. **Total:** 26 G.

GARY WILLIAMS Williams, Gary Leon 6′2″, 215 **WR**
Col: Ohio State *HS:* Wilmington [OH] B: 9/4/1959, Wilmington, OH
Drafted: 1983 Round 11 Cin
1984 Cin: 8 G; KR 1-0.

GEORGE WILLIAMS Williams, George Roger III 6′3″, 294 **DT**
Col: North Carolina State *HS:* Lakewood [Roseboro, NC]
B: 12/8/1975, Roseboro, NC
1998 NYG: 2 G.

VAN WILLIAMS Williams, George Van 6′0″, 208 **RB**
Col: East Tennessee State; Carson-Newman *HS:* All-Science [Johnson City, TN] B: 3/15/1959, Johnson City, TN *Drafted:* 1982 Round 4 Buf
1983 Buf: PR 1-0. **1984** Buf: Rec 5-46 9.2 1 TD. **1985** Buf: Rec 1-7 7.0. **1987** NYG: Rec 5-36 7.2. **Total:** Rec 11-89 8.1 1 TD; PR 1-0.

		Rushing				Kickoff Returns				
Year Team	**G**	**Att**	**Yds**	**Avg**	**TD**	**Ret**	**Yds**	**Avg**	**TD**	**Fum**
1983 Buf	16	3	11	3.7	0	25	550	22.0	0	2
1984 Buf	16	18	51	2.8	0	39	820	21.0	0	1
1985 Buf	2	0	0	—	0	1	20	20.0	0	0
1987 NYG	3	29	108	3.7	0	0	0	—	0	2
NFL Total	37	50	170	3.4	0	65	1390	21.4	0	5

GERALD WILLIAMS Williams, Gerald 6′3″, 290 **NT-DE-DT**
Col: Auburn *HS:* Valley [AL] B: 9/8/1963, Waycross, GA
Drafted: 1986 Round 2 Pit
1986 Pit: 16 G; 3.5 Sac. **1987** Pit: 9 G; 1 Sac. **1988** Pit: 16 G; 3.5 Sac. **1989** Pit: 16 G; 3 Sac. **1990** Pit: 16 G; 6 Sac. **1991** Pit: 16 G; 2 Sac. **1992** Pit: 10 G; 3 Sac. **1993** Pit: 10 G; 1 Sac. **1994** Pit: 11 G; 1 Fum TD; 6 Pt; 1.5 Sac. **1995** Car: 16 G. **1996** Car: 16 G; 1 Sac. **1997** Car-GB: 9 G. Car: 5 G. GB: 4 G. **Total:** 161 G; 1 Fum TD; 6 Pt; 25.5 Sac.

GERARD WILLIAMS Williams, Gerard Anthony 6′1″, 184 **DB**
Col: Langston *HS:* Northeast [Oklahoma City, OK] B: 5/25/1952, Oklahoma City, OK

		Interceptions			
Year Team	**G**	**Int**	**Yds**	**TD**	**Fum**
1976 Was	14	0	0	0	0
1977 Was	14	4	25	0	1
1978 Was	16	4	51	0	0
1979 SF	15	4	38	0	0
1980 SF-StL	9	1	28	0	0
1980 SF	5	1	28	0	0
1980 StL	4	0	0	0	0
NFL Total	68	13	142	0	1

GRANT WILLIAMS Williams, Grant James 6′7″, 323 **OT**
Col: Louisiana Tech *HS:* Clinton [MS] B: 5/10/1974, Hattiesburg, MS
1996 Sea: 8 G. **1997** Sea: 16 G. **1998** Sea: 16 G. **Total:** 40 G.

GREG WILLIAMS Williams, Gregory 5′11″, 185 **DB**
Col: Mississippi Delta CC; Mississippi State *HS:* Greenville Christian Academy [Greenville, MS] B: 8/1/1959, Greenville, MS
1982 Was: 9 G; PR 1-9 9.0; KR 1-2 2.0. **1983** Was: 16 G; KR 1-6 6.0; Int 2-25. **1984** Was: 16 G; PR 1-0. **1985** Was: 16 G. **Total:** 57 G; PR 2-9 4.5; KR 2-8 4.0; Int 2-25.

HARVEY WILLIAMS Williams, Harvey Lavance 6′2″, 226 **RB**
Col: Louisiana State *HS:* Hempstead [TX] B: 4/22/1967, Hempstead, TX *Drafted:* 1991 Round 1 KC
1991 KC: Pass 1-0. **1994** LARd: Scor 1 2XP. **1995** Oak: Pass 1-1 100.0%, 13 13.00 1 TD. **1996** Oak: Pass 2-1 50.0%, 18 9.00 1 TD. **1997** Oak: Scor 1 2XP. **1998** Oak: Pass 1-1 100.0%, 27 27.00.
Total: Pass 5-3 60.0%, 58 11.60 2 TD; Scor 2 2XP.

		Rushing				Receiving			
Year Team	**G**	**Att**	**Yds**	**Avg**	**TD**	**Rec**	**Yds**	**Avg**	**TD**
1991 KC	14	97	447	4.6	1	16	147	9.2	2
1992 KC	14	78	262	3.4	1	5	24	4.8	0
1993 KC	7	42	149	3.5	0	7	42	6.0	0
1994 LARd	16	282	983	3.5	4	47	391	8.3	3
1995 Oak	16	255	1114	4.4	9	54	375	6.9	0
1996 Oak	13	121	431	3.6	0	22	143	6.5	0
1997 Oak	14	18	70	3.9	3	16	147	9.2	2
1998 Oak	16	128	496	3.9	2	26	173	6.7	0
NFL Total	110	1021	3952	3.9	20	193	1442	7.5	7

	Kickoff Returns					Tot
Year Team	**Ret**	**Yds**	**Avg**	**TD**	**Fum**	**TD**
1991 KC	24	524	21.8	0	1	3
1992 KC	21	405	19.3	0	1	1
1993 KC	3	53	17.7	0	3	0
1994 LARd	8	153	19.1	0	4	7
1995 Oak	0	0	—	0	5	9
1996 Oak	0	0	—	0	3	0
1997 Oak	0	0	—	0	0	5
1998 Oak	0	0	—	0	3	2
NFL Total	56	1135	20.3	0	20	27

HENRY WILLIAMS Williams, Henry James 5′10″, 180 **DB**
Col: Hartnell Coll. CA (J.C.); San Diego State *HS:* Thomas Jefferson [Los Angeles, CA] B: 12/2/1956, Greensboro, AL *Drafted:* 1979 Round 6 Oak
1979 Oak: 16 G; Int 3-37. **1983** LARm-SD: 6 G. LARm: 5 G. SD: 1 G.
Total: 22 G; Int 3-37.

HENRY WILLIAMS Williams, Henry Lee 5′6″, 185 **WR**
(Gizmo) *Col:* Northwest Mississippi CC; East Carolina *HS:* Rosa Fort [Tunica, MS] B: 5/31/1962, Memphis, TN
1989 Phi: Rec 4-32 8.0; KR 14-249 17.8.

		Punt Returns				
Year Team	**G**	**Ret**	**Yds**	**Avg**	**TD**	**Fum**
1989 Phi	13	30	267	8.9	0	1

HERB WILLIAMS Williams, Herbert Earl 6′0″, 198 **DB**
Col: Southern University *HS:* McKinley [Baton Rouge, LA]
B: 8/30/1958, Lafayette, LA *Drafted:* 1980 Round 6 SF
1980 SF: 9 G. **1981** StL: 3 G. **1982** StL: 7 G. **Total:** 19 G.

HOWIE WILLIAMS Williams, Howard Lee 6′1″, 190 **DB**
Col: Howard *HS:* Carver [Spartanburg, SC] B: 12/4/1936, Spartanburg, SC

		Interceptions		
Year Team	**G**	**Int**	**Yds**	**TD**
1962 GB	1	0	0	0
1963 GB-SF	14	0	0	0
1963 GB	7	0	0	0
1963 SF	7	0	0	0
1964 Oak	12	1	0	0
1965 Oak	14	2	23	0
1966 Oak	14	3	51	0
1967 Oak	13	4	96	0
1968 Oak	13	2	66	0
1969 Oak	14	2	4	0
NFL Total	95	14	240	0

IKE WILLIAMS Williams, Ivan Andy 5′10″, 180 **HB**
Col: Georgia Tech *HS:* Little Rock Central [AR] B: 1903
1929 SI: 6 G.

TEX WILLIAMS Williams, Jack Gressert 5′11″, 193 **C-LB**
Col: Auburn *HS:* Georgia Vocational & Trade School [Walker Park, GA]
B: 8/21/1919, Lancaster, PA
AAFC **1946** MiaA: 6 G; Int 1-3.

NFL **1942** Phi: 5 G.

JAKE WILLIAMS Williams, Jacob Crawford 6′0″, 205 **T-E-G-C**
Col: Texas Christian B: 1904
1929 ChiC: 8 G. **1930** ChiC: 9 G. **1931** ChiC: 8 G. **1932** ChiC: 8 G; Rec 1-15 15.0. **1933** ChiC: 11 G. **Total:** 44 G; Rec 1-15 15.0.

JAMAL WILLIAMS Williams, Jamal 6′3″, 305 **DT**
Col: Oklahoma State *HS:* Archbishop Carroll [Washington, DC]
B: 4/28/1976, Washington, DC
1998 SD: 9 G; Int 1-14 1 TD; 6 Pt.

JAMEL WILLIAMS Williams, Jamel Ishmael 5′11″, 205 **DB**
Col: Nebraska *HS:* Merrillville [IN] B: 12/22/1973, Merrillville, IN
Drafted: 1997 Round 5 Was
1997 Was: 16 G. **1998** Was: 16 G. **Total:** 32 G.

JAMES WILLIAMS Williams, James Earl 5′10″, 180 **DB**
Col: Fresno State *HS:* Coalinga [CA] B: 3/30/1967, Osceola, AR
Drafted: 1990 Round 1 Buf

		Interceptions		
Year Team	G	Int	Yds	TD
1990 Buf	16	2	0	0
1991 Buf	8	1	0	0
1992 Buf	15	2	15	0
1993 Buf	15	2	11	0
1994 Ariz	15	4	48	0
1996 SF	1	0	0	0
NFL Total	70	11	74	0

JIM WILLIAMS Williams, James Edward 5′10″, 210 **RB**
Col: Taft Coll. CA (J.C.); Fresno State *HS:* Brunswick [GA]
B: 11/22/1963, Brunswick, GA
1987 Sea: 1 G.

JAMES WILLIAMS Williams, James Edward 6′0″, 236 **LB**
Col: Mississippi State *HS:* Natchez [MS] B: 10/10/1968, Natchez, MS
Drafted: 1990 Round 6 NO
1990 NO: 14 G. **1991** NO: 16 G; 1 Sac. **1992** NO: 16 G. **1993** NO: 16 G; 2 Sac. **1994** NO: 16 G; Int 2-42 1 TD; 6 Pt. **1995** Jac: 12 G; Int 2-19. **1997** SF: 16 G. **1998** SF: 15 G. **Total:** 121 G; Int 4-61 1 TD; 6 Pt; 3 Sac.

JIMMY WILLIAMS Williams, James Henry 6′3″, 228 **LB**
Col: Nebraska *HS:* Woodrow Wilson [Washington, DC] B: 11/15/1960, Washington, DC *Drafted:* 1982 Round 1 Det
1983 Det: 1 Sac. **1984** Det: 2 Sac. **1985** Det: 7.5 Sac. **1986** Det: 2 Sac. **1987** Det: 4 Sac. **1988** Det: 2 Sac. **1989** Det: 4 Sac. **1990** Det-Min: 1 Fum TD; 3 Sac. Det: 1 Fum TD; 3 Sac. **1992** TB: 2 Sac.
Total: 1 Fum TD; 27.5 Sac.

		Interceptions		
Year Team	G	Int	Yds	TD
1982 Det	6	1	4	0
1983 Det	16	0	0	0
1984 Det	16	0	0	0
1985 Det	16	0	0	0
1986 Det	10	2	12	0
1987 Det	12	2	51	0
1988 Det	5	1	5	0
1989 Det	16	5	15	0
1990 Det-Min	14	0	0	0
1990 Det	10	0	0	0
1990 Min	4	0	0	0
1991 Min	14	0	0	0
1992 TB	16	2	4	0
1993 TB	11	0	0	0
NFL Total	152	13	91	0

JAMES WILLIAMS Williams, James Otis 6′7″, 329 **OT-DE-DT**
(Big Cat) *Col:* Cheyney *HS:* Allderdice [Pittsburgh, PA] B: 3/29/1968, Pittsburgh, PA
1991 ChiB: 14 G; 1 Sac. **1992** ChiB: 5 G. **1993** ChiB: 3 G. **1994** ChiB: 16 G. **1995** ChiB: 16 G. **1996** ChiB: 16 G. **1997** ChiB: 16 G. **1998** ChiB: 16 G. **Total:** 102 G; 1 Sac.

JAMIE WILLIAMS Williams, Jamie Earl 6′4″, 240 **TE**
Col: Nebraska *HS:* Central [Davenport, IA] B: 2/25/1960, Vero Beach, FL *Drafted:* 1983 Round 3 NYG
1984 Hou: KR 1-0. **1985** Hou: KR 2-21 10.5. **1990** SF: KR 2-7 3.5. **1994** LARd: KR 1-0. **Total:** KR 6-28 4.7.

		Receiving				
Year Team	G	Rec	Yds	Avg	TD	Fum
1983 StL	1	0	0	—	0	0
1984 Hou	16	41	545	13.3	3	2
1985 Hou	16	39	444	11.4	1	1
1986 Hou	16	22	227	10.3	1	0
1987 Hou	12	13	158	12.2	3	0
1988 Hou	16	6	46	7.7	0	0
1989 SF	3	3	38	12.7	0	0
1990 SF	16	9	54	6.0	0	0
1991 SF	16	22	235	10.7	1	0
1992 SF	16	7	76	10.9	1	1
1993 SF	16	16	132	8.3	1	0
1994 LARd	16	3	25	8.3	0	1
NFL Total	160	181	1980	10.9	11	5

JARVIS WILLIAMS Williams, Jarvis Eric 5′11″, 200 **DB**
Col: Florida *HS:* Palatka [FL] B: 5/16/1965, Palatka, FL *Drafted:* 1988 Round 2 Mia
1988 Mia: PR 3-29 9.7; KR 8-159 19.9. **1989** Mia: KR 1-21 21.0; 1 Sac. **1990** Mia: PR 1-0; 2 Sac. **1991** Mia: KR 1-7 7.0. **1992** Mia: PR 1-0. **Total:** PR 5-29 5.8; KR 10-187 18.7; 3 Sac.

		Interceptions			
Year Team	G	Int	Yds	TD	Fum
1988 Mia	16	4	62	0	0
1989 Mia	16	2	43	0	0
1990 Mia	16	5	82	1	0
1991 Mia	11	1	0	0	0
1992 Mia	16	2	29	0	1
1993 Mia	16	0	0	0	0
1994 NYG	13	2	10	0	0
NFL Total	104	16	226	1	1

INKY WILLIAMS Williams, Jay Mayo 5′11″, 174 **OE**
Col: Brown *HS:* Monmouth [IL] B: 7/25/1894 D: 1/2/1980, Chicago, IL
1921 Can-Ham: 6 G. Can: 1 G. Ham: 5 G. **1922** Ham: 6 G. **1923** Ham: 6 G; 1 Fum TD; 6 Pt. **1924** Ham-Day: 4 G. Ham: 3 G. Day: 1 G. **1925** Ham-Cle: 12 G. Ham: 3 G. Cle: 9 G. **1926** Ham: 3 G. **Total:** 37 G; 1 Fum TD; 6 Pt.

JAY WILLIAMS Williams, Jay Omar 6′3″, 277 **DE**
Col: Wake Forest *HS:* St. John's [Washington, DC] B: 10/13/1971, Washington, DC
1995 StL: 7 G. **1996** StL: 2 G. **1997** StL: 16 G; KR 1-10 10.0; 1 Sac. **1998** StL: 16 G; 1 Sac. **Total:** 41 G; KR 1-10 10.0; 2 Sac.

JEFF WILLIAMS Williams, Jeffrey Scott 6′4″, 256 **OG-OT**
Col: Rhode Island *HS:* Gloucester [MA] B: 4/15/1955, Gloucester, MA
Drafted: 1977 Round 5 LARm
1977 LARm: 1 G. **1978** Was: 7 G. **1979** Was: 16 G. **1980** Was: 15 G. **1981** SD: 12 G. **1982** ChiB: 5 G. **Total:** 56 G.

JERMAINE WILLIAMS Williams, Jermaine Mequell 6′0″, 228 **RB**
Col: Houston *HS:* J.H. Rose [Greenville, NC] B: 7/3/1972, Greenville, NC
1998 Oak: 10 G.

JERROL WILLIAMS Williams, Jerrol Lynn 6′5″, 240 **LB**
Col: Purdue *HS:* Chaparral [Las Vegas, NV] B: 7/5/1967, Las Vegas, NV *Drafted:* 1989 Round 4 Pit
1989 Pit: 16 G; KR 4-31 7.8; 3 Sac. **1990** Pit: 16 G; KR 3-31 10.3; 1 Fum; 1 Sac. **1991** Pit: 16 G; KR 1-19 19.0; 1 Fum TD; 6 Pt; 9 Sac. **1992** Pit: 16 G; Int 1-4; 4.5 Sac. **1993** SD: 6 G. **1994** KC: 6 G; 0.5 Sac. **1996** Bal: 9 G; 1 Fum; 3 Sac. **Total:** 85 G; KR 8-81 10.1; Int 1-4; 1 Fum TD; 6 Pt; 2 Fum; 21 Sac.

JERRY WILLIAMS Williams, Jerry Ralph 5′10″, 175 **HB-DB**
Col: Idaho; Washington State *HS:* North Central [Spokane, WA]
B: 11/1/1923, Spokane, WA D: 12/31/1998, Chandler, AZ
1951 LARm: KR 6-133 22.2. **1953** Phi: KR 14-343 24.5. **Total:** KR 20-476 23.8.

		Rushing				Receiving			
Year Team	G	Att	Yds	Avg	TD	Rec	Yds	Avg	TD
1949 LARm	12	19	103	5.4	3	7	102	14.6	0
1950 LARm	12	13	108	8.3	1	4	21	5.3	1
1951 LARm	10	21	106	5.0	2	5	49	9.8	0
1952 LARm	12	11	65	5.9	0	0	0	—	0
1953 Phi	12	61	345	5.7	3	31	438	14.1	1
1954 Phi	11	47	183	3.9	1	44	668	15.2	3
NFL Total	69	172	910	5.3	10	91	1278	14.0	5

	Punt Returns				Interceptions				Tot
Year Team	Ret	Yds	Avg	TD	Int	Yds	TD	Fum	TD
1949 LARm	2	33	16.5	0	5	42	1	2	4
1950 LARm	6	35	5.8	0	3	39	0	0	2
1951 LARm	4	22	5.5	0	3	53	1	0	4
1952 LARm	1	9	9.0	0	4	41	0	0	0
1953 Phi	15	25	1.7	0	0	0	0	2	4
1954 Phi	23	153	6.7	0	0	0	0	7	4
NFL Total	51	277	5.4	0	15	175	2	11	18

JOE WILLIAMS Williams, Joe John 5′9″, 178 **HB**
(Jumpin' Joe) *Col:* Ohio State *HS:* Barberton [OH] B: 3/19/1915
1937 Cle: 1 G. **1939** Pit: 1 G. **Total:** 2 G.

JOEL WILLIAMS Williams, Joel 6'1", 222 **LB**
Col: Peru State; Wis.-La Crosse *HS:* North Miami [FL] B: 12/13/1956, Miami, FL
1979 Atl: 16 G. **1980** Atl: 16 G; Int 2-55; Scor **1** Saf; **1** Fum TD; 8 Pt. **1981** Atl: 10 G; Int 1-25; 1 Fum TD; 6 Pt. **1982** Atl: 9 G; 3 Sac. **1983** Phi: 16 G; 2.5 Sac. **1984** Phi: 16 G; 1.5 Sac. **1985** Phi: 7 G. **1986** Atl: 15 G; Int 2-18 1 TD; 6 Pt. **1987** Atl: 8 G. **1988** Atl: 14 G. **1989** Atl: 10 G. **Total:** 137 G; Int 5-98 1 TD; Scor 1 Saf; 2 Fum TD; Tot TD 3; 20 Pt; 7 Sac.

JOEL WILLIAMS Williams, Joel David 6'3", 242 **TE**
Col: Notre Dame *HS:* Gateway [Monroeville, PA] B: 3/16/1965, Pittsburgh, PA *Drafted:* 1987 Round 8 Mia
1987 Mia: 3 G.

JOEL WILLIAMS Williams, Joel Herschel 6'1", 220 **C-LB**
Col: Texas *HS:* San Angelo [TX] B: 3/18/1926, San Angelo, TX *Drafted:* 1948 Round 20 Was
AAFC **1948** SF-A: 14 G.

NFL **1950** Bal: 12 G; Rush 0-50 1 TD; 6 Pt.

JOHN WILLIAMS Williams, John Alan 5'11", 213 **RB**
Col: Wisconsin *HS:* Reeths Puffer [Muskegon, MI] B: 10/26/1960, Muskegon, MI
1985 Dal-Sea: 10 G; Rush 14-42 3.0; KR 6-129 21.5; 3 Fum. Dal: 8 G; Rush 13-40 3.1; KR 6-129 21.5; 3 Fum. Sea: 2 G; Rush 1-2 2.0. **1986** NO: 7 G; Rec 1-5 5.0. **1987** Ind: 2 G. **Total:** 19 G; Rush 14-42 3.0; Rec 1-5 5.0; KR 6-129 21.5; 3 Fum.

JOHNNY WILLIAMS Williams, John Elliot 5'11", 177 **DB-HB**
(Scooter) *Col:* Compton CC CA; USC *HS:* Huntington Park [CA] B: 6/30/1927, Los Angeles, CA *Drafted:* 1951 Round 26 Was
1952 Was: Rush 2-3 1.5; Rec 1-13 13.0. **Total:** Rush 2-3 1.5; Rec 1-13 13.0.

		Punt Returns				Kickoff Returns			
Year Team	G	Ret	Yds	Avg	TD	Ret	Yds	Avg	TD
1952 Was	12	24	366	15.3	**2**	20	486	24.3	0
1953 Was	12	18	172	9.6	0	9	224	24.9	0
1954 SF	11	0	0	—	0	0	0	—	0
NFL Total	35	42	538	12.8	2	29	710	24.5	0

	Interceptions				Tot
Year Team	Int	Yds	TD	Fum	TD
1952 Was	5	97	1	5	3
1953 Was	6	26	0	0	0
1954 SF	3	28	0	0	0
NFL Total	14	151	1	5	3

JOHN L. WILLIAMS Williams, John L 5'11", 231 **RB**
Col: Florida *HS:* Palatka [FL] B: 11/23/1964, Palatka, FL *Drafted:* 1986 Round 1 Sea
1993 Sea: Pass 1-0. **Total:** Pass 1-0.

		Rushing				Receiving					Tot
Year Team	G	Att	Yds	Avg	TD	Rec	Yds	Avg	TD	Fum	TD
1986 Sea	16	129	538	4.2	0	33	219	6.6	0	1	0
1987 Sea	12	113	500	4.4	1	38	420	11.1	3	2	4
1988 Sea	16	189	877	4.6	4	58	651	11.2	3	0	7
1989 Sea	15	146	499	3.4	1	76	657	8.6	6	2	7
1990 Sea	16	187	714	3.8	3	73	699	9.6	0	5	3
1991 Sea	16	188	741	3.9	4	61	499	8.2	1	2	5
1992 Sea	16	114	339	3.0	1	74	556	7.5	2	4	3
1993 Sea	16	82	371	4.5	3	58	450	7.8	1	2	4
1994 Pit	15	68	317	4.7	1	51	378	7.4	2	0	3
1995 Pit	11	29	110	3.8	0	24	127	5.3	1	2	1
NFL Total	149	1245	5006	4.0	18	546	4656	8.5	19	20	37

JOHN WILLIAMS Williams, John McKay 6'3", 256 **OT-OG-DE**
Col: Minnesota *HS:* Edward D. Libbey [Toledo, OH] B: 10/27/1945, Jackson, MS *Drafted:* 1968 Round 1 Bal
1968 Bal: 14 G. **1969** Bal: 13 G. **1970** Bal: 14 G. **1971** Bal: 14 G. **1972** LARm: 14 G. **1973** LARm: 14 G. **1974** LARm: 14 G. **1975** LARm: 14 G. **1976** LARm: 14 G. **1977** LARm: 14 G. **1978** LARm: 16 G. **1979** LARm: 11 G. **Total:** 166 G.

JOHN WILLIAMS Williams, John Wesley 5'7", 180 **DB**
Col: Southern University *HS:* Hammonds [LA] B: 7/26/1974, Hammonds, LA
1997 Bal: 4 G. **1998** Bal: 16 G. **Total:** 20 G.

JON WILLIAMS Williams, Jonathan 5'9", 205 **RB**
Col: Penn State *HS:* Somerville [NJ] B: 6/1/1961, Somerville, NJ *Drafted:* 1984 Round 3 NE
1984 NE: 9 G; KR 23-461 20.0.

JOE WILLIAMS Williams, Joseph Alford 6'0", 238 **G-E-FB**
Col: Lafayette *HS:* Hamilton Inst. [New York, NY] B: 3/3/1896, New York, NY D: 1/18/1949
1923 Can: 8 G. **1925** NYG: 10 G; Rush 1 TD; 6 Pt. **1926** NYG: 12 G. **Total:** 30 G; Rush 1 TD; 6 Pt.

JOE WILLIAMS Williams, Joseph Dennis 6'4", 237 **LB**
Col: Grambling State *HS:* McKinley [Baton Rouge, LA] B: 3/5/1965, Baton Rouge, LA
1987 Pit: 3 G; 1 Sac.

JOE WILLIAMS Williams, Joseph Harold 6'0", 193 **RB**
Col: Wyoming *HS:* Dunbar [Lufkin, TX] B: 3/30/1947, Center, TX *Drafted:* 1970 Round 12 Dal
1971 Dal: Rec 3-59 19.7; KR 1-12 12.0. **1972** NO: Rec 16-116 7.3; KR 2-23 11.5. **Total:** Rec 19-175 9.2; KR 3-35 11.7.

		Rushing				
Year Team	G	Att	Yds	Avg	TD	Fum
1971 Dal	12	21	67	3.2	1	3
1972 NO	14	31	72	2.3	0	4
NFL Total	26	52	139	2.7	1	7

KARL WILLIAMS Williams, Karl Daneil 5'10", 174 **WR**
Col: Texas A&M–Kingsville *HS:* Rowlett [TX] B: 4/10/1971, Rowlett, TX
1996 TB: Rush 1-(-3) -3.0. **1997** TB: Rush 1-5 5.0. **Total:** Rush 2-2 1.0.

		Receiving				Punt Returns			
Year Team	G	Rec	Yds	Avg	TD	Ret	Yds	Avg	TD
1996 TB	16	22	246	11.2	0	13	274	21.1	1
1997 TB	16	33	486	14.7	4	46	597	13.0	1
1998 TB	13	21	252	12.0	1	10	83	8.3	0
NFL Total	45	76	984	12.9	5	69	954	13.8	2

	Kickoff Returns					Tot
Year Team	Ret	Yds	Avg	TD	Fum	TD
1996 TB	14	383	27.4	0	2	1
1997 TB	15	277	18.5	0	5	5
1998 TB	0	0	—	0	0	1
NFL Total	29	660	22.8	0	7	7

KEITH WILLIAMS Williams, Keith 5'10", 173 **WR-RB**
Col: Southwest Missouri State *HS:* Sumner [St. Louis, MO] B: 9/30/1964, St. Louis, MO *Drafted:* 1986 Round 6 Atl
1986 Atl: 12 G; Rush 3-18 6.0; Rec 12-164 13.7 1 TD; KR 14-255 18.2; 6 Pt; 1 Fum.

KENDALL WILLIAMS Williams, Kendall Edwin 5'9", 190 **DB**
Col: Long Beach City Coll. CA (J.C.); Arizona State *HS:* Long Beach Polytechnic [CA] B: 2/7/1959, Long Beach, CA
1983 Bal: 16 G; PR 9-43 4.8; KR 20-490 24.5; Int 1-32; 2 Fum; 1 Sac.

KEVIN WILLIAMS Williams, Kevin 6'0", 190 **DB**
Col: Oklahoma State *HS:* Watson Chapel [Pine Bluff, AR] B: 8/4/1975, Pine Bluff, AR *Drafted:* 1998 Round 3 NYJ
1998 NYJ: 15 G; KR 11-230 20.9; Int 1-34.

KEVIN WILLIAMS Williams, Kevin Deleon 6'0", 208 **RB**
Col: UCLA *HS:* Spring [TX] B: 2/17/1970, Marshall, TX *Drafted:* 1993 Round 5 Den
1993 GB: 3 G.

KEVIN WILLIAMS Williams, Kevin J 5'9", 169 **DB**
Col: San Diego City Coll. CA (J.C.); Iowa State *HS:* Crawford [San Diego, CA] B: 11/28/1961, San Diego, CA
1985 Was: 12 G. **1986** Buf: 1 G. **1988** Was: 5 G. **Total:** 18 G.

KEVIN WILLIAMS Williams, Kevin Lewis 5'8", 164 **WR**
Col: USC *HS:* San Fernando [CA] B: 1/7/1958, Los Angeles, CA D: 2/1/1996, Cajon Junction, CA *Drafted:* 1981 Round 7 NO
1981 Bal: 11 G; KR 20-399 20.0; 4 Fum.

KEVIN WILLIAMS Williams, Kevin Ray 5'9", 195 **WR**
Col: Miami (Fla.) *HS:* Franklin D. Roosevelt [Dallas, TX] B: 1/25/1971, Dallas, TX *Drafted:* 1993 Round 2 Dal

		Rushing				Receiving			
Year Team	G	Att	Yds	Avg	TD	Rec	Yds	Avg	TD
1993 Dal	16	7	26	3.7	2	20	151	7.6	2
1994 Dal	15	6	20	3.3	0	13	181	13.9	0
1995 Dal	16	10	53	5.3	0	38	613	16.1	2
1996 Dal	10	4	11	2.8	0	27	323	12.0	1
1997 Ariz	16	1	-2	-2.0	0	20	273	13.7	1
1998 Buf	16	5	46	9.2	0	29	392	13.5	1
NFL Total	89	33	154	4.7	2	147	1933	13.1	7

	Punt Returns				Kickoff Returns					Tot
Year Team	Ret	Yds	Avg	TD	Ret	Yds	Avg	TD	Fum	TD
1993 Dal	36	381	10.6	**2**	31	689	22.2	0	8	6
1994 Dal	39	349	8.9	1	43	1148	26.7	1	4	2
1995 Dal	18	166	9.2	0	49	1108	22.6	0	3	2
1996 Dal	2	17	8.5	0	21	471	22.4	0	0	1
1997 Ariz	40	462	11.6	0	59	**1458**	24.7	0	3	1
1998 Buf	37	369	10.0	0	47	1059	22.5	0	3	1
NFL Total	172	1744	10.1	3	250	5933	23.7	1	21	13

BROOKS WILLIAMS Williams, Kim Brooks 6'4", 226 **TE**
Col: North Carolina *HS:* Frank W. Cox [Virginia Beach, VA]
B: 12/7/1954, Baltimore, MD *Drafted:* 1978 Round 8 NO
1979 NO: KR 2-12 6.0. **1981** NO-ChiB: KR 1-35 35.0. ChiB: KR 1-35 35.0. **Total:** KR 3-47 15.7.

Year Team	G	Receiving Rec	Yds	Avg	TD	Fum
1978 NO	16	0	0	—	0	0
1979 NO	16	2	22	11.0	0	0
1980 NO	12	26	351	13.5	2	1
1981 NO-ChiB	12	8	82	10.3	0	0
1981 NO	7	5	50	10.0	0	0
1981 ChiB	5	3	32	10.7	0	0
1982 ChiB	9	0	0	—	0	0
1983 NE	13	1	0	0.0	0	0
NFL Total	78	37	455	12.3	2	1

LAMANZER WILLIAMS Williams, Lamanzer Deshan 6'4", 276 **DE**
Col: Minnesota *HS:* Willow Run [Ypsilanti, MI] B: 11/17/1974, Greensboro, AL *Drafted:* 1998 Round 6 Jac
1998 Jac: 2 G.

LARRY WILLIAMS Williams, Lawrence Richard II 6'5", 292 **OG-C**
Col: Notre Dame *HS:* Mater Dei [Santa Ana, CA] B: 7/3/1963, Orange, CA *Drafted:* 1985 Round 10 Cle
1986 Cle: 16 G. **1987** Cle: 12 G. **1988** Cle: 14 G. **1991** NO: 6 G. **1992** NE: 13 G. **Total:** 61 G.

LEE WILLIAMS Williams, Lee Eric 6'6", 270 **DE-DT**
Col: Bethune-Cookman *HS:* Stranahan [Fort Lauderdale, FL]
B: 10/15/1962, Fort Lauderdale, FL *Drafted:* 1984 Supplemental Round 1 SD
1984 SD: 8 G; Int 1-66 1 TD; 6 Pt; 1 Sac. **1985** SD: 16 G; Int 1-17; 9 Sac. **1986** SD: 16 G; 15 Sac. **1987** SD: 12 G; Scor **1** Saf; 2 Pt; 8 Sac. **1988** SD: 16 G; 11 Sac. **1989** SD: 16 G; 14 Sac. **1990** SD: 16 G; 7.5 Sac. **1991** Hou: 10 G; 3 Sac. **1992** Hou: 16 G; 11 Sac. **1993** Hou: 14 G; 3 Sac. **Total:** 140 G; Int 2-83 1 TD; Scor 1 Saf; 8 Pt; 82.5 Sac.

LEONARD WILLIAMS Williams, Leonard Jr. 6'0", 205 **RB**
Col: Western Carolina *HS:* Eastern Guilford [Gibsonville, NC]
B: 6/27/1960, Man, WV
1987 Buf: 2 G; Rush 9-25 2.8; Rec 1-5 5.0.

LESTER WILLIAMS Williams, Lester 6'3", 275 **NT-DE**
Col: Miami (Fla.) *HS:* Miami Carol City [Miami, FL] B: 1/19/1959, Miami, FL *Drafted:* 1982 Round 1 NE
1982 NE: 9 G; 2 Sac. **1983** NE: 15 G; 1 Sac. **1984** NE: 7 G; 1.5 Sac. **1985** NE: 9 G; 1 Sac. **1986** SD: 4 G. **1987** Sea: 2 G; 1 Sac. **Total:** 46 G; 6.5 Sac.

BEN WILLIAMS Williams, Lewis Ben 6'2", 265 **DT**
Col: Minnesota *HS:* Humphreys Co. [Belzoni, MS] B: 5/28/1970, Belzoni, MS
1998 Min: 1 G.

MARK WILLIAMS Williams, Mark Anthony 6'3", 240 **LB**
Col: Ohio State *HS:* Bishop McNamara [Forestville, MD] B: 5/17/1971, Camp Springs, MD
1994 GB: 16 G. **1995** Jac: 11 G. **1996** StL: 2 G. **Total:** 29 G.

MARVIN WILLIAMS Williams, Marvin Lee 6'3", 233 **TE**
Col: Coll. of Marin CA (J.C.); Cal State-Fullerton *HS:* Santa Rosa [CA]
B: 10/11/1963
1987 Was: 2 G.

MOE WILLIAMS Williams, Maurece Jabari 6'1", 206 **RB**
Col: Kentucky *HS:* William H. Spencer [Columbus, GA] B: 7/26/1974, Columbus, GA *Drafted:* 1996 Round 3 Min
1996 Min: 9 G. **1997** Min: 14 G; Rush 22-59 2.7 1 TD; Rec 4-14 3.5; KR 16-388 24.3; 6 Pt. **1998** Min: 12 G; Rec 1-64 64.0; KR 2-19 9.5; 1 Fum. **Total:** 35 G; Rush 22-59 2.7 1 TD; Rec 5-78 15.6; KR 18-407 22.6; 6 Pt; 1 Fum.

MAXIE WILLIAMS Williams, Maxie Foy 6'4", 250 **OG-OT**
Col: Southeastern Louisiana *HS:* Granite Falls [NC] B: 6/28/1940, Granite Falls, NC *Drafted:* 1965 Round 10 Hou
1965 Hou: 14 G; KR 1-23 23.0. **1966** Mia: 14 G. **1967** Mia: 14 G. **1968** Mia: 14 G. **1969** Mia: 14 G. **1970** Mia: 13 G. **Total:** 83 G; KR 1-23 23.0.

GEROME WILLIAMS Williams, Meltrix Gerome 6'2", 210 **DB**
Col: Houston *HS:* Kempner [Houston, TX] B: 7/9/1973, Houston, TX
1997 SD: 6 G. **1998** SD: 16 G. **Total:** 22 G.

MIKE WILLIAMS Williams, Michael 6'4", 249 **TE**
Col: Alabama A&M *HS:* Lafayette [AL] B: 8/27/1959, Lafayette, AL
Drafted: 1982 Round 5 Was
1982 Was: 6 G; Rec 3-14 4.7. **1983** Was: 7 G. **1984** Was: 1 G. **Total:** 14 G; Rec 3-14 4.7.

MICHAEL WILLIAMS Williams, Michael 6'2", 220 **RB**
Col: Northeast Mississippi CC; Mississippi College *HS:* Escambia Co. [Altmore, AL] B: 7/16/1961, Altmore, AL *Drafted:* 1983 Round 4 Phi
1983 Phi: KR 3-59 19.7. **1987** Atl: KR 2-15 7.5. **Total:** KR 5-74 14.8.

Year Team	G	Rushing Att	Yds	Avg	TD	Receiving Rec	Yds	Avg	TD	Fum
1983 Phi	15	103	385	3.7	0	17	142	8.4	0	1
1984 Phi	16	33	83	2.5	0	7	47	6.7	0	1
1987 Atl	3	14	49	3.5	0	9	70	7.8	0	0
NFL Total	34	150	517	3.4	0	33	259	7.8	0	2

MIKE WILLIAMS Williams, Michael Anthony 6'3", 222 **FB-TE**
Col: New Mexico *HS:* Parkland [El Paso, TX] B: 10/14/1957, New Kingston, PA *Drafted:* 1979 Round 8 KC
1979 KC: Rec 16-129 8.1 2 TD. **1980** KC: Rec 2-9 4.5 1 TD; KR 4-79 19.8. **1981** KC: Rec 1-3 3.0; KR 1-7 7.0. **Total:** Rec 19-141 7.4 3 TD; KR 5-86 17.2.

Year Team	G	Rushing Att	Yds	Avg	TD	Fum	Tot TD
1979 KC	14	69	261	3.8	1	2	3
1980 KC	16	0	0	—	0	0	1
1981 KC	3	2	0	0.0	0	0	0
NFL Total	33	71	261	3.7	1	2	4

MICHAEL WILLIAMS Williams, Michael Dean 5'10", 185 **DB**
Col: UCLA *HS:* Crenshaw [Los Angeles, CA] B: 5/28/1970, Los Angeles, CA
1995 SF: 4 G.

MIKE WILLIAMS Williams, Michael J 5'10", 177 **WR**
Col: Northeastern *HS:* John Jay [Katonah, NY] B: 10/9/1966, Mount Kisco, NY *Drafted:* 1989 Round 10 LARm
1992 Mia: Rec 3-43 14.3. **1993** Mia: Rec 1-11 11.0. **1994** Mia: Rec 15-221 14.7. **1995** Mia: Rec 2-17 8.5. **Total:** Rec 21-292 13.9.

Year Team	G	Kickoff Returns Ret	Yds	Avg	TD	Fum
1989 Det	1	0	0	—	0	0
1991 Mia	3	0	0	—	0	0
1992 Mia	15	19	328	17.3	0	1
1993 Mia	13	8	180	22.5	0	1
1994 Mia	15	2	9	4.5	0	0
1995 Mia	12	0	0	—	0	0
NFL Total	59	29	517	17.8	0	2

MIKE WILLIAMS Williams, Mikell Herman 5'10", 181 **DB**
Col: Louisiana State *HS:* Covington [LA] B: 11/22/1953, New Orleans, LA *Drafted:* 1975 Round 1 SD
1976 SD: PR 5-23 4.6. **1977** SD: PR 1-0. **1978** SD: PR 1-0. **1979** SD: PR 3-19 6.3. **Total:** PR 10-42 4.2.

Year Team	G	Interceptions Int	Yds	TD	Fum
1975 SD	14	4	67	0	0
1976 SD	14	4	76	0	0
1977 SD	10	3	36	0	1
1978 SD	16	3	23	0	1
1979 SD	16	4	55	0	0
1980 SD	14	1	0	0	0
1981 SD	14	3	0	0	0
1982 SD	9	2	12	0	0
1983 LARm	2	0	0	0	0
NFL Total	109	24	269	0	2

NEWTON WILLIAMS Williams, Newton Dennis 5'10", 204 **RB**
Col: Arizona State *HS:* North Mecklenburg [Huntersville, NC]
B: 5/10/1959, Charlotte, NC *Drafted:* 1982 Round 5 SF
1983 Bal: Rec 4-46 11.5. **Total:** Rec 4-46 11.5.

Year Team	G	Rushing Att	Yds	Avg	TD
1982 SF	6	0	0	—	0
1983 Bal	16	28	77	2.8	0
NFL Total	22	28	77	2.8	0

OLIVER WILLIAMS Williams, Oliver Lavell Jr. 6'3", 194 **WR**
Col: Los Angeles Harbor Coll. CA (J.C.); Illinois *HS:* Junipero Serra [Gardena, CA] B: 10/17/1960, Chicago, IL *Drafted:* 1983 Round 12 ChiB
1985 Ind: 8 G; Rec 9-175 19.4 1 TD; KR 3-44 14.7; 6 Pt; 2 Fum. **1986** Ind: 3 G; KR 1-15 15.0; 1 Fum. **1987** Hou: 3 G; Rec 11-165 15.0 1 TD; 6 Pt; 1 Fum. **Total:** 14 G; Rec 20-340 17.0 2 TD; KR 4-59 14.8; 12 Pt; 4 Fum.

PAT WILLIAMS Williams, Patrick 6'3", 270 **DT**
Col: Navarro Coll. TX (J.C.); Northeastern State (Okla.); Texas A&M
HS: Woosman [Monroe, LA] B: 10/24/1972, Monroe, LA
1997 Buf: 1 G. **1998** Buf: 13 G; 3.5 Sac. **Total:** 14 G; 3.5 Sac.

PERRY WILLIAMS Williams, Perry Andrew 6'2", 219 **RB**
Col: Purdue *HS:* Withrow [Cincinnati, OH] B: 12/11/1946, Cincinnati, OH *Drafted:* 1969 Round 4 GB
1969 GB: KR 1-0. **1970** GB: KR 1-20 20.0. **1971** GB: KR 2-41 20.5. **1972** GB: KR 1-9 9.0. **1973** GB: KR 1-24 24.0. **Total:** KR 6-94 15.7.

		Rushing				Receiving				
Year Team	G	Att	Yds	Avg	TD	Rec	Yds	Avg	TD	Fum
1969 GB	14	18	55	3.1	0	4	63	15.8	0	1
1970 GB	13	17	44	2.6	0	3	11	3.7	0	1
1971 GB	14	3	4	1.3	0	0	0	—	0	0
1972 GB	14	33	139	4.2	0	0	0	—	0	1
1973 GB	14	32	87	2.7	1	5	44	8.8	0	1
1974 ChiB	14	74	218	2.9	1	25	167	6.7	0	2
NFL Total	83	177	547	3.1	2	37	285	7.7	0	6

PERRY WILLIAMS Williams, Perry Lamar 6'2", 203 **DB**
Col: North Carolina State *HS:* Richmond [Rockingham, NC] B: 5/12/1961, Hamlet, NC *Drafted:* 1983 Round 7 NYG
1985 NYG: 2 Sac. **1986** NYG: 1 Sac. **1988** NYG: 2 Sac. **Total:** 5 Sac.

		Interceptions			
Year Team	G	Int	Yds	TD	Fum
1984 NYG	16	3	7	0	0
1985 NYG	16	2	28	0	0
1986 NYG	16	4	31	0	0
1987 NYG	10	1	-5	0	0
1988 NYG	16	1	0	0	0
1989 NYG	16	3	14	0	1
1990 NYG	16	3	4	0	0
1991 NYG	16	0	0	0	0
1992 NYG	16	1	0	0	0
1993 NYG	8	0	0	0	0
NFL Total	146	18	79	0	1

PERRY WILLIAMS Williams, Perry Michael 6'1", 200 **DB**
Col: Clemson *HS:* St.Matthews [Adairsville, GA] B: 4/12/1964, Cartersville, GA
1987 NE: 3 G; Int 1-0.

PRYOR WILLIAMS Williams, Pryor Allen 6'1", 226 **G-C**
(Pig Iron) *Col:* Auburn; Vanderbilt *HS:* Greene School [Athens, AL] B: 12/26/1893, Athens, AL D: Birmingham, AL
1921 Det: 3 G.

RALPH WILLIAMS Williams, Ralph 6'3", 280 **OT-OG**
Col: Southern University *HS:* West [Monroe, LA] B: 3/27/1958, Monroe, LA
1982 Hou: 7 G. **1983** Hou: 1 G. **1985** NO: 16 G. **1986** NO: 6 G. **Total:** 30 G.

RAY WILLIAMS Williams, Raymond Darrell 5'9", 170 **RB**
Col: Washington State *HS:* San Fernando [CA] B: 9/22/1958, Welch, WV *Drafted:* 1980 Round 12 Det
1980 Det: Rush 2-17 8.5 1 TD; Rec 10-146 14.6 1 TD; KR 9-228 25.3 **1** TD.

		Punt Returns				Tot
Year Team	G	Ret	Yds	Avg	TD	TD
1980 Det	6	27	259	9.6	0	3

RAY WILLIAMS Williams, Raymond Michael 5'11", 180 **DB**
Col: Rhode Island *HS:* Bishop Hendrickson [Werwick, RI] B: 11/9/1965, Providence, RI
1987 Pit: 1 G; Int 1-0.

REGGIE WILLIAMS Williams, Reginald 6'1", 228 **LB**
Col: Dartmouth *HS:* Southwestern [Flint, MI] B: 9/19/1954, Flint, MI *Drafted:* 1976 Round 3 Cin
1977 Cin: PR 1-0. **1980** Cin: PR 1-0; Scor **1** Saf. **1982** Cin: Scor **1** Saf; 4.5 Sac. **1983** Cin: 1 Fum TD; 7.5 Sac. **1984** Cin: 9 Sac. **1985** Cin: 3.5 Sac. **1986** Cin: 4.5 Sac. **1987** Cin: 6 Sac. **1988** Cin: 2.5 Sac. **1989** Cin: 3.5 Sac. **Total:** PR 2-0; Scor 2 Saf; 1 Fum TD; 41 Sac.

		Interceptions				Tot
Year Team	G	Int	Yds	TD	Fum	TD
1976 Cin	14	1	17	0	0	0
1977 Cin	14	3	67	**1**	1	2
1978 Cin	16	1	11	0	0	0
1979 Cin	12	2	5	0	0	0
1980 Cin	14	2	8	0	1	0
1981 Cin	16	4	33	0	0	0
1982 Cin	9	1	20	0	0	0
1983 Cin	16	0	0	0	0	1
1984 Cin	16	2	33	0	0	0
1985 Cin	16	0	0	0	0	0
1986 Cin	16	0	0	0	0	0
1987 Cin	15	0	0	0	0	0
1988 Cin	16	0	0	0	0	0
1989 Cin	16	0	0	0	0	0
NFL Total	206	16	194	1	2	3

REX WILLIAMS Williams, Rex B 6'2", 203 **C-LB**
(Pinky) *Col:* Texas Tech *HS:* Sherman [TX] B: 7/16/1916, Bonham, TX D: 11/1980, Rogers, AR *Drafted:* 1940 Round 5 NYG
1940 ChiC: 2 G. **1945** Det: 1 G. **Total:** 3 G.

RICHARD WILLIAMS Williams, Richard Jr. 5'11", 170 **WR**
Col: Abilene Christian *HS:* Gainesville [FL] B: 1/30/1952, Campville, FL *Drafted:* 1974 Round 4 Cin
1974 NO: 2 G.

RICHARD WILLIAMS Williams, Richard Keith 6'0", 205 **RB**
Col: Memphis *HS:* Eustis [FL] B: 8/13/1960, Eustis, FL *Drafted:* 1983 Round 2 Was
1983 Atl: Rush 1-5 5.0. **Total:** Rush 1-5 5.0.

		Kickoff Returns				
Year Team	G	Ret	Yds	Avg	TD	Fum
1983 Atl	14	23	461	20.0	0	1
1984 Atl-Hou	8	5	84	16.8	0	0
1984 Atl	1	0	0	—	0	0
1984 Hou	7	5	84	16.8	0	0
NFL Total	22	28	545	19.5	0	1

RICKY WILLIAMS Williams, Ricky C 6'1", 195 **RB**
Col: Santa Monica Coll. CA (J.C.); Langston *HS:* Santa Monica [CA] B: 4/27/1960, Santa Monica, CA
1985 LARd: 2 G. **1987** LARd: 1 G. **Total:** 3 G.

BOB WILLIAMS Williams, Robert Allen 6'1", 197 **QB**
Col: Notre Dame *HS:* Loyola [Towson, MD] B: 1/2/1930, Cumberland, MD *Drafted:* 1951 Round 1 ChiB
1951 ChiB: Punt 4-145 36.3. **1952** ChiB: Punt 2-90 45.0. **1955** ChiB: Punt 13-508 39.1. **Total:** Punt 19-743 39.1.

		Passing							
Year Team	G	Att	Comp	Comp%	Yds	YPA	TD	Int	Rating
1951 ChiB	8	33	14	42.4	146	4.42	1	2	40.7
1952 ChiB	11	87	45	51.7	579	6.66	6	5	72.0
1955 ChiB	10	40	15	37.5	256	6.40	3	5	45.4
NFL Total	29	160	74	46.3	981	6.13	10	12	55.8

	Rushing				
Year Team	Att	Yds	Avg	TD	Fum
1951 ChiB	5	0	0.0	0	2
1952 ChiB	11	33	3.0	0	3
1955 ChiB	13	79	6.1	0	0
NFL Total	29	112	3.9	0	5

ROBERT WILLIAMS Williams, Robert Anthony 5'11", 202 **DB**
Col: Eastern Illinois *HS:* Dunbar [Chicago, IL] B: 9/26/1962, Chicago, IL
1984 Pit: 2 G.

ROBERT WILLIAMS Williams, Robert Cole 5'10", 190 **DB**
Col: Baylor *HS:* Ball [Galveston, TX] B: 10/2/1962, Galveston, TX
1987 Dal: 11 G. **1988** Dal: 16 G; Int 2-18. **1989** Dal: 13 G. **1990** Dal: 16 G; Int 1-0. **1991** Dal: 16 G; Int 1-24; 6 Pt; 1 Sac. **1992** Dal: 9 G; 6 Pt. **1993** Dal: 4 G. **Total:** 85 G; Int 4-42; 12 Pt; 1 Sac.

BEN WILLIAMS Williams, Robert Jerry 6'3", 251 **DE-NT**
Col: Mississippi *HS:* Yazoo City [MS] B: 9/1/1954, Yazoo City, MS *Drafted:* 1976 Round 3 Buf
1976 Buf: 13 G. **1977** Buf: 14 G. **1978** Buf: 16 G. **1979** Buf: 16 G. **1980** Buf: 16 G. **1981** Buf: 16 G; Int 1-0; Scor **1** Saf; 2 Pt. **1982** Buf: 9 G; Int 1-20; 4 Sac. **1983** Buf: 16 G; 10 Sac. **1984** Buf: 15 G; 2 Sac. **1985** Buf: 16 G; 1.5 Sac. **Total:** 147 G; Int 2-20; Scor 1 Saf; 2 Pt; 17.5 Sac.

ROBERT WILLIAMS Williams, Robert M 5'10", 177 **DB**
Col: North Carolina *HS:* Shelby [NC] B: 5/29/1977, Shelby, NC *Drafted:* 1998 Round 5 KC
1998 KC: 16 G; 0.5 Sac.

RODNEY WILLIAMS Williams, Rodney Allen 6'0", 185 **WR**
Col: Pierce Coll. CA (J.C.); Arizona *HS:* Palmdale [CA] B: 8/15/1973, Santa Monica, CA
1998 Oak: 1 G; KR 4-63 15.8; 1 Fum.

ROGER WILLIAMS Williams, Roger J 5'10", 180 **DB-WR**
Col: Grambling State *HS:* Moley [Jeanerette,LA] B: 7/1/1945, Jeanerette, LA *Drafted:* 1969 Round 13 LARm
1971 LARm: 4 G; KR 4-100 25.0; 1 Fum. **1972** LARm: 14 G; KR 6-141 23.5; 1 Fum. **Total:** 18 G; KR 10-241 24.1; 2 Fum.

ROLAND WILLIAMS Williams, Roland Lamar 6'5", 269 **TE**
Col: Syracuse *HS:* East [Rochester, NY] B: 4/27/1975, Rochester, NY *Drafted:* 1998 Round 4 StL
1998 StL: 13 G; Rec 15-144 9.6 1 TD; 6 Pt.

ROLLIE WILLIAMS Williams, Rolland Franklin 5'8", 170 **WB-BB**
Col: Wisconsin *HS:* Edgerton [WI] B: 10/11/1897, Edgerton, WI D: 4/5/1968, North Liberty, IA
1923 Rac: 2 G; Rush 1 TD; 6 Pt.

RONNIE WILLIAMS Williams, Ronald 6'3", 262 **TE**
Col: Oklahoma State *HS:* S.H. Rider [Wichita Falls, TX] B: 1/19/1966, Wichita Falls, TX
1993 Mia: 11 G. **1994** Mia: 14 G; Rec 2-26 13.0; KR 2-25 12.5. **1995** Mia: 16 G; Rec 3-28 9.3; KR 2-20 10.0. **1996** Sea: 14 G; Rec 5-25 5.0 1 TD; 6 Pt. **Total:** 55 G; Rec 10-79 7.9 1 TD; KR 4-45 11.3; 6 Pt.

ROY WILLIAMS Williams, Roy Orville 6'7", 265 **DT**
Col: U. of Pacific *HS:* Pasco [WA] B: 4/30/1937, Moorhead, MN
Drafted: 1963 Round 2 Det
1963 SF: 7 G.

SAM WILLIAMS Williams, Samuel Charles 6'2", 192 **DB**
Col: New Mexico Highlands; California *HS:* Rockdale [TX]
B: 7/22/1952, Cameron, TX *Drafted:* 1974 Round 12 SD
1974 SD: 13 G; Int 1-25. **1975** SD: 11 G; Int 1-0. **1976** Hou: 4 G. **Total:** 28 G; Int 2-25.

SAM WILLIAMS Williams, Samuel F 6'5", 235 **DE-OE-LB**
Col: Michigan State *HS:* Dansville [MI] B: 3/9/1931, Dansville, MI
Drafted: 1956 Round 24 LARm
1959 LARm: 12 G; Scor **1** Saf; 2 Pt. **1960** Det: 12 G. **1961** Det: 12 G; Rec 1-10 10.0; KR 1-4 4.0. **1962** Det: 13 G; Int 1-22 **1** TD; **1** Fum TD; Tot TD 2; 12 Pt. **1963** Det: 14 G. **1964** Det: 14 G; 1 Fum TD; 6 Pt. **1965** Det: 14 G. **1966** Atl: 14 G. **1967** Atl: 14 G. **Total:** 119 G; Rec 1-10 10.0; KR 1-4 4.0; Int 1-22 1 TD; Scor 1 Saf; 2 Fum TD; Tot TD 3; 20 Pt.

SHAUN WILLIAMS Williams, Shaun LeJon 6'2", 215 **DB**
Col: UCLA *HS:* Crespi [Encino, CA] B: 10/10/1976, Los Angeles, CA
Drafted: 1998 Round 1 NYG
1998 NYG: 13 G; Int 2-6.

SHERMAN WILLIAMS Williams, Sherman Cedric 5'8", 198 **RB**
Col: Alabama *HS:* Mattie T. Blount [Prichard, AL] B: 8/13/1973, Mobile, AL *Drafted:* 1995 Round 2 Dal
1996 Dal: Pass 1-0. **1998** Dal: KR 4-103 25.8. **Total:** Pass 1-0; KR 4-103 25.8.

		Rushing				Receiving				
Year Team	G	Att	Yds	Avg	TD	Rec	Yds	Avg	TD	Fum
1995 Dal	11	48	205	4.3	1	3	28	9.3	0	2
1996 Dal	16	69	269	3.9	0	5	41	8.2	0	2
1997 Dal	16	121	468	3.9	2	21	159	7.6	0	5
1998 Dal	16	64	220	3.4	1	11	104	9.5	0	0
NFL Total	59	302	1162	3.8	4	40	332	8.3	0	9

SID WILLIAMS Williams, Sidney 6'2", 235 **LB**
Col: Southern University *HS:* Phillis Wheatley [Houston, TX]
B: 3/24/1942, Shreveport, LA *Drafted:* 1964 Round 16 Cle
1964 Cle: 14 G; PR 1-0; KR 1-0; 6 Pt. **1965** Cle: 14 G; Int 1-0. **1966** Cle: 13 G. **1967** Was: 10 G. **1968** Bal: 12 G. **1969** Pit: 7 G. **Total:** 70 G; PR 1-0; KR 1-0; Int 1-0; 6 Pt.

STAN WILLIAMS Williams, Stanley Neil 6'2", 195 **DB-OE**
Col: Baylor *HS:* Cisco [TX] B: 12/5/1929, Callahan Co., TX
Drafted: 1952 Round 8 Cle
1952 Dal: 12 G; Rec 9-123 13.7; Int 5-84; 1 Fum TD; 6 Pt; 1 Fum.

STEPFRET WILLIAMS Williams, Stepfret 6'0", 170 **WR**
Col: Northeast Louisiana *HS:* Minden [LA] B: 6/14/1973, Minden, LA
Drafted: 1996 Round 3 Dal
1997 Dal: PR 2-14 7.0. **1998** Cin: PR 2-16 8.0; KR 1-20 20.0.
Total: PR 4-30 7.5; KR 1-20 20.0.

		Receiving			
Year Team	G	Rec	Yds	Avg	TD
1996 Dal	5	1	32	32.0	0
1997 Dal	16	30	308	10.3	1
1998 Cin	5	6	81	13.5	1
NFL Total	26	37	421	11.4	2

STEVEN WILLIAMS Williams, Steven Ford 6'6", 260 **DE**
Col: Western Carolina *HS:* Eau Claire [Columbia, SC] B: 1/12/1951, Columbia, SC *Drafted:* 1972 Round 10 SF
1974 Bal: 12 G.

TERRY WILLIAMS Williams, Terrance 5'11", 197 **DB**
Col: Bethune-Cookman *HS:* South Dade [Homestead, FL]
B: 10/14/1965, Homestead, FL *Drafted:* 1988 Round 2 NYJ
1988 NYJ: 8 G. **1989** NYJ: 3 G. **Total:** 11 G.

TED WILLIAMS Williams, Theodore Patrick 5'11", 183 **FB-LB-HB-DB**
Col: Notre Dame; Boston College *HS:* Gloucester [MA] B: 6/3/1916, Bay Bulls, Canada D: 10/30/1993, Gloucester, MA *Drafted:* 1942 Round 3 Phi
1942 Phi: Rec 9-58 6.4; KR 3-58 19.3. **1944** Bos: Pass 6-0, 2 Int; Rec 6-28 4.7; PR 1-13 13.0; KR 6-82 13.7; Int 1-54. **Total:** Pass 6-0, 2 Int; Rec 15-86 5.7; PR 1-13 13.0; KR 9-140 15.6; Int 1-54.

		Rushing			
Year Team	G	Att	Yds	Avg	TD
1942 Phi	11	50	183	3.7	2
1944 Bos	10	52	13	0.3	1
NFL Total	21	102	196	1.9	3

TOBY WILLIAMS Williams, Tobias 6'3", 264 **DT-NT**
Col: Nebraska *HS:* Woodrow Wilson [Washington, DC] B: 11/19/1959, Washington, DC *Drafted:* 1983 Round 10 NE
1983 NE: 16 G; 2 Sac. **1984** NE: 16 G; 6 Sac. **1985** NE: 5 G; 2 Sac. **1986** NE: 16 G; 0.5 Sac. **1987** NE: 12 G; 4.5 Sac. **1988** NE: 15 G. **Total:** 80 G; 15 Sac.

TONY WILLIAMS Williams, Tony Demetric 6'1", 288 **DT**
Col: Memphis *HS:* Oakhaven [Memphis, TN]; Germantown HS [TN]
B: 7/9/1975, Germantown, TN *Drafted:* 1997 Round 5 Min
1997 Min: 6 G. **1998** Min: 14 G; 1 Sac. **Total:** 20 G; 1 Sac.

TRAVIS WILLIAMS Williams, Travis 6'1", 210 **RB**
(Roadrunner) *Col:* Contra Costa Coll. CA (J.C.); Arizona State
HS: Harry Ellis [Richmond, CA] B: 1/14/1946, El Dorado, AR
D: 2/17/1991, Martinez, CA *Drafted:* 1967 Round 4 GB
1969 GB: PR 8-189 23.6 **1** TD. **1970** GB: PR 4-20 5.0. **1971** LARm: PR 1-4 4.0. **Total:** PR 13-213 16.4 1 TD.

		Rushing				Receiving			
Year Team	G	Att	Yds	Avg	TD	Rec	Yds	Avg	TD
1967 GB	14	35	188	5.4	1	5	80	16.0	1
1968 GB	14	33	63	1.9	0	5	48	9.6	0
1969 GB	13	129	536	4.2	4	27	275	10.2	3
1970 GB	7	74	276	3.7	1	12	127	10.6	1
1971 LARm	14	18	103	5.7	0	3	68	22.7	0
NFL Total	62	289	1166	4.0	6	52	598	11.5	5

	Kickoff Returns					Tot
Year Team	Ret	Yds	Avg	TD	Fum	TD
1967 GB	18	739	**41.1**	**4**	1	6
1968 GB	28	599	21.4	0	3	0
1969 GB	21	517	24.6	**1**	5	9
1970 GB	10	203	20.3	0	0	2
1971 LARm	25	743	**29.7**	1	3	1
NFL Total	102	2801	27.5	**6**	12	18

TRAVIS WILLIAMS Williams, Travis Bill 6'0", 200 **WB-T**
(Bull; Bill) *Col:* Indiana *HS:* Boonville [IN] B: 1/5/1892, Boonville, IN
D: Evansville, IN
1921 Eva: 3 G; Rush 1 TD; 6 Pt. **1922** Eva: 1 G. **Total:** 4 G; Rush 1 TD; 6 Pt.

TYRONE WILLIAMS Williams, Tyrone M 6'4", 292 **DE**
Col: Wyoming *HS:* La Vista [Papillon, NE] B: 10/22/1972, Philadelphia, PA
1997 ChiB: 3 G.

TYRONE WILLIAMS Williams, Tyrone Robert 6'5", 220 **WR**
Col: Western Ontario (Canada) *HS:* George Harvey Sec. School [Toronto, Canada];Queen Elizabeth Sec. Sch. [Halifax] B: 3/26/1970, Halifax, Canada *Drafted:* 1992 Round 9 Pho
1993 Dal: 5 G; Rec 1-25 25.0.

TYRONE WILLIAMS Williams, Upton Tyrone 5'11", 192 **DB**
Col: Nebraska *HS:* Manatee [Bradenton, FL] B: 5/31/1973, Bradenton, FL *Drafted:* 1996 Round 3 GB
1996 GB: 16 G. **1997** GB: 16 G; Int 1-0. **1998** GB: 16 G; Int 5-40.
Total: 48 G; Int 6-40.

VAUGHN WILLIAMS Williams, Vaughn Aaron 6'2", 193 **DB**
Col: Stanford *HS:* George Washington [Denver, CO] B: 12/14/1961, Denver, CO
1984 Ind: 10 G.

VINCE WILLIAMS Williams, Vincent Bernard 6'0", 231 **RB**
Col: Oregon *HS:* Mount Tahoma [Tacoma, WA] B: 10/24/1959, Tacoma, WA *Drafted:* 1982 Round 6 SF
1982 SF: 2 G; Rush 20-68 3.4; Rec 4-33 8.3. **1983** SF: 1 G. **Total:** 3 G; Rush 20-68 3.4; Rec 4-33 8.3.

WALLY WILLIAMS Williams, Wally James Jr. 6'2", 305 **C**
Col: Florida A&M *HS:* James S. Rickards [Tallahassee, FL]
B: 2/19/1971, Tallahassee, FL
1993 Cle: 2 G. **1994** Cle: 11 G. **1995** Cle: 16 G. **1996** Bal: 15 G. **1997** Bal: 10 G. **1998** Bal: 13 G. **Total:** 67 G.

WALT WILLIAMS Williams, Walter 6'1", 185 **DB**
Col: Ashland; New Mexico State *HS:* Hillcrest [Bedford Hills, NY]
B: 7/10/1954, Bedford Hills, NY *Drafted:* 1977 Round 2 Det
1977 Det: 14 G. **1978** Det: 15 G; PR 1-1 1.0; Int 1-2. **1979** Det: 12 G; Int 2-39 1 TD; 6 Pt. **1980** Det: 16 G; Int 1-19. **1981** Min: 16 G; Scor **1** Saf; 2 Pt. **1982** Min-ChiB: 5 G. Min: 1 G. ChiB: 4 G. **1983** ChiB: 15 G.
Total: 93 G; PR 1-1 1.0; Int 4-60 1 TD; Scor 1 Saf; 8 Pt.

WALTER WILLIAMS Williams, Walter L 6'2", 195 **DB-TB-HB**
Col: Boston U. B: 2/12/1919 D: 8/8/1990
AAFC **1946** ChiA: 14 G; Pass 30-13 43.3%, 226 7.53 1 TD 5 Int; Rush 21-19 0.9 1 TD; Rec 1-3 3.0; PR 1-6 6.0; KR 1-18 18.0; Int 2-148 1 TD; Punt 24-998 41.6; Tot TD 2; 12 Pt.

NFL **1947** Bos: 10 G; Pass 1-0, 1 Int; Rec 1-2 2.0; PR 1-14 14.0.

WANDY WILLIAMS Williams, Wanqalin Jacob 6'1", 189 **RB**
Col: Kansas; Hofstra *HS:* Malverne [NY] B: 1/3/1946, Brooklyn, NY
Drafted: 1969 Round 6 Den
1969 Den: 11 G; Rush 10-18 1.8 1 TD; Rec 5-56 11.2; KR 23-574 25.0; 6 Pt. **1970** Den: 1 G. **Total:** 12 G; Rush 10-18 1.8 1 TD; Rec 5-56 11.2; KR 23-574 25.0; 6 Pt.

WARREN WILLIAMS Williams, Warren Jr. 6'0", 209 **RB**
Col: Miami (Fla.) *HS:* North Fort Myers [FL] B: 7/29/1965, Fort Myers, FL *Drafted:* 1988 Round 6 Pit
1988 Pit: KR 1-10 10.0. **1992** Pit: KR 1-0. **Total:** KR 2-10 5.0.

		Rushing				Receiving					Tot
Year Team	**G**	**Att**	**Yds**	**Avg**	**TD**	**Rec**	**Yds**	**Avg**	**TD**	**Fum**	**TD**
1988 Pit	15	87	409	4.7	0	11	66	6.0	1	3	1
1989 Pit	5	37	131	3.5	1	6	48	8.0	0	0	1
1990 Pit	14	68	389	5.7	3	5	42	8.4	1	5	4
1991 Pit	16	57	262	4.6	4	15	139	9.3	0	2	4
1992 Pit	16	2	0	0.0	0	1	44	44.0	0	0	0
1993 Ind	5	0	0	—	0	0	0	—	0	0	0
NFL Total	71	251	1191	4.7	8	38	339	8.9	2	10	10

TOM WILLIAMS Williams, William Thomas 6'4", 250 **DT-DE**
Col: California-Davis *HS:* Rancho Cordova [CA] B: 7/21/1948, Hempstead, NY *Drafted:* 1970 Round 2 SD
1970 SD: 14 G. **1971** SD: 13 G. **Total:** 27 G.

WILLIE WILLIAMS Williams, Willie 6'6", 300 **OT**
Col: Louisiana State *HS:* Phillis Wheatley [Houston, TX] B: 8/6/1967, Houston, TX *Drafted:* 1990 Supplemental Round 9 Pho
1991 Pho: 16 G; Rec 1-3 3.0 1 TD; 6 Pt. **1994** NO: 16 G; Rec 1-7 7.0. **Total:** 32 G; Rec 2-10 5.0 1 TD; 6 Pt.

WILLIE WILLIAMS Williams, Willie Albert 6'0", 190 **DB**
Col: Grambling State *HS:* Archer [Atlanta, GA] B: 12/29/1942, Atlanta, GA *Drafted:* 1965 Round 8 NYG
1965 NYG: PR 18-28 1.6; KR 5-113 22.6. **1966** Oak: KR 2-52 26.0. **1967** NYG: PR 6-28 4.7. **1968** NYG: KR 1-0; Punt 10-291 29.1. **1969** NYG: KR 6-96 16.0. **Total:** PR 24-56 2.3; KR 14-261 18.6; Punt 10-291 29.1.

		Interceptions			
Year Team	**G**	**Int**	**Yds**	**TD**	**Fum**
1965 NYG	14	1	0	0	2
1966 Oak	6	0	0	0	0
1967 NYG	6	1	44	0	0
1968 NYG	14	**10**	103	0	1
1969 NYG	14	4	19	0	0
1970 NYG	14	6	114	0	0
1971 NYG	10	5	58	0	0
1972 NYG	14	4	42	0	0
1973 NYG	14	4	82	0	0
NFL Total	106	35	462	0	3

WILLIE WILLIAMS Williams, Willie James Jr. 5'9", 180 **DB**
Col: Western Carolina *HS:* Spring Valley [Columbia, SC]
B: 12/26/1970, Columbia, SC *Drafted:* 1993 Round 6 Pit
1993 Pit: KR 1-19 19.0. **1996** Pit: 1 Sac. **Total:** KR 1-19 19.0; 1 Sac.

		Interceptions		
Year Team	**G**	**Int**	**Yds**	**TD**
1993 Pit	16	0	0	0
1994 Pit	16	0	0	0
1995 Pit	16	7	122	1
1996 Pit	15	1	1	0
1997 Sea	16	1	0	0
1998 Sea	14	2	36	1
NFL Total	93	11	159	2

CARLTON WILLIAMSON Williamson, Carlton 6'0", 204 **DB**
Col: Pittsburgh *HS:* Brown [Atlanta, GA] B: 6/12/1958, Atlanta, GA
Drafted: 1981 Round 3 SF
1984 SF: 1 Sac. **Total:** 1 Sac.

		Interceptions		
Year Team	**G**	**Int**	**Yds**	**TD**
1981 SF	16	4	44	0
1982 SF	8	0	0	0
1983 SF	9	4	51	0
1984 SF	15	2	42	0
1985 SF	16	3	137	**1**
1986 SF	16	3	3	0
1987 SF	8	1	17	0
NFL Total	88	17	294	1

ERNIE WILLIAMSON Williamson, Ernest Warriner 6'4", 245 **T**
Col: North Carolina *HS:* Crewe [VA] B: 9/9/1922, Crewe, VA
Drafted: 1947 Round 8 Was
AAFC **1949** LA-A: 12 G.

NFL **1947** Was: 9 G; KR 1-28 28.0. **1948** NYG: 2 G. **Total:** 11 G; KR 1-28 28.0.

FRED WILLIAMSON Williamson, Frederick Robert 6'3", 219 **DB**
(Hammer) *Col:* Northwestern *HS:* Froebel [Gary, IN] B: 3/5/1937, Gary, IN
1962 Oak: PR 1-3 3.0. **1966** KC: PR 1-10 10.0. **Total:** PR 2-13 6.5.

		Interceptions		
Year Team	**G**	**Int**	**Yds**	**TD**
1960 Pit	11	0	0	0
1961 Oak	14	5	58	0
1962 Oak	14	8	**151**	**1**
1963 Oak	14	6	44	0
1964 Oak	14	6	40	0
1965 KC	14	6	89	0
1966 KC	12	4	20	0
1967 KC	11	1	77	1
NFL Total	104	36	479	2

GREG WILLIAMSON Williamson, Gregory Scott 5'11", 185 **DB**
Col: Cerritos Coll. CA (J.C.); Fresno State *HS:* R.A. Millikan [Long Beach, CA] B: 5/11/1964, Long Beach, CA
1987 LARm: 3 G; Int 1-28.

J.R. WILLIAMSON Williamson, John Robert 6'2", 220 **LB-C**
Col: Louisiana Tech *HS:* El Dorado [AR] B: 10/9/1941, El Dorado, AR
Drafted: 1964 Round 9 Oak
1964 Oak: 14 G. **1965** Oak: 14 G. **1966** Oak: 13 G. **1967** Oak: 13 G; Int 2-9. **1968** Bos: 14 G. **1969** Bos: 14 G. **1970** Bos: 11 G; Int 1-2. **Total:** 93 G; Int 3-11.

MATT WILLIG Willig, Matthew Joseph 6'7", 315 **OT**
Col: USC *HS:* St. Paul [Santa Fe Springs, CA] B: 1/21/1969, La Mirada, CA
1993 NYJ: 3 G. **1994** NYJ: 16 G. **1995** NYJ: 15 G. **1996** Atl: 12 G. **1997** Atl: 16 G. **1998** GB: 16 G. **Total:** 78 G.

LARRY WILLINGHAM Willingham, Larry Levi 6'0", 190 **DB**
Col: Auburn *HS:* Banks [Birmingham, AL] B: 12/22/1948, Cullman, AL
Drafted: 1971 Round 4 StL
1971 StL: 9 G; PR 10-84 8.4; KR 6-125 20.8; 2 Fum. **1972** StL: 11 G; PR 9-41 4.6; KR 9-194 21.6; 2 Fum. **Total:** 20 G; PR 19-125 6.6; KR 15-319 21.3; 4 Fum.

CHESTER WILLIS Willis, Chester O'Neal 5'11", 195 **RB**
Col: Auburn *HS:* Johnson [Gainesville, GA] B: 5/2/1958, Elberton, GA
Drafted: 1981 Round 11 Oak
1981 Oak: Rec 1-24 24.0; KR 15-309 20.6. **1982** LARd: KR 1-11 11.0. **1984** LARd: KR 1-13 13.0. **Total:** Rec 1-24 24.0; KR 17-333 19.6.

		Rushing				
Year Team	**G**	**Att**	**Yds**	**Avg**	**TD**	**Fum**
1981 Oak	15	16	54	3.4	1	1
1982 LARd	8	6	15	2.5	0	2
1983 LARd	13	5	0	0.0	0	1
1984 LARd	16	5	4	0.8	0	0
NFL Total	52	32	73	2.3	1	4

DONALD WILLIS Willis, Donald Kirk 6'3", 330 **OG**
Col: Washington; North Carolina A&T *HS:* Cabrillo [Lompoc, CA]
B: 7/15/1973, Goleta, CA
1996 NO: 4 G.

FRED WILLIS Willis, Frederick Francis III 6'0", 212 **RB**
Col: Boston College *HS:* Kimball Union Acad. [Meriden, NH]
B: 12/9/1947, Natick, MA *Drafted:* 1971 Round 4 Cin
1971 Cin: Pass 2-1 50.0%, 8 4.00; KR 4-81 20.3. **1972** Cin-Hou: Pass 4-1 25.0%, 16 4.00 1 Int. Cin: Pass 1-1 100.0%, 16 16.00. Hou: Pass 3-0, 1 Int. **1973** Hou: Pass 1-0. **Total:** Pass 7-2 28.6%, 24 3.43 1 Int; KR 4-81 20.3.

		Rushing				Receiving					Tot
Year Team	**G**	**Att**	**Yds**	**Avg**	**TD**	**Rec**	**Yds**	**Avg**	**TD**	**Fum**	**TD**
1971 Cin	14	135	590	4.4	7	24	223	9.3	0	3	7
1972 Cin-Hou	13	134	461	3.4	0	45	297	6.6	2	3	2
1972 Cin	5	42	127	3.0	0	9	46	5.1	0	1	0
1972 Hou	8	92	334	3.6	0	36	251	7.0	2	2	2
1973 Hou	14	171	579	3.4	4	57	371	6.5	1	5	5
1974 Hou	10	74	239	3.2	3	25	130	5.2	1	0	4
1975 Hou	13	118	420	3.6	2	20	104	5.2	0	7	2
1976 Hou	13	148	542	3.7	2	32	255	8.0	1	3	3
NFL Total	77	780	2831	3.6	18	203	1380	6.8	5	21	23

JAMAL WILLIS Willis, Jamalsikou Leirus 6'2", 218 **RB**
Col: Brigham Young *HS:* Bonanza [Las Vegas, NV] B: 12/12/1972, Lawton, OK
1995 SF: 11 G; Rush 12-35 2.9; Rec 3-8 2.7; KR 17-427 25.1.

JAMES WILLIS Willis, James Edward III 6'2", 237 **LB**
Col: Auburn *HS:* J.O. Johnson [Huntsville, AL] B: 9/2/1972, Huntsville, AL *Drafted:* 1993 Round 5 GB
1993 GB: 13 G. **1994** GB: 12 G; Int 2-20; 1 Fum. **1995** Phi: 5 G. **1996** Phi: 16 G; Int 1-14. **1997** Phi: 15 G; Int 1-0; 2 Sac. **1998** Phi: 16 G. **Total:** 77 G; Int 4-34; 1 Fum; 2 Sac.

KEITH WILLIS Willis, Keith 6'1", 260 **DE-NT**
Col: Northeastern *HS:* Malcolm X Shabazz [Newark, NJ] B: 7/29/1959, Newark, NJ
1982 Pit: 9 G; 1 Sac. **1983** Pit: 14 G; 14 Sac. **1984** Pit: 12 G; 5 Sac. **1985** Pit: 16 G; 5.5 Sac. **1986** Pit: 16 G; 12 Sac. **1987** Pit: 11 G; 3 Sac. **1989** Pit: 16 G; 6.5 Sac. **1990** Pit: 16 G; Int 1-5; 5 Sac. **1991** Pit: 16 G; 7 Sac. **1992** Buf: 12 G. **1993** Was: 1 G. **Total:** 139 G; Int 1-5; 59.0 Sac.

LARRY WILLIS Willis, Larry Lee 5'11", 171 **DB**
Col: Texas-El Paso *HS:* South Mountain [Phoenix, AZ] B: 7/18/1948, Phoenix, AZ
1973 Was: 1 G.

LEONARD WILLIS Willis, Leonard Leroy 5'11", 183 **WR**
Col: Nebraska Southern JC; Ohio State *HS:* Roosevelt [Washington, DC] B: 3/4/1953, Washington, DC *Drafted:* 1976 Round 4 Min
1978 Buf: Rec 2-41 20.5. **Total:** Rec 2-41 20.5.

		Punt Returns				Kickoff Returns				
Year Team	**G**	**Ret**	**Yds**	**Avg**	**TD**	**Ret**	**Yds**	**Avg**	**TD**	**Fum**
1976 Min	14	30	207	6.9	0	24	552	23.0	0	4
1977 NO-Buf	11	1	0	0.0	0	8	148	18.5	0	0
1977 NO	7	0	0	—	0	8	148	18.5	0	0
1977 Buf	4	1	0	0.0	0	0	0	—	0	0
1978 Buf	4	0	0	—	0	1	0	0.0	0	0
1979 Buf	7	0	0	—	0	4	92	23.0	0	0
NFL Total	36	31	207	6.7	0	37	792	21.4	0	4

MITCH WILLIS Willis, Otis Mitchell 6'8", 278 **NT-DT**
Col: Southern Methodist *HS:* Lamar [Arlington, TX] B: 3/16/1962, Dallas, TX *Drafted:* 1984 Round 7 LARd
1985 LARd: 11 G; 2 Sac. **1986** LARd: 16 G. **1987** LARd: 10 G. **1988** LARd-Atl: 10 G. LARd: 1 G. Atl: 9 G. **1990** Dal: 4 G. **Total:** 51 G; 2 Sac.

PETER TOM WILLIS Willis, Peter Tom 6'2", 188 **QB**
Col: Florida State *HS:* Mortimer Jordan [Morris, AL] B: 1/4/1967, Morris, AL *Drafted:* 1990 Round 3 ChiB
1991 ChiB: Rush 2-6 3.0. **1992** ChiB: Rush 1-2 2.0. **1993** ChiB: Rush 2-6 3.0. **Total:** Rush 5-14 2.8.

		Passing								
Year Team	**G**	**Att**	**Comp**	**Comp%**	**Yds**	**YPA**	**TD**	**Int**	**Rating**	**Fum**
1990 ChiB	3	13	9	69.2	106	8.15	1	1	87.3	0
1991 ChiB	4	18	11	61.1	171	9.50	1	1	88.0	0
1992 ChiB	9	92	54	58.7	716	7.78	4	8	61.7	0
1993 ChiB	5	60	30	50.0	268	4.47	0	5	27.6	2
NFL Total	21	183	104	56.8	1261	6.89	6	15	54.9	2

KEN WILLIS Willis, Robert Kenneth II 5'11", 190 **K**
Col: Kentucky *HS:* Owensboro [KY] B: 10/6/1966, Owensboro, KY

		Scoring						
Year Team	**G**	**Pts**	**FG**	**FGA**	**FG%**	**XK**	**XKA**	**XK%**
1990 Dal	16	80	18	25	72.0	26	26	100.0
1991 Dal	16	118	27	39	69.2	37	37	100.0
1992 TB-NYG	15	57	10	16	62.5	27	27	100.0
1992 TB	9	44	8	14	57.1	20	20	100.0
1992 NYG	6	13	2	2	100.0	7	7	100.0
NFL Total	47	255	55	80	68.8	90	90	100.0

BILL WILLIS Willis, William Karnet 6'2", 213 **DG-OG**
Col: Ohio State *HS:* East [Columbus, OH] B: 10/5/1921, Columbus, OH *HOF:* 1977
AAFC **1946** CleA: 13 G. **1947** CleA: 13 G. **1948** CleA: 14 G. **1949** CleA: 12 G; Int 1-6. **Total:** 52 G; Int 1-6.

NFL **1950** Cle: 12 G. **1951** Cle: 12 G. **1952** Cle: 12 G. **1953** Cle: 11 G. **Total:** 47 G.

LADELL WILLS Wills, Ladell P 6'3", 240 **LB**
Col: Jackson State *HS:* Northwestern [Flint, MI] B: 5/30/1962, Flint, MI
1987 NYJ: 3 G.

JOE WILLSON Willson, Joseph Putnam 5'11", 185 **G-FB**
Col: Pennsylvania *HS:* Cazenovia Seminary [NY] B: 1902
1926 Buf: 6 G. **1927** Buf: 1 G. **Total:** 7 G.

DIDDIE WILLSON Willson, Osborn Putnam 5'10", 196 **G-OE-DE**
Col: Pennsylvania *HS:* Corning Acad. [NY] B: 1/17/1911, Crosby, PA D: 1/19/1961, Phelps, NY
1933 Phi: 7 G. **1934** Phi: 11 G. **1935** Phi: 10 G. **Total:** 28 G.

RAY WILMER Wilmer, Bonnie Raymond 6'2", 190 **DB**
Col: Louisiana Tech *HS:* Marksville [LA] B: 6/27/1962, Pineville, LA
1984 Sea: 3 G.

TREVOR WILMOT Wilmot, Trevor Richard 6'2", 220 **LB**
Col: Indiana *HS:* Evanston Twp. [Evanston, IL] B: 10/30/1972, Evanston, IL
1995 Ind: 7 G.

KLAUS WILMSMEYER Wilmsmeyer, Klaus Jr. 6'2", 210 **P**
Col: Louisville *HS:* Lorne Park Sec. School [Mississauga, Canada] B: 12/4/1967, Mississauga, Canada *Drafted:* 1992 Round 12 TB
1992 SF: Rush 2-0. **1993** SF: Rush 2-0. **1995** NO: Pass 1-1 100.0%, 18 18.00. **1996** NO: Scor 1 2XP. **Total:** Pass 1-1 100.0%, 18 18.00; Rush 4-0; Scor 1 2XP.

		Punting			
Year Team	**G**	**Punts**	**Yds**	**Avg**	**Fum**
1992 SF	15	49	1918	39.1	1
1993 SF	15	42	1718	40.9	2
1994 SF	16	54	2235	41.4	0
1995 NO	16	73	2965	40.6	0
1996 NO	16	87	3551	40.8	0
1998 Mia	16	93	3949	42.5	0
NFL Total	94	398	16336	41.0	3

JEFF WILNER Wilner, Jeffrey Scott 6'5", 250 **TE**
Col: Wesleyan *HS:* Phillips Exeter Acad. [Exeter, NH] B: 12/31/1971, East Meadowbrook, NY
1994 GB: 11 G; Rec 5-31 6.2. **1995** GB: 2 G. **Total:** 13 G; Rec 5-31 6.2.

FRANK WILSBACH Wilsbach, Frank Ferdinand 6'0", 215 **G**
Col: Bucknell *HS:* Harrisburg Tech [PA] B: 4/23/1904, Harrisburg, PA D: 12/16/1959, Bellevue Park, PA
1925 Fra: 4 G.

WILSON Wilson 215 **T-G-TB**
Col: Carnegie Mellon
1923 Akr: 5 G. **1924** Akr: 2 G. **Total:** 7 G.

DRIP WILSON Wilson, ? 1 **C**
Col: No College
1931 Cle: 1 G.

ABE WILSON Wilson, Abraham Y 5'10", 192 **G**
Col: Washington *HS:* Everett [WA] B: 10/6/1899 D: 5/1981, Everett, WA
1927 Prov: 14 G. **1928** Prov: 9 G. **1929** Prov: 10 G. **Total:** 33 G.

BEN WILSON Wilson, Benjamin Ivery 6'0", 225 **FB**
Col: USC *HS:* Carver [Houston, TX] B: 3/9/1939, Houston, TX *Drafted:* 1962 Round 5 LARm
1963 LARm: KR 1-17 17.0. **1965** LARm: Pass 1-1 100.0%, 8 8.00; KR 3-66 22.0. **Total:** Pass 1-1 100.0%, 8 8.00; KR 4-83 20.8.

		Rushing				Receiving					Tot
Year Team	**G**	**Att**	**Yds**	**Avg**	**TD**	**Rec**	**Yds**	**Avg**	**TD**	**Fum**	**TD**
1963 LARm	13	109	394	3.6	1	9	173	19.2	1	4	2
1964 LARm	14	159	553	3.5	5	15	116	7.7	1	3	6
1965 LARm	14	60	189	3.2	1	9	110	12.2	0	2	1
1967 GB	14	103	453	4.4	2	14	88	6.3	0	4	2
NFL Total	55	431	1589	3.7	9	47	487	10.4	2	13	11

BOBBY WILSON Wilson, Bobby 6'2", 297 **DT**
Col: Northeastern Oklahoma A&M (J.C.); Michigan State *HS:* Austin [Chicago, IL] B: 3/4/1968, Chicago, IL *Drafted:* 1991 Round 1 Was
1991 Was: 16 G; 4.5 Sac. **1992** Was: 5 G; 2 Sac. **1993** Was: 12 G; 2 Sac. **1994** Was: 9 G; 2.5 Sac. **Total:** 42 G; 11 Sac.

BRENARD WILSON Wilson, Brenard Kenric 6'0", 178 **DB**
Col: Vanderbilt *HS:* Father Lopez [Daytona Beach, FL] B: 8/15/1955, Daytona Beach, FL
1979 Phi: KR 2-0. **Total:** KR 2-0.

		Interceptions		
Year Team	**G**	**Int**	**Yds**	**TD**
1979 Phi	14	4	70	0
1980 Phi	16	6	79	0
1981 Phi	15	5	73	0
1982 Phi	8	1	0	0
1983 Phi	16	0	0	0
1984 Phi	16	1	28	0
1985 Phi	16	0	0	0
1986 Phi	16	0	0	0
1987 Phi-Atl	9	0	0	0
1987 Phi	1	0	0	0

1987 Atl	8	0	0	0
NFL Total	126	17	250	0

BRETT WILSON Wilson, Brett Allan 6'0", 220 **RB**
Col: Illinois *HS:* Lyons Twp. [La Grange, IL] B: 12/29/1960, La Grange, IL
1987 Min: 3 G; Rush 5-16 3.2; Rec 2-14 7.0.

CHARLES WILSON Wilson, Charles Joseph II 5'9", 180 **WR**
Col: Memphis *HS:* Amos P. Godby [Tallahassee, FL] B: 7/1/1968, Tallahassee, FL *Drafted:* 1990 Round 5 GB
1991 GB: Rush 3-3 1.0. **1993** TB: Rush 2-7 3.5. **1994** TB: Rush 2-15 7.5. **Total:** Rush 7-25 3.6.

		Receiving				Kickoff Returns					Tot
Year Team	**G**	**Rec**	**Yds**	**Avg**	**TD**	**Ret**	**Yds**	**Avg**	**TD**	**Fum**	**TD**
1990 GB	15	7	84	12.0	0	35	798	22.8	0	0	0
1991 GB	15	19	305	16.1	1	23	522	22.7	**1**	4	2
1992 TB	2	0	0	—	0	1	23	23.0	0	0	0
1993 TB	15	15	225	15.0	0	23	454	19.7	0	1	0
1994 TB	14	31	652	21.0	6	10	251	25.1	0	0	6
1995 NYJ	15	41	484	11.8	4	0	0	—	0	1	4
NFL Total	76	113	1750	15.5	11	92	2048	22.3	1	6	12

WADE WILSON Wilson, Charles Wade 6'3", 210 **QB**
(Whiskey) *Col:* Texas A&M-Commerce *HS:* Commerce [TX]
B: 2/1/1959, Greenville, TX *Drafted:* 1981 Round 8 Min
1986 Min: Punt 2-76 38.0. **Total:** Punt 2-76 38.0.

		Passing							
Year Team	**G**	**Att**	**Comp**	**Comp%**	**Yds**	**YPA**	**TD**	**Int**	**Rating**
1981 Min	3	13	6	46.2	48	3.69	0	2	16.3
1983 Min	1	28	16	57.1	124	4.43	1	2	50.3
1984 Min	8	195	102	52.3	1019	5.23	5	11	52.5
1985 Min	4	60	33	55.0	404	6.73	3	3	71.8
1986 Min	9	143	80	55.9	1165	8.15	7	5	84.4
1987 Min	12	264	140	53.0	2106	**7.98**	14	13	76.7
1988 Min	14	332	204	**61.4**	2746	8.27	15	9	91.5
1989 Min	14	362	194	53.6	2543	7.02	9	12	70.5
1990 Min	6	146	82	56.2	1155	7.91	9	8	79.6
1991 Min	5	122	72	59.0	825	6.76	3	10	53.5
1992 Atl	9	163	111	68.1	1366	8.38	13	4	110.1
1993 NO	14	388	221	57.0	2457	6.33	12	15	70.1
1994 NO	4	28	20	71.4	172	6.14	0	0	87.2
1995 Dal	7	57	38	66.7	391	6.86	1	3	70.1
1996 Dal	3	18	8	44.4	79	4.39	0	1	34.3
1997 Dal	7	21	12	57.1	115	5.48	0	0	72.5
1998 Oak	5	88	52	59.1	568	6.45	7	4	85.8
NFL Total	125	2428	1391	57.3	17283	7.12	99	102	75.6

	Rushing				
Year Team	**Att**	**Yds**	**Avg**	**TD**	**Fum**
1981 Min	0	0	—	0	2
1983 Min	3	-3	-1.0	0	1
1984 Min	9	30	3.3	0	2
1986 Min	13	9	0.7	1	3
1987 Min	41	263	6.4	5	3
1988 Min	36	136	3.8	2	4
1989 Min	32	132	4.1	1	5
1990 Min	12	79	6.6	0	3
1991 Min	13	33	2.5	0	3
1992 Atl	15	62	4.1	0	0
1993 NO	31	230	7.4	0	9
1994 NO	7	15	2.1	0	1
1995 Dal	10	12	1.2	0	1
1996 Dal	4	5	1.3	0	0
1997 Dal	6	-2	-0.3	0	0
1998 Oak	7	24	3.4	0	1
NFL Total	239	1025	4.3	9	38

DARRELL WILSON Wilson, Darrell Kenton 5'11", 180 **DB**
Col: Connecticut *HS:* Pennsauken [NJ] B: 7/28/1958, Camden, NJ
1981 NE: 1 G.

DARRYAL WILSON Wilson, Darryal Edgar 6'0", 182 **WR**
Col: Tennessee *HS:* Virginia [Bristol, VA] B: 9/19/1960, Florence, AL
Drafted: 1983 Round 2 NE
1983 NE: 9 G.

DAVID WILSON Wilson, David Alan 5'10", 192 **DB**
Col: California *HS:* Reseda [Los Angeles, CA] B: 6/10/1970, Los Angeles, CA *Drafted:* 1992 Round 7 Min
1992 NE-Min: 4 G. NE: 1 G. Min: 3 G. **Total:** 4 G.

DAVE WILSON Wilson, David Carlton 6'3", 206 **QB**
Col: Fullerton Coll. CA (J.C.); Illinois *HS:* Katella [Anaheim, CA]
B: 4/27/1959, Anaheim, CA *Drafted:* 1981 Supplemental Round 1 NO

		Passing							
Year Team	**G**	**Att**	**Comp**	**Comp%**	**Yds**	**YPA**	**TD**	**Int**	**Rating**
1981 NO	11	159	82	51.6	1058	6.65	1	11	46.1
1983 NO	8	112	66	58.9	770	6.88	5	7	68.7
1984 NO	5	93	51	54.8	647	6.96	7	4	83.9
1985 NO	10	293	145	49.5	1843	6.29	11	15	60.7
1986 NO	14	342	189	55.3	2353	6.88	10	17	65.8
1987 NO	4	24	13	54.2	243	10.13	2	0	117.2
1988 NO	1	16	5	31.3	73	4.56	0	1	21.1
NFL Total	53	1039	551	53.0	6987	6.72	36	55	63.8

	Rushing				
Year Team	**Att**	**Yds**	**Avg**	**TD**	**Fum**
1981 NO	5	1	0.2	0	4
1983 NO	5	3	0.6	1	5
1984 NO	3	-7	-2.3	0	2
1985 NO	18	7	0.4	0	6
1986 NO	14	19	1.4	1	8
NFL Total	45	23	0.5	2	25

DON WILSON Wilson, Donald Allen 6'2", 190 **DB**
Col: Ellsworth CC IA; North Carolina State *HS:* Cardozo [Washington, DC] B: 7/28/1961, Washington, DC
1985 Buf: Int 2-23; **1** Fum TD. **Total:** Int 2-23; 1 Fum TD.

		Punt Returns				Kickoff Returns					Tot
Year Team	**G**	**Ret**	**Yds**	**Avg**	**TD**	**Ret**	**Yds**	**Avg**	**TD**	**Fum**	**TD**
1984 Buf	16	33	297	9.0	1	34	576	16.9	0	3	1
1985 Buf	16	16	161	10.1	0	22	465	21.1	0	5	1
NFL Total	32	49	458	9.3	1	56	1041	18.6	0	8	2

EARL WILSON Wilson, Earl 6'4", 276 **DE**
Col: Kentucky *HS:* Atlantic City [NJ] B: 9/13/1958, Long Branch, NJ
1985 SD: 16 G; 3 Sac. **1986** SD: 16 G; 5.5 Sac. **1987** SD: 1 G.
Total: 33 G; 8.5 Sac.

MARCUS WILSON Wilson, Edmond Marcus 6'1", 210 **RB**
Col: Virginia *HS:* Olympia [Rochester, NY] B: 4/16/1968, Rochester, NY *Drafted:* 1990 Round 6 LARd
1991 LARd: 1 G; Rush 6-21 3.5. **1992** GB: 6 G. **1993** GB: 16 G; Rush 6-3 0.5; Rec 2-18 9.0; KR 9-197 21.9; 1 Fum. **1994** GB: 12 G; KR 2-14 7.0; 1 Fum. **1995** GB: 14 G. **Total:** 49 G; Rush 12-24 2.0; Rec 2-18 9.0; KR 11-211 19.2; 2 Fum.

EDDIE WILSON Wilson, Edward Adair 6'0", 190 **QB-P**
Col: Arizona *HS:* Chandler [AZ] B: 8/14/1940, Redding, CA
Drafted: 1962 Round 3 DalT
1962 DalT: Rush 1-5 5.0. **1963** KC: Rush 8-45 5.6. **1964** KC: Rush 6-5 0.8 1 TD. **1965** Bos: Rush 8-4 0.5. **Total:** Rush 23-59 2.6 1 TD.

		Passing							
Year Team	**G**	**Att**	**Comp**	**Comp%**	**Yds**	**YPA**	**TD**	**Int**	**Rating**
1962 DalT	14	11	6	54.5	65	5.91	0	0	72.2
1963 KC	14	82	39	47.6	537	6.55	3	2	71.0
1964 KC	14	47	25	53.2	392	8.34	1	1	79.4
1965 Bos	14	46	20	43.5	257	5.59	1	3	41.7
NFL Total	56	186	90	48.4	1251	6.73	5	6	65.9

	Punting			
Year Team	**Punts**	**Yds**	**Avg**	**Fum**
1962 DalT	48	1681	35.0	0
1963 KC	1	43	43.0	2
1964 KC	1	32	32.0	4
1965 Bos	6	194	32.3	0
NFL Total	56	1950	34.8	6

ERIC WILSON Wilson, Eric Wendell 6'1", 247 **LB**
Col: Maryland *HS:* Charlottesville [VA] B: 10/17/1962, Charlottesville, VA
1985 Buf: 14 G; PR 1-0. **1987** Was: 3 G. **Total:** 17 G; PR 1-0.

MULE WILSON Wilson, Faye 5'11", 192 **WB-DB-FB-TB**
Col: Texas A&M B: 8/10/1903, Red Oak, TX D: 2/12/1991, Fort Worth, TX
1926 Buf: 9 G. **1927** NYG: 13 G; Rush 3 TD; Rec 2 TD; Int 1 TD; Tot TD **6**; 36 Pt. **1928** NYG: 13 G; Rush 1 TD; Scor 7, 1 XK. **1929** NYG: 9 G; Rush 1 TD; 6 Pt. **1930** NYG-SI-GB: 14 G. NYG: 10 G; Rush 1 TD; Rec 3 TD; Tot TD 4; 24 Pt. SI: 3 G. GB: 1 G. **1931** GB: 12 G; Pass 1 TD; Rush 2 TD; 12 Pt. **1932** Port: 10 G; Rush 5-9 1.8. **1933** Port: 5 G; Rush 3-10 3.3; Rec 1-8 8.0. **Total:** 85 G; Pass 1 TD; Rush 8-19 2.4 8 TD; Rec 1-8 8.0 5 TD; Int 1 TD; Tot TD 14.

FRANK WILSON Wilson, Frank Henry Jr. 6'2", 233 **TE-FB**
Col: Rice *HS:* A.S. Johnston [Austin, TX] B: 10/11/1958, Austin, TX
Drafted: 1981 Round 8 Pit
1982 Pit: 1 G.

MIKE WILSON Wilson, George Bownan Jr. 5'11", 185 **WB-TB-FB**
Col: Lafayette *HS:* Northeast [Philadelphia, PA]; Wyoming Seminary [Kingston, PA] B: 7/18/1905, Glenside, PA D: 5/3/1990, Bryn Mawr, PA
1929 Fra: 18 G.

BUTCH WILSON Wilson, George Marvin 6'2", 228 **TE**
Col: Alabama *HS:* Hueytown [AL] B: 9/18/1941, Birmingham, AL
Drafted: 1963 Round 2 Bal

		Receiving			
Year Team	G	Rec	Yds	Avg	TD
1963 Bal	2	0	0	—	0
1964 Bal	11	7	86	12.3	1
1965 Bal	14	1	38	38.0	0
1966 Bal	14	3	27	9.0	2
1967 Bal	13	0	0	—	0
1968 NYG	14	4	34	8.5	0
1969 NYG	14	10	132	13.2	0
NFL Total	82	25	317	12.7	3

WILDCAT WILSON Wilson, George Schly 5'11", 200 **TB**
Col: Washington *HS:* Everett [WA] B: 9/6/1901, Everett, WA
D: 12/27/1963, San Francisco, CA
1927 Prov: 14 G; Pass 4 TD; Rush 4 TD; 24 Pt. **1928** Prov: 11 G; Pass 5 TD; Rush 5 TD; 30 Pt. **1929** Prov: 12 G; Pass 3 TD; Rush 1 TD; 6 Pt. **Total:** 37 G; Pass 12 TD; Rush 10 TD; 60 Pt.

GEORGE WILSON Wilson, George William 6'1", 199 **OE-DE**
(Ducky) *Col:* Northwestern *HS:* Austin [Chicago, IL]; St.John's Mil. Acad. [Delafield,WI] B: 2/3/1914, Chicago, IL D: 11/23/1978, Detroit, MI
1942 ChiB: Int 1-2 **1** TD; **1** Fum TD. **1943** ChiB: Int 2-15. **1945** ChiB: PR 1-2 2.0. **Total:** PR 1-2 2.0; Int 3-17 1 TD; 1 Fum TD.

		Receiving					Tot
Year Team	G	Rec	Yds	Avg	TD	Fum	TD
1937 ChiB	11	1	20	20.0	0	0	1
1938 ChiB	11	4	81	20.3	1	0	1
1939 ChiB	11	5	66	13.2	0	0	0
1940 ChiB	11	4	90	22.5	1	0	1
1941 ChiB	11	4	75	18.8	0	0	0
1942 ChiB	11	9	89	9.9	0	0	2
1943 ChiB	10	21	293	14.0	5	0	5
1944 ChiB	10	24	265	11.0	4	0	4
1945 ChiB	9	28	259	9.3	3	1	3
1946 ChiB	11	11	104	9.5	1	0	1
NFL Total	106	111	1342	12.1	15	1	18

GEORGE WILSON Wilson, George William Jr. 6'2", 185 **QB**
Col: Notre Dame; Xavier (Ohio) *HS:* Sacred Heart [Detroit, MI]
B: 5/29/1943, Oak Park, IL *Drafted:* 1965 Redshirt Round 12 Buf
1966 Mia: Scor **1** 2XP.

		Passing							
Year Team	G	Att	Comp	Comp%	Yds	YPA	TD	Int	Rating
1966 Mia	14	112	46	41.1	764	6.82	5	10	42.4

	Rushing				Punting			
Year Team	Att	Yds	Avg	TD	Punts	Yds	Avg	Fum
1966 Mia	27	137	5.1	0	42	1772	42.2	3

JERRY WILSON Wilson, Gerald Roscoe 6'3", 238 **DE**
Col: Auburn *HS:* Phillips [Birmingham, AL] B: 12/9/1936, Birmingham, AL *Drafted:* 1959 Round 2 ChiC
1959 Phi: 12 G; KR 2-4 2.0. **1960** Phi-SF: 10 G; KR 1-0. Phi: 4 G; KR 1-0. SF: 6 G. **Total:** 22 G; KR 3-4 1.3.

GORDON WILSON Wilson, Gordon 6'0", 228 **G-T**
Col: Texas-El Paso B: 11/23/1915, Fort Towson, OK *Drafted:* 1941 Round 16 Cle
1941 Cle: 1 G. **1942** ChiC: 11 G. **1943** ChiC: 10 G; KR 1-6 6.0.
1944 Bos-Bkn: 8 G. Bos: 1 G. Bkn: 7 G. **1945** ChiC: 9 G. **Total:** 39 G; KR 1-6 6.0.

HARRY WILSON Wilson, Harry Edward 5'11", 204 **RB**
Col: Nebraska *HS:* Steubenville [OH] B: 9/28/1944, Steubenville, OH
Drafted: 1967 Round 3 Phi
1967 Phi: 3 G; Rec 2-20 10.0; KR 7-150 21.4. **1969** Phi: 2 G; Rush 4-7 1.8; Rec 1-6 6.0. **1970** Phi: 1 G. **Total:** 6 G; Rush 4-7 1.8; Rec 3-26 8.7; KR 7-150 21.4.

JACK WILSON Wilson, Jack William 6'0", 200 **HB**
Col: Baylor *HS:* Paris [TX] B: 11/20/1917, Paris, TX *Drafted:* 1942 Round 1 Cle
1946 LARm: 9 G; Rush 19-120 6.3; Rec 3-30 10.0 1 TD; PR 5-99 19.8; KR 6-145 24.2; Int 1-32; 6 Pt. **1947** LARm: 1 G; Rush 3-3 1.0; Rec 1-(-5) -5.0. **Total:** 10 G; Rush 22-123 5.6; Rec 4-25 6.3 1 TD; PR 5-99 19.8; KR 6-145 24.2; Int 1-32; 6 Pt.

JIM WILSON Wilson, James B 5'7", 155 **E**
Col: Cornell *HS:* Lafayette [Buffalo, NY] B: 7/8/1896, Buffalo, NY
D: 9/25/1986, Clarence, NY
1922 Buf: 4 G.

J.C. WILSON Wilson, James C 6'0", 178 **DB**
Col: Tampa; Pittsburgh *HS:* East [Cleveland, OH] B: 3/11/1956, Cleveland, OH *Drafted:* 1978 Round 8 Hou
1981 Hou: KR 2-27 13.5. **Total:** KR 2-27 13.5.

		Interceptions			
Year Team	G	Int	Yds	TD	Fum
1978 Hou	16	2	10	0	0
1979 Hou	16	6	135	1	0
1980 Hou	16	2	26	0	0
1981 Hou	16	1	1	0	1
1982 Hou	7	0	0	0	0
1983 Hou	13	0	0	0	0
NFL Total	84	11	172	1	1

JIM WILSON Wilson, James Milligan 6'3", 258 **OG-OT**
(Big Jim) *Col:* Georgia *HS:* Edgewood [Pittsburgh, PA] B: 6/12/1942, Pittsburgh, PA *Drafted:* 1964 Round 4 SF
1965 SF: 11 G. **1966** SF: 14 G. **1967** Atl: 7 G. **1968** LARm: 14 G. **Total:** 46 G.

REINARD WILSON Wilson, James Reinard 6'2", 261 **LB**
Col: Florida State *HS:* Columbia [Lake City, FL] B: 12/17/1973, Gainesville, FL *Drafted:* 1997 Round 1 Cin
1997 Cin: 16 G; 3 Sac. **1998** Cin: 16 G; 6 Sac. **Total:** 32 G; 9 Sac.

JERREL WILSON Wilson, Jerrel Douglas 6'2", 222 **RB-P**
Col: Pearl River CC MS; Southern Mississippi *HS:* S.S. Murphy [Mobile, AL] B: 10/4/1941, New Orleans, LA *Drafted:* 1963 Round 11 KC
1963 KC: Rush 9-41 4.6; Rec 2-21 10.5; KR 1-20 20.0. **1964** KC: Rush 1-(-10) -10.0; Rec 1-11 11.0. **1965** KC: Rush 2-4 2.0; Scor 1 2XP. **1966** KC: Rush 3-7 2.3; Rec 1-7 7.0; Scor **1** 2XP. **1967** KC: Rush 1-10 10.0. **1968** KC: Rush 5-1 0.2; Rec 1-14 14.0. **1972** KC: Pass 1-1 100.0%, 20 20.00. **1973** KC: Pass 1-1 100.0%, 9 9.00. **1974** KC: Pass 2-0. **1978** NE: Rush 1-0; Scor 0-1 XK. **Total:** Pass 4-2 50.0%, 29 7.25; Rush 22-53 2.4; Rec 5-53 10.6; KR 1-20 20.0; Scor 4, 0-1 XK, 2 2XP.

		Punting			
Year Team	G	Punts	Yds	Avg	Fum
1963 KC	14	61	2628	43.1	0
1964 KC	14	78	**3326**	42.6	1
1965 KC	14	69	3132	**45.4**	0
1966 KC	14	62	2715	43.8	0
1967 KC	10	41	1739	42.4	0
1968 KC	14	63	2841	**45.1**	0
1969 KC	14	68	3022	44.4	0
1970 KC	14	76	3415	44.9	1
1971 KC	14	64	2864	44.8	1
1972 KC	14	66	2960	**44.8**	0
1973 KC	14	80	**3642**	**45.5**	1
1974 KC	14	83	3462	41.7	0
1975 KC	11	54	2233	41.4	0
1976 KC	14	65	2729	42.0	0
1977 KC	14	88	3510	39.9	0
1978 NE	14	54	1921	35.6	1
NFL Total	217	1072	46139	43.0	5

JERRY WILSON Wilson, Jerry Lee Jr. 5'10", 187 **DB**
Col: Southern University *HS:* La Grange [Lake Charles, LA]
B: 7/17/1973, Alexandria, LA *Drafted:* 1995 Round 4 TB
1996 Mia: 2 G. **1997** Mia: 16 G; 2 Sac. **1998** Mia: 16 G; Int 1-0. **Total:** 34 G; Int 1-0; 2 Sac.

JOHNNY WILSON Wilson, John Samuel 6'3", 203 **OE-DE**
(Long John) *Col:* Case Western Reserve *HS:* Steubenville [OH]
B: 11/2/1915, Dover, OH

		Receiving				Tot
Year Team	G	Rec	Yds	Avg	TD	TD
1939 Cle	11	8	108	13.5	1	1
1940 Cle	10	7	93	13.3	1	1
1941 Cle	11	5	115	23.0	1	1
1942 Cle	3	6	113	18.8	1	2
NFL Total	35	26	429	16.5	4	5

JOE WILSON Wilson, Joseph 5'10", 210 **RB**
Col: Holy Cross *HS:* Jamaica Plain [MA] B: 8/11/1950, Raeford, NC
Drafted: 1973 Round 8 Cin
1973 Cin: KR 8-173 21.6. **1974** NE: Rec 3-38 12.7; KR 2-33 16.5. **Total:** Rec 3-38 12.7; KR 10-206 20.6.

		Rushing				
Year Team	G	Att	Yds	Avg	TD	Fum
1973 Cin	13	10	39	3.9	0	0
1974 NE	12	15	57	3.8	0	1
NFL Total	25	25	96	3.8	0	1

KARL WILSON Wilson, Karl Wendell 6′4″, 277 **DE-DT-LB**
Col: Louisiana State *HS:* Baker [LA] B: 9/10/1964, Amite, LA
Drafted: 1987 Round 3 SD
1987 SD: 7 G; 1 Sac. **1988** SD: 13 G; 0.5 Sac. **1989** Pho: 15 G; Scor **1** Saf; 2 Pt; 1 Sac. **1990** Mia: 16 G; 4 Sac. **1991** LARm: 13 G; 2 Sac. **1992** NYJ: 2 G. **1993** NYJ-Mia-SF: 12 G; 3 Sac. NYJ: 5 G. Mia: 2 G. SF: 5 G; 3 Sac. **1994** TB: 14 G; 2.5 Sac. **1995** Buf: 11 G; 1 Sac. **Total:** 103 G; Scor 1 Saf; 2 Pt; 15 Sac.

LARRY WILSON Wilson, Lawrence Frank 6′0″, 190 **DB**
Col: Utah *HS:* Rigby [ID] B: 3/24/1938, Rigby, ID *Drafted:* 1960 Round 7 StL *HOF:* 1978
1960 StL: PR 3-26 8.7; KR 6-115 19.2. **1961** StL: KR 4-83 20.8; Scor **1** Saf. **1963** StL: Rush 2-38 19.0 1 TD; **1** Fum TD. **1964** StL: Rush 2-(-14) -7.0. **1968** StL: Rush 1-12 12.0. **1969** StL: **1** Fum TD. **1970** StL: KR 1-0. **1972** StL: Pass 2-0. **Total:** Pass 2-0; Rush 5-36 7.2 1 TD; PR 3-26 8.7; KR 11-198 18.0; Scor 1 Saf; 2 Fum TD.

		Interceptions				Tot
Year Team	**G**	**Int**	**Yds**	**TD**	**Fum**	**TD**
1960 StL	11	2	4	0	1	0
1961 StL	11	3	36	0	0	0
1962 StL	14	2	59	**1**	0	1
1963 StL	14	4	67	0	0	2
1964 StL	14	3	44	1	0	1
1965 StL	10	6	153	1	0	1
1966 StL	14	**10**	180	**2**	0	2
1967 StL	14	4	75	0	0	0
1968 StL	14	4	14	0	0	0
1969 StL	14	2	15	0	0	1
1970 StL	13	5	72	0	0	0
1971 StL	14	4	46	0	0	0
1972 StL	12	3	35	0	1	0
NFL Total	169	52	800	5	2	8

LEE WILSON Wilson, Leland Moore 5′11″, 184 **E-WB**
Col: Cornell College B: 7/24/1905 D: 1/17/1970, Clarion, IA
1929 Min: 9 G. **1930** Min-Fra: 12 G. Min: 8 G. Fra: 4 G. **1931** Fra: 5 G. **Total:** 26 G.

MARC WILSON Wilson, Marc Douglas 6′6″, 205 **QB**
Col: Brigham Young *HS:* Shorecrest [Seattle, WA] B: 2/15/1957, Bremerton, WA *Drafted:* 1980 Round 1 Oak

		Passing							
Year Team	**G**	**Att**	**Comp**	**Comp%**	**Yds**	**YPA**	**TD**	**Int**	**Rating**
1980 Oak	2	5	3	60.0	31	6.20	0	0	77.9
1981 Oak	13	366	173	47.3	2311	6.31	14	19	58.9
1982 LARd	8	2	1	50.0	4	2.00	0	0	56.3
1983 LARd	10	117	67	57.3	864	7.38	8	6	82.0
1984 LARd	16	282	153	54.3	2151	7.63	15	17	71.7
1985 LARd	16	388	193	49.7	2608	6.72	16	21	62.7
1986 LARd	16	240	129	53.8	1721	7.17	12	15	67.4
1987 LARd	15	266	152	57.1	2070	7.78	12	8	84.6
1989 NE	14	150	75	50.0	1006	6.71	3	5	64.5
1990 NE	16	265	139	52.5	1625	6.13	6	11	61.6
NFL Total	126	2081	1085	52.1	14391	6.92	86	102	67.7

	Rushing				
Year Team	**Att**	**Yds**	**Avg**	**TD**	**Fum**
1980 Oak	1	3	3.0	0	0
1981 Oak	30	147	4.9	2	8
1983 LARd	13	122	9.4	0	4
1984 LARd	30	56	1.9	1	11
1985 LARd	24	98	4.1	2	8
1986 LARd	14	45	3.2	0	6
1987 LARd	17	91	5.4	0	1
1989 NE	7	42	6.0	0	2
1990 NE	5	7	1.4	0	6
NFL Total	141	611	4.3	5	46

MIKE WILSON Wilson, Michael DeForest 6′3″, 245 **OG-OT**
Col: Dayton *HS:* Wilmington [OH] B: 10/20/1947, Wilmington, OH
Drafted: 1969 Round 14 Cin
1969 Cin: 3 G. **1970** Cin: 14 G. **1971** Buf: 5 G. **1975** KC: 4 G. **Total:** 26 G.

MIKE WILSON Wilson, Michael Ruben 6′3″, 213 **WR**
Col: Washington State *HS:* Carson [CA] B: 12/19/1958, Los Angeles, CA *Drafted:* 1981 Round 9 Dal
1981 SF: KR 4-67 16.8. **1984** SF: KR 1-14 14.0. **1986** SF: KR 1-10 10.0. **1988** SF: KR 1-2 2.0. **1990** SF: PR 1-1 1.0. **Total:** PR 1-1 1.0; KR 7-93 13.3.

		Receiving				
Year Team	**G**	**Rec**	**Yds**	**Avg**	**TD**	**Fum**
1981 SF	16	9	125	13.9	1	0
1982 SF	6	6	80	13.3	1	0
1983 SF	15	30	433	14.4	0	1
1984 SF	13	17	245	14.4	1	0
1985 SF	16	10	165	16.5	2	0
1986 SF	11	9	104	11.6	1	0
1987 SF	11	29	450	15.5	5	0
1988 SF	16	33	405	12.3	3	0
1989 SF	16	9	103	11.4	1	2
1990 SF	16	7	89	12.7	0	0
NFL Total	136	159	2199	13.8	15	3

MIKE WILSON Wilson, Michael S 5′11″, 200 **DB**
Col: Western Illinois *HS:* Rochelle Twp. [Rochelle, IL] B: 11/19/1946, Washington, DC
1969 StL: 3 G; KR 4-66 16.5; 1 Fum.

NEMIAH WILSON Wilson, Nemiah 6′0″, 165 **DB**
Col: Grambling State *HS:* McKinley [Baton Rouge, LA] B: 4/6/1943, Baton Rouge, LA
1966 Den: PR 2-10 5.0; KR 10-309 30.9 1 TD. **1967** Den: KR 4-106 26.5. **1968** Oak: PR 1-0; KR 4-84 21.0. **Total:** PR 3-10 3.3; KR 18-499 27.7 1 TD.

		Interceptions				Tot
Year Team	**G**	**Int**	**Yds**	**TD**	**Fum**	**TD**
1965 Den	14	3	118	1	0	1
1966 Den	14	1	2	0	3	1
1967 Den	14	4	153	2	2	2
1968 Oak	1	0	0	0	1	0
1969 Oak	14	2	25	0	0	0
1970 Oak	14	2	7	0	0	0
1971 Oak	13	5	70	0	1	0
1972 Oak	14	4	48	0	0	0
1973 Oak	13	3	28	0	0	0
1974 Oak	12	3	35	0	0	0
1975 ChiB	7	0	0	0	0	0
NFL Total	130	27	486	3	7	4

GENE WILSON Wilson, Ollie Eugene 5′10″, 178 **DB-OE**
Col: Southern Methodist B: 6/24/1926, Arp, TX
1947 GB: 9 G; Rush 1-(-2) -2.0; Rec 3-34 11.3. **1948** GB: 12 G; Rec 2-23 11.5; Int 2-13. **Total:** 21 G; Rush 1-(-2) -2.0; Rec 5-57 11.4; Int 2-13.

OTIS WILSON Wilson, Otis Ray 6′2″, 227 **LB**
Col: Syracuse; Louisville *HS:* Thomas Jefferson [Brooklyn, NY] B: 9/15/1957, New York, NY *Drafted:* 1980 Round 1 ChiB
1982 ChiB: 2.5 Sac. **1983** ChiB: 2 Sac. **1984** ChiB: 6.5 Sac. **1985** ChiB: Scor 1 Saf; 10.5 Sac. **1986** ChiB: 8 Sac. **1987** ChiB: 6.5 Sac. **Total:** Scor 1 Saf; 36 Sac.

		Interceptions			
Year Team	**G**	**Int**	**Yds**	**TD**	**Fum**
1980 ChiB	16	2	4	0	1
1981 ChiB	15	0	0	0	0
1982 ChiB	9	2	39	**1**	0
1983 ChiB	16	1	6	0	0
1984 ChiB	15	0	0	0	0
1985 ChiB	16	3	35	**1**	0
1986 ChiB	15	2	31	0	0
1987 ChiB	7	0	0	0	0
1989 LARd	1	0	0	0	0
NFL Total	110	10	115	2	1

PERCE WILSON Wilson, Percy 150 **BB**
(Shorty) *Col:* No College *HS:* Western [Detroit, MI] B: 1890 D: 9/20/1936
1920 Det: 7 G.

BERNARD WILSON Wilson, Raphael Bernard 6′3″, 303 **DT-NT**
Col: Tennessee State *HS:* Maplewood [Nashville, TN] B: 8/17/1970, Nashville, TN
1993 TB: 13 G. **1994** TB-Ariz: 14 G; 1 Sac. TB: 1 G. Ariz: 13 G; 1 Sac. **1995** Ariz: 16 G; 1 Sac. **1996** Ariz: 16 G; 1 Sac. **1997** Ariz: 16 G; Int 1-66 1 TD; 6 Pt. **1998** Ariz: 16 G; 1 Sac. **Total:** 91 G; Int 1-66 1 TD; 6 Pt; 4 Sac.

MILT WILSON Wilson, Richard Milton 5′10″, 200 **G**
Col: Wis.-Oshkosh *HS:* Oshkosh [WI] Deceased
1921 GB: 6 G.

ROBERT WILSON Wilson, Robert 5′11″, 176 **WR**
Col: Florida A&M *HS:* Jefferson Co. [Monticello, FL] B: 6/23/1974, Tallahassee, FL
1998 Sea: 16 G; KR 1-16 16.0.

BOBBY WILSON Wilson, Robert Edward Jr. 5′9″, 147 **TB-DB**
Col: Southern Methodist *HS:* Corsicana [TX] B: 8/16/1913, Nacogdoches, TX *Drafted:* 1936 Round 5 Bkn
1936 Bkn: Pass 40-11 27.5%, 148 3.70 9 Int; Rec 1-12 12.0 1 TD.

		Rushing				Tot
Year Team	**G**	**Att**	**Yds**	**Avg**	**TD**	**TD**
1936 Bkn	12	104	505	4.9	3	4

ROBERT WILSON Wilson, Robert Eugene 6′0″, 250 **RB**
Col: Texas A&M *HS:* Evan E. Worthing [Houston, TX] B: 1/13/1969, South Park, TX *Drafted:* 1991 Round 3 TB
1991 TB: Rec 20-121 6.1 2 TD; KR 2-19 9.5. **1995** Mia: Rec 1-3 3.0. **1996** Mia: Rec 2-5 2.5 1 TD; KR 1-12 12.0. **Total:** Rec 23-129 5.6 3 TD; KR 3-31 10.3.

		Rushing				
Year Team	G	Att	Yds	Avg	TD	Fum
1991 TB	16	42	179	4.3	0	3
1994 Dal-Mia	4	1	-1	-1.0	0	0
1994 Dal	2	1	-1	-1.0	0	0
1994 Mia	2	0	0	—	0	0
1995 Mia	16	1	5	5.0	0	0
1996 Mia	15	1	0	0.0	0	0
NFL Total	51	45	183	4.1	0	3

MIKE WILSON Wilson, Samuel Marshall 5′10″, 167 **OE-BB**
Col: Lehigh *HS:* Northeast [Philadelphia, PA] B: 12/2/1896, Edge Hill, PA D: 5/16/1978, Boynton Beach, FL
1922 Roch: 1 G. **1923** RI: 8 G; Rec 1 TD; 6 Pt. **1924** RI: 8 G; Rec 1 TD; 6 Pt. **Total:** 17 G; Rec 2 TD; 12 Pt.

SHEDDRICK WILSON Wilson, Sheddrick Roderica 6′2″, 210 **WR**
Col: Louisiana State *HS:* Thomasville [GA] B: 11/23/1973, Thomasville, GA
1996 Hou: 11 G; Rec 2-24 12.0.

STANLEY WILSON Wilson, Stanley T 5′10″, 209 **RB**
Col: Oklahoma *HS:* Phineas Banning [Los Angeles, CA] B: 8/23/1961, Los Angeles, CA *Drafted:* 1983 Round 9 Cin
1983 Cin: KR 7-161 23.0. **Total:** KR 7-161 23.0.

		Rushing				Receiving					Tot
Year Team	G	Att	Yds	Avg	TD	Rec	Yds	Avg	TD	Fum	TD
1983 Cin	10	56	267	4.8	1	12	107	8.9	1	4	2
1984 Cin	1	17	74	4.4	0	2	15	7.5	0	0	0
1986 Cin	10	68	379	5.6	8	4	45	11.3	0	1	8
1988 Cin	15	112	398	3.6	2	9	110	12.2	1	3	3
NFL Total	36	253	1118	4.4	11	27	277	10.3	2	8	13

STEVEN WILSON Wilson, Steven Alan 6′4″, 265 **C-OG-OT**
Col: Georgia *HS:* Southwest [Macon, GA] B: 5/19/1954, Fort Sill, OK *Drafted:* 1976 Round 5 TB
1976 TB: 10 G. **1977** TB: 14 G. **1978** TB: 16 G. **1979** TB: 16 G. **1980** TB: 15 G. **1981** TB: 15 G. **1982** TB: 8 G. **1983** TB: 10 G. **1984** TB: 16 G; 1 Fum. **1985** TB: 5 G. **Total:** 125 G; 1 Fum.

STEVE WILSON Wilson, Steven Anthony 5′10″, 195 **DB-WR**
Col: Howard *HS:* Northern [Durham, NC] B: 8/24/1957, Los Angeles, CA
1979 Dal: Rec 3-76 25.3. **1984** Den: 0.5 Sac. **1986** Den: Rec 1-43 43.0 1 TD. **1987** Den: 1 Sac. **1988** Den: 2 Sac. **Total:** Rec 4-119 29.8 1 TD; 3.5 Sac.

		Punt Returns				Kickoff Returns			
Year Team	G	Ret	Yds	Avg	TD	Ret	Yds	Avg	TD
1979 Dal	16	35	236	6.7	0	19	328	17.3	0
1980 Dal	16	0	0	—	0	7	139	19.9	0
1981 Dal	16	0	0	—	0	2	32	16.0	0
1982 Den	8	0	0	—	0	6	123	20.5	0
1983 Den	16	0	0	—	0	24	485	20.2	0
1984 Den	15	1	0	0.0	0	0	0	—	0
1985 Den	14	0	0	—	0	0	0	—	0
1986 Den	16	0	0	—	0	0	0	—	0
1987 Den	11	0	0	—	0	0	0	—	0
1988 Den	12	0	0	—	0	0	0	—	0
NFL Total	140	36	236	6.6	0	58	1107	19.1	0

	Interceptions			
Year Team	Int	Yds	TD	Fum
1979 Dal	0	0	0	1
1980 Dal	4	82	0	0
1981 Dal	2	0	0	0
1982 Den	2	22	0	0
1983 Den	5	91	0	1
1984 Den	4	59	0	1
1985 Den	3	8	0	0
1986 Den	1	-5	0	0
1988 Den	1	7	0	0
NFL Total	22	264	0	3

TED WILSON Wilson, Ted 5′9″, 170 **WR**
Col: Central Florida *HS:* Zephyrhills [FL] B: 7/14/1964
1987 Was: 3 G; Rush 2-28 14.0 1 TD; Rec 5-112 22.4 1 TD; PR 8-143 17.9; KR 1-20 20.0; Tot TD 2; 12 Pt.

TOMMY WILSON Wilson, Thomas Lee 6′0″, 203 **HB-FB**
(Touchdown Tommy) *Col:* No College *HS:* Hillside [Durham, NC] B: 9/1/1932, Stamford, CT
1956 LARm: Pass 1-0; PR 2-0. **1957** LARm: PR 1-28 28.0. **1958** LARm: Pass 1-0, 1 Int. **Total:** Pass 2-0, 1 Int; PR 3-28 9.3.

		Rushing				Receiving			
Year Team	G	Att	Yds	Avg	TD	Rec	Yds	Avg	TD
1956 LARm	12	64	470	7.3	0	6	86	14.3	0
1957 LARm	11	127	616	4.9	3	7	95	13.6	1
1958 LARm	12	73	475	6.5	9	9	101	11.2	1
1959 LARm	12	40	210	5.3	0	12	83	6.9	1
1960 LARm	11	41	139	3.4	0	11	82	7.5	2
1961 LARm	11	44	220	5.0	1	1	12	12.0	0
1962 Cle	14	46	141	3.1	1	8	110	13.8	0
1963 Min	8	73	282	3.9	4	7	48	6.9	0
NFL Total	91	508	2553	5.0	18	61	617	10.1	5

	Kickoff Returns					Tot
Year Team	Ret	Yds	Avg	TD	Fum	TD
1956 LARm	15	477	**31.8**	**1**	2	1
1957 LARm	11	290	26.4	0	6	4
1958 LARm	16	324	20.3	0	7	10
1959 LARm	7	243	34.7	0	1	1
1960 LARm	2	48	24.0	0	1	2
1961 LARm	0	0	—	0	2	1
1962 Cle	11	307	27.9	0	2	1
1963 Min	0	0	—	0	2	4
NFL Total	62	1689	27.2	1	23	24

TIM WILSON Wilson, Timothy 6′3″, 226 **FB**
Col: Maryland *HS:* De La Warr [New Castle, DE] B: 1/14/1954, New Castle, DE Deceased *Drafted:* 1977 Round 3 Hou
1977 Hou: KR 2-33 16.5. **1978** Hou: KR 2-29 14.5. **1979** Hou: KR 2-30 15.0. **1981** Hou: KR 3-41 13.7. **1982** Hou: KR 2-40 20.0. **1984** NO: KR 1-16 16.0. **Total:** KR 12-189 15.8.

		Rushing				Receiving					Tot
Year Team	G	Att	Yds	Avg	TD	Rec	Yds	Avg	TD	Fum	TD
1977 Hou	10	99	343	3.5	3	20	107	5.4	0	1	3
1978 Hou	16	126	431	3.4	0	15	91	6.1	1	5	1
1979 Hou	16	84	319	3.8	2	29	208	7.2	1	2	3
1980 Hou	16	66	257	3.9	1	30	170	5.7	1	2	2
1981 Hou	16	13	35	2.7	0	5	33	6.6	0	2	0
1982 Hou	9	0	0	—	0	0	0	—	0	0	0
1983 NO	6	8	21	2.6	0	0	0	—	0	0	0
1984 NO	12	2	8	4.0	0	0	0	—	0	0	0
NFL Total	101	398	1414	3.6	6	99	609	6.2	3	12	9

TROY WILSON Wilson, Troy Anthony 5′10″, 170 **DB**
Col: Notre Dame *HS:* Thomas Jefferson [Frederick, MD] B: 9/19/1965, San Antonio, TX
1987 Cle: 3 G; PR 10-101 10.1; Int 1-0; 2 Fum.

TROY WILSON Wilson, Troy Ethan 6′4″, 257 **DE**
Col: Pittsburg State *HS:* Shawnee Heights [Tecumseh, KS] B: 11/22/1970, Topeka, KS *Drafted:* 1993 Round 7 SF
1993 SF: 10 G; 5.5 Sac. **1994** SF: 11 G; 2 Sac. **1995** Den: 3 G; 0.5 Sac. **1998** NO: 15 G; 1 Sac. **Total:** 39 G; 9 Sac.

WALTER WILSON Wilson, Walter James 5′10″, 185 **WR**
Col: East Carolina *HS:* Southern [Baltimore, MD] B: 10/6/1966, Baltimore, MD *Drafted:* 1990 Round 3 SD
1990 SD: 14 G; Rush 1-0; Rec 10-87 8.7.

CAMP WILSON Wilson, Warren Camp 6′2″, 201 **FB-LB**
Col: Tarleton State; Hardin-Simmons; Tulsa B: 3/29/1922, Pecos, TX
1946 Det: Rec 9-62 6.9; KR 1-12 12.0; Punt 22-868 39.5. **1947** Det: Rec 5-96 19.2; KR 3-46 15.3. **1948** Det: Rec 2-9 4.5; KR 10-228 22.8. **1949** Det: Rec 6-31 5.2. **Total:** Rec 22-198 9.0; KR 14-286 20.4; Punt 22-868 39.5.

		Rushing				
Year Team	G	Att	Yds	Avg	TD	Fum
1946 Det	10	64	207	3.2	3	6
1947 Det	12	89	412	4.6	0	2
1948 Det	11	157	612	3.9	2	6
1949 Det	12	68	222	3.3	1	3
NFL Total	45	378	1453	3.8	6	17

WAYNE WILSON Wilson, Wayne MacArthur 6′3″, 215 **RB**
Col: Shepherd *HS:* Howard [Ellicott City, MD] B: 9/4/1957, Montgomery Co., MD *Drafted:* 1979 Round 12 Hou

		Rushing				Receiving			
Year Team	G	Att	Yds	Avg	TD	Rec	Yds	Avg	TD
1979 NO	14	5	26	5.2	0	0	0	—	0
1980 NO	15	63	188	3.0	1	31	241	7.8	1
1981 NO	16	44	137	3.1	1	31	384	12.4	4
1982 NO	8	103	413	4.0	3	25	175	7.0	2

1983 NO	14	199	787	4.0	9	20	178	8.9	2
1984 NO	14	74	261	3.5	1	33	314	9.5	3
1985 NO	16	168	645	3.8	1	38	228	6.0	2
1986 Min-NO	12	10	19	1.9	0	1	-3	-3.0	0
1986 Min	7	8	14	1.8	0	0	0	—	0
1986 NO	5	2	5	2.5	0	1	-3	-3.0	0
1987 Was	2	18	55	3.1	2	2	16	8.0	0
NFL Total	111	684	2531	3.7	18	181	1533	8.5	14

	Kickoff Returns					Tot
Year Team	**Ret**	**Yds**	**Avg**	**TD**	**Fum**	**TD**
1979 NO	11	230	20.9	0	1	0
1980 NO	9	159	17.7	0	3	2
1981 NO	31	722	23.3	0	1	5
1982 NO	7	192	27.4	0	4	5
1983 NO	9	239	26.6	0	6	11
1984 NO	1	23	23.0	0	2	4
1985 NO	0	0	—	0	2	3
1986 Min-NO	2	33	16.5	0	0	0
1986 Min	2	33	16.5	0	0	0
1987 Was	2	32	16.0	0	1	2
NFL Total	72	1630	22.6	0	20	32

BILLY WILSON Wilson, William Gene 6′3″, 190 **OE-FL**
Col: San Jose State *HS:* Westmont [Campbell, CA] B: 2/3/1927, Sayre, OK *Drafted:* 1950 Round 22 SF
1951 SF: KR 1-0. **Total:** KR 1-0.

		Receiving				
Year Team	**G**	**Rec**	**Yds**	**Avg**	**TD**	**Fum**
1951 SF	9	18	268	14.9	3	0
1952 SF	9	23	304	13.2	3	1
1953 SF	12	51	840	16.5	**10**	1
1954 SF	12	**60**	830	13.8	5	1
1955 SF	12	53	831	15.7	7	0
1956 SF	12	**60**	889	14.8	5	1
1957 SF	11	**52**	757	14.6	6	0
1958 SF	9	43	592	13.8	5	0
1959 SF	10	44	540	12.3	4	0
1960 SF	4	3	51	17.0	1	0
NFL Total	100	407	5902	14.5	49	4

MIKE WILSON Wilson, William Michael 6′5″, 275 **OT**
Col: Georgia *HS:* Johnson [Gainesville, GA] B: 5/28/1955, Norfolk, VA *Drafted:* 1977 Round 4 Cin
1978 Cin: 9 G. **1979** Cin: 16 G. **1980** Cin: 16 G. **1981** Cin: 16 G. **1982** Cin: 9 G. **1983** Cin: 16 G. **1984** Cin: 16 G. **1985** Cin: 16 G. **1986** Sea: 16 G. **1987** Sea: 12 G. **1988** Sea: 16 G. **1989** Sea: 16 G. **Total:** 174 G.

BILLY WILSON Wilson, William Stanton 5′10″, 184 **OE-DE**
Col: Gonzaga *HS:* Lewiston [ID]; Rogers HS [Spokane, WA] B: 5/8/1911, Union, OR D: 12/1972, Renton, WA
1935 ChiC: 11 G. **1936** ChiC: 12 G; Rec 1-12 12.0. **1937** ChiC: 11 G; Rec 1-2 2.0. **1938** Pit-Phi: 5 G. Pit: 4 G. Phi: 1 G. **Total:** 39 G; Rec 2-14 7.0.

STU WILSON Wilson, William Stuart Jr. 6′2″, 209 **WB-TB-OE**
Col: Washington & Jefferson B: 7/1/1907 D: 9/15/1957, Elizabeth, NJ
1932 SI: 11 G; Pass 7-1 14.3%, 18 2.57 1 Int; Rush 7-(-9) -1.3; Rec 1 TD; Scor 12, 1 FG, 3 XK.

RAY WILSON Wilson, Wiltha Ray 6′1″, 202 **DB**
Col: Pearl River CC MS; New Mexico *HS:* A. Crawford Mosley [Lynn Haven, FL] B: 8/26/1971, Panama City, FL
1994 NO-GB: 6 G. NO: 3 G. GB: 3 G. **Total:** 6 G.

AB WIMBERLY Wimberly, Abner Perry 6′1″, 213 **DE-OE**
Col: Louisiana State *HS:* Oak Ridge [LA] B: 5/4/1926, Oak Ridge, LA D: 9/19/1976, Oak Ridge, LA *Drafted:* 1948 Round 10 Bos
AAFC **1949** LA-A: 12 G; Rec 3-22 7.3; Int 1-16 1 TD; Tot TD 2; 12 Pt.

NFL **1950** GB: 11 G; Rec 2-18 9.0; Int 1-0. **1951** GB: 12 G; Rec 1-10 10.0; KR 2-4 2.0; 1 Fum. **1952** GB: 12 G; Int 1-5. **Total:** 35 G; Rec 3-28 9.3; KR 2-4 2.0; Int 2-5; 1 Fum.

BY WIMBERLY Wimberly, Adlai Byron 6′2″, 200 **T-G**
Col: Washington & Jefferson B: 9/3/1892, Stevenson, AL D: 5/10/1956, Detroit, MI
1925 Det: 11 G.

DEREK WIMBERLY Wimberly, Derek Nathaniel 6′4″, 270 **DE**
Col: Purdue *HS:* American Senior [Hialeah, FL] B: 1/4/1964, Miami, FL
1987 Mia: 3 G; 0.5 Sac.

MARCUS WIMBERLY Wimberly, Marcus Juanald 5′11″, 192 **DB**
Col: Miami (Fla.) *HS:* East [Memphis, TN] B: 7/8/1974, Memphis, TN *Drafted:* 1997 Round 5 Atl
1997 Atl: 6 G.

GARY WIMMER Wimmer, Gary Edwin 6′2″, 225 **LB**
Col: Stanford *HS:* Capital [Boise, ID] B: 3/9/1961, Pocatello, ID
1983 Sea: 3 G.

JEFF WINANS Winans, Jeff Dow 6′5″, 265 **DE-OG-DT-OT**
Col: Modesto JC CA; USC *HS:* Turlock [CA] B: 10/12/1951, Turlock, CA *Drafted:* 1973 Round 2 Buf
1973 Buf: 9 G. **1975** Buf: 11 G. **1976** NO: 3 G. **1977** TB: 11 G. **1978** TB: 1 G. **Total:** 35 G.

TYDUS WINANS Winans, Tydus Oran 5′11″, 180 **WR**
Col: Fresno State *HS:* Carson [CA] B: 7/26/1972, Los Angeles, CA *Drafted:* 1994 Round 3 Was
1994 Was: 15 G; Rush 1-5 5.0; Rec 19-344 18.1 2 TD; Scor 1 2XP; 14 Pt. **1995** Was: 8 G; Rec 4-77 19.3; 1 Fum. **1996** Cin: 2 G. **Total:** 25 G; Rush 1-5 5.0; Rec 23-421 18.3 2 TD; Scor 1 2XP; 14 Pt; 1 Fum.

ERNIE WINBURN Winburn, Earnest 5′11″, 175 **E**
Col: Central Missouri State *HS:* Lees Summit [MO]; Wentworth Mil. School [Lexington, MO] B: 4/1897, Lees Summit, MO Deceased
1923 StL: 1 G.

BILL WINDAUER Windauer, William Joseph 6′4″, 250 **DT-NT**
Col: Iowa *HS:* Mendel [Chicago, IL] B: 11/22/1949, Chicago, IL *Drafted:* 1973 Round 8 Bal
1973 Bal: 2 G. **1974** Bal: 9 G. **1975** NYG: 4 G. **1976** Atl: 3 G. **Total:** 18 G.

JOE WINDBIEL Windbiel, Joseph C 6′1″, 220 **C**
Col: Dayton *HS:* U. of Dayton Prep [OH] B: 3/6/1897, IL D: 6/25/1971, Fort Lauderdale, FL
1921 Eva: 5 G.

SAMMY WINDER Winder, Sammy 5′11″, 203 **RB**
Col: Southern Mississippi *HS:* Ridgeland [MS] B: 7/15/1959, Madison, MS *Drafted:* 1982 Round 5 Den
1985 Den: Pass 1-0. **1988** Den: KR 1-11 11.0. **1990** Den: KR 4-55 13.8. **Total:** Pass 1-0; KR 5-66 13.2.

		Rushing				Receiving					Tot
Year Team	**G**	**Att**	**Yds**	**Avg**	**TD**	**Rec**	**Yds**	**Avg**	**TD**	**Fum**	**TD**
1982 Den	8	67	259	3.9	1	11	83	7.5	0	1	1
1983 Den	14	196	757	3.9	3	23	150	6.5	0	7	3
1984 Den	16	296	1153	3.9	4	44	288	6.5	2	5	6
1985 Den	14	199	714	3.6	8	31	197	6.4	0	4	8
1986 Den	16	240	789	3.3	9	26	171	6.6	5	2	14
1987 Den	12	196	741	3.8	6	14	74	5.3	1	5	7
1988 Den	16	149	543	3.6	4	17	103	6.1	1	1	5
1989 Den	16	110	351	3.2	2	14	91	6.5	0	1	2
1990 Den	15	42	120	2.9	2	17	145	8.5	0	2	2
NFL Total	127	1495	5427	3.6	39	197	1302	6.6	9	28	48

DAVID WINDHAM Windham, David Rogers 6′2″, 240 **LB**
Col: Jackson State *HS:* C.F. Vigor [Prichard, AL] B: 3/14/1961, Mobile, AL
1987 Was: 3 G.

BOB WINDSOR Windsor, Robert Edward 6′4″, 220 **TE**
Col: Montgomery Coll. MD (J.C.); Kentucky *HS:* Montgomery Blair [Silver Spring, MD] B: 12/19/1942, Washington, DC *Drafted:* 1966 Round 2 SF
1967 SF: Rush 1-7 7.0; KR 1-21 21.0; **1** Fum TD. **1969** SF: Rush 5-39 7.8. **1970** SF: KR 1-0. **1971** SF: Rush 1-21 21.0; KR 4-66 16.5. **1972** NE: Rush 1-(-4) -4.0. **1973** NE: Rush 1-(-6) -6.0; KR 1-0. **Total:** Rush 9-57 6.3; KR 7-87 12.4; 1 Fum TD.

		Receiving					Tot
Year Team	**G**	**Rec**	**Yds**	**Avg**	**TD**	**Fum**	**TD**
1967 SF	14	21	254	12.1	2	1	3
1968 SF	14	8	146	18.3	2	0	2
1969 SF	14	49	597	12.2	2	0	2
1970 SF	14	31	363	11.7	2	0	2
1971 SF	13	2	32	16.0	0	1	0
1972 NE	14	33	383	11.6	1	1	1
1973 NE	13	23	348	15.1	4	2	4
1974 NE	7	12	127	10.6	1	0	1
1975 NE	14	6	57	9.5	0	0	0
NFL Total	117	185	2307	12.5	14	5	15

VERN WINFIELD Winfield, Vernon Hall 6′2″, 248 **OG**
Col: Minnesota *HS:* South [Minneapolis, MN] B: 8/27/1949, Norfolk, VA *Drafted:* 1972 Round 6 Phi
1972 Phi: 9 G; PR 1-12 12.0; KR 3-9 3.0. **1973** Phi: 5 G. **Total:** 14 G; PR 1-12 12.0; KR 3-9 3.0.

CHUCK WINFREY Winfrey, Carl LeNell 6′0″, 230 **LB**
Col: Wisconsin *HS:* DuSable [Chicago, IL] B: 3/27/1949, Chicago, IL
1971 Min: 14 G. **1972** Pit: 1 G. **Total:** 15 G.

STAN WINFREY Winfrey, Stanley 5′11″, 223 **RB**
Col: Arkansas State *HS:* Forrest City [AR] B: 2/20/1953, Forrest City, AR *Drafted:* 1975 Round 2 Mia
1975 Mia: KR 1-25 25.0. **1976** Mia: Rec 6-55 9.2 1 TD; KR 2-24 12.0. **Total:** Rec 6-55 9.2 1 TD; KR 3-49 16.3.

Year Team	G	Rushing Att	Yds	Avg	TD	Fum	Tot TD
1975 Mia	11	3	10	3.3	0	0	0
1976 Mia	14	52	205	3.9	1	1	2
1977 TB-Mia	5	0	0	—	0	0	0
1977 TB	2	0	0	—	0	0	0
1977 Mia	3	0	0	—	0	0	0
NFL Total	30	55	215	3.9	1	1	2

CHRIS WING Wing, Christopher R 6′2″, 235 **LB**
Col: Boise State *HS:* Redmond [WA] B: 5/28/1971, Redmond, WA
1997 NYJ: 2 G.

ELMER WINGATE Wingate, Elmer Horsey Jr. 6′3″, 230 **DE**
Col: Maryland *HS:* Baltimore Polytechnic Inst. [MD] B: 10/26/1928, Baltimore, MD *Drafted:* 1951 Round 4 NYY
1953 Bal: 12 G.

HEATH WINGATE Wingate, Heath L 6′2″, 240 **C**
(Gate) *Col:* Bowling Green State *HS:* Whitmer [Toledo, OH]
B: 12/5/1944, Toledo, OH *Drafted:* 1966 Round 13 Was
1967 Was: 3 G.

LEONARD WINGATE Wingate, Leonard Junior 6′3″, 265 **DT**
Col: South Carolina State *HS:* Burke [Charleston, SC] B: 11/3/1961, Charleston, SC
1987 Atl: 1 G.

BLAKE WINGLE Wingle, Blake Leo 6′2″, 267 **OG**
Col: Ventura Coll. CA (J.C.); Cal Poly-S.L.O.; UCLA *HS:* Rio Mesa [Oxnard, CA] B: 4/17/1960, Pottsville, CA *Drafted:* 1983 Round 9 Pit
1983 Pit: 16 G. **1984** Pit: 15 G. **1985** Pit-GB: 5 G. Pit: 3 G. GB: 2 G. **1987** Cle: 3 G. **Total:** 39 G.

RICH WINGO Wingo, Richard Allen 6′1″, 230 **LB**
Col: Alabama *HS:* Elkhart Central [IN] B: 7/16/1956, Elkhart, IN
Drafted: 1979 Round 7 GB
1979 GB: 16 G; Int 2-13. **1981** GB: 16 G; Int 1-38; Scor **1** 1XP; 1 Pt. **1982** GB: 5 G; Int 1-0; 1 Sac. **1983** GB: 16 G. **1984** GB: 16 G. **Total:** 69 G; Int 4-51; Scor 1 1XP; 1 Pt; 1 Sac.

DEAN WINK Wink, Dean Albert 6′4″, 246 **DE-DT**
Col: Yankton *HS:* Woodbury Central [Molville, IA] B: 9/25/1944, Moville, IA
1967 Phi: 5 G. **1968** Phi: 7 G. **Total:** 12 G.

BOB WINKEL Winkel, Bob Alexander 6′4″, 253 **DT-DE**
Col: Kentucky *HS:* Oak Ridge [KY] B: 10/23/1955, Paducah, KY
Drafted: 1979 Round 7 Min
1979 NYJ: 15 G. **1980** NYJ: 16 G; KR 1-4 4.0. **Total:** 31 G; KR 1-4 4.0.

BEN WINKELMAN Winkelman, Ben Hartwell 6′1″, 190 **OE-WB-FB-TB**
Col: Arkansas *HS:* Fayetteville [AR] B: 2/28/1899, Fayetteville, AR
D: 12/18/1981, Citrus Heights, CA
1922 Mil: 1 G. **1923** Mil: 13 G; Rush 1 TD; Rec 1 TD; Int **1** TD; Scor 45, 6 FG, 9 XK; Tot TD 3. **1924** Mil: 13 G; Rush 1 TD; Rec 1 TD; Scor 15, 1 FG; Tot TD 2. **Total:** 27 G; Rush 2 TD; Rec 2 TD; Int 1 TD; Scor 60, 7 FG, 9 XK; Tot TD 5.

BERNIE WINKLER Winkler, Bernard Arthur 6′1″, 232 **T**
Col: Millsaps; Texas Tech *HS:* Temple [TX] B: 12/5/1925, The Grove, TX D: 6/28/1990, New Braunfels, TX
AAFC **1948** LA-A: 4 G.

FRANCIS WINKLER Winkler, Francis Michael 6′3″, 230 **DE**
(Bubba) *Col:* Memphis *HS:* Memphis Catholic [TN] B: 10/20/1946, Memphis, TN *Drafted:* 1968 Round 5 GB
1968 GB: 7 G; KR 1-0. **1969** GB: 14 G. **Total:** 21 G; KR 1-0.

JIM WINKLER Winkler, James Carl 6′2″, 250 **DT-OG**
Col: Texas A&M *HS:* Temple [TX] B: 7/21/1927, Moody, TX Deceased
Drafted: 1949 Round 3 LARm
1951 LARm: 12 G. **1952** LARm: 11 G. **1953** Bal: 9 G; 1 Fum. **Total:** 32 G; 1 Fum.

JOE WINKLER Winkler, Joseph C 6′1″, 200 **C-LB**
Col: Purdue *HS:* Catholic Central [Hammond, IN] B: 3/9/1922, Hammond, IN *Drafted:* 1945 Round 12 Cle
1945 Cle: 8 G; Int 1-5.

RANDY WINKLER Winkler, Randolph Stanley 6′5″, 255 **OT-OG**
Col: Tarleton State *HS:* Belton [TX] B: 7/18/1943, Temple, TX
Drafted: 1966 Round 12 Det
1967 Det: 8 G. **1968** Atl: 12 G. **1971** GB: 7 G. **Total:** 27 G.

BRYANT WINN Winn, Bryant M 6′4″, 231 **LB**
Col: Houston *HS:* Hamilton [Memphis, TN] B: 11/7/1961, Memphis, TN
1987 Den: 3 G.

BILL WINNESHICK Winneshick, William 5′8″, 180 **C**
Col: Carlisle B: 1894, NC Deceased
1922 Oor: 5 G.

DOUG WINSLOW Winslow, Charles Douglas 5′11″, 181 **WR**
Col: Drake *HS:* Southeast Polk [Runnels, IA] B: 7/19/1951, Des Moines, IA *Drafted:* 1973 Round 8 NO
1973 NO: 12 G; Rec 4-45 11.3; PR 5-47 9.4. **1976** Was: 5 G; KR 2-32 16.0; 1 Fum. **Total:** 17 G; Rec 4-45 11.3; PR 5-47 9.4; KR 2-32 16.0; 1 Fum.

GEORGE WINSLOW Winslow, George Arthur 6′4″, 205 **P**
Col: Wisconsin; Villanova *HS:* La Salle Prep [Philadelphia, PA]
B: 7/28/1963, Philadelphia, PA
1987 Cle: 5 G; Punt 18-616 34.2. **1989** NO: 5 G; Rush 1-0; Punt 16-595 37.2; 1 Fum. **Total:** 10 G; Rush 1-0; Punt 34-1211 35.6; 1 Fum.

KELLEN WINSLOW Winslow, Kellen Boswell 6′5″, 251 **TE**
Col: Missouri *HS:* East St. Louis [IL] B: 11/5/1957, St. Louis, MO
Drafted: 1979 Round 1 SD *HOF:* 1995
1981 SD: Pass 2-0. **1982** SD: Pass 1-0. **1986** SD: KR 2-11 5.5.
Total: Pass 3-0; KR 2-11 5.5.

Year Team	G	Receiving Rec	Yds	Avg	TD	Fum
1979 SD	7	25	255	10.2	2	1
1980 SD	16	**89**	1290	14.5	9	2
1981 SD	16	**88**	1075	12.2	10	2
1982 SD	9	54	721	13.4	6	1
1983 SD	16	88	1172	13.3	8	3
1984 SD	7	55	663	12.1	2	1
1985 SD	10	25	318	12.7	0	0
1986 SD	16	64	728	11.4	5	0
1987 SD	12	53	519	9.8	3	1
NFL Total	109	541	6741	12.5	45	11

PAUL WINSLOW Winslow, Paul Lawrence Jr. 5′11″, 200 **DB**
Col: North Carolina Central *HS:* P.W. Moore [Elizabeth City, NC]
B: 2/28/1938, Elizabeth City, NC *Drafted:* 1960 Round 13 GB
1960 GB: 12 G; Rush 2-(-3) -1.5; 6 Pt.

BOB WINSLOW Winslow, Robert E 6′2″, 205 **DE**
Col: Modesto JC CA; USC *HS:* Inglewood [CA] B: 9/18/1916, Rifle, CO D: 1/11/1994, Fallbrook, CA *Drafted:* 1940 Round 5 Det
1940 Det-Bkn: 10 G. Det: 8 G. Bkn: 2 G. **Total:** 10 G.

CHARLIE WINSTON Winston, Charles Soudder 6′1″, 185 **G**
(Chuck) *Col:* Purdue *HS:* Washington [IN] B: 6/1890, Washington, IN
D: 11/11/1944, Chicago, IL
1920 Day: 5 G.

DENNIS WINSTON Winston, Dennis Edward 6′0″, 228 **LB**
(Dirt) *Col:* Arkansas *HS:* Robert E. Lee [Marianna, AR]
B: 10/25/1955, Forrest City, AR *Drafted:* 1977 Round 5 Pit
1980 Pit: KR 1-13 13.0. **1982** NO: 0.5 Sac. **1983** NO: 1 Sac. **1984** NO: 0.5 Sac. **Total:** KR 1-13 13.0; 2 Sac.

Year Team	G	Interceptions Int	Yds	TD	Fum	Tot TD
1977 Pit	13	2	7	0	0	0
1978 Pit	16	0	0	0	0	0
1979 Pit	16	3	48	1	0	1
1980 Pit	14	0	0	0	0	1
1981 Pit	14	1	1	0	0	0
1982 NO	9	2	-2	0	0	0
1983 NO	16	3	21	0	1	0
1984 NO	16	2	90	**2**	0	2
1985 NO-Pit	12	0	8	0	0	0
1985 NO	2	0	8	0	0	0
1985 Pit	10	0	0	0	0	0
1986 Pit	16	0	0	0	0	0
NFL Total	142	13	173	3	1	4

DEMOND WINSTON Winston, Edward DeMond 6′2″, 239 **LB**
Col: Vanderbilt *HS:* Central Catholic [Lansing, MI] B: 9/14/1968, Birmingham, AL *Drafted:* 1990 Round 4 NO
1990 NO: 16 G. **1992** NO: 15 G. **1993** NO: 16 G. **1994** NO: 3 G.
Total: 50 G.

KELTON WINSTON Winston, Kelton Earl 6′0″, 195 **DB**
(Scooter) *Col:* Wiley *HS:* Terrell [TX] B: 10/22/1940, Corsicana, TX
D: 11/30/1980, Los Angeles, CA *Drafted:* 1962 Round 9 ChiB
1967 LARm: 9 G; PR 1-12 12.0; KR 3-65 21.7. **1968** LARm: 11 G.
Total: 20 G; PR 1-12 12.0; KR 3-65 21.7.

LLOYD WINSTON Winston, Lloyd Leonard 6′2″, 215 **FB**
Col: Santa Monica Coll. CA (J.C.); USC *HS:* Merced [CA] B: 9/22/1939
1962 SF: Rec 1-2 2.0; KR 3-67 22.3. **1963** SF: Rec 2-13 6.5.
Total: Rec 3-15 5.0; KR 3-67 22.3.

Year Team	G	Rushing Att	Yds	Avg	TD	Fum
1962 SF	2	1	-15	-15.0	0	1
1963 SF	4	27	127	4.7	1	0
NFL Total	6	28	112	4.0	1	1

ROY WINSTON Winston, Roy Charles 5′11″, 222 LB
(Moonie) *Col:* Louisiana State *HS:* Istrouma [Baton Rouge, LA]
B: 9/15/1940, Baton Rouge, LA *Drafted:* 1962 Round 4 Min
1963 Min: **1** Fum TD. **1966** Min: KR 1-2 2.0. **1970** Min: 1 Fum TD.
1973 Min: Scor 1 Saf. **Total:** KR 1-2 2.0; Scor 1 Saf; 2 Fum TD.

		Interceptions			Tot
Year Team	G	Int	Yds	TD	TD
1962 Min	13	0	0	0	0
1963 Min	14	1	0	0	1
1964 Min	14	3	24	0	0
1965 Min	14	0	0	0	0
1966 Min	12	0	0	0	0
1967 Min	14	0	0	0	0
1968 Min	14	0	0	0	0
1969 Min	14	3	17	0	0
1970 Min	14	1	13	0	1
1971 Min	14	1	29	1	1
1972 Min	13	3	55	0	0
1973 Min	13	0	0	0	0
1974 Min	12	0	0	0	0
1975 Min	9	0	0	0	0
1976 Min	7	0	0	0	0
NFL Total	191	12	138	1	3

BLAISE WINTER Winter, Blaise 6′3″, 278 DE-DT-NT
Col: Syracuse *HS:* Tappan Zee [Orangeburg, NY] B: 1/31/1962, Blauvelt, NY *Drafted:* 1984 Round 2 Ind
1984 Ind: 16 G; 2 Sac. **1986** SD: 4 G. **1987** SD: 3 G; 4 Sac. **1988** GB: 16 G; KR 1-7 7.0; 5 Sac. **1989** GB: 16 G; 2 Sac. **1990** GB: 13 G. **1992** SD: 16 G; 6 Sac. **1993** SD: 16 G; 2 Sac. **1994** SD: 2 G. **Total:** 102 G; KR 1-7 7.0; 21 Sac.

BILL WINTER Winter, William Ross 6′3″, 220 LB
Col: St. Olaf *HS:* Spring Valley [MN] B: 1/28/1940, Milbank, SD
D: 5/29/1995 *Drafted:* 1962 Round 18 NYG
1962 NYG: 11 G. **1963** NYG: 10 G; Int 1-38. **1964** NYG: 12 G. **Total:** 33 G; Int 1-38.

LEON WINTERNHEIMER Winternheimer, Leon 6′1″, 240 G-T
Col: No College Deceased
1921 Eva: 1 G. **1922** Eva: 2 G. **Total:** 3 G.

CHET WINTERS Winters, Chester 5′11″, 205 RB
Col: Oklahoma *HS:* Jacksonville [AR] B: 10/22/1960, Chicago, IL
1983 GB: 4 G; KR 3-28 9.3.

FRANK WINTERS Winters, Frank Mitchell 6′3″, 291 C
Col: Western Illinois *HS:* Emerson [Union City, NJ] B: 1/23/1964, Hoboken, NJ *Drafted:* 1987 Round 10 Cle
1987 Cle: 12 G; 1 Fum. **1988** Cle: 16 G. **1989** NYG: 15 G. **1990** KC: 16 G. **1991** KC: 16 G. **1992** GB: 16 G; 1 Fum. **1993** GB: 16 G. **1994** GB: 16 G; 1 Fum. **1995** GB: 16 G. **1996** GB: 16 G. **1997** GB: 13 G. **1998** GB: 13 G. **Total:** 181 G; 3 Fum.

SONNY WINTERS Winters, Lindell 5′7″, 155 TB
Col: Ohio Wesleyan *HS:* V. W. Scott [Toledo, OH] B: 1898 Deceased
1923 Col: 10 G; Pass 5 TD; Rush 2 TD; Rec 1 TD; Tot TD 3; 18 Pt.
1924 Col: 8 G; Pass 8 TD; Rush 1 TD; Scor 14, 1 FG, 5 XK. **Total:** 18 G; Pass 13 TD; Rush 3 TD; Rec 1 TD; Scor 32, 1 FG, 5 XK; Tot TD 4.

RICHARD WINTHER Winther, Richard Lew 6′4″, 261 C
(Wimpy) *Col:* Mississippi *HS:* Biloxi [MS] B: 10/22/1947, Charles City, IA *Drafted:* 1971 Round 4 NO
1971 GB: 11 G. **1972** NO: 5 G. **Total:** 16 G.

DON WIPER Wiper, Donald William 5′10″, 150 BB
Col: Ohio State *HS:* North [Columbus, OH] B: 7/8/1900, Columbus, OH D: 11/8/1961, Columbus, OH
1922 Col: 2 G.

DENNIS WIRGOWSKI Wirgowski, Dennis 6′5″, 257 DE-DT
Col: Purdue *HS:* Central [Bay City, MI] B: 9/20/1947, Bay City, MI
Drafted: 1970 Round 9 Bos
1970 Bos: 14 G. **1971** NE: 9 G. **1972** NE: 14 G; 1 Fum. **1973** Phi: 13 G; Int 1-0. **Total:** 50 G; Int 1-0; 1 Fum.

TERRENCE WISDOM Wisdom, Terrence Bancroft 6′4″, 300 OG
Col: Syracuse *HS:* Roosevelt [NY] B: 12/4/1971, Brooklyn, NY
1995 NYJ: 5 G.

MIKE WISE Wise, Michael Allen 6′6″, 271 DE
Col: California-Davis *HS:* San Marin [Novato, CA] B: 6/5/1964, Greenbrae, CA *Drafted:* 1986 Round 4 LARd
1986 LARd: 6 G. **1988** LARd: 16 G; 5 Sac. **1989** LARd: 16 G; 3.5 Sac.
1990 LARd: 12 G; 1 Sac. **1991** Cle: 3 G. **Total:** 53 G; 9.5 Sac.

PHILLIP WISE Wise, Phillip Vaughn 6′0″, 190 DB
Col: South Dakota; Nebraska-Omaha *HS:* Omaha Tech [NE]
B: 4/25/1949, Omaha, NE *Drafted:* 1971 Round 6 NYJ
1971 NYJ: 14 G; KR 8-210 26.3; Int 1-33. **1972** NYJ: 9 G; KR 9-211 23.4; 1 Fum. **1973** NYJ: 8 G; **1** Fum TD; 6 Pt. **1974** NYJ: 14 G. **1975** NYJ: 5 G; KR 1-20 20.0; Int 2-17. **1976** NYJ: 12 G; 1 Fum. **1977** Min: 13 G; Int 1-4. **1978** Min: 16 G; Int 2-21. **1979** Min: 1 G. **Total:** 92 G; KR 18-441 24.5; Int 6-75; 1 Fum TD; 6 Pt; 2 Fum.

GARY WISENER Wisener, Gary Gayle 6′1″, 206 DB
Col: Baylor *HS:* Fort Smith [AR] B: 8/24/1938, Warren, AR
Drafted: 1960 Round 1 Bos
1960 Dal: 10 G. **1961** Hou: 5 G. **Total:** 15 G.

JEFF WISKA Wiska, Jeffrey Rolland 6′3″, 265 OG
Col: Michigan State *HS:* Catholic Central [Redford, MI] B: 10/17/1959, Detroit, MI
1986 Cle: 1 G. **1987** Mia: 3 G. **Total:** 4 G.

LEO WISNIEWSKI Wisniewski, Leo Joseph 6′1″, 263 NT
Col: Penn State *HS:* Fox Chapel [PA] B: 11/6/1959, Hancock, MI
Drafted: 1982 Round 2 Bal
1982 Bal: 7 G; 2.5 Sac. **1983** Bal: 15 G; 5 Sac. **1984** Ind: 14 G; 7 Sac.
Total: 36 G; 14.5 Sac.

STEVE WISNIEWSKI Wisniewski, Stephen Adam 6′4″, 294 OG
Col: Penn State *HS:* Westfield [Houston, TX] B: 4/7/1967, Rutland, VT
Drafted: 1989 Round 2 Dal
1989 LARd: 15 G. **1990** LARd: 16 G. **1991** LARd: 15 G. **1992** LARd: 16 G. **1993** LARd: 16 G. **1994** LARd: 16 G. **1995** Oak: 16 G. **1996** Oak: 16 G. **1997** Oak: 16 G. **1998** Oak: 16 G. **Total:** 158 G.

ZEKE WISSINGER Wissinger, Zonar Albert 6′0″, 195 T
(Doc) *Col:* Pittsburgh *HS:* Johnstown [PA] B: 10/30/1902, Johnstown, PA D: 11/1963, PA
1926 Pott: 5 G.

PETE WISSMAN Wissman, Lawrence Peter 6′0″, 215 C-LB
Col: Miami (Ohio); Washington-St. Louis; St. Louis *HS:* Maplewood [MO] B: 10/9/1923, St. Louis, MO *Drafted:* 1949 Round 7 NYB
AAFC **1949** SF-A: 12 G; Int 1-12.

NFL **1950** SF: 12 G; Int 1-5. **1951** SF: 9 G; Int 2-12; 1 Fum. **1952** SF: 12 G. **1954** SF: 3 G. **Total:** 36 G; Int 3-17; 1 Fum.

AL WISTERT Wistert, Albert Alexander 6′1″, 214 OT-DT-OG
(Ox) *Col:* Michigan *HS:* Foreman [Chicago, IL] B: 12/28/1920, Chicago, IL *Drafted:* 1943 Round 5 Phi
1943 PhPt: 9 G. **1944** Phi: 8 G. **1945** Phi: 10 G. **1946** Phi: 9 G; Int 1-27.
1947 Phi: 12 G. **1948** Phi: 12 G. **1949** Phi: 12 G. **1950** Phi: 11 G. **1951** Phi: 12 G. **Total:** 95 G; Int 1-27.

GRANT WISTROM Wistrom, Grant 6′4″, 267 DE
Col: Nebraska *HS:* Webb City [MO] B: 7/3/1976, Webb City, MO
Drafted: 1998 Round 1 StL
1998 StL: 13 G; 3 Sac.

DICK WITCHER Witcher, Richard Vernon 6′3″, 204 WR-TE
Col: Bakersfield Coll. CA (J.C.); UCLA *HS:* Shafter [CA] B: 10/10/1944, Salinas, CA *Drafted:* 1966 Round 8 SF
1968 SF: **1** Fum TD. **Total:** 1 Fum TD.

		Receiving					Tot
Year Team	G	Rec	Yds	Avg	TD	Fum	TD
1966 SF	14	10	115	11.5	1	0	1
1967 SF	14	46	705	15.3	3	0	3
1968 SF	14	39	531	13.6	1	1	2
1969 SF	14	33	435	13.2	3	0	3
1970 SF	11	22	288	13.1	2	0	2
1971 SF	14	18	250	13.9	3	0	3
1972 SF	14	3	22	7.3	1	0	1
1973 SF	14	1	13	13.0	0	0	0
NFL Total	109	172	2359	13.7	14	1	15

AL WITCHER Witcher, Thomas Albert 6′1″, 200 OE
Col: Baylor *HS:* Lampasas [TX] B: 9/28/1936 *Drafted:* 1960 Round 1 Oak
1960 Hou: 14 G; Rec 4-34 8.5 1 TD; Int 1-0; 6 Pt.

DERRICK WITHERSPOON Witherspoon, Derrick Leon 5′10″, 196 RB
Col: Clemson *HS:* Sumter [SC] B: 2/14/1971, Sumter, SC
1995 Phi: Rush 2-7 3.5. **Total:** Rush 2-7 3.5.

		Kickoff Returns				
Year Team	G	Ret	Yds	Avg	TD	Fum
1995 Phi	15	18	459	25.5	1	0
1996 Phi	16	53	1271	24.0	**2**	1
1997 Phi	3	9	171	19.0	0	0
NFL Total	34	80	1901	23.8	3	1

CAL WITHROW Withrow, James Calvin 6′0″, 240 C
Col: Kentucky *HS:* Fairmont West [Kettering, OH] B: 7/4/1945, Portsmouth, OH
1970 SD: 4 G. **1971** GB: 14 G. **1972** GB: 14 G. **1973** GB: 14 G. **1974** StL: 12 G. **Total:** 58 G.

MIKE WITHYCOMBE Withycombe, William Michael 6′5″, 300 **OG-OT-C**
Col: Fresno State *HS:* Lemoore [CA] B: 11/18/1964, Meridian, MS
Drafted: 1988 Round 5 NYJ
1988 NYJ: 6 G. **1989** NYJ: 5 G. **1991** Pit: 2 G. Cin: 3 G. **1992** Cin: 14 G. **Total:** 30 G.

JOHN WITKOWSKI Witkowski, John Joseph 6′1″, 200 **QB**
Col: Nassau CC NY; Columbia *HS:* Lindenhurst [NY] B: 6/18/1962, Queens, NY *Drafted:* 1984 Round 6 Det
1984 Det: 3 G; Pass 34-13 38.2%, 210 6.18; Rush 7-33 4.7; 1 Fum. **1988** Det: 2 G; Pass 1-0; Rush 1-0; 1 Fum. **Total:** 5 G; Pass 35-13 37.1%, 210 6.00; Rush 8-33 4.1; 2 Fum.

JON WITMAN Witman, Jon Doyle 6′2″, 240 **RB**
Col: Penn State *HS:* Eastern [Wrightsville, PA] B: 6/1/1972, Wrightsville, PA *Drafted:* 1996 Round 3 Pit
1996 Pit: 16 G; Rush 17-69 4.1; Rec 2-15 7.5; KR 1-20 20.0. **1997** Pit: 16 G; Rush 5-11 2.2; Rec 1-3 3.0. **1998** Pit: 16 G; Rush 1-2 2.0; Rec 13-74 5.7. **Total:** 48 G; Rush 23-82 3.6; Rec 16-92 5.8; KR 1-20 20.0.

BILLY WITT Witt, Billy 6′5″, 258 **DE**
Col: North Alabama *HS:* Russellville [AL] B: 4/25/1964
1987 Buf: 2 G.

MEL WITT Witt, Hillery Melvin 6′3″, 250 **DE-DT**
Col: Texas-Arlington B: 11/23/1945, Fort Worth, TX *Drafted:* 1967 Round 5 Bos
1967 Bos: 1 G. **1968** Bos: 14 G; Int 1-4 1 TD; 6 Pt. **1969** Bos: 6 G. **1970** Bos: 14 G. **Total:** 35 G; Int 1-4 1 TD; 6 Pt.

EARL WITTE Witte, Earl John 6′0″, 188 **BB-DB**
Col: Gustavus Adolphus *HS:* St. Peter [MN] B: 12/12/1906, St. Peter, MN D: 11/1/1991
1934 GB: 5 G; Rush 8-22 2.8.

MARK WITTE Witte, Mark Steven 6′3″, 236 **TE**
Col: North Texas *HS:* San Marcos [TX] B: 12/3/1959, Corpus Christi, TX *Drafted:* 1983 Round 11 TB
1983 TB: 16 G; Rec 2-15 7.5. **1984** TB: 16 G. **1985** TB: 16 G; Rec 3-28 9.3. **1987** Det: 3 G; Rec 1-19 19.0. **Total:** 51 G; Rec 6-62 10.3.

MIKE WITTECK Witteck, Michael Robert 6′2″, 225 **LB**
Col: Northwestern *HS:* Valley Stream North [Franklin Square, NY] B: 2/21/1964, Queens, NY D: 3/15/1990, Floral Park, NY
1987 NYJ: 3 G.

JOHN WITTENBORN Wittenborn, John Otis 6′2″, 238 **OG-K**
(Jack; Otie) *Col:* Southeast Missouri State *HS:* Sparta [IL] B: 3/1/1936, Sparta, IL *Drafted:* 1958 Round 17 SF
1958 SF: 12 G; 1 Fum. **1959** SF: 12 G. **1960** SF-Phi: 12 G; Scor 0-3 FG. SF: 4 G; Scor 0-3 FG. Phi: 8 G. **1961** Phi: 13 G. **1962** Phi: 14 G; Scor 6, 2-4 50.0% FG. **1964** Hou: 5 G. **1965** Hou: 14 G. **1966** Hou: 14 G. **1967** Hou: 14 G; Scor 72, 14-28 50.0% FG, 30-30 100.0% XK. **1968** Hou: 6 G; Rec 1-(-8) -8.0; Scor 23, 4-13 30.8% FG, 11-11 100.0% XK. **Total:** 116 G; Rec 1-(-8) -8.0; Scor 101, 20-48 41.7% FG, 41-41 100.0% XK; 1 Fum.

RAY WITTER Witter, Ray Charles 5′10″, 183 **E-TB-BB-G**
Col: Syracuse; Alfred *HS:* Warsaw [NY] B: 2/19/1896, Perry, NY D: 8/4/1983, Batavia, NY
1920 Roch: 1 G. **1921** Roch: 5 G. **1922** Roch: 1 G. **1923** Roch: 3 G. **Total:** 10 G.

TOM WITTUM Wittum, Thomas Howard 6′1″, 190 **P**
Col: Northern Illinois *HS:* Round Lake [IL] B: 1/11/1950, Berwyn, IL *Drafted:* 1972 Round 8 SF
1973 SF: Rush 1-63 63.0. **1974** SF: Rush 1-13 13.0. **1975** SF: Rush 1-(-10) -10.0; Rec 2-29 14.5. **1977** SF: Pass 3-1 33.3%, 15 5.00; Scor 5, 1-2 50.0% FG, 2-4 50.0% XK. **Total:** Pass 3-1 33.3%, 15 5.00; Rush 3-66 22.0; Rec 2-29 14.5; Scor 5, 1-2 50.0% FG, 2-4 50.0% XK.

		Punting			
Year Team	**G**	**Punts**	**Yds**	**Avg**	**Fum**
1973 SF	14	79	3455	43.7	0
1974 SF	14	68	2800	41.2	0
1975 SF	14	67	2804	41.9	1
1976 SF	14	89	3634	40.8	0
1977 SF	14	77	2801	36.4	0
NFL Total	70	380	15494	40.8	1

SLUG WITUCKI Witucki, Casimir Leo 5′11″, 245 **OG**
Col: Indiana *HS:* Michael Washington [South Bend, IN] B: 5/26/1928, South Bend, IN *Drafted:* 1950 Round 21 Was
1950 Was: 12 G. **1951** Was: 12 G. **1953** Was: 11 G. **1954** Was: 12 G. **1955** Was: 2 G. **1956** Was: 5 G. **Total:** 54 G.

ALEX WIZBICKI Wizbicki, Alexander John 5′11″, 188 **DB-HB**
Col: Dartmouth; Holy Cross *HS:* Boys [Brooklyn, NY] B: 10/6/1921, Brooklyn, NY
AAFC **1947** BufA: 13 G; Rush 9-44 4.9; PR 9-105 11.7; KR 5-164 32.8 1 TD; 6 Pt. **1948** BufA: 9 G; PR 3-33 11.0; Int 3-49. **1949** BufA: 12 G; Rush 5-(-10) -2.0; KR 1-22 22.0; Int 1-1. **Total:** 34 G; Rush 14-34 2.4; PR 12-138 11.5; KR 6-186 31.0 1 TD; Int 4-50; 6 Pt.

NFL **1950** GB: 11 G; Int 2-38.

ERNIE WOERNER Woerner, Erwin 6′1″, 200 **T**
Col: Bucknell *HS:* Central [Newark, NJ] B: 5/26/1906 D: 12/26/1972, Atlantic Highlands, NJ
1930 Nwk: 8 G.

SCOTT WOERNER Woerner, Scott Allison 6′0″, 190 **DB**
Col: Georgia *HS:* Jonesboro [GA] B: 12/18/1958, Baytown, TX
Drafted: 1981 Round 3 Atl
1981 Atl: KR 10-210 21.0. **Total:** KR 10-210 21.0.

		Punt Returns			
Year Team	**G**	**Ret**	**Yds**	**Avg**	**TD**
1981 Atl	16	33	278	8.4	0
1987 NO	1	0	0	—	0
NFL Total	17	33	278	8.4	0

DAVE WOHLABAUGH Wohlabaugh, David Vincent 6′3″, 292 **C**
Col: Syracuse *HS:* Frontier [Hamburg, NY] B: 4/13/1972, Lackawanna, NY *Drafted:* 1995 Round 4 NE
1995 NE: 11 G. **1996** NE: 16 G. **1997** NE: 14 G. **1998** NE: 16 G. **Total:** 57 G.

RICHIE WOIT Woit, Richard Edward 5′8″, 175 **DB**
Col: Arkansas State *HS:* Carl Schurz [Chicago, IL] B: 7/5/1931, Chicago, IL *Drafted:* 1954 Round 25 Det
1955 Det: 1 G; KR 1-13 13.0; 1 Fum.

JOHN WOITT Woitt, John Merit 5′11″, 171 **DB**
Col: Mississippi State *HS:* Pascagoula [MS] B: 6/29/1946, Yakima, WA
1968 SF: 14 G. **1969** SF: 14 G; Int 1-57 1 TD; 6 Pt. **Total:** 28 G; Int 1-57 1 TD; 6 Pt.

ALEX WOJCIECHOWICZ Wojciechowicz, Alexander Francis 5′11″, 217 **C-LB**
(Wojey) *Col:* Fordham *HS:* South River [NJ] B: 8/12/1915, South River, NJ D: 7/13/1992, Forked River, NJ *Drafted:* 1938 Round 1 Det
HOF: 1968
1942 Det: Rec 4-44 11.0; KR 3-30 10.0. **1943** Det: KR 1-17 17.0. **Total:** Rec 4-44 11.0; KR 4-47 11.8.

		Interceptions			
Year Team	**G**	**Int**	**Yds**	**TD**	**Fum**
1938 Det	11	—	—	0	0
1939 Det	11	—	—	0	0
1940 Det	11	3	20	**1**	0
1941 Det	10	0	0	0	0
1942 Det	11	2	5	0	0
1943 Det	9	2	14	0	0
1944 Det	10	7	88	0	0
1945 Det	10	0	0	0	0
1946 Det-Phi	10	0	0	0	1
1946 Det	3	0	0	0	0
1946 Phi	7	0	0	0	1
1947 Phi	12	1	3	0	0
1948 Phi	10	1	2	0	0
1949 Phi	12	2	26	0	0
1950 Phi	7	1	4	0	0
NFL Total	134	19	162	1	1

JOHN WOJCIECHOWSKI Wojciechowski, John Stanley 6′4″, 272 **OT-OG**
Col: Michigan State *HS:* Fitzgerald [Warren, MI] B: 7/30/1963, Detroit, MI
1987 ChiB: 4 G. **1988** ChiB: 16 G. **1989** ChiB: 13 G. **1990** ChiB: 13 G. **1991** ChiB: 16 G. **1992** ChiB: 16 G. **1993** ChiB: 14 G. **Total:** 92 G.

GREGORY WOJCIK Wojcik, Gregory Steven 6′6″, 268 **DT**
Col: Orange Coast Coll. CA (J.C.); USC *HS:* Huntington Beach [CA] B: 1/27/1946, Jamestown, ND
1971 LARm: 10 G. **1972** SD: 7 G. **1973** SD: 10 G. **1975** SD: 6 G. **Total:** 33 G.

AL WOLDEN Wolden, Alan M 6′3″, 232 **RB**
Col: Bemidji State *HS:* Govnick-Trail [Govnick, MN] B: 4/11/1965, Govnick, MN
1987 ChiB: 3 G; Rush 2-8 4.0; Rec 1-26 26.0.

JIM WOLF Wolf, James Arthur Jr. 6′2″, 240 **DE**
Col: Prairie View A&M *HS:* Warren [TX] B: 4/4/1952, San Antonio, TX
Drafted: 1974 Round 6 Pit
1974 Pit: 11 G. **1976** KC: 14 G. **Total:** 25 G.

JOE WOLF Wolf, Joseph Francis Jr. 6'6", 293 **OG**
Col: Boston College *HS:* William Allen [Allentown, PA] B: 12/28/1966, Allentown, PA *Drafted:* 1989 Round 1 Pho
1989 Pho: 16 G. **1990** Pho: 15 G. **1991** Pho: 8 G. **1992** Pho: 3 G. **1993** Pho: 8 G. **1994** Ariz: 7 G. **1995** Ariz: 6 G. **1996** Ariz: 16 G. **1997** Ariz: 15 G. **Total:** 94 G.

DICK WOLF Wolf, Richard D 5'9", 160 **WB-BB-FB**
Col: Miami (Ohio) B: 8/29/1900, Versailles, OH D: 6/28/1967, Marion, IN
1923 Cle: 5 G; Rush 1 TD; 6 Pt. **1924** Cle: 6 G; Rush 1 TD; Rec 1 TD; Tot TD 2; 12 Pt. **1925** Cle: 14 G; Rec 1 TD; 6 Pt. **1927** Cle: 1 G. **Total:** 26 G; Rush 2 TD; Rec 2 TD; Tot TD 4; 24 Pt.

RED WOLFE Wolfe, Hugh Othello 6'0", 205 **FB-DB**
Col: Texas *HS:* Stephenville [TX] B: 6/13/1912, Mason, TX
Drafted: 1938 Round 2 Pit
1938 NYG: 8 G; Rush 15-19 1.3; Rec 2-23 11.5; Scor 0-1 XK.

WAYNE WOLFF Wolff, Wayne William 6'2", 243 **OG**
Col: Wake Forest *HS:* Greensburg [PA] B: 1/28/1938, Greensburg, PA
Drafted: 1961 Round 17 Buf
1961 Buf: 2 G.

CRAIG WOLFLEY Wolfley, Craig Alan 6'1", 265 **OG-OT**
Col: Syracuse *HS:* Orchard Park [NY] B: 5/19/1958, Buffalo, NY
Drafted: 1980 Round 5 Pit
1980 Pit: 16 G. **1981** Pit: 16 G. **1982** Pit: 9 G. **1983** Pit: 14 G. **1984** Pit: 9 G. **1985** Pit: 13 G. **1986** Pit: 9 G. **1987** Pit: 12 G. **1988** Pit: 16 G. **1989** Pit: 15 G. **1990** Min: 8 G. **1991** Min: 16 G. **Total:** 153 G.

RON WOLFLEY Wolfley, Ronald Paul 6'0", 226 **RB**
Col: West Virginia *HS:* Frontier [Hamburg, NY] B: 10/14/1962, Blasdell, NY *Drafted:* 1985 Round 4 StL
1985 StL: KR 13-234 18.0. **Total:** KR 13-228 17.5.

		Rushing				Receiving					Tot
Year Team	G	Att	Yds	Avg	TD	Rec	Yds	Avg	TD	Fum	TD
1985 StL	16	24	64	2.7	0	2	18	9.0	0	1	0
1986 StL	16	8	19	2.4	0	2	32	16.0	0	0	0
1987 StL	12	26	87	3.3	1	8	68	8.5	0	0	1
1988 Pho	16	9	43	4.8	0	2	11	5.5	0	0	0
1989 Pho	16	13	36	2.8	1	5	38	7.6	0	0	1
1990 Pho	13	2	3	1.5	0	0	0	—	0	0	0
1991 Pho	16	0	0	—	0	0	0	—	0	0	0
1992 Cle	15	1	2	2.0	0	2	8	4.0	1	0	1
1993 Cle	16	0	0	—	0	5	25	5.0	1	0	1
1995 StL	9	3	9	3.0	0	0	0	—	0	0	0
NFL Total	145	86	263	3.1	2	26	200	7.7	2	1	4

OSCAR WOLFORD Wolford, Oscar 6'0", 188 **G-C-OE**
Col: No College *HS:* None B: 3/14/1897, St. Clairsville, OH
D: 2/3/1977, Walnut Creek, OH
1920 Col: 7 G. **1921** Col: 8 G; 1 Fum TD; Tot TD 2; 12 Pt. **1922** Col: 8 G. **1924** Col: 4 G. **Total:** 27 G; 1 Fum TD; Tot TD 2; 12 Pt.

WILL WOLFORD Wolford, William Charles 6'5", 294 **OT-OG**
Col: Vanderbilt *HS:* St. Xavier [Louisville, KY] B: 5/18/1964, Louisville, KY *Drafted:* 1986 Round 1 Buf
1986 Buf: 16 G. **1987** Buf: 9 G. **1988** Buf: 16 G. **1989** Buf: 16 G. **1990** Buf: 14 G. **1991** Buf: 15 G. **1992** Buf: 16 G. **1993** Ind: 12 G. **1994** Ind: 16 G. **1995** Ind: 16 G. **1996** Pit: 16 G. **1997** Pit: 16 G. **1998** Pit: 13 G. **Total:** 191 G.

BILL WOLSKI Wolski, William Frank 5'11", 203 **FB**
Col: Notre Dame *HS:* Catholic Central [Muskegon, MI] B: 5/23/1944, Muskegon, MI *Drafted:* 1966 Round 5 Atl
1966 Atl: 2 G; KR 1-21 21.0.

WHITEY WOLTER Wolter, Herbert Max 5'10", 170 **WB-BB**
Col: Wis.-Milwaukee *HS:* North Division [Milwaukee, WI] B: 8/22/1899, Milwaukee, WI D: 4/1966, Los Angeles, CA
1924 Ken: 3 G.

CLEM WOLTMAN Woltman, Clement J 6'1", 214 **T**
Col: Purdue B: 12/4/1914, South Bend, IN D: 1/16/1988
Drafted: 1938 Round 6 Phi
1938 Phi: 10 G. **1939** Phi: 11 G. **1940** Phi: 10 G. **Total:** 31 G.

BRUCE WOMACK Womack, Bruce Larimore 6'3", 210 **OG**
(Dad) *Col:* West Texas A&M B: 5/12/1929, Floydada, TX
Drafted: 1951 Round 29 Det
1951 Det: 3 G.

JEFF WOMACK Womack, Jeffrey Allen 5'9", 188 **RB**
Col: Memphis *HS:* Warren Co. [McMinnville, TN] B: 6/26/1963, McMinnville, TN
1987 Min: 2 G; Rush 9-20 2.2; Rec 5-46 9.2 1 TD; KR 5-77 15.4; 6 Pt.

JOE WOMACK Womack, Joe Neil 5'9", 210 **HB**
Col: Los Angeles State *HS:* San Bernardino [CA] B: 12/10/1936, Fort Worth, TX
1962 Pit: Rec 6-57 9.5; KR 1-16 16.0.

		Rushing				
Year Team	G	Att	Yds	Avg	TD	Fum
1962 Pit	11	128	468	3.7	5	3

ROYCE WOMBLE Womble, Royce Cullen 6'0", 185 **HB-FL**
(Rolls Royce) *Col:* North Texas *HS:* Mansfield [TX] B: 8/12/1931, Webb, TX
1954 Bal: KR 9-170 18.9. **Total:** KR 9-170 18.9.

		Rushing				Receiving				
Year Team	G	Att	Yds	Avg	TD	Rec	Yds	Avg	TD	Fum
1954 Bal	12	60	174	2.9	0	30	338	11.3	3	1
1955 Bal	3	4	2	0.5	0	1	14	14.0	0	0
1956 Bal	12	20	72	3.6	0	9	180	20.0	2	0
1957 Bal	10	7	18	2.6	0	7	69	9.9	0	0
1960 LAC	14	0	0	—	0	32	316	9.9	4	0
NFL Total	51	91	266	2.9	0	79	917	11.6	9	1

BILL WONDOLOWSKI Wondolowski, William Walter 5'10", 168 **WR**
(Wondo) *Col:* Eastern Montana *HS:* Bayonne [NJ] B: 11/29/1946, Jersey City, NJ
1969 SF: 1 G.

KAILEE WONG Wong, Kailee Warner 6'2", 259 **LB**
Col: Stanford *HS:* North Eugene [OR] B: 5/23/1976, Eugene, OR
Drafted: 1998 Round 2 Min
1998 Min: 15 G; 1.5 Sac.

GEORGE WONSLEY Wonsley, George Ivory 5'10", 218 **RB**
Col: Mississippi State *HS:* Moss Point [MS] B: 11/23/1960, Moss Point, MS *Drafted:* 1984 Round 4 Ind
1984 Ind: KR 4-52 13.0. **1986** Ind: KR 2-31 15.5. **1987** Ind: KR 1-19 19.0. **1989** NE: KR 3-69 23.0. **Total:** KR 10-171 17.1.

		Rushing				Receiving				
Year Team	G	Att	Yds	Avg	TD	Rec	Yds	Avg	TD	Fum
1984 Ind	14	37	111	3.0	0	9	47	5.2	0	0
1985 Ind	16	138	716	5.2	6	30	257	8.6	0	4
1986 Ind	16	60	214	3.6	1	16	175	10.9	0	1
1987 Ind	11	18	71	3.9	1	5	48	9.6	0	1
1988 Ind	16	26	48	1.8	1	0	0	—	0	0
1989 NE	5	2	-2	-1.0	0	0	0	—	0	0
NFL Total	78	281	1158	4.1	9	60	527	8.8	0	6

NATHAN WONSLEY Wonsley, Nathan Jr. 5'10", 190 **RB**
Col: Mississippi *HS:* Moss Point [MS] B: 12/7/1963, Moss Point, MS
1986 TB: Rec 8-57 7.1; KR 10-208 20.8.

		Rushing				
Year Team	G	Att	Yds	Avg	TD	Fum
1986 TB	10	73	339	4.6	3	2

OTIS WONSLEY Wonsley, Otis 5'10", 214 **RB**
Col: Alcorn State *HS:* Moss Point [MS] B: 8/13/1957, Pascaquola, MS
Drafted: 1980 Round 9 NYG
1981 Was: Rec 1-5 5.0; KR 6-124 20.7. **1982** Was: Rec 1-1 1.0 1 TD; KR 1-14 14.0. **1983** Was: KR 2-36 18.0. **1985** Was: KR 2-26 13.0. **Total:** Rec 2-6 3.0 1 TD; KR 11-200 18.2.

		Rushing					Tot
Year Team	G	Att	Yds	Avg	TD	Fum	TD
1981 Was	15	3	11	3.7	0	1	0
1982 Was	9	11	36	3.3	0	0	1
1983 Was	16	25	88	3.5	0	0	0
1984 Was	16	18	38	2.1	4	0	4
1985 Was	16	4	8	2.0	0	0	0
NFL Total	72	61	181	3.0	4	1	5

WOOD Wood **FB**
Col: No College Deceased
1920 Det: 2 G.

BO WOOD Wood, Charles Henry 6'3", 235 **DE**
Col: North Carolina *HS:* Haddon Heights [NJ] B: 1/24/1945, Camden, NJ *Drafted:* 1967 Round 6 NO
1967 Atl: 14 G; KR 1-9 9.0.

DUANE WOOD Wood, Duane Scott 6'1", 200 **DB**
Col: Oklahoma State *HS:* Wilburton [OK] B: 9/20/1937, Wilburton, OK

		Interceptions			Tot
Year Team	G	Int	Yds	TD	TD
1960 DalT	9	4	85	1	1
1961 DalT	14	4	31	0	0
1962 DalT	14	4	81	0	0
1963 KC	14	3	23	0	1
1964 KC	14	5	27	0	0
NFL Total	65	20	247	1	2

GARY WOOD Wood, Gary Fay 5'11", 192 **QB**
Col: Cornell *HS:* Cortland [NY] B: 2/5/1942, Taylor, NY D: 3/2/1994, Dix Hills, NY *Drafted:* 1964 Round 8 NYG
1965 NYG: Scor **1** 1XP. **Total:** Scor 1 1XP.

		Passing							
Year Team	G	Att	Comp	Comp%	Yds	YPA	TD	Int	Rating
1964 NYG	12	143	66	46.2	952	6.66	6	**3**	73.5
1965 NYG	9	36	15	41.7	190	5.28	1	2	44.9
1966 NYG	14	170	81	47.6	1142	6.72	6	13	49.7
1967 NO	2	11	5	45.5	62	5.64	0	0	63.4
1968 NYG	14	24	9	37.5	123	5.13	0	5	15.1
1969 NYG	12	16	10	62.5	106	6.63	1	0	102.6
NFL Total	63	400	186	46.5	2575	6.44	14	23	55.4

	Rushing				
Year Team	Att	Yds	Avg	TD	Fum
1964 NYG	39	158	4.1	3	5
1965 NYG	5	68	13.6	0	1
1966 NYG	28	196	7.0	3	4
1968 NYG	2	0	0.0	0	0
1969 NYG	1	3	3.0	0	0
NFL Total	75	425	5.7	6	10

JOHN WOOD Wood, John Curtis 6'3", 249 **DT**
Col: Louisiana State *HS:* Lake Charles [LA] B: 1/20/1951, Lake Charles, LA *Drafted:* 1973 Round 3 Den
1973 NO: 2 G.

DICK WOOD Wood, Malcolm Richard 6'5", 205 **QB**
Col: Auburn *HS:* Lanett [AL] B: 2/29/1936, Lanett, AL *Drafted:* 1959 Round 12 Bal

		Passing							
Year Team	G	Att	Comp	Comp%	Yds	YPA	TD	Int	Rating
1962 SD-Den	7	97	41	42.3	655	6.75	4	7	49.1
1962 SD	6	97	41	42.3	655	6.75	4	7	49.1
1962 Den	1	0	0	—	0	—	0	0	—
1963 NYJ	12	352	160	45.5	2204	6.26	18	19	60.6
1964 NYJ	13	358	169	47.2	2298	6.42	17	25	54.9
1965 Oak	14	157	69	43.9	1003	6.39	8	**6**	66.4
1966 Mia	14	230	83	36.1	993	4.32	4	14	30.6
NFL Total	60	1194	522	43.7	7153	5.99	51	71	52.9

	Rushing				
Year Team	Att	Yds	Avg	TD	Fum
1962 SD-Den	1	0	0.0	0	2
1962 SD	1	0	0.0	0	2
1963 NYJ	7	17	2.4	1	6
1964 NYJ	9	6	0.7	1	4
1965 Oak	4	16	4.0	1	0
1966 Mia	5	6	1.2	1	2
NFL Total	26	45	1.7	4	14

MARV WOOD Wood, Marvin 6'1", 195 **WB-FB-OE**
(Sam) *Col:* California B: 11/28/1900, Borden, IN D: 12/18/1973, Bloomington, IN
1924 Ken: 4 G.

MIKE WOOD Wood, Michael Stephen 5'11", 199 **K**
Col: Southeast Missouri State *HS:* Kirkwood [MO] B: 9/3/1954, Kirkwood, MO *Drafted:* 1978 Round 8 Min
1978 Min-StL: Pass 1-1 100.0%, 29 29.00. StL: Pass 1-1 100.0%, 29 29.00. **1982** Bal: Pass 1-1 100.0%, 5 5.00 1 TD. **Total:** Pass 2-2 100.0%, 34 17.00 1 TD.

		Punting		
Year Team	G	Punts	Yds	Avg
1978 Min-StL	15	82	3019	36.8
1978 Min	7	31	1100	35.5
1978 StL	8	51	1919	37.6
1979 StL-SD	12	0	0	—
1979 StL	3	0	0	—
1979 SD	9	0	0	—
1980 SD	1	0	0	—
1981 Bal	16	0	0	—
1982 Bal	6	0	0	—
NFL Total	50	82	3019	36.8

	Scoring						
Year Team	Pts	FG	FGA	FG%	XK	XKA	XK%
1979 StL-SD	73	13	21	61.9	34	38	89.5
1979 StL	12	2	7	28.6	6	7	85.7
1979 SD	61	11	14	78.6	28	31	90.3
1981 Bal	59	10	18	55.6	29	33	87.9
1982 Bal	24	6	10	60.0	6	6	100.0
NFL Total	156	29	49	59.2	69	77	89.6

RICHARD WOOD Wood, Richard Marlon 6'2", 224 **LB**
(Batman) *Col:* USC *HS:* Thomas Jefferson [Elizabeth, NJ] B: 5/31/1953, Elizabeth, NJ *Drafted:* 1975 Round 3 NYJ
1975 NYJ: 14 G; KR 3-27 9.0. **1976** TB: 13 G. **1977** TB: 14 G; Int 4-86 **1** TD; 1 Fum TD; Tot TD 2; 12 Pt. **1978** TB: 16 G. **1979** TB: 16 G; Int 2-37. **1980** TB: 16 G; Int 3-76 1 TD; 6 Pt. **1981** TB: 16 G. **1982** TB: 9 G. **1983** TB: 16 G. **1984** TB: 16 G; KR 5-43 8.6. **Total:** 146 G; KR 8-70 8.8; Int 9-199 2 TD; 1 Fum TD; Tot TD 3; 18 Pt.

BOBBY WOOD Wood, Robert Harry 6'2", 230 **T**
Col: Alabama *HS:* Batesville [MS] B: 1/14/1916, McComb, MS D: 10/22/1973, McComb, MS *Drafted:* 1940 Round 4 Cle
1940 ChiC-GB: 3 G. ChiC: 1 G. GB: 2 G. **Total:** 3 G.

BILL WOOD Wood, William Rodgers 5'11", 190 **DB**
Col: West Virginia Wesleyan B: 4/17/1939, Allentown, PA
1963 NYJ: 1 G.

WILLIE WOOD Wood, William Vernell 5'10", 190 **DB**
Col: West Hills CC CA (J.C.); USC *HS:* Armstrong [Washington, DC] B: 12/23/1936, Washington, DC *HOF:* 1989
1963 GB: KR 1-20 20.0. **1964** GB: Scor 7, 0-1 FG, 1-1 100.0% XK. **1966** GB: KR 1-0. **1967** GB: KR 1-0. **Total:** KR 3-20 6.7; Scor 25, 0-1 FG, 1-1 100.0% XK.

		Punt Returns				Interceptions				Tot
Year Team	G	Ret	Yds	Avg	TD	Int	Yds	TD	Fum	TD
1960 GB	12	16	106	6.6	0	0	0	0	2	0
1961 GB	14	14	225	**16.1**	**2**	5	52	0	1	2
1962 GB	14	23	273	11.9	0	**9**	132	0	0	0
1963 GB	14	19	169	8.9	0	5	67	0	0	0
1964 GB	14	19	252	13.3	0	3	73	1	1	1
1965 GB	14	13	38	2.9	0	6	65	0	0	0
1966 GB	14	22	82	3.7	0	3	38	1	0	1
1967 GB	14	12	3	0.3	0	4	60	0	0	0
1968 GB	14	26	126	4.8	0	2	54	0	1	0
1969 GB	14	8	38	4.8	0	3	40	0	0	0
1970 GB	14	11	58	5.3	0	7	110	0	1	0
1971 GB	14	4	21	5.3	0	1	8	0	0	0
NFL Total	166	187	1391	7.4	2	48	699	2	6	4

AL WOODALL Woodall, Frank Alley 6'5", 205 **QB**
Col: Duke *HS:* Erwin [NC] B: 12/7/1945, Erwin, NC *Drafted:* 1969 Round 2 NYJ

		Passing							
Year Team	G	Att	Comp	Comp%	Yds	YPA	TD	Int	Rating
1969 NYJ	4	9	4	44.4	67	7.44	0	2	30.6
1970 NYJ	10	188	96	51.1	1265	6.73	9	9	68.7
1971 NYJ	5	97	42	43.3	395	4.07	0	2	46.5
1973 NYJ	9	201	101	50.2	1228	6.11	9	8	67.8
1974 NYJ	3	8	3	37.5	15	1.88	0	2	6.3
NFL Total	31	503	246	48.9	2970	5.90	18	23	60.3

	Rushing				
Year Team	Att	Yds	Avg	TD	Fum
1969 NYJ	4	13	3.3	0	0
1970 NYJ	28	110	3.9	0	2
1971 NYJ	13	26	2.0	0	3
1973 NYJ	13	68	5.2	0	1
1974 NYJ	2	-3	-1.5	0	0
NFL Total	60	214	3.6	0	6

LEE WOODALL Woodall, Lee Artis 6'1", 224 **LB**
Col: West Chester *HS:* Carlisle [PA] B: 10/31/1969, Carlisle, PA *Drafted:* 1994 Round 6 SF
1994 SF: 15 G; 1 Sac. **1995** SF: 16 G; Int 2-0; **1** Fum TD; 6 Pt; 3 Sac. **1996** SF: 16 G; 2.5 Sac. **1997** SF: 16 G; Int 2-55. **1998** SF: 15 G; Int 1-4. **Total:** 78 G; Int 5-59; 1 Fum TD; 6 Pt; 6.5 Sac.

KEN WOODARD Woodard, Kenneth Emil 6'1", 218 **LB**
Col: Tuskegee *HS:* Martin Luther King [Detroit, MI] B: 1/22/1960, Detroit, MI *Drafted:* 1982 Round 10 Den
1982 Den: 9 G. **1983** Den: 16 G; 2 Sac. **1984** Den: 16 G; Int 1-27 1 TD; 6 Pt; 3 Sac. **1985** Den: 16 G; Int 1-18; 3 Sac. **1986** Den: 16 G; **1** Fum TD; 6 Pt; 3 Sac. **1987** Pit: 7 G. **1988** SD: 8 G. **1989** SD: 16 G. **Total:** 104 G; Int 2-45 1 TD; 1 Fum TD; Tot TD 2; 12 Pt; 11 Sac.

MARC WOODARD Woodard, Marc Sionn 6'0", 234 **LB**
Col: Mississippi State *HS:* Kosciusko [MS] B: 2/21/1970, Kosciusko, MS *Drafted:* 1993 Round 5 Pit
1994 Phi: 16 G. **1995** Phi: 16 G; 1.5 Sac. **1996** Phi: 16 G. **Total:** 48 G; 1.5 Sac.

RAY WOODARD Woodard, Raymond Lee Jr. 6'6", 290 **DE**
Col: Texas *HS:* Corrigan-Camden [Corrigan, TX] B: 8/20/1961, Corrigan, TX *Drafted:* 1984 Round 8 SD
1987 Den-KC: 9 G; 0.5 Sac. Den: 3 G; 0.5 Sac. KC: 6 G. **Total:** 9 G; 0.5 Sac.

DICK WOODARD Woodard, Richard Ernest 6'2", 224 **LB-C**
Col: Iowa *HS:* Fort Dodge [IA] B: 7/26/1926, Britt, IA *Drafted:* 1948 Round 21 NYG
AAFC **1949** LA-A: 12 G; Int 2-39 1 TD; 6 Pt.

NFL **1950** NYG: 12 G; Int 1-11; **1** Fum TD; 6 Pt. **1951** NYG: 11 G; Int 2-13; 1 Fum. **1952** Was: 12 G. **1953** NYG: 12 G; Int 1-10. **Total:** 47 G; Int 4-34; 1 Fum TD; 6 Pt; 1 Fum.

DENNIS WOODBERRY Woodberry, Dennis Earl 5'10", 183 **DB**
Col: Southern Arkansas *HS:* Arkansas [Texarkana, AR] B: 4/22/1961, Texarkana, AR *Drafted:* 1984 Supplemental Round 3 Atl
1986 Atl: 7 G; Int 2-14. **1987** Was: 12 G. **1988** Was: 12 G. **Total:** 31 G; Int 2-14.

JOHN WOODCOCK Woodcock, John Maurer 6'3", 246 **DT**
Col: New Mexico; Hawaii *HS:* Washington [Fremont, CA] B: 3/19/1954, Eureka, CA *Drafted:* 1976 Round 3 Det
1976 Det: 14 G. **1977** Det: 14 G; KR 1-12 12.0. **1978** Det: 16 G. **1980** Det: 8 G. **1981** SD: 12 G. **1982** SD: 6 G. **Total:** 70 G; KR 1-12 12.0.

SHAWN WOODEN Wooden, Shawn Anthony 5'11", 205 **DB**
Col: Notre Dame *HS:* Abington [PA] B: 10/23/1973, Willow Grove, PA *Drafted:* 1996 Round 6 Mia
1996 Mia: 16 G; Int 2-15. **1997** Mia: 16 G; Int 2-10; 1 Fum. **1998** Mia: 2 G. **Total:** 34 G; Int 4-25; 1 Fum.

TERRY WOODEN Wooden, Terrence Tylon 6'3", 239 **LB**
Col: Syracuse *HS:* Farmington [CT] B: 1/14/1967, Hartford, CT *Drafted:* 1990 Round 2 Sea
1990 Sea: 8 G. **1991** Sea: 16 G; 2 Sac. **1992** Sea: 8 G; Int 1-3. **1993** Sea: 16 G; 2.5 Sac. **1994** Sea: 16 G; Int 3-78 1 TD; 6 Pt; 1.5 Sac. **1995** Sea: 16 G; Int 1-9. **1996** Sea: 9 G; Int 1-13. **1997** KC: 15 G; 2 Sac. **1998** Oak: 16 G; Int 1-14; 2 Sac. **Total:** 120 G; Int 7-117 1 TD; 6 Pt; 10 Sac.

TOM WOODESHICK Woodeshick, Thomas 6'0", 225 **RB**
Col: West Virginia *HS:* Hanover Twp. [Wilkes-Barre, PA] B: 12/3/1941, Wilkes-Barre, PA *Drafted:* 1963 Round 8 Phi
1963 Phi: KR 3-72 24.0. **Total:** KR 3-72 24.0.

		Rushing				Receiving					Tot
Year Team	**G**	**Att**	**Yds**	**Avg**	**TD**	**Rec**	**Yds**	**Avg**	**TD**	**Fum**	**TD**
1963 Phi	14	5	18	3.6	0	1	-3	-3.0	0	1	0
1964 Phi	13	37	180	4.9	2	4	12	3.0	0	1	2
1965 Phi	13	28	145	5.2	0	6	86	14.3	0	0	0
1966 Phi	14	85	330	3.9	4	10	118	11.8	1	2	5
1967 Phi	14	155	670	4.3	6	34	391	11.5	4	3	10
1968 Phi	14	217	947	4.4	3	36	328	9.1	0	7	3
1969 Phi	12	186	831	4.5	4	22	177	8.0	0	6	4
1970 Phi	6	52	254	4.9	2	6	28	4.7	0	2	2
1971 Phi	11	66	188	2.8	0	6	36	6.0	1	2	1
1972 StL	4	5	14	2.8	0	1	2	2.0	0	0	0
NFL Total	115	836	3577	4.3	21	126	1175	9.3	6	24	27

WHITEY WOODIN Woodin, Howard Lee 5'10", 208 **G-T**
Col: Marquette *HS:* Fort Atkinson [WI]; St. John Acad. [Green Bay, WI] B: 11/29/1894, Fort Atkinson, WI D: 2/9/1974, Green Bay, WI
1922 Rac-GB: 10 G. Rac: 4 G. GB: 6 G. **1923** GB: 10 G. **1924** GB: 11 G. **1925** GB: 11 G. **1926** GB: 13 G; Scor 1, 1 XK. **1927** GB: 7 G. **1928** GB: 10 G. **1929** GB: 6 G. **1930** GB: 10 G. **1931** GB: 2 G; Int **1** TD; Scor 9, 3 XK. **Total:** 90 G; Int 1 TD.

DAVID WOODLEY Woodley, David Eugene 6'2", 204 **QB**
Col: Louisiana State *HS:* C.E. Byrd [Shreveport, LA] B: 10/25/1958, Shreveport, LA *Drafted:* 1980 Round 8 Mia
1982 Mia: Rec 1-15 15.0 1 TD. **1983** Mia: Rec 1-6 6.0. **Total:** Rec 2-21 10.5 1 TD.

		Passing							
Year Team	**G**	**Att**	**Comp**	**Comp%**	**Yds**	**YPA**	**TD**	**Int**	**Rating**
1980 Mia	13	327	176	53.8	1850	5.66	14	17	63.1
1981 Mia	15	366	191	52.2	2470	6.75	12	13	69.8
1982 Mia	9	179	98	54.7	1080	6.03	5	8	63.5
1983 Mia	5	89	43	48.3	528	5.93	3	4	59.6
1984 Pit	7	156	85	54.5	1273	8.16	8	7	79.9
1985 Pit	9	183	94	51.4	1357	7.42	6	14	54.8
NFL Total	58	1300	687	52.8	8558	6.58	48	63	65.7

	Rushing					Tot
Year Team	**Att**	**Yds**	**Avg**	**TD**	**Fum**	**TD**
1980 Mia	55	214	3.9	3	3	3
1981 Mia	63	272	4.3	4	9	4
1982 Mia	36	207	5.8	2	2	3
1983 Mia	19	78	4.1	0	4	0
1984 Pit	11	14	1.3	0	5	0
1985 Pit	17	71	4.2	2	8	2
NFL Total	201	856	4.3	11	31	12

RICHARD WOODLEY Woodley, Richard L 5'9", 180 **DB**
Col: Texas Christian *HS:* La Marque [TX] B: 1/13/1972, Texas City, TX
1996 Det: 11 G.

DOUG WOODLIEF Woodlief, Douglas Eugene 6'3", 225 **LB**
Col: Chipola JC FL; Memphis *HS:* Marianna [FL] B: 9/4/1943, Marianna, FL *Drafted:* 1965 Round 5 LARm
1965 LARm: 14 G. **1966** LARm: 14 G. **1967** LARm: 13 G; Int 2-24. **1968** LARm: 14 G. **1969** LARm: 14 G; Int 4-29. **Total:** 69 G; Int 6-53.

JOHN WOODRING Woodring, John 6'2", 232 **LB**
Col: Brown *HS:* Springfield [PA] B: 4/4/1959, Phildelphia, PA *Drafted:* 1981 Round 6 NYJ
1981 NYJ: 12 G. **1982** NYJ: 9 G. **1983** NYJ: 14 G; 1 Sac. **1984** NYJ: 15 G. **1985** NYJ: 2 G. **Total:** 52 G; 1 Sac.

TONY WOODRUFF Woodruff, Anthony DeWayne 6'0", 178 **WR**
Col: Kings River CC CA; Los Angeles Harbor Coll. CA (J.C.); Fresno State *HS:* Roosevelt [Fresno, CA] B: 11/12/1958, Hazen, AR *Drafted:* 1982 Round 9 Phi

		Receiving				
Year Team	**G**	**Rec**	**Yds**	**Avg**	**TD**	**Fum**
1982 Phi	1	0	0	—	0	0
1983 Phi	6	6	70	11.7	2	1
1984 Phi	16	30	484	16.1	3	0
NFL Total	23	36	554	15.4	5	1

DWAYNE WOODRUFF Woodruff, Dwayne Donzell 5'11", 198 **DB**
Col: Louisville *HS:* New Richmond [OH] B: 2/18/1957, Bowling Green, KY *Drafted:* 1979 Round 6 Pit
1982 Pit: 1 Sac. **1983** Pit: 1 Sac. **1984** Pit: **1** Fum TD. **1989** Pit: 1 Fum TD. **Total:** 2 Fum TD; 2 Sac.

		Interceptions				Tot
Year Team	**G**	**Int**	**Yds**	**TD**	**Fum**	**TD**
1979 Pit	16	1	31	0	0	0
1980 Pit	16	1	0	0	0	0
1981 Pit	16	1	17	0	1	0
1982 Pit	9	5	53	0	0	0
1983 Pit	15	3	85	0	0	0
1984 Pit	16	5	56	1	0	2
1985 Pit	12	5	80	0	0	0
1987 Pit	12	5	91	1	0	1
1988 Pit	14	4	109	1	0	1
1989 Pit	16	4	57	0	0	1
1990 Pit	15	3	110	0	0	0
NFL Total	157	37	689	3	1	5

JIM WOODRUFF Woodruff, James L 6'3", 210 **E-T-TB**
Col: No College B: 8/3/1903 D: Atlanta, GA
1926 ChiC: 1 G. **1929** Buf: 6 G; Pass 1 TD. **Total:** 7 G; Pass 1 TD.

LEE WOODRUFF Woodruff, Lee Thornton 6'0", 202 **FB-LB-DB-TB**
(Cowboy) *Col:* Mississippi *HS:* Batesville [MS] B: 1909, Batesville, MS Deceased
1931 Prov: 11 G; Rush 4 TD; Scor **1** 1XP; 25 Pt. **1932** Bos: 7 G; Rec 2-35 17.5. **1933** Phi: 9 G; Pass 1-0, 1 Int; Rush 22-74 3.4 1 TD; Rec 3-57 19.0; Int **1** TD; Tot TD 2; 12 Pt. **Total:** 27 G; Pass 1-0, 1 Int; Rush 22-74 3.4 5 TD; Rec 5-92 18.4; Int 1 TD; Scor 1 1XP; Tot TD 6; 37 Pt.

ROB WOODS Woods, Alex Robert 6'5", 295 **OT**
Col: Santa Barbara City Coll. CA (J.C.); Eastern Washington; California-Santa Barbara *HS:* Dos Pueblos [Goleta, CA] B: 10/3/1965, Fayetteville, NC *Drafted:* 1989 Round 4 Cin
1991 Cle: 2 G.

CARL WOODS Woods, Carl Frank 5'11", 200 **RB**
Col: Vanderbilt *HS:* Gallatin [TN] B: 10/22/1964, Gallatin, TN
1987 NE: 2 G; Rush 4-20 5.0 1 TD; 6 Pt.

CHRIS WOODS Woods, Christopher Wyatt 5'11", 190 **WR**
Col: Auburn *HS:* A.H. Parker [Birmingham, AL] B: 7/19/1962, Birmingham, AL *Drafted:* 1984 Supplemental Round 1 LARd
1987 LARd: Rec 1-14 14.0; KR 3-55 18.3. **1988** LARd: KR 1-20 20.0. **1989** Den: KR 1-17 17.0. **Total:** Rec 1-14 14.0; KR 5-92 18.4.

		Punt Returns				
Year Team	**G**	**Ret**	**Yds**	**Avg**	**TD**	**Fum**
1987 LARd	9	26	189	7.3	0	2
1988 LARd	2	0	0	—	0	0
1989 Den	1	2	6	3.0	0	0
NFL Total	12	28	195	7.0	0	2

GLENN WOODS Woods, Clarence Glenn 6'4", 250 **DE**
Col: Prairie View A&M *HS:* C.B. Dansby [Kilgore, TX] B: 1/7/1946, Kilgore, TX *Drafted:* 1969 Round 8 Hou
1969 Hou: 7 G.

TONY WOODS Woods, Clinton Anthony 6'5", 265 **DT**
Col: Rose State Coll. OK (J.C.); Oklahoma *HS:* Harrison [Colorado Springs, CO] B: 3/14/1966, Fort Lee, VA *Drafted:* 1989 Round 8 ChiB
1989 ChiB: 15 G; 1 Sac.

DON WOODS Woods, Donald Ray 6'1", 210 **RB**
Col: New Mexico Highlands; New Mexico *HS:* Fred Moore [Denton, TX]
B: 2/17/1951, Denton, TX *Drafted:* 1974 Round 6 GB
1974 SD: Pass 3-1 33.3%, 28 9.33 1 TD 1 Int; KR 3-61 20.3. **1976** SD: Pass 2-1 50.0%, 11 5.50 1 TD. **1977** SD: Pass 1-0; KR 1-27 27.0. **1978** SD: KR 2-37 18.5. **1979** SD: KR 0-10. **1980** SD-SF: Pass 2-1 50.0%, 6 3.00. SF: Pass 2-1 50.0%, 6 3.00. **Total:** Pass 8-3 37.5%, 45 5.63 2 TD 1 Int; KR 6-135 22.5.

		Rushing				Receiving					Tot
Year Team	G	Att	Yds	Avg	TD	Rec	Yds	Avg	TD	Fum	TD
1974 SD	12	227	1162	5.1	7	26	349	13.4	3	4	10
1975 SD	5	87	317	3.6	2	13	101	7.8	0	1	2
1976 SD	11	126	450	3.6	3	34	224	6.6	1	1	4
1977 SD	14	118	405	3.4	1	18	218	12.1	1	2	2
1978 SD	16	151	514	3.4	3	34	295	8.7	0	5	3
1979 SD	15	0	0	—	0	0	0	—	0	0	0
1980 SD-SF	12	54	239	4.4	0	20	171	8.6	0	2	0
1980 SD	2	4	10	2.5	0	0	0	—	0	0	0
1980 SF	10	50	229	4.6	0	20	171	8.6	0	2	0
NFL Total	85	763	3087	4.0	16	145	1358	9.4	5	15	21

ICKEY WOODS Woods, Elbert L 6'2", 231 **RB**
Col: Nevada-Las Vegas *HS:* Edison [CA] B: 2/28/1966, Fresno, CA
Drafted: 1988 Round 2 Cin

		Rushing				Receiving				
Year Team	G	Att	Yds	Avg	TD	Rec	Yds	Avg	TD	Fum
1988 Cin	16	203	1066	**5.3**	15	21	199	9.5	0	8
1989 Cin	2	29	94	3.2	2	0	0	—	0	1
1990 Cin	10	64	268	4.2	6	20	162	8.1	0	1
1991 Cin	9	36	97	2.7	4	6	36	6.0	0	2
NFL Total	37	332	1525	4.6	27	47	397	8.4	0	12

FLASH WOODS Woods, Gerald E 6'0", 180 **WB**
(Nig) *Col:* Butler *HS:* Greenfield [IN] B: 4/26/1902 D: 10/20/1989
1926 Col: 2 G.

JIMMY WOODS Woods, James 5'9", 196 **G-T-C**
Col: No College B: 5/5/1894 D: Salamanca, NY
1920 Roch: 9 G. **1921** Roch: 3 G. **1922** Roch: 1 G. **1923** Roch: 4 G. **1924** Roch: 5 G. **Total:** 22 G.

JEROME WOODS Woods, Jerome 6'2", 207 **DB**
Col: Northeast Mississippi CC; Memphis *HS:* Melrose [Memphis, TN]
B: 3/17/1973, Memphis, TN *Drafted:* 1996 Round 1 KC
1997 KC: Int 4-57; 1 Sac. **1998** KC: Int 2-47. **Total:** Int 6-104; 1 Sac.

		Kickoff Returns				
Year Team	G	Ret	Yds	Avg	TD	Fum
1996 KC	16	25	581	23.2	0	1
1997 KC	16	0	0	—	0	0
1998 KC	16	0	0	—	0	0
NFL Total	48	25	581	23.2	0	1

JERRY WOODS Woods, Jerry Lee 5'10", 187 **DB**
Col: Northern Michigan *HS:* Washington Park [Racine, WI]
B: 2/13/1966, Dyersburg, TN *Drafted:* 1989 Round 7 Det
1989 Det: 2 G; KR 2-28 14.0; 1 Fum. **1990** GB: 16 G. **Total:** 18 G; KR 2-28 14.0; 1 Fum.

LARRY WOODS Woods, Larry Dobie 6'6", 260 **DT**
Col: Tennessee State *HS:* Lauderdale Co. [Rogersville, AL]
B: 5/11/1948, Florence, AL *Drafted:* 1971 Round 4 Det
1971 Det: 1 G. **1972** Det: 12 G. **1973** Mia: 3 G. **1974** NYJ: 13 G. **1975** NYJ: 12 G. **1976** Sea: 6 G. **Total:** 47 G.

MIKE WOODS Woods, Michael Jay 6'2", 233 **LB**
Col: Ellsworth CC IA; Tampa; Cincinnati *HS:* Benedictine [Cleveland, OH] B: 11/1/1954, Cleveland, OH *Drafted:* 1978 Round 2 Bal
1979 Bal: 16 G. **1980** Bal: 13 G; Int 1-13. **1981** Bal: 7 G. **Total:** 36 G; Int 1-13.

RICK WOODS Woods, Rick L 6'0", 196 **DB**
Col: Boise State *HS:* Boise [ID] B: 11/16/1959, Boise, ID
Drafted: 1982 Round 4 Pit
1983 Pit: 1 Fum TD. **1985** Pit: 1 Sac. **1986** Pit: KR 1-17 17.0.
Total: KR 1-17 17.0; 1 Fum TD; 1 Sac.

		Punt Returns				Interceptions			
Year Team	G	Ret	Yds	Avg	TD	Int	Yds	TD	Fum
1982 Pit	5	13	142	10.9	0	1	12	0	2
1983 Pit	15	5	46	9.2	0	5	53	0	0
1984 Pit	15	6	40	6.7	0	2	0	0	0
1985 Pit	16	13	46	3.5	0	0	0	0	0
1986 Pit	15	33	294	8.9	0	3	26	0	2
1987 TB	5	0	0	—	0	2	63	0	1
NFL Total	71	70	568	8.1	0	13	154	0	5

ROBERT WOODS Woods, Robert Christopher 5'7", 170 **WR**
Col: Grambling State *HS:* George Washington Carver [New Orleans, LA]
B: 7/3/1955, New Orleans, LA *Drafted:* 1978 Round 5 KC
1978 Hou: 3 G; Rush 2-4 2.0; Rec 6-96 16.0 2 TD; PR 9-82 9.1; KR 3-59 19.7; 12 Pt; 1 Fum. **1979** Det: 1 G; PR 2-12 6.0; KR 2-34 17.0. **Total:** 4 G; Rush 2-4 2.0; Rec 6-96 16.0 2 TD; PR 11-94 8.5; KR 5-93 18.6; 12 Pt; 1 Fum.

ROBERT WOODS Woods, Robert Earl 6'3", 255 **OT-OG**
Col: Tennessee State *HS:* Lauderdale Co. [Rogersville, AL]
B: 7/26/1950, Florence, AL *Drafted:* 1973 Round 2 NYJ
1973 NYJ: 14 G. **1974** NYJ: 14 G. **1975** NYJ: 14 G. **1976** NYJ: 10 G. **1977** NYJ-NO: 6 G. NYJ: 2 G. NO: 4 G. **1978** NO: 16 G. **1979** NO: 15 G. **1980** NO: 10 G. **Total:** 99 G.

TONY WOODS Woods, Stanley Anthony 6'4", 269 **DE-LB**
Col: Pittsburgh *HS:* Seton Hall Prep [South Orange, NJ]
B: 10/11/1965, Newark, NJ *Drafted:* 1987 Round 1 Sea
1987 Sea: 12 G. **1988** Sea: 16 G; 5 Sac. **1989** Sea: 16 G; KR 1-13 13.0; 1 Fum; 3 Sac. **1990** Sea: 16 G; 3 Sac. **1991** Sea: 14 G; 2 Sac. **1992** Sea: 15 G; 3 Sac. **1993** LARm: 14 G; 1 Sac. **1994** Was: 15 G; 4.5 Sac. **1995** Was: 16 G; **1** Fum TD; 6 Pt; 2 Sac. **1996** Was: 13 G; 1 Sac.
Total: 147 G; KR 1-13 13.0; 1 Fum TD; 6 Pt; 1 Fum; 24.5 Sac.

KEITH WOODSIDE Woodside, Keith A 5'11", 203 **RB**
Col: Texas A&M *HS:* Vidalia [LA] B: 7/29/1964, Natchez, MS
Drafted: 1988 Round 3 GB
1988 GB: KR 19-343 18.1. **1989** GB: KR 2-38 19.0. **Total:** KR 21-381 18.1.

		Rushing				Receiving					Tot
Year Team	G	Att	Yds	Avg	TD	Rec	Yds	Avg	TD	Fum	TD
1988 GB	16	83	195	2.3	3	39	352	9.0	2	3	5
1989 GB	16	46	273	5.9	1	59	527	8.9	0	4	1
1990 GB	16	46	182	4.0	1	24	184	7.7	0	2	1
1991 GB	16	84	326	3.9	1	22	185	8.4	0	3	1
NFL Total	64	259	976	3.8	6	144	1248	8.7	2	12	8

ABE WOODSON Woodson, Abraham Benjamin 5'11", 188 **DB-HB**
(Gum) *Col:* Illinois *HS:* Austin [Chicago, IL] B: 2/15/1934, Jackson, MS *Drafted:* 1957 Round 2 SF
1958 SF: Rush 2-12 6.0. **1960** SF: Rush 4-4 1.0. **1961** SF: Rush 14-23 1.6; Rec 8-74 9.3. **1962** SF: **1** Fum TD. **Total:** Rush 20-39 2.0; Rec 8-74 9.3; 1 Fum TD.

		Punt Returns				Kickoff Returns			
Year Team	G	Ret	Yds	Avg	TD	Ret	Yds	Avg	TD
1958 SF	9	7	53	7.6	0	11	239	21.7	0
1959 SF	12	15	143	9.5	0	13	382	**29.4**	**1**
1960 SF	12	13	**174**	**13.4**	0	17	498	29.3	0
1961 SF	14	16	172	10.8	1	27	782	29.0	**1**
1962 SF	14	19	179	9.4	**1**	**37**	**1157**	**31.3**	0
1963 SF	14	13	95	7.3	0	29	935	**32.2**	**3**
1964 SF	14	22	133	6.0	0	32	880	27.5	0
1965 StL	13	18	7	0.4	0	27	665	24.6	0
1966 StL	14	0	0	—	0	0	0	—	0
NFL Total	116	123	956	7.8	2	193	5538	28.7	5

	Interceptions				Tot
Year Team	Int	Yds	TD	Fum	TD
1958 SF	1	44	0	1	0
1959 SF	4	20	0	2	1
1960 SF	2	0	0	1	0
1961 SF	1	2	0	3	2
1962 SF	2	31	0	2	2
1963 SF	3	61	0	2	3
1964 SF	2	1	0	3	0
1965 StL	0	0	0	2	0
1966 StL	4	47	0	1	0
NFL Total	19	206	0	17	8

CHARLES WOODSON Woodson, Charles 6'0", 200 **DB**
Col: Michigan *HS:* Ross [Fremont, OH] B: 10/7/1976, Fremont, OH
Drafted: 1998 Round 1 Oak
1998 Oak: 16 G; Int 5-118 1 TD; 6 Pt.

DARREN WOODSON Woodson, Darren Ray 6'1", 219 **DB**
Col: Arizona State *HS:* Maryvale [Phoenix, AZ] B: 4/25/1969, Phoenix, AZ *Drafted:* 1992 Round 2 Dal
1992 Dal: 1 Sac. **1996** Dal: 3 Sac. **1997** Dal: 2 Sac. **1998** Dal: 3 Sac.
Total: 9 Sac.

		Interceptions			
Year Team	G	Int	Yds	TD	Fum
1992 Dal	16	0	0	0	0
1993 Dal	16	0	0	0	0
1994 Dal	16	5	140	1	0
1995 Dal	16	2	46	1	0
1996 Dal	16	5	43	0	1
1997 Dal	14	1	14	0	1

1998 Dal	16	1	1	0	0
NFL Total	110	14	244	2	2

FREDDIE WOODSON Woodson, Frederick 6′2″, 255 **OG-DT-DE**
Col: Florida A&M *HS:* Tompkins [Savannah, GA] B: 6/9/1944, Savannah, GA
1967 Mia: 12 G. **1968** Mia: 14 G; KR 1-0. **1969** Mia: 1 G. **Total:** 27 G; KR 1-0.

MARV WOODSON Woodson, Marvin Lewis 6′1″, 190 **DB-HB**
Col: Indiana *HS:* Rowan [Hattiesburg, MS] B: 9/19/1941, Hattiesburg, MS *Drafted:* 1964 Round 1 Bal
1964 Pit: PR 1-0; KR 5-178 35.6. **1965** Pit: KR 2-45 22.5. **1966** Pit: KR 6-113 18.8. **1969** Pit-NO: KR 1-18 18.0. Pit: KR 1-18 18.0. **Total:** PR 1-0; KR 14-354 25.3.

		Interceptions		
Year Team	**G**	**Int**	**Yds**	**TD**
1964 Pit	4	0	0	0
1965 Pit	13	3	87	1
1966 Pit	14	4	91	1
1967 Pit	14	7	49	0
1968 Pit	14	3	23	0
1969 Pit-NO	13	1	0	0
1969 Pit	8	1	0	0
1969 NO	5	0	0	0
NFL Total	72	18	250	2

ROD WOODSON Woodson, Roderick Kevin 6′0″, 200 **DB**
Col: Purdue *HS:* R. Nelson Snider [Fort Wayne, IN] B: 3/10/1965, Fort Wayne, IN *Drafted:* 1987 Round 1 Pit
1988 Pit: 0.5 Sac. **1991** Pit: 1 Sac. **1992** Pit: 6 Sac. **1993** Pit: Rush 1-0; 2 Sac. **1994** Pit: 3 Sac. **1996** Pit: **1** Fum TD; 1 Sac. **Total:** Rush 1-0; 1 Fum TD; 13.5 Sac.

		Punt Returns				Kickoff Returns			
Year Team	**G**	**Ret**	**Yds**	**Avg**	**TD**	**Ret**	**Yds**	**Avg**	**TD**
1987 Pit	8	16	135	8.4	0	13	290	22.3	0
1988 Pit	16	33	281	8.5	0	37	850	23.0	**1**
1989 Pit	15	29	207	7.1	0	36	982	**27.3**	**1**
1990 Pit	16	38	398	10.5	**1**	35	764	21.8	0
1991 Pit	15	28	320	11.4	0	**44**	880	20.0	0
1992 Pit	16	32	364	11.4	1	25	469	18.8	0
1993 Pit	16	42	338	8.0	0	15	294	19.6	0
1994 Pit	15	39	319	8.2	0	15	365	24.3	0
1995 Pit	1	0	0	—	0	0	0	—	0
1996 Pit	16	0	0	—	0	0	0	—	0
1997 SF	14	1	0	0.0	0	0	0	—	0
1998 Bal	16	0	0	—	0	0	0	—	0
NFL Total	164	258	2362	9.2	2	220	4894	22.2	2

	Interceptions				Tot
Year Team	**Int**	**Yds**	**TD**	**Fum**	**TD**
1987 Pit	1	45	1	3	1
1988 Pit	4	98	0	3	1
1989 Pit	3	39	0	3	1
1990 Pit	5	67	0	3	1
1991 Pit	3	72	0	3	0
1992 Pit	4	90	0	2	1
1993 Pit	8	138	1	2	1
1994 Pit	4	109	2	2	2
1996 Pit	6	121	1	1	2
1997 SF	3	81	0	0	0
1998 Bal	6	108	2	0	2
NFL Total	47	968	7	22	12

SCOTT WOOLF Woolf, Rodney Scott 6′1″, 190 **QB**
Col: Ohio State; Mount Union *HS:* West Branch [Beloit, IA] B: 12/26/1961, Salem, OH
1987 LARd: 1 G.

BUTCH WOOLFOLK Woolfolk, Harold E 6′1″, 210 **RB**
Col: Michigan *HS:* Westfield [NJ] B: 3/1/1960, Milwaukee, WI *Drafted:* 1982 Round 1 NYG

		Rushing				Receiving			
Year Team	**G**	**Att**	**Yds**	**Avg**	**TD**	**Rec**	**Yds**	**Avg**	**TD**
1982 NYG	9	112	439	3.9	2	23	224	9.7	2
1983 NYG	16	246	857	3.5	4	28	368	13.1	0
1984 NYG	15	40	92	2.3	1	9	53	5.9	0
1985 Hou	16	103	392	3.8	1	80	814	10.2	4
1986 Hou	10	23	57	2.5	0	28	314	11.2	2
1987 Det	12	12	82	6.8	0	19	166	8.7	0
1988 Det	3	1	4	4.0	0	0	0	—	0
NFL Total	81	537	1923	3.6	8	187	1939	10.4	8

	Kickoff Returns				Tot
Year Team	**Ret**	**Yds**	**Avg**	**TD**	**Fum**	**TD**
1982 NYG	20	428	21.4	0	5	4
1983 NYG	2	13	6.5	0	8	4
1984 NYG	14	232	16.6	0	1	1
1985 Hou	0	0	—	0	5	5
1986 Hou	2	38	19.0	0	0	2
1987 Det	11	219	19.9	0	1	0
1988 Det	4	99	24.8	0	1	0
NFL Total	53	1029	19.4	0	21	16

DONNELL WOOLFORD Woolford, Donnell 5′9″, 192 **DB**
Col: Clemson *HS:* Douglas Byrd [Fayetteville, NC] B: 1/6/1966, Baltimore, MD *Drafted:* 1989 Round 1 ChiB
1989 ChiB: PR 1-12 12.0. **1990** ChiB: 2 Sac. **1991** ChiB: 1 Sac. **1992** ChiB: PR 12-127 10.6. **1994** ChiB: KR 1-28 28.0. **Total:** PR 13-139 10.7; KR 1-28 28.0; 3 Sac.

		Interceptions			
Year Team	**G**	**Int**	**Yds**	**TD**	**Fum**
1989 ChiB	11	3	0	0	0
1990 ChiB	13	3	18	0	0
1991 ChiB	15	2	21	0	0
1992 ChiB	16	7	67	0	2
1993 ChiB	16	2	18	0	0
1994 ChiB	16	5	30	0	1
1995 ChiB	9	4	21	0	0
1996 ChiB	15	6	37	1	0
1997 Pit	15	4	91	0	0
NFL Total	126	36	303	1	3

GARY WOOLFORD Woolford, Gary Steven 6′0″, 180 **DB**
Col: Western Illinois; Florida State *HS:* West [Joliet, IL] B: 5/4/1954, Cairo, IL *Drafted:* 1977 Round 6 Hou
1980 NYG: 12 G; Int 2-0.

ROLAND WOOLSEY Woolsey, Roland Bert 6′1″, 182 **DB**
(Rolly) *Col:* Boise State *HS:* Grandview [ID] B: 8/11/1953, Provo, UT *Drafted:* 1975 Round 6 Dal
1975 Dal: KR 12-247 20.6. **1976** Sea: Int 4-19. **1977** Cle: KR 1-2 2.0; Int 1-0. **1978** StL: KR 1-25 25.0. **Total:** KR 14-274 19.6; Int 5-19.

		Punt Returns				
Year Team	**G**	**Ret**	**Yds**	**Avg**	**TD**	**Fum**
1975 Dal	14	4	25	6.3	0	4
1976 Sea	14	2	5	2.5	0	1
1977 Cle	14	32	290	9.1	0	2
1978 StL	2	1	4	4.0	0	0
NFL Total	44	39	324	8.3	0	7

JOHN WOOTEN Wooten, John B 6′2″, 235 **OG**
Col: Colorado *HS:* Carlsbad [NM] B: 12/5/1936, Clarksville, TX *Drafted:* 1959 Round 5 Cle
1959 Cle: 12 G. **1960** Cle: 12 G. **1961** Cle: 14 G. **1962** Cle: 14 G. **1963** Cle: 14 G. **1964** Cle: 14 G. **1965** Cle: 14 G. **1966** Cle: 14 G. **1967** Cle: 14 G. **1968** Was: 14 G. **Total:** 136 G.

MIKE WOOTEN Wooten, Michael Carroll 6′3″, 260 **C**
Col: Virginia Military *HS:* Smithfield-Selma [Smithfield, NC] B: 10/23/1962, Roanoke, VA
1987 Was: 3 G.

RON WOOTEN Wooten, Ronald John 6′4″, 274 **OG**
Col: North Carolina *HS:* Kinston [NC] B: 6/28/1959, Bourne, MA *Drafted:* 1981 Round 6 NE
1982 NE: 9 G. **1983** NE: 16 G. **1984** NE: 16 G. **1985** NE: 14 G. **1986** NE: 16 G. **1987** NE: 13 G. **1988** NE: 14 G. **Total:** 98 G.

TITO WOOTEN Wooten, Tito J 6′0″, 191 **DB**
Col: North Carolina; Northeast Louisiana *HS:* Goldsboro [NC] B: 12/12/1971, Goldsboro, NC
1994 NYG: 16 G. **1995** NYG: 16 G; Int 1-38; **1** Fum TD; 6 Pt. **1996** NYG: 13 G; Int 1-35; Scor 1 Saf; **1** Fum TD; 8 Pt. **1997** NYG: 16 G; Int 5-146 1 TD; 6 Pt; 1 Fum. **1998** NYG: 14 G; 3 Sac. **Total:** 75 G; Int 7-219 1 TD; Scor 1 Saf; 2 Fum TD; Tot TD 3; 20 Pt; 1 Fum; 3 Sac.

BARRY WORD Word, Barry Quentin 6′2″, 242 **RB**
Col: Virginia *HS:* Halifax Co. [South Boston, VA] B: 1/17/1963, Long Island, VA *Drafted:* 1986 Round 3 NO
1987 NO: KR 3-100 33.3. **1990** KC: KR 1-10 10.0. **Total:** KR 4-110 27.5.

		Rushing				Receiving				
Year Team	**G**	**Att**	**Yds**	**Avg**	**TD**	**Rec**	**Yds**	**Avg**	**TD**	**Fum**
1987 NO	12	36	133	3.7	2	6	54	9.0	0	1
1988 NO	2	0	0	—	0	0	0	—	0	0
1990 KC	16	204	1015	5.0	4	4	28	7.0	0	4
1991 KC	16	160	684	4.3	4	2	13	6.5	0	1
1992 KC	12	163	607	3.7	4	9	80	8.9	0	2
1993 Min	13	142	458	3.2	2	9	105	11.7	0	3
1994 Ariz	1	0	0	—	0	0	0	—	0	0
NFL Total	72	705	2897	4.1	16	30	280	9.3	0	11

ROSCOE WORD Word, Roscoe 5'11", 170 **DB**
Col: Jackson State *HS:* Dollarway [Pine Bluff, AR] B: 7/24/1952, Pine Bluff, AR *Drafted:* 1974 Round 3 NYJ
1974 NYJ: KR 4-69 17.3; Int 2-19. **1975** NYJ: KR 1-22 22.0; Int 1-0. **1976** NYJ-Buf-NYG-TB: KR 2-36 18.0. Buf: KR 2-36 18.0. **Total:** KR 7-127 18.1; Int 3-19.

		Punt Returns				
Year Team	G	Ret	Yds	Avg	TD	Fum
1974 NYJ	14	38	301	7.9	0	1
1975 NYJ	14	0	0	—	0	0
1976 NYJ-Buf-NYG-TB	9	1	-8	-8.0	0	1
1976 NYJ	2	0	0	—	0	0
1976 Buf	1	1	-8	-8.0	0	1
1976 NYG	4	0	0	—	0	0
1976 TB	2	0	0	—	0	0
NFL Total	37	39	293	7.5	0	2

JIM WORDEN Worden, James Crawford 5'10", 180 **HB-DB**
Col: Waynesburg *HS:* Lorain [OH] B: 6/21/1915, Lorain, OH D: 6/7/1983, Lorain, OH
1945 Cle: 5 G; Rush 4-3 0.8.

NEIL WORDEN Worden, Neil James 5'10", 198 **FB**
(Bull) *Col:* Notre Dame *HS:* Pulaski [Milwaukee, WI] B: 7/1/1931, Milwaukee, WI *Drafted:* 1954 Round 1 Phi
1954 Phi: Rec 7-63 9.0. **1957** Phi: Rec 1-3 3.0; KR 4-63 15.8. **Total:** Rec 8-66 8.3; KR 4-63 15.8.

		Rushing				
Year Team	G	Att	Yds	Avg	TD	Fum
1954 Phi	12	58	128	2.2	1	3
1957 Phi	12	42	133	3.2	0	0
NFL Total	24	100	261	2.6	1	3

STU WORDEN Worden, Stuart Barrett 6'0", 210 **G-T-C-LB**
Col: Hampden-Sydney *HS:* Greenbrier Mil. Acad. [Lewisburg, WV] B: 5/6/1907, Abingdon, VA D: 3/17/1978, Elkton, VA
1930 Bkn: 11 G. **1932** Bkn: 12 G. **1933** Bkn: 10 G. **1934** Bkn: 11 G. **Total:** 44 G.

JOE WORK Work, Joseph Ranisa 5'10", 177 **OE-WB**
Col: Miami (Ohio) *HS:* Homestead [PA] B: 1899, PA Deceased
1923 Cle: 7 G. **1924** Cle: 8 G; Rec 1 TD; 6 Pt. **1925** Cle: 4 G. **Total:** 19 G; Rec 1 TD; 6 Pt.

BLAKE WORKMAN Workman, Blake 5'11", 185 **DB-TB-BB**
(Sheriff) *Col:* Tulsa B: 8/12/1908 D: 6/1983, Opelousas, LA
1933 Cin: 4 G; Pass 6-0; Rush 7-11 1.6; Rec 2-19 9.5. **1934** StL: 3 G. **Total:** 7 G; Pass 6-0; Rush 7-11 1.6; Rec 2-19 9.5.

HOGE WORKMAN Workman, Harry Hall 5'11", 173 **TB-QB-BB-WB**
(Sonny) *Col:* Ohio State *HS:* Huntington [WV] B: 9/25/1899, Huntington, WV D: 5/20/1972, Fort Myers, FL
1924 Cle: 9 G; Pass **9** TD; Scor 25, 3 FG, 16 XK. **1931** Cle: 9 G; Scor 2, 2 XK. **1932** NYG: 1 G; Rush 1-1 1.0. **Total:** 19 G; Pass 9 TD; Rush 1-1 1.0; Scor 27, 3 FG, 18 XK.

VINCE WORKMAN Workman, Vincent Innocent Jr. 5'10", 200 **RB**
Col: Ohio State *HS:* Dublin [OH] B: 5/9/1968, Buffalo, NY *Drafted:* 1989 Round 5 GB
1991 GB: PR 1-0. **1995** Car-Ind: Pass 1-0. Car: Pass 1-0. **Total:** Pass 1-0; PR 1-0.

		Rushing				Receiving			
Year Team	G	Att	Yds	Avg	TD	Rec	Yds	Avg	TD
1989 GB	15	4	8	2.0	1	0	0	—	0
1990 GB	15	8	51	6.4	0	4	30	7.5	1
1991 GB	16	71	237	3.3	7	46	371	8.1	4
1992 GB	10	159	631	4.0	2	47	290	6.2	0
1993 TB	16	78	284	3.6	2	54	411	7.6	2
1994 TB	15	79	291	3.7	0	11	82	7.5	0
1995 Car-Ind	10	44	165	3.8	1	13	74	5.7	0
1995 Car	9	35	139	4.0	1	13	74	5.7	0
1995 Ind	1	9	26	2.9	0	0	0	—	0
1996 Ind	9	24	70	2.9	0	4	36	9.0	0
NFL Total	106	467	1737	3.7	13	179	1294	7.2	7

	Kickoff Returns					Tot
Year Team	Ret	Yds	Avg	TD	Fum	TD
1989 GB	33	547	16.6	0	1	1
1990 GB	14	210	15.0	0	0	1
1991 GB	8	139	17.4	0	3	11
1992 GB	1	17	17.0	0	4	2
1993 TB	5	67	13.4	0	2	4
1994 TB	0	0	—	0	2	0
1995 Car-Ind	0	0	—	0	0	1
1995 Car	0	0	—	0	0	1
NFL Total	61	980	16.1	0	12	20

TIM WORLEY Worley, Timothy Ashley 6'2", 228 **RB**
Col: Georgia *HS:* Lumberton [NC] B: 9/24/1966, Lumberton, NC *Drafted:* 1989 Round 1 Pit
1993 Pit-ChiB: KR 6-121 20.2. Pit: KR 4-85 21.3. ChiB: KR 2-36 18.0. **1994** ChiB: KR 4-52 13.0. **Total:** KR 10-173 17.3.

		Rushing				Receiving				
Year Team	G	Att	Yds	Avg	TD	Rec	Yds	Avg	TD	Fum
1989 Pit	15	195	770	3.9	5	15	113	7.5	0	9
1990 Pit	11	109	418	3.8	0	8	70	8.8	0	6
1991 Pit	2	22	117	5.3	0	0	0	—	0	1
1993 Pit-ChiB	15	120	470	3.9	2	11	62	5.6	0	3
1993 Pit	5	10	33	3.3	0	3	13	4.3	0	0
1993 ChiB	10	110	437	4.0	2	8	49	6.1	0	3
1994 ChiB	5	9	17	1.9	1	1	8	8.0	0	1
NFL Total	48	455	1792	3.9	8	35	253	7.2	0	20

BARRON WORTHAM Wortham, Barron Winfred 5'11", 244 **LB**
Col: Texas-El Paso *HS:* Everman [TX] B: 11/1/1969, Fort Worth, TX *Drafted:* 1994 Round 6 Hou
1994 Hou: 16 G. **1995** Hou: 16 G; KR 1-(-3) -3.0; 1 Sac. **1996** Hou: 15 G; 2 Sac. **1997** Ten: 16 G. **1998** Ten: 13 G. **Total:** 76 G; KR 1-(-3) -3.0; 3 Sac.

NAZ WORTHEN Worthen, Nasrallah Onea 5'8", 177 **WR**
Col: North Carolina State *HS:* Jean Ribault [Jacksonville, FL] B: 3/27/1966, Jacksonville, FL *Drafted:* 1989 Round 3 KC
1989 KC: Rec 5-69 13.8; KR 5-113 22.6. **1990** KC: KR 11-226 20.5. **Total:** Rec 5-69 13.8; KR 16-339 21.2.

		Punt Returns				
Year Team	G	Ret	Yds	Avg	TD	Fum
1989 KC	10	19	133	7.0	0	1
1990 KC	9	25	180	7.2	0	1
NFL Total	19	44	313	7.1	0	2

KEITH WORTMAN Wortman, Keith Delane 6'2", 260 **OG-OT-C**
Col: Rio Hondo Coll. CA (J.C.); Nebraska *HS:* Whittier [CA] B: 7/20/1950, Billings, MT *Drafted:* 1972 Round 10 GB
1972 GB: 13 G; KR 1-0. **1973** GB: 8 G. **1974** GB: 12 G. **1975** GB: 13 G. **1976** StL: 3 G. **1977** StL: 14 G; KR 1-15 15.0. **1978** StL: 14 G. **1979** StL: 13 G. **1980** StL: 2 G. **1981** StL: 4 G. **Total:** 96 G; KR 2-15 7.5.

JOE WOSTOUPAL Wostoupal, Joseph Jr. 6'3", 208 **C**
Col: Nebraska *HS:* West Point [NE] B: 8/10/1903, West Point, NE Deceased
1926 KC: 5 G. **1928** Det: 8 G. **1929** NYG: 15 G. **1930** NYG: 15 G. **Total:** 43 G.

JOHN WOUDENBERG Woudenberg, John William Jr. 6'3", 226 **T**
(Dutch) *Col:* Denver; St. Mary's (Cal.) *HS:* South [Denver, CO] B: 5/25/1918, Denver, CO *Drafted:* 1940 Round 4 ChiB
AAFC **1946** SF-A: 14 G. **1947** SF-A: 14 G; KR 1-2 2.0. **1948** SF-A: 14 G. **1949** SF-A: 12 G. **Total:** 54 G; KR 1-2 2.0.

NFL **1940** Pit: 7 G. **1941** Pit: 11 G. **1942** Pit: 11 G; Rec 1-(-1) -1.0. **Total:** 29 G; Rec 1-(-1) -1.0.

MIKE WOULFE Woulfe, Michael Jerome 6'2", 225 **LB**
Col: Bakersfield Coll. CA (J.C.); Colorado *HS:* Mendel [Chicago, IL] B: 8/14/1939, Chicago, IL *Drafted:* 1962 Round 15 Phi
1962 Phi: 13 G; KR 2-5 2.5.

JOHN WOZNIAK Wozniak, John Edward 6'0", 218 **OG-LB**
Col: Alabama *HS:* Marion [Fairhope, PA] B: 8/2/1921, Arnold City, PA D: 8/1982, Tuscaloosa, AL
AAFC **1948** BknA: 14 G; Rush 0-13; Int 1-7. **1949** NY-A: 12 G. **Total:** 26 G; Rush 0-13; Int 1-7.

NFL **1950** NYY: 12 G. **1951** NYY: 12 G; Rec 1-4 4.0; 1 Fum. **1952** Dal: 12 G; Rec 1-(-1) -1.0; KR 1-4 4.0. **Total:** 36 G; Rec 2-3 1.5; KR 1-4 4.0; 1 Fum.

LUD WRAY Wray, James R. Ludlow 6'0", 180 **C**
Col: Pennsylvania *HS:* Chestnut Hill Acad. [Philadelphia, PA] B: 2/7/1894, Philadelphia, PA D: 7/24/1967, Philadelphia, PA
1920 Buf: 11 G. **1921** Buf: 7 G. **Total:** 18 G.

DARRYL WREN Wren, Darryl Tyrone 6'1", 188 **DB**
Col: Pittsburg State *HS:* Will Rogers [Tulsa, OK] B: 1/25/1967, Tulsa, OK *Drafted:* 1991 Round 3 Buf
1993 NE: 12 G; Int 3-(-7). **1994** NE: 8 G. **Total:** 20 G; Int 3-(-7).

JUNIOR WREN Wren, Lowe Jr. 6'0", 192 **DB**
Col: Missouri *HS:* Central [Kansas City, MO] B: 12/10/1929, Kansas City, MO *Drafted:* 1952 Round 24 Cle
1956 Cle: Scor **1** Saf. **1958** Cle: PR 1-0; Punt 1-38 38.0. **1959** Cle: Punt 27-996 36.9; **1** Fum TD. **1961** NYT: Punt 8-271 33.9. **Total:** PR 1-0; Punt 36-1305 36.3; Scor 1 Saf; 1 Fum TD.

		Interceptions		
Year Team	G	Int	Yds	TD
1956 Cle	12	1	0	0

1957 Cle	12	2	73	0
1958 Cle	12	3	36	0
1959 Cle	12	5	39	0
1960 Pit	12	2	0	0
1961 NYT	2	1	2	0
NFL Total	62	14	150	0

ADRIAN WRIGHT Wright, Adrian Douglas 6′1″, 230 **RB**
Col: Virginia Union *HS:* Virgina Union [Richmond, VA] B: 10/13/1961, Charleston, WV
1987 TB: Rec 13-98 7.5 1 TD; KR 1-17 17.0.

		Rushing				
Year Team	G	Att	Yds	Avg	TD	Fum
1987 TB	3	37	112	3.0	0	1

AB WRIGHT Wright, Albert Owen 6′1″, 190 **TB**
Col: Oklahoma State *HS:* Stillwater [OK] B: 11/16/1905, Terlton, OK
D: 5/23/1995, Muskogee, OK
1930 Fra: 4 G; Pass 1 TD.

ALEXANDER WRIGHT Wright, Alexander 6′0″, 192 **WR**
Col: Auburn *HS:* Albany [GA] B: 7/19/1967, Albany, GA
Drafted: 1990 Round 2 Dal
1990 Dal: Rush 3-26 8.7. **1991** Dal: Rush 2-(-1) -0.5. **1995** StL: Rush 1-17 17.0. **Total:** Rush 6-42 7.0.

		Receiving				Kickoff Returns					Tot
Year Team	G	Rec	Yds	Avg	TD	Ret	Yds	Avg	TD	Fum	TD
1990 Dal	15	11	104	9.5	0	12	276	23.0	1	1	1
1991 Dal	16	10	170	17.0	0	21	514	24.5	**1**	0	1
1992 Dal-LARd	13	12	175	14.6	2	26	442	17.0	0	1	2
1992 Dal	3	0	0	—	0	8	117	14.6	0	0	0
1992 LARd	10	12	175	14.6	2	18	325	18.1	0	1	2
1993 LARd	15	27	462	17.1	4	10	167	16.7	0	0	4
1994 LARd	16	16	294	18.4	2	10	282	28.2	0	0	2
1995 StL	8	23	368	16.0	2	0	0	—	0	0	2
1996 StL	3	2	24	12.0	0	0	0	—	0	0	0
NFL Total	86	101	1597	15.8	10	79	1681	21.3	2	2	12

ALVIN WRIGHT Wright, Alvin 6′2″, 274 **NT-DT-DE**
Col: Jacksonville State *HS:* Randolph Co. [Wedowee, AL] B: 2/5/1961, Wedowee, AL
1986 LARm: 4 G. **1987** LARm: 15 G; 2 Sac. **1988** LARm: 16 G; 2 Sac. **1989** LARm: 16 G; 3 Sac. **1990** LARm: 16 G; 1 Sac. **1991** LARm: 13 G. **1992** LARm-Cle: 4 G. LARm: 1 G. Cle: 3 G. **Total:** 84 G; 8 Sac.

CHARLES WRIGHT Wright, Charles James 5′9″, 178 **DB**
Col: Tulsa *HS:* Carthage [MO] B: 4/5/1964, Carthage, MO
Drafted: 1987 Round 10 StL
1987 StL: 3 G. **1988** Dal-TB: 5 G. Dal: 3 G. TB: 2 G. **Total:** 8 G.

DANA WRIGHT Wright, Dana Jerome 6′1″, 219 **RB**
Col: Kent State; Findlay *HS:* Theodore Roosevelt [Kent, OH]
B: 6/2/1963, Ravenna, OH *Drafted:* 1987 Round 9 NYG
1987 Cin: 5 G; Rush 24-74 3.1; Rec 4-28 7.0; KR 13-266 20.5; 1 Fum.

ELMO WRIGHT Wright, Elmo 6′0″, 190 **WR**
Col: Houston *HS:* Sweeny [TX] B: 7/3/1949, Brazoria, TX
Drafted: 1971 Round 1 KC
1971 KC: Rush 1-(-10) -10.0. **1972** KC: Rush 1-24 24.0. **1973** KC: Rush 5-29 5.8. **1974** KC: Rush 3-26 8.7 1 TD. **Total:** Rush 10-69 6.9 1 TD.

		Receiving					Tot
Year Team	G	Rec	Yds	Avg	TD	Fum	TD
1971 KC	14	26	528	20.3	3	1	3
1972 KC	7	11	81	7.4	0	0	0
1973 KC	11	16	252	15.8	2	1	2
1974 KC	13	13	209	16.1	1	0	2
1975 Hou-NE	6	4	46	11.5	0	0	0
1975 Hou	2	0	0	—	0	0	0
1975 NE	4	4	46	11.5	0	0	0
NFL Total	51	70	1116	15.9	6	2	7

ERIC WRIGHT Wright, Eric Cortez 6′1″, 183 **DB**
Col: Missouri *HS:* Assumption [East St. Louis, IL] B: 4/18/1959, St. Louis, MO *Drafted:* 1981 Round 2 SF

		Interceptions		
Year Team	G	Int	Yds	TD
1981 SF	16	3	26	0
1982 SF	7	1	31	0
1983 SF	16	7	**164**	**2**
1984 SF	16	2	0	0
1985 SF	16	1	0	0
1986 SF	2	0	0	0
1987 SF	2	0	0	0
1988 SF	15	2	-2	0
1989 SF	11	2	37	0
1990 SF	9	0	0	0
NFL Total	110	18	256	2

ERIC WRIGHT Wright, Eric LaMon 6′0″, 196 **WR**
Col: Stephen F. Austin St. *HS:* Pittsburg [TX] B: 8/4/1969, Pittsburg, TX
1991 ChiB: Postseason only. **1992** ChiB: 13 G; Rec 5-56 11.2.

ERNIE WRIGHT Wright, Ernest Henry 6′4″, 270 **OT**
Col: Ohio State *HS:* V. W. Scott [Toledo, OH] B: 11/6/1939, Toledo, OH
1960 LAC: 14 G. **1961** SD: 14 G. **1962** SD: 14 G. **1963** SD: 14 G. **1964** SD: 14 G; KR 1-0. **1965** SD: 14 G. **1966** SD: 13 G. **1967** SD: 14 G. **1968** Cin: 14 G. **1969** Cin: 14 G. **1970** Cin: 14 G. **1971** Cin: 7 G. **1972** SD: 14 G. **Total:** 174 G; KR 1-0.

FELIX WRIGHT Wright, Felix Carl 6′2″, 190 **DB**
Col: Highland CC KS; Fort Scott CC KS; Drake *HS:* Carthage [MO]
B: 6/22/1959, Carthage, MO
1993 KC: Postseason only.

		Interceptions				Tot
Year Team	G	Int	Yds	TD	Fum	TD
1985 Cle	16	2	11	0	0	0
1986 Cle	16	3	33	0	0	1
1987 Cle	12	4	152	1	0	1
1988 Cle	16	5	126	0	1	0
1989 Cle	16	**9**	91	1	0	1
1990 Cle	16	3	56	0	0	0
1991 Min	16	2	3	0	0	0
1992 Min	13	1	20	0	0	0
NFL Total	121	29	492	2	1	3

GEORGE WRIGHT Wright, George Wayne 6′3″, 265 **DT**
Col: Sam Houston State *HS:* C.E. King [Houston, TX] B: 3/3/1947, Houston, TX *Drafted:* 1969 Round 9 Bal
1970 Bal: 2 G. **1971** Bal: 10 G. **1972** Cle: 4 G. **Total:** 16 G.

GORDON WRIGHT Wright, Gordon Arnold 6′3″, 248 **OG**
Col: Delaware State *HS:* Freeport [NY] B: 12/15/1943, East Meadow, NY
1967 Phi: 3 G. **1969** NYJ: 2 G. **Total:** 5 G.

JIM WRIGHT Wright, James Earl 5′11″, 190 **DB**
Col: Memphis *HS:* Stephen D. Lee [Columbus, MS] B: 3/27/1939, Columbus, MS
1964 Den: 10 G; Int 1-11.

JAMES WRIGHT Wright, James Willie 6′3″, 240 **TE**
Col: Blinn Coll. TX (J.C.); Texas Christian *HS:* Brenham [TX]
B: 9/1/1956, Fort Hood, TX *Drafted:* 1978 Round 7 Atl
1978 Atl: KR 2-31 15.5. **1981** Den: Rush 1-11 11.0. **1982** Den: Rush 1-(-4) -4.0. **1983** Den: Rush 1-(-11) -11.0. **Total:** Rush 3-(-4) -1.3; KR 2-31 15.5.

		Receiving				
Year Team	G	Rec	Yds	Avg	TD	Fum
1978 Atl	15	2	26	13.0	0	0
1980 Den	1	0	0	—	0	0
1981 Den	16	3	22	7.3	1	0
1982 Den	9	9	120	13.3	1	0
1983 Den	6	13	134	10.3	0	2
1984 Den	16	11	118	10.7	1	0
1985 Den	16	28	246	8.8	1	0
NFL Total	79	66	666	10.1	4	2

JEFF WRIGHT Wright, Jeff Dee 6′2″, 274 **NT**
Col: Coffeyville CC KS; Tulsa; Central Missouri State *HS:* Lawrence [KS]
B: 6/13/1963, San Bernardino, CA *Drafted:* 1988 Round 8 Buf
1988 Buf: 15 G; 5 Sac. **1989** Buf: 15 G; Int 1-0; 3 Sac. **1990** Buf: 16 G; 5 Sac. **1991** Buf: 9 G; 6 Sac. **1992** Buf: 16 G; 6 Sac. **1993** Buf: 15 G; 4.5 Sac. **1994** Buf: 12 G; 2 Sac. **Total:** 98 G; Int 1-0; 31.5 Sac.

JEFF WRIGHT Wright, Jeffrey Ralph 5′11″, 190 **DB**
Col: Minnesota *HS:* Edina [MN] B: 6/13/1949, Edina, MN
Drafted: 1971 Round 15 Min
1973 Min: PR 2-0; KR 1-0. **1975** Min: PR 1-22 22.0. **Total:** PR 3-22 7.3; KR 1-0.

		Interceptions			
Year Team	G	Int	Yds	TD	Fum
1971 Min	14	0	0	0	0
1972 Min	13	3	31	0	0
1973 Min	14	3	31	0	2
1974 Min	11	4	60	0	0
1975 Min	3	0	0	0	0
1976 Min	14	1	5	0	0
1977 Min	14	1	5	0	0
NFL Total	83	12	132	0	2

JIM WRIGHT Wright, Jim Sid 6′1″, 222 **G**
Col: Texas-Arlington; Southern Methodist *HS:* Sulphur Springs [TX]
B: 9/12/1921, Sulphur Springs, TX *Drafted:* 1944 Round 13 Bkn
1947 Bos: 12 G.

JOHNNIE WRIGHT Wright, John Lee 6′2″, 210 **RB**
Col: South Carolina *HS:* Cypress Lake [Fort Myers, FL] B: 9/13/1958, Fort Myers, FL *Drafted:* 1982 Round 12 Bal
1982 Bal: 7 G; Rush 1-3 3.0; Rec 1-12 12.0.

JOHN WRIGHT Wright, John Oliver 5′11″, 225 **FB-LB**
(Red) *Col:* Maryland; Georgia *HS:* Baltimore City College [MD]
B: 7/13/1921, Baltimore, MD
AAFC **1947** BalA: Int 1-5.

		Rushing			
Year Team	**G**	**Att**	**Yds**	**Avg**	**TD**
1947 BalA	13	38	113	3.0	0

JOHN WRIGHT Wright, John William 6′0″, 197 **WR**
Col: Illinois *HS:* Central [Wheaton, IL] B: 1/11/1946, Oak Park, IL
Drafted: 1968 Round 2 Atl
1968 Atl: 5 G. **1969** Det: 14 G; Rec 12-130 10.8 2 TD; **1** Fum TD; Tot TD 3; 18 Pt. **Total:** 19 G; Rec 12-130 10.8 2 TD; 1 Fum TD; Tot TD 3; 18 Pt.

RAYFIELD WRIGHT Wright, Larry Rayfield 6′6″, 255 **OT-TE**
Col: Fort Valley State *HS:* Fairmont [Griffin, GA] B: 8/23/1945, Griffin, GA *Drafted:* 1967 Round 7 Dal
1967 Dal: 10 G. **1968** Dal: 14 G; Rush 1-(-10) -10.0; Rec 1-15 15.0 1 TD; 6 Pt. **1969** Dal: 14 G; Rec 1-12 12.0. **1970** Dal: 14 G. **1971** Dal: 14 G. **1972** Dal: 14 G. **1973** Dal: 12 G. **1974** Dal: 14 G. **1975** Dal: 13 G. **1976** Dal: 14 G. **1977** Dal: 2 G. **1978** Dal: 15 G. **1979** Dal: 16 G. **Total:** 166 G; Rush 1-(-10) -10.0; Rec 2-27 13.5 1 TD; 6 Pt.

LONNIE WRIGHT Wright, Lawrence 6′2″, 205 **DB**
Col: Colorado State *HS:* South Side [Newark, NJ] B: 1/23/1945, Newark, NJ
1966 Den: 14 G; Rec 1-(-2) -2.0; Int 1-15. **1967** Den: 12 G; Int 4-22. **Total:** 26 G; Rec 1-(-2) -2.0; Int 5-37.

LAWRENCE WRIGHT Wright, Lawrence D III 6′2″, 209 **DB**
Col: Florida *HS:* North Miami [FL]; Valley Forge Mil. Acad. [Wayne, PA]
B: 9/6/1973
1997 Cin: 4 G.

LOUIS WRIGHT Wright, Louis Donnel 6′2″, 200 **DB**
Col: Bakersfield Coll. CA (J.C.); Arizona State; San Jose State
HS: Bakersfield [CA] B: 1/31/1953, Gilmer, TX *Drafted:* 1975 Round 1 Den
1979 Den: **1** Fum TD. **1982** Den: 1 Sac. **1983** Den: PR 1-0; 1 Sac. **1984** Den: **1** Fum TD. **Total:** PR 1-0; 2 Fum TD; 2 Sac.

		Interceptions				Tot
Year Team	**G**	**Int**	**Yds**	**TD**	**Fum**	**TD**
1975 Den	11	2	9	0	1	0
1976 Den	14	0	32	0	0	0
1977 Den	14	3	128	**1**	0	1
1978 Den	16	2	2	0	1	0
1979 Den	16	2	20	0	0	1
1980 Den	15	0	0	0	0	0
1981 Den	8	0	0	0	0	0
1982 Den	9	2	18	0	0	0
1983 Den	16	6	50	0	1	0
1984 Den	16	1	1	0	0	1
1985 Den	15	5	44	0	0	1
1986 Den	16	3	56	0	0	0
NFL Total	166	26	360	1	3	4

NATE WRIGHT Wright, Nathaniel 5′11″, 180 **DB**
Col: Monterey Peninsula Coll. CA (J.C.); San Diego State *HS:* Monterey [CA] B: 12/21/1946, Madison, FL
1969 Atl-StL: PR 4-21 5.3. Atl: PR 4-21 5.3. **1970** StL: KR 8-156 19.5. **1974** Min: Rec 1-6 6.0. **1977** Min: 1 Fum TD. **Total:** Rec 1-6 6.0; PR 4-21 5.3; KR 8-156 19.5; 1 Fum TD.

		Interceptions			
Year Team	**G**	**Int**	**Yds**	**TD**	**Fum**
1969 Atl-StL	13	2	41	0	1
1969 Atl	3	0	0	0	1
1969 StL	10	2	41	0	0
1970 StL	14	1	0	0	0
1971 Min	3	0	0	0	0
1972 Min	14	1	10	0	0
1973 Min	14	3	6	0	1
1974 Min	14	6	91	0	0
1975 Min	14	0	0	0	0
1976 Min	14	7	47	0	0
1977 Min	14	3	0	0	0
1978 Min	16	5	58	0	0
1979 Min	10	4	44	0	0
1980 Min	16	2	16	0	0
NFL Total	156	34	313	0	2

RALPH WRIGHT Wright, Ralph 6′0″, 230 **T**
Col: Kentucky *HS:* Sturgis [KY] B: 1/16/1908, Sturgis, KY Deceased
1933 Bkn: 6 G.

RANDY WRIGHT Wright, Randall Steven 6′2″, 200 **QB**
Col: Wisconsin *HS:* St. Charles [IL] B: 1/12/1961, St. Charles, IL
Drafted: 1984 Round 6 GB

		Passing							
Year Team	**G**	**Att**	**Comp**	**Comp%**	**Yds**	**YPA**	**TD**	**Int**	**Rating**
1984 GB	8	62	27	43.5	310	5.00	2	6	30.4
1985 GB	5	74	39	52.7	552	7.46	2	4	63.6
1986 GB	16	492	263	53.5	3247	6.60	17	23	66.2
1987 GB	9	247	132	53.4	1507	6.10	6	11	61.6
1988 GB	8	244	141	57.8	1490	6.11	4	13	58.9
NFL Total	46	1119	602	53.8	7106	6.35	31	57	61.4

	Rushing				
Year Team	**Att**	**Yds**	**Avg**	**TD**	**Fum**
1984 GB	8	11	1.4	0	1
1985 GB	8	8	1.0	0	5
1986 GB	18	41	2.3	1	8
1987 GB	13	70	5.4	0	3
1988 GB	8	43	5.4	2	6
NFL Total	55	173	3.1	3	23

STEVE WRIGHT Wright, Stephen Hough 6′6″, 271 **OT-OG-TE**
Col: Northern Iowa *HS:* Wayzata [MN] B: 4/8/1959, St. Louis, MO
1981 Dal: 16 G. **1982** Dal: 9 G. **1983** Bal: 13 G. **1984** Ind: 12 G. **1987** LARd: 9 G. **1988** LARd: 15 G. **1989** LARd: 16 G. **1990** LARd: 16 G. **1991** LARd: 16 G. **1992** LARd: 7 G. **Total:** 129 G.

STEVE WRIGHT Wright, Stephen Thomas 6′6″, 250 **OT**
Col: Alabama *HS:* Manual [Louisville, KY] B: 7/17/1942, Birmingham, AL *Drafted:* 1964 Round 5 GB
1964 GB: 14 G. **1965** GB: 14 G. **1966** GB: 14 G. **1967** GB: 14 G. **1968** NYG: 10 G. **1969** NYG: 2 G. **1970** Was: 14 G. **1971** ChiB: 14 G. **1972** StL: 5 G. **Total:** 101 G.

SYLVESTER WRIGHT Wright, Sylvester L 6′2″, 258 **LB**
Col: Kansas *HS:* MacKenzie [Detroit, MI] B: 12/30/1971, Detroit, MI
1995 Phi: 6 G. **1996** Phi: 16 G. **Total:** 22 G.

TERRY WRIGHT Wright, Terry Leon 6′0″, 195 **DB**
Col: Scottsdale CC AZ; Temple *HS:* South Mountain [Phoenix, AZ]
B: 7/17/1964, Phoenix, AZ
1987 Ind: 13 G; KR 10-187 18.7; 1 Sac. **1988** Ind: 8 G; KR 1-22 22.0; 0.5 Sac. **Total:** 21 G; KR 11-209 19.0; 1.5 Sac.

TOBY WRIGHT Wright, Toby Lin 5′11″, 212 **DB**
Col: Phoenix Coll. AZ (J.C.); Nebraska *HS:* Dobson [Mesa, AZ]
B: 11/19/1970, Phoenix, AZ *Drafted:* 1994 Round 2 LARm
1994 LARm: 16 G; 1 Fum TD; 6 Pt. **1995** StL: 16 G; Rush 1-9 9.0; Int 6-79; **1** Fum TD; 6 Pt; 1 Sac. **1996** StL: 12 G; Int 1-19 1 TD; 6 Pt. **1997** StL: 11 G. **1998** StL: 3 G; 1 Sac. **Total:** 58 G; Rush 1-9 9.0; Int 7-98 1 TD; 2 Fum TD; Tot TD 3; 18 Pt; 2 Sac.

TED WRIGHT Wright, Weldon H 6′0″, 185 **WB-DB-BB-LB**
(Cowboy) *Col:* North Texas *HS:* Sherman [TX] B: 11/8/1913, Savoy, TX
1934 Bos: Pass 4-1 25.0%, 25 6.25 1 Int; Rec 1-25 25.0; Scor 8, 2 XK. **1935** Bos-Bkn: Pass 18-4 22.2%, 51 2.83 1 Int; Scor 1, 1 XK. Bos: Pass 18-4 22.2%, 51 2.83 1 Int; Scor 1, 1 XK. **Total:** Pass 22-5 22.7%, 76 3.45 2 Int; Rec 1-25 25.0.

		Rushing			
Year Team	**G**	**Att**	**Yds**	**Avg**	**TD**
1934 Bos	10	19	123	6.5	1
1935 Bos-Bkn	9	15	43	2.9	0
1935 Bos	6	15	43	2.9	0
1935 Bkn	3	0	0	—	0
NFL Total	19	34	166	4.9	1

KEITH WRIGHT Wright, William Keith 5′10″, 172 **WR**
Col: Memphis *HS:* Warren Central [Vicksburg, MS] B: 1/30/1956, Mercedes, TX *Drafted:* 1978 Round 5 Cle
1978 Cle: Rec 8-76 9.5. **1979** Cle: Rec 1-13 13.0. **1980** Cle: Rec 3-62 20.7 3 TD. **Total:** Rec 12-151 12.6 3 TD.

		Punt Returns				Kickoff Returns				
Year Team	**G**	**Ret**	**Yds**	**Avg**	**TD**	**Ret**	**Yds**	**Avg**	**TD**	**Fum**
1978 Cle	16	37	288	7.8	0	30	789	26.3	0	6
1979 Cle	5	12	50	4.2	0	15	402	26.8	0	0
1980 Cle	12	29	129	4.4	0	25	576	23.0	0	2
NFL Total	33	78	467	6.0	0	70	1767	25.2	0	8

WILLIE WRIGHT Wright, Willie Don 6′4″, 239 **TE**
Col: Wyoming *HS:* Riverton [WY] B: 3/9/1968, Riverton, WY
1992 Pho: 9 G.

TIM WRIGHTMAN Wrightman, Timothy John 6′3″, 237 **TE**
Col: UCLA *HS:* Mary Star of the Sea [San Pedro, CA] B: 3/27/1960, Los Angeles, CA *Drafted:* 1982 Round 3 ChiB

Year Team	G	Rec	Yds	Avg	TD	Fum
		Receiving				
1985 ChiB	16	24	407	17.0	1	0
1986 ChiB	16	22	241	11.0	0	1
NFL Total	32	46	648	14.1	1	1

DANNY WUERFFEL Wuerffel, Daniel Carl 6′1″, 212 **QB**
Col: Florida *HS:* Fort Walton Beach [FL] B: 5/27/1974, Fort Walton Beach, FL *Drafted:* 1997 Round 4 NO
1997 NO: Rush 6-26 4.3. **1998** NO: Rush 11-60 5.5. **Total:** Rush 17-86 5.1.

Year Team	G	Att	Comp	Comp%	Yds	YPA	TD	Int	Rating	Fum
		Passing								
1997 NO	7	91	42	46.2	518	5.69	4	8	42.3	2
1998 NO	5	119	62	52.1	695	5.84	5	5	66.3	1
NFL Total	12	210	104	49.5	1213	5.78	9	13	55.9	3

AL WUKITS Wukits, Albert Robert 6′3″, 218 **LB-C-G**
(Buckets) *Col:* Duquesne *HS:* Millvale [PA] B: 12/16/1917, Millvale, PA D: 10/15/1978, Pittsburgh, PA *Drafted:* 1943 Round 9 Pit
AAFC **1946** BufA-MiaA: 15 G; Int 2-26.

NFL **1943** PhPt: 10 G; Int 1-7; **1** Fum TD; 6 Pt. **1944** ChPt: 10 G. **1945** Pit: 3 G; 2 Fum. **Total:** 23 G; Int 1-7; 1 Fum TD; 6 Pt; 2 Fum.

JIM WULFF Wulff, James Francis 5′10″, 184 **DB**
Col: Michigan State *HS:* St. George [Evanston, IL] B: 3/22/1936, Chicago, IL *Drafted:* 1958 Round 6 Cle
1960 Was: 9 G. **1961** Was: 8 G; Rec 1-6 6.0; Int 3-11. **Total:** 17 G; Rec 1-6 6.0; Int 3-11.

JERRY WUNSCH Wunsch, Gerald 6′6″, 333 **OT**
Col: Wisconsin *HS:* West [Wausau, WI] B: 1/21/1974, Eau Claire, WI *Drafted:* 1997 Round 2 TB
1997 TB: 16 G. **1998** TB: 16 G. **Total:** 32 G.

HARRY WUNSCH Wunsch, Harry Frederick 5′11″, 212 **G**
Col: Notre Dame *HS:* South Bend Central [IN] B: 11/20/1910, Chicago, IL D: 4/1954
1934 GB: 2 G.

FRED WYANT Wyant, Frederick Mount Jr. 6′0″, 200 **QB**
Col: West Virginia *HS:* Weston [WV] B: 4/26/1934, Weston, WV *Drafted:* 1956 Round 3 Was
1956 Was: 10 G; Pass 2-1 50.0%, 17 8.50.

ALVIN WYATT Wyatt, Alvin B 5′10″, 184 **DB**
Col: Bethune-Cookman *HS:* Matthew W. Gilbert [Jacksonville, FL] B: 12/13/1947, Jacksonville, FL *Drafted:* 1970 Round 6 Oak
1971 Buf: Int 1-30. **1972** Buf: Int 4-52 1 TD. **Total:** Int 5-82 1 TD.

Year Team	G	Ret	Yds	Avg	TD	Ret	Yds	Avg	TD	Fum	Tot TD
		Punt Returns				Kickoff Returns					
1970 Oak	11	25	231	9.2	**1**	13	286	22.0	0	4	1
1971 Buf	14	23	188	8.2	**1**	30	762	25.4	0	5	1
1972 Buf	14	11	85	7.7	0	17	432	25.4	0	0	1
1973 Hou	4	0	0	—	0	0	0	—	0	0	0
NFL Total	43	59	504	8.5	2	60	1480	24.7	0	9	3

ANTWUAN WYATT Wyatt, Antwuan Bernard 5′10″, 193 **WR**
Col: Bethune-Cookman *HS:* Mainland [Daytona Beach, FL] B: 7/18/1975, Daytona Beach, FL *Drafted:* 1997 Round 6 Phi
1997 Phi: 1 G; PR 2-(-2) -1.0; KR 2-50 25.0.

DOUG WYATT Wyatt, John Douglas 6′1″, 195 **DB**
Col: Tulsa *HS:* John Tyler [Tyler, TX] B: 10/18/1946, Tyler, TX *Drafted:* 1970 Round 17 NO
1970 NO: 14 G; PR 1-15 15.0; Int 4-45. **1971** NO: 12 G; Int 4-84 1 TD; 6 Pt. **1972** NO: 14 G; **1** Fum TD; 6 Pt. **1973** Det: 6 G. **1974** Det: 12 G. **Total:** 58 G; PR 1-15 15.0; Int 8-129 1 TD; 1 Fum TD; Tot TD 2; 12 Pt.

KERVIN WYATT Wyatt, Kervin Doran 6′1″, 235 **LB**
Col: Maryland *HS:* Potomac [Oxon Hill, MD] B: 10/17/1957, Washington, DC
1980 NYG: 4 G; KR 1-0.

KEVIN WYATT Wyatt, Kevin Michael 5′10″, 199 **DB**
Col: Arkansas *HS:* Rockhurst [Kansas City, MO] B: 3/14/1964, Norfolk, VA *Drafted:* 1986 Round 5 Mia
1986 SD: 16 G; KR 5-74 14.8. **1987** KC: 2 G; PR 2-4 2.0; KR 5-121 24.2; 1 Fum. **Total:** 18 G; PR 2-4 2.0; KR 10-195 19.5; 1 Fum.

WILLIE WYATT Wyatt, Willie Porter 5′11″, 275 **NT**
Col: Alabama *HS:* Gardendale [AL] B: 9/27/1967, Birmingham, AL
1990 TB: 7 G.

SAM WYCHE Wyche, Samuel David 6′4″, 218 **QB**
Col: Furman *HS:* North Fulton [Atlanta, GA] B: 1/5/1945, Atlanta, GA
1968 Cin: Rec 1-5 5.0. **Total:** Rec 1-5 5.0.

Year Team	G	Att	Comp	Comp%	Yds	YPA	TD	Int	Rating
		Passing							
1968 Cin	3	55	35	63.6	494	8.98	2	2	89.5
1969 Cin	7	108	54	50.0	838	7.76	7	4	82.3
1970 Cin	14	57	26	45.6	411	7.21	3	2	73.1
1971 Was	1	0	0	—	0	—	0	0	—
1972 Was	7	0	0	—	0	—	0	0	—
1974 Det	14	1	0	0.0	0	0.00	0	1	0.0
1976 StL	1	1	1	100.0	5	5.00	0	0	87.5
NFL Total	47	222	116	52.3	1748	7.87	12	9	79.6

Year Team	Att	Yds	Avg	TD	Fum
	Rushing				
1968 Cin	12	74	6.2	0	2
1969 Cin	12	107	8.9	1	1
1970 Cin	19	118	6.2	2	3
1971 Was	1	4	4.0	0	0
1974 Det	1	0	0.0	0	0
NFL Total	45	303	6.7	3	6

FRANK WYCHECK Wycheck, Frank John 6′3″, 241 **TE**
Col: Maryland *HS:* Archbishop Ryan [Philadelphia, PA] B: 10/14/1971, Philadelphia, PA *Drafted:* 1993 Round 6 Was
1994 Was: KR 4-84 21.0. **1995** Hou: Rush 1-1 1.0 1 TD. **1996** Hou: Rush 2-3 1.5; KR 2-5 2.5. **1997** Ten: KR 1-3 3.0; Scor 1 2XP. **1998** Ten: KR 1-10 10.0. **Total:** Rush 3-4 1.3 1 TD; KR 8-102 12.8; Scor 1 2XP.

Year Team	G	Rec	Yds	Avg	TD	Fum	Tot TD
		Receiving					
1993 Was	9	16	113	7.1	0	1	0
1994 Was	9	7	55	7.9	1	0	1
1995 Hou	16	40	471	11.8	1	0	2
1996 Hou	16	53	511	9.6	6	2	6
1997 Ten	16	63	748	11.9	4	0	4
1998 Ten	16	70	768	11.0	2	2	2
NFL Total	82	249	2666	10.7	14	5	15

CRAIG WYCINSKY Wycinsky, Craig Peter 6′3″, 243 **OG**
Col: Michigan State *HS:* North Farmington [Farmington, MI] B: 1/4/1948, Detroit, MI *Drafted:* 1970 Round 7 Cle
1972 Cle: 6 G.

DOUG WYCOFF Wycoff, Stephen Douglas 6′0″, 206 **FB-DB-TB-BB**
Col: Georgia Tech *HS:* Little Rock Central [AR] B: 9/16/1903, St. Louis, MO D: 10/27/1981, Atlanta, GA
1927 NYG: Int 1 TD; Scor 19, 1 XK. **1931** NYG: Int **1** TD. **Total:** Int 2 TD.

Year Team	G	Att	Comp	Comp%	Yds	YPA	TD	Int	Rating
		Passing							
1927 NYG	11	—	—	—	—	—	0	—	—
1929 SI	9	—	—	—	—	—	2	—	—
1930 SI	12	—	—	—	—	—	5	—	—
1931 NYG	12	—	—	—	—	—	0	—	—
1932 SI	12	31	10	32.3	140	4.52	0	2	20.9
1934 Bos	12	30	6	20.0	93	3.10	1	7	11.5
NFL Total	68	61	16	26.2	233	3.82	8	9	43.0

Year Team	Att	Yds	Avg	TD	Tot TD
	Rushing				
1927 NYG	—	—	—	2	3
1929 SI	—	—	—	2	2
1930 SI	—	—	—	4	4
1931 NYG	—	—	—	1	2
1932 SI	135	454	3.4	1	1
1934 Bos	106	326	3.1	1	1
NFL Total	241	780	3.2	11	13

FRANK WYDO Wydo, Frank 6′4″, 225 **OT-DT**
Col: Duquesne; Cornell *HS:* German Twp. [McClellandtown, PA] B: 6/15/1924, Footedale, PA D: 2/17/1979, Uniontown, PA *Drafted:* 1947 Round 3 Pit
1947 Pit: 12 G. **1948** Pit: 12 G. **1949** Pit: 12 G; Rec 2-21 10.5. **1950** Pit: 12 G; KR 1-7 7.0; 1 Fum. **1951** Pit: 12 G; KR 1-0; 1 Fum. **1952** Phi: 12 G. **1953** Phi: 12 G. **1954** Phi: 12 G. **1955** Phi: 12 G. **1956** Phi: 12 G; 1 Fum. **1957** Phi: 12 G; KR 1-2 2.0; Int 1-25. **Total:** 132 G; Rec 2-21 10.5; KR 3-9 3.0; Int 1-25; 3 Fum.

JOHN WYHONIC Wyhonic, John N 6′0″, 213 **G**
(AKA John N. Wyhowanec) *Col:* Alabama B: 12/23/1919, Tiltonville, OH D: 7/19/1989, Arcadia, FL *Drafted:* 1942 Round 14 Phi
AAFC **1948** BufA: 13 G. **1949** BufA: 3 G. **Total:** 16 G.

NFL **1946** Phi: 11 G. **1947** Phi: 12 G. **Total:** 23 G.

LEE WYKOFF Wykoff, Lee Arlo 6′1″, 195 **FB-HB**
Col: Washburn *HS:* Osborne [KS] B: 3/10/1898, Marietta, KS D: 4/30/1974, Kansas City, KS
1923 StL: 4 G.

PUDGE WYLAND Wyland, Guido B 5'10", 180 G
Col: Iowa *HS:* Moline [IL] B: 6/5/1891, Minden, IA D: 12/8/1974, Moline, IL
1920 RI: 9 G.

ARNIE WYMAN Wyman, Arnold Douglas 5'11", 172 FB
Col: Minnesota *HS:* East [Minneapolis, MN] B: 8/20/1895, Minneapolis, MN Deceased
1920 RI: 6 G.

DAVID WYMAN Wyman, David Matthew 6'2", 241 LB
Col: Stanford *HS:* Earl Wooster [Reno, NV] B: 3/31/1964, San Diego, CA *Drafted:* 1987 Round 2 Sea
1987 Sea: 4 G. **1988** Sea: 16 G; 2.5 Sac. **1989** Sea: 16 G. **1990** Sea: 8 G; Int 2-24; 1 Sac. **1991** Sea: 6 G. **1992** Sea: 11 G. **1993** Den: 16 G; Rec 1-1 1.0 1 TD; Int 1-9; 6 Pt; 2 Sac. **1994** Den: 4 G. **1995** Den: 11 G. **Total:** 92 G; Rec 1-1 1.0 1 TD; Int 3-33; 6 Pt; 5.5 Sac.

DEVIN WYMAN Wyman, Devin Edward 6'7", 290 DT
Col: Coll. of San Mateo CA (J.C.); Kentucky State *HS:* Carlmont [Belmont, CA] B: 8/29/1973, East Palo Alto, CA *Drafted:* 1996 Round 6 NE
1996 NE: 9 G; 1 Sac. **1997** NE: 6 G. **Total:** 15 G; 1 Sac.

RENALDO WYNN Wynn, Renaldo Levalle 6'3", 289 DE-DT
Col: Notre Dame *HS:* De La Salle [Chicago, IL] B: 9/3/1974, Chicago, IL *Drafted:* 1997 Round 1 Jac
1997 Jac: 16 G; 2.5 Sac. **1998** Jac: 15 G; 1 Sac. **Total:** 31 G; 3.5 Sac.

WILL WYNN Wynn, William 6'4", 245 DE
Col: Tennessee State *HS:* Huntington [Newport News, VA] B: 1/15/1949, Apex, NC *Drafted:* 1973 Round 7 Phi
1973 Phi: 12 G; **1** Fum TD; 6 Pt. **1974** Phi: 14 G; 1 Fum TD; 6 Pt. **1975** Phi: 14 G. **1976** Phi: 14 G. **1977** Was: 1 G. **Total:** 55 G; 2 Fum TD; 12 Pt.

CHET WYNNE Wynne, Chester Allen 6'0", 180 TB-FB
Col: Notre Dame *HS:* Norton [KS] B: 11/23/1898 D: 7/17/1967, Chicago, IL
1922 Roch: 2 G.

ELMER WYNNE Wynne, Elmer Burton 6'1", 193 FB
Col: Nebraska; Notre Dame *HS:* Norton [KS] B: 1/20/1901, Long Island, KS D: 11/9/1989, Brush, CO
1928 ChiB: 10 G. **1929** Day: 5 G. **Total:** 15 G.

HARRY WYNNE Wynne, Harry Clayton 6'4", 203 OE-DE
Col: Arkansas *HS:* West Memphis [AR] B: 7/10/1920, Senatobia, MS D: 11/28/1989 *Drafted:* 1943 Round 22 Pit
1944 Bos: 10 G; Rec 10-205 20.5; KR 1-11 11.0. **1945** NYG: 5 G; Rec 2-25 12.5. **Total:** 15 G; Rec 12-230 19.2; KR 1-11 11.0.

PETE WYSOCKI Wysocki, Peter Joseph 6'1", 224 LB
Col: Western Michigan *HS:* Garden City [MI] B: 10/3/1948, Detroit, MI
1975 Was: 13 G. **1976** Was: 14 G; KR 1-0; 1 Fum. **1977** Was: 13 G. **1978** Was: 16 G. **1979** Was: 16 G; Int 1-9. **1980** Was: 16 G. **Total:** 88 G; KR 1-0; Int 1-9; 1 Fum.

IZZY YABLOCK Yablock, Julius 5'10", 172 BB-TB
(Indian) *Col:* Colgate *HS:* Boys [Brooklyn, NY] B: 7/28/1907, Brooklyn, NY D: 8/15/1983, Encino, CA
1930 Bkn: 7 G; Pass 1 TD. **1931** Bkn-SI: 13 G. Bkn: 6 G. SI: 7 G. **Total:** 20 G; Pass 1 TD.

VINNIE YABLONSKI Yablonski, Ventan Constantine 5'8", 195 FB-LB
Col: Fordham; Columbia *HS:* Worcester Classical [MA] B: 3/4/1923, Worcester, MA *Drafted:* 1946 Round 12 ChiC
1948 ChiC: Rec 1-13 13.0; Scor 3, 1-4 25.0% FG. **1949** ChiC: Rec 6-35 5.8; Scor 16, 5-6 83.3% FG, 1-1 100.0% XK. **1950** ChiC: Rec 7-71 10.1; Scor 19, 2-3 66.7% FG, 7-7 100.0% XK. **1951** ChiC: Rec 1-8 8.0; Scor 14, 2-5 40.0% FG, 8-8 100.0% XK. **Total:** Rec 15-127 8.5; Scor 52, 10-18 55.6% FG, 16-16 100.0% XK.

		Rushing				
Year Team	**G**	**Att**	**Yds**	**Avg**	**TD**	**Fum**
1948 ChiC	12	48	233	4.9	0	0
1949 ChiC	12	32	97	3.0	0	1
1950 ChiC	12	30	110	3.7	1	1
1951 ChiC	4	14	20	1.4	0	0
NFL Total	40	124	460	3.7	1	2

JOHN YACCINO Yaccino, John Nino 6'0", 190 DB
Col: Pittsburgh *HS:* Hazleton [PA] B: 6/27/1940, Hazleton, PA
1962 Buf: 3 G.

JOE YACKANICH Yackanich, Joseph Peter 5'10", 205 G
Col: Fordham *HS:* Hazelton [PA]; Seton Hall Prep [South Orange, NJ] B: 3/31/1922 D: 8/1969, Lansing, IL
AAFC **1946** NY-A: 11 G. **1947** NY-A: 14 G. **1948** NY-A: 1 G. **Total:** 26 G.

RAY YAGIELLO Yagiello, Raymond Walter 6'0", 220 G-LB
(Mike) *Col:* Franklin & Marshall; Catawba *HS:* Kearny [NJ] B: 9/21/1923, Orange, NJ *Drafted:* 1948 Round 20 LARm
1948 LARm: 12 G. **1949** LARm: 12 G. **Total:** 24 G.

RAY YAKAVONIS Yakavonis, Raymond 6'4", 250 NT
Col: East Stroudsburg *HS:* Hanover Area [Wilkes-Barre, PA] B: 1/20/1957, Wilkes-Barre, PA *Drafted:* 1980 Round 6 Min
1981 Min: 15 G. **1982** Min: 2 G. **1983** Min-KC: 4 G. Min: 2 G. KC: 2 G. **Total:** 21 G.

BILL YANCHAR Yanchar, William J Jr. 6'3", 251 DT
Col: Purdue *HS:* Euclid [OH] B: 3/25/1948, Euclid, OH *Drafted:* 1970 Round 10 Cle
1970 Cle: 5 G.

CARLOS YANCY Yancy, Carlos Delaino 6'2", 190 DB
Col: Georgia *HS:* Laurinburg Inst. [NC]; Sarasota [FL] B: 6/26/1970, Sarasota, FL *Drafted:* 1995 Round 7 NE
1995 NE: 4 G.

RON YANKOWSKI Yankowski, Ronald William 6'5", 244 DE
Col: Northeastern Oklahoma A&M (J.C.); Kansas State *HS:* Picher [OK] B: 10/23/1946, Arlington, MA *Drafted:* 1971 Round 8 StL
1971 StL: 12 G. **1972** StL: 10 G. **1973** StL: 14 G. **1974** StL: 14 G; 1 Fum TD; 6 Pt. **1975** StL: 13 G. **1976** StL: 5 G. **1977** StL: 14 G. **1978** StL: 16 G. **1979** StL: 16 G. **1980** StL: 14 G. **Total:** 128 G; 1 Fum TD; 6 Pt.

ERIC YARBER Yarber, Eric Lamone 5'8", 156 WR
Col: Los Angeles Valley Coll. CA (J.C.); Idaho *HS:* Crenshaw [Los Angeles, CA] B: 9/22/1963, Chicago, IL *Drafted:* 1986 Round 12 Was
1987 Was: Rec 1-5 5.0. **Total:** Rec 1-5 5.0.

		Punt Returns				
Year Team	**G**	**Ret**	**Yds**	**Avg**	**TD**	**Fum**
1986 Was	2	9	143	15.9	0	0
1987 Was	12	37	273	7.4	0	1
NFL Total	14	46	416	9.0	0	1

RYAN YARBOROUGH Yarborough, Ryan Kenneth 6'2", 195 WR
Col: Wyoming *HS:* Rich East [Park Forest, IL] B: 4/26/1971, Baltimore, MD *Drafted:* 1994 Round 2 NYJ

		Receiving				
Year Team	**G**	**Rec**	**Yds**	**Avg**	**TD**	**Fum**
1994 NYJ	13	6	42	7.0	1	0
1995 NYJ	16	18	230	12.8	2	0
1997 Bal	16	16	183	11.4	0	3
1998 Bal	6	4	39	9.8	0	0
NFL Total	51	44	494	11.2	3	3

JIM YARBROUGH Yarbrough, James Edward 6'0", 195 DB
Col: Murray State *HS:* Fulton [Knoxville, TN] B: 11/20/1963
1987 NYG: 3 G.

JIM YARBROUGH Yarbrough, James Kelley 6'5", 265 OT
Col: Florida *HS:* DeSoto [Arcadia, FL] B: 10/28/1946, Charlotte, NC *Drafted:* 1969 Round 2 Det
1969 Det: 14 G; KR 1-0; 1 Fum. **1970** Det: 12 G. **1971** Det: 14 G. **1972** Det: 13 G. **1973** Det: 10 G. **1974** Det: 12 G. **1975** Det: 13 G. **1976** Det: 11 G. **1977** Det: 13 G. **Total:** 112 G; KR 1-0; 1 Fum.

GEORGE YARNO Yarno, George Anthony 6'2", 260 OG-C-OT
Col: Washington State *HS:* East [Archorage, AK]; Joel E. Ferris HS [Spokane, WA] B: 8/12/1957, Spokane, WA
1979 TB: 15 G. **1980** TB: 16 G. **1981** TB: 16 G. **1982** TB: 9 G; KR 1-14 14.0. **1983** TB: 14 G; Scor 1, 1-1 100.0% XK. **1985** TB: 12 G. **1986** TB: 16 G. **1987** TB: 11 G. **1988** Atl: 16 G. **1989** Hou: 11 G. **Total:** 136 G; KR 1-14 14.0; Scor 1, 1-1 100.0% XK.

JOHN YARNO Yarno, John Richard 6'5", 251 C
Col: Idaho *HS:* Gonzaga Prep [Spokane, WA]; Joel E. Ferris [Spokane, WA] B: 12/17/1954, Spokane, WA *Drafted:* 1977 Round 4 Sea
1977 Sea: 10 G. **1978** Sea: 13 G. **1979** Sea: 16 G. **1980** Sea: 15 G. **1981** Sea: 11 G. **1982** Sea: 9 G. **Total:** 74 G.

TOMMY YARR Yarr, Thomas Cornelius 5'10", 205 C-LB
Col: Notre Dame *HS:* Chimacum Prep [WA] B: 12/4/1908, Dabob, WA D: 12/24/1941, Chicago, IL
1933 ChiC: 8 G.

RON YARY Yary, Anthony Ronald 6'5", 255 OT
Col: Cerritos Coll. CA (J.C.); USC *HS:* Bellflower [CA] B: 7/16/1946, Chicago, IL *Drafted:* 1968 Round 1 Min
1968 Min: 14 G. **1969** Min: 11 G. **1970** Min: 14 G. **1971** Min: 14 G. **1972** Min: 14 G. **1973** Min: 14 G. **1974** Min: 14 G. **1975** Min: 14 G. **1976** Min: 14 G. **1977** Min: 14 G. **1978** Min: 16 G. **1979** Min: 16 G. **1980** Min: 14 G; Rec 1-5 5.0; KR 1-3 3.0. **1981** Min: 16 G. **1982** LARm: 8 G. **Total:** 207 G; Rec 1-5 5.0; KR 1-3 3.0.

BOB YATES Yates, Robert E 6'1", 240 OT-C
Col: Syracuse *HS:* Montpelier [VT] B: 11/20/1938 *Drafted:* 1960 Round 1 Den
1961 Bos: 14 G. **1962** Bos: 14 G. **1963** Bos: 14 G; KR 1-0. **1964** Bos: 12 G; KR 1-0. **1965** Bos: 14 G. **Total:** 68 G; KR 2-0.

HOWIE YEAGER Yeager, Howard Leon 5′11″, 173 WB-DB
Col: California-Santa Barbara *HS:* John Muir [Pasadena, CA]
B: 2/19/1915, Orosi, CA
1941 NYG: 10 G; Rush 22-67 3.0 1 TD; Rec 11-220 20.0 3 TD; PR 2-40 20.0; KR 3-89 29.7; Tot TD 4; 24 Pt.

JIM YEAGER Yeager, James Roland 6′1″, 230 T-G
(Dutch) *Col:* Lehigh *HS:* Reading [PA]; Schuylkill Acad. [Reading, PA]
B: 9/21/1903, Reading, PA D: 1/13/1972, Reading, PA
1926 Bkn: 11 G.

BILL YEARBY Yearby, William M 6′3″, 235 DE
Col: Michigan *HS:* East Detroit [Eastpointe, MI] B: 7/24/1944, Birmingham, AL *Drafted:* 1966 Round 1 NYJ
1966 NYJ: 9 G.

JEFF YEATES Yeates, Jeffrey Lee 6′3″, 248 DE-DT-OG
Col: Boston College *HS:* Cardinal O'Hara [Tonawanda, NY]
B: 8/3/1951, Buffalo, NY *Drafted:* 1973 Round 4 Buf
1974 Buf: 10 G. **1975** Buf: 13 G. **1976** Buf-Atl: 5 G. Buf: 3 G. Atl: 2 G. **1977** Atl: 13 G. **1978** Atl: 16 G. **1979** Atl: 16 G. **1980** Atl: 16 G; Int 1-5. **1981** Atl: 16 G. **1982** Atl: 9 G; 1 Sac. **1983** Atl: 16 G; 4 Sac. **1984** Atl: 8 G; 2 Sac. **Total:** 138 G; Int 1-5; 7 Sac.

JAMES YEATS Yeats, James Melvin 6′4″, 245 TE
Col: Florida *HS:* Roy Miller [Corpus Christi, TX] B: 1936
1960 Hou: 1 G.

PHIL YEBOAH-KODIE Yeboah-Kodie, Philip Anthony 6′2″, 220 LB
Col: Penn State *HS:* Vanier Coll. [Montreal, Canada] B: 1/22/1971, Ghana *Drafted:* 1995 Round 5 Den
1996 Ind: 2 G.

DON YEISLEY Yeisley, Donald Lee 6′1″, 185 E
Col: Chicago *HS:* Cedar Rapids [IA] B: 1/21/1904, Chelsea, IA
D: 10/1971, Victor, IA
1928 ChiC: 3 G.

BILL YELVERTON Yelverton, William Grover 6′4″, 220 DE
Col: Mississippi *HS:* Central [Jackson, MS] B: 5/19/1933, Taylorsville, MS *Drafted:* 1956 Round 18 SF
1960 Den: 10 G; Int 1-20 1 TD; 6 Pt.

DICK YELVINGTON Yelvington, Richard Joseph Jr. 6′2″, 232 OT
Col: Georgia *HS:* Mainland [Daytona Beach, FL] B: 7/27/1928, Titusville, FL *Drafted:* 1951 Round 23 NYG
1952 NYG: 7 G. **1953** NYG: 12 G. **1954** NYG: 12 G. **1955** NYG: 11 G. **1956** NYG: 12 G. **1957** NYG: 8 G. **Total:** 62 G.

GARO YEPREMIAN Yepremian, Garabed Sarkis 5′8″, 175 K
Col: No College *HS:* American Acad. [Larnaca, Cyprus] B: 6/2/1944, Larnaca, Cyprus

		Scoring						
Year Team	**G**	**Pts**	**FG**	**FGA**	**FG%**	**XK**	**XKA**	**XK%**
1966 Det	9	50	13	22	59.1	11	11	100.0
1967 Det	8	28	2	6	33.3	22	23	95.7
1970 Mia	13	97	22	29	**75.9**	31	31	**100.0**
1971 Mia	14	**117**	28	40	70.0	33	33	100.0
1972 Mia	14	115	24	37	64.9	43	**45**	95.6
1973 Mia	14	113	25	37	67.6	38	38	100.0
1974 Mia	14	67	8	15	53.3	43	43	100.0
1975 Mia	14	79	13	16	**81.3**	40	46	**87.0**
1976 Mia	14	77	16	23	69.6	29	31	93.5
1977 Mia	14	67	10	22	45.5	37	40	92.5
1978 Mia	16	98	19	23	**82.6**	41	45	**91.1**
1979 NO	14	75	12	16	75.0	39	40	97.5
1980 TB	16	79	16	23	69.6	31	32	96.9
1981 TB	3	12	2	4	50.0	6	6	100.0
NFL Total	177	1074	210	313	67.1	444	464	95.7

HOWARD YERGES Yerges, Howard E 5′9″, 155 TB
(Littleboy) *Col:* Ohio State *HS:* North [Columbus, OH] B: 1896
Deceased
1920 Col: 1 G.

TOM YEWCIC Yewcic, Thomas 5′11″, 185 QB-P-HB
(Kibby) *Col:* Michigan State *HS:* Conemaugh Twp. [Davidsville, PA]
B: 5/9/1932, Conemaugh, PA *Drafted:* 1954 Round 27 Pit
1961 Bos: Rec 6-56 9.3. **1965** Bos: Rec 1-13 13.0. **Total:** Rec 7-69 9.9.

		Passing							
Year Team	**G**	**Att**	**Comp**	**Comp%**	**Yds**	**YPA**	**TD**	**Int**	**Rating**
1961 Bos	14	8	3	37.5	25	3.13	1	2	46.4
1962 Bos	14	126	54	42.9	903	7.17	7	5	69.6
1963 Bos	14	70	29	41.4	444	6.34	4	5	52.3
1964 Bos	14	1	1	100.0	2	2.00	0	0	79.2
1965 Bos	14	1	0	0.0	0	0.00	0	0	39.6
1966 Bos	7	0	0	—	0	—	0	0	—
NFL Total	77	206	87	42.2	1374	6.67	12	12	60.2

	Rushing				Punting			
Year Team	**Att**	**Yds**	**Avg**	**TD**	**Punts**	**Yds**	**Avg**	**Fum**
1961 Bos	11	51	4.6	1	64	2406	37.6	0
1962 Bos	33	215	6.5	2	69	2654	38.5	8
1963 Bos	22	161	7.3	1	74	2880	38.9	3
1964 Bos	5	2	0.4	0	73	2787	38.2	1
1965 Bos	0	0	—	0	76	3094	40.7	0
1966 Bos	1	-5	-5.0	0	21	732	34.9	1
NFL Total	72	424	5.9	4	377	14553	38.6	13

JOHN YEZERSKI Yezerski, John G 6′4″, 240 T
Col: St. Mary's (Cal.) *HS:* Washington [Portland, OR] B: 9/22/1914
D: 1/1979, Boring, OR
1936 Bkn: 9 G.

DAVE YOHN Yohn, John David 6′0″, 220 LB
Col: Gettysburg *HS:* Palmyra [PA] B: 10/10/1937
1962 Bal: 4 G. **1963** NYJ: 14 G. **Total:** 18 G.

MACK YOHO Yoho, Mack 6′2″, 230 DE-K
Col: Miami (Ohio) *HS:* East Canton [OH] B: 6/14/1936, Reader, WV
1960 Buf: 14 G; Int 1-15 1 TD; Scor 12, 2-5 40.0% FG. **1961** Buf: 14 G; Int 1-0; Scor 0-4 FG. **1962** Buf: 14 G; Scor 23, 1-3 33.3% FG, 20-22 90.9% XK. **1963** Buf: 14 G; Scor 62, 10-24 41.7% FG, 32-35 91.4% XK. **Total:** 56 G; Int 2-15 1 TD; Scor 97, 13-36 36.1% FG, 52-57 91.2% XK.

FRANK YOKAS Yokas, Frank P 5′11″, 210 G
(Yogi) *Col:* No College *HS:* Rock Island [IL] B: 2/27/1924, Rock Island, IL D: 5/12/1994, Los Angeles, CA
AAFC **1946** LA-A: 12 G. **1947** BalA: 13 G. **Total:** 25 G.

JOHN YONAKOR Yonakor, John Joseph 6′5″, 222 DE-OE-DT
Col: Notre Dame *HS:* Mechanic Arts [Boston, MA] B: 8/4/1921, Boston, MA
AAFC **1946** CleA: 14 G; Rec 7-98 14.0 2 TD; 12 Pt. **1947** CleA: 14 G; Rec 6-95 15.8 2 TD; KR 1-0; 12 Pt. **1948** CleA: 14 G; Rec 5-27 5.4; Int 1-1. **1949** CleA: 12 G; PR 1-1 1.0. **Total:** 54 G; Rec 18-220 12.2 4 TD; PR 1-1 1.0; KR 1-0; Int 1-1; 24 Pt.

NFL **1950** NYY: 8 G; Int 1-10. **1952** Was: 12 G. **Total:** 20 G; Int 1-10.

WALLY YONAMINE Yonamine, Wallace 5′9″, 180 HB-DB
Col: No College *HS:* Farrington [Honolulu, HI] B: 6/1925, Maui, HI
AAFC **1947** SF-A: 12 G; Rush 19-74 3.9; Rec 3-40 13.3; PR 2-29 14.5; KR 7-127 18.1; Int 1-20.

JIM YOUEL Youel, James Stewart 6′0″, 175 QB-DB
Col: Iowa *HS:* Fort Madison [IA] B: 2/13/1922, Vinton, IA
1946 Was: PR 13-150 11.5; KR 2-29 14.5; Int 2-0; Punt 2-68 34.0. **1947** Was: Punt 2-35 17.5. **1948** Bos-Was: Rec 1-20 20.0; Punt 2-65 32.5. Bos: Punt 2-65 32.5. Was: Rec 1-20 20.0. **Total:** Rec 1-20 20.0; PR 13-150 11.5; KR 2-29 14.5; Int 2-0; Punt 6-168 28.0.

		Passing							
Year Team	**G**	**Att**	**Comp**	**Comp%**	**Yds**	**YPA**	**TD**	**Int**	**Rating**
1946 Was	9	48	20	41.7	352	7.33	2	3	55.2
1947 Was	6	62	21	33.9	398	6.42	3	3	53.0
1948 Bos-Was	8	36	9	25.0	99	2.75	2	4	18.5
1948 Bos	6	25	6	24.0	63	2.52	2	3	26.7
1948 Was	2	11	3	27.3	36	3.27	0	1	2.8
NFL Total	23	146	50	34.2	849	5.82	7	10	42.3

	Rushing				
Year Team	**Att**	**Yds**	**Avg**	**TD**	**Fum**
1946 Was	16	60	3.8	1	3
1947 Was	10	44	4.4	1	2
1948 Bos-Was	19	79	4.2	1	3
1948 Bos	15	63	4.2	0	3
1948 Was	4	16	4.0	1	0
NFL Total	45	183	4.1	3	8

MAURY YOUMANS Youmans, Maurice Edward 6′4″, 251 DE
Col: Syracuse *HS:* North Syracuse [NY] B: 10/18/1936, Eagle Bay, NY
Drafted: 1959 Round 9 ChiB
1960 ChiB: 8 G. **1961** ChiB: 14 G. **1962** ChiB: 6 G. **1964** Dal: 14 G. **1965** Dal: 14 G. **Total:** 56 G.

LEN YOUNCE Younce, Leonard Alonzo 6′1″, 208 G-LB
Col: Oregon State *HS:* Roosevelt [Portland, OR] B: 1/8/1917, Dayton, OR *Drafted:* 1941 Round 6 NYG
1943 NYG: Scor 6, 0-1 FG. **1947** NYG: KR 1-0; Scor 4, 1-1 100.0% FG, 1-1 100.0% XK. **1948** NYG: Scor 39, 1-7 14.3% FG, 36-37 97.3% XK. **Total:** KR 1-0; Scor 49, 2-9 22.2% FG, 37-38 97.4% XK.

		Interceptions			Punting		
Year Team	**G**	**Int**	**Yds**	**TD**	**Punts**	**Yds**	**Avg**
1941 NYG	11	2	25	0	0	0	—
1943 NYG	10	1	30	**1**	20	851	42.6
1944 NYG	10	3	16	0	**48**	**1941**	40.4
1946 NYG	11	1	0	0	1	10	10.0
1947 NYG	12	3	44	0	1	43	43.0

1948 NYG	11	0	0	0	0	0	—
NFL Total	65	10	115	1	70	2845	40.6

AL YOUNG Young, Alfred L 6'1", 195 **WR**
Col: South Carolina State *HS:* Booker T. Washington [Columbia, SC]
B: 8/24/1949, Norway, SC *Drafted:* 1971 Round 13 Pit
1971 Pit: 1 G. **1972** Pit: 14 G; Rec 6-86 14.3. **Total:** 15 G; Rec 6-86 14.3.

ALMON YOUNG Young, Almon Jr. 6'3", 290 **OG**
Col: Bethune-Cookman *HS:* Umatilla [FL] B: 7/3/1962, Eustis, FL
1987 Hou: 3 G.

ANDRE YOUNG Young, Andre Benoise 6'0", 199 **DB**
Col: Louisiana Tech *HS:* West Monroe [LA] B: 11/22/1960, West Monroe, LA *Drafted:* 1982 Round 10 SD
1982 SD: 8 G; KR 4-45 11.3; Int 2-9; 1 Fum. **1983** SD: 15 G; KR 3-41 13.7; Int 2-49 1 TD; 6 Pt; 1 Sac. **1984** SD: 13 G; Int 2-31; 1 Fum; 1 Sac. **Total:** 36 G; KR 7-86 12.3; Int 6-89 1 TD; 6 Pt; 2 Fum; 2 Sac.

ANTHONY YOUNG Young, Anthony Ricardo 5'11", 187 **DB**
Col: Temple *HS:* Pemberton Twp. [Pemberton, NJ] B: 10/8/1963, Columbia, SC *Drafted:* 1985 Round 3 Ind
1985 Ind: 14 G; KR 2-15 7.5; Int 1-0; **1** Fum TD; 6 Pt.

BEN YOUNG Young, Benjamin 6'4", 225 **TE**
Col: Texas-Arlington *HS:* Perry Meridian [Indianapolis, IN]
B: 1/13/1960, Toledo, OH
1983 Atl: 11 G; Rec 6-74 12.3 1 TD; 6 Pt.

BRYANT YOUNG Young, Bryant Colby 6'2", 279 **DT**
Col: Notre Dame *HS:* Bloom [Chicago Heights, IL] B: 1/27/1972, Chicago Heights, IL *Drafted:* 1994 Round 1 SF
1994 SF: 16 G; 6 Sac. **1995** SF: 12 G; 6 Sac. **1996** SF: 16 G; Scor **2** Saf; 4 Pt; 11.5 Sac. **1997** SF: 12 G; 4 Sac. **1998** SF: 12 G; 9.5 Sac.
Total: 68 G; Scor 2 Saf; 4 Pt; 37 Sac.

CHARLE YOUNG Young, Charle Edward 6'4", 234 **TE**
Col: USC *HS:* Edison [Fresno, CA] B: 2/5/1951, Fresno, CA
Drafted: 1973 Round 1 Phi
1973 Phi: Rush 4-24 6.0 1 TD. **1974** Phi: Rush 6-38 6.3. **1975** Phi: Rush 2-1 0.5. **1976** Phi: Rush 1-6 6.0. **1978** LARm: Rush 2-6 3.0. **1980** SF: KR 1-14 14.0. **1984** Sea: Rush 1-5 5.0. **Total:** Rush 16-80 5.0 1 TD; KR 1-14 14.0.

		Receiving					Tot
Year Team	**G**	**Rec**	**Yds**	**Avg**	**TD**	**Fum**	**TD**
1973 Phi	14	55	854	15.5	6	0	7
1974 Phi	14	63	696	11.0	3	4	3
1975 Phi	14	49	659	13.4	3	0	3
1976 Phi	14	30	374	12.5	0	1	0
1977 LARm	14	5	35	7.0	1	0	1
1978 LARm	16	18	213	11.8	0	1	0
1979 LARm	15	13	144	11.1	2	2	2
1980 SF	16	29	325	11.2	2	0	2
1981 SF	16	37	400	10.8	5	0	5
1982 SF	9	22	189	8.6	0	1	0
1983 Sea	16	36	529	14.7	2	1	2
1984 Sea	15	33	337	10.2	1	1	1
1985 Sea	14	28	351	12.5	2	1	2
NFL Total	187	418	5106	12.2	27	12	28

CHARLEY YOUNG Young, Charles Lee 6'1", 213 **RB**
Col: North Carolina State *HS:* William G. Enloe [Raleigh, NC]
B: 10/13/1952, Raleigh, NC *Drafted:* 1974 Round 1 Dal
1974 Dal: KR 8-161 20.1. **1975** Dal: KR 3-54 18.0. **Total:** KR 11-215 19.5.

		Rushing				Receiving					Tot
Year Team	**G**	**Att**	**Yds**	**Avg**	**TD**	**Rec**	**Yds**	**Avg**	**TD**	**Fum**	**TD**
1974 Dal	14	33	205	6.2	0	11	73	6.6	0	2	0
1975 Dal	12	50	225	4.5	2	18	184	10.2	1	1	3
1976 Dal	11	48	208	4.3	0	11	134	12.2	1	1	1
NFL Total	37	131	638	4.9	2	40	391	9.8	2	4	4

BUDDY YOUNG Young, Claude Henry 5'4", 175 **HB-DB-FB**
Col: Illinois *HS:* Englewood [Chicago, IL];Wendell Phillips HS [Chicago, IL] B: 1/5/1926, Chicago, IL D: 9/4/1983, Terrell, TX
AAFC **1947** NY-A: Pass 2-1 50.0%, 13 6.50; PR 8-127 15.9 1 TD.
1948 NY-A: PR 2-11 5.5. **1949** NY-A: PR 9-171 19.0. **Total:** Pass 2-1 50.0%, 13 6.50; PR 19-309 16.3 1 TD.

		Rushing				Receiving			
Year Team	**G**	**Att**	**Yds**	**Avg**	**TD**	**Rec**	**Yds**	**Avg**	**TD**
1947 NY-A	14	116	712	6.1	3	27	303	11.2	2
1948 NY-A	12	70	245	3.5	1	21	259	12.3	4
1949 NY-A	12	76	495	6.5	5	12	171	14.3	2
AAFC Total	38	262	1452	5.5	9	60	733	12.2	8

	Kickoff Returns				Tot
Year Team	**Ret**	**Yds**	**Avg**	**TD**	**TD**
1947 NY-A	12	332	27.7	1	7
1948 NY-A	12	303	25.3	0	5
1949 NY-A	11	316	28.7	1	8
AAFC Total	35	951	27.2	2	20

NFL **1952** Dal: Pass 3-0, 1 Int. **Total:** Pass 3-0, 1 Int.

		Rushing				Receiving			
Year Team	**G**	**Att**	**Yds**	**Avg**	**TD**	**Rec**	**Yds**	**Avg**	**TD**
1950 NYY	12	76	334	4.4	1	20	302	15.1	1
1951 NYY	12	46	165	3.6	1	31	508	16.4	3
1952 Dal	12	71	243	3.4	3	22	269	12.2	2
1953 Bal	10	40	135	3.4	0	12	201	16.8	3
1954 Bal	10	70	311	4.4	2	15	272	18.1	3
1955 Bal	11	32	87	2.7	1	19	426	22.4	1
NFL Total	67	335	1275	3.8	8	119	1978	16.6	13

	Punt Returns				Kickoff Returns					Tot
Year Team	**Ret**	**Yds**	**Avg**	**TD**	**Ret**	**Yds**	**Avg**	**TD**	**Fum**	**TD**
1950 NYY	9	54	6.0	0	20	536	26.8	0	6	2
1951 NYY	12	231	**19.3**	1	14	427	30.5	**1**	3	6
1952 Dal	6	35	5.8	0	**23**	**643**	28.0	0	5	5
1953 Bal	6	9	1.5	0	11	378	34.4	**1**	6	4
1954 Bal	14	60	4.3	0	13	308	23.7	0	1	5
1955 Bal	1	0	0.0	0	9	222	24.7	0	1	2
NFL Total	48	389	8.1	1	90	2514	27.9	2	22	24

DUANE YOUNG Young, Curtis Duane 6'3", 270 **TE**
Col: Michigan State *HS:* Kalamazoo Central [MI] B: 5/29/1968, Kalamazoo, MI *Drafted:* 1991 Round 5 SD

		Receiving			
Year Team	**G**	**Rec**	**Yds**	**Avg**	**TD**
1991 SD	7	2	12	6.0	0
1992 SD	16	4	45	11.3	0
1993 SD	16	6	41	6.8	2
1994 SD	14	17	217	12.8	1
1995 SD	16	9	90	10.0	0
1998 Buf	4	0	0	—	0
NFL Total	73	38	405	10.7	3

DAVE YOUNG Young, David Joseph 6'5", 242 **TE**
Col: Purdue *HS:* East [Akron, OH] B: 2/9/1959, Akron, OH
Drafted: 1981 Round 2 NYG
1981 NYG: 11 G; Rec 5-49 9.8 1 TD; 6 Pt. **1983** Bal: 1 G. **1984** Ind: 13 G; Rec 14-164 11.7 2 TD; 12 Pt. **Total:** 25 G; Rec 19-213 11.2 3 TD; 18 Pt.

FLOYD YOUNG Young, Floyd Alexander 6'0", 170 **DB**
Col: Scottsdale CC AZ; Texas A&M–Kingsville *HS:* Joseph S. Clark [New Orleans, LA] B: 11/23/1975, New Orleans, LA
1997 TB: 12 G. **1998** TB: 11 G. **Total:** 23 G.

FREDD YOUNG Young, Frederick Kimball 6'1", 233 **LB**
Col: New Mexico State *HS:* Woodrow Wilson [Dallas, TX]
B: 11/14/1961, Dallas, TX *Drafted:* 1984 Round 3 Sea
1984 Sea: 16 G; 1 Sac. **1985** Sea: 16 G; 3 Sac. **1986** Sea: 15 G; 6 Sac. **1987** Sea: 13 G; Int 1-50 1 TD; 6 Pt; 9 Sac. **1988** Ind: 15 G. **1989** Ind: 15 G; Int 2-2; 2 Sac. **1990** Ind: 11 G. **Total:** 101 G; Int 3-52 1 TD; 6 Pt; 21 Sac.

GEORGE YOUNG Young, George Donald 6'3", 214 **DE-OE**
Col: Baldwin-Wallace; Georgia *HS:* Wilkes-Barre [PA] B: 5/10/1924, Wilkes-Barre, PA D: 9/21/1969, Chicago, IL
AAFC **1946** CleA: 13 G; Rec 3-37 12.3. **1947** CleA: 13 G. **1948** CleA: 14 G; Rec 2-20 10.0; 6 Pt. **1949** CleA: 9 G. **Total:** 49 G; Rec 5-57 11.4; 6 Pt.

NFL **1950** Cle: 12 G. **1951** Cle: 12 G; 1 Fum TD; 6 Pt. **1952** Cle: 12 G; Scor **1** Saf; 2 Pt. **1953** Cle: 12 G; KR 1-0. **Total:** 48 G; KR 1-0; Scor 1 Saf; 1 Fum TD; 8 Pt.

GLEN YOUNG Young, Glen Edward 6'2", 205 **WR**
Col: Mississippi State *HS:* Greenwood [MS] B: 10/11/1960, Greenwood, MS *Drafted:* 1983 Round 3 Phi
1983 Phi: Rec 3-125 41.7 1 TD; PR 14-93 6.6. **1984** Cle: Rec 1-47 47.0. **1985** Cle: Rec 5-111 22.2 1 TD. **1988** Cle: Rec 2-34 17.0.
Total: Rec 11-317 28.8 2 TD; PR 14-93 6.6.

		Kickoff Returns				
Year Team	**G**	**Ret**	**Yds**	**Avg**	**TD**	**Fum**
1983 Phi	16	26	547	21.0	0	2
1984 Cle	2	5	134	26.8	0	0
1985 Cle	15	35	898	25.7	0	1
1987 Cle	10	18	412	22.9	0	0
1988 Cle	15	29	635	21.9	0	0
NFL Total	58	113	2626	23.2	0	3

GLEN YOUNG Young, Glen H 6'3", 235 **LB**
Col: Syracuse *HS:* Neil McNeil Sec. School [Toronto, Canada]; St. Michael's School [Toronto,Canada] B: 5/2/1969, Scarborough, Canada
1995 SD: 16 G; 1 Sac. **1996** SD: 6 G; Int 1-(-1). **Total:** 22 G; Int 1-(-1); 1 Sac.

GLENN YOUNG Young, Glenn Charles 6'2", 205 **DB**
(Buster) *Col:* Purdue *HS:* Maine West [Des Plaines, IL]
B: 12/22/1929, Woodstock, IL
1956 GB: 4 G.

HERM YOUNG Young, Herman DeVerne 5'11", 178 **OE**
Col: Detroit Mercy *HS:* Flint [MI] B: 3/21/1906, Flint, MI
D: 6/16/1985, Bradenton, FL
1930 Prov: 3 G; Rec 1 TD; 6 Pt.

JIM YOUNG Young, James Alexander 6'2", 260 **DE**
Col: Texas Southern *HS:* Phillis Wheatley [Houston, TX] B: 7/8/1950, Houston, TX
1977 Hou: 13 G; Scor **2** Saf; 4 Pt. **1978** Hou: 16 G. **1979** Hou: 5 G.
Total: 34 G; Scor 2 Saf; 4 Pt.

JIM YOUNG Young, James Norman 6'0", 205 **HB**
Col: Queens (Canada) B: 6/6/1943, Hamilton, Canada
1965 Min: 2 G; Rush 3-4 1.3; PR 4-7 1.8; KR 4-78 19.5; 1 Fum. **1966** Min: 4 G; PR 2-7 3.5; KR 5-105 21.0. **Total:** 6 G; Rush 3-4 1.3; PR 6-14 2.3; KR 9-183 20.3; 1 Fum.

AL YOUNG Young, John Allen 5'10", 180 **WB-FB-TB-BB**
Col: California B: 4/28/1902 D: 3/14/1980, Corning, CA
1926 LA: 7 G.

STEVE YOUNG Young, Jon Steven 6'2", 205 **QB**
Col: Brigham Young *HS:* Greenwich [CT] B: 10/11/1961, Salt Lake City, UT *Drafted:* 1984 Supplemental Round 1 TB
1993 SF: Rec 2-2 1.0. **1996** SF: Scor 1 2XP. **Total:** Rec 2-2 1.0; Scor 1 2XP.

		Passing							
Year Team	**G**	**Att**	**Comp**	**Comp%**	**Yds**	**YPA**	**TD**	**Int**	**Rating**
1985 TB	5	138	72	52.2	935	6.78	3	8	56.9
1986 TB	14	363	195	53.7	2282	6.29	8	13	65.5
1987 SF	8	69	37	53.6	570	8.26	10	0	120.8
1988 SF	11	101	54	53.5	680	6.73	3	3	72.2
1989 SF	10	92	64	69.6	1001	10.88	8	3	120.8
1990 SF	6	62	38	61.3	427	6.89	2	0	92.6
1991 SF	11	279	180	64.5	2517	**9.02**	17	8	**101.8**
1992 SF	16	402	268	**66.7**	3465	**8.62**	**25**	7	**107.0**
1993 SF	16	462	314	68.0	4023	**8.71**	**29**	16	**101.5**
1994 SF	16	461	324	**70.3**	3969	**8.61**	**35**	10	**112.8**
1995 SF	11	447	299	**66.9**	3200	7.16	20	11	92.3
1996 SF	12	316	214	**67.7**	2410	7.63	14	**6**	**97.2**
1997 SF	15	356	241	**67.7**	3029	**8.51**	19	6	**104.7**
1998 SF	15	517	322	62.3	4170	8.07	**36**	12	101.1
NFL Total	166	4065	2622	**64.5**	32678	8.04	229	103	**97.6**

	Rushing				
Year Team	**Att**	**Yds**	**Avg**	**TD**	**Fum**
1985 TB	40	233	5.8	1	4
1986 TB	74	425	5.7	5	11
1987 SF	26	190	7.3	1	0
1988 SF	27	184	6.8	1	5
1989 SF	38	126	3.3	2	2
1990 SF	15	159	10.6	0	1
1991 SF	66	415	6.3	4	3
1992 SF	76	537	7.1	4	9
1993 SF	69	407	5.9	2	8
1994 SF	58	293	5.1	7	4
1995 SF	50	250	5.0	3	3
1996 SF	52	310	6.0	4	3
1997 SF	50	199	4.0	3	4
1998 SF	70	454	6.5	6	9
NFL Total	711	4182	5.9	43	66

JOE YOUNG Young, Joseph Albert 6'3", 245 **DE**
Col: Marquette; Arizona *HS:* Kelly [Chicago, IL] B: 8/3/1933, Chicago, IL *Drafted:* 1955 Round 24 ChiB
1960 Den: 14 G. **1961** Den: 6 G. **Total:** 20 G.

KEVIN YOUNG Young, Kevin 6'5", 265 **DE**
Col: Pasadena City Coll. CA (J.C.); Tulane; Utah State *HS:* George Washington Carver [New Orleans, LA] B: 11/8/1964, New Orleans, LA
1987 NO: 1 G.

LLOYD YOUNG Young, Lloyd 6'2", 192 **G-C-T-OE**
Col: Macalester; North Dakota *HS:* Austin [MN] B: 5/27/1903, Austin, MN D: 6/10/1978, Austin, MN
1925 Prov: 11 G. **1926** Prov: 13 G. **1927** Prov: 1 G. **1929** Min: 8 G.
1930 Min: 2 G. **Total:** 35 G.

LONNIE YOUNG Young, Lonnie R 6'1", 189 **DB**
Col: Michigan State *HS:* Beecher [Flint, MI] B: 7/18/1963, Flint, MI
Drafted: 1985 Round 12 StL
1986 StL: 1.5 Sac. **1993** NYJ: 1 Sac. **1994** SD: 1 Sac. **Total:** 3.5 Sac.

		Interceptions		
Year Team	**G**	**Int**	**Yds**	**TD**
1985 StL	16	3	0	0
1986 StL	13	0	0	0
1987 StL	12	1	0	0
1988 Pho	12	1	2	0
1989 Pho	10	1	32	0
1990 Pho	16	2	8	0
1991 NYJ	12	1	15	0
1992 NYJ	13	0	0	0
1993 NYJ	9	1	6	0
1994 SD	12	0	0	0
1995 NYJ	7	0	0	0
1996 NYJ	15	1	0	0
NFL Total	147	11	63	0

ADRIAN YOUNG Young, Matthew Adrian Jr. 6'1", 232 **LB**
Col: USC *HS:* Bishop Amat [La Puente, CA] B: 1/31/1946, Dublin, Ireland *Drafted:* 1968 Round 3 Phi
1968 Phi: 10 G. **1969** Phi: 13 G; Int 1-0. **1970** Phi: 14 G; Int 2-19.
1971 Phi: 2 G. **1972** Phi-Det: 11 G. Phi: 1 G. Det: 10 G. **1973** ChiB: 2 G.
Total: 52 G; Int 3-19.

MIKE YOUNG Young, Michael David 6'1", 187 **WR**
Col: UCLA *HS:* Mount Whitney [Visalia, CA] B: 2/21/1962, Hanford, CA *Drafted:* 1985 Round 6 LARm

		Receiving				
Year Team	**G**	**Rec**	**Yds**	**Avg**	**TD**	**Fum**
1985 LARm	15	14	157	11.2	0	1
1986 LARm	16	15	181	12.1	3	2
1987 LARm	12	4	56	14.0	1	0
1988 LARm	8	2	27	13.5	0	0
1989 Den	16	22	402	18.3	2	0
1990 Den	16	28	385	13.8	4	0
1991 Den	16	44	629	14.3	2	1
1992 Den	3	1	11	11.0	0	0
1993 Phi	10	14	186	13.3	2	0
1994 KC	2	0	0	—	0	0
NFL Total	114	144	2034	14.1	14	4

MITCHELL YOUNG Young, Mitchell 6'4", 260 **DE**
Col: Northwest Mississippi CC; Arkansas State *HS:* North Panola [Sardis, MS] B: 7/18/1961, Coldwater, MS
1987 Atl: 1 G.

PAUL YOUNG Young, Paul Wesley 6'4", 195 **C-LB**
Col: Oklahoma *HS:* Norman [OK] B: 12/7/1908, Melrose, NM
D: 10/19/1978, Cambridge, NE
1933 GB: 2 G.

RANDY YOUNG Young, Randall Louis 6'5", 250 **OT**
Col: Iowa State *HS:* Miami Carol City [Miami, FL] B: 7/4/1954, Montgomery, AL *Drafted:* 1976 Round 12 Mia
1976 TB: 9 G.

RANDY YOUNG Young, Randolph 6'0", 175 **OE**
Col: Millikin *HS:* Stephen Decatur [Decatur, IL] B: 1898 D: 11/1/1975
1920 Sta: 1 G.

RENARD YOUNG Young, Renard F 5'10", 184 **DB**
Col: Los Angeles Southwest Coll. CA (J.C.); San Diego State; Nevada-Las Vegas *HS:* Verbum Dei [Los Angeles, CA] B: 7/31/1961, Los Angeles, CA
1987 Sea: 3 G.

DICK YOUNG Young, Richard 5'11", 210 **FB-HB**
Col: Tennessee-Chattanooga *HS:* Trumbull [CT] B: 8/25/1930, Trumbull, CT *Drafted:* 1954 Round 18 ChiC
1955 Bal: Rec 2-15 7.5; PR 1-3 3.0; KR 2-37 18.5. **1956** Bal: KR 3-40 13.3. **1957** Pit: Rec 4-38 9.5. **Total:** Rec 6-53 8.8; PR 1-3 3.0; KR 5-77 15.4.

		Rushing				
Year Team	**G**	**Att**	**Yds**	**Avg**	**TD**	**Fum**
1955 Bal	11	17	39	2.3	0	2
1956 Bal	12	5	7	1.4	0	0
1957 Pit	11	56	153	2.7	2	1
NFL Total	34	78	199	2.6	2	3

RICKEY YOUNG Young, Rickey Dornial 6'2", 196 **RB**
Col: Jackson State *HS:* C.F. Vigor [Prichard, AL] B: 12/7/1953, Mobile, AL *Drafted:* 1975 Round 7 SD
1975 SD: KR 15-323 21.5. **1978** Min: KR 1-8 8.0. **1981** Min: KR 1-15 15.0.
1983 Min: KR 3-27 9.0. **Total:** KR 20-373 18.7.

		Rushing				Receiving					Tot
Year Team	**G**	**Att**	**Yds**	**Avg**	**TD**	**Rec**	**Yds**	**Avg**	**TD**	**Fum**	**TD**
1975 SD	14	138	577	4.2	5	21	166	7.9	1	5	6
1976 SD	14	162	802	5.0	4	47	441	9.4	1	2	5
1977 SD	14	157	543	3.5	4	48	423	8.8	0	4	4
1978 Min	16	134	417	3.1	1	**88**	704	8.0	5	6	6
1979 Min	16	188	708	3.8	3	72	519	7.2	4	2	7
1980 Min	16	130	351	2.7	3	64	499	7.8	2	2	5
1981 Min	16	47	129	2.7	0	43	296	6.9	2	4	2

1982 Min	9	16	49	3.1	1	4	44	11.0	1	0	2
1983 Min	16	39	90	2.3	2	21	193	9.2	0	0	2
NFL Total	131	1011	3666	3.6	23	408	3285	8.1	16	25	39

BOB YOUNG Young, Robert Allen 6'1", 270 **OG-DT**
Col: Texas; Southwest Texas State; Howard Payne *HS:* Brownwood [TX] B: 9/3/1942, Marshall, TX D: 6/17/1995, Missouri City, TX
1966 Den: 11 G. **1967** Den: 5 G. **1968** Den: 14 G. **1969** Den: 14 G. **1970** Den: 14 G. **1971** Hou: 14 G. **1972** StL: 14 G. **1973** StL: 13 G. **1974** StL: 9 G. **1975** StL: 12 G. **1976** StL: 14 G. **1977** StL: 14 G. **1978** StL: 16 G. **1979** StL: 13 G. **1980** Hou: 15 G. **1981** NO: 2 G. **Total:** 194 G.

ROBERT YOUNG Young, Robert E 6'6", 273 **DE-DT**
Col: Mississippi State *HS:* Carthage [MS] B: 1/29/1969, Jackson, MS
Drafted: 1991 Round 5 LARm
1991 LARm: 16 G; 1 Sac. **1992** LARm: 11 G; 2 Sac. **1993** LARm: 6 G; 7 Sac. **1994** LARm: 16 G; 6.5 Sac. **1995** StL: 14 G. **1996** Hou: 15 G; 4 Sac. **Total:** 78 G; 20.5 Sac.

RODNEY YOUNG Young, Rodney Menard 6'0", 210 **DB**
Col: Louisiana State *HS:* Ruston [LA] B: 1/25/1973, Grambling, LA
Drafted: 1995 Round 3 NYG
1995 NYG: 10 G; PR 1-0; 1 Fum. **1996** NYG: 12 G. **1997** NYG: 9 G. **1998** NYG: 2 G. **Total:** 33 G; PR 1-0; 1 Fum.

ROY YOUNG Young, Roy O 6'2", 215 **T**
Col: Texas A&M B: 9/11/1917, Abbeville, LA D: 5/5/1987, Scottsdale, AZ *Drafted:* 1938 Round 5 Was
1938 Was: 9 G.

ROYNELL YOUNG Young, Roynell 6'1", 181 **DB**
Col: Alcorn State *HS:* Walter L. Cohen [New Orleans, LA]
B: 12/1/1957, New Orleans, LA *Drafted:* 1980 Round 1 Phi
1983 Phi: KR 1-18 18.0. **Total:** KR 1-18 18.0.

		Interceptions		
Year Team	**G**	**Int**	**Yds**	**TD**
1980 Phi	16	4	27	0
1981 Phi	13	4	35	0
1982 Phi	9	4	0	0
1983 Phi	16	1	0	0
1984 Phi	7	0	0	0
1985 Phi	14	1	0	0
1986 Phi	16	6	9	0
1987 Phi	11	1	30	0
1988 Phi	15	2	5	0
NFL Total	117	23	106	0

RUSS YOUNG Young, Russell Charles 6'0", 190 **FB**
Col: No College *HS:* Stivers [Dayton, OH] B: 9/15/1899, Bryan, OH
D: 5/13/1984, Roseville, CA
1925 Day: 4 G.

SAM YOUNG Young, Samuel Leslie 6'1", 190 **HB**
(Les) *Col:* Macalester; North Dakota *HS:* Austin [MN] B: 2/11/1905, Austin, MN D: 12/1/1991, Glendale, AZ
1927 Prov: 2 G.

STEVE YOUNG Young, Steven Russell 6'8", 272 **OT**
Col: Colorado *HS:* Chaffey [Ontario, Canada] B: 7/18/1953, Spokane, WA *Drafted:* 1976 Round 3 TB
1976 TB: 13 G. **1977** Mia: 14 G. **Total:** 27 G.

THEO YOUNG Young, Theo Thomas 6'2", 237 **TE**
Col: Arkansas *HS:* Remmel Park [Newport, AR] B: 4/25/1965, Newport, AR *Drafted:* 1987 Round 12 Pit
1987 Pit: 12 G; Rec 2-10 5.0.

TYRONE YOUNG Young, Tyrone Donnive 6'6", 190 **WR**
Col: Florida *HS:* Forest [Ocala, FL] B: 4/29/1960, Ocala, FL

		Receiving				
Year Team	**G**	**Rec**	**Yds**	**Avg**	**TD**	**Fum**
1983 NO	16	7	85	12.1	3	0
1984 NO	16	29	597	20.6	3	1
NFL Total	32	36	682	18.9	6	1

WADDY YOUNG Young, Walter Roland 6'3", 205 **OE-DE**
Col: Oklahoma *HS:* Ponca City [OK] B: 9/4/1916, Ponca City, OK
D: 1/9/1945, Tokyo, Japan *Drafted:* 1939 Round 3 Bkn
1939 Bkn: 11 G; Rec 8-100 12.5. **1940** Bkn: 11 G; Rush 1-1 1.0; Rec 7-85 12.1. **Total:** 22 G; Rush 1-1 1.0; Rec 15-185 12.3.

WILBUR YOUNG Young, Wilbur Eugene Jr. 6'6", 285 **DE-DT**
Col: William Penn *HS:* James Monroe [Bronx, NY] B: 4/20/1949, New York, NY *Drafted:* 1971 Round 2 KC
1971 KC: 13 G; Int 1-3. **1972** KC: 14 G. **1973** KC: 13 G. **1974** KC: 14 G; Int 1-52 1 TD; 6 Pt. **1975** KC: 13 G. **1976** KC: 14 G. **1977** KC: 13 G. **1978** SD: 10 G. **1979** SD: 16 G; Scor **1** Saf; **1** Fum TD; 8 Pt. **1980** SD: 12 G. **1981** Was-SD: 12 G. Was: 7 G. SD: 5 G. **1982** SD: 9 G; 1 Sac. **Total:** 153 G; Int 2-55 1 TD; Scor 1 Saf; 1 Fum TD; Tot TD 2; 14 Pt; 1 Sac.

BILL YOUNG Young, William A Jr. 6'1", 247 **T**
(Bubbles) *Col:* Alabama *HS:* North Little Rock [AR] B: 5/20/1914, Argenta, AR D: 1/21/1994, Jacksonville Beach, FL
1937 Was: 6 G. **1938** Was: 11 G; Rec 1-62 62.0 1 TD; 6 Pt. **1939** Was: 8 G. **1940** Was: 10 G. **1941** Was: 6 G. **1942** Was: 10 G. **1946** Was: 8 G. **Total:** 59 G; Rec 1-62 62.0 1 TD; 6 Pt.

BILLY YOUNG Young, William George 5'10", 210 **G**
Col: Ohio State *HS:* Kenton [OH] B: 12/17/1901 D: 7/29/1971, Kenton, OH
1929 GB: 2 G.

WILLIE YOUNG Young, William Joseph Lull 6'0", 265 **OT**
(Sugar Bear) *Col:* Grambling State *HS:* Lincoln [LA] B: 6/27/1943, Ruston, LA
1966 NYG: 14 G; KR 2-6 3.0. **1967** NYG: 14 G; Rush 0-2. **1968** NYG: 14 G; Rush 2-(-2) -1.0. **1969** NYG: 14 G; Rec 1-8 8.0. **1970** NYG: 13 G. **1971** NYG: 14 G. **1972** NYG: 14 G. **1973** NYG: 14 G; Rec 1-(-5) -5.0. **1974** NYG: 12 G. **1975** NYG: 12 G. **Total:** 135 G; Rush 2-0; Rec 2-3 1.5; KR 2-6 3.0.

WILLIE YOUNG Young, Willie 6'4", 270 **OT**
Col: Alcorn State *HS:* Brinkley [Jackson, MS] B: 11/12/1947, Jefferson, MS
1971 Buf: 14 G. **1972** Buf: 1 G. **1973** Mia: 1 G. **Total:** 16 G.

GEORGE YOUNGBLOOD Youngblood, George Alton 6'3", 205 **DB**
Col: Los Angeles State *HS:* David Starr Jordan [Los Angeles, CA]
B: 1/4/1945, Los Angeles, CA *Drafted:* 1966 Round 7 LARm
1966 LARm: 14 G. **1967** Cle-NO: 12 G; PR 1-0; 1 Fum. Cle: 11 G; PR 1-0; 1 Fum. NO: 1 G. **1968** NO: 4 G. **1969** ChiB: 14 G; Int 3-22 1 TD; 6 Pt. **Total:** 44 G; PR 1-0; Int 3-22 1 TD; 6 Pt; 1 Fum.

JACK YOUNGBLOOD Youngblood, Herbert Jackson III 6'4", 247 **DE**
Col: Florida *HS:* Jefferson Co. [Monticello, FL] B: 1/26/1950, Jacksonville, FL *Drafted:* 1971 Round 1 LARm
1971 LARm: 14 G; KR 2-36 18.0. **1972** LARm: 14 G. **1973** LARm: 14 G. **1974** LARm: 14 G. **1975** LARm: 14 G; Scor **1** Saf; 2 Pt. **1976** LARm: 14 G. **1977** LARm: 14 G. **1978** LARm: 16 G. **1979** LARm: 16 G. **1980** LARm: 16 G. **1981** LARm: 16 G. **1982** LARm: 9 G; 4 Sac. **1983** LARm: 16 G; Scor 1 Saf; 2 Pt; 10.5 Sac. **1984** LARm: 15 G; 9.5 Sac. **Total:** 202 G; KR 2-36 18.0; Scor 2 Saf; 4 Pt; 24.0 Sac.

JIM YOUNGBLOOD Youngblood, James Lee 6'3", 235 **LB**
Col: Tennessee Tech *HS:* Jonesville [SC] B: 2/23/1950, Union, SC
Drafted: 1973 Round 2 LARm
1974 LARm: KR 1-0. **Total:** KR 1-0.

		Interceptions		
Year Team	**G**	**Int**	**Yds**	**TD**
1973 LARm	14	1	15	0
1974 LARm	14	0	0	0
1975 LARm	14	0	0	0
1976 LARm	14	2	28	0
1977 LARm	14	2	27	**1**
1978 LARm	16	2	50	0
1979 LARm	16	5	89	**2**
1980 LARm	15	1	33	1
1981 LARm	16	1	20	0
1982 LARm	7	0	0	0
1983 LARm	7	0	0	0
1984 Was-LARm	9	0	0	0
1984 Was	4	0	0	0
1984 LARm	5	0	0	0
NFL Total	156	14	262	4

SID YOUNGELMAN Youngelman, Sidney 6'3", 257 **DT-DE**
Col: Alabama *HS:* Abraham Lincoln [Brooklyn, NY] B: 12/1/1931, Newark, NJ D: 12/21/1991, Lake Hiawatha, NY *Drafted:* 1954 Round 7 SF
1955 SF: 10 G. **1956** Phi: 12 G. **1957** Phi: 12 G; Rush 0-3. **1958** Phi: 5 G. **1959** Cle: 12 G. **1960** NYT: 14 G. **1961** NYT: 14 G. **1962** Buf: 14 G. **1963** Buf: 14 G. **Total:** 107 G; Rush 0-3.

PAUL YOUNGER Younger, Paul Lawrence 6'3", 225 **FB-LB-HB**
(Tank) *Col:* Grambling State *HS:* Grambling [LA] B: 6/25/1928, Grambling, LA
1951 LARm: Int 1-0. **1952** LARm: Int 2-0. **1953** LARm: KR 1-24 24.0. **1957** LARm: Pass 1-0, 1 Int. **Total:** Pass 1-0, 1 Int; KR 1-24 24.0; Int 3-0.

		Rushing				Receiving					Tot
Year Team	**G**	**Att**	**Yds**	**Avg**	**TD**	**Rec**	**Yds**	**Avg**	**TD**	**Fum**	**TD**
1949 LARm	12	52	191	3.7	0	7	119	17.0	0	4	0
1950 LARm	12	8	28	3.5	2	0	0	—	0	0	2
1951 LARm	12	36	223	6.2	1	5	72	14.4	0	0	1
1952 LARm	12	63	331	5.3	1	12	73	6.1	0	3	1
1953 LARm	12	84	350	4.2	8	20	259	13.0	1	4	9
1954 LARm	8	91	610	6.7	8	8	76	9.5	0	2	8
1955 LARm	8	138	644	4.7	5	6	51	8.5	0	3	5
1956 LARm	12	114	518	4.5	3	18	268	14.9	0	8	3
1957 LARm	12	96	401	4.2	3	8	61	7.6	0	2	3

1958 Pit	12	88	344	3.9	3	16	188	11.8	0	3	3
NFL Total	112	770	3640	4.7	34	100	1167	11.7	1	29	35

FRANK YOUNGFLEISH Youngfleish, Frank Whiting 5′9″, 190 **C-G**
(Yank) *Col:* Villanova *HS:* Pottsville [PA] B: 5/7/1896, Pottsville, PA D: 7/1958, Pottsville, PA
1926 Pott: 9 G. **1927** Pott: 6 G. **Total:** 15 G.

SWEDE YOUNGSTROM Youngstrom, Adolf Frederick 6′1″, 187 **G-T-E-C**
Col: Dartmouth *HS:* Waltham [MA] B: 5/24/1897, Waltham, MA D: 8/5/1968, Boston, MA
1920 Buf: 11 G. **1921** Buf-Can: 13 G; Rec 1 TD; 6 Pt. Buf: 12 G; Rec 1 TD; 6 Pt. Can: 1 G. **1922** Buf: 10 G. **1923** Buf: 12 G. **1924** Buf: 11 G. **1925** Buf-Cle: 10 G. Buf: 9 G. Cle: 1 G. **1926** Fra: 16 G; Int **1** TD; Tot TD 2; 12 Pt. **1927** Fra: 13 G. **Total:** 96 G; Rec 1 TD; Int 1 TD; Tot TD 3; 18 Pt.

MIKE YOUNT Yount, Myron Edwin 6′1″, 205 **T**
Col: Franklin (Ind.) *HS:* Greenwood [IN] B: 4/18/1894, Pleasant Twp., IN D: 1/25/1964, Indianapolis, IN
1921 Mun: 2 G.

FRANK YOUSO Youso, Frank Michael 6′4″, 257 **OT-DT**
(Mocus) *Col:* Minnesota *HS:* Falls [International Falls, MN] B: 7/5/1936, International Falls, MN *Drafted:* 1958 Round 2 NYG
1958 NYG: 12 G. **1959** NYG: 12 G. **1960** NYG: 12 G; KR 1-7 7.0. **1961** Min: 14 G. **1962** Min: 13 G. **1963** Oak: 4 G. **1964** Oak: 14 G; Rush 0-4. **1965** Oak: 11 G. **Total:** 92 G; Rush 0-4; KR 1-7 7.0.

JOHN YOVICSIN Yovicsin, John Michael 6′3″, 195 **DE**
Col: Gettysburg *HS:* Steelton [PA] B: 10/17/1918, Steelton, PA D: 9/13/1989, Hyannis, MA
1944 Phi: 1 G.

WALT YOWARSKY Yowarsky, Walter Robert 6′2″, 234 **DE-OT**
Col: Kentucky *HS:* Lincoln [Cleveland, OH] B: 5/10/1928, Cleveland, OH *Drafted:* 1951 Round 3 Was
1951 Was: 11 G. **1954** Was: 11 G; KR 1-13 13.0. **1955** Det-NYG: 12 G; KR 3-0. Det: 2 G. NYG: 10 G; KR 3-0. **1956** NYG: 11 G. **1957** NYG: 11 G. **1958** SF: 8 G. **Total:** 64 G; KR 4-13 3.3.

JOHN YURCHEY Yurchey, John Henry 5′11″, 188 **HB-DB**
Col: Duquesne *HS:* Bridgeville [PA] B: 11/12/1917, Bridgeville, PA D: 6/1/1944, Bridgeville, PA
1940 Pit: 1 G; Punt 3-121 40.3.

STEVE ZABEL Zabel, Steven Gregory 6′4″, 235 **LB-TE**
Col: Oklahoma *HS:* Thornton [CO] B: 3/20/1948, Minneapolis, MN *Drafted:* 1970 Round 1 Phi
1970 Phi: 14 G; Rec 8-119 14.9 1 TD; 6 Pt. **1971** Phi: 14 G; Rush 1-(-5) -5.0; Rec 2-4 2.0 2 TD; KR 1-0; Int 1-4; 12 Pt. **1972** Phi: 7 G. **1973** Phi: 11 G; Int 2-13. **1974** Phi: 14 G; Int 2-12. **1975** NE: 13 G. **1976** NE: 14 G; Scor 1, 1-1 100.0% XK. **1977** NE: 11 G. **1978** NE: 11 G; Int 1-0. **1979** Bal: 15 G. **Total:** 124 G; Rush 1-(-5) -5.0; Rec 10-123 12.3 3 TD; KR 1-0; Int 6-29; Scor 19, 1-1 100.0% XK.

KEN ZACHARY Zachary, Kenneth R 6′0″, 222 **RB**
Col: Oklahoma State *HS:* Sapulpa [OK] B: 11/19/1963, Sapulpa, OK
1987 SD: 3 G; Rush 1-3 3.0; KR 1-2 2.0; 1 Fum.

TONY ZACKERY Zackery, Anthony Eugene 6′2″, 195 **DB**
Col: Washington *HS:* Franklin [Seattle, WA] B: 11/20/1966, Seattle, WA *Drafted:* 1989 Round 8 NE
1989 Atl: 1 G; Int 1-3. **1990** NE: 2 G. **1991** NE: 16 G; PR 1-0; 1 Fum. **Total:** 19 G; PR 1-0; Int 1-3; 1 Fum.

FRANK ZADWORNEY Zadworney, Frank Stanley 6′0″, 202 **HB-DB**
Col: Ohio State B: 11/2/1916 D: 3/24/1979, Westerville, OH *Drafted:* 1940 Round 8 Bkn
1940 Bkn: 3 G; Rush 2-5 2.5.

PAUL ZAESKE Zaeske, Paul Alan 6′2″, 200 **WR**
Col: North Park *HS:* Sterling Twp. [Sterling, IL] B: 12/4/1945, Sioux City, IA
1969 Hou: 6 G. **1970** Hou: 5 G. **Total:** 11 G.

BERT ZAGERS Zagers, Albert Aldon 5′10″, 185 **HB-DB**
Col: Michigan State *HS:* Cadillac [MI] B: 1/30/1933, Fremont, MI D: 9/2/1992, Traverse City, MI *Drafted:* 1955 Round 7 Det
1955 Was: Rec 14-306 21.9. **1957** Was: Int 2-29. **1958** Was: Rec 3-50 16.7; Int 2-59. **Total:** Rec 17-356 20.9; Int 4-88.

		Rushing				Punt Returns			
Year Team	**G**	**Att**	**Yds**	**Avg**	**TD**	**Ret**	**Yds**	**Avg**	**TD**
1955 Was	11	89	395	4.4	2	7	125	17.9	1
1957 Was	11	0	0	—	0	14	**217**	**15.5**	**2**
1958 Was	10	27	82	3.0	1	7	41	5.9	0
NFL Total	32	116	477	4.1	3	28	383	13.7	3

	Kickoff Returns					Tot
Year Team	**Ret**	**Yds**	**Avg**	**TD**	**Fum**	**TD**
1955 Was	11	280	25.5	0	5	3
1957 Was	15	348	23.2	0	1	2
1958 Was	0	0	—	0	1	1
NFL Total	26	628	24.2	0	7	6

ERNIE ZALEJSKI Zalejski, Ernest Raymond 6′0″, 185 **DB-HB**
Col: Notre Dame *HS:* Michael Washington [South Bend, IN] B: 11/23/1925, South Bend, IN *Drafted:* 1950 Round 5 ChiB
1950 Bal: 11 G; Rush 7-(-2) -0.3 1 TD; Rec 1-1 1.0; PR 3-17 5.7; KR 7-101 14.4; Int 2-81 1 TD; Tot TD 2; 12 Pt; 2 Fum.

JOHN ZAMBERLIN Zamberlin, John 6′2″, 230 **LB**
Col: Pacific Lutheran *HS:* Woodrow Wilson [Tacoma, WA] B: 2/13/1956, Tacoma, WA *Drafted:* 1979 Round 5 NE
1979 NE: 16 G. **1980** NE: 16 G. **1981** NE: 16 G; Int 1-11. **1982** NE: 8 G; 1 Sac. **1983** KC: 14 G. **1984** KC: 8 G. **Total:** 78 G; Int 1-11; 1 Sac.

CARL ZANDER Zander, Carl August 6′2″, 235 **LB**
Col: Tennessee *HS:* West Morris [Mendham, NJ] B: 4/12/1963, Mendham, NJ *Drafted:* 1985 Round 2 Cin
1985 Cin: 16 G; KR 1-19 19.0; 2 Sac. **1986** Cin: 16 G; Int 1-18; 3.5 Sac. **1987** Cin: 12 G; 1 Sac. **1988** Cin: 16 G; Int 1-3. **1989** Cin: 16 G; 1.5 Sac. **1990** Cin: 16 G; Int 1-12. **1991** Cin: 14 G. **Total:** 106 G; KR 1-19 19.0; Int 3-33; 8 Sac.

EMANUEL ZANDERS Zanders, Emanuel 6′1″, 251 **OG**
Col: Jackson State *HS:* U.S. Jones [Demopolis, AL] B: 7/31/1951, Demopolis, AL
1974 NO: 10 G. **1975** NO: 14 G. **1976** NO: 14 G. **1977** NO: 14 G. **1978** NO: 3 G. **1979** NO: 16 G. **1980** NO: 16 G. **1981** ChiB: 12 G; Rec 1-7 7.0. **Total:** 99 G; Rec 1-7 7.0.

MIKE ZANDOFSKY Zandofsky, Michael Leslie 6′2″, 300 **OG**
Col: Washington *HS:* Corvallis [OR] B: 11/30/1965, Corvallis, OR *Drafted:* 1989 Round 3 Pho
1989 Pho: 15 G. **1990** SD: 13 G. **1991** SD: 10 G. **1992** SD: 15 G. **1993** SD: 16 G. **1994** Atl: 16 G. **1995** Atl: 12 G. **1996** Atl: 14 G. **1997** Phi: 5 G. **Total:** 116 G.

SILVIO ZANINELLI Zaninelli, Silvio David 5′10″, 207 **BB-DB-LB-FB**
Col: Duquesne *HS:* Avella [PA] B: 12/9/1913, Reading, PA D: 1/29/1979, Weirton, WV
1934 Pit: Pass 1-0; Rec 2-14 7.0. **1935** Pit: Pass 8-1 12.5%, 4 0.50 2 Int; Rec 1-7 7.0. **1936** Pit: Pass 6-1 16.7%, 2 0.33 1 Int; Rec 2-12 6.0. **1937** Pit: Rec 2-12 6.0. **Total:** Pass 15-2 13.3%, 6 0.40 3 Int; Rec 7-45 6.4.

		Rushing			
Year Team	**G**	**Att**	**Yds**	**Avg**	**TD**
1934 Pit	11	24	60	2.5	0
1935 Pit	11	22	15	0.7	0
1936 Pit	12	31	61	2.0	1
1937 Pit	10	4	14	3.5	0
NFL Total	44	81	150	1.9	1

WILLIE ZAPALAC Zapalac, William Frank Jr. 6′4″, 225 **LB-DE**
Col: Texas *HS:* McCallum [Austin, TX] B: 9/1/1948, Bellville, TX *Drafted:* 1971 Round 4 NYJ
1971 NYJ: 14 G. **1972** NYJ: 6 G; KR 1-8 8.0. **1973** NYJ: 13 G. **Total:** 33 G; KR 1-8 8.0.

JOE ZAPUSTAS Zapustas, Joseph John 6′0″, 198 **OE-DE**
Col: Fordham *HS:* South Boston [MA]; St. Anselm's Prep [Washington, DC] B: 7/25/1907, South Boston, MA
1933 NYG: 2 G; Rec 1-26 26.0.

GUST ZARNAS Zarnas, Gustave Constantine 5′10″, 220 **G**
Col: Ohio State *HS:* Bethlehem [PA]; Kiski School [Saltsburg, PA] B: 12/16/1913, Ikaris, Greece *Drafted:* 1938 Round 3 ChiB
1938 ChiB: 10 G. **1939** Bkn-GB: 9 G. Bkn: 4 G. GB: 5 G. **1940** GB: 9 G. **Total:** 28 G.

CARROLL ZARUBA Zaruba, Carroll Robert 5′9″, 210 **DB**
Col: Nebraska *HS:* Fullerton [NE] B: 1934, Fullerton, NE *Drafted:* 1960 Round 1 DalT
1960 DalT: 7 G.

ROB ZATECHKA Zatechka, Robert Brett 6′4″, 313 **OG**
Col: Nebraska *HS:* Lincoln East [NE] B: 12/1/1971, Lansing, MI *Drafted:* 1995 Round 4 NYG
1995 NYG: 16 G; KR 1-5 5.0. **1996** NYG: 15 G. **1997** NYG: 16 G. **Total:** 47 G; KR 1-5 5.0.

ROGER ZATKOFF Zatkoff, Roger 6′2″, 216 **LB-DE**
Col: Michigan *HS:* Hamtramck [MI] B: 3/25/1931, Hamtramck, MI *Drafted:* 1953 Round 5 GB
1953 GB: 12 G. **1954** GB: 12 G; Int 1-0. **1955** GB: 12 G; Int 3-25; 1 Fum. **1956** GB: 12 G. **1957** Det: 12 G. **1958** Det: 12 G. **Total:** 72 G; Int 4-25; 1 Fum.

GODFREY ZAUNBRECHER Zaunbrecher, Godfrey William 6′2″, 240 **C**
Col: Louisiana State *HS:* St. Michael's [Crowley, LA] B: 12/17/1946, Crowley, LA *Drafted:* 1970 Round 11 Min
1971 Min: 4 G. **1972** Min: 7 G. **1973** Min: 5 G. **Total:** 16 G.

JERRY ZAWADZKAS Zawadzkas, Gerald A 6′4″, 220 **TE**
Col: Columbia *HS:* Torrington [CT] B: 1/3/1946, Torrington, CT
Drafted: 1967 Round 16 Det
1967 Det: 2 G; KR 1-0.

DAVE ZAWATSON Zawatson, David Francis 6′5″, 275 **OG-OT**
Col: California *HS:* Fairview [Fairview Park, OH]; Ygnacio Valley HS [Concord, CA] B: 4/13/1966, Cleveland, OH *Drafted:* 1989 Round 2 ChiB
1989 ChiB: 4 G. **1990** NYJ: 16 G. **1991** Mia: 2 G. **Total:** 22 G.

RICH ZECHER Zecher, Richard Frederick 6′2″, 255 **DT-OT**
Col: Contra Costa Coll. CA (J.C.); Utah State *HS:* Alameda [CA]
B: 10/14/1943, Alameda, CA *Drafted:* 1965 Round 9 Oak
1965 Oak: 14 G. **1966** Mia: 14 G. **1967** Mia-Buf: 12 G. Mia: 7 G. Buf: 5 G. **Total:** 40 G.

HENRY ZEHRER Zehrer, Henry Christian 175 **FB-WB**
(Zip) *Col:* No College *HS:* New Britain [CT] B: 12/20/1905, New Britain, CT D: 3/16/1955, Putnam, CT
1926 Har: 7 G.

ERIC ZEIER Zeier, Eric Royce 6′1″, 205 **QB**
Col: Georgia *HS:* American School [Heidelberg, Germany]; Marietta [GA] B: 9/6/1972, Pensacola, FL *Drafted:* 1995 Round 3 Cle
1995 Cle: Scor 1 2XP. **Total:** Scor 1 2XP.

		Passing							
Year Team	G	Att	Comp	Comp%	Yds	YPA	TD	Int	Rating
1995 Cle	7	161	82	50.9	864	5.37	4	9	51.9
1996 Bal	1	21	10	47.6	97	4.62	1	1	57.0
1997 Bal	5	116	67	57.8	958	8.26	7	1	101.1
1998 Bal	10	181	107	59.1	1312	7.25	4	3	82.0
NFL Total	23	479	266	55.5	3231	6.75	16	14	75.4

	Rushing				
Year Team	Att	Yds	Avg	TD	Fum
1995 Cle	15	80	5.3	0	3
1996 Bal	2	8	4.0	0	2
1997 Bal	10	17	1.7	0	3
1998 Bal	11	17	1.5	0	2
NFL Total	38	122	3.2	0	10

DUSTY ZEIGLER Zeigler, Curtis Dustin 6′5″, 298 **C-OG**
Col: Notre Dame *HS:* Effingham Co. [Springfield, GA] B: 9/27/1973, Rincon, GA *Drafted:* 1996 Round 6 Buf
1996 Buf: 2 G. **1997** Buf: 13 G; 1 Fum. **1998** Buf: 16 G; 3 Fum. **Total:** 31 G; 4 Fum.

MIKE ZELE Zele, Michael Robert 6′3″, 239 **NT-DT**
Col: Kent State *HS:* St. Joseph [Cleveland, OH] B: 7/3/1956, Cleveland, OH *Drafted:* 1979 Round 5 Atl
1979 Atl: 13 G. **1980** Atl: 11 G. **1981** Atl: 14 G. **1982** Atl: 9 G; 1 Sac. **1983** Atl: 5 G; 1 Sac. **Total:** 52 G; 2 Sac.

CONNIE ZELENCIK Zelencik, Conrad James 6′4″, 245 **C**
Col: Purdue *HS:* Thornton Fractional North [Calumet City, IL]
B: 4/3/1955, Calumet City, IL *Drafted:* 1977 Round 11 ChiB
1977 Buf: 14 G; 1 Fum.

FRANK ZELENCIK Zelencik, Frank 6′1″, 220 **T**
Col: Oglethorpe *HS:* Theodore Roosevelt [East Chicago, IL]
B: 1/17/1915, Chicago, IL D: 3/1976, Newark, AR
1939 ChiC: 9 G.

RAY ZELLARS Zellars, Raymond Mark 5′11″, 233 **RB**
Col: Notre Dame *HS:* David B. Oliver [Pittsburgh, PA] B: 3/25/1973, Pittsburgh, PA *Drafted:* 1995 Round 2 NO

		Rushing				Receiving				
Year Team	G	Att	Yds	Avg	TD	Rec	Yds	Avg	TD	Fum
1995 NO	12	50	162	3.2	2	7	33	4.7	0	1
1996 NO	9	120	475	4.0	4	9	45	5.0	0	2
1997 NO	16	156	552	3.5	4	31	263	8.5	0	6
1998 NO	11	56	162	2.9	1	10	50	5.0	0	2
NFL Total	48	382	1351	3.5	11	57	391	6.9	0	11

JERRY ZELLER Zeller, Gerald T 5′11″, 170 **WB-BB**
Col: Purdue; Illinois B: 6/3/1898, OH D: 11/1968, Columbus, OH
1921 Eva: 4 G; Rec 1 TD; 6 Pt.

JOE ZELLER Zeller, Joseph Thomas 6′1″, 203 **G-OE-DE**
Col: Indiana *HS:* Washington [East Chicago, IN] B: 5/2/1908, East Chicago, IN D: 9/23/1983, Chicago, IL
1932 GB: 14 G. **1933** ChiB: 11 G; Rec 2-44 22.0 1 TD; 6 Pt. **1934** ChiB: 11 G. **1935** ChiB: 12 G. **1936** ChiB: 11 G. **1937** ChiB: 11 G. **1938** ChiB: 11 G; Int **1** TD; 6 Pt. **Total:** 81 G; Rec 2-44 22.0 1 TD; Int 1 TD; Tot TD 2; 12 Pt.

BOB ZEMAN Zeman, Edward Robert 6′1″, 200 **DB**
Col: Wisconsin *HS:* Wheaton [IL] B: 2/22/1937, Geneva, IL
1961 SD: PR 1-12 12.0. **1962** Den: PR 5-59 11.8. **Total:** PR 6-71 11.8.

		Interceptions				Tot
Year Team	G	Int	Yds	TD	Fum	TD
1960 LAC	12	2	25	0	0	0
1961 SD	14	8	89	0	0	1
1962 Den	14	6	133	**1**	0	1
1963 Den	14	1	23	0	1	0
1965 SD	14	0	0	0	0	0
1966 SD	14	0	0	0	0	0
NFL Total	82	17	270	1	1	2

ED ZEMAN Zeman, Edward Robert II 6′1″, 195 **DB**
Col: Cerritos Coll. CA (J.C.); Fort Lewis *HS:* Monte Vista [Cupertino, CA]
B: 9/25/1963, Denver, CO
1987 LARm: 3 G.

TONY ZENDEJAS Zendejas, Anthony Guerrero 5′8″, 165 **K**
Col: Nevada-Reno *HS:* Don Antonio Lugo [Chino, CA] B: 5/15/1960, Curimeo, Mexico *Drafted:* 1984 Supplemental Round 1 Was
1985 Hou: Pass 1-1 100.0%, -7 -7.00. **1986** Hou: Punt 1-36 36.0.
1989 Hou: Pass 1-0, 1 Int. **Total:** Pass 2-1 50.0%, -7 3.50 1 Int; Punt 1-36 36.0.

		Scoring						
Year Team	G	Pts	FG	FGA	FG%	XK	XKA	XK%
1985 Hou	14	92	21	27	77.8	29	31	93.5
1986 Hou	15	94	22	27	81.5	28	29	96.6
1987 Hou	13	92	20	26	76.9	32	33	97.0
1988 Hou	16	114	22	34	64.7	48	50	96.0
1989 Hou	16	115	25	37	67.6	40	40	100.0
1990 Hou	7	41	7	12	58.3	20	21	95.2
1991 LARm	16	76	17	17	**100.0**	25	26	**96.2**
1992 LARm	16	83	15	20	75.0	38	38	100.0
1993 LARm	16	71	16	23	69.6	23	25	92.0
1994 LARm	16	82	18	23	78.3	28	28	100.0
1995 Atl-SF	4	14	3	6	50.0	5	6	83.3
1995 Atl	1	6	2	3	66.7	0	0	—
1995 SF	3	8	1	3	33.3	5	6	83.3
NFL Total	149	874	186	252	73.8	316	327	96.6

JOAQUIN ZENDEJAS Zendejas, Joaquin [Campos] Jr. 5′11″, 176 **K**
Col: La Verne *HS:* Don Antonio Lugo [Chino, CA] B: 1/14/1960, Curimeo, Mexico
1983 NE: 2 G; Scor 3, 0-1 FG, 3-4 75.0% XK.

LUIS ZENDEJAS Zendejas, Luis Fernando [Campos] 5′9″, 175 **K**
Col: Arizona State *HS:* Don Antonio Lugo [Chino, CA] B: 10/22/1961, Mexico City, Mexico

		Scoring						
Year Team	G	Pts	FG	FGA	FG%	XK	XKA	XK%
1987 Dal	2	19	3	4	75.0	10	10	100.0
1988 Dal-Phi	14	95	20	27	74.1	35	36	97.2
1988 Dal	2	8	1	3	33.3	5	5	100.0
1988 Phi	12	87	19	24	79.2	30	31	96.8
1989 Phi-Dal	15	75	14	24	58.3	33	33	100.0
1989 Phi	8	50	9	15	60.0	23	23	100.0
1989 Dal	7	25	5	9	55.6	10	10	100.0
NFL Total	31	189	37	55	67.3	78	79	98.7

MAX ZENDEJAS Zendejas, Maximiano Javier [Campos] 5′11″, 184 **K**
Col: Arizona *HS:* Don Antonio Lugo [Chino, CA] B: 9/2/1963, Curimeo, Mexico *Drafted:* 1986 Round 4 Dal

		Scoring						
Year Team	G	Pts	FG	FGA	FG%	XK	XKA	XK%
1986 Was	9	50	9	14	64.3	23	28	82.1
1987 GB	10	61	16	19	84.2	13	15	86.7
1988 GB	8	44	9	16	56.3	17	19	89.5
NFL Total	27	155	34	49	69.4	53	62	85.5

COLEMAN ZENO Zeno, Coleman Joseph Jr. 6′4″, 210 **WR**
Col: Grambling State *HS:* Lincoln [Marrero, LA] B: 11/18/1946, New Orleans, LA *Drafted:* 1971 Round 17 NYG
1971 NYG: 2 G; Rush 2-10 5.0; Rec 5-97 19.4; 1 Fum.

JOE ZENO Zeno, Joseph H 5′10″, 234 **G-T**
Col: Holy Cross *HS:* Waltham [MA] B: 6/14/1919, Brooklyn, NY
D: 1/8/1992, Sacramento, CA *Drafted:* 1942 Round 3 Was
1942 Was: 9 G. **1943** Was: 10 G. **1944** Was: 10 G. **1946** Bos: 11 G; Int 1-0. **1947** Bos: 2 G. **Total:** 42 G; Int 1-0.

LANCE ZENO Zeno, Lance Michael 6′4″, 279 **C**
Col: UCLA *HS:* Fountain Valley [CA] B: 4/15/1967, Los Angeles, CA
1992 Cle: 3 G. **1993** Cle-TB-GB: 7 G. Cle: 2 G. GB: 5 G. **Total:** 10 G.

MIKE ZENTIC Zentic, Michael Lee 6′3″, 255 **C**
Col: Northwest Missouri State; Oklahoma State *HS:* Lincoln East [NE]
B: 11/22/1963
1987 Dal: 3 G.

HAROLD ZERBE Zerbe, Harold 165 **E**
Col: No College *HS:* McKinley [Canton, OH] B: 1901 Deceased
1926 Can: 1 G.

JEFF ZGONINA Zgonina, Jeffrey Marc 6′2″, 290 **DT**
Col: Purdue *HS:* Carmel [Lake Grove, IL] B: 5/24/1970, Long Grove, IL
Drafted: 1993 Round 7 Pit
1993 Pit: 5 G. **1994** Pit: 16 G; KR 2-8 4.0; 1 Fum. **1995** Car: 2 G. **1996** Atl: 8 G; 1 Sac. **1997** StL: 15 G; KR 1-5 5.0; 2 Sac. **1998** Ind: 2 G. **Total:** 48 G; KR 3-13 4.3; 1 Fum; 3 Sac.

FRANK ZIEGLER Ziegler, Frank Richard 5′11″, 175 **HB-DB**
Col: Georgia Tech *HS:* College Park [GA] B: 10/1/1923, College Park, GA *Drafted:* 1949 Round 3 Phi
1949 Phi: PR 2-20 10.0; KR 1-21 21.0; Int 1-16. **1950** Phi: PR 3-20 6.7; KR 10-204 20.4. **1952** Phi: KR 4-82 20.5. **1953** Phi: Pass 1-0.
Total: Pass 1-0; PR 5-40 8.0; KR 15-307 20.5; Int 1-16.

		Rushing				Receiving					Tot
Year Team	G	Att	Yds	Avg	TD	Rec	Yds	Avg	TD	Fum	TD
1949 Phi	10	84	283	3.4	1	3	33	11.0	0	4	1
1950 Phi	12	172	733	4.3	1	13	216	16.6	2	10	3
1951 Phi	12	113	418	3.7	2	8	59	7.4	0	6	2
1952 Phi	11	67	172	2.6	2	8	120	15.0	2	1	4
1953 Phi	12	83	320	3.9	5	15	211	14.1	0	2	5
NFL Total	57	519	1926	3.7	11	47	639	13.6	4	23	15

PAUL ZIEGLER Ziegler, Paul K 5′10″, 185 **FB-TB-WB**
Col: No College *HS:* East [Columbus, OH] B: 9/1898, Kenton, OH Deceased
1922 Col: 6 G.

DAVE ZIFF Ziff, David 6′0″, 195 **OE**
Col: Syracuse; Carson-Newman *HS:* Northampton [MA] B: 1/18/1902, MA D: 10/17/1977, New York, NY
1925 Roch: 4 G. **1926** Bkn: 7 G. **Total:** 11 G.

JACK ZILLY Zilly, John Jynus 6′2″, 212 **DE-OE**
Col: Notre Dame *HS:* Lewis [Southington, CT]; Cheshire Acad. [CT] B: 11/11/1921, Waterbury, CT *Drafted:* 1945 Round 4 Cle
1947 LARm: 12 G; Rec 7-75 10.7; KR 1-10 10.0. **1948** LARm: 12 G; Rec 13-169 13.0 4 TD; 24 Pt; 1 Fum. **1949** LARm: 12 G; Rec 3-35 11.7; KR 1-0. **1950** LARm: 12 G. **1951** LARm: 4 G. **1952** Phi: 12 G. **Total:** 64 G; Rec 23-279 12.1 4 TD; KR 2-10 5.0; 24 Pt; 1 Fum.

GENO ZIMMERLINK Zimmerlink, Eugene Franklin Jr. 6′3″, 222 **TE**
Col: Virginia *HS:* Spotswood [NJ] B: 3/26/1963, Milltown, NJ
1987 Atl: 3 G.

CORL ZIMMERMAN Zimmerman, Corl James 6′0″, 185 **G-T**
Col: Mount Union *HS:* Central [Akron, OH] B: 2/22/1899, Akron, OH D: 6/30/1959, Akron, OH
1927 Day: 5 G. **1928** Day: 4 G. **1929** Day: 4 G. **Total:** 13 G.

DON ZIMMERMAN Zimmerman, Donald 6′3″, 195 **WR**
Col: Arkansas-Pine Bluff; Northeast Louisiana *HS:* Richwood [Monroe, LA] B: 11/22/1949, Monroe, LA *Drafted:* 1972 Round 12 Phi
1974 Phi: KR 1-0. **1976** Phi-GB: Rush 1-3 3.0. GB: Rush 1-3 3.0.
Total: Rush 1-3 3.0; KR 1-0.

		Receiving				
Year Team	G	Rec	Yds	Avg	TD	Fum
1973 Phi	14	22	220	10.0	3	1
1974 Phi	14	30	368	12.3	2	0
1975 Phi	10	0	0	—	0	0
1976 Phi-GB	3	1	13	13.0	0	0
1976 Phi	1	0	0	—	0	0
1976 GB	2	1	13	13.0	0	0
NFL Total	41	53	601	11.3	5	1

GARY ZIMMERMAN Zimmerman, Gary Wayne 6′6″, 294 **OT**
Col: Oregon *HS:* Walnut [CA] B: 12/13/1961, Fullerton, CA
Drafted: 1984 Supplemental Round 1 NYG
1986 Min: 16 G. **1987** Min: 12 G. **1988** Min: 16 G. **1989** Min: 16 G. **1990** Min: 16 G. **1991** Min: 16 G. **1992** Min: 16 G. **1993** Den: 16 G. **1994** Den: 16 G. **1995** Den: 16 G. **1996** Den: 14 G. **1997** Den: 14 G. **Total:** 184 G.

GIFF ZIMMERMAN Zimmerman, Gifford Guy 5′10″, 180 **WB-TB**
Col: Syracuse *HS:* Central [Akron, OH] B: 8/25/1900, Akron, OH D: 11/27/1968, Akron, OH
1924 Akr: 2 G. **1925** Can: 6 G; Rush 1 TD; Rec 1 TD; Tot TD 2; 12 Pt.
Total: 8 G; Rush 1 TD; Rec 1 TD; Tot TD 2; 12 Pt.

ROY ZIMMERMAN Zimmerman, Henry Leroy Jr. 6′2″, 201 **QB-K**
Col: San Jose State *HS:* Monrovia [CA] B: 2/20/1918, Tonganoxie, KS D: 8/22/1997, Madera, CA *Drafted:* 1940 Round 5 Was
1940 Was: Scor 0-1 XK. **1941** Was: Rec 5-36 7.2. **1942** Was: KR 1-25 25.0; Scor 4, 1-1 100.0% FG, 1-1 100.0% XK. **1943** PhPt: KR 3-55 18.3; Scor 35, 1-6 16.7% FG, 26-28 92.9% XK. **1944** Phi: Scor 62, 4-8 **50.0**% FG, 32-34 **94.1**% XK. **1945** Phi: PR 1-7 7.0; Scor 47, 4-8 50.0% FG, 29-33 87.9% XK. **1946** Phi: Scor 14, 2-4 50.0% FG, 2-2 100.0% XK. **1947** Det: Scor 51, 5-11 45.5% FG, 30-31 96.8% XK. **1948** Bos: Scor 16, 1-4 25.0% FG, 13-15 86.7% XK. **Total:** Rec 5-36 7.2; PR 1-7 7.0; KR 4-80 20.0; Scor 229, 18-42 42.9% FG, 133-145 91.7% XK.

		Passing							
Year Team	G	Att	Comp	Comp%	Yds	YPA	TD	Int	Rating
1940 Was	6	12	4	33.3	53	4.42	0	3	8.7
1941 Was	9	1	0	0.0	0	0.00	0	0	39.6
1942 Was	7	10	2	20.0	13	1.30	0	2	0.0
1943 PhPt	10	124	43	34.7	846	6.82	9	17	44.0
1944 Phi	10	105	39	37.1	785	7.48	8	10	50.0
1945 Phi	10	127	67	52.8	991	7.80	9	8	75.9
1946 Phi	11	79	41	51.9	597	7.56	4	8	54.1
1947 Det	12	138	57	41.3	867	6.28	7	9	52.4
1948 Bos	9	107	46	43.0	649	6.07	7	13	45.4
NFL Total	84	703	299	42.5	4801	6.83	44	70	47.3

	Rushing				Interceptions		
Year Team	Att	Yds	Avg	TD	Int	Yds	TD
1940 Was	31	127	4.1	0	0	0	0
1941 Was	20	54	2.7	0	0	0	0
1942 Was	12	56	4.7	0	0	0	0
1943 PhPt	33	-41	-1.2	1	5	19	0
1944 Phi	26	-84	-3.2	2	4	36	0
1945 Phi	29	-11	-0.4	1	**7**	90	0
1946 Phi	23	43	1.9	1	3	58	0
1947 Det	13	28	2.2	1	0	0	0
1948 Bos	13	72	5.5	0	0	0	0
NFL Total	200	244	1.2	6	19	203	0

	Punting				Tot
Year Team	Punts	Yds	Avg	Fum	TD
1940 Was	7	256	36.6	0	0
1941 Was	14	594	42.4	0	0
1942 Was	4	202	50.5	0	0
1943 PhPt	44	1521	34.6	0	1
1944 Phi	39	1531	39.3	0	3
1945 Phi	47	1778	37.8	3	1
1946 Phi	23	890	38.7	3	1
1947 Det	49	2078	42.4	8	1
1948 Bos	51	2215	43.4	4	0
NFL Total	278	11065	39.8	18	7

JEFF ZIMMERMAN Zimmerman, Jeffrey Alan 6′3″, 320 **OG**
Col: Florida *HS:* Evans [Orlando, FL] B: 1/10/1963, Enid, OK
Drafted: 1987 Round 3 Dal
1987 Dal: 11 G. **1988** Dal: 1 G. **1989** Dal: 16 G. **1990** Dal: 6 G. **Total:** 34 G.

BOB ZIMNY Zimny, Robert John 6′1″, 233 **T**
Col: Indiana *HS:* St. Rita [Chicago, IL] B: 12/11/1921, Chicago, IL
1945 ChiC: 10 G; KR 1-12 12.0; 1 Fum. **1946** ChiC: 11 G. **1947** ChiC: 7 G. **1948** ChiC: 12 G. **1949** ChiC: 12 G. **Total:** 52 G; KR 1-12 12.0; 1 Fum.

WALT ZIRINSKY Zirinsky, Walter John 5′11″, 187 **HB-DB**
Col: Lafayette *HS:* Northampton [PA] B: 8/1/1920, Northampton, PA
Drafted: 1942 Round 12 Cle
1945 Cle: 5 G; Rush 3-3 1.0.

VINCE ZIZAK Zizak, Vincent Augustine 5′8″, 208 **G-T**
Col: Villanova *HS:* La Salle Prep [Philadelphia, PA] B: 8/8/1908, Camden, NJ D: 8/1973, Upper Darby, PA
1934 ChiB-Phi: 8 G. ChiB: 2 G. Phi: 6 G. **1935** Phi: 4 G. **1936** Phi: 10 G. **1937** Phi: 2 G. **Total:** 24 G.

MICKEY ZOFKO Zofko, Michael Joseph 6′3″, 195 **RB**
Col: Auburn *HS:* Melbourne [FL] B: 6/8/1949, Melbourne, FL
Drafted: 1971 Round 9 Det
1972 Det: Rush 7-28 4.0; Rec 2-14 7.0; Scor **1** 1XP. **1973** Det: Pass 1-1 100.0%, 35 35.00; Rush 11-33 3.0; Rec 2-16 8.0. **1974** Det-NYG: Rush 3-6 2.0; Rec 3-15 5.0. Det: Rush 3-6 2.0; Rec 3-15 5.0.
Total: Pass 1-1 100.0%, 35 35.00; Rush 21-67 3.2; Rec 7-45 6.4; Scor 1 1XP.

		Kickoff Returns				
Year Team	G	Ret	Yds	Avg	TD	Fum
1971 Det	11	0	0	—	0	0
1972 Det	14	26	616	23.7	0	3
1973 Det	8	1	7	7.0	0	0
1974 Det-NYG	11	3	33	11.0	0	1
1974 Det	4	2	19	9.5	0	0
1974 NYG	7	1	14	14.0	0	1
NFL Total	44	30	656	21.9	0	4

JON ZOGG Zogg, Jon Frederick 6′4″, 290 **OG**
Col: Boise State *HS:* Watsonville [CA] B: 11/19/1960, San Jose, CA
1987 LARd: 1 G.

CLYDE ZOIA Zoia, Clyde John 5′7″, 175 **G**
Col: Notre Dame *HS:* Woodstock [IL] B: 5/1896, MN Deceased
1920 ChiC: 8 G. **1921** ChiC: 8 G. **1922** ChiC: 7 G. **1923** ChiC: 11 G. **Total:** 34 G.

SCOTT ZOLAK Zolak, Scott David 6'5", 230 **QB**
Col: Maryland *HS:* Ringgold [Monongahela, PA] B: 12/13/1967, Pittsburgh, PA *Drafted:* 1991 Round 4 NE

Year Team	G	Passing Att	Comp	Comp%	Yds	YPA	TD	Int	Rating
1992 NE	6	100	52	52.0	561	5.61	2	4	58.8
1993 NE	3	2	0	0.0	0	0.00	0	0	39.6
1994 NE	16	8	5	62.5	28	3.50	0	0	68.8
1995 NE	16	49	28	57.1	282	5.76	1	0	80.5
1996 NE	3	1	1	100.0	5	5.00	0	0	87.5
1997 NE	4	9	6	66.7	67	7.44	2	0	128.2
1998 NE	6	75	32	42.7	371	4.95	3	3	54.9
NFL Total	54	244	124	50.8	1314	5.39	8	7	65.8

Year Team	Rushing Att	Yds	Avg	TD	Fum
1992 NE	18	71	3.9	0	5
1993 NE	1	0	0.0	0	0
1994 NE	1	-1	-1.0	0	0
1995 NE	4	19	4.8	0	4
1996 NE	4	-3	-0.8	0	0
1997 NE	3	-3	-1.0	0	0
1998 NE	5	0	0.0	0	1
NFL Total	36	83	2.3	0	10

CARL ZOLL Zoll, Carl Francis 5'9", 215 **G**
Col: No College *HS:* Green Bay West [WI] B: 1/29/1899, Howard, WI D: 10/19/1973, Green Bay, WI
1922 GB: 1 G.

MARTY ZOLL Zoll, Martin A 5'8", 185 **G**
Col: No College *HS:* Green Bay West [WI] B: 11/12/1900, Howard, WI D: 10/14/1968, Green Bay, WI
1921 GB: 1 G.

DICK ZOLL Zoll, Richard Archibald 5'11", 218 **G-T**
Col: Indiana *HS:* Green Bay West [WI] B: 12/10/1913, Green Bay, WI D: 9/6/1985, Green Bay, WI
1937 Cle: 11 G. **1938** Cle: 11 G; Scor 1, 1-1 100.0% XK. **1939** GB: 1 G. **Total:** 23 G; Scor 1, 1-1 100.0% XK.

ERIC ZOMALT Zomalt, Eric Lee 5'11", 197 **DB**
Col: California *HS:* Canyon Springs [Moreno Valley, CA] B: 8/9/1972, Los Angeles, CA *Drafted:* 1994 Round 3 Phi
1994 Phi: 12 G. **1995** Phi: 15 G. **1996** Phi-NYJ: 13 G. Phi: 3 G. NYJ: 10 G. **Total:** 40 G.

JOE ZOMBEK Zombek, Joseph A 6'1", 195 **OE**
Col: Pittsburgh *HS:* Scott Twp. [North Braddock, PA] B: 12/24/1932 D: 1/13/1996, McDonald, PA *Drafted:* 1954 Round 9 Pit
1954 Pit: 8 G. **1955** Pit: 1 G; Punt 5-201 40.2. **Total:** 9 G; Punt 5-201 40.2.

LOU ZONTINI Zontini, Louis Rogers 5'9", 189 **HB-LB-DB-BB**
Col: Notre Dame *HS:* Sherman [Seth, WV] B: 8/30/1917, Whitesville, WV D: 8/6/1986, Cleveland, OH
AAFC **1946** BufA: Pass 1-0; Rush 13-36 2.8; KR 1-19 19.0; Int 1-2; Scor 42, 4-8 50.0% FG, 30-31 96.8% XK.

Year Team	G	Punting Punts	Yds	Avg
1946 BufA	14	44	1595	36.3

NFL **1940** ChiC: Int 1-20; Punt 2-92 46.0; Scor 16, 2-5 40.0% FG, 10-10 100.0% XK. **1941** ChiC: Rec 1-22 22.0; Punt 12-446 37.2; Scor 5, 0-4 FG, 5-7 71.4% XK. **1944** Cle: Pass 2-2 100.0%, 18 9.00; Rec 3-88 29.3 1 TD; PR 4-47 11.8; KR 3-66 22.0; Int 2-14; Scor 47, 3-6 **50.0**% FG, 14-16 **87.5**% XK. **Total:** Pass 2-2 100.0%, 18 9.00; Rec 4-110 27.5 1 TD; PR 4-47 11.8; KR 3-66 22.0; Int 3-34; Punt 14-538 38.4; Scor 68, 5-15 33.3% FG, 29-33 87.9% XK.

Year Team	G	Rushing Att	Yds	Avg	TD	Tot TD
1940 ChiC	8	1	1	1.0	0	0
1941 ChiC	8	1	-9	-9.0	0	0
1944 Cle	10	33	105	3.2	3	4
NFL Total	26	35	97	2.8	3	4

JOHN ZOOK Zook, John Eldon 6'4", 243 **DE**
Col: Kansas *HS:* Larned [KS] B: 9/24/1947, Garden City, KS *Drafted:* 1969 Round 4 LARm
1969 Atl: 14 G; Int 2-22. **1970** Atl: 14 G; Int 1-24. **1971** Atl: 14 G; Scor 1 Saf; 2 Pt. **1972** Atl: 14 G; **1** Fum TD; 6 Pt; 1 Fum. **1973** Atl: 14 G. **1974** Atl: 14 G; Int 1-14. **1975** Atl: 14 G. **1976** StL: 13 G. **1977** StL: 12 G. **1978** StL: 16 G. **1979** StL: 5 G. **Total:** 144 G; Int 4-60; Scor 1 Saf; 1 Fum TD; 8 Pt; 1 Fum.

FRANK ZOPPETTI Zoppetti, Frank 5'11", 185 **TB-DB**
Col: Duquesne *HS:* Cherry Valley [PA] B: 4/15/1916 D: 6/1985, Burgettstown, PA
1941 Pit: 4 G; Pass 1-0.

MIKE ZORDICH Zordich, Michael Edward 6'1", 207 **DB**
Col: Penn State *HS:* Chaney [Youngstown, OH] B: 10/12/1963, Youngstown, OH *Drafted:* 1986 Round 9 SD
1987 NYJ: 1 Sac. **1989** Pho: 1 Sac. **1994** Phi: KR 1-0; 1 Sac. **1995** Phi: **1** Fum TD; 1 Sac. **1997** Phi: 2 Sac. **Total:** KR 1-0; 1 Fum TD; 6 Sac.

Year Team	G	Interceptions Int	Yds	TD	Tot TD
1987 NYJ	10	0	0	0	0
1988 NYJ	16	1	35	1	1
1989 Pho	16	1	16	1	1
1990 Pho	16	1	25	0	0
1991 Pho	16	1	27	0	0
1992 Pho	16	3	37	0	0
1993 Pho	16	1	0	0	0
1994 Phi	16	4	39	1	1
1995 Phi	15	1	10	0	1
1996 Phi	16	4	54	0	0
1997 Phi	16	1	21	0	0
1998 Phi	16	2	18	0	0
NFL Total	185	20	282	3	4

CHRIS ZORICH Zorich, Christopher Robert 6'1", 278 **DT**
Col: Notre Dame *HS:* Chicago Vocational [IL] B: 3/13/1969, Chicago, IL *Drafted:* 1991 Round 2 ChiB
1991 ChiB: 12 G. **1992** ChiB: 16 G; 1 Fum TD; 6 Pt; 2 Sac. **1993** ChiB: 16 G; 7 Sac. **1994** ChiB: 16 G; 5.5 Sac. **1995** ChiB: 16 G; 1 Sac. **1997** ChiB-Was: 8 G; 1 Sac. ChiB: 3 G. Was: 5 G; 1 Sac. **Total:** 84 G; 1 Fum TD; 6 Pt; 16.5 Sac.

GEORGE ZORICH Zorich, George 6'2", 213 **G-LB**
Col: Northwestern *HS:* Wakefield [MI] B: 11/24/1915, Wakefield, MI D: 10/14/1967, Rensselaer, IN
AAFC **1946** MiaA: 6 G; PR 1-18 18.0. **1947** BalA: 11 G. **Total:** 17 G; PR 1-18 18.0.

NFL **1944** ChiB: 10 G; Int 1-4. **1945** ChiB: 8 G. **Total:** 18 G; Int 1-4.

JIM ZORN Zorn, James Arthur 6'2", 200 **QB**
Col: Cal Poly-Pomona *HS:* Gahr [Cerritos, CA] B: 5/10/1953, Whittier, CA
1982 Sea: Rec 1-27 27.0. **Total:** Rec 1-27 27.0.

Year Team	G	Passing Att	Comp	Comp%	Yds	YPA	TD	Int	Rating
1976 Sea	14	**439**	208	47.4	2571	5.86	12	27	49.5
1977 Sea	10	251	104	41.4	1687	6.72	16	19	54.3
1978 Sea	16	443	248	56.0	3283	7.41	15	20	72.1
1979 Sea	16	505	285	56.4	3661	7.25	20	18	77.7
1980 Sea	16	488	276	56.6	3346	6.86	17	20	72.3
1981 Sea	13	397	236	59.4	2788	7.02	13	**9**	82.4
1982 Sea	9	245	126	51.4	1540	6.29	7	11	61.9
1983 Sea	16	205	103	50.2	1166	5.69	7	7	64.8
1984 Sea	16	17	7	41.2	80	4.71	0	2	16.4
1985 GB	13	123	56	45.5	794	6.46	4	6	57.4
1987 TB	1	36	20	55.6	199	5.53	0	2	48.3
NFL Total	140	3149	1669	53.0	21115	6.71	111	141	67.3

Year Team	Rushing Att	Yds	Avg	TD	Fum
1976 Sea	52	246	4.7	4	7
1977 Sea	25	141	5.6	1	1
1978 Sea	59	290	4.9	6	11
1979 Sea	46	279	6.1	2	6
1980 Sea	44	214	4.9	1	12
1981 Sea	30	140	4.7	1	2
1982 Sea	15	113	7.5	1	5
1983 Sea	30	71	2.4	1	4
1984 Sea	7	-3	-0.4	0	0
1985 GB	10	9	0.9	0	3
1987 TB	4	4	1.0	0	3
NFL Total	322	1504	4.7	17	54

VIC ZUCCO Zucco, Victor A 6'0", 187 **DB**
Col: Wayne State (Mich.); Michigan State *HS:* Plum [Pittsburgh, PA] B: 9/4/1935, Renton, PA *Drafted:* 1957 Round 5 ChiB
1957 ChiB: KR 8-224 28.0; Int 3-20; 1 Fum TD. **1958** ChiB: KR 3-63 21.0; Int 3-13. **1960** ChiB: KR 1-17 17.0; Int 2-52. **Total:** KR 12-304 25.3; Int 8-85; 1 Fum TD.

Year Team	G	Punt Returns Ret	Yds	Avg	TD	Fum
1957 ChiB	12	11	58	5.3	0	2
1958 ChiB	12	15	35	2.3	0	1
1959 ChiB	2	1	0	0.0	0	0
1960 ChiB	12	10	83	8.3	0	0
NFL Total	38	37	176	4.8	0	3

DAVE ZUIDMULDER Zuidmulder, David C 5′10″, 175 **TB**
Col: St. Ambrose; Georgetown *HS:* Green Bay East [WI] B: 2/4/1906, New Franken, WI D: 6/8/1978, Green Bay, WI
1929 GB: 1 G. **1930** GB: 4 G. **1931** GB: 2 G. **Total:** 7 G.

CHARLIE ZUNKER Zunker, Charles A 6′4″, 227 **T**
Col: Southwest Texas State *HS:* San Marcos Acad. [TX] B: 8/24/1908, Henley, TX D: 6/11/1963, San Antonio, TX
1934 Cin: 3 G.

AL ZUPEK Zupek, Albert Ernest 6′1″, 205 **BB-DE**
Col: Lawrence *HS:* Racine [WI] B: 1/12/1922, Racine, WI D: 6/16/1980, Burlington, IA
1946 GB: 3 G.

MERLE ZUVER Zuver, Merle Dale 6′1″, 198 **G-C**
Col: Nebraska *HS:* Adams [NE] B: 1/25/1905, Adams, NE D: 3/25/1969, Phoenix, AZ
1930 GB: 10 G.

TONY ZUZZIO Zuzzio, Anthony Joseph 5′11″, 210 **G**
(Zu) *Col:* Muhlenberg *HS:* Belleville [NJ] B: 8/5/1916, Irvington, NJ
1942 Det: 2 G.

JIM ZYNTELL Zyntell, Ignatius James 6′1″, 200 **G**
(Iggy) *Col:* Holy Cross *HS:* Boston English [MA] B: 4/27/1910, Boston, MA D: 11/13/1992, Brighton, MA
1933 NYG-Phi: 10 G. NYG: 2 G. Phi: 8 G. **1934** Phi: 8 G. **1935** Phi: 7 G. **Total:** 25 G.

The Draft

Jim J. Campbell, Beau Riffenburgh, Joel Bussert, and Bob Carroll

The format of the NFL draft has changed many times since the brainchild of former NFL Commissioner and club owner Bert Bell was accepted by the league owners on May 19, 1935. Bell's idea was to help the weaker teams by allowing them first choice of the top college players. Teams would draft in an inverse order of their finish, with the league champion selecting last, regardless of its record. Prior to that time, players had been able to sign with any club. Open signing tended to make the strong get stronger.

The initial draft was held February 8, 1936, at the Ritz-Carlton Hotel in Philadelphia. The first player chosen was Heisman Trophy winner Jay Berwanger, a halfback from the University of Chicago. But Berwanger never signed with either the Eagles, who selected him, or the Bears, after they traded for his rights. The first drafted player who did play was the number-two pick, halfback Riley Smith of Alabama, who was selected by the Boston Redskins.

It took only one year for the format of the draft to change. The December 1936 draft had 10 rounds, one more than the first year. In 1939, the draft increased to 20 rounds; at the start of World War II, it was expanded to 30 rounds, the assumption being that many of those drafted also would be drafted by the Armed Forces. During the war, the NFL voted to stop using the term "draft" and referred to players as being on the "preferred negotiations list."

Following World War II, The All-American Football Conference operated for four years, and held drafts prior to three of them, 1947-49. Those drafts are included after the NFL drafts of the same years.

From 1947-1958, the bonus pick rule was in effect. Each year one team received the first pick in the draft, usually in exchange for its thirtieth-round choice. In 1949 and 1950, the bonus pick was a true bonus. In each of those years, the team selecting didn't lose its final-round choice; Philadelphia had a twenty-fifth-round selection in 1949 (when, for one year, the draft dropped to 25 rounds), and Detroit had a thirtieth-round choice in 1950. Each team was eligible for the bonus pick only once, and it was selected by lottery.

When the AFL was founded prior to the 1960 season, the two leagues began drafting many of the same players. That same season the NFL draft was shortened to 20 rounds. After its initial draft, the AFL varied the length of its drafts from 34 to 20 rounds.

Part of the merger agreement between the AFL and the NFL was to hold a combined draft, which started in 1967 and was shortened to 17 rounds. The draft was further reduced to 12 rounds in 1977, the same year it was moved to late April or May.

The format of the following all-time draft list changes several times. In the early years of the draft, the league kept only scant records, listing each team's order of selection, from first pick to thirtieth. But those picks didn't necessarily correspond to rounds 1 through 30. In several years, the teams that finished in the bottom half of the league standings received either more selections, or more selections higher in the draft, than teams in the top half of the standings. Records from other early years make it difficult to determine the round in which a player was chosen. Thus, from 1936-1947, the numbers before each player generally indicate only the best available information. Numbers after picks names are the order of selection for the draft whenever known.

In the 1930s, it was common for a team to trade an established player for the rights to sign a draftee, who had been selected with that team in mind. Teams also traded actual draft positions for players, as is done today. But for the 1942 draft, rules were passed prohibiting the sale or trading of a team's first two draft positions or of a team's first two selections until one playing season after that selection. Shortly thereafter, the rule involving draft positions was expanded to include all rounds, and in that form remained in effect until 1947, when the Chicago Bears received two draft choices in trades, the Chicago Cardinals' third-round and Philadelphia's fourth-round. Again because of inadequate records, the trading of draft positions isn't always indicated prior to 1947, except in 1939.

Throughout the first four decades of the draft, players occasionally (or in some years frequently) were selected who hadn't completed their college eligibility. These players were divided into two groups — "future picks" and players ineligible for the draft.

The future pick was based on the old NFL rule that a player could be chosen if his class had graduated even if he hadn't completed his eligibility. Thus, if a player had been redshirted in college, had sat out a year while transferring from one school to another, or otherwise would have completed his four years of eligibility in five years, he could be drafted after his fourth year, and his rights would remain with the team that selected him, even if he didn't sign for a year.

Most early future picks were not recorded as such, but

they were made as long ago as 1949. In the 1960s, with the AFL and NFL each trying to get a draft advantage, future picks became more and more frequent; in 1965 and 1966, the AFL actually held separate drafts for futures. At the time of the merger, in 1967, the leagues agreed to eliminate future picks.

Today a player is no longer required to have graduated or to have completed his eligibility before he can be drafted.

In the unusual circumstance that a player loses his eligibility after the draft, a supplemental draft can be held. In the same order as the previous draft, each team has the opportunity to offer its first-round pick of the next year for the athlete. The process continues through the rounds until he is chosen.

In the draft list, a future pick is indicated by an "F" at the end of his entry. No future picks are shown prior to 1949. Those obtainable for the NFL, such as all that were made by San Francisco, are indicated through 1961. All AFL future picks and those of the NFL from 1962-66 are indicated.

Through the years, many players were selected who still had college eligibility remaining but weren't eligible to be drafted as futures. These selections basically were mistakes that were made before scouting became as exact as it is today. Generally, these players were drafted again the next year, sometimes even by the same team. A selection that was voided by the league because the player who was drafted was ineligible is indicated by + at the end of the information about the player.

Notes included with each year refer only to that year, unless otherwise indicated.

* - Player's record in Register

1936

Held February 8, 1936

BOSTON 1936
1. *Smith, Riley, B, Alabama, 2
2. Topping, Keith, E, Stanford, 11
3. *Smith, Ed, B, NYU, 20
4. Tangora, Paul, G, Northwestern, 29
5. Groseclose, Wilson, T, TCU, 38
6. Lutz, Larry, T, California, 47
7. *Irwin, Don, B, Colgate, 56
8. *Millner, Wayne, E, Notre Dame, 65
9. Saunders, Marcel, G, Loyola (CA), 74

BROOKLYN 1936
1. *Crayne, Dick, B, Iowa, 4
2. LeVoir, Vernal (Babe), B, Minnesota, 13
3. *Jorgenson, Wagner, C, St. Mary's (CA), 22
4. Bryant, Paul (Bear), E, Alabama, 31
5. *Wilson, Bob, B, SMU, 40
6. *Maniaci, Joe, B, Fordham, 49
7. Schreiber, Herb, B, St. Mary's (CA), 58
8. Hamilton, Bob (Bones), B, Stanford, 67
9. *Moscrip, Jim (Monk), E, Stanford, 76

CHICAGO BEARS 1936
1. *Stydahar, Joe, T, West Virginia, 6
2. *Michaels, Eddie, G, Villanova, 14
3. Roscoe, George, B, Minnesota, 24
4. *Allman, Bob, E, Michigan State, 32
5. *Oech, Vern, T, Minnesota, 42
6. Christofferson, Ted, B, Washington State, 50
7. Smith, Dick, T, Minnesota, 60
8. Sylvester, John, E, Rice, 68
9. *Fortmann, Dan, G, Colgate, 78

CHICAGO CARDINALS 1936
1. *Lawrence, Jim, B, TCU, 5
2. Jones, Gomer, C, Ohio State, 15
3. Erdelalz, Eddie, E, St. Mary's (CA), 23
4. *Brett, Ed, E, Washington State, 33
5. Riordan, Stan, E, Oregon, 41
6. Antonini, Ettore, E, Indiana, 51
7. Dennis, Tack, B, Tulsa, 59
8. *Carter, Ross, G, Oregon, 69
9. Larsen, Niels, T, Stanford, 77

DETROIT 1936
1. *Wagner, Sid, G, Michigan State, 8
2. Cheshire, Chuck, B, UCLA, 17
3. Pilney, Andy, B, Notre Dame, 26
4. Biese, Sheldon, B, Minnesota, 35
5. Francis, Kavanaugh, C, Alabama, 44
6. Mickal, Abe, B, LSU, 53
7. Wasicek, Charlie. T, Colgate, 62
8. Rennebohn, Dale, C, Minnesota, 71
9. Train, Bob (Choo-Choo), E, Yale, 80

GREEN BAY 1936
1. *Letlow, Russ, G, San Francisco, 7
2. Wheeler, J.W., T, Oklahoma, 16
3. *Scherer, Bernie, E, Nebraska, 25
4. Ward, Theron, B, Idaho, 34
5. *Lester, Darrell, C, TCU, 43
6. *Reynolds, Bob, T, Stanford, 52
7. Fromhart, Wally, B, Notre Dame, 61
8. Cruice, Wally, B, Northwestern, 70
9. Wetsel, J.C., G, SMU, 79

NEW YORK GIANTS 1936
1. *Lewis, Art, T, Ohio U., 9
2. *Leemans, Alphonse (Tuffy), B, Geo. Washington, 18
3. Loebs, Frank (Butch), E, Purdue, 27
4. *Rose, Gene, E, Tennessee, 36
5. Jontos, Ed, G, Syracuse, 45
6. Durner, Gus, T, Duke, 54
7. Peeples, Bob, T, Marquette, 63
8. Heekin, Dick, B, Ohio State, 72
9. Flanagan, Phil, G, Holy Cross, 81

PHILADELPHIA 1936
1. Berwanger, Jay, B, Chicago, 1
2. McCauley, John, B, Rice, 10
3. Muller, Wes, C, Stanford, 19
4. Wallace, Bill, B, Rice, 28
5. Shuford, Harry, B, SMU, 37
6. Barabas, Al, B, Columbia, 46
7. Weller, Jack, G, Princeton, 55
8. Constable, Pepper, B, Princeton, 64
9. Pauk, Paul, B, Princeton, 73

PITTSBURGH 1936
1. Shakespeare, Bill, B, Notre Dame, 3
2. *Barnum, Len, B, West Virginia Wesleyan, 12
3. Grayson, Bobby, B, Stanford, 21
4. Spain, Truman, T, SMU, 30
5. *Sandefur, Wayne, B, Purdue, 39
6. Orr, Maurice, T, SMU, 48
7. Peters, Marty, E, Notre Dame, 57
8. *Karpowich, Ed, T, Catholic, 66
9. Meglen, Joe, B, Georgetown (DC), 75

1937

Held December 12, 1936

President Joe Carr stated at the draft meeting that because there was a possibility of adding a tenth franchise to the league prior to the opening of the season, 10 players should be drafted for the new team. It was decided that the league would draft for the new franchise, selecting in last place in each round. It was agreed that if no additional team was admitted, the players selected by the league were to revert to the remaining clubs, with preference for selection being given in the same order as in the regular draft. Before the 1937 season, the Cleveland Rams were admitted as the tenth team in the league.

BOSTON 1937
1. *Baugh, Sammy, B, TCU, 6
2. *Falaschi, Nello, B, Santa Clara, 16
3. Eldar, Maurice, B, Kansas State, 26
4. *Bassi, Dick, G, Santa Clara, 36
5. *Bond, Chuck, T, Washington, 46
6. Cain, Jimmie, B, Washington, 56
7. Holland, Rotta, G, Kansas State, 66
8. Eaves, Joel, E, Auburn, 76
9. Docherty, Bill, T, Temple, 86
10. *Cara, Dom Mac, E, North Carolina State, 96

BROOKLYN 1937
1. *Goddard, Ed, B, Washington State, 2
2. *Parker, Clarence (Ace), B, Duke, 13
3. Starcevich, Max, G, Washington, 22
4. Kurlish, Bill, B, Penn, 33
5. *Johnson, Bert, B, Kentucky, 42
6. *Golemgeske, John, T, Wisconsin, 53
7. Funk, Fred, B, UCLA, 62
8. Reid, Steve, G, Northwestern, 73
9. Nowogrowski, Ed, B, Washington, 82
10. Kuhn, Gil, T, USC, 93

CHICAGO BEARS 1937
1. *McDonald, Les, E, Nebraska, 8
2. Stewart, Marv, C, LSU, 18
3. *Plasman, Dick, E, Vanderbilt, 28
4. *Hammond, Henry, E, Southwestern (KS), 38
5. *Conkright, Bill (Red), C, Oklahoma, 48
6. *Bjork, Del, T, Oregon, 58
7. Friedman, J.W. (Buck), B, Rice, 68
8. Toth, Steve, B, Northwestern, 78
9. Guepe, Al, B, Marquette, 88
10. Wade, Ed (Red), T, Utah State, 98

CHICAGO CARDINALS 1937
1. *Buivid, Ray (Buzz), B, Marquette, 3
2. *Tinsley, Gaynell, E, LSU, 12
3. Guepe, Art, B, Marquette, 23
4. Bryan, H.K. (Bucky), B, Tulane, 32
5. *Harmon, Harn, C, Tulsa, 43
6. Dickens, Phil, B, Tennessee, 52
7. Dickerson, Herm, B, Virginia Tech, 63
8. *Reynolds, John, C, Baylor, 72
9. Hafeli, Dwight, E, Washington (StL) 83
10. Fitzsimmons, Middleton, G, Georgia Tech, 92

DETROIT 1937
1. *Cardwell, Lloyd, B, Nebraska, 7
2. Hamrick, Charley, T, Ohio State, 17
3. *Huffman, Vern, B, Indiana, 27
4. Glassford, Bill, G, Pittsburgh, 37
5. *Patt, Maury, E, Carnegie Mellon, 47
6. Bell, George, G, Purdue, 57
7. Sprague, John, E, SMU, 67
8. Sayre, Elvin, C, Illinois, 77
9. Kelley, Larry, E, Yale, 87
10. *Bell, Kay, T, Washington State, 97

GREEN BAY 1937
1. *Jankowski, Eddie, B, Wisconsin, 9
2. *Daniell, Ave, T, Pittsburgh, 19
3. Wilkinson, Charles (Bud), T, Minnesota, 29
4. *Svendsen, Earl, C, Minnesota, 39
5. Gibson, Dewitt, T, Northwestern, 49
6. Wendt, Merle, E, Ohio State, 59
7. Baldwin, Marv, T, TCU, 69
8. Chapman, Les, T, Tulsa, 79
9. Dahlgren, Gordon, G, Michigan State, 89
10. Gavin, Dave, T, Holy Cross, 99

NEW YORK GIANTS 1937
1. *Widseth, Ed, T, Minnesota, 4
2. *White, Arthur (Tarzan), G, Alabama, 14
3. *Dennerlein, Gerry, T, St, Mary's (CA), 24
4. *Cuff, Ward, B, Marquette, 34
5. *Kobrosky, Mickey, B, Trinity (CT), 44
6. Farley, Jim, G, Virginia Military, 54
7. *Poole, Jim, E, Mississippi, 64
8. Meyers, Gene, G, Kentucky, 74
9. Scheyer, Dwight, T, Washington State, 84
10. *Gelatka, Chuck, E, Mississippi State, 94

PHILADELPHIA 1937
1. *Francis, Sam, B, Nebraska, 1
2. *Murray, Franny, B, Penn, 11
3. *Ellis, Drew, T, TCU, 21
4. Gilbert, Walt, B, Auburn, 31
5. Drobnitch, Alex, G, Denver, 41
6. Guckeyson, Bill, B, Maryland, 51
7. Barna, Herb, E, West Virginia, 61
8. Hennon, Nestor, E, Carnegie-Mellon, 71
9. Fanning, Paul, T, Kansas State, 81
10. Antil, Ray, E, Minnesota, 91

PITTSBURGH 1937
1. *Basrak, Mike, C, Duquesne, 5
2. Finley, Bob, B, SMU, 15
3. *Breeden, Bill, E, Oklahoma, 25
4. Hewes, Elmo (Bo), B, Oklahoma, 35
5. Frye, Jack, B, Missouri, 45
6. Roach, Walt, E, TCU, 55
7. *Haines, Byron, E, Washington, 65
8. Kordick, Marty, G, St. Mary's (CA), 75
9. Patanelli, Matt, E, Michigan, 85
10. Nevers, Stan, T, Kentucky, 95

LEAGUE 1937
1. *Drake, Johnny, B, Purdue, 10
2. *Alfonse, Jules, B, Michigan, 20
3. LaRue Bobby, B, Pittsburgh, 30
4. *Wiatrak, John, C, Washington, 40
5. Smith, Inwood, G, Ohio State, 50
6. Del Sasso, Chris, T, Indiana, 60
7. Schoen, Norm, B, Baldwin-Wallace, 70
8. *Schmarr, Herm, E, Catholic, 80
9. *Johnson, Ray, B, Denver, 90
10. Holt, Solon, G, TCU, 100

1938

Held December 12,1937

After each team made its first-round selection, only the five teams that finished lowest in the 1937 standings made second-round selections. The same process was repeated in round 4.

BROOKLYN 1938
1. *Brumbaugh, Boyd, B, Duquesne, 3
2. Kilgrow, Joe, B, Alabama, 13
3. *Kinard, Frank (Bruiser), T, Mississippi, 18
4. *Moore, Gene, C, Colorado, 28
5. *Merlin, Ed, G, Vanderbilt, 33
6. *Schwartz, Perry, E, California, 43
7. Monsky, Leroy, G, Alabama, 53
8. *Noyes, Len, T, Montana, 63
9. Stringham, John, B, BYU, 73
10. *Sivell, Jim, G, Auburn, 83
11. *Druze, Johnny, E, Fordham, 93
12. *Mark, Lou, C, North Carolina State, 103

CHICAGO BEARS 1938
1. Gray, Joe, B, Oregon State, 10
3. *Famiglietti, Gary, B, Boston U., 25
5. *Zarnas, Gust, G, Ohio State, 40
6. *Masterson, Bob, E, Miami (FL), 50
7. *Ramsey, Frank, G, Oregon State, 60
8. Sims, Fletcher, B, Georgia Tech, 70
9. Schwarz, Alex, T, San Francisco, 80
10. Wager, John, T, Butler, 90
11. Mickovsky, Ray, B, Case Western Reserve, 100
12. *Dreher, Ferd, E, Denver, 110

CHICAGO CARDINALS 1938
1. *Robbins, Jack, B, Arkansas, 5
2. *Popovich, Milt, B, Montana, 15
3. *Patrick, Frank, B, Pittsburgh, 20
4. Herwig, Bob, C, California, 30
5. *Babartsky, Al, T, Fordham, 35
6. Brunansky, Joe, T, Duke, 45
7. *Cherry, Ed, B, Hardin-Simmons, 55
8. Lavington, Leon, E, Colorado, 65
9. *Dougherty, Phil, C, Santa Clara, 75
10. *Sloan, Dwight, B, Arkansas, 85
11. Kenderdine, Bob, E, Indiana, 95
12. Mautner, Bob, C, Holy Cross, 105

CLEVELAND 1938
1. *Davis, Corbett, B, Indiana, 1
2. *Benton, Jim, E, Arkansas, 11
3. Routt, Joe, G, Texas A&M, 16
4. *Markov, Vic, T, Washington, 26
5. *Franco, Ed, G, Fordham, 31
6. *Hamilton, Ray, G, Arkansas, 41
7. *Chesbro, Marcel (Red), G, Colgate, 51
8. Mayberry, Walt (Tiger), B, Florida, 61
9. *Ream, Chuck, E, Ohio State, 71
10. *Maras, Joe, T, Duquesne, 81
11. *Hoptowit, Al, T, Washington State, 91
12. *Spadaccini, Vic, B, Minnesota, 101

DETROIT 1938
1. *Wojciechowicz, Alex, C, Fordham, 6
3. Smith, Pete, E, Oklahoma, 21
5. Bershak, Andy, E, North Carolina, 36
6. Schleckman, Karl, T, Utah, 46
7. *Szakash, Paul, B, Montana, 56
8. *Nardi, Dick, B, Ohio State, 66
9. Sirtosky, Jim, G, Indiana, 76
10. Wolf, Ralph, C, Ohio State, 86
11. Douglass, Clarence, B, Kansas, 96
12. Frank, Clint, B, Yale, 106

GREEN BAY 1938
1. *Isbell, Cecil, B, Purdue, 7
3. Schreyer, Marty, T, Purdue, 22
5. Sweeney, Chuck, E, Notre Dame, 37
6. *Uram, Andy, B, Minnesota, 47
7. *Kovatch, Johnny, E, Northwestern, 57
8. *Ragazzo, Phil, T, Case Western Reserve, 67
9. *Howell, Johnny, B, Nebraska, 77
10. Barnhart, Frank, G, Northern Colorado, 87
11. *Tinsley, Pete, G, Georgia, 97
12. *Falkenstein, Tony, B, St. Mary's (CA), 107

NEW YORK GIANTS 1938
1. *Karamatic, George, B, Gonzaga, 8
3. *Vanzo, Fred, B, Northwestern, 23
5. Konemann, Marion (Dutch), B, Georgia Tech, 38
6. *Souchak, Frank, E, Pittsburgh, 48
7. *Moan, Kelly, B, West Virginia, 58
8. *Doyle, Ted, T, Nebraska, 68
9. *Mellus, John, T, Villanova, 78
10. Grimstead, Bob, T, Washington State, 88
11. *Oldershaw, Doug, G, Cal-Santa Barbara, 98
12. Hackney, Elmore, B, Duke, 108

PHILADELPHIA 1938
1. *McDonald, Jim, B, Ohio State, 2
2. *Riffle, Dick, B, Albright, 12
3. *Bukant, Joe, B, Washington (StL), 17
4. Meek, John, B, California, 27
5. *Shirey, Fred, T, Nebraska, 32
6. *Ramsey, Herschel, E, Texas Tech, 42
7. Lannon, Bob, E, Iowa, 52
8. *Woltman, Clem, T, Purdue, 62
9. *Kolberg, Elmer, B, Oregon State, 72
10. *Kriel, Emmett, T, Baylor, 82
11. Hinkle, Carl, C, Vanderbilt, 92
12. Michelosen, Johnny, B, Pittsburgh, 102

PITTSBURGH 1938
1. *White, Byron (Whizzer), B, Colorado, 4
2. *Filchock, Frank, B, Indiana, 14
3. *Wolfe, Hugh, B, Texas, 19
4. *Matisi, Tony, T, Pittsburgh, 29
5. *Midler, Lou, T, Minnesota, 34
6. *Platukis, George, E, Duquesne, 44
7. King, Ray, E, Minnesota, 54
8. *Burnette, Tom, B, North Carolina, 64
9. *McDonough, Paul, E, Utah, 74
10. McCarty, Pat, C, Notre Dame, 84
11. *Krause, Bill, T, Baldwin-Wallace, 94
12. *Kuharich, Joe, G, Notre Dame, 104

WASHINGTON 1938
1. *Farkas, Andy, B, Detroit, 9
3. Chapman, Sam, B, California, 24
5. Price, Dave, C, Mississippi State, 39
6. Dohrmann, Elmer, E, Nebraska, 49
7. *Young, Roy, T, Texas A&M, 59
8. *Hartman, Bill, B, Georgia, 69
9. *Parks, Ed, C, Oklahoma, 79
10. Abbitt, Jack, B, Elon, 89
11. Johnston, Dick, E, Washington, 99
12. *Bartos, Henry, G, North Carolina, 109

1939

Held December 9, 1938

As in 1938, the second and fourth rounds were limited to the five teams with the poorest records.

BROOKLYN 1939
1. *MacLeod, Bob, B, Dartmouth, 5
2. *Manders, Clarence (Pug), B, Drake [from Pittsburgh], 11
   *Haak Bob, T, Indiana, 15
3. *Young, Waddy, E, Oklahoma, 20
4. Bottari, Vic, B, California, 30
5. Kinnison, Jack, C, Missouri, 35
6. *Janiak, Len, B, Ohio U., 45
   *Beinor, Ed, T, Notre Dame [from Chicago Bears], 46
7. *Schoenbaum, Alex, T, Ohio State, 55
8. Hill, Dan (Tiger), C, Duke, 65
9. Kline, Forrest, G, TCU, 75
10. Bradley, Kimble, B, Mississippi, 85
11. *Lenc, George, E, Augustana (IL), 95
12. *Heikkenen, Ralph, G, Michigan, 105
   *Kaplanoff, Carl, T, Ohio State [from Green Bay], 109
13. Gembis, George, B, Wayne State, 115
14. *Carnelly, Ray, B, Carnegie-Mellon, 125
15. Trunzo, Lou, G, Wake Forest, 135
16. Gross, Charley, G, Bradley, 145
17. *Siegel, Johnny, E, Columbia, 155
18. Morin, Paul, T, Iowa State, 165
19. Anderson, Ferrel, G, Kansas, 175
20. *Popp,Tony, E, Toledo, 185

CHICAGO BEARS 1939
1. *Luckman, Sid, QB, Columbia [from Pittsburgh], 2
   *Osmanski, Bill, B, Holy Cross, 6
3. Wysocki, John, E, Villanova, 21
5. Delaney, Joe, T, Holy Cross, 36
6. Choice to Brooklyn
7. *Heileman, Charlie, E, Iowa State, 56
8. Dannies, Bob, C, Pittsburgh, 66
9. *Bray, Ray, G, Western Michigan, 76
10. Wood, Walt, B, Tennessee, 86
11. Braga, Al, B, San Francisco, 96
12. Roise, Hal, B, Idaho, 106
13. Bock, Ed, G, Iowa State, 116
14. *Stolfa, Anton, B, Luther, 126
15. Voigts, Bob, T, Northwestern, 136
16. Armstrong, Ken, T, Tarkio, 146
17. Masters, Raphael, E, Newberry, 156
18. *Sherman, Solly, B, Chicago, 166
19. Simonich, Ed, B, Notre Dame, 176
20. Vogeler, George, C, Oklahoma State, 186
21. *Forte, Aldo, T, Montana, 191
22. Kircher, Everett, B, Iowa State, 196

CHICAGO CARDINALS 1939
1. *Aldrich, Ki, C, TCU, 1
2. *Goldberg, Marshall (Biggie), B, Pittsburgh, 12
3. Wolff, Alvord, T, Santa Clara, 16
4. Stebbins, Hal (Curly), B, Pittsburgh, 27
5. *Daddio, Bill, E, Pittsburgh, 31
6. *Faust, George, B, Minnesota, 42
7. Dwyer, Bill, B, New Mexico, 51
8. Hinkebein, Sherm, C, Kentucky, 62
9. Brown, Earl, E, Notre Dame, 71
10. *Crowder, Earl, QB, Oklahoma, 82
11. Wyatt, Bowden, E, Tennessee, 91
12. *Thomas, Jim, G, Oklahoma, 102
13. *Sabodos, Andy, G, Citadel, 111
14. Miatovich, Blase, T, San Francisco, 122
15. Clarke, Russ, G, Santa Clara, 131
16. Goins, Gus, E, Clemson, 142
17. *Elkins, Everett, B, Marshall, 151
18. *Huffman, Frank, E, Marshall, 162
19. *Kochel, Mike, G, Fordham, 171
20. Rice, Tom, T, San Francisco, 182

CLEVELAND 1939
1. *Hall, Parker, B, Mississippi, 3
2. *Smith, Gaylon, B, Southwestern, 13
3. Tarbox, Elmer, B, Texas Tech, 18
4. Garard, Wally, T, St. Mary's (CA), 28
5. Gallo, Eddie, T, LSU, 33
6. *McGarry, Bernie, T, Utah, 43
7. *Dowd, Gerry, C, St. Mary's (CA), 53
8. Brunner, Warren (Bronco), B, Tulane, 63
9. *Bostick, Lew, G, Alabama, 73
10. Petrick, Frank, E, Indiana, 83
11. Roth, Sid, G, Cornell, 93
12. *Adams, Chet, T, Ohio U., 103
13. *Hitt, Joel, E, Mississippi College, 113
14. Ryland, John, C, UCLA, 123
15. *Friend, Ben, T, LSU, 133
16. Reupke, Gordon, B, Iowa State, 143
17. *Perrie, Mike, B, St. Mary's (CA), 153
18. *Atty, Alex, G, West Virginia, 163
19. Lane, Bill, B, Bucknell, 173
20. Graham, Paul, B, Indiana, 183

DETROIT 1939
1. *Pingel, John, B, Michigan State, 7
3. *Weiss, Howie, B, Wisconsin, 22
5. *Maronic, Steve, T, North Carolina, 37
6. Wendlick, Joe, E, Oregon State, 47
7. *Tutty, Darrell, B, East Texas State, 57
8. Trzuskowski, Dick, T, Idaho, 67
9. *Callihan, Bill, B, Nebraska, 77
10. *George, Ray, T, USC, 87
11. *Calvelli, Tony, C, Stanford, 97
12. Coughlan, Jim, E, Santa Clara, 107
13. Hutchins, Prescott, G, Oregon State, 117
14. Means, Art, G, Washington., 127
15. Hodge, Gene, E, East Texas State, 137
16. *Lazetich, Bill, B, Montana, 147
17. *Neihaus, Ralph, T, Dayton, 157
18. Niemant, Dutch, B, New Mexico, 167
19. *Tonelli, Amerigo (Tony), G, USC, 177
20. McDonald, Jim, C, Illinois, 187
21. Waters, Merrill, E, BYU, 192
22. Howe, Al, T, Xavier, 197

GREEN BAY 1939
1. *Buhler, Larry, B, Minnesota, 9
3. *Brock, Charley, C, Nebraska, 24
5. Hovland, Lynn, G, Wisconsin, 39
6. *Craig, Larry, E, South Carolina, 49
7. *Twedell, Francis, T, Minnesota, 59
8. Kell, Paul, T, Notre Dame, 69
9. *Hall, John, B, TCU, 79
10. Gavre, Vince, B, Wisconsin, 89
11. Sprague, Charley, E, SMU, 99
12. Choice to Brooklyn
13. Elmer, Dan, C, Minnesota, 119
14. Badgett, Bill, T, Georgia, 129
15. *Greenfield, Tom, C, Arizona, 139
16. Bellin, Roy, B, Wisconsin, 149
17. Yerby, John, E, Oregon, 159
18. *Balasz, Frank, B, Iowa, 169
19. *Brennan, Jack, G, Michigan, 179
20. *Schultz, Charley, T, Minnesota , 189
21. Hofer, Willard, B, Notre Dame, 194
22. Gunther, Bill, B, Santa Clara, 199

NEW YORK GIANTS 1939
1. *Neilson, Walt, B, Arizona, 10
3. *Chickerneo, John (Chick), B, Pittsburgh, 25
5. Willis, Don, B, Clemson, 40
6. *Ginney, Jerry, G, Santa Clara, 50
7. Woodell, Lloyd, C, Arkansas, 60
8. Zagar, Pete, T, Stanford, 70
9. Mills, Bob, T, Nebraska, 80
10. *Roberts, Tom, T, DePaul, 90
11. Miller, Merl, B, Washington, 100
12. Schroeder, Bruno, E, Texas A&M, 110
13. Allis, Sam, B, Centenary, 120
14. Watson, George, B, North Carolina, 130
15. *Duggan, Gil, T, Oklahoma, 140
16. Panish, Ted, B, Bradley, 150
17. *Sanders, Jack, T, SMU, 160
18. Dolman, Will, E, California, 170
19. Paulman, Bill, B, Stanford, 180
20. Smith, Lyle, G, Tulane, 190
21. *Tonelli, Mario, B, Notre Dame, 195
22. Rhodes, Jack, G, Texas, 200

PHILADELPHIA 1939
1. *O'Brien, Davey, B, TCU, 4
2. *Newton, Charlie, B, Washington, 14
3. *Mihal, Joe, T, Purdue, 19
4. *Dewell, Bill, E, SMU, 29
5. *Costen, Fred, G, Texas A&M, 34
6. *Schuehle, Carl, B, Rice, 44
7. *Ippolito, Tony, B, Purdue, 54
8. *Somers, George, T, LaSalle, 64
9. *Britt, Rankin, E, Texas A&M, 74
10. McKeever, Bill, T, Cornell, 84
11. *Humphrey, Paul, C, Purdue, 94
12. Kraynick, Jack, B, North Carolina, 104
13. *White, Thomas (Allie), T, TCU, 114
14. Aleskus, Joe, T, Ohio State, 124
15. *Watkins, Forrest, B, West Texas State Teachers, 134
16. *Hall, Irv, B, Brown, 144
17. Riddell, Bob, E, South Dakota State, 154
18. *Gainor, Charley, E, North Dakota, 164
19. White, Morris, B, Tulsa, 174
20. Gormley, Dick, C, LSU, 184

PITTSBURGH 1939
1. Choice to Chicago Bears
2. Choice to Brooklyn
3. *Patterson, Bill, B, Baylor, 17
4. *McCullough, Hugh, B, Oklahoma, 26
5. *Wheeler, Ernie, B, No. Dakota State, 32
6. *Boyd, Sam, E, Baylor, 41
7. Palumbo, Eddie, B, Detroit, 52
8. Nelson, Ole, E, Michigan State, 61
9. *Petro, Steve, G, Pittsburgh, 72
10. *Lee, Jack, B, Carnegie-Mellon, 81
11. *Tomasetti, Lou, B, Bucknell, 92
12. Cochran, Denny, B, St. Louis U., 101
13. Hoffman, Fabian, E, Pittsburgh, 112
14. Clary, Ed, B, South Carolina, 121
15. *Tosi, John, C, Niagara, 132
16. Lezouski, Al, G, Pittsburgh, 141
17. Longhi, Ed, C, Notre Dame, 152
18. Shirk, Dave, E, Kansas, 161
19. Peters, Frank, E, Washington, 172
20. Sheldrake, Tom, E, Washington, 181

WASHINGTON 1939
1. Hale, I.B., T, TCU, 8
3. Holm, Charley, B, Alabama, 23
5. *Todd, Dick, B, Texas A&M, 38
6. Anderson, Dave, B, California, 48
7. Lumpkin, Quinton, C, Georgia, 58
8. *Russell, Torrance (Bo), T, Auburn, 68
9. *Moore, Wilbur, B, Minnesota, 78
10. *Johnston, Jimmy, B, Washington, 88
11. *German, Jim, B, Centre, 98
12. *O'Mara, Bob, B, Duke, 108
13. *Slivinski, Steve, G, Washington, 118
14. *Hoffman, Bob, B, USC, 128
15. Tipton, Eric, B, Duke, 138
16. *Farman, Dick, T, Washington State, 148
17. *Shugart, Clyde, T, Iowa State, 158
18. *Morgan, Boyd, B, USC, 168
19. Smith, Phil, T, St. Benedict's, 178
20. Coop, Paul, T, Centre, 188
21. *Kuber, Matt, G, Villanova, 193
22. Cruver, Al, B, Washington State, 198

1940

Held December 9, 1939

The format of limiting the second and fourth rounds to those five teams with the poorest records was continued for the third year.

BROOKLYN 1940
1. *McFadden, Banks, B, Clemson, 4
2. Kinnick, Nile, B, Iowa, 14
3. *Shetley, Rhoten, B, Furman, 19
4. *Bailey, Edgar (Bill), E, Duke, 29
5. *Merrill, Walt, T, Alabama, 34
6. Murray, Jack, C, Wisconsin, 44
7. *Coon, Ed (Ty), T, North Carolina State, 54
8. *Zadworney, Frank, B, Ohio State, 64
9. *Jocher, Art, T, Manhattan, 74
10. Turner, Jim, G, Holy Cross, 84
11. Cutlich, Nick, T, Northwestern, 94
12. Dougherty, George, B, Howard, 104
13. *Gussie, Mike, G, West Virginia, 114
14. Coffman, Len, B, Tennessee, 124
15. Conlin, Jim, C, NYU, 134
16. Donovan, Dennis, B, Oregon, 144
17. Funair, Frank, B, Bucknell, 154
18. Strosser, Walt, B, St. Vincent, 164
19. Hydock, Steve, E, Albright, 174
20. Howell, Milt, G, Auburn, 184

CHICAGO BEARS 1940
1. *Turner, Clyde (Bulldog), C, Hardin-Simmons, 7
3. *Kavanaugh, Ken, E, LSU, 22
5. *Kolman, Ed, T, Temple, 37
6. *Woudenberg, John, T, Denver, 47
7. *Akin, Leonard, G, Baylor, 57
8. *Fordham, Jim, B, Georgia, 67
9. *Pool, Hampton, E, Stanford, 77
10. Pace, Tom, B, Utah, 87
11. *Artoe, Lee, T, California, 97
12. McCubbin, Bill, E, Kentucky, 107
13. *Clark, Harry, B, West Virginia, 117
14. Crisci, Frank, T, Case Western Reserve, 127
15. Barnes, Sherm, E, Baylor, 137
16. Christianson, Al, B, Knox, 147
17. White, Wilbur, T, Bradley, 157
18. Schlosser, Ralph, C, Gonzaga, 167
19. Popov, John, B, Cincinnati, 177
20. *Bussey, Young, B, LSU, 187
21. *McLean, Ray (Scooter), B, St. Anselm's, 192
22. *Kichefski, Walt, E, Miami (FL), 197

CHICAGO CARDINALS 1940
1. *Cafego, George, B, Tennessee, 1
2. Stirnweiss, George (Snuffy), B, North Carolina, 11
3. *Madden, Lloyd, B, Colorado Mines, 16
4. *Shirk, Cecil (Jack), E, Oklahoma, 26
5. *Christiansen, Marty, B, Minnesota, 31
6. Reginato, Vic, E, Oregon, 41
7. *Chisick, Andy, C, Villanova, 51
8. *Kish, Ben, B, Pittsburgh, 61
9. Pappas, Luke, T, Utah, 71
10. Roche, Jack, B, Santa Clara, 81
11. *Davis, Bill, T, Texas Tech, 91
12. *Anderson, Stan, T, Stanford, 101
13. *Coppage, Alton, E, Oklahoma, 111
14. Hudson, Judson, B, Davis & Elkins, 121
15. Ziembra, Joe, E, St. Benedict's, 131
16. *Clark, Beryl, B, Oklahoma, 141
17. *Foster, Ralph, T, Oklahoma A&M, 151
18. Bryant, Lowell, B, Clemson, 161
19. Buckley, Russ, B, Gustavus-Adolphus, 171
20. *Pate, Rupert, T, Wake Forest, 181

CLEVELAND 1940
1. *Cordill, Olie, B, Rice, 5
2. *Condit, Merl, B, Carnegie-Mellon, 15
3. *Haman, Johnny, C, Northwestern, 20
4. *Wood, Bob, T, Alabama, 30
5. Myers, Park, T, Texas, 35
6. *Heineman, Ken, B, Texas-El Paso, 45
7. *Nowaskey, Bob, E, Geo. Washington, 55
8. Anahu, Bob, E, Santa Clara, 65
9. *Thorpe, Wilfrid, G, Arkansas, 75
10. Smith, Herb, B, St. Mary's (CA), 85
11. *Clay, Boyd, T, Tennessee, 95
12. *Goolsby, Jim, C, Mississippi State, 105
13. *Gregory, Jack, T, Tennessee-Chattanooga, 115
14. Bogden, Pete, E, Utah, 125
15. *Goodnight, Owen, B, Hardin-Simmons, 135
16. Kohler, Morris, B, Oregon State, 145
17. *Nix, Jack, B, Mississippi State, 155
18. *Stevenson, Ralph, G, Oklahoma, 165
19. *Magnani, Dante, B, St. Mary's (CA), 175
20. *Lindon, Luke, T, Kentucky, 185

DETROIT 1940
1. Nave, Doyle, B, USC, 6
3. *Fisk, Bill, E, USC, 21
5. *Smith, Harry, G, USC, 36
6. Rike, Jim, C, Tennessee, 46
7. *Winslow, Bob, E, USC, 56
8. Tranavitch, Bill, B, Rutgers, 66
9. Haas, Bob, T, Missouri, 76
10. DeWitte, Leon, B, Purdue, 86
11. Prasse, Erwin, E, Iowa, 96
12. Binder, Ken, B, Carroll, 106
13. Bowers, Justin, T, Oklahoma, 116
14. *Morlock, Jack, B, Marshall, 126
15. *Rouse, Stillman, E, Missouri, 136
16. Padley, Jack, B, Dayton, 146
17. *Hackenbruck, John, T, Oregon State, 156
18. *Ribar, Frank, G, Duke, 166
19. McCarthy, Herb, B, Denver, 176
20. Parten, Dub, T, Centenary, 186
21. Morgan, Malvern, C, Auburn, 191
22. Orf, Bob, E, Missouri, 196

GREEN BAY 1940
1. *Van Every, Hal, B, Minnesota, 9
3. *Brock, Lou, B, Purdue, 24
5. Sarkkinen, Esco, E, Ohio State, 39
6. *Cassiano, Dick, B, Pittsburgh, 49
7. White, Millard, T, Tulane, 59
8. *Seeman, George, E, Nebraska, 69
9. Manley, J.R., G, Oklahoma, 79
10. Brown, Jack, B, Purdue, 89
11. Guritz, Don, G, Northwestern, 99
12. Gaspar, Phil, T, USC, 109
13. Schindler, Ambrose, B, USC, 119
14. Kerr, Bill, E, Notre Dame, 129
15. Brewer, Mel, G, Illinois, 139
16. Andrus, Ray, B, Vanderbilt, 149
17. Kodros, Archie, C, Michigan, 159
18. *Gillette, Jim, B, Virginia, 169
19. *Matuza, Al, C, Georgetown, 179
20. Reeder, Jim, T, Illinois, 189
21. Eichler, Vince, B, Cornell, 194
22. Luebcke, Henry, T, Iowa, 199

NEW YORK GIANTS 1940
1. *Lansdell, Grenny, B, USC, 10
3. *McLaughry, John, B, Brown, 25
5. *Tomaselli, Carl, E, Scranton, 40
6. Smith, Lou, B, California, 50
7. *Williams, Rex, C, Texas Tech, 60
8. *Pederson, Win, T, Minnesota, 70
9. *Principe, Dom, B, Fordham, 80
10. Clark, Earl, B, TCU, 90
11. McKibben, John, E, Tulsa, 100
12. *McGee, Ed, G, Temple, 110
13. Payne, Joe, G, Clemson, 120
14. Smith, Bob, B, Oregon, 130
15. Turner, Othel, T, Tulsa, 140
16. Swan, Ned, C, Drake, 150
17. *Rogalia, John, B, Scranton, 160

18. *Edwards, Bennett (Monk), T, Baylor, 170
19. Walden, Cecil, G, Oregon, 180
20. Sullivan, John, E, San Francisco, 190
21. Bynum, Weenie, B, Centenary, 195
22. Claxton, Myron, T, Whittier, 200

PHILADELPHIA 1940
1. *McAfee, George, B, Duke, 2
2. *Schiechl, Johnny, C, Santa Clara, 13
3. Favor, Dick, B, Oklahoma, 17
4. *Schultz, Eberle, G, Oregon State, 28
5. *Emmons, Frank, B, Oregon, 32
6. Singer, Saul, T, Arkansas, 43
7. Pegg, Hal (Mike), C, Bucknell, 52
8. *Looney, Don, E, TCU, 63
9. Jones, Don, B, Washington, 72
10. *Maher, Frank, B, Toledo, 83
11. *Hackney, Elmer, B, Kansas State, 92
12. Hoerner, Durward, E, TCU, 103
13. Hennis, Ted, B, Purdue, 112
14. Bunsen, Bill, B, Kansas, 123
15. Crumbaker, Don, E, Kansas State, 132
16. Green, J.R., T, Rice, 143
17. Molnar, Jim, B, Bradley, 152
18. Schwartzer, Ernie, G, Boston College, 163
19. Schneller, Bill, B, Mississippi, 172
20. Debord, Bill, T, Kansas State, 183

PITTSBURGH 1940
1. *Eakin, Kay, B, Arkansas, 3
2. *Wenzel, Ralph, E, Tulane, 12
3. *Kiick, George, B, Bucknell, 18
4. *Ivy, Frank (Pop), E, Oklahoma, 27
5. *Goff, Clark, T, Florida, 33
6. *Bykowski, Frank, G, Purdue, 42
7. Cignetti, Pete, B, Boston College, 53
8. *Nery, Carl, G, Duquesne, 62
9. Boisseau, Dick, T, Washington & Lee, 73
10. Shu, Paul, B, VMI, 82
11. Cox, Cary, C, Alabama, 93
12. *Pirro, Rocco, B, Catholic U., 102
13. *Noppenberg, John, B, Miami (FL), 113
14. Stublar, Nick, T, Santa Clara, 122
15. McCarthy, Ray, B, Santa Clara, 133
16. Gajecki, Leon, C, Penn State, 142
17. Sullivan, Mike, E, North Carolina State, 153
18. Daly, Seaton, T, Gonzaga. 162
19. Harvey, Thad, T, Notre Dame, 173
20. Katzenstein, Marvin, T, Colorado Mines, 182

WASHINGTON 1940
1. Boell, Ed, B, NYU, 8
3. Banker, Burt (Buddy), B, Tulane, 23
5. Kirchem, Bill, T, Tulane, 38
6. Boyd, Joe, T, Texas A&M, 48
7. *Zimmerman, Roy, B, San Jose State, 58
8. Orf, Roland (Bud), E, Missouri, 68
9. *Hoffman, Bob, B, USC, 78
10. *Seymour, Bob, B, Oklahoma, 88
11. Stoecker, Howard, T, USC, 98
12. Johnson, Allen, G, Duke, 108
13. *Bartholomew, Sam, B, Tennessee, 118
14. Lain, Ernie, B, Rice, 128
15. *Sanford, Hayward, E, Alabama, 138
16. *Perdue, Willard (Bolo), E, Duke, 148
17. *Andrako, Steve, C, Ohio State, 158
18. Graybeal, Jay, B, Oregon, 168
19. Slagle, Charley, B, North Carolina, 178
20. Murphy, F.W. (Buck), B, Georgia Tech, 188
21. Wetzel, Mel, T, Missouri, 193
22. Sitko, Steve, B, Notre Dame, 198

1941

Held December 10, 1940

Each team was permitted to draft 20 players, including Pittsburgh and Philadelphia which had traded two choices each to the Chicago Bears. Only the five teams that had finished lowest in 1940 were permitted to draft in rounds two and four.

BROOKLYN 1941
1. *McAdams, Dean, B, Washington, 8
3. *Stasica, Leo, B, Colorado, 24
5. *Frick, Ray, C, Penn, 38
6. *Rucinski, Eddie, E, Indiana, 49
7. Newman, Hal, E, Alabama, 58
8. Jackson, Glenn, C, Texas, 69
9. Toczylowski, Henry, B, Boston College, 78
10. Langhurst, Jim, B, Ohio State, 89
11. *Weiner, Bernie, T, Kansas State, 98
12. Johnson, Harvey, B, Mississippi State, 109
13. *Kinard, George, G, Mississippi, 118
14. *Cheatham, Lloyd, B, Auburn, 129
15. *Jurich, Mike, T, Denver, 138
16. *Alfson, Warren, G, Nebraska, 149
17. McGowen, Dick, B, Auburn, 158
18. McCurry, Lonnie, G, Texas Tech, 169
19. *Parker, Dave, E, Hardin-Simmons, 178
20. *Ungerer, Joe, T, Fordham, 189
21. *Koshlap, Jules, B, Georgetown (DC), 193
22. *Whitlow, Ken, C, Rice, 199

CHICAGO BEARS 1941
1. *Tom Harmon, B, Michigan [from Philadelphia], 1
   *Norm Standlee, B, Stanford [from Pittsburgh], 3
   Scott, Don, B, Ohio State, 9
3. *Gallarneau, Hugh, B, Stanford, 23
5. *O'Rourke, Charley, B, Boston College, 39
6. O'Boyle, Tom, G, Tulane, 48
7. *Federovich, John, T, Davis & Elkins, 59
8. *Hartman, Fred, T, Rice [from Philadelphia], 61
   Rankin, Dave, E, Purdue [from Pittsburgh], 62
   *Matuza, Al, C, Georgetown (DC), 68
9. *Lahar, Hal, G, Oklahoma, 79
10. Lalanne, Jim (Sweet), B, North Carolina, 88
11. Hardin, Jim, E, Kentucky, 99
12. *Morrow, Bob, B, Illinois Wesleyan, 108
13. Johnson, Jim, B, Santa Clara, 119
14. *Martin, Johnny, B, Oklahoma, 128
15. Mulkey, Jack, E, Fresno State, 139
16. Osterman, Bob, C, Notre Dame, 148
17. Glenn, Bill, B, East Illinois Teachers, 159
18. Hahnenstein, Ollie, B, Northwestern, 168
19. Alex Winterson, T, Duke, 179 - Disallowed
20. Jack Odle, QB, TCU, 188 - Disallowed
21. Hunter Corbern, G, Mississippi State, 194 - Disallowed
22. Dave Buck, T, Colgate, 198 - Disallowed (At the completion of the draft, the Bears had selected 24 players instead of the mandated 20. Chicago's last four selections were disallowed.)

CHICAGO CARDINALS 1941
1. *Kimbrough, John, B, Texas A&M, 2
2. *Christman, Paul, QB, Missouri, 13
3. Foxx, Bob, B, Tennessee, 17
4. *Clement, John, B, SMU, 28
5. *Apolskis, Ray, C, Marquette, 32
6. *Robnett, Marshall, G, Texas A&M, 43
7. *Kuzman, John, T, Fordham, 52
8. *Kracum, George, B, Pitt, 63
9. Vargo, Tom, E, Penn State, 72
10. *Mallouf, Ray, B, SMU, 83
11. *Sommers, Jack, C, UCLA, 92
12. *Armstrong, Charley, B, Mississippi College, 103
13. Pitts, Wayne, B, Arizona State, 112
14. *Lokanc, Joe, G, Northwestern, 123
15. White, Claude, C, Ohio State, 132
16. Kimball, Gates, T, North Carolina, 143
17. Schultz, Ray, G, Missouri, 152
18. Harris, Fred, T, SMU, 163
19. Aussieker, Mel, B, St. Louis, 172
20. Platt, Frank, T, Penn State, 183

CLEVELAND 1941
1. *Mucha, Rudy, C, Washington, 4
2. *Shires, Marshall (Abe), T, Tennessee, 14
3. *MacDowell, Jay, E, Washington, 19
4. Luther, Walt (Butch), B, Nebraska, 29
5. Haliska, Chet, B, Oregon, 34
6. Kisselburgh, Jim, B, Oregon State, 44
7. *Prochaska, Ray, E, Nebraska, 54
8. *Gallovich, Tony, B, Wake Forest, 64
9. *Simington, Milt, G, Arkansas, 74
10. Pendergast, John, C, Wake Forest, 84
11. Drahos, Nick, T, Cornell, 94
12. Punches, Harold, G, Colorado, 104
13. McMurray, Bill, E, Murray State, 114
14. Elmore, Bill, B, California, 124
15. Desmore, Warren, C, Toledo, 134
16. *Wilson, Gordon, G, Texas-El Paso, 144
17. *Hershey, Kirk, E, Cornell, 154
18. Lee, Cobbie, B, Murray State, 164
19. Hursh, Harold, B, Indiana, 174
20. Barnes, Leo, T, LSU, 184

DETROIT 1941
1. *Thomason, Jim, B, Texas A&M, 5
2. Goodreault, Gene, E, Boston College, 15
3. *Hopp, Harry, B, Nebraska, 20
4. *Lio, Augie, G, Georgetown (DC), 30
5. *Nelson, Bob, C, Baylor, 35
6. *Tripson, John, T, Mississippi State, 45
7. *Jett, John, E, Wake Forest, 55
8. *Manzo, Joe, T, Boston College, 65
9. Davis, Jasper, B, Duke, 75
10. *Pavelec, Ted, T, Detroit, 85
11. *Piepul, Milt, B, Notre Dame, 95
12. *Jefferson, Billy, B, Mississippi State, 105
13. *Britt, Maurice, E, Arkansas, 115
14. *Schibanoff, Alex, T, Franklin & Marshall, 125
15. *Scott, Perry, E, Muhlenberg, 135
16. Sarres, George, C, Providence, 145
17. Gage, Fred, B, Wisconsin, 155
18. Ishmael, Charlie, B, Kentucky, 165
19. Isberg, Len, B, Oregon, 175
20. Friedlander, Paul, B, Carnegie-Mellon, 185

GREEN BAY 1941
1. *Paskvan, George, B, Wisconsin, 7
3. *Paffrath, Bob, B, Minnesota, 21
5. *Frutig, Ed, E, Michigan, 37
6. *Rohrig, Herman, B, Nebraska, 46
7. Telesmanic, Bill, E, San Francisco, 57
8. *Kuusisto, Bill, G, Minnesota, 66
9. *Canadeo, Tony, B, Gonzaga, 77
10. Byelene, Mike, B, Purdue, 86
11. Heimenz, Paul, C, Northwestern, 97
12. Enich, Mike, T, Iowa, 106
13. Heffernan, Ed, B, St. Mary's (CA), 117
14. *Lyman, Del, T, UCLA, 126
15. Frieberger, Johnny, E, Arkansas, 137
16. *Pannell, Ernie, T, Texas A&M, 146
17. Saggau, Bob, B, Notre Dame, 157
18. Pukema, Heige, G, Minnesota, 166
19. Hayes, Bob, E, Toledo, 177
20. *Strasbaugh, Jim, B, Ohio State, 186
21. Bailey, Joe, C, Kentucky, 192
22. Malinowski, Bruno, B, Holy Cross, 196

NEW YORK GIANTS 1941
1. *Franck, George, B, Minnesota, 6
3. *Reagan, Frankie, B, Penn, 22
5. *Eshmont, Len, B, Fordham, 36
6. *DeFilippo, Lou, C, Fordham, 47
7. *Vosberg, Don, E, Marquette, 56
8. *Younce, Len, G, Oregon State, 67
9. *Sohn, Ben, G, USC, 76
10. Matuszczak, Walt, B, Cornell, 87
11. Peoples, Bobby, B, USC, 96
12. *Marefos, Andy, B, St. Mary's (CA), 107
13. Brovarney, Cass, G, Detroit, 116
14. Moore, Arnie, E, Mississippi State, 127
15. Black, Johnny, B, Arizona, 136
16. Lucas, Wilson, E, Baylor, 147
17. Anderson, Jack, T, Baylor, 156
18. Allerdice, Dave, B, Princeton, 167
19. Peters, Chuck, B, Penn State, 176
20. Stone, Earl, C, Washington State, 187
21. Dungan, Jack, T, Arizona, 191
22. Fisher, Ted, E, Carnegie-Mellon, 197

PHILADELPHIA 1941
1. Choice to Chicago Bears
2. *Jones, Art, B, Richmond, 11
3. *Pugh, Marion, B, Texas A&M, 16
4. Ghesquiere, Al, B, Detroit, 26
5. *Kahler, Royal, T, Nebraska, 31
6. *Hickey, Howard (Red), E, Arkansas, 41
7. Battista, Julius, (Mush), G, Florida, 51
8. Choice to Chicago Bears
9. Rogers, P.K., B, East Texas State, 71
10. *Williams, Don, T, Texas, 81
11. Stenstrom, Marshall, B, Oregon, 91
12. *Patrick, John, B, Penn State, 101
13. *Hoague, Joe, B, Colgate, 111
14. *Dodson, Les, B, Mississippi, 121
15. Lukachick, Alex, E, Boston College, 131
16. Conatser, Bill, B, Texas A&M, 141
17. Yauckoes, John, T, Boston College, 151
18. McFadden, Joe, B, Georgetown (DC), 161
19. *Shonk, John, E, West Virginia, 171
20. Russell, L.B., B, Hardin-Simmons, 181
21. Henke, Charley, G, Texas A&M, 201
22. Fernella, Mike, T, Akron, 203

PITTSBURGH 1941
1. Choice to Chicago Bears
2. *Gladchuck, Chet, C, Boston College, 12
3. *Knolla, Johnny, B, Creighton, 18
4. Ringgold, Jim, B, Wake Forest, 27
5. *Sears, Vic, T, Oregon State, 33
6. *Suffridge, Bob, G, Tennessee, 42
7. Roberts, Jim, C, Marshall, 53
8. Choice to Chicago Bears
9. *Elrod, Ervin (Buddy), E, Mississippi State, 73
10. *Fritz, Ralph, G, Michigan, 82
11. *Uremovich, Emil, T, Indiana, 93
12. Severin, Paul, E, North Carolina, 102
13. *Cotton, Russ, B, Texas-El Paso, 113
14. Goree, J.W., G, LSU, 122
15. *Eibner, John, T, Kentucky, 133
16. *McAfee, Wes, B, Duke, 142
17. *Fox, Terry, B, Miami (FL), 153
18. Cornwall, Bill, T, Furman, 162
19. Kerr, George, G, Boston College, 173
20. *Bjorcklund, Bob, E, Minnesota, 182
21. *Castiglia, Jim, B, Georgetown (DC), 202
22. *Landsberg, Mort, B, Cornell, 204

WASHINGTON 1941
1. Evashevski, Forest, B, Michigan, 10
3. *Davis, Fred, T, Alabama, 25
5. *Stuart, Jim, T, Oregon, 40
6. *Cifers, Ed, E, Tennessee, 50
7. *Krueger, Al, E, USC, 60
8. Wilder, Henry, B, Iowa State, 70
9. Grimmett, Bill, E, Tulsa, 80
10. Hickerson, Ed, G, Alabama, 90
11. *Aguirre, Joe, E, St. Mary's (CA), 100
12. *Banta, Herbert (Jack), B, USC, 110
13. Conn, Roy, T, Arizona, 120
14. Tornell, Deward, B, San Jose State, 130
15. Buckingham, Morris, C, San Jose State, 140
16. *Dow, Ken, B, Oregon State, 150
17. *McRae, Stan, E, Michigan State, 160
18. *Osmanski, Joe, B, Holy Cross, 170
19. Fullilove, Earl, T, Georgetown (DC), 180
20. Hiestand, Ed, E, Vanderbilt, 190
21. Riggs, Tom, T, Illinois, 195
22. *Gentry, Lee, B, Tulsa, 200

1942

Held December 22, 1941

Each team drafted 20 players but only the five teams with the poorest records in 1941 drafted in the second and fourth rounds.

BROOKLYN 1942
1. *Robertson, Bob, B, USC, 7
3. *Mechan, Curt, B, Oregon, 22
5. Francis, Vike, B, Nebraska, 37
6. *Stanton, Henry, E, Arizona, 47
7. Goldsmith, Wayne, B, Emporia State, 57
8. Flanagan, Preston, E, Texas, 67
9. *Gifford, Bob, B, Denver, 77
10. Petro, Joe, G, Muhlenberg, 87
11. Donlan, Fraser (Pat), T, Manhattan, 97
12. *Thibaut, Jim, B, Tulane, 107
13. *Deremer, Art, C, Niagara, 117
14. Gervelis, Stan, E, Pittsburgh, 127
15. Davis, Gene, B, Penn, 137
16. Masloski, Ed, B, Scranton, 147
17. Pitts, R.C., E, Arkansas, 157
18. Miller, Ralph, B, Kansas, 167
19. Elliott, Wilson, T, Tenn.-Chattanooga, 177
20. Polantonio, Bill, G, Elon, 187
21. Hayes, Bert, B, Wichita, 192
22. *Fedora, Walt (Fuzzy), B, Geo. Washington, 197

CHICAGO BEARS 1942
1. *Albert, Frankie, B, Stanford, 10
3. Boratyn, Joe, B, Holy Cross, 25
5. *Ruby, Martin, T, Texas A&M, 40
6. Burrus, H.C., E, Hardin-Simmons, 50
7. *Jeffries, Bob, G, Missouri, 60
8. *Maznicki, Frank, B, Boston College, 70
9. *Petty, John, B, Purdue, 80
10. *Mullins, Noah (Moon), B, Kentucky, 90
11. *Geyer, Bill, B, Colgate, 100
12. *Daniell, Jim, T, Ohio State, 110
13. *Hunt, Jack, B, Marshall, 120
14. *Gude, Henry (Bob), C, Vanderbilt, 130
15. Krutulis, Joe, E, Miami (FL), 140
16. Abel, George, G, Nebraska, 150
17. Edmiston, Don, T, Tennessee, 160
18. Rast, Holt, E, Alabama, 170
19. *Jones, Edgar (Special Delivery), B, Pittsburgh, 180
20. Tessendorf, Bill, T, Gonzaga, 190
21. *Kissell, Adolph, B, Boston College, 195
22. *Clarkson, Stu, C, Texas A&I, 200

CHICAGO CARDINALS 1942
1. *Lach, Steve, B, Duke, 4
2. *Cheatham, Lloyd, B, Auburn, 14
3. *Schwenk, Wilson (Bud), B, Washington (StL), 19
4. *Banonis, Vince, C, Detroit, 29
5. *Reinhard, Bob, T, California, 34
6. Daniel, Chal, G, Texas, 44
7. *Thornton, Rupe, G, Santa Clara, 54
8. Renzel, Doug, B, Marquette, 64
9. *Wetterlund, Chet, B, Illinois Wesleyan, 74
10. Ringer, Jud, E, Minnesota, 84
11. Fitzharris, Jim, E, St. Thomas (MN), 94
12. Brye, Dick, T, Marquette, 104
13. Givler, Charley, G, Wake Forest, 114
14. Swink, Hugh, T, Oklahoma State, 124
15. Harshman, Marv, B, Pacific Lutheran, 134
16. Arabian, George, B, St. Mary's (CA), 144
17. Crain, Jackie, B, Texas, 154
18. Suntheimer, Carl, C, North Carolina, 164
19. *Nelson, Jimmy, B, Alabama, 174
20. Wallach, Norvell, T, Missouri, 184

CLEVELAND 1942
1. *Wilson, Jack, B, Baylor, 2
2. *Jacobs, (Indian) Jack B, Oklahoma, 12
3. *Eason, Roger, T, Oklahoma, 17
4. *Levy, Len, G, Minnesota, 27
5. Matthews, Orville, B, Oklahoma, 32
6. Sweeney, Mike, E, Texas, 42
7. Rossi, Italo, T, Purdue, 52
8. *Brumley, Bob, B, Rice, 62
9. *Ulrich, Hubert, E, Kansas, 72
10. *deLauer, Bob, T, USC, 82
11. *Hightower, Ben, E, Sam Houston State, 92
12. *Zirinsky, Walt, B, Lafayette, 102
13. Bradfield, Ray, E, Santa Clara, 112
14. Greene, Tom, T, Georgia, 122
15. Peel, Ike, B, Tennessee, 132
16. Henicle, Glenn, G, Tulsa, 142
17. Clawson, Don, B, Northwestern, 152
18. Graf, Jack, B, Ohio State, 162
19. Regner, Bill, E, Oregon, 172
20. Conley, Gene, T, Washington, 182

DETROIT 1942
1. *Westfall, Bob, B, Michigan, 5
2. *Bauman, Alf, T, Northwestern, 15
3. Dethman, Bob, B, Oregon State, 20
4. *Sanzotta, Dom, B, Case Western Reserve, 30
5. Blalock, Joe, E, Clemson, 35
6. *Evans, Murray, B, Hardin-Simmons, 45
7. *Colella, Tommy, B, Canisius, 55
8. Franceski, Joe, T, Scranton, 65
9. *Banjavic, Emil, B, Arizona, 75
10. Diehl, Bill, C, Iowa, 85
11. *Polansky, John, B, Wake Forest, 95
12. *Stringfellow, Joe, E, Southern Mississippi, 105
13. *Arena, Tony, C, Michigan State, 115
14. Heinberg, Wolf, T, Cal-Santa Barbara, 125
15. *Speedie, Mac, E, Utah, 135
16. Bynum, Firman, T, Arkansas, 145
17. Fisher, Dick, B, Ohio State, 155
18. *Speth, George, T, Murray State, 165
19. Heaton, Blair, E, Susquehanna, 175
20. Collins, Ben, B, West Texas State, 185

GREEN BAY 1942
1. *Odson, Urban, T, Minnesota, 9
3. *Frankowski, Ray, G, Washington, 24
5. Green, Bill, B, Iowa, 39
6. *Krivonak, Joe, G, South Carolina, 49
7. *Johnston, Preston, B, SMU, 59
8. Rogers, Joe, E, Michigan, 69
9. Langdale, Noah, T, Alabama, 79
10. Flick, Gene, C, Minnesota, 89
11. *Farris, Tom, B, Wisconsin, 99
12. Richardson, Jimmy, B, Marquette, 109
13. *Smith, Bruce, B, Minnesota, 119
14. Applegate, Bill, G, South Carolina, 129
15. Trimble, Jim, T, Indiana, 139
16. Kinkade, Tom, B, Ohio State, 149

17. Preston, Fred, E, Nebraska, 159
18. *Ingalls, Bob, C, Michigan, 169
19. *Benson, George, B, Northwestern, 179
20. Young, Horace (Deacon), B, SMU, 189
21. Woronicz, Henry, E, Boston College, 194
22. Adams, Woody, T, TCU, 199

NEW YORK GIANTS 1942
1. *Hapes, Merle, B, Mississippi, 8
3. *Sweiger, Bob, B, Minnesota, 23
5. *Blozis, Al, T, Georgetown (DC), 38
6. Glass, Bob, B, Tulane, 48
7. Prothro, Tommy, B, Duke, 58
8. *Kearns, Tom, T, Miami (FL), 68
9. Merker, Bob, E, Millikin, 78
10. Kopcik, Mike, E, Georgetown (DC), 88
11. Solic, John, C, St. Francis (NY), 98
12. Krouse, Len, B, Penn State, 108
13. Barnett, Bob, C, Duke, 118
14. *Layden, Pete, B, Texas, 128
15. *Jungmichel, Buddy, G, Texas, 138
16. Doggett, Keith, T, Wichita State, 148
17. Miller, Verne, T, Harvard, 158
18. *Hovious, John (Junie), B, Mississippi, 168
19. Price, Owen, B, Texas-El Paso, 178
20. Kretowicz, Adam, E, Holy Cross, 188
21. *Blumenstock, Jim (Blackie), B, Fordham, 193
22. Hull, Milt, T, Florida, 198

PHILADELPHIA 1942
1. *Kmetovic, Pete, B, Stanford, 3
2. *Lindskog, Vic, C, Stanford, 13
3. *Williams, Ted, B, Boston College, 18
4. *Paschka, Gordon, G, Minnesota, 28
5. *Blandin, Ernie, T, Tulane, 33
6. Younglove, Earl, E, Washington, 43
7. Sewell, Billy, B, Washington State , 53
8. *Halverson, Bill, G, Oregon State, 63
9. *Graves, Ray, C, Tennessee, 73
10. *Stackpool, Jack, B, Washington, 83
11. *Doss, Noble, B, Texas, 93
12. *Meyer, Fred, E, Stanford, 103
13. Brenton, Bob, T, Missouri, 113
14. *Wyhonic, John, G, Alabama, 123
15. Griffin, O'Dell, G, Baylor, 133
16. Smaltz, Bill, B, Penn State, 143
17. Meiners, Arnie, E, Stanford, 153
18. Braun, Bill, T, Santa Clara, 163
19. Dvoracek, Charley, B, Texas Tech, 173
20. Tommervik, Marv, B, Pacific Lutheran, 183

PITTSBURGH 1942
1. *Dudley, (Bullet) Bill, B, Virginia, 1
2. *Martin, Vern, B, Texas, 11
3. *Casanega, Ken, B, Santa Clara, 16
4. *Kutner, Mal, E, Texas, 26
5. *Sandig, Curt, B, St. Mary's (TX), 31
6. Greene, Charley, T, Tulsa, 41
7. *Butler, Johnny, B, Tennessee, 51
8. Spendlove, Floyd, T, Utah, 61
9. Chase, Rayburn, B, Missouri, 71
10. *Steele, Ernie, B, Washington, 81
11. Wood, Thornley, B, Columbia, 91
12. Roach, Bill, E, TCU, 101
13. Holt, Wayne, G, Tulsa, 111
14. *Mosher, Clure, C, Louisville, 121
15. *Law, Hubbard, B, Sam Houston State, 131
16. *Tomasic, Andy, B, Temple, 141
17. *Chamberlain, Garth, T, BYU, 151
18. *Rokisky, John, E, Duquesne, 161
19. Jenkins, Ray (Earthquake), B, Colorado, 171
20. Kapriva, Frank, G, Wake Forest, 181

WASHINGTON 1942
1. *Sanders, Orban (Spec), B, Texas, 6
3. *Deal, Rufus, B, Auburn, 21
5. *Zeno, Joe, G, Holy Cross, 36
6. *McCollum, Harley, T, Tulane, 46
7. Fitch, Bob, E, Minnesota, 56
8. Peters, George, B, Oregon State, 66
9. Swiger, Frank, B, Duke, 76
10. *Goodyear, Johnny, B, Marquette, 86
11. *DeMao, Al, C, Duquesne, 96
12. Ahwesh, Phil, B, Duquesne, 106
13. *Kovatch, John, E, Notre Dame, 116
14. *deCorrevant, Bill, B, Northwestern, 126
15. *Whited, Marvin, B, Oklahoma, 136
16. Chipman, Dean (Dee), B, BYU, 146
17. *Watts, George, T, Appalachian State, 156
18. Stewart, Gene, B, Willamette, 166
19. *Timmons, Charlie, B, Clemson, 176
20. *Croft, Milburn (Tiny), T, Ripon, 186
21. *Juzwik, Steve, B, Notre Dame, 191
22. *Couppee, Al, B, Iowa, 196

1943

Held April 8, 1943

Although the Philadelphia and Pittsburgh franchises merged for the 1943 season, at the time of the draft they were still independent franchises, and each selected separately. Neither gave up its rights to any players while the merger was in effect. The Cleveland franchise participated in the draft, but then was granted permission to suspend operations for one year. It retained the rights to the players it had selected.

Each team drafted 30 players but only the five teams with the poorest records in 1942 were allowed to draft in the second and fourth rounds. The five teams with the best records then drafted alone in the final rounds.

BROOKLYN 1943
1. *Governali, Paul, B, Columbia, 4
2. *Black, John (Blondy), B, Mississippi State, 13
3. Ceithaml, George, B, Michigan, 19
4. *Domnanovich, Joe, C, Alabama, 28
5. *Comer, Marty, E, Tulane, 34
6. *Johnson, Harvey (Stud), B, William & Mary, 43
7. *Matisi, John, T, Duquesne, 54
8. Ferguson, John, E, California, 63
9. Rason, Ray G, SMU, 74
10. *Schleich, Vic, T, Nebraska, 83
11. *Sabasteanski, Joe, C, Fordham, 94
12. Thomas, Lou, B, Tulane, 103
13. Stiff, Bert, B, Penn, 114
14. *Fekete, John, B, Ohio U., 123
15. *Rhea, Floyd, G, Oregon, 134
16. Burkett, Bill, E, Iowa, 143
17. Onofrio, Al, B, Arizona State, 154
18. Schoonover, Ken, T, Penn State, 163
19. Barnette, Quentin, B, West Virginia, 174
20. Bledsoe, Bill, E, USC, 183
21. Coutchie, Bob, E, Arizona, 194
22. *Reece, Don (Bull), B, Missouri, 203
23. Gibson, W.J., E, North Carolina State, 214
24. Dent, Lou (Dude), B, Colorado State, 223
25. *Lee, Gene, C, Florida, 234
26. Hardy, Harvey, G, Georgia Tech, 243
27. Green, Bob, T, Arkansas, 254
28. Poleshuk, Steve, G, Colgate, 263
29. Sabo, Al, B, Alabama, 274
30. Allshouse, George, C, Pittsburgh, 283

CHICAGO BEARS 1943
1. *Steuber, Bob, B, Missouri, 9
3. *Evans, Fred (Dippy), B, Notre Dame, 24
5. Stamm, Ed, T, Stanford, 39
6. *Palmer, Derrell, T, TCU, 49
7. *Vucinich, Milt, C, Stanford, 59
8. *Beals, Alyn, E, Santa Clara, 69
9. Jurkovich, Jim, B, California, 79
10. *Lamb, Walt (Dub), E, Oklahoma, 89
11. Hammett, Ray (Duke), B, Stanford, 99
12. Zikmund, Al, B, Nebraska, 109
13. Wood, Clark, T, Kentucky, 119
14. *Arms, Loyd, T, Oklahoma State, 129
15. Sturdy, Lyle, B, Wichita State, 139
16. Tomlinson, Buddy, T, Hardin-Simmons, 149
17. *Preston, Pat, T, Wake Forest, 159
18. *Norberg, Hank, E, Stanford, 169
19. Lyons, Pat, E, Wisconsin, 179
20. Butler, Marion, B, Clemson, 189
21. Santucci, Al, C, Santa Clara, 199
22. Johnson, Orville, G, SMU, 209
23. Boudreau, Wally, B, Boston College, 219
24. Baumann, Bob, T, Wisconsin, 229
25. Holtscher, Elwood, C, Shurtleff, 239
26. Keller, Ben, G, Duquesne, 249
27. Block, Charley, E, Shurtleff, 259
28. Brannon, Ted, T, Rice, 269
29. Wayne, Lou, E, Texas, 279
30. Creevy, Dick, B, Notre Dame, 289
31. Buffington, Bill, B, Purdue, 294
32. Peterson, Woody, B, Utah, 299

CHICAGO CARDINALS 1943
1. *Dobbs, Glenn, B, Tulsa, 3
2. *Grigas, Johnny, B, Holy Cross, 14
3. *Currivan, Don, E, Boston College, 18
4. *Hust, Al, E, Tennessee, 29
5. *Hecht, George, G, Alabama, 33
6. *Klug, Al, T, Marquette, 44
7. *Mauldin, Stan, T, Texas, 53
8. *Godwin, Bill, C, Georgia, 64
9. Storer, Moffatt, B, Duke, 73
10. *Mitchell, Fondren, B, Florida, 84
11. Lussow, Emil, E, Dubuque, 93
12. Hirsbrunner, Paul, T, Wisconsin, 104
13. *Baumgartner, Bill, E, Minnesota, 113
14. *Ramsey, Garrard (Buster), G, William & Mary, 124
15. Doloway, Earl, B, Indiana, 133
16. Burke, Nick, G, Northwestern, 144
17. *Campbell, Bill, B, Oklahoma, 153
18. *Booth, Clarence, T, SMU, 164
19. Simmons, Elvis (Boots), E, Texas A&M, 173
20. Ericson, Roy, G, Villanova, 184
21. *Smith, George (Locomotive), B, Villanova, 193
22. *Sutch, George, B, Temple, 204
23. Kimsey, Cliff, B, Georgia, 213
24. *Humble, Weldon, G, Rice, 224
25. *Purdin, Cal, B, Tulsa, 233
26. McGovern, Eddie, B, Illinois, 244
27. *Drulis, Al, G, Temple, 253
28. MacDonald, Ken, C, Rutgers, 264
29. Edwards, Bill, G, LSU, 273
30. Hecomovich, Pete, B, Idaho, 284

CLEVELAND 1943
1. *Holovak, Mike, B, Boston College, 5
2. *Farmer, Tom, B, Iowa , 15
3. *Naumetz, Fred, C, Boston College, 20
4. *Taylor, Chuck, G, Stanford, 30
5. *Johnson, Clyde, T, Kentucky, 35
6. *Horvath, Les, B, Ohio State, 45
7. Henderson, Bill, E, Texas A&M, 55
8. Parker, Bill, E, Iowa, 65
9. Solari, Al, B, UCLA, 75
10. Simmons, Homer, T, Oklahoma, 85
11. Roblin, Tom, B, Oregon, 95
12. Vickroy, Bill, C, Ohio State, 105
13. *Alberghini, Tom, G, Holy Cross, 115
14. Sharp, Sam, E, Alabama, 125
15. Kieppe, Dick, B, Michigan State, 135
16. *Rogers, Cullen, B, Texas A&M, 145
17. Ruark, Walt, G, Georgia, 155
18. Davis, Bert, C, Utah, 165
19. Fidler, Jay, T, Brown, 175
20. Falk, Carl, T, Washington, 185
21. Coll, Tom, E, St. Mary's (CA), 195
22. McCorkle, Mark, B, Washington, 205
23. Moshofsky, Ed, T, Oregon, 215
24. Adams, Hal, B, Missouri, 225
25. Shephard, Jim, E, Oregon, 235
26. Stetler, Jack, B, Pittsburgh, 245
27. Davis, Jeff, C, Missouri, 255
28. *Pritko, Steve, E, Villanova, 265
29. *Konetsky, Floyd, G, Florida, 275
30. Miller, Willie, G, LSU, 285

DETROIT 1943
1. *Sinkwich, Frank, B, Georgia, 1
2. Schreiner, Dave, E, Wisconsin, 11
3. Ashcom, Dick, T, Oregon, 16
4. Hamer, Ralph, B, Furman, 26
5. *Wickett, Lloyd, T, Oregon State, 31
6. *Jones, Casey, B, Union (TN), 41
7. Sizemore, Paul. E, Furman, 51
8. Poschner, George, E, Georgia, 61
9. Irish, Jack, T, Arizona, 71
10. Fenton, Jack, B, Michigan State, 81
11. *Renfro, Dick, B, Washington State, 91
12. *Kolesar, Bob, G, Michigan, 101
13. Huntsinger, Del, B, Portland, 111
14. Dernoncourt, Ellard, E, St. Louis, 121
15. Woodward, Dick, E, Colorado, 131
16. Bass, Marv, T, William & Mary, 141
17. Peelish, Vic, G, West Virginia, 151
18. *Maeda, Chet, B, Colorado State, 161
19. *Kuszynski, Bernie E, Penn, 171
20. Scanland, Al, B, Oklahoma State, 181
21. Lohry, Royal (Ace), B, Iowa State, 191
22. Holland, Percy, G, LSU, 201
23. Fitzgerald, Mike, G, Missouri, 211
24. *Remington, Will, C, Washington State, 221
25. Hamm, Huel, B, Oklahoma, 231
26. Konopka, Irv, T, Idaho, 241
27. Fears, Chuck, T, UCLA, 251
28. Ekern, Bert, E, Missouri, 261
29. Wagner, Virgil, B, Millikin, 271
30. Kaplan, Manny, B, Western Maryland, 281

GREEN BAY 1943
1. *Wildung, Dick, T, Minnesota, 8
3. *Comp, Irv, B, St. Benedictine, 23
5. *McKay, Roy Dale, B, Texas, 38
6. *Susoeff, Nick, E, Washington State, 48
7. *Snelling, Ken, B, UCLA, 58
8. *Gatewood, Les, C, Baylor, 68
9. *Verry, Norm, T, USC, 78
10. *Barnett, Solon (Bobo), G, Baylor, 88
11. *Forte, Bob, B, Arkansas, 98
12. *Davis, Van, E, Georgia, 108
13. Brock, Tom, C, Notre Dame, 118
14. Tate, Ralph, B, Oklahoma State, 128
15. Carlson, Don, T, Denver, 138
16. Welch, Mike, B, Minnesota, 148
17. Thomas, Ron, G, USC, 158
18. Powers, Jim, T, St. Mary's (CA), 168
19. *Prescott, Harold (Ace), E, Hardin-Simmons, 178
20. *Forrest, Eddie, C, Santa Clara, 188
21. *Wasserbach, Lloyd, T, Wisconsin, 198
22. Hoskins, Mark, B, Wisconsin, 208
23. *Bennett, Earl (Jug), G, Hardin-Simmons, 218
24. Zellick, George, E, Oregon State, 228
25. Bierhaus, Gene, E, Minnesota, 238
26. Makris, George, G, Wisconsin, 248
27. Susick, Pete, B, Washington, 258
28. Hasse, Bud, E, Northwestern, 268
29. Thornally, Dick, T, Wisconsin, 278
30. Ray, Bob, B, Wisconsin, 288
31. Christensen, Brunel, T, California, 293
32. *Roskie, Ken, B, USC, 298

NEW YORK GIANTS 1943
1. *Filipowicz, Steve, B, Fordham, 6
3. *Proctor, Dewey, B, Furman, 21
5. Culwell, Val, G, Oregon, 36
6. *Reynolds, Jim, B, Auburn, 46
7. *Palazzi, Lou, C, Penn State, 56
8. *Visnic, Larry, G, St. Benedictine, 66
9. Caraway, Doyle, G, Texas Tech, 76
10. *Piccolo, Bill, C, Canisius, 86
11. Knox, Glenn, E, William & Mary, 96
12. Domina, Walt, B, Norwich, 106
13. *McCafferty, Don, T, Ohio State, 116
14. Stoves, Jay, B, Washington State, 126
15. Currie, Howard, T, Geneva, 136
16. Keithley, N.A., B, Tulsa, 146
17. Lister, Jack, E, Missouri, 156
18. Holshouser, Dwight, B, Catawba, 166
19. Lushine, Jim, T, Minnesota, 176
20. Berllus, Veto, E, Idaho, 186
21. Marshall, Fred, G, North Carolina, 196
22. Korczowski, John, B, William & Mary, 206
23. Hoeman, Gene, E, Oklahoma State, 216
24. *Beebe, Keith, B, Occidental, 226
25. *Brown, Dave, B, Alabama, 236
26. Hail, Maurice, G, Tulsa, 246
27. McNamara, Ed, T, Holy Cross, 256
28. Drake, Dick, T, Ohio Wesleyan, 266
29. Ritinski, Stan, E, Fordham, 276
30. Mollenhoff, Clark, T, Drake, 286
31. *Adams, Verlin, G, Morris Harvey, 291
32. Brundage, Bob, B, Penn, 296

PHILADELPHIA 1943
1. *Muha, Joe, B, VMI, 2
2. *Davis, Lamar (Racehorse), B, Georgia, 12
3. *Gafford, Roy (Monk), B, Auburn, 17
4. *Kennedy, Bob, B, Washington State, 27
5. *Wistert, Al, T, Michigan, 32
6. *Banducci, Bruno, G, Stanford, 42
7. Harrison, Walt, C, Washington, 52
8. *Alford, Bruce, E, TCU, 62
9. *Canale, Rocco, G, Boston College, 72
10. *Conoly, Bill, T, Texas, 82
11. *Billman, John, G, Minnesota, 92
12. Donaldson, Jack, T, Penn, 102
13. Erickson, Bill, C, Georgetown (DC), 112
14. *Weeks, George, E, Alabama, 122
15. *Craft, Russ, B, Alabama, 132
16. Darling, Paul, B, Iowa State, 142
17. *Gorinski, Walt, B, LSU, 152
18. *Friedman, Bob, T, Washington, 162
19. Bezemes, Johnny, B, Holy Cross, 172
20. *Mutryn, Chet, B, Xavier, 182
21. *Manzini, Baptiste, C, St. Vincent's, 192
22. Gillespie, Bernie, E, Scranton, 202
23. Lawhon, Jay (Mule), T, Arkansas, 212
24. Zachem, Vince, C, Morehead State (KY), 222
25. Schwarting, Joe, E, Texas, 232
26. Neff, Bob, T, Notre Dame, 242
27. *Macioszczyk, Art, B, Western Michigan, 252
28. Arata, Jim, T, Xavier, 262
29. Scott, Wally, E, Texas, 272
30. Jaworowski, Stan, T, Georgetown (DC), 282

PITTSBURGH 1943
1. *Daley, Bill, B, Minnesota, 7
3. *Russell, Jack E, Baylor, 22
5. *Connolly, Harry, B, Boston College, 37
6. *Sossamon, Lou, C, South Carolina, 47
7. Ratto, Al, C, St. Mary's (CA), 57
8. Curry, Ray, E, St. Mary's (CA), 67
9. Murphy, Ed, E, Holy Cross, 77
10. Dwelle, Dick, B, Rice, 87
11. *Wukits, Al, C, Duquesne, 97
12. *Repko, Joe, T, Boston College, 107
13. Boltrek, Pete, T, North Carolina State, 117
14. Shiekman, Mort, G, Penn, 127
15. *Crain, Milt, B, Baylor, 137
16. *Kielbasa, Max, B, Duquesne, 147
17. *Skorich, Nick, G, Cincinnati, 157
18. Field, Jackie, B, Texas, 167
19. *Bucek, Felix, G, Texas A&M, 177
20. Welsh, Johnny, B, Penn, 187
21. *Compagno, Tony, B, St. Mary's (CA), 197
22. Zapalac, Willie, B, Texas A&M, 207
23. Bain, George, T, Oregon State, 217
24. *Wynne, Harry, T, Arkansas, 227
25. *Cibulas, Joe, T, Duquesne, 237
26. Yambrick, Bill, C, Western Michigan, 247
27. *Freeman, Jack, G, Texas, 257
28. Goode, Joe, B, Duquesne, 267
29. *Durishan, Jack, T, Pittsburgh, 277
30. Lobpries, Fritz, G, Texas, 287
31. Jones, Art, B, Haverford, 292
32. Ruman, Bob, B, Arizona, 297

WASHINGTON 1943
1. *Jenkins, Jack, B, Vanderbilt, 10
3. *Dutton, Bill, B, Pittsburgh, 25
5. *Dove, Bob, E, Notre Dame, 40
6. Ziemba, Wally, C, Notre Dame, 50
7. *Rymkus, Lou, T, Notre Dame, 60
8. *Leon, Tony, G, Alabama, 70
9. *Motl, Bob, E, Northwestern, 80
10. *McDonald, Walt, B, Tulane, 90
11. *Perpich, George, T, Georgetown (DC), 100
12. Wood, Dan, C, Mississippi, 110
13. Wright, Harry, G, Notre Dame, 120
14. *Britt, Oscar, G, Mississippi, 130
15. Weber, Dick, G, Syracuse, 140
16. Day, Joe, B, Oregon State, 150
17. Dornfield, Frank, B, Georgetown (DC), 160
18. Baklarz, John, T, Arizona State, 170
19. Mogus, Leo, E, Youngstown State, 180
20. Secrest, Dick, B, Rochester, 190
21. *Nolander, Don, C, Minnesota, 200
22. Barrett, Johnny B, Georgetown (DC), 210
23. Vohs, Tom, T, Colgate, 220
24. Yancey, Charlie, B, Mississippi State, 230
25. *Bentz, Roman, T, Tulane, 240
26. Berthold, Paul (Swifty), E, Syracuse, 250
27. *Pacewic, Vince, B, Loyola (LA), 260
28. Riccardi, Joe, T, Ohio U., 270
29. *Jaffurs, Johnny, G, Penn State, 280
30. *Akins, Frank, B, Washington State, 290
31. Corry, Bill (Mother), B, Florida, 295
32. Bogovich, Bo, G, Delaware, 300

1944

Held April 19, 1944

Although the Pittsburgh and Chicago Cardinals franchises merged for the 1944 season, at the time of the draft they still were independent franchises, and each selected separately. Neither gave up its rights to any players while the merger was in effect. Philadelphia and Pittsburgh, which had been merged in 1943, alternately selected fourth (for their fifth-place finish) and ninth (last of the teams playing the previous season). Cleveland, which was given permission to resume operations for 1944, selected tenth. The expansion Boston Yanks franchise had the first overall selection in the draft and then selected last in each following round. Again, some teams were given extra picks in the second and fourth rounds.

BOSTON 1944
1. *Bertelli, Angelo, QB, Notre Dame, 1
3. *Dimancheff, Boris (Babe) B, Purdue, 27
5. Rice, Larry, C, Tulane, 43
6. Parker, John (Butch), T, Loyola (LA), 54
7. Andrews, Mike, E, North Carolina State, 65
8. Musick, Bob, B, USC, 76
9. *Warrington, Caleb (Tex), C, Auburn, 87
10. Sisti, Angelo, T, Boston College, 98
11. Long, Gene, G, Kansas, 109
12. *Fiorentino, Ed, E, Boston College, 120
13. Zeleznak, Mike, B, Kansas State, 131
14. *Maskas, John, T, Virginia Tech, 142
15. Bond, John, B, TCU, 153
16. Antaya, Roger, G, Dartmouth, 164
17. *Shurnas, Marshall, E, Missouri, 175
18. Bennett, Reldon, T, LSU, 186
19. *Faircloth, Art, B, North Carolina State, 197
20. Bilotti, Tony, G, St.Mary's (CA), 208
21. Furman, Bill, T, Washington & Lee, 219
22. Morford, Clare, G, Oklahoma, 230
23. Richmond, Dilton, E, LSU, 241
24. Lawlor, Courtney, B, Richmond, 252
25. Debus, Howard, B, Nebraska, 263
26. Portwood, Bill, E, Kentucky, 274
27. Collins, Harold, G, Southwestern (TX), 285
28. Gill, Aubrey, C, Texas, 296
29. Wasilewski, Chet, B, Holy Cross, 307
30. Letchas, Gus, B, Georgia, 318
31. *Calcagni, Ralph, T, Penn, 324
32. Roberts, Walton, B, Texas, 330

BROOKLYN 1944
1. Miller, Creighton, B, Notre Dame, 3
2. *Callahan, Jim, B, Texas, 13
3. Park, Ralph, B, Texas, 18
4. *Sikich, Rudy, T, Minnesota, 29
5. Ullom, Verne, E, Cincinnati, 34
6. McDonald, Bruce, E, Illinois State, 45
7. Graiziger, Bob, G, Minnesota, 56
8. *Sachse, Jack, C, Texas, 67
9. *Olenski, Mitch, T, Alabama, 78
10. Cenci, Aldo, B, Penn State, 89
11. Bicaninch, John, G, Minnesota, 100
12. *Tyree, Jim, E, Oklahoma, 111
13. *Wright, Jim, C, SMU, 122
14. Genis, John, T, Illinois, 133
15. Murphy, Billie (Spook), B, Mississippi State, 144
16. Essick, Doug, E, USC, 155
17. *Maley, Howard (Red), B, SMU, 166
18. Willer, Don, T, USC, 177
19. Callanan, Howard, B, USC, 188
20. *Doherty, George, T, Louisiana Tech, 199
21. Mihalic, Mike. G, Mississippi State, 210
22. *Cook, Ted, E, Alabama, 221
23. Gillenwater, Bucky, T, Texas, 232
24. *Baldwin, Jack, C, Centenary, 243
25. Manning, Dick, B, USC, 254
26. Grierson, Ray, E, Illinois, 265
27. *Golding, Joe, B, Oklahoma, 276
28. *Zimny, Bob, T, Indiana, 287
29. Frohm, Marty, T, Mississippi State, 298
30. Blose, Howard, B, Cornell, 309

CHICAGO BEARS 1944
1. *Evans, Ray, B, Kansas, 9
3. *Smeja, Rudy, E, Michigan, 24
5. *Croft, Abe, E, SMU, 40
6. *Stanley, C.B., T, Tulsa, 51
7. Seeley, Darwin, C, Stanford, 62
8. Fawcett, Randall (Buck), B, Stanford, 73
9. *Morton, Jack, E, Missouri, 84
10. Starford, Bill, C, Wake Forest, 95
11. *Houston, Lin, G, Ohio State, 106
12. Moore, J.P., B, Vanderbilt, 117
13. Duffey, Bill, E, Georgetown (DC), 128
14. Hartley, Joe, T, LSU, 139
15. *Milner, Bill, G, Duke, 150
16. *Hirsch, Ed (Buckets), B, Northwestern, 161
17. Ryckeley, Ed, E, Georgia Tech, 172
18. Plasman, Howdy, B, Miami, 183
19. *French, Barry (Bear), T, Purdue, 194
20. Taylor, Paul, B, USC, 205
21. *Margarita, Hank, B, Brown, 216
22. Davis, Ed, B, Oklahoma, 227
23. Jamison, Dick, T, USC, 238
24. Bortka, Jack, B, Kansas State, 249
25. *Ruskusky, Roy, E, St. Mary's (CA), 260
26. Franck, Harry, B, Northwestern, 271
27. McKewan, Jack, T, Alabama, 282
28. *Mitchell, Charley, B, Tulsa, 293
29. Boyle, Pat, G, Wisconsin, 304
30. Pepper, Bernie, T, Missouri, 315
31. Vogt, Karl, T, Villanova, 321
32. Endres, Bob, T, Colgate, 327

CHICAGO CARDINALS 1944
1. *Harder, Pat, B, Wisconsin, 2
2. *Mitchell, Paul, T, Minnesota, 12
3. *Judd, Saxon, E, Tulsa, 17
4. *Tavener, Jack, C, Indiana, 28
5. *Blackburn, Bill, C, Rice, 33
6. *Garnaas, Bill, B, Minnesota, 44
7. Smith, Rodger, B, Texas Tech, 55
8. *Cochran, John (Red), B, Wake Forest, 66
9. Scanlan, Frank, B, Loyola (LA), 77
10. *Saban, Lou, B, Indiana, 88
11. Griffin, Fran, T, Holy Cross, 99
12. Daniels, Leo, B, Texas A&M, 110
13. Dobbs, Bobby, B, Tulsa, 121
14. Hall, Van, B, TCU, 132
15. *Carpenter, Jack, T, Missouri, 143
16. Csuri, Charley, T, Ohio State, 154
17. *Magliolo, Joe, B, Texas, 165
18. *Szot, Walt, T, Bucknell, 176
19. Adams, Jack, E, Presbyterian, 187
20. *Kuffel, Ray, E, Marquette, 198
21. West, Jack, E, Texas, 209
22. Esorcia, Jack, B, Illinois State, 220
23. Buffmire, Don, B, Northwestern, 231
24. Nanni, Bob, T, Duke, 242
25. McGinnis, John, E, Notre Dame, 253
26. Hodges, Warren, T, Kansas, 264
27. Earley, Bill, B, Notre Dame, 275
28. Davis, Bob, G, Oregon, 286
29. DiFrancesca, Vince, T, Northwestern, 297
30. Ott, Lloyd, C, North Carolina State, 308

CLEVELAND 1944
1. Butkovich, Tony, B, Illinois, 11
3. *Bouley, Gil, T, Boston College, 26
5. *Waterfield, Bob, B, UCLA, 42
6. *Akins, Al, B, Washington State, 53
7. *Cheverko, George, B, Fordham, 64
8. *Stasica, Stan, B, South Carolina, 75
9. *Boensch, Fred, T, Stanford, 86
10. *Shaw, Bob, E, Ohio State, 97
11. Andrejco, Joe, B, Fordham, 108
12. Filley, Pat, G, Notre Dame, 119
13. Erickson, Bob, B, Washington, 130
14. *Maceau, Mel, C, Marquette, 141
15. *Hubbell, Frank (Bud), E, Tennessee, 152
16. Aguirre, John, T, USC, 163
17. Clayton, Aubrey, B, Auburn, 174
18. Zamlynski, Ziggy, B, Villanova, 185
19. McBride, Bob, G, Notre Dame, 196
20. *Yackanich, Joe, T, Fordham, 207
21. Creevey, John, B, Notre Dame, 218
22. Jones, David Paul, B, Arkansas, 229
23. Pharr, Jim, C, Auburn, 240
24. Warlick, Joe, B, Mississippi State, 251
25. Gianelli, Bert, G, Santa Clara, 262
26. Kuhn, Charley, B, Kentucky, 273
27. *Smith, Jim, T, Colorado, 284
28. Donelli, Ray, B, Duquesne, 295
29. Hughes, John, E, Mississippi State, 306
30. McPhee, Dick, B, Georgia, 317
31. McLeod, Jim, E, LSU, 323
32. Kudlacz, Stan, C, Notre Dame, 329

DETROIT 1944
1. *Graham, Otto, B, Northwestern, 4
2. *Cifers, Bob, B, Tennessee, 14
3. *Heywood, Ralph, E, USC, 19
4. Betteridge, George, B, Utah, 30
5. *Greene, John, T, Michigan, 35
6. Alliquie, Ed, T, Santa Clara, 46
7. *Briggs, Paul, T, Colorado, 57
8. Giske, Red, G, Washington State, 68
9. Bolger, Matthew, E, Notre Dame, 79
10. Hein, Herb, E, Minnesota, 90
11. *White, Paul, B, Michigan, 101
12. Lescoulie, Jack, G, UCLA, 112
13. Rehor, Doug, B, Dickinson, 123
14. Pritula, Bill, C, Michigan, 134
15. Molich, Jim, E, Fresno State, 145
16. Yakapovich, Jules, B, Colgate, 156
17. *Helms, Jack, T, Georgia Tech, 167
18. *Madarik, Elmer (Tippy), B, Detroit, 178
19. Eubank, Bill, E, Mississippi State, 189
20. Ahlstrom, Ray, B, St. Mary's (CA), 200
21. *Kapter, Alex, G, Northwestern, 211
22. Clark, Vic, B, Texas (El Paso), 222
23. Fischer, Max, C, Oklahoma, 233
24. Jacoby, Chuck, B, Indiana, 244
25. McCarthy, Bob, E, St. Mary's (CA), 255
26. Hendrickson, Stan, E, Colorado, 266
27. *Bouldin, Fred, B, Missouri, 277
28. McElwee, Dick, B, West Virginia, 288
29. Derleth, Bob, T, Michigan, 299
30. Dick, George, E, Kansas, 310

GREEN BAY 1944
1. *Pregulman, Merv, G, Michigan, 7
3. Kuzma, Tom, B, Michigan, 22
5. McPartland, Bill, T, St.Mary's (CA), 38
6. McCardle, Mickey, B, USC, 49
7. Tracy, Jack, E, Washington, 60
8. *Agase, Alex, G, Illinois, 71
9. Whitmire, Don, T, Alabama, Navy, 82
10. Koch, Bob, B, Oregon, 93
11. Johnson, Virgil, E, Arkansas, 104
12. Giusti, Roy, B, St. Mary's (CA), 115
13. Baughman, Bill, C, Alabama, 126
14. *Griffin, Don, B, Illinois, 137
15. Gissler, Bert, E, Nebraska, 148
16. Shelton, Lou, B, Oregon State, 159
17. Cusick, Charley, G, Colgate, 170
18. Cox, Hugh, B, North Carolina, 181
19. Davis, Kermit, E, Mississippi State, 192
20. Johnson, Bob, C, Purdue, 203
21. *Cox, Jim, T, Stanford, 214
22. Anderson, Cliff, E, Minnesota, 225
23. Perry, John Wesley, B, Duke, 236
24. DeMaria, Pete, G, Purdue, 247
25. Liss, Len, T, Marquette, 258
26. Jordan, Ray, B, North Carolina, 269
27. Grubaugh, Al, T, Nebraska, 280
28. Howard, A.B., E, Mississippi State, 291
29. Paladino, Paul, G, Arkansas, 302
30. Butchofsky, Bob, B, Texas A&M, 313
31. Deal, Russ, G, Indiana, 319
32. Gonzales, Abel (Frito), B, SMU, 325

NEW YORK GIANTS 1944
1. *Hillenbrand, Billy, B, Indiana, 6
2. *Blount, Lamar, B, Mississippi State, 16
3. Flowers, Clyde, T, TCU, 21
4. *Kane, Herb, T, East Central (OK), 32
5. Maitland, Vic, T, Hobart, 37
6. Okland, Jack, T, Utah State, 48
7. Frickey, Herm, B, Minnesota, 59
8. *Clay, Roy, B, Colorado State, 70
9. *Sanchez, Johnny, T, San Francisco, 81
10. Beamer, Ernie, E, Duke, 92
11. *Grate, Carl, G, Georgia, 103
12. *Mont, Tommy, B, Maryland, 114
13. *Poole, Ray, E, Mississippi, 125
14. *Corley, Bert, C, Mississippi State, 136
15. *Poole, Ollie, E, Mississippi, 147
16. Ellsworth, Ralph, B, Texas, 158
17. Schneider, Ed, T, Washburn, 169
18. Gres, Marcel, T, Texas, 180
19. Brooks, Neil, B, Washington, 191
20. Kane, Pete, B, Geneva, 202
21. Kittrell, M.L. (Kit), B, Baylor, 213
22. Renfro, Roy, G, Fresno State, 224
23. Dubzinski, John, G, Boston College, 235
24. Beyer, Howard, C, Michigan State, 246
25. Babula, Ben, B, Fordham, 257
26. Fitanides, Ted, B, New Hampshire, 268
27. Bires, Andy, E, Alabama, 279
28. Rock, Tom, E, Columbia, 290
29. Cyhel, Walt, T, Creighton, 301
30. Nelson, Francis, B, Baylor, 312

PHILADELPHIA 1944
1. *Van Buren, Steve, B, LSU, 5
3. LaPrade, Loren, G, Stanford , 20
5. *Parker, Joe, E, Texas, 36
6. Horne, Hillary, T, Mississippi State, 52
7. *Kulbitski, Vic, B, Minnesota, 58
8. *Phillips, George, B, UCLA, 74
9. *Sarringhaus, Paul, B, Ohio State, 80
10. *Perko, John, G, Minnesota, 96
11. *Ormsbee, Elliott, B, Bradley, 102
12. *Parsons, Earle, B, USC, 118
13. Hanzlik, Bob, E, Wisconsin, 124
14. Talley, Jim, C, LSU, 140
15. Fusci, Dom, T, South Carolina, 146
16. *Green, Johnny, E, Tulsa, 162
17. Freeman, Jackie, B, William & Mary, 168
18. Kane, Joe, B, Penn, 184
19. Schiro, Tony, G, Santa Clara, 190
20. Michael, Norm, B, Syracuse, 206
21. Kulakowski, Eddie, T, West Virginia, 212
22. *Postus, Al, B, Villanova, 228
23. *Smith, Milt, E, UCLA, 234
24. *Klapstein, Earl, T, Pacific, 250
25. Frisbee, Bob, B, Stanford, 256
26. *Eiden, Ed, B, Scranton, 272
27. Burdick, Barney, E, Creighton, 278
28. *Daukas, Nick, T, Dartmouth, 294
29. Darone, Pasquale, G, Boston College, 300
30. Clark, Bill, T, Colorado College, 316
31. Pasko, Pete, E, East Stroudsburg, 322
32. Majewski, Myron, T, American International, 328

PITTSBURGH 1944
1. Podesto, Johnny, B, St. Mary's (CA), 10
2. Odell, Bob, E, Penn, 15
3. Gantt, Bob, E, Duke, 25
4. *McCaffray, Art, T, Pacific, 31
5. Owen, George, G, Wake Forest, 41
6. Savage, Dan, B, Brown, 47
7. *Frietas, Jesse, B, Santa Clara, 63
8. *Titus, George, C, Holy Cross, 69
9. *Stofko, Ed, B, St. Francis, 85
10. *Jansante, Val, E, Duquesne, 91
11. *Buda, Carl, G, Tulsa, 107
12. *Gray, Sam, E, Tulsa, 113
13. Longacre, Bob, B, William & Mary, 129
14. Zetty, Les, E, Muhlenberg, 135
15. Myers, Jim, G, Tennessee, 151
16. Gottlieb, Joe, B, Duquesne, 157
17. Davis, Hugh, B, Michigan State, 173
18. Sullivan, Bill, E, Villanova, 179
19. Woodside, Jimmy, C, Temple, 195
20. Miller, Bill, B, Penn, 201
21. Lawson, Bob, E, Holy Cross, 217
22. Caver, Hank, B, Presbyterian, 223
23. Carter, Paul, T, Michigan State, 239
24. Holben, Dick, T, Muhlenberg, 245
25. Tippee, Howard, B, Iowa State, 261
26. Malmberg, Charley, T, Rice, 267
27. Ashbaugh, Russ, B, Notre Dame, 283
28. Petroski, Pat, G, Miami (FL), 289
29. Tosti, Joe, E, Scranton, 305
30. Seelinger, Len, B, Wisconsin, 311

WASHINGTON 1944
1. *Micka, Mike, B, Colgate, 8
3. *Audet, Earl, T, USC, 23
5. Doherty, Ed, B, Boston College, 39
6. Fellows, Jackie, B, Fresno State, 50
7. Fischer, Hal, G, Texas, 61
8. White, Cliff, T, Murray State, 72
9. Ogdahl, Ted, B, Willamette, 83
10. *Sneddon, Bob, B, St. Mary's (CA), 94
11. Aldworth, Bill, T, Minnesota, 105
12. Joslyn, Bill, B, Stanford, 116
13. Walker, Charley, C, Kentucky, 127
14. Clement, Boyd, C, Oregon State, 138
15. *Gaffney, Jim, B, Tennessee, 149
16. *Ossowski, Ted, T, Oregon State, 160
17. Davis, Tom, B, Duke, 171
18. *Batorski, John, E, Colgate, 182
19. *Ehrhardt, Clyde, C, Georgia, 193
20. Brown, Dave, E, UCLA, 204
21. Ivy, Bill, T, Northwestern, 215
22. Babcock, Bruce, B, Rochester, 226
23. *Reinhard, Bill, B, California, 237
24. Bauer, Ed, G, South Carolina, 248
25. Martin, Joe (Smokey), B, Cornell, 259
26. Gustafson, Lee, B, Oregon State, 270
27. Pappas, Nick, T, Utah, 281
28. Bowen, Lindsey, E, Rice, 292
29. Gustafson, Bill, T, Washington State, 303
30. Yablonski, Bill, C, Holy Cross, 314
31. Hollingbery, Buster, C, Washington State, 320
32. Sheller, Willard, B, Stanford, 326

1945

Held April 8, 1945

Although the Boston and Brooklyn franchises merged for the 1945 season, at the time of the draft they still were independent franchises, and each selected separately. Neither gave up its rights to any players while the merger was in effect. Pittsburgh and the Chicago Cardinals which had been merged in 1944, alternately selected first, second, and third (with Brooklyn) for their last-place finish the previous season.

In 1944, the league had passed a special one-year rule allowing a handful of players who still had college eligibility to play one year in the NFL and then to be returned to the preferred negotiations list in 1945. This rule primarily was aimed at those players who were unable to play collegiate ball because their programs had dropped football, but also included some who had left school but then had been ineligible to serve in the Armed Forces. In 1945, three such players were selected after a year in the NFL: Paul Duhart (Pittsburgh, second round), Russ Lowther (Detroit, sixth round), and John Morelli (Boston, twenty-eighth round). One other player — John Itzel (Pittsburgh, seventeenth round) — was granted special permission to be selected and to play in 1945, returning to the preferred negotiations list in 1946.

BOSTON 1945
1. *Prokop, Eddie, B, Georgia Tech, 4
2. *Dean, Tom, T, SMU, 15
3. *Tassos, Damon, G, Texas A&M, 20
4. *Deeks, Don, T, Washington, 31
5. *Strzykalski, Johnny (Strike), B, Marquette, 36 +
6. *Mello, Jim, B, Notre Dame, 47
7. Silovich, Marty, C, Marquette, 58
8. *Jones, Ellis, G, Tulsa, 69
9. Lambert, Earl, B, Manhattan, 80
10. Kasprzak, Don, B, Dartmouth, 91
11. Jones, Ben, E, Arkansas, 102
12. *Coleman, Herb, C, Notre Dame, 113
13. Pezelski, Joe, B, Villanova, 124
14. DiGangi, John, T, Holy Cross, 135
15. Highsmith, Chan, C, North Carolina, 146
16. Costello, Mike, E, Georgetown (DC), 157
17. Dromgoole, Paul, E, Manhattan, 168
18. Czekala, Dolph, T, Syracuse, 179
19. Drumm, Joe, T, Georgetown (DC), 190
20. *Gianelli, Mario, T, Boston College, 201
21. Jamison, Eric, T, San Francisco, 212
22. Kretz, Walt, B, Cornell, 223
23. Grbovaz, Marty, E, San Francisco, 234 +
24. Gory, Ziggy, C, Villanova, 245
25. Iancelli, Bill, E, William & Mary, 256 +
26. Kull, Al, T, Fordham, 267
27. Mangene, Bob, B. Boston College, 278
28. *Morelli, John, G, Georgetown (DC), 289
29. Fisher, John, C, Harvard, 300
30. Oberto, Elmer, G, Georgetown (DC), 311

BROOKLYN 1945
1. Renfroe, Joe, B, Tulane, 3
2. Williams, Wayne, B, Minnesota, 13
3. Gray, Cecil, C, Oregon, 17
4. *Erich, Steve, G, Marquette, 30
5. *Kowalski, Al, QB, Tulsa, 34
6. *Barwegen, Dick, G, Purdue, 44
7. Futrell, Louie, B, Fresno State, 57
8. Dodds, John, G, California, 67
9. Johnson, Elting, B, Bucknell, 77
10. Cross, Roy, E, Tennessee, 90
11. Haury, Earl, T, Kansas State, 100
12. Martin, John, B, East Tennessee State, 110
13. McDonald, George, T, South Carolina, 123
14. Self, Hal, B, Alabama, 133
15. Reilly, Tom, G, Fordham, 143
16. Harrison, Skimp, E, South Carolina, 156
17. *Weinmeister, Arnie, E, Washington, 166
18. *Eikenberg, Virgil, B, Rice, 176
19. Kasulin, Al, B, Villanova, 189
20. Lively, Charley, T, Arkansas, 199
21. Curran, Ted, B, Iowa, 209
22. Fabling, Don, B, Colorado, 222
23. Crittenden, Wally, B, USC, 232
24. Taddie, Jules, C, Rochester, 242
25. Whitney, Jerry, B, USC, 255
26. Trapani, Felix, G, LSU, 265
27. Finney, Hal, B, USC, 275
28. Fauble, Don, B, Oklahoma, 288
29. Studen, Nick, B, Denver, 298
30. Dykstra, LaMar, B, Colorado, 308

CHICAGO BEARS 1945
1. Lund, Don, B, Michigan, 7
3. Allen, Charley, B, SMU, 22
5. *Masterson, Forest, C, Iowa, 40
6. Shaw, Wayne, B, SMU, 50
7. *Burgeis, Glen, T, Tulsa, 60
8. O'Brien, Pat, T, Purdue, 73
9. Mayther, Bill, C, Oregon, 83
10. Poe, Bill, B, Clemson, 93
11. Avery, Chuck, B, Minnesota, 106
12. Boyd, Jack, B, UCLA, 116
13. Ellsworth, Ralph, B, Texas, 126
14. *Mattioli, Frank, G, Pittsburgh, 139
15. Gibson, Merle, E, TCU, 149
16. Creevey, John, B, Notre Dame, 159
17. *Sacrinty, Nick, B, Wake Forest, 172
18. *Keane, Jim, E, Iowa, 182
19. *Niedziela, Bruno, T, Iowa, 192
20. Williams, Broughton, E, Florida, 205
21. *Stickel, Walt, T, Penn, 215
22. *Livingston, Bob, B, Notre Dame, 225
23. Vargon, Mike, E, Kansas State, 238
24. Wright, Charley, G, Iowa Stale, 248
25. Green, Jack, G, Alabama, 258
26. *Gambino, Lu, B, Maryland, 271
27. Jones, Ray, B, Texas, 281
28. Hary, Bob, B, Minnesota, 291
29. *Forkovich, Nick, B, William & Mary, 304
30. Robinson, Don, B, Michigan, 314
31. Johnston, Wayne (Rusty), B, Marquette, 319
32. *Groves, George, C, Marquette, 327

CHICAGO CARDINALS 1945
1. *Trippi, Charley, B, Georgia, 1
2. *Collins, Paul, B, Missouri, 14
3. *Watt, Walt, B, Miami, 18
4. *Dobelstein, Bob, G Tennessee, 28
5. Chronister, Zeke, E, TCU, 35
6. *Clatt, Corwin, B, Notre Dame, 45
7. *Czarobski, Ziggy, T, Notre Dame, 55
8. *Harrington, John, E, Marquette, 68
9. Meeks, Gene, B, Kentucky, 78
10. Huber, Bill, E, Notre Dame, 88
11. Heard, Halley, T, LSU, 101
12. *Cowan, Bob, B, Indiana, 111
13. Luper, Elmore (Buddy), B, Duke, 121
14. *Barnett, Solon (Bobo), G, Baylor, 134
15. Carver, Gordon, B, Duke, 144
16. *Cannady, John, B, Indiana, 154 +
17. Cittadino, Ben, E, Duke, 167
18. Strayhorn, Ralph, G, North Carolina, 177
19. Andretich, John, B, Purdue, 187
20. *Kramer, John, T, Marquette, 200
21. Cheek, J.D. (Red), G, Baylor, 210 +
22. Grant, Fred, B, Wake Forest, 220
23. Cook, Johnny, B, Georgia, 233 +
24. McClure, Ardie, T, Georgia, 243
25. Norige, Hugo, B, Wooster, 253
26. Knight, Gene (Red), B, LSU, 266 +
27. Fambrough, Don, B, Texas, 276
28. Williams, Garland (Bulldog), T, Duke, 286
29. Dusek, Ed, B, Texas A&M, 299
30. Payne, Otto, B, Texas A&M, 309

CLEVELAND 1945
1. *Hirsch, Elroy (Crazylegs), B, Michigan, Wisconsin, 5
2. *Lazetich, Milan, T, Michigan, 16
3. Wooten, W.G. (Dub), E, Oklahoma, 21
4. *Zilly, Jack, E, Notre Dame, 32
5. *Harding, Roger, C, California, 37
6. *Cowhig, Jerry, B, Notre Dame, 48
7. *Negus, Fred, C, Wisconsin, 59
8. August, Johnny, B, Alabama, 70
9. *Huffman, Dick, T, Tennessee, 81
10. Walters, Vern, B, Alma, 92
11. *Fears, Tom, E, UCLA, 103
12. *Winkler, Joe, C, Purdue, 114
13. Aland, Jack, T, Alabama, 125
14. Uknes, Chuck, B, Iowa, 136
15. *Lund, Bill, B, Case Western Reserve, 147 +
16. Barton, Bob, E, Holy Cross, 158
17. *Hoerner, Dick, B, Iowa, 169
18. Kennon, Lee, T, Oklahoma, 180
19. Matulich, Eagle, B, Mississippi State, 191
20. Griffin, Bill, T, Kentucky, 202
21. Erickson, Leroy, B, Oregon, 213
22. *Evans, Ray, T, Texas-El Paso, 224 +
23. *Higgins, Luke, T, Notre Dame, 235
24. Nowak, Stan, E, South Carolina, 246
25. Konopka, Gene, G, Villanova, 257
26. Florek, Ray, B, Illinois, 268
27. Perry, Russ, B, Wake Forest, 279
28. *West, Pat, B, USC, 290
29. Davis, Bill, B, Oregon, 301
30. Compton, Charley, T, Alabama, 312

DETROIT 1945
1. *Szymanski, Frank, C, Notre Dame, 6
3. Mohrbacher, Stan, G, Iowa, 24
5. *Wiese, Bob, B, Michigan, 39
6. *Fekete, Gene, B, Ohio State, 49
7. *Jarmoluk, Mike, T, Temple, 62
8. *Lowther, Russ, B, Detroit, 72
9. Joop, Les, T, Illinois, 82
10. *Walker, Paul, E, Yale, 95
11. Hansen, Howie, T, Utah State, 105
12. *Kasap, Mike, T, Illinois, 115
13. Hopp, Wally, B, Nebraska, 128
14. Trickey, Ben, B, Iowa, 138
15. *Williams, Windell, E, Rice, 148
16. Flanigan, Wayne, E, Denver, 161
17. Key, O.J., B, Tulane, 171
18. McWhorter, Jim, B, Alabama, 181
19. *LeForce, Clyde, B, Tulsa, 194
20. Castronis, Mike, G, Georgia, 204
21. Currier, Ken, G, Wisconsin, 214
22. Verutti, Jack, B, St, Mary's (CA), 227
23. Olsen, Ray, B, Tulane, 237
24. *Morrow, Russ, C Tennessee, 247
25. Green, Stan, T, Oklahoma, 260
26. *Ivory, Bob, G, Detroit, 270
27. Taylor, Dell, B, Tulsa, 280
28. Ciesla, Len, B, Creighton, 293
29. Lopp, Frank, T, Wisconsin, 303
30. Limont, Paul, E, Notre Dame, 313
31. Schadler, Ben, B, Northwestern, 321 +
32. Dorais, Tom, B, Detroit, 326

GREEN BAY 1945
1. *Schlinkman, Walt, B, Texas Tech, 11
3. *Goodnight, Clyde, E, Tulsa, 27
5. Graham, Joe, E, Florida, 43
6. *Wells, Don, T, Georgia, 54
7. Stephenson, Casey, B, Tennessee, 65
8. Collins, Toby, T, Tulsa, 76
9. Dingler, Lamar, E, Arkansas, 87
10. Helscher, Hal, B, LSU, 98
11. Hammond, Ralph, C, Pittsburgh, 109
12. Podgorski, Ed, T, Lafayette, 120
13. Hackett, Bill, G, Ohio State, 131
14. Lindsey, Marv, B, Arkansas, 142
15. *McClure, Robert (Buster), T, Nevada-Reno, 153 +
16. Pieper, Harry, C, California, 164
17. Kula, Bob, B, Minnesota, 175
18. Hazard, Frank, G, Nebraska, 186
19. *Jeffers, Ed, T, Oklahoma State, 197
20. Prentice, Bill, B, Santa Clara, 208
21. Fuller, Warren, E, Fordham, 219
22. Neilsen, Fred, T, St. Mary's (CA), 230
23. Gilmore, Bob, B, Washington, 241
24. *Baxter, Lloyd, C, SMU, 252
25. *Luhn, Nolan, E, Tulsa, 263
26. Blanco, Nestor, G, Colorado Mines, 274
27. Chestnut, Bill, B, Kansas, 285
28. Thompson, Jim, B, Washington State, 296
29. Evans, Jim, E, Idaho, 307
30. *Nichols, Ham, G, Rice, 318
31. Priday, John, B, Ohio State, 324
32. Aldridge, Billy Joe, B, Oklahoma State, 330

NEW YORK GIANTS 1945
1. *Barbour, Elmer, B, Wake Forest, 10
3. Appleby, Gordon, C, Ohio State, 26
5. Castleberry, Ed, B, West Texas State, 42
6. *Poole, Barney, E, Mississippi, Army, 53
7. *Mead, Jack, E, Wisconsin, 64
8. Vodick, Nick, B, Northwestern, 75
9. Rudan, John, B, Marquette, 86
10. Smith, Vic, B, UCLA, 97
11. Young, Jim, T, Arkansas, 108
12. Bevis, Billy, B, Tennessee, 119
13. Boozer, Bob, T, Arkansas, 130
14. Rhoades, Stan, B, Mississippi State, 141
15. Wink, Jack, B, Wisconsin, 152
16. *Little, Jim, T, Kentucky, 163
17. Jabbusch, Bob, G, Ohio State, 174
18. Byrd, Bill, C, Maryland, 185
19. Morries, Glenn, T, Texas, 196
20. Davis, Pete, B, Santa Clara, 207
21. *Vacanti, Sam, B, Iowa, 218
22. Oliver, Vern, C, Washington State, 229
23. Chadwell, Jim, T, Tennessee, 240
24. Mroz, Vince, E, Michigan State, 251
25. Kita, George, B, Drake, 262
26. Graham, Doug, T, Stanford, 273
27. Dillon, Jack, E, Texas Tech, 284
28. Anthony, Charley, B, Brown, 295
29. Pipkin, Ray, B, Arkansas, 306
30. Wolf, Joe, C, USC, 317
31. Broderick, Bill, T, Utah, 323
32. Staples, John, G, Alabama, 329

PHILADELPHIA 1945
1. *Yonaker, John, E, Notre Dame, 9
3. Dark, Alvin, B, LSU, 25
5. *Pihos, Pete, E, Indiana, 41
6. Dellago, Chuck, G, Minnesota, 52
7. *Morales, Gonzalo, B, St, Mary's (CA), 63
8. Robinson, Sam, B, Washington, 74
9. *Hall, Forrest, B, San Francisco, 85
10. Sadonis, Joe, T, Fordham, 96
11. *Mobley, Rudy, B, Hardin-Simmons, 107
12. Newmeyer, Jim, T, St, Vincent, 118
13. *Chambers, Bill, T, UCLA, 129
14. Duda, John, B, Virginia, 140 +
15. *Montgomery, Bill, B, LSU, 151
16. Werner, Howard, E, Syracuse, 162
17. Austin, Jim, B, Missouri, 173
18. *Klenk, Quentin, T, USC, 184
19. *Spencer, Joe, T, Oklahoma State, 195
20. Pratt, Leo, T, Oklahoma State, 206
21. Teschner, Phil, T, Brown, 217
22. *Magee, Johnny, G, Rice, 228
23. *Mosley, Norm (Monk), B, Alabama, 239
24. Brown, Blair, G, Oklahoma State, 250
25. Hall, Bob, E, Stanford, 261
26. *Talcott, Don, T, Nevada-Reno, 272
27. Thompson, Bill, T, New Mexico, 283
28. Fleming, Al, C, Wichita State, 294
29. Benjamin, Leo, C, West Virginia, 305
30. Dougherty, Jim, B, Miami (OH), 316
31. *Reese, Ken, B, Alabama, 322
32. Braner, Loren, C, Pittsburgh, 328

PITTSBURGH 1945
1. *Duhart, Paul, B, Florida, 2
2. *Dugger, Jack, E, Ohio State, 12
3. Dellastatious, Bill, B, Missouri, 19 +
4. Adams, Roger, C, Florida, 29 +
5. *Mehelich, Chuck, E, Duquesne, 33
6. *Browning, Greg, E, Denver, 46
7. Wolak, Mike, B, Duquesne, 56
8. Hughes, Tom, T, Missouri, 66
9. *Pense, Leon, B, Arkansas, 79
10. *Brandau, Art, C, Tennessee, 89
11. Ball, Ray, B, Holy Cross, 99
12. Basilone, Frank, B, Duquesne, 112
13. Monahan, John, E, Dartmouth, 122
14. *Odelli, Mel, B, Duquesne, 132
15. *Connor, George, T, Notre Dame, 145 +
16. Ungles, Jim, B, Kansas State, 155
17. *Itzel, John, B, Pittsburgh, 165
18. *Wizbicki, Alex, B, Holy Cross, 178
19. *Landrigan, Jim, T, Dartmouth, 188
20. Lilienthal, Bill, T, Villanova, 198
21. Price, Art, B, Rutgers, 211
22. Malmberg, Don, B, UCLA, 221
23. Hartwell, Everett, E, Auburn, 231
24. Cain, Ed, B, Rice, 244
25. Carlaccini, Angelo, B, Pittsburgh, 254
26. Burns, Ed, B, Boston College, 264
27. *Stough, Glen, T, Duke, 277
28. Marsh, Jim, T, Oklahoma State, 287
29. Grant, Ralph, B, Bucknell, 297 +
30. *Kondrla, John, T, St. Vincent, 310

WASHINGTON 1945
1. *Hardy, Jim, QB, USC, 8
3. *Adams, John (Tree), T, Notre Dame, 23
5. Bujan, George, C Oregon, 38
6. *North, Johnny, E, Vanderbilt, 51
7. *Steber, John, G, Georgia Tech, 61
8. Porter, Art, E, Tulane, 71
9. Kuykendall, Curt, B, Auburn, 84
10. Brogger, Frank, E, Michigan State, 94
11. Creger, Mack, B, Northwestern, 104
12. *McKee, Paul, E, Syracuse, 117
13. *Conerly, Charlie, QB, Mississippi, 127
14. Putnik, John, E, Utah State, 137
15. *Saenz, Eddie, B, USC, 150
16. Fusci, Dom, T, South Carolina, 160
17. Jenkins, Bobby Tom, B, Alabama, 170
18. *Stacco, Ed, T, Colgate, 183 +
19. Bradshaw, Jim, C, Auburn, 193
20. Shipkey, Bill, B, Stanford, 203
21. Halliday, Sid, T, SMU, 216
22. Davidson, Chick, T, Cornell, 226 +
23. Martin, Gabby, E, SMU, 236
24. McCurdy, Jim, C, Stanford, 249
25. *Souders, Cecil (Cy), E, Ohio State, 259
26. Wall, Ben, B, Western Michigan, 269 +
27. Hillery, George, E, Texas-El Paso,282
28. Dreblow, Milford, B, USC, 292
29. Irwin, Frank, T, Duke, 302 +
30. Diner, Leon, E, Denver, 315
31. Cummings, Bob, C, Vanderbilt, 320
32. *Nolander, Don, T, Minnesota, 325

1946

Held January 14, 1946

BOSTON 1946
1. *Dancewicz, Frank (Boley), QB, Notre Dame, 1
2. *Scollard, Nick, E, St, Joseph's (IN), 12
3. *McClure, Robert (Buster), T, Nevada-Reno, 17
4. Breslin, Jack, B, Michigan State, 27
5. Bourgeois, Gaston, B, Tulane, 32
6. Tigart, Thurman, G, Oklahoma, 42
7. *Mieszkowski, Ed, T, Notre Dame, 52
8. Lipka, Chet, E, Boston College, 62
9. *Dekdebrun, Al, B, Cornell, 72
10. John, Rex, T, Wisconsin, 82
11. West, Bob, B, Colorado, 92
12. Dodge, Max, E, Nevada-Reno, 102
13. Kirkland, Joe, T, Virginia, 112
14. Ventresco, Ralph, B, Penn State, 122
15. Furey, John, T, Boston College, 132
16. *Swiacki, Bill, E, Columbia, 142
17. Tiedeman, Charley, B, Brown, 152
18. Alverez, Don, G, Dartmouth, 162
19. Burns, Jack, B, Temple, 172
20. Ruggerio, Frank, B, Notre Dame, 182
21. Price, Jack, B, Baylor, 192
22. Igleheart, Elliot (Ike), G, Tulane, 202
23. Levitt, Bill, C, Miami (FL), 212
24. *Karmazin, Mike, E, Duke, 222
25. Latcham, Chet, G, Denver, 232
26. Botsford, Gordon, E, Boston U., 242
27. Kauffman, John, G, Oregon, 252
28. Glaesner, Don, E, Maryland, 262
29. McKinnon, Carl, G, Dartmouth, 272
30. *Klutka, Nick, E, Florida, 282

CHICAGO BEARS 1946
1. *Lujack, Johnny, QB, Notre Dame, 4
2. *Rykovich, Julie, B, Illinois, 14
3. Broyles, Frank, QB, Georgia Tech, 19
4. Knotts, Ernie, G, Duke, 29
5. Schneider, Don, B, Penn, 34
6. *Scruggs, Ted, E, Rice, 44
7. Beard, Wendell, T, California, 54
8. Ziegler, John, B, Colorado, 64
9. Dropo, Walt, E, Connecticut, 74
10. Harris, Bill, C, Auburn, 84
11. *Allen, Eddie, B, Penn, 94
12. Bauman, Frank, E, Illinois, 104
13. Nostrum, Reed, T, Utah, 114
14. Chatterton, Dick, B, BYU, 124
15. Timko, Johnny, C, Temple, 134
16. *Hazelwood, Ted, T, North Carolina, 144
17. Johnson, Dick, C, Baylor, 154
18. Boettcher, Art, B, Shurtleff, 164
19. Gallagher, Tom, B, Illinois, 174
20. Adams, Johnny, B, Denver, 184
21. Widseth, Dean, T, Bemidji State, 194
22. Kochins, George, T, Bucknell, 204
23. Hoisch, Al, B, Stanford, 214
24. *Grgich, Visco, E, Santa Clara, 224
25. Richards, Allen, B, Cincinnati, 234
26. Tunstill, Jess, B, Kentucky, 244
27. Smock, Ken, B, Purdue, 254
28. Weldon, Howard, G, North Carolina, 264
29. Cook, Johnny, B, Georgia, 274
30. Franck, Harry, B, Northwestern, 284

CHICAGO CARDINALS 1946
1. *Jones, Dub, B, Tulane, 2
2. Wenskunas, Mac, C, Illinois, 11
3. *Angsman, Elmer, B, Notre Dame, 16
4. *Nichols, Ham, G, Rice, 26
5. *Golding, Joe, B, Oklahoma, 31
6. Dickey, Len, T, Texas A&M, 41
7. Lenshan, Pat, E, Tennessee, 51
8. Tinsley, Phil, E, Alabama, 61
9. *Colhouer, J.C., G, Oklahoma State, 71
10. Barber, Tom, T, Tennessee-Chattanooga, 81
11. *Loepfe, Dick, T, Wisconsin, 91
12. *Yablonski, Venton, B, Columbia, 101
13. Lewis, Lee, B, Washington, 111
14. Russell, Bob, B, Miami (OH), 121
15. Rovai, Fred, G, Notre Dame, 131
16. *Evans, Ray, T, Texas-El Paso, 141
17. Loubie, Bob, B, Miami (OH), 151
18. Irwin, Frank, T, Duke, 161
19. Ratteree, Pride, G, Wake Forest, 171
20. Heywood, Bill, B, Notre Dame, 181
21. Traught, Al, B, Miami (OH), 191
22. Andrulewicz, Clem, T, Villanova, 201
23. Rakowski, Adam, E, Penn, 211
24. McKenzie, Jack, B, Northwestern, 221
25. Worthington, Tom, T, Tulsa, 231
26. Vugrin, Jim, G, Tennessee, 241
27. Herschbarger, Jesse, E, SMU, 251
28. Ledbetter, Newman, T, Texas Tech, 261
29. *Baldwin, Alton, E, Arkansas, 271
30. LaRue, Jim, B, Duke, 281

DETROIT 1946
1. Dellastatious, Bill, B, Missouri, 8
3. *Thomas, Russ, T, Ohio State, 22 +
5. Harris, Dave, E, Wake Forest, 38
6. Eddins, Joe, G, Auburn, 47
7. *Berezney, Pete, T, Notre Dame, 58
8. DeCourcey, Keith, B, Washington, 67
9. Hedges, Bill, T, West Texas State, 78
10. Dixon, Thornton, T, Ohio State, 87
11. Stevens, Bob, B, Oregon State, 98
12. Farris, Pat, T, Texas Tech, 107
13. Copoulos, Paul, B, Marquette, 118
14. Irby, Ty, B, Auburn, 127
15. Thrash, Pat, E, South Carolina, 138
16. *Mote, Kelly, E, Duke, 147
17. Scrugg, Bill, B, Rice, 158
18. Wall, Ben, B, Central Michigan, 167
19. Kispert, Merlin, B, Minnesota, 178
20. Malmberg, Don, T, UCLA, 187
21. Maloney, Norm, E, Purdue, 198
22. *Simmons, Jack, B, Detroit, 207
23. Pulte, Joe, E, Detroit, 218
24. Funderberg, Bob, B, Northwestern, 227
25. *Stacco, Ed, T, Colgate, 238
26. Anderson, Roger, G, Oregon State, 247
27. Murdock, Chuck, E, Georgia Tech, 258
28. Van Duesen, Dick, C, Minnesota, 267
29. Agnew, Bill, B, California, 278
30. Panos, Tom, G, Utah, 287
31. Palesse, Orlando, E, Marquette, 293
32. Schellstede, Otis, G, Oklahoma State, 297

GREEN BAY 1946
1. *Strzykalski, Johnny (Strike), B, Marquette, 6
3. *Nussbaumer, Bob, B, Michigan, 21
5. *Cody, Ed, B, Purdue, 36
6. Ferraro, John, T, USC, 46
7. Renner, Art, E, Michigan, 56
8. Cole, Bert, T, Oklahoma State, 66
9. Darnell, Grant, G, Texas A&M, 76

10. McAfee, Joe, B, Holy Cross, 86
11. Conroy, Steve, B, Holy Cross, 96
12. Hildebrand, Billy, E, Mississippi State, 106
13. Hand, Tom, C, Iowa, 116
14. Hills, George, G, Georgia Tech, 126
15. Hough, Jim, B, Clemson, 136
16. Gaines, Dean, T, Georgia Tech, 146
17. Miller, J.P., G, Georgia, 156
18. Morse, Boyd, E, Arizona, 166
19. Bradford, Joe, C, USC, 176
20. DeRosa, Bill, B, Boston College, 186
21. Grant, Ralph, B, Bucknell, 196
22. *Brown, Howard, G, Indiana, 206
23. Kosmac, Andy, C, LSU, 216
24. Stacy, Maurice, B, Washington, 226
25. Davidson, Chick, T, Cornell, 236
26. Norton, John, B, Washington, 246
27. Holtsinger, Ed, B, Georgia Tech, 256
28. Campbell, Joe, E, Holy Cross, 266
29. Saunders, Francis, T, Clemson, 276
30. *Sparlis, Al, G, UCLA, 286
31. Clymer, Ralph, G, Purdue, 291
32. Henderson, Joervin, C, Missouri, 296

LOS ANGELES RAMS 1946
1. *Sitko, Emil (Red), B, Notre Dame, 10
3. *Samuel, Don, B, Oregon State, 25
5. *Paul, Don, C, UCLA, 40 +
6. Oestreich, Newell (Ace), B, California, 50
7. *King, Lafayette (Dolly), E, Georgia, 60
8. Whisler, Joe, B, Ohio State, 70
9. Schumchyk, Mike, E, Arkansas, 80
10. *Signaigo, Joe, G, Notre Dame, 90
11. Phillips, Tom, B, Ohio State, 100
12. Strojny, Ted, T, Holy Cross, 110
13. *Strohmeyer, George, C, Notre Dame, 120
14. Palladino, Bob, B, Notre Dame, 130
15. Lorenz, Dick, E, Oregon State, 140
16. Bouley, Larry, B, Georgia, 150
17. *Urban, Gasper, G, Notre Dame, 160
18. Wise, Bob, G, Colorado, 170
19. Ford, Jerry, E, Notre Dame, 180
20. Albrecht, Bob, B, Marquette, 190
21. *Lewis, Cliff, B, Duke, 200
22. Richardson, Bob, T, Marquette, 210
23. Lebow, Derald, B, Oklahoma, 220
24. Lippincott, Bill, B, Washington St., 230
25. Jamison, Kay, E, Florida, 240
26. Gambrell, D.J., C, Alabama, 250
27. Dickey, Joe Ben, B, Colorado, 260
28. Grbovaz, Marty, E, San Francisco, 270
29. Perrin, Jay, T, USC, 280
30. Plant, Frank, C, Georgia, 290
31. Cowan, Dale, T, Kansas State, 295
32. West, John, B, Oklahoma, 300

NEW YORK GIANTS 1946
1. *Connor, George, T, Notre Dame, 5
2. *Jones, Elmer, (Buck), G, Wake Forest, 15
3. *Rodgers, Hosea, B, North Carolina, 20
4. *Duke, Paul, C, Georgia Tech, 30
5. *Stout, Pete, B, TCU, 35
6. Lalikos, Jim, T, Brown, 45
7. Plyler, Jim, T, Texas, 55
8. *Roberts, Gene (Choo-Choo), B, Tenn.-Chat., 65
9. Harris, Mike, G, Mississippi State, 75
10. *Clay, Walt, B, Colorado, 85
11. Amling, Warren, G, Ohio State, 95
12. Bush, Al, T, Duke, 105
13. Reiman, Bob, B, Oregon State, 115
14. *Hazelhurst, Bob, B, Denver, 125
15. Stapley, Stan, T, Utah, 135
16. Terlizzi, Nick, T, Alabama, 145
17. Justak, Ray, G, Northwestern, 155
18. Morris, Bob, B, USC, 165
19. Loflin, Tom, E, LSU, 175
20. *Kelly, Dick, B, Minnesota, 185
21. Patton, Mel, B, Santa Clara, 195
22. Stiers, Bill, B, UCLA, 205
23. Hare, Vernon, B, Santa Clara, 215
24. Scully, Neil, B, Dayton, 225
25. Miller, George, T, Denver, 235
26. White, Barney, E, Tulsa, 245
27. Kalens, Butch, G, Illinois, 255
28. Ellis, Charlie, B, Virginia, 265
29. Lucas, Steve, E, Duke, 275
30. Voris, Bill, B, North Carolina, 285

PHILADELPHIA 1946
1. Riggs, Leo, B, USC, 7
3. Gray, Gordon, E, USC, 23
5. *Slater, Walt, B, Tennessee, 37
6. *Prewitt, Felto, C, Tulsa, 48
7. Robotham, George, E, UCLA, 57
8. Lecture, Jim, G, Northwestern, 68
9. *Lewis, Ernie, B, Colorado, 77
10. *Vandeweghe, Al, E, William & Mary, 88
11. Iancelli, Bill, E, Franklin & Marshall, 97
12. *McHugh, Pat, B, Georgia Tech, 108
13. Wingender, John, B, Washington, 117
14. *Paine, Homer, T, Tulsa, 128
15. Kerns, John, T, Ohio U., 137
16. Hubbard, Buddy, B, William & Mary, 148
17. Smith, Allen, B, Tulsa, 157
18. Millham, Bernie, E, Fordham, 168
19. Mauss, Lawrence, C, Utah, 177
20. Butcher, Dave, B, William & Mary, 188
21. Fabling, Don, B, Colorado, 197
22. Feldman, George, B Tufts, 208
23. Cameron, Ed, G, Miami (OH), 217
24. Steed, Charley, B, Arkansas-Monticello, 228
25. Grygiel, Ed, B, Dartmouth, 237
26. *Raimondi, Ben, B, Indiana, 248 +
27. *Bailey, Sam, E, Georgia, 257
28. *Long, Bob, B, Tennessee, 268
29. Fisher, Bill, T, Harvard, 277
30. Slusser, George, B, Ohio State, 288
31. *Itzel, John, B, Pittsburgh, 292
32. Kirkman, Larry, B, Boston U., 298

PITTSBURGH 1946
1. Blanchard, Felix (Doc), B, Army, 3
2. Clark, George, B, Duke, 13
3. *Rowe, Harmon, B, San Francisco, 18
4. Tepsic, Joe, B, Penn State, 28
5. Seiferling, Jack, B, Utah State, 33
6. Woods, Marion, G, Clemson, 43
7. Reinhardt, Tom, T, Minnesota, 53
8. Ponsetto, Joe, B, Michigan, 63
9. Evans, Bob, B, Penn , 73
10. Bonwell, Mel, B, Central (IA), 83
11. Holloway, Doc, G, William & Mary, 93
12. Owen, Carroll, B, Catawba, 103
13. Poppin, George, T, New Mexico, 113
14. *McCain, Bob, E, Mississippi, 123
15. Tallchief, Tom, T, Oklahoma, 133
16. Perl, Al, B, Youngstown State, 143
17. Lopez, Russ, C, West Virginia, 153
18. Garrison, Charles (Buck), G, Wake Forest, 163
19. Cloud, Bill, T, Temple, 173
20. Garbinski, Mike, B, Penn State, 183
21. Loiacano, Charley, C, Lafayette, 193
22. Johnson, George, T, Pittsburgh, 203
23. Leitheiser, Bill, G, Duke, 213
24. Adams, Roger, C, Florida, 223
25. Verkins, Bob, B, Tulsa, 233
26. Castle, Clarence, B, Mississippi, 243
27. Marino, Marchi, T, Penn State, 253
28. Hansen, Bob, E, UCLA, 263
29. Graves, Larry, T, Newberry, 273
30. *Bruce, Gail, E, Washington, 283

WASHINGTON 1946
1. Rossi, Cal, B, UCLA, 9 +
3. *Koslowski, Stan, B, Holy Cross, 24
5. Adelt, Gay B, Utah, 39
6. Trojanowski, Walt, B, Connecticut, 49
7. *Hendren, Bob, T, USC, 59
8. Callanan, George, B, USC, 69
9. *Skoglund, Bob, E, Notre Dame, 79
10. *Leicht, Jake, B, Oregon, 89
11. *Maggioli, Achille (Chick), B, Illinois, 99
12. Moncrief, Monte, T, Texas A&M, 109 +
13. *Tereshinski, Joe, E, Georgia, 119
14. Sprague, Stan, E, Illinois, 129
15. Adelman, Harry, E, USC, 139
16. Butchofsky, Bob, B, Texas A&M, 149 +
17. Prashaw, Mike, T, Michigan, 159
18. *Robnett, Ed, B, Texas Tech, 169
19. Dykstra, LaMar, B, Colorado, 179
20. Ward, Bob, B, San Jose State, 189
21. Pehar, John, T, USC, 199
22. Robinson, Roger, B, Syracuse, 209
23. Cadenhead, Charley, C, Mississippi State, 219
24. Rodas, Bob, G, Santa Clara, 229
25. Webb, Charlie, E, LSU, 239
26. Flanagan, Marion, B, Texas A&M, 249
27. Phillips, Roland, T, Georgia Tech, 259
28. Hallmark, Jim, B, Texas A&M, 269
29. Mills, Fay, T, Alabama, 279
30. Ritter, William (Tex), B, Georgia Tech, 289
31. Takesian, Sarkis, B, California, 294
32. Campbell, Mike, E, Mississippi, 299

1947 NFL

Held December 16, 1946

The first choice of the draft was made a Bonus Selection, with teams drawing lots for the right to it. In succeeding seasons, teams that already had been awarded a Bonus Selection no longer were eligible for the draw. The Chicago Bears were awarded the first Bonus Selection in 1947 and chose Bob Fenimore. The second and fourth rounds were limited to the Detroit Lions and Boston Yanks.

BOSTON 1947
1. *Barzilauskas, Fritz, G, Yale, 3
2. *Heap, Walt, B, Texas, 13
3. *Rapacz, John, C, Oklahoma, 15
4. *Baldwin, Alton, E, Arkansas, 25
5. *Vogelaar, Carroll, T, San Francisco, 27
6. *Sullivan, George, T, Notre Dame, 37
7. *Watt, Joe, B, Syracuse, 47
8. *Chipley, Bill, E, Washington & Lee, 57
9. *Malinowski, Gene, C, Detroit, 67
10. *Hazelhurst, Bob, B, Denver, 77
11. *Sidorik, Al, T, Mississippi State, 87
12. Roberts, Wally, E, Holy Cross, 97
13. *Sullivan, Bob, B, Iowa, 107
14. Long, Leo, B, Duke, 117
15. Parker, Frank, T, Holy Cross, 127
16. *Marcolini, Hugo, B, St. Bonaventure, 137
17. *Shirley, Marion, T, Oklahoma City, 147
18. *Nabors, Roland, C, Texas Tech, 157
19. Kennelly, Pat, E, Southeastern Louisiana, 167
20. Waller, Darrell, B, Washington State, 177
21. Hart, Paul, B, Delaware, 187
22. Lamoure, Gene, G, Fresno State, 197
23. Kolaskinski, Hank, B, Wyoming, 207
24. Heap, Ed, T, Texas, 217
25. Polzin, John, G, TCU, 227
26. Bloxom, Dave, B, TCU, 237
27. *Stautzenberger, Odell, G, Texas A&M, 247
28. Chatterton, Dick, B, BYU, 257
29. *Rodgers, Tom, T, Bucknell, 267
30. *Prchlik, John, G, Yale, 277

CHICAGO BEARS 1947

BONUS CHOICE: *Fenimore, Bob, B, Oklahoma State, 1
1. *Kindt, Don, B, Wisconsin, 11
3. *Minini, Frank, B, San Jose State, 23
5. Merriman, Lloyd, B, Stanford [from Chicago Cardinals], 32
   *Canady, Jim, B, Texas, 35
6. Stephens, Roger, B, Cincinnati [from Philadelphia], 42
   *Wetz, Harlan, T, Texas, 45
7. Moseley, Reid, E, Georgia, 55
8. *Smith, Houston Allen, E, Mississippi, 65
9. Eddleman, Dwight (Dike), B, Illinois, 75
10. Tucker, Arnold, B, Army, 85
11. Hatch, Larry, B, Washington, 95
12. *Adamle, Tony, C, Ohio State, 105
13. Fritz, Emil, G, Maryland, 115
14. Turner, Jim, T, California, 125
15. Goodall, Wayne, E, Oklahoma City, 135
16. Gagne, Verne, E, Minnesota, 145
17. *Dreyer, Wally, B, Wisconsin, 155
18. Pupa, Walt, B, North Carolina, 165
19. McLellan, John, T, Montana State, 175
20. Cromer, Bill, B, Texas, 185
21. *Reader, Russ, B, Michigan State, 195
22. Batchelor, Jim, B, East Texas State, 205
23. *Lawler, Allen, B, Texas, 215
24. Berlin, Gordon, C, Washington, 225
25. Cunningham, John, E, California, 235
26. *Morris, Max, B, Northwestern, 245
27. Morris, Bill, E, Oklahoma, 255
28. Baumgardner, Joe Bill, B, Texas, 265
29. McCarthy, Jerry, E, Penn, 275
30. Pierce, Jack, B, Illinois, 285
31. Ehlers, Ed, B, Purdue. 293

CHICAGO CARDINALS 1947
1. *Coulter, DeWitt (Tex), T, Army, 7
3. *Allen, Ermal, B, Kentucky, 18
5. Choice to Chicago Bears
6. *Raimondi, Ben, B, Indiana, 41
7. Turner, Howard, B, North Carolina State, 50
8. Maddock, George, T, Northwestern, 60
9. Dufelmeier, Art, B, Illinois, 70
10. *Ramsey, Ray, B, Bradley, 82
11. Wallace, Dave, B, Oklahoma, 90
12. *Sarratt, Charley, B, Oklahoma, 101
13. Cooper, Hardin, T, Tulsa, 112
14. Russ, Carl, B, Rice, 120 +
15. Mulligan, Buddy, B, Duke, 131
16. *Smith, Charlie, B, Georgia, 142
17. *Ravensburg, Bob, E, Indiana, 150
18. Barnett, Barney, E, Northeastern Oklahoma, 162
19. Deeds, Scotty, B, BYU, 171
20. Esser, Clarence, T, Wisconsin, 180
21. Ballard, Shelton, C, LSU, 192
22. Walker, Wade, T, Oklahoma, 201
23. Carroll, Tom, T, Minnesota, 210
24. Dorsey, Tom, B, Brown, 222
25. *Schnellbacher, Otto, E, Kansas, 231
26. *Joe, Larry, B, Penn State, 240
27. Abrams, Dick, B, Washington State, 252
28. *Smith, Joe, E, Texas Tech, 260
29. Rotunno, Tony, B, St. Ambrose, 270
30. *Lindsey, Clyde, E, LSU, 282
31. *Callahan, Bob, C, Michigan, 289
32. Karamigios, Johnny, B, Denver, 296

DETROIT 1947
1. *Davis, Glenn, B, Army, 2
2. *Thomas, Russ, T, Ohio State, 12
3. *Kekeris, Jim, T, Missouri, 14
4. Hoover, Charley, C, Vanderbilt, 24
5. *Chappuis, Bob, B, Michigan, 26
6. *Gallagher, Bernie, T, Penn, 36
7. *Grain, Ed, G, Penn, 46
8. James, Harvey, C, Miami (FL), 56
9. Alexander, Kale, T, South Carolina, 66
10. Elliott, Chalmers (Bump), B, Michigan, 76
11. Sullivan, Pete, T, Detroit, 86
12. Camaratta, LaVerne, B, Iowa State, 96
13. *Vezmar, Walt, G, Michigan State, 106
14. Hagen, Dick, E, Washington, 116
15. Meeks, J.W., B, East Texas State, 126
16. *Nilsen, Reed, C BYU, 136
17. *James, Tommy, B, Ohio State, 146
18. Maugham, Ralph, E, Utah State, 156
19. Baty, Buryl, B, Texas A&M, 166
20. *Madar, Elmer, E, Michigan, 176
21. White, J.T., E, Michigan, 186
22. *Schuette, Carl, B, Marquette, 196
23. Cipot, Steve, T, St. Bonaventure, 206
24. Cadenhead, Bill, B, Alabama, 216
25. Cody, Jim, T, East Texas State, 226
26. *Maves, Earl, B, Wisconsin, 236
27. *Hillman, Bill, B, Tennessee, 246
28. Kelly, Arch, E, Detroit, 256
29. Tulis, Bob, T, Texas A&M, 266
30. McAfee, Howard, T, Tulane, 276

GREEN BAY 1947
1. *Case, Ernie, B, UCLA, 6
3. *Baldwin, Burr, E, UCLA, 20
5. *Burns, Paul (Buddy), G, Oklahoma, 31
6. *Wilson, Gene, E, SMU, 40
7. Connors, Dick, B, Northwestern, 52
8. Moncrief, Monte, T, Texas A&M, 62
9. McDougal, Bob, B, Miami (FL), 72
10. *Kelly, Bob, B, Notre Dame, 81
11. Moulton, Tom, C, Oklahoma State, 92
12. Hills, George, G, Georgia Tech, 100
13. *Skoglund, Bob, E, Notre Dame, 111
14. Mitchell, Jack, B, Oklahoma, 122
15. *Crawford, Denver, T, Tennessee, 130
16. Callanan, Jim, E, USC, 141
17. *Scalissi, Ted, B, Ripon, 151
18. Goodman, Jim, T, Indiana, 160
19. Miller, Dick, G, Lawrence, 172
20. *Ecklund, Brad (Whitey), C, Oregon, 181
21. West, Bob, B, Colorado, 190
22. Reilly, Maurice (Tex), B, Colorado, 202
23. Sockolov, Ron, T, California, 211
24. *St. John, Herb, G, Georgia, 220
25. Redeker, Fred, B, Cincinnati, 232
26. Lubker, Herm, E, Arkansas, 241
27. Palladino, Bob, B, Notre Dame, 250
28. Baxter, Jerrell, T, North Carolina, 262
29. Sellers, Ray, E, Georgia, 271
30. Carle, Jerry, B, Northwestern, 280
31. Hogan, Bill, B, Kansas, 290
32. *Olsen, Ralph, E, Utah, 297

LOS ANGELES RAMS 1947
1. *Wedemeyer, Herman, B, St. Mary's (CA), 9
3. *Paul, Don, C, UCLA, 21
5. Gray, Gordon, B, USC, 33
6. *Evenson, Paul, T, Oregon State, 43
7. *Smyth, Bill, T, Cincinnati, 53
8. McGovern, Bill, C, Washington, 63
9. Partin, Max, B, Tennessee, 73
10. *Samuelson, Carl, T, Nebraska, 83
11. Steger, Russ, B, Illinois, 93
12. *Lavelli, Dante, E, Ohio State, 103
13. Dimitro, Mike, G, UCLA, 113
14. *Kissell, John, T, Boston College, 123
15. Fuchs, George, B, Wisconsin, 133
16. Chubb, Ralph, B, Michigan, 143
17. Hardy, Don, E, USC, 153
18. *Champagne, Ed, T, LSU, 163
19. *Dewar, Jimmy, B, Indiana, 173
20. Reiges, Bernie, B, UCLA, 183
21. *McLaughlin, Leon, C, UCLA, 193
22. *Elliott, Chuck, T, Oregon, 203
23. *Levanti, Lou, C, Illinois, 213
24. Cheek, J.D., T, Oklahoma State, 223 +
25. Dal Porto, Bob, B, California, 233
26. Standefer, Gene, B, Texas Tech, 243
27. *David, Bob, B, Villanova, 253
28. Hunnicutt, Jim, B, South Carolina, 263
29. Comer, John, B, Holy Cross, 273
30. *Dean, Hal, G, Ohio State, 283
31. Atwell, James, B, South Carolina, 291
32. Prymuski, Bob, G, Illinois, 299

NEW YORK GIANTS 1947
1. *Schwall, Vic, B, Northwestern, 10
3. *Cannady, John, C, Indiana, 22
5. *Greene, Nelson, T, Tulsa, 34
6. *Davis, Bob, T, Georgia Tech, 44
7. *Iversen, Chris (Duke), B, Oregon, 54
8. *Muelheuser, Frank, B, Colgate, 64
9. Novitsky, John, T, Oklahoma City, 74
10. Mullis, Fred, B, Tennessee-Chattanooga, 84
11. *Hoernschemeyer, Bob (Hunchy), B, Indiana, 94
12. *Brown, Hardy (Thumper), B, Tulsa, 104 +
13. *Hachten, Bill, G, Stanford, 114
14. Fuson, Herschel (Ug), B, Army, 124
15. Fallon, John, T, Notre Dame, 134
16. Orlando, Bob, G, Colgate, 144
17. Pullatie, Frank, B, SMU, 154
18. Brinkley, Dick, B, Wake Forest, 164
19. Guess, Frank, B, Texas, 174
20. *Landry, Tom, B, Texas, 184 F
21. Ponsetto, Joe, B, Michigan, 194
22. *Donovan, Art, T, Boston College, 204
23. *Shoener, Hal, E, Iowa, 214
24. Moll, Bill, B, Connecticut, 224
25. Thomas, Dick, G, Southern Mississippi, 234
26. *Stewart, Ralph, C, Notre Dame, 244
27. Bibighaus, George, E, Muhlenberg, 254
28. Carrington, Jim, G, Navy, 264
29. Harrison, Claude, B, South Carolina, 274
30. *Wright, John, B, Maryland, 284
31. *Shuler, Bill, E, Yale, 292
32. Clayton, Don, B, North Carolina, 300

PHILADELPHIA 1947
1. *Armstrong, Neill, E, Oklahoma State, 8
3. *Mackrides, Bill, B, Nevada-Reno, 19
5. *Savitsky, George, T, Penn, 30
6. Choice to Chicago Bears
7. Yovicsin, Tony, E, Miami (FL), 51
8. *Satterfield, Alf, T, Vanderbilt, 61
9. *Leonetti, Bob, G, Wake Forest, 71
10. Cornogg, Ulysses, T, Wake Forest, 80
11. Sarkisian, Alex, C, Northwestern, 91
12. D'Arcy, Jerry, C, Tulsa, 102
13. Hamberger, John, T, SMU, 110
14. *Johnson, Alvin, B, Hardin-Simmons, 121
15. Cook, Joe, B, Hardin-Simmons, 132
16. *Durkota, Jeff, B, Penn State, 140 F
17. *Shurtz, Hubert, T, LSU, 152
18. Bell, Hal, B, Muhlenberg, 161
19. *Campion, Tom, T, Southeastern Louisiana, 170
20. Hall, Fred, G, LSU, 182
21. Clayton, Jim, T, Wyoming, 191
22. Blomquist, George, E, North Carolina State, 200
23. *Haynes, Joe, G, Tulsa, 212
24. Hense, Stanton, E, Xavier, 221

25. Kelly, Johnny, B, Rice, 230
26. Roberts, H.J., G, Rice, 242
27. Cutchin, Phil, B, Kentucky, 251
28. Wakefield, Charley, T, Stanford, 261
29. Lagenbeck, Dick, T, Cincinnati, 272
30. *Winkler, Bernie, T, Texas Tech, 281
31. Stephens, Bill, T, Baylor, 288
32. Kalash, Mike, E, Wisconsin-La Crosse, 298

PITTSBURGH 1947
1. *Bechtol, Hub, E, Texas, 5
3. *Mastrangelo, John, G, Notre Dame, 16
5. *Wydo, Frank, T, Cornell, 29
6. *Aschenbrenner, Frank, B, Northwestern, 38
7. *Meeks, Bryant (Meatball), C, South Carolina, 49
8. *Shipkey, Jerry, B, UCLA, 58
9. Vander Clute, Bert, G, Wesleyan, 69
10. *Gibson, Paul, E, North Carolina State, 78
11. Medd, Jack, C, Wesleyan, 89
12. Fitch, Jack, B, North Carolina, 98
13. *Parseghian, Ara, B, Miami (OH), 109 F
14. *Moore, Bill (Red), T, Penn State, 118
15. Bruno, Larry, B, Geneva, 129
16. Jenkins, Ralph, C, Clemson, 138
17. *Nickel, Elbie, E, Cincinnati, 149
18. *Cregar, Bill, C, Holy Cross, 158
19. *Mulready, Jerry, B, North Dakota State, 169
20. Smith, Warren, T, Kansas Wesleyan, 178
21. Hamilton, Fred, T, Vanderbilt, 189
22. Taylor, Fred, E, TCU, 198
23. Bushmaier, Binks, B, Vanderbilt, 209
24. *Davis, Paul, B, Otterbein, 218
25. *Kalmanir, Tommy, B, Nevada-Reno, 229 F
26. Mohr, Don, E, Baldwin-Wallace, 238
27. Young, Art, G, Dartmouth, 249
28. *Sazio, Ralph, T, William & Mary, 258
29. Pitzer, Dick, E, Army, 269
30. Stalloni, Tom, T, Delaware, 278
31. DiFrancesca, Vince, G, Northwestern, 287
32. *Lahr, Warren, B, Case Western Reserve, 294

WASHINGTON 1947
1. Rossi, Cal, B, UCLA, 4
3. Knight, Gene (Red), B, LSU, 17
5. *Foldberg, Hank, E, Army, 28
6. *Garzoni, Mike, G, USC, 39
7. *Gray, Bill, C, Oregon State, 48
8. *Harris, Hank, T, Texas, 59
9. *Karrasch, Roy, E, UCLA, 68
10. Williamson, Ernie, T, North Carolina, 79
11. Carmody, L.G., B, Central Washington, 88
12. Savage, U.S., E, Richmond, 99
13. Steckroth, Bob, E, William & Mary, 108
14. *Edwards, Weldon, T, TCU, 119
15. Wheeler, Earl, C, Arkansas, 128
16. Gold, Billy, B, Tennessee, 139
17. Hart, Jack, T, Detroit, 148
18. Nichols, Tom, B, Richmond, 159
19. *Dowda, Harry, B, Wake Forest, 168
20. Webb, Charlie, E, LSU, 179
21. Bond, Elmo, T, Washington State, 188
22. Hefti, Jim, B, St. Lawrence, 199
23. Dudley, Tom, E, Virginia, 208
24. *Smith, Jim, B, Iowa, 219
25. Mullins, Hal, T, Duke, 228
26. Bocoka, Francis, E, Washington State, 239
27. Sacrinty, Otis, B, Wake Forest, 248
28. Dropo, Milt, C, Connecticut, 259
29. Brownson, Lynn, B, Stanford, 268
30. Colone, Joe, B, Penn State, 279
31. *Shoener, Herb, E, Iowa, 286
32. Plevo, Bob, T, Purdue, 295

1947 AAFC

Held December 20-21, 1946

The AAFC's first draft was held in the same manner as the NFL draft—teams drafting in inverse order of finish. Buffalo, which had finished the 1946 season with the same record as Brooklyn, drafted second in each round, however, with Brooklyn drafting third. Although Miami was no longer in the league by the time the 1947 season was played, it was at the time of the draft. Miami's selections later were granted to the new Baltimore Colts. Prior to the regular draft, "special selections" were made. It is not known why these selections weren't part of the regular draft or in what order they were made. All teams had two, except Buffalo, which had five, and the Los Angeles Dons and San Francisco, which had one each. Most likely, Los Angeles and San Francisco each traded one of its choices to Buffalo. The regular draft was 15 rounds, followed by a "supplemental draft," in which various teams didn't get choices. From rounds 16 through 20, Cleveland and the New York Yankees didn't make selections. From rounds 21 through 25, Cleveland, New York, San Francisco, and Los Angeles didn't receive selections. Like current NFL drafts, the AAFC drafts indicated an overall order of selection, which is shown by a number after each player's school.

BROOKLYN 1947
Blanchard, Felix (Doc), FB, Army
*Roberts, Gene (Choo-Choo), B, Tennessee-Chattanooga
1. *Armstrong, Neill, E, Oklahoma Stale, 3
2. *Conerly, Charlie, QB, Mississippi, 11
3. *Barzilauskas, Fritz, G, Yale, 19
4. *Wright, Jim, G, SMU, 27
5. *Wetz, Harlan, T, Texas, 35
6. Bushmaier, Binks, B, Vanderbilt, 43
7. *Williams, Garland, T, Georgia, 51
8. Hefti, Jim, B, St. Lawrence, 59
9. *Burris, Paul (Buddy), G, Oklahoma, 67
10. *Milner, Bill, G, Duke, 75
11. *Smith, Jim, T, Colorado, 83
12. Goodman, Marv, E, Willamette, 91
13. *Scruggs, Ted, E, Rice, 99
14. *Nelsen, Reed, C, BYU, 107
15. Shannon, Gus, G, Colorado, 115
16. Cook, Joe, B, Hardin-Simmons, 123
17. *Laurinaitas, Frank, G, Richmond, 129
18. *Gustafson, Ed, C, Geo. Washington, 135
19. Hagen, Dick, E, Washington, 141
20. *Foldberg, Hank, E, Army, 147
21. Furman, Harry, T, Cornell, 153
22. Kretz, Walt, B, Cornell, 157
23. Monahan, John, E, Dartmouth, 161
24. Bailey, Bruce, B, Virginia, 165
25. *Evans, Ray, B, Texas-El Paso, 169

BUFFALO 1947
*Fenimore, Bob, B, Oklahoma State
*Aschenbrenner, Frank, B, Northwestern
Richardson, Cal, E, Tulsa
*Cochran, John (Red), B, Wake Forest
1. *Baldwin, Alton, E, Arkansas, 2
2. *Davis, Bob, T, Georgia Tech, 10
3. *Kuffel, Ray, E, Marquette, 18
4. Andrejko, Joe, B, Fordham, 26
5. *Mastrangelo, John, G, Notre Dame, 34
6. *Corley, Bert, C, Mississippi State, 42
7. Knotts, Ernie, G, Duke, 50
8. *Watt, Joe, B, Syracuse, 58
9. *Gibson, Paul, E, North Carolina State, 66
10. *Maskas, John, T, Virginia Tech, 74
11. Jarrell, Baxter, T, North Carolina, 82
12. Liptka, Chet, T, Boston College, 90
13. Sowinski, Joe, G, Indiana, 98
14. *Chipley, Bill, E, Washington & Lee, 106
15. Kosanovich, Bronco, C, Penn State, 114
16. * Kosikowski, Frank, E, Notre Dame, 122
17. *Serini, Washington, T, Kentucky, 128
18. *Yablonski, Ventan, B, Columbia, 134
19. Compton, Chuck, T, Alabama, 140
20. *Swiacki, Bill, E, Columbia, 146
21. *Nichols, Hamil, G, Rice, 152
22. Furey, John, T, Boston College, 156
23. *Schneider, Don, B, Penn, 160
24. Highsmith, Chan, C, North Carolina, 164
25. *Wydo, Frank, T, Cornell, 168

CHICAGO ROCKETS 1947
*Lujack, Johnny, QB, Notre Dame
*Gallagher, Bernie, T, Penn
1. *Sullivan, George, T, Notre Dame, 4
2. Manieri, Ray, B, Wake Forest, 12
3. Derleth, Bob, T, Michigan, 20
4. Reagan, Johnny, B, Montana State, 28
5. Pharr, Jim, C, Auburn, 36
6. Sandberg, Bob, B, Minnesota, 44
7. *Allen, Eddie, B, Penn, 52
8. Bolger, Matt, E, Notre Dame, 60
9. *Eikenberg, Charlie, B, Rice, 68
10. *Allen, Ermal, QB, Kentucky, 76
11. Chaves, Marty, G, Oregon State, 84
12. Jernigan, George, G, Georgia, 92
13. Jordan, R.J., E, Georgia Tech, 100
14. *Livingston, Bob, B, Notre Dame, 108
15. Ivy, Bill, T, Northwestern, 116
16. *Niedziela, Bruno, T, Iowa, 124
17. *Mackrides, Bill, QB, Nevada-Reno, 130
18. Wenskunas, Mac, C, Illinois, 136
19. Graham, Tony, C, St. Mary's (MN), 142
20. Benda, Russ, G, Iowa, 148
21. Watkins, George, T, Texas, 154
22. *Vacanti, Sam, B, Nebraska, 158
23. Zenkevitch, Len, T, Idaho, 162
24. Day, Dave, G, Iowa, 166
25. Franks, Bill, T, Illinois, 170

CLEVELAND 1947
*Hoerner, Dick, B, Iowa
Rice, Robert Lawrence, C, Tulane
1. *Chappuis, Bob, B, Michigan, 8
2. *Cowhig, Gerry, B, Notre Dame, 16
3. *Carpenter, Jack, T, Missouri, Michigan, 24
4. *Cowan, Bob, B, Indiana, 32
5. Griffen, Bill, T, Kentucky, 40
6. Bush, Jack, T, Georgia, 48
7. *Rapacz, John, C, Oklahoma, 56
8. *Hazelhurst, Bob, B, Denver, 64
9. Ellsworth, Ralph, B, Texas, 72
10. Dewar, Jimmy, H, Indiana, 80
11. Huber, Bill, E, Illinois, 88
12. *Giannelli, Mario, G, Boston College, 96
13. *Shumas, Marshall, E, Missouri, 104
14. *Signaigo, Joe, B, Notre Dame, 112
15. Widseth, Dean, T, Minnesota, 120

LOS ANGELES DONS 1947
*Wedemeyer, Herman, B, St. Mary's (CA)
1. *Baldwin, Burr, E, UCLA, 5
2. *Skipkey, Jerry, B, UCLA, 13
3. Merriman, Lloyd, B, Stanford, 21
4. Rossi, Cal, B, UCLA, 29
5. Clement, Boyd, T, Oregon State, 37
6. Zapalac, Willie, B, Texas A&M, 45
7. *Savitsky, George, T, Penn, 53
8. *Paul, Don, C, UCLA, 61
9. Hart, Paul, B, Delaware, 69
10. *Heap, Walt, QB, Texas, 77
11. Dimitro, Mike, G, UCLA, 85
12. *Moore, Bill (Red), T, Penn State, 93
13. Martin, Joe, B, Cornell, 101
14. *Wilson, Gene, E, SMU, 109
15. *Muelheuser, Frank, B, Colgate, 117
16. *Cody, Ed (Cat Foot), B, Purdue, 125
17. *Sullivan, Bob, B, Iowa, 131
18. Cullen, Louis, B, New Mexico, 137
19. Killelea, John, B, Boston College, 143
20. Andros, Dee, G, Oklahoma, 149

MIAMI 1947
Tucker, Arnold, QB, Army
*Case, Ernie, B, UCLA
1. *Madar, Elmer, E, Michigan, 1
2. *Bechtol, Hub, E, Texas, 9
3. *Mont, Tommy, B, Maryland, 17
4. *Humble, Weldon, G, Rice, 25
5. Deal, Russ, T, Indiana, 33
6. Malmberg, Don, T, UCLA, 41
7. *Schwall, Vic, B, Northwestern, 49
8. Turner, Howard, B, North Carolina State, 57
9. *Hubbell, Frank, E, Tennessee, 65
10. Burgeois, Gaston, G, Tulane, 73
11. Brieske, Jim, C, Michigan, 81
12. *Mobley, Rudy, B, Hardin-Simmons, 89
13. Doherty Gerry, B, Delaware, 97
14. *Baumgartner, Bill, E, Minnesota, 105
15. *Kekeris, Jim, T, Missouri, 113
16. *North, Johnny, E, Vanderbilt, 121
17. *Canady, Jim, B, Texas, 127
18. *Brown, Howard, G, Indiana, 133
19. Sims, John, B, Tulane, 139
20. Vanderclutte, Bert, G, Wesleyan, 145
21. Stalloni, Tony, T, Delaware, 151
22. Lamoure, Gene, G, Fresno State, 155
23. Daniels, Leo, B, Texas A&M, 159
24. Reilly, Tex, B, Colorado, 163
25. *Landrigan, Jim, T, Dartmouth, 167

NEW YORK YANKEES 1947
*Young, Claude (Buddy), B, Illinois
*Trippi, Charley, B, Georgia
1. *Raimondi, Ben, B, Indiana, 7
2. Moncreif, Monte, T, Texas A&M, 15
3. *Collins, Bill (Spot), G, Texas, 23
4. *Tereshinski, Joe, E, Georgia Tech, 31
5. *Durishan, Jack, T, Pittsburgh, 39
6. Dropo, Walt, E, Connecticut, 47
7. *Nabors, Roland, C, Texas Tech, 55
8. *Strohmeyer, George, C, Notre Dame, 63
9. *Ossowski, Ted, T, Oregon State, 71
10. Werder, Dick, G, Georgetown (DC), 79
11. Healey, Bill, G, Georgia Tech, 87
12. Sikorski, Ed, B, Muhlenberg, 95
13. *Miklich, Bill, B, Idaho, 103
14. *Elliott, Chuck, T, Oregon, 111
15. *Grain, Ed, G, Penn, 119

SAN FRANCISCO 1947
*Davis, Glenn, B, Army
1. *LeForce, Clyde, B, Tulsa, 6
2. *Wiese, Bob, B, Michigan, 14
3. *Duke, Paul, C, Georgia Tech, 22
4. *Samuel, Don, B, Oregon State, 30
5. *Satterfield, Alf, T, Vanderbilt, 38
6. *Zilly, Jack, E, Notre Dame, 46
7. Knight, Gene (Red), B, LSU, 54
8. Malmberg, Charlie, T, Rice, 62
9. *Leonetti, Bob, G, Wake Forest, 70
10. Broyles, Frank, QB, Georgia Tech, 78
11. *Tyree, Jim, E, Oklahoma, 86
12. *Robnett, Ed, B, Texas Tech, 94
13. *Slater, Walt, B, Tennessee, 102
14. Wheeler, Earl, C, Arkansas, 110
15. Proctor, Les, G, Texas, 118
16. *DeRogatis, Al, T, Duke, 126
17. Tullos, Earl, T, LSU, 132
18. *Meeks, Bryant, C, South Carolina, 138
19. *Royston, Ed, G, Wake Forest, 144
20. *Bumgardner, Max, E, Texas, 150

1948 NFL

Held December 19, 1947

BOSTON 1948
1. *Mancha, Vaughn, C, Alabama, 5
3. *Nolan, John, T, Penn State [from New York Giants], 14
Cook, Earl, G, SMU, 17
5. Healey, Bill, G, Georgia Tech, 29
6. *Slosburg, Phil, B, Temple, 39
7. Choice to Los Angeles Rams
8. Furse, Robert (Tex), B, Yale, 59
9. Burton, Jim, E, Wesleyan, 69
10. Forbes, Bob, B, Florida, 79
11. *Roman, George, T, Case Western Reserve, 89
12. *Wimberly, Abner, E, LSU, 99
13. *Jensen, Bob, E, Iowa St., 109
14. Entsminger, Hal (Bus), B, Missouri, 119
15. Ragonese, Carmen, B, New Hampshire, 129
16. *Ratterman, George, QB, Notre Dame, 139
17. Trotter, Nute, T, Oklahoma, 149
18. Mendel, Jack, E, Canisius, 159
19. Jowell, Mel, G, McMurry, 169
20. *Nelson, Frank, B, Utah, 179
21. *Lukens, Jim, E, Washington & Lee, 189
22. O'Brien, Fran, B, Dartmouth, 199
23. Zito, Jim, T, Michigan State, 209
24. Roderick, Jack, E, Yale, 219
25. Sikorski, Eddie, B, Muhlenberg, 229
26. Mather, Bruce, B, New Hampshire, 239
27. Shoaf, Jim, T, Iowa, 249 +
28. McCary, Joe, B, Virginia, 259
29. Sica, Al, B, Penn, 269
30. Bonk, Harry, B, Maryland, 279
31. Langsjoen, Bernor, B Gustavus Adolphus, 287
32. Neff, George, B, Virginia, 294

CHICAGO BEARS 1948
1. *Layne, Bobby, QB, Texas [from Detroit thru Pittsburgh], 3
*Baumgardner, Max, E, Texas, 10
3. *Garrett, Dub, T, Mississippi State, 21
5. *Ramsey, Knox, G, William & Mary, 32
6. Brugge, Bob, B, Ohio State, 44
7. Choice to Detroit
8. *McWilliams, Tom (Shorty), B, Mississippi State, 62
9. Mills, Malachi, T, Virginia Military, 74
10. *Flanagan, Dick, E, Ohio State, 83
11. McDowell, Jim, G, William & Mary, 92
12. Sheehan, Mel, E, Missouri, 104
13. Scott, Dick, C, Navy, 113
14. *Cline, Ollie, B, Ohio State, 122
15. *Goode, Rob, B, Texas A&M, 134 +
16. Grimenstein, Clyde, E, Purdue, 143
17. Fallon, John, G, Notre Dame, 152
18. Brown, Ray, B, Virginia, 164
19. Hileman, Bob, C, California, 173
20. Gay, Thurman, T, Oklahoma State, 182
21. Blount, Ralph (Peppy), E, Texas, 194
22. *Boone, J.R., B, Tulsa, 203
23. *Duncan, Jim, E, Wake Forest, 212
24. Gatewood, Jimmy, B, Georgia, 224
25. Brumm, George, C, Pacific, 233
26. Dietzel, Paul, C, Miami (OH), 242
27. Clasby, Ed, B, Boston College, 254
28. Hardison, Fred, E, Duke, 263
29. Van Deren, Frank, E, California, 272
30. Pietkiewicz, Al, E, San Francisco, 284
31. *Cox, Norm, B, TCU, 291
32. *Smith, Truett, B, Mississippi State, 297 +

CHICAGO CARDINALS 1948
1. *Spavital, Jim, B, Oklahoma State, 11
3. *Smith, Bill, T, North Carolina, 23
5. Smith, Jay, E, Southern Mississippi, 35
6. Choice to Pittsburgh
7. *Cason, Jim, B, LSU, 55
8. *Camp, Jim, B, North Carolina, 65
9. Choice to New York Giants
10. Weisner, Carl, E, St. Louis, 85
11. Corum, Gene, G, West Virginia, 95
12. *Self, Clarence, B, Wisconsin, 105
13. *Hollar, John, B, Appalachian State, 115
14. *Hanlon, Bob, B, Loras, 125
15. *Petrovich, George, T, Texas, 135
16. *Still, Jim, B, Georgia Tech, 145
17. Davis, Clay, C, Oklahoma State, 155
18. Caughron, Harry, T, William & Mary, 165
19. *Davis, Jerry, B, Southeastern Louisiana, 175
20. Dwyer, Gene, E, St. Ambrose, 185
21. Waters, Harry, B, Colorado College, 195
22. Monroe, Dick, C, Kansas, 205
23. Reynolds, H.M. (Hindu), E, Southern Mississippi, 215
24. *Wedel, Dick, G, Wake Forest, 225
25. *Shoults, Paul, B, Miami (OH), 235
26. Wendt, Fred, B, Texas-El Paso, 245
27. Belden, Doug, B, Florida, 255
28. Stackhouse, Ray, T, Xavier, 265
29. Reid, Bernie, G, Georgia, 275
30. Powell, Jim, E, Tennessee, 285
31. Polidor, Bob, B, Villanova, 293
32. *Fischer, Bill, G, Notre Dame, 300 +

DETROIT 1948
1. Choice to Chicago Bears thru Pittsburgh
*Tittle, Y.A., QB, LSU [from Los Angeles Rams], 6
2. Quist, George, B, Stanford, 13
3. *Bingaman, Les, T, Illinois, 15
4. Minor, Jim, T, Arkansas, 25
5. Choice to Green Bay
6. Williamson, Bob, T, Hobart, 37
7. *Enke, Fred, B, Arizona, 47
Schwab, Moroni, T, Utah St. [from Chicago Bears], 53
8. Choice to NY Giants
9. *Doll, Don, B, USC, 67
10. *Cleary, Paul, E, USC, 77
11. *Land, Fred, T, LSU, 87
12. Choice to NY Giants
13. Steger, Russ, B, Illinois, 107 +
14. Enstice, Hal, B, Union (NY), 117
15. Elliott, Pete, B, Michigan, 127 F
16. Templeton, Dave, G, Ohio State, 137
17. Sickels, Quentin, G, Michigan, 147
18. *Spruill, Jim, T, Rice, 157
19. *Hafen, Barney, E, Utah, 167

20. Dellosobelle, Aldo, T, Loyola (CA), 177
21. Dill, Dean, B, USC, 187
22. McEwen, Jack, B, Colorado, 197
23. *Steiner, Roy (Rebel), E, Alabama, 207 +
24. Saurez, Joe, G, St. Mary's (CA), 217
25. McGee, Coy, B, Notre Dame, 227
26. Alexander, Phil, T, South Carolina, 237
27. Pizza, Frank, T, Toledo, 247
28. Schutte, George, T, USC, 257
29. Pabalis, Tony, B, Central Michigan, 267
30. McCurry, Bob, C, Michigan State, 277

GREEN BAY 1948
1. *Girard, Earl (Jug), B, Wisconsin, 7
3. *Smith, Oscar, B, Texas-El Paso, 19
5. Richards, Don, T, Arkansas [from Detroit], 27
   Sellers, Weyman, E, Georgia, 31
6. *Olsonoski, Larry G, Minnesota, 41
7. *Rhodemyre, Jay, C, Kentucky, 51
8. Cunz, Bob, T, Illinois, 61
9. Choice to NY Giants
10. Walmsley, George, B, Rice, 81
11. Hodges, Bob, T, Bradley, 91
12. Rennebohm, Bob, E, Wisconsin, 101
13. *Moss, Perry, B, Illinois, 111
14. *Provo, Fred, B, Washington, 121
15. Agase, Lou, T, Illinois, 131
16. Raven, Travis, B, Texas, 141
17. Choice to Washington
18. Balge, Ken, E, Michigan State, 161
19. Tatom, Charley, T, Texas, 171
20. Thomas, Floyd, C, Arkansas, 181
21. *St. John, Herb, G, Georgia, 191
22. Anderson, Don (Red), B, Rice, 201
23. Kling, Fred, B, Missouri, 211
24. Biggers, Clyde, T, Catawba, 221
25. *Heath, Stan, QB, Nevada-Reno, 231
26. Allen, Aubrey, T, Colorado, 241
27. Gorski, Stan, E, St. Mary's (MN), 251
28. Sharp, Don, C, Tulsa, 261
29. *Panelli, John (Pep), B, Notre Dame, 271 +
30. *McGeary, Clarence (Clink), T, North Dakota State, 281
31. Mills, Gayland (Mike), E, BYU, 289
32. *Earhart, Ralph, E, Texas Tech, 296

LOS ANGELES RAMS 1948
1. Choice to Detroit
3. *Keane, Tom, B, West Virginia, 18
5. Bailey, Bruce, B, Virginia, 30
6. *Grimes, George, B, Virginia, 40
7. Ruszkowski, Gene, T, Ohio U. [from Boston], 49
   Cudd, Noel, T, West Texas St., 50
8. Walker, Bob, B, Colorado Mines, 60
9. *Graham, Mike, B, Cincinnati, 70
10. *Johnson, Glenn, T, Arizona State, 80
11. Zisch, Johnny, E, Colorado, 90
12. Phleger, Atherton (Pinky), T, Stanford, 100
13. *Heck, Bob, E, Purdue, 110
14. *Schroll, Bill, B, LSU, 120
15. Dement, Bob, T, Southern Mississippi, 130
16. Schoenherr, Charley, B, Wheaton, 140
17. *Brink, Larry, E, Northern Illinois, 150
18. *O'Connor, Bill (Zeke), G, Notre Dame, 160
19. Nelson, Bill, B, Montana State, 170
20. Rees, Jim, T, North Carolina State, 180
21. Borneman, Ray, B, Texas, 190
22. *Yagiello, Ray, T, Catawba, 200
23. Pesek, John, E, Nebraska, 210
24. DeAutremont, Charlie, B, Southern Oregon, 220
25. Levenhagen, Bob, G, Washington, 230
26. Cooper, Leon, T, Hardin-Simmons, 240
27. *Wade, Jim, B, Oklahoma City, 250
28. Sinofsky, Ken, G, Nevada-Reno, 260
29. Stuart, Bobby Jack, B, Tulsa, Army, 270
30. Crum, Hilliard (Junior), E, Arizona, 280
31. Kunkiewicz, Tony, B, Trinity (CT), 288
32. Taylor, Bill, E, Rice, 295

NEW YORK GIANTS 1948
1. *Minisi, Tony (Skippy), B, Penn, Navy, 2
2. *Scott, Joe, B, San Francisco, 12
3. Choice to Boston
4. *Gehrke, Bruce, E, Columbia, 24
5. Wolosky, Johnny, C, Penn State, 26
6. *Erickson, Bill, T, Mississippi, 36
7. *Pfohl, Bob, B, Purdue, 46
8. *Hutchinson, Ralph, T, Tennessee-Chattanooga, 56
   *Coates, Ray, B, LSU, [from Detroit], 57
9. *Ottele, Dick, B, Washington, 66
   Wiltgen, Ken, E, Northwestern [from Green Bay], 71
   *Royston, Ed, G, Wake Forest [from Chicago Cardinals], 75
10. Magdziak, Stan, B, William & Mary, 76
11. Lanzl, Pete, E, Youngstown State, 86
12. Modzeleski, Len, T, Scranton, 96
    Brieske, Jim, C, Michigan [from Detroit], 97
13. Hatch, Bob, B, Boston U., 106
14. Hansel, John, G, Guilford, 116
15. *Garza, Dan, E, Oregon, 126
16. Yovetich, Dan, E, Montana State, 136
17. Grothus, Joe, G, Iowa, 146
18. Mathews, George, B, Georgia Tech, 156
19. *Ettinger, Don (Red Dog), G, Kansas, 166
20. *Williams, Frank, B, Utah State, 176
21. *Woodward, Dick, C, Iowa, 186
22. *Kisiday, George, T, Columbia, 196
23. Roberts, Theron, G, Arkansas, 206
24. *McCormick, Walt, C, USC, 216
25. *Wilkins, Dick, E, Oregon, 226
26. Marotta, Vince, B, Mount Union, 236
27. Salisbury, Tom, T, Clemson, 246
28. Lilja, Roy, C, Colorado College, 256
29. *Greenhalgh, Bobby, B, San Francisco, 266
30. *Kelley, Ed, T, Texas, 276

PHILADELPHIA 1948
1. *Scott, Clyde (Smackover), B, Arkansas, Navy, 8
3. Campbell, Paul, QB, Texas, 22
5. *Myers, Jack (Moose), B, UCLA, 33
6. Duncan, Howard, C, Ohio State, 42
7. *Tinsley, Buddy, T, Baylor, 54
8. *Wendell, Marty, G, Notre Dame, 63
9. Beasley, Scott, E, Nevada-Reno, 72
10. *Richeson, Ray, G, Alabama, 84
11. *Johnson, Gil, QB, SMU, 93
12. Wyman, Bill, T, Rice, 102 +
13. Waithall, Jim, B, West Virginia, 114
14. Kempthorn, Dick, B, Michigan, 123
15. *Rifenburg, Dick, E, Michigan, 132
16. Stanton, Don, T, Oregon, 144
17. Kohl, Ralph, T, Michigan, 153
18. *Fowler, Aubrey, B, Arkansas, 162
19. Krall, Rudy, B, New Mexico, 174
20. Claunch, Ed, C, LSU, 183
21. Norton, Negley, T, Penn State, 192
22. Frizzell, Lockwood, C, Virginia, 204
23. Swaner, Jack, B, California, 213
24. Littleton, Art, E, Penn, 222
25. *Parmer, Jim, B, Oklahoma State, 234
26. *Creekmur, Lou, T, William & Mary, 243
27. *Stanton, Bill, E, North Carolina State, 252
28. Ellender, Benny, B, Tulane, 264
29. *Grossman, Rex, B, Indiana, 273
30. Kitchens, A.B., T, Tulsa, 282
31. *Statuto, Art, C, Notre Dame, 292
32. Novak, Tom, C, Nebraska, 298

PITTSBURGH 1948
1. *Edwards, Dan, E, Georgia, 9
3. *Nuzum, Jerry, B, New Mexico State, 20
5. *Wozniak, John, G, Alabama, 34
6. *Gasparella, Joe, B, Notre Dame, 43
   O'Reilly, Phil, T, Purdue, [from Chicago Cardinals], 45
7. Luongo, Bill, B, Pennsylvania, 52
8. *Cooper, Jim, C, North Texas State, 64
9. *Ryan, Ed, E, St, Mary's (CA), 73
10. Deranek, Dick, B, Indiana, 82
11. Redfield, Paul, T, Colgate, 94
12. *Papach, George, B, Purdue, 103
13. Finical, Tom, E, Princeton, 112
14. *Lane, Clayton, T, New Hampshire, 124
15. Mazuca, Dick, G, Canisius, 133
16. *McPeak, Bill, E, Pittsburgh, 142
17. Messoline, Frank, B, Scranton, 154
18. Lane, Tom, T, Muhlenburg, 163
19. *Barbolak, Pete, T, Purdue, 172
20. Folger, Fred, B, Duke, 184
21. Snyder, Charley, T, Marshall, 193
22. Stevens, Tally, E, Utah, 202
23. Norman, Dike, C, Washington & Lee, 214
24. *Simmons, Floyd, B, Notre Dame, 223
25. Hausser, Paul, T, Wichita State, 232
26. Ramsey, Bob, B, SMU, 244
27. Whitlow, Felton, T, North Texas State, 253
28. Bowen, Dinky, B, Georgia Tech, 262
29. *Gibron, Abe, G, Purdue, 274
30. Hilkene, Bruce, T, Michigan, 283
31. Zuchowski, Ted, T, Toledo, 290
32. DeMattea, Tony, B, Pittsburgh, 299

WASHINGTON 1948
BONUS CHOICE: *Gilmer, Harry, B, Alabama, 1
1. *Tew, Lowell, B, Alabama, 4
3. *Thompson, Tommy, C, William & Mary, 16
5. *Sandifer, Dan, B, LSU, 28
6. Weisenburger, Jack, B, Michigan, 38
7. Kurkowski, Jack, B, Detroit, 48
8. Cady, Jerry, T, Gustavus Adolphus, 58
9. Anderson, Bob, B, Stanford, 68
10. *Katrishen, Mike, T, Southern Mississippi, 78
11. Marshall, Ed, T, Penn, 88
12. Andrus, Ted, G, Southwestern Louisiana, 98
13. Russ, Carl, B, Rice, 108
14. *Jagade, Harry (Chick), B, Indiana, 118
15. *Quirk, Eddie, B, Missouri, 128
16. Pollard, Art, B, Arizona, 138
17. Newman, Chuck, E, Louisiana Tech, 148
    Schwartzkopf, Dale, E, Texas [from Green Bay], 151
18. Pearcy, Ray, C, Oklahoma, 158
19. Veilela, Gene, T, Scranton, 168
20. *Box, Cloyce, B, West Texas State, 178
21. Bell, Bryan, B, Washington & Lee, 188
22. *Williams, Joel, C, Texas, 198
23. Hoitsma, Lou, E, William & Mary, 208
24. Lawhorn, Floyd, G, Texas Tech, 218
25. West, Dick, B, Princeton, 228
26. Oakes, Roland, E, Missouri, 238
27. Watkins, Ed, T, Idaho, 248
28. *Corbitt, Don, C, Arizona, 258
29. Bowen, Buddy, B, Mississippi, 268
30. Paulson, Vic, E, Cal-Santa Barbara, 278
31. Welch, Barney, B, Texas A&M, 286

1948 AAFC

Held December 16, 1947

The draft increased to 30 rounds, and the best teams from the preceding season again received fewer choices, but this year those lost selections were earlier in the draft than in 1947. Each team selected in the first round. The next nine rounds varied greatly. In the second round, only the Chicago Rockets and Baltimore received a choice. In the third, seventh, and ninth rounds, each team made a selection. In the fourth and sixth rounds, Cleveland and the New York Yankees didn't receive selections. In the fifth round, only the Rockets, Baltimore, and Brooklyn received picks. And in the eighth and tenth rounds, only the Rockets, Baltimore, Brooklyn, and the Los Angeles Dons received picks. After the tenth round, each team made selections throughout the next 20 rounds.

BALTIMORE 1948
1. *Layne, Bobby, QB, Texas, 2
2. *Garrett, Dub, T, Mississippi State, 10
3. Cooke, Earl, G, SMU, 12
4. *Sandifer, Don, B, LSU, 20
5. *Smith, Joe, E, Texas Tech, 26
6. Raczkowski, Gene, T, Ohio U, 29
7. Batchelor, Jim, B, East Texas State, 35
8. Olson, Rex, B, BYU, 43
9. *Fowler, Aubrey, B, Arkansas, 47
10. Fitch, Jack, B, North Carolina, 55
11. *Ettinger, Don (Red Dog), G, Kansas, 59
12. Redfield, Paul, T, Colgate, 67
13. Madgziak, Stan, B, William & Mary, 75
14. Deranek, Dick, B, Indiana, 83
15. Norman, Dike, B, Washington & Lee, 91
16. Working, Dick, B, Washington & Lee, 99
17. Sparter, George, C, North Carolina, 107
18. Prather, Rollin, E, Kansas State, 115
19. *Mosely, Monk, B, Alabama, 123
20. Ragonese, Carmen, B, New Hampshire, 131
21. Walker, Bob, B, Colorado Mines, 139
22. Borneman, Ray, B, Texas, 147
23. *Tillman, Al (Pete), C, Oklahoma, 155
24. *Pfohl, Bob, B, Purdue, 163
25. *Levanti, Lou, C, Illinois, 171
26. Zatkoff, Sam, E, Illinois, 179
27. *Jagade, Harry (Chick), B, Indiana, 187
28. Bendrick, Ben, B, Wisconsin, 195
29. *Grossman, Rex, B, Indiana, 203
30. Reinking, Dick, E, SMU, 211

BROOKLYN 1948
1. *Gilmer, Harry, QB, Alabama, 3
3. *Edwards, Dan, E, Georgia, 13
4. *Spencer, Joe, T, Oklahoma State, 21
5. *Binganan, Les, T, Illinois, 27
6. Smith, Jim, E, Southern Mississippi, 30
7. *Paine, Homer, T, Oklahoma, 36
8. *Gehrke, Bruce, E, Columbia, 44
9. Minor, Jim, T, Arkansas, 48
10. *St. John, Herb, G, Georgia, 56
11. Newman, Chuck, E, Louisiana Tech, 60
12. *Camp, Jim, B, North Carolina, 68
13. Koch, Bob, B, Oregon, 76
14. White, John, C, Michigan, 84
15. Terry, Bob, B, Texas A&M, 92
16. *Wozniak, John, G, Alabama, 100
17. *Jensen, Bob, E, Iowa State, 108
18. Jurich, Joe, E, West Chester, 116
19. Cromer, Bill, B, North Texas State, 124
20. Scott, Dick, C, Navy, 132
21. Marusa, Walt, G, Delaware, 140
22. Dobkins, Knute, E, Buller, 148
23. Westphal, Fred, E, Cornell, 156
24. Dinkins, Merle, E, Oklahoma, 164
25. Pupa, Walt, B, North Carolina, 172
26. *Richeson, Ray, G, Alabama, 180
27. Hurrle, Ott, C, Butler, 188
28. Lowans, Warren, T, West Chester, 196
29. Littleton, Art, E, Penn, 204
30. *McGeary, Clarence (Clink), T, North Dakota State, 212

BUFFALO 1948
1. *Scott, Clyde (Smackover), B, Arkansas, Navy, 6
3. *Gompers, Bill, B, Notre Dame, 16
4. *O'Connor, Bill (Zeke), E, Notre Dame, 24
6. *Wendell, Marty, G, Notre Dame, 33
7. Brugge, Bob, B, Ohio State, 39
9. King, Lou, B, Iowa, 51
11. Finney, John, B, Compton J.C., 63
12. Johnson, Dick, G, Baylor, 71
13. *Grimes, George, B, Virginia, 79
14. *Joe, Larry, B, Penn State, 87
15. Ballard, Frank, G, Virginia Tech, 95
16. Waithall, Jim, B, West Virginia, 103
17. *Coates, Ray, B, LSU, 111
18. Waybright, Dud, E, Notre Dame, 119
19. Walker, Wade, T, Oklahoma, 127
20. Stephens, Roger, B, Cincinnati, 135
21. Duncan, Howard, C, Ohio State, 143
22. *Sazio, Ralph, T, William & Mary, 151
23. Bloomquist, George, E, North Carolina St., 159
24. Cheek, J.D., T, Oklahoma State, 167
25. Rennebohm, Bob, E, Wisconsin, 175
26. Andrus, Ted, G, Southwestern Louisiana, 183
27. Brown, Ray, B, Virginia, 191
28. Corriere, Lou, B, Buffalo, 199
29. Wosloski, John, C, Penn State, 207
30. Stevens, Talley, E, Utah State, 215 +

CHICAGO ROCKETS 1948
1. *Minisi, Tony (Skippy), B, Penn, 1
2. *Samuelson, Carl, T, Nebraska, 9
3. *Nolan, John, T, Penn State, 11
4. *Cleary, Paul, E, USC, 19
5. *Walsh, Bill, C, Notre Dame, 25 +
6. DiFrancisca, Vince, G, Northwestern, 28
7. *Rhodemyer, Jay, C, Kentucky, 34
8. Turner, Jim, T, California, 42
9. Miller, Myron, C, Oklahoma State, 46
10. *Slosburg, Phil, B, Temple, 54
11. Swaner, Jack, B, California, 58
12. Gay, Thurman, T, Oklahoma State, 66
13. Parker, Frank, T, Holy Cross, 74 +
14. Agase, Lou, T, Illinois, 82
15. McCarthy, J.F., E, Penn, 90
16. Krall, Rudy, B, New Mexico, 98
17. *Flanagan, Dick, B, Ohio State, 106
18. *Ryan, Ed, E, St, Mary's (CA), 114
19. Gillory, Byron, B, Texas, 122 +
20. *Doll, Don, B, USC, 130
21. *Provo, Fred, B, Washington, 138
22. Tinsley, Phil, E, UCLA, 146
23. Treichler, Glen, B, Colgate, 154
24. Owen, Ike, E, Illinois, 162
25. Sockalov, Ron, T, California, 170
26. Corum, Gene, G, West Virginia, 178
27. Daniels, John, C, Cal-Santa Barbara, 186
28. Hoisch, Al, B, UCLA, 194
29. *Wedel, Dick, G, Wake Forest, 202
30. Finical, Tom, E, Princeton, 210

CLEVELAND 1948
1. *Durkota, Jeff, B, Penn State, 8
3. *Cline, Ollie, B, Ohio State, 18
7. *Thompson, Tommy, C, William & Mary, 41
9. *Smith, Bill, T, North Carolina, 53
11. Maughan, Ralph, C, Utah State, 65
12. *Sensenbaugher, Dean, B, Ohio State, 73
13. Rubish, Mike, E, North Carolina, 81 +
14. Sarkesian, Alex, C, Northwestern, 89
15. *Dworsky, Dan, B, Michigan, 97 +
16. Beasley, Scott, E, Nevada-Reno, 105
17. Steqer, Russ, B, Illinois 113
18. Hoistma, Lou, E, William & Mary, 121
19. Ashbaugh, Pete, B, Notre Dame, 129
20. Templeton, Dave, G, Ohio State, 137
21. Eddleman, Dwight (Dike), B, Illinois, 145
22. *Gambino, Lou, B, Maryland, 153
23. McDowell, Jim, G, William & Mary, 161
24. Fowle, Heywood, T, North Carolina, 169
25. *Parseghian, Ara, B, Miami (OH), 177
26. Saylor, Todd, E, Lafayette, 185
27. Caughron Harry, T, William & Mary, 193
28. Lanzi, Pete, E, Youngstown State, 201
29. *Roman, George, T, Case Western Reserve, 209
30. Sheehan, Mel, E, Missouri, 217

LOS ANGELES DONS 1948
1. *Mancha, Vaughn, C, Alabama, 4
3. *Ford, Len, E, Michigan, 14
4. Novitsky, John, T, Oklahoma City, 22
6. *Sexton, Lin, B, Wichita State, 31
7. *Edwards, Weldon, T, TCU, 37
8. *Spavital, Jim, B, Oklahoma State, 45
9. *Ramsey, Knox, G, William & Mary, 49
10. Mills, Malachi, G, Virginia Military, 57
11. *Mihajlovich, Lou, E, Indiana, 61
12. *Davis, Harper, B, Mississippi State, 69
13. *Graham, Mike, B, Cincinnati, 77
14. *Winkler, Bernie, T, Texas Tech, 85
15. *Erickson, Bill, T, Mississippi, 93
16. *McWilliams, Tom (Shorty), B, Mississippi State, 101
17. Levenhagen, Bob, G, Washington, 109
18. Sellers, Wayman, E, Georgia, 117
19. *Wimberly, Abner, E, LSU, 625
20. *Ziegler, Frank, B, Georgia Tech, 133
21. Smith, Ed, B, Texas-El Paso, 141
22. Mortelello, Paul, G, Florida, 149
23. Kenfield, Ted, B, California, 157
24. Mulligan, Buddy, B, Duke, 165
25. Lambert, George, T, Mississippi, 173
26. *Still, Jim, QB, Georgia Tech, 181
27. Tatom, Charley, G, Texas, 189
28. *Creekmur, Lou, T, William & Mary, 197
29. *McLaughlin, Leon, C, UCLA, 205
30. Kitchens, A.B., T, Tulsa, 213

NEW YORK YANKEES 1948
1. *Tew, Lowell, B, Alabama, 7
3. *Schnellenbacher, Otto, E, Kansas, 17
7. *Stout Pete, B, TCU, 40
9. *Poole, Barney, E, Army, Mississippi, 52, F
11. Weisenberger, Jack, B, Michigan, 64
12. *Hendren, Bob, T, USC, 72
13. *Ottele, Dick, B, Washington, 80
14. *McKissack, Dick, B, SMU, 88
15. Magliolo, Joe, B, Texas, 96
16. Ramsey, Bob, B, SMU, 104
17. Wright, Charles, E, Texas A&M, 112
18. *Shirley, Marion, T, Oklahoma City, 120
19. *Landry, Tom, B, Texas, 128
20. Forbes, Bobby, B, Florida, 136
21. Russ, Carl, B, Rice, 144
22. *Enke, Fred, B, Arizona, 152 +
23. Cunningham, John, E, California, 160
24. Ognovich, Nick, B, Wake Forest, 168
25. Zelezanak, Mike, B, Kansas State, 176
26. *Panelli, John (Pep), B, Notre Dame, 184 +
27. *Girard, Earl (Jug), B, Wisconsin, 192

28. *Collins, Albin (Rip), B, LSU, 200 *
29. *Nelson, Frank, B, Utah, 208
30. Clements, Bill, E, UCLA, 216

SAN FRANCISCO 1948
1. *Scott, Joe, B, San Francisco, 5
3. *Cason, Jim, B, LSU, 15
4. *McCormick, Walt, C, USC, 23
6. *Land, Fred, T, LSU, 32
7. O'Reilly, Phil, T, Purdue, 38
9. Luongo, Bill, B, Penn, 50
11. Steckroth, Bob, E, William & Mary, 62
12. *Malinowski, Gene, C, Detroit, 70
13. Modzelski, Len, T, Scranton, 78
14. Rideout, Les, T, Bowling Green, 86
15. *Olsonoski, Larry, T, Purdue, 94
16. Matulich, Wally, B, Mississippi State, 102
17. *Ravensberg, Bob, E, Indiana, 110
18. Pritula, Bill, T, Michigan, 118
19. Fitzgerald, Art, B, Yale, 126
20. *Barbolak, Pete, T, Purdue, 134
21. *Loepfe, Dick, T, Wisconsin, 142
22. *Heck, Bob, E, Purdue, 150
23. Lanhorne, Floyd, G, Texas Tech, 158
24. Bryant, Goble, T, Army, 166
25. Talarico, Bill, B, Penn, 174
26. Marshall, Everett, T, Penn, 182
27. *Moss, Perry, B, Illinois, 190
28. Bell, Bill, QB, Muhlenberg, 198
29. *Siegert, Herb, G, Illinois, 206
30. *Williams, Frank, B, Utah State, 214

1949 NFL

Held December 21, 1948

Before the start of the 1949 season Ted Collins returned his Boston franchise to the league and received another in New York, which he named the Bulldogs. He retained the rights to his Boston players and the draft rights to the players selected in this draft when his franchise was still the one in Boston.

BOSTON 1949
1. *Walker, Doak, B, SMU, 3
2. *DeMoss, Bob, B, Purdue, 13
3. Colella, Phil, B, St. Bonaventure, 23
   Chewning, Lynn, B, Hampden-Sydney [from Chicago Cardinals], 30
4. Keeney, Huey, B, Rice, 33
5. *Boyda, Mike, B, Washington & Lee, 44
6. *Collins, Albin (Rip), B, LSU, 53
   *Tamburo, Sam, E, Penn State, [from Philadelphia], 61
7. *Wissman, Pete, C, St. Louis, 64
8. Rubish, Mike, E, North Carolina, 73
9. Craig, Bernie, T, Denver, 84
10. Geary, John, T, Wesleyan, 93
11. Mencotti, Edo, B, Detroit, 104
12. Maenhout, Mornane, E, St. John's (MN), 113
13. Dieckelman, Jim, E, Holy Cross, 124
14. Toscani, Ed, B, Dayton, 133
15. Ramacorti, George, G, Boston U., 144
16. Bruce, Jack, B, William & Mary, 153
17. *Beson, Warren, C, Minnesota, 164
18. Gould, Albie, E, Boston College, 173
19. Reich, Bob, T, Colgate, 184
20. *Gaul, Frank, T, Notre Dame, 193
21. Pierce, Sammy, B, Baylor, 204
22. Lail, Jim, B, Wake Forest, 213
23. Lanza, Nick, B, Rice, 224
24. Ponsalle, Joe, T, Trinity (CT), 233
25. Girolamo, Paul, B, Cornell, 244

CHICAGO BEARS 1949
1. Harris, Dick, C, Texas, 11
2. *Grimes, Billy, B, Oklahoma State, 20
3. *O'Quinn, Johnny (Red), E, Wake Forest, 31 F
4. Bendrick, Ben, B, Wisconsin, 39
5. *Hoffman, John, B, Arkansas, 49
6. *Krall, Jerry, B, Ohio State, 59 F
7. Jones, Wally (Wah-Wah), E, Kentucky, 69
8. *Weatherly, Gerry (Bones), C, Rice, [from Detroit], 72
   *Wightkin, Bill, E, Notre Dame, 79 F
9. Tokarczyk, Dolph, G, Penn, 89
10. Malley, Lee, B, Vanderbilt, 99
11. Tiblier, Jerry, B, Mississippi, 109
12. *Blanda, George, QB, Kentucky, 119
13. *Taliaferro, George, B, Indiana, 129
14. Keily, Ernie, G, Texas-El Paso, 139 +
15. *Faverty, Hal, G, Wisconsin, 149
16. Wahl, Al, T, Michigan, 159 +
17. Corbisiero, John, B, Middlebury, 169
18. Moran, Jim, B, John Carroll, 179
19. Mitten, Bob, G, North Carolina, 189
20. Heck, Bob, B, Pacific, 199
21. *Duncan, Jim, E, Duke, 209
22. Bertuzzi, Dick, B, Kansas, 219
23. Kane, Harry, C, Pacific, 229 +
24. Smith, Bernie, T, Texas-El Paso, 239
25. Marczyk, Stan, T, North Carolina, 249

CHICAGO CARDINALS 1949
1. *Fischer, Bill, G, Notre Dame, 10
2. *McKissack, Dick, B, SMU, 21 +
3. Choice to Boston
4. *Goldsberry, John, T, Indiana, 40
5. *Wham, Tom, E, Furman, 50
6. Hanula, Bernie, T, Wake Forest, 60
7. Greathouse, Myrl, B, Oklahoma [from Detroit], 62
   *Cain, Jim, E, Alabama, 70
8. Brown, Joe E, B, Georgia Tech, 80
9. *Herring, Hal, C, Auburn, 90
10. *Hecker, Bob, B, Baldwin-Wallace, 100
11. Flowers, Stan, E, Redlands, 110
12. *Stone, Billy, B, Bradley, 120
13. Todd, Bob, T, Louisville, 130
14. *Klimek, Tony, E, Illinois, 140 F
15. McQuade, Bob, B, Xavier, 150
16. Murdock, Tom, B, Appalachian State, 160
17. Rupp, Eddie, B, Denison, 170
18. Halbert, Webb, B, Iowa, 180
19. Laun, Dean, E, Iowa State, 190
20. Rowan, Earl, T, Hardin-Simmons, 200 +
21. Joslin, Leon, B, TCU, 210
22. Sprang, Bill, C, Purdue, 220
23. Cox, Bob, E, North Carolina, 230
24. Szymakowski, Stan, B, Lehigh, 240
25. Choice to NY Giants

DETROIT 1949
1. *Rauch, Johnny, QB, Georgia, 2
2. *Panelli, John (Pep), B, Notre Dame, 12
3. *Kusserow, Lou, B, Columbia, 22
4. Sullivan, Joe, B, Dartmouth, 32
5. Brodnax, George, E, Georgia Tech, 42
6. Meinert, Bob, B, Oklahoma State, 52
7. Choice to Chicago Cardinals
8. Choice to Chicago Bears
9. *Drazenovich, Chuck, B, Penn State, 82 F
10. Davis, Bill, G, Duke, 92
11. Settembre, Ernie, T, Miami, 102
12. Boteler, Virgil, C, New Mexico , 112
13. *Russas, Al, E, Tennessee, 122
14. Panter, Dale, T, Utah State, 132
15. *Pifferini, Bob, C, San Jose State, 142
16. Merrill, Kimball, T, BYU, 152
17. Thigpen, Zealand, B, Vanderbilt, 162
18. Wehr, Bill, C, Denison, 172
19. *Triplett, Wally, B, Penn State, 182
20. Romano, Joe, T, North Carolina, 192
21. *Lininger, Jack, C, Ohio State, 202
22. Tobler, Gil, B, Utah, 212
23. Patterson, R.B., G, Mississippi State, 222
24. Clark, Oswald, E, Michigan, 232
25. *Cowan, Les, E, McMurry, 242

GREEN BAY 1949
1. *Heath, Stan, QB, Nevada-Reno, 5
2. *Dworsky, Dan, C, Michigan, 15
3. *Ferry, Lou, T, Villanova, 25
4. *Summerhays, Bob, B, Utah, 34
5. Lewis, Glenn, B, Texas Tech, 43
6. *Ethridge, Joe, T, SMU, 54
7. Choice to Los Angeles Rams
8. *Orlich, Dan, E, Nevada-Reno, 74
9. Faunce, Everett, B, Minnesota, 83
10. Choice to Los Angeles Rams thru Detroit
11. Larche, Harry, T, Arkansas State, 103
12. *Steiner, Roy (Rebel), E, Alabama, 114
13. Mastrangeli, Al, C, Illinois, 123
14. Williams, Bobby, C, Texas Tech, 134
15. *Cooper, Ken, G, Vanderbilt, 143
16. Remenar, Gene, T, West Virginia, 154
17. Devine, Paul, B, Heidelberg, 163
18. Lewis, Floyd, G, SMU, 174
19. Folsom, Bobby, E, SMU, 183
20. Cooney, Larry, B, Penn State, 194
21. *Kranz, Ken, B, Wisconsin-Milwaukee, 203
22. Kordick, John, B, USC, 214
23. Kelly, Bill, E, Texas Tech, 223
24. Ford, Jimmy, B, Tulsa, 234
25. Lambright, Frank, G, Arkansas, 243

LOS ANGELES RAMS 1949
1. *Thomason, Bobby, B, Virginia Military, 7
2. *Sims, George, B, Baylor, 17
3. *Winkler, Jim, T, Texas A&M, 27
4. *Van Brocklin, Norm, QB, Oregon, 37
5. *Howell, Earl (Dixie), B, Mississippi, 47
6. Reynolds, Charles, B, Texas Tech, 57
7. *Williams, Jerry, B, Washington State [from Green Bay], 63
   *Baker, Jon, G, California, 67
8. Waldrum, John, G, Sul Ross, 77
9. Smith, Johnny, E, Arizona, 87 +
10. *Buksar, George, B, Purdue [from Green Bay thru Detroit], 94
    Minnich, Max, B, Bowling Green, 97
11. Cozad, Jim, T, Iowa, 107
12. Renna, Bill, C, Santa Clara, 117
13. *Barry, Paul, B, Tulsa, 127
14. Carmichael, Ed, T, Oregon State, 137
15. Dodd, J.C., B, Sul Ross, 147
16. *Morgan, Joe, G, Southern Mississippi, 157
17. Sheffield, Dick, E, Tulane, 167
18. Chollet, Hillary, B, Cornell, 177
19. Leonard, Joe, T, Virginia, 187
20. Eisenberg, Lloyd, T, Duke, 197
21. Teufel, George, B, Lock Haven, 207
22. Hamilton, Ed, E, Arkansas, 217
23. Kersulis, Walt, E, Illinois, 227 +
24. Klemenok, Fred, B, San Francisco, 237
25. *Matthews, Clay, T, Georgia Tech, 247

NEW YORK GIANTS 1949
1. *Page, Paul, B, SMU, 4
2. *DeRogatis, Al, T, Duke, 14
3. Olson, Bill, B, Columbia, 24
4. Kay, Bill, T, Iowa, 35
5. Cheek, J.D., G, Oklahoma State, 46
6. *Gibron, Abe, G, Purdue, 55
7. *LoVuolo, Frank, E, St. Bonaventure, 66
8. *Salscheider, John, B, St. Thomas (MN), 75
9. *Soboleski, Joe, G, Michigan, 86
10. Rossides, Gene, B, Columbia, 95
11. *Hensley, Dick, E, Kentucky, 106
12. Sundheim, George, B, Northwestern, 115
13. *Austin, Bill, T, Oregon State, 126
14. Adams, Norb, B, Purdue, 135
15. Pickelsimer, Ralph, C, Otterbein, 146
16. Morrical, Jerry, T, Indiana, 155
17. Teninga, Wally, B, Michigan, 166
18. Nutt, Dick, B, North Texas State, 175
19. McCall, Ken, B, Georgia, 186
20. O'Sullivan, Pat, C, Alabama, 195
21. Cate, A.D., G, North Texas State, 206
22. Fetzer, Tom, B, Wake Forest, 215
23. *Fischer, Cletus, B, Nebraska, 226
24. McAuliffe, Don, B, Notre Dame, 235
25. Degyanski, Gene, E, Baldwin-Wallace, 246
    Doran, Ralph, B, Iowa [from Chicago Cardinals], 250

PHILADELPHIA 1949
BONUS CHOICE: *Bednarik, Chuck, C, Penn, 1
1. *Tripucka, Frank, QB, Notre Dame, 9
2. Burns, Frank, B, Rutgers, 19
3. *Ziegler, Frank, B, Georgia Tech, 29
4. *Panciera, Don, B, San Francisco, 41
5. Brennan, Terry, B, Notre Dame, 51
6. Huey, Warren, E, Michigan State, [from Washington], 58
   Choice to Boston
7. Gillespie, Frank, G, Clemson, 71
8. Dean, Bob, B, Cornell, 81
9. *Jenkins, Jonathan, T, Dartmouth, 91
10. Lester, Roy, E, West Virginia, 101
11. Wilson, Bobby, B, Mississippi, 111
12. Armstrong, Dale, E, Dartmouth, 121
13. Button, Lyle, T, Illinois, 131 +
14. Lund, Bobby, B, Tennessee, 141
15. Copp, Carl, T, Vanderbilt, 151
16. Reno, Frank, E, West Virginia, 161
17. *Skladany, Leo, E, Pittsburgh, 171
18. Strait, Russ, B, Muhlenberg, 181
19. Odom, Paul, G, Rollins, 191
20. Brinkman, Lloyd, B, Missouri, 201
21. Futrell, Lou, B, USC, 211
22. Kingry, Harvey, B, Colorado Mines, 221
23. Kalver, Hank T, Oklahoma City, 231
24. Leon, Fred, T, Nevada-Reno, 241
25. *Schweder, John (Bull), G, Penn, 251

PITTSBURGH 1949
1. *Gage, Bobby, B, Clemson, 6
2. *Davis, Harper, B, Mississippi State, 16
3. *Walsh, Bill, C, Notre Dame, 26
4. *Geri, Joe, B, Georgia, 36
5. *Long, Bill, E, Oklahoma State, 45
6. Brightwell, Doug, C, TCU, 56
7. Talarico, Bill, B, Penn, 65
8. *Brown, George, G, TCU, 76
9. Brennan, Tom, T, Boston College, 85
10. Hood, Bob, E, Alabama, 96
11. Sanders, Al, C, Southern Mississippi, 105
12. *Finks, Jim, B, Tulsa, 116
13. Walston, R.R., G, North Texas State, 125
14. Moon, Dave, B, SMU, 136
15. Sobczak, Ed, E, Michigan, 145
16. Snell, Denvard, T, Auburn, 156
17. *Kissell, Veto, B, Holy Cross, 165
18. Shipman, Clint, T, East Texas State, 176
19. McBride, Jack, E, Rice, 185
20. Mann, Ben, G, Mississippi, 196
21. Jackura, Joe, C, Georgia, 205
22. Johnson, Lloyd, B, West Texas State, 216
23. *Owens, Jim, E, Oklahoma, 225
24. Snowden, Ivan, T, Texas A&I, 236
25. Gaff, Bobby, B, Texas A&M, 245

WASHINGTON 1949
1. *Goode, Rob, B, Texas A&M, 8
2. *Niemi, Laurie, T, Washington State, 18
3. *Szafaryn, Len, T, North Carolina, 28
4. DeNoia, Mike, B, Scranton, 38
5. *Berrang, Eddie, E, Villanova, 48
6. Choice to Philadelphia
7. Fritz, Chet, G, Missouri, 68
8. Kennedy, Bob, B, North Carolina, 78
9. McNeil, Ed, E, Michigan, 88
10. *Vasicek, Vic, G, Texas, 98
11. *Hobbs, Homer, G, Georgia, 108
12. Varner, Harry, T, Arizona, 118
13. *Henke, Ed, T, USC, 128
14. Haggerty, Pat, E, William & Mary, 138
15. Frassetto, Gene, T, California, 148
16. Flowers, Dick, T, Alabama, 158
17. Pritchard, Ross, B, Arkansas, 168
18. *Siegert, Herb, G, Illinois, 178
19. Hainlen, Bob, B, Colorado State, 188
20. Fletcher, Ollie, E, USC, 198
21. Hughes, Tommy, B, Duke, 208
22. Clements, Bill, E, UCLA, 218
23. Pattee, Frank, B, Kansas, 228
24. *Cullom, Jim, G, California, 238 +
25. *Sebek, Nick, B, Indiana, 248

1949 AAFC SECRET

Held July 8, 1948

A secret, two-round draft was held for players who were to be seniors in the 1948 season. The purpose was for the struggling AAFC to be able to get a jump on wooing the top college players before the NFL teams could talk to them. Two of the selections were voided by AAFC Commissioner O.O. Kessing because the players were not seniors and had college eligibility remaining for the 1949 season. Dick Harris, the first selection of Baltimore, later was assigned to Cleveland by the Commissioner.

BALTIMORE
1. Harris, Dick, C, Texas
2. Jackson, Levi, B, Yale +

BROOKLYN
1. *Bednarik, Chuck, C, Penn
2. Choice to New York Yankees

BUFFALO
1. *Gibron, Abe, G, Purdue
2. *Tripucka, Frank, QB, Notre Dame

CHICAGO ROCKETS
1. Brennan, Terry, B, Notre Dame
   Elliott, Pete, B, Michigan, [from New York Yankees]
2. *Fisher, Bill, G, Notre Dame

CLEVELAND
1. Derricotte, Gene, B, Michigan
2. Kempthorn, Dick, B, Michigan

LOS ANGELES DONS
1. *Dworsky, Dan, C, Michigan
2. Price, Jack, B, Baylor

NEW YORK YANKEES
1. Choice to Chicago Rockets
2. *Kusserow, Lou, B, Columbia, [from Brooklyn Dodgers (AAFC)]
   *Rauch, Johnny, QB, Georgia

SAN FRANCISCO
1. *Stautner, Ernie, T, Boston College +
2. *Winkler, Jim, T, Texas A&M

1949 AAFC

Held December 21, 1948

In determining the draft order, the divisional playoff game between Buffalo and Baltimore was added to the regular season finish. This made the order of selection for the three teams that had tied during the regular season Baltimore (7-8), the Los Angeles Dons (7-7), and Buffalo (8-7). For the first time in the AAFC, there were several trades for selections. There were 29 rounds, and again the teams with a lower finish in 1948 received more selections. Each team received a first-round choice. The Chicago Rockets, the New York Yankees, and Baltimore received a second-round selection, and Brooklyn received a third-round pick. Every team then selected in each round through the sixteenth. Everyone but Cleveland and San Francisco made choices from rounds 17 through 21, and then just Chicago, Brooklyn, and New York from rounds 22 through 24. Each selected again in round 25, and each team except Chicago, Brooklyn, and New York from rounds 26 through 30.

BALTIMORE 1949
1. *Sims, George, B, Baylor, 4
2. *Gage, Bobby, B, Clemson, 14
4. Kohl, Ralph, T, Michigan, 25
5. Jones, Wally (Wah-Wah), E, Kentucky, 33
6. Pattee, Frank, B, Kansas, 41
7. Folger, Frank, B, Duke, 49
8. Prymuski, Bob, T, Illinois, 57
9. Faunce, Everett, B, Minnesota, 65
10. Alexander, Kale, T, South Carolina, 73
11. *Page, Paul, B, SMU, 81
12. *Owens, Jim, E, Oklahoma, 89
13. *Beson, Warren, C, Minnesota, 97
14. Moon, David, B, SMU, 105
15. *Jenkins, Jon, T, Dartmouth, 113
16. *O'Quinn, Johnny (Red), E, Wake Forest, 121
17. Geary, Clyde, T, Connecticut Wesleyan, 129
18. Sanders, Al, T, Southern Mississippi, 135
19. Sundheim, Guy, C, Northwestern, 141 +
20. Lazier, Mernie, B, Illinois, 147
21. Larche, Harry, T, Arkansas State, 153
25. Grothus, Joe, G, Iowa, 168
26. Gillory, Byron, B, Texas, 173
27. Cox, Bob, E, North Carolina, 178

28. *DeMoss, Bob, B, Purdue, 183
29. Pryor, George, F, Wake Forest, 188

BROOKLYN 1949
1. Sullivan, Joe, B, Dartmouth, 2
2. *Szafaryn, Len, T, North Carolina, 10
*Walsh, Bill, C, Notre Dame, 11
*Ferry, Lou, T, Villanova, 12
3. *Triplett, Wally, B, Penn State, 16
4. Tokarczyk, Dolph, G, Penn, 23
5. Quinn, Joe, G. Cornell, 31
6. *Skladany, Leo, E, Pittsburgh, 39
7. Chewning, Lynn, B, Hampden-Sydney, 47
8. McCurry, Bob, C, Michigan State, 55
9. Klemovitch, Chuck, G, Columbia, 63
10. Duncan, Bob, E, Duke, 71
11. Chollet, Hilary, B, Cornell, 79 +
12. Davis, Bill, G, Duke, 87
13. *Dale, Roland, T, Mississippi, 95
14. Alexander, Murry, E, Mississippi State, 103
15. Derrick, Howard, B, Tennessee-Chattanooga, 111
16. Armstrong, Dale, E, Dartmouth, 119
17. *Younger, Paul (Tank), B, Grambling, 127
18. Holgren, Mitchell, T, Hartford, 133
19. Weaver, Frank, B, Moravian, 139
20. *Price, Eddie, B, Tulane, 145
21. Geosits, John, T, Bucknell, 151
22. Brennan, Tom, G, Boston College, 157
23. Mc Bride, Jack, E, Rice, 160
24. Folson, Bobby, E, SMU, 163
25. *Long, Bill, E, Oklahoma State, 166

BUFFALO 1949
1. Kay, Bill, T, Iowa, 6
3. Keeney, Hugh, B, Rice [from Chicago Rockets (AAFC)], 15
*Kissell, Vito, B, Holy Cross, 19
4. *Volz, Wilbur, B, Missouri, 27
5. *Gaul, Frank, G, Notre Dame, 35
6. Guess, Frank, B, Texas, 43
7. Ensminger, Harold, QB Missouri, 51
8. *Vasicek, Vic, G, Texas, 59
9. Verdova, Alex, B, Ohio State, 67
10. *Russas, Al, E, Tennessee, 75
11. Settembre, Ernie, T, Miami, 83
12. Kormarnicki, Milt, C, Villanova, 91 +
13. *Songin, Butch, QB, Boston College, 99 +
14. Cooper, Leon, T, Hardin-Simmons, 107
15. *Tonnemaker, Clayton, C, Minnesota, 115 +
16. *Goode, Rob, B, Texas A&M, 123
17. *Donovan, Art, G, Boston College, 131
18. Goodman, Jim, T, Maryland, 137
19. London, Merlin, E, Oklahoma State, 143
20. Breen, Marty, C, Canisius, 149
21. Simon, John, G, Penn State, 155
25. Hanula, Bernie, T, Wake Forest, 170
26. Deuber, Bobby, B, Penn, 175
27. Lewis, Floyd, G, SMU, 180
28. *Cochran, Tom, B, Auburn, 185
29. Leonard, Joe, T, Virginia, 190 +

CHICAGO HORNETS 1949
1. *Heath, Stan, QB, Nevada-Reno, 1
2. *Blanda, George, QB, Kentucky, 9
3. Choice to Buffalo
4. *Finks, Jim, QB, Tulsa, 22
5. Falcone, Carmen, B, Penn, 30
6. *Tamburo, Sam, B, Penn State, 38
7. *Hutchinson, Ralph, T, Tennessee-Chattanoga, 46
8. *Cain, Jim, E, Alabama, 54
9. *Sabucco, Tino, C, San Francisco, 62 +
10. Huey, Warren, E, Michigan State, 70
11. *Van Brocklin, Norm, QB, Oregon, 78
12. Van Noy, Jay, B, Utah State, 86 +
13. *Wham, Tom, E, Furman, 94
14. Snowden, Ivan, T, Texas A&I, 102
15. Reynolds, Abbie, B, Texas Tech, 110 +
16. Monroe, Dick, C, Kansas, 118
17. Guerre, George, B, Michigan State, 126
18. Phillips, John, B, Southern Mississippi, 132 +
19. *Smith, Verda (Vitamin), B, Abilene Christian, 138
20. Davis, Clayton, C, Oklahoma State, 144
21. Benigni, George, E, Georgetown (D.C.), 150
22. Patterson, R.M., T, McMurry, 156
23. Kemplin, Bill, E, No. Texas State, 159 +
24. Cadenhead, Bill, B, Alabama, 162 +
25. Poole, Phil, G, Mississippi, 165

CLEVELAND 1949
1. Mitchell, Jack, QB, Oklahoma, 8
3. *Collins, Albin (Rip), B, LSU, 21
4. McLellan, Bill, T, Brown, 29
5. McNeill, Ed, E, Michigan, 37
6. *O'Malley, Tom, B, Cincinnati, 45
7. Alexander, Phil, T, South Carolina, 53
8. Cannevino, Mike, B, Ohio State, 61
9. *Walker, Doak, B, SMU, 69, F
10. Adams, Norb, B, Purdue, 77
11. Norton, Negley, T, Penn State, 85
12. Burns, Frank, B, Rutgers, 93
13. *Self, Clarence, B, Wisconsin, 101
14. Kersulis, Walt, E, Illinois, 109
15. Stuart, Bobby Jack, B, Army, 117
16. Bowen, Dinky, B, Georgia Tech, 125
25. Cooney, Larry, B, Penn State, 172
26. *Lininger, Jack, C, Ohio State, 177
27. Gagne, Verne, E, Minnesota, 182
28. Moran, Jim, B, John Carroll, 187
29. *Soboleski, Joe, T, Michigan, 192

LOS ANGELES DONS 1949
1. *Taliaferro, George, B, Indiana, 5
3. *Rodgers, Hosea, B, North Carolina, 18
4. Meinert, Bob, B, Oklahoma State, 26
5. *Grimes, Billy, B, Oklahoma State, 34
6. *Geri, Joe, B, Georgia, 42
7. Renna, Bill, C, Santa Clara, 50
8. *Austin, Bill, T, Oregon St., 58
9. Rubish, Mike, E, North Carolina, 66
10. *Krall, Jerry, B, Ohio State, 74
11. *Drazenovich, Chuck, B, Penn State, 82
12. Klosterman, Larry, G, North Carolina, 90
13. *Blake, Tom, G, Cincinnati, 98
14. Lorenz, Dick, E, Oregon St., 106
15. Bastian, Bob, G, USC, 114
16. Steffen, Art, B, UCLA, 122
17. Gannon, Tom (Chip), B, Harvard, 130
18. Hatch, Larry, B, Washington, 136
19. Tiblier, Jerry, B, Mississippi, 142
20. Frasseto, Gene, T, California, 148
21. Clark, Jim, G, Mississippi, 154
25. Ralston, Ed, B, Richmond, 169
26. *Donaldson, John, B, Georgia, 174
27. Eisenberg, Lloyd, T, Duke, 179
28. Pastre, George, T, UCLA, 184
29. *Ethridge, Joe, G, SMU, 189

NEW YORK YANKEES 1949
1. *Thomason, Bobby, QB, Virginia Military, 3
2. *Panelli, John (Pep), B, Notre Dame, 13
3. *Howard, Sherman, B, Nevada-Reno, 17
4. *Rifenburg, Dick, E, Michigan, 24
5. Maddock, George, T, Northwestern, 32
6. *Panciera, Don, QB, San Francisco, 40
7. *Garza, Dan, E, Oregon, 48
8. Bell, Brian, B, Washington & Lee, 56
9. Mastrangeli, Al, C, Illinois, 64
10. *Goldsberry, John, T, Indiana, 72
11. Bendrick, Ben, B, Wisconsin, 80
12. Van Deren, Frank, E, California, 88 +
13. *Berrang, Eddie, E, Villanova, 96
14. Doormink, Bob, T, Washington State, 104
15. Glenn, Jack, T, Georgia Tech, 112
16. Bruce, Jack, B, William & Mary, 120
17. *Johnson, Gil, B, SMU, 128
18. *Hafen, Barney, E, Utah, 134
19. Jensen, Hal, B, San Francisco, 140
20. *Kalmanir, Tommy, B, Nevada, 146
21. Beasley, Al, G, St. Mary's (CA), 152
22. Tolman, Ernie, E, USC, 158
23. Morrical, Gerry, T, Indiana, 161
24. Hood, Bob, E, Alabama, 164
25. *Nagel, Ross, T, St. Louis, 167

SAN FRANCISCO 1949
1. Fritz, Chester, T, Missouri, 7
3. *LoVuolo, Frank, E, St. Bonaventure, 20
4. De Noia, Mike, B, Scranton, 28
5. Brodnax, George, E, Georgia Tech, 36
6. Hamberger, John, T, SMU, 44
7. Steigman, Dan, C, North Carolina, 52
8. Reid, Bernie, G, Georgia, 60
9. Wendt, Fred, B, Texas-El Paso, 68
10. Flowers, Dick, T, Alabama, 78
11. Lund, Bob, B, Tennessee, 84
12. *Baker, Jon, G, California, 92
13. Reichert, Jim, G, Arkansas, 100
14. *Garlin, Don, B, California, 108
15. *Wissman, Pete, C, St. Louis, 116
16. *Hobbs, Homer, G, Georgia, 124
25. *Shoults, Paul, B, Miami (OH), 171
26. Kelly, Jack, T, Louisiana Tech, 176
27. Flanakin, Jasper, E, Baylor, 181
28. Smith, Rudy, T, Louisiana Tech, 186
29. Long, Gordon, B, Arkansas, 191

1950

Held January 21-22, 1950

When the NFL and the AAFC merged on December 9, 1949, the NFL draft increased by three teams—the Baltimore Colts, the Cleveland Browns, and the San Francisco 49ers. At the draft, members of the 1949 New York Bulldogs' active roster and reserve list were eligible to be selected along with the college seniors. Such players have New York Bulldogs in parentheses after their school.

Shortly after the draft, the New York Yankees of the AAFC were divided between the New York Giants and the Bulldogs. The rest of the AAFC players went into a special allocation pool from which they were selected by the NFL teams. Each team received 10 choices in the allocation draft, except for Baltimore, which received 15. Before the start of the 1950 season, the Bulldogs-Yankees team was renamed the New York Yanks.

BALTIMORE 1950
1. *Burk, Adrian, QB, Baylor, 2
2. *Campbell, Leon (Muscles), B, Arkansas, 15
3. *Colo, Don, T, Brown, 28
4. *Murray, Earl, G, Purdue, 41
5. *Halliday, Jack, G, SMU, 54
6. *Rich, Herb, B, Vanderbilt, 67
7. Bok, Art, B, Dayton, 80
8. Harris, Dick, C, Texas, 93
9. Bass, Bill, B, Arkansas, 106
10. Fry, Errol, G, Texas, 119
11. Romanosky, Joe, T, St. Bonaventure, 132
12. Dey, Bill, B, Dartmouth, 145
13. Stone, Ray, E, Texas, 158
14. Smiarowski, Mitch, C, St. Bonaventure, 171
15. *Spinney, Art, E, Boston College, 184
16. Fisher, Dave, B, Southwestern Louisiana, 197
17. Murphy, Ralph, G, Rice, 210
18. Schoolmaster, Charley, C, Western Michigan, 223
19. Waddail, Bill, B, Auburn, 236
20. Dunlap, Sheldon, G, Cincinnati, 249
21. Phillips, Tom, B, Baldwin-Wallace, 262
22. Armstrong, Chip, C, Occidental, 275
23. Weittlaufer, Harry, E, Pennsylvania, 288
24. Petroski, Bill, T, Holy Cross, 301
25. Pepper, Jim, G. Syracuse, 314
26. *Mazzanti, Gino, B, Arkansas, 327
27. Johnson, Mitford, B, Baylor, 340
28. Adcock, John, T, Auburn, 353
29. Graham, Bob (Snakey), B, Pennsylvania, 366
30. Blake, Tom, G, Cincinnati , 379

CHICAGO BEARS 1950
1. *Hunsinger, Chuck, B, Florida [from New York Bulldogs], 3
*Morrison, Fred (Curly), B, Ohio State, 10
2. *Dottley, John (Kayo), B, Mississippi, 24
3. *Romanik, Steve, B, Villanova, 36
4. Novak, Tom, C, Nebraska [from Pittsburgh], 48
Papaleo, Dom, G, Boston College, 50
5. *Zalejski, Ernie, B, Notre Dame, 62
6. Perricone, Gaspar, B, Northwestern [from New York Giants], 72
*Hansen, Wayne, C, Texas-El Paso, 76
7. Prather, Rollin, E, Kansas State, 88
8. Nevills, Sam, T, Oregon, 102
9. *Reid, Floyd (Breezy), B, Georgia [from New York Bulldogs], 107
Braznell, Dick, B, Missouri, 114
10. Wahl, Al, T, Michigan, 128
11. *Helwig, John, G, Notre Dame, 140
12. Roof, Kenny, B, Oklahoma State, 154
13. *Dempsey, Frank, T, Florida, 166
14. Hover, Al, G, LSU, 180
15. Glisson, Jimmy, B, Tulane, 192
16. *Bradley, Ed, E, Wake Forest, 206
17. Janaszek, Ray, B, Dayton, 218
18. Andrews, Rupert, B, Stanford, 232
19. Bye, Billy, B, Minnesota, 244
20. Crawford, Jim (Tank), G, Mississippi, 258
21. *Angie, Bob, B, Iowa State, 270
22. Byler, Jim, G, North Carolina State, 284
23. Bigham, Bill, T, Harding, 296
24. Polenske, Walt, B, Pacific, 310
25. Samuels, Perry, B, Texas, 322
26. Sella, George, B, Princeton, 336
27. Davis, Wilton (Hook), B, Hardin-Simmons, 348
28. Kenary, Jim, B, Harvard, 362
29. Nadherny, Ferd, B, Yale, 374
30. Markert, Allen, T, Minnesota, 388

CHICAGO CARDINALS 1950
1. Choice to Los Angeles Rams
2. *Jennings, Jack, T, Ohio State, 21
3. *Svoboda, Bill, B, Tulane [from New York Bulldogs], 29
*Polsfoot, Fran, E, Washington State, 35
4. *Paul, Don, B, Washington State, 47
5. Kiilsgaard, Carl, T, Idaho, 61
6. Wood, Warren, G, Puget Sound, 73
7. *Gay, Billy, B, Notre Dame [from New York Giants], 85 F
*Bagdon, Eddie, G, Michigan State, 87
8. *Hock, John, T, Santa Clara, 99
9. Ragazzo, Vito, E, William & Mary, 113
10. Grothaus, Walt, C, Notre Dame, 125
Lavigne, Milt, B, Southeastern Louisiana [from Pittsburgh], 126
11. Ison, J.D., E, Baylor, 139
12. Wallheiser, Frank, E, Western Kentucky, 151
Sharpe, Bob, G, Davidson [from Pittsburgh], 152
13. *Hennessey, Jerry, E, Santa Clara, 165
14. Andros, Dee, G, Oklahoma, 177
15. Langford, Al, B, Howard Payne, 191
16. Bierman, Harry, E, Furman, 203
17. *Palmer, Tom, T, Wake Forest, 217
18. Espenan, Ray, E, Notre Dame, 229
19. Day, Loran, B, Northwestern, 243
20. Halbert, Webb, B, Iowa State, 255
21. Blumhardt, Howard, B, South Dakota, 269
22. Lipinski, Jim, T, Fairmont State, 281
23. Montgomery, Bill, B, Fresno State, 295
24. *Gambold, Bob, B, Washington State, 307 F
25. Truman, Lee, B, Kentucky, 321
26. Pittman, Jim, B, Mississippi State, 333
27. *Bienemann, Tom, E, Drake, 347
28. Jones, Sonny, B, Wyoming, 359
29. Montagne, Bill, B, California, 373
30. Banonis, Vic, C, Georgetown (D.C.), 385

CLEVELAND 1950
1. *Carpenter, Ken, B, Oregon State, 13
2. *Sandusky, John, T, Villanova [from Detroit], 18
*Martin, Jim, E, Notre Dame, 26
3. Robinson, Jimmy Joe, B, Pittsburgh, 39
4. Wilson, Bob (Red), C, Wisconsin, 52
5. *Phelps, Don (Dopey), B, Kentucky, 65
6. *Gorgal, Ken, B, Purdue, 78
7. Carter, Win, B, Missouri, 91
8. Frizzell, Russ, T, Tulsa, 104
9. *Duncan, Jim, E, Wake Forest, 117
10. O'Pella, Frank, B, William & Mary, 130
11. Plotz, Bob, G, Pittsburgh, 143
12. *Cole, Emerson, B, Toledo, 156
13. Wright, Rupe, G, Baylor, 169
14. Harrington, Packard, C, St. Mary's (CA), 182
15. Meland, Ted, G, Oregon, 195
16. King, Art, G, Ball State, 208
17. McKinney, Hal, G, Missouri Valley, 221
18. Travue, Joe, B, Louisville, 234
19. *Songin, Butch, B, Boston College, 247
20. Hackney, John, G, Murray State, 260
21. Vogts, Leroy, G, Washington (St. Louis), 273
22. Dowling, Jim, G, Santa Clara, 286
23. *Moselle, Don, B, Wisconsin-Superior, 299
24. Woodland, Jack, B, Bowling Green, 312
25. Brasher, Jim, C, Maryland, 325
26. *Toogood, Charley, T, Nebraska, 338 +
27. Gray, Dick, B, Oregon State, 351
28. Pyle, Billy, B, Texas, 364
29. *Schnelker, Bob, E, Bowling Green, 377
30. Massey, Jim, B, Detroit, 390

DETROIT 1950
BONUS CHOICE: *Hart, Leon, E, Notre Dame, 1
1. *Watson, Joe, C, Rice, 5
2. Choice to Cleveland
*McGraw, Thurman (Fum), T, Colorado St. [from Philadelphia], 27
3. *Murakowski, Art, B, Northwestern, 31
4. Kiely, Ernie, G, Texas-El Paso, 44
5. Fitkin, Hal, B, Dartmouth, 57
6. *Jaszewski, Floyd, T, Minnesota, 70
7. Leverman, Bill, B, St. Edward's, 83
8. McAllister, Ralph, B, Minnesota, 96
9. Wood, Ed, G, Detroit, 109
10. Malcolm, Roland, B, Gustavus Adolphus, 122
11. Wilson, Jack, T, Ohio State, 135
12. Walters, Bucky, T, Brown, 148
13. Ryan, Jim, B, San Francisco, 161
14. Squires, Cliff, C, Nebraska Wesleyan, 174
15. Worthington, Tom, B, Northwestern, 187
16. Greiner, Jerry, C, Detroit, 200
17. Callahan, Connie, B, Morningside, 213
18. *Stansauk, Don, T, Denver, 226
19. *Cifelli, Gus, T, Notre Dame, 239
20. Davis, Fred, E, Maryland, 252
21. Brewer, George, B, Oklahoma, 265
22. Tate, Jim, T, Purdue, 278
23. Heller Irv, T, Boston U., 291
24. McDowell, Jim, G, William & Mary, 304
25. Glick, Gene, B, Michigan State, 317
26. Lee, Bobby Coy, B, Texas, 330
27. Johnson, Elbert, E, Texas Tech, 343
28. *Karras, Johnny, B, Illinois, 356 +
29. Steger, Russ, B, Illinois, 369
30. DeRoin, Rube, C, Oklahoma Slate, 382

GREEN BAY 1950
1. *Tonnemaker, Clayton, C, Minnesota, 4
2. *Rote, Tobin, QB, Rice, 17
3. *Soltau, Gordy, E, Minnesota, 30
4. *Coutre, Larry, B, Notre Dame, 43
5. Choice to Pittsburgh
6. *Cloud, Jack, B, William & Mary, 69
7. *Manley, Leon, G, Oklahoma, 82
8. Szulborski, Harry, B, Purdue, 95
9. Wilson, Roger, E, South Carolina, 108
10. Mealey, Bob, T, Minnesota, 121
11. Lorendo, Gene, E, Georgia, 134
12. Pavich, Andy, E, Denver, 147
13. Elliott, Carlton, E, Virginia, 160
14. Leon, Fred, T, Nevada-Reno, 173
15. Huebner, Gene, C, Baylor, 186
16. Kuzma, Frank, B, Minnesota, 199
17. Otterback, Hal, G, Wisconsin, 212
18. *Galiffa, Arnold, QB, Army, 225
19. Rowan, Earl, T, Hardin-Simmons, 238
20. Howe, Jim, B, Kentucky, 251
21. Evans, Gene, B, Wisconsin, 264
22. Beatty, Chuck, C, Penn State, 277
23. Mattey, George, G, Ohio State, 290
24. Delph, Don, B, Dayton, 303
25. Waters, Frank, B, Michigan State, 316
26. Radtke, Claude, E, Lawrence, 329
27. Osborne, Bill, B, Nevada-Reno, 342
28. Hering, Herm, B, Rutgers, 355
29. Zaranka, Ben, E, Kentucky, 368
30. *Mallouf, Ray, B, SMU (New York Bulldogs), 381

LOS ANGELES RAMS 1950
1. *Pasquariello, Ralph, B, Villanova [from Chicago Cardinals], 9
*West, Stan, G, Oklahoma, 12
2. Fuchs, Bob, C, Missouri, 25
3. Murray, Don, T, Penn State, 38
4. Proctor, Ben, E, Texas, 51
5. *McKissack, Dick, B, SMU, 64
6. Langrell, Orville, T, Oklahoma City, 77
7. Coggin, Cliff, E, Southern Mississippi, 90
8. *Lewis, Woodley, B, Oregon, 103
9. *Cowan, Les, E, McMurry, 116 F
10. Van Noy, Jay, B, Utah State, 129
11. Roundy, Jay, B, USC [from New York Giants], 137
Stuvek, Fred, G, West Virginia, 142
12. Lunney, John, G, Arkansas, 155

13. Winbigler, Tom, B, College of Idaho, 168
14. Trautwein, Bill, T, Ohio State, 181
15. *Stephenson, Dave (Trapper), C, West Virginia, 194
16. Maloney, Jim, E, Fordham, 207
17. Neugold, Harry, T, Rensselaer, 220
18. *Collier, Bobby, T, SMU, 233 F
19. Smith, Johnny, E, Arizona, 246
20. Young, Bill, B, Hillsdale, 259
21. Klein, Bill, E, Hanover, 272
22. Barber, Doug, B, Dakota Wesleyan, 285
23. Bird, Jim, T, USC, 298
24. Joiner, Joe, E, Austin, 311
25. *Towler, Dan (Deacon), B, Washington & Jeff., 324
26. Haldy, Otto, T, Mankato State, 337
27. Kilman, Hal, T, TCU, 350
28. Morgan, Junior, E, San Jose State, 363
29. Heck, Bob, B, Pacific, 376
30. *Lange, Bill, G, Dayton, 389

NEW YORK BULLDOGS 1950

1. Choice to Chicago Bears
2. *Weiner, Art, E, North Carolina, 16
3. Choice to Chicago Cardinals
4. *Toth, Zollie, B, LSU, 42
5. *Swistowicz, Mike, B, Notre Dame, 55
6. *Aldridge, Ben, B, Oklahoma State, 68
7. Narrell, Don, T, TCU, 81
8. Archer, Jack, B, TCU, 94
9. Choice to Chicago Bears
10. Lyle, Melvin, E, LSU, 120
11. McAuley, Roger, G, TCU, 133
12. Hillhouse, Andy, E, Texas A&M, 146
13. Morton, Jack, B, West Virginia, 159
14. Carmichael, Ed, G, Oregon State, 172
15. Messeroll, Norm, T, Tennessee, 185
16. Stetter, Bill, C, Holy Cross, 198
17. Tidwell, Joe Dean, B, Harding (TN), 211
18. *Champion, Jim, T, Mississippi State, 224
19. *Griffin, Bob, B, Baylor, 237
20. Royal, Darrell, B, Oklahoma, 250
21. French, Bud, B, Kansas, 263
22. Johnson, R.V., T, St. Mary's (CA), 276
23. Sheffield, Dick, E, Tulane, 289
24. DeYoung, Bill, B, Stanford, 302
25. Dotur, Steve, G, Oregon, 315
26. Noonan, Red, B, Alabama, 328
27. Olson, Chuck, E, Washington, 341
28. Petty, Ed, C, Hardin-Simmons, 354
29. Jasonek, Ed, B, Furman, 367
30. Poulos, John, B, Pacific, 380

NEW YORK GIANTS 1950

1. *Tidwell, Travis, B, Auburn, 7
2. *Price, Eddie, B, Tulane, 20
3. *Clay, Randy, B, Texas, 33
4. Payne, Porter, G, Georgia, 46
5. *Griffith, Forrest, B, Kansas, 59
6. Choice to Chicago Bears
7. Choice to Chicago Cardinals
8. *Van Buren, Ebert, B, LSU, 98 +
9. Cisterna, Vince, E, Northern Arizona, 111
10. *Wilkinson, Bob, E, UCLA, 124 F
11. Choice to Los Angeles Rams
12. *Wietecha, Ray, C, Northwestern, 150
13. Kelly, Joe, C, Wisconsin, 163
14. Fritz, Gene, T, Minnesota, 176
15. Roberson, Bill, T, Stephen F. Austin, 189
16. Jackson, Bob (Stonewall), B, North Carolina A&T, 202
17. Hatfield, Steve, B, Shippensburg, 215
18. *Roman, Geo., T, Case West.Res.(New York Bulldogs), 228
19. *Barzilauskas, Fritz, G, Yale (New York Bulldogs), 241
20. Tangaro, Joe, T, Utah, 254
21. *Stribling, Bill, E, Mississippi, 267 F
22. *DeMoss, Bob, B, Purdue (New York Bulldogs), 280
23. Davis, Warren, C, Colgate, 293
24. *Finnin, Tom, T, Detroit, 306
25. Beiersdorf, Ken, B, Minnesota, 319
26. Copp, Carl, T, Vanderbilt, 332
27. Sweet, Art, B, Baylor, 345
28. McAuliffe, Don, B, Michigan State, 358 F
29. *Boyda, Mike, B, Wash. & Lee (New York Bulldogs), 371
30. *Tanner, Hampton, T, Georgia, 384

PHILADELPHIA 1950

1. *Grant, Harry (Bud), E, Minnesota, 14
2. Choice to Detroit
3. Sanders, Bob, B, Oregon, 40
4. *McChesney, Bob, E, Hardin-Simmons, 53
5. Kaysserian, Mike, B, Detroit, 66
6. McDermott, Lloyd, T, Kentucky, 79
7. Olix, Mel, B, Miami (OH), 92
8. O'Hanlon, Dick, T, Ohio State, 105
9. Wilson, Bobby, B, Mississippi, 118
10. Johnson, Ernie, B, UCLA, 131
11. Lantrip, Bobby, B, Rice, 144
12. Mahoney, Frank, E, Brown, 157
13. *Willey, Norm (Wildman), B, Marshall, 170
14. *Hix, Billy, E, Arkansas, 183
15. Carey, Herb, B, Dartmouth, 196
16. Marck, Jim, T, Xavier, 209
17. Taylor, Jerry, C, Mississippi State, 222
18. Tunnicliff, Ed, B, Northwestern, 235
19. Robinson, Darrell, E, Oregon, 248
20. *Pregulman, Merv, G, Michigan (New York Bulldogs), 261
21. Cross, Marv, B, Washington State, 274
22. Hague, Jim, E, Ohio State, 287
23. Lesko, Al, T, St. Bonaventure, 300
24. DeSylvia, Tom, G, Oregon State, 313
25. Eagles, Jim, C, North Texas State, 326
26. Franz, Rod, G, California, 339
27. Martin, Bill, B, USC, 352
28. Burson, Don, B, Northwestern, 365
29. Curtier, Wes, T, Richmond, 378
30. Parker, Dud, B, Baylor, 391

PITTSBURGH 1950

1. *Chandnois, Lynn, B, Michigan State, 8
2. *Stautner, Ernie, T, Boston College, 22
3. *Hughes, George, G, William & Mary, 34
4. Choice to Chicago Bears
5. Rowe, Tom, E, Dartmouth [from Green Bay], 56
   *Allen, Lou, T, Duke, 60
6. Mattson, Ed, B, Trinity (TX), 74
7. *Smith, Truett, B, Mississippi State, 86
8. *Rogel, Fran, B, Penn State, 100
9. Druen, Max, T, Tulane, 112
10. Choice to Chicago Cardinals
11. Williams, Charley, E, Sam Houston State, 138
12. Choice to Chicago Cardinals
13. Norton, Negley, T, Penn State, 164
14. Kynes, Jim, C, Florida, 178
15. Russell, Harry, B, San Jose State, 190
16. Barkouskie, Bernie, G, Pittsburgh, 204
17. Bodine, Al, B, Georgia, 216
18. Powell, Kenneth, E, North Carolina, 230
19. *Gaul, Frank, T, Notre Dame, 242
20. DeNoia, Mike, B, Scranton, 256
21. *Tomlinson, Dick, G, Kansas, 268
22. Burak, Stan, B, George Washington, 282
23. Kersulis, Walt, E, Illinois, 294
24. *Weaver, John, G, Miami (OH), 308
25. Numbers, Bob, C, Lehigh, 320
26. Vaccaro, Nick, B, Florida, 334
27. Kreiser, Elmer, E, Bloomsburg, 346
28. Diehl, Jerry, B, Idaho, 360
29. DePasqua, Carl, B, Pittsburgh, 372
30. Hudak, Ed, T, Notre Dame, 386

SAN FRANCISCO 1950

1. *Nomellini, Leo, T, Minnesota, 11
2. *Campora, Don, T, Pacific, 23
3. *Collins, Ray, T, LSU, 37
4. Bailey, Morris, E, TCU, 49
5. Kane, Harry, C, Pacific, 63
6. Van Pool, Don, E, Oklahoma State, 75
7. Berry, Lindy, B, TCU, 89
8. *Williams, Ellery, E, Santa Clara, 101
9. Zinach, Pete, B, West Virginia, 115
10. *Celeri, Bob, B, California, 127
11. *Dow, Harley, T, San Jose State, 141
12. *Burke, Don, B, USC, 153
13. Cecconi, Lou (Bimbo), B, Pittsburgh, 167
14. Payne, Tom, E, Santa Clara, 179
15. Crampsey, Leo, E, St. Bonaventure, 193
16. *Shaw, Charley, G, Oklahoma State, 205
17. Van Meter, Cliff, B, Tulane, 219
18. Genito, Ralph, B, Kentucky, 231
19. Klein, Forest, G, California, 245
20. Nix, Jack, E, USC, 257
21. Alker, Guerin, C, Loyola (CA), 271
22. *Wilson, Billy, E, San Jose State, 283 F
23. Williams, Jim (Froggy), E, Rice, 297
24. Wyman, Bill, T, Rice, 309
25. Dunn, Bob, G, Dayton, 323
26. *Powers, Jim, B, USC, 335
27. Johnson, Ken, G, Pacific, 349
28. Hall, Charley, B, Arizona, 361
29. Whelan, Bob, B, Boston U., 375
30. Stillwell, Bob, E, USC, 387

WASHINGTON 1950

1. *Thomas, George B, Oklahoma, 6
2. *Haynes, Hall, B, Santa Clara, 19
3. *Karras, Lou, T, Purdue, 32
4. *Ulinski, Harry, C, Kentucky, 45
5. *Spaniel, Frank, B, Notre Dame, 58
6. *Pepper, Gene, G, Missouri, 71
7. *Houghton, Jerry, T, Washington State, 84
8. Rohde, John, E, Pacific, 97
9. Winslow, Don, T, Iowa, 110
10. *LeBaron, Eddie, QB, Pacific, 123
11. *Brown, Dan, E, Villanova, 136
12. Chauncey, Bill, B, Iowa State, 149
13. Davis, Clay, C, Oklahoma State, 162
14. Button, Lyle, T, Illinois, 175
15. *Loyd, Alex, E, Oklahoma State, 188
16. *Justice, Charlie (Choo-Choo), B, North Carolina, 201
17. *Cullom, Jim, G, California, 214
18. Duke, Alvin, B, Arkansas, 227
19. White, Ed, E, Alabama, 240
20. Bayer, George, T, Washington, 253
21. *Witucki, Cas (Slug), G, Indiana, 266
22. deLaurentis, John, T, Waynesburg, 279
23. Zuravleff, Joe, E, Northwestern, 292
24. Tilton, Dick, T, Neveda-Reno, 305
25. Stewart, Art, B, Southeastern Oklahoma, 318
26. Roth, Earl, B, Maryland, 331
27. Lee, Ed, T, Kansas, 344
28. Shoaf, Ralph, B, West Virginia, 357
29. Lundin, Johnny, G, Minnesota, 370
30. Noppinger, Bob, E, Georgetown (D.C), 383

1951

Held January 18-19, 1951

After the Baltimore franchise disbanded following the 1950 season, players from its active roster and reserve list were made eligible for the draft along with college seniors. Such players have Baltimore in parentheses after their school. Additionally, two teams were owed draft choices by the defunct Colts. The addition of those two choices brought the total number of players drafted to 362.

CHICAGO BEARS 1951

1. *Williams, Bob, QB, Notre Dame [from Baltimore], 2
   *Stone, Billy, B, Bradley and New York Yanks [from Baltimore], 10
   *Schroeder, Gene, E, Virginia, 12
2. *George, Bill, T, Wake Forest, 23
3. *White, Wilford (Whizzer), B, Arizona State, 36
4. *Moser, Bob, C, Pacific, 47
   *Jelley, Tom, E, Miami (FL) [from New York Giants], 49
5. *Rowland, Brad, B, McMurry, 60
6. Falkenberg, Herb, B, Trinity (Texas), 71
7. *Lea, Paul, T, Tulane, 84
8. Mayes, Clair, G, Oklahoma, 95
9. Gregus, Bill, B, Wake Forest, 108
10. Sherrill, J.W., B, Tennessee, 120
11. Hardiman, Tom, B, Georgetown (D.C.), 133
12. Hairston, Lawrence (Punjab), T, Nevada-Reno, 144
13. Wright, Charley, B, West Texas State, 157
14. Woods, Bailey, B, Abilene Christian, 168
15. Hall, Sid, C, Pacific, 181
16. Volm, Frank, E, Marquette, 192
17. Dufek, Don, B, Michigan, 205
18. Brown, Chuck, G, Illinois, 216
19. Lisak, Ed, B, Oklahoma, 229
20. Smith, Larry, C, South Carolina, 240
21. Higgins, Larry, B, Fordham, 253
22. Hanson, Bob, G, Montana, 264
23. Hlavac, Rene, T, Nebraska-Omaha, 277
24. Dokas, Pete, E, Mansfield, 288
25. Miller, Johnny, B, Northwestern, 301
26. Rogers, Buddy, B, Arkansas, 312
27. Taylor, Jerry, C, Wyoming, 325
28. *Campbell, Leon (Muscles), B, Arkansas [from Baltimore], 336
29. Justice, John, G, Santa Clara, 349
30. Butler, Charley, E, Geo.Washington, 360

CHICAGO CARDINALS 1951

1. *Groom, Jerry, C, Notre Dame, 6
2. *Joyce, Don, T, Tulane, 18
3. *Stonesifer, Don, E, Northwestern, 30
4. Doyne, Dick, B, Lehigh, 42
5. *Lynch, Lynn, G, Illinois [from Washington], 51
   Choice to San Francisco
6. Jasonek, Ed, B, Furman, 66
7. Punches, Dick, T, Colorado, 78
8. *Sanford, Leo, C, Louisiana Tech, 90
9. Schmidt, Neil, B, Purdue, 102
10. *Cooper, Ken, G, Vanderbilt [from Baltimore], 115
11. *Bienemann, Tom, E, Drake, 127
12. Landry, Jack, B, Notre Dame, 139
13. *Peters, Volney, T, USC, 151
14. Leskovar, Bill, B, Kentucky, 163
15. Simcic, John, G, Wisconsin, 175
16. Miller, Gene, B, Northwestern, 187
17. May, Henry, C, Southwest Missouri State, 199
18. Pomeroy, Russ, T, Stanford, 211
19. Ackerman, Gene, E, Missouri, 223
20. *Wallner, Fred, G, Notre Dame, 235
21. Bunting, Dick, E, Drake, 247
22. *Whitman, S.J., B, Tulsa, 259
23. *Owens, Jim, E, Oklahoma [from Baltimore], 271
24. *Cross, Billy, B, West Texas State, 283
25. Quick, Vernon, G, Wofford, 295
26. Fleischmann, Jeff, B, Cornell, 307
27. *Huxhold, Ken, T, Wisconsin, 319
28. Martin, Dick, B, Kentucky, 331
29. *Livingston, Bob, B, Notre Dame [from Baltimore], 343
30. Root, Leon, B, Rutgers, 355

CLEVELAND 1951

1. *Konz, Kenny, B, LSU, 14
2. Curtis, Bucky, E, Vanderbilt, 26
3. *Helluin, Jerry, T, Tulane, 38 F
4. *Oristaglio, Bob, E, Penn [from San Francisco] [from Baltimore], 39
   *Smith, Bob, B, Texas A&M [from Green Bay], 41
   *Donovan, Art, T, Boston College [from Baltimore], 50
5. *Loomis, Ace, B, Wisconsin-La Crosse, 62
6. *Rogas, Dan, G, Tulane, 74
7. Holdash, Irv, C, North Carolina, [from New York Yankees], 82
   *Michaels, Walt, B, Washington & Lee, 86
8. *Spinney, Art, E, Boston College [from Green Bay] [from Baltimore], 88
   *Clark, Max, B, Houston, 98
9. Toler, Burl, G, San Francisco [from Detroit], 105
   *Shula, Don, B, John Carroll, 110
10. Gierula, Chet, G, Maryland, 123
11. Custis, Bernie, B, Syracuse, 135
12. Seillers, Milan, B, Florida State [from Detroit], 142
    Kirtley, Stew, E, Morehead State, 147
13. Voskuhl, Bob, C, Georgetown (KY), 159
14. Cernoch, Rudy, T, Northwestern, 171
15. *Skibinski, Joe, G, Purdue, 183 F
16. Pasky, Ed, B, South Carolina, 195
17. Ka-Ne, Leroy, B, Dayton, 207
18. DeRoin, Rube, C, Oklahoma State, 219
19. Solari, Ray, G, California, 231
20. Crocher, Jack, B, Tulsa, 243
21. Stone, Ray, E, Texas, 255
22. *Taseff, Carl, B, John Carroll, 267
23. Champion, Johnny, B, SMU, 279
24. Benner, Wayne, B, Florida State, 291
25. Knispel, John, T, Wisconsin-LaCrosse, 303
26. *Williams, Fred, T, Arkansas, 315 F
27. Jones, Jack, B, Livingston, 327
28. Thrift, Roger, B, East Carolina, 339
29. Driver, Bill, B, Florida State, 351
30. *Averno, Sisto, G, Muhlenberg [from Baltimore], 362

DETROIT 1951

1. Choice to Philadelphia
2. *Stanfel, Dick, G, San Francisco, 19
3. *Dibble, Dorne, E, Michigan State, 33
4. *D'Alonzo, Pete, B, Villanova, 44
5. *Doran, Jim, E, Iowa State, 55
   *Torgeson, LaVern, C, Washington St., [from New York Yanks], 58
6. *Christiansen, Jack, B, Colorado State, 69
7. *Momsen, Bob, T, Ohio State, 80
8. Raklovits, Dick, B, Illinois, 91
9. Choice to Cleveland
10. Shoaf, Jim, G, LSU, 117
11. Anderson, Frankie, E, Oklahoma, 128
12. Choice to Cleveland
13. *Siegert, Wayne, T, Illinois, 153
14. Wittmer, Lee, T, Detroit, 164
15. *Hill, Jimmie, B, Tennessee, 178
16. Geremsky, Ted, E, Pittsburgh, 189
17. *Meisenheimer, Darrell, B, Oklahoma State, 200
18. Wolgast, Eddie, B, Arizona, 214
19. Hanson, Gordy, T, Washington State, 225
20. Gibbons, Harry, B, South Dakota State, 236
21. Block, King, B, Idaho, 250
22. Foldberg, Dan, E, Army, 261
23. Gabriel, Dick, B, Lehigh, 272
24. *Buksar, George, B, Purdue [from Baltimore], 286
25. Harris, Dick, C, Texas [from Baltimore], 297
26. Kazmierski, Frank, C, West Virginia, 308
27. Allis, Harry, E, Michigan, 322
28. Peot, Dick, T, South Dakota State, 333
29. *Womack, Bruce, T, West Texas State, 344
30. Horwath, Ron, B, Detroit, 358

GREEN BAY 1951

1. *Gain, Bob, T, Kentucky, 5
2. *Collins, Albin (Rip), B, LSU [from Baltimore], 16
3. *Cone, Fred, B, Clemson, 27
4. Choice to Cleveland
5. Stinson, Wade, B, Kansas, 52
6. Holowenko, Sig, T, John Carroll, 63
7. Sutherland, Bill, E, St. Vincent, 77
8. Choice to Cleveland
9. McWilliams, Dick, T, Michigan, 99
10. Noppinger, Bob, T, Georgetown (D.C.), 114
11. Rooks, George, B, Morgan State, 125
12. Kreager, Carl, C, Michigan, 136
13. Stephens, Ed, B, Missouri, 150
14. Bauer, Ray, E, Montana, 161
15. Ernst, Joe, B, Tulane, 172
16. *Afflis, Dick (The Bruiser), T, Nevada-Reno, 186
17. *Pelfrey, Ray, B, Eastern Kentucky, 197
18. Petela, Ed, B, Boston College, 208
19. Liber, Jim, B, Xavier, 222
20. Johnson, Dick, T, Virginia, 233
21. Edling, Art, E, Minnesota, 244
22. *Felker, Art, E, Marquette, 258
23. Chamberlain, Tubba, G, Wisconsin-Eau Claire, 269
24. Christie, Dick, B, Nebraska-Omaha, 280
25. Monte, Charlie, B, Hillsdale, 294
26. Miller, Bill, T, Ohio State, 305
27. Bossons, Bob, C, Georgia Tech, 316
28. Ayre, Bill, B, Abilene Christian, 330
29. Fieler, Ralph, E, Miami, 341
30. Withers, Ed, B, Wisconsin, 352

LOS ANGELES RAMS 1951

1. *McFadin, Bud, G, Texas, 11
2. *Rich, Herb, B, Vanderbilt [from Baltimore], 24
3. *Toogood, Charley, T, Nebraska, 35
4. *Kinek, George, B, Tulane, 48
5. *Momsen, Tony, C, Michigan, 59
6. *Hecker, Norb, E, Baldwin-Wallace, 72
7. Egler, Alan, B, Colgate, 83
8. Primiani, Hugo, T, Boston U., 96
9. Lang, Nolan, B, Oklahoma, 107
10. Kirkby, Roland, B, Washington, 121
11. Natyshak, John, B, Tampa, 132
12. Hardey, Don, B, Pacific, 145
13. *Reid, Joe, C, LSU, 156
14. McCoy, Rob, B, Georgia Tech, 169
15. Posey, Obie, B, Southern, 180
16. Robertson, Bill, E, Memphis State, 193
17. Riley, Hal, E, Baylor, 204
18. *Daugherty, Dick, G, Oregon, 217
19. *Robustelli, Andy, E, Arnold, 228
20. Nutter, Jim, B, Wichita State, 241
21. Stelle, Earl, B, Oregon, 252

22. *Baggett, Billy, B, LSU, 265
23. Thomas, Dean, T, Michigan State, 276
24. Abeltin, Harry, T, Colgate, 289
25. Calvert, Jackie, T, Clemson, 300
26. *Ruetz, Howie, T, Loras, 313
27. *Brosky, Al, B, Illinois, 324 F
28. Wingo, Sterling, B, Virginia Tech, 337
29. Jackson, Earl, B, Texas Tech, 348
30. Hanley, Alvin, B, Kentucky State, 361

NEW YORK GIANTS 1951

BONUS CHOICE: *Rote, Kyle, B, SMU, 1
1. *Spavital, Jim, B, Oklahoma State [from Baltimore], 13
2. *Krouse, Ray, T, Maryland, 25
3. *Grandelius, Sonny, B, Michigan State, 37
4. Choice to Chicago Bears
5. *Stroud, Jack, T, Tennessee, 61
6. *Hannah, Herb, T, Alabama, 73
7. *Williams, Joel, C, Texas [from Baltimore], 85
8. *Benners, Fred, B, SMU, 97 F
9. Donan, Holland, T, Princeton, 109
10. *Murray, Earl, G, Purdue [from Baltimore], 122
11. Bagnell, Reds, B, Pennsylvania, 134
12. *Hudson, Bob, E, Clemson, 146
13. Douglass, Paul, B, Illinois, 158
14. Flanagan, Pat, T, Marquette, 170
15. Vykukal, Gene, T, Texas, 182
16. Pfeifer, Alan, E, Fordham, 194
17. *Sherrod, Bud, E, Tennessee, 206
18. Smith, Frank, B, Miami, 218
19. Conn, Billy, B, Auburn, 230
20. *Albright, Bill, T, Wisconsin, 242
21. Lemonick, Bernie, G, Pennsylvania, 254
22. Binkley, Waldo, T, Austin Peay, 266
23. *Yelvington, Dick, T, Georgia, 278
24. Kuh, Dick, G, Michigan State, 290
25. *Lagod, Chet, T, Tennessee-Chattanooga, 302
26. Armstrong, Quincy, C, North Texas State, 314
27. Hubbard, Charley, E, Morris Harvey, 326
28. Quinn, Hal, G, SMU, 338
29. Considine, John, T, Purdue, 350

NEW YORK YANKS 1951

1. Choice to Chicago Bears
2. *Jackson, Ken, T, Texas, 22
3. *McCormack, Mike, T, Kansas, 34
4. *Wingate, Elmer, E, Maryland, 46
5. Choice to Detroit
6. Musacco, George, B, Loyola (CA), 70
7. Choice to Cleveland
8. *Lauer, Larry, C, Alabama, 94
9. *Colo, Don, T, Brown [from Baltimore], 106
10. *Thomas, Jesse, B, Michigan State, 119
11. Wyndham, Steve, B, Clemson, 131
12. Lary, Al, E, Alabama, 143
13. Thomas, John, E, Oregon State, 155
14. Rapp, Charley, B, Duquesne, 167
15. Wanamaker, Bill, G, Kentucky, 179
16. Fray, Bill, T, Idaho, 191
17. Rowan, Dick, C, Texas, 203
18. Watson, Bob, E, UCLA, 215
19. Longmore, Ralph, B, Duquesne, 227
20. Price, Jerrell, T, Texas Tech, 239
21. *Pollard, Al, B, Army, 251
22. *King, Eddie, C, Boston College [from Baltimore], 263
23. Cunningham, Dave, B, Utah, 275
24. *Stroschein, Breck, E, UCLA, 287
25. Boudreaux, Roy, T, Southwestern Louisiana, 299
26. *Sherman, Will, B, St. Mary's (CA), 311
27. Price, Ed, B, Texas Tech, 323
28. Chadband, Jim, B, Idaho, 335
29. *Kissell, Veto, B, Holy Cross [from Baltimore], 347
30. Shinn, Joe, E, Tulane, 359

PHILADELPHIA 1951

1. *Van Buren, Ebert, B, LSU, 7
   *Mutryn, Chet, B, Xavier [from Detroit] [from Baltimore], 8
2. Choice to Washington
3. Bruno, Al, E, Kentucky, 32
4. Nagle, Fran, B, Nebraska, 43
5. *Dwyer, Jack, B, Loyola (CA), 57
6. *Farragut, Ken, C, Mississippi, 68
7. Boydston, Frank, B, Baylor, 79
8. Richards, Jack, E, Arkansas, 93
9. Doyle, Denny, G, Tulane, 104
10. Schaufele, Louis, B, Arkansas, 116
11. Pope, Bob, T, Kentucky, 130
12. Rich, Henry, B, Arizona State, 141
13. Mastellone, Pete, C, Miami, 152
14. *Walston, Bobby, E, Georgia, 166
15. North, Bobby, B, Georgia Tech, 177
16. Hatfield, Hal, E, USC, 188
17. Waggoner, Hal, B, Tulane, 202
18. Weeks, Bill, B, Iowa State, 213
19. Bove, Jack, T, West Virginia, 224
20. Glorioso, John, B, Missouri, 238
21. Franklin, Neal, T, SMU, 249
22. Rucker, Jack, B, Mississippi State, 260
23. *Bighead, Jack, E, Pepperdine, 274 +
24. Kotowski, Tony, E, Mississippi State, 285
25. Drahn, Glenn, B, Iowa, 296
26. Stewart, Billy, B, Mississippi State, 310
27. Winship, Bob, T, Rice, 321
28. Stendel, Marv, E, Arkansas, 332
29. *Hansen, Roscoe, T, North Carolina, 346
30. Ford, John (Model-T), QB, Hardin-Simmons, 357

PITTSBURGH 1951

1. *Avinger, Clarence (Butch), B, Alabama, 9
2. *Ortmann, Chuck, B, Michigan, 20
3. *Sulima, George, E, Boston U., 31
4. *French, Barry (Bear), T, Purdue [from Baltimore], 45
5. Sampson, Floyd, B, McMurry, 56
6. *Dodrill, Dale, G, Colorado State, 67
7. *Mathews, Ray, B, Clemson, 81
8. *Minarik, Hank, E, Michigan State, 92
9. *Schweder, John (Bull), G, Penn [from Baltimore], 103
10. *Salata, Paul, E, USC [from Baltimore], 118
11. McCutcheon, Joe, C, Washington & Lee, 129
12. *Brandt, Jim (Popcorn), B, St. Thomas (MN), 140
13. Szabo, Bill, T, Bucknell, 154
14. Mizerany, Mike, G, Alabama, 165
15. Webb, Clay, B, Kentucky, 176
16. Oberg, Lambert, C, Trinity (CT), 190
17. Gehlmann, Ted, T, William & Mary, 201
18. Field, Pat, B, Georgia, 212
19. Pavlikowski, Bill, B, Boston U., 226
20. Donnelly, Tom (Tex), T, Holy Cross, 237
21. *Cheatam, Ernie, T, Loyola (CA), 248
22. *Hendley, Dick, B, Clemson, 262
23. Minor, Joe, E, John Carroll, 273
24. Alois, Art, C, San Francisco, 284
25. *Calvin, Tommy, B, Alabama, 298
26. Pearman, Bill (Pug), G, Tennessee, 309
27. Radcliffe, Bob, B, Wisconsin, 320
28. Hansen, Howie, B, UCLA, 334
29. Smith, Fred, E, Tulsa, 345
30. Gruble, John, E, Tennessee, 356

SAN FRANCISCO 1951

1. *Tittle, Y.A., QB, LSU [from Baltimore], 3
2. *Schabarum, Pete, B, California, 17
3. *Mixon, Bill, B, Georgia, 28
4. Choice to Cleveland
5. *Steere, Dick, T, Drake, 53
   *Carapella, Al, T, Miami [from Chicago Cardinals], 54
6. *Strickland, Bishop, B, South Carolina, 64
7. Forbes, Dick, E, St. Ambrose, 75
8. *Arenas, Joe, B, Nebraska-Omaha, 89
9. Van Alstyne, Bruce, E, Stanford, 100
10. *Feher, Nick, G, Georgia, 112
11. *Jessup, Bill, E, USC, 126
12. *Monachino, Jim, B, California, 137
13. Harvin, Dick, E, Georgia Tech, 148
14. *Berry, Rex, B, BYU, 162
15. *Sparks, Dave, G, South Carolina, 173
16. *White, Bob, B, Stanford, 184
17. *Michalik, Art, G, St. Ambrose, 198
18. Murphy, Jim, T, Xavier, 209
19. Phillips, John, B, Southern Mississippi, 220
20. Tate, Al, T, Illinois, 234
21. *Brown, Hardy, B, Tulsa [from Baltimore], 245
22. Winslow, Dwight, B, Boise J.C., 256
23. Brunswald, Wally, B, Gustavus Adolphus, 270
24. Kingsford, Tom, B, Montana, 281
25. Peterson, Mike, E, Denver, 292
26. Carpenter, Keith, T, San Jose State, 306
27. Lung, Ray, G, Oregon, 317
28. Rohan, Jack, B, Loras, 328
29. Garnett, S.P., T, Kansas, 342
30. Faske, Jerry, B, Iowa, 353

WASHINGTON 1951

1. *Heath, Leon, B, Oklahoma, 4
2. Salem, Eddie, B, Alabama, 15
   Staton, Jim, T, Wake Forest [from Philadelphia], 21
3. *Yowarsky, Walt, T, Kentucky, 29
4. Giroski, Paul, T, Rice, 40
5. Choice to Chicago Cardinals
6. *Martinkovic, Jonn, E, Xavier, 65
7. *Papit, Johnny, B, Virginia, 76
8. *Cox, Billy, B, Duke, 87
9. Rowden, Jake, C, Maryland, 101
10. Janosek, James, T, Purdue [from Baltimore], 111
    *Jensen, Bob, E, Iowa State [from Baltimore], 113
11. DeChard, Bill, B, Holy Cross, 124
12. Applegate, Al, G, Scranton, 138
13. Campbell, Dick, B, Wyoming, 149
14. *Burk, Adrian, QB, Baylor [from Baltimore], 160
15. Thomas, Vic, T, Colorado, 174
16. Bates, Bob, C, Texas A&M, 185
17. *Brito, Gene, E, Loyola (CA), 196
18. *Fucci, Dom, B, Kentucky, 210
19. *Brown, Buddy, G, Arkansas, 221
20. Kerestes, John, B, Purdue, 232
21. Marable, Clarence, T, TCU, 246
22. Speed, Elliot, C, Alabama, 257
23. Martin, Cecil, B, North Texas State, 268
24. Powers, Tom, B, Duke, 282
25. Chubb, Bob, E, Shippensburg, 293
26. *Williams, Johnny, B, USC, 304
27. Johnson, Bill, B, Stetson, 318
28. Kadlec, John, G, Missouri, 329
29. Stewart, Art, B, Southeastern Oklahoma, 340
30. *Bolkovac, Nick, T, Pittsburgh, 354

1952

Held January 17, 1952

Two days after the draft, Ted Collins sold his New York Yanks franchise back to the league for $100,000. The franchise and assets were granted to a Dallas, Texas, group. The team originally was known as the Texas Football Rangers but changed later to the Dallas Texans.

CHICAGO BEARS 1952

1. *Dooley, Jim, B, Miami (FL), 8
2. *Macon, Eddie, B, Pacific, 20
3. *McColl, Bill, E, Stanford, 32
4. *Clark, Herman, T, Oregon State, 44
5. *Hoffman, Jack, E, Xavier [from Pittsburgh], 54
   *Williams, Fred, T, Arkansas, 56
6. *Brown, Ed, B, San Francisco, 68
7. *Fortunato, Joe, B, Mississippi State, 80
8. *Bishop, Bill, T, North Texas State [from Pittsburgh], 90
   Jurney, Billy, E, Arkansas, 92
9. *Cross, Bobby, T, Stephen F. Austin, 104
10. Choice to Green Bay
11. Miller, Bill, B, Wake Forest, 128
12. Kozar, Andy, B, Tennessee, 140
13. Athan, Rich, B, Northwestern, 152
14. Galloway, Gale, C, Baylor, 164
15. Kazmaier, Dick, B, Princeton, 176
16. Spears, Bob, B, Yale, 188
17. Carroll, John, T, Houston, 200
18. *O'Connell, Tommy, B, Illinois, 212 F
19. Reidenbach, Ken, T, Drake, 224
20. *Lesane, Jimmy, B, Virginia, 236
21. *Daffer, Ted, G, Tennessee, 248
22. Gregory, Dick, B, Minnesota, 260
23. Nestor, Paul, T, Maryland, 272
24. Mundinger, Dick, T, Minnesota, 284
25. Stoddard, Bob, T, Utah State, 296
26. *McElroy, Bucky, B, Southern Mississippi, 308 +
27. Reid, Bob, B, Baylor, 320
28. Scioscia, Karney, B, Maryland, 332
29. Riggs, Teddy, B, Rice, 344
30. Shemonski, Bob, B, Maryland, 356

CHICAGO CARDINALS 1952

1. *Matson, Ollie, B, San Francisco, 3
2. *Karras, Johnny, B, Illinois, 16
   *Brewster, Darrel (Pete), E, Purdue [from Detroit], 21
3. Choice to San Francisco
4. Choice to Los Angeles Rams
5. *Fugler, Dick, T, Tulane, 51
6. Hancock, John, G, Baylor, 64
7. Jabbusch, Harry, C, South Carolina, 75
8. Coleman, Don, G, Michigan State, 88
9. Cook, Malcolm, B, Georgia, 99
10. Feltch, John, T, Holy Cross, 112
11. *Sugar, Leo, E, Purdue, 123
12. Masnaghetti, Joe, T, Marquette, 136
13. Massucco, Mel, B, Holy Cross, 147
14. Tofaute, Tom, C, North Carolina State, 160
15. Davis, John, B, Indiana, 171
16. *Mergen, Mike, G, San Francisco, 184
17. Crawford, Darrell, B, Georgia Tech, 195
18. Pyron, Bill, T, Mississippi State, 208
19. *Listopad, Ed, T, Wake Forest, 219
20. Fischel, Frank, E, Arkansas, 232
21. Musgrove, Wade, G, Hardin-Simmons, 243
22. Lippman, Glenn, B, Texas A&M, 256
23. *Stephens, Louis (Red), G, San Francisco, 267
24. Moore, E.J., G, Abilene Christian, 280
25. *Anderson, Cliff, E, Indiana, 291
26. Fry, Charley, T, Maryland, 304
27. Moses, Sam, T, Texas A&M, 315
28. Lutz, Harold, E, Alabama, 328
29. Kasperan, Don, B, Purdue, 339
30. Stolk, Will, B, Miami, 352

CLEVELAND 1952

1. *Rechichar, Bert, B, Tennessee [from Detroit], 10
   Agganis, Harry, QB, Boston U., 12 F
2. Hughes, Bill, C, Michigan State, 24
3. *Klosterman, Don, QB, Loyola (CA) [from New York Yankees], 26
   *Campanella, Joe, T, Ohio State, 36
4. Costa, Elmer, G, North Carolina State [from Green Bay], 39
   *Renfro, Ray, B, North Texas State, 48
5. *Jankovich, Keever, E, Pacific, 60
6. *Shields, Burrell, B, John Carroll, 72
7. Pace, John, T, Mississippi State, 84
8. *Williams, Stan, E, Baylor [from New York Yankees], 86
   *Forester, Herschel, G, SMU, 96
9. Finnell, Bob, B, Xavier, 108
10. Ribiero, Pat, T, Pacific, 120
11. *Logan, Dick, T, Ohio State, 132
12. Thompson, Roy, B, Florida State, 144
13. Cosgrove, Tom, C, Maryland, 156 F
14. *Ruzich, Steve, G, Ohio State, 168
15. Alpin, Holly, E, Tampa, 180
16. Neathery, Herb, B, Illinois [from Detroit], 189
    Rowland, Ed, T, Oklahoma, 192
17. Sheets, Stew, T, Penn State, 204
18. Mirchi, Ken, G, Santa Clara, 216
19. Talarico, Sam, T, Indiana [from San Francisco], 225
    Maccioli, Mike, B, Purdue, 228
20. Brandenberry, Bob, B, Kansas, 240
21. Calhoun, Dick, G, Baylor, 252
22. Johnson, Howard (Corky), T, Cal-Santa Barbara, 264
23. Robertson, Bobby, B, Indiana, 276
24. *Wren, Junior, B, Missouri, 288
25. Reddell, Billy, B, Florida, 300
26. Vernasco, Joe, E, Illinois, 312
27. Maletzky, Bill, G, Maryland, 324 F
28. Pietro, John, G, Brown, 336
29. Klevay, Walt, B, Ohio State, 348
30. Saban, John, B, Xavier, 360

DETROIT 1952

1. Choice to Cleveland
2. Choice to Chicago Cardinals
3. *Lary, Yale, B, Texas A&M, 34
4. *Summerall, Pat, E, Arkansas, 45
5. *Miller, Bob, T, Virginia, 58
6. Cooper, Gordon, E, Denver, 69
7. Gardner, Wes, C, Utah, 82
8. *Dublinski Tom, B, Utah, 93
9. *Gandee, Sherwin (Sonny), E, Ohio State, 106
10. *Dowden, Steve, T, Baylor, 117
11. *Flowers, Keith, C, TCU, 130
12. Roshto, Jim, B, LSU, 141
13. McDonald, Carroll, C, Florida, 154
14. Oliverson, Ray, B, BYU, 165
15. Burgamy, John, G, Georgia, 178
16. Choice to Cleveland
17. *Lauricella, Hank, B, Tennessee, 202
18. *Campbell, Stan, G, Iowa State, 213
19. *Earon, Blaine, E, Duke, 226
20. *Mains, Gil, T, Murray State, 237
21. Boykin, Arnold (Showboat), B, Mississippi, 250
22. *David, Jim, E, Colorado State, 261
23. Maxwell, Hal, E, Mississippi, 274
24. Werckle, Bob, T, Vanderbilt, 285
25. *Bailey, By, B, Washington State, 298
26. Terry, Buddy, E, Stephen F. Austin, 309
27. Trout, Bob, E, Baylor, 322
28. *Turner, Hal, E, Tennessee State, 333
29. Hudson, Art, B, Western Illinois, 346
30. Dillon, Ray Don, B, Prairie View A&M, 357

GREEN BAY 1952

1. *Parilli, Vito (Babe), QB, Kentucky, 4
2. *Howton, Billy, E, Rice, 15
3. *Dillon, Bobby, B, Texas, 28
4. Choice to Cleveland
5. *Hanner, Dave (Hawg), T, Arkansas, 52
6. *Johnson, Tom, T, Michigan, 63
7. *Reichardt, Bill, B, Iowa, 76
8. Becket, Mel, C, Indiana, 87
9. *Teteak, Deral, G, Wisconsin, 100
10. Kleinschmidt, Art, G, Tulane, 111
    *Roffler, Bud, B, Washington State [from Chicago Bears], 116
11. Burkhalter, Billy, B, Rice, 124
12. Wilson, Bill, T, Texas, 135
13. Hair, Billy, B, Clemson, 148
14. Morgan, Jack, T, Michigan State, 159
15. *Floyd, Bobby Jack, B, TCU, 172
16. Coatta, Johnny, B, Wisconsin, 183
17. Peterson, Don, B, Michigan, 196
18. Tisdale, Howard, T, Stephen F. Austin, 207
19. Pont, Johnny, B, Miami (OH), 220
20. Boerio, Chuck, C, Illinois, 231
21. Zimmerman, Herb, G, TCU, 244
22. Kluckhohn, Karl, E, Colgate, 255
23. Kapral, Frank, G, Michigan State, 268
24. Schuetzner, John, E, South Carolina, 279
25. LaPradd, Charlie, T, Florida, 292
26. Stokes, Charlie, T, Tennessee, 303
27. Russell, I.D., B, SMU, 316
28. Barrett, Billy, B, Notre Dame, 327
29. Stratton, Bill, B, Lewis, 340
30. Fulkerson, Jack, T, Southern Mississippi, 351

LOS ANGELES RAMS 1952

BONUS CHOICE: *Wade, Bill, QB, Vanderbilt, 1
1. *Carey, Bob, E, Michigan State, 13
2. *Griffin, Bob, T, Arkansas, 25
3. *McConnell, Dewey, E, Wyoming, 37
4. *Casner, Ken, T, Baylor [from Chicago Cardinals], 40
   *Quinlan, Volney (Skeet), B, San Diego State, 49
5. *Polofsky, Gordon, B, Tennessee, 61
6. *Putnam, Duane, G, Pacific [from Pittsburgh], 66
   Price, Jerrell, T, Texas Tech, 73
7. *Delevan, Burt, T, Pacific, 85 F
8. *McCormick, Tom, B, Pacific, 97 F
9. Townsend, Byron, B, Texas, 109
10. Welch, Luke, T, Baylor, 121
11. *Baker, Sam, B, Oregon State, 133 F
12. Roberts, Jake, B, Tulsa, 145
13. Phillips, Aubrey (Red), C, Texas Tech, 157
14. *Moss, Joe, T, Maryland, 169
15. *Hegarty, Bill, T, Villanova, 181 F
16. Hooks, Bob, E, USC, 193
17. Griggs, John, C, Kentucky, 205
18. *Dees, Bob, T, Southwest Missouri State, 217
19. Geldien, Harry, B, Wyoming, 229
20. Weber, Ed, B, William & Mary, 241
21. Preston, Art, B, San Diego State, 253
22. Pahr, Joe, B, Valparaiso, 265
23. Greene, Don, T, Miami (OH), 277
24. Kelnhofer, Rich, G, St. Ambrose, 289
25. *Teeuws, Len, T, Tulane, 301
26. *Fuller, Frank, T, Kentucky, 313 F
27. Meyer, Hugh, C, Texas A&M, 325
28. Hart, Granville, B, Southern Mississippi, 337
29. *Perry, Gerry, T, California, 349 F

NEW YORK GIANTS 1952
1. *Gifford, Frank, B, USC, 11
2. *Beck, Ray, G, Georgia Tech, 23
3. *Heinrich, Don, QB, Washington, 35 F
4. *Hodel, Merwin, B, Colorado [from Dallas], 38
   *Menasco, Don, E, Texas, 47
5. *Patton, Bob, T, Clemson, 59
6. MacKenzie, Jim, T, Kentucky, 71
7. *Walker, Val Joe, B, SMU, 83 F
8. *Shipp, Billy, T, Alabama, 95 F
9. Kastan, John, B, Boston U., 107
10. *Knight, Pat, E, SMU, 119
11. Harris, Charlie, C, California, 131
12. Ochoa, Dick, B, Texas, 143
13. *Brady, Pat, B, Nevada-Reno, 155
14. *Mitchell, Hal, T, UCLA, 167
15. Bischoff, Paul, E, West Virginia, 179
16. Burns, Paul, G, Notre Dame, 191
17. Karpe, Bob, T, California, 203
18. Little, Gene, G, Rice, 215
19. Cahill, Frank, E, Northern Illinois, 227
20. *Boggan, Rex, T, Mississippi, 239 F
21. Creamer, Jim, C, Michigan State, 251
22. Raley, Bob, B, Texas, 263
23. Bickel, Bob, B, Duke, 275
24. Mitchell, Wes, E, Pacific, 287
25. Kelley, Bill, C, Pacific, 299
26. Lavery, Tom, E, Boston U., 311
27. Morrison, Duane, B, Arizona State, 323
28. Patterson, Alton, T, McMurry, 335
29. Dillon, Jim, B, California, 347
30. Arnold, Joe, G, Texas, 359

NEW YORK YANKS 1952
1. *Richter, Les, G, California, 2
2. *Marchetti, Gino, T, San Francisco, 14
3. Choice to Cleveland
4. Choice to New York Giants
5. Jorgenson, Jack, T, Colorado, 50
   Sinquefield, Mel, C, Mississippi [from Philadelphia], 53
6. Cianelli, Dave, C, Maryland, 62
7. *Petitbon, John, B, Notre Dame, 74
8. Choice to Cleveland
9. *Lansford, Jim, T, Texas, 98
10. Hammond, Jim, B, Wisconsin, 110
11. *Cannamela, Pat, G, USC, 122
12. *Mutscheller, Jim, E, Notre Dame, 134
13. Ward, Bill, G, Arkansas, 146
14. Williams, Paul, E, Texas, 158
15. *Bighead, Jack, E, Pepperdine, 170
16. Kaseta, Vince, E, Tennessee, 182
17. *Horn, Dick, B, Stanford, 194
18. Molnar, Les, T, Buffalo, 206
19. *Felker, Gene, E, Wisconsin, 218
20. Adams, John, E, Texas, 230
21. *Hugasian, Harry, B, Stanford, 242
22. Schneider, Dean, B, USC, 254
23. Freeman, Chet, B, LSU, 266
24. Ward, Bob, G, Maryland, 278
25. Monihan, Jim, B, Rutgers, 290
26. Young, George, T, Bucknell, 302
27. Bartosh, Gil, B, TCU, 314
28. Moseley, Doug, C, Kentucky, 326
29. Hudeck, Russ, T, Texas A&M, 338
30. Suchy, Ray, G, Nevada-Reno, 350

PHILADELPHIA 1952
1. Bright, Johnny, B, Drake, 5
2. *Weatherall, Jim, T, Oklahoma, 17
3. *Snyder, Lum, T, Georgia Tech, 29
4. *Ulrich, Chuck, T, Illinois, 41
5. Choice to Texas
6. Lemmon, Dick, B, California, 65
7. *Thomas, John, E, Oregon State, 77
8. *Robinson, Wayne, C, Minnesota, 89
9. *Nipp, Maury, G, Loyola (CA), 101
10. McGinley, Gerry, G, Pennsylvania, 113
11. *Goldston, Ralph. B, Youngstown State, 125
12. Blount, Jack, T, Mississippi State, 137
13. Hamilton, Ed, B, Kentucky, 149
14. *Stringer, Bob, B, Tulsa, 161
15. Schmidt, Malcolm, E, Iowa State, 173
16. Brewer, Jim, G, North Texas State, 185
17. Weigle, John, E, Oklahoma State, 197
18. Romanowski, Ed, B, Scranton, 209
19. Trammell, Talbott, E, Washington & Lee, 221
20. Blaik, Bobby, B, Army, Colorado College, 233
21. Wheeler, Les, G, Abilene Christian, 245
22. Turco, Johnny, B, Holy Cross, 257
23. Schnell, Maury, B, Iowa State, 269
24. *Tyrrell, Joe, G, Temple, 281
25. *Kelley, Bob, C, West Texas State, 293
26. Albert, Bob, B, Bucknell, 305
27. Hill, Chuck, B, New Mexico, 317
28. *Brewer, Johnny, B, Louisville, 329
29. Morocco, Tony (Zippy), B, Georgia, 341
30. *Stevens, Don, B, Illinois, 353

PITTSBURGH 1952
1. *Modzelewski, Ed, B, Maryland, 6
2. *Tarasovic, George, C, LSU, 18
3. Wadiak, Steve, B, South Carolina, 30
4. Gearding, Jack, T, Xavier, 42
5. Choice to Chicago Bears
6. Choice to Los Angeles Rams
7. *Hipps, Claude, B, Georgia, 78
8. Choice to Chicago Bears
9. Payne, Hal (Herky), B, Tennessee, 102
10. Gilmartin, George, B, Xavier, 114
11. *Spinks, Jack, B, Alcorn State, 126
12. *McFadden, Marv, T, Michigan State, 138
13. Flood, Dave, B, Notre Dame, 150
14. Davis, June, G, Texas, 162
15. Pivirotto, Dick, B, Princeton, 174
16. *Ladygo, Pete, G, Maryland, 186
17. Smithwick, Pat, E, St. Norbert, 198
18. MacDonald, Andy, B, Central Michigan, 210
19. *Kerkorian, Gary, QB, Stanford, 222
20. Simeone, Dan, T, Villanova, 234
21. *Babcock, Harry, E, Georgia, 246 +
22. Byrne, Bob, B, Montana State, 258
23. Pollock, Vic, B, Army, 270
24. Bestwick, Bob, B, Pittsburgh, 282
25. *Robinson, Bill, B, Lincoln (MO), 294
26. Wilson, Bobby, B, Alabama, 306
27. *Doyle, Dick (Skippy), B, Ohio State, 318 F
28. Hanifan, Jerry, B, St. Bonaventure, 330
29. Warriner, Chris, E, Pittsburgh, 342
30. *Kissell, Ed, B, Wake Forest, 354

SAN FRANCISCO 1952
1. *McElhenny, Hugh (The King), B, Washington, 9
2. *Toneff, Bob, T, Notre Dame, 22
3. Shannon, Gene, B, Houston [from Chicago Cardinals], 27
   *Tidwell, Billy, B, Texas A&M, 33
4. *Campbell, Marion, T, Georgia, 46
5. *O'Donahue, Pat, E, Wisconsin, 57
6. Beasley, Jim, C, Tulsa, 70
7. Robison, Don, B, California, 81
8. *Smith, Jerry, T, Wisconsin, 94
9. Christian, Glen, B, Idaho, 105
10. West, Carl, B, Mississippi, 118
11. *Kimmel, J.D., T, Army, Houston, 129
12. Snyder, Fred, E, Loyola (CA), 142
13. Yeager, Rudy, T, LSU, 153
14. Simons, Frank, E, Nebraska, 166
15. Norman, Haldo, E, Gustavus Adolphus, 177
16. Meyers, Bob, B, Stanford, 190
17. Baldock, Al, E, USC, 201
18. Carey, Bill, E, Michigan State, 214
19. Choice to Cleveland
20. Yates, Jess, E, LSU, 238
21. Offield, Gene, C, Hardin-Simmons, 249
22. Cozad, Jim, T, Santa Clara, 262
23. Glazier, Bill, E, Arizona, 273
24. Kreuger, Ralph, T, California, 286
25. *Laughlin, Bud, B, Kansas, 297 F
26. Kane, Dick, G, Cincinnati, 310
27. Schaaf, Waldo, T, Oklahoma State, 321
28. Palumbo, Joe, G, Virginia, 334
29. Mosher, Chuck, E, Colorado, 345
30. Patrick, Dick, C, Oregon, 358

WASHINGTON 1952
1. Isbell, Larry, B, Baylor, 7
2. *Davis, Andy, B, George Washington, 19
3. *Dorow, Al, B, Michigan State, 31
4. Hightower, Dick, C, SMU, 43
5. *Clark, Jim, G, Oregon State, 55
6. Kensler, Ed, G, Maryland, 67
7. *Janowicz, Vic, B, Ohio State, 79
8. Johnston, Hubert, T, Iowa, 91
9. *Alban, Dick, B, Northwestern, 103
10. *Ostrowski, Chet, E, Notre Dame, 115
11. Mazza, Orlando, E, Michigan State, 127
12. Middendorf, Frank, C, Cincinnati, 139
13. Potter, Ray, T, LSU, 151
14. Conway, Doug, T, TCU, 163
15. Wittman, Julius, T, Ohio State, 175
16. Berschet, Marv, T, Illinois, 187
17. Bocetti, Gil, B, Washington & Lee, 199
18. Bartlett, Ed, E, California, 211
19. Marvin, Joe, B, UCLA, 223
20. Kinson, Roger, C, Missouri, 235
21. Jenkins, Dick, T, Illinois, 247
22. O'Rourke, Jim, B, North Carolina State, 259
23. *Barfield, Ken, T, Mississippi, 271
24. Kirkland, Ted, E, Vanderbilt, 283
25. Gero, Sal, T, Elon, 295
26. Goode, Dunny, B, Hardin-Simmons, 307
27. White, Ben, E, SMU, 319
28. Engel, Ron, B, Minnesota, 331
29. Pappa, John, B, California, 343
30. Linn, Bob, B, Case Western Reserve, 355

1953

Held January 22, 1953

The Baltimore Colts didn't officially enter the NFL until January 23, 1953, the day after the draft. The Colts' selections were made by their coaching and scouting staff, however.

BALTIMORE 1953
1. *Vessels, Billy, B, Oklahoma, 2
2. *Flowers, Bernie, E, Purdue, 14
3. *McPhail, Buck, B, Oklahoma, 26
4. *Catlin, Tom, C, Oklahoma, 38
5. *Little, Jack, T, Texas A&M, 50
6. *Sears, Jim, B, USC, 62
7. Athey, Bill, G, Baylor, 74
8. Prewett, Jim, T, Tulsa, 86
9. Blair, Bob, E, TCU, 98
10. Cole, John, B, Arkansas, 110
11. Rossi, Gene, B, Cincinnati, 122
12. Vaughn, Kaye, G, Tulsa, 134
13. Morehead, Bobby, B, Georgia Tech, 146
14. Continetti, Frank, G, George Washington, 158
15. Sutton, Buddy, B, Arkansas, 170
16. Currin, Jim, E, Dayton, 182
17. Rambour, George, T, Dartmouth, 194
18. Labat, LeRoy, B, LSU, 206
19. Powell, Bill, B, California, 218
20. Russo, Pete, T, Indiana, 230
21. Kirby, Frank, T, Bucknell, 242
22. Gish, Merlin, C, Kansas, 254
23. Housepian, Mike, G, Tulane, 266
24. *Brethauer, Monte, E, Oregon, 278
25. Szombathy, Joe, E, Syracuse, 290
26. Prescott, Scott, C, Minnesota, 302
27. Graves, Ray, B, Texas A&M, 314
28. Sabol, Joe, B, UCLA, 326
29. Alessandrini, Jack, G, Notre Dame, 338
30. Roche, Tom, T, Northwestern, 350

CHICAGO BEARS 1953
1. *Anderson, Billy, B, Compton J.C., 6
2. *Bratkowski, Zeke, QB, Georgia, 17 F
3. Rowekamp, Bill, B, Army, Missouri, 30
4. Koch, Joe, B, Wake Forest, 41
5. *Jones, Stan, T, Maryland, 54 F
6. *DeCarlo, Art, B, Georgia, 65
   *Gilbert, Kline, T, Mississippi [from San Francisco], 68
7. *McElroy, Bucky, B, Southern Miss [from Washington], 75
   *Bingham, Don, B, Sul Ross, 78
8. *Kreamcheck, John, T, William & Mary, 89
9. Ashley, Bruno, T, East Texas State, 102
10. Moore, Jimmy, B, Florida A&M, 113
11. Charney, Ralph, B, Kentucky [from Pittsburgh], 125
    Slowey, Jim, C, Georgetown (Wash., DC), 126
12. Lawrence, Jim, T, Duke, 137
13. *Strickland, Larry, C, North Texas State, 150
14. *Carl, Harland, B, Wisconsin, 161
15. *Jecha, Ralph, G, Northwestern, 174
16. *Hatley, John, T, Sul Ross, 185
17. Beal, Bob, E, California, 198
18. Shirley, Jim, B, Clemson, 209
19. Byrus, Bill, T, Iowa State, 222
20. Mahin, Tom, T, Purdue, 233
21. Martin, Wayne, E, TCU, 246
22. Wood, Wayne, T, Memphis State, 257
23. Mask, Jim, E, Mississippi, 270
24. Hatcher, Paul, C, Arkansas City J.C., 281
25. Pickard, Clyde, G, Wake Forest, 294
26. Evans, Bob, T, Pennsylvania, 305
27. Wahlin, Marvin, B, Arizona State, 318
28. Caldwell, Jim, T, Tennessee State, 329
29. Lewis, Jack, E, Wake Forest, 342
30. Brehany, Bill, QB, Virginia Military, 353

CHICAGO CARDINALS 1953
1. *Olszewski, Johnny, B, California, 4
2. *Psaltis, Jim, B, USC, 15
3. Samuels, Dale, QB, Purdue, 28
4. Martin, Gerdes (Buck), E, Georgia Tech, 39
5. Shalosky, Bill, G, Cincinnati, 52
6. *Curcillo, Tony, B, Ohio State, 63
   *Higgins, Tom, T, North Carolina [from Philadelphia], 70
7. Choice to Philadelphia
8. *Watford, Jerry, G, Alabama, 87
9. *Husmann, Ed, G, Nebraska [from Washington], 99
   *Stone, Avatus, B, Syracuse, 100
10. Berndt, Charley, T, Wisconsin, 111
11. Woodsum, Ed, E, Yale, 124
12. Spaulding, Chuck, B, Wyoming, 135
13. *McPhee, Frank, E, Princeton [from Washington], 147
    Morris, Ronnie, B, Tulsa, 148
14. Sprague, Dick, B, Washington, 159
15. *Chickillo, Nick, G, Miami, 172
16. Lear, Jimmy, B, Mississippi, 183
17. Heninger, Earl, B, Purdue, 196
18. Yukica, Joe, E, Penn State, 207
19. Donahue, Tom, C, Wake Forest, 220
20. D'Errico, Len, G, Boston U., 231
21. Curtis, Joe, E, Alabama, 244
22. Lokovsek, Hal, T, Washington State, 255
23. *Root, Jim, B, Miami (OH), 268
24. Glass, Brad, G, Princeton, 279
25. Sullivan, Haywood, B, Florida, 292
26. Ringe, Don, T, Idaho, 303
27. Brocato, C.O., C, Baylor, 316
28. Prokopiak, Mike, B, New Mexico, 327
29. Wrightenberry, Earl, T, Clemson, 340
30. Gaudreau, Bill, B, Notre Dame, 351

CLEVELAND 1953
1. *Atkins, Doug, T, Tennessee, 11
2. *Reynolds, Billy, B, Pittsburgh, 23
3. *Bruney, Fred, B, Ohio State, 35
   *Donaldson, Gene, G, Kentucky [from Detroit], 37
4. Tamburo, Dick, C, Michigan State, 47
5. *Van Doren, Bob, E, USC, 59
6. Steinbrunner, Don, E, Washington State, 71
7. *Filipski, Gene, B, Army, Villanova, 83 F
8. *Massey, Carlton, E, Texas, 95 F
9. *McNamara, Bob, B, Minnesota, 107
10. Natali, Elmo, B, California (PA), 119
11. Hilinski, Dick, T, Ohio State, 131 F
12. Willhoite, Elmer, G, USC, 143
13. *Fiss, Galen, B, Kansas, 155
14. *Nagler, Gern, E, Santa Clara, 167
15. *Carson, Johnny, E, Georgia, 179 F
16. Kuykendall, Eric, B, Illinois, 191
17. Bean, George, B, Utah, 203
18. Batten, Dick, T, Pacific, 215
19. Cain, Tom, G, Colorado, 227
20. *Noll, Chuck, T, Dayton, 239
21. Crockett, Bill, G, Rice, 251
22. Looper, Byrd, B, Duke, 263
23. Kent, Ronnie, B, Tulane, 275
24. Labenda, John, T, Wittenberg, 287
25. Ellis, Jim, B, Michigan State, 299
26. Hoag, Charley, B, Kansas, 311
27. Sisco, Jack, C, Baylor, 323
28. Verkirk, Ray, T, North Texas State, 335
29. Hobson, Clell, B, Alabama, 347
30. Myers, Andy, G, Tennessee, 358

DETROIT 1953
1. *Sewell, Harley, G, Texas, 13
2. *Gedman, Gene, B, Indiana, 25
3. Choice to Cleveland
4. *Ane, Charlie, T, USC, 49
5. Choice to Philadelphia
6. *Spencer, Ollie, T, Kansas, 73
7. *Schmidt, Joe, C, Pittsburgh, 85
8. *Carpenter, Lew, B, Arkansas, 97
9. McCormick, Carlton, C, TCU, 109
10. Gaskin, Dreher, E, Clemson, 121
11. Messenger, Elmer, G, Washington State, 133
12. Spencer, Larry, B, Wake Forest, 145
13. Thomas, Bob, E, Washington & Lee, 157
14. Barger, Jack, T, New Mexico, 169
15. *Topor, Ted, B, Michigan, 181
16. Volonnino, Bob, G, Army, Villanova, 193
17. Green, Ray, T, Duke, 205
18. *Mioduszewski, Ed, B, William & Mary, 217
19. *Held, Paul, B, San Diego State, 229 F
20. Hart, Gerry, T, Army, Mississippi State, 241
21. Tata, Bob, B, Virginia, 253
22. *Retzlaff, Pete, B, South Dakota State, 265
23. *Karilivacz, Carl, B, Syracuse, 277
24. Grant, Truett, T, Duke, 289
25. *Brown, Marv, B, East Texas State, 301
26. Dooley, Jim, C, Penn State, 313
27. Parker, Jackie, B, Mississippi State, 325 +
28. Pepper, Laurin, B, Southern Mississippi, 337 +
29. Rector, Harley, T, Wayne State (NE), 349
30. Maus, Hal, E, Montana, 360

GREEN BAY 1953
1. *Carmichael, Al, B, USC, 7
2. Reich, Gil, B, Army, Kansas, 19
3. *Forester, Bill, T, SMU, 31
4. *Dawson, Gib, B, Texas, 43
5. *Zatkoff, Roger, T, Michigan, 55
6. Kennedy, Bob, G, Wisconsin, 67
7. *Ringo, Jim, C, Syracuse, 79
8. Hargrove, Lauren, B, Georgia, 91
9. Harrawood, Floyd, T, Tulsa, 103
10. Rimkus, Vic, G, Holy Cross, 115
11. *Johnson, Joe, B, Boston College, 127 F
12. Curran, Dick, B, Arizona State, 139
13. Orders, Bob, C, Army, West Virginia, 151
14. Wrenn, Charley, T, TCU, 163
15. Helwig, Gene, B, Tulsa, 175
16. Hlay, John, B, Ohio State, 187
17. Georges, Bill, E, Texas, 199
18. Philbee, Jim, B, Bradley, 211
19. *Lucky, Bill, T, Baylor, 223 +
20. Harville, John, B, TCU, 235
21. Conway, Bob, B, Alabama, 247
22. Turnbeaugh, Bill, T, Auburn, 259
23. Murray, Bill, E, American International, 271
24. Haslam, Jim, T, Tennessee, 283
25. Jones, Ike, E, UCLA, 295
26. Bozanic, George, B, USC, 307
27. McConaughey, Jim, E, Houston, 319
28. Jordan, Zack, B, Colorado, 331
29. O'Brien, Henry, G, Boston College, 343
30. *Barry, Al, G, USC, 355

LOS ANGELES RAMS 1953
1. Moomaw, Donn, C, UCLA [from Philadelphia], 9
   *Barker, Ed, E, Washington State, 12
2. *Bukich, Rudy, B, USC, 24
3. *Fry, Bob, T, Kentucky, 36
4. Roberts, Willie, E, Tulsa, 48
5. *Scott, Tom, E, Virginia, 60
6. *Miller, Paul, T, LSU [from Washington], 64 F
   Waugh, Howie, B, Tulsa, 72
7. Reynolds, Bobby, B, Nebraska, 84
8. *Morgan, Bob, T, Maryland, 96 F
9. *Myers, Brad, B, Bucknell, 108
10. Lakos, Mick, B, Vanderbilt, 120
11. Bailey, Jim, B, Miami (OH), 132
12. Doud, Chuck, G, UCLA, 144
13. Matto, Andy, T, Cincinnati, 156
14. James, Frank, G, Houston, 168
15. Carroll, Tom, B, Oklahoma, 180
16. DeLoe, Ben, T, Mississippi State, 192
17. *Svare, Harland, E, Washington State, 204
18. Jones, Lew, T, Wabash, 216
19. *Ellena, Jack, T, UCLA, 228 F
20. Morford, Bob, B, College of Idaho, 240
21. Gordon, Dick, T, Toledo, 252
22. Porter, George, T, Southwest Texas State, 264
23. Willoughby, Larry, B, Fresno State, 276
24. Gudmundson, Marlow, B, North Dakota State, 288
25. Clemens, Ed, C, Dayton, 300
26. Yourkowski, Louie, T, Washington, 312
27. Welsh, Lou, C, USC, 324
28. Murray, Jim, T, Montana, 336
29. Lewis, Ray, E, Boise J.C., 348
30. Phren, Fritz, B, College of the Ozarks, 359

NEW YORK GIANTS 1953
1. Marlow, Bobby, B, Alabama, 8
2. Crowder, Eddie, QB, Oklahoma, 22
3. Roberts, Cal, T, Gustavus Adolphus, 33
4. Douglas, Everett, T, Florida, 44
5. *Long, Buford, B, Florida, 58

6. *Peviani, Bob, G, USC, 69
7. Branby, Don, E, Colorado, 80
8. Beck, Don, B, Army, Notre Dame, 94
9. Gray, Jim, B, Panola J.C., 105
10. Cooper, Darrow, E, Texas A&M [from Washington], 112
Maloy, Charlie, QB, Holy Cross, 116
11. Ruehl, Jim, C, Ohio State, 130
12. *Matesic, Joe, T, Arizona State, 141
13. McShulski, Jack, E, Army, Kansas State, 152
14. Hall, J.L., B, Florida, 166
15. Bowman, Dick, G, Oklahoma, 177
16. Skyinskus, Bill, G, Syracuse, 188
17. Rhoden, Don, C, Rice, 202
18. Suwall, Phil, B, Western Maryland, 213
19. Lehman, Hal, T, Southern Mississippi, 224
20. Christiansen, Dick, E, Arizona, 238
21. Bullard, Gene, T, Louisiana College, 249
22. Kelley, Mike, E, Florida, 260
23. Kukowski, Ted, C, Navy, Syracuse, 274
24. Kubes, Charley, G, Minnesota, 285
25. Drake, Dan, B, Rice, 296
26. Wetzel, Bill, B, Syracuse, 310
27. *Brown, Roosevelt (Rosey), T, Morgan State, 321
28. *Ramona, Joe, G, Santa Clara, 332
29. Griffis, Bob, G, Furman, 346
30. Canakes, Stavros, G, Minnesota, 356

PHILADELPHIA 1953
1. Choice to Los Angeles Rams
2. Conway, Al, B, Army, William Jewell, 20
3. *Johnson, Don, B, California, 34
4. *Mrkonic, George, G, Kansas, 45
5. *Bell, Eddie, E, Pennsylvania, 56
Smith, Rex, E, Illinois [from Detroit], 61
6. Choice to Chicago Cardinals
7. Erickson, Jack, T, Army, Beloit [from Chicago Cardinals], 76
Malavasi, Ray, G, Army, Mississippi State, 81
8. *Richardson, Jess, T, Alabama, 92
9. French, Roger, E, Minnesota, 106
10. *Brookshier, Tom, B, Colorado, 117
11. Pollard, Bob, B, Penn State, 128
12. Porter, George, T, San Jose State, 142
13. Westort, Ray, G, Utah, 153
14. Bailey, Roy, B, Tulane, 164
15. *Irvin, Willie, E, Florida A&M, 178
16. Wallace, Bud, B, North Carolina, 189
17. Rados, Tony, B, Penn State, 200
18. Trauth, Marv T, Mississippi, 214
19. Bachouros, Pete, B, Illinois, 225
20. Arns, Rollie, C, Iowa State, 236
21. Brooks, Hal, T, Washington & Lee, 250
22. LeClaire, Laurie, B, Michigan, 261
23. Knox, Jeff, E, Georgia Tech, 272
24. Romero, Eli, B, Wichita State, 286
25. *Michels, Johnny, G, Tennessee, 297
26. Achziger, Harvey, T, Colorado State, 308
27. Hersh, Earl, B, West Chester, 322
28. Gratson, Joe, B, Penn State, 333
29. Paolone, Ralph, B, Kentucky, 344
30. Hren, Chuck, B, Northwestern, 357

PITTSBURGH 1953
1. *Marchibroda, Ted, QB, Detroit, 5
2. *Johnson, John Henry, B, Arizona State, 18
3. *Matuszak, Marv, T, Tulsa, 29
4. *Colteryahn, Lloyd, E, Maryland, 42
5. *Gaona, Bob, T, Wake Forest, 53
6. Barton, Tom, G, Clemson, 66
7. *Alderton, John, E, Maryland, 77
8. *Perry, Lowell, E, Michigan, 90
9. Sarnese, Pat, T, Temple, 101
10. Holohan, Frank, T, Tennessee, 114
11. Choice to Chicago Bears
12. Robertson, Jerry, B, Kansas, 138
13. Davis, Leo, E, Bradley, 149
14. Montgomery, Charley, T, Mississippi, 162
15. *O'Neil, Bob, E, Notre Dame, 173
16. Zachary, John, B, Miami (OH), 186
17. Quinn, Reed, B, Florida, 197
18. Holben, Carl, T, Duke, 210
19. Williams, Jim, B, Louisville, 221
20. Hayley, Will Lee, E, Auburn, 234
21. Earley, Don, G, South Carolina, 245
22. O'Connor, Ed, T, Maryland, 258
23. Correll, Ray, G, Kentucky, 269
24. Schneidenbach, Bob, B, Miami (FL), 282
25. Hampel, Vic, E, Houston, 293
26. *McClairen, Jack (Goose), E, Bethune-Cookman, 306
27. Delaney, Jack, B, Cincinnati, 317
28. Cimini, Joe, T, Mississippi State, 330
29. Massaro, Art, B, Washington & Jefferson, 341
30. *Tepe, Lou, C, Duke, 354

SAN FRANCISCO 1953
BONUS CHOICE: *Babcock, Harry, E, Georgia, 1
1. *Stolhanske, Tom, E, Texas, 10
2. *Morris, George, C, Georgia Tech, 21
3. *St Clair, Bob, T, San Francisco, 32
4. *Fullerton, Ed, B, Maryland, 46
5. *Miller, Hal, T, Georgia Tech, 57
6. Choice to Chicago Bears
7. *Carr, Paul, B, Houston, 82 +
8. *Hogland, Doug, T, Oregon State, 93
9. *Ledyard, Hal, B, Tennessee-Chattanooga, 104
10. *Brown, Pete, G, Georgia Tech, 118
11. Charlton, Al, B, Washington State, 129
12. Leach, Carson (Red), G, Duke, 140
13. Earley, Bill, B, Washington, 154
14. Fletcher, Tom, B, Arizona State, 165
15. Genthner, Charley, T, Texas, 176
16. Durig, Fred, E, Bowling Green, 190
17. Latham, Hugh, T, San Diego State, 201
18. Wacholz, Stan, E, San Jose State, 212
19. DuClos, King, T, Texas-El Paso, 226
20. Huizinga, Ray, T, Northwestern, 237
21. Bahnsen, Ken, E, North Texas State, 248
22. Robbins, Laverne, G, Midwestern State (TX), 262
23. Hunt, Travis, T, Alabama, 273
24. Morgan, Ed, B, Tennessee, 284
25. Stockert, Ernie, E, UCLA, 298
26. Cooper, Harley, B, Arizona State, 309
27. McCleod, Ralph, E, LSU, 320
28. Novikoff, Tom, B, Oregon, 334
29. Stillwell, Don, E, USC, 345

WASHINGTON 1953
1. *Scarbath, Jack, B, Maryland, 3
2. *Modzelewski, Dick, T, Maryland, 16
3. *Dekker, Paul, E, Michigan State, 27
4. *Boll, Don, G, Nebraska, 40
5. Carras, Nick, B, Missouri, 51
6. Choice to Los Angeles Rams
7. Choice to Chicago Bears
8. Weidensaul, Lew, E, Maryland, 88
9. Choice to Chicago Cardinals
10. Choice to New York Giants
11. *Webster Alex, B, North Carolina State, 123
12. *Nutter, Madison (Buzz), C, Virginia Tech, 136
13. Choice to Chicago Cardinals
14. Timmerman, Ed, B, Michigan State, 160
15. *Suminski, Dave, T, Wisconsin, 171
16. Slay, Jim, E, Mississippi, 184
17. Haner, Bob, B, Villanova, 195
18. Turner, Jim, B, Texas Tech, 208
19. Flyzik, Tom, T, George Washington, 219
20. Link, Bill, G, Wake Forest, 232
21. Dublinski, Jim, C, Utah, 243
22. Pucci, Ed, G, USC, 256
23. Bierne, Ed, E Detroit, 267
24. Butterworth, Stan, B, Bucknell, 280
25. Hurd, Art, G, Maryland, 291
26. Ashcratt, Walt, T, USC, 304
27. Zanetti, John, T, John Carroll, 315
28. Buckley, Bob, B, USC, 328
29. Shires, Pat, B, Tennessee, 339
30. Mathias, Bob, B, Stanford, 352

1954

Held January 28, 1954

BALTIMORE 1954
1. *Davidson, Cotton, QB, Baylor, 5
2. Grigg, Larry, B, Oklahoma, 16
3. Choice to Los Angeles Rams
4. Choice to Green Bay
5. Ellis, Don, B, Texas A&M, 53
6. Choice to Cleveland
7. Turner, Glenn, B, Georgia Tech, 77
8. McCotter, Dennis, G, Detroit, 88
9. Adams, Bob, G, Shippensburg, 101
10. Schoonmaker, Bob, B, Missouri, 112
11. *Leberman, Bob, B, Syracuse, 125
12. *Chelf, Don, T, Iowa, 136
13. McMillan, Chuck, B, John Carroll, 149
14. *Braase, Ordell, T, South Dakota, 160
15. D'Agostino, Joe, G, Florida, 173
16. *Sandusky, Alex, E, Clarion, 184
17. Adkins, Tommy, C, Kentucky, 197
18. Shinaut, Dick, B, Texas-El Paso, 208
19. Wenzlau, Charley, E, Miami (OH), 221
20. *Berry, Raymond, E, SMU, 232 F
21. Lade, Bob, G, Wayne State, 245
22. Meyer, Bob, T, Ohio State, 256
23. Hardeman, Leon, B, Georgia Tech, 269
24. Kerlin, Don, B, Concordia (MN), 280
25. Rodgers, Pepper, B, Georgia Tech, 293
26. Esparza, Jesus, T, New Mexico State, 304
27. Sennett, Bill, E, Georgia Tech, 317
28. Ecstrom, Ray, C, Westminster (PA), 328
29. Taliaferro, Claude, B, Illinois, 341
30. Abbruzzi, Pat, B, Rhode Island, 352 +

CHICAGO BEARS 1954
1. *Wallace, Stan, B, Illinois, 6
2. *Casares, Rick, B, Florida, 18
3. *Meadows, Ed, T, Duke, 30
4. Paterra, Fran, B, Notre Dame, 42
5. Griffis, Bob, G, Furman, 54
6. Hudson, John, G, Rice, 66
7. Cecere, Ralph, B, Villanova, 78
8. Garlington, Tom, T, Arkansas, 90
9. Giel, Paul, B, Minnesota, 102
10. Andrews, D.C., E, Hardin-Simmons, 114
11. Wallin, Ron, B, Minnesota, 126
12. Faragalli, Joe, G, Villanova, 138
13. Seaholm, Julius, G, Texas, 150
14. Miller, Ken, B, Illinois, 162
15. *Hill, Harlon, E, North Alabama, 174
16. Lindley, Earl, B, Utah State, 186
17. Woodard, Lou, C, Sam Houston State, 198
18. *Moore, McNeil, B, Sam Houston State, 210
19. Lum, Jim, T, Louisiana Tech, 222
20.*Ladd, Jim, E, Bowling Green, 234
21. Cleere, Sonny, T, Abilene Christian, 246
22. *Sumner, Charlie, B, William & Mary, 258
23. *Lee, Herman, T, Florida A&M, 270
24. Jarrett, Bill, B, West Virginia, 282
25. *Feamster, Tom, E, Florida State, 294 +
26. Petroka, Lou, B, Boston U., 306
27. *Oniskey, Dick, C, Tennessee-Chattanooga, 318
28. Underwood, P.W., G, Mississippi State, 330
29. Beale, Alvin, B, Trinity (TX), 342
30. *Haluska, Jim, B, Wisconsin, 354

CHICAGO CARDINALS 1954
1. *McHan, Lamar, QB, Arkansas, 2
2. *Knafelc, Gary, E, Colorado, 14
3. Cavazos, Bobby, B, Texas Tech, 26
4. *Bredde, Bill, B, Oklahoma State, 38
5. Dohoney, Don, E, Michigan State, 50
6. McHugh, Tom, B, Notre Dame, 62
7. *Mann, Dave, B, Oregon State, 74
8. *Larson, Paul, B, California, 86 F
9. Chambers, Dean, T, Washington, 98
10. Lewis, Tommy, B, Alabama, 110
11. Smith, Homer, B, Princeton, 122
12. Pitt, Howard, E, Duke, 134
13. *Goble, Les, B, Alfred, 146
14. Dumas, Sammy, G, Arkansas, 158
15. Harp, Cecil, E, Pacific, 170
16. Kilgore, Al, T, Kent State, 182
17. Troxell, Jack, B, Arkansas, 194
18. *Young, Dick, B, Tennessee-Chattanooga, 206
19. Sazio, Jerry, T, William & Mary, 218
20. Huntsman, Stan, B, Wabash, 230
21. Stander, Jim, T, Colorado, 242
22. *Fanucchi, Ledio, T, Fresno State, 254
23. *Oakley, Charley, B, LSU, 266
24. Sawchik, Lou, E, Ohio U., 278
25. Marchand, Jerry, B, LSU, 290
26. Carrigan, Ralph, C, Alabama, 302
27. Culver, John, B, Harvard, 314
28. Koller, Tom, B, William & Mary, 326
29. Albrecht, Bill, B, Washington, 338
30. Burl, Alex, B, Colorado State, 350

CLEVELAND 1954
BONUS CHOICE: *Garrett, Bobby, QB, Stanford, 1
1. *Bauer, John, G, Illinois, 12
2. *Hanulak, Chet (The Jet), B, Maryland, 24
3. *Bassett, Maurice, B, Langston, 36
4. Hilgenberg, Jerry, C, Iowa, 48
5. *Lucky, Bill, T, Baylor, 60
6. *Smith, Jim Ray, G, Baylor [from Baltimore], 64
Jenkins, Asa, B, Toledo, 72
7. *Miller, Don, B, SMU, 84
8. Barbish, Bill, B, Tennessee [from San Francisco], 95
Harris, Charlie, B, Georgia, 96
9. *Jones, Tom, T, Miami (OH), 108 F
10. *Goss, Don, G, SMU [from San Francisco], 119
Pagna, Tom, B, Miami (OH), 120
11. Schuebel, Max, T, Rice, 132
12. Bruenich, Tom, T, Maryland, 144
13. Cummins, George, T, Tulane, 156
14. Head, Jim, B, Iowa, 168
15. Lyssy, Chet, B, Hardin-Simmons, 180
16. Raidel, Rich, G, Kent State, 192
17. Chapman, Howard, T, Florida, 204
18. Wohrman, Bill, B, South Carolina, 216
19. Taylor, John, C, Austin, 228
20. Pierce, Hugh, C, North Carolina State, 240
21. Baughman, Jim, G, Illinois, 252
22. Caudle, Lloyd, B, Duke, 264
23. *Mischak, Bob, E, Army, 276
24. Grambling, Johnny, B, South Carolina, 288
25. Hughes, Tom, T, Virginia Tech, 300
26. Lundy, Joe, G, Kansas, 312
27. Mapp, Johnny, B, Virginia Military, 324
28. Vergara, Vince, B, Syracuse, Army, 336
29. Carter, Troy, B, Virginia Military, 348

DETROIT 1954
1. Chapman, Dick, T, Rice, 13
2. Neal, Jim, C, Michigan State, 25
3. *Bowman, Bill, B, William & Mary, 37
4. *Stits, Bill, B, UCLA [from Washington], 44
McCants, Howard, E, Washington State, 49
5. Parozzo, George, T, William & Mary, 61
6. Dacus, Pence, B, Southwest Texas St. [from Green Bay], 63
*Kercher, Dick, B, Tulsa, 73
7. Cross, Jack, B, Utah, 85
8. *Davis, Milt, B, UCLA, 97
9. Lawson, Bob, B, Cal Poly-SLO, 109
10. Carroll, Jack, E, Holy Cross, 121
11. Schwenk, Milt, T, Washington State, 133
12. Hartman, Bob, T, Oregon State, 145
13. Swierczek, Jim, B, Marshall, 157
14. Novak, Ray, B, Nebraska, 169
15. Hinderlider, Kirk, E, Colorado State, 181
16. Chuoke, Bob, T, Houston, 193
17. Kaser, Rick, B, Toledo, 205
18. Hayes, Norm, T, Idaho, 217
19. Graves, Buster, T, Arkansas, 229
20. Durrant, Jim, G, Utah, 241
21. Kistler, Jack, B, Duke, 253
22. *Brundage, Dewey, E, BYU, 265
23. Shanafelt, Jack, T, Pennsylvania, 277
24. Burrows, Bobby, G, Duke, 289
25. *Woit, Dick, B, Arkansas State, 301
26. George, Jim, T, Syracuse, 313
27. Rzeszut, Dick, C, Benedictine, 325
28. Rutschman, Dolph, B, Linfield, 337
29. Bertrand, Mel, C, Idaho, 349
30. Horton, Ellis, B, Eureka (IL), 360

GREEN BAY 1954
1. *Hunter, Art, T, Notre Dame, 3
*Switzer, Veryl, B, Kansas State [from New York Giants], 4
2. Fleck, Bob, T, Syracuse, 15
3. *Timberlake, George, G, USC, 27
4. Choice to Washington
Allman, Tommy, B, West Virginia [from Baltimore], 40
5. *McGee, Max, B, Tulane, 51
6. Choice to Detroit
7. Marshall, Sam, T, Florida A&M, 75
8. Williams, Jimmie, T, Texas Tech, 87
9. Davis, Dave, E, Georgia Tech, 99
10. *Knutson, Gene, E, Michigan, 111
11. Hall, Ken, E, North Texas State, 123
12. Oliver, Bill, B, Alabama, 135
13. Takacs, Mike, G, Ohio State, 147
14. Johnson, Dave (Kosse), B, Rice, 159
15. Choice to San Francisco
16. Koch, Des, B, USC, 183
17. Roberts, J.D., G, Oklahoma, 195
18. *Barnes, Emery, E, Oregon, 207
19. Hall, Ken, C, Springfield, 219
20. Herbert, Lowell, G, Pacific, 231
21. Liebscher, Art, B, Pacific, 243
22. Buford, Willie, T, Morgan State, 255
23. Sathrum, Clint, B, St. Olaf, 267
24. Tennefoss, Marv, E, Stanford, 279
25. Smalley, John, T, Alabama, 291
26. Baierl, Ralph, T, Maryland, 303
27. Sims, Hosea, E, Marquette, 315
28. Slonac, Evan, B, Michigan State, 327
29. Dufek, Jerry, T, St. Norbert, 339
30. Campbell, Terry, B, Washington State, 351

LOS ANGELES RAMS 1954
1. *Beatty, Ed, C, Mississippi, 10
2. Gillioz, Buddy, T, Houston, 22
3. Kincaid, Jim, B, South Carolina [from Baltimore], 29
Nickoloff, Tom, E, USC [from Washington], 32
Hair, Henry, E, Georgia Tech, 34
4. McClelland, Lester, T, Syracuse [from Pittsburgh], 43
Nygaard, Norm, B, San Diego State, 46
5. Allen, Charlie, T, San Jose State [from Philadelphia], 57
*Hauser, Art, T, Xavier, 58
6. *Panfil, Ken, T, Purdue, 70 F
7. Weeks, Charley, T, USC, 82
8. Black, George, E, Washington, 94
9. *Bravo, Alex, B, Cal Poly-SLO, 106
10. *Hughes, Ed, B, Tulsa [from Philadelphia], 117
*Katchik, Joe, E, Notre Dame, 118
11. *Wardlow, Duane, T, Washington, 130
12. Maultsby, Jack, T, North Carolina, 142
13. Hensley, Sam, E, Georgia Tech, 154
14. Johnson, Mitchell, B, Bishop, 166
15. Elliot, Ed, B, Richmond, 178
16. Frey, Roger, T, Georgia Tech, 190
17. Wilhelm, Ed, C, Houston, 202
18. *Sheriff, Stan, C, Cal Poly-SLO, 214
19. Givens, Frank, T, Georgia Tech, 226
20. *Dougherty, Bob, B, Cincinnati, 238
21. Cooper, Jerry, T, West Virginia, 250
22. Pacer, Ray, T, Purdue, 262
23. Marks, Don, B, California, 274
24. Brookman, Ed, T, West Virginia, 286
25. Miller, Dick, B, Baldwin-Wallace, 298
26. *Holtzman, Glen, T, North Texas State, 310
27. Shine, Entee, E, Notre Dame, 322
28. Mann, Dick, B, Case Western Reserve, 334
29. Dietrick, Dick, E, Pittsburgh, 346
30. Metzke, Frank, T, Marquette, 358

NEW YORK GIANTS 1954
1. Choice to Green Bay
2. Buck, Ken, E, Pacific, 17
3. Bennett, Clyde, E, South Carolina, 28
4. *Nolan, Dick, B, Maryland, 41
5. Putman, Earl, T, Arizona State, 52
6. Jacoby, George, T, Ohio State, 65
7. *Berry, Wayne, B, Washington State, 76
8. Starkey, Ralph, T, West Virginia, 89
9. O'Garra, Pete, E, UCLA, 100
10. Steinberg, John, E, Stanford, 113
11. Fitzpatrick, Tom, G, Villanova, 124
12. Gulseth, Wendell, T, Wisconsin, 137
13. *Topp, Bob, E, Michigan, 148
14. *Epps, Bobby, B, Pittsburgh, 161
15. Swan, Jim, G, Denver, 172
16. Rice, George, B, Iowa, 185
17. Parker, Jackie, B, Mississippi State, 196
18. Mims, Crawford, G, Mississippi, 209
19. King, Bob, G, South Carolina, 220
20. Snipes, Gene, E, Austin, 233
21. Corless, Rex, B, Michigan State, 244
22. Collier, Joe, E, Northwestern, 257
23. Mangum, Pete, B, Mississippi, 268
24. Harris, Bill, T, LSU, 281
25. Baker, Bill, B, Washburn, 292
26. Van Zandt, George, B, Long Beach C.C., 305
27. *Clatterbuck, Bobby, B, Houston, 316
28. Partridge, Jim, B, Tulane, 329
29. Mote, Bill, T, Florida State, 340
30. Gibson, Jim, T, USC, 353

PHILADELPHIA 1954
1. *Worden, Neil, B, Notre Dame, 9
2. *Ryan, Rocky, E, Illinois, 21
3. Connor, Ted, T, Nebraska, 33
4. *Mavraides, Menil (Minnie), G, Notre Dame, 45
5. Choice to Los Angeles Rams
6. Lambert, Hal, T, TCU, 69
7. *Norton, Jerry, B, SMU, 81
8. Hunter, Dan, T, Florida, 93
9. Branch, Phil, G, Texas, 105

10. Choice to Los Angeles Rams
11. McLaughlin, Dave, E, Dartmouth, 129
12. Clasby, Dick, B, Harvard, 141
13. Mehalick, Joe, T, Virginia, 153
14. Patterson, Hal, B, Kansas, 165
15. McKown, Ray, B, TCU, 177
16. Grant, Charlie, C, Utah, 189
17. Knowles, Bob, T, Baylor, 201
18. Mrvos, Sam, G, Georgia, 213
19. Clem, Jerry, G, SMU, 225
20. Bailes, Tommy, B, Houston, 237
21. Crouch, Johnny, E, TCU, 249 +
22. Wojciehowski, Jim, E, Purdue, 261
23. Lofton, Harold, B, Mississippi, 273
24. Gressette, Nate, T, Clemson, 285
25. Zambiasi, Ray, B, Detroit, 297
26. Smith, Charley, B, Baylor, 309
27. Addiego, Ben, B, Villanova, 321
28. Gerdes, John, T, Cornell, 333
29. Stone, Jack, B, West Virginia, 345
30. Woodlee, Tommy, B, South Carolina, 357

PITTSBURGH 1954
1. *Lattner, Johnny, B, Notre Dame, 7
2. Stark, Pat, B, Syracuse, 19
3. *Miner, Tom, E, Tulsa, 31
4. Choice to Los Angeles Rams
5. Choice to San Francisco
6. Pepper, Laurin, B, Southern Mississippi, 67
7. *O'Brien, Jack, E, Florida, 79
8. *Cameron, Paul, B, UCLA, 91
9. *Zombek, Joe, E, Pittsburgh, 103
10. Fisher, Bob, T, Tennessee, 115
11. Cimarolli, Lou, B, Pittsburgh, 127
12. Fritz, Don, E, Cincinnati, 139
13. Lattimer, Charley, C, Maryland, 151
14. Bradford, Roger, E, Waynesburg, 163
15. Drake, Tom, G, Tennessee-Chattanooga, 175
16. Krol, Cas, T, Detroit, 187
17. Fulwyler, Joe, C, Oregon State, 199
18. Penza, Don, E, Notre Dame, 211
19. Rydalch, Don, B, Utah, 223
20. Prender, Fred, B, West Chester, 235
21. Tassotti, Dan, T, Miami, 247
22. Lapsley, John, G, Northeastern, 259
23. Pascarella, Joe, T, Penn State, 271
24. Flanagan, Jack, E, Detroit, 283
25. Barron, Jim, T, Mississippi State, 295
26. Varaitis, Joe, B, Pennsylvania, 307
27. *Yewcic, Tom, QB, Michigan State, 319
28. Bush, Joe, G, Notre Dame, 331
29. Fagan, Joe, T, John Carroll, 343
30. Sweatte, Juel, B, Oklahoma, 355

SAN FRANCISCO 1954
1. Faloney, Bernie, B, Maryland, 11
2. *Rucka, Leo, C, Rice, 23
3. Korcheck, Steve, C, George Washington, 35
4. Boxhold, Charlie, B, Maryland, 47
5. *Hantla, Bob, G, Kansas [from Pittsburgh], 55
   Mincevich, Frank, G, South Carolina, 59
6. *Sagely, Floyd, E, Arkansas, 71
7. *Youngelman, Sid, T, Alabama, 83
8. Choice to Cleveland
9. *Connolly, Ted, G, Tulsa, 107
10. Choice to Cleveland
11. Skocko, John, E, USC, 131
12. Easterwood, Hal, C, Mississippi State, 143
13. Williams, Morgan, G, TCU, 155
14. Williams, Sammy, B, California, 167
15. Gossage, Ed, T, Georgia Tech [from Green Bay], 171
   *Palumbo, Sam, G, Notre Dame, 179 +
16. Fiveash, Bobby, B, Florida State, 191
17. Kautz, Carl, T, Texas Tech, 203
18. Kay, Morris, E, Kansas, 215
19. Edmiston, Bob, T, Temple, 227
20. DePietro, Frank, B, Georgia, 239
21. Alsup, Howard, T, Middle Tennessee State, 251
22. Reynolds, Ralph, B, North Texas State, 263
23. Fenstemaker, LeRoy, B, Rice, 275
24. Daniels, Jerry, T, Tennessee Tech, 287
25. Platt, John, B, Elon, 299
26. Bello, Pete, C, Pasadena C.C., 311
27. Baker, Gayford, G, Nebraska-Omaha, 323
28. Garbrecht, Bob, B, Rice, 335
29. Dunn, Ted, B, Murray State, 347
30. Folks, Don, E, Houston, 359

WASHINGTON 1954
1. *Meilinger, Steve, E, Kentucky, 8
2. *Schrader, Jim, C, Notre Dame, 20
3. Choice to Los Angeles Rams
4. *Felton, Ralph, B, Maryland [from Green Bay], 39
   Choice to Detroit
5. *Wells, Billy, B, Michigan State, 56
6. McHenry, Bill, C, Washington & Lee, 68
7. *Jagielski, Harry, T, Indiana, 80
8. Marker, Bill, E, West Virginia, 92
9. Minnick, Jerry, T, Nebraska, 104
10. Green, Merrill, B, Oklahoma, 116
11. Wilson, Gene, B, South Carolina, 128
12. Dunkerly, Ben, T, West Virginia, 140
13. Dornburg, Roger, B, Wisconsin, 152
14. Nelson, Roger, T, Oklahoma, 164
15. Merck, Hugh, T, South Carolina, 176
16. Spring, Gilmer, E, Texas, 188
17. Coody, Jerry, B, Baylor, 200
18. *Cudzik, Walt, C, Purdue, 212
19. Witt, Jerry, B, Wisconsin, 224
20. Morley, Sam, E, Stanford, 236
21. Cavaglieri, John, T, North Texas State, 248
22. Schmaling, Max, B, Purdue, 260
23. Carrieri, Pete, G, Villanova, 272
24. *Renfro, Will, E, Memphis State, 284
25. *Rosso, George, B, Ohio State, 296
26. Gibson, Dorsey, B, Oklahoma State, 308
27. Yarborough, Ken, E, North Carolina, 320
28. *Hansen, Ron, T, Minnesota, 332
29. Kress, Ted, B, Michigan, 344
30. Rondou, Don, B, Northwestern, 356

1955

Held January 27-28, 1955

BALTIMORE 1955

BONUS CHOICE: *Shaw, George, B, Oregon, 1
1. *Ameche, Alan (The Horse), B, Wisconsin, 3
2. *Szymanski, Dick, C, Notre Dame, 16
3. *Dupre, L.G. (Long Gone), B, Baylor, 27
4. Choice to Los Angeles Rams
   *Patera, Jack, G, Oregon [from New York Giants], 44
5. *Preas, George, G, Virginia Tech, 51
6. Lewis, Leo, B, Lincoln (MO), 64
7. McDonald, Frank, E, Miami, 75
8. *Meinert, Dale, G, Oklahoma State, 88
9. Walter, Bryan, B, Texas Tech, 99
   Evans, Bill, G, Miami (OH) [from New York Giants], 104
10. Choice to Los Angeles Rams
11. Radik, Emil, B, Nebraska-Omaha, 123
12. Chorovich, Dick, T, Miami (OH), 136
13. Abbruzzi, Pat, B, Rhode Island, 147
14. Lee, John, B, Georgia Tech, 160
15. *Peterson, Gerry, T, Texas, 171 F
16. Laswell, Dick, T, TCU, 184
17. Clark, Wes, T, Southern Mississippi, 195
18. *Shephard, Charley, B, North Texas State, 208
19. Cobb, Jim, T, Abilene Christian, 219
20. Cianciola, Charley, E, Lawrence, 232
21. Manych, Nick, E, Eastern Michigan, 243
22. Welch, Jerry, B, South Dakota State, 256
23. McNamara, Dick, B, Minnesota, 267
24. Esquivel, Alex, B, Mexico City College, 280
25. Grann, Dick, T, Rhode Island, 291
26. Minker, Marion, T, Bucknell, 304
27. Locke, Jim, T, Virginia Tech, 315
28. Meyer, Bob, T, Ohio State, 328
29. Waters, Bill, T, Austin, 339

CHICAGO BEARS 1955
1. *Drzewiecki, Ron, B, Marquette, 11
2. *Watkins, Bobby, B, Ohio State, 23
3. Choice to Cleveland
4. *O'Malley, Joe, E, Georgia, 47
5. Kendall, Leland, T, Oklahoma State, 59
6. Shannon, Dan, E, Notre Dame [from Washington], 63
   *Mosely, Henry, B, Morris Brown, 71
7. Sturgess, Bruce, B, William & Mary, 83
8. Verkerk, Gene, T, North Texas State, 95
9. Lavery, Jim, B, Scranton, 107
10. Allen, John, E, Arizona State, 119
11. Redfield, Tom, E, Delaware, 131
12. Bratt, Clarence, B, Wisconsin, 143
13. Cash, Norm, B, Sul Ross, 155
14. *Nickla, Ed, G, Tennessee, 167
15. *Smith, J.D., B, North Carolina A&T, 179
16. Choice to Chicago Cardinals
17. Harrison, Mel, C, Sam Houston State, 203
18. Roach, Claude, G, TCU, 215
19. Jones, Allen, B, Baylor, 227
20. James, Joe, T, Howard Payne, 239
21. Hall, Choyce, C, Midwestern State (TX), 251
22. Allison, Carl, B, Oklahoma, 263
23. Barger, Jerry, B, Duke, 275
24. Young, Joe, E, Marquette, 287
25. Dees, Charley, T, Tyler J.C., 299
26. *Jeter, Perry, B, Cal Poly-SLO, 311
27. Kinley, Joel, G, Tennessee, 323
28. Wright, Charley, E, Prairie View A&M, 335
29. *Klein, Dick, T, Iowa, 347
30. Fouts, Jerry, B, Midwestern State (TX), 358

CHICAGO CARDINALS 1955
1. *Boydston, Max, E, Oklahoma, 2
2. *Crow, Lindon, B, USC, 14
3. *Hammack, Mal, B, Florida, 26
   *Pasquesi, Tony, T, Notre Dame [from New York Giants], 32
4. *Bernardi, Frank, B, Colorado, 38
5. De Ra, Mario, T, USC, 50
6. Bowersox, Jack, G, Maryland, 62
7. *Leggett, Dave, B, Ohio State, 74
8. Irvine, Sam, C, Maryland, 86
9. McGinty, Charlie, E, North Texas State, 98
10. Scaffidi, Frank, T, Marquette, 110
11. Pepsin, Tom, E, Miami (FL), 122
12. Sandstrom, Dale, B, Concordia (MN), 134
13. McLuckie, Tom, G, Maryland, 146
14. Brown, Gordy, E, Louisiana Tech, 158
15. *Brubaker, Dick, E, Ohio State, 170
16. Herndon, Bob, B, Oklahoma, 182
   Dennis, Al, E, Middlebury [from Chicago Bears], 191
17. White, Larry, C, New Mexico, 194
18. Campbell, Fred, T, Duke, 206
19. Coy, Dick, T, St. John's (MN), 218
20. Burst, Jim, B, Washington (St. Louis), 230
21. Wright, Howie, B, Virginia Tech, 242
22. Berra, Vic, E, Montana State, 254
23. Bays, Karl, T, Eastern Kentucky, 266
24. Pierce, Max, B, Utah, 278
25. Scott, Bob, E, Evansville, 290
26. Hooper, Billy, B, Baylor, 302
27. Schwager, Bruce, T, Merchant Marine, 314
28. Ems, Bob, B, Southern Illinois, 326
29. Renzi, Gene, T, Northeastern, 338
30. Sweet, Bob, B, Trinity (TX), 350

CLEVELAND 1955
1. Burris, Kurt, C, Oklahoma, 13
2. *Renfro, Dean, B, North Texas State, 25
3. *Hall, John, T, Iowa [from Chicago Bears], 35
   *Freeman, Bobby, B, Auburn, 37
4. Reynolds, Paul, B, Notre Dame [from Green Bay], 41
   *Palumbo, Sam, C, Notre Dame, 49
5. Dandoy, Aramis, B, USC, 61
6. *Bolden, Leroy, B, Michigan State, 73
7. Locklear, Jack, C, Auburn, 85
8. Choice to Detroit
9. *Ford, Henry, B, Pittsburgh, 109
10. Dillon, Glen, E, Pittsburgh, 121
11. Knebel, Eric, T, SMU, 133
12. Eaton, Jack, T, New Mexico, 145
13. *Borton, Johnny, QB, Ohio State, 157
14. *Robinson, Fred, G, Washington, 169 F
15. *Smith, Bob, B, Nebraska, 181
16. Suchy, Don, C, Iowa, 193
17. Leonard, Bob, B, Purdue, 205
18. Champlin, Steve, T, Oklahoma, 217
19. Ebert, Tom, E, Kansas State, 229
20. Proctor, Bill, T, Florida State, 241
21. Spinks, Rick, B, Texas Tech, 253
22. Stone, Jerry, T, Southeastern Louisiana, 265
23. Greer, Jim, E, Elizabeth City State, 277
24. Matsock, John, B, Michigan State, 289
25. Lindo, Ernie, B, Pacific, 301
26. Fife, Don, C, Purdue, 313
27. Baldwin, Bobby, B, Sam Houston State, 325
28. Tokus, Ed, E, Georgia, 337
29. Robinson, Ted (Tex), B, Temple, 349
30. Leachman, Lamar, C, Tennessee, 360

DETROIT 1955
1. *Middleton, Dave, B, Auburn, 12
2. *Salsbury, Jim, G, UCLA, 24
3. *McCord, Darris, T, Tennessee, 36
   Malloy, Gordon, B, Miami [from Washington], 39
   *Riley, Lee, B, Detroit, 48
5. Brooks, Bud, G, Arkansas, 60
6. Childers, Elijah, T, Prairie View A&M, 72
7. *Zagers, Bert, B, Michigan State, 84
8. *Cunningham, Leon, G, South Carolina [from Pittsburgh], 90
   Walker, Bill, E, Maryland, 96
   Holland, Lamoine, E, Rice [from Cleveland], 97
9. *Jenkins, Walt, T, Wayne State, 108
10. Gastall, Tom, B, Boston U., 120
11. McDermott, Herb, T, Iowa State, 132
12. Goist, Dick, B, Cincinnati, 144
13. Henderson, Don, T, Utah, 156
14. Gajda, Jerry, B, St. Benedict's (KS), 168
15. *Atkins, George, G, Auburn, 180
16. Marr, Al, E, Bradley, 192
17. Daly, Don, B, Eastern Kentucky, 204
18. Oleksiak, Pat, B, Tennessee, 216
19. Muller, Bob, C, Eastern Kentucky, 228
20. Mahaffey, Fred, B, Denver, 240
21. Walters, Jim, T, Mississippi, 252
22. Albrecht, George, B, Maryland, 264
23. Galuska, George, B, Wyoming, 276
24. Flacke, Bob, G, Holy Cross, 288
25. Miller, Dick, T, Illinois, 300
26. McDonald, Duncan, B, Michigan, 312
27. Troka, Mike, B, Trinity (CT), 324
28. Lovell, Harry, G, South Carolina, 336
29. Dearing, Bill, B, Florida, 348
30. Hatch, Charley, E, Utah State, 359

GREEN BAY 1955
1. *Bettis, Tom, G, Purdue, 5
2. *Temp, Jim, E, Wisconsin, 17
3. Leake, Buddy, B, Oklahoma, 29
4. Choice to Cleveland
5. *Bullough, Hank, G, Michigan State, 53
6. *Amundsen, Norm, G, Wisconsin, 65
7. *Clemens, Bob, B, Georgia, 77
8. Crouch, Johnny, E, TCU, 89
9. *Culpepper, Ed, T, Alabama, 101
10. Rogers, George, T, Auburn, 113
11. Clark, Ron, B, Nebraska, 125
12. Walker, Art, T, Michigan, 137
13. Adams, Ed, B, South Carolina, 149
14. Baer, Fred, B, Michigan, 161
15. Machoukas, George, C, Toledo, 173
16. *Brackins, Charley, QB, Prairie View A&M, 185
17. Beightol, Lynn, B, Maryland, 197
18. *Nix, Doyle, B, SMU, 209
19. Carter, Bob, T, Grambling, 221
20. Bolt, Carl, B, Southern Mississippi, 233
   Antkowiak, Bob, E, Bucknell [from New York Giants], 236
21. Isbell, Lavell, T, Houston, 245
22. Brunner, Bill, B, Arkansas Tech, 257
23. Shaw, Elton, T, LSU, 269
24. Bryant, Charley, G, Nebraska, 281
25. *Borden, Nate, E, Indiana, 293
26. *Jennings, Jim, E, Missouri, 305
27. Peringer, Bob, E, Washington State, 317
28. Spears, Jack, T, Tennessee-Chattanooga, 329
29. Pino, Sam, B, Boston U., 341
30. Saia, Bob, B, Tulane, 352

LOS ANGELES RAMS 1955
1. *Morris, Larry, C, Georgia Tech, 7
2. *Waller, Ron, B, Maryland [from Washington], 15
   *Long, Bob, B, UCLA [from Pittsburgh], 18
   Taylor, Corky, B, Kansas State, 19
   *Fournet, Sid, T, LSU [from New York Giants], 20
3. Choice to New York Giants
4. *Feamster, Tom, E, Florida State [from Baltimore], 40
   Fouch, Ed, T, USC, 43
5. *Kelley, Ed, B, Texas, 55
6. *Tharp, Tom (Corky), B, Alabama, 67
7. Clayton, Frank, B, USC, 79
8. Teas, Billy, B, Georgia Tech, 91
9. Witte, John, T, Oregon State, 103
10. Arnelle, Jesse, E, Penn State [from Baltimore], 112
   Harland, Claude, E, Texas Tech, 115
11. Ray, Joe, T, UCLA, 127
12. Hanifan, Jim, E, California, 139
13. Parkinson, Dave, B, Texas, 151
14. Elliot, George, B, Northeastern Oklahoma, 163
15. Hoerning, Bob, B, St. Norbert, 175
16. Coates, Charley, T, Tulane, 187
17. *Mitcham, Gene, E, Arizona State, 199
18. Sweeney, Clyde, T, West Virginia, 211
19. Davis, John, E, Miles, 223
20. Muldowney, Jack, T, Dayton, 235
21. Cvengros, Jerry, T, Wisconsin, 247
22. Elmore, Ken, T, Texas Tech, 259
23. Medved, George, T, Florida, 271
24. Andrews, Bill, B, Trinity (TX), 283
25. Cook, Ralph, T, Ball State, 295
26. Hallow, Lou, C, Wake Forest, 307
27. Nevitt, Bruce, C, Washington State, 319
28. Hoffman, Jim, B, Cincinnati, 331
29. Howe, Bob, B, Cincinnati, 343
30. Jones, K.C., E, San Francisco, 354

NEW YORK GIANTS 1955
1. *Heap, Joe, B, Notre Dame, 8
2. Choice to Los Angeles Rams
3. *Grier, Roosevelt (Rosey), T, Penn St. [from Los Angeles Rams], 31
   Choice to Chicago Cardinals
4. Choice to Baltimore
5. *Triplett, Mel, B, Toledo, 56
6. Locklin, Ron, E, Wisconsin, 68
7. Choice to Washington
8. *Patton, Jimmy, B, Mississippi, 92
9. Choice to Baltimore
10. Paslay, Lea, B, Mississippi, 116
11. Hillen, Bill, E, West Virginia, 128
12. *Burnine, Hank, E, Missouri, 140 F
13. *Damore, John, C, Northwestern, 152
14. Kettler, Elwood, B, Texas A&M, 164
15. Stowers, Ed, E, Wake Forest, 176
16. Kragthorpe, Dave, G, Utah State, 188
17. Bills, Bob, B, BYU, 200
18. Stout, Joe, B, Temple, 212
19. Jacobs, John, E, Colby, 224
20. Choice to Green Bay
21. Dilby, Gary, C, LSU, 248
22. Doggett, Al, B, LSU, 260
23. Callahan, Jerry, B, Colorado State, 272
24. Vujevich, Matt, B, San Jose State, 284
25. Dement, Ken, T, Southeast Missouri State, 296
26. *Cohen, Abe, G, Tennessee-Chattanooga, 308
27. Blanda, Paul, B, Pittsburgh, 320
28. *Crow, Al, T, William & Mary, 332
29. Jackson, Harold, B, Southern, 344
30. Toole, Bill, B, Oregon, 355

PHILADELPHIA 1955
1. *Bielski, Dick, B, Maryland, 9
2. *Lansford, Alex (Buck), T, Texas, 22
3. Eidom, Frank, B, SMU, 33
4. Dugger, Dean, E, Ohio State, 46
5. Lamone, Gene, G, West Virginia, 57
6. Quinn, Billy, B, Texas, 70
7. McKenna, Bill, E, Brandeis, 81
8. Watson, Herman, T, Vanderbilt, 94
9. Morgan, Von, E, Abilene Christian, 105
10. Washington, Talmadge, (Duke), B, Wash. State, 118
11. Hardy, Bob, B, Kentucky, 129
12. *Nacrelli, Andy, E, Fordham, 142
13. Krisher, Jerry, C, Ohio State, 153
14. Bell, Tommy, B, Army, 166
15. Brougher, Don, C, Maryland, 177
16. White, Clyde, G, Clemson, 190
17. Maravic, Nick, B, Wake Forest, 201
18. Nutt, Duane, B, SMU, 214
19. Fails, Terry, E, Vanderbilt, 225
20. Wade, Jimmy, B, Tennessee, 238
21. Anderson, John, E, Kansas, 249
22. Lewis, Ernie, G, Arizona, 262
23. Ingram, Cecil, B, Alabama, 273
24. Postula, Vic, (Hootie), B, Michigan State, 286
25. Pavich, Frank, G, USC, 297
26. Palahunik, George, G, Maryland, 310
27. Gringrass, Bob, B, Wisconsin, 321
28. Avery, Wingo, C, Clemson, 334
29. Lloyd, Ron, T, Bucknell, 345
30. Finney, Dave, B, TCU, 357

PITTSBURGH 1955
1. *Varrichione, Frank, T, Notre Dame, 6
2. Choice to Los Angeles Rams
3. *Bernet, Ed, E, SMU, 30
4. *Broussard, Fred, C, Northwestern State (LA), 42
5. Mason, George, T, Alabama, 54
6. *Harkey, Lem, B, Emporia State, 66
7. Reeve, Hal, T, Oregon, 78
8. Choice to Detroit

9. *Unitas, Johnny, QB, Louisville, 102
10. Boyle, Terry, T, Cincinnati, 114
11. *Eaton, Vic, B, Missouri, 126
12. Cooke, Jim, E, Lincoln (PA), 138
13. Whitmer, Jim, B, Purdue, 150
14. Byrne, John (Buck), G, John Carroll, 162
15. Duckett, Ellis, B, Michigan State, 174
16. Vincent, Frank, C, Glenville State, 186
17. Merchant, Ed, B, Miami (OH), 198
18. Maier, Albie, G, Marshall, 210
19. Smith, Ed, B, Texas Southern, 222
20. Matykiewicz, Lou, E, Iowa, 234
21. Phenix, Rees, T, Georgia Tech, 246
22. *McCabe, Richie, B, Pittsburgh, 258
23. *Holz, Gordy, T, Minnesota, 270
24. Mayock, Mike, E, Villanova, 282
25. Bull, Charlie, G, Missouri, 294
26. Soltau, Jim, E, Minnesota, 306
27. Sanford, Bill, B, Hofstra, 318
28. Williams, Dave, G, Ohio State, 330
29. Sinclair, Bernie, E, Texas A&M, 342
30. Caruzzi, Jim, B, Marquette, 353

SAN FRANCISCO 1955

1. *Moegle, Dickie, B, Rice, 10
2. *Morze, Frank, C, Boston College, 21
3. *Hardy, Carroll, B, Colorado, 34
4. *Hazeltine, Matt, C, California, 45
5. *Kraemer, Eldred, T, Pittsburgh, 58
6. *Luna, Bobby, B, Alabama, 69
7. Dean, Johnny, B, Virginia Tech, 82
8. Meyers, Freddie, B, Oklahoma State, 93 F
9. Preziosio, Fred, T, Purdue, 106 F
10. Aschbacker, Ron, E, Oregon State, 117
11. Rotella, Rudy, E, Nebraska-Omaha, 130
12. *Palatella, Lou, T, Pittsburgh, 141 F
13. Gaskell, Richie, E, George Washington, 154
14. McKeithan, Nick, B, Duke, 165
15. Hess, Burdette, G, Idaho, 178
16. Hall, Jim, E, Auburn, 189
17. Newton, Bob, G, San Diego State, 202
18. Pheister, Ron, C, Oregon, 213
19. Garzoli, John, T, California, 226
20. Dyer, Glen, B, Texas, 237
21. *Maderos, George, E, Cal State-Chico, 250
22. Vann, Pete, QB, Army, 261
23. Gunnari, Tom, E, Washington State, 274 F
24. Heaston, Bob, G, Cal Poly-SLO, 285
25. Wade, Dewey, E, Kansas State, 298
26. Kerr, Johnny, E, Purdue, 309
27. Shockey, Dick, B Marquette, 322 F
28. Sanders, Don, B, Stanford, 333
29. Kniedinger, Otto, T, Penn State, 346 F
30. Gongola, Bob, B, Illinois, 356 F

WASHINGTON 1955

1. *Guglielmi, Ralph QB, Notre Dame, 4
2. Choice to Los Angeles Rams
3. Perkins, Ray, B, Syracuse, 28
4. Choice to Detroit
5. Glantz, Don, T, Nebraska, 52
6. Choice to Chicago Bears
7. *Christensen, Erik, E, Richmond, 76
*Marciniak, Ron, G, Kansas State [from New York Giants], 80
8. *Allen, Johnny, C, Purdue, 87
9. Miller, John, T, Boston College, 100 F
10. *Louderback, Tom, G, San Jose State, 111
11. Parker, Larry, B, North Carolina, 124
12. Barish, John, T, Waynesburg, 135
13. Oniskey, Len, T, Cornell, 148
14. *Braatz, Tom, E, Marquette, 159
15. Horton, Charley, B, Vanderbilt, 172
16. *Norris, Hal, B, California, 183
17. Shea, Don, G, Georgia, 196
18. Bailey, Don, B, Penn State, 207
19. *Dee, Bob, E, Holy Cross, 220
20. Geyer, Ron, T, Michigan, 231
21. George, Buck, B, Clemson, 244
22. Boland, Joe, B, George Washington, 255
23. Donaldson, Chick, C, West Virginia, 268
24. Ready, Bob, T, Notre Dame, 279
25. Radella, Frank, C, Wyoming, 292
26. *Houston, Walt, G, Purdue, 303
27. Baker, A.J., B, Arkansas, 316
28. Cassidy, Arch, T, Florida, 327
29. Bordier, Bing, E, USC, 340
30. Petty, Tom, E, Virginia Tech, 351

1956

Held November 29, 1955 (Rounds 1-3 and January 17, 1956 (Rounds 4-30)

The first three rounds were held two months earlier than recent drafts in order to give NFL teams an even start with the Canadian Football League in signing top players. The CFL had been attempting to build its popularity by signing big-name players from the United States. Rounds 4-30 were held in January. The NFL also had early drafts the next two years, when the first four rounds were picked in November or December.

BALTIMORE 1956

1. *Moore, Lenny, B, Penn State, 9
2. Donlin, Dick, E, Hamline, 21
3. Pascal, Bob, B, Duke, 33
4. Inabinet, Ben, T, Clemson, 43
5. Gray, Herb, E, Texas, 55
6. Schmidt, Don, B, Texas Tech, 67
7. Waters, Bill, T, Austin, 79
8. *Koman, Bill, G, North Carolina, 91
9. Lewis, John, E, Michigan State, 103
10. Scott, Gene, B, Centre, 115
11. Shaw, Dennis, E, North Texas State, 127
12. *Myrha, Steve, G, North Dakota, 139
13. *Hill, Jack, B, Utah State, 151
14. Schwanger, Ted, B, Tennessee Tech, 163
15. Polzer, John, QB, Virginia, 175
16. Hendrik, Gene (Moose), B, Drake, 187
17. *Danenhauer, Bill, E, Emporia State, 199
18. Looman, Earl, G, Stetson, 211
19. Fyvie, Bob, T, Lafayette, 223
20. Hill, Bob, B, Jackson State, 235
21. *Harness, Jim, B, Mississippi State, 247
22. Del Vicaro, Pat, G, Southern Mississippi, 259
23. Stephenson, Al (Bear), T, Idaho State, 271
24. Fox, Bobby, QB, East Texas State, 283
25. Mills, Brad, B, Kentucky, 295
26. Lohr, Jim, T, Southwest Missouri State, 307
27. Hartwell, Herb, B, Virginia, 319
28. Shearer, John, QB, Shepherd, 331
29. Rusher, Jim, E, Kansas State, 343
30. Sweeney, Terry, B, Middle Tennessee State, 354

CHICAGO BEARS 1956

1. Schriewer, Menan (Tex), E, Texas, 10
2. *Brackett, M.L., T, Auburn, 22
3. Choice to Cleveland
4. *Mellekas, John, T, Arizona, 47
5. *Galimore, Willie, B, Florida A&M, 58
6. Choice to Cleveland
7. *Caroline, J.C., B, Illinois, 82
8. *Klawitter, Dick, C, South Dakota State, 95
9. Vargo, Ken, C, Ohio State, 106
10. *Lucas, Dick, E, Boston College, 119
11. Jankans, John, E, Arizona State, 130
12. Cruze, Buddy, E, Tennessee, 143
13. Grogg, Dick, G, Minnesota, 154
14. *Graham, Milt, E, Colgate, 167
15. Fitzgerald, Dick, B, Notre Dame, 178
16. Brown, Ray, B, Florida, 191
17. Adams, Tom, E, UCLA, 202
18. Payton, Earl, B, Prairie View A&M, 215
19. Smith, John, B, UCLA, 226
20. Maxime, Charley, G, Auburn, 239
21. Waddell, Jimmy, B, Compton J.C., 250
22. Billings, Joe, T, Memphis State, 263
23. Holt, Lou, E, Howard Payne, 274
24. *Castete, Jess, B, McNeese State, 287
25. Hentschel, Jerry, T, Sam Houston State, 298
26. Orr, Don, B, Vanderbilt, 311
27. Buchanan, Waylon, E, East Texas State, 322
28. Alexander, Bob, B, Trinity (CT), 335
29. Krietemeyer, Billy, B, Vanderbilt, 346
30. Buckler, Jim, G, Alabama, 358

CHICAGO CARDINALS 1956

1. *Childress, Joe, B, Auburn, 7
2. *Masters, Norm, T, Michigan State, 18
3. *Roach, John, QB, SMU, 31
4. Salerno, Sam, T, Coloraoo, 42
5. Choice to Los Angeles Rams
6. *Dupre, Charlie, B, Baylor, 66
Dittrich, John, T, Wisconsin [from Washington], 70 F
7. *Konovsky, Bob, T, Wisconsin, 77
8. *Lunceford, Dave, T, Baylor, 90 F
9. Lovely, Bob, T, Tampa, 101
10. Towne, Willis, E, Wichita State, 114
11. James, Fob, B, Auburn, 125
12. Walker, Jerry, T, Texas Tech, 138
13. Bolinger, Bo, G, Oklahoma, 149
14. Neuman, Carnell, B, Illinois, 162
15. *Anderson, Charley, E, Louisiana Tech, 173
Spiers, Tom, QB, Arkansas State [from Washington], 179
16. Welsh, George, QB, Navy, 186
17. Beagle, Ron, E, Navy, 197
18. Brown, Jim, G, UCLA, 210
19. Zagar, Ray, B, Marquette, 221
20. Mattison, Dickie, B, Georgia Tech, 234
21. Herr, Ronnie, B, Texas Tech, 245
22. Murphy, Jim, T, Stephen F. Austin, 258
23. Branoff, Tony, B, Michigan, 269
24. *Trask, Orville, T, Rice, 282
25. Wheeler, Bill, T, Kentucky, 293
26. Zickefoose, Chuck, E, Kansas State, 306
27. Hutchinson, Jack, T, Oklahoma State, 317
28. Miller, Jim, QB, Wisconsin, 330
29. Troglio, Jim, B, Northwestern, 341
30. Kucera, Bill, T, Colorado, 353

CLEVELAND 1956

1. *Carpenter, Preston, B, Arkansas, 13
2. *Kinard, Billy, B, Mississippi, 25
3. Ross, Larry, E, Denver [from Chicago Bears], 34
*Quinlan, Billy, E, Michigan State, 37
4. Moss, Bobby, B, West Virginia, 49
5. *Clarke, Frank, E, Colorado, 61 F
6. *Plunkett, Sherman, E, Maryland-Eastern Shore [from Chicago Bears], 71
*Wiggin, Paul, E, Stanford, 73 F
7. Griffith, Chuck, E, USC, 85
8. Hellyer, Len, B, Marshall, 97
9. Hecker, Jack, E, Bowling Green, 109
10. Rayburn, Eddie, T, Rice, 121
11. Underdonk, Bill, T, West Virginia, 133
12. Javernick, Harry, T, Colorado, 145
13. *Furey, Jim, C, Kansas State, 157
14. Sidwell, Charlie, B, William & Mary, 169
15. *Davis, Willie, E, Grambling, 181
16. *Cooper, Thurlow, E, Maine, 193
17. West, Eddie, QB, North Carolina State, 205
18. Carroll, Hal (Candy), B, Case Western Reserve, 217
19. Sebest, John, E, Eastern Kentucky, 229
20. Mobra, Joe, E, Oklahoma, 241
21. Kapish, Gene, E, Notre Dame, 253
22. Brown, Sam (First Down), B, UCLA, 265
23. Althouse, Don, E, Syracuse, 277
24. Hughes, Jim, G, San Jose State, 289
25. Davenport, Bob, B, UCLA, 301
26. Kammerman, Jack, E, Utah, 313
27. Dwyer, Ed, E, Purdue, 325
28. Sparks, Ollie, G, Iowa State, 337
29. Battos, John, E, Vanderbilt, 349
30. Bartholomew, Bob, T, Wake Forest, 360

DETROIT 1956

1. *Cassady, Howard (Hopalong), B, Ohio State, 3
2. Choice to Los Angeles Rams
3. *McIlhenny, Don, B, SMU, 27
4. *Reichow, Jerry, QB, Iowa, 38
5. *Tracy, Tom (The Bomb), B, Tennessee, 50
6. *Lusk, Bob, C, William & Mary, 62
7. *Cronin, Gene, G, Pacific, 74
8. Powell, Jack, T, Texas A&M, 86
9. Jones, Calvin, G, Iowa, 98
10. Silas, Joe, DE, South Carolina, 110
11. Wacker, Lew, B, Richmond, 122
Selep, Tom, B, Maryland [from Pittsburgh], 124
12. *Nunnery, Bob, T, LSU, 134
13. Ferguson, O.K., B, LSU, 146
14. Falls, Ronnie, LB, Duke, 158
15. Allert, Horace (Buzzy), DE, Southwest Texas St., 170
16. Zyzda, Len, DE, Purdue, 182
17. Wind, Ken, E, Houston, 194
18. Petrarca, Emidio, B, Boston College, 206
19. Vaughn, Dale, B, Virginia Military, 218
20. Stephenson, Joe, E, Vanderbilt, 230
21. Blechen, Bob, C, Whittier, 242
22. Marazza, Dick, T, Clemson, 254
23. Garrard, Bob, B, Georgia, 266
24. Walz, Jarv, E, Central Michigan, 278
25. Hall, Jerry, B, Rice, 290
26. Walden, Joe, B, West Texas State, 302
27. Bunthorne, Bryan, G, Tulane, 314
28. Smith, John, G, Northwestern, 326
29. Peters, Doug, B, UCLA, 338
30. Gibbens, John, T, Southwest Texas State, 350

GREEN BAY 1956

1. *Losch, Jack, B, Miami (FL), 8
2. *Gregg, Forrest, T, SMU, 20
3. Choice to Los Angeles Rams
4. Morris, Cecil, G, Oklahoma, 44
5. *Skoronski, Bob, T, Indiana, 56
6. Burris, Bob, B, Oklahoma, 68
7. *Gremminger, Hank, E, Baylor, 80
8. Dennis, Russ, E, Maryland, 92
9. Duvall, Gordy, B, USC, 104
10. Laugherty, Bob, B, Maryland, 116
11. *Hudock, Mike, C, Miami, 128
12. Burnett, Max, B, Arizona, 140
13. Mense, Jim, C, Notre Dame, 152
14. Thomas, Charlie, B, Wisconsin, 164
15. *Alliston, Warren (Buddy), G, Mississippi, 176
16. Lynch, Curtis, T, Alabama, 188
17. *Starr, Bart, QB, Alabama, 200
18. Intihar, Stan, E, Cornell, 212
19. Vakey, Ken, E, Texas Tech, 224
20. Letbetter, Clyde, T, Baylor, 236
21. O'Brien, Hal, B, SMU, 248
22. Popson, Johnny, B, Furman, 260
23. Birchfield, Jesse, G, Duke, 272
24. Wilson, Don, C, Rice, 284
25. Koeneke, Franz, E, Minnesota, 296
26. Goehe, Dick, T, Mississippi, 308
27. Kolian, Dick, E, Wisconsin, 320
28. Lance, Bobby, QB, Florida, 332
29. Newcomb, Vester, C, Southwest J.C. (MS), 344
30. Hermes, Rod, QB, Beloit, 355

LOS ANGELES RAMS 1956

1. *Marconi, Joe, B, West Virginia [from New York Giants], 6
Horton, Charlie, B, Vanderbilt, 11
2. *Clarke, Leon, E, USC [from Detroit], 14
*Pitts, Hugh, C, TCU, 23
3. *Williams, A.D., DE, Pacific [from Green Bay], 32
Marshall, John, B, SMU, 35
4. *Berzinski, Willie, B, Wisc.-La Crosse [from Washington], 46
Carmichael, Jim, E, California, 48
5. Freeman, Jim, E, Iowa [from San Francisco], 51
Nakken, Herb, B, Utah [from Chicago Cardinals], 53
*Whittenton, Jesse, DB, Texas-El Paso, 60
6. Vincent, Eddie, B, Iowa, 72
7. *Morris, Jack, B, Oregon, 84 F
8. Boyer, George, LB, Florida State, 96
9. Woolford, Maury, T, Louisville, 108
10. Sticka, Charlie, B, Trinity (CT), 120
11. Decker, Jim, B, UCLA, 132
12. Lindbeck, Em, QB, Illinois, 144
13. Norcia, Mike, B, Kent State, 156
14. *Runnels, Tom, B, North Texas State, 168
15. Shatto, Dick, B, Kentucky, 180
16. Pelluer, Arnie, E, Washington State, 192
17. Butler, Jack, T, Kentucky, 204
18. *Klotz, Jack, T, Widener, 216
19. Dees, Charlie, T, McNeese State, 228
20. Coyne, John, T, West Chester, 240
21. Robichaux, Milt, E, Trinity (TX), 252
22. Fouts, Dick, E, Missouri, 264
23. Paulson, Al, B, Washington State, 276
24. *Williams, Sam, DE, Michigan State, 288 F
25. Tunning, Glen, G, Pittsburgh, 300
26. Cureton, Hardiman, T, UCLA, 312
27. Siesel, Roger, T, Miami (OH), 324
28. *Morrow, John, T, Michigan, 336
29. Bates, Mickey, B, Illinois, 348
30. Kackmeister, Dick, C, Central Michigan, 359

NEW YORK GIANTS 1956

1. Choice to Los Angeles Rams
2. Moore, Henry, B, Arkansas, 19
3. *Huff, Sam, T, West Virginia, 30
4. *Katcavage, Jim, E, Dayton, 45
5. *Chandler, Don, B, Florida, 57
6. Cason, Fred, B, Florida, 69
7. *Nery, Ron, T, Kansas State, 81
8. Holleder, Don, E, Army, 93
9. Braden, Ken, C, East Texas State, 105
10. *Herman, Johnny, B, UCLA, 117
11. Moloney, Dick, B, Kentucky, 129
12. Choice to Washington
13. *Crawford, Eddie, B, Mississippi, 153 F
14. *McMullen, John, G, Notre Dame, 165
15. Melnik, Ron, T, Army, 177
16. Portney, Al, T, Missouri, 189
17. Mooney, Tom, T, Miami (OH), 201
18. Boone, Matt, B, North Carolina Central, 213
19. Dettring, Ray, B, Missouri, 225
20. *Falls, Mike, G, Minnesota, 237
21. *McComb, Don, E, Villanova, 249
22. Harkrader, Jerry, B, Ohio State, 261
23. McCool, Bob (Slick), B, Mississippi, 273
24. *Huth, Gerry, G, Wake Forest, 285
25. Speers, Harry, B, Florida, 297
26. Buller, Bev, B, Kansas, 309
27. Nesbitt, Gerry, B, Arkansas, 321
28. Fuller, Bill, T, Arkansas, 333
29. Nelson, Jim, G, Duke, 345
30. Williams, Wayne, E, Southern Illinois, 356

PHILADELPHIA 1956

1. *Pellegrini, Bob, C, Maryland, 4
2. *D'Agoslino, Frank, T, Auburn, 16
3. *Schaffer, Don, B, Notre Dame, 28
4. Choice to Washington
5. *Thurston, Fred (Fuzzy), G, Valparaiso, 54
6. Burton, Tirrel, B, Miami (OH), 65
7. Waedekin, John, T, Hardin-Simmons, 78
8. Payne, Elroy, B, McMurry, 89
9. *Bredice, Johnny, E, Boston U., 102
10. *Dimmick, Tom, C, Houston, 113
11. *Keller, Kenny, B, North Carolina, 126
12. Harkins, Tommy, E, Vanderbilt, 137
13. Sides, James, B, Texas Tech, 150
14. Relch, Frank, C, Penn State, 161
15. Brant, Don, B, Montana, 174
16. Hix, Billy,T, Middle Tennessee State, 185
17. Mastrogiovanni, Joe, B, Wyoming, 198
18. Consoles, Nick, 08, Wake Forest, 209
19. Womack, Delano B, Texas, 222
20. Glover, Darrell, T, Maryland-Eastern Shore, 233
21. Adams, Jack, T, San Jose State, 246
22. Miller, Joe, B, Cincinnati, 257
23. Spencer, Chet, E, Oklahoma State, 270
24. Parham, John, B, Wake Forest, 281
25. Grogan, Johnny, T, Dayton, 294
26. Lunsford, Earl, B, Oklahoma State, 305
27. Ellett, Al, T, Alabama, 318
28. Strawn, Bill, LB, Western Kentucky, 329
29. Hughes, Bob, B, Southern Mississippi, 342
30. Ulm, Joe, B, San Jose State, 352

PITTSBURGH 1956

BONUS CHOICE: *Glick, Gary, QB, Colorado State, 1
1. *Davis, Art, B, Mississippi State, 5
2. *Krupa, Joe, T, Purdue, 17
3. *Taylor, Jim, C, Baylor, 29
4. *Murley, Dick, G, Purdue, 39
5. Murakowski, Bill, B, Purdue, 52
6. Taylor, Ray, B, TCU, 63
7. Gaspari, Dick, C, George Washington, 76
8. Wellman, Vere, G, Wichita State, 87
9. Edmonds, Wayne, G, Notre Dame, 100
10. *Baldacci, Lou, B, Michigan, 111
Nolan, Bob, E, Miami [from Washington], 118
11. Choice to Detroit
12. Tarasovic, Phil, E, Yale, 135
13. Holley, Weldon, B, Baylor, 148
14. Emmons, Jim, T, Alabama, 159
15. Choice to San Francisco
16. Reed, Lionel, B, Central State (OK), 183
17. Schmidt, Bill, G, Pittsburgh, 196
18. Stephens, John, QB, Holy Cross, 207
19. Jacobs, Jerry, G, Florida State, 220
20. *Glatz, Fred, E, Pittsburgh, 231
21. Martell, Gene, T, Notre Dame, 244
22. DiPasquale, Ray, B, Pittsburgh, 255
23. Neft, Pete, QB, Pittsburgh, 268
24. Engram, Bryan, E, TCU, 279
25. O'Dell, Bill, B, Clemson, 292
26. Sweeney, Frank, G, Xavier, 303
27. Benson, Buddy, B, Arkansas, 316
28. DeGraaf, Bill, B, Cornell, 327
29. Thompson, Wes, T, Alabama, 340

SAN FRANCISCO 1956
1. *Morrall, Earl, QB, Michigan State, 2
2. *Bosley, Bruce, T, West Virginia, 15
3. *Herchman, Bill, T, Texas Tech, 26
4. Pajaczkowski, Frank, B, Richmond, 40
5. Choice to Los Angeles Rams
6. *Sardisco, Tony, LB, Tulane, 64
7. *Barnes, Larry, B, Colorado State, 75 F
8. *Smith, Charley, E, Abilene Christian, 88
9. Cox, Jim, E, Cal Poly-SLO, 99
10. Zaleski, Jerry, B, Colorado State, 112
11. Pell, Stew, T, North Carolina, 123
12. Swedberg, Roger, T, Iowa, 136
13. Moody, Ralph, B, Kansas, 147
14. *Owens, R.C., E, College of Idaho, 160 F
15. Henderson, Reed, T, Utah State, 171
Boyd, Gene, B, Abilene Christian [from Pittsburgh], 172
16. *Herring, George, QB, Southern Mississippi, 184
17. Weiss, Dick, T, Mississippi, 195
18. *Yelverton, Billy, T, Mississippi, 208 F
19. Arrigoni, Pete, B, Arizona, 219
20. Scarbrough, Bob, C, Auburn, 232
21. *Joyner, L.C., E, Contra Costa J.C., 243
22. Wessman, Clarence, E, San Jose State, 256
23. Monroe, Mike, B, Washington, 267
24. Wallace, Ed, T, San Diego J.C., 280
25. *Goad, Paul, B, Abilene Christian, 291
26. *Loudd, Rommie, E, UCLA, 304
27. Gustafson, Jerry, QB, Stanford, 315
28. Drew, Jerry, B, California, 328 F
29. Benson, Dean, G, Willamette, 339
30. Mitchell, Bob, T, Puget Sound, 351 F

WASHINGTON 1956
1. *Vereb, Ed, B, Maryland, 12
2. *Paluck, John, E, Pittsburgh, 24
3. *Wyant, Fred, B, West Virginia, 36
4. Machinsky, Fran, T, Ohio State [from Philadelphia], 41
Choice to Los Angeles Rams
5. *Lowe, Gary, B, Michigan State, 59
6. Choice to Chicago Cardinals
7. Caraway, Donnie, B, Houston, 83
8. *James, Dick, B, Oregon, 94
9. Rouviere, Francis (Whitey), B, Miami (FL), 107
10. Choice to Pittsburgh
11. Powell, Tom, G, Colgate, 131
12. *Planutis, Gerry, B, Michigan State [from New York Giants], 141
Moreno, Gil, T, UCLA, 142
13. Ward, Jerry, G, Dayton, 155
14. Uebel, Pat, B, Army, 166
15. Choice to Chicago Cardinals
16. Gray, Wells, G, Wisconsin, 190
17. *Day, Eagle, OB, Mississippi, 203
18. Pyburn, Jim, E, Auburn, 214
19. *Lemek, Ray, G, Notre Dame, 227
20. Gonzales, Vince, B, LSU, 238
21. Schnellenberger, Howard, E, Kentucky, 251
22. Nicula, George, T, Notre Dame, 262
23. St. John, Don, B, Xavier, 275
24. Tatum, Johnny, C, Texas, 286
25. Brooks, Franklin, G, Georgia Tech, 299
26. Burnham, Dave, B, Wheaton, 310
27. Flippin, Royce, B, Princeton, 323
28. Hicks, Billy, B, North Alabama, 334
29. Bisceglia, Pat, G, Notre Dame, 347
30. Nystrom, Buck, G, Michigan State, 357

1957

Held November 27, 1956 (Rounds 1-4) and January 31, 1957 (Rounds 5-30)

BALTIMORE 1957
1. *Parker, Jim, G, Ohio State, 8
2. *Shinnick, Don, LB, UCLA, 20
3. *Owens, Luke, T, Kent State, 32
4. *Simpson, Jackie, B, Florida, 44
5. Underwood, Ronnie, B, Arkansas, 54
6. *Pricer, Billy, B, Oklahoma, 65
7. Saage, Reuben, B, Baylor, 79
8. Harmon, Jack, E, Eastern Oregon, 90
9. White, Bob, T, Otterbein, 101
10. Grisham, Joe, E, Austin Peay, 115
11. *Nelson, Andy, QB, Memphis State, 126
12. Simonic, Don, T, Tennessee Tech, 137
13. *Call, Jack, B, Colgate, 151
14. Guido, Joe, B, Youngstown State, 162
15. *Whitley, Hall, C, Texas A&I, 173
16. *Canavino, Joe, HB, Ohio State [from Pittsburgh], 185
Prelock, Ed, T, Kansas, 187
17. Wisniewski, Dan, G, Pittsburgh, 198
18. Villa, Jim, B, Allegheny, 209
19. Froehle, Charlie, G, St. John's (MN), 223
20. *Livingston, Walt, B, Heidelberg, 234
21. Mulholland, Owen, B, Houston, 245
22. Van Atta, Chet, T, Kansas, 259
23. Baird, Connie, E, Hardin-Simmons, 270
24. Hoeft, Harwood, E, South Dakota State, 281
25. Geach, Harlan, T, College of Idaho, 295
26. Unitas, Joe, T, Louisville, 306
27. DeMalon, Len, G, St. Vincent, 317
28. Schnieter, Walt, T, Colorado, 331
29. Rasmussen, Bob, G, Minnesota, 342
30. Bailey, Bob, E, Thiel, 352

CHICAGO BEARS 1957
1. *Leggett, Earl, T, LSU, 13
2. *Swink, Jim, B, TCU, 25
3. *Knox, Ronnie, QB, UCLA, 37
4. *Johnson, Jack, B, Miami, 49
5. *Zucco, Vic, B, Michigan State, 60
6. *Dickinson, Bo, B, Southern Mississippi, 72
7. *DeLuca, Gerry, T, Middle Tennessee State, 84
8. Ward, Al, B, Yale [from Pittsburgh], 91
*Kilcullen, Bob, T, Texas Tech, 96
9. *Brown, Bill, G, Syracuse, 108
10. Murphy, Bill, E, Fresno State, 120
11. Hampton, Roger, B, McNeese State, 132
12. Sorenson, Larry, T, Utah State, 144
13. Williams, Don, B, Texas Tech, 156
14. Schmidt, Bob, B, Memphis State, 168
15. Hosek, Tony, E, West Virginia, 180
16. Heuring, Ed, E, Maryland, 192
17. Heine, Don, E, Murray State, 204
18. Wharton, Al, G, Maryland, 216
19. Hermsen, Lee, B, Marquette, 228
20. *Frazier, Al, B, Florida A&M, 240
21. Janes, Jerry, E, LSU, 252
22. Dalzell, Tom, T, Virginia Tech, 264
23. Peroyea, Don, T, Southeastern Louisiana, 276
24. Lutterback, Ken, B, Evansville, 288
25. *Ryan, Joe, C, Villanova, 300
26. Harris, Gehrig, B, Grambling, 312
27. Brown, Nick, G, Fresno State, 324
28. Emerson, Tom, G, Oklahoma, 336
29. Caraway, Donnie, B, Houston, 348 +
30. Wesley, Sam, B, Oregon State, 359

CHICAGO CARDINALS 1957
1. *Tubbs, Jerry, C, Oklahoma, 10
2. Maentz, Tom, E, Michigan, 22
3. *Hudson, Bill, T, Clemson, 34
4. Choice to San Francisco
5. *Bock, Wayne, T, Illinois, 58
6. Choice to Green Bay
7. Choice to Cleveland thru New York Giants
8. Choice to Los Angeles Rams
9. McCumby, Don, T, Washington, 106
10. *Carouthers, Don, E, Bradley, 118
11. Kraus, Bob, G, Kansas, 130
12. Derrick, Bob, B, Oklahoma, 142
13. Ritt, Ed, T, Montana State, 154
14. Fee, Bob, B, Indiana, 166
15. Livingston, Bill, C, SMU, 178
16. Hurley, Terry, E, Montana, 190
17. Terry, Buddy, T, Houston, 202
18. *Smith, Hal, B, UCLA, 214
19. Barrington, Paul, G, Minnesota, 226
20. Homer, Tom, T, Kansas, 238
21. Kopnisky, Joe, E, West Virginia, 250
22. Sizemore, Don, B, Hardin-Simmons, 262
23. Konicek, Milt, T, Duke, 274
24. Klim, Ron, C, West Virginia, 286
25. Volz, Ray, B, Denison, 298
26. Rohde, Ted, B, Kansas, 310
27. Butorovich, Bob, T, Montana State, 322
28. Husser, Hugh, E, Southeastern Louisiana, 334
29. Corso, Lee, B, Florida State, 346
30. Gibson, Frank, T, Kansas, 357

CLEVELAND 1957
1. *Brown, Jim, B, Syracuse, 6
2. *Plum, Milt, QB, Penn State, 17
3. Walker, George, B, Arkansas, 28
4. Camera, Paul, E, Stanford, 42
5. *Jordan, Henry, T, Virginia [from Green Bay], 52
*Campbell, Milt, B, Indiana, 53
6. *Amstutz, Joe, C, Indiana [from Green Bay], 63
Martin, Harley, T, California, 67
7. *Hickerson, Gene, T, Mississippi, 78 F
Rotunno, Mike, C, Michigan [from Chicago Cardinals thru New York Giants], 82
8. *Gills, Don, C, Rice, 89
9. Comstock, Don, B, Alabama, 103
10. Reinhart, Bob, B, San Jose State, 114
11. Cummings, Bill, T, Ohio State, 125
12. Spitzenberger, Rudy, G, Houston, 139
13. Sansom, Jerry, E, Auburn, 150
14. Feller, Don, B, Kansas, 161
15. Kaiser, Dave, E, Michigan State, 175
16. Bayuk, John (The Beast), B, Colorado, 186
17. Tamburello, Frank, B, Maryland, 197
18. *Torczon, Laverne, G, Nebraska, 211
19. Ploen, Kenny, QB, Iowa, 222
20. Stillwell, Jack, E, North Carolina, 233
21. Juneau, Curry, E, Southern Mississippi, 247
22. Winters, Bob, QB, Utah State, 258
23. Frazer, Jim, T, Hampden-Sydney, 269
24. Napolean, Allen, B, Stanford, 283
25. *Dimitroff, Tom, B, Miami (OH), 294
26. Bliss, Allen, E, Miami (OH), 305
27. Okulovich, Andy, B, Ohio State, 319
28. *Cockrell, Gene, T, Hardin-Simmons, 330
29. Trozzo, Bill, T, West Virginia, 341
30. McKiever, Bob, B, Northwestern, 354

DETROIT 1957
1. *Glass, Bill, G, Baylor, 12
2. *Gordy, John, T, Tennessee, 24
3. *Barr, Terry, B, Michigan, 36
4. *Junker, Steve, E, Xavier, 48
5. Barrow, John, G, Florida, 59
6. Russell, Ken, T, Bowling Green, 71
7. *Leahy, Gerry, E, Colorado, 83
8. *Liddick, Dave, T, George Washington, 95
9. Nikkel, John, E, TCU, 107
10. *Rychlec, Tom, E, American International, 119
11. Osterich, Carl, C, Missouri, 131
12. O'Brien, Charlie, E, Valparaiso, 143
13. West, Bill, B, Eastern Oregon, 155
14. Smith, Phil, B, Jacksonville State, 167
15. Alderton, Gene, C, Maryland, 179
16. Olson, Hillmer, C, Virginia Tech, 191
17. *Kemp, Jack, QB, Occidental, 203
18. Weenig, Jay, G, BYU, 215
19. *Gunderman, Bob, E, Virginia, 227
20. Lazzerino, Alex, T, South Carolina, 239
21. *Meredith, Dudley, T, Lamar, 251
22. Schulte, Tom, E, Eastern Kentucky, 263
23. Gillar, George, B, Texas A&M, 275
24. Scales, Joe, B, Vanderbilt, 287
25. Johnson, Carl, B, South Dakota, 299
26. *Muelhaupt, Ed, G, Iowa State, 311
27. Trafas, Dick, E, St. Thomas (MN), 323
28. Smith, Joe, B, Houston, 335
29. Martin, Hugh, G, Pomona, 347
30. Shill, Mike, T, Furman, 358

GREEN BAY 1957
BONUS CHOICE: *Hornung, Paul, QB, Notre Dame, 1
1. *Kramer, Ron, E, Michigan, 4
2. *Wells, Joel, B, Clemson, 18
3. *Truax, Dalton, T, Tulane, 29
4. *Vereen, Carl, T, Georgia Tech, 41
5. Choice to Cleveland
6. Choice to Cleveland
*Nisby, John, G, Pacific [from Chicago Cardinals], 70
7. Gilliam, Frank, E, Iowa, 76
8. *Belotti, George, C, USC, 87
9. Wineberg, Ken, B, TCU, 100
10. Gustafson, Gary, G, Gustavus Adolphus, 111
11. Roseboro, Jim, B, Ohio State, 124
12. Sullivan, Ed, C, Notre Dame, 135
Bestor, Glenn, B, Wisconsin [from New York Giants], 145
13. Morse, Jim, B, Notre Dame, 148
14. Schoendorf, Rudy, T, Miami (OH), 159
15. Hinton, Pat, G, Louisiana Tech, 172
16. Buckingham, Ed, T, Minnesota, 183
17. Boudreaux, Don, T, Houston, 196
18. Green, Credell, B, Washington, 207
19. *Danjean, Ernie, G, Auburn, 220
20. Oliver, Percy, G, Illinois, 231
21. Mehrer, Chuck, T, Missouri, 244
22. Quillian, Ronnie, QB, Tulane, 255
23. *Symank, John, B, Florida, 268
24. Leyendecker, Charlie, T, SMU, 279
25. Johnson, Jerry, T, St. Norbert, 292
26. Bass, Buddy, E, Duke, 303
27. Booher, Marty, T, Wisconsin, 316
28. Herbold, Dave, G, Minnesota, 327
29. Dare, Howie, B, Maryland, 340

LOS ANGELES RAMS 1957
1. *Arnett, Jon, B, USC, 2
*Shofner, Del, B, Baylor [from New York Giants], 11
2. *Pardee, Jack, B, Texas A&M, 14
3. *Smith, Billy Ray, T, Arkansas, 26
*Strugar, George, T, Washington [from San Francisco], 27
4. Cox, Bobby, QB, Minnesota, 38
*Lundy, Lamar, E, Purdue [from New York Giants], 47
5. *Derby, Dean, B, Washington, 51
Enright, Dick, G, USC [from Washington], 57
6. *Wilkins, Roy, E, Georgia, 64
7. Gray, Ed, T, Oklahoma, 75
8. *Hord, Roy, T, Duke, 88
*Bradshaw, Charlie, T, Baylor [from Chicago Cardinals], 94 F
9. Mitchell, John, C, TCU, 99
10. Spragg, Warren, T, Hillsdale, 112
11. Smith, Don, T, Miami (OH), 123
12. Klochak, Don, B, North Carolina, 136
13. Wolfenden, Bob, B, Virginia Tech, 147
14. Lazzarino, Joe, T, Maryland, 160
15. Hinman, Ed, B, Wichita State, 171
16. Luck, John, T, Georgia, 184
17. Trippett, Dave, T, Hillsdale, 195
18. Cook, Clarence, E, Nebraska, 208
19. Zuhowski, Bill, T, Arizona State, 219
20. *Beams, Byron, T, Notre Dame, 232
21. Pinkston, Pat, E, UCLA, 243
22. *Cothren, Paige, B, Mississippi, 256
23. *Allen, Dalva, T, Houston, 267
24. Rogers, Darryl, B, Fresno State, 280
25. *Orr, Jimmy, B, Georgia, 291
26. Blakely, Dick, B, Minnesota, 304
27. *Osborne, Clancy, E, Arizona State, 315
28. Gudath, Bob, E, Compton J.C., 328
29. Maas, Dean, C, Minnesota, 339
30. Williams, Lee, B, Ohio State, 351

NEW YORK GIANTS 1957
1. Choice to Los Angeles Rams
2. *DeLuca, Sam, T, South Carolina, 23
3. Mendyk, Dennis, B, Michigan State, 35
4. Choice to Los Angeles Rams
5. Wesley, Larry, T, Florida, 61
6. Hobert, Bob, T Minnesota, 73
7. Curtis, Chuck, QB, TCU, 85
8. *Bookman, John, B, Florida, 97
9. *Maynard, Don, B, Texas-El Paso, 109
10. Massa, Gordon, C, Holy Cross, 121
11. Burke, Pat, G, Michigan State, 133
12. Choice to Green Bay
13. Bennett, Ron, E, Mississippi State, 157
14. Hesse, Dean, T, East Texas State, 169
15. Derrick, Julius, E, South Carolina, 181
16. Deutschmann, Lou, B, LSU, 193
17. Stone, Jerry, C, Mississippi, 205
18. Eaton, Jim, E, Florida, 217
19. Morris, Ronnie, B, Tulsa, 229
20. Roberts, Laneair, E, Georgia, 241
21. Smaltz, Joe, B, John Carroll, 253
22. Niemann, Jim, B, Cincinnati, 265
23. Healy, Jack, B, Maryland, 277
24. Hicks, Don, T, Florida, 289
25. Goebel, Jerry, C, Michigan, 301
26. Zalenka, Emmett, G, Tulane, 313
27. Brawley, Carl, T, Sul Ross, 325
28. Gaines, Corky, G, South Carolina, 337
29. Bowman, Mike, G, Princeton, 349
30. Gest, Don, E, Washington State, 360

PHILADELPHIA 1957
1. *Peaks, Clarence, B, Michigan State, 7
2. *Barnes, Billy Ray, B, Wake Forest, 19
3. *McDonald, Tommy, B, Oklahoma, 31
4. *Jurgensen, Sonny, QB, Duke, 43
5. *Harris, Jimmy, QB, Oklahoma, 50
6. Choice to San Francisco
7. *Saidock, Tom, T, Michigan State, 74
8. McElhaney, Hal, B, Duke, 86
9. Davis, Hal, B, Westminster (PA), 98
10. Bruhns, Don, C, Drake, 110
11. Shoaf, Gil, T, Wabash, 122
12. Dike, Buddy, B, TCU, 134
13. *Bobo, Hubert, B, Ohio State, 146
14. Cashman, Jerry, T, Syracuse, 158
15. Moriarity, Mort, E, Texas, 170
16. *Nocera, John, B, Iowa, 182
17. Radakovich, Dan, C, Penn State, 194
18. Kelley, Billy, T, Baylor, 206
19. Harasimowicz, Paul, T, Vermont, 218
20. Thompson, Leroy, B, Butler, 230
21. Brooks, Charley, E, Michigan, 242
22. *Simerson, John, T, Purdue, 254
23. Lovely, Lou, G, Boston U., 266
24. McGill, Dennis, B, Yale, 278
25. Ratliff, Bob, B, West Texas State, 290
26. *Richardson, Alvin, T, Grambling, 302
27. Hall, Frank, B, USC, 314
28. Corona, Clem, G, Michigan, 326
29. Niznik, John, E, Wake Forest, 338
30. Hubbard, Larry, E, Marquette, 350

PITTSBURGH 1957
1. *Dawson, Len, QB, Purdue, 5
2. *Michael, Bill, T, Ohio State, 16
3. *Owens, Don, T, Southern Mississippi, 30
4. Choice to Washington
5. *Richards, Perry, E, Detroit, 55
6. Volkert, George, B, Georgia Tech, 66
7. *Johnson, Curley, B, Houston, 77
8. Choice to Chicago Bears
9. Hutchings, Charley, T, Miami, 102
10. Jelic, Ralph, B, Pittsburgh, 113
11. *Hughes, Dick, B, Tulsa, 127
12. Ellison, Vern, G, Oregon State, 138
13. Underwood, Dwaine, T, Oklahoma State, 149
14. *Crawford, Jim, B, Wyoming, 163
15. Canil, Herman, T, Pittsburgh, 174
16. Choice to Baltimore
17. Salvaterra, Corny, QB, Pittsburgh, 199
18. Bigbee, Len, E, East Texas State, 210
19. *Bennett, Phil, E, Miami (FL), 221
20. Szuehan, John, T, North Carolina State, 235
21. Cichowski, Gene, QB, Indiana, 246
22. Thomas, Aurelius, G, Ohio State, 257
23. Pollock, Bob, T, Pittsburgh, 271
24. Francis, Gary, E, Illinois, 282
25. Hinesley, Jim, E, Michigan State, 293
26. Swann, Bob, T, Vanderbilt, 307
27. Konkoly, Bob, B, Xavier, 318
28. Kolinsky, Frank, T, Tennessee, 329
29. Ramage, Tom, G, Utah State, 343
30. Serier, Don, E, Arkansas State, 353

SAN FRANCISCO 1957
1. *Brodie, John, QB, Stanford, 3
2. *Woodson, Abe, B, Illinois, 15
3. Choice to Los Angeles Rams
4. *Ridlon, Jim, B, Syracuse, 39
*Sandusky, Mike, T, Maryland [from Chicago Cardinals], 46
5. *Rubke, Karl, C, USC, 56
6. Rhodes, Bill, B, Western State (CO) [from Philadelphia], 62
Hunter, Jim, B, Missouri, 68
7. *Dugan, Fred, E, Dayton, 80 F
8. Pitts, Ernie, E, Denver, 92
9. *Brueckman, Charlie, C, Pittsburgh, 104 F
10. Hurst, Jerry, E, Middle Tennessee State, 116 F
11. *Davis, Tommy, B, LSU, 128 F
12. Sington, Fred, T, Alabama, 140 F
13. Mackey, Charley, E, Arizona State, 152
14. *Warzeka, Ron, T, Montana State, 164
15. Kaiser, Earl, B, Houston, 176 F
16. Kristopaitis, Vic, B, Dayton, 188
17. Kuhn, Dave, C, Kentucky, 200
18. Guy, Dick, G, Ohio State, 212
19. *Babb, Gene, B, Austin, 224
20. DeLoatch, Sid, G, Duke, 236
21. Wilcox, Fred, B, Tulane, 248
22. Tripp, Paul, T, Idaho State, 260
23. *Thomas, John, E, Pacific, 272
24. Ladner, John, E, Wake Forest, 284
25. Meyer, Ray, B, Lamar, 296
26. Topping, Tom, T, Duke, 308 F
27. Vicic, Don, B, Ohio State, 320
28. Curtis, Bill, B, TCU, 332
29. Hallbeck, Vern, B, TCU, 344
30. Parks, George, B, Lamar, 355

WASHINGTON 1957
1. *Bosseler, Don, B, Miami (FL), 9
2. *Walton, Joe, E, Pittsburgh, 21
3. *Sutton, Eddie, B, North Carolina, 33
4. *Podoley, Jim, B, Central Michigan [from Pittsburgh], 40
   Scorsone, Vince, G, Pittsburgh, 45
5. Choice to Los Angeles Rams
6. Frankenberger, J.T., T, Kentucky, 69
7. Merz, Wally, T, Colorado, 81
8. Lopata, Paul, E, Yale, 93
9. *Laack, Galen, G, Pacific, 105
10. Dobrino, Don, B, Iowa, 117
11. Foster, Dick, T, Idaho, 129
12. Mitchell, Wade, QB, Georgia Tech, 141
13. Austin, Claude, B, George Washington, 153
14. Rice, George, T, Wofford, 165
15. Bomba, Brad, E, Indiana, 177
16. Brodsky, Joe, B, Florida, 189
17. Brock, Fred, B, Wheaton, 201
18. Sakach, Ed, G, George Washington, 213
19. Bauer, John, B, Villanova, 225
20. Frick, Buddy, E, South Carolina, 237
21. Owen, Sam, B, Georgia Tech, 249
22. *Voytek, Ed, G, Purdue, 261
23. Viola, Al, G, Northwestern, 273
24. Jennings, Bob, C, Furman, 285
25. Sassels, Dick, T, Catawba, 297
26. Rotenberry, Paul, B, Georgia Tech, 309
27. Anderson, Ormand, T, Georgia Tech, 321
28. Martin, Guy, B, Colgate, 333
29. Benedict, George, E, Springfield, 345
30. Luppino, Art, B, Arizona, 356

1958

Held December 2, 1957 (Rounds 1-4) and January 28, 1958 (Rounds 5-30)

BALTIMORE 1958
1. *Lyles, Lenny, B, Louisville, 11
2. *Stransky, Bob, B, Colorado, 24
3. Nicely, Joe, G, West Virginia, 35
4. *Walters, Les, E, Penn State, 48
5. *Brown, Ray, B, Mississippi [from Chicago Cardinals], 50
   Choice to New York Giants
6. Taylor, Bob, E, Vanderbilt, 69
7. *Sample, Johnny, B, Maryland-Eastern Shore [from Pittsburgh], 79
   *Diehl, John, T, Virginia, 82
8. *Peters, Floyd, G, Cal State-San Francisco, 93
9. Bullard, Hal, B, Lenoir-Rhyne, 106
10. Schamber, Ray, E, South Dakota, 117
11. Jordan, Bobby, B, Virginia Military, 130
12. *Addison, Tommy, G, South Carolina, 141
13. *Richardson, Jerry, E, Wofford, 154
14. *Hall, Ken, B, Texas A&M, 165
15. Carney, Les, B, Ohio U., 178
16. *Matsos, Archie, G, Michigan State, 189 F
17. Reese, Jim, B, Minnesota, 202
18. *Lloyd, Dave, C, Georgia, 213 +
19. Murnen, John, G, Bowling Green, 226
20. Forrestal, Tom, QB, Navy, 237
21. Faulk, Jim, B, TCU, 250
22. McKee, Bob, E, Monmouth, 261
23. Parslow, Phil, B, UCLA, 274
24. Sandlin, Bobby, B, Tennessee, 285
25. Rountree, Jim, B, Florida, 298
26. Grimes, Bob, T, Central Michigan, 309
27. Dintiman, George, B, Lock Haven, 322
28. Murphy, Jim, T, East Tennessee State, 333
29. Padgett, Doug, E, Duke, 346
30. Lund, Gary, G, Utah State, 356

CHICAGO BEARS 1958
1. *Howley, Chuck, G, West Virginia, 7
2. *Dewveall, Willard, E, SMU, 18
3. *Cooke, Ed, E, Maryland, 29
   *Healy, Don, T, Maryland [from Cleveland], 37
4. *Barnes, Erich, B, Purdue, 42
5. *Jewett, Bob, E, Michigan State, 53
6. *Douglas, Merrill, B, Utah, 65
7. Bentley, Gene, B, Texas Tech, 77
8. Rutsch, Ed, T, George Washington, 89
9. *Anderson, Ralph, E, Cal State-Los Angeles, 101
10. Lewis, Aubrey, B, Notre Dame, 113
11. Cinelli, Rocco, T, Wisconsin, 125
12. *Morris, Johnny, B, Cal-Santa Barbara, 137
13. Choice to New York Giants
14. Melnik, Bill, T, Army, 161
15. Harryman, Jim, B, Compton J.C., 173
16. Pleger, Ken, T, Capital, 185
17. Eaton, Dick, C, Richmond, 197
18. Dupler, Phil, B, Duke, 209
19. *Roehnelt, Bill, G, Bradley [from Green Bay], 219
    Chancey, Bill, E, West Virginia, 221
20. Rutledge, Les, T, Michigan State, 233
21. *Miller, Bill, T, New Mexico Highlands, 245
22. Carter, Al, B, Tennessee, 257
23. Daw, Ken, B, Sam Houston State, 269
24. Moon, Russ, T, Virginia Tech, 281
25. Barron, Bob, C, St. Norbert, 293
26. Lyles, Bob, B, Memphis State, 305
27. Napolski, Ben, E, Northwestern, 317
28. Main, Wilbur, B, Maryland, 329
29. Hakes, Glen, G, New Mexico, 341
30. Halum, Bobby, B, Middle Tennessee State, 352

CHICAGO CARDINALS 1958
BONUS CHOICE: *Hill, King, QB, Rice, 1
1. *Crow, John David, B Texas A&M, 2
2. McCusker, Jim, T, Pittsburgh, 14
   Oliver, Bobby Jack, T, Rice [from Detroit], 21
3. Cowart, Larry, C, Baylor, 26
4. Choice to Los Angeles Rams
5. Choice to Baltimore
6. *Gordon, Bobby, B, Tennessee, 63
7. *Jelacic, Jon, E, Minnesota, 74
8. Choice to San Francisco
9. Keelan, John, T, Kansas State, 98
10. Robertshaw, Gil, T, Brown, 111
11. *Philpot, Dean, B, Fresno State, 122
12. Hinton, Bill, G, Louisiana Tech, 135
13. *Jackson, Charlie, B, SMU, 146
14. *Schmidt, Bob, T, Minnesota, 159
15. Dunlap, Ray, B, Marshall, 170
16. Patterson, Wade, E, Idaho, 183
17. Starnes, Mac, C, Abilene Christian, 194
18. Cheppo, Mario, E, Louisville, 207
19. *Randle, Ulmo (Sonny), B, Virginia, 218 F
20. Matheny, Jim, C, UCLA, 231
21. Toole, Ray, B, North Texas State, 242
22. Aloisio, Tony, E, Indiana, 255
23. Harbour, John, T, Southeast Missouri State, 266
24. Soesbe, Eric, T, Vanderbilt, 279
25. Riekenberg, J.C., B, Northwestern State (LA), 290
26. Masters, Ray, B, SMU, 303
27. Lewis, Will, B, Tennessee-Chattanooga, 314
28. McGinty, Gale, B, West Texas State, 327
29. Irby, Ken, T, Mississippi State, 338

CLEVELAND 1958
1. *Shofner, Jim, B, TCU, 13
2. Mitchell, Charley, G, Florida, 25
3. *Guy, Melwood (Buzz), T, Duke [from Detroit], 34
   Choice to Chicago Bears
4. *Ninowski, Jim, QB, Michigan State, 49
5. Funston, Farrell, E, Pacific, 60
   *Gibbons, Jim, E, Iowa [from Detroit], 61
6. *Wulff, Jim, B, Michigan State, 72 F
7. *Mitchell, Bobby, B, Illinois, 84
8. Lattimore, Bert, E, Duke, 96
9. *Parrish, Bernie, B, Florida, 108
10. Russavage, Leo, T, North Carolina, 120
11. Bowermaster, Russ, E, Ohio State, 132
12. *Brodhead, Bob, B, Duke, 144
13. *Williams, Hal, B, Miami (OH), 156
14. Miller, Ken, T, TCU, 168
15. Hoelscher, Howard, B, Rice, 180
16. *Cornelison, Jerry, T, SMU, 192
17. Osborne, Roddy, B, Texas A&M, 204
18. Johnson, Alvin, T, Idaho, 216
19. Brown, Ed, G, Arizona, 228
20. Serieka, Ed, B, Xavier, 240
21. Martin, Bill, E, Iowa State, 252
22. *Renn, Bob, B, Florida State, 264
23. Verhey, Dan, T, Washington State, 276
24. O'Connor, Jim, T, Marshall, 288
25. Peters, Bobby, B, Baylor, 300
26. Thompson, Frank, T, Wake Forest, 312
27. Thelen, Dave, B, Miami (OH), 324
28. Boykin, Bill, T, Michigan State, 336
29. Czapla, Frank, T, Missouri, 348
30. Svendsen, Bern, C, Minnesota, 359

DETROIT 1958
1. *Karras, Alex, T, Iowa, 10
2. Choice to Chicago Cardinals
3. Choice to Cleveland
4. *Walker, Wayne, C, Idaho, 45
5. Choice to Cleveland
6. *Lewis, Danny, B, Wisconsin, 73
7. Pfeifer, Ralph, B, Kansas State [from San Francisco], 83
   Outten, Hal, T, Virginia, 85
8. Koepfer, Karl, G, Bowling Green [from Pittsburgh], 92
   *Blazer, Phil, T, North Carolina, 97
9. Loftin, Jim, B, Alabama [from Pittsburgh], 103
   *Paolucci, Ben, T, Wayne State, 109
10. *Schaubach, Elliot, T, William & Mary, 121
11. Chaney, Claude, B, Dayton, 133
12. Boutte, Hal, E, San Jose State, 145
13. Maroney, Barry, B, Cincinnati, 157
14. *Webb, Ken, B, Presbyterian, 169
15. Scheldrup, John, E, Iowa State [from San Francisco], 179
    Mohlman, Jerry, B, Benedictine, 181
16. Ringquist, Gordon, T, Central Michigan, 193
17. Gurasich, Walt, G, USC, 205
18. Austin, Bill, C, Auburn [from Pittsburgh], 212
    Carrier, Larry, B, Kansas, 217
19. Bottos, Dave, B, Murray State, 229
20. Curry, Bill, T, Western Kentucky, 241
21. *Wagstaff, Jim, B, Idaho State, 253
22. Nidiffer, Buddy, E, South Carolina, 265
23. Destino, Frank, B, South Carolina, 277
24. *Whitsell, Dave, B, Indiana, 289
25. Cook, Jim, B, Auburn, 301
26. Bruce, Joe, T, Middle Tennessee State, 313
27. Agers, Don, T, Missouri-Rolla, 325
28. Pitt, Jack, E, South Carolina, 337
29. Herzog, Henry, B, Kentucky, 349
30. Bronson, Tommy, B, Tennessee, 360

GREEN BAY 1958
1. *Currie, Dan, C, Michigan State, 3
2. *Taylor, Jim, B, LSU, 15
3. *Christy, Dick, B, North Carolina State, 27
   *Nitschke, Ray, B, Illinois [from New York Giants], 36
4. *Kramer, Jerry, G, Idaho, 39
5. *Francis, Joe, B, Oregon State, 51
6. *Gray, Ken, T, Howard Payne, 62
7. Mainson, Doug, B, Hillsdale, 75
8. Bill, Mike, C, Syracuse, 86
9. Jarock, Norm, B, St. Norbert, 99
10. Johnson, Carl, T, Illinois, 110
11. Horton, Harry, E, Wichita State, 123
12. Miller, Wayne, E, Baylor, 134
13. Cook, Gene, E, Toledo, 147
14. Hauffe, Harry T, South Dakota, 158
15. Newell, Tom, B, Drake, 171
16. Finley, Arley, T, Georgia Tech, 182
17. Reese, Joe, E, Arkansas Tech, 195
18. Strid, Chuck, G, Syracuse, 206
19. Choice to Chicago Bears
20. DuBose, John, B, Trinity (TX), 230
21. Kershner, Jerry, T, Oregon, 243
22. Maggard, Dick, B, College of Idaho, 254
23. Ashton, Jack, G, South Carolina, 267
24. Jereck, John, T, Detroit, 278
25. Plenty, Larry, B, Boston College, 291
26. Harris, Esker, G, UCLA, 302
27. Habig, Neil, C, Purdue, 315
28. Crowell, Dave, G, Washington State, 326
29. Haynes, Bob, T, Sam Houston State, 339
30. Peters, John, T, Houston, 350

LOS ANGELES RAMS 1958
1. *Michaels, Lou, T, Kentucky [from Washington], 4
   *Phillips, Jim (Red), E, Auburn, 5
2. *Thomas, Clendon, B, Oklahoma, 19
3. *Jones, Jim, B, Washington, 30
4. *Henry, Urban, T, Georgia Tech [from Chicago Cardinals], 38
   *Guzik, John, G, Pittsburgh, 41 F
   Woidzik, Frank, T, Buffalo [from Pittsburgh], 44
5. *Ryan, Frank, QB, Rice [from Pittsburgh], 55
   *Baker, John, T, North Carolina Central, 56
6. *Iglehart, Floyd, B, Wiley, 67
7. *Jobko, Bill, G, Ohio State, 80
8. Marks, Bobby, B, Texas A&M, 91
9. *Selawski, Gene, T, Purdue, 104 F
10. Jacks, Al, QB, Penn State, 115
11. Schweitzer, Gerry, E, Pacific, 128
12. Clairborne, Ron, T, Kansas, 139
13. Kolodziej, Tony, E, Michigan State, 152
14. Mason, Bill, B UCLA, 163
15. Johnston, Dick, C, Southern Mississippi, 176
16. Westemeyer, Clint, E, St. Ambrose, 187
17. Thomas, Bill, C, Clemson, 200
18. Scott, Coy, T, McNeese State, 211
19. *Dorsey, Dick, E, USC, 224
20. Colbert, George, B, Denver, 235
21. Parrish, Ron, B, Linfield, 248
22. Steiger, Bill, E, Washington State, 259
23. Berry, Gary, B, East Texas State, 272
24. Harding, Larry, E, Michigan State, 283
25. Atkins, Bill, T, San Jose State, 296
26. Bridges, Corky, B, Central Washington, 307
27. Vereen, Alonzo, B, Florida A&M, 320
28. Morrow, Gordy, E, Michigan, 331
29. Bourgeois, O'Jay, B, Arizona State, 344
30. Fondren, Walt, B, Texas, 354

NEW YORK GIANTS 1958
1. *King, Phil, B, Vanderbilt, 12
2. *Youso, Frank, T, Minnesota, 23
3. Choice to Green Bay
4. Caraway, Donnie, B, Houston, 47
5. Day, Dick, T, Washington, 57
   Conrad, Bobby Joe, B, Texas A&M [from Baltimore], 58
6. *Lott, Billy, B, Mississippi, 70
7. Vaughn, Vernon, E, Maryland-Eastern Shore, 81
8. *Sutherin, Don, B, Ohio State, 94
9. Kissell, Ron, T, Pittsburgh, 105
10. Drummond, Herb, B, Central State (OH), 118
11. Williams, Sid, B, Wisconsin, 129
12. Hershey, Gerry, T, Syracuse, 142
13. Kurker, George, T, Tufts [from Chicago Bears], 149
    Herndon, Don, B, Tampa, 153
14. *Roberts, C.R., B, USC, 166
15. Sixta, Norm, T, Minnesota, 177
16. West, John, T, Mississippi, 190
17. Harrison, Jack, C, Duke, 201
18. Fusco, Dick, T, Middlebury, 214
19. Jackson, Ernie, B, Syracuse, 225
20. Clements, Joe, B, Texas, 238
21. Hansen, Charlie, C Tulane, 249
22. Wester, Cleve, T, Auburn, 262
23. Hurst, Billy, B, Mississippi, 273
24. Brod, Max, B, Texas Tech, 286
25. Haensel, Wayne, T, South Dakota, 297
26. Burkholder, Dave, G, Minnesota, 310
27. Bronson, Dick, T, USC, 321
28. *Watters, Bob, E, Lincoln (MO), 334
29. Pitney, Lou, C, New Haven State, 345
30. Lumpkin, Billy, E, North Alabama, 357

PHILADELPHIA 1958
1. *Kowalczyk, Walt, B, Michigan State, 6
2. *Jacobs, Proverb, T, California, 17
3. Choice to Washington
4. Rigney, Frank, T, Iowa, 43
5. Mulgado, Bobby, B, Arizona State, 52
6. Kersey, John, T, Duke, 64
7. Mansfield, Len, T, Pittsburg State, 76
8. *Striegel, Bill, LB, Pacific, 88
9. Choice to Pittsburgh
10. *Sapp, Theron, B, Georgia, 112 F
11. Dillard, Mel, B, Purdue, 124
12. Crabtree, Jack, B, Oregon, 136
13. Trimarki, Mickey, QB, West Virginia, 148
14. *Lapham, Bill, C, Iowa, 160
15. Hinos, Stan, T, Mississippi Valley State, 172
16. Meatheringham, Mike, T, Georgia, 184
17. Van Buren, Bill, C, Iowa, 196
18. Burroughs, John, T, Iowa, 208
19. *Sabal, Ron, G, Purdue, 220
20. Lovelace, Kent, B, Mississippi, 232
21. Madden, John, T, Cal Poly-SLO, 244
22. Sherwood, George, E, St. Joseph's (IN), 256
23. Templeton, Billy, E, Mississippi, 268
24. Padgett, Jim, C, Clemson, 280
25. Divine, Hal, T, Memphis State, 292
26. MacLean, Neil, B, Wake Forest, 304
27. Wall, Hindman, E, Auburn, 316
28. *Gossage, Gene, T, Northwestern, 328
29. *McDonald, Don, B, Houston, 340
30. Thompson, Jim, E, Temple, 351

PITTSBURGH 1958
1. Choice to San Francisco
2. *Krutko, Larry, B, West Virginia, 20
3. *Krisher, Bill, G, Oklahoma, 32
4. Choice to Los Angeles Rams
5. Choice to Los Angeles Rams
6. *Lasse, Dick, E, Syracuse, 68
7. Choice to Baltimore, 79
8. Choice to Detroit
9. *Henry, Mike, T, USC [from Philadelphia], 100
   Choice to Detroit
10. *Campbell, Dick, C, Marquette, 116
11. Aldrich, Larry, E, Idaho, 127
12. Reed, Leroy, B, Mississippi, 140
13. Choice to San Francisco
14. Jennings, Doyle, T, Oklahoma, 164
15. Sears, Ed, B, Florida, 175
16. Perkins, John, T, Southern Mississippi, 188
17. *Lewis, Joe, T, Compton J.C., 199
18. Choice to Detroit
19. Keady, Gene, B, Kansas State, 223
20. Johnson, George, T, Wake Forest, 236
21. Jones, Everett, G, Utah, 247
22. Thompson, Bill, E, Duke, 260
23. Trowbridge, Ken, B, North Carolina State, 271
24. Roberts, Norm, E, East Texas State, 284
25. Groce, Bill, B, North Texas State, 295
26. *Evans, Jon, E, Oklahoma State, 308
27. Dellinger, Floyd, B, Texas Tech, 319
28. Akin, Dean, E, Jacksonville State, 332
29. Fuquay, Mert, E, Baylor, 343
30. Scherer, Dick, E, Pittsburgh, 355

SAN FRANCISCO 1958
1. *Pace, Jim, B, Michigan [from Pittsburgh], 8
   *Krueger, Charlie, T, Texas A&M, 9
2. Newman, Bob, B, Washington State, 22 F
3. Hoppe, Bob, B, Auburn, 33
4. Varone, John, B, Miami (FL), 46
5. *Atkins, Billy, B, Auburn, 59
6. *Schmidt, Henry, T, USC, 71
7. Choice to Detroit
8. *Burton, Leon, B, Arizona State [from Chicago Cardinals], 87 F
   Mills, Ron, B, West Texas State, 95
9. Troutman, George, T, Capital, 107
10. Heckman, Vel, T, Florida, 119 F
11. *Wharton, Hogan, T, Houston, 131 F
12. Williams, Pete, T, Lehigh, 143
13. Yore, Jim, B, Indiana [from Pittsburgh], 151
    Dukes, Hal, E, Michigan State, 155
14. Fields, Max, B, Whittier, 167
15. Choice to Detroit
16. *Shirkey, George, T, Stephen F. Austin, 191
17. *Wittenborn, John, T, Southeast Missouri State, 203
18. *Morris, Dennit, B, Oklahoma, 215
19. Mushatt, Ronnie, C, Grambling, 227
20. *Mertens, Jerry, E, Drake, 239
21. Christian, Don, B, Arkansas, 251
22. Hartman, Bruce, T, Luther, 263
23. Fields, Larry, B, Utah, 275
24. *Mackey, Dee, E, East Texas State, 287 F
25. Kaczmarek, Bill, C, Southwest Missouri State, 299
26. Hill, Hillard, E, USC, 311 F
27. Witucki, Bob, E, Texas Tech, 323
28. Warren, Garland, C, North Texas State, 335
29. Hodges, Herman, B, Sam Houston State, 347
30. Stahura, Ted, T, Kansas State, 358 F

WASHINGTON 1958
1. Choice to Los Angeles Rams
2. *Sommer, Mike, B, George Washington, 16
3. Flowers, Stan, B, Georgia Tech, 28
   *Anderson, Bill, B, Tennessee [from Philadelphia], 31
4. Nolan, Dan, QB, Lehigh, 40
5. Van Pelt, Jim, QB, Michigan, 54
6. *Lynch, Dick, B, Notre Dame, 66
7. Bennett, Leon, T, Boston College, 78
8. Payne, Buddy, E, North Carolina, 90
9. *Kuchta, Frank, C, Notre Dame, 102
10. Preston, Ben, T, Auburn, 114
11. *Dess, Darrell, T, North Carolina State, 126
12. Michaels, Eddie, G, Villanova, 138
13. Ford, Ken (Model-T), QB, Hardin-Simmons, 150
14. Farls, Jack, E, Penn State, 162
15. *Davis, Jack, T, Arizona, 174
16. Polzer, Fred, E, Virginia, 186
17. Wilt, Fred, T, Richmond, 198
18. King, Lennie, B, Connecticut, 210
19. Stephenson, Don, C, Georgia Tech, 222

20. Pelham, Lou, E, Florida, 234
21. *Simpson, Jackie, G, Mississippi, 246
22. Sanders, Charley, B, West Texas State, 258
23. Schomburger, Ron, E, Florida State, 270
24. Hanson, Rod, E, Illinois, 282
25. Groom, John, G, TCU, 294
26. Bloomquist, Frank, G, Iowa, 306
27. Gehring, Perry, E, Minnesota, 318
28. Biggs, Joe, G, Hardin-Simmons, 330
29. Coffin, Ed, B, Syracuse, 342
30. Smith, Ted, E, Georgia Tech, 353

1959

Held December 2, 1958 (Rounds 1-4) and January 21, 1959 (Rounds 5-30)

BALTIMORE 1959

1. *Burkett, Jackie, C, Auburn, 12
2. *Sherer, Dave, E, SMU, 24
3. Choice to Detroit
4. *Smith, Zeke, G, Auburn, 48
5. *Churchwell, Don, G, Mississippi, 60
6. *Pyle, Palmer, T, Michigan State, 72
7. *Lewis, Hal, B, Houston, 84
8. Coffey, Tommy Joe, B, West Texas State, 96
9. Brown, Tom, G Minnesota, 108
10. Stewart, Don, E, SMU, 120
11. *Stephens, Tom, B, Syracuse, 132
12. *Wood, Dick, QB, Auburn, 144
13. Smith, Rudi, T, Mississippi, 156
14. Burket, Ferdie, B, Southeastern Oklahoma, 168
15. Foret, Ted, T, Auburn, 180
16. Keller, Morris, T, Clemson, 192
17. Bergan, Leroy, T, South Dakota State, 204
18. Bandy, Opie, T, Tulsa, 216
19. Crain, Milt, C, Mississippi, 228
20. Balonick, Paul, C, North Carolina State, 240
21. Hernstein, John, B, Michigan, 252
22. Leatherman, Lonny, E, TCU, 264
23. Davis, Bob, B, Houston, 276
24. Novagratz, Bob, G, Army, 288
25. Kieffer, Ed, B, Syracuse, 300
26. Lorio, Rene, B, Southern Mississippi, 312
27. Thurman, Terry, B, Rice, 324
28. Long, Fred, B, Iowa, 336
29. McGriff, Perry, E, Florida, 348
30. Weese, Blair, B, West Virginia Tech, 360

CHICAGO BEARS 1959

1. Clark, Don, B, Ohio State, 7
2. *Petitbon, Richie, QB, Tulane, 21
3. *Johnson, Pete, B, Virginia Military, 32
4. Choice to Los Angeles Rams
5. *Adams, John, B, Cal State-Los Angeles, 57
6. *Cole, Fred, G, Maryland, 68
7. Tucker, Jim, E, Tennessee-Chattanooga [from Philadelphia], 75
   Choice to Washington
8. Clark, Dick, B, Baylor, 92
   *Smith, Willie, T, Michigan [from New York Giants], 94
9. *Youmans, Maury, T, Syracuse, 105
10. *Coronado, Bobby, E, Pacific, 116
11. Gray, Ed, T, North Texas State, 129
12. *Rowland, Justin, E, TCU, 140
13. *Jones, Gene, B, Rice, 153
14. *Robb, Joe, T, TCU, 164
15. *LeClerc, Roger, C, Trinity (CT), 177, F
16. Redding, Don, T, North Carolina, 188
17. Neal, Willie, B, Jackson State, 201
18. Asbury, Ken, B, Missouri Valley, 212
19. Plain, Chris, T, Stanford, 225
20. Carcaterra, Tony, E, Elon, 236
21. *Stone, Donnie, B, Arkansas, 249
22. Rubal, Lennie, B, William & Mary, 260
23. Haller, Bob, T, Northwest Missouri State, 273
24. Spain, Bob, T, Baylor, 284
25. Huhn, Tom, C, St. Joseph's (IN), 297
26. Kunde, Bob, T, Capital, 308
27. *Aveni, John, E, Indiana, 321
28. Williams, Bob, B, Notre Dame, 332
29. Southern, Eddie, E, Texas, 345
30. Jackson, Cliff, B, North Carolina Central, 356

CHICAGO CARDINALS 1959

1. *Stacy, Billy, B, Mississippi State, 3
2. *Wilson, Jerry, E, Auburn, 14
3. Butler, Jimmy, B, Vanderbilt, 27
4. *Beck, Ken, T, Texas A&M, 38
5. *Schleicher, Maury, E, Penn State, 50
   *Bates, Ted, T, Oregon State [from Washington], 52
6. *Redmond, Tom, T, Vanderbilt, 63
   *Lewis, Mac, T, Iowa [from Detroit], 64
7. Choice to San Francisco
8. Choice to Cleveland
9. Ferguson, Gary, T, SMU, 98
10. DeCantis, Emil, B, North Carolina, 111
11. Faucette, Floyd, B, Georgia Tech, 122
12. Edmondson, Ted, E, Hardin-Simmons, 135
13. *Lamberti, Pat, E, Richmond, 146
14. Bobo, Bob, T, Texas-El Paso, 159
15. Schroeder, John, E, North Carolina, 170
16. Dingens, John, T, Detroit, 183
17. *Hart, Pete, B, Hardin-Simmons, 194
18. DeDecker, Darrell, T, Illinois, 207
19. Dunn, Billy, B, SMU, 218
20. Murphy, Jerry Lee, T, Ohio State, 231
21. *Memmelaar, Dale, G, Wyoming, 242
22. Shamblin, Glenn, B, West Virginia, 255
23. *Glick, Freddie, B, Colorado State, 266
24. Reed, Jim, G, East Texas State, 279
25. Jeffery, Jim, T, Auburn, 290
26. Chuha, Joe, C, USC, 303
27. Corrigan, Bob, G, Indiana, 314
28. *Fleming, Don, B, Florida, 327
29. O'Connor, Jim, C, Marshall, 338
30. Walton, Rabe, B, North Carolina, 351

CLEVELAND 1959

1. *Kreitling, Rich, E, Illinois, 11
2. *Schafrath, Dick, G, Ohio State, 23
3. *O'Brien, Fran, T, Michigan State, 35
4. Prahst, Gary, E, Michigan [from Green Bay], 37
   *Lloyd, Dave, C, Georgia, 47
5. *Wooten, John, G, Colorado [from Detroit], 53
   *LeBeau, Dick, B, Ohio State, 58
6. *Prestel, Jim, T, Idaho [from New York Giants], 70
   *Denton, Bob, E, Pacific, 71
7. Miller, Gene, T, Rice, 82
8. *Ptacek, Bob, QB, Michigan [from Chicago Cardinals], 87
   Choice to Green Bay, 95
9. Wilson, Kirk, B, UCLA, 106
10. *Zeman, Bob, B, Wisconsin, 119
11. King, Jerry, G, Kent State, 130
12. Palandrani, Frank, T, North Carolina State, 143
13. Reese, Ray, B, Bowling Green, 154
14. *Dubenion, Elbert (Golden Wheels), B, Bluffton, 167
15. Salwocki, Tom, C, Pittsburgh, 178
16. *Caleb, Jamie, B, Grambling, 191
17. Schmittan, Homer, E, Tennessee Tech, 202
18. Hill, Ed, G, Miami (OH), 215
19. Schroeder, Joe, T, Xavier, 226
20. McClain, Al, T, Shaw, 239
21. *Fraser, Jim, G, Wisconsin, 250
22. Wenzel, Joe, E, Lehigh, 263
23. Gardner, Jim, T, Duke, 274
24. Goings, Russ, G, Xavier, 287
25. Spycholski, Ernie, T, Ohio State, 298
26. Floyd, Homer, B, Kansas, 311
27. *Baker, Larry, T, Bowling Green, 322
28. Abadie, Pete, E, Tulane, 335
29. Nietupski, Ron, T, Illinois, 346
30. Ketchie, Carl, B, Washington State, 359

DETROIT 1959

1. *Pietrosante, Nick, B, Notre Dame, 6
2. Horton, Charley, G, Baylor, 18
   *Rabold, Mike, T, Indiana [from Pittsburgh], 19
3. Koes, Ron, C, North Carolina, 30
   Luciano, Ron, T, Syracuse [from Baltimore], 36
4. Brandriff, Art, B, Virginia Military, 42
   *Grottkau, Bob, G, Oregon State [from New York Giants], 46
5. Choice to Cleveland
6. Choice to Chicago Cardinals
   *Guesman, Dick, T, West Virginia [from Pittsburgh], 67
7. *Donnell, Ben, C, Vanderbilt, 77
8. Lenden, Jim, T, Oregon, 88
9. *Smith, Carl, B, Tennessee, 101
10. *Laraway, Jack, B, Purdue, 112
11. *Jacobs, Harry, G, Bradley, 125
12. *Stehouwer, Ron, T, Colorado State, 136
13. *Steffen, Jim, B, UCLA, 149
14. Baldwin, Jim, C, McMurry, 160
15. *Maher, Bruce, B, Detroit, 173
16. *McGee, George, T, Southern, 184
17. *Rudolph, Jack, E, Georgia Tech, 197
18. Holden, Dave, T, Cal State-Los Angeles, 208
19. *Granderson, Rufus, T, Prairie View A&M, 221
20. *McGrew, Dan, C, Purdue, 232
21. Davis, Buddy, B, Richmond, 245
22. *Shields, Lebron, T, Tennessee, 256 F
23. Cesario, Sal, T, Denver, 269
24. Riddle, Fred, B, Pittsburgh, 280
25. *Chamberlain, Dan, E, Cal State-Sacramento, 293
26. Bradley, Jim, B, Lincoln (MO), 304
27. Jerry, Bill, T, South Carolina, 317
28. Matthews, Vince, B, Texas, 328
29. Sime, Dave, E, Duke, 341
30. Stover, Ron, E, Oregon, 352

GREEN BAY 1959

1. *Duncan, Randy, QB, Iowa, 1
2. *Hawkins, Alex, B, South Carolina, 13
3. *Dowler, Boyd, B, Colorado, 25
4. Choice to Cleveland
5. Choice to Washington
   *Cverko, Andy, C, Northwestern [from Pittsburgh], 55
6. Taylor, Willie, C, Florida A&M, 61
7. *Jackson, Bobby, B, Alabama, 73
   Raid, Gary, T, Willamette [from New York Giants], 83
8. Mayfield, Buddy, E, South Carolina, 85
   *Laraba, Bob, B, Texas-El Paso [from Cleveland], 95
9. Dixon, George, B, Bridgeport, 97
10. Tuccio, Sam, T, Southern Mississippi, 109
11. Webb, Bob, B, St. Ambrose, 121
12. Hall, Larry, G, Missouri Valley, 133
13. Hurd, Jim, B, Albion, 145
14. Kerr, Ken, G, Arizona State, 157
15. Teteak, Dick, G, Wisconsin, 169
16. Edgington, Dan, E, Florida, 181
17. Secules, Tom, B, William & Mary, 193
18. Nearents, Dick, T, Eastern Washington, 205
19. *Butler, Bill, B, Tennessee-Chattanooga, 217
20. Sample, Charley, B, Arkansas, 229
21. *Smith, Dave, B, Ripon, 241
22. Anderson, Charlie, E, Drake, 253
23. Lawver, Ben, T, Lewis & Clark, 265
24. *Hergert, Joe, C, Florida, 277
25. Hardee, Leroy, B, Florida A&M, 289
26. Higginbotham, Ken, E, Trinity (TX), 301
27. *Brown, Timmy, B, Ball State, 313
28. Epps, Jerry, G, West Texas State, 325
29. Flara, Jack, B, Pittsburgh, 337
30. Emerich, Dick, T, West Chester, 349

LOS ANGELES RAMS 1959

1. *Bass, Dick, B, Pacific [from Philadelphia], 2
   *Dickson, Paul, T, Baylor, 9
2. *Humphrey, Buddy, QB, Baylor [from Washington], 16
   *Brown, Don, B, Houston, 20
3. *Hickman, Larry, B, Baylor, 31
   *Franckhauser, Tom, E, Purdue [from Pittsburgh], 33
4. *Martin, Blanche, B, Michigan State, 43
   *Tracey, John, E, Texas A&M [from Chicago Bears], 44
   *Reifsnyder, Bob, T, Navy [from Pittsburgh], 45
5. Lands, John, E, Montana State, 56
6. Painter, Dave, C, Tulane, 69
7. *Meador, Eddie, B, Arkansas Tech, 80
8. Conner, Bill, E, Jackson State, 93
9. Cundiff, Larry, T, Michigan State, 104
10. *Goldstein, Alan, E, North Carolina, 117
11. Kelly, Joe, B, New Mexico State, 128
12. *Connelly, Mike, C, Utah State, 141
13. *Witcher, Al, E, Baylor, 152
14. *Davidson, Pete, T, Citadel, 165
15. Kelly, Walt, B, Houston, 176
16. Royal, Ted, C, Duke, 189
17. Wilemon, Dave, T, SMU, 200
18. Van Metre, Dave, E, Colorado College, 213
19. *Shannon, Carver, B, Southern Illinois, 224
20. Coyle, Ross, E, Oklahoma, 237
21. Bergmann, Marv, T, Washington, 248
22. Meglen, Bill, G, Utah State, 261
23. Deiderich, George, G, Vanderbilt, 272
24. Campbell, Tom, B, Indiana, 285
25. Borah, Bob, E, Houston, 296
26. Strumke, Bill, B, Georgia, 309
27. *Kroll, Alex, C, Rutgers, 320 F
28. Johnson, Rafer, B, UCLA, 333
29. Moore, Ernie, E, Alabama State, 344
30. Millich, Don, B, Washington, 357

NEW YORK GIANTS 1959

1. *Grosscup, Lee, QB, Utah, 10
2. *Dial, Buddy, E, Rice, 22
3. *Morrison, Joe, B, Cincinnati, 34
4. Choice to Detroit
5. *Kelly, Ellison, G, Michigan State, 59
6. Choice to Cleveland
7. Choice to Green Bay
8. Choice to Chicago Bears
9. Delveaux, Jack, B, Illinois, 107
10. Pepe, Bob, E, North Carolina State, 118
11. *Sawyer, Bob, B, Wyoming, 131
12. *Flowers, Charlie, B, Mississippi, 142
13. *Kompara, John, T, South Carolina, 155
14. *Ellis, Roger, C, Maine, 166
15. *Bercich, Bob, B, Michigan State, 179
16. *Soltis, Bob, B, Minnesota, 190
17. *Gonsoulin, Austin (Goose), E, Baylor, 203 +
18. Ecuyer, Al, G, Notre Dame, 214
19. *Scott, George, B, Miami (OH), 227
20. Shetler, Jerry, G, Minnesota, 238
21. Swearingen, Fred, G, North Carolina, 251
22. Gibson, Gale, E, Iowa State, 262
23. Kremblas, Frank, QB, Ohio State, 275
24. James, Charley, B, Missouri, 286
25. Reale, Lou, C, Buffalo, 299
26. Doretti, Frank, C, California, 310
27. *Biscaha, Joe, E, Richmond, 323
28. Williams, Dolphus, T, Morgan State, 334
29. Christopher, Henry, E, SMU, 347
30. Sington, Dave, T, Alabama, 358

PHILADELPHIA 1959

1. Choice to Los Angeles Rams
2. *Smith, J.D., T, Rice, 15
3. *Carlton, Wray, B, Duke, 26
4. Grazione, Jim, QB, Villanova, 39
5. *Mumley, Nick, T, Purdue, 51
6. Benecick, Al, G, Syracuse, 62
7. Choice to Chicago Bears
8. *Fowler, Wilmer, B, Northwestern, 86
9. *Johnson, Gene, B, Cincinnati, 99
10. West, Rollie, B, Villanova, 110
11. *Powell, Art, E, San Jose State, 123
12. *Keys, Howard, T, Oklahoma State, 134
13. Stillwagon, Dick, B, Purdue, 147
14. Smith, Jack, T, Clemson, 158
15. Poteete, Jim, C, Mississippi State, 171
16. Paduch, Ken, T, Auburn, 182
17. Craig, Bill, T, Villanova, 195
18. Benson, Jim, B, Georgia Tech, 206
19. *Miller, Alan, B, Boston College, 219
20. Payne, Jim, G, Clemson, 230
21. Salerno, Bob, G, Colorado, 243
22. Bowie, Jim, T, Kentucky, 254
23. Williams, Dick, E, Southern, 267
24. Benn, Gerry, T, Oklahoma State, 278
25. *Jamieson, Dick, QB, Bradley, 291
26. Burks, Jim, T, Virginia Tech, 302
27. Jenkins, Lowell, T, Wisconsin, 315
28. Sexton, Leo, E, Auburn, 326
29. Stolte, John, T, Kansas State, 339
30. Mosca, Angelo, T, Notre Dame, 350

PITTSBURGH 1959

1. Choice to San Francisco
2. Choice to Detroit
3. Choice to Los Angeles Rams
4. Choice to Los Angeles Rams
5. Choice to Green Bay
6. Choice to Detroit
7. Choice to Washington
8. *Barnett, Tom, B, Purdue, 91
9. Davis, Hal, G, Houston, 103
10. *Gunnels, Riley, T, Georgia, 115
11. Curtis, Overton, B, Utah State, 127
12. Pavliska, Bill, B, Baylor, 139
13. *Bohling, Dewey, B, Hardin-Simmons, 151
14. Peppercorn, John, E, Kansas, 163
15. *Brodnax, J.W. (Red), B, LSU, 175
16. Carrico, Bill, G, North Texas State, 187
17. Leeka, Bill, T, UCLA, 199
18. Seinturier, John, T, USC, 211
19. *Kocourek, Dave, E, Wisconsin, 223
20. *Hayes, Rudy, B, Clemson, 235
21. *Green, Johnny, QB, Tennessee-Chattanooga, 247
22. Polk, Burley, T, Hardin-Simmons, 259
23. Davis, Ernye, B, McMurry, 271
24. Farmer, Wayne, T, Purdue, 283
25. Miller, Ron, E, Vanderbilt, 295
26. *Scott, John, T, Ohio State, 307
27. *Tolar, Charley, B, Northwestern State (LA), 319
28. *Hall, Ronnie, B, Missouri Valley, 331
29. Loncar, Dick, T, Notre Dame, 343
30. Fjerstad, Willus, B, Minnesota, 355

SAN FRANCISCO 1959

1. *Baker, Dave, QB, Oklahoma, 5
   *James, Dan, C, Ohio State [from Pittsburgh], 8
2. *Harrison, Bob, C, Oklahoma, 17
3. *Dove, Eddie, B, Colorado, 29
4. *Clark, Monte, T, USC, 41
5. Geremia, Frank, T, Notre Dame, 54
6. Bavaro, Tony, T, Holy Cross, 66
7. *Rogers, Don, T, South Carolina [from Chicago Cardinals], 74
   *Colchico, Dan, E, San Jose State, 78 F
8. Aiken, Lew, E, Vanderbilt, 90
9. *Green, Bobby Joe, B, Florida, 102
10. Nagurski, Bronko, T, Notre Dame, 114
11. Hayes, Jack, B, Trinity (TX), 126
12. Korutz, Bill, C, Dayton, 138
13. *Lopasky, Bill, G, West Virginia, 150
14. *Dukes, Mike, B, Clemson, 162
15. Belland, Joe, B, Arizona State, 174
16. Cook, Bob, B, Idaho State, 186
17. Jurczak, Jerome, C, Benedictine, 198
18. Cowley, Jack, T, Trinity (TX), 210
19. Osborne, Tom, B, Hastings, 222 F
20. Deese, Toby, T, Georgia Tech, 234 F
21. Carr, Luther, B, Washington, 246
22. McQueen, Burnio, E, North Carolina A&T, 258
23. Dollahan, Bruce, T, Illinois, 270
24. Chudy, Craig, E, UCLA, 282
25. Gee, Roy, G, Trinity (TX), 294 F
26. Young, Ed, E, Louisville, 306
27. Semenko, Mel, T, Colorado, 318
28. McCluskey, Mike, B, Washington, 330
29. Bolton, Jack, T, Puget Sound, 342
30. Carter, Bob, T, Denver, 354

WASHINGTON 1959

1. *Allard, Don, QB, Boston College, 4
2. Choice to Los Angeles Rams
3. *Karas, Emil, T, Dayton, 28
4. Wood, Jim, E, Oklahoma State, 40
5. *Wetoska, Bob, T, Notre Dame [from Green Bay], 49
   Choice to Chicago Cardinals
6. McFalls, Jim, T, Virginia Military, 65
7. *Lawrence, Don, T, Notre Dame, 76
   Ogiego, Mitch, QB, Iowa [from Pittsburgh], 79
   Kenney, Jim, E, Boston U. [from Chicago Bears], 81
8. O'Pella, Gene, E, Villanova, 89
9. *Haley, Dick, B, Pittsburgh, 100
10. Toth, Ron, B, Notre Dame, 113
11. Marciniak, Gerry, G, Michigan, 124
12. Wypyszynski, Roger, T, St. Norbert, 137
13. Shoemake, Billy, E, LSU, 148
14. Schwarz, Kurt, G, Maryland, 161
15. Hood, Fred, E, Northeastern Oklahoma, 172
16. Splain, Dick, T, New Haven, 185
17. Healy, Jim, G, Holy Cross, 196
18. *Kapp, Joe, QB, California, 209
19. Lauder, Bobby, B, Auburn, 220
20. Brewer, Billy, B, Mississippi, 233
21. Reight, Mel, B, West Virginia, 244
22. *Gob, Art, E, Pittsburgh, 257
23. Alexander, Clarence, B, Southeastern Louisiana, 268
24. Darrah, George, B, Franklin & Marshall, 281
25. Sargent, Bob, T, Colby, 292
26. *Grabosky, Gene, T, Syracuse, 305
27. Odyniec, Norm, B, Notre Dame, 316
28. Austin, Billy, B, Rutgers, 329
29. Lockwood, Don, G, Tulane, 340
30. *Colclough, Jim, B, Boston College, 353

1960 NFL

Date unknown

The NFL held an early secret draft so that its teams could get a jump on the new AFL teams in signing players, and so that the AFL teams couldn't use the NFL draft list to help them sign quality players. Although the Cardinals played the 1960 season in St. Louis, at the time of the draft the franchise still was located in Chicago.

The expansion Dallas Rangers were admitted to the league too late to participate in the 1960 draft. Owner Clint Murchison did sign two players—Don Meredith of SMU and Don Perkins of New Mexico—to personal services contracts before the draft, however. At the draft, the Chicago Bears drafted Meredith in the third round so that, according to George Halas, no other teams would draft him and cause trouble over the contract. The Colts, apparently unaware of Perkins's status, drafted him in the ninth round. The Rangers retained both players, but had to give up their third-round and ninth-round choices in 1962 to the Bears and Colts, respectively.

On March 13, 1960, the Rangers selected 36 players in an expansion draft. Each of the other 12 NFL teams froze 25 players from its 36-man roster. The Rangers then were given 24 hours to pick three veterans from those unfrozen by each other team. Murchison changed the name of his team from the Rangers to the Cowboys before the start of the 1960 season.

BALTIMORE 1960
1. *Mix, Ron, T, USC, 10
2. *Floyd, Don, T, TCU, 23
 *Terrell, Marvin (Bo), G, Mississippi [from New York Giants] 24
3. *Welch, Jim, HB, SMU, 34
4. *Schwedes, Gerhard, HB, Syracuse, 47
5. Lasater, Marv, B, TCU, 58
6. *Bansavage, Al, G, USC, 71
7. Beabout, Jerry, T, Purdue, 82
8. *Colvin, Jim (Rocky), T-E, Houston, 95
9. Hall, Bob, T, Army [from Philadelphia] 103
 *Perkins, Don, B, New Mexico, 106
10. *Barnes, Ernie, T, N.Car.Central [from Washington] 112
 *Boyd, Bobby, B, Oklahoma, 119
11. Wehking, Bob, C, Florida, 130
12. Bucek, Bill, HB, Rice, 143
13. Nemeth, Jim, C, South Carolina, 154
14. Johannsen, Dale, T, Augustana (SD), 167
15. *Grantham, Larry, E, Mississippi, 178
16. *Boynton, George, B, North Texas State, 191
17. *Beaver, Jim, T, Florida, 202
18. Sheehan, Dan, T, Tennessee-Chattanooga, 215
19. Carpenter, Bill, E, Army, 226
20. Hogue, Bob, T, Shepherd, 239

CHICAGO BEARS 1960
1. *Davis, Roger, G, Syracuse, 7
2. Choice to Washington, 21
3. *Meredith, Don, QB, SMU, 32
4. *Martin, Billy, B, Minnesota, 43
5. *Norman, Dick, QB, Stanford, 57
6. *Kovac, Ed, B, Cincinnati, 68
7. *Bivins, Charley, B, Morris Brown, 79
8. *Manning, Pete, E, Wake Forest, 93
9. *Kirk, Ken, C, Mississippi, 104
10. Choice to Pittsburgh, 115
11. *Fanning, Stan, T, Idaho [from Philadelphia] 128
 *Shaw, Glenn, HB, Kentucky, 129
12. *Budrewicz, Tom, T, Brown, 140
13. Spada, Bob, E, Duke, 151
14. *Sorey, Jim, T, Texas Southern, 165
15. Lashua, Warren, B, Whitworth, 176
16. *Farrington, John (Bo), E, Prairie View A&M, 187
17. Hanna, Jim, E, USC, 201
18. *King, Claude, B, Houston, 212
19. Roberts, Lloyd, T, Georgia, 223
20. *Coia, Angelo, B, USC, 237

CHICAGO CARDINALS 1960
1. *Izo, George, B, Notre Dame, 2
2. *Olson, Harold, T, Clemson, 13
 *McGee, Mike, G, Duke [from Los Angeles Rams] 14
3. *McInnis, Hugh, E, Southern Mississippi, 26
 *Ellzey, Charley, C, Southern Mississippi [from Green Bay] 29
4. *West, Willie, HB, Oregon, 37
 Woods, Silas, E, Marquette [from Los Angeles Rams] 38
5. Burrell, Bill, LB, Illinois, 50
 Phelps, George, B, Cornell College (IA) [from Pittsburgh] 54
 *Mazurek, Ed, T, Xavier [from New York Giants] 60
6. *Lee, Jacky, QB, Cincinnati, 61
7. *Wilson, Larry, HB, Utah, 74
8. *Crow, Wayne, HB, California, 85
9. Hoopes, Dewitt, T, Northwestern, 98
10. *Johnson, Charley, QB, New Mexico State, 109 F
 *Oglesby, Paul, T, UCLA [from Green Bay] 113
11. *Towns, Bobby, HB, Georgia, 122
12. Chapman, Tom, E, Detroit, 133
13. Jones, Vic, HB, Indiana, 146
14. *DeMarco, Bob, T, Dayton, 157 F
15. *Mestnik, Frank, FB, Marquette, 170
16. *Hunt, Jim (Earthquake), T, Prairie View A&M, 181
17. Davis, Joe, T, Citadel, 194
18. Haas, Bob, HB, Missouri, 205
19. Alexander, Herman, T, Findlay, 218
20. *Day, Tom, G, North Carolina A&T, 229

CLEVELAND 1960
1. *Houston, Jim, E, Ohio State, 8
2. *Stephens, Larry, T, Texas [from Pittsburgh] 18
 *Gautt, Prentice, FB, Oklahoma, 19
3. *Fichtner, Ross, B, Purdue, 33
4. *Brewer, Johnny, E, Mississippi [from Green Bay] 41
 *Marshall, Jim, T, Ohio State, 44
5. Jarus, Bob, FB, Purdue [from Green Bay] 53
 Choice to Pittsburgh, 55
6. *Khayat, Bob, G, Mississippi, 69
7. *Anderson, Taz, FB, Georgia Tech, 80
8. *White, Bob, B, Ohio State, 91
9. *Burford, Chris, E, Stanford, 105
10. *Washington, Clyde, HB, Purdue, 116
11. *Franklin, Bobby, B, Mississippi, 127
12. *Mostardo, Rich, B, Kent State, 141
13. Grecni, Rich, C, Ohio U., 152
14. Dumbauld, Bill, T, West Virginia, 163
15. *Watkins, Tom, HB, Iowa State, 177
16. Waldon, Jim, QB, Wyoming, 188
17. Coleman, Lovell, B, Western Michigan, 199
18. Hanlon, Jack, B, Pennsylvania, 213
19. Campbell, Jack, E, Toledo, 224
20. Nelson, Bob, C, Wisconsin, 235

DALLAS RANGERS (Expansion) 1960
*Ane, Charlie, C, USC [from Detroit]
*Barry Al, G, USC [from New York Giants]
*Bielski, Dick, TE, Maryland [from Philadelphia]
*Bolden, Leroy, HB, Michigan State [from Cleveland]
*Borden, Nate, DE, Indiana [from Green Bay]
*Braatz, Tom, LB, Marquette [from Washington]
*Butler, Bill, S, Tennessee-Chattanooga [from Green Bay]
*Clarke, Frank, TE-FL, Colorado [from Cleveland]
*Cronin, Gene, LB, Pacific [from Detroit]
*Cross, Bobby, T, Stephen F. Austin [from Chicago Cardinals]
*DeLucca, Jerry, T, Tennessee [from Philadelphia]
*Doran, Jim, SE, Iowa State [from Detroit]
*Dugan, Fred, SE, Dayton [from San Francisco]
*Dupre, L.G., HB, Baylor [from Baltimore]
*Fisher, Ray, DT, Eastern Illinois [from Pittsburgh]
*Franckhauser, Tom, DB, Purdue [from Los Angeles Rams]
*Fry, Bob, T, Kentucky [from Los Angeles Rams]
*Gonzaga, John, DE [from San Francisco]
*Guy, Buzz, G, Duke [from New York Giants]
*Healy, Don, DT, Maryland [from Chicago Bears]
*Heinrich, Don, QB, Washington [from New York Giants]
*Husmann, Ed, DT, Nebraska [from Chicago Cardinals]
*Johnson, Jack, QB, Miami [from Chicago Bears]
*Johnson, Pete, DB, Virginia Military [from Chicago Bears]
*Krouse, Ray, DT, Maryland [from Baltimore]
*Luna, Bobby, DB, Alabama [from Pittsburgh]
*Mathews, Ray, FL, Clemson [from Pittsburgh]
*McIlhenny, Don, HB, SMU [from Green Bay]
*Modzelewski, Ed, FB, Maryland [from Cleveland]
Nicely, Joe, G, West Virginia [from Washington]
*Nix, Doyle, DB, SMU [from Washington]
*Patera, Jack, LB, Oregon [from Chicago Cardinals]
*Putnam, Duane, G, Pacific [from Los Angeles Rams]
*Sherer, Dave, P, SMU [from Baltimore]
*Striegel, Bill, G, Pacific [from Philadelphia]
*Tubbs, Jerry, LB, Oklahoma [from San Francisco]

DETROIT 1960
1. *Robinson, Johnny, HB, LSU, 3
2. *Rabb, Warren, QB, LSU, 15
3. *Scholtz, Bob, C, Notre Dame, 27
4. Andreotti, Jim, C, Northwestern, 39
 *Brown, Roger, T, Maryland-E.Shore [from Pittsburgh] 42
5. Choice to Green Bay, 51
6. *Cogdill, Gail, E, Washington State, 63
7. *Norton, Jim, E, Idaho, 75
8. Choice to Washington, 87
9. *Messner, Max, T, Cincinnati, 99
10. *Alderman, Grady, T, Detroit, 111
 O'Brien, Jim, T, Boston College [from Philadelphia] 117
11. Aucerman, Ted, E, Indiana, 123
12. *Ross, Dave, E, Cal State-Los Angeles, 135
13. Tunney, Pete, HB, Occidental, 147
14. Glasgow, Jim, T, Jacksonville State, 159
15. *Harper, Darrell, HB, Michigan, 171
16. Rasso, Steve, B, Cincinnati, 183
17. Hudson, Bob, E, Louisiana Tech, 195
18. Walton, Frank, HB, John Carroll, 207
19. *Prebola, Gene, E, Boston U., 219
20. *Look, Dean, QB, Michigan State, 231

GREEN BAY 1960
1. *Moore, Tom, B Vanderbilt, 5
2. *Jeter, Bob, HB, Iowa, 17
3. Choice to Chicago Cardinals, 29
4. Choice to Cleveland, 41
5. *Hackbart, Dale, B, Wisconsin [from Detroit] 51
 Choice to Cleveland
6. Wright, Mike, T, Minnesota, 65
7. Phares, Kirk, G, South Carolina, 77
8. Hitt, Don, C, Oklahoma State, 89
9. Brixius, Frank, T, Minnesota, 101
10. Choice to Chicago Cardinals
11. Ray, Ron, T, Howard Payne, 125
12. Ball, Harry, T, Boston College, 137
13. *Winslow, Paul, B, North Carolina Central, 149
14. *Gilliam, Jon, C, East Texas State, 161
15. Henley, Garney, B, Huron, 173
16. Littlejohn, John, B, Kansas State, 185
17. Gomes, Joe, B, South Carolina, 197
18. Whittington, Royce, T, SW Louisiana, 209
19. Brooks, Rich, E, Purdue, 221
20. Lewis, Gilmer, T, Oklahoma, 233

LOS ANGELES RAMS 1960
1. *Cannon, Billy, B, LSU, 1
2. Choice to Chicago Cardinals
3. *Britt, Charley, QB, Georgia, 25
 *Atkins, Pervis, HB, New Mexico State [from Pittsburgh] 30
4. Choice to Chicago Cardinals
5. *Janerette, Charley, T, Penn State, 49
6. *Stalcup, Jerry, G, Wisconsin, 62
 *Ellersick, Don, E, Washington State [from Pittsburgh] 66
7. Morrison, Ron, T, New Mexico, 73
8. *Dale, Carroll, E, Virginia Tech, 86
9. Luster, Marv, E, UCLA, 97
10. *McClinton, Curtis, HB, Kansas, 110
11. Young, Ken, HB, Valparaiso, 121
12. *Brown, Doug Pat, G, Fresno State, 134 F
13. Jones, James, E, SMU, 145
14. Stanger, Harold, C, North Texas State, 158
15. Rakowski, Harry, C, Citadel, 169
16. Kaczmarek, Don, T, North Dakota, 182
17. Congedo, Emanuel, E, Villanova, 193
18. Gates, Tom, B, San Bernardino Valley Col., 206
19. *Boeke, Jim, T, Heidelberg, 217
20. Shelton, Royce, HB, Stephen F. Austin, 230

NEW YORK GIANTS 1960
1. *Cordileone, Lou, T, Clemson, 12
2. Choice to Baltimore
3. *Leo, Jim, E, Cincinnati, 36
4. Choice to Washington
5. Choice to Chicago Cardinals
6. *Blair, George, B, Mississippi, 72
7. *Yates, Bob, T, Syracuse, 84
8. *Hageman, Fred, C Kansas, 96
9. *Anderson, Bob, HB, Army, 108
10. *Simms, Bob, E, Rutgers, 120
11. Rems, Dale, T, Purdue, 132
12. *Hall, Pete, QB, Marquette, 144
13. Varnado, Jim, FB, Southern, 156
14. *Cline, Doug, FB, Clemson, 168
15. *Beach, Walter, HB, Central Michigan, 180
16. Beck, Bill, T, Gustavus Adolphus, 192
17. Baker, Dave, E, Syracuse, 204
18. Polychronis, Tony, T, Utah, 216
19. Webster, Jim, HB, Marquette, 228
20. Gorman, Bill, T, McMurry, 240

PHILADELPHIA 1960
1. *Burton, Ron, HB, Northwestern, 9
2. *Baughan, Maxie, C, Georgia Tech, 20
3. *Merz, Curt, E, Iowa, 31
4. *Dean, Ted, B, Wichita State [from Washington] 40
 Cummings, Jack, QB, North Carolina, 45
5. *Norton, Don, E, Iowa, 56
6. Wilson, Emmett, T, Georgia Tech, 67
7. Wilkins, John, T, USC, 81
8. *Lee, Monte, E, Texas, 92
9. Choice to Baltimore
10. Choice to Detroit
11. Choice to Chicago Bears
12. Grosz, Dave, QB, Oregon, 139
13. *Graham, Dave, E, Virginia, 153
14. Petersen, Ray, B, West Virginia, 164
15. *Wilcox, John, T, Oregon, 175
16. Lancaster, Larry, T, Georgia, 189
17. Graney, Mike, E, Notre Dame, 200
18. Turner, Emory, G, Rurdue, 211
19. Hain, Bob, T, Iowa, 225
20. *Armstrong, Ramon, G, TCU, 236

PITTSBURGH 1960
1. *Spikes, Jack, FB, TCU, 6
2. Choice to Cleveland
3. Choice to Los Angeles Rams
4. Choice to Detroit
5. Choice to Chicago Cardinals
 *Haynes, Abner, B, North Texas State [from Cleveland] 55
6. Choice to Los Angeles Rams
7. Wilson, Leonard, B, Purdue [from Washington] 76
 Dennis, Lonnie, G, BYU, 78
8. *Lanphear, Dan, T, Wisconsin, 90
9. Harris, Marshall, HG, TCU, 102
10. *Kapele, John, T, BYU, 114
 Martin, Arvie, C, TCU [from Chicago Bears] 115
11. Choice to San Francisco
12. Butler Earl, T, North Carolina, 138
13. *Womack, Joe, HB, Cal State-Los Angeles, 150
14. *Keyes, Brady, HB, Colorado State, 162
15. Essenmacker, Larry, T, Alma, 174
16. *Ames, Dave, B, Richmond, 186
17. Chamberlain, Dale, FB, Miami (OH), 198
18. Lee, Charley, T, Iowa, 210
19. Turley, Howard, E, Louisville, 222
20. Hershberger, George, T, Wichita State, 234

SAN FRANCISCO 1960
1. *Stickles, Monty, E, Notre Dame, 11
2. *Magac, Mike, G, Missouri [from Washington] 16
 *Kammerer, Carl, G, Pacific, 22 F
3. *Breedlove, Rod, G, Maryland, 35
4. *Norton, Ray, HB, San Jose State, 46
5. *Rohde, Len, T, Utah State, 59
6. *Murchison, Ola Lee, E, Pacific, 70
7. *Waters, Bobby, QB, Presbyterian, 83
8. *Mathis, Bill, HB, Clemson [from Washington] 88
 Fugler, Max, C, LSU, 94
9. Wasden, Bobby, E, Auburn, 107
10. *Branch, Mel, E, LSU, 118
11. Pitts, Ed, T, South Carolina [from Pittsburgh] 126
 Hansen, Ernie, C, Northern Arizona, 131 F
12. Williams, Jim, G, North Carolina, 142
13. Hinshaw, Dean, T, Stanford, 155 F
14. Campbell, Gary, B, Whittier, 166
15. *Dowdle, Mike, B, Texas, 179
16. Heinke, Jim, T, Wisconsin, 190
17. *Gonsoulin, Austin (Goose), B, Baylor, 203
18. Robinson, Carl, T, South Carolina State, 214
19. Pate, Bobby, B, Presbyterian, 227
20. Woodward, Jim, T, Lamar, 238

WASHINGTON 1960
1. *Lucas, Richie, QB, Penn State, 4
2. Choice to San Francisco
 *Homer, Sam, HB, Virginia Military [from Chicago Bears] 21
3. *Stynchula, Andy, T, Penn State, 28
4. Choice to Philadelphia
 *Promuto, Vince, G, Holy Cross [from New York Giants] 48
5. *Stallings, Don, T, North Carolina, 52
6. Hudson, Dave, E, Florida, 64
7. Choice to Pittsburgh
8. Kohlhaas, Earl, G, Penn State [from Detroit] 87
 Choice to San Francisco
9. Bumgarner, Dwight, E, Duke, 100
10. Choice to Baltimore
11. *Eifrid, Jim, C, Colorado State, 124
12. *Crotty, Jim, HB, Notre Dame, 136
13. Herron, Bill, E, Georgia, 148
14. *Milstead, Charley, B, Texas A&M, 160
15. *Darre, Bernie, G, Tulane, 172
16. *Kulbacki, Joe, B, Purdue, 184
17. Roland, Billy, G, Georgia, 196
18. Lawrence, John, G, North Carolina State, 208
19. Maltony, Ron, G, Purdue, 220
20. Wolf, Jimmy, HB, Panhandle State, 232

1960 AFL

Held November 22, 1959 (First selections) and December 2, 19S9 (Second selections)

When the first AFL draft was held, no front offices or coaching staffs were yet complete. No more than half of the eight teams even had any scouts or personnel staff. In order to be equitable to all eight teams, all information on college players was pooled. The four people responsible for the information used in the draft were Don Rossi, the general manager of the Dallas Texans; Dean Griffing, the general manager of the Denver Broncos; John Breen, the director of player personnel for the Houston Oilers; and Frank Leahy, the general manager of the Los Angeles Chargers.

To begin the draft, each team received one territorial, or bonus, pick. The purpose of the selection was to gain the rights to a player who not only would be one of the main building blocks of the team, but who, being a star of regional or national scope, would help sell tickets and assure the financial success of the franchise. The territorial picks were not made in any order. They were agreed upon unanimously by the clubs. The territorial picks were as follows: Boston, Gerhard Schwedes, HB, Syracuse; Buffalo, Richie Lucas, QB, Penn State; Dallas Texans, Don Meredith, QB, SMU; Denver, Roger LeClerc, C, Trinity (CT); Houston, Billy Cannon, HB, LSU; Los Angeles Chargers, Monty Stickles, E, Notre Dame; Minneapolis, Dale Hackbart, QB, Wisconsin; and New York Titans, George Izo, QB, Notre Dame.

After the territorial picks, a consensus was reached by Rossi, Griffing, Breen, and Leahy as to who were the best eight players in the country at each offensive position. (Due to limited substitution rules at the time, college football players generally were listed only by their offensive positions.) The names of each position were put into a box and drawn for by each club. If a club already had a player at a certain position due to its territorial pick, it was left out of the first selection for that position. For example, the first time ends were selected, only seven names instead of eight were placed in the box and drawn, and Los Angeles didn't receive a choice. When each team had completed a full offensive team, the process was repeated, with the players deemed the ninth through sixteenth best in the country. This selection process continued through 33 selections per team, or three full offensive platoons.

Shortly after the draft was completed, the teams decided there was a need for a wider base from which to attempt to sign players. Two weeks after the first selections, a second draft was held. The second draft consisted of 20 rounds and was conducted under the same guidelines. Occasionally the lists of players at each position didn't work out to be evenly divisible by eight. Therefore, although each team received 20 picks, some received a player more at one position than did others.

Since there was no real order of priority for the players selected, they were listed in alphabetical order under the headings "First selections" and "Second selections." Since the players selected simply were rated as the top collegians in the country, some of them were juniors, and were selected as future picks. One, Doug Pat Brown of Fresno State, was a sophomore, but his selection by the Dallas Texans was upheld despite not following traditional guidelines of future picks.

Shortly after the draft, Minneapolis was offered a franchise in the NFL, and, on January 27, 1960, withdrew from the AFL. Three days later, Oakland was admitted as the eighth AFL team, and the new club inherited Minneapolis' draft list. In the interim period, however, AFL clubs had signed a number of players drafted by Minneapolis. In order to stock the Oakland franchise with players, the AFL held an allocation draft. The other seven teams froze 11 players, after which Oakland chose a varying number of players from each unfrozen list, totaling 24 players.

BOSTON 1960
(First Selections)
Allen, Buddy, HB, Utah State
*Burton, Ron, HB, Northwestern
Chamberlain, Dale, FB, Miami (OH)
Christopher, Henry, E, SMU
*Colchicco, Dan, E, San Jose State
Cummings, Jack, QB, North Carolina State
Davis, James, C, Oklahoma
Fazio, Serafino (Foge), C, Pittsburgh
Fugler, Max, C, LSU
Gardner, Tim, T, Duke
Goodyear, James, T-G, Wake Forest
Harris, Dave, HB, Kansas
Henderson, Al, T, Colorado State
Hickman, Jim, T-G, Penn State
Kranz, Bob, FB, Penn State
Kulbacki, Joe, HB, Purdue
*Mackey Dee, E, East Texas State
Manley, Leon, G, West Texas State
Manning, Cliff, T-G, Hardin-Simmons
*Manning, Pete, E, Wake Forest
Mazurek, Ed, T, Xavier
Meglen, Bill, G, Utah State
*Mestnik, Frank, FB, Marquette
*Mix, Ron, T, USC
Nikolai, Irv, E, Stanford
*Prestel, Jim, T, Idaho
Salerno, Bob, G, Colorado
*Schwedes, Gerhard, HB, Syracuse
Soergel, Dick, QB, Oklahoma State
Wagner, Larry, T, Vanderbilt
*White, Harvey, QB, Clemson
Wilemon, Tirey, HB, SMU
Wisener, Gary E, Baylor
(Second Selections)
Ames, Dave, HB, Richmond
*Boeke, Jim, T-G, Heidelberg
Brewer, Billy, QB, Mississippi
Congedo, Emanuel, T-G, Villanova
Dye, Pat, T-G, Georgia
*Farrington, John (Bo), E, Prairie View A&M
Grecni, Rich, C, Ohio U., F
Jones, Bud, E, SMU
Kacmarek, Don, T-G, North Dakota
Lawrence, John, T-G, North Carolina State
Maltony, Ron, T-G, Purdue, F
Pate, Bobby, HB, Presbyterian
*Rudolph, Jack, LB, Georgia Tech
Sally, Frank, T-G, California
Spada, Bob, E, Duke, F
Tunney, Pete, HB, Occidental
Webster, Jim, HB, Marquette
*Wilcox, John, T-G, Oregon

BUFFALO 1960
(First selections)
Arnold, Birtho, T-G, Ohio State
*Bivins, Charlie, HB, Morris Brown
Black, Don, E, New Mexico
Burrell, Bill, G, Illinois
Choquette, Paul, FB, Brown
Connelly, Mike, C, Utah State
Conroy, Jim, FB, USC
Coogan, Bob, T-G, Utah
*Cordileone, Lou, T, Clemson
*Dean, Ted, FB, Wichita State
Evans, Willie, HB, Buffalo
*Fichtner, Ross, QB, Purdue
Gilliam, Jon, C, East Texas State
Goldstein, Al, E, North Carolina
*Houston, Jim, E, Ohio State
Jauch, Ray, HB, Iowa
*Khayat, Bob, T, Mississippi
Kirk, Ken, C, Mississippi
*Leo, Jim, E, Cincinnati
*Lucas, Richie, QB, Penn State
McMurtry Chuck, T-G, Whittier
Meyer, Bubba, E, TCU
Miller, Ron, E, Vanderbilt
Oliver, Gale, T, Texas A&M
Olson, Harold, T, Clemson
Peterson, Ray, HB, West Virginia
*Promuto, Vince, G, Holy Cross
Ramirez, Rene, HB, Texas
*Rohde, Len, T, Utah State
Schaffer, Joe, T, Tennessee
Schneider, Wayne, HB, Colorado State
Toncic, Ivan, QB, Pittsburgh
*Wilson, Larry, HB, Utah
(Second Selections)
Bumgarner, Dwight, E, Duke, F
*Day, Tom, T-G, North Carolina A&T
Dreymala, Babe, T-G, Texas
Gomes, Joe, HB, South Carolina
Graney, Mike, E, Notre Dame
*Hall, Pete, QB, Marquette
Hanna, Jim, E, USC
Hanson, Ernie, C, Northern Arizona, F
Harper, Darrell, HB, Michigan, F
Littlejohn, John, HB, Kansas State
Luster, Marv, E, UCLA, F
Nichols, Dwight, HB, Iowa State
Priddy, Merlin, HB, TCU
Rakowski, Harry, HB, Citadel, F
Rems, Dale, T-G, Purdue, F
Robison, Carl, T-G, South Carolina State
Sliva, Bob, T-G, Stephen F. Austin
Sorey, James, T-G, Texas Southern
Thompson, Jerry, T-G, Oklahoma
Whittington, Royce, T-G, Southeastern Louisiana, F

DALLAS TEXANS 1960
(First Selections)
Atcheson, Jack, E, Western Illinois
Boone, George, T, Kentucky
*Burford, Chris, E, Stanford
Butler, Earl Ray, T, North Carolina
*Cogdill, Gail, E, Washington State
Crotty, Jim, HB, Notre Dame
Ferguson, Gary T, SMU
Glynn, Tom, C, Boston College, F
*Gossage, Gene T, Northwestern
Heineke, Jim, T, Wisconsin
Jerry, William, T-G, South Carolina
*Kapele, John, T, BYU
Kelley, Louis, FB, New Mexico State
Lewis, Gilmer, T-G, Oklahoma
Malmberg, John, T-G, Knox
Martin, Arvie, C, TCU, F
*Meredith, Don, QB, SMU
*Moore, Tom, HB, Vanderbilt
Murchison Ola Lee, E, Pacific
Nelson, Bob, C, Wisconsin
*Norton, Jim, E, Idaho
*Rabb, Warren, QB, LSU
Ringwood, Howard, HB, BYU
Robinson, Johnny, HB, LSU
Saunders, John, FB, South Carolina
Shaw, Glenn, FB, Kentucky
Speer, Gordon, HB, Rice
Stone, Jack, G, Oregon
Terrell, Marvin (Bo), G, Mississippi
Turner, Emery, G, Purdue
Vader, Joe, E, Kansas State
Zaruba, Carroll, HB, Nebraska
(Second Selections)
*Alderman, Grady, T-G, Detroit
Alexander, Herman, T-G, Findlay
*Anderson, Taz, HB, Georgia Tech, F
Beaver, Jim, T-G, Florida
Beck, Bill, T-G, Gustavus Adolphus, F
Brown, Doug Pat, T-G, Fresno State, F
Campbell, Gary, HB, Whittier
Cole, Vernon, QB, North Texas State
Deese, Toby, T-G, Georgia Tech
Dumbald, Carl, T-G, West Virginia
Elizey, Charley, C, Southern Mississippi
Gates, Tom, HB, San Bernardino Valley College
*Gonsoulin, Austin (Goose), HB, Baylor
Holden, Clark, HB, USC
Hoopes, Dewitt, T-G, Northwestern
Leebern, Don, T-G, Georgia
Thompson, Bill, C, Georgia
Tranum, Billy, E, Arkansas
Vickers, Jim, E, Georgia
Ward, Larry, E, Lamar
*Winslow, Paul, HB, North Carolina Central

DENVER 1960
(First Selections)
Ball, Harry, T, Boston College
*Britt, Charley, QB, Georgia
Canary, Dave, E, Cincinnati
Candro, Paul, HB, Boston U.
Carrico, Bill, G, North Texas State
Cundiff, Larry, C, Michigan State
Darre, Bernard, T, Tulane, F
*Davis, Roger, T, Syracuse
Dennis, Lonnie, G, BYU
Dingens, John, T-G, Detroit
Doke, Maurice, G, Texas
*Dowdle, Mike, FB, Texas
*Hawkins, Wayne, T, Pacific
Huber, Gary, C, Miami (OH)
Hudson, Dave, E, Florida
King, Claude, HB, Houston
Klochak, Don, FB, North Carolina
*LeClerc, Roger, C, Trinity (CT)
*Look, Dean, QB, Michigan State
*Mathis, Bill, HB, Clemson
McNeece, Ken, T-G, San Jose State
Monroe, James, QB, Arkansas
*Norton, Ray, HB, San Jose State
Rosbaugh, Bob, HB, Miami (FL)
Semenko, Mel, E, Colorado, F
*Shields, Lebron, T, Tennessee
*Spikes, Jack, FB, TCU
Turley, Howard, E, Louisville
Walden, Jim, QB, Wyoming
*West, Willie, HB, Oregon
Willener, John, G, Oregon
Yates, Bob, T, Syracuse
Young, Ken, E, Valparaiso
Zimpfer, Bob, T-G, Bowling Green
(Second Selections)
*Branch, Mel, T-G, LSU
Cain, Ronnie, E, Kentucky
Campbell, Jack, E, Toledo, F
Chapman, Tom, E, Detroit
Coleman, LeVelle, HB, Western Michigan
*Colvin, Jim (Rocky), T-G, Houston
Foret, Teddy, T-G, Auburn
*Green, Bobby Joe, HB, Florida
Hanlon, Jack, HB, Penn State
Hershberger, George, T-G, Wichita State
*Horner, Sam, HB, Virginia Military
Hudson, Bob, E, Lamar
Jones, Vic, HB, Indiana
Luplow, Billy, T-G, Arkansas
Phelps, George, HB, Cornell College (IA)
Roberts, Tom, T-G, Georgia Tech
Stenger, Sam, C, Denver
Treadway, Olin, QB, Iowa
Wilkins, John, T-G, USC, F
Wilson, Emmet, T-G, Georgia Tech

HOUSTON 1960
(First Selections)
Arena, Pete, G, Northwestern
*Bass, Dick, HB, Pacific
Bohler, Bill, E-T, State Ambrose
Cadwell, Larry, G-T, Louisville
*Cannon, Billy, HB, LSU
*Cline, Doug, FB, Clemson
Coleman, DeJustice, HB, Illinois
Crandall, Bob, HB, New Mexico
Drinnon, Cleatus, C, Hardin-Simmons
Gremer, John, G, Illinois
Herring, George, G-T, North Texas State
Hitt, Don, C, Oklahoma State
Johnson, Steve, QB, Pepperdine
Lands, John, E, Montana
*Lee, Jacky, QB, Cincinnati
Maher, Bruce, HB, Detroit
Mattson, Don, T, USC
*McGee, Mike, G, Duke
McInnis, Hugh, E, Southern Mississippi
*Messner, Max, T, Cincinnati
Mulholland, George, E, New Mexico State
O'Steen, Gary, HB, Alabama
Prebola, Gene, E, Boston U.
*Pyle, Palmer, T, Michigan State
Roach, William, T, TCU
*Simms, Bob, E, Rutgers
Snowden, Philip, QB, Missouri
Underwood, Don, G-T, McNeese State
Whetstone, Duane, FB, George Washington
*White, Bob, FB, Ohio State
*Youmans, Maury, T, Syracuse
(Second Selections)
Branch, Clair, HB, Texas
Chamberlain, Dave, HB, Miami (OH)
Cochran, Don, T-G, Alabama
*Fanning, Stan, T-G, Idaho
Glasgow, Jim, T-G, Jackson State
*Graham, Dave, E, Virginia
Haas, Bob, HB, Missouri
Hughes, Lowell, QB, Kent State
Johannson, Dale, T-G, Augustana (SD), F
*Marshall, Jim, T-G, Ohio State
Morrison, Ron, T-G, New Mexico
Muennink, Jerry, C, Texas
*Oglesby, Paul, T-G, UCLA
Peppercorn, John, E, Kansas
Peterson, Bob, C, Oregon
*Talamini, Bob, T-G, Kentucky
Towns, Bob, E, Georgia
Wasden, Bob, E, Auburn
*Welch, Jim, HB, SMU
Wolff, Jim, HB, Panhandle State

LOS ANGELES CHARGERS 1960
(First Selections)
Aucreman, Ted, E, Indiana
Bercich, Bob, HB, Michigan State
Berlinger, Barney, E, Penn
Boone, Charley, C, Richmond
*Boyd, Bobby, QB, Oklahoma
Bradfute, Byron, T-G, Southern Mississippi
*Breedlove, Rod, G, Maryland
Budrewicz, Tom, T, Brown
Cameron, Jim, C, East Texas State
Crouthamel, Jake, HB, Dartmouth
Davidson, Pete, T-G, Citadel
Faucette, Floyd, HB, Georgia Tech
*Franklin, Bobby, QB, Mississippi
*Flowers, Charley, FB, Mississippi
Horn, Don, FB, Iowa
*Jeter, Bob, HB, Iowa
Lindner, Bill, T, Pittsburgh
Locklin, Billy Ray, T, New Mexico State
Lopasky, Bill, G, West Virginia
*Maguire, Paul, E, Citadel
*McDaniel, Edward (Wahoo), E, Oklahoma
*Milstead, Charley, QB, Texas A&M
Pitts, Ed, T, South Carolina
Serieka, Ed, FB, Xavier
*Schlotz, Bob, C, Notre Dame
Sloan, Russ, E, Missouri
Stehouwer, Ron, T, Colorado
Stewart, Wayne, G, Citadel
*Stickles, Monty, E, Notre Dame
Stolte, John, T, Kansas City
Wilson, Leonard, HB, Purdue
*Zeman, Bob, HB, Wisconsin
(Second Selections)
Beabout, Jerry, T-G, Purdue, F
Blair, George, HB, Mississippi, F
Brixius, Frank, T-G, Minnesota, F
Davis, Joe, T-G, Citadel
*DeMarco, Bob, T-G, Dayton, F
Hain, Bob, T-G, Iowa
Janssen, Chuck, T-G, Tulsa
*Kelley, Gordon, E, Georgia
Lancaster, Larry, G-T, Georgia
Lasater, Marv, HB, TCU
Lashua, Warren, E, Whitworth
McGriff, Perry, E, Florida
Phares, Kirk, T-G, South Carolina
Rawson, Lamar, HB, Auburn
Ray, Ronald, T-G, Howard Payne
Talkington, Ken, QB, Texas Tech
Talley, John, QB, Northwestern
*Waters, Bobby, HB, Presbyterian
Wehking, Bob, C, Florida
Womack, Larry, HB, Colorado State

MINNEAPOLIS 1960
(First Selections)
Andreotti, Jim, C, Northwestern
*Baughan, Maxie, C, Georgia Tech
Blanch, George, HB, Texas
Boyette, Cloyd, T-G, Texas Southern
Boykin, Willie, T, Michigan State
Cavelli, Carmen, E, Richmond
Chastain, Jim, T-G, Michigan State

Curci, Fran, QB, Miami (FL)
*Carroll, Dale, E, Virginia Tech
Daniels, Purcell, FB, Pepperdine
Deskin, Don, T, Michigan
Dumbroski, Leon, T-G, Delaware
Fitch, Ken, T, Kansas
*Hackbart, Dale, QB, Wisconsin
*Haynes, Abner, HB, North Texas State
Hogan, Vin, HB, Boston College
Jarus, Bob, HB, Purdue
Kohlhaas, Earl, G, Penn State
Lackey, Bobby, QB, Texas
MacLean, Neil, FB, Wake Forest
Muff, Larry, E, Benedictine
*Norton, Don, E, Iowa
O'Brien, Jim, T, Boston College
*Otto, Jim, C, Miami (FL)
Pollard, Chuck, E, Rice
Roland, Billy, G, Georgia
Smith, Ray, FB, UCLA
Smith, Wade, HB, North Carolina
Stalcup, Jerry, G, Wisconsin
*Wilcox, John, T, Oregon
Witcher, Al, E, Baylor
Woods, Silas, HB, Marquette
Wright, Mike, T, Minnesota
(Second Selections)
Alexander, C.J., HB, Southeastern
*Atkins, Pervis, HB, New Mexico State, F
*Bansavage, Al, T-G, USC
*Beach, Walter, HB, Central Michigan
*Brewer, Johnny, E, Mississippi, F
Edington, Don, E, Florida
Evans, Howard, C, Houston
Hageman, Fred, C, Kansas, F
Herron, Bill, E, Georgia
Hogue, Bob, T-G, Shepherd, F
Lambert, Gerald, T-G, Texas A&I
McCord, Sam, QB, East Texas State
*Mostardo, Rich, HB, Kent State
Parker, Bob, T-G, East Texas State
Polychronis, Tony, T-G, Utah, F
Sheehan, Dan, T-G, Tennessee-Chattanooga, F
Turley, Howard, E, Louisville
Williams, Jim, T-G, North Carolina
Woodward, Jim, T-G, Lamar

NEW YORK TITANS 1960
(First Selections)
Akin, Lewis, E, Vanderbilt
Allen, Chuck, T, Alabama
Bucek, Bill, HB, Rice
*Burkett, Jackie, C, Auburn
*Coia, Angelo, HB, USC
Eifrid, Jim, C, Colorado State
Ellersick, Don, E, Washington State
*Floyd, Don, T, ICU
*Gautt, Prentice, FB, Oklahoma
Genyk, George, G, Michigan
*Grantham, Larry, E, Mississippi
Graybeal, Joe, C, Eastern Kentucky
Groner, Jack, QB, Washington & Lee
*Izo, George, QB, Notre Dame
Kaohelaulii, Ed, T, Oregon State
Kovac, Ed, HB, Cincinnati
*Magac, Mike, T, Missouri
Martin, Blanche, FB, Michigan State
*Merz, Curt, E, Iowa
Meyer, Eddie, T-G, West Texas State
Miller, Gene, T-G, Rice
Mooty, Jim, HB, Arkansas
Morin, Mike, HB, Knox
Patella, Nick, G, Wake Forest
*Perkins, Don, HB, New Mexico
Ross, David, E, Cal State-Los Angeles
Smith, Roger (Zeke), G, Auburn
Stallings, Don, T, North Carolina State
*Stephens, Larry, T-G, Texas
State Clair, Jim, QB, Cal-Santa Barbara
Stinnette, Jim, FB, Oregon State
Wilemon, David, T, SMU
(Second Selections)
Abadie, Pete, E, Tulane
Armstrong, Ramon, T-G, TCU
Baker, Dave, E, Syracuse, F
Brooks, Richard, E, Purdue
*Brown, Roger, T-G, Maryland-Eastern Shore
Budrewicz, Tom, T-G, Brown
Colburn, Bob, QB, Bowling Green
Essenmacker, Larry, T-G, Alma
Gorman, Bill, T-G, McMurry
Hall, Bob, T-G, Kent State, F
Harris, Marshall, HB, TCU
Henley, Garney, HB, Huron
Hunt, Jim, T-G, Purdue
Leboeuf, Gordon, HB, Texas A&M
Nemeth, Jim, C, South Carolina, F
Rasso, Steve, HB, Cincinnati
Shelton, Royce, HB, Stephen F. Austin, F
Sknoeckni, Gary, E, Syracuse
*Stynchula, Andy, T-G, Penn State
Walton, Frank, HB, John Carroll

OAKLAND (Allocation) 1960
Armstrong, Ramon, T, TCU [from New York Titans]
Blanch, George, HB, Texas [from Houston]
Cannivino, Joe, DB, Ohio State [from Buffalo]
Carr, Luther, T, Washington [from Los Angeles Chargers]
Cavalli, Carmen, DE, Richmond [from Buffalo]
Churchwell, Don, G Mississippi [from Houston]
Curci, Fran, QB, Miami (FL) [from Houston]
Daniels, Purcell, DB, Pepperdine [from Houston]
Deskins, Don, G, Michigan [from Los Angeles Chargers]
Edington, Don, E, Florida [from Boston]
Epps, Jerry, G, West Texas State [from New York Titans]
Goldstein, Al, E, North Carolina [from Buffalo]
Harrison, Bob, LB, Arizona State [from Los Angeles Chargers]
*Hawkins, Wayne, G, Pacific [from Denver]
Holden, Clark, HB, USC [from Dallas Texans]
Jones, Stan, G, Maryland-Eastern Shore [from Dallas Texans]
Lancaster, Larry, G-T, Georgia [from Los Angeles Chargers]
Lott, Billy, HB, Mississippi [from Houston]
Nelson, Bob, C, Wisconsin [from Boston]
Newhouse, Ron, LB, Michigan [from New York Titans]
Peterson, Ray, HB, West Virginia [from Buffalo]
Prebola, Gene, E, Boston U. [from Houston]
Starnes, Mack, DB, USC [from Houston]
Woodward, Jim, G, North Carolina Central [from Houston]

1961 NFL

Held December 27-28, 1960

The expansion Minnesota Vikings received the first choice in each round. The draft consisted of 280 selections. In February, the Vikings selected 36 players in an expansion draft. Each of the other 13 NFL teams, except Dallas, froze 30 players from its 38-man roster. The Vikings chose three players per team from those remaining.

BALTIMORE 1961
1. *Matte, Tom, HB, Ohio State, 7
2. *Gilburg, Tom, T, Syracuse, 21
3. *Hill, Jerry, FB, Wyoming, 35
4. *Gregory, Ken, E, Whittier, 49
5. Dyas, Ed, B, Auburn [from Pittsburgh] 62
   Osborne, Ron, T, Clemson, 63
6. Kern, Don, HB, Virginia Military, 77
7. Grimsley, Ike, HB, Michigan State, 91
8. Terhes, Paul, B, Bucknell, 105
9. *Nicklas, Pete, T, Baylor, 119
10. *Clemens, Bob, B Pittsburgh, 133
11. White, Ralph, T, Bowling Green, 147
12. Reynolds, Dick, T, North Carolina State, 161
13. Garber, Dallas, B, Marietta, 175
14. Hunt, Bob, T, SMU, 189
15. Sims, E.A., E, New Mexico State, 203
16. Weisner, Tom, B, Wisconsin, 217
17. Jastrzembski, Steve, B, Pittsburgh, 231
18. Allison, Wilson, T, Baylor, 245
19. *Novsek, Joe, T, Tulsa, 259
20. Kimbrough, Albert, B, Northwestern, 273

CHICAGO BEARS 1961
1. *Ditka, Mike, E, Pittsburgh, 5
2. *Brown, Bill, B, Illinois, 20
3. *Gibson, Claude (Hoot), B, North Carolina State, 33
4. *Ladd, Ernie, T, Grambling, 48
5. *Lincoln, Keith, B, Washington State, 61
6. *Fleming, George, B, Washington, 76
7. *Pyle, Mike, C, Yale, 89
8. Ryan, Ed, B, Michigan State, 104
9. *Bethune, Bob, B, Mississippi State, 117
10. Harness, Jason, E, Michigan State, 132
11. Fewell, Sam, T, South Carolina, 145
12. Dyer, Howard, QB, Virginia Military, 160
13. *McLeod, Bob, E, Abilene Christian, 173
14. *Tyrer, Jim, T, Ohio State, 188
15. Linning, Chuck, T, Miami (FL), 201
16. *Frazier, Wayne, C Auburn, 216
17. Barfield, Rossie, E, North Carolina Central, 229
18. Finn, John, T, Louisville, 244
19. Charles, Ben, QB, South Carolina, 257
20. Mason, Gordon, B, Tennessee Tech, 272

CLEVELAND 1961
1. *Crespino, Bobby, E, Mississippi [from Detroit] 10
   Choice to Dallas
2. *Nutting, Ed, T, Georgia Tech, 27
3. Choice to Los Angeles Rams
4. *Brown, John, T, Syracuse, 55, F
5. *Lucci, Mike, C, Tennessee, 69, F
6. *Parker, Frank, T, Oklahoma State [from Detroit] 79
   Choice to St. Louis
7. *Powell, Preston, B, Grambling, 97
8. *Cox, Fred, HB, Pittsburgh [from Green Bay] 110, F
   *Frongillo, John, T, Baylor, 111, F
9. Gibbs, Jake, QB, Mississippi, 125
10. *Wolff, Wayne, G, Wake Forest [from Washington] 129
    Ericson, Ken, E, Syracuse, 139
11. *Gault, Billy, B, TCU, 153
12. *Lage, Dick, E, Lenoir-Rhyne, 167
13. Wilson, Jack, B, Duke, 181
14. Lohman, Phil, C, Oklahoma, 195
15. Taylor, Charley, B, Mississippi, 209
16. *Shoals, Roger, T, Maryland, 223
17. *Bird, Calvin, B, Kentucky, 237
18. Morris, Ed, T, Indiana, 251
19. Minihane, Bob, G, Boston U., 265
20. Baker, Charlie, T, Tennessee, 279, F

DALLAS COWBOYS 1961
1. Choice to Washington
   *Lilly, Bob, T, TCU [from Cleveland] 13
2. *Holub, E.J., C, Texas Tech, 16
3. *Barber, Stew, G, Penn State, 30
4. Davis, Arnold, E, Baylor, 44
5. Choice to San Francisco
6. Choice to Washington
7. Gilmore, Art, B, Oregon State, 86
8. *Talbert, Don, T, Texas, 100, F
9. *Gregory, Glynn, B, SMU, 114
10. Choice to Green Bay
11. Stevenson, Norris, B, Missouri, 142
12. Shingler, Lowndes, QB, Clemson, 156
13. Goodman, Don, B, Florida, 170
14. *Shaw, Billy, T, Georgia Tech, 184
15. Varnado, Julius, T, Cal State-San Francisco, 198
16. Steffen, Jerry, B, Colorado, 212
17. Cloud, Everett, B, Maryland, 226
18. Williams, Randy, B, Indiana, 240
19. *Hoyem, Lynn, C, Long Beach State, 254
20. Morgan, Jerry, B, Iowa State, 268

DETROIT 1961
1. Choice to Cleveland
2. *LaRose, Danny, E, Missouri, 23
3. *Mills, Dick T, Pittsburgh [from Pittsburgh] 34
   *Antwine, Houston, G, Southern Illinois, 38
4. Hartline, Ron, FB, Oklahoma, 51
5. *Faison, Earl, E, Indiana, 66
   Puckett, Ron, T, Cal State-Los Angeles [from Philadelphia] 70
6. Choice to Cleveland
7. Choice to St. Louis
8. Muff, Larry, E, Benedictine, 107
9. *Brooks, Bob, FB, Ohio U., 122
10. *Linden, Errol, E, Houston, 135
11. *Vargo, Larry, E, Detroit, 150, F
12. Rodgers, Tom, B, Kentucky, 163
13. Hodge, Paul, LB, Pittsburgh, 178
14. Bowers, Charley, HB, Arizona State, 191
15. Lauber, Mike, E, Wisconsin-River Falls, 206
16. Krantz, Gus, T, Northern Michigan, 219
17. *Goode, Tom, LB, Mississippi State, 234
18. Gregor, John, T, Montana, 247
19. Valesano, Gene, B, Northern Michigan, 262
20. Lewis, Tom, B, Lake Forest, 275

GREEN BAY 1961
1. *Adderley, Herb, B, Michigan State, 12
2. *Kostelnik, Ron, T, Cincinnati, 26
3. *Nugent, Phil, B, Tulane, 40
4. *Dudley, Paul, B, Arkansas, 54
   LeSage, Joe, G, Tulane [from Philadelphia] 56
5. Novak, Jack, G, Miami, 68
6. *Folkins, Lee, E, Washington, 82
7. Johnson, Lewis, B, Florida A&M, 96
8. Choice to Cleveland
9. Flanagan, Vester, T, Cal State-Humboldt, 124
10. *Hagberg, Roger, B, Minnesota [from Dallas] 128
    McLeod, Buck, T, Baylor, 138
11. *Keckin, Val, B, Southern Mississippi, 152
12. *Denvir, John, T, Colorado, 166
13. *Pitts, Elijah, B, Philander Smith, 180
14. *Toburen, Nelson, E, Wichita State, 194
15. Lardani, Ray, T, Miami, 208
16. Mason, Clarence, E, Bowling Green, 222
17. *Brewington, Jim, T, North Carolina Central, 236
18. Sims, Arthur, B, Texas A&M, 250
19. Bondhus, Leland, T, South Dakota State, 264
20. *Ratkowski, Ray, B, Notre Dame, 278

LOS ANGELES RAMS 1961
1. *McKeever, Marlin, LB, USC, 4
2. *Kimbrough, Elbert, E, Northwestern, 18
3. Beaty, Harold, G, Oklahoma State, 32
   *Miller, Ron, QB, Wisconsin [from Cleveland] 41, F
4. *Cowan, Charlie, T, N.Mex. Highlands [from Washington] 45
   Choice to New York Giants
5. *Hector, Willie, G, Pacific, 60
6. Olderman, Bruce, T, Allegheny, 74
   Wood, Larry, B, Northwestern [from Pittsburgh] 75
7. *Smith, Bobby, B, UCLA, 88, F
8. *Carolan, Reg, E, Idaho, 102, F
9. *Allen, Duane, E, Santa Ana JC, 116
10. *Scibelli, Joe, T, Notre Dame, 130
11. *Lane, Bob, E, Baylor, 144, F
12. Mince, Walt, B, Arizona, 158
13. McKeever, Mike, G, USC, 172
14. *Jones, David (Deacon), T, South Carolina State, 186
15. *Wright, Ernie, T, Ohio State, 200
16. Zeno, Mike, G, Virginia Tech, 214
17. *Allen, Chuck, G, Washington, 228
18. Williamson, Bill, T, Bakersfield JC, 242
19. Zivkovich, Lou, T, New Mexico State, 256
20. Lederle, Al, E, Georgia Tech, 270

MINNESOTA 1961
1. *Mason, Tommy, HB, Tulane, 1
2. *Hawkins, Rip, LB, North Carolina, 15
3. *Tarkenton, Fran, QB, Georgia, 29
4. *Lamson, Chuck, HB, Wyoming, 43, F
5. *Sharockman, Ed, HB, Pittsburgh, 57
6. *Burch, Jerry, E, Georgia Tech, 71
7. Ferrie, Allan, E, Wagner, 85
8. *Lindquist, Paul, T, New Hampshire, 99
9. Sheehan, Dan, T, Tennessee-Chattanooga, 113
10. *Mayberry, Doug, FB, Utah State, 127
11. *Mays, Jerry, T, SMU, 141
12. *Stonebreaker, Steve, E, Detroit, 155, F
13. *Hayes, Ray, FB, Central State (OK), 169
14. *Peterson, Ken, T, Utah, 183
15. *Mercer, Mike, E, Arizona State, 197
16. Karpowicz, Ted, HB, Detroit, 211
17. *Jones, Willie, B, Purdue, 225
18. *Voight, Bob, T, Cal State-Los Angeles, 239, F
19. Hill, Bill, FB, Presbyterian, 253
20. McFarland, Mike, QB, Western Illinois, 267

MINNESOTA (Expansion) 1961
*Alderman, Grady, G, Detroit [from Detroit]
*Barnett, Tom, HB, Purdue [from Pittsburgh]
*Beams, Byron, T, Notre Dame [from Pittsburgh]
*Beck, Ken, DT, Texas A&M [from Green Bay]
*Bishop, Bill, DT, North Texas State [from Chicago Bears]
*Boll, Don, T, Nebraska [from New York Giants]
*Culpepper, Ed, DT, Alabama [from St. Louis]
*Ellersick, Don, FL, Washington State [from Los Angeles Rams]
*Haley, Dick, DB, Pittsburgh [from Washington]
*Huth, Gerry, G, Wake Forest [from Philadelphia]
*Janerette, Charlie, G, Penn State [from Los Angeles Rams]
*Johnson, Gene, DB, Cincinnati [from Philadelphia]
*Joyce, Don, DE, Tulane [from Baltimore]
*Kimber, Bill, E, Florida State [from New York Giants]
*Lapham, Bill, C, Iowa [from Philadelphia]
*McElhenny, Hugh, HB, Washington [from San Francisco]
*Middleton, Dave, E, Auburn [from Detroit]
Morris, Jack, DB, Oregon [from Pittsburgh]
*Mostardi, Rich, DB, Kent State [from Cleveland]
*Murphy, Fred, E, Georgia Tech [from Cleveland]
*Osborne, Clancy, LB, Arizona State [from San Francisco]
*Pesonen, Dick, DB, Minnesota-Duluth [from Green Bay]
*Rabold, Mike, G, Indiana [from St. Louis]
*Richards, Perry, SE, Detroit [from St. Louis]
*Roehnelt, Bill, LB, Bradley [from Washington]
*Rubke, Karl, LB, USC [from San Francisco]
*Selawski, Gene, T, Purdue [from Cleveland]
*Shaw, Glenn, FB, Kentucky [from Chicago Bears]
*Shields, Lebron, DT, Tennessee [from Baltimore]
*Smith, Zeke, LB, Auburn [from Baltimore]
*Stalcup, Jerry, LB, Wisconsin [from Los Angeles Rams]
*Stephens, Louis (Red), G, San Francisco [from Washington]
*Sumner, Charlie, DB, William & Mary [from Chicago Bears]
*Whitsell, Dave, DB, Indiana [from Detroit]
*Winslow, Paul, HB, North Carolina Central [from Green Bay]
*Youso, Frank, T, Minnesota [from New York Giants]

NEW YORK GIANTS 1961
1. Choice to San Francisco thru Baltimore
2. *Gaiters, Bob, B, New Mexico State [from Washington] 17
   *Tarbox, Bruce, G, Syracuse, 25
3. Choice to Washington
4. *Davidson, Ben, T, Washington [from Los Angeles Rams] 46
   Choice to Philadelphia
5. Daniels, Jerry, E, Mississippi, 67
6. *Larson, Greg, C, Minnesota, 81
7. *Collier, Jimmy, E, Arkansas, 95
8. *Green, Allen, C, Mississippi, 109
9. *Gray, Moses, T, Indiana, 123
10. Knight, Glen, E, Shaw, 137
11. Benton, Bob, T, Mississippi, 151
12. Moynihan, Jack, QB, Holy Cross, 165
13. *Fields, Jerry, B, Ohio State, 179
14. *White, Eugene, B, Florida A&M, 193
15. Binkley, Cody, C, Vanderbilt, 207
16. Vishneski, Bernie, T, Virginia Tech, 221
17. Cooper, Sylvester, T, Bakersfield JC, 235
18. DesMarais, Ken, C, Holy Cross, 249
19. Reublin, Bob, B, Bowling Green, 263
20. McKeta, Don, B, Washington, 277

PHILADELPHIA 1961
1. *Baker, Art, FB, Syracuse, 14
2. Strange, Bo, C, LSU, 28
3. *Wright, Jim, QB, Memphis State [from St. Louis] 36, F
   *Oakes, Don, T, Virginia Tech, 42
4. *Ficca, Dan, G, USC [from New York Giants] 53
   Choice to Green Bay
5. Choice to Detroit
6. Balme, Ben, G, Yale, 84
7. *Cross, Irv, B, Northwestern, 98
8. *Beaver, Jim, G, Florida, 112
9. *Fontes, Wayne, HB, Michigan State, 126, F
10. *Hayes, Luther, E, USC, 140
11. Hicks, L.E., T, Florida, 154
12. *Majors, Billy, B, Tennessee, 168
13. *Jonas, Don, QB, Penn State, 182
14. Fleming, Willie, HB, Iowa, 196
15. *Richards, Bobby, T, LSU, 210
16. Clapp, G.W., G, Auburn, 224
17. Lavery, Larry, T, Illinois, 238
18. Maravich, Nick, T, North Carolina State, 252
19. Wilson, Dick, C, Penn State, 266

20. *MacKinnon, Jacque, B, Colgate, 280

PITTSBURGH 1961
1. Choice to San Francisco
2. *Pottios, Myron, LB, Notre Dame, 19
3. Choice to Detroit
4. Choice to San Francisco
5. Mautino, Fred, E, Syracuse [from Washington] 59
Choice to Baltimore
6. Choice to Los Angeles Rams
7. *Hoak, Dick, B, Penn State, 90
8. Balthazar, George, T, Tennessee State, 103
9. Choice to San Francisco
10. *Mack, Bill (Red), B, Notre Dame, 131
11. *Clement, Henry, B, North Carolina, 146
12. *Jackunas, Frank, T, Detroit, 159, F
13. Choice to San Francisco
14. *Schmitz, Bob, G, Montana State, 187
15. McCown, Ray, B, West Texas State, 202
16. *Scott, Wilbert, B, Indiana, 215
17. *Nofsinger, Terry, QB, Utah, 230
18. Simko, John, E, Augustana (ND), 243
19. Wyatt, Bernard, B, Iowa, 258
20. Jones, Mike, QB, San Jose State, 271

ST. LOUIS 1961
1. *Rice, Ken, T, Auburn, 8
2. *Arbanas, Fred, E, Michigan State, 22
3. Wilson, Billy, T, Auburn [from Washington] 31 F
Choice to Philadelphia
4. *McDole, Ron, T, Nebraska, 50
5. *Bass, Glen, E, East Carolina, 64
6. *Evans, Dale, B, Kansas State, 78
Thornton, Dick, QB, Northwestern [from Cleveland] 83 F
7. *Hultz, George, T, Southern Mississippi, 92
*Bemiller, Al, C, Syracuse [from Detroit] 94
8. *Starks, Marshall, HB, Illinois, 106
9. Graning, Chick, HB, Georgia Tech, 120, F
10. King, Jimmy, T, Clemson, 134, F
11. Kinnune, Bill, G, Washington, 148
12. Stock, Mike, B, Northwestern, 162
13. *McMillan, Ernie, E, Illinois, 176
14. Elliot, Bob, FB, North Carolina, 190
15. *West, Mel, B, Missouri, 204
16. Bradley, Jake, T, Florida A&M, 218
17. *Fischer, Pat, B, Nebraska, 232
18. Browning, Art, G, Duke, 246
19. Schnell, Dick, T, Wyoming, 260
20. Reed, Leo, E, Colorado State, 274

SAN FRANCISCO 1961
1. *Johnson, Jimmy B, UCLA [from Pittsburgh] 6
*Casey, Bernie, B, Bowling Green, 9
*Kilmer, Billy, B, UCLA [from Baltimore] 11
2. *Lakes, Roland, C, Wichita State, 24
3. *Cooper, Bill, B, Muskingum, 37
4. *Thomas, Aaron, E, Oregon State [from Pittsburgh] 47
*Messer, Dale, B, Fresno State, 52
5. *Miller, Clark, T, Utah State [from Dallas] 58, F
*McCreary, Bob, T, Wake Forest, 65
6. *McClellan, Mike, B, Oklahoma, 80, F
7. Purdin, Ray, B, Northwestern, 93
8. Plumley, Neill, T, Oregon, 108
9. *Donahue, Leon, T, San Jose State [from Pittsburgh] 118, F
Nino, Everisto, T, East Texas State, 121
10. *Hynes, Paul, FB, Louisiana Tech, 136
11. Parrilli, Tony, G, Illinois, 149
12. *Coffey, Don, E, Memphis State, 164, F
13. Hackler, Tommy, E, Tennessee Tech [from Pittsburgh] 174
Fincke, Julius, T, McNeese State, 177, F
14. Worrell, Bill, T, Georgia, 192
15. Sams, Bob, T, Central State (OK), 205
16. *Fuller, Charlie, HB, Cal State-San Francisco, 220
17. Jewell, Tom, T, Idaho State, 233
18. *McFarland, Kay, HB, Colorado State, 248, F
19. Simpson, Tom, T, Davidson, 261
20. Perry, Jerry, G, Central State (OK), 276

WASHINGTON 1961
1. *Snead, Norm, QB, Wake Forest [from Dallas] 2
*Rutgens, Joe, T, Illinois, 3
2. Choice to New York Giants
3. Choice to St. Louis
*Cunningham, Jim, B, Pittsburgh [from New York Giants] 39
4. Choice to Los Angeles Rams
5. Choice to Pittsburgh
6. *Krakoski, Joe, B, Illinois [from Dallas] 72
O'Day, John, T, Miami (FL), 73
7. *Kerr, Jim, B, Penn State, 87
8. *Barnes, Charley, E, Northeast Louisiana, 101
9. Arrington, Joel, B, Duke, 115
10. Choice to Cleveland
11. *Mattson, Riley, T, Oregon, 143
12. *Coolbaugh, Bob, E, Richmond, 157
13. *Elmore, Doug, B, Mississippi, 171, F
14. *Schick, Doyle, B, Kansas, 185
15. Johnson, Bob, E, Michigan, 199
16. Petty, Ron, T, Louisville, 213
17. *Bellino, Joe, B, Navy, 227
18. Tolford, George, T, Ohio State, 241
19. *Romeo, Tony, E, Florida State, 255
20. Ingram, Mike, G, Ohio State, 269

1961 AFL

Held November 23, 1960 (Rounds 1-6) and December 5, 1960 (Rounds 7-30)

The AFL established the same draft format as the NFL used-teams drafting in an inverse order of finish. One difference from the NFL was that no future picks could be made until the fourteenth round. Each team could protect two players within its geographical territory through the first two rounds, in order to assure itself the right to players whose signing might help the financial success of the franchise. The territorial draft rule was used again in the 1962 draft, before being eliminated on January 8, 1962. Although the Chargers played the 1961 season in San Diego, at the time of the draft, the franchise still was located in Los Angeles.

BOSTON 1961
1. *Mason, Tommy, HB, Tulane
2. *Hawkins, Rip, C, North Carolina
3. *LaRose, Danny, E, Missouri
4. Zeno, Mike, G, Virginia Tech
5. *Tarkenton, Fran, QB, Georgia
6. *Eisenhauer, Larry, T, Boston College
7. Terhes, Paul, QB, Bucknell
8. *Long, Charley, G, Tennessee-Chattanooga
9. *Lakes, Roland, C, Wichita State
10. Mueller, Dick, E, Kentucky
11. *West, Mel, HB, Missouri
12. Harris, Wayne, C, Arkansas
13. Underwood, Dan, T, McNeese State
14. *Wright, James Earl, QB, Memphis State, F
15. Choice to Dallas Texans
16. Balthazar, George, T, Tennessee State
17. *Ratkowski, Ray, HB, Notre Dame
18. Rodgers, Tom, HB, Kentucky
19. *Bellino, Joe, HB, Navy
20. *Childs, Clarence, HB, Florida A&M
21. *Oakes, Dan, G, Virginia Tech
22. Johnson, Bob, E, Michigan
23. DeDecker, Darrel, C, Illinois
24. *Webb, Don, HB, Iowa State
25. Minihane, Bob, T, Boston U.
26. *Granger, Charles, T, Southern
27. Huxhold, Terry, T, Wisconsin
28. Harvard, Bryant, QB, Auburn
29. *McMillan, Ernie, T, Illinois
30. *Hultz, George, T, Southern Mississippi, F

BUFFALO 1961
1. *Rice, Ken, T, Auburn
2. *Shaw, Billy, T, Georgia Tech
3. *Baker, Art, FB, Syracuse
*Gilburg, Tom, T, Syracuse [from New York Titans]
4. *Barber, Stew, T, Penn State
5. *Snead, Norm, QB, Wake Forest
6. *Brown, Fred, HB, Georgia
7. *Bemiller, Al, C, Syracuse
8. Linning, Chuck, T, Miami (FL)
9. *Majors, Billy, HB, Tennessee
10. Kern, Don, HB, Virginia Military
11. Wall, Roy (Milam), HB, North Carolina
12. Powers, Floyd, G, Mississippi State
13. Causey, Tom, E, Louisiana Tech
14. *Kostelnik, Ron, T, Cincinnati
15. Frye, Jerry, E, South Carolina
16. Scott, Vince, E, Maryland
17. *Wolff, Wayne, T, Wake Forest
18. Bodkin, John, G, South Carolina
19. *Barnes, Charley, E, Northeast Louisiana
20. Cloud, Everett, HB, Maryland
21. *Vargo, Larry, E, Detroit, F
22. Baker, Charlie, T, Tennessee F
23. *Mack, Bill (Red), HB, Notre Dame
24. *Jackunas, Frank, C, Detroit, F
25. Harbaugh, Jack, HB, Bowling Green
26. Stanford, Lorenzo, T, North Carolina A&I
27. Allen, Bob, E, Wake Forest
28. Harness, Jason, E, Michigan State
29. Stock, Mike, HB, Northwestern
30. Martin, Billy, HB, Minnesota

DALLAS TEXANS 1961
1. *Holub, E.J., C, Texas Tech
2. *Lilly, Bob, T, TCU
3. *Tyrer, Jim, T, Ohio State
4. Moorman, Claude, E, Duke
5. *Mays, Jerry, T, SMU
6. Choice to Los Angeles Chargers
7. *Arbanas, Fred, E, Michigan State
8. O'Day, John, T, Miami (FL)
9. *Mills, Dick, T, Pittsburgh
10. Daniels, Jerry, E, Mississippi
11. Tibbets, Marvin, HB, Georgia Tech
12. *Hynes, Paul, HB, Louisiana Tech
13. *Gregory, Glynn, HB, SMU
14. *McClinton, Curtis, HB, Kansas, F
15. *Nutting, Ed, T, Georgia Tech [from Boston]
Rambo, Roy Lee, G, TCU
16. *Thomas, Aaron, E, Oregon State
17. Williams, Jarrell, HB, Arkansas
18. Hartline, Ron, FB, Oklahoma
19. Jackson, Frank, HB, SMU
20. *Lane, Bob, E, Baylor, F
21. Thornton, Dick, QB, Northwestern, F
22. *Sharockman, Ed, HB, Pittsburgh
23. Zivkovich, Lou, T, New Mexico State, F
24. Dye, Pat, G, Georgia
25. Ramsey, Ray, QB, Adams State
26. House, Danny, HB, Davidson
27. Schloredt, Bob, QB, Washington
28. Stine, Bill, G, Michigan
29. Caddell, Lonnie, FB, Rice, F
30. Price, Cedric, E, Kansas State

DENVER 1961
1. *Gaiters, Bob, HB, New Mexico State
2. *Hill, Jerry, HB, Wyoming
3. Strange, Bo, C, LSU
4. *McDole, Ron, T, Nebraska
*Davis, Sonny, E, Baylor [from New York Titans]
5. *Cowan, Charlie, E, New Mexico Highlands
6. *Evans, Dale, HB, Kansas State
7. Patchen, Pat, E, Florida
8. Choice to Oakland
9. *Nugent, Phil, QB, Tulane
10. Sturgeon, Charley, HB, Kentucky
11. Simko, John, E, Augustana (SD)
12. Miller, Jerry, E, Howard Payne
13. Greene, Ron, G, Washington State
14. *Cooper, Bill, FB, Muskingum
15. Crafts, Willie, G, Texas A&I
16. Larkin, Jim, T, Hillsdale
17. Weiss, Chuck, FB, Colorado
18. Graning, Chick, HB, Georgia Tech, F
19. Hobbs, John, G, Maryland-Eastern Shore
20. McLeod, Buck, T, Baylor
21. Morgan, Jim, HB, Iowa State
22. Hackler, Tom, E, Tennessee Tech
23. Jewel, Tom, T, Idaho State
24. Simms, E.A., E, New Mexico State
25. Samms, Pete, T, Central State (OK)
26. Smith, Sam, HB, North Alabama
27. Olson, Don, HB, Nebraska
28. Lee, Wayne, G, Colorado State
29. Cobb, Archie, T, Nebraska, F
30. Mills, Dave, HB, Northeast Missouri State

HOUSTON 1961
1. *Ditka, Mike, E, Pittsburgh
2. *Goode, Tom, C, Mississippi State
3. *Suggs, Walt, T, Mississippi State
4. *Walden, Bobby, HB, Georgia
5. *Lee, Monte, G, Texas
6. Gibbs, Jake, QB, Mississippi
7. Reynolds, Dick, T, North Carolina State
8. *Antwine, Houston, G, Southern Illinois
9. White, Ralph, T, Bowling Green
10. Lee, Charley, C, Iowa
11. Bird, Bob, G, Bowling Green
12. *McLeod, Bob, E, Abilene Christian
13. Hinton, Gerald, G, Louisiana Tech
14. King, Jimmy, T, Clemson, F
15. Ferriter, Dennis, C, Marquette
16. Wood, Larry, HB, Northwestern
17. Fewell, Sam, T, South Carolina
18. Grimsley, Ike, HB, Michigan State
19. Pearson, Myron, HB, Colorado State
20. Johnson, Lewis, HB, Florida A&M
21. *Miller, Ron, QB, Wisconsin, F
22. *Kelly, Bob, E, New Mexico State
23. Anderson, Jim, FB, Mississippi
24. *Gregory, Ken, E, Whittier
25. Kreider, Jack, HB, Tulsa, F
26. Fuell, Don, QB, Southern Mississippi, F
27. King, Boyd, C, Rice
28. *Frongillo, John, T, Baylor, F
29. Lewis, Tom, E, Lake Forest [from New York Titans]
*Linden, Errol, E, Houston
30. Stroud, Jim, T, Rice

LOS ANGELES CHARGERS 1961
1. *Faison, Earl, E, Indiana
2. *Lincoln, Keith, HB, Washington State
3. *McKeever, Marlin, E, USC
4. *Johnson, Jimmy, HB, UCLA
5. *Kilmer, Billy, HB-QB, UCLA
6. Bird, Calvin, HB, Kentucky [from Dallas Texans]
*Roberts, Cliff, T, Illinois
7. *Gibson, Claude (Hoot), HB, North Carolina State
8. *Johnson, Charley, QB, New Mexico State
9. *Scarpitto, Bob, HB, Notre Dame
10. *Hector, Willie, G, Pacific
11. *Larson, Greg, C, Minnesota
12. *Braxton, Hezekiah, FB, Virginia Union
13. *Messer, Dale, FB, Fresno State
14. Wilson, Billy, T, Auburn, F
15. *Ladd, Ernie, T, Grambling
16. *Whitehead, Bud, HB, Florida State
17. *Carolan, Reg, E, Idaho, F
18. Dyas, Ed, FB, Auburn
19. Espenship, Jack, HB, Florida
20. *Lucci, Mike, C, Tennessee, F
21. Gaines, Gene, HB, UCLA
22. *Brown, John, T, Syracuse, F
23. *Bass, Glenn, HB, East Carolina
24. Balme, Ben, G, Yale
25. *Coffey, Don, E, Memphis State, F
26. Kinnune, Bill, G, Washington
27. *Hayes, Luther, E, USC
28. *Allen, Chuck, G, Washington
29. *Ficca, Dan, T, USC
30. McKeever, Mike, G, USC

NEW YORK TITANS 1961
1. Brown, Tom, G, Minnesota
2. *Adderley, Herb, HB, Michigan State
3. Choice to Buffalo
4. Choice to Denver
5. *Matte, Tom, QB, Ohio State
6. *Brown, Bill, FB, Illinois
7. Mautino, Fred, E, Syracuse
8. Beaty, Harold, T, Oklahoma State
9. *Casey, Bernie, FB, Bowling Green
10. *Scibelli, Joe, T, Notre Dame
11. *Gilmore, Art, HB, Oregon State
12. Stevenson, Norris, HB, Missouri
13. *Wendryhoski, Joe, T, Illinois
14. *Cunningham, Jim, FB, Pittsburgh
15. *Cross, Irv, E, Northwestern
16. Steffen, Jerry, HB, Colorado
17. *Pyle, Mike, T, Yale
18. Bentley, Alfred, E, Arkansas State
19. *Kerr, Jim, HB, Penn State
20. Plumley, Neil, T, Oregon State
21. *Brooks, Bob, FB, Ohio U.
22. *Fontes, Wayne, HB, Michigan State, F
23. *Walker, Mickey, LB, Michigan State
24. Dyer, Howard, QB, Virginia Military
25. Griffith, Andy, HB, American International
26. *Smith, Bobby, HB, UCLA, F
27. *Gray, Moses, T, Indiana
28. *Cox, Fred, HB, Pittsburgh, F
29. Choice to Houston
30. Minnerly, Bill, HB, Connecticut

OAKLAND 1961
1. *Rutgens, Joe, T, Illinois
2. *Fleming, George, HB, Washington
3. *Pottios, Myron, G, Notre Dame
4. *Kimbrough, Elbert, E, Northwestern
5. *Norman, Dick, QB, Stanford
6. *Crespino, Bobby, HB, Mississippi
7. Purdin, Ray, HB, Northwestern
8. *Watkins, Tom, HB, Iowa State [from Denver]
Price, Dick, G, Mississippi
9. Shingler, Lowndes, QB, Clemson
10. *Peterson, Ken, T, Utah
11. *Mayberry, Doug, FB, Utah State
12. *Schmitz, Bob, G, Montana State
13. *Burch, Gerald, E, Georgia Tech
14. *Miller, Clark, T, Utah State, F
15. *Coolbaugh, Bob, E, Richmond
16. *Lamson, Chuck, HB, Wyoming, F
17. *Novsek, Joe, T, Tulsa
18. *Krakoski, Joe, HB, Illinois
19. Fuller, Charles, HB, Cal State-San Francisco
20. *Powell, Preston, FB, Grambling
21. Jones, Mike, QB, San Jose State
22. Jones, Blayne, G, Idaho State
23. Fisher, Roger, C, Utah State
24. Novak, Jack, G, Miami (FL)
25. Yanke, Paul, E, Northwestern
26. Hinshaw, Dean, T, Stanford
27. Appledoorn, Clair, E, San Jose State
28. Grosz, Dave, QB, Oregon
29. Morris, Ed, T, Indiana
30. Face, Bill, HB, Stanford

1962 NFL

Held December 4, 1961

BALTIMORE 1962
1. *Harris, Wendell, B, LSU, 9
2. *Saul, Bill, LB, Penn State, 23
3. *Sullivan, Dan, T, Boston College, 37
4. Dillard, Jim, B, Oklahoma State, 51
5. Croft, Jerry, G, Bowling Green [from Pittsburgh] 61
Choice to Green Bay
6. Choice to Green Bay
7. *Miller, Fred, T, LSU, 93, F
8. Brokaw, Pete, B, Syracuse, 107
9. Walker, Roy, FB, Purdue [from Dallas] 116, F
Rappold, Walt, QB, Duke, 121, F
10. *Moore, Fred, T, Memphis State, 135, F
11. Tyler, Scott, B, Miami (OH), 149, F
12. *Turner, Bake, HB, Texas Tech, 163
13. Holmes, Charles, FB, Maryland-Eastern Shore, 177
14. Jones, Stinson, B, Virginia Military, 191
15. Monte, Joe, G, Furman, 205, F
16. *Abruzzeze, Ray, HB, Alabama, 219
17. Knocke, Bill, HB, Fresno State, 233, F
18. Rideout, Mel, QB, Richmond, 247, F
19. *Gillett, Fred, B, Cal State-Los Angeles, 261
20. McKee, Herm, B, Washington State, 275, F

CHICAGO BEARS 1962
1. *Bull, Ronnie, B, Baylor, 7
2. *Brock, Clyde, T, Utah State [from Pittsburgh] 20
*McRae, Bennie, B, Michigan, 21
3. Bates, Jim, E, USC [from Dallas] 32
*Hull, Bill, E, Wake Forest, 35
4. *Cadile, Jim, T, San Jose State, 49
5. Burton, Mac, E, San Jose State [from Washington] 57
Tunnicliff, Bill, FB, Michigan, 63
6. Choice to Philadelphia
7. *O'Bradovich, Ed, E, Illinois, 91
8. Reynolds, Ed, T, Tulane, 105, F
Onesti, Larry, C, Northwestern [from New York Giants] 110
9. *Winston, Kelton, HB, Wiley, 119
10. Weaver, LeRoy, B, Adams State, 133
11. *Robinson, Jerry, HB, Grambling, 147
12. Watts, Bill, T, Miami (FL), 161
13. Perkowski, Joe, B, Notre Dame, 175

14. *Von Sonn, Andy, C, UCLA, 189, F
15. Martin, Kent, T, Wake Forest, 203, F
16. Nelson, John, C, Xavier, 217
17. *Glass, Glenn, HB, Tennessee, 231
18. *Neck, Tommy, B, LSU, 245
19. Kellum, Bill, T, Tulane, 259, F
20. Roberts, Jack, T, Ohio State, 273

CLEVELAND 1962
1. *Collins, Gary, E, Maryland [from Dallas] 4
   *Jackson, Leroy, B, Western Illinois, 11
2. *Hinton, Chuck, T, N. Carolina Central [from Minnesota] 17
   Stephens, Sandy, B, Minnesota, 25
3. Choice to Dallas
   *Furman, John, QB, Texas-El Paso [from Green Bay] 42
4. *Sczurek, Stan, G, Purdue, 53
5. *Rivera, Henry, HB, Oregon State, 67
6. *Tidmore, Sam, E, Ohio State, 81
7. Havlicek, John, E, Ohio State, 95
8. Choice to Detroit
9. Dickerson, Charles, T, Illinois, 123, F
10. Goerlitz, Jerry, C, Northern Michigan [from Minnesota] 129
    White, Albert, B, Capital, 137
11. Meyers, Ronnie, E, Villanova [from Minnesota] 142
    *McNeil, Clifton, E, Grambling, 151
12. Stute, Ted, E, Ohio U., 165
13. Gardner, Frank, T, North Carolina Central, 179
14. *Shorter, Jim, B, Detroit, 193
15. *Goosby, Tom, G, Baldwin-Wallace, 207, F
16. *Biodrowski, Dennis, E, Memphis State, 221, F
17. Harlan, Herbert, E, Baylor, 235, F
18. *Bishop, Sonny, G, Fresno State, 249
19. Anabo, John, QB, Fresno State, 263
20. *Flatley, Paul, B, Northwestern, 277

DALLAS COWBOYS 1962
1. Choice to Cleveland
2. *Gibbs, Sonny, QB, TCU, 18, F
3. Choice to Chicago Bears
   Plummer, Bobby, T, TCU [from Cleveland] 39
4. Choice to San Francisco
5. Choice to Los Angeles Rams
6. *Davis, Donnie, E, Southern, 74
   *Andrie, George, E, Marquette [from New York Giants] 82
7. Choice to Los Angeles Rams
8. Tureaud, Ken, B, Michigan, 102
9. Choice to Baltimore
10. Longmeyer, John, G, Southern Illinois, 130
11. Hudas, Larry, E, Michigan State, 144
12. Choice to Green Bay
13. Moses, Bob, E, Texas, 172
14. *Hays, Harold, G, Southern Mississippi, 186, F
15. *Reese, Guy, T, SMU, 200
16. Johnston, Bob, T, Rice, 214
17. *Jacobs, Ray, T, Howard Payne, 228
18. *Cloutier, Dave, B, Maine, 242
19. Holmes, Paul, T, Georgia, 256, F
20. *Bullocks, Amos, B, Southern Illinois, 270

DETROIT 1962
1. *Hadl, John, B, Kansas, 10
2. Wilson, Eddie, QB, Arizona, 24
3. *Thompson, Bobby, HB, Arizona, 38
4. *Lomakoski, John, T, Western Mich. [from Pittsburgh] 48
   *Ferguson, Larry, B, Iowa, 52, F
5. *Birdwell, Dan, C, Houston, 66
6. *Bundra, Mike, T, USC, 80
7. *Hall, Tom, E, Minnesota, 94
8. Hooper, Murdock, T, Houston, 108
   Imperiale, Frank, G, Southern Illinois [from Cleveland] 109
9. Grant, Todd, C, Michigan, 122
10. Archer, Jerry, C, Pittsburg State, 136, F
11. Anderson, Karl, T, Bowling Green, 150
12. Sprute, Gale, C, Winona State, 164
13. Knight, Sherlock, T, Central State (OH), 178
14. Davidson, Jim, B, Maryland, 192
15. Broadbent, Dick, E, Delaware, 206
16. *Sestak, Tom, E, McNeese State, 220
17. Wickline, Rucker, C, Marshall, 234
18. Zuger, Joe, QB, Arizona State, 248
19. Bernhardt, Jim, T, Linfield, 262
20. Brown, Bob, E, Michigan, 276 F

GREEN BAY 1962
1. *Gros, Earl, B, LSU, 14
2. *Blaine, Ed, G, Missouri, 28
3. *Barnes, Gary, E, Clemson [from New York Giants] 41
   Choice to Cleveland
4. *Gassert, Ron, T, Virginia, 56
5. Morris, Chuck, B, Mississippi [from Baltimore] 65, F
   Schopf, Jon, G, Michigan, 70
6. *Sutro, John, T, San Jose State [from Baltimore] 79
   *Donahue, Oscar, E, San Jose State, 84
7. *Cutsinger, Gary, T, Oklahoma State, 98
8. Tullis, Jim, B, Florida A&M, 112, F
9. Schenck, Peter, B, Washington State, 126
10. Weidner, Gale, QB, Colorado, 140
11. Thrush, Jim, T, Xavier, 154, F
12. Thorne, Joe, B, South Dakota State [from Dallas] 158
    *Pennington, Tom, B, Georgia, 168
13. Kepner, Tom, T, Villanova, 182
14. *Green, Ernie, B, Louisville, 196
15. Holdinsky, Roger, B, West Virginia, 210
16. Field, Jimmy, B, LSU, 224, F
17. *Buchannan, Buck, T, Grambling, 238
18. Joiner, Bob, QB, Presbyterian, 252
19. Scattini, Jerry, B, California, 266
20. Snodgrass, Mike, C, Western Michigan, 280

LOS ANGELES RAMS 1962
1. *Gabriel, Roman, QB, N.Carolina State [from Minnesota] 2
   *Olsen, Merlin, T, Utah State, 3
2. *Carollo, Joe, T, Notre Dame, 16
3. *Meyers, John, T, Washington, 31
   Cornett, John, T, Rice [from Pittsburgh] 33
4. *Perkins, Art, FB, North Texas State, 44
5. Choice to New York Giants
   Smith, Jim, T, Penn State [from Dallas] 60
   Wilson, Ben, FB, USC [from Philadelphia] 68, F
6. Choice to New York Giants
7. Thorson, Sherwyn, G, Iowa, 87
   *Bakken, Jim, QB, Wisconsin [from Dallas] 88
8. Farris, Dick, G, North Texas State, 100, F
9. *Lassiter, Ike, T, State Augustine, 115
10. *Norris, Jim, T, Houston, 128
11. *Wilder, Bert, T, North Carolina State, 143, F
12. *Marinovich, Marv, T, USC, 156, F
13. Fearnside, Bob, HB, Bowling Green, 171
14. Henson, Gary, E, Colorado, 184
15. Nikirk, Walter, T, Houston, 199, F
16. Skufca, Ron, T, Purdue, 212, F
17. Steadman, Dave, T, Georgia Tech, 227, F
18. Furlow, Charlie, QB, Mississippi State, 240, F
19. Barto, Gerard, T, Drake, 255, F
20. Andersen, Foster, T, UCLA, 268

MINNESOTA 1962
1. Choice to Los Angeles Rams
2. Choice to Cleveland
3. *Miller, Bill, E, Miami (FL), 30
4. *Winston, Roy, G, LSU, 45
5. Choice to New York Giants
6. *Bowie, Larry, T, Purdue, 73
7. Choice to Philadelphia
8. White, Paul, HB, Florida, 101
9. Shirk, Marshall, T, UCLA, 114
10. Choice to Cleveland
11. Choice to Cleveland
12. Fallon, Gary, HB, Syracuse, 157
13. Van Cleef, Roger, T, Southwestern Oklahoma, 170
14. Russ, Patrick, T, Purdue, 185
15. Guilford, Larry, E, Pacific, 198
16. *Contoulis, John, T, Connecticut, 213, F
17. Staley, Ron, E, Wisconsin, 226
18. Hawthorne, Junior, T, Kentucky, 241, F
19. *Minter, Tommy, B, Baylor, 254
20. Cagaanan, Terry, B, Utah State, 269, F

NEW YORK GIANTS 1962
1. *Hillebrand, Jerry, E, Colorado, 13
2. Bill, Bob, T, Notre Dame, 26
3. Choice to Green Bay
4. *Griffing, Glynn, QB, Mississippi, 54, F
5. *Bolin, Bookie, G, Mississippi [from Minnesota] 58
   Miranda, Curtis, C, Florida A&M [from Los Angeles Rams] 59
   Choice to St. Louis
6. *Triplett, Bill, B, Miami (OH) [from Los Angeles Rams] 72
   Choice to Dallas
7. *Byers, Ken, T, Cincinnati, 97
8. Choice to Chicago Bears
9. *Bohovich, Reed, T, Lehigh, 125
10. Williams, J.R., C, Fresno State, 138, F
11. Bishop, Dave, B, Connecticut, 153
12. *Gursky, Al, HB, Penn State, 166, F
13. Booth, Billy Joe, T, LSU, 181
14. Mather, Greg, E, Navy, 194
15. *Taylor, Joe, HB, North Carolina A&T, 209
16. Johnson, Roger, HB, Oregon State, 222
17. Schaffer, Ken, T, Marquette, 237
18. *Winter, Bill, FB, St. Olaf, 250
19. Stern, Bob, C, Syracuse, 265
20. Moss, Jim, T, South Carolina, 278

PHILADELPHIA 1962
1. Choice to St. Louis
2. *Case, Pete, T, Georgia, 27
3. *Holmes, Pat, T, Texas Tech, 40
4. *Byrne, Bill, G, Boston College, 55
5. Choice to Los Angeles Rams
6. Gonzales, Gus, G, Tulane [from Chicago Bears] 77
   *McGeever, John, HB, Auburn, 83
7. *Perkins, Jim, T, Colorado [from Minnesota] 86
   *Budd, Frank, B, Villanova, 96
8. *Smith, Ralph (Catfish), E, Mississippi, 111
9. *Butler, Bob, T, Kentucky, 124
10. *Skaggs, Jim, G, Washington, 139
11. Horne, George, T, BYU, 152
12. Thompson, Larry, C, Tulane, 167
13. McKinney, George, B, Arkansas, 180
14. Schwab, Jim, E, Penn State, 195
15. *Woulfe, Mike, G, Colorado, 208, F
16. *Mazzanti, Jerry, T, Arkansas, 223, F
17. Martin, Mike, T, Washington State, 236
18. Larscheid, Tom, B, Utah State, 251
19. Ericksen, Harold, G, Georgia Tech, 264
20. Turner, Ron, E, Wichita State, 279

PITTSBURGH 1962
1. *Ferguson, Bob, B, Ohio State, 5
2. Choice to Chicago Bears
3. Choice to Los Angeles Rams
4. Choice to Detroit
5. Choice to Baltimore
6. Choice to San Francisco
7. Collins, Jack, HB, Texas, 89
8. *Ballman, Gary, B, Michigan State, 104
9. *Powers, John, E, Notre Dame, 117
10. Vignali, Larry, G, Pittsburgh, 132
11. Wills, Bob, E, California, 145
12. Mudie, Sam, B, Rutgers, 160
13. Woodward, Dave, T, Auburn, 173
14. Whitaker, Jim, E, Nevada-Reno, 188
15. Hatch, Vern, E, North Carolina Central, 201
16. *Ply, Bobby, B, Baylor, 216
17. Tucker, Nat, B, Florida A&M, 229
18. Yarbrough, Ferrell, T, Northwestern State (LA), 244
19. Kuprok, John, E, Pittsburgh, 257
20. Knight, John, B, Valparaiso, 272

ST. LOUIS 1962
1. *Echols, Fate, T, Northwestern, 6
   *Goode, Irv, C, Kentucky [from Philadelphia] 12
2. *Jackson, Bob, FB, New Mexico State, 19
3. *Bryant, Chuck, E, Ohio State, 34
4. *Kochman, Roger, HB, Penn State, 47, F
5. Choice to San Francisco
   Rice, Bill, E, Alabama [from New York Giants] 69
6. *Elwell, John, E, Purdue, 75
7. *Kirchiro, Bill, G, Maryland, 90
8. Gross, George, T, Auburn, 103, F
9. Hollis, Wilburn, QB, Iowa, 118
10. Francovitch, George, G, Syracuse, 131
11. *Saxton, James, B, Texas, 146
12. O'Billovich, Bob, B, Montana State, 159
13. *Diamond, Bill, G, Miami (FL), 174
14. Mans, George, E, Michigan, 187
15. Barlund, Dick, E, Maryland, 202
16. *Wegener, Bill, G, Missouri, 215
17. Kasso, Don, HB, Oregon State, 230
18. Donatelli, Don, C, Florida State, 243
19. Smith, Don, B, Langston, 258
20. Dickson, Judge, B, Minnesota, 271

SAN FRANCISCO 1962
1. *Alworth, Lance, B, Arkansas, 8
2. *Pine, Ed, C, Utah, 22
3. Adams, Billy Ray, FB, Mississippi, 36
4. *Sieminski, Chuck, T, Penn State [from Dallas] 46, F
   Dean, Floyd, T, Florida, 50, F
5. Woods, Ted, HB, Colorado [from St. Louis] 62
   *Lind, Mike, HB, Notre Dame, 64, F
6. Luhnow, Keith, B, Santa Ana [from Washington] 71
   Brown, Jerry, G, Mississippi [from Pittsburgh] 76
   Winter, Bill, T, West Virginia, 78
7. *Burrell, John, E, Rice, 92
8. *Vollenweider, Jim, B, Miami (FL), 106
9. Roberts, Jim, T, Mississippi, 120, F
10. Coustillac, Regis, G, Pittsburgh, 134
11. Jepson, Larry, C, Furman, 148
12. McPike, Milt, E, Kirksville, 162
13. Pierovich, George, B, California, 176
14. Easterly, Dick, B, Syracuse, 190
15. Osborne, Ray, T, Mississippi State, 204
16. Frank, Ron, T, South Dakota State, 218
17. Foltz, Wally, E, De Pauw, 232
18. Brown, Gary, T, Illinois, 246
19. Burton, Bob, T, Murray State, 260
20. McFarland, Roger, B, Kansas, 274, F

WASHINGTON 1962
1. Davis, Ernie, B, Syracuse, 1
2. *Hernandez, Joe, B, Arizona, 15
3. *Mitinger, Bob, E, Penn State, 29
4. *Neighbors, Billy, T, Alabama, 43
5. Choice to Chicago Bears
6. Choice to San Francisco
7. *Coan, Bert, HB, Kansas, 85, F
8. *Hatcher, Ron, FB, Michigan State, 99
9. Viti, Dave, E, Boston U., 113
10. Childress, John, G, Arkansas, 127
11. Palazzo, Carl, T, Adams State, 141
12. Terrebonne, Terry, HB, Tulane, 155, F
13. Whisler, Bill, E, Iowa, 169
14. Costen, Jim, HB, South Carolina, 183
15. Velia, Len, T, Georgia, 197
16. *Brooker, Tommy, E, Alabama, 211
17. *Miller, Alan, G, Ohio U., 225
18. *Charon, Carl, B, Michigan State, 239
19. *Crabb, Claude, B, Colorado, 253
20. Trancygier, Ed, QB, Florida State, 267, F

1962 AFL

Held December 2, 1961 (Rounds 1-25) and December 16, 1961 (Rounds 26-34)

The AFL initially held its 25-round draft as planned. Two days later, however, the NFL draft included many future picks that the AFL teams had not made. In order to be competitive with the NFL teams for those players chosen by the NFL as future picks, the AFL teams selected nine more rounds of future picks in a continuation of their earlier draft.

BOSTON 1962
1. *Collins, Gary, E, Maryland, 6
2. *Jackson, Leroy, HB, Western Illinois, 14
3. Thorson, Sherwyn, G, Iowa, 22
4. Choice to Houston
5. Hull, Bill, E, Wake Forest, 38
6. *Neighbors, Billy, T, Alabama, 46
7. Schopf, John, T, Michigan, 54
8. *McRae, Benny, HB, Michigan, 62
9. *Triplett, Bill, FB, Miami (OH), 70
10. Knight, John, HB, Valparaiso, 78
11. Choice to Buffalo
12. Choice to Oakland
13. *Buoniconti, Nick, G, Notre Dame, 102
14. *Sieminski, Chuck, T, Penn State, 110, F
15. Goerlitz, Gerry, C, Northern Michigan, 118
16. *Byers, Ken, G, Cincinnati, 126
17. Maentz, Scott, E, Michigan, 134
18. Chandler, Tom, T, Florida A&M, 142
19. Meyers Ron, E, Villanova, 150
20. *Neck, Tommy, HB, LSU, 158
21. Traynham, John, HB, Virginia Military, 166
22. Asack, Bob, T, Columbia, 174
23. Crate, Walt, HB, Widener, 182
24. Christman, Don, C, Richmond, 190
25. Stern, Bob, C, Syracuse, 198
26. Field, Jimmy, QB, LSU, 206, F
27. *Gursky, Al, HB, Penn State, 214, F
28. Dickerson, Charlie, T, Illinois, 222, F
29. Fincke, Julius, T, McNeese State, 230, F
30. Finn, John, T, Louisville, 238, F
31. Ingram, Mike, G, Ohio State, 246, F
32. Taylor, Charley, HB, Mississippi, 254, F
33. Jastrzembski, Steve, E, Pittsburgh, 262, F
34. Lardani, Ray, T, Miami, 270, F

BUFFALO 1962
1. Davis, Ernie, HB, Syracuse, 4
2. *Glass, Glenn, HB, Tennessee, 12
3. *Elwell, John, E, Purdue, 20
4. Choice to Dallas Texans
5. Dellinger, Tom, HB, North Carolina State, 36
6. Viti, Dave, E, Boston U., 44
7. LeCompte, Jim, G, North Carolina, 52
8. White, Paul, HB, Florida, 60
9. *Saul, Bill, C, Penn State, 68
10. *Bullocks, Amos, HB, Southern Illinois, 76
11. Croft, Jerry, G, Bowling Green, 84
    *Pennington, Tom, E, Georgia [from Boston] 86
12. Choice to Oakland
13. *Gassert, Ron, T, Virginia [from Dallas Texans] 99
    *Stratton, Mike, E, Tennessee, 100
14. Scufca, Ron, T, Purdue, 108, F
15. *Kochman, Roger, HB, Penn State, 116, F
16. Imperiale, Frank, T, Southern Illinois, 124
17. *Sestak, Tom, E, McNeese State, 132
18. Kehoe, Joe, E, Virginia, 140 +
19. Johnson, Bill, LB, Southeastern Louisiana, 148
20. *Tidmore, Sam, E, Ohio State, 156
21. *Henley, Carey, HB, Tennessee-Chattanooga, 164
22. *Hall, Tom, E, Minnesota, 172
23. *Abruzzese, Ray, HB, Alabama, 180
24. Sczurek, Stan, G, Purdue, 188
25. Gash, Dave, E, Kentucky, 196, F
26. Reynolds, Ed, T, Tulane, 204, F
27. *Crabb, Claude, HB, Colorado, 212, F
28. Walker, Roy, FB, Purdue, 220, F
29. *Beaver, Jim, G, Florida, 228, F
30. Binkley, Cody, C, Vanderbilt, 236, F
31. *Collier, Jim, E, Arkansas, 244, F
32. Erickson, Ken, E, Syracuse, 252, F
33. Parilli, Tony, G, Illinois, 260, F
34. Charles, Ben, QB, USC, 268, F

DALLAS TEXANS 1962
1. *Bull, Ronnie, HB, Baylor, 3
2. *Miller, Bill, E, Miami (FL), 11
3. *Wilson, Eddie, QB, Arizona, 19
4. *Hinton, Chuck, T, North Carolina Central, 27
   *Goode, Irv, C, Kentucky [from Buffalo] 28
5. Plummer, Bobby, T, TCU, 35
6. Hinton, Al, E, Iowa, 43
7. Choice to San Diego
8. *Bowie, Larry, T, Purdue, 59
9. Shirk, Marshall, T, UCLA, 67
10. *Saxton, James, HB, Texas, 75
11. *Hunt, Bobby, QB, Auburn [from Oakland] 81
    *Reese, Guy, T, SMU, 83
12. *Thompson, Bobby, HB, Arizona, 91
13. Choice to Buffalo
14. *Bolin, Bookie, G, Mississippi, 107, F
15. *Graham, Dave, T, Virginia, 115, F
16. *Norman, Pettis, E, Johnson C. Smith, 123
17. *Brooker, Tommy, E, Alabama, 131
18. *Carollo, Joe, T, Notre Dame, 139
19. Welch, Lee, HB, Mississippi State, 147
20. Semcheski, Mike, G, Lehigh, 155
21. Martin, Kent, T, Wake Forest, 163, F
22. Bernhardt, Jim, T, Linfield, 171
23. Foret, Russ, T, Georgia Tech, 179
24. Trammell, Pat, QB, Alabama, 187
25. Burrell, John, E, Rice, 195
26. Rappold, Walt, QB, Duke, 203, F
27. Tyler, Scott, HB, Miami (OH), 211, F
28. Thrush, Jim, T, Xavier, 219, F
29. Ryan, Ed, HB, Michigan State, 227, F
30. Goodman, Don, HB, Florida, 235, F

31. Nino, Everisto, T, East Texas State, 243, F
32. Arrington, Joel, HB, Duke, 251, F
33. Wilson, Jack, HB, Duke, 259, F
34. *Shoals, Rodger, C, Maryland, 267, F

DENVER 1962
1. *Olsen, Merlin, T, Utah State, 2
2. *Hillebrand, Jerry, E, Colorado, 10
3. Holmes, Charles, FB, Maryland-Eastern Shore, 18
4. *Furman, John, QB, Texas-El Paso, 26
5. Choice to San Diego
6. Choice to San Diego
7. *McGeever, John, HB, Auburn, 50
8. Harris, Elbert, HB, Southeastern Louisiana, 58
9. Jepson, Larry, C, Furman, 66
10. Weidner, Gale, QB, Colorado, 74
11. Kline, Mike, G, Oregon State, 82
12. Choice to New York Titans
13. Cegelski, Bob, C, Montana State, 98
14. *Gibbs, Sonny, QB, TCU, 106, F
15. Louden, Bill, G, Benedictine, 114
16. *Ballman, Gary, HB, Michigan State, 122
17. *Tarr, Jerry, E, Oregon, 130
18. Schenk, Pete, E, Washington State, 138
19. Choice to Oakland
20. Martin, Mike, E, Washington State, 154
21. *Perkins, Jim, T, Colorado, 162
22. Kasso, Don, HB, Oregon State, 170
23. Tureaud, Ken, HB, Michigan, 178
24. Thomas, Neil, G, Hillsdale, 186
25. *Edwards, Dave, E, Auburn, 194
26. Roberts, Jim, T, Mississippi, 202, F
27. *Von Sonn, Andy, C, UCLA, 210, F
28. Holmes, Paul, T, Georgia, 218, F
29. *Hoyem, Lynn, C, Long Beach State, 226, F
30. Mince, Walt, HB, Arizona, 234, F
31. Williamson, Bill, T, Bakersfield J.C., 242, F
32. Flanagan, Vester, T, Cal Stale-Humboldt, 250, F
33. *Allen, Duane, E, Santa Ana J.C., 258, F
34. *Stonebreaker, Steve, E, Detroit, 264, F

HOUSTON 1962
1. *Jacobs, Ray, T, Howard Payne, 7
2. *Gros, Earl, FB, LSU, 15
3. *Case, Pete, T, Georgia, 23
4. *Cutsinger, Gary, T, Oklahoma State [from Boston] 30
   Choice to San Diego
5. Rice, Bill, E, Alabama, 39
6. Pinion, Ray, G, TCU, 47
7. Gonzales, Gus, G, Tulane, 55
8. *Brock, Clyde, T, Utah State, 63
9. *Onesti, Larry, C, Northwestern, 71
10. Moses, Bob, E, Texas, 79
11. Thomas, John, G, McMurry, 87
12. Collins, Jack, HB, Texas, 95
13. Cassell, Royce, E, New Mexico State, 103
14. *Griffing, Glynn, QB, Mssssippi, 111, F
15. Shaffer, Ken, T, Marquette, 119
16. Adams, Billy Ray, FB, Mississippi, 127
17. *Miller, Bill, T, New Mexico Highlands, 135
18. *Perkins, Art, FB, North Texas State, 143
19. *Jancik, Bobby, HB, Lamar, 151
20. *Isbell, Joe Bob, G, Houston, 159
21. Jackson, Roland, FB, Rice, 167
22. Bolin, Kenny, HB, Houston, 175
23. Van Buren, Bill, C, Iowa, 183
24. Melvin, Boyd, T, Northwestern, 191
25. Johnson, Bob, T, Rice, 199
26. *Hays, Harold, G, Southern Mississippi, 207, F
27. McFarland, Roger, HB, Kansas, 215, F
28. *Henson, Gary, E, Colorado, 223, F
29. Osborne, Ron, T, Clemson, 231, F
30. *Clemens, Bob, HB, Pittsburgh, 239, F
31. *Kimbrough, Al, HB, Northwestern, 247, F
32. Wyatt, Bernard, HB, Iowa, 255, F
33. Lerderle, Al, E, Georgia Tech, 263, F
34. *Talbert, Don, T, Texas, 271, F

NEW YORK TITANS 1962
1. Stephens, Sandy, QB, Minnesota, 5
2. *Kroll, Alex, C, Rutgers, 13
3. *Echols, Fate, T, Northwestern, 21
4. *Blaine, Ed, G, Missouri, 29
5. *Ply, Bobby, QB, Baylor, 37
6. Melin, Mel, QB, Washington State, 45
7. Mans, George, E, Michigan, 53
8. Lomakoski, John, T, Western Michigan, 61
9. *Barnes, Gary, E, Clemson, 69
10. Stute, Ted, T, Ohio U., 77
11. Miranda, Curtis, C, Florida A&M, 85
12. Winter, Bill, T, West Virginia [from Denver] 90
    Choice to San Diego
13. Hollis, Wilburn, QB, Iowa, 101
14. *Wilder, Bert, T, North Carolina State, 109, F
15. Mudie, Sam, HB, Rutgers, 117
16. Smith, Jim, T, Penn State, 125
17. *Miller, Allen, G, Ohio U., 133
18. Iles, Buddy, E, TCU, 141
19. *Bohovich, Reed, T, Lehigh, 149
20. Dickson, Judge, FB, Minnesota, 157
21. Hatcher, Ron, FB, Michigan State, 165
22. Nolan, Tom, T, Widener, 173
23. Kuprok, John, E, Pittsburgh, 181
24. *Counts, Johnny, HB, Illinois, 189
25. Warren, Russ, HB, Columbia, 197
26. Morris, Chuck, HB, Mississippi, 205, F
27. Archer, Jerry, C, Pittsburg State, 213, F
28. Nikirk, Walter, T, Houston, 221, F
29. *Parker, Frank, T, Oklahoma State, 229, F
30. *McClellan, Mike, HB, Oklahoma, 237, F
31. Hicks, L.E., T, Florida, 245, F
32. *Jonas, Don, HB, Penn State, 253, F
33. Maravich, Nick, T, North Carolina State, 261, F
34. Wilson, Dick, C, Penn State, 267, F

OAKLAND 1962
1. *Gabriel, Roman, QB, North Carolina State, 1
2. *Alworth, Lance, HB, Arkansas, 9
3. *Pine, Ed, C, Utah, 17
4. *Meyers, John, T, Washington, 25
5. *Hernandez, Joe, HB, Arizona, 33
6. *Birdwell, Dan, C, Houston, 41
7. *Norris, Jim, T, Houston, 49
8. Yarborough, Ferrell, E, Northwestern State (LA), 57
9. Dillard, Jim, HB, Oklahoma State, 65
10. *Rivera, Henry, HB, Oregon State, 73
11. Choice to Dallas Texans
12. *Skaggs, Jim, G, Washington, 89
    Schwertfeger, Gary, LB, Montana [from Buffalo] 92
    Donahue, Oscar, E, San Jose State [from Boston] 94
13. Pierovich, George, FB, California, 97
14. *Coan, Bert, HB, Kansas, 105, F
15. *Dean, Floyd, E, Florida, 113, F
16. Russ, Pat, T, Purdue, 121
17. *Ferguson, Larry, HB, Iowa, 129, F
18. *Vollenweider, Jim, FB, Miami (FL), 137
19. Spurlock, Dennis, QB, Whitworth, 145
    Horne, Kent, T, BYU [from Denver] 146
20. Sutro, John, G, San Jose State, 153
21. Tunnicliff, Bill, FB, Michigan, 161
22. *Cadile, Jim, E, San Jose State, 169
23. Basham, Elvin, G, Kansas, 177
24. Bruce, Mickey, HB, Oregon, 185
25. Cagaanan, Tom, HB, Utah State, 193, F
26. *Miller, Fred, T, LSU, 201, F
27. Luhnow, Keith, FB, Santa Ana J.C., 209, F
28. *Marinovich, Marv, T, USC, 217, F
29. *Donahue, Leon, E, San Jose State, 225, F
30. Nicklas, Pete, T, Baylor, 233, F
31. Elliott, Bob, FB, North Carolina, 241, F
32. *Richards, Bob, T, LSU, 249, F
33. White, Eugene, HB, Florida A&M, 257, F
34. Worrell, Bill, T, Georgia, 265, F

SAN DIEGO 1962
1. *Ferguson, Bob, FB, Ohio State, 8
2. *Hudson, Dick, T, Memphis State, 16
3. *Hadl, John, QB, Kansas, 24
4. Bill, Bob, T, Notre Dame [from Houston] 31
   Burton, Mack, HB, San Jose State, 32
5. Mitinger, Bob, E, Penn State [from Denver] 34
   Cornett, John, T, Rice, 40
6. *Winston, Roy, G, LSU [from Denver] 42
   *Buncom, Frank, LB, USC, 48
7. *Harris, Wendell, HB, LSU [from Dallas] 51
   *Jackson, Bob, FB, New Mexico State, 56
8. *Robinson, Jerry, HB, Grambling, 64
9. *Minter, Tom, HB, Baylor, 72
10. *Sullivan, Dan, T, Boston College, 80
11. Bishop, Irv, G, Fresno State, 88
12. *Smith, Ralph, E, Mississippi [from New York Titans] 93
    *Andrie, George, E, Marquette, 96
13. *Bryant, Charles, E, Ohio State, 104
14. Bates, Jim, HB, USC, 112, F
15. *Moore, Fred, T, Memphis State, 120, F
16. Gross, George, T, Auburn, 128, F
17. Gardner, Frank, T, North Carolina Central, 136
18. *Biodrowski, Dennis, E, Memphis State, 144, F
19. *Lind, Mike, FB, Notre Dame, 152, F
20. Herman, Ron, QB, Bradley, 160
21. Williams, Jesse, C, Fresno State, 168, F
22. *Thibert, Jim, E, Toledo, 176, F
23. Farris, Dick, G, North Texas State, 184, F
24. *Jones, Homer, HB, Texas Southern, 192, F +
25. *Gruneisen, Sam, E, Villanova, 200
26. *Woulfe, Mike, G, Colorado, 208, F
27. Rideout, Mel, QB, Richmond, 216, F
28. *Wilson, Ben, FB, USC, 224, F
29. *Dudley, Paul, HB, Arkansas, 232, F
30. *Denvir, John, T, Colorado, 240, F
31. *Elmore, Doug, HB, Mississippi, 248, F
32. *Frazier, Wayne, C, Auburn, 256, F
33. *MacKinnon, Jacque, HB, Colgate, 264, F
34. Lohman, Phil, C, Oklahoma, 272, F

1963 NFL

Held December 3, 1962

BALTIMORE 1963
1. *Vogel, Bob, T, Ohio State, 5
2. *Mackey, John, E, Syracuse, 19
   *Wilson, Butch, B, Alabama [from Pittsburgh] 24
3. Choice to St. Louis
4. *Logan, Jerry, B, West Texas State, 47
   Fullwood, Harlow, G-T, Virginia [from Chicago Bears] 53
5. Ventura, Bill, T-E, Richmond, 61
6. Cook, Jerry, B, Texas, 75
7. *Richardson, Willie, E, Jackson State, 89
8. Hayes, Dave, B, Penn State, 103
9. *Trull, Don, QB, Baylor, 117, F
10. Sierkerskl, Bill, G-T, Missouri, 131
11. *Hill, Winston, T, Texas Southern, 145
12. *Maples, Jimmy, C-LB, Baylor, 159
13. Watters, Paul, T, Miami (OH), 173, F
14. *Petties, Neil, E-B, San Diego State, 187 F
15. Mavity, Leon, DB, Colorado, 201, F
16. Quast, Dick, G, Memphis State, 215, F
17. *Carson, Kern, B, San Diego State, 229, F
18. Woodruff, Luther, T, North Carolina A&T, 243, F
19. Berzansky, Steve, B, West Virginia, 257, F
20. Hurd, D.L., E, Cal State-San Francisco, 271

CHICAGO BEARS 1963
1. Choice to Los Angeles Rams
   *Behrman, Dave, C, Michigan State [from Pittsburgh] 11
2. *Barnett, Steve, T, Oregon [from Dallas] 20
   *Jencks, Bob, E, Miami (OH), 25
3. *Glueck, Larry, DB, Villanova, 38
4. Sanders, Stan, E, Whittier [from San Francisco], 49
   *Mitchell, Charley, HB, Washington [from Pittsburgh] 52
   Choice to Baltimore
5. Choice to San Francisco
6. *Johnson, John, T, Indiana [from Pittsburgh] 80
   Mathieson, Dave, QB, Washington State, 81, F
7. Underhill, Paul, B, Missouri, 94, F
8. Harmon, Dennis, DB, Southern Illinois, 109
9. Day, Monte, T, Fresno State [from Dallas] 118, F
   *Watson, Dave, LB, Georgia Tech, 122
10. Hoerster, Ed, LB, Notre Dame, 137
11. Tullis, James, DB, Florida A&M, 150, F
12. Drummond, Dick, B, George Washington, 165, F
13. Szumczyk, John, B, Trinity (CT), 178
14. Banks, Gordon, B, Fisk, 193
15. Dentel, Bob, C-LB, Miami (FL), 206
16. *Caylor, Lowell, DB, Miami (OH), 221
17. *Sisk, John, B, Miami (FL), 234, F
18. Slabaugh, Jeff, E, Indiana, 249
19. Yaksick, Bob, DB, Rutgers, 262
20. Gregory, John, E, Baldwin-Wallace, 277

CLEVELAND 1963
1. *Hutchinson, Tom, E, Kentucky, 9
2. *Kanicki, Jim, T, Michigan State, 23
3. Choice to Los Angeles Rams
4. Munsey, Bill, B, Minnesota, 51
5. Choice to Pittsburgh then San Francisco
   Baker, Frank, B, Toledo [from Detroit] 68
6. Borghetti, Ernie, T, Pittsburgh [from Minnesota] 72, F
   Bloom, Tom, B, Purdue [from Philadelphia] 74
   Choice to Los Angeles Rams
7. Choice to Green Bay
8. *Sweeney, Walt, E, Syracuse, 107
9. *Raimey, Dave, B, Michigan, 121
10. Bobbitt, Jim, G, Michigan State, 135
11. *Graham, Art, E, Boston College, 149
12. Infante, Lindy, B, Florida, 163
13. Katterhenrich, Dave, B, Ohio State, 177
14. *Faulkner, Staley, T, Texas, 191, F
15. Reade, Lynn, T, USC, 205, F
16. Kelly, Dick, G, Georgia, 219, F
17. Anderson, Dick, E, Penn State, 233, F
18. Garvin, Bobby, T, Mississippi State, 247
19. Sherman, Gary, LB, Bowling Green, 261
20. Shaw, Steve, B, Vanderbilt, 275, F

DALLAS COWBOYS 1963
1. *Jordan, Lee Roy, LB, Alabama, 6
2. Choice to Chicago Bears
3. *Price, Jim, LB, Auburn, 34
4. Hall, Whaley, T, Mississippi, 48, F
5. Choice to New York Giants
6. Choice to Green Bay
7. Clothier, Marv, G, Kansas, 90
8. Choice to Green Bay
9. Choice to Chicago Bears
10. Scheyer, Rod, T, Washington, 132
11. *Schoenke, Ray, C, SMU, 146
12. *Perkins, Bill, FB, Iowa, 160
13. Wicker, Paul, T, Fresno State, 174, F
14. Cioci, Lou, LB, Boston College, 188
15. *Overton, Jerry, DB, Utah, 202
16. Golden, Dennis, T, Holy Cross, 216
17. Parks, Ernie, G, McMurry, 230, F
18. *Frank, Bill, T, Colorado, 244
19. *Stiger, Jim, B, Washington, 258
20. Lucas, Tommy, E, Texas, 272

DETROIT 1963
1. *Sanders, Daryl, T, Ohio State, 12
2. *Williams, Roy, T, Pacific, 27
3. Choice to Philadelphia
4. *Walton, Chuck, G, Iowa State, 55
5. Choice to Clevelandveland
6. King, Don, HB, Syracuse, 83
7. Gamble, John, G, Pacific, 96
8. *Gaubatz, Dennis, LB, LSU, 111
9. Dill, Ken, LB, Mississippi, 124, F
10. *Ryder, Nick, B, Miami (FL), 139
11. *Kassulke, Karl, B, Drake, 152
12. *Janik, Tom, B, Texas A&I, 167
13. *Clark, Ernie, LB, Michigan State, 180
14. O'Brien, Bill, T, Xavier, 195
15. *Simon, Jim, E-LB, Miami (FL), 208
16. Johnson, Charlie, T, Villanova, 223
17. Frantz, Gene, B, BYU, 236
18. *Greer, Al, E, Jackson State, 251
19. *Reeberg, Lucian, T, Hampton, 264
20. Scarborough, Gordon, B, East Texas State, 279, F

GREEN BAY 1963
1. *Robinson, Dave, E, Penn State, 14
2. *Brown, Tom, B, Maryland, 28
3. *Claridge, Dennis, B, Nebraska [from Pittsburgh] 39, F
   *Liscio, Tony, T, Tulsa, 42
4. *Aldridge, Lionel, G, Utah State [from New York Giants] 54
   Simons, Carlton, C, Stanford, 56
5. Cverko, Jack, G, Northwestern [from Washington] 63, F
   *Grimm, Dan, T, Colorado, 70
6. Simmons, John, E, Tulsa [from Dallas] 76, F
   *Barrett, Jan, E, Fresno State, 84
7. *Kroner, Gary, B, Wisconsin [from Cleveland] 93
   Hill, Olin, T, Furman [from Pittsburgh] 95
   Todd, Turnley, LB, Virginia, 98, F
8. *Kinderman, Keith, B, Florida State [from Dallas] 104
   Rettino, Louis, B, Villanova, 112
9. Freeman, Bill, T, Southern Mississippi, 126, F
10. McQuiston, Earl, G, Iowa, 140
11. *Fleming, Marv, E, Utah, 154
12. *Lamonica, Daryle, QB, Notre Dame, 168
13. Kellum, Bill, T, Tulane, 182, F
14. *Holler, James (Punkey), LB, South Carolina, 196
15. *Breen, Gene, T, Virginia Tech, 210, F
16. Hunt, Coolidge, B, Texas Tech, 224
17. Walker, Thurman, E, Illinois, 238
18. Hernandez, Luis, G, Texas-El Paso, 252
19. Hamp, Herman, B, Fresno State, 266, F
20. *Brezina, Bobby, B, Houston, 280

LOS ANGELES RAMS 1963
1. *Baker, Terry, B, Oregon State, 1
   Guthrie, Rufus, G, Georgia Tech [from Chicago Bears] 10
2. *Nomina, Tom, T, Miami (OH), 15
3. *Costa, Dave, G, Utah, 29
   *Baker, John, LB, Mississippi State [from Cleveland] 37
4. *Griffin, John, B, Memphis State, 43
5. *Auer, Joe, B, Georgia Tech, 57, F
   Benson, Roland, T, Miami [from Philadelphia] 60, F
   *Chuy, Don, T, Clemson [from Pittsburgh] 67
6. *Saimes, George, B, Michigan State, 71
   Monaghan, Terry, T, Penn State [from Cleveland] 79, F
7. Zorn, Bill, T, Michigan State, 85
8. *Peters, Anton, T, Florida, 99
9. Profit, Mel, E, UCLA, 113, F
10. *Farrier, Curt, T, Montana State, 127
11. Theisen, Dave, B, Nebraska, 141, F
12. Moody, Billy, B, Arkansas, 155
13. Hildebrand, Al, T, Stanford, 169, F
14. Arbuse, Alan, T, Rhode Island, 183
15. Campbell, Larry, E, Toledo, 197, F
16. Burden, Walter, LB, McNeese State, 211
17. *Wilson, Jerrel, LB-K, Southern Mississippi, 225
18. Soefker, Buddy, B, LSU, 239, F
19. Nelson, Dornel, B, Arizona State, 253
20. Redell, Bill, DHB, Occidental, 267, F

MINNESOTA 1963
1. *Dunaway, Jim, T, Mississippi, 3
2. *Bell, Bobby, T, Minnesota, 16
3. *Poage, Ray, B, Texas, 31
4. *Flatley, Paul, E, Northwestern, 44
5. Kaltenbach, Gary, T, Pittsburgh, 59
6. Choice to Clevelandveland
7. Choice to New York Giants
8. O'Mahoney, Jim, LB, Miami (FL), 100
9. Hoover, Bob, B, Florida, 115
10. *Kosens, Terry, B, Hofstra, 128
11. *Campbell, John, LB, Minnesota, 143
12. *Sklopan, John, B, Southern Mississippi, 156
13. *O'Brien, Dave, T, Boston College, 171
14. Ferrisi, Ralph, B, Southern Connecticut State, 184
15. Murio, John, E, Whitworth, 199
16. Mirich, Rex, T, Northern Arizona, 212, F
17. Munsey, Tom, B, Concord, 227
18. McIntyre, Tom, T, State John's (MN), 240
19. Horvath, Frank, B, Youngstown State, 255
20. Kent, Mailon, B, Auburn, 268, F

NEW YORK GIANTS 1963
1. Choice to St. Louis
2. *Lasky, Frank, T, Florida, 26, F
3. Skelly, Dick, B, Florida, 41
4. Choice to Green Bay
5. *Hill, Dave, T, Auburn [from Dallas] 62
   *Slaby, Lou, B, Pittsburgh, 69
6. *Petrich, Bob, T, West Texas State, 82
7. Hoppmann, Dave, B, Iowa State [from Minnesota] 87
   Petkus, Burt, G, Northwestern, 97
8. *Herman, Dave, G, Michigan State, 110, F
9. *Taylor, Bob, T, Maryland-Eastern Shore, 125
10. *Taliaferro, Mike, QB, Illinois, 138, F
11. *McKinnon, Don, C, Dartmouth, 153
12. *Adamchik, Ed, G, Pittsburgh, 166, F
13. Moss, Jim, B, West Virginia, 181
14. Williams, Joe, B, Iowa, 194
15. *Howell, Lane, C, Grambling, 209
16. *Killett, Charlie, B, Memphis State, 222, F
17. *McAdams, Bob, T, North Carolina Central, 237
18. *Pashe, Bill, B, George Washington, 250
19. *Buchanan, Buck, T, Grambling, 265
20. *Jones, Homer, B, Texas Southern, 278, F

PHILADELPHIA 1963
1. *Budde, Ed, T, Michigan State, 4
2. *Mansfield, Ray, T, Washington, 18
3. *Crossan, Dave, G-C, Maryland, 32
   *Guy, Louis, B, Mississippi [from Detroit] 40
4. Choice to San Francisco
5. Choice to Los Angeles Rams
6. Choice to Clevelandveland
7. *Caffey, Lee Roy, B-LB, Texas A&M, 88
8. *Woodeshick, Tom, B, West Virginia, 102
   *Sykes, Gene, B, LSU [from Washington] 106
9. Ward, Dennis, T, Oklahoma, 116
10. *Liske, Pete, B, Penn State, 130, F
11. *Heck, Ralph, LB, Colorado, 144
12. *Gill, Roger, B, Texas Tech, 158, F
13. Iacone, Joe, B, West Chester, 172
14. *Ramsey, Nate, B, Indiana, 186
15. Heard, George, E, New Mexico, 200
16. *Goodwin, Ronnie, B, Baylor, 214
17. Rush, Gordon, B, Tulane, 228
18. Mathews, Rudy, T, TCU, 242
19. Wasdovich, Mike, G, Indiana, 256
20. Rizzo, Ben, B, Miami (FL), 270

PITTSBURGH 1963
1. Choice to Chicago Bears
2. Choice to Baltimore
3. Choice to Green Bay
4. Choice to Chicago Bears
5. Choice to Los Angeles Rams
6. Choice to Chicago Bears
7. Choice to Green Bay
8. *Atkinson, Frank, T, Stanford, 108
9. Carrington, Gene, T, Boston College, 123
10. *Nelsen, Bill, QB, USC, 136
11. *Dixon, Hewritt, B, Florida A&M, 151
12. *Curry, Roy, B, Jackson State, 164, F
13. Gray, Harold, LB, Cal State-Los Angeles, 179
14. Dickerson, Robert, E, Bethune-Cookman, 192
15. Szykowny, Matt, B, Iowa, 207
16. *Russell, Andy, B, Missouri, 220
17. Stein, Tim, C, Miami (OH), 235, F
18. *Bradshaw, Jim, B, Tennessee-Chattanooga, 248
19. Berg, Roger, T, State Thomas (MN), 263
20. Traficant, Jim, B, Pittsburgh, 276

ST. LOUIS 1963
1. *Stovall, Jerry, B, LSU, 2
   *Brumm, Don, DE, Purdue [from New York Giants] 13
2. *Reynolds, Bob, T, Bowling Green, 17
3. *Brabham, Danny, DE, Arkansas, 30
   Fracchia, Mike, B, Alabama [from Baltimore] 33, F
4. *Estes, Don, T, LSU, 45
5. *Thornton, Bill (Thunder), B, Nebraska, 58
6. *Paremore, Bob, B, Florida A&M, 73
7. Moss, Jim, T, South Carolina, 86
8. Cook, Jim, G, Oklahoma, 101
9. *Crenshaw, Willis, B, Kansas State, 114, F
10. *Smith, Jackie, E, Northwestern State (LA), 129
11. *Burson, Jim, B, Auburn, 142
12. *Walker, Chuck, G, Duke, 157, F
13. Zyskowski, Alex, B, Wichita State, 170
14. Lea, Paul, B, Oklahoma, 185
15. *Scrutchins, Ed, E, Toledo, 198
16. Slafkosky, John, T, Notre Dame, 213
17. *Meggyesy, Dave, LB, Syracuse, 226
18. *Stallings, Larry, T, Georgia Tech, 241
19. Haney, Darnell, T, Utah State, 254
20. Clay, Bill, E, Arkansas, 269, F

SAN FRANCISCO 1963
1. *Alexander, Kermit, B, UCLA, 8
2. *Rock, Walter, G, Maryland, 21
3. *Lisbon, Don, B, Bowling Green, 36
4. *Rosdahl, Harrison, G, Penn State [from Philadelphia] 46, F
   Choice to Chicago Bears
   Campbell, Hugh, E, Washington State [from Washington] 50
5. *Burke, Vern, E, Oregon State, 64, F
   Pilot, Jim (Preacher), B, New Mex State [from Cleveland thru Pittsburgh] 65, F
   Moeller, Gary, G-LB, Ohio State [from Chicago Bears] 66
6. Emerick, Pat, G, Western Michigan, 77
7. DeCourley, Ernest, T, Moorhead State, 92
8. Locke, Roger, E, Arizona State, 105, F
9. *Maczuzak, John, T, Pittsburgh, 120, F
10. Lopour, Dick, B, Huron, 133
11. Shafer, Steve, B, Utah State, 148
12. Benton, Bob, T, Mississippi State, 161
13. Schultz, Dick, T, Ohio, 176
14. *Tobin, Bill, B, Missouri, 189
15. Ross, Oliver, B, West Texas State, 204, F
16. Bogdalek, Jim, T, Toledo, 217
17. Reed, Ken, G, Tulsa, 232
18. Sellers, John, T, Bakersfield J.C., 245, F
19. Price, Bob, G, North Texas State, 260
20. Davis, Don, B, McMurry, 273

WASHINGTON 1963
1. *Richter, Pat, E, Wisconsin, 7
2. *Sanders, Lonnie, B, Michigan State, 22
3. *Snidow, Ron, T, Oregon, 35
4. Choice to San Francisco
5. Choice to Green Bay
6. Nickoson, Charley, T, Ohio U., 78
7. *Francis, Dave, B, Ohio State, 91
8. Choice to Philadelphialadelphia
9. *Joe, Billy, B, Villanova, 119
10. Foster, Rod, G, Ohio State, 134
11. Schau, Allen, E, Western Michigan, 147
12. Caldwell, Bob, C, Georgia Tech, 162
13. Greiner, John, E, Purdue, 175
14. Winingder, Tom, B, Georgia Tech, 190
15. *Butsko, Harry, LB, Maryland, 203
16. Adams, Dave, G, Arkansas, 218, F
17. Whaley, Ron, DHB, Tenn.-Chattanooga, 231, F
18. Roberts, Drew, E, Cal State-Humboldt, 246
19. *Turner, Jim, QB, Utah State, 259
20. Baughan, Joe, T, Auburn, 274

1963 AFL

Held December 1, 1962

Although the two franchises played the 1963 season as the Kansas City Chiefs and the New York Jets, at the time of the draft they still were known as the Dallas Texans and the New York Titans, respectively. Boston became the only franchise ever to select the same player twice in the same draft. In the thirteenth round, the Patriots chose Dave Adams of Arkansas as a future, but the selection was voided because future picks couldn't be made until the fourteenth round. The Patriots again chose Adams in the twenty-seventh round, when he was eligible as a future pick.

BOSTON 1963
1. *Graham, Art, E, Boston College, 7
2. *Jordan, Lee Roy, C, Alabama, 14
3. *Vogel, Bob, T, Ohio State, 23
4. *Reynolds, Bob, T, Bowling Green, 30
5. Cioci, Lou, G, Boston College, 39
6. *Silas, Sam, T, Southern Illinois, 46
7. Williamson, Dick, E, Alabama, 55
8. Foster, Rod, G, Ohio State, 62
9. *Simon, Jim, E, Miami (FL), 71
10. *McKinnon, Don, C, Dartmouth, 79
11. Hayes, Dave, FB, Penn State [from Houston] 86
    *Watson, Dave, G, Georgia Tech, 87
12. *Gambrell, Billy, HB, South Carolina [from Buffalo] 92
    Gauntner, Tim, HB, John Carroll, 94
13. Adams, Dave, T, Arkansas [from Buffalo] 100, F +
    Ferrissi, Ralph, FB, Southern Connecticut State, 103
14. Hall, Whaley, T, Mississippi, 110, F
15. Dentel, Bob, C, Miami (FL), 119
16. Bryant, Wes, T, Arkansas, 126
17. Neumann, Tom, HB, Michigan, 135
18. O'Brien, Dave, T, Boston College, 142
19. McCarthy, Pat, QB, Holy Cross, 151
20. Bradshaw, Jim, HB, Tennessee-Chattanooga, 158
21. Sherman, Gary, B, Bowling Green, 167
22. Craddock, Nate, FB, Parsons, 174
23. Snyder, Al, HB, Holy Cross, 183
24. Schultz, Dick, T, Ohio U., 190
25. *Gaubatz, Dennis, G, LSU, 199
26. Tullis, Jim, HB, Florida A&M, 206, F
27. Adams, Dave, T, Arkansas, 215, F
28. Whaley, Ron, HB, Tennessee-Chattanooga, 222, F
29. Kelly, Dick, G, Georgia, 231, F

BUFFALO 1963
1. *Behrman, Dave, C, Michigan State, 4
2. *Dunaway, Jim, T, Mississippi [from Oakland] 9
   *Hutchinson, Tom, E, Kentucky, 12
3. *Brown, Tom, HB, Maryland, 20
4. *Woodeshick, Tom, HB, West Virginia, 28
5. *Jencks, Bob, E, Miami (OH), 36
6. Moss, Jim, LB, South Carolina, 44
7. *Kanicki, Jim, T, Michigan State, 52
8. Choice to Denver
9. *Stallings, Larry, LB, Georgia Tech, 68
10. *Snidow, Ron, T, Oregon, 76
11. Goodwin, Ronnie, HB, Baylor [from New York Titans] 83
    Choice to Houston
12. Choice to Boston
13. Choice to Boston
14. Simmons, J B., E, Tulsa, 108, F
15. Underhill, Paul, FB, Missouri, 116, F
16. Hoerster, Ed, LB, Notre Dame, 124
17. Slabaugh, Jeff, T, Indiana, 132
18. *Paterra, Herb, LB, Michigan State, 140
19. *Sykes, Gene, E, LSU, 148
20. Fullwood, Harlow, T, Virginia, 156
21. *Adamchik, Ed, T, Pittsburgh, 164, F
22. *Walker, Chuck, T, Duke, 172, F
23. Middleton, Bob, E, Ohio State, 180
24. *Lamonica, Daryle, QB, Notre Dame, 188
25. Carlson, Ron, E, Wisconsin, 196
26. *Crenshaw, Willis, FB, Nebraska, 204, F
27. Quast, Dick, G, Memphis State, 212., F
28. Mavity, Leon, HB, Colorado, 220, F
29. Killett, Charlie, HB, Memphis State, 228, F

DALLAS TEXANS 1963
1. *Buchanan, Buck, T, Grambling [from Oakland] 1
   *Budde, Ed, T, Michigan State, 8
2. *Rock, Walter, T, Maryland, 16
3. *Brumm, Don, T, Purdue, 24
4. *Sanders, Daryl, G, Ohio State, 32
5. *Campbell, John, E, Minnesota, 40
6. *Saimes, George, FB, Michigan State, 48
7. *Bell, Bobby, T, Minnesota, 56
8. *Sklopan, John, HB, Southern Mississippi, 64
9. *Barrett, Jan, E, Fresno State, 72
10. *Farrier, Curt, T, Montana State, 80
11. *Infante, Lindy, HB, Florida [from Oakland] 81
    *Wilson, Jerrel, FB, Southern Mississippi, 88
12. Choice to New York Titans
13. Ward, Dennis, G, Oklahoma, 104
14. Johnson, Stone, HB, Grambling [from Oakland] 105
    Pilot, Jim (Preacher), HB, New Mexico State, 112, F
15. *Auer, Joe, HB, Georgia Tech, 120, F
16. Profit, Mel, E, UCLA, 128, F
17. Moore, Billy, QB, Arkansas, 136
18. Freeman, Bill, T, Southern Mississippi, 144
19. Starling, Bruce, DB, Florida, 152
20. Vaught, Lowell, T, Southwestern Louisiana, 160, F
21. Borghetti, Ernie, T, Pittsburgh, 168, F
22. Maczuzak, John, T, Pittsburgh, 176, F
23. Adams, Dave, G, Arkansas, 184
24. *Hill, Dave, T, Auburn, 192
25. Hughes, John, G, SMU, 200, F
26. Todd, Tumley, C, Virginia, 208, F
27. Clay, Billy, E, Arkansas, 216, F
28. Scarborough, Gordon, E, East Texas State, 224, F
29. *Sisk, John, HB, Miami (FL), 232, F

DENVER 1963
1. *Alexander, Kermit, HB, UCLA, 5
2. *Poage, Ray, FB, Texas [from New York Titans] 11
   *Nomina, Tom, T, Miami (OH), 13
3. *Janik, Tom, HB, Texas A&I, 21
4. *Slaby, Lou, LB, Pittsburgh, 29
5. *Mansfield, Ray, C, Washington, 37
6. *Peters, Anton, T, Florida, 45
7. *Slaughter, Mickey, QB, Louisiana Tech [from San Diego] 50
   *Flatley, Paul, E, Northwestern, 53
8. *Dixon, Hewritt, FB, Florida A&M [from Buffalo] 60
   Griffin, John, HB, Memphis State, 61
9. *Fleming, Marv, E, Utah, 69
10. *Sanders, Lonnie, HB, Michigan State, 77
    *Richter, Pat, E, Wisconsin [from Houston] 78
11. *Joe, Billy, FB, Villanova, 85
12. Gamble, John, E, Pacific, 93
13. *Maples, Butch, C, Baylor, 101
14. Choice to San Diego
15. Freeman, Winston, E, North Texas State, 117
16. *Crossan, Dave, G, Maryland, 125
17. *Paremore, Bob, HB, Florida A&M, 133
18. *Mitchell, Charley, HB, Washington, 141
19. Baker, Frank, FB, Toledo, 149
20. *Grimm, Dan, G, Colorado, 157
21. Nolan, Ross, E, Northeast Louisiana, 165
22. Mathiesen, Dave, QB, Washington State, 173, F
23. Moody, Billy, HB, Arkansas, 181
24. Simons, C.B., LB, Stanford, 189
25. Farmer, Forest, LB, Purdue, 197
26. Day, Monte, T, Fresno State, 205, F
27. Sellers, John, T, Bakersfield J.C., 213, F
28. Reddell, Bill, HB, Occidental, 221, F
29. Carson, Kern, HB, San Diego State, 229, F

HOUSTON 1963
1. *Brabham, Danny, FB, Arkansas, 6
2. Estes, Don, T, LSU, 15
3. Cook, Jerry, HB, Texas, 22
4. *Caffey, Lee Roy, FB, Texas A&M [from Oakland] 25
   Hopkins, Jerry, C, Texas A&M, 31
5. *Jones, Homer, HB, Texas Southern [from Oakland] 33
   *Chuy, Don, T, Clemson, 38
6. *Aldridge, Lionel, T, Utah State, 47
7. *Baker, John, E, Mississippi State, 54
8. *Burson, Jim, HB, Auburn, 63
9. Burke, Ed, T, Notre Dame, 70
10. Choice to Den
11. Brown, Tom, G, Pittsburgh [from Buffalo] 84
    Choice to Boston
12. Choice to Oaklandland
13. Choice to Oaklandland
14. *Trull, Don, QB, Baylor, 111, F
15. *Looney, Joe Don, HB, Oklahoma, 118 +
16. Benson, Rex, T, Miami, 127, F
17. Griffin, Jerry, E, Louisiana Tech, 134
18. Lea, Paul, HB, Oklahoma, 143
19. Hoover, Bob, HB, Florida, 150
20. Lee, Wayne, C, Oklahoma, 159
21. *Faulkner, Staley, T, Texas, 166, F
22. Byer, Sam, FB, Texas A&M, 175
23. Raesz, Gene, E, Rice, 182
24. Burton, Bob, T, Grambling, 191
25. Kaltenbach, Gary, T, Pittsburgh, 198
26. Thiesen, Dave, HB, Nebraska, 207, F
27. Hildebrand, Al, T, Stanford, 214, F
28. Stein, Tim, C, Miami (OH), 223, F
29. Ross, Oliver, T, West Texas State, 230, F

NEW YORK TITANS 1963
1. *Stovall, Jerry, HB, LSU, 3
2. Choice to Den
3. *Richardson, Willie, E, Jackson State, 19
4. *Contoulis, John, T, Connecticut, 27
5. *Mackey, John, E, Syracuse, 35
6. *Price, Jim, LB, Auburn, 43
7. *Guy, Lou, HB, Mississippi, 51
8. King, Bill, QB, Dartmouth, 59
9. Sanders, Stan, E, Whittier, 67
10. *Liscio, Tony, T, Tulsa, 75
11. Choice to Buffalo
12. Craver, Joe, LB, North Carolina, 91
    Lucas, Tommy, E, Texas [from Dallas Texans] 96
13. Hill, Olin, T, Furman, 99
14. Choice to San Diego
15. *Liske, Pete, QB, Penn State, 115, F
16. Ryder, Nick, HB, Miami (FL), 123
17. Johnson, Charley, G, Villanova, 131
18. Munsey, Bill, HB, Minnesota, 139
19. *Kroner, Gary, HB, Wisconsin, 147
20. Johnson, John, T, Indiana, 155
21. *VanderKelen, Ron, QB, Wisconsin, 163
22. *Thornton, Bill (Thunder), FB, Nebraska, 171
23. Rettino, Lou, FB, Villanova, 179
24. *Caylor, Lowell, HB, Miami (OH), 187
25. Baughan, Joe, T, Auburn, 195
26. Monaghan, Terry, T, Penn State, 203, F
27. *Herman, Dave, G, Michigan State, 211, F
28. *Taliaferro, Mike, QB, Illinois, 219, F
29. Wicker, Paul, T, Fresno State, 227, F

OAKLAND 1963
1. Choice to Dallas Texans
2. Choice to Buffalo
3. Choice to San Diego
4. Choice to Houston
5. Choice to Houston
6. *Wilson, Butch, HB, Alabama, 41
7. *Costa, Dave, T, Utah, 49
8. Locke, Roger, E, Arizona State, 57
9. *Logan, Jerry, HB, West Texas State, 65
10. *Schoenke, Ray, G, SMU, 73
11. Choice to Dallas Texans
12. Burdin, Walt, LB, McNeese State, 89
    Branson, Doyle, HB, Southern Oregon [from Houston] 95
13. Haney, Darnel, E, Utah State, 97
    Roberts, Drew, E, Cal State-Humboldt [from Houston] 102
14. Choice to Dallas Texans
15. *Burke, Vern, E, Oregon, 113, F
16. Moss, Jim, HB, West Virginia, 121
17. Murio, John, HB, Whitworth, 129
18. *Dillon, Terry, HB, Montana, 137
    Hogan, George, G, Texas A&M [from San Diego] 138
19. Fiorentino, Tony, G, UCLA, 145
20. *Mirich, Rex, T, Arizona State, 153, F
21. *Petties, Neal, HB, San Diego State, 161, F
22. Campbell, Hugh, E, Washington State, 169
23. Anabo, Jon, QB, Fresno State, 177
24. Peters, Dick, T, Whittier, 185
25. McFarland, Bill, FB, Oklahoma State, 193
26. *Claridge, Dennis, QB, Nebraska, 201, F
27. Skelly, Dick, HB, Florida, 209, F
28. Campbell, Larry, FB, Utah State, 217, F
29. Anderson, Dick, E, Penn State, 225, F

SAN DIEGO 1963
1. *Sweeney, Walt, E, Syracuse, 2
2. Guthrie, Rufus, G, Georgia Tech, 10
3. *Robinson, Dave, E, Penn State [from Oakland] 17
   *Kinderman, Keith, HB, Florida State, 18
4. *Williams, Roy, T, Pacific, 26
5. *Glueck, Larry, HB, Villanova, 34
6. Emerick, Pat, LB, Western Michigan, 42
7. Choice to Denver
8. *Heeter, Gene, E, West Virginia, 58
9. *Barnett, Steve, T, Oregon, 66
10. Scott, Don, T, Tampa, 74
11. *Petrich, Bob, T, West Texas State, 82
12. *Baker, Terry, QB, Oregon State, 90
13. *Walton, Chuck, G, Iowa State, 98
14. *Lasky, Frank, T, Florida, 106, F
    *Rosdahl, Harrison, G, Penn State [from New York Jets] 107, F
    Cverko, Jack, G, Northwestern [from Denver] 109, F
15. Fracchia, Mike, HB, Alabama, 114, F
16. *Breen, Gene, LB, Virginia Tech, 122, F
17. Drummond, Dick, HB, George Washington, 130, F
18. Choice to Oaklandland
19. *Park, Ernie, T, McMurry, 146
20. Soefker, Buddy, LB, LSU, 154, F
21. Points, Dan, T, Cincinnati, 162, F
22. *Gill, Roger, HB, Texas Tech, 170, F
23. Watters, Paul, T, Miami (OH), 178, F
24. *Frank, Bill, T, Colorado, 186
25. *Mazzanti, Jerry, T, Arkansas, 194
26. Dill, Ken, C, Mississippi, 202, F
27. *Butsko, Harry, G, Maryland, 210, F
28. Berzansky, Steve, FB, West Virginia, 218, F
29. Hamp, Herman, HB, Fresno State, 226, F

1964 NFL

Held December 2, 1963

BALTIMORE 1964
1. *Woodson, Marv, HB, Indiana, 8
2. *Lorick, Tony, HB, Arizona State, 22
3. Choice to Green Bay

4. *Davis, Ted, E-LB, Georgia Tech, 50
5. *Lothamer, Ed, T, Michigan State, 64
6. Mazurek, Jim, T, Syracuse, 78
7. Sugarman, Ken, T, Whitworth, 92
8. *Williamson, John, LB, Louisiana Tech, 106
9. *Turner, Vince, B, Missouri, 120
10. Choice to Detroit
11. Paglio, John, T, Syracuse, 148
12. *Graham, Kenny, HB, Washington State, 162
13. *Parker, Charlie, T, Southern Mississippi, 176
14. Case, John, E, Clemson, 190
15. Kramer, Larry, T, Nebraska, 204, F
16. Lopes, Roger, FB, Michigan State, 218
17. Green, Don, HB, Susquehanna, 232
18. *Haymond, Alvin, HB, Southern, 246
19. Dejanovich, Owen, T, Northern Arizona, 260
20. Butler, John, FB, San Diego State, 274, F

CHICAGO BEARS 1964
1. *Evey, Dick, T, Tennessee, 14
2. Choice to Pittsburghtsburgh
   *Martin, Billy, E, Georgia Tech [from Los Angeles Rams] 21
   Crain, Pat, HB, Clemson [from Pittsburgh] 23, F
3. *Blanks, Sid, HB, Texas A&I, 42
4. *Reilly, Mike, LB, Iowa [from Minnesota] 47
   *Budka, Frank, HB, Notre Dame, 56
5. *Conners, Dan, T, Miami (FL), 70
6. *Jones, Jimmy, E, Wisconsin, 84, F
7. *Logan, Chuck, E, Northwestern, 98
8. *Rakestraw, Larry, QB, Georgia, 112
9. Wilkinson, Jay, HB, Duke, 126
10. Brown, Mike, B, Delaware, 140
11. *Leeuwenberg, Dick, T, Stanford, 154, F
12. *Horton, Bob, FB, Boston U., 168
13. Webb, Cloyd, E, Iowa, 182
14. Francisco, Kent, T, UCLA, 196, F
15. *Burman, George, T, Northwestern, 210
16. Butler, Roderick, HB, Eastern Illinois, 224
17. Kasapis, Constantinos, T, Iowa, 238
18. Batts, Bob, HB, Texas Southern, 252
19. Whitehead, Jim, T, Georgia, 266, F
20. Niglio, Dick, FB, Yale, 280, F

CLEVELAND 1964
1. *Warfield, Paul, HB, Ohio State, 11
2. *Truax, Billy, DE, LSU, 26
3. Choice to Los Angeles Rams
4. *Shackelford, Don, T, Pacific, 54
5. Klein, Dick, T, Wichita State, 67, F
6. Choice to Dallas
7. *Odom, Sammy, LB, Northwestern State (LA), 95
8. *Kelly, Leroy, HB, Morgan State, 110
9. Briscoe, John, LB, Arizona, 123, F
10. Robinson, Bobby, G, Mississippi [from Pittsburgh] 135, F
    *Van Raaphorst, Dick, K, Ohio State, 138
11. Versprille, Eddie, FB, Alabama, 151
12. *Mitchell, Ed, T, Southern, 166, F
13. Meehan, Bob, G, Syracuse, 179
14. Sieg, Terry, HB, Virginia, 194, F
15. Houtman, John, T, Michigan, 207
16. *Williams, Sid, E, Southern, 222
17. Bartolameolli, Larry, T, Western Michigan, 235, F
18. *Lewis, Sherman, HB, Michigan State, 250
19. Higgins, Jim, G, Xavier, 263
20. Archer, Dave, T, Syracuse, 278, F

DALLAS 1964
1. *Appleton, Scott, T, Texas, 4
2. *Renfro, Mel, B, Oregon, 17
3. Choice to Los Angeles Rams
4. *Dunn, Perry Lee, QB, Mississippi, 45
5. Choice to Green Bay
6. *Lothridge, Billy, QB, Georgia Tech, 73
   Curry, Jim, E, Cincinnati [from Cleveland] 82
   *Evans, Jim, E, Texas-El Paso [from Green Bay] 83
7. *Hayes, Bob, HB, Florida A&M, 88, F
8. Geverink, Al, HB, UCLA, 101
9. *Kupp, Jake, E, Washington, 116
10. *Staubach, Roger, QB, Navy, 129, F
11. Crenshaw, Bob, G, Baylor, 144
12. Norman, Johnny, E, Northwestern State (LA), 157
13. *Rhome, Jerry, QB, Tulsa, 172, F
14. Worden, Jim, LB, Wittenberg, 185
15. Van Burkleo, Bill, B, Tulsa, 200, F
16. Cercel, Paul, C, Pittsburgh, 213, F
17. *Abell, Bud, E, Missouri, 228, F
18. *Viltz, Theo, DB, USC, 241, F +
19. Murphy, H.D., B, Oregon, 256
20. Hughes, John, LB, SMU, 269

DETROIT 1964
1. *Beathard, Pete, QB, USC, 5
2. *Snorton, Matt, E, Michigan State, 20
3. *Batten, Pat, HB, Hardin-Simmons [from Philadelphia] 30
   *Philbin, Gerry, T, Buffalofalo, 33
4. *Hilgenberg, Wally, G, Iowa, 48
5. *Nelson, Benny, HB, Alabama, 61
6. *Hilton, John, E, Richmond, 76, F
7. Parcells, Bill, T, Wichita State, 89
8. Choice to St. Louis
9. *Rasmussen, Wayne, HB, South Dakota State, 117
10. *Hand, Larry, T, Appalachian State, 132, F
    Holton, Glenn, HB, West Virginia [from Baltimore] 134
11. Hyne, Don, T, Baldwin-Wallace, 145
12. *Wells, Warren, E, Texas Southern, 160
13. Miller, John, T, Idaho State, 173
14. Bickle, Doug, E, Hillsdale, 188, F
15. *LaLonde, Roger, T, Muskingum, 201
16. Robinson, Allan, HB, BYU, 216, F
17. Provenzano, Joe, T, Kansas State, 229
18. Langley, Willis, T, LSU, 244
19. Zellmer, Bruce, HB, Winona State, 257
20. Barilla, Steve, T, Wichita State, 272

GREEN BAY 1964
1. *Voss, Lloyd, T, Nebraska, 13
2. *Morris, Jon, C, Holy Cross, 27
3. *Burrell, Ode, B, Mississippi State [from Baltimore] 36
   *O'Donnell, Joe, G, Michigan [from New York Giants] 40
   *Crutcher, Tommy, B, TCU, 41
4. *Long, Bob, E, Wichita State [from Philadelphia] 44
   *Costa, Paul, T, Notre Dame, 55, F
5. Carlisle, Duke, B, Texas [from Dallas] 60
   *Wright, Steve, T, Alabama, 69
6. Choice to Dal
7. Herzing, Dick, T, Drake, 97, F
8. *Bowman, Ken, C, Wisconsin, 111
9. *McDowell, John, T, State John's (MN), 125
10. *Jacobs, Allen, B, Utah, 139, F
11. Petersen, Jack, T, Nebraska-Omaha, 153
12. Bean, Dwain, B, North Texas State, 167
13. Mauro, Jack, T, Northern Michigan, 181
14. O'Grady, Tom, E, Northwestern, 195
15. Zenko, Alex, T, Kent State, 209, F
16. Ireland, Andrew, B, Utah, 223, F
17. *State Jean, Len, E, Northern Michigan, 237
18. Hicks, Mike, G, Marshall, 251
19. *Baker, John, E, Norfolk State, 265
20. *Curry, Bill, C, Georgia Tech, 279, F

LOS ANGELES RAMS 1964
1. *Munson, Bill, QB, Utah State, 7
2. Choice to Chicago Bears
3. Mims, John, T, Rice [from Washington] 31
   *Brown, Willie, B, USC [from Dallas] 32
   *Richardson, Jerry, B, West Texas State, 35
   *Pillath, Roger, T, Wisconsin [from Cleveland] 39
4. Choice to New York Giants
5. Henson, Ken, C, TCU, 63, F
6. Johnson, Herman, HB, Michigan State, 77, F
7. Varnell, John, T, West Texas State, 91
8. *Pope, Bucky, E, Catawba, 105
9. Burton, Jerry, B, Northwestern State (LA), 119
10. *Smith, Ron, QB, Richmond [from Minnesota] 131, F
    *Larsen, Gary, T, Concordia (MN), 133
11. *Farris, John, T, San Diego State, 147, F
12. *Dawson, Bill, E, Florida State, 161, F
13. *Harris, Marvin, C, Stanford, 175
14. Garrett, John, LB, Oklahoma, 189, F
15. Mayne, Mike, E, Idaho, 203, F
16. Zera, Phil, B, St. Joseph's (IN), 217, F
17. Galmin, Jim, E, Tampa, 231
18. Smith, Tom, G, Villanova, 245, F
19. Cherry, Bob, E, Wittenberg, 259
20. *Hohn, Bob, HB, Nebraska, 273, F

MINNESOTA 1964
1. *Eller, Carl, T, Minnesota, 6
2. *Bedsole, Hal, E, USC, 19
3. *Rose, George, HB, Auburn, 34
4. Choice to Chicago Bears
   *Keating, Tom, T, Michigan [from New York Giants] 53
5. *Kirby, John, LB, Nebraska, 62
6. *Lacey, Bob, E, North Carolina, 75
7. Bryant, Wes, T, Arkansas, 90
8. *McWatters, Bill, FB, North Texas State, 103
9. *Lester, Darrell, FB, McNeese State, 118
10. Choice to Los Angeles Rams
11. Estes, H.O., G, East Central (OK), 146
12. Sands, Sandy, E, Texas, 159, F
13. Vollmer, Russ, HB, Memphis State, 174
14. *Michel, Tom, HB, East Carolina, 187
15. Kiffin, Monte, T, Nebraska, 202
16. *Oats, Carlton, E, Florida A&M, 215, F
17. McClurg, Jerry, E, Colorado, 230, F
18. Robinson, Carl, T, Prairie View A&M, 243
19. Schott, Dick, E, Louisville, 258, F
20. *Sunde, Milt, T, Minnesota, 271

NEW YORK GIANTS 1964
1. *Looney, Joe Don, B, Oklahoma, 12
2. *Thurlow, Steve, HB, Stanford, 25
3. Choice to Green Bay
4. *Snell, Matt, FB, Ohio State [from Los Angeles Rams] 49
   *Seals, George, E, Missouri [from St. Louis] 52
   Choice to Min
5. *DiMidio, Tony, T, West Chester, 68
6. *Schichtle, Henry, QB, Wichita State, 81
7. *Anderson, Roger, T, Virginia Union, 96
8. Popp, Ray, G, Pittsburgh [from Philadelphia] 100, F
   *Wood, Gary, QB, Cornell, 109
9. Bitsko, Mickey, LB, Dayton, 124, F
10. *Moran, Jim, T, Idaho, 137
11. *Condren, Glen, T, Oklahoma, 152, F
12. McNaughton, Jim, E, Utah State, 165
13. Deibert, John, T, Penn State, 180, F
14. *Harris, Bill, HB, Colorado, 193
15. *Hinton, Chuck, G, Mississippi, 208, F
16. Lembright, Wynn, T, Toledo, 221
17. Humenik, Dave, T, Notre Dame, 236, F
18. *Garrett, Jim, HB, Grambling, 249
19. Kinard, Frank, HB, Mississippi, 264, F
20. Gibbons, Tony, T, John Carroll, 277

PHILADELPHIA 1964
1. *Brown, Bob, G, Nebraska, 2
2. *Concannon, Jack, QB, Boston College, 16
3. Choice to Det
4. *Kubala, Ray, C, Texas A&M [from Washington] 46
   Choice to Green Bay
5. Babb, Mickey, E-LB, Georgia, 58
6. *Denson, Al, E, Florida A&M, 72
7. Goimarac, Pete, C, West Virginia, 86
8. Choice to New York Giants
9. Smith, Larry, B, Mississippi, 114
10. Boris, Tom, B, Purdue, 128
11. *Berry, Bob, QB, Oregon, 142, F
12. Sapinsky, John, T, William & Mary, 156
13. *Kindig, Howard, C, Cal State-L.A., 170, F
14. Arizzi, Ernie, B, Maryland, 184
15. Burrows, Bob, T, East Texas State, 198, F
16. Radosevich, Will, T, Wyoming, 212., F
17. *Morgan, Mike, E, LSU, 226
18. *Lang, Izzy, B, Tennessee State, 240, F
19. Bowe, Dick, T, Rice, 254, F
20. Lucas, Tommy, G, Mississippi, 268, F

PITTSBURGH 1964
1. *Martha, Paul, HB, Pittsburgh, 10
2. Choice to Chicago Bears
   *Kelly, Jim, E, Notre Dame [from Chicago Bears] 28
3. *Baker, Ralph, LB, Penn State, 38
4. *McGee, Ben, T, Jackson State, 51
5. Alley, T.W., T, William & Mary, 66
6. Gibson, Tom, G, South Carolina, 79
7. *Smith, Bobby, HB, North Texas State, 94
8. Currington, Bobby, HB, North Carolina Central, 107
9. *Nichols, Bob, T, Stanford, 122, F
10. Choice to Cleveland
11. *Soleau, Bob, G, William & Mary, 150
12. *Sherman, Bob, HB, Iowa, 163
13. Baker, Glenn, T, Washington State, 178
14. Jenkins, Tom, G, Ohio State, 191
15. *Brown, Barry, E, Florida, 206, F
16. Kesler, Ed, FB, North Carolina, 219, F
17. Shaw, Dennis, C, Detroit, 234
18. *Dobbins, Oliver, HB, Morgan State, 247
19. Marshall, Don, T, Lehigh, 262
20. Generalovich, Bryan, E, Pittsburgh, 275, F

ST. LOUIS 1964
1. *Kortas, Ken, T, Louisville, 9
2. *Turner, Herschel, G, Kentucky, 24
3. *Prudhomme, Remi, T, LSU, 37, F
4. Choice to New York Giants
5. Brooks, Charley, E, Memphis State, 65, F
6. Bowman, Dick, E, Syracuse, 80
7. Lamb, Jerry, E, Arkansas, 93, F
8. Bednar, George, G, Notre Dame [from Detroit] 104
   Johnson, Bob, E, Wisconsin, 108
9. *Ross, Willie, B, Nebraska, 121
10. Lawrence, Tony, T, Bowling Green, 136, F
11. Hard, Richard, T, Wenatchee Valley J.C., 149
12. *Sortun, Rick, G, Washington, 164
13. Adams, Jake, E, Virginia Tech, 177
14. Slaby, Len, C, Syracuse, 192
15. Stallings, Cliff, B, New Mexico, 205
16. Ankerson, Jack, QB, Ripon, 220
17. Evans, John, T, Memphis State, 233, F
18. Hoover, Dave, B, Iowa State, 248
19. *Young, Bob, T, Howard Payne, 261, F
20. Kubinski, Ralph, G, Missouri, 276

SAN FRANCISCO 1964
1. *Parks, Dave, E, Texas Tech, 1
2. *Mira, George, QB, Miami, 15
3. *Wilcox, Dave, DE, Oregon, 29
4. *Wilson, Jim, G, Georgia, 43, F
5. *Johnson, Rudy, B, Nebraska, 57
6. *Lewis, Gary, B, Arizona State, 71
7. *Clarke, Hagood, B, Florida, 85
8. *Daugherty, Bob, B, Tulsa, 99, F
   *Poole, Bob, E, Clemson [from Washington] 102
9. *Mudd, Howard, G, Hillsdale, 113
10. Polser, Fred, T, East Texas State, 127, F
11. Almquist, Dennis, G, Idaho, 141
12. Long, Jim, B, Fresno State, 155, F
13. *Brown, Bob, T, Arkansas A&M, 169
14. *Beard, Ed, T, Tennessee, 183
15. Griffin, Jim, E, Grambling, 197
16. *Gordon, Cornell, B, North Carolina A&T, 211, F
17. Brusven, Ken, T, Oregon State, 225, F
18. Cole, Jerry, E, Southwest Texas State, 239, F
19. Rawson, Larry, B, Auburn, 253
20. Baker, Gene, G, Whitworth, 267

WASHINGTON 1964
1. *Taylor, Charley, HB, Arizona State, 3
2. *Krause, Paul, B, Iowa, 18
3. Choice to Los Angeles Rams
4. Choice to Philadelphia
5. *Snowden, Jim, FB, Notre Dame, 59, F
6. Brown, Russ, E, Florida, 74
7. *Shiner, Dick, QB, Maryland, 87
8. Choice to San Francisco
9. *Hauss, Len, C, Georgia, 115
10. Leeson, Rick, B, Pittsburgh, 130
11. *Donaldson, Gene, LB, Purdue, 143
12. *Zvolerin, Bob, T, Tennessee, 158
13. MacDonald, Tom, B, Notre Dame, 171
14. Urbanik, Tom, B, Penn State, 186, F
15. Evers, Dick, T, Colorado State, 199, F
16. *Walters, Tommy, B, Southern Mississippi, 214
17. *Clay, Ozzie, B, Iowa State, 227
18. Jones, Bob, G, Nebraska, 242
19. *Seedborg, John, G, Arizona State, 255
20. Guest, Gordon, B, Arkansas, 270 F

1964 AFL

Held November 30, 1963

BOSTON 1964
1. *Concannon, Jack, QB, Boston College, 1
2. *Kelly, Jim, E, Notre Dame, 13
3. Choice to Den
4. *Morris, Jon, E, Holy Cross, 29
5. Choice to San Diego
6. Mazurek, Jim, G, Syracuse, 45
7. Alley, T.W., T, William & Mary, 52
8. *Garrett, J.D., HB, Grambling [from Buffalo] 60
   *LaLonde, Roger, T, Muskingum, 61
9. *State Jean, Len, E, Northern Michigan, 68
10. Choice to Buffalo
11. Barrett, John, HB, Boston College, 84
12. Choice to Kansas City
13. *Scarpati, Joe, DB, North Carolina State, 100
14. *Wilson, Jim, T, Georgia, 109, F
15. Gibbons, Tony, T, John Carroll, 116
16. Pedro, Pete, HB, West Texas State, 124
17. *Wood, Gary, Q-HB, Cornell, 132
18. Tiller, Joe, T, Montana State, 140
19. *Dawson, Bill, E, Florida State, 148, F
20. *Farmer, Lonnie, LB, Tenn.-Chattanooga, 156
21. Lawrence, Tony, T, Bowling Green, 164, F
22. Archer, Dave, T, Syracuse, 172, F
23. Humenik, Dave, T, Notre Dame, 180, F
24. Bartolameoli, Larry, T, Western Michigan, 188, F
25. Generalovich, Bryan, E, Pittsburgh, 196, F
26. Niglio, Dick, HB, Yale, 204, F

BUFFALO 1964
1. *Eller, Carl, T, Minnesota, 5
2. *Evey, Dick, DE, Tennessee, 12
3. *Rose, George, DB, Auburn, 21
4. *Byrd, Butch, HB, Boston U. [from Denver] 25
   *Warfield, Paul, HB, Ohio State, 28
5. *Reilly Mike, LB, Iowa, 37
6. Choice to Kansas City
7. *Pillath, Roger, T, Wisconsin, 53
8. Choice to Boston
9. *Martha, Paul, HB, Pittsburgh, 69
10. *Simpson, Howard, E, Auburn, 76
    Lattimer, Earl, FB-LB, Mich. State [from Boston] 77
11. *Smith, Bobby, HB, N.Texas State [from Denver] 81
    Webb, Cloyd E, Iowa, 85
12. *Ross, Willie, HB, Nebraska [from Kansas City] 90
    *Gogolak, Pete, K, Cornell, 92
13. *O'Donnell, Joe, G-LB, Michigan, 101
14. *Prudhomme, Remi, T, LSU, 108, F
15. Simpson, Bill, T, Baylor, 117, F
16. *Hilton, John, E, Richmond, 125, F
17. Kramer, Larry, T, Nebraska, 133, F
18. *Clarke, Hagood, HB, Florida, 141
19. Montgomery, Don, E, N.Carolina State, 149
20. Dugan, Bob, T, Mississippi State, 157
21. Deibert, John, T, Penn State, 165, F
22. Briscoe, John, LB, Arizona, 173, F
23. Evans, John, T, Memphis State, 181, F
24. Schott, Dick, T, Louisville, 189, F
25. Urbanik, Tom, DB, Penn State, 197, F
26. *Jacobs, Allen, FB, Utah, 205, F

DENVER 1964
1. *Brown, Bob, T, Nebraska, 4
2. Choice to Houston
3. *Woodson, Marv, DB, Indiana, 17
   *Snorton, Matt, E, Michigan State [from Boston] 20
4. Choice to Buffalo
5. Choice to Houston
6. *Shackleford, Don, T, Pacific, 41
   *Denson, Al, FL, Florida A&M [from Oakland] 47
7. *Kubala, Ray, C-T, Texas A&M, 49
   *Richardson, Jerry, LB, W.Texas State [from Houston] 54
8. *Hilgenberg, Wally, G-LB, Iowa, 57
9. Mims, John, T, Rice, 65
10. Choice to Kansas City
11. Choice to Buffalo
12. *Krause, Paul, DB, Iowa, 89
13. *Parker, Charlie, G, Southern Mississippi, 97
14. *Hayes, Bob, HB, Florida A&M, 105, F
15. *Logan, Chuck, E, Northwestern, 113
16. Cherry, Bob, E, Wittenburg, 121
17. McNaughton, Jim, E, Utah State, 129
18. *Mira, George, QB, Miami (FL), 137
19. *Barry, Odell, FL, Findlay, 145
20. Choice to Kansas City
21. Herzing, Dick, T, Drake, 161, F
22. *Lewis, Gary, HB, Arizona State, 169, F
23. Brusvan, Ken, T, Oregon State, 177, F
24. Bitsko, Mickey, LB, Dayton, 185, F
25. Jones, Jim, E, Wisconsin, 193, F
26. *Berry, Bob, QB, Oregon, 201, F

HOUSTON 1964
1. *Appleton, Scott, T, Texas, 6

2. *Taylor, Charley, HB, Arizona State [from Denver] 9
*Truax, Billy, DE, LSU, 14
3. Crenshaw, Bobby, T, Baylor, 22
4. *Burrell, Ode, HB, Mississippi State, 30
5. Varnell, John, T, W.Texas State [from Denver] 33
*Blanks, Sid, HB, Texas A&I, 38
6. *Wilcox, Dave, G, Oregon, 46
7. Choice to Denver
8. Seals, Ezell, HB, Prairie View A&M, 62
9. Burton, Jerry, HB, Northwestern State (LA), 70
10. *Odom, Sammy, LB, Northwestern State (LA), 78
11. Dejanovich, Owen, G, Northern Arizona, 86
12. *Nelson, Benny, DB, Alabama, 94
13. Choice to Kansas City
14. *Henson, Ken, C, TCU, 110, F
15. Crain, Pat, FB, Clemson, 118, F
16. *Munson, Bill, QB, Utah State, 126
17. *Leeuwenburg, Dick, T, Stanford, 134, F
18. *Nichols, Bob, T, Stanford, 142, F
19. Robinson, Carl, T, Prairie View A&M, 150
20. *Jaquess, Pete, HB, Eastern New Mexico, 158
21. Cole, Jerry, HB, Southwest Texas State, 166, F
22. Kessler, Ed, FB, North Carolina, 174, F
23. Whitehead, Jim, T, Georgia, 182, F
24. Garrett, John, LB, Oklahoma, 190, F
25. Bowe, Dick, T, Rice, 198, F
26. Zenko, Alex, T, Kent State, 206, F

KANSAS CITY 1964
1. *Beathard, Pete, QB, USC, 2
2. *Martin, Billy, E, Georgia Tech, 10
3. *Kortas, Ken, T, Louisville, 18
4. *Lothamer, Ed, T, Michigan State, 26
5. *Keating Tom, T, Michigan, 34
6. Carlisle, Duke, DB, Texas, 42
*Looney, Joe Don, HB, Oklahoma [from Buffalo] 44
7. Simon, John, E, Notre Dame, 50
8. *Bedsole, Hal, E, USC, 58
9. *DiMidio, Tony, T, West Chester, 66
10. Stephens, Clay, E, Notre Dame [from Denver] 73
Choice to San Diego
11. *Crutcher, Tommy, LB, TCU, 82
12. Adams, Jack, E, Virginia Tech [from Boston] 93
13. Hudson, Orville, E, East Texas State, 98
Wilkinson, Jay, HB, Duke [from Houston] 102
14. *Costa, Paul, HB, Notre Dame, 106, F
15. *Snowden, Jim, FB, Notre Dame, 114, F
16. *Staubach, Roger, QB, Navy, 122, F
17. Peterson, Jack, T, Nebraska-Omaha, 130
18. Knoll, Jerry, T, Washington, 138, F
19. Lamb, Jerry, E, Arkansas, 146, F
20. Sands, Sandy, E, Texas [from Denver] 153, F
*Hohn, Bob, HB, Nebraska, 154, F
21. Burrows, Bob, T, East Texas State, 162, F
22. Evers, Dick, T, Colorado State, 170, F
23. *Abell, Bud, E, Missouri, 178, F
24. Young, Bob, T, Austin, 186, F
25. McClurg, Jerry, T, Colorado, 194, F
26. Zera, Phil, HB, State Joseph's (IN), 202, F

NEW YORK JETS 1964
1. *Snell, Matt, FB, Ohio State, 3
2. *Voss, Lloyd, T, Nebraska, 11
3. *Philbin, Gerry, LB, Buffalo, 19
4. *Evans, Jim, FL, Texas-El Paso, 27
5. *McGee, Ben, DT, Jackson State, 35
6. *Baker, Ralph, LB, Penn State, 43
7. Choice to San Diego
8. *Wright, Steve, T, Alabama, 59
9. *Lewis, Sherman, HB, Michigan State, 67
10. *Bowman, Ken, C, Wisconsin, 75
11. Lacey, Bob, E, North Carolina, 83
12. Johnson, Rudy, FB, Nebraska, 91
13. Ware, Jeff, LB, Pittsburgh, 99
14. Brooks, Charley, E, Memphis State, 107, F
15. Johnson, Herman, DB, Michigan State, 115, F
16. Popp, Ray, LB, Pittsburgh, 123, F
17. Lehman, Bob, G-LB, Notre Dame, 131
18. Scott, Bill, G, Memphis State, 139
19. *Condren, Glenn, T, Oklahoma, 147, F
20. *Shiner, Dick, QB, Maryland, 155
21. *Hand, Larry, T, Appalachian State, 163, F
22. Radosevich, Will, T, Wyoming, 171, F
23. *Gordon, Cornell, HB, N.Carolina A&T, 179, F
24. Mayne, Mike, E, Idaho, 187, F
25. *Rhome, Jerry, QB, Tulsa, 195, F
26. Butler, John, FB, San Diego State, 203, F

OAKLAND 1964
1. *Lorick, Tony, HB, Arizona State, 7
2. *Conners, Dan, T, Miami, 15
3. Bednar, George, T, Notre Dame, 23
4. *Budness, Bill, LB, Boston U., 31
5. Green, Don, DB, Susquehanna, 39
6. Choice to Denver
7. Sapinsky, John, T, William & Mary, 55
8. Petno, Vince, DB, Citadel, 63
9. *Williamson, J.R., G, Louisiana Tech, 71
*Turner, Herschel, T, Kentucky [from San Diego] 72
10. *Renfro, Mel, HB, Oregon, 79
11. *Rakestraw, Larry, QB, Georgia, 87
12. *Lothridge, Billy, QB, Georgia Tech, 95
13. Babb, Mickey, E, Georgia, 103
14. Polser, Fred, G, East Texas State, 111, F
15. Geirs, Mike, T, USC, 119, F
16. Wilkening, Ron, HB, North Dakota, 127, F
17. Lewis, Fred, HB, Massachusetts, 135, F
18. Calcagno, Ron, QB, Santa Clara, 143
19. *Michel, Tom, FB, East Carolina, 151
20. *Beard, Ed, T, Tennessee, 159
21. *Oates, Carlton, E, Florida A&M, 167, F
22. Long, Jim, FB, Fresno State, 175, F
23. *Curry, Bill, C, Georgia Tech, 183, F
24. Francisco, Kent, T, UCLA, 191, F
25. Sieg, Terry, HB, Virginia, 199, F
26. Guest, Gordon, QB, Arkansas, 207, F

SAN DIEGO 1964
1. *Davis, Ted, E, Georgia Tech, 8
2. *Kirby, John, LB, Nebraska, 16
3. *Dunn, Perry Lee, DB, Mississippi, 24
4. *Parks, Dave, E, Texas Tech, 32
5. Goimarac, Pete, C, West Virginia [from Boston] 36
*Kirner, Gary, T, USC, 40
6. *Brown, Willie, HB, USC, 48
7. *Anderson, Roger, T, Virginia Union [from New York Jets] 51
*Batten, Pat, FB, Hardin-Simmons, 56
8. *Seals, George, DE, Missouri, 64
9. Choice to Oaklandland
10. *Long, Bob, E, Wichita State [from Kansas City] 74
Bowman, Dick, E, Syracuse, 80
11. *Horton, Bob, FB, Boston U., 88
12. *Carpenter, Ron, E, Texas A&M, 96
13. *Graham, Kenny, HB, Washington State, 104
14. *Kindig, Howard, C, Cal State-Los Angeles, 112, F
15. *Mitchell, Ed, T, Southern, 120, F
16. *Daugherty, Bob, HB, Tulsa, 128, F
17. *Farris, John, T, San Diego State, 136, F
18. Robinson, Bob, G-LB, Mississippi, 144, F
19. Cercel, Paul, C-LB, Pittsburgh, 152, F
20. Klein, Dick, T, Wichita State, 160, F
21. Robinson, Allen, HB, BYU, 168, F
22. *Hinton, Charles, C, Mississippi, 176, F
23. *Smith, Ron, QB, Richmond, 184, F
24. Van Burkleo, Bill, HB, Tulsa, 192, F
25. Lucas, Tommy, G, Mississippi, 200, F
26. Kinard, Frank, FB, Mississippi, 208, F

1965 NFL

Held November 28, 1964

BALTIMORE 1965
1. *Curtis, Mike, LB, Duke, 14
2. *Neely, Ralph, T, Oklahoma, 28
3. *Ressler, Glenn, C, Penn State [from Minnesota] 36
Choice to San Francisco
4. *Schottenheimer, Marty, LB, Pittsburgh [from Washington] 49
Johnson, Dave, E, San Jose State, 56
5. McGuire, John, E, Syracuse, 70, F
6. *Felts, Bobby, HB, Florida A&M [from New York Giants] 71
*Atkinson, Al, T, Villanova, 84
7. Kolocek, John, T, Corpus Christi State, 98
8. *Davis, Roosevelt, T, Tennessee State, 112
9. *Bleick, Tom, B, Georgia Tech, 126, F
10. *Harold, George, B, Allen, 140
11. Richardson, Lamar, E, Fisk, 154
12. Rodosovich, Ted, G, Cincinnati, 168
13. Airheart, Bruce, HB, North Dakota State, 182
14. Fishman, Jerry, LB, Maryland, 196
15. *Hilton, Roy, FB, Jackson State, 210
16. *Tensi, Steve, QB, Florida State, 224
17. Reichardt, Rick, HB, Wisconsin, 238
18. *King, Charley, HB, Purdue, 252, F
19. *Brown, Barry, E-LB, Florida, 266, F
20. Johnson, Ray, C, Prairie V. A&M [from Washington] 273, F
*Haffner, George, QB, McNeese State, 280, F

CHICAGO BEARS 1965
1. *Butkus, Dick, LB, Illinois [from Pittsburgh] 3
*Sayers, Gale, HB, Kansas, 4
*DeLong, Steve, T, Tennessee [from Washington] 6
2. Choice to Cleveland
3. Choice to Cleveland
4. *Nance, Jim, FB, Syracuse, 45
5. Choice to Los Angeles Rams
6. Carey, Tony, HB, Notre Dame, 73, F
7. *Gordon, Dick, HB, Michigan State, 88
*Sutton, Mickey, B, Auburn [from Washington] 90
8. *Schweda, Brian, T, Kansas, 101
9. Ambrusko, Ken, B, Maryland, 116, F
10. *Murphy, Dennis, T, Florida, 129
11. *Cornish, Frank, T, Grambling, 144, F
12. Cox, Steve, T, South Carolina, 157, F
13. *Daniels, Dave, T, Florida A&M, 172, F
14. *Pivec, Dave, E, Notre Dame, 185
15. Robinson, Art, B, Cal State-Los Angeles, 200
16. *Pitts, Frank, E, Southern, 213
17. LaFramboise, Tom, QB, Louisville, 228
18. Schwager, Mike, T, Northwestern, 241
19. Bobich, Lou, K, Michigan State, 256
20. *Kurek, Ralph, FB, Wisconsin, 269

CLEVELAND 1965
1. Choice to San Francisco
2. *Garcia, Jim, T, Purdue [from Chicago Bears] 17
*Bussell, Gerry, HB, Georgia Tech [from Los Angeles Rams] 22
*Johnson, Walter, DT, Cal State-Los Angeles, 27
3. *Scott, Bo, HB, Ohio State [from Chicago Bears] 32
*Maples, Bobby, LB, Baylor, 41
4. Choice to Minnesota
5. Irwin, Bill, T, Mississippi, 69
6. *Simkus, Arnie, T, Michigan [from San Francisco] 72
Aldredge, Corwyn, E, Northwestern State (LA), 83
7. *Lindsey, Dale, LB, Western Kentucky, 97
8. *Howell, Mike, B, Grambling, 111
9. *Lane, Gary, QB, Missouri, 125, F
10. Screen, Pat, QB, LSU, 139, F
11. *Cordill, Olie, B, Memphis State, 153, F
12. *Canale, Justin, G, Mississippi State, 167
13. Pickett, Henry, HB, Baylor, 181, F
14. Simrell, Dan, QB, Toledo, 195
15. *Gagner, Larry, T, Florida, 209, F
16. Anthony, Mel, FB, Michigan, 223
17. Boyette, John, T, Clemson, 237, F
18. Arrington, Dick, G, Notre Dame, 251, F
19. Orazen, Ed, G, Ohio State, 265
20. Goldberg, Frank, LB, Central Michigan, 279

DALLAS 1965
1. *Morton, Craig, QB, California, 5
2. *Walker, Malcolm, LB, Rice, 19
3. Choice to New York Giants thru Green Bay
4. *Sidle, Jimmy, HB, Auburn, 47
*Svihus, Bob, T, USC, [from Detroit] 53
5. Pettee, Roger, LB, Florida, 61
6. Utz, Sonny, FB, Virginia Tech, 75
7. *Owens, Brig, QB, Cincinnati, 89
8. *Wayt, Russell, LB, Rice, 103
9. Zanios, Jim, FB, Texas Tech, 117
10. McCullough, Gaylon, C, Alabama, 131
11. *Pugh, Jethro, T, Elizabeth City State, 145
12. *Kellerman, Ernie, QB, Miami (OH), 159
13. Schraub, Jack, E California, 173
14. *Porterfield, Gary, E, Tulsa, 187
15. *Foster, Gene, B, Arizona State, 201
16. McDougal, Doug, E, Oregon State, 215
17. *Johnson, Mitch, T, UCLA, 229
18. *Amsler, Marty, T, Evansville, 243
19. Rettenmund, Marv, HB, Ball State, 257
20. Barlow, Don, T, Kansas State, 271

DETROIT 1965
1. *Nowatzke, Tom, FB, Indiana, 11
2. *Rush, Jerry, T, Michigan State, 25
3. *Biletnikoff, Fred, FL, Florida State, 39
4. Choice to Dallas
*Myers, Tommy, QB, Northwestern [from Pittsburgh] 46
5. *Vaughn, Tommy, B, Iowa State [from New York Giants] 57
*Flanagan, Ed, C, Purdue [from Minnesota] 64
Flynn, John, E, Oklahoma, 67
6. Hawkins, Earl, B, Emory & Henry, 81
7. *Kent, Gregg, T, Utah [from Minnesota] 92, F
*Kowalkowski, Bob, G, Virginia, 95, F
8. Harbin, Larry, B, Appalachian State, 109
9. *McLenna, Bruce, B, Hillsdale, 123, F
10. Pennie, Frank, T, Florida, 137, F
11. *Kearney, Jim, B, Prairie View A&M, 151
12. Moore, Jim, LB, North Texas State, 165
13. *Jacobson, Jack, B, Oklahoma State, 179
14. Brown, Larry, B, Oklahoma, 193, F
15. *Dickey, Wallace, E, Southwest Texas State, 207
16. Smith, John, T, Maryland-Eastern Shore, 221
17. Odom, Sonny, HB, Duke, 235, F
18. *Sweetan, Karl, QB, Wake Forest, 249
19. Love, Preston, B, Nebraska, 263
20. *Wilson, George, QB, Xavier, 277, F

GREEN BAY 1965
1. *Anderson, Donny, HB, Texas Tech [from Philadelphia] 7, F
*Elkins, Lawrence, E, Baylor, 10
2. *Dotson, Alphonse, T, Grambling, 24
3. *Brown, Allen, E, Mississippi, 38
4. Mahle, Wally, B, Syracuse, 52
5. *Harvey, Jim, T, Mississippi [from Pittsburgh] 59, F
*Goodwin, Doug, FB, Maryland-Eastern Shore, 66
6. *Koeper, Rich, T, Oregon State [from Pittsburgh] 74
Symons, Bill, HB, Colorado, 80
7. Roberts, Jerry, B, Baldwin,Wallace [from New York Giants] 85
Jacobazzi, Roger, T, Wisconsin [from San Francisco] 86
*Coffey, Junior, FB, Washington, 94
8. Shinn, Mike, E, Kansas, 108, F
9. Bulaich, Larry, B, TCU, 122
10. *Marshall, Bud, T, Stephen F. Austin, 136
11. *Weatherwax, Jim, T, Cal State-Los Angeles, 150, F
12. *Jeter, Gene, HB, Arkansas-Pine Bluff, 164
13. *Schmidt, Roy, G, Long Beach State, 178, F
14. Putnam, John, FB, Drake, 192
15. *Hurston, Chuck, T, Auburn, 206
16. *Vandersea, Phil, FB, Massachusetts, 220, F
17. Clark, Steve, K, Oregon State, 234
18. White, Jeff, E, Texas Tech, 248, F
19. Sears, Len, T, South Carolina, 262, F
20. Chandler, Jim, FB, Benedictine, 276

LOS ANGELES RAMS 1965
1. *Williams, Clancy, HB, Washington State, 9
2. Choice to Cleveland
3. *Brown, Fred, E-LB, Miami (FL), 37
4. *Strofolino, Mike, LB, Villanova, 50
5. *Marchlewski, Frank, C, Minnesota [from Chicago Bears] 60
*Woodlief, Doug, E, Memphis State, 65
6. Harrison, Bill, E, Elon, 78
7. *Guillory, Tony, G, Lamar, 93
8. Dzura, Stan, T, California, 106, F
9. *Caveness, Ronnie, LB, Arkansas, 121
10. Burt, Jim, HB, Western Kentucky, 134
11. Walet, Merlin, FB, McNeese State, 149, F
12. *Werl, Bob, E, Miami (FL), 162, F
13. Berry, Brent, T, San Jose State, 177, F
14. Robertson, Bill, E, Austin, 190
15. *Davis, Marvin, E, Wichita State, 205, F
16. Brown, Charlie, T, Tulsa, 218, F
17. Blecksmith, Ed, B, USC, 233, F
18. Lowery, Leo, FB, Texas Tech, 246, F
19. *Anderson, Billy Guy, QB, Tulsa, 261, F
20. Scott, Billy, E, Northeast Oklahoma, 274, F

MINNESOTA 1965
1. *Snow, Jack, E, Notre Dame, 8
2. *Sutton, Archie, T, Illinois [from New York Giants] 15
*Rentzel, Lance, HB, Oklahoma, 23
3. Choice to Bal
4. *Whalen, Jim, E, Boston College, 51
*Harris, Jim, T, Utah State [from Cleveland] 55
5. Choice to Det
6. Grisham, Jim, B, Oklahoma, 79
7. Choice to Det
8. Hankinson, John, QB, Minnesota [from San Francisco] 100, F
*Jordon, Jeff, B, Tulsa, 107
9. McClendon, Frank, T, Alabama, 120
10. Schweiger, Jerald, T, Wisconsin-Superior, 135
11. Thomas, John, E, USC, 148, F
12. *Tilleman, Mike, T, Montana, 163
13. *Osborn, Dave, B, North Dakota, 176
14. *Leetzow, Max, E, Idaho, 191
15. Morgan, Phillip, B, East Tennessee State, 204
16. Labinski, Paul, T, St. John's (MN), 219
17. Smith, Veran, B, Utah State, 232
18. *Kotite, Rich, E, Wagner, 247, F
19. *Johnson, Ellis, HB, Southeastern Louisiana, 260
20. *Iacavazzi, Cosmo, B, Princeton, 275

NEW YORK GIANTS 1965
1. *Frederickson, Tucker, B, Auburn, 1
2. Choice to Min
3. Choice to San Francisco
*Mercein, Chuck, FB, Yale [from Pittsburgh] 31
*Timberlake, Bob, QB, Michigan [from Dallas thru Green Bay] 33
4. *Carr, Henry, HB, Arizona State, 43
5. Choice to Det
*Lambert, Frank, E, Mississippi [from Washington] 62
6. Choice to Baltimore
7. Choice to Green Bay
8. *Williams, Willie, B, Grambling, 99
9. Frick, John, E, Ohio U., 113
10. Crenshaw, Ben, B, Jackson State, 127
11. *Koy, Ernie, B, Texas, 141
12. *Carroll, Jim, LB, Notre Dame, 155
13. *Lockhart, Carl, B, North Texas State, 169
14. *Underwood, Olin, E, Texas, 183
15. Giers, Mike, G, USC, 197
16. *Good, Tom, B, Marshall, 211., F
17. Powless, Dave, G, Illinois, 225
18. *Ciccolella, Mike, LB, Dayton, 239, F
19. *Reed, Smith, B, Alcorn State, 253
20. Torok, John, QB, Arizona State, 267

PHILADELPHIA 1965
1. Choice to Green Bay
2. *Rissmiller, Ray, T, Georgia, 20
3. *Nelson, Al, HB, Cincinnati, 35
4. *Hill, Fred, E, USC, 48
5. *Henderson John, E, Michigan, 63
6. *Huarte, John, QB, Notre Dame, 76
*Garrison, Gary, E, San Diego State [from Washington] 77, F
7. *Will, Erwin, T, Dayton, 91
8. Piraino, Al, T, Wisconsin, 104
9. *Hudlow, Floyd, B, Arizona, 119
10. Redman, Rick, C, Washington, 132
11. James, Louis, HB, Texas-El Paso, 147
12. Kuznieski, John, HB, Purdue, 161, F
13. Fouse, John, E, Arizona, 175
14. *Longo, Tom, B, Notre Dame, 188, F
15. *Taylor, Otis, B, Prairie View A&M, 203
16. *Gray, Jim, B, Toledo, 216
17. Austin, Dave, E, Georgia Tech, 231, F
18. Marcordes, Bill, E, Bradley, 244
19. Englehart, Charley, T, John Carroll, 259
20. *Shann, Bobby, E, Boston College, 272

PITTSBURGH 1965
1. Choice to Chicago Bears
2. Jefferson, Roy, HB, Utah, 18
3. Choice to New York Giants
4. Choice to Detroit
5. Choice to Green Bay
6. Choice to Green Bay
7. *Browning, Charley, B, Washington, 87
8. Howley, Bill, E, Pittsburgh, 102

9. *Neville, Tom, T, Mississippi State, 115
10. *Tobey, Dave, C, Oregon, 130, F
11. *Molden, Frank, T, Jackson State, 143
12. Lofquist, Craig, B, Minnesota, 158
13. *Wilburn, J.R., B, South Carolina, 171, F
14. *Butler, Jim (Cannonball), B, Edward Waters, 186
15. *Carrell, John, T, Texas Tech, 199, F
16. Dusenbury, Doug, K, Kansas State, 214
17. *Canale, Whit, FB, Tennessee, 227
18. Howard, Bob, B, Stanford, 242
19. Price, Lonnie, B, Southwestern Louisiana, 255, F
20. Fertig, Craig, QB, USC, 270

ST. LOUIS 1965
1. *Namath, Joe, QB, Alabama, 12
2. *Simmons, Dave, LB, Georgia Tech, 26
3. *Ogden, Ray, E, Alabama, 40
4. *Roland, Johnny, HB, Missouri, 54, F
5. Bonds, Bob, HB, San Jose State, 68
6. *Hines, Glen Ray, T, Arkansas, 82, F
7. *Roy, Frank, E, Utah, 96
8. *Meyer, John, LB, Notre Dame, 110
9. *Heidel, Jimmy, B, Mississippi, 124, F
10. Drulis, Chuck, E, Duke, 138, F
11. French, Bud, B, Alabama, 152
12. Sasser, Glen, E, North Carolina State, 166
13. Murphy, Steve, HB, Northwestern, 180
14. *Alford, Mike, C, Auburn, 194
15. Lane, Harlan, B, Baylor, 208, F
16. *Silvestri, Carl, B, Wisconsin, 222
17. *Melinkovich, Mike, T, Gray's Harbor J.C., 236
18. *McQuarters, Ed, G, Oklahoma, 250
19. *Shivers, Roy, HB, Utah State, 264, F
20. Giacobazzi, Tony, E, Iowa, 278

SAN FRANCISCO 1965
1. *Willard, Ken, FB, North Carolina, 2
   *Donnelly, George, B, Illinois [from Cleveland] 13
2. *Cerne, Joe, C, Northwestern, 16
3. *Schweickert, Bob, B, Virginia Tech [from New York Giants] 29
   *Norton, Jim, T, Washington, 30
   *Chapple, Jack, LB, Stanford [from Baltimore] 42
4. *Todd, Larry, FL, Arizona State, 44
5. *McCormick, Dave, T, LSU, 58, F
6. Choice to Cleveland
7. Choice to Green Bay
8. Choice to Min
9. *Swinford, Wayne, HB, Georgia, 114
10. *Cappadona, Bob, FB, Northeastern, 128, F
11. Mass, Steve, T, Detroit, 142, F
12. *Plump, Dave, HB, Fresno State, 156, F
13. *Schumacher, Gregg, E, Illinois, 170
14. Andruski, Frank, HB, Utah, 184
15. Pabian, Joe, T, West Virginia, 198
16. *Hettema, Dave, T, New Mexico, 212, F
17. Frketich, Len, E, Oregon State, 226
18. Standridge, Leon, E, San Diego State, 240, F
19. Ford, Dale, HB, Washington State, 254
20. Duncan, Dennis, B, Louisiana College, 268

WASHINGTON 1965
1. Choice to Chicago Bears
2. *Breitenstein, Bob, T, Tulsa, 21
3. *McCloughan, Kent, B, Nebraska, 34
4. Choice to Bal
5. Choice to New York Giants
6. Choice to Philadelphia
7. Choice to Chicago Bears
8. *Croftcheck, Don, G-LB, Indiana, 105
9. *Smith, Jerry, E, Arizona State, 118
10. *Briggs, Bob, FB, Central State (OK), 133
11. *Adams, Willie, G, New Mexico State, 146
12. Strohmeyer, John, T, Nebraska, 160, F
13. Bracy, Biff, HB, Duke, 174, F
14. Estrada, Dave, HB, Arizona State, 189
15. Baldwin, Ben, B, Vanderbilt, 202
16. *Reed, Robert, G, Tennessee A&I, 217
17. Hart, Gary, E, Vanderbilt, 230
18. *Hanburger, Chris, C-LB, North Carolina, 245
19. Ellerbe, Roosevelt, B, Iowa State, 258, F
20. Choice to Baltimore

1965 AFL

Held November 28, 1964

BOSTON 1965
1. *Rush, Jerry, T, Michigan State
2. Choice to Houston
3. *Whalen, Jim, E, Boston College
4. *Johnson, Ellis, HB, Southeastern Louisiana
5. Aldredge, Corwyn, E, Northwestern State (LA)
6. *Canale, Justin, G, Mississippi State
7. Neville, Tom, T, Mississippi State
8. *Brown, Fred, E, Miami (FL)
9. Malone, Bob, T, Louisiana Tech
10. Choice to Buffalo
11. Frechette, John, T, Boston College
12. Weatherly, Jim, DB, Mississippi
13. *Green, Charlie, QB, Wittenberg
14. *Cunningham, Jay, HB, Bowling Green
15. Rodosevitch, Ted, G, Cincinnati
16. *Pyne, George, T, Olivet
17. *Graves, White, DB, LSU
   *Lee, David, E, Louisiana Tech [from New York Jets]
18. *Meixler, Ed, LB, Boston U.
19. *Nance, Jim, FB, Syracuse
20. Fugazzi, Fred, FB, Missouri Valley

BUFFALO 1965
1. Davidson, Jim, T, Ohio State
2. Choice to Kansas City
3. *Atkinson, Alan, T, Villanova
4. Choice to Kansas City
5. *Simmons, Dave, LB, Georgia Tech
6. *Rentzel, Lance, HB, Oklahoma
7. *Schottenheimer, Marty, LB, Pittsburgh
8. *Rissmiller, Ray, T, Georgia
9. *Nelson, Al, DB, Cincinnati
10. *Mercein, Chuck, FB, Yale
   *Hudlow, Floyd, DB, Arizona [from Boston]
11. *Goodwin, Doug, FB, Maryland-Eastern Shore
12. *Hurston, Chuck, T, Auburn
   *Mills, Pete, HB, Wichita State [from Oakland]
13. *Timberlake, Bob, QB, Michigan
14. Hart, Lyn, DB, Virginia State
15. *Meyer, John, LB, Notre Dame
16. Airheart, Bruce, HB, North Dakota State
17. *Henderson, John, E, Michigan
18. Hinze, Ray, T, Texas A&M
   Fouse, John, E, Arizona [from Denver]
19. *Marchlewski, Frank, LB, Minnesota
20. Henry, John, DT, Boston U.

DENVER 1965
1. Choice to New York Jets
2. *Butkus, Dick, LB, Illinois
3. Ressler, Glenn, C, Penn State
4. *Donnelly, George, DB, Illinois
5. *Breitenstein, Bob, T, Tulsa
   *Leetzow, Max, DT, Idaho [from Oakland]
6. Wilhelm, Tom, T, Syracuse
7. *Garcia, Jim, DE, Purdue
8. Hohman, John, G, Wisconsin
9. *Bussell, Jerry, DB, Georgia Tech
10. *Jeter, Gene, LB, Arkansas-Pine Bluff
11. *Vaughn, Tommy, HB, Iowa State
12. *Myers, Tommy, QB, Northwestern
13. *Strofalino, Mike, LB, Villanova
14. Frick, John, G, Ohio U.
15. *Jordan, Jeff, DB, Tulsa
16. *Schweda, Brian, T, Kansas
17. Choice to Boston
18. Dupree, Larry, HB, Florida [from New York Jets]
   Choice to Buffalo
19. Oelschlager, Ron, HB, Kansas
20. Metchner, Terry, G, Albion

HOUSTON 1965
1. *Elkins, Lawrence, E, Baylor
2. *Walker, Malcolm, LB, Rice
   *Neely, Ralph, T, Oklahoma [from Boston]
3. *Koy, Ernie, FB, Texas
4. Maples, Bobby, LB, Baylor
5. *Molden, Frank, T, Jackson State
6. *Murphy, Dennis, T, Florida
   Wayt, Russ, LB, Rice [from Oakland]
7. Choice to Kansas City
8. *Ogden, Ray, FB, Alabama
   Hilton, Roy, LB, Jackson State [from Oakland]
9. Kinney, George, DE, Wiley
10. *Williams, Maxie, T, Southeastern Louisiana
11. McCloughan, Kent, HB, Nebraska
12. Reed, Bob, G, Tennessee State
13. *Felts, Bob, DB, Florida A&M
14. Evans, Norm, T, TCU
15. *Guillory, Tony, T, Lamar
16. *Coffey, Junior, HB, Washington
17. Grisham, Jim, FB, Oklahoma
18. Mundy, Russ, HB, West Texas State
19. Fox, Frank, T, Sam Houston State
20. *Brezina, Gus, G, Houston

KANSAS CITY 1965
1. *Sayers, Gale, HB, Kansas
2. *Chapple, Jack, G, Stanford
   *Caveness, Ronnie, LB, Arkansas [from Buffalo]
3. *Curtis, Mike, FB, Duke
4. *Taylor, Otis, E, Prairie View A&M
   *Pitts, Frank, HB, Southern [from Buffalo]
5. *Reed, Smith, HB, Alcorn State
6. *Sutton, Mickey, DB, Auburn
7. *Richardson, Gloster, E, Jackson State [from Houston]
   Bobich, Lou, DB-K, Michigan State
8. Thomas, Danny, QB-K, SMU
9. *Cerne, Joe, C, Northwestern
10. Howard, Bob, DB, Stanford
11. Piraino, Al, T, Wisconsin
12. Cox, Mike, LB, Iowa State
13. Bonds, Bob, DB-E, San Jose State
14. Dolson, Fred, DB, Wiley
15. Powless, Dave, G, Illinois
16. Irvine, Stan, T, Colorado
17. *Croftcheck, Don, LB, Indiana
18. *Smith, Jerry, E, Arizona State
19. Alford, Mike, C, Auburn
20. Symons, Bill, HB, Colorado

NEW YORK JETS 1965
1. *Namath, Joe, QB, Alabama [from Denver]
   *Nowatzke, Tom, FB, Indiana
2. *Huarte, John, QB, Notre Dame
3. Biggs, Verlon, T, Jackson State
4. *Schweickert, Bob, HB, Virginia Tech
5. Sasser, Glenn, DE, North Carolina State
6. Hoovler, Don LB, Ohio U.
7. *Harris, Jim, DT, Utah State
   *Roberts, Archie, QB, Columbia [from Oakland]
8. McCurdy, Rick, DE, Oklahoma
9. *Sidle, Jimmy, HB, Auburn
10. *Lambert, Frank, K-E, Mississippi
11. *Gray, Jim, DB, Toledo
12. Berrington, John, LB-C, Iowa State
13. Utz, Sonny, FB, Virginia Tech
14. Plumlee, Gary, DT-DE, New Mexico
15. Burt, Jim, DB, Western Kentucky
16. Cartwright, Seth, DT, Prairie View A&M
17. *Browning, Charles, DB, Washington
18. Choice to Den
19. *Dudek, Frank, G, Xavier
20. Allen, Troy, DB, Western Michigan

OAKLAND 1965
1. *Schuh, Harry, T, Memphis State
2. *Biletnikoff, Fred, E, Florida State
3. *Svihus, Bob, T, USC
4. *Otto, Gus, FB, Missouri
5. Choice to Den
6. Choice to Houston
7. Choice to New York Jets
8. Choice to Houston
9. *Zecher, Rich, T, Utah State
10. *Morton, Craig, QB, California
11. Minor, Bill, LB, Illinois
12. Choice to Buffalo
13. Mahle, Wally, DB, Syracuse
14. Hawley, Loren, DB, California
15. *Cronin, Bill, DE, Boston College
16. *Hill, Fred, E, USC
17. *Porterfield, Gary, E, Tulsa
18. Dugan, John, T, Holy Cross
19. McClendon, Frank, T, Alabama
20. *Scott, Bo, HB, Ohio State

SAN DIEGO 1965
1. *DeLong, Steve, G, Tennessee
2. Jefferson, Roy, E, Utah
3. *Brown, Allen, E, Mississippi
4. *Tensi, Steve, QB, Florida State
5. *Redman, Rick, LB, Washington
6. Beasley, Will, FB, North Carolina A&T
7. Snow, Jack, E, Notre Dame
8. *Williams, Clancy, HB, Washington
9. Whelchel, Jerry, QB, Massachusetts
10. *Foster, Gene, HB, Arizona State
11. Smith, Veran, G, Utah State
12. *Allison, Jim, FB, San Diego State
13. Quigley, Bill, LB, Villanova
14. Floyd, Don, E, Florida State
15. *Howell, Mike, DB, Grambling
16. Godden, John, LB, San Diego State
17. Hardy, Leon, T, Texas Southern
18. *Evans, Bobby, T, Texas A&M
19. *Beck, Braden, K, Stanford
20. Edwards, Jack, C, Florida State

1965 AFL REDSHIRT

Held November 28, 1984

A separate, 12-round redshirt draft was held, and no future picks were made in the regular draft The AFL repeated the redshirt draft in 1966.

BOSTON 1965
1. *McCormick, Dave, T, LSU
2. *Kowalkowski, Bob, T, Virginia
3. *Cappadonna, Bob, FB, Northwestern
4. Arrington, Dick, G, Notre Dame
5. Smith, Dennis, DE, Cincinnati
6. Ezell, Billy, DB, LSU
7. Hankinson, John, QB, Minnesota
8. Colle, Beau, DB, LSU
9. Brown, Charley, T, Tulsa
10. *Hettema, Dave, T, New Mexico
11. Schmidt, Roy, G, Long Beach State
12. Standridge, Leon, E, San Diego State

BUFFALO 1965
1. Ambrusko, Ken, HB, Maryland
2. Lane, Gary, QB, Missouri
3. Kuzniewski, John, FB, Purdue
4. Davis, Roger, HB, Virginia
5. Boyette, John, T, Clemson
6. Strohmeyer, John, DE, Nebraska
7. Wilburn, J.R., E, South Carolina
8. *King, Charley, DB, Purdue
9. Hawkins, Earl, HB, Emory & Henry
10. Odom, Sonny, HB, Duke
11. Johnson, Ray, G, Prairie View A&M
12. *Wilson, George, QB, Xavier

DENVER 1965
1. *Farr, Miller, HB, Wichita State
2. *Johnson, Walter, G, Cal State-Los Angeles
3. *Davis, Marvin, DE, Wichita State
4. *Brown, Barry, E, Florida
5. *Tilleman, Mike, T, Montana State
6. *Inman, Jerry, T, Oregon
7. *Tobey, Dave, LB, Oregon
8. Maddox, John, E, Mississippi
9. *Vandersea, Phil, FB, Massachusetts
10. Walet, Merlin, FB, McNeese State
11. Fishman, Jerry, LB, Maryland
12. Bracy, Biff, HB, Duke

HOUSTON 1965
1. *Anderson, Donny, HB, Texas Tech
2. *Hines, Glen Ray, T, Arkansas
3. Shinn, Mike, DE, Kansas
4. *Cordill, Ollie, QB, Memphis State
5. Crumpler, Jerry, T, Mississippi
6. *Daniels, Dave, T, Florida A&M
7. Lowery, Leo, HB, Texas Tech
8. Sears, Len, T, South Carolina
9. *Bleick, Tom, HB, Georgia Tech
10. Hafner, George, QB, McNeese State
11. *Anderson, Billy Guy, QB, Tulsa
12. Lane, Harlan, FL, Baylor

KANSAS CITY 1965
1. *Dotson, Alphonse, T, Grambling
2. *Cornish, Frank, DT, Grambling
3. *Carr, Henry, HB, Arizona State
4. Cox, Steve, T, South Carolina
5. Thomas, John, E, USC
6. *Wilburn, John, G, Stanford
7. Moore, Bill, HB, Mississippi State
8. Ellerbe, Roosevelt, DB, Iowa State
9. *McLenna, Bruce, HB, Hillsdale
10. Drulis, Chuck, E, Duke
11. Scott, Bill, E, Northeastern Oklahoma
12. Price, Lonnie, HB, Southwestern Louisiana

NEW YORK JETS 1965
1. *Roland, Johnny, HB, Missouri
2. McGuire, John, TE-DE, Syracuse
3. *Heidel, Jimmy, DB, Mississippi
4. *Werl, Bob, DE, Miami (FL)
5. *Sauer, George, FL, Texas
6. *Lindsey, Dale, LB, Western Kentucky
7. Barlow, Ron, FB, Kansas State
8. Mallendick, Bob, T, Hillsdale
9. *Kotite, Rich, E, Wagner
10. Austin, Dave, E, Georgia Tech
11. Marshall, Richard, T, Stephen F Austin
12. Screen, Pat, QB, LSU

OAKLAND 1965
1. *Todd, Larry, HB, Arizona State
2. *Harvey, Jim, T, Mississippi
3. Mass, Steve, T, Detroit
4. Cox, Mickey, T, LSU
5. Taylor, Bob, G, Cincinnati
6. *Kent, Gregg, T, Utah
7. Carroll, John, T, Texas Tech
8. Pickett, Henry, HB, Baylor
9. Pennie, Frank, T, Florida State
10. Berry, Brent, T, San Jose State
11. *Longo, Tom, DB, Notre Dame
12. Duncan, Dennis, HB, Louisiana College

SAN DIEGO 1965
1. *Garrison, Gary, E, San Diego State
2. *Martin, Larry, T, San Diego State
3. Dzura, Stan, T-DE, California
4. *Woodlief, Doug, LB, Memphis State
5. *Weatherwax, Jim, T, Cal State-Los Angeles
6. *Good, Tom, LB, Marshall
7. Waff, Wayne, E, East Tennessee State
8. *Shivers, Roy, HB, Utah
9. Carey, Tony, HB, Notre Dame
10. *Plump, Dave, HB, Fresno State
11. White, Jeff, E, Texas Tech
12. *Cicollella, Mike, LB, Dayton

1966 NFL

Held November 27, 1965

The expansion Atlanta Falcons received the first and last choices in each of the first five rounds, and the first choice in rounds 6-20. The draft consisted of 305 selections.

On February 15, the Falcons selected 42 players in an expansion draft. Each of the other 14 NFL teams froze 29 players from its 40-man roster. The Falcons chose one player from those remaining on each team. Then the other teams froze two additional players, leaving eight on each list from which the Falcons chose two more each.

ATLANTA 1966
1. *Nobis, Tommy, LB, Texas, 1
   *Johnson, Randy, QB, Texas A&I, 16
2. *Rassas, Nick, DB, Notre Dame, 17
   *Jones, Jerry, T, Bowling Green, 32
3. *Dennis, Mike, HB, Mississippi, 33
   Sheridan, Phil, E, Notre Dame, 48
4. *Reaves, Ken, DB, Virginia State, 49
   *Asbury, Willie, HB, Kent State, 64
5. *Wolski, Bill, HB, Notre Dame, 65
   Kahn, Martin, T, North Texas State, 80
6. Casey, Charley, FL, Florida, 81
7. Johnson, William, FB, University of the South, 96
8. Goss, Bill, LB, Tulane, 111
9. *Sanders, Bob, C, North Texas State, 126
10. Bender, Mike, G, Arkansas, 141
11. *Sloan, Steve, QB, Alabama, 156
12. Hollister Ken, T, Indiana, 171
13. Collins, Bob, T, South Carolina, 186
14. Ecker, Steve, K, Shippensburg, 201
15. *Tolleson, Tom, FL, Alabama, 216
16. Vining, Jim, G, Rice, 231
17. Archambeau, Lurley, C, Toledo, 246
18. Korver, Doug, C, Northern Iowa, 261
19. Mainer, Walt, DB, Xavier, 276
20. *Riggle, Bob, DB, Penn State, 291

ATLANTA (Expansion) 1966
*Anderson, Roger, DT [from New York Giants]
*Benz, Larry, S, Northwestern [from Cleveland]
*Calland, Lee, DB, Louisville [from Minnesota]
*Claridge, Dennis, QB, Nebraska [from Green Bay]
*Coffey, Junior, FB, Washington [from Green Bay]
*Cook, Ed, G, Notre Dame [from St. Louis]
*Crossan, Dave, C, Maryland [from Washington]
*Dunn, Perry Lee, HB, Mississippi [from Dallas]
*Franklin, Bobby, S, Mississippi [from Cleveland]
*Grimm, Dan, G, Colorado [from Green Bay]
*Hawkins, Alex, FL, South Carolina [from Baltimore]
*Heck, Ralph, LB, Colorado [from Philadelphia]
*Jencks, Bob, TE-K, Miami (OH) [from Washington]
*Jobko, Bill, LB, Ohio State [from Minnesota]
*Johnson, Rudy, HB, Nebraska [from San Francisco]
*Lasky, Frank, T, Florida [from New York Giants]
*Lewis, Danny, FB, Wisconsin [from Washington]
*Linden, Errol, T, Houston [from Minnesota]
*Mack, Bill (Red), FL, Notre Dame [from Pittsburgh]
*Marchlewski, Frank, C, Minnesota [from Los Angeles Rams]
*Martin, Billy, TE, Georgia Tech [from Chicago Bears]
*Memmelaar, Dale, G, Wyoming [from Cleveland]
*Messer, Dale, FL, Fresno State [from San Francisco]
*Messner, Max, LB, Cincinnati [from Pittsburgh]
*Murphy, Dennis, DT, Florida [from Chicago Bears]
*Petties, Neal, SE, San Diego State [from Baltimore]
*Powell, Tim, DE, Northwestern [from Los Angeles Rams]
*Recher, Dave, C, Iowa [from Philadelphia]
*Reese, Guy, T, SMU [from Baltimore]
*Richards, Bob, DE, LSU [from Philadelphia]
*Richardson, Jerry, DB, West Texas State [from Los Angeles Rams]
*Rushing, Marion, LB, Southern Illinois [from St. Louis]
*Sherman, Bob, DB, Iowa [from Pittsburgh]
*Sieminski, Chuck, DT, Penn State [from San Francisco]
*Silvestri, Carl, DB, Wisconsin [from St. Louis]
*Simon, Jim, G-T, Miami [from Detroit]
*Smith, Ron, DB, Wisconsin [from Chicago Bears]
*Talbert, Don, T, Texas [from Dallas]
*Wheelwright, Ernie, FB, Southern Illinois [from New York Giants]
*Whitlow, Bob, C, Arizona [from Detroit]
*Williams, Sam, DE, Michigan State [from Detroit]
*Youmans, Maury, DE, Syracuse [from Dallas]

BALTIMORE 1966
1. *Ball, Sam, T, Kentucky, 15
2. *Allison, Butch, T, Missouri, 31
3. Kestner, Rick, FL, Kentucky, 47
4. *Sherman, Rod, FL, USC [from Dallas] 54, F
   *Granger, Hoyle, FB, Mississippi State, 63
5. Choice to Dallas
6. Maliszewski, Stas, LB, Princeton, 95
7. Ellis, Dave, DE-T, North Carolina State [from San Francisco] 105
   *Perkins, Ray, E, Alabama, 110, F
8. *Allen, Jerry, HB, Nebraska-Omaha [from Minnesota] 12.0
   White, Jack, QB, Penn State, 125, F
9. Gross, Jerry, HB, Auburn, 140
10. *Brownlee, Claude, DE, Benedictine, 155
11. *Crabtree, Eric, HB, Pittsburgh, 170
12. Carter, Jim, G, Tennessee State, 185
13. Hadrick, Bob, E, Purdue, 200
14. *Ward, Jim, QB, Gettysburg, 215
15. Garner, Lee, LB, Mississippi, 230, F
16. Stewart, Rod, E, Duke, 245
17. Matson, Randy, T, Texas A&M, 260, F
18. *Toner, Ed, T, Massachusetts, 275, F
19. Duke, Ken, HB, Morgan State, 290
20. *Carr, Tom, T, Morgan State, 305

CHICAGO BEARS 1966
1. *Rice, George, T, LSU, 12
2. *Brown, Charlie, DB, Syracuse, 28
3. *Pickens, Bob, T, Nebraska, 44, F
4. *Jackson, Randy, T, Florida [from Pittsburgh] 51
   *Buffalofone, Doug, LB, Louisville, 60
5. Choice to Min
6. Brewster, Dennis, T, BYU [from Washington] 85
   *McRae, Franklin, DT, Tennessee State, 92
7. *Meyer, Ron, QB, South Dakota State, 107
8. McFalls, Doug, DB, Georgia, 122
9. *Greenlee, Fritz, E, Northern Arizona, 137, F
10. *Burnett, Bobby, HB, Arkansas, 152
11. *Owens, Terry, E, Jacksonville State, 167
12. Page, Wayne, DE, Clemson, 182
13. Becker, Wayne, T, Montana, 197, F
14. Buckner, Mike, DB, Northwestern, 212.
15. Kollman, Jim, G, Oregon, 227, F
16. Senkbeil, Lynn, LB, Nebraska, 242, F
17. *Gentry, Curtis, DB, Maryland-Eastern Shore, 257
18. Kines, Charley, T, Michigan, 272
19. Haberer, Roger, HB, Eastern Illinois, 287
20. *Sellers, Goldie, HB, Grambling, 302

CLEVELAND 1966
1. *Morin, Milt, E, Massachusetts, 14
2. *Norton, Rick, QB, Kentucky, 29
3. Choice to Green Bay
4. *Duranko, Pete, DE-LB, Notre Dame, 61, F
5. *Schultz, Randy, FB, Northern Iowa [from Detroit] 74
   Fulford, Dan, E, Auburn, 78, F
6. *Battle, Jim, DE, Southern [from New York Giants] 90
   *Hoaglin, Fred, C, Pittsburgh, 93
7. Carter, Leroy, FL, Grambling, 109, F
8. Talaga, Tom, E, Notre Dame, 123
9. *Gregory, Jack, DE, Delta State, 139, F
10. *Ledbetter, Monty, E, Northwestern State (LA), 153
11. Fire, Tony, T, Bowling Green, 169
12. Czap, Rich, T, Nebraska, 183, F
13. *Boudreaux, Jim, T, Louisiana Tech, 199
14. *Lammons, Pete, E, Texas, 213
15. Ellis, Bob, DE, Massachusetts, 229
16. *Ray, David, E, Alabama, 243
17. Modzelewski, Gene, T, New Mexico State, 259
18. *Harraway, Charley, FB, San Jose State, 273
19. *Singer, Karl, T, Purdue, 289
20. Petro, Joe, DB, Temple, 303

DALLAS 1966
1. *Niland, John, G, Iowa, 5
2. *Townes, Willie, T, Tulsa, 22
3. Choice to San Francisco
4. Choice to Baltimore
5. Choice to San Francisco
   *Garrison, Walt, HB, Oklahoma State [from Baltimore] 79
6. Dunlevy, Bob, E, West Virginia, 86
7. Robinson, Arthur, E, Florida A&M, 100
8. Kunit, Don, HB, Penn State, 116
9. Elam, Darrell, E, West Virginia Tech, 130
10. Mitchell, Mason, HB, Washington, 146
11. *Denny, Austin, E, Tennessee, 160, F
12. *Shy, Les, DB, Long Beach State [from Pittsburgh] 173
   *Baynham, Craig, HB, Georgia Tech, 176, F
13. *Lamb, Ron, HB, South Carolina, 190
14. Turner, Lewis, HB, Norfolk State, 206
15. Gartung, Mark, T, Oregon State, 220, F
16. Piggee, Tom, HB, Cal State-San Francisco, 236
17. *Allen, George, T, West Texas State, 250
18. Orr, Steve, T, Washington, 266
19. Johnson, Byron, T, Central Washington, 280
20. Hudson, Lou, FL, Minnesota, 296

DETROIT 1966
1. Choice to Green Bay
2. *Eddy, Nick, HB, Notre Dame, 24, F
3. *Malinchak, Bill, E, Indiana, 39
4. *Van Horn, Doug, G, Ohio State [from New York Giants] 55
   *Walker, Willie, FL, Tennessee State, 59
5. *Cody, Bill, LB, Auburn [from Pittsburgh] 67
   Choice to Cleveland
6. *De Sutter, Wayne, T, Western Illinois [from Minnesota] 87
   Choice to Philadelphia
7. *Robinson, Johnnie, E, Tennessee State, 103
8. Pincavage, John, HB, Virginia, 117
9. *Cunningham, Dick, G, Arkansas, 136, F
10. Yates, Bruce, T, Auburn [from Minnesota] 148
   Brigham, Tom, DE, Wisconsin, 150
11. O'Billovich, Jack, LB, Oregon State, 164
12. *Winkler, Randy, T, Tarleton State, 178, F
13. Maselter, Bill, T, Wisconsin, 192
14. *Moore, Denis, T, USC, 211, F
15. Sullivan, Bill, DE, West Virginia, 225
16. Gendron, Jerry, E, Wisconsin-Eau Claire, 239
17. Dunlap, Ralph, DE, Baylor, 253
18. *Johnson, Bill, E, Livingston, 267
19. Baier, Bob, T, Simpson, 286
20. *Smith, Allen, HB, Findlay, 300, F

GREEN BAY 1966
1. *Grabowski, Jim, FB, Illinois [from Detroit] 9
   *Gillingham, Gale, T, Minnesota, 13
2. *Cichowski, Tom, T, Maryland, 30, F
3. *Heron, Fred, T, San Jose State, 45
   *Jeter, Tony, E, Nebraska [from Cleveland] 46
4. *Roderick, John, FL, SMU, 62
5. Choice to Los Angeles Rams
6. Choice to Was
7. Miller, Ray, DE, Idaho, 108, F
8. McLean, Ken, FL, Texas A&M, 124
9. *Rector, Ron, HB, Northwestern, 138
10. Montgomery, Sam, DE, Southern, 154
11. *Wenzel, Ralph, G, San Diego State, 168
12. *Mankins, Jim, FB, Florida State, 184, F
13. King, Ed, LB, USC, 198, F
14. Hanson, Ron, FL, North Dakota State, 214
15. Bolton, Grady, T, Mississippi State, 228
16. Schultz, Bob, DE, Wisconsin-Stevens Point, 244
17. *Hathcock, David, DB, Memphis State, 258
18. Jones, Jim, DE, Nebraska-Omaha, 274
19. Moton, Dave, E, USC, 288
20. Maras, Ed, E, South Dakota State, 304

LOS ANGELES RAMS 1966
1. *Mack, Tom, T, Michigan, 2
2. *Garrett, Mike, HB, USC, 18
3. *Tyson, Dick, G, Tulsa, 34
4. *Dyer, Henry, FB, Grambling, 50
5. *Talbert, Diron, T, Texas, 66, F
   *Arndt, Dick, T, Idaho [from Green Bay] 77, F
6. *Anderson, Bruce, T, Willamette, 82
7. *Youngblood, George, DB, Cal State-Los Angeles, 97
8. *Ezerins, Vilnis, HB, Wisconsin-Whitewater, 112
9. Matthies, Burton, HB, Wayne State, 127
10. Capshaw, Mike, T, Abilene Christian, 142
11. Hoover, Darrell, HB, Arizona, 157
12. Clayton, George, DB, Fairmont State, 172
13. David, Jake, HB, Lamar, 187, F
14. Parks, Terry, T, Cal State-Los Angeles, 202, F
15. Sullivan, Mike, E, Oregon State, 217, F
16. O'Brien, Joe, E, Texas-Arlington, 232, F
17. Gilbert, Dan, T, Arkansas Tech, 247
18. Johnson, Ray, LB, Whitworth, 262
19. Williams, Homer, FL, USC, 277, F
20. Harrington, Bud, FB, Tulsa, 292, F

MINNESOTA 1966
1. *Shay, Jerry, T, Purdue, 7
2. *Lindsey, Jim, HB, Arkansas, 27
3. *Hansen, Don, LB, Illinois, 42
4. *Acks, Ron, DE, Illinois, 57
5. *Davis, Doug, T, Kentucky, 72
   Hall, Bob, DB, Brown [from Chicago Bears] 76
6. Aylor, Wilbur, T, Southwest Texas State [from Pittsburgh] 83
   Choice to Detroit
7. Meers, Bob, E, Massachusetts, 106
8. Choice to Baltimore
9. *Green, Ron, FL, North Dakota, 134
10. Choice to Detroit
11. Quintana, Stan, DB, New Mexico, 162
12. *Petrella, Bob, DB, Tennessee, 181
13. *Martin, Larry, T, San Diego State, 195
14. *Twilley, Howard, E, Tulsa, 209
15. Wright, Hugh, HB, Adams State, 223, F
16. *Williams, Jim, DE, Arkansas, 237
17. Beard, Monroe, HB, Virginia Union, 256
18. Greco, Dale, DT, Illinois, 270
19. *Stokes, Jessie, HB, Corpus Christi State, 284
20. Choice to Philadelphia

NEW YORK GIANTS 1966
1. *Peay, Francis, T, Missouri, 10
2. *Davis, Don, T, Cal State-Los Angeles, 25
3. Fisher, Tom, LB, Tennessee, 40, F
4. Choice to Detroit
5. *Briggs, Bill, DE, Iowa, 75
6. Choice to Cleveland
7. *Harris, Phil, HB, Texas, 104
8. *Harper, Charlie, T, Oklahoma State [from Pittsburgh] 11.3
   *Matan, Bill, E, Kansas State, 118
9. *White, Freeman, E, Nebraska, 132
10. *Smith, Jeff, LB, USC, 151
11. Wilder, Cliff, E, Iowa, 165
12. *Avery, Ken, LB, Southern Mississippi, 179, F
13. Fulgham, Jim, T, Minnesota, 193
14. McCard, Howard, G, Syracuse, 207
15. *Bowman, Steve, HB, Alabama, 226
16. *Price, Sam, HB, Illinois, 240
17. Eickman, Gary, T, Illinois, 254
18. Anderson, Kai, C, Illinois, 268, F
19. *Crockett, Bobby, E, Arkansas, 282
20. *Minniear, Randy, HB, Purdue, 301

PHILADELPHIA 1966
1. *Beisler, Randy, DE, Indiana, 4
2. *Pettigrew, Gary, DE, Stanford, 20
3. *Hawkins, Ben, FL, Arizona State, 36
4. *Emanuel, Frank, LB, Tennessee, 52
5. Berry, Dan, HB, California, 68, F
6. *Sherlag, Bob, DB, Memphis State, 84
   *Tom, Mel, LB, San Jose State [from Detroit] 89, F
7. *Lince, David, T, North Dakota, 99
8. Mason, John, E, Stanford, 114, F
9. *Todd, Jim, HB, Ball State, 129
10. Osmond, John, C, Tulsa, 144
11. Walton, Welford, DE, Nevada-Reno, 159
12. *Van Dyke, Bruce, G, Missouri, 174
13. Bohl, Jim, HB, New Mexico State, 189, F
14. *Medved, Ron, HB, Washington, 204
15. Day, Harry, T, Memphis State, 219
16. *Vasys, Arunas, LB, Notre Dame, 234
17. *Kelley, Ike, LB, Ohio State, 249
18. Moorer, Bill, C, Georgia Tech, 264, F
19. *Reed, Taft, DB, Jackson State, 279
20. Risio, Bill, T, Boston College, 294, F
   Circo, Gerald, K, Cal State-Chico [from Minnesota] 298

PITTSBURGH 1966
1. *Leftridge, Dick, FB, West Virginia, 3
2. *Gagner, Larry, G, Florida, 19
3. *Killorin, Pat, C, Syracuse, 35
4. Choice to Chicago Bears
5. Choice to Detroit
6. Choice to Minnesota
7. *Boozer, Emerson, HB, Maryland-Eastern Shore, 98
8. Choice to New York Giants
9. Stewart, Dale, DE, Pittsburgh, 128
10. *Marion, Jerry, DB, Wyoming, 143, F
11. Washington, Charley, HB, Grambling, 158
12. Choice to Dal
13. *Dial, Benjy, QB, Eastern New Mexico, 188
14. Novogratz, Joe, LB, Pittsburgh, 203
15. Dobson, Joe, T, Idaho, 218
16. Long, Jim, E, Purdue, 233
17. Brundage, Mike, QB, Oregon, 248, F
18. Lucas, Ken, QB, Pittsburgh, 263
19. Neilson, Dave, QB, Albion, 278
20. Springer, Ron, T, Albion, 293

ST. LOUIS 1966
1. *McAdams, Carl, LB, Oklahoma, 8
2. Lucas, Harold, T, Michigan State, 23
3. *Long, Dave, DE, Iowa, 43
4. Snook, Gary, QB, Iowa, 58
5. *Clancy, Jack, FL, Michigan, 73, F
6. *Van Galder, Tim, QB, Iowa State, 88, F
7. Arkwright, Charley, T, Georgia, 102, F
8. *Goich, Dan, E, California, 121, F
9. *Bryant, Charlie, FL, Allen, 135
10. Ringer, Mike, HB, Oklahoma, 149
11. *Williams, Bobby, HB, Central State (OK), 163
12. Johnson, Rickey, T, Clemson, 177
13. Brown, Jim, G, Nebraska, 196
14. Pratt, LaVerle, LB, Idaho, 210, F
15. Alleman, Darryl, E, Wyoming, 224
16. *Kasperek, Dick, C, Iowa State, 238
17. *Russell, Benny, QB, Louisville, 252, F
18. *Jones, Willie, DE, Kansas State, 271
19. Golmont, Tony, DB, North Carolina State, 285
20. Gallagher, Tom, DE, Indiana, 299

SAN FRANCISCO 1966
1. *Hindman, Stan, T, Mississippi, 11
2. *Windsor, Bob, E, Kentucky, 26, F
3. *Randolph, Al, HB, Iowa [from Dallas] 37
   Bland, Dan, DB, Mississippi State, 41
4. *Parker, Don, G, Virginia, 56, F
5. *Phillips, Mel, DB, North Carolina A&T [from Dallas] 69
   *Smith, Steve, E, Michigan, 71
6. *Johnson, Charlie, DT, Louisville, 91
7. Choice to Baltimore
8. *Witcher, Dick, E, UCLA, 119
9. *Kramer, Kent, E, Minnesota, 133
10. *Sbranti, Ron, DE, Utah State, 147
11. *Ridlehuber, Preston, HB, Georgia, 166
12. Loebach, Lyle, T, Simpson, 180
13. *Jackson, Jim, HB, Western Illinois, 194, F
14. *Collett, Elmer, C, Cal State-San Francisco, 208, F
15. *Saffold, Saint, E, San Jose State, 222, F
16. *LeClair, Jim, QB, C.W Post, 241
17. Breeland, Jim, C, Georgia Tech, 255, F
18. Parson, Ron, E, Austin Peay, 269, F
19. Fitzgerald, Dick, T, Nebraska, 283, F
20. Walker, Willie, E, Baylor, 297, F

WASHINGTON 1966
1. *Gogolak, Charlie, K, Princeton, 6
2. *Barnes, Walter, T, Nebraska, 21
3. *Barrington, Tom, FB, Ohio State, 38
4. *Clay, Bill, DB, Mississippi, 53
5. Lemay, Dick, T, Vanderbilt, 70
6. Choice to Chicago Bears
   Yates, Earl, T, Duke [from Green Bay] 94
7. Patton, George, T, Georgia, 101, F
8. *Mitchell, Stan, FB, Tennessee, 115
9. Shinholser, Jack, LB, Florida State, 131
10. *Belser, Caesar, DB, Arkansas-Pine Bluff, 145
11. Reding, Dick, FL, Northwestern State (LA), 161, F
12. Stipech, John, LB, Utah, 175, F
13. *Wingate, Heath, C, Bowling Green, 191, F
14. Lovelace, Jerry, HB, Texas Tech, 205, F
15. Seymour, Hal, HB-K, Florida, 221
16. *Wantland, Hal, HB, Tennessee, 235
17. Zalnasky, Mitch, E, Pittsburgh, 251
18. Burson, Joe, HB, Georgia, 265
19. *White, Andre, E, Florida A&M, 281, F
20. Kelly, John, C, Florida A&M, 295

1966 AFL

Held November 28, 1965

The expansion Miami Dolphins received the first two choices in the first round and the first choice in each subsequent round. The draft consisted of 181 selections.

On January 15, 1966, the Dolphins selected 32 players in an expansion draft, four from each of the other eight AFL teams.

BOSTON 1966
1. *Singer, Karl, T, Purdue
2. *Boudreaux, Jim, T, Louisiana Tech
3. Lucas, Harold, T, Michigan State
4. Choice to New York Jets
5. *Mangum, John, T, Southern Mississippi
6. Irby, Dan, T, Louisiana Tech
7. *Battle, Jim, T, Southern
8. Montgomery, Sam, DB, Southern
9. *Satcher, Doug, LB, Southern Mississippi
10. Brewster, Dennis, T, BYU
11. Choice to New York Jets
12. Fugere, Dick, LB, Cincinnati
13. Carr, Tom, FB, Bates
14. Hall, Bob, DB, Brown
15. Laird, Billy, QB, Louisiana Tech
16. *Owens, Buddy, G, Michigan State
17. *Capp, Dick, DE, Boston College
18. Pincavage, John, E-DB, Virginia
19. Novogratz, Joe, G, Pittsburgh
20. Soule, Paul, HB, Bowdoin

BUFFALO 1966
1. *Dennis, Mike, HB, Mississippi
2. *Lindsey, Jim, HB, Arkansas

3. *Jackson, Randy, T, Florida
4. *Burnett, Bobby, HB, Arkansas
5. *Sherlag, Bob, DB, Memphis State
6. Johnson, Bill, HB, University of the South
7. Choice to Denver
8. *Guidry, Paul, E, McNeese State
9. Carter, Jim, DE, Tennessee State
10. *Crockett, Bobby, E, Arkansas
11. Stewart, Dale, HB, Pittsburgh
12. *DeSutter, Wayne, T, Western Illinois
13. McFarlane, Al, HB-K, Louisville
14. Golmont, Tony, DB, North Carolina State
15. Smith, Allen, HB, Fort Valley State
16. Russell, Ed, T, Illinois
17. Earhart, Bill, DT, Bowling Green
18. Lashutka, Greg, E, Ohio State
19. *Phillips, Mel, HB, North Carolina A&T
20. McLean, Ken, E, Texas A&M

DENVER 1966
1. *Shay, Jerry, T, Purdue
2. *White, Freeman, E, Nebraska
3. Hadrick, Bob, E, Purdue
4. *Johnson, Randy, QB, Texas A&I
5. *Clay, Billy, DB, Mississippi
6. Fulgham, James, T, Minnesota
7. *Jones, Jerry, G, Bowling Green
   *Glacken, Scotty, QB, Duke [from Buffalo]
8. *Sellers, Goldie, DB, Grambling
9. *Sbranti, Ron, LB, Utah State
10. Cox, Larry, T, Abilene Christian
11. Burns, James, G, Northwestern
12. Choice to New York Jets
13. *Crabtree, Eric, DB, Pittsburgh
14. Forseberg, Fred, DT, Washington
15. Ringer, Mike, DB, Oklahoma
16. Rogers, Frank, K, Colorado
17. Eickman, Gary, DE, Illinois
18. Talaga, Tom, T, Notre Dame
19. Coughlin, Tom, DE, Miami
20. Hysell, Cliff, T, Montana State

HOUSTON 1966
1. *Nobis, Tommy, LB, Texas
2. *Hindman, Stan, G, Mississippi
3. *Rice, George, T, LSU
4. *Allen, George, T, West Texas State
5. *Granger, Hoyle, FB, Mississippi State
6. Long, Dave, DE-LB, Iowa
7. *Menefee, Hartwell, DB, New Mexico State
8. Bland, Dan, HB, Mississippi State
9. Suffel, Dick, DB, Southwest Texas State
10. Aylor, Wilbur, DT, Southwest Texas State
11. *Ledbetter, Monty, E, Northwestern State (LA)
12. Day, Harry, DE, Memphis State
13. Zimmerman, Fred, LB, Toledo
14. *Lince, Butch, DT, North Dakota
15. Dillard, Tom, T, Austin Peay
16. Smith, Steve, DE, Michigan
17. Loebach, Lyle, T, Simpson
18. Buzzell, Ed, QB, Ottawa
19. Fuller, Frank, DT, Drake
20. Odegaard, Dave, C, Bemidji State

KANSAS CITY 1966
1. *Brown, Aaron, E, Minnesota
2. *Peay, Francis, T, Missouri
3. *Barnes, Walter, G, Nebraska
4. Gibson, Elijah, HB, Bethune-Cookman
5. *Van Horn, Doug, G, Ohio State
6. Osmond, John, C, Tulsa
7. *Gogolak, Charlie, K, Princeton
8. *Smith, Fletcher, DB, Tennessee State
9. *Smith, Dick, E-DB, Northwestern
10. Dawston, Fred, DB, South Carolina State
11. Smith, Willie Ray, DB, Kansas
12. Bonds, Bill, DB, McMurry
13. *Walker, Wayne, E-K, Northwestern State (LA)
14. *Harraway, Charley, FB, San Jose State
15. *Van Dyke, Bruce, G, Missouri
16. *Barrington, Tom, FB, Ohio State
17. *Garrison, Walt, FB, Oklahoma State
18. Seymour, Hal, DB, Florida
19. Dunlevy, Bob, E, West Virginia
20. *Garrett, Mike, HB, USC

MIAMI 1966
1. *Grabowski, Jim, FB, Illinois
   *Norton, Rick, QB, Kentucky
2. *Emanuel, Frank, LB, Tennessee
3. *Gagner, Larry, G, Florida
4. *Leftridge, Dick, FB, West Virginia
5. Bolton, Grady, T, Mississippi State
6. *Weisacosky, Ed, LB, Miami
7. *Hansen, Don, LB, Illinois
8. *Petrella, Bob, HB, Tennessee
9. *Matan, Bill, DE, Kansas State
10. *Killorin, Pat, C, Syracuse
11. *Price, Sam, HB, Illinois
12. *Twilley, Howard, E, Tulsa
13. *Kramer, Kent, E, Minnesota
14. Scoggin, Phil, K, Texas A&M
15. Oliver, Jerry, T, Southwest Texas State
16. Lorenz, Don, DE, Stephen F. Austin
17. Bender, Mike, G, Arkansas
18. Kestner, Rich, E, Kentucky
19. *Moreau, Doug, E-K, LSU
20. Tooker, John, DB, Adams State

MIAMI (Expansion) 1966
*Branch, Mel, DE, LSU [from Kansas City]
*Caveness, Ronnie, LB, Arkansas [from Kansas City]
*Cooke, Ed, DE, Maryland [from Denver]
Davidson, Jim, T, Ohio State [from Buffalo]
*Dotson, Al, DT, Grambling [from Kansas City]
*Erlandson, Tom, LB, Washington State [from Denver]
*Evans, Norm, T, TCU [from Houston]
*Goode, Tom, C, Mississippi State [from Houston]
Huddock, Mike, C, Miami [from New York Jets]
*Jackson, Frank, WR, SMU [from Kansas City]
*Joe, Billy, FB, Villanova [from Buffalo]
*Kocourek, Dave, TE, Wisconsin [from San Diego]
*McDaniel, Edward (Wahoo), LB, Oklahoma [from New York Jets]
*McGeever, John, S, Auburn [from Denver]
*Mingo, Gene, K, No College [from Oakland]
*Neighbors, Billy, G, Alabama [from Boston]
*Nomina, Tom, DT, Miami (OH) [from Denver]
*O'Hanley, Ross, S, Boston College [from Boston]
*Park, Ernie, G, McMurry [from San Diego]
*Rice, Ken, G, Auburn [from Oakland]
*Roberson, Bo, WR, Cornell [from Buffalo]
*Rudolph, Jack, LB, Georgia Tech [from Boston]
*Simpson, Howard, DT, Auburn [from Buffalo]
*Spikes, Jack, FB, TCU [from Houston]
*Torczon, Laverne, DE, Nebraska [from New York Jets]
*Warren, Jimmy, CB, Illinois [from San Diego]
*West, Willie, S, Oregon [from New York Jets]
*Westmoreland, Dick, CB, North Carolina A&T [from San Diego]
*Williams, Maxie, T, Southeastern Louisiana
*Wilson, Eddie, QB, Arizona [from Boston]
*Wood, Dick, QB, Auburn [from Oakland]
*Zecher, Rich, DT, Utah State [from Oakland]

NEW YORK JETS 1966
1. *Yearby, Bill, T, Michigan
2. *Ball, Sam, T, Kentucky
3. *McAdams, Carl, LB, Oklahoma
4. *Waskiewicz, Jim, C-LB, Wichita State [from Boston]
   Sheridan, Phil, E, Notre Dame
5. *Hawkins, Ben, E, Arizona State
6. *Boozer, Emerson, FB, Maryland-Eastern Shore
   Lemay, Dick, G, Vanderbilt [from Oakland]
7. Dobson, Joe, T, Idaho
8. *Lammons, Pete, E, Texas
9. Jones, James, E, Nebraska-Omaha
10. *Wolski, Bill, HB, Notre Dame
11. *Allen, Gerry, HB, Nebraska-Omaha [from Boston]
    Walton, Bob, T, Auburn
12. *Chomyszak, Steve, DT, Syracuse [from Denver]
    Hollister, Ken, DE, Indiana
13. Maliszewski, Stas, LB, Princeton
14. Quintana, Stan, DB, New Mexico
15. *Cody, Steve, LB, Auburn
16. *Acks, Ron, DB, Illinois
17. *Tolleson, Tom, DB, Alabama
18. Mosher, Gerry, E, California
19. *Ridlehuber, Preston, HB, Georgia
20. *Schultz, Randy, HB, Iowa State

OAKLAND 1966
1. *Bird, Rodger, HB, Kentucky
2. Allison, Butch, T, Missouri
3. *Mitchell, Tom, E, Bucknell
4. Tyson, Richard, G, Tulsa
5. *Banaszak, Pete, HB, Miami
6. Choice to New York Jets
7. McRae, Franklin, T, Tennessee State
8. Choice to Denver
9. Kinney, Clifton, LB, San Diego State
10. *Jeter, Tony, E, Nebraska
11. Labruzzo, Joe, HB, LSU
12. Foster, Wayne, T, Washington State
13. *Niland, John, G, Iowa
14. Johnson, Mike, HB, Kansas
15. Renko, Steve, FB, Kansas
16. Ritchey, Craig, DB, Stanford
17. Holman, Ted, DB, Syracuse
18. Robinson, Art, E, Florida A&M
19. Shinholser, Jack, LB, Florida State
20. *Bowman, Steve, FB, Alabama

SAN DIEGO 1966
1. *Davis, Don, T, Cal State-Los Angeles
2. *Rassas, Nick, HB, Notre Dame
3. *Morin, Milt, E, Massachusetts
4. *Brown, Charlie, HB, Syracuse
5. *Smith, Russ, HB, Miami
6. *Pettigrew, Gary, DE, Stanford
7. *Tolbert, Jim, E, Lincoln (MO)
8. *Buffalofone, Doug, LB, Louisville
9. *Reed, Taft, E-DB, Jackson State
10. Pride, Danny, LB, Tennessee State
11. *Owens, Terry, E, Jacksonville State
12. Jones, Ray, HB, Cal State-Los Angeles
13. *Ridge, Houston, DE, San Diego State
14. *London, Mike, E, Wisconsin
15. Novack, Shelly, E, Long Beach State
16. *Scott, Bill, DB, Idaho
17. Ogle, Ron, DT, Long Beach State
18. *Travis, John, HB, San Jose State
19. Bell, Jerome, E-K, Central State (OK)
20. McDowell, Bill, LB, Florida State

1966 AFL REDSHIRT

Held November 28, 1965

BOSTON 1966
1. *Townes, Willie, T, Tulsa
2. *Avery, Ken, LB, Southern Mississippi
3. *Toner, Ed, G, Massachusetts
4. *Wingate, Heath, T, Bowling Green
5. *Perkins, Ray, E, Alabama
6. *Avezzano, Joe, G, Florida State
7. Caston, Brent, DB, Mississippi
8. Schaefer, Tom, FB, Tennessee-Chattanooga
9. White, Jack, QB, Penn State
10. Ellis, Bob, HB, Massachusetts
11. *Marion, Jerry, HB, Wyoming

BUFFALO 1966
1. *Gregory, Jack, E, Tennessee-Chattanooga
2. *Robinson, John, E, Tennessee State
3. *King, Tony, E, Findlay
4. *Cunningham, Dick, LB, Arkansas
5. Czap, Dick, T, Nebraska
6. Carter, Leroy, HB, Grambling
7. Weeks, Dick, B, Texas-El Paso
8. Phelps, Monroe, HB, Missouri
9. King, Ed, LB, USC
10. Moorer, Bill, C, Georgia Tech
11. *Russell, Benny, QB, Louisville

DENVER 1966
1. *Eddy, Nick, HB, Notre Dame
2. Duranko, Pete, E, Notre Dame
3. *Arndt, Dick, T, Idaho
4. Gartung, Mark, T, Oregon State
5. Hatfield, Art, E, Cal State-Los Angeles
6. Durling, Jerald, T, Wyoming
7. Mason, John, E, Stanford
8. *Sorrell, Henry, LB, Tennessee-Chattanooga
9. Harrington, Bud, FB, Tulsa
10. *White, Andre, E, Florida A&M
11. Sullivan, Mike, E, Oregon State

HOUSTON 1966
1. Fisher, Tom, LB, Tennessee
2. *Van Galder, Tim, QB, Iowa State
3. Dunlap, Ralph, DT, Baylor
4. Davis, Bill, QB, Lamar
5. Glover, Richard, T, Virginia State
6. Gary, John, DT, Grambling
7. Pettaway, Clyde, T, North Carolina A&T
8. Marshall, Roger, QB, Baylor
9. Garner, Lee, LB, Mississippi
10. Goich, Dan, T, California
11. Arkwright, Charley, T, Georgia

KANSAS CITY 1966
1. *Youngblood, George, E-DB, Cal State-Los Angeles
2. *Pickens, Bob, T, Nebraska
3. *Stenerud, Jan, K, Montana State
4. Berry, Dan, HB, California
5. Senkbeil, Lynn, LB, Nebraska
6. Reding, Dick, DB, Northwestern State (LA)
7. Ogle, Bill, T, Stanford
8. Myricks, Melvin, DB, Washburn
9. Parks, Perry, DT, Cal State-Los Angeles
10. *Collett, Elmer, C, Cal State-San Francisco
11. *Moore, Denis, T, USC

MIAMI 1966
1. *Roderick, John, E, SMU
2. Fulford, Harold, E, Auburn
3. *Clancy, Jack, E, Michigan
4. *Mankins, Jim, FB, Florida
5. *Greenlee, Fritz, E, Arizona
6. *Darnell, Bill, DB, North Carolina
7. Williams, Don, DT, Wofford
8. *Brittenum, Jon, QB, Arkansas
9. *Baynham, Craig, E, Georgia Tech
10. *Winkler, Randy, T, Tarleton State
11. Anderson, Kai, C, Illinois

NEW YORK JETS 1966
1. *Parker, Don, E, Virginia
2. Denney, Austin, E, Tennessee
3. Lovelace, Jerry, HB, Texas Tech
4. Burnett, Tom, E, Arkansas
5. Miller, Ray, T, Idaho
6. *Smith, Allen, HB, Findlay
7. Smith, Randy, LB, Clemson
8. Campbell, Joe, DB, Auburn
9. Stipech, John, T, Utah
10. Fitzgerald, Dick, T, Nebraska
11. Kollman, Jim, G, Oregon

OAKLAND 1966
1. *Sherman, Rod, HB, USC
2. *Cichowski, Tom, T, Maryland
3. Parson, Ron, E, Austin Peay
4. Crumbacher, John, T, Tennessee
5. Patton, George, T, Georgia
6. *Archer, Dan, T, Oregon
7. Thomas, Bill, HB, Oklahoma
8. *Schmautz, Ray, LB, San Diego State
9. *Tom, Mel, LB, San Jose State
10. O'Brien, Joe, FB, Texas-Arlington
11. Brundage, Mike, QB, Oregon

SAN DIEGO 1966
1. *Windsor, Bob, E, Kentucky
2. *Talbert, Diron, T, Texas
3. *Staggs, Jeff, LB, San Diego State
4. Pratt, LaVerle, LB, Idaho
5. Nixon, Rhome, E, Southern
6. *Beauchamp, Joe, E-DB, Iowa
7. *Saffold, S.T., E, San Jose State
8. *Hubbert, Brad, HB, Arizona
9. Page, Wayne, DB, Clemson
10. Becker, Wayne, T, Montana
11. Wright, Hugh, FB, Adams State

1967

Held March 14, 1967

The first combined AFL-NFL draft was held. A player's order of selection among the 445 players drafted was designated by a number after his college. The expansion New Orleans Saints received first and last choices in each round and one additional choice at the end of the second, third, and fourth rounds.

On February 10, the Saints selected 42 players in an expansion draft, using the same procedures as in the formation of the Atlanta Falcons in 1966. The Falcons were exempted from the expansion draft in 1967, thus leaving 14 teams from whom the Saints selected players.

ATLANTA 1967
1. Choice to San Francisco
2. Carroll, Leo, DE, San Diego State, 31
3. *Jordan, Jim, HB, Florida, 57
4. Choice to Cleveland
5. Delaney, Bill, TE, American International, 112
   Matson, Randy, DT, Texas A&M [from San Francisco] 12.0
6. Choice to Bal
   Snipes, Eugene, H, Elizabeth City [from Los Angeles Rams] 148
   Bircher, Martine, DB, Arkansas [from Baltimore] 151
7. Colehour, Corey, QB, North Dakota, 162
8. Choice to Was
9. *Moten, Bob, FL, Bishop, 215
10. Schafroth, Dick, T, Iowa State, 240
11. Walker, John, LB, Jackson State, 268
12. Gentry, Bill, LB, North Carolina State, 293
13. Szabo, Sandor, K, Ithaca, 317
14. Bryan, Tom, FB, Auburn, 346
15. Nicholas, Al, FB, Cal State-Sacramento, 371
16. Chester, Larry, DB, Allen, 396
17. Buckner, Bill, QB, Delta State, 424

BALTIMORE 1967
1. *Smith, Bubba, DT, Michigan State [from New Orleans] 1
   Detwiler, Jim, HB, Michigan, 20
2. *Volk, Rick, DB, Michigan, 45
3. *Davis, Norman, T, Grambling [from New Orleans] 54
   Ward, Leon, LB, Oklahoma State, 71
4. *Stukes, Charlie, HB, Maryland-Eastern Shore, 100
5. *Porter, Ron, LB, Idaho, 126
6. Southall, Terry, QB, Baylor [from Atlanta] 137
   Choice to Atlanta
7. Rein, Bo, FL, Ohio State, 179
8. Anderson, Lee, T, Bishop [from St. Louis] 202
   *Johnson, Cornelius, LB, Virginia Union, 204
9. Kirkland, Ron, HB, Nebraska, 229
10. Gilbert, Leigh, TE, Northern Illinois, 258
11. Reed, Herman, T, St. Augustine, 290
12. *Pearson, Preston, DB, Illinois [from Pittsburgh] 298
    Christian, J.B., G, Oklahoma State, 307
13. Allen, Marc, DE, West Texas State, 335
14. Conley, Pat, LB, Purdue, 359
15. Wade, Bob, DB, Morgan State, 385
16. *Alley, Don, FL, Adams State, 413
17. Choice to NO

BOSTON 1967
1. *Charles, John, DB, Purdue, 21
2. Choice to Kansas City
3. Choice to New York Jets
4. *Philpott, Ed, DE, Miami (OH), 101
5. *Witt, Melvin, DE, Texas-Arlington, 128
6. Medlen, Ron, DE, SMU, 154
7. *Leo, Bobby, HB, Harvard, 180
8. *Fussell, Tom, DT, LSU, 206
9. Thornhill, Charlie, DB, Michigan State, 232
10. Runnels, John, LB, Penn State, 257
11. *Mitchell, Leroy, FL, Texas Southern, 283
12. Davis, Dave, T, Harvard, 310
13. *Ilg, Ray, LB, Colgate, 336
14. Beaird, Bobby, DB, Auburn, 361
15. Folliard, Tom, LB, Mississippi State, 388
16. Nocera, Dick, HB, Southern Connecticut, 414
17. *Nichols, Bobby, TE, Boston U., 440

BUFFALO 1967
1. *Pitts, John, FL-DB, Arizona State, 22
2. *LeMoine, Jim, TE, Utah State [from Oakland] 42
   Choice to San Diego
3. Rhoads, Tom, DE, Notre Dame [from Oakland thru Denver] 70
   Choice to Oakland
4. *Bugenhagen, Gary, T, Syracuse, 102
5. Choice to Mia
6. Wilkerson, Bill, DE, Texas-El Paso [from Oakland] 149
   Choice to Oakland
7. *Gaiser, George, T, SMU, 181

8. *Luke, Tommy, DB, Mississippi, 207
9. Seither, Gerald, E, Kent State, 233
10. Croft, Tom, DB, Louisiana Tech, 259
11. Tomich, Paul, T, Drake, 284
12. Ames, Ernie, DT, Kent State [from Houston] 292
Bonner, Bob, DT, Southern, 311
13. Finley, Howard, DB, Tennessee State [from Miami] 318
Carter, George, HB, St. Bonaventure [from Houston] 319
Wheeler, Randy, HB, Georgia, 337
14. Moore, Vern, HB, Central State (OK), 362
15. Martinsen, Grant, DB, Utah State, 389
16. Irwin, Mike, HB, Penn State, 415
17. Smith, Grover, HB, Port Valley State, 441

CHICAGO BEARS 1967
1. *Phillips, Loyd, DE, Arkansas, 10
2. *Jones, Bob, DB, San Diego State, 36
3. *Lyle, Gary, HB, George Washington, 63
4. *Dodd, Al, DB, Northwestern State (LA), 90
Greenlee, Tom, DB, Washington [from Los Angeles Rams] 95
5. *Alford, Bruce, K, TCU, 119
6. *Carter, Virgil, QB, BYU, 142
*Kriewald, Doug, G, West Texas State, 143
7. Truitt, John, E, Indiana State, 169
8. Murphy, Roger, E, Northwestern, 195
Griffin, Jerry, LB, SMU, 200
9. Cass, Greg, C, Washington, 221
10. Choice to Washington
11. Mayo, Earl, HB, Morgan State, 273
12. Green, Bruce, E, Midland Lutheran, 299
13. Carstens, Kaye, DB, Nebraska, 326
14. Nesbitt, Lynn, G, Wake Forest, 351
15. Oakes, Terry, DE, Cal State-San Francisco, 377
16. Rogers, Bill, DB, Weber State, 403 +
17. Myers, Jack, LB, Western State (CO), 429

CLEVELAND 1967
1. *Matheson, Bob, LB, Duke, 18
2. *Conjar, Larry, FB, Notre Dame, 46
3. *Cockroft, Don, K, Adams State [from New York Giants] 55
*Barney, Eppie, E, Iowa State, 72
4. *Ward, Carl, HB, Michigan [from Atlanta] 83
*Taffoni, Joe, T, Tennessee-Martin, 98
5. Choice to Houston thru Dallas
6. *Demarie, John, DE, LSU, 152
7. House, Bill, T, Youngstown State, 177
8. Devrow, Bill, DB, Southern Mississippi, 205
9. Dowdy, Cecil, LB, Alabama, 230
10. *Copeland, Jim, G, Virginia, 255
11. *Sabatino, Bill, DE, Colorado, 282
12. Fowler, Charlie, T, Houston, 308
13. *Andrews, Billy, LB, Southeastern Louisiana, 333
14. Rogers, Floyd, T, Clemson, 360
15. Williamson, Dennis, DB, Wisconsin-Whitewater, 386
16. Williams, Don, E, Akron, 411
17. *Davis, Ben, HB, Defiance, 439

DALLAS 1967
1. Choice to Houston
2. Choice to Houston
3. *Clark, Phil, DB, Northwestern, 76
4. Marker, Curtis, G, Northern Michigan, 103
5. Choice to Green Bay
6. *Stokes, Sims, FL, Northern Arizona, 157
7. *Wright, Rayfield, DT, Fort Valley State, 182
8. Laub, Steve, QB, Illinois Wesleyan, 208
9. Morgan, Byron, DB, Findlay, 234
10. Bowens, Eugene, HB, Tennessee State, 260
11. Riley, Pat, FL, Kentucky, 285
12. *Deters, Harold, K, North Carolina State, 312
13. Kerkian, Al, DE, Akron, 338
14. Boyd, Tommy, G, Tarleton State, 364
15. David, Leavie, DB, Edward Waters, 390
16. Brothers, Paul, QB, Oregon State, 416
17. Adams, George, LB, Morehead State, 442

DENVER 1967
1. *Little, Floyd, HB, Syracuse, 6
2. *Beer, Tom, TE, Houston, 32
3. *Current, Mike, T, Ohio State [from Miami] 58
*Goeddeke, George, C, Notre Dame, 59
4. *Cunningham, Carl, DE, Houston, 85
5. *Lynch, Fran, FB, Hofstra [from Miami] 110
*Huard, John, LB, Maine, 113
6. *Sweeney, Neal, E, Tulsa, 139
7. *Richter, Frank, G, Georgia, 165
8. *Cassese, Tom, E, C.W. Post, 191
9. *Summers, Jim, DB, Michigan State, 217
10. Krause, Paul, QB, Dubuque, 243
11. *Andrus, Lou, DE, BYU, 269
12. Choice to Miami
13. Furjanic, Dennis, DE, Houston, 321
14. Francisco, Tom, HB, Virginia Tech, 347
15. *Smith, Don, G, Florida A&M, 373
16. *Lentz, Jack, QB, Holy Cross, 399
17. Valley, Wayne, T, Oregon State, 425

DETROIT 1967
1. *Farr, Mel, HB, UCLA, 7
2. *Barney, Lem, DB, Jackson State, 34
3. *Naumoff, Paul, LB, Tennessee, 60
4. *Kamanu, Lew, DE, Weber State, 88
5. Choice to Philadelphia
6. Jones, Tim, QB, Weber State, 141
*McCambridge, John, DE, Northwestern [from Washington] 144
7. Tuinstra, Ted, T, Iowa State, 166
8. Choice to St. Louis
9. *Weger, Mike, DB, Bowling Green, 218
10. Hayhoe, Jerry, G, USC, 245
11. Shirley, Ray, T, Arizona State, 270
12. Watts, Eric, DB, San Jose State, 297
13. Wright, Lamar, G, Georgia Tech, 322
14. Robinson, Cleveland, DE, South Carolina State, 349
15. Burke, Sam, DB, Georgia Tech, 374
16. *Zawadzkas, Jerry, TE, Columbia, 401
17. Ramsey, Ken, DT, Northwestern, 426

GREEN BAY 1967
1. *Hyland, Bob, G, Boston College, 9
*Horn, Don, QB, San Diego State, 25
2. *Dunaway, Dave, FL, Duke [from Los Angeles Rams] 41
*Flanigan, Jim, LB, Pittsburgh, 51
3. *Rowser, John, DB, Michigan, 78
4. *Williams, Travis, HB, Arizona State [from Washington] 93
Choice to St. Louis
5. Hood, Dwight, DT, Baylor [from Pittsburgh] 116
Tate, Richard, DB, Utah [from Dallas] 130
*Bachman, Jay, C, Cincinnati, 132
6. Williams, Stew, FB, Bowling Green, 158
7. Ziolkowski, Bob, T, Iowa [from New York Giants] 161
Powell, Bill, LB, Missouri, 184
8. Miles, Clarence, DT, Trinity (TX), 210
9. Reed, Harlan, TE, Mississippi State, 236
10. Shear, Bill, K, Cortland State, 262
11. Bennett, Dave, QB, Springfield, 287
12. *Bass, Mike, DB, Michigan, 314
13. Brown, Keith, FL, Central Missouri State, 340
14. *James, Claudis, HB, Jackson State, 366
15. Schneider, Jim, DT, Colgate, 392
16. Cassidy, Fred, HB, Miami, 418
17. Elias, Jeff, TE, Kansas, 444

HOUSTON 1967
1. *Webster, George, LB, Michigan State, 5
*Regner, Tom, G, Notre Dame [from Dallas] 23
2. *Davis, Bob, QB, Virginia, 30
*Hopkins, Roy, HB, Texas Southern [from Dallas] 49
3. *Carwell, Larry, DB, Iowa State, 56
4. *Stith, Carel, T, Nebraska, 85
5. *Johns, Peter, DB, Tulane, 111
*Parker, Willie, DT, Arkansas-Pine Bluff [from Washington thru Dallas] 11.8
Moore, Zeke, DB, Lincoln (MO) [from Cleveland thru Dallas] 127
6. *Barnes, Pete, LB, Southern, 136
7. *Carrington, Ed, FL, Virginia, 164
8. Brunson, John, HB, Benedictine, 189
Washington, Sharon, FL, Northeast Missouri State [from Oakland] 201
9. *Houston, Ken, DB, Prairie View A&M, 214
10. *Campbell, Woody, HB, Northwestern, 242
Sheehan, Tim, C, Stanford [from Kansas City] 261
11. Decker, Harold, DE, Kalamazoo, 267
12. Choice to Buffalo
13. Choice to Buffalo
14. Hailstock, Henry, G, Lincoln (MO), 345
15. McQueen, Marvin, LB, Mississippi, 370
16. Keeling, Rex, FL, Samford, 398
17. Lee, Larry, FL, Texas A&M, 423

KANSAS CITY 1967
1. *Trosch, Gene, DT, Miami, 24
2. *Lynch, Jim, LB, Notre Dame [from Boston] 47
*Lanier, Willie, LB, Morgan State, 50
3. *Masters, Billy, TE, LSU, 77
4. Zwernemann, Ron, G, East Texas State, 104
5. Choice to Oakland thru Buffalofalo
6. *Smith, Noland, HB, Tennessee State, 156
7. Erickson, Dick, C, Wisconsin-Stout, 183
8. Altemeier, Tom, T, Luther, 209
9. Pope, Ed, DT, Jackson State, 235
10. Choice to Houston
11. Braswell, Bill, G, Auburn, 286
12. Kolonski, Dick, C, Lake Forest [from San Diego] 303
Lashley, Kent, FL, Northeastern Oklahoma, 313
13. Simmons, Linwood, FB, Edward Waters, 339
14. Bishop, John, DT, Delta State, 365
15. Caponi, Dennis, FB, Xavier, 391
16. Noggle, Charlie, HB, North Carolina State, 417
17. Lattin, Dave, FL, Texas-El Paso, 443

LOS ANGELES RAMS 1967
1. Choice to Minnesota
2. *Ellison, Willie, HB, Texas Southern [from Minnesota] 33
Choice to Green Bay
3. Choice to Philadelphia
4. Choice to Chicago Bears
5. *Shaw, Nate, DB, USC, 122
6. Choice to Atlanta
7. Choice to Philadelphia
8. Choice to Chicago Bears
9. *Smith, Tommie, HB, San Jose State, 226
10. Moore, Leon, DB, Tennessee State, 252
11. Horak, Frank, DB, TCU, 278
12. Badjek, Pat, LB, Franklin, 304
13. Erisman, John, E, Miami (OH), 330
14. Richardson, Walt, DT, Fresno State, 356
15. Bunker, Steve, TE, Oregon, 382
16. Sack, Allen, LB, Notre Dame, 408
17. Barnes, Bill, C, Washington, 434

MIAMI 1967
1. *Griese, Bob, QB, Purdue, 4
2. *Riley, Jim, T, Oklahoma, 29
3. Choice to Denver
4. Greenlee, Bob, T, Yale, 84
5. Choice to Denver
*Tucker, Gary, HB, Tennessee-Chattanooga [from Buffalo] 129
6. Norris, Bud, TE, Washington State, 138
7. *Seiple, Larry, HB, Kentucky, 163
8. Choice to Oakland
9. *Richardson, John, DT, UCLA, 216
10. *Beier, Tom, DB, Miami, 241
11. *Pyburn, Jack, T, Texas A&M, 266
12. Juk, Stan, LB, South Carolina, 294
Whitaker, Jim, DB, Missouri [from Denver] 295
13. Choice to Buffalo
14. Stikes, Charles, DB, Kent State, 344
15. Ferro, Jake, LB, Youngstown State, 372
16. Calhoun, Maurice, FB, Central State (OH), 397
17. Kissam, Larry, T, Florida State, 422

MINNESOTA 1967
1. *Jones, Clint, HB, Michigan State [from New York Giants] 2
Washington, Gene, FL, Michigan State, 8
*Page, Alan, DE, Notre Dame [from Los Angeles Rams] 15
2. Grim, Bob, HB, Oregon State [from New York Giants] 28
Choice to Los Angeles Rams
3. *Denny, Earl, FL, Missouri, 61
4. *Coleman, Alvin, DB, Tennessee A&I, 87
5. Last, Ken, E, Minnesota, 115
6. Choice to Pittsburgh
7. *Bryant, Bobby, DB, South Carolina, 167
8. Choice to Pittsburgh
*Beasley, John, TE, California [from Washington] 197
9. Morris, Bill, G, Holy Cross, 219
10. *Tatman, Pete, FB, Nebraska, 244
11. Trygstad, Bob, DT, Washington State, 271
12. Cremer, Fred, G, St. John's (MN), 296
13. Hardt, Charley, DB, Tulsa, 323
14. *Hargrove, Jimmy, LB, Howard Payne, 348
15. Shea, Jimmy, DB, Eastern New Mexico, 375
16. Beard, Gene, DB, Virginia Union, 400
17. Wagoner, Dick, DB, Bowling Green, 427

NEW ORLEANS 1967
1. Choice to Baltimore
*Kelley, Les, HB, Alabama, 26
2. *Burris, Bo, QB-DB, Houston, 27
*Gilliam, John, FL, South Carolina State, 52
*Rowe, Dave, T, Penn State, 53
3. Choice to Bal
Williams, Del, C, Florida State, 79
*Hart, Ben, HB, Oklahoma, 80
4. *Widby, Ron, K, Tennessee, 81
Carr, Bill, C, Florida, 106
Stangle, Tom, T, Dayton, 107
5. *McCall, Don, HB, USC, 108
*Douglas, John, DB, Texas Southern, 133
6. *Harvey, George, G, Kansas, 134
*Wood, Bo, LB, North Carolina, 159
7. Hertzog, Gary, G, Willamette, 160
McKelvey, Bob, HB, Northwestern, 185
8. Harris, Sam, TE, Colorado, 186
Siler, Barry, LB, Albion, 211.
9. Lavens, Tim, TE, Idaho, 212.
Ross, Eugene, DB, Oklahoma, 237
10. *Brown, Charlie, FL, Missouri, 238
Robertson, Roosevelt, FL, North Carolina Central, 263
11. Benson, Jim, C, Florida, 264
Corbin, Bernard, DB, Alabama A&M, 288
12. Pack, Ronnie, G, Texas Tech, 289
*Robinson, John, FL, Tennessee State, 315
13. *Stetz, Bill, LB, Boston College, 316
Grossnickle, Gary, DB, Missouri, 341
14. *Hester, Jim, TE, North Dakota, 342
Stetter, George, DB, Virginia, 367
15. Snow, John, T, Wake Forest, 368
Johnson, Darrell, HB, Lamar, 393
16. Rhoden, Marcus, FL, Mississippi State, 394
*Cortez, Bruce, DB, Parsons, 419
17. *Abramowicz, Dan, HB, Xavier, 420
Stewart, Billy Bob, LB, SMU [from Baltimore] 438
Walker, Jimmy, E, Providence, 445

NEW ORLEANS (Expansion) 1967
*Barrington, Tom, FB, Ohio State [from Washington]
*Battle, Jim, T, Southern [from Cleveland]
*Bradshaw, Charlie, T, Baylor [from Pittsburgh]
*Burkett, Jackie, LB, Auburn [from Baltimore]
*Cahill, Dave, DT, Arizona State [from Philadelphia]
*Cody, Bill, LB, Auburn [from Detroit]
*Croftcheck, Don, G, Indiana [from Washington]
*Curry, Bill, C, Georgia Tech [from Green Bay]
*Davis, Ted, LB, Georgia Tech [from Baltimore]
*Garcia, Jim, DE, Cal State-Chico [from New York Giants]
*Hall, Tom, FL, Minnesota [from Minnesota]
*Heckard, Steve, FL, Davidson [from Los Angeles Rams]
*Heidel, Jimmy, DB, Mississippi [from St. Louis]
*Hornung, Paul, HB, Notre Dame [from Green Bay]
*Kilmer, Billy, QB, UCLA [from San Francisco]
*Kimbrough, Elbert, DB, Northwestern [from San Francisco]
*Kramer, Kent, TE, Minnesota [from San Francisco]
*Kupp, Jake, G, Washington [from Washington]
*Leggett, Earl, DT, LSU [from Los Angeles Rams]
*Logan, Obert, DB, Trinity (TX) [from Dallas]
*Mattson, Riley, T, Oregon [from Chicago Bears]
*Morrow, John, C, Michigan [from Cleveland]
*Ogden, Ray, TE, Alabama [from St. Louis]
*Rissmiller, Ray, T, Georgia [from Philadelphia]
*Roberts, Walter (The Flea), FL, San Jose State [from Cleveland]
*Rose, George, DB, Auburn [from Minnesota]
*Sandeman, Bill, T, Pacific [from Dallas]
*Scholtz, Bob, T, Notre Dame [from New York Giants]
*Schweda, Brian, DE, Kansas [from Chicago Bears]
*Simmons, Dave, LB, Georgia Tech [from St. Louis]
*Simmons, Jerry, SE, Bethune-Cookman [from Pittsburgh]
*Smith, Bob, HB, North Texas State [from Pittsburgh]
*Smith, Bobby Lee, DB, UCLA [from Detroit]
*Stephens, Larry, DT, Texas [from Dallas]
*Stonebreaker, Steve, LB, Detroit [from Baltimore]
*Tilleman, Mike, DT, Montana [from Minnesota]
*Vandersea, Phil, LB, Massachusetts [from Green Bay]
*Walker, Willie, SE, Tennessee State [from Detroit]
*Wendryhoski, Joe, G, Illinois [from Los Angeles Rams]
*Whitsell, Dave, DB, Indiana [from Chicago Bears]
*Whittingham, Fred, LB, Cal Poly-SLO [from Philadelphia]
*Wood, Gary, QB, Cornell [from New York Giants]

NEW YORK GIANTS 1967
1. Choice to Minnesota
2. Choice to Minnesota
3. Choice to Cleveland
4. Thompson, Louis, DT, Alabama, 82
5. *Lewis, Dave, QB, Stanford, 109
6. Choice to Was thru Minnesota
7. Choice to Green Bay
8. *Eaton, Scott, DB, Oregon State, 187
9. Freeman, Fred, T, Mississippi Valley State, 213
10. Stebbins, Dick, E, Grambling, 239
11. Pifer, Pete, FB, Oregon State, 265
12. Shortal, Bob, LB, Dayton, 291
13. Stidham, Tom, K, Oklahoma, 320
14. Bates, Bill, K, Missouri, 343
15. Reale, Tom, T, Southern Connecticut State, 369
16. Seman, Bill, G, Northeast Missouri State, 395
17. Rowe, Gary, HB, North Carolina State, 421

NEW YORK JETS 1967
1. *Seiler, Paul, G, Notre Dame, 12
2. Sheron, Rich, TE, Washington State, 37
3. Randall, Dennis, DE, Oklahoma State, 66
*King, Henry, DB, Utah State [from Boston] 74
4. Gray, Julian, DB, Grambling, 92
5. Jackson, Louis, DB, Grambling, 117
6. *Richardson, Jeff, DE, Michigan State, 146
7. *Elliott, John, G, Texas, 171
8. Bledsoe, Gene, G, Texas, 196
9. Scott, Ray, DE, Prairie View A&M, 224
10. Brown, Raymond, OS, Alcorn State, 249
11. Slattery, Herb, G, Delaware, 274
12. *Rasmussen, Randy, G, Kearney State, 302
13. Emmer, Jack, FL, Rutgers, 327
14. *Stromberg, Mike, LB, Temple, 352
15. Schweberger, Jack, FL, Vermont, 380
16. Archibald, Doug, DB, Tennessee, 405
17. Biletnikoff, Bob, QB, Miami, 430

OAKLAND 1967
1. *Upshaw, Gene, G-T, Texas A&I, 17
2. Choice to Buffalo
3. Choice to Buffalo thru Denver
*Fairband, Bill, LB, Colorado [from Buffalo] 75
4. Jackson, James Roy, E, Oklahoma, 96
5. Warfield, Gerald, HB, Mississippi, 124
*Hibler, Mike, LB, Stanford [from Buffalo thru Kansas City] 131
6. Choice to Buffalo
Egloff, Rick, QB, Wyoming [from Buffalo] 155
7. Lewellen, Ron, DT, Tennessee-Martin, 176
8. *Banks, Estes, HB, Colorado [from Miami] 188
Choice to Houston
9. Devilling, Mark, LB, Muskingum, 228
10. *Sligh, Richard, T, North Carolina Central, 253
11. *Benson, Dwayne, LB, Hamline, 280
12. *Kruse, Bob, T, Wayne State, 306
13. Kleinpeter, Len, E, Southwestern Louisiana, 332
14. Boyett, Casey, E, BYU, 363 +
15. Woodson, Ben, HB, Utah, 384
16. Bruce, Don, G, Virginia Tech, 409
17. Cullin, Mike, DE, Slippery Rock, 436

PHILADELPHIA 1967
1. *Jones, Harry, HB, Arkansas, 19
2. Brooks, John, G, Kent State, 44
3. *Wilson, Harry, HB, Nebraska [from Los Angeles Rams] 68
Choice to Pittsburgh

4. *Hughes, Chuck, FL, Texas-El Paso, 99
5. Van Pelt, Bob, C, Indiana [from Detroit] 114
   *Absher, Dick, TE, Maryland, 125
6. *Hughes, Bob, DE, Jackson State, 153
7. Williams, John, DB, San Diego State [from Los Angeles Rams] 174
   Crenshaw, Bob, G, New Mexico State, 178
8. Klacking, Don, FB, Wyoming, 203
9. Stancell, Harold, DB, Tennessee, 231
10. Bates, Maurice, DE, Northern State (SD), 256
11. Parker, Omar, G, Washington, 281
12. Monroe, Ben, QB, New Mexico, 309
13. Downs, Bill, DT, Louisville, 334
14. Kenney, Dick, K, Michigan State, 358
15. Poche, David, T, McNeese State, 387
16. Baker, Lynn, DB, Colorado, 412.
17. Catavolos, George, DB, Purdue, 437

PITTSBURGH 1967
1. Choice to Green Bay
2. *Shy, Don, HB, San Diego State, 35
3. Choice to San Francisco
   *Freitas, Rockne, C, Oregon State [from Philadelphia] 73
4. *May, Ray, LB, USC, 89
5. Choice to Green Bay
6. *Haggerty, Mike, T, Miami [from Minnesota] 140
   Choice to Chicago Bears thru Atlanta
7. Choice to Washington
8. *Foruria, John, QB, Idaho [from Minnesota] 192
   Barnes, Mike, T, Purdue, 194
9. Otis, Paul, DT, Houston, 221
10. Wilsey, Bill, LB, Fresno State, 246
11. Whitcomb, Jim, FL, Emporia State, 272
12. Choice to Baltimore
13. Homan, Jim, G, USC, 324
14. *Anderson, Chet, TE, Minnesota, 350
15. Love, Mike, FB, Abilene Christian, 376
16. Smith, Bill, C, Oregon, 402
17. Davenport, Mike, FB, Wyoming, 428

ST. LOUIS 1967
1. *Williams, Dave, FL, Washington, 16
2. Rowe, Bob, DE, Western Michigan, 43
3. Carlin, Vidal, QB, North Texas State, 69
4. Barnes, Mike, DB, Texas-Arlington, 97
   *Bowling, Andy, LB, Virginia Tech [from Green Bay] 105
5. Rivers, Jamie, TE, Bowling Green, 123
6. *Campbell, Mike, HB, Lenoir-Rhyne, 150
7. Randall, Joe, K, Brown, 175
8. Gold, Mike, T, Utah State [from Detroit] 193
   Choice to Baltimore
9. *Wheeler, Ted, TE, West Texas State, 227
10. Barrs, Lavern, DB, Furman, 255
11. *Marcontell, Ed, G, Lamar, 279
12. Dundas, Steve, FL, Pomona, 305
13. Duncum, Bob, T, West Texas State, 331
14. *Hickey, Bo, FB, Maryland, 357
15. Wosilius, Bill, LB, Syracuse, 383
16. *Spiller, Phil, DB, Cal State-Los Angeles, 410
17. Bacigalupo, Terry, DE, Oklahoma State, 435

SAN DIEGO 1967
1. *Billingsley, Ron, DT, Wyoming, 14
2. *McCall, Ron, LB, Weber State, 40
   *Howard, Bob, DB, San Diego State [from Buffalo] 48
3. *Akin, Harold, T, Oklahoma State, 67
4. *Post, Dickie, HB, Houston, 94
5. *Erickson, Bernard, LB, Abilene Christian, 121
6. Johns, Nate, FL, San Diego State, 147
7. Conway, David, K, Texas, 173
8. Mills, John, E, Tennessee, 199
9. *Newell, Steve, E, Long Beach State, 225
10. Ossmo, Torre, T, Western Michigan, 251
11. Jarvis, Carroll, HB, Virginia, 277
12. Choice to Kansas City
13. Carr, Leon, DB, Prairie View A&M, 329
14. *Baccaglio, Martin, DT, San Jose State, 355
15. Scoggins, Craig, E, San Diego State, 381
16. Phillips, Paul, T, South Carolina, 407
17. Gibbs, John, HB, South Carolina State, 433

SAN FRANCISCO 1967
1. *Spurrier, Steve, QB, Florida [from Atlanta] 3
   *Banaszek, Cas, TE-LB, Northwestern, 11
2. *Holzer, Tom, T, Louisville, 39
3. *Nunley, Frank, LB, Michigan [from Pittsburgh] 62
   *Tucker, Bill, HB, Tennessee State, 65
4. *Trimble, Wayne, DB, Alabama, 91
5. Choice to Atlanta
6. *Cunningham, Doug, HB, Mississippi, 145
7. Jackson, Milt, DB, Tulsa, 170
8. *Johnson, Walter, LB, Tuskegee, 198
9. *Briggs, Bob, T, Heidelberg, 223
10. Myers, Phil, FL, Northwestern Oklahoma, 248
11. Carmann, Ken, DT, Kearney State, 276
12. Hall, James, LB, Tuskegee, 301
13. Gibbs, Rich, DB, Iowa, 325
14. Leblanc, Dalton, FL, Northeast Louisiana, 354
15. Spencer, Clarence, FL, Louisville, 379 +
16. Templeman, Bart, C, Eastern Montana, 404
17. Talbott, Danny, QB, North Carolina, 432

WASHINGTON 1967
1. *McDonald, Ray, FB, Idaho, 13
2. Musgrove, Spain, DT, Utah State, 38
3. Belcher, Curg, DB, BYU, 64
4. Choice to Green Bay
5. Choice to Houston thru Dallas
6. *Bandy, Don, T, Tulsa [from New York Giants thru Minnesota] 135
   Choice to Detroit
7. Matte, Bruce, QB-HB, Miami (OH) [from Pittsburgh] 168
   *Love, John, FL, North Texas State, 172
8. *Hendershot, Larry, G-LB, Arizona State [from Atlanta] 190
   Choice to Minnesota
9. *Larsen, Pete, HB, Cornell, 222
10. Houlton, Tim, DT, St. Norbert [from Chicago Bears] 247
    Sullivan, Bruce, DB, Illinois, 250
11. Brown, Bill, C, Texas-El Paso, 275
12. Sepic, Ron, E, Ohio State, 300
13. Rodwell, Bob, LB, Eastern Michigan, 328
14. Socha, Andy, HB, Marshall, 353
15. *Breding, Ed, G, Texas A&M, 378
16. Avila, Alfredo, DB, Sul Ross, 406
17. Baucom, Lyle, T, Cal State-San Francisco, 431

1968

Held January 30-31, 1968

Minnesota had the first selection in the draft due to a trade with the New York Giants. Despite a 7-7 record in 1967, under the merger agreement the Giants had received the first choice overall as compensation for accepting the Jets as a New York entry into the merged league. The expansion Cincinnati Bengals received the first and last choices in each round (the second choice in the first round): one additional choice at the end of the second, third, and fourth rounds: and all AFL sixth-round selections except Miami's. Atlanta, with the worst record in pro football in 1967, received the third pick in the first round and the second in each subsequent round.

On January 21, the Bengals selected 40 players in an expansion draft, taking five from each AFL team except the Miami Dolphins.

ATLANTA 1968
1. *Humphrey, Claude, DE, Tennessee State, 3
2. *Dabney, Carlton, DE, Morgan State, 29
   *Wright, John, FL, Illinois [from Green Bay thru Los Angeles Rams] 53
3. Choice to Chicago Bears
4. Choice to St. Louis
5. Choice to Washington
6. Hagle, Jim, RB, SMU, 140
   Wynns, Joe, DB, South Carolina State [from Pittsburgh] 147
   *Eber, Rick, FL, Tulsa [from Baltimore] 162
7. Choice to Minnesota
8. Jeffords, Ray, TE, Georgia, 194
9. Holland, Henry, C, North Texas State, 221
10. Tomasini, Mike, DT, Colorado State, 248
11. *Brezina, Greg, LB, Houston, 275
12. Vaughn, A.J., RB, Wayne State, 302
13. *Harris, Bill, RB, Colorado, 329
14. Polk, Joe, RB, Livingstone, 356
15. Bean, Don, FL, Houston, 383
16. Hall, Roy, T, San Jose State, 410
17. Schmidt, Jim, DB, Cal State-San Francisco, 437

BALTIMORE 1968
1. *Williams, John, T, Minnesota, 23
2. *Grant, Bob, LB, Wake Forest, 50
3. O'Hara, Rich, FL, Northern Arizona, 78
4. *Duncan, Jim, RB, Maryland-Eastern Shore, 107
5. *Elzey, Paul, LB, Toledo [from New York Giants] 126
   Choice to Cleveland
6. Choice to Atl
7. Andrews, Anthony, RB, Hampton, 188
8. Davis, Tommy, G, Tennessee State, 216
9. *Cole, Terry, RB, Indiana, 242
10. *Austin, Ocie, DB, Utah State [from Washington] 257
    Tomlin, Ed, RB, Hampton, 270
11. Pickens, Bill, G, Houston, 296
12. Jackson, James, T, Jackson State, 324
13. Tennebar, Howard, T, Kent State, 350
14. Mitchell, Charles, TE, Alabama State, 378
15. Beaver, Jeff, QB, North Carolina, 404
16. Blackledge, Walt, FL, San Jose State, 432
17. Pederson, Roy, LB, Northern Iowa, 458

BOSTON 1968
1. *Byrd, Dennis, DT, North Carolina State, 6
2. *Funchess, Tom, T, Jackson State, 32
3. *Marsh, Aaron, FL, Eastern Kentucky, 60
4. *Gamble, R.C., RB, South Carolina State, 88
5. Smithberger, Jim, DB, Notre Dame, 116
6. Choice to Cincinnati
7. Schneider, John, QB, Toledo, 170
8. *Johnson, Daryl, DB, Morgan State, 197
9. Choice to Houston
10. Outlaw, Johnny, DB, Jackson State, 249
11. *Feldhausen, Paul, T, Northland, 278
12. *Cheyunski, Jim, LB, Syracuse, 305
13. Huber, Max, T, BYU, 332
14. McKay, Henry, E, Guilford, 358
15. *McMahon, Art, DB, North Carolina State, 385
16. Fulton, Charley, RB, Tennessee, 413
17. *Koontz, Ed, LB, Catawba, 440

BUFFALO 1968
1. *Moses, Haven, E, San Diego State, 9
2. Tatareck, Bob, DT, Miami, 34
3. *Trapp, Richard, E, Florida, 83
4. *Chandler, Edgar, T-K, Georgia [from Denver] 86
   Choice to Kansas City
5. *Gregory, Ben, RB, Nebraska [from Denver thru Cincinnati] 114
   *McBath, Mike, DE, Penn State 119
   *Anderson, (Mini) Max, RB, Arizona State [from Kansas City] 132
6. Choice to Cincinnati
7. *Richardson, Pete, DB, Dayton, 173
8. *Kalsu, Bob, T, Oklahoma, 199
9. *McDermott, Gary, RB, Tulsa, 227
10. Lawson, Jerome, DB, Utah, 251
11. Plagge, Dick, RB, Auburn, 281
12. Pipes, Greg, LB, Baylor, 306
13. *Darragh, Dan, QB, William & Mary, 336
14. *DeVliegher, Chuck, DT, Memphis State, 361
15. Gilmore, John, DT, Peru State, 389
16. *Frantz, John, C, California, 415
17. Hines, Dick, DT, Kentucky State, 443

CHICAGO BEARS 1968
1. *Hull, Mike, RB, USC, 16
2. *Wallace, Bob, E, Texas-El Paso, 46
3. *Hazelton, Major, DB, Florida A&M [from Atlanta] 57
   Choice to Dal
4. *Mass, Wayne, T, Clemson, 99
   Bush, Alan, G, Mississippi [from Los Angeles Rams] 106
5. *Turner, Cecil, FL, Cal Poly-SLO, 127
6. *Schmedding, Jim, C, Weber State, 154
7. Holmon, Willie, DE, South Carolina State, 181
8. Bell, Wayne, RB, Lenoir-Rhyne, 208
9. Moore, Sam, T, Mississippi Valley State, 235
10. Davis, Fred, G, Doane, 262
11. *Coady, Rich, TE, Memphis State, 289
12. *Vallez, Emilio, LB, New Mexico, 316
13. Dearion, Willie, FL, Prairie View A&M, 343
14. Gargus, Harold, DT, New Mexico State, 370
15. Jaeger, Rich, C, Gustavus Adolphus, 397
16. Murphy, Jim, K, Utah State, 424
17. Layton, Gene, DT, Colorado State, 451

CINCINNATI 1968
1. *Johnson, Bob, C, Tennessee, 2
   Choice to Mia
2. *Staley, Bill, DE, Utah State, 28
   Choice to Miami
   *Smiley, Tom, RB, Lamar, 55
3. Davis, Gary, QB, Vanderbilt, 56
   Robinson, Paul, RB, Arizona, 82
   *Livingston, Dale, K, Western Michigan, 83
4. *Phillips, Jess, DB, Michigan State, 84
   *McVea, Warren, RB, Houston, 109
   Choice to Den
5. *Middendorf, Dave, G, Washington State, 112
   Beauchamp, Al, LB, Southern, 138
6. *Fest, Howard, T, Texas, 139
   Kendricks, Billy, T, Alabama A&M [from Boston] 143
   *Neidert, John, LB, Louisville [from Buffalo] 145
   *Warren, Dewey, QB, Tennessee [from San Diego] 155
   *Johnson, Essex, DB, Grambling [from New York Jets] 156
   Maple, Elmo, FL, Southern [from Kansas City] 158
   Ellis, Sidney, DB, Jackson State [from Houston] 160
   Williams, Charles, RB, Arkansas-Pine Bluff [from Oakland] 163
   Johnson, James, DB, South Carolina State, 165
7. Smith, Steve, TE, Miami, 166
   Bean, Wes, LB, Grambling, 192
8. *Gunner, Harry, LB, Oregon State, 193
   Brantley, Ed, T, North Texas State, 219
9. Johnson, Phil, DB, Long Beach State, 220
   Hanrahan, Steve, DT, Weber State, 246
10. *Patrick, Wayne, RB, Louisville, 247
    Russell, James, E, North Texas State, 273
11. Scott, Wally, DB, Arizona, 274
    Banks, Jeff, LB, Pacific, 300
12. *Trumpy, Bob, TE, Utah, 301
    *Jones, Harold, T, Grambling, 327
13. Bivins, James, LB, Texas Southern, 328
    *Washington, Teddy, RB, San Diego State, 354
14. Webster, Les, RB, Iowa State, 355
    Lewicke, Steve, E, Texas-El Paso, 381
15. Palmore, Harvey, G, Morgan State, 382
    Mira, Joe, FL, Miami, 408
16. *Williams, Monk, DB, Alcorn State, 409
    Marks, Brown, LB, Indiana, 435
17. Manning, Don, LB, UCLA, 436
    Smith, Jimmy, TE, Jackson State, 462

CINCINNATI (Expansion) 1968
*Archer, Dan, T, Oregon [from Oakland]
*Banks, Estes, RB, Colorado [from Oakland]
*Bellino, Joe, RB, Navy [from Boston]
*Boudreaux, Jim, DT, Louisiana Tech [from Boston]
*Brabham, Danny, LB, Arkansas [from Houston]
*Brannen, Solomon, DB, Morris Brown [from New York Jets]
Brown, Bill, T, Texas-El Paso [from New York Jets]
*Bugenhagen, Gary, T, Syracuse [from Buffalo]
*Buncom, Frank, LB, USC [from San Diego]
*Burford, Chris, SE, Stanford [from Kansas City]
*Burnett, Bobby, RB, Arkansas [from Buffalo]
*Garrett, J.D., RB, Grambling [from Boston]
*Gilchrist, Cookie, RB [from Denver]
*Graves, White, DB, LSU [from Boston]
*Griffin, Jim, DE, Grambling [from San Diego]
*Hall, Ron, DB, Missouri Valley [from Boston]
*Headrick, Sherrill, LB, TCU [from Kansas City]
*Hunt, Bobby, DB, Auburn [from Kansas City]
*Isbell, Joe Bob, G, Houston [from Houston]
Johns, Nate, RB, San Diego State [from Oakland]
*Jones, Willie, DE, Kansas State [from Houston]
*Kellogg, Mike, RB, Santa Clara [from Denver]
*King, Charley, DB, Purdue [from Buffalo]
*Marsh, Frank, RB, Oregon State [from San Diego]
*Matlock, John, C, Miami [from New York Jets]
*Matson, Pat, G, Oregon [from Denver]
*Perreault, Pete, G, Boston U. [from New York Jets]
*Poole, Bob, TE, Clemson [from Houston]
*Reynolds, Al, G, Tarkio [from Kansas City]
*Rice, Andy, DT, Texas Southern [from Houston]
*Schmidt, Bob, T, Minnesota [from Buffalo]
Sherman, Rod, FL, USC [from Oakland]
*Sligh, Richard, DT, North Carolina Central [from Oakland]
*Smith, Fletcher, DB, Tennessee [from Kansas City]
*Sorrell, Henry, LB, Tennessee-Chattanooga [from Denver]
*Van Raaphorst, Dick, K, Ohio State [from San Diego]
*Waskiewicz, Jim, C-LB, Wichita State [from New York Jets]
*Wright, Ernie, T, Ohio State [from San Diego]
*Wright, Lonnie, DB, Colorado State [from Denver]
*Zecher, Rich, DT, Utah State [from Buffalo]

CLEVELAND 1968
1. Upshaw, Marvin, DE, Trinity (TX), 21
2. *Garlington, John, LB, LSU, 47
3. Olszewski, Harry, G, Clemson [from Pittsburgh] 64
   Morrison, Reece, RB, Southwest Texas State [from Washington] 66
   Choice to Detroit thru Los Angeles Rams
4. *Meylan, Wayne, LB, Nebraska, 104
5. Wempe, Mike, T, Missouri, 131
   Jackson, Jackie, RB, Clemson [from Baltimore] 134
6. *James, Nathaniel, DB, Florida A&M [from New York Giants] 152
7. Brady, Dale, RB, Memphis State, 186
8. *Schoen, Tom, DB, Notre Dame, 212
9. Porter, David, DT, Michigan, 238
10. Greer, James, DE, Stephen F Austin [from Pittsburgh] 255
    *Mitchell, Alvin, FL, Morgan State, 267
11. Alcorn, Jim, QB, Clarion, 293
12. *Beutler, Tom, LB, Toledo, 319
13. Sellers, Terry, DB, Georgia, 348
14. Whipps, Edgar, RB, Jackson State, 374
15. Baxter, Bob, FL, Memphis State, 400
16. Sievert, Dick, DE, Wisconsin-River Falls, 429
17. McDuffie, Wayne, C, Florida State, 455

DALLAS 1968
1. *Homan, Dennis, E, Alabama, 20
2. *McDaniels, Dave, E, Mississippi Valley State, 45
3. Harmon, Ed, LB, Louisville [from Chicago Bears] 71
   Choice to Minnesota
4. *Douglas, John, LB, Missouri [from New York Giants] 97
   Choice to New Orleans
5. Nye, Blaine, T, Stanford, 130
6. *Lewis, D.D., LB, Mississippi State, 159
7. Taucher, Bob, T, Nebraska, 185
8. Brown, Frank, DT, Albany State, 211
9. Kmiec, Ken, DB, Illinois, 241
10. Olison, Ben, FL, Kansas, 266
11. Shotts, Ron, RB, Oklahoma, 292
12. Whitty, Wilson, LB, Boston U., 321
13. Lord, Carter, FL, Harvard, 347
14. Williams, Ron, DB, West Virginia, 373
15. Lunceford, Tony, K, Auburn, 402
16. *Cole, Larry, T, Hawaii, 428
17. Nordgren, George, RB, Houston, 454

DENVER 1968
1. Choice to San Diego
2. *Culp, Curley, DE, Arizona State, 31
3. *Ford, Garrett, RB, West Virginia, 58
   *Vaughn, Bob, T, Mississippi [from Kansas City] 75
4. Choice to Buffalo
   *Lambert, Gordon, LB, Tennessee-Martin [from Miami] 91
   *Garrett, Drake, DB, Michigan State [from

Kansas City] 102
*Holloman, Gus, DB, Houston [from Cincinnati] 111
5. Choice to Buffalo thru Cincinnati
6. Choice to Miami
7. Choice to Oakland
8. Holloway, Steve, DB, Weber State, 196
9. *Smith, Paul, LB, New Mexico, 222
10. Langford, Bob, T, Middle Tennessee State, 252
11. Choice to Oakland
12. Hendrix, Bobby, T, Mississippi, 304
13. *Greer, Charlie, DB, Colorado, 330
14. *Briscoe, Marlin, RB, Nebraska-Omaha, 357
15. Kuhman, Jeff, LB, Vermont, 386
16. Brown, Adin, LB, William & Mary, 412
17. Grady, Steve, RB, USC, 438

DETROIT 1968
1. *Landry, Greg, QB, Massachusetts, 11
*McCullouch, Earl, E, USC [from Los Angeles Rams] 24
2. DePoyster, Jerry, K, Wyoming, 37
3. Choice to San Francisco
*Sanders, Charlie, TE, Minnesota [from Cleveland thru Los Angeles Rams] 74
4. *Mooney, Ed, LB, Texas Tech, 93
5. *Odle, Phil, E, BYU, 120
6. Spitzer, Mike, DE, San Jose State, 148
7. Choice to New Orleans
8. *Miller, Terry, LB, Illinois, 202
9. *Barton, Greg, QB, Tulsa, 229
10. Liggins, Granville, LB, Oklahoma, 256
11. Little, Dwight, G, Kentucky, 283
12. Caruthers, Ed, DB, Arizona, 310
13. Bailey, Chuck, T, Cal State-Humboldt, 337
14. Davis, Richie, E, Upsala, 364
15. Oliver, Jim, RB, Colorado State, 391
16. Rokita, Bob, DE, Arizona State, 418
17. Choice to Minnesota

GREEN BAY 1968
1. *Carr, Fred, LB, Texas-El Paso [from New Orleans] 5
*Lueck, Bill, G, Arizona, 26
2. Choice to Atlanta thru Los Angeles Rams
3. *Stevens, Billy, QB, Texas-El Paso [from St. Louis] 67
*Himes, Dick, T, Ohio State, 81
4. *McCarthy, Brendan, RB, Boston College [from Pittsburgh] 92
*Robinson, John, FL, Tennessee State, 108
5. *Duich, Steve, T, San Diego State [from Pittsburgh] 12.1
*Winkler, Francis, DE, Memphis State, 137
6. Chadwick, Walter, RB, Tennessee, 164
7. Beath, Andy, DB, Duke, 191
8. Owens, Tom, G, Missouri-Rolla, 218
9. Apisa, Bob, RB, Michigan State, 245
10. Cash, Rick, T, Northeast Missouri State [from New York Giants] 260
Worthen, Ron, C, Arkansas State, 272
11. *Rule, Gordon, DB, Dartmouth, 299
12. Porter, Dennis, T, Northern Michigan, 325
13. Geiselman, Frank, FL, Rhode Island, 353
14. Farler, John, E, Colorado, 380
15. Gibson, Ridley, DB, Baylor, 407
16. Groves, Al, T, St, Norbert, 434
17. Rota, Ken, RB, North Dakota State, 461

HOUSTON 1968
1. Choice to Kansas City
2. *Haik, Mac, E, Mississippi, 49
3. *Bethea, Elvin, T, North Carolina A&T, 77
4. *Beirne, Jim, E, Purdue, 105
5. *Longo, Bob, E, Pittsburgh, 137
6. Choice to Cincinnati
7. Toscano, Paul, DB, Wyoming, 187
8. Choice to New York J
9. *Robertson, Bob, C, Illinois [from Boston] 224
Choice to Mia
10. Peace, Joe, LB, Louisiana Tech [from San Diego] 263
*Domres, Tom, DE, Wisconsin, 268
11. Halley, Bill, E, La Verne, 295
12. Lischner, Barry, RB, Missouri, 322
13. Dousay, Jimmy, RB, LSU, 349
14. *Stotter, George, G, Houston, 376
15. Choice to San Diego
16. *Smith, Bob, DB, Miami (OH), 430
17. Alsbrooks, Billy, DB, North Carolina Central, 457

KANSAS CITY 1968
1. *Moorman, Mo, G, Texas A&M, 19
*Daney, George, G, Texas-El Paso [from Houston] 22
2. *Livingston, Mike, QB, SMU, 48
3. Choice to Denver
4. *McCarty, Mickey, TE, TCU [from Buffalo] 90
Choice to Denver
5. Choice to Buffalo
6. Choice to Cincinnati
7. Grezaffi, Sammy, DB, LSU, 184
8. Endsley, Lindon, C, North Texas State, 213
9. *McClure, Wayne, LB, Mississippi, 239
10. *Gehrke, Jack, FL, Utah, 265
11. Nosewicz, Tom, DE, Tulane, 294
12. Johns, Bobby, DB, Alabama, 320
13. Kavanagh, Jim, FL, Boston College, 346
14. *Holmes, Robert, RB, Southern, 375
15. Chambless, Bill, G, Miami, 401
16. Talbert, Pat, T, Southwest Missouri State, 427
17. Williams, Wesley, LB, Texas Southern, 456

LOS ANGELES RAMS 1968
1. Choice to Detroit
2. *Beban, Gary, QB, UCLA [from New Orleans] 30
*La Hood, Mike, G, Wyoming, 51
3. Choice to Pittsburgh
4. Choice to Chicago Bears
5. Martin, Don, K, Washington, 135
6. Webb, Bobby, C, Southern Mississippi, 161
7. Choice to Pittsburgh
8. Williams, Joe, FL, Florida A&M, 215
9. Richardson, Bob, T, Washington, 243
10. Marcelin, Allen, FL, Parsons, 269
11. *Pergine, John, LB, Notre Dame, 297
12. *Jackson, Harold, FL, Jackson State, 323
13. *Halverson, Dean, LB, Washington, 351
14. Jackson, Cephus, DB, Jackson State, 377
15. Yell, Dennis, T, Moorhead State, 405
16. *Raye, Jimmy, QB-DB, Michigan State, 431
17. Choice to Philadelphia

MIAMI 1968
1. *Csonka, Larry, RB, Syracuse, 8
*Crusan, Doug, T, Indiana [from Cincinnati] 27
2. Keyes, Jimmy, LB-K, Mississippi, 35
*Cox, Jim, E, Miami [from Cincinnati] 54
3. *Urbanek, Jim, T, Mississippi, 62
*Anderson, Dick, DB, Colorado [from San Diego] 73
4. Choice to Denver
5. *Kiick, Jim, RB, Wyoming, 118
6. *Hammond, Kim, QB, Florida State [from Denver] 142
*Hines, Jimmy, FL, Texas Southern, 146
7. *Boynton, John, T, Tennessee, 172
8. Choice to New York Jets
Edmonds, Randall, LB, Georgia Tech [from Oakland] 217
9. McDowell, Sam, T, Southwest Missouri State, 226
Paciorek, Tom, DB, Houston [from Houston] 240
10. Mirto, Joe, T, Miami, 253
11. Cooper, Cornelius, T, Prairie View A&M, 280
12. Paxton, Paul, T, Akron, 307
13. *Joswick, Bob, DT, Tulsa, 334
14. Blunk, Ray, TE, Xavier, 362
15. Corbin, Ken, LB, Miami, 388
16. Still, Henry, DT, Bethune-Cookman, 416
17. Nemeth, Bill, C, Anizona, 442

MINNESOTA 1968
1. *Yary, Ron, T, USC [from New York Giants] 1
Choice to NO
2. *West, Charlie, DB, Texas-El Paso, 33
3. Choice to Pittsburgh
*McGill, Mike, LB, Notre Dame [from Dallas] 76
4. *Freeman, Mike, DB, Fresno State, 89
5. Choice to Washington
6. *Goodridge, Bob, FL, Vanderbilt, 144
7. *Reed, Oscar, Colorado State [from Atlanta] 167
Snow, Lenny, RB, Georgia Tech, 171
8. Urbanowicz, Hank, DT, Miami, 198
9. *Donohoe, Mike, TE, San Francisco, 225
10. Sakal, Tom, DB, Minnesota, 250
11. Haas, Bill, E, Nebraska-Omaha, 279
12. Small, Howie, C, Rhode Island, 308
13. Wherry, Rich, E, Northern State (SD), 333
14. Evans, Don, T, Arkansas-Pine Bluff, 360
15. Haynie, Jim, QB, West Chester, 387
16. Kuharich, Larry, DB, Boston College, 414
17. *Lee, Bob, QB, Pacific, 441
Hull, Bill, G, Tennessee Tech [from Detroit] 445

NEW ORLEANS 1968
1. Choice to Green Bay
*Hardy, Kevin, DE, Notre Dame [from Minnesota] 7
2. Choice to Los Angeles Rams
3. *Szymakowski, Dave, E, West Texas State, 59
4. Crittendon, Willie, DT, Tulsa, 85
*Sartin, Dan, T, Mississippi [from Dallas] 103
5. *South, Ronnie, QB, Arkansas, 115
6. Choice to San Francisco
7. Phillips, Ray, G, Michigan, 169
*Howard, Eugene, FL, Langston [from Detroit] 175
8. Southland, Dick, G-T, Notre Dame, 195
9. Blake, Joe, T, Tulsa, 223
10. Robinson, Doug, DB, Iowa State, 254
11. Blocker, Bennie, RB, South Carolina State, 276
12. Beck, John, DB, San Diego State, 303
13. Trepanier, K.O., DE, Montana State, 331
14. Covington, Herb, RB, Memphis State, 359
15. Cooks, Wilmer, RB, Colorado, 384
16. Ghattas, Elie, G, Ball State, 411
17. *Ferguson, Jim, LB, USC, 439

NEW YORK GIANTS 1968
1. Choice to Minnesota
2. *Buzin, Rich, T, Penn State, 41
3. *Duhon, Bobby, RB, Tulane, 70
4. Choice to Dallas
5. Choice to Baltimore
6. Choice to Cleveland
7. Chatman, Doug, DE, Jackson State, 180
8. Choice to San Francisco
9. *Koontz, Joe, E, Cal State-San Francisco, 234
10. Choice to Green Bay
11. *Davis, Henry, DE, Grambling, 288
12. *Holifield, Jimmy, DB, Jackson State, 314
13. Gallagher, John, DE, Boston U., 342
14. Moreman, Bill, RB, Florida State, 368
15. *Boston, McKinley, G, Minnesota, 396
16. *Parker, Ken, DB, Fordham, 422
17. Kohn, Larry, TE, Georgia, 450

NEW YORK JETS 1968
1. *White, Lee, RB, Weber State, 17
2. *Thompson, Steve, DE, Washington, 44
3. *Walton, Sam, T, East Texas State, 72
4. Magner, Gary, DT, USC, 101
5. Jacobsen, Lee, LB, Kearney State, 128
6. Choice to Cin
7. Lubke, Oscar, T, Ball State, 182
8. Taylor, Bob, RB, Maryland-Eastern Shore [from Miami] 200
*Richards, Jim, DB, Virginia Tech, 210
*Henke, Karl, DT, Tulsa [from Houston] 214
9. Houser, Gary, TE-K, Oregon State, 236
10. *D'Amato, Mike, DB, Hofstra, 264
11. Owens, Henry, FL, Weber State, 290
12. Hayes, Ray, DT, Toledo, 318
13. Myslinski, Tom, G, Maryland, 344
14. *Nairn, Harvey, RB, Southern, 372
15. Ehrig, Ronnie, DB, Texas, 398 +
16. Bilotta, Tom, G, Adams State, 426
17. Strasser, Myles, RB, Wisconsin-Oshkosh, 452

OAKLAND 1968
1. *Dickey, Eldridge, QB, Tennessee State, 25
2. *Stabler, Ken, QB, Alabama, 52
3. *Shell, Art, T, Maryland-Eastern Shore, 80
4. *Smith, Charlie, RB, Utah, 110
5. Naponic, John, T, Virginia, 136
6. Choice to Cincinnati
7. Harper, John, C, Adams State [from Denver] 168
Atkinson, George, DB, Morris Brown, 190
8. Choice to Miami
9. *Eason, John, TE, Florida A&M, 244
10. Owens, Rick, DB, Pennsylvania, 271
11. *Hubbard, Marv, TE, Colgate [from Denver] 277
Oliver, Ralph (Chip), LB, USC, 298
12. Plantz, Larry, FL, Colorado, 326
13. Blackstone, Larry, RB, Fairmont State, 352
14. Carlson, Ray, LB, Hamline, 379
15. Leinert, Mike, RB, Texas Tech, 406
16. Morrison, David, DB, Southwest Texas State, 433
17. Berry, Steve, E, Catawba, 460

PHILADELPHIA 1968
1. *Rossovich, Tim, DE, USC, 14
2. *Pinder, Cyril, RB, Illinois, 39
3. *Young, Adrian, LB, USC, 68
4. McNeil, Len, G, Fresno State, 95
5. *Dirks, Mike, T, Wyoming [from Washington] 122
*Nordquist, Mark, T, Pacific, 124
6. Randle, Thurman, T, Texas-El Paso, 150
*Martin, Dave, DB, Notre Dame [from Cleveland] 157
7. Przybycki, Joe, G, Michigan State, 178
8. *Lavan, Al, DB, Colorado State, 204
9. *Evans, Mike, C, Boston College, 232
10. *Mallory, John, DB, West Virginia, 258
11. Persin, Len, DE, Boston College, 286
12. Taylor, Thurston, TE, Florida State, 312.
13. Barron, George, T, Mississippi State, 340
14. Williamson, Dan, LB, West Virginia, 366
15. Graham, Joe, G, Tennessee, 394
16. Creel, Phil, Northwestern State (LA), 420
17. Forzani, Joe, LB, Utah Stare, 448
Antonini, Frank, RB, Parsons [from Los Angeles Rams] 459

PITTSBURGH 1968
1. *Taylor, Mike, T, USC, 10
2. *Ruple, Ernie, T, Arkansas, 36
3. *Henderson, John, DB, Colorado State [from Minnesota] 61
Choice to Cleveland
*Hebert, Ken, FL-K, Houston [from Los Angeles Rams] 79
4. Choice to Green Bay
5. Choice to Green Bay
6. Choice to Atlanta
7. Dalton, Doug, RB, New Mexico State, 174
Glennon, Bill, DT, Washington [from Los Angeles Rams] 189
8. Holman, Danny, QB, San Jose State, 201
9. Knight, John, DE, Weber State, 228
10. Choice to Cleveland
11. King, Kim, QB, Georgia Tech, 282
12. Wheeler, Sam, LB, Wisconsin, 309
13. Roundy, Joe, G, Puget Sound, 335
14. *Harris, Lou, DB, Kent State, 363
15. Lanning, Bob, DE, Northern Montana, 390
16. *Bleier, Rocky, RB, Notre Dame, 417
17. *Cole, Bob, LB, South Carolina, 444

ST. LOUIS 1968
1. *Lane, MacArthur, RB, Utah State, 13
2. *Hyatt, Freddie, FL, Auburn, 40
*Atkins, Bob, DB, Grambling [from San Francisco] 42
3. Choice to Green Bay
4. Fitzgerald, Don, RB, Kent State [from Atlanta] 87
Schniesing, Joe, LB, New Mexico State, 96
5. *Rosema, Rocky, LB, Michigan, 123
6. Lane, Frank, LB, Stephen F Austin, 151
7. Henry, Ken, FL, Wake Forest, 177
8. *Daanen, Jerry, FL, Miami, 205
9. Sinkule, Billy, DE, Central Michigan, 231
10. Busch, Tom, FL-K, Iowa State, 259
11. Slagle, Larry, G, UCLA, 285
12. *Emerson, Vernon, T, Minnesota-Duluth, 313
13. *Sauls, Mack, DB, Southwest Texas State, 339
14. Bender, Vic, C, Northeast Louisiana, 367
15. Lovich, Dave, DE, Northwestern State (LA), 393
16. Lankas, Dan, LB, Kansas State, 421
17. *Lee, Bob, FL, Minnesota, 447

SAN DIEGO 1968
1. *Washington, Russ, T, Missouri [from Denver] 4
*Hill, Jim, DB, Texas A&I, 18
2. *Lenkaitis, Bill, C, Penn State, 43
3. Choice to Miami
4. *Dyer, Ken, FL, Arizona State, 100
5. Perry, Bill, TE, Kent State, 129
6. Choice to Cincinnati
7. *Fenner, Lane, FL, Florida State, 183
8. Gammage, Elliot, TE, Tennessee, 209
9. Harris, Grundy, RB, Southern, 237
10. Choice to Houston
11. *Partee, Dennis, K, SMU, 291
12. *Queen, Jeff, LB, Morgan State, 317
13. Combs, Fred, DB, North Carolina State, 345
14. *Campbell, Jim, LB, West Texas State, 371
15. Kramarczyk, Dan, T, Dayton, 399
*Wells, Robert, T, Johnson C. Smith [from Houston] 403
16. *Farley, Dick, DB, Boston U., 425
17. Andrews, Dan, TE, West Texas State, 453

SAN FRANCISCO 1968
1. *Blue, Forrest, C, Auburn, 15
2. Choice to St. Louis
3. *Olssen, Lance, T, Purdue [from Detroit] 65
*Vanderbundt, Skip, LB, Oregon State, 69
4. *Fuller, Johnny, E, Lamar, 98
5. *Lee, Dwight, RB, Michigan State, 125
6. Jonnson, Leo, FL, Tennessee State [from New Orleans] 141
*Belk, Bill, DE, Maryland-Eastern Shore, 153
7. Richardson, Jerry, LB, Mississippi, 179
8. Brown, Charley, T, Augustana (SD) [from New York Giants] 206
Gray, Tom, FL, Morehead State, 207
9. Boyett, Casey, E, BYU, 233 +
10. *Hart, Tommy, LB, Morris Brown, 261
11. Fitzgibbons, Dennis, G, Syracuse, 287
12. Johnson, Henry, QB, Fisk, 315
13. Mitrakos, Tom, C, Pittsburgh, 341
14. *Moore, Alex, RB, Norfolk State, 369
15. Spencer, Clarence, FL, Louisville, 395
16. Rosenow, Tom, DT, Northern Illinois, 423
17. *Patera, Dennis, K, BYU, 449

WASHINGTON 1968
1. *Smith, Jim (Yazoo), DB, Oregon, 12
2. Roussel, Tom, LB, Southern Mississippi, 38
3. Choice to Cleveland
4. *Crane, Dennis, DT, USC, 94
5. *Barefoot, Ken, TE, Virginia Tech [from Atlanta] 113
*Bragg, Mike, K, Richmond [from Minnesota] 117
Choice to Philadelphia
6. *Banks, Willie, G, Alcorn State, 149
7. *Brunet, Bob, RB, Louisiana Tech, 176
8. Magnuson, Brian, RB, Montana, 203
9. Liberatore, Frank, DB, Clemson, 230
10. Choice to Baltimore
11. Garretson, Tom, DB, Northwestern, 284
12. Weedman, Dave, DT, Western Washington, 311
13. St. Louis, Mike, T, Central Missouri State, 338
14. Zivich, Dave, T, Cal-Santa Barbara, 365
15. Coverson, Coger, G, Texas Southern, 392
16. Turner, Willie, RB, Jackson State, 419
17. *Bosch, Frank, DT, Colorado, 446

1969

Held January 28-29, 1969

ATLANTA 1969
1. *Kunz, George, T, Notre Dame, 2
2. *Gipson, Paul, RB, Houston, 29
3. Snider, Malcolm, T, Stanford, 54
Sandstrom, Jon, G, Oregon State [from New York Giants thru Los Angeles Rams] 67
4. *Mitchell, Jim, TE, Prairie View A&M, 81
*Lyons, Dickie, DB, Kentucky [from Baltimore] 103
5. Choice to Minnesota
Pleviak, Tony, DE, Illinois [from Dallas thru Baltimore] 127
6. Choice to Los Angeles Rams
Oyler, Wally, DB, Louisville [from Detroit] 137
7. Enderle, Dick, G, Minnesota, 158
Cottrell, Ted, LB, Delaware Valley [from Detroit] 164
8. Callahan, Jim, FL, Temple, 185
9. Choice to Baltimore
10. *Stanciel, Jeff, RB, Mississippi Valley State, 237
11. *Van Note, Jeff, LB, Kentucky, 262
12. Samples, Denver, DT, Texas-El Paso, 289
13. Carpenter, Harry, T, Tennessee State, 313
14. Hunt, Billy, DB, Kansas, 341

15. *Weatherford, Jim, DB, Tennessee, 366
16. Hughes, Ed, RB, Texas Southern, 393
17. Williams, Paul, RB, California, 418

BALTIMORE 1969
1. *Hinton, Eddie, FL, Oklahoma, 25
2. *Hendricks, Ted, LB, Miami [from New Orleans] 33
*Maxwell, Tom, DB, Texas A&M, 51
3. *Nelson, Dennis, T, Illinois State, 77
4. Stewart, Jacky, RB, Texas Tech [from Washington] 87
Choice to Atlanta
5. Dunlap, King, DT, Tennessee State, 129
6. Fortier, Bill, T, LSU, 154
7. Fleming, Gary, DE, Samford [from New Orleans] 163
*Moss, Roland, RB, Toledo, 181
8. *Havrilak, Sam, QB, Bucknell, 207
9. *Wright, George, DT, Sam Houston State [from Atlanta] 210
Good, Larry, QB, Georgia Tech, 232
10. Griffin, Marion, TE, Purdue, 259
11. Delaney, Ken, T, Akron, 285
12. Riley, Butch, LB, Texas A&I, 310
13. *Mauck, Carl, LB, Southern Illinois, 337
14. Bartelt, Dave, LB, Colorado, 363
15. Thompson, George, DB, Marquette, 389
16. McMillan, Jim, RB-FL, Citadel, 415
17. Cowan, Joe, FL, Johns Hopkins, 441

BOSTON 1969
1. *Sellers, Ron, SE, Florida State, 6
2. *Montler, Mike, G, Colorado, 32
3. *Garrett, Carl, RB, New Mexico Highlands, 58
4. Choice to Denver thru Kansas City
5. Jackson, Onree, QB, Alabama A&M, 110
6. Choice to Oakland
7. Hackley, Rick, T, New Mexico State, 162
8. *Gladieux, Bob, RB, Notre Dame, 188
9. *Alexakos, Steve, G-LB, San Diego State [from Buffalo] 209
Walker, Joe, DE, Albany State, 214
10. Devlin, Dennis, DB, Wyoming, 240
11. Gallup, Barry, SE, Boston College, 266
12. Lee, Richard, DT, Grambling, 292
13. Leasy, Joe, LB, Alcorn State, 318
14. *Cagle, John, LB, Clemson, 344
15. Conley, Brant, RB-P, Tulsa, 370
16. Vuono, Jim, LB, Adams State, 396
17. Muse, George, LB-DB, Grambling, 422

BUFFALO 1969
1. *Simpson, O.J., RB, USC, 1
2. *Enyart, Bill, RB, Oregon State, 27
3. *Nunamaker, Julian, DE, Tennessee-Martin, 53
4. *Richey, Mike, T, North Carolina, 79
5. *Mayes, Ben, DT, Duke, 105
6. Choice to Denver
7. Helton, John, DE, Arizona State, 157
8. *Harvey, Waddey, T, Virginia Tech, 183
*Harris, James, QB, Grambling [from Denver] 192
9. Choice to Boston
10. Baines, Ron, FL, Montana, 235
11. Hall, Bobby, RB, North Carolina State, 261
12. *Pate, Lloyd, RB, Cincinnati, 287
13. Lovelace, Leon, T, Texas Tech, 312
14. *Thornton, Bubba, FL, TCU, 339
15. Wilson, Karl, RB, Olivet, 365
16. Kirk, Robert, G, Indiana, 391
17. Lineberry, Wayne, LB, East Carolina, 417

CHICAGO BEARS 1969
1. *Mayes, Rufus, T, Ohio State, 14
2. *Douglass, Bobby, QB, Kansas, 41
3. *Montgomery, Ross, RB, TCU, 66
4. *Redmond, Rudy, DB, Pacific, 91
5. *Winegardner, Jim, TE, Notre Dame, 119
6. Nicholson, Bill, DE, Stanford, 144
7. *Copeland, Ron, FL, UCLA, 169
8. Hubbell, Webb, G, Arkansas, 197
9. Aluise, Joe, RB, Arizona, 222
10. Pearson, Ron, TE-LB, Maryland, 247
11. Campbell, Sam, DT, Iowa State, 275
12. *Hale, Dave, DE, Ottawa, 300
13. Quinn, Tom, DB, Notre Dame, 325
14. Ehrig, Ronnie, DB, Texas, 353
15. Coble, Bob, P, Kansas State, 378
16. Stydahar, Dave, G, Purdue, 403
17. Long, Bob, SE, Texas A&M, 431

CINCINNATI 1969
1. *Cook, Greg, QB, Cincinnati, 5
2. *Bergey, Bill, LB, Arkansas State, 31
3. *Thomas, Louis (Speedy), SE, Utah, 57
4. *Turner, Clem, RB, Cincinnati, 83
5. *Dennis, Guy, G, Florida, 109
6. *Riley, Ken, DB, Florida A&M, 135
7. *Berry, Royce, DE, Houston, 161
8. *Buchanan, Tim, LB, Hawaii, 187
9. Stripling, Mike, RB, Tulsa, 213
10. Howell, Steve, TE, Ohio State, 239
11. Stewart, Mark, DB, Georgia, 265
12. Paige, Lonnie, DT, North Carolina Central, 291
13. Benson, Chuck, SE, Southern Illinois, 316
14. *Wilson, Mike, RB, Dayton, 343
15. Shoemaker, Bill, K, Stanford, 369
16. Schmidt, Bill, LB, Missouri, 395
17. Story, Terry, T, Georgia Tech, 421

CLEVELAND 1969
1. *Johnson, Ron, RB, Michigan, 20
2. Choice to Washington
3. *Jenkins, Al, G, Tulsa [from Philadelphia] 55
*Glass, Chip, TE, Florida State, 72
4. *Summers, Freddie, DB, Wake Forest, 98
5. *Hooker, Fair, FL, Arizona State, 124
6. Adams, Larry, DT, TCU [from New York Giants] 145
*Righetti, Joe, DT, Waynesburg, 150
7. *Sumner, Walt, DB, Florida State, 176
8. *Reynolds, Chuck, C, Tulsa, 202
9. Kamzelski, Ron, DT, Minnesota, 228
10. Shelly, Greg, G, Virginia, 254
11. *Jones, Dave, FL, Kansas State, 280
12. *Davis, Dick, RB, Nebraska, 306
13. *Boutwell, Tommy, QB, Southern Mississippi, 332
14. Smaha, Jiggy, DT, Georgia, 358
15. Stevenson, Joe, TE, Georgia Tech, 384
16. Lowe, James, FL, Tuskegee, 410
17. *Oliver, Bob, DE, Abilene Christian, 436

DALLAS 1969
1. *Hill, Calvin, RB, Yale, 24
2. *Flowers, Richmond, FL, Tennessee, 49
3. *Stinic, Tom, LB, Michigan [from San Francisco] 68
*Hagen, Halvor, DT, Weber State, 74
4. Choice to New Orleans
5. Kyle, Chuck, LB, Purdue [from Los Angeles Rams] 125
Choice to Atlanta thru Baltimore
6. Shaw, Rick, FL, Arizona State, 152
7. Bales, Larry, FL, Emory & Henry, 180
8. Benhardt, Elmer, LB, Missouri, 205
9. *Welch, Claxton, RB, Oregon, 230
10. Gottlieb, Stuart, T, Weber State, 258
11. *Williams, Clarence, DT, Prairie View A&M, 283
12. *Belden, Bob, QB, Notre Dame, 308
13. Matison, Rene, FL, New Mexico, 336
14. Lutri, Gerald, T, Northern Michigan, 361
15. Justus, Bill, DB, Tennessee, 386
16. Kerr, Floyd, DB, Colorado State, 414
17. Bailey, Bill, DT, Lewis & Clark, 439

DENVER 1969
1. Choice to San Diego
2. *Cavness, Grady, DB, Texas-El Paso, 36
3. *Thompson, Billy, DB, Maryland-Eastern Shore, 61
4. *Schnitker, Mike, LB, Colorado [from Boston thru Kansas City] 84
*Hayes, Ed, DB, Morgan State, 88
5. Quayle, Frank, RB, Virginia, 113
6. *Williams, Wendy, RB, Hofstra [from Buffalo] 131
Coleman, Mike, RB, Tampa, 140
7. Giffin, Al, TE, Auburn, 165
8. Choice to Buffalo
9. *Jones, Henry, RB, Grambling, 217
10. *Smith, Jim, DB, Utah State, 244
11. *Pastrana, Alan, QB, Maryland, 270
12. Plummer, Wes, DB, Arizona State, 196
13. Sias, Johnny, SE, Georgia Tech, 321
14. *Crane, Gary, LB, Arkansas State, 348
15. Kahoun, Errol, G, Miami (OH), 373
16. Woods, Billy, DB, North Texas State, 400
17. O'Brien, Buster, QB, Richmond, 425

DETROIT 1969
1. Choice to Los Angeles Rams
2. *Taylor, Altie, RB, Utah State, 34
*Yarbrough, Jim, TE, Florida [from Los Angeles Rams] 47
3. *Walton, Larry, FL, Arizona State [from New Orleans] 59
Choice to New York Giants
4. Choice to San Francisco
5. Choice to Minnesota thru Pittsburgh
6. Choice to Atlanta
7. Choice to Atlanta
8. Carr, Jim, T, Jackson State, 190
9. *Rasley, Rocky, G, Oregon State, 216
10. Bergum, Bob, DE, Wisconsin-Platteville, 242
11. Walker, Ron, DE, Morris Brown, 268
12. Hadlock, Bob, DT, George Fox, 294
13. Bowie, Wilson, RB, USC, 320
14. *Hoey, George, FL, Michigan, 346
15. Gough, Fred, LB, Texas-Arlington, 372
16. Spain, Ken, DE, Houston, 398
Stahl, John, G, Fresno State [from Minnesota] 407
17. Steele, Gary, TE, Army, 424

GREEN BAY 1969
1. *Moore, Rich, DT, Villanova, 12
2. *Bradley, Dave, T, Penn State, 38
3. *Spilis, John, FL, Northern Illinois, 64
4. *Williams, Perry, RB, Purdue, 90
5. *Hayhoe, Bill, DT, USC, 116
6. *Jones, Ron, TE, Texas-El Paso [from Pittsburgh] 134
*Vinyard, Kenny, K, Texas Tech, 142
7. Agajanian, Larry, DT, UCLA, 168
8. Gosnell, Doug, CT, Utah State, 194
9. *Hampton, Dave, RB, Wyoming, 220
10. Nelson, Bruce, T, North Dakota State, 246
11. *Harden, Lee, DB, Texas-El Paso, 272
12. *Buckman, Tom, TE, Texas A&M, 298
13. Koinzan, Craig, LB, Doane, 324
14. Voltzke, Rich, RB, Minnesota, 350
15. Eckstein, Dan, DB, Presbyterian, 376
16. Hewins, Dick, FL, Drake, 402
17. Mack, John, RB, Central Missouri State, 428

HOUSTON 1969
1. *Pritchard, Ron, LB, Arizona State, 15
2. *LeVias, Jerry, FL, SMU, 40
3. *Drungo, Elbert, T, Tennessee State, 65
*Johnson, Rich, RB, Illinois [from New York Jets] 78
4. *Joiner, Charlie, DB, Grambling, 93
*Gerela, Roy, P, New Mexico State [from San Diego] 96
5. *Peacock, John, DB, Houston, 118
6. *Grate, Willie, FL, South Carolina State, 143
7. Richardson, Mike, RB, SMU, 171
8. *Woods, Glenn, DE, Prairie View A&M, 196
9. *Watson, Ed, LB, Grambling, 221
10. Pryor, Joe, DE, Boston College, 249
*Naponic, Bob, QB, Illinois [from Oakland] 256
11. May, Terry, C, SMU, 274
12. Resley, George, DT, Texas A&M, 299
13. Pickens, Richard, RB, Tennessee, 327
14. *Reeves, Roy, DB, South Carolina, 352
15. Tyszlewicz, John, G, Tennessee-Chattanooga, 377
16. *Wainscott, Loyd, DT, Texas, 405
17. *Autry, Hank, C, Southern Mississippi, 430

KANSAS CITY 1969
1. *Marsalis, Jim, DB, Tennessee State, 23
2. *Podolak, Ed, RB, Iowa, 48
3. *Stroud, Morris, TE, Clark, 76
4. *Rudnay, Jack, C, Northwestern, 101
5. *Stein, Bob, LB, Minnesota, 126
6. Pleasant, John, RB, Alabama State, 155
7. Nettles, Tom, FL, San Diego State, 179
8. King, Clanton, T, Purdue, 204
LeBlanc, Maurice, DB, LSU [from Oakland] 206
9. Klepper, Dan, G, Nebraska-Omaha, 231
10. Sponheimer, John, DT, Cornell, 257
11. Wupper, Skip, DE, C.W Post, 282
12. Lavin, John, LB, Notre Dame, 309
13. Piland, Rick, G, Virginia Tech, 335
14. Bream, Al, DB, Iowa, 360
15. Winston, Leland, T, Rice, 388
16. Johnson, Eural, DB, Prairie View A&M, 413
17. Jenkins, Ralph, DB, Tuskegee, 438

LOS ANGELES RAMS 1969
1. *Smith, Larry, RB, Florida [from Detroit] 8
*Seymour, Jim, SE, Notre Dame [from Washington] 10
*Klein, Bob, TE, USC, 21
2. Choice to Detroit
3. Choice to St. Louis thru Detroit
4. *Zook, John, DE, Kansas, 99
5. Choice to Dallas
6. Drones, A.Z., T, West Texas State [from Atlanta] 133
*Curran, Pat, LB, Lakeland, 151
7. Hawkins, James, DB, Nebraska, 177
8. *Harvey, Richard, DB, Jackson State, 203
9. Foote, Mike, LB, Oregon State, 229
10. Gordon, Jerry, T, Auburn, 255
11. Svendsen, Dave, FL, Eastern Washington, 281
12. Carr, Tim, QB, C.W Post, 307
13. *Williams, Roger, DB, Grambling, 333
14. Stephens, Ray, RB, Minnesota, 359
15. Jugum, George, LB, Washington, 385
16. Hipps, Henry, LB, North Carolina State, 411
17. Thorpe, Jim, DB, Hofstra, 437

MIAMI 1969
1. *Stanfill, Bill, DE, Georgia, 11
2. *Heinz, Bob, T, Pacific, 37
3. *Morris, Eugene (Mercury), RB, West Texas State, 63
4. *McBride, Norm, LB, Utah, 89
5. Pearson, Willie, DB, North Carolina A&T, 115
*Kremser, Karl, K, Tennessee [from Oakland] 128
6. Tuck, Ed, G, Notre Dame, 141
7. Eagan, John, C, Boston College, 167
Kulka, John, C, Penn State [from San Diego] 174
8. Weinstein, Bruce, TE, Yale, 193
9. *Powell, Jesse, LB, West Texas State, 219
10. *Mertens, Jim, TE, Fairmont State, 245
11. Berdis, Mike, T, North Dakota State, 271
12. *McCullers, Dale, LB, Florida State, 297
13. Ayres, Amos, DB, Arkansas-Pine Bluff, 323
14. Thompson, Glenn, T, Troy State, 349
15. McGeehan, Chick, FL, Tennessee, 375
16. *Mumphord, Lloyd, DB, Texas Southern, 401
17. Krallman, Tom, DE, Xavier, 427

MINNESOTA 1969
1. Choice to New Orleans
2. *White, Ed, G, California [from New York Giants] 39
Murphy, Volly, FL, Texas-El-Paso, 43
3. Choice to Philadelphia
4. McCaffrey, Mike, LB, California, 95
5. Barnes, Jim, G, Arkansas [from Atlanta] 106
O'Shea, Mike, SE, Utah State [from Detroit thru Pittsburgh] 112
Davis, Cornelius, RB, Kansas State, 121
6. Bates, Marion, DB, Texas Southern, 148
7. Choice to Washington
8. Wood, Harris, FL, Washington, 199
9. Fink, Tom, G, Minnesota, 225
10. McCauley, Tom, SE, Wisconsin, 253
11. *Dowling, Brian, QB, Yale, 277
12. Jenke, Noel, LB, Minnesota, 303
13. Moylan, Jim, DT, Texas Tech, 329
14. Head, Tommy, C, Southwest Texas State, 355
15. Mosley, Eugene, TE, Jackson State, 381
16. Choice to Detroit
17. Housely, Wendell, RB, Texas A&M, 433

NEW YORK GIANTS 1969
1. *Dryer, Fred, DE, San Diego State, 13
2. Choice to Minnesota
3. *Vanoy, Vernon, DE, Kansas [from Detroit] 60
Choice to Atlanta thru Los Angeles Rams
4. *Houston, Rich, FL, East Texas State, 92
5. Choice to New Orleans
6. Choice to Cleveland
7. *Brenner, Al, DB, Michigan State, 170
8. Irby, George, RB, Tuskegee, 195
9. *Hickl, Ray, LB, Texas A&I, 223
10. Galiardi, Lou, DT, Dayton, 248
11. *Fuqua, John (Frenchy), RB, Morgan State, 273
12. Blackney, Harry, RB, Maryland, 301
13. Perrin, Richard, DB, Bowling Green, 326
14. Smith, Steve, K, Weber State, 351
15. *Herrmann, Don, FL, Waynesburg, 379
16. Jones, Byron, LB, West Texas State, 404
17. *Riley, Ken, LB, Texas-Arlington, 429

NEW YORK JETS 1969
1. *Foley, Dave, T, Ohio State, 26
2. *Woodall, Al, QB, Duke, 52
3. Choice to Houston
4. *Jones, Ezell, T, Minnesota, 104
5. Gilbert, Chris, RB, Texas, 130
6. *Jones, Jimmy, LB, Wichita State, 156
7. Larson, Cliff, DE, Houston, 182
8. *Leonard, Cecil, DB, Tuskegee, 208
9. *Peters, Frank, T-C, Ohio U., 233
10. Hall, Mike, LB, Alabama, 260
11. *Roberts, Gary, G, Purdue, 286
12. *Battle, Mike, DB, USC, 311.
13. *O'Neal, Steve, P, Texas A&M, 338
14. *Finnie, Roger, DE, Florida A&M, 364
15. *Stewart, Wayne, TE, California, 390
16. *Nock, George, RB, Morgan State, 416
17. Zirkle, Fred, DT, Duke, 442

NEW ORLEANS 1969
1. Choice to San Francisco
*Shinners, John, G, Xavier [from Minnesota] 17
2. Choice to Baltimore
*Neal, Richard, DE, Southern [from St. Louis] 45
3. Choice to Detroit
4. Hale, Dennis, DB, Minnesota, 85
Hudspeth, Bob, T, Southern Illinois [from Dallas] 102
5. Kyasky, Tony, DB, Syracuse, 111
Christensen, Keith, T, Kansas [from New York Giants] 117
6. Miller, Bob, TE, USC, 138
7. Choice to Baltimore
8. Lawrence, Jim, FL, USC, 189
9. *Owens, Joe, LB, Alcorn State, 215
10. Reynolds, McKinley, RB, Hawaii, 241
11. Morel, Tommy, FL, LSU, 267
12. Broadhead, Tom, RB, Cal-Santa Barbara, 293
13. Robillard, Joe, DB, Linfield, 319
14. Loyd, Gary, K, California Lutheran, 345
15. Waller, Bill, FL, Xavier, 371
16. *Hargett, Ed, QB, Texas A&M, 397
17. Kurzawski, Chico, DB, Northwestern, 423

OAKLAND 1969
1. *Thoms, Art, DT, Syracuse, 22
2. *Buehler, George, G, Stanford, 50
3. *Edwards, Lloyd, TE, San Diego State, 75
4. Jackson, Ruby, T, New Mexico State, 100
5. Choice to Miami
6. Newfield, Ken, RB, LSU [from Boston] 136
*Allen, Jackie, DB, Baylor, 153
7. Taylor, Finnis, DB, Prairie View A&M, 178
8. Choice to Kansas City
9. *Buie, Drew, E, Catawba, 234
10. Choice to Houston
11. *Rice, Harold, LB, Tennessee State, 284
12. Goddard, Al, DB, Johnson C. Smith, 317
13. Husted, Dave, LB, Wabash, 334
14. Busby, Harold, E, UCLA, 362
15. Presnell, Alvin, RB, Alabama A&M, 387
16. Davis, Bill, LB, Alabama, 412
17. Austin, Billy, TE, Arkansas-Pine Bluff, 440

PHILADELPHIA 1969
1. *Keyes, Leroy, RB, Purdue, 3
2. *Calloway, Ernie, LB, Texas Southern, 28
3. Choice to Cleveland
*Bradley, Bill, DB, Texas [from Minnesota] 69
4. *Kuechenberg, Bob, G, Notre Dame, 80
5. Anderson, Jim, G, Missouri, 107
6. Barnhorst, Dick, TE, Xavier, 132
7. *Schmeising, Mike, RB, St. Olaf, 159
8. *Hobbs, Bill, LB, Texas A&M, 184
9. *Lawrence, Kent, FL, Georgia, 211
Buss, Lynn, LB, Wisconsin [from Washington] 218
10. Wade, Sonny, QB, Emory & Henry, 236
Shanklin, Donnie, RB, Kansas [from Washington] 243
11. Marcum, Jim, DB, Texas-Arlington, 263
12. Adams, Gary, DB, Arkansas, 288
13. *Key, Wade, TE, Southwest Texas State, 314
14. Ross, Jim, T, Bishop, 340
15. Angevine, Leon, SE, Penn State, 367
16. McClinton, Tom, DB, Southern, 392
17. Haack, Bob, T, Linfield, 419

PITTSBURGH 1969
1. *Greene, Joe, DT, North Texas State, 4
2. *Hanratty, Terry, QB, Notre Dame, 30
*Bankston, Warren, RB, Tulane [from San Francisco thru Cleveland] 42
3. *Kolb, Jon, C, Oklahoma State, 56
4. Campbell, Bob, RB, Penn State, 82
5. Choice to St. Louis
6. Choice to Green Bay
7. *Beatty, Charles, DB, North Texas State, 160
Brown, Chadwick, T, East Texas State [from St. Louis thru Minnesota] 175
8. Cooper, Joe, FL, Tennessee State, 186
9. *Sodaski, John, DB, Villanova, 212
10. *Greenwood, L.C., DE, Arkansas-Pine Bluff, 238
11. Washington, Clarence, DT, Arkansas-Pine Bluff, 264
12. Fisher, Doug, LB, San Diego State, 290
13. Lynch, John, LB, Drake, 315
14. Houmard, Bob, RB, Ohio U., 342
15. Liberto, Ken, SE, Louisiana Tech, 368
16. Mosley, Dock, FL, Alcorn State, 394
17. Eppright, Bill, K, Kent State, 420

ST. LOUIS 1969
1. *Wehrli, Roger, DB, Missouri, 19
2. *Krueger, Rolf, DT, Texas A&M [from Washington] 35
Choice to New Orleans
3. *Healy, Chip, LB, Vanderbilt, 71
*Brown, Terry, DB, Oklahoma State [from Los Angeles Rams thru Det] 73
4. Rhodes, Bill, G, Florida State, 97
5. Shockley, Walt, RB, San Jose State [from Pittsburgh] 108
*Huey, Gene, FL, Wyoming, 123
6. Van Pelt, Amos, RB, Ball State, 149
7. Choice to Pittsburgh thru Minnesota
8. *Mulligan, Wayne, C, Clemson, 201
9. *Snowden, Cal, DE, Indiana, 227
10. Warren, Gerald, K, North Carolina State, 252
11. Kerl, Gary, LB, Utah, 279
12. Taylor, Howard, RB, New Mexico State, 305
13. Heinz, Dick, DT, Cal-Santa Barbara, 331
14. Roseborough, Ed, QB, Arizona State, 356
15. Latham, Fritz, T, Tuskegee, 383
16. Riggins, Junior, RB, Kansas, 409
17. Hummer, George, C, Arizona State, 435

SAN DIEGO 1969
1. *Domres, Marty, QB, Columbia [from Denver] 9
*Babich, Bob, LB, Miami (OH), 18
2. *Sayers, Ron, RB, Nebraska-Omaha, 44
3. *Ferguson, Gene, T, Norfolk State, 70
4. Choice to Houston
5. Orszulak, Harry, FL, Pittsburgh, 122
6. Swarn, Terry, FL, Colorado State, 147
7. Choice to Miami
8. *Cotton, Craig, FL, Youngstown State, 200
9. Williams, Joe, DB, Southern, 226
10. Arnold, David, G, Northwestern State (LA), 251
11. Norwood, Willie, TE, Alcorn State, 278
12. White, Jim, RB, Arkansas-Pine Bluff, 304
13. *Simpson, M.H., DB, Houston, 330
14. Ackman, Bill, DT, New Mexico State, 356
15. Jarvis, Charlie, RB, Army, 382
16. Davenport, Willie, FL, Southern, 408
17. *Rentz, Larry, DB, Florida, 434

SAN FRANCISCO 1969
1. *Kwalick, Ted, TE, Penn State [from New Orleans] 7
*Washington, Gene, FL, Stanford, 18
2. Choice to Pittsburgh thru Cleveland
3. Choice to Dallas
4. *Sniadecki, Jim, LB, Indiana [from Detroit] 86
*Moore, Gene, RB, Occidental, 94
5. *Edwards, Earl, DT, Wichita State, 120
6. *Thomas, Jimmy, RB, Texas-Arlington, 146
7. Van Sinderen, Steve, T, Washington State, 172
8. Loper, Mike, T, BYU, 198
9. *Crawford, Hilton, DB, Grambling, 224
10. *Chapple, Dave, K, Cal-Santa Barbara, 250
11. Peake, Willie, T, Alcorn State, 276
12. O'Malley, Jack, T, USC, 302
13. Champlin, Paul, DB, Eastern Montana, 328
14. Black, Tom, FL, East Texas State, 354
15. Golden, Gary, DB, Texas Tech, 380
16. *Hoskins, Bob, LB, Wichita State, 406
17. Rushing, Joe, LB, Memphis State, 432

WASHINGTON 1969
1. Choice to Los Angeles Rams
2. Choice to St. Louis
Epps, Eugene, DB, Texas-El Paso [from Cleveland] 46
3. Cross, Ed, RB, Arkansas-Pine Bluff, 62
4. Choice to Baltimore
5. Kishman, Bill, DB, Colorado State, 114
6. *McLinton, Harold, LB, Southern, 139
7. Anderson, Jeff, RB, Virginia, 166
*Didion, John, C, Oregon State [from Minnesota] 173
8. *Brown, Larry, RB, Kansas State, 191
9. Choice to Philadelphia
10. Choice to Philadelphia
11. Norri, Eric, DT, Notre Dame, 269
12. Shannon, Bob, DB, Tennessee State, 295
13. Shook, Mike, DB, North Texas State, 322
14. Brand, Rick, DT, Virginia, 347
15. Rogers, Paul, T, Virginia, 374
16. Washington, Mike, LB, Southern, 399
17. Dobbert, Rich, DE, Springfield, 426

1970

Held January 27-28, 1970

ATLANTA 1970
1. *Small, John, LB, Citadel, 12
2. *Malone, Art, RB, Arizona State, 39
3. *Maurer, Andy, G, Oregon, 64
*Snyder, Todd, WR, Ohio U. [from New York Giants] 65
4. Reed, Paul, T, Johnson C. Smith [from Philadelphia] 84
Choice to St. Louis
5. Van Ness, Bruce, RB, Rutgers [from Philadelphia thru New York Giants] 112
*Mendenhall, Ken, C, Oklahoma, 116
6. *Herron, Mack, RB, Kansas State, 143
Butcher, Jade, WR, Indiana [from Washington] 147
*Marshall, Randy, DE, Linfield [from Los Angeles Rams] 152
7. Choice to Los Angeles Rams
Orcutt, Gary, WR, USC [from New York Giants] 169
8. Brewer, Larry, TE, Louisiana Tech [from New York Giants] 194
Miller, Seth, DB, Arizona State, 195
9. Robinson, Roy, DB, Montana, 220
10. Hatcher, Jim, DB, Kansas, 246
11. *Brunson, Mike, RB, Arizona State, 272
12. Holton, Lonnie, RB, Northern Michigan, 298
13. Stepanek, Rich, DT, Iowa, 324
14. Wald, Chuck, WR, North Dakota State, 351
15. Mauney, Keith, DB, Princeton, 376
16. Parnell, Steve, WR, Massachusetts, 403
17. *Bell, Bill, K, Kansas, 428

BALTIMORE 1970
1. *Bulaich, Norm, RB, TCU, 18
2. *Bailey, Jim, DT, Kansas, 44
3. *O'Brien, Jim, WR, Cincinnati, 70
*Person, Ara, TE, Morgan State [from Los Angeles Rams thru Philadelphia] 74
4. Smear, Steve, LB, Penn State [from Washington] 95
Choice to Green Bay
5. *Newsome, Billy, DE, Grambling, 122
6. *Gardin, Ron, DB, Arizona, 148
7. Slade, Gordon, QB, Davidson, 174
8. Bouley, Bob, T, Boston College, 199
9. Harris, Barney, DB, Texas A&M, 226
10. *Palmer, Dick, LB, Kentucky, 252
11. Edwards, George, RB, Fairmont State, 278
12. Burrell, Don, WR, Angelo State, 304
13. Polak, Dave, LB, Bowling Green, 330
14. *Curtis, Tom, DB, Michigan, 356
15. Gary, Philip, DE, Kentucky State, 382
16. *Maitland, Jack, RB, Williams, 408
17. Pearman, Alvin, WR, Colgate, 434

BOSTON 1970
1. *Olsen, Phil, DT, Utah State, 4
2. Choice to Houston
3. *Ballou, Mike, LB, UCLA, 56
4. *Ray, Eddie, DB, LSU, 83
5. Olson, Bob, LB, Notre Dame [from Miami] 107
Choice to New York Jets
6. Choice to Buffalo
7. *Lawson, Odell, RB, Langston, 160
8. Choice to New York Jets
9. *Wirgowski, Dennis, DE, Purdue, 212
10. Brown, Henry, K-WR, Missouri, 239
11. Bramlett, Dennis, T, Texas-El Paso, 264
12. Roero, Greg, DT, New Mexico Highlands, 291
13. Shelley, Ronnie, DB, Troy State, 316
14. Craw, Garvie, RB-TE, Michigan, 343
15. Schoolfield, Kent, WR, Florida A&M, 368
16. McDaniel, Otis, DE, Tuskegee, 395
17. Killingsworth, Joe, WR, Oklahoma, 420

BUFFALO 1970
1. *Cowlings, Al, DE, USC, 5
2. *Shaw, Dennis, QB, San Diego State, 30
3. *Reilly, Jim, G, Notre Dame, 57
*Alexander, Glenn, DB, Grambling [from San Diego] 67
4. *Gantt, Jerry, DE, North Carolina Central, 82
5. Starnes, Steve, LB, Tampa, 109
6. Edwards, Ken, RB, Virginia Tech, 134
*Guthrie, Grant, K, Florida State [from Boston] 135
7. *Fowler, Wayne, T, Richmond, 161
8. *Cheek, Richard, T, Auburn, 186
9. Bridges, Bill, G, Houston, 213
10. Dixon, Willie, DB, Albany State, 238
11. Williams, Terry, RB, Grambling, 265
12. Simpson, Dave, T, Drake, 290
13. Schroeder, Stefan, K, Pacific, 317
14. Costen, Bill, T, Morris Brown, 342
15. Farris, Dave, TE, Central Michigan, 369
16. Davis, Larry, WR, Rice, 394
17. Bevan, George, DB, LSU, 421

CHICAGO BEARS 1970
1. Choice to Green Bay
2. Choice to Dallas
3. *Farmer, George, WR, UCLA, 54
4. *Larson, Lynn, T, Kansas State, 79
*Brupbacher, Ross, LB, Texas A&M [from Los Angeles Rams] 100
5. Choice to New Orleans
6. Cutburth, Bobby, QB, Oklahoma State, 133
*Curchin, Jeff, T, Florida State [from St. Louis] 139
7. Choice to Philadelphia
8. Stephenson, Dana, DB, Nebraska, 183
9. *Cole, Linzy, TCU, 210
10. *Holloway, Glen, G, North Texas State, 235
11. Rose, Ted, TE, Northern Michigan, 262 +
12. *Davis, Butch, DB, Missouri, 287
13. *Gunn, Jimmy, DB, USC, 314
14. Morgan, Jim, WR, Henderson State, 339
15. Abraira, Phil, DB, Florida State, 366
16. Helterbran, Bob, G, North Texas State, 390
17. Brunson, Joe, DT, Furman, 416

CINCINNATI 1970
1. *Reid, Mike, DT, Penn State, 7
2. *Carpenter, Ron, DT, North Carolina State, 32
3. Bennett, Chip, LB, Abilene Christian, 60
4. Stephen, Joe, G, Jackson State, 85
*Hayes, Billie, DB, San Diego State [from Kansas City] 104
5. Choice to Houston thru New York Jets
6. *Durko, Sandy, DB, USC, 137
7. *Parrish, Lemar, DB, Lincoln (MO), 163
8. Trout, Bill, DT, Miami, 188
9. Bolden, Bill, RB, UCLA, 216
10. *Roman, Nick, DE, Ohio State, 241
11. Wallace, Sam, LB, Grambling, 266
12. Truesdell, Tom, DT, Ohio Wesleyan, 294
13. *Dunn, Paul, WR, U.S. International, 319
14. Johnson, Joe, WR, Johnson C. Smith, 344 +
15. Weeks, Marvin, DB, Alcorn State, 372
16. *Ely, Larry, LB, Iowa, 397
17. Smith, Dick, RB, Washington State, 422

CLEVELAND 1970
1. *Phipps, Mike, QB, Purdue [from Miami] 3
*McKay, Bob, T, Texas, 21
2. *Jones, Joe, DE, Tennessee State [from New Orleans] 36
*Sherk, Jerry, DT, Oklahoma State, 47
3. Choice to Dallas
4. *Stevenson, Ricky, DB, Arizona, 99
5. *Engel, Steve, DB, Colorado, 125
6. Cilek, Mike, QB, Iowa, 151
7. *Wycinsky, Craig, G, Michigan, 177
8. Davidson, Honester, DB, Bowling Green, 203
9. Brown, Geoff, LB, Pittsburgh, 229
10. *Yanchar, Bill, DT, Purdue, 255
11. Benner, Gene, WR, Maine, 281
12. Sanders, Jerry, K, Texas Tech, 307
13. Roberts, Larry, RB, Central Missouri State, 333
14. Tharpe, Jim, LB, Lincoln (MO), 359
15. Homoly, Guy, DB, Illinois State, 385
16. Redebough, John, TE, Bemidji State, 410
17. Tabb, Charles, RB, McMurry, 436

DALLAS 1970
1. *Thomas, Duane, RB, West Texas State, 23
2. *Asher, Bob, T, Vanderbilt [from Chicago Bears] 27
*Adkins, Margene, WR, Henderson J.C., 49
3. *Waters, Charlie, DB, Clemson [from Houston thru Cleveland] 66
*Kiner, Steve, LB, Tennessee [from Cleveland] 73
Fox, Denton, DB, Texas Tech, 75
4. *Fitzgerald, John, T, Boston College, 101
5. Choice to St. Louis
6. *Toomay, Pat, DE, Vanderbilt, 153
7. Abbey, Don, LB, Penn State, 179
8. Dossey, Jerry, G, Arkansas, 205
9. *Andrusyshyn, Zenon, K, UCLA, 231
10. *Athas, Pete, DB, Tennessee, 257
11. Southerland, Ivan, T, Clemson, 283
12. *Williams, Joe, RB, Wyoming, 309
13. *Washington, Mark, DB, Morgan State, 335
14. Martin, Julian, WR, North Carolina Central, 361
15. DeLong, Ken, TE, Tennessee, 387
16. Hill, Seabern, DB, Arizona State, 411
17. Patterson, Glenn, C, Nebraska, 438

DENVER 1970
1. *Anderson, Bobby, RB, Colorado, 11
2. *Roche, Alden, DE, Southern, 37
3. Kohler, John, T, South Dakota, 63
4. *Hendren, Jerry, WR, Idaho, 89
5. *McKoy, Bill, LB, Purdue, 115
6. *Mosier, John, TE, Kansas, 141
7. *Montgomery, Randy, DB, Weber State, 67
8. Choice to Kansas City
*Porter, Lewis, RB, Southern [from Kansas City] 208
9. *Washington, Dave, LB, Alcorn State, 219
10. Fullerton, Maurice, DT, Tuskegee, 247
11. Bryant, Cleve, DB, Ohio U., 271
12. Jones, Greg, RB, Wisconsin-Whitewater, 301
13. McKoy, Jim, DB, Parsons, 323
14. Slipp, Jeff, DE, BYU, 349
15. Barakat, Maher, K, South Dakota Tech, 375
16. Stewart, Bobby, QB, Northern Arizona, 401
17. Kalfoss, Frank, K, Montana State, 427

DETROIT 1970
1. *Owens, Steve, RB, Oklahoma, 19
2. *Parson, Ray, DE, Minnesota, 45
3. *Mitchell, Jim, DE, Virginia State, 71
4. Choice to New York Giants
5. Parker, Bob, G, Memphis State, 123
6. Terry, Tony, DT, USC, 149
7. *Geddes, Ken, LB, Nebraska, 175
8. Choice to St. Louis
9. *Weaver, Herman, P, Tennessee, 227
10. *Maxwell, Bruce, RB, Arkansas, 253
11. Laird, Roger, DB, Kentucky State, 279
12. Murrell, Emanuel, DB, Cal Poly-SLO, 305
13. *Haverdick, Dave, DT, Morehead State, 331
14. *Brown, Charlie, WR, Northern Arizona, 357
15. Haney, Bob, T, Idaho, 383
16. Todd, Jerry, DB, Memphis State, 409
17. Marshall, Jesse, DT, Centenary, 435

GREEN BAY 1970
1. *McCoy, Mike, DT, Notre Dame [from Chicago Bears] 2
*McGeorge, Rich, TE, Elon, 16
2. *Matthews, Al, DB, Texas A&M, 41
3. *Carter, Jim, LB, Minnesota, 68
4. *Ellis, Ken, WR, Southern, 93
*Butler, Skip, K, Texas-Arlington [from Baltimore] 96
5. Pryor, Cecil, DE, Michigan, 120
6. *Hunt, Ervin, DB, Fresno State, 145
7. *Walker, Cleo, C, Louisville, 172
8. Mjos, Tim, RB, North Dakota State, 197
9. Reinhard, Bob, G, Stanford, 224
10. Melby, Russ, DT, Weber State, 248
*Patrick, Frank, TE, Nebraska [from Washington] 251
11. Hook, Dan, LB, Cal State-Humboldt, 276
12. Foreman, Frank, WR, Michigan State, 300
13. *Smith, Dave, RB, Utah, 328
14. Lints, Bob, G, Eastern Michigan, 353
15. Carter, Mike, WR, Cal State-Sacramento, 380
16. Heacock, Jim, DB, Muskingum, 405
17. *Krause, Larry, RB, St. Norbert, 432

HOUSTON 1970
1. *Wilkerson, Doug, G, North Carolina Central, 14
2. *Brooks, Lee, DT, Texas [from Boston] 31
*Dusenbery, Bill, RB, Johnson C. Smith, 40
3. Choice to Dallas thru Cleveland
4. *Jones, John (Spike), P, Georgia, 92
5. *Saul, Ron, G, Michigan State [from Cincinnati thru New York Jets] 110
Duley, Ed, DT, Northern Arizona, 118
6. *Johnson, Benny, DB, Johnson C. Smith, 144
7. Olson, Charley, DB, Concordia (MN), 170
8. McClish, Mike, T, Wisconsin, 196
9. Blossoms, Charley, DE, Texas Southern, 222
10. *Dawkins, Joe, RB, Wisconsin, 249
11. Morris, Bob, C, Duke, 274
12. Dawkins, Richard, TE, Johnson C. Smith, 299 +
13. *Lewis, Jess, LB, Oregon State, 326
14. Rasmussen, Clair, G, Wisconsin-Oshkosh, 352
15. Sharp, Dave, T, Stanford, 378
16. Myers, Chris, WR, Kenyon, 404 +
17. *Fagan, Julian, P, Mississippi, 430

KANSAS CITY 1970
1. *Smith, Sid, T, USC, 26
2. *Werner, Clyde, LB, Washington, 52
3. Barnett, Billy Bob, DE, Texas A&M [from San Francisco] 61
*Hadley, David, DB, Alcorn State, 78
4. Choice to Cincinnati
5. *Oriard, Mike, C, Notre Dame, 130
6. *Hews, Bob, T, Princeton, 156
7. *Glossen, Clyde, WR, Texas-El Paso, 182
8. *Barry, Fred, DB, Boston U. [from Denver] 193
Choice to Denver
9. Evans, Charley, T, Texas Tech, 234
10. Stankovich, Bob, G, Arkansas, 259
11. O'Neal, Bill, RB, Grambling, 285
12. Fedorchak, Rod, G, Pittsburgh, 312
13. Patridge, Troy, DE, Texas-Arlington, 338
14. Dumont, Glen, RB, American International, 364
15. *Liggett, Bob, DB, Nebraska, 389
16. Ross, Randy, LB, Kansas State, 413
17. Jenkins, Rayford, DB, Alcorn State, 442

LOS ANGELES RAMS 1970
1. *Reynolds, Jack, LB, Tennessee, 22
2. *Williams, Donnie, WR, Prairie View A&M, 35
Choice to San Francisco thru Philadelphia
3. Choice to Baltimore thru Philadelphia
4. Choice to Chicago Bears
5. Choice to New Orleans
6. Choice to Atlanta
7. *Provost, Ted, DB, Ohio State [from Philadelphia] 162
*Nelson, Bill, DT, Oregon State [from Atlanta] 168
Choice to Washington
8. *Saul, Rich, LB, Michigan State, 204
9. Graham, Dave, T, New Mexico Highlands, 230
10. Opalsky, Vince, RB, Miami, 256
11. Bookert, David, RB, New Mexico, 282
12. Arnold, Larry, QB, Hawaii, 308
13. Jones, Melvin, WR, Florida A&M, 334
14. *Geddes, Bob, LB, UCLA, 360
15. Azam, Dag, G, West Texas State, 386
16. Reichardt, Roland, K, West Texas State, 412
17. Crenshaw, Don, DB, USC, 437

MIAMI 1970
1. Choice to Cleveland
2. *Mandich, Jim, TE, Michigan, 29
3. *Foley, Tim, DB, Purdue, 55
4. *Johnson, Curtis, DB, Toledo, 81
5. Choice to Boston

6. Campbell, Dave, DE, Auburn, 132
7. *Scott, Jake, DB, Georgia, 159
8. Chavers, Narvel, RB, Jackson State, 185
9. *Ginn, Hubert, RB, Florida A&M, 211
10. Nittenger, Dick, G, Tampa, 237
11. Wheless, Brownie, T, Rice, 263 +
12. *Kolen, Mike, LB, Auburn, 289
13. Buddington, Dave, RB, Springfield, 315
14. Brackett, Gary, G, Holy Cross, 341
15. Hauser, Pat, WR, East Tennessee State, 367
16. Williams, Charlie, G, Tennessee State, 393
17. Myles, George, DT, Morris Brown, 419

MINNESOTA 1970
1. *Ward, John, T, Oklahoma State, 25
2. *Cappleman, Bill, QB, Florida State, 51
3. Burgoon, Chuck, LB, North Park, 77
4. Choice to Washington thru Los Angeles Rams and New Orleans
5. *Jones, Greg, RB, UCLA, 129
6. Choice to Pittsburgh
7. *Farber, Hap, LB, Mississippi, 181
8. Carroll, Mike, G, Missouri, 206
9. Morrow, George, DE, Mississippi, 233
10. *Voight, Stu, TE, Wisconsin, 260
11. *Zaunbrecher, Godfrey, C, LSU, 286
12. Holland, James, DB, Jackson State, 311
13. Pearce, Bob, DB, Stephen F. Austin, 337
14. Spinks, Tommy, WR, Louisiana Tech, 363
15. Francis, Bennie, DE, Chadron State, 388
16. Cerone, Bruce, WR, Emporia State, 417
17. Healy, Brian, DB, Michigan, 441

NEW ORLEANS 1970
1. *Burrough, Ken, WR, Texas Southern, 10
2. Choice to Cleveland
3. *Swinney, Clovis, DE, Arkansas State, 62
4. *Howell, Delles, DB, Grambling, 88
5. Cannon, Glenn, DB, Mississippi [from Chicago Bears] 106
   Choice to Washington
   *Ramsey, Steve, QB, North Texas State [from Los Angeles Rams] 126
6. Easley, Mel, DB, Oregon State, 140
7. Woodard, Lon, DE, San Diego State, 166
8. *Estes, Lawrence, DE, Alcorn State, 192
9. *Otis, Jim, RB, Ohio State, 218
10. Brumfield, Jim, RB, Indiana State, 244
11. Klahr, Gary, LB, Arizona, 270
12. Davenport, Willie, DB, Southern, 296
13. Miller, Ralph, TE, Alabama State, 322 +
14. *Sutherland, Doug, DE, Wisconsin-Superior, 348
15. Vest, Jim, DE, Washington State, 374
16. Gaspar, Cliff, DT, Grambling, 400
17. *Wyatt, Doug, DB, Tulsa, 426

NEW YORK GIANTS 1970
1. *Files, Jim, LB, Oklahoma, 13
2. Choice to St. Louis
3. Choice to Atlanta
4. Choice to Pittsburgh
   *Grant, Wes, DE, UCLA [from Detroit] 97
5. Brumfield, Claude, G, Tennessee State, 117
6. Miller, Duane, WR, Drake, 142
7. Choice to Atlanta
8. Choice to Atlanta
9. *Hughes, Pat, C, Boston U., 221
10. Fortier, Matt, DE, Fairmont State, 245
11. Pitcaithley, Alan, RB, Oregon, 273
12. Nels, Larry, LB, Wyoming, 297
13. Inskeep, Gary, T, Wisconsin-Stout, 325
14. Brand, Rodney, C, Arkansas, 350
15. Muir, Warren, RB, South Carolina, 377
16. Nolting, Vic, DB, Xavier, 402
17. Breaux, Walter, DT, Grambling, 429

NEW YORK JETS 1970
1. *Tannen, Steve, DB, Florida, 20
2. *Caster, Richard, WR, Jackson State, 46
3. *Onkotz, Dennis, LB, Penn State, 72
4. *Ebersole, John, DE, Penn State, 98
5. *McClain, Cliff, RB, South Carolina State [from Boston] 108
   *Arthur, Gary, TE, Miami (OH), 124
6. Stewart, Terry, DB, Arkansas, 150
7. Williams, Jim, DB, Virginia State, 176
8. *Porter, Jack, G, Oklahoma [from Boston] 187
   *Lomas, Mark, DE, Northern Arizona, 202
9. *Bell, Eddie, WR, Idaho State, 228
10. Dickerson, Cleve, RB, Miami (OH), 254
11. *Thomas, Earlie, DB, Colorado State, 280
12. Pierson, Bill, C-G, San Diego State, 306
13. Groth, Walter, DT, Baylor, 332
14. *Little, John, LB, Oklahoma State, 358
15. *Bayless, Tom, DT, Purdue, 384
16. Herard, Claude, DT, Mississippi, 418
17. Beard, Dick, RB, Kentucky, 440

OAKLAND 1970
1. *Chester, Raymond, TE, Morgan State, 24
2. *Koy, Ted, RB, Texas, 50
3. *Irons, Gerald, DE-DT, Maryland-Eastern Shore, 76
4. *Cline, Tony, LB, Miami, 102
5. *Laster, Art, T, Maryland-Eastern Shore, 128
6. *Wyatt, Alvin, DB, Bethune-Cookman, 154
7. Svitak, Steve, LB, Boise State, 180
8. Wynn, Mike, DE-DT, Nebraska, 207
9. *Hill, Ike, DB, Catawba, 232
10. Bosserman, Gordon, T, UCLA, 258
11. Hicks, Emery, LB, Kansas, 284
12. De Loach, Gerry, G, Cal-Davis, 310
13. *Highsmith, Don, RB, Michigan State, 336
14. Riley, John, K-P, Auburn, 362
15. Moore, Fred, WR, Washington State, 392
16. Roth, Tim, DB, South Dakota State, 414
17. Stolberg, Eric, WR, Indiana, 439

PHILADELPHIA 1970
1. *Zabel, Steve, TE, Oklahoma, 6
2. *Jones, Ray, DB, Southern, 34
3. *Bouggess, Lee, RB, Louisville, 59
4. Choice to Atlanta
5. Choice to Atlanta thru New York Giants
6. Choice to St. Louis
7. Brennan, Terry, T, Notre Dame [from Chicago Bears] 158
   Choice to Los Angeles Rams
8. *Gordon, Ira, T, Kansas State, 190
9. King, David, LB, Stephen F. Austin, 215
10. Jaggard, Steve, DB, Memphis State, 240
11. *Walik, Billy, DB, Villanova, 268
12. Jones, Robert, DT, Grambling, 293
13. *Stevens, Richard, T, Baylor, 318
14. *Moseley, Mark, K, Stephen F. Austin, 346
15. Carlos, John, WR, San Jose State, 371
16. Uperesa, Tuufuli, T, Montana, 396
17. Sizelove, Mike, TE, Idaho, 424

PITTSBURGH 1970
1. *Bradshaw, Terry, QB, Louisiana Tech, 1
2. *Shanklin, Ronnie, WR, North Texas State, 28
3. *Blount, Mel, DB, Southern, 53
4. *George, Ed, T, Wake Forest, 80
   Evenson, Jim, RB, Oregon [from New York Giants] 90
5. *Staggers, Jon, DB, Missouri, 105
6. Barrera, Manuel, LB, Kansas State, 131
   Kegler, Clarence, T, South Carolina State [from Minnesota] 155
7. Griffin, Danny, RB, Texas-Arlington, 157
8. *Smith, Dave, WR, Indiana State, 184
9. *Crennel, Carl, LB, West Virginia, 209
10. Brown, Isaiah, DB, Stanford, 236
11. *Hunt, Calvin, C, Baylor, 261
12. *Sharp, Vaughan, T, Washington, 288
13. Main, Billy, RB, Oregon State, 313
14. *Askson, Bert, LB, Texas Southern, 340
15. Keppy, Glen, DT, Wisconsin-Platteville, 365
16. Yanossy, Frank, DT, Tennessee, 391
17. Key, Harry, TE, Mississippi Valley State, 415

ST. LOUIS 1970
1. *Stegent, Larry, RB, Texas A&M, 8
2. Corrigall, Jim, LB, Kent State, 33
   *Hutchison, Chuck, G, Ohio State [from New York Giants] 38
3. *Pittman, Charlie, RB, Penn State, 58
   Harris, Eric, DB, Colorado [from Washington] 69
4. *Lens, Greg, DT, Trinity (TX), 86
   *Parish, Don, LB, Stanford [from Atlanta] 91
5. Lloyd, Tom, T, Bowling Green, 111
   Pierson, Barry, DB, Michigan [from Dallas] 127
6. Manuel, James, T, Toledo [from Philadelphia] 136
   Choice to Chicago Bears
7. *McFarland, Jim, TE, Nebraska, 164
8. *Banks, Tom, C, Auburn, 189
   Holmgren, Mike, QB, USC [from Detroit] 201
9. *White, Paul, RB, Texas-El Paso, 214
10. *Plummer, Tony, DB, Pacific, 242
11. *Siwek, Mike, DT, Western Michigan, 267
12. Collins, Charles, WR, Kansas State, 292
13. Thomas, Jack, G, Mississippi State, 320
14. Groth, Ray, WR, Utah, 345
15. Wilson, Ron, WR, West Illinois, 370
16. Fowler, Gary, RB, California, 398
17. Powell, Cliff, LB, Arkansas, 423

SAN DIEGO 1970
1. *Gillette, Walker, WR, Richmond, 15
2. *Williams, William, DT, Cal-Davis, 42
3. Choice to Buffalo
4. Maddox, Bill, TE, Syracuse, 94
5. Farrar, Pettus, RB, Norfolk State, 119
6. *Parks, Billy, WR, Long Beach State, 146
7. Fabish, Jim, DB, Texas-El Paso, 171
8. *Clark, Wayne, QB, U,S, International, 198
9. *Fletcher, Chris, DB, Temple, 213
10. Steen, Mac, G, Florida, 250
11. *Protz, John, LB, Syracuse, 275
12. Gravelle, Howard, TE, Cal-Davis, 302
13. Bradley, Bernard, DB, Utah State, 327
14. Caldwell, Tyrone, DT, South Carolina State, 354
15. Childs, Eugene, RB, Texas-El Paso, 379
16. Green, Mike, RB, Nebraska, 406
17. Sanks, Dave, G, Louisville, 431

SAN FRANCISCO 1970
1. *Hardman, Cedrick, DE, North Texas State, 9
   *Taylor, Bruce, DB, Boston U. [from Washington] 17
2. Choice to Los Angeles Rams
   *Isenbarger, John, RB, Indiana [from Los Angeles Rams thru Philadelphia] 48
3. Choice to Kansas City
4. *Washington, Vic, WR, Wyoming, 87
5. McArthur, Gary, T, USC, 113
6. Clark, Rusty, QB, Houston, 138
7. *Strong, Jim, RB, Houston, 165
8. *Campbell, Carter, LB, Weber State, 191
9. *Riley, Preston, DB-WR, Memphis State, 217
10. *Schreiber, Larry, RB, Tennessee Tech, 243
11. Crockett, Dan, WR, Toledo, 269
12. Tant, Bill, T, Dayton, 295
13. Vanderslice, Jim, LB, TCU, 321
14. King, Jack, G, Clemson, 347
15. Delsignore, Dave, WR, Youngstown State, 373
16. Perkins, Produs, DB, Livingstone, 399
17. Culton, Mike, P, La Verne, 425

WASHINGTON 1970
1. Choice to St. Louis
2. *Brundige, Bill, DE, Colorado, 43
3. Choice to St. Louis
4. Choice to Baltimore
   *Laaveg, Paul, T, Iowa [from Minnesota thru Los Angeles Rams and New Orleans] 103
5. *Sistrunk, Manny, DT, Arkansas-Pine Bluff [from New Orleans] 114
   *Pierce, Danny, RB, Memphis State, 121
6. Choice to Atlanta
7. Merritt, Roland, WR, Maryland, 173
   *Harris, Jimmy, DB, Howard Payne [from Los Angeles Rams] 178
8. Johnson, Paul, DB, Penn State, 200
9. Sonntag, Ralph, T, Maryland, 225
10. Choice to Green Bay
11. *Alston, Mack, TE, Maryland-Eastern Shore, 277
12. Kates, Jim, LB, Penn State, 303
13. Patterson, Joe, T, Lawrence, 329
14. Moro, Tony, RB, Dayton, 355
15. Lewandowski, Vic, C, Holy Cross, 381
16. Bushore, Steve, WR, Emporia State, 407
17. Maxfield, Earl, DT, Baylor, 433

1971

Held January 28-29, 1971

Although the Patriots' franchise played the 1971 season as New England, at the time of the draft it still was located in Boston.

ATLANTA 1971
1. *Profit, Joe, RB, Northeast Louisiana, 7
2. *Burrow, Ken, WR, San Diego State, 33
3. *Hart, Leo, QB, Duke, 59
4. Potchad, Mike, T, Pittsburg State (KS), 85
5. *Jarvis, Ray, WR, Norfolk State, 111
6. *Hayes, Tom, DB, San Diego State, 137
   *Brown, Ray, DB, West Texas State [from New York Giants] 148
7. *Chesson, Wes, WR, Duke, 163
8. *Havig, Dennis, G, Colorado, 189
9. Griffin, Alvin, WR, Tuskegee, 215
10. *Tillman, Faddie, DE, Boise State, 241
11. *Shears, Larry, DB, Lincoln (MO), 267
12. Lowe, Ronnie, WR, Ft. Valley State, 293
13. Crooks, Dan, DB, Wisconsin, 319
14. Comer, Deryl, TE, Texas, 345
15. Clark, Wallace, RB, Auburn, 371
16. James, Lindsey, RB, San Diego State, 397
17. Martin, Willie, RB, Johnson C. Smith, 423

BALTIMORE 1971
1. *McCauley, Don, RB, North Carolina [from Miami] 22
   *Dunlap, Leonard, DB, North Texas State, 26
2. *Atessis, Bill, DE, Texas, 52
3. Douglas, Karl, QB, Texas A&I, 78
4. Choice to Pittsburgh
5. *Andrews, John, TE, Indiana, 130
6. Frith, Ken, DT, Northeast Louisiana, 156
7. *Bowdell, Gordon, WR, Michigan State, 182
8. Bogan, Willie, DB, Dartmouth, 207
9. Burnett, Bill, RB, Arkansas, 234
10. *Kern, Rex, QB, Ohio State, 260
11. Jones, Dave, LB, Baylor, 286
12. Wuensch, Bobby, T, Texas [from Pittsburgh] 294
    Triplett, Bill, WR, Michigan State, 312
13. Neville, Tom, LB, Yale, 338
14. Mikolayunas, Mike, RB, Davidson, 364
15. Hogan, Mike, LB, Michigan State, 390
16. Harrington, Rich, DB, Houston, 416
17. *Nottingham, Don, RB, Kent State, 441

BOSTON 1971
1. *Plunkett, Jim, QB, Stanford, 1
2. *Adams, Julius, DT, Texas Southern, 27
3. Choice to Buffalo thru Oakland
4. Choice to Denver
5. Kelly, Tim, LB, Notre Dame, 105
6. Hardt, David, TE, Kentucky, 131
7. Choice to Oakland
8. Choice to Buffalo
9. *Ashton, Josh, RB, Tulsa, 209
10. McDowell, Layne, T, Iowa, 235
11. Schneiss, Dan, TE, Nebraska, 261
12. Rodman, John, T, Northwestern, 287
13. Swain, Lewis, DB, Alabama A&M, 313
14. *Sykes, Alfred, WR, Florida A&M, 339
15. McGarry, Nick, TE, Massachusetts, 365
16. Zikmund, Jim, DB, Kearney State, 391
17. Leigh, Ronald, DE, Elizabeth City State, 417

BUFFALO 1971
1. *Hill, J.D., WR, Arizona State, 4
2. *White, Jan, TE, Ohio State, 29
3. *Jarvis, Bruce, C, Washington [from Boston thru Oakland] 53
   *Braxton, Jim, RB, West Virginia, 57
4. Choice to New Orleans
5. *Green, Donnie, T, Purdue, 107
   *Beamer, Tim, DB, Johnson C. Smith [from Denver] 113
6. Choice to Chicago Bears
   *McKinley, Bill, DE, Arizona [from Cincinnati] 145
7. *Chandler, Bob, WR, USC, 160
8. *Ross, Louis, DE, South Carolina State [from Boston] 183
   Walls, Tyrone, RB, Missouri, 185
9. Strickland, Bob, LB, Auburn, 213
10. Choice to Oakland
11. Browder, Andy, T, Texas A&I, 263
12. Sheffield, Jim, K, Texas A&M, 291
13. Underwood, Busty, QB, TCU, 316
14. Hoots, Jim, DE, Missouri Southern, 341
15. Cole, Charley, RB, Toledo, 369
16. Hunter, Billy, DB, Utah, 394
17. Morrison, Pat, TE, Arkansas, 419

CHICAGO BEARS 1971
1. *Moore, Joe, RB, Missouri, 11
2. *Harrison, Jim, RB, Missouri [from New Orleans] 28
   *Ford, Charles, DB, Houston, 36
3. *McGee, Tony, DE, Bishop, 64
   *Newton, Bob, T, Nebraska [from Los Angeles Rams] 71
4. *Moore, Jerry, DB, Arkansas, 89
5. Choice to San Francisco
6. *Thomas, Earl, TE, Houston [from Buffalo] 135
7. Lee, Buddy, QB, LSU, 167
   Ferris, Dennis, RB, Pittsburgh [from Los Angeles Rams] 176
8. Weiss, Karl, T, Vanderbilt, 192
9. McClain, Lester, WR, Tennessee, 220
10. *Rowden, Larry, LB, Houston, 245
11. *Hardy, Cliff, DB, Michigan State, 270
12. Booras, Steve, DE, Mesa J.C., 298 +
13. Nicholas, Ed, T, North Carolina State, 323
14. Lewis, Willie, RB, Arizona, 347
15. Maciejowski, Ron, QB, Ohio State, 376
16. Bailey, Sid, DE, Texas-Arlington, 401
17. Garganes, Ray, LB, Millersville, 426

CINCINNATI 1971
1. *Holland, Vernon, T, Tennessee State, 15
2. *Lawson, Steve, G, Kansas, 41
3. *Anderson, Ken, QB, Augustana (IL), 67
4. *Willis, Fred, RB, Boston College, 93
5. *May, Arthur, DE, Tuskegee [from New York Jets] 110
   Choice to San Diego
6. Choice to Buffalo
7. *Craig, Neal, DB, Fisk, 171
8. Herring, Fred, DB, Tennessee State, 197
9. Gustafson, Gary, LB, Montana State, 223
10. Stambaugh, Jack, G, Oregon, 249
11. *Marshall, Ed, WR, Cameron, 275
12. Hayden, James, DE, Memphis State, 301
13. Knapman, David, TE, Central Washington, 327
14. *Mallory, Irvin, DB, Virginia Union, 353
15. Thomas, Bob, RB, Arizona State, 379
16. Debevc, Mark, LB, Ohio State, 405
17. Pearson, Sam, DB, Western Kentucky, 432

CLEVELAND 1971
1. *Scott, Clarence, DB, Kansas State, 14
2. *Cornell, Bo, RB, Washington, 40
3. *Staroba, Paul, WR, Michigan, 66
   *Hall, Charlie, LB, Houston [from Kansas City] 68
4. *Pena, Bubba, G, Massachusetts, 92
5. *Brown, Stan, WR, Purdue, 118
6. *Dieken, Doug, T, Illinois [from Chicago Bears] 142
   Dixon, Jay, DE, Boston U., 144
7. Jacobs, Bob, K, Wyoming, 170
8. Zelina, Larry, RB, Ohio State, 196
9. Levels, Wilmur, DB, North Texas State, 222
10. Casteel, Steve, LB, Oklahoma, 248
11. *Sikich, Mike, G, Northwestern, 274
12. Blanchard, Tony, TE, North Carolina, 300
13. Jamula, Thad, T, Lehigh, 326
14. *Kingrea, Rick, LB, Tulane, 352
15. Green, Bill, DB, Western Kentucky, 378
16. Smith, Dave, WR, Mississippi State, 404
17. Dillon, Leo, C, Dayton, 430

DALLAS 1971
1. *Smith, Tody, DE, USC, 25
2. *Thomas, Ike, DB, Bishop, 51
3. *Scarber, Sam, RB, New Mexico [from St. Louis] 69
   *Gregory, Bill, DT, Wisconsin, 77
4. Carter, Joe, TE, Grambling [from New Orleans] 80
   Mitchell, Adam, T, Mississippi, 103
5. *Kadziel, Ron, LB, Stanford, 129
6. Maier, Steve, WR, Northern Arizona, 155
7. Griffin, Bill, T, Catawba, 181
8. *Jessie, Ron, WR, Kansas, 206
9. *Jackson, Honor, WR, Pacific, 233
10. *Wallace, Rodney, DT, New Mexico, 259
11. Bonwell, Ernest, DT, Lane, 285
12. Goepel, Steve, QB, Colgate, 311
13. *Ford, Jim, RB, Texas Southern, 337
14. Covey, Tyrone, DB, Utah State, 363
15. Young, Bob, TE, Delaware, 389
16. Brennan, John, T, Boston College, 415
17. Bomer, John, C, Memphis State, 440

DENVER 1971
1. Choice to Green Bay
   *Montgomery, Marv, T, USC [from Green Bay] 12
2. *Harrison, Dwight, WR, Texas A&I, 35
3. Choice to St. Louis
4. *Alzado, Lyle, DE, Yankton [from Boston] 79

Johnson, Cleo, DB, Alcorn State, 87
5. Choice to Buffalo
6. Phillips, Harold, DB, Michigan State, 139
7. *Adams, Doug, LB, Ohio State, 165
8. *Beard, Tom, C, Michigan State [from Houston] 187
Choice to Kansas City
9. Handy, John, LB, Purdue, 217
10. Harris, Carlis, WR, Idaho State, 243
11. Roitsch, Roger, DT, Rice, 269
12. Franks, Floyd, WR, Mississippi, 295
13. Blackford, Craig, QB, Evansville, 321
14. *Lyons, Tommy, C, Georgia, 350
15. James, Larry, RB, Norfolk State, 373
16. Thompson, Steve, DT, Minnesota, 399
17. Simcsak, Jack, K, Virginia Tech, 425

DETROIT 1971
1. *Bell, Bob, DT, Cincinnati, 21
2. *Thompson, Dave, C-G, Clemson [from Philadelphia] 30
*Weaver, Charlie, LB, USC, 48
3. *Clark, Al, DB, Eastern Michigan, 72
4. *Woods, Larry, DT, Tennessee State, 100
5. Newell, Pete, G, Michigan, 125
6. Harris, Frank, QB, Boston College [from Los Angeles Rams thru Philadelphia] 150
Franklin, Herman, WR, USC, 152
7. Wheless, Brownie, T, Rice, 177
8. *Lee, Ken, LB, Washington, 204
9. *Zofko, Mickey, RB, Auburn, 229
10. Choice to Philadelphia
11. Webb, Phil, DB, Colorado State, 281
12. Pilconis, Bill, WR, Pittsburgh, 308
13. Abercrombie, David, RB, Tulane, 332
14. Lorenz, Tom, TE, Iowa State, 360
15. Coates, Ed, WR, Central Missouri State, 385
16. Kutchinski, Tom, DB, Michigan State, 411
17. *Jolley, Gordon, T, Utah, 436

GREEN BAY 1971
1. *Brockington, John, RB, Ohio State [from Denver] 9
Choice to Denver
2. Choice to San Francisco
*Robinson, Virgil, RB, Grambling [from Los Angeles Rams] 46
3. *Hall, Charlie, DB, Pittsburgh, 62
4. Choice to Los Angeles Rams
5. Choice to San Diego
*Smith, Donnell, DE, Southern [from Washington] 116
Stillwagon, Jim, LB, Ohio State [from Los Angeles Rams thru Washington] 124
6. *Hunter, Scott, QB, Alabama, 140
7. *Davis, Dave, WR, Tennessee State, 168
Johnson, James, WR, Bishop [from Oakland] 175
8. Headley, Win, C, Wake Forest, 193
9. Mayer, Barry, RB, Minnesota, 216
10. *Hunt, Kevin, T, Doane, 246
11. Lanier, John, RB, Parsons, 271
12. Hendren, Greg, G, California, 296
13. Martin, Jack, RB, Angelo State, 324
14. Spears, LeRoy, DE, Moorhead State, 348
15. *Garrett, Len, TE, New Mexico Highlands, 374
16. O'Donnell, Jack, G, Central State (OK), 402
17. Johnson, Monty, DB, Oklahoma, 427

HOUSTON 1971
1. *Pastorini, Dan, QB, Santa Clara, 3
2. Choice to New Orleans
3. *Dickey, Lynn, QB, Kansas City, 56
4. *Jackson, Larron, T, Missouri, 81
5. Armstrong, Willie, RB, Grambling, 109
6. *Alexander, Willie, DB, Alcorn State, 134
7. *Croyle, Phil, LB, California, 159
Watson, Larry, T, Morgan State [from New York Giants] 174
8. Choice to Denver
9. *Rice, Floyd, TE-LB, Alcorn State, 212 +
10. Price, Russell, DE, North Carolina Central, 237
11. Hughes, Macon, WR, Rice, 265
12. Thompson, John, G, Minnesota, 290
13. Hoing, Joe, G, Arkansas Tech, 315
14. Adams, Dick, DB, Miami (OH), 343
15. *Hopkins, Andy, RB, Stephen F. Austin, 368
16. Denson, Moses, RB, Maryland-Eastern Shore, 393 +
17. Fox, Calvin, LB, Michigan State, 421

KANSAS CITY 1971
1. *Wright, Elmo, WR, Houston, 16
2. *Young, Wilbur, DT, William Penn [from San Diego] 39
Lewis, Scott, DE, Grambling, 42
3. Choice to Cleveland
4. Robinson, David, TE, Jacksonville State, 94
5. *Adamle, Mike, RB, Northwestern, 120
6. *Reardon, Kerry, DB, Iowa, 146
7. Choice to New Orleans
8. *Sensibaugh, Mike, DB, Ohio State [from Denver] 191
Telander, Rick, DB, Northwestern, 198
9. Hawes, Alvin, T, Minnesota, 224
10. *Jankowski, Bruce, WR, Ohio State, 250
11. *Allen, Nate, DB, Texas Southern, 276
12. Esposito, Tony, RB, Pittsburgh, 302
13. Hixson, Chuck, QB, SMU, 328
14. *Bergey, Bruce, DE, UCLA, 354
15. Montgomery, Mike, DB, Southwest Texas State, 380
16. Jansonius, Darrell, G, Iowa State, 406
17. Hill, Travis, DB, Prairie View A&M, 431 +

LOS ANGELES RAMS 1971
1. *Robertson, Isiah, LB, Southern [from Washington] 10
*Youngblood, Jack, DE, Florida, 20
2. Choice to Green Bay
3. *Elmendorf, Dave, DB, Texas A&M [from Washington] 63
Choice to Chicago Bears
4. Worster, Steve, RB, Texas [from Green Bay] 90
Choice to New Orleans
5. Choice to Green Bay thru Washington
6. Choice to Detroit thru Philadelphia
7. Choice to Chicago Bears
8. Garay, Tony, DE, Hofstra, 202
9. Schmidt, Joe, WR, Miami, 228
10. Popplewell, Don, C, Colorado, 254
11. Richards, Charlie, QB, Richmond, 280
12. Behrendt, Kirk, T, Wisconsin-Whitewater, 306
13. Harrison, Russell, RB, Kansas State, 331
14. Coleman, Lionel, DB, Oregon, 358
15. Kos, Gary, G, Notre Dame, 384
16. Boice, Ross, LB, Pacific Lutheran, 409
17. *Vataha, Randy, WR, Stanford [from New Orleans] 418
*Sweet, Joe, WR, Tennessee State, 435

MIAMI 1971
1. Choice to Baltimore
2. *Stowe, Otto, WR, Iowa State, 47
3. *Farley, Dale, LB, West Virginia, 74
4. *Theismann, Joe, QB, Notre Dame, 99
5. Choice to Pittsburgh
6. Coleman, Dennis, LB, Mississippi, 151
7. Dickerson, Ron, DB, Kansas State, 178
8. Choice to Pittsburgh
9. *Den Herder, Vern, DE, Central Iowa, 230
10. Maree, Ron, DT, Purdue, 255
11. Surma, Vic, T, Penn State, 282
12. Byars, Leroy, RB, Alcorn State, 307
13. *Hepburn, Lonnie, DB, Texas Southern, 333
14. Vaughn, David, TE, Memphis State, 359
15. Richards, Bob, G, California, 386
16. Myers, Chris, WR, Kenyon, 410
17. Mark, Curt, LB, Mayville, 437

MINNESOTA 1971
1. *Hayden, Leo, RB, Ohio State, 24
2. Choice to Philadelphia
3. Hackett, Eddie, WR, Alcorn State, 76
4. *Clements, Vince, RB, Connecticut, 102
5. Choice to Pittsburgh
6. Choice to Philadelphia
7. Mack, Gene, LB, Texas-El Paso, 180
8. Farley, John, DE, Johnson C. Smith, 208
9. Sullivan, Tim, RB, Iowa, 232
10. *Morris, Chris, G, Indiana, 258
11. *Walker, Joseph, LB, Tulane, 284
12. Holmes, Reggie, DB, Wisconsin-Stout, 310
13. Fry, Benny, C, Houston, 336
14. Gallagher, Jim, LB, Yale, 362
15. *Wright, Jeff, DB, Minnesota, 388
16. Edmonds, Greg, WR, Penn State, 413
17. *Duncan, Ken, P, Tulsa, 439

NEW ORLEANS 1971
1. *Manning, Archie, QB, Mississippi, 2
2. Choice to Chicago Bears
*Holden, Sam, G, Grambling [from Houston] 31
3. *Lee, Bivian, DB, Prairie View A&M, 54
4. Choice to Dallas
*Bell, Carlos, RB, Houston [from Buffalo] 82
*Winther, Wimpy, C, Mississippi [from Washington] 88
*Martin, D'Artagnan, DB, Kentucky State [from San Diego] 91
*Morrison, Don, T, Texas-Arlington [from Los Angeles Rams] 98
5. Choice to Pittsburgh
6. Moorhead, Don, RB, Michigan, 132
7. DiNardo, Larry, G, Notre Dame, 158
*Newland, Bob, WR, Oregon [from Kansas City] 172
8. Choice to Pittsburgh
Elder, Jimmy, DB, Southern [from Washington] 194
*Gresham, Bob, RB, West Virginia [from Oakland] 201
9. Williams, Tom, DB, Willamette, 210
10. Choice to San Francisco
Pamplin, Rocky, RB, Hawaii [from Philadelphia] 239
11. *Pollard, Bob, DE, Weber State, 262
12. Gathright, Ron, DB, Morehead State, 288
13. *Burchfield, Don, TE, Ball State, 314
14. *Scott, Bobby, QB, Tennessee, 340
15. Graves, Bart, T-DE, Tulane, 366
16. *Robinson, Craig, T, Houston, 392
17. Choice to Los Angeles Rams
Eben, Hermann, WR, Oklahoma State [from Washington] 428

NEW YORK GIANTS 1971
1. *Thompson, Rocky, WR, West Texas State, 18
2. *Walton, Gerald, T, Abilene Christian, 44
3. *Hornsby, Ronnie, LB, Southeastern Louisiana, 70
4. *Tipton, Dave, DT, Stanford, 96
5. Choice to San Francisco
6. Choice to Atlanta
7. Choice to Houston
8. Gregory, Ted, DE-LB, Delaware, 200
9. Thomas, Ed, LB, Lebanon Valley, 226
10. *Reed, Henry, LB, Weber State, 252
11. *Ellison, Mark, G, Dayton, 278
12. *Blanchard, Tom, QB-K, Oregon, 304
13. *Roller, Dave, DT, Kentucky, 330
14. *Evans, Charlie, RB, USC, 356
15. Wright, Jim, LB, Notre Dame, 382
16. Gibbs, Dick, TE, Texas-El Paso, 408
17. *Zeno, Coleman, WR, Grambling, 434

NEW YORK JETS 1971
1. *Riggins, John, RB, Kansas, 6
2. *Mooring, John, T, Tampa, 32
3. *Farasopoulos, Chris, DB, BYU, 58
4. *Zapalac, Bill, LB, Texas, 84
5. Choice to Cincinnati
6. *Wise, Phil, TE, Nebraska-Omaha, 136
7. *Palmer, Scott, DT, Texas, 162
8. *Kirksey, Roy, G, Maryland-Eastern Shore, 188
9. Curtis, John, TE, Springfield, 214
10. Bettis, Jim, DB, Michigan, 240
11. *Studdard, Vern, WR, Mississippi, 266
12. *Sowells, Rich, DB, Alcorn State, 292
13. Eggold, John, DE, Arizona, 318
14. Harpring, John, G, Michigan 344
15. Dyches, Dan, C, South Carolina, 370
16. Harky, Steve, RB, Georgia Tech, 396
17. Flaska, Greg, DE, Western Michigan, 422

OAKLAND 1971
1. *Tatum, Jack, DB, Ohio State, 19
2. *Villapiano, Phil, LB, Bowling Green, 45
3. *Koegel, Warren, C, Penn State, 73
4. *Davis, Clarence RB, USC, 97
5. *Moore, Bob, TE, Stanford, 123
6. *Slough, Greg, LB, USC, 149
7. *Martin, Don, DB, Yale [from Boston] 157
Choice to Green Bay
8. Choice to New Orleans
9. Garnett, Dave, RB, Pittsburgh, 227
10. *West, Bill, DB, Tennessee State [from Buffalo] 238
Oesterling, Tim, DT, UCLA, 253
11. Poston, Jim, DT, South Carolina, 279
12. *Jones, Horace, DT, Louisville, 305
13. Natzel, Mick, DB, Central Michigan, 334
14. *Gipson, Tom, DT, North Texas State, 357
15. Giles, Andy, DE, William & Mary, 383
16. Stawarz, Tony, DB, Miami, 412
17. Hill, Charles, WR, Sam Houston State, 442

PHILADELPHIA 1971
1. *Harris, Richard, DE, Grambling, 5
2. Choice to Detroit
*Allison, Hank, G, San Diego State [from Minnesota] 50
3. Choice to San Francisco
4. *Feller, Happy, K, Texas, 83
5. Shellabarger, Tom, T, San Diego State, 108
6. *Smith, Jack, DB, Troy State, 133
Neely, Wyck, DB, Mississippi [from Minnesota] 154
7. *Carmichael, Harold, WR, Southern, 161
8. *Gotshalk, Len, C, Cal State-Humboldt, 186
9. Pettigrew, Len, LB, Ashland, 211
10. Choice to New Orleans
*Bailey, Tom, Florida State [from Detroit] 256
11. *Davis, Albert, RB, Tennessee State, 264
12. Saathoff, Rich, DE, Northern Arizona, 289
13. Lester, Danny, DB, Texas, 317
14. *Creech, Robert, LB, TCU, 342
15. Fisher, Ed, G, Prairie View, 367
16. James, Bruce, LB, Arkansas, 395
17. Sage, John, LB, LSU, 420

PITTSBURGH 1971
1. *Lewis, Frank, WR, Grambling, 8
2. *Ham, Jack, LB, Penn State, 34
3. *Davis, Steve, RB, Delaware State, 60
4. *Mullins, Gerry, TE, USC, 86
*White, Dwight, DE, East Texas State [from Baltimore] 104
5. *Brown, Larry, TE, Kansas [from New Orleans] 106
*Holmes, Mel, T, North Carolina A&T, 112
*Anderson, Ralph, DB, West Texas State [from Miami] 126
Brister, Fred, LB, Mississippi [from Minnesota] 128
6. *Hanneman, Craig, T, Oregon State, 138
7. McClure, Worthy, T-G, Mississippi, 164
8. *Crowe, Larry, RB, Texas Southern [from New Orleans] 184
Rogers, Paul, K, Nebraska, 190
*Holmes, Ernie, DT, Texas Southern [from Miami] 203
9. Anderson, Mike, LB, LSU, 216
10. O'Shea, Jim, TE, Boston College, 242
11. *Wagner, Mike, DB, Western Illinois, 268
12. Choice to Baltimore
13. *Young, Al, WR, South Carolina State, 320
14. Evans, McKinney, DB, New Mexico Highlands, 346
15. Makin, Ray, G, Kentucky, 372
16. Huntley, Walter, DB, Trinity (TX), 398
17. Ehle, Danny, RB, Howard Payne, 424

ST. LOUIS 1971
1. *Thompson, Norm, DB, Utah, 17
2. *Dierdorf, Dan, T, Michigan, 43
3. Livesay, Jim, WR, Richmond [from Denver] 61
Choice to Dallas
4. *Willingham, Larry, DB, Auburn, 95
5. Wallace, Rocky, LB, Missouri, 121
6. *Gray, Mel, WR, Missouri, 147
7. Cooch, James, DB, Colorado, 173
8. *Yankowski, Ron, DE, Kansas State, 199
9. Savoy, Mike, WR, Black Hills State, 225
10. Miller, Ron, T, McNeese State, 251
11. *Ogle, Dick, LB, Colorado, 277
12. Von Dulm, Tim, QB, Portland State, 303
13. *Allen, Jeff, DB, Iowa State, 329
14. Klausen, Doug, T, Arizona, 355
15. Heiskell, Ted, RB, Houston, 381
16. Brame, Lawrence, LB, Western Kentucky, 407
17. Watkins, Preston, WR, Bluefield, 433

SAN DIEGO 1971
1. *Burns, Leon, RB, Long Beach State, 13
2. Choice to Kansas City
3. *Montgomery, Mike, RB, Kansas State, 65
4. Choice to New Orleans
5. *Salter, Bryant, DB, Pittsburgh [from Green Bay] 115
*White, Ray, LB, Syracuse, 117
Asack, Phil, DE, Duke [from Cincinnati] 119
6. Mayes, Jacob, RB, Tennessee State, 143
7. *Dicus, Chuck, WR, Arkansas, 169
8. Van Gorkum, Leon, DE, San Diego State, 195
9. *Tanner, John, TE, Tennessee Tech, 221
10. *Nowak, Gary, TE, Michigan State, 247
11. Pinson, Don, DB, Tennessee State, 273
12. Garnett, Wes, WR, Utah State, 299
13. Milner, Sammy, WR, Mississippi State, 325
14. O'Daniel, Edward, DE, Texas Southern, 351
15. Humston, Eric, LB, Muskingum, 377
16. Foote, Ed, C, Hawaii, 403
17. Kell, Chip, C, Tennessee, 429

SAN FRANCISCO 1971
1. *Anderson, William Tim, DB, Ohio State, 23
2. *Janet, Ernie, G, Washington [from Green Bay] 37
*Orduna, Joe, RB, Nebraska, 49
3. Dickerson, Sam, WR, USC [from Philadelphia] 55
*Parker, Willie, C, North Texas State, 75
4. *Harris, Tony, RB, Toledo, 101
5. Shaternick, Dean, T, Kansas State [from Chicago Bears] 114
Wells, George, LB, New Mexico State [from New York Giants] 122
*Huff, Marty, LB, Michigan, 127
6. Bresler, Al, WR, Auburn, 153
7. *Watson, John, T, Oklahoma, 179
8. *McCann, Jim, K, Arizona State, 205
9. Couch, Therman, LB, Iowa State, 231
10. Cardo, Ron, RB, Wisconsin-Oshkosh [from New Orleans] 236
Jennings, Ernie, WR, Air Force, 257
11. *Reed, Joe, QB, Mississippi State, 283
12. Bunch, Jim, DT, Wisconsin-Platteville, 309
13. Bullock, John, RB, Purdue, 335
14. *Dunstan, Bill, DE, Utah State, 361
15. Lennon, John, T, Colgate, 387
16. Purcell, Dave, DT, Kentucky, 414
17. Charlton, Leroy, DB, Florida A&M, 438 +

WASHINGTON 1971
1. Choice to Los Angeles Rams
2. *Speyrer, Cotton, WR, Texas, 38
3. Choice to Los Angeles Rams
4. Choice to New Orleans
5. Choice to Green Bay
6. *Hayman, Conway, G, Delaware, 141
7. *Germany, Willie, DB, Morgan State, 166
8. Choice to New Orleans
9. *Fanucci, Mike, DE, Arizona State, 219
10. *Taylor, Jessie, RB, Cincinnati, 244
11. *Starke, George, T, Columbia, 272
12. *Severson, Jeff, DB, Long Beach State, 297
13. *Ryczek, Dan, C, Virginia, 322
14. Bynum, Bill, QB, Western New Mexico, 349
15. Christnovich, Anthony, G, Wisconsin-LaCrosse, 375
16. Tucker, Glenn, LB, North Texas State, 400
17. Choice to New Orleans

1972

Held February 1-2, 1972

ATLANTA 1972
1. *Ellis, Clarence, DB, Notre Dame, 15
2. *Sullivan, Pat, QB, Auburn [from Philadelphia thru Detroit] 40
*Okoniewski, Steve, T, Montana [from Detroit] 41
*Manning, Roosevelt, DT, Northeastern Oklahoma, 42
3. *Goodman, Les, RB, Yankton, 67
4. Howard, Andrew, DT, Grambling, 94
5. Taylor, Billy, RB, Michigan [from Houston thru Denver and Buffalo] 109
*Cindrich, Ralph, LB, Pittsburgh, 119
6. Perfetti, Mike, DB, Minnesota [from New England thru New York Giants] 40
Riley, Fred, WR, Idaho, 146
7. Moon, Lance, RB, Wisconsin, 171
8. Brandon, Henry, RB, Southern, 198
9. *Easterling, Ray, DB, Richmond, 223
10. Choice to St. Louis
11. Phillips, Jack, WR, Grambling, 275
12. *Mialik, Larry, TE, Wisconsin, 302
13. Sovio, Henry, TE, Hawaii, 327
14. Chandler, Tom, LB, Minnesota, 354
15. Jenkins, Oscar, DB, Virginia Union, 379
16. Butler, Larry, LB, Stanford, 406
17. Holland, Bill, RB, USC, 431

BALTIMORE 1972
1. *Drougas, Tom, T, Oregon, 22
2. *Mildren, Jack, DB, Oklahoma [from Oakland] 46
   *Doughty, Glenn, WR, Michigan [from Washington] 47
   *Mitchell, Lydell, RB, Penn State, 48
3. Choice to New Orleans thru Oakland
4. Choice to Oakland
   Allen, Eric, WR, Michigan State [from Dallas thru New Orleans and San Diego] 104
5. *Croft, Don, DT, Texas-El Paso [from New England] 115
   Choice to New Orleans
6. *Laird, Bruce, DB, American International, 152
7. *Sykes, John, RB, Morgan State [from New York Jets thru Washington] 169
   Choice to Oakland
8. Qualls, Al, LB, Oklahoma, from San Diego, 191
   Brownson, Van, QB, Nebraska, 204
9. Hambell, Gary, DT, Dayton [from Green Bay] 215
   Choice to Cleveland
10. Schilling, Dave, RB, Oregon State [from New England] 256
11. *DeBernardi, Fred, DE, Texas-El Paso, 282
12. Theiler, Gary, TE, Tennessee, 308
13. Washington, Herb, WR, Michigan, 334
14. Morris, John, C, Missouri Valley, 359
15. Parkhouse, Robin, LB, Alabama, 386
16. Wichard, Gary, QB, C.W. Post, 412
17. *White, Stan, LB, Ohio State, 438

BUFFALO 1972
1. *Patulski, Walt, DE, Notre Dame, 1
2. *McKenzie, Reggie, G, Michigan, 27
3. Swendsen, Fred, DE, Notre Dame, 53
4. *Jackson, Randy, RB, Wichita State, 79
5. *Garror, Leon, DB, Alcorn State, 105
   *Penchion, Bob, G, Alcorn State [from Denver] 108
6. Choice to Oakland
7. Stepaniak, Ralph, DB, Notre Dame, 157
8. *Gibson, Paul, WR, Texas-El Paso, 183
9. Vogel, Steve, LB, Boise State, 209
10. *Tyler, Maurice, DB, Morgan State, 235
11. Light, Bill, LB, Minnesota, 271
12. Baker, Jeff, WR, U.S. International, 287
13. *Moss, Ed, RB, Southeast Missouri State, 313
14. Salb, Karl, DT, Kansas, 340
15. Choice to Oakland
16. Linstrom, Brian, QB, Arizona, 391
17. Shelley, John, DB, Oklahoma, 417

CHICAGO BEARS 1972
1. *Antoine, Lionel, T, Southern Illinois [from New York Giants] 3
   *Clemons, Craig, DB, Iowa, 12
2. Choice to Philadelphia
3. *Musso, Johnny, RB, Alabama, 62
4. Choice to Los Angeles Rams
5. *Parsons, Bob, TE, Penn State, 117
6. *Pifferini, Bob Jr., LB, UCLA [from Cincinnati] 133
   Choice to Green Bay
7. Fassel, Jim, QB Long Beach State, 167
   *Osborne, Jim, DT Southern [from Dallas] 182
8. Wirtz, Ralph, WR, North Dakota State, 192
9. *Horton, Larry, DE, Iowa, 219
10. Turnbull, Jack, C, Oregon State, 247
11. Wimberly, Ed, DB, Jackson State, 272
12. Neill, Doug, RB, Texas A&M, 297
13. Rood, Jay, T, South Dakota-Springfield, 322
14. Brown, Bob, WR, Rice, 347
15. *Lawson, Roger, RB, Western Michigan, 377
16. *McKinney, Bill, LB, West Texas State, 402
17. Dickinson, LaVerne, DB, Southern, 427

CINCINNATI 1972
1. *White, Sherman, DE, California, 2
2. *Casanova, Tommy, DB, LSU, 29
3. *LeClair, Jim, LB, North Dakota, 54
4. *Jackson, Bernard, DB, Washington State, 81
5. *DeLeone, Tom, C, Ohio State, 106
6. Choice to Chicago Bears
7. *Conley, Steve, RB, Kansas, 158
8. *Kratzer, Dan, WR, Missouri Valley, 185
9. *Walters, Stan, T, Syracuse, 210
10. Foster, Brian, DB, Colorado, 237
11. Pederson, Kent, TE, Cal-Santa Barbara, 261
12. Wegis, Fredrick, DB, Cal Poly-SLO, 289
13. Hamilton, James, QB, Arkansas State, 314
14. Porter, Steve, WR, Indiana, 341
15. Minnieweather, Hosea, DT, Jackson State, 366
16. Wiegmann, John, WR, Cal Poly-Pomona, 393
17. *Green, David, K, Ohio U., 418

CLEVELAND 1972
1. *Darden, Thom, DB, Michigan, 18
2. *Brooks, Clifford, DB, Tennessee State, 45
   Sims, Lester, DE, Alabama [from Miami] 51
3. Choice to Los Angeles Rams
4. Choice to Kansas City
5. *Hunt, George, K, Tennessee, 122
   Kucera, Greg, RB, Northern Colorado [from Minnesota thru Los Angeles Rams] 128
6. Forey, Leonard, G, Texas A&M, 149
7. Wesley, Don, T, Maryland-Eastern Shore, 174
8. *McKinnis, Hugh, RB, Arizona State, 201
9. McKee, Larry, G, Arizona, 226
   *LeFear, Billy, WR-RB, Henderson State [from Baltimore] 230
10. Mosier, Herschell, DT, Northwestern Oklahoma, 253
11. *Long, Mel, LB, Toledo, 278
12. Chapman, Bernie, DB, Texas-El Paso, 305
13. *Sipe, Brian, QB, San Diego State, 330
14. Stewart, Ed, G, East Central (OK), 357
15. McCullar, Jewel, LB, Cal State-Chico, 382
16. Wakefield, Dick, WR, Ohio State, 409
17. Portz, Bill, DB, Sterling, 434

DALLAS 1972
1. *Thomas, Bill, RB, Boston College, 26
2. *Newhouse, Robert, RB, Houston [from New England Patriots] 35
   *Babinecz, John, LB, Villanova [from New York Jets thru Oakland and New Orleans] 39
   McKee, Charlie, WR, Arizona, 52
3. *Keller, Mike, LB, Michigan [from New England Patriots] 64
   *Bateman, Marv, K, Utah, 78
4. *Kearney, Tim, LB, North Michigan [from Denver thru New Orleans] 83
   *West, Robert, WR, San Diego State [from New England] 90
   Zapiec, Charlie, LB, Penn State [from Detroit] 93
   Choice to Bal thru New Orleans and San Diego
5. Choice to San Diego
6. Bolden, Charles, DB, Iowa, 156
7. Choice to Chicago Bears
8. *Coleman, Ralph, LB, North Carolina A&T, 208
9. Bell, Roy, RB, Oklahoma, 234
10. *Amman, Richard, DE, Florida State, 260
11. Leonard, Lonnie, DE, North Carolina A&T, 286
12. Harris, Jimmy, WR, Ohio State, 312
13. *Fugett, Jean, TE, Amherst, 338
14. Thompson, Alan, RB, Wisconsin, 363
15. Alvarez, Carlos, WR, Florida, 390
16. Longmire, Gordon, QB, Utah, 416
17. Cain, Alfonso, DT, Bethune-Cookman, 442

DENVER 1972
1. *Odoms, Riley, TE, Houston, 5
2. Choice to Los Angeles Rams thru San Diego
3. Phillips, Bill, LB, Arkansas State, 58
4. Choice to Dal thru New Orleans
   *Graham, Tom, LB, Oregon [from Minnesota] 102
5. Choice to Buffalo
   *Krieg, Jim, WR, Washington [from Philadelphia] 118
6. Choice to Houston
7. Choice to Miami
8. Estay, Ronnie, DT-LE, LSU, 186
9. Priester, Floyd, DB, Boston U., 214
10. Wilkins, Richard, DE, Maryland-Eastern Shore, 239
11. *Brunson, Larry, WR, Colorado, 263
12. McDougall, Randy, WR-DB, Weber State, 292
13. Warner, Bob, RB, Bloomsburg, 317
14. Kundich, Jerome, G, Texas-El Paso, 342
15. Parmenter, Harold, DT, Massachusetts, 370
16. Bougus, Tom, RB, Boston College, 395
17. Harris, Lou, RB, USC, 420

DETROIT 1972
1. *Orvis, Herb, DE, Colorado, 16
2. Choice to Atlanta
3. *Sanders, Ken, DE, Howard Payne [from Philadelphia] 65
   Choice to Philadelphia
4. Choice to Dallas
5. Choice to Los Angeles Rams
6. *Potts, Charlie, DB, Purdue, 145
7. Stoudamire, Charles, WR, Portland State, 172
8. *Stuckey, Henry, DB, Missouri, 197
9. McClintock, Bill, DB, Drake, 224
10. *Teal, Jim, LB, Purdue, 249
11. Waldron, Bob, DT, Tulane, 276
12. Bradley, Paul, WR, SMU, 301
13. Kirschner, John, TE, Memphis State, 328
14. Kelly, Eric, T, Whitworth, 353
15. Roach, Steve, LB, Kansas, 380
16. *Jenkins, Leon, DB, West Virginia, 405
17. Tyler, Mike, DB, Rice, 432

GREEN BAY 1972
1. *Buchanon, Willie, DB, San Diego State, 7
   *Tagge, Jerry, QB, Nebraska [from San Diego] 11
2. *Marcol, Chester, K, Hillsdale, 34
3. Choice to Minnesota
4. Patton, Eric, LB, Notre Dame, 86
5. Choice to New Orleans
6. Ross, Nathaniel, DB, Bethune-Cookman, 138
   *Pureifory, Dave, LB, Eastern Michigan [from Chicago Bears] 142
   *Hudson, Robert, RB, Northeastern Oklahoma [from Los Angeles Rams] 147
7. Bushong, Bill, DT, Kentucky, 163
8. *Glass, Leland, WR, Oregon, 190
9. Choice to Baltimore
10. *Wortman, Keith, G, Nebraska, 242
11. Bailey, David, WR, Alabama, 266
12. Rich, Mike, RB, Florida, 294
13. Lakes, Jesse, RB, Central Michigan, 319
14. *Hefner, Larry, LB, Clemson, 346
15. Thone, Rich, WR, Arkansas Tech, 371
16. Burrell, Charles, DT, Arkansas-Pine Bluff, 398
17. Choice to San Diego

HOUSTON 1972
1. *Sampson, Greg, DE, Stanford, 6
2. Choice to New Orleans
3. *Jolley, Lewis, RB, North Carolina, 56
   *Freelon, Solomon, G, Grambling [from Kansas City] 75
4. Choice to St. Louis
5. Choice to Atlanta thru Denver and Buffalo
6. Bullard, Joe, DB, Tulane 134
   Allen, Elmer, LB, Mississippi [from Denver] 136
7. Hutchinson, Eric, DB, Northwestern, 162
8. *Roberts, Guy, LB, Maryland, 187
9. PoSt. Louiser, Willie T, Montana, 212
10. *Dawson, Rhett, WR, Florida State, 240
    Butler Jim, TE, Tulsa [from Miami] 259
11. Evans, Ron, T, Baylor, 264
12. *Rodgers, Willie, RB Kentucky State, 290
13. Roberts, Willie, DB, Houston, 318
14. Crockett, Gary, C, Lamar, 343
15. Choice to Pittsburgh
16. *Murdock, Guy, C, Michigan, 396
17. Cochrane, Kelly, QB, Miami, 421

KANSAS CITY 1972
1. *Kinney, Jeff, RB, Nebraska, 23
2. Choice to New England
3. Choice to Houston
4. *Hamilton, Andy, WR, LSU [from Cleveland] 97
   Choice to New Orleans
5. Davis, Milt, DE, Texas-Arlington, 127
6. Kahler, John, DE, Long Beach State, 153
7. *Carlson, Dean, QB, Iowa State, 179
8. Mahoney, Scott, G, Colorado, 205
9. Taylor, Dave, DT, Weber State, 231
10. Ruppert, Rich, T, Hawaii, 257
11. Walker, Elbert, T, Wisconsin, 283
12. Williams, Mike, DT, Oregon, 309
13. Hellams, Tyler, DB, South Carolina, 335
14. Chaney, Dave, LB, San Jose State, 360
15. *Marshall, Larry, DB, Maryland-Eastern Shore, 387
16. Johnson, Bob, DE, Hanover, 413
17. *Washington, Ted, LB, Mississippi Valley State, 439

LOS ANGELES RAMS 1972
1. Choice to New York Giants thru New England
2. *Bertelsen, Jim, RB, Texas [from Denver thru San Diego] 30
   Choice to Oakland
3. Choice to New York Giants
   *McCutcheon, Lawrence, RB, Colorado State [from Cleveland] 70
4. *Saunders, John, DB, Toledo [from Chicago Bears] 87
   Phillips, Eddie, DB, Texas, 95
5. Childs, Bob, G, Kansas [from Detroit] 120
   Choice to New York Giants thru Washington
   *Christiansen, Bob, TE, UCLA [from Washington] 125
6. Choice to Green Bay
   Herbert, Eddie, DT, Texas Southern [from Washington] 151
7. Choice to Oakland
8. Graham, Tom, WR, Baldwin-Wallace, 199
9. *Howard, Harry, DB, Ohio State, 225
10. *Massey, Jim, DB, Linfield, 251
11. Choice to Oakland
    Schmidt, Albert, RB, Pittsburg State [from Oakland] 280
12. Hoot, Dave, DB, Texas A&M, 303
13. Nunez, Jaime, K, Weber State, 329
14. *Brooks, Larry, T, Virginia State, 355
15. Page, Kenny, LB, Kansas, 381
16. Kirby, Jim, WR, Long Beach State, 407
17. Palmer, Luther, TE, Virginia Union, 433
    McKean, John, C, Oregon [from Oakland] 436

MIAMI 1972
1. *Kadish, Mike, DT, Notre Dame, 25
2. Choice to Cleveland
3. *Kosins, Gary, RB, Dayton, 77
4. *Ball, Larry, DE, Louisville [from San Diego] 91
   Benton, Al, T, Ohio U., 103
5. *Babb, Charlie, DB, Memphis State, 129
6. Nettles, Ray, LB, Tennessee, 155
7. *Adams, Bill, G, Holy Cross [from Denver] 161
   Harrell, Calvin, RB, Arkansas State, 180
8. Curry, Craig, QB, Minnesota, 207
9. Johnson, Greg, DB, Wisconsin, 233
10. Choice to Houston
11. *Jenkins, Ed, WR, Holy Cross, 285
12. Bell, Ashley, TE, Purdue, 311
13. Robinson, Archie, DB, Hillsdale, 337
14. Jones, Willie, LB, Tampa, 362
15. Davis, Bill, DT, William & Mary, 389
16. Hannah, Al, WR, Wisconsin, 415
17. Brown, Vern, DB, Western Michigan, 441

MINNESOTA 1972
1. *Siemon, Jeff, LB, Stanford [from New England] 10
   Choice to New York Giants
2. *Marinaro, Ed, RB, Cornell, 50
3. *Buetow, Bart, T, Minnesota [from Green Bay] 59
   Choice to Philadelphia
4. Choice to Denver
5. Choice to Cleveland thru Los Angeles Rams
6. *Martin, Amos, LB, Louisville, 154
7. Slater, Bill, DE, Western Michigan, 181
8. *Demery, Calvin, WR, Arizona State, 206
9. *Goodrum, Charles, G, Florida A&M, 232
10. Aldridge, Willie, RB-DB, South Carolina State, 258
11. McKelton, Willie, DB, Southern, 284
12. Banaugh, Bob, DB, Montana State, 310
13. Roberts, Franklin, RB, Alcorn State, 336
14. *Owens, Marv, WR-RB, San Diego State, 361
15. Sivert, Mike, G, East Tennessee State, 388
16. *Graff, Neil, QB, Wisconsin, 414
17. Schmalz, Dick, WR, Auburn, 440

NEW ENGLAND 1972
1. Choice to Minnesota
2. Choice to Dallas
   *Reynolds, Tom, WR, San Diego State [from Kansas City] 49
3. Choice to Dallas
   *White, Jim, DE, Colorado State [from Washington thru Los Angeles Rams] 73
4. Choice to Dallas
5. Choice to Baltimore
   *Bolton, Ron, DB, Norfolk State [from Oakland] 124
6. Choice to Atlanta thru New York Giants
7. *Hoss, Clark, TE, Oregon State, 165
   *Tarver, John, RB, Colorado [from San Diego] 186
8. Beyrle, Steve, G, Kansas State, 195
9. Kelson, Mike, T, Arkansas, 220
10. Caraway, Mel, DB, Northwestern Oklahoma, 245
11. Cason, Rodney, T, Angelo State, 269
12. Booras, Steve, DE, Mesa J.C., 296
13. Elmore, Sam, DB, Eastern Michigan, 325
14. Rideout, Eddie, WR, Boston College, 350
15. Klimek, Joel, TE, Pittsburgh, 375
16. Dahl, Eric, DB, San Jose State, 400
17. Ah You, Junior, LB, Arizona State, 425

NEW ORLEANS 1972
1. *Smith, Royce, G, Georgia, 8
2. *Hall, Willie, LB, USC [from Houston] 31
   Choice to Oakland
3. *Kuziel, Bob, C, Pittsburgh, 60
   *Myers, Tommy, DB, Syracuse [from Baltimore thru Oakland] 74
4. *Crangle, Mike, DE, Tennessee-Martin, 85
   *Federspiel, Joe, LB, Kentucky [from Washington thru Los Angeles Rams and Philadelphia] 99
   Coleman, Mike, DE, Knoxville [from Kansas City] 101
5. *Butler, Bill, RB, Kansas State [from Green Bay] 111
   *Johnson, Carl, T, Nebraska, 112
   Davies, Bob, DB, South Carolina [from Baltimore] 126
6. Dorton, Wayne, G, Arkansas State, 137
   Watson, Curt, RB, Tennessee [from Oakland] 150
7. *Jackson, Ernie, DB, Duke, 164
8. Vinson, Ron, WR, Abilene Christian, 189
9. *Branstetter, Kent, DT, Houston, 216
10. Kupp, Andy, G, Idaho, 241
11. Dongieux, Paul, LB, Mississippi, 267
12. Lockhart, Steve, TE, Arkansas State, 293
13. *Weatherspoon, Cephus, WR, Ft. Lewis, 320
14. Barrios, Steve, WR, Tulane, 345
15. Lachaussee, Rusty, QB, Tulane, 372
16. Balthrop, Joe, G, Tennessee, 397
17. Graham, Dick, R, Oklahoma State, 424

NEW YORK GIANTS 1972
1. Choice to Chicago Bears
   *Small, Eldridge, DB, Texas A&I, from Los Angeles Rams thru New England Patriots] 17
   *Jacobson, Larry, DE, Nebraska [from Minnesota] 24
2. Choice to San Francisco
3. *Mendenhall, John, T, Grambling, 55
   Mozisek, Tommy, RB, Houston [from Los Angeles Rams] 69
4. Choice to Pittsburgh
5. *Gatewood, Tom, WR, Notre Dame, 107
   Edwards, Larry, LB, Texas A&I [from Los Angeles Rams thru Washington] 121
6. *Hill, John, C, Lehigh, 132
7. Choice to Pittsburgh
   Zikas, Mike, DT, Notre Dame [from Washington] 177
8. Mabry, Tom, T, Arkansas, 184
9. Richardson, Ed, RB, Southern, 211
10. Odom, John, DB, Texas Tech, 236
11. Robertson, John, DB, Kansas State, 262
12. Anderson, Jay, DT, Mayville, 288
13. Heard, Chuck, DE, Georgia, 315
14. Evans, James, LB, South Carolina State, 339
15. Kavanaugh, Ken, TE, LSU, 367
16. Greyer, Neova, DB, Wisconsin, 392
17. Seyferth, Fritz, RB, Michigan, 419

NEW YORK JETS 1972
1. *Barkum, Jerome, WR, Jackson State, 9
   *Taylor, Mike, LB, Michigan [from Washington] 20
2. Choice to Dallas thru New Orleans and Oakland

3. *Hammond, Gary, WR, SMU, 66
4. *Galigher, Ed, DE, UCLA, 89
5. Harris, Dick, DB, South Carolina, 114
6. *Jackson, Joe, DE, New Mexico State, 139
7. Choice to Baltimore thru Washington
8. Latimore, Marion, G, Kansas State, 194
9. Ford, Jeff, DB, Georgia Tech, 218
10. *Turner, Harley, DB, Tennessee-Chattanooga, 244
11. Stevenson, Robert, LB, Tennessee State, 268
12. *Bjorklund, Hank, RB, Princeton, 299
13. Sullivan, Steve, T, North Texas State, 324
14. Age, Louis, G, Southwestern Louisiana, 349
15. Sullivan, Phil, DB, Georgia, 374
16. Kipfmiller, Gary, C, Nebraska-Omaha, 399
17. Gamble, Ken, P, Fayetteville, 429

OAKLAND 1972
1. *Siani, Mike, WR, Villanova, 21
2. *Korver, Kelvin, T, Northwestern (IA) [from New Orleans] 33
   Choice to Baltimore
   *Vella, John, T, USC [from Los Angeles Rams] 43
3. *Lunsford, Mel, DT, Central State (OH), 72
4. *Branch, Cliff, WR, Colorado, 98
   *Dalby, Dave, C, UCLA [from Baltimore] 100
5. Choice to New England
6. *Medlin, Dan, DT, North Carolina State [from Buffalo] 131
   Choice to New Orleans
7. Jamieson, Ray, RB, Memphis State [from Los Angeles Rams] 173
   *Thomas, Alonzo (Skip), DB, USC, 176
   Pete, Dennis, DB, Cal State-San Francisco [from Baltimore] 178
8. Brown, Jackie, RB, Stanford, 202
9. Bigler, Dave, RB, Morningside, 228
10. Price, Phillip, DB, Idaho State, 254
11. *Carroll, Joe, LB, Pittsburgh [from Los Angeles Rams] 277
    Choice to Los Angeles Rams
12. *Gaydos, Kent, TE, Florida State, 306
13. Covington, Ted, WR, Cal State-Northridge, 333
14. *Cambal, Dennis, RB, William & Mary, 358
15. Hester, Charles, RB, Central State (OH) [from Buffalo] 364
    Snesrud, Dave, LB, Hamline, 384
16. Wright, Willie, TE, North Carolina A&T, 410
17. Choice to Los Angeles Rams

PHILADELPHIA 1972
1. *Reaves, John, QB, Florida, 14
2. Yochum, Dan, T, Syracuse [from Chicago Bears] 37
   Choice to Atlanta thru Detroit
3. Choice to Detroit
   *Luken, Tom, G, Purdue [from Detroit] 68
   *Majors, Bobby, DB, Tennessee [from Minnesota] 76
4. *James, Ron (Po), RB, New Mexico State, 92
5. Choice to Denver
6. *Winfield, Vern, G, Minnesota, 144
7. *Foster, Will, LB, Eastern Michigan, 170
8. Ratcliff, Larry, RB, Eastern Michigan, 196
9. *Gibbs, Pat, DB, Lamar, 222
10. *Bunting, John, LB, North Carolina, 248
11. Sweeney, Dennis, DE, Western Michigan, 274
12. *Zimmerman, Don, WR, Northeast Louisiana, 300
13. Carpenter, Preston, DE, Mississippi, 326
14. *Overmyer, Bill, LB, Ashland, 352
15. *Sullivan, Tom, RB, Miami, 378
16. Bielenberg, Steve, LB, Oregon State, 404
17. Nash, Tom, T, Georgia, 430

PITTSBURGH 1972
1. *Harris, Franco, RB, Penn State, 13
2. *Gravelle, Gordon, T, BYU, 38
3. *McMakin, John, TE, Clemson, 63
4. Brinkley, Lorenzo, DB, Missouri [from New York Giants] 80
   *Bradley, Ed, LB, Wake Forest, 88
5. *Furness, Steve, DE, Rhode Island, 113
6. *Meyer, Dennis, DE, Arkansas State, 143
7. Colquitt, Joe DE, Kansas State [from New York Giants] 159
   Kelly, Robert, DB, Jackson State, 168
8. Vincent, Stahle, RB, Rice, 193
9. Kelley, Don, DB, Clemson, 217
10. Brown, Bob, DT, Tampa, 243
11. *Gilliam, Joe, QB, Tennessee State, 273
12. Curl, Ron, T, Michigan State, 298
13. Messmer, Ernie, T, Villanova, 323
14. Durrance, Tommy, RB, Florida, 348
15. Hulecki, John, G, Massachusetts [from Houston] 368
    Harrington, Charles, G, Wichita State, 373
16. *Hawkins, Nate, WR, Nevada-Las Vegas, 403
17. Linehan, Ron, LB, Idaho, 428

ST. LOUIS 1972
1. *Moore, Bobby, (Ahmad Rashad), RB-WR, Oregon, 4
2. *Arneson, Mark, LB, Arizona, 32
3. *Beckman, Tom, DE, Michigan, 57
4. *Lyman, Jeff, LB, BYU, 82
   *Imhof, Martin, DT, San Diego State [from Houston] 84
5. *Dobler, Conrad, G, Wyoming, 110
6. *Heater, Don, RB, Montana Tech, 135
7. *Rudolph, Council, DE, Kentucky State, 160
8. *Wicks, Bob, WR, Utah State, 188
9. Macken, Gene, C, South Dakota, 213
10. *Washington, Eric, DB, Texas-El Paso, 238
    Franks, Mike, QB, Eastern New Mexico [from Atlanta] 250
11. Jones, Ron, LB, Arkansas, 265
12. Gay, Tommy, DT, Arkansas-Pine Bluff, 291
13. Campana, Tom, DB, Ohio State, 316
14. McTeer, Pat, K, New Mexico State, 344
15. Herman, Mark, TE, Yankton, 369
16. Alford, Henry, DE, Pittsburgh, 394
17. *Carter, Kent, LB, USC, 422

SAN DIEGO 1972
1. Choice to Green Bay
2. *Lazetich, Pete, DE, Stanford, 36
3. *McClard, Bill, K, Arkansas, 61
4. Choice to Miami
5. Bishop, Jim, TE, Tennessee Tech, 116
   Gooden, Harry, DE, Alcorn State [from Dallas] 130
6. Ward, Bruce, G, San Diego State, 141
7. Choice to New England
8. Choice to Baltimore
9. Schmitz, Fran, DT, St. Norbert, 221
10. Kolstad, Lon, LB, Wisconsin-Whitewater, 246
11. Turner, John, TE, Long Beach State, 270
12. Key, Sam, LB, Elon 295
13. *Selfridge, Andy, LB, Virginia, 321
14. Van Reenen, John, DE, Washington State, 351
15. Neugent, Charles, DB, Tuskegee, 376
16. Shaw, James, DB, Tulsa, 401
17. *Dragon, Oscar, RB, Arizona State [from Green Bay] 423
    Tackett, Bob, T, Texas-El Paso, 426

SAN FRANCISCO 1972
1. *Beasley, Terry, WR, Auburn, 19
2. *McGill, Ralph, RB, Tulsa [from New York Giants] 28
   *Barrett, Jean, T, Tulsa, 44
3. *Dunbar, Allen, WR, Southern, 71
4. *Hall, Windlan, DB, Arizona State, 96
5. Greene, Mike, LB, Georgia, 123
6. Walker, Jackie, DB, Tennessee, 148
7. *Hardy, Edgar, G, Jackson State, 175
8. *Wittum, Tom, K, Northern Illinois, 200
9. Brown, Jerry, DB, Northwestern, 227
10. *Williams, Steve, DT, Western Carolina, 252
11. Laputka, Tom, DE, Southern Illinois, 279
12. Setzler, Steve, DE, St. John's (MN), 304
13. Pettigrew, Leon, T, Cal State-Northridge, 331
14. Guthrie, Eric, QB, Boise State, 356
15. Maddox, Bob, DE, Frostburg State, 383
16. *Davis, Ron, G, Virginia State, 408
17. Alexander, Ted, RB, Langston, 435

WASHINGTON 1972
1. Choice to New York Jets
2. Choice to Baltimore
3. Choice to New England thru Los Angeles Rams
4. Choice to New Orleans thru Los Angeles Rams and Philadelphia
5. Choice to Los Angeles Rams
6. Choice to Los Angeles Rams
7. Choice to New York Giants
8. *Denson, Moses, RB, Maryland-Eastern Shore, 203
9. Boekholder, Steve, DE, Drake, 229
10. Oldham, Mike, WR, Michigan, 255
11. Welch, Jeff, DB, Arkansas Tech, 281
12. Bunce, Don, QB, Stanford, 307
13. *Grant, Frank, WR, Southern Colorado, 332
14. O'Quinn, Mike, G, McNeese State, 365
15. Taibi, Carl, DE, Colorado, 385
16. Higginbotham, Steve, DB, Alabama, 411
17. Clemente, Kevin, LB, Boston College, 437

1973

Held January 30-31, 1973

ATLANTA 1973
1. Choice to Houston
2. *Marx, Greg, DT, Notre Dame, 39
3. Choice to San Diego thru Oakland
4. Choice to Detroit
   *Geredine, Tom, WR, Northeast Missouri State [from New York Giants] 94
5. Choice to Washington
6. *Bebout, Nick, T, Wyoming, 142
7. *Campbell, George, DB, Iowa State, 170
8. Reed, Tom, G, Arkansas, 195
9. Ingram, Russell, C, Texas Tech, 220
10. *Mike-Mayer, Nick, K, Temple, 248
11. Buelow, Byron, DB, Wisconsin-LaCrosse, 273
12. Samples, Mike, LB, Drake, 298
13. Stecher, Chris, T, Claremont-Mudd-Scripps, 326
14. Madeya, John, QB, Louisville, 351
15. Gage, Thomas, DB, Lamar, 376
16. Ferguson, Rufus, RB, Wisconsin, 404
17. Hodge, Jim, WR, Arkansas, 428

BALTIMORE 1973
1. *Jones, Bert, QB, LSU [from New Orleans] 2
   *Ehrmann, Joe, DT, Syracuse, 10
2. *Barnes, Mike, DE, Miami, 35
3. *Olds, Bill, RB, Nebraska [from Denver thru Houston] 61
   Rotella, Jamie, LB, Tennessee, 62
4. *Palmer, Gery, T, Kansas [from Chicago Bears thru Philadelphia] 83
   *Smith, Ollie, WR, Tennessee State [from San Diego] 85
   Choice to New Orleans
5. *Taylor, David, G, Catawba, 114
6. Choice to Min thru New Orleans
7. Choice to Denver
8. *Oldham, Ray, DB, Middle Tennessee State [from San Diego] 189
   *Windauer, Bill, G, Iowa, 191
9. Choice to Washington
10. Choice to New York Jets
11. *Neal, Dan, C, Kentucky, 270
12. Thomas, Bernard, DE, Western Michigan, 295
13. Pierantozzi, Tom, QB, West Chester, 322
14. Williams, Ed, RB, West Virginia, 347
15. Brown, Jackie, DB, South Carolina, 374
16. Januszkiewicz, Marty, RB, Syracuse, 399
17. Falkenhagen, Guy, T, Northern Michigan, 426

BUFFALO 1973
1. *Seymour, Paul, T, Michigan, 7
   *DeLamielleure, Joe, G, Michigan State [from Miami] 26
2. *Winans, Jeff, DT, USC, 32
3. *Ferguson, Joe, QB, Arkansas, 57
   *Kampa, Bob, DT, California [from Washington] 77
4. *Walker, Don, DB, Central State (OH), 87
   *Yeates, Jeff, DT, Boston College [from Washington] 103
5. *Francis, Wallace, WR, Arkansas-Pine Bluff [from San Diego] 110
   Choice to Miami
6. *Skorupan, John, LB, Penn State, 136
7. *McConnell, Brian, LB, Michigan State, 162
   Ford, John, TE, Henderson State [from Washington] 181
8. Fobbs, Lee, RB, Grambling, 190
9. *Reppond, Mike, WR, Arkansas, 215
10. Reed, Matthew, QB, Grambling, 240
    LeHeup, John, LB, South Carolina [from Washington] 259
11. Earl, Richard, T, Tennessee, 265
12. *Carroll, Ron, DT, Sam Houston State, 294
13. Choice to Denver
14. *Krakau, Merv, LB, Iowa State, 344
15. *Rizzo, Joe, LB, Merchant Marine, 369
    O'Neil, Vince, RB, Kansas [from Kansas City] 379
16. Choice to Denver
17. Stearns, John (Bad Dude), DB, Colorado, 423

CHICAGO BEARS 1973
1. *Chambers, Wally, DE, Eastern Kentucky, 8
2. *Huff, Gary, QB, Florida State, 33
   *Hrivnak, Gary, DT, Purdue [from Dallas] 48
3. Choice to Detroit
4. Choice to Baltimore thru Philadelphia
5. *Ellis, Allan, DB, UCLA [from Philadelphia] 107
   Choice to San Francisco
6. Creaney, Mike, C, Notre Dame, 138
7. Choice to Los Angeles Rams
8. Graham, Conrad, DB, Tennessee, 187
9. Deutsch, Mike, RB, North Dakota, 216
10. Barry, Bill, WR, Mississippi, 241
11. Seigler, Ed, K, Clemson, 266
12. Griffin, Mike, G, Arkansas, 291
13. Cieszkowski, John, RB, Notre Dame, 320
14. *Juenger, Dave, WR, Ohio U., 345
15. *Rives, Don, LB, Texas Tech, 370
16. Hart, Bill, C, Michigan, 395
17. Roach, Larry, DB, Oklahoma, 424

CINCINNATI 1973
1. *Curtis, Isaac, WR, San Diego State, 15
2. *Chandler, Al, TE, Oklahoma, 43
3. *George, Tim, WR, Carson-Newman, 68
4. Choice to Cleveland thru Baltimore
5. *McCall, Bob, RB, Arizona, 121
6. *Jones, Bob, DB, Virginia Union, 146
7. *Maddox, Robert, DE, Frostburg, 171
8. *Wilson, Joe, RB, Holy Cross, 199
9. Dampeer, John, G, Notre Dame, 224
10. *Elliott, Lenvil, RB, Northeast Missouri State, 249
11. Montgomery, William, DB, Morehouse, 277
12. *Clark, Boobie, RB, Bethune-Cookman, 302
13. West, Brooks, DT, Texas-El Paso, 327
14. *Scales, Hurles, DB, North Texas State, 355
15. McNulty, Ted, QB, Indiana, 380
16. Unger, Harry, RB, Auburn, 405
17. Estabrook, Wayne, QB, Whittier, 433

CLEVELAND 1973
1. *Holden, Steve, WR, Arizona State [from New York Giants] 16
   *Adams, Pete, T, USC, 22
2. *Pruitt, Greg, RB, Oklahoma [from New England Patriots thru New York Giants] 30
   *Stienke, Jim, DB, Southwest Texas State, 47
3. *Crum, Bob, DE, Arizona [from Kansas City thru Baltimore] 67
4. *Dorris, Andy, LB, New Mexico State [from Cincinnati thru Baltimore] 93
   Mattingly, Randy, QB, Evansville, 100
5. Choice to San Diego
6. *Green, Van, DB, Shaw, 150
7. Choice to Miami
8. Choice to Detroit
9. Wester, Curtis, G, East Texas State, 228
10. *Humphrey, Tom, T, Abilene Christian, 256
11. *Barisich, Carl, DT, Princeton, 281
12. Simmons, Stan, TE, Lewis & Clark, 306
13. *Romaniszyn, Jim, RB, Edinboro, 334
14. Popelka, Robert, DB, SMU, 359
15. *Sullivan, Dave, WR, Virginia, 384
16. Greenfield, George, RB, Murray State, 412
17. McClowry, Robert, C, Michigan State, 437

DALLAS 1973
1. *Dupree, Billy Joe, TE, Michigan State, 20
2. *Richards, Golden, WR, Hawaii [from Green Bay] 46
   Choice to Chicago Bears
3. *Martin, Harvey Banks, DE, East Texas State [from Houston thru New Orleans] 53
   Choice to New England
4. Scrivener, Drane, DB, Tulsa, 98
5. *Walton, Bruce, T, UCLA, 126
6. Leyen, Bob, G, Yale, 151
7. *Barnes, Rodrigo, LB, Rice, 176
8. Werner, Dan, QB, Michigan State, 204
9. White, Mike, DB, Minnesota, 229
10. Johnson, Carl, LB, Tennessee, 254
11. Caswell, Gerald, G, Colorado State, 282
12. *Arneson, Jim, G, Arizona, 307
13. Smith, John, WR, UCLA, 332
14. Thornton, Bob, G, North Carolina, 360
15. Baisy, Walt, LB, Grambling, 385
16. Conley, John, TE, Hawaii, 410
17. *Strayhorn, Les, RB, East Carolina, 438

DENVER 1973
1. *Armstrong, Otis, RB, Purdue, 9
2. *Chavous, Barney, DE, South Carolina State, 36
3. *Howard, Paul, G, BYU [from New Orleans thru Washington and Cleveland] 54
   Choice to Baltimore thru Houston
   *Wood, John, DT, LSU [from San Francisco thru Washington and San Diego] 70
4. *Jackson, Tom, LB, Louisville, 88
5. McTorry, Charles, DB, Tennessee State, 113
6. Choice to Pittsburgh
7. *Askea, Mike, T, Stanford, 165
   *Grant, John, DE, USC [from Baltimore] 166
8. Choice to Pittsburgh
9. *Blackwood, Lyle, DB, TCU, 217
10. *Marshall, Al, WR, Boise State, 244
11. Brown, Elton, DE, Utah State, 269
12. *O'Malley, Jim, LB, Notre Dame, 296
13. *Smith, Ed, DE, Colorado College [from Buffalo] 319
    White, Ed, RB, Tulsa, 321
14. *Hufnagel, John, QB, Penn State, 348
15. *Jones, Calvin, DB, Washington, 373
16. *Ross, Oliver, RB, Alabama A&M [from Buffalo] 398
    Muhlbeier, Ken, C, Idaho, 200
17. Morgan, Kenneth, TE, Elon, 425

DETROIT 1973
1. *Price, Ernie, DE, Texas A&I, 17
2. *Crosswhite, Leon, RB, Oklahoma, 44
3. Brady, John, TE, Washington [from Chicago Bears] 58
   *Laslavic, Jim, LB, Penn State, 71
   *Johnson, Levi, DB, Texas A&I [from Oakland thru Los Angeles Rams] 75
4. *Hennigan, Mike, LB, Tennessee Tech [from New Orleans] 81
   *Jauron, Dick, RB, Yale [from Atlanta] 91
   *Hooks, Jim, RB, Central State (OK), 96
5. Choice to San Diego thru Washington
6. Choice to St. Louis
7. *Andrews, John, DT, Morgan State, 175
8. *McCray, Prentice, DB, Arizona State, 200
   Bledsoe, John, RB, Ohio State [from Cleveland] 203
9. Dean, Ira, DB, Baylor, 227
10. Bonner, Ray, DB, Middle Tennessee State, 252
11. Freeman, Scott, WR, Wyoming, 279
12. Scott, Tom, WR, Washington, 304
13. Moss, John, LB, Pittsburgh, 331
14. Corey, Jay, T, Santa Clara, 356
15. Hansen, Dan, DB, BYU, 383
16. Nickels, Larry, WR, Dayton, 408
17. Belgrave, Earl, T, Ohio State, 435

GREEN BAY 1973
1. *Smith, Barry, WR, Florida State, 21
2. Choice to Dallas
3. *MacLeod, Tom, LB, Minnesota, 74
4. Choice to Los Angeles Rams
5. Choice to Oakland
6. *Toner, Tom, LB, Idaho State, 152
7. Muller, John, T, Iowa, 177
8. *Austin, Hise, DB, Prairie View A&M, 202
9. Brown, Rick, LB, South Carolina, 230
10. Allen, Larry, LB, Illinois, 255
11. Engle, Phil, DT, South Dakota State, 280
12. *McCarren, Larry, C, Illinois, 308
13. Alderson, Tim, DB, Minnesota, 333
14. Anderson, James, DT, Northwestern, 358
15. Echols, Reggie, WR, UCLA, 386
16. Pretty, Keith, TE, Western Michigan, 411
17. Sampson, Harold, DT, Southern, 436

HOUSTON 1973
1. *Matuszak, John, DE, Tampa, 1
   *Amundson, George, RB, Iowa State [from Atlanta] 14
2. Choice to Kansas City
3. Choice to Dallas thru New Orleans
4. *Bingham, Gregg, LB, Purdue, 79
5. Garrison, Edesel, WR, USC, 105

6. *Mayo, Ron, TE, Morgan State, 131
7. *Jordan, Shelby, T, Washington, (St. Louis), 157
8. *Blahak, Joe, DB, Nebraska, 183
9. Williams, Mark, K-P, Rice, 209
10. Vaughn, Darrell, DT, Northern Colorado, 235
11. *Eaglin, Lawrence, DB, Stephen F. Austin, 261
12. Lyman, Brad, WR, UCLA, 287
13. Martin, Willie, G, Northeastern Oklahoma, 313
14. *Lou, Ron, C, Arizona State, 339
15. Goree, Roger, LB, Baylor, 365
16. Dameron, Tim, WR, East Carolina, 390
17. Braband, Randy, LB, Texas, 417

KANSAS CITY 1973
1. Choice to Detroit thru Chicago Bears
2. *Butler, Gary, TE, Rice [from Houston] 27
   Choice to Los Angeles Rams
3. Choice to Cleveland thru Baltimore
   Krause, Paul, T, Central Michigan [from Cleveland] 72
4. *Lohmeyer, John, DE, Emporia State [from Minnesota] 89
   Choice to Los Angeles Rams
5. Grambau, Fred, DE, Michigan, 120
6. *Jones, Doug, DB, Cal State-Northridge, 145
7. Smith, Donn, T, Purdue, 173
8. *Palewicz, Al, LB, Miami, 197
9. *Story, Bill, DT, Southern Illinois, 223
10. *Osley, Willie, DB, Illinois, 251
11. *Eley, Monroe, RB, Arizona State, 276 +
12. Ramsey, Tom, DT, Northern Arizona, 301
13. Metallo, Paul, DB, Massachusetts, 329
14. White, Albert, WR, Fort Valley State, 354
15. Choice to Buffalo
16. Grooms, Wilbur, LB, Tampa, 407
17. Korver, Clayton, TE, SMU, 431

LOS ANGELES RAMS 1973
1. Choice to New England
2. *Bryant, Cullen, DB, Colorado [from San Diego] 31
   *Jaworski, Ron, QB, Youngstown State, 37
   *Youngblood, Jim, LB, Tennessee Tech [from Kansas City] 42
3. *Stokes, Tim, T, Oregon [from San Diego] 60
   Choice to St. Louis
4. Choice to Oakland
   *McMillan, Eddie, DB, Florida State [from Kansas City] 95
   *Nelson, Terry, TE, Arkansas-Pine Bluff [from Green Bay] 99
5. *Jones, Steve, RB, Duke, 115
   *Jones, Cody, DE, San Jose State [from Washington] 129
6. *Peterson, Jim, DE, San Diego State [from New Orleans thru Washington] 133
   Caldwell, Jason, WR, North Carolina Central, 141
7. Brown, Steve, LB, Oregon State [from Chicago Bears] 161
   *DuLac, Bill, G, Eastern Michigan, 167
8. Choice to Washington
9. *Nicholson, Jim, T, Michigan State, 219
10. Choice to Washington
11. *Inmon, Jeff, RB, North Carolina Central, 271
    Jackson, Willie, WR, Florida [from Washington] 285
12. Storck, Robert, DT, Wisconsin, 297
13. Milburn, Rod, WR, Southern, 323
    Spearman, Clint, LB, Michigan [from Oakland] 335
14. Rhone, Walter, DB, Central State (MO), 349
15. Bond, Jerry, DB, Weber State, 375
    Matter, Kurt, DE, Washington [from Washington] 393
16. Cherry, Fuller, DB, Arkansas-Monticello, 401
17. Henry, Fred, RB, New Mexico, 427

MIAMI 1973
1. Choice to Buffalo
2. *Bradley, Chuck, C, Oregon, 52
3. *Gray, Leon, T, Jackson State, 78
4. *Rather, Bo, WR, Michigan, 104
5. *Strock, Don, QB, Virginia Tech [from Buffalo] 111
   *McCurry, Dave, DB, Iowa State, 130
6. *Newman, Ed, G, Duke, 156
7. *Reilly, Kevin, LB, Villanova [from New England] 160
   Shepherd, Benny, RB, Arkansas Tech [from San Diego] 163
   Hatter, Willie, WR, Northern Illinois [from Cleveland] 178
   *Smith, Tom, RB, Miami, 182
8. Pearmon, Archie, DE, Northeastern Oklahoma, 208
9. *Lorch, Karl, DE, USC, 234
10. *Fernandes, Ron, DE, Eastern Michigan, 260
11. Kete, Chris, C, Boston College, 286
12. Mullen, Mike, LB, Tulane, 312
13. Booker, Joe, RB, Miami (OH), 338
14. *Boyd, Greg, RB, Arizona, 364
15. Palmer, Bill, TE, St. Thomas (MN), 389
16. Jackson, James, DE, Norfolk State, 416
17. *Wade, Charlie, WR, Tennessee State, 442

MINNESOTA 1973
1. *Foreman, Chuck, RB, Miami, 12
2. *Wallace, Jackie, DB, Arizona [from St. Louis] 34
   Choice to New York Giants
3. *Lash, Jim, WR, Northwestern, 65
4. *Wells, Mike, QB, Illinois [from Philadelphia] 80
   Choice to Kansas City
5. *McClanahan, Brent, RB, Arizona State, 118
6. *Kingsriter, Doug, TE, Minnesota [from Baltimore thru New Orleans] 139
   Abbott, Fred, LB, Florida, 143
7. Brown, Josh, RB, Southwest Texas State, 168
8. Darling, Craig, T, Iowa, 196
9. Dibbles, Larry, DE, New Mexico, 221
10. Lee, Randy, DB-P, Tulane [from Philadelphia] 236
    *Mason, Dave, DB, Nebraska, 246
11. Murdock, Geary, G, Iowa State, 274
12. Spencer, Alan, WR, Pittsburg State (KS), 299
13. Just, Ron, G, Minot Slate, 324
14. Bishop, Eddie, DB, Southern, 352 +
15. Chandler, Tony, RB, Missouri Valley, 377
16. Smiley, Larry, DE, Texas Southern, 402
17. Winfield, Dave, TE, Minnesota, 429

NEW ENGLAND 1973
1. *Hannah, John, G, Alabama, 4
   *Cunningham, Sam, RB, USC [from Los Angeles Rams] 11
   *Stingley, Darryl, WR, Purdue [from Chicago Bears] 19
2. Choice to Cleveland thru New York Giants
3. *Dusek, Brad, DB, Texas A&M, 56
   Davis, Charles, RB, Alcorn State [from Dallas] 73
4. *Gallagher, Allen, T, USC, 82
5. *Dumler, Doug, C, Nebraska, 108
6. Choice to New Orleans
7. Choice to Miami
8. Brown, Isaac, RB, Western Kentucky, 186
9. Callaway, David, T, Texas A&M, 212
10. Ruster, Dan, DB, Oklahoma, 238
11. May, Homer, TE, Texas A&M, 264
12. *Barnes, Bruce, P, UCLA, 290
13. Lowry, Alan, DB, Texas, 316
14. *Hamilton, Ray (Sugar Bear), LB, Oklahoma, 342
15. Pugh, Condie, RB, Norfolk State, 368
16. Kutter, Mike, DE, Concordia, 394
17. McAshan, Eddie, QB-DB, Georgia Tech, 420

NEW ORLEANS 1973
1. Choice to Baltimore
2. *Moore, Derland, DE, Oklahoma, 29
   *Baumgartner, Steve, DE, Purdue [from Washington thru New York Jets] 51
3. Choice to Denver thru Washington and Cleveland
   *Van Valkenburg, Pete, RB, BYU [from New York Jets] 66
4. Choice to Detroit
   *Merlo, Jim, LB, Stanford [from Baltimore] 86
5. Choice to Pittsburgh thru Denver
6. Choice to Los Angeles Rams thru Washington
   Shuford, Marty, RB, Arizona [from New England] 134
7. *Cahill, Bill, DB, Washington, 158
8. Peterson, Bob, G, Utah, 185
   *Winslow, Charles, WR, Drake [from Washington] 207
9. *Fink, Mike, DB, Missouri, 210
10. Horsley, Jeff, RB, North Carolina Central, 237
11. Owens, James, RB, Auburn, 262
12. Orndorff, Paul, RB, Tampa, 289
13. Watkins, Richard, DT, Weber State, 314
14. *Fersen, Paul, T, Georgia, 341
15. Evenson, Mike, C, North Dakota State, 366
16. *Stevens, Howard, RB, Louisville, 392
17. Garner, Bobby, TE, Winston-Salem, 418

NEW YORK GIANTS 1973
1. Choice to Cleveland
2. *Van Pelt, Brad, LB, Michigan State [from Minnesota] 40
   Choice to San Francisco
3. *Glover, Rich, DT, Nebraska, 69
4. Choice to Atlanta
5. *McQuay, Leon, RB, Tampa, 119
6. Brantley, Wade, DT, Troy State, 147
7. Freeman, Rod, TE, Vanderbilt, 172
8. *Hasenohrl, George, DT, Ohio State, 198
9. Paine, Ty, QB, Washington State, 225
10. *Love, Walter, DB, Westminster (UT), 250
11. Wideman, William, DT, North Carolina A&T, 275
12. *Lumpkin, Ron, DB, Arizona State, 303
13. Davis, Clifton, RB, Alcorn State, 328
14. *Kelley, Brian, LB, California Lutheran, 353
15. *Schaukowitch, Carl, G, Penn State, 381
16. Nitka, Ben, K, Colorado College, 406
17. Billizon, John, DE, Grambling, 430

NEW YORK JETS 1973
1. *Owens, Burgess, DB, Miami, 13
2. *Woods, Robert, T, Tennessee State, 38
3. Choice to New Orleans
4. *Ferguson, Bill, LB, San Diego State, 90
5. *Bannon, Bruce, LB, Penn State, 116
6. *Roach, Travis, G, Texas, 144
   *Harrell, Rick, C, Clemson [from Washington] 155
7. Haggard, Mike, WR, South Carolina, 169
8. Seifert, Rick, DB, Ohio State, 194
9. *Spicer, Robin, LB, Indiana, 222
10. Carbone, Joe, LB, Delaware [from Baltimore] 243
    Krempin, James, T, Texas A&I, 247
11. *Knight, David, WR, William & Mary, 272
12. *Puetz, Garry, T, Valparaiso, 300
13. Parrish, Robert, DT, Duke, 325
14. Schwartz, Joe, RB, Toledo, 350
15. Williams, Mahlon, TE, North Carolina Central, 378
16. Cerwinski, John, T, Bowling Green, 403
17. *Foote, Jim, P, Delaware Valley, 432

OAKLAND 1973
1. *Guy, Ray, K-P, Southern Mississippi, 23
2. *Johnson, Monte, DT, Nebraska, 49
3. Choice to Det thru Los Angeles Rams
4. *Smith, Perry, DB, Colorado State [from Los Angeles Rams] 92
   Wylie, Joe, WR, Oklahoma, 101
5. *Neal, Louis, WR, Prairie View A&M [from Green Bay] 124
   *Mikolajczyk, Ron, T, Tampa, 127
6. Myers, Brent, T, Purdue, 153
7. *Weaver, Gary, LB, Fresno State, 179
8. *Rae, Mike, QB, USC, 205
9. *Sweeney, Steve, TE, California, 231
10. Allen, Leo, RB, Tuskegee, 257
11. List, Jerry, RB, Nebraska, 283
12. Krapf, Jim, G-LB, Alabama, 309
13. Choice to Los Angeles Rams
14. Polen, Bruce, DB, William Penn, 361
15. Leffers, Dave, C, Vanderbilt, 387
16. Gadlin, Jerry, WR, Wyoming, 413
17. Ryan, Mike, G, USC, 439

PHILADELPHIA 1973
1. *Sisemore, Jerry, T, Texas, 3
   *Young, Charle, TE, USC [from San Diego] 6
2. *Morriss, Guy, G TCU, 28
3. *Logan, Randy, DB, Michigan, 55
4. Choice to Minnesota
5. Choice to Chicago Bears
6. *Picard, Bob, WR, Eastern Washington, 132
7. *Wynn, Will, DE, Tennessee State, 159
8. Lintner, Dan, DB, Indiana, 184
9. Nokes, John, LB, Northern Illinois, 211
10. Choice to Minnesota
11. Van Elst, Gary, DT, Michigan State, 263
12. *Lavender, Joe, DB, San Diego State, 288
13. *Davis, Stan, WR, Memphis State, 315
14. Sacra, Ralph, T, Texas A&M, 340
15. Schlezes, Ken, DB, Notre Dame, 367
16. Dowsing, Frank, DB, Mississippi State, 391
17. *Oliver, Greg, RB, Trinity (TX), 419

PITTSBURGH 1973
1. *Thomas, J.T., DB, Florida State, 24
2. Phares, Ken, DB, Mississippi State, 50
3. *Bernhardt, Roger, G, Kansas, 76
4. *Clark, Gail, LB, Michigan State, 102
5. *Reavis, Dave, DE, Arkansas [from New Orleans thru Washington] 106
   Clark, Larry, LB, Northern Illinois, 128
6. Bell, Ron, RB, Illinois State [from Denver] 140
   *Scolnik, Glen, WR, Indiana, 154
7. *Dorsey, Nate, DE, Mississippi Valley State, 180
8. *Toews, Loren, LB, California [from Denver] 192
   Janssen, Bill, T, Nebraska, 206
9. Bonham, Bracey, G, North Carolina Central, 232
10. Wunderly, Don, DT, Arkansas, 258
11. White, Bob, DB, Arizona, 284
12. Lee, Willie, RB, Indiana State, 310
13. Fergerson, Rick, WR, Kansas State, 336
14. Cowan, Roger, DE, Stanford, 362
15. Cross, Charles, DB, Iowa, 388
16. Nardi, Glen, DT, Navy, 414
17. Shannon, Mike, DT, Oregon State, 440

ST. LOUIS 1973
1. *Butz, Dave, DT, Purdue, 5
2. Choice to Minnesota
   *Keithley, Gary, QB, Texas-El Paso [from San Francisco] 45
3. *Sturt, Fred, G, Bowling Green, 59
   *Metcalf, Terry, RB, Long Beach State [from Los Angeles Rams] 63
4. Choice to San Diego thru Chicago Bears
5. *Brahaney, Tom, C, Oklahoma, 109
6. *Crump, Dwayne, DB, Fresno State, 137
   Andre, Phil, DB, Washington [from Detroit] 148
7. Jones, Ken, T, Oklahoma, 164
8. Garrett, Ken, RB, Wake Forest, 188
9. King, Ken, LB, Kentucky, 213
10. *Sloan, Bonnie, T, Austin Peay, 242
11. Sanspree, Dan, DE, Auburn, 267
12. Unruh, Dean, T, Oklahoma, 292
13. Robinson, Ed, DB, Lamar, 317
14. *Peiffer, Dan, G, Southeast Missouri State, 346
15. Parker, Mel, LB, Duke, 371
16. Hann, Jim, LB, Montana, 396
17. Crone, Eric, QB, Harvard, 421

SAN DIEGO 1973
1. Choice to Philadelphia
   *Rodgers, Johnny, WR, Nebraska [from Washington thru Baltimore] 25
2. Choice to Los Angeles Rams
3. Choice to Los Angeles Rams
   *Fouts, Dan, QB, Oregon [from Atlanta thru Oakland] 84
4. *Thaxton, James, TE, Tennessee State [from St. Louis thru Chicago Bears] 84
   Choice to Baltimore
   *Singletary, Bill, LB, Temple [from San Francisco thru Washington] 97
5. Choice to Buffalo
   *McGee, Willie, WR, Alcorn State [from Detroit thru Washington] 123
   Knoble, Jon, LB, Weber State [from Cleveland] 125
6. Roberts, Marvin, C, Michigan State, 135
7. Choice to Miami thru New England
8. Choice to Baltimore
9. Bennett, Tab, LB, Illinois, 214
10. Burnett, Cliff, DE, Montana, 239
11. *Douglas, Jay, C, Memphis State, 268
12. Ahrens, Lynn, T, Eastern Montana, 293
13. Reese, Alfred, RB, Tennessee State, 318
14. *Adams, Tony, QB, Utah State, 343
15. *Parris, Gary, TE, Florida State, 372
16. Petty, Joe, DB, Arizona State, 397
17. *Darrow, Barry, T, Montana, 422

SAN FRANCISCO 1973
1. *Holmes, Mike, DB, Texas Southern, 18
2. *Harper, Willie, LB, Nebraska [from New York Giants] 41
   Choice to St. Louis
3. Choice to Denver thru Washington and San Diego
4. Choice to San Diego thru Washington
5. Fulk, Mike, LB, Indiana [from Chicago Bears] 112
   *Beverly, Ed, WR, Arizona State, 122
6. *Moore, Arthur, DT, Tulsa, 149
7. Mitchell, John, LB, Alabama, 174
8. *Atkins, Dave, RB, Texas-El Paso, 201
9. Praetorius, Roger, RB, Syracuse, 226
10. *Hunt, Charlie, LB, Florida State, 253
11. Dahlberg, Tom, RB, Gustavus Adolphus, 278
12. Pettus, Larry, T, Tennessee State, 305
13. Kelso, Alan, C, Washington, 330
14. *Morrison, Dennis, QB, Kansas State, 357
15. *Bettiga, Mike, WR, Cal State-Humboldt, 382
16. Oven, Mike, TE, Georgia Tech, 409
17. Erickson, Bob, G, North Dakota State, 434

WASHINGTON 1973
1. Choice to San Diego thru Baltimore
2. Choice to New Orleans thru New York Jets
3. Choice to Buffalo
4. Choice to Buffalo
5. Cantrell, Charley, G, Lamar [from Atlanta] 117
   Choice to Los Angeles Rams
6. Choice to New York Jets
7. Choice to Buffalo
8. Choice to New Orleans
   *Hancock, Mike, TE, Idaho State [from Los Angeles Rams] 193
9. Galbos, Rich, RB, Ohio State [from Baltimore] 218
   Sheats, Eddie, LB, Kansas, 233
10. *Stone, Ken, DB, Vanderbilt [from Los Angeles Rams] 245
11. Choice to Los Angeles Rams
12. Webster, Ernie, G, Pittsburgh, 311
13. *Johnson, Dennis, DT, Delaware, 337
14. Marshall, Herb, DB, Cameron, 363
15. Choice to Los Angeles Rams
16. Wedman, Mike, K, Colorado, 415
17. Davis, Jeff, RB, Mars Hills, 441

1974

Held January 29-30, 1974

ATLANTA 1974
1. Choice to Minnesota
2. *Tinker, Gerald, WR, Kent State, 44
3. *McQuilkin, Kim, QB, Lehigh, 69
   *Spencer, Thurmon (Mo), DB, North Carolina Central [from Oakland thru New Orleans] 71
4. *Kendrick, Vince, RB, Florida, 96
5. *Childs, Henry, TE, Kansas State [from Baltimore thru Detroit] 109
   Choice to New Orleans
   *Eley, Monroe, RB, Arizona State [from Los Angeles Rams thru Minnesota and Philadelphia] 128
6. Orange, Doyle, RB, Southern Mississippi, 147
7. Coode, James, T-G, Michigan, 173
8. Choice to Green Bay thru New Orleans
9. *Bailey, Larry, DT, Pacific, 225
10. *Ryczek, Paul, C, Virginia, 252
11. Wilson, Eddie, WR, Albany State, 277
12. *Koegel, Vic, LB, Ohio State, 304
13. Powell, Ralph, RB, Nebraska, 329
14. Givens, John, G, Villanova, 356
15. Jones, Willie, WR, Iowa State, 381
16. *McGee, Sylvester, RB, Rhode Island, 408
17. Davis, Al, G-T, Boise State, 433

BALTIMORE 1974
1. *Dutton, John, DE, Nebraska, 5
   *Carr, Roger, WR, Louisiana Tech [from Los Angeles Rams] 24
2. *Cook, Fred, DE, Southern Mississippi, 32
   Shuttlesworth, Ed. RB, Michigan [from Philadelphia] 37
3. *Robinson, Glenn, LB-DE, Oklahoma State, 57
   *Pratt, Robert, G, North Carolina [from Denver] 67
4. Bell, Tony, DB, Bowling Green, 84
5. Choice to Atl thru Detroit
   *Nettles, Doug, DB, Vanderbilt [from

Minnesota] 129
6. Choice to Miami
*Rhodes, Danny, LB, Arkansas [from New England] 140
7. *Jackson, Noah, G, Tampa, 161
*Dickel, Dan, LB, Iowa [from Denver] 170
*Scott, Freddie, WR, Amherst [from Buffalo] 174
8. *Latta, Greg, TE, Morgan State, 188
Miles, Paul, Bowling Green [from Denver] 198
9. Choice to Los Angeles Rams thru Washington
10. *Van Duyne, Bob, G, Idaho, 240
Ellis, Glenn, DT, Elon [from Los Angeles Rams] 257
11. *Rudnick, Tim, DB, Notre Dame, 265
12. *Simonson, Dave, T, Minnesota, 292
Bobrowski, Bo, QB, Purdue [from Washington] 307
13. *Hall, Randy, DB, Idaho, 317
14. Collins, Ed, WR, Rice, 344
15. Kelly, Pat, LB, Richmond, 369
16. Margavage, Dave, T, Kentucky, 396
17. *Berra, Tim, WR, Massachusetts, 421
Lewis, Buzzy, DB, Florida State [from Washington] 436

BUFFALO 1974
1. *Gant, Reuben, TE, Oklahoma State, 18
2. *Allen, Doug, LB, Penn State [from Houston] 27
Choice to San Diego
3. *Marangi, Gary, QB, Boston College, 70
4. Crumpler, Carlester, RB, East Carolina, 95
5. *Hayman, Gary, WR, Penn State [from San Diego] 106
Guy, Tim, T, Oregon, 122
6. Choice to Cleveland
7. Choice to Baltimore
8. Choice to Cleveland
Hare, Gregg, QB, Ohio State [from Washington] 203
9. Doherty, Brian, P, Notre Dame, 226
10. Cameron, Art, TE, Albany State (GA) [from St. Louis] 241
*Calhoun, Don, RB, Kansas State [from Cleveland] 249
Choice to St. Louis thru Denver
11. Kirby, Rod, LB, Pittsburgh, 278
12. *Means, Dave, DE, Southeast Missouri State, 303
13. Gatewood, Ed, LB, Tennessee State, 331
14. Lamm, Paul, DB, North Carolina [from Houston] 339
Gurbada, Phil, DB, Mayville State, 355
15. Williams, Ken, LB, Southwestern Louisiana, 382
16. Quale, Sanford, T, North Dakota State, 406
17. Casola, Sal, K, Cincinnati, 434

CHICAGO BEARS 1974
1. *Bryant, Waymond, LB, Tennessee State, 4
*Gallagher, Dave, DE-DT, Michigan [from Was thru Los Angeles Rams] 20
2. Choice to New England
3. *Wheeler, Wayne, WR, Alabama [from San Diego] 54
*Horton, Greg, G-T, Colorado, 56
*Taylor, Cliff, RB, Memphis State [from New England thru Washington] 62
4. Choice to Pittsburgh thru New England
5. Choice to Philadelphia
6. Choice to Green Bay
7. Ettinger, Jack, WR, Arkansas, 160
8. Chadwick, Alan, QB, East Tennessee State, 186
*Grandberry, Ken, RB, Washington [from New England] 190
9. Choice to Miami
10. Choice to Cleveland
11. *Hodgins, Norm, DB, LSU, 264
12. *Sevy, Jeff, DT, California, 290
13. *Barnes, Joe, QB, Texas Tech, 316
14. Vellano, Paul, DT, Maryland, 342
15. Alexander, Oliver, TE, Grambling, 368
16. Geist, Randy, DB, Colorado, 394
17. Holland, Craig, QB, Texas-Arlington, 420

CINCINNATI 1974
1. *Kollar, Bill, DT, Montana State, 23
2. *Davis, Charlie, RB, Colorado, 48
3. *Lapham, Dave, G, Syracuse [from New Orleans] 61
*Jolitz, Evan, LB, Cincinnati, 73
4. *Boryla, Mike, QB, Stanford [from New England] 87
*White, Daryl, G, Nebraska, 98
*Williams, Richard Jr., WR, Abilene Christian [from Minnesota] 103
5. *Stanback, Haskel, RB, Tennessee [from New Orleans] 114
*Bishop, Richard, DT, Louisville, 127
6. Sinclair, Robin, DB, Washington State, 152
*Byrant, William, DB, Grambling [from Washington thru New Orleans] 153
7. *Sawyer, Ken, DB, Syracuse, 177
8. *McDaniel, John, WR, Lincoln (MO), 202
9. Johnson, Ed, DE, SMU, 231
10. Herd, Charles, WR, Penn State, 256
11. Kezirian, Ed, T, UCLA, 281
12. McClinon, Rudy, DB, Xavier, 306
13. Jornov, Ted, LB, Iowa State, 335
14. Phillips, Mike, T, Cornell, 360
15. Jackson, Isaac, RB, Kansas State, 385
16. Bishop, Darryl, DB, Kentucky, 410
17. Smith, Jim, RB, North Carolina Central, 439 +

CLEVELAND 1974
1. Choice to San Diego
2. Corbett, Billy, T, Johnson C. Smith, 40
3. Choice to Denver
4. Choice to Oakland
5. *Ilgenfritz, Mark, DE, Vanderbilt, 118
6. *Pritchett, Billy, RB, West Texas State [from Buffalo] 146
Choice to Pittsburgh thru Denver
7. Herrick, Bob, WR, Purdue [from St. Louis] 163
*Sullivan, Gerry, C-T, Illinois, 171
8. Choice to Washington
*Brown, Eddie, DB, Tennessee [from Buffalo] 199
9. Scott, Dan, G, Ohio State, 224
10. Puestow, Mike, WR, North Dakota State [from Chicago Bears] 238
Choice to Buffalo
11. Gooden, Tom, K, Harding, 274
12. McNeil, Ron, DE, North Carolina Central, 302
13. *Seifert, Mike, DE, Wisconsin, 327
14. *Hunt, Bob, RB, Heidelberg, 352
15. Terrell, Ransom, LB, Arizona, 380
16. *Anderson, Preston, DB, Rice, 407
17. Buchanan, Carlton, DT, Southwestern Oklahoma, 430

DALLAS 1974
1. *Jones, Ed (Too Tall), DE, Tennessee State [from Houston] 1
*Young, Charley, RB, North Carolina State, 22
2. Choice to Mia
3. *White, Danny, QB, Arizona State [from Houston] 53
*Peterson, Cal, LB, UCLA, 72
4. *Hutcherson, Ken, LB, Livingston [from Oakland] 97
Andrade, Andy, RB, Northern Michigan, 101
5. Kelsey, Jon, T, Missouri, 126
6. Bright, Jimmy, DB, UCLA, 151
7. Nester, Raymond, LB, Michigan State, 176
8. Holt, Mike, DB, Michigan State, 205
9. Dulin, Bill, T, Johnson C. Smith, 230
10. *Morgan, Dennis, RB, Western Illinois, 255
11. McGee, Harvey, WR, Southern Mississippi, 280
12. Bobo, Keith, QB, SMU, 209
13. Lima, Fred, K, Colorado, 334
14. Richards, Doug, DB, BYU, 359
15. Craft, Bruce, T, Geneva, 384
16. *Killian, Gene, G-T, Tennessee, 413
17. Skolrood, Lawrie, T, North Dakota, 438

DENVER 1974
1. *Gradishar, Randy, LB, Ohio State, 14
2. *Wafer, Carl, DT, Tennessee State, 42
3. Choice to Baltimore
*Minor, Claudie, T, San Diego State [from Cleveland] 68
4. Collier, Ozell, DB, Colorado, 92
5. Choice to Minnesota
6. Winesberry, John, WR, Stanford, 145
7. Choice to Baltimore
8. Choice to Baltimore
9. Choice to Pittsburgh
10. Johnson, Charlie, DB, Southern, 248
11. Buchanan, Steve, RB, Holy Cross, 276
12. Cameron, Larry, LB, Acorn State, 301
13. Clerkley, John, DT, Fort Valley State, 326
14. Marks, Rich, DB, Northern Illinois, 354
15. Pennington, Piel, QB, Massachusetts, 379
16. *Austin, Darrell, T, South Carolina, 404
17. *Brown, Boyd, TE, Alcorn State, 432

DETROIT 1974
1. *O'Neil, Ed, LB, Penn State [from New Orleans] 8
Choice to New Orleans
2. *Howard, Billy, DT, Alcorn State, 39
3. *Bussey, Dexter, RB, Texas-Arlington, 65
4. Choice to St. Louis
5. *Capria, Carl, DB, Purdue, 117
6. Burden, Willie, RB, North Carolina State [from New Orleans] 139
Davis, Jim, G, Alcorn State, 143
7. *Herrera, Efren, K, UCLA, 169
8. Denimarck, Mike, LB, Emporia State, 195
9. Choice to Los Angeles Rams
10. Wooley, David, RB, Central State (OK), 247
11. *Blair, T.C., TE, Tulsa, 273
12. Wakefield, Mark, WR, Tampa, 299
13. *Rothwell, Fred, C, Kansas State, 325
14. Jones, David, DB, Howard Payne, 351
15. Wells, John, G, Kansas State, 377
16. Wilson, Myron, DB, Bowling Green, 403
17. Temple, Collis, DE, LSU, 429

GREEN BAY 1974
1. *Smith, Barty, RB, Richmond, 12
2. Choice to Miami
3. Choice to Minnesota thru San Diego
4. Choice to San Francisco
5. *Odom, Steve, WR, Utah, 116
6. *Woods, Don, RB, New Mexico [from Chicago Bears] 134
*Payne, Ken, WR, Langston, 142
7. Purvis, Bart, T, Maryland, 168
8. Doris, Monte, LB, USC, 194
Guillet, Ned, DB, Boston College [from Atlanta thru New Orleans] 200
9. Holton, Harold, G, Texas-El Paso, 220
10. Troszak, Doug, DT, Michigan, 246
11. *Torkelson, Eric, RB, Connecticut, 272
12. *Walker, Randy, K, Northwestern State (LA), 298
13. Armstrong, Emanuel, LB, San Jose State, 324
14. Neloms, Andrew, DT, Kentucky State, 350
15. Wannstedt, Dave, T, Pittsburgh, 376
16. *Cooney, Mark, LB, Colorado, 402
17. Woodfield, Randy, WR, Portland State, 428

HOUSTON 1974
1. Choice to Dallas
2. Choice to Buffalo
3. Choice to Dallas
4. Manstedt, Steve, LB, Nebraska, 79
5. Choice to San Diego thru Washington
6. Choice to Kansas City thru New Orleans
*Brown, Booker, G, USC [from Los Angeles Rams] 154
7. *Fairley, Leonard, DB, Alcorn State, 157
8. McCoy, Mike, DB, Western Kentucky, 183
9. Choice to New England
10. Choice to New Orleans
11. Taylor, Steve, C, Auburn, 261
12. Browne, Ricky, LB, Florida, 287
13. Dixon, Dan, G, Boise State, 313
14. Choice to Buffalo
15. *Johnson, Billy (White Shoes), WR, Widener, 365
16. Williams, Mathew, RB, Northeast Louisiana, 391
17. Hedge, Bill, T, Northeast Missouri State, 417

KANSAS CITY 1974
1. *Green, Woody, RB, Arizona State, 16
2. *Getty, Charlie, T, Penn State, 41
3. *Jaynes, David, QB, Kansas, 66
4. *Herkenhoff, Matt, T, Minnesota, 94
5. Choice to New York Giants
6. Washington, Jim, RB, Clemson [from Houston thru New Orleans] 13
Choice to Washington
7. Hegge, Leroy, DE, South Dakota-Springfield, 172
8. Choice to New York Jets
9. Jennings, Jim, RB, Rutgers, 222
10. *Condon, Tom, G, Boston College, 250
11. *Thornbladh, Bob, RB, Michigan, 275
12. Brown, Carl, WR, West Texas State, 300
13. Romagnoli, Norm, LB, Kentucky State, 328
14. Pomarico, Frank, G, Notre Dame, 353
15. *Burnham, Lem, LB, U.S. International, 378
16. Beers, Barry, G, William & Mary, 405
17. Langner, David, DB, Auburn, 431

LOS ANGELES RAMS 1974
1. *Cappelletti, John, RB, Penn State [from Philadelphia] 11
Choice to Baltimore
2. *Simpson, Bill, DB, Michigan State, 50
3. Oliver, Al, T, UCLA, 76
4. *Weese, Norris, DB, Mississippi [from Washington] 99
Johnson, Frank, T, Cal-Riverside, 102
5. Choice to Atlanta thru Minnesota and Philadelphia
6. Choice to Houston
7. Harvey, John, RB, Texas-Arlington [from San Diego] 158
Choice to Washington
8. Choice to San Diego
9. Hutt, Don, WR, Boise State [from Baltimore thru Washington] 213
Williams, Derek, DB, Cal-Riverside [from Detroit] 221
Choice to Washington
10. Choice to Baltimore
11. Hayes, Rick, T, Washington, 284
12. Freberg, Roger, G, UCLA, 310
13. Solverson, Pete, T, Drake, 336
14. Carson, Ananias, WR, Langston, 362
15. *Thomas, Bob, K, Notre Dame, 388
16. Ottmar, Dave, P, Stanford, 414
17. Townsend, Willie, WR, Notre Dame, 440

MIAMI 1974
1. *Reese, Don, DE, Jackson State, 26
2. *Tillman, Andre, TE, Texas Tech [from Green Bay] 38
*Malone, Benny, RB, Arizona State [from Dallas] 47
*White, Jeris, DB, Hawaii, 52
3. *Moore, Nat, WR, Florida, 78
4. Stevenson, Bill, D, Drake, 104
5. Vann, Cleveland, LB, Oklahoma State, 130
6. *Crowder, Randy, DE, Penn State [from Baltimore] 136
Wolfe, Bob, T, Nebraska, 156
7. Swierc, Carl, WR, Rice [from New Orleans] 164
Sullivan, Joe, G, Boston College, 182
8. *Baker, Melvin, WR, Texas Southern, 208
9. *Wickert, Tom, G, Washington State [from Chicago Bears] 212
*Lally, Bob, LB, Cornell, 234
10. Valbuena, Gary, QB, Tennessee, 260
11. Roberts, Gerry, DE, UCLA, 286
12. Revels, Jim, DB, Florida, 312
13. *Heath, Clayton, RB, Wake Forest, 338
14. Johnson, Sam, LB, Arizona State, 364
15. Cates, Larry, DB, Western Michigan, 390
16. Wolf, Jessie, DT, Prairie View A&M, 416
17. Dickerson, Ken, DB, Tuskegee, 442

MINNESOTA 1974
1. *McNeill, Fred, LB, UCLA [from Atlanta] 1
*Riley, Steve, T, USC, 25
2. *Holland, John, WR, Tennessee State [from San Diego] 29
*Blair, Matt, LB, Iowa State, 51
3. *Craig, Steve, TE, Northwestern [from Green Bay thru San Diego] 64
*Anderson, Scott, C, Missouri, 77
4. Townsend, Mike, DB, Notre Dame [from New Orleans] 86
Choice to Cincinnati
5. Ferguson, Jim, DB, Stanford [from Denver] 120
Choice to Baltimore
6. *Kellar, Mark, RB, Northern Illinois, 155
7. Tabron, Fred, RB, Southwest Missouri State, 181
8. Simmons, Berl, K, TCU, 207
9. *McCullum, Sam, WR, Montana State, 232
10. Reed, Barry, RB, Peru State, 259
11. *Boone, Dave, DE, Eastern Michigan, 285
12. *Poltl, Randy, DB, Stanford, 311
13. Keller, Gary, DT, Utah, 337
14. Dixon, Alan, RB, Harding, 363
15. Wachtler, Kurt, DT, St. John's (MN), 289
16. Goebel, John, RB, St. Thomas (MN), 415
17. Garrett, Earl, DB, Massachusetts-Boston, 441

NEW ENGLAND 1974
1. Choice to San Francisco
2. *Corbett, Steve, G, Boston College [from Chicago Bears] 30
*Nelson, Steve, LB, North Dakota State, 34
3. Choice to Chicago Bears thru Washington
4. Choice to Cincinnati
5. *Johnson, Andy, RB, Georgia, 113
Battle, Charlie, LB-DE, Grambling [from Washington thru New Orleans] 124
6. Choice to Baltimore
*Ramsey, Chuck, P, Wake Forest [from Philadelphia] 141
7. Choice to Pittsburgh
*Damkroger, Maury, LB, Nebraska [from Washington] 178
8. Choice to Chicago Bears
9. McCartney, Ed, LB, Northwestern Oklahoma [from Houston] 209
Choice to Washington
10. Choice to Pittsburgh
11. Gibson, Archie, RB, Utah State, 268
12. Foster, Eddie, T, Oklahoma, 296
13. Bennett, Phil, RB, Boston College, 321
14. Bowens, Cecil, RB, Kentucky, 346
15. *Hunt, Sam, LB, Stephen F. Austin, 374
16. Selmon, Lucious, DT, Oklahoma, 399
17. Hudson, Gary, DB, Boston College, 424

NEW ORLEANS 1974
1. Choice to Detroit
*Middleton, Rick, LB, Ohio State [from Detroit] 13
2. *Seal, Paul, TE, Michigan, 36
3. Choice to Cincinnati
4. Choice to Minnesota
*McNeill, Rod, RB, USC [from San Francisco] 88
5. *Parker, Joel, WR, Florida [from San Francisco] 113
Choice to Cincinnati
*Schmidt, Terry, DE, Ball State [from Atlanta] 121
6. Choice to Detroit
7. Choice to Miami
8. Choice to New York Jets
*Maxson, Alvin, RB, SMU [from Oakland] 201
9. *La Porta, Phil, T, Penn State, 217
10. Anderson, Frosty, WR, Nebraska [from Houston] 235
Thibodeaux, Tommy, G, Tulane, 242
11. Merritt, Kent, WR, Virginia, 270
12. Buckmon, James, DE, Pittsburgh, 295
13. Truax, Mike, LB, Tulane, 320
14. Marshall, Kent, DB, TCU, 348
15. *Cipa, Larry, QB, Michigan, 373
16. *Coleman, Don, LB, Michigan, 398
17. Williams, Marvin, WR, Western Illinois, 426

NEW YORK GIANTS 1974
1. *Hicks, John, G, Ohio State, 3
2. *Mullen, Tom, G, Southwest Missouri State, 28
3. *Dvorak, Rick, DE-LB, Wichita State, 55
4. *Summerell, Carl, QB, East Carolina, 80
5. *Clune, Don, WR, Penn State, 107
*Powers, Clyde, DB, Oklahoma [from Kansas City] 119
6. *Pietrzak, Jim, T, Eastern Michigan, 132
7. Woolbright, Marty, TE, South Carolina, 159
8. Bilbbs, Ezil, DE, Grambling, 184
9. Rathje, Jim, RB, Northern Michigan, 211
10. *Rhodes, Ray, WR, Tulsa, 236
11. *Brooks, Bobby, DB, Bishop, 263
12. *Sims, James, DB, USC, 288
13. Colvin, Dennis, T, Southwest Texas State, 315
14. Hayes, Mike, T, Virginia State, 340
15. *Jones, Larry, WR, Northeast Missouri State, 367
16. Brown, Buddy, G, Alabama, 392
17. *Crosby, Steve, RB, Ft. Hays State, 419

NEW YORK JETS 1974
1. *Barzilauskas, Carl, DT, Indiana, 6
2. *Browne, Gordon, T, Boston College, 31

3. *Turk, Godwin, LB, Southern, 58
*Word, Roscoe, DB, Jackson State [from Washington] 74
4. Choice to San Francisco thru New Orleans
5. Baccus, Gary, LB, Oklahoma, 110
6. Wyman, Bill, C, Texas, 135
Jones, Wayne, RB, Mississippi State [from St. Louis] 137
7. Veazey, Burney, TE, Mississippi, 162
8. *Gantt, Greg, K, Alabama, 187
Lightfoot, Larry, RB, Livingston [from New Orleans] 192
*Rydalch, Ron, DT, Utah [from Kansas City] 197
9. *Burns, Robert, RB, Georgia, 214
10. Baker, Sam, G, Georgia, 239
11. Bird, Eugene, DB, Southern Mississippi, 266
Buckley, Bill, WR, Mississippi State [from St. Louis] 267
12. Ricca, John, DE, Duke, 291
13. Tate, John, LB, Jackson State, 318 +
14. Fountain, Greg, G, Mississippi State, 343
15. *Brister, Willie, TE, Southern, 370
16. *Jackson, Clarence, RB, Western Kentucky, 395
17. Lowrey, Doug, G-C, Arkansas State, 422

OAKLAND 1974
1. *Lawrence, Henry, T, Florida A&M, 19
2. *Casper, Dave, TE, Notre Dame, 45
3. Choice to Atl thru New Orleans
*van Eeghen, Mark, RB, Colgate [from Pittsburgh] 75
4. *Bradshaw, Morris, RB, Ohio State [from Cleveland] 93
Choice to Dallas
5. Wessel, Pete, DB, Northwestern, 128
6. *McAlister, James, RB, UCLA, 148
7. Garcia, Rod, K, Stanford, 175
8. Choice to New Orleans
9. *Pope, Kenith, DB, Oklahoma, 227
10. Arnold, Chris, DB, Virginia State, 253
11. *Hart, Harold, RB, Texas Southern, 279
12. *Gonzalez, Noe, RB, Southwest Texas State, 305
13. *Dennery, Mike, LB, Southern Mississippi, 330
14. Willingham, Don, RB, Wisconsin-Milwaukee, 357
15. Mathis, Greg, DB, Idaho State, 383
16. Robinson, Delario, WR, Kansas, 409
17. Morris, James, DT, Missouri Valley, 435

PHILADELPHIA 1974
1. Choice to Los Angeles Rams
2. Choice to Baltimore
3. *Sutton, Mitch, DT, Kansas, 63
4. *LeMaster, Frank, LB, Kentucky, 89
5. *Cagle, Jim, DT, Georgia [from Chicago Bears] 108
*Krepfle, Keith, TE, Iowa State, 115
6. Choice to New England
7. *Cullars, Willie, DE, Kansas, 167
8. Woods, Robert, LB, Howard Payne, 193
9. Sheridan, Mark, WR, Holy Cross, 219
10. Polak, Phil, RB, Bowling Green, 245
11. Brittain, Bill, C, Kansas State, 271
12. *Parker, Artimus, DB, USC, 297
13. Ditley, Lars, DE, South Dakota Tech, 323
14. Smith, Dave, LB, Oklahoma, 349
15. Bond, Sid, T, TCU, 375
16. Smith, Jim, LB, Monmouth, 401
17. Brown, Cliff, RB, Notre Dame, 427

PITTSBURGH 1974
1. *Swann, Lynn, WR, USC, 21
2. *Lambert, Jack, LB, Kent State, 46
3. Choice to Oakland
4. *Stallworth, John, WR, Alabama A&M [from Chicago Bears thru New England] 82
*Allen, Jimmy, DB, UCLA, 100
5. *Webster, Mike, C, Wisconsin, 125
6. *Wolf, James, DE, Prairie View A&M [from Cleveland thru Denver] 149
*Druschel, Rick, G, North Carolina State, 150
7. Sitterle, Allen, T, North Carolina State [from New England] 165
Garske, Scott, TE, Eastern Michigan, 179
8. Gefert, Mark, LB, Purdue, 204
9. *Reamon, Tommy, RB, Missouri [from Denver] 223
*Davis, Charlie, T, TCU, 229
10. Kregel, Jim, G, Ohio State [from New England] 243
Atkinson, Dave, DB, BYU, 254
11. Morton, Dickie, RB, Arkansas, 283
12. Lickiss, Hugh, LB, Simpson, 308
13. Kolch, Frank QB, Eastern Michigan, 333
14. Henley, Bruce, DB, Rice, 358
15. Hunt, Larry, DT, Iowa State, 387
16. Morgan, Octavus, LB, Illinois, 412
17. Moore, Larry, DE, Angelo State, 437

ST. LOUIS 1974
1. *Cain, J.V., TE, Colorado, 7
2. *Kindle, Greg, T, Tennessee State, 33
3. Choice to San Diego
*George, Steve, DT, Houston [from San Francisco] 60
4. *Keeton, Durwood, DB, Oklahoma, 85
*Harris, Ike, WR, Iowa State [from Detroit] 91
5. *Neils, Steve, LB, Minnesota, 111
6. Choice to New York Jets
7. Choice to Cleveland
8. *Albert, Sergio, K, U.S. International, 189
9. *Harrison, Reggie, RB, Cincinnati, 215
10. Choice to Buffalo
*Hartle, Greg, LB, Newberry [from Buffalo thru Denver] 251
11. Choice to New York Jets
12. *Wallace, Roger, WR, Bowling Green, 293
13. Poulos, Jimmy, RB, Georgia, 319
14. Smith, Charles, RB, Yankton, 345
15. Ancell, Vincent, DB, Arkansas State, 371
16. Emery, Alonzo, RB, Arizona State, 397
17. Moseley, John, DB, Missouri, 423

SAN DIEGO 1974
1. *Matthews, Bo, RB, Colorado, 2
*Goode, Don, LB, Kansas [from Cleveland] 15
2. Choice to Minnesota
*Markovich, Mark, C, Penn State [from Buffalo] 43
3. Choice to Chicago Bears
Rudder, Bill, RB, Tennessee [from St. Louis] 59
4. *Davis, Harrison, WR, Virginia, 81
5. *Teerlinck, John, DT, Western Illinois [from Houston thru Washington] 105
Choice to Buffalo
6. *Freitas, Jesse, QB, San Diego State, 133
7. Choice to Los Angeles Rams
8. *Forrest, Tom, G, Cincinnati, 185
*Boatwright, Bon, T, Oklahoma State [from Los Angeles Rams] 206
9. *Colbert, Danny, DB, Tulsa, 210
10. Ketchoyian, John, LB Santa Clara, 237
11. *Grannell, Dave, TE, Arizona State, 262
12. *Williams, Sam, DB, California, 289
13. *Vertefeuille, Brian, T, Idaho State, 314
14. Bailey, Greg, DB, Long Beach State, 341
15. *Anthony, Charles, LB, USC, 366
Meczka, Greg, TE, Bowling Green [from Washington] 386
16. Skarin, Neal, DE, Arizona State, 393
17. *DeJurnett, Charles, DT, San Jose State, 418

SAN FRANCISCO 1974
1. *Jackson, Wilbur, RB, Alabama [from New England] 9
*Sandifer, Bill, DT, UCLA, 10
2. *Fahnhorst, Keith, TE, Minnesota, 35
*Williams, Delvin, RB, Kansas [from Washington] 49
3. Choice to St. Louis
4. *Haslerig, Clint, WR, Michigan [from New York Jets thru New Orleans] 83
Choice to New Orleans
*Johnson, Sammy, RB, North Carolina [from Green Bay] 90
5. Choice to New Orleans
6. *Raines, Mike, DT, Alabama, 138
7. *Johnson, Kermit, RB, UCLA, 166
8. Schneitz, Jim, G, Missouri, 191
9. *Moore, Manfred, RB, USC, 216
10. Gaspard, Glen, LB, Texas, 244
11. Battle, Greg, DB, Colorado State, 269
12. *Hull, Tom, LB, Penn State, 294
13. *Owen, Tom, QB, Wichita State, 322
14. Williamson, Walt, DE, Michigan, 347
15. Gray, Leonard, TE, Long Beach State, 372
16. Conners, Jack, DB, Oregon, 400
17. Stanley, Levi, G, Hawaii, 425

WASHINGTON 1974
1. Choice to Chicago Bears thru Los Angeles Rams
2. Choice to San Francisco
3. Choice to New York Jets
4. Choice to Los Angeles Rams
5. Choice to New England thru New Orleans
6. *Keyworth, Jon, TE, Colorado [from Kansas City] 144
Choice to Cin thru New Orleans
7. Choice to New England
*Varty, Mike, LB, Northwestern [from Los Angeles Rams] 180
8. Robinson, Darwin, RB, Dakota State (San Diego) [from Cleveland] 196
Choice to Buffalo
9. Sens, Mark, DE, Colorado [from New England] 218
Flater, Mike, K, Colorado Mines, 228
*Kennedy, Jim, TE, Colorado State [from Los Angeles Rams] 233
10. Vann, Johnny, DB, South Dakota, 258
11. Miller, Joe, T, Villanova, 282
12. Choice to Baltimore
13. *O'Dell, Stu, LB, Indiana, 332
14. Van Galder, Don, QB, Utah, 361
15. Choice to San Diego
16. Anderson, Nate, RB, Eastern Illinois, 411
17. Choice to Baltimore

1975

Held January 28-29, 1975

ATLANTA 1975
1. *Bartkowski, Steve, QB, California [from Baltimore] 1
Choice to Baltimore
2. *Ortega, Ralph, LB, Florida, 29
3. Choice to Cincinnati
*Thompson, Woody, RB, Miami [from Houston] 65
4. Nessel, John, G, Penn State, 81
5. Choice to Denver
*McCrary, Greg, TE, Clark [from Buffalo] 123
6. *Kuykendall, Fulton, LB, UCLA [from Baltimore] 132
Payton, Doug, G, Colorado, 133
7. *Esposito, Mike, RB, Boston College, 159
8. *Adams, Brent, T, Tennessee-Chattanooga, 185
9. *Davis, Brad, RB, LSU, 211
10. Mills, Marshall, WR, West Virginia, 237
11. *Merrow, Jeff, DT, West Virginia, 263
12. Pickett, Monzo, T-G, Texas Southern, 289
13. *Russ, Carl, LB, Michigan, 315
14. Robinson, Steve, DT, Tuskegee, 340
15. *Robinson, Jim, WR, Georgia Tech, 367
16. *Knutson, Steve, T, USC, 393
17. Anderson, Mitch, QB, Northwestern, 418

BALTIMORE 1975
1. Choice to Atlanta
*Huff, Ken, G, North Carolina [from Atlanta] 3
2. Choice to Los Angeles Rams thru Green Bay
3. *Washington, Mike, DB, Alabama, 53
*Pear, Dave, DT, Washington [from Chicago Bears] 56
4. *Johnson, Marshall, RB, Houston, 80
Linford, Paul, DT, BYU [from New York Jets] 93
5. *Leaks, Roosevelt, RB, Texas, 105
6. Choice to Atlanta
*Westbrook, Don, WR, Nebraska [from New York Giants] 131
7. *Jones, Kim, RB, Colorado State, 157
*Joachim, Steve, QB, Temple [from Chicago Bears] 160
*Luce, Derrel, LB, Baylor [from New York Jets thru Chicago Bears] 166
8. Bushong, John, DE, Western Kentucky, 184
Denboer, Greg, TE, Michigan [from Chicago Bears thru Denver] 187
Cage, Mario, RB, Northwestern State (LA) [from Green Bay]192
9. *McKinney, Royce, DB, Kentucky State, 209
10. Waganheim, Phil, P, Maryland, 236
11. Hazel, Dave, WR, Ohio State, 261
12. Storm, Brad, LB, Iowa State, 288
13. *Roman, John, G, Idaho State, 313
14. Smith, Mike, C, SMU 339
15. Goodie, John, RB, Langston, 365
16. Malouf, Bill, QB, Mississippi, 392
Evavold, Mike, DT, Macalester [from San Francisco] 399
Smith, Robert, DB, Maryland [from Oakland] 419
17. McKnight, David, LB, Georgia, 416
Bengard, Mike, DE, Northwestern (IA) [from San Francisco] 426
Russel, Frank, WR, Maryland [from Oakland] 440

BUFFALO 1975
1. *Ruud, Tom, LB, Nebraska, 19
2. Choice to Oakland
*Nelson, Bob, LB, Nebraska [from Philadelphia] 42
Lott, Glenn, DB, Drake [from Oakland] 50
3. Choice to San Francisco
4. Choice to Cincinnati
*Donchez, Tom, RB, Penn State [from Washington] 102
5. Choice to Atlanta
*McCrumbly, John, LB, Texas A&M [from Houston thru Oakland] 115
6. Choice to New Orleans
7. *Chapman, Gil, RB, Michigan [from San Francisco] 166
Cherry, Reggie, RB, Houston [from Denver] 174
Banks, Harry, DB, Michigan, 175
8. Hill, John, DT, Duke, 201
9. Choice to Cincinnati
10. *Hooks, Roland, RB, North Carolina State, 253
11. Drake, Tom, DB, Michigan, 279
12. *Johnson, Mark, DE, Missouri, 305
13. Dienhart, Mark, T, St. Thomas (MN), 331
14. Evans, Robert, WR, Morris Brown, 350
15. Kupec, Chris, QB, North Carolina, 383
16. Fine, Tom, TE, Notre Dame, 408
17. Turcotte, Jeff, DE, Colorado, 435

CHICAGO BEARS 1975
1. *Payton, Walter, RB, Jackson State, 4
2. *Hartenstine, Mike, DE, Penn State, 31
3. Choice to Baltimore
4. *Livers, Virgil, DB, Western Kentucky, 83
5. Choice to Washington
*Sorey, Revie, G, Illinois [from New Orleans] 110
6. *Avellini, Bob, QB, Maryland, 135
*Hicks, Tom, LB, Illinois [from Los Angeles Rams thru San Diego] 151
7. Choice to Baltimore
*Douthitt, Earl, DB, Iowa [from Washington thru St. Louis] 178
8. Choice to Baltimore thru Denver
*Harris, Joe, LB, Georgia Tech [from New England] 197
9. *Stillwell, Roger, DT, Stanford, 212
10. Choice to Miami
Julius, Mike, G, St. Thomas (MN) [from Los Angeles Rams] 254
11. Dean, Mike, K, Texas, 264
12. *Plank, Doug, DB, Ohio State, 291
13. McDaniel, Charles, RB, Louisiana Tech, 316
14. Hartfield, Walter, RB, Southwest Texas State, 342
15. Marcantonio, Steve, WR, Miami, 368
16. Beckman, Witt, WR, Miami, 395
17. *Harper, Roland, RB, Louisiana Tech, 420

CINCINNATI 1975
1. *Cameron, Glenn, LB, Florida, 14
2. *Krevis, Al, T, Boston College, 39
3. *Burley, Gary, DE, Pittsburgh [from Atlanta] 55
Sheide, Gary, QB, BYU, 64
*Harris, Bo, LB, LSU [from Minnesota] 77
4. Choice to Minnesota
*Fritts, Stan, RB, North Carolina State [from Buffalo] 97
5. *McInally, Pat, WR, Harvard, 120
*West, Jeff, TE-P, Cincinnati [from Dallas] 122
6. Shuman, Tom, QB, Penn State [from Philadelphia] 142
Smith, Rollen, DB, Arkansas, 145
7. *Devlin, Chris, LB, Penn State, 170
8. *Davis, Ricky, DB, Alabama, 195
9. *Dubinetz, Greg, G-C, Yale, 220
Williams, Lofell, WR, Virginia Union [from Buffalo] 227
10. Felker, Rocky, DB, Mississippi State, 245
11. *Cobb, Marvin, DB, USC, 276
12. *Novak, Jack, TE, Wisconsin, 301
13. Rosenberg, Ron, LB, Montana, 326
14. Haywood, Frank, DT, North Carolina State, 351
15. Enright, Greg, K, Southern Oregon, 376
16. Tuttle, John, WR, Kansas State, 401
17. Charity, Elvin, DB, Yale, 432

CLEVELAND 1975
1. *Mitchell, Mack, DE, Houston, 5
2. Choice to San Diego
3. *Roan, Oscar, WR, SMU, 57
4. *Peters, Tony, DB, Oklahoma, 82
5. Zimba, John, DE, Villanova, 109
*Cope, Jim, LB, Ohio State [from Detroit] 119
6. Choice to San Diego
Miller, Charles, DB, West Virginia [from Washington] 150
*Hynoski, Henry, RB, Temple [from Oakland] 154
7. Wang, Merle, T, TCU, 161
8. Santini, Barry, TE, Purdue, 186
9. *Poole, Larry, RB, Kent State, 213
Hogan, Floyd, DB, Arkansas [from Kansas City] 215
10. *Lewis, Stan, DE, Wayne, 238
11. Marinelli, Tom, G, Boston College, 265
12. *Ambrose, Dick, LB, Virginia, 290
13. Armstead, Willie, WR, Utah, 317
14. Barrett, Tim, RB, John Carroll, 341
15. Moore, Willie, DT, Johnson C. Smith, 369
16. *McKay, John (J.K.), WR, USC, 394
17. *Graf, Dave, LB, Penn State, 421

DALLAS 1975
1. *White, Randy, LB, Maryland [from New York Giants] 2
*Henderson, Thomas, LB, Langston, 18
2. *Lawless, Burton, G, Florida, 44,
3. *Breunig, Bob, LB, Arizona State, 70
4. *Donovan, Pat, DE, Stanford [from Houston] 90
*Hughes, Randy, DB, Oklahoma, 96
5. *Davis, Kyle, C, Oklahoma [from Green Bay] 113
Choice to Cincinnati
6. *Woolsey, Rolly, DB, Boise State, 148
7. *Hegman, Mike, LB, Tennessee State, 173
8. *Hoopes, Mitch, P, Arizona, 200
9. *Jones, Ed, DB, Rutgers, 226
10. Booker, Dennis, RB, Millersville, 252
11. Krpalek, Greg, C, Oregon State, 278
12. Bland, Chuck, DB, Cincinnati, 304
13. *Scott, Herbert, G, Virginia Union, 330
14. *Laidlaw, Scott, RB, Stanford, 356
15. Hamilton, Willie, RB, Arizona, 382
16. Clark, Pete, TE, Colorado State, 407
17. Testerman, Jim, TE, Dayton, 434

DENVER 1975
1. *Wright, Louis, DB, San Jose State, 17
2. Smith, Charles, DE, North Car. Central, 43
3. *Franckowiak, Mike, QB, Central Michigan [from New York Giants] 54
*Mahalic, Drew, LB, Notre Dame, 69
4. Taylor, Steve, DB, Georgia [from Kansas City] 84
*Upchurch, Rick, WR, Minnesota, 95
5. *Rogers, Stan, T, Maryland [from Atlanta] 107
*Carter, Rubin, DT, Miami, 121
6. Choice to Washington
7. Choice to Buffalo
8. *Foley, Steve, QB, Tulane, 199
9. Williams, Roussell, DB, Arizona, 225
10. Engelhardt, Hank, C, Pacific [from Kansas City] 240
*Haggerty, Steve, WR, Nevada-Las Vegas, 251
11. Choice to Washington
12. Walters, Harry, LB, Maryland, 303
13. Penick, Eric, RB, Notre Dame, 329
14. Arnold, Jerry, G, Oklahoma, 355
15. Shelton, Ken, TE, Virginia, 381
16. Bridges, Bubba, DT, Colorado, 409
17. Sherman, Lester, RB, Albany State, 433

DETROIT 1975
1. *Boden, Lynn, G, South Dakota State, 13
2. *English, Doug, DT, Texas, 38
3. Choice to New Orleans thru Min
4. *Hertwig, Craig, T, Georgia, 94
5. Choice to Cleveland
6. Cooper, Fred, DB, Purdue [from New

Orleans] 138
*King, Horace, RB, Georgia [from New England] 141
*Franklin, Dennis, QB-WR, Michigan, 144
7. Murphy, Mike, WR, Drake, 169
8. *Thompson, Leonard, RB, Oklahoma State, 194
9. Strinko, Steve, LB, Michigan, 219
10. Boyd, Brad, TE, LSU, 250
11. Myers, Steve, G, Ohio State, 275
12. Roundtree, Andre, LB, Iowa State, 300
13. Smith, Jim, RB, North Carolina Central, 325
14. McMillan, Jim, QB, Boise State, 350
15. Green, Rudy, RB, Yale, 375
16. Chaves, Les, DB, Kansas State, 406
17. Lancaster, Mark, G, Tulsa, 431

GREEN BAY 1975
1. Choice to Los Angeles Rams
2. Choice to Miami
*Bain, Bill, G, USC [from Washington] 47
3. Choice to Los Angeles Rams
*Harrell, Willard, RB, Pacific [from San Diego] 58
4. *Luke, Steve, DB, Ohio State, 88
5. Choice to Dallas
6. Choice to Los Angeles Rams
7. Giaquinto, Tony, WR, Central Connecticut State, 165
8. Choice to Baltimore
9. Hodgin, Jay Lynn, RB, South Carolina, 217
10. *Cooke, William, DE, Massachusetts, 244
11. Martin, Bob, DE, Washington, 269
12. *Brown, Carlos, QB, Pacific, 296
13. Fuhriman, Bob, DB, Utah State, 321
14. Blackmon, Stan, TE, North Texas State, 348
15. Allen, Randy, WR, Southern, 373
16. *McCaffrey, Bob, C, USC, 400
17. Ray, Tom, DB, Central Michigan, 425

HOUSTON 1975
1. *Brazile, Robert, LB, Jackson State [from Kansas City] 6
*Hardeman, Don, RB, Texas A&I, 15
2. *Edwards, Emmett, WR, Kansas, 40
3. Choice to Atlanta
4. Choice to Dallas
5. Choice to Buffalo thru Oakland
6. O'Neal, Jesse, DE, Grambling, 146
7. Biehle, Mike, T, Miami (OH) [from Kansas City] 162
*Cotney, Mark, DB, Cameron, 171
8. Lawrence, Jerry, DT, South Dakota State, 196
9. *Bruer, Bob, TE, Mankato State, 221
10. *Pringle, Alan, K, Rice, 246
11. *Sawyer, John, TE, Southern Mississippi, 271
12. *Miller, Willie, WR, Colorado State, 302
13. Scales, Ricky, WR, Virginia Tech, 327
14. Medford, Jody, G, Rice, 352
15. *Holmes, Jack, RB, Texas Southern, 377
16. Lambert, Ken, DB, Virginia Tech, 402
17. Seeker, Ricky, C, Texas A&M, 427

KANSAS CITY 1975
1. Choice to Houston
2. Stephens, Elmore, TE, Kentucky, 34
3. Walker, Cornelius, DT, Rice, 59
4. Choice to Denver
5. Choice to Los Angeles Rams
6. *LaGrand, Morris, RB, Tampa, 137
Wasick, Dave, LB, San Jose State [from San Francisco] 139
7. Choice to Houston
8. Choice to Pittsburgh
Hoffman, Wayne, TE, Oklahoma [from San Diego thru Washington] 189
9. Choice to Cleveland
10. Choice to Denver
11. Hegland, Dale, G, Minnesota, 268
12. Rackley, James, RB, Florida A&M, 293
13. Snider, John, LB, Stanford, 318
14. Moshier, Gene, G, Vanderbilt, 346
15. Choice to Pittsburgh
16. Peterson, Mark, DE, Illinois, 396
17. Bulino, Mike, DB, Pittsburgh, 424

LOS ANGELES RAMS 1975
1. *Fanning, Mike, DT, Notre Dame [from Green Bay] 9
*Harrah, Dennis, T, Miami [from Philadelphia] 11
*France, Doug, T, Ohio State, 20
2. *Jackson, Monte, DB, San Diego State [from Baltimore thru Green Bay] 28
*Jones, Leroy, DE, Norfolk State, 48
3. Choice to San Diego thru Chicago Bears
*Reece, Geoff, C, Washington State [from Green Bay] 61
*Nugent, Dan, TE, Auburn [from Philadelphia] 67
4. *Perry, Rod, DB, Colorado, 98
5. *Hammond, Wayne, DT, Montana State [from Kansas City] 112
*Nuzum, Fred, C, Kentucky, 126
6. Choice to Chicago Bears thru San Diego
McCarthy, Darius, WR, South Carolina State [from Green Bay] 140
7. *Haden, Pat, QB, USC, 176
8. Washington, John, DB, Tulane, 204
9. Riegel, Gordy, LB, Stanford, 229
10. Choice to Chicago Bears
11. Strickland, Howard, RB, California, 281
12. Williams, Chandler, WR, Lincoln (MO), 307
13. Jacobs, A.J., DB, Louisville, 332
14. Allen, Arthur, WR, Clark, 360
15. White, Alvin, QB, Oregon State, 385
16. Reynolds, Francis, RB, Alcorn State, 410
17. Boyd, Skip, P, Washington, 438

MIAMI 1975
1. *Carlton, Darryl, T, Tampa, 23
2. *Solomon, Fredde, QB, Tampa [from Green Bay] 36
*Winfrey, Stan, RB, Arkansas State, 49
3. Hill, Gerald, LB, Houston, 75
4. *Elia, Bruce, LB, Ohio State, 100
5. *Owens, Morris, WR, Arizona State [from New York Giants] 106
*Hill, Barry, DB, Iowa State, 127
6. Choice to New York Jets
*Towle, Steve, LB, Kansas [from New York Jets] 143
7. Kent, Phillip, RB, Baylor, 179
8. Crawford, Barney, DT, Harding, 205
9. Wilson, James, G, Clark, 231
10. Russell, Clyde, RB, Oklahoma [from Chicago Bears] 239
Jackson, Joe, TE, Penn State [from Washington] 256
*Danelo, Joe, K, Washington State, 257
11. Dilworth, John, DB, Northwestern State (LA), 283
12. Yancey, Joe, T, Henderson State, 309
13. Isabell, Leonard, WR, Tulsa, 334
14. Lewis, James, DB, Tennessee State [from New York Giants] 338
Graham, John, QB, Colorado State, 361
15. Johns, Skip, RB, Carson-Newman, 387
16. Smith, Vernon, C, Georgia, 413
17. Copeland, Dwaine, RB, Middle Tennessee State, 439

MINNESOTA 1975
1. *Mullaney, Mark, DE, Colorado State, 25
2. Riley, Art, DT, USC, 52
3. Choice to Cincinnati
4. *Henson, Harold (Champ), RB, Ohio State [from Cincinnati] 89
Adams, Bruce, WR, Kansas, 103
5. *Miller, Robert, RB, Kansas, 129
6. Broussard, Bubba, LB, Houston, 155
7. Greene, Henry, RB, Southern, 181
8. Hollimon, Joe, DB, Arkansas State, 207
9. Passananti, John, G, Western Illinois, 233
10. *Clabo, Neil, P, Tennessee, 258
11. Spencer, Ike, RB, Utah, 285
12. *Beamon, Autry, DB, East Texas State, 311
13. Hurd, Mike, WR, Michigan State, 336
14. Strickland, Mike, RB, Eastern Michigan, 363
15. Bakken, Ollie, LB, Minnesota, 388
16. Goedjen, Tom, K, Iowa State, 414
17. Bellizeare, Adolph, RB, Pennsylvania, 441

NEW ENGLAND 1975
1. *Francis, Russ, TE, Oregon, 16
2. *Shoate, Rod, LB, Oklahoma, 41
3. *Cusick, Pete, DT, Ohio State, 66
4. *Carter, Allen, RB, USC [from San Diego thru Cleveland] 86
*Burks, Steve, WR, Arkansas State, 91
5. *Grogan, Steve, QB, Kansas State, 116
*Freeman, Steve, DB, Mississippi State [from Philadelphia] 117
6. Choice to Detroit
7. *Williams, Lawrence, WR, Texas Tech, 172
8. Choice to Chicago Bears
9. Choice to Pittsburgh
10. Choice to Pittsburgh
11. Garnett, Rene, DB, Idaho State, 272
12. Kendon, Matt, DT, Idaho State, 297
Holloway, Condredge, QB-DB, Tennessee [from Washington] 306
13. Harvey, Joe, DE, Northern Michigan, 328
14. Gossom, Tom, WR, Auburn, 353
15. Clayton, Don, RB, Murray State, 378
16. Marbury, Kerry, RB, West Virginia, 403
17. Horton, Myke, T, UCLA, 428

NEW ORLEANS 1975
1. *Burton, Larry, WR, Purdue, 7
*Schumacher, Kurt, T, Ohio State [from New York Jets] 12
2. *Gross, Lee, C, Auburn, 32
3. *Jones, Andrew, RB, Washington State, 60
*Grooms, Elois, DE, Tennessee Tech [from Detroit thru Minnesota] 63
4. Choice to San Francisco
Starkebaum, John, DB, Nebraska [from Philadelphia] 92
Hall, Charlie, DE, Tulane [from St. Louis] 99
5. Choice to Chicago Bears
6. Choice to Detroit
*Lemon, Mike, LB, Kansas [from Buffalo] 149
7. *Rogers, Steve, RB, LSU, 163
8. Choice to St. Louis
9. *Strachan, Mike, RB, Iowa State, 216
10. Heater, Chuck, RB, Michigan, 241
11. Lee, Danny, P, Northeast Louisiana, 266
12. Gustafson, Ron, WR, North Dakota, 294
13. Upchurch, Jim, RB, Arizona, 319
14. Rhino, Randy, DB, Georgia Tech, 343
15. Burget, Grant, RB, Oklahoma, 372
16. *McDonald, Mike, LB, Catawba, 397
17. *Westbrooks, Greg, LB, Colorado, 422

NEW YORK GIANTS 1975
1. Choice to Dallas
2. *Simpson, Al, T, Colorado State, 27
3. Choice to Denver
*Buggs, Danny, WR, West Virginia [from San Francisco] 62
4. *Giblin, Robert, DB, Houston, 79
5. Choice to Miami
6. Choice to Baltimore
7. *Obradovich, Jim, TE, USC, 158
8. *Tate, John, LB, Jackson State, 183
9. Mahoney, Mike, WR, Richmond, 210
10. McClowry, Terry, LB, Michigan State, 235
11. *Martin, George, DE, Oregon, 262
12. *White, Marsh, RB, Arkansas, 287
13. Townsend, Ricky, K, Tennessee, 314
14. Choice to Miami
15. O'Connor, Jim, RB, Drake, 366
16. Micklos, Jim, TE, Ball State, 391
17. *Colbert, Rondy, DB, Lamar, 417

NEW YORK JETS 1975
1. Choice to New Orleans
2. *Davis, Anthony, RB, USC, 37
3. *Wood, Richard, LB, USC, 68
4. Choice to Baltimore
5. Wysocki, Joe, G, Miami, 118
6. Choice to Miami
*Alward, Tom, G, Nebraska [from Miami] 153
7. Choice to Baltimore thru Chicago Bears
8. *Scott, James, WR, Henderson J.C., 193
9. Taylor, Everett, DB, Memphis State, 224
10. James, Charles, DB, Jackson State, 249
11. Bradford, Jon, RB, Central State (OH), 274
12. *Cooper, Bert, LB, Florida State, 299
13. Spivey, Dan, DT, Georgia, 324
14. *Fields, Joe, C, Widener, 349
15. *Manor, Brison, DT, Arkansas, 380
16. Wells, Greg, G, Albany State, 405
17. Bartoszek, Mike, TE, Ohio State, 430

OAKLAND 1975
1. *Colzie, Neal, DB, Ohio State, 24
2. *Phillips, Charles, DB, USC [from Buffalo] 45
Choice to Buffalo
3. *Carter, Louis, RB, Maryland, 76
4. Choice to San Diego
5. *Humm, David, QB, Nebraska, 128
6. Choice to Cleveland
7. Daniels, James, DB, Texas A&M, 180
8. Choice to San Diego
9. Knight, Harry, QB, Richmond, 232
10. *Sylvester, Steve, T, Notre Dame, 259
11. Choice to San Diego
12. Magee, Jack, C, Boston College, 310
13. Choice to San Diego
14. Doyle, Tom, QB, Yale, 362
15. Careathers, Paul, RB, Tennessee, 389
16. Choice to Baltimore
17. Choice to Baltimore

PHILADELPHIA 1975
1. Choice to Los Angeles Rams
2. Choice to Buffalo
3. Choice to Los Angeles Rams
4. Choice to New Orleans
5. Choice to New England
6. Choice to Cincinnati
7. Capraun, Bill, T, Miami, 167
8. *Bleamer, Jeff, T, Penn State, 198
9. Choice to San Francisco
10. *Schroy, Ken, DB, Maryland, 248
11. Rowen, Keith, G, Stanford, 273
12. Pawlewicz, Dick, RB, William & Mary, 298
13. *Ehlers, Tom, LB, Kentucky, 324
14. O'Rourke, Larry, DT, Ohio State, 355
15. Korver, Clayton, DE, Northwestern (IA), 379 +
16. Jones, Calvin, WR, Texas Tech, 404
17. Webb, Gary, DE, Temple, 429

PITTSBURGH 1975
1. *Brown, Dave, DB, Michigan, 26
2. *Barber, Bob, DE, Grambling, 51
3. *White, Walter, TE, Maryland, 78
4. Evans, Harold, LB, Houston, 104
5. *Sexton, Russell, DB, Elon, 130
6. Crenshaw, Marvin, T, Nebraska, 156
7. Mattingly, Wayne, T, Colorado, 185
8. Kropp, Tom, LB, Kearney State [from Kansas City] 190
Humphrey, Al, DE, Tulsa, 208
9. Clark, Eugene, G, UCLA [from New England] 222
Reimer, Bruce, RB, North Dakota State, 234
10. Heyer, Kirt, DT, Kearney State [from New England] 247
Gray, Archie, WR, Wyoming, 260
11. Little, Randy, TE, West Liberty, 286
12. Murphy, Greg, DE, Penn State, 312
13. *Gaddis, Bob, WR, Mississippi Valley State, 337
14. *Collier, Mike, RB, Morgan State, 364
15. Thatcher, James, WR, Langston [from Kansas City] 371
*Smith, Marty, DT, Louisville, 390
16. Bassler, Miller, TE, Houston, 415
17. Hegener, Stan, G, Nebraska, 442

ST. LOUIS 1975
1. *Gray, Tim, DB, Texas A&M, 21
2. Germany, Jim, RB, New Mexico State, 46
3. Choice to San Francisco
4. Choice to New Orleans
5. *Goodman, Harvey, T, Colorado, 124
6. *Jameson, Larry, DT, Indiana, 152
7. Beaird, Steve, RB, Baylor, 177
8. Adams, John, DT, West Virginia [from New Orleans] 188
Lauriano, Louis, DB, Long Beach State, 202
9. Choice to San Francisco
10. *McGraw, Mike, LB, Wyoming, 255
11. *Latin, Jerry, RB, Northern Illinois, 280
12. Jones, Ben, WR, LSU, 308
13. Lindgren, Steve, DE, Hamline, 333
14. Bahe, Ritch, WR, Nebraska, 358
15. Franklin, Ron, DT, Boise State, 386
16. Miller, Mark, WR, Missouri, 411
17. Monroe, Ken, RB, Indiana State, 436

SAN DIEGO 1975
1. *Johnson, Gary, DT, Grambling, 8
*Williams, Mike, DB, LSU [from Washington] 22
2. *Kelcher, Louie, DT, SMU [from Cleveland] 30
*Dean, Fred, LB, Louisiana Tech, 33
3. Choice to Green Bay
*Fuller, Mike, DB, Auburn [from Los Angeles Rams thru Chicago Bears] 73
4. Choice to New England thru Cleveland
*Bernich, Ken, LB, Auburn [from Oakland] 101
5. Nosbusch, Kevin, DT, Notre Dame, 111
Waddell, Charles, TE, North Carolina [from Was thru Los Angeles Rams and Buffalo] 125
6. Carroll, John, WR, Oklahoma [from Cleveland] 134
*Shields, Billy, T, Georgia Tech, 136
7. *Young, Rickey, RB, Jackson State, 164
8. Choice to Kansas City thru Washington
Collier, Barry, T, Georgia [from Washington] 203
*Peretta, Ralph, G, Purdue [from Oakland] 206
9. *Keller, Larry, LB, Houston, 214
10. Bradley, Otha, DT, USC, 242
11. Phason, Vince, DB, Arizona, 267
McBee, Ike, WR, San Jose State [from Oakland] 284
12. Dahl, Jerry, LB, North Dakota State, 292
13. Demmerle, Pete, WR, Notre Dame, 320
Printers, Glen, RB, South Colorado State [from Oakland] 335
14. Barnett, Reggie, DB, Notre Dame, 345
15. Roush, John, G, Oklahoma, 370
16. Salvestrini, Chip, G, Yankton, 398
17. *Jeffrey, James, QB, Baylor, 423

SAN FRANCISCO 1975
1. *Webb, Jimmy, DT, Mississippi State, 10
2. *Collins, Greg, LB, Notre Dame, 35
3. Choice to New York Giants
*Hart, Jeff, T, Oregon State [from Buffalo] 71
*Mike-Mayer, Steve, K, Maryland [from Washington] 72
*Baker, Wayne, DT, BYU [from New Orleans] 74
4. *Elam, Cleveland, DE, Tennessee State [from New Orleans] 85
*Oliver, Frank, DB, Kentucky State, 87
5. Bullock, Wayne, RB, Notre Dame, 114
6. Choice to Kansas City
7. Choice to Buffalo
8. Kendrick, Preston, LB, Florida, 191
9. Johnson, James, DB, Tennessee State, 218
Natale, Dan, TE, Penn State [from Philadelphia] 223
Douglas, Caesar, T, Illinois Weslyan [from St. Louis] 230
10. Layton, Donnie, RB, South Carolina State, 243
11. Hernandez, Gene, DB, TCU, 270
12. Worley, Rick, QB, Howard Payne, 295
13. *Mitchell, Dale, LB, USC, 322
14. Henson, David, WR, Abilene Christian, 347
15. Lavin, Rich, TE, Western Illinois, 374
16. Choice to Baltimore
17. Choice to Baltimore

WASHINGTON 1975
1. Choice to San Diego
2. Choice to Green Bay
3. Choice to San Francisco
4. Choice to Buffalo
5. Choice to San Diego thru Los Angeles Rams and Buffalo
*Thomas, Mike, RB, Nevada-Las Vegas [from Chicago Bears] 108
6. Choice to Cleveland
Doak, Mark, T, Nebraska [from Denver] 147
7. Choice to Chicago Bears thru St. Louis
8. Choice to San Diego
9. *Hickman, Dallas, DE, California, 228
10. Choice to Miami
11. Johnson, Ardell, DB, Nebraska [from Denver] 277
Hackenbruck, Jerry, DE, Oregon State, 282
12. Choice to New England
13. McKie, Morris, DB, North Carolina A&T, 344
14. Benson, Dave, LB, Weber State, 359
15. *Kuehn, Art, C, UCLA, 384
16. Pavelka, Dennis, G, Nebraska, 412
17. Taylor, Carl, DE, Memphis State, 437

1976

Held April 8-9, 1976

There were 487 selections instead of 492. Five teams forfeited choices: the Chicago Bears and New York Giants each a sixth-round pick, Washington a seventh-round pick, and Atlanta and the

New York Jets each a tenth-round pick.

The expansion Tampa Bay Buccaneers and Seattle Seahawks alternated making the first and second selections of each round. Each new team also received two choices at the end of the second, third, fourth, and fifth rounds.

On March 30-31, Tampa Bay and Seattle each selected 39 players in an expansion draft. Each of the other 26 teams froze 29 players from its roster. Tampa Bay and Seattle alternated making selections from the remaining pool of players. When the first player was chosen from each team, that team then froze two additional players. Tampa Bay and Seattle continued making their selections until three players had been chosen from each existing team.

ATLANTA 1976

1. *Bean, Bubba, RB, Texas A&M, 9
2. *Collins, Sonny, RB, Kentucky, 36
3. *Scott, Dave, T, Kansas, 71
4. Brett, Walt, G-T, Montana, 102
5. Choice to Minnesota
   Choice to Buffalo
6. Varner, Stan, DT-DE, BYU [from Denver] 169
7. *Farmer, Karl, WR, Pittsburgh, 193
8. *Reed, Frank, DB, Washington, 219
9. *McKinnely, Phil, T, UCLA, 246
10. Choice forfeited
11. Brislin, Chuck, T, Mississippi State, 302
12. Bolton, Pat, K, Montana State, 329
13. Williams, Mike, T, Florida, 356
14. Husfloen, Mark, DE, Washington State, 383
15. Olson, Ron, DB, Washington, 414
16. Curto, Pat, LB, Ohio State, 441
17. Green, Tony, DB, Texas Tech, 468

BALTIMORE 1976

1. *Novak, Ken, DT, Purdue, 20
2. Choice to Pittsburgh
3. *Simonini, Ed, LB, Texas A&M, 81
   *Lee, Ron, RB, West Virginia [from Tampa Bay] 90
4. Choice to Pittsburgh
5. *Shiver, Sanders, LB, Carson-Newman [from Chicago Bears thru Mia and Chicago Bears] 134
   *Kirkland, Mike, QB, Arkansas, 143
6. Choice to Buffalo
7. Choice to New Orleans thru Chicago Bears and Oakland
8. *Thompson, Rick, WR, Baylor, 228
9. Levenick, Stu, T, Illinois, 258
10. *Baylor, Tim, DB, Morgan State, 283
11. Gibney, Rick, DT, Georgia Tech, 310
12. Stavroff, Frank, K, Indiana, 339
13. Choice to Oakland
14. Cummings, Jeremiah, DE, Albany State, 394
15. Alexander, Gary, T, Clemson, 424
16. Fuhrman, Mike, TE, Memphis State [from Washington thru Baltimore and San Francisco] 449
   Ludwig, Steve, C, Miami, 451
17. Choice to Oakland

BUFFALO 1976

1. *Clark, Mario, DB, Oregon, 18
2. *Jones, Ken, G, Arkansas State, 45
   *Devlin, Joe, T, Iowa [from St. Louis] 52
3. *Williams, Ben, DT, Mississippi, 78
4. *Jilek, Dan, LB, Michigan, 78
5. *Coleman, Fred, TE, Northeast Louisiana, 142
6. Benson, Leslie, DE, Baylor [from Atlanta] 164
   *Piper, Scott, WR, Arizona, 171
   *Powell, Darnell, RB, Tennessee-Chattanooga [from Baltimore] 175
7. Williams, Jackie, DB, Texas A&M [from New York Giants] 195
   Choice to New York Jets
8. Gardner Scott, QB, Virginia [from Cleveland] 215
   Easter, Bobby Joe, RB, Middle Tennessee State, 226
   Meadowcroft, Art, G, Minnesota [from Washington thru Atlanta] 227
9. Turner, Jeff, LB, Kansas [from San Diego] 241
   Kotzur, Bob, DT, Southwest Texas State, 255
10. *Moody, Keith, DB, Syracuse, 280
11. Smith, Forry, WR, Iowa State, 309
12. Lowery, Joe, RB, Jackson State, 336
13. Wilcox, Will, G, Texas, 365
14. Williams, Tony, WR, Middle Tennessee State, 392
15. Robinson, Arnold, LB, Bethune-Cookman, 421
16. Gorrell, Gary, LB, Boise State, 448
17. Berg, Bob, K, New Mexico, 477

CHICAGO BEARS 1976

1. *Lick, Dennis, T, Wisconsin [from Green Bay thru Los Angeles Rams and Detroit] 8
   Choice to Detroit
2. Choice to Pittsburgh
3. *Baschnagel, Brian, RB-WR, Ohio State [from New England] 66
   Choice to Detroit
4. *Sciarra, John, DB, UCLA, 103
   Rhodes, Wayne, DB, Alabama [from Detroit thru Miami] 108
5. Choice to Baltimore thru Miami and Chicago Bears
6. *Jiggetts, Dan, T, Harvard [from Cleveland] 161
   Choice forfeited
7. *Muckensturm, Jerry, LB, Arkansas State, 190
8. Choice to Oakland thru San Diego
9. Choice to Philadelphia
10. Choice to Washington
11. Andersen, Norm, WR, UCLA, 299
12. O'Leary, John, RB, Nebraska, 330
13. Kasowski, Dale, RB, North Dakota, 357
14. Cuie, Ron, RB, Oregon State, 384
15. *Meyers, Jerry, DT, Northern Illinois, 411
16. Parker, Ronald, TE, TCU, 442
17. Malham, Mike, LB, Arkansas State, 469

CINCINNATI 1976

1. *Brooks, Billy, WR, Oklahoma [from Philadelphia] 11
2. *Griffin, Archie, RB, Ohio State, 24
   *Bujnoch, Glenn, Texas A&M [from Philadelphia] 38
3. *Bahr, Chris, K, Penn State, 51
   *Reece, Danny, DB, USC [from Philadelphia] 69
   *Williams, Reggie, LB, Dartmouth, 82
4. *Davis, Tony, RB, Nebraska [from Kansas City] 106
   *Fairchild, Greg, G, Tulsa, 116
5. *Shelby, Willie, DB, Alabama [from San Francisco] 138
   *Perry, Scott, DB, Williams, 147
6. Nelson, Orlando, TE, Utah State, 176
7. Bateman, Bob, QB, Brown [from New England] 187
   Rome, Pete, DB, Miami (OH) [from Green Bay] 192
   Kuhn, Ken, LB, Ohio State, 205
   *Hunt, Ron, T, Oregon, 232
9. Allgood, Lonnie, WR, Syracuse, 259
10. Klaban, Tom, K, Ohio State, 287
11. *Morgan, Melvin, Mississippi Valley State, 314
12. Harris, Joe Dale, WR, Alabama, 340
13. Walker, Randy, RB, Miami (OH), 371
14. *Coleman, Greg, P, Florida A&M, 398
15. Hieber, Lynn, QB, Indiana (PA), 425
16. Demopoulos, George, C, Miami, 455
17. Dannelley, Scott, G, Ohio State, 482

CLEVELAND 1976

1. *Pruitt, Mike, RB, Purdue, 7
2. Choice to Oakland
3. *Logan, Dave, WR-TE, Colorado, 65
4. Swick, Gene, QB, Toledo [from New England thru Philadelphia] 97
   *St. Clair, Mike, DE, Grambling, 99
5. *Sheppard, Henry, T, SMU, 130
6. Choice to Chicago Bears
7. Cassidy, Steve, DT, LSU, 189
8. Choice to Buffalo
9. Reed, James, RB, Mississippi, 242
   Nagel, Craig, QB, Purdue [from Oakland] 261
10. Kleber, Doug, T, Illinois, 271
11. Celek, Doug, DE, Kent State, 297
12. Choice to Houston
13. Murray, Brian, T, Arizona, 354
14. Smalzer, Joe, TE, Illinois, 381
15. Philyaw, Luther, DB, Loyola (Los Angeles), 408
16. Lorenzen, Chris, DT, Arizona State, 438
17. Fleming, Tom, WR, Dartmouth, 464

DALLAS 1976

1. *Kyle, Aaron, DB, Wyoming, 27
2. *Jensen, Jim, RB, Iowa [from New York Giants] 40
   *Eidson, Jim, G, Mississippi State, 55
3. *Fergerson, Duke, WR, San Diego State [from San Francisco] 73
   Smith, John, RB, Boise State [from Denver] 75
   *Johnson, Butch, WR, Cal-Riverside, 87
4. *Rafferty, Tom, G, Penn State, 119
5. *Pesuit, Wally, T, Kentucky, 151
6. McGuire, Greg, T, Indiana, 181
7. *Schaum, Greg, DT, Michigan State [from San Diego] 186
   *Williams, Dave, RB, Colorado, 208
8. Laws, Henry, DB, South Carolina, 236
9. *Reece, Beasley, DB, North Texas State, 264
10. Cook, Leroy, DE, Alabama, 290
11. Greene, Cornelius, QB, Ohio State, 317
12. *McShane, Charles, LB, California Lutheran, 346
13. Driscoll, Mark, QB, Colorado State, 374
14. Mushinskie, Larry, TE, Nebraska, 402
15. Curry, Dale, LB, UCLA, 430
16. Costanzo, Rick, T, Nebraska, 458
17. Woodfill, Stan, K, Oregon, 486

DENVER 1976

1. *Glassic, Tom, G, Virginia, 15
2. *Knoff, Kurt, DB, Kansas, 43
3. Choice to Dallas
4. *Penrose, Craig, QB, San Diego State, 107
5. *Perrin, Lonnie, RB, Illinois, 139
6. Choice to Atlanta
7. Choice to Houston
8. *Betterson, James, RB, North Carolina, 224
9. Czirr, Jim, C, Michigan, 252
   Lisko, Jim, LB, Arkansas State [from St. Louis] 260
10. Gilliam, Art, DE, Grambling, 278
11. Pittman, Greg, LB, Iowa State, 306
12. *Moore, Randy, DT, Arizona, 334
13. McGraw, Donnie, RB, Houston, 362
14. *Evans, Larry, LB, Mississippi College, 390
15. *Summers, Wilbur, P, Louisville, 418
16. *Huddleston John, LB, Utah, 446
17. Cozens, Randy, DE, Pittsburgh, 474

DETROIT 1976

1. *Hunter, James, DB, Grambling [from Chicago Bears] 10
   *Gaines, Lawrence, RB, Wyoming, 16
2. *Long, Ken, G, Purdue, 44
   *Hill, David, TE, Texas A&I [from Washington thru San Diego] 46
3. *Bolinger, Russ, T, Long Beach State [from Chicago Bears] 68
   *Woodcock, John, DT, Hawaii, 76
4. Choice to Chicago Bears thru Miami
5. Choice to San Francisco
   Scavella, Steadman, LB, Miami [from Miami] 145
   Choice to New England
7. *Ten Napel, Garth, LB, Texas A&M, 198
8. Sorenson, Rich, K, Cal State-Chico [from Philadelphia thru New England] 217
   Braswell, Charles, DB, West Virginia, 225
9. Jones, Leanell, TE, Long Beach State, 253
10. Bowerman, Bill, QB, New Mexico State, 279
11. Shugrue, Gary, DE-LB, Villanova, 307
12. McCabe, Mike, C, South Carolina, 335
13. Jacobs, Mel, WR-KR, San Diego State, 363
14. Elston, Leonard, WR, Kentucky State, 391
15. Smock, Trent, WR, Indiana, 419
16. McCurdy, Craig, LB, William & Mary, 447
17. Meeks, Jim, DB, Boise State, 475

GREEN BAY 1976

1. Choice to Chicago Bears thru Los Angeles Rams and Detroit
   *Koncar, Mark, T, Colorado [from Oakland] 23
2. Choice to Los Angeles Rams
3. Choice to Pittsburgh
   *McCoy, Mike, DB, Colorado [from Kansas City] 72
4. *Perko, Tom, LB, Pittsburgh, 101
5. *Thompson, Aundra, RB, East Texas State, 132
6. Choice to Kansas City thru Houston
7. Choice to Cincinnati
8. *Burrow, Jim, DB, Nebraska, 218
9. *Gueno, Jim, LB, Tulane, 245
10. *Green, Jessie, WR, Tulsa, 274
11. *Leak, Curtis, WR, Johnson C. Smith, 301
12. *Jackson, Mel, G, USC, 328
13. Bowman, Bradley, DB, Southern Mississippi, 355
14. Henson, John, RB, Cal Poly-SLO, 386
15. *Dandridge, Jerry, LB, Memphis State, 413
16. Timmermans, Mike, G, Northern Iowa, 440
17. Hall, Ray, TE, Cal Poly-SLO, 467

HOUSTON 1976

1. Choice to New England thru San Francisco
2. *Barber, Mike, TE, Louisiana Tech, 48
3. Choice to Kansas City
4. Choice to San Diego thru Oakland
   *Largent, Steve, WR, Tulsa [from Los Angeles Rams thru Philadelphia and Green Bay] 117
5. Choice to Kansas City
6. Simonsen, Todd, T, South Dakota State, 173
7. *Harris, Larry, DT, Oklahoma State [from Denver] 197
   Choice to New England
8. *Simon, Bobby, T, Grambling, 229
9. *Stringer, Art, LB, Ball State, 256
10. Kincannon, Steve, QB, Cal State-Humboldt, 284
11. Walker, Skip, RB, Texas A&M, 311
12. Bell, Larry, DT, East Texas State [from Cleveland] 324
   Choice to San Diego
13. O'Rourke, Dan, WR, Colorado, 368
14. Reimer, John, T, Wisconsin, 395
15. Byars, Bobby, DB, Cheyney, 422
16. Johnson, Claude, LB, Florida A&M, 452
17. Misher, Allen, WR, LSU, 479

KANSAS CITY 1976

1. *Walters, Wayne, G, Iowa, 14
2. *Frazier, Cliff, DT, UCLA, 41
3. *Simons, Keith, DT, Minnesota [from New Orleans thru San Francisco] 63
   Choice to Green Bay
   *Barbaro, Gary, DB, Nicholls State [from New York Giants thru Green Bay] 74
   *Marshall, Henry, WR, Missouri [from Houston] 79
4. Choice to Cincinnati
5. *Lee, Willie, DT, Bethune-Cookman, 137
   *Elrod, Jimbo, LB, Oklahoma [from Houston] 144
6. *Taylor, Steve, DB, Kansas [from Green Bay thru Houston] 166
   Gregolunas, Bob, LB, Northern Illinois, 167
   Harper, Calvin, T, Illinois State [from Washington] 172
7. Wellington, Rod, RB, Iowa, 196
8. *Olsen, Orrin, C, BYU, 222
9. *Collier, Tim, East Texas State, 249
10. *Paul, Whitney, DE, Colorado, 277
11. Squires, Bob, TE, Hastings, 304
12. Porter, Harold, WR, Southwestern Louisiana, 331
13. Bruner, Joe, QB, Northeast Louisiana, 361
14. Thurman, Rick, T, Texas, 388
15. *Rozumek, Dave, LB, New Hampshire, 415
16. Anderson, Dennis, P-DB, Arizona, 445
17. *McNeil, Pat, RB, Baylor, 472

LOS ANGELES RAMS 1976

1. *McLain, Kevin, LB, Colorado State, 26
2. *Thomas, Pat, DB, Texas A&M [from Green Bay] 39
   *McCartney, Ron, LB, Tennessee, 53
3. *Slater, Jackie, G, Jackson State, 86
4. Taylor, Gerald, WR, Texas A&I [from Tampa Bay] 96
   Choice to Houston thru Phi and Green Bay
5. *Ekern, Carl, LB, San Jose State [from San Diego] 128
   *Bordelon, Ken, DE, LSU, 149
   *Scales, Dwight, WR, Grambling [from Tampa Bay] 155
6. Choice to Washington
7. Buie, Larry, DB, Mississippi State, 207
8. Choice to Washington
9. Church, Jeb, DB, Stanford, 263
10. *Johns, Freeman, WR, SMU, 288
11. Nemeth, Brian, TE, South Carolina, 316
12. *Jodat, Jim, RB, Carthage, 344
13. Hamilton, Steve, QB, Emporia State, 373
14. Burleson, Al, DB, Washington, 400
15. Campbell, Malcolm, WR, Cal State-Los Angeles, 429
16. Gage, Rick, WR, Arkansas Tech, 456
17. Shaw, Gary, DB, BYU, 485

MIAMI 1976

1. *Gordon, Larry, LB, Arizona State [from Washington] 17
   *Bokamper, Kim, LB, San Jose State, 18
2. *McCreary, Loaird, TE, Tennessee State, 49
3. *Harris, Duriel, WR, New Mexico State, 80
4. *Mitchell, Melvin, G, Tennessee State [from New York Jets thru Chicago Bears] 98
   Choice to Philadelphia
5. Choice to Detroit
6. *Davis, Gary, RB, Cal Poly-SLO, 174
7. Ingersoll, Joe, G, Nevada-Las Vegas [from New Orleans] 185
   Owens, John, DE, Tennessee State, 200
8. *Simpson, Bob, T, Colorado, 230
9. *Thomas, Norris, DB, Southern Mississippi, 257
10. *Fencik, Gary, DB, Yale [from Washington] 281
   *Testerman, Don, RB, Clemson, 282
11. Pride, Dexter, RB, Minnesota, 312
12. *Young, Randy, T, Iowa State, 338
   Brandford, Darryl, DT, Northwestern [from St. Louis] 341
13. Head, Bernie, C, Tulsa, 366
14. Gissler, Bob, LB, South Dakota State, 396
15. Holmes, Ron, Utah State, 423
16. Green, Mike, K, Ohio U., 450
17. Grantz, Jeff, QB, South Carolina, 480

MINNESOTA 1976

1. *White, James (Duck), DT, Oklahoma State, 25
2. *White, Sammy, WR, Grambling, 54
3. *Hamilton, Wes, G, Tulsa, 85
4. *Willis, Leonard, WR, Ohio State, 118
5. *Wagner, Steve, DB, Wisconsin [from Atlanta] 133
   Barnette, Keith, RB, Boston College, 150
6. Egerdahl, Terry, DB, Minnesota-Duluth, 180
7. *Brune, Larry, DB, Rice, 206
8. Choice to New England
9. *Hagins, Isaac, WR, Southern, 262
10. Salmon, Bill, QB, Northern Iowa, 289
11. Kracher, Steve, RB, Montana State, 318
12. Sparks, Robert, DB, Cal State-San Francisco, 345
13. Pauson, Gary, DE, Colorado State, 372
14. Stapleton, Jeff, T, Purdue, 401
15. *Groce, Ron, RB, Macalester, 428
16. Hickel, Randy, DB, Montana State, 457
17. Lukowski, Rich, West Virginia, 484

NEW ENGLAND 1976

1. *Haynes, Mike, DB, Arizona State, 5
   *Brock, Pete, C, Colorado [from San Francisco] 12
   *Fox, Tim, DB, Ohio State [from Hou thru San Francisco] 21
2. *Forte, Ike, RB, Arkansas, 35
3. Choice to Chicago Bears
4. Choice to Cleveland thru Philadelphia
5. Choice to San Diego
6. Choice to New York Giants
   *Boyd, Greg, DE, San Diego State, 170
7. Choice to Cincinnati
   *Brooks, Perry, DT, Southern [from Houston] 202
8. Choice to Philadelphia
   Betts, Stu, RB, Northern Michigan [from

Minnesota] 235
9. *Beaudoin, Doug, DB, Minnesota, 243
10. *Feacher, Ricky, WR, Mississippi Valley State, 270
11. *Thomas, Donnie, LB, Indiana, 298
12. Bell, Nathaniel, DT, Tulane, 325
13. Jones, James, DB, Central Michigan, 352
14. Quehl, Dave, WR, Holy Cross, 382
15. Coleman, Bernard, WR, Bethune-Cookman, 409
16. Brown, Clifford, DT, Tuskegee, 436
17. Anderson, Todd, C, Stanford, 465

NEW ORLEANS 1976
1. *Muncie, Chuck, RB, California, 3
2. *Galbreath, Tony, RB, Missouri, 32
3. Choice to Kansas City from San Francisco
*Simmons, Bob, T, Texas [from Washington thru San Diego] 77
4. *Owens, Tinker, WR, Oklahoma, 95
5. *Parrish, Scott, T, Utah State, 127
6. *Stieve, Terry, G, Wisconsin, 160
7. Choice to Miami
Bauer, Ed, G, Notre Dame [from Baltimore thru Chicago Bears and Oakland] 201
8. *Cassady, Craig, DB, Ohio State, 213
9. Peiffer, Warren, DT, Iowa, 240
10. Hardin, Junior, LB, Eastern Kentucky, 269
11. Kokal, Greg, QB, Kent State, 294
12. Butts, Milton, T, North Carolina, 323
13. Downing, Kenny, DB, Missouri, 350
14. Hucke, Rich, DE, Western Montana, 379
15. Seminoff, Steve, DT, Wichita State, 406
16. Jones, Gene, T, Bowling Green, 435
17. MacDonald, Scott, TE, West Virginia, 462

NEW YORK GIANTS 1976
1. *Archer, Troy, DE, Colorado, 13
2. Choice to Dallas
3. Choice to Kansas City thru Green Bay
4. *Bell, Gordon, RB, Michigan [from San Francisco] 104
*Carson, Harry, LB, South Carolina State, 105
5. Wilson, Melvin, DB, Cal State-Northridge, 136
6. *Lloyd, Dan, LB, Washington [from New England] 162
Choice forfeited
7. Choice to Buffalo
8. Jordan, John, DT, Indiana, 221
9. Choice to San Diego
10. Thomas, John, RB, Valley City, 276
11. Brantley, Craig, WR, Clemson, 303
12. *Golsteyn, Jerry, QB, Northern Illinois, 333
13. Caswell, Rick, KR, Western Kentucky, 360
14. Mullane, Jerry, LB, Lehigh, 387
15. Morgan, Eddie, DT, Arkansas State, 417
16. Lawson, Dave, K, Air Force, 444
17. Curnutte, Steve, DB, Vanderbilt, 471

NEW YORK JETS 1976
1. *Todd, Richard, QB, Alabama, 6
2. *Suggs, Shafer, DB, Ball State, 33
3. *Buttle, Greg, LB, Penn State, 67
4. Choice to Miami thru Chicago Bears
5. King, Steve, T, Michigan, 129
6. *Martin, Bob, LB, Nebraska, 163
7. *Faulk, Larry, (Abdul Salaam), DE, Kent State, 188
Richards, James, RB, Florida [from Buffalo] 199
8. Davis, Joe, G, USC [from Tampa Bay] 211
*Giammona, Louie, RB, Utah State, 214
9. Moore, Ronnie, WR, Virginia Military, 244
10. Choice forfeited
11. *Pillers, Lawrence, LB, Alcorn State, 296
12. *Buckey, Don, WR, North Carolina State, 326
Buckey, Dave, QB, North Carolina State [from Philadelphia] 327
13. Choice to Philadelphia
14. Gluchoski, Al, C, West Virginia, 380
15. Faulk, Rick, P, Cal State-San Francisco, 410
16. Godwin, James, RB, Fayetteville State, 437
17. Willie, Darwin, TE, Tulane, 466

OAKLAND 1976
1. Choice to Green Bay
2. *Philyaw, Charles, DT, Texas Southern [from Cleveland] 34
*Blount, Jeb, QB, Tulsa, 50
3. *Bonness, Rik, LB, Nebraska, 84
4. *McMath, Herb, LB, Morningside [from Washington thru San Diego] 110
Choice to San Diego
5. *Steinfort, Fred, K, Boston College, 146
6. Choice to San Diego
7. *Chapman, Clarence, WR, Eastern Michigan, 204
8. *Dove, Jerome, DB, Colorado State [from Chicago Bears thru San Diego] 220
*Kunz, Terry, RB, Colorado, 231
9. Choice to Cleveland
10. Lewis, Dwight, DB, Purdue, 286
11. *Jennings, Rick, RB, Maryland, 313
12. *Brown, Cedric DB, Kent State, 343
13. Crnick, Craig, DE, Idaho [from Baltimore] 367
Young, Mark, T, Washington State, 370
14. Young, Calvin, RB, Fresno State, 397
15. Hargrave, Carl, DB, Upper Iowa, 427
16. Hogan, Doug, DB, USC, 454
17. Tate, Buddy, DB, Tulsa [from Baltimore] 478
Beasley, Nate, RB, Delaware, 481

PHILADELPHIA 1976
1. Choice to Cincinnati
2. Choice to Cincinnati
3. Choice to Cincinnati
4. Choice to San Francisco
Smith, Mike, DE, Florida [from Miami] 111
5. *Johnson, Greg, DT, Florida State, 135
6. Johnson, Kirk, T, Howard Payne, 165
7. *Hairston, Carl, DE, Maryland-Eastern Shore, 191
8. La Fargue, Richard, C, Arkansas [from New England] 216
Choice to Detroit thru New England
9. *Hogan, Mike, RB, Tennessee-Chattanooga [from Chicago Bears] 247
*Osborne, Richard, TE, Texas A&M, 248
10. *Lusk, Herb, RB, Long Beach State, 273
11. Gilbert, Mike, DT-DE, San Diego State, 300
12. Choice to New York Jets
13. *Tautolo, Terry, LB, UCLA [from New York Jets] 353
Ebbecke, Steve, DB, Villanova, 358
14. Shy, Melvin, DB, Tennessee State, 385
15. White, Brett, P, UCLA, 412
16. Campassi, Steve, RB, Kentucky, 439
17. Terry, Anthony, DB, Cal-Davis, 470

PITTSBURGH 1976
1. *Cunningham, Bennie, TE, Clemson, 28
2. *Pinney, Ray, C, Washington [from Chicago Bears] 37
*Kruczek, Mike, QB, Boston College [from Baltimore] 47
Files, James, C, McNeese State, 56
3. *Coder, Ron, DT, Penn State [from Green Bay] 70
*Pough, Ernest, WR, Texas Southern, 88
4. *Monds, Wonder, DB, Nebraska [from Baltimore] 112
*Bell, Theo, WR, Arizona, 120
5. Norton, Rodney, LB, Rice, 152
6. *Dunn, Gary, DT, Miami [from San Diego thru St. Louis] 159
*Deloplaine, Jack, RB, Salem, 182
7. Burton, Barry, TE, Vanderbilt, 209
8. *McAleney, Ed, DT, Massachusetts, 237
9. *Gaines, Wentford, DB, Cincinnati, 265
10. *Campbell, Gary, LB, Colorado, 291
11. Fuchs, Rolland, RB, Arkansas, 319
12. Carroll, Bill, WR, East Texas State, 347
13. Kain, Larry, TE, Ohio State, 375
14. Fields, Wayne, DB, Florida, 403
15. Davis, Mel, DE, North Texas State, 431
16. Butts, Randy, RB, Kearney State, 459
17. Kirk, Kelvin, WR, Dayton, 487

ST. LOUIS 1976
1. *Dawson, Mike, DT, Arizona, 22
2. Choice to Buffalo
3. *Oates, Brad, T, BYU, 82
4. *Tilley, Pat, WR, Louisiana Tech, 114
5. *Morris, Wayne, RB, SMU [from Washington] 141
Choice to Washington
6. Choice to San Francisco
7. Rogers, Phil, RB, Virginia Tech, 203
8. *Burks, Randy, WR, Southeastern Oklahoma, 233
9. Choice to Denver
10. Walker, Randy, RB, Bethune-Cookman, 285
11. Akins, Marty, DB, Texas, 315
12. Choice to Miami
13. Brewton, Greg, DT, Michigan State, 369
14. Crosier, Raymond, DE, Abilene Christian, 399
15. Choice to Washington
*Nelson, Lee, DB, Florida State [from Washington] 420
16. Beaird, Cecil, WR, Fisk, 453
17. Myers, Dan, DB, Georgia Tech, 483

SAN DIEGO 1976
1. *Washington, Joe, RB, Oklahoma, 4
2. *Macek, Don, G, Boston College, 31
3. *Dorsey, Larry, WR, Tennessee State, 64
4. *Horn, Bob, LB, Oregon State, 94
*Singleton, Ron, TE, Grambling [from Hou thru Oakland] 13
*Owens, Artie, WR, West Virginia [from Oakland] 115
5. Choice to Los Angeles Rams
*Lowe, Woodrow, LB, Alabama [from New England] 131
6. Choice to Pittsburgh thru St. Louis
Lane, Calvin, DB, Fresno State [from Oakland] 178
7. Choice to Dallas
8. DiRienzo, Tony, K, Oklahoma, 212
9. Choice to Buffalo
*Harrison, Glynn, RB, Georgia [from New York Giants] 251
10. Perlinger, Jeff, DE, Michigan, 268
11. *Preston, Ray, LB, Syracuse, 295
12. Lee, Ron, DB, Oregon, 322
Harris, Herman, DB, Mississippi Valley State [from Houston] 337
13. *Lee, John, DT, Nebraska, 351
14. Jones, Ed, G, Cincinnati, 378
15. Hoffman, Jack, DT-DE, Indiana, 407
16. Harrison, Jack, G, California, 434
17. *Sanders, Clarence, LB, Cincinnati, 463

SAN FRANCISCO 1976
1. Choice to New England
2. *Cross, Randy, C, UCLA, 42
*Lewis, Eddie, DB, Kansas [from Tampa Bay] 57
3. Choice to Dallas
4. *Rivera, Steve, WR, California [from Philadelphia] 100
Choice to New York Giants
5. Choice to Cincinnati
*Leonard, Anthony, DB, Virginia Union [from Detroit] 140
6. *Pennywell, Robert, LB, Grambling, 168
*Bull, Scott, QB, Arkansas [from St. Louis] 177
7. Chesley, Jay, DB, Vanderbilt, 194
8. *Ayers, John, T, West Texas State, 223
9. *Harrison, Kenny, WR, SMU, 250
10. Ross, Robin, T, Washington State, 275
11. *Hofer, Paul, RB, Mississippi, 305
12. Loper, Gerald, G, Florida, 332
13. Brumfield, Larry, DB, Indiana State, 359
14. *Miller, Johnny, LB, Livingstone, 389
15. *Stidham, Howard, LB, Tennessee Tech, 416
16. *Lewis, Reggie, DE, San Diego State, 443
17. Jenkins, Darryl, RB, San Jose State, 473

SEATTLE 1976
1. *Niehaus, Steve, DT, Notre Dame, 2
2. *Green, Sammy, LB, Florida, 29
*Smith, Sherman, RB, Miami (OH), 58
*Raible, Steve, WR, Georgia Tech, 59
3. *Lloyd, Jeff, DE, West Texas State, 62
*Engles, Rick, P, Tulsa, 89
*Bitterlich, Don, K, Temple, 92
4. *Myer, Steve, QB, New Mexico, 93
*Johnson, Randy, G, Georgia, 122
*Bolton, Andy, RB, Fisk, 123
5. *Dufek, Don, DB, Michigan, 126
*Jones, Ernie, DB, Miami, 153
Bates, Larry, RB, Miami, 156
6. *Darby, Alvis, TE, Florida, 157
7. Dixon, Lodie, DT, Arkansas State, 184
8. Shipp, Larry, WR, LSU, 210
9. Bos, Bob, T, Iowa State, 239
10. *Coffield, Randy, LB, Florida State, 266
11. Muehr, Keith, P, Southwestern Louisiana, 293
12. Barnett, Ronnie, WR, Texas-Arlington, 320
13. *Reid, Andy, RB, Georgia, 349
14. Blinks, Jarvis, DB, Northwestern State (LA), 376
15. Smith, Dan, T, Washington State, 405
16. Urczyk, Jeff, G, Georgia Tech, 432
17. Rowland, Chris, QB, Washington, 461

SEATTLE (Expansion) 1976
*Baker, Wayne, DT, BYU [from San Francisco]
*Barisch, Carl, DT, Princeton [from Cleveland]
*Bebout, Nick, T, Wyoming [from Atlanta]
*Blackwood, Lyle, DB, TCU [from Cincinnati]
*Bradley, Ed, LB, Wake Forest [from Pittsburgh]
*Brown, Dave, DB, Michigan [from Pittsburgh]
*Clune, Don, WR, Pennsylvania [from New York Giants]
*Colbert, Rondy, DB, Lamar [from New York Giants]
*Crump, Dwayne, DB, Fresno State [from St. Louis]
*Curtis, Mike, LB, Duke [from Baltimore]
*Davis, Jerry, DB, Morris Brown [from New York Jets]
*Demarie, John, G, LSU [from Cleveland]
*Evans, Norm, T, TCU [from Miami]
*Geddes, Ken, LB, Nebraska [from Los Angeles Rams]
*Graff, Neil, QB, Wisconsin [from New England]
*Hansen, Don, LB, Illinois [from Atlanta]
*Hayman, Gary, RB, Penn State [from Buffalo]
*Hoaglin, Fred, C, Pittsburgh [from Houston]
*Howard, Ron, TE, Seattle [from Dallas]
*Hutcherson, Ken, LB, Livingston State [from Green Bay]
*Jolley, Gordon, T, Utah [from Detroit]
*Keithley, Gary, QB, Texas-El Paso [from St. Louis]
*Kuehn, Art, C, UCLA [from Washington]
Marbury, Kerry, RB, West Virginia [from New England]
*Matthews, Al, DB, Texas A&I [from Green Bay]
*McCullum, Sam, WR, Montana State [from Minnesota]
*McMakin, John, TE, Clemson [from Detroit]
*McMillan, Eddie, DB, Florida State [from Los Angeles Rams]
*Olds, Bill, RB, Nebraska [from Baltimore]
O'Neal, Jesse, DE, Grambling [from Houston]
*Owens, Joe, DE, Alcorn State [from New Orleans]
*Penchion, Bob, G, Alcorn State [from San Francisco]
*Picard, Bob, WR, Eastern Washington State [from Philadelphia]
*Rasley, Rocky, G, Oregon State [from Kansas City]
*Taylor, Steve, DB, Kansas [from Denver]
*Tipton, Dave, DE, Stanford [from San Diego]
*Waddell, Charles, TE, North Carolina [from San Diego]
*Woods, Larry, DT, Tennessee State [from New York Jets]
*Woolsey, Rolly, DB, Boise State [from Dallas]

TAMPA BAY 1976
1. *Selmon, Lee Roy, DE, Oklahoma, 1
2. *DuBose, Jimmy, RB, Florida, 30
Choice to San Francisco
*Selmon, Dewey, DT, Oklahoma, 60
3. *Young, Steve, T, Colorado, 61
Choice to Baltimore
Maughan, Steve, LB, Utah State, 91
4. Choice to Los Angeles Rams
Appleby, Richard, WR, Georgia, 121
*Little, Everett, G, Houston, 124
5. Kelson, Mishael, DB, West Texas State, 125
*Wilson, Steve, T, Georgia, 154
Choice to Los Angeles Rams
6. *Jordan, Curtis, DB, Texas Tech, 158
7. *Dickinson, Parnell, QB, Mississippi Valley State, 183
8. Choice to New York Jets
9. Welch, Bruce, G, Texas A&M, 238
10. Smith, Sid, LB, BYU, 267
11. Washington, Melvin, DB, Colorado State, 297
12. *Ragsdale, George, RB, North Carolina A&T, 321
13. Jenkins, Brad, TE, Nebraska, 348
14. *Roaches, Carl, KR, Texas A&M, 377
15. Dzierzak, Bob, DT, Utah State, 404
16. West, Tommy, LB, Tennessee, 433
17. Berry, Jack, QB, Washington & Lee, 460

TAMPA BAY (Expansion) 1976
*Ball, Larry, LB, Louisville [from Detroit]
*Blahak, Joe, DB, Nebraska [from Minnesota]
Bridges, Bubba, DT, Colorado [from Denver]
*Broussard, Bubba, LB, Houston [from Chicago Bears]
*Carter, Louis, RB, Maryland [from Oakland]
*Colavito, Steve, LB, Wake Forest [from Philadelphia]
*Cotney, Mark, DB, Cameron State [from Houston]
*Current, Mike, T, Ohio State [from Denver]
*Davis, Anthony, RB, USC [from New York Jets]
Davis, Ricky, DB, Alabama [from Cincinnati]
*Douthitt, Earl, DB, Iowa [from Chicago Bears]
*Elia, Bruce, LB, Ohio State [from Miami]
*Ely, Larry, LB, Iowa [from Chicago Bears]
*Fest, Howard, G, Texas [from Cincinnati]
*Gordon, Ira, G, Kansas State [from San Diego]
*Gunn, Jimmy, LB, USC [from New York Giants]
*Hart, Harold, RB, Texas Southern [from Oakland]
*Keeton, Durwood, DB, Oklahoma [from New England]
*Kendrick, Vince, RB, Florida [from Atlanta]
*LaGrand, Morris, RB, Tampa [from New Orleans]
*McGee, Willie, WR, Alcorn State [from Los Angeles Rams]
*McKay, John (J.K.), WR, USC [from Cleveland]
*Moore, Bob, TE, Stanford [from Oakland]
*Moore, Manfred, RB, USC [from San Francisco]
*Oliver, Frank, DB, Kentucky State [from Buffalo]
*Pear, Dave, DT, Washington [from Baltimore]
*Peterson, Cal, LB, UCLA [from Dallas]
*Reavis, Dave, T, Arkansas [from Pittsburgh]
*Rudolph, Council, DE, Kentucky State [from St. Louis]
*Ryczek, Dan, C, Virginia [from Washington]
*Smith, Barry, WR, Florida State [from Green Bay]
*Stone, Ken, DB, Vanderbilt [from Washington]
*Swift, Doug, LB, Amherst [from Miami]
*Thompson, Dave, T-C, Clemson [from New Orleans]
*Toomay, Pat, DE, Vanderbilt [from Buffalo]
*Ward, John, C-G, Oklahoma State [from Minnesota]
*Williams, Lawrence, WR, Texas Tech [from Kansas City]
*Yochum, Dan, T, Syracuse [from Philadelphia]

WASHINGTON 1976
1. Choice to Miami
2. Choice to Detroit thru San Diego
3. Choice to New Orleans thru San Diego
4. Choice to Oakland thru San Diego
5. Choice to St. Louis
Hughes, Mike, G, Baylor [from St. Louis] 148
6. Choice to Kansas City
*Marvaso, Tom, DB, Cincinnati [from Los Angeles Rams] 179
7. Choice forfeited
8. Choice to Buffalo thru Atlanta
*Fryer, Bryan, WR, Alberta [from Los Angeles Rams] 234 +
9. Akins, Curtis, G-C, Hawaii, 254
10. Strohmeier, Paul, LB, Washington [from Chicago Bears] 272
Choice to Miami
11. Gissler, Dean, DE, Nebraska, 308
12. *Tullis, Walter, DB, Delaware State, 342
13. Britt, Waymon, DB-WR, Michigan, 364
14. Buckner, Quinn, DB, Indiana, 393 +
15. Choice to St. Louis
Monroe, John, RB, Bluefield [from St. Louis] 426
16. Choice to Baltimore thru Baltimore and San Francisco
17. Wills, Chuck, DB, Oregon, 476

1977

Held May 3-4, 1977

There were 335 selections instead of 336. Houston forfeited its fifth-round choice.

ATLANTA 1977
1. *Bryant, Warren, T, Kentucky, 6
*Faumina, Wilson, DT, San Jose State [from St. Louis] 20
2. *Thielemann, R.C., C, Arkansas, 36
3. *Fields, Edgar, DT, Texas A&M, 63
4. *Leavitt, Allan, K, Georgia, 89
5. *Diggs, Shelton, RB, USC, 120

6. Choice to San Diego
Jenkins, Keith, DB, Cincinnati [from Washington] 161
7. Choice to Cleveland
8. *Packer, Walter, WR, Mississippi State, 203
9. Maxwell, John, T, Boston College, 230
Speer, Robert, DE, Arkansas State [from Washington] 242
10. *Ryckman, Billy, WR, Louisiana Tech, 257
11. *Farmer, Dave, RB, USC, 287
12. *Parrish, Don, DE, Pittsburgh, 314

BALTIMORE 1977
1. *Burke, Randy, WR, Kentucky, 26
2. *Ozdowski, Mike, DE, Virginia, 53
3. Choice to St. Louis
4. Choice to Cleveland thru Washington, Miami, and Chicago Bears
5. Choice to New Orleans
6. *O'Neal, Calvin, LB, Michigan, 163
7. *Carter, Blanchard, T, Nevada-Las Vegas, 193
8. Helvis, Ken, T-C, Georgia, 220
9. Capriola, Glen, RB, Boston College, 247
10. *Baker, Ron, G, Oklahoma State, 277
11. Ruff, Brian, LB, Citadel, 304
12. Deutsch, Bill, RB, North Dakota, 331

BUFFALO 1977
1. Choice to Cincinnati
2. *Dokes, Phil, DT, Oklahoma State [from Detroit] 12
Choice to Seattle thru Dallas
3. *Brown, Curtis, RB, Missouri, 59
*Kimbrough, John, WR, St. Cloud State [from Cleveland] 73
4. *Dean, Jimmy, DT, Texas A&M, 86
5. Besana, Fred, QB, California, 115
*O'Donoghue, Neil, K, Auburn [from San Francisco] 127
6. Choice to San Francisco
Pruitt, Ron, DE, Nebraska [from Cleveland] 157
7. *Nelms, Mike, DB, Baylor, 170
8. *Morton, Greg, DT, Michigan, 197
9. Choice to Kansas City
10. Choice to Pittsburgh
11. Jackson, Nate, RB, Tennessee State, 282
12. *Romes, Charles, DB, North Carolina Central, 309

CHICAGO BEARS 1977
1. *Albrecht, Ted, T, California, 15
2. *Spivey, Mike, DB, Colorado, 43
3. *Earl, Robin, RB, Washington [from New York Giants] 61
Choice to Miami
4. Choice to Pittsburgh
5. Choice to Oakland
6. *Evans, Vince, QB, USC [from Tampa Bay] 140
Choice to Philadelphia
7. Butler, Gerald, WR, Nicholls State, 182
8. Choice to New York Jets
9. Buonamici, Nick, DT, Ohio State, 238
10. Breckner, Dennis, DE, Miami, 266
11. *Zelencik, Connie, C, Purdue, 294
12. Irvin, Terry, DB, Jackson State, 322

CINCINNATI 1977
1. *Edwards, Eddie, DT, Miami [from Buffalo] 3
*Whitley, Wilson, DT, Houston [from Philadelphia] 8
*Cobb, Mike, TE, Michigan State, 22
2. *Johnson, Pete, RB, Ohio State, 49
3. *Voight, Mike, RB, North Carolina, 76
4. *Walker, Rick, TE, UCLA [from Tampa Bay] 85
*Wilson, Mike, T, Georgia, 103
*Anderson, Jerry, DB, Oklahoma [from St. Louis] 105
5. *Phillips, Ray, LB, Nebraska, 133
6. *Duniven, Tommy, QB, Texas Tech, 160
7. *Breeden, Louis, DB, North Carolina Central, 187
*Corbett, Jim, TE, Pittsburgh [from Minnesota] 194
8. St. Victor, Jose, G, Syracuse, 214
9. Zachary, Willie, WR, Central State (OH), 245
10. Bialik, Bob, P, Hillsdale, 272
11. Parrish, Joel, G, Georgia [from San Diego] 292
*Allen, Carl, DB, Southern Mississippi, 299
12. Percival, Alex, WR, Morehouse, 326

CLEVELAND 1977
1. *Jackson, Robert, LB, Texas A&M, 17
2. *Skladany, Tom, P-K, Ohio State, 46
3. Choice to Buffalo
4. *Davis, Oliver, DB, Tennessee State, 102
*Sims, Robert, DT, South Carolina State [from Baltimore thru Washington, Miami, and Chicago Bears] 110
5. Choice to San Diego
6. Choice to Buffalo
7. Randle, Kenny, WR, SMU [from Atlanta] 173
*Smith, Blane, TE, Purdue, 184
*Lingenfelter, Bob, T, Nebraska [from St. Louis] 188
8. Armstrong, Bill, DB, Wake Forest, 213
9. Brown, Daryl, DB, Tufts, 240
10. Burkett, Tom, T, North Carolina, 269
11. Nash, Charles, WR, Arizona, 296
12. *Tierney, Clarence, C, Georgia Tech, 325

DALLAS 1977
1. *Dorsett, Tony, RB, Pittsburgh [from Seattle] 2
Choice to San Diego
2. *Carano, Glenn, QB, Nevada-Las Vegas, 54
3. *Hill, Tony, WR, Stanford [from Philadelphia] 62
Belcher, Val, G, Houston, 81
4. *Brown, Guy, LB, Houston, 108
5. *Frederick, Andy, DT, New Mexico, 137
6. *Cooper, Jim, T, Temple, 164
7. *Stalls, Dave, DE, Northern Colorado, 191
8. Cleveland, Al, DE, Pacific [from San Diego] 208
Williams, Fred, RB, Arizona State, 221
9. Cantrell, Mark, C, North Carolina, 248
10. *DeBerg, Steve, QB, San Jose State, 275
11. Wardlow, Don, TE, Washington, 305
12. Peters, Greg, G, California, 332

DENVER 1977
1. *Schindler, Steve, G, Boston College, 18
2. *Lytle, Rob, RB, Michigan, 45
3. Choice to Green Bay
4. *Bryan, Billy, C, Duke, 101
5. Choice to New York Jets
6. Choice to Los Angeles Rams
7. *Swider, Larry, P, Pittsburgh, 185
8. Culliver, Calvin, RB, Alabama, 212
9. *Jackson, Charles, DT, Washington, 241
10. *Middlebrook, Oren, WR, Arkansas State, 268
11. Heck, Phil, LB, California, 297
12. Levenhagen, Scott, TE, Western Illinois, 324

DETROIT 1977
1. Choice to Buffalo
2. *Williams, Walt, DB, New Mexico State, 42
3. *Kane, Rick, RB, San Jose State, 69
4. *Blue, Luther, WR, Iowa State, 96
5. *Crosby, Ron, LB, Penn State [from Seattle] 114
Choice to Pittsburgh
6. Choice to San Diego
*Pinkney, Reggie, DB, East Carolina [from Minnesota thru New England] 166
7. *Black, Tim, LB, Baylor, 179
8. Griffin, Mark, T, North Carolina, 209
9. Mathieson, Steve, QB, Florida State, 236
10. *Anderson, Gary, G, Stanford, 263
11. *Daykin, Tony, LB, Georgia Tech, 293
12. Greenwood, Dave, G-C, Iowa State, 320

GREEN BAY 1977
1. *Butler, Mike, DE, Kansas, 9
*Johnson, Ezra, DE, Morris Brown [from Oakland] 28
2. *Koch, Greg, DT, Arkansas, 39
3. Choice to Houston
Scribner, Rick, G, Idaho State [from Denver] 74
4. Choice to Pittsburgh
5. *Simpson, Nate, RB, Tennessee State, 122
6. *Moresco, Tim, DB, Syracuse, 149
7. *Gofourth, Derrel, C, Oklahoma State [from New York Giants] 172
Tipton, Rell, G, Baylor, 176
8. *Whitehurst, David, QB, Furman, 206
9. Mullins, Joel, T, Arkansas State, 233
10. *Culbreath, Jim, RB, Oklahoma, 260
11. *Randolph, Terry, DB, American International, 290
12. Choice to Oakland

HOUSTON 1977
1. *Towns, Morris, T, Missouri, 11
2. *Reihner, George, G, Penn State, 38
3. Choice to San Francisco
*Wilson, Tim, RB, Maryland [from Green Bay] 66
*Giles, Jimmie, TE, Alcorn State [from Miami] 70
*Carpenter, Rob, RB, Miami (OH) [from Oakland thru Buffalo]
4. Choice to Kansas City
*Anderson, Warren, WR, West Virginia State [from San Diego thru Miami] 98
5. Choice forfeited
6. *Woolford, Gary, DB, Florida State, 148
*Carter, David, C, Western Kentucky [from New England] 165
7. Choice to New York Giants
8. Davis, Steve, WR, Georgia [from Seattle] 198
*Foster, Eddie, WR, Houston, 205
9. *Currier, Bill, DB, South Carolina, 232
10. Hull, Harvey, LB, Mississippi State, 262
11. Romano, Al, LB, Pittsburgh, 289
12. *Johansson, Ove, K, Abilene Christian, 316

KANSAS CITY 1977
1. *Green, Gary, DB, Baylor, 10
2. *Reed, Tony, RB, Colorado, 37
3. *Howard, Thomas, LB, Texas Tech, 67
4. *Bailey, Mark, RB, Long Beach State [from Philadelphia] 92
*Samuels, Tony, TE, Bethune-Cookman, 94
*Helton, Darius, G, North Carolina Central [from Houston] 95
*Harris, Eric, DB, Memphis State [from Washington] 104
5. Choice to Pittsburgh
6. Burleson, Rick, DE, Texas, 150
Herrera, Andre, RB, Southern Illinois [from Oak thru Tampa Bay and Chicago Bears] 167
7. *Golub, Chris, DB, Kansas, 177
8. Olsonoski, Ron, LB, St. Thomas (MN), 204
Smith, Waddell, WR, Kansas [from Washington] 215
9. Glanton, Derrick, DE, Bishop [from Buffalo] 226
Green, Dave, T, New Mexico, 235
10. Vitali, Mark, QB, Purdue, 261
11. Mitchell, Maurice, WR, Northern Michigan, 288
12. *Burks, Raymond, LB, UCLA, 318

LOS ANGELES RAMS 1977
1. *Brudzinski, Bob, LB, Ohio State, 23
2. *Cromwell, Nolan, DB, Kansas [from Seattle] 31
*Waddy, Billy, RB-WR, Colorado [from Washington thru San Diego] 50
Choice to Seattle
3. *Fulton, Ed, G, Maryland [from San Diego] 68
*Tyler, Wendell, RB, UCLA, 79
4. *Ferragamo, Vince, QB, Nebraska [from New Orleans] 91
Jones, Eary, DE, Memphis State, 107
5. *Hickman, Donnie, G, USC [from Washington] 130
*Williams, Jeff, G, Rhode Island, 134
6. *Best, Art, RB, Kent State [from Denver] 156
Choice to New Orleans
7. Choice to Washington
8. Bockwoldt, Rod, DB, Weber State, 218
9. Choice to Washington
10. Petersen, Don, TE, Boston College, 274
11. *Long, Carson, K, Pittsburgh, 302
12. Caudill, Barry, C, Southern Mississippi, 330

MIAMI 1977
1. *Duhe, A.J., DT, LSU, 13
2. *Baumhower, Bob, DT, Alabama, 40
3. Choice to Houston
Watson, Mike, T, Miami (OH) [from Chicago Bears] 71
4. Choice to Washington
5. *Michel, Mike, K, Stanford [from Tampa Bay] 113
*Harris, Leroy, RB, Arkansas State, 123
6. Choice to New York Giants
7. *Herron, Bruce, LB, New Mexico, 180
8. *Perkins, Horace, DB, Colorado, 207
9. *Turner, Robert, RB, Oklahoma State, 237
10. Carter, Mark, T, Eastern Michigan, 264
11. *Alexander, John, DE, Rutgers, 291
12. *Anderson, Terry, WR, Bethune-Cookman, 321

MINNESOTA 1977
1. *Kramer, Tommy, QB, Rice, 27
2. *Swilley, Dennis, G, Texas A&M, 55
3. *Hannon, Tom, DB, Michigan State, 83
4. Choice to Seattle
5. *Moore, Ken, TE, Northern Illinois, 138
6. Choice to Detroit thru New England
7. Choice to Cincinnati
8. Strozier, Clint, DB, USC, 222
9. *Studwell, Scott, LB, Illinois, 250
10. Beaver, Dan, K, Illinois, 278
11. *Hartwig, Keith, WR, Arizona, 306
12. Kelleher, Jim, RB, Colorado, 335

NEW ENGLAND 1977
1. *Clayborn, Raymond, DB, Texas [from San Francisco] 16
*Morgan, Stanley, WR, Tennessee, 25
2. *Ivory, Horace, RB, Oklahoma [from San Francisco] 44
*Hasselbeck, Don, TE, Colorado, 52
3. *Brown, Sidney, DB, Oklahoma, 82
4. *Skinner, Gerald, T, Arkansas, 109
5. Choice to St. Louis
6. Choice to Houston
7. Smith, Ken, WR, Arkansas-Pine Bluff, 192
8. *Benson, Brad, G, Penn State, 219
9. Vogele, Jerry, LB, Michigan, 249
10. Rasmussen, John, T, Wisconsin, 276
Alexander, Giles, DE, Tulsa [from Oakland] 279
11. *Costict, Ray, LB, Mississippi State, 303
12. *Preston, Dave, RB, Bowling Green, 333

NEW ORLEANS 1977
1. *Campbell, Joe, DE, Maryland, 7
2. *Fultz, Mike, DT, Nebraska, 34
3. *Watts, Bob, LB, Boston College, 64
4. Choice to Los Angeles Rams
5. *Lafary, Dave, T, Purdue, 118
*Hubbard, Dave, T, BYU [from Baltimore] 136
6. *Parsley, Cliff, P, Oklahoma State, 147
Shick, Tom, G, Maryland [from Los Angeles Rams] 162
7. *Boykin, Greg, RB, Northwestern, 174
8. *Stewart, Jim, DB, Tulsa, 201
9. Knowles, Dave, T, Indiana, 231
10. *Septien, Rafael, K, Southwestern Louisiana, 258
11. Blain, John, T, San Jose State, 285
12. *Dalton, Oakley, DE, Jackson State, 315

NEW YORK GIANTS 1977
1. *Jeter, Gary, DT, USC, 5
2. *Perkins, Johnny, WR, Abilene Christian, 32
3. Choice to Chicago Bears
4. Vaughan, Mike, T, Oklahoma, 88
5. *Dean, Randy, QB, Northwestern, 117
6. Jordan, Bob, T, Memphis State, 143
*Moorehead, Emery, WR-RB, Colorado [from Miami] 153
7. Choice to Green Bay
*Dixon, Al, TE, Iowa State [from Houston] 178
8. Rice, Bill, DT, BYU, 199
Rodgers, Otis, LB, Iowa State [from San Francisco] 211
9. Mullins, Ken, DE, Florida A&M, 228
10. Jones, Mike, WR, Minnesota, 255
11. Helms, Bill, TE, San Diego State, 284
12. Simmons, Elmo, RB, Texas-Arlington, 311

NEW YORK JETS 1977
1. *Powell, Marvin, T, USC, 4
2. *Walker, Wesley, WR, California, 33
3. Choice to Pittsburgh
*Marshall, Charles (Tank), DE, Texas A&M [from San Francisco] 72
4. *Dierking, Scott, RB, Purdue, 90
5. *Griggs, Perry, WR, Troy State, 116
Gregory, Gary, T, Baylor [from Denver] 129
6. *Klecko, Joe, DT, Temple, 144
7. *White, Charles, RB, Bethune-Cookman [from Tampa Bay] 168
*Grupp, Bob, DB, Duke, 171
*Long, Kevin, RB, South Carolina [from Oakland] 195
8. *Alexander, Dan, DT, LSU, 200
Thompson, Ed, LB, Ohio State [from Chicago Bears] 210
9. *Robinson, Matt, QB, Georgia, 227
10. *Hennessy, John, DE, Michigan, 256
11. Choice to Philadelphia
Butterfield, Dave, DB, Nebraska [from Oakland] 307
12. Gargis, Phil, RB-DB, Auburn, 312
Conrad, Dave, T, Maryland [from Philadelphia] 313

OAKLAND 1977
1. Choice to Green Bay
2. *Davis, Mike, DB, Colorado [from Philadelphia] 35
*McKnight, Ted, RB, Minnesota-Duluth, 57
3. Choice to Houston thru Buffalo
4. *Marvin, Mickey, G, Tennessee, 112
5. *Hayes, Lester, DB, Texas A&M [from Chicago Bears] 126
*Barnes, Jeff, LB, California, 139
6. Choice to Kansas City thru Tampa Bay and Chicago Bears
7. *Martini, Rich, WR, Cal-Davis [from Washington thru Houston and New York Giants] 190
Choice to New York Jets
8. *Robiskie, Terry, RB, LSU, 223
9. Choice to Tampa Bay
10. Choice to New England
11. Choice to New York Jets
12. *Martin, Rod, LB, USC [from Green Bay] 317
*Benirschke, Rolf, K, Cal-Davis, 334

PHILADELPHIA 1977
1. Choice to Cincinnati
2. Choice to Oakland
3. Choice to Dallas
4. Choice to Kansas City
5. Sharp, Skip, DB, Kansas, 119
6. Russell, Kevin, DB, Tennessee State, 145
*Montgomery, Wilbert, RB, Abilene Christian [from Chicago Bears] 154
*Mitchell, Martin, DB, Tulane [from St. Louis thru Washington] 158
7. *Johnson, Charlie, DT, Colorado, 175
8. *Franklin, Cleveland, RB, Baylor, 202
9. Humphreys, T.J., G, Arkansas State, 229
10. Mastronardo, John, WR, Villanova, 259
11. *Moore, Rocco, T, Western Michigan [from New York Jets] 283
Cordova, Mike, QB, Stanford, 286
12. Choice to New York Jets

PITTSBURGH 1977
1. *Cole, Robin, LB, New Mexico, 21
2. *Thornton, Sidney, RB, Northwestern State (LA), 48
3. *Beasley, Tom, DT, Virginia Tech [from New York Jets] 60
*Smith, Jim, WR, Michigan, 75
4. *Petersen, Ted, C, Eastern Illinois [from Green Bay] 93
*Smith, Laverne, RB, Kansas [from Chicago Bears] 99
*Audick, Dan, G, Hawaii, 106
5. *Stoudt, Cliff, QB, Youngstown State [from Kansas City] 121
*Courson, Steve, G, South Carolina [from Detroit] 125
*Winston, Dennis, LB, Arkansas, 132
6. *Harris, Paul, LB, Alabama, 159
7. Frisch, Randy, DT, Missouri, 186
8. August, Phil, WR, Miami, 217
9. Kelly, Roosevelt, TE, Eastern Kentucky, 244
10. Cowans, Alvin, DB, Florida [from Buffalo] 253
*LaCrosse, Dave, LB, Wake Forest, 271
11. West, Lou, DB, Cincinnati, 298
12. Stephens, Jimmy, TE, Florida [from Seattle] 310
Choice to Seattle

ST. LOUIS 1977
1. *Pisarkiewicz, Steve, QB, Missouri [from Washington] 19
Choice to Atlanta
2. *Franklin, George, RB, Texas A&I, 47
3. *Allerman, Kurt, LB, Penn State, 78
*Middleton, Terdell, RB, Memphis State [from Baltimore] 80
4. Choice to Cincinnati
5. Lee, Ernest, DT, Texas, 131

*Spiva, Howard, LB, Tennessee [from New England] 135
6. Choice to Philadelphia thru Washington
7. Choice to Cleveland
8. *Williams, Eric, LB, USC, 216
9. *Jackson, Johnny, DT, Southern, 243
10. LeJay, Jim, WR, San Jose State, 270
11. Lee, Greg, DB, Western Illinois, 301
12. Fenlaw, Rick, LB, Texas, 328

SAN DIEGO 1977
1. Choice to Seattle thru Dallas
2. *Rush, Bob, C, Memphis State [from Dallas] 24
2. Choice to Seattle thru Dallas
3. Choice to Los Angeles Rams
*King, Keith, DB, Colorado State [from Washington] 77
4. Choice to Houston thru Miami
5. *Williams, Clarence, RB, South Carolina, 124
*Olander, Cliff, QB, New Mexico State [from Cleveland] 128
6. *Lindstrom, Dave, DE, Boston U. [from Atlanta] 146
Barnes, Larry, RB, Tennessee State, 151
*Shaw, Pete, DB, Northwestern [from Detroit] 152
7. Bush, Ron, DB, USC, 181
8. Choice to Dallas
9. *Washington, Gene, WR, Georgia, 234
10. *Townsend, Curtis, LB, Arkansas, 265
11. Choice to Cincinnati
12. Stansik, Jim, TE, Eastern Michigan, 319

SAN FRANCISCO 1977
1. Choice to New England
2. Choice to New England
3. *Boyd, Elmo, WR, Eastern Kentucky [from Houston] 65
Choice to New York Jets
4. *Black, Stan, DB, Mississippi State, 100
5. Choice to Buffalo
6. *Burns, Mike, DB, USC [from Buffalo] 141
*Harlan, Jim, C, Howard Payne, 155
7. *Van Wagner, Jim, RB, Michigan Tech, 183
8. Choice to New York Giants
9. *Posey, David, K, Florida, 239
10. Choice to Tampa Bay
11. Billick, Brian, TE, BYU, 295
12. Martin, Scott, G, North Dakota, 323

SEATTLE 1977
1. Choice to Dallas
*August, Steve, G, Tulsa [from San Diego thru Dallas] 14
2. *Lynch, Tom, T, Boston College [from Buffalo thru Dallas] 30
Choice to Los Angeles Rams
*Beeson, Terry, LB, Kansas [from San Diego thru Dallas] 41
*Cronan, Pete, LB, Boston College [from Los Angeles Rams] 51
3. *Boyd, Dennis, DE, Oregon State, 58
4. *Yarno, John, C, Idaho, 87
Seivers, Larry, WR, Tennessee [from Minnesota] 111
5. Choice to Detroit
6. *Benjamin, Tony, RB, Duke, 142
7. *Sims, David, RB, Georgia Tech, 169
8. Choice to Houston
9. Adzick, George, DB, Minnesota, 225
10. *Adkins, Sam, QB, Wichita State, 254
11. Westbeld, Bill, T, Dayton, 281
12. Choice to Pittsburgh
Wilson, I.V., DT, Tulsa [from Pittsburgh] 329

TAMPA BAY 1977
1. *Bell, Ricky, RB, USC, 1
2. *Lewis, David, LB, USC, 29
3. *Hannah, Charley, DE, Alabama, 56
4. Choice to Cincinnati
5. Choice to Miami
6. Choice to Chicago Bears
7. Choice to New York Jets
8. *Hedberg, Randy, QB, Minot State, 196
9. Hemingway, Byron, LB, Boston College, 224
*Mucker, Larry, WR, Arizona State [from Oakland] 251
10. Morgan, Robert, RB, Florida, 252
Ball, Aaron, LB, Cal State-Fullerton [from San Francisco] 267
11. Rodgers, Chuck, DB, North Dakota State, 280
12. Sheffield, Chip, WR, Lenoir-Rhyne, 308

WASHINGTON 1977
1. Choice to St. Louis
2. Choice to Los Angeles Rams thru San Diego
3. Choice to San Diego
4. McColl, Duncan, DE, Stanford [from Miami] 97
Choice to Kansas City
5. Choice to Los Angeles Rams
6. Choice to Atlanta
7. Choice to Oakland thru Houston and New York Giants
*Haynes, Reggie, TE, Nevada-Las Vegas [from Los Angeles Rams] 189
8. Choice to Kansas City
9. Choice to Atlanta
Northington, Mike, RB, Purdue [from Los Angeles Rams] 246
10. Sykes, James, RB, Rice, 273
11. *Harris, Don, DB, Rutgers, 300
12. Kirkland, Curtis, DE, Missouri, 327

1978

Held May 2-3, 1978

There were 334 selections instead of 336. Seattle gave up its fourth-round choice in a 1977 supplemental draft. Green Bay forfeited its fourth-round pick.

ATLANTA 1978
1. *Kenn, Mike, T, Michigan, 13
2. *Stewart, Steve, LB, Minnesota, 43
3. *Waldemore, Stan, G, Nebraska, 70
4. *Cabral, Brian, LB, Colorado, 95
5. *Pearson, Dennis, WR, San Diego State, 125
6. *Parker, Rodney, WR, Tennessee State, 152
7. *Jackson, Alfred, WR, Texas [from Tampa Bay] 167
*Wright, James, TE, TCU, 179
8. Adkins, David, LB, Ohio State, 209
Williams, David, DB, Tennessee-Martin [from Washington] 216
9. *Pridemore, Tom, DB, West Virginia, 236
10. *Patton, Ricky, RB, Jackson State [from Philadelphia] 257
*Strong, Ray, RB, Nevada-Las Vegas, 263
11. Reed, Milton, DB, Baylor, 293
12. Butler, Daria, LB, Oklahoma State, 320

BALTIMORE 1978
1. *McCall, Reese, TE, Auburn, 25
2. *Woods, Mike, LB, Cincinnati, 52
3. Choice to San Francisco
4. Choice to Detroit
5. *Myers, Frank, T, Texas A&M [from San Francisco] 117
Choice to Kansas City
6. *Garry, Ben, RB, Southern Mississippi, 161
7. Logan, Jeff, RB, Ohio State, 191
8. Anthony, Monte, RB, Nebraska, 218
9. *Studdard, Dave, T, Texas, 245
10. Owens, Dallas, DB, Kentucky, 275
11. Mason, Henry, WR, Central Missouri, 302
12. Allen, Bruce, P, Richmond, 329

BUFFALO 1978
1. *Miller, Terry, RB, Oklahoma State, 5
2. *Hardison, Dee, DE, North Carolina, 32
*Hutchinson, Scott, DE, Florida [from San Francisco] 38
3. *Johnson, Dennis, RB, Mississippi State, 59
*Fulton, Danny, WR, Nebraska-Omaha [from San Francisco] 65
4. *Sanford, Lucius, LB, Georgia Tech, 89
5. Spaeth, Ken, TE, Nebraska, 114
6. Choice to New York Jets
Smith, Eric, T, Southern Mississippi [from Philadelphia] 145
7. *Celotto, Mario, LB, USC, 171
*Powell, Steve, RB, Northeast Missouri State [from Houston] 183
8. Choice to New England thru Philadelphia
9. Choice to New York Jets
10. *Grant, Will, C, Kentucky, 255
11. *Blanton, Jerry, LB, Kentucky, 282
12. Crump, Richard, RB, Northeastern Oklahoma, 308

CHICAGO BEARS 1978
1. Choice to Los Angeles Rams thru Cleveland
2. Choice to San Francisco
3. *Shearer, Sterling, DT, Texas, 74
4. Choice to Kansas City
5. Choice to Cincinnati
6. *Skibinski, John, RB, Purdue [from Kansas City] 139
*Leremia, Mekeli, DE, BYU, 158
7. Jones, Herman, WR, Ohio State, 185
8. Freitas, George, TE, California, 212
9. Martin, Mike, LB, Kentucky, 244
10. Zambiasi, Ben, LB, Georgia, 271
11. Underwood, Walt, DE, USC, 298
12. Sibley, Lew, LB, LSU, 325

CINCINNATI 1978
1. *Browner, Ross, DT, Notre Dame [from Philadelphia] 8
*Bush, Blair, C, Washington, 16
2. *Griffin, Ray, DB, Ohio State [from Philadelphia] 35
*Turner, Dave, RB, San Diego State, 45
3. *Vincent, Ted, DT, Wichita State, 72
*Bass, Dan, WR, Houston [from Denver] 83
4. *Law, Dennis, WR, East Tennessee State, 99
5. *Dinkel, Tom, LB, Kansas, 126
*Hertel, Bob, QB, USC [from Chicago Bears] 131
6. Geise, Steve, RB, Penn State, 155
7. Branson, Joe, DB, Livingstone, 182
Bass, Dan, G, Elon [from Denver] 193
8. Miller, Bill, T, Western Illinois, 211
9. *Shumon, Ron, LB, Wichita State, 238
10. *DePaso, Tom, LB, Penn State, 267
11. Prince, Calvin, RB, Louisville [from St. Louis] 293
*Donahue, Mark, G, Michigan, 294
12. Featsent, Kim, WR, Kent State, 323

CLEVELAND 1978
1. *Matthews, Clay, LB, USC, 12
*Newsome, Ozzie, WR, Alabama [from Los Angeles Rams] 23
2. *Evans, Johnny, P-QB, North Carolina State, 39
3. *Collins, Larry, RB, Texas A&I [from Detroit] 67
*Miller, Mark, QB, Bowling Green, 68
4. Choice to Miami
Pullara, Pete, G Tennessee-Chattanooga [from Washington thru Los Angeles Rams] 103
5. *Wright, William, WR, Memphis State, 122
6. Pitts, Al, C, Michigan State, 149
7. Choice to Miami
8. *Turnbow, Jesse, DT, Tennessee, 205
9. Kramer, Jon, G, Baylor, 234
10. Watson, Brent, T, Tennessee, 261
11. Gillard, Larry, DT, Mississippi State, 290
12. *Biedermann, Leo, T, California, 317

DALLAS 1978
1. *Bethea, Larry, DE, Michigan State, 28
2. *Christensen, Todd, RB, BYU, 56
3. Hudgens, Dave, DT, Oklahoma, 84
4. *Blackwell, Alois, RB, Houston, 110
5. Rosen, Rich, G, Syracuse, 138
6. Randolph, Harold, LB, East Carolina, 166
7. *Randall, Tom, DT-DE, Iowa State, 194
8. Butler, Homer, WR, UCLA, 222
9. Williams, Russ, DB, Tennessee, 250
10. Tomasetti, Barry, G, Iowa, 278
11. *Thurman, Dennis, DB, USC, 306
12. Washburn, Lee, G, Montana State, 334

DENVER 1978
1. *Latimer, Don, DT, Miami, 27
2. *Gay, William, TE, USC, 55
3. Choice to Cincinnati
4. Choice to Detroit
5. Choice to New York Giants
6. Choice to Detroit
7. Choice to Cincinnati
8. Smith, Frank, T, Alabama A&M, 221
9. Choice to San Francisco
10. *Kinney, Vince, WR, Maryland, 277
11. Brumley, Lacy, T, Clemson, 305
12. Choice to Miami

DETROIT 1978
1. *Bradley, Luther, DB, Notre Dame, 11
2. *Baker, Al, DE, Colorado State, 40
3. Choice to Cleveland
4. *Fifer, William, T, West Texas State, 94
*Elias, Homer, G, Tennessee State [from Baltimore] 107
5. *Tearry, Larry, C, Wake Forest [from Denver] 109
*Fowler, Amos, G, Southern Mississippi, 121
*Gray, Dan, DE, Rutgers [from San Diego] 123
6. *Hicks, Dwight, DB, Michigan, 150
*Ardizzone, Tony, G, Northwestern [from San Diego] 153
*Thompson, Jesse, WR, California [from Denver] 165
7. Gibson, Bruce, RB, Pacific, 177
8. *Breech, Jim, K, California, 206
9. Choice to San Francisco
10. Arrington, Fred, LB, Purdue, 262
11. Murray, Richard, DT, Oklahoma, 289
12. Patterson, Mark, DB, Washington State, 318

GREEN BAY 1978
1. *Lofton, James, WR, Stanford, 6
*Anderson, John, LB, Michigan [from Oakland] 26
2. *Hunt, Mike, LB, Minnesota, 34
3. *Hood, Estus, DB, Illinois State, 62
4. Choice forfeited
5. *Douglass, Mike, LB, San Diego State, 116
Wilder, Willie, RB, Florida [from Pittsburgh] 128
6. *Harris, Leotis, G, Arkansas, 144
7. Plasketes, George, LB, Mississippi, 172
8. *Sproul, Dennis, QB, Arizona State, 200
9. Myers, Keith, QB, Utah State, 228
10. Key, Larry, RB, Florida State, 256
Totten, Mark, C, Florida [from New York Giants] 259
11. *Jones, Terry, DT, Alabama, 284
12. *Ramson, Eason, TE, Washington State, 312

HOUSTON 1978
1. *Campbell, Earl, RB, Texas [from Tampa Bay] 1
Choice to Tampa Bay
2. Choice to Tampa Bay
3. *Nielsen, Gifford, QB, BYU, 73
4. *Renfro, Mike, WR, TCU, 98
5. Choice to San Francisco thru Kansas City and Chicago Bears
6. *Rucker, Conrad, TE, Southern, 154
7. Choice to Buffalo
8. *Wilson, J.C., DB, Pittsburgh, 210
9. Mol, Jim, DE, Morningside, 239
10. Young, Steve, TE, Wake Forest, 266
11. Thicklen, Willie, WR, Alabama State, 295
12. *Schuhmacher, John, G, USC, 322

KANSAS CITY 1978
1. *Still, Art, DE, Kentucky, 2
2. *Hicks, Sylvester, DE, Tennessee State, 29
3. *Spani, Gary, LB, Kansas State, 58
4. *Johnson, Danny, LB, Tennessee State, 85
Woods, Pete, QB, Missouri [from Chicago Bears] 104
5. *McRae, Jerrold, WR, Tennessee State, 112
Carey, Dwight, DT, Texas-Arlington [from Philadelphia] 118
*Woods, Robert, WR-KR, Grambling [from Baltimore] 134
6. Choice to Chicago Bears
7. *Odom, Ricky, DB, USC, 168
*Kellar, Bill, WR, Stanford [from Washington] 184
8. White, John Henry, RB, Louisiana Tech, 195
9. *Brown, Larry, T, Miami, 224
10. Bryant, Eart, DE, Jackson State, 251
11. *Milo, Ray, DB, New Mexico State, 280
12. *Brock, Willie, C, Colorado, 310

LOS ANGELES RAMS 1978
1. *Peacock, Elvis, RB, Oklahoma [from Chicago Bears thru Cleveland] 20
Choice to Cleveland
2. *Johnson, Stan, DT, Tennessee State [from Washington] 46
*Smith, Ronnie, WR, San Diego State, 53
3. *Corral, Frank, P, UCLA [from Washington] 78
White, Leon, C, Colorado, 80
4. *Manges, Mark, QB, Maryland, 105
5. Choice to San Diego
6. Choice to Tampa Bay
7. *Doss, Reggie, DE, Hampton, 189
8. Choice to Washington
9. Anderson, Andre, DE, New Mexico State, 246
10. Peal, Charles, T, Indiana, 273
11. Hostetler, Ron, LB, Penn State, 303
12. *Coppens, Gus, T, UCLA, 330

MIAMI 1978
1. Choice to San Francisco
2. *Benjamin, Guy, QB, Stanford, 51
3. *Smith, Lyman, DT, Duke [from New York Giants] 64
*Cefalo, Jimmy, WR, Penn State, 81
4. *Small, Gerald, DB, San Jose State [from Cleveland] 93
*Laasko, Eric, T, Tulane, 106
5. *Burgmeier, Ted, DB, Notre Dame [from Tampa Bay] 111
Choice to San Francisco
6. *Betters, Doug, DE, Nevada-Reno, 163
7. *Baldischwiler, Karl, T, Oklahoma [from Cleveland] 178
Henry, Lloyd, WR, Northeast Missouri State, 190
8. *Clancy, Sean, LB, Amherst, 217
9. *Hardy, Bruce, TE, Arizona State, 247
10. *Dennard, Mark, C, Texas A&M, 274
11. Choice to Seattle
12. Moore, Mike, RB, Middle Tennessee, 331
*Kenney, Bill, QB, Northern Colorado [from Denver] 333

MINNESOTA 1978
1. *Holloway, Randy, DE, Pittsburgh, 21
2. *Turner, John Jr., DB, Miami, 48
3. *Walton, Whip, LB, San Diego State, 75
4. *Hough, Jim, C, Utah State, 100
5. Choice to New York Giants
6. Choice to Washington thru San Francisco
7. Choice to Philadelphia
8. *Wood, Mike, K, Southeast Missouri State [from Seattle] 204
Choice to New York Jets
9. Deutsch, Mike, P, Colorado State, 240
10. Shaw, Hughie, RB, Texas A&I, 272
11. Harris, Ron, RB, Colorado State, 299
12. Morrow, Jeff, T, Minnesota, 326

NEW ENGLAND 1978
1. *Cryder, Bob, G, Alabama, 18
2. *Cavanaugh, Matt, QB, Pittsburgh, 50
3. *Pennywell, Carlos, WR, Grambling, 77
4. *Wheeler, Dwight, T, Tennessee State, 102
5. *Matthews, Bill, LB, South Dakota State, 129
6. Coleman, Kem, LB, Mississippi, 156
7. *Hawkins, Mike, LB, Texas A&I, 188
8. *Falcon, Terry, G, Montana [from Buffalo thru Philadelphia] 198
*Tatupu, Mosi, RB, USC, 215
9. Petersen, Tim, LB, Arizona State, 242
10. Ferguson, Bryan, DB, Miami, 269
11. Williams, Charlie, LB, Florida, 296
12. Gibney, John, C, Colgate, 328

NEW ORLEANS 1978
1. *Chandler, Wes, WR, Florida, 3
2. *Taylor, James, T, Missouri, 33
3. *Bennett, Barry, DT, Concordia (MN), 60
4. *Schwartz, Don, DB, Washington State, 87
5. *Felton, Eric, DB, Texas Tech, 115
6. Rieker, Mike, QB, Lehigh, 141
*Chesley, Francis, LB, Wyoming [from Washington thru Houston] 157
7. Choice to New York Jets
8. *Williams, Brooks, TE, North Carolina, 199
9. Carter, Richard, DB, North Carolina State, 226
10. Choice to New York Giants
11. Besaint, Nathan, DT, Southern, 283
Riley, Dave, RB, West Virginia [from Seattle] 285
12. *Hardy, Larry, TE, Jackson State, 309

NEW YORK GIANTS 1978
1. *King, Gordon, T, Stanford, 10
2. *McKinney, Odis, DB, Colorado, 37
3. Choice to Miami
4. *Taylor, Billy, RB, Texas Tech, 90
5. *Jackson, Terry, DB, San Diego State, 120
*Krahl, Jim, DT, Texas Tech [from Minnesota] 132
*DeRoo, Brian, WR, Redlands [from Denver]

137
6. Pass, Randy, G-C, Georgia Tech, 147
7. *Doornink, Dan, RB, Washington State, 174
8. Grady, Jeff, LB, Florida A&M, 201
9. Swiacki, Bill, TE, Amherst, 232
10. Jorgensen, Greg, G, Nebraska [from New Orleans] 253
Choice to Green Bay
11. Heim, Dennis, DT, Southwest Missouri State, 286
12. Lawson, Greg, RB, Western Illinois, 313

NEW YORK JETS 1978
1. *Ward, Chris, T, Ohio State, 4
2. *Merrill, Mark, LB, Minnesota, 31
3. *Shuler, Mickey, TE, Penn State, 61
4. Donnell, Dodie, RB, Nebraska, 88
5. Sidler, Randy, LB, Penn State, 113
6. *Jackson, Bobby, DB, Florida State [from Buffalo] 140
*Robinson, Gregg, DT, Dartmouth, 142
7. Armstrong, Levi, DB, UCLA [from New Orleans] 169
*Earley, James, RB, Michigan State, 170
8. *Gaffney, Derrick, WR, Florida, 197
*Mock, Mike, P-LB, Texas Tech [from Philadelphia] 203
Eppes, Roy, DB, Clemson [from Minnesota] 213
9. *Grant, Reggie, DB, Oregon [from Buffalo] 225
Hutton, Neil, DB, Penn State, 227
10. Richardson, Louis, DE, Florida State, 254
11. *Ryan, Pat, QB, Tennessee, 281
12. Williams, Alan, P, Florida, 311

OAKLAND 1978
1. Choice to Green Bay
2. *Browning, Dave, DE, Washington, 54
3. *Jensen, Derrick, RB, Texas-Arlington [from Tampa Bay] 57
*Mason, Lindsey, T, Kansas, 82
4. *Harvey, Maurice, DB, Ball State [from Tampa Bay] 86
*Stewart, Joe, WR, Missouri, 108
5. *Ramsey, Derrick, TE, Kentucky, 136
6. Davis, Tom, C, Nebraska [from Tampa Bay] 143
*Levenseller, Mike, WR, Washington State, 164
7. *Whittington, Arthur, RB, SMU [from Philadelphia] 176
*Inmon, Earl, LB, Bethune-Cookman, 192
8. *Nichols, Mark, DE, Colorado State [from San Diego] 207
Choice to San Diego
9. Choice to San Diego
10. Choice to Pittsburgh thru Tampa Bay
11. Jones, Dean, DB, Fresno State [from San Diego] 291
*Glazebrook, Bob, DB, Fresno State, 304
12. Conron, Joe, WR, Pacific, 332

PHILADELPHIA 1978
1. Choice to Cincinnati
2. Choice to Cincinnati
3. *Wilkes, Reggie, LB, Georgia Tech, 66
4. *Harrison, Dennis, DT, Vanderbilt, 92
5. Choice to Kansas City
Banks, Norris, RB, Kansas [from Washington] 130
6. Choice to Buffalo
7. Choice to Oakland
*Marshall, Greg, DT, Oregon State [from Minnesota] 186
8. Choice to New York Jets
9. *Williams, Charles, DB, Jackson State, 230
10. Choice to Atlanta
11. *Campfield, Bill, RB, Kansas, 288
12. *Slater, Mark, C, Minnesota, 315

PITTSBURGH 1978
1. *Johnson, Ron, DB, Eastern Michigan, 22
2. Fry, Willie, DE, Notre Dame, 49
3. *Colquitt, Craig, P, Tennessee, 76
4. *Anderson, Larry, DB, Louisiana Tech, 101
5. Choice to Green Bay
6. *Reutershan, Randy, WR, Pittsburgh, 160
7. Dufresne, Mark, TE, Nebraska, 187
8. *Moser, Rich, RB, Rhode Island [from St. Louis] 208
Keys, Andre, WR, Cal Poly-SLO, 214
9. Reynolds, Lance, T, BYU, 241
10. *Becker, Doug, LB, Notre Dame, 268
*Jurich, Tom, K, Northern Arizona [from Oak thru Tampa Bay] 276
11. *Terry, Nat, DB, Florida State [from Tampa Bay] 279
Brzoza, Tom, C, Pittsburgh, 300
12. Carr, Brad, LB, Maryland, 327

ST. LOUIS 1978
1. *Little, Steve, K, Arkansas, 15
*Greene, Ken, DB, Washington State [from Washington] 19
2. *Barefield, John, LB, Texas A&I, 42
3. *Greene, Doug, DB, Texas A&I, 69
4. Collins, George, G, Georgia [from San Diego] 96
*Childs, Jim, WR, Cal Poly-SLO, 97
5. *Carr, Earl, RB, Florida, 124
6. Williams, Jack, DE, Bowling Green, 151
7. *Stief, Dave, WR, Portland State, 181
8. Choice to Pittsburgh
9. Mosley, Joe, TE, Central State (OH), 235
10. *Gill, Randy, LB, San Jose State, 265
11. Choice to Cincinnati
12. Clay, Anthony, LB, South Carolina State, 319

SAN DIEGO 1978
1. *Jefferson, John, WR, Arizona State, 14
2. *Hardaway, Buddy, T, Oklahoma State, 41
3. *Anderson, Rickey, RB, South Carolina State, 71
4. Choice to St. Louis
5. Choice to Detroit
*Choma, John, G, Virginia [from Los Angeles Rams] 135
6. Choice to Detroit
7. Featherstone, Cliff, DB, Colorado State, 180
8. Choice to Oakland
Hedrick, Gavin, P, Washington State [from Oakland] 220
9. *Bradley, Henry, DT, Alcorn State, 237
*Whitlatch, Blake, LB, LSU [from Oakland] 248
10. Price, Charles, TE, Cincinnati, 264
11. Choice to Oakland
12. *Bell, Kevin, WR, Lamar, 321

SAN FRANCISCO 1978
1. *MacAfee, Ken Jr., TE, Notre Dame, 7
*Bunz, Dan, LB, Long Beach State [from Miami] 24
2. Choice to Buffalo
*Downing, Walt, G, Michigan [from Chicago Bears] 47
3. Choice to Buffalo
*Hughes, Ernie, G, Notre Dame [from Baltimore] 79
4. *LeCount, Terry, WR, Florida, 91
5. Choice to Baltimore
*Reese, Archie, DT, Clemson [from Hou thru Kansas City and Chicago Bears] 127
*Threadgill, Bruce, DB, Mississippi State [from Miami] 133
6. *Walker, Elliott, RB, Pittsburgh, 148
7. *Quillan, Fred, C, Oregon, 175
8. Choice to Washington
9. Redden, Herman, DB, Howard, 229
*Moore, Dean, LB, Iowa [from Detroit] 233
McDaniels, Steve, T, Notre Dame [from Denver] 249
10. *Connell, Mike, P, Cincinnati, 260
11. *McCray, Willie, DE, Troy State, 287
12. Irons, Dan, T, Texas Tech, 314

SEATTLE 1978
1. *Simpson, Keith, DB, Memphis State, 9
2. *Butler, Keith, LB, Memphis State, 36
3. *Jury, Bob, DB, Pittsburgh, 63
4. Choice exercised in 1977 supplemental draft (Hunter, Al, RB, Notre Dame)
5. *Bullard, Louis, T, Jackson State, 119
6. Starks, Glenn, WR, Texas A&I, 146
7. *Harris, John, DB, Arizona State, 173
8. Choice to Minnesota
9. Grimmett, Rich, T, Illinois, 231
10. Stewart, Rob, WR, Lafayette, 258
11. Choice to New Orleans
Halas, George, LB, Miami [from Miami] 301
12. Bergeron, Jeff, RB, Lamar, 316

TAMPA BAY 1978
1. Choice to Houston
*Williams, Doug, QB, Grambling [from Houston] 17
2. *Davis, Johnny, RB, Alabama, 30
*Moritz, Brett, G, Nebraska [from Houston] 44
3. Choice to Oakland
4. Choice to Oakland
5. Choice to Miami
6. Choice to Oakland
Marshall, Elijah, WR, North Carolina State [from Los Angeles Rams] 162
7. Choice to Atlanta
8. McGriff, John, LB, Miami, 196
9. *Taylor, Willie, WR, Pittsburgh, 223
10. *Brown, Aaron, LB, Ohio State, 252
11. Choice to Pittsburgh
12. McLee, Kevin, RB, Georgia, 307

WASHINGTON 1978
1. Choice to St. Louis
2. Choice to Los Angeles Rams
3. Choice to Los Angeles Rams
4. Choice to Cleveland thru Los Angeles Rams
5. Choice to Philadelphia
6. Choice to New Orleans thru Hou
*Green, Tony, RB, Florida [from Min thru San Francisco] 159
7. Choice to Kansas City
8. Lee, Walker, WR, North Carolina [from San Francisco] 202
Choice to Atlanta
*Hover, Don, LB, Washington State [from Los Angeles Rams] 219
9. Hurley, John, QB, Santa Clara, 243
10. Hertenstein, Scott, DE, Azusa Pacific, 270
11. Williams, Mike, DB, Texas A&M, 297
12. McCabe, Steve, G, Bowdoin, 324

1979

Held May 3-4, 1979

There were 330 selections instead of 336. Houston gave up its tenth-round choice and San Francisco its twelfth-round pick in 1978 supplemental drafts. Four teams forfeited choices: Minnesota and Pittsburgh each a third-round pick, the Los Angeles Rams a fifth-round pick, and New England a seventh-round pick.

ATLANTA 1979
1. *Smith, Don, DE, Miami, 17
2. *Howell, Pat, G, USC, 49
3. *Mayberry, James, RB, Colorado, 75
*Andrews, William, RB, Auburn [from Miami] 79
4. *Cain, Lynn, RB, USC [from Philadelphia] 100
*Johnson, Charles, DB, Grambling, 101
5. *Zele, Mike, DT, Kent State, 127
6. *Moroski, Mike, QB, Cal-Davis, 154
7. Westlund, Roger, T, Washington, 186
8. Miller, Keith, LB, Northeastern Oklahoma, 212
9. *Parkins, Dave, DB, Utah State, 239
10. *Beekley, Bruce, LB, Oregon, 266
11. Leer, Bill, C, Colorado State, 292
12. Walker, Stuart, LB, Colorado, 323

BALTIMORE 1979
1. *Krauss, Barry, LB, Alabama, 6
2. Choice to Tampa Bay
3. Choice to Tampa Bay
*Anderson, Kim, DB, Arizona State [from Washington thru Houston] 69
4. Choice to Detroit
5. *Braziel, Larry, DB, USC, 115
6. Choice to Buffalo
*Moore, Jimmy, T, Ohio State [from Washington] 150
7. Choice to Houston
8. *Heimkreiter, Steve, LB, Notre Dame, 197
*Glasgow, Nesby, DB, Washington [from Minnesota] 207
9. Henderson, Russ, P, Virginia, 224
10. *Stephens, Steve, TE, Oklahoma State, 254
11. Priestner, John, LB, Western Ontario, 280
12. Green, Charlie, WR, Kansas State, 306

BUFFALO 1979
1. *Cousineau, Tom, LB, Ohio State [from San Francisco] 1
*Butler, Jerry, WR, Clemson, 5
2. *Smerlas, Fred, DT, Boston College, 32
*Haslett, Jim, LB, Indiana (PA) [from Denver] 51
3. *Borchardt, Jon, T, Montana State, 62
4. *Johnson, Ken, DE, Knoxville [from San Francisco] 83
*Nixon, Jeff, DB, Richmond, 87
5. *Kush, Rod, DB, Nebraska-Omaha, 114
*Manucci, Dan, QB, Kansas State [from Tampa Bay thru Sea] 116
6. Choice to Houston
Burrow, Mike, G, Auburn [from Baltimore] 141
7. *Mullady, Tom, TE, Southwestern (Memphis), 170
8. Choice to Philadelphia
9. Baker, Kevin, DE, William Penn, 226
10. Marler, David, QB, Mississippi State, 253
11. Lawler, Paul, DB, Colgate, 279
12. Harris, Mike, RB, Arizona State, 308

CHICAGO BEARS 1979
1. *Hampton, Dan, DT, Arkansas [from Tampa Bay] 4
*Harris, Al, DE, Arizona State, 9
2. *Watts, Rickey, WR, Tulsa, 39
3. *McClendon, Willie, RB, Georgia, 66
4. Choice to Cincinnati
5. Choice to Dallas
6. *Sullivan, John, LB, Illinois, 147
7. *Kunz, Lee, LB, Nebraska, 174
8. Moss, Rick, DB, Purdue, 203
9. Heavens, Jerome, RB, Notre Dame, 230
10. Restic, Joe, DB, Notre Dame, 257
11. Wright, Bob, T, Cincinnati, 286
12. *Becker, Dave, DB, Iowa, 312

CINCINNATI 1979
1. *Thompson, Jack, QB, Washington State, 3
*Alexander, Charles, RB, LSU [from Washington] 12
2. *Ross, Dan, TE, Northeastern, 30
3. *Cotton, Barney, G, Nebraska, 59
4. *White, Mike, DT, Albany State, 84
*Lusby, Vaughn, DB, Arkansas [from Chicago Bears] 91
5. *Merrill, Casey, DE, Cal-Davis, 113
6. *Kreider, Steve, WR, Lehigh, 139
7. *Montoya, Max, T, UCLA, 168
8. *Kurnick, Howie, LB, Cincinnati, 194
9. *Burk, Scott, DB, Oklahoma State, 223
10. *Poole, Nathan, RB, Louisville, 250
11. *Bungarda, Ken, DT, Missouri, 278
12. *Browner, Jim, DB, Notre Dame, 304

CLEVELAND 1979
1. Choice to San Diego
*Adams, Willis, WR, Houston [from San Diego] 20
2. *Johnson, Lawrence, DB, Wisconsin, 40
*Claphan, Sam, T, Oklahoma [from San Diego] 47
3. *Ramey, Jim, DE, Kentucky, 70
4. *Miller, Matt, T, Colorado, 95
5. Choice to Los Angeles Rams
*Dimler, Rich, DT, USC [from Washington thru Los Angeles Rams] 124
6. *Burrell, Clinton, DB, LSU, 151
Ronan, Jim, DT, Minnesota [from Los Angeles Rams] 163
7. Choice to Philadelphia
*Risien, Cody, T, Texas A&M [from Oakland] 183
8. Perkov, Kent, DE, San Diego State, 204
9. *McGee, Carl, LB, Duke, 234
*Weathers, Curtis, TE, Mississippi [from Oakland] 241
10. *Smith, John, WR, Tennessee State, 261
11. Poeschl, Randy, DE, Nebraska, 287
12. Choice to Oakland
Methvin, Dewitt, C, Tulane [from Washington] 315

DALLAS 1979
1. *Shaw, Robert, C, Tennessee, 27
2. *Mitchell, Aaron, DB, Nevada-Las Vegas, 55
3. *Cosbie, Doug, TE, Santa Clara [from Seattle] 76
Choice to San Francisco thru Seattle
4. *DeLoach, Ralph, DE, California, 109
5. Hukill, Bob, G, North Carolina [from Chicago Bears] 121
*Anderson, Curtis, DE, Central State (OH) [from Seattle] 128
*Springs, Ron, RB, Ohio State, 136
6. Lavender, Tim, DB, USC [from Seattle] 155
Salzano, Mike, G, North Carolina [from Denver] 160
*De France, Chris, WR, Arizona State, 164
7. Fitzpatrick, Greg, LB, Youngstown State, 191
8. *Thornton, Bruce, DT, Illinois, 219
9. *Cobb, Garry, LB, USC, 247
10. *Calhoun, Mike, DT, Notre Dame, 274
11. Choice to Detroit
12. *Lowry, Quentin, LB, Youngstown State, 329

DENVER 1979
1. *Clark, Kelvin, T, Nebraska, 22
2. Choice to Buffalo
3. *Radford, Bruce, DE, Grambling, 77
4. *Jefferson, Charles, DB, McNeese State, 105
5. Leach, Rick, QB, Michigan, 132
6. *McIntyre, Jeff, LB, Arizona State [from Detroit] 148
Choice to Dallas
7. *Prestridge, Luke, P, Baylor, 188
8. Choice to Miami
9. Taylor, Charlie, WR, Rice, 242
10. Choice to New England
11. *Dixon, Zachary, RB, Temple, 297
12. *Jacobs, Dave, K, Syracuse, 325

DETROIT 1979
1. *Dorney, Keith, T, Penn State, 10
2. *Fantetti, Ken, LB, Wyoming, 37
3. *Robinson, Bo, RB, West Texas State, 67
4. *Norris, Ulysses, TE, Georgia [from Baltimore] 88
*Brooks, Jon, LB, Clemson, 92
5. Choice to San Francisco
Brown, Walt, C, Pittsburgh [from San Diego thru Baltimore] 131
6. Choice to Denver
7. Choice to Oakland thru Cleveland
8. Choice to New York Giants
*Mohring, John, LB, C.W. Post [from Seattle] 213
9. *Komlo, Jeff, QB, Delaware, 231
10. Choice to Miami
11. Choice to New York Giants
*Cole, Eddie, LB, Mississippi [from Dallas] 302
12. Forster, Bob, C-G, Brown, 313
Sweeney, Bryan, WR, Texas A&I [from New England] 326

GREEN BAY 1979
1. *Ivery, Eddie Lee, RB, Georgia Tech, 15
2. *Atkins, Steve, RB, Maryland, 44
3. *Johnson, Charles, DT, Maryland, 71
4. Choice to New York Jets
5. Choice to New York Jets
6. *Simmons, Dave, LB, North Carolina, 153
7. *Monroe, Henry, DB, Mississippi State, 180
*Wingo, Rich, LB, Alabama [from San Diego] 184
8. *Cassidy, Ron, WR, Utah State [from San Francisco] 193
*Partridge, Rick, P, Utah, 208
9. *Thompson, John, TE, Utah State, 235
10. *Lockett, Frank, WR, Nebraska, 264
11. Thorson, Mark, DB, Ottawa, 290
12. Moats, Bill, P, South Dakota, 318

HOUSTON 1979
1. Choice to Kansas City
2. *Stensrud, Mike, DE Iowa State [from Kansas City] 31
*Baker, Jesse, DE, Jacksonville State, 50
3. *King, Kenny, RB, Oklahoma [from Oak thru Baltimore] 72
Choice to Tampa Bay
4. Choice to San Diego
5. Choice to Tampa Bay
6. *Hunt, Darryl, LB, Oklahoma [from Buffalo] 143
*Murphy, Mike, LB, Southwest Missouri State, 159
7. Ries, Tim, DB, Southwest Missouri State

[from Baltimore] 171
Choice to New York Jets
8. *Hartwig Carter, DB, USC, 214
9. *Ellender, Richard, WR, McNeese State, 243
10. Choice exercised in 1978 supplemental draft (Dirden, Johnnie, WR, Sam Houston State)
11. Taylor, Mike, T, Georgia Tech, 298
12. *Wilson, Wayne, RB, Shepherd, 324

KANSAS CITY 1979
1. *Bell, Mike, DE, Colorado State, 2
*Fuller, Steve, QB, Clemson [from Houston] 23
2. Choice to Houston
3. Choice to Los Angeles Rams
4. *Manumaleuga, Frank, LB, San Jose State, 85
5. *Gant, Earl, RB, Missouri, 112
6. Gaines, Robert, WR, Washington, 140
7. *Kremer, Ken, DE, Ball State, 167
8. *Williams, Mike, RB, New Mexico, 195
Brewer, Robert, G, Temple [from Los Angeles Rams thru St. Louis] 218
9. Folston, James, TE, Cameron, 222
Robinson, Joe, T, Ohio State [from New Orleans] 229
10. DuPree, Mike, LB, Florida, 251
*Jackson, Gerald, DB, Mississippi State [from Washington] 260
11. *Rome, Stan, WR, Clemson, 277
12. Forrest, Michael, RB, Arkansas, 305

LOS ANGELES RAMS 1979
1. *Andrews, George, LB, Nebraska [from Oakland] 19
*Hill, Kent, T, Georgia Tech, 26
2. *Hill, Eddie, RB, Memphis State, 54
3. *Moore, Jeff, WR, Tennessee [from Kansas City] 58
*Wellman, Mike, C, Kansas [from New England] 81
Choice to Tampa Bay thru Washington, Miami, and Oakland
4. Tucker, Derwin, DB, Illinois [from San Diego] 99
*Wilkinson, Jerry, DT, Oregon State, 108
5. Choice forfeited
*Hicks, Victor, TE, Oklahoma [from Cleveland] 122
6. Choice to Cleveland
7. *Delaney, Jeff, DB, Pittsburgh, 190
8. Choice to Kansas City
9. *Rutledge, Jeff QB, Alabama, 246
10. Willis, Larry, WR, Alcorn State [from Kansas City] 268
Ebensberger, Grady, DT, Houston, 273
11. Deramus, Jesse, DT, Tennessee State, 301
12. *Hill, Drew, WR, Georgia Tech, 328

MIAMI 1979
1. *Giesler, Jon, T, Michigan, 24
2. *Toews, Jeff, T, Washington, 53
3. *Nathan, Tony, RB, Alabama [from Tampa Bay] 61
*Land, Mel, LB, Michigan State [from New York Giants] 63
*Lee, Ron, TE, Baylor [from New Orleans] 65
Choice to Atlanta
4. *Howell, Steve, RB, Baylor, 107
5. *Bessillieu, Don, DB, Georgia Tech, 134
6. Lindquist, Steve, G, Nebraska, 162
7. *von Schamann, Uwe, K, Oklahoma, 189
8. *Groth, Jeff, WR, Bowling Green [from Washington] 206
Choice to Tampa Bay
*Blackwood, Glenn, DB, Texas [from Denver] 215
9. *Weston, Jeff, DT, Notre Dame, 244
10. Stanton, Jerome, DB, Michigan State [from Detroit] 258
*Kozlowski, Mike, RB, Colorado, 272
11. Blanton, Mike, DE, Georgia Tech, 299
12. Fortner, Larry, QB, Miami (OH), 327

MINNESOTA 1979
1. *Brown, Ted, RB, North Carolina State, 16
2. *Huffman, Dave, C, Notre Dame, 43
3. Choice forfeited
4. *Dils, Steve, QB, Stanford, 97
5. Meter, Jerry, LB, Michigan, 129
6. *Senser, Joe, TE, West Chester, 152
7. *Winkel, Bob, DT, Kentucky, 181
8. Choice to Baltimore
9. Diggs, Billy, WR, Winston-Salem State, 236
10. Choice to New York Jets
11. Nelson, Brian, WR, Texas Tech, 291
12. Stephens, David, LB, Kentucky, 317

NEW ENGLAND 1979
1. *Sanford, Rick, DB, South Carolina, 25
2. *Golic, Bob, LB, Notre Dame, 52
3. Choice to Los Angeles Rams
4. *Hare, Eddie, P, Tulsa, 106
5. *Zamberlin, John, LB, Pacific Lutheran, 135
6. Choice to Pittsburgh
7. *Flint, Judson, DB, Memphis State [from Washington] 177
Choice forfeited
8. *Love, Randy, RB, Houston, 216
9. *Spagnola, John, TE, Yale, 245
10. Cox, Martin, WR, Vanderbilt [from Denver] 270
*Clark, Allan, RB, Northern Arizona, 271
11. Choice to Washington
12. Choice to Detroit

NEW ORLEANS 1979
1. *Erxleben, Russell, K-P, Texas, 11
2. *Mathis, Reggie, LB, Oklahoma, 38
3. Choice to Miami
4. *Kovach, Jim, LB, Kentucky, 93
5. *Huckleby, Harlan, RB, Michigan, 120
6. *Ray, Ricky, DB, Norfolk State, 146
7. Sytsma, Stan, LB, Minnesota, 176
8. Panfil, Doug, G, Tulsa, 202
9. Choice to Kansas City
10. Choice to Oakland
11. Hall, David, WR, Missouri-Rolla, 285
12. Finch, Kelsey, RB, Tennessee, 311

NEW YORK GIANTS 1979
1. *Simms, Phil, QB, Morehead State, 7
2. *Gray, Earnest, WR, Memphis State, 36
3. Choice to Miami
4. Tabor, Phil, DE, Oklahoma, 90
5. *Jackson, Cleveland, TE, Nevada-Las Vegas, 117
6. *Torrey, Bob, RB, Penn State, 145
*Hicks, Eddie, RB, East Carolina [from Philadelphia] 158
7. *Alvers, Steve, TE, Miami, 172
8. Perry, D.K., DB, SMU, 200
*Simmons, Roy, G, Georgia Tech [from Detroit] 201
9. Rusk, Tom, LB, Iowa, 227
10. *Fowler, Dan, G, Kentucky, 256
11. Mince, Mike, DB, Fresno State, 282
*Johnson, Ken, RB, Miami [from Detroit] 284
12. Gillespie, Tim, G, North Carolina State, 310

NEW YORK JETS 1979
1. *Lyons, Marty, DE, Alabama, 14
2. *Gastineau, Mark, DE, East Central (OK), 41
3. *Dykes, Donald, DB, Southeastern Louisiana, 68
4. *Cunningham, Eric, G, Penn State, 96
*Lynn, Johnny, DB, UCLA [from Green Bay] 98
5. *Kirchbaum, Kelly, LB, Kentucky, 123
*Blinka, Stan, LB, Sam Houston State [from Green Bay] 125
6. Dufek, Bill, G, Michigan, 149
7. King, Emmett, RB, Houston, 179
Brown, Keith, Minnesota [from Houston] 187
8. *Harris, Marshall, DT, TCU [from Tampa Bay] 198
Beamon, Willie, LB, Boise State, 205
9. Sprattler, Gordy, RB, North Dakota State, 232
10. Sybeldon, Steve, T, North Dakota, 262
*McGlasson, Ed, C, Youngstown State [from Minnesota] 263
11. Sanders, Dan, QB, Carson-Newman, 288
12. *Darby, Paul, WR, Southwest Texas State, 314

OAKLAND 1979
1. Choice to Los Angeles Rams
2. *Jones, Willie, DE, Florida State [from Washington thru St. Louis] 42
Choice to St. Louis
3. Choice to Houston thru Baltimore
4. Choice to Washington
5. Choice to St. Louis
6. *Matthews, Ira, KR, Wisconsin [from Tampa Bay] 142
*Williams, Henry, DB, San Diego State, 156
7. Matia, Jack, T, Drake [from Detroit thru Cleveland] 175
Choice to Cleveland
8. Hawkins, Robert, RB, Kentucky, 209
9. Choice to Cleveland
*Rourke, Jim, T, Boston College [from Philadelphia] 238
10. Choice to Kansas City
Smith, Ricky, DB, Tulane [from New Orleans] 259
11. *Davis, Bruce, T, UCLA, 294
12. Abernathy, Dirk, DB, Bowling Green [from Cleveland] 316
*Kinlaw, Reggie, DT, Oklahoma, 320

PHILADELPHIA 1979
1. *Robinson, Jerry, LB, UCLA, 21
2. *Perot, Petey, G, Northwestern State (LA), 48
3. *Franklin, Tony, K, Texas A&M, 74
4. Cowins, Ben, RB, Arkansas [from Washington] 94
Choice to Atlanta
5. *Fitzkee, Scott, WR, Penn State, 126
6. Choice to New York Giants
7. Swafford, Don, T, Florida [from Cleveland] 178
Bunche, Curtis, DE, Albany State, 185
8. *Correal, Chuck, C, Penn State [from Buffalo] 196
*Runager, Max, P, South Carolina, 211
9. Choice to Oakland
10. Choice to San Diego
11. *Chesley, Al, LB, Pittsburgh, 296
12. Choice to Pittsburgh

PITTSBURGH 1979
1. *Hawthorne, Greg, RB, Baylor, 28
2. *Valentine, Zack, LB, East Carolina, 56
3. Choice forfeited
4. *Davis, Russell, RB, Michigan [from Tampa Bay thru Det] 86
*Sweeney, Calvin, WR, USC, 110
5. *Board, Dwaine, DE, North Carolina A&T, 137
6. *Murrell, Bill, TE, Winston-Salem State [from San Diego] 157
*Woodruff, Dwayne, DB, Louisville [from New England] 161
*Bahr, Matt, K, Penn State, 165
7. *Kimball, Bruce, G, Massachusetts, 192
8. *Graves, Tom, LB, Michigan State, 220
9. Kirk, Richard, DE, Denison, 248
10. Thompson, Tod, TE, BYU, 275
11. Moore, Charlie, C, Wichita State, 303
12. *Smith, Ed, LB, Vanderbilt [from Philadelphia] 322
Almond, Mike, WR, Northwestern State (LA), 330

ST. LOUIS 1979
1. *Anderson, Ottis, RB, Miami, 8
2. *Brown, Theotis, RB, UCLA, 35
*Favron, Calvin, LB, Southeastern Louisiana [from Oakland] 46
3. *Bostic, Joe, T, Clemson, 64
4. *Green, Roy, DB, Henderson State, 89
5. *Henry, Steve, DB, Emporia State, 118
*Bell, Mark, R., WR, Colorado State [from Oakland] 130
6. *Lott, Thomas, RB, Oklahoma, 144
7. Gibson, Kirk, WR, Michigan State, 173
8. Miller, Larry, LB, BYU, 199
9. *Rozier, Bob, DE, California, 228
10. Holloway, Jerry, TE, Western Illinois, 255
11. Henderson, Nate, T, Florida State, 283
12. McBride, Ricky, LB, Georgia, 309

SAN DIEGO 1979
1. *Winslow, Kellen, TE, Missouri [from Cleveland] 13
Choice to Cleveland
2. Choice to Cleveland
3. *Thrift, Cliff, LB, East Central (OK), 73
4. Choice to Los Angeles Rams
*Floyd, John, WR, Northeast Louisiana [from Houston] 104
5. Choice to Detroit
6. Choice to Pittsburgh
7. Choice to Green Bay
8. *Haslip, Wilbert, RB, Hawaii, 210
9. *Garrett, Alvin, WR, Angelo State, 237
10. Petruccio, Tony, DT, Penn State [from Philadelphia] 265
Green, Al, DB, LSU, 269
11. Rader, Dave, QB, Tulsa, 295
12. *Duncan, Frank, DB, Cal State-San Francisco, 321

SAN FRANCISCO 1979
1. Choice to Buffalo
2. *Owens, James, WR, UCLA, 29
3. Choice to Seattle
*Montana, Joe, QB, Notre Dame [from Dal thru Seattle] 82
4. Choice to Buffalo
5. *Seabron, Tom, LB, Michigan, 111
*Aldridge, Jerry, RB, Angelo State [from Detroit] 119
6. *Vaughan, Ruben, DT, Colorado, 138
7. *Francis, Phil, RB, Stanford, 166
8. Choice to Green Bay
9. Hamilton, Steve, DT, Missouri, 221
10. *Clark, Dwight, WR, Clemson, 249
Ballage, Howard, DB, Colorado [from Tampa Bay] 252
11. McBride, Billy, DB, Tennessee State, 276
12. Choice exercised in 1978 supplemental draft (Connors, Rod, RB, USC)

SEATTLE 1979
1. *Tuiasosopo, Manu, DT, UCLA, 18
2. *Norman, Joe, LB, Indiana, 45
3. *Jackson, Michael, LB, Washington [from San Francisco] 57
Choice to Dallas
4. *Bell, Mark E., TE, Colorado State, 102
5. Choice to Dallas
6. Choice to Dallas
7. *Polowski, Larry, LB, Boise State [from Tampa Bay thru Washington] 169
Choice to Washington
8. Choice to Detroit
9. Tate, Ezra, RB, Mississippi College, 240
10. *Hardy, Robert, DT, Jackson State, 267
11. Hinesly, Jim, G, Michigan State, 293
12. *Moore, Jeff, RB, Jackson State, 319

TAMPA BAY 1979
1. Choice to Chicago
2. *Roberts, Greg, G, Oklahoma [from Baltimore] 33
*Jones, Gordon, WR, Pittsburgh, 34
3. *Eckwood, Jerry, RB, Arkansas [from Baltimore] 60
Choice to Miami
*Lewis, Reggie, DE, North Texas State [from Houston] 78
*Berns, Rick, RB, Nebraska [from Los Angeles Rams thru Washington, Miami, and Oakland] 80
4. Choice to Pittsburgh thru Detroit
5. Choice to Buffalo
*Fusina, Chuck, QB, Penn State [from Houston] 133
6. Choice to Oakland
7. Choice to Seattle thru Washington
8. *Sanders, Eugene, DT, Texas A&M [from Miami] 217
Choice to New York Jets
9. Vereen, Henry, WR, Nevada-Las Vegas, 225
10. Choice to San Francisco
11. Rippentrop, Bob, TE, Fresno State, 281
12. *Logan, David, DT, Pittsburgh, 307

WASHINGTON 1979
1. Choice to Cincinnati
2. Choice to Oakland thru St. Louis
3. Choice to Baltimore thru Houston
4. Choice to Philadelphia
*Warren, Don, TE, San Diego State [from Oakland thru Green Bay] 103
5. Choice to Cleveland
6. Choice to Baltimore
7. Choice to New England
*Milot, Rich, LB, Penn State [from Seattle] 182
8. Choice to Miami
9. *Haines, Kris, WR, Notre Dame, 233
10. *Coleman, Monte, LB, Central Arkansas, 289
11. Hall, Tony, WR, Knoxville [from New England] 300
12. Choice to Cleveland

1980

Held April 29-30, 1980

There were 333 selections instead of 336. Buffalo gave up its sixth-round choice in a 1979 supplemental draft. Philadelphia and Oakland forfeited their third-round and fourth-round choices, respectively.

ATLANTA 1980
1. *Miller, Junior, TE, Nebraska, 7
2. *Curry, Buddy, LB, North Carolina, 36
3. *Jones, Earl, DB, Norfolk State, 63
4. *Laughlin, Jim, LB, Ohio State, 91
*Hipp, I.M., RB, Nebraska [from Philadelphia] 104
5. Vassar, Brad, LB, Pacific, 117
*Johnson, Kenny, DB, Mississippi State [from Los Angeles Rams thru Washington] 137
6. Davis, Mike, DB, Colorado, 146
7. *Smith, Mike, WR, Grambling, 172
8. *Richardson, Al, LB, Georgia Tech, 201
9. Keller, Glen, C, West Texas State, 228
10. Bellamy, Walt, DB, Virginia Military, 257
11. Babb, Mike, DB, Oklahoma, 284
12. Jones, Quinn, RB, Tulsa, 313

BALTIMORE 1980
1. *Dickey, Curtis, RB, Texas A&M, 5
*Hatchett, Derrick, DB, Texas [from Dallas] 24
2. *Donaldson, Ray, C, Georgia, 32
*Foley, Tim, T, Notre Dame [from Dallas] 51
3. Choice to Detroit
4. *Butler, Raymond, WR, USC, 88
5. Choice to Kansas City
6. *Foote, Chris, C, USC, 144
7. *Roberts, Wesley, DE, TCU, 170
8. Walter, Ken, T, Texas Tech [from Detroit] 195
Choice to Denver
9. Bright, Mark, RB, Temple, 227
10. Stewart, Larry, T, Maryland, 254
11. Whitley, Eddy, TE, Kansas State, 280
12. Bielski, Randy, K, Towson State, 311
*Sims, Marvin, RB, Clemson [from Denver] 324

BUFFALO 1980
1. Choice to Seattle
*Ritcher, Jim, C, North Carolina State [from Seattle] 16
2. *Cribbs, Joe, RB, Auburn [from San Francisco] 29
Bradley, Gene, QB, Arkansas State, 37
3. *Brammer, Mark, TE, Michigan State, 67
Schmeding, John, G, Boston College [from Seattle] 71
4. *Parker, Ervin, LB, South Carolina State, 93
5. Pyburn, Jeff, DB, Georgia, 119
*Lee, Keith, DB, Colorado State [from Washington] 129
6. Choice exercised in 1979 supplemental draft (Stewart, Rod, RB, Kentucky)
7. Choice to San Diego
8. Krueger, Todd, QB, Northern Michigan, 202
9. Davis, Kent, DB, Southeast Missouri State, 231
10. *Cater, Greg, P, Tennessee-Chattanooga, 259
11. Gordon, Joe, DT, Grambling, 286
12. Lapham, Roger, TE, Maine, 316

CHICAGO BEARS 1980
1. *Wilson, Otis, LB, Louisville, 19
2. *Suhey, Matt, RB, Penn State, 46
3. Choice to Dallas
4. *Thompson, Arland, G, Baylor, 103
5. *Tabor, Paul, C, Oklahoma, 130
6. Guess, Mike, DB, Ohio State, 156
7. Tolbert, Emanuel, WR, SMU, 183
8. *Clark, Randy, G, Northern Illinois, 215
9. *Schonert, Turk, QB, Stanford, 242
10. Stephens, Willie, DB, Texas Tech, 269
11. Judge, Chris, DB, TCU, 296
12. *Fisher, Robert, TE, SMU, 323

CINCINNATI 1980
1. *Munoz, Anthony, T, USC, 3
2. *Criswell, Kirby, LB, Kansas, 31
3. *Horn, Rod, DT, Nebraska, 59
4. *Glass, Bill, G, Baylor, 86
5. *Hicks, Bryan, DB, McNeese State, 113
6. *Heath, Jo Jo, DB, Pittsburgh, 141
*Melontree, Andrew, LB, Baylor [from Tampa Bay] 159

7. *Simpkins, Ron, LB, Michigan [from San Francisco] 167
Johnson, Gary Don, DT, Baylor, 168
8. Lyles, Mark, RB, Florida State, 196
9. *Bright, Greg, DB, Morehead State, 224
10. *Vitiello, Sandro, K, Massachusetts, 252
11. *Alexis, Alton, WR, Tulane, 281
12. Wright, Mike, QB, Vanderbilt, 308

CLEVELAND 1980
1. Choice to Los Angeles Rams
*White, Charles, RB, USC [from Los Angeles Rams] 27
2. Choice to Denver
*Crosby, Cleveland, DE, Arizona [from San Diego thru Los Angeles Rams] 54
3. *Odom, Cliff, LB, Texas-Arlington, 72
4. *Crews, Ron, DE, Nevada-Las Vegas, 99
*McDonald, Paul, QB, USC [from Los Angeles Rams] 109
5. *Franks, Elvis, DE, Morgan State [from Green Bay thru Los Angeles Rams] 116
Choice to Oakland
6. Choice to San Diego
7. Choice to New York Giants
8. Copeland, Jeff, LB, Texas Tech, 209
9. Dewalt, Roy, RB, Texas-Arlington, 236
10. Fidel, Kevin, C, San Diego State, 263
11. Sales, Roland, RB, Arkansas, 294
12. Jackson, Marcus, DT, Purdue, 321

DALLAS 1980
1. Choice to Baltimore
2. Choice to Baltimore
3. *Roe, Bill, LB, Colorado [from Chicago Bears] 78
*Jones, James Jr., RB, Mississippi State, 80
4. *Petersen, Kurt, DE, Missouri, 105
5. *Hogeboom, Gary, QB, Central Michigan, 133
6. *Newsome, Timmy, RB, Winston-Salem State, 162
7. Brown, Lester, RB, Clemson, 189
8. Savage, Larry, LB, Michigan State, 216
9. Flowers, Jackie, WR, Florida State, 246
10. *Teague, Matthew, DE, Prairie View A&M, 273
11. Padjen, Gary, LB, Arizona State, 300
12. *Wells, Norm, DE, Northwestern, 330

DENVER 1980
1. Choice to San Francisco thru New York Jets
2. *Jones, Rulon, DE, Utah State [from Cleveland] 42
Choice to New York Jets
3. Carter, Larry, DB, Kentucky, 74
4. *Parros, Rick, RB, Utah State, 107
5. *Harden, Mike, DB, Michigan, 131
*Short, Laval, DT, Colorado [from San Diego thru Washington and Cleveland] 136
6. *Bishop, Keith, G, Baylor, 157
7. Havekost, John, G, Nebraska, 184
8. Coleman, Don, WR, Oregon [from Baltimore] 197
Choice to St. Louis
9. *Bracelin, Greg, LB, California, 243
10. *Seay, Virgil, WR, Troy State, 270
11. Farris, Phil, WR, North Carolina, 297
12. Choice to Baltimore

DETROIT 1980
1. *Sims, Billy, RB, Oklahoma, 1
2. Choice to Min thru San Francisco
3. *Turnure, Tom, C, Washington, 57
*Friede, Mike, WR, Indiana [from Baltimore] 62
4. *Hipple, Eric, QB, Utah State, 85
5. Streeter, Mark, DB, Arizona, 111
*Ginn, Tommie, G, Arkansas [from Kansas City] 120
6. *Dieterich, Chris, T, North Carolina State, 140
7. *Murray, Ed, K, Tulane, 166
8. Choice to Baltimore
9. Jett, DeWayne, WR, Hawaii, 222
*Tuinei, Tom, DT, Hawaii [from San Francisco thru Kansas City] 223
10. Henderson, Henry (Donnie), DB, Utah State, 251
11. *Smith, Wayne, DB, Purdue, 278
12. *Williams, Ray, KR, Washington State, 307

GREEN BAY 1980
1. *Clark, Bruce, DE, Penn State, 4
*Cumby, George, LB, Oklahoma [from San Diego] 26
2. *Lee, Mark, DB, Washington, 34
3. *Kitson, Syd, G, Wake Forest, 61
4. *Nixon, Fred, WR, Oklahoma, 87
5. Choice to Cleveland thru Los Angeles Rams
6. *Swanke, Karl, G, Boston College, 143
7. *Aydelette, Buddy, T, Alabama, 169
8. Smith, Tim, DB, Oregon State, 199
9. *Saalfeld, Kelly, C, Nebraska, 226
10. White, Jafus, DB, Texas A&I, 253
11. Skiles, Ricky, LB, Louisville, 283
12. Stewart, James, DB, Memphis State, 310

HOUSTON 1980
1. Choice to New England
2. *Fields, Angelo, T, Michigan State [from Kansas City] 38
*Skaugstad, Daryle, DT, California, 52
3. *Smith, Tim, WR-P, Nebraska, 79
4. *Combs, Chris, TE, New Mexico, 106
5. *Corker, John, LB, Oklahoma State, 134
6. Choice to New England
7. *Bradshaw, Craig, QB, Utah State [from Oakland] 182
Choice to New York Jets
8. *Bailey, Harold, RB, Oklahoma State, 217
9. Harris, Ed, RB, Bishop, 244
10. Choice to Seattle
11. Preston, Eddie, WR, Western Kentucky, 301
12. Pitts, Wiley, WR, Temple, 328

KANSAS CITY 1980
1. *Budde, Brad, G, USC, 11
2. Choice to Houston
3. *Hadnot, James, RB, Texas Tech, 66
4. *Klug, Dave, LB, Concordia, 94
5. *Carson, Carlos, WR, LSU [from Baltimore] 114
Pensick, Dan, DT, Nebraska [from St. Louis] 115
Choice to Detroit
6. *Garcia, Bubba, WR, Texas-El Paso, 147
*Heater, Larry, RB, Arizona [from Los Angeles Rams] 164
7. Choice to Los Angeles Rams
8. Stepney, Sam, LB, Boston U., 203
9. *Donovan, Tom, WR, Penn State, 230
10. Martinovich, Rob, T, Notre Dame, 261
11. *Markham, Dale, DT, North Dakota, 287
12. Brewington, Mike, LB, East Carolina, 314

LOS ANGELES RAMS 1980
1. *Johnson, Johnnie, DB, Texas [from Cleveland] 17
Choice to Cleveland
2. *Pankey, Irv, T, Penn State [from Washington] 50
Choice to Washington
3. *Thomas, Jewerl, RB, San Jose State [from San Francisco] 58
*Irvin, LeRoy, DB, Kansas [from Oakland] 70
*Murphy, Phil, DT, South Carolina State, 82
4. Choice to Cleveland
5. Choice to Atl thru Was
6. *Guman, Mike, RB, Penn State [from New England thru Cleveland] 154
Choice to Kansas City
7. *Collins, Kirk, DB, Baylor [from Kansas City] 176
*Ellis, Gerry, RB, Missouri, 192
8. Pettigrew, Tom, T, Eastern Illinois, 220
9. *Farmer, George, WR, Southern, 248
10. *Gruber, Bob, T, Pittsburgh, 276
11. *Greer, Terry, WR, Alabama State, 304
12. Scanlon, Kevin, QB, Arkansas, 332

MIAMI 1980
1. *McNeal, Don, DB, Alabama, 21
2. *Stephenson, Dwight, C, Alabama, 48
3. *Barnett, Bill, DE, Nebraska, 75
4. *Bailey, Elmer, WR, Minnesota, 100
5. Choice to Seattle thru Washington
6. Byrd, Eugene, WR, Michigan State, 158
7. *Rose, Joe, TE, California, 185
8. *Allen, Jeff, DB, Cal-Davis, 212
*Woodley, David, QB, LSU [from Washington] 214
9. *Goodspeed, Mark, T, Nebraska, 239
10. Lantz, Doug, C, Miami (OH), 271
Long, Ben, LB, South Dakota [from Philadelphia] 272
11. Driscoll, Phil, DE, Mankato State [from San Francisco] 279
Choice to Philadelphia
12. Stone, Chuck, G, North Carolina State, 325

MINNESOTA 1980
1. *Martin, Doug, DT, Washington, 9
2. *Teal, Willie, DB, LSU [from Detroit thru San Francisco] 30
Choice to San Francisco
3. Choice to San Francisco
*Boyd, Brent, C, UCLA [from New Orleans] 68
4. *Johnson, Dennis, LB, USC, 92
5. *Paschal, Doug, RB, North Carolina, 121
Jones, Paul, RB, California [from New Orleans] 122
6. *Yakavonis, Ray, DE, East Stroudsburg, 148
7. *Johnson, Henry, LB, Georgia Tech, 174
8. Choice to Seattle
9. Mosley, Dennis, RB, Iowa, 232
10. Brown, Kenny, WR, Nebraska, 258
11. *Harrell, Sam, RB, East Carolina, 288
12. Lane, Thomas, DB, Florida A&M, 315

NEW ENGLAND 1980
1. *James, Roland, DB, Tennessee, 14
*Ferguson, Vagas, RB, Notre Dame [from Houston] 25
2. *McGrew, Larry, LB, USC, 45
3. *McMichael, Steve, DT, Texas, 73
4. Choice to San Francisco thru Los Angeles Rams
5. *McDougald, Doug, DE-DT, Virginia Tech, 124
6. Choice to Los Angeles Rams thru Cle
*Brown, Preston, WR, Vanderbilt [from Houston] 160
7. Kearns, Tom, G, Kentucky, 180
8. House, Mike, TE, Pacific, 208
9. Burget, Barry, LB, Oklahoma, 235
10. Daniel, Tom, C, Georgia Tech, 266
11. *Hubach, Mike, P, Kansas, 293
12. Jordan, Jimmy, QB, Florida State, 320

NEW ORLEANS 1980
1. *Brock, Stan, T, Colorado, 12
2. *Waymer, Dave, DB, Notre Dame, 41
3. Choice to Minnesota
4. *Jolly, Mike, DB, Michigan, 96
5. Choice to Minnesota
6. Boyd, Lester, LB, Kentucky, 150
7. Morucci, Mike, RB, Bloomsburg, 177
8. *Evans, Chuck, LB, Stanford, 206
9. Mordica, Frank, RB, Vanderbilt, 233
10. Webb, Tanya, DE, Michigan State, 262
11. Woodard, George, RB, Texas A&M, 289
12. Lewis, Kiser, LB, Florida A&M, 318

NEW YORK GIANTS 1980
1. *Haynes, Mark, DB, Colorado, 8
2. Choice to Pittsburgh
3. *Lapka, Myron, DT, USC, 64
4. *Pittman, Danny, WR, Wyoming, 90
5. *Blount, Tony, DB, Virginia, 118
6. *Brunner, Scott, QB, Delaware, 145
7. Choice to Oakland
*Hebert, Bud, DB, Oklahoma [from Seattle] 179
*Linnin, Chris, DE, Washington [from Cleveland] 181
8. Harris, Ken, RB, Alabama, 200
9. *Wonsley, Otis, RB, Alcorn State, 229
10. Sanford, Joe, T, Washington, 256
11. Bernish, Steve, DE, South Carolina, 285
12. *Lansford, Mike, K, Washington, 312

NEW YORK JETS 1980
1. *Jones, Johnny (Lam), WR, Texas [from San Francisco] 2
Choice to San Francisco
2. *Ray, Darrol, DB, Oklahoma, 40
*Clayton, Ralph, WR-RB, Michigan [from Denver] 47
3. *Mehl, Lance, LB, Penn State, 69
4. *Johnson, Jesse, DB, Colorado, 95
5. Zidd, Jim, LB, Kansas, 123
6. *Visger, George, DE-DT, Colorado, 149
Schremp, Tom, DE-DT, Wisconsin [from Oakland] 152
7. *Batton, Bob, RB, Nevada-Las Vegas, 178
Leverett, Bennie, RB, Bethune-Cookman [from Houston] 190
8. Dziama, Jeff, LB, Boston College, 205
9. Peters, Joe, DT, Arizona State, 234
10. *Bingham, Guy, C, Montana, 260
11. Zachery, James, LB, Texas A&M, 290
12. Dumars, David, DB, Northeast Louisiana, 317

OAKLAND 1980
1. *Wilson, Marc, QB, BYU, 15
2. *Millen, Matt, LB, Penn State, 43
3. Choice to Los Angeles Rams
4. Choice forfeited
5. *Lewis, Kenny, LB, Virginia Tech [from Cleveland] 125
Adams, John, LB, LSU, 126
Bowens, William, LB, North Alabama [from Tampa Bay] 128
6. Choice to New York Jets
7. *Barnwell, Malcolm, WR, Virginia Union [from New York Giants] 173
Choice to Houston
8. *Hill, Kenny, DB, Yale [from San Francisco] 194
Choice to San Francisco
9. Choice to San Francisco
10. *Carter, Walter, DT, Florida State, 264
11. Massey, Mike, LB, Arkansas, 291
12. *Muhammad, Calvin, WR, Texas Southern, 322

PHILADELPHIA 1980
1. *Young, Roynell, DB, Alcorn State, 23
2. *Harrington, Perry, RB, Jackson State, 53
3. Choice forfeited
4. Choice to Atlanta
5. *Rivers, Nate, WR, South Carolina State, 135
6. *Murtha, Greg, T, Minnesota, 161
7. Ward, Terrell, DB, San Diego State, 188
8. *Curcio, Mike, LB, Temple, 218
9. Harris, Bob, T, Bowling Green, 245
10. Choice to Miami
11. Jukes, Lee, WR, North Carolina State [from Miami] 298
*Brown, Thomas, DE, Baylor, 302
12. Fields, Howard, DB, Baylor, 329

PITTSBURGH 1980
1. *Malone, Mark, QB, Arizona State, 28
2. *Kohrs, Bob, LB, Arizona State [from New York Giants] 35
*Goodman, John, DE, Oklahoma, 56
3. Sydnor, Ray, TE, Wisconsin, 83
4. *Hurley, Bill, QB, Syracuse, 110
5. *Wolfley, Craig, G, Syracuse, 138
6. *Ilkin, Tunch, C, Indiana State, 165
7. *Johnson, Nate, WR, Hillsdale, 193
8. Walton, Ted, DB, Connecticut, 221
9. McCall, Ron, WR, Arkansas-Pine Bluff, 249
10. Wilson, Woodrow, DB, North Carolina State [from San Francisco] 250
Fritz, Ken, G, Ohio State, 277
11. *Pollard, Frank, RB, Baylor, 305
12. Vaclavik, Charles, DB, Texas [from San Francisco] 306
*McGriff, Tyrone, G, Florida A&M, 333

ST. LOUIS 1980
1. *Greer, Curtis, DE, Michigan, 6
2. *Marsh, Doug, TE, Michigan, 33
3. *Sinnott, John, T, Brown, 60
*Baker, Charlie, LB, New Mexico [from San Diego] 81
4. *Lisch, Rusty, QB, Notre Dame, 89
5. Choice to Kansas City
6. *Acker, Bill, DT, Texas, 142
7. *Apuna, Ben, LB, Arizona State, 171
8. Branch, Dupree, DB, Colorado State, 198
Hudson, Grant, DT, Virginia [from Denver] 211
9. *Mays, Stafford, DE, Washington, 225
10. *Brown, Rush, DT, Ball State, 255
11. Brown, Delrick, DB, Houston, 282
12. Gray, Tyrone, WR, Washington State, 309

SAN DIEGO 1980
1. Choice to Green Bay
2. Choice to Cleveland thru Los Angeles Rams
3. Choice to St. Louis
4. *Luther, Ed, QB, San Jose State [from Tampa Bay] 101
*Gregor, Bob, DB, Washington State, 108
5. Choice to Denver thru Washington and Cleveland
6. *Harrington, LaRue, RB, Norfolk State [from Cleveland] 151
Hamilton, Wayne, LB, Alabama, 163
7. *Loewen, Chuck, G, South Dakota State [from Buffalo] 175
Dodds, Stuart, P, Montana State, 191
8. Sirmones, Curtis, RB, North Alabama, 219
9. Whitman, Steve, RB, Alabama, 247
10. Choice to Tampa Bay
11. Singleton, John, DE, Texas-El Paso, 303
12. Price, Harry, WR, McNeese State, 331

SAN FRANCISCO 1980
1. Choice to New York Jets
*Cooper, Earl, RB, Rice [from New York Jets] 13
*Stuckey, Jim, DT, Clemson [from Den thru New York Jets] 20
2. Choice to Buffalo
*Turner, Keena, LB, Purdue [from Minnesota] 39
3. Choice to Los Angeles Rams
*Miller, Jim, P, Mississippi [from Minnesota] 65
*Puki, Craig, LB, Tennessee [from Was thru Los Angeles Rams] 77
4. *Churchman, Ricky, DB, Texas, 84
Hodge, David, LB, Houston [from New England thru Los Angeles Rams] 98
5. *Times, Kenneth, DT, Southern, 112
6. *Williams, Herb, DB, Southern, 139
7. Choice to Cincinnati
8. Choice to Oakland
*Leopold, Bobby, LB, Notre Dame [from Oakland] 210
9. Choice to Det thru Kansas City
Hartwig, Dan, QB, California Lutheran [from Oakland] 237
10. Choice to Pittsburgh
11. Choice to Miami
12. Choice to Pittsburgh

SEATTLE 1980
1. *Green, Jacob, DE, Texas A&M [from Buffalo] 10
Choice to Buffalo
2. *Hines, Andre, T, Stanford, 44
3. Choice to Buffalo
4. *Dion, Terry, DE, Oregon, 97
5. Steele, Joe, RB, Washington, 127
Jacobs, Daniel, DE, Winston-Salem State [from Miami thru Washington] 132
6. McNeal, Mark, DE, Idaho, 153
7. Choice to New York Giants
8. *Minor, Vic, DB, Northeast Louisiana [from Minnesota] 204
Cosgrove, Jack, C, Pacific, 207
9. Swift, Jim, T, Iowa, 238
10. *Essink, Ron, T, Grand Valley State, 265
Reaves, Billy, WR, Morris Brown [from Houston] 274
11. Ena, Tali, RB, Washington State, 292
12. Gilbert, Presnell, DB, U.S. International, 319

TAMPA BAY 1980
1. *Snell, Ray, G, Wisconsin, 22
2. *House, Kevin, WR, Southern Illinois, 49
3. *Brantley, Scot, LB, Florida, 76
4. Choice to San Diego
*Flowers, Larry, DB, Texas Tech [from Washington] 102
5. Choice to Oakland
6. Choice to Cincinnati
7. *Leonard, Jim, C, Santa Clara, 186
8. Goodard, Derrick, DB, Drake, 213
9. *Carter, Gerald, WR, Texas A&M, 240
10. *Hawkins, Andy, LB, Texas A&I, 267
Davis, Brett, RB, Nevada-Las Vegas [from San Diego] 275
11. Jones, Terry, DE, Central State (OK), 299
12. Coleman, Gene, DB, Miami, 326

WASHINGTON 1980
1. *Monk, Art, WR, Syracuse, 18
2. Choice to Los Angeles Rams
*Mendenhall, Mat, DE, BYU [from Los Angeles Rams] 55
3. Choice to San Francisco thru Los Angeles Rams
4. Choice to Tampa Bay
5. Choice to Buffalo
6. Bell, Farley, LB, Cincinnati, 155
7. *Jones, Melvin, G, Houston, 187

8. Choice to Miami
9. McCullough, Lawrence, WR, Illinois, 241
10. Walker, Lewis, RB, Utah, 268
11. Matocha, Mike, DE, Texas-Arlington, 295
12. Emmett, Marcene, DB, North Alabama, 327

1981

Held April 28-29, 1981

There were 332 selections instead of 336. Atlanta gave up its seventh-round pick and San Diego its ninth-round choice In 1980 supplemental drafts. Denver and Oakland forfeited their third-round and fifth-round choices, respectively.

ATLANTA 1981
1. *Butler, Bobby, DB, Florida State, 25
2. *White, Lyman, LB, LSU, 54
3. *Woerner, Scott, DB, Georgia, 80
4. *Scully, John, C, Notre Dame, 109
5. *Sanders, Eric, T, Nevada-Reno, 136
6. *Stanback, Harry, DT, North Carolina, 164
7. Choice exercised in 1980 supplemental draft (Teague, Matthew, DE, Prairie View A&M)
8. Toney, Clifford, DB, Auburn, 219
9. Fance, Calvin, RB, Rice, 245
10. Murphy, Robert, DB, Ohio State, 274
11. Chappelle, Keith, WR, Iowa, 301
12. McCants, Mark, DB, Temple, 330

BALTIMORE 1981
1. *McMillan, Randy, RB, Pittsburgh, 12
 *Thompson, Donnell, DT, North Carolina [from Minnesota] 18
2. Choice to Minnesota
3. *Van Divier, Randy, T, Washington, 68
4. *Sherwin, Tim, TE, Boston College, 94
5. Choice to Minnesota
6. *Green, Bubba, DT, North Carolina State, 149
7. *Ariri, Obed, K, Clemson, 178
8. Sitton, Ken, DB, Oklahoma, 204
 *Taylor, Hosea, DT, Houston [from Philadelphia] 220
9. Gooch, Tim, DT, Kentucky, 233
10. Gerken, Gregg, LB, Northern Arizona [from San Francisco] 256
 *Bryant, Trent, DB, Arkansas, 259
11. *Smith, Holden, WR, California, 288
12. Scoggins, Eric, LB, USC, 315

BUFFALO 1981
1. Choice to Oakland
 *Moore, Booker, RB, Penn State [from Oakland] 28
2. *Williams, Chris, DB, LSU [from Cleveland] 49
 *Franklin, Byron, WR, Auburn, 50
3. *Mosley, Mike, WR, Texas A&M, 76
 Geathers, Robert, DT, South Carolina State [from Oakland] 83
4. Choice to Los Angeles Rams
5. Clark, Calvin, DE, Purdue, 135
6. *Holt, Robert, WR, Baylor, 161
7. Doolittle, Steve, LB, Colorado, 188
8. Choice to New Orleans
9. *Riddick, Robb, RB, Millersville, 241
10. *Cross, Justin, T, Western Colorado, 272
11. *Barnett, Buster, TE, Jackson State, 299
12. Clark, Keith, LB, Memphis State, 326

CHICAGO BEARS 1981
1. *Van Horne, Keith, T, USC, 11
2. *Singletary, Mike, LB, Baylor [from San Francisco] 38
 Choice to San Francisco
3. *Margerum, Ken, WR, Stanford, 67
4. *Bell, Todd, DB, Ohio State, 95
5. Choice to San Francisco
6. *Henderson, Reuben, DB, San Diego State, 150
7. *Fisher, Jeff, DB, USC, 177
8. Zettek, Scott, DT, Notre Dame, 205
9. Ditta, Frank, G, Baylor, 232
10. Clifford, Tim, QB, Indiana, 260
11. Johnson, Lonnie, RB, Indiana, 287
12. Shupryt, Bob, LB, New Mexico, 316

CINCINNATI 1981
1. *Verser, David, WR, Kansas, 10
2. *Collinsworth, Cris, WR, Florida, 37
3. *Simmons, John, DB, SMU, 64
4. *Frazier, Guy, LB, Wyoming, 93
5. Pryor, Benjie, TE, Pittsburgh, 120
6. *Robinson, Rex, K, Georgia, 146
7. *Schuh, Jeff, LB, Minnesota, 176
8. *Kemp, Bobby, DB, Cal State-Fullerton, 202
9. *Hannula, Jim, T, Northern Illinois, 229
 Samoa, Samoa, RB, Washington State [from San Francisco] 230
10. Simpson, Hubert, RB, Tennessee, 258
11. *Jackson, Robert, DB, Central Michigan, 285
12. O'Connell, Mark, QB, Ball State, 312

CLEVELAND 1981
1. *Dixon, Hanford, DB, Southern Mississippi, 22
2. Choice to Buffalo
3. Choice to Kansas City lhru Den
4. Choice to San Diego
 *Robinson, Mike, DE, Arizona [from Washington] 92
5. *Cox, Steve, K, Arkansas, 134
6. Simmons, Ron, DT, Florida State, 160
7. *Johnson, Eddie, LB, Louisville, 187
8. Choice to New York Jets
9. Schleusener, Randy, G, Nebraska, 244
10. *Prater, Dean, DE, Oklahoma State, 271
11. *Friday, Larry, DB, Mississippi State, 298
12. McGill, Kevin, T, Oregon, 325

DALLAS 1981
1. *Richards, Howard, T, Missouri, 26
2. *Donley, Doug, WR, Ohio State, 53
3. *Titensor, Glen, DE, BYU, 81
4. *Pelluer, Scott, LB, Washington State [from San Francisco] 91
 *Nelson, Derrie, LB, Nebraska, 108
5. *Spradlin, Danny, LB, Tennessee, 137
6. Skillings, Vince, DB, Ohio State, 163
7. *Fellows, Ron, DB, Missouri [from Tampa Bay] 173
 Miller, Ken, DB, Eastern Michigan, 191
8. Piurowski, Paul, LB, Florida State, 218
9. *Wilson, Mike, WR, Washington State, 246
10. Graham, Pat, DT, California, 273
11. Morrison, Tim, G, Georgia, 302
12. Lundy, Nate, WR, Indiana, 329

DENVER 1981
1. *Smith, Dennis, DB, USC, 15
2. *Brown, Clay, TE, BYU, 42
3. Choice forfeited
4. *Herrmann, Mark, QB, Purdue, 98
5. *Lanier, Ken, T, Florida State, 125
6. Lewis, Alvin, RB, Colorado State, 151
7. *Busick, Steve, LB, USC, 181
8. Choice to New York Giants
9. Olsen, Rusty, DE, Washington, 234
10. Choice to St. Louis
11. Walker, Pat, WR, Miami, 290
12. Hankerd, John, LB, Notre Dame, 317
 Robinson, Mandel, RB, Wyoming [from Detroit] 321

DETROIT 1981
1. *Nichols, Mark, WR, San Jose State, 16
2. *Green, Curtis, DE, Alabama State, 46
3. *Greco, Don, G, Western Illinois, 72
4. *Porter, Tracy, WR, LSU, 99
5. *Lee, Larry, G, UCLA, 129
6. Johnson, Sam, DB, Maryland, 155
7. Spivey, Lee, T, SMU, 182
8. *Niziolek, Bob, TE, Colorado, 211
9. Jernigan, Hugh, DB, Arkansas, 238
 *Martin, Dave, DB, Villanova [from New England] 240
10. Cannavino, Andy, LB, Michigan, 264
11. Jackson, Willie, DB, Mississippi State, 294
12. Choice to Denver

GREEN BAY 1981
1. *Campbell, Rich, QB, California, 6
2. *Lewis, Gary, TE, Texas-Arlington, 35
3. *Stachowicz, Ray, P, Michigan State, 62
 Choice to Washington
4. *Turner, Richard, DT, Oklahoma [from Los Angeles Rams thru Washington] 105
5. *Braggs, Byron, DT, Alabama, 117
6. Choice to New York Giants
7. *Whitaker, Bill, DB, Missouri, 172
8. Werts, Larry, LB, Jackson State, 200
9. *Huffman, Tim, T, Notre Dame, 227
10. Hall, Nickie, QB, Tulane, 255
11. Valora, Forrest, LB, Oklahoma, 282
12. *Lewis, Cliff, LB, Southern Mississippi, 311

HOUSTON 1981
1. Choice to Oakland
2. Choice to Oakland
3. *Holston, Michael, WR, Morgan State, 79
4. *Eyre, Nick, T, BYU, 106
5. Fowler, Delbert, LB, West Virginia, 133
6. *Kay, Bill, DB, Purdue, 159
7. Choice to Seattle
 Washington, Don, DB, Texas A&I [from Oakland] 193
8. *Tullis, Willie, WR, Troy State, 217
9. *Riley, Avon, LB, UCLA, 243
10. Jones, Larry, RB, Colorado State, 270
11. Mathews, Claude, G, Auburn, 297
12. *Capece, Bill, K, Florida State, 324

KANSAS CITY 1981
1. *Scott, Willie, TE, South Carolina, 14
2. *Delaney, Joe, RB, Northwestern State (LA), 41
3. *Harvey, Marvin, TE, Southern Mississippi, 70
 *Taylor, Roger, T, Oklahoma State [from Cleveland thru Denver] 75
 *Burruss, Lloyd, DB, Maryland [from Los Angeles Rams] 78
4. Washington, Ron, WR, Arizona State, 97
5. *Thomas, Todd, T, North Dakota, 124
6. Luckie, Dock, DT, Florida, 153
7. *Jackson, Billy, RB, Alabama, 180
8. Dorn, David, WR, Rutgers, 206
9. Vereen, Anthony, DB, Southeastern Louisiana, 237
10. *Studdard, Les, G, Texas, 262
11. *Case, Frank, DE, Penn State, 289
12. *Gagliano, Bob, QB, Utah State, 319

LOS ANGELES RAMS 1981
1. *Owens, Mel, LB, Michigan [from Washington] 9
 Choice to Washington
2. Choice to Minnesota thru Washington and Baltimore
 *Collins, Jim, LB, Syracuse [from Miami] 43
3. Choice to Kansas City
 *Meisner, Greg, DT, Pittsburgh [from Tampa Bay] 63
 *Cobb, Robert, DE, Arizona [from Washington] 66
4. *Lilja, George, C, Michigan [from Buffalo] 104
 Choice to Green Bay thru Washington
5. Choice to Washington
6. Daniels, William, DT, Alabama State, 158
7. *Battle, Ron, TE, North Texas State [from Washington] 175
 *Clark, Mike, DE, Florida, 190
8. *Plunkett, Art, T, Nevada-Las Vegas, 216
9. Seawell, Ron, LB, Portland State, 242
10. *Alexander, Robert, RB, West Virginia, 269
11. *Greene, Marcellus, DB, Arizona, 296
12. *Penaranda, Jairo, RB, UCLA, 328

MIAMI 1981
1. *Overstreet, David, RB, Oklahoma, 13
2. Choice to Los Angeles Rams
 *Franklin, Andra, RB, Nebraska [from Oakland thru Los Angeles Rams] 56
3. Choice to Los Angeles Rams
4. Greene, Sam, WR, Nevada-Las Vegas [from New Orleans] 84
 Wright, Brad, QB, New Mexico, 96
5. *Poole, Ken, DE, Northeast Louisiana, 126
 *Vigorito, Tommy, RB, Virginia [from Philadelphia] 138
6. *Moore, Mack, DE, Texas A&M, 152
 *Walker, Fulton, DB, West Virginia [from Minnesota] 154
7. Daum, Mike, T, Cal Poly-SLO, 179
8. *Judson, William, DB, South Carolina State, 208
9. Noonan, John, WR, Nebraska, 235
10. *Folsom, Steve, TE, Utah, 261
11. *Jensen, Jim, QB, Boston U., 291
12. Alford, John, DT, South Carolina State, 318

MINNESOTA 1981
1. Choice to Baltimore
2. *McDole, Mardye, WR, Mississippi State [from Baltimore] 39
 *Sendlein, Robin, LB, Texas, 45
 *Redwine, Jarvis, RB, Nebraska [from Los Angeles Rams thru Washington and Baltimore] 52
3. Choice to New Orleans
 *Irwin, Tim, T, Tennessee [from New England] 74
4. *Swain, John, DB, Miami, 101
5. Choice to New Orleans
 Ray, Wendell, DE, Missouri [from Baltimore] 123
6. Choice to Miami
7. Shaver, Don, RB, Kutztown, 184
8. *Wilson, Wade, QB-P, East Texas State, 210
9. Choice to Seattle
10. *Murphy, James, WR, Utah State, 266
11. Stephanos, Bill, T, Boston College, 293
12. *Williams, Brian, TE, Southern, 320

NEW ENGLAND 1981
1. *Holloway, Brian, T, Stanford, 19
2. *Collins, Tony, RB, East Carolina, 47
3. Choice to Minnesota
4. *Blackmon, Don, LB, Tulsa, 102
5. *Clark, Steve, DT, Kansas State, 130
6. *Wooten, Ron, G, North Carolina, 157
7. *Toler, Ken, WR, Mississippi, 185
8. Naber, Ken, K-P, Stanford [from New Orleans] 194
 *Dawson, Lin, TE, North Carolina State, 212
9. Choice to Detroit
10. Choice to Cleveland
11. Buckley, Brian, QB, Harvard, 295
12. *Crissy, William, DB, Princeton, 323

NEW ORLEANS 1981
1. *Rogers, George, RB, South Carolina, 1
2. *Gary, Russell, DB, Nebraska, 29
 *Jackson, Rickey, LB, Pittsburgh [from San Diego] 51
3. *Warren, Frank, DE, Auburn, 57
 *Brenner, Hoby, TE, USC [from Minnesota] 71
4. Choice to Miami
5. *Oubre, Louis, T, Oklahoma, 112
 *Boyarsky, Jerry, DT, Pittsburgh [from Minnesota] 128
6. *Hudson, Nat, G, Georgia, 139
 *Poe, Johnnie, DB, Missouri [from Tampa Bay] 144
 *Redd, Glen, LB, BYU [from Oakland] 166
7. *Williams, Kevin, WR, USC, 167
8. Choice to New England
 Gladys, Gene, LB, Penn State [from Buffalo] 214
 Evans, Kevin, DB, Arkansas [from San Diego] 215
9. *Tyler, Toussaint, RB, Washington, 222
10. *Gajan, Hokie, RB, LSU, 249
11. Mickens, Lester, WR, Kansas, 277
12. *Wilks, Jim, DT, San Diego State, 305

NEW YORK GIANTS 1981
1. *Taylor, Lawrence, LB, North Carolina, 2
2. *Young, Dave, TE, Purdue, 32
3. *Mistler, John, WR, Arizona State, 59
4. *Chatman, Clifford, RB, Central State (OK), 85
5. *Neill, Bill, DT, Pittsburgh, 115
6. Choice to San Diego
 *Hoover, Mel, WR, Arizona State [from Green Bay] 145
 O'Neal, Edward, RB, Tuskegee, 165
7. *Jackson, Louis, RB, Cal Poly-SLO, 168
8. Powers, John, G, Michigan, 197
 *Reed, Mark, QB, Moorhead State [from Denver] 207
 *Ard, Billy, G, Wake Forest [from Oakland] 221
9. *Hunt, Byron, LB, SMU, 224
10. Barker, Mike, DT, Grambling, 250
11. Choice to San Diego
12. Maher, Mike, TE, Western Illinois, 307

NEW YORK JETS 1981
1. *McNeil, Freeman, RB, UCLA, 3
2. *Barber, Marion, RB, Minnesota, 30
3. *Rudolph, Ben, DT, Long Beach State, 60
4. *Washington, Al, LB, Ohio State, 86
5. *Keys, Tyrone, DE, Mississippi State, 113
6. *Woodring, John, LB, Brown, 142
7. *Neil, Kenny, DE, Iowa State, 169
8. Jones, Lloyd, WR, BYU, 195
 Watts, J.C., DB, Oklahoma [from Cleveland] 213
9. Larry, Admiral Dewey, DB, Nevada-Las Vegas, 225
10. Wetzel, Marty, LB, Tulane, 251
11. Gall, Ed, DT, Maryland, 278
12. Moeller, Mike, T, Drake, 308

OAKLAND 1981
1. *Watts, Ted, DB, Texas Tech [from Houston] 21
 *Marsh, Curt, T, Washington [from Buffalo] 23
 Choice to Buffalo
2. *Long, Howie, DT, Villanova [from Houston] 48
 Choice to Miami thru Los Angeles Rams
3. Choice to Buffalo
4. *Robinson, Johnny, DT, Louisiana Tech, 111
5. *Davis, James, DB, Southern [from Tampa Bay] 118
 Choice forfeited
6. Choice to New Orleans
7. Choice to Houston
8. Choice to New York Giants
9. Mohl, Curt, T, UCLA, 248
10. *Hawkins, Frank, RB, Nevada-Reno, 276
11. *Willis, Chester, RB, Auburn, 304
12. Nelson, Phil, TE, Delaware, 332

PHILADELPHIA 1981
1. *Mitchell, Leonard, DE, Houston, 27
2. *Miraldi, Dean, G, Utah, 55
3. *LaFleur, Greg, TE, LSU, 82
4. *Murray, Calvin, RB, Ohio State, 110
5. Choice to Miami
6. Choice to New York Giants
7. Duncan, Alan, K, Tennessee [from San Francisco] 174
 *Field, Doak, LB, Baylor, 192
8. Choice to Baltimore
9. *Commiskey, Chuck, C, Mississippi, 247
10. *Oliver, Hubie, RB, Arizona, 275
11. Davis, Gail, OT, Virginia Union, 303
12. *Ellis, Ray, DB, Ohio State, 331

PITTSBURGH 1981
1. *Gary, Keith, DE, Oklahoma, 17
2. *Washington, Anthony, DB, Fresno State, 44
3. *Donnalley, Rick, C-G, North Carolina, 73
4. *Martin, Robbie, WR, Cal Poly-SLO, 100
5. Martin, Ricky, WR, New Mexico, 127
6. *Hinkle, Bryan, LB, Oregon, 156
7. *Little, David, LB, Florida, 183
8. *Wilson, Frank, RB, Rice, 209
9. *Hunter, James, T, USC, 239
10. *Mayock, Mike, DB, Boston College, 265
11. *Trocano, Rick, QB, Pittsburgh, 292
12. Choice to San Francisco

ST. LOUIS 1981
1. *Junior, E.J., LB, Alabama, 5
2. *Lomax, Neil, QB, Portland State, 33
3. *Griffin, Jeff, DB, Utah, 61
4. Rhodes, Steve, WR, Oklahoma, 88
5. *Gillen, John, LB, Illinois, 116
6. *Ahrens, Dave, LB, Wisconsin, 143
7. *Donnalley, Kevin, DB, North Dakota State, 171
8. *Fisher, Mike, WR, Baylor, 198
9. *Mitchell, Stump, RB, Citadel, 226
10. Mallard, James, WR, Alabama, 253
 Joiner, Jim, WR, Miami [from Denver] 263
11. Sherrod, Mike, TE, Illinois, 281
12. Adams, Joe, G, Nebraska, 309

SAN DIEGO 1981
1. *Brooks, James, RB, Auburn, 24
2. Choice to New Orleans
3. *Phillips, Irvin, DB, Arkansas Tech, 77
4. *Lawrence, Amos, RB, North Carolina, 103
 *Sievers, Eric, TE, Maryland [from Cleveland] 107
5. *Ferguson, Keith, LB, Ohio State, 131
6. *Gissinger, Andrew, T, Syracuse [from New York Giants] 141
 *Duckworth, Bobby, WR, Arkansas, 162
7. *Holohan, Pete, TE, Notre Dame, 189
8. Choice to New Orleans
9. Choice exercised in 1980 supplemental draft (Mullins, Billy, WR, USC)
10. Parham, Robert, RB, Grambling, 268
11. Petrzelka, Matt, T, Iowa [from New York

Giants] 280
*Bradley, Carlos, LB, Wake Forest, 300
12. Charles, Stacy, WR, Bethune-Cookman, 327

SAN FRANCISCO 1981
1. *Lott, Ronnie, DB, USC, 8
2. *Harty, John, DT, Iowa [from Washington] 36
Choice to Chicago Bears
*Wright, Eric, DB, Missouri [from Chicago Bears] 40
3. *Williamson, Carlton, DB, Pittsburgh, 65
4. Choice to Dallas
5. Thomas, Lynn, DB, Pittsburgh, 121
*Jones, Arrington, RB, Winston-Salem State [from Chicago Bears] 122
6. *Kugler, Pete, DT, Penn State, 147
7. Choice to Philadelphia
8. White, Garry, RB, Minnesota, 203
9. Choice to Cincinnati
10. Choice to Baltimore
11. DeBose, Ronnie, TE, UCLA, 286
12. Ogilvie, Major, RB, Alabama, 313
Adams, Joe, QB, Tennessee State [from Pittsburgh] 322

SEATTLE 1981
1. *Easley, Kenny, DB, UCLA, 4
2. *Hughes, David, RB, Boise State, 31
3. *Dugan, Bill, G, Penn State, 58
4. Phillips, Scott, WR, BYU, 87
5. *Bailey, Edwin, G, South Carolina State, 114
6. *Durham, Steve, DE, Clemson, 140
7. *Johnson, Ron, WR, Long Beach State, 170
Scovill, Brad, TE, Penn State [from Houston] 186
8. *Lane, Eric, RB, BYU, 196
9. Stone, Jim, RB, Notre Dame, 223
Whatley, Jim, WR, Washington State [from Minnesota] 236
10. Dawson, Ken, RB, Savannah State, 252
11. Olander, Lance, RB, Colorado, 279
12. Bednarek, Jeff, DT, Pacific, 306

TAMPA BAY 1981
1. *Green, Hugh, LB, Pittsburgh, 7
2. *Wilder, James, RB, Missouri, 34
3. Choice to Los Angeles Rams
4. *Holt, John, DB, West Texas State, 89
5. Choice to Oakland
6. Choice to New Orleans
7. Choice to Dallas
8. Johnson, Denver, T, Tulsa, 199
9. Ford, Mike, QB, SMU, 228
10. McCune, Ken, DE, Texas, 254
11. *Smith, Johnny Ray, DB, Lamar, 283
12. *White, Brad, DT, Tennessee, 310

WASHINGTON 1981
1. Choice to Los Angeles Rams
*May, Mark, T, Pittsburgh [from Los Angeles Rams] 20
2. Choice to San Francisco
3. Choice to Los Angeles Rams
*Grimm, Russ, C, Pittsburgh [from Mia thru Los Angeles Rams] 69
4. *Flick, Tom, QB, Washington [from Green Bay] 90
Choice to Cleveland
5. *Manley, Dexter, DE, Oklahoma State, 119
Sayre, Gary, G, Cameron [from Los Angeles Rams] 132
6. *Kubin, Larry, LB, Penn State, 148
7. Choice to Los Angeles Rams
8. *Brown, Charlie, WR, South Carolina State, 201
9. *Grant, Darryl, G, Rice, 231
10. Kessel, Phil, QB, Northern Michigan, 257
*Kennedy, Allan, T, Washington State [from New England thru Cleveland] 267
11. Hill, Jerry, WR, North Alabama, 284
12. *Didier, Clint, WR, Portland State, 314

1982

Held April 27-28, 1982

There were 334 selections instead of 336. New Orleans gave up its first-round pick and New England its eleventh-round pick in 1981 supplemental drafts. Although the Raiders played the 1982 season in Los Angeles, at the time of the draft, the franchise still was located in Oakland.

ATLANTA 1982
1. *Riggs, Gerald, RB, Arizona State, 9
2. *Rogers, Doug, DE, Stanford, 36
3. *Bailey, Stacey, WR, San Jose State, 63
4. *Brown, Reggie, RB, Oregon, 95
5. *Mansfield, Von, DB, Wisconsin, 122
6. *Kelley, Mike, QB, Georgia Tech, 149
7. Toloumu, David, RB, Hawaii, 176
8. Eberhardt, Ricky, DB, Morris Brown, 203
9. *Horan, Mike, P, Long Beach State, 235
10. Stowers, Curtis, LB, Mississippi State, 262
11. Keller, Jeff, WR, Washington State, 288
12. *Levenick, Dave, LB, Wisconsin, 315

BALTIMORE 1982
1. *Cooks, Johnie, LB, Mississippi State, 2
*Schlichter, Art, QB, Ohio State [from Los Angeles Rams] 4
2. *Wisniewski, Leo, DT, Penn State, 28
*Stark, Rohn, P, Florida State [from Los Angeles Rams] 34
3. *Burroughs, James, DB, Michigan State, 57
4. *Pagel, Mike, QB, Arizona State, 84
5. *Crouch, Terry, G, Oklahoma, 113
6. *Beach, Pat, TE, Washington State, 140
7. *Jenkins, Fletcher, DT, Washington, 169
8. Loia, Tony, G, Arizona State, 196
9. Berryhill, Tony, C, Clemson, 225
10. Deery, Tom, DB, Widener, 252
11. Meacham, Lamont, DB, Western Kentucky, 280
12. *Wright, Johnnie, RB, South Carolina, 307

BUFFALO 1982
1. *Tuttle, Perry, WR, Clemson [from Denver] 19
Choice to Denver
2. *Kofler, Matt, QB, San Diego State, 48
3. *Marve, Eugene, LB, Saginaw Valley State [from Cleveland] 59
Choice to Seattle
4. *Williams, Van, RB, Carson-Newman [from St. Louis] 93
Choice to Denver
5. Choice to Washington
6. Chivers, DeWayne, TE, South Carolina, 160
7. *Anderson, Gary, K, Syracuse [from Cleveland] 171
Choice to Det thru Los Angeles Rams
8. Tousignant, Luc, QB, Fairmont State, 218
9. Edwards, Dennis, DT, USC, 245
10. James, Vic, DB, Colorado, 272
11. Kalil, Frank, G, Arizona, 298
12. Suber, Tony, DT, Gardner-Webb, 329

CHICAGO BEARS 1982
1. *McMahon, Jim, QB, BYU, 5
2. Choice to Tampa Bay
3. *Wrightman, Tim, TE, UCLA, 62
4. *Gentry, Dennis, RB, Baylor, 89
5. *Hartnett, Perry, G, SMU, 116
Tabron, Dennis, DB, Duke [from San Diego] 134
6. *Becker, Kurt, G, Michigan, 146
7. *Waechter, Henry, DT, Nebraska, 173
8. *Doerger Jerry, T, Wisconsin, 200
9. Hatchett, Mike, DB, Texas, 230
10. Turner, Joe, DB, USC, 257
11. Boliaux, Guy, LB, Wisconsin, 283
12. Young, Ricky, LB, Oklahoma State, 313

CINCINNATI 1982
1. *Collins, Glen, DE, Mississippi State, 26
2. *Weaver, Emanuel, DT, South Carolina, 54
3. *Holman, Rodney, TE, Tulane, 82
4. *Tate, Rodney, RB, Texas, 110
5. Sorensen, Paul, DB, Washington State, 138
6. King, Arthur, DT, Grambling, 166
7. Needham, Ben, LB, Michigan, 194
8. Yli-Renko, Kari, T, Cincinnati, 222
9. Bennett, James, WR, Northwestern State (LA), 250
10. Hogue, Larry, DB, Utah State, 278
11. Davis, Russell, RB, Idaho, 350
12. Feraday, Dan, QB, Toronto, 333

CLEVELAND 1982
1. *Banks, Chip, LB, USC, 3
2. *Baldwin, Keith, DE, Texas A&M, 31
3. Choice to Buffalo
4. *Walker, Dwight, WR, Nicholls State, 87
5. *Baab, Mike, C, Texas, 115
6. Choice to Dal
*Whitwell, Mike, WR, Texas A&M [from Denver] 162
7. Choice to Buffalo
8. *Kafentzis, Mark, DB, Hawaii, 199
Heflin, Van, TE, Vanderbilt [from Oakland] 204
*Jackson, Bill, DB, North Carolina [from Washington] 211
9. Baker, Milton, TE, West Texas State, 227
10. Floyd, Ricky, RB, Southern Mississippi, 255
11. Michuta, Steve, QB, Grand Valley State, 282
12. *Nicolas, Scott, LB, Miami, 310

DALLAS 1982
1. *Hill, Rod, DB, Kentucky State, 25
2. *Rohrer, Jeff, LB, Yale, 53
3. *Eliopulos, Jim, LB, Wyoming, 81
4. *Carpenter, Brian, DB, Michigan [from Tampa Bay] 101
5. *Hunter, Monty, DB, Salem (WV), 109
*Pozderac, Phil, T, Notre Dame, 137
6. Hammond, Ken, G, Vanderbilt [from Cleveland] 143
Daum, Charles, DT, Cal Poly-SLO, 165
7. Purifoy, Bill, DE, Tulsa, 193
8. *Peoples, George, RB, Auburn [from Denver thru Buffalo] 216
Sullivan, Dwight, RB, North Carolina State, 221
9. Gary, Joe, DT, UCLA, 249
10. Eckerson, Todd, T, North Carolina State, 277
11. Thompson, George, WR, Albany State (GA) [from Tampa Bay] 295
Whiting, Mike, RB, Florida State, 304
12. Burtness, Rich, G, Montana, 332

DENVER 1982
1. Choice to Buffalo
*Willhite, Gerald, RB, San Jose State [from Buffalo] 21
2. *McDaniel, Orlando, WR, LSU, 50
3. Choice to Houston thru Los Angeles Rams
4. Choice to Kansas City
Plater, Dan, WR, BYU [from Buffalo] 106
5. *Winder, Sammy, RB, Southern Mississippi, 131
6. Choice to Cleveland
7. Ruben, Alvin, DE, Houston, 189
8. Choice to Dal thru Buf
9. *Uecker, Keith, T, Auburn, 243
10. *Woodard, Ken, LB, Tuskegee, 274
11. Yatsko, Stuart, G, Oregon, 300
12. Clark, Brian, G, Clemson, 327

DETROIT 1982
1. *Williams, Jimmy, LB, Nebraska, 15
2. *Watkins, Bobby, DB, Southwest Texas State, 42
3. *Doig, Steve, LB, New Hampshire, 69
4. *McNorton, Bruce, DB, Georgetown (KY), 96
5. *Graham, William, DB, Texas, 127
6. *Machurek, Mike, QB, Idaho State, 154
7. Bates, Phil, RB, Nebraska [from Houston] 175
Choice to Los Angeles Rams
Simmons, Victor, WR, Oregon State [from Buffalo thru Los Angeles Rams] 187
8. *Moss, Martin, DE, UCLA, 208
9. *Wagoner, Danny, DB, Kansas [from Oak thru Los Angeles Rams] 231
Choice to Miami
10. *Barnes, Roosevelt, LB, Purdue, 266
11. Lee, Edward, WR, South Carolina State, 292
12. *Porter, Ricky, RB, Slippery Rock, 319
*Rubick, Rob, TE, Grand Valley State [from San Diego] 326

GREEN BAY 1982
1. Choice to New Orleans thru San Diego
*Hallstrom, Ron, G, Iowa [from San Diego] 22
2. Choice to New England thru San Diego
3. *Rodgers, Del, RB, Utah, 71
4. *Brown, Robert, LB, Virginia Tech, 98
5. *Meade, Mike, RB, Penn State, 126
6. *Parlavecchio, Chet, LB, Penn State, 152
7. Whitley, Joey, DB, Texas-El Paso, 183
8. *Boyd, Thomas, LB, Alabama, 210
9. Riggins, Charles, DE, Bethune-Cookman, 237
10. *Garcia, Eddie, K, SMU, 264
11. *Macaulay, John, C, Stanford, 294
12. *Epps, Phillip, WR, TCU, 321

HOUSTON 1982
1. *Munchak, Mike, G, Penn State, 8
2. Choice to Oakland
*Luck, Oliver, QB, West Virginia [from Tampa Bay thru Miami and Los Angeles Rams] 44
3. Choice to Los Angeles Rams
*Edwards, Stan, RB, Michigan [from New York Giants] 72
*Abraham, Robert, LB, North Carolina State [from Denver thru Los Angeles Rams] 77
4. *Bryant, Steve, WR, Purdue, 94
5. *Taylor, Malcolm, DE, Tennessee State, 121
6. *Allen, Gary, RB, Hawaii, 148
7. Choice to Detroit
8. Choice to Los Angeles Rams
9. Bradley, Matt, DB, Penn State, 234
10. Reeves, Ron, QB, Texas Tech, 261
11. Campbell, Jim, TE, Kentucky, 287
12. *Craft, Donnie, RB, Louisville, 314

KANSAS CITY 1982
1. *Hancock, Anthony, WR, Tennessee [from St. Louis] 11
Choice to St. Louis
2. *Daniels, Calvin, LB, North Carolina, 46
3. Choice to St. Louis
4. *Haynes, Louis, LB, North Texas State, 100
*Anderson, Stuart, LB, Virginia [from Denver] 104
5. *Thompson, Delbert, RB, Texas-El Paso, 130
6. *Roquemore, Durwood, DB, Texas A&I, 157
7. Smith, Greg, DT, Kansas, 184
8. *DeBruijn, Case, P-K, Idaho State, 214
9. Byford, Lyndle, T, Oklahoma, 241
10. Brodsky, Larry, WR, Miami, 268
11. Carter, Bob, WR, Arizona, 297
12. Miller, Mike, DB, Southwest Texas State, 324

LOS ANGELES RAMS 1982
1. Choice to Baltimore
*Redden, Barry, RB, Richmond [from Washington] 14
2. Choice to Baltimore
3. Choice to Washington
Bechtold, Bill, C, Oklahoma [from Houston] 67
4. Gaylord, Jeff, LB, Missouri, 88
5. *Kersten, Wally, T, Minnesota [from Seattle] 117
*Barnett, Doug, DE, Azusa Pacific, 118
6. *Locklin, Kerry, TE, New Mexico State, 145
7. Choice to Pittsburgh thru Washington
*Shearin, Joe, G, Texas [from Detroit] 181
8. *Jones, A.J. (Jam), RB, Texas, 202
*Reilly, Mike, DE, Oklahoma [from Houston] 207
9. Speight, Bob, T, Boston U., 229
10. *McPherson, Miles, DB, New Haven, 256
11. Coffman, Ricky, WR, UCLA, 285
12. Coley, Raymond, DT, Alabama A&M, 312

MIAMI 1982
1. *Foster, Roy, G, USC, 24
2. *Duper, Mark, WR, Northwestern State (LA), 52
3. *Lankford, Paul, DB, Penn State, 80
4. *Bowser, Charles, LB, Duke, 108
5. *Nelson, Bob, DT, Miami [from Minnesota] 120
*Diana, Rich, RB, Yale, 136
6. *Tutson, Tom, DB, South Carolina State [from San Diego] 161
*Hester, Ron, LB, Florida State, 164
7. *Johnson, Dan, TE, Iowa State [from New Orleans] 170
*Cowan, Larry, RB, Jackson State, 192
8. *Randle, Tate, DB, Texas Tech, 220
9. *Clark, Steve, DE, Utah [from Detroit] 239
*Boatner, Mack, RB, Southeastern Louisiana, 248
10. Fisher, Robin, LB, Florida [from Philadelphia] 271
*Jones, Wayne, T, Utah, 276
11. Crum, Gary, T, Wyoming, 303
12. Rodrique, Mike, WR, Miami, 331

MINNESOTA 1982
1. *Nelson, Darrin, RB, Stanford, 7
2. *Tausch, Terry, T, Texas, 39
3. Choice to New Orleans
4. *Fahnhorst, Jim, LB, Minnesota, 92
5. Choice to Miami
6. Storr, Greg, LB, Boston College, 147
7. *Jordan, Steve, TE, Brown, 179
8. Harmon, Kirk, LB, Pacific, 206
9. *Howard, Bryan, DB, Tennessee State, 233
10. Lucear, Gerald, WR, Temple, 260
11. *Rouse, Curtis, G, Tennessee-Chattanooga, 286
12. Milner, Hobson, RB, Cincinnati, 318

NEW ENGLAND 1982
1. *Sims, Ken, DE, Texas, 1
*Williams, Lester, DT, Miami [from San Francisco] 27
2. Choice to San Francisco
*Weathers, Robert, RB, Arizona State [from Green Bay thru San Diego] 40
*Tippett, Andre, LB, Iowa [from Washington thru San Francisco] 41
*Haley, Darryl, T, Utah [from San Francisco] 55
3. *Jones, Cedric, WR, Duke, 56
*Weishuhn, Clayton, LB, Angelo State [from Seattle] 60
4. *Crump, George, DE, East Carolina, 85
*Ingram, Brian, LB, Tennessee [from San Francisco] 111
5. *Marion, Fred, DB, Miami, 112
6. *Smith, Ricky, DB, Alabama State, 141
7. Roberts, Jeff, LB, Tulane, 168
8. Collins, Ken, LB, Washington State, 197
9. Murdock, Kelvin, WR, Troy State, 224
10. *Clark, Brian, K, Florida, 253
11. Choice exercised in 1981 supplemental draft (Davidson, Chy, WR, Rhode Island)
12. Sandon, Steve, QB, Northern Iowa [from New York Giants] 296
Taylor, Greg, KR, Virginia, 308

NEW ORLEANS 1982
1. Choice exercised in 1981 supplemental draft (Wilson, Dave, QB, Illinois)
*Scott, Lindsay, WR, Georgia [from Green Bay thru San Diego] 13
2. *Edelman, Brad, C, Missouri, 30
3. *Lewis, Rodney, DB, Nebraska, 58
*Goodlow, Eugene, WR, Kansas State [from Minnesota] 66
*Duckett, Kenny, WR, Wake Forest [from Washington] 68
*Krimm, John, DB, Notre Dame [from San Diego] 76
4. *Andersen, Morten, K, Michigan State, 86
5. *Elliott, Tony, DE, North Texas State, 114
6. *Lewis, Marvin, RB, Tulane, 142
7. Choice to Miami
8. *Slaughter, Chuck, T, South Carolina, 198
9. Choice to Washington
10. Choice to Washington
11. Choice to Washington
12. Choice to Washington

NEW YORK GIANTS 1982
1. *Woolfolk, Butch, RB, Michigan, 18
2. *Morris, Joe, RB, Syracuse, 45
3. Choice to Houston
4. Raymond, Gerry, G, Boston College, 102
5. *Umphrey, Rich, C, Colorado, 129
6. Nicholson, Darrell, LB, North Carolina, 156
7. Wiska, Jeff, G, Michigan State, 186
8. Hubble, Robert, TE, Rice, 213
9. Higgins, John, DB, Nevada-Las Vegas, 240
10. *Baldinger, Rich, T, Wake Forest, 270
11. Choice to New England
12. Seale, Mark, DT, Richmond, 323

NEW YORK JETS 1982
1. *Crable, Bob, LB, Notre Dame, 23
2. *McElroy, Reggie, T, West Texas State, 51
3. *Crutchfield, Dwayne, RB, Iowa State, 79
4. *Floyd, George, DB, Eastern Kentucky, 107
5. *Jerue, Mark, LB, Washington, 135
6. Phea, Lonell, WR, Houston, 163
7. *Coombs, Tom, TE, Idaho, 191
8. Texada, Lawrence, RB, Henderson State, 219

9. *Klever, Rocky, RB, Montana, 247
10. *Hemphill, Darryl, DB, West Texas State, 275
11. Parmelee, Perry, WR, Santa Clara, 302
12. Carlstrom, Tom, G, Nebraska, 330

OAKLAND 1982
1. *Allen, Marcus, RB, USC, 10
2. *Squirek, Jack, LB, Illinois [from Houston] 35
*Romano, Jim, C, Penn State, 37
3. *McElroy, Vann, DB, Baylor, 64
4. *Muransky, Ed, T, Michigan, 91
5. Jackson, Ed, LB, Louisiana Tech, 123
6. Choice to San Francisco
7. Jackson, Jeff, DE, Toledo, 177
8. Choice to Cleveland
9. Choice to Det thru Los Angeles Rams
10. D'Amico, Rich, LB, Penn State, 263
11. Turner, Willie, WR, LSU, 289
12. Smith, Randy, WR, East Texas State, 316

PHILADELPHIA 1982
1. *Quick, Mike, WR, North Carolina State, 20
2. *Sampleton, Lawrence, TE, Texas, 47
3. *Kab, Vyto, TE, Penn State, 78
4. *Griggs, Anthony, LB, Ohio State, 105
5. *DeVaughn, Dennis, DB, Bishop, 132
6. Grieve, Curt, WR, Yale, 159
7. *Armstrong, Harvey, DT, SMU, 190
8. *Fritzsche, Jim, T, Purdue, 217
9. *Woodruff, Tony, WR, Fresno State, 244
10. Choice to Miami
11. Ingram, Ron, WR, Oklahoma State, 301
12. *Taylor, Rob, T, Northwestern, 328

PITTSBURGH 1982
1. *Abercrombie, Walter, RB, Baylor, 12
2. Meyer, John, T, Arizona State, 43
3. *Merriweather, Mike, LB, Pacific, 70
4. *Woods, Rick, DB, Boise State, 97
5. *Dallafior, Ken, T, Minnesota, 124
6. *Perko, Mike, DT, Utah State, 155
*Bingham, Craig, LB, Syracuse [from San Francisco thru New Orleans] 167
7. *Nelson, Edmund, DT, Auburn [from Los Angeles Rams] 172
*Boures, Emil, C, Pittsburgh, 182
8. *Goodson, John, P, Texas, 209
9. Hirn, Mike, TE, Central Michigan, 236
10. Sunseri, Sal, LB, Pittsburgh, 267
11. Sorboor, Mikal Abdul, G, Morgan State, 293
12. Hughes, Al, DE, Western Michigan, 320

ST. LOUIS 1982
1. Choice to Kansas City
*Sharpe, Luis, T, UCLA [from Kansas City] 16
2. *Galloway, David, DT, Florida, 38
3. *Perrin, Benny, DB, Alabama, 65
*Guilbeau, Rusty, DE, McNeese State [from Kansas City] 73
4. *Robbins, Tootie, T, East Carolina [from Seattle] 90
5. Bedford, Vance, DB, Texas, 119
*Ferrell, Earl, RB, East Tennessee State [from Washington] 125
6. *Shaffer, Craig, LB, Indiana State, 150
7. Sebro, Bob, C, Colorado, 178
8. *Lindstrom, Chris, DT, Boston U., 205
9. Dailey, Darnell, LB, Maryland, 232
10. *McGill, Eddie, TE, Western Carolina, 259
11. Williams, James, DE, North Carolina A&T, 290
12. Atha, Bob, K, Ohio State, 317

SAN DIEGO 1982
1. Choice to Green Bay
2. Choice to Washington thru Los Angeles Rams
3. Choice to New Orleans
4. Choice to Tampa Bay
5. Choice to Chicago Bears
6. Choice to Miami
7. Hall, Hollis, DB, Clemson, 188
8. *Buford, Maury, P, Texas Tech, 215
9. Lyles, Warren, DT, Alabama, 246
10. *Young, Andre, DB, Louisiana Tech, 273
11. Watson, Anthony, DB, New Mexico State, 299
12. Choice to Detroit

SAN FRANCISCO 1982
1. Choice to New England
2. *Paris, Bubba, T, Michigan [from New England] 29
Choice to New England
3. Choice to Tampa Bay thru San Diego
4. Choice to New England
5. *Williams, Newton, RB, Arizona State, 139
6. Choice to Pittsburgh thru New Orleans
*Williams, Vince, RB, Oregon [from Oakland] 151
7. *Ferrari, Ron, LB, Illinois, 195
8. Choice to Washington thru New Orleans
9. Clark, Bryan, QB, Michigan State, 251
10. *McLemore, Dana, KR, Hawaii [from Tampa Bay] 269
Barbian, Tim, DT, Western Illinois, 279
11. Gibson, Gary, LB, Arizona, 306
12. *Washington, Tim, DB, Fresno State, 334

SEATTLE 1982
1. *Bryant, Jeff, DE, Clemson, 6
2. *Scholtz, Bruce, LB, Texas, 33
3. Choice to New England
*Metzelaars, Pete, TE, Wabash [from Buffalo] 75
4. Choice to St. Louis
5. Choice to Los Angeles Rams
6. *Campbell, Jack, T, Utah, 144
7. *Williams, Eugene, LB, Tulsa, 174
8. Cooper, Chester, WR, Minnesota, 201
9. Jefferson, David, LB, Miami, 228
10. Austin, Craig, LB, South Dakota, 258
11. *Clancy, Sam, DE-DT, Pittsburgh, 284
12. Naylor, Frank, C, Rutgers, 311

TAMPA BAY 1982
1. *Farrell, Sean, G, Penn State, 17
2. Choice to Houston thru Mia and Los Angeles Rams
*Reese, Booker, DE, Bethune-Cookman [from Chicago Bears] 32
3. *Bell, Jerry, TE, Arizona State, 74
*Cannon, John, DE, William & Mary [from San Francisco thru San Diego] 83
4. Choice to Dallas
*Barrett, Dave, RB, Houston [from San Diego] 103
5. *Davis, Jeff, LB, Clemson, 128
6. *Tyler, Andre, WR, Stanford, 158
7. *Morris, Tom, DB, Michigan State, 185
8. *Atkins, Kelvin, LB Illinois, 212
9. Lane, Bob, QB, Northeast Louisiana, 242
10. Choice to San Francisco
11. Choice to Dallas
12. *Morton, Michael, KR, Nevada-Las Vegas, 325

WASHINGTON 1982
1. Choice to Baltimore thru Los Angeles Rams
2. Choice to New England thru San Francisco
*Dean, Vernon, DB, San Diego State [from San Diego thru Los Angeles Rams] 49
3. Powell, Carl, WR, Jackson State [from Los Angeles Rams] 61
Choice to New Orleans
4. *Liebenstein, Todd, DE, Nevada-Las Vegas, 99
5. Choice to St. Louis
*Williams, Michael, TE, Alabama A&M [from Buffalo] 133
6. Jeffers, Lamont, LB, Tennessee, 153
7. Schachtner, John, LB, Northern Arizona, 180
8. Choice to Cleveland
Warthen, Ralph, DT, Gardner-Webb [from San Francisco thru New Orleans] 223
9. *Coffey, Ken, DB, Southwest Texas State [from New Orleans] 226
Trautman, Randy, DT, Boise State, 238
10. Smith, Harold, DE, Kentucky State [from New Orleans] 254
Daniels, Terry, DB, Tennessee, 265
11. *Miller, Dan, K, Miami [from New Orleans] 281
*Holly, Bob, QB, Princeton, 291
12. *Laster, Don, T, Tennessee State [from New Orleans] 309
Goff, Jeff, LB, Arkansas, 322

1983

Held April 26-27, 1983

There were 335 selections instead of 336. Detroit gave up its ninth-round pick in a 1982 supplemental draft.

ATLANTA 1983
1. *Pitts, Mike, DE, Alabama, 16
2. *Britt, James, DB, LSU, 43
3. *Provence, Andrew, DE, South Carolina, 75
4. *Harper, John, LB, Southern Illinois, 102
5. *Miller, Brett, T, Iowa, 129
6. *Allen, Anthony, WR, Washington, 156
7. Turk, Jeff, DB, Boise State, 183
8. *Rade, John, LB, Boise State, 215
9. Choice to Baltimore
10. *Giacomarro, Ralph, P, Penn State, 268
11. Salley, John, DB, Wyoming, 295
12. *Matthews, Allama, TE, Vanderbilt, 322

BALTIMORE 1983
1. *Elway, John, QB, Stanford, 1
2. *Maxwell, Vernon, LB, Arizona State, 29
3. *Achica, George, DT, USC, 57
4. *Smith, Phil, WR, San Diego State, 85
5. *Abramowitz, Sid, T, Tulsa, 113
6. Choice to San Diego
*Feasel, Grant, C, Abilene Christian [from San Diego] 161
7. *Moore, Alvin, RB, Arizona State, 169
8. Choice to Denver
9. *Mills, Jim, T, Hawaii, 225
Rose, Chris, T, Stanford [from Atlanta] 241
10. Hopkins, Ronald, DB, Murray State, 252
11. *Taylor, Jim Bob, QB, Georgia Tech, 280
12. Williams, Carl, WR, Texas Southern, 308

BUFFALO 1983
1. *Hunter, Tony, TE, Notre Dame, 12
*Kelly, Jim, QB, Miami [from Cleveland] 14
2. *Talley, Darryl, LB, West Virginia, 39
3. Choice to New Orleans thru St. Louis
4. *Junkin, Trey, LB, Louisiana Tech, 93
Payne, Jimmy, DE, Georgia [from Was thru New Orleans] 112
5. Vandenboom, Matt, DB, Wisconsin, 126
6. Choice to New York Giants through Los Angeles Rams
7. Brown, Gurnest, DT, Maryland, 180
8. Durham, James, DB, Houston, 207
9. Parker, George, RB, Norfolk State, 234
10. Tharpe, Richard, DT, Louisville, 260
11. White, Larry, DE, Jackson State, 293
12. *Dawkins, Julius, WR, Pittsburgh, 320

CHICAGO BEARS 1983
1. *Covert, Jim, T, Pittsburgh, 6
*Gault, Willie, WR, Tennessee [from Tampa Bay] 18
2. *Richardson, Mike, DB, Arizona State, 33
3. *Duerson, Dave, DB, Notre Dame, 64
4. *Thayer, Tom, C, Notre Dame, 91
*Dunsmore, Pat, TE, Drake [from San Diego] 107
5. Choice to New England
6. Choice to Cleveland
7. Choice to Cleveland
8. *Dent, Richard, DE, Tennessee State, 203
*Bortz, Mark, DT, Iowa [from San Diego] 219
9. *Fada, Rob, G, Pittsburgh, 230
Zavagnin, Mark, LB, Notre Dame [from Cleveland thru San Francisco] 235
10. *Hutchison, Anthony, RB, Texas Tech, 256
11. Worthy, Gary, RB, Wilmington, 286
12. *Williams, Oliver, WR, Illinois [from San Francisco] 313
Choice to San Diego

CINCINNATI 1983
1. *Rimington, Dave, C, Nebraska, 25
2. *Horton, Ray, DB, Washington, 53
3. *Turner, Jim, DB, UCLA, 81
4. *Maidlow, Steve, LB, Michigan State, 109
5. *Christensen, Jeff, QB, Eastern Illinois, 137
6. *DeAyala, Kiki, LB, Texas [from New Orleans] 152
*Kinnebrew, Larry, RB, Tennessee State, 165
7. *Griffin, James, DB, Middle Tennessee State, 193
8. *Martin, Mike, WR, Illinois, 221
9. *Wilson, Stanley, RB, Oklahoma, 248
10. *Krumrie, Tim, DT, Wisconsin, 276
11. *Williams, Gary, WR, Ohio State, 304
12. Young, Andre, LB, Bowling Green, 332

CLEVELAND 1983
1. Choice to Buffalo
2. *Brown, Ron, WR, Arizona State, 41
3. *Camp, Reggie, DE, California, 68
4. Choice to San Diego
5. *Contz, Bill, T, Penn State, 122
6. *Stracka, Tim, TE, Wisconsin [from Chicago Bears] 145
*Puzzuoli, Dave, DT, Pittsburgh, 149
7. *Belk, Rocky, WR, Miami [from Chicago Bears] 176
Choice to Philadelphia
8. McClearn, Mike, G, Temple, 209
9. Choice to Chicago Bears thru San Francisco
10. *Hopkins, Thomas, T, Alabama A&M, 262
11. *Green, Boyce, RB, Carson-Newman, 288
McAdoo, Howard, LB, Michigan State [from Los Angeles Raiders] 305
12. *Farren, Paul, T, Boston U., 316

DALLAS 1983
1. *Jeffcoat, Jim, DE, Arizona State, 23
2. *Walter, Mike, DE, Oregon, 50
3. *Caldwell, Bryan, DE, Arizona State, 77
4. *Faulkner, Chris, TE, Florida, 108
5. *McSwain, Chuck, RB, Clemson, 135
6. *Collier, Reggie, QB, Southern Mississippi, 162
7. *Schultz, Chris, T, Arizona, 189
8. *Ricks, Lawrence, RB, Michigan, 220
9. *Gross, Al, DB, Arizona, 246
10. *Moran, Eric, T, Washington, 273
11. Taylor, Dan, T, Idaho State, 300
12. Bouier, Lorenzo, RB, Maine, 331

DENVER 1983
1. *Hinton, Chris, G, Northwestern, 4
2. *Cooper, Mark, T, Miami, 31
3. *Sampson, Clint, WR, San Diego State, 60
4. Choice to Los Angeles Rams thru San Francisco
5. Harris, George, LB, Houston, 116
Baldwin, Bruce, DB, Harding [from New Orleans] 125
6. *Heflin, Victor, DB, Delaware State, 143
7. *Dupree, Myron, DB, North Carolina Central, 172
8. *Kubiak, Gary, QB, Texas A&M [from Baltimore] 197
Choice to Pittsburgh
9. Hawkins, Brian, DB, San Jose State, 228
10. *Bowyer, Walt, DE, Arizona State, 254
11. *Bailey, Don, C, Miami, 283
12. *Mecklenburg, Karl, DT, Minnesota, 310

DETROIT 1983
1. *Jones, James, RB, Florida, 13
2. *Strenger, Rich, T, Michigan, 40
3. *Cofer, Mike, DE, Tennessee, 67
4. *Curley, August, LB, USC, 94
5. *Johnson, Demetrious, DB, Missouri [from Los Angeles Rams] 115
*Mott, Steve, C, Alabama, 121
6. Brown, Todd, WR, Nebraska, 154
7. *Black, Mike, P, Arizona State, 181
8. Stapleton, Bill, DB, Washington, 208
9. Choice used in 1982 supplemental draft (Robinson, Kevin, DB, North Carolina A&T)
10. Laube, Dave, G, Penn State, 261
11. Tate, Ben, RB, North Carolina Central, 287
12. Lane, Jim, C, Idaho State, 321

GREEN BAY 1983
1. *Lewis, Tim, DB, Pittsburgh [from New Orleans] 11
Choice to San Diego
2. *Drechsler, Dave, G, North Carolina, 48
3. Choice to Miami through Houston
4. *Miller, Mike, WR, Tennessee, 104
5. Thomas, Bryan, RB, Pittsburgh, 132
6. *Sams, Ron, G, Pittsburgh, 160
7. *Clark, Jessie, RB, Arkansas, 188
8. Briscoe, Carlton, DB, McNeese State, 216
9. Ham, Robin, C, West Texas State, 243
10. *Williams, Byron, WR, Texas-Arlington [from Houston] 253
Thomas, Jimmy, DB, Indiana, 271
11. *Scribner, Bucky, P, Kansas, 299
12. Harvey, John, DT, USC, 327

HOUSTON 1983
1. Choice to Los Angeles Rams
*Matthews, Bruce, T, USC [from Seattle] 9
2. *Salem, Harvey, T, California, 30
*Bostic, Keith, DB, Michigan [from Seattle] 42
3. *Joiner, Tim, LB, LSU, 58
*Dressel, Chris, TE, Stanford [from Seattle] 69
*Brown, Steve, DB, Oregon [from Miami] 83
4. *Hill, Greg, DB, Oklahoma State, 86
*McCloskey, Mike, TE, Penn State [from Los Angeles Rams] 88
5. *Moriarty, Larry, RB, Notre Dame, 114
*Foster, Jerome, DT, Ohio State [from Miami] 139
6. *Haworth, Steve, DB, Oklahoma, 142
7. *Walls, Herkie, WR, Texas, 170
8. *Thompson, Robert, LB, Michigan, 198
9. *Potter, Kevin, DB, Missouri, 226
10. Choice to Green Bay
11. Choice to New York Giants
12. Choice to New York Giants

KANSAS CITY 1983
1. *Blackledge, Todd, QB, Penn State, 7
2. *Lutz, Dave, T, Georgia Tech, 34
3. *Lewis, Albert, DB, Grambling, 61
4. *Wetzel, Ron, TE, Arizona State, 92
5. *Arnold, Jim, P, Vanderbilt, 119
6. *Gardner, Ellis, T, Georgia Tech, 146
7. *Thomas, Ken, RB, San Jose State, 173
Posey, Daryl, RB, Mississippi College [from New Orleans] 179
8. *Eatman, Irv, T, UCLA, 204
9. *Lingner, Adam, C, Illinois, 231
10. *Shumate, Mark, DT, Wisconsin, 257
11. Jackson, DeWayne, DE, South Carolina State, 284
12. Jones, Ken, T, Tennessee, 315

LOS ANGELES RAIDERS 1983
1. *Mosebar, Don, T, USC, 26
2. *Pickel, Bill, DT, Rutgers, 54
3. *Caldwell, Tony, LB, Washington, 82
4. *Townsend, Greg, DE, TCU, 110
5. *Williams, Dokie, WR, UCLA, 138
6. Choice to Washingtonhington
7. McCall, Jeff, RB, Clemson, 194
8. Dotterer, Mike, RB, Stanford, 222
9. Jordan, Kent, TE, St. Mary's (CA), 249
10. *Fernandez, Mervyn, WR, San Jose State, 277
11. Choice to Cleveland
12. Lindquist, Scott, QB, Northern Arizona, 333

LOS ANGELES RAMS 1983
1. *Dickerson, Eric, RB, SMU [from Houston] 2
Choice to Seattle thru Houston
2. *Ellard, Henry, WR, Fresno State, 32
*Wilcher, Mike, LB, North Carolina [from San Francisco] 36
3. Choice to San Francisco
4. *Nelson, Chuck, K, Washington [from Denver thru San Francisco] 87
Choice to Houston
*Newsome, Vince, DB, Washington [from New York Giants] 97
*Reed, Doug, DT, San Diego State [from Miami] 111
5. Choice to Detroit
*Grant, Otis, WR, Michigan State [from San Diego] 134
6. *Kowalski, Gary, T, Boston College, 144
7. *Simmons, Jeff, WR, USC, 171
8. West, Troy, DB, USC, 200
9. Belcher, Jack, C, Boston College, 227
10. Choice to Minnesota
11. Triplett, Danny, LB, Clemson, 282
12. Casper, Clete, QB, Washington State, 311

MIAMI 1983
1. *Marino, Dan, QB, Pittsburgh, 27
2. *Charles, Mike, DT, Syracuse, 55
3. *Benson, Charles, DE, Baylor [from Green Bay thru Houston] 76
Choice to Houston
4. Choice to Los Angeles Rams
5. Choice to Houston
6. *Roby, Reggie, P, Iowa, 167
7. Woetzel, Keith, LB, Rutgers, 195
8. *Clayton, Mark, WR, Louisville, 223
9. *Brown, Mark, LB, Purdue, 250
10. Reed, Anthony, RB, South Carolina State, 278
11. Lukens, Joe, G, Ohio State, 306
12. *Carter, Anthony, WR, Michigan, 334

MINNESOTA 1983
1. *Browner, Joey, DB, USC, 19
2. Choice to Philadelphia
3. *Ashley, Walker Lee, LB, Penn State, 73
4. Rush, Mark, RB, Miami, 100
5. Stewart, Mark, LB, Washington, 127
6. *Jones, Mike, WR, Tennessee State, 159
7. *Lee, Carl, DB, Marshall, 186
8. *Brown, Norris, TE, Georgia, 213
9. Achter, Rod, WR, Toledo, 239
10. Brown, Melvin, DB, Mississippi [from Los Angeles Rams] 255
Tate, Walter, C, Tennessee State, 266
11. Butcher, Brian, G, Clemson, 298
12. *Turner, Maurice, RB, Utah State, 325

NEW ENGLAND 1983
1. *Eason, Tony, QB, Illinois, 15
2. *Wilson, Darryal, WR, Tennessee, 47
3. *Starring, Steven, WR, McNeese State, 74
*Moore, Steve, G, Tennessee State [from San Diego] 80
4. *Rembert, Johnny, LB, Clemson, 101
5. *Creswell, Smiley, DE, Michigan State [from Chicago Bears] 118
*Lewis, Darryl, TE, Texas-Arlington, 128
6. Bass, Mike, K, Illinois, 155
7. *James, Craig, RB, SMU, 187
8. *Lippett, Ronnie, DB, Miami, 214
9. Williams, Ricky, RB, Langston [from New Orleans] 233
*Keel, Mark, TE, Arizona, 240
10. Williams, James, TE, Wyoming [from New York Giants] 264
*Williams, Toby, DE, Nebraska [from New Orleans] 265
*Ramsey, Tom, QB, UCLA, 267
11. Parker, Steve, WR, Abilene Christian [from New Orleans] 292
Eason, Calvin, DB, Houston, 294
12. Kelly, Waddell, RB, Arkansas State [from New Orleans] 319
*Ekern, Andy, T, Missouri, 326

NEW ORLEANS 1983
1. Choice to Green Bay
2. *Korte, Steve, G, Arkansas, 38
3. *Tice, John, TE, Maryland, 65
*Austin, Cliff, RB, Clemson [from Buffalo thru St. Louis] 66
4. *Lewis, Gary, NT, Oklahoma State, 98
5. Choice to Denver
6. Choice to Cincinnati
7. Choice to Kansas City
8. *Greenwood, David, DB, Wisconsin, 206
9. Choice to New England
10. Choice to New England
11. Choice to New England
12. Choice to New England

NEW YORK GIANTS 1983
1. *Kinard, Terry, DB, Clemson, 10
2. *Marshall, Leonard, DT, LSU, 37
3. *Williams, Jamie, TE, Nebraska [from San Francisco thru Los Angeles Rams] 63
*Nelson, Karl, T, Iowa State, 70
4. Choice to Los Angeles Rams
5. *Scott, Malcolm, TE, LSU, 124
6. Patterson, Darrell, LB, TCU, 151
*Belcher, Kevin, G, Texas-El Paso [from Buffalo thru Los Angeles Rams] 153
7. *Williams, Perry, DB, North Carolina State, 178
8. *Headen, Andy, LB, Clemson, 205
9. *Haji-Sheikh, Ali, K, Michigan, 237
10. Choice to New England
11. Jenkins, Lee, DB, Tennessee [from Houston] 281
Pierson, Clenzie, DT, Rice, 291
12. *Jones, Robbie, LB, Alabama [from Houston] 309
Magwood, Frank, WR, Clemson, 318
*Tuggle, John, RB, California [from Washington] 335

NEW YORK JETS 1983
1. *O'Brien, Ken, QB, Cal-Davis, 24
2. *Hector, Johnny, RB, Texas A&M, 51
3. *Townsell, Jo-Jo, WR, UCLA, 78
4. Howell, Wes, TE, California, 105
5. Walker, John, DT, Nebraska-Omaha, 136
6. White, Vincent, RB, Stanford, 163
7. Newbold, Darrin, LB, Southwest Missouri State, 190
8. *Mullen, Davlin, DB, Western Kentucky, 217
9. *Humphery, Bobby, WR, New Mexico State, 247
10. *Fike, Dan, T, Florida, 274
11. *Harmon, Mike, WR, Mississippi, 301
12. Crum, Stu, K, Tulsa, 328

PHILADELPHIA 1983
1. *Haddix, Michael, RB, Mississippi State, 8
2. *Hopkins, Wes, DB, SMU, 35
*Schulz, Jody, LB, East Carolina [from Minnesota] 46
3. *Young, Glen, WR, Mississippi State, 62
4. *Williams, Michael, RB, Mississippi College, 89
5. *Darby, Byron, DT, USC, 120
6. *Oatis, Victor, WR, Northwestern State (LA), 147
7. Edgar, Anthony, RB, Hawaii, 174
Schultheis, Jon, G, Princeton [from Cleveland] 182
8. *Kraynak, Rich, LB, Pittsburgh, 201
9. Pelzer, Rich, T, Rhode Island, 232
10. *Strauthers, Thomas, DE, Jackson State, 258
11. Sebahar, Steve, C, Washington State, 285
12. Mangrum, David, QB, Baylor, 312

PITTSBURGH 1983
1. *Rivera, Gabriel, DT, Texas Tech, 21
2. *Capers, Wayne, WR, Kansas, 52
3. *Seabaugh, Todd, LB, San Diego State, 79
4. *Metcalf, Bo Scott, DB, Baylor, 106
5. *Skansi, Paul, WR, Washington, 133
*Garrity, Gregg, WR, Penn State [from Washington] 140
6. *Williams, Eric, DB, North Carolina State, 164
7. *Kirchner, Mark, G, Baylor, 191
8. *Odom, Henry, RB, South Carolina State [from Denver] 199
*Dunaway, Craig, TE, Michigan, 218
9. *Wingle, Blake, G, UCLA, 244
10. Straughter, Roosevelt, DB, Northeast Louisiana, 275
11. Raugh, Mark, TE, West Virginia, 302
12. Wiley, Roger, RB, Sam Houston State, 330

ST. LOUIS 1983
1. *Smith, Leonard, DB, McNeese State, 17
2. *Mack, Cedric, DB, Baylor, 44
3. *Dardar, Ramsey, DT, LSU, 71
4. *Duda, Mark, DT, Maryland [from Seattle] 96
*Washington, Lionel, DB, Tulane, 103
5. *Bird, Steve, WR, Eastern Kentucky, 130
6. *Schmitt, George, DB, Delaware, 157
7. *Scott, Carlos, C, Texas-El Paso, 184
8. *Harris, Bob, DB, Auburn, 211
9. Brown, Otis, RB, Jackson State, 242
10. *Lucas, Tim, LB, California, 269
11. Williams, Aaron, WR, Washington, 296
12. Lane, James, LB, Alabama State, 323

SAN DIEGO 1983
1. *Smith, Billy Ray Jr., LB, Arkansas [from San Francisco] 5
*Anderson, Gary, WR-RB, Arkansas [from Green Bay] 20
*Byrd, Gill, DB, San Jose State, 22
2. Choice to San Francisco
3. Choice to New England
4. *Walters, Danny, DB, Arkansas [from Cleveland] 95
Choice to Chicago Bears
5. Choice to Los Angeles Rams
6. *Johnson, Trumaine, WR, Grambling [from Baltimore] 141
Choice to Baltimore
7. *Elko, Bill, DT, LSU, 192
8. *Jackson, Earnest, RB, Texas A&M [from San Francisco] 202
Choice to Chicago Bears
9. *Green, Mike, LB, Oklahoma State, 245
10. *Mathison, Bruce, QB, Nebraska, 272
11. *Kearse, Tim, WR, San Jose State, 303
*Spencer, Tim, RB, Ohio State [from Washington] 307
12. Blaylock, Billy, DB, Tennessee Tech [from Chicago Bears] 314
*Ehin, Chuck, DT, BYU, 329

SAN FRANCISCO 1983
1. Choice to San Diego
2. Choice to Los Angeles Rams
*Craig, Roger, RB, Nebraska [from San Diego] 49
3. *Montgomery, Blanchard, LB, UCLA [from Los Angeles Rams] 59
Choice to New York Giants thru Los Angeles Rams
4. *Holmoe, Tom, DB, BYU, 90
5. *Ellison, Riki, LB, USC, 117
6. Choice to Tampa Bay
7. *Moten, Gary, LB, SMU, 175
8. Choice to San Diego
9. *Mularkey, Mike, TE, Florida, 229
10. Merrell, Jeff, DT, Nebraska, 259
11. *Sapolu, Jesse, G, Hawaii, 289
12. Choice to Chicago Bears

SEATTLE 1983
1. *Warner, Curt, RB, Penn State [from Los Angeles Rams thru Houston] 3
Choice to Houston
2. Choice to Houston
3. Choice to Houston
4. Choice to St. Louis
5. *Castor, Chris, WR, Duke, 123
6. Gipson, Reginald, RB, Alabama A&M, 150
7. *Merriman, Sam, LB, Idaho, 177
8. *Hernandez, Matt, T, Purdue, 210
9. *Clasby, Bob, T, Notre Dame, 236
10. Speros, Pete, G, Penn State, 263
11. Mayberry, Bob, G, Clemson, 290
12. Dow, Don, T, Washington, 317

TAMPA BAY 1983
1. Choice to Chicago Bears
2. *Grimes, Randy, C, Baylor, 45
3. *Castille, Jeremiah, DB, Alabama, 72
4. *Thomas, Kelly, T, USC, 99
5. *Chickillo, Tony, DT, Miami, 131
6. *Branton, Gene, WR, Texas Southern [from San Francisco] 148
*Kaplan, Ken, T, New Hampshire, 158
7. Ledbetter, Weldon, RB, Oklahoma, 185
8. Samuelson, John, LB, Azusa Pacific, 212
9. *Arbubakrr, Hasson, DT, Texas Tech, 238
10. Durham, Darius, WR, San Diego State, 270
11. *Witte, Mark, TE, North Texas State, 297
12. Higgenbotham, John, DT, Northeastern Oklahoma, 324

WASHINGTON 1983
1. *Green, Darrell, DB, Texas A&I, 28
2. *Williams, Richard, RB, Memphis State, 56
3. *Mann, Charles, DE, Nevada-Reno, 84
4. Choice to Buffalo thru New Orleans
5. Choice to Pittsburgh
6. Winckler, Bob, T, Wisconsin [from Los Angeles Raiders] 166
*Laufenberg, Babe, QB, Indiana, 168
7. *Bryant, Kelvin, RB, North Carolina, 196
8. Hallstrom, Todd, T, Minnesota, 224
9. Gilbert, Marcus, RB, TCU, 251
10. Gandy, Geff, LB, Baylor, 279
11. Choice to San Diego
12. Choice to New York Giants

1984

Held May 1-2, 1984

ATLANTA 1984
1. *Bryan, Rick, DT, Oklahoma, 9
2. *Case, Scott, DB, Oklahoma [from Philadelphia] 32
*Benson, Thomas, LB, Oklahoma, 36
3. *McSwain, Rod, DB, Clemson, 63
4. *Malancon, Rydell, LB, LSU, 94
5. Choice to San Francisco
*Benson, Cliff, TE, Purdue, [from Denver thru San Francisco] 132
6. *Bennett, Ben, QB, Duke, 148
*Ralph, Dan, DT, Oregon [from San Francisco] 163
7. *Dodge, Kirk, LB, Nevada-Las Vegas, 175
8. *Jackson, Jeff, LB, Auburn, 206
9. *Howe, Glen, T, Southern Mississippi, 233
10. Franklin, Derrick, DB, Fresno State, 260
11. Norman, Tommy, WR, Jackson State, 287
12. *Holmes, Don, WR, Mesa, 318

BUFFALO 1984
1. Choice to Miami
*Bell, Greg, RB, Notre Dame [from Miami] 26
2. *Richardson, Eric, WR, San Jose State, 41
3. Choice to New Orleans
*Bellinger, Rodney, DB, Miami [from Cleveland] 77
*McNanie, Sean, DE, San Diego State [from Pittsburgh thru Miami] 79
*Neal, Speedy, RB, Miami [from Miami] 82
4. *Brookins, Mitchell, WR, Illinois, 95
5. *Kidd, John, P, Northwestern, 128
6. *Slaton, Tony C, USC, 155
7. *David, Stan, DB, Texas Tech, 182
8. Rayfield, Stacy, DB, Texas-Arlington, 209
9. Howell, Leroy, DE, Appalachian State, 236
10. *Azelby, Joe, LB, Harvard, 263
11. *White, Craig, WR, Missouri, 299
12. Davis, Russell, WR, Maryland, 322

CHICAGO BEARS 1984
1. *Marshall, Wilber, LB, Florida, 11
2. *Rivera, Ron, LB, California, 44
3. *Humphries, Stefan, G, Michigan, 71
4. *Andrews, Tom, G, Louisville, 98
5. Choice to Washington thru San Diego, Seattle, and New York Giants
6. Choice to Dallas
7. Robertson, Dakita, RB, Central Arkansas, 179
8. *Anderson, Brad, WR, Arizona, 212
9. Choice to San Francisco
Casale, Mark, QB, Montclair State [from Cleveland] 244
10. Vestman, Kurt, TE, Idaho, 266
*Gayle, Shaun, DB, Ohio State [from Cleveland] 271
11. Choice to Los Angeles Rams
Butkus, Mark, DT, Illinois [from Cleveland] 297
12. Choice to Miami thru San Francisco
*Jordan, Donald, RB, Houston [from Cleveland] 330

CINCINNATI 1984
1. *Hunley, Ricky, LB, Arizona, 7
*Koch, Pete, Maryland [from New England] 16
*Blados, Brian, T, North Carolina [from Los Angeles Raiders thru New England] 28
2. *Esiason, Boomer, QB, Maryland, 38
3. *Jennings, Stanford, RB, Furman, 85
4. *Farley, John, RB, Cal State-Sacramento, 92
5. *Bussey, Barney, DB, South Carolina State, 119
6. *Kern, Don, TE, Arizona State 150
7. *Barker, Leo, LB, New Mexico State, 177
8. *Reimers, Bruce, T, Iowa State, 204
9. *Kozerski, Bruce, C, Holy Cross, 231
10. Jackson, Aaron, LB, North Carolina, 262
Ziegler, Brent, RB, Syracuse [from New England] 265
11. McKeaver, Steve, RB, Central State (OK), 289
12. Raquet, Steve, LB, Holy Cross, 316

CLEVELAND 1984
1. *Rogers, Don, DB, UCLA, 18
2. *Rockins, Chris, DB, Oklahoma State [from Los Angeles Rams] 48
*Davis, Bruce, WR, Baylor, 50
3. Choice to Buffalo
4. *Bolden, Rickey, TE, SMU [from New Orleans thru Denver] 96
*Brennan, Brian, WR, Boston College, 104
5. Piepkorn, Dave, T, North Dakota State, 131
6. *Nugent, Terry, QB, Colorado State, 158
7. *Dumont, Jim, LB, Rutgers, 190
8. Choice to New York Jets
9. Jones, Don, WR, Texas A&M [from Philadelphia] 227
Choice to Chicago Bears
10. Choice to Chicago Bears
*Byner, Earnest, RB, East Carolina [from Los Angeles Raiders] 280
11. Choice to Chicago Bears
12. Choice to Chicago Bears

DALLAS 1984
1. *Cannon, Billy Jr., LB, Texas A&M, 25
2. *Scott, Victor, DB, Colorado [from Minnesota thru Houston] 40
Choice to Houston
3. *Cornwell, Fred, TE, USC, 81
4. *DeOssie, Steve, LB, Boston College, 110
5. *Pelluer, Steve, QB, Washington [from Tampa Bay] 113
*Granger, Norm, RB, Iowa, 137
6. *Lockhart, Eugene, LB, Houston [from Chicago Bears] 152
Levelis, Joe, G, Iowa, 166
7. Martin, Ed, LB, Indiana State, 193
8. Revell, Mike, RB, Bethune-Cookman, 222
9. *Hunt, John, G, Florida [from Indianapolis] 232
Maune, Neil, G, Notre Dame, 249
10. *Salonen, Brian, TE, Montana, 278
11. *Aughtman, Dowe, DT, Auburn, 304
12. Lewis, Carl, WR, Houston, 334

DENVER 1984
1. Choice to Indianapolis
2. *Townsend, Andre, DE, Mississippi, 46
3. *Lilly, Tony, DB, Florida, 78
4. *Robbins, Randy, DB, Arizona [from San Diego thru Tampa Bay] 89
Choice to New York Giants
5. Choice to Atlanta thru San Francisco
6. *Smith, Aaron, LB, Utah State, 159
7. *Kay, Clarence, TE, Georgia, 186
8. *Hood, Winford, T, Georgia [from Green Bay] 207
*Garnett, Scott, DT, Washington, 218
9. *Brewer, Chris, RB, Arizona, 245
10. *Micho, Bobby, TE, Texas, 272
11. *Lang, Gene, RB, LSU, 298
12. Jarmin, Murray, WR, Clemson, 326

DETROIT 1984
1. *Lewis, David, TE, California, 20
2. *Mandley, Pete, WR, Northern Arizona, 47
3. *Williams, Eric, DT, Washington State [from San Diego thru St. Louis] 62
Anderson, Ernest, RB, Oklahoma State, 74
*Baack, Steve, DE, Oregon [from Los Angeles Rams] 75
4. *D'Addio, Dave, RB, Maryland, 106
5. Choice to Los Angeles Rams
6. *Witkowski, John, QB, Columbia, 160
7. Carter, Jimmie, LB, New Mexico [from Indianapolis] 178
Atkins, Renwick, T, Kansas, 187
8. *Jones, David, C, Texas, 214
9. Hollins, Rich, WR, West Virginia, 246
10. *Frizzell, William, DB, North Carolina Central [from Indianapolis] 259
Thaxton, James, DB, Louisiana Tech, 273
11. *Saxon, Mike, P, San Diego State, 300
12. Streno, Glenn, C, Tennessee, 327

GREEN BAY 1984
1. *Carreker, Alphonso, DE, Florida State, 12
2. Choice to New York Jets thru San Diego
3. *Humphrey, Donnie, DT, Auburn, 72
4. *Dorsey, John, LB, Connecticut, 99
5. *Flynn, Tom, DB, Pittsburgh, 126
6. *Wright, Randy, QB, Wisconsin, 153
7. *Jones, Daryll, DB, Georgia, 181
8. Choice to Denver
9. Choice to Kansas City
10. *Hoffman, Gary, T, Santa Clara, 267
11. *Cannon, Mark, C, Texas- Arlington, 294
12. *Taylor, Lenny, WR, Tennessee [from San Diego] 313
Emans, Mark, LB, Bowling Green, 323

HOUSTON 1984
1. *Steinkuhler, Dean, T, Nebraska, 2
2. *Smith, Doug, DE, Auburn, 29
*Eason, Bo, DB, Cal-Davis [from Dallas] 54
3. *Meads, Johnny, LB, Nicholls State, 58
4. *Studaway, Mark, DE, Tennessee, 85
*Allen, Patrick, DB, Utah State [from Minnesota] 100
5. *Lyles, Robert, LB, TCU, 114
6. *Grimsley, John, LB, Kentucky, 141
*Mullins, Eric, WR, Stanford [from Los Angeles Rams] 161
7. *Joyner, Willie, RB, Maryland, 170
8. Baugh, Kevin, WR, Penn State, 197
9. *Donaldson, Jeff, DB, Colorado, 226
*Johnson, Mike, DE, Illinois [from New York Giants] 228
Russell, Mike, LB, Toledo [from Los Angeles Raiders] 252
10. Choice to Los Angeles Rams
11. Choice to Los Angeles Raiders
12. Choice to Los Angeles Rams

INDIANAPOLIS 1984
1. *Coleman, Leonard, DB, Vanderbilt, 8
*Solt, Ron, G, Maryland [from Denver] 19
2. *Winter, Blaise, DT, Syracuse, 35

3. *Scott, Chris, DT, Purdue, 66
4. *Curry, Craig, DB, Texas, 93
*Wonsley, George, RB, Mississippi State [from Seattle] 103
5. Tate, Golden, WR, Tennessee State, 120
*Call, Kevin, T, Colorado State [from Seattle] 130
6. Beverly, Dwight, RB, Illinois, 147
7. Choice to Det
8. *Daniel, Eugene, DB, LSU, 205
9. Choice to Dal
10. Choice to Det
11. Stowe, Bob, T, Illinois, 290
12. *Hathaway, Steve, LB, West Virginia, 317

KANSAS CITY 1984
1. *Maas, Bill, DT, Pittsburgh, 5
*Alt, John, T, Iowa [from Los Angeles Rams] 21
2. *Radecic, Scott, LB, Penn State, 34
3. *Heard, Herman, RB, Southern Colorado, 61
4. *Robinson, Mark, DB, Penn State, 90
5. *Holle, Eric, DE, Texas, 117
*Paine, Jeff, LB, Texas A&M [from Los Angeles Rams] 134
6. Stevens, Rufus, WR, Grambling, 146
7. *Ross, Kevin, DB, Temple, 173
8. *Clark, Randy, DB, Florida, 202
9. *Auer, Scott, T, Michigan State, 229
Hestera, Dave, TE, Colorado [from Green Bay] 240
10. *Wenglikowski, Al, LB, Pittsburgh, 258
11. Johnson, Bobby, RB, San Jose State, 285
12. Lang, Mark, LB, Texas, 314

LOS ANGELES RAIDERS 1984
1. Choice to Cin thru NE
2. *Jones, Sean, DE, Northeastern [from San Francisco] 51
Choice to San Francisco
3. *McCall, Joe, RB, Pittsburgh, 84
4. Choice to Tampa Bay
5. *Parker, Andy, TE, Utah [from Minnesota] 127
Choice to Minnesota
6. *Toran, Stacey, DB, Notre Dame, 168
7. *Willis, Mitch, DE, SMU [from New Orleans] 183
Choice to Minnesota
8. *Seale, Sam, WR, Western State (CO), 224
9. Choice to Houston
10. Choice to Cleveland
11. *Williams, Gardner, DB, St. Mary's (CA) [from Houston] 282
Choice to Minnesota
12. Essington, Randy, QB, Colorado, 336

LOS ANGELES RAMS 1984
1. Choice to Kansas City
2. Choice to Cleveland
3. Choice to Detroit
4. Choice to Washington thru Houston
5. *Stephens Hal, DE, East Carolina [from Detroit] 133
Choice to Kansas City
6. Choice to Houston
7. *Radachowsky, George, DB, Boston College, 188
8. *Brady, Ed, LB, Illinois, 215
9. Reynolds, George, P, Penn State, 242
10. *Vann, Norwood, TE, East Carolina [from Houston] 253
Dooley, Joe, C, Ohio State, 274
11. *Harper, Michael, RB, USC [from Chicago Bears] 293
Love, Dwayne, RB, Houston, 301
12. Fisher, Rod, DB, Oklahoma State [from Houston] 309
Bias, Moe, LB, Illinois, 328

MIAMI 1984
1. *Shipp, Jackie, LB, Oklahoma [from Buffalo] 14
Choice to Buffalo
2. *Brophy, Jay, LB, Miami, 53
3. Choice to Buffalo
4. *Carter, Joe, RB, Alabama, 109
5. *May, Dean, QB, Louisville, 138
6. Tatum, Rowland, LB, Ohio State, 165
7. Carvalho, Bernard, G, Hawaii, 194
8. Landry, Ronnie, RB, McNeese State, 221
9. *Boyle, Jim, T, Tulane, 250
10. *Chesley, John, TE, Oklahoma State, 277
11. *Brown, Bud, DB, Southern Mississippi, 305
12. Devane, William, DT, Clemson [from Chicago Bears thru San Francisco] 320
Weingrad, Mike, LB, Illinois, 333

MINNESOTA 1984
1. *Millard, Keith, DE, Washington State, 13
2. Choice to Dallas thru Houston
3. *Anderson, Alfred, RB, Baylor, 67
4. Choice to Houston
5. Choice to Los Angeles Raiders
*Rice, Allen, RB, Baylor [from Los Angeles Raiders] 140
6. *Collins, Dwight, WR, Pittsburgh, 154
7. *Haines, John, DT, Texas, 180
Lewis, Loyd, G, Texas A&I [from Los Angeles Raiders] 196
8. Sverchek, Paul, DT, Cal Poly-SLO, 208
9. Kidd, Keith, WR, Arkansas, 235
10. Spencer, James, LB, Oklahoma State, 268
11. Pickett, Edgar, LB, Clemson, 295
Thompson, Lawrence, WR, Miami [from Los Angeles Raiders] 308
12. Jones, Mike, RB, North Carolina A&T, 321

NEW ENGLAND 1984
1. *Fryar, Irving, WR, Nebraska [from TB thru Cincinnati] 1
Choice to Cincinnati
2. *Williams, Ed, LB, Texas, 43
3. *Williams, Jon, RB, Penn State, 70
4. Choice to New Orleans
5. *Fairchild, Paul, G, Kansas, 124
6. *Gibson, Ernest, DB, Furman, 151
7. Kallmeyer, Bruce, K, Kansas, 184
*Williams, Derwin, WR, New Mexico [from San Francisco] 192
8. Keyton, James, T, Arizona State, 211
9. Bolzan, Scott, T, Northern Illinois, 238
Windham, David, LB, Jackson State [from Washington] 251
10. Choice to Cincinnati
11. Flager, Charlie, G, Washington State, 292
12. Howell, Harper, TE, UCLA, 319

NEW ORLEANS 1984
1. Choice to New York Jets
2. *Geathers, James, DE, Wichita State, 42
3. *Hoage, Terry, DB, Georgia [from Buffalo] 68
*Anthony, Tyrone, RB, North Carolina, 69
4. Choice to Cleveland thru Den
*Hilgenberg, Joel, C, Iowa [from New England] 97
5. *Fields, Jitter, DB, Texas, 123
6. *Thorp, Don, DT, Illinois, 156
7. Choice to Los Angeles Raiders
8. Terrell, Clemon, RB, Southern Mississippi, 210
9. *Hansen, Brian, P, Sioux Falls, 237
10. *Gray, Paul, LB, Western Kentucky, 264
11. Bourgeau, Michel, DE, Boise State, 291
12. Nelson, Byron, T, Arizona, 324

NEW YORK GIANTS 1984
1. *Banks, Carl, LB, Michigan State, 3
*Roberts, William, T, Ohio State [from Washington] 27
2. Choice to Washington
3. *Hostetler, Jeff, QB, West Virginia, 59
4. *Goode, Conrad, T, Missouri, 87
*Reasons, Gary, LB, Northwestern State (LA) [from Denver] 105
5. Harris, Clint, DB, East Carolina, 115
6. Scott, Jim, DE, Clemson, 143
7. *Manuel, Lionel, WR, Pacific, 171
8. Choice to San Diego
9. Choice to Houston
10. *Jordan, David, G, Auburn, 255
Golden, Heyward, DB, South Carolina State [from San Diego] 257
11. *Cephous, Frank, RB, UCLA, 283
12. Green, Lawrence, LB, Tennessee-Chattanooga, 311

NEW YORK JETS 1984
1. *Carter, Russell, DB, SMU, 10
*Faurot, Ron, DE, Arkansas [from New Orleans] 15
2. *Sweeney, Jim, C, Pittsburgh, 37
*Dennison, Glenn, TE, Miami [from Green Bay thru San Diego] 39
3. *Clifton, Kyle, LB, TCU, 64
4. *Bell, Bobby Jr., LB, Missouri, 91
5. Armstrong, Tron, WR, Eastern Kentucky, 122
6. *Paige, Tony, RB, Virginia Tech, 149
7. *Hamilton, Harry, DB, Penn State, 176
8. *Griggs, Billy, TE, Virginia, 203
Wright, Brett, P, Southeastern Louisiana [from Cleveland] 217
9. *Baldwin, Tom, DT, Tulsa, 234
10. Cone, Ronny, RB, Georgia Tech, 261
11. Martin, Dan, T, Iowa State, 288
12. Roberson, David, WR, Houston, 315

PHILADELPHIA 1984
1. *Jackson, Kenny, WR, Penn State, 4
2. Choice to Atlanta
3. *Russell, Rusty, T, South Carolina, 60
4. *Cooper, Evan, DB, Michigan, 88
5. *Hardy, Andre, RB, St. Mary's (CA), 116
6. Raridon, Scott, T, Nebraska, 145
7. *Hayes, Joe, RB, Central State (OK), 172
8. Matsakis, Manny, K, Capital, 200
9. Choice to Cleveland
10. Thomas, John, DB, TCU, 256
11. Robertson, John, T, East Carolina, 284
12. *McFadden, Paul, K, Youngstown State, 312

PITTSBURGH 1984
1. *Lipps, Louis, WR, Southern Mississippi, 23
2. *Kolodziejski, Chris, TE, Wyoming, 52
3. Choice to Buffalo thru Mia
4. *Thompson, Weegie, WR, Florida State, 108
*Long, Terry, G, East Carolina [from Washington] 111
5. *Hughes, Van, DT, Southwest Texas State, 135
6. *Brown, Chris, DB, Notre Dame, 164
7. *Campbell, Scott, QB, Purdue, 191
8. *Rasmussen, Randy, C, Minnesota, 220
9. *Erenberg, Rich, RB, Colgate, 247
10. McJunkin, Kirk, T, Texas, 276
11. *Veals, Elton, RB, Tulane, 303
12. *Gillespie, Fernandars, RB, William Jewell, 332

ST. LOUIS 1984
1. *Duncan, Clyde, WR, Tennessee, 11
2. *Dawson, Doug, G, Texas, 45
3. Choice to San Francisco
*McIvor, Rick, QB, Texas [from San Francisco] 80
4. *Bayless, Martin, DB, Bowling Green, 101
5. *Leiding, Jeff, LB, Texas, 129
*Goode, John, TE, Youngstown State [from San Francisco] 136
6. Clark, Rod, LB, Southwest Texas State, 157
7. *Walker, Quentin, RB, Virginia, 185
8. *Noga, Niko, LB, Hawaii [from San Diego] 201
Paulling, Bob, K, Clemson, 213
9. Walker, John, RB, Texas, 241
10. Smythe, Mark, DT, Indiana, 269
11. *Mackey, Kyle, QB, East Texas State, 296
12. Parker, Paul, G, Oklahoma, 325

SAN DIEGO 1984
1. *Cade, Mossy, DB, Texas, 6
2. *Guendling, Mike, LB, Northwestern, 33
3. Choice to Det thru St. Louis
4. Choice to Denver thru TB
5. *James, Lionel, KR, Auburn, 118
6. *Guthrie, Keith, DT, Texas A&M, 144
7. *Bendross, Jesse, WR, Alabama, 174
8. *Woodard, Ray, DT, Texas [from New York Giants] 199
Choice to St. Louis
Craighead, Bob, RB, Northeast Louisiana [from San Francisco] 219
9. Barnes, Zack, DT, Alabama State, 230
10. Choice to New York Giants
11. *McGee, Buford, RB, Mississippi, 286
12. Choice to Green Bay
Harper, Maurice, WR, LaVerne [from San Francisco] 331

SAN FRANCISCO 1984
1. *Shell, Todd, LB, BYU, 24
2. Choice to Los Angeles Raiders
*Frank, John, TE, Ohio State [from Los Angeles Raiders] 56
3. *McIntyre, Guy, G, Georgia [from St. Louis] 73
Choice to St. Louis
4. Choice to Tampa Bay thru San Diego
5. *Carter, Michael, DT, SMU [from Atlanta] 121
Choice to St. Louis
*Fuller, Jeff, LB, Texas A&M [from Washington thru Los Angeles Raiders] 139
6. Choice to Atlanta
7. Choice to New England
8. Choice to San Diego
9. Miller, Lee, DB, Cal State-Fullerton [from Chicago Bears] 239
*Harmon, Derrick, RB, Cornell, 248
10. Moritz, Dave, WR, Iowa, 275
11. Pendleton, Kirk, WR, BYU, 307
12. Choice to San Diego

SEATTLE 1984
1. *Taylor, Terry, DB, Southern Illinois, 22
2. *Turner, Darryl, WR, Michigan State, 49
3. *Young, Fred, LB, New Mexico State, 76
*Hagood, Rickey, DT, South Carolina [from Tampa Bay thru San Francisco] 86
4. Choice to Indianapolis
5. Choice to Indianapolis
6. *Kaiser, John, LB, Arizona, 162
7. Slater, Sam, T, Weber State, 189
8. Puzar, John, C, Long Beach State, 216
9. *Schreiber, Adam, G, Texas, 243
10. *Morris, Randall, RB, Tennessee, 270
11. Gemza, Steve, T, UCLA, 302
12. Windham, Theodis, DB, Utah State, 329

TAMPA BAY 1984
1. Choice to New England thru Cin
2. *Browner, Keith, LB, USC, 30
3. *Acorn, Fred, DB, Texas, 57
4. Choice to Seattle thru San Francisco
*Gunter, Michael, RB, Tulsa [from San Francisco thru San Diego] 107
*Heller, Ron, T, Penn State [from Los Angeles Raiders] 112
5. Choice to Dallas
6. *Washington, Chris, LB, Iowa State, 142
7. *Carroll, Jay, TE, Minnesota, 169
8. *Robinson, Fred, DE, Miami, 198
9. *Mallory, Rick, G, Washington, 225
10. *Gallery, Jim, K, Minnesota, 254
11. *Kiel, Blair, QB, Notre Dame, 281
12. Jemison, Thad, WR, Ohio State, 310

WASHINGTON 1984
1. Choice to New York Giants
2. Slater, Bob, DT, Oklahoma [from New York Giants] 31
*Hamilton, Steve, DE, East Carolina, 55
3. *Schroeder, Jay, QB, UCLA, 83
4. Smith, Jimmy, RB, Elon [from Los Angeles Rams thru Houston] 102
Choice to Pittsburgh
5. Pegues, Jeff, LB, East Carolina [from Chicago Bears thru San Diego, Sea, and New York Giants] 125
Choice to San Francisco thru Los Angeles Raiders
6. *Singer, Curt, T, Tennessee, 167
7. Smith, Mark, WR, North Carolina, 195
8. Smith, Jeff, DB, Missouri, 223
9. Choice to New England
10. *Griffin, Keith, RB, Miami, 279
11. *Jones, Anthony, TE, Wichita State, 306
12. *Thomas, Curtland, WR, Missouri, 335

1984 SUPPLEMENTAL

Held June 5, 1984

A supplemental draft was held for those players who had been eligible to be drafted by NFL teams, but who hadn't been due to contracts with other professional leagues. The draft gave NFL teams the league rights to the players should they ever become free agents.

ATLANTA 1984
1. *Jones, Joey, WR, Alabama, 9 (Birmingham)
2. McInnis, Mike, DT, Arkansas-Pine Bluff, 36 (Philadelphia)
3. *Woodberry, Dennis, DB, Southern Arkansas, 63 (Birmingham)

BUFFALO 1984
1. *Drane, Dwight, DB, Oklahoma, 14 (Los Angeles Express)
2. Hart, Darryl, DB, Lane, 41 (Oakland)
3. Corbin, Don, T, Kentucky, 68 (Pittsburgh)

CHICAGO 1984
1. Choice to Cleveland
2. Choice to Cleveland
3. Choice to Cleveland

CINCINNATI 1984
1. Peace, Wayne, QB, Florida, 7 (Tampa Bay)
2. *Johnson, Bill, RB, Arkansas State, 38 (Denver)
3. Kilkenny, Tom, LB, Temple, 65 (Chicago Blitz)

CLEVELAND 1984
1. *Mack, Kevin, RB, Clemson, [from Chicago Bears, 11 (Los Angeles Express)
*Johnson, Mike, LB, Virginia Tech, 18 (Philadelphia)
2. *McNeil, Gerald, WR, Baylor, [from Chicago Bears, 44 (Houston)
*Robison, Tommy, T, Texas A&M, 50 (Houston)
3. West, Doug, LB, UCLA, [from Chicago Bears, 71 (Jacksonville)
Bond, John, QB, Mississippi State, 77 (Saskatchewan)

DALLAS 1984
1. *Fowler, Todd, TE, Stephen F. Austin, 25 (Houston)
2. *Moore, Malcolm, WR, USC, 54 (Los Angeles Express)
3. *Spek, Jeff, TE, San Diego State, 81 (New Jersey)

DENVER 1984
1. *Gilbert, Freddie, DE, Georgia, 19 (New Jersey)
2. *Massie, Rick, WR, Kentucky, 48 (Calgary)
3. *Smith, Reggie, T, Kansas, 78 (Tampa Bay)

DETROIT 1984
1. *Williams, Alphonso, WR, Nevada-Reno, 20 (Oklahoma)
2. *Jamison, George, LB, Cincinnati, 47 (Philadelphia)
3. *Hollie, Doug, DE, SMU, 74 (Pittsburgh)

GREEN BAY 1984
1. *Jordan, Buford, RB, McNeese State, 12 (New Orleans)
2. *Clanton, Chuck, DB, Auburn, 39 (Birmingham)
3. *Sullivan, John, DB, California, 72 (Oakland)

HOUSTON 1984
1. *Rozier, Mike, RB, Nebraska, 2 (Pittsburgh)
2. *Maggs, Don, T, Tulane, 29, (Pittsburgh)
3. *Madsen, Lynn, DT, Washington, 58, (New Jersey)

INDIANAPOLIS 1984
1. Bergmann, Paul, TE, UCLA, 8 (Jacksonville)
2. *Bentley, Albert, RB, Miami, 35 (Michigan)
3. *Smith, Byron, DT, California, 66 (Saskatchewan)

KANSAS CITY 1984
1. *Adickes, Mark, T, Baylor, 5 (Los Angeles Express)
2. *Sanchez, Lupe, DB, UCLA, 34 (Arizona)
3. *Lane, Garcia, DB, Ohio State, 61 (Philadelphia)

LOS ANGELES RAIDERS 1984
1. *Woods, Chris, WR, Auburn, 28 (Edmonton)
2. Hill, Stewart, LB, Washington, 56 (Edmonton)
3. Farr, James, G, Clemson, 84 (Washington)

LOS ANGELES RAMS 1984
1. *Fuller, William, DE, North Carolina, 21 (Philadelphia)
2. Johnson, Rick, QB, Southern Illinois, 48 (Oklahoma)
3. Byrne, Jim, DT, Wisconsin-LaCrosse, 75 (New Jersey)

MIAMI 1984
1. Knight, Danny, WR, Mississippi State, 26 (New Jersey)
2. Forte, Dewey, DE, Bethune-Cookman, 53 (Los Angeles Express)
3. Hanks, Duan, WR, Stephen F. Austin, 82 (Philadelphia)

MINNESOTA 1984
1. Smith, Allanda, DB, TCU, 13 (Los Angeles Express)
2. *Smith, Robert, DE, Grambling, 40 (Arizona)
3. *Howard, Davie, LB, Long Beach State, 67 (Los Angeles Express)

NEW ENGLAND 1984
1. *Sanders, Ricky, WR-PR, Southwest Texas State, 16 (Houston)
2. Jordan, Eric, RB, Purdue, 43 (Oakland)
3. Lewis, Walter, QB, Alabama, 70 (Memphis)

NEW ORLEANS 1984
1. *Johnson, Vaughan, LB, North Carolina State, 65 (Jacksonville)
2. *Gray, Mel, RB, Purdue, 42 (Los Angeles Express)
3. Bearden, Steve, LB, Vanderbilt, 69 (Memphis)

NEW YORK GIANTS 1984
1. *Zimmerman, Gary, G, Oregon, 3 (Los Angeles Express)
2. Robinson, James, DT, Clemson, 31 (Los Angeles Express)
3. Warren, Kirby, RB, Pacific, 59 (Los Angeles Express)

NEW YORK JETS 1984
1. Hobart, Ken, QB, Idaho, 10 (Denver)
2. Sandusky, Jim, WR, San Diego State, 37 (British Columbia)
3. Gill, Turner, QB, Nebraska, 64 (Montreal)

PHILADELPHIA 1984
1. *White, Reggie, DE, Tennessee, 4 (Memphis)
2. *Goodlow, Darryl, LB, Arizona, 32 (Oklahoma)
3. Carter, Thomas, LB, San Diego State, 60 (Oakland)

PITTSBURGH 1984
1. Gunn, Duane, WR, Indiana, 23 (Los Angeles Express)
2. Dixon, Tom, C, Michigan, 52 (Michigan)
3. Boren, Phillip, T, Arkansas, 79 (Birmingham)

SEATTLE 1984
1. *Hudson, Gordon, TE, BYU, 22 (Los Angeles Express)
2. *Powell, Alvin, G, Winston-Salem State, 49 (Oklahoma)
3. *Seurer, Frank, QB, Kansas, 76 (Los Angeles Express)

ST. LOUIS 1984
1. *Ruether, Mike, C, Texas, 17 (Los Angeles Express)
2. *Kennard, Derek G, Nevada-Reno, 45 (Los Angeles Express)
3. *Riordan, Tim, QB, Temple, 73 (Philadelphia)

SAN DIEGO 1984
1. *Williams, Lee, DE, Bethune-Cookman, 6 (Los Angeles Express)
2. Smith, Steve, QB, Michigan, 33 (Montreal)
3. *Collins, Clarence, WR, Illinois State, 62 (New Jersey)

SAN FRANCISCO 1984
1. *Crawford, Derrick, WR, Memphis State, 24 (Memphis)
2. Conwell, Joe, T, North Carolina, 51 (Philadelphia)
3. Schellen, Mark, RB, Nebraska, 80 (New Orleans)

TAMPA BAY 1984
1. *Young, Steve, QB, BYU, 1 (Los Angeles Express)
2. Nelson, Kevin, RB, UCLA, 30 (Los Angeles Express)
3. Clark, Alex, DB, LSU, 57 (New Orleans)

WASHINGTON 1984
1. *Zendejas, Tony, K, Nevada-Reno, 27 (Los Angeles Express)
2. *Clark, Gary, WR, James Madison, 55 (Jacksonville)
3. *Verdin, Clarence, WR, Southwestern Louisiana, 83 (Houston)

1985

Held April 30-May 1, 1985

ATLANTA 1985
1. *Fralic, Bill, T, Pittsburgh [from Houston thru Minnesota] 2
   Choice to Minnesota
2. Choice to Washington
   *Gann, Mike, DE, Notre Dame [from St. Louis] 45
3. Choice to Minnesota
4. *Harry, Emile, WR, Stanford, 89
5. Choice to St. Louis
6. Choice to Miami
   *Pleasant, Reggie, DB, Clemson [from New Orleans] 152
7. Choice to Cincinnati
8. Lee, Ashley, DB, Virginia Tech, 201
   *Washington, Ronnie, LB, Northeast Louisiana [from New England] 215
9. Moon, Micah, LB, North Carolina, 228
10. Martin, Brent, C, Stanford, 257
11. Ayres, John, DB Illinois, 284
12. *Whisenhunt, Ken, TE, Georgia Tech, 313

BUFFALO 1985
1. *Smith, Bruce, DE, Virginia Tech, 1
   *Burroughs, Derrick, DB, Memphis State [from Green Bay] 14
2. *Traynowicz, Mark, T, Nebraska, 29
   *Burkett, Chris, WR, Jackson State [from Green Bay] 42
3. *Reich, Frank, QB, Maryland, 57
   *Garner, Hal, LB, Utah State [from Cleveland] 63
4. *Reed, Andre, WR, Kutztown, 86
   *Hellestrae, Dale, T, SMU [from San Francisco] 112
5. Choice to Los Angeles Rams
   *Teal, Jimmy, WR, Texas A&M [from Dallas] 130
6. *Hamby, Mike, DT, Utah State, 141
7. *Pitts, Ron, DB, UCLA, 169
8. Robinson, Jacque, RB, Washington, 197
9. Jones, Glenn, DB, Norfolk State, 225
10. Babyar, Chris, G, Illinois, 253
11. Seawright, James, LB, South Carolina, 282
12. Choice to Washington
    Woodside, Paul, K, West Virginia [from Seattle] 333

CHICAGO BEARS 1985
1. *Perry, William, DT, Clemson, 22
2. *Phillips, Reggie, DB, SMU, 49
3. *Maness, James, WR, TCU, 78
4. *Butler, Kevin, K, Georgia, 105
5. Choice to New York Jets
6. Choice to Los Angeles Rams
7. *Bennett, Charles, DE, Southwestern Louisiana, 190
8. Buxton, Steve, T, Indiana State, 217
9. *Sanders, Thomas, RB, Texas A&M, 250
10. Coryatt, Pat, DT, Baylor, 273
11. *Morrissey, Jim, LB, Michigan State, 302
12. Choice to San Diego

CINCINNATI 1985
1. *Brown, Eddie, WR, Miami, 13
   *King, Emanuel, LB, Alabama [from Seattle] 25
2. *Zander, Carl, LB, Tennessee, 43
3. *Thomas, Sean, DB, TCU, 70
4. *Tuggle, Anthony, DB, Nicholls State, 97
5. *Degrate, Tony, DT, Texas, 127
   *Davis, Lee, DB, Mississippi, [from New England] 129
6. Stokes, Eric, T, Northeastern [from Tampa Bay] 148
   *Lester, Keith, TE, Murray State, 154
7. Locklin, Kim, RB, New Mexico State [from Atlanta] 172
   *Walter, Joe, T, Texas Tech, 181
8. Strobel, Dave, LB, Iowa, 211
9. Cruise, Keith, DE, Northwestern, 238
10. King, Bernard, LB, Syracuse, 265
11. Stanfield, Harold, TE, Mississippi College, 296
12. Garza, Louis, T, New Mexico State, 322

CLEVELAND 1985
1. Choice to Green Bay thru Buffalo
2. *Allen, Greg, RB, Florida State, 35
3. Choice to Buffalo
4. Choice to Miami
5. Choice to Dallas thru Buffalo
6. *Krerowicz, Mark, G, Ohio State, 147
7. *Langhorne, Reggie, WR, Elizabeth City State, 175
8. *Banks, Fred, WR, Liberty Baptist, 203
9. Choice to Philadelphia
10. *Williams, Larry, G, Notre Dame, 259
11. *Tucker, Travis, TE, Southern Connecticut, 287
12. *Swanson, Shane, WR, Nebraska, 315

DALLAS 1985
1. *Brooks, Kevin, DE, Michigan, 17
2. *Penn, Jesse, LB, Virginia Tech, 44
3. *Ker, Crawford, G, Florida, 76
4. *Lavette, Robert, RB, Georgia Tech, 103
5. *Walker, Herschel, RB, Georgia [from Houston] 114
   Darwin, Matt, C, Texas A&M [from Cleveland thru Buffalo] 119
   Choice to Buffalo
6. *Ploeger, Kurt, DE, Gustavus Adolphus [from Indianapolis] 144
   Moran, Matt, G, Stanford, 157
7. *Powe, Karl, WR, Alabama State [from New York Jets thru Kansas City] 178
   Herrmann, Jim, DE, BYU, 184
8. *Gonzalez, Leon (Speedy), WR, Bethune-Cookman, 216
9. Strasburger, Scott, LB, Nebraska, 243
10. Jones, Joe, TE, Virginia Tech, 270
11. Dellocono, Neal, LB, UCLA, 297
12. Jordan, Karl, LB, Vanderbilt, 324

DENVER 1985
1. *Sewell, Steve, RB, Oklahoma, 26
2. *Johnson, Vance, WR, Arizona [from Houston] 31
   *Fletcher, Simon, DE, Houston, 54
3. Choice to Houston
4. *McGregor, Keli, TE, Colorado State, 110
5. Choice to Houston
   Hinson, Billy, G, Florida [from Miami] 139
6. Choice to New York Jets
7. Cameron, Dallas, NT, Miami, 194
8. Riley, Eric, DB, Florida State, 222
9. Smith, Daryl, DB, North Alabama, 249
10. Funck, Buddy, QB, New Mexico [from New England] 269
    Anderson, Ron, LB, SMU, 278
11. Rolle, Gary, WR, Florida, 306
12. Lynch, Dan, G, Washington State, 334

DETROIT 1985
1. *Brown, Lomas, T, Florida, 6
2. *Glover, Kevin, C, Maryland, 34
3. *Johnson, James, LB, San Diego State, 62
4. *Hancock, Kevin, LB, Baylor, 90
5. McIntosh, Joe, RB, North Carolina State, 118
6. Short, Stan, G, Penn State, 146
7. Staten, Tony, DB, Angelo State, 174
8. *Caldwell, Scotty, RB, Texas-Arlington, 202
9. *James, June, LB, Texas, 230
10. Beauford, Clayton, WR, Auburn, 258
11. Harris, Kevin, DB, Georgia, 286
12. Weaver, Mike, G, Georgia, 314

GREEN BAY 1985
1. *Ruettgers, Ken, T, USC [from Cleveland thru Buffalo] 7
   Choice to Buffalo
2. Choice to Buffalo
3. *Moran, Rich, G, San Diego State, 71
4. *Stanley, Walter, WR, Mesa, 98
5. *Noble, Brian, LB, Arizona State, 125
6. *Lewis, Mark, TE, Texas A&M, 155
7. Wilson, Eric, LB, Maryland [from Minnesota] 171
   *Ellerson, Gary, RB, Wisconsin, 182
8. *Stills, Ken, DB, Wisconsin, 209
9. Johnson, Morris, G, Alabama A&M, 239
10. *Burgess, Ronnie, DB, Wake Forest, 266
11. *Shield, Joe, QB, Trinity (CT), 294
12. Meyer, Jim, P, Arizona State, 323

HOUSTON 1985
1. Choice to Atlanta thru Min
   *Childress, Ray, DE, Texas A&M [from Minnesota] 3
   *Johnson, Richard, DB, Wisconsin [from New Orleans] 11
2. Choice to Denver
   *Byrd, Richard, DE, Southern Mississippi [from Tampa Bay thru Denver] 36
3. Choice to New York Giants
   *Kelley, Mike, C, Notre Dame [from Denver] 82
4. *Briehl, Tom, LB, Stanford, 87
5. Choice to Dal
   *Bush, Frank, LB, North Carolina State [from Los Angeles Rams thru Kansas City] 133
   *Johnson, Lee, K, BYU [from Denver] 138
6. Choice to Los Angeles Raiders
   *Krakoski, Joe, LB, Washington [from Kansas City] 153
7. *Akiu, Mike, WR, Hawaii, 170
8. *Thomas, Chuck, C, Oklahoma, 199
9. *Tasker, Steve, KR, Northwestern, 226
10. *Golic, Mike, DE, Notre Dame, 255
11. *Drewrey, Willie, KR, West Virginia, 281
12. Vonder Haar, Mark, DT, Minnesota, 311

INDIANAPOLIS 1985
1. *Bickett, Duane, LB, USC, 5
2. *Anderson, Don, DB, Purdue, 32
3. *Young, Anthony, DB, Temple, 61
4. *Broughton, Willie, DE, Miami, 88
5. *Caron, Roger, T, Harvard, 117
6. Choice to Dallas
7. *Harbour, James, WR, Mississippi, 173
8. *Nichols, Ricky, WR, East Carolina, 200
9. *Boyer, Mark, TE, USC, 229
10. Pinesett, Andre, DT, Cal State-Fullerton, 256
11. Choice to Los Angeles Rams
12. *Burnette, Dave, T, Central Arkansas, 312

KANSAS CITY 1985
1. *Horton, Ethan, RB, North Carolina, 15
2. *Hayes, Jonathan, TE, Iowa, 41
3. Choice to San Diego
4. *Olderman, Bob, G, Virginia, 99
5. *King, Bruce, RB, Purdue, 126
6. *Bostic, Jonathan, DB, Bethune-Cookman [from Philadelphia] 149
   Choice to Houston
7. Thomson, Vince, DE, Missouri Western [from San Diego] 180
   Heffernan, Dave, G, Miami, 183
8. *Hillary, Ira, WR, South Carolina, 210
9. Armentrout, Mike, DB, Southwest Missouri State, 237
10. *Smith, Jeff, RB, Nebraska, 267
11. Jackson, Chris, C, SMU, 293
12. *LeBel, Harper, C, Colorado State, 321

LOS ANGELES RAIDERS 1985
1. *Hester, Jessie, WR, Florida State, 23
2. Choice to New England
3. *Moffett, Tim, WR, Mississippi, 79
   *Adams, Stefon, DB, East Carolina [from Was thru Houston] 80
4. *Kimmel, Jamie, LB, Syracuse [from Washington] 107
   Choice to New England
5. *Reeder, Dan, RB, Delaware, 135
6. *Hilger, Rusty, QB, Oklahoma State [from Houston] 143
   Choice to Minnesota
7. *Belcher, Kevin, T, Wisconsin [from New York Giants] 186
   *Pattison, Mark, WR, Washington [from New England] 188
   *Clark, Bret, DB, Nebraska, 191
   *Haden, Nick, C, Penn State [from Was thru New England] 192
8. Wingate, Leonard, DT, South Carolina State, 220
9. Sydnor, Chris, DB, Penn State, 246
10. *McKenzie, Reggie, LB, Tennessee [from Washington] 275
    Myres, Albert, DB, Tulsa, 276
11. *Strachan, Steve, RB, Boston College, 303
12. Polk, Raymond, DB, Oklahoma State, 332

LOS ANGELES RAMS 1985
1. *Gray, Jerry, DB, Texas, 21
2. *Scott, Chuck, WR, Vanderbilt, 50
3. *Hatcher, Dale, P, Clemson, 77
4. Choice to Minnesota
5. *Greene, Kevin, LB, Auburn [from Buffalo] 113
   Choice to Houston thru Kansas City
6. *Young, Mike, WR, UCLA [from Chicago Bears] 161
   *Johnson, Damone, TE, Cal Poly-SLO, 162
7. *Bradley, Danny, RB, Oklahoma, 189
8. McIntyre, Marlon, RB, Pittsburgh, 218
9. Swanson, Gary, LB, Cal Poly-SLO, 245
10. *Love, Duval, G, UCLA, 274
11. *Flutie, Doug, QB, Boston College [from Indianapolis] 285
    Brown, Kevin, DB, Northwestern, 301
12. Choice to Tampa Bay

MIAMI 1985
1. *Hampton, Lorenzo, RB, Florida, 27
2. Choice to San Diego
3. *Little, George, DT, Iowa [from Philadelphia] 65
   *Moyer, Alex, LB, Northwestern, 83
4. *Smith, Mike, DB, Texas-El Paso [from Cleveland] 91
   *Dellenbach, Jeff, T, Wisconsin, 111
5. Choice to Denver
6. *Shorthose, George, WR, Missouri [from Atl] 145
   *Davenport, Ron, RB, Louisville, 167
7. *Reveiz, Fuad, K, Tennessee, 195
8. Sharp, Dan, TE, TCU, 223
9. Hinds, Adam, DB, Oklahoma State, 251
10. Pendleton, Mike, DB, Indiana, 279
11. Jones, Mike, RB, Tulane, 307
12. Noble, Ray, DB, California, 335

MINNESOTA 1985
1. Choice to Houston
   *Doleman, Chris, LB, Pittsburgh [from Atlanta] 4
2. *Holt, Issiac, DB, Alcorn State, 30
3. *Lowdermilk, Kirk, C, Ohio State, 59
   *Meamber, Tim, LB, Washington [from Atlanta] 60
   *Long, Tim, T, Memphis State [from San Diego] 66
4. *Rhymes, Buster, WR, Oklahoma, 85
   *Morrell, Kyle, DB, BYU [from Los Angeles Rams] 106
5. *MacDonald, Mark, G, Boston College, 115
6. *Bono, Steve, QB, UCLA, 142
   *Newton, Tim, NT, Florida [from Los Angeles Raiders] 164
7. Choice to Green Bay
8. Blair, Nikita, LB, Texas-El Paso, 198
9. Covington, Jaime, RB, Syracuse, 227
10. Johnson, Juan, WR, Langston, 254
11. Williams, Tim, DB, North Carolina A&T, 283
12. Jones, Byron, NT, Tulsa, 310

NEW ENGLAND 1985
1. Choice to San Francisco
   *Matich, Trevor, C, BYU [from San Francisco] 28
2. *Veris, Garin, DE, Stanford, 48
   *Bowman, Jim, DB, Central Michigan [from Los Angeles Raiders] 52
   *Thomas, Ben, DE, Auburn [from San Francisco] 56
3. Choice to San Francisco
   *McMillian, Audray, DB, Houston [from San Francisco] 84
4. *Toth, Tom, T, Western Michigan, 102
   Phelan, Gerard, WR, Boston College [from Los Angeles Raiders] 108
5. Choice to Cincinnati
6. Choice to Philadelphia
7. Choice to Los Angeles Raiders
8. Choice to Atlanta
   *Hodge, Milford, DT, Washington State [from San Francisco] 224
9. Choice to Pittsburgh
10. Choice to Denver
11. Lewis, Paul, RB, Boston U., 295
12. *Mumford, Tony, RB, Penn State, 328

NEW ORLEANS 1985
1. Choice to Houston
   *Toles, Alvin, LB, Tennessee [from

Washington] 24
2. *Gilbert, Daren, T, Cal State-Fullerton, 38
3. *Del Rio, Jack, LB, USC, 68
4. Allen, Billy, DB, Florida State, 95
5. Choice to Washington
6. Choice to Atlanta
7. *Martin, Eric, WR, LSU, 179
8. *Kohlbrand, Joe, DE, Miami, 206
9. *Johnson, Earl, DB, South Carolina, 236
10. Choice to Washington
11. Choice to Washington
12. Songy, Treg, DB, Tulane, 320

NEW YORK GIANTS 1985
1. *Adams, George, RB, Kentucky, 19
2. *Robinson, Stacy, WR, North Dakota State, 46
3. *Davis, Tyrone, DB, Clemson [from Houston] 58
   *Johnston, Brian, C, North Carolina, 73
4. *Bavaro, Mark, TE, Notre Dame, 100
5. Henderson, Tracy, WR, Iowa State, 132
6. *Oliver, Jack, G, Memphis State, 159
   Pembrook, Mark, DB, Cal State-Fullerton [from Seattle] 165
7. Choice to Los Angeles Raiders
8. *Rouson, Lee, RB, Colorado, 213
9. Wright, Frank, NT, South Carolina, 240
10. Dubroc, Gregg, LB, LSU, 272
11. Young, Allen, DB, Virginia Tech, 299
12. *Welch, Herb, DB, UCLA, 326

NEW YORK JETS 1985
1. *Toon, Al, WR, Wisconsin, 10
2. *Lyles, Lester, DB, Virginia, 40
3. *Elder, Donnie, DB, Memphis State, 67
4. Allen, Doug, WR, Arizona State, 94
5. *Benson, Troy, LB, Pittsburgh [from Tampa Bay] 120
   Luft, Brian, DT, USC, 124
   Smith, Tony, WR, San Jose State [from Chicago Bears] 134
6. Deaton, Jeff, G, Stanford, 151
   *Miano, Rich, DB, Hawaii [from Denver] 166
7. Choice to Dal thru Kansas City
8. *Monger, Matt, LB, Oklahoma State, 208
9. *Waters, Mike, RB, San Diego State, 235
10. *Glenn, Kerry, DB, Minnesota, 262
11. White, Brad, DE, Texas Tech, 292
12. Wallace, Bill, WR, Pittsburgh, 319

PHILADELPHIA 1985
1. *Allen, Kevin, T, Indiana, 9
2. *Cunningham, Randall, QB-P, Nevada-Las Vegas, 37
3. Choice to Miami
4. Naron, Greg, G, North Carolina, 93
5. *Jiles, Dwayne, LB, Texas Tech, 121
6. Choice to Kansas City
   *Reeves, Ken, T, Texas A&M [from New England] 156
7. Choice to Washington
8. *Polley, Tom, LB, Nevada-Las Vegas, 205
9. Toub, Dave, C, Texas-El Paso [from Cleveland] 231
   *Drake, Joe, DT, Arizona, 233
10. *Kelso, Mark, DB, William & Mary, 261
11. *Hunter, Herman, RB, Tennessee State, 289
12. Russell, Todd, DB, Boston College, 317

PITTSBURGH 1985
1. *Sims, Darryl, DE, Wisconsin, 20
2. *Behning, Mark, T, Nebraska, 47
3. *Hobley, Liffort, DB, LSU, 74
4. *Turk, Dan, C, Wisconsin, 101
5. Choice to Seattle
   *Jacobs, Cam, LB, Kentucky [from Washington] 136
6. *Carr, Gregg, LB, Auburn, 160
7. Andrews, Alan, TE, Rutgers, 187
8. *Newsome, Harry, P, Wake Forest, 214
9. *Small, Fred, LB, Washington, 241
   Harris, Andre, DB, Minnesota [from New England] 242
10. White, Oliver, TE, Kentucky, 268
11. Matichak, Terry, DB, Missouri, 300
12. Sanchez, Jeff, DB, Georgia, 327

ST. LOUIS 1985
1. *Nunn, Freddie Joe, LB, Mississippi, 18
2. Choice to Atlanta
   *Bergold, Scott, T, Wisconsin [from Washington thru Atlanta] 51
3. *Smith, Lance, T, LSU, 72
4. *Wolfley, Ron, RB, West Virginia, 104
5. *Dunn, K.D., TE, Clemson [from Atlanta] 116
   Wong, Louis, G, BYU, 131
6. *Novacek, Jay, WR, Wyoming, 158
7. Choice to Washington thru Kansas City
8. *Monaco, Rob, G, Vanderbilt, 212
9. *Williams, Scott, TE, Georgia, 244
10. Williams, Dennis, RB, Furman, 271
11. Anderson, Ricky, K, Vanderbilt, 298
12. *Young, Lonnie, DB, Michigan State, 325

SAN DIEGO 1985
1. *Lachey, Jim, G, Ohio State, 12
2. Davis, Wayne, DB, Indiana State, 39
   *Dale, Jeffery, DB, LSU [from Miami] 55
3. Choice to Minnesota
   *Hendy, John, DB, Long Beach State [from Kansas City] 69
4. *Mojsiejenko, Ralf, K, Michigan State, 96
5. Choice to Seattle
6. *Lewis, Terry, DB, Michigan State, 150
7. Choice to Kansas City
   *Fellows, Mark, LB, Montana State [from San Francisco] 196
8. *Adams, Curtis, RB, Central Michigan, 207
9. Berner, Paul, QB, Pacific, 234
   *Remsberg, Dan, T, Abilene Christian [from San Francisco] 252
10. *King, David, DB, Auburn, 264
11. Smith, Jeff, NT, Kentucky, 291
12. *Simmons, Tony, DE, Tennessee, 318
    Pearson, Bret, TE, Wisconsin [from Chicago Bears] 329

SAN FRANCISCO 1985
1. *Rice, Jerry, WR, Mississippi Valley State [from New England] 16
   Choice to New England
2. Choice to New England
3. *Moore, Ricky, RB, Alabama [from New England] 75
   Choice to New England
4. Choice to Buffalo
5. *Collie, Bruce, T, Texas-Arlington, 140
6. Barry, Scott, QB, Cal-Davis, 168
7. Choice to San Diego
8. Choice to New England
9. Choice to San Diego
10. Choice to Seattle
11. Wood, David, DE, Arizona, 308
12. Chumley, Donald, DT, Georgia, 336

SEATTLE 1985
1. Choice to Cincinnati
2. *Gill, Owen, RB, Iowa, 53
3. *Greene, Danny, WR, Washington, 81
4. Davis, Tony, TE, Missouri, 109
5. Napolitan, Mark, C, Michigan State [from San Diego] 123
   *Brown, Arnold, DB, North Carolina Central [from Pittsburgh] 128
   Jones, Johnnie, RB, Tennessee, 137
6. Choice to New York Giants
7. *Mattes, Ron, T, Virginia, 193
8. Lewis, Judious, WR, Arkansas State, 221
9. *Otto, Bob, DE, Idaho State, 248
10. Conner, John, QB, Arizona, 277
    Bowers, James, DB, Memphis State [from San Francisco] 280
11. *Cooper, Louis, LB, Western Carolina, 305
12. Choice to Buffalo

TAMPA BAY 1985
1. *Holmes, Ron, DE, Washington, 8
2. Choice to Houston thru Denver
3. *Randle, Ervin, LB, Baylor, 64
4. Heaven, Mike, DB, Illinois, 92
5. Choice to New York Jets
6. Choice to Cincinnati
7. *Prior, Mike, DB, Illinois State, 176
8. *Freeman, Phil, WR, Arizona, 204
9. Calabria, Steve, QB, Colgate, 232
10. *Igwebuike, Donald, K, Clemson, 260
11. Williams, James, RB, Memphis State, 288
12. *Rockford, Jim, DB, Oklahoma, 316
    Melka, Jim, LB, Wisconsin [from Los Angeles Rams] 330

WASHINGTON 1985
1. Choice to New Orleans
2. *Nixon, Tory, DB, San Diego State [from Atlanta] 33
   Choice to St. Louis thru Atlanta
3. Choice to Los Angeles Raiders thru Houston
4. Choice to Los Angeles Raiders
5. *Cherry, Raphel, RB, Hawaii [from New Orleans] 122
   Choice to Pittsburgh
6. *Lee, Danzell, TE, Lamar, 163
7. Harris, Jamie, KR, Oklahoma State [from Philadelphia] 177
   *Vital, Lionel, RB, Nicholls State [from St. Louis thru Kansas City] 185
   Choice to Los Angeles Raiders thru New England
8. *Wilburn, Barry, DB, Mississippi, 219
9. Geier, Mitch, G, Troy State, 247
10. *Orr, Terry, RB, Texas [from New Orleans] 263
    Choice to Los Angeles Raiders
11. *McKenzie, Raleigh, G, Tennessee [from New Orleans] 290
    *Kimble, Garry, DB, Sam Houston State, 304
12. *Hamel, Dean, DT, Tulsa [from Buffalo] 309
Winn, Bryant, LB, Houston, 331

1986

Held April 29-30, 1986

There were 333 choices instead of 336. Cleveland gave up a first-round choice and San Francisco a ninth-round choice in 1985 supplemental drafts. New England forfeited its fourth-round selection.

ATLANTA 1986
1. *Casillas, Tony, NT, Oklahoma, 2
   *Green, Tim, LB, Syracuse [from Washington] 17
2. Choice to Washington
3. Choice to Cincinnati
4. Choice to Los Angeles Raiders
5. Choice to Washington
6. Choice to Kansas City thru Washington
   *Dixon, Floyd, WR, Stephen F. Austin [from Cleveland thru Buffalo] 154
   *Williams, Keith, RB, Southwest Missouri State [from Washington] 159
7. Choice to Philadelphia
8. Hudgens, Kevin, DE, Idaho State, 197
9. Starks, Kevin, TE, Minnesota, 224
10. *Baker, Tony, RB, East Carolina, 252
11. Hegg, Chris, QB, Northeast Missouri State, 280
12. *Griffin, Steve, WR, Purdue, 308

BUFFALO 1986
1. Choice to Cleveland
   *Harmon, Ronnie, RB, Iowa [from Cleveland] 16
   *Wolford, Will, T, Vanderbilt [from Dal thru San Francisco] 20
2. Choice to Det thru San Francisco
3. Choice to San Francisco
   *Burton, Leonard, C, South Carolina State [from Los Angeles Rams] 77
4. Choice to Green Bay
5. *Byrum, Carl, RB, Mississippi Valley State, 111
6. Choice to Dallas
7. Choice to Cleveland
   Williams, Bob, TE, Penn State [from Tampa Bay] 168
   *Pike, Mark, DT, Georgia Tech [from Detroit] 178
   *Rolle, Butch, TE, Michigan State [from Seattle] 180
8. Choice to Kansas City
   *Furjanic, Tony, LB, Notre Dame [from Kansas City] 202
9. *Bynum, Reggie, WR, Oregon State, 222
10. Teafatiller, Guy, NT, Illinois, 251
11. Garbarczyk, Tony, NT, Wake Forest, 278
    Witt, Billy, DE, North Alabama [from Indianapolis] 282
12. Choice to Dallas
    *McClure, Brian, QB, Bowling Green [from Kansas City] 313
    Christian, Derek, LB, West Virginia [from Green Bay] 331

CHICAGO BEARS 1986
1. *Anderson, Neal, RB, Florida, 27
2. *Jackson, Vestee, DB, Washington, 55
3. *Williams, David, WR, Illinois, 82
4. *Blair, Paul, T, Oklahoma State, 110
5. *Barnes, Lew, WR, Oregon, 138
6. *Powell, Jeff, RB, Tennessee, 166
7. *Jones, Bruce, DB, North Alabama, 194
8. *Douglass, Maurice, DB, Kentucky, 221
9. *Teltschik, John, P, Texas, 249
10. Hundley, Barton, DB, Kansas State, 277
11. *Kozlowski, Glen, WR, BYU, 305
12. Choice to San Diego

CINCINNATI 1986
1. *Kelly, Joe, LB, Washington, 11
   *McGee, Tim, WR, Tennessee [from Denver] 21
2. *Billups, Lewis, DB, North Alabama, 38
3. *Skow, Jim, DE, Nebraska [from Atlanta] 58
   *Hammerstein, Mike, DT, Michigan, 65
   *Fulcher, David, DB, Arizona State [from Denver] 78
4. *Kattus, Eric, TE, Michigan, 91
   *Gaynor, Doug, QB, Long Beach State [from Seattle] 99
5. *White, Leon, LB, BYU, 123
6. *Hunt, Gary, DB, Memphis State, 152
7. *Franklin, Pat, RB, Southwest Texas State, 177
8. *Douglas, David, G, Tennessee, 204
9. Whittingham, Cary, LB, BYU, 230
10. Shaw, Jeff, NT, Salem (WV), 262
11. Stone, Tim, T, Kansas State, 289
    *Flaherty, Tom, LB, Northwestern [from Green Bay] 294
12. *Bradley, Steve, QB, Indiana, 316

CLEVELAND 1986
1. Choice exercised in 1985 supplemental draft (Kosar, Bernie, QB, Miami) [from Buffalo]
   Choice to Buffalo
2. *Slaughter, Webster, WR, San Diego State, 43
3. Choice to Detroit
4. Choice to San Francisco thru Los Angeles Rams
5. *Miller, Nick, LB, Arkansas, 127
6. Choice to Atlanta thru Buffalo
7. *Meyer, Jim, T, Illinois State [from Buffalo] 167
   *Norseth, Mike, QB, Kansas [from Kansas City] 174
   Choice to Seattle
8. Choice to Philadelphia
9. Taylor, Danny, DB, Texas-El Paso, 238
10. Smith, Willie, TE, Miami, 265
11. Dausin, Randy, G, Texas A&M, 292
12. Simmons, King, DB, Texas Tech, 319

DALLAS 1986
1. *Sherrard, Mike, WR, UCLA [from San Francisco] 18
   Choice to Buffalo thru San Francisco
2. *Clack, Darryl, RB, Arizona State [from Indianapolis] 33
   Choice to Indianapolis
3. *Walen, Mark, DT, UCLA, 74
4. *Zendejas, Max, K, Arizona, 100
5. Choice to San Francisco
6. *Chandler, Thornton, TE, Alabama [from Buffalo] 140
   *Gelbaugh, Stan, QB, Maryland [from Detroit] 150
   Yancey, Lloyd, G, Temple, 158
7. *Holloway, Johnny, WR, Kansas, 185
8. Clemons, Topper, RB, Wake Forest, 212
9. Ionata, John, G, Florida State, 242
10. Chester, Bryan, G, Texas, 269
11. *Jax, Garth, LB, Florida State, 296
12. *Duliban, Chris, LB, Texas [from Buffalo] 307
    Flack, Tony, DB, Georgia, 322

DENVER 1986
1. Choice to Cincinnati
2. Choice to New York Giants
3. Choice to Cincinnati
4. *Juriga, Jim, T, Illinois, 104
5. *Colorito, Tony, NT, USC, 134
6. *Mobley, Orson, TE, Salem (WV) [from Green Bay] 151
   *Jackson, Mark, WR, Purdue, 161
7. *Phillips, Raymond, LB, North Carolina State, 188
8. *Klosterman, Bruce, LB, South Dakota State, 217
9. Thomas, Joe, WR, Mississippi Valley State, 244
10. Hall, Victor, TE, Jackson State, 271
11. Dendy, Thomas, RB, South Carolina, 301
12. Choice to Los Angeles Rams

DETROIT 1986
1. *Long, Chuck, QB, Iowa, 12
2. *James, Garry, RB, LSU [from Buffalo thru San Francisco] 29
   Choice to San Francisco
3. *Milinichik, Joe, T, North Carolina State [from Cleveland] 69
   Choice to Los Angeles Rams thru San Francisco
4. *Mitchell, Devon, DB, Iowa, 92
5. *Smith, Oscar, RB, Nicholls State, 119
6. Choice to Dallas
7. Choice to Buffalo
8. Griffin, Allyn, WR, Wyoming, 205
9. Pickens, Lyle, DB, Colorado, 231
10. Johnson, Tracy, LB, Morningside, 258
11. Melvin, Leland, WR, Richmond, 290
12. Durden, Allan, DB, Arizona, 317

GREEN BAY 1986
1. Choice to Minnesota thru San Diego
2. *Davis, Kenneth, RB, TCU, 41
3. Bosco, Robbie, QB, BYU, 72
4. *Harris, Tim, LB, Memphis State [from Buffalo] 84
   Knight, Dan, T, San Diego State, 98
5. *Koart, Matt, DT, USC, 125
6. *Dent, Burnell, LB, Tulane [from St. Louis] 143
   Choice to Denver
7. *Berry, Ed, DB, Utah State, 183
8. Cline, Michael, NT, Arkansas State, 210
9. *Moore, Brent, DT, USC, 236
10. Spann, Gary, LB, TCU, 263
11. Choice to Cincinnati
12. Choice to Buffalo

HOUSTON 1986
1. *Everett, Jim, QB, Purdue, 3
2. *Givins, Ernest, WR, Louisville, 34
3. *Pinkett, Allen, RB, Notre Dame, 61
4. Choice to Kansas City
5. *Parks, Jeff, TE, Auburn, 114
6. *Wallace, Ray, RB, Purdue, 145
7. Choice to Indianapolis thru Los Angeles Rams
8. *Griffin, Larry, DB, North Carolina, 199
9. Sebring, Bob, LB, Illinois, 225
10. Sommer, Don, G, Texas-El Paso, 256
11. Cochran, Mark, T, Baylor, 283
12. *Banks, Chuck, RB, West Virginia Tech, 310

INDIANAPOLIS 1986
1. *Hand, Jon, DE, Alabama [from New Orleans] 4
   Choice to New Orleans
2. Choice to Dallas
   *Trudeau, Jack, QB, Illinois [from Dallas] 47
3. Choice to New Orleans
4. *Brooks, Bill, WR, Boston U., 86
5. *Kellar, Scott, DE, Northern Illinois, 117
   Walker, Gary, C, Boston U. [from San Diego] 124
6. Choice to Los Angeles Rams
7. O'Malley, Steve, NT, Northern Illinois, 171
   White, Chris, K, Illinois [from Hou thru Los Angeles Rams] 172
   *Sims, Tommy, DB, Tennessee [from Los Angeles Rams] 190
8. Hooper, Trell, DB, Memphis State, 198
9. *Brotzki, Bob, T, Syracuse, 228
10. Choice to St. Louis
    Anderson, Pete, G, Georgia [from San Diego] 266
11. Choice to Buffalo
12. Wade, Steve, DT, Vanderbilt, 309
    Williams, Isaac, DT, Florida State [from Los Angeles Rams] 326

KANSAS CITY 1986
1. *Jozwiak, Brian, T, West Virginia, 7
2. *Hackett, Dino, LB, Appalachian State, 35
3. *Griffin, Leonard, DE, Grambling, 63
4. *Baugh, Tom, C, Southern Illinois [from

Houston] 87
*Fox, Chas, WR, Furman, 90
5. Choice to San Diego
6. Hagood, Kent, RB, South Carolina [from Atlanta thru Washington] 141
Choice to Washington
7. Choice to Cleveland
8. *Colbert, Lewis, P, Auburn [from Buffalo] 196
Choice to Buffalo
9. *Baldinger, Gary, DE, Wake Forest, 229
10. *Readon, Ike, NT, Hampton, 257
11. *Pearson, Aaron, LB, Mississippi State, 285
12. Choice to Buffalo

LOS ANGELES RAIDERS 1986
1. *Buczkowski, Bob, DE, Pittsburgh, 24
2. Choice to New York Giants thru Minnesota
3. Cochran, Brad, DB, Michigan, 80
4. *Wise, Mike, DE, Cal-Davis [from Atlanta] 85
*Mueller, Vance, RB, Occidental [from New York Giants] 103
*McCallum, Napoleon, RB, Navy, 108
5. Choice to Pittsburgh
6. *Marrone, Doug, T, Syracuse, 164
7. *Lewis, Bill, C, Nebraska, 191
8. Mauntel, Joe, LB, Eastern Kentucky, 219
9. *Lee, Zeph, RB, USC, 246
10. *Reinke, Jeff, DE, Mankato State, 275
11. Webster, Randell, LB, Southwestern Oklahoma, 302
12. Shepherd, Larry, WR, Houston, 330

LOS ANGELES RAMS 1986
1. *Schad, Mike, T, Queen's (Ontario), 23
2. *Newberry, Tom, G, Wisconsin-La Crosse, 50
3. *Millen, Hugh, QB, Washington [from Detroit thru San Francisco] 71
Choice to Buffalo
4. Choice to Philadelphia
5. Choice to San Diego
6. *Jenkins, Robert (born Cox), T, UCLA [from Indianapolis] 144
Williams, Lynn, RB, Kansas, 160
7. Choice to Indianapolis
8. Jarecki, Steve, LB, UCLA [from Tampa Bay] 195
*Goebel, Hank, T, Cal State-Fullerton, 216
9. *Watts, Elbert, DB, USC, 243
10. Breeland, Garrett, LB, USC, 273
11. Schwanke, Chul, RB, South Dakota, 300
12. Choice to Indianapolis
*Dupree, Marcus, RB, Oklahoma [from Denver] 327

MIAMI 1986
1. Choice to Tampa Bay
2. *Offerdahl, John, LB, Western Michigan, 52
3. *Turner, T.J., DT, Houston, 81
4. *Pruitt, James, WR, Cal State-Fullerton, 107
5. *Wyatt, Kevin, DB, Arkansas, 136
6. Sowell, Brent, DT, Alabama, 163
7. *Kolic, Larry, LB, Ohio State, 193
8. Stuart, John, T, Texas, 218
9. *Thompson, Reyna, DB, Baylor, 247
10. Wickersham, Jeff, QB, LSU, 274
11. Franklin, Arnold, TE, North Carolina, 303
12. Isom, Rickey, RB, North Carolina State, 329

MINNESOTA 1986
1. Choice to San Diego
*Robinson, Gerald, DE, Auburn [from Green Bay thru San Diego] 14
2. Choice to Tampa Bay thru Mia
3. Choice to San Diego
4. *Phillips, Joe, DT, SMU, 93
5. *Jones, Hassan, WR, Florida State, 120
6. Rooks, Thomas, RB, Illinois, 147
7. *Hilton, Carl, TE, Houston, 179
8. Schippang, Gary, T, West Chester, 206
9. Slaton, Mike, DB, South Dakota, 232
10. Cormier, Joe, WR, USC, 259
11. Armstrong, John, DB, Richmond, 286
12. *Solomon, Jesse, LB, Florida State, 318

NEW ENGLAND 1986
1. *Dupard, Reggie, RB, SMU, 26
2. *Ruth, Mike, NT, Boston College [from Seattle] 42
*Glenn, Vencie, DB, Indiana State, 54
3. Forfeited
4. Gieselman, Scott, TE, Boston College, 109
5. *Robinson, Greg, G, Cal State-Sacramento, 137
6. Choice to Tampa Bay
7. McDonald, Ray, WR, Florida [from San Francisco] 187
*Williams, Brent, DE, Toledo, 192
8. *Baty, Greg, TE, Stanford, 220
9. *Colton, George, G, Maryland, 248
10. Jones, Cletis, RB, Florida State, 276
11. Thomas, Gene, WR, Pacific, 304
12. McAulay, Don, K, Syracuse, 332

NEW ORLEANS 1986
1. Choice to Indianapolis
*Dombrowski, Jim, T, Virginia [from Indianapolis] 6
2. *Hilliard, Dalton, RB, LSU, 31
3. *Mayes, Rueben, RB, Washington State [from Tampa Bay] 57
*Swilling, Pat, LB, Georgia Tech [from Indianapolis] 60
*Word, Barry, RB, Virginia, 62
4. *Edwards, Kelvin, WR, Liberty Baptist, 88
5. *Sutton, Reggie, DB, Miami, 115
6. *Thompson, Robert, WR, Youngstown State, 142
7. *Fenerty, Gill, RB, Holy Cross, 173
8. Mokofisi, Filipo, LB, Utah, 200
9. Jones, Merlon, LB, Florida A&M, 226
10. *Dumbauld, Jon, DE, Kentucky, 253
11. *Swoopes, Pat, NT, Mississippi State, 284
12. Brown, Sebastian, WR, Bethune-Cookman, 311

NEW YORK GIANTS 1986
1. *Dorsey, Eric, DE, Notre Dame, 19
2. *Collins, Mark, DB, Cal State-Fullerton [from San Diego thru Minnesota] 44
*Howard, Erik, NT, Washington State, 46
*Johnson, Pepper, LB, Ohio State [from Denver] 51
*Lasker, Greg, DB, Arkansas [from Los Angeles Raiders thru Minnesota] 53
3. *Washington, John, DE, Oklahoma State, 73
4. Choice to Los Angeles Raiders
5. *Warren, Vince, WR, San Diego State, 130
6. *Brown, Ron, WR, Colorado [from Tampa Bay thru Denver] 139
*Miller, Solomon, WR, Utah State, 157
7. *Francis, Jon, RB, Boise State, 184
8. *Cisowski, Steve, T, Santa Clara, 214
9. Luebbers, Jim, DE, Iowa State, 241
10. Kimmel, Jerry, LB, Syracuse, 268
11. Lynch, Len, G, Maryland, 295
12. Choice to Philadelphia

NEW YORK JETS 1986
1. *Haight, Mike, T, Iowa, 22
2. *Williams, Doug, T, Texas A&M, 49
3. Crawford, Tim, LB, Texas Tech, 79
4. *Alexander, Rogers, LB, Penn State, 105
5. *Hadley, Ron, LB, Washington, 132
6. Choice to San Francisco
7. *White, Bob, T, Rhode Island, 189
8. *Ducksworth, Robert, DB, Southern Mississippi, 215
9. *Faaola, Nuu, RB, Hawaii, 245
10. *Carr, Carl, LB, North Carolina, 272
11. Amoia, Vince, RB, Arizona State, 299
12. *Cesario, Sal, T, Cal Poly-SLO, 328

PHILADELPHIA 1986
1. *Byars, Keith, RB, Ohio State, 10
2. *Toney, Anthony, RB, Texas A&M, 37
*Johnson, Alonzo, LB, Florida [from Washington thru Los Angeles Raiders] 48
3. Choice to San Francisco
4. Choice to San Diego
*Darwin, Matt, C, Texas A&M [from Los Angeles Rams] 106
5. *Criswell, Ray, P, Florida, 121
*McMillen, Dan, DE, Colorado [from Was thru Atlanta] 128
6. *Landsee, Bob, C, Wisconsin, 149
7. *Redick, Corn, WR, Cal State-Fullerton [from Atlanta] 169
*Lee, Byron, LB, Ohio State, 176
8. Choice to San Francisco
*Joyner, Seth, LB, Texas-El Paso [from Cleveland] 208
9. *Simmons, Clyde, DE, Western Carolina, 233
10. *Tautalatasi, Taivale (Junior), RB, Washington State, 261
11. Bogdalek, Steve, G, Michigan State, 288
12. *Singletary, Reggie, DE, North Carolina State, 315
*Howard, Bobby, RB, Indiana [from New York Giants] 325

PITTSBURGH 1986
1. *Rienstra, John, G, Temple, 9
2. *Williams, Gerald, DE, Auburn, 36
3. *Brister, Walter (Bubby), QB, Northeast Louisiana, 67
4. *Callahan, Bill, DB, Pittsburgh, 94
5. *Tucker, Erroll, DB, Utah, 122
*Jones, Brent, TE, Santa Clara [from Los Angeles Raiders] 135
6. *Bryant, Domingo, DB, Texas A&M, 148
7. *Carter, Rodney, RB, Purdue, 175
8. *Boso, Cap, TE, Illinois, 207
9. *Henton, Anthony, LB, Troy State, 234
10. *Seitz, Warren, WR, Missouri, 260
11. *Station, Larry, LB, Iowa, 287
12. Williams, Mike, LB, Tulsa, 314

ST. LOUIS 1986
1. *Bell, Anthony, LB, Michigan State, 5
2. *Lee, John, K, UCLA, 32
3. *Chilton, Gene, C, Texas, 59
4. *Carter, Carl, DB, Texas Tech, 89
5. *Tupper, Jeff, DE, Oklahoma, 116
6. Choice to Green Bay
7. *Swanson, Eric, WR, Tennessee, 170
8. *Brown, Ray, G, Arkansas State, 201
9. Kafentzis, Kent, DB, Hawaii, 227
10. *Sikahema, Vai, RB, BYU, 254
Smith, Wes, WR, East Texas State [from Indianapolis] 255
11. Dillard, Wayne, LB, Alcorn State, 281
12. *Austin, Kent, QB, Mississippi, 312

SAN DIEGO 1986
1. *O'Neal, Leslie, DE, Oklahoma State [from Minnesota] 8
*Fitzpatrick, James, T, USC, 13
2. Choice to New York Giants thru Minnesota
3. *Unrein, Terry, DE, Colorado State [from Minnesota] 66
4. *Walker, Jeff, T, Memphis State, 70
*Allert, Ty, LB, Texas [from Philadelphia] 95
Taylor, Tommy, LB, UCLA, 97
5. Landry, Doug, LB, Louisiana Tech [from Kansas City] 118
Choice to Indianapolis
*Brown, Donald, DB, Maryland [from San Francisco] 129
Johnson, Matt, DB, USC [from Los Angeles Rams] 133
6. Pardridge, Curt, WR, Northern Illinois, 155
7. Smalls, Fred, LB, West Virginia, 182
8. Perrino, Mike, T, Notre Dame, 209
9. *Zordich, Mike, DB, Penn State, 235
10. Choice to Indianapolis
11. *Sanders, Chuck, RB, Slippery Rock, 293
Smetana, Drew, T, Oregon [from San Francisco] 298
12. Sprowls, Jeff, DB, BYU, 320
Travis, Mike, DB, Georgia Tech [from Chicago Bears] 333

SAN FRANCISCO 1986
1. Choice to Dallas
2. *Roberts, Larry, DE, Alabama [from Detroit] 39
Choice to Washington
3. *Rathman, Tom, RB, Nebraska [from Buffalo] 56
*McKyer, Tim, DB, Texas-Arlington [from Philadelphia] 64
*Taylor, John, WR, Delaware State, 76
4. *Haley, Charles, LB, James Madison [from Cleveland thru Los Angeles Rams] 96
*Wallace, Steve, T, Auburn [from Washington thru Los Angeles Rams] 101
*Fagan, Kevin, DT, Miami, 102
5. Choice to San Diego
*Miller, Patrick, LB, Florida [from Dallas] 131
6. Choice to Washington
*Griffin, Don, DB, Middle Tennessee State [from New York Jets] 162
7. Choice to New England
8. Popp, Jim, TE, Vanderbilt [from Philadelphia] 203
Choice exercised in 1985 supplemental draft (Snipes, Roosevelt, RB, Florida State)
9. *Cherry, Tony, RB, Oregon, 240
10. Stinson, Elliston, WR, Rice, 267
Hallman, Harold, LB, Auburn [from Washington] 270
11. Choice to San Diego
12. Choice to Tampa Bay

SEATTLE 1986
1. *Williams, John L., RB, Florida, 15
2. Choice to New England
3. *Hunter, Patrick, DB, Nevada-Reno, 68
4. Choice to Cincinnati
5. *Edmonds, Bobby Joe, WR, Arkansas, 126
6. *Anderson, Eddie, DB, Fort Valley State, 153
7. Choice to Buffalo
Miles, Paul, RB, Nebraska [from Cleveland] 181
8. *Mitz, Alonzo, DE, Florida, 211
9. *Black, Mike, T, Cal State-Sacramento, 237
10. Fairbanks, Don, DE, Colorado, 264
11. Norrie, David, QB, UCLA, 291
12. McVeigh, John, LB, Miami, 321

TAMPA BAY 1986
1. Jackson, Bo, RB, Auburn, 1
*Jones, Roderick, DB, SMU [from Miami] 25
2. *Walker, Jackie, LB, Jackson State, 28
*Murphy, Kevin, LB, Oklahoma [from Minnesota thru Miami] 40
3. Choice to New Orleans
4. *Swoope, Craig, DB, Illinois, 83
5. *Maarleveld, J.D., T, Maryland, 112
6. Choice to New York Giants thru Den
*Walker, Kevin, DB, East Carolina [from New England] 165
7. Choice to Buffalo
8. Choice to Los Angeles Rams
9. *Barnhardt, Tommy, P, North Carolina, 223
10. Reed, Benton, DE, Mississippi, 250
11. Drenth, Mark, T, Purdue, 279
12. *Miller, Clay, G, Michigan, 306
Crawford, Mike, RB, Arizona State [from San Francisco] 324

WASHINGTON 1986
1. Choice to Atlanta
2. *Koch, Markus, DE, Boise State [from Atlanta] 30
*Murray, Walter, WR, Hawaii [from San Francisco] 45
Choice to Philadelphia thru Los Angeles Raiders
3. *Walton, Alvin, DB, Kansas, 75
4. Choice to San Francisco thru Los Angeles Rams
5. *Caldwell, Ravin, LB, Arkansas [from Atlanta] 113
Choice to Philadelphia thru Atlanta
6. *Rypien, Mark, QB, Washington State [from Kansas City] 146
Huddleston, Jim, G, Virginia [from San Francisco] 156
Choice to Atlanta
7. *Badanjek, Rick, RB, Maryland, 186
8. *Gouveia, Kurt, LB, BYU, 213
9. Asberry, Wayne, DB, Texas A&M, 239
10. Choice to San Francisco
11. Fells, Kenny, RB, Henderson State, 297
12. *Yarber, Eric, WR, Idaho, 323

1987

Held April 28-29, 1987

ATLANTA 1987
1. *Miller, Chris, QB, Oregon, 13
2. *Flowers, Kenny, RB, Clemson [from Green Bay] 31
Choice to Green Bay
3. Choice to Green Bay
4. Van Dyke, Ralph, T, Southern Illinois, 97
5. *Mraz, Mark, DE, Utah State, 125
6. *Kiser, Paul, G, Wake Forest, 153
7. *Reid, Michael, LB, Wisconsin, 181
8. Taliaferro, Curtis, LB, Virginia Tech, 208
9. *Anthony, Terrence, DB, Iowa State, 236
10. Reese, Jerry, TE, Illinois, 264
11. *Shelley, Elbert, DB, Arkansas State, 292
12. *Emery, Larry, RB, Wisconsin, 320

BUFFALO 1987
1. Choice to Houston
*Conlan, Shane, LB, Penn State [from Houston] 8
2. *Odomes, Nate, DB, Wisconsin [from Tampa Bay] 29
*Mitchell, Roland, DB, Texas Tech, 33
3. *Brandon, David, LB, Memphis State, 60
*Mueller, Jamie, RB, Benedictine [from San Francisco] 78
4. Choice to Tampa Bay
*Seals, Leon, DE, Jackson State [from Washington] 109
5. Choice to Washington
6. Choice to Washington
7. *Porter, Kerry, RB, Washington State, 171
8. Choice to Indianapolis
*Mesner, Bruce, NT, Maryland [from Los Angeles Raiders] 209
9. *McKeller, Keith, TE, Jacksonville State, 227
10. Choice to Los Angeles Raiders
11. *Ballard, Howard, T, Alabama A&M, 283
12. *McGrail, Joe, DT, Delaware, 311

CHICAGO 1987
1. *Harbaugh, Jim, QB, Michigan, 26
2. *Morris, Ron, WR, Southern Methodist, 54
3. Choice to Cleveland thru Los Angeles Rams
4. *Smith, Sean, DE, Grambling [from Los Angeles Rams] 101
Choice to Los Angeles Raiders
5. *Bryan, Steve, DE, Oklahoma [from Houston thru Washington and Los Angeles Raiders] 120
*Johnson, Will, LB, Northeast Louisiana, 138
6. *Adickes, John, C, Baylor [from Los Angeles Raiders] 154
Choice to Los Angeles Rams
7. *Harris, Archie, T, William & Mary, 193
8. *Migliazzo, Paul, LB, Oklahoma, 221
9. *Heimuli, Lakei, RB, Brigham Young, 249
10. *Chapura, Dick, DT, Missouri, 277
11. *Jessie, Tim, RB, Auburn, 305
12. *Jeffries, Eric, DB, Texas, 333

CINCINNATI 1987
1. *Buck, Jason, DE, Brigham Young, 17
2. *Thomas, Eric, DB, Tulane, 49
3. *Bell, Leonard, DB, Indiana, 76
*McClendon, Skip, DE, Arizona State [from Seattle] 77
4. *Riggs, Jim, TE, Clemson, 103
5. *Logan, Marc, RB, Kentucky, 130
*Horne, Greg, P, Arkansas [from Denver] 139
6. *Gordon, Sonny, DB, Ohio State, 157
7. Thatcher, Chris, G, Lafayette, 188
8. *Wilcots, Solomon, DB, Colorado, 215
9. Raddatz, Craig, LB, Wisconsin, 242
10. *McCluskey, David, RB, Georgia, 269
11. Warne, Jim, T, Arizona State, 296
12. *Holifield, John, RB, West Virginia, 328

CLEVELAND 1987
1. *Junkin, Mike, LB, Duke [from San Diego] 5
Choice to San Diego
2. *Rakoczy, Gregg, C, Miami [from San Diego] 32
Choice to San Diego
3. *Manoa, Tim, RB, Penn State, 80
*Jaeger, Jeff, K, Washington [from Chicago Bears thru Los Angeles Rams] 82
4. Choice to Los Angeles Rams
5. Choice to Los Angeles Rams
6. *Braggs, Stephen, DB, Texas, 165
7. Choice to Green Bay
8. Bullitt, Steve, LB, Texas A&M, 220
9. Choice to Indianapolis
10. *Winters, Frank, C, Western Illinois, 276
11. Brewton, Larry, DB, Temple, 303
12. Choice to Los Angeles Rams

DALLAS 1987
1. *Noonan, Danny, DT, Nebraska, 12
2. *Francis, Ron, DB, Baylor, 39
3. *Zimmerman, Jeff, G, Florida, 68
4. *Martin, Kelvin, WR, Boston College, 95
5. *Gay, Everett, WR, Texas, 124
6. Onosai, Joe, G, Hawaii, 151
7. *Sweeney, Kevin, QB, Fresno State, 180
8. *Gogan, Kevin, T, Washington, 206
9. *Blount, Alvin, RB, Maryland, 235
10. *Jones, Dale, LB, Tennessee, 262
11. Ward, Jeff, K, Texas, 291
12. Armstrong, Scott, LB, Florida, 318

DENVER 1987
1. *Nattiel, Ricky, WR, Florida, 27
2. Choice to New York Giants
3. *Brooks, Michael, LB, Louisiana State, 86
4. *Munford, Marc, LB, Nebraska, 111
5. Choice to Cincinnati
6. *Marshall, Warren, RB, James Madison, 167
7. *Strozier, Wilbur, TE, Georgia, 194
8. Morgan, Dan, G, Penn State, 222
9. *Plummer, Bruce, DB, Mississippi State, 250
10. Wilkinson, Rafe, LB, Richmond, 278
11. Roberts, Steve, DE, Washington [from Los Angeles Rams] 299
Neal, Tommy, RB, Maryland, 306
12. *Braxton, Tyrone, DB, North Dakota State, 334

DETROIT 1987
1. *Rogers, Reggie, DE, Washington, 7
2. Choice to Tampa Bay thru Hou and Buf
3. *Ball, Jerry, NT, Southern Methodist, 63
4. *Rivers, Garland, DB, Michigan, 92
5. Choice to Seattle
6. *Lockett, Danny, LB, Arizona, 148
7. *Saleaumua, Dan, DT, Arizona State, 175
8. *Gibson, Dennis, LB, Iowa State, 203
9. *Calhoun, Rick, RB, Cal State-Fullerton, 230
10. *Brown, Raynard, WR, South Carolina, 259
11. Siverling, Brian, TE, Penn State, 286
12. *Lee, Gary, WR, Georgia Tech, 315

GREEN BAY 1987
1. *Fullwood, Brent, RB, Auburn, 4
2. Choice to Atlanta
*Holland, Johnny, LB, Texas A&M [from Atlanta] 41
3. *Crosten, Dave, T, Iowa, 61
*Stephen, Scott, LB, Arizona State [from Atlanta] 69
*Neal, Frankie, WR, Fort Hays State [from Los Angeles Raiders] 71
4. *Freeman, Lorenzo, DT, Pittsburgh, 89
5. Choice to San Diego
6. Marshall, Willie, WR, Temple, 145
7. *Leiker, Tony, DT, Stanford, 172
Smith, Bill, P, Mississippi [from Cleveland] 191
8. *Drost, Jeff, DT, Iowa, 198
9. Harris, Gregg, G, Wake Forest, 228
10. *Majkowski, Don, QB, Virginia, 255
11. *Scott, Patrick, WR, Grambling, 282
12. Choice to Seattle
*Jefferson, Norman, DB, Louisiana State [from New York Giants] 335

HOUSTON 1987
1. *Highsmith, Alonzo, RB, Miami [from Buffalo] 3
Choice to Buffalo
*Jeffires, Haywood, WR, North Carolina State [from Los Angeles Rams] 20
2. Choice to Kansas City
*Johnson, Walter, LB, Louisiana Tech [from Kansas City] 46
3. *Carlson, Cody, QB, Baylor, 64
4. Choice to Los Angeles Rams
*Dusbabek, Mark, LB, Minnesota [from Kansas City] 105
5. Choice to Chicago Bears thru Was and Los Angeles Raiders
*Tillman, Spencer, RB, Oklahoma [from Los Angeles Rams] 133
6. *Smith, Al, LB, Utah State, 147
*Caston, Toby, LB, Louisiana State [from Kansas City] 159
7. *Banks, Robert, DT, Notre Dame, 176
8. James, Michel, WR, Washington State, 202
9. Neighbors, Wes, C, Alabama, 231
10. *Duncan, Curtis, WR, Northwestern, 258
11. *Davis, John, G, Georgia Tech, 287
12. *Valentine, Ira, RB, Texas A&M, 314

INDIANAPOLIS 1987
1. *Bennett, Cornelius, LB, Alabama, 2
2. Choice to Washington
3. *Gambol, Chris, T, Iowa, 58
4. *Dixon, Randy, T, Pittsburgh, 85
5. Banks, Roy, WR, Eastern Illinois, 114
6. *Robinson, Freddie, DB, Alabama, 142
7. *Bellini, Mark, WR, Brigham Young, 170
8. Choice to Tampa Bay
*Miller, Chuckie, DB, UCLA [from Buffalo] 200
9. Choice to New York Giants
*Ontko, Bob, LB, Penn State [from Cleveland] 247
10. *Goode, Chris, DB, Alabama, 253
11. Reynosa, Jim, DE, Arizona State, 281
12. *Adams, David, RB, Arizona, 309

KANSAS CITY 1987
1. *Palmer, Paul, RB, Temple, 19
2. *Okoye, Christian, RB, Azusa Pacific [from Houston] 35
Choice to Houston
3. *Howard, Todd, LB, Texas A&M, 73
4. Choice to Houston
5. *Taylor, Kitrick, WR, Washington State [from Minnesota thru Miami] 128
Choice to Miami
6. Choice to Houston
7. *Hudson, Doug, QB, Nicholls State, 186
8. Choice to Miami
*Clemons, Michael, RB, William & Mary [from New England] 218
9. *Watts, Randy, DE, Catawba, 244
10. *Evans, James, RB, Southern, 271
11. Richardson, Craig, WR, Eastern Washington, 298
12. *Holmes, Bruce, LB, Minnesota, 325

LOS ANGELES RAIDERS 1987
1. *Clay, John, T, Missouri, 15
2. Choice to New York Jets
*Wilkerson, Bruce, T, Tennessee [from Washington] 52
3. Choice to Green Bay
*Smith, Steve, RB, Penn State [from Was thru New England] 81
4. Choice to New England
*Beuerlein, Steve, QB, Notre Dame [from Chicago Bears] 110
5. Choice to St. Louis
6. Choice to Chicago Bears
7. *Jackson, Bo, RB, Auburn, 183
8. Choice to Buffalo
9. *Eccles, Scott, TE, Eastern New Mexico, 238
10. *Harrison, Rob, DB, Cal State-Sacramento [from Buffalo] 254
*Gesek, John, G, Cal State-Sacramento, 265
*Ellis, Jim, LB, Boise State [from San Francisco thru Buffalo] 273
11. *McLemore, Chris, RB, Arizona [from Phi thru San Francisco] 288
*Perry, Mario, TE, Mississippi, 294
12. Choice to New York Giants

LOS ANGELES RAMS 1987
1. Choice to Houston
2. *Evans, Donald, DE, Winston-Salem, 47
3. *Hicks, Cliff, DB, Oregon, 74
4. *Bartlett, Doug, NT, Northern Illinois [from Houston] 91
Choice to Chicago Bears
*Kelm, Larry, LB, Texas A&M [from Cleveland] 108
5. Choice to Houston
*Mersereau, Scott, DT, Southern Connecticut [from Cleveland] 136
6. Choice to New York Giants
*Embree, Jon, TE, Colorado [from Chicago Bears] 166
7. Choice exercised in 1986 Supplemental Draft by Philadelphia (Crawford, Charles, RB, Oklahoma)
8. *Stewart, Michael, DB, Fresno State, 213
9. Ham, Tracy, RB, Georgia Southern, 240
10. Smith, David, LB, Northern Arizona, 272
11. Choice to Denver
12. Williams, Alonzo, RB, Mesa (CO), 326
*Stokes, Fred, DE, Georgia Southern [from Cleveland] 332

MIAMI 1987
1. Choice to Minnesota
*Bosa, John, DE, Boston College [from Minnesota] 16
2. *Graf, Rick, LB, Wisconsin, 43
*Schwedes, Scott, WR, Syracuse [from New York Giants thru St. Louis] 56
3. Choice to St. Louis
4. *Stradford, Troy, RB, Boston College, 99
5. Choice to St. Louis
*Conlin, Chris, T, Penn State [from Kansas City] 132
6. Sellers, Lance, LB, Boise State, 155
7. *Brown, Tom, RB, Pittsburgh, 182
8. *Williams, Joel, TE, Notre Dame, 210
*Dennis, Mark, T, Illinois [from Kansas City] 212
9. *Pidgeon, Tim, LB, Syracuse, 237
10. Taylor, Bobby, DB, Wisconsin, 266
11. Mann, Terence, NT, Southern Methodist, 293
12. Karsatos, Jim, QB, Ohio State, 322

MINNESOTA 1987
1. *Dozier, D.J., RB, Penn State [from Miami] 14
Choice to Miami
2. *Berry, Ray, LB, Baylor, 44
3. *Thomas, Henry, NT, Louisiana State, 72
4. *Mustafaa, Najee (Reggie Rutland), DB, Georgia Tech, 100
5. Choice to Kansas City thru Mia
6. *Richardson, Greg, WR, Alabama, 156
7. Choice to Seattle
8. *Fenney, Rick, RB, Washington, 211
9. *Jones, Leonard, DB, Texas Tech, 239
10. *Riley, Bob, T, Indiana, 267
11. *Pease, Brent, QB, Montana, 295
12. Williams, Keith, DT, Florida, 323

NEW ENGLAND 1987
1. *Armstrong, Bruce, T, Louisville, 23
2. Choice to Tampa Bay
3. *Perryman, Bob, RB, Michigan, 79
4. *Gannon, Rich, QB, Delaware [from Los Angeles Raiders] 98
Beasley, Derrick, DB, Winston-Salem [from New York Jets thru Los Angeles Raiders] 102
*Jordan, Tim, LB, Wisconsin, 107
5. *Villa, Danny, T, Arizona State [from Tampa Bay] 113
*Gibson, Tom, DE, Northern Arizona [from San Diego] 116
6. *Taylor, Gene, WR, Fresno State, 163
7. Choice to Tampa Bay
8. Choice to Kansas City
9. Choice to Tampa Bay
10. Choice to San Francisco thru Buf
11. Reveiz, Carlos, K, Tennessee, 302
12. *Davis, Elgin, RB, Central Florida, 330

NEW ORLEANS 1987
1. *Knight, Shawn, DT, Brigham Young, 11
2. *Hill, Lonzell, WR, Washington, 40
3. *Adams, Mike, DB, Arkansas State, 67
4. *Trapilo, Steve, G, Boston College, 96
5. *Mack, Milton, DB, Alcorn State, 123
6. *Henley, Thomas, WR, Stanford, 152
7. *Atkins, Gene, DB, Florida A&M, 179
8. *Cook, Toi, DB, Stanford, 207
9. *Leach, Scott, LB, Ohio State, 234
10. *Clark, Robert, WR, North Carolina Central, 263
11. Wells, Arthur, TE, Grambling, 290
12. Sorrells, Tyrone, G, Georgia Tech, 319

NEW YORK GIANTS 1987
1. *Ingram, Mark, WR, Michigan State, 28
2. *White, Adrian, DB, Florida [from Denver] 55
Choice to Miami thru St. Louis
3. *Baker, Stephen, WR, Fresno State, 83
4. *Turner, Odessa, WR, Northwestern State (LA), 112
5. *O'Connor, Paul, G, Miami, 140
6. Richardson, Tim, RB, Pacific [from Los Angeles Rams] 160
*Riesenberg, Doug, T, California, 168
7. Choice to St. Louis
8. *Jones, Rod, TE, Washington, 223
9. Parker, Stan, G, Nebraska [from Indianapolis] 225
*Wright, Dana, RB, Findlay, 251
10. *Faucette, Chuck, LB, Maryland, 279
11. *Walter, Dave, QB, Michigan Tech, 307
12. *Berthusen, Bill, DT, Iowa State [from Los Angeles Raiders] 321
Stark, Chad, RB, North Dakota State [from San Francisco thru Los Angeles Raiders] 329
Choice to Green Bay

NEW YORK JETS 1987
1. *Vick, Roger, RB, Texas A&M, 21
2. *Gordon, Alex, LB, Cincinnati [from Los Angeles Raiders] 42
Choice to Washington thru Los Angeles Raiders
3. *Elam, Onzy, LB, Tennessee State, 75
4. Choice to New England thru Los Angeles Raiders
5. *Jackson, Kirby, DB, Mississippi State, 129
6. *Martin, Tracy, WR, North Dakota, 161
7. *Nichols, Gerald, NT, Florida State, 187
8. *Hunter, Eddie, RB, Virginia Tech [from Tampa Bay] 196
Rice, Mike, P, Montana, 214
9. *McLean, Ron, DE, Cal State-Fullerton, 241
10. *Lewis, Sid, DB, Penn State, 268
11. Timmer, Kirk, LB, Montana State, 300
12. Ransdell, Bill, QB, Kentucky, 327

PHILADELPHIA 1987
1. *Brown, Jerome, DT, Miami, 9
2. Choice to San Francisco
3. *Tamburello, Ben, C, Auburn, 65
4. *Evans, Byron, LB, Arizona, 93
5. *Alexander, David, G, Tulsa, 121
6. Moten, Ron, LB, Florida, 149
*Pike, Chris, DT, Tulsa [from Seattle] 158
7. Williams, Brian, T, Central Michigan, 177
Choice [from Los Angeles Rams, exercised in 1986 Supplemental Draft (Crawford, Charles, RB, Oklahoma State)
8. Choice to San Diego
9. Lambiotte, Ken, QB, William & Mary, 232
10. Carberry, Paul, DT, Oregon State, 260
11. Choice to Los Angeles Raiders thru San Francisco
12. *Morse, Bobby, RB, Michigan State, 316

PITTSBURGH 1987
1. *Woodson, Rod, DB, Purdue, 10
2. *Hall, Delton, DB, Clemson, 38
3. *Lockett, Charles, WR, Long Beach State, 66
4. *Everett, Thomas, DB, Baylor, 94
5. *Nickerson, Hardy, LB, California, 122
6. *Johnson, Tim, NT, Penn State [from Tampa Bay] 141
*Lloyd, Greg, LB, Fort Valley State, 150
7. *Kelley, Chris, TE, Akron, 178
8. *Buchanan, Charles, DE, Tennessee State, 205
9. *Clinkscales, Joey, WR, Tennessee, 233
10. *Hoge, Merril, RB, Idaho State, 261
11. *Oswald, Paul, C, Kansas, 289
12. *Young, Theo, TE, Arkansas, 317

ST. LOUIS 1987
1. *Stouffer, Kelly, QB, Colorado State, 6
2. *McDonald, Tim, DB, Southern California, 34
3. *Awalt, Robert, TE, San Diego State, 62
*Scotts, Colin, DT, Hawaii [from Miami] 70
4. *Saddler, Rod, DT, Texas A&M, 90
5. *Swarn, George, RB, Miami (OH), 118
*Bruno, John, P, Penn State [from Miami] 126
*Jarostchuk, Ilia, LB, New Hampshire [from Los Angeles Raiders] 127
6. *Garalczyk, Mark, DT, Western Michigan, 146
7. Peoples, Tim, DB, Washington, 174
*Harris, William, TE, Bishop College [from New York Giants] 195
8. *Alvord, Steve, DT, Washington, 201
9. *Davis, Wayne, LB, Alabama, 229
10. *Wright, Charles, DB, Tulsa, 257
11. *Peat, Todd, G, Northern Illinois, 285
12. Choice to Tampa Bay

SAN DIEGO 1987
1. Choice to Cleveland
*Bernstine, Rod, TE, Texas A&M [from Cleveland] 24
2. Choice to Cleveland
*Brock, Louis, DB, Southern California [from Cleveland] 53
3. *Wilson, Karl, DE, Louisiana State, 59
4. *Vlasic, Mark, QB, Iowa, 88
5. Jones, Nelson, DB, North Carolina State [from Green Bay] 115
Choice to New England
6. Choice to Tampa Bay
7. *Holland, Jamie, WR, Ohio State, 173
8. MacEsker, Joe, T, Texas-El Paso, 199
*Brown, Ron, LB, Southern California [from Philadelphia] 204
9. Wilcher, Thomas, RB, Michigan, 226
10. *Anderson, Anthony, DB, Grambling, 256
11. *Goebel, Joe, C, UCLA, 284
12. Greenwood, Marcus, RB, UCLA, 310

SAN FRANCISCO 1987
1. *Barton, Harris, T, North Carolina, 22
*Flagler, Terrence, RB, Clemson [from Washington] 25
2. *Bregel, Jeff, G, Southern California [from Philadelphia] 37
Choice to Tampa Bay
3. Choice to Buffalo
4. Choice to Tampa Bay
5. Jokisch, Paul, WR, Michigan, 134
6. White, Bob, LB, Penn State, 162
7. *DeLine, Steve, K, Colorado State, 189
8. *Grayson, Dave, LB, fresno State, 217
9. Shelley, Jonathan, DB, Mississippi, 245
10. Choice to Los Angeles Raiders thru Buffalo
Paye, John, QB, Stanford [from New England thru Los Angeles Raiders] 275
11. *Nicholas, Calvin, WR, Grambling, 301
12. Choice to New York Giants thru Los Angeles Raiders

SEATTLE 1987
1. *Woods, Tony, LB, Pittsburgh, 18
2. *Wyman, Dave, LB, Stanford, 45
3. Choice to Cincinnati
4. *Moore, Mark, DB, Oklahoma State, 104
5. *Agee, Tommie, R, Auburn [from Detroit] 119
*Rodriguez, Ruben, P, Arizona, 131
6. Choice to Phi
7. *Barbay, Roland, NT, Louisiana State [from Minnesota] 184
*Tennell, Derek, TE, UCLA, 185
8. *Garza, Sammy, QB, Texas-El Paso, 216
9. *Johnson, M.L., LB, Hawaii, 243
10. *Clark, Louis, WR, Mississippi State, 270
11. *Oliver, Darryl, RB, Miami, 297
12. *Dove, Wes, DE, Syracuse [from Green Bay] 312
*Burse, Tony, RB, Middle Tennessee State, 324

TAMPA BAY 1987
1. *Testaverde, Vinny, QB, Miami, 1
2. Choice to Buffalo
*Reynolds, Ricky, DB, Washington State [from Detroit thru Houston and Buffalo] 36
*Moss, Winston, LB, Miami [from San Francisco] 50
*Smith, Don, RB, Mississippi State [from New England] 51
3. *Carrier, Mark, WR, Nicholls State, 57
4. *Graham, Don, LB, Penn State, 84
*Hall, Ron, TE, Hawaii [from Buffalo] 87
*Hill, Bruce, WR, Arizona State [from San Francisco] 106
5. Choice to New England
*Rolling, Henry, LB, Nevada-Reno [from New England] 135
Mayes, Tony, DB, Kentucky [from Washington] 137
6. Choice to Pittsburgh
*Bartalo, Steve, RB, Colorado State [from San Diego] 143
7. *Jarvis, Curt, NT, Alabama, 169
*Swayne, Harry, DE, Rutgers [from New England] 190
8. Choice to New York Jets
Mataele, Stan, NT, Arizona [from Indianapolis] 197
9. Armentrout, Joe, RB, Wisconsin, 224
*Davis, Greg, P, Citadel [from New England] 246
10. *Simmonds, Mike, G, Indiana State, 252
11. Taylor, Reggie, RB, Cincinnati, 280
12. Cooper, Scott, DT, Kearney State, 308
Shula, Mike, QB, Alabama [from St. Louis] 313

WASHINGTON 1987
1. Choice to San Francisco
2. *Davis, Brian, DB, Nebraska [from Indianapolis] 30
Kleine, Wally, T, Notre Dame [from New York Jets thru Los Angeles Raiders] 48
Choice to Los Angeles Raiders
3. Choice to Los Angeles Raiders thru NE
4. Choice to Buffalo
5. *Smith, Timmy, RB, Texas Tech [from Buffalo] 117
Choice to Tampa Bay
6. *Gage, Steve, DB, Tulsa [from Buffalo] 144
*Simmons, Ed, T, Eastern Washington, 164

7. *Thomas, Johnny, DB, Baylor, 192
8. *Vaughn, Clarence, DB, Northern Illinois, 219
9. Jenkins, Alfred, RB, Arizona, 248
10. Wilson, Ted, WR, Central Florida, 274
11. *Brown, Laron, WR, Texas, 304
12. *Hitchcock, Ray, C, Minnesota, 331

1988

Held April 24-25, 1988

ATLANTA 1988
1. *Bruce, Aundray, LB, Auburn, 1
2. *Cotton, Marcus, LB, Southern California, 28
3. *Higdon, Alex, TE, Ohio State, 56
4. Choice to Tampa Bay thru Philadelphia
5. *Dimry, Charles, DB, Nevada-Las Vegas, 110
6. *Thomas, George, WR, Nevada-Las Vegas, 138
   *Hoover, Houston, G, Jackson State [from Tampa Bay] 140
7. *Haynes, Michael, WR, Northern Arizona, 166
8. Brown, Phillip, LB, Alabama, 194
9. *Primus, James, RB, UCLA, 222
10. *Clayton, Stan, T, Penn State, 250
11. *Milling, James, WR, Maryland, 278
12. Wiley, Carter, DB, Virginia Tech, 306

BUFFALO 1988
1. Choice to Los Angeles Rams
2. *Thomas, Thurman, RB, Oklahoma State, 40
3. *Ford, Bernard, WR, Central Florida, 65
4. Choice to San Diego
5. Gadson, Ezekial, DB, Pittsburgh, 123
   Roach, Kirk, K, Western Carolina [from San Francisco] 135
6. *Murray, Dan, LB, East Stroudsburg, 150
7. Borcky, Tim, T, Memphis State, 177
   Wright, Bo, RB, Alabama [from San Diego] 184
8. *Hagy, John, DB, Texas, 204
   *Wright, Jeff, NT, Central Missouri [from Indianapolis] 213
9. *Bailey, Carlton, NT, North Carolina, 235
10. *Mayhew, Martin, DB, Florida State, 262
11. Curkendall, Pete, NT, Penn State, 289
12. Driscoll, John, T, New Hampshire [from Kansas City] 309
   *Erlandson, Tom Jr., LB, Washington, 316

CHICAGO BEARS 1988
1. *Muster, Brad, RB, Stanford, 23
   *Davis, Wendell, WR, Louisiana State [from Washington] 27
2. *Jones, Dante, LB, Oklahoma, 51
3. Jarvis, Ralph, DE, Temple, 78
4. *Thornton, Jim, TE, Cal State-Fullerton, 105
5. *Johnson, Troy, LB, Oklahoma, 133
6. *Stinson, Lemuel, DB, Texas Tech, 161
7. *Rentie, Caesar, T, Oklahoma, 189
8. *Tate, David, DB, Colorado [from New England] 208
   Harvey, Reed, RB, Howard, 217
9. Magee, Rogie, WR, Louisiana State, 245
10. Porter, Joel, G, Baylor, 273
11. Forch, Steve, LB, Nebraska, 301
12. *Clark, Greg, LB, Arizona State, 329

CINCINNATI 1988
1. *Dixon, Rickey, DB, Oklahoma, 5
2. *Woods, Ickey, DB, Nevada-Las Vegas, 31
3. *Walker, Kevin, LB, Maryland, 57
4. *Grant, David, NT, West Virginia, 84
5. Wester, Herb, T, Iowa, 114
6. *Jetton, Paul, G, Texas, 141
7. *Romer, Rich, LB, Union (NY), 168
8. *Maxey, Wilson, NT, Grambling, 195
9. Wells, Brandy, DB, Notre Dame, 226
10. *Dillahunt, Ellis, DB, East Carolina, 253
11. Hickert, Paul, K, Murray State, 280
12. *Parker, Carl, WR, Vanderbilt, 307

CLEVELAND 1988
1. *Charlton, Clifford, LB, Florida, 21
2. *Perry, Michael Dean, DT, Clemson, 50
3. *Waiters, Van, LB, Indiana, 77
4. *Blaylock, Anthony, DB, Winston-Salem State, 103
5. Choice to Phoenix
6. Choice to Philadelphia
7. *Gash, Thane, DB, East Tennessee State, 188
8. *Birden, J.J., WR, Oregon, 216
9. *Copeland, Danny, DB, Eastern Kentucky, 244
10. *Washington, Brian, DB, Nebraska, 272
11. Hawkins, Hendley, WR, Nebraska, 300
12. Slayden, Steve, QB, Duke, 328

DALLAS 1988
1. *Irvin, Michael, WR, Miami, 11
2. *Norton, Ken Jr., LB, UCLA, 41
3. Hutson, Mark, G, Oklahoma, 67
4. *Widell, Dave, T, Boston College, 94
5. Choice to Pho thru Sea
6. *Secules, Scott, QB, Virginia, 151
7. Hooven, Owen, T, Oregon State, 178
8. *Higgs, Mark, RB, Kentucky, 205
9. Bedford, Brian, WR, California, 232
10. *Owens, Billy, DB, Pittsburgh, 263
11. *Hennings, Chad, DE, Air Force, 290
12. Hummel, Ben, LB, UCLA, 317

DENVER 1988
1. *Gregory, Ted, NT, Syracuse, 26
2. *Perry, Gerald, T, Southern U. [from Minnesota] 45
   Choice to Minnesota
3. *Guidry, Kevin, DB, Louisiana State [from New Orleans] 79
   Choice to New Orleans
4. Choice to Minnesota
5. Ervin, Corris, DB, Central Florida, 136
6. Choice to Minnesota
7. *Kelly, Pat, TE, Syracuse [from Los Angeles Rams] 174
   Frank, Garry, G, Mississippi State, 192
8. Choice to Miami
9. *Farr, Mel Jr., RB, UCLA, 248
10. Williams, Channing, RB, Arizona State [from Pittsburgh] 268
   Choice to New Orleans
11. Calvin, Richard, RB, Washington State, 304
12. Carter, Johnny, NT, Grambling, 332

DETROIT 1988
1. Choice to Kansas City
   *Blades, Bennie, DB, Miami [from Kansas City] 3
2. *Spielman, Chris, LB, Ohio State [from Kansas City] 29
   *Carter, Pat, TE, Florida State, 32
3. *Roundtree, Ray, WR, Penn State, 58
4. *White, William, DB, Ohio State, 85
5. *Andolsek, Eric, G, Louisiana State, 111
6. *Painter, Carl, RB, Hampton Institute, 142
7. James, Jeff, WR, Stanford, 169
8. *Hadd, Gary, DE, Minnesota, 196
9. *Corrington, Kip, DB, Texas A&M, 223
   Irvin, Todd, T, Mississippi [from Philadelphia] 234
10. *Craig, Paco, WR, UCLA, 254
11. McCoin, Danny, QB, Cincinnati, 281
12. Choice to Indianapolis

GREEN BAY 1988
1. *Sharpe, Sterling, WR, South Carolina, 7
2. *Patterson, Shawn, DT, Arizona State, 34
3. *Woodside, Keith, RB, Texas A&M, 61
4. *Putzier, Rollin, DT, Oregon [from Los Angeles Raiders] 88
   *Cecil, Chuck, DB, Arizona, 89
5. Reed, Darrell, LB, Oklahoma, 116
6. *Hill, Nate, DE, Auburn, 144
7. *Richard, Gary, DB, Pittsburgh, 173
8. *Collins, Patrick, RB, Oklahoma, 200
9. Wilkinson, Neal, TE, James Madison, 228
10. Keyes, Bud, QB, Wisconsin, 256
11. Choice to Seattle
12. *Bolton, Scott, WR, Auburn, 312

HOUSTON 1988
1. *White, Lorenzo, RB, Michigan State, 22
2. *Jones, Quintin, DB, Pittsburgh, 48
3. *Montgomery, Greg, P, Michigan State [from San Diego] 72
   Choice to New York Jets thru Los Angeles Raiders
4. Choice to San Francisco thru Los Angeles Raiders
5. *Dishman, Cris, DB, Purdue [from San Diego] 125
   *Verhulst, Chris, TE, Cal State-Chico, 130
6. Crain, Kurt, LB, Auburn, 157
7. *Eaton, Tracey, DB, Portland State, 187
8. *Viaene, Dave, C, Minnesota-Duluth, 214
9. Spradlin, David, LB, Texas Christian, 241
10. Johnson, Marco, WR, Hawaii, 271
11. *Franklin, Jethro, DE, Fresno State, 298
12. *Brantley, John, LB, Georgia, 325

INDIANAPOLIS 1988
1. Choice to Los Angeles Rams
2. Choice to Los Angeles Rams
3. *Chandler, Chris, QB, Washington, 76
4. *Ball, Michael, DB, Southern U., 104
5. *Baylor, John, DB, Southern Mississippi, 129
6. Choice to Washington
7. Choice to New York Giants
8. Choice to Buffalo
9. *Herrod, Jeff, LB, Mississippi, 243
10. *Alston, O'Brien, LB, Maryland, 270
11. *Dee, Donnie, TE, Tulsa, 297
12. Kenney, Aatron, WR, Wisconsin-Stevens Point [from Detroit] 308
   Vesling, Tim, K, Syracuse, 327

KANSAS CITY 1988
1. *Smith, Neil, DE, Nebraska [from Detroit] 2
   Choice to Detroit
2. Choice to Detroit
3. *Porter, Kevin, DB, Auburn, 59
4. Choice to Tampa Bay
   Ambrose, J.R., WR, Mississippi [from Pittsburgh] 96
5. Choice to New Orleans
6. *Saxon, James, RB, San Jose State, 139
7. *Stedman, Troy, LB, Washburn, 170
8. *Roberts, Alfredo, TE, Miami, 197
9. Abdur-Ra'Oof, Azizuddin, WR, Maryland, 224
10. *Gamble, Kenny, RB, Colgate, 251
11. McManus, Danny, QB, Florida State, 282
12. Choice to Buffalo

LOS ANGELES RAIDERS 1988
1. *Brown, Tim, WR, Notre Dame, 6
   *McDaniel, Terry, DB, Tennessee [from Los Angeles Rams thru Houston] 9
   *Davis, Scott, DE, Illinois [from San Francisco] 25
2. Choice to San Francisco
3. Choice to San Diego thru Houston
4. Choice to Green Bay
   *Rother, Tim, DT, Nebraska [from New York Jets] 90
5. Choice to New England
   *Price, Dennis, DB, UCLA [from Sea thru San Francisco and New York Jets] 131
6. Grabisna, Erwin, LB, Case Western, 143
7. *Crudup, Derrick, DB, Oklahoma, 171
8. *Alexander, Mike, WR, Penn State, 199
9. Ware, Reggie, RB, Auburn, 227
   Tabor, Scott, P, California [from New York Giants] 229
10. Harrell, Newt, T, West Texas State, 255
11. Weber, David, QB, Carroll (WI), 283
12. Kunkel, Greg, G, Kentucky, 311

LOS ANGELES RAMS 1988
1. Choice to Los Angeles Raiders thru Houston
   *Green, Gaston, RB, UCLA [from Buffalo] 14
   *Cox, Aaron, WR, Arizona State [from Indianapolis] 20
2. *Newman, Anthony, DB, Oregon, 35
   *Anderson, Willie (Flipper), WR, UCLA [from San Diego] 46
   *Strickland, Fred, LB, Purdue [from Indianapolis] 47
3. Choice to Washington
   *Piel, Mike, DT, Illinois [from Washington] 82
4. Choice to San Diego
5. *Delpino, Robert, RB, Missouri, 117
   *Washington, James, DB, UCLA [from Washington] 137
6. *Jones, Keith, RB, Nebraska, 147
   Knapton, Jeff, DT, Wyoming [from Washington] 165
7. Choice to Denver
8. Franklin, Darryl, WR, Washington, 201
9. Foster, Pat, DT, Montana, 231
10. Mullin, R.C., T, Southwest Louisiana, 258
11. Choice to San Diego
12. Choice to Washington
   Beathard, Jeff, WR, Southern Oregon [from Washington] 333

MIAMI 1988
1. *Kumerow, Eric, DE, Ohio State, 16
2. *Williams, Jarvis, DB, Florida, 42
3. *Edmunds, Ferrell, TE, Maryland, 73
4. *Johnson, Greg, T, Oklahoma, 99
5. *Thomas, Rodney, DB, Brigham Young, 126
6. Bratton, Melvin, RB, Miami, 153
   Cooper, George, RB, Ohio State [from Minnesota] 156
7. Bell, Kerwin, QB, Florida, 180
8. *Galbreath, Harry, G, Tennessee, 212
   *Cheek, Louis, T, Texas A&M [from Denver] 220
9. *Cross, Jeff, DE, Missouri, 239
10. Jackson, Artis, NT, Texas Tech, 266
11. Kelleher, Tom, RB, Holy Cross, 292
12. *Kinchen, Brian, TE, Louisiana State, 320

MINNESOTA 1988
1. *McDaniel, Randall, G, Arizona State, 19
2. Choice to Denver
   *Edwards, Brad, DB, South Carolina [from Denver] 54
3. *Noga, Al, DT, Hawaii, 71
4. Choice to New England
   *Kalis, Todd, G, Arizona State [from Denver] 108
5. *Fullington, Darrell, DB, Miami, 124
6. Choice to Miami
   White, Derrick, DB, Oklahoma [from Denver] 164
7. *Beckman, Brad, TE, Nebraska-Omaha, 183
8. *Cain, Joe, LB, Oregon Tech, 210
9. McGowan, Paul, LB, Florida State, 237
10. *Habib, Brian, DT, Washington, 264
11. Floyd, Norman, DB, South Carolina, 296
12. Choice to New York Giants

NEW ENGLAND 1988
1. *Stephens, John, RB, Northwestern State (LA), 17
2. *Brown, Vincent, LB, Mississippi Valley State, 43
3. *Rehder, Tom, T, Notre Dame, 69
4. *Goad, Tim, NT, North Carolina [from Tampa Bay] 87
   *Martin, Sammy, WR, Louisiana State [from Minnesota] 97
   *Garcia, Teddy, K, Northeast Louisiana, 100
5. Wolkow, Troy, G, Minnesota [from Los Angeles Raiders] 115
   Choice to Washington
6. *Johnson, Steve, TE, Virginia Tech, 154
7. Usher, Darryl, WR, Illinois, 181
8. Choice to Chicago
9. Galbraith, Neil, DB, Central State, (OK), 240
10. Lossow, Rodney, C, Wisconsin, 267
11. *Allen, Marvin, RB, Tulane, 294
12. Nugent, Dave, NT, Boston College, 321

NEW ORLEANS 1988
1. *Heyward, Craig, RB, Pittsburgh, 24
2. *Perriman, Brett, WR, Miami, 52
3. Choice to Denver
   Stephens, Tony, NT, Clemson [from Denver] 81
4. *Carr, Lydell, RB, Oklahoma, 106
5. *Scales, Greg, TE, Wake Forest [from Kansas City] 112
   *Taylor, Keith, DB, Illinois, 134
6. Sims, Bob, G, Florida, 162
7. *Forde, Brian, LB, Washington State, 190
8. *Derby, Glen, T, Wisconsin, 218
9. Nunn, Clarence, DB, San Diego State, 246
10. Santos, Todd, QB, San Diego State, 274
   Fizer, Vincent, LB, Southern U. [from Denver] 276
11. Couch, Gary, WR, Minnesota, 302
12. Jurgensen, Paul, DE, Georgia Tech, 330

NEW YORK GIANTS 1988
1. *Moore, Eric, T, Indiana, 10
2. *Elliott, John, T, Michigan, 36
3. *White, Sheldon, DB, Miami (OH), 62
4. *Shaw, Ricky, LB, Oklahoma State, 92
5. *Carter, Jon, DE, Pittsburgh, 118
6. Houle, David, G, Michigan State, 145
7. Perez, Mike, QB, San Jose State, 175
   *Whitaker, Danta, TE, Mississippi Valley State [from Indianapolis] 186
8. *Lilly, Sammy, DB, Georgia Tech, 202
9. Choice to Los Angeles Raiders
10. Hickerson, Eric, DB, Indiana, 259
   Wilkes, Steve, TE, Appalachian State [from San Diego] 265
11. Harris, Greg, WR, Troy State, 286
12. Futrell, David, NT, Brigham Young, 313
   McCormack, Brendan, DT, South Carolina [from Minnesota] 323

NEW YORK JETS 1988
1. *Cadigan, Dave, T, Southern California, 8
2. *Williams, Terry, DB, Bethune-Cookman, 37
3. *McMillan, Erik, DB, Missouri, 63
   *Hasty, James, DB, Washington State [from Houston thru Los Angeles Raiders] 74
4. Choice to Los Angeles Raiders
5. *Withycombe, Mike, T, Fresno State, 119
6. *Frase, Paul, DE, Syracuse, 146
7. Patton, Gary, RB, Eastern Michigan, 172
8. *Neubert, Keith, TE, Nebraska, 203
9. *Tamm, Ralph, G, West Chester U., 230
10. *Booty, John, DB, Texas Christian, 257
11. *Galvin, John, LB, Boston College, 287
12. Goss, Albert, NT, Jackson State, 314

PHILADELPHIA 1988
1. *Jackson, Keith, TE, Oklahoma, 13
2. *Allen, Eric, DB, Arizona State [from Tampa Bay] 30
   Choice to San Francisco thru Tampa Bay
3. Patchan, Matt, T, Miami, 64
4. Choice exercised in 1987 Supplemental Draft (Carter, Cris, WR, Ohio State)
5. *Everett, Eric, DB, Texas Tech, 122
6. McPherson, Don, QB, Syracuse, 149
   Sterling, Rob, DB, Maine [from Cleveland] 160
7. White, Todd, WR, Cal State-Fullerton, 176
8. Smith, David, RB, Western Kentucky, 207
9. Choice to Det
10. Schuster, Joe, DT, Iowa, 261
11. *Jenkins, Izel, DB, North Carolina State, 288
12. *Kaufusi, Steve, DE, Brigham Young, 319

PHOENIX 1988
1. *Harvey, Ken, LB, California, 12
2. *Jeffery, Tony, RB, Texas Christian, 38
3. *Tupa, Tom, P, Ohio State, 68
4. *Brim, Michael, DB, Virginia Union, 95
5. *Gaines, Chris, LB, Vanderbilt [from Dallas thru Seattle] 120
   Choice to Pittsburgh
   *Jordan, Tony, RB, Kansas State [from Cleveland] 132
6. Phillips, Jon, G, Oklahoma, 148
7. *Jones, Ernie, WR, Indiana, 179
8. Moore, Tim, LB, Michigan State, 206
9. *Dill, Scott, G, Memphis State, 233
10. *Schillinger, Andy, WR, Miami (OH), 260
11. McCoy, Keith, DB, Fresno State, 291
12. Carrier, Chris, DB, Louisiana State, 318

PITTSBURGH 1988
1. *Jones, Aaron, DE, Eastern Kentucky, 18
2. *Dawson, Dermontti, G, Kentucky, 44
3. *Lanza, Chuck, C, Notre Dame, 70
4. Choice to Kansas City
5. *Jordan, Darin, LB, Northeastern [from Phoenix] 121
   *Reese, Jerry, NT, Kentucky, 128
6. *Williams, Warren, RB, Miami, 155
7. Zeno, Marc, WR, Tulane, 182
8. Nichols, Mark, NT, Michigan State, 209
   *Hinnant, Mike, TE, Temple [from San Diego] 211
9. Lockbaum, Gordie, RB, Holy Cross, 236
10. *Jackson, John, T, Eastern Kentucky [from Tampa Bay] 252
   Choice to Denver
11. Dawson, Bobby, DB, Illinois, 295
12. Earle, James, LB, Clemson, 322

SAN DIEGO 1988
1. *Miller, Anthony, WR, Tennessee, 15
2. Choice to Los Angeles Rams
3. *Early, Quinn, WR, Iowa [from Los Angeles Raiders thru Houston] 60
   Choice to Houston
4. *Campbell, Joe, DE, New Mexico State [from Los Angeles Rams] 91
   Searels, Stacy, T, Auburn [from Buffalo] 93
   *Richards, David, T, UCLA, 98
5. Choice to Houston
6. *Figaro, Cedric, LB, Notre Dame, 152
7. Choice to Buffalo
8. Choice to Pittsburgh
9. *Howard, Joey, T, Tennessee, 238

10. Choice to New York Giants
11. Miller, Ed, C, Pittsburgh [from Los Angeles Rams] 285
*Hinkle, George, NT, Arizona, 293
12. Phillips, Wendell, DB, North Alabama, 324

SAN FRANCISCO 1988
1. Choice to Los Angeles Raiders
2. *Stubbs, Danny, DE, Miami [from Los Angeles Raiders] 33
*Holt, Pierce, DT, Angelo State [from Philadelphia thru Tampa Bay] 39
Choice to Tampa Bay
3. *Romanowski, Bill, LB, Boston College, 80
4. *Helton, Barry, P, Colorado [from Houston thru Los Angeles Raiders] 102
Choice to Tampa Bay
5. Choice to Buffalo
6. Choice to Tampa Bay
7. Bryant, Kevin, LB, Delaware State, 191
8. Clarkson, Larry, T, Montana, 219
9. *Bonner, Brian, LB, Minnesota, 247
10. Foley, Tim, K, Georgia Southern, 275
11. *Brooks, Terrance, DB, Texas A&M, 303
12. Mira, George Jr., LB, Miami, 331

SEATTLE 1988
1. Choice exercised in 1987 Supplemental Draft (Bosworth, Brian, LB, Oklahoma)
2. *Blades, Brian, WR, Miami, 49
3. *Kane, Tommy, WR, Syracuse, 75
4. *Harmon, Kevin, RB, Iowa, 101
5. Choice to Los Angeles Raiders thru San Francisco and New York Jets
6. *Hart, Roy, NT, South Carolina, 158
7. Jackson, Ray, DB, Ohio State, 185
8. *Tyler, Robert, TE, South Carolina State, 215
9. Wise, Deatrich, NT, Jackson State, 242
10. Jones, Derwin, DE, Miami, 269
11. McLeod, Rick, T, Washington [from Green Bay] 284
*Harper, Dwayne, DB, South Carolina State, 299
12. Des Rochers, Dave, T, San Diego State, 326

TAMPA BAY 1988
1. *Gruber, Paul, T, Wisconsin, 4
2. Choice to Philadelphia
*Tate, Jamel, RB, Georgia [from San Francisco] 53
3. Choice exercised in 1987 Supplemental Draft (Sileo, Dan, DT, Miami)
4. *Goff, Robert, DT, Auburn [from Atlanta thru Philadelphia] 83
*Bruhin, John, G, Tennessee [from Kansas City] 86
Choice to New England
Robbins, Monte, P, Michigan [from San Francisco] 107
5. *Howard, William, RB, Tennessee, 113
6. Choice to Atlanta
*Lee, Shawn, DT, North Alabama [from San Francisco] 163
7. *Goode, Kerry, RB, Alabama, 167
8. Simpson, Anthony, RB, East Carolina, 198
9. *Davis, Reuben, DT, North Carolina, 225
10. Choice to Pittsburgh
11. *Pillow, Frank, WR, Tennessee State, 279
12. *Jones, Victor, LB, Virginia Tech, 310

WASHINGTON 1988
1. Choice to Chicago Bears
2. *Lohmiller, Chip, K, Minnesota, 55
3. *Oliphant, Mike, KR, Puget Sound [from Los Angeles Rams] 66
Choice to Los Angeles Rams
4. *Morris, Jamie, RB, Michigan, 109
5. Mims, Carl, DB, Sam Houston State [from New England] 127
Choice to Los Angeles Rams
6. *Humphries, Stan, QB, Northeast Louisiana [from Indianapolis] 159
Choice to Los Angeles Rams
7. Hicks, Harols, DB, San Diego State, 193
8. McGill, Darryl, RB, Wake Forest, 221
9. Peterson, Blake, LB, Mesa College (CO), 249
10. Brown, Henry, T, Ohio State, 277
11. Koch, Curt, DE, Colorado, 305
12. Ross, Wayne, P, San Diego State [from Los Angeles Rams] 315
Choice to Los Angeles Rams

1989

Held April 23-24, 1989

ATLANTA 1989
1. *Sanders, Deion, DB, Florida State, 5
*Collins, Shawn, WR, Northern Arizona [from Cincinnati] 27
2. Choice to Cincinnati
*Norwood, Ralph, T, Louisiana State [from Los Angeles Raiders thru Washington], 38
3. *Jones, Keith, RB, Illinois, 62
4. Choice to Cincinnati
5. Choice to Dal thru Los Angeles Raiders
6. *Sadowski, Troy, TE, Georgia, 145
7. Johnson, Undra, RB, West Virginia, 172
8. Singer, Paul, QB, Western Illinois, 202
9. Dunn, Chris, LB, Cal Poly-San Luis Obispo, 229
10. Choice to Cincinnati
11. *Paterra, Greg, RB, Slippery Rock, 286
12. *Bowick, Tony, NT, Tennessee-Chattanooga, 313

BUFFALO 1989
1. Choice to Los Angeles Rams
2. Choice to Los Angeles Rams
3. *Beebe, Don, WR, Chadron (NE), 82
4. Kolesar, John, WR, Michigan, 109
5. Andrews, Michael, DB, Alcorn State, 137
6. Doctor, Sean, RB, Marshall, 164
7. *Jordan, Brian, DB, Richmond [from Tampa Bay] 173
*Hale, Chris, DB, Southern California, 193
8. Choice to Kansas City
9. Rabold, Pat, DT, Wyoming, 249
10. Cheattom, Carlo, DB, Auburn, 276
11. *Harvey, Richard, LB, Tulane, 305
12. Marshall, Derrell, T, Southern California, 332

CHICAGO BEARS 1989
1. *Woolford, Donnell, DB, Clemson [from Los Angeles Raiders] 11
*Armstrong, Trace, DE, Florida [from Washington] 12
Choice to Miami
2. *Roper, John, LB, Texas A&M [from Miami] 36
*Zawatson, Dave, T, California, 54
3. *Fontenot, Jerry, G, Texas A&M [from Miami] 65
Choice to Philadelphia
4. *Paul, Markus, DB, Syracuse [from Los Angeles Raiders] 95
Choice to Washington thru Los Angeles Raiders
5. *Green, Mark, RB, Notre Dame [from Philadelphia] 130
Gilbert, Greg, LB, Alabama, 136
6. Choice to New England thru Los Angeles Raiders
7. Brothers, Richard, DB, Arkansas [from Philadelphia] 189
Snyder, Brent, QB, Utah State, 192
8. *Woods, Tony, DT, Oklahoma [from Philadelphia] 216
*Dyko, Chris, T, Washington State, 221
9. *Harper, LaSalle, LB, Arkansas [from Philadelphia] 243
Sanders, Byron, RB, Northwestern, 248
10. Millikan, Todd, TE, Nebraska [from Philadelphia] 270
Simpson, John, WR, Baylor, 277
11. Nelms, Joe, DT, California [from Philadelphia] 297
*Streeter, George, DB, Notre Dame, 304
12. Weygand, Freddy, WR, Auburn [from Philadelphia] 330
Phillips, Anthony, G, Oklahoma, 333

CINCINNATI 1989
1. Choice to Atlanta
2. *Ball, Eric, RB, UCLA [from Atlanta] 35
*Childress, Freddie, G, Arkansas, 55
3. *Wilhelm, Erik, QB, Oregon State, 83
4. Owens, Kerry, LB, Arkansas [from Atlanta] 89
*Woods, Rob, T, Arizona, 111
5. *Tuatagaloa, Natu, DT, California, 138
6. *Taylor, Craig, RB, West Virginia, 166
7. *Smith, Kendal, WR, Utah State, 194
8. Chenault, Chris, LB, Kentucky, 222
9. Stephens, Richard, T, Tulsa, 250
10. *Holloway, Cornell, DB, Pittsburgh [from Atlanta] 256
Jean, Bob, QB, New Hampshire, 278
11. *Wells, Dana, DT, Arizona, 306
12. *Jones, Scott, T, Washington, 334

CLEVELAND 1989
1. *Metcalf, Eric, RB, Texas [from Denver] 13
Choice to Denver
2. *Tillman, Lawyer, WR, Auburn [from Green Bay] 31
Choice to Denver
3. Choice to Green Bay
4. *Stewart, Andrew, DE, Cincinnati, 107
5. *Kramer, Kyle, DB, Bowling Green [from Green Bay] 114
*Joines, Vernon, WR, Maryland [from Kansas City] 116
Choice to Denver
6. Wilkerson, Gary, DB, Penn State, 160
7. *Graybill, Mike, T, Boston U., 187
8. Aeilts, Rick, TE, Southeastern Missouri, 214
9. Choice to Denver
10. Buddenberg, John, T, Akron, 274
11. Plocki, Dan, K, Maryland, 301
12. Brown, Marlon, LB, Memphis State, 328

DALLAS 1989
1. *Aikman, Troy, QB, UCLA, 1
2. Choice to Los Angeles Raiders
*Johnston, Daryl, RB, Syracuse [from Washington thru Los Angeles Raiders] 39
3. *Stepnoski, Mark, G, Pittsburgh, 57
*Weston, Rhondy, DE, Florida [from Los Angeles Raiders] 68
4. *Tolbert, Tony, DE, Texas-El Paso, 85
5. *Jennings, Keith, TE, Clemson, 113
*Crockett, Willis, LB, Georgia Tech [from Atlanta thru Los Angeles Raiders] 119
Roth, Jeff, DT, Florida [from Denver] 125
6. Choice to Los Angeles Raiders
7. Peterson, Kevin, LB, Northwestern, 168
8. Foger, Charvez, RB, Nevada-Reno, 196
9. *Jackson, Tim, DB, Nebraska, 224
10. Carter, Rod, LB, Miami, 252
11. *Shannon, Randy, LB, Miami, 280
12. *Ankrom, Scott, WR, Texas Christian, 308

DENVER 1989
1. Choice to Cleveland
*Atwater, Steve, DB, Arkansas [from Cleveland] 20
2. *Widell, Doug, G, Boston College, 41
*Powers, Warren, DE, Maryland [from Cleveland] 47
3. *Hamilton, Darrell, T, North Carolina, 69
4. *McCullough, Richard, DE, Clemson, 97
5. Choice to Dallas
*Carrington, Darren, DB, Northern Arizona [from Cleveland]134
6. Stafford, Anthony, WR, Oklahoma, 152
7. *Bratton, Melvin, RB, Miami, 180
8. *Green, Paul, TE, Southern California, 208
9. *Smith, Monte, G, North Dakota, 236
Williams, Wayne, RB, Florida [from Cleveland] 241
10. Butts, Anthony, DT, Mississippi State, 264
11. *Shelton, Richard, DB, Liberty U., 292
12. Javis, John, WR, Howard, 320

DETROIT 1989
1. *Sanders, Barry, RB, Oklahoma State, 3
2. *Ford, John, WR, Virginia, 30
3. *Utley, Mike, G, Washington State, 59
4. *Crockett, Ray, DB, Baylor, 86
5. *Pete, Lawrence, DT, Nebraska, 115
6. *Peete, Rodney, QB, Southern California, 141
7. *Woods, Jerry, DB, Northern Michigan, 170
8. Parker, Chris, DT, West Virginia, 197
9. MacCready, Derek, DE, Ohio State, 226
10. *Phillips, Jason, WR, Houston, 253
11. *Kapinski, Keith, LB, Penn State, 282
12. *Cribbs, James, DE, Memphis State, 309

GREEN BAY 1989
1. *Mandarich, Tony, T, Michigan State, 2
2. Choice to Cleveland
3. *Brock, Matt, DE, Oregon, 58
*Dilweg, Anthony, QB, Duke [from Cleveland] 74
4. Graham, Jeff, QB, Long Beach State, 87
5. Choice to Cleveland
*Query, Jeff, WR, Millikin [from Washington] 124
*Workman, Vince, RB, Ohio State [from New England thru Cleveland] 127
6. *Jacke, Chris, K, Texas-El Paso, 142
7. *Hall, Mark, DE, Southwestern Louisiana, 169
8. King, Thomas, DB, Southwestern Louisiana, 198
Shulman, Brian, P, Auburn [from Washington] 206
9. Kirby, Scott, T, Arizona State, 225
10. Jessie, Ben, DB, Southwest Texas State, 254
11. Stallworth, Cedric, DB, Georgia Tech, 281
12. Shiver, Stan, DB, Florida State, 310

HOUSTON 1989
1. *Williams, David, T, Florida, 23
2. *Kozak, Scott, LB, Oregon, 50
3. *McDowell, Bubba, DB, Miami, 77
4. *Harris, Rod, WR, Texas A&M, 104
5. *Montgomery, Glenn, NT, Houston, 131
6. *Orlando, Bo, DB, West Virginia, 157
7. *Rogers, Tracy, LB, Fresno State, 190
8. *Mays, Alvoid, DB, West Virginia, 217
9. *Mrosko, Bob, TE, Penn State, 244
10. *Johnson, Tracy, RB, Clemson, 271
11. Smider, Brian, T, West Virginia, 298
12. Hartlieb, Chuck, QB, Iowa, 325

INDIANAPOLIS 1989
1. Choice to Seattle
*Rison, Andre, WR, Michigan State [from Philadelphia] 22
2. Choice to Los Angeles Rams
3. *Benson, Mitchell, DT, Texas Christian, 72
4. *Tomberlin, Pat, G, Florida State, 99
5. Choice to Washington
6. *McDonald, Quintus, LB, Penn State, 155
7. *Hunter, Ivy Joe, RB, Kentucky, 182
*Washington, Charles, DB, Cameron [from New York Giants] 185
8. *Larson, Kurt, LB, Michigan State, 212
9. Mackall, William, WR, Tennessee-Martin, 239
10. Thompson, Jim, T, Auburn, 266
11. Johnson, Wayne, QB, Georgia, 296
12. DuBose, William, RB, S. Carolina State [from Tampa Bay] 314
Taylor, Steve, QB, Nebraska, 323

KANSAS CITY 1989
1. *Thomas, Derrick, LB, Alabama, 4
2. *Elkins, Mike, QB, Wake Forest, 32
3. *Worthen, Naz, WR, North Carolina State, 60
4. *Petry, Stanley, DB, Texas Christian, 88
5. Choice to Cleveland
6. *Thomas, Robb, WR, Oregon State, 143
7. Sancho, Ron, LB, Louisiana State, 171
8. Tobey, Bryan, RB, Grambling, 199
*McNair, Todd, RB, Temple [from Buffalo] 220
9. Phillips, Jack, DB, Alcorn State, 227
10. *McGovern, Rob, LB, Holy Cross, 255
11. *Turner, Marcus, DB, UCLA, 283
12. *Jones, Bill, RB, Southwest Texas State, 311

LOS ANGELES RAIDERS 1989
1. Choice to Chicago Bears
2. *Wisniewski, Steve, G, Penn State, 29 [from Dallas] 29
Choice to Atlanta thru Washington
3. Choice to Dallas
4. Choice to Chicago Bears
5. Choice to San Francisco
6. *Francis, Jeff, QB, Tennessee [from Dallas] 140
Choice to New York Jets
*Lloyd, Doug, RB, North Dakota State [from New England] 156
7. Choice to New England
8. *Gainer, Derrick, RB, Florida A&M, 205
9. Gooden, Gary, DB, Indiana, 235
10. Jackson, Charles, DT, Jackson State, 262
11. Choice to San Francisco
12. Choice to San Francisco

LOS ANGELES RAMS 1989
1. *Hawkins, Bill, DE, Miami, 21
*Gary, Cleveland, RB, Miami [from Buffalo] 26
2. *Stams, Frank, LB, Notre Dame [from Indianapolis] 45
*Smith, Brian, LB, Auburn, 48
*Henley, Darryl, DB, UCLA [from Buffalo] 53
3. *Robbins, Kevin, T, Michigan State, 75
4. *Carlson, Jeff, QB, Weber State, 102
5. *Jackson, Alfred, WR, San Diego State, 135
6. *Kaumeyer, Thom, DB, Oregon [from San Diego] 148
*Messner, Mark, LB, Michigan, 161
7. *Bethune, George, LB, Alabama, 188
8. *Wheat, Warren, T, Brigham Young, 215
9. Kirk, Vernon, TE, Pittsburgh, 242
10. *Williams, Mike, WR, Northeastern, 269
11. Choice to Tampa Bay
12. Choice to Tampa Bay

MIAMI 1989
1. *Smith, Sammie, RB, Florida State, 9
*Oliver, Louis, DB, Florida [from Chicago Bears] 25
2. Choice to Chicago Bears
3. Choice to Chicago Bears
4. Holmes, David, DB, Syracuse, 92
5. *Uhlenhake, Jeff, C, Ohio State, 121
6. *Pritchett, Wes, LB, Notre Dame, 147
7. Zdelar, Jim, T, Youngstown, 176
8. *Stoyanovich, Pete, K, Indiana, 203
9. Batiste, Dana, LB, Texas A&M, 232
10. Glover, Deval, WR, Syracuse, 259
Ross, Greg, NT, Memphis State [from Minnesota] 275
11. *Weidner, Bert, DT, Kent State, 288
12. *Brown, J.B., DB, Maryland, 315

MINNESOTA 1989
1. Choice to Pittsburgh
2. *Braxton, David, LB, Wake Forest, 52
3. *Hunter, John, T, Brigham Young, 80
4. *Ingram, Darryl, TE, California, 108
5. Choice exercised in 1988 Supplemental Draft (Bethea, Ryan, WR, South Carolina)
6. *Mickel, Jeff, T, Eastern Washington, 163
7. *Roland, Benji, DT, Auburn, 191
8. Stewart, Alex, DE, Cal State-Fullerton, 219
9. Choice to New England
10. Choice to Miami
11. *Baxter, Brad, RB, Alabama State, 303
12. Woodson, Shawn, LB, James Madison, 331
Ross, Everett, WR, Ohio State [from San Francisco thru Los Angeles Raiders] 335

NEW ENGLAND 1989
1. *Dykes, Hart Lee, WR, Oklahoma State, 16
2. *Coleman, Eric, DB, Wyoming, 43
3. *Cook, Marv, TE, Iowa [from Tampa Bay] 63
*Gannon, Chris, DE, Southwestern Louisiana, 73
4. *Hurst, Maurice, DB, Southern U. [from Washington] 96
*Timpson, Michael, WR, Penn State, 100
5. Choice to Green Bay thru Cleveland
6. Choice to Los Angeles Raiders
Mitchel, Eric, RB, Oklahoma [from Chicago Bears thru Los Angeles Raiders] 165
7. Lindstrom, Eric, LB, Boston College [from Los Angeles Raiders] 178
Choice to San Diego
8. *Rice, Rodney, DB, Brigham Young, 210
*Zackery, Tony, DB, Washington [from San Francisco thru Los Angeles Raiders] 223
9. Norris, Darron, RB, Texas, 240
Wilson, Curtis, C, Missouri [from Minnesota] 247
10. *McNeil, Emanuel, DT, Tennessee-Martin, 267
11. Hinz, Tony, RB, Harvard, 294
12. Chubb, Aaron, LB, Georgia, 324

NEW ORLEANS 1989
1. *Martin, Wayne, DE, Arkansas, 19
2. *Massey, Robert, DB, North Carolina Central, 46
3. *Phillips, Kim, DB, North Texas State, 79
4. *Mayes, Mike, DB, Louisiana State, 106
5. *Haverdink, Kevin, T, Western Michigan, 133
6. *Turner, Floyd, WR, Northwest Louisiana, 159
7. *Griggs, David, LB, Virginia, 186
8. Hadley, Fred, WR, Mississippi State, 213
9. Leggett, Jerry, LB, Cal State-Fullerton, 246
10. Henderson, Joe, RB, Iowa State, 273
11. *Nicholson, Calvin, DB, Oregon State, 300
12. Cadore, Mike, WR, Eastern Kentucky, 327

NEW YORK GIANTS 1989
1. *Williams, Brian, G, Minnesota, 18
2. Choice to San Diego
3. *Kratch, Bob, G, Iowa [from San Diego] 64
*Jackson, Greg, DB, Louisiana State, 78

4. *Tillman, Lewis, RB, Jackson State [from San Diego] 93
*Henke, Brad, NT, Arizona, 105
5. *Meggett, Dave, RB, Towson State, 132
6. *Cross, Howard, TE, Alabama, 158
7. Popp, Dave, T, Eastern Illinois [from San Diego] 175
Choice to Indianapolis
8. *Guyton, Myron, DB, Eastern Kentucky, 218
9. Greene, A.J., DB, Wake Forest, 245
10. Lowe, Rodney, DE, Mississippi, 272
11. Rinehart, Jerome, LB, Tennessee-Martin, 299
12. Smith, Eric, LB, UCLA, 326

NEW YORK JETS 1989
1. *Lageman, Jeff, LB, Virginia, 14
2. *Byrd, Dennis, DE, Tulsa, 42
3. *Mott, Joe, LB, Iowa, 70
4. *Stallworth, Ron, DE, Auburn, 98
5. *Martin, Tony, WR, Mesa (CO), 126
6. *Washington, Marvin, DE, Idaho [from Los Angeles Raiders] 151
*Dixon, Titus, WR, Troy State, 153
7. *Moore, Stevon, DB, Mississippi, 181
8. *Brown, Anthony, RB, West Virginia, 209
9. Marlatt, Pat, DT, West Virginia, 237
10. *Bob, Adam, LB, Texas A&M, 265
11. Holmes, Artie, DB, Washington State, 293
12. Snead, Willie, WR, Florida, 321

PHILADELPHIA 1989
1. Choice to Indianapolis
2. *Small, Jessie, LB, Eastern Kentucky, 49
3. *Drummond, Robert, RB, Syracuse, 76
*Hager, Britt, LB, Texas [from Chicago Bears] 81
4. Choice to Seattle
5. Choice to Chicago Bears
6. *Sherman, Heath, RB, Texas A&I, 162
7. Choice to Chicago Bears
8. Choice to Chicago Bears
9. Choice to Chicago Bears
10. Choice to Chicago Bears
11. Choice to Chicago Bears
12. Choice to Chicago Bears

PHOENIX 1989
1. *Hill, Eric, LB, Louisiana State, 10
*Wolf, Joe, G, Boston College [from Seattle] 17
2. *Reeves, Walter, TE, Auburn, 40
3. *Zandofsky, Mike, G, Washington, 67
4. *Wahler, Jim, DT, UCLA, 94
5. *Tardits, Richard, LB, Georgia, 123
Edeen, David, DE, Wyoming [from Seattle] 128
6. *Taylor, Jay, DB, San Jose State, 150
7. *Royal, Rickey, DB, Sam Houston State, 177
8. Burch, John, RB, Tennessee-Martin, 207
9. Trainor, Kendall, K, Arkansas, 234
10. Becker, Chris, P, Texas Christian, 261
11. *Hunter, Jeffrey, DE, Albany State (GA), 291
12. Nelson, Todd, G, Wisconsin, 318

PITTSBURGH 1989
1. *Worley, Tim, RB, Georgia, 7
*Ricketts, Tom, T, Pittsburgh [from Minnesota] 24
2. *Lake, Carnell, DB, UCLA, 34
3. *Hill, Derek, WR, Arizona, 61
4. *Williams, Jerrol, LB, Purdue, 91
5. *Arnold, David, DB, Michigan, 118
6. *Stock, Mark, WR, Virginia Military, 144
7. *Johnson, D.J., DB, Kentucky, 174
8. Asbeck, Chris, NT, Cincinnati, 201
9. *Jenkins, A.J., DE, Cal State-Fullerton, 228
10. *Olsavsky, Jerry, LB, Pittsburgh, 258
11. Slater, Brian, WR, Washington, 285
12. *Haselrig, Carlton, DE, Pitt-Johnstown, 312

SAN DIEGO 1989
1. *Grossman, Burt, DE, Pittsburgh, 8
2. *Hall, Courtney, C, Rice, 37
*Tolliver, Billy Joe, QB, Texas Tech [from New York Giants] 51
3. Choice to New York Giants
4. Choice to New York Giants
5. *Smith, Elliot, DB, Alcorn State, 120
6. Choice to Los Angeles Rams
7. Choice to New York Giants
*Butts, Marion, RB, Florida State [from New England] 183
Jones, Terrence, QB, Tulane [from San Francisco] 195
8. *Brinson, Dana, WR, Nebraska, 204
9. Davis, Pat, TE, Syracuse, 231
10. *Andrews, Ricky, LB, Washington, 260
11. *Floyd, Victor, RB, Florida State, 287
12. Choice to Washington

SAN FRANCISCO 1989
1. *DeLong, Keith, LB, Tennessee, 28
2. *Walls, Wesley, TE, Mississippi, 56
3. *Henderson, Keith, RB, Georgia, 84
4. *Barber, Mike, WR, Marshall, 112
5. *Jackson, Johnny, DB, Houston [from Los Angeles Raiders] 122
Choice to Washington thru LA Raiders
6. *Hendrickson, Steve, LB, California, 167
7. Choice to San Diego
8. Choice to New England thru LA Raiders
9. Harmon, Rudy, LB, Louisiana State, 251
10. Sinclair, Andy, C, Stanford, 279
11. Bell, Jim, RB, Boston College [from Los Angeles Raiders] 289
McGee, Norm, WR, North Dakota, 307
12. *Goss, Antonio, LB, North Carolina [from Los Angeles Raiders] 319
Choice to Minnesota thru Los Angeles Raiders

SEATTLE 1989
1. *Heck, Andy, T, Notre Dame [from Indianapolis] 15
Choice to Phoenix
2. *Tofflemire, Joe, C, Arizona, 44
3. *Harris, Elroy, RB, Eastern Kentucky, 71
4. *McNeal, Travis, TE, Tennessee-Chattanooga, 101
Henry, James, DB, S. Mississippi [from Philadelphia] 103
5. Choice to Phoenix
6. Choice to Tampa Bay
7. Nettles, Mike, DB, Memphis State, 184
8. Williams, Martin, DE, Western Illinois, 211
9. Franks, David, G, Connecticut, 238
10. *Fenner, Derrick, RB, North Carolina, 268
11. Baum, Mike, DE, Northwestern 295
12. *Kors, R.J., DB, Long Beach State, 322

TAMPA BAY 1989
1. *Thomas, Broderick, LB, Nebraska, 6
2. *Peebles, Danny, WR, North Carolina State, 33
3. Choice to New England
4. Florence, Anthony, DB, Bethune-Cookman, 90
5. *Lawson, Jamie, RB, Nicholls State, 117
6. *Mohr, Chris, P, Alabama, 146
Little, Derrick, LB, South Carolina [from Seattle] 154
7. Choice to Buffalo
8. *Bax, Carl, G, Missouri, 200
9. *Egu, Patrick, RB, Nevada-Reno, 230
10. Granger, Ty, T, Clemson, 257
11. Mounts, Rod, G, Texas A&I, 284
Griffin, Willie, DE, Nebraska [from Was thru Los Angeles Rams] 290
Duncan, Herb, WR, Northern Arizona [from Los Angeles Rams] 302
12. Choice to Indianapolis
Young, Terry, DB, Georgia Southern [from Los Angeles Rams] 329

WASHINGTON 1989
1. Choice to Chicago Bears
2. Choice to Dallas thru Los Angeles Raiders
3. *Rocker, Tracy, DT, Auburn, 66
4. Choice to New England
*Affholter, Erik, WR, Southern California [from Chicago Bears thru Los Angeles Raiders] 110
5. Choice to Green Bay
Smiley, Tim, DB, Arkansas State [from Indianapolis] 129
*Robinson, Lybrant, DE, Delaware State [from San Francisco thru Los Angeles Raiders] 139
6. *Johnson, A.J., DB, Southwest Texas State, 149
7. Hendrix, Kevin, LB, South Carolina, 179
8. Choice to Green Bay
9. Darrington, Charles, TE, Kentucky, 233
10. *Schlereth, Mark, C, Idaho, 263
11. Choice to Tampa Bay thru Los Angeles Rams
12. Johnson, Jimmie, TE, Howard [from San Diego] 316
*Mickles, Joe, RB, Mississippi, 317

1990

Held April 22-23, 1990

ATLANTA 1990
1. Choice to Indianapolis
*Broussard, Steve, RB, Washington State [from Washington] 20
2. *Conner, Darion, LB, Jackson State, 27
3. *Barnett, Oliver, DE, Kentucky, 55
4. Choice to Indianapolis
5. Choice to Denver thru Washington and New England
*Redding, Reggie, TE, Cal State-Fullerton [from Indianapolis] 121
6. *Pringle, Mike, RB, Cal State-Fullerton, 139
7. Choice to New York Jets
8. *Epps, Tory, NT, Memphis State, 195
9. Jordan, Darrell, LB, Northern Arizona, 222
10. Salum, Donnie, LB, Arizona, 250
11. Ellison, Chris, DB, Houston, 278
12. McCarthy, Shawn, P, Purdue, 305

BUFFALO 1990
1. *Williams, James, DB, Fresno State, 16
2. *Gardner, Carwell, RB, Louisville, 42
3. *Parker, Glenn, T, Arizona, 69
4. *Fuller, Eddie, RB, Louisiana State, 100
5. Choice to Kansas City
6. *Nies, John, P, Arizona, 154
7. Griffith, Brent, G, Minnesota-Duluth [from Dallas thru New England] 166
Collins, Brent, LB, Carson-Newman [from New England] 170
*DeRiggi, Fred, NT, Syracuse, 181
8. *Patton, Marvcus, LB, UCLA [from Kansas City] 208
Choice exercised in 1989 Supplemental Draft (Young, Brett, DB, Oregon)
9. Hines, Clarkston, WR, Duke, 238
10. *Lodish, Mike, DT, UCLA, 265
11. *Edwards, Al, WR, Northwest Louisiana, 292
12. Choice to New England

CHICAGO BEARS 1990
1. *Carrier, Mark, DB, Southern California, 6
2. *Washington, Fred, DT, Texas Christian, 32
*Cox, Ron, LB, Fresno State [from San Diego] 33
3. *Ryan, Tim, DT, Southern California, 61
*Willis, Peter Tom, QB, Florida State [from Los Angeles Raiders] 63
4. Moss, Tony, WR, Louisiana State, 88
5. *Chaffey, Pat, RB, Oregon State, 117
6. *Mangum, John, DB, Alabama, 144
7. Choice to Los Angeles Raiders
Anderson, Bill, C, Iowa [from Los Angeles Raiders] 176
8. *Rouse, James, RB, Arkansas, 200
9. *Bailey, Johnny, RB, Texas A&I, 228
10. *Price, Terry, DT, Texas A&M, 255
11. White, Brent, DE, Michigan, 284
Matusz, Roman, T, Pittsburgh [from Minnesota thru Los Angeles Raiders] 298
12. Cooney, Anthony, DB, Arkansas, 310

CINCINNATI 1990
1. *Francis, James, LB, Baylor, 12
2. *Green, Harold, RB, South Carolina, 38
3. *Clark, Bernard, LB, Miami, 65
4. *Brennan, Mike, T, Notre Dame, 91
5. *James, Lynn, WR, Arizona State, 122
6. *Odegard, Don, DB, Nevada-Las Vegas, 150
7. *Ogletree, Craig, LB, Auburn, 177
8. *Wellsandt, Doug, TE, Washington State, 204
9. *Price, Mitchell, DB, Tulane, 234
10. Crigler, Eric, T, Murray State, 261
11. O'Connor, Tim, T, Virginia, 288
12. Riley, Andre, WR, Washington, 314

CLEVELAND 1990
1. Choice to Green Bay
2. *Hoard, Leroy, RB, Michigan, 45
3. *Pleasant, Anthony, DE, Tennessee State, 73
4. *Barnett, Harlon, DB, Michigan State, 101
5. *Burnett, Rob, DE, Syracuse, 129
6. *Hilliard, Randy, DB, Northwest Louisiana, 157
7. *Galbraith, Scott, TE, Southern California [from Miami] 178
Choice to San Diego
8. *Jones, Jock, LB, Virginia Tech, 212
9. *Rowell, Eugene, WR, Southern Mississippi, 240
10. Wallace, Michael, DB, Jackson State, 268
11. Gordon, Clemente, QB, Grambling, 296
12. Simien, Kerry, WR, Texas A&I, 323

DALLAS 1990
1. Choice exercised in 1989 Supplemental Draft (Walsh, Steve, QB, Miami)
*Smith, Emmitt, RB, Florida [from Pittsburgh] 17
2. *Wright, Alexander, WR, Auburn, 26
3. Choice to Minnesota
*Jones, Jimmie, DT, Miami [from Seattle thru New England] 64
4. Choice to Denver
5. Choice to New England thru Washington
*Smagala, Stan, DB, Notre Dame [from Los Angeles Raiders] 123
6. Choice to San Diego
7. Choice to Buffalo thru New England
8. Choice to Detroit
9. *Gant, Kenneth, DB, Albany State (GA), 221
10. Choice to Minnesota
11. *Harper, Dave, LB, Humboldt State, 277
12. Choice exercised in 1989 Supplemental Draft (Lowman, Mike, RB, Coffeyville JC)

DENVER 1990
1. Choice exercised in 1989 Supplemental Draft (Humphrey, Bobby, RB, Alabama)
2. *Montgomery, Alton, DB, Houston, 52
3. Choice to New England thru Dallas
4. *Robinson, Jeroy, LB, Texas A&M [from Dallas] 82
Choice to Tampa Bay
5. *Davidson, Jeff, G, Ohio State [from Atlanta thru Washington and New England] 111
*Lang, Le-Lo, DB, Washington, 136
6. *Haliburton, Ronnie, TE, Louisiana State, 164
7. *Sharpe, Shannon, WR, Savannah State, 192
8. *Leggett, Brad, C, Southern California, 219
9. Ellis, Todd, QB, South Carolina, 247
10. *Szymanski, James, DE, Michigan State [from Indianapolis thru Dallas and Los Angeles Raiders] 259
*Thompson, Anthony, LB, East Carolina, 275
11. Choice to Los Angeles Raiders
12. Choice to Phoenix

DETROIT 1990
1. *Ware, Andre, QB, Houston, 7
2. *Owens, Dan, DE, Southern California, 35
3. *Spindler, Marc, DE, Pittsburgh, 62
4. Hinckley, Rob, LB, Stanford, 90
*Oldham, Chris, DB, Oregon [from Los Angeles Rams] 105
5. *Campbell, Jeff, WR, Colorado, 118
6. *Henry, Maurice, LB, Kansas State, 147
7. *Hayworth, Tracy, LB, Tennessee, 174
8. *Green, Willie, WR, Mississippi [from Dallas] 194
*Fortin, Roman, G, San Diego State, 203
9. *Linn, Jack, T, West Virginia, 229
10. Miller, Bill, WR, Illinois State, 258
11. Warnsley, Reginald, RB, Southern Mississippi, 285
12. *Claiborne, Robert, WR, San Diego State, 313

GREEN BAY 1990
1. *Bennett, Tony, LB, Mississippi [from Cleveland] 18
*Thompson, Darrell, RB, Minnesota, 19
2. *Butler, LeRoy, DB, Florida State, 48
3. *Houston, Bobby, LB, North Carolina State, 75
4. *Harris, Jackie, TE, Northeast Louisiana, 102
5. *Wilson, Charles, WR, Memphis State, 132
6. *Paup, Bryce, LB, Northern Iowa, 159
7. *Archambeau, Lester, DE, Stanford, 186
8. *Brown, Roger, DB, Virginia Tech, 215
9. Baumgartner, Kirk, QB, Wisconsin-Stevens Point, 242
10. Martin, Jerome, DB, Western Kentucky, 269
11. Jackson, Harry, RB, St. Cloud (MN), 299
12. Maggio, Kirk, P, UCLA, 325

HOUSTON 1990
1. *Lathon, Lamar, LB, Houston, 15
2. *Alm, Jeff, DT, Notre Dame, 41
3. *Peguese, Willis, DE, Miami, 72
4. Still, Eric, G, Tennessee, 99
5. *Newbill, Richard, LB, Miami, 126
6. *Jones, Tony, WR, Texas, 153
7. Murray, Andy, RB, Kentucky, 184
8. Tucker, Brett, DB, Northern Illinois, 211
9. *Coleman, Pat, WR, Mississippi, 237
10. *Thomas, Dee, DB, Nicholls State, 264
11. *Banes, Joey, T, Houston, 295
12. Slack, Reggie, QB, Auburn, 321

INDIANAPOLIS 1990
1. *George, Jeff, QB, Illinois [from Atlanta] 1
2. *Johnson, Anthony, RB, Notre Dame, 36
3. Choice to San Diego
4. *Simmons, Stacey, WR, Florida [from Atlanta] 83
*Schultz, Bill, G, Southern California, 94
*Grant, Alan, DB, Stanford [from Washington] 103
*Cunningham, Rick, T, Texas A&M [from Philadelphia] 106
5. Choice to Atlanta
6. *Walker, Tony, LB, Southeast Missouri, 148
7. Singletary, James, LB, East Carolina, 179
8. *Clark, Ken, RB, Nebraska, 206
Wilson, Harvey, DB, Southern U. [from Washington] 213
9. *Huffman, Darvell, WR, Boston U., 232
10. Choice to Denver thru Dallas and Los Angeles Raiders
11. Smith, Carnel, DE, Pittsburgh, 290
12. Benhart, Gene, QB, Western Illinois [from San Diego] 311
Brown, Dean, G, Notre Dame, 316

KANSAS CITY 1990
1. *Snow, Percy, LB, Michigan State, 13
2. *Grunhard, Tim, C, Notre Dame, 40
3. Choice to San Francisco thru Dallas
4. *Jones, Fred, WR, Grambling, 96
5. *Graham, Derrick, T, Appalachian State, 124
Hackemack, Ken, T, Texas [from Buffalo] 127
6. *Sims, Tom, DT, Pittsburgh, 152
7. *Szott, Dave, G, Penn State, 180
8. Choice to Buffalo
9. Owens, Michael, RB, Syracuse, 235
10. Hudson, Craig, TE, Wisconsin, 263
11. Thompson, Ernest, RB, Georgia Southern, 291
12. Jeffery, Tony, WR, San Jose State, 318

LOS ANGELES RAIDERS 1990
1. *Smith, Anthony, DE, Arizona, 11
2. *Wallace, Aaron, LB, Texas A&M, 37
3. Choice to Chicago Bears
4. *Dorn, Torin, DB, North Carolina, 95
5. Choice to Dallas
6. *Wilson, Marcus, RB, Virginia, 149
7. *Lewis, Garry, DB, Alcorn State [from Chicago Bears] 173
Choice to Chicago Bears
8. *Jimerson, Arthur, LB, Norfolk State [from New England Patriots thru Dallas] 197
Choice to New Orleans
9. Perry, Leon, RB, Oklahoma [from Seattle thru Dallas] 230
Choice to New Orleans
10. Choice to New Orleans
11. Choice to New Orleans
Lewis, Ron, WR, Jackson State [from Denver] 303
Jones, Myron, DB, Fresno State [from San Francisco thru Dallas] 304
12. Harris, Major, QB, West Virginia, 317
Davis, Demetrius, TE, Nevada-Reno [from San Francisco] 331

LOS ANGELES RAMS 1990
1. *Brostek, Bern, C, Washington, 23
2. *Terrell, Pat, DB, Notre Dame, 49
3. *Berry, Latin, RB, Oregon, 78
4. Choice to Detroit
5. Choice to New York Jets
6. *Stallworth, Tim, WR, Washington State, 161
7. Elmore, Kent, P, Tennessee, 190
8. Savage, Ray, LB, Virginia [from Tampa Bay] 198

*Crawford, Elbert, C, Arkansas, 216
9. *Lomack, Tony, WR, Florida, 245
10. Bates, Steve, DE, James Madison, 272
11. *Goldberg, Bill, DT, Georgia, 301
12. *Lang, David, RB, Northern Arizona, 328

MIAMI 1990
1. *Webb, Richmond, T, Texas A&M, 9
2. *Sims, Keith, G, Iowa State, 39
3. *Oglesby, Alfred, DT, Houston, 66
4. *Mitchell, Scott, QB, Utah, 93
5. Choice to New England thru Dallas
   Holt, Leroy, RB, Southern California [from San Francisco thru Los Angeles Raiders and Washington] 137
6. *Vanhorse, Sean, DB, Howard, 151
7. Choice to Cleveland
8. Woods, Thomas, WR, Tennessee, 205
9. Ross, Phil, TE, Oregon State, 231
10. Choice to Washington
11. Choice to San Francisco
12. *Harden, Bobby, DB, Miami, 315

MINNESOTA 1990
1. Choice to Pittsburgh thru Dallas
2. Choice to San Francisco thru Dallas
3. *Jones, Mike, TE, Texas A&M [from Dallas] 54
   *Hobby, Marion, DE, Tennessee, 74
4. *Hampton, Alonzo, DB, Pittsburgh, 104
5. Thornton, Reggie, WR, Bowling Green [from San Diego thru Dal] 116
   *Smith, Cedric, RB, Florida, 131
6. Choice to New Orleans thru Dallas and Los Angeles Raiders
7. Levelis, John, LB, C.W. Post, 188
8. Schlichting, Craig, DE, Wyoming, 214
9. *Allen, Terry, RB, Clemson, 241
10. *Newman, Pat, WR, Utah State [from Dallas] 249
    *Smith, Donald, DB, Liberty, 271
11. Choice to Chicago Bears thru Los Angeles Raiders
12. Goetz, Ron, LB, Minnesota, 324

NEW ENGLAND 1990
1. Choice to Seattle
   *Singleton, Chris, LB, Arizona [from Seattle] 8
   *Agnew, Ray, DE, North Carolina State [from Indianapolis thru Seattle] 10
2. Choice to Seattle
3. *Hodson, Tommy, QB, Louisiana State, 59
   *McMurtry, Greg, WR, Michigan [from Denver thru Dallas] 80
4. Choice to Washington
5. *Robinson, Junior, DB, East Carolina [from Dal thru Washington] 110
   *Melander, Jon, T, Minnesota, 113
   Gray, James, RB, Texas Tech [from Miami thru Dallas] 120
6. Choice to San Diego thru Dallas
7. Choice to Buffalo
8. Choice to Los Angeles Raiders thru Dallas
9. *Bouwens, Shawn, G, Nebraska Wesleyan, 226
10. Landry, Anthony, RB, Stephen F. Austin, 253
11. *Smith, Sean, DE, Georgia Tech, 280
12. Donelson, Ventson, DB, Michigan State, 309
    Rose, Blaine, G, Maryland [from Buffalo] 322

NEW ORLEANS 1990
1. *Turnbull, Renaldo, DE, West Virginia, 14
2. *Buck, Vince, DB, Central State (OH), 44
3. *Smeenge, Joel, DE, Western Michigan, 71
4. *Winston, DeMond, LB, Vanderbilt, 98
5. *Arbuckle, Charles, TE, UCLA, 125
6. *Buck, Mike, QB, Maine, 156
   *Williams, James, LB, Mississippi State [from Minnesota thru Dallas and Los Angeles Raiders] 158
7. Hough, Scott, G, Maine, 183
8. Gdowski, Gerry, QB, Nebraska [from Los Angeles Raiders] 207
   Carr, Derrick, DE, Bowling Green, 210
9. Graves, Broderick, RB, Winston-Salem State [from Los Angeles Raiders] 233
   Brockman, Lonnie, LB, West Virginia, 236
10. Cooper, Gary, WR, Clemson [from Los Angeles Raiders] 260
    *Spears, Ernest, DB, Southern California, 267
11. Burnett, Webbie, NT, Western Kentucky [from Los Angeles Raiders] 287
    Choice to Philadelphia
12. *Port, Chris, G, Duke, 320

NEW YORK GIANTS 1990
1. *Hampton, Rodney, RB, Georgia, 24
2. *Fox, Mike, DT, West Virginia, 51
3. *Mark, Greg, DE, Miami, 79
4. *Whitmore, David, DB, Stephen F. Austin, 107
5. *Kupp, Craig, QB, Pacific Lutheran, 135
6. Choice to San Diego thru Dal
7. Emanuel, Aaron, RB, Southern California, 191
8. Voorhees, Barry, T, Cal State-Northridge, 218
9. James, Clint, DE, Louisiana State, 246
10. Moore, Otis, DT, Clemson, 274
11. Downing, Tim, DE, Washington State, 302
12. *Stover, Matt, K, Louisiana Tech, 329

NEW YORK JETS 1990
1. *Thomas, Blair, RB, Penn State, 2
2. *Rembert, Reggie, WR, West Virginia, 28
3. *Stargell, Tony, DB, Tennessee State, 56
4. *Taylor, Troy, QB, California, 84
5. *Savage, Tony, DT, Washington State, 112
   McWright, Robert, DB, Texas Christian [from Los Angeles Rams] 134
6. *Mathis, Terance, WR, New Mexico, 140
7. *White, Dwayne, G, Alcorn State [from Atlanta] 167
   Proctor, Basil, LB, West Virginia, 168
8. *Duffy, Roger, C, Penn State, 196
9. *Dawkins, Dale, WR, Miami, 223
10. Quast, Brad, LB, Iowa, 251
11. Kelson, Derrick, DB, Purdue, 279
12. *Davis, Darrell, LB, Texas Christian, 306

PHILADELPHIA 1990
1. *Smith, Ben, DB, Georgia, 22
2. *Bellamy, Mike, WR, Illinois, 50
3. *Barnett, Fred, WR, Arkansas State, 77
4. Choice to Indianapolis
5. *Williams, Calvin, WR, Purdue, 133
6. Thompson, Kevin, DB, Oklahoma, 162
7. Strouf, Terry, T, Wisconsin-LaCrosse, 189
8. Dykes, Curt, T, Oregon, 217
9. *Gray, Cecil, DT, North Carolina, 244
10. Adams, Orlando, DT, Jacksonville State, 273
11. *Hudson, John, C, Auburn [from New Orleans] 294
    Watson, Tyrone, WR, Tennessee State, 300
12. Garrett, Judd, RB, Princeton, 327

PHOENIX 1990
1. Choice exercised in 1989 Supplemental Draft (Rosenbach, Timm, QB, Washington State)
2. *Thompson, Anthony, RB, Indiana, 31
3. *Proehl, Ricky, WR, Wake Forest, 58
4. *Davis, Travis, DT, Michigan State, 85
5. *Centers, Larry, RB, Stephen F. Austin, 115
6. Shavers, Tyrone, WR, Lamar, 142
7. *Johnson, Johnny, RB, San Jose State, 169
8. *Washington, Mickey, DB, Texas A&M, 199
9. *Bavaro, David, LB, Syracuse, 225
10. Elle, Dave, TE, South Dakota, 252
11. Norman, Dempsey, WR, St. Francis (IL), 282
12. Riley, Donnie, RB, Central Michigan, 308
    McMichel, Ken, DB, Oklahoma [from Denver] 330

PITTSBURGH 1990
1. Choice to Dallas
   *Green, Eric, TE, Liberty [from Minnesota thru Dallas] 21
2. *Davidson, Kenny, DE, Louisiana State, 43
3. *O'Donnell, Neil, QB, Maryland, 70
   *Veasey, Craig, DT, Houston [from San Francisco thru Dallas] 81
4. *Calloway, Chris, WR, Michigan, 97
5. *Foster, Barry, RB, Arkansas, 128
6. Heard, Ronald, WR, Bowling Green, 155
7. Grayson, Dan, LB, Washington State, 182
8. Dunbar, Karl, DT, Louisiana State, 209
9. *Jones, Gary, DB, Texas A&M, 239
10. *Miles, Eddie, LB, Minnesota, 266
11. *Strzelczyk, Justin, T, Maine, 293
12. *Bell, Richard, RB, Nebraska, 319

SAN DIEGO 1990
1. *Seau, Junior, LB, Southern California, 5
2. Choice to Chicago Bears
3. *Mills, Jeff, LB, Nebraska [from Tampa Bay] 57
   *Goeas, Leo, G, Hawaii, 60
   *Wilson, Walter, WR, East Carolina [from Indianapolis] 67
4. Choice to San Francisco thru Los Angeles Raiders
5. Choice to Minnesota thru Dallas
6. *Friesz, John, QB, Idaho [from Dallas] 138
   *Cornish, Frank, C, UCLA [from New England thru Dallas] 143
   *Pool, David, DB, Carson-Newman, 145
   *Walker, Derrick, TE, Michigan [from New York Giants thru Dallas] 163
7. Novak, Jeff, G, S.W. Texas State, 172
   *Staysniak, Joe, T, Ohio State [from Cleveland] 185
   *Lewis, Nate, WR, Oregon Tech [from Washington] 187
   Collins, Keith, DB, Appalachian State [from San Francisco] 193
8. Flannigan, J.J., RB, Colorado, 201
9. Goetz, Chris, G, Pittsburgh, 227
10. Berry, Kenny, DB, Miami, 256
11. Stowers, Tommie, TE, Missouri, 283
12. Choice to Indianapolis
    Searcy, Elliott, WR, Southern U. [from Washington] 326

SAN FRANCISCO 1990
1. *Carter, Dexter, RB, Florida State, 25
2. *Brown, Dennis, DT, Washington [from Minnesota thru Dallas] 47
   *Davis, Eric, DB, Jacksonville State, 53
3. *Lewis, Ronald, WR, Florida State [from Kansas City thru Dallas] 68
   Choice to Pittsburgh thru Dallas
4. *Caliguire, Dean, C, Pittsburgh [from San Diego thru Los Angeles Raiders] 92
   Choice to Washington thru Los Angeles Raiders
5. Choice to Miami thru Los Angeles Raiders and Washington
6. *Pollack, Frank, T, Northern Arizona, 165
7. Choice to San Diego
8. Pickens, Dwight, WR, Fresno State, 220
9. *Haggins, Odell, DT, Florida State, 248
10. *Harrison, Martin, DE, Washington, 276
11. *Shelton, Anthony, DB, Tennessee State [from Miami] 289
    Choice to Los Angeles Raiders thru Dallas
12. Choice to Los Angeles Raiders

SEATTLE 1990
1. *Kennedy, Cortez, DT, Miami [from New England] 3
   Choice to New England
2. *Wooden, Terry, LB, Syracuse [from New England] 29
   *Blackmon, Robert, DB, Baylor, 34
3. Choice to Dallas thru New England
4. *Warren, Chris, RB, Ferrum (VA), 89
5. *Hayes, Eric, DT, Florida State, 119
6. *Bolcar, Ned, LB, Notre Dame, 146
7. Kula, Bob, T, Michigan State, 175
8. *Hitchcock, Bill, T, Purdue, 202
9. Choice to Los Angeles Raiders thru Dallas
10. Morris, Robert, DE, Valdosta State, 257
11. Reed, Daryl, DB, Oregon, 286
12. Gromos, John, QB, Vanderbilt, 312

TAMPA BAY 1990
1. *McCants, Keith, LB, Alabama, 4
2. *Cobb, Reggie, RB, Tennessee, 30
3. Choice to San Diego
4. *Anderson, Jesse, TE, Mississippi State, 87
   *Mayberry, Tony, C, Wake Forest [from Denver] 108
5. *Beckles, Ian, G, Indiana, 114
6. *Douglas, Derrick, RB, Louisiana Tech, 141
7. *Gardner, Donnie, DE, Kentucky, 171
8. Choice to Los Angeles Rams
9. Cook, Terry, DE, Fresno State, 224
10. Busch, Mike, TE, Iowa State, 254
11. *Anthony, Terry, WR, Florida State, 281
12. Hammel, Todd, QB, Stephen F. Austin, 307

WASHINGTON 1990
1. Choice to Atlanta
2. *Collins, Andre, LB, Penn State, 46
3. *Elewonibi, Mohammed, G, Brigham Young, 76
4. *Conklin, Cary, QB, Washington [from New England] 86
   Choice to Indianapolis
   Labbe, Rico, DB, Boston College [from San Francisco thru Los Angeles Raiders] 109
5. *Mitchell, Brian, RB, Southwestern Louisiana, 130
6. *Wells, Kent, DT, Nebraska, 160
7. Choice to San Diego
8. Choice to Indianapolis
9. Moxley, Tim, G, Ohio State, 243
10. Francisco, D'Juan, DB, Notre Dame [from Miami] 262
    *Rayam, Thomas, DT, Alabama, 270
11. Leverenz, Jon, LB, Minnesota, 297
12. Choice to San Diego

1991

Held April 21-22, 1991

ATLANTA 1991
1. *Pickens, Bruce, DB, Nebraska, 3
   *Pritchard, Mike, WR, Colorado [from Indianapolis] 13
2. *Favre, Brett, QB, Southern Mississippi, 33
3. Choice to Miami
4. *Gardner, Moe, NT, Illinois, 87
5. Goode, James, LB, Oklahoma, 114
6. *Pegram, Erric, RB, North Texas State, 145
7. *Mitchell, Brian, DB, Brigham Young, 172
   Tucker, Mark, C, Southern California [from Seattle] 186
8. Austin, Randy, TE, UCLA, 199
9. *Logan, Ernie, DE, East Carolina, 226
10. Sutton, Walter, WR, Southwest Minnesota, 256
    Lucas, Pete, T, Wisconsin-Stevens Point [from Detroit] 258
11. *Sims, Joe, NT, Nebraska, 283
12. *Christian, Bob, RB, Northwestern, 310

BUFFALO 1991
1. *Jones, Henry, DB, Illinois, 26
2. *Hansen, Phil, DE, North Dakota State, 54
3. *Wren, Darryl, DB, Pittsburg (KS), 82
4. Choice to Dallas thru New England
5. Wilbourn, Shawn, DB, Long Beach State, 138
6. Hamilton, Millard, WR, Clark, 166
7. Rasul, Amir, RB, Florida A&M, 194
8. *Lamb, Brad, WR, Anderson (IN), 222
9. *Maddox, Mark, LB, Northern Michigan, 249
10. De Lorenzo, Tony, G, New Mexico State, 277
11. Kirkland, Dean, G, Washington, 305
12. Clark, Stephen, TE, Texas, 333

CHICAGO 1991
1. *Thomas, Stan, T, Texas, 22
2. *Zorich, Chris, DT, Notre Dame, 49
3. *Gardocki, Chris, P-K, Clemson, 78
4. Johnson, Joe, DB, North Carolina State, 105
5. *Morgan, Anthony, WR, Tennessee, 134
6. *Lewis, Darren, RB, Texas A&M, 161
7. *Justin, Paul, QB, Arizona State, 190
8. Horton, Larry, DB, Texas A&M, 217
9. *Stonebreaker, Mike, LB, Notre Dame, 245
10. Backes, Tom, DE, Oklahoma, 272
11. Long, Stacy, G, Clemson, 301
12. Cook, John, DT, Washington, 328

CINCINNATI 1991
1. *Williams, Alfred, LB, Colorado, 18
2. Choice to San Francisco
   *Rogers, Lamar, DT, Auburn [from Miami thru San Francisco] 52
3. *Dahl, Bob, DT, Notre Dame, 72
4. *Hollas, Donald, QB, Rice, 99
   *Carpenter, Rob, WR, Syracuse [from San Francisco] 109
5. *Arthur, Mike, C, Texas A&M, 130
6. *Fain, Richard, DB, Florida, 157
7. *Vinson, Fernandus, DB, North Carolina State, 184
8. *Dingle, Mike, RB, South Carolina, 211
9. *Garrett, Shane, WR, Texas A&M, 241
10. Lavin, Jim, G, Georgia Tech, 268
11. Smith, Chris, TE, Brigham Young, 295
12. *Bennett, Antoine, DB, Florida A&M, 322

CLEVELAND 1991
1. *Turner, Eric, DB, UCLA, 2
2. *King, Ed, G, Auburn, 29
3. *Jones, James, NT, Northern Iowa, 57
4. *Sagapolutele, Pio, NT, San Diego State, 85
5. Choice to Miami
6. *Jackson, Michael, WR, Southern Mississippi, 141
7. Choice to Green Bay
8. *Conover, Frank, DT, Syracuse, 197
9. Irvin, Raymond, DB, Central Florida, 225
   Wiggins, Shawn, WR, Wyoming [from Seattle] 239
10. Greenfield, Brian, P, Pittsburgh, 252
11. Jones, Todd, G, Henderson, (AR), 280
12. Austin, Elijah, NT, North Carolina State, 308

DALLAS 1991
1. *Maryland, Russell, DT, Miami [from New England] 1
   *Harper, Alvin, WR, Tennessee, 12
   *Pritchett, Kelvin, DT, Mississippi [from Washington] 20
2. *Edwards, Dixon, LB, Michigan State [from Detroit] 37
   Choice to New England
3. *Myles, Godfrey, LB, Florida [from San Diego] 62
   Richards, James, G, California [from Detroit] 64
   Choice to Minnesota
   *Williams, Erik, T, Central State (OH) [from New Orleans] 70
4. *Richards, Curvin, RB, Pittsburgh, 97
   *Musgrave, Bill, QB, Oregon [from Kansas City] 106
   *Hill, Tony, DE, Tennessee-Chattanooga [from Miami thru Washington and Detroit] 108
   Harris, Kevin, DE, Texas Southern [from Buffalo thru New England] 110
5. Choice to New England thru Los Angeles Raiders
   *Brownlow, Darrick, LB, Illinois [from Washington] 132
6. *Sullivan, Mike, G, Miami, 153
7. *Lett, Leon, DT, Emporia State [from Denver] 173
   Choice to Minnesota thru Los Angeles Raiders
8. Choice to Phoenix
9. *Mays, Damon, WR, Missouri, 235
10. *Love, Sean, G, Penn State, 264
11. Boles, Tony, RB, Michigan, 291
12. *Brown, Larry, DB, Texas Christian, 320

DENVER 1991
1. *Croel, Mike, LB, Nebraska, 4
2. *Johnson, Reggie, TE, Florida State, 30
3. *Traylor, Keith, LB, Central State, (OK), 61
4. Choice to Pit thru New England
   *Russell, Derek, WR, Arkansas [from Los Angeles Rams] 89
5. *Lewis, Greg, RB, Washington, 115
6. *Subis, Nick, T, San Diego State, 142
7. Choice to Dallas
8. *Walker, Kenny, DE, Nebraska, 200
9. Gibson, Don, NT, Southern California, 227
10. Mayfield, Curtis, WR, Oklahoma State, 253
11. *Moore, Shawn, QB, Virginia, 284
12. Choice to Los Angeles Rams

DETROIT 1991
1. *Moore, Herman, WR, Virginia, 10
2. Choice to Dallas
3. *Barrett, Reggie, WR, Texas-El Paso [from Los Angeles Rams] 58
   Choice to Dallas
4. *Scott, Kevin, DB, Stanford, 91
5. *Conover, Scott, G, Purdue, 118
6. Andrews, Richie, K, Florida State, 151
7. Thomas, Franklin, TE, Grambling, 178
8. *Jackson, Cedric, RB, Texas Christian, 205
9. *Milburn, Darryl, DE, Grambling, 231
10. Choice to Atlanta
11. Watkins, Slip, KR, Louisiana State, 285
12. Alexander, Zeno, LB, Arizona, 318

GREEN BAY 1991
1. Choice to Philadelphia
   *Clark, Vinnie, DB, Ohio State [from Philadelphia] 19
2. *Tuaolo, Esera, NT, Oregon State, 35
3. Choice to New York Jets

*Davey, Don, DE, Wisconsin [from New York Jets] 67
*Webb, Chuck, RB, Tennessee [from San Francisco] 81
4. Choice to San Francisco
5. Choice to San Francisco
Fite, Jeff, P, Memphis State [from Miami] 135
6. *Dean, Walter, RB, Grambling, 149
Garten, Joe, C, Colorado [from Miami] 164
7. Blevins, Frank, LB, Oklahoma [from Cleveland] 169
*Burnette, Reggie, LB, Houston, 176
8. Walker, Johnny, WR, Texas, 203
9. Witkowski, Dean, LB, North Dakota, 229
10. Porter, Rapier, TE, Arkansas-Pine Bluff, 262
11. Wierenga, J.J., DE, Central Michigan, 289
12. Collins, Linzy, WR, Missouri, 316

HOUSTON 1991
1. Choice to Washington thru New England and Dallas
2. *Dumas, Mike, DB, Indiana [from New England] 28
*Lewis, Darryll, DB, Arizona [from Minnesota thru Dallas] 38
*Flannery, John, C, Syracuse, 44
3. *Jackson, Steve, DB, Purdue, 71
*Donnalley, Kevin, T, North Carolina [from Miami] 79
4. *Rocker, David, DT, Auburn [from Seattle thru New England] 101
*Robertson, Marcus, DB, Iowa State, 102
5. *Wellman, Gary, WR, Southern California, 129
6. Choice to Philadelphia
7. Freeman, Kyle, LB, Angelo State, 183
8. *Brown, Gary, RB, Penn State, 214
9. *Jefferson, Shawn, WR, Central Florida, 240
10. Moore, Curtis, LB, Kansas, 267
11. Smith, James, DB, Richmond, 294
12. *Johnson, Alex, WR, Miami, 325

INDIANAPOLIS 1991
1. Choice to Atlanta
2. *Curry, Shane, DE, Miami, 40
3. *McCloughan, Dave, DB, Colorado, 69
4. *Vander Poel, Mark, T, Colorado, 96
5. *Cash, Kerry, TE, Texas, 125
6. *Agee, Mel, DT, Illinois, 152
7. Bradley, James, WR, Michigan State, 181
8. Bruton, Tim, TE, Missouri, 208
9. *Griffith, Howard, RB, Illinois, 237
10. *Giannetti, Frank, DE, Penn State, 263
11. *Crafts, Jerry, T, Louisville, 292
12. Luedeke, Rob, C, Penn State, 319

KANSAS CITY 1991
1. *Williams, Harvey, RB, Louisiana State, 21
2. *Valerio, Joe, T, Pennsylvania, 50
3. *Barnett, Tim, WR, Jackson State, 77
4. Choice to Dallas
5. *Mincy, Charles, DB, Washington, 133
6. *Malone, Darrell, DB, Jacksonville State, 162
7. Ellison, Bernard, DB, Nevada-Reno, 189
8. *Dohring, Tom, T, Michigan, 218
9. Keen, Robbie, K, California, 244
10. Ramsey, Eric, DB, Auburn, 273
11. Olive, Bobby, WR, Ohio State, 300
12. Shipley, Ron, G, New Mexico, 329

LOS ANGELES RAIDERS 1991
1. *Marinovich, Todd, QB, Southern California, 24
2. *Bell, Nick, RB, Iowa [from Seattle] 43
Choice to Seattle
3. Choice to Tampa Bay
4. *Ismail, Raghib, WR, Notre Dame [from Pittsburgh thru New England] 100
Choice to Los Angeles Rams
5. Choice to Tampa Bay
6. *Harrison, Nolan, DT, Indiana [from Min] 146
Choice to Minnesota
7. Choice to San Diego
8. *Jones, Brian, LB, Texas [from Seattle] 213
Woulard, Todd, LB, Alabama A&M, 219
9. *Lewis, Tahaun, DB, Nebraska, 247
10. *Glover, Andrew, TE, Grambling, 274
11. Choice to New England thru San Diego
12. Johnson, Dennis, WR, Winston-Salem State, 330

LOS ANGELES RAMS 1991
1. *Lyght, Todd, DB, Notre Dame, 5
2. *Phifer, Roman, LB, UCLA, 31
3. Choice to Detroit
4. Choice to Denver
*Bailey, Robert, DB, Miami [from Los Angeles Raiders] 107
5. *Young, Robert, DE, Mississippi State, 116
6. Fort, Neal, T, Brigham Young, 143
7. Shelton, Tyrone, RB, William & Mary, 170
8. Tyrance, Pat, LB, Nebraska, 201
9. Fields, Jeff, NT, Arkansas State, 228
10. Choice to San Diego
11. *Crews, Terry, LB, Western Michigan, 281
12. *Pahukoa, Jeff, T, Washington [from Denver] 311
*Thompson, Ernie, RB, Indiana, 312

MIAMI 1991
1. *Hill, Randal, WR, Miami, 23
2. Choice to Cincinnati thru San Francisco
3. *Craver, Aaron, RB, Fresno State [from Atlanta] 60
Choice to Houston
4. Choice to Dallas thru Washington and Detroit
5. *Cox, Bryan, LB, Western Illinois [from Cleveland] 113
*Williams, Gene, G, Iowa State [from New York Jets thru Green Bay] 121
Choice to Green Bay
6. Choice to Green Bay
7. *Green, Chris, DB, Illinois, 191
8. Smith, Roland, DB, Miami, 220
9. *Miller, Scott, WR, UCLA, 246
10. Titley, Michael, TE, Iowa, 275
11. Rogers, Ernie, G, California, 302
12. Brunson, Joe, DT, Tennessee-Chattanooga, 331

MINNESOTA 1991
1. Choice to New England thru Dallas
2. Choice to Houston thru Dallas
3. *Jenkins, Carlos, LB, Michigan State, 65
*Reed, Jake, WR, Grambling [from Dallas] 68
4. *Baldwin, Randy, RB, Mississippi, 92
5. *Thome, Chris, C, Minnesota, 119
6. Choice to Los Angeles Raiders
*Scott, Todd, DB, Southwestern Louisiana [from Los Angeles Raiders] 163
7. Reagan, Scotty, DT, Humboldt State, 179
*Welborne, Tripp, DB, Michigan [from Dal thru Los Angeles Raiders] 180
8. Johnson, Reggie, DE, Arizona, 206
9. Hudson, Gerald, RB, Oklahoma State, 232
10. Pierce, Brady, T, Wisconsin, 259
11. *Caesar, Ivan, LB, Boston College, 286
12. Hughes, Darren, WR, Carson-Newman, 313

NEW ENGLAND 1991
1. Choice to Dallas
*Harlow, Pat, T, Southern California [from Minnesota thru Dallas] 11
*Russell, Leonard, RB, Arizona State [from New Orleans thru Dallas] 14
2. Choice to Houston
*Henderson, Jerome, DB, Clemson [from Dallas] 41
3. *Stephens, Calvin, G, South Carolina, 56
4. *Zolak, Scott, QB, Maryland, 84
5. *Vaughn, Jon, RB, Michigan, 112
*Coates, Ben, TE, Livingstone [from Dal thru Los Angeles Raiders] 124
6. *Key, David, DB, Michigan, 140
7. Miller, Blake, C, Louisiana State, 168
8. *Colon, Harry, DB, Missouri, 196
9. Glenn, O'Neil, G, Maryland, 224
10. Bethel, Randy, TE, Miami, 251
11. Moore, Vince, WR, Tennessee, 279
Alsbury, Paul, P, Southwest Texas State [from Los Angeles Raiders thru San Diego] 303
12. *Edwards, Tim, DT, Delta State, 307

NEW ORLEANS 1991
1. Choice to New England thru Dallas
2. *Carroll, Wesley, WR, Miami, 42
3. Choice to Dallas
4. Choice to Seattle thru Los Angeles Raiders
5. *Jones, Reginald, DB, Memphis State, 126
6. *McAfee, Fred, RB, Mississippi College, 154
7. Haynes, Hayward, G, Florida State, 182
8. *Wainright, Frank, TE, Northern Colorado, 210
9. Wallace, Anthony, RB, California, 237
10. Choice to Tampa Bay
11. *Ross, Scott, LB, Southern California, 293
12. Drabczak, Mark, G, Minnesota, 321

NEW YORK GIANTS 1991
1. *Bunch, Jarrod, RB, Michigan, 27
2. *McGhee, Kanavis, LB, Colorado, 55
3. *McCaffrey, Ed, WR, Stanford, 83
4. *Jones, Clarence, T, Maryland, 111
5. Moss, Anthony, LB, Florida State, 139
6. *Miller, Corey, LB, South Carolina, 167
7. Carter, Simmie, DB, Southern Mississippi, 195
8. *McGriggs, Lamar, DB, Western Illinois, 223
9. Bouldin, Jerry, WR, Mississippi State, 250
10. Cristobal, Luis, G, Miami, 278
11. Popson, Ted, TE, Portland State, 306
12. Wanke, Larry, QB, John Carroll, 334

NEW YORK JETS 1991
1. Choice exercised in 1990 Supplemental Draft (Moore, Rob, WR, Syracuse)
2. *Nagle, Browning, QB, Louisville, 34
3. *Lewis, Morris, LB, Georgia [from Green Bay] 63
Choice to Green Bay
4. *Gunn, Mark, DT, Pittsburgh, 94
5. Choice to Miami thru Green Bay
6. Bryant, Blaise, RB, Iowa State, 148
Riley, Mike, DB, Tulane [from Philadelphia] 160
7. Parrish, Doug, DB, San Francisco State, 175
8. James, Tim, DB, Colorado, 202
9. Glonek, Paul, DT, Arizona, 234
10. Baker, Al, RB, Kentucky, 261
11. Keeton, Rocen, LB, UCLA, 288
12. Hayes, Mark, T, Arizona State, 315

PHILADELPHIA 1991
1. *Davis, Antone, T, Tennessee [from Green Bay] 8
Choice to Green Bay
2. *Campbell, Jesse, DB, North Carolina State, 48
3. *Selby, Rob, T, Auburn, 75
4. *Thomas, William, LB, Texas A&M, 104
5. *Erickson, Craig, QB, Miami, 131
6. *Harmon, Andy, DE, Kent State [from Houston] 156
Choice to New York Jets
7. *Joseph, James, RB, Auburn, 187
8. *Kowalkowski, Scott, LB, Notre Dame, 216
9. *Weatherspoon, Chuck, RB, Houston, 242
10. Harmon, Eric, G, Clemson, 271
11. *Flores, Mike, DE, Louisville, 298
12. Beavers, Darrell, DB, Morehead State, 327

PHOENIX 1991
1. *Swann, Eric, DE, No College, 6
2. *Jones, Mike, DE, North Carolina State, 32
3. *Williams, Aeneas, DB, Southern University, 59
4. *Davis, Dexter, DB, Clemson, 86
5. Hammond, Vance, DT, Clemson, 117
6. Vega, Eduardo, T, Memphis State, 144
7. *Brown, Ivory Lee, RB, Arkansas-Pine Bluff, 171
8. Amsler, Greg, RB, Tennessee, 198
Evans, Jerry, TE, Toledo [from San Diego] 204
*Evans, Scott, DT, Oklahoma [from Dallas] 209
9. Choice exercised in 1990 Supplemental Draft (Williams, Willie, TE, Louisiana State)
10. *Anderson, Herbie, DB, Texas A&I, 255
11. LaDuke, Nathan, DB, Arizona State, 282
12. Bridewell, Jeff, QB, Cal-Davis, 309

PITTSBURGH 1991
1. *Richardson, Huey, DE, Florida, 15
2. *Graham, Jeff, WR, Ohio State, 46
3. *Mills, Ernie, WR, Florida, 73
4. *Walker, Sammy, DB, Texas Tech [from Denver thru New England] 88
Choice to Los Angeles Raiders thru New England
*Cooper, Adrian, TE, Oklahoma [from Washington] 103
5. Choice to San Diego thru New England
6. *Thompson, Leroy, RB, Penn State, 158
7. *Jones, Andre, LB, Notre Dame, 185
8. Dingman, Dean, G, Michigan, 212
9. *McGonnigal, Bruce, TE, Virginia, 238
10. *Solomon, Ariel, T, Colorado, 269
11. Thomas, Efrum, DB, Alabama, 296
12. *Brady, Jeff, LB, Kentucky, 323

SAN DIEGO 1991
1. *Richard, Stanley, DB, Texas, 9
2. *Thornton, George, DT, Alabama, 36
*Bieniemy, Eric, RB, Colorado [from Tampa Bay] 39
*Moten, Eric, G, Michigan State [from Washington] 47
3. Choice to Dallas
4. *Thigpen, Yancey, WR, Winston-Salem State, 90
5. *Young, Duane, TE, Michigan State, 123
*Fields, Floyd, DB, Arizona State [from Pittsburgh thru New England] 127
6. Laister, Jimmy, T, Oregon Tech, 150
7. *Jones, David, WR, Delaware State, 177
Beauford, Terry, G, Florida A&M [from Los Angeles Raiders] 177
8. Choice to Phoenix
9. Katoa, Andy, LB, Southern Oregon, 230
10. Poles, Ronald, RB, Tennessee [from Los Angeles Rams] 254
Heldt, Mike, C, Notre Dame, 257
11. Weinberg, Joachim, WR, Johnson C. Smith, 290
12. *Samuels, Chris, RB, Texas, 317

SAN FRANCISCO 1991
1. *Washington, Ted, DT, Louisville, 25
2. *Watters, Ricky, RB, Notre Dame [from Cincinnati] 45
*Johnson, John, LB, Clemson, 53
3. Choice to Green Bay
4. *Donahue, Mitch, LB, Wyoming [from Green Bay] 95
Choice to Cincinnati
5. *Hanks, Merton, DB, Iowa [from Green Bay] 122
*Boatswain, Harry, T, New Haven, 137
6. Bowles, Scott, T, North Texas State, 165
7. *Canley, Sheldon, RB, San Jose State, 193
8. *Hargain, Tony, WR, Oregon, 221
9. *Riddick, Louis, DB, Pittsburgh, 248
10. Holdbrooks, Byron, NT, Alabama, 276
11. Slaughter, Bobby, WR, Louisiana Tech, 304
12. Confer, Cliff, DE, Michigan State, 332

SEATTLE 1991
1. *McGwire, Dan, QB, San Diego State, 16
2. Choice to Los Angeles Raiders
*Thomas, Doug, WR, Clemson [from Los Angeles Raiders] 51
3. *Daniels, David, WR, Penn State, 74
4. *Kasay, John, K, Georgia [from New Orleans thru Los Angeles Raiders] 98
Choice to Houston thru New England
5. Davis, Harlan, DB, Tennessee, 128
6. *Sinclair, Mike, DE, Eastern New Mexico, 155
7. Choice to Atlanta
8. Choice to Los Angeles Raiders
9. Choice to Cleveland
10. Ringoen, Erik, LB, Hofstra, 266
11. Stewart, Tony, RB, Iowa, 297
12. Harris, Ike, G, South Carolina, 324

TAMPA BAY 1991
1. *McRae, Charles, T, Tennessee, 7
2. Choice to San Diego
3. *Dawsey, Lawrence, WR, Florida State, 66
*Wilson, Robert, RB, Texas A&M [from Los Angeles Raiders] 80
4. *Covington, Tony, DB, Virginia, 93
5. Bagsby, Terry, LB, East Texas State, 120
*Ryan, Tim, G, Notre Dame [from Los Angeles Raiders] 136
6. *Hall, Rhett, DT, California, 147
7. *Tiggle, Calvin, LB, Georgia Tech, 174
8. *Carter, Marty, DB, Middle Tennessee State, 207
9. Taylor, Treamelle, WR, Nevada-Reno, 233
10. O'Hara, Pat, QB, Southern California, 260
Hickson, Hyland, RB, Michigan State [from New Orleans] 265
11. Sunvold, Mike, DT, Minnesota, 287
12. *Chamblee, Al, LB, Virginia Tech, 314

WASHINGTON 1991
1. *Wilson, Bobby, DT, Michigan State [from Houston thru New England and Dallas] 17
Choice to Dallas
2. Choice to San Diego
3. *Ervins, Ricky, RB, Southern California, 76
4. Choice to Pittsburgh
5. Choice to Dallas
6. Ransom, Dennis, TE, Texas A&M, 159
7. *Cash, Keith, WR, Texas, 188
8. *Spencer, Jimmy, DB, Florida, 215
9. Bell, Charles, DB, Baylor, 243
10. Shale, Cris, P, Bowling Green, 270
11. *Gulledge, David, DB, Jacksonville State, 299
12. *McCardell, Keenan, WR, Nevada-Las Vegas, 326

1992

Held April 26-27, 1992

ATLANTA 1992
1. *Whitfield, Bob, T, Stanford, 8
*Smith, Tony, RB, Southern Mississippi, 19
2. Choice to Phoenix thru New England
*Smith, Chuck, DE, Tennessee [from Dallas] 51
3. *Dinkins, Howard, LB, Florida State, 73
4. *Smith, Frankie, DB, Baylor, 104
5. Choice to San Diego
6. *Ray, Terry, DB, Oklahoma, 158
7. Paulk, Tim, LB, Florida [from Miami] 182
Choice to Los Angeles Raiders thru Miami
8. *Moore, Derrick, RB, Northeast Oklahoma, 216
Dwight, Reggie, TE, Troy State [from Dallas] 217
9. *Alex, Keith, T, Texas A&M, 243
10. *Hardy, Darryl, LB, Tennessee, 270
11. Jones, Robin, DE, Baylor, 297
12. Choice to Miami

BUFFALO 1992
1. *Fina, John, T, Arizona, 27
2. *Patton, James, NT, Texas, 55
3. *Goganious, Keith, LB, Penn State, 83
4. Kmet, Frank, DE, Purdue, 111
5. *Darby, Matt, DB, UCLA, 139
6. *Turner, Nate, TE, Nebraska, 167
7. *Schulz, Kurt, DB, Eastern Washington, 195
8. *Humphries, Leonard, DB, Penn State, 223
9. *Walsh, Chris, WR, Stanford, 251
10. *Rose, Barry, WR, Wisconsin-Stevens Point, 279
11. *Marrow, Vince, TE, Toledo, 307
12. Rodgers, Matt, QB, Iowa, 335

CHICAGO BEARS 1992
1. *Spellman, Alonzo, DE, Ohio State, 22
2. *Auzenne, Troy, T, California, 49
3. *Lincoln, Jeremy, DB, Tennessee, 80
4. *Furrer, Will, QB, Virginia Tech, 107
5. *Harrison, Todd, TE, North Carolina State, 134
6. Berry, Mark, DB, Texas, 161
7. Brown, John, WR, Houston, 192
8. Choice to New York Jets
9. Jurkovic, Mirko, G, Notre Dame, 246
10. Fisher, Nikki, RB, Virginia, 273
11. *Age, Louis, T, Southwestern Louisiana, 304
12. Wilson, Chris, LB, Oklahoma, 331

CINCINNATI 1992
1. Choice to Washington
*Klingler, David, QB, Houston [from San Diego thru Washington] 6
*Williams, Darryl, DB, Miami [from Washington] 28
2. *Pickens, Carl, WR, Tennessee, 31
3. Choice to Dallas thru Washington
*Wheeler, Leonard, DB, Troy State [from Washington] 84
4. *McDonald, Ricardo, LB, Pittsburgh, 88
5. *Thompson, Craig, TE, North Carolina A&T, 115
6. Burns, Chris, DT, Middle Tennessee State, 142
7. Olberding, Lance, T, Iowa, 172
8. *Nix, Roosevelt, DE, Central State (OH), 199
9. *Miles, Ostell, RB, Houston, 226
10. Smith, Horace, DB, Oregon Tech, 256
11. Earle, John, T, Western Illinois, 283
12. *Shaw, Eric, LB, Louisiana Tech, 310

CLEVELAND 1992
1. *Vardell, Tommy, RB, Stanford, 9

2. Choice to Dallas
*Rowe, Patrick, WR, San Diego State [from New Orleans thru Dallas] 52
3. *Johnson, Bill, DT, Michigan State, 65
*Dixon, Gerald, LB, South Carolina [from Dallas] 78
4. Choice to Philadelphia
5. Choice to Dallas
6. *Smith, Rico, WR, Colorado [from Tampa Bay] 143
Choice to Tampa Bay
Williams, George, DT, Notre Dame [from Dallas] 163
7. *Jones, Selwyn, DB, Colorado State, 177
8. Choice to New England
9. Hill, Tim, DB, Kansas, 233
10. Lowe, Marcus, DT, Baylor, 260
11. Olobia, Augustin, WR, Washington State, 289
12. McCant, Keithen, QB, Nebraska, 316
*Simpson, Tim, C-G, Illinois [from Dallas] 329

DALLAS 1992
1. *Smith, Kevin, DB, Texas A&M [from Philadelphia thru Green Bay and Atlanta] 17
*Jones, Robert, LB, East Carolina, 24
2. *Smith, Jimmy, WR, Jackson State [from Cleveland] 36
*Woodson, Darren, DB, Arizona State [from New England] 37
Choice to Atlanta
3. *Holmes, Clayton, DB, Carson-Newman [from Cincinnati thru Washington] 58
Choice to Cleveland
*Brown, James, T, Virginia State [from Detroit] 82
4. Choice to Indianapolis thru Los Angeles Raiders
*Myslinski, Tom, G-C, Tennessee [from Detroit] 109
5. *Briggs, Greg, DB, Texas Southern [from NE thru Atl] 120
*Milstead, Rod, G, Delaware State [from Cleveland] 121
Choice to Houston
6. Wacasey, Fallon, TE, Tulsa [from New England] 149
Choice to Cleveland
7. Choice to Green Bay thru Los Angeles Raiders
8. Choice to Atlanta
9. Kirtman, Nate, DB, Pomona-Pitzer, 248
*Hall, Chris, DB, East Carolina [from Detroit] 250
10. Terry, John, G, Livingstone, 275
11. Daniel, Tim, WR, Florida A&M, 302
12. Harris, Don, DB, Texas Tech [from New England] 317
Choice to Cleveland

DENVER 1992
1. *Maddox, Tommy, QB, UCLA, 25
2. *Dronett, Shane, DE, Texas, 54
3. Choice to Detroit
4. *Johnson, Chuck, G, Texas, 110
5. *Robinson, Frank, DB, Boise State, 137
6. Choice to New York Jets
7. *Geater, Ron, DE, Iowa [from Tampa Bay] 170
Johnson, Jim, T, Michigan State [from New York Jets] 181
Bostick, Jon, WR, Nebraska, 193
8. Lockridge, Dietrich, G, Jackson State [from New York Jets] 208
Choice to Tampa Bay thru Dallas and Cleveland
9. *Oliver, Muhammad, DB, Oregon, 249
10. *Meeks, Bob, C, Auburn, 278
11. *Tillman, Cedric, WR, Alcorn State, 305
12. *Granby, John, DB, Virginia Tech, 334

DETROIT 1992
1. *Porcher, Robert, DE, South Carolina State, 26
2. *Scroggins, Tracy, LB, Tulsa, 53
*Hanson, Jason, K, Washington, 56
3. *McLemore, Thomas, TE, Southern [from Denver] 81
Choice to Dallas
4. Choice to Dallas
5. Choice to New Orleans
6. *Tharpe, Larry, T, Tennessee State [from Phoenix thru New England] 145
Choice to New England
7. Choice to New England
8. *Clay, Willie, DB, Georgia Tech, 221
9. Choice to Dallas
10. Choice to New England
11. *Tillison, Ed, RB, Northwest Missouri, 306
12. Choice to New England

GREEN BAY 1992
1. *Buckley, Terrell, DB, Florida State, 5
2. *D'Onofrio, Mark, LB, Penn State, 34
3. *Brooks, Robert, WR, South Carolina, 62
4. Choice to San Francisco
*Bennett, Edgar, RB, Florida State [from San Francisco] 103
5. *McNabb, Dexter, RB, Florida, 119
McKay, Orlando, WR, Washington [from San Francisco] 130
6. Choice to Phoenix
*Chmura, Mark, TE, Boston College [from San Francisco] 157
7. Choice to Los Angeles Raiders
Holder, Christopher, WR, Tuskegee [from Dal thru Los Angeles Raiders] 190
8. Choice to Pittsburgh thru San Francisco
9. *Detmer, Ty, QB, Brigham Young, 230
Bradley, Shazzon, NT, Tennessee [from Los Angeles Raiders] 240
10. Oberg, Andrew, T, North Carolina, 257
11. Mokwuah, Gabe, LB, American International, 287
12. *Collins, Brett, LB, Washington, 314

HOUSTON 1992
1. Choice to San Diego
2. *Robinson, Eddie, LB, Alabama State, 50
3. *Harris, Corey, WR, Vanderbilt, 77
4. *Mooney, Mike, T, Georgia Tech, 108
5. *Bowden, Joe, LB, Oklahoma [from New Orleans] 133
*Brown, Tony, DB, Fresno State, 135
*Roberts, Tim, DT, Southern Mississippi [from Dallas] 136
6. Bailey, Mario, WR, Washington, 162
7. Turner, Elbert, WR, Illinois, 189
8. *Richardson, Bucky, QB, Texas A&M, 220
9. *Dafney, Bernard, T, Tennessee, 247
10. Johnson, Dion, WR, East Carolina, 274
11. *Davis, Anthony, LB, Utah, 301
12. Wood, Joe, K, Air Force, 332

INDIANAPOLIS 1992
1. *Emtman, Steve, DT, Washington, 1
*Coryatt, Quentin, LB, Texas A&M [from Tampa Bay] 2
2. *Ambrose, Ashley, DB, Mississippi Valley State, 29
3. Choice to Los Angeles Rams
4. *Culver, Rodney, RB, Notre Dame, 85
*McCoy, Tony, DT, Florida [from Dal thru Los Angeles Raiders] 105
5. Toy, Maury, RB, UCLA, 113
6. Habersham, Shoun, WR, Tennessee-Chattanooga, 141
7. Steele, Derek, DE, Maryland, 169
8. *Belser, Jason, DB, Oklahoma, 197
*Humphrey, Ronald, RB, Mississippi Valley State [from Los Angeles Raiders] 212
9. *Miller, Eddie, WR, South Carolina, 225
10. *Grant, Steve, LB, West Virginia, 253
11. Choice to Los Angeles Rams
12. *Brandon, Mike, DE, Florida, 309

KANSAS CITY 1992
1. *Carter, Dale, DB, Tennessee, 20
2. *Blundin, Matt, QB, Virginia [from Minnesota thru Dallas] 40
Choice to Washington thru Dallas
3. Choice to Washington thru Dallas
4. *Evans, Mike, DE, Michigan, 101
5. Choice to Tampa Bay
6. Smith, Tony, WR, Notre Dame, 159
7. *Anderson, Erick, LB, Michigan, 186
8. Jennings, Jim, G, San Diego State, 213
9. *Leeuwenburg, Jay, C, Colorado, 244
10. Ostroski, Jerry, G, Tulsa, 271
11. Rigby, Doug, DE, Wyoming, 298
12. Williams, Corey, DB, Oklahoma State, 325

LOS ANGELES RAIDERS 1992
1. *McGlockton, Chester, DE, Clemson, 16
2. *Skrepenak, Greg, T, Michigan [from Tampa Bay] 32
Choice to Tampa Bay
3. Choice to New Orleans thru Tampa Bay
4. Choice to Phoenix thru New England
5. *Hoskins, Derrick, DB, Southern Mississippi, 128
6. Rowell, Tony, C, Florida, 156
7. Cotton, Curtis, DB, Nebraska [from Green Bay] 173
Choice to Tampa Bay
*Smith, Kevin, RB, UCLA [from Atlanta thru Miami] 185
8. Choice to Indianapolis
9. Choice to Green Bay
10. *White, Alberto, LB, Texas Southern, 268
11. Choice to Miami
12. Roth, Tom, G, Southern Illinois, 324

LOS ANGELES RAMS 1992
1. *Gilbert, Sean, DE, Pittsburgh, 3
2. *Israel, Steve, DB, Pittsburgh, 30
3. *Boutte, Marc, DT, Louisiana State [from Indianapolis] 57
*Kinchen, Todd, WR, Louisiana State, 60
4. *Harper, Shawn, T, Indiana, 87
5. *Crooms, Chris, DB, Texas A&M, 114
6. Campbell, Joe, RB, Middle Tennessee State, 144
7. *Ashmore, Darryl, T, Northwestern, 171
8. Jones, Ricky, QB, Alabama State, 198
9. *Rubley, T.J., QB, Tulsa, 228
10. *Lester, Tim, RB, Eastern Kentucky, 255
11. *Townsend, Brian, LB, Michigan [from Indianapolis] 281
Thomas, Brian, WR, Southern, 282
12. Harris, Kelvin, C, Miami, 312

MIAMI 1992
1. *Vincent, Troy, DB, Wisconsin [from Phoenix] 7
*Coleman, Marco, LB, Georgia Tech, 12
2. Blake, Eddie, DT, Auburn, 43
3. *Webster, Larry, DT, Maryland, 70
4. *Hollier, Dwight, LB, North Carolina, 97
5. Perez, Christopher, T, Kansas, 124
6. *Collins, Roosevelt, LB, Texas Christian, 155
7. Choice to Atlanta
*Moore, Dave, TE, Pittsburgh [from New Orleans thru Los Angeles Raiders] 191
8. Powell, Andre, LB, Penn State, 209
9. Tellington, Tony, DB, Youngstown, 236
10. Spears, Raoul, RB, Southern California, 267
11. Miles, Lee, WR, Baylor, 294
Barsotti, Mark, QB, Fresno State [from Los Angeles Raiders] 296
12. Biggins, Milton, TE, Western Kentucky, 321
Bell, Kameno, RB, Illinois [from Atlanta] 328

MINNESOTA 1992
1. Choice to New England thru Dallas
2. *Harris, Robert, DE, Southern [from Seattle] 39
Choice to Kansas City thru Dallas
3. Choice to New England thru Dallas
4. *Barker, Roy, DT, North Carolina, 98
5. *McDaniel, Ed, LB, Clemson, 125
6. Gaddis, Mike, RB, Oklahoma, 152
7. *Wilson, David, DB, California, 183
8. Fisher, Luke, TE, East Carolina, 210
9. *Johnson, Brad, QB, Florida State [from Tampa Bay] 227
*West, Ronnie, WR, Pittsburg (KS), 237
10. *Culpepper, Brad, DT, Florida, 264
11. *Evans, Charles, RB, Clark (GA), 295
12. Randolph, Joe, WR, Elon, 322

NEW ENGLAND 1992
1. Choice to Atlanta
*Chung, Eugene, T, Virginia Tech [from Minnesota thru Dallas] 13
2. *Smith, Rod, DB, Notre Dame [from Phoenix] 35
Choice to Dallas
3. *Collins, Todd, LB, Carson-Newman, 64
*Turner, Kevin, RB, Alabama, from Minnesota thru Dallas] 71
4. *Lambert, Dion, DB, UCLA [from San Diego] 90
*Anderson, Darren, DB, Toledo, 93
5. *Sabb, Dwayne, LB, New Hampshire [from Tampa Bay] 116
Choice to Dallas thru Atlanta
6. Choice to Dallas
Boyd, Tracy, G, Elizabeth City State [from Detroit] 165
7. Hawkins, Wayne, WR, Southwest Minnesota, 176
Gray, Jim, DT, West Virginia [from Detroit] 194
8. *Lockwood, Scott, RB, Southern California [from Cleveland] 204
*Gash, Sam, RB, Penn State, 205
9. *Dixon, David, DT, Arizona State, 232
10. Baur, Turner, TE, Stanford, 261
Gordon, Steve, C, California [from Detroit] 277
11. Petko, Mike, LB, Nebraska, 288
12. Choice to Dallas
Baysinger, Freeman, WR, Humboldt State [from Detroit] 333

NEW ORLEANS 1992
1. *Dunbar, Vaughn, RB, Indiana, 21
2. Choice to Cleveland thru Dallas
3. *Legette, Tyrone, DB, Nebraska, from Los Angeles Raiders thru Tampa Bay] 72
Choice to Tampa Bay
4. *McGuire, Gene, C, Notre Dame [from Seattle] 95
*Lumpkin, Sean, DB, Minnesota, 106
5. Choice to Houston
*Small, Torrance, WR, Alcorn State [from Detroit] 138
6. Vincent, Kary, DB, Texas A&M, 164
7. Choice to Miami thru Los Angeles Raiders
8. Stewart, Robert, NT, Alabama, 218
9. *Jones, Donald, LB, Washington, 245
10. *Dowdell, Marcus, WR, Tennessee State, 276
11. *Gisler, Mike, G, Houston, 303
12. Adell, Scott, T, North Carolina State, 330

NEW YORK GIANTS 1992
1. *Brown, Derek, TE, Notre Dame, 14
2. *Sparks, Phillippi, DB, Arizona State, 41
3. *Pierce, Aaron, TE, Washington, 69
4. *Hamilton, Keith, DT, Pittsburgh, 99
5. Wright, Michael, DB, Washington State, 126
6. *Dillard, Stacey, NT, Oklahoma, 153
7. *Widmer, Corey, NT, Montana State, 180
8. *Graham, Kent, QB, Ohio State, 211
9. *Prior, Anthony, DB, Washington State, 238
10. Rooks, George, NT, Syracuse, 265
11. *Singleton, Nate, WR, Grambling, 292
12. *Swann, Charles, WR, Indiana State, 323

NEW YORK JETS 1992
1. *Mitchell, Johnny, TE, Nebraska, 15
2. *Barber, Kurt, LB, Southern California, 42
3. *Malamala, Siupeli, T, Washington, 68
4. *Coleman, Keo, LB, Mississippi State, 96
5. *Dixon, Cal, C, Florida, 127
6. *Cadrez, Glenn, LB, Houston, 154
*Blake, Jeff, QB, East Carolina [from Denver] 166
7. Choice to Denver
8. Choice to Denver
Brownlee, Vincent, WR, Mississippi [from Chicago Bears] 219
9. Choice to Phoenix
10. *Johnson, Mario, DT, Missouri, 266
11. Boles, Eric, WR, Central Washington, 293
12. Choice to Seattle

PHILADELPHIA 1992
1. Choice to Dallas thru Green Bay and Atl
2. *Stacy, Siran, RB, Alabama, 48
3. *Jeter, Tommy, DT, Texas, 75
4. *Brooks, Tony, RB, Notre Dame [from Cleveland] 92
*Weldon, Casey, QB, Florida State, 102
5. *Barlow, Corey, DB, Auburn, 129
6. *Sydner, Jeff, WR, Hawaii, 160
7. Boatwright, William, G, Virginia Tech, 187
8. *Bullough, Chuck, LB, Michigan State, 214
9. *Bartley, Ephesians, LB, Florida, 241
10. *McMillian, Mark, DB, Alabama, 272
11. Tudors, Pumpy, P, Tennessee-Chattanooga, 299
12. Houston, Brandon, T, Oklahoma, 326

PHOENIX 1992
1. Choice to Miami
2. Choice to New England
*Sacca, Tony, QB, Penn State [from Atlanta thru New England] 46
3. *Cunningham, Ed, C, Washington, 61
4. *Christy, Jeff, T, Pittsburgh, 91
*Bankston, Michael, NT, Sam Houston State [from Los Angeles Raiders thru New England] 100
5. Choice to Tampa Bay thru New Orleans
6. Choice to Detroit thru New England
Brauninger, Brian, T, Oklahoma [from Green Bay] 146
7. *Ware, Derek, TE, Central State, (OK), 175
8. *Blount, Eric, WR, North Carolina, 202
9. Henson, David, NT, Central Arkansas, 229
*Williams, Tyrone, WR, Western Ontario [from New York Jets] 239
10. Yarbrough, Reggie, RB, Cal State-Fullerton, 259
11. *Baxley, Rob, T, Iowa, 286
12. Wilson, Lance, NT, Texas, 313

PITTSBURGH 1992
1. *Searcy, Leon, T, Miami, 11
2. *Kirkland, Levon, LB, Clemson, 38
3. *Steed, Joel, NT, Colorado, 67
4. *Davenport, Charles, WR, North Carolina State, 94
5. *Haller, Alan, DB, Michigan State, 123
6. Choice to San Francisco
7. *Campbell, Russ, TE, Kansas State, 179
*Graham, Scottie, RB, Ohio State [from San Francisco] 188
8. *Perry, Darren, DB, Penn State [from Green Bay thru San Francisco] 203
Ismail, Hesham, G, Florida, 206
Williams, Nate, DT, Mississippi State [from San Francisco] 215
9. *Webster, Elnardo, LB, Rutgers, 235
10. Saunders, Mike, RB, Iowa, 262
11. *Gammon, Kendall, G, Pittsburg (KS), 291
12. Benton, Cornelius, QB, Connecticut, 318

SAN DIEGO 1992
1. Choice to Cincinnati thru Washington
*Mims, Chris, DE, Tennessee [from Houston] 23
2. *Pope, Marquez, DB, Fresno State, 33
3. *Ethridge, Ray, WR, Pasadena C.C., 63
4. Choice to New England
5. *Whitley, Curtis, C, Clemson, 117
Little, Kevin, LB, North Carolina A&T [from Atlanta] 131
*Jonassen, Eric, T, Bloomsburg [from Washington] 140
6. *White, Reggie, DT, North Carolina A&T, 147
7. *May, Deems, TE, North Carolina, 174
8. *Fuller, James, DB, Portland State, 201
9. *Barnes, Johnnie, WR, Hampton, 231
10. Paul, Arthur, DT, Arizona State, 258
11. McAfee, Keith, RB, Texas A&M, 285
12. *Huerta, Carlos, K, Miami, 315

SAN FRANCISCO 1992
1. *Hall, Dana, DB, Washington, 18
2. *Lee, Amp, RB, Florida State, 45
3. *Bollinger, Brian, G, North Carolina, 76
4. *Thomas, Mark, DE, North Carolina State [from Green Bay] 89
Choice to Green Bay
5. Choice to Green Bay
6. *Russell, Damien, DB, Virginia Tech [from Pittsburgh] 151
Choice to Green Bay
7. Choice to Pittsburgh
8. Choice to Pittsburgh
9. Hagan, Darian, QB, Colorado, 242
10. *Mayfield, Corey, DE, Oklahoma, 269
11. Covington, Tom, TE, Georgia Tech, 300
12. *LaBounty, Matt, DE, Oregon, 327

SEATTLE 1992
1. *Roberts, Ray, T, Virginia, 10
2. Choice to Minnesota
3. *Spitulski, Bobby, LB, Central Florida, 66
4. Choice to New Orleans
5. Dandridge, Gary, DB, Appalachian State, 122
6. *Bates, Michael, WR, Arizona, 150
7. *Frier, Mike, DT, Appalachian State, 178
8. Shamsid-Deen, Muhammad, RB, Tennessee-Chattanooga, 207
9. Stayner, Larry, TE, Boise State, 234
10. Hamlet, Anthony, DE, Miami, 263
11. Rongen, Kris, G, Washington, 290
12. Fraley, Chico, LB, Washington, 319
MacNeill, John, DE, Michigan State [from New York Jets] 320

TAMPA BAY 1992
1. Choice to Indianapolis
2. Choice to Los Angeles Raiders
 *Hawkins, Courtney, WR, Michigan State [from Los Angeles Raiders] 44
3. *Wheeler, Mark, DT, Texas A&M, 59
 *Armstrong, Tyji, TE, Mississippi [from New Orleans] 79
4. *Erickson, Craig, QB, Miami, 86
5. Choice to New England
 *Green, Rogerick, DB, Kansas State [from Pho thru New Orleans] 118
 *Dotson, Santana, DE, Baylor [from Kansas City] 132
6. Choice to Cleveland
 Malone, James, LB, UCLA [from Cleveland] 148
7. Choice to Denver
 Swilling, Ken, DB, Georgia Tech [from Los Angeles Raiders] 184
8. *McDowell, Anthony, RB, Texas Tech, 200
 Pawlawski, Mike, QB, California [from Den thru Dallas and Cleveland] 222
9. Choice to Minnesota
10. *Alexander, Elijah, LB, Kansas State, 254
11. *Royster, Mazio, RB, Southern California, 284
12. *Wilmsmeyer, Klaus, P, Louisville, 311

WASHINGTON 1992
1. *Howard, Desmond, WR, Michigan [from Cincinnati] 4
 Choice to Cincinnati
2. *Collins, Shane, DE, Arizona State [from Kansas City thru Dallas] 47
 Choice to Detroit thru Dallas
3. Siever, Paul, G, Penn State [from Kansas City thru Dallas] 74
 Choice to Cincinnati
4. Hakel, Chris, QB, William & Mary, 112
5. Choice to San Diego
6. *Rowe, Ray, TE, San Diego State, 168
7. Holmes, Calvin, DB, Southern California, 196
8. *Moore, Darryl, G, Texas-El Paso, 224
9. Powell, Boone, LB, Texas, 252
10. *Barker, Tony, LB, Rice, 280
11. Smith, Terry, WR, Penn State, 308
12. *Elliott, Matt, C, Michigan, 336

1993

Held April 25-26, 1993

#Compensatory Pick

ATLANTA 1993
1. *Kennedy, Lincoln, T, Washington, 9
2. *Harper, Roger, DB, Ohio State, 38
3. *Alexander, Harold, P, Appalachian State, 67
4. Choice to Dallas thru Green Bay
5. *George, Ron, LB, Stanford, 121
6. *Lyons, Mitch, TE, Michigan State, 151
7. *Walker, Darnell, DB, Oklahoma, 178
8. *Baker, Shannon, WR, Florida State, 205

BUFFALO 1993
1. *Smith, Thomas, DB, North Carolina, 28
2. *Parrella, John, DT, Nebraska, 55
3. Choice to Cleveland thru Atl and Den
4. *Copeland, Russell, WR, Memphis State, 111
5. *Devlin, Mike, C, Iowa [from Philadelphia] 136
 *Savage, Sebastian, DB, North Carolina State, 139
6. *Lacina, Corbin, T, Augustana (San Diego), 167
7. Harris, Willie, WR, Mississippi State, 195
8. Luneberg, Chris, T, West Chester (PA), 223

CHICAGO BEARS 1993
1. *Conway, Curtis, WR, Southern California, 7
2. *Simpson, Carl, DT, Florida State, 35
3. *Gedney, Chris, TE, Syracuse, 61
4. Choice to Indianapolis
 *Perry, Todd, G, Kentucky [from Cleveland] 97
 *Baker, Myron, LB, Louisiana Tech [from Indianapolis] 100
 *Fontenot, Albert, DE, Baylor [from Dallas thru Green Bay] 112
5. Choice to Green Bay
6. *Hoffmann, Dave, LB, Washington, 146
7. *Johnson, Keshon, DB, Arizona, 173
8. Choice to Seattle

CINCINNATI 1993
1. *Copeland, John, DE, Alabama, 5
2. *McGee, Tony, TE, Michigan, 37
3. *Tovar, Steve, LB, Ohio State [from New York Jets] 59
 *Parten, Ty, DT, Arizona, 63
4. *Simmons, Marcello, DB, Southern Methodist, 90
5. *Duckett, Forey, DB, Nevada-Reno, 117
6. *Scott, Tom, T, East Carolina, 148
7. *Gunn, Lance, DB, Texas, 175
8. *Pelfrey, Doug, K, Kentucky, 202

CLEVELAND 1993
1. Choice to Denver
 *Everitt, Steve, C, Michigan [from Denver] 14
2. *Footman, Dan, DE, Florida State, 42
3. Choice to Detroit
 *Caldwell, Mike, LB, Middle Tennessee State [from Buffalo thru Atlanta and Denver] 83
4. Choice to Chicago Bears
5. *Arvie, Herman, T, Grambling, 124
6. *McKenzie, Rich, LB, Penn State, 153
7. *Hill, Travis, LB, Nebraska, 180
8. Choice to Los Angeles Rams

DALLAS 1993
1. Choice to Green Bay
2. *Williams, Kevin, WR, Miami [from Green Bay] 46
 *Smith, Darrin, LB, Miami [from San Francisco thru Green Bay] 54
3. Choice to Los Angeles Raiders thru San Francisco
 Middleton, Mike, DB, Indiana, 84
4. *Lassic, Derrick, RB, Alabama [from Atlanta thru Green Bay] 94
 *Stone, Ron, T, Boston College [from Los Angeles Raiders] 96
 Choice to Chicago Bears thru Green Bay
5. Choice to Pittsburgh
6. *Minter, Barry, LB, Tulsa, 168
7. *Marion, Brock, DB, Nevada-Reno, 196
8. *Thomas, Dave, DB, Tennessee [from Tampa Bay] 203
 Givens, Reggie, DB, Penn State [from Green Bay] 213
 Choice to Tampa Bay

DENVER 1993
1. *Williams, Dan, DE, Toledo [from Cleveland] 11
 Choice to Cleveland
2. *Milburn, Glyn, RB, Stanford, 43
3. *Jones, Rondell, DB, North Carolina [from Los Angeles Raiders] 69
 *Elam, Jason, P-K, Hawaii, 70
4. *Robinson, Jeff, DE, Idaho, 98
5. *Williams, Kevin, RB, UCLA, 126
6. *Bonner, Melvin, WR, Baylor, 154
7. *Williams, Clarence, TE, Washington State [from New England Patriots thru Atlanta] 169
 *Kimbrough, Antonius, WR, Jackson State, 182
8. Stablein, Brian, WR, Ohio State, 210

DETROIT 1993
1. Choice to New Orleans
2. *McNeil, Ryan, DB, Miami [from New York Jets] 33
 Choice to New York Jets
3. *London, Antonio, LB, Alabama, 62
 *Compton, Mike, C, West Virginia [from Cleveland] 68
4. Choice to New Orleans
5. Choice to New York Jets
6. *Jeffries, Greg, DB, Virginia, 147
7. *Hallock, Ty, LB, Michigan State, 174
8. *Miniefield, Kevin, DB, Arizona State, 201

GREEN BAY 1993
1. *Simmons, Wayne, LB, Clemson, 15
 *Teague, George, DB, Alabama [from Dallas] 29
2. Choice to Dallas
3. Choice to Los Angeles Raiders
 *Dotson, Earl, T, Texas A&I [from New Orleans thru San Francisco and Los Angeles Raiders] 81
4. Choice to San Diego thru New England
5. *Brunell, Mark, QB, Washington [from Tampa Bay] 118
 *Willis, James, LB, Auburn [from Chicago Bears] 119
 Choice to New York Jets
6. *Evans, Doug, DB, Louisiana Tech [from Seattle] 141
 *Hutchins, Paul, T, Western Michigan [from Los Angeles Raiders] 152
 *Watson, Tim, DB, Howard, 156
7. *Kuberski, Robert, DE, Navy, 183
8. Choice to Dallas

HOUSTON 1993
1. *Hopkins, Brad, T, Illinois [from Philadelphia] 13
 Choice to Philadelphia
2. *Barrow, Micheal, LB, Miami, 47
3. Choice to Philadelphia
4. *Hannah, Travis, WR, Southern California, 102
5. *Mills, John Henry, TE, Wake Forest, 131
6. *Bradley, Chuck, T, Kentucky, 158
7. *Robinson, Patrick, WR, Tennessee State, 187
8. *Bishop, Blaine, DB, Ball State, 214

INDIANAPOLIS 1993
1. *Dawkins, Sean, WR, California, 16
2. Choice to Pittsburgh
 *Potts, Roosevelt, RB, Northeast Louisiana [from Pittsburgh] 49
3. *Buchanan, Ray, DB, Louisville [from Los Angeles Rams] 65
 Choice to Los Angeles Rams
4. *Gray, Derwin, DB, Brigham Young [from Chicago Bears] 92
 Choice to Chicago Bears
 *McDonald, Devon, LB, Notre Dame [from San Diego thru Pittsburgh] 107
5. Choice to Los Angeles Rams
6. *Etheredge, Carlos, TE, Miami, 157
7. Lewis, Lance, RB, Nebraska, 184
8. Thomas, Marquise, LB, Mississippi, 211

KANSAS CITY 1993
1. Choice to Phoenix thru San Francisco
2. Choice exercised in 1992 Supplemental Draft
3. *Shields, Will, G, Nebraska, 74
4. *Fields, Jaime, LB, Washington, 103
5. *Knapp, Lindsay, G, Notre Dame, 130
6. Turner, Darius, RB, Washington, 159
7. *Hughes, Danan, WR, Iowa, 186
8. Choice to Phoenix

LOS ANGELES RAIDERS
1. *Bates, Patrick, DB, Texas A&M, 12
2. Choice to San Diego thru San Francisco
3. *Hobert, Billy Joe, QB, Washington [from Dallas thru San Francisco] 58
 Choice to Denver
 *Trapp, James, DB, Clemson [from Green Bay] 72
4. Choice to Dallas
5. *Truitt, Olanda, WR, Mississippi State, 125
6. Choice to Green Bay
7. *Biekert, Greg, LB, Colorado, 181
8. *Robinson, Greg, RB, Northeast Louisiana, 208

LOS ANGELES RAMS 1993
1. *Bettis, Jerome, RB, Notre Dame, 10
2. *Drayton, Troy, TE, Penn State, 39
3. Choice to Indianapolis
 *White, Russell, RB, California [from Indianapolis] 73
4. Choice to San Diego
5. *LaChapelle, Sean, WR, UCLA, 122
 *Belin, Chuck, G, Wisconsin [from Indianapolis] 127
6. *Boykin, Deral, DB, Louisville, 149
7. *Fichtel, Brad, C, Eastern Illinois, 179
8. Buffaloe, Jeff, P, Memphis State, 206
 *Tanuvasa, Maa, DT, Hawaii [from Cleveland] 209

MIAMI 1993
1. *McDuffie, O.J., WR, Penn State, 25
2. Choice to New England
3. *Kirby, Terry, RB, Virginia, 78
4. *Bradford, Ronnie, DB, Colorado, 105
5. *Gray, Chris, G, Auburn, 132
6. *O'Neal, Robert, DB, Clemson, 164
7. *Merritt, David, LB, North Carolina State, 191
8. *Gordon, Dwayne, LB, New Hampshire, 218

MINNESOTA 1993
1. *Smith, Robert, RB, Ohio State, 21
2. *Ismail, Qadry, WR, Syracuse, 52
3. *Gerak, John, G, Penn State [from Seattle] 57
 *Brown, Gilbert, DT, Kansas, 79
4. *Sheppard, Ashley, LB, Clemson, 106
5. *Lindsay, Everett, T, Mississippi, 133
6. Choice to Washington
7. *Torretta, Gino, QB, Miami, 192
8. Choice to San Francisco

NEW ENGLAND 1993
1. *Bledsoe, Drew, QB, Washington State, 1
2. *Slade, Chris, DE, Virginia, 31
3. *Rucci, Todd, T, Penn State [from Miami] 51
 *Brisby, Vincent, WR, Northeast Louisiana, 56
4. *Johnson, Kevin, NT, Texas Southern, 86
 *Brown, Corwin, DB, Michigan [from San Francisco thru San Diego] 110
5. *Sisson, Scott, K, Georgia Tech, 113
 *Griffith, Richard, TE, Arizona [from San Francisco thru San Diego] 138
6. Hatch, Lawrence, DB, Florida, 142
7. Choice to Denver thru Atl
8. *Brown, Troy, KR, Mashall, 198

NEW ORLEANS 1993
1. *Roaf, William, T, Louisiana Tech [from Detroit] 8
 *Smith, Irv, TE, Notre Dame [from Phoenix thru San Francisco] 20
 Choice to San Francisco
2. *Freeman, Reggie, LB, Florida State, 53
3. Choice to Green Bay thru San Francisco and Los Angeles Raiders
4. *Neal, Lorenzo, RB, Fresno State [from Detroit] 89
 *Brown, Derek, RB, Nebraska, 109
5. *Hughes, Tyrone, DB, Nebraska, 137
6. *Dixon, Ronnie, NT, Cincinnati, 165
7. *Henderson, Othello, DB, UCLA, 193
8. Kirksey, Jon, NT, Cal State-Sacramento, 221

NEW YORK GIANTS 1993
1. Choice exercised in 1992 Supplemental Draft
2. *Strahan, Michael, DE, Texas Southern, 40
3. *Buckley, Marcus, LB, Texas A&M, 66
4. *Bishop, Greg, T, Pacific, 93
5. Thigpen, Tommy, LB, North Carolina, 123
6. *Davis, Scott, G, Iowa, 150
7. *Peterson, Todd, K, Georgia, 177
8. *Armstead, Jessie, LB, Miami, 207

NEW YORK JETS 1993
1. Choice to Phoenix
 *Jones, Marvin, LB, Florida State [from Phoenix] 4
2. Choice to Detroit
 *Rudolph, Coleman, DE, Georgia Tech [from Detroit] 36
3. Choice to Cincinnati
4. Ware, David, T, Virginia, 88
5. *Baxter, Fred, TE, Auburn, 115
 *Murrell, Adrian, RB, West Virginia [from Detroit] 120
 *Shedd, Kenny, WR, Northern Iowa [from Green Bay] 129
6. *Anderson, Richie, RB, Penn State, 144
7. Millen, Alec, T, Georgia, 171
8. *Hentrich, Craig, K, Notre Dame, 200

PHILADELPHIA 1993
1. #Choice to Houston
 *Holmes, Lester, T, Jackson State [from Houston] 19
 *Renfro, Leonard, DT, Colorado, 24
2. *Bailey, Victor, WR, Missouri, 50
3. *Frazier, Derrick, DB, Texas A&M [from Houston] 75
 *Reid, Mike, DB, North Carolina State, 77
4. Choice to Tampa Bay thru San Diego
5. Choice to Buffalo
6. *Oden, Derrick, LB, Alabama, 163
7. *Mickey, Joey, TE, Oklahoma, 190
8. *Skene, Doug, T, Michigan, 217

PHOENIX 1993
1. *Hearst, Garrison, RB, Georgia [from New York Jets] 3
 Choice to New York Jets
 *Dye, Ernest, T, South Carolina [from Kansas City thru San Francisco] 18
 #Choice to New Orleans thru San Francisco
2. *Coleman, Ben, T, Wake Forest, 32
3. Choice to Tampa Bay
4. *Moore, Ronald, RB, Pittsburg (KS), 87
5. Choice to San Francisco
6. *Wallerstedt, Brett, LB, Arizona State, 143
7. White, Will, DB, Florida, 172
8. *Brown, Chad, DE, Mississippi, 199
 *Anderson, Steve, WR, Grambling [from Kansas City] 215

PITTSBURGH 1993
1. *Figures, Deon, DB, Colorado, 23
2. *Brown, Chad, LB, Colorado [from Indianapolis] 44
 Choice to Indianapolis
3. *Hastings, Andre, WR, Georgia, 76
4. *Henry, Kevin, DE, Mississippi State, 108
5. *Palelei, Lonnie, G, Nevada-Las Vegas, 135
 Woodard, Marc, LB, Mississippi State [from Dallas] 140
6. *Williams, Willie, DB, Western Carolina, 162
7. *Zgonina, Jeff, DT, Purdue [from Washington] 185
 *Keith, Craig, TE, Lenoir-Rhyne, 189
8. *Van Pelt, Alex, QB, Pittsburgh, 216

SAN DIEGO 1993
1. *Gordon, Darrien, DB, Stanford, 22
2. *Means, Natrone, RB, North Carolina [from Los Angeles Raiders thru San Francisco] 41
 Choice to San Francisco
3. *Cocozzo, Joe, G, Michigan [from Tampa Bay] 64
 Choice to Washington
4. *Johnson, Raylee, DE, Arkansas [from Los Angeles Rams] 95
 *Bush, Lewis, LB, Washington State [from Green Bay thru New England] 99
 Choice to Indianapolis thru Pit
5. Dunson, Walter, WR, Middle Tennessee State, 134
6. *Castle, Eric, DB, Oregon, 161
7. *Miller, Doug, LB, South Dakota State, 188
8. Choice to Tampa Bay
 Green, Trent, QB, Indiana [from San Francisco] 222

SAN FRANCISCO 1993
1. *Stubblefield, Dana, DT, Kansas [from New Orleans] 26
 *Kelly, Todd, DE, Tennessee, 27
2. *Hardy, Adrian, DB, Northwest Louisiana [from San Diego] 48
 Choice to Dallas thru Green Bay
3. Choice to Tampa Bay thru San Diego
4. Choice to New England thru San Diego
5. *Smith, Artie, DT, Louisiana Tech [from Phoenix] 116
 Choice to New England thru San Diego
6. *Dalman, Chris, G, Stanford, 166
7. *Wilson, Troy, LB, Pittsburg (KS), 194
8. *Grbac, Elvis, QB, Michigan [from Minnesota] 219
 Choice to San Diego

SEATTLE 1993
1. *Mirer, Rick, QB, Notre Dame, 2
2. *Gray, Carlton, DB, UCLA, 30
3. Choice to Minnesota
4. *Wells, Dean, LB, Kentucky, 85
5. *Warren, Terrence, WR, Hampton, 114
6. Choice to Green Bay
7. *McCrary, Michael, DE, Wake Forest, 170
8. *Blackshear, Jeff, G, Northeast Louisiana, 197
 *Edwards, Antonio, DE, Valdosta State [from Chicago Bears]204

TAMPA BAY 1993
1. *Curry, Eric, DE, Alabama, 6
2. *DuBose, Demetrius, LB, Notre Dame, 34
3. *Thomas, Lamar, WR, Miami [from Phoenix] 60
 Choice to San Diego

*Lynch, John, DB, Stanford [from San Francisco thru San Diego] 82
4. *Harris, Rudy, RB, Clemson, 91
*Copeland, Horace, WR, Miami [from Philadelphia thru San Diego] 104
5. Choice to Green Bay
6. *Ahanotu, Chidi, DT, California, 145
7. *Davis, Tyree, WR, Central Arkansas, 176
8. Choice to Dallas
Branch, Darrick, WR, Hawaii [from San Diego] 220
Alcorn, Daron, K, Akron [from Dallas] 224

WASHINGTON 1993
1. *Carter, Tom, DB, Notre Dame, 17
2. *Brooks, Reggie, RB, Notre Dame, 45
3. *Hamilton, Rick, LB, Central Florida, 71
Bunn, Ed, P, Texas-El Paso [from San Diego] 80
4. *Palmer, Sterling, DE, Florida State, 101
5. *Huntington, Greg, C, Penn State, 128
6. *Morrison, Darryl, DB, Arizona, 155
*Wycheck, Frank, TE, Maryland [from Minnesota] 160
7. Choice to Pittsburgh
8. *Hollinquest, Lamont, LB, Southern California, 212

1994

Held April 24-25, 1994

#Compensatory Pick

ARIZONA 1994
1. *Miller, Jamir, LB, UCLA 10
2. *Levy, Chuck, RB, Arizona, 38
#Choice to Miami
3. *Braham, Rich, G, West Virginia, 76
*England, Eric, DE, Texas A&M [from Green Bay thru Miami] 89
4. *Carter, Perry, DB, Southern Mississippi [from New England] 107
*Reece, John, DB, Nebraska, 113
*Irving, Terry, LB, McNeese State [from San Diego thru Miami] 115
5. *Redmon, Anthony, G, Auburn, 139
6. *Samuels, Terry, TE, Kentucky, 172
7. *Harvey, Frank, RB, Georgia, 204

ATLANTA 1994
1. Choice to San Francisco thru Ind and Los Angeles Rams
2. Choice to Philadelphia
#*Emanuel, Bert, WR, Rice [from Minnesota] 45
3. *Phillips, Anthony, DB, Texas A&M-Kingsville, 72
#Choice to Los Angeles Rams thru Indianapolis
Kalaniuvalu, Alai, G, Oregon State [from Dal thru San Francisco and Denver] 99
4. *Klein, Perry, QB, C.W. Post, 111
Davis, Mitch, LB, Georgia [from Philadelphia] 118
5. Houston, Harrison, WR, Florida, 138
6. Choice to Green Bay thru Los Angeles Raiders
7. *Anderson, Jamal, RB, Utah, 201

BUFFALO 1994
1. *Burris, Jeff, DB, Notre Dame, 27
2.#*Brooks, Bucky, WR, North Carolina, 48
*Johnson, Lonnie, TE, Florida State, 61
#*Rogers, Sam, LB, Colorado, 64
3.#*Perry, Marlo, LB, Jackson State, 81
*Louchiey, Corey, T, South Carolina, 98
4. Crocker, Sean, DB, North Carolina, 130
5. Ofodile, A.J., TE, Missouri, 158
6. Abrams, Kevin, DE, Clark (GA), 188
#*Knox, Kevin, WR, Florida State, 192
7. *Johnson, Filmel, DB, Illinois, 221

CHICAGO BEARS 1994
1. *Thierry, John, DE, Alcorn State, 11
2. *Spears, Marcus, T, Northwest Louisiana, 39
3. *Flanigan, Jim, DT, Notre Dame, 74
4. *Harris, Raymont, RB, Ohio State, 114
5. Choice to Pittsburgh
6. Hill, Lloyd, WR, Texas Tech, 170
7. Collier, Dennis, DB, Colorado, 205

CINCINNATI 1994
1. *Wilkinson, Dan, DT, Ohio State, 1
2. *Scott, Darnay, WR, San Diego State, 30
3. *Cothran, Jeff, RB, Ohio State, 66
#Shine, Steve, LB, Northwestern, 86
4. *Sawyer, Corey, DB, Florida State, 104
5. *Pollard, Trent, T, Eastern Washington, 132
6. *Von Oelhoffen, Kimo, DT, Boise State, 162
*Reynolds, Jerry, T, Nevada-Las Vegas [from Los Angeles Raiders] 184
7. *Stallings, Ramondo, DE, San Diego State, 195

CLEVELAND 1994
1. *Langham, Antonio, DB, Alabama, 9
#*Alexander, Derrick, WR, Michigan [from Philadelphia] 29
2. Choice to Minnesota thru Phi and Atl
3. *Bandison, Romeo, DT, Oregon, 75
4. Choice to Miami
5. *Booth, Issac, DB, California, 141
6. Strait, Robert, RB, Baylor, 171
7. Hewitt, Andre, T, Clemson, 203

DALLAS 1994
1. *Carver, Shante, DE, Arizona State [from San Francisco] 23
Choice to San Francisco
2.#*Allen, Larry, G, Sonoma State, 46
Choice to San Francisco
3. Choice to Atlanta thru San Francisco and Den
#*Hegamin, George, T, North Carolina State, 102
4. *Jackson, Willie, WR, Florida [from Tampa Bay] 109
*Dotson, DeWayne, LB, Mississippi, 131
5. Choice to Los Angeles Raiders
6. Choice to Los Angeles Rams
#*Studstill, Darren, DB, West Virginia [from Los Angeles Rams] 191
7. *McIntosh, Toddrick, DT, Florida State [from Los Angeles Raiders] 216
Choice to New England

DENVER 1994
1. Choice to Minnesota
2. *Aldridge, Allen, LB, Houston, 51
3. Choice to San Francisco
4. *Fuller, Randy, DB, Tennessee State, 123
5. Choice to Green Bay thru San Francisco
6. Choice to Minnesota
7. *Burns, Keith, LB, Oklahoma State, 210
*By'not'e, Butler, RB, Ohio State [from Green Bay] 212
*Nalen, Tom, C, Boston College [from New York Giants] 218

DETROIT 1994
1. *Morton, Johnnie, WR, Southern California, 21
2. *Malone, Van, DB, Texas, 57
3. *Bonham, Shane, DT, Tennessee, 93
4. Bryant, Vaughn, DB, Stanford, 124
5. *Semple, Tony, G, Memphis State, 154
6. *Borgella, Jocelyn, DB, Cincinnati, 183
7. *Beer, Tom, LB, Wayne State (MI), 215

GREEN BAY 1994
1. *Taylor, Aaron, T, Notre Dame [from Miami] 16
Choice to Miami
2. Choice to San Francisco
3.*Johnson, LeShon, RB, Northern Illinois [from San Francisco] 84
Choice to Arizona thru Miami
4. Choice to Los Angeles Raiders
*Wilkins, Gabe, DE, Gardner-Webb [from San Francisco thru Los Angeles Raiders] 126
5. *Mickens, Terry, WR, Florida A&M, 146
*Levens, Dorsey, RB, Georgia Tech [from Denver thru San Francisco] 149
6. Kearney, Jay, WR, West Virginia [from Atlanta thru Los Angeles Raiders] 169
*Hamilton, Ruffin, LB, Tulane [from San Diego thru San Francisco] 175
Schroeder, Bill, WR, Wisconsin-LaCrosse, 181
#*Duckworth, Paul, LB, Connecticut [from Philadelphia thru San Francisco] 190
7. Choice to Denver

HOUSTON 1994
1. *Ford, Henry, DE, Arkansas, 26
2. *Nunley, Jeremy, DE, Alabama, 60
3. Choice to Washington
#*Seabron, Malcolm, WR, Fresno State, 101
4. *Davis, Michael, DB, Cincinnati [from Minnesota] 119
Jackson, Sean, RB, Florida State, 129
5. *Lewis, Roderick, TE, Arizona, 157
#*Reid, Jim, T, Virginia, 161
6. Gissendaner, Lee, WR, Northwestern, 187
#*Wortham, Barron, LB, Texas-El Paso, 194
7. *Hall, Lemanski, LB, Alabama, 220

INDIANAPOLIS 1994
1. *Faulk, Marshall, RB, San Diego State, 2
*Alberts, Trev, LB, Nebraska [from Los Angeles Rams] 5
2. *Mahlum, Eric, G, California, 32
3. *Mathews, Jason, T, Texas A&M, 67
4. *Banta, Brad, TE, Southern California, 106
5. *Covington, John, DB, Notre Dame, 133
6. *Warren, Lamont, RB, Colorado, 164
7. *Teichelman, Lance, DT, Texas A&M, 196

KANSAS CITY 1994
1. *Hill, Greg, RB, Texas A&M, 25
2. *Bennett, Donnell, RB, Miami, 58
3. *Dawson, Lake, WR, Notre Dame [from San Francisco] 92
*Penn, Chris, WR, Tulsa, 96
4. *Walker, Bracey, DB, North Carolina, 127
5. *Burton, James, DB, Fresno State [from Minnesota] 151
*Waldrop, Rob, DT, Arizona, 156
6. *Daigle, Anthony, RB, Fresno State, 185
7. Matthews, Steve, QB, Memphis State [from Los Angeles Rams] 199
*Greene, Tracy, TE, Grambling, 219

LOS ANGELES RAIDERS 1994
1. *Fredrickson, Rob, LB, Michigan State, 22
2. *Folston, James, DE, Northeast Louisiana [from Minnesota] 52
Choice to Minnesota
3. *Jones, Calvin, RB, Nebraska [from New York Jets] 80
Choice to New York Jets
4. *Robbins, Austin, DT, North Carolina [from Green Bay] 120
Choice to Minnesota
5. Choice to New York Jets
Patterson, Roosevelt, G, Alabama [from Dallas] 159
6. Choice to Cincinnati
7. Choice to Dallas
*Holmberg, Rob, LB, Penn State [from San Francisco thru Dallas] 217

LOS ANGELES RAMS 1994
1. Choice to Indianapolis
*Gandy, Wayne, T, Auburn [from San Diego thru San Francisco] 15
2. *Bruce, Isaac, WR, Memphis State, 33
#*Wright, Toby, DB, Nebraska, 49
*Ottis, Brad, DT, Wayne State (NE) [from San Francisco] 56
3. *Lyle, Keith, DB, Virginia, 71
#Bostic, James, RB, Auburn [from Atlanta thru Indianapolis] 83
#*Jones, Ernest, LB, Oregon [from Philadelphia thru San Francisco] 100
4. *Brantley, Chris, WR, Rutgers, 108
5. Choice to New England thru Ariz
6. *Brady, Rickey, TE, Oklahoma, 167
Edwards, Ronald, T, North Carolina A&T [from Dallas] 189
#Choice to Dallas
7. Choice to Kansas City

MIAMI 1994
1. Choice to Green Bay
*Bowens, Tim, DT, Mississippi [from Green Bay] 20
2. *Beavers, Aubrey, LB, Oklahoma, 54
#*Ruddy, Tim, C, Notre Dame [from Arizona] 65
3. Choice to New England
4. Woolfork, Ronnie, LB, Colorado [from Cleveland] 112
Choice to New England thru Arizona
5. *Gaines, William, DT, Florida, 147
6. *Boyer, Brant, LB, Arizona, 177
7. *Hill, Sean, DB, Montana State, 214

MINNESOTA 1994
1. *Washington, DeWayne, DB, North Carolina State [from Denver] 18
*Steussie, Todd, T, California, 19
2. *Palmer, David, WR, Alabama [from Cleveland thru Philadelphia and Atlanta] 40
#Choice to Atlanta
Choice to Los Angeles Raiders
*Smith, Fernando, DE, Jackson State [from Los Angeles Raiders] 55
3. Choice to Pittsburgh
4. Choice to Houston
*Wells, Mike, DT, Iowa [from Los Angeles Raiders] 125
5. *Hammonds, Shelly, DB, Penn State [from Washington] 134
Choice to Kansas City
6. *Jordan, Andrew, TE, Western Carolina [from Denver] 179
Choice to Pittsburgh
7. *Bercich, Pete, LB, Notre Dame, 211

NEW ENGLAND 1994
1. *McGinest, Willie, DE, Southern California, 4
2. *Lee, Kevin, WR, Alabama, 35
3. Choice to San Diego
Collier, Ervin, NT, Florida A&M [from San Diego] 78
Burch, Joe, C, Texas Southern [from Miami] 90
4. Choice to Arizona
*Burke, John, TE, Virginia Tech [from Miami thru Arizona] 121
5. *O'Neill, Pat, P, Syracuse [from Los Angeles Rams thru Arizona] 135
Choice to San Diego
6. *Hawkins, Steve, WR, Western Michigan, 166
*Lane, Max, T, Navy [from Seattle] 168
7. Walker, Jay, QB, Howard, 198
*Moore, Marty, LB, Kentucky [from Dallas] 222

NEW ORLEANS 1994
1. Choice to New York Jets
*Johnson, Joe, DE, Louisville [from New York Jets] 13
2. *Bates, Mario, RB, Arizona State, 44
3. *Tubbs, Winfred, LB, Texas, 79
4. *Nussmeier, Doug, QB, Idaho, 116
5. *Carroll, Herman, DE, Mississippi State, 142
*Novitsky, Craig, G, UCLA [from New York Jets] 143
6. *Mitchell, Derrell, WR, Texas Tech, 176
7. Lundberg, Lance, T, Nebraska, 213

NEW YORK GIANTS 1994
1. *Lewis, Thomas, WR, Indiana, 24
2.#*Randolph, Thomas, DB, Kansas State, 47
*Sehorn, Jason, DB, Southern California, 59
3. *Downs, Gary, RB, North Carolina State, 95
4. *Maumalanga, Chris, DT, Kansas, 128
5. *Bratzke, Chad, DE, Eastern Kentucky, 155
6. Winrow, Jason, G, Ohio State, 186
7. Choice to Denver

NEW YORK JETS 1994
1. *Glenn, Aaron, DB, Texas A&M [from New Orleans] 12
Choice to New Orleans
2. *Yarborough, Ryan, WR, Wyoming, 41
3. Choice to Los Angeles Raiders
*Benfatti, Lou, DT, Penn State [from Los Angeles Raiders] 94
4. *Parker, Orlando, WR, Troy State, 117
5. Choice to New Orleans
Morris, Horace, LB, Tennessee [from Los Angeles Raiders] 152
6. Lester, Fred, RB, Alabama A&M, 173
7. *Foley, Glenn, QB, Boston College, 208

PHILADELPHIA 1994
1. *Williams, Bernard, T, Georgia, 14
#Choice to Cleveland
2. *Walker, Bruce, DT, UCLA [from Atlanta] 37
*Garner, Charlie, RB, Tennessee, 42
3. *Panos, Joe, G, Wisconsin, 77
#Choice to Los Angeles Rams thru San Francisco
#*Zomalt, Eric, DB, California, 103
4. Choice to Atlanta
5. Goodwin, Marvin, DB, UCLA, 144
6. McCoy, Ryan, LB, Houston, 174
#Choice to Green Bay thru San Francisco
#*Berger, Mitch, P, Colorado, 193
7. Montgomery, Mark, RB, Wisconsin, 206

PITTSBURGH 1994
1. *Johnson, Charles, WR, Colorado, 17
2. *Buckner, Brentson, DE, Clemson, 50
3. *Gildon, Jason, LB, Oklahoma State [from Minnesota] 88
*Morris, Bam, RB, Texas Tech, 91
4. *Faumui, Taase, DE, Hawaii, 122
5. *Bell, Myron, DB, Michigan State [from Chicago Bears] 140
*Brown, Gary, T, Georgia Tech, 148
6. *Miller, Jim, QB, Michigan State, 178
*Ravotti, Eric, LB, Penn State [from Minnesota] 180
7. Abrams, Brice, RB, Michigan State, 209

SAN DIEGO 1994
1. Choice to Los Angeles Rams thru San Francisco
2. *Davis, Isaac, G, Arkansas, 43
#*Parker, Vaughn, G, UCLA, 63
3. *Coleman, Andre, WR, Kansas State [from New England] 70
Choice to New England
#*Clark, Willie, DB, Notre Dame, 82
4. Choice to Arizona thru Miami
5. *Laing, Aaron, TE, New Mexico State [from New England] 137
*Harrison, Rodney, DB, Western Illinois, 145
Krein, Darren, DE, Miami [from Seattle] 150
#Vinson, Tony, RB, Towson State, 160
6. Choice to Green Bay thru San Francisco
7. Beehn, Zane, LB, Kentucky, 207

SAN FRANCISCO 1994
1. *Young, Bryant, DT, Notre Dame [from Atlanta thru Ind and Los Angeles Rams] 7
Choice to Dallas
*Floyd, William, RB, Florida State [from Dallas] 28
2. *Mitchell, Kevin, LB, Syracuse [from Green Bay] 53
Choice to Los Angeles Rams
*Drakeford, Tyronne, DB, Virginia Tech [from Dallas] 62
3. #Choice to Green Bay
#*Brien, Doug, K, California, 85
*Fleming, Cory, WR, Tennessee [from Denver] 87
Choice to Kansas City
4. Choice to Green Bay thru Los Angeles Raiders
5. *Peterson, Anthony, LB, Notre Dame, 153
6. *Woodall, Lee, LB, West Chester (PA), 182
7. Choice to Los Angeles Raiders thru Dallas

SEATTLE 1994
1. *Adams, Sam, DT, Texas A&M, 8
2. *Mawae, Kevin, C, Louisiana State, 36
3. *Smith, Lamar, RB, Houston, 73
4. *Whigham, Larry, DB, Northeast Louisiana, 110
5. Choice to San Diego
6. Choice to New England
7. *Crumpler, Carlester, TE, East Carolina, 202

TAMPA BAY 1994
1. *Dilfer, Trent, QB, Fresno State, 6
2. *Rhett, Errict, RB, Florida, 34
3. *Bishop, Harold, TE, Louisiana State, 69
4. Choice to Dallas
5. *Pierson, Pete, T, Washington, 136
6. *Carter, Bernard, LB, East Carolina, 165
7. *Pyne, Jim, C, Virginia Tech, 200

WASHINGTON 1994
1. *Shuler, Heath, QB, Tennessee, 3
2. *Johnson, Tre, T, Temple, 31
3. *Winans, Tydus, WR, Fresno State, 68
*Patton, Joe, G, Alabama A&M [from Houston] 97
4. *Haws, Kurt, TE, Utah, 105
5. Choice to Minnesota
6. *Nottage, Dexter, DE, Florida A&M, 163
7. *Frerotte, Gus, QB, Tulsa, 197

1995

Held April 22-23, 1995

On February 15, 1995, Carolina and Jacksonville participated in an expansion draft. Jacksonville, which had the first pick, chose 31 players. Carolina chose 35. In the April draft, each of the expansion teams had two picks per round.

Although the Raiders played the 1995 season in Oakland, the franchise still was in Los Angeles at the time of the draft.

#Compensatory Pick

ARIZONA 1995
1. Choice to New York Jets
2. *Sanders, Frank, WR, Auburn, 47
3. *Case, Stoney, QB, New Mexico, 80
4. Choice to Buffalo
5. Davis, Cedric, DB, Tennessee State, 150
   #Scott, Lance, C, Utah, 165
   #*Paul, Tito, DB, Ohio State, 167
6. Choice to Detroit
   #Bridges, Anthony, DB, North Texas, 205
7. *Williams, Billy, WR, Tennessee [from Washington] 212
   *Leasy, Wesley, LB, Mississippi State, 224
   #Eaton, Chad, DT, Washington State, 241

ATLANTA 1995
1. Choice to San Francisco thru Cle
   *Bush, Devin, DB, Florida State [from Cleveland] 26
2. *Davis, Ronald, DB, Tennessee [from Tampa Bay thru Dallas] 41
   Choice to Dallas
3. *Styles, Lorenzo, LB, Ohio State, 77
4. Choice to Dallas
5. *Preston, Roell, WR, Mississippi, 145
6. *Hall, Travis, DT, Brigham Young, 181
7. Choice to Denver
   #*Burrough, John, DE, Wyoming, 245

BUFFALO 1995
1. *Brown, Ruben, G, Pittsburgh, 14
2. *Collins, Todd, QB, Michigan, 45
3. *Kerner, Marlon, DB, Ohio State, 76
   #*Covington, Damien, LB, North Carolina State, 96
4. *Irvin, Ken, DB, Memphis State, 109
   *Armour, Justin, WR, Stanford [from Arizona] 113
   #*Cline, Tony, TE, Stanford, 131
5. *Holecek, John, LB, Illinois, 144
6. *Clavelle, Shannon, DE, Colorado, 185
7. *Nutten, Tom, C, Western Michigan, 221
   #*Holmes, Darick, RB, Portland State, 244

CAROLINA 1995
1. Choice to Cincinnati
   *Collins, Kerry, QB, Penn State [from Cincinnati] 5
   *Poole, Tyrone, DB, Fort Valley State [from Green Bay] 22
   *Brockermeyer, Blake, T, Texas [from San Diego] 29
   Choice to Green Bay
2. Choice to San Diego
   *King, Shawn, DE, Northeast Louisiana [from Cincinnati] 36
   Forfeited choice
3. Choice to Green Bay
   Choice to San Diego
4. Choice to San Diego
   *Garcia, Frank, C, Washington, 132
5. *Senters, Michael, DB, Northwestern, 135
   *Peterson, Andrew, T, Washington, 171
6. Choice to Green Bay
   Strahan, Steve, DT, Baylor [from Green Bay] 188
   Colquitt, Jerry, QB, Tennessee [from Kansas City] 191
   Forfeited choice
7. *Cota, Chad, DB, Oregon, 209
   *Reed, Michael, DB, Boston College, 249

CAROLINA (Expansion) 1995
*Smith, Rod, CB, Notre Dame [from New England]
*Boatswain, Harry, T, New Haven [from San Francisco]
*Haws, Kurt, TE, Utah [from Washington]
*Rodgers, Tyrone, DE. Washington [from Seattle]
*Thomas, Mark, DE, North Carolina State [from San Francisco]
*McKyer. Tim, CB, Texas-Arlington [from Pittsburgh]
*Whitley, Curtis, C, Clemson [from San Diego]
*Griffith, Howard, RB, Illinois [from Los Angeles Rams]
*Kragen, Greg, NT, Utah State [from Kansas City]
*Brabham, Cary, DB, Southern Methodist [from Los Angeles Raiders]
*Garnett, Dave, LB, Stanford [from Minnesota]
*Powell, Andre, LB, Penn State [from New York Giants]
*Brewer, Dewell, RB, Oklahoma [from Indianapolis]
*Christian, Bob, RB, Northwestern [from Chicago Bears]
*Foggie, Fred, DB, Minnesota [from Pittsburgh]
*Carrier, Mark, WR, Nicholls State [from Cleveland]
*Rodenhauser, Mark, C, Illinois State [from Detroit]
*Hawkins, Steve, WR, Western Michigan [from New England]
*O'Neal, Brian, RB, Penn State [from Philadelphia]
*Lassic, Derrick, RB, Alabama [from Dallas]
*Buchanan, Richard, WR, Northwestern [from Los Angeles Rams]
*Pederson, Doug, QB, N.E. Louisiana [from Miami]
*Marrow, Vince, TE, Toledo [from Buffalo]
*Ryans, Larry, WR, Clemson [from Detroit]
*Rollins, Baron, G, Louisiana Tech [from New Orleans]
*Sims, Williams, LB, Southwestern Louisiana [from Minnesota]
*Butcher, Paul, LB, Wayne State [from Indianapolis]
*Trudeau, Jack, QB, Illinois [from New York Jets]
*Swann, Charles, WR, Indiana State [from Denver]
*Mims, David, WR, Baylor [from Atlanta]
*Price, Shawn, DE, Pacific [from Tampa Bay]
*Quliford, Eric, WR, Aruona State [from Minnesota]
*Goldberg, Bill, DT, Georgia [from Atlanta]
*'Ball, Eric, RB, UCLA [from Cincinnati]
*Teeter, Mike, DT, Michigan [from Houston]

CHICAGO BEARS 1995
1. *Salaam, Rashaan, RB, Colorado, 21
2. *Riley, Patrick, DE, Miami, 52
   *Sauerbrun, Todd, P, West Virginia [from Miami] 56
3. *Harris, Sean, LB, Arizona, 83
   *Pilgrim, Evan, G, Brigham Young [from Miami] 87
4. *Jackson, Jack, WR, Florida, 116
5. Choice to Pittsburgh
6. Gales, Kenny, DB, Wisconsin, 193
   *Reeves, Carl, DE, North Carolina State [from Dallas] 198
7. Cox, Jamal, LB, Georgia Tech, 229

CINCINNATI 1995
1. *Carter, Ki-Jana, RB, Penn State [from Car] 1
   Choice to Carolina
2. Choice to Carolina
3. *Tuten, Melvin, T, Syracuse, 69
4. *Shade, Sam, DB, Alabama, 102
5. *Dunn, David, WR, Fresno State, 139
6. Grigson, Ryan, T, Purdue, 175
7. *Walsh, John, QB, Brigham Young, 213

CLEVELAND 1995
1. Choice to Atlanta
   *Powell, Craig, LB, Ohio State [from San Francisco] 30
2. Choice to Philadelphia
3. *Zeier, Eric, QB, Georgia [from Green Bay] 84
   Choice to Green Bay
   *Frederick, Mike, DE, Virginia [from San Francisco] 94
4. Choice to Jacksonville
5. Pupua, Tau, DT, Weber State [from Jac] 136
   Miller, Mike, WR, Notre Dame [from Philadelphia] 147
   Choice to Green Bay
6. Choice to San Diego
7. Tellison, A.C., WR, Miami [from New England] 231
   Choice to New England

DALLAS 1995
1. Choice to Tampa Bay
2. *Williams, Sherman, RB, Alabama [from Atlanta] 46
   *Watkins, Kendell, TE, Mississippi State, 59
   #Hannah, Shane, G, Michigan State [from Phi thru Tampa Bay] 63
3. *Williams, Charlie, DB, Bowling Green, 92
4. *Bjornson, Eric, WR, Washington [from Atlanta] 110
   Choice to Denver thru St. Louis
   #*Brice, Alundis, DB, Mississippi, 129
   #Harden, Linc, LB, Oklahoma State, 130
5. Choice exercised in 1994 Supplemental Draft
   #*Edward, WR, Southern California, 166
   #*Howard, Dana, LB, Illinois, 168
6. Choice to Chicago Bears
7. *Sturgis, Oscar, DE, North Carolina, 236

DENVER 1995
1. Choice to Minnesota thru Atlanta
2. Choice to Minnesota
3. Choice to Philadelphia
4. Choice to Minnesota
   *Brown, Jamie, T, Florida A&M [from Minnesota] 121
   *Brown, Ken, LB, Virginia Tech [from Dallas thru St. Louis] 124
5. *Yeboah-Kodie, Phil, LB, Penn State, 146
6. Fequiere, Fritz, G, Iowa, 182
   *Davis, Terrell, RB, Georgia [from Minnesota] 196
7. Russ, Steve, LB, Air Force, 218
   *Chamberlain, Byron, WR, Wayne State (NE) [from Atlanta] 222

DETROIT 1995
1. *Elliss, Luther, DT, Utah, 20
2. Choice to San Diego
3. *Sloan, David, TE, New Mexico [from St. Louis] 70
   Choice to St. Louis
4. Choice to St. Louis
5. *Boyd, Stephen, LB, Boston College [from Seattle] 141
   *McCorvey, Kez, WR, Florida State, 156
   *Cherry, Ronald, T, McNeese State [from San Francisco] 163
6. *Hickman, Kevin, TE, Navy [from Arizona] 186
   *Schlesinger, Cory, RB, Nebraska, 192
7. *Hempstead, Hessley, G, Kansas, 228

GREEN BAY 1995
1. Choice to Carolina
   *Newsome, Craig, DB, Arizona State [from Carolina] 32
2. Choice to Miami
3. *Holland, Darius, DT, Colorado [from Carolina] 65
   *Henderson, William, RB, North Carolina [from Jacksonville] 66
   *Williams, Brian, LB, Southern California [from Seattle] 73
   Choice to Cleveland
   *Freeman, Antonio, WR, Virginia Tech [from Cleveland] 90
4. Miller, Jeff, T, Mississippi, 117
5. Choice to Washington thru Oak
   Barker, Jay, QB, Alabama [from Cleveland] 160
   *Jervey, Travis, RB, Citadel [from Jacksonville] 170
6. Simmons, Charlie, WR, Georgia Tech [from Carolina] 173
   Choice to Carolina
7. *Timmerman, Adam, G, South Dakota State, 230

HOUSTON 1995
1. *McNair, Steve, QB, Alcorn State, 3
2. *Cook, Anthony, DT, South Carolina State, 35
3. *Sanders, Chris, WR, Ohio State, 67
   *Thomas, Rodney, RB, Texas A&M [from Minnesota] 89
   #*Hunter, Torey, DB, Washington State, 95
4. *Roan, Michael, TE, Wisconsin, 101
5. Choice to Washington
   *Walker, Gary, DE, Auburn [from New England] 159
6. *El-Mashtoub, Hicham, C, Arizona, 174
7. *Richardson, C.J., DB, Miami, 211

INDIANAPOLIS 1995
1. *Johnson, Ellis, DT, Florida, 15
2. *Dilger, Ken, TE, Illinois, 48
3. *Crockett, Zack, RB, Florida State, 79
4. *McElroy, Ray, DB, Eastern Illinois, 114
5. *West, Derek, T, Colorado, 149
6. Gelzheiser, Brian, LB, Penn State, 187
7. Cox, Jessie, LB, Texas Southern, 223

JACKSONVILLE 1995
1. *Boselli, Tony, T, Southern California, 2
   *Stewart, James, RB, Tennessee [from Kansas City] 19
   Choice to Kansas City
2. Choice to New York Jets
   *DeMarco, Brian, T, Michigan State [from New York Jets] 40
   *Schwartz, Bryan, LB, Augustana (San Diego), 64
3. Choice to Green Bay
   *Hudson, Chris, DB, Colorado [from New York Jets] 71
   Choice to Kansas City
4. *Johnson, Rob, QB, Southern California, 99
   *Thompson, Mike, DT, Wisconsin [from Cleveland] 123
   Choice to Kansas City
5. Choice to Cleveland
   #*Christopherson, Ryan, RB, Wyoming [from Philadelphia] 169
   Choice to Green Bay
6. Price, Marcus, T, Louisiana State, 172
   Choice to Philadelphia
7. Choice to Philadelphia
   *Marsh, Curtis, WR, Utah [from Philadelphia] 219
   Choice to Philadelphia

JACKSONVILLE (Expansion) 1995
*Beuerlein, Steve, QB, Notre Dame [from Arizona]
*Raymond, Corey, CB, Louisiana State [from New York Giants]
*Novak, Jeff, T, Southwest Texas State [from Miami]
*Duff, John, DE, New Mexico [from Los Angeles Raiders]
*Goganious, Keith, LB, Penn State [from Buffalo]
*Williams, Mark, LB, Ohio State [from Green Bay]
*Jackson, Al, CB, Georgia [from Philadelphia]
*Tucker, Mark, C-G, Southern California [from Arizona]
*Frase, Paul, T, Syracuse [from New York Jets]
*Myslinski, Tom, G, Tennessee [from Chicago Bears]
*Jackson, Willie. WR, Florida [from Dallas]
*Henderson, Othello, DB, UCLA [from New Orleans]
*Stephens, Santo, LB, Temple [from Cincinnati]
*Carrington, Darren, S, Northern Arizona [from San Diego]
*Davis, Michael, CB, Cincinnati [from Houston]
*Thomas, Dave, C8, Tennessee [from Dallas]
*Royster, Mazio, RB, USC [from Tampa Bay]
*Maston, Le'Shai, RB, Baylor [from Houston]
*Davenport, Charles, WR, North Carolina State, [from Pittsburgh]
*Grow, Monty, S, Florida [from Kansas City]
*Wilson, Marcus, RB, Virginia [from Green Bay]
*Boyer, Brant, LB, Arizona [from Miami]
*Colon, Harry, S, Missouri [from Detroit]
*Brown, Derek, TE, Notre Dame [from New York Giants]
*Williams, James, LB, Mississippi State [from New Orleans]
*Chung, Eugene, G, Virginia Tech [from New England]
*Cobb, Reggie, RB, Tennessee [from Green Bay]
*Howard, Desmond, WR, Michigan [from Washington]
*Martin, Kelvin, WR, Boston College [from Seattle]
*Tillman, Cedric, WR, Alcorn State [from Denver]
*Green, Rogerick, CB, Kansas State [from Tampa Bay]

KANSAS CITY 1995
1. Choice to Jacksonville
   *Jenkins, Trezelle, T, Michigan [from Jacksonville] 31
2. Choice to Philadelphia
3. *Vanover, Tamarick, WR, Florida State, 81
   *Dumas, Troy, LB, Nebraska [from Jacksonville] 97
4. Choice to Philadelphia thru San Francisco and Cle
   *Stenstrom, Steve, QB, Stanford [from Jacksonville] 134
5. Pelton, Mike, DT, Auburn, 155
   #*Willard, Jerrott, LB, California, 164
6. Choice to Carolina
   #*Bryan, DT, Arizona State, 202
   #*Barndt, Tom, C, Pittsburgh, 207
7. Choice to Tampa Bay

MIAMI 1995
1. *Milner, Billy, T, Houston, 25
2. *Greene, Andrew, G, Indiana [from Green Bay] 53
   Choice to Chicago Bears
3. Choice to Chicago Bears
4. *Mitchell, Pete, TE, Boston College, 122
5. *Hand, Norman, DT, Mississippi, 158
6. *Kopp, Jeff, LB, Southern California, 194
7. Swinson, Corey, DT, Hampton, 233
   #Myers, Shannon, WR, Lenoir-Rhyne, 246

MINNESOTA 1995
1. *Alexander, Derrick, DE, Florida State [from Den thru Atl] 11
   *Stringer, Korey, T, Ohio State, 24
2. *Thomas, Orlando, DB, Southwestern Louisiana [from Denver] 42
   *Fuller, Corey, DB, Florida State, 55
3. Choice to Houston
4. *May, Chad, QB, Kansas State [from Denver] 111
   Choice to Denver
5. *Stewart, James, RB, Miami, 157
6. Solomon, John, LB, Sam Houston State [from New York Giants] 189
   Choice to Denver
7. *White, Jose, LB, Howard, 232
   #*Fisk, Jason, DT, Stanford, 243

NEW ENGLAND 1995
1. *Law, Ty, DB, Michigan, 23
2. *Johnson, Ted, LB, Colorado, 57
3. *Martin, Curtis, RB, Pittsburgh [from Philadelphia] 74
   *Hitchcock, Jimmy, DB, North Carolina, 88
4. *Wohlabaugh, Dave, C, Syracuse [from Philadelphia thru Kansas City] 112
   Choice to Pittsburgh
5. Choice to Houston
6. *Philyaw, Dino, RB, Oregon, 195
7. Choice to Cleveland
   *Yancy, Carlos, DB, Georgia [from Cleveland] 234

NEW ORLEANS 1995
1. *Fields, Mark, LB, Washington State, 13
2. *Zellars, Ray, RB, Notre Dame, 44
3. *Verstegen, Mike, T, Wisconsin, 75
4. *Jeffries, Dameian, DE, Alabama, 108
5. *Strong, William, DB, North Carolina State, 148
6. *DeRamus, Lee, WR, Wisconsin, 184
7. Choice to St. Louis
   #*Davis, Travis, DB, Notre Dame, 242

NEW YORK GIANTS 1995
1. *Wheatley, Tyrone, RB, Michigan, 17
2. *Gragg, Scott, T, Montana, 54
3. *Young, Rodney, DB, Louisiana State, 85
4. Choice exercised in 1994 Supplemental Draft
   #*Zatechka, Rob, G, Nebraska, 128
   #*Talley, Ben, LB, Tennessee, 133
5. *Mullen, Roderick, DB, Grambling State, 153
6. Choice to Minnesota
   #*Duff, Jamal, DE, San Diego State, 204
   #*Way, Charles, RB, Virginia, 206
7. Diehl, Bryne, P, Alabama, 225

NEW YORK JETS 1995
1. *Brady, Kyle, TE, Penn State, 9
   *Douglas, Hugh, DE, Central State (OH) [from Arizona] 16
2. *O'Dwyer, Matt, T, Northwestern [from Jacksonville] 33
   Choice to Jacksonville
3. Choice to Jacksonville

4. *Hayes, Melvin, T, Mississippi State [from Seattle thru Arizona] 106
   *Davis, Tyrone, WR, Virginia, 107
5. *Greenwood, Carl, DB, UCLA, 142
6. *Mason, Eddie, LB, North Carolina, 178
7. *Ceaser, Curtis, WR, Grambling State, 217

OAKLAND 1995
1. *Kaufman, Napoleon, RB, Washington, 18
2. *Robbins, Barret, C, Texas Christian, 49
3. *Aska, Joe, RB, Central State (OK), 86
4. *Morton, Mike, LB, North Carolina, 118
5. *Dyson, Matt, LB, Michigan [from Washington] 138
   *Kysar, Jeff, T, Arizona State, 154
6. Herring, Eli, T, Brigham Young, 190
7. Choice to Washington

PHILADELPHIA 1995
1. *Mamula, Mike, DE, Boston College [from Tampa Bay] 7
   Choice to Tampa Bay
2. Choice to Tampa Bay
   *Taylor, Bobby, DB, Notre Dame [from Kansas City] 50
   *Brooks, Barrett, T, Kansas State [from Cleveland] 58
   #Choice to Dallas thru Tampa Bay
3. *Jefferson, Greg, DE, Central Florida [from Tampa Bay] 72
   Choice to New England
   *Jones, Chris T., WR, Miami [from Denver] 78
4. Choice to New England thru Kansas City
   *Barr, Dave, QB, California [from Kansas City thru San Francisco and Cleveland] 119
5. Choice to Cleveland
   Choice to Jacksonville
6. Choice to San Diego
   *McCrary, Fred, RB, Mississippi State [from Jacksonville] 208
7. Bouie, Kevin, RB, Mississippi State [from Jacksonville] 210
   Choice to Jacksonville
   *Smothers, Howard, T, Bethune-Cookman [from Jacksonville] 248

PITTSBURGH 1995
1. *Bruener, Mark, TE, Washington, 27
2. *Stewart, Kordell, QB, Colorado, 60
3. *Stai, Brenden, G, Nebraska, 91
4. *Gibson, Oliver, DE, Notre Dame [from New England] 120
   *Jones, Donta, LB, Nebraska, 125
5. *Flowers, Lethon, DB, Georgia Tech [from Chicago Bears] 151
   *Brown, Lance, DB, Indiana, 161
6. Miles, Barron, DB, Nebraska, 199
7. *Bailey, Henry, WR, Nevada-Las Vegas, 235
   #*Ford, Cole, K, Southern California, 247

ST. LOUIS 1995
1. *Carter, Kevin, DE, Florida, 6
2. *Wiegert, Zach, T, Nebraska, 38
   *James, Jesse, G, Mississippi State [from San Francisco] 62
3. Choice to Detroit
   *McLaughlin, Steve, K, Arizona [from Detroit] 82
4. Choice to San Diego
   *Pinkney, Lovell, TE, Texas [from Detroit] 115
5. *Scurlock, Mike, DB, Arizona, 140
6. Choice to San Diego
7. *McBurrows, Gerald, DB, Kansas, 214
   *O'Berry, Herman, DB, Oregon [from New Orleans] 220
   #*Miller, Bronzell, DE, Utah, 239
   #*Thomas, Johnny, WR, Arizona State, 240

SAN DIEGO 1995
1. Choice to Carolina
2. *Shaw, Terrance, DB, Stephen F. Austin [from Carolina] 34
   *Fletcher, Terrell, RB, Wisconsin [from Detroit] 51
   *Oliver, Jimmy, WR, Texas Christian, 61
3. *Sasa, Don, DT, Washington State, 93
   Harrison, Preston, LB, Ohio State [from Carolina] 98
4. Cowart, Chris, LB, Florida State [from Carolina] 100
   *Hayden, Aaron, RB, Tennessee [from St. Louis] 104
   Choice to Seattle
5. *Ellison, O'Mar, WR, Florida State, 162
6. *Sienkiewicz, Troy, G, New Mexico State [from St. Louis] 177
   Harrison, Brandon, WR, Howard Payne [from Philadelphia] 183
   *Whelihan, Craig, QB, Pacific [from Cleveland] 197
   *Berti, Tony, T, Colorado, 200
7. *Montreuil, Mark, DB, Concordia, Canada, 237

SAN FRANCISCO 1995
1. *Stokes, J.J., WR, UCLA [from Atlanta thru Cleveland] 10
   Choice to Cleveland
2. Choice to St. Louis
3. Choice to Cleveland
4. *Hanshaw, Tim, G, Brigham Young, 127
5. Choice to Detroit
6. *Armstrong, Antonio, DE, Texas A&M, 201
7. Coleman, Herbert, DE, Trinity (IL), 238

SEATTLE 1995
1. *Galloway, Joey, WR, Ohio State, 8
2. *Fauria, Christian, TE, Colorado, 39
3. Choice to Green Bay
4. Choice to New York Jets thru Arizona
   *Kyle, Jason, LB, Arizona State [from San Diego] 126
5. Choice to Detroit
6. *McMillian, Henry, DT, Florida, 180
   #Goines, Eddie, WR, North Carolina State, 203
7. Bryant, Keif, DE, Rutgers, 216

TAMPA BAY 1995
1. Choice to Philadelphia
   *Sapp, Warren, DT, Miami [from Philadelphia] 12
   *Brooks, Derrick, LB, Florida State [from Dallas] 28
2. Choice to Atlanta thru Dallas
   *Johnson, Melvin, DB, Kentucky [from Philadelphia] 43
3. Choice to Philadelphia
4. *Wilson, Jerry, DB, Southern, 105
5. *Abraham, Clifton, DB, Florida State, 143
6. *Rouse, Wardell, LB, Clemson, 179
7. *Ingram, Steve, G, Maryland, 215
   Rodgers, Jeff, DE, Texas A&M-Kingsville [from Kansas City] 227

WASHINGTON 1995
1. *Westbrook, Michael, WR, Colorado, 4
2. *Raymer, Cory, C, Wisconsin, 37
3. *Pounds, Darryl, DB, Nicholls State, 68
4. Jones, Larry, RB, Miami, 103
5. *Asher, Jamie, TE, Louisville [from Houston] 137
   Choice to Oakland
   *Owens, Rich, DE, Lehigh [from Green Bay thru Oakland] 152
6. *Thure, Brian, T, California, 176
7. Choice to Arizona

*Turner, Scott, DB, Illinois [from Oakland] 226

1996

Held April 20-21, 1996

Carolina and Jacksonville were given extra picks after the second round.

#Compensatory Pick

ARIZONA 1996
1. *Rice, Simeon, DE, Illinois, 3
2. *McElroy, Leeland, RB, Texas A&M, 32
3. *McWilliams, Johnny, TE, Southern California, 64
4. Choice to Minnesota
   *Graham, Aaron, C, Nebraska [from Minnesota] 112
5. Choice to Kansas City
   *Dexter, James, T, South Carolina [from New York Giants thru Min] 137
   Stamps, Harry, T, Oklahoma [from Green Bay thru Kansas City] 161
   McGee, Dell, DB, Auburn [from Kansas City] 162
6. Foley, Mike, DT, New Hampshire, 169
7. *Hayes, Jarius, TE, North Alabama, 212

ATLANTA 1996
1. Choice to Indianapolis
2. Choice to Houston thru Oakland
3. Brown, Shannon, DT, Alabama, 84
4. Huntley, Richard, RB, Winston-Salem, 117
   *Bolden, Juran, DB, Mississippi Delta [from Dallas] 127
5. Choice to Baltimore
   Bandy, Gary, DE, Baylor [from Dallas] 164
6. *Sauer, Craig, LB, Minnesota, 188
7. Brooks, Ethan, T, Williams, 229

BALTIMORE 1996
1. *Ogden, Jonathan, T, UCLA, 4
   *Lewis, Ray, LB, Miami [from San Francisco] 26
2. Choice to Tampa Bay
   *Jenkins, DeRon, DB, Tennessee [from Det thru Denver] 55
3. Choice to Denver
4. Choice to Denver
5. Choice to New Orleans
   *Lewis, Jermaine, WR, Maryland [from Atlanta] 153
6. Daniels, Dexter, LB, Florida, 172
   Roe, James, WR, Norfolk State [from Jacksonville] 186
7. Choice to Denver
   Stark, Jon, QB, Trinity (IL) [from Philadelphia] 238

BUFFALO 1996
1. *Moulds, Eric, WR, Mississippi State, 24
2. *Northern, Gabe, DE, Louisiana State, 53
3. *Stevens, Matt, DB, Appalachian State, 87
4. *Moran, Sean, DE, Colorado State, 120
5. *Jackson, Raymond, DB, Colorado State, 156
6. Neal, Leon, RB, Washington, 196
   #Zeigler, Dusty, C, Notre Dame, 202
7. Brandenburg, Dan, DE, Indiana State, 237
   #Riemersma, Jay, TE, Michigan, 244
   #*Smedley, Eric, DB, Indiana, 249

CAROLINA 1996
1. *Biakabutuka, Tim, RB, Michigan, 8
2. *Muhammad, Muhsin, WR, Michigan State, 43
3. *Oliver, Winslow, RB, New Mexico, 73
   Price, J.C., DT, Virginia Tech, 88
4. *Garrido, Norberto, T, Southern California, 106
   *McDaniel, Emmanuel, DB, East Carolina [from Denver] 111
   Choice to Denver
5. Smith, Marquette, RB, Central Florida, 142
   Choice to Denver
6. Choice to Kansas City
   Choice to San Diego thru Pittsburgh
   *Greene, Scott, RB, Michigan State, 193
7. Baker, Donnell, WR, Southern, 217
   Hicks, Kerry, DE, Colorado, 234
   Choice to Denver

CHICAGO BEARS 1996
1. *Harris, Walt, DB, Mississippi State [from St. Louis] 13
   Choice to St. Louis
2. *Engram, Bobby, WR, Penn State, 52
3. Choice to St. Louis
4. *Grasmanis, Paul, DT, Notre Dame, 116
5. *Villarrial, Chris, G, Indiana (PA), 152
6. *Clark, Jon, T, Temple, 187
7. Keyes, Marcus, DT, North Alabama, 233
   #*Hicks, Michael, RB, South Carolina State, 253

CINCINNATI 1996
1. *Anderson, Willie, T, Auburn, 10
2. *Battaglia, Marco, TE, Rutgers, 39
3. *Blackman, Ken, T, Illinois, 69
4. *Langford, Jevon, DE, Oklahoma State, 108
5. *Myers, Greg, DB, Colorado State, 144
6. *Tumulty, Tom, LB, Pittsburgh, 178
7. *Jones, Rod, T, Kansas, 219

DALLAS 1996
1. Choice to Washington
2. *Pittman, Kavika, DE, McNeese State [from Washington] 37
   *Godfrey, Randall, LB, Georgia [from Miami] 49
   Choice to Jacksonville thru Miami
3. *Shiver, Clay, C, Florida State [from Washington] 67
   Choice exercised in 1995 Supplemental Draft
   #*Williams, Stepfret, WR, Northeast Louisiana, 94
   #*Ulufale, Mike, DT, Brigham Young, 95
4. Choice to Atlanta
5. McDaniel, Kenneth, T, Norfolk State [from Philadelphia thru Baltimore] 157
   Choice to Atlanta
   #*Campos, Alan, LB, Louisville, 167
6. Choice to St. Louis thru Chicago Bears
   #*Wendell, DB, Oklahoma, 207
7. Wood, Ryan, RB, Arizona State, 243

DENVER 1996
1. *Mobley, John, LB, Kutztown, 15
2. *James, Tory, DB, Louisiana State, 44
3. *Smith, Detron, RB, Texas A&M [from Baltimore] 65
   Campbell, Mark, DT, Florida, 78
4. Lewis, Jeff, QB, Northern Arizona [from Baltimore] 100
   Choice to Carolina
   *Johnson, Darrius, DB, Oklahoma [from Carolina] 122
5. Choice to Philadelphia
   *Jeffers, Patrick, WR, Virginia [from Carolina] 159
6. Veland, Tony, DB, Nebraska, 181
7. Ratliffe, Leslie, T, Tennessee [from Baltimore] 213
   Banks, Chris, G, Kansas, 226
   Levine, L.T., RB, Kansas [from Carolina] 235
   Gragert, Brian, P, Wyoming [from Detroit] 236

DETROIT 1996
1. *Brown, Reggie, LB, Texas A&M [from Oakland thru Houston and Seattle] 17
   *Hartings, Jeff, G, Penn State, 23
2. Choice to Baltimore thru Denver
3. *Stewart, Ryan, DB, Georgia Tech [from Oakland thru New England] 76
   Choice to New England
4. Choice to New England
   #*Ford, Brad, DB, Alabama, 129
5. *Waldroup, Kerwin, DT, Central State (OH), 158
6. Choice to New England
7. Choice to Denver

GREEN BAY 1996
1. *Michels, John, T, Southern California, 27
2. *Mayes, Derrick, WR, Notre Dame, 56
3. Flanagan, Mike, C, UCLA, 90
   #*Williams, Tyrone, DB, Nebraska, 93
4. Darkins, Chris, RB, Minnesota, 123
5. Choice to Arizona thru Kansas City
6. Choice to Philadelphia
   #Rivera, Marco, G, Penn State, 208
7. Wachholtz, Kyle, QB, Southern California, 240
   #*McKenzie, Keith, LB, Ball State, 252

HOUSTON 1996
1. Choice to Oakland
   *George, Eddie, RB, Ohio State [from Seattle] 14
2. *Mix, Bryant, DE, Alcorn State, 38
   *Layman, Jason, T, Tennessee [from Atlanta thru Oakland] 48
3. *Killens, Terry, LB, Penn State, 74
4. *Burton, Kendrick, DE, Alabama, 107
   *Runyan, Jon, T, Michigan [from Oakland] 109
5. *Stewart, Rayna, DB, Northern Arizona, 143
6. *Dorsett, Anthony, DB, Pittsburgh, 177
7. *Archie, Mike, RB, Penn State, 218

INDIANAPOLIS 1996
1. *Harrison, Marvin, WR, Syracuse [from Atlanta] 19
   Choice to Tampa Bay
2. *Mathis, Dedric, DB, Houston, 51
3. *Slutzker, Scott, TE, Iowa, 82
4. *Milne, Brian, RB, Penn State, 115
5. *Martin, Steve, DT, Missouri, 151
6. Conlin, Keith, T, Penn State, 191
   #Cawley, Mike, QB, James Madison, 205
7. Robinson, Adrian, DB, Baylor, 232

JACKSONVILLE 1996
1. *Hardy, Kevin, LB, Illinois, 2
2. *Brackens, Tony, DE, Texas, 33
   *Cheever, Michael, C, Georgia Tech [from Dallas thru Miami] 60
3. *Beasley, Aaron, DB, West Virginia, 63
   Choice to Miami
4. Choice to Kansas City thru Miami
   *Barlow, Reggie, WR, Alabama State [from Seattle] 110
   Choice to Miami thru Kansas City
5. Choice to Miami
   Herndon, Jimmy, T, Houston [from Seattle] 146
   Choice to Miami
6. Fisher, John, DB, Missouri Western, 170
   Doering, Chris, WR, Florida, 185
   Choice to Baltimore
7. Choice to Kansas City thru Pittsburgh
   Jones, Clarence, WR, Tennessee State, 227
   Spann, Gregory, WR, Jackson State, 228

KANSAS CITY 1996
1. *Woods, Jerome, DB, Memphis, 28
2. *Tongue, Reggie, DB, Oregon State, 58
3. *Browning, John, DE, West Virginia [from New England] 68
   Choice to Seattle thru Detroit
4. *Edwards, Donnie, LB, UCLA [from Jacksonville thru Miami] 98
   Choice to Miami
5. *Horn, Joe, WR, Itawamba JC [from Arizona] 135
   Choice to Arizona
6. *Jells, Dietrich, WR, Pittsburgh [from Carolina] 176
   Choice to Philadelphia
7. Lynch, Ben, C, California [from Jacksonville thru Pittsburgh] 211
   Smith, Jeff, C, Tennessee, 241
   #Williams, Darrell, DB, Tennessee State, 245

MIAMI 1996
1. *Gardener, Daryl, DT, Baylor, 20
2. Choice to Dallas
3. *Brew, Dorian, DB, Kansas [from Jacksonville] 79
   *Abdul-Jabbar, Karim, RB, UCLA, 80
4. Pointer, Kirk, DB, Austin Peay [from Jacksonville thru Kansas City] 113
   *Pritchett, Stanley, RB, South Carolina, 118
   *Jones, LaCurtis, LB, Baylor [from Kansas City] 125
5. *McPhail, Jerris, RB, East Carolina [from Jacksonville] 134
   *Burton, Shane, DT, Tennessee [from Jacksonville] 150
   *Thomas, Zach, LB, Texas Tech, 154
6. *Wooden, Shawn, DB, Notre Dame, 189
7. *Buckey, Jeff, T, Stanford, 230
   #Hunter, Brice, WR, Georgia, 251

MINNESOTA 1996
1. *Clemons, Duane, DE, California, 16
2. Manley, James, DT, Vanderbilt, 45
3. *Williams, Moe, RB, Kentucky, 75
4. *Goodwin, Hunter, TE, Texas A&M [from Arizona] 97
   Choice to Arizona
5. Boyd, Sean, DB, North Carolina, 148
6. Choice to New York Giants
7. Merrill, Jon, G, Duke, 223

NEW ENGLAND 1996
1. *Glenn, Terry, WR, Ohio State, 7
2. *Milloy, Lawyer, DB, Washington, 36
3. Choice to Kansas City
   *Bruschi, Tedy, LB, Arizona [from Detroit] 86
4. Irwin, Heath, G, Colorado, 101
   *Sullivan, Chris, DE, Boston College [from Detroit] 119
   Barber, Kantroy, RB, West Virginia [from San Francisco thru Oakland] 124
5. Elmore, John, G, Texas, 139
   Peter, Christian, NT, Nebraska [from Oakland] 149
6. Griffin, Chris, TE, New Mexico, 173
   *Grier, Marrio, RB, Tennessee-Chattanooga [from Detroit] 195
   *Wyman, Devin, DT, Kentucky State, 206

7. *Purnell, Lovett, TE, West Virginia, 216
Conrad, J.R., G, Oklahoma, 247

NEW ORLEANS 1996
1. *Molden, Alex, DB, Oregon, 11
2. *Cherry, Je'Rod, DB, California, 40
3. *Smith, Brady, DE, Colorado State, 70
4. *Whittle, Ricky, RB, Oregon, 103
5. *Hayes, Mercury, WR, Michigan [from Baltimore] 136
*Ackerman, Tom, G, Eastern Washington, 145
#Guess, Terry, WR, Gardner-Webb, 165
6. Hills, Keno, T, Southwestern Louisiana, 179
#Malone, Toderick, WR, Alabama, 204
7. Choice to Oakland
#*Lusk, Henry, TE, Utah, 246

NEW YORK GIANTS 1996
1. *Jones, Cedric, DE, Oklahoma, 5
2. *Toomer, Amani, WR, Michigan, 34
3. Oben, Roman, T, Louisville, 66
4. Choice to Seattle thru Dallas, Miami, and Jacksonville
#*Kanell, Danny, QB, Florida State, 130
5. Choice to Arizona thru Minnesota
6. *Colman, Doug, LB, Nebraska, 171
*Galyon, Scott, LB, Tennessee [from Minnesota] 182
7. *Hamilton, Conrad, DB, Eastern New Mexico, 214

NEW YORK JETS 1996
1. *Johnson, Keyshawn, WR, Southern California, 1
2. *Van Dyke, Alex, WR, Nevada, 31
3. *Mickens, Ray, DB, Texas A&M, 62
4. Choice to Tampa Bay
5. *Coleman, Marcus, DB, Texas Tech, 133
6. Hunter, Hugh, DE, Hampton, 168
7. Hayes, Chris, DB, Washington State, 210

OAKLAND 1996
1. *Dudley, Rickey, TE, Ohio State [from Houston] 9
Choice to Detroit thru Houston and Seattle
2. Choice to San Francisco
*Johnstone, Lance, DE, Temple, from San Francisco thru New England] 57
3. Choice to Detroit thru New England
4. Choice to Houston
5. Choice to New England
#*Glover, La'Roi, DT, San Diego State, 166
6. *Hall, Tim, RB, Robert Morris, 183
7. *Clark, Sedric, LB, Tulsa [from New Orleans] 220
Smith, Darius, C, Sam Houston State, 224
#Wylie, Joey, G, Stephen F. Austin, 248

PHILADELPHIA 1996
1. *Mayberry, Jermane, T, Texas A&M-Kingsville, 25
2. *Dunn, Jason, TE, Eastern Kentucky, 54
#*Dawkins, Brian, DB, Clemson, 61
3. *Hoying, Bobby, QB, Ohio State, 85
4. *Farmer, Ray, LB, Duke, 121
5. Marshall, Whit, LB, Georgia [from Denver] 147
Choice to Dallas thru Baltimore
6. *White, Steve, LB, Tennessee, 194
*Johnson, Tony, TE, Alabama [from Green Bay] 197
*Riley, Phillip, WR, Florida State [from Kansas City] 199
7. Choice to Baltimore

PITTSBURGH 1996
1. *Stephens, Jamain, T, North Carolina A&T, 29
2. Choice to St. Louis
3. *Conley, Steven, LB, Arkansas [from St. Louis] 72
*Witman, Jon, RB, Penn State, 92
4. *Holmes, Earl, LB, Florida A&M, 126
#*Arnold, Jahine, WR, Fresno State, 132
5. *Raybon, Israel, DE, North Alabama, 163
6. *Roye, Orpheus, DE, Florida State, 200
#Fischer, Spence, QB, Duke, 203
7. *Emmons, Carlos, LB, Arkansas State, 242

ST. LOUIS 1996
1. *Phillips, Lawrence, RB, Nebraska [from Washington] 6
Choice to Chicago Bears
*Kennison, Eddie, WR, Louisiana State [from Chicago Bears] 18
2. *Banks, Tony, QB, Michigan State, 42
*Conwell, Ernie, TE, Washington [from Pittsburgh] 59
3. Choice to Pittsburgh
*Moore, Jerald, RB, Oklahoma [from Chicago Bears] 83
4. *Gaskins, Percell, LB, Kansas State, 105
5. *Miller, Fred, T, Baylor, 141
6. *Harris, Derrick, RB, Miami, 175
*Clay, Hayward, TE, Texas A&M [from Dal thru Chicago Bears] 201
7. *Osborne, Chuck, DT, Arizona, 222

SAN DIEGO 1996
1. Choice to Seattle thru Detroit
2. *Still, Bryan, WR, Virginia Tech [from Tampa Bay] 41
*Sapp, Patrick, LB, Clemson, 50
3. *Roche, Brian, TE, San Jose State, 81
4. *Jones, Charlie, WR, Fresno State, 114
5. Soli, Junior, DT, Arkansas, 155
6. *Mills, Jim, T, Idaho, 190
*Stoltenberg, Bryan, C, Colorado [from Carolina thru Pittsburgh] 192
7. *Bradley, Freddie, RB, Sonoma State, 231

SAN FRANCISCO 1996
1. Choice to Baltimore
2. *Ifeanyi, Israel, DE, Southern California [from Oakland] 46
Choice to Oakland thru New England
3. *Owens, Terrell, WR, Tennessee-Chattanooga, 89
4. Choice to New England thru Oakland
#*Price, Daryl, DE, Colorado, 128
5. *Uwaezuoke, Iheanyi, WR, California, 160
6. Pitts, Stephen, RB, Penn State, 198
7. *Manuel, Sean, TE, New Mexico State, 239
#Manuel, Sam, LB, New Mexico State, 254

SEATTLE 1996
1. Choice to Houston
*Kendall, Pete, T, Boston College [from San Diego thru Detroit] 21
2. *Thomas, Fred, DB, Tennessee-Martin, 47
3. Barr, Robert, T, Rutgers, 77
*Brown, Reggie, RB, Fresno State [from Kansas City thru Detroit] 91
4. *Daniels, Phillip, DE, Georgia [from New York Giants thru Dallas, Mia, and Jacksonville] 99
Choice to Jacksonville
#*Unverzagt, Eric, LB, Wisconsin, 131
5. Choice to Jacksonville
6. Green, Reggie, G, Florida, 184
#*Cunningham, T.J., DB, Colorado, 209
7. Church, Johnie, DE, Florida, 225

TAMPA BAY 1996
1. *Upshaw, Regan, DE, California, 12
*Jones, Marcus, DT, North Carolina [from Indianapolis] 22
2. *Alstott, Mike, RB, Purdue [from Baltimore] 35
Choice to San Diego
3. *Abraham, Donnie, DB, East Tennessee State, 71
4. *Odom, Jason, T, Florida [from New York Jets] 96
*Austin, Eric, DB, Jackson State, 104
5. *Maniecki, Jason, DT, Wisconsin, 140
6. *Silvan, Nilo, WR, Tennessee, 180
7. *Rusk, Reggie, DB, Kentucky, 221

WASHINGTON 1996
1. Choice to St. Louis
Johnson, Andre, T, Penn State [from Dallas] 30
2. Choice to Dallas
3. Choice to Dallas
4. *Davis, Stephen, RB, Auburn, 102
5. *Evans, Leomont, DB, Clemson, 138
6. Kinney, Kelvin, DE, Virginia State, 174
7. Asher, Jeremy, LB, Oregon, 215
#Maxwell, DeAndre, WR, San Diego State, 250

1997

Held April 19-20, 1997

#- Compensatory selection based on free agent losses from 1996

ARIZONA 1997
1. *Knight, Tom, DB, Iowa, 9
2. *Plummer, Jake, QB, Arizona State, 42
3. Choice to Philadelphia
*Howard, Ty, DB, Ohio State [from Philadelphia] 84
4. *Dishman, Chris, G, Nebraska, 106
5. Carpenter, Chad, WR, Washington State, 139
6. Brown, Rod, RB, North Carolina State, 175
*McCombs, Tony, LB, Eastern Kentucky [from Philadelphia] 188
7. *Smith, Mark, DE, Auburn, 212

ATLANTA 1997
1. Choice to Seattle
*Booker, Michael, DB, Nebraska [from Chicago Bears thru Seattle] 11
2. *Davis, Nathan, DE, Indiana, 32
*Hanspard, Byron, RB, Texas Tech [from Seattle] 41
3. Choice to Seattle
*Santiago, O.J., TE, Kent [from Seattle] 70
4. Choice to Houston
*Crockett, Henri, LB, Florida State [from Baltimore thru Seattle] 100
5. *Wimberly, Marcus, DB, Miami, 133
6. Choice to Houston
*Collins, Calvin, C, Texas A & M [from Washington] 180
7. *Graziani, Tony, QB, Oregon, 204
Bayne, Chris, DB, Fresno State [from Washington] 222

BALTIMORE 1997
1. *Bouleware, Peter, DE, Florida State, 4
2. *Sharper, Jamie, LB, Virginia, 34
*Herring, Kim, DB, Penn State [from Denver] 58
3. *Graham, Jay, RB, Tennessee, 64
4. Choice to Seattle
*McCloud, Tyrus, LB, Louisville [from Dallas] 118
5. Mitchell, Jeff, C, Florida, 134
6. Lee, Steve, RB, Indiana, 167
#*Brown, Cornell, DE, Virginia Tech, 194
7. *Ward, Chris, DE, Kentucky, 205
#Richardson, Wally, QB, Penn State, 234
#*Staten, Ralph, DB, Alabama, 236
#*Taylor, Leland, DT, Louisville, 238

BUFFALO 1997
1. *Smith, Antowain, RB, Houston, 23
2. *Wiley, Marcellus, DE, Columbia, 52
3. Choice to Oakland
4. *Nails, Jamie, T, Florida A&M, 120
5. Woodson, Sean, DB, Jackson State, 153
6. *Spriggs, Marcus, T, Houston, 185
7. Fitzgerald, Pat, TE, Texas, 226

CAROLINA 1997
1. *Carruth, Rae, WR, Colorado, 27
2. *Minter, Mike, DB, Nebraska, 56
3. *Tatum, Kinnon, LB, Notre Dame, 87
4. *Saleh, Tarek, LB, Wisconsin, 122
5. Choice to Oakland
6. Finkes, Matt, DE, Ohio State, 189
7. *Mangum, Kris, TE, Mississippi, 228

CHICAGO BEARS 1997
1.Choice to Seattle
2. *Allred, John, TE, USC [from St. Louis] 38
Choice to St. Louis
3. Sapp, Bob, G, Washington, 69
4. *Autry, Darnell, RB, Northwestern [from Seattle] 105
Robinson, Marcus, WR, South Carolina, 108
5. *Hiles, Van, DB, Kentucky, 141
6. Choice to St. Louis
#Swayda, Shawn, DE, Arizona State, 196
#Hogans, Richard, LB, Memphis, 200
#Parker, Ricky, DB, San Diego State, 201
7. Miano, Mike, DT, Southwest Missouri State, 210
#Thomas, Marvin, DE, Memphis, 233

CINCINNATI 1997
1. *Wilson, Reinard, LB, Florida State, 14
2. *Dillon, Corey, RB, Washington, 43
3. Payne, Rod, C, Michigan, 76
4. *Mack, Tremain, DB, Miami, 111
5. *Purvis, Andre, DT, North Carolina, 144
6. *Curtis, Canute, LB, West Virginia, 176
7. Carr, William, DT, Michigan, 217

DALLAS 1997
1. *LaFleur, David, TE, LSU [from Philadelphia] 22
Choice to Philadelphia
2. Choice to Detroit
3. *Coakley, Dexter, LB, Appalachian State [from Detroit] 65
*Scifires, Steve, T, Wyoming, 83
#*Wheaton, Kenny, DB, Oregon, 94
4. *Anderson, Antonio, DT, Syracuse [from Detroit] 101
Choice to Baltimore
#Brooks, Macey, WR, James Madison, 127
#*Sualua, Nicky, RB, Ohio State, 129
5. Choice to Philadelphia
6. Vaughn, Lee, DB, Wyoming, 187
7. *Stoutmire, Omar, DB, Fresno State, 224

DENVER 1997
1. *Pryce, Trevor, DT, Clemson, 28
2. Choice to Baltimore
3. *Neil, Dan, C, Texas [from St. Louis thru New York Jets] 67
Choice to New York Jets
4. Gilliard, Corey, DB, Ball State, 124
5. Choice to St. Louis
6. Choice to New York Jets
7. Choice to New York Jets

DETROIT 1997
1. *Westbrook, Bryant, DB, Texas, 5
2. *Roque, Juan, G, Arizona State, 35
*Abrams, Kevin, DB, Syracuse [from Dallas] 54
3. Choice to Dallas
4. Choice to Dallas
#*Russell, Matt, LB, Colorado
5. *Chryplewicz, Pete, TE, Notre Dame, 135
#Ashman, Duane, DE, Virginia, 161
6. *Ramirez, Tony, T, Northern Colorado, 168
7. Battle, Terry, RB, Arizona State, 206
#Harris, Marcus, WR, Wyoming, 232
#Jordan, Richard, LB, Mississippi Southern, 239

GREEN BAY 1997
1. *Verba, Ross, T, Iowa, 30
2. *Sharper, Darren, DB, William & Mary, 60
3. Conway, Brett, PK, Penn State, 90
4. *Smith, Jermaine, DT, Georgia, 126
5. Hicks, Anthony, LB, Arkansas, 160
6. Choice to Oakland
7. Miller, Chris, WR, Southern California [from Oakland] 213
Sowell, Jerald, RB, Tulane, 231
#McAda, Ron, QB, Army, 240

HOUSTON 1997
1. Choice to Kansas City
*Holmes, Kenny, DE, Miami [from Kansas City] 18
2. *Kent, Joey, WR, Tennessee, 46
3. *Walker, Denard, DB, LSU, 75
*Sanderson, Scott, T, Washington State [from Kansas City] 81
4. *Mason, Derrick, WR, Michigan State [from Atlanta] 98
*Lyons, Pratt, DE, Troy State [from Oakland thru New Orleans] 107
Choice to Kansas City
5. Choice to Washington
*McCullough, George, DB, Baylor, 143
6. Choice to St. Louis
*Stallings, Dennis, LB, Illinois [from Kansas City] 181
7. *Williams, Armon, DB, Arizona, 216

INDIANAPOLIS 1997
1. *Glenn, Tarik, T, California, 19
2. *Meadows, Adam, T, Georgia, 48
3. Choice to San Francisco
*Berry, Bert, LB, Notre Dame [from San Francisco] 86
4. *Montgomery, Delmonico, DB, Houston, 117
5. *Jacquet, Nate, WR, San Diego State, 150
*Powell, Carl, DE, Louisville [from San Francisco] 156
6. *Von Der Ahe, Scott, LB, Arizona State, 182
7. Thompson, Clarence, DB, Knoxville, 219

JACKSONVILLE 1997
1. *Wynn, Renaldo, DT, Notre Dame, 21
2. *Logan, Mike, DB, West Virginia, 50
3. *Hamilton, James, LB, North Carolina, 79
4. *Payne, Seth, DT, Cornell, 114
5. *Jones, Damon, TE, Southern Illinois, 147
6. *Shelton, Daimon, RB, Cal State-Sacramento, 184
7. Hesse, Jon, LB, Nebraska, 221

KANSAS CITY 1997
1. *Gonzalez, Tony, TE, California [from Houston] 13
Choice to Houston
2. *Lockett, Kevin, WR, Kansas State, 47
3. Choice to Houston
4. Barnes, Pat, QB, California [from Houston] 110
Choice to Houston
5. Choice to Miami
#Henley, June, RB, Kansas, 163
6. Choice to Houston
#Byrd, Isaac, WR, Kansas, 195
7. Parks, Nathan, T, Stanford [from Miami] 214
Choice to Pittsburgh

MIAMI 1997
1. Green, Yatil, WR, Miami, 15
2. *Madison, Sam, DB, Louisville, 44
3. *Taylor, Jason, DE, Akron, 73
#*Rodgers, Derrick, LB, Arizona State, 92
#*Ward, Ronnie, LB, Kansas, 93
#Smith, Brent, T, Mississippi State, 96
4. Choice to St. Louis
Daniels, Jerome, T, Northeastern [from Pittsburgh thru St. Louis] 121
5. Choice to New York Jets
*Tanner, Barron, DT, Oklahoma [from Kansas City] 149
Lopez, Nicholas, DE, Texas Southern [from Carolina thru Oakland] 157
6. Fiala, John, LB, Washington [from New Orleans thru Oakland] 166
*Manning, Brian, WR, Stanford [from St. Louis] 170
*Crawford, Mike, LB, Nevada [from Chicago Bears thru St. Louis] 173
*Perry, Ed, TE, James Madison, 177
7. Ismaeli, Hudhaifa, DB, Northwestern [from New Orleans thru Oakland] 203
Choice to Kansas City

MINNESOTA 1997
1. *Rudd, Dwayne, LB, Alabama, 20
2. *Gray, Torrian, DB, Virginia Tech, 49
3. *Colinet, Stalin, DE, Boston College, 78
4. Banks, Antonio, DB, Virginia Tech, 113
5. *Williams, Tony, DT, Memphis, 151
6. *Tate, Robert, WR, Cincinnati, 183
7. Ulmer, Artie, LB, Valdosta State, 220
#*Hatchette, Matthew, WR, Langston, 235

NEW ENGLAND 1997
1. *Canty, Chris, DB, Kansas State, 29
2. *Mitchell, Brandon, DT, Texas A & M, 59
3. *Shaw, Sedrick, RB, Iowa [from New York Jets] 61
*Carter, Chris, DB, Texas, 89
4. *Denson, Damon, G, Michigan [from New York Jets] 97
*Ellis, Ed, T, Buffalo, 125
5. *Crawford, Vernon, LB, Florida State, 159
6. Gaiter, Tony, WR, Miami, 192
7. *Rehberg, Scott, T, Central Michigan, 230

NEW ORLEANS 1997
1. Choice to Oakland
*Naeole, Chris, G, Colorado [from Oakland] 10
2. *Kelly, Rob, DB, Ohio State, 33
*Tomich, Jared, DE, Nebraska [from Oakland] 39
3. *Davis, Troy, RB, Iowa State, 62
4. *Wuerffel, Danny, QB, Florida, 99
*Poole, Keith, WR, Arizona State [from Kansas City thru Houston] 116
5. Choice to Washington
6. *Savoie, Nicky, TE, LSU [from Atlanta thru Houston] 165
Choice to Oakland
7. Choice to Oakland

NEW YORK GIANTS 1997
1. *Hilliard, Ike, WR, Florida, 7
2. *Barber, Tiki, RB, Virginia, 36
3. *Phillips, Ryan, LB, Idaho, 68
#*Maynard, Brad, P, Ball State, 95
4. *Monty, Pete, LB, Wisconsin, 103
5. *Garnes, Sam, DB, Cincinnati, 136
6. *Cherry, Mike, QB, Murray State, 171
7. Keneley, Matt, DT, USC, 208

NEW YORK JETS 1997
1. Choice to St. Louis
*Farrior, James, LB, Virginia [from Tampa Bay] 8
2. *Terry, Rick, DT, North Carolina, 31
3. Choice to New England
*Ward, Dedric, WR, Northern Iowa [from Denver] 88
4. Choice to New England
*Day, Terry, DE, Mississippi State [from St. Louis] 102
*Johnson, Leon, RB, North Carolina [from Tampa Bay] 104
5. *Burns, Lamont, G, East Carolina, 131
*Austin, Raymond, DB, Tennessee [from Miami] 145
6. Scharf, Tim, LB, Northwestern, 164
*Clements, Chuck, QB, Houston [from Denver] 191
7. Rosga, Steve, DB, Colorado, 202
*Ferguson, Jason, DT, Georgia [from Denver] 229

OAKLAND 1997
1. *Russell, Darrell, DT, USC [from New Orleans] 2
Choice to New Orleans
2. Choice to New Orleans
3. *Treu, Adam, G, Nebraska, 72
Kohn, Tim, T, Iowa State [from Buffalo] 85
4. Choice to New Orleans
*Levitt, Chad, RB, Cornell [from San Francisco thru Miami] 123
5. Choice to Atlanta
6. *Branch, Calvin, RB, Colorado State, 172
*Jackson, Grady, DE, Knoxville [from Green Bay] 193
7. Choice to Green Bay

PHILADELPHIA 1997
1. Choice to Dallas
*Harris, Jon, DE, Virginia [from Dallas] 25
2. Choice to San Francisco
*Darling, James, LB, Washington State [from San Francisco] 57
3. *Staley, Duce, RB, South Carolina [from Arizona] 71
Choice to Arizona
4. Robinson, Damien, DB, Iowa, 119
5. *Kalu, Ndukwe, DE, Rice, 152
Broughton, Luther, TE, Furman [from Dallas] 155
6. Choice to Arizona
*Wyatt, Antwuan, WR, Bethune-Cookman [from San Francisco] 190
#*Jasper, Edward, DT, Texas A & M, 198
7. *Detmer, Koy, QB, Colorado [from St. Louis thru New York Jets] 207
Capers, Byron, DB, Florida State, 225
*Brown, Deauntae, DB, Central State (OH) [from San Francisco] 227

PITTSBURGH 1997
1. *Scott, Chad, DB, Maryland, 24
2. *Blackwell, Will, WR, San Diego State, 53
3. *Wiggins, Paul, T, Oregon, 82
#*Vrabel, Mike, DE, Ohio State, 91
4. Choice to St. Louis
5. *Jones, George, RB, San Diego State, 154
6. Porter, Daryl, DB, Boston College, 186
#*Manuel, Rod, DE, Oklahoma, 199
7. *Adams, Michael, WR, Texas 223

ST. LOUIS 1997
1. *Pace, Orlando, T. Ohio State [from New York Jets] 1
2. Choice to Tampa Bay
*McCleon, Dexter, DB, Clemson [from Chicago Bears] 40
3. Choice to New York Jets
4. Choice to New York Jets
*Tucker, Ryan, C, TCU [from Miami] 112
5. Choice to San Diego
*Allen, Taje, DB, Texas [from Denver] 158
6. Choice to Miami
*Kazadi, Muadianvita, LB, Tulsa [from Houston] 179
7. Choice to New York Jets
White, Cedric, DE, North Carolina A & T [from San Diego] 215

SAN DIEGO 1997
1. Choice to Tampa Bay
2. *Jones, Freddie, TE, North Carolina, 45
3. *Hamilton, Michael, LB, North Carolina A&T, 74
4. Roundtree, Raleigh, T, South Carolina State, 109
5. *Bynum, Kenny, RB, South Carolina State [from St. Louis] 138
*Bradford, Paul, DB, Portland State, 146
6. Palmer, Daniel, C, Air Force, 178
7. James, Toran, LB, North Carolina A&T [from Kansas City thru Pittsburgh] 218
#Corbin, Tony, QB, Cal State-Sacramento, 237

SAN FRANCISCO 1997
1. *Druckenmiller, Jim, QB, Virginia Tech, 26
2. *Edwards, Marc, FB, Notre Dame [from Philadelphia] 55
3. *Clark, Greg, TE, Stanford [from Ind] 77
Choice to Indianapolis
4. Choice to Miami
5. Choice to Indianapolis
6. Choice to Philadelphia
7. Choice to Philadelphia

SEATTLE 1997
1. *Springs, Shawn, CB, Ohio State [from Atlanta] 3
*Jones, Walter, T, Florida State [from St. Louis thru New York Jets and Tampa Bay] 6
Choice to Tampa Bay
2. Choice to Atlanta
3. Choice to Atlanta
4. Choice to Chicago Bears
5. *Stokes, Eric, DB, Nebraska, 142
6. Mili, Itula, TE, Brigham Young, 174
7. Jones, Carlos, DB, Miami, 211

TAMPA BAY 1997
1. Choice to New York Jets
*Dunn, Warrick, RB, Florida State [from Seattle] 12
*Anthony, Reidel, WR, Florida [from San Diego] 16
2. *Wunsch, Jerry, T, Wisconsin, 37
3. *Middleton, Frank, G, Arizona [from Atlanta thru Seattle] 62
*Barber, Ronde, DB, Virginia, 66
4. Choice to New York Jets
#*Singleton, Alshermond, LB, Temple, 128
5. *Hape, Patrick, TE, Alabama, 137
6. Harris, Al, DB, Texas A&M-Kingsville, 169
#Carter, Nigea, WR, Michigan State, 197
7. DeGrate, Anthony, DT, Stephen F. Austin, 209

WASHINGTON 1997
1. *Lang, Kenard, DE, Miami, 17
2. *Jones, Greg, LB, Colorado, 51
3. *Smith, Derek, LB, Arizona, State, 80
4. *Connell, Albert, WR, Texas A & M, 115
5. *Williams, Jamel, DB, Nebraska [from Houston] 132
*Thibodeaux, Keith, DB, Northwestern State [from Oakland thru Atlanta] 140
*Russell, Twan, LB, Miami, 148
#*Badger, Brad, G, Stanford, 162
6. Choice to Atlanta
7. Choice to Atlanta

1998

Held April 18-19

#Compensatory Selection

ARIZONA 1998
1. Choice to San Diego
*Wadsworth, Andre, DE, Florida State [from San Diego] 3
2. *Chavous, Corey, DB, Vanderbilt [from San Diego] 33
*Clement, Anthony, T, Southwestern Louisiana, 36
3. Choice to St. Louis thru New York Jets
4. *Pittman, Michael, RB, Fresno State, 95
5. *Hardy, Terry, TE, Southern Mississippi, 125
6. *Walz, Zach, LB, Dartmouth, 158
7. Savoy, Phil, WR, Colorado, 193
Cousins, Jomo, DE, Florida A&M [from New York Jets] 209
#*Tillman, Pat, DB, Arizona State, 226
#Janes, Ron, RB, Missouri, 233

ATLANTA 1998
1. *Brooking, Keith, LB, Georgia Tech, 12
2. Choice to Tampa Bay
*Hallen, Bob, C, Kent State [from Tampa Bay] 53
3. *German, Jammi, WR, Miami, 74
4. *Brown, Omar, DB, North Carolina, 103
*Dwight, Tim, WR, Iowa [from Tampa Bay] 114
5. Choice to Pit
6. *Williams, Elijah, DB, Florida, 166
7. Salaam, Ephraim, T, San Diego State [from Baltimore thru Pittsburgh] 199
*Oxendine, Ken, RB, Virginia Tech, 201
*Slay, Henry, DT, West Virginia [from Carolina thru Pittsburgh] 203

BALTIMORE RAVENS 1998
1. *Starks, Duane, DB, Miami, 10
2. *Johnson, Pat, WR, Oregon, 42
3. Choice to Indianapolis
4. Choice to Tampa Bay
5. Chase, Martin, DT, Oklahoma [from Indianapolis] 124
*Sutter, Ryan, DB, Colorado, 133
6. Rogers, Ron, LB, Georgia Tech [from Indianapolis] 154
Williams, Sammy, T, Oklahoma, 164
7. Choice to Atlanta thru Pittsburgh
#Quayle, Cam, TE, Weber State, 241

BUFFALO 1998
1. Choice to Jacksonville
2. *Cowart, Sam, LB, Florida State, 39
3. *Hicks, Robert, T, Mississippi State, 68
4. Choice to Jacksonville
5. *Linton, Jonathan, RB, North Carolina, 131
6. Coleman, Fred, WR, Washington, 160
7. Allotey, Victor, G, Indiana, 198
#*Loud, Kamil, WR, Cal Poly-San Luis Obispo, 238

CAROLINA 1998
1. *Peter, Jason, DT, Nebraska, 14
2. Choice to Miami
3. Wiley, Chuck, DE, Louisiana State [from Indianapolis] 62
Marrow, Mitch, DE, Pennsylvania, 73
4. *Hayes, Donald, WR, Wisconsin, 106
5. *Jensen, LB, Washington, 136
6. *Richardson, Damien, DB, Arizona State, 165
7. Maumau, Viliami, DT, Colorado [from New Orleans] 196
Choice to Atlanta thru Pittsburgh
#Turner, Jim, WR, Syracuse, 228

CHICAGO BEARS 1998
1. *Enis, Curtis, RB, Penn State, 5
2. *Parrish, Tony, DB, Washington, 35
3. *Kreutz, Olin, C, Washington, 64
4. *Mayes, Alonzo, TE, Oklahoma State, 94
5. Choice to Kansas City
6. *Draft, Chris, LB, Stanford, 157
#*Mannelly, Patrick, T, Duke, 189
7. Choice to Jacksonville
Overhauser, Chad, T, UCLA [from San Francisco] 217
#*Moreno, Moses, QB, Colorado State, 232

CINCINNATI 1998
1. *Spikes, Takeo, LB, Auburn, 13
*Simmons, Brian, LB, North Carolina [from Washington] 17
2. *Hawkins, Artrell, DB, Cincinnati, 43
3. *Foley, Steve, LB, Northeast Louisiana, 75
*Goff, Mike, G, Iowa [from Washington] 78
4. *Steele, Glen, DT, Michigan, 105
5. Choice to Indianapolis
6. Tucker, Jason, WR, Texas Christian, 167
7. Parker, Marcus, RB, Virginia Tech, 202
#Vaughn, Damian, TE, Miami (OH), 222

DALLAS 1998
1. *Ellis, Greg, DE, North Carolina, 8
2. *Adams, Flozell, T, Michigan State, 38
3. Choice to New York Giants thru Philadelphia
4. *Myers, Michael, DT, Alabama, 100
5. *Hambrick, Darren, LB, South Carolina, 130
*Ross, Oliver, T, Iowa State [from Seattle] 138
6. Choice to Seattle
#*Reese, Izell, DB, Alabama-Birmingham, 188
7. Choice to Seattle
#Smith, Tarik, RB, California, 223
#Fleming, Antonio, G, Georgia, 227
#Monroe, Rodrick, TE, Cincinnati, 237

DENVER 1998
1. *Nash, Marcus, WR, Tennessee, 30
2. *Brown, Eric, DB, Mississippi State, 61
3. *Griese, Brian, QB, Michigan, 91
4. Alexander, Curtis, RB, Alabama, 122
5. *Howard, Chris, RB, Michigan, 153
6. Choice to New York Jets
7. Teague, Trey, T, Tennessee [from Philadelphia] 200
*Wayne, Nate, LB, Mississippi, 219

DETROIT 1998
1. *Fair, Terry, DB, Tennessee, 20
2. *Crowell, Germane, WR, Virginia, 50
*Batch, Charlie, QB, Eastern Michigan [from Green Bay thru Miami] 60
3. Choice to Miami
4. Choice to Washington thru Oakland
5. Choice to Miami
6. Choice to Miami
Alexander, Jamaal, DB, Southern Mississippi, 185
7. *Liwienski, Chris, T, Indiana, 207

GREEN BAY 1998
1. *Holliday, Vonnie, DT, North Carolina [from Miami] 19
Choice to Miami
2. Choice to Detroit thru Miami
3. *Brown, Jonathan, DE, Tennessee, 90
4. *Blackmon, Roosevelt, DB, Morris Brown, 121
5. *Bradford, Corey, WR, Jackson State [from Kansas City] 150
Choice to Oakland
6. *McGarrahan, Scott, DB, New Mexico [from Oakland] 156
Choice to Jacksonville
#Hasselbeck, Matt, QB, Boston College, 187
7. Watson, Edwin, RB, Purdue, 218

INDIANAPOLIS 1998
1. *Manning, Peyton, QB, Tennessee, 1
2. *Pathon, Jerome, WR, Washington, 32
3. Choice to Carolina
*Green, E.G., WR, Florida State [from Baltimore] 71
4. *McKinney, Steve, G, Texas A&M, 93
5. Choice to Baltimore
*Jordon, Antony, LB, Vanderbilt [from Cincinnati] 135
6. Choice to Baltimore
7. Taylor, Aaron, G, Nebraska, 190
#Gaines, Corey, DB, Tennessee, 231

JACKSONVILLE 1998
1. *Taylor, Fred, RB, Florida [from Buffalo] 9
*Darius, Donovin, DB, Syracuse, 25
2. *Taylor, Cordell, DB, Hampton, 57
3. *Quinn, Jonathan, QB, Middle Tennessee State, 86
4. *Banks, Tavian, RB, Iowa [from Buffalo] 101
Deligianis, Harry, DT, Youngstown State, 118
5. *Wade, John, C, Marshall, 148
6. *Williams, Lamanzer, DE, Minnesota, 179
McLeod, Kevin, RB, Auburn [from Green Bay] 182
7. *Whitted, Alvis, WR, North Carolina State [from Chicago Bears] 192
Tolbert, Brandon, LB, Georgia, 214

KANSAS CITY 1998
1. *Riley, Victor, T, Auburn, 27
2. Choice to San Diego thru Oakland and Tampa Bay
3. *Shehee, Rashaan, RB, Washington, 88
4. *Favors, Greg, LB, Mississippi State, 120
5. *Williams, Robert, DB, North Carolina [from Chicago Bears] 128
Choice to Green Bay
6. *Ransom, Derrick, DT, Cincinnati, 181
7. *Warfield, Eric, DB, Nebraska, 216
#Blackwell, Ernest, RB, Missouri, 224

MIAMI 1998
1. Choice to Green Bay
*Avery, John, RB, Mississippi [from Green Bay] 29
2. *Surtain, Patrick, DB, Southern Mississippi [from Carolina] 44
*Mixon, Kenny, DE, Louisiana State, 49
3. Jackson, Brad, LB, Cincinnati [from Detroit] 79
Shannon, Larry, WR, East Carolina, 82
4. *Bromell, Lorenzo, DE, Clemson [from Philadelphia] 102
Choice to Philadelphia
5. Choice to Philadelphia
*Shaw, Scott, G, Michigan State [from Detroit] 143
6. Strikwerda, Nathan, C, Northwestern, 171
Dutton, John, QB, Nevada [from Detroit] 172
7. Bundren, Jim, G, Clemson, 210

MINNESOTA 1998
1. *Moss, Randy, WR, Marshall, 21
2. *Wong, Kailee, LB, Stanford, 51
3. *McDonald, Ramos, DB, New Mexico, 80
4. *Mays, Kivuusama, LB, North Carolina, 110
5. *Cooks, Kerry, DB, Iowa, 144
6. *Birk, Matt, T, Harvard, 173
7. *Burnett, Chester, LB, Arizona, 208
#Darden, Tony, DB, Texas Tech, 225

NEW ENGLAND 1998
1. *Edwards, Robert, RB, Georgia [from New York Jets] 18
*Jones, Tebucky, DB, Syracuse, 22
2. *Simmons, Tony, WR, Wisconsin [from New York Jets] 52
*Rutledge, Rod, TE, Alabama, 54
3. *Floyd, Chris, RB, Michigan [from New York Jets] 81
*Spires, Greg, DE, Florida State, 83
4. *Rheams, Leonta, DT, Houston, 115
5. Merkerson, Ron, LB, Colorado, 145
6. *Shaw, Harold, RB, Southern Mississippi, 176
7. Andersen, Jason, C, Brigham Young, 211

NEW ORLEANS 1998
1. *Turley, Kyle, T, San Diego State, 7
2. *Cleeland, Cameron, TE, Washington, 40
3. Choice to Washington
4. *Weary, Fred, DB, Florida [from Oakland] 97
*Pittman, Julian, DE, Florida State, 99
5. Perry, Wilmont, RB, Livingstone College, 132
6. *Bordano, Chris, LB, Southern Methodist, 161
7. Choice to Car
McCullough, Andy, WR, Tennessee [from Seattle] 204
#*Wamer, Ron, LB. Kansas, 239

NEW YORK GIANTS 1998
1. *Williams, Shaun, DB, UCLA, 24
2. *Jurevicius, Joe, WR, Penn State, 55
3. *Alford, Brian, WR, Purdue [from Dallas thru Philadelphia] 70
Choice to Philadelphia
4. Choice to Philadelphia
5. Myles, Toby, T, Jackson State, 147
6. Pollack, Todd, TE, Boston College, 177
7. Fricke, Ben, C, Houston, 213

NEW YORK JETS 1998
1. Choice to New England
2. Choice to New England
*Boose, Dorian, DE, Washington State [from Philadelphia] 56
3. *Frost, Scott, DB, Nebraska [from St. Louis] 67
Choice to New England
*Williams, Kevin, DB, Oklahoma State [from Pittsburgh] 87
4. *Fabini, Jason, T, Cincinnati, 111
5. Dailey, Casey, LB, Northwestern [from Philadelphia] 134
Karczewski, Doug, G, Virginia, 141
*Spence, Blake, TE, Oregon [from Tampa

Bay] 146
Bateman, Eric, T, Brigham Young [from Pittsburgh] 149
6. *Ogbogu, Eric, DE, Maryland [from Philadelphia] 163
Brazzell, Chris, WR, Angelo State, 174
Johnson, Dustin, RB, Brigham Young [from Denver] 183
7. Hart, Lawrence, TE, Southern [from St. Louis] 195
Choice to Arizona

OAKLAND 1998
1. *Woodson, Charles, DB, Michigan, 4
*Collins, Mo, T, Florida [from Tampa Bay] 23
2. #Bender, Leon, DT, Washington State, 31
Choice to Tampa Bay
3. *Ritchie, Jon, RB, Stanford, 63
4. Choice to New Orleans
DiNapoli, Gennaro, G, Virginia Tech [from Washington] 109
5. *Brigham, Jeremy, TE, Washington, 127
*Smith, Travian, LB, Oklahoma [from Green Bay] 152
6. Choice to Green Bay
7. Choice to Washington
#*Amey, Vince, DE, Arizona State, 230
#Sanders, David, DE, Arkansas, 235

PHILADELPHIA 1998
1. *Thomas, Tra, T, Florida State, 11
2. Choice to Pittsburgh thru New York Jets
3. *Trotter, Jeremiah, LB, Stephen F. Austin, 72
*Rossum, Allen, DB, Notre Dame [from New York Giants] 85
4. Choice to Miami
*Whiting, Brandon, DT, California [from Miami] 112
*Love, Clarence, DB, Toledo [from New York Giants] 116
5. Choice to New York Jets
*Reese, Ike, LB, Michigan State [from Miami] 142
6. Choice to New York Jets
7. Choice to Denver
#Akins, Chris, DT, Texas, 220
#Thomas, Melvin, G, Colorado, 240

PITTSBURGH 1998
1. *Faneca, Alan, G, Louisiana State, 26
2. *Staat, Jeremy, DE, Arizona State [from Philadelphia thru New York Jets] 41
Choice to New York Jets
3. *Conrad, Chris, T, Fresno State [from San Diego] 66
Choice to New York Jets
#*Ward, Hines, WR, Georgia, 92
4. *Townsend, Deshea, DB, Alabama, 117
#*King, Carlos, RB, North Carolina State, 123
5. *Simmons, Jason, DB, Arizona State [from Atlanta] 137
Choice to New York Jets
6. *Fuamatu-Ma'afala, Chris, RB, Utah, 178
#Olson, Ryan, LB, Colorado, 186
7. Choice to San Francisco thru Atlanta
#Rubio, Angel, DE, Southeast Missouri State, 221

ST. LOUIS 1998
1. *Wistrom, Grant, DE, Nebraska, 6
2. *Holcombe, Robert, RB, Illinois, 37
3. *Little, Leonard, LB, Tennessee [from Arizona thru New York Jets] 65
Choice to New York Jets
4. *Hakim, Az-Zahir, WR, San Diego State [from San Diego] 96
*Williams, Roland, TE, Syracuse, 98
5. Priester, Raymond, RB, Clemson, 129
6. Rountree, Glenn, G, Clemson, 159
7. Choice to New York Jets
#*Chorak, Jason, DE, Washington, 236

SAN DIEGO 1998
1. *Leaf, Ryan, QB, Washington State [from Arizona] 2
Choice to Arizona
2. Choice to Arizona
*Ricks, Mikhael, WR, Stephen F. Austin [from Kansas City thru Oak and Tampa Bay] 59
3. Choice to Pittsburgh
4. Choice to St. Louis
5. Harden, Cedric, DE, Florida A&M, 126
6. Ivory, Clifford, DB, Troy State, 155
7. *Haskins, Jon, LB, Stanford, 194
#Sanford, Kio, WR, Kentucky, 234

SAN FRANCISCO 1998
1. *McQuarters, R.W., DB, Oklahoma State, 28
2. Newberry, Jeremy, C, California, 58
3. *Ruhman, Chris, T, Texas A&M, 89
4. *Schulters, Lance, DB, Hofstra, 119
5. Ostrowski, Phil, G, Penn State, 151
6. *Beasley, Fred, RB, Auburn, 180
7. *Thelwell, Ryan, WR, Minnesota [from Pittsburgh thru Atlanta] 215
Choice to Chicago Bears

SEATTLE 1998
1. *Simmons, Anthony, LB, Clemson, 15
2. *Weiner, Todd, T, Kansas State, 47
3. *Green, Ahman, RB, Nebraska, 76
4. *Myles, DeShone, LB, Nevada, 108
5. Choice to Dallas
6. *Hansen, Carl, DE, Stanford [from Dallas] 162
Shaw, Bobby, WR, California, 169
7. *McEndoo, Jason, C, Washington State [from Dallas] 197
Choice to New Orleans

TAMPA BAY 1998
1. Choice to Oakland
2. *Green, Jacquez, WR, Florida [from Oakland] 34
*Kelly, Brian, DB, Southern California [from Atlanta] 45
Choice to Atlanta
3. *Duncan, Jamie, LB, Vanderbilt, 84
4. *Washington, Todd, C, Virginia Tech [from Baltimore] 104
Choice to Atlanta
5. Choice to New York Jets
6. *Cannida, James, DT, Nevada, 175
#*Smith, Shevin, DB, Florida State, 184
7. McCarty, Chance, DE, Texas Christian, 212

TENNESSEE 1998
1. *Dyson, Kevin, WR, Utah, 16
2. *Rolle, Samari, DB, Florida State, 46
3. *Dainon, Sidney, DB, Alabama-Birmingham, 77
4. *Salave'a, Joe, DT, Arizona, 107
5. *Olson, Benji, G, Washington, 139
6. Wiggins, Lee, DB, South Carolina, 168
7. *Sprotte, Jimmy, LB, Arizona, 205
#*Long, Kevin, C, Florida State, 229

WASHINGTON 1998
1. Choice to Cincinnati
2. *Alexander, Stephen, TE, Oklahoma, 48
3. *Hicks, Skip, RB, UCLA [from New Orleans] 69
Choice to Cincinnati
4. Choice to Oakland
*Barber, Shawn, LB, Richmond [from Detroit thru Oakland] 113
5. *Fischer, Mark, C, Purdue, 140
6. Palmer, Patrick, WR, Northwestern State (LA), 170
7. Terrell, David, DB, Texas-El Paso [from Oakland] 191
*Ponds, Antwaune, LB, Syracuse, 206

1999

Held April 17-18, 1999

On February 9, 1999, Cleveland participated in an expansion draft. The Browns had a total of 150 veteran players—five per team—from which to choose. An existing club could recall one player from its list after one of its players was selected; after another of its players was selected, the club had the option to pull back its remaining players.

In the April draft, the Browns had the first pick in each round and also received supplementary selections (+).

Compensatory selections

ARIZONA 1999
1. Boston, David, WR, Ohio State [from San Diego] 8
Shelton, L.J., T, Eastern Michigan, 21
2. Rutledge, Johnny, LB, Florida, 51
3. Burke, Tom, DE, Wisconsin, 83
4. Makovicka, Joel, RB, Nebraska, 116
5. Johnson, Paris, DB, Miami (OH), 155
#Scott, Yusuf, G, Arizona, 168
6. Rhinehart, Jacoby, DB, Southern Methodist, 190
#Bradley, Melvin, LB, Arkansas, 202
#McKinley, Dennis, RB, Mississippi State, 206
7. Choice to Pittsburgh
#Greisen, Chris, QB, Northwest Missouri, 239

ATLANTA 1999
1. Kerney, Patrick, DE, Virgina, 30
2. Kelly, Reggie, TE, Mississippi State [from Baltimore] 42
Choice to San Diego
3. Paulk, Jeff, RB, Arizona State, 92
4. Carty, Johndale, DB, Utah State, 126
5. Baker, Eugene, WR, Kent, 164
6. Kelly, Jeff, LB, Kansas State [from San Francisco] 198
Thigpen, Eric, DB, Iowa, 200
7. McClure, Todd, C, Louisiana State, 237
#Menendez, Rondel, WR, Eastern Kentucky, 247

BALTIMORE 1999
1. McAlister, Chris, DB, Arizona, 10
2. Choice to Atlanta
3. Choice to Miami thru Detroit
4. Stokley, Brandon, WR, Southwestern Louisiana, 105
#Mulitalo, Edwin, G, Arizona, 129
5. Choice to St. Louis
6. Choice to New England
7. Poindexter, Anthony, DB, Virginia, 216

BUFFALO 1999
1. Winfield, Antoine, DB, Ohio State, 23
2. Price, Peerless, WR, Tennessee, 53
3. Bryson, Shawn, RB, Tennessee, 86
4. Newman, Keith, LB, North Carolina, 119
Collins, Bobby, TE, North Alabama [from Green Bay] 122
5. Foreman, Jay, LB, Nebraska, 156
6. Hatcher, Armon, DB, Oregon State, 194
7. Jackson, Sheldon, TE, Nebraska, 230
#Fisher, Bryce, DE, Air Force, 248

CAROLINA 1999
1. Choice to New Orleans thru Washington
2. Terry, Chris, T, Georgia [from Indianapolis] 34
Rucker, Mike, DE, Nebraska, 38
3. Choice to Denver
4. Navies, Hannibal, LB, Colorado, 100
5. Choice to Seattle thru Dallas
6. Daniel, Robert, DE, Northwestern State (LA), 175
7. Booth, Tony, DB, James Madison, 211

CHICAGO 1999
1. Choice to Washington
McNown, Cade, QB, UCLA [from New Orleans thru Washington] 12
2. Choice to Washington
Davis, Russell, DT, North Carolina [from Oakland] 48
3. Tucker, Rex, G, Texas A&M, 66
Bates, D'Wayne, WR, Northwestern [from New Orleans thru Washington]
Booker, Marty, WR, Northeast Louisiana [from Oakland] 78
4. Choice to Oakland
Holdman, Warrick, LB, Texas A&M [from Washington] 106
Colvin, Rosevelt, DE, Purdue [from Oakland] 111
5. Choice to San Diego
Wisne, Jerry, G, Notre Dame [from Washington] 143
Samuel, Khari, LB, Massachusetts [from New Orleans thru Washington] 144
Azumah, Jerry, RB, New Hampshire [from Kansas City] 147
6. Choice to Cleveland
Cook, Rashard, DB, Southern California [from Cleveland] 184
7. Choice to Green Bay
Sanford, Sulecio, WR, Middle Tennessee [from Cleveland] 221
#Finn, Jim, RB, Pennsylvania [from Cleveland] 253

CINCINNATI 1999
1. Smith, Akili, QB, Oregon, 3
2. Fisher, Charles, DB, West Virginia, 33
3. Hall, Cory, DB, Fresno State, 65
4. Yeast, Craig, WR, Kentucky, 98
5. Williams, Nick, RB, Miami, 135
6. Gregg, Kelly, DT, Oklahoma, 173
7. Coats, Tony, G, Washington, 209
#Covington, Scott, QB, Miami, 245
#Broomfield, Donald, DT, Clemson, 249

CLEVELAND 1999
1. Couch, Tim, QB, Kentucky, 1
2. Johnson, Kevin, WR, Syracuse, 32
(+)Abdullah, Rahim, LB, Clemson, 45
3. McCutcheon, Daylon, DB, Southern California, 62
(+)Smith, Marquis, DB, California, 76
4. Choice to Indianapolis thru San Francisco
Choice to San Francisco
Rainer, Wali, LB, Virginia [from San Francisco] 124
5. Choice to Miami thru San Francisco
+Chiaverini, Darrin, WR, Colorado, 148
6. Choice to Seattle
Spriggs, Marcus, DT, Troy State [from Chicago Bears] 174
Choice to Chicago Bears
Ogle, Kendall, LB, Maryland [from Seattle] 187
Dearth, James, TE, Tarleton State [from New England thru Seattle] 191
7. Hill, Madre, RB, Arkansas, 207
Choice to Chicago Bears
#Choice to Chicago Bears

CLEVELAND (Expansion) 1999
1. Pyne, Jim, C, from Detroit
2. McCormack, Hurvin, DE, from Dallas
3. Rehberg, Scott, T, from New England
4. Gibson, Damon, WR, from Cincinnati
5. Gordon, Steve, C, from San Francisco
6. Saleh, Tarek, LB, from Carolina
7. Buckey, Jeff, G, from Miami
8. Kyle, Jason, LB, from Seattle
9. Manuel, Rod, DE, from Pittsburgh
10. Jones, Lenoy, LB, from Tennessee
11. McTyer, Tim, CB, from Philadelphia
12. Alexander, Elijah, LB, from Indianapolis
13. Swanson, Pete, T, from Kansas City
14. Williams, Gerome, S, from San Diego
15. Forbes, Marlon, S, from Chicago Bears
16. Armour, Justin, WR, from Denver
17. Wiggins, Paul, T, from Washington
18. Butler, Duane, S, from Minnesota
19. Brock, Fred, WR, from Arizona
20. Blackwell, Kory, CB, from New York Giants
21. Devine, Kevin, CB, from Jacksonville
22. Jackson, Ray, CB, from Buffalo
23. Bundren, Jim, G, from New York Jets
24. Cavil, Ben, G, from Baltimore
25. Blair, Michael, RB, from Green Bay
26. Anderson, Antonio, DT, from Dallas
27. Bobo, Orlando, G, from Minnesota
28. Williams, James, LB, from San Francisco
29. Milanovich, Scott, QB, from Tampa Bay
30. Stokes, Eric, S, from Seattle
31. Moore, Ronald, RB, from Miami
32. Williams, Clarence, RB, from Buffalo
33. Solomon, Freddie, WR, from Philadelphia
34. Sanders, Brandon, S, from New York Giants
35. Thompson, Mike, DT, from Cincinnati
36. McPhail, Jerris, WR, from Detroit
37. Langham, Antonio, CB, from San Francisco

DALLAS 1999
1. Ekuban, Ebenezer, DE, North Carolina [from New England thru Seattle] 20
Choice to Seattle
2. Page, Solomon, T, West Virginia, 55
3. Nguyen, Dat, LB, Texas A&M, 85
4. McGarity, Wane, WR, Texas, 118
#Zellner, Peppi, DE, Fort Valley State, 132
5. Choice to Denver
6. Jenkins, MarTay, WR, Nebraska-Omaha, 193
7. Lucky, Mike, TE, Arizona, 229
#Garmon, Kelvin, G, Baylor, 243

DENVER 1999
1. Wilson, Al, LB, Tennessee, 31
2. Reagor, Montae, DE, Texas Tech [from San Francisco] 58
Friedman, Lennie, G, Duke, 61
3. Watson, Chris, DB, Eastern Illinois [from Carolina] 67
McGriff, Travis, WR, Florida, 93
4. Gary, Olandis, RB, Georgia, 127
5. Bowens, David, DE, Western Illinois [from Dallas] 158
Choice to Washington
#Brown, Darwin, DB, Texas Tech, 167
6. Clark, Desmond, TE, Wake Forest [from New Orleans thru Washington] 179
Choice to Philadelphia
#Plummer, Chad, WR, Cincinnati, 204
7. Miller, Billy, WR, Southern California [from New Orleans thru Washington] 218
Swift, Justin, TE, Kansas State, 238

DETROIT 1999
1. Claiborne, Chris, LB, Southern California, 9
Gibson, Aaron, T, Wisconsin [from San Francisco thru Miami] 27
2. Choice to Miami
3. DeVries, Jared, DE, Iowa, 70
4. Irvin, Sedrick, RB, Michigan State, 103
5. Talton, Tyree, DB, Northern Iowa [from Philadelphia] 137
Choice to Miami
6. Kriewaldt, Clint, LB, Wisconsin-Stevens Point, 177
7. Pringley, Mike, DE, North Carolina, 215

GREEN BAY 1999
1. Edwards, Antwan, DB, Clemson, 25
2. Vinson, Fred, DB, Vanderbilt [from Seattle] 47
Choice exercised in 1998 Supplemental Draft (Wahle, Mike, T, Navy)
3. McKenzie, Mike, DB, Memphis, 87
#Hunt, Cletidus, DT, Kentucky State, 94
4. Choice to Buffalo
#Brooks, Aaron, QB, Virginia, 131
#Bidwell, Josh, P, Oregon, 133
5. Parker, De'Mond, RB, Oklahoma, 159
Heimburger, Craig, C, Missouri [from Minnesota thru Pittsburgh and Oakland] 163
6. Miller, Dee, WR, Ohio State, 196
#Curry, Scott, T, Montana, 203
7. Akins, Chris, DB, Arkansas-Pine Bluff [from St. Louis] 212
Driver, Donald, WR, Alcorn State [from Chicago Bears] 213
Choice to Miami thru Detroit

INDIANAPOLIS 1999
1. James, Edgerrin, RB, Miami (FL), 4
2. Choice to Carolina
Peterson, Mike, LB, Florida [from St. Louis] 36
3. Burlsworth, Brandon, G, Arkansas, 63
4. Miranda, Paul, DB, Central Florida [from Cleveland thru San Francisco] 96
Choice to San Francisco
5. Choice to Pittsburgh
Scioli, Brad, DE, Penn State [from St. Louis] 138
6. Choice to San Francisco
7. Smith, Hunter, P, Notre Dame, 210
#Terry, Corey, LB, Tennessee, 250

JACKSONVILLE 1999
1. Bryant, Fernando, DB, Alabama, 26
2. Smith, Larry, DT, Florida State, 56
3. Cesario, Anthony, G, Colorado State, 88
4. Landolt, Kevin, DT, West Virginia, 121
5. Craft, Jason, DB, Colorado State, 160
6. Leroy, Emarlos, DT, Georgia [from Kansas City thru Tampa Bay] 182
Choice to Tampa Bay
7. Choice to Tampa Bay
#Moronkola, Dee, DB, Washington State, 242
#White, Chris, DE, Southern, 246

KANSAS CITY 1999
1. Tait, John, T, Brigham Young, 14
2. Choice to Miami
   Cloud, Mike, RB, Boston College [from Miami] 54
3. Stills, Gary, LB, West Virginia, 75
   Atkins, Larry, DB, UCLA [from Miami] 84
4. Parker, Larry, WR, Southern California, 108
5. Choice to Chicago Bears
6. Choice to Jacksonville thru Tampa Bay
7. King, Eric, G, Richmond, 220

MIAMI 1999
1. Choice to San Francisco
2. Johnson, James, RB, Mississippi State [from Detroit] 39
   Konrad, Rob, RB, Syracuse [from Kansas City] 43
   Choice to Kansas City
3. Ruegamer, Grey, C, Arizona State [from Baltimore thru Detroit] 72
   Choice to Kansas City
4. Choice to Minnesota
5. Collins, Cecil, RB, McNeese State [from Cleveland thru San Francisco] 134
   Jones, Bryan, LB, Oregon State [from Detroit] 142
   Choice to San Francisco
6. Bartholomew, Brent, P, Ohio State, 192
7. Choice to New York Giants
   Haley, Jermaine, DT, Butte J.C. [from Green Bay thru Detroit] 232
   #Wong, Joe, T, Brigham Young, 244

MINNESOTA 1999
1. Culpepper, Daunte, QB, Central Florida [from Washington] 11
   Underwood, Dimitrius, DE, Michigan State, 29
2. Kleinsasser, Jim, TE, North Dakota [from Pittsburgh] 44
   Choice to Pittsburgh
3. Choice to New England
4. Wright, Kenny, DB, Northwestern State (LA) [from Miami] 120
   Humphrey, Jay, T, Texas, 125
5. Choice to Green Bay thru Pittsburgh and Oakland
   #Jones, Chris, LB, Clemson, 169
6. Sawyer, Talance, DE, UNLV [from Tampa Bay thru Baltimore] 185
   Dalton, Antico, LB, Hampton, 199
7. Scarlett, Noel, DT, Langston (OK), 236

NEW ENGLAND 1999
1. Woody, Damien, C, Boston College [from Seattle] 17
   Choice to Dallas thru Seattle
   Katzenmoyer, Andy, LB, Ohio State [from New York Jets] 28
2. Faulk, Kevin, RB, Louisiana State [from Tennessee] 46
   Choice to Tennessee
3. Choice to Seattle
   George, Tony, DB, Florida [from Minnesota] 91
4. Choice to Tennessee
5. Fletcher, Derrick, G, Baylor, 154
6. Washington, Marcus, DB, Colorado [from Baltimore], 180
   Choice to Cleveland thru Seattle
7. Bishop, Michael, QB, Kansas State, 227
   #Morey, Sean, WR, Brown, 241

NEW ORLEANS 1999
1. Williams, Ricky, RB, Texas [from Carolina thru Washington] 5
   Choice to Chicago Bears thru Washington
2. Choice to St. Louis
3. Choice to Chicago Bears thru Washington
4. Choice to Washington
5. Choice to Chicago Bears thru Washington
6. Choice to Denver thru Washington
7. Choice to Denver thru Washington

NEW YORK GIANTS 1999
1. Petitgout, Luke, T, Notre Dame, 19
2. Montgomery, Joe, RB, Ohio State, 49
3. Campbell, Dan, TE, Texas A&M, 79
4. Bennett, Sean, RB, Northwestern, 112
5. Rosenthal, Mike, T, Notre Dame, 149
6. West, Lyle, DB, San Jose State, 189
   #Weathers, Andre, DB, Michigan, 205
7. Hale, Ryan, DT, Arkansas, 225
   Childress, O.J., LB, Clemson [from Miami] 231

NEW YORK JETS 1999
1. Choice to New England
2. Thomas, Randy, G, Mississippi State, 57
3. Loverne, David, T, San Jose State, 90
4. Wiltz, Jason, DT, Nebraska, 123
5. Jones, Jermaine, DB, Northwestern State (LA), 162
6. Megna, Marc, LB, Richmond [from Pittsburgh] 183
   Machado, J.P., G, Illinois, 197
7. Young, Ryan, T, Kansas State [from Seattle] 223
   Syvrud, J.J., DE, Jamestown, 235

OAKLAND 1999
1. Stinchcomb, Matt, T, Georgia, 18
2. Bryant, Tony, DE, Florida State [from Washington thru Chicago Bears] 40
   Choice to Chicago Bears
3. Choice to Chicago Bears
4. Douglas, Dameane, WR, California [from Chicago Bears] 102
   Choice to Chicago Bears
5. Barton, Eric, LB, Maryland [from Pittsburgh] 146
   Coleman, Roderick, LB, East Carolina, 153
6. Yancy, Daren, DT, Brigham Young, 188
7. Armour, JoJuan, LB, Miami (OH), 224

PHILADELPHIA 1999
1. McNabb, Donovan, QB, Syracuse, 2
2. Gardner, Barry, LB, Northwestern, 35
3. Brzezinski, Doug, G, Boston College, 64
4. Welbourn, John, T, California, 97
   #Moore, Damon, DB, Ohio State, 128
   #Brown, Na, WR, North Carolina, 130
5. Choice to Detroit
6. Martin, Cecil, RB, Wisconsin, 172
   Smith, Troy, WR, East Carolina [from Denver] 201
7. Weaver, Jed, TE, Oregon, 208
   #Davis, Pernell, DT, Alabama-Birmingham, 251

PITTSBURGH 1999
1. Edwards, Troy, WR, Louisiana Tech, 13
2. Choice to Minnesota
   Shields, Scott, DB, Weber State [from Minnesota] 59
3. Porter, Joey, LB, Colorado State [from Washington thru Minnesota] 73
   Farris, Kris, T, UCLA, 74
   #Zereoue, Amos, RB, West Virginia, 95
4. Smith, Aaron, DE, Northern Colorado, 109
5. Tuman, Jerame, TE, Michigan [from Indianapolis] 136
   Choice to Oakland
   #Johnson, Malcolm, WR, Notre Dame, 166
6. Choice to New York Jets
7. Dingle, Antonio, DT, Virginia [from San Diego] 214
   Kelsay, Chad, LB, Nebraska, 219
   Brown, Kris, K, Nebraska [from Arizona] 228

ST. LOUIS 1999
1. Holt, Torry, WR, North Carolina State, 6
2. Choice to Indianapolis
   Bly, Dre', DB, North Carolina [from New Orleans] 41
3. Coady, Richard, DB, Texas A&M, 68
4. Germaine, Joe, QB, Ohio State, 101
5. Choice to Indianapolis
   Spikes, Cameron, G, Texas A&M [from Baltimore] 145
6. Barnes, Lionel, DE, Northeast Louisiana, 176
7. Choice to Green Bay
   #Williams, Rodney, P, Georgia Tech, 252

SAN DIEGO 1999
1. Choice to Arizona
2. Choice exercised in 1998 Supplemental Draft (Williams, Jamal, DT, Oklahoma State)
   Fazande, Jermaine, RB, Oklahoma [from Atlanta] 60
3. Heiden, Steve, TE, South Dakota State, 69
4. Perry, Jason, DB, North Carolina State, 104
5. Dingle, Adrian, DE, Clemson [from Chicago Bears] 139
   Nelson, Reggie, G, McNeese State, 141
6. Bell, Tyrone, DB, North Alabama, 178
7. Choice to Pittsburgh

SAN FRANCISCO 1999
1. McGrew, Reggie, DT, Florida [from Miami] 24
   Choice to Detroit thru Miami
2. Choice to Denver
3. Okeafor, Chike, DE, Purdue, 89
4. Parker, Anthony, DB, Weber State [from Indianapolis] 99
   Prioleau, Pierson, DB, Virginia Tech [from Cleveland] 110
   Choice to Cleveland
5. Jackson, Terry, RB, Florida [from Miami] 157
   Hopson, Tyrone, T, Eastern Kentucky, 161
6. Streets, Tai, WR, Michigan [from Indianapolis] 171
   Choice to Atlanta
7. Minor, Kory, LB, Notre Dame, 234

SEATTLE 1999
1. Choice to New England
   King, Lamar, DE, Saginaw Valley [from Dallas] 22
2. Choice to Green Bay
3. Huard, Brock, QB, Washington, 77
   Bailey, Karsten, WR, Auburn [from New England] 82
4. Cochran, Antonio, DE, Georgia, 115
5. Wedderburn, Floyd, T, Penn State [from Carolina thru Dallas] 140
   Rogers, Charlie, WR, Georgia Tech, 152
6. Johnson, Steve, DB, Tennessee [from Cleveland] 170
   Choice to Cleveland
7. Choice to New York Jets

TAMPA BAY 1999
1. McFarland, Anthony, DT, Louisiana State, 15
2. King, Shaun, QB, Tulane, 50
3. Gramatica, Martin, K, Kansas State, 80
4. Jackson, Dexter, DB, Florida State, 113
5. McLaughlin, John, DE, California, 150
6. Choice to Minnesota thru Baltimore
   Glenn, Lamarr, RB, Florida State [from Jacksonville] 195
7. Hunt, Robert, G, Virginia, 226
   Denson, Autry, RB, Notre Dame [from Jacksonville] 233
   #McDonald, Darnell, WR, Kansas State, 240

TENNESSEE 1999
1. Kearse, Jevon, DE, Florida, 16
2. Choice to New England
   Thornton, John, DT, West Virginia [from New England] 52
3. Piller, Zach, G, Florida, 81
4. Ware, Brad, DB, Auburn, 114
   Mitchell, Donald, DB, Southern Methodist [from New England] 117
5. Daft, Kevin, QB, California-Davis, 151
6. Hall, Darran, WR, Colorado State, 186
7. Glover, Phil, LB, Utah, 222

WASHINGTON 1999
1. Bailey, Champ, DB, Georgia [from Chicago Bears] 7
   Choice to Minnesota
2. Jansen, Jon, T, Michigan [from Chicago Bears] 37
   Choice to Oakland thru Chicago Bears
3. Choice to Pittsburgh thru Minnesota
4. Choice to Chicago Bears
   Stimson, Nate, LB, Georgia Tech [from New Orleans] 107
5. Choice to Chicago Bears
   Smith, Derek, T, Virginia Tech [from Denver] 165
6. Hall, Jeff, K, Tennessee, 181
7. Alexander, Tim, WR, Oregon State, 217

Draft-Day Surprises

Beau Riffenburgh

The key event in player development every year is the draft, where the top college players in the country are divided among all 31 NFL teams. The selections in the NFL draft once were made right out of *Street & Smith's College Football* magazine, and some of the choices reflected the folly of this approach. So today, with huge amounts of money poured into the system and the use of computers and physical and psychological testing, the situation has improved and there are no more surprises, right?

Well, as a matter of fact, no. The selection of players remains one of the most subjective and least understood aspects of the game.

This less-than-perfect system for providing new players has been marked through the years by unbelievable surprises, both positive and negative. Players such as Tucker Frederickson, Terry Baker, Tom Cousineau, and Walt Patulski failed in their NFL careers after being the first player selected. Other players didn't impress the scouts enough to be taken at the front end of the draft but eventually starred in the NFL.

The Pro Football Hall of Fame includes many players who were low draft selections and then went on to star in the league. Emlen Tunnell, Dick (Night Train) Lane, and Willie Wood were not drafted, and Colts wide receiver Raymond Berry was taken in the twentieth round of the 1954 draft as a "future." (A future pick was based on the old NFL rule that a player could be chosen if his class had graduated, even if he hadn't completed his eligibility.) The rule applied to players who had been "redshirted," that is, who had sat out a year. Under the "future rule," a player could be drafted after his fourth year, and his rights would remain with the team that selected him even if he didn't sign for a year or more.

Berry was a future, and, of course, went on to become the primary receiver for Johnny Unitas with the Colts; he led the NFL in receiving three times and finished his 13-year career with 631 receptions, then the pro football record. He later became a coach and led the New England Patriots to their first Super Bowl appearance.

Speaking of Unitas, despite a successful career at Louisville, even he didn't get much respect at draft time. He was left unclaimed until the ninth round in 1955, when Pittsburgh selected him. But he was cut without even getting into a preseason game. Owner Art Rooney's sons called him "the best quarterback in camp, but the only people they let him throw to is us."

Arguably the greatest NFL quarterback of all time, Unitas played for the semipro Bloomfield Rams of the Greater Pittsburgh League for six dollars a game until Colts general manager Don Kellett signed him as a backup to George Shaw in 1956. When Shaw was injured, Unitas quickly established himself as the starter and went on to pass for 40,239 yards and 290 touchdowns in his 18-year career. A three-time NFL most valuable player, he went on to demonstrate as much poise and control of the clock as any other quarterback in football history.

One of Unitas's great rivals, Bart Starr, also was overlooked in the draft. He had been a star at Alabama, and as a freshman had led the Crimson Tide to a 61-6 victory over Syracuse in the Orange Bowl. Starr had a standout sophomore year, but coach Harold (Red) Drew eventually lost confidence in him, and Starr lasted until the seventeenth round in 1956, when the Packers selected him. (Of the other quarterbacks in Starr's class that year, only Earl Morrall distinguished himself as an NFL quarterback.)

Vince Lombardi took over as the Packers' coach in 1959. Lombardi traded for quarterback Lamar McHan, and when McHan separated a shoulder, Joe Francis became the starter. The Packers lost five consecutive games before Starr got his chance against the Redskins, and led Green Bay to a 21-0 victory. Starr blossomed under Lombardi's tutelage and went on to lead the NFL in passing three times. He guided the Packers to five NFL titles, plus victories in the first two Super Bowls. (He was named the MVP in both.)

Throughout most of the careers of Unitas and Starr, one team—the Los Angeles Rams—was far ahead of most teams in its selection techniques. Rams owner Daniel F. Reeves had a passion for the draft. He developed many of the scouting techniques all teams eventually utilized, and it was Reeves who broke the color barrier in the NFL with the signing of Kenny Washington and Woody Strode in 1946. He also signed the first player from a predominantly black college, Paul (Tank) Younger of Grambling in 1949.

Under Reeves's direction, the Rams often traded established veterans for draft choices. An example was one of the Rams' most successful selections, Andy Robustelli, who had been a two-way lineman at tiny Arnold College, which doesn't exist today. Robustelli, who was selected in the nineteenth round of the 1951 draft, was a Pro Bowl defensive end twice in five seasons in Los Angeles.

Then the Rams abruptly traded him (along with Ed Hughes) to the Giants for draft choices that were used to select three players who would go on to be named to the Pro Bowl: fullback Joe Marconi; split end Del Shofner;

and, defensive end Lamar Lundy, who became part of the defensive line known as the Fearsome Foursome.

One of Lundy's colleagues on that fabled line was another masterful Reeves selection—Pro Football Hall of Fame defensive end David (Deacon) Jones, taken in the fourteenth round of the 1961 draft from Mississippi Vocational (now known as Mississippi Valley State). While Reeves and his coaches looked at film of a running back from a small southern school, they were more impressed with Jones, who had the speed and tenacity to catch the back in the open field and tackle him on several plays. At the time, Jones was playing defensive tackle at South Carolina State prior to transferring to Mississippi Vocational. Jones switched to end, coined the term "sack," and became one of the greatest defensive linemen in NFL history.

Of course, even Reeves's Rams were not infallible in finding draft-day gems. In 1965, the Los Angeles personnel director wanted to use a late-round selection to obtain a multitalented quarterback from South Carolina, a player who also happened to be named Dan Reeves. "There is only one Dan Reeves with the Los Angeles Rams," the owner snapped, "and that is all there will ever be." The other Dan Reeves signed a free-agent contract with the Cowboys, for whom he played eight years before becoming a successful coach.

The same year Reeves finished his college career, so did another quarterback, Roger Staubach of the U.S. Naval Academy. Again, the Cowboys showed remarkable foresight. In 1964, following Staubach's Heisman Trophy winning junior season, they selected him in the tenth round of the draft as a future. Unlike a usual future pick, Staubach owed the Navy four years of service after his graduation. Waiting five years for him to play pro football was a longshot. The gamble paid off, of course, as Staubach joined the Cowboys in 1969, gained a starting position two years later, and went on to lead the NFL in passing four times while quarterbacking Dallas to four Super Bowl appearances.

The Rams' Reeves died in 1971, around the time that Pittsburgh succeeded Los Angeles as the most innovative team on draft day. Through much of the 1970s, the Steelers spent more time scouting—and had more success selecting players from—primarily black colleges than any other team in the NFL. This led to a huge influx of players who went on to be key figures in the Steelers' four Super Bowl championships, including L.C. Greenwood of Arkansas-Pine Bluff, Mel Blount of Southern, Frank Lewis of Grambling, Joe Gilliam of Tennessee State, and John Stallworth of Alabama A&M.

Even as scouting techniques improved through the 1970s and into the 1980s, the computers continued to miss players who would go on to be giants of the game. In 1979, the 49ers, with only their second selection of the draft, were able to grab quarterback Joe Montana in the third round. Montana led Notre Dame to a national championship in his junior year, and thus was not someone who had been hidden from national view, but somehow Jack Thompson of Washington State, Steve Fuller of Clemson, and Phil Simms of Morehead State went in the first round while personnel folks ignored Montana.

Four years later, a similar scenario unfolded. Dan Marino, who would go on to throw more passes for more completions, more yards, and more touchdowns than any other player in NFL history, was selected in the first round, but not until five other quarterbacks had been taken before the University of Pittsburgh standout. Granted, one of those was John Elway, whom Baltimore grabbed with the first pick of the draft before trading him to Denver. And three of the other first-rounders—Jim Kelly of Miami (to Buffalo), Tony Eason of Illinois (to New England), and Ken O'Brien of California-Davis (to the New York Jets) — went on to productive NFL careers, leaving only Todd Blackledge of Penn State (taken by Kansas City) as a true disappointment. But still, five quarterbacks before Marino?

Of course, if a team felt strongly about Marino, it could always have traded up in order to obtain him. Such a move happens frequently, when one team is intent on drafting a specific player and is willing to trade extra draft picks or players for the right to secure that selection with an earlier pick.

In 1985, for example, San Francisco coach Bill Walsh was desperate to draft wide receiver Jerry Rice of Mississippi Valley State. "Rice was considered to have marginal speed for a starting NFL wide receiver by virtually every team in the NFL," Walsh wrote later. "The only exceptions were the New York Jets, the Dallas Cowboys, and the San Francisco 49ers." The Jets were due to select tenth, the Cowboys seventeenth, and the 49ers twenty-eighth. It appeared that there was no way to make a trade with the Jets, and the 49ers' personnel team had to hold its breath until New York made wide receiver Al Toon of Wisconsin its initial choice.

Then San Francisco had to worry about Dallas taking the man who would go on to become arguably the greatest receiver in pro football history. The 49ers offered to trade New England their first- , second- , and third-round selections for the Patriots' first- and third-round choices. A deal was struck. The Patriots gained a high selection, the 49ers moved up to sixteenth in the first round, and Rice went to San Francisco.

"There is a public perception that the NFL draft is a very technical, scientific kind of enterprise," Gil Brandt, the former personnel guru of the Cowboys, once said. "However, it is actually as much an art as a science. You need to take all of the data that you compile and then use it creatively for the benefit of your team. Those franchises that approach the draft with no creativity are destined to remain mediocre, while those that use it in original, thinking ways will have a much better chance of getting to the top of the pro football world."

Colleges That Produced the Pros

The pro game evolved out of the college game, and, not surprisingly, the vast majority of professional football players have come from colleges. It should also not come as much of a surprise that Notre Dame has produced more NFL players than any other school. Through the 1998 season, 429 pros had played college ball in South Bend, compared with 359 from USC and 288 from Ohio State.

Many schools other than the football powerhouses have prepared players for the NFL. Players from small private schools, community colleges, and junior colleges alike have made it to the pros. For example, three different Trinity Colleges (in Connecticut, Illinois, and Texas) have students that made it to the NFL, along with another 16 players who attended Trinity Valley Community College.

Colleges outside the U.S. have also contributed to the NFL talent pool. College students from Austria, Canada, Serbia, and Wales have also found places in the NFL.

Note also that, when a player has attended more than one school (like Troy Aikman), all the schools are listed.

Abilene Christian (24)

Larry Cox
Bernie Erickson
Grant Feasel
Greg Feasel
Paul Goad
Tom Humphrey
Mark Jackson
Steve Jacobson
Ove Johansson
Thurman Jones
Clint Longley
Reggie McGowan
Bob McLeod
Cleo Montgomery
Wilbert Montgomery
Tipp Mooney
Bob Oliver
Johnny Perkins
Dan Remsberg
Charlie Smith
Vitamin Smith
Dick Stovall
Wayne Walton
Richard Williams

Acadia (Canada) (1)

Jerome Pathon

Adams State (4)

Don Alley
Don Cockroft
Pat Epperson
Ken Marchiol

Air Force (9)

Sid Abramowitz
Shane Bonham
Larry Cole
Ron George
Chad Hennings
Bill Line
Mike Rengel
Steve Russ
Jeff Smith

Akron (15)

Scotty Bierce
James Black
Spark Clark
Red Daum
Victor Green
Ed Grimsley
Art Haley
Chris Kelley
Robert Lyons
Ara Parseghian
Ron Pasquale
Jason Taylor
Mike Teifke
Shawn Vincent
Ralph Waldsmith

Alabama (204)

Ray Abruzzese
Don Avery
Butch Avinger
Buddy Aydelette
Bob Baumhower
Albert Bell
Jesse Bendross
Cornelius Bennett
George Bethune
Lew Bostick
Jim Bowdoin
Steve Bowman
Tom Boyd
Byron Braggs
Tommy Brooker
Dave Brown
Bill Buckler
Kendrick Burton
Jim Cain
Tom Calvin
Paul Ott Carruth
Joe Carter
Jeremiah Castille
Bill Chambers
Thornton Chandler
Jackie Cline
Ted Cook
John Copeland
Russ Craft
Paul Crane
Tiny Croft
Sylvester Croom
Howard Cross
Bob Cryder
Ed Culpepper
Eric Curry
Wayne Davis
Fred Davis
Johnny Davis
Ricky Davis
Chuck DeShane
Joe Domnanovich
Jess Eberdt
Randy Edwards
Leon Fichman
Brad Ford
Greg Gantt
Woody Gerber
Harry Gilmer
Chris Goode
Kerry Goode
Preston Gothard
George Gulyanics
Lemanski Hall
Jon Hand
Charley Hannah
Herb Hannah
John Hannah
Patrick Hape
Paul Harris
George Hecht
Tony Holm
Dennis Homan
Dixie Howell
Bobby Humphrey
Ben Hunt
Scott Hunter
Tom Hupke
Don Hutson
Billy Jackson
Bobby Jackson
Wilbur Jackson
Curt Jarvis
Dameian Jeffries
Hoss Johnson
Tommy Johnson
Tony Johnson
Joey Jones
Ralph Jones
Bruce Jones
Robbie Jones
Terry Jones
Lee Roy Jordan
E.J. Junior
Les Kelley
Emanuel King
Bo Kirkland
Larry Knorr
Barry Krauss
Antonio Langham
Derrick Lassic
Larry Lauer
Kevin Lee
Bill Lee
Tony Leon
Antonio London
Woodrow Lowe
Bobby Luna
Marty Lyons
Ken MacAfee
Vaughn Mancha
John Mangum
Kris Mangum
Frank Martin
Keith McCants
Joel McCoy
Willie McCray
Charlie McGibbony
Curtis McGriff
Mark McMillian
Don McNeal
Walt Merrill
Chris Mohr
Ricky Moore
Norman Mosley
Russ Mosley
Steve Mott
Johnny Musso
Michael Myers
Joe Namath
Tony Nathan
Billy Neighbors
Benny Nelson
Jimmy Nelson
Ozzie Newsome
Jeremy Nunley
Derrick Oden
Ray Ogden
Mitch Olenski
Bill Oliver
Norm Olsen
David Palmer
Ray Perkins
Benny Perrin
Claude Perry
Mike Pitts
Mike Raines
David Ray
Thomas Rayam
Ken Reese
Greg Richardson
Jess Richardson
Ray Richeson
Charlie Rieves
Larry Roberts
Freddie Robinson
Hosea Rodgers
Mike Rodriguez
Andre Royal
Dwayne Rudd
Jeff Rutledge
Rod Rutledge
Ed Salem
Sandy Sanford
Willard Scissum
Randy Scott
Bill Searcey
Sam Shade
Willie Shelby
Billy Shipp
Steve Sloan
Anthony Smith
Ben Smith
Riley Smith
Irving Spikes
Ken Stabler
Siran Stacy
Bart Starr
Ralph Staten
Rebel Steiner
Dwight Stephenson
Vaughn Stewart
John Sullins
George Teague
Lowell Tew
Corky Tharp
Derrick Thomas
Ricky Thomas
George Thornton
Van Tiffin
Richard Todd
Tommy Tolleson
Deshea Townsend
Wayne Trimble
Paul Tripoli
Bob Trocolor
Kevin Turner
Mike Washington
Jerry Watford
George Weeks
Bull Wesley
Jim Whatley
Wayne Wheeler
Tarzan White
Sherman Williams
Butch Wilson
Rich Wingo
Bobby Wood
John Wozniak
Steve Wright
Willie Wyatt
John Wyhonic
Bill Young
Sid Youngelman

Alabama A&M (14)

Howard Ballard
Ricky Blake
Ronnie Coleman
Ernest French
Mike Hegman
Thomas Hopkins
Bill Kindricks
Wayne Mosley
Joe Patton
Oliver Ross
Franky Smith
John Stallworth
Barry Wagner
Mike Williams

Alabama State (13)

Reggie Barlow
Brad Baxter
Reggie Brown
Buddy Davis
Curtis Green
Terry Greer
Emanuel Martin
Ralph Miller
Zefross Moss
Karl Powe
Eddie Robinson
Ricky Smith
Rodell Thomas

Alabama-Birmingham (3)

Josh Evans
Izell Reese
Dainon Sidney

Albany State (Ga.) (7)

Steve Carter
Kenneth Gant
Arthur Green
Jeff Hunter
Dan Land
Chris Sheffield
Mike White

Albion (1)

Joe Felton

Albright (5)

Knuckles Boyle
Leo Disend
John Durko
Stan Kosel
Dick Riffle

Alcorn State (46)

Willie Alexander
Willie Banks
Milton Barney
Henry Bradley
Boyd Brown
Robert Brown
Arnold Campbell
Charles Coleman
Larry Estes
Leonard Fairley
Elbert Foules
Leslie Frazier
Larry Friday
Leon Garror
Jimmie Giles
David Hadley
Mark Harper
Marcus Hinton
Issiac Holt
Billy Howard
Mike Jones
Garry Lewis
Milton Mack
Willie McGee
Steve McNair
Bryant Mix
Joe Owens
Bob Penchion
Lawrence Pillers
Elex Price
Frank Purnell
Smith Reed
Floyd Rice
Torrance Small
Elliot Smith
Rich Sowells
Jack Spinks
John Thierry
Cedric Tillman
Dave Washington
Robert Washington
Larry Watkins
Dwayne White
Otis Wonsley
Roynell Young
Willie Young

Alfred (3)

Les Goble
Frank Trigilio
Ray Witter

Allan Hancock Coll. CA (J.C.) (7)

Brian Allred
Israel Byrd
Sheldon Canley
Johnnie Gray
Wymon Henderson
Mike Vanderjagt
Nat Whitmyer

Allegany CC MD (1)

George Small

Allegheny (3)

Ronnie Anderson
Babe Parnell
Eddie Wall

Allen (4)

Charlie Bryant
John Cash
Sam Davis
George Harold

Allentown College (1)

Jamie Kurisko

Alma (1)

Mark Konecny

Alvin CC TX (2)

Gary Keithley
Andre Ware

Amarillo Coll. TX (J.C.) (3)

Kevin Brown
Ed Cherry
Odis Crowell

American Coll. of Physical Education (1)

Lenny Sachs

American International (8)

Brian Carey
Bruce Laird
Jon Norris
Terry Randolph
Tom Rychlec
Joe Scibelli
George Sergienko
Chris Williams

American River Coll. CA (J.C.) (5)

Fred Brown
Curt DiGiacomo
Tony Eason
James Saxon
Gerald Willhite

Amherst (5)

Sean Clancy
Jean Fugett
Kid Hill
Freddie Scott
Doug Swift

Anahuac (Mexico) (1)

Sergio Albert

Anderson (Ind.) (2)

Brad Lamb
Tim Mooney

Angelina Coll. TX (J.C.) (1)

Tony Jones

Angelo State (9)

Jerry Aldridge
Alvin Garrett
Shawn Hollingsworth
Pierce Holt
Ken Kennard
Andre President
Wylie Turner
Clayton Weishuhn
Charlie West

Antelope Valley Coll. CA (J.C.) (4)

John Janata
Tony Reed
Vern Valdez
Larrye Weaver

Appalachian State (19)

Harold Alexander
Jimmy Armstrong
Dexter Coakley
Tommy Dawkins
George Demko
Mike Frier
Derrick Graham
Dino Hackett
Larry Hand
John Hollar
Rico Mack
Bjorn Nittmo
Russell Payne
Mark Royals
Darryl Russell
John Settle
Struggy Smith
Matt Stevens
George Watts

Arizona (118)

David Adams
Brad Anderson
Jim Arneson
Mark Arneson
Emil Banjavic
Rod Barksdale
Michael Bates
Theo Bell
Steve Boadway
Tony Bouie
Greg Boyd
Brant Boyer
Chris Brewer
Tedy Bruschi
Chester Burnett
Chuck Cecil
Bob Cobb
Don Corbitt
Cleveland Crosby
Bob Crum
Jack Davis
Mike Dawson
Bill Demory
Charlie Dickey
Curt DiGiacomo
Joe Drake
Hicham El-Mashtoub
Fred Enke
Byron Evans
John Fina
Mike Freeman
Phil Freeman
Frank Garcia
Ron Gardin
Marsharne Graves
Marcellus Greene
Tom Greenfield
Rich Griffith
Al Gross
Rickie Harris
Sean Harris
Keith Hartwig
Larry Heater
Brad Henke
Joe Hernandez
Derek Hill
George Hinkle
Harry Holt
Mitch Hoopes
Brad Hubbert
Floyd Hudlow
Lamonte Hunley
Ricky Hunley
Keshon Johnson
Vance Johnson
John Kaiser
Abe Karnofsky
Mark Keel
Jeff Kiewel
Chuck Levy
Darryll Lewis
Roderick Lewis
Warren Livingston
Danny Lockett
Bill Lueck
Stan Mataele
Bob McCall
Bill McKinley
Steve McLaughlin
Chris McLemore
John Mellekas
Frank Middleton
Josh Miller
Darryl Morrison
Walt Nielsen
John Nies
Tory Nixon
Earl Nolan
Jim Oldham
Hubie Oliver
Chuck Osborne
Glenn Parker
Ty Parten
Francis Peay
Scott Piper
Jose Portilla
Randy Robbins
Mike Robinson
Paul Robinson
Ruben Rodriguez
Martin Rudolph
Joe Salave'a
Brandon Sanders
Chris Schultz
Mike Scurlock
Chris Singleton
Branko Smilanich
Tommie Smiley
Anthony Smith
Jimmy Sprotte
Henry Stanton
Ricky Stevenson
Bobby Thompson
Rusty Tillman
Joe Tofflemire
Van Tuinei
Mark Walczak
Rob Waldrop
Jackie Wallace
Robert Weathers
Dana Wells
Bob Whitlow
Armon Williams
Rodney Williams
Eddie Wilson
Rob Woods
Joe Young
Max Zendejas

Arizona State (183)

Eric Allen
Vincent Amey
Kim Anderson
Max Anderson
Ben Apuna
Trace Armstrong
Jon Baker
Mario Bates
Jerry Bell
Ed Beverly
Mike Black
Walt Bowyer
Bob Breunig
Ray Brown
Ron Brown
Mike Brunson
Tim Buchanan
Leon Burton
Steve Bush
Eddie Cade
Bryan Caldwell
Henry Carr
Shante Carver
Darryl Clack
Greg Clark
Lee Cole
Shane Collins
Darren Comeaux
Aaron Cox
Mike Crawford
Curley Culp
Anthony Daigle
Jerone Davison
Chris DeFrance
Calvin Demery
David Dixon
Mike Douglass
Oscar Dragon
George Duarte
Mark Duckens
Ken Dyer
Monroe Eley
Bill Elko
Mike Fanucci
Floyd Fields
Ed Fisher
George Flint
Gene Foster
David Fulcher
Duane Galloway
Frank Garcia
Mark Gastineau
Larry Gordon
Dave Grannell
Woody Green
Eric Guliford
Windlan Hall
Bruce Hardy
Al Harris
Darryl Harris
John Harris
Stacy Harvey
Ben Hawkins
Mike Haynes
Larry Hendershot
Bernard Henry
Mark Hicks
Bruce Hill
J.D. Hill
Steve Holden
Todd Hons
Fair Hooker
Melvin Hoover
Lynn James
Jim Jeffcoat
John Jefferson
Greg Joelson
Glenn Johnson
John Henry Johnson
Doug Jones
Paul Justin
Todd Kalis
Kani Kauahi
Bill Kenney
Don Kern
Jon Kirksey
Bob Kohrs
Stein Koss
Jason Kyle
Jeff Kysar
Kit Lathrop
Bob Lee
Gary Lewis
Hal Lewis
Tony Lorick
Ron Lou
Joey Lumpkin
Ron Lumpkin
Art Malone
Benny Malone
Mark Malone
Derrick Martin
Joe Matesic
Vernon Maxwell
Jim McCann
Brent McClanahan
Skip McClendon
Prentice McCray
Randall McDaniel
Lenny McGill
Jeff McIntyre
Hugh McKinnis
Sean McNanie
Mike Mercer
Kevin Miniefield
Rex Mirich
John Mistler
Gene Mitcham
Alvin Moore
Randy Moore
Paul Moyer
Larry Mucker
Craig Newsome
Brian Noble
Clancy Osborne
Sandy Osiecki
Morris Owens
Gary Padjen
Mike Pagel
Anthony Parker
Shawn Patterson
Bruce Perkins
John Pitts
Jake Plummer
Keith Poole
Ron Pritchard
Bryan Proby
Earl Putman
Bryan Reeves
Damien Richardson
Mike Richardson
Gerald Riggs
Billy Robinson
Hank Rockwell
Derrick Rodgers
Juan Roque
Leonard Russell
Dan Saleaumua
John Seedborg
Mark Shupe
Jason Simmons
Derek Smith
Gordon Smith
Jerry Smith
Phillippi Sparks
Dennis Sproul
Jeremy Staat
Israel Stanley
Scott Stephen
Norris Steverson
Shawn Swayda
Charley Taylor
J.T. Thomas
Kevin Thomas
Bob Thomas
Pat Tillman
Larry Todd
Jeff Van Raaphorst
Danny Villa
Scott Von der Ahe
Brett Wallerstedt
Larry Walton
Jim Warne
Morrie Warren
Ron Wetzel
Danny White
Whizzer White
Kendall Williams
Newton Williams
Travis Williams
Darren Woodson
Louis Wright
Luis Zendejas

Arizona Western Coll. (J.C.) (20)

Woody Bennett
Reggie Berry
Ken Bungarda
Steve Conley
Eddie Edwards
Stan Eisenhooth
Jerry Keeble
Karl Lorch
Lamar McGriggs
Chuck Muncie
Reggie Pierson
Bernard Russ
Ricky Siglar
Skip Thomas
Bobby Thompson
Leonard Thompson
Faddie Tillman
Charlie Weaver
Emanuel Weaver
Lee White

Arkansas (149)

Neal Adams
Lance Alworth
Gary Anderson
Steve Atwater
Herm Bagby
Al Baldwin
Hubert Barker
Jim Benton
Kirk Botkin
Danny Brabham
Freddie Bradley
Robert Brannon
Maurice Britt
Jon Brittenum
Bud Brooks
Buddy Brown
Trent Bryant
Scott Bull
Bobby Burnett
Dave Burnette
Ravin Caldwell
Leon Campbell
Lew Carpenter
Preston Carpenter
Ronnie Carroll
Daryl Cato
Ronnie Caveness
Mike Cherry
Freddie Childress
Jessie Clark
Jim Collier
Steven Conley
Ed Conti
Chuck Corgan
Steve Cox
Reggie Craig
Elbert Crawford
Milan Creighton
Bobby Crockett
Dick Cunningham
Isaac Davis
Ron Dickerson
Chuck Dicus
Freddie Douglas
Jay Douglas
Bobby Duckworth
Paul Dudley
Kay Eakin
Jerry Eckwood
Bobby Joe Edmonds
Glenn Ellison
Ron Faurot
Joe Ferguson
Henry Ford
Ike Forte
Bob Forte
Barry Foster
Aubrey Fowler
Weldon Gentry
Tommie Ginn
Oscar Gray
Bob Griffin
Jack Haden
Ray Hamilton
Dan Hampton
Dave Hanner
LaSalle Harper
Leotis Harris
Ken Hayden
Chuck Herman
Red Hickey
Glen Ray Hines
Billy Hix
John Hoffman
Derek Holloway
Greg Horne
Jim Lee Howell
Darwin Ireland
Lefty Jamerson
Raylee Johnson
Harry Jones
Todd Jones
Rabbit Keen
Carl Kidd
Keith Kidd
Mike Kirkland
Greg Koch
Steve Korte
Greg Lasker
Doc Ledbetter
Jim Lindsey
Steve Little
Kayo Lunday
Vaughn Lusby
Brison Manor
Wayne Martin
Bruce Maxwell
Geno Mazzanti
Jerry Mazzanti
Bill McClard
Lamar McHan
Nick Miller
Charlie Moore
Henry Moore
Jerry Moore
Jim Mooty
Tom Murphy
Limbo Parks
Leon Pense
Loyd Phillips
Joyce Pipkin
Dave Reavis
Mike Reppond
Danny Rhodes
Jack Robbins
James Rouse
Ernie Ruple
Derek Russell
Floyd Sagely
Howard Sampson
Clyde Scott
James Shibest
Milt Simington
Gerald Skinner
Dwight Sloan
Billy Ray Smith Jr.
Billy Ray Smith Sr.
Ronnie Lee South
Ray Spillers
Donnie Stone
Pat Summerall
Clovis Swinney
R.C. Thielemann
Derrick Thomas
Wilfred Thorpe
Curtis Townsend
Clyde Van Sickle
Jimmy Walker
Danny Walters
Chuck Washington
Orlando Watters
Tim Webster
Marsh White
Fred Williams
Ben Winkelman
Dennis Winston
Kevin Wyatt
Harry Wynne
Theo Young

Arkansas State (32)

Michael Adams
Fred Barnett
Vincent Barnett
Bill Bergey
Ray Brown
Kendricke Bullard
Steve Burks
Maurice Carthon
Gary Crane
Tom Dean
Ferd Dreher
Carlos Emmons
Jeff Fields
Dick Folk
Stacy Gore
Leroy Harris
Bill Johnson
Tyrone Jones
Ken Jones
Greg Lee
Dennis Meyer
Oren Middlebrook
Jerry Muckensturm
Stacy Price
Kyle Richardson
Elbert Shelley
Clovis Swinney
Corey Walker
Sammy Weir
Stan Winfrey
Richie Woit
Mitchell Young

Arkansas Tech (7)

Ray Burnett
Aubrey Fowler
Bruce Livingston
Ed Meador
Irvin Phillips
Sandy Sanford
Chuck Taylor

Arkansas-Monticello (2)

Mike Nichols
Steve Rhem

Arkansas-Pine Bluff (18)

Ceasar Belser
Gregg Briggs
Ivory Lee Brown
Robert Brown
Wally Francis
Willie Frazier
L.C. Greenwood
Gene Jeter
Mike Lewis
Cleo Miller
Ray Nealy
Terry Nelson
Willie Parker
Rickey Parks
Manny Sistrunk
Clarence Washington
Monk Williams
Don Zimmerman

Army (26)

Bob Anderson
Chris Cagle
Glen Carberry
Tex Coulter
Glenn Davis
Jack Dibb
Eddie Doyle
Gene Filipski
Hank Foldberg
Walt French
Arnie Galiffa
Herb Johnson
J.D. Kimmel
Karl Kremser
Hal McPhail
Shorty McWilliams
Lou Merillat
Bob Mischak
Brett Moritz
Elmer Oliphant
Al Pollard
Hamp Pool
Barney Poole
Dean Sensanbaugher
Harry Stafford
Gene Vidal

Arnold (2)

Andy Robustelli
Allan Webb

Ashland (3)

Ray Novotny
Bill Overmyer
Walt Williams

Auburn (162)

Tommie Agee
Mike Alford
Willie Anderson
William Andrews
Gump Ariail
George Atkins
Billy Atkins
Dowe Aughtman
Thomas Bailey
Tom Banks
Corey Barlow
Fred Baxter
Fred Beasley
Terry Beasley
Clayton Beauford
Kenneth Bernich
David Beverly
Forrest Blue
Scott Bolton
James Bostic
M.L. Brackett
Dieter Brock
James Brooks
Steve Broussard
Aundray Bruce
Chet Bulger
Jackie Burkett
Jimmy Burson
Gregg Carr
Lloyd Cheatham
Richard Cheek
Joe Childress
Chuck Clanton
Leon Cochran
Bill Cody
Lewis Colbert
Ted Cremer
Joe Cribbs
Frank D'Agostino
Ernie Danjean
Stephen Davis
Rufus Deal
Al Del Greco
Moon Ducote
Dave Edwards
Eric Floyd
Charlie Fowler
Byron Franklin
Wayne Frazier
Tucker Frederickson
Bobby Freeman
Mike Fuller
Brent Fullwood
Monk Gafford
Wayne Gandy
Frank Gatski
Vern Ghersanich
Robert Goff
Chris Gray
Kevin Greene
Andy Gross
George Gross
Lee Gross
Anthony Harris
Bob Harris
Max Harrison
Hal Herring
Dave Hill
Nate Hill
John Hudson
Donnie Humphrey
Bobby Hunt
Chuck Hurston
Fred Hyatt
Calvin Jackson
Jeff Jackson
Bo Jackson
Lionel James
Tim Jessie
Chuckie Johnson
David Jordan
James Joseph
Jon Kilgore
David King
Ed King
John Klasnic
Mike Kolen
Rich Kreitling
Chris Martin
Reese McCall
Dell McGee
John McGeever
Secdrick McIntyre
Bob Meeks
Dave Middleton
Ron Middleton
Alvin Mitchell
Harold Morrow
Ed Nelson
Dan Nugent
Neil O'Donoghue
Craig Ogletree
Jeff Parks
George Peoples
Jim Phillips
Kevin Porter
Jim Price
Anthony Redmon
Walter Reeves
Jim Reynolds
Ken Rice
Tony Richardson
Victor Riley
Gerald Robinson
David Rocker
Tracy Rocker
Lamar Rogers
Benji Roland
George Rose
Herb Roton
Bo Russell
Frank Sanders
Bill Schuler
Rob Selby
Chris Shelling
Jimmy Sidle
Howard Simpson
Jim Sivell
Billy Ray Smith
Brian Smith
Doug Smith
Mark Smith
Zeke Smith
Takeo Spikes
Ron Stallworth
Curtis Stewart
Pat Sullivan
Ricky Sutton
Mickey Sutton
Ben Tamburello
Erk Taylor
Ben Thomas
Jack Thornton
Travis Tidwell
Lawyer Tillman
Keith Uecker
Gary Walker
Steve Wallace
Frank Warren
Tex Warrington
Ed West
Gerald Williams
Pryor Williams
Tex Williams
Larry Willingham
Chester Willis
James Willis
Jerry Wilson
Dick Wood
Chris Woods
Alexander Wright
Mickey Zofko

Augsburg (3)

Steve Nelson

Jim Pederson
David Warnke

Augustana (Ill.) (2)

Ken Anderson
George Lenc

Augustana (S.D.) (5)

Tom Brown
Les Josephson
Corbin Lacina
Karl Mecklenburg
Bryan Schwartz

Aurora (1)

Don Beebe

Austin (8)

Gene Babb
Billy Bookout
Joe Carter
Joe Coomer
Tex Grigg
Maurice Harper
Leonard Harris
Barnes Milam

Austin CC TX (1)

Mike Baab

Austin Peay State (7)

Boris Byrd
Scott Fox
Jeff Gooch
Percy Howard
Ron Shegog
Bonnie Sloan
Michael Swift

Austria Tech School (1)

Toni Linhart

Azusa Pacific (2)

Doug Barnett
Christian Okoye

Baker (2)

Roger Farmer
Charley Hill

Bakersfield Coll. CA (J.C.) (28)

Jon Baker
Mike Bundra
Vern Burke
Chris DeFrance
David Dunn
George Fields
Frank Gifford
Joe Hernandez
Don Johnson
George Jones
Jon Kirksey
Spain Musgrove
Richard Newbill
Mark Nichols
Rocky Rasley
Gary Richard
Leroy Sledge
Charlie Smith
Jeremy Staat
Michael Stewart
Jim Stiger
Jerry Tarr
John Tarver
Deacon Turner
Mike Waters
Dick Witcher
Mike Woulfe
Louis Wright

Baldwin-Wallace (10)

Bob Barrett
Herb Bauer
Fred Cardinal
Tom Goosby
Norb Hecker
Robert Hecker
Bill Krause
George Morris
Ed Schenk
George Young

Ball State (24)

Blaine Bishop
Michael Blair
Mark Boggs
Rush Brown
Timmy Brown
Don Burchfield
Corey Croom
Jerome Davis
John Diettrich
Cory Gilliard
Maurice Harvey
Jonathan Hoke
Ed Konopasek
Ken Kremer
Brad Maynard
Keith McKenzie
Bernie Parmalee
Mike Patanelli
Eugene Riley
Brad Saar
Terry Schmidt
Art Stringer
Shafer Suggs
Jim Todd

Baltimore City CC MD (2)

Wayne Fowler
Maurice Tyler

Barstow Coll. CA (J.C.) (1)

Greg Feasel

Bates (2)

Rico Corsetti
Fritz Pollard

Baylor (149)

Walter Abercrombie
John Adickes
Mark Adickes
Len Akin
Jackie Allen
Alfred Anderson
Solon Barnett
Charles Benson
Ray Berry
Riley Biggs
Keith Bishop
Tim Black
Robert Blackmon
Russ Blailock
Melvin Bonner
Sam Boyd
Charlie Bradshaw
Wes Bradshaw
Carl Brazell
Ben Bronson
Thomas Brown
Ronnie Bull
Adrian Burk
Cody Carlson
Ken Casner
Mark Cochran
Anthony Coleman
Lincoln Coleman
Kirk Collins
Dobie Craig
Milt Crain
Ray Crockett
Cotton Davidson
Bruce Davis
Preston Davis
Sonny Davis
Paul Dickson
Santana Dotson
Leland Douglas
Steve Dowden
Charlie Dupre
L.G. Dupre
Monk Edwards
Larry Elkins
Thomas Everett
Doak Field
Mike Fisher
Al Fontenot
James Francis
Ron Francis
Malcolm Frank
Cleveland Franklin
John Frongillo
Daryl Gardener
Les Gatewood
Dennis Gentry
William Glass
Bill Glass
Brad Goebel
Goose Gonsoulin
Aubrey Goodman
Ron Goodwin
Gary Green
Hank Gremminger
Bobbie Griffin
Randy Grimes
Malcolm Hamilton
Kevin Hancock
Bug Hartzog
Johnny Hatley
Greg Hawthorne
Larry Hickman
Dalton Hoffman
Darrell Hogan
Robert Holt
Steve Howell
Buddy Humphrey
Calvin Hunt
Neal Jeffrey
Byron Johnson
Harvey Jones
LaCurtis Jones
Mark Kirchner
George Kirk
George Koch
Emmett Kriel
Bobby Lane
Ronnie Lee
Derrel Luce
Bill Lucky
Jack Lummus
Dave Lunceford
Cedric Mack
Bobby Maples
Butch Maples
Bud Marshall
Bob Masters
Le'Shai Maston
Derrick McAdoo
Len McCormick
George McCullough
Vann McElroy
Gerald McNeil
Pat McNeil
Andrew Melontree
Bo Metcalf
Fred Miller
David Mims
Tom Minter
Mike Nelms
Shane Nelson
Robert Nelson
Pete Nicklas
Ox Parry
Billy Patterson
Ralph Pittman
Bobby Ply
Frank Pollard
Luke Prestridge
Ervin Randle
Joe Reed
John Reynolds
Allen Rice
Don Robinson
Harmon Rowe
Jack Russell
Broderick Sargent
Buzz Sawyer
Tom Sestak
Del Shofner
George Sims
Mike Singletary
Frankie Smith
Jim Ray Smith
Dick Stevens
Ralph Stockemer
Jim Taylor
Johnny Thomas
Arland Thompson
Reyna Thompson
Ricky Thompson
Buddy Tinsley
Don Trull
Cop Weathers
Robert Williams
Stan Williams
Jack Wilson
Gary Wisener
Al Witcher

Belgrade (Serbia) (1)

Momcilo Gavric

Beloit (9)

Mush Crawford
George Dahlgren
Boob Darling
Stan Kuick
Jack McAuliffe
Walt McGaw
Pid Purdy
Elmer Rhenstrom
Rex Smith

Bemidji State (1)

Al Wolden

Benedict (1)

Claude Brownlee

Benedictine (4)

Irv Comp
Charlie Huneke
Jamie Mueller
Larry Visnic

Bergen CC NJ (1)

Bruce Harper

Bethany (KS) (1)

Milt Rehnquist

Bethany (W.V.) (9)

Roy Adkins
Arda Bowser
Karl Broadley
Sid Gepford
Walt LeJeune
Kile MacWherter
Emil Mayer
Harry Randolph
Hub Shoemake

Bethune-Cookman (34)

Terry Anderson
Rudy Barber
Anthony Bass
John Bostic
Albert Burton
Rickey Claitt
Boobie Clark
Steve Collier
Charles Cornelius
Brian Dudley
Anthony Florence
Leon Gonzalez
Al Haywood
Earl Inmon
Mark Irvin
Roger Jackson
Willie Lee
Larry Little
Jack McClairen
Maulty Moore
Jeff Parker
Reno Patterson
Booker Reese
Charles Riggins
Tony Samuels
Jerry Simmons
Dick Washington
Remi Watson
Charlie White
Lee Williams
Terry Williams
Alvin Wyatt
Antwuan Wyatt
Almon Young

Birmingham-Southern (3)

Erm Davis
John McMichaels
Charlie Ware

Bishop (12)

Bobby Brooks
Dennis DeVaughn
William Harris
Louis Haynes
Will Hill
Harry Hooligan
Leroy Howard
Tony Martin
Tony McGee
Bobby Moten
Emmitt Thomas
Ike Thomas

Blinn Coll. TX (J.C.) (11)

Lyle Blackwood
Scott Boucher
Eric Brown
Kirk Collins
Tim Denton
Buddy Hardaway
Ray Hickl
Steve Jacobson
Shane Nelson
Marquis Walker
James Wright

Bliss College (2)

Frank Glassman
Babe Houck

Bloomsburg (3)

Red Griffiths
Eric Jonassen
Bob Tucker

Bluffton (1)

Elbert Dubenion

Boise State (27)

Darrel Aschbacher
Barry Black
Chuck Butler
Chuck Compton
Jim Ellis
Jon Francis
Rashid Gayle
David Hughes
Jerry Inman
Carl Keever
Markus Koch
Alva Liles
Al Marshall
Cedric Minter
Larry Polowski
John Rade
Frank Robinson
Lance Sellers
Don Summers
Faddie Tillman
Kimo von Oelhoffen
Dave Wilcox
John Wilcox
Chris Wing
Rick Woods
Roland Woolsey
Jon Zogg

Boston College (152)

Don Allard
Vito Ananis
Alec Anderson
Ken Bell
John Bosa
Gil Bouley
Stephen Boyd
Brian Brennan
Gordie Browne
Jim Browne
Bill Budness
Bill Byrne
Ivan Caesar
Rocco Canale
Al Cannava
Dick Capp
Mark Chmura
Jim Colclough
Stalin Colinet
Jack Concannon
Tom Condon
Harry Connolly
Steve Corbett
Pete Cronan
Jack Cronin
Bill Cronin
Bill Cronin
Harry Crump
Don Currivan
Fred DaGata
Steve DeOssie
Joe DiVito
Jack Donahue
Art Donovan
Walt Dubzinski
Larry Eisenhauer
Terry Erwin
Mike Esposito
Mike Evans
Al Fiorentino
Ed Fiorentino
John Fitzgerald
Darren Flutie
Doug Flutie
Glenn Foley
John Galvin
Mario Gianelli
Chet Gladchuk
Chuck Gorecki
Art Graham
David Green
Dimp Halloran
Shawn Halloran
Dick Hardy
Ed Harrison
Dick Harrison
Mike Holovak
Bob Hyland
Joe Johnson
Pete Kendall
Jimmy Kennedy
Ed King
Lou Kirouac
Adolph Kissell
John Kissell
Steve Kobolinski
Gary Kowalski
Joe Kozlowsky
Al Krevis
Mike Kruczek
Gordon Laro
Steve Levanitis
Steve Lubischer
Dick Lucas
Tom Lynch
Mark MacDonald
Don Macek
Mike Mamula
Joe Manzo
Gary Marangi
Kelvin Martin
Mike Mayock
Frank Maznicki
Brendan McCarthy
Warren McGuirk
Tom McManus
Alan Miller
Johnny Miller
Pete Mitchell
Tim Morabito
Frank Morrissey
Frank Morze
Tom Nalen
Joe Nash
Fred Naumetz
Con O'Brien
Dave O'Brien
Grat O'Connell
Dan O'Connor
Ross O'Hanley
Ed O'Hearn
Jeff Oliver
Charlie O'Rourke
Tom Porell
Daryl Porter
George Radachowsky
Michael Reed
Dan Reeder
Shawn Regent
Joe Repko
Frank Robotti
Ben Roderick
Bill Romanowski
Mark Roopenian
Jim Rourke
Mike Ruth
Brian Saxton
Steve Schindler
Bob Shann
Tim Sherwin
Fred Smerlas
Butch Songin
Art Spinney
Ernie Stautner
Fred Steinfort
Bill Stetz
Ron Stone
Greg Storr
Erik Storz
Steve Strachan
Troy Stradford
Chris Sullivan
Dan Sullivan
Karl Swanke
George Tarasovic
Bill Thomas
Ed Toner
Flavio Tosi
Steve Trapilo
Ray Trowbridge
Bill Turner
Darren Twombly
Luke Urban
Tom Waddle
Robert Watts
Jim Whalen
Dave Widell
Doug Widell
Ted Williams
Fred Willis
Joe Wolf
Jeff Yeates

Boston U. (34)

Fred Barry
John Bredice
Bill Brooks
Butch Byrd
Brad Costello
Art Dorfman
Carl Etelman
Gary Famiglietti
Dick Farley
Paul Farren
Dennis Gadbois
Mike Graybill
Bob Horton
Darvell Huffman
Pat Hughes
Jim Jensen
Karl Kaimer
Lou Koplow
Pete Lamana
Chris Lindstrom
Dave Lindstrom
Bob Marques
Ralph Marston
Ed Meixler
Frank Morris
Bobby Nichols
Pete Perreault
Gene Prebola
Barry Pryor
Reggie Rucker
George Sulima
Bruce Taylor
Gary Walker
Walter Williams

Bowie State (2)

Victor Jackson
Marco Tongue

Bowling Green State (41)

Larry Baker
Martin Bayless
Ed Bettridge
Carlos Brooks
Bernie Casey
Jay Cunningham
Sean Dykes
Mike Estep
Joe Green
Jeff Groth
Stan Hunter
Jerry Jones
Karl Koepfer
Kyle Kramer
Jim Ladd
Don Lisbon
Brian McClure
Greg Meehan
Art Mergenthal
Mark Miller
Tom Moriarty
Mark Nelson
Mike Obrovac
Kevin O'Neill
Mike Patanelli
Dave Preston
Bob Reynolds
Jamie Rivers
Tim Ross
Ken Russell
Bob Schnelker
Doug Smith
Fred Sturt
Reggie Thornton
Stuart Tolle
Vince Villanucci
Phil Villapiano
Roger Wallace
Mike Weger
Charlie Williams
Heath Wingate

Bradley (12)

Pat Brady
Roy Carlson
Don Carothers
Shorty Elness
Harry Jacobs
Dick Jamieson
Elliott Ormsbee
Marcus Pollard
Joe Prokop
Ray Ramsey
Bill Roehnelt
Billy Stone

Brandeis (1)

Mike Long

Brevard CC FL (1)

John Tanner

Bridgeport (2)

Bill Brown
Nick Giaquinto

Brigham Young (94)

Brad Anderson
Lou Andrus
David Aupiu
Wayne Baker
Mark Bellini
Eric Bergeson
Rex Berry
Phil Brady
Clay Brown
Scott Brumfield
Dewey Brundage
Jason Buck
Virgil Carter
Garth Chamberlain
Todd Christensen
Ty Detmer
Chuck Ehin
Mohammed Elewonibi
Nick Eyre
Chris Farasopoulos
Dick Felt
Kurt Gouveia
Gordon Gravelle
Derwin Gray
Travis Hall
Bruce Hansen
Tim Hanshaw
Lakei Heimuli
Tom Holmoe
Paul Howard
Dave Hubbard
Gordon Hudson
John Hunter
Mekeli Ieremia
Lee Johnson
John Kapele
Steve Kaufusi
Mike Keim
Doug Kellermeyer
Shawn Knight
Glen Kozlowski
Mike Kozlowski
Eric Lane
Chad Lewis
Jeff Lyman
Chris Matau
Jason Mathews
Trevor Match
Nyle McFarlane
Kaipo McGuire
Jim McMahon
Tim McTyer
Mat Mendenhall
Itula Mili
Brian Mitchell
Larry Moore
Kyle Morrell
Gifford Nielsen
Reed Nilsen
Bart Oates
Brad Oates
Ronnie O'Bard

Phil Odle
Orrin Olsen
Robert Parker
Dennis Patera
Craig Patterson
Evan Pilgrim
Glen Redd
Spencer Reid
Rodney Rice
Golden Richards
Bill Ring
Burle Robison
Steve Rogers
Todd Shell
Vai Sikahema
Jeff Staggs
Vince Stroth
Rodney Thomas
Glen Titensor
Casey Tiumalu
Peter Tuipulotu
Mike Ulufale
Morris Unutoa
Pete Van Valkenberg
Warren Wheat
Leon White
Cary Whittingham
Fred Whittingham
Kyle Whittingham
Jamal Willis
Marc Wilson
Steve Young

British Columbia (Canada) (4)

Brant Bengen
Bill Crawford
Rick Goltz
Ed Ryan

Brockport State (1)

Mike Jones

Brooklyn College (2)

Waddy MacPhee
Allie Sherman

Brown (44)

Dunc Annan
Keiron Bigby
Bill Brace
Hal Broda
Tom Budrewicz
Bruce Caldwell
Don Colo
Al Cornsweet
Dolph Eckstein
Bud Edwards
Ed Fiorentino
Mike Gulian
Irv Hall
Andy Hillhouse
Jimmy Jemail
Steve Jordan
Jack Keefer
Ed Lawrence
Bob Margarita
Ed McCrillis
John McLaughry
Dave Mishel
Curly Oden
John Pohlman
Fritz Pollard
Bob Priestley
Mike Purdy
Quentin Reynolds
Seneca Samson
Joe Schein
Jim Sheldon
Bert Shurtleff
John Sinnott
Orland Smith
Butch Spagna
Jack Spellman
Spike Staff
Bill Stephens
Jim Stifler
Fred Sweet
John Talbot
Thurston Towle
Inky Williams
John Woodring

Bucknell (39)

Earl Beecham
Eddie Bollinger
Arda Bowser
Justin Brumbaugh
Ed Conti
Harry Dayhoff
Jack Dempsey
Wally Diehl
John Dooley
Bill Edgar
Bud Ellor
Wally Foster
Harry Fry
Earl Goodwin
Myrl Goodwin
Eddie Halicki
Ernie Hambacher
Sam Havrilak
Johnny Hendren
Brian Henesey
Clarke Hinkle
Gene Hubka
Ken Jenkins
Potsy Jones
Frank Jordan
George Kiick
Tony Kostos
Felix McCormick
Ted Mitchell
Tom Mitchell
Brad Myers
Jim Ostendarp
Max Reed
Tom Rodgers
Stu Smith
Walt Szot
Lou Tomasetti
Frank Wilsbach
Ernie Woerner

Buena Vista (1)

Jim Doran

Buffalo (7)

Jim Ailinger
Bill Ellenbogen
Ed Ellis
Roy Martineau
Gerry Philbin
Red Seick
John Stofa

Burlington Co. Coll. NJ (J.C.) (1)

Henry Carr

Butler (10)

John Cavosie
Babe Dimancheff
Earl Elser
Hal Griggs
Dick Hall
Curly Hinchman
Joe Kodba
Arnold Mickens
Lou Reichel
Flash Woods

Butler County CC KS (11)

Roger Bernhardt
Ron Fellows
Robert Goff
Jamie Holland
Johnny Holloway
Reggie Jones
Kwamie Lassiter
Skip McClendon
Bruce Perkins
Jerry Quick
Dave Thomas

Butte Coll. CA (J.C.) (2)

Vashone Adams
Larry Allen

C.W. Post (8)

Tom Cassese
Joe Chetti
Sean Dowling
James Eaddy
Perry Klein
Jim LeClair
John Mohring
Al Steinfeld

CCNY (2)

Willie Halpern
Roy Ilowit

Cabrillo Coll. CA (J.C.) (4)

Obafemi Ayanbadejo
Sherman Cocroft
Scott Eccles
Sam Kennedy

Cal Poly-Pomona (11)

Patrick Cain
Glenn Davis
Fred Ford
David Grayson
Ron Hall
J.C. Pearson
Joe Prokop
Ev Sharp
Al Smith
Vern Valdez
Jim Zorn

Cal Poly-S.L.O. (22)

Alex Bravo
Sal Cesario
Jimmy Childs
Gary Davis
Karl Finch
Bob Howard
Louis Jackson
Perry Jeter
Damone Johnson
Mel Kaufman
Kamil Loud
Robbie Martin
LeCharls McDaniel
Don Milan
Dana Nafziger
Brian Roche
Stan Sheriff
Paul Sverchek
Chris Thomas
Cecil Turner
Fred Whittingham
Blake Wingle

Cal State-Chico (6)

Tony Bertuca
Eddie Butts
Doug Dressler
George Maderos
Chris Pane
Chris Verhulst

Cal State-Fullerton (23)

Vince Abbott
Rick Calhoun
M.L. Carter
Mark Collins
Mike Ernst
Alex Espinoza
Vince Gamache
Daren Gilbert
Hank Goebel
Johnnie Gray
A.J. Jenkins
Bobby Kemp
Wade Lockett
Ron McLean
Paul Moyer
Mike Pringle
James Pruitt
Reggie Redding
Corn Redick
Grady Richardson
Lucious Smith
Jim Thornton
Marvin Williams

Cal State-Hayward (3)

Greg Blankenship
Sandy LaBeaux
Joe Terry

Cal State-Northridge (10)

Daved Benefield
Lon Boyett
Bill Butler
Max Choboian
Ron Foster
Alvin Hooks
Doug Jones
Bruce Lemmerman
Chris Pacheco
Bryan Wagner

Calgary (Canada) (1)

Brian Belway

California (153)

Chidi Ahanotu
Ted Albrecht
Lee Artoe
Troy Auzenne
Mark Bailey
Jon Baker
Jeff Barnes
Dave Barr
Steve Bartkowski
Fred Beach
John Beasley
Leo Biedermann
David Binn
Fred Boensch
Issac Booth
Matt Bouza
Greg Bracelin
Jim Breech
Doug Brien
Mike Caldwell
Reggie Camp
Rich Campbell
Bob Celeri
Je'Rod Cherry
Duane Clemons
Ferric Collons
Joe Cooper
Jim Cox
Wayne Crow
Phil Croyle
Jim Cullom
Isaac Curtis
Sean Dawkins
Ralph DeLoach
Kevin Devine
Rich Dixon
Clarence Duren
Lou Eaton
Floyd Eddings
Herman Edwards
Jack Evans
Vince Ferragamo
Jim Fetherston
Jack Frantz
Dwight Garner
Gale Gilbert
Tarik Glenn
Dan Goich
Tony Gonzalez
Steve Gordon
Bill Hachten
Rhett Hall
Roger Harding
John Hardy
Ken Harvey
Matt Hazeltine
Steve Hendrickson
Dallas Hickman
Stan Holloway
Del Hufford
Tut Imlay
Darryl Ingram
Proverb Jacobs
Don Johnson
Sidney Johnson
Bob Kampa
Joe Kapp
Keith Kartz
Perry Klein
Ronnie Knox
Paul Larson
David Lewis
Greg Loberg
Ryan Longwell
Tim Lucas
Mick Luckhurst
Eric Mahlum
Doug Mayberry
Mike McCaffrey
Jack McCarthy
Jack McQuary
Dan Melville
Jim Monachino
Craig Morton
Brick Muller
Chuck Muncie
Don Newmeyer
Tom Newton
Hardy Nickerson
Don Noble
Hal Norris
Mike O'Brien
Johnny Olszewski
Dwayne O'Steen
Gerry Perry
Gary Plummer
Hamp Pool
James Reed
Bill Reinhard
Bob Reinhard
Les Richter
Doug Riesenberg
Ron Rivera
Steve Rivera
Joe Rose
Bob Rozier
Mike Rusinek
Harvey Salem
Buck Saunders
Pete Schabarum
Pete Schaffnit
Perry Schwartz
Jeff Sevy
Daryle Skaugstad
Byron Smith
George Smith
Holden Smith
Rich Stachowski
Chuck Steele
Todd Steussie
Wayne Stewart
Scott Stringer
John Sullivan
Steve Sweeney
Bob Swenson
Troy Taylor
Jesse Thompson
Brian Thure
Loren Toews
Mack Travis
Brian Treggs
Natu Tuatagaloa
John Tuggle
Godwin Turk
Miles Turpin
Regan Upshaw
Iheanyi Uwaezuoke
Wesley Walker
Anthony Washington
Tim Washington
Ray Wersching
Ed White
Russell White
Sherman White
Brandon Whiting
Jim Wilks
Jerrott Willard
Sam Williams
David Wilson
Marv Wood
Al Young
Dave Zawatson
Eric Zomalt

California (Pa.) (7)

John Bristor
Judson Flint
Brendan Folmar
Perry Kemp
Bob McDonough
Terry O'Shea
Fran Rogel

California Lutheran (9)

Hank Bauer
Andy Dickerson
Phil Frye
Darren Gottschalk
Brian Kelley
Charles McShane
Ralph Miller
Kent Sullivan
Bryan Wagner

California Western (1)

Jesse Murdock

California-Davis (11)

Jeffrey Allen
Rolf Benirschke
Bo Eason
Chris Mandeville
Rich Martini
Casey Merrill
Mike Moroski
Ken O'Brien
Kermit Schmidt
Tom Williams
Mike Wise

California-Riverside (5)

Michael Basinger
Russ Bolinger
Dan Bunz
Butch Johnson
Calvin Sweeney

California-Santa Barbara (8)

Royal Cathcart
Sam Cathcart
Dave Chapple
Jason Franci
Johnny Morris
Doug Oldershaw
Rob Woods
Howie Yeager

Cameron (15)

John Brandes
Mark Cotney
Ron Gardin
Joe Gibson
Ed Hughes
Joe Don Looney
Ed Marshall
Riley Matheson
Pep Menefee
Jerry Nuzum
Francis Peay
Spec Sanders
Tony Stricker
Tony Sumpter
Charles Washington

Campion (2)

Clarke Fischer
Adolph Spiegel

Canisius (15)

Russ Burt
Tom Colella
Harry Collins
Ed Doyle
Lou Feist
Chick Guarnieri
John Mahoney
Joe McClain
Elmer McCormick
Mike Panepinto
Bill Piccolo
Dick Poillon
Sam Salemi
Mike Trainor
Jerry Whalen

Carleton (3)

Bill Fleckenstein
Verne Miller
Henry Willegale

Carlisle (19)

Napoleon Barrel
Lo Boutwell
Fred Broker
Elmer Busch
Pete Calac
Xavier Downwind
Birdie Gardner
Joe Guyon
Bob Hill
Nick Lassa
Joe Little Twig
Frank Lone Star
Bill Newashe
Stan Powell
Ted St. Germaine
Stillwell Saunooke
Jim Thorpe
Woodchuck Welmas
Bill Winneshick

Carnegie Mellon (21)

Don Campbell
Ray Carnelly
Merl Condit
Cliff Dolaway
Bill Donohoe
Latham Flanagan
Bull Karcis
George Kavel
Jack Lee
Phil Marshall
Saul Mielziner
Joe Mills
Hap Moran
Obie Newman
Maury Patt
Bill Rieth
James Robertson
John Schmidt
Hugh Sprinkle
Ray Tesser
Wilson

Carroll (Mont.) (1)

Dave Romasko

Carroll (Wis.) (13)

Walt Ambrose
Herb Bizer
Moxie Dalton
Carl George
Rudy Gollomb
Bill Hempel
Kirk Hershey
Frank Hertz
Ivan Quinn
Ed Sparr
Gil Sterr
Biff Taugher
Buff Wagner

Carson-Newman (13)

Don Bramlett
Charlie Burgess
Todd Collins
Joe Fishback
Tim George
Boyce Green
Robert Hardy
Clayton Holmes
David Pool
Sanders Shiver
Vernon Turner
Van Williams
Dave Ziff

Carthage (5)

Steve Hanson
Jim Jodat
Rick Kehr
John Wager
Adam Walker

Case Western Reserve (15)

John Badaczewski
Steve Belichick
Dick Booth
Frank Civiletto
Red Kirkman
Warren Lahr
Andy Logan
Bill Lund
Phil Ragazzo
Mike Rodak
George Roman
Mickey Sanzotta
Stan Skoczen
Sol Weinberg
Johnny Wilson

Catawba (13)

Drew Buie
Ken Hartley
Ike Hill
Ed Koontz
Emerson Martin
Mike McDonald
Bucky Pope
Greg Quick
Gil Robinson
David Taylor
Army Tomaini
Randy Watts
Ray Yagiello

Catholic (19)

John Ambrose
Gene Augusterfer
Bill Connor
Beanie Eberts
Clarke Fischer
Tom Gormley
Bill Howell
Bill Joyce
Ed Karpowich
Leo Katalinas
George Kerr
Bill Lajousky
Ed Lynch
Emil Mayer
Fred Mazurek
George Mulligan
Rocco Pirro
Herm Schmarr
Tommy Whelan

Centenary (12)

Conway Baker
Jack Baldwin
Dan Barnhart
Mack Flenniken
Murrell Hogue
Cal Hubbard
Lou Jennings
Jack May
Buddy Parker
Paul Rebsamen
Ted Schwarzer
Dixie Stokes

Central Arkansas (8)

Ray Burnett
Dave Burnette
Curtis Burrow
Monte Coleman
Tyree Davis
Willie Davis
David Evans
Charlie McGibbony

Central Coll. (Iowa) (8)

Jeff Allen
Tyji Armstrong
Vern Den Herder
Creig Federico
David Frisch
Ron Hallstrom
Mike St. Clair
Troy Stedman

Central Connecticut State (1)

Joe Costello

Central Florida (9)

Elgin Davis
Bernard Ford
Mike Gruttadauria
Rick Hamilton
Greg Jefferson
Shawn Jefferson
Ed Schenk
Bob Spitulski
Ted Wilson

Central Michigan (16)

Curtis Adams
Walter Beach
Ray Bentley
Novo Bojovic
Jim Bowman
John Cameron
James Capers
Tom Edwards
Tony Elliott
Fred Failing
Mike Franckowiak
Brock Gutierrez
Gary Hogeboom

Robert Jackson
Jim Podoley
Scott Rehberg

Central Missouri State (4)

Dan Garza
Phil Grimes
Ernie Winburn
Jeff Wright

Central Oklahoma (20)

Joe Aska
Charles Barnard
Bob Briggs
Obie Bristow
Chetti Carr
Cliff Chatman
Ray Clemons
Joe Hayes
Ray Hayes
Jim Hooks
George Hughley
Scott Leggett
J.W. Lockett
John Preston
Alvin Ross
Hal Springer
John Sterling
Keith Traylor
Derek Ware
Bobby Williams

Central State (Ohio) (20)

Curtis Anderson
DeAuntae Brown
Orlando Brown
Vince Buck
Vince Carreker
Hugh Douglas
Darrell Grymes
Brandon Hayes
Vince Heflin
Charles Hope
Alonzo Johnson
Marlon Jones
Mel Lunsford
Roosevelt Nix
Jerry Parker
Victor Simmons
Kerwin Waldroup
Donnie Walker
Dave West
Erik Williams

Central Washington (3)

James Hasty
Jon Kitna
Jim North

Centre (17)

Norris Armstrong
Earl Bartlett
Gene Bedford
Jimmy German
Dick Gibson
Gus King
Marty Kottler
Cliff Lemon
Max MacCollum
Bo McMillin
Sully Montgomery
Tom Moran
Stan Robb
Red Roberts
Lou Smyth
John Tanner
Red Weaver

Cerritos Coll. CA (J.C.) (19)

Dick Degen
Mike Ernst
John Farris
Jim Ferguson
John Frongillo
Sidney Johnson
Bobby Lane
Bill Nelsen
Bob Newton
Pete Nicklas
Chris Pacheco
Dave Ross
Rico Smith
Guy Teafatiller
Broderick Thompson
Ray Wersching
Greg Williamson
Ron Yary
Ed Zeman

Chabot Coll. CA (J.C.) (16)

Jeff Barnes
Curtis Bledsoe
Dennis Bragonier
Mike Burke
Chuck Butler
Darryl Byrd
Herschel Currie
Manny Fernandez
Ed Galigher
Chris Geile
Robert Jenkins
Eric Lane
Jim LeMoine
Lorenzo Lynch
Ken O'Neal
Junior Tautalatasi

Chadron State (3)

Don Beebe
Dub Miller
Joe Planansky

Chaffey Coll. CA (J.C.) (1)

Glenn Cadrez

Chapman (2)

Matt George
Fred Orns

Charles Stewart Mott CC MI (2)

Leon Burton
Nate Johnson

Charleston (WV) (7)

Verlin Adams
Jimmy Carr
Billy Jones
Rich Mostardo
Harry Seltzer
Al Thacker
Frank Turbert

Chemeketa CC OR (1)

Joe Phillips

Cheyney (2)

Andre Waters
James Williams

Chicago (25)

Dunc Annan
Johnny Bryan
Moose Cochran
Davis
Shorty Des Jardien
Art Engstrom
Art Folz
Gene Francis
Aubrey Goodman
Harry Hall
Dick Halladay
George Hartong
Fred Hobscheid
John Hurlburt
Red Jackson
Graham Kernwein
Ralph King
Paul Leatherman
Harry O'Connell
Milt Romney
Solly Sherman
Jimmy Tays
John Thomas
Buck Weaver
Don Yeisley

Chipola JC FL (1)

Doug Woodlief

Chowan Coll. NC (8)

Fred Banks
Robert Brown
David Green
Jerry Holmes
George Koonce
Mark Royals
Jody Schulz
Curtis Whitley

Christian Brothers (Mo.) (3)

Charlie Essman
Walt Rogers
Norb Sacksteder

Cincinnati (74)

Jay Bachman
Teddy Bailey
Bob Bell
Tom Blake
Vaughn Booker
Jocelyn Borgella
Ken Byers
Jim Capuzzi
Vince Carreker
Toney Catchings
Bob Cobb
Mike Connell
Greg Cook
Mike Crangle
Mike Davis
Nate Dingle
Ronnie Dixon
Bob Dougherty
Jason Fabini
Bill Feldhaus
Tom Forrest
Wentford Gaines
Sam Garnes
Antonio Gibson
Don Goodman
Alex Gordon
Mike Graham
Reggie Harrison
Allen Harvin
Artrell Hawkins
Chris Hewitt
George Jamison
Melvin Jenkins
Al Johnson
Gene Johnson
Evan Jolitz
Rich Karlis
Ron Kostelnik
Ed Kovac
Howie Kurnick
Anthony Ladd
Greg Lathan
Jacky Lee
Jim Leo
Tommy Marvaso
Max Messner
Joe Morrison
Al Nelson
Elbie Nickel
Rob Niehoff
Ray Nolting
Jim O'Brien
Tom O'Malley
Brig Owens
Lloyd Pate
Mike Perrotti
Rod Phillips
Errol Prisby
Dan Rains
Derrick Ransom
Clarence Sanders
Jon Sawyer
Dan Sileo
Nick Skorich
Bill Smyth
Jerry Stautberg
Andrew Stewart
Jake Sweeney
Robert Tate
Jesse Taylor
John Thornton
Clem Turner
Jeff West
Mike Woods

Cisco JC TX (13)

Joe Aska
Tomur Barnes
John Booty
Wayne Coffey
John Davis
Harry Gunner
Mark Johnson
Garry Kimble
John Love
Buster Mitchell
Hurles Scales
Marquis Walker
Fred Washington

Citrus Coll. CA (J.C.) (2)

Paul Carr
Lionel Manuel

Clarion (3)

Bruce Gossett
Alex Sandusky
Bret Shugarts

Clark Atlanta (5)

Chuck Evans
Walt Landers
Greg McCrary
Elijah Nevett
Morris Stroud

Clark Coll. WA (J.C.) (1)

Bill Swain

Clarkson (1)

Bill Bucher

Clemson (121)

Terry Allen
Obed Ariri
Cliff Austin
Bob Baldwin
Mike Barber
Gary Barnes
Dan Benish
Jeff Bostic
Joe Bostic
Lorenzo Bromell
Jon Brooks
Jeff Bryant
Brentson Buckner
Jerry Butler
Johnny Cagle
Ken Callicutt
Bill Chipley
Don Chuy
Dwight Clark
Doug Cline
James Coley
Fred Cone
Lou Cordileone
Bennie Cunningham
Dexter Davis
Jeff Davis
Tyrone Davis
Billy Davis
Brian Dawkins
Stacey Driver
Mike Dukes
K.D. Dunn
Steve Durham
Leomont Evans
Terrence Flagler
Kenny Flowers
George Fritts
Steve Fuller
Bobby Gage
Chris Gardocki
Marrio Grier
Steve Griffin
Delton Hall
Rick Harrell
Rudy Harris
Dale Hatcher
Rudy Hayes
Andy Headen
Larry Hefner
Jerome Henderson
Dick Hendley
Tony Horne
Bob Hudson
Bill Hudson
Donald Igwebuike
Keith Jennings
John Johnson
Tracy Johnson
Steve Kenney
Terry Kinard
Levon Kirkland
Al Latimer
Kevin Mack
Terence Mack
Wayne Mass
Ray Mathews
Bill Mathis
Jim McCanless
Dexter McCleon
Jake McCullough
Ed McDaniel
Banks McFadden
Chester McGlockton
John McMakin
Chuck McSwain
Rod McSwain
Eldridge Milton
Wayne Mulligan
Harold Olson
Robert O'Neal
Jimmy Orr
Joe Pagliei
Robert Patton
Michael Dean Perry
William Perry
Reggie Pleasant
Bob Poole
Daddy Potts
Trevor Pryce
Archie Reese
Marion Reeves
Johnny Rembert
Jim Riggs
Stan Rome
Wardell Rouse
Larry Ryans
Patrick Sapp
Charley Sarratt
Ashley Sheppard
Anthony Simmons
Wayne Simmons
Marvin Sims
Darnell Stephens
Jim Stuckey
Don Testerman
Doug Thomas
Dave Thompson
Charlie Timmons
Sid Tinsley
James Trapp
David Treadwell
Perry Tuttle
Henry Walls
Joey Walters
Charlie Waters
Joel Wells
Harvey White
Curtis Whitley
Perry Williams
Derrick Witherspoon
Donnell Woolford

Cleveland State CC TN (1)

Craig Colquitt

Coahoma CC MS (3)

James Haynes
Simon Shanks
Willie Walker

Coast Guard (1)

Curt Knight

Coe (1)

Carey Bender

Coffeyville CC KS (25)

Steve Ache
Lynwood Alford
Joe Aska
Jerry Baker
Albert Bell
Will Cokeley
Wendell Davis
Mel Gray
Dean Hamel
Dave Kalina
Bob LeBlanc
Tony Leiker
Leonard Little
Pete Mills
Jim Bob Morris
Limbo Parks
Bruce Pickens
Mike Rozier
Henry Schichtle
Tracy Scroggins
Ron Springs
Siran Stacy
Keith Traylor
Ted Watts
Jeff Wright

Colgate (68)

Frank Abruzzino
Ockie Anderson
Winnie Anderson
John Batorski
Larry Cabrelli
Jack Call
Bart Carroll
Red Chesbro
Rae Crowther
Saville Crowther
Joe Davidson
Tommy Dowler
Joe Duckworth
Rich Erenberg
Danny Fortmann
Kenny Gamble
Charlie Gauer
Bill Geyer
Hank Gillo
Bob Gillson
Milt Graham
Hoot Haines
Les Hart
Charlie Havens
Joe Hoague
Steamer Horning
Marv Hubbard
Ray Ilg
Don Irwin
Al Jamison
Matt Jaworski
George Kershaw
Jon Kimmel
Carl Kinscherf
Babe Kraus
Jim Laird
Jim Leonard
Johnny Long
Jacque MacKinnon
Carl Mankat
Greg Manusky
Mike Micka
Fran Morelli
Frank Muehlheuser
Mark Murphy
Clem Neacy
Babe Parnell
Ted Plumridge
Ruel Redinger
Wooky Roberts
Eugene Robinson
Erik Rosenmeier
Bob Rowe
Art Schiebel
Vin Shekleton
Ed Stacco
Charlie Stewart
Charlie Strack
Mike Stramiello
Barney Traynor
Eddie Tryon
Mark van Eeghen
Elmer Volgenau
Charlie Weber
Jim Welsh
Don Wemple
Belf West
Izzy Yablock

Coll. of the Redwoods CA (J.C.) (3)

Mike Bettiga
Rob Harrison
Gary Thompson

Coll. of DuPage IL (J.C.) (4)

Aaron Bailey
Mike Bellamy
Bill Lobenstein
Roosevelt Nix

Coll. of Eastern Utah (J.C.) (3)

Rex Berry
Donald Miller
Mark Stevens

Coll. of Emporia (2)

Lem Harkey
Jim Jacquith

Coll. of Idaho (1)

R.C. Owens

Coll. of Lake Co. IL (J.C.) (1)

Brad Saar

Coll. of Marin CA (J.C.) (6)

Marty Baccaglio
Doug Dressler
Honor Jackson
Ted Popson
Roger Stillwell
Marvin Williams

Coll. of San Mateo CA (J.C.) (8)

Paul Bradford
Tony Calvelli
Clyde Conner
Frank Duncan
Tony Plummer
Bill Ring
Jim Schmedding
Devin Wyman

Coll. of Southern Idaho (J.C.) (1)

Ben Bangs

Coll. of the Canyons CA (J.C.) (3)

Terry Love
Aaron Mitchell
Avon Riley

Coll. of the Desert CA (J.C.) (2)

Reggie Brown
Bryan Robinson

Coll. of the Sequoias CA (J.C.) (12)

Hank Allison
Wilson Alvarez
Ryan Benjamin
Trent Collins
Dick Handley
Alvin Horn
John Kaiser
Danny Lockett
Darren Long
Ruben Rodriguez
Bob Rosenstiel
Martin Sartin

Coll. of the Siskiyous CA (J.C.) (1)

Duke Schamel

Colorado (171)

Bobby Anderson
Dick Anderson
Troy Archer
Bill Bain
Estes Banks
Mitch Berger
Frank Bernardi
Tony Berti
Greg Biekert
Eric Bieniemy
Frank Bosch
Kevin Bowman
Ronnie Bradford
Cliff Branch
Paul Briggs
Pete Brock
Stan Brock
Willie Brock
Tom Brookshier
Chad Brown
Ron Brown
Bill Brundige
Larry Brunson
Cullen Bryant
Brian Cabral
J.V. Cain
Gary Campbell
Jeff Campbell
Roland Caranci
Rae Carruth
Frank Clarke
Shannon Clavelle
Walt Clay
Mark Cooney
Eric Coyle
Claude Crabb
T.J. Cunningham
Charlie Davis
Mike Davis
John Denvir
Dan DeRose
Koy Detmer
Jeff Donaldson
Eddie Dove
Boyd Dowler
Jon Embree
Steve Engel
Keith English
Bill Fairband
Don Fairbanks
Christian Fauria
George Figner
Deon Figures
Bill Frank
Harvey Goodman
Charlie Greer
Dan Grimm
George Grosvenor
Steve Haggerty
Carroll Hardy
Billy Harris
Don Hasselbeck
Dennis Havig
Mark Haynes
Ralph Heck
Barry Helton
Gary Henson
Kerry Hicks
Jerry Hillebrand
Merwin Hodel
Darius Holland
Don Holmes
Greg Horton
Garry Howe
Chris Hudson
Heath Irwin
Charles Johnson
Charlie Johnson
Jesse Johnson
Kelley Johnson
Richard Johnson
Ted Johnson
Greg Jones
Vance Joseph
Rick Kay
Jon Keyworth
Gary Knafelc
Jeff Knapple
Mark Koncar
Mike Kozlowski
Terry Kunz
Jerry Leahy
Jay Leeuwenburg
Matt Lepsis
Ernie Lewis
Dave Logan
Bo Matthews
James Mayberry
Dave McCloughan
Mike McCoy
Bob McCullough
Kanavis McGhee
Odis McKinney
Chris McLemore
Dan McMillen
Matt Miller
Mike Montler
Gene Moore
Emery Moorehead
Chris Naeole
Bob Niziolek
Erik Norgard
Rick Ogle
Herb Orvis

Whitney Paul
Craig Penrose
Horace Perkins
Jim Perkins
Rod Perry
Lyle Pickens
Daryl Price
Mike Pritchard
Mickey Pruitt
Vince Rafferty
Dan Ralph
Tony Reed
Leonard Renfro
Del Ritchhart
Bill Roe
Sam Rogers
Tom Rouen
Lee Rouson
Matt Russell
Bill Sabatino
Rashaan Salaam
Mike Schnitker
Victor Scott
Laval Short
Bob Simpson
Jim Smith
Rico Smith
Ariel Solomon
Mike Spivey
Walter Stanley
Leo Stasica
Joel Steed
Kordell Stewart
Bryan Stoltenberg
Bob Stransky
Tony Stricker
Ryan Sutter
John Tarver
David Tate
Rich Umphrey
Mark Vander Poel
Ruben Vaughan
George Visger
Billy Waddy
Ward Walsh
Lamont Warren
Teddy Washington
Derek West
Michael Westbrook
Greg Westbrooks
Whizzer White
Solomon Wilcots
Alfred Williams
Dave Williams
John Wooten
Mike Woulfe
Steve Young

Colorado College (2)

Dutch Clark
Ed Smith

Colorado Mines (2)

Jack Colahan
Lloyd Madden

Colorado State (78)

Al Baker
Larry Barnes
Steve Bartalo
Sanjay Beach
Mark Bell
Mark Bell
Mike Bell
Randy Beverly
Calvin Branch
Sam Brunelli
Alex Burl
Don Burroughs
Kevin Call
Jack Christiansen
Roy Clay
Jim David
Steve DeLine
Rick Dennison
Dale Dodrill
Jerome Dove
Jim Eifrid
Jon Francis
Sherwood Fries
David Frisch
Fred Glick
Gary Glick
Jim Hartman
Jon Henderson
John Ivlow
Raymond Jackson
Kim Jones
Selwyn Jones
Jimmie Kennedy
Brady Keys
Linden King
Bob Kruse
Bill Larson
Al Lavan
Harper LeBel
Keith Lee
Chet Maeda
Lawrence McCutcheon
Kay McFarland
Thurman McGraw
Keli McGregor
Kevin McLain
Jim McMillin
Mark Miller
Willie Miller
Sean Moran
Moses Moreno
Glen Morris
Mark Mullaney
Greg Myers
Mark Nichols
Ben Norman
Terry Nugent
Jim Opperman
Mitch Palmer
Greg Primus
Roy Ratekin
Leo Reed
Oscar Reed
Adrian Ross
Tom Rouen
Al Simpson
Brady Smith
Perry Smith
Ron Stehouwer
Greg Stemrick
Kelly Stouffer
Earlie Thomas
Terry Unrein
Louie Walker
Harry Washington
Jim White
Wilbur White
Lonnie Wright

Columbia (36)

Mal Bleeker
John Chirico
Ernie Cuneo
Bill Daley
Fred DeStefano
Marty Domres
Lou Feist
Eddie Fisher
Bill Garnjost
Jason Garrett
John Garrett
Bruce Gehrke
Paul Governali
Ken Harris
Leon Johnson
Tom Kerrigan
George Kisiday
Walt Koppisch
Lou Kusserow
Sid Luckman
Herb Maack
Cliff Montgomery
George Pease
Harry Robb
Archie Roberts
Ben Roderick
Sam Salemi
John Siegal
George Starke
Bruce Stephens
Bill Swiacki
Ray Wagner
Marcellus Wiley
John Witkowski
Vinnie Yablonski
Jerry Zawadzkas

Columbia Basin Coll. WA (J.C.) (7)

Smiley Creswell
Clint Didier
Billy Donckers
Ron East
Lyndell Jones
Mark Kafentzis
Dennis Patera

Columbus State CC OH (1)

Vince Carreker

Compton CC CA (29)

Ben Agajanian
Billy Anderson
Charlie Ane
Don Bandy
Eddie Bell
Bob Boyd
Larry Braziel
Royal Cathcart
John Embree
Carl Fennema
Dick Horne
Joe Lewis
John LoVetere
Paul Lowe
Hugh McElhenny
Charlie McNeil
Solomon Miller
John Morton
Dan Orlich
Joe Perry
Gerry Perry
Volney Peters
Bobby Smith
Ernie Smith
J.D. Smith
Bobby Thompson
Bev Wallace
Bob Whitlow
Johnny Williams

Concordia (Ill.) (1)

Gary Larsen

Concordia (Minn.) (6)

Barry Bennett
Todd Black
Kim Bokamper
Jim Christopherson
Dave Klug
Cleve Wester

Concordia (Quebec) (1)

Mark Montreuil

Concordia (Wis.) (1)

John Scardina

Connecticut (20)

Glenn Antrum
Vince Clements
John Contoulis
Bill Cooke
Mark Didio
John Dorsey
Nick Giaquinto
Ching Hammill
Brian Herosian
Brian Kozlowski
Bob Leahy
Booth Lusteg
Jim Merritts
Eric Naposki
Red O'Neil
Vic Radzievitch
Pete Rostosky
Eric Torkelson
Pop Williams
Darrell Wilson

Contra Costa Coll. CA (J.C.) (11)

Mike Burns
Kenny Daniel
Curt Frazier
Jim Harris
Joe Koontz
Frank Lockett
Larry McGrew
Ray Strong
Gene Taylor
Travis Williams
Rich Zecher

Cooke Co. Coll. TX (J.C.) (16)

Willis Brennan
Joe Carey
Frank Coughlin
Dick Fencl
Bob Koehler
Louis Kolls
Tim Moynihan
Harry O'Connell
Bill O'Neill
Carmen Scardine
Frank Seliger
Ron Shanklin
Dick Stahlman
Johnny Wiatrak
Charlie Winston
Frank Zelencik

Copiah-Lincoln CC MS (5)

Gregg Briggs
Toney Catchings
Victor Green
Stephen Hobbs
Allen Smith

Cornell (36)

Greg Bloedorn
Ralph Calcagni
Tex Coulter
Lou Daukas
Al Dekdebrun
Hal Ebersole
Furlong Flynn
Fred Gillies
Pete Gogolak
Derrick Harmon
Kirk Hershey
Reno Jones
Eddie Kaw
Bob Lally
Mort Landsberg
Pete Larson
Chad Levitt
Ed Marinaro
Hal McCullough
Tom McHale
Lou Molinet
Bob Morris
Bill Murphy
Bob Nash
Jack O'Hearn
Seth Payne
Bo Roberson
Harry Shaub
Murray Shelton
Charlie Stewart
Ken Stofer
John Tagliaferri
Ken Talton
Jim Wilson
Gary Wood
Frank Wydo

Cornell College (1)

Lee Wilson

Corpus Christi (1)

Jesse Stokes

Cowley Co. CC KS (2)

Bob Layden
Johnny Rembert

Creighton (10)

Ed Allen
Jim Bertoglio
Fred Borak
Carl Buda
Tony Cemore
Paul Fitzgibbon
Chuck Gayer
Johnny Knolla
Ike Mahoney
Ralph Maillard

Crowder College MO (J.C.) (1)

Robert Brannon

Culver-Stockton (2)

Bob Hendren
Jason Kaiser

Cypress Coll. CA (J.C.) (1)

Tom Morris

Dakota Wesleyan (1)

Paul Sheeks

Dallas Co. CC TX (1)

Ken Jolly

Dana (1)

Lawrence White

Dartmouth (39)

Phil Bower
Johnny Bryan
Chick Burke
Jake Crouthamel
Joe Crowley
Nick Daukas
Joe DuSossoit
Jay Fiedler
Milt Ghee
Ed Gustafson
Charlie Guy
Vern Hagenbuckle
Les Haws
Ed Healey
Bill Hutchinson
Jon Jenkins
Jeff Kemp
Bob Krieger
Jim Landrigan
Lloyd Lee
Nick Lowery
Bob MacLeod
Ray MacMurray
Red Maloney
Don McKinnon
Joe Murphy
Bill Roberts
Gregg Robinson
Gordon Rule
John Shelburne
David Shula
Gustave Sonnenberg
Karl Thielscher
George Tully
Zack Walz
Tom Whelan
Reggie Williams
Alex Wizbicki
Swede Youngstrom

Darton Coll. GA (J.C.) (1)

Derrick Moore

Davidson (6)

Billy Crouch
Kevin Donnalley
Steve Heckard
Mike Kelly
Johnny Mackorell
Derrick Taylor

Davis & Elkins (9)

Red Corzine
John Federovitch
Tex Irvin
Ove Johansson
Buster Mitchell
Dick Powell
Neil Rengel
Emmett Ruh
Wayne Underwood

Dayton (38)

Sneeze Achiu
Johnnie Becker
Bill Belanich
Jack Brown
Augie Cabrinha
Mike Ciccolella
Tom Costello
Fest Cotton
Bob DeMarco
Pat Duffy
Fred Dugan
Mark Ellison
Tony Furst
Sam Hipa
Emil Karas
Jim Katcavage
Larry Knorr
Gary Kosins
Bill Lange
Al Mahrt
Armin Mahrt
Johnny Mahrt
Lou Mahrt
Coley McDonough
Ralph Niehaus
Chuck Noll
Dunc Obee
Bob Print
Jim Raiff
Pete Richardson
Norb Sacksteder
Dick Schuster
Jim Spencer
Aubrey Strosnider
Red Werder
Erwin Will
Mike Wilson
Joe Windbiel

De Anza Coll. CA (J.C.) (6)

Jahine Arnold
Doug Cosbie
Mervyn Fernandez
Randy Kirk
Frank Manumaleuga
Jeff Sevy

Dean Coll. MA (J.C.) (3)

Zachary Dixon
Ken Hartley
Bubba Pena

DePaul (15)

Chuck Apolskis
Bill Boedeker
Hal Carlson
Harold Cherne
Chet Chesney
Bill Daley
Pat Dowling
Egan
Max Fiske
Ted Lapka
Bill Muellner
Red O'Connor
Tom Roberts
John Scanlon
Dick Stahlman

DePauw (10)

Al Bloodgood
Bourbon Bondurant
Lyle Burton
Winnie Denton
Dave Finzer
Dutch Hendrian
Wilfrid Smith
Bob Steuber
Dick Sturtridge
Greg Werner

Defiance (1)

Ben Davis

Del Mar Coll. TX (J.C.) (2)

Don Gillis
Dudley Meredith

Delaware (15)

Scott Brunner
Leon Dombrowski
Rich Gannon
Conway Hayman
Tim Jacobs
Dennis Johnson
Jeff Komlo
Joe McGrail
Joe McHale
Jeff Modesitt
Bob Patton
Dan Reeder
George Schmitt
Ivory Sully
Hal Thompson

Delaware State (14)

Steve Coleman
Steve Davis
Victor Heflin
Chris Jones
David Jones
Tim King
Al Lawson
Rod Milstead
Frank Nicholson
Lybrant Robinson
John Taylor
Walter Tullis
Clarence Weathers
Gordon Wright

Delaware Valley (2)

Ted Cottrell
Bill Cottrell

Delgado CC LA (1)

Ken Karcher

Delta State (7)

George Chesser
Tim Edwards
Jack Gregory
Arrike James
Aubrey Matthews
Wilbur Myers
Aubrey Rozzell

Denison (11)

Johnnie Becker
Eric Calhoun
Mike Gregory
Tommy McMahon
Wilkie Moody
Dave Reese
George Roudebush
Nelson Rupp
Fritz Slackford
Dutch Thiele
Dave Thompson

Denver (12)

Bob Balog
Gregg Browning
Ferd Dreher
Sam Etcheverry
Tom Fena
Bob Gifford
Robert Hazelhurst
Ray Johnson
Mike Jurich
Don Stansauk
Morgan Tiller
John Woudenberg

Des Moines CC IA (1)

Kink Richards

Detroit J.C. (2)

Wayne Brenkert
Tom Dickinson

Detroit Mercy (62)

Grady Alderman
Lynn Allen
Sig Andrusking
Rip Bachor
Pete Bahan
Vince Banonis
John Barrett
Tom Beer
Tom Beier
Frank Bucher
Wes Carlson
Walt Cassidy
Walt Clago
Hal Cooper
George Daney
Walt Ellis
Andy Farkas
Tom Finnin
France Fitzgerald
Ernie Fritsch
Joe Gillis
Norm Harvey
Dutch Hendrian
Paul Hogan
Tom Hogan
Bob Ivory
Frank Jackunas
Bob Keene
Jimmy Kelly
Ty Krentler
Dutch Lauer
Harvey Long
Jackie Lowther
Elmer Madarik
Birdie Maher
Bruce Maher
Gene Malinowski
Ted Marchibroda
Leo McCausland
Elmer McCormick
Tom McNamara
Eddie Moegle
Doug Nott
Bill O'Neill
Tip O'Neill
Ted Pavelec
Charlie Payne
Peter Rajkovich
Perry Richards
Lee Riley
Sod Ryan
Eddie Scharer
Jim Shorter
Jack Simmons
Jimmy Simpson
Alex Smail
Gustave Sonnenberg
Steve Stonebreaker
Lou Usher
Larry Vargo
Tillie Voss
Herm Young

Detroit Tech (1)

Michael Kostiuk

Diablo Valley Coll. CA (J.C.) (7)

Steve Alexakos
Leo Biedermann
Daniel Colchico
John Gesek
Jim McMillin
Anthony Spears
Altie Taylor

Dickinson (3)

Bull Behman
Bob Books
Len Supulski

Dixie Coll. UT (J.C.) (5)

Scott Brumfield
Corey Dillon
Larry Heater
Ron McCall
Alfred Pupunu

Doane (2)

Kevin Hunt
Mike Ulmer

Dodge City CC KS (4)

Larry Brown
Robert Delpino
Willard Goff
Steve Tasker

Drake (25)

Tom Bienemann
Walt Brindley
Versil Deskin
Waldo Don Carlos
Pat Dunsmore
Matt Hanousek
Rudy Holmes
Garry Howe
Karl Kassulke

Al Krueger
Bill Lapham
Bob Mahan
Pug Manders
Bob McClure
Dennis McKnight
Jerry Mertens
Dick Nesbitt
Ron Shearer
Boris Shlapak
Oak Smith
Glen Spear
Dick Steere
Dan Turk
Doug Winslow
Felix Wright

Dubuque (5)

John Armstrong
Sol Butler
Waddy Kuehl
Walter Lowe
Eugene Rowell

Duke (81)

Lou Allen
Bill Bailey
Brian Baldinger
Tony Benjamin
Ben Bennett
Lamar Blount
Greg Boone
Charles Bowser
Bob Brodhead
Dave Brown
Billy Bryan
Joe Cardwell
Wray Carlton
Chris Castor
Wes Chesson
Billy Cox
Fred Crawford
Mike Curtis
Randy Cuthbert
Al DeRogatis
Anthony Dilweg
Dave Dunaway
Jim Duncan
Blaine Earon
Ray Farmer
John Farquhar
Carl Gersbach
Scotty Glacken
Billy Granville
Bob Grupp
Buzz Guy
Leo Hart
Howard Hartley
Bernard Holsey
Roy Hord
Ernie Jackson
Robert Jackson
Cedric Jones
Steve Jones
Mike Junkin
Sonny Jurgensen
Mike Karmazin
John Kerns
Steve Lach
Cliff Lewis
Patrick Mannelly
Bob Matheson
Ben Mayes
George McAfee
Wes McAfee
Bob McDonough
Bob McDougal
Carl McGee
Mike McGee
Ed Meadows
Ted Million
Bill Milner
Brandon Moore
Kelley Mote
Ed Newman
Brad Oates
Ace Parker
Joel Patten
Bolo Perdue
Alex Piasecky
Bucky Pope
Chris Port
Pat Preston
Frank Ribar
Tawambi Settles
Ed Sharkey
Frank Sinkovitz
Lyman Smith
Glen Stough
Lou Tepe
Corey Thomas
Emmett Tilley
J.T. Turner
Chuck Walker
Garland Williams
Al Woodall

Duquesne (49)

Mike Basrak
John Binotto
Boyd Brumbaugh
Joe Cibulas
Ben Ciccone
Tom Corbo
Nick DeCarbo
Al DeMao
Henry DePaul
Al Donelli
Leo Elter
George Gonda
Bruce Gossett
Ted Grabinski
Forrest Hall
Val Jansante
George Kakasic
John Karrs
Ray Kemp
Max Kielbasa
George Kisiday
Joe Malkovich
Joe Maras
John Matisi
Jim McDonald
Charley Mehelich
Carl Nery
Armand Niccolai
John Nosich
Mel O'Delli
Bob O'Neil
John Perko
John Petchel
George Platukis
George Rado
John Rokisky
Bernie Semes
Joe Setcavage
Steve Sinko
George Sirochman
Art Strutt
Vic Vidoni
Henry Weinberg
Joe Wiehl
Al Wukits
Frank Wydo
John Yurchey
Silvio Zaninelli
Frank Zoppetti

Earlham (2)

John Beasley
Jeff Smith

East Carolina (45)

Stefon Adams
Tony Baker
Tommy Barnhardt
Glenn Bass
Jeff Blake
Reggie Branch
Lamont Burns
Earnest Byner
Bernard Carter
Tony Collins
George Crump
Carlester Crumpler
Ellis Dillahunt
Mitchell Galloway
Chris Hall
Steve Hamilton
Sam Harrell
Eddie Hicks
Kevin Ingram
John Jett
Robert Jones
George Koonce
Ernie Logan
Terry Long
Emmanuel McDaniel
Jerris McPhail
Tom Michel
Ricky Nichols
Reggie Pinkney
Tootie Robbins
Junior Robinson
Jody Schulz
Tom Scott
Walter Scott
Vinson Smith
Hal Stephens
Les Strayhorn
Carl Summerell
Anthony Thompson
Zack Valentine
Norwood Vann
Kevin Walker
Randy Watts
Henry Williams
Walter Wilson

East Central (OK) (5)

Bill Capps
Mark Gastineau
Herb Kane
Dewey McClain
Cliff Thrift

East Central CC MS (1)

Alex Sidorik

East Los Angeles Coll. CA (J.C.) (18)

Frank Buncom
Lynn Cain
Ron Copeland
Ben Davidson
Clarence Davis
Mike Davis
George Fleming
David Gray
Jimmie Jones
Kerry Justin
Brady Keys
Steve Knutson
Tony Lorick
Norm McBride
Henry Schmidt
Ron Spears
Tom Watkins
Elbert Watts

East Mississippi CC (4)

Orlando Bobo
Willie Gillespie
Virgil Seay
Antowain Smith

East Stroudsburg (5)

Chris Gerhard
Mike Lush
Dan Murray
Mike Reichenbach
Ray Yakavonis

East Tennessee State (11)

Donnie Abraham
Ken Bowen
Jerry Butler
Mack Cummings
Earl Ferrell
Phil Forney
Thane Gash
Dennis Law
Steve Parker
Dainon Sidney
Van Williams

Eastern Arizona Coll. (J.C.) (8)

Jeff Colter
Sean Dykes
Roger Farmer
Mark Gastineau
Michael Haynes
Bronzell Miller
Paul Robinson
Jerry Smith

Eastern Illinois (19)

Evan Arapostathis
Roy Banks
Mel Black
Greg Brown
Jeff Christensen
Rob DeVita
Brad Fichtel
Ray Fisher
Chris Geile
Bill Glenn
Jeff Gossett
Kevin Gray
Lennie High
John Jurkovic
Ray McElroy
Sean Payton
Ted Petersen
Bob Rosenstiel
Robert Williams

Eastern Kentucky (24)

Steve Bird
Keith Bosley
Elmo Boyd
Chad Bratzke
Wally Chambers
Danny Copeland
Dale Dawson
Jason Dunn
George Floyd
Myron Guyton
Elroy Harris
David Hoelscher
Joe Hollingsworth
Byron Ingram
John Jackson
Aaron Jones
John Klingel
Tim Lester
Aaron Marsh
Tony McCombs
Buddy Moor
Ray Pelfrey
Jessie Small
David Wilkins

Eastern Michigan (28)

Vashone Adams
John Banaszak
Charlie Batch
Dave Boone
Duane Butler
Rick Byas
Clarence Chapman
Al Clark
Lional Dalton
Al Day
Bill DuLac
Ron Fernandes
Anthony Fields
Will Foster
Reggie Garrett
Garry Grady
Chuck Hanneman
Ron Johnson
Dale Livingston
David Marshall
Ed Opalewski
Brett Petersmark
Jim Pietrzak
Dave Pureifory
Ron Rice
Keith Rucker
Chuck Shonta
Barry Stokes

Eastern Montana (2)

Rick Duncan
Bill Wondolowski

Eastern New Mexico (7)

George Boynton
Benjy Dial
Scott Eccles
Conrad Hamilton
Derrick Harden
Pete Jaquess
Michael Sinclair

Eastern Washington (11)

Tom Ackerman
Mark Gehring
Jeff Mickel
Jeff Ogden
Bob Picard
Trent Pollard
Eric Riley
Kevin Sargent
Kurt Schulz
Ed Simmons
Rob Woods

Edinboro (2)

David Green
Jim Romaniszyn

Edmonton (Canada) (1)

Brian Fryer

Edward Waters (1)

Cannonball Butler

El Camino Coll. CA (J.C.) (23)

Jim Allison
Joe Caravello
Paul Carmichael
Curtis Conway
Aaron Craver
Anthony Daigle
Chris Darrington
Derrick Deese
Fred Dryer
Rick Eber
Paul Held
Todd Hons
Lynn Hoyem
Andrew Jackson
Suge Knight
Terry Mendenhall
Jim Obradovich
Latario Rachal
Bryan Reeves
Tom Reynolds
Jimmy Sears
Ken Stills
Stan Talley

Elizabeth City State (8)

Tim Cofield
Bobby Futrell
Jim Greer
Reggie Langhorne
Everett McIver
Jethro Pugh
Carlton Thomas
John Walton

Ellendale State ND (J.C.) (1)

Pete Retzlaff

Ellsworth CC IA (9)

Dale Carter
Paul Fairchild
Derrick Harden
Mike Lemon
Herb McMath
Dan Peiffer
John Teerlinck
Don Wilson
Mike Woods

Elmhurst (2)

Steve Finch
Swede Johnston

Elon (9)

Quinton Ballard
Jack Boone
Hal Bradley
Joey Hackett
Bob LeBlanc
Rich McGeorge
Tony Settles
Brent Sexton
Jimmy Smith

Emporia State (14)

Dale Burnett
Glenn Campbell
Eldon Danenhauer
Bill Danenhauer
John Davis
Wen Goldsmith
Kelly Goodburn
Steve Henry
Jiggs Kline
Bob Leahy
Leon Lett
John Lohmeyer
George Munday
Bud Widick

Evangel (2)

Derrick Clark
Tony Dollinger

Evansville (2)

Bibbles Bawel
Ken Smith

Everett CC WA (3)

Terry Metcalf
Randy Montgomery
Steve Okoniewski

Fairmont State (3)

Jim Lipinski
Jim Mertens
Don Overton

Fayetteville State (2)

Moses Ford
Blenda Gay

Ferris State (4)

Monty Brown
Dave Gagnon
Ricky Patton
Ed Philion

Ferrum (13)

Chuck Banks
Michael Durrette
Wentford Gaines
Keith Gary
Ed George
Bruce Gossett
Jim Kitts
Leander Knight
Al Latimer
Larry Robinson
Don Testerman
Don Thompson
Chris Warren

Findlay (8)

Odell Barry
Keith Cupp
Tony King
George McDuffie
Allen Smith
Dutch Strassner
Ed Susteric
Dana Wright

Fisk (4)

Andy Bolton
Neal Craig
Robert James
John Jones

Flagler (1)

Scott Player

Florida (171)

Tremayne Allen
Neal Anderson
Reidel Anthony
Trace Armstrong
Ephesians Bartley
Jim Beaver
Kerwin Bell
Michael Brandon
Scot Brantley
Larry Brinson
Barry Brown
Lomas Brown
Carl Brumbaugh
Glenn Cameron
Mark Campbell
Earl Carr
Kevin Carter
Rick Casares
Don Chandler
Wes Chandler
Clifford Charlton
Brian Clark
Mike Clark
Randy Clark
Hagood Clarke
Greg Cleveland
Mo Collins
Cris Collinsworth
Clyde Crabtree
Ray Criswell
Derrick Crudup
Brad Culpepper
Ivory Curry
Dexter Daniels
Al Darby
Floyd Dean
Frank Dempsey
Guy Dennis
Cal Dixon
Dwayne Dixon
Chris Doering
Everett Douglas
Jimmy DuBose
Paul Duhart
Ricky Easmon
Shayne Edge
Richard Fain
Chris Faulkner
Dan Fike
Don Fleming
Derrick Gaffney
Larry Gagner
William Gaines
David Galloway
Lewis Gilbert
Clark Goff
Tim Golden
Royce Goodbread
Tony Green
Bobby Joe Green
Jacquez Green
Sammy Green
Monty Grow
Darren Hambrick
Mal Hammack
Lorenzo Hampton
Ben Hanks
Jack Harper
James Harrell
Roy Harris
Joe Hergert
Bob Hewko
Ike Hilliard
Eric Hodges
Chuck Hunsinger
John Hunt
Scott Hutchinson
Jack Jackson
Randy Jackson
Willie Jackson
John James
Alonzo Johnson
Ellis Johnson
James Jones
Jimmy Jordan
Vince Kendrick
Crawford Ker
Nick Klutka
Floyd Konetsky
Mark Korff
Frank Lasky
Burton Lawless
Terry LeCount
Gene Lee
Tony Lilly
David Little
Tony Lomack
Buford Long
Anthone Lott
Wilber Marshall
Shane Matthews
Fred McCallister
Tony McCoy
Lee McGriff
Vito McKeever
Henry McMillian
Dexter McNabb
Dudley Meredith
Darren Mickell
Pat Miller
Ernie Mills
Fondren Mitchell
Jeff Mitchell
Alonzo Mitz
Nat Moore
Mike Moten
Mike Mularkey
Dennis Murphy
Mark Murray
Godfrey Myles
Ricky Nattiel
Frankie Neal
Tim Newton
Jack O'Brien
Jason Odom
Louis Oliver
Ralph Ortega
Joel Parker
Bernie Parrish
Leon Pennington
Anton Peters
David Posey
John Reaves
Larry Rentz
Errict Rhett
Huey Richardson
Ed Robinson
Al Romine
Stacey Simmons
Jackie Simpson
Cedric Smith
Emmitt Smith
John Smith
Larry Smith
Del Speer
Jimmy Spencer
Steve Spurrier
Kay Stephenson
John Symank
Steve Tannen
Fred Taylor
Ron Tilton
Allen Trammel
Richard Trapp
Harmon Wages
Dale Waters
Fred Weary
Rhondy Weston
Adrian White
Cy Williams
David Williams
Elijah Williams
Jarvis Williams
John L. Williams
Lawrence Wright
Danny Wuerffel
Jim Yarbrough
James Yeats
Tyrone Young
Jack Youngblood
Jeff Zimmerman

Florida A&M (64)

Ray Alexander
Gene Atkins
Antoine Bennett
Lewis Bennett
Tony Bland
Ronnie Blye
Jamie Brown
Rufus Brown
Thornton Chandler
Clarence Childs
Greg Coleman
Dave Daniels
Al Denson
Hewritt Dixon
John Eason
Glen Edwards
William Evers
Chad Fann
Bobby Felts
Roger Finnie
Al Frazier
Derrick Gainer
Willie Galimore
Hubert Ginn
Charlie Goodrum
Clarence Hawkins
Bob Hayes
Major Hazelton
Buzz Highsmith
Ralph Hill
Earl Holmes
Johnny Holmes
Willie Irvin
Nate James
Ken Johnson
Preston Johnson
John Kelly
Henry Lawrence
Herman Lee
Frank Marion
Willie McClung
Tyrone McGriff
Terry Mickens
Frank Middleton
Bob Mike

Gene Milton
Riley Morris
Jamie Nails
Nate Newton
Dexter Nottage
Carleton Oats
Bob Paremore
Ken Riley
Mel Rogers
Don Smith
Vernice Smith
Al Sykes
Gene Thomas
Eric Truvillion
Andre White
Gene White
Wally Williams
Robert Wilson
Freddie Woodson

Florida Atlantic (1)

Ed Newman

Florida CC at Jacksonville (1)

Scott Player

Florida State (150)

Clifton Abraham
Derrick Alexander
Greg Allen
Dick Amman
Terry Anthony
Joe Avezzano
Tom Bailey
Shannon Baker
Ed Beckman
Edgar Bennett
Scott Bentley
Louis Berry
Fred Biletnikoff
Peter Boulware
Leon Bright
Derrick Brooks
Terrell Buckley
Devin Bush
LeRoy Butler
Bobby Butler
Marion Butts
Bill Capece
Bill Cappleman
Alphonso Carreker
Duane Carrell
Dexter Carter
Walter Carter
Pat Carter
Derrick Clark
Harvey Clayton
Randy Coffield
Bert Cooper
Sam Cowart
Vernon Crawford
Henri Crockett
Zack Crockett
Jeff Curchin
Lawrence Dawsey
Rhett Dawson
Bill Dawson
Howard Dinkins
Dedrick Dodge
Jamie Dukes
Warrick Dunn
'Omar Ellison
Tom Feamster
Lane Fenner
Victor Floyd
William Floyd
Dan Footman
Todd Fordham
Reggie Freeman
Corey Fuller
Steve Gabbard
Kent Gaydos
Chip Glass
Hector Gray
E.G. Green
Grant Guthrie
Odell Haggins
Kim Hammond
Eric Hayes
Jim Hendley
Dick Hermann
Jessie Hester
Ron Hester
Gary Huff
Charlie Hunt
Bobby Jackson
Garth Jax
Greg Johnson
Brad Johnson
Lonnie Johnson
Reggie Johnson
Fred Jones
Hassan Jones
Marvin Jones
Walter Jones
Willie Jones
Danny Kanell
Bill Kimber
Keith Kinderman
Kevin Knox
Ken Lanier
Amp Lee
Keith Lester
Ron Lewis
Kevin Long
Kim Mack
Joe Majors
Jim Mankins
Martin Mayhew
Kez McCorvey
Dale McCullers
Toddrick McIntosh
Dennis McKinnon
Scott McLean
Eddie McMillan
Mike Mercer
Mark Meseroll
Orson Mobley
Randy Moss
Zeke Mowatt
Les Murdock
Lee Nelson
Gerald Nichols
Lee Paige
Sterling Palmer
Gary Parris
Julian Pittman
Scott Player
Dave Ponder
Bob Renn
Phillip Riley
James Roberson
Samari Rolle
Tony Romeo
Orpheus Roye
Deion Sanders
Corey Sawyer
Stanley Scott
Ron Sellers
Eric Shaw
Clay Shiver
Mike Shumann
Carl Simpson
Barry Smith
Sammie Smith
Shevin Smith
Jesse Solomon
Greg Spires
Rohn Stark
Walt Sumner
Steve Tensi
Nat Terry
J.T. Thomas
Tra Thomas
Weegie Thompson
Pat Tomberlin
Rick Tuten
Tamarick Vanover
Andre Wadsworth
Casey Weldon
Max Wettstein
Bud Whitehead
Clarence Williams
Del Williams
Peter Tom Willis
Reinard Wilson
Gary Woolford

Foothill Coll. CA (J.C.) (4)

Bill Munson
Mike Perko
John Travis
Ralph Wenzel

Fordham (65)

John Alexander
Al Babartsky
Paul Berezney
Frank Bissell
Jim Blumenstock
Les Borden
Sam Bowers
Speed Braney
Matt Brennan
Ralph Buckley
John Cannella
George Cheverko
Bunny Corcoran
Ed Danowski
Lou DeFilippo
Johnny Dell Isola
Vince Dennery
Johnny Druze
Jim Dufft
Joe DuMoe
Len Eshmont
Bill Feaster
Steve Filipowicz
Ed Franco
George Grandinette
Dimp Halloran
Tom Hogan
Harry Jacunski
Art Johnson
George Kane
Bill Kellagher
Harry Kloppenberg
Mike Kochel
John Kuzman
Tom Leary
Bull Lowe
Joe Maniaci
Jim Manning
Tommy Myers
Andy Nacrelli
Jerry Noonan
Kenny Parker
Dom Principe
Ray Riddick
Bill Ryan
Joe Sabasteanski
Frank Sacco
Tony Sarausky
Larry Sartori
Ed Shedlosky
Tony Siano
Kurt Sohn
Cliff Steele
Bill Stein
Art Stevenson
Leif Strand
Fred Sweetland
Joe Ungerer
Walt Uzdavinis
George Vergara
Larry Walbridge
Alex Wojciechowicz
Vinnie Yablonski
Joe Yackanich
Joe Zapustas

Fort Hays State (5)

Vashone Adams
Steve Crosby
Les Miller
Frankie Neal
Bill Reissig

Fort Lewis (3)

Herman Heard
Cephus Weatherspoon
Ed Zeman

Fort Scott CC KS (9)

Curtis Brown
Gerry Ellis
Cliff Frazier
Mel Gray
Leroy Harris
Frank Middleton
Tommy Reamon
Mitch Sutton
Felix Wright

Fort Valley State (8)

Eddie Anderson
Dean Brown
Darryl Holmes
Greg Lloyd
Leroy Moore
Tyrone Poole
Allen Smith
Rayfield Wright

Franklin & Marshall (8)

Mike Caterbone
Tom Caterbone
Rob Jamieson
Elmer Jones
Ken Jones
Alex Schibanoff
Steve Uhrinyak
Ray Yagiello

Franklin (Ind.) (3)

Paul Franklin
Hugh Lowery
Mike Yount

Franklin (Ohio) (1)

Ralph Isselhardt

Frederick CC MD (1)

Wade Traynham

Fresno City Coll. CA (J.C.) (19)

Greg Boyd
Dwayne Crump
Ledio Fanucchi
Tom Flores
Brad Ford
Mike Freeman
Doug Gaynor
Bob Glazebrook
Keshon Johnson
Jim Merlo
Anthony Mosley
Rod Perry
Daimon Shelton
David Sloan
Andrew Stewart
Damon Thomas
Anthony Washington
Tim Washington
Ryan Wetnight

Fresno State (72)

Jahine Arnold
Stephen Baker
Jan Barrett
Rich Bartlewski
Chris Bayne
Sonny Bishop
Doug Brown
Reggie Brown
Tony Brown
Victor Burnett
James Burton
Floyd Collier
Chris Conrad
Ron Cox
Aaron Craver
Dwayne Crump
Anthony Daigle
Trent Dilfer
David Dunn
Henry Ellard
Ledio Fanucchi
Malcolm Floyd
Jethro Franklin
Curt Frazier
Mike Freeman
Bob Garner
Mike Garzoni
Bob Glazebrook
Clyde Glover
David Grayson
Courtney Griffin
Dick Handley
Cliff Hannemann
Gary Hayes
Wyatt Henderson
Ervin Hunt
Charlie Jones
Len Masini
Jack Mattox
Dale Messer
Mike Moffitt
Anthony Mosley
Lorenzo Neal
Tom Neville
Chris Pacheco
Stephone Paige
Nick Papac
Dean Philpott
Michael Pittman
Dave Plump
Marquez Pope
Latario Rachal
Greg Ramsey
Ron Rivers
Bryan Robinson
Tracy Rogers
Michael Stewart
Omar Stoutmire
Kevin Sweeney
Gene Taylor
Lavale Thomas
Marty Thompson
Anthony Washington
Tim Washington
Gary Weaver
Jack Wender
James Williams
Jim Williams
Greg Williamson
Tydus Winans
Mike Withycombe
Tony Woodruff

Frostburg State (3)

Bob Maddox
Sean McInerney
Murray Wichard

Fullerton Coll. CA (J.C.) (18)

Dean Barnett
Ron Cassidy
Robert Coons
Steve DeBerg
Kirk Dodge
Mike Horan
Howie Livingston
Kevin McLain
Chuck McMurtry
Brian Noble
Brig Owens
J.C. Pearson
Floyd Rhea
Hank Rockwell
Ted Rosnagle
Ron Smith
Larrye Weaver
Dave Wilson

Furman (11)

Luther Broughton
Chas Fox
Ernest Gibson
Stanford Jennings
Jerome Norris
Dewey Proctor
Rhoten Shetley
Tommy Southard
Tom Wham
David Whitehurst
Sam Wyche

Garden City CC KS (10)

Kevin Bouie
Derrick Clark
Steve Collier
Dwayne Crutchfield
Corey Dillon
Mike Friede
Frank Ori
Phillip Riley
Kelly Stouffer
Jabbar Threats

Gardner-Webb (3)

Derrick Fenner
Terry Guess
Gabe Wilkins

Gavilan Coll. CA (J.C.) (6)

Dave Bruno
Rhett Hall
Don Holmes
Bob Kampa
Carl Monroe
Dave Tipton

General Motors Inst (1)

Vince Lensing

Geneseo State (1)

Jim Leonard

Geneva (8)

Sam Cooper
David Cullen
Red Davis
Mack Flenniken
Max Hicks
Cal Hubbard
Al Maglisceau
Ernie Meyer

George Washington (23)

Jim Bryant
Carl Butkus
Andy Davis
Walt Fedora
Hank Goodman
Scott Gudmundson
Ed Gustafson
Ray Hanken
Denny Hughes
Heinie Jawish
Charlie Jones
Duce Keahey
John Koniszewski
Tuffy Leemans
Dave Liddick
Garry Lyle
Bob Nowaskey
Bill Pashe
Dale Prather
Frank Seno
Mike Sommer
Lee Tevis
Jay Turner

Georgetown (60)

Dan Ahern
Alec Anderson
Earl Audet
Jim Barron
Al Blozis
Jim Castiglia
Rudy Comstock
Babe Connaughton
Bunny Corcoran
Sam Cordovano
Wayne Davenport
John Doolan
Maury Dubofsky
Bob Dwyer
Jim Flaherty
Jack Flavin
Paul Florence
Joe Frank
Lou Ghecas
Johnny Gilroy
Gene Golsen
Tom Golsen
Tom Gormley
Larry Green
Jack Hagerty
Ching Hammill
Jack Itzel
Heinie Jawish
Bill Kenyon
Bob Kercher
Julie Koshlap
John Lascari
Dutch Leighty
Augie Lio
Paul Liston
Mickey Livers
Walter Lowe
Al Matuza
Frank McGrath
Johnny McQuade
Lou Metzger
Jim Mooney
John Morelli
Mickey Murtagh
Dan O'Connor
George Perpich
Tony Plansky
Ken Provencial
Jim Ricca
Johnny Scalzi
Fred Sheehan
Ed Skoronski
Metz Smeach
Ross Sorce
Clem Stralka
Johnny Tomaini
Carl Waite
Dick Werder
Tom Whelan
Dave Zuidmulder

Georgetown (Ky.) (2)

Louie Fritsch
Bruce McNorton

Georgia (174)

Scott Adams
Jim Auer
Harry Babcock
Bob Balog
Larry Bowie
John Brantley
Zeke Bratkowski
Charley Britt
Fred Brown
Norris Brown
Bob Burns
Kevin Butler
Jim Cagle
Marion Campbell
Johnny Carson
Dale Carver
Pete Case
Edgar Chandler
Bob Clemens
Charlie Clemons
George Collins
Todd Collins
Mel Conger
Dick Conn
Phillip Daniels
Lamar Davis
Terrell Davis
Van Davis
Art DeCarlo
Bucky Dilts
John Donaldson
Ray Donaldson
Andy Dudish
Dan Edwards
Robert Edwards
Clyde Ehrhardt
Gene Ellenson
Bob Etter
Nick Feher
Jason Ferguson
Paul Fersen
Jim Fordham
Mike Garrett
Cleveland Gary
Joe Geri
Freddie Gilbert
Randall Godfrey
Bill Godwin
Bill Goldberg
Hason Graham
Carl Grate
Riley Gunnels
Rodney Hampton
Glynn Harrison
Bill Hartman
Frank Harvey
Andre Hastings
Len Hauss
Garrison Hearst
Bill Hegarty
Keith Henderson
Craig Hertwig
Claude Hipps
Terry Hoage
Homer Hobbs
Pat Hodgson
Joe Hollingsworth
Winford Hood
Nat Hudson
Dennis Hughes
Brice Hunter
Al Jackson
Andy Johnson
Randy Johnson
Smiley Johnson
Daryll Jones
Spike Jones
John Kasay
Clarence Kay
Gorden Kelley
Ken Keuper
Horace King
Fay King
Dick Klein
Kent Lawrence
Milt Leathers
Allan Leavitt
Mo Lewis
Nate Lewis
Dave Lloyd
Tommy Lyons
Jim Magee
Gene Malinowski
Arthur Marshall
Whit Marshall
Willie McClendon
David McCluskey
Herdis McCrary
Guy McIntyre
Adam Meadows
Bryant Meeks
Shannon Mitchell
Billy Mixon
Gary Moss
Buster Mott
Tom Nash
Ulysses Norris
Joe O'Malley
Jimmy Orr
Tom Pennington
Victor Perry
Todd Peterson
Alex Piasecky
Wayne Radloff
Larry Rakestraw
Johnny Rauch
Andy Reid
Breezy Reid
Owen Reynolds
Frank Richter
Preston Ridlehuber
Ray Rissmiller
Jack Roberts
Matt Robinson
Rex Robinson
Troy Sadowski
Herb St. John
Theron Sapp
Jake Scott
Lindsay Scott
Bob Sedlock
Frankie Sinkwich
Ben Smith
Charles Smith
Gene Smith
Jermaine Smith
Royce Smith
Bill Stanfill
Mack Strong
Wilbur Strozier
Wayne Swinford
Hamp Tanner
Richard Tardits
Fran Tarkenton
Lars Tate
Joe Tereshinski
Charlie Timmons
Pete Tinsley
Bobby Towns
Greg Tremble
Charlie Trippi
Darrell Tully
Bobby Walden
Herschel Walker
Bobby Walston
Hines Ward
Gene Washington
Don Wells
Jodie Whire
Gene White
Roy Wilkins
Bernard Williams
Garland Williams
Scott Williams
Jim Wilson
Steven Wilson
Mike Wilson
Scott Woerner
Tim Worley
John Wright
Carlos Yancy
Dick Yelvington
George Young
Eric Zeier

Georgia Mil. Coll. (J.C.) (5)

Dutch Elston
Terry Guess
Bill Hartman
Jermaine Smith
Allen Williams

Georgia Southern (1)

Fred Stokes

Georgia Tech (112)

Taz Anderson
Joe Auer
Maxie Baughan
Craig Baynham
Scott Beavers
Ray Beck

William Bell
Don Bessillieu
Tom Bleick
Johnny Brewer
Keith Brooking
Gary Brown
Pete Brown
Jerry Burch
Gerry Bussell
Bill Chambers
Michael Cheever
Willie Clay
Marco Coleman
Willis Crockett
Shane Curry
Bill Curry
John Davis
Ted Davis
Bob Davis
Tony Daykin
Paul Duke
Randy Edmunds
Lethon Flowers
Elliott Fortune
Russ Freeman
Bill Fulcher
Ellis Gardner
Bill Giaver
Walt Godwin
Jerry Green
Joe Guyon
Steve Harkey
Joe Harris
Anthony Harrison
Jack Helms
David Hendrix
Urban Henry
Drew Hill
Kent Hill
Eddie Lee Ivery
Henry Johnson
Shawn Jones
Mike Kelley
Robert Lavette
Gary Lee
Dorsey Levens
Sammy Lilly
Billy Lothridge
Father Lumpkin
Dave Lutz
Ralph Malone
Billy Martin
Clay Matthews
Jerry Mays
Frank McConnell
Pat McHugh
Hal Miller
Warner Mizell
Mike Mooney
Pat Moriarty
George Morris
Larry Morris
Fred Murphy
Najee Mustafaa
Ed Nutting
Bill Paschal
Don Patterson
Mark Pike
Eddie Prokop
Steve Raible
Al Richardson
Jim Robinson
Coleman Rudolph
Jack Rudolph
Lucius Sanford
Billy Shaw
Billy Shields
Dave Simmons
Roy Simmons
David Sims
Scott Sisson
Sean Smith
Lum Snyder
Larry Stallings
John Steber
Rod Stephens
Ryan Stewart
Jim Still
Rick Strom
Pat Swilling
Jim Bob Taylor
Tom Taylor
Stumpy Thomason
Leo Tierney
Calvin Tiggle
Ben Utt
Carl Vereen
Gordon Watkins
Dave Watson
Ken Whisenhunt
Reggie Wilkes
Gary Wilkins
Clyde Williams
Ike Williams
Doug Wycoff
Frank Ziegler

Gettysburg (5)

Rip Kyle
Jim Nicely
Jim Ward
Dave Yohn
John Yovicsin

Glendale CC AZ (6)

Brian Davis
Chris Hale
Damon Mays
Randy McClanahan
Muhammad Oliver
Phillippi Sparks

Glendale CC CA (14)

Wes Bender
Bruce Bergey
Leo Carroll
Keith Franklin
Bob Gagliano
Mike Hull
Allen Jacobs
Tom Kennedy
Brett Miller
Dick Moje
Bill Schultz
George Smith
Bob Titchenal
Bob White

Golden Valley Lutheran Coll. MN (J.C.) (1)

Dan Johnson

Golden West Coll. CA (J.C.) (8)

Don Fielder
Mark Lomas
Dan MacDonald
Tom Morris
Mark Nichols
Rick Partridge
Van Tuinei
Randy Vataha

Gonzaga (21)

Roger Ashmore
Bob Bellinger
Bill Brian
Mal Bross
Tiny Cahoon
Tony Canadeo
Hec Cyre
Ray Flaherty
Dick Flaherty
Cece Hare
Ray Hare
Ed Justice
George Karamatic
Max Krause
Mike Perko
Ike Peterson
Phil Poth
Gil Skeate
Hust Stockton
Tim Waldron
Billy Wilson

Gordon Coll. GA (J.C.) (3)

Tommy Pharr
Ken Roskie
Stan Stasica

Graceland (1)

Jeff Criswell

Grambling State (99)

Glenn Alexander
Anthony Anderson
Stevie Anderson
Herman Arvie
Bob Atkins
Marvin Ayers
Bob Barber
Garland Boyette
Jason Bratton
Willie Brown
Bill Bryant
Buck Buchanan
Jamie Caleb
Curtis Ceaser
Al Clark
Frank Cornish
Hilton Crawford
Henry Davis
Norman Davis
Willie Davis
Walter Dean
Al Dennis
Al Dotson
Henry Dyer
Greg Fields
Solomon Freelon
J.D. Garrett
Andrew Glover
Tracy Greene
Jim Griffin
Leonard Griffin
James Harris
Michael Harris
Richard Harris
Sam Holden
Delles Howell
Lane Howell
Mike Howell
James Hunter
Charles Johnson
Essex Johnson
Gary Johnson
Trumaine Johnson
Charlie Joiner
Fred Jones
Henry Jones
Ernie Ladd
Albert Lewis
Frank Lewis
Curtis Maxey
Clifton McNeil
John Mendenhall
Darryl Milburn
Roderick Mullen
Derrick Ned
Billy Newsome
Calvin Nicholas
Kerry Parker
Carlos Pennywell
Robert Pennywell
Woody Peoples
Preston Powell
Guy Prather
Bruce Radford
Jake Reed
Albert Reese
Al Richardson
Vern Roberson
Jerry Robinson
Virgil Robinson
Mike St. Clair
Michael Samson
Dwight Scales
Ed Scott
Patrick Scott
Goldie Sellers
Leon Simmons
Nate Singleton
Ron Singleton
Charlie Smith
Mike Smith
Robert Smith
Sean Smith
Rosey Taylor
Sammie Taylor
Bennie Thompson
Everson Walls
Ed Watson
Arthur Wells
Sammy White
Doug Williams
Joe Williams
Roger Williams
Willie Williams
Nemiah Wilson
Robert Woods
Willie Young
Paul Younger
Coleman Zeno

Grand Rapids CC MI (2)

Bob Lurtsema
Carl Powell

Grand Valley State (7)

Jeff Chadwick
Ron Essink
Rick Johnson
Eric Lynch
Frank Miotke
Rob Rubick
Mike Sheldon

Grays Harbor Coll. WA (J.C.) (4)

Mike Melinkovich
Bob Rozier
Jerry Sherk
Harry Washington

Grinnell (2)

Ben Douglas
Hap Moran

Grossmont Coll. CA (J.C.) (10)

Evan Arapostathis
Robert Claiborne
Brad Daluiso
Bill Ferguson
Dan Melville
Larry Moore
Ronnie O'Bard
Brian Sipe
Jay Taylor
Casey Tiumalu

Grove City (10)

Don Batchelor
Harry Brian
Larry Critchfield
Butch Gibson
Ben Jones
Mose Lantz
Alec Sofish
Dave Tallant
Leo Tobin
Eddie Wall

Guilford (2)

Art Faircloth
Sam Venuto

Gulf Coast CC FL (1)

Nicky Savoie

Gustavus Adolphus (8)

Wendell Butcher
Tom Harmon
Bob Lundell
LaDue Lurth
Bernie Nygren
Lloyd Parsons
Kurt Ploeger
Earl Witte

Hagerstown JC MD (1)

Mike Holston

Hamline (10)

Duane Benson
Carl Cramer
Don Eliason
Ira Haaven
Ave Kaplan
Cully Lidberg
Marty Norton
Les Scott
John Simons
Hal Truesdell

Hampden-Sydney (3)

Tom Miller
Harry Myles
Stu Worden

Hampton (14)

Clarence Bailey
Johnnie Barnes
Tom Casey
Reggie Doss
Mike Jenkins
Emerson Martin
Carl Painter
Ike Readon
Lucien Reeberg
Mike Robinson
Donovan Rose
Torin Smith
Cordell Taylor
Terrence Warren

Hardin-Simmons (28)

Pat Batten
Jug Bennett
Dewey Bohling
Harry Burrus
Ed Cherry
Gene Cockrell
Ogden Compton
Odis Crowell
Wayne Davenport
Murray Evans
Owen Goodnight
Billy Harris
Pete Hart
Al Johnson
Bob McChesney
Mike Mercer
Rudy Mobley
Dave Parker
Swede Pittman
Hal Prescott
Dave Ribble
Dave Ryan
Ed Sprinkle
Harold Stephens
John Treadaway
Bulldog Turner
Pete Tyler
Camp Wilson

Harford CC MD (2)

Randy McMillan
Greg Paterra

Harold Washington Coll. IL (J.C.) (1)

Wayne Smith

Hartnell Coll. CA (J.C.) (8)

Ed Brown
Don Burke
Greg Cox
Greg Fields
Jim Mankins
Rocky Thompson
Anthony Toney
Henry Williams

Harvard (24)

Joe Azelby
Matt Birk
Stanley Burnham
Roger Caron
Eddie Casey
Charlie Clark
Bill Craven
Harrie Dadmun
John Dockery
Carl Etelman
Earl Evans
Herman Gundlach
Arnie Horween
Ralph Horween
Dan Jiggetts
Dick King
Bobby Leo
Joe McGlone
Pat McInally
Al Miller
Joe Murphy
Joseph Pellegrini
Red Steele
Richie Szaro

Haskell Indian (19)

Ted Buffalo
Alvro Casey
Bob Choate
Orien Crow
Chief Elkins
Lou Jennings
Larry Johnson
Buck Jones
Nick Lassa
Nat McCombs
Firpo McGilbra
Chief McLain
Emmett McLemore
Chief Mullen
George Nix
Joe Pappio
Stan Powell
David Ward
Rabbit Weller

Hastings (2)

Jerry Drake
Tom Osborne

Hawaii (59)

Sneeze Achiu
Theo Adams
Charles Aiu
Mike Akiu
Gary Allen
Jim Asmus
Dan Audick
Kerry Brady
Tim Buchanan
James Burton
Raphel Cherry
Larry Cole
Paul Dombroski
Jim Dombrowski
Jason Elam
Nuu Faaola
Ta'ase Faumui
Harry Field
Blane Gaison
Leo Goeas
John Gordon
Ron Hall
Wilbert Haslip
John Hoffman
Thad Jefferson
M.L. Johnson
Lyndell Jones
June Jones
Kurt Kafentzis
Mark Kafentzis
Kani Kauahi
Dana McLemore
Rich Miano
Jim Mills
Arnold Morgado
Walter Murray
Johnny Naumu
Al Noga
Niko Noga
Peter Noga
Bernard Quarles
Mike Rengel
Golden Richards
Jesse Sapolu
Jerry Scanlan
Henry Schichtle
Colin Scotts
Jack Sims
Art Smith
Hal Stringert
Jeff Sydner
Maa Tanuvasa
Johnny Taylor
Mel Tom
Mark Tuinei
Tom Tuinei
Kimo von Oelhoffen
Jeris White
John Woodcock

Heidelberg (10)

Jim Boeke
Bob Briggs
Bill Groman
Bob Hunt
Merle Hutson
Walt LeJeune
Walt Livingston
Al Michaels
David Nelson
Otto Vokaty

Henderson State (7)

Marvell Burgess
Roy Green
Daniel Hunter
Todd Jones
Billy Lefear
Earnest Rhone
Robert Thomas

Hibbing CC MN (2)

Joseph Chrape
Joe Maras

Highland CC KS (3)

Jeff George
Terry Joyce
Felix Wright

Hillsdale (4)

Nate Johnson
Chester Marcol
Bruce McLenna
Howard Mudd

Hinds CC MS (18)

Ray Abruzzese
Corey Bradford
John Copeland
Zack Crockett
Jeff Fields
Antonio Gibson
Hason Graham
Grady Jackson
Melvin Jenkins
Earl Leggett
Leon Lett
Bucky McElroy
Michael Myers
Mark Smith
Marcus Spriggs
Jim Taylor
Gary Walker
Marvin Washington

Hiram (2)

Jimmie Kennedy
Bob Spiers

Hobart (4)

George Barna
Don Dimmick
Fred King
Babe Kraus

Hofstra (11)

Frank Bianchini
Wayne Chrebet
Lou D'Agostino
Mike D'Amato
Dave Fiore
Don Gault
Terry Kosens
Fran Lynch
John Schmitt
Lance Schulters
Wandy Williams

Holmes CC MS (8)

Randy Baldwin
Ode Burrell
Terry Day
Willie Fears
Clarence Harmon
Walter Jones
Greg Robinson
Duane Starks

Holy Cross (71)

Bill Adams
Tom Alberghini
Alec Anderson
Fritz Barzilauskas
Peter Bove
Phil Branon
Ed Brawley
Leo Brennan
Eddie Britt
Bernard Buzyniski
Ronnie Cahill
Charlie Carton
Stu Clancy
George Connor
Doug Cosbie
Bill Cregar
Bob Dee
Mark Devlin
Bernie Digris
Gill Fenerty
Bernie Finn
Jim Fitzgerald
Harry Flaherty
Franny Garvey
Frank Gaziano
Denny Gildea
Archie Golembeski
Tom Greene
John Grigas
Tom Hennessey
Ken Holley
Ed Jenkins
Bill Joyce
Jimmy Kennedy
Vito Kissell
Paul Kittredge
Bruce Kozerski
Stan Kozlowski
Ted Kucharski
Jim Landrigan
Jack Lentz
Tony Manfreda
Frank Mattiace
Jerry McCabe
Rob McGovern
Dick McGrath
Harry McMahon
Ed McNamara
Ray Monaco
Jim Moran
Jon Morris
Andy Natowich
John Nolan
Frank O'Connor
Joe Osmanski
Bill Osmanski
Rob Porter
Vince Promuto
George Pyne
Hop Riopel
Tony Rovinski
Ken Simendinger
Al Snyder
Bob Sullivan
Bill Swiacki
George Titus
Si Titus
Joe Wilson
Alex Wizbicki
Joe Zeno
Jim Zyntell

Holy Cross (Ind.) (1)

Tony Brooks

Houston (111)

Willis Adams
Allen Aldridge
Dalva Allen
Earl Allen
Kimble Anders
Joey Banes
Dave Barrett
Don Bass
Tom Beer
Carlos Bell
Royce Berry
Dan Birdwell
Alois Blackwell
Kent Branstetter
Greg Brezina
Bobby Brezina
Charlie Brown
Chuck Brown
Don Brown
Guy Brown
Reggie Burnette
Bo Burris
Glenn Cadrez
Paul Carr
Bobby Clatterbuck
Chuck Clements
Mike Clendenen
Jim Colvin
Carl Cunningham
Tom Dimmick
James Dixon
Wiley Feagin
Simon Fletcher
Don Flynn
Charlie Ford
Eddie Foster
Charlie Fowler
Pat Franklin

Steve George
Robert Giblin
Paul Gipson
Mike Gisler
Charlie Hall
Jim Harris
Ken Hebert
Jimmy Herndon
Carl Hilton
Gus Hollomon
Joe Bob Isbell
Johnnie Jackson
Curley Johnson
Marshall Johnson
Melvin Jones
Donald Jordan
Larry Keller
Billy Kidd
J.D. Kimmel
Claude King
David Klingler
Lamar Lathon
Hal Lewis
Errol Linden
Everett Little
Eugene Lockhart
Randy Love
Dedric Mathis
Don McDonald
Audray McMillian
Warren McVea
Ostell Miles
Billy Milner
Leonard Mitchell
Mack Mitchell
Alton Montgomery
Glenn Montgomery
Monty Montgomery
Don Mullins
Robert Newhouse
Jim Norris
Riley Odoms
Alfred Oglesby
Johnny Peacock
Jason Phillips
Dickie Post
Leonta Rheams
Charlie Rieves
Hal Roberts
Willie Roberts
Craig Robinson
Larry Rowden
Mike Simpson
Antowain Smith
Lamar Smith
Marcus Spriggs
Richard Stotter
Jim Strong
Pat Studstill
Hosea Taylor
Earl Thomas
Ed Thomas
T.J. Turner
Craig Veasey
Andre Ware
Chuck Weatherspoon
Hogan Wharton
Wilson Whitley
Daryl Wilkerson
Gerome Williams
Jermaine Williams
Bryant Winn
Elmo Wright

Howard (15)

Derrick Faison
Rupert Grant
Gary Harrell
Billy Jenkins
Jimmie Johnson
Troy Kyles
Ron Mabra
Ted St. Germaine
Robert Sowell
Sean Vanhorse
Jay Walker
Tim Watson
Jose White
Howie Williams
Steve Wilson

Howard Coll. TX (J.C.) (1)

Jim Evans

Howard Payne (13)

Howard Carson
Dobie Craig
Keith Crawford
Ken Gray
Jim Hargrove
Jim Harlan
Jim Harris
Ray Jacobs
Ernest Kirk
Michael Mitchell
Ken Sanders
Buck White
Bob Young

Hudson Valley CC NY (1)

Leander Knight

Humboldt State (6)

Richard Ashe
Mike Bettiga
Len Gotshalk
Dave Harper
Wendell Hayes
R.W. Hicks

Hutchinson CC KS (5)

Gordon Brown
Jerome Dove
Mack Herron
Aaron Manning
Curtis Townsend

Idaho (52)

Art Anderson
Dick Arndt
Brant Bengen
Ted Bucklin
Richard Carey
Reggie Carolan
Larry Coombs
Tom Coombs
Charlie Diehl
Stan Fanning
Bob Fitzke
Spencer Folau
John Foruria
Ralph Foster
John Friesz
Randy Hall
Jerry Hendren
Mike Hollis
Eddie Howard
Kevin Juma
Jerry Kramer
Max Leetzow
Calvin Loveall
Sherriden May
Ray McDonald
Sam Merriman
Bill Miklich
Jim Mills
Jim Moran
John Norby
Jim Norton
Doug Nussmeier
Ronnie O'Bard
Steve Parker
Stan Pavkov
Joe Pellegrini
Ryan Phillips
Ron Porter
Jim Prestel
Jeff Robinson
Mark Schlereth
Bill Scott
Wee Willie Smith
Ray Stephens
Joe Taibi
Bob Van Duyne
John Vesser
Wayne Walker
Marvin Washington
Jerry Williams
Eric Yarber
John Yarno

Idaho State (19)

Shawn Beals
Eddie Bell
Mike Busch
Matt Courtney
Case deBruijn
Jamie Fitzgerald
Will Grant
Mike Hancock
Merril Hoge
Dan MacDonald
Mike Machurek
Donald Miller
Joe Moreino
Ken O'Neal
Bob Otto
John Roman
Tom Toner
Brian Vertefeuille
Jim Wagstaff

Illinois (210)

Ron Acks
Earnest Adams
Alex Agase
Mel Agee
Derek Allen
Paul Anderson
Clarence Applegran
Kelvin Atkins
John Bauer
Tim Beamer
Mike Bellamy
George Bernhardt
Gil Berry
Marv Berschet
Dwight Beverly
Les Bingaman
Ken Blackman
Wayne Bock
Chuck Boerio
Ron Bohm
Cap Boso
Jim Bradshaw
Ed Brady
Earl Britton
Mitchell Brookins
Al Brosky
Bill Brown
Darrick Brownlow
Lloyd Burdick
Dick Butkus
Darryl Byrd
Chuck Carney
James Caroline
Len Charpier
Steve Collier
Dave Cook
Johnny Counts
Jack Crangle
Mush Crawford
Russ Daugherity
Scott Davis
Mark Dennis
Jack Depler
Wayne DeSutter
Doug Dieken
Ken Dilger
George Donnelly
Ty Douthard
Clarence Drayer
Tony Eason
Dave Edwards
Greg Engel
Ron Ferrari
Dave Finzer
Moe Gardner
Curtis Garrett
Jeff George
Alec Gibson
John Gillen
Willard Goff
Lou Gordon
Jim Grabowski
Gardie Grange
Red Grange
African Grant
Chris Green
Vee Green
Don Greenwood
Don Griffin
Howard Griffith
George Halas
Dick Hall
Harry Hall
Bernie Halstrom
Don Hansen
Dave Harbour
Kevin Hardy
Lance Harkey
Frank Hartley
Tom Hicks
Robert Holcombe
John Holecek
Brad Hopkins
Dana Howard
Burt Ingwersen
T.J. Jackson
John Janata
Filmel Johnson
Mike Johnson
Nate Johnson
Rich Johnson
Henry Jones
Keith Jones
Jim Juriga
Johnny Karras
Mike Kasap
Chuck Kassel
Eddie Kawal
Scott Kehoe
Tony Klimek
Oscar Knop
Sam Knox
Eddie Kotal
Bill Kovacsy
Ren Kraft
Joe Krakoski
Rich Kreitling
Jake Lanum
Lou Levanti
Adam Lingner
Lynn Lynch
Chick Maggioli
Jeff Markland
Mike Martin
Larry McCarren
Jim McCarthy
Wally McIlwain
Ernie McMillan
Jim McMillen
Terry Miller
Bobby Mitchell
Max Morris
Perry Moss
Vern Mullen
Bob Naponic
Packie Nelson
Sid Nichols
Ray Nitschke
Tim Norman
Ed O'Bradovich
Tommy O'Connell
Russ Oltz
Vince Osby
Willie Osley
Ike Owens
Paul Patterson
Preston Pearson
Pete Perez
Lonnie Perrin
Frosty Peters
Larry Petty
Ross Petty
Mike Piel
Steve Pierce
Bert Piggott
Cyril Pinder
Paul Podmajersky
Eli Popa
Sammy Price
Dick Reichle
Simeon Rice
Ted Richards
Harry Richman
Cliff Roberts
Bob Robertson
Swede Rundquist
Joe Rutgens
Rocky Ryan
Julie Rykovich
Rick Schulte
Gregg Schumacher
Bud Schwenk
Mike Scully
Hub Shoemake
Herb Siegert
Wayne Siegert
Rich Siler
Tim Simpson
Russ Smith
Revie Sorey
Jack Squirek
Dennis Stallings
Basil Stanley
Marshall Starks
Stan Stasica
Dutch Sternaman
Joey Sternaman
Don Stevens
Scott Studwell
Jerry Sturm
Steve Sucic
Gerry Sullivan
John Sullivan
Archie Sutton
Craig Swoope
Mike Taliaferro
Keith Taylor
Guy Teafatiller
Calvin Thomas
Bruce Thornton
Don Thorp
Jack Trudeau
Bob Trumpy
Scott Turner
Chuck Ulrich
Darryl Usher
Stan Wallace
Bill Waller
Laurie Walquist
Jimmy Warren
Mike Wells
Joe Wendryhoski
David Williams
Oliver Williams
Brett Wilson
Dave Wilson
Abe Woodson
John Wright
Buddy Young
Jerry Zeller

Illinois Benedictine (1)

Rob DeVita

Illinois State (17)

Duane Butler
Clarence Collins
Creig Federico
Brian Gant
Curtis Garrett
Jeff George
Estus Hood
Jason Johnson
Jim Meyer
Dennis Nelson
Tony Office
Larry Petty
Mike Prior
Mark Rodenhauser
Peter Shorts
Joe Washington
Steve Wilburn

Illinois Tech (4)

Joe Carey
Lou Merillat
George Schmidt
Joe Vodicka

Illinois Wesleyan (8)

Tony Blazine
Dick Folk
Tony Kaska
Bill Larson
Mike Mergen
Bob Morrow
Bob Neuman
Chet Wetterlund

Imperial Valley Coll. CA (J.C.) (2)

Ron Jessie
Joe Lavender

Independence CC KS (8)

Levert Carr
Bobby Johnson
Bruce McCray
Bobby Morgan
Reggie Rembert
Warren Thompson
Dick Tyson
Ron Warner

Indian Hills CC IA (6)

Tony Galbreath
Larry Horton
Wonder Monds
Eddie Moss
Ricky Stevenson
Rick Upchurch

Indiana (157)

Abe Addams
Kevin Allen
Marty Amsler
Joe Amstutz
Cliff Anderson
John Andrews
John Aveni
Richie Badar
Carl Barzilauskas
Ian Beckles
Randy Beisler
Ed Bell
Len Bell
Chuck Bennett
Dan Bernoske
Nate Borden
Nate Borders
Steve Bradley
Howie Brown
Lance Brown
Mike Bucchianeri
Art Bultman
Milt Campbell
John Cannady
Chick Cichowski
Terry Cole
Bob Cowan
Don Croftcheck
Doug Crusan
Slats Dalrymple
Doc Davis
Nathan Davis
Corby Davis
Stacey Dawsey
Bob DeMarco
Jim Dewar
Troy Drake
Mike Dumas
Vaughn Dunbar
Joey Eloms
Archie Erehart
Earl Faison
Frank Filchock
George Fisher
Mike Friede
Lu Gambino
Chris Gartner
Gene Gedman
John Goldsberry
Earl Goldsmith
Ralph Goldston
Moses Gray
Trent Green
Alex Green
Andrew Greene
Mel Groomes
Rex Grossman
Bob Haak
Duke Hanny
Shawn Harper
Nolan Harrison
Russ Hathaway
Wally Hess
Billy Hillenbrand
Bob Hoernschemeyer
Bobby Howard
Tubby Howard
Vern Huffman
John Isenbarger
Chick Jagade
Harry Jagielski
Larry Jameson
John Johnson
Ken Johnson
Bobby Jones
Ernie Jones
Tim Jorden
Walt Jurkiewicz
Ted Karras
George Karstens
Rudy Kuechenberg
Johnny Kyle
Babe Laufenberg
Chuck Leo
John Leonard
Thomas Lewis
Ted Livingston
Chris Liwienski
Jim Logan
Hugh Lowery
Don Luft
Chick Maggioli
Bill Malinchak
Larry Marks
Joe Matesic
Charlie Mathys
Bill McCaw
Hurvin McCormack
Mike McCurry
Dustin McDonald
Arnold Mickens
Lou Mihajlovich
Lamar Mills
Eric Moore
Chris Morris
Joe Norman
Tom Nowatzke
Stu O'Dell
Vince Oliver
Pete Pihos
Spencer Pope
Mike Rabold
Ken Radick
Ben Raimondi
Clare Randolph
Am Rascher
Bob Ravensberg
Bob Riley
Carroll Ringwalt
Elliot Risley
Eddie Rucinski
Lou Saban
Charlie Scales
Glenn Scolnik
Wilbert Scott
Nick Sebek
Mike Sikora
Bob Skoronski
Eric Smedley
Jim Sniadecki
Cal Snowden
Rob Spicer
Pete Stoyanovich
Dan Stryzinski
Kywin Supernaw
George Taliaferro
John Tavener
Donnie Thomas
Anthony Thompson
Ernie Thompson
Joe Tofil
Emil Uremovich
Van Waiters
Craig Walls
Damon Watts
Gene White
Bob Whitlow
Dave Whitsell
Bernard Whittington
Elmer Wilkens
Travis Williams
Trevor Wilmot
Slug Witucki
Marv Woodson
Joe Zeller
Bob Zimny
Dick Zoll

Indiana (Pa.) (10)

Jim Angelo
Milo Gwosden
Jim Haslett
Ben Jones
Bill Kellogg
Ben Lawrence
Harry Malcolm
Bret Shugarts
Dave Smith
Chris Villarrial

Indiana State (11)

John Bock
Dan Brandenburg
Jim Brumfield
Wayne Davis
Vencie Glenn
Fred Graham
Tunch Ilkin
Nate Ramsey
Craig Shaffer
Mike Simmonds
Charles Swann

Indianapolis (1)

Dick Nyers

Iona (1)

Laz Chavez

Iowa (174)

John Alt
Frank Balasz
Tavian Banks
Rob Baxley
Rick Bayless
Dave Becker
Les Belding
Nick Bell
Mark Bortz
Hal Bradley
Harold Bradley
Bill Briggs
Richard Brown
Rudy Bukich
Don Chelf
Craig Clemons
Marv Cook
Kerry Cooks
Al Couppee
Dick Crayne
Dave Croston
Scott Davis
John Derby
Joe Devlin
Mike Devlin
Dan Dickel
Earl Douthitt
Jeff Drost
Randy Duncan
Tim Dwight
Quinn Early
Harold Ely
Larry Ely
Dick Evans
Tom Farmer
Larry Ferguson
Karl Finch
Darrell Fisher
Greg Fitzgerald
Bill Fleckenstein
Bob Fosdick
Wes Fry
Nick Gallery
Chris Gambol
Ron Geater
Jim Gibbons
Damon Gibson
Owen Gill
Bill Glassgow
Mike Goff
Norm Granger
Glenn Greenwood
Hal Griffen
Harry Gunderson
Horse Hagerty
Mike Haight
John Hall
Ron Hallstrom
Merton Hanks
Kevin Harmon
Ronnie Harmon
John Harty
Jonathan Hayes
Jack Heldt
Jay Hilgenberg
Joel Hilgenberg
Wally Hilgenberg
Dick Hoerner
Larry Horton
Walt Housman
Sherman Howard
Danan Hughes
Tom Humphrey
Jim Jensen
Leo Jensvold
Ernie Jessen
Bob Jeter
Max Kadesky
Alex Karras
Jim Keane
Matt Kelsch
Nick Kerasiotis
Dick Klein
Bruce Klosterman
Tom Knight
Bob Kratch
Paul Krause
Paul Laaveg
Bill Lapham
Pete Lauer
Larry Lawrence
Joe Laws
Mac Lewis
George Little
Chuck Long
Dave Long
Forrest Masterson
Gus Mastrogany
Dan McGwire
Chief McLain
Bill McWilliams
Bus Mertes
Curt Merz
Brett Miller
Jim Miller
Paul Minick
Devon Mitchell
Charlie Mockmore
Dean Moore
Joe Mott

Denny Myers
Don Nelson
Bruno Niedziela
John Niland
Jerry Niles
John Nocera
Karl Noonan
Don Norton
Jay Norvell
Clem Nugent
Forrest Olson
Glenn Olson
Lowell Otte
Oran Pape
Bill Perkins
Carl Pignatelli
Paul Podmajersky
Ed Podolak
Derek Price
Kenny Price
Al Randolph
Kerry Reardon
Dave Recher
Bill Reichardt
Jerry Reichow
Mike Reilly
Fred Roberts
Damien Robinson
Reggie Roby
Jon Roehlk
George Rogge
Ollie Sansen
Zud Schammel
Vin Schleusner
Herm Schneidman
Sedrick Shaw
Bob Sherman
Hal Shoener
Herbert Shoener
Ken Sims
Duke Slater
Scott Slutzker
Bob Smith
Tom Smith
Larry Station
Mike Stoops
Bob Sullivan
John Synhorst
Ryan Terry
George Thompson
Andre Tippett
Chuck Tollefson
Emlen Tunnell
Sam Vacanti
Ross Verba
Mark Vlasic
Scott Von der Ahe
Rod Walters
Mike Wells
Casey Wiegmann
Bill Windauer
Dick Woodard
Pudge Wyland
Jim Youel

Iowa Central CC (3)

John Matuszak
Henry Reed
Charlie White

Iowa State (74)

Jeff Allen
George Amundson
Terrence Anthony
David Archer
Tony Baker
Dick Barker
Eppie Barney
Joe Beauchamp
Bill Berthusen
Matt Blair
Luther Blue
Carl Brettschneider
Stan Campbell
Tommy Campbell
Dean Carlson
Larry Carwell
Ozzie Clay
Hal Crisler
Dwayne Crutchfield
Pat Curran
Troy Davis
Al Dixon
Jim Doran
Todd Doxzon
Alex Espinoza
Mike Fitzgerald
Dennis Gibson
Kelly Goodburn
Buddy Hardeman
Ike Harris
Charles Heileman
Brad Henke
Barry Hill
Chuck Hill
Andrew Jackson
Vince Jasper
Bob Jensen
Dan Johnson
Dick Kasperek
Merv Krakau
Keith Krepfle
Chuck Lamson

Greg Liter
Roy Longstreet
Aaron Manning
Frank Mayer
Dave McCurry
Chuck Muelhaupt
Kenny Neil
Karl Nelson
Mark Nelson
Tony Norman
Tom Randall
Lew Reeve
Bruce Reimers
Guy Roberts
Marcus Robertson
Oliver Ross
Clyde Shugart
Keith Sims
Mike Stensrud
Otto Stowe
Mike Strachan
Eli Strand
Viv Vanderloo
Tim Van Galder
Tom Vaughn
Chuck Walton
Chris Washington
Tom Watkins
Don Webb
Gene Williams
Kevin Williams
Randy Young

Iowa Wesleyan (1)

Sandy Sandberg

Isothermal CC NC (1)

Percy Howard

Itawamba CC MS (9)

Tim Bowens
Ernest Dye
Jason Ferguson
Norman Hand
Joe Horn
Oren Middlebrook
Aaron Pearson
Wardell Rouse
Duce Staley

Ithaca (1)

Joe D'Orazio

Ivy Tech State-SW IN (J.C.) (1)

Marty Amsler

Jackson State (85)

Eric Austin
Coy Bacon
Jerome Barkum
Buster Barnett
Tim Barnett
Lem Barney
Roy Bennett
Verlon Biggs
Corey Bradford
Robert Brazile
Louis Bullard
Chris Burkett
Reggie Carr
Rich Caster
Al Coleman
Darion Conner
Larry Cowan
Roy Curry
Bobby Curtis
Oakley Dalton
Speedy Duncan
Larry Franklin
Tom Funchess
Leon Gray
Al Greer
Ed Hardy
Larry Hardy
Robert Hardy
Perry Harrington
James Harvey
Richard Harvey
Jim Hayes
Roy Hilton
Jim Holifield
Lester Holmes
Houston Hoover
Bill Houston
Bob Hughes
Harold Jackson
Claudis James
Mike Jones
Tony Kimbrough
James Marshall
Steve Martin
Ben McGee
Paul McJulien
Stacey Mobley
Frank Molden
Fred Molden

Wilbert Montgomery
Jeff Moore
Leonard Moore
John Outlaw
Ricky Patton
Eddie Payton
Walter Payton
Marlo Perry
Vernon Perry
Rod Phillips
Dan Pride
Taft Reed
Don Reese
Ernie Richardson
Gloster Richardson
Tom Richardson
Willie Richardson
Leon Seals
Cleo Simmons
Jackie Slater
Fernando Smith
Jimmy Smith
Sylvester Stamps
Robert Staten
Thomas Strauthers
Frank Sutton
John Tate
Lee Thomas
Lewis Tillman
Jackie Walker
Charles Williams
Ladell Wills
David Windham
Roscoe Word
Rickey Young
Emanuel Zanders

Jacksonville State (10)

Jesse Baker
Ralph Battle
Dieter Brock
Walter Broughton
Eric Davis
David Gulledge
Darrell Malone
Keith McKeller
Terry Owens
Alvin Wright

James Madison (6)

Gary Clark
Dion Foxx
Charles Haley
Warren Marshall
Scott Norwood
Ed Perry

Jamestown (1)

John Thomas

John Carroll (10)

Graham Armstrong
Ed Ecker
London Fletcher
Pat Lahey
Chuck McMillan
Ted Rosequist
Burrell Shields
Don Shula
Gene Stringer
Carl Taseff

Johnson C. Smith (10)

Tim Beamer
Greg Clifton
Kelvin Davis
Bill Dusenbery
Benny Johnson
Donnell Johnson
Harris Jones
Tim Newman
Pettis Norman
Bob Wells

Johnson Co. CC KS (1)

Ken Jolly

Joliet JC IL (3)

Cap Boso
Ken Knapczyk
Derrell Mitchell

Jones Co. JC MS (6)

George Gulyanics
George Herring
Marcus Keyes
James Logan
Orpheus Roye
Larry Suchy

Kalamazoo (4)

John Cameron

Mike Casteel
Marty Conrad
Frank Fausch

Kansas (123)

John Amberg
Jim Bailey
Chris Banks
Frank Bausch
Jim Bausch
Terry Beeson
Bill Bell
Roger Bernhardt
Charlie Black
Tony Blevins
Deral Boykin
Dorian Brew
Gilbert Brown
Larry Brown
Fred Bukaty
Hal Burt
Mike Butler
Isaac Byrd
Sylvester Byrd
Billy Campfield
Wayne Capers
Bert Coan
Jeff Colter
Steve Conley
Kirby Criswell
Nolan Cromwell
Dick Davis
Don Davis
John Detwiller
Tom Dinkel
Bobby Douglass
Emmett Edwards
Richard Estell
Don Ettinger
Ray Evans
Paul Fairchild
Galen Fiss
Matt Gay
Chris Golub
Don Goode
Forrest Griffith
John Hadl
Fred Hageman
Bob Hantla
George Harvey
Hessley Hempstead
June Henley
Johnny Holloway
Mike Hubach
LeRoy Irvin
David Jaynes
Ron Jessie
Bobby Johnson
Mike Johnson
E.J. Jones
Rod Jones
George Kennard
Kurt Knoff
Zvonimir Kvaternik
Kwamie Lassiter
Bud Laughlin
Steve Lawson
Mike Lemon
Eddie Lewis
Keith Loneker
Mike Loyd
Lindsey Mason
Chris Maumalanga
Gerald McBurrows
Curtis McClinton
Mike McCormack
Pete Mehringer
Monte Merkel
Robert Miller
John Mosier
George Mrkonic
Steve Nave
Mike Norseth
Paul Oswald
Gery Palmer
Elvis Patterson
Don Pierce
Jerry Quick
John Riggins
Tom Robertson
Gale Sayers
Elmer Schaake
Doyle Schick
Otto Schnellbacher
Brian Schweda
Dave Scott
Bucky Scribner
Frank Seurer
Greg Smith
Hugh Smith
Laverne Smith
Quintin Smith
Reggie Smith
Waddell Smith
Ollie Spencer
Sims Stokes
Dana Stubblefield
Mitch Sutton
Harry Sydney
Steve Taylor
Doug Terry
Broderick Thompson
Dick Tomlinson
Steve Towle
Hub Ulrich

Vern Vanoy
David Verser
Dan Wagoner
Alvin Walton
Ronnie Ward
Ron Warner
Frank Wattelet
Mike Wellman
Bobby Whitten
Delvin Williams
Wandy Williams
Sylvester Wright
John Zook

Kansas State (97)

Elijah Alexander
Gerald Alphin
Eric Bailey
Monte Bennett
Greg Best
Keith Best
Barrett Brooks
Greg Brown
Larry Brown
Tom Bushby
Bill Butler
Don Calhoun
Russ Campbell
Chris Canty
Henry Childs
Steven Clark
Paul Coffman
Will Cokeley
Andre Coleman
Tim Colston
Willis Crenshaw
Doc Cronkhite
Steve Crosby
Willie Cullars
Lynn Dickey
Bob Douglas
Jack Epps
Dale Evans
Tiny Feather
DeShawn Fogle
Jerrell Franklin
Scott Fulhage
Jim Furey
Percell Gaskins
Eugene Goodlow
Ira Gordon
Rogerick Green
Steve Grogan
Elmer Hackney
Ray Hahn
Homer Hanson
M.L. Harris
Larry Hartshorn
Maurice Henry
Mack Herron
Doug Hoppock
Jeff Hurd
Tim Jackson
Kendyl Jacox
Clyde Johnson
Damian Johnson
Jason Johnson
Al Jolley
Dave Jones
Willie Jones
Tony Jordan
Jerry Krysl
Lynn Larson
Ted Livingston
Kevin Lockett
Babe Lyon
Buster Maddox
Dan Manucci
Ron Marciniak
Bill Matan
Harry McGee
Les Miller
Mike Montgomery
Jim Bob Morris
Dennis Morrison
Lyle Munn
Ron Nery
Quentin Neujahr
Ralph Nichols
Mike Osborn
Bert Pearson
Norbert Raemer
Proc Randels
Thomas Randolph
Ray Romero
Fred Rothwell
Doug Russell
Clarence Scott
Dick Sears
Lee Shaffer
Michael Smith
Gary Spani
Art Strozier
Marvin Switzer
Veryl Switzer
Cookie Tackwell
Corky Taylor
James Walker
Dutch Webber
Bernie Weiner
Todd Weiner
Ron Yankowski

Kemper Mil. School MO (J.C.) (1)

Tim Hall

Kennedy King Coll. IL (J.C.) (1)

Kevin Gray

Kent State (32)

Willie Asbury
Joe Barbee
Art Best
Robert Brannon
Cedric Brown
Todd Feldman
Pat Gucciardo
Bob Hallen
Andy Harmon
Lou Harris
Bob Hein
Scott Hernandez
Keno Hills
Van Jakes
Jack Lambert
Mike McGruder
Mike McKibben
Pete Mikolajewski
Rich Mostardo
Don Nottingham
Luke Owens
Larry Poole
Abdul Salaam
O.J. Santiago
Timothy Starks
Gerald Tinker
Ray Wagner
Ken Walter
Bert Weidner
Eric Wilkerson
Dana Wright
Mike Zele

Kentucky (118)

George Adams
Ermal Allen
Sam Ball
Oliver Barnett
Rodger Bird
George Blanda
Jerry Blanton
Chuck Bradley
Jeff Brady
Warren Bryant
Cornell Burbage
Randy Burke
Bob Butler
Sonny Collins
Doug Davis
Bob Davis
Dermontti Dawson
Gene Donaldson
Thom Dornbrook
Bob Dougherty
Maurice Douglass
Jon Dumbauld
Tom Ehlers
John Eibner
Joe Federspiel
Don Fielder
Dan Fowler
Bob Fry
Dom Fucci
Frank Fuller
Bob Gain
Carwell Gardner
Donnie Gardner
Irv Goode
Will Grant
Edd Gregg
John Grimsley
Herb Gruber
Russell Hairston
Steve Hall
Dick Hensley
Mark Higgs
Van Hiles
Ivy Joe Hunter
Tom Hutchinson
Cam Jacobs
Bert Johnson
Clyde Johnson
D.J. Johnson
Melvin Johnson
Shipwreck Kelly
Ralph Kercheval
Don King
Kelly Kirchbaum
Doug Kotar
Jim Kovach
Bill Leach
Frank LeMaster
Joe Lindahl
Luke Lindon
Dale Lindsey
Jim Little
Marc Logan
Dicky Lyons
Pete Marcus
Rick Massie
Tony Mayes
Bubba McCollum

Lloyd McDermott
John McVeigh
Steve Meilinger
Lou Michaels
Marty Moore
Mo Moorman
Noah Mullins
Dan Neal
Bill Netherton
Rick Norton
Rick Nuzum
Dick Palmer
Babe Parilli
Doug Pelfrey
Todd Perry
Wally Pesuit
Don Phelps
Joe Phillips
Jim Ramey
Derrick Ramsey
Jerry Reese
Jay Rhodemyre
Dick Richards
Tom Richey
Dave Roller
Spencer Rork
Reggie Rusk
Terry Samuels
Larry Seiple
Wash Serini
John Shannon
Glenn Shaw
Larry Smith
Art Still
Bob Talamini
Herschel Turner
Harry Ulinski
Jeff Van Note
Chris Ward
Pete Wathen
Dean Wells
Mark Wheeler
Moe Williams
Ken Willis
Earl Wilson
Bob Windsor
Bob Winkel
Cal Withrow
Ralph Wright
Walt Yowarsky

Kentucky State (10)

Sugarfoot Anderson
Rod Hill
Tom Jones
John Kenerson
Dee Martin
Royce McKinney
Frank Oliver
Willie Rodgers
Council Rudolph
Devin Wyman

Kenyon (1)

Herb Stock

Kilgore Coll. TX (J.C.) (11)

George Benyola
Curtis Buckley
Adrian Burk
Bobby Cross
Jorge Diaz
Lenny Dunlap
Glenn Holtzman
Tony Hutson
Buddy Jungmichel
Nolan Luhn
Robbie Tobeck

King Alfred's (England) (1)

John Smith

Kings Point (3)

Bob Pfohl
Bobby Post
Joe Rizzo

Kings River CC CA (7)

Doug Fisher
Dallas Hickman
Goran Lingmerth
Dave Morton
Houston Ridge
Danny Villanueva
Tony Woodruff

Kirkwood CC IA (1)

Troy Stedman

Knox (3)

Lane Bridgford
Bob Prout
Bill Senn

Knoxville (2)

Grady Jackson
Ken Johnson

Kutztown (6)

Doug Dennison
Robert DiRico
Bruce Harper
Michael Kullman
John Mobley
Andre Reed

La Salle (2)

Mike Mandarino
George Somers

La Verne (1)

Joaquin Zendejas

Lafayette (26)

Ed Baker
Al Bedner
Charlie Berry
Matt Brennan
Johnny Budd
Art Deibel
Joe DuMoe
Doc Elliott
Jack Ernst
Adrian Ford
Frank Grube
Frank Kirkleski
Nick Kowgios
Bull Lowe
Bob Millman
Dinty Moore
Milt O'Connell
Vic Reuter
Johnny Scott
George Seasholtz
Johnny Thompson
Larry Walbridge
Bodie Weldon
Joe Williams
Mike Wilson
Walt Zirinsky

Lake City CC FL (1)

Charles Romes

Lake Forest (4)

John Biolo
Mush Crawford
Gar Leaf
Hub Shoemake

Lakeland (2)

Pat Curran
Ron Ferrari

Lakewood CC MN (2)

Rick Danmeier
Doug Greene

Lamar (23)

Billy Bell
Kevin Bell
Chris Brown
Rondy Colbert
Chris Ford
Johnny Fuller
Pat Gibbs
Tony Guillory
Herbert Harris
Bobby Jancik
Danzell Lee
Ed Marcontell
Kevin McArthur
Larry McCoy
Dudley Meredith
Wayne Moore
Keith Powe
Colin Ridgway
Eugene Seale
Tyrone Shavers
Tommie Smiley
Johnny Ray Smith
Bucky White

Lamar CC CO (1)

Andre President

Lane (1)

Fred Lane

Laney Coll. CA (J.C.) (10)

Al Andrews
Leon Burns
Mel Carver
Ray Crouse
Ken Harvey
Sean Manuel
Reggie Redding
Brian Taylor
Norm Thompson
Sherman White

Langston (9)

Mo Bassett
Matt Hatchette
Tom Henderson
Gene Howard
Odell Lawson
Ken Payne
Ed Williams
Gerard Williams
Ricky Williams

Lassen Coll. CA (J.C.) (1)

Jack Ellena

Lawrence (8)

Myrt Basing
Champ Boettcher
Eddie Glick
Eddie Kotal
John McDonald
Rip Owens
Red Smith
Al Zupek

Lebanon Valley (6)

Bull Behman
Hinkey Haines
Two-Bits Homan
Roy Lechthaler
Ken Longenecker
Roy Mackert

Lees-McRae JC NC (5)

Tommy Dawkins
Clark Gaines
Robert Hardy
Calvin Tiggle
Leonard Wheeler

Lehigh (27)

Reed Bohovich
Leo Douglass
John Hill
Bill Hoffman
Marty Horn
Kevin Jefferson
Sam Kaplan
Steve Kreider
Buck MacDonald
Al Maginnes
Dave Maginnes
Joe Mattern
Don McCarthy
Hugh McGoldrick
Kim McQuilken
Ed O'Hearn
Rich Owens
Jack Rizzo
Jim Sanford
Roy Scholl
Herbert Shoener
Ken Simendinger
Butch Spagna
Bill Springsteen
Jack Storer
Mike Wilson
Jim Yeager

Lenoir-Rhyne (5)

Mike Campbell
Craig Keith
Dick Lage
Wes Phillips
Don Testerman

Lewis & Clark (1)

Jon Jaqua

Liberty (11)

Fred Banks
Sebastian Barrie
Dwayne Carswell
Steve Clark
Kelvin Edwards
Eric Green
Wayne Haddix
Mark Mathis
James McKnight
Richard Shelton
Donald Smith

Lincoln (Mo.) (11)

John Arp
Elmer Bailey
Johnnie McDaniel
Zeke Moore
Lemar Parrish
Bill Robinson
John Scardina
Larry Shears
Jim Sullivan
Jim Tolbert
Bob Watters

Lincoln College (1)

Ray MacMurray

Linfield (6)

Paul Dombroski
Howard Glenn
Doug Hire
Randy Marshall
Jim Massey
Wilkie Moody

Livingstone (3)

Ben Coates
Johnny Miller
Wilmont Perry

Lock Haven (2)

John Eisenhooth
Bret Shugarts

Lombard (5)

Swede Hummell
Roddy Lamb
Bill Strickland
Evar Swanson
Alvie Thompson

Lon Morris Coll. TX (J.C.) (1)

John Treadaway

Long Beach City Coll. CA (J.C.) (22)

Greg Barton
Mike Battle
Victor Burnett
Sam Cathcart
Charles Clinton
Gary Garrison
Darryl Hall
Bob Humphreys
Bill Jessup
Charles Jordan
Chris Matau
Gerry McDougall
Charles McShane
Bill Reid
Frank Roy
Don Sasa
Jeff Severson
Terry Tautolo
George Timberlake
Greg Townsend
Erroll Tucker
Kendall Williams

Long Beach State (35)

Mark Bailey
Reggie Berry
Russ Bolinger
Dan Bunz
Leon Burns
Scott Byers
Terrell Davis
Dick Degen
Steve Folsom
Sheldon Gaines
Doug Gaynor
Kwante Hampton
John Hendy
Mike Horan
David Howard
Lynn Hoyem
Ron Johnson
Sidney Justin
R.J. Kors
Charles Lockett
Darren Long
Herb Lusk
Terry Metcalf
Dean Miraldi
Steve Newell
John O'Callaghan
Billy Parks
Darrell Pattillo
Ben Rudolph
Martin Sartin
Roy Schmidt
Mark Seay
Jeff Severson
Les Shy
Jay Walker

Long Island University (2)

Bernie Kapitansky
Bob Trocolor

Loras (6)

Tommy Cronin
Moxie Dalton
Carl George
Bob Hanlon
Ray Oberbroekling
Howie Ruetz

Los Angeles City Coll. CA (J.C.) (17)

Don Bishop
Kent Carter
Milt Davis
Joe Dawkins
Mike Douglass
Clarence Duren
Jack Dwyer
Vince Evans
Harvey Goodman
Reggie Haynes
Woodley Lewis
Rod Martin
Ray May
Don McCall
Hank Rivera
John Sanchez
Harry Thompson

Los Angeles Harbor Coll. CA (J.C.) (9)

Lloyd Edwards
Don Horn
Richard Johnson
Haven Moses
Jimmy Sims
Glen Walker
David Williams
Oliver Williams
Tony Woodruff

Los Angeles Southwest Coll. CA (J.C.) (18)

Larry Brown
Mark Brown
Steve Bryant
Bernard Dafney
James Davis
Karl Farmer
Mark Fields
Cleveland Jackson
Samuel Johnson
Sidney Justin
Jeff McIntyre
Tim McTyer
Chris Mims
Bryan Proby
Ron Scoggins
Waddell Smith
Alonzo Williams
Renard Young

Los Angeles State (14)

John Adams
Ralph Anderson
Don Davis
Fred Gillett
Mitch Johnson
Walter Johnson
Tom Kennedy
Howard Kindig
Dave Ross
Philip Spiller
Bob Voight
Jim Weatherwax
Joe Womack
George Youngblood

Los Angeles Valley Coll. CA (J.C.) (16)

Vernon Dean
Pat Epperson
Brian Goodman
Wyatt Henderson
Floyd Hodge
Holbert Johnson
Kelley Johnson
Charlie Kendall
Odis McKinney
Marv Montgomery
Darrell Pattillo
Jairo Penaranda
Lyle Pickens
Rock Richmond
Jack Steptoe
Eric Yarber

Los Medanos Coll. CA (J.C.) (1)

Jack Larscheid

Louisiana Coll. (1)

Mike Sutton

Louisiana State (190)

Charles Alexander
Dan Alexander
Eric Andolsek
Mitch Andrews
Billy Baggett
Roland Barbay
Walt Barnes
Jeff Barrett
Brett Bech
Karl Bernard
Joe Bernstein
Harold Bishop
Ben Bordelon
Ken Bordelon
Marc Boutte
George Brancato
Mel Branch
Jim Britt
J.W. Brodnax
Michael Brooks
Jeff Burkett
Shawn Burks
Clinton Burrell
Young Bussey
Billy Cannon
Warren Capone
Carlos Carson
Tommy Casanova
Jim Cason
Toby Caston
Ed Champagne
Ricky Chatman
Ray Coates
Pat Coffee
Ray Collins
Rip Collins
Bill Crass
Jeffery Dale
Eugene Daniel
Ramsey Dardar
Kenny Davidson
Brad Davis
Tommy Davis
Wendell Davis
John Demarie
A.J. Duhe
Karl Dunbar
Bill Elko
Don Estes
Alan Faneca
Herman Fontenot
Sid Fournet
Ben Friend
Eddie Fuller
Tom Fussell
Hokie Gajan
John Garlington
Dennis Gaubatz
Joe Glamp
Walt Gorinski
White Graves
Earl Gros
Kevin Guidry
Paul Guidry
Ronnie Haliburton
Andy Hamilton
Karl Hankton
Bo Harris
Wendell Harris
Charley Hennigan
Tom Henry
Eric Hill
Dalton Hilliard
Lifford Hobley
Norm Hodgins
Tom Hodson
Stan Humphries
Greg Jackson
Rusty Jackson
Steve Jackson
Garry James
Tory James
Garland Jean-Batiste
Norman Jefferson
Kerry Jenkins
Tim Joiner
Bert Jones
Reggie Jones
Victor Jones
Ken Kavanaugh
Eddie Kennison
Brian Kinchen
Todd Kinchen
Shawn King
Wayne Kingery
Ken Konz
David LaFleur
Greg LaFleur
Fred Land
Gene Lang
Jamie Lawson
Earl Leggett
Rube Leisk
Darrell Lester
Rydell Malancon
Tilly Manton
Anthony Marshall
Leonard Marshall
Eric Martin
Sammy Martin
Billy Masters
Kevin Mawae
Bill May
Michael Mayes
Dave McCormick
Orlando McDaniel
Blake Miller
Fred Miller
Nate Miller
Paul Miller
Kenny Mixon
Bill Montgomery
Doug Moreau
Mike Morgan
Jesse Myles
Ed Neal
Tommy Neck
Gabe Northern
Ralph Norwood
R.B. Nunnery
Charley Oakley
Tracy Porter
Marcus Price
Remi Prudhomme
Marcus Quinn
Warren Rabb
Eddie Ray
Corey Raymond
Rock Reed
Steve Rehage
Joe Reid
M.C. Reynolds
George Rice
Bobby Richards
Wade Richey
Alan Risher
Tom Robertson
Johnny Robinson
Terry Robiskie
Steven Rogers
Justin Rukas
Dan Sandifer
Nicky Savoie
Bill Schroll
Malcolm Scott
Hubert Shurtz
Eric Smith
Lance Smith
Raymond Smoot
Jerry Stovall
Eugene Sykes
George Tarasovic
Jim Taylor
Willie Teal
Henry Thomas
Gus Tinsley
Jess Tinsley
Y.A. Tittle
Charley Tolar
Jack Torrance
Zollie Toth
Billy Truax
Mike Turner
Ebert Van Buren
Steve Van Buren
Denard Walker
Lyman White
Blake Whitlatch
Chris Williams
Harvey Williams
Mike Williams
Willie Williams
Karl Wilson
Sheddrick Wilson
Ab Wimberly
Roy Winston
John Wood
David Woodley
Rodney Young
Godfrey Zaunbrecher

Louisiana Tech (44)

Charlie Anderson
Larry Anderson
Myron Baker
Mike Barber
Lloyd Baxter
George Benyola
Chris Boniol
Jim Boudreaux
Barry Bowman
Cloyce Box
Craig Bradshaw
Terry Bradshaw
Bob Brunet
Roger Carr
Jessie Clark
Fred Dean
George Doherty
Derrick Douglas
Doug Evans
Bobby Fowler
Wimpy Giddens
Garland Gregory
Roland Harper
Paul Hynes
Walter Johnson
Trey Junkin
David Lee
Caleb Martin
Eldonta Osborne
Willie Roaf
Johnny Robinson
John Rodgers
Billy Ryckman
Glenell Sanders
Leo Sanford
Eric Shaw
Mickey Slaughter
Artie Smith
Matt Stover
Pat Tilley
Grant Williams
J.R. Williamson
Ray Wilmer
Andre Young

Louisville (73)

David Akers
Tom Andrews
Bruce Armstrong
Jamie Asher
Aaron Bailey
Larry Ball
Matt Battaglia
Richard Bishop
John Bock
Lee Bouggess
Deral Boykin
John Brewer
Charlie Brinkman
Jeff Brohm
Ray Buchanan
Doug Buffone
Lee Calland
Alan Campos
Rico Clark
Mark Clayton
Anthony Copeland
Donnie Craft
Jerry Crafts
Ron Davenport
Mike Flores
Salem Ford
Carwell Gardner
Ernest Givins
Ernie Green
Jim Hanna
Ed Harmon
Tom Holzer
Tom Jackson
Joe Jacoby
Curtis Jeffries
Charlie Johnson
Eddie Johnson
Joe Johnson
Horace Jones
Ken Kortas
Lenny Lyles
Sam Madison
Amos Martin
Dean May
Pete McCartney
Tyrus McCloud
Eddie Meeks
Kevin Miller
Frank Minnifield
Clure Mosher
Browning Nagle
John Neidert
Roman Oben
Garin Patrick
Wayne Patrick
Nathan Poole
Carl Powell
Steve Reese
Ed Rubbert
Benny Russell
Mark Sander
Joey Smith
Marty Smith
Howard Stevens
Wilbur Summers
Leland Taylor
Richard Tharpe
Johnny Unitas
Cleo Walker
Ted Washington
Klaus Wilmsmeyer
Otis Wilson
Dwayne Woodruff

Loyola (Balt.) (1)

Marne Intrieri

Loyola (Chicago) (10)

Ed Berwick
Chuck Braidwood
Phil Brennan
Ray Bush
Paul Florence
Ed Greene
Larry Jackson
Charlie Knight
George Knight
Les Malloy

Loyola (N.O.) (2)

Bucky Moore
Frank Sullivan

Loyola Marymount (16)

Bob Boyd
Gene Brito
Ernie Cheatham
Jack Dwyer

Earl Elsey
Neil Ferris
Hal Giancanelli
Frank Hrabetin
Don Klosterman
Dick Moje
Maury Nipp
Vince Pacewic
Al Pollard
Eddie Saenz
Carroll Vogelaar
Bob Wilkinson

Luther (3)

Cliff Hansen
Ossie Orwoll
Anton Stolfa

Luzerne Co. CC PA (1)

Jack Bravyak

MacMurray (1)

Olindo Mare

Macalester (5)

Ron Groce
Lee Nystrom
Bill Stein
Lloyd Young
Sam Young

Maine (11)

Mike Buck
Dave Cloutier
Thurlow Cooper
Roger Ellis
Mike Flynn
John Huard
Dan Jones
Chris Keating
Clay Pickering
Justin Strzelczyk
Manch Wheeler

Manchester (4)

Herb Banet
Don Lieberum
Mike Patanelli
Paul Shenefelt

Manhattan (5)

Frank Damiani
Art Jocher
Sal Marone
Red Seick
Dick Tuckey

Manitoba (Canada) (1)

Les Lear

Mankato State (5)

Larry Brown
Bob Bruer
Ted Elliott
Mark Hanson
Jeff Reinke

Marietta (9)

Gene Carroll
Dane Dastillung
Mel Doherty
Dud Harris
Dosey Howard
Al Jolley
Peck Reiter
Red Shurtliffe
Mac White

Marion Mil. Inst. AL (J.C.) (3)

Jerry Baker
Steve Broussard
Bernard Ford

Marquette (68)

George Andrie
Ray Apolskis
Frank Aschenbrenner
Ed Aspatore
Wayland Becker
Al Bentzin
Dick Bilda
Frank Bohlmann
Tom Braatz
Dave Braden
Ray Buivid
Art Bultman
Ray Busler
Dick Campbell
Jim Capuzzi
Tommy Cronin
Ward Cuff
Don Curtin
Pahl Davis
Lavvie Dilweg
Ron Drzewiecki
Dukes Duford
Red Dunn
Steve Enich
Earl Evans
John Fahay
Clarke Fischer
Dick Flaherty
Eddie Glick
John Goodyear
George Groves
Pete Hall
Bo Hanley
John Harrington
Norb Hayes
Les Hearden
Johnny Heimsch
Swede Johnston
Al Klug
Frank Kosikowski
Jack Kramer
Ray Kuffel
Joe LaFleur
Oxie Lane
Irv Langhoff
Frank Linnan
Jerry Lunz
Mel Maceau
George McGill
Larry McGinnis
Frank Mestnik
Jab Murray
Ken Radick
Herb Roedel
Fritz Roeseler
Gene Ronzani
Roy Schoemann
Carl Schuette
Vin Shekleton
John Sisk
Johnny Sisk
Johnny Strzykalski
Biff Taugher
Milt Trost
Don Vosberg
Ken Wendt
Whitey Woodin
Joe Young

Marshall (28)

Bob Adkins
Michael Barber
Jim Barton
Mike Bartrum
Troy Brown
Terry Echols
Ev Elkins
Frank Gatski
Tom Good
Alan Huff
Frank Huffman
Jack Hunt
Ramey Hunter
Eric Kresser
Carl Lee
Billy Lyon
Sam Manos
Jack Mattiford
Ron Mikolajczyk
Jack Morlock
Randy Moss
Chris Parker
Jim Pearcy
Johnny Stephens
Ed Ulinski
Wayne Underwood
John Wade
Norm Willey

Marshalltown CC IA (2)

Richard Bishop
Ray Phillips

Maryland (139)

Dick Absher
John Alderton
O'Brien Alston
Steve Atkins
Jess Atkinson
Bob Avellini
Rick Badanjek
Dick Bielski
Alvin Blount
Rod Breedlove
Untz Brewer
Donald Brown
J.B. Brown
Tom Brown
Lloyd Burruss
Harry Butsko
Joe Campbell
Louis Carter
Ted Chapman
Tom Cichowski
Fred Cole
Gary Collins
Lloyd Colteryahn
George Colton
Ed Cooke
King Corcoran
Joe Coster
Dave Crossan
Dave D'Addio
Jack Davis
Darren Drozdov
Mark Duda
Ferrell Edmunds
Boomer Esiason
Chuck Faucette
Ron Fazio
Ralph Felton
Andy Fletcher
Ed Fullerton
Ed Fulton
Lu Gambino
Stan Gelbaugh
Kevin Glover
Tony Greene
Chet Hanulak
Don Healy
Bo Hickey
Eric Hicks
Steve Ingram
Ben Jefferson
Rick Jennings
Barry Johnson
Charles Johnson
Vernon Joines
Clarence Jones
Stan Jones
Willie Joyner
Dan Kecman
Vince Kinney
Bill Kirchiro
Mike Kiselak
Pete Koch
Ray Krouse
Pete Ladygo
Jermaine Lewis
John Lookabaugh
J.D. Maarleveld
Roy Mackert
Mark Manges
Larry Marshall
Ed McGlasson
Tom McHale
Jim Meade
Bruce Mesner
Steve Mike-Mayer
Scott Milanovich
James Milling
Charlie Mills
Dick Modzelewski
Ed Modzelewski
Tommy Mont
Bob Morgan
Joe Moss
Chip Myrtle
Renaldo Nehemiah
Ed Nickla
Dick Nolan
Jack Norris
Neil O'Donnell
Eric Ogbogu
Neal Olkewicz
Dave Pacella
Chuck Pastrana
Bob Pellegrini
Phil Perlo
Warren Powers
Bob Raba
Don Ratliff
Frank Reich
Guy Roberts
Walt Rock
Jeff Rodenberger
Stan Rogers
Mike Sandusky
Jack Scarbath
Scott Schankweiler
Ken Schroy
John Schultz
Chad Scott
Sean Scott
Ben Scotti
Henry Shank
Dick Shiner
Roger Shoals
Eric Sievers
Dan Sileo
Jack Simmons
Snitz Snyder
Ron Solt
Ratcliff Thomas
John Tice
Mike Tice
Steve Trimble
Billy Van Heusen
Ed Vereb
Kevin Walker
Al Wallace
Ron Waller
Larry Webster
Randy White
Walter White
Allen Williams
Eric Wilson
Tim Wilson
Elmer Wingate
John Wright
Kervin Wyatt
Frank Wycheck
Scott Zolak

Maryland East. Shore (24)

Mack Alston
Bill Belk
Willie Belton
Emerson Boozer
Roger Brown
Earl Christy
Marshall Cropper
Moses Denson
Jim Duncan
Curt Gentry
Doug Goodwin
Carl Hairston
Ray Hayes
Gerald Irons
Anthony Jones
Roy Kirksey
Art Laster
Sherman Plunkett
Johnny Sample
Art Shell
Charles Stukes
Bob Taylor
Billy Thompson
Erwin Williams

Massachusetts (17)

Tim Berra
Kory Blackwell
Bill Cooke
Harry Curran
Mike Dwyer
Bruce Kimball
Greg Landry
Ed McAleney
John McCormick
Joe McLaughlin
Milt Morin
Bubba Pena
Steve Schubert
Terry Swanson
Ed Toner
Phil Vandersea
Sandro Vitiello

McCook CC NE (3)

Ray Parson
Al Simpson
Freddie Summers

McMurry (5)

Dick Compton
Les Cowan
Ernie Park
Brad Rowland
Mule Stockton

McNeese State (22)

Don Breaux
Zack Bronson
Jesse Castete
Rich Ellender
Chris Fontenot
Paul Guidry
Rusty Guilbeau
Dick Harris
Bryan Hicks
Terry Irving
Charles Jefferson
Flip Johnson
Buford Jordan
Kerry Joseph
Wayne Kingery
Darrell Lester
Joe Morgan
Keith Ortego
Kavika Pittman
Tom Sestak
Leonard Smith
Stephen Starring

McPherson (1)

Jack Vetter

Memphis (78)

Rick Ackerman
Stan Adams
Charlie Babb
Denny Biodrowski
Dennis Borcky
Don Bramlett
John Bramlett
David Brandon
Ray Brown
Isaac Bruce
Derrick Burroughs
Keith Butler
Billy Cesare
Rich Coady
Don Coffey
Russell Copeland
Olie Cordill
Derrick Crawford
James Cribbs
Stan Davis
Chuck DeVliegher
Scott Dill
Jay Douglas
Ken Dunek
Donnie Elder
Tory Epps
Eric Fairs
Billy Fletcher
Judson Flint
Earnest Gray
John Griffin
Eric Harris
Tim Harris
Dave Hathcock
Eddie Hill
Marcus Holliday
Trell Hooper
Dick Hudson
Gary Hunt
Ken Irvin
Enis Jackson
Reggie Jones
Charlie Killett
James Logan
Tim Long
Edwin Lovelady
Steve Matthews
Terdell Middleton
Fred Moore
Andy Nelson
Darrell Nelson
Jack Oliver
Danny Pierce
Will Renfro
Preston Riley
Glenn Rogers
Bob Rush
Harry Schuh
Tony Semple
Bob Sherlag
Keith Simpson
Jack Smith
Dave Strickland
Cliff Taylor
Ed Taylor
Marvin Thomas
James Thompson
Gerald Tinker
Jeff Walker
Richard Williams
Tony Williams
Charles Wilson
Francis Winkler
Jeff Womack
Doug Woodlief
Jerome Woods
Jim Wright
Keith Wright

Menlo Coll. CA (J.C.) (3)

Burt Delevan
Tom McCormick
Kaulana Park

Merced Coll. CA (J.C.) (7)

Chuck Compton
Duke Fergerson
Mark Gunn
A.J. Jenkins
Rodney Rice
Jon Sawyer
Herman Smith

Mercer (3)

Dutch Irwin
Les Olsson
Al Owen

Mercyhurst (1)

Matt Hatchette

Merritt Coll. CA (J.C.) (9)

Charlie Brown
John Guillory
Anthony Howard
MacArthur Lane
Clark Miller
Roy Shivers
Henry Stuckey
Elton Veals
Ron Wheeler

Mesa (11)

Larry Brunson
Mike Brunson
Don Holmes
Ken Marchiol
Tony Martin
Mark Miller
Perry Smith
Walter Stanley
Jeff Tootle
Greg Westbrooks
Alonzo Williams

Mesa CC AZ (14)

Ben Apuna
Tony Banks
Anthony Brown
Bryan Caldwell
Willie Franklin
Kurt Haws
Mike Hold
Mike Keim
Dan Manucci
Derek Price
Bob Thomas
Jim Warne
Cephus Weatherspoon
Walter White

Mesabi CC (MN) (1)

Bree Cuppoletti

Miami (Fla.) (190)

Steve Alvers
Ottis Anderson
Jessie Armstead
Joe Auer
Don Bailey
Robert Bailey
Pete Banaszak
Mike Barnes
Micheal Barrow
Robert Bass
Tom Beier
Rocky Belk
Coleman Bell
Rodney Bellinger
Donnell Bennett
Phil Bennett
Woody Bennett
Albert Bentley
Bennie Blades
Brian Blades
Johnny Bookman
Don Bosseler
Mel Bratton
Jay Brophy
Willie Broughton
Andre Brown
Eddie Brown
Fred Brown
Jerome Brown
Larry Brown
Selwyn Brown
James Burgess
Mike Burke
Jim Burt
Al Carapella
Wesley Carroll
Rubin Carter
Billy Cesare
Tony Chickillo
Nick Chickillo
Bernard Clark
Tony Cline
Dan Conners
Charles Cook
Mark Cooper
Horace Copeland
Walt Corey
Julio Cortes
Tom Costello
Jim Cox
Shane Curry
Jerry Daanen
Dale Dawkins
Jack Del Bello
Mario DeMarco
Glenn Dennison
Bill Diamond
Charley Diamond
Andy Dickerson
Jim Dooley
Gary Dunn
Eddie Edwards
Craig Erickson
Carlos Etheredge
Leon Evans
Kevin Fagan
Jeff Feagles
Chuck Foreman
Terry Fox
Frank Frazier
Bill Frohbose
Darrell Fullington
Tony Gaiter
Cleveland Gary
Jammi German
Gary Greaves
Keith Griffin
Mike Haggerty
Bobby Harden
Dennis Harrah
Derrick Harris
Bill Hawkins
Dave Heffernan
Ted Hendricks
Charles Henry
Alonzo Highsmith
Randal Hill
Kenny Holmes
Mike Hudock
Carlos Huerta
Michael Irvin
Tom Jelley
Alex Johnson
Jack Johnson
Ken Johnson
Chris T. Jones
Ernie Jones
Jimmie Jones
Dave Kalina
Tom Kearns
Jim Kelly
Cortez Kennedy
Walt Kichefski
Joe Kohlbrand
Bernie Kosar
Rich Kotite
Kenard Lang
Eric Larkin
Don Latimer
Larry Lawrence
Ray Lewis
Ronnie Lippett
Earl Little
Jack Losch
Tremain Mack
Fred Marion
Greg Mark
Russell Maryland
Bob Masterson
John Matlock
Bob McDougal
Bubba McDowell
Ryan McNeil
John McVeigh
Danny Miller
Bill Miller
George Mira
Victor Morris
Winston Moss
Speedy Neal
Bob Nelson
Richard Newbill
Scott Nicolas
John Noppenberg
Paul O'Connor
Darryl Oliver
Jim O'Mahoney
Jim Otto
Burgess Owens
Al Palewicz
Willis Peguese
Brett Perriman
Gregg Rakoczy
C.J. Richardson
Pat Riley
Alfredo Roberts
Fred Robinson
Twan Russell
Nick Ryder
Warren Sapp
Leon Searcy
Dexter Seigler
Stanley Shakespeare
Randy Shannon
Rex Shiver
Dan Sileo
Jim Simon
John Sisk
Darrin Smith
Don Smith
Russ Smith
Tom Smith
Willie Smith
Darryl Spencer
Duane Starks
James Stewart
Danny Stubbs
Mike Sullivan
Tom Sullivan
Reggie Sutton
John Swain
Bob Tatarek
Vinny Testaverde
Lamar Thomas
Woody Thompson
Gino Torretta
Gene Trosch
John Turner
Rick Tuten
Kipp Vickers
Jim Vollenweider
Steve Walsh
Walt Watt
Ed Weisacosky
Bob Werl
Darryl Williams
Kevin Williams
Lester Williams
Warren Williams
Marcus Wimberly

Miami (Ohio) (56)

Gary Arthur
Bob Babich
Ferris Beekley
Eric Beverly
Dave Brown
Steve Buchanan
Rob Carpenter
Ron Carpenter
Lowell Caylor
Dick Chorovich
Brad Cousino
Ken Crawford
Tom Dimitroff
Guy Early

Bob Emerick
Steve Fitzhugh
Al Gansberg
Alvin Hall
Earl Hauser
Walt Houston
Bob Jencks
Tom Jones
Red Joseph
Zip Joseph
Ernie Kellermann
George Munns
Tom Nomina
Henry Orth
Ara Parseghian
Ed Philpott
Brian Pillman
David Pyles
Peck Reiter
Jim Root
Clive Rush
Ed Sauer
Ollie Savatsky
Andy Schillinger
Walt Schupp
George Scott
Paul Shoults
Bob Smith
Ken Smith
Sherman Smith
Kirk Springs
Red Steele
Milt Stegall
George Swarn
Lee Tevis
Bill Triplett
John Weaver
Sheldon White
Pete Wissman
Dick Wolf
Joe Work
Mack Yoho

Miami-Dade CC FL (2)

Pete Athas
Craig Jay

Miami-Dade CC North FL (3)

Ernie Jones
Nat Moore
David Rackley

Michigan (256)

Bobby Abrams
Derrick Alexander
Earl Allen
Erick Anderson
John Anderson
David Arnold
Howie Auer
Lou Baldacci
Terry Barr
Mike Bass
Kurt Becker
Tom Beckman
Gordon Bell
Chuck Bernard
Tim Biakabutuka
Keith Bostic
Don Bracken
Jack Brennan
Kevin Brooks
Corwin Brown
Dave Brown
Jarrod Bunch
Bob Callahan
Chris Calloway
Brian Carpenter
Jack Carpenter
Anthony Carter
Milt Carthens
Gil Chapman
Bob Chappuis
Larry Cipa
Jack Clancy
Ralph Clayton
Joe Cocozzo
Don Coleman
Todd Collins
Evan Cooper
Bob Cowan
Tom Curtis
Bill Daley
Thom Darden
Carl Davis
Russell Davis
Fred Dawley
Damon Denson
Robert Derleth
Don Deskins
Dan Dierdorf
Jerry Diorio
Tom Dohring
Mark Donahue
Glenn Doughty
Walt Downing
Leo Draveling
Wally Dreyer
Don Dufek
Craig Dunaway
Dan Dworsky
Matt Dyson
Stan Edwards
Tom Edwards
Jumbo Elliott
Matt Elliott
Mike Evans
Steve Everitt
Chris Floyd
Len Ford
Bill Fortune
Dennis Franklin
Dennis Franks
Benny Friedman
Ralph Fritz
Ed Frutig
Dave Gallagher
Jon Giesler
Chris Godfrey
Paul Goebel
Gus Goetz
Elvis Grbac
John Greene
Curtis Greer
Bruce Gregory
Brian Griese
Charlie Grube
Thomas Guynes
Ali Haji-Sheikh
Mike Hammerstein
Jim Harbaugh
Mike Harden
Tommy Harmon
Darrell Harper
Clint Haslerig
Mercury Hayes
Ralph Heikkinen
John Henderson
John Hennessy
Bill Hewitt
Dwight Hicks
Ivan Hicks
Crazy Legs Hirsch
Leroy Hoard
Mike Hoban
George Hoey
Lin Houston
Chris Howard
Desmond Howard
Harlan Huckleby
Marty Huff
Tommy Hughitt
Stefan Humphries
Bob Ingalls
Trezelle Jenkins
Dan Jilek
Ed Johns
Farnham Johnson
Gilvanni Johnson
Ron Johnson
Tom Johnson
Mike Jolly
Damon Jones
Mike Jones
Fred Julian
Jack Karwales
Eric Kattus
Tom Keating
Bill Keating
Jack Keefer
Mike Keller
Mike Kenn
David Key
Gene Knutson
Bob Kolesar
Ron Kramer
Walt Kreinheder
Tony LaBissoniere
Gordon Laro
Bill Laskey
Ty Law
Mike Lazetich
Burnie Legette
George Lilja
Earl Little
Randy Logan
Alvin Loucks
Rob Lytle
Tom Mack
Elmer Madar
Jim Mandich
Bob Mann
Dutch Marion
Doug Marsh
Earl Maves
Tony McGee
Reggie McKenzie
Bruce McLenna
Greg McMurtry
Paul McNulty
Bennie McRae
Mark Messner
Clay Miller
Bo Molenda
Tony Momsen
Jamie Morris
Doc Morrison
Steve Morrison
John Morrow
Greg Morton
Stan Muirhead
Ed Muransky
Guy Murdock
Fred Negus
Harry Newman
Wally Niemann
Frank Nunley
Bob Nussbaumer
Joe O'Donnell
Calvin O'Neal
Chuck Ortmann
Mel Owens
James Pace
Bubba Paris
Ricky Patton
Rod Payne
Jack Perrin
Lowell Perry
Bob Perryman
Dick Pierce
Ricky Powers
Merv Pregulman
Trevor Pryce
Bob Ptacek
Jerry Quaerna
Dave Raimey
Bo Rather
Fred Ratterman
Russ Reader
Dan Rice
Lawrence Ricks
Jay Riemersma
Dick Rifenburg
Jon Ritchie
Garland Rivers
Doug Roby
Rudy Rosatti
Carlton Rose
Rocky Rosema
John Rowser
Jon Runyan
Carl Russ
Todd Schlopy
Thomas Seabron
Paul Seal
Paul Seymour
Arnie Simkus
Ron Simpkins
Doug Skene
Greg Skrepenak
Rudy Smeja
Jim Smith
Pat Smith
Steve Smith
Willie Smith
Joe Soboleski
Sylvester Stanley
Paul Staroba
Glen Steele
Thomas Stincic
Rich Strenger
Michael Taylor
Mike Teeter
Robert Thompson
Bob Thornbladh
Dick Thornton
Bob Timberlake
Amani Toomer
Ted Topor
Bob Topp
Brian Townsend
Eddie Usher
Jon Vaughn
Ernie Vick
Rick Volk
Kerwin Waldroup
Derrick Walker
Carl Ward
Tripp Welborne
Bob Westfall
Tyrone Wheatley
Gerald White
Paul White
Bob Wiese
Al Wistert
Charles Woodson
Butch Woolfolk
Bill Yearby
Roger Zatkoff

Michigan State (210)

Flozell Adams
Herb Adderley
Bob Allman
Morten Andersen
Charlie Ane
Fred Arbanas
Tony Arena
Scott Auer
Ed Bagdon
Gary Ballman
Carl Banks
Tony Banks
Harlon Barnett
Tom Beard
Art Beckley
Dave Behrman
Veno Belk
Anthony Bell
Myron Bell
Bob Bercich
Larry Bethea
Tom Birney
Hugh Blacklock
Leroy Bolden
Willie Bouyer
Gordon Bowdell
Mark Brammer
Al Brenner
Les Bruckner
Ed Budde
Chuck Bullough
Hank Bullough
Derek Bunch
James Burroughs
Art Buss
Frank Butler
Bob Carey
Lynn Chandnois
Carl Charon
Koester Christensen
Bryan Clark
Ernie Clark
Gail Clark
Mike Cobb
George Cooper
Brad Costello
Smiley Creswell
Dan Currie
Fred Danziger
Jerry DaPrato
Travis Davis
Paul Dekker
Joe DeLamielleure
Brian DeMarco
Dorne Dibble
Dave Diehl
Tony Discenzo
Roger Donnahoo
Al Dorow
Billy Joe DuPree
Jim Earley
Dixon Edwards
Blake Ezor
Angelo Fields
Wayne Fontes
Rob Fredrickson
Bob Friedlund
Drake Garrett
Pete Gent
Ron Goovert
Dick Gordon
Sonny Grandelius
Otis Grant
Tom Graves
Scott Greene
Roger Grove
Alan Haller
Ty Hallock
Tom Hannon
Dale Hansen
Cliff Hardy
Ron Hatcher
Courtney Hawkins
Dave Herman
Don Highsmith
Ray Hill
Bill Horrell
Vivian Hultman
Mike Iaquaniello
Mark Ingram
Cleveland Jackson
Carlos Jenkins
Bob Jewett
Ed Johns
Bill Johnson
Clint Jones
Jim Kanicki
Ellison Kelly
Bill Kennedy
Alex Ketzko
Mike Kinek
Ed Klewicki
Walt Kowalczyk
Todd Krumm
Mel Land
Kurt Larson
Russ Lay
Dwight Lee
Sherman Lewis
Terry Lewis
Dean Look
Ed Lothamer
Gary Lowe
Mitch Lyons
Steve Maidlow
Tony Mandarich
Dave Manders
Blanche Martin
Derrick Mason
Norm Masters
Archie Matsos
Henry Matthews
Brian McConnell
Marv McFadden
Jim Miller
John Miller
Blake Miller
Henry Minarik
Ralf Mojsiejenko
Bob Monnett
Greg Montgomery
Arnold Morgado
Earl Morrall
Tom Morris
Jim Morrissey
Bobby Morse
Eric Moten
Howard Mudd
Muhsin Muhammad
Jim Nicholson
Hans Nielsen
Jim Ninowski
Gary Nowak
Fran O'Brien
Herb Paterra
Clarence Peaks
Jess Phillips
Johnny Pingel
Jerry Planutis
Paul Podmajersky
Palmer Pyle
Bill Quinlan
Kelly Quinn
Jimmy Raye
Russ Reader
Travis Reece
Ike Reese
Jeff Richardson
Don Ridler
Andre Rison
Kevin Robbins
Paul Rochester
Lyle Rockenbach
Butch Rolle
Paul Rudzinski
Jerry Rush
Tom Saidock
George Saimes
Lonnie Sanders
Rich Saul
Ron Saul
Greg Schaum
Scott Shaw
Boris Shlapak
Steve Sieradzki
Bill Simpson
Bubba Smith
Tody Smith
Matt Snorton
Percy Snow
Harry Speelman
Ray Stachowicz
Bob Suci
Jim Summers
Jim Szymanski
Jesse Thomas
Jabbar Threats
Willie Thrower
Daryl Turner
Matt Vanderbeek
Brad Van Pelt
Walt Vezmar
Sid Wagner
Mickey Walker
Gene Washington
George Webster
Billy Wells
Lorenzo White
Ray Wietecha
Sam Williams
Bobby Wilson
Jeff Wiska
John Wojciechowski
Jim Wulff
Craig Wycinsky
Tom Yewcic
Duane Young
Lonnie Young
Bert Zagers
Vic Zucco

Michigan Tech (4)

Bob Lurtsema
Porky Rundquist
James Van Wagner
Dave Walter

MidAmerica Nazarene (1)

Ken Jolly

Middle Georgia Coll. (J.C.) (1)

Spike Jones

Middle Tennessee State (13)

Tony Burse
Mike Caldwell
Marty Carter
Bill Cherry
Jerry DeLucca
Don Griffin
James Griffin
Kelly Holcomb
Dave Little
Ray Oldham
Jonathan Quinn
Dwight Stone
Ken Tippins

Middlebury (2)

Phil Bower
Stone Hallquist

Middlesex Co. Coll. NJ (J.C.) (1)

Mark Meserol

Midland Coll. TX (J.C.) (1)

Larry Linne

Midwestern State (2)

Dudley Meredith
Ray Gene Smith

Miles (1)

Ed McCall

Millersville (3)

Chris Johnson
Will Lewis
Robb Riddick

Millikin (12)

Roy Adkins
Aric Anderson
Joe Carpe
George Corbett
Sid Gepford
Bobby Jones
Jake Lanum
Kile MacWherter
George Musso
Jim Perryman
Jeff Query
Randy Young

Millsaps (2)

Ed Khayat
Bernie Winkler

Milton (2)

Dave Kraayeveld
Dave Krieg

Minnesota (199)

George Abramson
Julie Alfonse
Chet Anderson
Mel Anderson
Elmer Bailey
Marion Barber
Bert Baston
Bill Baumgartner
Doug Beaudoin
Bobby Bell
Warren Beson
John Billman
Bob Bjorklund
Brian Bonner
McKinley Boston
Aaron Brown
Bob Bruggers
Hubie Bryant
Bart Buetow
Larry Buhler
Anthony Burke
John Campbell
Gino Cappelletti
Ralph Capron
Jay Carroll
Tony Carter
Jim Carter
Marty Christiansen
Bill Daley
Ken Dallafior
Chris Darkins
Omar Douglas
Tony Dungy
Pat Dunnigan
Mark Dusbabek
Ben Dvorak
Gus Eckberg
Carl Eller
Dick Enderle
Jim Fahnhorst
Keith Fahnhorst
Mike Falls
George Faust
Paul Faust
Paul Flinn
Fred Foggie
George Franck
Jim Gallery
Bill Garnaas
Chet Gay
George Gibson
Gale Gillingham
Kerry Glenn
Bud Grant
Gary Hadd
Roger Hagberg
Tom Hall
Carl Hanke
Hal Hansen
Ron Hansen
Hal Hanson
Ed Hawthorne
Ken Haycraft
Matt Herkenhoff
Ray Hitchcock
Jim Hobbins
Mike Hohensee
Bruce Holmes
Gordy Holz
Mike Hunt
Tony Hunter
Floyd Jaszewski
Jon Jelacic
Noel Jenke
Herb Joesting
Bill Johnson
Dick Johnson
Ezell Jones
Larry Joyner
Rube Juster
Ike Kakela
Jerry Keeble
Kevin Kellin
Wally Kersten
Wally Kilbourne
Doug Kingsriter
Stan Kostka
Kent Kramer
Vic Kulbitski
Bill Kuusisto
Greg Larson
Ed Lechner
Bobby Lee
Len Levy
Cully Lidberg
Chip Lohmiller
Sean Lumpkin
Dewey Lyle
Tom MacLeod
Al Maeder
Jack Manders
Frank Marchlewski
Bobby Marshall
Billy Martin
Joe Mattern
Clarence McGeary
Bob McNamara
Karl Mecklenburg
Jon Melander
Mike Mercer
Mark Merrill
Lou Midler
Eddie Miles
Paul Mitchell
Wilbur Moore
Jerry Mulready
Greg Murtha
Steve Myhra
Bronko Nagurski
Pete Najarian
Steve Neils
Don Nolander
Leo Nomellini
Mally Nydall
Jack O'Brien
Dick O'Donnell
Urban Odson
Vern Oech
Earl Ohlgren
Larry Olsonoski
Bob Paffrath
Ray Parson
Lloyd Parsons
Gordon Paschka
Win Pedersen
John Perko
Dick Pesonen
Art Pharmer
Warren Plunkett
Randy Rasmussen
Pete Regnier
Alan Reid
Mike Rengel
Neil Rengel
Steve Rhem
Wayne Robinson
Charlie Sanders
Craig Sauer
Bob Schmidt
Joe Schmiesing
Jeff Schuh
Charlie Schultz
Rudy Sikich
Keith Simons
Dave Simonson
Mark Slater
Donovan Small
Bruce Smith
Gordie Soltau
Robert Soltis
Vic Spadaccini
Randy Staten
Bob Stein
Joe Stepanek
Mac Stephens
Steve Stewart
Leif Strand
Milt Sunde
Bud Svendsen
George Svendsen
Bob Sweiger
Stan Sytsma
Bob Tanner
Al Teeter
Bob Tenner
Ryan Thelwell
Chris Thome
Darrell Thompson
Steve Thompson
Tuffy Thompson
Festus Tierney
Steven Tobin
Clayton Tonnemaker
George Tuttle
Frank Twedell
Rick Upchurch
Andy Uram
Hal Van Every
Fred Vant Hull

Ed Widseth
Dick Wildung
Brian Williams
John Williams
Lamanzer Williams
Ben Williams
Vern Winfield
Jeff Wright
Arnie Wyman
Frank Youso

Minnesota-Crookston (2)

Ira Haaven
Ed Widseth

Minnesota-Duluth (6)

Tom Adams
Lou Barle
Vern Emerson
Ted McKnight
Dick Pesonen
David Viaene

Minot State (2)

Terry Falcon
Randy Hedberg

Mira Costa Coll. CA (J.C.) (3)

Willie Buchanon
Mike Kozlowski
Bill Sandifer

Miramonte J.C. (GA) (1)

Mickey Colmer

Mississippi (149)

Buddy Alliston
Tyji Armstrong
Kent Austin
John Avery
Randy Baldwin
Ken Barfield
Ed Beatty
Tony Bennett
Dave Bernard
Jonathan Bilbo
Dwight Bingham
George Blair
Rex Boggan
Bookie Bolin
Tim Bowens
Billy Brewer
Johnny Brewer
Alundis Brice
Lester Brinkley
Oscar Britt
Allen Brown
Chad Brown
Ray Brown
Lonny Calicchio
George Chesser
Don Churchwell
Billy Clay
Eddie Cole
Dennis Coleman
Pat Coleman
Chuck Commiskey
Charlie Conerly
Paige Cothren
Eddie Crawford
Bob Crespino
Doug Cunningham
Roland Dale
Lee Davis
Eagle Day
Mike Dennis
Les Dodson
DeWayne Dotson
John Dottley
Jim Dunaway
Perry Lee Dunn
Doug Elmore
Bill Erickson
Julian Fagan
Chad Fann
Hap Farber
Ken Farragut
Charlie Flowers
John Fourcade
Keith Fourcade
Bobby Franklin
Kline Gilbert
Larry Grantham
Allen Green
Willie Green
Duke Greenich
Wade Griffin
Glynn Griffing
Louis Guy
Mac Haik
Parker Hall
Norman Hand
Merle Hapes
James Harbour
Mike Harmon
Jim Harvey
Jimmy Heidel
Jeff Herrod
Gene Hickerson
Stan Hindman
Chuck Hinton
Paul Hofer
Junie Hovious
Earl Howell
Dou Innocent
Joe Johnson
Charlie Kempinska
Jimmy Keyes
Bob Khayat
Billy Kinard
Bruiser Kinard
George Kinard
Ken Kirk
Chet Kozel
Frank Lambert
Skip Lane
Everett Lindsay
Billy Lott
Michael Lowery
Tommy Luke
Pete Mangum
John Mangum
Kris Mangum
Archie Manning
Bob McCain
Wayne McClure
Buford McGee
Joe Mickles
Jim Miller
Russell Mitchell
Tim Moffett
Tyrone Montgomery
Stevon Moore
Harvey Murphy
Freddie Joe Nunn
Darrick Owens
Jimmy Patton
Leon Perry
Mario Perry
Barney Poole
Jim Poole
Ollie Poole
Ray Poole
Roell Preston
Kelvin Pritchett
Ben Reed
Bill Reynolds
Lake Roberson
Dan Sartin
Jonathan Shelley
Jackie Simpson
Allen Smith
Ralph Smith
Bill Stribling
Vern Studdard
Marvin Terrell
Ray Terrell
Andre Thomas
Fred Thomas
Kenneth Toler
Andre Townsend
Guy Turnbow
Jim Urbanek
Bob Vaughn
Wesley Walls
Nate Wayne
Curtis Weathers
Norris Weese
Leonard Wheeler
Barry Wilburn
Ben Williams
Richard Winther
Nathan Wonsley
Lee Woodruff
Bill Yelverton

Mississippi College (7)

Charlie Armstrong
Larry Evans
Major Everett
Joel Hitt
Fred McAfee
Larry Suchy
Michael Williams

Mississippi Delta CC (5)

Michael Adams
Vincent Barnett
Charles Bennett
Juran Bolden
Greg Williams

Mississippi Gulf Coast CC (9)

Tommy Boutwell
Wendell Davis
Mark Hall
Tyrone Jones
Ed Khayat
Aubrey Matthews
Calvin Miller
Melvin Morgan
Jim Still

Mississippi State (97)

Jesse Anderson
Johnny Baker
Earnest Barnes
Bobby Bethune
Blondy Black
Stan Black
Richard Blackmore
Lamar Blount
Kevin Bouie
Eric Brown
Ode Burrell
Justin Canale
Herman Carroll
Jim Champion
Louis Clark
Keo Coleman
Glen Collins
Johnie Cooks
Bert Corley
Ray Costict
Willie Daniel
Art Davis
Harper Davis
Terry Day
Jim Eidson
Clifton Eley
Greg Favors
Joe Fortunato
Steve Freeman
Larry Friday
Dub Garrett
Chuck Gelatka
Tom Goode
Shag Goolsby
Hoyle Granger
Michael Haddix
Clarence Harmon
Jim Harness
Amos Harris
Walt Harris
Gran Harrison
Melvin Hayes
Kevin Henry
Robert Hicks
Kent Hull
Brian Hutson
Gerald Jackson
Kirby Jackson
Jesse James
Billy Jefferson
Dennis Johnson
Kenneth Johnson
Kenny Johnson
James Jones
Tyrone Keys
Andy Kowalski
Wesley Leasy
D.D. Lewis
Jack Manley
Fred McCrary
Mardye McDole
Shorty McWilliams
John Miller
Henry Monroe
Dana Moore
Eric Moulds
Tom Neville
Jack Nix
Walter Packer
Mike Patrick
Aaron Pearson
Tommy Pharr
Danny Pierce
Bruce Plummer
Joe Reed
Corey Sears
Alex Sidorik
Michael Simmons
Don Smith
Brent Smith
Truett Smith
Billy Stacy
Walt Suggs
Patrick Swoopes
Art Tait
Bruce Threadgill
John Tripson
Olanda Truitt
Kendell Watkins
Jimmy Webb
Greg Williams
James Williams
John Woitt
George Wonsley
Marc Woodard
Glen Young
Robert Young

Mississippi Valley State (26)

Ashley Ambrose
Fred Bohannon
Vincent Brown
Carl Byrum
Phil Darns
Parnell Dickinson
Nate Dorsey
Ricky Feacher
Robert Gaddis
James Haynes
Ronald Humphrey
Deacon Jones
Dave McDaniels
Melvin Morgan
Lloyd Mumphrey
Freddie Parker
Lou Rash
Jerry Rice
Jeff Stanciel
Fred Thomas
Joe Thomas
Willie Totten
Sam Washington
Ted Washington
Louis Watson
Danta Whitaker

Missouri (133)

Bud Abell
Scott Anderson
Bob Armstrong
Carl Bacchus
Victor Bailey
Carl Bax
Norm Beal
Bobby Bell
Ed Blaine
Herb Blumer
Jeff Brockhaus
Charlie Brown
Curtis Brown
Ken Bungarda
Hank Burnine
Bob Callahan
Jack Carpenter
Rick Cash
James Caver
Byron Chamberlain
Dick Chapura
Paul Christman
John Clay
Paul Collins
Harry Colon
Jeff Cross
Butch Davis
Robert Delpino
Earl Denny
John Douglas
Vic Eaton
Brad Edelman
Andy Ekern
Gerry Ellis
Ron Fellows
Mike Fink
David Frisch
Tony Galbreath
Earl Gant
Chris Garlich
Andy Gibler
Mack Gladden
Conrad Goode
Mel Gray
Don Greenwood
Jim Harrison
Pete Jackson
Larron Jackson
Bob Jeffries
Jim Jennings
Demetrious Johnson
Herbert Johnson
Mario Johnson
Mark Johnson
Curtis Jones
Mike Jones
Jim Kekeris
Gary Lane
Dan LaRose
Babe Laufenberg
Biff Lee
Bob Lee
Leo Lewis
Rick Lyle
Mike Magac
Henry Marshall
Steve Martin
John Matuszak
Damon Mays
Ron McBride
Adrian McBride
Len McGirl
Erik McMillan
Joe Moore
Jack Morton
A.J. Ofodile
Brock Olivo
Gus Otto
Jim Palermo
Francis Peay
Gene Pepper
Kurt Petersen
Phil Pettey
Steve Pisarkiewicz
Johnnie Poe
Kevin Potter
Ed Quirk
Tommy Reamon
Don Reece
Howard Richards
Cameron Riley
Johnny Roland
Stillman Rouse
Andy Russell
Jerome Sally
Randy Sealby
George Seals
Warren Seitz
George Shorthose
Marshall Shurnas
Clyde Smith
Gordon Smith
Otis Smith
Ray Smith
Dave Smukler
Hugh Sprinkle
Jon Staggers
Bob Steuber
Mark Stevenson
Joe Stewart
Ralph Stewart
Tommie Stowers
Henry Stuckey
Jim Tarr
J.T. Taylor
Curtland Thomas
Bill Tobin
Morris Towns
Brick Travis
Vince Turner
Bruce Van Dyke
Chase Van Dyne
Wilbur Volz
Russ Washington
Bucky Wegener
Roger Wehrli
Mel West
Bill Whitaker
Craig White
James Wilder
Kellen Winslow
Junior Wren
Eric Wright

Missouri Southern State (7)

Bruce Cortez
Curtis Jones
Richard Jordan
Terry Joyce
Mike Loyd
Rod Smith
James Thrash

Missouri Valley (3)

Ron Hall
Dan Kratzer
Moses Regular

Missouri-Rolla (3)

Charlie Copley
Dick Thornton
Eric Wiegand

Moberly Area CC (1)

Howard Kindig

Modesto JC CA (9)

Karl Finch
Proverb Jacobs
Verl Lillywhite
Gino Marchetti
Bob Pifferini
John Rade
Paul Wiggin
Jeff Winans
Bob Winslow

Monmouth (Ill.) (1)

Keith Molesworth

Monmouth (N.J.) (2)

Jug Earp
Ned Scott

Monroe CC NY (1)

Tommy Campbell

Montana (33)

Raul Allegre
Chris Bentz
Doug Betters
Guy Bingham
Tiny Cahoon
Barry Darrow
Terry Dillon
Terry Falcon
Aldo Forte
Scott Gragg
Mike Hagen
Tim Hauck
Ted Illman
Wild Bill Kelly
Rocky Klever
Mike Lazetich
Bill Lazetich
Jack McAuliffe
Blaine McElmurry
Len Noyes
Vern Oech
Steve Okoniewski
Brent Pease
Frosty Peters
Russ Peterson
Milt Popovich
Brian Salonen
Kirk Scrafford
Steve Sullivan
Mickey Sutton
Paul Szakash
Mike Tilleman
Tuufuli Uperesa

Montana State (19)

Tony Boddie
Jon Borchardt
Don Cosner
Ron East
Curt Farrier
Mark Fellows
Wayne Hammond
Sean Hill
Jim Kalafat
Bill Kollar
Sam McCullum
Mark McGrath
Mike McLeod
Larry Rubens
Bob Schmitz
Jan Stenerud
Kirk Timmer
Ron Warzeka
Corey Widmer

Montana Tech (2)

Don Heater
Craig Kupp

Montclair State (6)

Walter Briggs
Eddie Chavis
Amod Field
Leander Knight
Sam Mills
Tony Sweet

Monterey Peninsula Coll. CA (J.C.) (6)

M.L. Carter
Claude Crabb
Herman Edwards
Herb Lusk
Eric Richardson
Nate Wright

Montgomery Coll. MD (J.C.) (1)

Bob Windsor

Moorhead State (1)

Ted Nemzek

Moorpark Coll. CA (J.C.) (4)

Freddie Bradley
Mike Crawford
Sheldon Gaines
Curtis Marsh

Moraine Valley CC IL (1)

Dave Bruno

Moravian (1)

Jack Finn

Morehead State (9)

Adrian Breen
Greg Bright
Randy Frazier
Dave Haverdick
Nick Nighswander
Billy Poe
Mark Reed
Gary Shirk
Phil Simms

Morehouse (1)

David Graham

Morgan State (35)

John Andrews
Tim Baylor
Rosey Brown
Tom Carr
Stan Cherry
Raymond Chester
Mike Collier
Carlton Dabney
Ollie Dobbins
Len Ford
Elvis Franks
John Fuqua
Willie Germany
Cornell Gowdy
Bobby Hammond
Elmore Harris
Ed Hayes
Mike Holston
Daryl Johnson
Leroy Kelly
Willie Lanier
Greg Latta
Ron Mayo
Dave Meggett
Alvin Mitchell
Kelvin Moore
George Nock
Ara Person
Jeff Queen
Charley Robinson
Clarence Scott
John Sykes
Maurice Tyler
Bob Wade
Mark Washington

Morningside (7)

Anthony Fieldings
Jerry Johnson
Gayle Knief
Herb McMath
Vic Menefee
Harry Webber
Obe Wenig

Morris Brown (12)

Butch Atkinson
Charlie Bivins
Roosevelt Blackmon
Solomon Brannan
Fernanza Burgess
Herb Christopher
Jerry Davis
Tommy Hart
Alfred Jenkins
Ezra Johnson
Aaron Mitchell
Henry Mosley

Mount Hood CC OR (3)

Willie Brock
Randy Gill
Stafford Mays

Mount Olive Coll. NC (J.C.) (1)

Jerris McPhail

Mount San Antonio Coll. CA (J.C.) (21)

Duane Allen
Jim Asmus
Sammie Burroughs
Norberto Davidds-Garrido
Herb Dobbins
Teddy Farmer
Tommy Haynes
Mike Hohensee
Eddie Howard
Nate Jacquet
Bob Jones
Claudie Minor
Steve Myer
Leonard Russell
Clint Sampson
Dennis Shaw
Don Shy
Bob Voight
Don Warren
Jim Weatherly
Troy West

Mount San Jacinto Coll. CA (J.C.) (2)

Max Montoya
Alvin Walton

Mount Senario (1)

Craig Jay

Mount St. Mary's (2)

Fritz Ferko
Joe Lamas

Mount Union (3)

Wilmer Fleming
Scott Woolf
Corl Zimmerman

Muhlenberg (11)

Sisto Averno
Howard Berry
Nick Borelli

Charlie Copley
Mickey Fallon
Scrapper Farrell
Pete Gorgone
Orian Rice
Perry Scott
Reds Weiner
Tony Zuzzio

Murray State (13)

Melvin Aldridge
Mike Cherry
Daniel Coleman
Derrick Cullors
Stan Fritts
Pete Gudauskas
Keith Lester
Terry Love
Gil Mains
Bill McRaven
George Speth
Rocky Ugucccioni
Jim Yarbrough

Murray State Coll. OK (J.C.) (1)

Mike Barnes

Muskingum (5)

Bill Cooper
Roger LaLonde
Greg Ours
Doug Russell
Dave Tallant

Nassau CC NY (17)

Mike Alexander
Brian Baldinger
Robert Bass
Rich Borresen
Donny Brady
Gary Brown
Nick Bruckner
Tony Garbarczyk
Clayton Heath
Rich Mauti
John Nies
Tom O'Connor
Dameon Reilly
Lance Schulters
Kurt Sohn
Sandro Vitiello
John Witkowski

Navarro Coll. TX (J.C.) (23)

Willis Adams
Eddie Brown
Keith Burns
Keo Coleman
Edgar Fields
Al Fontenot
Aaron Glenn
Tim Gray
Earnest Hunter
Horace Ivory
Ray Jacobs
Reggie Mathis
Ramos McDonald
Fred Robinson
Glenn Robinson
Corey Sears
Emil Slovacek
Ken Smith
Mark Smith
Karl Sweetan
Bubba Thornton
Mark Wheeler
Pat Williams

Navy (26)

Joe Bartos
Joe Bellino
Art Carney
Ben Chase
Fred Denfeld
Dick Duden
Kevin Hickman
Bob Hoernschemeyer
Rob Holmberg
Jimmy Jemail
Bob Kelly
Bob Kuberski
Max Lane
Jack Martin
Napoleon McCallum
Phil McConkey
Skippy Minisi
Todd Peterson
Bob Reifsnyder
Wooky Roberts
Jim Schuber
Clyde Scott
Russ Smith
Ed Sprinkle
Roger Staubach
Mike Wahle

Nebraska (252)

Nick Adduci
Trev Alberts
Warren Alfson
Tom Alward
George Andrews
Cliff Ashburn
Walt Barnes
Bill Barnett
Henry Bassett
Mark Behning
Richard Bell
Rick Berns
Jay Berquist
Keith Bishop
Joe Blahak
Brian Blankenship
Al Bloodgood
Don Boll
Rik Bonness
Michael Booker
Dana Brinson
Marion Broadstone
Charley Brock
Bob Brown
Derek Brown
Ed Burns
Jim Burrow
Joe Byler
Bill Callihan
Lloyd Cardwell
Guy Chamberlin
Dennis Claridge
Bret Clark
Kelvin Clark
Ken Clark
Doug Colman
Reggie Cooper
Barney Cotton
Roger Craig
Mike Croel
Maury Damkroger
Brian Davis
Dick Davis
Tony Davis
Bob DeFruiter
Herb DeWitz
Rufe DeWitz
Chris Dishman
Ted Doyle
Doug DuBose
Troy Dumas
Doug Dumler
John Dutton
Chief Elkins
LeRoy Etienne
Vince Ferragamo
Clete Fischer
Pat Fischer
Dick Frahm
Todd Frain
Sam Francis
Andra Franklin
Scott Frost
Irving Fryar
Danny Fulton
Mike Fultz
Russell Gary
Ken Geddes
Bill Glassgow
Rich Glover
Mark Goodspeed
Aaron Graham
Ahman Green
Ben Gregory
Tony Guillory
Chris Hale
Willie Harper
Jon Hesse
Travis Hill
I.M. Hipp
Bob Hohn
Steve Hokuf
Tony Holloway
Harry Hopp
Rod Horn
John Howell
Tyrone Hughes
David Humm
Ed Husmann
Tim Jackson
Larry Jacobson
Ted James
Tony Jeter
Carl Johnson
Monte Johnson
Rudy Johnson
Billy Johnson
Calvin Jones
Donta Jones
Keith Jones
Bob Kahler
Royal Kahler
Jeff Kinney
John Kirby
Mike Knox
Mitch Krenk
Lee Kunz
Jeff Lee
John Lee
Oudious Lee
Tyrone Legette
Verne Lewellen
Bill Lewis
Rodney Lewis
Tahaun Lewis
Bob Liggett
Bob Lingenfelter
Frank Lockett
Terry Luck
Allen Lyday
Link Lyman
Bob Martin
Dave Mason
Bernie Masterson
Bruce Mathison
Kent McCloughan
Ron McDole
Les McDonald
Jim McFarland
Danny McMullen
Forrest McPherson
Wayne Meylan
Junior Miller
Jeff Mills
Mike Minter
Johnny Mitchell
Wonder Monds
Brett Moritz
Marc Munford
Bob Nelson
Derrie Nelson
Keith Neubert
Bob Newton
Dave Noble
Danny Noonan
Gail O'Brien
Arnie Oehlrich
Bill Olds
Joe Orduna
Greg Orton
Rip Owens
John Parrella
Frank Patrick
Jerry Patton
Lawrence Pete
Christian Peter
Jason Peter
Carl Peterson
Lawrence Phillips
Ray Phillips
Bruce Pickens
Bob Pickens
Warren Powers
Glenn Presnell
Ray Prochaska
Tom Rathman
Jarvis Redwine
John Reece
Hughie Rhea
Ray Richards
Speed Riddell
Dave Rimington
Johnny Rodgers
Herm Rohrig
Willie Ross
Tim Rother
Mike Rozier
Reb Russell
Tom Ruud
Kelly Saalfeld
Carl Samuelson
George Sauer
Bernie Scherer
Vic Schleich
Cory Schlesinger
Bob Schmit
George Seeman
Ed Shaw
Will Shields
Fred Shirey
Joe Sims
Jim Skow
Bob Smith
Jeff Smith
Neil Smith
Tim Smith
Brenden Stai
Anthony Steels
Dean Steinkuhler
Carel Stith
Eric Stokes
Shane Swanson
Jerry Tagge
Pete Tatman
Broderick Thomas
Alvie Thompson
Russ Thompson
Fred Thomsen
Bill Thornton
Mick Tingelhoff
Jared Tomich
Charlie Toogood
LaVerne Torczon
Mark Traynowicz
Adam Treu
Nate Turner
Sam Vacanti
Ted Vactor
Tony Veland
Gene Vidal
Lloyd Voss
Henry Waechter
Stan Waldemore
Kenny Walker
Eric Warfield
Brian Washington
Joe Weir
Ed Weir
Bub Weller
Kent Wells
Tom Welter
Ad Wenke
Donald Westbrook
Daryl White
David White
Freeman White
Zach Wiegert
Hal Wilder
Jamel Williams
Jamie Williams
Jimmy Williams
Toby Williams
Tyrone Williams
Harry Wilson
Grant Wistrom
Keith Wortman
Joe Wostoupal
Toby Wright
Elmer Wynne
Carroll Zaruba
Rob Zatechka
Merle Zuver

Nebraska Southern JC (1)

Leonard Willis

Nebraska Wesleyan (4)

Shawn Bouwens
Guy Chamberlin
Ossie Wiberg
Hal Wilder

Nebraska-Kearney (3)

Paul Blessing
John Marrow
Randy Rasmussen

Nebraska-Omaha (10)

Jerry Allen
Joe Arenas
Brad Beckman
Brian Blankenship
Marlin Briscoe
Danny Fulton
Rod Kush
Ron Sayers
John Walker
Phillip Wise

Nevada-Las Vegas (53)

Harvey Allen
Henry Bailey
Dean Barnett
Bobby Batton
Tony Blue
Glenn Carano
Blanchard Carter
Mel Carver
Mike Crawford
Ron Crews
Ray Crouse
Randall Cunningham
Charles Dimry
Kirk Dodge
Frank Garcia
Tony Gladney
Steve Haggerty
Nate Hawkins
Reggie Haynes
Wymon Henderson
Dave Hollis
Alvin Horn
Cleveland Jackson
Keyvan Jenkins
Kirk Jones
Suge Knight
Daryl Knox
Mike Lee
Todd Liebenstein
Keenan McCardell
Dan McQuaid
Aaron Mitchell
Ken Mitchell
Aaron Moog
Michael Morton
Ted Nelson
Don Odegard
Lonnie Palelei
Art Plunkett
Tom Polley
Shar Pourdanesh
Floyd Raglin
Jerry Reynolds
Ken Rose
Ron Scoggins
Jeff Spek
Ray Strong
George Thomas
Mike Thomas
Keith Washington
Charles Wiley
Ickey Woods
Renard Young

Nevada-Reno (42)

Dick Afflis
Rob Awalt
Bill Bass
Doug Betters
Jim Bradshaw
Pat Brady
James Cannida
Victor Carroll
Pots Clark
Anthony Corley
Forey Duckett
Patrick Egu
Horace Gillom
Bill Gutteron
Bob Hamm
Frank Hawkins
Stan Heath
Terry Hermeling
Sherman Howard
Patrick Hunter
Tom Kalmanir
Derek Kennard
Dave Kilson
Bill Mackrides
Charles Mann
Brock Marion
Bob McClure
Marion Motley
DeShone Myles
Dan Orlich
Joe Peterson
Bryan Reeves
Elston Ridgle
Greg Robinson
Henry Rolling
Eric Sanders
Ed Sharkey
Don Smerek
Dan Talcott
Alex Van Dyke
Al Williams
Tony Zendejas

New Hampshire (16)

Dutch Connor
Scott Curtis
Steve Doig
Paul Dufault
David Gamble
Dwayne Gordon
Red Howard
Bruce Huther
Ilia Jarostchuk
Ken Kaplan
Sam Knox
Clayton Lane
Paul Lindquist
Dave Rozumek
Dwayne Sabb
Cy Wentworth

New Haven (4)

Harry Boatswain
Fred DiRenzo
Roger Graham
Miles McPherson

New Mexico (41)

Ben Agajanian
Walt Arnold
Billy Austin
Charles Baker
Ken Brown
Jimmie Carter
Stoney Case
Robin Cole
Chris Combs
Preston Dennard
John Duff
Andy Frederick
Frank Giddens
Bruce Herron
Dave Hettema
Shawn Hollingsworth
Eric Jack
Terance Mathis
Ramos McDonald
Scott McGarrahan
Avery Monfort
Bobby Morgan
Ron Morrison
Steve Myer
Winslow Oliver
Don Perkins
Randy Rich
Sam Scarber
David Sloan
Ken Smith
Paul Smith
Jon Sutton
Willie Turral
Emilio Vallez
Rodney Wallace
David Ward
Derwin Williams
Mike Williams
Ray Wilson
John Woodcock
Don Woods

New Mexico Highlands (11)

Mark Cotney
Charley Cowan
Monte Crockett
Anthony Edwards
Carl Garrett
Len Garrett
Reggie Garrett
Bill Miller
Lionel Taylor
Sam Williams
Don Woods

New Mexico Mil. Inst. (J.C.) (11)

Wilson Alvarez
Dave Atkins
John Carrell
Jack Chapple
Bob Daugherty
Conrad Hamilton
Joe Hernandez
Eddie Miller
Dave Sherer
Roger Staubach
Tim Van Galder

New Mexico State (36)

Willie Adams
Al Andrews
Pervis Atkins
Ted Bachman
Leo Barker
Al Barnes
Joseph Campbell
Andy Dorris
Darryl Ford
Bob Gaiters
Roy Gerela
Duriel Harris
Bobby Humphery
Bobby Jackson
Joey Jackson
Po James
Charley Johnson
Holbert Johnson
Walter Johnson
Bob Kelly
Aaron Laing
Billy Locklin
Kerry Locklin
Sean Manuel
Pep Menefee
Eddie Miller
Ray Milo
Lincoln Minor
Jerry Nuzum
Cliff Olander
Joe Pisarcik
Joe Schmiesing
Troy Sienkiewicz
Danny Villanueva
Walt Williams
Fredd Young

New York Tech (2)

Chris Brown
James Eaddy

New York U. (29)

Bob Barrabee
Frank Briante
Fred Brown
John Bunyan
George Chalmers
Rick Concannon
Bob Dunn
Bernie Feibish
Beryl Follet
Len Grant
Rosie Grant
Joe Hugret
Basilio Marchi
Charley Marshall
Bing Miller
Dave Myers
Jerry Nemecek
Mike Riordan
Ollie Satenstein
Babe Scheuer
Jack Shapiro
Dave Skudin
Ed Smith
Ken Strong
Phil Swiadon
Bill Tanguay
Chief Toorock
Bill Wexler
Ralph White

Newberry (2)

Greg Hartle
Herb Spencer

Newport (Wales) (1)

Allan Watson

Niagara (8)

Art Deremer
Dan DeSantis
Chick Guarnieri
Al Gutknecht
Paul Hogan
Roman Piskor
Bob Stefik
John Tosi

Nicholls State (16)

Sheldon Andrus
Gary Barbaro
Mark Carrier
Terrence Cooks
Greg Harding
Doug Hudson
Jamie Lawson
Johnny Meads
Jay Pennison
Darryl Pounds
Rusty Rebowe
Oscar Smith
Dee Thomas
Anthony Tuggle
Lionel Vital
Dwight Walker

Norfolk State (14)

John Baker
Joe Bell
Ron Bolton
Gene Ferguson
Willie Gillus
LaRue Harrington
Ray Jarvis
A.J. Jimerson
Earl Jones
Leroy Jones
Alex Moore
Ricky Ray
Ken Reaves
James Roe

Normandale CC MN (3)

Wally Kersten
Mark Nelson
Tom Polley

North Alabama (16)

Lewis Billups
Chris Goode
Jarius Hayes
Harlon Hill
Stephen Hobbs
Bruce Jones
Marcus Keyes
Shawn Lee
Ronald McKinnon
Israel Raybon
Al Romine
Tyrone Rush
Brian Satterfield
Daryl Smith
Robert Steele
Billy Witt

North Carolina (147)

Ethan Albright
Edward Anthony
Frank Aschenbrenner
Carlton Bailey
Roy Barker
Troy Barnett
Tommy Barnhardt
Harris Barton
Hank Bartos
James Betterson
Terry Billups
Brian Blados
Phil Blazer
Eric Blount
Brian Bollinger
Sean Boyd
Ray Bray
Bucky Brooks
Omar Brown
Kelvin Bryant
John Bunting
Danny Burmeister
Tom Burnette
Ron Burton
Alan Caldwell
Jim Camp
Carl Carr
Reggie Clark
Henry Clement
Joe Conwell
Buddy Curry
Calvin Daniels
Bill Darnall
Paul Davis
Reuben Davis
Greg DeLong
Jim DeRatt
Kevin Donnalley

Rick Donnalley
Torin Dorn
Dave Drechsler
Mike Dulaney
Greg Ellis
Bill Erickson
Howard Feggins
Derrick Fenner
Arnold Franklin
William Fuller
Frank Gallagher
Tim Goad
Al Goldstein
Antonio Goss
Cecil Gray
Larry Griffin
George Grimes
Darrell Hamilton
James Hamilton
Chris Hanburger
Roscoe Hansen
Dee Hardison
Bernardo Harris
Vic Harrison
Rip Hawkins
Jeff Hayes
Ted Hazelwood
William Henderson
Tom Higgins
Jimmy Hitchcock
Corey Holliday
Vonnie Holliday
Dwight Hollier
Ethan Horton
Ken Huff
Don Jackson
Bill Jackson
Ray Jacobs
Sammy Johnson
Leon Johnson
Bill Johnson
Brian Johnston
Lewis Jolley
Freddie Jones
Marcus Jones
Rondell Jones
Randy Jordan
Charlie Justice
Eddie Kahn
Ken Keller
Bob Kennedy
John Kerns
Bill Koman
Bob Lacey
Amos Lawrence
Jonathan Linton
Jim Magner
Steve Maronic
John Maskas
Eddie Mason
Deems May
Kivuusama Mays
Don McCauley
Tom McCauley
Natrone Means
Andy Miketa
Bill Moore
Tim Morrison
Mike Morton
Riddick Parker
Doug Paschal
Chris Pike
Barney Poole
Ollie Poole
Ray Poole
Bob Pratt
Jack Protz
Andre Purvis
Mike Richey
Austin Robbins
Shelton Robinson
Hosea Rodgers
Brian Simmons
Dave Simmons
Thomas Smith
Bill Smith
Don Stallings
Harry Stanback
Scott Stankavage
Eric Streater
Oscar Sturgis
Ed Sutton
Len Szafaryn
George Tandy
Lawrence Taylor
Rick Terry
Donnell Thompson
Dave Truitt
Mike Voight
Bracey Walker
Art Weiner
Mike Wilcher
Ken Willard
Brooks Williams
Robert Williams
Ernie Williamson
Bo Wood
Ron Wooten
Tito Wooten

North Carolina A&T (22)

Chris Barber
Elvin Bethea
Dwaine Board
Jessie Britt
Ralph Coleman
Tom Day
Cornell Gordon
Michael Hamilton
Mel Holmes
Bob Jackson
Toran James
Willie Pearson
Mel Phillips
George Ragsdale
George Small
J.D. Smith
Jamain Stephens
Joe Taylor
Craig Thompson
Dick Westmoreland
Reggie White
Donald Willis

North Carolina Central (25)

John Baker
Ernie Barnes
Louis Breeden
Jim Brewington
Arnold Brown
John Brown
Robert Clark
Buddy Crutchfield
Myron Dupree
William Frizzell
Jerry Gantt
Darius Helton
Chuck Hinton
Luther Jeralds
Aaron Martin
Robert Massey
Bob McAdams
Charles Romes
Richard Sligh
Reggie Smith
Mo Spencer
Franklin Tate
Ernie Warlick
Doug Wilkerson
Paul Winslow

North Carolina State (97)

Robert Abraham
Ray Agnew
Ricky Bell
Connie Mack Berry
Ralph Britt
Michael Brooks
Ted Brown
Don Buckey
Brian Bulluck
Frank Bush
Dennis Byrd
Jesse Campbell
Mac Cara
Ron Carpenter
Dick Christy
Mike Cofer
Ty Coon
Martin Cornelson
Damien Covington
Bill Cowher
Charles Davenport
Lin Dawson
Darrell Dess
Harold Deters
Chris Dieterich
Gary Downs
Rich Druschel
Johnny Evans
Art Faircloth
Vinnie Farrar
Stan Fritts
Roman Gabriel
Claude Gibson
Paul Gibson
Bubba Green
Skip Hamilton
Frank Harris
Kenny Harris
Todd Harrison
George Hegamin
Andy Hendel
Tom Higgins
D.D. Hoggard
Roland Hooks
Bobby Houston
Johnnie Hudson
Ed Hughes
John Huzvar
Rickey Isom
Haywood Jeffires
Izel Jenkins
Vaughan Johnson
Mike Jones
Carlos King
Erik Kramer
Reggie Lawrence
Bill Leach
Tom London
Lou Mark
Joe McIntosh
Art McMahon
Dan Medlin
David Merritt
Joe Milinichik
Neal Musser
Dennis Owens
Les Palmer
Danny Peebles
Ray Phillips
Mike Quick
Carl Reeves
Mike Reid
Jim Ritcher
Sebastian Savage
Joe Scarpati
Reggie Singletary
Kurt Sohn
Jack Stanton
Bill Stanton
Tremayne Stephens
William Strong
Jack Sullivan
Jess Tatum
Derrick Taylor
Pat Teague
Mark Thomas
Fernandus Vinson
Dewayne Washington
Alex Webster
Alvis Whitted
Bert Wilder
Eric Williams
George Williams
Perry Williams
Don Wilson
Naz Worthen
Charley Young

North Central (3)

Levert Carr
Fritz Roeseler
Ron Selesky

North Dakota (24)

Nip Felber
Charlie Gainor
Ron Green
Don Gulseth
Jimmy Hester
Marshall Jones
Cy Kahl
Irv Kupcinet
Jim LeClair
Dave Lince
Jack Mackenroth
Stu MacMillan
Errol Mann
Dale Markham
Tracy Martin
Steve Myhra
Dave Osborn
Monte Smith
Gregg Swartwoudt
Jim Talbott
Todd Thomas
Tuffy Thompson
Lloyd Young
Sam Young

North Dakota State (18)

Robert Blakely
Tyrone Braxton
Jim Dick
Kevin Donnalley
Phil Hansen
Dick Hanson
Doug Lloyd
Clarence McGeary
Jerry Mulready
Steve Nelson
Stacy Robinson
Rudy Rosatti
Cliff Rothrock
Scott Schutt
Chad Stark
Cecil Sturgeon
Lyle Sturgeon
Ernie Wheeler

North Dakota State Coll. of Science (JC) (1)

Joe Schmiesing

North Florida CC FL (1)

Jesse Solomon

North Greenville Coll. SC (J.C.) (1)

Andrew Jordan

North Hennepin CC MN (1)

Jeff Schuh

North Idaho Coll. (J.C.) (1)

Steve Parker

North Iowa Area CC (3)

Shawn Harper
Chuck Harris
Mark Tigges

North Park (1)

Paul Zaeske

North Texas (58)

Joe Abbey
Quincy Armstrong
Ken Bahnsen
Tomur Barnes
Ron Battle
Chuck Beatty
Craig Birdsong
Bill Bishop
Rayford Cooks
Jim Cooper
Greg Davidson
Lenny Dunlap
Tony Elliott
Dan Garza
Tom Gipson
Toby Gowin
Joe Greene
Cedrick Hardman
Abner Haynes
Louis Haynes
Glen Holloway
Glenn Holtzman
Curt Knight
Reggie Lewis
Carl Lockhart
John Lott
John Love
Lloyd Lowe
Bill McWatters
Michael Minter
Donnie Joe Morris
Garvin Mugg
Buddy Parker
Willie Parker
Erric Pegram
Art Perkins
Kim Phillips
Perry Pruett
Steve Ramsey
Beasley Reece
Ray Renfro
Dean Renfro
Tommy Runnels
Bob Sanders
Hurles Scales
Ron Shanklin
Charlie Shepard
J.T. Smith
Bobby Smith
John Starnes
Larry Strickland
Dennis Swilley
Fred Washington
Creston Whitaker
A.D. Whitfield
Mark Witte
Royce Womble
Ted Wright

Northeast CC NE (1)

Ted Doyle

Northeast Louisiana (35)

Charlie Barnes
Jeff Blackshear
Orlando Bobo
Scott Boucher
Vincent Brisby
Bubby Brister
Conrad Clarks
Fred Coleman
Joe Driskill
Jimmy Edwards
John Floyd
Steve Foley
James Folston
Teddy Garcia
Jackie Harris
Stan Humphries
Will Johnson
Bob Kellogg
Shawn King
Vic Minor
Doug Pederson
Ken Poole
Roosevelt Potts
Joe Profit
Steve Rhem
Greg Robinson
Tag Rome
Irving Spikes
Smokey Stover
Hugh Taylor
Ronnie Washington
Larry Whigham
Stepfret Williams
Tito Wooten
Don Zimmerman

Northeast Mississippi CC (4)

Jeff Blackshear
Dave Strickland
Michael Williams
Jerome Woods

Northeast Missouri State (9)

Rick Cash
Lenvil Elliott
Russell Evans
Tom Geredine
Larry Jones
Mike Morris
Leo Petree
Steve Powell
Jack Robinson

Northeastern (10)

Bob Cappadona
Jerome Daniels
Sean Jones
Darin Jordan
Dan Ross
Todd Sandham
Eric Stokes
Sid Watson
Mike Williams
Keith Willis

Northeastern Illinois (1)

Ron Daugherty

Northeastern JC CO (4)

Dave Costa
Paul Costa
Sam Scarber
Jim White

Northeastern Oklahoma A&M (J.C.) (32)

Jerry Anderson
Matt Blair
Larry Bowie
Marion Butts
Scott Case
Alvro Casey
Charlie Clemons
Jack Epps
Jerrell Franklin
Ernest Givins
Reggie Harrison
Joey Howard
Darrell Irvin
LeShon Johnson
Carl Kidd
Frank Lasky
Nate Lewis
Ralph McGill
Eric Moore
Darrick Owens
Robert Parker
Chris Penn
Tony Peters
Don Pumphrey
Chuck Smith
Kywin Supernaw
Greg Tremble
Ronnie West
James Wilder
Billy Williams
Bobby Wilson
Ron Yankowski

Northeastern State (Okla.) (9)

Ira Albright
Vaughn Dunbar
Bob Hudson
Tony Hutson
Rosie Manning
Wes Matthews
Derrick Moore
Dan Smith
Pat Williams

Northern Arizona (29)

Charlie Brown
Dave Cahill
Sonny Campbell
Phil Cancik
Darren Carrington
Al Clark
Allan Clark
Shawn Collins
Jack DeGrenier
George Duarte
Tom Gibson
Fritz Greenlee
Michael Haynes
Ed Judie
Tom Jurich
Dan Kratzer
David Lang
Jeff Lewis
Goran Lingmerth
Mark Lomas
Pete Mandley
Lee Mulleneaux
Frank Pollack
Willard Reaves
Elston Ridgle
DeJuan Robinson
Rayna Stewart
Sims Stokes
Rusty Tillman

Northern Colorado (8)

Steve Gaunty
Andy Haase
Bill Kenney
Jeff Knapple
Tony Ramirez
Loren Snyder
Dave Stalls
Frank Wainright

Northern Illinois (31)

Carl Aikens
Jim Avery
Doug Bartlett
Bill Bealles
Chuck Behan
Larry Brink
Randy Clark
Brian Glasgow
Jerry Golsteyn
Jim Hannula
Steve Hirsch
Mitch Jacoby
Toimi Jarvi
LeShon Johnson
Mark Kellar
Scott Kellar
Jerry Latin
Jerry Meyers
Ken Moore
Reino Nori
Curt Pardridge
Todd Peat
David Petway
Dan Rosado
Pete Roth
Reggie Sims
John Spilis
Hollis Thomas
Tim Tyrrell
Clarence Vaughn
Tom Wittum

Northern Iowa (16)

Bill Bealles
Willie Beamon
Joe Fuller
Steve Harris
James Jones
Ken Knapczyk
Larry Miller
Frank Ori
Bryce Paup
Dennis Remmert
Randy Schultz
Kenny Shedd
Dedric Ward
Kurt Warner
Kevin Webster
Steve Wright

Northern Michigan (9)

Steve Avery
Tim Kearney
Chuck Klingbeil
Bob Kroll
Mark Maddox
Tom Neumann
Bill Rademacher
Len St. Jean
Jerry Woods

Northern Oklahoma Coll. (J.C.) (1)

Swede Ellstrom

Northern State (1)

Chris Bentz

Northern Virginia CC (1)

John Leypoldt

Northland CC MN (2)

Paul Feldhausen
Don Harris

Northwest Mississippi CC (17)

John Armstrong
John Avery
Leonard Burton
Lonny Calicchio
Roy Hart
Bill Houston
Cortez Kennedy
Bryant Mix
Alton Montgomery
Roell Preston
Ron Shegog
Eric Smith
Fred Thomas
Tommy Thompson
Leonard Wheeler
Henry Williams
Mitchell Young

Northwest Missouri State (3)

Ivan Schottel
Ed Tillison
Mike Zentic

Northwestern (132)

Mike Adamle
Dick Alban
Tony Ardizzone
Doug Asad
Frank Aschenbrenner
Darryl Ashmore
Darnell Autry
Frank Baker
Cas Banaszek
Alf Bauman
Sid Bennett
George Benson
Larry Benz
Rich Borresen
Greg Boykin
Jim Browne
Hank Bruder
Richard Buchanan
George Burman
Ron Burton
Woody Campbell
Hal Carlson
Joe Cerne
Bob Christian
Phil Clark
Leon Cook
Clyde Crabtree
Steve Craig
Irv Cross
Andy Cvercko
John Damore
Randy Dean
Bill deCorrevont
Fred DeStefano
Paddy Driscoll
Curtis Duncan
Fate Echols
Tiny Engebretsen
Dick Erdlitz
Mickey Erickson
Dick Fencl
Tom Flaherty
Paul Flatley
Dick Flowers
Willmer Fowler
Bob Gonya
Gene Gossage
Otto Graham
Ted Grefe
Mike Guendling
Chuck Hajek
Jack Haman
Ed Herman
Chris Hinton
Buckets Hirsch
Johnny Holloway
Walt Holmer
Thomas Homco
John Ivlow
Paul Janus
Ralph Jecha
Carroll Johnson
Don Johnson
Luke Johnsos
Mark Johnson
Alex Kapter
Ted Karras
Jim Keane
Doc Kelley
Mike Kerrigan
John Kidd
Elbert Kimbrough
Bob Koehler
Johnny Kovatch
Irv Kupcinet
Jim Lash
Jim Lecture
Tiny Lewis
Chuck Logan
Joe Lokanc
Angelo Loukas
Dennis Lundy

Glen Magnusson
Eggs Manske
Rube Marquardt
Chris Martin
Barney Mathews
John McCambridge
Skip McClendon
Bill McElwain
Al Moore
Max Morris
Bob Motl
Alex Moyer
Art Murakowski
Tom Myers
Matt O'Dwyer
Larry Onesti
Dan Orlich
Chuck Palmer
Barry Pearson
Tim Powell
Ron Rector
Pug Rentner
Jack Riley
Jack Rudnay
Reb Russell
Vic Schwall
Pete Shaw
Jules Siegle
Mike Sikich
Dick Smith
Dick Stahlman
Don Stonesifer
Eddie Sutter
Bob Swisher
Willie Sydnor
Joe Szczecko
Steve Tasker
Rob Taylor
Jim Turner
Fred Vanzo
Mike Varty
Pete Volz
Hal Weldin
Norm Wells
Chet Widerquist
Ray Wietecha
Fred Williamson
George Wilson
Mike Witteck
George Zorich

Northwestern (Ia) (1)

Kelvin Korver

Northwestern Coll. OH (J.C.) (1)

Joe Beauchamp

Northwestern Okla. State (4)

Chetti Carr
Percell Gaskins
Chip Myers
Brian Sochia

Northwestern State-Louisiana (34)

Fred Broussard
Joe Delaney
Al Dodd
Mark Duper
Al Edwards
Willie Fears
Jerry Fowler
Paul Frazier
Ross Gwinn
James Hall
Adrian Hardy
Bobby Hebert
Charley Hennigan
Randy Hilliard
Monte Ledbetter
Kevin Lewis
Robert Moore
Vic Nyvall
Victor Oatis
Sammy Odom
Petey Perot
Gary Reasons
Larry Robinson
Jackie Smith
Marcus Spears
John Stephens
Keith Thibodeaux
Sidney Thornton
Charley Tolar
Darrel Toussaint
Floyd Turner
Odessa Turner
Randy Walker
Wayne Walker

Norwich (4)

Beau Almodobar
Frank Liebel
Jim Luscinski
Gus Redman

Notre Dame (429)

John Adams
Ken Adamson
Arnold Ale
Jeff Alm
Eddie Anderson
Hunk Anderson
Elmer Angsman
Steve Bagarus
Pete Bahan
Pat Ballage
Steve Banas
Robert Banks
Norm Barry
Harry Baujan
Mark Bavaro
Byron Beams
Doug Becker
Ed Beinor
Greg Bell
Pete Bercich
Pete Berezney
Bert Berry
Angelo Bertelli
Art Best
Jerome Bettis
Steve Beuerlein
Rocky Bleier
Johnny Blood
Ronnie Blye
Ned Bolcar
Luther Bradley
Mike Brennan
Reggie Brooks
Tony Brooks
Chris Brown
Derek Brown
Tim Brown
Jim Browner
Ross Browner
Jim Brutz
Junior Bryant
Frank Budka
Nick Buoniconti
Ted Burgmeier
Max Burnell
Jeff Burris
Dave Butler
Frank Butler
Mike Calhoun
Al Cannava
Bob Cappadona
Glen Carberry
Fred Cardinal
John Carney
Joe Carollo
Rob Carpenter
Jim Carroll
Tom Carter
Dave Casper
Pete Chryplewicz
Gus Cifelli
Willie Clark
Bob Clasby
Corwin Clatt
Tom Clements
Lyron Cobbins
Stan Cofall
Herb Coleman
Lincoln Coleman
Greg Collins
Vince Commisa
Larry Conjar
Ward Connell
George Connor
Ed Cook
James Cook
Mike Corgan
Paul Costa
Fod Cotton
Danny Coughlin
Frank Coughlin
Larry Coutre
John Covington
Gerry Cowhig
Bob Crable
Ron Crews
Bernie Crimmins
Jim Crotty
Jim Crowley
Al Culver
Rodney Culver
Ziggy Czarobski
Bob Dahl
Boley Dancewicz
Bob David
Travis Davis
Mike Davlin
Lake Dawson
Cy DeGree
Rick DiBernardo
Eric Dorsey
Bob Dove
Demetrius DuBose
Dave Duerson
Eddie Duggan
Pete Duranko
Ray Ebli
Nick Eddy
Cap Edwards
Marc Edwards
Ray Eichenlaub
Pat Eilers
Clarence Ellis
Rex Enright
Fred Evans
Mike Fanning
Al Feeney
Vagas Ferguson
Cedric Figaro
Bill Fischer
Freeman Fitzgerald
Jim Flanigan
Tim Foley
Tony Furjanic
Mike Gann
Hec Garvey
Joe Gasparella
Tom Gatewood
Frank Gaul
Billy Gay
Oliver Gibson
Bob Gladieux
George Goeddeke
Mike Golic
Bob Golic
Bill Gompers
Kent Graham
Paul Grasmanis
Mark Green
Norm Greeney
Bob Greenhalgh
Jerry Groom
Tim Grunhard
Ralph Guglielmi
Kris Haines
Bob Hanlon
Terry Hanratty
Kevin Hardy
Leon Hart
Dave Hayes
Joe Heap
Tom Hearden
Andy Heck
Pat Heenan
Shawn Heffern
Steve Heimkreiter
John Helwig
Craig Hentrich
Luke Higgins
Paul Hogan
Pete Holohan
Paul Hornung
John Huarte
Dave Huffman
Tim Huffman
Ernie Hughes
Al Hunter
Art Hunter
Tony Hunter
Raghib Ismail
George Izo
Anthony Johnson
Joe Johnson
Andre Jones
Jerry Jones
Steve Juzwik
Mike Kadish
Joe Kantor
Ken Karcher
Cy Kasper
Joe Katchik
Emmett Keefe
Paul Kell
Mike Kelley
Bob Kelly
Jim Kelly
Bill Kerr
Blair Kiel
Roger Kiley
Bucko Kilroy
Randy Kinder
Greg Knafelc
Lindsay Knapp
Mike Koken
Frank Kosikowski
Mike Kovaleski
John Kovatch
Scott Kowalkowski
John Krimm
Frank Kuchta
Bob Kuechenberg
Ray Kuffel
Joe Kuharich
Vic Kulbitski
George Kunz
Joe Kurth
Curly Lambeau
Daryle Lamonica
Chuck Lanza
Ojay Larson
Johnny Lattner
John Law
Don Lawrence
Bernie Leahy
Ray Lemek
Jim Leonard
Bill Leonard
Bobby Leopold
Dorsey Levens
Mike Lind
Rusty Lisch
Bob Livingstone
Tom Longo
Johnny Lujack
Todd Lyght
Jim Lynch
Dick Lynch
J.D. Maarleveld
Ken MacAfee
Red Mack
Bob Maddock
Chick Maggioli
Drew Mahalic
Grover Malone
Ray Marelli
Dave Martin
Jim Martin
Greg Marx
John Mastrangelo
Menil Mavraides
Joey Maxwell
Frank Mayer
Derrick Mayes
Gene Mayl
Oscar McBride
Mike McCoy
Devon McDonald
Karmeeleyah McGill
Mike McGill
Gene McGuire
Tom McLaughlin
John McMullan
Paul McNulty
Bill McPeak
Jack Meagher
Harry Mehre
Jim Mello
Art Mergenthal
John Meyer
Ed Mieszkowski
Don Miller
John Miller
Wayne Millner
Rick Mirer
Johnny Mohardt
Joe Montana
Larry Moriarty
Emmett Mortell
Tim Moynihan
Fred Mundee
Jim Mutscheller
Peaches Nadolney
Steve Nemeth
Steve Niehaus
Jerry Noonan
Harry O'Boyle
Tommy O'Connell
Bill O'Connor
Jim O'Malley
Bob O'Neil
Mike Oriard
Chet Ostrowski
Alan Page
Sam Palumbo
John Panelli
Tony Pasquesi
Walt Patulski
Dud Pearson
John Pergine
John Perko
Mike Perrino
Tony Peterson
Johnny Petitbon
Bob Phelan
Milt Piepul
Nick Pietrosante
Allen Pinkett
Joe Pivarnik
Dave Pivec
Ron Plantz
Joe Pliska
Bull Polisky
Myron Pottios
John Powers
Phil Pozderac
Wes Pritchett
Joe Prokop
Andy Puplis
Steve Quinn
Nick Rassas
Brian Ratigan
Ray Ratkowski
George Ratterman
Tom Regner
Tom Rehder
Jim Reilly
Charley Riffle
John Rogers
Allen Rossum
Tim Ruddy
Tim Rudnick
Joe Ruetz
Ed Rutkowski
Tim Ryan
Frank Rydzewski
Julie Rykovich
Lou Rymkus
Joe Savoldi
Bob Scarpitto
Don Schaefer
Eddie Scharer
Tom Schoen
Bob Scholtz
Jim Schrader
Joe Scibelli
Vin Scott
John Scully
Paul Seiler
Si Seyfrit
Jim Seymour
Alec Shellogg
Joe Signaigo
Floyd Simmons
Emil Sitko
Bob Skoglund
Fritz Slackford
Stan Smagala
Chris Smith
Irv Smith
Red Smith
Rod Smith
Bill Smyth
Jack Snow
Jim Snowden
Frank Spaniel
Frank Stams
Basil Stanley
Art Statuto
Bill Steinkemper
Brian Stenger
Mark Stevenson
Ralph Stewart
Monty Stickles
Mike Stonebreaker
George Streeter
George Strohmeyer
Harry Stuhldreher
George Sullivan
Richard Swatland
Mike Swistowicz
Steve Sylvester
Frank Szymanski
Dick Szymanski
Kinnon Tatum
Aaron Taylor
Bobby Taylor
George Terlep
Pat Terrell
Tom Thayer
Joe Theismann
Bob Thomas
George Tobin
Bob Toneff
Mario Tonelli
Stacey Toran
George Trafton
Frank Tripucka
Gasper Urban
Dom Vairo
Frank Varrichione
Arunas Vasys
George Vergara
John Wallace
Fred Wallner
Bill Walsh
Ricky Watters
Dave Waymer
Ron Weissenhofer
Marty Wendell
Jeff Weston
Bob Wetoska
Tom Whelan
Ray Whipple
Jim White
Mike Whittington
Bill Wightkin
Bob Williams
Joel Williams
Larry Williams
Ted Williams
George Wilson
Troy Wilson
Bill Wolski
Shawn Wooden
Neil Worden
Harry Wunsch
Renaldo Wynn
Chet Wynne
Elmer Wynne
Tommy Yarr
John Yonakor
Bryant Young
Ernie Zalejski
Dusty Zeigler
Ray Zellars
Jack Zilly
Clyde Zoia
Lou Zontini
Chris Zorich

Oberlin (1)

Herb Henderson

Occidental (7)

Keith Beebe
Ron Botchan
Steve Brooks
Jack Kemp
Gene Moore
Vance Mueller
Jim Steffen

Oglethorpe (2)

Ted Fulton
Frank Zelencik

Ohio Dominican (1)

Dom Albanese

Ohio Northern (3)

Don Batchelor
Stacey Hairston
Paul Lynch

Ohio State (288)

Tony Adamle
Doug Adams
Dick Anderson
William Anderson
Steve Andrako
Tom Barrington
Brian Baschnagel
Todd Bell
Greg Bellisari
John Bettridge
Harry Bliss
Hubert Bobo
John Borton
Morris Bradshaw
Hi Brigham
John Brockington
Aaron Brown
Dick Brubaker
Bob Brudzinski
Carl Brumbaugh
Fred Bruney
Chuck Bryant
Sam Busich
Keith Byars
Butler By'Not'e
Joe Campanella
Joe Cannavino
Cris Carter
Craig Cassady
Hopalong Cassady
George Cheroke
Frank Clair
Algy Clark
Vinnie Clark
Ollie Cline
Neal Colzie
Ray Conlin
Jim Cope
Jeff Cothran
Tom Cousineau
Frank Cumiskey
Cookie Cunningham
Tony Curcillo
Mike Current
Pete Cusick
Jim Daniell
LeShun Daniels
Jeff Davidson
Glenn Davis
Hal Dean
Allen DeGraffenreid
Tom DeLeone
Spiro Dellerba
Raymond DiPierro
Dick Dobeleit
Doug Donley
Dick Doyle
Rickey Dudley
Jack Dugger
Gary Dulin
Howard Duncan
Byron Eby
Bruce Elia
Ray Ellis
Gene Fekete
Bob Ferguson
Keith Ferguson
Jerry Fields
Matt Finkes
Dick Flanagan
Jim Flower
Dave Foley
Jerome Foster
Sam Fox
Tim Fox
Doug France
Dave Francis
John Frank
Joey Galloway
Sonny Gandee
Bob Gaudio
Shaun Gayle
Eddie George
Horace Gillom
Jim Gilmore
Terry Glenn
Sam Goldman
Sonny Gordon
Flop Gorrill
Randy Gradishar
Scottie Graham
Jeff Graham
Kent Graham
Rory Graves
Archie Griffin
Ray Griffin
Anthony Griggs
Lou Groza
Al Hadden
Ray Hanson
Chic Harley
Roger Harper
Dud Harris
Raymont Harris
George Hasenohrl
Leo Hayden
Herb Henderson
Champ Henson
Luther Henson
John Hicks
Alex Higdon
Dick Himes
Jamie Holland
Charlie Honaker
Les Horvath
Jim Houston
Lin Houston
Harry Howard
Ty Howard
Bobby Hoying
Iolas Huffman
Chuck Hutchison
Wilmer Isabel
Dan James
Tommy James
Bruce Jankowski
Vic Janowicz
Jack Jennings
Bill Jobko
Pete Johnson
Pepper Johnson
Red Joseph
Mike Kabealo
John Kacherski
Carl Kaplanoff
Bob Karch
Jim Karcher
Tom Keane
Ike Kelley
Rob Kelly
Rex Kern
Marlon Kerner
Alan Kline
Vic Koegel
Larry Kolic
Gerry Krall
Mark Krerowicz
Howie Kriss
Eric Kumerow
Rudy Kutler
Jim Lachey
Garcia Lane
Jim Laughlin
Dante Lavelli
Scott Leach
Dick LeBeau
Byron Lee
Dave Leggett
Jack Lininger
Dick Logan
Tom Long
Kirk Lowdermilk
Orlando Lowry
Steve Luke
Doug Mackie
Wade Manning
Vic Marino
Jim Marshall
Tom Matte
Rufus Mayes
Don McCafferty
Jim McDonald
Bill Michael
Rich Michael
Al Michaels
Rick Middleton
Bob Momsen
Regis Monahan
Jimmy Moore
Fred Morrison
Calvin Murray
Truck Myers
Bob Myers
Dick Nardi
Andy Nemecek
John Nichols
Ike Nonnenmaker
Bobby Olive
Tom Orosz
Jim Otis
Orlando Pace
Bob Padan
Max Padlow
Fred Pagac
Jim Parker
Tito Paul
Dwight Peabody
Pete Perini
Mike Perrotti
Boni Petcoff
Stan Pincura
Doug Plank
Craig Powell
Ted Provost
Leo Raskowski
Chuck Ream
Chris Riehm
William Roberts
Nick Roman
Ted Rosequist
George Rosso
Ev Rowan
Steve Ruzich
Chris Sanders
Daryl Sanders
Paul Sarringhaus
Cedric Saunders
Dick Schafrath
Herb Schell
Art Schlichter
Kurt Schumacher
Jack Scott
Bo Scott
Dean Sensanbaugher
Mike Sensibaugh
Bob Shaw
Tom Skladany
Bill Slyker
Dick Smith

Doug Smith
Robert Smith
Matt Snell
Cecil Souders
Alonzo Spellman
Tim Spencer
Chris Spielman
Bob Spiers
Ron Springs
Shawn Springs
Brian Stablein
Joe Staysniak
Pete Stinchcomb
Jimmy Strausbaugh
Korey Stringer
Lorenzo Styles
Nicky Sualua
Don Sutherin
Jack Tatum
Tarzan Taylor
Russ Thomas
Sam Tidmore
Mike Tomczak
Steve Tovar
Tom Tupa
Tiny Turner
Jim Tyrer
Jeff Uhlenhake
Doug Van Horn
Dick Van Raaphorst
Bob Vogel
Tim Vogler
Mike Vrabel
Chris Ward
Paul Warfield
Al Washington
Bobby Watkins
Tad Weed
Hal Wendler
Buzz Wetzel
Jan White
Bob White
Stan White
William White
Dan Wilkinson
Gary Williams
Joe Williams
Mark Williams
Leonard Willis
Bill Willis
Don Wiper
Scott Woolf
Hoge Workman
Vince Workman
Ernie Wright
Howard Yerges
Billy Young
Frank Zadworney
Gust Zarnas

Ohio U. (29)

Chet Adams
Bob Brooks
Reggie Brown
Jason Carthen
Vince Costello
Earl Duvall
John Fekete
Russ Finsterwald
Tom Gerhart
Dick Grecni
Dave Green
John Guzik
Paul Halleck
Bob Harrison
George Hastings
Len Janiak
Dave Juenger
John Kerns
Earl Krieger
Jack LeVeck
Art Lewis
Al Miller
Harry Newman
Clete Patterson
Frank Peters
Walt Rogers
Bob Snyder
Bull Snyder
Todd Snyder

Ohio Wesleyan (13)

Dick Brubaker
Fred Day
Deke Edler
Babe Frump
Ray Hanson
Buck Lamme
Don Nelson
Harley Pearce
Keith Rucker
Olin Smith
John Turley
Ed Westfall
Sonny Winters

Oklahoma (233)

Kevin Adkins
Troy Aikman
Stephen Alexander
James Allen
Joe Allton
Jerry Anderson
Vickey Ray Anderson
Plato Andros
Dave Baker
Karl Baldischwiler
Reggie Barnes
Aubrey Beavers
Jason Belser
Thomas Benson
Scott Blanton
Billy Bookout
Brian Bosworth
Joe Bowden
Bobby Boyd
Max Boydston
Danny Bradley
Rickey Brady
Tom Brahaney
Bill Breeden
Dewell Brewer
Obie Bristow
Billy Brooks
Sonny Brown
Donald Brown
Sidney Brown
Rick Bryan
Steve Bryan
Buddy Burris
Dexter Bussey
Bill Campbell
Lydell Carr
Scott Case
Tony Casillas
Tom Catlin
Ben Cavil
Al Chandler
Cliff Chatman
Sam Claphan
Beryl Clark
Gene Cockrell
Patrick Collins
Glen Condren
Bill Conkright
J.R. Conrad
Adrian Cooper
Al Coppage
Ross Coyle
Jerry Crafts
Leon Crosswhite
Terry Crouch
Earl Crowder
Derrick Crudup
Jim Culbreath
George Cumby
Kyle Davis
Wendell Davis
Tim Denton
Stacey Dillard
Rickey Dixon
Dick Dorsey
Dwight Drane
Gil Duggan
Bob Dunlap
Marcus Dupree
Roger Eason
Van Edmondson
Jimmy Edwards
Swede Ellstrom
Jimbo Elrod
Scott Evans
Jim Files
Willie Franklin
Keith Gary
Prentice Gautt
Weldon Gentry
Joe Golding
Darryl Goodlow
John Goodman
Roy Guffey
Ray Hamilton
Jimmy Harris
Bob Harrison
Ben Hart
Steve Haworth
Leon Heath
Bud Hebert
Zac Henderson
Victor Hicks
Cowboy Hill
Eddie Hinton
Randy Hughes
Daryl Hunt
Darrell Irvin
Horace Ivory
Frank Ivy
Keith Jackson
Jack Jacobs
Ed Jeffers
Darrius Johnson
Greg Johnson
Troy Johnson
Cedric Jones
Dante Jones
Bob Kalsu
Durwood Keeton
Bobby Kimball
Kenny King
Reggie Kinlaw
Billy Krisher
Hal Lahar
Walt Lamb
Tim Lashar
Biff Lee
Scott Leggett
Joe Don Looney
Thomas Lott
Jim Mankins
Leon Manley
Rod Manuel
Dick Marsh
Johnny Martin
Reggie Mathis
Corey Mayfield
Carl McAdams
Mike McClellan
Hugh McCullough
Wahoo McDaniel
Flip McDonald
Tommy McDonald
Buck McPhail
Ed McQuarters
Ken Mendenhall
Joey Mickey
Paul Migliazzo
Glyn Milburn
Jack Mildren
Derland Moore
Jerald Moore
Dennit Morris
Lee Morris
Kevin Murphy
Ralph Neely
Fred Nixon
Louis Oubre
David Overstreet
Jim Owens
Steve Owens
Tinker Owens
Homer Paine
Mickey Parks
Harold Paul
Elvis Peacock
Lindy Pearson
Tony Peters
Tyrell Peters
Mike Pleasant
Ken Pope
Jack Porter
Clyde Powers
Lee Presley
Billy Pricer
Greg Pruitt
Johnny Rapacz
Kenyon Rasheed
Darrol Ray
Terry Ray
Jerry Reese
Mike Reilly
Caesar Rentie
Lance Rentzel
Buster Rhymes
Jim Riley
Greg Roberts
Jim Rockford
Tyrone Rodgers
Jimmy Rogers
Dave Rolle
Alvin Ross
Charley Sarratt
Dewey Selmon
Lee Roy Selmon
Steven Sewell
Bob Seymour
Derrick Shepard
Jackie Shipp
John Shirk
Rod Shoate
Travis Simpson
Billy Sims
Elmer Slough
Travian Smith
Cliff Speegle
Red Stacy
Ralph Stevenson
Paul Tabor
Philip Tabor
Barron Tanner
Chuck Thomas
Clendon Thomas
George Thomas
Jim Thomas
Mike Thomas
Bobby Thompson
Pete Tillman
Spencer Tillman
Keith Traylor
Jerry Tubbs
Jeff Tupper
Richard Turner
Jim Tyree
Billy Vessels
Uwe von Schamann
Darnell Walker
Joe Washington
John Watson
Elbert Watts
Jim Weatherall
Mike Weddington
Stan West
Phil White
Marv Whited
Firpo Wilcox
Stanley Wilson
Chet Winters
Tony Woods
Paul Young
Waddy Young
Steve Zabel

Oklahoma Baptist (2)

Clark Craig
Ewell Phillips

Oklahoma City (10)

Ace Gutowsky
Hal Hilpert
Jim Kamp
Ralph Schilling
Ray Schwab
Marion Shirley
Hugh Taylor
Orville Tuttle
Jim Wade
Basil Wilkerson

Oklahoma Mil. Acad. (J.C.) (1)

Fran Lynch

Oklahoma Panhandle State (1)

Frank Beede

Oklahoma State (119)

Harold Akin
Bennie Aldridge
Loyd Arms
Neill Armstrong
David Bailey
Harold Bailey
Ron Baker
Tony Banfield
Paul Blair
Stanley Blair
Cary Blanchard
Bon Boatwright
Harry Bolton
Bill Bredde
Terry Brown
Harry Buffington
Scott Burk
Randy Burks
Keith Burns
Derek Burton
John Chesley
Jake Colhouer
Kelly Cook
John Corker
Charles Crawford
Gary Cutsinger
Joe Davidson
Phil Dokes
Charlie Durkee
Hart Lee Dykes
Donnie Echols
Jon Evans
Bob Fenimore
Ralph Foster
Wendall Gaines
Reuben Gant
Thurman Garrett
Walt Garrison
Jason Gildon
Jon Gilliam
Derrel Gofourth
Mike Green
Billy Grimes
Buddy Hardaway
Charlie Harper
Reuben Henderson
Rusty Hilger
Greg Hill
Mike Hudson
Leonard Jackson
Jack Jacobson
Ed Jeffers
Gregg Johnson
Howard Keys
Joe King
Jon Kolb
Jevon Langford
Toy Ledbetter
Gary Lewis
Sonny Liles
Garrett Limbrick
John Little
Bill Long
Alex Loyd
Dexter Manley
Wes Matthews
Alonzo Mayes
Lamar McGriggs
R.W. McQuarters
Dale Meinert
Darrel Meisenheimer
Ed Merkle
Calvin Miller
Terry Miller
Matt Monger
Mark Moore
Leslie O'Neal
Bill Owen
Frank Parker
Jim Parmer
Cliff Parsley
Gordon Peery
Reggie Pierson
Dean Prater
Dennis Randall
Jim Reynolds
Bobby Riley
Glenn Robinson
Mike Robinson
Chris Rockins
Barry Sanders
Charlie Shaw
Ricky Shaw
Jerry Sherk
Marion Shirley
Jim Spavital
Joe Spencer
Steve Stephens
Charlie Strack
Roger Taylor
Thurman Thomas
David Thompson
Leonard Thompson
Warren Thompson
Jim Turner
Robert Turner
Scott Tyner
John Ward
John Washington
James White
Demise Williams
Jeff Williams
Jamal Williams
Kevin Williams
Ronnie Williams
Duane Wood
Ab Wright
Ken Zachary
Mike Zentic

Olivet (2)

George Pyne
Ernest Watson

Olympic Coll. WA (J.C.) (2)

Mark Gehring
Mark Keel

Orange Coast Coll. CA (J.C.) (7)

Israel Ifeanyi
James Johnson
Cliff Livingston
Clancy Oliver
Benny Ricardo
Philip Spiller
Gregory Wojcik

Oregon (142)

Dan Archer
LeFrancis Arnold
Darrel Aschbacher
Steve Baack
Romeo Bandison
Derrick Barnes
Emery Barnes
Lew Barnes
Steve Barnett
Jack Beckett
Bruce Beekley
Latin Berry
Bob Berry
Lyle Bigbee
J.J. Birden
Del Bjork
Tom Blanchard
Chuck Bradley
Monte Brethauer
Matt Brock
Reggie Brown
Steve Brown
Len Burnett
Ross Carter
Tim Casey
Wendell Cason
Eric Castle
Tony Cherry
Max Choboian
George Christensen
Mario Clark
Chad Cota
Bree Cuppoletti
Dick Daugherty
Terry Dion
Dale Dorning
Bill Drake
Tom Drougas
Alex Eagle
Brad Ecklund
Charlie Elliott
Neil Elshire
Frank Emmons
Teddy Farmer
Roman Fortin
Dan Fouts
Russ Francis
Mike Gaechter
Roy Gagnon
Dan Garza
Leland Glass
Tom Graham
Reggie Grant
Dave Grayson
Tony Graziani
Bob Grottkau
Kwante Hampton
Steve Hardin
Tony Hargain
Ronnie Harris
Cliff Hicks
Bryan Hinkle
Scott Holman
Dick Horne
Bernie Hughes
Ron Hunt
Jerry Inman
Duke Iverson
Dick James
Pat Johnson
Ernest Jones
June Jones
Rick Kane
Thom Kaumeyer
Dutch Kitzmiller
Stan Kostka
Scott Kozak
Matt LaBounty
Tuffy Leemans
Jake Leicht
Reggie Lewis
Woodley Lewis
Joe Lillard
Derek Loville
George Martin
Pat Matson
Riley Mattson
Andy Maurer
Curt Mecham
Mike Mikulak
Chris Miller
Alex Molden
Bill Morgan
Jack Morris
Butch Morse
Bill Musgrave
Bob Newland
Anthony Newman
Terry Obee
Herman O'Berry
Chris Oldham
Muhammad Oliver
Jack Patera
Dino Philyaw
Rollin Putzier
Fred Quillan
Dan Ralph
Ahmad Rashad
Mel Renfro
Floyd Rhea
Rock Richmond
Jim Shanley
George Shaw
Mike Sikora
Jim Smith
Ron Snidow
Blake Spence
Timothy Stokes
Jack Stone
Jeff Stover
Jim Stuart
Bill Swain
Jerry Tarr
Willy Tate
Mark Temple
Jeff Thomason
Tommy Thompson
Dave Tobey
Norm Van Brocklin
Michael Walter
Claxton Welch
Willie West
Kenny Wheaton
Ricky Whittle
Paul Wiggins
Dave Wilcox
John Wilcox
Josh Wilcox
Dick Wilkins
Kevin Willhite
Vince Williams
Gary Zimmerman

Oregon State (102)

Fred Anderson
Juddy Ash
Bill Austin
Sam Baker
Terry Baker
Ted Bates
Gil Bergerson
Johnny Biancone
Dennis Boyd
Jerome Boyd
Darrick Brilz
Mike Burke
Vern Burke
Reggie Bynum
John Cadwell
Zuck Carlson
Ken Carpenter
Pat Chaffey
Herman Clark
Jim Clark
Tuffy Conn
Herschel Currie
John Didion
Ken Dow
Don Durdan
Scott Eaton
Bill Enyart
Dave Etherly
Paul Evansen
Harry Field
Joe Francis
Red Franklin
Rocky Freitas
Bill Gray
David Gray
Bob Grim
Harry Gunner
Johnny Hackenbruck
Bill Halverson
Craig Hanneman
Jeff Hart
Ron Heller
Doug Hogland
Bob Horn
Clark Hoss
David Howard
Honolulu Hughes
Kerry Justin
Carl Keever
Dick Koeper
Elmer Kolberg
Jess Lewis
Paul Lowe
Dave Mann
Howie Maple
Amos Marsh
Frank Marsh
Chuck Marshall
Greg Marshall
Pellom McDaniels
Bill McKalip
John Misko
Hal Moe
David Montagne
Rob Nairne
Bill Nelson
Calvin Nicholson
Tom Oberg
Don Odegard
Ted Ossowski
Hal Pangle
Dainard Paulson
Joe Phillips
Steve Preece
Hal Puddy
Frank Ramsey
Rocky Rasley
Jarvis Redwine
Hank Rivera
Steve Rogers
Reggie Rust
Don Samuel
Elbie Schultz
Ade Schwammel
Lew Scott
Vic Sears
James Stinnette
George Svendsen
Brian Taylor
Ken Taylor
Aaron Thomas
Robb Thomas
Reggie Tongue
Sam Tsoutsouvas
Esera Tuaolo
Skip Vanderbundt
Joe Wendlick
Craig Whelihan
Lloyd Wickett
Erik Wilhelm
Jerry Wilkinson
Len Younce

Oregon Tech (3)

Joe Cain
Nate Lewis
Don Summers

Ottawa (Ks) (2)

Dave Hale
Jack Knapper

Otterbein (6)

Bob Agler
Paul Davis
Dick Faust
Bob Padan
Steve Schnarr
Ed Seibert

Ouachita Baptist (5)

Carl Allen
Cliff Harris
Bill LaFitte
Ed Neal
Chuck Taylor

Pacific (Ore) (2)

Dick Daniels
Tim Hauck

Pacific Lutheran (3)

Craig Kupp
Sig Sigurdson
John Zamberlin

Paducah CC KY (1)

Ken Dunek

Palo Verde Coll. CA (J.C.) (1)

Monroe Eley

Palomar Coll. CA (J.C.) (4)

Tom Dempsey
Brad Henke
Thom Kaumeyer
Steve Rogers

Paris JC TX (1)

Cecil Johnson

Park (1)

Ken Jolly

Parsons (3)

Bruce Cortez
Nate Craddock
Mike Hennigan

Pasadena City Coll. CA (J.C.) (30)

Kim Anderson
Hasson Arbubakrr
Reggie Brown
Ron Brown
Don Burroughs
Victor Carroll
Dwayne Crump
Mike Dennis
Ray Ethridge
Dick Frey
Dave Hettema
Al Hoisington
Darick Holmes
Mark Korff
Mike Lansford
Jake Leicht
Bob Meyers
Ostell Miles
Anthony Miller
Jack Nix
Vince Osby
Danny Pittman
Grady Richardson
Mike Saxon
Don Stansauk
Eric Thomas
Jay Walker
Jim Wilks
Ellery Williams
Kevin Young

Paul Quinn (1)

Walter Napier

Pearl River CC MS (7)

Conrad Clarks
Danny Pierce
Jeff Posey
Tom Walters
Larry Whigham
Jerrel Wilson
Ray Wilson

Penn State (264)

Mike Alexander
Rogers Alexander
Doug Allen
Kurt Allerman
Richie Anderson
Mike Archie
Walker Lee Ashley
Chris Bahr
Matt Bahr
Ralph Baker
Bruce Bannon
Stew Barber
Clarence Beck
Lou Benfatti
Brad Benson
Todd Blackledge
Jeff Bleamer
Dave Bradley
Kyle Brady
Gary Brown
John Bruno
Todd Burger
Greg Buttle
Rich Buzin
Bob Campbell
John Cappelletti
Ki-Jana Carter
Frank Case
Jimmy Cefalo
Chuck Cherundolo
Bruce Clark
Stan Clayton
Duffy Cobbs
Ron Coder
Andre Collins
Kerry Collins
Shane Conlan
Chris Conlin
Larry Conover
Bobby Joe Conrad
Bill Contz
Brett Conway
Bud Cooper
Chuck Correal
Chuck Crist
Ron Crosby
Randy Crowder
Rae Crowther
Saville Crowther
Ernie Cuneo
Eric Cunningham
David Daniels
Bob Davis
Tom DePaso
Chris Devlin
Tom Donchez
Mark D'Onofrio
Tom Donovan
Keith Dorney
D.J. Dozier
Troy Drayton
Chuck Drazenovich
Roger Duffy
Bill Dugan
Jeff Durkota
John Ebersole
Bobby Engram
Curtis Enis
Herb Eschbach
Sean Farrell
Jack Filak
Scott Fitzkee
Mark Flythe
Marlon Forbes
Brian Franco
Mitch Frerotte
Len Frketich
Chuck Fusina
Gregg Garrity
Sam Gash
John Gerak
Charlie Getty
Ralph Giacomarro
Frank Giannetti
Reggie Givens
Keith Goganious
Dave Graf
Don Graham
Bucky Greeley
Donn Greenshields
Rosey Grier
Red Griffiths
Mike Guman
Al Gursky
Nick Haden
Hinkey Haines
Galen Hall
Jack Ham
Steve Hamas
Harry Hamilton
Shelly Hammonds
Franco Harris
Mike Hartenstine
Jeff Hartings
Gary Hayman
Ron Heller
Kim Herring
Bob Higgins
Dick Hoak
Rob Holmberg
Jeff Hostetler
John Hufnagel
Tom Hull
Leonard Humphries
Greg Huntington
Ray Isom
Kenny Jackson
Tyoka Jackson
Johnny Jaffurs
Chuck Janerette
Steve Joachim
Larry Joe
Andre Johnson
Tim Johnson
Don Jonas
Eric Jonassen
Joe Jurevicius
Vyto Kab
Keith Karpinski
Jim Kerr
Terry Killens
Glenn Killinger
Roger Kochman
Warren Koegel
Rudy Kraft
Larry Kubin
Pete Kugler
Ted Kwalick
Paul Lankford
Ron LaPointe
Phil LaPorta
Jim Laslavic
Bill Lenkaitis
Sid Lewis
Pete Liske
Sean Love
Richie Lucas
Lew Luce
Roger Mahoney
Massimo Manca
Tim Manoa
Mark Markovich
Rich Mauti
Mike McBath
Ernie McCann
Mike McCloskey
Quintus McDonald
O.J. McDuffie
Rich McKenzie
Mike Meade
Lance Mehl
Mike Michalske
Matt Millen
Stan Mills
Brian Milne
Rich Milot
Lydell Mitchell
Bob Mitinger
Greg Montgomery
Booker Moore
Lenny Moore
Red Moore
Dan Morgan
Bob Mrosko
Tony Mumford
Mike Munchak
Jim Nelson
Leo Nobile
John Nolan
Al Olszewski
Brian O'Neal
Ed O'Neil
Dennis Onkotz
Bob Ontko
Dave Opfar
Dan Orlich
Duke Osborn
Lou Palazzi
Mike Palm
Tony Panaccion
Irvin Pankey
Chet Parlavecchio
Bob Parsons
John Patrick
Darren Perry
Pepper Petrella
Charlie Pittman
Milt Plum
Andre Powell
Bill Pritchard
Keith Radecic
Scott Radecic
Tom Rafferty
Dick Rauch
Eric Ravotti
Ruel Redinger
Mike Reid
George Reihner
Glenn Ressler
Wally Richardson
Bob Riggle
Marco Rivera
Harry Robb
Dave Robinson
Mark Robinson
Johnny Roepke
Fran Rogel
Jim Romano
Hatch Rosdahl
James Rosecrans
Ray Roundtree
Dave Rowe
Todd Rucci
Brad Saar
Tony Sacca
Bill Saul
Carl Schaukowitch
Maury Schleicher
Dick Schuster
Freddie Scott
Bob Scrabis
Tom Sherman
Mickey Shuler
Chuck Sieminski
John Skorupan
Steve Smith
Bill Smyth
George Snell
Andy Stynchula
Matt Suhey
Steve Suhey
David Szott
Sam Tamburo
Jimmy Tays
Blair Thomas
Whitey Thomas
Leroy Thompson
Michael Timpson
Elgie Tobin
Bob Torrey
Wally Triplett
Greg Truitt
Jiggs Ullery
Les Walters
Curt Warner
Charlie Way
Bob Wear
Barney Wentz
Jon Williams
Leo Wisniewski
Steve Wisniewski
Jon Witman
Phil Yeboah-Kodie
Mike Zordich

Pennsylvania (55)

Eddie Allen
Chuck Bednarik
Eddie Bell
Jim Bryant
George Burrell
Ralph Calcagni
Don Clune
Clark Craig
Jim Crocicchia
Ben Derr
Wally Diehl
Herb Dieter
Fred Doelling
Bill Fiedler
Ray Frick
Bernie Gallagher
Ed Grain
Tex Hamer
Mark Iwanowski
Florian Kempf
Bert Kuczynski
Al Leith
Lou Little
Walt Masters
Neil Mathews
Tim Mazzetti
Ed McGinley
Heinie Miller
Skippy Minisi
Franny Murray
Herb Nelson
Brent Novoselsky
Bob Oristaglio
Pard Pearce
Frank Quillen
Bill Raffel
Frank Reagan
Jay Repko
Paul Riblett
Charley Rogers
George Savitsky
Don Schneider
John Schweder
Stan Sieracki
Bob Sponaugle
Walt Stickel
George Sullivan
Carl Thomas
Enid Thomas
John Thurman
Joe Valerio
Bill Ward
Joe Willson
Diddie Willson
Lud Wray

Pensacola JC FL (2)

Lee Nelson
Benny Russell

Pepperdine (5)

Tom Bedore
Jack Bighead
Mel Embree
Gerry Perry
Frank Williams

Peru State (2)

Joe Krejci
Joel Williams

Philander Smith (1)

Elijah Pitts

Phillips (10)

Dick Marsh
Joe Milam
Chuck O'Neil
Steve Owen
Bill Owen
Doug Roby
Harvey Sark
Len Sedbrook
Dutch Strauss
Orville Tuttle

Phoenix Coll. AZ (J.C.) (11)

Fred Carr
Ira Gordon
Carl Johnson
Lynn Larson
Andy Livingston
Jim McCann
Darryl Morrison
Tory Nixon
Damon Pieri
Morrie Warren
Toby Wright

Pierce Coll. CA (J.C.) (13)

Jimmy Allen
Hal Bedsole
Rick Duncan
Bernard Jackson
Erik Kramer
Babe Laufenberg
Jeff Markland
Chris Mims
Mark Nordquist
Alan Reid
Neal Sweeney
Tom Taylor
Rodney Williams

Pittsburg State (10)

Roy Andrews
Eldon Danenhauer
Ralph Earhart
Kendall Gammon
Emmett McLemore
Ronald Moore
Bob Tarrant
Ronnie West
Troy Wilson
Darryl Wren

Pittsburgh (239)

Ed Adamchik
Henry Adams
Rudy Andabaker
Curtis Anderson
Steve Apke
Bill Ashbaugh
Tom Barndt
Troy Benson
Karl Bohren
Nick Bolkovac
Jim Bond
Ernie Bonelli
Emil Boures
Jerry Boyarsky
A.B. Brown
Jesse Brown
Ruben Brown
Tom Brown
Tony Brown
Doc Bruder
Charlie Brueckman
Bob Buczkowski
Gary Burley
Dean Caliguire
Bill Callahan
Joe Carroll
Jon Carter
Dick Cassiano
Matt Cavanaugh
John Cenci
Mike Chalenski
Ralph Chase
Al Chesley
John Chickerneo
Greg Christy
Jeff Christy
Ralph Cindrich
Sam Clancy
James Clark
Bob Clemens
Dwight Collins
Paul Collins
Robert Coons
James Corbett
Jim Covert
Fred Cox
Eric Crabtree
Paul Cuba
Jim Cunningham
Bill Daddio
Ted Dailey
Ave Daniell
Billy Davis
Julius Dawkins
Jeff Delaney
Mike Ditka
Randy Dixon
Chris Doleman
Anthony Dorsett
Tony Dorsett
Jack Durishan
Bill Dutton
Bill Edgar
Bobby Epps
Rob Fada
Karl Farmer
Ralph Fife
Hoot Flanagan
Jim Flanigan
Tom Flynn
Henry Ford
Bill Fralic
Lorenzo Freeman
Sean Gilbert
Charles Gladman
Fred Glatz
Art Gob
Marshall Goldberg
Hugh Green
Russ Grimm
Burt Grossman
Bob Gruber
Mark Gunn
John Guzik
Milo Gwosden
Mike Halapin
Dick Haley
Charlie Hall
Keith Hamilton
Alonzo Hampton
Sandy Hastings
Jo Jo Heath
Warren Heller
Dutch Hendrian
Pat Herron
Craig Heyward
Hal Hinte
Fred Hoaglin
Bob Hoel
Tom Holleran
Ron Holliday
Cornell Holloway
Randy Holloway
Frank Hood
John Huzvar
Glenn Hyde
Steve Israel
Jack Itzel
Rickey Jackson
Dietrich Jells
John Jenkins
Cecil Johnson
Walt Johnson
Gordon Jones
Quintin Jones
Special Delivery Jones
Bob Jury
Tom Kalmanir
Bill Kern
Ben Kish
George Kracum
Eldred Kraemer
Rich Kraynak
Frank Kristufek
Bob Kuziel
Lindy Lauro
John Lewis
Tim Lewis
Vernon Lewis
David Logan
Carson Long
Mike Lucci
Bill Maas
Jim MacMurdo
John Maczuzak
Dan Marino
Paul Martha
Curtis Martin
Ed Matesic
Tony Matisi
Frank Mattioli
Mark May
Fred Mazurek
Richie McCabe
Joe McCall
Jim McCusker
Ricardo McDonald
Randy McMillan
Bill McPeak
Greg Meisner
Elmer Merkovsky
Dick Mills
Mike Mohring
Dave Moore
Jim Morrow
Bill Neill
Mike Nixon
Stan Olejniczak
Jerry Olsavsky
Al Olszewski
Billy Owens
Lou Palatella
John Paluck
Doc Parkinson
Don Parrish
Frank Patrick
Larry Peace
Red Pearlman
Tom Perko
Steve Petro
Barry Pettyjohn
Joe Pierre
Bill Priatko
Dave Puzzuoli
Jess Quatse
George Radosevich
John Reger
Randy Reutershan
Billy Reynolds
Gary Richard
Curvin Richards
Paul Rickards
Tom Ricketts
Louis Riddick
Mike Roussos
Jack Sack
Andy Salata
Bryant Salter
Ron Sams
Joe Schmidt
Theodore Schmitt
Marty Schottenheimer
Eric Schubert
Mike Sebastian
Red Seidelson
Ed Sharockman
Herb Sies
Don Silvestri
Tom Sims
Tony Siragusa
Vinnie Sites
Joe Skladany
Leo Skladany
Lou Slaby
Frank Souchak
Marc Spindler
Jake Stahl
Herb Stein
Mark Stepnoski
John Stock
Joe Stydahar
Jim Sweeney
Larry Swider
Willie Taylor
Lynn Thomas
Tiny Thornhill
Bob Thurbon
Keith Tinsley
Rick Trocano
David Trout
Olanda Truitt
Tom Tumulty
Alex Van Pelt
Adam Walker
Elliot Walker
Frank Walton
Joe Walton
Izzy Weinstock
Heinie Weisenbaugh
Gibby Welch
Al Wenglikowski
Pat West
Walter West
Carlton Williamson
J.C. Wilson
Zeke Wissinger
Tony Woods
John Yaccino
Joe Zombek

Pittsburgh-Johnstown (1)

Carlton Haselrig

Plymouth State (1)

Joe Dudek

Porterville Coll. CA (J.C.) (2)

Ted Bachman
John Misko

Portland (4)

Emmett Barrett
Larry Beil
Elwyn Dunstan
Karl McDade

Portland CC OR (1)

Kerry Brady

Portland State (20)

Paul Bradford
Sammie Burroughs
Clint Didier
Tracey Eaton
Dave Etherly
James Fuller
Darick Holmes
James Hundon
June Jones
Rich Lewis
Neil Lomax
Doug Mikolas
Fred Nordgren
Tom Oberg
Ted Popson
Ted Rosnagle
Jon Shields
Herman Smith
Anthony Spears
Dave Stief

Potomac State Coll. WV (J.C.) (1)

Pete Ladygo

Prairie View A&M (29)

Sam Adams
Allen Aldridge
Fred Anderson
Hise Austin
Sebastian Barrie
Charlie Brackins
Otto Brown
Leroy Clark
Clem Daniels
Bo Farrington
Claude Harvey

Ken Houston
Jim Hunt
Samuel Johnson
Jim Kearney
Bivian Lee
Jim Mitchell
Louis Neal
Alvin Reed
Stacy Robinson
Otis Taylor
Matthew Teague
Charley Warner
Dave Webster
C.L. Whittington
Donnie Williams
Sweeny Williams
Jim Wolf
Glenn Woods

Pratt CC KS (5)

Willie Cullars
Lee Harden
Bill Larson
Brison Manor
Bucky Scribner

Presbyterian (8)

Jim Elliott
Charles Huff
Lawrence Jackson
Paul Moore
Jimmie Turner
Bob Waters
Ken Webb
Larry Weldon

Princeton (25)

Carl Barisich
Bob Beattie
Hank Bjorklund
Karl Chandler
Cris Crissy
Fred DeStefano
Ted Drews
Keith Elias
Bernie Gallagher
Jason Garrett
John Garrett
Charlie Gogolak
Dutch Hendrian
Bob Hews
Bob Holly
Red Howard
Cosmo Iacovazzi
Stan Keck
Waddy MacPhee
Jack Martin
Tim McCann
Frank McPhee
Chip Nuzzo
Frank Perantoni
Bob Perina

Principia (1)

John Butler

Providence (5)

Chuck Avedisian
Bill Connor
Fred DaGata
Hank Soar
Jack Triggs

Puget Sound (2)

Tom Coombs
Mike Oliphant

Purdue (209)

Dick Abrell
Dick Afflis
Alex Agase
Brian Alford
Johnny Allen
Mike Alstott
Don Anderson
Otis Armstrong
Mike Augustyniak
Don Baldwin
Pete Barbolak
Erich Barnes
Roosevelt Barnes
Tom Barnett
Dick Barwegan
Steve Baumgartner
Tom Bayless
Jim Beirne
Cliff Benson
Bobby Berns
Tom Bettis
Gregg Bingham
George Bolan
Larry Bowie
Pete Brewster
Lou Brock
Mark Brown
Stan Brown
Don Brumm
Steve Bryant
George Buksar
Forrest Burmeister
Larry Burton
Dave Butz
Frank Bykowski
Scott Campbell
Carl Capria
Ed Carman
Rodney Carter
John Charles
Ralph Claypool
Ed Cody
Bill Combs
Scott Conover
Cleveland Crosby
Walt Cudzik
Gary Danielson
Chris Davis
Len Dawson
Lou DeFilippo
Bob DeMoss
Scott Dierking
Babe Dimancheff
Cris Dishman
Gene Donaldson
Johnny Drake
Herb Duggins
Jack Elwell
Jim Everett
Ross Fichtner
Mark Fischer
Ed Flanagan
Jack Fleischmann
Bernie Flowers
Tim Foley
Tom Franckhauser
Barry French
Jim Fritzsche
David Frye
John Galvin
Jim Garcia
Jeff George
Abe Gibron
Wayne Gift
Ken Gorgal
Mel Gray
Donnie Green
Bob Griese
Steve Griffin
Ted Hazelwood
Bob Heck
Carl Heldt
Matt Hernandez
Mark Herrmann
Jeff Hill
Bill Hitchcock
Roy Horstmann
Walt Houston
Gary Hrivnak
Ken Huffine
Paul Humphrey
Jack Hutton
Tony Ippolito
Cecil Isbell
Marcus Jackson
Mark Jackson
Steve Jackson
Clarence Janecek
Tom Jelesky
Pat Johnson
Willie Jones
Larry Kaminski
Lou Karras
Mike Kasap
Bill Kay
Leroy Keyes
Bruce King
Charlie King
Jerome King
Matt Kinzer
Bill Knox
Joe Kodba
Joe Krupa
Joe Kulbacki
Dave Lafary
Jack Laraway
Jim Letsinger
Ken Long
Sam Longmire
Jim Looney
Tom Luken
Lamar Lundy
Ned Maloney
Marc May
Shawn McCarthy
Dan McGrew
Bill McKoy
Joe Mihal
Candy Miller
Ookie Miller
Randy Minniear
Jack Morton
Paul Moss
Nick Mumley
Dick Murley
Bill Murray
Ken Novak
Cap Oehler
Elmer Oliphant
Lance Olssen
Lonnie Palelei
Ken Panfil
George Papach
Paul Pardonner
Ralph Perretta
John Petty
Bob Pfohl
Mike Phipps
Lew Pope
Charlie Potts
Mike Pruitt
John Quast
Ed Rate
Gus Redman
Ed Risk
Gary Roberts
Tom Roggeman
Jermaine Ross
Pat Russ
Ron Sabal
Dick Sandefur
Jim Schwantz
Chris Scott
Stan Sczurek
Chris Sedoris
Gene Selawski
Jerry Shay
John Simerson
Karl Singer
Joe Skibinski
John Skibinski
Lew Skinner
Ed Skoronski
Red Sleight
Blane Smith
Jimmy Smith
Marv Smith
Wayne Smith
Pat Snyder
Mark Stevens
Darryl Stingley
Fred Strickland
Leo Sugar
Jim Teal
Jim Tiller
Ray Trowbridge
Keena Turner
Sam Vacanti
Tony Vinson
Scott Virkus
Ed Voytek
Ray Wallace
Clyde Washington
Harold Wells
Calvin Williams
Jerrol Williams
Perry Williams
Derek Wimberly
Joe Winkler
Charlie Winston
Dennis Wirgowski
Clem Woltman
Rod Woodson
Bill Yanchar
Dave Young
Glenn Young
Connie Zelencik
Jerry Zeller
Jeff Zgonina

Queens (Canada) (2)

Mike Schad
Jim Young

Rancho Santiago Coll. CA (J.C.) (25)

Duane Allen
Pervis Atkins
Mel Black
George Brancato
Bob Bryant
Lem Burnham
Al Carmichael
Dan Clark
Paul Cleary
Don Davis
Keith Denson
Ollie Fletcher
David Frye
Bob Gaiters
Merle Hapes
Keever Jankovich
Jerry Lawson
Vic Lindskog
Joe Margucci
Craig McEwen
Earle Parsons
John Pitts
Jim Steffen
Rick Walker
Johnny Ward

Randolph-Macon (2)

Jim Camp
Howard Stevens

Ranger Coll. TX (J.C.) (10)

Elmer Arterburn
George Boynton
Vince Courville
Will Hill
Ed Marshall
Greg Oliver
Johnny Perkins
Allen Rice
Dan Sharp
Del Thompson

Redlands (4)

Brian DeRoo
John Houser
John Sanchez
Don Thompson

Regis (1)

Arnie Herber

Rhode Island (16)

Duke Abbruzzi
Bill Connor
Armand Cure
Lou D'Agostino
Chy Davidson
Tony DeLuca
Mike Dwyer
Steve Furness
Molly McGee
Al McIntosh
Rick Moser
Dameon Reilly
Kevin Smith
Bob White
Jeff Williams
Ray Williams

Rhodes (3)

Henry Hammond
Tom Mullady
Gaylon Smith

Rice (68)

Preston Anderson
Bob Armstrong
Tony Barker
Rodrigo Barnes
Bill Blackburn
Shirley Brick
O.J. Brigance
Bob Brumley
Larry Brune
John Burrell
Gary Butler
Trevor Cobb
Earl Cooper
Olie Cordill
Vince Courville
Douglas Cunningham
Buddy Dial
Michael Downs
Virgil Eikenberg
Bert Emanuel
Hosea Fortune
Spencer George
Don Gillis
Darryl Grant
Courtney Hall
James Hamrick
Fred Hartman
King Hill
Donald Hollas
Hugo Hollas
Billy Howton
Weldon Humble
Larry Izzo
Roland Jackson
Gene Jones
Ndukwe Kalu
Randy Kerbow
Tommy Kramer
Chuck Latourette
John Magee
Don Maynard
Primo Miller
Dicky Moegle
McNeil Moore
Hamilton Nichols
Alan Pringle
Rex Proctor
Tobin Rote
Leo Rucka
Frank Ryan
Jake Schuehle
Ted Scruggs
J.D. Smith
Jim Spruill
Seaman Squyres
Frank Steen
Orville Trask
Dwain Turner
John Underwood
Malcolm Walker
Dale Walters
Eric Washington
Joe Watson
Russell Wayt
Bones Weatherly
Ken Whitlow
Win Williams
Frank Wilson

Richmond (31)

Dave Ames
John Armstrong
Shawn Barber
Joe Biscaha
Bob Bleier
Mike Bragg
Carmen Cavalli
Erik Christensen
Bob Coolbaugh
Ray Easterling
Reggie Evans
Wayne Fowler
Andy Fronczek
Walker Gillette
Bruce Gossett
Lyle Graham
Marvin Hargrove
John Hilton
Dick Humbert
Art Jones
Brian Jordan
Matt Joyce
Pat Lamberti
Frank Laurinaitis
Bert Milling
Jeff Nixon
Barry Redden
Barty Smith
Ron Smith
Don Thompson
Brendan Toibin

Richmond CC NC (1)

Louis Breeden

Ricks Coll. ID (J.C.) (5)

Jason Buck
Greg Clark
David Dixon
Mark Harris
Jose Portilla

Rider (1)

Les Maynard

Rio Hondo Coll. CA (J.C.) (3)

Troy Archer
Mike Katolin
Keith Wortman

Ripon (11)

Tiny Croft
Boob Darling
George Glennie
Tubby Howard
Charlie Mathys
Charlie Rutkowski
Ted Scalissi
Champ Seibold
Wally Sieb
Dave Smith
Cowboy Wheeler

Riverside CC CA (12)

Sonny Bishop
Bob Boyd
Tony Cherry
Frank Corral
Bob Geddes
Alonzo Hampton
Billie Hayes
Tom Hayes
Bobby Jackson
Rudy Redmond
Derrick Rodgers
Calvin Sweeney

Robert Morris (1)

Tim Hall

Rochester (5)

Ben Forsyth
Paul McKee
Joe McShea
George Sutch
Gordon Wallace

Rogers State Coll. OK (J.C.) (1)

Frank Strom

Rose Hulman Tech (2)

Joe Engelhard
Owen Floyd

Rose State Coll. OK (J.C.) (2)

Alonzo Mayes
Tony Woods

Rowan (2)

Dino Hall
Steve Rhem

Rust Coll. MS (J.C.) (1)

Bob Hughes

Rutgers (42)

John Alexander
John Alexander
Marco Battaglia
Jay Bellamy
Heinie Benkert
Chris Brantley
Joe Burke
Alcides Catanho
Deron Cherry
Jerry Cronin
Bernie Crowl
Jim Dufft
Jim Dumont
Walt French
Budge Garrett
Lee Getz
Dan Gray
Ben Greenberg
Jack Grossman
Don Harris
John Hasbrouck
Bill Hill
Carl Howard
James Jenkins
Ed Jones
Alex Kroll
Jack Lord
Ray Lucas
Dino Mangiero
Bob Nash
Bill Pellington
Bill Pickel
Nick Prisco
Paul Robeson
Stan Rosen
Anthony Sagnella
Bob Simms
Tyronne Stowe
Harry Swayne
Rashod Swinger
Carl Waite
Elnardo Webster

Rutgers-Camden (1)

Joe Fields

Sacramento City Coll. CA (J.C.) (12)

Rob Awalt
Issac Booth
Kevin Bowman
James Campen
Rick Cunningham
Dave Kilson
Carl Littlefield
Stan Mataele
Perry Schwartz
Sean Thomas
Alex Van Dyke
Derek Ware

Sacramento State (14)

Brian Allred
Mike Black
Mike Carter
Dan Chamberlain
John Farley
John Gesek
Rob Harrison
Angelo James
Jon Kirksey
Lorenzo Lynch
Ken O'Brien
Greg Robinson
Daimon Shelton
Bob Wear

Saddleback Coll. CA (J.C.) (8)

John Duff
Rudy Holmes
Bill Kenney
Scott Miller
Stephone Paige
Mike Piel
Chuck Steele
Scott Von der Ahe

Saginaw Valley State (2)

Tom Beer
Eugene Marve

Salem (3)

Jack Deloplaine
Monty Hunter
Orson Mobley

Salem (NC) (5)

Tom Gerhart
Scott Hilton
George McDuffie
Larry Riley
Jess Rodriguez

Sam Houston State (19)

Michael Bankston
Stan Blinka
Ronnie Carroll
Tim Denton
Johnnie Dirden
Odie Harris
Ben Hightower
Jimmy Hill
Ed Kallina
Garry Kimble
Hubbard Law
Guido Merkens
McNeil Moore
Mike Nelms
Ricky Royal
Ralph Ruthstrom
Howard Satterwhite
Julian Spence
George Wright

Samford (10)

Norm Cooper
Ray Davis
Sam Goldman
Pat Harrison
Harold Hill
Herman Hodges
Rex Keeling
Slick Lollar
Nate Schenker
Jimmy Tarrant

Sampson CC NC (1)

Bob Logel

San Bernardino Valley Coll. CA (J.C.) (12)

Chris Bayne
Lee Cole
Dennis Crane
Tony Gaiter
Lance Harkey
Perry Jeter
Paul Lavine
Avery Monfort
Craig Newsome
Eric Swanson
J.T. Thomas
Mike Ulufale

San Diego (2)

Matt Maslowski
Vern Valdez

San Diego City Coll. CA (J.C.) (20)

Bill Bain
Paul Dunn
Bill Frank
Bill Gay
Dave Grayson
Andre Hardy
Wally Henry
Terry Jackson
Doug Jones
Dave Lewis
Mike Machurek
Saladin Martin
Dwight McDonald
Claudie Minor
Chip Oliver
Art Powell
Greg Slough
Ernie Smith
Jeff Staggs
Kevin Williams

San Diego Mesa Coll. CA (J.C.) (10)

Lew Barnes
Steve Duich
Cliff Hicks
Monte Jackson
Matt Kofler
Greg Lathan
Jim Peterson
Doug Reed
Ken Thompson
Bob West

San Diego State (138)

Hank Allison
Jim Allison

Mike Ariey
Doug Aronson
Rob Awalt
Obafemi Ayanbadejo
Will Blackwell
Curtis Bledsoe
Greg Boyd
Richard Brown
Willie Buchanon
Ken Burrow
Leo Carroll
Kern Carson
Robert Claiborne
Trent Collins
David Croudip
Isaac Curtis
Tom Dahms
Brad Daluiso
Chris Davis
Vernon Dean
Keith Denson
Herb Dobbins
Billy Donckers
Mike Douglass
Fred Dryer
Phil DuBois
Jamal Duff
Steve Duich
Herman Edwards
Lloyd Edwards
Craig Ellis
John Farris
Brett Faryniarz
Marshall Faulk
Duke Fergerson
Bill Ferguson
Doug Fisher
Roman Fortin
Jesse Freitas
Gary Garrison
La'Roi Glover
David Gray
Robert Griffith
Az-zahir Hakim
Darryl Hall
Rob Harrison
Billie Hayes
Tom Hayes
Reuben Henderson
Don Horn
Bob Howard
Martin Imhof
Alfred Jackson
Monte Jackson
Terry Jackson
Nate Jacquet
Chris Johnson
James Johnson
George Jones
Bob Jones
Bob Keyes
Randy Kirk
Matt Kofler
Mike Kozlowski
Jim Laughton
Joe Lavender
Reggie Lewis
Matt Long
Larry Martin
Saladin Martin
Lloyd McCoy
Dwight McDonald
Dan McGwire
Sean McNanie
Terry Mendenhall
Mario Mendez
John Milks
Anthony Miller
Claudie Minor
Rich Moran
Haven Moses
Tory Nixon
John O'Callaghan
Dave Ogas
Clancy Oliver
Marv Owens
Ricky Parker
Dennis Pearson
Craig Penrose
Jim Peterson
Neal Petties
Duane Pettitt
Damon Pieri
Skeets Quinlan
Jimmy Raye
Doug Reed
Tom Reynolds
Benny Ricardo
Houston Ridge
Patrick Rowe
Ray Rowe
Pio Sagapolutele
Ephraim Salaam
Clint Sampson
Mike Saxon
Ray Schmautz
Darnay Scott
Todd Seabaugh
Dennis Shaw
Don Shy
Brian Sipe
Webster Slaughter
Lucious Smith
Phil Smith
Ron Smith
Ron Spears
Jeff Spek
Jeff Staggs
Ramondo Stallings
Nick Subis
Eric Sutton
Kyle Turley
Deacon Turner
Whip Walton
Don Warren
Vince Warren
Teddy Washington
Mike Waters
Carl Weathers
Mike Wells
Ralph Wenzel
Bob West
Jim Wilks
Henry Williams
Nate Wright
Renard Young

San Francisco (30)

Ernie Barber
Jim Barber
Roy Barni
Ed Brown
George Buksar
Mike Davlin
Mike Donohoe
Pete Franceschi
Bob Greenhalgh
Forrest Hall
Russ Letlow
Gino Marchetti
Ollie Matson
Ken McAlister
Mike Mergen
Dave Olerich
Vince Pacewic
Don Panciera
Ray Peterson
Harmon Rowe
Tino Sabuco
Bob St. Clair
John Sanchez
Joe Scott
Joe Scudero
Larry Siemering
Dick Stanfel
Red Stephens
Ralph Thomas
Carroll Vogelaar

San Francisco City Coll. CA (J.C.) (16)

Mike Carter
Vernon Crawford
Oscar Donahue
Doug Hollie
James Hundon
Henry King
Bob Lee
Gary Lewis
Ollie Matson
Mack Moore
Reggie Rusk
O.J. Simpson
Carl Sullivan
Mike Taylor
Mel Tom
Scott Virkus

San Francisco State (14)

Pervis Atkins
Bill Baird
Elmer Collett
Frank Duncan
Maury Duncan
Paul Dunn
Al Endress
Charley Fuller
Joe Jackson
Carl Kammerer
Joe Koontz
Floyd Peters
Bruce Rhodes
Willie Simpson

San Jacinto Coll. TX (J.C.) (1)

Orville Trask

San Joaquin Delta Coll. CA (J.C.) (6)

Bob Denton
Bob Heinz
Bill Sandeman
Webster Slaughter
Jimmy Smith
Scott Stringer

San Jose City Coll. CA (J.C.) (6)

Kim Bokamper
Mervyn Fernandez
Jethro Franklin
Chon Gallegos
Steve Kinney
Tom Newton

San Jose State (89)

Steve Alexakos
Marty Baccaglio
Stacey Bailey
Bill Benjamin
Keith Birlem
Kim Bokamper
Kevin Bowman
Gill Byrd
Jim Cadile
Sheldon Canley
M.L. Carter
Dan Clark
Kevin Clark
Charles Clinton
Sherman Cocroft
Daniel Colchico
Floyd Collier
Greg Cox
Hal Crisler
Kenny Daniel
Steve DeBerg
Charles DeJurnett
David Diaz-Infante
Oscar Donahue
Leon Donohue
Harley Dow
Carl Ekern
Wilson Faumuina
Mervyn Fernandez
Tracy Franz
Chon Gallegos
Randy Gill
Charlie Hardy
Charlie Harraway
Paul Held
Fred Heron
Bud Hubbard
Eric Hurt
Johnny Johnson
Marvin Johnson
Cody Jones
Rick Kane
Mike Katolin
Tim Kearse
Sam Kennedy
Art Kuehn
Tom Louderback
Ed Luther
Frank Manumaleuga
Derrick Martin
Keith McDonald
Frank Minini
Kenny Nash
Joe Nedney
Mark Nichols
Ray Norton
Bernie Nygren
Dwayne O'Steen
Bill Peterson
Bob Pifferini
Art Powell
Jim Psaltis
Jerry Reese
Eric Richardson
Walter Roberts
Brian Roche
Saint Saffold
James Saxon
Ricky Siglar
Gerald Small
Tommie Smith
Carl Sullivan
John Sutro
Bob Sykes
Jay Taylor
Tony Teresa
Jewerl Thomas
Ken Thomas
Gary Thompson
Bob Titchenal
Mel Tom
John Travis
Mitch Ucovich
Jim Walsh
Ralph Wenzel
Gerald Willhite
Billy Wilson
Louis Wright
Roy Zimmerman

Santa Barbara City Coll. CA (J.C.) (4)

Booker Brown
Craig Ellis
Larry Moriarty
Rob Woods

Santa Clara (40)

Lee Artoe
Bullet Baker
Bryan Barker
Dick Bassi
Alyn Beals
Don Brown
Ken Casanega
Steve Cisowski
Ted Connolly
Frank Cope
Doug Cosbie
Phil Dougherty
Nello Falaschi
John Faylor
Tom Fears
Ev Fisher
Eddie Forrest
Jesse Freitas
Mike Garzoni
Jerry Ginney
Visco Grgich
Hall Haynes
Jerry Hennessy
John Hock
Gary Hoffman
Brent Jones
Mike Kellogg
Jim Leonard
Art McCaffray
Bob McGee
Gern Nagler
John Nolan
Mike Nott
Dan Pastorini
Joe Ramona
John Schiechl
Ed Storm
Rupe Thornton
Paul Vinnola
Ellery Williams

Santa Monica Coll. CA (J.C.) (28)

John Adams
Ralph Anderson
Mike Ballou
Jerome Boyd
Isaac Bruce
Dick Dorsey
Earl Elsey
George Farmer
Duane Galloway
Wes Grant
Lee Grosscup
John Harris
Daryl Hobbs
Jim Johnson
Gary Kirner
Daryl Knox
Keith Lee
Marv Marinovich
Keith McDonald
Fred Miller
Kelvin Moore
Billy Parks
Junior Thurman
Elbert Watts
A.D. Williams
Alonzo Williams
Ricky Williams
Lloyd Winston

Santa Rosa JC CA (9)

Bobby Batton
Barry Black
Jason Franci
Len Gotshalk
Tom Louderback
Hugh Millen
Karl Rubke
Jack Sims
Larry Steele

Saskatchewan (Canada) (1)

Joe Kraker

Savannah State (4)

Eric Brown
Bobby Curtis
Shannon Sharpe
Tim Walker

Schreiner Coll. (7)

Winnie Baze
Raymond Berry
Fred Hartman
Tex Irvin
Charley Johnson
Len McCormick
Joe Smith

Schuylkill (2)

Ralph Barkman
Marty Kostos

Scottsdale CC AZ (8)

Charlie Dickey
Jeff Feagles
Greg Meehan
Josh Miller
Mike Rusinek
Cornell Webster
Terry Wright
Floyd Young

Scranton (6)

Ed Eiden
Joe Koons
Patsy Martinelli
John Rogalla
Carl Tomasello
Doug Turley

Seattle (1)

Ron Howard

Seward Co. CC KS (1)

Marcus Pollard

Shasta Coll. CA (J.C.) (3)

Mike Humiston
Bob Rosenstiel
Jason Sehorn

Shaw (1)

Van Green

Shepherd (1)

Wayne Wilson

Sherman Indian (2)

Reggie Attache
Elmer Busch

Shippensburg (1)

Rob Davis

Shoreline CC WA (1)

Halvor Hagen

Sierra Coll. CA (J.C.) (1)

Shawn Price

Simon Fraser (Canada) (2)

Doug Brown
Rick Goltz

Simpson (2)

Ken Mercer
Kink Richards

Sioux Falls (2)

Rick Danmeier
Brian Hansen

Slippery Rock (4)

Greg Paterra
Ricky Porter
Chuck Sanders
Enid Thomas

Snow Coll. UT (J.C.) (8)

David Archer
Brad Badger
Brant Boyer
Mohammed Elewonibi
Frank Harris
Mike Norseth
Derek Smith
Brian Walker

Solano C.C. CA (1)

Jerone Davison

Sonoma State (2)

Larry Allen
Freddie Bradley

South Carolina (86)

Tom Addison
Darrell Austin
Brandon Bennett
Hal Blackwell
Robert Brooks
Ray Brown
Bobby Bryant
Leonard Burton
Matt Campbell
Dave Cloutier
Chris Corley
Steve Courson
Terry Cousin
Larry Craig
Leon Cunningham
Bill Currier
Sam DeLuca
James Dexter
Mike Dingle
Ernest Dixon
Gerald Dixon
Ernest Dye
Brad Edwards
Dutch Elston
Keith Franklin
Billy Gambrell
Rusty Ganas
Harold Green
Al Grygo
Scott Hagler
Rickey Hagood
Chuck Hajek
Darren Hambrick
Zip Hanna
Roy Hart
Alex Hawkins
Ira Hillary
Mike Hold
Ed Holler
Jim Hunnicutt
Earl Johnson
Jack Keenan
Jim Kincaid
John Kompara
Joe Krivonak
Ron Lamb
Kevin Long
Corey Louchiey
Zion McKinney
Bryant Meeks
Corey Miller
Eddie Miller
Bill Milner
Ron Monaco
Kelley Mote
Chris Norman
Tom O'Connor
Daren Parker
Stanley Pritchett
Andrew Provence
Dan Reeves
Roy Reeves
Marcus Robinson
Don Rogers
George Rogers
Ken Roskie
Max Runager
Rusty Russell
Jay Saldi
Rick Sanford
Willie Scott
Sterling Sharpe
Chuck Slaughter
Lou Sossamon
Dave Sparks
Duce Staley
Stan Stasica
Calvin Stephens
Bishop Strickland
Henry Taylor
Bill Troup
Alex Urban
Paul Vogel
J.R. Wilburn
Clarence Williams
Johnnie Wright

South Carolina State (45)

Rickey Anderson
Edwin Bailey
Rufus Bess
James Black
Charlie Brown
Orlando Brown
Barney Bussey
Kenny Bynum
Harry Carson
Barney Chavous
Dextor Clinkscale
Anthony Cook
R.C. Gamble
John Gilliam
Charles Glaze
Willie Grate
Dwayne Harper
Michael Hicks
Willie Holman
Jim Johnson
Deacon Jones
William Judson
Angelo King
Edward Lee
Marvin Marshall
Cliff McClain
Marion Motley
Phil Murphy
Henry Odom
Ervin Parker
Robert Porcher
Nate Rivers
Louis Ross
Raleigh Roundtree
Donnie Shell
Mickey Sims
Freddie Solomon
Zach Thomas
Wendell Tucker
Tom Tutson
Robert Tyler
Remi Watson
Emanuel Weaver
Leonard Wingate
Al Young

South Dakota (14)

Ordell Braase
George Burnside
Joe Crakes
Hal Hanson
Les Lane
Frank McCormick
Deac Sanders
Duke Schamel
Paul Sheeks
Mike Slaton
Rodney Tweet
Gene Vidal
Robb White
Phillip Wise

South Dakota State (22)

Al Arndt
Mark Barber
Lynn Boden
Mike Busch
Doug Eggers
Wuert Engelmann
Ray Jennison
Frank Kelley
Dick Klawitter
Bruce Klosterman
Jim Langer
Chuck Loewen
Bill Matthews
Ron Meyer
Doug Miller
Paul Miller
Bob Pylman
Wayne Rasmussen
Pete Retzlaff
Brian Sisley
Adam Timmerman
Adam Vinatieri

South Texas J.C. (1)

Carlos Bell

Southampton (England) (1)

John Smith

Southeast Missouri State (11)

Ted Banker
Ken Iman
David Jackson
Brian Lattimore
Dave Means
Eddie Moss
Dan Peiffer
Marquis Walker
Tony Walker
John Wittenborn
Mike Wood

Southeastern Louisiana (14)

Wilson Alvarez
Billy Andrews
Horace Belton
Mack Boatner
T.J. Campion
Jerry Davis
Donald Dykes
Calvin Favron
Ron Hornsby
Ellis Johnson
Troy Johnson
Oscar Lofton
Albie Reisz
Maxie Williams

Southeastern Oklahoma State (3)

Stanley Blair
Randy Burks
Earnest Hunter

Southern Arkansas (3)

Ken Brown
David Ward
Dennis Woodberry

Southern Colorado (5)

Dan DeRose
Frank Grant

Herman Heard
Joe Taibi
John Trahan

Southern Connecticut State (10)

Joseph Andruzzi
Ricky Atkinson
Mark Carlson
Anthony Corvino
Nick DeFelice
David Hendley
Jamie Kurisko
Scott Mersereau
Pat Morrison
Travis Tucker

Southern Illinois (28)

Lionel Antoine
Houston Antwine
Jim Battle
Tom Baugh
Amos Bullocks
Fabray Collins
John Harper
Jim Hart
Kevin House
Damon Jones
Yonel Jourdain
Mike Kaczmarek
Abe Martin
Carl Mauck
Marion Rushing
Carver Shannon
Sam Silas
Dave Smith
Russ Smith
Sebron Spivey
Bill Story
Terry Taylor
Jim Thompson
Tommy Thompson
Ralph Van Dyke
Clarence Walker
Ernie Wheelwright
Adrian White

Southern Methodist (123)

Dwayne Anderson
Harvey Armstrong
Marvin Ayers
Jerry Ball
Lloyd Baxter
Gene Bedford
Fred Benners
Ed Bernet
Raymond Berry
Rickey Bolden
Clarence Booth
Chris Bordano
Cary Brabham
Maury Bray
Hardy Brown
John Burleson
Michael Carter
Russell Carter
Joe Carter
Putt Choate
Johnny Clement
Bobby Collier
Jerry Cornelison
Chris Cortemeglia
Abe Croft
Tom Dean
Bill Dewell
Willard Dewveall
Anthony Dickerson
Eric Dickerson
Cornelius Dozier
Brian Duncan
Reggie Dupard
Vernon Edwards
Joe Ethridge
Jake Fawcett
Bob Fisher
Bill Forester
Herschel Forester
Ray Fuqua
George Gaiser
Eddie Garcia
Don Goss
Forrest Gregg
Glynn Gregory
Jack Halliday
Gary Hammond
Kenny Harrison
Perry Hartnett
Dale Hellestrae
Doug Hollie
Wes Hopkins
Byron Hunt
Charlie Jackson
Frank Jackson
Craig James
Lynn James
Freeman Johns
Bill Johnson
Gil Johnson
Pres Johnston
Bill Jones
Rod Jones
Louie Kelcher
Don King
Heinie Kirkgard
Pat Knight
Jerry LeVias
Bill Line
Mike Livingston
Louie Long
Howie Maley
Ray Mallouf
Alvin Maxson
Jerry Mays
Clint McClain
Don McIlhenny
Dick McKissack
Don Meredith
Don Miller
Ron Morris
Wayne Morris
Gary Moten
Doyle Nix
Jerry Norton
Paul Page
Howie Parker
Dennis Partee
Joe Pasqua
Joe Phillips
Reggie Phillips
Marquis Pleasant
Mitchell Price
Buster Raborn
Keith Ranspot
Guy Reese
Jerry Rhome
David Richards
Mike Richardson
John Roach
Oscar Roan
John Roderick
Kyle Rote
Ralph Ruthstrom
Jack Sanders
Ray Schoenke
Henry Sheppard
Dave Sherer
John Simmons
Marcello Simmons
Eric Smith
Jim Bob Taylor
Ted Thompson
Bill Vaughn
Doak Walker
Val Joe Walker
Jim Welch
Ricky Wesson
Art Whittington
Mitch Willis
Gene Wilson
Bobby Wilson
Jim Wright

Southern Mississippi (75)

Vincent Alexander
Carl Allen
Lyneal Alston
Hank Autry
Ken Avery
John Baylor
Tommy Boutwell
Byron Bradfute
Fred Brock
Steve Broussard
Bud Brown
Jack Brumfield
Tim Bryant
Richard Byrd
Perry Carter
Sidney Coleman
Reggie Collier
Fred Cook
Mike Dennery
Bo Dickinson
Hanford Dixon
Robert Ducksworth
Charley Ellzey
Brett Favre
Amos Fowler
Ben Garry
Ray Guy
Bobby Hamilton
Terry Hardy
Marvin Harvey
Harold Hays
George Herring
Derrick Hoskins
Glen Howe
George Hultz
Don Hultz
Michael Jackson
Mike Katrishen
Val Keckin
William Kirksey
Mike Landrum
Cliff Lewis
Louis Lipps
John Mangum
Larry Mason
Bucky McElroy
Hugh McInnis
Fred Molden
Joe Morgan
Tommy Morrow
Maurice Oliver
Don Owens
Charlie Parker
Perry Phenix
Jeff Posey
Vic Purvis
Tim Roberts
Tom Roussel
Eugene Rowell
Doug Satcher
John Sawyer
Harold Shaw
John Sklopan
Tony Smith
Robert Stallings
Joe Stringfellow
Patrick Surtain
Norris Thomas
Willie Tullis
Art Van Tone
Joe Vetrano
Tom Walters
Terry Wells
Jerrel Wilson
Sammy Winder

Southern University (66)

Jeff Alexander
Michael Ball
Pete Barnes
Jim Battle
Al Beauchamp
Mel Blount
Malik Boyd
Willie Brister
Jerry Broadnax
Perry Brooks
Harold Carmichael
Andre Davis
Donnie Davis
James Davis
Marvin Davis
Matthew Dorsett
Jubilee Dunbar
Ken Ellis
James Evans
George Farmer
Jeff Faulkner
Jerrell Franklin
Charley Granger
Cleveland Green
Isaac Hagins
Skip Hamilton
Robert Harris
Alvin Haymond
Mack Lee Hill
Robert Holmes
Maurice Hurst
Johnny Jackson
Rich Jackson
Phillip James
Troy Johnson
Ray Jones
Tyrone Jones
Calvin Magee
George McGee
Thomas McLemore
Harold McLinton
Ed Mitchell
Richard Neal
Jim Osborne
Gerald Perry
Frank Pitts
Lew Porter
Rufus Porter
Floyd Raglin
Isiah Robertson
Alden Roche
Conrad Rucker
Ronald Scott
Kendel Shello
Donnell Smith
Ken Times
Anthony Tuggle
Godwin Turk
Aeneas Williams
Brian Williams
Clyde Williams
Herb Williams
John Williams
Ralph Williams
Sid Williams
Jerry Wilson

Southern Utah (2)

Mark Harris
Len Walterscheid

Southwest Mississippi CC (1)

Billy Milner

Southwest Missouri State (7)

Steve Ache
Bob Dees
Charlie Mitchell
Tom Mullen
Mike Murphy
Jason Whittle
Keith Williams

Southwest Texas State (26)

Eric Cobble
Ken Coffey
Wayne Coffey
Paul Darby
Wallace Dickey
Pat Franklin
Noe Gonzalez
Van Hughes
A.J. Johnson
Bill Jones
Ed Kallina
Wade Key
Kevin Meuth
Reece Morrison
Jeff Novak
Reggie Rivers
Booker Russell
Ricky Sanders
Mack Sauls
Jim Stienke
Henry Thomas
Joe Vance
Charles Vatterott
Bobby Watkins
Bob Young
Charlie Zunker

Southwestern (Ks) (2)

Vic Baltzell
Bob Layden

Southwestern (Tex.) (9)

Solon Barnett
Bill Collins
Zuehl Conoly
R.W. Hicks
Carlton Massey
Len McCormick
Jim O'Neal
Jack Sachse
Rat Watson

Southwestern Coll. CA (J.C.) (4)

Scott Byers
Robert Claiborne
Steve Pierce
Oliver Ross

Southwestern Louisiana (31)

Louis Age
Patrise Alexander
James Atkins
John Bandura
Charles Bennett
Karl Bernard
Bill Blackburn
Chris Cagle
Anthony Clement
Kenyon Cotton
Willie Culpepper
Richie Cunningham
Joe DeForest
Virgil Eikenberg
Chris Gannon
Mark Hall
Keno Hills
Weldon Humble
Saxon Judd
John Magee
Randy McClanahan
Brian Mitchell
Dwaine Morris
Lance Poimbeouf
John Roveto
Todd Scott
Rafael Septien
William Sims
Orlando Thomas
Clarence Verdin
Win Williams

Southwestern Oklahoma State (9)

Carl Birdsong
Gary Bolden
Chief Elkins
Mike Gibbons
Gordon Gore
Perry Jackson
Arnie Shockley
Jim Simmons
Pete Tillman

Southwestern Oregon CC (1)

Ross Carter

Spokane CC WA (2)

Dave Browning
Anthony Davis

Spring Hill (1)

Ed McEvoy

Springfield (6)

Ted Alflen
Frank Civiletto
Harold Hall
Vic Obeck
Jack Peavey
Len Watters

St. Ambrose (9)

Frank DeClerk
Les Hearden
Nick Kerasiotis
Louis Kolls
Waddy Kuehl
Ted Lapka
Art Michalik
John Oelerich
Dave Zuidmulder

St. Anselm (2)

Ray McLean
Johnny Spirida

St. Augustine's (1)

Ike Lassiter

St. Bernard (1)

Neil O'Donoghue

St. Bonaventure (12)

Jack Butler
Mike Gavagan
Johnny Gildea
Hank Goodman
George Hays
Al Kaporch
George Kenneally
John Ksionzyk
Frank LoVuolo
Ted Marchibroda
Hugo Marcolini
George Nicksich

St. Cloud State (7)

Len Johnson
John Kimbrough
Mike Lambrecht
Mick Luckhurst
Keith Nord
Neil Rengel
Doc Williams

St. Edmonds (1)

Charlie Knox

St. Edward's (3)

Bull Polisky
Al Sarafiny
Mel Stuessy

St. Francis (Pa.) (7)

Tony Bova
George Magulick
John McCarthy
Archie Milano
John Naioti
Joe Restic
Ed Stofko

St. John's (Minn.) (4)

Ricky Bell
Johnny Blood
Irv Carlson
John McDowell

St. John's (N.Y.) (8)

Dennis Bligen
Lester Caywood
Tom Cobb
Joe McClain
Ted Plumridge
Pat Ragusa
Sam Salemi
Rex Thomas

St. Joseph's (Ind.) (3)

Blaine Bishop
John McGarry
Nick Scollard

St. Joseph's (Pa) (3)

John Cole
Ted Laux
Vince Papale

St. Lawrence (3)

Dave Jennings
Bill Leckonby
Shag Sheard

St. Leo (1)

Sankar Montoute

St. Louis (19)

Arnie Arenz
Jack Corcoran
Hoot Drury
Jim Finnegan
Doc Gorman
Carl Kane
Jimmy Kelly
Henry Krause
Benny LaPresta
Pat Leahy
Joe Lintzenich
Russ McLeod
George Meinhardt
Bill Montgomery
Ross Nagel
Manny Rapp
Dick Schweidler
Dick Weber
Pete Wissman

St. Mary's (Cal.) (58)

Joe Aguirre
Jim Austin
Dan Barnhart
Bunny Belden
Larry Bettencourt
Angie Brovelli
Frank Cassara
Ray Clemons
Tony Compagno
Gerry Conlee
Paul Crowe
Jerry Dennerlein
Jerry Dowd
Harry Ebding
Al Endress
Tony Falkenstein
Jack Flagerman
Ike Frankian
Dale Gentry
Jack Giannoni
Ducky Grant
Andre Hardy
Hoot Herrin
John Henry Johnson
Bud Jorgensen
Wayne Jorgensen
Clarence Kellogg
Mike Klotovich
Jim Lankas
Dante Magnani
Andy Marefos
Harry Mattos
Tuffy Maul
Jack McArthur
Frank McNally
Dick Mesak
Gonzalo Morales
Al Nichelini
Mike Perrie
Bobby Robertson
Roy Ruskusky
Ed Ryan
Will Sherman
Butch Simas
Bob Sneddon
Basil Stanley
Ben Starret
Stud Stennett
Mike Steponovich
Red Strader
Frank Szymanski
Bud Toscani
Buzz Trebotich
Herman Wedemeyer
Willie Wilkin
Gardner Williams
John Woudenberg
John Yezerski

St. Mary's (Canada) (1)

Ken Clark

St. Mary's (Kansas) (2)

Lew Lane
Tommy Murphy

St. Mary's (Minn.) (9)

Frank Billock
Fritz Cronin
Chuck Gayer
John Madigan
Bill McNellis
Tony Mehelich
Verne Miller
Ben Oas
Clint Wager

St. Mary's (Tex.) (3)

Charlie Huneke
George Koch
Curt Sandig

St. Norbert (4)

Ted Fritsch
Larry Krause
Joe LaFleur
Tip O'Neill

St. Olaf (4)

Hal Erickson
Fred Putzier
Pete Saumer
Bill Winter

St. Thomas (21)

Adrian Baril
Jim Brandt
Jack Corcoran
Danny Coughlin
John Fahay
Chief Franta
Neal Guggemos
Jim Gustafson
Bill Houle
Walt Kiesling
Tony LaBissoniere
John Madigan
Jimmy Manion
Louie Mohs
Jim Murphy
Jock Murray
Chuck Reichow
Jack Salscheider
Don Simensen
Larry Steinbach
Roy Vassau

St. Viator (2)

Vince McCarthy
Am Rascher

St. Vincent (6)

Vern Foltz
John Kondrla
John Macerelli
Bap Manzini
John Popovich
Joe Ratica

Stanford (161)

Frankie Albert
Stan Andersen
Gary Anderson
Lester Archambeau
Justin Armour
Dick Arndt
Corrie Artman
Mike Askea
Frank Atkinson
Brad Badger
Bruno Banducci
Gordon Banks
Benny Barnes
Greg Baty
Braden Beck
Guy Benjamin
Fred Boensch
George Bogue
Mike Boryla
Dennis Bragonier
Tom Briehl
John Brodie
Jeff Buckey
George Buehler
Chris Burford
Ernie Caddel
Joe Cain
Tony Calvelli
Gordy Ceresino
Jack Chapple
Greg Clark
Tony Cline
Greg Comella
Toi Cook
Jim Cox
Ed Cummings
Chris Dalman
Steve Dils
Pat Donovan
Chris Draft
Chris Dressel
Kwame Ellis

John Elway
Chuck Evans
Jason Fisk
Phil Francis
Jesse Freitas
Scott Frost
Hugh Gallarneau
Dave Garnett
Bobby Garrett
Ron George
Rick Gervais
Darrien Gordon
Alan Grant
John Guillory
Bill Hachten
Carl Hansen
Mark Harris
Marv Harris
Walter Harris
Emile Harry
Jon Haskins
Thomas Henley
Wilbur Henry
Mike Hibler
Don Hill
Tony Hill
Andre Hines
Brian Holloway
Dick Horn
Steve Hoyem
Harry Hugasian
Ron Kadziel
Bill Kellar
Gary Kerkorian
Gordon King
Pete Kmetovic
Scott Laidlaw
Kevin Lamar
Babe Laufenberg
Jim Lawson
Pete Lazetich
Dick Leeuwenburg
Tony Leiker
Dave Lewis
Vic Lindskog
James Lofton
John Lynch
John Macaulay
Brian Manning
Don Manoukian
Ken Margerum
Ed McCaffrey
Milt McColl
Bill McColl
Jim Merlo
Fred Meyer
Bob Meyers
Mike Michel
Glyn Milburn
Bob Mitchell
Bob Moore
Sam Morley
Monk Moscrip
Eric Mullins
Brad Muster
Darrin Nelson
Ernie Nevers
Bob Nichols
Mike Noble
Hank Norberg
Al Norgard
Dick Norman
Blaine Nye
Bob O'Connor
John Olenchalk
Don Parish
Kaulana Park
Gary Pettigrew
Jim Plunkett
Randy Poltl
Hamp Pool
Jim Price
Bill Reid
Terry Rennaker
Bob Reynolds
Jon Ritchie
Doug Rogers
Greg Sampson
Reggie Sanderson
Turk Schonert
Kevin Scott
Kevin Scott
Jeff Siemon
Mike Simone
Jack Smith
Mal Snider
Norm Standlee
Steve Stenstrom
Roger Stillwell
Chuck Taylor
Steve Thurlow
Dave Tipton
Lou Tsoutsouvas
Andre Tyler
Tommy Vardell
Randy Vataha
Garin Veris
Milt Vucinich
Chris Walsh
Gene Washington
Ryan Wetnight
Bob White
Bob Whitfield
Paul Wiggin
John Wilbur
Vaughn Williams
Gary Wimmer
Kailee Wong
David Wyman

Stephen F. Austin St. (28)

Bruce Alexander
Leo Araguz
Billy Autrey
Larry Centers
Bobby Cross
Floyd Dixon
Larry Eaglin
John Evans
Todd Fowler
Andy Hopkins
Sam Hunt
Michael LeBlanc
Bud Marshall
Tom McNeill
Mark Moseley
Bob Neff
Tony Newsom
James Noble
Mike Quinn
Mikhael Ricks
James Ritchey
Terrance Shaw
George Shirkey
Emil Slovacek
Jeremiah Trotter
David Whitmore
Todd Whitten
Eric Wright

Sterling (1)

Ed Hiemstra

Still (1)

Jim Regan

Suffolk Co. CC NY (1)

Chris Dieterich

Sul Ross State (3)

Gene Alford
Don Bingham
Johnny Hatley

Swarthmore (5)

Les Asplundh
Ben Clime
Charlie Lungren
Pete Richards
Ned Wilcox

Syracuse (186)

Faye Abbott
Kevin Abrams
Vannie Albanese
Doc Alexander
Lynwood Alford
Antonio Anderson
Gary Anderson
Will Anderson
Julie Archoska
Sam Babcock
Art Baker
John Barsha
David Bavaro
John Bayley
Reaves Baysinger
Vic Bellamy
Al Bemiller
Mil Berner
Craig Bingham
Speed Braney
Bob Brotzki
Bill Brown
Charlie Brown
Jim Brown
John Brown
Matt Brown
Nick Bruckner
Gary Bugenhagen
Rob Burnett
Rob Carpenter
Harlan Carr
Mike Charles
Jim Cheyunski
Steve Chomyszak
Ken Clarke
Alf Cobb
Jim Collins
Frank Conover
Irv Constantine
Dana Cottrell
Gerry Courtney
Jaime Covington
Larry Csonka
Frank Culver
Kirby Dar Dar
Donovin Darius
Roger Davis
Jim Del Gaizo
Fred DeRiggi
Tom Dickinson
John Dooley
Wes Dove
Robert Drummond
Joe DuMoe
Roddy Dunn
Les Dye
Joe Ehrmann
Larry Ellis
Mickey Fallon
Gerry Feehery
Russ Finsterwald
Dick Fishel
John Flannery
Jim Foley
Ben Forsyth
Fred Foster
Paul Frase
Jim Frugone
Chris Gedney
Tom Gilburg
Andrew Gissinger
Gene Grabosky
Tim Green
Ted Gregory
Ken Harris
Marvin Harrison
Garland Hawkins
Red Heater
Nate Hemsley
Jack Hinkle
Billy Hunter
Bill Hurley
Qadry Ismail
Dave Jacobs
George Jakowenko
Paul Jappe
Len Johnson
Daryl Johnston
Tony Jones
Tebucky Jones
Dwayne Joseph
Tommy Kane
Al Kanya
Carl Karilivacz
Bill Kellogg
Patrick Kelly
Pat Killorin
Jamie Kimmel
Jerry Kimmel
Dave Lapham
Dick Lasse
Gar Leaf
Bob Leberman
Harvey Levy
Floyd Little
John Mackey
Olindo Mare
Doug Marrone
Roy Martineau
Frank Matteo
Jack McBride
Paul McKee
Dave Meggyesy
Bill Meisner
Kevin Mitchell
Art Monk
Keith Moody
Rob Moore
Tim Moresco
Larry Morris
Joe Morris
Vince Mulvey
Tom Myers
Jim Nance
Jim Noble
Henry Obst
Pat O'Neill
Emile Palmer
Markus Paul
Todd Philcox
Tim Pidgeon
Hank Piro
Antwaune Ponds
Ray Preston
Jack Protz
Billy Rafter
Ray Reckmack
Roger Remo
Orian Rice
Terry Richardson
Jimmy Ridlon
Jim Ringo
Harry Robertson
Tam Rose
Guy Ruff
Herm Sawyer
Ken Sawyer
Gerhard Schwedes
Scott Schwedes
Sam Sebo
Mike Siano
Kaseem Sinceno
Walt Singer
Cliff Steele
Jim Steen
Thomas Stephens
Avatus Stone
Walt Sweeney
Willie Sydnor
Bruce Tarbox
Tiny Thompson
Art Thoms
Herb Titmas
Tommy Tomlin
Melvin Tuten
Lou Usher
Stan Walters
Joe Watt
Larry Weltman
Frank Whitcomb
Ray White
Vic Whitmarsh
Boyd Williams
Roland Williams
Otis Wilson
Blaise Winter
Terrence Wisdom
Ray Witter
Dave Wohlabaugh
Craig Wolfley
Terry Wooden
Bob Yates
Maury Youmans
Glen Young
Dave Ziff
Giff Zimmerman

Tabor (1)

Rolland Lawrence

Taft Coll. CA (J.C.) (13)

Steve Alvers
Blake Ezor
Jon Francis
Izel Jenkins
Bobby Kemp
R.J. Kors
Jim Krieg
David Nelson
Jason Phillips
Dino Philyaw
Tracy Rogers
Otis Smith
Jim Williams

Tampa (14)

Darryl Carlton
Jim Del Gaizo
Ted Greene
M.L. Harris
Don Herndon
Noah Jackson
Morris LaGrand
John Matuszak
Leon McQuay
Ron Mikolajczyk
John Mooring
Freddie Solomon
J.C. Wilson
Mike Woods

Tarkio (2)

Al Reynolds
Brick Travis

Tarleton State (4)

Marv Brown
Walter Bryan
Camp Wilson
Randy Winkler

Tarrant Co. JC TX (2)

Mike Baab
Mike Nelms

Taylor (1)

Wade Russell

Tekarkana Coll. TX (J.C.) (1)

Randy Jackson

Temple (73)

Anthony Anderson
Stan Batinski
Don Bitterlich
Todd Bowles
Larry Brahm
Jack Bravyak
Larry Chester
Jon Clark
Wayne Colman
Jim Cooper
Eric Coss
Mike Curcio
Bill Davidson
Wendell Davis
Zachary Dixon
Al Drulis
Chuck Drulis
Chris Fletcher
Glenn Frey
Gorham Getchell
Les Grace
Tom Graham
Randy Grossman
Len Gudd
Swede Hanson
James Harris
Mike Hinnant
Gene Hubka
Henry Hynoski
Mike Jarmoluk
Ralph Jarvis
Steve Joachim
Lorne Johnson
Maurice Johnson
Tre' Johnson
Lance Johnstone
Bucko Kilroy
Joe Klecko
Ed Kolman
John Kusko
John Lipski
Ed McGee
Todd McNair
Nick Mike-Mayer
Allen Nichols
Paul Palmer
James Parrish
Joe Pilconis
Shelley Poole
Hank Reese
John Rienstra
Tim Riordan
Kevin Ross
Jim Russell
Leslie Shepherd
Johnny Shultz
Bill Singletary
Alshermond Singleton
Phil Slosburg
Dave Smukler
Santo Stephens
Pete Stevens
Mike Stromberg
George Sutch
Joe Sutton
John Sylvester
Alphonso Taylor
Tim Terry
Andy Tomasic
Joe Tyrrell
Steve Watson
Terry Wright
Anthony Young

Tennessee (213)

Brent Adams
Bill Anderson
Pete Athas
Doug Atkins
Raymond Austin
Howard Bailey
Sam Bartholomew
Bill Bates
Ed Beard
Tom Blake
Shane Bonham
Dirk Borgognone
John Boynton
Art Brandau
Eddie Brown
Jonathan Brown
Laron Brown
John Bruhin
Shane Burton
Johnny Butler
George Cafego
Whit Canale
Dale Carter
Ed Cifers
Bob Cifers
Neil Clabo
Boyd Clay
Joey Clinkscales
Reggie Cobb
Joe Cofer
Mike Cofer
Todd Collins
Craig Colquitt
Jimmy Colquitt
Richard Cooper
Denny Crawford
Ted Daffer
Bernard Dafney
Antone Davis
Ron Davis
Keith DeLong
Steve DeLong
Jerry DeLucca
Austin Denney
Bob Dobelstein
David Douglas
Clyde Duncan
Frank Emanuel
Dick Evey
Terry Fair
Beattie Feathers
Cory Fleming
Richmond Flowers
Jeff Francis
Ken Frost
Jim Gaffney
Greg Gaines
Harry Galbreath
Scott Galyon
Charlie Garner
Willie Gault
Glenn Glass
Bobby Gordon
John Gordy
Sam Graddy
Jay Graham
Ray Graves
Anthony Hancock
Darryl Hardy
Alvin Harper
Aaron Hayden
Tracy Hayworth
Tim Hendrix
Herman Hickman
Jim Hill
Bill Hillman
Marion Hobby
Marc Hogan
Anthony Howard
Joey Howard
William Howard
Ian Howfield
Frank Hubbell
Dick Huffman
George Hunt
Al Hust
Tom Hutton
Brian Ingram
Tim Irwin
Roland James
DeRon Jenkins
Bob Johnson
Dale Jones
Todd Kelly
Joey Kent
Gene Killian
Steve Kiner
Steve Knight
Karl Kremser
Eric Lane
Hank Lauricella
Jason Layman
Cotton Letner
Jeremy Lincoln
Paul Lipscomb
Leonard Little
Bob Long
Corey Louchiey
Mike Lucci
Billy Majors
Bobby Majors
Peyton Manning
Tal Maples
Mickey Marvin
Steve Matthews
Adrian McBride
Ronnie McCartney
J.J. McCleskey
Darris McCord
Terry McDaniel
Tim McGee
Raleigh McKenzie
Reggie McKenzie
Charles McRae
Art Mergenthal
John Michels
Anthony Miller
Bubba Miller
Darrin Miller
Mike Miller
Chris Mims
Stan Mitchell
Jeff Moore
Anthony Morgan
Stanley Morgan
Randall Morris
Russ Morrow
Tom Myslinski
Marcus Nash
Paul Naumoff
Ed Nickla
Bob Petrella
Carl Pickens
Gordon Polofsky
Steve Poole
Jeff Powell
Craig Puki
Van Rayburn
Bert Rechichar
Lloyd Reese
Fuad Reveiz
Jack Reynolds
Larry Robinson
Tony Robinson
Gene Rose
John Rowan
Al Russas
Pat Ryan
Joe Schaffer
Bobby Scott
Robert Shaw
Bud Sherrod
Lebron Shields
Abe Shires
Heath Shuler
Nilo Silvan
Tony Simmons
Len Simonetti
Kevin Simons
Tommy Sims
Curt Singer
Walt Slater
Carl Smith
Chuck Smith
Daryle Smith
Jeff Smith
Jeff Smith
Andy Spiva
Danny Spradlin
Haskel Stanback
Dave Stephenson
James Stewart
Mike Stratton
Jack Stroud
Mark Studaway
Bob Suffridge
Eric Swanson
Ben Talley
Jimmy Tarrant
Lenny Taylor
Harry Thayer
Dave Thomas
Alvin Toles
Tom Tracy
Jesse Turnbow
Pug Vaughan
Hal Wantland
Buss Warren
John Warren
Dewey Warren
Jim Weatherford
Herman Weaver
Chuck Webb
Burr West
Brad White
Reggie White
Chris White
Steve White
Ron Widby
Bruce Wilkerson
Billy Williams
Darryal Wilson
Carl Zander

Tennessee Mil. Acad. (J.C.) (3)

Jerry Butler
Willie Green
Dale Jones

Tennessee State (98)

Brent Alexander
Larry Barnes
Bill Bass
Cliff Brooks
Waymond Bryant
Charles Buchanan
Darryl Caldwell
Alex Carter
Willie Carter
Al Coleman
Dave Davis
Oliver Davis
Rosey Davis
Sonny Davis
Richard Dent
Eldridge Dickey
Larry Dorsey
Marcus Dowdell
Elbert Drungo
Cid Edwards
Cleveland Elam
Onzy Elam
Homer Elias
Charley Ferguson
Randy Fuller
Chuck Gavin
George Gilchrist
Joe Gilliam
Steve Griffin
Steve Hawkins
Mike Hegman
Sylvester Hicks
John Holland
Vern Holland
Steve Holloway
Bryan Howard
Claude Humphrey
Herman Hunter
Johnny Jackson
Danny Johnson
Lee Johnson
Stan Johnson
Joe Jones
Mike Jones
Roger Jones
Too Tall Jones
Jim Kelly
Greg Kindle
Larry Kinnebrew
Mack Lamb
Izzy Lang
Don Laster
Larry Mallory
Jim Marsalis
Loaird McCreary
Frank McRae
Jerrold McRae
Mel Mitchell
Willie Mitchell
Steve Moore
McDonald Oden
Rod Parker
Frank Pillow
Anthony Pleasant
David Pool
Robert Porcher
Dan Pride
Robert Reed
Harold Rice
Johnnie Robinson
Patrick Robinson
Simon Shanks
Anthony Shelton
Nate Simpson
Fletcher Smith
John Smith

Noland Smith
Ollie Smith
Tony Stargell
Joe Sweet
Malcolm Taylor
Ryan Terry
Larry Tharpe
Jim Thaxton
Charlie Thomas
Bill Tucker
Hal Turner
Charlie Wade
Carl Wafer
Willie Walker
Riley Walton
Bill West
Dwight Wheeler
Dan Williams
Bernard Wilson
Larry Woods
Robert Woods
Will Wynn

Tennessee Tech (8)

Wentford Gaines
Elois Grooms
Mike Hennigan
Larry Schreiber
Howard Stidham
John Tanner
Lonnie Warwick
Jim Youngblood

Tennessee Wesleyan (2)

Aaron Grant
Ray Graves

Tennessee-Chattanooga (43)

Tony Bowick
Jim Bradshaw
Chuck Braidwood
Bill Butler
Malcolm Carson
Greg Cater
Howard Clark
Abe Cohen
Jerry Ellison
Lonnie Farmer
Fred Getz
Willie Gillespie
Aaron Grant
Johnny Green
Jack Gregory Jr.
Jack Gregory Sr.
Marrio Grier
Frank Grigonis
Carey Henley
Tony Hill
Mike Hogan
Ralph Hutchinson
Brent Johnson
Spider Johnson
Art Koeninger
Joe Kopcha
Chet Lagod
Hal Ledyard
Charley Long
Travis McNeal
Randall Mitchell
Greg Moore
Mike Nease
Terrell Owens
Darnell Powell
Fred Rayhle
Harold Ricks
Choo-Choo Roberts
Curtis Rouse
Henry Sorrell
Gary Tucker
Rocky Turner
Dick Young

Tennessee-Martin (7)

Mike Crangle
Bobby Fowler
Gordon Lambert
Emanuel McNeil
Julian Nunamaker
Joe Taffoni
Fred Thomas

Texas (208)

Joe Abbey
Bill Acker
Fred Acorn
Tony Adams
Mike Adams
Raul Allegre
Don Allen
Taje Allen
Ty Allert
Scott Appleton
Jay Arnold
Bill Atessis
John Ayers
Mike Baab
Don Barton
Joe Billy Baumgardner
Hub Bechtol
Vance Bedford
Jim Bertelsen
Glenn Blackwood
Tony Brackens
Bill Bradley
Stephen Braggs
Blake Brockermeyer
Lee Brooks
Laron Brown
Bob Bryant
Max Bumgardner
Mossy Cade
Jim Callahan
Earl Campbell
Jim Canady
Chris Carter
Keith Cash
Kerry Cash
Mike Chapman
Gene Chilton
Ricky Churchman
Darryl Clark
Randy Clay
Raymond Clayborn
Bill Collins
Zuehl Conoly
Dave Conway
Craig Curry
Doug Dawson
Gib Dawson
Kiki DeAyala
Tony Degrate
Bobby Dillon
Sonny Doell
Noble Doss
Mike Dowdle
Shane Dronett
Chris Duliban
Ox Eckhardt
John Elliott
Ox Emerson
Doug English
Russell Erxleben
Staley Faulkner
Wiley Feagin
Happy Feller
Howard Fest
Jitter Fields
Bob Flowers
Jack Freeman
Everett Gay
John Goodson
William Graham
Jerry Gray
Tex Grigg
Lance Gunn
Britt Hager
John Hagy
John Haines
Hank Harris
Phil Harris
William Harris
Derrick Hatchett
Walt Heap
Lew Holder
Eric Holle
Priest Holmes
Jim Hudson
Bill Hughes
Alfred Jackson
Ken Jackson
June James
Mike January
Eric Jeffries
Tommy Jeter
Paul Jetton
Bobby Johnson
Chuck Johnson
Johnnie Johnson
A.J. Jones
Brian Jones
David Jones
Lam Jones
Tony Jones
Buddy Jungmichel
Ray Keeling
Gary Keithley
Ed Kelley
Edward Kelley
Wade Key
Curt Knight
Ernie Koy
Ted Koy
Mal Kutner
Pete Lammons
Tom Landry
Buck Lansford
Jim Lansford
Carl Larpenter
Al Lawler
Pete Layden
Bobby Layne
Roosevelt Leaks
Monte Lee
Jeff Leiding
Larry Linne
Louie Long
Joe Don Looney
Joe Magliolo
Van Malone
Vern Martin
Carlton Massey
Stan Mauldin
Carl Mayes
Lew Mayne
Bud McFadin
Rick McIvor
Bob McKay
Roy McKay
Steve McMichael
Don Menasco
Eric Metcalf
Bobby Micho
Bryan Millard
Dan Neil
Tommy Nobis
Terry Orr
Scott Palmer
Joe Parker
James Patton
Jerry Peterson
Les Peterson
George Petrovich
Lovell Pinkney
Ray Poage
Stanley Richard
Travis Roach
Al Rose
Mike Ruether
Jack Sachse
Lawrence Sampleton
Chris Samuels
Spec Sanders
George Sauer
Jimmy Saxton
Bruce Scholtz
Adam Schreiber
Robin Sendlein
Harley Sewell
Brad Shearer
Joe Shearin
Deck Shelley
Bob Simmons
Kenneth Sims
Jerry Sisemore
Lou Smyth
Cotton Speyrer
Harry Stafford
Larry Stephens
Tom Stolhandske
Dave Studdard
Les Studdard
Diron Talbert
Don Talbert
Rodney Tate
Terry Tausch
John Teltschik
Stan Thomas
Del Thompson
Tony Tillmon
Winfred Tubbs
Buddy Tynes
Olen Underwood
Joe Vance
Vic Vasicek
Tommy Wade
Loyd Wainscott
Alex Waits
Herkie Walls
Charles Washington
Rat Watson
Don Weedon
Bryant Westbrook
Harlan Wetz
Don Williams
Ed Williams
Joel Williams
Red Wolfe
Ray Woodard
Bob Young
Willie Zapalac

Texas A&M (195)

Sam Adams
Keith Alex
Grady Allen
Neely Allison
Adger Armstrong
Antonio Armstrong
Mike Arthur
Keith Baker
Keith Baldwin
Patrick Bates
Bubba Bean
Ken Beck
Rod Bernstine
Adam Bob
Ed Breding
Rankin Britt
Chet Brooks
Fred Broussard
Reggie Brown
Ross Brupbacher
Domingo Bryant
Ray Bucek
Marcus Buckley
Tom Buckman
Glenn Bujnoch
Lee Roy Caffey
Billy Cannon
Ron Carpenter
Gerald Carter
Louis Cheek
Ray Childress
Mike Clark
Hayward Clay
Calvin Collins
Albert Connell
Kip Corrington
Quentin Coryatt
Zed Coston
Tex Coulter
Chris Crooms
John David Crow
Rick Cunningham
Matt Darwin
Jimmy Dean
Mark Dennard
Curtis Dickey
Brad Dusek
Herb Ellis
Dave Elmendorf
Eric England
Bob Evans
Edgar Fields
Hank Foldberg
Jerry Fontenot
Tony Franklin
Derrick Frazier
Dick Frey
Jeff Fuller
Shane Garrett
Aaron Glenn
Rob Goode
Hunter Goodwin
Tim Gray
Jacob Green
Donovan Greer
Clif Groce
Keith Guthrie
Ken Hall
David Hardy
Edd Hargett
Rod Harris
Lester Hayes
Johnny Hector
Greg Hill
Bill Hobbs
Johnny Holland
Jerry Hopkins
Todd Howard
Clarence Howell
Barlow Irvin
Earnest Jackson
Robert Jackson
Steve Jacobson
Tom Janik
Edward Jasper
Bill Johnson
Gary Jones
Jeff Jones
Mike Jones
Larry Kelm
Jim Kendrick
John Kimbrough
Kelvin Korver
Charlie Krueger
Rolf Krueger
Ray Kubala
Gary Kubiak
Yale Lary
Darren Lewis
Mark Lewis
Jack Little
Steve Lofton
Chuck Malone
Tank Marshall
Jason Mathews
Fran Mattingly
Tommy Maxwell
John McCrumbly
Leeland McElroy
Danny McIlhany
James McKeehan
Steve McKinney
Ray Mickens
Russ Mikeska
Charlie Milstead
Brandon Mitchell
Keith Mitchell
Jim Montgomery
Al Moore
Mack Moore
Mo Moorman
Mark Moseley
Mike Mosley
Cap Murrah
Frank Myers
Steve O'Neal
Richard Osborne
Jeff Paine
Ernie Pannell
Jack Pardee
Jim Parmer
Roger Powell
Cotton Price
Terry Price
Marion Pugh
Jack Pyburn
Ken Reeves
Bucky Richardson
Cody Risien
Carl Roaches
Jeroy Robinson
Tommy Robison
Marshall Robnett
Ed Robnett
Cullen Rogers
John Roper
Martin Ruby
Chris Ruhman
Rod Saddler
Chris Sanders
Gene Sanders
Thomas Sanders
Buzz Sawyer
Tom Sestak
Rich Siler
Ed Simonini
Detron Smith
Kevin Smith
Bob Smith
Al Sparkman
Odell Stautzenberger
Larry Stegent
Gil Steinke
George Strohmeyer
Karl Sweetan
Dennis Swilley
Damon Tassos
Jimmy Teal
Lance Teichelman
Garth Ten Napel
Pat Thomas
Rodney Thomas
William Thomas
Jim Thomason
Billy Tidwell
Dick Todd
Anthony Toney
Jack Tracey
Ira Valentine
Roger Vick
Aaron Wallace
Derek Ware
Mickey Washington
Richmond Webb
Joe Wellborn
Mark Wheeler
Mike Whitwell
George Wilde
Doug Williams
Pat Williams
Mule Wilson
Robert Wilson
Jim Winkler
Keith Woodside
Roy Young

Texas A&M-Commerce (23)

Autry Beamon
George Boynton
Marv Brown
Curtis Buckley
Tim Collier
Will Cureton
Jon Gilliam
Rich Houston
Cecil Johnson
Jay Johnson
Dee Mackey
Kyle Mackey
Harvey Martin
Kevin Mathis
Marshall Robnett
Wes Smith
Aundra Thompson
Jim Thrower
Darrell Tully
Alan Veingrad
Sam Walton
Dwight White
Wade Wilson

Texas A&M-Kingsville (45)

Herbie Anderson
Johnny Bailey
John Barefield
Sid Blanks
Stu Clarkson
Larry Collins
Paschall Davis
Jorge Diaz
Kevin Dogins
Earl Dotson
Mike Dyal
John Fletcher
George Franklin
Hunter Goodwin
Darrell Green
Doug Greene
Don Hardeman
Al Harris
Dwight Harrison
Andy Hawkins
Mike Hawkins
Joe Hayes
Ray Hickl
David Hill
Jim Hill
Tom Janik
James Jefferson
Levi Johnson
Randy Johnson
Richard Jones
Al Matthews
Jermane Mayberry
Anthony Phillips
Ernie Price
John Randle
Butch Riley
Durwood Roquemore
Heath Sherman
Eldridge Small
Emmuel Thompson
Gene Upshaw
Ray Waddy
Hall Whitley
Karl Williams
Floyd Young

Texas Christian (110)

Ki Aldrich
Bruce Alford Jr.
Bruce Alford Sr.
Egypt Allen
Scott Ankrom
Ray Armstrong
Sammy Baugh
Mitchell Benson
Kelly Blackwell
Lyle Blackwood
John Booty
Ben Boswell
George Brown
Larry Brown
Norm Bulaich
David Caldwell
Cy Casper
Kyle Clifton
Bert Coan
Danny Colbert
Linzy Cole
Roosevelt Collins
Jim Cooper
Norm Cox
Bob Creech
Tommy Crutcher
Derrick Cullors
Charles Davis
Darrell Davis
Kenneth Davis
Kevin Dean
Weldon Edwards
Drew Ellis
Hunter Enis
Phil Epps
Greg Evans
Lon Evans
Norm Evans
Keith Flowers
Bobby Jack Floyd
Don Floyd
Billy Gault
Donnie Gibbs
Sonny Gibbs
Johnny Hall
Phil Handler
Marshall Harris
Sherrill Headrick
Ken Henson
Grassy Hinton
Foster Howell
Cedric Jackson
Tony Jeffery
Lenoy Jones
Frank Kring
Jimmy Lawrence
Darrell Lester
Bob Lilly
Aubrey Linne
Joe Don Looney
Don Looney
Robert Lyles
James Maness
Tilly Manton
Mickey McCarty
Ross Montgomery
Guy Morriss
John Morton
Emery Nix
Kent Nix
Davey O'Brien
Jim O'Neal
Derrell Palmer
Cliff Patton
Stan Petry
Hugh Pitts
John Preston
Skeets Quinlan
Alan Reid
Mike Renfro
Chuck Reynolds
Ray Rhodes
Rollin Roach
Joe Robb
Barret Robbins
Wes Roberts
Glynn Rogers
Justin Rowland
Dan Sharp
Jim Shofner
Fred Shook
Tracy Simien
Brad Smith
Gary Spann
Jack Spikes
Pete Stout
Jim Swink
Stan Talley
Sean Thomas
Bubba Thornton
Greg Townsend
Ryan Tucker
Ted Vaught
Will Walls
Fred Washington
Allie White
George Wilde
Jake Williams
Richard Woodley
James Wright

Texas Southern (57)

Julius Adams
Nate Allen
Bert Askson
Keith Baker
Melvin Baker
Raymond Baylor
Warren Bone
Gene Branton
Gregg Briggs
Ken Burrough
Ernie Calloway
B.W. Cheeks
Darrell Colbert
Vince Courville
Arthur Cox
Larry Crowe
Fred Dean
John Douglas
Willie Ellison
James Ford
Charley Frazier
Harold Hart
Lonnie Hepburn
W.K. Hicks
Winston Hill
Jimmy Hines
Ernie Holmes
Jack Holmes
Mike Holmes
Roy Hopkins
Kevin Johnson
Nate Johnson
Boyd Jones
Homer Jones
Allen Lyday
Brett Maxie
Dave Mays
Leroy Mitchell
Will Moore
Calvin Muhammad
Lloyd Mumphord
Harold Paul
Willis Perkins
Charles Philyaw
Bob Pollard
Willie Porter
Ernest Pough
David Rackley
Andy Rice
Jim Sorey
Art Strahan
Michael Strahan
Leon Thomasson
Warren Wells
Alberto White
John White
Jim Young

Texas Tech (91)

Gene Alford
Glen Amerson
Donny Anderson
Hasson Arbubakrr
Elmer Arterburn
Joe Barnes
Winnie Baze
Hub Bechtol
Bill Brown
Walter Bryan
Bob Bryant
Maury Buford
Victor Burnett
Jim Callahan
John Carrell
Carl Carter
Marcus Coleman
Tim Crawford
Stan David
Gaines Davis
Bill Davis
Mule Dowell
Tom Duniven
Ralph Earhart
Lin Elliott
Eric Everett
Eric Felton
Larry Flowers
Bob Flowers
Roger Gill
Jim Hadnot
Byron Hanspard
Leonard Harris
Bill Herchman
Tex Holcomb
Pat Holmes
E.J. Holub
Tom Howard
Van Hughes
Anthony Hutchison
Charles Jackson
Dwayne Jiles
Leonard Jones
Lew Jones
Curtis Jordan
Bill Kelley
Bob Kilcullen
Jim Krahl

Dave Lloyd
Anthony Lynn
Jodie Marek
Anthony McDowell
Monte McGuire
Derrell Mitchell
Roland Mitchell
Mike Mock
Ed Mooney
Bam Morris
Roland Nabors
Jim Neill
Pete Owens
Dave Parks
Mac Percival
Red Ramsey
Tate Randle
Walt Rankin
Gabe Rivera
Don Rives
Ed Robnett
Frank Sachse
Walt Schlinkman
Prince Scott
King Simmons
Joe Smith
Timmy Smith
Dick Stafford
Lemuel Stinson
Billy Taylor
Zach Thomas
Andre Tillman
Billy Joe Tolliver
Bake Turner
Ken Vinyard
Sammy Walker
Wayne Walker
Joe Walter
Ted Watts
George Webb
Lawrence Williams
Rex Williams
Bernie Winkler

Texas-Arlington (25)

Mike Barnes
Dexter Bussey
Skip Butler
Scott Caldwell
Mark Cannon
Bruce Collie
Jack DeGrenier
Weldon Edwards
Mal Hammack
Doug Hart
Steve Jackson
Derrick Jensen
Darryl Lewis
Gary Lewis
Howie Maley
Tim McKyer
Don Morrison
Cliff Odom
Pete Stout
John Symank
Jimmy Thomas
Byron Williams
Mel Witt
Jim Wright
Ben Young

Texas-El Paso (57)

J.B. Andrews
Dave Atkins
Victor Bailey
Reggie Barrett
Kevin Belcher
Fred Carr
Grady Cavness
Russ Cotton
Don Croft
George Daney
Fred DeBernardi
Jim Evans
Ray Evans
Bobby Fowler
Bubba Garcia
Sammy Garza
Paul Gibson
Clyde Glosson
Wayne Hansen
Lee Harden
John Harvey
Ken Heineman
Chuck Hughes
Chris Jacke
Ron Jones
Seth Joyner
Gary Keithley
Bob Keseday
Bob Laraba
Larry Linne
Riley Matheson
Lindy Mayhew
Don Maynard
Darryl Moore
Raymond Morris
Jack Oliver
Jim O'Neal
Keith Powe
Carlos Scott
Pete Shufelt
Mike Smith
Ed Smith
Don Sommer
Billy Stevens
Del Thompson
Tony Tolbert
Bob Wallace
Eric Washington
Marvin Washington
Charlie West
Jeff White
Paul White
Jesse Whittenton
Albert Williams
Larry Willis
Gordon Wilson
Barron Wortham

The Citadel (12)

Al Bansavage
Bobby Curtis
Pete Davidson
Greg Davis
Travis Jervey
Brad Keeney
Jimmy Lesane
Paul Maguire
Stump Mitchell
Andy Sabados
John Small
Byron Walker

Thiel (3)

Floyd Christman
Al Mitchell
Woodie Pippens

Thornton CC IL (1)

Tom Baldwin

Toledo (38)

Darren Anderson
Bob Beemer
Tom Beutler
Tommie Boyd
Tyrone Brown
Dexter Clark
Emerson Cole
Gene Cook
Paul Elzey
Jerry Evans
Jim Gray
Tony Harris
Ray Hayes
Tim Inglis
Curtis Johnson
Bryant Jones
Mike Kennedy
Mel Long
Clarence Love
Frank Maher
Lou Marotti
Vince Marrow
Andy McCollum
Darryl Meadows
Roland Moss
Ken Moyer
Tubby Rousch
Chuck Sample
John Saunders
Ed Scrutchins
Marty Slovak
Jim Thibert
John Thomas
Mel Triplett
Emlen Tunnell
Mike Varajon
Brent Williams
Dan Williams

Toronto (Canada) (1)

Dean Dorsey

Towson State (6)

Marc Brown
Stan Eisenhooth
Sean Landeta
Dave Meggett
Chad Scott
Tony Vinson

Treasure Valley CC OR (1)

Carter Campbell

Trinidad State JC CO (5)

Randy Beverly
Frank Clarke
Cody Jones
Larry Walton
Gary Weaver

Trinity (Conn.) (6)

George Brickley
Mickey Kobrosky
Roger LeClerc
Dick Noble
Swede Nordstrom
Joe Shield

Trinity (Ill.) (1)

Karl Hankton

Trinity (Tex.) (13)

Wes Bradshaw
Pete Cole
Jim Higgins
Irv Hill
Darrell Hogan
Heinie Kirkgard
Greg Lens
Obert Logan
Ralph Nairan
Greg Oliver
Henry Schmidt
Al Swain
Marv Upshaw

Trinity Valley CC TX (16)

Margene Adkins
Max Anderson
Darren Benson
Linzy Cole
Paschall Davis
Anthony Dickerson
Todd Fowler
Jessie Green
Al Harris
Robert Jackson
Richard Jones
Ron Jones
Perry Phenix
John Randle
James Scott
Scott Tyner

Triton CC IL (1)

Steve Ache

Troy State (17)

Sherrill Busby
Titus Dixon
Perry Griggs
Anthony Henton
Kerry Jenkins
Reggie Lowe
Pratt Lyons
Larry Mason
Willie McCray
Derrick Moore
Orlando Parker
Jack Peavey
Virgil Seay
Jack Smith
Shawn Stuckey
Willie Tullis
Leonard Wheeler

Truckee Meadows CC NV (1)

Dirk Borgognone

Tufts (9)

Mark Buben
Harrie Dadmun
Dinger Doane
Carl Etelman
Joe Gillis
Doc Haggerty
Tom McNamara
Nate Share
Pete Watson

Tulane (83)

Alton Alexis
Marvin Allen
Marcus Anderson
Curt Baham
Jerry Baker
Warren Bankston
Michael Batiste
Roman Bentz
Ernie Blandin
Maury Bodenger
Jim Boyle
Bubby Brister
James Campen
Joe Caravello
Rusty Chambers
Marty Comer
Bernie Darre
Burnell Dent
Corey Dowden
Bobby Duhon
Steve Foley
Nolan Franz
Dick Fugler
Les Gatewood
Fred Gloden
Jim Gueno
Ruffin Hamilton
Richard Harvey
Jerry Helluin
Ray Hester
Rodney Holman
Bill Hornick
Pete Johns
Dub Jones
Don Joyce
Ken Karcher
Bob Kellogg
Ed Khayat
George Kinek
Ellsworth Kingery
Rick Kingrea
Eric Laakso
Paul Lea
Marvin Lewis
Don Maggs
Lonnie Marts
Tommy Mason
Harley McCollum
Walt McDonald
Max McGee
Sylvester McGrew
Mark Mitchell
Eddie Murray
Ed Neal
Phil Nugent
Richie Petitbon
Chuck Pitcock
Eddie Price
Mitchell Price
Jonathan Quinn
Freeman Rexer
Dan Rogas
Tony Sardisco
John Scafide
Leroy Schneider
Darin Shoulders
Joe Silipo
Treg Songy
Jerald Sowell
Bill Svoboda
Hugh Taylor
Len Teeuws
Jim Thibaut
Eric Thomas
Ron Tilton
Dalton Truax
Elton Veals
Mike Walker
Lionel Washington
Jeff Wenzel
Ralph Wenzel
Marty Wetzel
Kevin Young

Tulsa (142)

Sid Abramowitz
David Alexander
Billy Anderson
Dunstan Anderson
Rick Arrington
Josh Ashton
Steve August
Tom Baldwin
Don Bandy
Jean Barrett
Paul Barry
Greg Barton
Joe Bernstein
Stub Blackman
Don Blackmon
Thomas Blair
Dick Blanchard
Jeb Blount
J.R. Boone
Wade Bosarge
Bob Breitenstein
Eric Brown
Gordon Brown
Hardy Brown
Carl Buda
Tony Buford
Glenn Burgeis
Buddy Burris
Dennis Byrd
Leo Carroll
Sedric Clark
Danny Colbert
Ted Connolly
Steve Cox
Bob Daugherty
Donnie Dee
Joe Dixon
Glenn Dobbs
Ken Duncan
Rick Eber
Rick Engles
Greg Fairchild
Jim Finks
Gus Frerotte
Steve Gage
Lee Gentry
Joe Gibson
Clyde Goodnight
Tim Gordon
Les Graham
Sam Gray
Jessie Green
John Green
Frank Greene
Nelson Greene
Chubby Grigg
Mike Gunter
Dean Hamel
Wes Hamilton
Eddie Hare
Ham Harmon
Joe Haynes
Karl Henke
Bob Holladay
Ed Hughes
Dick Hughes
Al Jenkins
Paul Johns
Al Jolley
Ellis Jones
Jeff Jordan
Bob Joswick
Saxon Judd
Muadianvita Kazadi
Dick Kercher
Steve King
Adolph Kowalski
Ken Lacy
Steve Largent
Clyde LeForce
Kevin Lilly
Tony Liscio
Mike Loyd
Nolan Luhn
John Lyons
Marv Matuszak
Gary McDermott
Ralph McGill
Tom Miner
Barry Minter
Charlie Mitchell
Art Moore
Perry Moss
Robbie Nichols
Joe Novsek
Jerry Ostroski
Homer Paine
Drew Pearson
Chris Penn
Kirk Phillips
Chris Pike
Garry Porterfield
Felto Prewitt
Cal Purdin
Chuck Reynolds
Homer Reynolds
Ray Rhodes
Jerry Rhome
Tom Robertson
T.J. Rubley
Bob St. Clair
Tracy Scroggins
Ed Shedlosky
Bob Smith
Ray Smith
Gene Spangler
C.B. Stanley
Jason Staurovsky
Richard Stephens
Jimmy Stewart
Walt Stickel
Terry Stoepel
Bob Stringer
Roy Stuart
Neal Sweeney
Cal Thomas
Rex Thomas
Tommy Thompson
Willie Townes
Howard Twilley
Dick Tyson
Bill Volok
Xavier Warren
Rickey Watts
Cornell Webster
S.J. Whitman
Eugene Williams
Camp Wilson
Blake Workman
Charles Wright
Jeff Wright
Doug Wyatt

Tuskegee (8)

Gerald Bess
Leon Crenshaw
Walter Johnson
Ricky Jones
Ken Jordan
Cecil Leonard
Art May
Ken Woodard

Tyler JC TX (27)

Ira Albright
Allen Aldridge
Melvin Aldridge
Ken Bahnsen
Mitch Berger
Kent Branstetter
Ben Bronson
Ivory Lee Brown
Gerald Carter
Ken Coffey
Earl Dotson
Ike Forte
LaSalle Harper
Bill Herchman
Cedric Jackson
Paul Johns
Bill Johnson
Charlie Johnson
Marvin Lewis
Dave Lunceford
Dee Mackey
John McCrumbly
Andrew Melontree
Tyrone Montgomery
Darryl Moore
Charley Quilter
Tyrone Shavers

UCLA (221)

Karim Abdul-Jabbar
John Adams
Troy Aikman
Arnold Ale
Kermit Alexander
Jimmy Allen
Flipper Anderson
Zenon Andrusyshyn
Charles Arbuckle
Bill Armstrong
Burr Baldwin
Eric Ball
Mike Ballou
Bruce Barnes
Rich Baska
Gary Beban
Tommy Bennett
Bruce Bergey
Steve Bono
Brent Boyd
Verdi Boyer
Theotis Brown
Ray Burks
Paul Cameron
Leo Cantor
Ernie Case
Frank Cephous
Mike Chalenski
Bill Chambers
Bob Christiansen
Ron Copeland
Gus Coppens
Frank Cornish
Frank Corral
Paco Craig
Randy Cross
Willie Curran
Dave Dalby
Brad Daluiso
Matt Darby
Bruce Davis
Milt Davis
Alan Dial
Dan Dufour
Kenny Easley
Irv Eatman
Keith Eck
Donnie Edwards
Jack Ellena
Allan Ellis
Bert Emanuel
George Farmer
Mel Farr Jr.
Mel Farr Sr.
Mike Farr
Tom Fears
Chuck Fenenbock
Bob Ferrell
Jack Finlay
Mike Flanagan
Cliff Frazier
Ed Galigher
Bob Geddes
Joe Goebel
Brian Goodman
Wes Grant
Carlton Gray
Gaston Green
Carl Greenwood
Mike Haffner
Othello Henderson
Darryl Henley
Wally Henry
Johnny Hermann
Efren Herrera
Skip Hicks
Sale Isaia
Robert Jenkins
Jim Johnson
Kermit Johnson
Mitch Johnson
Norm Johnson
Brian Jones
Greg Jones
Jimmie Jones
Kevin Jordan
Joe Keeble
Charlie Kendall
Billy Kilmer
Travis Kirschke
Jeff Knapple
Ronnie Knox
Art Kuehn
Roy Kurrasch
Fulton Kuykendall
Sean LaChapelle
Carnell Lake
Dion Lambert
John Lee
Larry Lee
Cliff Livingston
Mike Lodish
Bob Long
Rommie Loudd
Duval Love
Del Lyman
Johnny Lynn
Tommy Maddox
Frank Manumaleuga
Ned Mathews
James McAlister
Bob McChesney
Gerry McDougall
Phil McKinnely
Leon McLaughlin
Freeman McNeil
Fred McNeill
Bob Mike
Chuckie Miller
Jamir Miller
Scott Miller
Hal Mitchell
Blanchard Montgomery
Max Montoya
Reynaud Moore
Karl Morgan
Dave Morton
Martin Moss
Jack Myers
Ray Nagel
Rick Neuheisel
David Norrie
Trusse Norris
Ken Norton
Craig Novitsky
Jonathan Ogden
Paul Oglesby
Carl Olson
James Owens
Vaughn Parker
Marvcus Patton
Don Paul
Jairo Penaranda
John Pentecost
Cal Peterson
Roman Phifer
George Phillips
Bob Pifferini
Ron Pitts
Dennis Price
James Primus
Bernard Quarles
Tom Ramsey
David Richards
Bob Richardson
John Richardson
Paul Richardson
Avon Riley
Oscar Roan
Jerry Robinson
Don Rogers
Craig Rutledge
Jim Salsbury
Lupe Sanchez
Bill Sandifer
Jay Schroeder
John Sciarra
Rob Scribner
Luis Sharpe
Mike Sherrard
Don Shinnick
Jerry Shipkey
Hal Smith
Kevin Smith
Milt Smith
Bobby Smith
Ken Snelling
Jack Sommers
Al Sparlis
Scott Stauch
Jim Steffen
Matt Stevens
Bill Stits
J.J. Stokes
Woody Strode
James Stroschein
John Tautolo
Terry Tautolo
Derek Tennell
Jewerl Thomas
Harry Thompson
Glen Titensor
Jo-Jo Townsell
Manu Tuiasosopo
Mark Tuinei
Eric Turner
Jimmy Turner
Marcus Turner
Wendell Tyler
Andy Von Sonn
Jim Wahler
Mark Walen
Bruce Walker
Rick Walker
Bruce Walton
Phillip Ward
James Washington
Kenny Washington
Bob Waterfield
Cornell Webster
Herb Welch
Bob Wilkinson
Dokie Williams
Kevin Williams
Michael Williams
Shaun Williams
Blake Wingle
Dick Witcher
Tim Wrightman
Mike Young
Lance Zeno

Ulster County CC NY (1)

Jerry Drake

Union (N.Y.) (2)

Fred Brumm
Rich Romer

Union (Tenn.) (2)

Jim Jones
Ralph Jones

U. of Pacific (59)

Bob Adams
Larry Bailey
Norm Bass
Dick Bass
Ryan Benjamin
Greg Bishop
Dirk Borgognone
Carlos Brown
Don Campora
Clyde Conner
Bob Coronado
Bruce Coslet
Gene Cronin
Burt Delevan
Bob Denton
Tom Flores
Willard Harrell
Wayne Hawkins
Willie Hector
Bob Heinz
Daryl Hobbs
Honor Jackson
Keever Jankovich
Carl Kammerer
Earl Klapstein
Galen Laack
Jack Larscheid
Paul Latzke
Eddie LeBaron
Bob Lee
Eddie Macon
Lionel Manuel
Phil Martinovich
Art McCaffray
Tom McCormick
Mike Merriweather
Fred Miller
Bob Moser
Lee Murchison
John Nisby
Mark Nordquist
Brian Peets
Tony Plummer
Shawn Price
Duane Putnam
Rudy Redmond
Bobby Reed
Bill Sandeman
Don Shackelford
Bill Striegel
John Thomas
Kevin Turner
Herm Urenda
Henry Wallace
Jim Watson
Craig Whelihan
Mike Whited
A.D. Williams
Roy Williams

University of the South (TN) (1)

Fred Benners

Upper Iowa (2)

Les Belding
Mike Eischeid

Upsala (3)

Jim Apple
Walt Housman
Jimmy Norris

Ursinus (5)

Reds Bassman
Tom Gormley
Earl Potteiger
Jay Repko
Dean Steward

USC (359)

George Achica
Pete Adams
Erik Affholter
Marcus Allen
John Allred
Charlie Ane
Sam Anno
Charles Anthony
Marger Apsit
Jon Arnett
Chuck Arrobio
Earl Audet
Don Avery
Red Badgro
Bill Bain
Bullet Baker
Chip Banks
Al Bansavage
Brad Banta
Jack Banta
Kurt Barber
Nate Barragar
Al Barry
Mike Battle
Pete Beathard
Hal Bedsole
Ricky Bell
George Belott
Wes Bender
Duane Bickett
Mel Bleeker
Tony Boselli
Bill Bowers
Mark Boyer
Larry Braziel
Jeff Bregel
Hoby Brenner
Lou Brock
Booker Brown
Ron Brown
Willie Brown
Joey Browner
Keith Browner
Brad Budde
Rudy Bukich
Frank Buncom
Mike Bundra
Don Burke
Mike Burns
Steve Busick
Ray Butler
Mac Byrd
Dave Cadigan
Lynn Cain
Jack Campbell
Pat Cannamela
Al Carmichael
Mark Carrier
Kent Carter
Allen Carter
Mario Celotto
Bob Chandler
Tom Chantiles
Don Clark
Monte Clark
Leon Clarke
Paul Cleary
Cal Clemens
Garry Cobb
Marvin Cobb
Angelo Coia
Floyd Collier
Tony Colorito
Curtis Conway
Joe Cormier
Fred Cornwell
Marcus Cotton
Al Cowlings
Tom Cox
Dennis Crane
Joel Crisman
Lindon Crow
Sam Cunningham
August Curley
Dick Danehe
Byron Darby
Norberto Davidds-Garrido
Anthony Davis
Clarence Davis
Joe Davis
Derrick Deese
Bob deLauer
Jack Del Rio
Shelton Diggs
Rich Dimler
Don Doll
Dick Dorsey
Bob Downs
Coye Dunn
Sandy Durko
Dennis Edwards
Riki Ellison
Ricky Ervins
Charlie Evans
Vince Evans
Dave Farmer
Jim Ferguson
Orlando Ferrante
Dan Ficca
Scott Fields
Gary Finneran
Jeff Fisher
Bob Fisher
Bill Fisk
James FitzPatrick
Ollie Fletcher
Chris Foote
Cole Ford
Roy Foster
Scott Galbraith
Allen Gallaher
Don Garlin
Mike Garrett
Mike Garzoni
Bill Gay
Byron Gentry
Ray George
Frank Gifford
John Grant
Bill Gray
Paul Green
Homer Griffith
Jimmy Gunn
Pat Haden
Chris Hale
Willie Hall
Dick Handley
Travis Hannah
Jim Hardy
Pat Harlow
Michael Harper
Carter Hartwig
Luther Hayes
Bill Hayhoe
Tommy Haynes
Steve Heckard
Bob Hendren
Ed Henke
Mike Henry
Rob Hertel
Ralph Heywood
Jesse Hibbs
Donnie Hickman
Fred Hill
Gary Hill
John Hoffman
Bob Hoffman
Lamont Hollinquest
Neil Hope
Darrel Hopper
Pat Howell
Mike Hull
James Hunter
Israel Ifeanyi
Andrew Jackson
John Jackson
Melvin Jackson
Bill Jessup
Gary Jeter
Dennis Johnson
Keyshawn Johnson
Rob Johnson
Rex Johnston
Steve Jordan
Mort Kaer
John Kamana
Brian Kelly
Jack Kirby
Gary Kirner
Bob Klein
Quentin Klenk
Sammy Knight
Steve Knutson
Matt Koart
Jeff Kopp
R.J. Kors
Al Krueger
Grenny Lansdell
Myron Lapka
Zeph Lee
Brad Leggett
Dave Lewis
Verl Lillywhite
Scott Lockwood
Karl Lorch
Ronnie Lott
Duval Love
Greg Marderian
Joe Margucci
Marv Marinovich
Todd Marinovich
Rod Martin
Bruce Matthews
Clay Matthews
Ray May
Bob McCaffrey
Don McCall
Walt McCormick
Earl McCullouch
James McDonald
Mike McDonald
Paul McDonald
Tim McDonald
Willie McGinest
Larry McGrew
John McKay
Marlin McKeever
Rod McNeill
Johnny McWilliams
John Michels
Ron Miller
Johnny Milton
Dale Mitchell
Ron Mix
Marv Montgomery
Brent Moore
Denis Moore
Malcolm Moore
Manfred Moore
Boyd Morgan
Bob Morris
Johnnie Morton
Don Mosebar
Don Moses
Gerry Mullins
Anthony Munoz
George Murphy
Joe Murray
Jim Musick
Johnny Naumu
Bill Nelsen
Jack Nix
Jim Obradovich
Ricky Odom
Chip Oliver
Ted Ossowski
Dan Owens
Artimus Parker
Earle Parsons
Rodney Peete
Volney Peters
Bob Peviani
Charlie Phillips
Ernie Pinckert
Marvin Powell
Jim Powers
Jim Psaltis
Dave Purling
Marc Raab
Bill Radovich
Mike Rae
Danny Reece
Steve Riley
C.R. Roberts
Bobby Robertson
Jim Rorison
Scott Ross
Tim Rossovich
Mazio Royster
Karl Rubke
Ken Ruettgers
Darrell Russell
Tim Ryan
Eddie Saenz
Paul Salata
Sean Salisbury
Mike Salmon
Russ Saunders
Henry Schmidt
John Schuhmacher
Bill Schultz
Eric Scoggins
Jimmy Sears
Junior Seau
Jason Sehorn
Dennis Shaw
Jesse Shaw
Nate Shaw
Pat Shea
Rod Sherman
Will Sherman
Jerry Shipkey
Joseph Shipp
Jeff Simmons
O.J. Simpson
Jimmy Sims
Tony Slaton
Greg Slough
Dennis Smith
Ernie Smith
Harry Smith
Jeff Smith
Sid Smith
Tody Smith
Ben Sohn
Ernest Spears
Todd Spencer
Tony Steponovich
John Stonebraker
Deon Strother
Bob Svihus
Lynn Swann
Calvin Sweeney
Mosi Tatupu
Mike Taylor
Skip Thomas
Kelly Thomas
Dennis Thurman
Junior Thurman
George Timberlake
Scott Tinsley
Howie Tipton
Tony Tonelli
Jerry Traynham
Mark Tucker
Bob Van Doren
Keith Van Horne
Vic Vasicek
John Vella
Jim Vellone
Norm Verry
Theo Viltz
Lowell Wagner
Glen Walker
Johnny Ward
Timmie Ware
Dave Washington
Elbert Watts
Charlie Weaver
Ray Wehba
Gary Wellman
Pat West
Troy West
Charles White
Brian Williams
Eric Williams
Johnny Williams
Kevin Williams
Matt Willig
Ben Wilson
Jeff Winans
Bob Winslow
Lloyd Winston
Gregory Wojcik
Richard Wood
Willie Wood
Ron Yary
Adrian Young
Charle Young

U.S. International (7)

Sergio Albert
Lem Burnham
Wayne Clark
Vernon Dean
Paul Dunn
Bob Gagliano
Dwight McDonald

Utah (84)

Jamal Anderson
Monk Bailey
Marv Bateman
Anthony Brown
Jack Campbell
Frank Christensen
Steve Clark
Wayne Clark
Dave Costa
Win Croft
Dave Cullity
Anthony Davis
Dan Doubiago
Merrill Douglas
Tom Dublinski
Kevin Dyson
Luther Elliss
Charlie Evans
Manny Fernandez
Marv Fleming
Steve Folsom
Chris Fuamatu-Ma'afala
Fred Gehrke
Jack Gehrke
Jeff Griffin
Lee Grosscup
Barney Hafen
Darryl Haley
Carl Harry
Kurt Haws
Manny Hendrix
Floyd Hodge
John Huddleston
Allen Jacobs
Roy Jefferson
Jack Johnson
Gordon Jolley
Marv Jonas
Wayne Jones
John Kapele
Greg Kent
Jerry Lawson
Henry Lusk
Curtis Marsh
Norm McBride
Walt McDonald
Paul McDonough
Craig McEwen
Barney McGarry
Bronzell Miller
Dean Miraldi
Scott Mitchell
Carl Monroe
Frank Nelson
Terry Nofsinger
Steve Odom
Ralph Olsen
Jerry Overton
Andy Parker
Rick Partridge
Ken Petersen
Ed Pine
Kevin Reach
Reggie Richardson
Aldo Richins
Del Rodgers
Milt Romney
Frank Roy
Ron Rydalch
Lance Scott
Charlie Smith
Dave Smith
Dennis Smith
Roland Solomon
Mac Speedie
Jack Steptoe
Mark Stevens
Bob Summerhays
Speedy Thomas
Norm Thompson
Bob Trumpy
Erroll Tucker
Rich Umphrey
Larry Wilson

Utah State (83)

Tony Adams
Louie Aguiar
Lionel Aldridge
Kevin Alexander
Buddy Allen
Patrick Allen
Ocie Austin
Willie Beecher
Ed Berry
Craig Bradshaw
Clyde Brock
Ken Burrow
Chuck Butler
Israel Byrd
Ron Cassidy
Mike Connelly
Chuck Detwiler
Jed DeVries
Bill Dunstan
Phil Frye
Bob Gagliano
Hal Garner
Louie Giammona
Cornell Green
Russ Griffith
Mike Hamby
Matt Hanousek
Jim Harris
Jack Hill
Eric Hipple
Jim Hough
Samuel Johnson
Rulon Jones
Henry King
Steve Kinney
Greg Kragen
MacArthur Lane
Paul Lavine
Jim LeMoine
Pratt Lyons
Earsell Mackbee
Doug Mayberry
Ron McCall
Donald Miller
Clark Miller
Shawn Miller
Solomon Miller
Mel Montalbo
Mark Mraz
Carl Mulleneaux
Bill Munson
James Murphy
Spain Musgrove
Pat Newman
Merlin Olsen
Phil Olsen
Dave Parkin
Rick Parros
Mike Perko
Len Rohde
Rip Ryan
Paul Sanders
Ronald Sbranti
Roy Shivers
Greg Sinnott
Aaron Smith
Al Smith
Jimmy Smith
Kendal Smith
Glen Sorenson
Bill Staley
Altie Taylor
John Thompson
Ken Thompson
Navy Tuiasosopo
Jim Turner
Maurice Turner
Rich Tylski
Elmer Ward
Bob Wicks
Frank Williams
Kevin Young
Rich Zecher

Utah Valley State (J.C.) (1)

Chad Lewis

Valdosta State (7)

Mark Catano
Antonio Edwards
Don Pumphrey
Dominique Ross
Dallis Smith
Jessie Tuggle
Ronnie West

Valencia CC FL (1)

Olindo Mare

Vallejo JC CA (4)

Bob Coronado
Earsell Mackbee
Dave Plump
Bobby Reed

Valley Forge J.C. PA (1)

Karl Hankton

Valparaiso (8)

Steve Bradley
Lloyd Cearing
Abe Gibron
Wally Gilbert
Garry Puetz
Dewey Scanlon
Fuzzy Thurston
Buck White

Vanderbilt (62)

Sam Agee
Jim Arnold
Bob Asher
Lynn Bomar
Preston Brown
Tim Bryant
Charlie Carman
Corey Chavous
Leonard Coleman
Gerald Collins
Ken Cooper
Dick Davis
Allen DeGraffenreid
Ben Donnell
Jamie Duncan
John Ellis
Chris Gaines
Paul Goad
Bob Goodridge
Henry Gude
Corey Harris
Dennis Harrison
Larry Hayes
Chip Healy
Alan Herline
Roy Huggins
Mark Ilgenfritz
Jack Jenkins
Antony Jordon
Phil King
Tex Leyendecker
James Manley
Allama Matthews
Ed Merlin
Rob Monaco
Tom Moore
Doug Nettles
John North
Carl Parker
Jim Peebles
Dick Plasman
John Pointer
Shelton Quarles
Baby Ray
Tom Redmond
Herb Rich
Pat Saindon
Al Satterfield
Chuck Scott
Ed Smith
John Steber
Ken Stone
Pat Toomay
Gary Tucker
Eric Vance
Billy Wade
Hubert Wiggs
Pryor Williams
Brenard Wilson
DeMond Winston
Will Wolford
Carl Woods

Ventura Coll. CA (J.C.) (11)

Don Burroughs
Pat Cannamela
David Croudip
Alec Gibson
Ed Henke
Karl Henke
Bobby Kimball
Mike Michel
Todd Seabaugh
Sam Tsoutsouvas
Blake Wingle

Vermont (6)

Leo Douglass
Art Harms
Oscar Johnson
Lou Little
Frank Seyboth
Frank Trigilio

Victoria Coll. TX (J.C.) (1)

Wallace Dickey

Villanova (75)

Teddy Andrulewicz
Al Atkinson
Sky August
John Babinecz
Nick Basca
Ed Berrang
Sam Brazinsky
Matt Brennan
Chuck Brodnicki
Dan Brown
Frank Budd
Gene Ceppetelli
Andy Chisick
Pete D'Alonzo
Bob David
Dave diFilippo
Leo Elter
Nick Farina
Lou Ferry
Gene Filipski
Jack Finn
Dutch Forst
Stan Galazin

Jim Gilmore
Larry Glueck
Tom Gormley
Anthony Griggs
Sam Gruneisen
Ching Hammill
Bill Hegarty
Val Jansante
Billy Joe
Frank Jordan
Ed Kasky
Ed Korisky
Paul Kuczo
Fungy Lebengood
Bernie Lee
Tom Lomasney
Howie Long
Paul Longua
Jim Magee
David Martin
Don McComb
John Mellus
Eddie Michaels
Rich Moore
Dick Moynihan
Walt Nowak
Willie Oshodin
Ralph Pasquariello
Louie Pessolano
Al Postus
Bill Potts
Steve Pritko
Chet Pudloski
Kevin Reilly
Joe Restic
Bill Rogers
Steve Romanik
Sal Rosato
Joe Ryan
John Sandusky
Rick Sapienza
Mike Siani
George Smith
John Sodaski
Paul Stenn
Mike Strofolino
Willie Sydnor
Vince Thompson
Billy Walik
George Winslow
Frank Youngfleish
Vince Zizak

Virginia (97)

Dick Ambrose
Stuart Anderson
George Baldwin
Tiki Barber
Ronde Barber
Tony Blount
Matt Blundin
Joe Bock
Will Brice
Ed Carrington
Russ Carroccio
John Choma
Jim Copeland
Tony Covington
Germane Crowell
Gary Cuozzo
Harrison Davis
Bob Davis
Tyrone Davis
John Diehl
Mark Dixon
Jim Dombrowski
Bill Dudley
Carl Elliott
Percy Ellsworth
James Farrior
Kevin Ferguson
John Ford
Mike Frederick
Jeff Gaffney
Ron Gassert
Jim Gillette
Tom Glassic
Dave Graham
David Griggs
Billy Griggs
George Grimes
Bob Gunderman
Jon Harris
Chris Harrison
Jim Huddleston
Michael Husted
Patrick Jeffers
Greg Jeffries
Henry Jordan
Terry Kirby
Bob Kowalkowski
Ryan Kuehl
Jeff Lageman
Jimmy Lesane
Keith Lyle
Lester Lyles
Don Majkowski
Ron Mattes
Frank McConnell
Bruce McGonnigal
Lee McLaughlin
Bob Miller
Herman Moore
Shawn Moore
Steve Morse
Randy Neal
Bobby Neely
Bob Olderman
Mike Ozdowski
Johnny Papit
Don Parker
Ray Perkins
Steve Potter
Frank Quayle
Sonny Randle
Jim Reid
Ed Reynolds
Ray Roberts
Joe Rowe
Bob Rowley
Dan Ryczek
Paul Ryczek
Ted Rzempoluch
Gene Schroeder
Tom Scott
Scott Secules
Andy Selfridge
Jamie Sharper
Chris Slade
Dave Sullivan
Russ Swan
Greg Taylor
Bill Troup
Scott Urch
Tommy Vigorito
Quentin Walker
Chris Warren
Charles Way
Marcus Wilson
Barry Word
Geno Zimmerlink

Virginia Military (14)

Greg Clifton
Joe Fortunato
Sam Horner
Pete Johnson
Sam Mason
Joe Muha
Bosh Pritchard
Vince Ragunas
Ray Reutt
George Robison
Mark Stock
Bobby Thomason
Bill Walker
Mike Wooten

Virginia State (8)

Larry Brooks
James Brown
Rufus Crawford
Ron Davis
Kelvin Kinney
Leo Miles
Jim Mitchell
Ben Whaley

Virginia Tech (59)

Antonio Banks
Ken Barefoot
Tom Beasley
Andy Bowling
Gene Breen
Cornell Brown
Ken Brown
Robert Brown
Roger Brown
John Burke
Al Chamblee
Eugene Chung
Bill Conaty
John Cowne
Ray Crittenden
Carroll Dale
Tyronne Drakeford
Jim Druckenmiller
Bill Ellenbogen
Mickey Fitzgerald
Antonio Freeman
Will Furrer
John Granby
Torrian Gray
Jay Hagood
Billy Hardee
Waddey Harvey
Vaughn Hebron
Eddie Hunter
Waverly Jackson
Mike Johnson
Steve Johnson
Jock Jones
Joe Jones
Victor Jones
Kenny Lewis
John Maskas
Doug McDougald
Buzz Nutter
Don Oakes
Ken Oxendine
Tony Paige
Jesse Penn
George Preas
Jim Pyne
Rick Razzano
Bill Renner
Jim Richards
George Roberts
Damien Russell
Bob Schweickert
Dave Smigelsky
Bruce Smith
Gary Smith
Donald Snell
Bryan Still
Don Strock
Don Testerman
Todd Washington

Virginia Union (13)

Roger Anderson
John Baker
Malcolm Barnwell
Carl Bland
Hez Braxton
Michael Brim
Cornelius Johnson
Bob Jones
Tony Leonard
Irvin Mallory
Bobby Phillips
Herbert Scott
Adrian Wright

Wabash (9)

Frank Bacon
Knute Caldwell
Slats Dalrymple
Menz Lindsey
Ward Meese
Pete Metzelaars
Century Milstead
Ray Neal
Basil Stanley

Wabash Valley Coll. IL (J.C.) (1)

Jerome Davis

Wagner (1)

Rich Kotite

Wake Forest (75)

Billy Ard
Gary Baldinger
Rich Baldinger
Elmer Barbour
Billy Barnes
Carlos Bradley
Ed Bradley
Ed Bradley
David Braxton
Jim Brim
Ronnie Burgess
Jim Clack
Topper Clemons
Red Cochran
George Coghill
Steve Colavito
Ben Coleman
Clem Crabtree
Jack Dolbin
Harry Dowda
Kenny Duckett
Jim Duncan
Marshall Edwards
Mike Elkins
Clark Gaines
Tony Gallovich
Bob Gaona
Tony Garbarczyk
Ed George
Bill George
Bob Grant
A.J. Greene
Steve Hammond
Jim Hargrove
Clayton Heath
Bill Hull
Jerry Huth
John Jett
Elmer Jones
Paul Kiser
Ed Kissell
Syd Kitson
Dave LaCrosse
Bob Leonetti
Ed Listopad
Pete Manning
Tony Mayberry
Michael McCrary
Bob McCreary
Jerris McPhail
Gil Meyer
John Henry Mills
Harry Newsome
Red O'Quinn
Jimmy Orr
Tom Palmer
Rupert Pate
Brian Piccolo
John Polanski
Pat Preston
Ricky Proehl
Chuck Ramsey
Walter Rasby
Ed Royston
Tony Rubino
Nick Sacrinty
Greg Scales
Ron Smith
Norm Snead
Jim Staton
Karl Sweetan
Larry Tearry
Dick Wedel
Jay Williams
Wayne Wolff

Waldorf JC (6)

Ian Beckles
Dwayne Crutchfield
Bruce Klosterman
George McDuffie
Joe Stepanek
Henry Waechter

Walla Walla CC WA (10)

Dorian Boose
Dale Dorning
James Fuller
Clyde Glover
Mike Hagen
Kevin Juma
Brent Pease
Mike Sellers
Jon Shields
Kimo von Oelhoffen

Washburn (5)

Arthur Fletcher
Larry McGinnis
Troy Stedman
Spencer Thomas
Lee Wykoff

Washington (209)

Vince Abbott
Fred Abel
Al Akins
Vince Albritton
Ink Aleaga
Anthony Allen
Chuck Allen
Steve Alvord
Ricky Andrews
Mike Baldassin
Eric Bjornson
Chuck Bond
Rink Bond
Glen Bonner
Jeremy Brigham
Bern Brostek
Dennis Brown
Charlie Browning
Dave Browning
Gail Bruce
Mark Bruener
Mark Brunell
Beno Bryant
Tim Burnham
Blair Bush
Hillary Butler
Denny Cahill
Tony Caldwell
Rich Camarillo
Chris Chandler
Jason Chorak
Cameron Cleeland
Junior Coffey
Brett Collins
Cary Conklin
Ernie Conwell
Bo Cornell
Ed Cunningham
Ben Davidson
Don Deeks
Dean Derby
Corey Dillon
Robin Earl
Steve Emtman
Bud Erickson
Walden Erickson
Tom Erlandson
D'Marco Farr
Carl Fennema
Rick Fenney
Bill Ferguson
John Fiala
Jaime Fields
George Fleming
Tom Flick
Lee Folkins
Fred Forsberg
Jamal Fountaine
Ray Frankowski
Bob Friedman
Frank Garcia
Scott Garnett
Nesby Glasgow
Kevin Gogan
Danny Greene
Lee Grosscup
Brian Habib
Ron Hadley
By Haines
Dana Hall
Darryl Hall
Dean Halverson
Dick Hanley
Martin Harrison
Harald Hasselbach
Don Heinrich
Lonzell Hill
Billy Joe Hobert
Dave Hoffmann
Ron Holmes
Jay Hornbeak
Ray Horton
Damon Huard
Ted Isaacson
Charles Jackson
Michael Jackson
Vestee Jackson
Jeff Jaeger
Ernie Janet
Bruce Jarvis
Fletcher Jenkins
Jerry Jensen
Mark Jerue
Herb Johnson
Jimmy Johnston
Calvin Jones
Don Jones
Jim Jones
Scott Jones
Rod Jones
Jeff Jordan
Napoleon Kaufman
Joe Kelly
Lincoln Kennedy
Dave Kopay
Joe Krakoski
Olin Kreutz
Jim Krieg
Jake Kupp
Le-Lo Lang
Mike Lansford
Ken Lee
Mark Lee
Greg Lewis
Chris Linnin
Dan Lloyd
Lamar Lyons
Jay MacDowell
Lynn Madsen
Siupeli Malamala
Rick Mallory
Ray Mansfield
Vic Markov
Curt Marsh
Doug Martin
Stafford Mays
Dean McAdams
Walt McCormick
Hugh McElhenny
Tim Meamber
Ron Medved
Mike Melinkovich
John Meyers
Hugh Millen
Lawyer Milloy
Charles Mincy
Charley Mitchell
Warren Moon
Eric Moran
Rudy Mucha
Leon Neal
Chuck Nelson
Vince Newsome
Chuck Newton
Dave Nisbet
Jim Norton
Steve Okoniewski
Benji Olson
Dick Ottele
Jeff Pahukoa
Shane Pahukoa
Steve Parker
Tony Parrish
Jerome Pathon
Mark Pattison
Dave Pear
Dennis Pearson
J.C. Pearson
Steve Pelluer
Dean Perriman
Andrew Peterson
Aaron Pierce
Pete Pierson
Ray Pinney
Fred Provo
Rick Redman
Frank Reed
Mike Reed
David Richie
Thron Riggs
Fred Robinson
Jacque Robinson
Tyrone Rodgers
Reggie Rogers
Gene Sanders
Bob Sapp
Rick Sharp
Rashaan Shehee
Jim Skaggs
Paul Skansi
Steve Slivinski
Fred Small
Bill Smith
Benny Sohn
Rick Sortun
Jack Stackpool
Ernie Steele
Mark Stewart
Jim Stiger
George Strugar
Garth Thomas
Steve Thompson
Jeff Toews
Tom Turnure
Toussaint Tyler
Randy Van Divier
Bill Ward
Duane Wardlow
Arnie Weinmeister
Clyde Werner
Ron Wheeler
Nat Whitmyer
Johnny Wiatrak
Dave Williams
Donald Willis
Abe Wilson
Wildcat Wilson
Tony Zackery
Mike Zandofsky

Washington & Jefferson (40)

Bill Berrehsem
Homer Bliss
Wayne Brenkert
Bird Carroll
Chase Clements
Al Crook
George Demas
Jap Douds
Bill Edgar
Hal Erickson
Ed Gallagher
Charlie Guy
Al Hadden
Pete Henry
Paul Hogan
Red Kirkman
Ed Loucks
Harry Malcolm
Dutch Marion
Frank McNeil
Ray Neal
Fanny Niehaus
Will Norman
Tony Paulekas
Frank Pauly
Don Rhodes
George Shaffer
Fred Shirey
Orville Siegfried
Russ Stein
Bill Stobbs
Don Straw
Dan Towler
Dick Vick
Ralph Vince
Al Wesbecher
Chet Widerquist
Joe Wiehl
Stu Wilson
By Wimberly

Washington & Lee (11)

Johnny Barrett
Mike Boyda
Bill Chipley
Pike Johnson
Jim Lukens
Marv Mattox
Walt Michaels
Buck Miles
Al Pierotti
Fred Sweetland
Charlie Van Horn

Washington (Md) (2)

Ed Keenan
Freddie Summers

Washington State (131)

Al Akins
Frank Akins
Mike Akiu
Tuineau Alipate
Byron Bailey
Ben Bangs
Ed Barker
Pat Beach
Kay Bell
Wayne Berry
Drew Bledsoe
Ed Blount
Dorian Boose
Jim Boylan
Jeep Brett
Steve Broussard
Cedrick Brown
Joe Burks
John Burrough
Lewis Bush
Brett Carolan
Ron Childs
Gail Cogdill
Mike Connelly
Joe Danelo
James Darling
Dan Doornink
Chris Dyko
Chad Eaton
Turk Edwards
Don Ellersick
Tom Erlandson
Dick Farman
Duke Fergerson
Mark Fields
Ray Flaherty
Brian Flones
Brian Forde
Bob Gambold
Dale Gentry
Ed Goddard
Herb Godfrey
Kenny Graham
Ken Grandberry
Ken Greene
Bob Gregor
Ray Hall
Dick Hanley
Jason Hanson
Tim Harris
James Hasty
Henry Hayduk
Chris Hayes
Mel Hein
Milford Hodge
Al Hoptowit
Don Horn
Jerry Houghton
Don Hover
Erik Howard
Torey Hunter
George Hurley
John Hurley
Bernard Jackson
Eric Johnson
Andrew Jones
Allan Kennedy
Bob Kennedy
John Klumb
Fritz Kramer
Porter Lainhart
Ryan Leaf
Mike Levenseller
Gary Lewis
Ron Lewis
Keith Lincoln
Carl Littlefield
Cliff Marker
Rueben Mayes
Charlie McBride
Jason McEndoo
Butch Meeker
Dave Middendorf
Keith Millard
Singor Mobley
Laurie Niemi
Don Paul
Scott Pelluer
Fran Polsfoot
Kerry Porter
Mike Pringle
Anthony Prior
Eason Ramson
Geoff Reece
Bill Remington
Dick Renfro
Ricky Reynolds
Bill Roffler
Timm Rosenbach
Mark Rypien
Scott Sanderson
Phil Sarboe
Don Sasa
Tony Savage
Donald Schwartz
Elmer Schwartz
Howie Slater
Tim Stallworth
Don Steinbrunner
Frank Stojack
Nick Susoeff
Harland Svare
Junior Tautalatasi
Kitrick Taylor
Jack Thompson
Rico Tipton
Robbie Tobeck
Lavern Torgeson
Ricky Turner
Mike Utley
Brian Walker
Bill Ward
Doug Wellsandt
Tom Wickert
Clarence Williams
Clancy Williams
Eric Williams
Jerry Williams
Ray Williams
Mike Wilson
George Yarno

Washington-St. Louis (14)

Libby Bertagnolli
Joe Bukant
Ed Comstock
Jimmy Conzelman
Shelby Jordan
Ollie Kraehe
Jim Lecture

Al Lindow
Bob Mahan
Bill Murphy
Skippy Scheib
Bud Schwenk
Bill Singleton
Pete Wissman

Wayne State (Mich.) (11)

Tom Beer
Paul Butcher
Rick Byas
Jack Crittendon
Walt Jenkins
Tom Kennedy
Bob Langas
Ben Paolucci
Tino Sabuco
John Sokolosky
Vic Zucco

Wayne State (Neb.) (8)

Ron Berger
Byron Chamberlain
Bob Kruse
Stan Lewis
Joe Lindahl
Ruben Mendoza
Brad Ottis
Damon Thomas

Waynesburg (11)

John Bristor
Gene Carroll
Paul Frank
Don Herrmann
Frank Pastin
Joe Righetti
Mike Scarry
Dave Smith
Harry Theofiledes
Jack Wiley
Jim Worden

Weatherford Coll. TX (J.C.) (1)

Lew Jones

Weber State (23)

Carter Campbell
Jeff Carlson
Chris Darrington
Russ Griffith
Halvor Hagen
Andre Hardy
Mike Humiston
Lew Kamanu
Al Lolotai
Jamie Martin
Ron McCall
Randy Montgomery
Tom Neville
Darryl Pollard
Bob Pollard
Alfred Pupunu
Henry Reed
Roger Ruzek
Jim Schmedding
Bob Sneddon
John Thompson
Phil Tuckett
Lee White

Wenatchee Valley Coll. WA (J.C.) (3)

Tony Bertuca
Lew Kamanu
Johnny Taylor

Wesley (3)

Clarence Bailey
Steve Colavito
Mark Meserol

Wesleyan (1)

Jeff Wilner

West Alabama (6)

Ken Hutcherson
Steve Hyche
Bill Johnson
Fletcher Louallen
Charles Martin
Johnny Shepherd

West Chester (11)

Ken Campbell
Tony DiMidio
Robert DiRico
Fritz Ferko
Carl Gersbach
Merritt Kersey
Joe Senser
Bill Shockley
Ralph Tamm
Chuck Weber
Lee Woodall

West Georgia (2)

Angelo Snipes
Cornell Thomas

West Hills CC CA (J.C.) (4)

Dan Goich
Angelo James
Sam Rogers
Willie Wood

West Liberty State (3)

Bob Campiglio
Mark Murphy
Lou Piccone

West Los Angeles Coll. CA (J.C.) (10)

Stephen Baker
Charles DeJurnett
R.W. Hicks
Keyshawn Johnson
Ron Lewis
Mike McCoy
Calvin Nicholson
Sam Rogers
Junior Thurman
Marcellus Wiley

West Texas A&M (38)

George Allen
Ralph Anderson
John Ayers
Cloyce Box
Kevin Brown
Ray Brown
Jim Campbell
Billie Cross
Woody Dow
Bob Duncum
Bill Fifer
Willard Goff
Earl Goodwin
Myrl Goodwin
Darryl Hemphill
John Holt
Bob Kelley
Doug Kriewald
Jeff Lloyd
Jerry Logan
Reggie McElroy
Bill McKinney
Eddie Meyer
Tex Mooney
Mercury Morris
Bob Petrich
Jesse Powell
Billy Pritchett
Jerry Richardson
Bo Robinson
Dave Szymakowski
Duane Thomas
Ken Thompson
Rocky Thompson
Foster Watkins
Jim Weatherwax
Ted Wheeler
Bruce Womack

West Valley Coll. CA (J.C.) (3)

Chris Farasopoulos
Don Kern
Kit Lathrop

West Virginia (126)

Robert Alexander
Bill Anderson
Alex Atty
Russ Bailey
Al Baisi
Pete Barnum
Scott Barrows
Charlie Baumann
Aaron Beasley
Carl Beck
Bruce Bosley
Rich Braham
Jim Braxton
Walt Brewster
A.B. Brown
John Browning
Doc Bruder
Danny Buggs
Rex Bumgardner
Mark Burke
Red Chenoweth
Harry Clarke
Mike Compton
Carl Crennel
Canute Curtis
Travis Curtis
Carl Davis
John Denvir
Dick Dolly
Willie Drewrey
Michael Durrette
Walt Easley
Gus Eckberg
Charles Emanuel
Dale Farley
Garrett Ford
Dennis Fowlkes
Mike Fox
Kenny Fryer
Hank Goodman
Tod Goodwin
Fred Graham
David Grant
Steve Grant
Bob Gresham
Dick Guesman
Mike Gussie
Swede Hagberg
Chuck Harris
Harry Harris
Steve Hathaway
Gene Heeter
Ken Herock
John Holifield
Jerry Holmes
Jeff Hostetler
Chuck Howley
Sam Huff
Leon Jenkins
James Jett
Undra Johnson
Brian Jozwiak
Bill Karr
Tom Keane
Frank Kimble
Rip King
Larry Krutko
Gordon Lambert
Ron Lee
Dick Leftridge
Jack Linn
Mike Logan
Bill Lopasky
Jeff Lucas
John Lucente
Oliver Luck
Walter Mahan
Armin Mahrt
John Mallory
Joe Marconi
Harry Marker
Alvoid Mays
Russ Meredith
Jim Merritts
Jeff Merrow
Kelly Moan
Gary Mullen
Adrian Murrell
Browning Nagle
Nick Nardacci
Aaron Oliker
Bo Orlando
Artie Owens
Bill Parriott
Tom Pridemore
Lovett Purnell
John Ray
Reggie Rembert
Bernard Russ
Cassy Ryan
Todd Sauerbrun
Charlie Seabright
Ed Seibert
Joe Setron
John Shonk
Henry Slay
Fred Smalls
Matt Smith
Bill Sortet
Dave Stephenson
Darren Studstill
Joe Stydahar
Steve Superick
Joe Taffoni
Darryl Talley
John Talley
Craig Taylor
Elgie Tobin
Renaldo Turnbull
Calvin Turner
Mike Vanderjagt
Fulton Walker
Robert Walker
Ron Wolfley
Tom Woodeshick
Fred Wyant

West Virginia State (5)

Warren Anderson
Jim Bailey
Reggie Branch
Torin Clark
Walter Holman

West Virginia Tech (3)

Chuck Banks
Alex Rado
Calvin Wallace

West Virginia Wesleyan (20)

Chalmers Ault
Len Barnum
Cliff Battles
Tom Blondin
Gale Bullman
Pete Calac
Ed Comstock
Hoot Flanagan
Harry Harris
Billy Jones
John Kellison
Jim Miller
Ken Moore
Vern Mullen
Nels Peterson
Kelly Rodriguez
Skippy Scheib
Rich Thomaselli
Chalmers Tschappat
Bill Wood

Westchester CC NY (2)

Sam Bowers
Marc Brown

Western Carolina (12)

Dean Biasucci
Louis Cooper
Fred Davis
George Greene
Tony Jones
Andrew Jordan
Eddie McGill
David Patten
Clyde Simmons
Leonard Williams
Steven Williams
Willie Williams

Western Illinois (28)

Jack Atchason
Todd Auer
Don Beebe
Fabien Bownes
Cyron Brown
Steve Carpenter
Bryan Cox
Wayne DeSutter
Booker Edgerson
Larry Garron
Don Greco
Rodney Harrison
Jim Jackson
Leroy Jackson
Bruce McCray
Lamar McGriggs
Dennis Morgan
John Stadnik
Mark Stevenson
Bill Strickland
John Teerlinck
Mark Tigges
Dave Tipton
Gunnard Twyner
Mike Wagner
Mike Wilson
Frank Winters
Gary Woolford

Western Kentucky (11)

Carl Brazley
David Carter
Paul Gray
Jazz Jackson
Mark Johnson
Dale Lindsey
Virgil Livers
Tim Mooney
Davlin Mullen
Keith Paskett
Pete Walters

Western Maryland (11)

Harry Benson
Nick Campofreda
Joe Coster
Charlie Havens
Bernie Kaplan
Lou Lassahn
Jack Norris
Mike Phillips
Bill Rieth
Bill Shepherd
Frank Sillin

Western Michigan (34)

Ray Bray
Charley Carr
Ed Chlebek
Jerald Collins
Terry Crews
Vern Davis
Mark Garalczyk
Gene Hamlin
Kevin Haverdink
Steve Hawkins
Paul Hutchins
Jeff Kacmarek
Ty Krentler
Roger Lawson
Dale Livingston
John Lomakoski
Bob Lurtsema
Art Macioszczyk
Joel Mason
Jack Matheson
Rocco Moore
Tom Nutten
John Offerdahl
Mike Prindle
Johnny Rapacz
Rudy Rosatti
Bob Rowe
Herman Seborg
Tom Sims
Mike Siwek
Joel Smeenge
Warren Smith
Tom Toth
Pete Wysocki

Western Montana (1)

Barry Darrow

Western Nebraska CC-Scottsbluff (2)

Night Train Lane
Ed Mooney

Western Ontario (Canada) (4)

Joe Krol
Dave Sparenberg
Tim Tindale
Tyrone Williams

Western State (Colo.) (3)

Justin Cross
Tyrone Johnson
Sam Seale

Western Washington (1)

Ken Sager

Westminster (1)

Lowell Lander

Westminster (Mo.) (2)

Bill Boyd
Jim Eliopulos

Westminster (Pa.) (2)

Wade McRoberts
Eric Stocz

Westminster (Ut.) (1)

Walt Love

Wharton Co. JC TX (9)

Cliff Branch
Gary Burley
Ray Butler
Bobby Jancik
Tom McNeill
Willie Parker
Jerry Peterson
Allen Rice
Ray Waddy

Wheaton (1)

Doug Rothschild

Whittier (5)

Bull Finch
Ken Gregory
Elvin Hutchison
Chuck McMurtry
Doug Mooers

Whitworth (2)

Doug Long
Paul Ward

Wichita State (39)

Margene Adkins
Sam Adkins
Jim Bausch
Hal Brill
Patrick Cain
Anthony Copeland
Marvin Davis
Ted Dean
Carmine DePascal
Mark Duckens
Len Dugan
Rick Dvorak
Earl Edwards
Miller Farr
Jumpy Geathers
Bob Hoskins
Bob Humphreys
Randy Jackson
Anthony Jones
Jimmie Jones
Terry Joyce
Marv Kellum
Elmo Kelly
Roland Lakes
Bob Long
Doug McEnulty
Charlie McLaughlin
Kelvin Middleton
Pete Mills
Tom Owen
Jerry Quick
Kevin Robbins
Henry Schichtle
Lin Sexton
Ron Shumon
Tony Sumler
Nelson Toburen
Ted Vincent
Jim Waskiewicz

Widener (7)

Joe Fields
Billy Johnson
Eddie Kawal
Jack Klotz
Jim Magner
Red Pollock
Ed Walsh

Wiley (5)

Floyd Iglehart
George Kinney
Mike Lewis
Lee Thomas
Kelton Winston

Willamette (4)

Bruce Anderson
Greg Joelson
Hal Stringert
Dick Weisgerber

William & Mary (43)

Bill Bowman
Tom Brown
Dennis Cambal
John Cannon
Win Charles
Steve Christie
Mike Clemons
Jack Cloud
John Clowes
Lou Creekmur
Al Crow
Dan Darragh
Otis Douglas
Tom Feamster
Nick Forkovitch
Robert Green
Isham Hardy
Archie Harris
Dan Henning
George Hughes
Harvey Johnson
Mark Kelso
David Knight
John Kreamcheck
Bob Lusk
Art Matsu
Tom Mikula
Denver Mills
Ed Mioduszewski
Jeff Powell
Ben Raimondi
Buster Ramsey
Knox Ramsey
Jim Ryan
Ralph Sazio
Darren Sharper
Steve Shull
Robert Soleau
Charlie Sumner
Tommy Thompson
Al Vandeweghe
Jude Waddy
Tex Warrington

William Jewell (3)

Fernandars Gillespie
Ike Martin
John Strada

William Paterson (1)

Derrick Foster

William Penn (2)

Warren Loving
Wilbur Young

William Rainey Harper Coll. IL (J.C.) (3)

Shane Matthews
Steve Matthews
Tim Tyrrell

Williams (6)

Benny Boynton
Ethan Brooks
Alex Clement
Gil Gregory
Jack Maitland
Scott Perry

Wilmington (2)

Dick Egan
Frank Glassman

Wilmington (Del.) (2)

Elliott Bonowitz
Chuck Weimer

Winona State (1)

Jim Althoff

Winston-Salem State (12)

Anthony Blaylock
Jack Cameron
Donald Evans
Donald Frank
Oronde Gadsden
Richard Huntley
Arrington Jones
Bill Murrell
Timmy Newsome
Alvin Powell
Bob Shaw
Yancey Thigpen

Wisconsin (198)

Dave Ahrens
Art Albrecht
Bill Albright
Alan Ameche
Norm Amundsen
John Atwood
Jim Bakken
Tom Baldwin
Shorty Barr
Kevin Belcher
Chuck Belin
Scott Bergold
Lee Bernet
Adolph Bieberstein
Brian Bonner
Kyle Borland
Ken Bowman
Donny Brady
Roman Brumm
Cub Buck
Jason Burns
George Burnside
Len Calligaro
Lamar Campbell
Larry Canada
Harland Carl
Irv Carlson
Daryl Carter
Chad Cascadden
John Cavosie
Bill Collins
Ken Criter
Boob Darling
Don Davey
Ralph Davis
Joe Dawkins
Jim DeLisle
Jeff Dellenbach
Lee DeRamus
Glenn Derby
John Dittrich
Jerry Doerger
Tom Domres
Wally Dreyer
Bob Eckl
Ron Egloff
Gary Ellerson
Al Elliott
Tony Elliott
Larry Emery

Derek Engler
Clarence Esser
Tom Farris
Hal Faverty
Gene Felker
Terrell Fletcher
Jim Fraser
Milt Gantenbein
Moose Gardner
Jug Girard
Buckets Goldenberg
John Golemgeske
Rudy Gollomb
Rick Graf
Neil Graff
David Greenwood
Bill Gregory
Paul Gruber
Dale Hackbart
John Hall
Jim Haluska
Pat Harder
Jack Harris
Donald Hayes
Stan Heath
George Hekkers
Arnie Herber
Crazy Legs Hirsch
John Hohman
Tubby Howard
Ken Huxhold
Ed Jankowski
Farnham Johnson
Lawrence Johnson
Richard Johnson
Jim Jones
Tim Jordan
Greg Kent
Don Kindt
Polly Koch
Dave Kocourek
Bob Konovsky
Joe Kresky
Gary Kroner
Tim Krumrie
Ralph Kurek
Joe Kurth
Curly Lambeau
Bob Landsee
Dan Lanphear
Wes Leaper
Dave Levenick
Dan Lewis
Dennis Lick
Bill Lobenstein
Dick Loepfe
Mike London
Lou Lubratovich
Jason Maniecki
Von Mansfield
Ira Matthews
Earl Maves
Thad McFadden
Jack Mead
James Melka
Paul Meyers
Larry Mialik
Ron Miller
Sankar Montoute
Pete Monty
Mike Morgan
Emmett Mortell
Brent Moss
Jock Mungavin
Don Murry
Fred Negus
Jim Nettles
Tom Neumann
Dave Noble
Jack Novak
Nate Odomes
Pat O'Donahue
Joe Panos
George Paskvan
Phil Peterson
Bob Pickens
Roger Pillath
Art Price
Jim Purnell
Cory Raymer
Michael Reid
Pat Richter
Michael Roan
Rafael Robinson
Tubby Rohsenberger
Gene Rose
Joe Rudolph
Tarek Saleh
Bob Schmitz
John Schneller
Bill Schroeder
Karl Schuelke
Paul Schuette
Ralph Scott
Champ Seibold
Mike Seifert
Clarence Self
Mark Shumate
Carl Silvestri
Tony Simmons
Eber Simpson
Darryl Sims
Jerry Smith
Len Smith
Ron Smith
Ray Snell
Philip Sobocinski
Jerry Stalcup
Ken Starch
Howie Stark
Terry Stieve
Ken Stills
Tim Stracka
Dave Suminski
Gus Tebell
Jim Temp
Deral Teteak
Mike Thompson
Clarence Tommerson
Al Toon
Dan Turk
Eric Unverzagt
Ron Vander Kelen
Mike Verstegen
Troy Vincent
Evan Vogds
Stu Voigt
Steve Wagner
Lloyd Wasserbach
Mike Webster
Howie Weiss
John Williams
Rollie Williams
Chuck Winfrey
George Winslow
Randy Wright
Jerry Wunsch
Bob Zeman

Wis.-Eau Claire (3)

Roman Brumm
Kevin Fitzgerald
Lee Weigel

Wis.-La Crosse (11)

Will Berzinski
Roman Brumm
George Dahlgren
Don Kindt
Ace Loomis
Ric Mathias
Tom Newberry
Bill Schroeder
Rex Smith
Wayne Smith
Joel Williams

Wis.-Milwaukee (5)

Ken Kranz
Paul Meyers
Clem Neacy
Mike Reinfeldt
Whitey Wolter

Wis.-Oshkosh (5)

Pahl Davis
Hal Robl
Eber Simpson
Len Smith
Milt Wilson

Wis.-Platteville (5)

Lee Croft
Mike Hintz
Phil Micech
Don Perkins
David Viaene

Wis.-River Falls (1)

Johnny Blood (McNally)

Wis.-Stevens Point (2)

Ted Fritsch
Barry Rose

Wis.-Stout (1)

Bob McRoberts

Wis.-Superior (6)

Herbert Clow
Dom Moselle
Jock Mungavin
Tom Murphy
Wally O'Neill
Doug Sutherland

Wis.-Whitewater (6)

Vilnis Ezerins
Dave Kraayeveld
Bill Lobenstein
Joe Panos
Stuart Rindy
Matt Turk

Wittenberg (9)

Earl Burgner
Ron Duncan
Charlie Green
Mack Hummon
Pesty Lentz
Dutch Miller
Ike Nonnenmaker
George Rohleder
Scott Watters

Wofford (1)

Jerry Richardson

Wooster (6)

Dan Callahan
Hank Critchfield
Willie Flattery
Johnnie Layport
Blake Moore
Ben Roderick

Worcester State (1)

Bruno Haas

Wyoming (53)

John Arnold
Nick Bebout
Ron Billingsley
Rob Bohlinger
John Burrough
Frank Chesley
Ryan Christopherson
Eric Coleman
Jim Crawford
Joe Cummings
Mitch Daum
Mike Dennis
Jerry DePoyster
Mike Dirks
Conrad Dobler
Mitch Donahue
Rick Donnelly
Jim Eliopulos
Ken Fantetti
Bob Fitzke
Guy Frazier
Lawrence Gaines
Dave Hampton
Jerry Hill
Gene Huey
Jim Kiick
Lee Kizzire
Chris Kolodziejski
Aaron Kyle
Mike LaHood
Chuck Lamson
Hub Lindsey
Jerry Marion
Dewey McConnell
Tony McGee
Mike McGraw
Dale Memmelaar
Nelson Munsey
Jay Novacek
Pat Ogrin
Danny Pittman
Paul Podmajersky
Steve Scifres
Truett Smith
Mark Smolinski
Dick Speights
Galand Thaxton
Vic Washington
Jack Weil
Joe Williams
Tyrone Williams
Willie Wright
Ryan Yarborough

Xavier (Ohio) (23)

Danny Abramowicz
Phil Bucklew
Dane Dastillung
Herb Davis
Mitch Dudek
Art Hauser
Jim Higgins
Jack Hoffman
Evan Jolitz
Steve Junker
Bill Knecht
John Martinkovic
Hal McPhail
Art Mergenthal
Chet Mutryn
Bob Pickard
Herb Rapp
John Shinners
Dom Sigillo
Hal Stotsberry
Socko Wiethe
Cole Willging
George Wilson

Yakima Valley CC WA (2)

Glen Bonner
Steve Sweeney

Yale (24)

Fritz Barzilauskas
Art Braman
Bruce Caldwell
Rich Diana
Brian Dowling
Greg Dubinetz
Joe Dufek
Gary Fencik
Chris Hetherington
Calvin Hill
Kenny Hill
Dick Jauron
Herb Kempton
Alex Kroll
Don Martin
Chuck Mercein
Century Milstead
John Prchlik
Gene Profit
Mike Pyle
Jeff Rohrer
Bill Schuler
John Spagnola
Paul Walker

Yankton (4)

Lyle Alzado
Les Goodman
Ruben Mendoza
Dean Wink

Youngstown State (18)

Tony Aiello
Al Campana
Craig Cotton
Lorenzo Davis
Slok Gill
Ralph Goldston
John Goode
Ron Jaworski
Bobby Jones
Larry Jordan
Quentin Lowry
Vince Marrow
Paul McFadden
Ed McGlasson
Frank Pokorny
Cliff Stoudt
Bob Thompson
Jeff Wilkins

Yuba Coll. CA (J.C.) (4)

Mike Hancock
Doug Mayberry
Sam Morley
Jim Watson

Team Rosters

Over the past eight decades, football has changed from a game of two-way players to one of specialization. Likewise, rosters have undergone alterations in size, number, and function. The early days of professional football often were a tug of war where one score, even a safety, sometimes was all that was needed as teams slugged it out with players who spent the entire game on the field and often were worn down by the time the game reached its climax. Players who came out of the game had to stay out for the rest of the quarter, so players either had to play both offense and defense or become benchwarmers. With only 16 players on an NFL active roster in 1925, there wasn't much room for substitutes.

The war-time substitution rule was instituted to help keep the NFL alive in 1943. A few teams briefly had to merge, including in-state rivals Pittsburgh and Philadelphia (nicknamed the "Steagles"), just to field a full squad of players. Active roster size diminished from 33 players to 28, but players freely could move on and off the field between plays for the first time. After World War II ended, the substitution rule went back into mothballs, but it returned for good three years later. With unlimited substitution, professional football was opened up to more players and those who played skill positions could concentrate on one facet of the game. In the 1950s, Cleveland coach Paul Brown switched guards on each play to send in the signals, and players haven't stopped shuttling on and off the field since.

Although two-way players still pop up occasionally, specialization remains the rule in the NFL. There are special teams, third-down specialists, nickel backs, pass-rushing specialists, and players whose sole job is to kick off, but each player has to excel in his given talent or find himself on the waiver wire. Modern football is a quick, complex game that forces split-second timing and decisions on the field. In other words, the names change, but the nature of the game remains the same. What follows are year-by-year rosters of every team since 1920. Until unlimited substitution, most offensive backs played defensive back as well. Fullbacks, centers and some guards and blocking backs played linebacker. For the years 1920-45, only players' offensive positions are given (unless a player appeared only on defense). Each player is listed by only his primary position.

1920 Akron

Russ Bailey - C
Scotty Bierce - E
Matt Brown - HB
Alf Cobb - G
Tuffy Conn - WB
Charlie Copley - T
Ken Crawford - FB
Budge Garrett - G
Harry Harris - BB
Tommy Holleran - BB
Pike Johnson - T
Rip King - TB
Frank McCormick - FB
Buck Miles - FB
Frank Moran - T
Bob Nash - E
Al Nesser - E
Al Pierotti - C
Fritz Pollard - WB
Bill Preston - T
Fred Sweetland - WB
Elgie Tobin - BB
Tommy Tomlin - G

1920 Buffalo

Ockie Anderson - TB
Jack Beckett - T
Bill Brace - G
Shirley Brick - E
Eddie Casey - TB
Buck Gavin - FB
Tommy Hughitt - BB
Jim Laird - WB
Barney Lepper - T
Lou Little - T
Heinie Miller - E
Charlie Mills - WB
Earl Potteiger - WB
John Rupp - G
Johnny Scott - TB
Murray Shelton - E
Pat Smith - FB
Butch Spagna - T
Karl Thielscher - FB
Tiny Thornhill - T
Voss - G
Bodie Weldon - WB
Red Werder - C
Lud Wray - C
Swede Youngstrom - G

1920 Canton

Cub Buck - T
Pete Calac - FB
Bunny Corcoran - E
Harrie Dadmun - G
Cap Edwards - G
Al Feeney - C
Birdie Gardner - T
Johnny Gilroy - BB
Tom Gormley - G
Larry Green - E
Tex Grigg - BB
Joe Guyon - WB
Doc Haggerty - G
Art Haley - WB
Johnny Hendren - TB
Pete Henry - T
Bob Higgins - E
John Kellison - G
Bull Lowe - E
Buck MacDonald - BB
Al Maginnes - C
Ike Martin - WB
Ralph Meadow - E
Joe Murphy - G
Dan O'Connor - G
Larry Petty - G
Lou Smyth - TB
Dutch Speck - G
Jim Thorpe - TB
Tom Whelan - E

1920 Chi. Cardinals

Willis Brennan - T
Joe Carey - T
Leon Chappell - G
Len Charpier - FB
Bill Clark - C
Harry Curran - WB
Paddy Driscoll - TB
Egan - WB
Paul Florence - E
Bill Fortune - G
Fred Gillies - T
Bernie Halstrom - BB
Charlie Knight - C
George Knight - T
Louis Kolls - C
Paul LaRosa - E
Nick McInerney - FB
Red O'Connor - E
Plunkett - FB
Lenny Sachs - E
Pete Schultz - FB
Bill Whalen - C
Clyde Zoia - G

1920 Chi. Tigers

Dunc Annan - TB
Johnny Barrett - TB
Sid Bennett - T
John Bosdett - E
Garland Buckeye - G
Ralph Capron - WB
Ben Derr - WB
Shorty Des Jardien - C
Alfred Eissler - FB
Guil Falcon - FB
Dick Falcon - G
Milt Ghee - BB
Emmett Keefe - G
Oscar Knop - E
Grover Malone - WB
Neil Mathews - T
Jack Meagher - E
Jock Mungavin - E
Dick Pierce - G
Lew Reeve - T
Frank Rydzewski - T
Walter Voight - G
Pete Volz - G

1920 Cleveland

Bert Baston - E
Harry Baujan - E
George Brickley - TB
Jim Bryant - BB
Stan Cofall - TB
Tuffy Conn - WB
Carl Cramer - FB
Mark Devlin - BB
Dinger Doane - FB
Moon Ducote - WB
Johnny Gilroy - BB
Tom Gormley - G
Doc Haggerty - G
Sandy Hastings - WB
Pat Herron - E
George Kerr - T
Phil Marshall - E
Joe Mattern - TB
Ed O'Hearn - G
Jack O'Hearn - WB
Red Pearlman - T
Leo Petree - FB
Al Pierotti - C
Frank Rydzewski - C
Herb Sies - T
Butch Spagna - T
Jake Stahl - G
Tiny Thornhill - T
Ray Trowbridge - E
Al Wesbecher - C

1920 Columbus

Beckwith - TB
Hi Brigham - G
John Davis - FB
Charlie Essman - G
Jim Flower - E
Hal Gaulke - BB
Babe Houck - G
Oscar Kuehner - T
Frank Lone Star - G
Wilkie Moody - WB
Joe Mulbarger - T
Frank Nesser - FB
Phil Nesser - G
Ted Nesser - T
Dwight Peabody - E
Homer Ruh - E
John Schneider - WB
Lee Snoots - TB
Will Waite - C
Oscar Wolford - G
Howard Yerges - TB

1920 Dayton

Dick Abrell - BB
Frank Bacon - WB
Max Broadhurst - T
Bill Clark - G
Harry Cutler - T
Doc Davis - G
Larry Dellinger - G
Guy Early - G
Lee Fenner - E
Russ Hathaway - T
Earl Hauser - T
Chuck Helvie - E
Hobby Kinderdine - C
Pesty Lentz - FB
Al Mahrt - BB
Lou Partlow - FB
Dave Reese - E
George Roudebush - TB
Norb Sacksteder - TB
Ed Sauer - T
Fritz Slackford - FB
Earl Stoecklein - G
Dutch Thiele - E
Glenn Tidd - G
Tiny Turner - G
Charlie Winston - G

1920 Decatur

Roy Adkins - G
Hugh Blacklock - T
Guy Chamberlin - E
Jimmy Conzelman - HB
Chuck Dressen - QB
Paddy Driscoll - HB
Andy Feichtinger - E
Sid Gepford - HB
George Halas - E
Lennie High - E
Burt Ingwersen - T
Jerry Jones - G
Bob Koehler - FB
Jake Lanum - HB
Kile MacWherter - FB
Walt May - G
Jake Mintun - C
Pard Pearce - QB
Ross Petty - G
Henry Shank - HB
Hub Shoemake - G
Dutch Sternaman - HB
George Trafton - C
Walt Veach - HB
Randy Young - E

1920 Detroit

Lynn Allen - TB
Clarence Applegran - G
Chris Bentz - T
Charlie Carman - G
Tom Dickinson - E
Pat Dunne FB
Russ Finsterwald - WB
Fitzgerald - E
Moose Gardner - G
Gates - G
Charlie Guy - G
Bo Hanley - WB
Steamer Horning - T
Stan Jacobs - TB
Marshall Jones - WB
Bill Joyce - BB
Jimmy Kelly - TB
King - WB
Ty Krentler - FB
Alvin Loucks - G
Hugh Lowery - T
Birdie Maher - E
McCoy - T
Blake Miller - E
Eddie Moegle - WB
Gil Runkel - C
Heinie Schultz - E
Don Straw - T
Ernest Watson - BB
Ray Whipple - E
Perce Wilson - BB
Wood - FB

1920 Hammond

Mose Bashaw - T
Brunswick - G
Tony Catalano - G
Davis - G
Guil Falcon - FB
Hank Gillo - FB
Wilbur Henderson - FB
Wally Hess - BB
Max Hicks - E
Carroll Johnson - E
Marshall Jones - TB
Dutch Kohl - E
Louis Kolls - C
Swede Larson - WB
Mathewson - WB
Klinks Meyers - BB
Frank Moran - C
Russ Oltz - G
Joe Pliska - WB
Mace Roberts - E
Frank Rydzewski - T
Walt Sechrist - G
Frank Seliger - T
Lew Skinner - G
Robert Specht - TB
Jim Talbott - BB
Ward - WB
Warren - BB

1920 Muncie

Cliff Baldwin - WB
Bobby Berns - T
Coonie Checkaye - BB
Doc Davis - T
Archie Erehart - WB
Owen Floyd - C
Russ Hathaway - T
Chuck Helvie - E
Ernie Hole - G
Mickey Hole - TB
Ken Huffine - FB
Spencer Pope - E
Jess Reno - E
Wilfred Smith - G

1920 Rochester

Bob Argus - TB
Joe Bachmaier - C
John Barsha - FB
Denny Cahill - G
Bart Carroll - T
Babe Clark - FB
Hal Clark - E
Fred Clarke - E
Ben Clime - G
Bill Connell - WB
Joe DuMoe - E
Ben Forsyth - C

Walt Frickey - E
Pete Heinlein - G
Dutch Irwin - WB
Jim Kane - G
Kwist - T
Jim Laird - FB
Darby Lowery - E
Dutch Mellody - G
Charlie Morrison - E
Elmer Oliphant - TB
Pepper - G
Mike Purdy - WB
Red Quigley - BB
Hank Smith - G
Charlie Stewart - G
George Tandy - E
Carl Thomas - WB
Vern Thomas - E
Lou Usher - T
Art Webb - G
Frank Whitcomb - G
Ray Witter - E
Jimmy Woods - G

1920 Rock Island

Walt Buland - T
Fred Chicken - TB
Fred Denfeld - T
Mark Devlin - BB
Freeman Fitzgerald - C
Frank Garden - E
Harry Gunderson - C
Ed Healey - T
Tom Henry - WB
Frank Jordan - WB
Polly Koch - T
Waddy Kuehl - TB
Dewey Lyle - G
George Magerkurth - T
Jerry Mansfield
Bobby Marshall - E
Charlie Mockmore - G
Sid Nichols - BB
Eddie Novak - WB
Paddy Quinn - FB
Speed Riddell - E
Loyal Robb - T
Ed Shaw - T
Oke Smith - E
Sullivan - F
John Synhorst - T
Rube Ursella - BB
Harry Webber - BB
Obe Wenig - E
Pudge Wyland - G
Arnie Wyman - FB

1921 Akron

Russ Bailey - C
Marty Beck - FB
Scotty Bierce - E
Alf Cobb - G
Charlie Copley - T
Bunny Corcoran - E
Carl Cramer - BF
Jim Flower - E
Bruno Haas - BB
Pike Johnson - T
Marshall Jones - WB
Rip King - TB
Frank McCormick - FB
Al Nesser - G
Fritz Pollard - WB
Roy Ratekin - E
Jack Read - G
Paul Robeson - E
Paul Sheeks - BB
Elgie Tobin - BB
Leo Tobin - G
Tommy Tomlin - G

1921 Buffalo

Ockie Anderson - TB
Carl Beck - TB
Bill Brace - G
Moose Gardner - G
Charlie Guy - C
Andy Hillhouse - WB
Steamer Horning - T
Tommy Hughitt - BB
Waddy Kuehl - WB
Jim Laird - FB
Lou Little - T
Heinie Miller - E
Bob Nash - T
Jack O'Hearn - WB
Elmer Oliphant - WB
Johnny Scott - BB
Pat Smith - FB
Butch Spagna - T
Herb Stein - G
Jack Sullivan - FB
Luke Urban - E
Eddie Usher - E
Tillie Voss - E
Bill Ward - T
Lud Wray - C
Swede Youngstrom - G

1921 Canton

Bird Carroll - E
Larry Conover - C
Cap Edwards - G
Guil Falcon - FB
Al Feeney - C
Red Griffiths - G
Tex Grigg - TB
Pete Henry - T
Bob Higgins - E
John Kellison - G
Herb Kempton - BB
Glenn Killinger - TB
Jim Laird - FB
Jim Morrow - WB
Duke Osborn - G
Harry Robb - BB
Ed Sauer - G
Fritz Slackford - WB
Marv Smith - TB
Lou Smyth - TB
Dutch Speck - G
Red Steele - E
Charlie Way - WB
Belf West - T
Inky Williams - E
Swede Youngstrom - G

1921 Chi. Cardinals

Norm Barry - BB
Ping Bodie - FB
Willis Brennan - G
Garland Buckeye - G
Leon Chappell - G
Harry Curran - WB
Paddy Driscoll - TB
Egan - BB
Fred Gillies - T
Bernie Halstrom - BB
Arnie Horween - BB
Ralph Horween - FB
Charlie Knight - C
Bob Koehler - FB
Paul LaRosa - E
Rube Marquardt - E
Nick McInerney - T
Red O'Connor - E
Earl Potteiger - WB
Frank Rydzewski - C
Lenny Sachs - E
John Scanlon - WB
Pete Steger - WB
Walter Voight - G
Clyde Zoia - G

1921 Chi. Staleys

Dick Barker - G
Hugh Blacklock - T
George Bolan - FB
Guy Chamberlin - E
Harry Englund - E
George Halas - E
Chic Harley - HB
Ken Huffine - FB
Jake Lanum - HB
Jake Mintun - C
Pard Pearce - QB
Ralph Scott - T
Russ Smith - G
Dutch Sternaman - HB
Pete Stinchcomb - HB
Tarzan Taylor - G
George Trafton - C
Lou Usher - T

1921 Cincinnati

Ferris Beekley - G
Ken Crawford - BB
Dane Dastillung - G
Fred Day - T
Mel Doherty - C
Guy Early - G
Earl Hauser - E
Shiner Knab - WB
Art Lewis - T
Lynch - G
Frank McCormick - FB
Tommy McMahon - FB
Tom Melvin - E
George Munns - TB
Ohmer - WB
Henry Orth - G
Walt Schupp - T
Dave Thompson - WB
Pete Volz - E

1921 Cleveland

Harry Baujan - E
Phil Bower - BB
Ed Brawley - G
Pete Calac - FB
Bunny Corcoran - E
Milt Ghee - BB
Joe Guyon - TB
Bruno Haas - WB
Johnny Hendren - FB
Bull Lowe - T
Moore - T
Joe Murphy - G
Dan O'Connor - T
Patterson - BB
Red Pearlman - G
Jake Stahl - G
George Tandy - C
Jim Thorpe - TB
Ralph Waldsmith - C
Tom Whelan - E

1921 Columbus

Harry Bliss - BB
Hal Gaulke - BB
Morris Glassman - E
Ted Hopkins - E
Babe Houck - G
Oscar Kuehner - T
Joe Mulbarger - T
Ted Murtha - G
Charlie Nesser - TB
Frank Nesser - FB
Fred Nesser - T
John Nesser - G
Phil Nesser - T
Ted Nesser - C
Walt Rogers - WB
Emmett Ruh - WB
Homer Ruh - E
Al Shook - G
Will Waite - G
Oscar Wolford - G

1921 Dayton

Faye Abbott - BB
Frank Bacon - TB
Larry Dellinger - G
Lee Fenner - E
Art Haley - TB
Russ Hathaway - T
Hobby Kinderdine - C
Al Mahrt - BB
John Miller - FB
Wilkie Moody - WB
Lou Partlow - FB
Gus Redman - WB
Dave Reese - E
George Roudebush - FB
Nelson Rupp - WB
Art Sampson - G
Ed Sauer - T
Herb Sies - G
Frank Sillin - WB
Jake Stahl - T
Dutch Thiele - E
Glenn Tidd - C
Chalmers Tschappatt - T

1921 Detroit

Butch Brandau - TB
Charlie Carman - G
Walt Clago - E
Frank Coughlin - T
Jerry DaPrato - FB
Cy DeGree - T
Pat Dunne - FB
Moose Gardner - G
Buck Gavin - FB
Charlie Guy - C
Steamer Horning - T
Earl Kreiger - TB
Waddy Kuehl - WB
Blake Miller - WB
Norb Sacksteder - TB
Bill Stobbs - BB
Don Straw - G
Tillie Voss - E
Vic Whitmarsh - E
Pryor Williams - G

1921 Evansville

Bourbon Bondurant - T
Frank Fausch - FB
Alec Fishman - G
Louie Fritsch - G
Bill Garnjost - G
Earl Goldsmith - E
Doc Gorman - E
Herb Henderson - TB
Mark Ingle - G
Red Jackson - T
Vince Lensing - G
Menz Lindsey - BB
John McDonald - T
Chief Mullen - E
Chuck O'Neil - E
Tubby Rohsenberger - T
Dick Spain - C
Adolph Spiegel - T
Earl Warweg - WB
Travis Williams - WB
Joe Windbiel - C
Leon Winternheimer - T
Jerry Zeller - WB

1921 Green Bay

Nate Abrams - E
Norm Barry - BB
Cub Buck - T
Joe Carey - G
James Cook - G
Frank Coughlin - T
Billy DuMoe - E
Dave Hayes - E
Tubby Howard - FB
Emmett Keefe - G
Fee Klaus - C
Adolph Kliebhan - BB
Wally Ladrow - HB
Curly Lambeau - TB
Grover Malone - HB
Herm Martell - E
Ray McLean - FB
Jab Murray - C
Sammy Powers - G
Art Schmaehl - FB
Warren Smith - G
Buff Wagner - HB
Cowboy Wheeler - E
Milt Wilson - G
Marty Zoll - G

1921 Hammond

Ken Crawford - BB
Jack Depler - C
Ben Derr - TB
Guil Falcon - FB
Hank Gillo - FB
Carl Hanke - E
George Hartong - G
Wally Hess - TB
Max Hicks - E
Red Jackson - T
Jones - TB
Dick King - FB
Oscar Knop - WB
Charlie Mathys - BB
Russ Oltz - G
Joe Pliska - WB
Rice - WB
Elliot Risley - T
Mace Roberts - E
Frank Seliger - G
Dave Tallant - T
Tommy Tomlin - G
Lou Usher - T
Walter Voight - C
Inky Williams - E

1921 Louisville

Chase Boldt - BB
Austin Brunklacher - G
Harper Card - T
Red Chenoweth - TB
Joe Engelhard - WB
Tom Ferguson - T
Herb Gruber - E
Fatty Harris - T
Austin Higgins - C
Karl Hower - FB
Bill Howser - G
Jim Irwin - FB
H. Lewis - G
Joe Martin - WB
Ted Moser - T
Bill Netherton - E
Harry Newland - E
Howard Stith - G
Jimmy Van Dyke - TB
Gene Wiggs - G
Hubert Wiggs - T

1921 Minneapolis

Oscar Christianson - E
Einar Cleve - E
Ben Dvorak - TB
Harold Erickson - T
Dutch Gaustad - G
Harry Gunderson - C
Bill Irgens - BB
Charlie Jonasen - E
George Kramer - G
John Norbeck - G
Mike Palmer - T
Sheepy Redeen - E
Pete Regnier - WB
Eber Sampson - FB
Rudy Tersch - G
Rube Ursella - BB

1921 Muncie

Cliff Baldwin - WB
Coonie Checkaye - BB
Owen Floyd - C
Ken Fulton - G
Chuck Helvie - E
Ernie Hole - G
Mickey Hole - FB
Kellogg - TB
Doc Ladorum - FB
Ray MacMurray - G
Mac McIndoo - E
Gus Redman - TB
Pete Slone - E
Wilfred Smith - T
Mike Yount - T

1921 NY Brickley Giants

Joe Bernstein - FB
Ed Brawley - G
George Brickley - FB
Harrie Dadmun - G
Mark Devlin - BB
Dinger Doane - FB
Jim Dufft - T
Joe DuSossoit - E
Tom Gormley - T
Doc Haggerty - G
Jimmy Jemail - BB
George Kane - G
George Kerr - T
Frank Leavitt - G
Buck MacDonald - G
Al Maginnes - G
Dave Maginnes - TB
Paul Meyers - E
Johnny Nagle - E
Jerry Noonan - BB
Con O'Brien - T
Ed O'Hearn - T
Al Pierotti - C
Mike Purdy - WB
Fred Sweetland - WB
Ray Trowbridge - E

1921 Rochester

Doc Alexander - C
Bob Argus - WB
Joe Bachmaier - G
Jim Barron - T
Howard Berry - TB
Benny Boynton - TB
Ben Clime - E
Jim Dufft - G
Joe DuMoe - E
Earl Ettenhaus - G
John Hasbrouck - FB
Jim Laird - FB
Darby Lowery - E
Frank Morrissey - G
Jerry Noonan BB
Billy Rafter - WB
Spin Roy - E
Hank Smith - G
Carl Thomas - T
Lou Usher - G
Frank Whitcomb - G
Ray Witter - E
Jimmy Woods - G

1921 Rock Island

Dick Barker - G
Lane Bridgeford - WB
Walt Brindley - BB
Walt Buland - T
Jimmy Conzelman - BB
Frank Coughlin - T
Eddie Duggan - FB
Jug Earp - C
Freeman Fitzgerald - C
Buck Gavin - FB
Hal Hanson - G
John Hasbrouck - WB
Dave Hayes - E
Ed Healey - T
Jerry Johnson - WB
Emmett Keefe - G
Dewey Lyle - G
Grover Malone - WB
Jerry Mansfield - FB
Vic Menefee - E
Sid Nichols - BB
Eddie Novak - TB
Paddy Quinn - FB
Oke Smith - E
Brick Travis - T
Viv Vanderloo - FB
Obe Wenig - E

1921 Tonawanda

Backnor - C
Fred Brumm - T
Cassidy - BB
Art Georke - E
Clarence Hosmer - G
Rudy Kraft - G
George Kuhrt - T
Buck MacDonald - G
Tom McLaughlin - FB
Bill Meisner - WB
Frank Primeau - BB
Tam Rose - TB
William Sanborn - E
Charles Tallman - T
Red Werder - C

1921 Washington

Dan Ahern - T
Alec Anderson - G
George Beyers - WB
Johnny Bleier - WB
Benny Boynton - TB
Pete Calac - FB
Joe Coster - T
Billy Crouch - C
Perry Dowrick - FB
Patsy Gerardi - E
Johnny Gilroy - TB
Tom Gormley - G
Joe Guyon - WB
Johnnie Hudson - WB
Sam Kaplan - E
Dutch Leighty - BB
Red Litkus - T
Mickey Livers - FB
Don McCarthy - E
Cy McDonald - G
Gordon Patterson - E
Metz Smeach - T
Jack Sullivan - FB
Buff Turner - T
Sam Turner - G
Pong Unitas - G
Ed Van Meter - G
Gene Vidal - FB
Bullets Walson - BB

1922 Akron

Marty Beck - WB
Scotty Bierce - E
Untz Brewer - WB
Charlie Copley - T
Bunny Corcoran - E
Carl Cramer - FB
Red Daum - E
Jim Flower - C
Al Jolley - T
Rip King - TB
Walt Kreinheder - C
Walt LeJeune - G
Leo McCausland - G
Joe Mills - WB
Ray Neal - G
Al Nesser - G
Ed Sauer - T
Paul Sheeks - BB
Bob Spiers - T
Cliff Steele - BB
Tillie Voss - E

1922 Buffalo

Ockie Anderson - TB
Bill Brace - G
Herb Dieter - G
Buck Gavin - FB
Gus Goetz - E
Charlie Guy - C
Tommy Hughitt - BB
Bill Kibler - TB
Glenn Knack - G
Waddy Kuehl - WB
Jim Laird - FB
Frank Morrissey - T
Jim Morrow - TB
Bob Nash - E
Bob Rawlings - FB
Johnny Scott - WB
Frank Spellacy - E
Carl Thomas - T
Luke Urban - E
Mike Wilson - E
Swede Youngstrom - G

1922 Canton

Don Batchelor - T
Arda Bowser - FB
Bird Carroll - E
Guy Chamberlin - E
Doc Elliott - FB
Tex Grigg - WB
Russ Hathaway - T
Pete Henry - T
Jim Kendrick - E
Link Lyman - T
Johnny McQuade - WB
Candy Miller - FB
William Murrah - C
Duke Osborn - G
Harry Robb - WB
Wooky Roberts - BB
Norb Sacksteder - TB
Ed Shaw - FB
Lou Smyth - TB
Dutch Speck - C
Tarzan Taylor - G
Ralph Waldsmith - G

1922 Chi. Bears

Hunk Anderson - G
Hugh Blacklock - T
George Bolan - FB
Bourbon Bondurant - G
Harry Englund - E
Hec Garvey - E
George Halas - E
Carl Hanke - E
Ed Healey - G
Joe LaFleur - G
Jake Lanum - HB
Ojay Larson - C
Pard Pearce - QB
Ralph Scott - T
Russ Smith - G
Dutch Sternaman - HB
Joey Sternaman - QB
Pete Stinchcomb - HB
Laurie Walquist - HB

1922 Chi. Cardinals

Eddie Anderson - E
Willis Brennan - G
Johnny Bryan - WB
Garland Buckeye - G
Paddy Driscoll - TB
Egan - E
Fred Gillies - T
Arnie Horween - BB
Ralph Horween - FB
Bob Koehler - FB
John Leonard - T
Nick McInerney - C
Johnny Mohardt - WB
Red O'Connor - E
Swede Rundquist - T
Lenny Sachs - E
Bill Whalen - C
Clyde Zoia - G

1922 Columbus

Burl Atcheson - E
Jack Beckett - T
Chuck Carney - T
Gene Carroll - E
John Conley - G
Doc Davis - G
Hal Gaulke - BB
Morris Glassman - E
Andy Gump - G
Ted Hopkins - E
Bob Karch - T
Earl Kreiger - E
Joe Mulbarger - T
Frank Nesser - G
Bob Rapp - WB
Walt Rogers - FB
Emmett Ruh - WB
Homer Ruh - E
Pete Schultz - FB
Lee Snoots - TB
Mark Stevenson - G
Don Wiper - BB
Oscar Wolford - C
Paul Ziegler - FB

1922 Dayton

Faye Abbott - BB
Frank Bacon - TB
Bobby Berns - G
Larry Dellinger - G
Lee Fenner - E
Bruno Haas - G
Russ Hathaway - T
Ken Huffine - FB
Hobby Kinderdine - C
Al Mahrt - BB
Tip O'Neill - WB
Lou Partlow - FB
Gus Redman - TB
Dave Reese - E
Ed Sauer - T
Herb Sies - G
Dutch Thiele - E
Glenn Tidd C
Jiggs Ullery - WB

1922 Evansville

Bourbon Bondurant - T
Slats Dalrymple - C
Winnie Denton - G
Vic Endress - BB
Frank Fausch - FB
Earl Goldsmith - WB
Tiny Ladson - G
Pete Lauer - TB
Chuck O'Neil - WB
Jess Reno - E
Spencer Rork - BB
Joe Sanders - G
Lew Skinner - T
Bill Slyker - E
Dick Spain - C
Adolph Spiegel - T
Steve Sullivan - TB
Pete Wathen - BB
Walker Whitehead - TB
Travis Williams - T
Leon Winternheimer - G

1922 Green Bay

Cub Buck - T
Tommy Cronin - HB
Pahl Davis - G
Pat Dunnigan - E
Jug Earp - T
Gus Gardella - FB
Moose Gardner - G
Eddie Glick - TB
Dave Hayes - E
Tubby Howard - E
Curly Lambeau - TB
Dutch Lauer - FB
Dewey Lyle - G
Charlie Mathys - BB
Stan Mills - FB
Jab Murray - T
Peaches Nadolney - G
Wally Niemann - C
Rip Owens - G
Pete Regnier - HB
Joe Second - C
Rex Smith - E
Biff Taugher - FB
Eddie Usher - HB
Cowboy Wheeler - E
Howard Woodin - G
Carl Zoll - G

1922 Hammond

Anderson - WB
George Berry - T
Teddy Besta - BB
Ed Carman - E
Lloyd Cearing - BB

Bill Giaver - WB
Carl Hanke - E
Wally Hess - TB
Oscar Knop - WB
Dutch Kohl - E
Tony LaBissoniere - C
Paul Leatherman - G
Elliot Risley - T
Mace Roberts - T
Frank Rydzewski - C
John Shelburne - FB
Bill Singleton - G
Steve Sullivan - TB
Dave Tallant - T
Festus Tierney - G
Willert - C
Inky Williams - E

1922 Louisville

Chase Boldt - BB
Austin Brunklacher - G
Harper Card - T
Joe Engelhard - TB
Salem Ford - TB
Dick Gibson - T
Edd Gregg - E
Herb Gruber - E
Austin Higgins - C
Jim Irwin - FB
Lou Jansing - FB
Charlie Lanham - T
Max MacCollom - E
Brian McGrath - G
Eddie Meeks - WB
Bill Netherton - E
Charlie Olmstead - G
Bo Otto - G
Bob Padan - WB
Wilfred Smith - T
Jimmy Van Dyke - TB
George Wanless - G
Hubert Wiggs - T

1922 Milwaukee

John Alexander - T
Norris Armstrong - FB
Norm Barry - WB
Sid Bennett - G
Lyle Bigbee - E
Moose Cochran - E
Bill Collins - E
Jimmy Conzelman - TB
Charlie Copley - T
Dinger Doane - FB
Jim Dufft - G
Mickey Fallon - G
Budge Garrett - E
Al Greene - WB
Emmett Keefe - G
Dick King - WB
Bo McMillin - BB
Ward Meese - E
George Mooney - WB
Al Pierotti - C
Fritz Pollard - TB
Earl Potteiger - WB
Mike Purdy - BB
Paul Robeson - E
George Seasholtz - TB
Duke Slater - T
Steve Sullivan - WB
Tommy Tomlin - G
Art Webb - T
Ben Winkelman - E

1922 Minneapolis

Oscar Christianson - E
Einar Cleve - WB
Shorty Des Jardien - E
Harold Erickson - T
Paul Flinn - E
Dutch Gaustad - G
Harry Gunderson - G
Bill Irgens - BB
Ren Kraft - E
George Kramer - G
John Madigan - C
Sam Mason - FB
Joe Mattern - BB
Harry Mehre - C
Louie Mohs - G
Marty Norton - TB
Eber Sampson - FB
Rudy Tersch - T
Otto Townsend - G

1922 Oorang

Reggie Attache - WB
Big Bear - E
E. Bobadash - E
Lo Boutwell - BB
Fred Broker - T
Elmer Busch - G
Pete Calac - E
Dick Deer Slayer - E
Xavier Downwind - C
Eagle Feather - FB
Joe Guyon - TB
Bob Hill - G
Horatio Jones - E
Nick Lassa - T
Joe Little Twig - E

Ted Lone Wolf - G
Ed Nason - E
Stilwell Sanooke - E
Ted St. Germaine - T
Jim Thorpe - TB
Baptiste Thunder - T
War Eagle - T
Bill Winneshick - C

1922 Racine

Buddy Baumann - T
George Berry - T
Art Braman - T
Moxie Dalton - BB
Chuck Dressen - BB
Al Elliott - TB
Bob Foster - TB
Karl George - G
Hank Gillo - FB
Norm Glockson - G
Earl Gorman - G
Norb Hayes - E
Fritz Heinisch - E
Jack Hueller - G
Jerry Johnson - TB
Irv Langhoff - WB
Frank Linnan - T
George McGill - G
Candy Miller - T
Jake Mintun - C
Jab Murray - G
Don Murry - T
Dud Pearson - BB
Elmer Rhenstrom - E
Fritz Roessler - E
Vin Shekleton - C
Wally Sieb - WB
Howard Woodin - T

1922 Rochester

Doc Alexander - C
Eddie Anderson - E
Bob Argus - WB
Joe Bachmaier - G
Eddie Bentz - E
Benny Boynton - BB
Hal Clark - E
John Dooley - G
Walt French - TB
Ralph Henricus - TB
Dick King - FB
Chris Lehrer - WB
Darby Lowery - T
Frank Matteo - T
Paul Meyers - E
Harry Robertson - T
Spin Roy - E
Herm Sawyer - WB
Hank Smith - T
Cliff Steele - BB
Tiny Thompson - G
Larry Weltman - BB
Mike Wilson - BB
Ray Witter - TB
Jimmy Woods - T
Chet Wynne - TB

1922 Rock Island

Lane Bridgeford - FB
Walt Brindley - BB
Mike Casteel - BB
Walt Clago - E
Jimmy Conzelman - TB
Jug Earp - C
Buck Gavin - FB
Ed Healey - T
Jerry Johnson - WB
Jerry Jones - G
Emmett Keefe - G
Louis Kolls - C
Ollie Kraehe - C
Dutch Lauer - WB
Dewey Lyle - G
Eddie Novak - WB
Duke Slater - T
Eddie Usher - WB
Tillie Voss - E
Obe Wenig - E

1922 Toledo

Dunc Annan - WB
Al Burgin - G
Marty Conrad - C
Cap Edwards - G
Guil Falcon - FB
Hippo Gozdowski - FB
Tom Holleran - BB
Steamer Horning - T
Reno Jones - G
John Kellison - T
Tex Kelly - G
Jim Kendrick - TB
Gus King - E
Truck Myers - E
Chuck O'Neil - FB
Dwight Peabody - E
Leo Petree - FB
Bob Phelan - BB
Red Roberts - TB
Tubby Rousch - WB
Buck Saunders - BB
Jimmy Simpson - BB

Herb Stein - G
Russ Stein - T
John Tanner - WB
Festus Tierney - G
Rat Watson - TB
Mac White - E

1923 Akron

Frank Bacon - WB
Wayne Brenkert - WB
George Brown - T
Carl Cramer - FB
Red Daum - E
Bill Edgar - G
Jim Flower - T
Art Haley - WB
Isham Hardy - G
Dutch Hendrian - BB
Walt LeJeune - G
Grover Malone - E
Al Michaels - TB
Joe Mills - C
Al Nesser - E
Red Roberts - E
Les Scott - G
Ed Shaw - FB
Hugh Sprinkle - T
Charlie Stewart - G
Dutch Wallace - G
Wilson - T

1923 Buffalo

Pete Bahan - TB
Scotty Bierce - E
Glen Carberry - E
Bunny Corcoran - WB
Frank Culver - C
Bill Edgar - FB
Jack Flavin - FB
Fred Foster - FB
Gil Gregory - FB
Mike Gulian - T
Tom Holleran - TB
Tommy Hughitt
Tex Kelly - G
John Mahoney - WB
Roy Martineau - FB
Elmer McCormick - C
Frank Morrissey - G
Vince Mulvey - FB
Bob Nash - T
Ben Roderick - TB
Johnny Scott - TB
Pat Smith - FB
Gustave Sonnenberg - T
Carl Thomas - T
Mike Trainor - WB
Luke Urban - E
Swede Youngstrom - G

1923 Canton

Bird Carroll - E
Guy Chamberlin - E
Rudy Comstock - G
Larry Conover - C
Doc Elliott - FB
Tex Grigg - WB
Dutch Hendrian - WB
Pete Henry - T
Ben Jones - FB
Link Lyman - T
Vern Mullen - E
Duke Osborn - G
Harry Robb - BB
Wooky Roberts - BB
Ben Roderick - WB
Ben Shaw - G
Russ Smith - G
Lou Smyth - TB
Dutch Speck - C
Joe Williams - G

1923 Chi. Bears

Hunk Anderson - G
Hugh Blacklock - T
George Bolan - FB
Johnny Bryan - QB
Gus Fetz - HB
Jim Flaherty - E
Hec Garvey - G
George Halas - E
Duke Hanny - E
Ed Healey - T
Oscar Knop - FB
Joe LaFleur - G
Jake Lanum - HB
Frank Rydzewski - C
Ralph Scott - T
Dutch Sternaman - HB
Joey Sternaman - QB
George Trafton - C
Lou Usher - T

1923 Chi. Cardinals

Eddie Anderson - E
Willis Brennan - G
Garland Buckeye - G
Jack Crangle - FB
Paddy Driscoll - TB
Egan - E
Art Folz - BB

Fred Gillies - T
Arnie Horween - BB
Ralph Horween - WB
Roger Kiley - E
Rip King - TB
Bob Koehler - FB
John Leonard - T
Nick McInerney - C
Johnny Mohardt - TB
Sully Montgomery - T
Wilfred Smith - G
Bill Whalen - C
Clyde Zoia - G

1923 Cleveland

Hunk Anderson - G
Pete Bahan - BB
Scotty Bierce - E
Arda Bowser - FB
Frank Civiletto - WB
Hal Ebersole - G
Deke Edler - WB
Cap Edwards - T
Frank Garden - E
Charlie Guy - C
Iolas Huffman - T
Ed Johns - G
Stan Keck - T
Johnny Kyle - FB
Bo McMillin - WB
Truck Myers - E
Lou Partlow - FB
Doug Roby - TB
Rudy Rosatti - T
Joe Setron - G
Pete Stinchcomb - WB
John Tanner - BB
Ralph Vince - G
Sol Weinberg - TB
Dick Wolf - FB
Joe Work - E

1923 Columbus

Elliott Bonowitz - BB
Paul Goebel - E
Gus Goetz - T
Ray Hanson - G
Jack Heldt - C
Wilmer Isabel - FB
Joe Mulbarger - T
Andy Nemecek - G
Bill Passuelo - G
Harry Randolph - BB
Bob Rapp - WB
Homer Ruh - E
Jack Sack - G
Lee Snoots - BB
Gustave Sonnenberg - T
Pete Stinchcomb - WB
Gus Tebell - E
Red Weaver - C
Sonny Winters - TB

1923 Dayton

Faye Abbott - BB
Frank Bacon - WB
John Beasley - G
Bobby Berns - G
Earl Burgner - BB
Ken Crawford - FB
Larry Dellinger - G
Lee Fenner - E
Russ Hathaway - T
Ken Huffine - FB
Al Jolley - G
Hobby Kinderdine - C
Walt Kinderdine - FB
Lou Partlow - TB
Dave Reese - E
Ed Sauer - T
Dutch Thiele - E
Glenn Tidd - G

1923 Duluth

Roddy Dunn - T
Wally Gilbert - WB
Ira Haaven - E
Ken Harris - FB
Art Johnson - T
Howard Kieley - T
Mickey MacDonnell - WB
John Madigan - C
Russ Method - WB
Red Morse - G
Dick O'Donnell - E
Joe Rooney - E
Bill Rooney - WB
Bill Stein - G
Joey Sternaman - BB
Doc Williams - G

1923 Green Bay

Myrt Basing - HB
Cub Buck - T
Jug Earp - T
Moose Gardner - G
Buck Gavin - FB
Jack Gray - E
Hal Hansen - FB
Norb Hayes - E

Curly Lambeau - TB
Wes Leaper - E
Dewey Lyle - G
Charlie Mathys - BB
Stan Mills - HB
Jab Murray - E
Wally Niemann - C
Cowboy Wheeler - E
Howard Woodin - G

1923 Hammond

Dunc Annan - FB
George Berry - G
Sol Butler - WB
Lloyd Cearing - WB
John Detwiller - FB
Carl Hanke - E
Wally Hess - TB
Oscar Knop - FB
Bill Kovascy - G
Swede Larson - BB
Russ Oltz - C
Fritz Pollard - BB
Elliot Risley - T
Ed Robinson - BB
Frank Rydzewski - C
Ed Seibert - G
Wilfred Smith - G
Steve Sullivan - WB
Dave Tallant - T
Lou Usher - T
Inky Williams - E

1923 Louisville

Chase Boldt - BB
Austin Brunklacher - G
Al Espie - T
Salem Ford - WB
Dick Gibson - T
Patsy Giugliano - BB
Herb Gruber - E
Austin Higgins - E
Bob Karch - T
Jim Kendrick - TB
Charlie Lanham - T
Russ Meredith - G
Charlie Olmstead - G
Bo Otto - C
John Quast - E
Earl Reiser - WB
John Rowan - TB
Jimmy Van Dyke - BB
George Wanless - WB
Bob White - E
Hubert Wiggs - FB

1923 Milwaukee

Russ Blailock - T
Jimmy Conzelman - TB
Dinger Doane - FB
Jim Dooley - G
Hal Erickson - WB
Frank Jordan - WB
Ojay Larson - C
Marv Mattox - BB
Larry McGinnis - G
Bo McMillin - TB
Johnny Milton - E
George Mooney - E
Peaches Nadolney - G
Al Pierotti - C
Ed Rate - BB
Dick Reichle - E
Lenny Sachs - E
Russ Smith - G
Bill Strickland - G
Jim Turner - BB
John Underwood - G
Roy Vassau - T
Ad Wenke - T
Chet Widerquist - T
Ben Winkelman - E

1923 Minneapolis

Adrian Baril - T
Oscar Christianson - E
Einar Cleve - BB
Danny Coughlin - WB
Paul Flinn - E
Bob Fosdick - G
Dutch Gaustad - G
Hal Hanson - C
Dick Hudson - FB
Bill Irgens - TB
Ave Kaplan - TB
George Kramer - T
Harry Mehre - C
Louie Mohs - E
Louie Pahl - WB
Eber Sampson - FB
Rudy Tersch - T
Festus Tierney - G

1923 Oorang

Arrowhead - E
Napoleon Barrel - C
Big Bear - T
Peter Black Bear - E
Lo Boutwell - BB
Ted Buffalo - T
Pete Calac - FB

Xavier Downwind - G
Eagle Feather - FB
Gray Horse - WB
Joe Guyon - TB
Al Jolley - T
Nick Lassa - C
Chim Lingrel - WB
Joe Little Twig - E
Ted Lone Wolf - G
Emmett McLemore - BB
Ed Nason - E
Bill Newashe - T
Joe Pappio - E
Stan Powell - G
Jack Thorpe - G
Jim Thorpe - TB
Woodchuck Welmas - E

1923 Racine

Shorty Barr - TB
A.C. Bauer - T
Jimmy Baxter - WB
Art Braman - T
Chuck Dressen - BB
Al Elliott - WB
Bob Foster - T
Hank Gillo - FB
Earl Gorman - G
Dick Halladay - E
George Hartong - G
Fritz Heinisch - E
Jack Hueller - G
Irv Langhoff - BB
Bill McCaw - G
Paul Meyers - E
Candy Miller - E
Jake Mintun - C
Al Pierotti - G
Fritz Roessler - E
Milt Romney - BB
Len Smith - T
Howie Stark - T
Rollie Williams - WB

1923 Rochester

Will Anderson - BB
Bob Argus - WB
Joe Bachmaier - G
Hugh Bancroft - E
Hal Clark - E
Red Emslie - G
Fred Foster - BB
Mike Gavagan - BB
Cy Kasper - G
Jim Leonard - G
Darby Lowery - T
Frank Matteo - T
Joe McShea - G
Jerry Noonan - BB
Leo Peyton - FB
Spin Roy - E
Shag Sheard - TB
Hank Smith - C
Gordon Wallace - FB
Jim Welsh - G
Ray Witter - BB
Jimmy Woods - C

1923 Rock Island

John Armstrong - BB
Joe Bernstein - G
Sol Butler - WB
Fod Cotton - T
Frank DeClerk - C
Bill Giaver - WB
Alex Gorgal - FB
Max Kadesky - E
Louis Kolls - C
Waddy Kuehl - TB
Walter Lowe - FB
Charlie Lungren - BB
Bob Phelan - FB
Herb Sies - G
Duke Slater - T
George Thompson - G
Harry Webber - E
Mike Wilson - E

1923 St. Louis

Roy Andrews - G
John Cardwell - HB
Pete Casey - HB
Jim Finnegan - E
Jack Gray - E
Dick King - FB
Ollie Kraehe - G
Walt Kreinheder - C
Ward Meese - E
George Meinhardt - G
Johnny Milton - E
William Murrah - G
Orville Siegfried - HB
Eber Simpson - QB
Brick Travis - T
Bub Weller - T
Hal Wilder - G
Ernie Winburn - E
Lee Wykoff - FB

1923 Toledo

Don Batchelor - T

Marty Conrad - C
Guil Falcon - FB
France Fitzgerald - BB
Joe Gillis - G
Cowboy Hill - TB
Steamer Horning - T
Ben Hunt - T
Cliff Jetmore - WB
Jerry Jones - G
Heinie Kirkgard - WB
Dutch Lauer - WB
Tom McNamara - G
Chuck O'Neil - E
Si Seyfrit - E
Dutch Strauss - FB
Tillie Voss - T
Rat Watson - BB
Mac White - E

1924 Akron

John Barrett - C
Marty Beck - WB
George Berry - G
Wayne Brenkert - BB
Sol Butler - WB
Carl Cardarelli - C
Carl Cramer - FB
Red Daum - E
Jim Flower - T
Paul Hogan - WB
Frank Hogue - BB
Al Michaels - TB
Joe Mills - E
Stan Mills - E
Al Nesser - G
Harry Newman - G
James Robertson - BB
Walt Sechrist - G
Dutch Speck - G
Hugh Sprinkle - T
Dick Stahlman - T
Dutch Wallace - G
Wilson - G
Giff Zimmerman - WB

1924 Buffalo

Jim Ailinger - G
Benny Boynton - BB
Russ Burt - WB
Pete Calac - FB
Glen Carberry - E
Harry Collins - G
Frank Culver - C
Lou Feist - T
Jack Flavin - FB
Gil Gregory - WB
Chick Guarnieri - E
Iolas Huffman - T
Tommy Hughitt - BB
Ken Jones - WB
Eddie Kaw - TB
Glenn Knack - G
Babe Kraus - T
Elmer McCormick - C
Al Mitchell - T
Frank Morrissey - T
Mike Trainor - WB
Len Watters - E
Swede Youngstrom - G

1924 Chi. Bears

Hunk Anderson - G
Hugh Blacklock - T
George Bolan - FB
Johnny Bryan - HB
George Halas - E
Duke Hanny - E
Ed Healey - T
Oscar Johnson - FB
Jim Kendrick - HB
Oscar Knop - FB
Joe LaFleur - G
Jake Lanum - FB
Jim McMillen - G
Vern Mullen - E
Harry O'Connell - T
Ralph Scott - T
Dutch Sternaman - HB
Joey Sternaman - QB
George Trafton - C
Laurie Walquist - HB

1924 Chi. Cardinals

Eddie Anderson - E
Willis Brennan - G
Garland Buckeye - G
Charlie Clark - G
Fred DeStefano - FB
Paddy Driscoll - TB
Art Folz - BB
Fred Gillies - T
Carl Hanke - E
George Hartong - T
Arnie Horween - BB
John Hurlburt - WB
Rip King - TB
Bob Koehler - FB
Bill McElwain - WB
Nick McInerney - C
Paul McNulty - E
Munger - T
Red O'Connor - E

Bill Ryan - T
Wilfred Smith - T
Bill Whalen - C

1924 Cleveland

Chalmers Ault - G
Scotty Bierce - E
Hal Burt - G
Guy Chamberlin - E
Rudy Comstock - G
Cap Edwards - T
Doc Elliott - FB
Charlie Honaker - E
Ben Jones - FB
Jerry Jones - G
Link Lyman - T
Stan Muirhead - T
Dave Noble - WB
Duke Osborn - C
Wooky Roberts - BB
Russ Smith - G
Olin Smith - T
John Tanner - FB
Dick Wolf - WB
Joe Work - E
Hoge Workman - TB

1924 Columbus

Earl Duvall - G
Walt Ellis - T
Paul Goebel - E
Neil Halleck - BB
Wilmer Isabel - BB
Johnnie Layport - G
Joe Mantell - G
Wilkie Moody - BB
Joe Mulbarger - G
Andy Nemecek - C
Boni Petcoff - T
Bob Rapp - WB
Homer Ruh - E
Herb Schell - WB
Herb Stock - BB
Gus Tebell - E
Buddy Tynes - FB
Sonny Winters - TB
Oscar Wolford - E

1924 Dayton

Faye Abbott - BB
Frank Bacon - E
Bobby Berns - G
Elliott Bonowitz - G
Dick Egan - G
Dick Faust - G
Lee Fenner - E
Russ Hathaway - T
Ken Huffine - FB
Hobby Kinderdine - C
Shine Kinderdine - G
Walt Kinderdine - WB
Waddy Kuehl - WB
Armin Mahrt - TB
Stan Muirhead - G
Lou Partlow - WB
Gus Redman - BB
Ed Sauer - T
Herb Sies - G
Glenn Tidd - C
Inky Williams - E

1924 Duluth

Eddie Bratt - E
Oke Carlson - T
Herbert Clow - FB
Art Engstrom - G
Wally Gilbert - TB
Art Johnson - T
Doc Kelley - TB
Howard Kieley - T
Allen MacDonald - WB
Russ Method - WB
Bill O'Toole - G
Cobb Rooney - BB
Joe Rooney - E
Bill Rooney - FB
Jim Sanford - T
Bill Stein - G
Leif Strand - C
Jack Underwood - E
Roy Vexall - FB
Doc Williams - G

1924 Frankford

Al Bedner - G
Bull Behman - T
Harry Dayhoff
Eddie Doyle - E
Jack Finn - BB
Mike Gulian - T
Tex Hamer - FB
Les Haws - BB
Bill Hoffman - G
Rob Jamieson - C
Bill Kellogg - TB
Milt O'Connell - E
Butch Spagna - G
Herb Stein - G
Russ Stein - T
Jack Storer - TB
George Sullivan - WB

Whitey Thomas - E
Charlie Way - WB
Jim Welsh - G

1924 Green Bay

Myrt Basing - HB
Cub Buck - T
Walt Buland - T
Dukes Duford - E
Jug Earp - C
Moose Gardner - G
Les Hearden - HB
Dutch Hendrian - FB
Curly Lambeau - TB
Verne Lewellen - HB
Charlie Mathys - BB
Jab Murray - E
Wally Niemann - C
Dick O'Donnell - E
Rudy Rosatti - T
Eddie Usher - HB
Tillie Voss - E
Howard Woodin - G

1924 Hammond

Dunc Annan - WB
George Berry - G
Teddy Besta - WB
Lyle Burton - G
Sol Butler - TB
John Detwiller - FB
Guil Falcon - FB
Bill Fortune - G
Wally Hess - BB
Ward Meese - E
Ray Neal - T
Russ Oltz - T
Mace Roberts - E
Ed Robinson - TB
Frank Rydzewski - C
Lenny Sachs - E
Si Seyfrit - E
Dick Stahlman - T
Steve Sullivan - E
Dave Tallant - T
Lou Usher - T
Rat Watson - BB
Inky Williams - E

1924 Kansas City

Roy Andrews - T
Henry Bassett - T
Jay Berquist - G
Jim Bradshaw - WB
Bob Choate - G
Chuck Corgan - E
Rufe DeWitz - WB
Charley Hill - FB
Cowboy Hill - TB
Jimmy Krueger - T
Lew Lane - TB
Emmett McLemore - BB
Johnny Milton - E
Steve Owen - G
Carl Peterson - C
Ivan Quinn - G
Milt Rehnquist - G
Dick Sears - T
Dick Stahlman - T
Dutch Strauss - FB
Steve Sullivan - TB
Eddie Usher - WB
Rat Watson - TB
Dutch Webber - E
Ralph Widick - T

1924 Kenosha

Jimmy Baxter - WB
Irv Carlson - WB
Walt Cassidy - E
Marty Conrad - C
George Dahlgren - G
Egan - E
Swede Erickson - E
Earl Gorman - G
Fritz Heinisch - E
Bill Hurst - T
Ray Oberbroekling - T
Clete Patterson - G
Pard Pearce - BB
Earl Potteiger
George Seasholtz - FB
Jimmy Simpson - BB
Dick Stahlman - G
Lou Usher - T
Dick Vick - TB
Whitey Wolter - WB
Marv Wood - WB

1924 Milwaukee

Jimmy Conzelman - TB
Dinger Doane - FB
Red Dunn - BB
Hal Erickson - WB
Bob Foster - G
Ojay Larson - C
Walt LeJeune - G
Larry McGinnis - C
George Mooney - FB
Frank Morrissey - G
Peaches Nadolney - G

Clem Neacy - E
Al Pierotti - T
Lenny Sachs - E
Russ Smith - G
Evar Swanson - E
Lou Usher - G
Bub Weller - T
Chet Widerquist - T
Ben Winkelman - WB

1924 Minneapolis

Adrian Baril - T
Oscar Christianson - E
Einar Cleve - WB
Pat Dunnigan - T
Beanie Eberts - G
Tom Hogan - C
Bill Houle - BB
Ed Johns - G
George Kramer - G
John Madigan - C
Louie Mohs - E
Marty Norton - TB
Eddie Novak - WB
Louie Pahl - FB
Fred Putzier - E
Les Scott - T
John Simons - FB
Festus Tierney - G

1924 Racine

Shorty Barr - FB
Al Bentzin - G
Roman Brumm - E
Lee Croft - G
Al Elliott - TB
Bill Giaver - WB
Hank Gillo - FB
Dick Halladay - E
Dick Hanley - WB
Jack Hueller - G
Ralph King - G
Jake Mintun - C
Johnny Mohardt - TB
Don Murry - T
Chuck Palmer - WB
Riley - G
Fritz Roessler - E
Milt Romney - BB
Len Smith - T
John Thomas - FB

1924 Rochester

Doc Alexander - T
Will Anderson - FB
Bob Argus - FB
Joe Bachmaier - G
Reaves Baysinger - E
Benny Boynton - TB
Hal Clark - E
Johnny Coaker - T
Frank Culver - E
John Dooley - T
Fred Foster - BB
Tex Grigg - TB
Darby Lowery - G
Roy Martineau - G
Frank Matteo - T
Bob Nash - T
Nielson - WB
Jerry Noonan - WB
Clem Nugent - FB
Red Pearlman - G
Leo Peyton - BB
Billy Rafter - BB
Spin Roy - E
Bill Ryan - T
Shag Sheard - TB
Hank Smith - C
Lou Smyth - WB
Elmer Volgenau - G
Gordon Wallace - C
Jimmy Woods - C

1924 Rock Island

John Armstrong - BB
Bill Ashbaugh - FB
Joe Bernstein - G
Wes Bradshaw - WB
Walt Buland - G
Frank DeClerk - C
Buck Gavin - FB
Joe Guyon - WB
Louis Kolls - C
Joe Kraker - G
Joe Little Twig - E
Vince McCarthy - WB
Bob Phelan - WB
Ned Scott - T
Duke Slater - T
Basil Stanley - G
George Thompson - G
Fred Thomsen - E
Jim Thorpe - TB
Rube Ursella - WB
Mike Wilson - E

1925 Akron

Dunc Annan - WB
John Barrett - C
George Berry - G

Scotty Bierce - E
Frank Bissell - E
Russ Blailock - G
Knute Caldwell - T
Chase Clements - T
Marty Conrad - G
Carl Cramer - FB
Red Daum - E
Guil Falcon - FB
Jim Flower - T
Fritz Henry - G
Joe Mills - C
Al Nesser - G
Obie Newman - E
Fanny Niehaus - TB
Fritz Pollard - TB
James Robertson - BB
Dick Stahlman - T

1925 Buffalo

Les Asplundh - FB
Ben Barber - T
Doc Bruder - WB
Russ Burt - WB
Ed Carman - T
Floyd Christman - FB
Harry Curzon - E
Lou Feist - E
Darrell Fisher - WB
Eddie Fisher - G
Wally Foster - BB
Chet Gay - G
Milo Gwosden - E
Norm Harvey - T
Jim Kendrick - TB
Jimmy Kennedy - WB
Walt Koppisch - WB
Elmer McCormick - G
Jim Noble - E
Max Reed - C
Chase Van Dyne - T
Swede Youngstrom - G

1925 Canton

Ray Brenner - WB
Pete Calac - FB
Bird Carroll - E
Rudy Comstock - G
Frank Culver - C
Willie Flattery - G
Wilmer Fleming - WB
Chick Guarnieri - E
Pete Henry - T
Paul Hogan - TB
Ben Jones - WB
Rip Kyle - T
Link Lyman - T
Wade McRoberts - C
Lou Merillat - E
Ruel Redinger - WB
Harry Robb - BB
Norb Sacksteder - BB
Dick Schuster - G
Dutch Speck - G
Dutch Strassner - E
Giff Zimmerman - TB

1925 Chi. Bears

Hunk Anderson - G
Hugh Blacklock - T
Earl Britton - FB
Johnny Bryan - HB
Mush Crawford - G
Bill Fleckenstein - G
Red Grange - HB
George Halas - E
Duke Hanny - E
Ed Healey - T
Ralph King - C
Oscar Knop - FB
Jim McMillen - G
Johnny Mohardt - HB
Vern Mullen - E
Don Murry - T
Milt Romney - HB
Ralph Scott - T
Russ Smith - C
Dutch Sternaman - HB
Joey Sternaman - QB
George Trafton - C
Laurie Walquist - HB
Buck White - FB

1925 Chi. Cardinals

Eddie Anderson - E
Herb Blumer - E
Willis Brennan - G
Ralph Claypool - C
Fred DeStefano - FB
Paddy Driscoll - TB
Red Dunn - BB
Hal Erickson - WB
Earl Evans - T
Art Folz - BB
Fred Gillies - T
John Hurlburt - WB
Bob Koehler - FB
Jerry Lunz - G
Mickey MacDonnell - WB
Ike Mahoney - BB
Nick McInerney - E

Paul McNulty - E
Lenny Sachs - E
Wilfred Smith - G
Evar Swanson - E
Jimmy Tays - TB
Bub Weller - T

1925 Cleveland

Chalmers Ault - T
George Baldwin - E
Herb Bauer - E
Phil Branon - T
Obie Bristow - TB
Karl Broadley - G
Glen Carberry - E
Carl Cardarelli - C
Chase Clements - T
Alf Cobb - T
Larry Conover - C
Gus Eckberg - FB
Doc Elliott - FB
Frank Garden - E
Walt Kreinheder - C
Rudy Kutler - G
Ed Loucks - E
Russ Meredith - T
Al Michaels - TB
Truck Myers - T
Nick Nardacci - TB
Al Nesser - G
Dave Noble - WB
Ray Norton - WB
Steve Owen - T
Milt Rehnquist - G
Wooky Roberts - BB
Walt Sechrist - T
Maury Segal - E
Bob Spiers - T
Hugh Sprinkle - T
Gene Stringer
Paul Suchy - E
Ralph Vince - G
Dutch Wallace - G
Dutch Webber - E
Inky Williams - E
Dick Wolf - BB
Joe Work - E
Swede Youngstrom - G

1925 Columbus

Dom Albanese - FB
Gale Bullman - E
Herb Davis - E
Earl Duvall - G
Ray Eichenlaub - FB
Walt Ellis - T
Paul Goebel - E
Tom Long - G
Paul Lynch - TB
Wilkie Moody - WB
Joe Mulbarger - G
Andy Nemecek - C
Frank Nesser - FB
Boni Petcoff - T
Bob Rapp - BB
Jim Regan - BB
George Rohleder - G
Homer Ruh - E
Lee Snoots - WB
Buddy Tynes - WB

1925 Dayton

Faye Abbott - BB
Frank Bacon - WB
Elliott Bonowitz - G
Dick Dobeleit - WB
Clarence Drayer - T
Lee Fenner - E
John Gabler - G
Al Graham - G
Charlie Guy - G
Ken Huffine - FB
Zip Joseph - G
Hobby Kinderdine - C
Walt Kinderdine - WB
Bill Knecht - T
Johnnie Layport - G
Armin Mahrt - TB
Johnny Mahrt - E
Gene Mayl - E
Lou Partlow - FB
Ed Sauer - T
Russ Young - FB

1925 Detroit

Bill Bucher - E
Jimmy Conzelman - BB
Al Crook - C
Dinger Doane - FB
Walt Ellis - T
Jack Fleischmann - G
Al Hadden - WB
Tom Hogan - T
Vivian Hultman - E
Dutch Lauer - BB
Dutch Marion - FB
Tom McNamara - G
Russ Smith - G
Gustave Sonnenberg - T
Ernie Vick - C
Dick Vick - TB
Tillie Voss - E

By Wimberly - T

1925 Duluth

Charlie Black - E
Oke Carlson - T
Fred Denfeld - G
Wally Gilbert - TB
Art Johnson - T
Doc Kelley - TB
Howard Kieley - T
Mike Koziak - G
Mickey MacDonnell - WB
Bobby Marshall - E
Russ Method - FB
Wally O'Neill - E
Cobb Rooney - BB
Bill Rooney - FB
Porky Rundquist - T
Bill Stein - C
Rex Tobin - E
Jack Underwood - E
Roy Vexall - FB
Doc Williams - G

1925 Frankford

Bull Behman - T
Doc Bruder - WB
Stanley Burnham
Charlie Carton - E
Guy Chamberlin - E
Alex Clement - WB
Clark Craig - E
Rae Crowther - E
Saville Crowther - G
Jug Earp - T
Bob Fitzke - WB
Tex Hamer - FB
Art Harms - T
Les Haws - BB
Bill Hoffman - G
Two-Bits Homan - BB
Ben Jones - FB
Walt LeJeune - T
Bull Lowe - E
Link Lyman - T
Elmer McCormick - G
Milt O'Connell - E
Walt Sechrist - T
Red Seidelson - G
Lou Smyth - TB
Butch Spagna - G
Bill Springsteen - C
Hust Stockton - TB
George Sullivan - TB
Jim Welsh - G
Frank Wilsbach - G

1925 Green Bay

George Abramson - G
Myrt Basing - FB
Cub Buck - T
Jim Crowley - TB
Jug Earp - T
Moose Gardner - G
Jack Harris - FB
Eddie Kotal - HB
Curly Lambeau - TB
Ojay Larson - C
Walt LeJeune - G
Verne Lewellen - TB
Charlie Mathys - BB
Marty Norton - HB
Dick O'Donnell - E
George Vergara - E
Elmer Wilkens - E
Howard Woodin - G

1925 Hammond

Dunc Annan - WB
Sol Butler - TB
Ed Carman - T
Ken Crawford - C
Harry Curzon - E
George Dahlgren - G
Wop Drumstead - G
Guil Falcon - FB
Bill Fortune - G
Bill Giaver - FB
Wally Hess - TB
Dick Hudson - WB
Merle Hunter - G
Jim Kendrick - BB
Rip King - TB
Glen Magnusson - G
McDonald - E
Ward Meese - E
Ray Neal - T
Russ Oltz - C
Fritz Pollard - WB
Ed Robinson - BB
Frank Rydzewski - G
Lenny Sachs - E
Dave Tallant - T
Rat Watson - FB
Inky Williams - E

1925 Kansas City

Roy Andrews - G
Bill Ashbaugh - WB
Al Bloodgood - BB

Obie Bristow - WB
Chuck Corgan - BB
Joe Guyon - WB
Charley Hill - WB
Cowboy Hill - WB
Dosey Howard - G
Joe Milam - G
Jake Mintun - C
Lyle Munn - E
Steve Owen - T
Jim Palermo - G
Milt Rehnquist - G
Alvie Thompson - T
Dutch Webber - E
Phil White - FB

1925 Milwaukee

Adrian Baril - T
Shorty Barr - BB
Roman Brumm - T
Johnny Bryan - TB
Jack Daniels - TB
Darroll DeLaPorte - BB
Pat Dunnigan - T
John Fahay - G
Hank Gillo - FB
Sam Mason - FB
Johnny (Blood) McNally - HB
Heinie Miller - G
Peaches Nadolney - G
Clem Neacy - E
Chuck Reichow - FB
Charlie Richardson - BB
Fritz Roessler - E
Bill Ryan - T
Frank Rydzewski - G
Jim Snyder - TB
Bill Thompson - C
Festus Tierney - G
Barney Traynor - C

1925 NY Giants

Doc Alexander - C
Al Bedner - T
Heinie Benkert - FB
Lynn Bomar - E
Matt Brennan - BB
Art Carney - G
Jim Frugone - TB
Hinkey Haines - WB
Dutch Hendrian - BB
Cowboy Hill - TB
Paul Jappe - E
Bill Kenyon - BB
Jack McBride - TB
Ed McGinley - T
Century Milstead - T
Tom Moran - BB
Tommy Myers - WB
Bob Nash - E
Swede Nordstrom - G
Mike Palm - BB
Babe Parnell - T
Earl Potteiger - BB
Owen Reynolds - E
Bill Rooney - WB
Jim Thorpe - TB
Tommy Tomlin - G
Larry Walbridge - C
Phil White - TB
Joe Williams - G

1925 Pottsville

Clarence Beck - T
Charlie Berry - E
Frank Bucher - E
Harry Dayhoff - WB
Eddie Doyle - E
Jack Ernst - BB
Hoot Flanagan - TB
Walt French - WB
Russ Hathaway - T
Denny Hughes - C
Tony Latone - WB
Fungy Lebengood - WB
Armin Mahrt - TB
Bob Millman - WB
Duke Osborn - G
Frank Racis - G
Dick Rauch - G
Ed Sauer - T
Herb Stein - C
Russ Stein - T
Barney Wentz - FB

1925 Providence

Speed Braney - G
Chick Burke - WB
Dutch Connor - FB
Jim Crowley - TB
Dolph Eckstein - C
Franny Garvey - E
Archie Golembeski - G
Mike Gulian - T
Ching Hammill - BB
Joe Kozlowsky - T
Jim Laird - FB
Bull Lowe - E
Red Maloney - E
Hugh McGoldrick - T
Al McIntosh - WB

Don Miller - WB
Curly Oden - BB
Pard Pearce - BB
John Pohlman - FB
Fritz Pollard - TB
Hop Riopel - TB
Nate Share - G
Fred Sheehan - G
Bert Shurtleff - G
Jack Spellman - T
Spike Staff - G
Fred Sweet - WB
John Thomas - FB
Cy Wentworth - TB
Lloyd Young - G

1925 Rochester

Bob Argus - FB
Gene Bedford - E
Hal Clark - E
Ham Connors - E
John Dooley - T
Guil Falcon - FB
Tex Grigg - BB
Jake Hoffman - FB
Bill Kellogg - FB
Tex Kelly - T
Jim Kendrick - WB
Darby Lowery - G
Ed Lynch - E
Roy Mackert - C
Roy Martineau - G
Frank Matteo - T
Spin Roy - E
Shag Sheard - WB
Hank Smith - C
Lou Smyth - TB
Dave Ziff - E

1925 Rock Island

Paul Anderson - G
John Armstrong - BB
Les Belding - E
Lyle Burton - G
Fod Cotton - T
George Dahlgren - G
Frank DeClerk - C
Buck Gavin - FB
Harry Hall - WB
Dutch Hendrian - WB
Ed Herman - E
Chuck Hill - WB
Jim Kendrick - E
Louis Kolls - C
Roddy Lamb - TB
Joe Little Twig - E
Vince McCarthy - WB
Eddie Novak - FB
Joe Rooney - E
Duke Slater - T
Evar Swanson - E
George Thompson - G
Jim Thorpe - TB
Rube Ursella - TB
Chet Widerquist - T

1926 Akron

Dunc Annan - TB
Marty Beck - FB
George Berry - C
Frank Bissell - E
Knute Caldwell - T
Alvro Casey - T
Ralph Chase - T
Carl Cramer - FB
Red Daum - E
Hal Griggs - BB
Isham Hardy - G
Joe Little Twig - E
Nat McCombs - G
Joe Mills - C
Al Nesser - G
Obie Newman - WB
Fritz Pollard - TB
George Rohleder - T
Red Seidelson - G
Rube Ursella - WB
Dutch Wallace - G
Hal Wendler - BB

1926 Brooklyn

Herm Bagby - WB
Hugh Blacklock - T
Jim Bond - G
Matt Brennan - BB
Earl Britton - FB
Dutch Connor - WB
Leo Douglass - FB
Ted Drews - E
Hec Garvey - C
Ed Harrison - E
Red Howard - G
Paul Jappe - T
Stan Kobolinski - C
Al Leith - BB
Dick McGrath - T
Bob Morris - G
Tommy Myers - BB
Swede Nordstrom - G
Ted Plumridge - C
Ed Reagen - T
Owen Reynolds - E
Quentin Reynolds - G
Bill Rooney - WB
Jim Sheldon - E
George Snell - FB
Bill Stephens - C
Art Stevenson - C
Harry Stuhldreher - TB
Tarzan Taylor - G
Rex Thomas - TB
Chief Toorock - WB
Charlie Weber - G
Jim Yeager - T
Dave Ziff - E

1926 Buffalo

Neely Allison - E
Wes Bradshaw - BB
Lester Caywood - T
Don Dimmick - WB
Van Edmondson - C
Lou Feist - E
Roy Guffey - E
Ben Hobson - FB
Barlow Irvin - G
Tex Kelly - G
Jim Kendrick - TB
George Kirk - C
Firpo McGilbra - T
Ralph Nairan - E
George Nix - G
Ralph Pittman - BB
Roger Powell - WB
Ted Schwarzer - G
Elmer Slough - BB
Al Swain - E
Bill Vaughn - FB
Cop Weathers - G
Firpo Wilcox - T
Joe Willson - G
Mule Wilson - WB

1926 Canton

Sam Babcock - WB
Sol Butler - FB
Pete Calac - FB
Hook Comber - FB
Art Deibel - T
Willie Flattery - G
Pete Henry - T
Rip Kyle - C
Joe Little Twig - E
Cliff Marker - E
Wade McRoberts - C
Don Nelson - T
John Nichols - G
Harry Robb - BB
Stan Robb - E
Guy Roberts - WB
Ben Roderick - WB
Jack Sack - G
Frank Seeds - WB
Dutch Speck - G
Russ Stein - E
Jim Thorpe - TB
Dick Vick - TB
Dutch Wallace - G
Harold Zerbe - E

1926 Chi. Bears

Johnny Bryan - HB
Bill Buckler - G
Paddy Driscoll - HB
Earl Evans - T
Bill Fleckenstein - C
George Halas - E
Duke Hanny - E
Ed Healey - T
Oscar Knop - FB
Cliff Lemon - E
Link Lyman - T
Jim McMillen - G
Vern Mullen - E
Don Murry - T
Milt Romney - QB
Bill Senn - HB
Dutch Sternaman - FB
George Trafton - C
Laurie Walquist - HB

1926 Chi. Cardinals

Herb Blumer - E
Willis Brennan - G
Ralph Claypool - C
Ward Connell - FB
Red Dunn - BB
Walt Ellis - T
Hal Erickson - WB
Gene Francis - FB
Fred Gillies - T
Ed Greene - G
Tom Hogan - G
Howard Kieley - G
Bob Koehler - FB
Roddy Lamb - TB
Jerry Lunz - G
Mickey MacDonnell
Ike Mahoney - BB
Bill McElwain - WB
Nick McInerney - E
Duke Slater - T
Mel Stuessy - T
Evar Swanson - E
Bub Weller - T
Chet Widerquist - G
Jim Woodruff - E

1926 Columbus

Pete Barnum - TB
Bill Berrehsem - T
Jim Bertoglio - FB
John Conley - T
Herb Davis - WB
Earl Duvall - T
Flop Gorrill - E
Jack Heldt - G
Len Johnson - BB
Joe Mulbarger - G
Tommy Murphy - BB
Frank Nesser - G
Ike Nonenmaker - E
Harley Pearce - E
Boni Petcoff - T
Earl Plank - E
Bob Rapp - WB
Lou Reichel - C
Flash Woods - WB

1926 Dayton

Faye Abbott - FB
Johnnie Becker - T
Art Beckley - BB
Jack Brown - G
Eric Calhoun - T
Dick Dobeleit - WB
Lee Fenner - E
Al Graham - G
Mack Hummon - E
Hobby Kinderdine - C
Johnnie Layport - T
Armin Mahrt - BB
Lou Mahrt - TB
Gene Mayl - E
Lou Partlow - TB
Peck Reiter - G
Ed Sauer - T

1926 Detroit

John Barrett - C
John Cameron - G
Jimmy Conzelman - BB
Al Crook - C
Dinger Doane - FB
Tom Edwards - T
Jack Fleischmann - G
Bruce Gregory - WB
Charlie Grube - E
Al Hadden - TB
Norm Harvey - T
Vivian Hultman - E
Dutch Lauer - E
Ed Lynch - E
Dutch Marion - FB
McDonald - WB
Tom McNamara - G
Eddie Scharer - TB
Gustave Sonnenberg - T
Dick Vick - BB

1926 Duluth

Walt Buland - T
Oke Carlson - G
Paul Fitzgibbon - WB
Chuck Gayer - T
Wally Gilbert - WB
Fritz Heinisch - E
Art Johnson - T
Doc Kelley - WB
Walt Kiesling - T
Louie Larson - BB
Jimmy Manion - G
Johnny (Blood) McNally - HB
Russ Method - WB
Jim Murphy - C
Jock Murray - E
Ernie Nevers - FB
Red Quam - BB
Cobb Rooney - BB
Joe Rooney - E
Porky Rundquist - G
Dewey Scanlon - WB
Bill Stein - C
Ray Suess - T
Hew Sullivan - G
Jack Underwood - E
Doc Williams - G

1926 Frankford

Bob Books - TB
Doc Bruder - WB
Johnny Budd - T
Joe Carpe - T
Guy Chamberlin - E
Rudy Comstock - G
Rae Crowther - E
Leo Douglass - FB
Fred Graham - E
Tex Hamer - FB
Bill Hoffman - G
Paul Hogan - WB
Two-Bits Homan - BB
Ben Jones - BB
Bull Lowe - E
Walter Mahan - G
Hap Moran - WB
Daddy Potts - T
Max Reed - C
Wooky Roberts - BB
Lou Smyth - TB
Bill Springsteen - E
Hust Stockton - TB
Ed Weir - T
Ned Wilcox - WB
Swede Youngstrom - G

1926 Green Bay

Myrt Basing - E
Adolph Bieberstein - G
Tiny Cahoon - T
Wes Carlson - G
Hec Cyre - T
Jug Earp - C
Rex Enright - FB
Dick Flaherty - E
Moose Gardner - G
Jack Harris - E
Eddie Kotal - TB
Curly Lambeau - TB
Walt LeJeune - C
Verne Lewellen - HB
Cully Lidberg - FB
Charlie Mathys - BB
Jack McAuliffe - HB
Walt McGaw - G
Dick O'Donnell - E
Pid Purdy - BB
Rudy Rosatti - T
Howard Woodin - G

1926 Hammond

Dunc Annan - WB
Gene Bedford - E
George Berry - G
Sol Butler - FB
Charley Carr - WB
Ralph Chase - T
George Dahlgren - T
George Fisher - T
Buck Gavin - FB
Ray Hahn - E
Dick Hudson - BB
Merle Hunter - T
Jack McKetes - BB
Bill Nagida - BB
Ray Neal - G
Don Nelson - C
Obie Newman - WB
Ed Robinson - BB
Frank Rydzewski - C
Walt Sechrist - G
Russ Smith - G
Rube Ursella - TB
Lou Usher - T
Hal Wendler - BB
Inky Williams - E

1926 Hartford

Eddie Barnikow - FB
Jack Bonadies - G
Harry Brian - WB
Chuck Corgan - BB
Dilly Dally - G
Jim Donlan - G
Furlong Flynn - G
Jim Foley - TB
Jake Friedman - E
Hec Garvey - T
Denny Gildea - C
Dimp Halloran - TB
John Harris - FB
Lefty Jamerson - E
Ed Keenan - G
Ed Lynch - E
Jim Manning - TB
Ernie McCann - T
Elmer McCormick - G
Ed McEvoy - WB
Harry McMahon - BB
Ralph Nichols - T
Dick Noble - G
Grat O'Connell - E
Frank O'Connor - T
Red O'Neil - C
Jack Perrin - BB
Vic Radzievitch - BB
Joseph Santone - G
Rocky Segretta - E
Stan Sieracki - T
Ken Simendinger - WB
Lou Smyth - FB
Enid Thomas - WB
Dutch Webber - E
Mule Werwaiss - T
Henry Zehrer - FB

1926 Kansas City

Roy Andrews - BB
Jay Berquist - G
Al Bloodgood - TB
Obie Bristow - BB
Tom Cobb - T
Chuck Corgan - BB
Rufe DeWitz - WB
Charley Hill - WB
Dosey Howard - G
Swede Hummell - FB
Jim Jacquith - BB
Lyle Munn - E
Tommy Murphy - BB
Bill Owen - T
Jim Palermo - G
Proc Randels - E
Milt Rehnquist - G
Clyde Smith - C
Glen Spear - FB
Alvie Thompson - T
Dutch Webber - E
Joe Wostoupal - C

1926 Los Angeles

Juddy Ash - G
Ben Bangs - WB
Fred Beach - G
Bull Finch - BB
Bill Gutteron - BB
Del Hufford - E
Tut Imlay - TB
Tuffy Maul - FB
Jack McArthur - C
Brick Muller - E
Don Newmeyer - T
John Nolan - G
Artie Sandberg - BB
Pete Schaffnit
Don Thompson - G
John Thurman - T
Ellery White - WB
Al Young - WB

1926 Louisville

Dan Bernoske - G
Ed Berwick - C
Ray Bush - E
Jim Eiden - T
Bill Flannigan - T
Al Gansberg - E
Bill Giaver - TB
Gene Golsen - FB
Tom Golsen - G
Vee Green - T
Glenn Greenwood - FB
Steve Hanson - E
Larry Jackson - C
Gar Leaf - T
Bill McCaw - G
John McDonald - T
Lou Metzger - FB
Omensky - G
Chuck Palmer - BB
Ed Robinson - WB
Lenny Sachs - E
John Scanlon - TB
Walt Sechrist - G
Gerry Sherry - FB
George Slagle - G
Pete Stinchcomb - TB
Pete Vainowski - G

1926 Milwaukee

Fred Abel - BB
Marion Ashmore - T
Johnny Bryan - HB
Joe Burks - C
Don Curtin - BB
Lavie Dilweg - E
Steve Douglas - G
Pat Dunnigan - G
Clarke Fischer - HB
Chet Gay - T
Stone Hallquist - BB
Johnny Heimsch - TB
Frank Hertz - E
Stan Kuick - G
Oxie Lane - T
Tom Murphy - TB
Clem Neacy - E
Ossie Orwoll - HB
Howie Slater - FB

1926 NY Giants

John Alexander - T
Doc Alexander - G
Al Bedner - G
Riley Biggs - C
Lynn Bomar - E
Art Carney - E
Tex Grigg - BB
Jack Hagerty - FB
Hinkey Haines - FB
Art Harms - T
Cowboy Hill - TB
Kid Hill - FB
Paul Hogan - WB
Glenn Killinger - TB
Walt Koppisch - WB
Jack McBride - TB
Mickey Murtagh - C
Al Nesser - G
Steve Owen - T
Mike Palm - BB
Babe Parnell - T
Earl Potteiger - E
Art Stevenson - C
Tommy Tomlin - G
Tillie Voss - E
Dutch Webber - E
Joe Williams - G

1926 Pottsville

Heinie Benkert - WB
Charlie Berry - E
Jesse Brown - TB
Frank Bucher - E
Jack Ernst - BB
Hoot Flanagan - WB
Russ Hathaway - T
Heinie Jawish - T
George Kenneally - E
Tony Latone - TB
Bob Millman - WB
Fanny Niehaus - WB
Aaron Oliker - E
Duke Osborn - G
Frank Racis - T
Herb Stein - C
Jim Welsh - G
Barney Wentz - FB
Zeke Wissinger - T
Frank Youngfleish - C

1926 Providence

Speed Braney - G
Jack Donahue - G
Dolph Eckstein - C
Carl Etelman - WB
Dutch Forst - FB
Franny Garvey - E
Archie Golembeski - E
Fred Graham - E
Mike Gulian - T
Vern Hagenbuckle - E
Swede Hummell - WB
Jack Keefer - TB
Lou Koplow - T
Joe Kozlowsky - T
Jim Laird - FB
Pinky Lester - E
Waddy MacPhee - WB
Jim Manning - TB
Ed McCrillis - G
Joe McGlone - BB
Al McIntosh - WB
Curly Oden - BB
Seneca Samson - BB
Bob Scott - C
Frank Seyboth - WB
Lou Smyth - TB
Jack Spellman - T
Jim Stifler - E
Fred Sweet - WB
John Talbot - E
Jack Triggs - FB
Cy Wentworth - WB
Bull Wesley - G
Lloyd Young - G

1926 Racine

Shorty Barr - BB
George Bernard - G
Adolph Bieberstein - G
Champ Boettcher - FB
Roman Brumm - G
George Burnsite - BB
Don Curtin - BB
John Fahay - E
Hank Gillo - FB
George Glennie - G
Dick Hardy - T
Fritz Heinisch - E
Fred Hobscheid - T
Graham Kernwein - TB
Frank Linnan - T
Roy Longstreet - C
Barney Mathews - E
Wally McIlwain - WB
Jake Mintun - C
Jim Murphy - E
Jim Oldham - E
Chuck Reichow - FB
Ed Sparr - T
Gil Sterr - BB

1927 Buffalo

Neely Allison - E
Karl Bohren - WB
Harlan Carr - TB
Ed Doyle - G
Norm Harvey - T
Russ Hathaway - T
Ken Hauser - FB
Ben Hobson - BB
Barlow Irvin - T
Jack McArthur - C
Frank McConnell - G
Paul Minick - G
Lowell Otte - E
Ben Roderick - WB
Spin Roy - E
George Snell - BB
Pinky Thompson - WB
Jack Underwood - E
Charlie Van Horn - FB
Norton Vedder - FB
Rat Watson - BB
Ralph White - E
Joe Willson - FB

1927 Chi. Bears

Johnny Bryan - QB
Bill Buckler - G
Paddy Driscoll - HB
Earl Evans - T
Bill Fleckenstein - G
George Halas - E
Duke Hanny - E
Ed Healey - T
Chuck Kassel - E
Oscar Knop - FB
Link Lyman - T
Jim McMillen - G
Don Murry - E
Clem Neacy - E
Milt Romney - QB
Bill Senn - HB
Dutch Sternaman - HB
Joey Sternaman - QB
George Trafton - C
Ernie Vick - C
Tillie Voss - E
Laurie Walquist - HB
Buck White - FB

1927 Chi. Cardinals

Jay Berquist - G
Herb Blumer - T
Willis Brennan - G
Ted Bucklin - FB
Guy Chamberlin - E
Ralph Claypool - C
Walt Ellis - T
Hal Erickson - TB
Aubrey Goodman - T
Paul Hogan - TB
Swede Hummell - G
Ben Jones - BB
Roddy Lamb - WB
Mickey MacDonnell - WB
Ike Mahoney - BB
Nick McInerney - G
Hap Moran - TB
Vern Mullen - E
Ray Risvold - WB
Rollin Roach - FB
Duke Slater - T
Bill Springsteen - C
Bill Stein - G
Red Strader - TB
Evar Swanson - E
John Vesser - E
Tim Waldron - G
Bub Weller - T

1927 Cleveland

Roy Andrews - T
Carl Bacchus - E
Herm Bagby - FB
Al Bloodgood - TB
Hal Broda - E
Lester Caywood - T
Tom Cobb - T
Cookie Cunningham - E
Herb DeWitz - BB
Tiny Feather - FB
Benny Friedman - TB
Dosey Howard - G
Frank Kelley - WB
Jerry Krysl - T
Harry McGee - G
Lyle Munn - E
Bill Owen - T
Gordon Peery - BB
Proc Randels - E
Milt Rehnquist - G
Jim Simmons - WB
Clyde Smith - C
Rex Thomas - WB
Dutch Webber - E
Ossie Wiberg - BB
Dick Wolf - WB

1927 Dayton

Faye Abbott - TB
Sneeze Achiu - WB
Johnnie Becker - T
Bill Belanich - T
Earl Britton - FB
Jack Brown - C
Augie Cabrinha - WB
Ebby DeWeese - G
Lee Fenner - E
Al Graham - G
Sam Hipa - E
Red Joseph - E
Zip Joseph - E
Hobby Kinderdine - C
Lou Mahrt - TB
Lou Partlow - TB
Peck Reiter - G
Ed Seibert - T
Frank Sillin - WB
Jimmy Tays - BB
Corl Zimmerman - G

1927 Duluth

Marion Ashmore - T
Bunny Belden - WB
Pots Clark - WB
Fritz Cronin - E
Walt Kiesling - G
Chick Lang - G

Jimmy Manion - G
Jack McCarthy - T
Johnny (Blood) McNally - HB
Bill McNellis - WB
Russ Method - WB
Clem Neacy - E
Ernie Nevers - FB
Cobb Rooney - BB
Joe Rooney - E
Bill Rooney - C
Shanley - T
Bill Stein - C
Ray Suess - G

1927 Frankford

Bull Behman - T
Earl Britton - FB
Pots Clark - T
Rudy Comstock - G
Babe Connaughton - G
Chris Cortemeglia - WB
Russ Daugherity - WB
Carl Davis - E
Bill Donohoe - BB
Jack Filak - T
Paul Fitzgibbon - WB
Adrian Ford - WB
Tex Grigg - WB
Tex Hamer - FB
Two-Bits Homan - BB
Chuck Kassel - E
Tony Kostos - E
Tom Leary - E
Cliff Marker - E
Joey Maxwell - C
Frank McGrath - E
Ken Mercer - TB
Lou Molinet - FB
Sully Montgomery - T
Hap Moran - TB
Dick Moynihan - BB
Max Reed - C
Pete Richards - C
Charley Rogers - WB
George Tully - E
Joe Weir - E
Ed Weir - T
Ned Wilcox - FB
Swede Youngstrom - T

1927 Green Bay

Myrt Basing - FB
Mal Bross - HB
Tiny Cahoon - T
Boob Darling - C
Lavie Dilweg - E
Red Dunn - BB
Jug Earp - C
Rex Enright - FB
Tom Hearden - HB
Bruce Jones - G
Eddie Kotal - HB
Curly Lambeau - TB
Verne Lewellen - HB
Frank Mayer - G
Dick O'Donnell - E
Claude Perry - T
Pid Purdy - BB
Rudy Rosatti - T
Gil Skeate - FB
Red Smith - G
George Tuttle - E
Howard Woodin - G

1927 NY Giants

Doc Alexander - G
Riley Biggs - C
Lester Caywood - G
Chuck Corgan - E
Hec Garvey - G
Joe Guyon - BB
Jack Hagerty - WB
Hinkey Haines - WB
Pete Henry - T
Red Howard - G
Cal Hubbard - E
Tut Imlay - WB
Paul Jappe - E
Jim Kendrick - E
Cliff Marker - E
Jack McBride - TB
Century Milstead - T
Mickey Murtagh - C
Al Nesser - G
Steve Owen - T
Babe Parnell - G
Earl Potteiger - BB
Dick Stahlman - T
Phil White - BB
Mule Wilson - FB
Doug Wycoff - BB

1927 NY Yankees

Red Badgro - E
Bullet Baker - TB
John Bayley - T
Bob Beattie - T
Mush Crawford - T
Jug Earp - T
Ray Flaherty - E
Wes Fry - FB

Red Grange - TB
Dick Hall - T
Norm Harvey - T
Wild Bill Kelly - BB
Louis Kolls - C
Fritz Kramer - G
Jim Lawson - E
Verne Lewellen - WB
Red Maloney - E
Larry Marks - WB
Jack McArthur - C
Mike Michalske - G
Bo Molenda - FB
Bill Oliver - G
Forrest Olson - G
Ralph Scott - T
Ray Stephens - C
Eddie Tryon - WB

1927 Pottsville

John Barrett - C
Johnny Budd - G
Joe Carpe - T
Harlan Carr - TB
Lester Caywood - T
Dinger Doane - FB
Walden Erickson - T
Jack Ernst - BB
Nick Farina - C
Adrian Ford - E
Pete Henry - T
Vivian Hultman - E
George Kenneally - E
Frank Kirkleski - TB
Tony Latone - WB
Walt LeJeune - T
Emil Mayer - E
Bob Millman - WB
Dinty Moore - WB
Vern Mullen - E
Duke Osborn - G
Frank Racis - G
Paul Rebseaman - C
Guy Roberts - WB
Eddie Scharer - BB
Jack Underwood - E
Barney Wentz - FB
Frank Youngfleish - C

1927 Providence

Jimmy Conzelman - BB
Jack Cronin - WB
Bill Cronin - WB
Dinger Doane - FB
Jack Fleischmann - G
Mike Gulian - T
Al Hadden - WB
Joe Kozlowsky - T
Jim Laird - G
Bull Lowe - E
Ed Lynch - E
Dave Mishel - TB
Grat O'Connell - E
Curly Oden - BB
Al Pierotti - C
Bill Pritchard - FB
Orland Smith - T
Gustave Sonnenberg - T
Jack Spellman - E
Jim Stifler - E
Bull Wesley - C
Abe Wilson - G
Wildcat Wilson - TB
Lloyd Young - FB
Sam Young - G

1928 Chi. Bears

Bill Buckler - G
Roy Carlson - E
Ted Drews - E
Paddy Driscoll - HB
Earl Evans - T
Bill Fleckenstein - G
Al Hadden - HB
George Halas - E
Ed Kallina - T
Link Lyman - T
Jim McMillen - G
Don Murry - T
Milt Romney - QB
Reggie Russell - E
Bill Senn - HB
Joey Sternaman - QB
Dick Sturtridge - HB
George Trafton - C
Ernie Vick - C
Tillie Voss - E
John Wallace - E
Laurie Walquist - HB
Buck White - FB
Elmer Wynne - FB

1928 Chi. Cardinals

Ed Allen - E
Homer Bliss - G
Herb Blumer - E
Hal Bradley - G
Ralph Claypool - C
Joe Davidson - G
Hal Erickson - WB
Paul Fitzgibbon - WB
Fred Gillies - T

Ducky Grant - BB
Ted Illman - FB
Ben Jones - FB
Lyons Killiher - G
Mickey MacDonnell - TB
Ike Mahoney - WB
Ray Marelli - G
Jim Murphy - BB
Clem Neacy - E
Ray Risvold - WB
Duke Slater - T
Bill Springsteen - E
Bill Stein - G
Charlie Strack - G
Jim Thorpe - E
Chet Widerquist - T
Don Yeisley - E

1928 Dayton

Faye Abbott - BB
Sneeze Achiu - WB
Johnnie Becker - T
Bill Belanich - T
Earl Britton - FB
Jack Brown - C
Win Charles - TB
Clair Cook - WB
Ebby DeWeese - BB
Dick Faust - T
Al Graham - G
Clarence Graham - WB
Sam Hipa - E
Mack Hummon - E
Jack Keefer - TB
Hobby Kinderdine - C
Carl Mankat - E
Art Matsu - BB
Ed Seibert - G
Frank Sillin - WB
Jim Spencer - G
Aubrey Strosnider - T
Corl Zimmerman - G

1928 Detroit

Carl Bacchus - E
Rip Bachor - T
John Barrett - C
Lester Caywood - G
Tom Cobb - T
Tiny Feather - FB
Benny Friedman - TB
Dosey Howard - G
Pete Jackson - FB
Lyle Munn - E
Bill Owen - T
Proc Randels - E
Eddie Scharer - TB
Len Sedbrook - WB
Rex Thomas - WB
Ernie Vick - G
Ossie Wiberg - BB
Chet Widerquist - G
Joe Wostoupal - C

1928 Frankford

Bull Behman - T
Rudy Comstock - G
Wally Diehl - FB
E.A. Dobrey - E
Chief Elkins - FB
Jack Filak - T
Hal Hanson - G
Two-Bits Homan - BB
Chuck Kassel - E
Tony Kostos - E
Roger Mahoney - C
Joey Maxwell - C
Ken Mercer - BB
Arnie Oehlrich - WB
Johnny Roepke - TB
Charley Rogers - TB
Hust Stockton - FB
Carl Waite - E
Ed Weir - T
Bub Weller - T

1928 Green Bay

Marion Ashmore - T
Bullet Baker - HB
Jim Bowdoin - G
Tiny Cahoon - T
Boob Darling - C
Lavie Dilweg - E
Red Dunn - BB
Jug Earp - C
Hal Griffen - C
Tom Hearden - HB
Bruce Jones - G
Eddie Kotal - HB
Curly Lambeau - BB
Verne Lewellen - TB
Slick Lollar - FB
Larry Marks - HB
Paul Minick - G
Bo Molenda - FB
Tom Nash - E
Harry O'Boyle - FB
Dick O'Donnell - E
Claude Perry - T
Dutch Webber - E
Howard Woodin - G

1928 NY Giants

Neely Allison - E
Al Bloodgood - BB
Bruce Caldwell - TB
Ox Eckhardt - FB
Ray Flaherty - E
Hec Garvey - G
Jack Hagerty - BB
Hinkey Haines - BB
Bug Hartzog - G
John Holman - T
Cal Hubbard - E
Paul Jappe - G
Jack McBride - TB
Century Milstead - T
Hap Moran - TB
Mickey Murtagh - C
Al Nesser - G
Steve Owen - T
Babe Parnell - G
Tony Plansky - FB
Earl Potteiger - BB
Max Reed - C
Rudy Rosatti - T
Paul Schuette - G
Red Smith - E
Bull Wesley - C
Mule Wilson - WB

1928 NY Yankees

Red Badgro - E
Jack Colahan - T
Hec Cyre - T
Jack Ernst - BB
Ray Flaherty - E
Ed Gallagher - T
Frank Grube - E
Murrell Hogue - G
Wild Bill Kelly - TB
Harvey Levy - T
Jack McArthur - C
Joe McClain - T
Frank McGrath - E
Mike Michalske - G
Bo Molenda - FB
Bill Pritchard - FB
Frank Racis - T
Dick Rauch - C
Cobb Rooney - TB
Sam Salemi - WB
Red Smith - BB
Art Stevenson - C
Gibby Welch - WB

1928 Pottsville

Johnny Budd - T
Joe Carpe - T
Jack Ernst - BB
Earl Goodwin - E
Myrl Goodwin - WB
Pete Henry - T
George Kenneally - E
Walt Kiesling - G
Tony Latone - FB
Johnny (Blood) McNally - HB
Hap Moran - TB
Will Norman - WB
Duke Osborn - G
Frank Racis - G
Joe Rooney - E
Herb Stein - C
Barney Wentz - FB

1928 Providence

Jimmy Conzelman - BB
Jack Cronin - WB
Bill Cronin - FB
Jack Fleischmann - G
Al Hadden - FB
Duke Hanny - E
Norm Harvey - E
Perry Jackson - T
Jim Laird - G
Curly Oden - BB
Milt Rehnquist - G
Jim Simmons - WB
Clyde Smith - C
Orland Smith - T
Gustave Sonnenberg - T
Jack Spellman - E
Pop Williams - FB
Abe Wilson - G
Wildcat Wilson - TB

1929 Boston

Joe Carpe - T
Bill Connor - G
Jack Ernst - BB
Bill Howell - E
George Kenneally - E
Paul Kittredge - HB
Joe Kozlowsky - T
Tony Latone - FB
Ed Lawrence - TB
Red Maloney - E
Ralph Marston - BB
Ed McCrillis - G
Al Miller - HB
Al Pierotti - C
Frank Racis - G

Dick Rauch - G
Roy Scholl - G
Arnie Shockley - T
Bert Shurtleff - C
Hust Stockton - TB
Thurston Towle - E
Cy Wentworth - BB

1929 Buffalo

Herb Bizer - E
Walt Brewster - T
Ulysses Comier - WB
Ed Comstock - G
Art Dorfman - C
Frank Glassman - G
Swede Hagberg - WB
Al Jolley - T
Bob Mahan - FB
Nat McCombs - G
Harry Myles - T
Earl Plank - E
Bob Rapp - WB
Jess Rodriguez - TB
Stan Rosen - BB
Cassy Ryan - BB
Red Shurtliffe - WB
Tillie Voss - E
Chuck Weimer - TB
Jim Woodruff - E

1929 Chi. Bears

Zuck Carlson - G
Cookie Cunningham - E
Paddy Driscoll - HB
Shorty Elness - HB
Earl Evans - T
Bill Fleckenstein - G
Gardie Grange - E
Red Grange - HB
Tom Hearden - HB
Walter Holmer - FB
Luke Johnsos - E
Joe Kopcha - G
Ojay Larson - C
Harvey Long - T
Ralph Maillard - T
Don Murry - T
Packie Nelson - T
Bert Pearson - C
Bull Polisky - G
Ted Richards - E
Harry Richman - G
Sod Ryan - T
Bill Senn - HB
Joey Sternaman - QB
Dick Sturtridge - HB
George Trafton - C
Laurie Walquist - HB
Buck White - FB

1929 Chi. Cardinals

Bullet Baker - BB
Herb Blumer - G
Earl Britton - FB
Eddie Butts - BB
Pat Dowling - E
Chief Elkins - WB
Don Hill - WB
Murrell Hogue - T
Chuck Kassel - E
Walt Kiesling - G
Chick Lang - E
Ojay Larson - C
Louie Larson - WB
Mickey MacDonnell - WB
Russ Method - BB
Ernie Nevers - FB
Cobb Rooney - WB
Bill Rooney - C
Gene Rose - WB
Duke Slater - T
Bill Stein - G
Jess Tinsley - T
Jack Underwood - G
Jake Williams - T

1929 Dayton

Faye Abbott - FB
Johnnie Becker - T
Bill Belanich - T
Johnny Brewer - WB
Jack Brown - C
Steve Buchanan - TB
Roy Carlson - E
John Depner - E
Pat Duffy - FB
Dick Faust - T
Lee Fenner - E
Al Graham - G
Bob Haas - BB
John Kauffman - T
Hobby Kinderdine - C
Carl Mankat - T
Lou Partlow - FB
Frank Sillin - BB
John Singleton - TB
Jim Spencer - G
Ed Tolley - G
Tillie Voss - T
John Wallace - E
Elmer Wynne - FB

Corl Zimmerman - G

1929 Frankford

George Barna - E
Bull Behman - T
Bill Capps - T
Rudy Comstock - G
Wally Diehl - FB
Chief Elkins - FB
Jack Filak - T
Eddie Halicki - FB
Hal Hanson - G
Two-Bits Homan - BB
Ted James - G
Wild Bill Kelly - BB
Tony Kostos - E
Marty Kostos - E
Al Maglisceau - T
Roger Mahoney - C
Harry Malcolm - T
Joey Maxwell - E
Ken Mercer - TB
Arnie Oehlrich - WB
Charley Rogers - WB
Johnny Thompson - G
Mike Wilson - WB

1929 Green Bay

Marion Ashmore - T
Bullet Baker - HB
Jim Bowdoin - G
Tiny Cahoon - T
Boob Darling - C
Lavie Dilweg - E
Red Dunn - BB
Jug Earp - C
Jack Evans - BB
Don Hill - HB
Cal Hubbard - T
Bill Kern - T
Eddie Kotal - HB
Curly Lambeau - TB
Verne Lewellen - TB
Cully Lidberg - FB
Hurdis McCrary - HB
Johnny (Blood) McNally - HB
Mike Michalske - G
Paul Minick - G
Bo Molenda - FB
Tom Nash - E
Dick O'Donnell - E
Claude Perry - T
Red Smith - BB
Howard Woodin - G
Billy Young - G
Dave Zuidmulder - TB

1929 Minneapolis

Joseph Chrape - G
Hal Erickson - HB
John Fahay - BB
Chief Franta - T
Al Gautsch - C
Ken Haycraft - E
Herb Joesting - FB
Fritz Lovin - G
Bob Lundell - E
LaDue Lurth - TB
Al Maeder - T
Tony Mehelich - G
Mally Nydall - TB
Ben Oas - C
Jack O'Brien - BB
Artie Sandberg - BB
Rube Ursella - HB
Chet Widerquist - T
Henry Willegale - BB
Lee Wilson - E
Lloyd Young - C

1929 NY Giants

Cliff Ashburn - G
Glenn Campbell - E
Lester Caywood - G
Tiny Feather - BB
Ray Flaherty - E
Benny Friedman - TB
Jack Hagerty - TB
Dosey Howard - G
Babe Lyon - T
Danny McMullen - G
Saul Mielziner - T
Hap Moran - BB
Lyle Munn - E
Mickey Murtagh - C
Steve Owen - T
Bill Owen - T
Tony Plansky - FB
Orian Rice - BB
Len Sedbrook - WB
Snitz Snyder - WB
Mule Wilson - FB
Joe Wostoupal - C

1929 Orange

Ralph Barkman - BB
Bob Beattie - T
Heinie Benkert - WB
Bill Clarkin - T
Ernie Cuneo - G

Jack Depler - T
Bob Dwyer - WB
Bill Feaster - T
Steve Hamas - FB
Ernie Hambacker - FB
Leon Johnson - E
Tex Kelly - T
Tom Kerrigan - G
Frank Kirkleski - TB
Paul Longua - E
John Lott - T
Ed Lynch - T
Jack McArthur - G
Felix McCormick - FB
Ted Mitchell - C
George Pease - BB
Andy Salata - G
Phil Scott - E
Johnny Tomaini - E
Charlie Van Horn - TB
Ray Wagner - E
Carl Waite - WB

1929 Providence

Jimmy Conzelman - BB
Jack Cronin - WB
Bill Cronin - E
Jack Fleischmann - G
Hec Garvey - G
Archie Golembeski - G
Al Hadden - FB
Duke Hanny - E
Norm Harvey - T
Perry Jackson - T
Lou Jennings - C
Jack McBride - FB
Warren McGuirk - T
Milt Rehnquist - C
Orland Smith - T
Jack Spellman - E
Hust Stockton - FB
Gibby Welch - BB
Pop Williams - WB
Abe Wilson - G
Wildcat Wilson - TB

1929 Staten Island

Frank Briante - TB
John Bunyan - G
Bob Dunn - C
Walt Godwin - G
Hinkey Haines - BB
Paul Kuczo - TB
Tom Leary - E
Tom Lomasney - E
Jack Lord - G
Hersh Martin - FB
Harry McGee - C
Bing Miller - T
Louie Pessolano - T
Mike Riordan - BB
Ollie Satenstein - G
Jack Shapiro - BB
Dave Skudin - G
Sammy Stein - E
Ken Strong - TB
Cy Williams - T
Ike Williams - HB
Doug Wycoff - FB

1930 Brooklyn

Mal Bleeker - G
Algy Clark - BB
Ed Comstock - G
Bernie Crowl - C
Ernie Cuneo - G
Hec Garvey - G
Fred Getz - E
Bob Gillson - G
Ben Greenberg - TB
Swede Hagberg - C
Horse Hagerty - FB
Hoot Haines - T
Al Jolley - T
Wild Bill Kelly - TB
Matt Kelsch - E
John Lott - T
Bob Mahan - E
Jack McArthur - C
Jack McBride - FB
Jim Miller - HB
Jim Mooney - T
Earl Plank - E
Ev Rowan - FB
Skippy Scheib - C
Jim Schuber - HB
Hal Stotsberry - T
Mike Stramiello - E
Rex Thomas - HB
Stumpy Thomason - DB
Johnny Tomaini - E
Chuck Weimer - TB
Stu Worden - T
Izzy Yablock - BB

1930 Chi. Bears

Stub Blackman - FB
Carl Brumbaugh - QB
Zuck Carlson - G
Hoot Drury - E
Bill Fleckenstein - E
Babe Frump - G

Gardie Grange - E
Red Grange - HB
Walter Holmer - HB
Luke Johnsos - E
Joe Lintzenich - HB
Link Lyman - T
Danny McMullen - G
Don Murry - T
Bronko Nagurski - FB
Dick Nesbitt - FB
Frank Pauly - T
Bert Pearson - C
Joe Savoldi - FB
Paul Schuette - G
Bill Senn - HB
Larry Steinbach - T
Joey Sternaman - QB
George Trafton - C
Laurie Walquist - HB

1930 Chi. Cardinals

Bullet Baker - BB
Bunny Belden - WB
Herb Blumer - G
George Bogue - WB
Bill Boyd - WB
Charlie Diehl - G
Mickey Erickson - C
Fred Failing - G
Mack Flenniken - FB
Lou Gordon - T
Phil Handler - G
Chuck Kassel - E
George Kenneally - E
Walt Kiesling - G
Mickey MacDonnell - WB
Howie Maple - WB
Ernie Nevers - FB
Joe Pappio - G
Clare Randolph - C
Cobb Rooney - BB
Gene Rose - WB
Duke Slater - T
Jess Tinsley - T
John Vesser - E
Buck Weaver - G
Jake Williams - T

1930 Frankford

Nate Barragar - C
Bull Behman - T
Eddie Bollinger - T
Bill Capps - T
Clyde Crabtree - BB
Wally Diehl - FB
Jack Ernst - TB
George Gibson - G
Royce Goodbread - WB
Eddie Halicki - TB
Hal Hanson - G
Charlie Havens - C
Two-Bits Homan - BB
Jack Hutton - E
Herb Joesting - FB
Potsy Jones - G
Tony Kostos - E
Harvey Long - T
Jerry Lunz - T
Roger Mahoney - G
Jack McArthur - T
Mally Nydall - BB
Tony Panaccion - T
Jim Pederson - WB
Art Pharmer - TB
Ken Provencial - E
Neil Rengel - FB
Ray Richards - T
Kelly Rodriguez - WB
Herman Seborg - WB
Johnny Shultz - WB
Gene Smith - G
Tony Steponovich - E
Cookie Tackwell - E
Bob Tanner - E
Clyde Van Sickle - G
Ed Wall - BB
Johnny Ward - T
Gordon Watkins - T
Lee Wilson - E
Ab Wright - TB

1930 Green Bay

Al Bloodgood - BB
Jim Bowdoin - G
Boob Darling - C
Lavie Dilweg - E
Red Dunn - BB
Jug Earp - C
Wuert Engelmann - HB
Paul Fitzgibbon - HB
Chief Franta - G
Duke Hanny - T
Ken Haycraft - E
Arnie Herber - BB
Cal Hubbard - T
Bill Kern - T
Verne Lewellen - TB
Cully Lidberg - FB
Hurdis McCrary - FB
Johnny (Blood) McNally - HB
Mike Michalske - G

Bo Molenda - FB
Tom Nash - E
Dick O'Donnell - E
Oran Pape - TB
Claude Perry - T
Ken Radick - E
Red Sleight - T
Mule Wilson - HB
Howard Woodin - G
Dave Zuidmulder - TB
Merle Zuver - G

1930 Minneapolis

Nate Barragar - C
Bill Capps - T
Jack Corcoran - C
Clyde Crabtree - HB
Hal Erickson - HB
Chief Franta - T
George Gibson - G
Royce Goodbread - HB
Eddie Halicki - TB
Hal Hanson - G
Ken Haycraft - E
Murrell Hogue - T
Herb Joesting - FB
Potsy Jones - G
Ike Kakela - C
Tony Kostos - E
Bob Lundell - E
Roger Mahoney - G
Verne Miller - HB
Ted Nemzek - T
Mally Nydall - TB
Oran Pape - HB
Jim Pederson - BB
Art Pharmer - TB
Kelly Rodriguez - HB
Herman Seborg - BB
Tony Steponovich - E
Cookie Tackwell - E
Hal Truesdell - T
Johnny Ward - T
Gordon Watkins - T
Lee Wilson - E
Lloyd Young - G

1930 NY Giants

Red Badgro - E
Dale Burnett - FB
Chris Cagle - TB
Glenn Campbell - E
Lester Caywood - G
Rudy Comstock - G
Tiny Feather - BB
Benny Friedman - TB
Butch Gibson - G
Len Grant - T
Jack Hagerty - TB
Hal Hilpert - E
Dosey Howard - G
Saul Mielziner - G
Hap Moran - TB
Mickey Murtagh - C
Steve Owen - T
Bill Owen - T
Len Sedbrook - WB
Dick Stahlman - T
Ossie Wiberg - FB
Mule Wilson - WB
Joe Wostoupal - C

1930 Newark

Teddy Andrulewicz - WB
Bob Beattie - T
Heinie Benkert - WB
George Bogue - FB
Nick Borelli - FB
Peter Bove - G
Phil Brennan - E
Frank Briante - TB
Stu Clancy - FB
Bill Connor - G
Sam Cordovano - G
Joe Davidson - C
John Dibb - T
Bud Ellor - G
Bill Feaster - T
Bernie Finn - BB
Paul Frank - BB
Les Grace - E
Ken Hauser - BB
Bruce Jones - G
Tom Kerrigan - G
Frank Kirkleski - TB
John Law - T
Tom Leary - E
Paul Liston - G
Paul Longua - E
Tony Manfreda - WB
Hersh Martin - FB
Jack McArthur - G
Felix McCormick - FB
Harry McGee - C
Ted Mitchell - C
Jim Mooney - T
Harry Myles - E
Andy Salata - G
Sam Sebo - FB
Don Smith - G
Red Smith - BB
Jimmy Tays - FB
Johnny Tomaini - E

Ray Wagner - E
Carl Waite - WB
Dutch Webber - E
Ernie Woerner - T

1930 Portsmouth

Walt Ambrose - G
Chuck Bennett - WB
Chuck Braidwood - E
Richard Brown - C
Koester Christensen - E
Ebby DeWeese - G
Jap Douds - T
Byron Eby - TB
Lee Fenner - E
Bill Fleckenstein - E
Bill Glassgow - TB
Al Graham - G
Aaron Grant - C
Hal Griffen - T
Duke Hanny - T
Dud Harris - T
George Hastings - T
Lou Jennings - E
Spider Johnson - T
Red Joseph - E
Cy Kahl - BB
Tiny Lewis - FB
Father Lumpkin - BB
Babe Lyon - T
Emil Mayer - E
Chief McLain - FB
Ernie Meyer - G
Ray Novotny - TB
Frosty Peters - TB
Carroll Ringwalt - G
Fred Roberts - G
Sod Ryan - T
Vin Schleusner - T
Ron Shearer - T
Gene Smith - C
Buck Weaver - G
Bull Wesley - C

1930 Providence

Jack Cronin - WB
Jap Douds - T
Bud Edwards - WB
Herb Eschbach - C
Weldon Gentry - G
Al Graham - G
Al Hadden - FB
Tony Holm - TB
Perry Jackson - T
Joe Kozlowsky - T
Ted Kucharski - E
Tony Latone - FB
Jack McArthur - C
Warren McGuirk - T
Butch Meeker - BB
Curly Oden - BB
Frosty Peters - TB
Frank Racis - G
Milt Rehnquist - G
Al Rose - E
Ray Smith - C
Gustave Sonnenberg - T
Jack Spellman - E
Dutch Webber - E
Pop Williams - WB
Herm Young - E

1930 Staten Island

Julie Archoska - E
Fred Brown - G
Ralph Buckley - BB
John Bunyan - G
John Demmy - T
Bernie Finn - BB
Jim Fitzgerald - C
Beryl Follet - HB
Willie Halpern - G
Wilbur Henry - G
Harry Kloppenberg - E
Ed Lawrence - HB
Bob Lundell - E
Bing Miller - T
Dave Myers - G
Jim Nicely - T
Herb Rapp - C
Ollie Satenstein - G
Snitz Snyder - BB
Sammy Stein - E
Ken Strong - FB
Jimmy Tays - HB
Bill Wexler - C
Firpo Wilcox - T
Cy Williams - T
Mule Wilson - HB
Doug Wycoff - TB

1931 Brooklyn

Frank Abruzzino - BB
Marger Apsit - WB
Art Bultman - C
Tommy Dowler - WB
Bill Fleckenstein - G
Ted Fulton - G
Bob Gillson - G
Lou Gordon - T
Hoot Haines - T
Swede Hanson - FB

Marv Jonas - G
Frank Kirkleski - TB
Harry Kloppenberg - E
Lou Lubratovich - T
Jack McBride - TB
Saul Mielziner - C
Warner Mizell - FB
Jim Mooney - T
Dave Myers - G
Jerry Nemecek - E
Dick O'Donnell - E
Claude Perry - T
Frosty Peters - BB
Ken Radick - G
Johnny Scalzi - BB
Bill Senn - WB
Mike Stramiello - E
Rex Thomas - WB
Stumpy Thomason - DB
Johnny Tomaini - E
Joe Vance - WB
Ray Wagner - E
Gordon Watkins - T
Izzy Yablock - BB

1931 Chi. Bears

Carl Brumbaugh - QB
Bill Buckler - G
Lloyd Burdick - T
Zuck Carlson - G
Hoot Drury - E
Bud Edwards - HB
Latham Flanagan - E
Paul Franklin - FB
Gardie Grange - E
Red Grange - HB
Jesse Hibbs - T
Leo Jensvold - HB
Herb Joesting - FB
Luke Johnsos - E
Eddie Kawal - C
Joe Lintzenich - HB
Link Lyman - T
Babe Lyon - T
Gus Mastrogany - E
Danny McMullen - G
Keith Molesworth - HB
Don Murry - T
Denny Myers - G
Bronko Nagurski - FB
Dick Nesbitt - HB
Bert Pearson - C
Paul Schuette - G
Bill Senn - HB
Larry Steinbach - T
Cookie Tackwell - T
George Trafton - C
Laurie Walquist - QB

1931 Chi. Cardinals

Bunny Belden - WB
Bill Boyd - WB
Lester Caywood - G
Tom Cobb - T
Milan Creighton - E
Charlie Diehl - G
Mickey Erickson - C
Latham Flanagan - E
Bill Glassgow - WB
Lou Gordon - T
Phil Handler - G
Irv Hill - BB
Walter Holmer - WB
Chuck Kassel - E
Walt Kiesling - G
Ike Mahoney - BB
Les Malloy - BB
Frank McNally - C
Ernie Nevers - FB
George Rogge - E
Gene Rose - WB
Jesse Shaw - G
Duke Slater - T
Larry Steinbach - T
Jess Tinsley - T
John Vesser - E
Jake Williams - T

1931 Cleveland

Chuck Braidwood - E
Algy Clark - HB
Al Cornsweet - FB
Hank Critchfield - C
David Cullen - G
Fred Danziger - FB
Doc Elliott - FB
Mike Gregory - G
Hoot Herrin - C
John Hurley - E
Merle Hutson - G
Leo Jensvold - HB
Ernie Jessen - T
Al Jolley - T
Red Joseph - E
Howie Kriss - HB
Buck Lamme - E
Biff Lee - G
Franklin Lewis - FB
Tiny Lewis - FB
Babe Lyon - T
Stu MacMillan - C
Dave Mishel - QB
George Munday - T

Al Nesser - E
Ray Novotny - HB
Carl Pignatelli - HB
Don Ridler - T
Jim Tarr - E
Otto Vokaty - FB
Dale Waters - E
Chuck Weimer - HB
Drip Wilson - C
Hoge Workman - QB

1931 Frankford

Marger Apsit - BB
Nate Barragar - C
Bull Behman - T
Justin Brumbaugh - TB
Bill Fleckenstein - E
Herb Joesting - FB
Potsy Jones - G
Mort Kaer - BB
Art Koeninger - T
Tony Kostos - E
Tom Leary - E
Mickey MacDonnell - WB
Jim Magner - TB
Warner Mizell - WB
Mally Nydall - TB
Jim Pederson - WB
Art Pharmer - FB
Frank Racis - T
Carroll Ringwalt - C
Herman Seborg - G
Cookie Tackwell - T
Lee Wilson - E

1931 Green Bay

Frank Baker - E
Nate Barragar - C
Jim Bowdoin - G
Hank Bruder - TB
Rudy Comstock - G
Boob Darling - C
Bill Davenport - HB
Lavie Dilweg - E
Waldo Don Carlos - C
Red Dunn - BB
Jug Earp - C
Wuert Engelmann - HB
Paul Fitzgibbon - BB
Milt Gantenbein - E
Roger Grove - BB
Arnie Herber - TB
Cal Hubbard - T
Ray Jenison - T
Swede Johnston - FB
Verne Lewellen - TB
Hurdis McCrary - FB
Johnny (Blood) McNally - HB
Mike Michalske - G
Bo Molenda - FB
Tom Nash - E
Claude Perry - T
Ken Radick - E
Russ Saunders - FB
Red Sleight - T
Dick Stahlman - T
Mule Wilson - TB
Howard Woodin - G
Dave Zuidmulder - TB

1931 NY Giants

Corrie Artman - T
Red Badgro - E
Marion Broadstone - T
Ted Bucklin - BB
Dale Burnett - WB
Chris Cagle - FB
Glenn Campbell - E
Lester Caywood - G
Tiny Feather - BB
Ray Flaherty - E
Mack Flenniken - TB
Benny Friedman - TB
Butch Gibson - G
Len Grant - T
Mel Hein - C
Dutch Kitzmiller - FB
Hap Moran - WB
George Munday - T
Mickey Murtagh - C
Steve Owen - T
Bill Owen - T
Milt Rehnquist - G
Harvey Sark - G
Ray Schwab - BB
Len Sedbrook - FB
Red Smith - TB
Sammy Stein - E
Doug Wycoff - BB

1931 Portsmouth

Gene Alford - WB
Bob Armstrong - G
Chuck Bennett - WB
Maury Bodenger - G
John Cavosie - BB
George Christensen - T
Dutch Clark - TB
Jap Douds - T
Harry Ebding - E

Ox Emerson - G
George Hastings - T
Tony Holm - FB
Cy Kahl - BB
Biff Lee - G
Louie Long - E
Father Lumpkin - BB
Bill McKalip - E
Chief McLain - FB
Dutch Miller - C
Buster Mitchell - E
Les Peterson - E
Glenn Presnell - TB
Clare Randolph - C
Fred Roberts - G
Vin Schleusner - T
Elmer Schwartz - FB
Deck Shelley - WB
Stud Stennett - WB
John Wager - C
Dale Waters - T

1931 Providence

Sky August - TB
Fred DaGata - FB
Bud Edwards - FB
Herb Eschbach - C
Weldon Gentry - G
Royce Goodbread - TB
Al Graham - G
Tex Irvin - T
Jack McArthur - T
Butch Meeker - BB
Curly Oden - BB
Oran Pape - WB
Lew Pope - TB
George Pyne - T
Milt Rehnquist - G
Al Rose - E
Joe Schein - T
Deck Shelley - TB
Ray Smith - C
Alec Sofish - G
Jack Spellman - E
Herb Titmas - BB
Pop Williams - WB
Lee Woodruff - FB

1931 Staten Island

Bullet Baker - BB
Bob Barabee - E
Stu Clancy - HB
Ed Comstock - T
Irv Constantine - HB
Cookie Cunningham - E
John Demmy - T
Tiny Feather - HB
Jim Fitzgerald - C
Beryl Follet - TB
Hec Garvey - G
Hoot Haines - T
Hinkey Haines - BB
Les Hart - BB
Al Kanya - T
Jim Laird - G
Charley Marshall - E
Chief McLain - FB
Bing Miller - T
Henry Obst - G
Doc Parkinson - FB
Herb Rapp - C
Ollie Satenstein - G
Ken Strong - TB
Erk Taylor - G
Izzy Yablock - BB

1932 Boston

Corrie Artman - T
Cliff Battles - TB
Algy Clark - BB
Paul Collins - E
Turk Edwards - T
Mickey Erickson - C
Nip Felber - E
Honolulu Hughes - BB
George Hurley - G
George Kenneally - E
Joe Kresky - G
Jim MacMurdo - T
Jim Musick - FB
Curly Oden - BB
Oran Pape - TB
Russ Peterson - T
Ernie Pinckert - WB
Tony Plansky - BB
Milt Rehnquist - G
Jack Roberts - FB
Reggie Rust - TB
Kermit Schmidt - E
Paul Schuette - G
Tony Siano - C
Jack Spellman - E
Dale Waters - T
Ed Westfall - TB
Basil Wilkerson - E
Lee Woodruff - WB

1932 Brooklyn

John Ambrose - C
Jim Bowdoin - G
John Bunyan - G
Lester Caywood - G

Jerry Cronin - E
Jess Eberdt - C
Harold Ely - T
Benny Friedman - TB
Ted Fulton - G
Donn Greenshields - T
Jack Grossman - FB
Buck Halperin - TB
Herman Hickman - G
Bruce Jones - G
Bull Karcis - BB
Lou Lubratovich - T
Babe Lyon - T
Jack McBride - TB
Frank McNeil - E
Saul Mielziner - C
Ray Novotny - TB
Bill Raffel - E
Paul Riblett - E
Ev Rowan - E
Ollie Sansen - HB
Sammy Stein - E
Mike Stramiello - E
Stumpy Thomason - DB
Bud Toscani - HB
Ossie Wiberg - HB
Pop Williams - HB
Cy Williams - T
Stu Worden - G

1932 Chi. Bears

Gil Bergerson - G
Carl Brumbaugh - QB
Bill Buckler - G
Lloyd Burdick - T
Zuck Carlson - G
George Corbett - HB
Al Culver - T
John Doehring - HB
Harold Ely - T
Tiny Engebretsen - T
Paul Franklin - FB
Red Grange - HB
Bill Hewitt - E
Herb Joesting - FB
Luke Johnsos - E
Joe Kopcha - G
Bernie Leahy - HB
Ookie Miller - C
Keith Molesworth - QB
Al Moore - HB
Don Murry - T
Bronko Nagurski - FB
Dick Nesbitt - HB
Bert Pearson - C
Jim Pederson - HB
Paul Schuette - G
Johnny Sisk - HB
Cookie Tackwell - E
George Trafton - C

1932 Chi. Cardinals

Chuck Braidwood - E
Joe Crakes - E
Milan Creighton - E
Jap Douds - T
Mickey Erickson - C
Bernie Finn - BB
Lou Gordon - T
Al Graham - G
Phil Handler - G
Irv Hill - FB
Tony Holm - FB
Walter Holmer - TB
Chuck Kassel - E
Walt Kiesling - G
Doc Ledbetter - FB
Joe Lillard - TB
Les Malloy - BB
Abe Martin - WB
Frank McNally - C
Bucky Moore - WB
Tim Moynihan - C
Frosty Peters - BB
Ed Risk - FB
George Rogge - E
Gene Rose - WB
Carmen Scardine - WB
Elmer Schwartz - FB
Deck Shelley - TB
Butch Simas - BB
Larry Steinbach - G
Stud Stennett - TB
Jess Tinsley - T
Bud Toscani - WB
Ken Wendt - G
Jake Williams - T

1932 Green Bay

Marger Apsit - BB
Nate Barragar - C
Hank Bruder - HB
Art Bultman - C
Rudy Comstock - G
Al Culver - T
Lavie Dilweg - E
Jug Earp - T
Wuert Engelmann - HB
Paul Fitzgibbon - BB
Milt Gantenbein - E
Roger Grove - BB
Arnie Herber - TB
Clarke Hinkle - FB

Cal Hubbard - T
Verne Lewellen - TB
Hurdis McCrary - FB
Johnny (Blood) McNally - HB
Mike Michalske - G
Bo Molenda - FB
Tom Nash - E
Harry O'Boyle - BB
Claude Perry - T
Les Peterson - E
Al Rose - E
Deck Shelley - HB
Dick Stahlman - T
Clyde Van Sickle - G
Joe Zeller - G

1932 NY Giants

Red Badgro - E
Jim Bowdoin - G
Dale Burnett - WB
Chris Cagle - FB
Glenn Campbell - E
Lester Caywood - G
Stu Clancy - FB
Maury Dubofsky - G
Tiny Feather - FB
Ray Flaherty - E
Butch Gibson - G
Len Grant - T
Jack Hagerty - TB
Mel Hein - C
Tex Irvin - T
Potsy Jones - G
Shipwreck Kelly - TB
Jack McBride - TB
Bo Molenda - BB
Hap Moran - TB
Lee Mulleneaux - BB
George Munday - T
Mickey Murtagh - C
Bill Owen - T
Dick Powell - E
Otto Vokaty - BB
Hoge Workman - BB

1932 Portsmouth

Gene Alford - WB
Bob Armstrong - T
Maury Bodenger - G
John Cavosie - FB
George Christensen - T
Dutch Clark - TB
Ray Davis - C
Harry Ebding - E
Ox Emerson - G
Hal Griffen - C
Ace Gutowsky - FB
Father Lumpkin - BB
Bill McKalip - E
Danny McMullen - G
Buster Mitchell - E
Glenn Presnell - TB
Clare Randolph - C
Am Rascher - T
Dave Ribble - T
Fred Roberts - G
John Wager - G
Mule Wilson - WB

1932 Staten Island

John Bunyan - G
Bob Campiglio - BB
Stu Clancy - TB
Rick Concannon - T
George Demas - G
Bernie Finn - BB
Dick Frahm - WB
Harry Fry - E
Rosie Grant - G
Swede Hanson - TB
Grassy Hinton - BB
Marne Intrieri - G
Jim Kamp - T
Al Kanya - T
Art Koeninger - C
Doc Ledbetter - FB
Charley Marshall - E
Les Maynard - E
Harry McGee - G
Jack Norris - E
Oran Pape - TB
Les Peterson - E
Leo Raskowski - T
Vic Reuter - C
Jack Roberts - FB
Ollie Satenstein - G
Art Schiebel - T
Ray Schwab - E
Mike Stramiello - E
Ken Strong - TB
Al Teeter - E
Basil Wilkerson - T
Stu Wilson - WB
Doug Wycoff - FB

1933 Boston

Marger Apsit - BB
Cliff Battles - WB
Bob Campiglio - WB
Harold Cherne - T
Paul Collins - E
Orien Crow - C
Turk Edwards - T
Ike Frankian - E
Irv Hill - WB
Steve Hokuf - BB
Walter Holmer - FB
Roy Horstmann - FB
George Hurley - G
Marne Intrieri - T
Larry Johnson - C
Jim Kamp - G
Benny LaPresta - BB
Jim MacMurdo - G
Jim Musick - FB
Ernie Pinckert - WB
Jack Riley - T
John Scafide - T
Dick Smith - C
Mike Steponovich - G
David Ward - E
Dale Waters - G
Rabbit Weller - WB
Ed Westfall - TB

1933 Brooklyn

Chris Cagle - TB
George Chalmers - C
Ben Douglas - WB
Harold Ely - T
Dick Fishel - BB
Benny Friedman - TB
Donn Greenshields - T
Herman Hickman - G
Bruce Jones - G
Bull Karcis - BB
Shipwreck Kelly - WB
Harry Kloppenberg - E
Lou Lubratovich - T
John Lyons - E
Saul Mielziner - T
Doc Morrison - C
Tom Nash - E
Les Peterson - E
Leo Raskowski - T
Van Rayburn - E
Hughie Rhea - G
Paul Riblett - E
Dick Richards - WB
Ollie Sansen - WB
Stumpy Thomason
Stu Worden - G
Ralph Wright - T

1933 Chi. Bears

Gil Bergerson - G
Carl Brumbaugh - QB
Bill Buckler - G
Zuck Carlson - G
George Corbett - HB
John Doehring - HB
Paul Franklin - FB
Red Grange - HB
Bill Hewitt - E
Luke Johnsos - E
Bill Karr - E
Joe Kopcha - G
Link Lyman - T
Jack Manders - FB
Ookie Miller - C
Keith Molesworth - QB
George Musso - T
Bronko Nagurski - FB
Dick Nesbitt - HB
Bert Pearson - C
Ray Richards - T
Gene Ronzani - HB
Johnny Sisk - HB
Dick Smith - C
Dick Stahlman - T
Cookie Tackwell - E
Joe Zeller - G

1933 Chi. Cardinals

Jim Bausch - FB
Chuck Bennett - BB
Gil Bergerson - G
Herb Blumer - G
Milan Creighton - E
Tiny Engebretsen - G
Lou Gordon - T
Al Graham - G
Phil Handler - G
Cliff Hansen - TB
Curly Hinchman - FB
Swede Johnston
Chuck Kassel - E
Walt Kiesling - G
Mike Koken - TB
Roddy Lamb - BB
Doc Ledbetter - FB
Joe Lillard - TB
Les Malloy - BB
Frank McNally - C
Hal Moe - WB
Tim Moynihan - C
Dick Nesbitt - FB
Dave Nisbet - E
Dave Ribble - G
George Rogge - E
Butch Simas - BB
Larry Steinbach - T
Jess Tinsley - T
Howie Tipton
Otto Vokaty - FB
Jake Williams - T
Tommy Yarr - C

1933 Cincinnati

Frank Abruzzino - C
Jim Bausch - TB
Mil Berner - C
Tom Blondin - G
Chuck Braidwood - E
Lloyd Burdick - T
John Burleson - T
Lester Caywood - G
Algy Clark - BB
Red Corzine - FB
Joe Crakes - E
Sonny Doell - T
Leo Draveling - T
Chief Elkins - WB
Rosie Grant - G
Hal Hilpert - E
Biff Lee - G
Gil LeFebvre - TB
Jim Mooney - E
Don Moses - BB
Lee Mulleneaux - LB
George Munday - T
Mike Palm - WB
Lew Pope - TB
Dick Powell - E
John Rogers - C
Kermit Schmidt - E
Bill Senn - TB
Seaman Squyres - TB
Cookie Tackwell - E
Ossie Wiberg - FB
Blake Workman - TB

1933 Green Bay

Larry Bettencourt - C
Hank Bruder - TB
Art Bultman - C
Rudy Comstock - G
Lavie Dilweg - E
Wuert Engelmann
Lon Evans - G
Milt Gantenbein - E
Buckets Goldenberg - FB
Norm Greeney - G
Roger Grove - BB
Arnie Herber - TB
Clarke Hinkle - FB
Cal Hubbard - T
Joe Kurth - T
Hurdis McCrary - FB
Johnny (Blood) McNally - HB
Mike Michalske - G
Bob Monnett - TB
Buster Mott - HB
Claude Perry - T
Jess Quatse - T
Al Rose - E
Al Sarafiny - C
Ben H. Smith - E
Clyde Van Sickle - G
Paul Young - C

1933 NY Giants

Red Badgro - E
Dale Burnett - WB
Glenn Campbell - E
John Cannella - G
Stu Clancy - TB
Tiny Feather
Ray Flaherty - E
Butch Gibson - G
Len Grant - T
Mel Hein - C
Tex Irvin - T
Potsy Jones - G
Max Krause - BB
Dick Marsh - G
Jack McBride - FB
Bo Molenda - BB
Hap Moran - WB
Bill Morgan - T
Harry Newman - TB
Steve Owen - G
Bill Owen - T
Hank Reese - G
Kink Richards - FB
Tony Rovinski - E
Reb Russell - BB
Ollie Satenstein - G
Ken Strong - FB
Joe Zapustas - E
Jim Zyntell - G

1933 Philadelphia

Howie Auer - T
Joe Carpe - T
Joe Carter - E
Paul Cuba - T
Red Davis - TB
Nip Felber - E
Dick Fencl - E
Bob Gonya - T
Swede Hanson - FB
George Kenneally - E
Red Kirkman - BB
Art Koeninger - C
Joe Kresky - G
Rick Lackman - HB
Porter Lainhart - BB
Milt Leathers - G
Roy Lechthaler - G
Tex Leyendecker - T
John Lipski - C
Harry O'Boyle - BB
Henry Obst - G
Nick Prisco - TB
Jack Roberts - HB
Ev Rowan - E
Reb Russell - HB
Ray Smith - C
Dick Smith - C
Larry Steinbach - T
Dick Thornton - BB
Guy Turnbow - T
Jodie Whire - FB
Diddie Willson - G
Lee Woodruff
Jim Zyntell - G

1933 Pittsburgh

Corrie Artman - T
Angie Brovelli - TB
John Burleson - G
James Clark - HB
Sam Cooper - T
Larry Critchfield - G
Ted Dailey - E
Nick DeCarbo - G
Jap Douds - T
Tiny Engebretsen - T
Tony Holm - FB
Walter Holmer - TB
Frank Hood - HB
Clarence Janecek - G
Mose Kelsch - HB
Ray Kemp - T
Marty Kottler
Mose Lantz - C
Jim Letsinger - G
Bucky Moore - HB
Paul Moss - E
Cap Oehler - C
Jess Quatse - T
Leo Raskowski - T
Don Rhodes - T
Gil Robinson - E
Elmer Schwartz
George Shaffer - BB
Bill Sortet - E
Bill Tanguay - TB
Ray Tesser - E
Harp Vaughan - TB
Ed Westfall - TB
Tommy Whelan - TB

1933 Portsmouth

Gene Alford - WB
Maury Bodenger - G
Ben Boswell - T
Jim Bowdoin - G
John Burleson - T
Ernie Caddel - WB
John Cavosie - FB
George Christensen - T
Ray Davis - G
Red Davis - TB
Harry Ebding - E
Earl Elser - T
Ox Emerson - G
Ace Gutowsky - FB
Ramey Hunter - E
Father Lumpkin - BB
Buster Mitchell - T
Glenn Presnell - TB
Clare Randolph - C
Elmer Schaake - FB
John Schneller - E
Harry Thayer - T
John Wager - C
Mule Wilson - WB

1934 Boston

Arnie Arenz - BB
Cliff Battles - WB
Frank Bausch - C
Ben Boswell - T
Paul Collins - E
Rick Concannon - G
Orien Crow - C
Turk Edwards - T
Swede Ellstrom - HB
Steve Hokuf - BB
Marne Intrieri - G
Larry Johnson - E
Chuck Malone - E
Hal McPhail - FB
Gail O'Brien - T
Les Olsson - G
Ernie Pinckert
Pug Rentner - WB
Phil Sarboe - BB
Steve Sinko - T
Flavio Tosi - E
Frank Walton - G
Ted Wright - WB
Doug Wycoff - FB

1934 Brooklyn

Gump Ariail - E
Wayland Becker - E
Jim Bowdoin - G
Chuck Brodnicki - G
Chris Cagle - TB
Doc Cronkhite - E
George Demas - G
Harold Ely - T
Tiny Engebretsen - T
Benny Friedman - TB
Jack Grossman - WB
Herman Hickman - G
Joe Hugret - E
Bruce Jones - T
Bull Karcis - BB
Shipwreck Kelly - TB
Ralph Kercheval - WB
Harry Kloppenberg - E
Lou Lubratovich - T
Saul Mielzner - T
Cliff Montgomery - TB
Doc Morrison - C
Tom Nash - E
Dick Nesbitt - BB
Phil Peterson - E
Paul Riblett - E
Ollie Sansen - WB
Tony Siano - C
Mike Stramiello - E
Stumpy Thomason - BB
Stu Worden - G

1934 Chi. Bears

Wayland Becker - E
Carl Brumbaugh - QB
Art Buss - T
Zuck Carlson - G
George Corbett - HB
John Doehring - HB
Beattie Feathers - HB
Red Grange - HB
Bill Hewitt - E
Luke Johnsos - E
Bill Karr - E
Eddie Kawal - C
Walt Kiesling - G
Joe Kopcha - G
Link Lyman - T
Jack Manders - FB
Bernie Masterson - QB
Ookie Miller - C
Keith Molesworth - HB
George Musso - T
Bronko Nagurski - FB
Bert Pearson - G
Gene Ronzani - HB
Ted Rosequist - T
Johnny Sisk - HB
Joe Zeller - G
Vince Zizak - G

1934 Chi. Cardinals

Dave Cook - WB
Milan Creighton - E
Bree Cuppoletti - G
Herb Duggins - E
Harry Field - T
Lou Gordon - T
Frank Greene - BB
Homer Griffith - TB
Phil Handler - G
Curly Hinchman - WB
Roy Horstmann - FB
Bernie Hughes - C
Ted Isaacson - T
Joe Krejci - E
Frank McNally - C
Pete Mehringer - T
Mike Mikulak - FB
Tom Murphy - BB
Bob Neuman - E
Paul Pardonner - BB
Doug Russell - TB
Phil Sarboe - BB
Paul Shenefelt - T
Bill Smith - E
Howie Tipton - G
Bill Volok - G

1934 Cincinnati

Gene Alford - WB
Gump Ariail - E
Ed Aspatore - T
Tom Bushby - WB
Lester Caywood - G
Algy Clark - BB
Red Corzine - FB
Earl Elser - T
Tiny Feather - WB
Rosie Grant - G
Homer Hanson - G
Foster Howell - T
Russ Lay - G
Biff Lee - G
Gil LeFebvre - TB
Bill Lewis - BB
Tal Maples - C
Jim Mooney - E
Cliff Moore - WB
Buster Mott - BB
Lee Mulleneaux
George Munday - T
Bill Parriott - FB
Lew Pope - TB
Ratterman - HB
John Rogers - C
Harvey Sark - G
Pete Saumer - TB
Benny Sohn - WB
Norris Steverson - TB
Cookie Tackwell - E
Otto Vokaty - FB
Cole Wilging - E
Basil Wilkerson - E
Charlie Zunker - T

1934 Detroit

Chuck Bernard - C
Maury Bodenger - G
Ernie Caddel - WB
Frank Christensen - FB
George Christensen - T
Dutch Clark - TB
Harry Ebding - E
Bob Emerick - T
Ox Emerson - G
Ace Gutowsky - FB
Curly Hinchman - BB
Tom Hupke - G
Jack Johnson - T
Sam Knox - T
Russ Lay - G
Father Lumpkin - BB
Bill McKalip - E
Bill McWilliams - WB
Buster Mitchell - E
Glenn Presnell - TB
Clare Randolph - C
Ray Richards - G
Bob Rowe - BB
John Schneller - E

1934 Green Bay

Nate Barragar - C
Hank Bruder - BB
Art Bultman - C
Frank Butler - C
Cy Casper - TB
Lavie Dilweg - E
Tiny Engebretsen - G
Lon Evans - T
Milt Gantenbein - E
Buckets Goldenberg - FB
Roger Grove - DB
Arnie Herber - TB
Clarke Hinkle - FB
Swede Johnston
Bob Jones - G
Bud Jorgensen - T
Joe Kurth - T
Joe Laws - HB
Mike Michalske - G
Bob Monnett - TB
Al Norgard - E
Claude Perry - T
Les Peterson - E
Al Rose - E
Ade Schwammel - T
Champ Seibold - G
Earl Witte - BB
Harry Wunsch - G

1934 NY Giants

Red Badgro - E
Bob Bellinger - G
Knuckles Boyle - T
Dale Burnett - WB
John Cannella - G
Stu Clancy - WB
Ed Danowski - TB
Johnny Dell Isola - C
Ray Flaherty - E
Ike Frankian - E
Butch Gibson - G
Len Grant - T
Mel Hein - C
Tex Irvin - T
Potsy Jones - G
Max Krause - BB
Jack McBride - TB
Bo Molenda - BB
Bill Morgan - T
Harry Newman - TB
John Norby - WB
Bill Owen - T
Hank Reese - G
Kink Richards - FB
Babe Scheuer - T
Wee Willie Smith - DB
Harry Stafford - WB
Ken Strong - FB

1934 Philadelphia

Dan Barnhart - TB
Joe Carter - E
Algy Clark - BB
Paul Cuba - T
Jack Dempsey - T
Swede Ellstrom - HB
Bob Gonya - T
Len Gudd - E
Chuck Hajek - C
Swede Hanson - FB
Lorne Johnson - FB
George Kavel - HB
George Kenneally - E
Red Kirkman - BB
Jack Knapper - HB
Joe Kresky - G
Rick Lackman - TB
Jim Leonard - BB
John Lipski - C
Jim MacMurdo - T
Ed Matesic - TB
Barnes Milam - G
John Norby - HB
Joe Pilconis - E
Phil Poth - G
Jack Roberts - HB
Ed Storm - FB
Guy Turnbow - T
Reds Weiner - FB
Diddie Willson - G
Vince Zizak - T
Jim Zyntell - G

1934 Pittsburgh

Angie Brovelli - DB
Ben Ciccone - C
James Clark - FB
Jack Dempsey - T
Jap Douds - G
Norm Greeney - G
Warren Heller - TB
George Kavel - HB
Mose Kelsch - FB
Zvonimir Kvaternik - G
Jim Levey - HB
Basilio Marchi - G
Harry Marker - BB
Johnny (Blood) McNally - HB
Buster Mott - BB
Armand Nicolai - T
Cap Oehler - C
Bill Potts - HB
Jess Quatse - T
Alex Rado - HB
Peter Rajkovich - FB
Dave Ribble - G
Jack Roberts - FB
Pete Saumer - FB
Joe Skladany - E
Ben H. Smith - E
Bull Snyder - G
Bill Sortet - E
Ray Tesser - E
Harp Vaughan - TB
Henry Weinberg - G
Silvio Zaninelli - BB

1934 St. Louis

Gene Alford - WB
Jaby Andrews - TB
Cy Casper - WB
Red Corzine - FB
Charlie Diehl - T
Earl Elser - T
Mack Gladden - E
Swede Johnston - FB
Benny LaPresta - BB
Russ Lay - G
Babe Lyon - T
Len McGirl - G
Charlie McLaughlin - TB
Russ McLeod - C
Bill Montgomery - G
Paul Moss - E
Lee Mulleneaux
George Munday - T
John Norby - WB
Manny Rapp - TB
Homer Reynolds - G
George Rogge - E
Sandy Sandberg - T
Bill Senn - TB
Hal Weldin - C
Blake Workman - BB

1935 Boston

Vic Baltzell - WB
Jim Barber - T
Cliff Battles - TB
Frank Bausch - C
Paul Collins - E
Rick Concannon - G
Turk Edwards - T
Dick Frahm - WB
Herman Gundlach - G
Steve Hokuf - FB
Larry Johnson - LB
Eddie Kahn - G
Chuck Malone - E
Hal McPhail - FB
Jim Moran - G
Jim Musick - FB
Doug Nott - TB
Gail O'Brien - T
Les Olsson - G
Ernie Pinckert - WB
Pug Rentner - TB
Mike Sebastian - HB
Bill Shepherd - TB
Larry Siemering - C
Steve Sinko - T

Flavio Tosi - E
Heinie Weisenbaugh - BB
Ted Wright - BB

1935 Brooklyn

Wayland Becker - E
Gil Bergerson - G
Win Croft - G
Alex Eagle - T
Red Franklin - TB
Ray Fuqua - E
Jack Grossman - TB
Henry Hayduk - G
Carl Heldt - T
Jay Hornbeak - BB
Bud Hubbard - E
Bull Karcis - FB
Ralph Kercheval - HB
Bo Kirkland - G
Stan Kostka - FB
Bill Lee - T
Lou Lubratovich - T
Father Lumpkin - BB
Walt McDonald - C
John Norby - BB
Cap Oehler - C
Paul Riblett - E
Jack Robinson - T
Ollie Sansen - HB
Frank Stojack - G
Stumpy Thomason - BB
Wilbur White - TB
Ted Wright - BB

1935 Chi. Bears

Art Buss - T
Zuck Carlson - G
George Corbett - QB
Fred Crawford - E
Bob Dunlap - QB
Beattie Feathers - HB
George Grosvenor - HB
Bill Hewitt - E
Luke Johnsos - E
Bill Karr - E
Eddie Kawal - C
Joe Kopcha - G
Jack Manders - FB
Bernie Masterson - QB
Forrest McPherson - G
Ookie Miller - C
Dub Miller - T
Keith Molesworth - HB
George Musso - T
Bronko Nagurski - FB
Red Pollock - HB
Ray Richards - G
Gene Ronzani - FB
Ted Rosequist - T
Johnny Sisk - HB
Frank Sullivan - C
Milt Trost - T
Buzz Wetzel - FB
Joe Zeller - G

1935 Chi. Cardinals

Gil Berry - TB
Tony Blazine - T
Dave Cook - WB
Milan Creighton - E
Bree Cuppoletti - G
Versil Deskin - E
Mule Dowell - FB
Harry Field - T
Lou Gordon - T
Phil Handler - G
Homer Hanson - G
Bernie Hughes - C
Ted Isaacson - T
Pete Mehringer - G
Mike Mikulak - FB
Jim Mooney - E
Bob Neuman - E
Al Nichelini - WB
Hal Pangle - BB
Paul Pardonner - BB
Bert Pearson - C
Ike Peterson - TB
Doug Russell - TB
Phil Sarboe - BB
Bill Smith - E
Howie Tipton - G
Bill Volok - G
Billy Wilson - E

1935 Detroit

Steve Banas - BB
Ernie Caddel - WB
Frank Christensen - BB
George Christensen - T
Dutch Clark - TB
Harry Ebding - E
Ox Emerson - G
Roy Gagnon - G
Ace Gutowsky - FB
Tom Hupke - G
Jack Johnson - T
Tony Kaska - FB
Ed Klewicki - E
Sam Knox - G
Gil LeFebvre - WB
Buster Mitchell - E
Regis Monahan - G
Butch Morse - E
Doug Nott - TB
Bill O'Neill - WB
Buddy Parker - FB
Glenn Presnell - TB
Clare Randolph - C
Aldo Richins - WB
John Schneller - E
Bill Shepherd - FB
Red Stacy - T
Jim Steen - T
Pug Vaughan - TB
Elmer Ward - C

1935 Green Bay

Nate Barragar - C
Hank Bruder - BB
Frank Butler - C
Tiny Engebretsen - G
Lon Evans - G
Milt Gantenbein - E
Buckets Goldenberg - BB
Roger Grove - HB
Arnie Herber - TB
Clarke Hinkle - FB
Cal Hubbard - T
Don Hutson - E
Swede Johnston - FB
Walt Kiesling - G
Joe Laws - HB
Buster Maddox - T
Dustin McDonald - G
Johnny (Blood) McNally - HB
Mike Michalske - G
Bob Monnett - TB
Bob O'Connor - G
Claude Perry - T
Al Rose - E
George Sauer - HB
Herm Schneidman - BB
Ade Schwammel - T
Champ Seibold - T
Ernie Smith - T
George Svendsen - C
Bob Tenner - E
Dom Vairo - E

1935 NY Giants

Red Badgro - E
Bob Bellinger - G
Les Borden - E
Dale Burnett - WB
Stu Clancy - FB
Red Corzine - BB
Ed Danowski - TB
Johnny Dell Isola - C
Ray Flaherty - E
Ike Frankian - E
Tod Goodwin - E
Len Grant - T
Mel Hein - C
Tex Irvin - T
Potsy Jones - G
Bernie Kaplan - G
Max Krause - FB
Johnny Mackorell - TB
Buster Mitchell - E
Bo Molenda - BB
Bill Morgan - T
Harry Newman - TB
Bill Owen - G
Jess Quatse - T
Kink Richards - FB
Tony Sarausky - TB
Lee Shaffer - WB
Walt Singer - E
Ken Strong - FB

1935 Philadelphia

Howard Bailey - T
Steve Banas - BB
Harry Benson - G
Bill Brian - T
Tom Bushby - WB
Glenn Campbell - E
Joe Carter - E
Paul Cuba - T
Dick Frahm - HB
Tom Graham - G
Homer Hanson - G
Swede Hanson - HB
Bud Jorgensen - T
George Kenneally - E
Red Kirkman - BB
Joe Kresky - T
Irv Kupcinet - BB
Rick Lackman - HB
Jim Leonard - FB
Jim MacMurdo - T
Eggs Manske - E
Ed Matesic - TB
Forrest McPherson - C
Max Padlow - E
Alabama Pitts - HB
Leo Raskowski - T
Hank Reese - C
Burle Robison - E
Bob Rowe - FB
Mike Sebastian - HB
Harry Shaub - G
Ed Storm - TB
Stumpy Thomason - BB
Izzy Weinstock - FB
Clyde Williams - T
Diddie Willson - G
Vince Zizak - G
Jim Zyntell - G

1935 Pittsburgh

Al Arndt - G
Gene Augusterfer - BB
Maury Bray - T
Glenn Campbell - E
Cy Casper - TB
Ben Ciccone - C
Thomas Cosgrove - HB
John Doehring - TB
Cliff Dolaway - E
Swede Ellstrom - FB
Johnny Gildea - TB
Norm Greeney - G
Henry Hayduk - G
Warren Heller - TB
Bob Hoel - G
Joe Kresky - G
Jim Levey - HB
Joe Malkovich - C
Lee Mulleneaux - C
Armand Niccolai - T
Mike Nixon - HB
Stan Olejniczak - T
Swede Pittman - C
George Rado - G
Dave Ribble - G
Sandy Sandberg - T
Mike Sebastian - HB
Ed Skoronski - C
Ben H. Smith - E
Bull Snyder - G
Bill Sortet - E
Art Strutt - HB
John Turley - BB
Vic Vidoni - E
Heinie Weisenbaugh - HB
Buzz Wetzel - FB
Joe Wiehl - T
Silvio Zaninelli - FB

1936 Brooklyn

Red Badgro - E
Jeff Barrett - E
Gil Bergerson - G
Johnny Biancone - TB
Verdi Boyer - G
Dave Cook - FB
Dick Crayne - FB
Red Franklin - TB
Ray Fuqua - E
Jim Hartman - E
Carl Heldt - T
Wayne Jorgensen - C
Tony Kaska - FB
Ralph Kercheval - HB
Bo Kirkland - G
Henry Krause - C
Bill Lee - T
Father Lumpkin - BB
Joe Maniaci - TB
Cap Oehler - C
Paul Riblett - E
Jack Robinson - T
Justin Rukas - G
Phil Sarboe - TB
Frank Stojack - G
Mark Temple - TB
Jim Whatley - T
Bobby Wilson - TB
John Yezerski - T

1936 Chi. Bears

Bob Allman - E
Carl Brumbaugh - QB
Zuck Carlson - G
George Corbett - QB
John Doehring - HB
Beattie Feathers - HB
Danny Fortmann - G
George Grosvenor - HB
Bill Hewitt - E
Luke Johnsos - E
Bill Karr - E
Eddie Kawal - C
Jack Manders - FB
Bernie Masterson - QB
Eddie Michaels - G
Ookie Miller - C
Keith Molesworth - HB
George Musso - T
Bronko Nagurski - FB
Ray Nolting - HB
Vern Oech - G
Red Pollock - E
Ray Richards - G
Gene Ronzani - HB
Ted Rosequist - E
Johnny Sisk - HB
Joe Stydahar - T
Frank Sullivan - C
Russ Thompson - T
Milt Trost - T
Joe Zeller - G

1936 Chi. Cardinals

Conway Baker - T
Tony Blazine - T
Jeep Brett - E
Ross Carter - G
Dave Cook - FB
Milan Creighton - E
Bree Cuppoletti - G
Hermit Davis - E
Versil Deskin - E
Mule Dowell - FB
Swede Ellstrom - FB
Harry Field - T
George Grosvenor - TB
Phil Handler - G
Homer Hanson - G
Bernie Hughes - C
Clarence Kellogg - FB
Jimmy Lawrence - WB
Charlie McBride - BB
Pete Mehringer - T
Mike Mikulak - BB
Dub Miller - G
Bob Neuman - E
Al Nichelini - WB
Hal Pangle - FB
Bert Pearson - C
Jack Robinson - T
Doug Russell - TB
Phil Sarboe - TB
Bill Smith - E
Howie Tipton - G
Pug Vaughan - TB
Bill Volok - G
Billy Wilson - E

1936 Detroit

Ernie Caddel - WB
Frank Christensen - BB
George Christensen - T
Dutch Clark - TB
Harry Ebding - E
Ox Emerson - G
Ace Gutowsky - FB
Tom Hupke - G
Jack Johnson - T
Ed Klewicki - E
Sam Knox - G
Joe Kopcha - G
Bill McKalip - E
Regis Monahan - G
Butch Morse - E
Buddy Parker - BB
Ike Peterson - WB
Glenn Presnell - TB
Clare Randolph - C
Del Ritchhart - C
John Schneller - E
Bill Shepherd - FB
Red Stacy - T
Jim Steen - T
Sid Wagner - G
Wilbur White - WB

1936 Green Bay

Wayland Becker - E
Hank Bruder - BB
Frank Butler - C
Cal Clemens - BB
Tiny Engebretsen - G
Lon Evans - G
Milt Gantenbein - E
Buckets Goldenberg - G
Lou Gordon - T
Arnie Herber - TB
Clarke Hinkle - FB
Don Hutson - E
Swede Johnston - FB
Walt Kiesling - G
Joe Laws - HB
Russ Letlow - G
Harry Mattos - TB
Johnny (Blood) McNally - HB
Paul Miller - HB
Bob Monnett - TB
Tony Paulekas - G
Al Rose - E
George Sauer - FB
Bernie Scherer - E
Herm Schneidman - E
Ade Schwammel - T
Champ Seibold - T
Ernie Smith - T
George Svendsen - C

1936 NY Giants

Winnie Anderson - E
Dale Burnett - WB
Red Corzine - BB
Ed Danowski - TB
Gaines Davis - G
Johnny Dell Isola - G
Len Dugan - C
Bob Dunlap - DB
Tod Goodwin - E
Len Grant - T
Jack Haden - T
Mel Hein - C
Cal Hubbard - T
Larry Johnson - C
Potsy Jones - G
Bernie Kaplan - G
Max Krause - WB
Tuffy Leemans - FB
Art Lewis - T
Tilly Manton - BB
Buster Mitchell - E
Bill Morgan - T
Bill Owen - T
Ewell Phillips - G
Kink Richards - FB
Gene Rose - E
Tony Sarausky - TB
Lee Shaffer - BB
Walt Singer - E
Bob Tarrant - E

1936 Philadelphia

Reds Bassman - TB
Bill Brian - T
Art Buss - T
Joe Carter - E
Glenn Frey - BB
Rudy Gollomb - G
Swede Hanson - TB
Don Jackson - TB
Carl Kane - HB
John Kusko - FB
Jim Leonard - BB
Jim MacMurdo - T
Eggs Manske - E
Walt Masters - TB
Forrest McPherson - G
George Mulligan - E
Max Padlow - E
Joe Pilconis - E
Joe Pivarnik - G
Hank Reese - C
Jim Russell - G
Dave Smukler - FB
Pete Stevens - C
Stumpy Thomason - DB
Vince Zizak - G

1936 Pittsburgh

Maury Bray - T
Jeep Brett - E
Win Croft - G
Max Fiske - TB
Johnny Gildea - BB
Warren Heller - HB
Cal Hubbard - G
George Kakasic - G
Bull Karcis - FB
Ed Karpowich - T
Bill Lajousky - G
Jim Levey - TB
Ed Matesic - TB
Lindy Mayhew - G
Jim McDonald - HB
Lee Mulleneaux - C
Armand Niccolai - T
Buster Raborn - C
George Rado - G
Sandy Sandberg - T
Dick Sandefur - FB
Vinnie Sites - E
Ed Skoronski - E
Bill Sortet - E
Art Strutt - HB
John Turley - BB
Vic Vidoni - E
Silvio Zaninelli - FB

1936 Boston

Jim Barber - T
Cliff Battles - TB
Frank Bausch - C
Eddie Britt - FB
Sam Busich - E
Victor Carroll - T
Rick Concannon - G
Turk Edwards - T
Don Irwin - FB
Ed Justice - WB
Eddie Kahn - G
Jim Karcher - G
Chuck Malone - E
Bob McChesney - E
Wayne Millner - E
Jim Moran - G
Jim Musick - FB
Gail O'Brien - T
Les Olsson - G
Ernie Pinckert - WB
Pug Rentner - FB
Larry Siemering - C
Steve Sinko - T
Ed Smith - FB
Riley Smith - BB
Mark Temple - TB
Flavio Tosi - E
Heinie Weisenbaugh - BB

1937 Brooklyn

Vannie Albanese - FB
Sig Andrusking - G
Jim Austin - E
Jeff Barrett - E
Carl Brumbaugh - TB
Norm Cooper - C
Dick Crayne - FB
Frank Cumiskey - E
Ave Daniell - T
Red Franklin - TB
Ed Goddard - TB
John Golemgeske - T
Pat Harrison - T
Roy Ilowit - T
Bert Johnson - HB
Wayne Jorgensen - C
Tony Kaska - BB
Shipwreck Kelly - TB
Ralph Kercheval - HB
Fred King - BB
Henry Krause - G
Bill Lee - T
Rube Leisk - G
Father Lumpkin - BB
Joe Maniaci - FB
Buster Mitchell - E
Don Nelson - G
Reino Nori - TB
Ace Parker - TB
Ray Reckmack - BB
Sandy Sandberg - T
Ed Skoronski - G
Jim Whatley - T

1937 Chi. Bears

Frank Bausch - C
Kay Bell - G
John Bettridge - FB
Del Bjork - T
Carl Brumbaugh - QB
Ray Buivid - QB
Bill Conkright - C
George Corbett - DB
John Doehring - HB
Beattie Feathers - HB
Danny Fortmann - G
Sam Francis - FB
Henry Hammond - E
Bill Karr - E
Jack Manders - HB
Eggs Manske - E
Bernie Masterson - QB
Les McDonald - E
Keith Molesworth - HB
George Musso - G
Bronko Nagurski - FB
Ray Nolting - HB
Vern Oech - G
Dick Plasman - E
Pug Rentner - HB
Gene Ronzani - QB
Joe Stydahar - T
Frank Sullivan - C
Russ Thompson - T
Milt Trost - T
George Wilson - E
Joe Zeller - G

1937 Chi. Cardinals

Conway Baker - T
Tony Blazine - T
Hal Carlson - G
Ross Carter - G
Pat Coffee - TB
Bill Crass - FB
Milan Creighton - E
Bree Cuppoletti - G
Versil Deskin - E
Len Dugan - C
George Grosvenor - TB
Ham Harmon - C
Bob Hoel - G
Jimmy Lawrence - WB
John Marrow - G
Bill May - BB
Dub Miller - T
Bill Muellner - E
Earl Nolan - T
Hal Pangle - FB
Buddy Parker - FB
Rock Reed - WB
John Reynolds - C
Jack Robinson - T
Doug Russell - WB
Bill Smith - E
Gus Tinsley - E
Howie Tipton - BB
Pete Tyler - BB
Bill Volok - G
Billy Wilson - E

1937 Cleveland

Julie Alfonse - WB
Mark Barber - FB
John Bettridge - FB
Carl Brumbaugh - BB
Phil Bucklew - E
Forrest Burmeister - G
Sam Busich - E
Chuck Cherundolo - C
Bud Cooper - TB
Johnny Drake - FB
Bob Emerick - T
Wayne Gift - BB
Ed Goddard - TB
Paul Halleck - E
Ralph Isselhardt - G
Ray Johnson - TB
Joe Keeble - TB
Ted Livingston - T
Harry Mattos - TB
Ookie Miller - G
Primo Miller - T
Bill O'Neill - TB
Stan Pincura - BB
Ted Rosequist - T
Ollie Savatsky - E
Mike Sebastian - WB
Ed Skoronski - T
Bob Snyder - TB
Jim Turner - C
Wayne Underwood - T
Walt Uzdavinis - E
Joe Williams - DB
Dick Zoll - G

1937 Detroit

Ernie Caddel - WB
Lloyd Cardwell - WB
Frank Christensen - BB
George Christensen - T
Dutch Clark - TB
Hal Cooper - G
Harry Ebding - E
Ox Emerson - G
Bill Feldhaus - G
Tom Fena - G
Ace Gutowsky - FB
Chuck Hanneman - E
Vern Huffman - BB
Tom Hupke - G
Ralph Isselhardt - G
Jack Johnson - T
Lee Kizzire - FB
Ed Klewicki - E
Regis Monahan - G
Butch Morse - E
Charlie Payne - WB
Ray Reckmack - BB
Bob Reynolds - T
Del Ritchhart - C
Bill Shepherd - FB
Red Stacy - T
Dixie Stokes - C
Sid Wagner - G

1937 Green Bay

Herb Banet - TB
Wayland Becker - E
Hank Bruder - BB
Ave Daniell - T
Tiny Engebretsen - G
Lon Evans - G
Milt Gantenbein - E
Buckets Goldenberg - BB
Lou Gordon - T
Arnie Herber - TB
Clarke Hinkle - FB
Don Hutson - E
Ed Jankowski - FB
Swede Johnston - FB
Joe Laws - HB
Bill Lee - T
Darrell Lester - C
Russ Letlow - G
Mike Michalske - G
Paul Miller - HB
Bob Monnett - TB
Ray Peterson - TB
George Sauer - FB
Zud Schammel - G
Bernie Scherer - E
Herm Schneidman - BB
Champ Seibold - T
Ed Smith - TB
Ernie Smith - T
Lyle Sturgeon - T
Bud Svendsen - C
George Svendsen - C

1937 NY Giants

Dale Burnett - WB
Pete Cole - G
Red Corzine - BB
Ward Cuff - WB
Ed Danowski - QB
Johnny Dell Isola - G
Jerry Dennerlein - T
Stan Galazin - C
Chuck Gelatka - E
Len Grant - T
Jack Haden - T
Ray Hanken - E
Mel Hein - C
Jim Lee Howell - E
Larry Johnson - C
Mickey Kobrosky - QB
Tuffy Leemans - FB
Kayo Lunday - G
Tilly Manton - BB
Jim Neill - FB
Ox Parry - T
Jim Poole - E
Kink Richards - FB
Tony Sarausky - QB
Lee Shaffer - BB
Hank Soar - FB
Orville Tuttle - G
Will Walls - E
Tarzan White - G
Ed Widseth - T

1937 Philadelphia

Jay Arnold - WB
Winnie Baze - WB
Art Buss - T
Joe Carter - E
Jack Dempsey - T
Fritz Ferko - T
Glenn Frey - BB
Swede Hanson - FB
Maurice Harper - C
Bill Hewitt - E
Tex Holcomb - T
Bill Hughes - G
Rabbit Keen - WB
Charlie Knox - T
John Kusko - BB
Jim Leonard - BB
Jim MacMurdo - T
Bob Masters - WB
Forrest McPherson - G
Emmett Mortell - TB
Joe Pilconis - E
George Rado - G
Hank Reese - C
Herb Roton - E
Jim Russell - G
Dave Smukler - FB
Ray Spillers - T
Mule Stockton - G
Vince Zizak - G

1937 Pittsburgh

Mike Basrak - C
Frank Billock - T
Bill Breeden - HB
Jeep Brett - E
Mac Cara - E
Joe Cardwell - T
Bill Davidson - HB
Max Fiske - TB
Byron Gentry - G
Johnny Gildea - TB
By Haines - HB
Billy Harris - E
Tex Holcomb - T
George Kakasic - G
Bull Karcis - FB
Ed Karpowich - T
Walt Kiesling - G
Lindy Mayhew - G
Johnny (Blood) McNally - HB
Armand Niccolai - T
John Perko - G
Buster Raborn - C
George Rado - G
Sandy Sandberg - T
Dick Sandefur - DB
Vinnie Sites - E
Stu Smith - FB
Bill Sortet - E
Tuffy Thompson - TB
Izzy Weinstock - FB
Silvio Zaninelli - BB

1937 Washington

Jim Barber - T
Cliff Battles - FB
Sammy Baugh - TB
Chuck Bond - T
Eddie Britt - FB
Victor Carroll - G
Turk Edwards - T
Dixie Howell - TB
Don Irwin - FB
Ed Justice - WB
Eddie Kahn - G
Jim Karcher - G
Eddie Kawal - C
Henry Krause - C
Max Krause - FB
Chuck Malone - E
Bob McChesney - E
Eddie Michaels - G
Wayne Millner - E
Les Olsson - G
Nels Peterson - WB
Ernie Pinckert - WB
Ben H. Smith - E
George Smith - C
Riley Smith - BB
Bill Young - T

1938 Brooklyn

Vannie Albanese - FB
Jim Austin - E
Jeff Barrett - E
Eddie Britt - DB
Boyd Brumbaugh - FB
Wendell Butcher
Norm Cooper - C
Leo Disend - T
Johnny Druze - E
Ox Emerson - G
Scrapper Farrell - FB
Beattie Feathers - HB
John Golemgeske - T
Harold Hill - E
Tony Kaska - BB
Ralph Kercheval - HB
Bruiser Kinard - T
Stan Kosel - FB
Joe Maniaci - FB
Lou Mark - C
Ed Merlin - G
Gene Moore - C
Len Noyes - G
Ace Parker - TB
Bill Reissig - BB
Tony Sarausky - TB
Perry Schwartz - E
Jim Sivell - G
Bill Waller - E
Jim Whatley - T

1938 Chi. Bears

Chuck Apolskis - E
Dick Bassi - G
Frank Bausch - C
Del Bjork - T
Carl Brumbaugh - QB
Ray Buivid - QB
Bill Conkright - C
George Corbett - QB
Ferd Dreher - E
Gary Famiglietti - FB
Danny Fortmann - G
Sam Francis - FB
Lou Gordon - T
Bert Johnson - FB
Bill Karr - E
Jack Manders - HB
Joe Maniaci - FB
Eggs Manske - E
Bernie Masterson - QB
Les McDonald - E
George Musso - G
Ray Nolting - HB
Reino Nori - QB
John Oelerich - HB
Dick Plasman - E
Gene Ronzani - QB
Dick Schweidler - HB
Joe Stydahar - T
Frank Sullivan - C
Bob Swisher - HB
Russ Thompson - T
Milt Trost - T
George Wilson - E
Gust Zarnas - G
Joe Zeller - G

1938 Chi. Cardinals

Sam Agee - FB
Al Babartsky - T
Conway Baker - T
Jonathan Bilbo - T
Tony Blazine - T
Ray Burnett - TB
Ross Carter - G
Ed Cherry - FB
Pat Coffee - TB
Bree Cuppoletti - G
Versil Deskin - E
Phil Dougherty - C
Len Dugan - C
Elwyn Dunstan - T
Ev Fisher - E
Bob Hoel - G
Jimmy Lawrence - WB
John Marrow - G
Bill May - BB
Bob McGee - T
Lee Mulleneaux - C
Earl Nolan - T
Hal Pangle - BB
Buddy Parker - FB
Frank Patrick - BB
Milt Popovich - FB
Jack Robbins - TB
Doug Russell - WB
Dwight Sloan - TB
Bill Smith - E
Gus Tinsley - E
Pete Tyler - BB
Bill Volok - G

1938 Cleveland

Julie Alfonse - WB
Jim Benton - E
Carl Brazell - BB
Phil Bucklew - E
Forrest Burmeister - G
Chuck Cherundolo - C
Red Chesbro - G
Gerry Conlee - C
Bob Davis - TB
Corby Davis - FB
Johnny Drake - FB
Jack Giannoni - E
Ed Goddard - TB
Ray Hamilton - E
Tom Hupke - G
Ray Johnson - TB
Johnny Kovatch - E
Bill Krause - T
Art Lewis - T
Carl Littlefield - TB
Ted Livingston - T
Vic Markov - G
Jack May - C
Primo Miller - T
Nels Peterson - WB
Stan Pincura - BB
Dale Prather - E
Phil Ragazzo - G
Chuck Ream - T
Jack Robinson - T
Bob Snyder - TB
Vic Spadaccini - BB
Johnny Stephens - E
Dick Tuckey - TB
Dick Zoll - G

1938 Detroit

Lou Barle - BB
Ernie Caddel - WB
Lloyd Cardwell - WB
George Christensen - T
Dutch Clark - TB
Bill Feldhaus - G
Les Graham - G
Ace Gutowsky - FB
Chuck Hanneman - E
Vern Huffman - TB
Jack Johnson - T
Ed Klewicki - E
Jack Mackenroth - C
Tony Matisi - T
Jim McDonald - BB
Regis Monahan - G
Butch Morse - E
Monk Moscrip - E
Dick Nardi - WB
Maury Patt - E
Bill Radovich - G
Bob Reynolds - T
Bill Rogers - T
Rip Ryan - WB
Bill Shepherd
Dixie Stokes - C
Paul Szakash - FB
Fred Vanzo - BB
Sid Wagner - G
Alex Wojciechowicz - C

1938 Green Bay

Wayland Becker - E
Fred Borak - E
Hank Bruder - BB
Frank Butler - T
Tiny Engebretsen - G
Milt Gantenbein - E
Buckets Goldenberg - G
Arnie Herber - TB
Clarke Hinkle - FB
John Howell - FB
Don Hutson - E
Cecil Isbell - TB
Ed Jankowski - FB
Swede Johnston - G
Potsy Jones - G
Leo Katalinas - T
Joe Laws - HB
Bill Lee - T
Darrell Lester - C
Russ Letlow - G
Ookie Miller - C
Paul Miller - HB
Bob Monnett - TB
Carl Mulleneaux - E
Lee Mulleneaux - C
Baby Ray - T
Bernie Scherer - E
Herm Schneidman - BB
Roy Schoemann - C
Champ Seibold - T
Pete Tinsley - G
Andy Uram - HB
Dick Weisgerber - BB

1938 NY Giants

Charles Barnard - E
Len Barnum - QB
Dale Burnett - WB
Pete Cole - G
Frank Cope - T
Ward Cuff - WB
Ed Danowski - QB
Johnny Dell Isola - G
Nello Falaschi - BB
Stan Galazin - C
Chuck Gelatka - E
Johnny Gildea - BB
Jack Haden - T
Ray Hanken - E
Mel Hein - C
Jim Lee Howell - E
Larry Johnson - C
Bull Karcis - FB
Tuffy Leemans - FB
Kayo Lunday - G
Tilly Manton - BB
John Mellus - T
Ox Parry - T
Jim Poole - E
Kink Richards - FB
Lee Shaffer - BB
Hank Soar - FB
Orville Tuttle - G
Will Walls - E
Tarzan White - G
Ed Widseth - T
Red Wolfe - FB

1938 Philadelphia

Jay Arnold - HB
Joe Bukant - FB
Tom Burnette - BB
Joe Carter - E
John Cole - BB
Woody Dow - BB
Drew Ellis - T
Fritz Ferko - T
Bill Fiedler - G
Wimpy Giddens - T
Maurice Harper - C
Bill Hewitt - E
Bill Hughes - G
Ray Keeling - T
Rabbit Keen - HB
John Kusko - HB
Bernie Lee - BB
Bob Masters - BB
Emmett Mortell - TB
Bob Pylman - T
George Rado - G
Red Ramsey - E
Hank Reese - C
Dick Riffle - TB
Theodore Schmitt - G
Dave Smukler - FB
Mule Stockton - G
Billy Wilson - E
Clem Woltman - T

1938 Pittsburgh

Mike Basrak - C
Tom Burnette - BB
Mac Cara - E
Joe Cardwell - T
Bill Davidson - HB
Bob Douglas - FB
Ted Doyle - T
Vinnie Farrar - G
Scrapper Farrell - FB
Frankie Filchock - TB
Max Fiske - TB
Byron Gentry - G
Swede Hanson - FB
George Kakasic - G
Bull Karcis - FB
Ed Karpowich - T
Walt Kiesling - G
Lou Lassahn - T
Bernie Lee - BB
Eggs Manske - E
Joe Maras - C
Lindy Mayhew - G
Karl McDade - C
Paul McDonough - E
Johnny (Blood) McNally - HB
Armand Niccolai - T
John Nosich - T
John Oelerich - HB
John Perko - G
George Platukis - E
Jack Robinson - T
Jim Rorison - T
Stu Smith - FB
Bill Sortet - E
Jess Tatum - E
Tuffy Thompson - HB
Clarence Tommerson - DB
Lou Tsoutsouvas - C
Izzy Weinstock - BB
Whizzer White - TB
Billy Wilson - E

1938 Washington

Jim Barber - T
Hank Bartos - G
Sammy Baugh - TB
Chuck Bond - T
Rink Bond - BB
Hal Bradley - E
Victor Carroll - C
Turk Edwards - T
Bud Erickson - C
Andy Farkas - FB
Frankie Filchock - TB
Bill Hartman - TB
Don Irwin - FB
Ed Justice - WB
George Karamatic - FB
Jim Karcher - G
Henry Krause - C
Max Krause - FB
Chuck Malone - E
Tilly Manton - BB
Bob Masterson - E
Bob McChesney - E
Wayne Millner - E
Les Olsson - G
Mickey Parks - C
Ernie Pinckert - WB
Riley Smith - BB
Clem Stralka - G
Dick Tuckey - TB
Jay Turner - BB
Willie Wilkin - T
Roy Young - T
Bill Young - T

1939 Brooklyn

Boyd Brumbaugh - FB
Wendell Butcher - BB
Ray Carnelly - TB
Leo Disend - T
Scrapper Farrell - FB
Beattie Feathers - HB
Dick Folk - FB
Sam Francis - FB
John Golemgeske - G
Ace Gutowsky - FB
Bob Haak - T
Ralph Heikkinen - G
Harold Hill - E
Herman Hodges - E
Paul Humphrey - C
Len Janiak - FB
Carl Kaplanoff - T
Ralph Kercheval - HB
Bruiser Kinard - T
Stan Kosel - BB
Les Lane - G
Bill Leckonby - TB
George Lenc - E
Pug Manders - FB
Lou Mark - C
Ed Merlin - G
Dick Nardi - HB
Ace Parker - TB
Joe Ratica - C
Bill Reissig - BB
Perry Schwartz - E
Alec Shellogg - T
Jim Sivell - G
John Tosi - C
Waddy Young - E
Gust Zarnas - G

1939 Chi. Bears

Chuck Apolskis - E
Dick Bassi - G
Frank Bausch - C
Ray Bray - G
Chet Chesney - C
Gary Famiglietti - FB
Aldo Forte - G
Danny Fortmann - G
Charles Heileman - E
Bert Johnson - FB
Sid Luckman - QB
Bob MacLeod - HB
Jack Manders - HB
Joe Maniaci - FB
Eggs Manske - E
Bernie Masterson - QB
Les McDonald - E
George Musso - G
Ray Nolting - HB
Bill Osmanski - FB
Billy Patterson - QB
Dick Plasman - E
Dick Schweidler - HB
Alec Shellogg - T
Solly Sherman - QB
John Siegal - E
Bob Snyder - QB
Anton Stolfa - QB
Joe Stydahar - T
Frank Sullivan - C
Bob Swisher - HB
Russ Thompson - T
Jack Torrance - T
Milt Trost - T
George Wilson - E

1939 Chi. Cardinals

Henry Adams - C
Sam Agee - FB
Ki Aldrich - C
Al Babartsky - T
Conway Baker - T
Jonathan Bilbo - T
Keith Birlem - E
Tony Blazine - T
Hal Bradley - E
Ross Carter - G
Ed Cherry - FB
Don Cosner - WB
Earl Crowder - BB
Versil Deskin - E
Len Dugan - C
Elwyn Dunstan - T
George Faust - BB
Ev Fisher - BB
Charlie Gainor - DE
Marshall Goldberg - FB
Frank Huffman - G
Bert Johnson - TB
John Klumb - E
Mike Kochel - G
Jimmy Lawrence - WB
Joel Mason - E
Coley McDonough - TB
Regis Monahan - G
Jim Neill - WB
Buddy Parker - BB
Frank Patrick - TB
Milt Popovich - WB
Rock Reed - WB
Jack Robbins - TB
Glynn Rogers - G
Doug Russell - WB
Andy Sabados - G
Bill Smith - E
Jim Thomas - G
Bill Volok - G
Ernie Wheeler - TB
Frank Zelencik - T

1939 Cleveland

Chet Adams - T
Alex Atty - G
Lou Barle - BB
Jim Benton - E
Lew Bostick - G
Chuck Cherundolo - C
Bill Conkright - C
Corby Davis - FB
Jerry Dowd - C
Johnny Drake - FB
Elwyn Dunstan - T
Ben Friend - T
Parker Hall - TB
Joel Hitt - E
Tom Hupke - G
Bill Lazetich - WB
Art Lewis - T
Ted Livingston - T
Riley Matheson - G
Paul McDonough - E
Barney McGarry - G
Bill McRaven - WB
Kelly Moan - TB
Ralph Niehaus - T
Maury Patt - E
Mike Perrie - BB
Phil Ragazzo - G
Mike Rodak - BB
Doug Russell - WB
Nate Schenker - T
Marty Slovak - TB
Bronko Smilanich - TB
Gaylon Smith - FB
Vic Spadaccini - BB
Johnny Wilson - E

1939 Detroit

Jim Austin - E
Connie Mack Berry - E
Hal Brill - TB
Tony Calvelli - C
Lloyd Cardwell - WB
Ray Clemons - G
Dave Diehl - E
Bill Feldhaus - G
Ray George - T
Gordon Gore - WB
Ray Hamilton - E
Chuck Hanneman - E
Elvin Hutchison - WB
Jack Johnson - T
Steve Maronic - T
Phil Martinovich - G
Jim McDonald - WB
Bill Moore - E
Monk Moscrip - E
Johnny Pingel - TB
Bill Radovich - G
Bill Rogers - T
Rip Ryan - WB
Bill Shepherd - FB
Dwight Sloan - TB
Dixie Stokes - C
Paul Szakash - BB
Cal Thomas - G
Tony Tonelli - C
Darrell Tully - TB
Fred Vanzo - BB
Howie Weiss - FB
Johnny Wiatrak - C
Socko Wiethe - G
Alex Wojciechowicz - C

1939 Green Bay

Frank Balasz - FB
John Biolo - G
Jack Brennan - G
Charley Brock - C
Hank Bruder - BB
Larry Buhler - HB
Larry Craig - BB
Tiny Engebretsen - G
Milt Gantenbein - E
Buckets Goldenberg - G
Tom Greenfield - C
Arnie Herber - TB
Clarke Hinkle - FB
Don Hutson - E
Cecil Isbell - TB
Harry Jacunski - E
Ed Jankowski - FB
Paul Kell - T
Wally Kilbourne - T
Jimmy Lawrence - TB
Joe Laws - HB
Bill Lee - T
Russ Letlow - G
Al Moore - DE
Carl Mulleneaux - E
Baby Ray - T
Herm Schneidman - BB
Charlie Schultz - T
Ernie Smith - T
Frank Steen - E
Bud Svendsen - C
Tuffy Thompson - HB
Pete Tinsley - G
Frank Twedell - G
Andy Uram - HB
Dick Weisgerber - BB
Gust Zarnas - G
Dick Zoll - G

1939 NY Giants

Len Barnum - QB
Dale Burnett - WB
Pete Cole - T
Frank Cope - T
Ward Cuff - WB
Ed Danowski - QB
Johnny Dell Isola - G
Nello Falaschi - BB
Stan Galazin - C
Chuck Gelatka - E
Mel Hein - C
Jim Lee Howell - E
Larry Johnson - C
Bull Karcis - FB
Jiggs Kline - E
Tuffy Leemans - FB
Kayo Lunday - G
John Mellus - T
Eddie Miller - QB
Doug Oldershaw - G
Al Owen - FB
Ox Parry - T
Jim Poole - E
Kink Richards - FB
Lee Shaffer - BB
Hank Soar - FB
Ken Strong - FB
Orville Tuttle - G
Will Walls - E
Tarzan White - G
Ed Widseth - T

1939 Philadelphia

Jay Arnold - BB
Rankin Britt - DE
Joe Bukant - FB
Joe Carter - E
Zed Coston - C
Bree Cuppoletti - G
Woody Dow - FB
Drew Ellis - T
Maurice Harper - C
Bill Hewitt - E
Bill Hughes - G
Ray Keeling - T
Elmer Kolberg - E
Emmett Kriel - G
Emmett Mortell - TB
Franny Murray - WB
Chuck Newton - BB
Davey O'Brien - TB
Bob Pylman - T
Red Ramsey - E
Hank Reese - G
Dick Riffle - WB
Theodore Schmitt - G
Jake Schuehle - LB
Dave Smukler - FB
George Somers - T
Allie White - G
Clem Woltman - T

1939 Pittsburgh

Earl Bartlett - HB
Wayland Becker - E
Rink Bond - BB
Sam Boyd - E
Boyd Brumbaugh - FB
Don Campbell - T
Ed Cherry - FB
Bill Davidson - HB
Ted Doyle - T
Len Dugan - C
Vinnie Farrar - G
Max Fiske - E
Sam Francis - FB
Byron Gentry - G
Ted Grabinski - C
Swede Johnston - FB
George Kakasic - G
Ed Karpowich - T
Jack Lee - BB
Carl Littlefield - FB
Joe Maras - C
Bob Masters - HB
Hugh McCullough - TB
Coley McDonough - TB
Lou Midler - G
Dick Nardi - HB
Armand Niccolai - T
Stan Pavkov - G
John Perko - G
George Platukis - E
Bernie Scherer - E
Karl Schuelke - FB
Bill Sortet - E
Frank Souchak - E
Lou Tomasetti - TB
Clarence Tommerson - HB
John Tosi - C
Ernie Wheeler - TB
Joe Williams - HB

1939 Washington

Jim Barber - T
Sammy Baugh - TB
Keith Birlem - WB
Hal Bradley - E
Victor Carroll - T
Turk Edwards - T

Bud Erickson - C
Andy Farkas - FB
Dick Farman - G
Frankie Filchock - TB
Jimmy German - TB
Don Irwin - FB
Jimmy Johnston - WB
Ed Justice - WB
Jim Karcher - G
Max Krause - BB
Chuck Malone - E
Bob Masterson - E
Bob McChesney - E
Jim Meade - FB
Wayne Millner - E
Wilbur Moore - FB
Boyd Morgan - WB
Mickey Parks - C
Ernie Pinckert - BB
Bo Russell - T
Clyde Shugart - G
Steve Slivinski - G
Johnny Spirida - BB
Clem Stralka - G
Dick Todd - WB
Jay Turner - BB
Steve Uhrinyak - G
Willie Wilkin - T
Bill Young - T

1940 Brooklyn

Bill Bailey - E
Sherrill Busby - DE
Wendell Butcher - BB
George Cafego - TB
Dick Cassiano - TB
Ty Coon - G
Sam Francis - FB
John Golemgeske - T
Mike Gussie - G
Rod Heater - T
Harold Hill - E
Herman Hodges - E
Art Jocher - G
Ralph Kercheval - TB
Bruiser Kinard - T
Ben Kish - BB
Frank Kristufek - T
Bill Leckonby - TB
Pug Manders - FB
Lou Mark - C
Banks McFadden - HB
Walt Merrill - T
Ace Parker - TB
Steve Petro - G
Perry Schwartz - E
Rhoten Shetley - BB
Jim Sivell - G
Bud Svendsen - C
Si Titus - C
Bob Winslow - DE
Waddy Young - E
Frank Zadworney - HB

1940 Chi. Bears

Lee Artoe - T
Al Baisi - G
Frank Bausch - C
Ray Bray - G
Chet Chesney - C
Harry Clarke - HB
Gary Famiglietti
Aldo Forte - G
Danny Fortmann - G
Ken Kavanaugh - E
Ed Kolman - T
Sid Luckman - QB
Jack Manders - HB
Joe Maniaci - FB
Eggs Manske - E
Phil Martinovich - G
Bernie Masterson - QB
George McAfee - HB
Ray McLean - HB
Joe Mihal - T
George Musso - G
Ray Nolting - HB
Bob Nowaskey - E
Bill Osmanski - FB
Dick Plasman - E
Hamp Pool - E
Solly Sherman - QB
John Siegal - E
Bob Snyder - QB
Joe Stydahar - T
Bob Swisher - HB
Jack Torrance - T
Bulldog Turner - C
George Wilson - E

1940 Chi. Cardinals

Ki Aldrich - C
Conway Baker - T
Ed Beinor - T
Tony Blazine - T
Ray Busler - T
Andy Chisick - C
Marty Christiansen - FB
Beryl Clark - TB
Al Coppage - E
Bill Davis - T
Bill Dewell - E
Ev Elkins - WB
Jimmy German - TB
Marshall Goldberg - FB
Johnny Hall - WB
Frank Huffman - G
Frank Ivy - E
Bert Johnson - BB
Ray Johnson - TB
Bob Kellogg - TB
John Klumb - E
Joe Kuharich - G
Lloyd Madden - WB
Hugh McCullough - TB
Bill Murphy - G
Buddy Parker - BB
Rupert Pate - G
Milt Popovich - FB
Keith Ranspot - E
Andy Sabados - G
Herm Schneidman - BB
John Shirk - E
Gus Tinsley - E
Mario Tonelli - FB
Tarzan White - G
Rex Williams - C
Bobby Wood - T
Lou Zontini - BB

1940 Cleveland

Chet Adams - T
Stan Andersen - T
Jim Benton - E
Connie Mack Berry - E
Boyd Clay - T
Bill Conkright - C
Olie Cordill - WB
Earl Crowder - BB
Johnny Drake - FB
Elwyn Dunstan - T
Fred Gehrke - TB
Jim Gillette - TB
Shag Goolsby - C
Pete Gudauskas - G
Parker Hall - TB
Jack Haman - C
Ken Heineman - TB
Len Janiak - FB
Mike Kinek - E
Ted Livingston - T
Dante Magnani - WB
Riley Matheson - G
Paul McDonough - WB
Barney McGarry - G
Harvey Murphy - E
Jack Nix - WB
Glenn Olson - BB
Maury Patt - E
Phil Ragazzo - T
Hank Rockwell - C
Mike Rodak - BB
Fred Shirey - T
Marty Slovak - TB
Gaylon Smith - BB
Vic Spadaccini - BB
Ralph Stevenson - G
Johnny Wilson - E

1940 Detroit

Bill Callihan - BB
Tony Calvelli - C
Lloyd Cardwell - WB
Clem Crabtree - T
Dave Diehl - E
Bill Feldhaus - G
Bill Fisk - E
Tony Furst - T
Johnny Hackenbruck - T
Chuck Hanneman - E
Jack Johnson - T
Steve Maronic - T
Les McDonald - E
Paul Moore - BB
Jack Morlock - WB
Glen Morris - E
Butch Morse - E
Cotton Price - TB
Bill Radovich - G
Bill Rogers - T
Stillman Rouse - E
Rip Ryan - WB
Bill Shepherd - FB
Dwight Sloan - TB
Harry Smith - T
Harry Speelman - G
Cal Thomas - G
Sam Tsoutsouvas - C
Fred Vanzo - BB
Howie Weiss - FB
Whizzer White - TB
Socko Wiethe - G
Bob Winslow - DE
Alex Wojciechowicz - C

1940 Green Bay

Bob Adkins - BB
Frank Balasz - FB
Connie Mack Berry - E
Charley Brock - C
Lou Brock - HB
Larry Buhler - FB
Larry Craig - BB
Leo Disend - T
Tiny Engebretsen - G
Dick Evans - E
Beattie Feathers - HB
Milt Gantenbein - E
Buckets Goldenberg - G
Tom Greenfield - C
Arnie Herber - TB
Clarke Hinkle - FB
Don Hutson - E
Cecil Isbell - TB
Harry Jacunski - E
Ed Jankowski - FB
Smiley Johnson - G
Paul Kell - T
Joe Laws - HB
Bill Lee - T
Russ Letlow - G
Lou Midler - G
Carl Mulleneaux - E
Baby Ray - T
Ray Riddick - E
Charlie Schultz - T
George Seeman - E
Champ Seibold - T
Fred Shirey - T
George Svendsen - C
Andy Uram - HB
Hal Van Every - TB
Dick Weisgerber - BB
Bobby Wood - T
Gust Zarnas - G

1940 NY Giants

Len Barnum - QB
Pete Cole - G
Frank Cope - T
Ward Cuff - WB
Johnny Dell Isola - G
Jerry Dennerlein - T
Gil Duggan - T
Kay Eakin - QB
Monk Edwards - T
Nello Falaschi - BB
Chuck Gelatka - E
Wen Goldsmith - C
Max Harrison - E
Mel Hein - C
Jack Hinkle - BB
Jim Lee Howell - E
Jiggs Kline - DE
Grenny Lansdell - QB
Tuffy Leemans - FB
Kayo Lunday - C
Ed McGee - T
John McLaughry - BB
John Mellus - T
Eddie Miller - QB
Ken Moore - G
Walt Nielsen - FB
Doug Oldershaw - G
Al Owen - BB
Bolo Perdue - E
Jim Poole - E
Dom Principe - FB
Lee Shaffer - WB
Hank Soar - FB
Carl Tomasello - DE
Orville Tuttle - G
Ed Widseth - T

1940 Philadelphia

Jay Arnold - HB
Dick Bassi - G
Joe Bukant - FB
Joe Carter - E
Chuck Cherundolo - C
John Cole - FB
Woody Dow - DB
Frank Emmons - FB
Ray George - T
Jerry Ginney - G
Elmer Hackney - FB
Maurice Harper - C
Bill Hughes - G
Elmer Kolberg - E
Don Looney - E
Les McDonald - E
Franny Murray - HB
Chuck Newton - HB
Davey O'Brien - QB
Phil Ragazzo - T
Red Ramsey - E
Dick Riffle - HB
Theodore Schmitt - C
Elbie Schultz - G
George Somers - T
Russ Thompson - T
Milt Trost - T
Foster Watkins - QB
Joe Wendlick - E
Clem Woltman - T

1940 Pittsburgh

Sam Boyd - E
Hank Bruder - BB
Boyd Brumbaugh - FB
Frank Bykowski - G
Don Campbell - T
Merl Condit - HB
Ted Doyle - T
Ev Fisher - BB
Clark Goff - T
Ted Grabinski - C
Frank Ivy - E
Swede Johnston - FB
Ed Karpowich - T
Walt Kichefski - E
George Kiick - FB
John Klumb - E
Carl Littlefield - FB
Joe Maras - C
Coley McDonough - TB
Carl Nery - G
Armand Niccolai - T
John Noppenberg - FB
Billy Patterson - TB
Stan Pavkov - G
John Perko - G
Rocco Pirro - HB
George Platukis - E
Jack Sanders - G
John Schmidt - C
Bill Sortet - E
Frank Sullivan - C
Tommy Thompson - TB
Lou Tomasetti - HB
John Woudenberg - T
John Yurchey - HB

1940 Washington

Steve Andrako - C
Jim Barber - T
Sammy Baugh - TB
Victor Carroll - T
Turk Edwards - T
Andy Farkas - FB
Dick Farman - G
Frankie Filchock - TB
Bob Fisher - T
Ray Hare - BB
Bob Hoffman - BB
Jimmy Johnston - FB
Ed Justice - WB
Max Krause - BB
Chuck Malone - E
Bob Masterson - E
Bob McChesney - E
Jim Meade - WB
Wayne Millner - E
Wilbur Moore - FB
Boyd Morgan - BB
Mickey Parks - C
Ernie Pinckert - BB
Bo Russell - T
Sandy Sanford - E
Bob Seymour - FB
Clyde Shugart - G
Steve Slivinski - G
Clem Stralka - G
Bob Titchenal - C
Dick Todd - WB
Willie Wilkin - T
Bill Young - T
Roy Zimmerman - TB

1941 Brooklyn

Warren Alfson - G
Bill Bailey - E
Wendell Butcher - BB
Merl Condit - HB
Ray Frick - C
Andy Fronczek - T
Herman Hodges - E
Thurman Jones - FB
Mike Jurich - T
Bruiser Kinard - T
George Kinard - G
Ben Kish - BB
Joe Koons - C
George Kracum - FB
Frank Kristufek - T
Bill Leckonby - TB
Pug Manders - FB
Dean McAdams - TB
Walt Merrill - T
Ace Parker - TB
Dave Parker - E
Larry Peace - HB
Steve Petro - G
Tom Robertson - C
Eddie Rucinski - E
Perry Schwartz - E
Rhoten Shetley - BB
Jim Sivell - G
Leo Stasica - TB
Bud Svendsen - C
Si Titus - C
Don Wemple - E

1941 Chi. Bears

Lee Artoe - T
Al Baisi - G
Ray Bray - G
Young Bussey - QB
Harry Clarke - HB
Gary Famiglietti
John Federovitch - T
Aldo Forte - G
Danny Fortmann - G
Hugh Gallarneau - HB
Bill Hughes - C
Ken Kavanaugh - E
Ed Kolman - T
Hal Lahar - G
Sid Luckman - QB
Joe Maniaci - FB
Al Matuza - C
George McAfee - HB
Ray McLean - HB
Joe Mihal - T
George Musso - G
Ray Nolting - HB
Bob Nowaskey - E
Bill Osmanski - FB
Dick Plasman - E
Hamp Pool - E
John Siegal - E
Bob Snyder - QB
Norm Standlee - FB
Joe Stydahar - T
Bob Swisher - HB
Bulldog Turner - C
George Wilson - E

1941 Chi. Cardinals

Ray Apolskis - C
Al Babartsky - T
Conway Baker - T
Frank Balasz - FB
Ed Beinor - T
Ray Busler - T
Andy Chisick - C
Johnny Clement - TB
Al Coppage - E
Bill Daddio - E
Bill Davis - T
Bill Dewell - E
Dick Evans - E
Marshall Goldberg - FB
Johnny Hall - WB
Jim Higgins - G
Frank Huffman - G
Frank Ivy - E
Bert Johnson - BB
Joe Kuharich - G
John Kuzman - T
Joe Lokanc - G
Ray Mallouf - TB
Johnny Martin - WB
Hugh McCullough - TB
Avery Monfort - WB
Bob Morrow - FB
Bill Murphy - G
Buddy Parker - BB
Milt Popovich - FB
Walt Rankin - FB
Seymour - E
Fred Shook - C
Fred Vanzo - BB
Tarzan White - G
Lou Zontini - BB

1941 Cleveland

Chet Adams - T
Stan Andersen - E
Graham Armstrong - T
Boyd Clay - T
Bill Conkright - C
Corby Davis - FB
Johnny Drake - FB
Elwyn Dunstan - T
Tony Gallovich - WB
Owen Goodnight - TB
Jack Gregory - G
Parker Hall - TB
Jack Haman - C
Chuck Hanneman - E
Kirk Hershey - E
Red Hickey - E
Len Janiak - FB
Michael Kostiuk - T
Del Lyman - T
Dante Magnani - WB
Frank Maher - DB
Riley Matheson - G
Paul McDonough - WB
Barney McGarry - G
George Morris - WB
Rudy Mucha - BB
Maury Patt - E
Ray Prochaska - E
Bill Rieth - C
Hank Rockwell - G
Charlie Seabright - BB
Fred Shirey - T
Milt Simington - G
Marty Slovak - TB
Gaylon Smith - FB
Wilfred Thorpe - G
Gordon Wilson - G
Johnny Wilson - E

1941 Detroit

Stan Andersen - E
Stan Batinski - G
Steve Belichick - FB
Dick Booth - WB
Maurice Britt - E
Bill Callihan - BB
Lloyd Cardwell - WB
Clem Crabtree - T
Bill Fisk - E
Tony Furst - T
Chuck Hanneman - E
Harry Hopp - FB
Billy Jefferson - TB
John Jett - E
Augie Lio - G
Andy Logan - T
Ned Mathews - WB
Jack Mattiford - G
Paul Moore - BB
Robert Nelson - C
John Noppenberg - HB
Dunc Obee - C
Lloyd Parsons - FB
Ted Pavelec - T
Milt Piepul - FB
Cotton Price - TB
Bill Radovich - G
Alex Schibanoff - T
Paul Szakash - E
Owen Thuerk - E
Lou Tomasetti - WB
John Tripson - T
Emil Uremovich - T
Fred Vanzo - BB
Whizzer White - TB
Socko Wiethe - G
Alex Wojciechowicz - C

1941 Green Bay

Bob Adkins - BB
Frank Balasz - FB
Charley Brock - C
Lou Brock - HB
Mike Bucchianeri - G
Larry Buhler - BB
Tony Canadeo - TB
Larry Craig - BB
Tiny Engebretsen - G
Ed Frutig - E
Buckets Goldenberg - G
Tom Greenfield - C
Clarke Hinkle - FB
Don Hutson - E
Cecil Isbell - TB
Harry Jacunski - E
Ed Jankowski - FB
Smiley Johnson - G
Bill Johnson - DE
Bill Kuusisto - G
Joe Laws - HB
Bill Lee - T
Russ Letlow - G
Del Lyman - T
Lee McLaughlin - G
Carl Mulleneaux - E
Ernie Pannell - T
George Paskvan - FB
Baby Ray - T
Ray Riddick - E
Herm Rohrig - HB
Charlie Schultz - T
George Svendsen - C
Pete Tinsley - G
Andy Uram - HB
Alex Urban - E
Hal Van Every - TB

1941 NY Giants

Tony Blazine - T
Frank Cope - T
Ward Cuff - WB
Ed Danowski - QB
Lou DeFilippo - C
Vince Dennery - E
Kay Eakin - QB
Monk Edwards - G
Len Eshmont - FB
Nello Falaschi - BB
George Franck - WB
Chet Gladchuk - C
Mel Hein - C
Dick Horne - DE
Jim Lee Howell - E
Tuffy Leemans - FB
Jack Lummus - E
Kayo Lunday - C
Andy Marefos - FB
Clint McClain - FB
John Mellus - T
Doug Oldershaw - G
Win Pedersen - T
Jim Poole - E
Dom Principe - BB
Marion Pugh - QB
Frank Reagan - FB
Lee Shaffer - BB
Hank Soar - FB
Ben Sohn - G
Orville Tuttle - G
Don Vosberg - E
Will Walls - E
Howie Yeager - WB
Len Younce - G

1941 Philadelphia

Jack Banta - HB
Len Barnum - QB
Sam Bartholomew - FB
Nick Basca - HB
Dick Bassi - G
Frank Bausch - C
Bob Bjorklund - C
Larry Cabrelli - E
Jim Castiglia - FB
Tony Cemore - G
Enio Conti - G
Dan DeSantis - HB
Dave diFilippo - G
John Eibner - T
Bernie Feibish - C
Jack Ferrante - E
Terry Fox - FB
Joe Frank - T
Ralph Fritz - G
Woody Gerber - G
Lou Ghecas - HB
Fred Gloden - HB
Lyle Graham - C
Gran Harrison - DE
Kirk Hershey - E
Jack Hinkle - HB
Dick Humbert - E
Bob Krieger - E
Mort Landsberg - HB
Wes McAfee - HB
Rupert Pate - G
Hank Piro - E
Phil Ragazzo - T
Vic Sears - T
John Shonk - E
Cecil Sturgeon - T
Bob Suffridge - G
Tommy Thompson - QB
Lou Tomasetti - HB
Foster Watkins - QB
Burr West - T

1941 Pittsburgh

Jay Arnold - BB
Boyd Brumbaugh - TB
Chuck Cherundolo - C
Joe Coomer - T
Les Dodson - TB
Dick Dolly - E
Al Donelli - TB
Ted Doyle - T
Elmer Hackney - FB
Red Hickey - E
Joe Hoague - FB
Art Jones - TB
Royal Kahler - T
Walt Kichefski - E
Elmer Kolberg - E
Don Looney - E
Frank Maher - DB
Coley McDonough - TB
Carl Nery - G
Armand Niccolai - T
John Noppenberg - HB
John Patrick - BB
Rocco Pirro - BB
George Platukis - E
Dick Riffle - FB
Jack Sanders - G
John Schiechl - C
Elbie Schultz - G
George Somers - T
Ben Starret - TB
Joe Wendlick - E
Don Williams - G
John Woudenberg - T
Frank Zoppetti - TB

1941 Washington

Joe Aguirre - E
Ki Aldrich - C
Jack Banta - HB
Jim Barber - T
Sammy Baugh - TB
Ed Beinor - T
Victor Carroll - C
Ed Cifers - E
Frank Clair - E
Fred Davis - T
Ken Dow - FB
Andy Farkas - FB
Dick Farman - G
Frankie Filchock - TB
Lee Gentry - FB
Cece Hare - BB
Ray Hare - BB
Bob Hoffman - BB
Ed Justice - WB
Al Krueger - E
Bob Masterson - E
Bob McChesney - E
Wayne Millner - E
Wilbur Moore - WB
Bob Seymour - FB
Clyde Shugart - G
Steve Slivinski - G
George Smith - C
Clem Stralka - G
Jim Stuart - T
Bob Titchenal - C
Dick Todd - FB
Willie Wilkin - T
Bill Young - T
Roy Zimmerman - WB

1942 Brooklyn

Wendell Butcher - BB
Merl Condit - HB
Gerry Courtney - TB
Art Deremer - C
Don Eliason - E
Walt Fedora - FB
Bob Gifford - BB
Herman Hodges - E
Billy Jefferson - HB
Bob Jeffries - G
Art Jocher - G
Thurman Jones - FB

Mike Jurich - T
Bernie Kapitansky - G
Duce Keahey - T
Bruiser Kinard - T
George Kinard - G
Pug Manders - FB
Dean McAdams - TB
Hal McCullough - TB
Curt Mecham - TB
Walt Merrill - T
Mike Nixon - WB
Don Pierce - C
Norbert Raemer - G
Bobby Robertson - HB
Tom Robertson - C
Eddie Rucinski - E
Perry Schwartz - E
Rhoten Shetley - BB
Jim Sivell - G
Bud Svendsen - G
Si Titus - C
Joe Tofil - E
Jack Vetter - HB
Bernie Weiner - T

1942 Chi. Bears

Len Akin - G
Lee Artoe - T
Connie Mack Berry - E
Ray Bray - G
Harry Clarke - HB
Stu Clarkson - C
Chuck Drulis - G
Gary Famiglietti - FB
Danny Fortmann - G
Hugh Gallarneau - HB
Bill Geyer - HB
Bill Hempel - T
Al Hoptowit - T
Nick Kerasiotis - G
Adolph Kissell - HB
Ed Kolman - T
Sid Luckman - QB
Al Matuza - C
Frank Maznicki - HB
Ray McLean - HB
Frank Morris - FB
George Musso - G
Ray Nolting - HB
Bob Nowaskey - E
Charlie O'Rourke - QB
Bill Osmanski - FB
John Petty - FB
Hamp Pool - E
John Siegal - E
Joe Stydahar - T
Bulldog Turner - C
Clint Wager - E
George Wilson - E

1942 Chi. Cardinals

Joe Allton - T
Ray Apolskis - C
Conway Baker - G
Vince Banonis - C
Libby Bertagnolli - G
Frank Bohlmann - G
Joe Bukant - TB
Chet Bulger - T
Lloyd Cheatham - WB
Ben Ciccone - C
Al Coppage - E
Bill Daddio - E
Gil Duggan - T
Ray Ebli - E
Dick Evans - E
Ralph Fife - G
Marshall Goldberg - FB
Frank Ivy - E
Johnny Knolla - TB
Steve Lach - WB
Bob Maddock - G
Johnny Martin - WB
Bob Morrow - FB
Ross Nagel - T
Carl Olson - T
Buddy Parker - BB
Milt Popovich - BB
Bud Schwenk - TB
Champ Seibold - T
Ernie Wheeler - DB
Gordon Wilson - G

1942 Cleveland

Chet Adams - T
Jim Benton - E
Jack Boone - WB
Lew Bostick - G
Larry Brahm - G
Boyd Clay - T
Bill Conkright - C
Corby Davis - FB
Dutch Elston - BB
Jake Fawcett - T
Joe Gibson - E
Herb Godfrey - E
Parker Hall - TB
Ben Hightower - E
Jack Jacobs - TB
Len Janiak - WB
Don Johnson - C
Bill Lazetich - WB
Dante Magnani - WB

Riley Matheson - G
Barney McGarry - G
Tex Mooney - T
George Morris - FB
Joe Pasqua - T
Maury Patt - DE
John Petchel - BB
George Platukis - E
Warren Plunkett - BB
Bosh Pritchard - HB
Manny Rapp - TB
Bill Rieth - C
Hank Rockwell - C
Gaylon Smith - FB
Roy Stuart - G
Wilfred Thorpe - G
Johnny Wilson - E

1942 Detroit

Tony Arena - C
Emil Banjavic - WB
Chuck Behan - E
Bill Callihan - BB
Lloyd Cardwell - WB
Tom Chantiles - T
Tom Colella - TB
Murray Evans - BB
Bill Fisk - E
Slok Gill - C
Hank Goodman - T
Frank Grigonis - FB
Elmer Hackney - FB
Johnny Hall - WB
Gran Harrison - E
Harry Hopp - TB
Bill Kennedy - DE
Larry Knorr - E
Augie Lio - G
Ned Mathews - TB
Ted Pavelec - T
John Polanski - FB
Keith Ranspot - E
Mickey Sanzotta - WB
Larry Sartori - G
Alex Schibanoff - T
John Schiechl - C
Perry Scott - E
Harry Seltzer - FB
George Speth - T
Joe Stringfellow
Paul Szakash - BB
Emil Uremovich - T
Chet Wetterlund - TB
Socko Wiethe - G
Alex Wojciechowicz - C
Tony Zuzzio - G

1942 Green Bay

Paul Berezney - T
Charley Brock - C
Lou Brock - FB
Tony Canadeo - TB
Joe Carter - E
Larry Craig - BB
Tiny Croft - T
Bob Flowers - C
Ted Fritsch - FB
Buckets Goldenberg - G
Hal Hinte - DE
Don Hutson - E
Bob Ingalls - C
Cecil Isbell - TB
Harry Jacunski - E
Bob Kahler - HB
Royal Kahler - T
Bill Kuusisto - G
Joe Laws - HB
Bill Lee - T
Russ Letlow - G
Joel Mason - E
Earl Ohlgren - DE
Ernie Pannell - T
Keith Ranspot - E
Baby Ray - T
Ray Riddick - E
Chuck Sample - FB
Ben Starret - BB
John Stonebraker - E
Pete Tinsley - G
Andy Uram - HB
Fred Vant Hull - G
Dick Weisgerber - BB

1942 NY Giants

Neal Adams - E
Chuck Avedisian - G
Hubert Barker - BB
Emmett Barrett - C
Kay Bell - T
Al Blozis - T
Harry Buffington - BB
Leo Cantor - FB
John Chickerneo - BB
Frank Cope - T
Ward Cuff - WB
Monk Edwards - G
Harold Hall - C
Merle Hapes - FB
Mel Hein - C
Ed Hiemstra - C
Jim Lee Howell - E
Bill Hutchinson - QB
Duce Keahey - T

Jiggs Kline - DE
John Lascari - E
Ed Lechner - G
Tuffy Leemans - QB
Frank Liebel - E
Don Lieberum - WB
Andy Marefos - QB
Al Owen - BB
Dom Principe - BB
Red Seick - G
Lee Shaffer - BB
Hank Soar - FB
Paul Stenn - T
Bob Trocolor - QB
Will Walls - E

1942 Philadelphia

Len Barnum - QB
John Binotto - HB
Leo Brennan - T
Larry Cabrelli - E
Bill Combs - E
Enio Conti - G
Leon Cook - T
Bob Davis - HB
John Eibner - T
Dick Erdlitz - HB
Joe Frank - T
Woody Gerber - G
Ray Graves - C
Irv Hall - FB
Bill Halverson - T
Ken Hayden - C
Frank Hrabetin - T
Billy Jefferson - HB
Bert Johnson - HB
Bernie Kaplan - G
Ed Kasky - T
Jim Lankas - FB
Steve Levanitis - T
Basilio Marchi - C
Bob Masters - HB
Fred Meyer - E
Bert Milling - G
Rupert Pate - G
Bob Priestley - E
Bosh Pritchard - HB
Vic Sears - T
Jack Smith - E
Jack Stackpool - FB
Ernie Steele - HB
Len Supulski - E
Al Thacker - DB
Tommy Thompson - QB
Lou Tomasetti - HB
Bob Wear - C
Ted Williams - FB
Tex Williams - C

1942 Pittsburgh

Art Albrecht - C
John Binotto - HB
Tony Bova - E
Tom Brown - E
Chuck Cherundolo - C
Russ Cotton - BB
Al Donelli - HB
Ted Doyle - T
Bill Dudley - TB
George Gonda - HB
Hal Hinte - DE
Joe Hoague - FB
Walt Kichefski - E
Joe Lamas - G
Hubbard Law - G
Don Looney - E
Vern Martin - BB
Clure Mosher - C
John Naioti - DB
Armand Niccolai - T
Frank Pastin - G
Dick Riffle - FB
Mike Rodak - G
Jack Sanders - G
Curt Sandig - HB
John Schiechl - C
Elbie Schultz - T
Milt Simington - G
George Sirochman - G
George Somers - T
Andy Tomasic - TB
Ralph Wenzel - DE
John Woudenberg - T

1942 Washington

Ki Aldrich - C
Sammy Baugh - TB
Ed Beinor - T
Victor Carroll - T
Ed Cifers - E
Fred Davis - T
Rufus Deal - FB
Andy Farkas - FB
Dick Farman - G
John Goodyear - WB
Cece Hare - BB
Ray Hare - BB
Ed Justice - WB
Steve Juzwik - FB
John Kovatch - E
Al Krueger - E
Chuck Malone - E
Bob Masterson - E

Bob McChesney - E
Wilbur Moore - WB
Dick Poillon - TB
Bob Seymour - FB
Clyde Shugart - G
Steve Slivinski - G
George Smith - C
Clem Stralka - G
Bob Titchenal - E
Dick Todd - WB
George Watts - T
Marv Whited - BB
Willie Wilkin - T
Bill Young - T
Joe Zeno - G
Roy Zimmerman - TB

1943 Brooklyn

Bill Armstrong - G
John Bandura - E
Bill Brown - BB
George Cafego - TB
Merl Condit - HB
Bill Conkright - C
Bill Davis - T
Marshall Edwards - FB
Jake Fawcett - T
George Grandinette - G
Al Gutknecht - G
Ken Heineman - TB
Cecil Johnson - TB
Lew Jones - G
Bruiser Kinard - T
Andy Kowalski - E
Pug Manders - FB
Tilly Manton - BB
Jodie Marek - FB
Frank Martin - HB
John Matisi - T
Dean McAdams - TB
Tex Mooney - T
Pete Owens - G
Keith Ranspot - E
Frank Sachse - TB
Herm Schmarr - DE
George Sergienko - T
Joe Setcavage - BB
Vaughn Stewart - C
Bud Svendsen - C
Phil Swiadon - G
George Webb - E
Ray Wehba - E

1943 Chi. Bears

Al Babartsky - T
Jim Benton - E
Connie Mack Berry - E
Harry Clarke - HB
Bernie Digris - T
Gary Famiglietti - FB
Danny Fortmann - G
Bill Geyer - HB
Pete Gudauskas - G
Al Hoptowit - T
Tony Ippolito - G
Jim Logan - G
Sid Luckman - QB
Dante Magnani - HB
Bob Masters - HB
Al Matuza - C
Doug McEnulty - HB
Ray McLean - HB
Monte Merkel - G
Fred Mundee - C
George Musso - G
Bronko Nagurski - T
Ray Nolting - HB
Bill Osmanski - FB
Hamp Pool - E
John Siegal - E
Dom Sigillo - T
Bob Snyder - QB
Bill Steinkemper - T
Bob Steuber - HB
Bulldog Turner - C
Joe Vodicka - HB
George Wilson - E

1943 Chi. Cardinals

Art Albrecht - T
Conway Baker - G
Clarence Booth - T
Joe Bukant - TB
Chet Bulger - T
Ronnie Cahill - TB
Don Currivan - E
Gil Duggan - T
Vern Ghersanich - G
Marshall Goldberg - WB
John Grigas - FB
Johnny Hall - WB
Lou Marotti - G
Johnny Martin - WB
Walt Masters - TB
Bob Morrow - FB
Buddy Parker - BB
Don Pierce - C
Andy Puplis - WB
Cal Purdin - WB
Walt Rankin - FB
Freeman Rexer - E
Floyd Rhea - G
Marshall Robnett - G

Eddie Rucinski - E
George Smith - FB
Vaughn Stewart - C
Dixie Stokes - C
Clint Wager - E
Gordon Wilson - G

1943 Detroit

Stan Batinski - G
Sam Busich - DE
Bill Callihan - BB
Lloyd Cardwell - WB
Tom Colella - TB
Gerry Conlee - C
Mike Corgan - FB
Murray Evans - BB
Chuck Fenenbock - TB
Bill Fisk - E
Elmer Hackney - FB
Ben Hightower - E
Harry Hopp - FB
Al Kaporch - T
Bob Keene - WB
Alex Ketzko - T
Bert Kuczynski - E
Bob Layden - DE
Sonny Liles - G
Augie Lio - G
Jack Matheson - E
Riley Matheson - G
Ned Mathews - WB
Ed Opalewski - T
Ted Pavelec - G
Lyle Rockenbach - G
Ernie Rosteck - C
Tony Rubino - G
Frankie Sinkwich - TB
Roy Stuart - G
Art Van Tone - WB
Lloyd Wickett - T
Alex Wojciechowicz - C

1943 Green Bay

Chet Adams - T
Paul Berezney - T
Charley Brock - C
Lou Brock - TB
Tony Canadeo - TB
Irv Comp - TB
Larry Craig - BB
Tiny Croft - T
Dick Evans - E
Tony Falkenstein - FB
Bob Flowers - C
Sherwood Fries - G
Ted Fritsch - FB
Buckets Goldenberg - G
Don Hutson - E
Harry Jacunski - E
Bob Kahler - HB
Bill Kuusisto - G
Jim Lankas - FB
Joe Laws - HB
Joel Mason - E
Forrest McPherson - C
Baby Ray - T
Ade Schwammel - T
Glen Sorenson - G
Ben Starret - BB
Pete Tinsley - G
Andy Uram - HB

1943 NY Giants

Neal Adams - E
Verlin Adams - T
Chuck Avedisian - G
Hubert Barker - BB
Al Blozis - T
Dave Brown - WB
Victor Carroll - T
Frank Cope - T
Ward Cuff - WB
Walt Dubzinski - G
Mel Hein - C
Bull Karcis - FB
Carl Kinscherf - FB
Tuffy Leemans - QB
Frank Liebel - E
Sal Marone - G
Emery Nix - QB
Bill Paschal - FB
Bill Piccolo - C
Steve Pritko - E
Tom Roberts - G
Lee Shaffer - BB
Hank Soar - WB
Joe Sulaitis - BB
Bob Trocolor - QB
Larry Visnic - G
Will Walls - E
Len Younce - G

1943 Phi.

Tony Bova - E
Johnny Butler - HB
Larry Cabrelli - E
Rocco Canale - G
Enio Conti - G
Ted Doyle - T
Joe Frank - T
Charlie Gauer - FB
Ray Graves - C

Bill Hewitt - E
Jack Hinkle - HB
Bucko Kilroy - T
Ben Kish - FB
Ted Laux - HB
Bob Masters - FB
Hugh McCullough - DB
Eddie Michaels - G
Tom Miller - E
Gordon Paschka - G
Ray Reutt - DE
Steve Sader - FB
Elbie Schultz - T
Vic Sears - T
Allie Sherman - QB
Ernie Steele - HB
Dean Steward - HB
Bob Thurbon - HB
Al Wistert - T
Al Wukits - C
Roy Zimmerman - QB

1943 Washington

Joe Aguirre - E
Frank Akins - FB
Sammy Baugh - TB
George Cafego - TB
Bill Conkright - C
Coye Dunn - WB
Andy Farkas - FB
Dick Farman - G
Al Fiorentino - G
Joe Gibson - BB
Ray Hare - BB
Ken Hayden - C
Jack Jenkins - FB
Ted Lapka - E
Tony Leon - G
Bob Masterson - E
Wilbur Moore - WB
Joe Pasqua - T
Alex Piasecky - E
Frank Ribar - G
Lou Rymkus - T
Frank Seno - WB
Bob Seymour - FB
Clyde Shugart - G
Steve Slivinski - G
George Smith - C
Jack Smith - E
Leo Stasica - TB
Willie Wilkin - T
Joe Zeno - T

1944 Boston

Art Albrecht - T
George Cafego - QB
Vince Commisa - G
Milt Crain - FB
Joe Crowley - E
Bob Davis - HB
Walt Dubzinski - C
Tony Falkenstein - FB
Ed Franco - T
Frank Gaziano - G
Wimpy Giddens - T
Sam Goldman - E
Scott Gudmundson - QB
Dick Harrison - E
Ed Korisky - C
Augie Lio - G
Jim Magee - C
Johnny Martin - HB
Ed McGee - T
Bob McRoberts - HB
John Morelli - G
Keith Ranspot - E
Freeman Rexer - E
Thron Riggs - T
Paul Sanders - HB
Frank Santora - QB
Dave Smukler - FB
Leo Stasica - QB
Ken Steinmetz - FB
Morgan Tiller - E
Frank Turbert - QB
Bill Walker - G
Ted Williams - HB
Gordon Wilson - G
Harry Wynne - E

1944 Brooklyn

Tony Aiello - HB
Bill Brown - BB
Johnny Butler - TB
Joe Carter - E
George Doherty - T
John Ellis - G
Tony Falkenstein - BB
Kenny Fryer - TB
Ray Hare - HB
Cecil Johnson - TB
Bruiser Kinard - T
Andy Kowalski - E
Bill LaFitte - E
Tony Leon - G
Pug Manders - FB
Steve Marko - TB
Frank Martin - HB
Bob Masterson - E
Flip McDonald - E
Charlie McGibbony - TB

John McMichaels - TB
Bill Reynolds - HB
Floyd Rhea - G
Frank Sachse - TB
George Sergienko - T
Jim Sivell - G
George Smith - C
Vaughn Stewart - C
Frank Strom - T
Chuck Taylor - BB
Bob Trocolor - HB
Rocky Uguccioni - E
Charlie Ware - T
George Weeks - DE
Gordon Wilson - G

1944 Chi. Bears

Al Babartsky - T
Connie Mack Berry - E
Max Burnell - HB
Abe Croft - E
Gary Famiglietti - FB
Jim Fordham - FB
Bill Glenn - QB
Duke Greenich - HB
Al Grygo - HB
Pete Gudauskas - G
Al Hoptowit - T
Elmo Kelly - DE
Johnny Long - QB
Sid Luckman - QB
Bob Margarita - HB
Bob Masters - FB
Doug McEnulty - HB
Ray McLean - HB
Tipp Mooney - HB
Fred Mundee - C
George Musso - G
Dick Plasman - E
Paul Podmajersky - G
Tom Roberts - T
Gene Ronzani - QB
Dom Sigillo - T
Rudy Smeja - E
Ed Sprinkle - G
Jake Sweeney - T
Bulldog Turner - C
George Wilson - E
George Zorich - G

1944 Chi.

Conway Baker - G
Vince Banonis - C
Clarence Booth - T
Tony Bova - QB
Chet Bulger - T
Johnny Butler - HB
Don Currivan - E
Ted Doyle - T
Gil Duggan - T
John Grigas - FB
Walt Kichefski - E
George Magulick - HB
Lou Marotti - G
Johnny Martin - HB
Walt Masters - QB
John McCarthy - QB
Coley McDonough - QB
Elmer Merkovsky - T
John Perko - G
John Popovich - HB
Walt Rankin - FB
Marshall Robnett - C
Eddie Rucinski - E
Elbie Schultz - T
Bernie Semes - HB
Bob Thurbon - HB
Clint Wager - E
Al Wukits - C

1944 Cleveland

Jim Benton - E
Dave Bernard - BB
Boyd Clay - T
Tom Colella - TB
Bill Conkright - C
Tom Corbo - G
Jake Fawcett - T
Joe Gibson - C
Jim Gillette - HB
Al Gutknecht - G
Ray Hamilton - E
Roy Huggins - FB
Harvey Jones - FB
Mike Kabealo - HB
John Karrs - BB
Floyd Konetsky - DE
Les Lear - G
Del Lyman - T
Riley Matheson - G
Norm Olsen - T
John Petchel - BB
Steve Pritko - E
Chet Pudloski - T
Albie Reisz - TB
Bill Rieth - C
Charley Riffle - G
Mike Scarry - C
Stan Skoczen - HB
Walter West - FB
Lou Zontini - HB

1944 Detroit

Tony Aiello - WB
Stan Batinski - G
Paul Blessing - E
Harry Bolton - T
Bill Callihan - BB
Wayne Clark - E
Fred Dawley - FB
Dave Diehl - E
Joe D'Orazio - T
Ed Eiden - C
Tony Furst - T
John Greene - BB
Elmer Hackney - FB
Dale Hansen - DE
Al Kaporch - G
Bob Keene - WB
Tom Kennedy - T
Sonny Liles - G
Luke Lindon - T
Jackie Lowther - TB
Jack Matheson - E
Ed Opalewski - T
Freeman Rexer - DE
Bill Rogers - T
Ernie Rosteck - C
Frankie Sinkwich - TB
George Sirochman - G
Buzz Trebotich - BB
Art Van Tone - WB
Bob Westfall - FB
Alex Wojciechowicz - C

1944 Green Bay

Paul Berezney - T
Dick Bilda - TB
Charley Brock - C
Lou Brock - HB
Mike Bucchianeri - G
Tony Canadeo - TB
Irv Comp - TB
Larry Craig - BB
Tiny Croft - T
Paul Duhart - HB
Bob Flowers - C
Ted Fritsch - FB
Buckets Goldenberg - G
Don Hutson - E
Harry Jacunski - E
Bob Kahler - DB
Bob Kercher - DE
Bill Kuusisto - G
Joe Laws - HB
Joel Mason - E
Roy McKay - TB
Forrest McPherson - C
Don Perkins - FB
Baby Ray - T
Ade Schwammel - T
Glen Sorenson - G
Ben Starret - BB
Pete Tinsley - G
Chuck Tollefson - G
Alex Urban - E
Ray Wehba - E

1944 NY Giants

Neal Adams - E
Verlin Adams - E
Chuck Avedisian - G
Hubert Barker - BB
Keith Beebe - BB
Al Blozis - T
Len Calligaro - BB
Roland Caranci - T
Victor Carroll - T
Roy Clay - WB
Frank Cope - T
Ward Cuff - WB
Frank Damiani - T
Mel Hein - C
Arnie Herber - QB
Herb Kane - T
Carl Kinscherf - FB
Frank Liebel - E
Howie Livingston - FB
Bill Paschal - FB
Bill Petrilas - WB
Bill Piccolo - C
Jim Sivell - G
Hank Soar - QB
Ken Strong - FB
Joe Sulaitis - QB
Frank Umont - G
Larry Visnic - BB
John Weiss - E
Len Younce - G

1944 Philadelphia

Bruno Banducci - G
Jack Banta - HB
Mel Bleeker - HB
Larry Cabrelli - E
Rocco Canale - T
Enio Conti - G
John Durko - E
Carl Fagiolo - G
Jack Ferrante - E
Bob Friedman - T
Charlie Gauer - E
Jack Hinkle - HB
Toimi Jarvi - HB
Bucko Kilroy - T
Ben Kish - FB
Ted Laux - HB
Vic Lindskog - C
Art Macioszczyk - FB
Mike Mandarino - G
Bap Manzini - C
Duke Maronic - G
Flip McDonald - E
Eddie Michaels - G
Tom Miller - E
Walt Nowak - E
Allie Sherman - QB
Ernie Steele - HB
Steve Van Buren - HB
Al Wistert - T
John Yovicsin - DE
Roy Zimmerman - QB

1944 Washington

Joe Aguirre - E
Frank Akins - FB
Sammy Baugh - QB
Tom Bedore - G
Nick Campofreda - C
Les Dye - E
Andy Farkas - FB
Frankie Filchock
Al Fiorentino - G
Vern Foltz - C
Larry Fuller - HB
Larry Johnson - C
Jack Keenan - T
Ted Lapka - E
Pete Marcus - DE
Ed Merkle - G
Mike Micka - FB
Ray Monaco - G
Wilbur Moore - HB
Andy Natowich - HB
Jim North - T
Alex Piasecky - E
Frank Seno - HB
Bob Seymour - FB
Ev Sharp - T
Clyde Shugart - G
Bob Sneddon - HB
Doug Turley - E
Mitch Ucovich - T
Joe Ungerer - T
Frank Walton - G
Larry Weldon - QB
Joe Zeno - T

1945 Boston

Bill Anderson - DE
George Cafego - QB
Joe Crowley - E
Don Currivan - E
Bob Davis - HB
Don Deeks - T
Babe Dimancheff - HB
George Doherty - T
Paul Duhart - HB
Al Fiorentino - G
John Grigas - FB
Scott Gudmundson - QB
Ellis Jones - G
Andy Kowalski - DE
Tony Leon - G
Augie Lio - G
Jim Magee - C
Pug Manders - FB
Lou Mark - DE
Frank Martin - WB
Johnny Martin - HB
Bob Masterson - E
Ned Mathews - HB
Hugh McCullough - QB
Ed McGee - T
Mike Micka - FB
John Morelli - G
Ace Parker - QB
Keith Ranspot - E
Floyd Rhea - G
Frank Sachse - QB
Jack Sachse - C
George Sergienko - T
George Smith - C
Ken Steinmetz - FB
Bill Walker - G

1945 Chi. Bears

Lee Artoe - T
Al Babartsky - T
Connie Mack Berry - E
Glenn Burgeis - T
Abe Croft - E
Jim Daniell - T
Chuck Drulis - G
Gary Famiglietti - FB
Jim Fordham - FB
Hugh Gallarneau - HB
Al Grygo - HB
Pete Gudauskas - G
Al Hoptowit - T
Jackie Hunt - HB
Special Delivery Jones - HB
Ken Kavanaugh - E
Nick Kerasiotis - G
Johnny Long - QB
Sid Luckman - QB
Bob Margarita - HB
Forrest Masterson - C
George McAfee - HB
Ray McLean - HB
Charlie Mitchell - DB
Tipp Mooney - HB
Jack Morton - HB
Rudy Mucha - G
Fred Mundee - C
Pete Perez - G
Don Perkins - FB
Frank Ramsey - T
Tom Roberts - T
Gene Ronzani - QB
John Schiechl - C
Rudy Smeja - E
Ed Sprinkle - G
Joe Stydahar - T
Bob Swisher - HB
Bulldog Turner - C
Joe Vodicka - HB
Milt Vucinich - C
George Wilson - E
George Zorich - G

1945 Chi. Cardinals

Ray Apolskis - C
Conway Baker - G
Frank Balasz - FB
Libby Bertagnolli - G
Hal Blackwell - HB
Ernie Bonelli - FB
Dave Braden - G
Les Bruckner - FB
Chet Bulger - T
Ray Busler - T
Bill Campbell - C
Leo Cantor - HB
Joe Carter - E
Paul Christman - QB
Paul Collins - QB
Bill Dewell - E
Al Drulis - FB
Gil Duggan - T
John Durko - DE
Bob Eckl - T
Steve Enich - G
Ralph Fife - G
Ralph Foster - T
Larry Fuller - LB
Frank Ivy - DE
Johnny Knolla - HB
Joe Kuharich - G
Al Lindow - HB
Chet Maeda - HB
Lou Marotti - G
Bus Mertes - HB
Bob Norman - C
Vic Obeck - G
Vince Oliver - QB
Jim Poole - E
Walt Rankin - FB
Freeman Rexer - E
Bill Reynolds - HB
Hal Robl - LB
Marshall Robnett - C
Eddie Rucinski - E
Frank Seno - HB
Cliff Speegle - C
Mitch Ucovich - T
Joe Vodicka - HB
Clint Wager - E
Walt Watt - HB
Gordon Wilson - G
Bob Zimny - T

1945 Cleveland

Graham Armstrong - T
Jim Benton - E
Dave Bernard - LB
Gil Bouley - T
Tom Colella - HB
Bob deLauer - C
Roger Eason - T
Fred Gehrke - HB
Jim Gillette - HB
Don Greenwood - FB
Ray Hamilton - E
Roger Harding - C
Red Hickey - E
Jack Jacobs - QB
Harvey Jones - HB
George Koch - HB
Floyd Konetsky - DE
Mike Lazetich - G
Les Lear - G
Len Levy - T
Sonny Liles - G
Riley Matheson - G
Art Mergenthal - G
Ray Monaco - G
Rudy Mucha - G
Steve Nemeth - QB
George Phillips - LB
Steve Pritko - E
Albie Reisz - QB
Bill Rieth - C
Ralph Ruthstrom - FB
Mike Scarry - C
Elbie Schultz - T
Bob Shaw - E
Rudy Sikich - T
Bob Waterfield - QB
Pat West - FB
Joe Winkler - C
Jim Worden - HB
Walt Zirinsky - HB

1945 Detroit

Stan Batinski - G
Dick Booth - WB
Bob Brumley - WB
Bill Callihan - BB
Chuck DeShane - BB
Dave Diehl - E
Andy Farkas - FB
Chuck Fenenbock - TB
Ed Frutig - E
John Greene - E
Ted Grefe - E
Elmer Hackney - FB
Al Kaporch - T
Bob Keene - WB
Larry Knorr - E
Michael Kostiuk - T
Frank Kring - LB
Joe Krol - DB
Sonny Liles - G
Luke Lindon - T
Elmer Madarik - WB
Joe Manzo - T
Jack Matheson - E
Vince Mazza - DE
Dick Mesak - T
Arch Milano - E
Garvin Mugg - T
Robert Nelson - C
Cotton Price - TB
Bill Radovich - G
Lake Roberson - DE
Dave Ryan - TB
Larry Sartori - G
Dom Sigillo - T
Bob Sneddon - WB
Frank Szymanski - C
Damon Tassos - G
Jim Thomason - WB
Buzz Trebotich - BB
Emil Uremovich - T
Art Van Tone - WB
Dick Weber - TB
Bob Westfall - FB
Rex Williams - C
Alex Wojciechowicz - C

1945 Green Bay

Bob Adkins - BB
Solon Barnett - T
Charley Brock - C
Lou Brock - TB
Mike Bucchianeri - G
Irv Comp - TB
Larry Craig - BB
Bernie Crimmins - G
Tiny Croft - T
Bob Flowers - C
Ray Frankowski - G
Ted Fritsch - FB
Ed Frutig - E
Buckets Goldenberg - G
Clyde Goodnight - E
Don Hutson - E
Ken Keuper - BB
Bill Kuusisto - G
Joe Laws - HB
Paul Lipscomb - T
Nolan Luhn - E
Joel Mason - DE
Roy McKay - TB
Forrest McPherson - T
Russ Mosley - HB
Carl Mulleneaux - E
Ed Neal - T
Ernie Pannell - T
Don Perkins - FB
Baby Ray - T
Chuck Sample - FB
Bruce Smith - HB
Ken Snelling - FB
Glen Sorenson - G
Ben Starret - BB
Pete Tinsley - G
Chuck Tollefson - G
Alex Urban - E

1945 NY Giants

Neal Adams - E
Verlin Adams - G
Elmer Barbour - BB
Hubert Barker - BB
Victor Carroll - T
Frank Cope - T
Ward Cuff - WB
Lou DeFilippo - C
John Doolan - WB
Lou Eaton - T
Steve Filipowicz - FB
Sam Fox - E
George Franck - WB
Bob Garner - G
Carl Grate - G
Mel Hein - C
Arnie Herber - QB
Junie Hovious - QB
Herb Kane - T
Tom Kearns - T
Mike Klotovich - WB
Frank Liebel - E
Joe Lindahl - G
Jim Little - T
Howie Livingston - FB
Frank Martin - WB
Bob Morrow - BB
Bill Paschal - FB
Win Pedersen - T
Bill Petrilas - DB
Bill Piccolo - C
Jim Poole - E
Marion Pugh - QB
Phil Ragazzo - T
Lee Shaffer - BB
Ed Shedlosky - WB
Jim Sivell - G
Hal Springer - E
Ken Strong - K
Joe Sulaitis - QB
Army Tomaini - T
Frank Umont - G
Larry Visnic - G
John Weiss - E
Tarzan White - G
Harry Wynne - E

1945 Philadelphia

Ben Agajanian - K
Bruno Banducci - G
Jack Banta - HB
Mel Bleeker - HB
Johnny Butler - HB
Larry Cabrelli - E
Rocco Canale - T
Jim Castiglia - FB
Enio Conti - G
Dick Erdlitz - HB
Jack Ferrante - E
Terry Fox - LB
George Fritts - T
Charlie Gauer - DE
Jack Hinkle - HB
Dick Humbert - E
Abe Karnofsky - HB
Bucko Kilroy - T
Ben Kish - FB
Vic Lindskog - C
Mike Mandarino - C
Bap Manzini - C
Duke Maronic - G
Flip McDonald - E
Fred Meyer - E
Eddie Michaels - G
Red Ramsey - DE
John Rogalla - FB
Jack Sanders - G
Vic Sears - T
Allie Sherman - QB
Abe Shires - T
John Smith - T
Milt Smith - DB
Ernie Steele - HB
Gil Steinke - HB
Bob Suffridge - G
Tommy Thompson - QB
Steve Van Buren - HB
Busit Warren - HB
Al Wistert - T
Roy Zimmerman - QB

1945 Pittsburgh

Ben Agajanian - K
Tom Alberghini - G
Tony Bova - E
Art Brandau - C
Carl Buda - G
Garth Chamberlain - G
Chuck Cherundolo - C
Joe Cibulas - T
Joe Coomer - T
Carmine DePascal - E
Henry DePaul - G
Dick Dolly - E
Ted Doyle - T
Bill Dudley - TB
Paul Duhart - HB
Vern Foltz - C
Len Frketich - T
Jack Itzel - FB
Toimi Jarvi - TB
Art Jones - HB
George Kiick - HB
Frank Kimble - E
John Kondria - T
Julie Koshlap - HB
Hubbard Law - G
Jackie Lowther - TB
John Lucente - FB
Ed McNamara - T
Elmer Merkovsky - G
John Naioti - HB
Allen Nichols - FB
Mel O'Delli - HB
Al Olszewski - E
John Patrick - BB
Leon Pense - BB
John Perko - G
John Petchel - BB
Pepper Petrella - HB
Joe Pierre - E
John Popovich - HB
Al Postus - TB
Ross Sorce - T
Ed Stofko - TB
Glen Stough - T
Morgan Tiller - E
Sid Tinsley - HB
Si Titus - C
Busit Warren - TB
Al Wukits - C

1945 Washington

John Adams - T
Joe Aguirre - E
Frank Akins - FB
Ki Aldrich - C
Vito Ananis - HB
Earl Audet - T
Steve Bagarus - HB
Ernie Barber - C
Sammy Baugh - QB
Merl Condit - HB
Fred Davis - T
Bill deCorrevont - HB
Bob DeFruiter - HB
Al DeMao - C
John Doolan - WB
Les Dye - E
Frankie Filchock - QB
Larry Fuller - LB
Jim Gaffney - HB
Zip Hanna - G
Cece Hare - HB
Jack Keenan - G
John Koniszewski - T
Reid Lennan - G
Al Lolotai - G
Mike Micka - FB
Tom Miller - E
Wayne Millner - E
Wilbur Moore - HB
Alex Piasecky - E
Lee Presley - C
Sal Rosato - FB
Bob Seymour - FB
Ev Sharp - T
Clem Stralka - G
Dick Todd - HB
Doug Turley - E
Joe Ungerer - T
Frank Walton - G
Jim Watson - C
Larry Weldon - DE
Marv Whited - G

1946 NFL

1946 Boston

Duke Abbruzzi - HB
John Badaczewski - G
Ralph Calcagni - T
Rocco Canale - G
Hal Crisler - E
Don Currivan - E
Boley Dancewicz - QB
Bob Davis - HB
Tom Dean - T
Don Deeks - T
Babe Dimancheff - HB
Joe Domnanovich - C
Don Eliason - E
Gary Famiglietti - FB
Jim Gillette - HB
Sam Goldman - E
Paul Governali - QB
John Grigas - FB
Joe Hoague - FB
Rube Juster - T
Abe Karnofsky - HB
Gene Lee - C
Tony Leon - G
Jim Magee - C
Howie Maley - QB
Ed McGee - T
Mike Micka - HB
Win Pedersen - T
Rudy Romboli - FB
Nick Scollard - E
Steve Sierocinski - T
Joe Sulaitis - LB
Joe Zeno - G

1946 Chi. Bears

Al Baisi - G
Connie Mack Berry - E
Ray Bray - G
Stu Clarkson - C
Fred Davis - T
Chuck Drulis - G
Tom Farris - QB
John Federovitch - T
Aldo Forte - G
Hugh Gallarneau - HB
Bill Geyer - HB
Mike Jarmoluk - T
Ken Kavanaugh - E
Jim Keane - E
Ed Kolman - T
Walt Lamb - E
Sid Luckman - QB
Dante Magnani - HB
Bob Margarita - HB
Frank Maznicki - HB
George McAfee - HB
Ray McLean - HB
Rudy Mucha - G
Noah Mullins - HB
Joe Osmanski - FB
Bill Osmanski - FB
Don Perkins - FB
Pat Preston - G
Lloyd Reese - FB
John Schiechl - C
Dick Schweidler - HB
Ed Sprinkle - E
Walt Stickel - T
Joe Stydahar - T
Bulldog Turner - C
George Wilson - E

1946 Chi. Cardinals

Elmer Angsman - HB
Ray Apolskis - G
Loyd Arms - G
Vince Banonis - C
Bill Blackburn - C
Chet Bulger - T
Bill Campbell - C
Paul Christman - QB
Jake Colhouer - G
Zuehl Conoly - G
Ward Cuff - HB
Bill Dewell - E
Al Drulis - FB
Ralph Foster - T
Marshall Goldberg - HB
Pat Harder - FB
Al Hust - E
Frank Ivy - E
Jimmy Johnston - HB
Tom Kearns - T
Mal Kutner - E
Bob Maddock - G
Ray Mallouf - QB
Stan Mauldin - T
Bill Montgomery - FB
Joe Parker - E
Dick Plasman - DE
Buster Ramsey - G
Walt Rankin - FB
Eddie Rucinski - E
Paul Sarringhaus - HB
Frank Seno - HB
Jimmy Strausbaugh - HB
George Sutch - HB
Walt Szot - T
Bob Zimny - T

1946 Detroit

Stan Batinski - G
Jim Callahan - TB
Bob Cifers - BB
Ted Cremer - E
Bill deCorrevont
Chuck DeShane - BB
Leon Fichman - T
Aldo Forte - G
Ed Frutig - E
John Greene - E
Elmer Hackney - LB
Jack Helms - DE
Jim Jones - TB
Ralph Jones - E
Walt Jurkiewicz - C
Elmer Madarik - TB
Jack Matheson - E
Vince Mazza - E
Joel McCoy - TB
Jim Montgomery - T
Tony Rubino - G
Dave Ryan - TB
Mickey Sanzotta - WB
Ivan Schottel - BB
Gene Spangler - WB
Frank Szymanski - C
Damon Tassos - G
Russ Thomas - T
Emil Uremovich - T
Walt Vezmar - G
Bob Westfall - FB
Lloyd Wickett - T
Camp Wilson - FB
Alex Wojciechowicz - C

1946 Green Bay

Cliff Aberson - TB
Solon Barnett - G
Jug Bennett - G
Charley Brock - C
Tony Canadeo - TB
Irv Comp - TB
Larry Craig - BB
Tiny Croft - T
Bob Flowers - C
Bob Forte - HB
Ted Fritsch - FB
Les Gatewood - C
Clyde Goodnight - E
Ken Keuper - BB
Bill Kuusisto - G
Bill Lee - T
Russ Letlow - G
Paul Lipscomb - T
Nolan Luhn - E
Roy McKay - FB
Tom Miller - E
Charlie Mitchell - DB
Russ Mosley - DB

Carl Mulleneaux - DE
Ed Neal - G
Bob Nussbaumer - HB
Urban Odson - T
Merv Pregulman - G
Hal Prescott - E
Baby Ray - T
Ray Riddick - DE
Herm Rohrig - HB
Walt Schlinkman - FB
Bruce Smith - TB
Al Sparlis - G
Chuck Tollefson - G
Don Wells - E
Dick Wildung - G
Al Zupek - BB

1946 LA Rams

Jack Banta - HB
Jim Benton - E
Gil Bouley - T
Bob deLauer - C
Roger Eason - G
Tom Farmer - HB
Jake Fawcett - T
Fred Gehrke - HB
Ray Hamilton - E
Roger Harding - C
Jim Hardy - QB
Tommy Harmon - HB
Red Hickey - E
Bob Hoffman - FB
Mike Holovak - FB
Clyde Johnson - T
Mike Lazetich - G
Les Lear - G
Len Levy - G
Riley Matheson - G
Art Mergenthal - G
Fred Naumetz - C
Joe Pasqua - T
Steve Pritko - E
Albie Reisz - DB
Ralph Ruthstrom - FB
Elbie Schultz - T
Bob Shaw - E
Woody Strode - E
Steve Sucic - FB
Kenny Washington - HB
Bob Waterfield - QB
Pat West - FB
Jack Wilson - HB

1946 NY Giants

Dave Brown - WB
Joe Byler - T
Victor Carroll - T
Frank Cope - T
Tex Coulter - T
Lou DeFilippo - C
Bob Dobelstein - G
John Doolan - WB
Monk Edwards - G
Frankie Filchock - QB
Steve Filipowicz - BB
George Franck - WB
Chet Gladchuk - C
Pete Gorgone - BB
Merle Hapes - FB
Cece Hare - BB
Jim Lee Howell - E
Frank Liebel - E
Howie Livingston - WB
Kayo Lunday - G
Don McCafferty - E
Jack Mead - E
Emery Nix - QB
Lou Palazzi - C
Bill Paschal - FB
Jim Poole - E
Phil Ragazzo - T
Frank Reagan - FB
Hank Soar - FB
Ken Strong - K
Orville Tuttle - G
John Weiss - E
Jim White - T
Len Younce - G

1946 Philadelphia

Mel Bleeker - HB
Larry Cabrelli - E
Jim Castiglia - FB
Russ Craft - HB
Otis Douglas - T
John Eibner - T
Jack Ferrante - E
Bob Friedlund - E
Ray Graves - C
Henry Gude - C
Jack Hinkle - HB
Dick Humbert - E
Bucko Kilroy - T
Ben Kish - FB
Pete Kmetovic - HB
Bob Krieger - E
Bert Kuczynski - E
Vic Lindskog - C
Augie Lio - G
Jay MacDowell - T
Duke Maronic - G
Flip McDonald - E
Bob McDonough - G

Eddie Michaels - G
Joe Muha - FB
Elliott Ormsbee - HB
Cliff Patton - G
Bosh Pritchard - HB
Vic Sears - T
Allie Sherman - QB
Rudy Smeja - E
Ernie Steele - HB
Gil Steinke - HB
Tommy Thompson - QB
Steve Van Buren - HB
Al Wistert - T
Alex Wojciechowicz - C
John Wyhonic - G
Roy Zimmerman - QB

1946 Pittsburgh

Ernie Bonelli - HB
Tony Bova - E
Art Brandau - C
Ray Bucek - G
Chuck Cherundolo - C
Johnny Clement - TB
Tony Compagno - FB
Merl Condit - HB
Joe Coomer - T
Bob Davis - E
Bill Dudley - TB
Bill Dutton - HB
Ralph Fife - G
Bill Garnaas - BB
Walt Gorinski - FB
Sam Gray - E
Val Jansante - E
Max Kielbasa - HB
Earl Klapstein - T
Steve Lach - FB
Frank Mattioli - G
Art McCaffray - T
Charley Mehelich - E
Elmer Merkovsky - T
John Patrick - BB
John Perko - G
Joe Repko - T
Jim Reynolds - DB
Cullen Rogers - HB
Charlie Seabright - BB
Nick Skorich - G
George Titus - C
Andy Tomasic - TB
Jack Wiley - T

1946 Washington

John Adams - T
Frank Akins - FB
Ki Aldrich - C
Don Avery - T
Steve Bagarus - HB
Sammy Baugh - QB
Oscar Britt - G
Ed Cifers - E
Al Couppee - G
Bob DeFruiter - HB
Al DeMao - C
Clyde Ehrhardt - C
Jim Gaffney - HB
Jack Jacobs - QB
Johnny Jaffurs - G
Jack Jenkins - FB
John Koniszewski - T
John Kovatch - E
Ted Lapka - E
John Lookabaugh - E
Wilbur Moore - HB
Jim Peebles - E
Dick Poillon - HB
Sal Rosato - FB
Eddie Saenz - HB
Ralph Schilling - E
John Steber - G
Paul Stenn - T
Clem Stralka - G
Dick Todd - HB
Doug Turley - E
Bill Ward - G
Jim Youel - QB
Bill Young - T

1946 AAFC

1946 Brooklyn

Neal Adams - E
Charlie Armstrong - TB
George Bernhardt - G
John Billman - G
Harry Buffington - G
Mickey Colmer - BB
Harry Connolly - TB
Bill Daley - FB
Nick Daukas - T
Joe Davis - E
Glenn Dobbs - TB
Jack Freeman - G
Monk Gafford - WB
Joe Gibson - C
Frank Hrabetin - T
Dub Jones - WB
Saxon Judd - E
Herb Maack - T
Phil Martinovich - G
Lew Mayne - TB

Bob McCain - E
Jim McCarthy - E
Walt McDonald - BB
Ed Mieszkowski - T
Russ Morrow - C
Vic Obeck - G
Bob Paffrath - BB
Bolo Perdue - DE
George Perpich - T
Dom Principe - FB
Cal Purdin - WB
Martin Ruby - T
George Sergienko - T
Rhoten Shetley - FB
Doyle Tackett - WB
Charlie Timmons - FB
Art Van Tone - WB
Tex Warrington - C

1946 Buffalo

John Batorski - E
Blondy Black - FB
Sam Brazinsky - C
Marty Comer - E
Bill Daddio - DE
Al Dekdebrun - QB
George Doherty - G
Andy Dudish - HB
Jack Dugger - T
Ray Ebli - E
John Fekete - HB
Chubby Grigg - T
Harry Hopp - QB
Pres Johnston - FB
Elmer Jones - G
Steve Juzwik - HB
Fay King - E
Quentin Klenk - T
Al Klug - G
Nick Klutka - E
Jack Kramer - T
Vic Kulbitski - FB
Hal Lahar - G
Jim Lecture - G
Patsy Martinelli - C
John Matisi - T
Chet Mutryn - HB
Herb Nelson - E
John Perko - G
Rocco Pirro - G
Felto Prewitt - C
Ben Pucci - T
Curt Sandig - HB
Ralph Schilling - E
C.B. Stanley - T
Ken Stofer - QB
Roy Stuart - G
George Terlep - QB
Jim Thibaut - FB
Bob Thurbon - HB
Lou Tomasetti - HB
Al Vandeweghe - E
Al Wukits - C
Lou Zontini - FB

1946 Chi. Rockets

Bill Boedeker - HB
Jim Brutz - T
Walt Clay - HB
Herb Coleman - C
Norm Cox - TB
Bob Dove - E
Don Griffin - HB
Ralph Heywood - E
Billy Hillenbrand - HB
Crazy Legs Hirsch - HB
Bob Hoernschemeyer - TB
Charlie Huneke - T
Bill Kellagher - FB
Quentin Klenk - T
Pat Lahey - E
Pete Lamana - FB
Ernie Lewis - FB
Ned Mathews - HB
Max Morris - E
Bob Motl - E
Steve Nemeth - TB
Jim O'Neal - G
Mickey Parks - C
Jim Pearcy - G
Frank Quillen - E
Joe Ruetz - G
Bill Schroeder - TB
Tony Sumpter - G
Norm Verry - T
Evan Vogds - G
Lloyd Wasserbach - T
Willie Wilkin - T
Walter Williams - TB

1946 Cleveland

Chet Adams - T
Al Akins - HB
Ernie Blandin - T
George Cheroke - G
Tom Colella - HB
Al Coppage - E
Jim Daniell - T
Fred Evans - HB
Gene Fekete - FB
Frank Gatski - C

Otto Graham - QB
Don Greenwood - HB
Lou Groza - T
John Harrington - E
Lin Houston - G
Special Delivery Jones
Alex Kapter - G
Bob Kolesar - G
Dante Lavelli - E
Cliff Lewis - QB
Bill Lund - HB
Mel Maceau - C
Marion Motley - FB
John Rokisky - E
Lou Rymkus - T
Lou Saban - FB
Mike Scarry - C
Bud Schwenk - QB
Gaylon Smith - FB
Mac Speedie - E
Bob Steuber - HB
Ray Terrell - HB
Ed Ulinski - G
Bill Willis - G
John Yonakor - E
George Young - E

1946 LA Dons

Joe Aguirre - E
Lee Artoe - T
Earl Audet - T
Angelo Bertelli - QB
Harry Clarke - HB
Gil Duggan - T
Earl Elsey - HB
Chuck Fenenbock - HB
Ray Frankowski - G
Dale Gentry - E
Bill Kerr - E
John Kimbrough - FB
Al Krueger - E
Al Lolotai - G
Andy Marefos - FB
Jack McQuary - HB
Bus Mertes - HB
Joe Mihal - T
Paul Mitchell - T
Bob Mitchell - QB
Jack Morton - E
Robert Nelson - C
Don Nolander - C
Bob Nowaskey - E
Bernie Nygren - HB
Charlie O'Rourke - QB
John Polanski - FB
Bill Radovich - G
Bob Reinhard - T
Hank Rockwell - C
Bob Seymour - HB
Bob Sneddon - HB
Frank Trigilio - FB
Paul Vinnola - HB
Frank Yokas - G

1946 Miami

Ed Bell - G
Paul Berezney - T
Lamar Blount - E
Daryl Cato - C
Bill Daley - FB
Lamar Davis - E
Bill Davis - T
Kay Eakin - QB
Gene Ellenson - T
Dick Erdlitz - HB
Terry Fox - FB
Monk Gafford - HB
Fred Gloden - HB
George Hekkers - T
Ken Holley - QB
Harry Hopp - QB
Dick Horne - E
Frank Hrabetin - T
Pres Johnston - FB
Dub Jones - HB
Buddy Jungmichel - G
Stan Kozlowski - FB
Joe Krivonak - G
Walt McDonald - QB
Fondren Mitchell - HB
Jimmy Nelson - HB
Mitch Olenski - T
Bob Paffrath - HB
Hamp Pool - E
Cotton Price - QB
Marion Pugh - QB
Cal Purdin - HB
Don Reece - FB
Jim Reynolds - FB
Prince Scott - E
Jim Sivell - G
Stan Stasica - HB
Jimmy Tarrant - QB
John Tavener - C
Chuck Taylor - G
Frank Trigilio - FB
Hub Ulrich - E
Johnny Vardian - HB
Ken Whitlow - C
Tex Williams - C
Al Wukits - C
George Zorich - G

1946 NY

Yankees

Bruce Alford - E
Jack Baldwin - C
Roman Bentz - T
Harry Burrus - E
Lloyd Cheatham - BB
Mel Conger - E
George Doherty - G
Ray Hare - BB
Harvey Johnson - FB
Nate Johnson - T
Mike Karmazin - G
Bob Kennedy - FB
Bruiser Kinard - T
George Kinard - G
Pug Manders - FB
Bob Masterson - E
Harley McCollum - T
Bob Morrow - BB
Derrell Palmer - T
Ace Parker - TB
Bob Perina - TB
Roman Piskor - T
Dewey Proctor - FB
Eddie Prokop - FB
Charley Riffle - G
Tom Robertson - C
Jack Russell - E
Spec Sanders - TB
Perry Schwartz - E
Frankie Sinkwich - TB
Lou Sossamon - C
Henry Stanton - E
Bob Sweiger - WB
Lowell Wagner - WB
Joe Yackanich - G

1946 San Francisco

Frankie Albert - QB
Ed Balatti - E
Bruno Banducci - G
Dick Bassi - G
Alyn Beals - E
Bob Bryant - T
Ken Casanega - HB
Gerry Conlee - C
Don Durdan - HB
Dutch Elston - C
Len Eshmont - HB
Bill Fisk - E
Eddie Forrest - C
Pete Franceschi - HB
Jesse Freitas - QB
Garland Gregory - G
Visco Grgich - G
Parker Hall - QB
John Kuzman - T
Ned Mathews - HB
John Mellus - T
Hank Norberg - E
Earle Parsons - HB
Charlie Pavlich - G
Bill Remington - C
Dick Renfro - FB
Ken Roskie - FB
Norm Standlee - FB
Johnny Strzykalski - HB
Nick Susoeff - E
Rupe Thornton - G
Bob Titchenal - E
Joe Vetrano - HB
John Woudenberg - T

1947 NFL

1947 Boston

John Badaczewski - G
Fritz Barzilauskas - G
Rocco Canale - T
Bill Chipley - E
Bill Collins - G
Hal Crisler - E
Don Currivan - E
Boley Dancewicz - QB
Tom Dean - T
Don Deeks - T
Joe Domnanovich - C
Ed Fiorentino - DE
Bill Godwin - C
Joe Golding - HB
Sam Goldman - E
Paul Governali - QB
John Grigas - FB
Bill Kennedy - G
Bob Long - HB
Howie Maley - QB
Frank Maznicki - HB
Bob McClure - G
Jim Mello - FB
Mike Micka - HB
Bill Paschal - FB
John Poto - HB
Tom Rodgers - T
Rudy Romboli - FB
Joe Sabasteanski - C
Nick Scollard - E
Frank Seno - HB
Alex Sidorik - T
Steve Sucic - FB
Carroll Vogelaar - T
Joe Watt - HB

Walter Williams - HB
Jim Wright - G
Joe Zeno - G

1947 Chi. Bears

Eddie Allen - FB
Ray Bray - G
Ed Cifers - E
Stu Clarkson - C
Fred Davis - T
Chuck Drulis - G
Ed Ecker - T
Tom Farris - QB
Bob Fenimore - HB
Hugh Gallarneau - HB
Thurman Garrett - C
George Gulyanics - HB
Fred Hartman - T
Mike Holovak - FB
Mike Jarmoluk - E
Bill Johnson - G
Ken Kavanaugh - E
Jim Keane - E
Don Kindt - HB
Ed Kolman - T
Sid Luckman - QB
Jack Matheson - E
George McAfee - HB
Ray McLean - HB
Bill Milner - G
Frank Minini - HB
Noah Mullins - HB
Joe Osmanski - FB
Bill Osmanski - FB
Pat Preston - G
Russ Reader - DB
Nick Sacrinty - QB
Allen Smith - DE
Ed Sprinkle - E
Walt Stickel - T
Bulldog Turner - C

1947 Chi. Cardinals

Plato Andros - G
Elmer Angsman - HB
Ray Apolskis - G
Loyd Arms - G
Vince Banonis - C
Bill Blackburn - C
Chet Bulger - T
Jeff Burkett - E
Bill Campbell - LB
Paul Christman - QB
Red Cochran - FB
Jake Colhouer - G
Joe Coomer - T
Bill deCorrevont - HB
Bill Dewell - E
Babe Dimancheff - HB
John Doolan - E
Clarence Esser - DE
Marshall Goldberg
Pat Harder - FB
Frank Ivy - DE
Jack Karwales - E
Mal Kutner - E
Ray Mallouf - QB
Caleb Martin - T
Stan Mauldin - T
Hamilton Nichols - G
Joe Parker - DE
Dick Plasman - T
Buster Ramsey - G
Walt Rankin - FB
Vic Schwall - HB
Charles Smith - HB
Walt Szot - T
Charlie Trippi - HB
Bob Zimny - T

1947 Detroit

Stan Batinski - G
Ben Chase - G
Ted Cook - E
Ted Cremer - E
Bob DeFruiter - HB
Robert Derleth - T
Chuck DeShane - G
Bill Dudley - HB
Jack Dugger - T
Leon Fichman - T
John Greene - E
George Hekkers - T
Ralph Heywood - E
Bill Hillman - FB
Bob Ivory - G
Tommy James - HB
Elmer Jones - G
Pete Kmetovic - HB
Les Lear - G
Clyde LeForce - QB
Elmer Madarik - HB
Joe Margucci - QB
Kelley Mote - E
Reed Nilsen - C
Bill O'Brien - HB
Mitch Olenski - T
Merv Pregulman - C
Ken Reese - HB
Floyd Rhea - G
Dave Ryan - TB
John Sanchez - T
Cecil Souders - E

Ed Stacco - T
Dick Stovall - C
Steve Sucic - FB
Frank Szymanski - C
Russ Thomas - T
Walt Vezmar - G
Bill Ward - G
Joe Watt - HB
Bob Westfall - FB
Bob Wiese - HB
Camp Wilson - FB
Roy Zimmerman - QB

1947 Green Bay

Ed Bell - G
Charley Brock - C
Tony Canadeo - HB
Ray Clemons - G
Ed Cody - FB
Irv Comp - QB
Larry Craig - E
Tiny Croft - T
Ward Cuff - HB
Ralph Davis - G
Bob Flowers - C
Aldo Forte - G
Bob Forte - HB
Ted Fritsch - HB
Les Gatewood - C
Jim Gillette - HB
Clyde Goodnight - E
Jack Jacobs - QB
Ken Keuper - HB
John Kovatch - DE
Paul Lipscomb - T
Nolan Luhn - E
Bob McDougal - FB
Roy McKay - HB
Ed Neal - G
Urban Odson - T
Baby Ray - T
Herm Rohrig - HB
Walt Schlinkman - FB
Bob Skoglund - DE
Bruce Smith - HB
Damon Tassos - G
Don Wells - DE
Dick Wildung - G
Gene Wilson - E

1947 LA Rams

Steve Bagarus - HB
Jack Banta - HB
Jim Benton - E
Mel Bleeker - HB
Gil Bouley - T
Ed Champagne - T
Gerry Cowhig - FB
Bob David - G
Hal Dean - G
Roger Eason - G
Jack Finlay - G
Fred GehrkeHB
Ray Hamilton - E
Jim Hardy - QB
Tommy Harmon - HB
Red Hickey - E
Dick Hoerner - FB
Bob Hoffman - FB
Les Horvath - HB
Frank Hubbell - E
Dick Huffman - T
Clyde Johnson - T
John Ksionzyk - QB
Mike Lazetich - G
Dante Magnani - HB
Jack Martin - C
Riley Matheson - G
Fred Naumetz - C
Steve Pritko - E
Elbie Schultz - T
Bill Smyth - T
Kenny Washington - HB
Bob Waterfield - QB
Pat West - FB
Jack Wilson - HB
Jack Zilly - E

1947 NY Giants

Jim Blumenstock - FB
Dave Brown - WB
Gregg Browning - E
John Cannady - BB
Victor Carroll - E
George Cheverko - WB
Frank Cope - T
Tex Coulter - E
Lou DeFilippo - C
Bob Dobelstein - G
Art Faircloth - QB
George Franck - WB
Chet Gladchuk - C
Paul Governali - QB
Bill Hachten - G
Jim Lee Howell - E
Duke Iverson - BB
Frank Liebel - E
Howie Livingston - WB
Kayo Lunday - G
Jack Mead - E
Bill Miklich - BB
Bob Morris - HB
Jerry Niles - QB

Lou Palazzi - C
Bill Paschal - FB
Gordon Paschka - FB
Ray Poole - E
Phil Ragazzo - T
Frank Reagan - QB
Choo-Choo Roberts - FB
Bill Schuler - T
Ken Strong - K
Joe Sulaitis - BB
George Tobin - G
John Weiss - E
Jim White - T
Len Younce - G

1947 Philadelphia

Neill Armstrong - E
Al Baisi - G
Alf Bauman - T
Larry Cabrelli - DE
T.G. Campion - T
Russ Craft - HB
Noble Doss - HB
Otis Douglas - T
Jack Ferrante - E
John Green - DE
Roger Harding - C
Jack Hinkle - HB
Dick Humbert - E
Jim Kekeris - T
Bucko Kilroy - G
Ben Kish - FB
Vic Lindskog - C
Jay MacDowell - T
Art Macioszczyk - FB
Bill Mackrides - QB
Duke Maronic - G
Pat McHugh - HB
Joe Muha - FB
Cliff Patton - G
Pete Pihos - E
Hal Prescott - E
Bosh Pritchard - HB
Vic Sears - T
Allie Sherman - QB
Ernie Steele - HB
Gil Steinke - HB
Dan Talcott - T
Tommy Thompson - QB
Steve Van Buren - HB
Don Weedon - G
Boyd Williams - C
Al Wistert - T
Alex Wojciechowicz - C
John Wyhonic - G

1947 Pittsburgh

Tony Bova - E
Ralph Calcagni - T
Chuck Cherundolo - C
Bob Cifers - HB
Johnny Clement - TB
Tony Compagno - FB
Bill Cregar - G
Paul Davis - FB
Bob Davis - E
Al Drulis - BB
Bill Garnaas - WB
Joe Glamp - HB
Sam Gray - DE
Bill Hornick - T
Gene Hubka - TB
Val Jansante - E
Steve Lach - FB
John Mastrangelo - G
Bryant Meeks - C
Charley Mehelich - E
Red Moore - G
Gonzalo Morales - TB
Elbie Nickel - E
John Perko - G
Joe Repko - T
Charlie Seabright - BB
Frank Sinkovitz - C
Nick Skorich - G
Walt Slater - TB
Paul Stenn - T
Bob Sullivan - HB
Paul White - HB
Jack Wiley - T
Frank Wydo - T

1947 Washington

John Adams - T
Ki Aldrich - C
Don Avery - T
Sammy Baugh - QB
Fred Boensch - G
Jim Castiglia - FB
Don Deeks - T
Bob DeFruiter - HB
Al DeMao - C
Joe Duckworth - E
Tom Farmer - HB
Mike Garzoni - G
Bill Gray - G
Hank Harris - G
Jack Jenkins - FB
Harvey Jones - HB
John Lookabaugh - E
Paul McKee - E
Tommy Mont - HB
Leo Nobile - G

Bob Nussbaumer - HB
Vince Pacewic - HB
Jim Peebles - E
Dick Poillon - HB
Sal Rosato - FB
Ralph Ruthstrom - FB
Eddie Saenz - HB
John Sanchez - T
Jack Sommers - C
John Steber - G
Hugh Taylor - E
Joe Tereshinski - E
Dick Todd - HB
Doug Turley - E
Bill Ward - G
George Wilde - HB
Ernie Williamson - T
Jim Youel - QB

1947 AAFC

1947 Baltimore

Bill Baumgartner - E
Hub Bechtol - E
Blondy Black - HB
Lamar Blount - E
Ernie Case - QB
Jim Castiglia - FB
Armand Cure - HB
Lamar Davis - E
Andy Dudish - HB
Barry French - G
John Galvin - QB
Gorham Getchell - E
Ed Grain - G
Dick Handley - C
George Hekkers - T
Luke Higgins - G
Billy Hillenbrand - HB
Ralph Jones - E
Mike Kasap - T
Al Klug - T
Joe Kodba - C
Floyd Konetsky - DE
Jim Landrigan - T
Augie Lio - G
Elmer Madar - E
Vic Marino - G
John Mellus - T
Bus Mertes - FB
Rudy Mobley - HB
Steve Nemeth - QB
George Perpich - T
Mike Phillips - C
Bud Schwenk - QB
Sig Sigurdson - E
Frankie Sinkwich - HB
Ray Terrell - HB
Buzz Trebotich - FB
Johnny Vardian - HB
John Wright - FB
Frank Yokas - G
George Zorich - G

1947 Brooklyn

Neal Adams - E
Al Akins - HB
George Benson - HB
George Bernhardt - G
Harry Buffington - G
Mickey Colmer - FB
Mel Conger - DE
Lou Daukas - C
Nick Daukas - T
Glenn Dobbs - QB
Monk Gafford - HB
Joe Gibson - LB
Ed Gustafson - C
Amos Harris - G
Elmore Harris - HB
Bob Hein - E
Bob Hoernschemeyer - TB
Charlie Huneke - T
Ed Jeffers - G
Dub Jones - TB
Billy Jones - G
Saxon Judd - E
Adolph Kowalski - BB
Frank Laurinaitis - LB
Phil Martinovich - G
Jim McCarthy - E
Walt McDonald - BB
Ed Mieszkowski - T
Russ Morrow - LB
Herb Nelson - E
Mike Patanelli - DE
Bob Perina - TB
Martin Ruby - T
Leroy Schneider - T
Ted Scruggs - E
Doyle Tackett - BB
Lee Tevis - FB
Hal Thompson - E
Tex Warrington - C
Harlan Wetz - T
Garland Williams - T

1947 Buffalo

Graham Armstrong - T
Al Baldwin - E
Lamar Blount - E

Jack Carpenter - T
Marty Comer - E
Al Coppage - E
Bert Corley - C
George Doherty - G
Gil Duggan - T
Fred Evans - HB
Paul Gibson - E
George Groves - G
Joe Haynes - C
Buckets Hirsch - FB
Steve Juzwik - HB
John Kerns - T
Fay King - E
George Koch - HB
Chet Kozel - T
Ray Kuffel - E
Vic Kulbitski - FB
Hal Lahar - G
Pug Manders - FB
John Maskas - G
Vince Mazza - E
Jack Morton - E
Chet Mutryn - HB
Rocco Pirro - G
Felto Prewitt - C
George Ratterman - QB
Albie Reisz - QB
Julie Rykovich - HB
Vin Scott - G
George Terlep - QB
Lou Tomasetti - HB
Alex Wizbicki - HB

1947 Chi. Rockets

Alex Agase - G
Bill Bass - HB
Alf Bauman - T
Connie Mack Berry - DE
Angelo Bertelli - QB
John Billman - G
Walt Clay - HB
Herb Coleman - C
Norm Cox - QB
Bill Daley - FB
Al Dekdebrun - QB
Bob Dove - E
Ray Ebli - E
Fred Evans - HB
Chubby Grigg - T
John Harrington - E
George Hecht - G
Crazy Legs Hirsch - HB
Bob Hoernschemeyer - TB
Charlie Huneke - T
Bill Kellagher - FB
John Kuzman - T
Pat Lahey - E
Pete Lamana - C
Ernie Lewis - FB
Fran Mattingly - G
Harley McCollum - T
Joe Mihal - T
Max Morris - E
Jerry Mulready - E
Fred Negus - C
Bruno Niedziela - T
Jim O'Neal - G
Jim Pearcy - G
Ben Pucci - T
Frank Quillen - E
Ray Ramsey - HB
John Rokisky - E
Cliff Rothrock - C
John Sanchez - T
Ted Scalissi - HB
Bill Schroeder - HB
Tony Sumpter - G
Sam Vacanti - QB
Norm Verry - T
Evan Vogds - G
Lloyd Wasserbach - T

1947 Cleveland

Tony Adamle - FB
Chet Adams - T
Ermal Allen - QB
Ernie Blandin - T
Bill Boedeker - HB
Tom Colella - HB
Bob Cowan - HB
Spiro Dellerba - FB
Jim Dewar - HB
Frank Gatski - C
Bob Gaudio - G
Horace Gillom - E
Otto Graham - QB
Don Greenwood - HB
Lou Groza - T
Lin Houston - G
Weldon Humble - G
Special Delivery Jones
Dante Lavelli - E
Cliff Lewis - QB
Bill Lund - HB
Mel Maceau - C
Lew Mayne - HB
Marion Motley - FB
Roman Piskor - T
Lou Rymkus - T
Lou Saban - LB
Mike Scarry - C

Marshall Shurnas - E
Len Simonetti - T
Mac Speedie - E
Ray Terrell - HB
Ed Ulinski - G
Bill Willis - G
John Yonakor - E
George Young - DE

1947 LA Dons

Ben Agajanian - K
Alex Agase - G
Joe Aguirre - E
Sugarfoot Anderson - E
Lee Artoe - T
Earl Audet - T
Burr Baldwin - E
Pete Berezney - T
John Brown - C
Harry Clarke - HB
Walt Clay - HB
Glenn Dobbs - QB
Chuck Fenenbock - HB
Ray Frankowski - G
Bernie Gallagher - G
Dale Gentry - E
Walt Heap - HB
Harry Hopp - FB
Bob Kelly - HB
John Kimbrough - FB
Mort Landsberg - HB
Reid Lennan - G
Len Levy - G
Al Lolotai - G
Paul Mitchell - T
Bob Mitchell - HB
Robert Nelson - C
Bob Nowaskey - E
Bernie Nygren - HB
Charlie O'Rourke - QB
Bert Piggott - HB
Bill Radovich - G
Bob Reinhard - FB
Bill Reinhard - QB
Jim Smith - T
Bob Steuber - FB
Bob Titchenal - E

1947 NY Yankees

Bruce Alford - E
Jack Baldwin - C
Dick Barwegen - G
Roman Bentz - G
Harry Burrus - WB
Fred Cardinal - LB
Lloyd Cheatham - BB
Van Davis - E
Paul Duke - C
Jack Durishan - T
Charlie Elliott - T
Ed Grain - G
Harvey Johnson - BB
Nate Johnson - T
Bob Kennedy - FB
Bruiser Kinard - T
Roy Kurrasch - E
Ted Ossowski - T
Derrell Palmer - T
Ollie Poole - E
Dewey Proctor - FB
Eddie Prokop - FB
Ben Raimondi - TB
Charley Riffle - G
Harmon Rowe - HB
Roy Ruskusky - DE
Jack Russell - E
Spec Sanders - TB
Vic Schleich - T
Ed Sharkey - G
Frankie Sinkwich - TB
Lou Sossamon - C
Henry Stanton - E
Ralph Stewart - C
Bob Sweiger - BB
John Sylvester - HB
Lowell Wagner - WB
Joe Yackanich - G
Buddy Young - FB

1947 San Francisco

Frankie Albert - QB
Ed Balatti - E
Jack Baldwin - C
Bruno Banducci - G
Dick Bassi - G
Alyn Beals - E
Bob Bryant - T
Tony Calvelli - C
Eddie Carr - HB
Gerry Conlee - C
Odis Crowell - T
Don Durdan - HB
Dutch Elston - G
Len Eshmont - HB
Bill Fisk - E
Eddie Forrest - G
Jesse Freitas - QB
Garland Gregory - G
Visco Grgich - T
Dick Horne - E
Len Masini - FB

Ned Mathews - HB
Hank Norberg - E
Earle Parsons - HB
Ed Robnett - FB
Al Satterfield - T
John Schiechl - C
George Smith - C
Norm Standlee - FB
Johnny Strzykalski - HB
Nick Susoeff - E
Rupe Thornton - T
Joe Vetrano - HB
Bev Wallace - QB
John Woudenberg - T
Wally Yonamine - HB

1948 NFL

1948 Boston

John Badaczewski - G
Fritz Barzilauskas - G
Stan Batinski - G
Bill Chipley - E
Don Currivan - E
Boley Dancewicz - QB
Bob Davis - T
Al Dekdebrun - TB
Joe Domnanovich - C
Bill Godwin - C
Joe Golding - HB
Robert Hazelhurst - HB
Ralph Heywood - E
Mike Jarmoluk - T
Gene Malinowski - TB
Vaughn Mancha - C
Bob McClure - G
Mike Micka - DB
Frank Muehlheuser - FB
Frank Nelson - TB
John Nolan - T
Bill Paschal - FB
John Poto - HB
Steve Pritko - E
George Roman - T
Rudy Romboli - FB
Dave Ryan - DB
Joe Sabasteanski - G
Nick Scollard - E
Frank Seno - HB
Phil Slosburg - TB
George Sullivan - E
Jim Tyree - E
Carroll Vogelaar - T
Jim Youel - QB
Roy Zimmerman - QB

1948 Chi. Bears

Joe Abbey - E
Alf Bauman - T
J.R. Boone - HB
Ray Bray - G
Jim Canady - HB
Ed Cifers - E
Stu Clarkson - C
George Connor - T
Fred Davis - T
Bill deCorrevont - HB
Chuck Drulis - G
Fred Evans - HB
Dick Flanagan - HB
Thurman Garrett - C
George Gulyanics - HB
Mike Holovak - FB
Ken Kavanaugh - E
Jim Keane - E
Don Kindt - FB
Al Lawler - HB
Bobby Layne - QB
Sid Luckman - QB
Johnny Lujack - QB
George McAfee - HB
Bill Milner - G
Frank Minini - HB
Noah Mullins - HB
Hank Norberg - E
Joe Osmanski - FB
Pat Preston - G
Wash Serini - G
Allen Smith - E
Ed Sprinkle - E
Paul Stenn - T
Walt Stickel - T
Bulldog Turner - C
Fred Venturelli - K

1948 Chi. Cardinals

Plato Andros - G
Elmer Angsman - HB
Ray Apolskis - G
Loyd Arms - G
John Badaczewski - G
Vince Banonis - C
Bill Blackburn - C
Chet Bulger - T
Bill Campbell - LB
Paul Christman - QB
Corwin Clatt - FB
Red Cochran - HB
Jake Colhouer - G
Joe Coomer - DG
Jerry Davis - HB
Bill Dewell - E

Babe Dimancheff - HB
John Doolan - DE
Bob Dove - DE
Virgil Eikenberg - QB
Marshall Goldberg - DB
Sam Goldman - DE
Bob Hanlon - HB
Pat Harder - FB
Marv Jacobs - T
Mal Kutner - E
Frank Liebel - E
Dick Loepfe - T
Ray Mallouf - QB
Stan Mauldin - T
Hamilton Nichols - G
Buster Ramsey - G
Bob Ravensberg - DB
Vic Schwall - HB
Walt Szot - T
Charlie Trippi - HB
Dick Wedel - G
Vinnie Yablonski - FB
Bob Zimny - T

1948 Detroit

Joe Baumgardner - HB
Les Bingaman - G
Paul Briggs - T
Howie Brown - G
Max Bumgardner - DE
Ted Cremer - E
Chuck DeShane - G
Andy Dudish - HB
Bill Dudley - HB
Jack Dugger - T
Howard Duncan - C
Larry Ellis - LB
Fred Enke - QB
Jim Gillette - HB
John Greene - E
George Grimes - WB
Mel Groomes - WB
Dale Hansen - T
Roger Harding - C
George Hekkers - T
Ralph Heywood - E
Jim Hunnicutt - G
Elmer Jones - G
Clyde LeForce - QB
Elmer Madarik
Bob Mann - E
Bap Manzini - C
Joe Margucci - WB
Earl Maves - DB
Bill Miklich - G
Kelley Mote - E
Merv Pregulman - C
Ken Roskie - FB
Charley Sarratt - QB
Paul Sarringhaus - HB
Ivan Schottel - DE
Cecil Souders - E
Dick Stovall - G
Steve Sucic - FB
Russ Thomas - T
Bill Ward - G
Joe Watt - HB
Bob Wiese - LB
Camp Wilson - FB

1948 Green Bay

Lloyd Baxter - C
Ed Bell - T
Tony Canadeo - HB
Ed Cody - FB
Irv Comp - QB
Ted Cook - E
Larry Craig - DE
Ted Cremer - DE
Ralph Davis - G
Don Deeks - G
Ralph Earhart - HB
Bob Flowers - C
Bob Forte - HB
Ted Fritsch - FB
Jug Girard - HB
Clyde Goodnight - E
Jack Jacobs - QB
Jim Kekeris - T
Paul Lipscomb - T
Nolan Luhn - E
Perry Moss - QB
Ed Neal - G
Urban Odson - T
Larry Olsonoski - G
Fred Provo - HB
Baby Ray - T
Jay Rhodemyre - C
Ken Roskie - FB
Walt Schlinkman - FB
Bruce Smith - HB
Ed Smith - HB
Damon Tassos - G
Evan Vogds - G
Don Wells - DE
Pat West - FB
Dick Wildung - T
Gene Wilson - DB

1948 LA Rams

Bob Agler - HB
Jack Banta - HB
Gil Bouley - T

Larry Brink - E
Ed Champagne - T
Joe Corn - HB
Gerry Cowhig - FB
Don Currivan - E
Bob David - G
Hal Dean - G
Bob DeFruiter - DB
Roger Eason - G
Tom Fears - E
Jack Finlay - G
Fred Gehrke - HB
Jim Hardy - QB
Red Hickey - E
Dick Hoerner - FB
Bob Hoffman - FB
Les Horvath - HB
Frank Hubbell - E
Dick Huffman - T
Tom Keane - HB
Mike Lazetich - G
Dante Magnani - HB
Jack Martin - C
Jim Mello - FB
Fred Naumetz - C
Don Paul - C
Joe Repko - T
Paul Rickards - QB
Bruce Smith - HB
Bill Smyth - E
Al Sparkman - T
Kenny Washington - HB
Bob Waterfield - QB
Pat West - FB
Ray Yagiello - G
Jack Zilly - E

1948 NY Giants

John Atwood - HB
Larry Beil - T
John Cannady - C
George Cheverko - HB
Ray Coates - HB
Charlie Conerly - QB
Tex Coulter - T
Bob Dobelstein - G
Bill Erickson - G
Don Ettinger - G
Art Faircloth - DB
Carl Fennema - C
Mike Garzoni - G
Bruce Gehrke - E
Paul Governali - QB
Joe Johnson - WB
Ken Keuper - DB
Bill Miklich - G
Skippy Minisi - HB
Joyce Pipkin - E
Ray Poole - E
Frank Reagan - DB
Choo-Choo Roberts - FB
Ed Royston - G
Bill Schuler - T
Joe Scott - HB
Jules Siegle - FB
Joe Sulaitis - BB
Bill Swiacki - E
John Treadaway - T
Emlen Tunnell - HB
Paul Walker - E
Jim White - T
Frank Williams - FB
Ernie Williamson - T
Len Younce - G

1948 Philadelphia

Neill Armstrong - E
Walt Barnes - G
Russ Craft - HB
Noble Doss - HB
Otis Douglas - T
Jack Ferrante - E
Mario Giannelli - G
John Green - E
Fred Hartman - T
Dick Humbert - E
Tom Johnson - QB
Bucko Kilroy - G
Ben Kish - FB
Vic Lindskog - C
Jay MacDowell - T
Bill Mackrides - QB
John Magee - G
Bap Manzini - C
Duke Maronic - G
Pat McHugh - HB
Joe Muha - FB
Jack Myers - FB
Les Palmer - HB
Jim Parmer - HB
Cliff Patton - G
Pete Pihos - E
Hal Prescott - E
Bosh Pritchard - HB
George Savitsky - T
Vic Sears - T
Ernie Steele - HB
Gil Steinke - HB
Frank Szymanski - C
Tommy Thompson - QB
Steve Van Buren - HB
Al Wistert - T
Alex Wojciechowicz - C

1948 Pittsburgh

Chuck Cherundolo - C
Bob Cifers - HB
Johnny Clement - TB
Tony Compagno - FB
Bill Cregar - G
Paul Davis - FB
Bob Davis - E
Ray Evans - TB
Bill Garnaas - WB
Joe Gasparella - BB
Joe Glamp - HB
Val Jansante - E
Roy Kurrasch - DE
John Mastrangelo - T
Bryant Meeks - C
Charley Mehelich - E
Red Moore - G
Gonzalo Morales - TB
Norman Mosley - TB
Elbie Nickel - E
Leo Nobile - G
Jerry Nuzum - HB
George Papach - FB
Ed Ryan - DE
Carl Samuelson - T
Charlie Seabright - BB
Jerry Shipkey - FB
Hubert Shurtz - T
Frank Sinkovitz - C
Nick Skorich - G
Steve Suhey - G
Jack Wiley - T
Frank Wydo - T

1948 Washington

John Adams - T
Steve Bagarus - HB
Sammy Baugh - QB
Fred Boensch - G
Carl Butkus - T
Jim Castiglia - FB
George Cheverko - HB
Don Corbitt - C
Hal Crisler - E
Al DeMao - C
Weldon Edwards - T
Clyde Ehrhardt - C
Tom Farmer - HB
Harry Gilmer - QB
Bill Gray - G
Hank Harris - G
Howard Hartley - HB
John Hollar - FB
Mike Katrishen - G
John Koniszewski - T
Howie Livingston - DB
Art Macioszczyk - FB
Elmer Madarik - HB
Paul McKee - E
Tommy Mont - QB
Bob Nussbaumer - HB
Jim Peebles - DE
Dick Poillon - HB
Ed Quirk - FB
Mike Roussos - T
Eddie Saenz - HB
John Sanchez - T
Dan Sandifer - HB
Herbert Shoener - DE
Ed Stacco - T
John Steber - G
Hugh Taylor - E
Joe Tereshinski - E
Dick Todd - HB
Doug Turley - E
Jim Youel - QB

1948 AAFC

1948 Baltimore

Lee Artoe - T
Dick Barwegen - G
Hub Bechtol - E
Pete Berezney - T
Ernie Blandin - T
Herb Coleman - C
Bert Corley - C
Lamar Davis - E
Spiro Dellerba - FB
Aubrey Fowler - HB
Lu Gambino - FB
Dub Garrett - G
Ed Grain - G
Rex Grossman - FB
George Groves - G
Billy Hillenbrand - HB
Al Klug - G
Jake Leicht - HB
Lew Mayne - HB
Len McCormick - C
John Mellus - T
Bus Mertes - FB
John North - E
Bob Nowaskey - E
Charlie O'Rourke - QB
Bob Pfohl - HB
Ollie Poole - E
Alex Sidorik - T
Jack Simmons - G
Joe Smith - E
Jim Spruill - T
Ralph Stewart - C
John Sylvester - DB
Y. A. Tittle - QB
Sam Vacanti - QB
Johnny Vardian - HB

1948 Brooklyn

Al Akins - HB
Carl Allen - WB
George Bernhardt - G
Hardy Brown - WB
Harry Buffington - G
Harry Burrus - E
Jim Camp - WB
Bob Chappuis - TB
John Clowes - T
Mickey Colmer - FB
Jim Cooper - C
Jim Dewar - WB
Dan Edwards - E
Hank Foldberg - E
Nick Forkovitch - FB
Monk Gafford - TB
Ed Gustafson - C
Amos Harris - G
Bob Hoernschemeyer - TB
Charlie Huneke - T
Saxon Judd - E
John Klasnic - WB
Bob Leonetti - G
Hugo Marcolini - WB
Walt McDonald - BB
Tom Mikula - FB
Max Morris - E
Herb Nelson - T
Ray Ramsey - WB
Martin Ruby - T
Ralph Sazio - T
Ted Scruggs - E
Bob Smith -
Joe Spencer - T
Herb St. John - G
George Strohmeyer - C
Bob Sullivan - FB
Doyle Tackett - BB
Lee Tevis - FB
Hal Thompson - E
Morrie Warren - FB
Tex Warrington - C
Garland Williams - T
John Wozniak - G

1948 Buffalo

Al Akins - HB
Graham Armstrong - T
Ed Balatti - DE
Al Baldwin - E
Jack Baldwin - C
Rex Bumgardner - HB
Bob Callahan - C
Jack Carpenter - T
Marty Comer - E
Paul Gibson - E
Bill Gompers - HB
Buckets Hirsch - LB
John Kerns - T
Ed King - G
George Kisiday - E
John Kissell - T
Chet Kozel - G
Vic Kulbitski - FB
Hal Lahar - G
Bob Leonetti - G
Chick Maggioli - HB
Vince Mazza - DE
Chet Mutryn - HB
Bill O'Connor - E
Rocco Pirro - G
Felto Prewitt - C
George Ratterman - QB
Julie Rykovich - HB
Don Schneider - HB
Carl Schuette - DB
Vin Scott - G
Bob Smith - WB
Art Statuto - C
Bob Stefik - DE
Bob Steuber - FB
Jim Still - QB
George Terlep - QB
Lou Tomasetti - HB
Jerry Whalen - C
Alex Wizbicki - DB
John Wyhonic - G

1948 Chi. Rockets

George Bernhardt - G
Angelo Bertelli - QB
Jim Brutz - T
Harry Burrus - E
Harry Clarke - HB
Herb Coleman - C
Ziggy Czarobski - T
Bob David - G
Ed Ecker - T
Charlie Elliott - T
Fred Evans - HB
Tom Farris - QB
Chuck Fenenbock - HB
Jesse Freitas - QB
Crazy Legs Hirsch - HB
Bob Jensen - E
Farnham Johnson - DE
Nate Johnson - T
Steve Juzwik - HB
Bill Kellagher - FB
Fay King - E
Chet Kozel - G
Ray Kuffel - E
Pete Lamana - C
Ernie Lewis - FB
Bob Livingstone - HB
Jim McCarthy - E
Jim Mello - FB
Fred Negus - C
Bob Perina - HB
Dewey Proctor - FB
Eddie Prokop - HB
Johnny Rapacz - C
Joe Ruetz - G
Julie Rykovich - HB
Floyd Simmons - HB
Bill Smith - T
Gasper Urban - G
Emil Uremovich - T
Sam Vacanti - QB

1948 Cleveland

Tony Adamle - FB
Chet Adams - T
Alex Agase - G
Bill Boedeker - HB
Ollie Cline - FB
Tom Colella - HB
Bob Cowan - HB
Frank Gatski - C
Bob Gaudio - G
Horace Gillom - E
Otto Graham - QB
Chubby Grigg - T
Lou Groza - T
Lin Houston - G
Weldon Humble - G
Tommy James - HB
Special Delivery Jones
Dub Jones - HB
Frank Kosikowski - DE
Dante Lavelli - E
Cliff Lewis - QB
Mel Maceau - C
Marion Motley - FB
Ara Parseghian - HB
Ben Pucci - T
Lou Rymkus - T
Lou Saban - LB
Dean Sensanbaugher - HB
Len Simonetti - T
Mac Speedie - E
George Terlep - QB
Ed Ulinski - G
Bill Willis - G
John Yonakor - E
George Young - E

1948 LA Dons

Ben Agajanian - K
Joe Aguirre - E
Earl Audet - T
Don Avery - T
Burr Baldwin - E
John Brown - C
Harry Clarke - HB
Walt Clay - HB
Glenn Dobbs - TB
Jeff Durkota - FB
Chuck Fenenbock - HB
Bill Fisk - E
Jack Flagerman - C
Len Ford - E
Ray Frankowski - G
Dale Gentry - E
Mike Graham - FB
Walt Heap - BB
Clyde Johnson - T
Bob Kelly - HB
John Kimbrough - FB
Len Levy - G
Al Lolotai - G
Len Masini - FB
Lou Mihajlovich - E
Paul Mitchell - T
Bob Mitchell - BB
Johnny Naumu - HB
Robert Nelson - C
Bob Nowaskey - E
Dick Ottele - BB
Mike Perrotti - T
Knox Ramsey - G
Bob Reinhard - FB
Bill Reinhard - TB
Hank Rockwell - G
Lin Sexton - HB
Bill Smith - T
Herman Wedemeyer - TB
Bernie Winkler - T

1948 NY Yankees

Bruce Alford - E
Ed Balatti - DE
Roman Bentz - G
Carl Butkus - T
Tom Casey - TB
Bill Chambers - T
Lloyd Cheatham - BB
Paul Cleary - E
Denny Crawford - T
Bill Daley - FB
Van Davis - E
Al Dekdebrun - TB
Mike Garzoni - G
Nelson Greene - T
Duke Iverson - WB
Glenn Johnson - T
Harvey Johnson - BB
Bob Kennedy - FB
Clayton Lane - T
Pete Layden - TB
Joe Magliolo - LB
Flip McDonald - E
Paul Mitchell - T
Roland Nabors - C
Derrell Palmer - T
Howie Parker - BB
Frank Perantoni - C
Charley Riffle - G
John Rokisky - DE
Harmon Rowe - DB
Jack Russell - E
Spec Sanders - TB
Otto Schnellbacher - E
Bud Schwenk - TB
Ed Sharkey - G
Marion Shirley - T
Steve Sieradzki - DB
Joe Signaigo - G
Lou Sossamon - C
Ralph Stewart - C
Bob Sweiger - BB
Lowell Tew - FB
Lowell Wagner - WB
Arnie Weinmeister - T
Dick Werder - G
Joe Yackanich - G
Buddy Young - FB

1948 San Francisco

Frankie Albert - QB
Ed Balatti - DE
Bruno Banducci - G
Alyn Beals - E
Roman Bentz - G
Gail Bruce - E
Bob Bryant - T
Eddie Carr - HB
Ken Casanega - HB
Jim Cason - HB
Don Clark - G
Floyd Collier - T
Jim Cox - G
Paul Crowe - HB
Charlie Elliott - T
Dutch Elston - C
Len Eshmont - HB
Paul Evansen - G
Visco Grgich - T
Forrest Hall - HB
Bill Johnson - C
Fred Land - T
Verl Lillywhite - HB
Ned Maloney - E
Len Masini - FB
Riley Matheson - G
Walt McCormick - C
Bob Mike - T
Joe Perry - FB
Hal Puddy - T
Hal Shoener - E
Norm Standlee - FB
Johnny Strzykalski - HB
Bob Sullivan - HB
Nick Susoeff - E
Joe Vetrano - HB
Bev Wallace - QB
Joel Williams - C
John Woudenberg - T

1949 NFL

1949 Chi. Bears

Alf Bauman - T
George Blanda - QB
J.R. Boone - HB
Ray Bray - G
Jim Canady - HB
Stu Clarkson - LB
Ed Cody - FB
George Connor - T
Fred Davis - T
Bill deCorrevont - DB
Wally Dreyer - HB
Chuck Drulis - G
Jack Dugger - E
Dick Flanagan - G
George Gulyanics - HB
John Hoffman - FB
Ken Kavanaugh - E
Jim Keane - E
Don Kindt - FB
Sid Luckman - QB
Johnny Lujack - QB
Dante Magnani - HB
George McAfee - HB
Bill Milner - DE
Joe Osmanski - FB
Bob Perina - HB
Pat Preston - G
Julie Rykovich - HB
Wash Serini - G
Ed Sprinkle - E
Paul Stenn - T
Walt Stickel - T
Frank Szymanski - C
Bulldog Turner - C

1949 Chi. Cardinals

Plato Andros - G
Elmer Angsman - HB
Ray Apolskis - G
Vince Banonis - C
Bill Blackburn - C
Chet Bulger - T
Jim Cain - DE
Bill Campbell - LB
Paul Christman - QB
Corwin Clatt - DB
Red Cochran - HB
Joe Coomer - T
Jerry Davis - DB
Bill Dewell - E
Babe Dimancheff - HB
Bob Dove - DE
Bill Fischer - T
John Goldsberry - T
Pat Harder - FB
Jim Hardy - QB
Mal Kutner - E
Dick Loepfe - T
Hamilton Nichols - G
Bob Nussbaumer - DB
George Petrovich - T
Buster Ramsey - G
Bob Ravensberg - E
Vic Schwall - HB
Clarence Self - HB
Charlie Trippi - HB
Tom Wham - E
Vinnie Yablonski - FB
Bob Zimny - T

1949 Detroit

Abe Addams - DE
Les Bingaman - DG
Cloyce Box - HB
Howie Brown - G
Mario DeMarco - G
Chuck DeShane - G
Don Doll - HB
Bill Dudley - HB
Fred Enke - QB
Sam Goldman - DE
John Greene - E
Mel Groomes - HB
Barney Hafen - E
George Hekkers - T
John Hollar - FB
George Karstens - C
Clyde LeForce - QB
Chick Maggioli - DB
Bob Mann - E
Jim Mello - DB
Kelley Mote - E
John Panelli - FB
Bob Sr. Pifferini - C
Ollie Poole - DE
John Prchlik - T
Hal Prescott - E
Mike Roussos - T
Al Russas - T
Jack Simmons - C
Bob Smith - HB
Cecil Souders - T
Russ Thomas - T
John Treadaway - T
Wally Triplett - HB
Frank Tripucka - QB
Bill Ward - G
Camp Wilson - FB

1949 Green Bay

Ed Bell - T
Buddy Burris - G
Tony Canadeo - HB
Bob Cifers - HB
Irv Comp - DB
Ted Cook - E
Larry Craig - DE
Ralph Earhart - HB
Roger Eason - G
Joe Ethridge - T
Lou Ferry - T
Bob Flowers - C
Bob Forte - HB
Ted Fritsch - FB
Jug Girard - QB
Clyde Goodnight - E
Roger Harding - C
Stan Heath - QB
Jack Jacobs - QB
Glenn Johnson - T
Bill Kelley - E
Jack Kirby - HB
Ken Kranz - DB
Paul Lipscomb - T
Nolan Luhn - E
Ed Neal - C
Urban Odson - T
Ralph Olsen - DE
Larry Olsonoski - G
Dan Orlich - E
Steve Pritko - E
Jay Rhodemyre - C
Walt Schlinkman - FB
Ed Smith - HB
Bob Summerhays - FB
Damon Tassos - G
Evan Vogds - G
Don Wells - DE
Dick Wildung - T

1949 LA Rams

Bob Agler - FB
Gil Bouley - T
Larry Brink - DE
Ed Champagne - T
Gerry Cowhig - FB
Don Currivan - E
Hal Dean - G
Tom Fears - E
Jack Finlay - G
Fred Gehrke - HB
Crazy Legs Hirsch - HB
Dick Hoerner - FB
Frank Hubbell - E
Dick Huffman - T
Tom Kalmanir - HB
Tom Keane - E
Mike Lazetich - G
Jack Martin - C
Fred Naumetz - C
Don Paul - LB
Joe Repko - T
Bob Shaw - E
George Sims - DB
Vitamin Smith - HB
Bill Smyth - E
Al Sparkman - T
Bobby Thomason - QB
Norm Van Brocklin - QB
Bob Waterfield - QB
Jerry Williams - HB
Ray Yagiello - G
Paul Younger - HB
Jack Zilly - E

1949 NY Bulldogs

Joe Abbey - E
Fritz Barzilauskas - G
Stan Batinski - G
Tom Blake - T
Mike Boyda - FB
Bill Campbell - LB
Jim Canady - HB
Bill Chipley - E
Bob DeMoss - QB
Joe Domnanovich - C
Herb Ellis - C
Frank Gaul - T
Joe Golding - HB
Roger Harding - C
Ralph Heywood - E
Mike Jarmoluk - T
Bobby Layne - QB
Frank Muehlheuser - FB
Frank Nelson - HB
John Nolan - T
Larry Olsonoski - G
Joe Osmanski - FB
Merv Pregulman - C
Hal Prescott - E
Steve Pritko - E
Johnny Rauch - QB
George Roman - T
Joe Sabasteanski - G
Nick Scollard - E
Dean Sensanbaugher - HB
Paul Shoults - HB
Phil Slosburg - HB
Ed Smith - HB
Bob Sponaugle - E
Sam Tamburo - DE
Carroll Vogelaar - T
Jim Wade - HB
Joe Watt - DB
John Weaver - G

1949 NY Giants

Ben Agajanian - K
Bill Austin - T
Jon Baker - G
Carl Butkus - T
John Cannady - LB
Ray Coates - HB
Jake Colhouer - G
Charlie Conerly - QB
Tex Coulter - C
Al DeRogatis - DT
Dick Duden - E
Don Ettinger - G
Carl Fennema - C
Clete Fischer - HB
Bob Greenhalgh - FB
Dick Hensley - E
Ralph Hutchinson - T
George Kershaw - DE
Ed Kolman - DT
Frank LoVuolo - E
Ray Mallouf - QB
Bus Mertes - FB
Noah Mullins - HB
Ray Poole - E
Choo-Choo Roberts - HB
Ed Royston - G
Jack Salscheider - HB
John Sanchez - T
Joe Scott - HB
Joe Sulaitis - FB
Bill Swiacki - E
Emlen Tunnell - HB
Jim White - T

1949 Philadelphia

Neill Armstrong - E
Walt Barnes - G
Chuck Bednarik - C
Russ Craft - HB
Otis Douglas - T
Jack Ferrante - E
Mario Giannelli - G
John Green - DE
Dick Humbert - DB
Mike Jarmoluk - T
Bucko Kilroy - G
Ben Kish - FB
Vic Lindskog - C
Jay MacDowell - DE
Bill Mackrides - QB
John Magee - G
Duke Maronic - G
Pat McHugh - HB
Joe Muha - FB
Jack Myers - FB
Jim Parmer - HB
Cliff Patton - G
Pete Pihos - E
Hal Prescott - E
Bosh Pritchard - HB
Frank Reagan - DB
George Savitsky - T
Clyde Scott - HB
Vic Sears - T
Leo Skladany - DE
Tommy Thompson - QB
Steve Van Buren - HB
Al Wistert - T
Alex Wojciechowicz - C
Frank Ziegler - HB

1949 Pittsburgh

Bob Balog - C
Pete Barbolak - T
Bob Davis - DE
Jim Finks - TB
Bobby Gage - TB
Joe Geri - TB
Joe Glamp - HB
Bob Hanlon - HB
Howard Hartley - DB
Darrell Hogan - G
Joe Hollingsworth - FB
Val Jansante - E
Bill Long - E
Bill McPeak - DE
Charley Mehelich - DE
Frank Minini - BB
Red Moore - G
Elbie Nickel - E
Leo Nobile - G
Jerry Nuzum - HB
George Papach - FB
Vince Ragunas - LB
Don Samuel - HB
Carl Samuelson - T
Charlie Seabright - BB
Jerry Shipkey - FB
Frank Sinkovitz - C
Steve Suhey - G
Walt Szot - T
Bill Walsh - C
Jack Wiley - T
Frank Wydo - T

1949 Washington

John Adams - T
John Badaczewski - G
Sammy Baugh - QB
Ed Berrang - E
Leon Cochran - FB
Hal Crisler - E
Al DeMao - C
Harry Dowda - HB
Clyde Ehrhardt - C
Harry Gilmer - QB
Rob Goode - HB
Clyde Goodnight - E
Bob Hendren - T
John Hollar - FB
Mike Katrishen - G
Howie Livingston - HB
Tommy Mont - QB
Laurie Niemi - T
Jim Peebles - DE
Dick Poillon - HB
Ed Quirk - FB
Mike Roussos - T
Eddie Saenz - HB
John Sanchez - T
Dan Sandifer - HB
Frank Seno - DB
Herbert Shoener - DE
Herb Siegert - G

Joe Soboleski - G
John Steber - G
Pete Stout - FB
Dick Stovall - G
Len Szafaryn - T
Hugh Taylor - E
Joe Tereshinski - E

1949 AAFC

1949 Baltimore

Dick Barwegen - G
Hub Bechtol - E
Warren Beson - C
Ernie Blandin - T
Ken Cooper - G
Bob Cowan - HB
Lamar Davis - E
Spiro Dellerba - LB
Barry French - G
Lu Gambino - FB
Dub Garrett - G
Rex Grossman - K
Chick Jagade - FB
Jon Jenkins - T
Bob Kelly - HB
Wayne Kingery - HB
Jake Leicht - HB
Bill Leonard - DE
John Mellus - T
Bus Mertes - FB
John North - E
Bob Nowaskey - DE
Charlie O'Rourke - QB
Paul Page - HB
Bob Pfohl - HB
Felto Prewitt - C
Ralph Ruthstrom - LB
Alex Sidorik - T
Jim Spruill - T
Billy Stone - HB
Pete Tillman - C
Y. A. Tittle - QB
Sam Vacanti - QB
Herman Wedemeyer - HB

1949 Buffalo

Chet Adams - T
Al Baldwin - E
Rex Bumgardner - HB
Jack Carpenter - T
Ollie Cline - FB
Tom Colella - HB
Jesse Freitas - QB
Abe Gibron - G
Paul Gibson - E
Hal Herring - C
Buckets Hirsch - LB
Larry Joe - HB
John Kerns - T
Ed King - G
John Kissell - T
Vito Kissell - FB
Bob Livingstone - HB
Bob Logel - DE
Jim Lukens - E
John Maskas - T
Vince Mazza - DE
Chet Mutryn - HB
Bob Oristaglio - E
Rocco Pirro - G
George Ratterman - QB
Bill Schroll - LB
Carl Schuette - C
Bill Stanton - DE
Art Statuto - C
Odell Stautzenberger - G
Jim Still - QB
Joe Sutton - HB
Lou Tomasetti - HB
Vic Vasicek - G
Wilbur Volz - HB
Alex Wizbicki - HB
John Wyhonic - G

1949 Chi. Rockets

Frank Aschenbrenner - FB
Jim Bailey - G
Hardy Brown - FB
George Buksar - FB
Bob Chappuis - TB
Paul Cleary - DE
Johnny Clement - TB
John Clowes - T
Rip Collins - FB
Ziggy Czarobski - T
Dan Edwards - E
Hank Foldberg - E
Ted Hazelwood - T
Bob Heck - DE
Bob Hoernschemeyer - TB
Bob Jensen - E
Nate Johnson - T
Fay King - E
Ray Kuffel - DE
Ernie Lewis - FB
Jim McCarthy - E
Walt McDonald - BB
Fred Negus - C
Homer Paine - T
Paul Patterson - WB
Jim Pearcy - G
Ray Ramsey - WB
Johnny Rapacz - C
Ray Richeson - G
Bob Smith - WB
Joe Soboleski - T
Herb St. John - G
George Strohmeyer - C
Bob Sweiger - BB
Marty Wendell - G

1949 Cleveland

Tony Adamle - FB
Alex Agase - G
Bill Boedeker - HB
Frank Gatski - C
Bob Gaudio - G
Horace Gillom - E
Otto Graham - QB
Chubby Grigg - T
Lou Groza - T
Les Horvath - HB
Lin Houston - G
Weldon Humble - G
Tommy James - HB
Special Delivery Jones
Dub Jones - HB
Warren Lahr - HB
Dante Lavelli - E
Cliff Lewis - QB
Marion Motley - FB
Bill O'Connor - DE
Derrell Palmer - T
Ara Parseghian - HB
Lou Rymkus - T
Lou Saban - LB
Mac Speedie - E
Joe Spencer - T
Ed Susteric - FB
Tommy Thompson - C
Ed Ulinski - G
Bill Willis - G
John Yonakor - DE
George Young - DE

1949 LA Dons

Joe Aguirre - E
Burr Baldwin - E
John Brown - C
Walt Clay - TB
Harper Davis - DB
Glenn Dobbs - TB
Bob Dobelstein - G
Dan Dworsky - BB
Ollie Fletcher - G
Len Ford - E
Billy Grimes - HB
Ed Henke - T
Bob Hoffman - BB
Lew Holder - E
Earl Howell - HB
Ed Kelley - T
Bob Kennedy - DB
Al Lolotai - G
Shorty McWilliams - DB
George Murphy - BB
Robert Nelson - C
Mike Perrotti - T
Joyce Pipkin - BB
Knox Ramsey - G
Bob Reinhard - T
Hosea Rodgers - FB
Jim Spavital - FB
George Taliaferro - TB
Ben Whaley - G
Dick Wilkins - E
Ernie Williamson - T
Ab Wimberly - E
Dick Woodard - C

1949 NY Yankees

Bruce Alford - E
George Brown - G
Bill Chambers - G
Mickey Colmer - FB
Van Davis - E
Noble Doss - HB
Brad Ecklund - C
Bill Erickson - G
Dan Garza - E
Sherman Howard - HB
Duke Iverson - HB
Gil Johnson - QB
Harvey Johnson - G
Bob Kennedy - FB
Lou Kusserow - FB
Tom Landry - HB
Pete Layden - HB
John Mastrangelo - G
Paul Mitchell - T
Don Panciera - QB
Frank Perantoni - C
Barney Poole - E
Dewey Proctor - FB
Eddie Prokop - FB
Harmon Rowe - DB
Martin Ruby - T
Jack Russell - E
Otto Schnellbacher - DB
Ed Sharkey - G
Marion Shirley - T
Joe Signaigo - G
Lowell Tew - HB
Arnie Weinmeister - T
John Wozniak - G
Buddy Young - HB

1949 San Francisco

Frankie Albert - QB
Bruno Banducci - G
Alyn Beals - E
Gail Bruce - E
Bob Bryant - T
Jack Carpenter - T
Eddie Carr - HB
Jim Cason - HB
Sam Cathcart - HB
Don Clark - G
Len Eshmont - HB
Ray Evans - T
Don Garlin - HB
Visco Grgich - G
Homer Hobbs - G
Bill Johnson - C
Verl Lillywhite - HB
Ned Maloney - E
Bob Mike - T
Joe Morgan - T
Joe Perry - FB
Charley Quilter - T
Tino Sabuco - C
Paul Salata - E
Hal Shoener - E
Norm Standlee - FB
Johnny Strzykalski - HB
Nick Susoeff - E
Joe Vetrano - HB
Lowell Wagner - HB
Bev Wallace - QB
Pete Wissman - C
John Woudenberg - T

1950 Baltimore

Sisto Averno - LB
George Blanda - DB
Ernie Blandin - T
Hardy Brown - DB
George Buksar - FB
Adrian Burk - QB
Leon Campbell - FB
Rip Collins - DB
Don Colo - DT
Ken Cooper - G
Hal Crisler - E
Art Donovan - T
Frankie Filchock - QB
Arthur Fletcher - G
Barry French - T
Rex Grossman - FB
Jon Jenkins - T
Bob Jensen - DE
Ed King - G
Vito Kissell - FB
Bob Livingstone - HB
Chick Maggioli - DB
Geno Mazzanti - HB
Bill Murray - G
Chet Mutryn - HB
Robert Nelson - LB
John North - E
Bob Nowaskey - DE
Bob Oristaglio - E
Jim Owens - E
Bob Perina - HB
Herb Rich - HB
Paul Salata - E
John Schweder - G
Frank Spaniel - HB
Jim Spavital - FB
Art Spinney - E
Billy Stone - HB
Y. A. Tittle - QB
Joel Williams - C
Ernie Zalejski - DB

1950 Chi. Bears

Dick Barwegen - G
Alf Bauman - DT
George Blanda - DB
J.R. Boone - HB
Ed Bradley - DE
Ray Bray - G
Al Campana - HB
Stu Clarkson - C
Ed Cody - DB
George Connor - LB
Fred Davis - T
Harper Davis - HB
Frank Dempsey - T
Dick Flanagan - LB
Dub Garrett - DT
George Gulyanics - HB
Wayne Hansen - LB
John Hoffman - LB
Chuck Hunsinger - HB
Ken Kavanaugh - E
Jim Keane - E
Don Kindt - FB
Sid Luckman - QB
Johnny Lujack - DB
George McAfee - HB
Fred Morrison - FB
Fred Negus - LB
Red O'Quinn - DB
Steve Romanik - QB
Julie Rykovich - HB
Wash Serini - G
Ed Sprinkle - E
Paul Stenn - T
Bulldog Turner - LB
Bones Weatherly - LB
Bill Wightkin - E

1950 Chi. Cardinals

Plato Andros - T
Elmer Angsman - HB
Ray Apolskis - G
Ed Bagdon - LB
Vince Banonis - C
Bill Blackburn - C
Gerry Cowhig - LB
Jerry Davis - DB
Babe Dimancheff - HB
Bob Dove - DE
Bill Fischer - T
Fred Gehrke - DB
John Goldsberry - DT
Pat Harder - FB
Jim Hardy - QB
Jerry Hennessy - DE
John Hock - T
Jack Jennings - T
Mal Kutner - DB
Jim Lipinski - T
Lloyd McDermott - DT
Bob Nussbaumer - DB
Don Paul - HB
George Petrovich - G
Fran Polsfoot - E
Buster Ramsey - G
Knox Ramsey - G
Ray Ramsey - E
Vic Schwall - HB
Bob Shaw - E
Bill Svoboda - LB
Mike Swistowicz - DB
Charlie Trippi - HB
Frank Tripucka - QB
Tom Wham - DE
Vinnie Yablonski - FB

1950 Cleveland

Tony Adamle - FB
Alex Agase - LB
Rex Bumgardner - HB
Ken Carpenter - HB
Emerson Cole - FB
Len Ford - DE
Frank Gatski - C
Abe Gibron - G
Horace Gillom - E
Ken Gorgal - DB
Otto Graham - QB
Chubby Grigg - DT
Lou Groza - T
Hal Herring - C
Lin Houston - G
Weldon Humble - G
Tommy James - HB
Dub Jones - HB
John Kissell - DT
Warren Lahr - DB
Dante Lavelli - E
Cliff Lewis - QB
Jim Martin - T
Dom Moselle - HB
Marion Motley - LB
Derrell Palmer - DT
Don Phelps - DB
Lou Rymkus - T
John Sandusky - DT
Mac Speedie - E
Tommy Thompson - LB
Bill Willis - DG
George Young - DE

1950 Detroit

Les Bingaman - DG
Cloyce Box - E
Howie Brown - G
Chet Bulger - T
Jim Cain - E
Gus Cifelli - T
Ollie Cline - FB
Lou Creekmur - DT
Don Doll - DB
Fred Enke - HB
Dick Flanagan - LB
John Greene - E
Rex Grossman - FB
Barney Hafen - E
Leon Hart - E
Bob Hoernschemeyer - HB
Floyd Jaszewski - T
Gerry Krall - HB
Bobby Layne - QB
Jack Lininger - C
Dante Magnani - HB
Lloyd McDermott - DT
Thurman McGraw - DT
Don Panciera - QB
John Panelli - FB
Lindy Pearson - HB
John Prchlik - DT
Dick Rifenburg - E
Dan Sandifer - HB
Bill Schroll - FB
Clarence Self - HB
Jack Simmons - C
Bob Smith - DB
Joe Soboleski - G
Wally Triplett - HB
Doak Walker - DB
Joe Watson - C

1950 Green Bay

Al Baldwin - DB
Bill Boedeker - HB
Buddy Burris - LB
Tony Canadeo - FB
Al Cannava - HB
Paul Christman - QB
Jack Cloud - FB
Ted Cook - E
Larry Coutre - HB
Raymond DiPierro - G
Wally Dreyer - HB
Chuck Drulis - LB
Ed Ecker - T
Bob Forte - HB
Ted Fritsch - FB
Jug Girard - HB
Billy Grimes - HB
Leon Manley - T
Bob Mann - E
Clarence McGeary - DT
Ed Neal - DG
Tom O'Malley - QB
Dan Orlich - DE
Steve Pritko - E
Breezy Reid - HB
Tobin Rote - QB
Carl Schuette - LB
Joe Spencer - DT
Don Stansauk - DT
Rebel Steiner - DB
Bob Summerhays - LB
Len Szafaryn - LB
Clayton Tonnemaker - C
Dick Wildung - T
Ab Wimberly - E
Alex Wizbicki - DB

1950 LA Rams

Paul Barry - HB
Gil Bouley - T
Bob Boyd - E
Larry Brink - DE
Ed Champagne - T
Glenn Davis - HB
Tom Fears - E
Jack Finlay - LB
Crazy Legs Hirsch - DB
Dick Hoerner - LB
Dick Huffman - T
Tom Kalmanir - HB
Tom Keane - E
Mike Lazetich - G
Woodley Lewis - DB
Fred Naumetz - LB
Ralph Pasquariello - FB
Don Paul - C
Bob Reinhard - DT
George Sims - DB
Vitamin Smith - HB
Bill Smyth - E
Art Statuto - C
Dave Stephenson - G
Harry Thompson - G
Dan Towler - FB
Norm Van Brocklin - QB
Vic Vasicek - G
Bob Waterfield - QB
Stan West - DG
Jerry Williams - HB
Paul Younger - HB
Jack Zilly - DE

1950 NY Giants

Bill Austin - G
Jon Baker - DG
John Cannady - LB
Randy Clay - DB
Charlie Conerly - QB
Al DeRogatis - DT
Jim Duncan - DE
Don Ettinger - G
Forrest Griffith - HB
Bob Jackson - FB
Tom Landry - DB
John Mastrangelo - G
Bob McChesney - E
Bill Milner - DG
Kelley Mote - E
Jim Ostendarp - HB
Ray Poole - DE
Eddie Price - FB
Johnny Rapacz - LB
Choo-Choo Roberts - HB
George Roman - T
Harmon Rowe - DB
John Sanchez - T
Otto Schnellbacher - DB
Joe Scott - HB
Leo Skladany - DE
Joe Sulaitis - BB
Bill Swiacki - E
Travis Tidwell - QB
Emlen Tunnell - DB
Arnie Weinmeister - DT
Jim White - T
Ellery Williams - E
Dick Woodard - C

1950 NY Yankees

Chet Adams - DT
Bennie Aldridge - DB
Bruce Alford - E
George Brown - G
Jim Champion - T
John Clowes - G
Joe Domnanovich - C
Brad Ecklund - LB
Dan Edwards - E
Joe Golding - HB
Sherman Howard - HB
Duke Iverson - DB
Jon Jenkins - T
Nate Johnson - DT
Bob Kennedy - LB
Lou Kusserow - FB
Pete Layden - DB
Paul Mitchell - DT
John Nolan - T
Barney Poole - E
George Ratterman - QB
Johnny Rauch - QB
Martin Ruby - DT
Jack Russell - E
Spec Sanders - HB
Ed Sharkey - G
Joe Signaigo - G
Mike Swistowicz - DB
George Taliaferro - HB
Zollie Toth - FB
Carroll Vogelaar - T
Art Weiner - E
John Wozniak - G
John Yonakor - DE
Buddy Young - HB

1950 Philadelphia

Neill Armstrong - DB
Walt Barnes - G
Chuck Bednarik - C
Bill Boedeker - HB
Russ Craft - HB
Jack Ferrante - E
Mario Giannelli - G
John Green - DE
Billy Hix - E
Mike Jarmoluk - T
Bucko Kilroy - T
Toy Ledbetter - DB
Vic Lindskog - C
Jay MacDowell - T
Bill Mackrides - QB
John Magee - G
Duke Maronic - G
Pat McHugh - HB
Joe Muha - LB
Jack Myers - LB
Jim Parmer - DB
Cliff Patton - G
Pete Pihos - E
Frank Reagan - HB
Dan Sandifer - HB
Clyde Scott - HB
Vic Sears - T
Walt Stickel - DT
Joe Sutton - HB
Tommy Thompson - QB
Steve Van Buren - HB
Norm Willey - DE
Al Wistert - T
Alex Wojciechowicz - C
Frank Ziegler - HB

1950 Pittsburgh

Lou Allen - T
Bob Balog - C
Lynn Chandois - WB
Bob Davis - DE
Jim Finks - TB
Bobby Gage - DB
Joe Gasparella - BB
Joe Geri - TB
Howard Hartley - WB
George Hays - DE
Darrell Hogan - LB
Joe Hollingsworth - FB
George Hughes - G
Val Jansante - E
Bill McPeak - DE
Shorty McWilliams - TB
Charley Mehelich - E
Elbie Nickel - E
George Nicksich - G
Jerry Nuzum - HB
Fran Rogel - FB
Don Samuel - DB
Carl Samuelson - DT
Charlie Seabright - BB
Jerry Shipkey - FB
Frank Sinkovitz - C
Truett Smith - BB
Ernie Stautner - DT
Walt Szot - DT
Dick Tomlinson - G
Bill Walsh - C
Jack Wiley - T
Frank Wydo - T

1950 San Francisco

Frankie Albert - QB
Bruno Banducci - G
Alyn Beals - E
Gail Bruce - E
Don Burke - LB
Don Campora - DT
Jim Cason - DB
Royal Cathcart - HB
Sam Cathcart - DB
Ray Collins - DT
Harley Dow - G
Ray Evans - G
Don Garlin - HB
Fred Gehrke - DB
Visco Grgich - LB
Homer Hobbs - G
Bill Johnson - LB
Verl Lillywhite - HB
Howie Livingston - HB
Alex Loyd - E
Clay Matthews - DT
Jack Nix - E
Leo Nomellini - T
Joe Perry - FB
Jim Powers - QB
Charley Quilter - T
Paul Salata - E
Dan Sandifer - HB
Charlie Shaw - G
Hal Shoener - DE
Emil Sitko - HB
Gordie Soltau - E
Norm Standlee - FB
Johnny Strzykalski - HB
Lowell Wagner - HB
Pete Wissman - C

1950 Washington

John Badaczewski - G
Joe Bartos - HB
Sammy Baugh - QB
Ed Berrang - E
Dan Brown - DE
Hardy Brown - DB
Roland Dale - DE
Al DeMao - C
Harry Dowda - HB
Chuck Drazenovich - FB
Bill Dudley - DB
Harry Gilmer - HB
Rob Goode - LB
Clyde Goodnight - E
Hall Haynes - HB
Bob Hendren - T
Jerry Houghton - T
Charlie Justice - HB
Lou Karras - DT
Paul Lipscomb - DT
Howie Livingston - HB
Laurie Niemi - T
Gene Pepper - T
Ed Quirk - C
Eddie Saenz - HB
Nick Sebek - QB
Herb Siegert - G
Frank Spaniel - HB
John Steber - G
Pete Stout - FB
Hugh Taylor - E
Joe Tereshinski - E
George Thomas - HB
Harry Ulinski - C
Slug Witucki - G

1951 Chi. Bears

Dick Barwegen - G
George Blanda - LB
J.R. Boone - HB
Ray Bray - DG
Al Campana - HB
Stu Clarkson - LB
George Connor - LB
Les Cowan - DT
Fred Davis - T
Frank Dempsey - G
John Dottley - FB
George Gulyanics - HB
Wayne Hansen - G
John Hoffman - LB
Chuck Hunsinger - HB
Jim Keane - E
Don Kindt - FB
Johnny Lujack - DB
Fred Morrison - FB
Bob Moser - C
Ed Neal - DG
Red O'Quinn - E
Steve Romanik - QB
Brad Rowland - HB
Julie Rykovich - HB
Gene Schroeder - E
Wash Serini - G
Ed Sprinkle - E
Jerry Stautberg - G
Paul Stenn - T
Billy Stone - HB

Bulldog Turner - G
Whizzer White - HB
Bill Wightkin - E
Bob Williams - QB

1951 Chi. Cardinals

Elmer Angsman - HB
Ed Bagdon - G
Tom Bienemann - E
Billy Cross - HB
Jerry Davis - HB
Bob Dove - DE
Lou Ferry - DT
Bill Fischer - T
Joe Gasparella - BB
Billy Gay - DB
Jerry Groom - LB
Jim Hardy - QB
Jerry Hennessy - DE
Jerry Houghton - LB
Jack Jennings - T
Don Joyce - DT
Tony Klimek - DE
Lindy Lauro - DB
Lynn Lynch - G
Lloyd McDermott - DT
John Panelli - FB
Ralph Pasquariello - FB
Cliff Patton - T
Don Paul - DB
Fran Polsfoot - E
Buster Ramsey - LB
Knox Ramsey - LB
Ray Ramsey - E
Leo Sanford - C
Jack Simmons - C
Emil Sitko - HB
Don Stonesifer - E
Bill Svoboda - FB
Charlie Trippi - QB
Frank Tripucka - QB
Fred Wallner - LB
Tom Wham - DE
S.J. Whitman - DB
Vinnie Yablonski - FB

1951 Cleveland

Tony Adamle - LB
Alex Agase - LB
Rex Bumgardner - HB
Ken Carpenter - HB
Emerson Cole - FB
Len Ford - DE
Frank Gatski - C
Bob Gaudio - G
Abe Gibron - G
Horace Gillom - E
Otto Graham - QB
Chubby Grigg - DT
Lou Groza - T
Hal Herring - C
Lin Houston - G
Chick Jagade - FB
Tommy James - DB
Dub Jones - HB
John Kissell - DT
Warren Lahr - DB
Dante Lavelli - E
Cliff Lewis - QB
Marion Motley - LB
Bob Oristaglio - E
Derrell Palmer - DT
Don Phelps - HB
Lou Rymkus - T
John Sandusky - T
Don Shula - DB
Mac Speedie - E
Carl Taseff - HB
Tommy Thompson - LB
Bill Willis - DG
George Young - DE

1951 Detroit

Vince Banonis - LB
Ed Berrang - DE
Les Bingaman - DG
Jack Christiansen - DB
Gus Cifelli - T
Ollie Cline - FB
Lou Creekmur - DT
Pete D'Alonzo - FB
Dorne Dibble - DB
Don Doll - DB
Jim Doran - E
Fred Enke - QB
Dick Flanagan - G
Barry French - G
Pat Harder - FB
Leon Hart - E
Jim Hill - DB
Bob Hoernschemeyer - HB
Floyd Jaszewski - T
Bobby Layne - QB
Jack Lininger - C
Jim Martin - T
Thurman McGraw - DT
Bob Momsen - G
Art Murakowski - FB
Lindy Pearson - HB
John Prchlik - DT
Dan Rogas - T
Clarence Self - DB
Bob Smith - DB
Bill Swiacki - E
Lavern Torgeson - C
Doak Walker - HB
Bruce Womack - G

1951 Green Bay

Dick Afflis - DG
Buddy Burris - LB
Tony Canadeo - HB
Jack Cloud - FB
Rip Collins - HB
Fred Cone - FB
Harper Davis - HB
Raymond DiPierro - G
Ed Ecker - T
Carl Elliott - E
Jug Girard - HB
Billy Grimes - HB
Val Jansante - E
Ace Loomis - HB
Leon Manley - G
Bob Mann - E
John Martinkovic - DE
Walt Michaels - LB
Dick Moje - E
Dom Moselle - DB
Ed Neal - DG
Hamilton Nichols - G
Bob Nussbaumer - DB
Dan Orlich - E
Ray Pelfrey - HB
Breezy Reid - HB
Jay Rhodemyre - C
Charley Robinson - G
Tobin Rote - QB
Howie Ruetz - DT
Bill Schroll - LB
Carl Schuette - C
Joe Spencer - T
Don Stansauk - DT
Rebel Steiner - DB
Dave Stephenson - G
Bob Summerhays - LB
Bobby Thomason - QB
Dick Wildung - T
Ab Wimberly - E

1951 NY Giants

Bill Albright - T
John Amberg - HB
Jon Baker - DG
Fritz Barzilauskas - G
John Cannady - LB
Charlie Conerly - QB
Tex Coulter - T
Al DeRogatis - DT
Jim Duncan - DE
Forrest Griffith - HB
Herb Hannah - T
Bob Hudson - E
Bob Jackson - FB
Ray Krouse - T
Tom Landry - DB
Duke Maronic - G
Bob McChesney - E
Kelley Mote - E
Bill Murray - G
Jim Ostendarp - HB
Ray Poole - DE
Eddie Price - FB
Bosh Pritchard - HB
Johnny Rapacz - C
Kyle Rote - HB
Harmon Rowe - DB
Otto Schnellbacher - DB
Joe Scott - HB
Bill Stribling - E
Joe Sulaitis - BB
Travis Tidwell - QB
Emlen Tunnell - DB
Arnie Weinmeister - DT
Bob Wilkinson - E
Dick Woodard - C

1951 NY Yankees

Bennie Aldridge - DB
Bruce Alford - E
Sisto Averno - LB
Bob Celeri - QB
Jim Champion - T
John Clowes - T
Don Colo - DT
Paul Crowe - HB
Jim Cullom - G
Joe Domnanovich - C
Art Donovan - DT
Brad Ecklund - C
Dan Edwards - E
Dan Garza - E
Joe Golding - DB
Bobby Griffin - DB
Sherman Howard - HB
Duke Iverson - DB
Harvey Johnson - LB
Mike McCormack - DT
Darrel Meisenheimer - DB
Paul Mitchell - DT
Ross Nagel - T
Bill O'Connor - E
Al Pollard - HB
Barney Poole - DE
George Ratterman - QB
Johnny Rauch - QB
Wayne Siegert - T
Joe Soboleski - G
Breck Stroschein - DE
Art Tait - DE
George Taliaferro - HB
Zollie Toth - FB
Bev Wallace - QB
John Wozniak - G
Buddy Young - HB

1951 LA Rams

Bob Boyd - E
Larry Brink - DE
Bobby Collier - T
Tom Dahms - T
Dick Daugherty - G
Glenn Davis - HB
Tom Fears - E
Jack Finlay - G
Jack Halliday - T
Norb Hecker - E
Crazy Legs Hirsch - HB
Dick Hoerner - FB
Marvin Johnson - HB
Tom Kalmanir - HB
Tom Keane - DB
Bill Lange - G
Woodley Lewis - DB
Leon McLaughlin - C
Don Paul - LB
Joe Reid - C
Herb Rich - DB
Andy Robustelli - DE
Don Simensen - T
Vitamin Smith - HB
Harry Thompson - DE
Charlie Toogood - DT
Dan Towler - FB
Norm Van Brocklin - QB
Bob Waterfield - QB
Stan West - G
Jerry Williams - HB
Jim Winkler - DT
Paul Younger - HB
Jack Zilly - DE

1951 Philadelphia

Neill Armstrong - E
Walt Barnes - G
Chuck Bednarik - C
Adrian Burk - QB
Gerry Cowhig - LB
Russ Craft - DB
Ken Farragut - C
Mario Giannelli - G
Bud Grant - E
John Green - DE
Roscoe Hansen - T
Mike Jarmoluk - DE
Bucko Kilroy - T
Vic Lindskog - C
Jay MacDowell - DE
Bill Mackrides - QB
John Magee - LB
Pat McHugh - DB
Red O'Quinn - E
Jim Parmer - DB
Pete Pihos - E
Al Pollard - HB
Bosh Pritchard - HB
Johnny Rauch - QB
Frank Reagan - DB
Ray Romero - G
Dan Sandifer - DB
Clyde Scott - HB
Vic Sears - T
Dick Steere - G
Walt Stickel - DT
Joe Sutton - DB
Ebert Van Buren - FB
Steve Van Buren - HB
Bobby Walston - E
Norm Willey - DE
Al Wistert - G
Frank Ziegler - HB

1951 Pittsburgh

Lou Allen - T
Jack Butler - DB
Lynn Chandois - TB
Dale Dodrill - LB
Jim Finks - TB
Joe Gasparella - BB
Joe Geri - TB
Howard Hartley - DB
George Hays - DT
Dick Hendley - BB
Darrell Hogan - LB
Joe Hollingsworth - FB
George Hughes - G
Val Jansante - E
Tom Jelley - E
Paul Lea - T
Ray Mathews - DB
Bill McPeak - DE
Charley Mehelich - DE
Henry Minarik - E
Tony Momsen - C
Elbie Nickel - E
Jerry Nuzum - HB
Chuck Ortmann - DB
Fran Rogel - FB
Carl Samuelson - DT
John Schweder - G
Jerry Shipkey - DB
Frank Sinkovitz - LB
Truett Smith - BB
Ernie Stautner - DT
Dick Tomlinson - G
Bill Walsh - C
Frank Wydo - T

1951 San Francisco

Frankie Albert - QB
Joe Arenas - HB
Bruno Banducci - G
Alyn Beals - E
Rex Berry - HB
Hardy Brown - LB
Gail Bruce - DE
Don Burke - G
Al Carapella - DT
Jim Cason - HB
Ray Collins - T
Bob Downs - G
Nick Feher - G
Visco Grgich - G
Ed Henke - DT
Bill Jessup - E
Bill Johnson - C
Verl Lillywhite - DB
Jim Monachino - HB
Leo Nomellini - T
Joe Perry - FB
Jim Powers - QB
Pete Schabarum - HB
Gordie Soltau - E
Dave Sparks - G
Norm Standlee - FB
Bishop Strickland - FB
Johnny Strzykalski - HB
Hamp Tanner - T
Y. A. Tittle - QB
Lowell Wagner - DB
Bob White - HB
Billy Wilson - E
Pete Wissman - C

1951 Washington

John Badaczewski - G
Sammy Baugh - QB
Ed Berrang - DE
Gene Brito - E
Buddy Brown - G
George Buksar - LB
Billy Cox - HB
Al DeMao - C
Harry Dowda - HB
Chuck Drazenovich - FB
Bill Dudley - DB
Jack Dwyer - DB
Neil Ferris - DB
Harry Gilmer - DB
Rob Goode - FB
Leon Heath - FB
Bob Hendren - T
Lou Karras - DT
Paul Lipscomb - DT
Laurie Niemi - T
Johnny Papit - HB
Jim Peebles - DE
Gene Pepper - G
Ed Quirk - LB
Jim Ricca - G
Eddie Saenz - HB
Ed Salem - QB
Herb Siegert - G
Jim Staton - DT
Hugh Taylor - E
Joe Tereshinski - LB
George Thomas - DB
Harry Ulinski - C
Slug Witucki - G
Walt Yowarsky - DE

1952 Chi. Bears

Dick Barwegen - G
Bill Bishop - DT
George Blanda - DB
Ed Bradley - G
Al Campana - HB
Leon Campbell - FB
Herman Clark - G
Emerson Cole - DB
George Connor - LB
Bobby Cross - T
Frank Dempsey - G
Babe Dimancheff - HB
Jim Dooley - HB
John Dottley - FB
Bill George - G
George Gulyanics - HB
Wayne Hansen - G
Jack Hoffman - DE
John Hoffman - E
Chuck Hunsinger - HB
Don Kindt - FB
Jimmy Lesane - HB
Eddie Macon - HB
Bill McColl - E
Fred Morrison - FB
Bob Moser - C
Steve Romanik - QB
Gene Schroeder - DB
Ed Sprinkle - E
Billy Stone - HB
Bulldog Turner - G
Bones Weatherly - LB
Whizzer White - HB
Bill Wightkin - E
Fred Williams - DT
Bob Williams - QB

1952 Chi. Cardinals

Cliff Anderson - E
Elmer Angsman - HB
Roy Barni - DB
Tom Bienemann - DE
Billy Cross - HB
Bob Dove - DE
Bill Fischer - G
Joe Geri - HB
Jerry Groom - C
Robert Hecker - DB
Jack Jennings - T
Don Joyce - DT
Johnny Karras - HB
Tony Klimek - DE
Ed Listopad - G
Ollie Matson - DB
Mike Mergen - DT
Denver Mills - DB
Don Panciera - QB
John Panelli - FB
Ralph Pasquariello - FB
Don Paul - HB
Ray Pelfrey - E
Volney Peters - T
Gordon Polofsky - G
Fran Polsfoot - E
Eli Popa - LB
Ray Ramsey - E
Leo Sanford - G
Mike Sikora - G
Jack Simmons - C
Emil Sitko - HB
Don Stonesifer - E
Bill Svoboda - LB
Ralph Thomas - E
Wally Triplett - HB
Charlie Trippi - HB
Frank Tripucka - QB
Fred Wallner - LB
S.J. Whitman - DB

1952 Cleveland

Pete Brewster - E
Rex Bumgardner - DB
Ken Carpenter - HB
Emerson Cole - DB
Len Ford - DE
Bob Gain - T
Frank Gatski - C
Abe Gibron - G
Horace Gillom - E
Otto Graham - QB
Lou Groza - T
Jerry Helluin - DT
Hal Herring - C
Lin Houston - G
Sherman Howard - HB
Chick Jagade - FB
Tommy James - DB
Dub Jones - HB
John Kissell - DT
Warren Lahr - DB
Dante Lavelli - E
Walt Michaels - LB
Marion Motley - LB
Derrell Palmer - DT
Don Phelps - DB
George Ratterman - QB
Bert Rechichar - DB
Ray Renfro - HB
John Sandusky - T
Ed Sharkey - G
Don Shula - DB
Joe Skibinski - G
Mac Speedie - E
Tommy Thompson - LB
Bill Willis - G
George Young - DE

1952 Dallas

Bennie Aldridge - HB
Sisto Averno - G
Billy Baggett - HB
Joe Campanella - DT
Pat Cannamela - LB
Bob Celeri - QB
Don Colo - DT
Jerry Davis - DB
Art Donovan - DT
Brad Ecklund - C
Dan Edwards - E
Gene Felker - E
Keith Flowers - C
Sonny Gandee - DE
Chubby Grigg - DT
Dick Hoerner - FB
Weldon Humble - G
Ken Jackson - T
Keever Jankovich - LB
Tom Keane - E
Jim Lansford - T
Hank Lauricella - HB
Gino Marchetti - T
Dick McKissack - DB
Chuck Ortmann - QB
Ray Pelfrey - E
Johnny Petitbon - HB
Barney Poole - E
Joe Reid - G
George Robison - G
Will Sherman - DB
Joe Soboleski - DT
Art Tait - DE
George Taliaferro - QB
Hamp Tanner - T
Zollie Toth - FB
Frank Tripucka - QB
Dick Wilkins - E
Stan Williams - E
John Wozniak - G
Buddy Young - HB

1952 Detroit

Byron Bailey - HB
Vince Banonis - C
Les Bingaman - G
Cloyce Box - E
Stan Campbell - G
Jack Christiansen - HB
Gus Cifelli - T
Ollie Cline - FB
Lou Creekmur - T
Pete D'Alonzo - FB
Jim David - DB
Don Doll - DB
Jim Doran - E
Tom Dublinski - QB
Blaine Earon - DE
Dick Flanagan - G
Keith Flowers - C
Sonny Gandee - DE
Jug Girard - HB
Pat Harder - FB
Jim Hardy - QB
Leon Hart - E
Jim Hill - DB
Bob Hoernschemeyer - HB
Yale Lary - DB
Bobby Layne - QB
Jim Martin - G
Thurman McGraw - DT
Bob Miller - T
Lindy Pearson - HB
John Prchlik - DT
Clyde Scott - HB
Bob Smith - HB
Dick Stanfel - G
Pat Summerall - E
Bill Swiacki - E
Lavern Torgeson - C
Doak Walker - HB

1952 Green Bay

Dick Afflis - T
Ed Berrang - DE
Chuck Boerio - LB
Ray Bray - G
Tony Canadeo - HB
Fred Cone - FB
Bob Dees - T
Bobby Dillon - DB
Steve Dowden - T
Carl Elliott - E
Hal Faverty - C
Bobby Jack Floyd - FB
Bob Forte - HB
Billy Grimes - HB
Dave Hanner - DT
Billy Howton - E
Marvin Johnson - DB
Tom Johnson - DT
Jim Keane - E
Dick Logan - DT
Ace Loomis - DB
Bob Mann - E
John Martinkovic - DE
Dom Moselle - DB
Babe Parilli - QB
Lindy Pearson - HB
Ray Pelfrey - E
Bill Reichardt - FB
Breezy Reid - HB
Jay Rhodemyre - C
Bill Robinson - HB
Tobin Rote - QB
Howie Ruetz - DT
Steve Ruzich - G
Dan Sandifer - DB
George Schmidt - C
Clarence Self - DB
Wash Serini - G
Dave Stephenson - G
Deral Teteak - G
Ab Wimberly - DE

1952 LA Rams

Paul Barry - HB
Larry Brink - DE
Bob Carey - E
Ken Casner - DT
Tom Dahms - T
Dick Daugherty - G
Jack Dwyer - DB
Tom Fears - E
Norb Hecker - E
Robert Hecker - DB
Crazy Legs Hirsch - E
Marvin Johnson - DB
Don Klosterman - QB
Night Train Lane - DB
Bill Lange - G
Woodley Lewis - HB
Carl Mayes - HB
Bud McFadin - G
Leon McLaughlin - C
Jack Myers - FB
Don Paul - C
Duane Putnam - G
Skeets Quinlan - HB
Herb Rich - DB
Andy Robustelli - DE
Don Simensen - T
Vitamin Smith - HB
Len Teeuws - T
Harry Thompson - DE
Charlie Toogood - DT
Dan Towler - FB
Norm Van Brocklin - QB
Bob Waterfield - QB
Stan West - G
Jerry Williams - HB
Jim Winkler - DT
Paul Younger - HB

1952 NY Giants

Bill Albright - G
John Amberg - HB
Jon Baker - LB
Ray Beck - G
Fred Benners - QB
John Cannady - LB
Charlie Conerly - QB
Tex Coulter - T
Al DeRogatis - DT
Jim Duncan - DE
Frank Gifford - DB
Bob Hudson - E
George Kennard - G
Pat Knight - DE
Ray Krouse - T
Tom Landry - QB
Bob McChesney - E
Don Menasco - DB
Hal Mitchell - G
Kelley Mote - E
Robert Patton - G
Ray Poole - DE
Eddie Price - FB
Johnny Rapacz - C
Kyle Rote - HB
Harmon Rowe - DB
Joe Scott - HB
Bud Sherrod - E
Bill Stribling - E
Joe Sulaitis - G
George Thomas - HB
Emlen Tunnell - DB
Arnie Weinmeister - DT
Bob Wilkinson - HB
Dick Yelvington - T

1952 Philadelphia

Bibbles Bawel - E
Chuck Bednarik - C
John Brewer - FB
Adrian Burk - QB
Russ Craft - DB
Fred Enke - QB
Ken Farragut - LB
Neil Ferris - HB
Ralph Goldston - HB
Bud Grant - E
Bill Horrell - G
John Huzvar - FB
Mike Jarmoluk - DT
Bucko Kilroy - T
John Magee - G
Maury Nipp - G
Bob Oristaglio - DE
Jim Parmer - FB
Pete Pihos - E
Al Pollard - HB
Knox Ramsey - LB
Joe Restic - DB
Wayne Robinson - C
Dan Rogas - G
Clyde Scott - HB
Vic Sears - DT
Lum Snyder - T
Don Stevens - HB
Bob Stringer - FB
Joe Sutton - DB
Bobby Thomason - QB
Joe Tyrrell - G
Ebert Van Buren - HB
Bobby Walston - E
Norm Willey - G
Frank Wydo - T
Frank Ziegler - HB
Jack Zilly - DE

1952 Pittsburgh

Rudy Andabaker - G
Pat Brady - QB
Jim Brandt - DB
Jack Butler - E
Tom Calvin - HB
Lynn Chandois - HB

Dale Dodrill - LB
Lou Ferry - DT
Jim Finks - QB
Dick Fugler - T
Howard Hartley - DB
George Hays - DE
Dick Hensley - E
Claude Hipps - DB
Darrell Hogan - LB
George Hughes - G
Gary Kerkorian - QB
Ed Kissell - DB
Pete Ladygo - LB
Lou Levanti - C
Ray Mathews - HB
Bill McPeak - DE
Ed Modzelewski - FB
Bill Murray - G
Elbie Nickel - E
Fran Rogel - FB
John Schweder - G
Jerry Shipkey - FB
Frank Sinkovitz - C
Alex Smail - LB
Jack Spinks - FB
Ernie Stautner - DT
George Sulima - E
George Tarasovic - DE
Bill Walsh - C

1952 San Francisco

Frankie Albert - QB
Bennie Aldridge - HB
Joe Arenas - HB
Bruno Banducci - G
Rex Berry - HB
J.R. Boone - DB
Hardy Brown - LB
Don Burke - G
Don Campora - DT
Al Carapella - T
Jim Cason - DB
Sam Cathcart - HB
Ray Collins - T
Al Endress - E
Nick Feher - G
Visco Grgich - G
Ed Henke - DE
Bill Jessup - E
Bill Johnson - C
Hugh McElhenny - HB
Bob Meyers - FB
Bob Momsen - G
Leo Nomellini - T
Pat O'Donahue - DE
Joe Perry - FB
Charley Powell - DE
Jim Powers - LB
Jerry Smith - LB
Gordie Soltau - E
Norm Standlee - FB
Johnny Strzykalski - HB
Y. A. Tittle - QB
Bob Toneff - T
Lowell Wagner - HB
Bob White - HB
Billy Wilson - E
Pete Wissman - C

1952 Washington

Dick Alban - DB
Ed Bagdon - G
Sammy Baugh - QB
Ed Berrang - DE
Gene Brito - E
Buddy Brown - G
George Buksar - FB
Jim Clark - G
Jack Cloud - FB
Billy Cox - HB
Andy Davis - DB
Al DeMao - C
Harry Dowda - HB
Chuck Drazenovich - FB
Ed Ecker - T
Neil Ferris - HB
Harry Gilmer - HB
Leon Heath - FB
Jerry Hennessy - DE
Charlie Justice - HB
Lou Karras - DT
Eddie LeBaron - QB
Paul Lipscomb - DT
Tony Momsen - C
Joe Moss - T
Laurie Niemi - T
Johnny Papit - HB
Gene Pepper - T
Knox Ramsey - LB
Jim Ricca - T
Julie Rykovich - HB
Bob Sykes - FB
Hugh Taylor - E
Joe Tereshinski - E
Sam Venuto - HB
Johnny Williams - HB
Dick Woodard - C
John Yonakor - DT

1953 Baltimore

Alex Agase - LB
Sisto Averno - LB
Dick Barwegen - G
Ernie Blandin - T
Monte Brethauer - DB
Joe Campanella - DT
Larry Coutre - HB
Jack Del Bello - QB
Art Donovan - DT
Brad Ecklund - C
Dan Edwards - E
Mel Embree - E
Fred Enke - QB
Tom Finnin - DT
Dick Flowers - QB
John Huzvar - FB
Ken Jackson - T
Tom Kalmanir - HB
Tom Keane - E
Bill Lange - G
Jack Little - T
Gino Marchetti - DT
Buck McPhail - FB
Ed Mioduszewski - QB
Bill Pellington - LB
Barney Poole - DE
Bert Rechichar - HB
Ed Sharkey - G
Don Shula - HB
Art Spinney - DE
George Taliaferro - QB
Carl Taseff - HB
Elmer Wingate - DE
Jim Winkler - G
Buddy Young - HB

1953 Chi. Bears

Billy Anderson - HB
Billy Autrey - C
John Badaczewski - G
Bill Bishop - DT
George Blanda - QB
Leon Campbell - FB
George Connor - G
Buddy Davis - T
Frank Dempsey - G
Jim Dooley - E
John Dottley - FB
George Figner - DB
Bobby Jack Floyd - FB
Bill George - G
Kline Gilbert - T
Wayne Hansen - T
Johnny Hatley - G
John Helwig - LB
Dick Hensley - E
John Hoffman - LB
Don Kindt - DB
John Kreamcheck - DT
Howie Livingston - DB
Lloyd Lowe - HB
Eddie Macon - HB
Bill McColl - E
Fred Morrison - HB
Bob Moser - C
Tommy O'Connell - QB
Rex Proctor - DB
Steve Romanik - QB
Jerry Shipkey - LB
Ed Sprinkle - DE
Billy Stone - HB
Willie Thrower - QB
Bones Weatherly - LB
S.J. Whitman - DB
Bill Wightkin - E
Fred Williams - DT

1953 Chi. Cardinals

Cliff Anderson - E
Roy Barni - DB
Tom Bienemann - DE
Al Campana - DB
Willie Carter - DB
Nick Chickillo - G
Billy Cross - HB
Tony Curcillo - HB
Bob Dove - DE
Bill Fischer - G
George Gilchrist - G
Jerry Groom - DT
Tom Higgins - T
Ed Husmann - LB
Keever Jankovich - DE
Jack Jennings - T
Don Joyce - DT
Ray Nagel - QB
Gern Nagler - E
Johnny Olszewski - FB
John Panelli - LB
Don Paul - HB
Volney Peters - T
Gordon Polofsky - G
Jim Psaltis - DB
Ray Ramsey - E
Steve Romanik - QB
Jim Root - QB
Dan Sandifer - DB
Leo Sanford - C
George Schmidt - DE
Jack Simmons - C
Jack Spinks - FB
Don Stonesifer - E
Dave Suminski - G
Pat Summerall - DE
Bill Svoboda - LB
Wally Triplett - HB
Charlie Trippi - HB
Jerry Watford - DE
S.J. Whitman - DB

1953 Cleveland

Doug Atkins - DE
Pete Brewster - E
Ken Carpenter - HB
Tom Catlin - C
Don Colo - DT
Gene Donaldson - G
Len Ford - DE
Frank Gatski - C
Abe Gibron - G
Horace Gillom - E
Ken Gorgal - DB
Otto Graham - QB
Lou Groza - T
Jerry Helluin - DT
Lin Houston - G
Sherman Howard - HB
Chick Jagade - FB
Tommy James - DB
Dub Jones - HB
Ken Konz - DB
Warren Lahr - DB
Dante Lavelli - E
Walt Michaels - LB
Marion Motley - LB
Chuck Noll - G
Derrell Palmer - DT
George Ratterman - QB
Ray Renfro - HB
Billy Reynolds - HB
John Sandusky - T
Don Steinbrunner - T
Tommy Thompson - LB
Bill Willis - G
George Young - DE

1953 Detroit

Charlie Ane - T
Vince Banonis - C
Les Bingaman - G
Cloyce Box - E
Jim Cain - DE
Lew Carpenter - DB
Jack Christiansen - DB
Ollie Cline - FB
Lou Creekmur - G
Jim David - DB
Dorne Dibble - E
Jim Doran - E
Bob Dove - DE
Tom Dublinski - QB
Blaine Earon - DE
Sonny Gandee - DE
Gene Gedman - HB
Jug Girard - HB
Pat Harder - FB
Leon Hart - E
Bob Hoernschemeyer - HB
Carl Karilivacz - DB
Yale Lary - DB
Bobby Layne - QB
Gil Mains - DT
Jim Martin - G
Thurman McGraw - DT
Bob Miller - T
John Prchlik - DT
Joe Schmidt - LB
Harley Sewell - LB
Bob Smith - HB
Bob Smith - FB
Ollie Spencer - T
Dick Stanfel - G
Lavern Torgeson - C
Doak Walker - HB

1953 Green Bay

Dick Afflis - G
Bennie Aldridge - DB
Byron Bailey - HB
Don Barton - DB
J.R. Boone - DB
Buddy Brown - G
Al Carmichael - HB
Gus Cifelli - T
Fred Cone - FB
Larry Coutre - HB
Gib Dawson - HB
Bobby Dillon - DB
Carl Elliott - E
Howie Ferguson - FB
Bill Forester - DT
Bob Forte - LB
Dave Hanner - DT
George Hays - DE
Billy Howton - E
Marvin Johnson - DB
Dick Logan - DT
Ace Loomis - DB
Bob Mann - E
John Martinkovic - DE
Johnny Papit - HB
Babe Parilli - QB
Breezy Reid - HB
Jim Ringo - C
Tobin Rote - QB
Howie Ruetz - DT
Clive Rush - E
Steve Ruzich - G
Dan Sandifer - DB
Dave Stephenson - G
Len Szafaryn - G
Deral Teteak - G
Clayton Tonnemaker - LB
Val Joe Walker - DB
Dick Wildung - DT
Roger Zatkoff - DE

1953 LA Rams

Ben Agajanian - K
Bob Boyd - DB
Larry Brink - DE
Rudy Bukich - QB
Tom Dahms - T
Dick Daugherty - G
Jack Dwyer - DB
Tom Fears - E
Neil Ferris - DB
Bob Fry - T
Frank Fuller - C
Bob Griffin - C
Norb Hecker - E
Crazy Legs Hirsch - E
John Hock - G
Night Train Lane - DB
Woodley Lewis - HB
Gene Lipscomb - DE
Tom McCormick - HB
Bud McFadin - LB
Leon McLaughlin - C
Brad Myers - HB
Don Paul - LB
Duane Putnam - G
Skeets Quinlan - HB
Herb Rich - DB
Andy Robustelli - DE
Vitamin Smith - HB
Harland Svare - LB
Len Teeuws - T
Harry Thompson - DE
Charlie Toogood - DT
Dan Towler - FB
Norm Van Brocklin - QB
Stan West - G
Paul Younger - LB

1953 NY Giants

Bill Albright - DT
Cliff Anderson - E
Bill Austin - G
Butch Avinger - FB
Rosey Brown - T
John Cannady - LB
Randy Clay - HB
Charlie Conerly - QB
Everett Douglas - T
Jim Duncan - DE
Arnie Galiffa - QB
Frank Gifford - DB
Sonny Grandelius - HB
Merwin Hodel - FB
George Kennard - G
Ray Krouse - DT
Chet Lagod - G
Tom Landry - DB
Buford Long - DB
Bill Mackrides - QB
Don Menasco - DB
Leo Miles - DB
Ray Pelfrey - E
Bob Peviani - LB
Eddie Price - FB
Joe Ramona - G
Johnny Rapacz - C
Kyle Rote - HB
Joe Scott - E
Bill Stribling - E
Jack Stroud - G
Joe Sulaitis - LB
Emlen Tunnell - DB
Arnie Weinmeister - DT
Ray Wietecha - C
Dick Woodard - C
Dick Yelvington - T

1953 Philadelphia

Chuck Bednarik - C
John Brewer - FB
Tom Brookshier - DB
Adrian Burk - QB
Russ Craft - DB
Ken Farragut - LB
Bob Gambold - QB
Hal Giancanelli - HB
Bob Hudson - DB
Willie Irvin - E
Mike Jarmoluk - DT
Don Johnson - HB
Bucko Kilroy - G
Toy Ledbetter - HB
John Magee - G
John Michels - G
George Mrkonic - T
Maury Nipp - G
Jim Parmer - DB
Pete Pihos - E
Al Pollard - FB
Jess Richardson - DT
Wayne Robinson - LB
Bob Schnelker - E
Tom Scott - DE
Vic Sears - DT
Lum Snyder - T
Bob Stringer - FB
Bobby Thomason - QB
Ebert Van Buren - LB
Bobby Walston - E
Norm Willey - DE
Jerry Williams - HB
Frank Wydo - T
Frank Ziegler - HB

1953 Pittsburgh

John Alderton - DE
Ed Barker - E
Nick Bolkovac - T
Pat Brady - QB
Jim Brandt - DB
Jack Butler - E
Tom Calvin - HB
Lynn Chandois - HB
Art DeCarlo - DB
Dale Dodrill - LB
Leo Elter - FB
Lou Ferry - DT
Jim Finks - QB
Dick Flanagan - LB
Ed Fullerton - DB
Bob Gaona - T
Bill Hegarty - DT
Claude Hipps - DB
Darrell Hogan - LB
George Hughes - G
Bill Mackrides - QB
Ted Marchibroda - QB
Ray Mathews - DB
Marv Matuszak - G
Marv McFadden - G
Bill McPeak - DE
Elbie Nickel - E
Tom Palmer - DT
Fran Rogel - FB
John Schweder - LB
Ernie Stautner - DT
George Sulima - E
George Tarasovic - DE
Lou Tepe - C
Bill Walsh - C

1953 San Francisco

Joe Arenas - DB
Harry Babcock - E
Ken Bahnsen - FB
Bruno Banducci - G
Rex Berry - DB
Hardy Brown - LB
Pete Brown - C
Fred Bruney - DB
Don Burke - G
Al Carapella - DT
Nick Feher - G
Doug Hogland - G
Bill Johnson - C
Hal Ledyard - QB
Jack Manley - C
Clay Matthews - DE
Hugh McElhenny - HB
Art Michalik - G
Hal Miller - T
Billy Mixon - DB
Jim Monachino - FB
John Morton - LB
Leo Nomellini - T
Joe Perry - FB
Charley Powell - DE
Jim Powers - DB
Pete Schabarum - DB
Jerry Smith - LB
Gordie Soltau - E
Bob St. Clair - T
Y. A. Tittle - QB
Bob Van Doren - DE
Lowell Wagner - HB
Billy Wilson - E

1953 Washington

Dick Alban - DB
Sam Baker - FB
Paul Barry - HB
Don Boll - T
Gene Brito - E
Don Campora - DT
Jim Clark - T
Jack Cloud - FB
Paul Dekker - E
Al DeMao - C
Don Doll - DB
Harry Dowda - HB
Chuck Drazenovich - FB
Bill Dudley - HB
Hall Haynes - HB
Ted Hazelwood - T
Leon Heath - FB
Bill Hegarty - DT
Jerry Hennessy - DE
Charlie Justice - HB
Eddie LeBaron - QB
Paul Lipscomb - DT
Dick Modzelewski - DT
Laurie Niemi - T
Johnny Papit - HB
Gene Pepper - T
Fran Polsfoot - E
Knox Ramsey - G
Jim Ricca - T
Julie Rykovich - HB
Jack Scarbath - QB
Dave Suminski - G
Hugh Taylor - E
Joe Tereshinski - LB
Harry Ulinski - C
Johnny Williams - DB
Slug Witucki - G

1954 Baltimore

Sisto Averno - LB
Dick Barwegen - G
Jack Bighead - E
Joe Campanella - T
Ernie Cheatham - DT
Lloyd Colteryahn - E
Cotton Davidson - QB
Art Donovan - DT
Dan Edwards - E
Doug Eggers - LB
Fred Enke - QB
Tom Finnin - DT
John Huzvar - FB
Ken Jackson - G
Don Joyce - DE
Tom Keane - HB
Gary Kerkorian - QB
Bob Langas - DE
Bob Leberman - DB
Jimmy Lesane - DB
Jack Little - T
Gino Marchetti - DE
Chuck McMillan - DB
Jim Mutscheller - E
Buzz Nutter - LB
Bill Pellington - LB
Gene Pepper - G
George Radosevich - C
Jim Raiff - T
Bert Rechichar - DB
Charley Robinson - G
Alex Sandusky - G
Don Shula - HB
Art Spinney - G
George Taliaferro - HB
Carl Taseff - DB
Zollie Toth - FB
Royce Womble - HB
Buddy Young - HB

1954 Chi. Bears

Billy Anderson - DB
Bill Bishop - DT
George Blanda - QB
Zeke Bratkowski - QB
Larry Brink - DE
Ed Brown - DB
Leon Campbell - FB
Herman Clark - LB
George Connor - LB
Ted Daffer - DE
Buddy Davis - T
Jim Dooley - E
Bill George - G
Kline Gilbert - G
Wayne Hansen - T
John Helwig - LB
Harlon Hill - E
John Hoffman - E
Chick Jagade - FB
Stan Jones - T
Don Kindt - HB
John Kreamcheck - DT
Jimmy Lesane - DB
Paul Lipscomb - DT
Lloyd Lowe - DB
Bill McColl - E
Bucky McElroy - HB
Ed Meadows - DE
McNeil Moore - DB
Pete Perini - FB
Gene Schroeder - E
Ray Gene Smith - HB
Ed Sprinkle - DE
Billy Stone - HB
Larry Strickland - C
Stan Wallace - DB
Bones Weatherly - C
S.J. Whitman - DB
Bill Wightkin - T
Fred Williams - G

1954 Chi. Cardinals

Elmer Arterburn - DB
Paul Barry - HB
Tom Bienemann - DE
George Brancato - DB
Bill Bredde - HB
Al Brosky - DB
Jack Crittendon - E
Mel Embree - E
Ledio Fanucchi - T
Dick Fugler - T
Les Goble - DB
Jerry Groom - DT
Johnny Hatley - G
Jack Jennings - T
George Kinek - E
Emmett King - HB
Ellsworth Kingery - DB
Gary Knafelc - E
Jim Ladd - E
Night Train Lane - E
Bill Lange - LB
Ollie Matson - DB
Lamar McHan - QB
Charley Oakley - DB
Johnny Olszewski - FB
Gordon Polofsky - G
Steve Romanik - QB
Leo Sanford - C
Jimmy Sears - DB
Jack Simmons - C
Don Stonesifer - E
Leo Sugar - DE
Pat Summerall - DE
Len Teeuws - T
Charlie Trippi - DB
Chuck Ulrich - DT
Fred Wallner - G
Jerry Watford - DE

1954 Cleveland

Tony Adamle - LB
Quincy Armstrong - C
Doug Atkins - DE
Mo Bassett - FB
Harold Bradley - G
Pete Brewster - E
Tom Catlin - C
Don Colo - DT
Len Ford - DE
Herschel Forester - G
Bob Gain - T
Frank Gatski - C
Abe Gibron - G
Horace Gillom - E
Ken Gorgal - DB
Otto Graham - QB
Lou Groza - T
Chet Hanulak - HB
Tommy James - HB
Dub Jones - HB
Don King - T
John Kissell - DT
Ken Konz - DB
Warren Lahr - HB
Dante Lavelli - E
Carlton Massey - DE
Mike McCormack - G
Walt Michaels - LB
Fred Morrison - FB
Chuck Noll - G
Don Paul - DB
George Ratterman - QB
Ray Renfro - HB
Billy Reynolds - HB
John Sandusky - T

1954 Detroit

Charlie Ane - T
Les Bingaman - G
Bill Bowman - FB
Cloyce Box - E
Jim Cain - DE
Lew Carpenter - FB
Jack Christiansen - DB
Lou Creekmur - T
Jim David - DB
Dorne Dibble - E
Jim Doran - E
Bob Dove - DE
Tom Dublinski - QB
Sonny Gandee - DE
Jug Girard - E
Leon Hart - E
Bob Hoernschemeyer - HB
Carl Karilivacz - DB
Dick Kercher - DB
Bobby Layne - QB
Gil Mains - DB
Jim Martin - G
Thurman McGraw - T
Andy Miketa - C
Bob Miller - T
Gerry Perry - DT
Joe Schmidt - LB
Harley Sewell - LB
Bob Smith - DB
Dick Stanfel - G
Bill Stits - DB
Lavern Torgeson - C
Hal Turner - DE
Doak Walker - HB

1954 Green Bay

Dick Afflis - T
Al Barry - G
Buddy Brown - G
Al Carmichael - HB
Fred Cone - FB
Bobby Dillon - DB
Carl Elliott - DE
Howie Ferguson - FB
Bill Forester - LB
Bobby Garrett - QB
Dave Hanner - DT
Jerry Helluin - DT
Billy Howton - E
Art Hunter - T
Joe Johnson - HB
Gary Knafelc - E
Gene Knutson - DE
Bob Mann - E
John Martinkovic - DE

Max McGee - E
Lou Mihajlovich - DE
Don Miller - HB
Jim Psaltis - DB
Breezy Reid - HB
Jim Ringo - C
Tobin Rote - QB
Steve Ruzich - T
Clarence Self - DB
Dave Stephenson - C
Veryl Switzer - DB
Len Szafaryn - T
Deral Teteak - LB
Clayton Tonnemaker - LB
Val Joe Walker - DB
Gene White - DE
Roger Zatkoff - LB

1954 LA Rams

Bill Bowers - DB
Bob Boyd - E
Bob Carey - E
Bobby Cross - T
Tom Dahms - T
Don Doll - DB
Jack Dwyer - DB
Tom Fears - E
Bob Griffin - LB
Art Hauser - DT
Hall Haynes - DB
Crazy Legs Hirsch - DB
Ed Hughes - DB
Woodley Lewis - DB
Gene Lipscomb - DT
Tom McCormick - HB
Bud McFadin - G
Leon McLaughlin - C
Paul Miller - C
Don Paul - C
Duane Putnam - G
Skeets Quinlan - HB
Les Richter - LB
Andy Robustelli - DE
Will Sherman - DB
Harland Svare - LB
Harry Thompson - G
Charlie Toogood - T
Dan Towler - FB
Norm Van Brocklin - QB
Billy Wade - QB
Duane Wardlow - DE
Stan West - G
Paul Younger - LB

1954 NY Giants

Ben Agajanian - K
Bill Albright - T
Bill Austin - G
John Bauer - G
Wayne Berry - HB
Rosey Brown - T
John Cannady - LB
Russ Carroccio - G
Bobby Clatterbuck - QB
Ray Collins - DT
Charlie Conerly - QB
Bobby Epps - FB
Frank Gifford - HB
Don Heinrich - QB
Herb Johnson - HB
George Kennard - G
Pat Knight - LB
Ray Krouse - DT
Tom Landry - DB
Cliff Livingston - DE
Buford Long - HB
Ken Sr. MacAfee - E
Pete Mangum - LB
Dick Nolan - DB
Barney Poole - DE
Eddie Price - FB
Johnny Rapacz - C
Herb Rich - DB
Kyle Rote - HB
Bob Schnelker - E
Billy Shipp - DT
Jack Stroud - G
Bill Svoboda - LB
Bob Topp - E
Emlen Tunnell - DB
Ray Wietecha - C
Dick Wilkins - E
Dick Yelvington - T

1954 Philadelphia

Roy Barni - DB
Chuck Bednarik - C
Adrian Burk - QB
Gus Cifelli - T
Harry Dowda - DB
Ken Farragut - LB
Hal Giancanelli - HB
Ralph Goldston - DB
Tom Higgins - T
Bob Hudson - DB
Ken Huxhold - G
Mike Jarmoluk - DT
Don Johnson - HB
Bucko Kilroy - G
Toy Ledbetter - HB
Don Luft - E
John Magee - G
Menil Mavraides - G
Don Miller - DB
Dom Moselle - DB
Jerry Norton - HB
Jim Parmer - FB
Pete Pihos - E
Jess Richardson - DT
Wayne Robinson - LB
Bill Roffler - DB
Tom Scott - DE
Ed Sharkey - T
Lum Snyder - T
Don Stevens - DB
Bobby Thomason - QB
Bobby Walston - E
Norm Willey - E
Jerry Williams - HB
Neil Worden - FB
Frank Wydo - T

1954 Pittsburgh

Rudy Andabaker - G
Nick Bolkovac - T
Pat Brady - K
Jim Brandt - DB
Dewey Brundage - DE
Jack Butler - E
Tom Calvin - HB
Paul Cameron - DB
Lynn Chandois - HB
Ernie Cheatham - DT
Gus Cifelli - T
Russ Craft - DB
Dale Dodrill - LB
Leo Elter - FB
Lou Ferry - DT
Jim Finks - QB
Dick Flanagan - LB
Bob Gaona - T
Paul Held - QB
George Hughes - T
Ed Kissell - DB
Pete Ladygo - G
Johnny Lattner - HB
Joe Matesic - T
Ray Mathews - HB
Dewey McConnell - E
Bill McPeak - DE
Elbie Nickel - E
Jack O'Brien - E
Tom Palmer - DT
Fran Rogel - FB
John Schweder - LB
Stan Sheriff - C
Burrell Shields - DB
Ernie Stautner - DT
George Sulima - E
Lou Tepe - C
Bill Walsh - C
Joe Zombek - DE

1954 San Francisco

Joe Arenas - DB
Harry Babcock - E
Bruno Banducci - G
Rex Berry - DB
Hardy Brown - LB
Pete Brown - C
Jack Brumfield - DE
Don Burke - G
Marion Campbell - T
Al Carapella - DT
Jim Cason - HB
Frank Cassara - FB
Ted Connolly - G
Maury Duncan - QB
Nick Feher - G
Arnie Galiffa - QB
Bob Hantla - LB
Doug Hogland - G
Bill Jessup - E
John Johnson - HB
Bill Johnson - C
Clay Matthews - DE
Hugh McElhenny - HB
Art Michalik - G
Billy Mixon - HB
Leo Nomellini - T
Joe Perry - FB
Floyd Sagely - E
Pete Schabarum - DB
Gordie Soltau - E
Bob St. Clair - T
Billy Tidwell - HB
Y. A. Tittle - QB
Bob Toneff - DT
Johnny Williams - DB
Billy Wilson - E
Pete Wissman - C

1954 Washington

Nick Adduci - LB
Dick Alban - DB
Dale Atkeson - FB
Ken Barfield - T
Ed Barker - E
Marv Berschet - DE
Don Boll - T
Johnny Carson - E
Walt Cudzik - C
Al Dorow - QB
Chuck Drazenovich - FB
Ralph Felton - FB
Harry Gilmer - DB
Rob Goode - FB
Ron Hansen - LB
Vic Janowicz - HB
Charlie Justice - HB
Jim Kincaid - DB
Paul Lipscomb - DT
Don Menasco - DB
Dick Modzelewski - DT
Bob Morgan - T
Sam Morley - E
Chet Ostrowski - DE
Volney Peters - DT
Jim Ricca - T
George Rosso - DB
Jack Scarbath - QB
Jim Schrader - T
Joe Scudero - HB
Dave Sparks - T
Hugh Taylor - E
Joe Tereshinski - DE
Harry Ulinski - C
Billy Wells - HB
Slug Witucki - G
Walt Yowarsky - DE

1955 Baltimore

Alan Ameche - FB
Raymond Berry - E
Monte Brethauer - E
Walter Bryan - HB
Joe Campanella - T
Dick Chorovich - T
Lloyd Colteryahn - E
Art Donovan - DT
L. G. Dupre - HB
Doug Eggers - LB
Tom Finnin - DT
Harry Hugasian - DB
Ken Jackson - T
Don Joyce - DE
Gary Kerkorian - QB
Gino Marchetti - DE
Jim Mutscheller - E
Bob Myers - DT
Buzz Nutter - LB
Jack Patera - G
Bill Pellington - LB
George Preas - G
George Radosevich - T
Bert Rechichar - DB
Dean Renfro - HB
Alex Sandusky - G
George Shaw - QB
Burrell Shields - HB
Don Shula - DB
Art Spinney - G
Dick Szymanski - C
Carl Taseff - HB
Jesse Thomas - DB
Bob White - DB
Royce Womble - HB
Buddy Young - HB
Dick Young - HB

1955 Chi. Bears

Doug Atkins - DE
Bill Bishop - DT
George Blanda - QB
Ed Brown - QB
Rick Casares - FB
Herman Clark - LB
George Connor - T
Ron Drzewiecki - DB
Joe Fortunato - LB
Bill George - LB
Kline Gilbert - T
Ken Gorgal - DB
Wayne Hansen - C
John Helwig - DE
Harlon Hill - E
Jack Hoffman - E
John Hoffman - FB
Harry Hugasian - DB
Chick Jagade - FB
Ralph Jecha - G
Stan Jones - G
Don Kindt - HB
John Kreamcheck - DT
Bill McColl - E
Henry Mosley - HB
Pete Perini - FB
Al Romine - DB
Gene Schroeder - E
Ray Gene Smith - HB
Ed Sprinkle - DE
Larry Strickland - C
Charlie Sumner - DB
Bobby Watkins - HB
Bill Wightkin - T
Fred Williams - DT
Bob Williams - QB

1955 Chi. Cardinals

Frank Bernardi - DB
Tom Bienemann - DE
Max Boydston - E
Dick Brubaker - E
Jimmy Carr - DB
Ogden Compton - QB
Lindon Crow - DB
Burt Delevan - T
Les Goble - DB
Jerry Groom - DT
Mal Hammack - FB
Larry Hartshorn - G
Johnny Hatley - G
Jimmy Hill - DB
Jack Jennings - T
Tom Keane - DB
Night Train Lane - E
Bill Lange - LB
Dave Leggett - DB
Dave Mann - HB
Ollie Matson - HB
Lamar McHan - QB
Frank McPhee - DB
Gern Nagler - E
Johnny Olszewski - FB
Tony Pasquesi - DT
Jim Psaltis - DB
Leo Sanford - C
Jack Simmons - C
Don Stonesifer - E
Leo Sugar - DE
Pat Summerall - DE
Len Teeuws - T
Harry Thompson - G
Charlie Trippi - DB
Chuck Ulrich - DT
Fred Wallner - LB

1955 Cleveland

Mo Bassett - FB
Harold Bradley - G
Pete Brewster - E
Don Colo - DT
Henry Ford - HB
Len Ford - DE
Herschel Forester - G
Bob Gain - G
Frank Gatski - C
Abe Gibron - G
Horace Gillom - E
Otto Graham - QB
Lou Groza - T
Tommy James - HB
Tom Jones - T
Dub Jones - HB
John Kissell - DT
Ken Konz - DB
Warren Lahr - DB
Dante Lavelli - E
Carlton Massey - DE
Mike McCormack - T
Walt Michaels - LB
Ed Modzelewski - FB
Fred Morrison - HB
Chuck Noll - LB
Sam Palumbo - C
Don Paul - DB
Pete Perini - FB
Johnny Petitbon - HB
George Ratterman - QB
Ray Renfro - HB
John Sandusky - T
Bob Smith - HB
Chuck Weber - G
Bob White - DB

1955 Detroit

Charlie Ane - T
George Atkins - G
Bud Brooks - G
Jim Cain - DE
Stan Campbell - G
Lew Carpenter - FB
Jack Christiansen - DB
Lou Creekmur - T
Leon Cunningham - C
Jim David - DB
Dorne Dibble - E
Jim Doran - E
Dom Fucci - DB
Sonny Gandee - LB
Harry Gilmer - QB
Jug Girard - E
Leon Hart - E
Bob Hoernschemeyer - HB
Walt Jenkins - DT
Carl Karilivacz - DB
Bobby Layne - QB
Bob Long - DE
Gil Mains - DT
Jim Martin - LB
Darris McCord - DT
Dave Middleton - E
Andy Miketa - C
Bob Miller - DT
Jim Ricca - T
Lee Riley - DB
Jim Salsbury - G
Joe Schmidt - LB
Harley Sewell - G
Dick Stanfel - G
Bill Stits - DB
Ted Topor - LB
Doak Walker - DB
Richie Woit - DB
Walt Yowarsky - DE

1955 Green Bay

Tom Bettis - LB
Billy Bookout - DB
Nate Borden - DE
Charlie Brackins - QB
Buddy Brown - G
Hank Bullough - G
Jim Capuzzi - QB
Al Carmichael - HB
Bob Clemens - FB
Fred Cone - FB
Tom Dahms - T
Dick Deschaine - K
Bobby Dillon - DB
Howie Ferguson - FB
Bill Forester - LB
Dave Hanner - DT
Paul Held - QB
Jerry Helluin - DT
Billy Howton - E
Jim Jennings - E
Joe Johnson - HB
Gary Knafelc - E
Bill Lucky - DT
John Martinkovic - DE
Doyle Nix - DB
Pat O'Donahue - DE
Breezy Reid - HB
Jim Ringo - C
Al Romine - DB
Tobin Rote - QB
Clarence Self - DB
Joe Skibinski - G
Jack Spinks - G
Dave Stephenson - C
Veryl Switzer - DB
Len Szafaryn - T
Deral Teteak - LB
George Timberlake - G
Val Joe Walker - DB
Roger Zatkoff - LB

1955 LA Rams

Jack Bighead - E
Bob Boyd - E
Don Burroughs - DB
Jim Cason - DB
Bobby Cross - T
Jack Dwyer - DB
Jack Ellena - G
Tom Fears - E
Sid Fournet - G
Frank Fuller - G
Bob Griffin - C
Art Hauser - DT
Hall Haynes - DB
Crazy Legs Hirsch - E
John Hock - G
Glenn Holtzman - T
Ed Hughes - DB
Woodley Lewis - E
Gene Lipscomb - DT
Bob Long - DE
Tom McCormick - HB
Bud McFadin - DT
Leon McLaughlin - C
Paul Miller - DE
Larry Morris - HB
Don Paul - LB
Duane Putnam - G
Skeets Quinlan - HB
Les Richter - LB
Andy Robustelli - DE
Will Sherman - DB
Corky Taylor - DB
Charlie Toogood - T
Dan Towler - FB
Norm Van Brocklin - QB
Billy Wade - QB
Ron Waller - HB
Paul Younger - FB

1955 NY Giants

Ben Agajanian - K
Bill Austin - G
Ray Beck - G
Rex Boggan - DT
Fred Broussard - C
Rosey Brown - T
Russ Carroccio - T
Bobby Clatterbuck - QB
Charlie Conerly - QB
Bobby Epps - FB
Frank Gifford - HB
Rosey Grier - DT
John Hall - DE
Joe Heap - HB
Don Heinrich - QB
George Kennard - G
Pat Knight - LB
Ray Krouse - DT
Tom Landry - DB
Cliff Livingston - DE
Buford Long - HB
Ken MacAfee Sr. - E
Dick Nolan - DB
Jimmy Patton - DB
Eddie Price - FB
Herb Rich - DB
Kyle Rote - HB
Bob Schnelker - E
Jack Stroud - G
Harland Svare - LB
Bill Svoboda - LB
Mel Triplett - FB
Emlen Tunnell - DB
Larrye Weaver - HB
Alex Webster - HB
Stan West - G
Ray Wietecha - C
Dick Yelvington - T
Walt Yowarsky - DE

1955 Philadelphia

Roy Barni - DB
Bibbles Bawel - E
Chuck Bednarik - C
Eddie Bell - DB
Dick Bielski - FB
Adrian Burk - QB
Russ Carroccio - T
Harry Dowda - DB
Hal Giancanelli - HB
Ralph Goldston - HB
Rob Goode - FB
Tom Higgins - G
Bob Hudson - LB
Ken Huxhold - G
Mike Jarmoluk - G
Don Johnson - HB
Bob Kelley - C
Bucko Kilroy - G
Buck Lansford - G
Toy Ledbetter - HB
John Magee - G
Jerry Norton - DB
Jim Parmer - HB
Pete Pihos - E
Jim Ricca - T
Jess Richardson - DT
Wayne Robinson - LB
Tom Scott - DE
Ed Sharkey - G
Lum Snyder - T
Bill Stribling - E
George Taliaferro - HB
Bobby Thomason - QB
Bobby Walston - HB
Jim Weatherall - T
Ted Wegert - HB
Norm Willey - E
Frank Wydo - T

1955 Pittsburgh

Ed Bernet - E
Fred Broussard - C
Jack Butler - DB
Tom Calvin - HB
Leon Campbell - FB
Lynn Chandois - HB
Dale Dodrill - LB
Dick Doyle - DB
Vic Eaton - QB
Nick Feher - G
Lou Ferry - DT
Jim Finks - QB
Dick Flanagan - C
Bob Gaona - T
Jim Hill - DB
Ted Marchibroda - QB
Ray Mathews - HB
Marv Matuszak - LB
Richie McCabe - DB
Jack McClairen - E
Willie McClung - DT
Bill McPeak - DE
Ed Meadows - DE
Art Michalik - LB
Dick Modzelewski - DT
Marion Motley - FB
Elbie Nickel - E
Jack O'Brien - E
Joe O'Malley - DE
John Reger - G
Fran Rogel - FB
John Schweder - LB
Ernie Stautner - G
Lou Tepe - C
Frank Varrichione - T
Sid Watson - HB
Tad Weed - K
Joe Zombek - E

1955 San Francisco

Joe Arenas - DB
Harry Babcock - E
Ed Beatty - C
Rex Berry - DB
Hardy Brown - LB
Marion Campbell - DT
Al Carapella - DT
Paul Carr - LB
Maury Duncan - QB
Bob Hantla - DE
Carroll Hardy - HB
Lem Harkey - FB
Matt Hazeltine - LB
Doug Hogland - G
John Johnson - DB
Bill Johnson - C
Eldred Kraemer - G
Bud Laughlin - FB
Bobby Luna - DB
George Maderos - DB
Clay Matthews - DE
Hugh McElhenny - HB
Dicky Moegle - HB
Leo Nomellini - T
Louis Palatella - LB
Joe Perry - FB
Charley Powell - DE
Ed Sharkey - G
Ernie Smith - HB
Gordie Soltau - E
Bob St. Clair - T
Tom Stolhandske - DE
Y. A. Tittle - QB
Bob Toneff - DT
Ted Vaught - E
Lowell Wagner - DB
Billy Wilson - E
Sid Youngelman - DT

1955 Washington

Nick Adduci - LB
Dick Alban - DB
Johnny Allen - C
Dale Atkeson - FB
Roy Barni - DB
Marv Berschet - G
Don Boll - T
Gene Brito - DE
Johnny Carson - E
Billy Cox - E
Mike Davlin - T
Al Dorow - QB
Chuck Drazenovich - FB
Leo Elter - HB
Ralph Felton - LB
Rob Goode - FB
Ralph Guglielmi - QB
Norb Hecker - E
Walt Houston - G
Vic Janowicz - HB
Charlie Jones - E
J. D. Kimmel - DT
Eddie LeBaron - QB
Ron Marciniak - G
Fred Miller - T
Jim Monachino - HB
Jim Norman - T
Hal Norris - LB
Chet Ostrowski - DE
Volney Peters - DT
Joe Scudero - HB
Red Stephens - G
Ralph Thomas - E
Lavern Torgeson - C
Harry Ulinski - C
Slug Witucki - G
Bert Zagers - HB

1956 Baltimore

Alan Ameche - FB
Raymond Berry - E
Joe Campanella - LB
Dick Chorovich - T
Lloyd Colteryahn - E
Art Donovan - DT
L. G. Dupre - HB
Doug Eggers - LB
Tom Feamster - DE
Tom Finnin - DT
Bernie Flowers - E
Jim Harness - DB
Johnny Hermann - DB
Ken Jackson - G
Tommy James - DB
Don Joyce - DE
Gary Kerkorian - QB
Bill Koman - LB
Gene Lipscomb - DT
Gino Marchetti - DE
Lenny Moore - HB
Jim Mutscheller - E
Buzz Nutter - C
Dick Nyers - DB
Jack Patera - LB
Bill Pellington - LB
Jerry Peterson - DT
George Preas - T
George Radosevich - T
Bert Rechichar - HB
Alex Sandusky - G
George Shaw - QB
Don Shula - DB
Art Spinney - G
Carl Taseff - HB
Jesse Thomas - DB
Johnny Unitas - QB
Billy Vessels - HB
Royce Womble - HB
Dick Young - FB

1956 Chi. Bears

Doug Atkins - DE
Don Bingham - HB
Bill Bishop - DT
George Blanda - QB
M.L. Brackett - DE
Ed Brown - QB
Harland Carl - HB
James Caroline - HB
Rick Casares - FB
Jesse Castete - DB
Herman Clark - G
Jim Dooley - E
Joe Fortunato - LB
Bill George - LB
Kline Gilbert - T
Ken Gorgal - DB
Jim Haluska - QB
Wayne Hansen - LB
John Helwig - DE

Harlon Hill - E
Jack Hoffman - DE
John Hoffman - FB
Perry Jeter - HB
Stan Jones - G
Dick Klawitter - C
Bill McColl - E
Ed Meadows - DE
John Mellekas - T
McNeil Moore - DB
Tom Roggeman - G
Gene Schroeder - E
J. D. Smith - DB
Ray Gene Smith - DB
Larry Strickland - C
Stan Wallace - DB
Bobby Watkins - HB
Bill Wightkin - T
Fred Williams - DT

1956 Chi. Cardinals

Charlie Anderson - E
Frank Bernardi - DB
Tom Bienemann - DE
Max Boydston - E
Carl Brettschneider - LB
Hardy Brown - LB
Alex Burl - HB
Joe Childress - FB
Lindon Crow - DB
Tom Dahms - T
Burt Delevan - T
John Dittrich - G
Jimmy Hill - DB
Doug Hogland - G
Ed Husmann - G
Harry Jagielski - T
Jack Jennings - T
Bob Konovsky - T
Night Train Lane - E
Woodley Lewis - DB
Dave Mann - E
Ollie Matson - HB
Lamar McHan - QB
Gern Nagler - E
Johnny Olszewski - FB
Tony Pasquesi - LB
John Roach - QB
Jim Root - QB
Leo Sanford - C
Jack Simmons - C
Julian Spence - DB
Don Stonesifer - E
Leo Sugar - DE
Pat Summerall - DE
Len Teeuws - DT
Chuck Ulrich - DT
Chuck Weber - DE
Stan West - G

1956 Cleveland

Mo Bassett - FB
Harold Bradley - G
Pete Brewster - E
Preston Carpenter - HB
Don Colo - DT
Galen Fiss - LB
Len Ford - DE
Herschel Forester - G
Bob Gain - DE
Frank Gatski - C
Abe Gibron - G
Horace Gillom - E
Don Goss - T
Lou Groza - T
Art Hunter - DE
Billy Kinard - HB
John Kissell - DT
Ken Konz - DB
Warren Lahr - DB
Dante Lavelli - E
John Macerelli - G
Carlton Massey - DE
Mike McCormack - T
Walt Michaels - LB
Ed Modzelewski - FB
Fred Morrison - HB
Chuck Noll - LB
Tommy O'Connell - QB
Sam Palumbo - C
Babe Parilli - QB
Don Paul - DB
Johnny Petitbon - DB
Skeets Quinlan - HB
George Ratterman - QB
Ray Renfro - HB
Jim Ray Smith - DE
Bob Smith - HB
Chuck Weber - DE
Junior Wren - DB

1956 Detroit

Charlie Ane - C
Bill Bowman - FB
Stan Campbell - G
Hopalong Cassady - HB
Jack Christiansen - DB
Lou Creekmur - T
Gene Cronin - G
Jim David - DB
Dorne Dibble - E
Jim Doran - E
Sonny Gandee - LB
Gene Gedman - HB
Harry Gilmer - QB
Jug Girard - E
Leon Hart - FB
Carl Karilivacz - DB
Ray Krouse - DT
Yale Lary - DB
Bobby Layne - QB
Bob Long - DE
Bob Lusk - C
Gil Mains - DT
Jim Martin - LB
Darris McCord - DT
Don McIlhenny - HB
Dave Middleton - E
Bob Miller - DT
Gerry Perry - DT
Jerry Reichow - E
Jim Salsbury - G
Joe Schmidt - LB
Harley Sewell - G
Ollie Spencer - T
Bill Stits - HB
Tom Tracy - FB

1956 Green Bay

Emery Barnes - DE
Tom Bettis - LB
Billy Bookout - DB
Nate Borden - DE
Buddy Brown - G
Jim Capuzzi - DB
Al Carmichael - HB
Fred Cone - FB
Dick Deschaine - K
Bobby Dillon - DB
Howie Ferguson - FB
Bill Forester - LB
Ken Gorgal - DB
Forrest Gregg - T
Hank Gremminger - DB
Dave Hanner - DT
Jerry Helluin - DT
Billy Howton - E
Joe Johnson - HB
Don King - T
Gary Knafelc - E
Gene Knutson - DE
Larry Lauer - C
Jack Losch - HB
John Martinkovic - DE
Breezy Reid - HB
Jim Ringo - C
Bill Roberts - HB
Tobin Rote - QB
John Sandusky - T
Joe Skibinski - G
Bob Skoronski - T
Jerry Smith - G
Jack Spinks - G
Bart Starr - QB
Len Szafaryn - G
Deral Teteak - LB
Val Joe Walker - DB
Glenn Young - DB
Roger Zatkoff - LB

1956 LA Rams

Bob Boyd - E
Rudy Bukich - QB
Don Burroughs - DB
Bob Carey - E
Jim Cason - DB
Jesse Castete - DB
Leon Clarke - E
Dick Daugherty - G
Jack Ellena - LB
Tom Fears - E
Sid Fournet - LB
Bob Fry - T
Bob Griffin - LB
Art Hauser - DT
Crazy Legs Hirsch - E
John Hock - G
Bob Holladay - DB
Glenn Holtzman - T
Joe Marconi - FB
Bud McFadin - DT
Paul Miller - DE
Ron Miller - E
Larry Morris - LB
John Morrow - G
Brad Myers - FB
Ken Panfil - T
Hugh Pitts - LB
Duane Putnam - G
Skeets Quinlan - HB
Les Richter - LB
Will Sherman - DB
Rex Shiver - DB
Charlie Toogood - T
Norm Van Brocklin - QB
Billy Wade - QB
Ron Waller - HB
Duane Wardlow - DE
Jesse Whittenton - DB
Tommy Wilson - HB
Paul Younger - FB

1956 NY Giants

Ben Agajanian - K
Bill Austin - G
Ray Beck - G
Rosey Brown - T
Hank Burnine - E
Don Chandler - HB
Bobby Clatterbuck - QB
Charlie Conerly - QB
Gene Filipski - HB
Frank Gifford - HB
Rosey Grier - DT
Don Heinrich - QB
Johnny Hermann - DB
Sam Huff - LB
Ed Hughes - DB
Jerry Huth - G
Jim Katcavage - DE
Cliff Livingston - LB
Ken Sr. MacAfee - E
Dick Modzelewski - DT
Henry Moore - HB
Dick Nolan - DB
Jimmy Patton - DB
Herb Rich - DB
Andy Robustelli - DE
Kyle Rote - E
Bob Schnelker - E
Jack Spinks - G
Jack Stroud - G
Harland Svare - LB
Bill Svoboda - LB
Mel Triplett - FB
Emlen Tunnell - DB
Alex Webster - HB
Ray Wietecha - C
Dick Yelvington - T
Walt Yowarsky - DE

1956 Philadelphia

Bibbles Bawel - DB
Chuck Bednarik - LB
Eddie Bell - DB
Will Berzinski - HB
Dick Bielski - FB
John Bredice - E
Tom Brookshier - DB
Adrian Burk - QB
Hank Burnine - E
Marion Campbell - DT
Frank D'Agostino - T
Tom Dimmick - C
Hal Giancanelli - HB
Abe Gibron - G
Ken Huxhold - G
Ken Keller - HB
Bob Kelley - C
Don King - T
Buck Lansford - T
Dick Murley - T
Maury Nipp - G
Jerry Norton - DB
Jim Parmer - FB
Bob Pellegrini - G
Pete Retzlaff - E
Jim Ricca - T
Jess Richardson - DT
Lee Riley - DB
Wayne Robinson - LB
Rocky Ryan - HB
Don Schaefer - FB
Tom Scott - DE
Bob Smith - HB
Bill Stribling - E
Bobby Thomason - QB
Bobby Walston - E
Jim Weatherall - DT
Ted Wegert - HB
Norm Willey - DE
Frank Wydo - T
Sid Youngelman - DT

1956 Pittsburgh

Dick Alban - DB
Lou Baldacci - HB
Fred Bruney - DB
Jack Butler - E
John Cenci - C
Lynn Chandois - HB
Art Davis - HB
Dale Dodrill - LB
Henry Ford - DB
Bob Gaona - T
Fred Glatz - E
Gary Glick - DB
Ralph Jecha - G
Joe Krupa - DT
Ted Marchibroda - QB
Ray Mathews - E
Marv Matuszak - LB
Jack McClairen - E
Willie McClung - T
Marv McFadden - G
Bill McPeak - DE
Art Michalik - LB
Dick Murley - T
Elbie Nickel - E
Jack O'Brien - E
Joe O'Malley - E
Bob O'Neil - DE
Lowell Perry - HB
John Reger - LB
Fran Rogel - FB
Jack Scarbath - QB
Charlie Shepard - HB
Ernie Stautner - DT
John Stock - E
George Tarasovic - C
Jim Taylor - C
Frank Varrichione - T
Sid Watson - HB

1956 San Francisco

Joe Arenas - HB
Ed Beatty - C
Rex Berry - DB
Bruce Bosley - DE
Fred Bruney - DB
Paul Carr - DB
Clyde Conner - E
Ted Connolly - G
Bobby Cross - T
Paul Goad - FB
John Gonzaga - DE
Matt Hazeltine - LB
Ed Henke - DE
Bill Herchman - DT
Bob Holladay - DB
Bill Jessup - FL
John Johnson - FB
Bill Johnson - C
George Maderos - DB
Tom McCormick - HB
Hugh McElhenny - HB
Dicky Moegle - HB
Earl Morrall - QB
George Morris - C
Leo Nomellini - DT
Louis Palatella - G
Joe Perry - FB
Charley Powell - DE
Leo Rucka - LB
Floyd Sagely - E
Tony Sardisco - LB
Ed Sharkey - G
Stan Sheriff - LB
Charlie Smith - DE
Ernie Smith - DB
J. D. Smith - DB
Jerry Smith - G
Gordie Soltau - E
Bob St. Clair - T
Y. A. Tittle - QB
Bob Toneff - G
Billy Wilson - E

1956 Washington

Johnny Allen - C
Dale Atkeson - FB
Sam Baker - FB
Roy Barni - DB
Don Boll - T
Gene Brito - DE
Johnny Carson - E
Erik Christensen - DE
Art DeCarlo - DB
Al Dorow - QB
Chuck Drazenovich - LB
Leo Elter - FB
Ralph Felton - LB
Bill Fulcher - LB
Norb Hecker - DB
Harry Jagielski - T
Dick James - DB
J. D. Kimmel - DT
Eddie LeBaron - QB
Gary Lowe - DB
Steve Meilinger - E
Johnny Miller - T
Hal Norris - LB
Chet Ostrowski - DE
John Paluck - DE
Volney Peters - DT
Jerry Planutis - HB
Tommy Runnels - HB
Tony Sardisco - LB
Jim Schrader - C
Joe Scudero - HB
Dick Stanfel - G
Red Stephens - G
Ralph Thomas - E
Lavern Torgeson - LB
Harry Ulinski - C
Billy Wells - HB
Slug Witucki - G
Fred Wyant - QB

1957 Baltimore

Alan Ameche - FB
Raymond Berry - E
Ordell Braase - DE
Jack Call - HB
Joe Campanella - LB
Cotton Davidson - QB
Milt Davis - DB
Art DeCarlo - DB
Art Donovan - DT
L. G. Dupre - HB
Doug Eggers - LB
Ken Jackson - G
Don Joyce - DE
Gene Lipscomb - DT
Gino Marchetti - DDE
Henry Moore - DB
Lenny Moore - HB
Jim Mutscheller - E
Steve Myhra - G
Andy Nelson - DB
Buzz Nutter - C
Dick Nyers - DB
Luke Owens - T
Jim Parker - T
Jack Patera - LB
Bill Pellington - LB
George Preas - T
Billy Pricer - FB
Bert Rechichar - DB
Alex Sandusky - G
George Shaw - QB
Don Shinnick - LB
Art Spinney - G
Dick Szymanski - LB
Carl Taseff - DB
Jesse Thomas - DB
Johnny Unitas - QB
Royce Womble - HB

1957 Chi. Bears

Doug Atkins - DE
Bill Bishop - DT
George Blanda - QB
M.L. Brackett - DE
Zeke Bratkowski - QB
Ed Brown - QB
James Caroline - HB
Rick Casares - FB
Herman Clark - G
John Damore - G
Jim Dooley - E
Ron Drzewiecki - HB
Joe Fortunato - FB
Willie Galimore - HB
Bill George - LB
Kline Gilbert - T
Wayne Hansen - LB
Harlon Hill - E
Jack Hoffman - DE
Perry Jeter - HB
Jack Johnson - DB
Stan Jones - G
Bob Kilcullen - T
Ronnie Knox - QB
Earl Leggett - DT
Bill McColl - E
Ed Meadows - DE
McNeil Moore - DB
Tom Roggeman - G
Gene Schroeder - E
Ray Gene Smith - HB
Larry Strickland - C
Stan Wallace - DB
Bobby Watkins - HB
Bill Wightkin - T
Fred Williams - DT
Vic Zucco - DB

1957 Chi. Cardinals

Frank Bernardi - HB
Wayne Bock - DT
Max Boydston - E
Carl Brettschneider - LB
Dick Brubaker - E
Jimmy Carr - DB
Joe Childress - HB
Lindon Crow - DB
Tom Finnin - DT
Mal Hammack - FB
Jimmy Hill - DB
Doug Hogland - G
Ed Husmann - G
Jack Jennings - T
Bob Konovsky - G
Night Train Lane - DB
Paul Larson - QB
Woodley Lewis - DB
Dave Lunceford - T
Dave Mann - E
Ted Marchibroda - QB
Ollie Matson - HB
Lamar McHan - QB
Gern Nagler - E
Johnny Olszewski - FB
Tony Pasquesi - DT
Earl Putman - C
Floyd Sagely - DB
Leo Sanford - C
Jimmy Sears - HB
Leo Sugar - DE
Pat Summerall - DE
Jim Taylor - LB
Len Teeuws - DT
Charlie Toogood - G
Jerry Tubbs - C
Chuck Ulrich - DT
Chuck Weber - LB
Stan West - C

1957 Cleveland

Joe Amstutz - C
John Borton - QB
Pete Brewster - E
Jim Brown - FB
Milt Campbell - HB
Lew Carpenter - HB
Preston Carpenter - E
Tom Catlin - LB
Frank Clarke - E
Don Colo - DT
Vince Costello - LB
Galen Fiss - LB
Len Ford - DE
Herschel Forester - G
Bobby Freeman - DB
Bob Gain - DT
Lou Groza - T
Chet Hanulak - HB
Art Hunter - C
Henry Jordan - DT
Ken Konz - DB
Warren Lahr - DB
Mike McCormack - T
Walt Michaels - LB
Ed Modzelewski - FB
Chuck Noll - LB
Tommy O'Connell - QB
Don Paul - DB
Milt Plum - QB
Bill Quinlan - DE
Ray Renfro - FL
Billy Reynolds - HB
Fred Robinson - G
Stan Sheriff - G
Jim Ray Smith - G
Paul Wiggin - DE
Junior Wren - DB

1957 Detroit

Charlie Ane - T
Terry Barr - DB
Marv Brown - HB
Stan Campbell - G
Hopalong Cassady - HB
Jack Christiansen - DB
Lou Creekmur - G
Gene Cronin - G
Jim David - DB
Dorne Dibble - E
Jim Doran - E
Frank Gatski - C
Gene Gedman - HB
John Gordy - T
Leon Hart - E
John Johnson - FB
Steve Junker - E
Carl Karilivacz - DB
Ray Krouse - DT
Yale Lary - DB
Bobby Layne - QB
Bob Long - LB
Gary Lowe - DB
Gil Mains - DT
Jim Martin - LB
Darris McCord - DT
Dave Middleton - E
Bob Miller - DT
Gerry Perry - DT
Jerry Reichow - QB
Tobin Rote - QB
Ken Russell - T
Joe Schmidt - LB
Harley Sewell - G
Tom Tracy - FB
Roger Zatkoff - LB

1957 Green Bay

Norm Amundsen - G
Al Barry - G
Tom Bettis - LB
Nate Borden - DE
Al Carmichael - HB
Fred Cone - FB
Ernie Danjean - LB
Dick Deschaine - K
Bobby Dillon - DB
Howie Ferguson - FB
Tom Finnin - DT
Bill Forester - LB
Hank Gremminger - DB
Dave Hanner - DT
Jerry Helluin - DT
Paul Hornung - FB
Billy Howton - E
Joe Johnson - HB
Billy Kinard - DB
Gary Knafelc - E
Ron Kramer - E
Larry Lauer - C
Carlton Massey - DE
Norm Masters - T
Max McGee - E
Don McIlhenny - HB
Sam Palumbo - LB
Babe Parilli - QB
Johnny Petitbon - DB
Frank Purnell - FB
Jim Ringo - C
Jim Salsbury - G
Ollie Spencer - T
Bart Starr - QB
John Symank - DB
Jim Temp - DE
Carl Vereen - T

1957 LA Rams

Jon Arnett - HB
Bob Boyd - E
Alex Bravo - DB
Don Burroughs - DB
Jesse Castete - DB
Leon Clarke - E
Paige Cothren - K
Dick Daugherty - LB
Bob Dougherty - LB
Bob Fry - T
Frank Fuller - DT
Bob Griffin - LB
Art Hauser - DT
Crazy Legs Hirsch - E
John Hock - G
Glenn Holtzman - DE
John Houser - G
Lamar Lundy - E
Joe Marconi - FB
Paul Miller - DE
Larry Morris - LB
Ken Panfil - T
Jack Pardee - LB
Duane Putnam - G
Les Richter - LB
Will Sherman - DB
Del Shofner - DB
Billy Ray Smith Sr. - DE
George Strugar - DT
Corky Taylor - DB
Norm Van Brocklin - QB
Billy Wade - QB
Ron Waller - HB
Jesse Whittenton - DB
Tommy Wilson - HB
Paul Younger - FB

1957 NY Giants

Ben Agajanian - K
Bill Austin - G
Ray Beck - G
Johnny Bookman - DB
Rosey Brown - T
Don Chandler - HB
Bobby Clatterbuck - QB
Charlie Conerly - QB
Ed Crawford - E
Bobby Epps - FB
Gene Filipski - HB
Frank Gifford - HB
Don Heinrich - QB
Sam Huff - LB
Ed Hughes - DB
Jim Katcavage - DT
Cliff Livingston - LB
Ken MacAfee Sr. - E
John Martinkovic - DT
Dick Modzelewski - DT
Dick Nolan - DB
Jimmy Patton - DB
Andy Robustelli - DE
Kyle Rote - E
Bob Schnelker - E
Jack Spinks - T
Jack Stroud - T
Harland Svare - LB
Bill Svoboda - LB
Mel Triplett - FB
Emlen Tunnell - DB
Alex Webster - HB
Ray Wietecha - C
Dick Yelvington - T
Walt Yowarsky - T

1957 Philadelphia

Billy Barnes - HB
Chuck Bednarik - C
Eddie Bell - DB
Dick Bielski - E
Tom Brookshier - DB
Hank Burnine - E
Marion Campbell - DT
Al Dorow - QB
Bob Gaona - T
Abe Gibron - G
Jimmy Harris - DB
Bob Hudson - DB
Ken Huxhold - G
Sonny Jurgensen - QB
Ken Keller - HB
Bill Koman - LB
Buck Lansford - T
Menil Mavraides - G
Tommy McDonald - FL
Jerry Norton - DB
Clarence Peaks - FB
Pete Retzlaff - FL
Rocky Ryan - E
Tom Saidock - DT
Tom Scott - DE
John Simerson - C
Bill Stribling - E
Len Szafaryn - T
Bobby Thomason - QB
Bobby Walston - E
Jim Weatherall - DT
Norm Willey - DE
Neil Worden - FB
Frank Wydo - DT
Sid Youngelman - DT

1957 Pittsburgh

Dick Alban - DB
Ed Beatty - C
Bill Bowman - FB
Fred Bruney - DB
Jack Butler - DB
Chick Cichowski - DB
Len Dawson - QB
Dean Derby - DB
Dale Dodrill - LB
Sid Fournet - G
Jug Girard - E
Gary Glick - DB
Bob Gunderman - E
Dick Hughes - HB

Jack Kemp - QB
Joe Krupa - DT
Jerry Leahy - T
Herman Lee - G
Dave Liddick - DT
Ray Mathews - E
Richie McCabe - DB
Jack McClairen - E
Willie McClung - T
Bill McPeak - DE
Bill Michael - G
Earl Morrall - QB
Elbie Nickel - E
John Nisby - G
Bob O'Neil - G
Bill Priatko - LB
John Reger - LB
Perry Richards - E
Fran Rogel - FB
Aubrey Rozzell - LB
Mike Sandusky - G
Ernie Stautner - DE
George Tarasovic - LB
Frank Varrichione - T
Sid Watson - HB
Billy Wells - HB
Dick Young - FB

1957 San Francisco

Joe Arenas - HB
Gene Babb - FB
Larry Barnes - FB
Bruce Bosley - G
John Brodie - QB
Paul Carr - DB
Clyde Conner - E
Ted Connolly - G
Bobby Cross - T
Tom Dahms - T
John Gonzaga - T
Matt Hazeltine - LB
Ed Henke - LB
Bill Herchman - DT
Bob Holladay - DB
Bill Jessup - E
Marv Matuszak - LB
Hugh McElhenny - HB
Dicky Moegle - HB
Frank Morze - C
Leo Nomellini - DT
R.C. Owens - E
Louis Palatella - G
Joe Perry - FB
Charley Powell - E
Jimmy Ridlon - DB
Karl Rubke - C
Stan Sheriff - G
J. D. Smith - DB
Gordie Soltau - E
Julian Spence - DB
Bob St. Clair - T
Bill Stits - DB
Y. A. Tittle - QB
Bob Toneff - DT
Val Joe Walker - DB
Billy Wilson - E

1957 Washington

Johnny Allen - C
Sam Baker - FB
Don Boll - T
Don Bosseler - FB
Tom Braatz - E
Gene Brito - DE
Rudy Bukich - QB
Johnny Carson - E
Art DeCarlo - DB
Bob Dee - DT
Chuck Drazenovich - LB
Leo Elter - FB
Ralph Felton - LB
Bill Fulcher - LB
Norb Hecker - DB
Dick James - HB
Ed Khayat - T
Eddie LeBaron - QB
Ray Lemek - T
Gary Lowe - DB
Steve Meilinger - E
Chet Ostrowski - DE
Don Owens - DT
Volney Peters - DT
Jim Podoley - HB
Will Renfro - DT
Tommy Runnels - HB
Jim Schrader - C
Joe Scudero - HB
Don Shula - DB
Dick Stanfel - G
Red Stephens - G
Ed Sutton - DB
Lavern Torgeson - LB
Ed Voytek - G
Joe Walton - E
Billy Wells - HB
Bert Zagers - DB

1958 Baltimore

Alan Ameche - FB
Raymond Berry - E
Ordell Braase - DE
Ray Brown - QB
Jack Call - HB
Milt Davis - DB
Art DeCarlo - E
Art Donovan - DT
L. G. Dupre - HB
Dick Horn - QB
Don Joyce - DE
Ray Krouse - DE
Gene Lipscomb - DT
Lenny Lyles - DB
Gino Marchetti - DE
Lenny Moore - HB
Jim Mutscheller - E
Steve Myhra - G
Andy Nelson - DB
Buzz Nutter - C
Jim Parker - T
Bill Pellington - LB
Sherman Plunkett - T
George Preas - T
Billy Pricer - FB
Bert Rechichar - E
Johnny Sample - DB
Alex Sandusky - G
Leo Sanford - LB
George Shaw - QB
Don Shinnick - LB
Jackie Simpson - DB
Art Spinney - G
Avatus Stone - HB
Dick Szymanski - C
Carl Taseff - DB
Fuzzy Thurston - G
Johnny Unitas - QB

1958 Chi. Bears

Ralph Anderson - E
Doug Atkins - DE
Erich Barnes - DB
Bill Bishop - DT
George Blanda - QB
Zeke Bratkowski - QB
Ed Brown - QB
Rudy Bukich - QB
Bob Carey - E
James Caroline - DB
Rick Casares - FB
Ed Cooke - DE
Merrill Douglas - HB
Joe Fortunato - LB
Willie Galimore - HB
Bill George - LB
Abe Gibron - G
Wayne Hansen - LB
Don Healy - G
Harlon Hill - E
Jack Hoffman - DE
Chuck Howley - LB
Bob Jewett - E
Jack Johnson - DB
Stan Jones - G
Bob Kilcullen - T
Dick Klein - T
Herman Lee - T
Earl Leggett - DT
Bill McColl - E
John Mellekas - C
Johnny Morris - HB
Bill Roehnelt - LB
Rocky Ryan - E
Larry Strickland - C
Charlie Sumner - DB
Stan Wallace - DB
Fred Williams - DT
Vic Zucco - DB

1958 Chi. Cardinals

Max Boydston - E
Carl Brettschneider - LB
Joe Childress - HB
Bobby Joe Conrad - DB
Ed Cook - T
Bobby Cross - T
John Crow - HB
Ed Culpepper - DT
Doug Eggers - LB
Don Gillis - C
Bobby Gordon - DB
Ken Gray - LB
Mal Hammack - FB
King Hill - QB
Doug Hogland - G
Ed Husmann - DE
Charlie Jackson - DB
Bob Konovsky - G
Lowell Lander - DB
Night Train Lane - DB
Woodley Lewis - E
Ollie Matson - HB
Jim McCusker - T
Lamar McHan - QB
Dale Meinert - T
Gern Nagler - E
Dick Nolan - DB
Luke Owens - DT
Jack Patera - LB
Dean Philpott - FB
M.C. Reynolds - QB
Jimmy Sears - HB
Leo Sugar - DE
Jim Taylor - LB
Jerry Tubbs - LB
Chuck Ulrich - DT
Bobby Watkins - HB
Chuck Weber - LB

1958 Cleveland

Leroy Bolden - HB
Pete Brewster - E
Jim Brown - FB
Lew Carpenter - HB
Preston Carpenter - E
Tom Catlin - LB
Frank Clarke - E
Don Colo - DT
Vince Costello - LB
Willie Davis - T
Dick Deschaine - K
Galen Fiss - LB
Bobby Freeman - HB
Bob Gain - DT
Lou Groza - T
Gene Hickerson - G
Art Hunter - C
Henry Jordan - DT
Ken Konz - DB
Warren Lahr - DB
Willie McClung - T
Mike McCormack - T
Walt Michaels - LB
Bobby Mitchell - HB
Ed Modzelewski - FB
Jim Ninowski - QB
Chuck Noll - C
Don Paul - DB
Milt Plum - QB
Bill Quinlan - DE
Ray Renfro - HB
Jim Shofner - DB
Jim Ray Smith - G
Paul Wiggin - DE
Junior Wren - DB

1958 Detroit

Charlie Ane - T
Terry Barr - DB
Stan Campbell - G
Hopalong Cassady - HB
Jack Christiansen - DB
Lou Creekmur - G
Gene Cronin - DE
Jim David - DB
Jim Doran - E
Gene Gedman - HB
Jim Gibbons - E
Bill Glass - T
Doug Hogland - G
John Johnson - FB
Alex Karras - DT
Karl Koepfer - G
Yale Lary - DB
Bobby Layne - QB
Dan Lewis - HB
Bob Long - LB
Gary Lowe - DB
Gil Mains - DT
Jim Martin - LB
Darris McCord - DE
Dave Middleton - E
Bob Miller - DT
Earl Morrall - QB
Gerry Perry - DT
Perry Richards - E
Tobin Rote - QB
Ken Russell - T
Tom Rychlec - E
Joe Schmidt - LB
Harley Sewell - G
Wayne Walker - LB
Ken Webb - FB
Dave Whitsell - DB
Roger Zatkoff - LB

1958 Green Bay

Tom Bettis - LB
Nate Borden - DE
Hank Bullough - G
Al Carmichael - HB
Dan Currie - LB
Bobby Dillon - DB
Howie Ferguson - FB
Len Ford - DE
Bill Forester - LB
Joe Francis - HB
Forrest Gregg - G
Hank Gremminger - DB
Dave Hanner - DT
Paul Hornung - HB
Billy Howton - E
Joe Johnson - FL
J. D. Kimmel - DT
Billy Kinard - HB
Gary Knafelc - E
Jerry Kramer - G
Carlton Massey - DE
Norm Masters - T
Marv Matuszak - LB
Max McGee - E
Don McIlhenny - HB
Steve Meilinger - E
Ray Nitschke - LB
Babe Parilli - QB
Jim Ringo - C
Al Romine - HB
Jim Salsbury - G
Jim Shanley - HB
Ollie Spencer - T
Bart Starr - QB
John Symank - DB
Jim Taylor - FB
Jim Temp - DE
Jesse Whittenton - DB

1958 LA Rams

Jon Arnett - HB
John Baker - T
Tom Braatz - E
Charlie Bradshaw - T
Alex Bravo - DB
Fred Bruney - DB
Don Burroughs - DB
Leon Clarke - E
Paige Cothren - K
Dick Daugherty - LB
Bob Fry - T
Frank Fuller - DT
Jimmy Harris - DB
Glenn Holtzman - DE
John Houser - C
Floyd Iglehart - DB
Bill Jobko - LB
Jim Jones - DB
Buck Lansford - G
Lamar Lundy - E
Joe Marconi - FB
Lou Michaels - DE
Jack Morris - DB
John Morrow - C
Ken Panfil - T
Jack Pardee - LB
Jim Phillips - E
Duane Putnam - G
Les Richter - LB
Frank Ryan - QB
Will Sherman - DB
Del Shofner - E
George Strugar - DT
Clendon Thomas - DB
Billy Wade - QB
Ron Waller - HB
Roy Wilkins - LB
Tommy Wilson - HB

1958 NY Giants

Al Barry - G
M.L. Brackett - DE
Rosey Brown - T
Don Chandler - HB
Charlie Conerly - QB
Lindon Crow - DB
Tom Dublinski - QB
Frank Gifford - HB
Rosey Grier - DT
Buzz Guy - G
Don Heinrich - QB
Sam Huff - LB
Ed Hughes - DB
Jon Jelacic - G
Carl Karilivacz - DB
Jim Katcavage - DE
Phil King - FB
Cliff Livingston - LB
Billy Lott - HB
Ken MacAfee Sr. - E
Don Maynard - HB
Bob Mischak - G
Dick Modzelewski - DT
Jimmy Patton - DB
Andy Robustelli - DE
Kyle Rote - E
Bob Schnelker - E
Jack Stroud - G
Pat Summerall - DE
Harland Svare - LB
Bill Svoboda - LB
Mel Triplett - FB
Emlen Tunnell - DB
Alex Webster - HB
Ray Wietecha - C
Frank Youso - T

1958 Philadelphia

Billy Barnes - HB
Chuck Bednarik - C
Eddie Bell - DB
Dick Bielski - E
Harold Bradley - G
Tom Brookshier - DB
Marion Campbell - DE
Ed Cooke - DE
Bob Hudson - LB
Ken Huxhold - G
Proverb Jacobs - T
Sonny Jurgensen - QB
Ed Khayat - DT
Bill Koman - LB
Walt Kowalczyk - DB
Galen Laack - G
Tom Louderback - G
Tommy McDonald - FL
Ed Meadows - DE
Gene Mitcham - E
Brad Myers - DB
Andy Nacrelli - E
Jerry Norton - DB
Don Owens - DT
Clarence Peaks - FB
Bob Pellegrini - LB
Volney Peters - DE
Pete Retzlaff - FL
Jess Richardson - DT
Lee Riley - DB
Rocky Ryan - E
Tom Scott - LB
John Simerson - C
Lum Snyder - T
Len Szafaryn - T
Norm Van Brocklin - QB
Bobby Walston - E
Billy Wells - HB
Sid Youngelman - DT

1958 Pittsburgh

Dick Alban - DB
Ed Beatty - C
Don Bishop - HB
Jack Butler - DB
Dick Campbell - LB
Dick Christy - HB
Len Dawson - QB
Dean Derby - DB
Darrell Dess - T
Dale Dodrill - LB
Bob Dougherty - LB
Leo Elter - FB
Jon Evans - E
Gary Glick - DB
Ted Karras - LB
Billy Krisher - G
Joe Krupa - DT
Larry Krutko - FB
Dick Lasse - LB
Bobby Layne - QB
Joe Lewis - DT
Dick Lucas - E
Ray Mathews - HB
Richie McCabe - DB
Jack McClairen - E
Tom Miner - K
Earl Morrall - QB
John Nisby - G
Jimmy Orr - E
John Reger - LB
Billy Reynolds - HB
Mike Sandusky - G
John Simerson - C
Billy Ray Smith Sr. - DE
Ernie Stautner - DE
George Tarasovic - DE
Tom Tracy - HB
Frank Varrichione - T
Paul Younger - FB

1958 San Francisco

Billy Atkins - DB
Gene Babb - FB
Bruce Bosley - G
John Brodie - QB
Clyde Conner - E
Ted Connolly - G
Fred Dugan - E
John Gonzaga - T
Matt Hazeltine - LB
Ed Henke - DE
Bill Herchman - DT
Bill Jessup - E
Marv Matuszak - LB
Hugh McElhenny - HB
Jerry Mertens - DB
Dicky Moegle - DB
Dennit Morris - LB
Frank Morze - C
Leo Nomellini - DT
R.C. Owens - E
James Pace - HB
Louis Palatella - G
Joe Perry - FB
Jimmy Ridlon - DB
Karl Rubke - C
J. D. Smith - FB
Gordie Soltau - E
Bob St. Clair - T
Bill Stits - DB
Tony Teresa - HB
John Thomas - T
Y. A. Tittle - QB
Bob Toneff - DE
Jerry Tubbs - LB
Billy Wilson - E
John Wittenborn - G
Abe Woodson - HB
Walt Yowarsky - DE

1958 Washington

Johnny Allen - LB
Bill Anderson - E
Sam Baker - K
Don Boll - T
Don Bosseler - FB
Tom Braatz - E
Gene Brito - DE
Charlie Brueckman - LB
Rudy Bukich - QB
Johnny Carson - E
Chick Cichowski - DB
Bob Dee - DE
Chuck Drazenovich - LB
Ralph Felton - LB
Bill Fulcher - LB
Ralph Guglielmi - QB
Dick James - HB
Frank Kuchta - LB
Eddie LeBaron - QB
Ray Lemek - T
Dick Lynch - DB
Johnny Miller - T
Doyle Nix - DB
Johnny Olszewski - FB
Chet Ostrowski - DT
Jim Podoley - HB
Will Renfro - T
Jim Schrader - C
Joe Scudero - HB
Mike Sommer - DB
Dick Stanfel - G
Red Stephens - G
Ed Sutton - HB
Ed Voytek - G
Les Walters - DB
Joe Walton - E
Sid Watson - HB
Jim Weatherall - DT
Bert Zagers - DB

1959 Baltimore

Alan Ameche - FB
Raymond Berry - E
Ordell Braase - DE
Ray Brown - QB
Ed Cooke - DE
Milt Davis - DB
Art DeCarlo - E
Art Donovan - DT
L. G. Dupre - HB
Alex Hawkins - HB
Don Joyce - DT
Ray Krouse - DE
Hal Lewis - DB
Gene Lipscomb - DT
Gino Marchetti - DE
Marv Matuszak - LB
Lenny Moore - HB
Jim Mutscheller - E
Steve Myhra - G
Andy Nelson - DB
Buzz Nutter - C
Jim Parker - T
Bill Pellington - LB
Sherman Plunkett - T
George Preas - T
Billy Pricer - FB
Bert Rechichar - LB
Jerry Richardson - FL
Johnny Sample - DB
Alex Sandusky - G
Dave Sherer - E
Don Shinnick - LB
Jackie Simpson - DB
Mike Sommer - HB
Art Spinney - G
Dick Szymanski - LB
Carl Taseff - DB
Johnny Unitas - QB

1959 Chi. Bears

John Adams - FB
Doug Atkins - DE
John Aveni - K
Erich Barnes - DB
Don Bishop - DB
Bill Bishop - DT
Zeke Bratkowski - QB
Ed Brown - QB
Rudy Bukich - QB
James Caroline - DB
Rick Casares - FB
John Damore - C
Willard Dewveall - E
Jim Dooley - FL
Merrill Douglas - FB
Joe Fortunato - LB
Willie Galimore - HB
Bill George - LB
Abe Gibron - G
Don Healy - G
Harlon Hill - E
Chuck Howley - LB
Jack Johnson - DB
Pete Johnson - DB
Stan Jones - G
Dick Klein - T
Herman Lee - T
Earl Leggett - DT
Bill McColl - E
John Mellekas - C
Johnny Morris - HB
Larry Morris - LB
Ed Nickla - T
Richie Petitbon - DB
Bill Roehnelt - LB
Larry Strickland - C
Charlie Sumner - DB
Lionel Taylor - FL
Fred Williams - DT
Vic Zucco - DB

1959 Chi. Cardinals

Ted Bates - LB
Carl Brettschneider - LB
Joe Childress - HB
Bobby Joe Conrad - HB
Ed Cook - G
Bobby Cross - T
John Crow - HB
Ed Culpepper - DT
Frank Fuller - DT
Don Gillis - C
Fred Glick - DB
Ken Gray - G
Ken Hall - HB
Mal Hammack - FB
Art Hauser - DT
Larry Hickman - FB
Jimmy Hill - DB
King Hill - QB
Ed Husmann - DT
Bill Koman - LB
Night Train Lane - DB
Mac Lewis - T
Woodley Lewis - E
Dale Meinert - G
Dale Memmelaar - T
Jerry Norton - DB
Luke Owens - DT
Ken Panfil - T
Jack Patera - LB
Sonny Randle - E
M.C. Reynolds - QB
Perry Richards - E
John Roach - DB
Marion Rushing - LB
Maury Schleicher - LB
Billy Stacy - DB
Leo Sugar - DE
Jack Tracey - E
Jim Wagstaff - DB

1959 Cleveland

Leroy Bolden - HB
Jim Brown - FB
Preston Carpenter - E
Frank Clarke - E
Vince Costello - LB
Willie Davis - T
Galen Fiss - LB
Bob Gain - DE
Lou Groza - T
Gene Hickerson - G
Billy Howton - E
Art Hunter - C
Ken Konz - DB
Rich Kreitling - E
Warren Lahr - DB
Dave Lloyd - C
Willie McClung - DT
Mike McCormack - T
Walt Michaels - LB
Bobby Mitchell - HB
Ed Modzelewski - FB
Jim Ninowski - QB
Chuck Noll - G
Fran O'Brien - DE
Bernie Parrish - DB
Floyd Peters - DT
Milt Plum - QB
Bob Ptacek - QB
Ray Renfro - FL
Dick Schafrath - DE
Jim Shofner - DB
Jim Ray Smith - G
Paul Wiggin - DE
John Wooten - G
Junior Wren - DB
Sid Youngelman - DT

1959 Detroit

Charlie Ane - T
Terry Barr - HB
Hopalong Cassady - HB
Gene Cook - E
Lou Creekmur - T
Gene Cronin - DE
Jim David - DB
Jim Doran - E
Jim Gibbons - E
Bill Glass - DE
John Gordy - T
Bob Grottkau - G
John Johnson - FB
Steve Junker - E
Alex Karras - DT
Yale Lary - DB
Dick LeBeau - DB
Dan Lewis - HB
Bob Long - LB
Gary Lowe - DB
Gil Mains - DT
Jim Martin - LB
Darris McCord - DE
Dave Middleton - E
Earl Morrall - QB
Ben Paolucci - DT
Gerry Perry - DT
Nick Pietrosante - FB
Mike Rabold - G
Jerry Reichow - E
Tobin Rote - QB
Ken Russell - T
Joe Schmidt - LB
Harley Sewell - G
Ollie Spencer - T
Jim Steffen - DB
Wayne Walker - LB
Jim Weatherall - DT
Ken Webb - FB
Dave Whitsell - DB

1959 Green Bay

Ken Beck - DT
Tom Bettis - LB
Nate Borden - DE

Timmy Brown - HB
Bill Butler - HB
Lew Carpenter - FB
Dan Currie - LB
Bobby Dillon - DB
John Dittrich - G
Boyd Dowler - E
Bill Forester - LB
Joe Francis - QB
Bobby Freeman - DB
Forrest Gregg - T
Hank Gremminger - DB
Dave Hanner - DT
Paul Hornung - HB
Henry Jordan - DT
Gary Knafelc - E
Jerry Kramer - G
Ron Kramer - E
Norm Masters - T
Max McGee - E
Lamar McHan - QB
Don McIlhenny - HB
Ray Nitschke - LB
Bill Quinlan - DE
Jim Ringo - C
Bob Skoronski - T
Bart Starr - QB
John Symank - DB
Jim Taylor - FB
Jim Temp - DE
Fuzzy Thurston - G
Emlen Tunnell - DB
Jesse Whittenton - DB
A.D. Williams - E

1959 LA Rams

Jon Arnett - FL
John Baker - DT
Charlie Bradshaw - T
Gene Brito - DE
Don Burroughs - DB
Leon Clarke - E
Paul Dickson - T
Tom Franckhauser - DB
Bob Fry - G
John Guzik - LB
John Houser - G
Buddy Humphrey - QB
Bill Jobko - LB
Carl Karilivacz - DB
Buck Lansford - G
John LoVetere - DT
Lamar Lundy - E
Joe Marconi - FB
Ollie Matson - FB
Ed Meador - DB
Lou Michaels - DE
Jack Morris - DB
John Morrow - C
Jack Pardee - LB
Jim Phillips - E
Duane Putnam - G
Les Richter - LB
Frank Ryan - QB
Gene Selawski - T
Will Sherman - DB
Del Shofner - E
George Strugar - DT
Clendon Thomas - DB
Billy Wade - QB
Roy Wilkins - LB
Sam Williams - E
Tommy Wilson - HB

1959 NY Giants

Al Barry - G
Joe Biscaha - E
Rosey Brown - T
Don Chandler - HB
Charlie Conerly - QB
Lindon Crow - DB
Darrell Dess - G
Frank Gifford - HB
Rosey Grier - DT
Buzz Guy - T
Art Hauser - DT
Don Heinrich - QB
Sam Huff - LB
Jim Katcavage - DE
Ellison Kelly - G
Bill Kimber - E
Phil King - HB
Cliff Livingston - LB
Dick Lynch - DB
Dick Modzelewski - DT
Joe Morrison - DB
Dick Nolan - DB
Jimmy Patton - DB
Andy Robustelli - DE
Kyle Rote - E
Bob Schmidt - C
Bob Schnelker - E
George Scott - HB
Tom Scott - DE
George Shaw - QB
Bill Stits - DB
Jack Stroud - G
Pat Summerall - E
Don Sutherin - DB
Harland Svare - LB
Mel Triplett - FB
Alex Webster - HB
Ray Wietecha - C
Frank Youso - T

1959 Philadelphia

Darrel Aschbacher - G
Billy Barnes - HB
Chuck Bednarik - C
Dick Bielski - E
Tom Brookshier - DB
Marion Campbell - DE
Stan Campbell - G
Jimmy Carr - DB
Tom Catlin - LB
Paige Cothren - K
Jerry DeLucca - T
Jerry Huth - G
Gene Johnson - DB
Sonny Jurgensen - QB
Ed Khayat - DE
Walt Kowalczyk - FB
Tom Louderback - C
Ken MacAfee Sr. - E
Jim McCusker - T
Tommy McDonald - FL
John Nocera - LB
Don Owens - T
Joe Pagliei - FB
Clarence Peaks - FB
Bob Pellegrini - LB
Art Powell - DB
Pete Retzlaff - E
Jess Richardson - DT
Lee Riley - DB
Joe Robb - DE
Theron Sapp - HB
J.D. Smith - T
Bill Striegel - G
Norm Van Brocklin - QB
Bobby Walston - E
Chuck Weber - LB
Jerry Wilson - DE

1959 Pittsburgh

Dick Alban - DB
Tom Barnett - DB
Byron Beams - T
Ed Beatty - C
Don Bishop - DB
Pete Brewster - E
Jack Butler - DB
Jack Call - HB
Dick Campbell - LB
Len Dawson - QB
Dean Derby - DB
Buddy Dial - E
Dale Dodrill - LB
Leo Elter - FB
Ray Fisher - G
Gary Glick - DB
Ron Hall - DB
Rudy Hayes - LB
Mike Henry - LB
Ted Karras - T
Joe Krupa - DT
Larry Krutko - FB
Dick Lasse - LB
Bobby Layne - QB
Joe Lewis - DT
Bobby Luna - DB
Ray Mathews - FL
Jack McClairen - E
Gern Nagler - E
John Nisby - G
Jimmy Orr - E
John Reger - LB
Mike Sandusky - G
Billy Ray Smith Sr. - DE
Ernie Stautner - DE
Don Sutherin - DB
George Tarasovic - C
Tom Tracy - HB
Frank Varrichione - T

1959 San Francisco

Billy Atkins - DB
Dave Baker - DB
Bruce Bosley - G
John Brodie - QB
Monte Clark - DT
Clyde Conner - E
Ted Connolly - G
Tommy Davis - K
Eddie Dove - DB
Fred Dugan - E
John Gonzaga - T
Bob Harrison - LB
Matt Hazeltine - LB
Ed Henke - LB
Bill Herchman - DT
Charlie Krueger - DE
Lenny Lyles - HB
Hugh McElhenny - HB
Jerry Mertens - DB
Dicky Moegle - HB
Frank Morze - DT
Leo Nomellini - DT
Clancy Osborne - LB
R.C. Owens - E
Joe Perry - FB
Jimmy Ridlon - DB
C. R. Roberts - FB
Karl Rubke - C
Henry Schmidt - DT
J. D. Smith - FB
Bob St. Clair - T
John Thomas - T

Y. A. Tittle - QB
Jerry Tubbs - LB
Billy Wilson - FL
John Wittenborn - G
Abe Woodson - DB

1959 Washington

Bill Anderson - E
Sam Baker - FB
Don Boll - G
Don Bosseler - FB
Tom Braatz - LB
Johnny Carson - E
Don Churchwell - DT
Chick Cichowski - DB
Eagle Day - QB
Chuck Drazenovich - LB
Ralph Felton - LB
Gary Glick - DB
Art Gob - DE
Ralph Guglielmi - QB
Dick Haley - DB
Bob Hudson - DB
Dick James - DB
Emil Karas - DE
Frank Kuchta - C
Don Lawrence - G
Eddie LeBaron - QB
Ray Lemek - T
Ken MacAfee Sr. - E
Richie McCabe - DB
Ed Meadows - DE
Johnny Miller - T
Doyle Nix - DB
Johnny Olszewski - HB
Chet Ostrowski - DT
John Paluck - DE
Jim Podoley - HB
Will Renfro - DT
Jim Schrader - C
Ben Scotti - DB
Mike Sommer - HB
Red Stephens - G
Bill Stits - DB
Ed Sutton - HB
Bob Toneff - DT
Joe Walton - E

1960 NFL

1960 Baltimore

Alan Ameche - FB
Raymond Berry - E
Bobby Boyd - DB
Ordell Braase - DE
Ray Brown - QB
Jim Colvin - G
Milt Davis - DB
Art DeCarlo - DB
Art Donovan - DT
Alex Hawkins - HB
Don Joyce - DT
Ed Kovac - HB
Gene Lipscomb - DT
Gino Marchetti - DE
Marv Matuszak - LB
Lenny Moore - HB
Jim Mutscheller - E
Steve Myhra - G
Andy Nelson - DB
Buzz Nutter - C
Jim Parker - T
Bill Pellington - LB
Sherman Plunkett - T
George Preas - T
Billy Pricer - FB
Palmer Pyle - G
Jerry Richardson - HB
Johnny Sample - HB
Alex Sandusky - G
Lebron Shields - DE
Don Shinnick - LB
Jackie Simpson - DB
Zeke Smith - DE
Mike Sommer - HB
Art Spinney - G
Dick Szymanski - LB
Carl Taseff - HB
Johnny Unitas - QB
Jim Welch - HB

1960 Chi. Bears

John Adams - FB
Doug Atkins - DE
John Aveni - K
Erich Barnes - DB
Bill Bishop - T
Charlie Bivins - HB
Zeke Bratkowski - QB
Ed Brown - QB
James Caroline - DB
Rick Casares - FB
Angelo Coia - E
Roger Davis - G
Willard Dewveall - E
Jim Dooley - E
Merrill Douglas - FB
Stan Fanning - T
Bo Farrington - E
Joe Fortunato - LB
Willie Galimore - HB
Bill George - LB

Harlon Hill - E
Stan Jones - G
Ted Karras - G
Bob Kilcullen - T
Ken Kirk - LB
Roger LeClerc - C
Herman Lee - T
Earl Leggett - DE
Pete Manning - DB
John Mellekas - C
Johnny Morris - HB
Larry Morris - LB
Richie Petitbon - DB
Justin Rowland - DB
Glenn Shaw - HB
Charlie Sumner - DB
Bob Wetoska - T
Fred Williams - DT
Maury Youmans - T
Vic Zucco - DB

1960 Cleveland

Sam Baker - K
Jim Brown - FB
Jamie Caleb - FB
Leon Clarke - E
Vince Costello - LB
Len Dawson - QB
Bob Denton - T
Ross Fichtner - DB
Galen Fiss - LB
Don Fleming - DB
Bobby Franklin - DB
Bob Gain - DT
Prentice Gautt - HB
Gene Hickerson - G
Jim Houston - DE
Rich Kreitling - E
Dave Lloyd - C
Jim Marshall - DE
Mike McCormack - T
Walt Michaels - LB
Bobby Mitchell - HB
John Morrow - C
Rich Mostardo - DB
Fred Murphy - E
Gern Nagler - E
Bernie Parrish - DB
Floyd Peters - DT
Milt Plum - QB
Jim Prestel - DT
Ray Renfro - FL
Dick Schafrath - T
Gene Selawski - T
Jim Shofner - DB
Jim Ray Smith - G
Larry Stephens - DT
Paul Wiggin - DE
A.D. Williams - E
John Wooten - G

1960 Dallas

Gene Babb - FB
Bob Bercich - DB
Dick Bielski - E
Don Bishop - DB
Nate Borden - DE
Tom Braatz - LB
Byron Bradfute - T
Bill Butler - DB
Frank Clarke - E
Fred Cone - K
Mike Connelly - C
Gene Cronin - DE
Paul Dickson - T
Fred Doelling - DB
Jim Doran - E
Mike Dowdle - FB
Fred Dugan - E
L. G. Dupre - HB
Mike Falls - G
Tom Franckhauser - DB
Bob Fry - T
John Gonzaga - DE
Buzz Guy - G
Wayne Hansen - LB
Don Healy - DT
Don Heinrich - QB
Bill Herchman - DT
John Houser - C
Billy Howton - E
Ed Husmann - DT
Dick Klein - T
Walt Kowalczyk - FB
Eddie LeBaron - QB
Woodley Lewis - E
Ray Mathews - FL
Don McIlhenny - HB
Don Meredith - QB
Jim Mooty - DB
Jack Patera - LB
Duane Putnam - G
Dave Sherer - E
Jerry Tubbs - LB
Gary Wisener - E

1960 Detroit

Grady Alderman - G
Terry Barr - HB
Carl Brettschneider - LB
Roger Brown - DT
Hopalong Cassady - HB
Gail Cogdill - E

Glenn Davis - E
Jim Gibbons - E
Bill Glass - DE
John Gordy - G
Bob Grottkau - G
Steve Junker - E
Alex Karras - DT
Night Train Lane - DB
Yale Lary - DB
Dick LeBeau - DB
Dan Lewis - HB
Gary Lowe - DB
Bruce Maher - DB
Gil Mains - DE
Jim Martin - LB
Willie McClung - T
Darris McCord - T
Max Messner - LB
Dave Middleton - E
Earl Morrall - QB
Jim Ninowski - QB
Nick Pietrosante - FB
Warren Rabb - QB
Joe Schmidt - LB
Bob Scholtz - C
Harley Sewell - G
Ollie Spencer - C
Jim Steffen - DB
Wayne Walker - LB
Jim Weatherall - DT
Ken Webb - FB
Dave Whitsell - DB
Sam Williams - LB

1960 Green Bay

Ken Beck - DE
Tom Bettis - LB
Lew Carpenter - E
Dan Currie - LB
Andy Cvercko - G
Willie Davis - DE
Boyd Dowler - FL
Bill Forester - LB
Forrest Gregg - T
Hank Gremminger - DB
Dale Hackbart - DB
Dave Hanner - DT
Larry Hickman - FB
Paul Hornung - HB
Ken Iman - C
Henry Jordan - DT
Gary Knafelc - E
Jerry Kramer - G
Ron Kramer - E
Norm Masters - T
Max McGee - E
Lamar McHan - QB
Steve Meilinger - E
Johnny Miller - DE
Tom Moore - HB
Ray Nitschke - LB
Dick Pesonen - DB
Bill Quinlan - DE
Jim Ringo - C
Bob Skoronski - T
Bart Starr - QB
John Symank - DB
Jim Taylor - FB
Jim Temp - DE
Fuzzy Thurston - G
Emlen Tunnell - DB
Jesse Whittenton - DB
Paul Winslow - HB
Willie Wood - DB

1960 LA Rams

Jon Arnett - HB
John Baker - DT
Dick Bass - HB
Jim Boeke - T
Charlie Bradshaw - T
Gene Brito - DE
Charley Britt - DB
Carroll Dale - E
Don Ellersick - DB
John Guzik - G
Roy Hord - G
Buddy Humphrey - QB
Art Hunter - C
Chuck Janerette - G
Bill Jobko - LB
Carl Karilivacz - DB
John Kenerson - DE
Buck Lansford - G
Bob Long - LB
John LoVetere - DT
Lamar Lundy - DE
Joe Marconi - FB
Ollie Matson - FL
Ed Meador - DB
Lou Michaels - DE
Jack Morris - DB
Jack Pardee - LB
Jim Phillips - E
Les Richter - LB
Frank Ryan - QB
Will Sherman - DB
Del Shofner - DB
Jerry Stalcup - G
George Strugar - DT
Clendon Thomas - DB
Vern Valdez - DB
Danny Villanueva - K
Billy Wade - QB

Tommy Wilson - HB

1960 NY Giants

Don Boll - T
Rosey Brown - T
Don Chandler - HB
Charlie Conerly - QB
Lou Cordileone - G
Bill Crawford - G
Lindon Crow - DB
Darrell Dess - G
Frank Gifford - HB
Rosey Grier - DT
Lee Grosscup - QB
Sam Huff - LB
Proverb Jacobs - DT
Jim Katcavage - DE
Bill Kimber - E
Phil King - HB
Jim Leo - LB
Cliff Livingston - LB
Dick Lynch - DB
Dick Modzelewski - DT
Joe Morrison - HB
Dick Nolan - DB
Jimmy Patton - DB
Lee Riley - DB
Andy Robustelli - DE
Kyle Rote - E
Bob Schmidt - T
Bob Schnelker - E
Tom Scott - LB
George Shaw - QB
Bob Simms - E
Bill Stits - DB
Jack Stroud - G
Pat Summerall - E
Ed Sutton - HB
Harland Svare - LB
Mel Triplett - FB
Alex Webster - HB
Ray Wietecha - C
Frank Youso - T

1960 Philadelphia

Billy Barnes - HB
Maxie Baughan - LB
Chuck Bednarik - C
Tom Brookshier - DB
Timmy Brown - HB
Don Burroughs - DB
Marion Campbell - DE
Stan Campbell - G
Jimmy Carr - DB
Ted Dean - FB
Bobby Freeman - DB
Gene Gossage - DT
Riley Gunnels - DT
Jerry Huth - G
Bobby Jackson - DB
Gene Johnson - DB
Sonny Jurgensen - QB
Howard Keys - C
Ed Khayat - DE
Bill Lapham - C
Dick Lucas - E
Jim McCusker - T
Tommy McDonald - FL
John Nocera - LB
Don Owens - DT
Clarence Peaks - FB
Bob Pellegrini - G
Jerry Reichow - E
Pete Retzlaff - E
Jess Richardson - DT
Joe Robb - LB
Theron Sapp - HB
J.D. Smith - T
Norm Van Brocklin - QB
Bobby Walston - FL
Chuck Weber - LB
John Wilcox - DE
Jerry Wilson - LB
John Wittenborn - G

1960 Pittsburgh

Tom Barnett - DB
Byron Beams - T
Ed Beatty - C
Pete Brewster - E
Rudy Bukich - QB
Dick Campbell - LB
Preston Carpenter - HB
Dean Derby - DB
Buddy Dial - FL
Bobby Joe Green - K
Rudy Hayes - LB
Mike Henry - LB
Dan James - C
John Johnson - FB
Rex Johnston - HB
John Kapele - T
Joe Krupa - DT
Larry Krutko - FB
Bobby Layne - QB
Joe Lewis - DT
Ken Longenecker - DT
Jack McClairen - E
Dicky Moegle - DB
Jack Morris - DB
John Nisby - G
Jimmy Orr - FL
Bert Rechichar - DB

John Reger - LB
Will Renfro - DE
Mike Sandusky - G
Charlie Scales - FB
Joe Scudero - DB
Billy Ray Smith Sr. - DE
Ernie Stautner - DT
Ron Stehouwer - T
Don Sutherin - DB
George Tarasovic - DE
Tom Tracy - FB
Frank Varrichione - T
Fred Williamson - DB
Junior Wren - DB

1960 St. Louis

Ted Bates - LB
Joe Childress - HB
Bobby Joe Conrad - HB
Ed Cook - T
John Crow - HB
Ed Culpepper - DT
Tom Day - G
Joe Driskill - DB
Charley Ellzey - C
Ernie Fritsch - LB
Frank Fuller - DT
Don Gillis - C
Fred Glick - DB
Ken Gray - G
Mal Hammack - FB
Jimmy Hill - DB
King Hill - QB
George Izo - QB
Bill Koman - LB
Mike McGee - G
Hugh McInnis - E
Dale Meinert - LB
Dale Memmelaar - T
Frank Mestnik - FB
Jerry Norton - DB
Don Owens - DT
Luke Owens - DE
Ken Panfil - T
Gerry Perry - DE
Mike Rabold - G
Sonny Randle - E
Tom Redmond - DT
Perry Richards - E
John Roach - QB
Billy Stacy - DB
Leo Sugar - DE
Bobby Towns - HB
Jack Tracey - LB
Willie West - HB
Larry Wilson - DB

1960 San Francisco

Dave Baker - DB
Bruce Bosley - G
John Brodie - QB
Monte Clark - DT
Daniel Colchico - DE
Clyde Conner - E
Ted Connolly - G
Tommy Davis - K
Eddie Dove - DB
Bob Harrison - LB
Matt Hazeltine - LB
Ed Henke - DE
Gorden Kelley - LB
Charlie Krueger - DE
Lenny Lyles - DB
Dee Mackey - E
Mike Magac - G
Hugh McElhenny - HB
Jerry Mertens - DB
Frank Morze - DT
Leo Nomellini - DT
Ray Norton - HB
Clancy Osborne - LB
R.C. Owens - E
Joe Perry - FB
Jimmy Ridlon - DB
C. R. Roberts - FB
Len Rohde - T
Karl Rubke - C
Henry Schmidt - DT
J. D. Smith - FB
Bob St. Clair - T
Monty Stickles - E
John Thomas - T
Y. A. Tittle - QB
Bob Waters - QB
Jerry Wilson - LB
Billy Wilson - FL
John Wittenborn - G
Abe Woodson - HB

1960 Washington

Bill Anderson - E
Don Bosseler - FB
Rod Breedlove - LB
Billy Brewer - DB
Jim Crotty - DB
Eagle Day - QB
Ralph Felton - LB
Gary Glick - HB
Art Gob - DE
Ralph Guglielmi - QB
Dick Haley - HB
Pat Heenan - E
Sam Horner - DB

Dick James - DB
Bob Khayat - G
Ray Krouse - DT
Dick Lasse - LB
Don Lawrence - T
Ray Lemek - T
Fran O'Brien - G
Johnny Olszewski - FB
Tom Osborne - E
John Paluck - DE
Jim Podoley - E
Vince Promuto - G
M.C. Reynolds - QB
Bill Roehnelt - LB
Jim Schrader - C
Ben Scotti - DB
Don Stallings - DE
Red Stephens - G
Andy Stynchula - C
Bob Toneff - DT
Ed Vereb - HB
Joe Walton - E
Bob Whitlow - G
Roy Wilkins - LB
Jim Wulff - DB

1960 AFL

1960 Boston

Tom Addison - LB
Jack Atchason - E
Walter Beach - HB
Phil Bennett - LB
Joe Biscaha - E
Bill Brown - LB
Fred Bruney - DB
Ron Burton - HB
Gino Cappelletti - E
Dick Christy - HB
Abe Cohen - G
Jim Colclough - E
Jim Crawford - FB
Bobby Cross - T
Jake Crouthamel - HB
Al Crow - DT
Walt Cudzik - C
Bill Danenhauer - DE
Jack Davis - G
Bob Dee - DE
Jerry DeLucca - T
Tom Dimitroff - QB
Tony Discenzo - T
Larry Garron - HB
Jerry Green - HB
Tom Greene - QB
Art Hauser - DT
Jim Hunt - DT
Harry Jacobs - DE
Harry Jagielski - DT
Joe Johnson - E
Bill Larson - FB
Bob Lee - G
Chuck Leo - G
Walt Livingston - HB
Oscar Lofton - E
Mike Long - E
Don McComb - DE
George McGee - T
Alan Miller - FB
Ross O'Hanley - DB
Al Richardson - DE
Jack Rudolph - LB
Tony Sardisco - LB
Gerhard Schwedes - HB
Chuck Shonta - DB
Hal Smith - DT
Robert Soltis - DB
Butch Songin - QB
Thomas Stephens - E
Bill Striegel - T
Clyde Washington - DB
Billy Wells - HB
Harvey White - QB

1960 Buffalo

Billy Atkins - HB
Bob Barrett - E
Phil Blazer - G
Bob Brodhead - QB
Dick Brubaker - E
Bernard Buzyniski - LB
Wray Carlton - FB
Dan Chamberlain - E
Don Chelf - G
Monte Crockett - E
Tony Discenzo - T
Elbert Dubenion - HB
Fred Ford - HB
Willmer Fowler - HB
Gene Grabosky - DT
Johnny Green - QB
Darrell Harper - HB
Joe Hergert - LB
Al Hoisington - E
Jack Johnson - DB
Billy Kinard - DB
Joe Kulbacki - HB
Jack Laraway - LB
Hal Lewis - HB
Richie Lucas - HB
Archie Matsos - LB
Richie McCabe - DB
Dan McGrew - C
Chuck McMurtry - DT
Eddie Meyer - T
Leroy Moore - DE
Chuck Muelhaupt - G
Tommy O'Connell - QB
Harold Olson - T
Sam Palumbo - LB
Dennis Remmert - LB
Charlie Rutkowski - DE
Tom Rychlec - E
Joe Schaffer - LB
Jack Scott - DT
Bob Sedlock - T
Carl Smith - FB
Jim Sorey - DT
LaVerne Torczon - DE
Jim Wagstaff - DB
Ted Wegert - HB
Mack Yoho - DE

1960 Dallas

Jim Barton - C
Ed Bernet - E
Johnny Bookman - DB
Max Boydston - E
Mel Branch - DE
Bob Bryant - E
Chris Burford - E
Ray Collins - DT
Walt Corey - LB
Jerry Cornelison - T
Clem Daniels - HB
Cotton Davidson - QB
Charley Diamond - T
Bo Dickinson - FB
Tom Dimmick - C
Hunter Enis - QB
Don Flynn - DB
Sid Fournet - G
Dick Frey - DE
Rufus Granderson - DT
Ted Greene - LB
Jimmy Harris - DB
Abner Haynes - HB
Sherrill Headrick - LB
Bob Hudson - LB
Charlie Jackson - DB
Curley Johnson - HB
Billy Krisher - G
Paul Miller - DE
Walter Napier - DT
R.B. Nunnery - T
Al Reynolds - G
Johnny Robinson - HB
Paul Rochester - DT
Jack Spikes - FB
Jack Stone - T
Smokey Stover - LB
Jim Swink - HB
Marvin Terrell - G
Dave Webster - DB
Duane Wood - DB
Carroll Zaruba - DB

1960 Denver

Ken Adamson - G
Don Allen - FB
Buddy Alliston - LB
Henry Bell - HB
Frank Bernardi - DB
J.W. Brodnax - FB
Fred Broussard - C
Hardy Brown - LB
Al Carmichael - HB
Don Carothers - E
Ken Carpenter - HB
Eldon Danenhauer - T
Bill Danenhauer - DE
Jack Davis - G
Al Day - LB
Dick Doyle - DB
Tom Dublinski - QB
Pat Epperson - E
Chuck Gavin - DE
Goose Gonsoulin - DB
Jim Greer - E
Johnny Hatley - DT
George Herring - QB
Gordy Holz - T
Bob Hudson - LB
Bill Jessup - E
Don King - T
Frank Kuchta - C
Carl Larpenter - G
Pete Mangum - LB
Bud McFadin - DT
Bob McNamara - HB
Gene Mingo - HB
Mike Nichols - C
Johnny Pyeatt - DB
Dave Rolle - FB
Al Romine - DB
Hal Smith - DT
Willie Smith - T
Bob Stransky - HB
Dave Strickland - G
Lionel Taylor - E
Frank Tripucka - QB
Ted Wegert - HB
Bill Yelverton - DE
Joe Young - DE

1960 Houston

Dalva Allen - DE
Jack Atchason - E
Tony Banfield - DB
George Belotti - C
George Blanda - QB
Don Brown - HB
Billy Cannon - HB
Johnny Carson - E
Doug Cline - FB
Pete Davidson - DT
Mike Dukes - LB
Don Floyd - DE
Bobby Gordon - DB
Gary Greaves - T
Bill Groman - E
Ken Hall - HB
Jerry Helluin - DT
Charley Hennigan - E
Al Jamison - T
Mark Johnston - DB
Charlie Kendall - DB
Dan Lanphear - DE
Jacky Lee - QB
Joe Majors - DB
Jim McCanless - G
Wahoo McDaniel - G
Rich Michael - T
Charlie Milstead - QB
Dennit Morris - LB
Ron Morrison - DT
Jim Norton - DB
Phil Perlo - LB
Hugh Pitts - LB
George Shirkey - DT
John Simerson - C
Dave Smith - FB
Julian Spence - DB
Bob Talamini - G
Charley Tolar - HB
Orville Trask - DT
Fred Wallner - G
Hogan Wharton - G
John White - E
Bob White - FB
Al Witcher - E
James Yeats - TE

1960 LA Chargers

Ben Agajanian - K
Ralph Anderson - E
Al Bansavage - LB
Al Barry - G
Hubert Bobo - LB
Ron Botchan - LB
Charlie Brueckman - LB
Dick Chorovich - T
Howard Clark - E
Bobby Clatterbuck - QB
Fred Cole - G
Sam DeLuca - T
Ben Donnell - DE
Howie Ferguson - FB
Orlando Ferrante - G
Gary Finneran - DT
Charlie Flowers - FB
Fred Ford - HB
Bob Garner - DB
Art Gob - DE
Dick Harris - DB
Emil Karas - LB
Jack Kemp - QB
Charlie Kempinska - G
Dave Kocourek - E
John Kompara - DT
Bob Laraba - LB
Rommie Loudd - LB
Paul Lowe - HB
Paul Maguire - E
Blanche Martin - FB
Charlie McNeil - DB
Ron Mix - DB
Ron Nery - DE
Doyle Nix - DB
Trusse Norris - E
Don Norton - E
Volney Peters - DT
Don Rogers - C
Maury Schleicher - DE
Jimmy Sears - HB
Jesse Thomas - DB
Henry Wallace - DB
Ron Waller - HB
Royce Womble - FL
Ernie Wright - T
Bob Zeman - DB

1960 NY Titans

Larry Baker - T
Ernie Barnes - T
Eddie Bell - DB
Dewey Bohling - HB
Leon Burton - HB
Dan Callahan - G
Ken Campbell - E
Gene Cockrell - T
Ed Cooke - DE
Thurlow Cooper - E
Frank D'Agostino - G
Leon Dombrowski - LB
Roger Donnahoo - DB
Al Dorow - QB
Charlie Dupre - DB
Roger Ellis - LB
Dick Felt - DB
Howard Glenn - G
Larry Grantham - LB
Dick Guesman - DT
Pete Hart - FB
Don Herndon - HB
Mike Hudock - C
Dick Jamieson - QB
Fred Julian - DB
Joe Katchik - DT
Jack Klotz - T
Bob Marques - LB
Blanche Martin - FB
Bill Mathis - FB
Don Maynard - E
John McMullan - G
Bob Mischak - G
Nick Mumley - T
Joe Pagliei - FB
Art Powell - E
Bob Reifsnyder - DE
Bill Robinson - HB
Dave Ross - E
Joe Ryan - DE
Tom Saidock - DT
Rick Sapienza - HB
Gerhard Schwedes - HB
Bob Scrabis - QB
Bill Shockley - HB
Corky Tharp - DB
Ted Wegert - HB
Hall Whitley - LB
Sid Youngelman - DT

1960 Oakland

Ray Armstrong - DT
Doug Asad - E
Joe Barbee - DT
Larry Barnes - DE
Alex Bravo - DB
Joe Cannavino - DB
Carmen Cavalli - DE
Don Churchwell - T
Wayne Crow - DB
Don Deskins - G
John Dittrich - G
Bob Dougherty - LB
George Fields - DE
Tom Flores - QB
Al Goldstein - E
Charlie Hardy - E
John Harris - HB
Wayne Hawkins - G
Al Hoisington - E
L. C. Joyner - DB
Bob Keyes - HB
Jack Larscheid - HB
Paul Larson - QB
Billy Locklin - LB
Billy Lott - FB
Tom Louderback - LB
Eddie Macon - DB
Don Manoukian - G
Nyle McFarlane - HB
Riley Morris - LB
Paul Oglesby - DT
Jim Otto - C
Babe Parilli - QB
Charley Powell - DE
Gene Prebola - E
Billy Reynolds - HB
Ron Sabal - G
J.D. Smith - FB
Bill Striegel - T
Tony Teresa - HB
Dalton Truax - T
Ron Warzeka - DT

1961 NFL

1961 Baltimore

Raymond Berry - E
Bobby Boyd - DB
Ordell Braase - DE
Jackie Burkett - C
Jim Colvin - DE
John Diehl - DT
Art Donovan - DT
Wiley Feagin - G
Tom Gilburg - T
Gary Glick - DB
Ken Gregory - E
Bob Harrison - DB
Alex Hawkins - HB
Jerry Hill - HB
Joe Lewis - DT
Aubrey Linne - E
Lenny Lyles - DB
Dee Mackey - E
Gino Marchetti - DE
Tom Matte - HB
Marv Matuszak - LB
Lamar McHan - QB
Lenny Moore - HB
Jim Mutscheller - E
Steve Myhra - G
Andy Nelson - DB
Jimmy Orr - E
Jim Parker - T
Bill Pellington - LB
Joe Perry - FB
George Preas - T
Palmer Pyle - G
Alex Sandusky - G
Don Shinnick - LB
Billy Ray Smith Sr. - DT
Mark Smolinski - FB
Mike Sommer - HB
Dick Szymanski - C
Carl Taseff - DB
Johnny Unitas - QB
Jim Welch - HB

1961 Chi. Bears

John Adams - FB
Art Anderson - T
Doug Atkins - DE
Charlie Bivins - HB
Ed Brown - QB
Bill Brown - FB
James Caroline - DB
Rick Casares - FB
Angelo Coia - E
Roger Davis - G
Mike Ditka - E
Jim Dooley - E
Stan Fanning - T
Bo Farrington - E
Joe Fortunato - LB
Willie Galimore - HB
Bill George - LB
Harlon Hill - DB
Bobby Jackson - DB
Stan Jones - G
Ted Karras - G
Bob Kilcullen - DE
Ken Kirk - C
Roger LeClerc - C
Herman Lee - T
Pete Manning - DB
John Mellekas - DT
Johnny Morris - FL
Larry Morris - LB
Don Mullins - DB
Dick Norman - QB
Richie Petitbon - DB
Mike Pyle - C
J.D. Smith - HB
Rosey Taylor - DB
Billy Wade - QB
Bob Wetoska - G
Dave Whitsell - DB
Fred Williams - DT
Maury Youmans - DE

1961 Cleveland

Sam Baker - K
Johnny Brewer - DE
Jim Brown - FB
Leon Clarke - E
Vince Costello - LB
Bob Crespino - E
Len Dawson - QB
Charley Ferguson - E
Ross Fichtner - DB
Galen Fiss - LB
Don Fleming - DB
Bobby Franklin - DB
Bob Gain - DT
Lou Groza - T
Jim Houston - DE
Rich Kreitling - E
Errol Linden - T
Dave Lloyd - C
Mike McCormack - T
Walt Michaels - LB
Bobby Mitchell - HB
John Morrow - C
Gern Nagler - E
Ed Nutting - T
Bernie Parrish - DB
Floyd Peters - DT
Milt Plum - QB
Preston Powell - FB
Duane Putnam - G
Ray Renfro - FL
Dick Schafrath - T
Jim Shofner - DB
Jim Ray Smith - G
Larry Stephens - DT
Tom Watkins - HB
Paul Wiggin - DE
John Wooten - G

1961 Dallas

Gene Babb - FB
Bob Bercich - DB
Dick Bielski - E
Don Bishop - DB
Nate Borden - DE
Byron Bradfute - T
Frank Clarke - E
Mike Connelly - C
Andy Cvercko - G
Sonny Davis - LB
Jim Doran - E
Merrill Douglas - HB
Mike Dowdle - LB
L. G. Dupre - HB
Mike Falls - G
Tom Franckhauser - DB
Ken Frost - DT
Bob Fry - T
Charley Granger - T
Allen Green - K
Glynn Gregory - DB
Bob Grottkau - G
Jimmy Harris - DB
Don Healy - DT
Bill Herchman - DT
John Houser - G
Chuck Howley - LB
Billy Howton - E
Buddy Humphrey - QB
Eddie LeBaron - QB
Bob Lilly - DE
Warren Livingston - DB
J. W. Lockett - FB
Amos Marsh - FB
Bob McCreary - T
Don McIlhenny - HB
Don Meredith - QB
Dicky Moegle - DB
Lee Murchison - E
Jack Patera - LB
Don Perkins - HB
Jerry Tubbs - LB

1961 Detroit

Terry Barr - FL
Carl Brettschneider - LB
Roger Brown - DT
Hopalong Cassady - HB
Gail Cogdill - E
Glenn Davis - E
Jim Gibbons - E
Bill Glass - DE
John Gonzaga - DT
John Gordy - T
Alex Karras - DT
Night Train Lane - DB
Dan LaRose - T
Yale Lary - DB
Dick LeBeau - DB
Dan Lewis - HB
Gary Lowe - DB
Bruce Maher - DB
Gil Mains - DT
Jim Martin - LB
Willie McClung - T
Darris McCord - DE
Max Messner - LB
Dick Mills - G
Earl Morrall - QB
Jim Ninowski - QB
Johnny Olszewski - FB
Nick Pietrosante - FB
Joe Schmidt - LB
Bob Scholtz - C
Harley Sewell - G
Ollie Spencer - G
Jim Steffen - DB
Pat Studstill - FL
Wayne Walker - LB
Paul Ward - DT
Ken Webb - FB
Bob Whitlow - G
Sam Williams - E

1961 Green Bay

Herb Adderley - DB
Ben Agajanian - K
Tom Bettis - LB
Lew Carpenter - HB
Dan Currie - LB
Ben Davidson - DE
Willie Davis - DE
Boyd Dowler - FL
Lee Folkins - E
Bill Forester - LB
Forrest Gregg - T
Hank Gremminger - DB
Dale Hackbart - DB
Dave Hanner - DT
Paul Hornung - HB
Ken Iman - C
Henry Jordan - DT
Gary Knafelc - E
Ron Kostelnik - DT
Jerry Kramer - G
Ron Kramer - E
Norm Masters - T
Max McGee - E
Tom Moore - HB
Ray Nitschke - LB
Elijah Pitts - HB
Bill Quinlan - DE
Jim Ringo - C
John Roach - QB
Bob Skoronski - T
Bart Starr - QB
John Symank - DB
Jim Taylor - FB
Fuzzy Thurston - G
Nelson Toburen - LB
Emlen Tunnell - DB
Jesse Whittenton - DB
Willie Wood - DB

1961 LA Rams

Duane Allen - E
Jon Arnett - HB
Pervis Atkins - HB
John Baker - DT
Dick Bass - FB
Jim Boeke - T
Zeke Bratkowski - QB
Charley Britt - DB
Charley Cowan - G
Ross Coyle - DB
Lindon Crow - DB
Carroll Dale - E
Alvin Hall - DB
Willie Hector - T
Urban Henry - DT
Roy Hord - G
Art Hunter - C
Bill Jobko - LB
Deacon Jones - DE
Elbert Kimbrough - DB
Bob Long - LB
John LoVetere - DT
Lamar Lundy - DE
Joe Marconi - FB
Ollie Matson - HB
Marlin McKeever - LB
Ed Meador - DB
Jack Pardee - LB
Jim Phillips - E
Les Richter - LB
Frank Ryan - QB
Joe Scibelli - G
George Strugar - DT
Bruce Tarbox - G
Clendon Thomas - DB
Frank Varrichione - T
Danny Villanueva - K
Frank Williams - FB
Tommy Wilson - HB

1961 Minnesota

Grady Alderman - G
Bill Bishop - DT
Jamie Caleb - HB
Ed Culpepper - DT
Bob Denton - T
Dean Derby - DB
Paul Dickson - T
Billy Gault - HB
Dick Grecni - LB
Dick Haley - FL
Rip Hawkins - LB
Ray Hayes - FB
Jerry Huth - G
Gene Johnson - DB
Don Joyce - DE
Bill Lapham - C
Jim Leo - DE
Jim Marshall - DE
Tommy Mason - HB
Doug Mayberry - FB
Hugh McElhenny - HB
Mike Mercer - K
Dave Middleton - E
Jack Morris - DB
Rich Mostardo - DB
Fred Murphy - E
Clancy Osborne - LB
Dick Pesonen - DB
Ken Petersen - G
Jim Prestel - DT
Mike Rabold - G
Jerry Reichow - E
Justin Rowland - DB
Karl Rubke - C
Bob Schnelker - E
Ed Sharockman - DB
George Shaw - QB
Will Sherman - HB
Lebron Shields - DE
Gordon Smith - E
Charlie Sumner - DB
Fran Tarkenton - QB
Mel Triplett - FB
A.D. Williams - E
Frank Youso - T

1961 NY Giants

Erich Barnes - HB
Rosey Brown - T
Don Chandler - HB
Charlie Conerly - QB
Darrell Dess - G
Bob Gaiters - HB
Rosey Grier - DT
Lee Grosscup - QB
Pete Hall - E
Larry Hayes - LB
Sam Huff - LB
Chuck Janerette - T
Gene Johnson - DB
Jim Katcavage - DE
Phil King - HB
Greg Larson - T
Cliff Livingston - LB
Dick Lynch - DB
Dick Modzelewski - DT
Joe Morrison - DB
Dick Nolan - DB
Jimmy Patton - DB
Andy Robustelli - DE
Kyle Rote - E
Tom Scott - LB
Del Shofner - E
Bob Simms - LB
Zeke Smith - G
Bill Stits - DB
Jack Stroud - G
Pat Summerall - K
Y. A. Tittle - QB
Mickey Walker - G

Joe Walton - E
Allan Webb - HB
Alex Webster - FB
Joel Wells - HB
Ray Wietecha - C

1961 Philadelphia

Glen Amerson - DB
Billy Barnes - HB
Maxie Baughan - LB
Chuck Bednarik - LB
Tom Brookshier - DB
Timmy Brown - HB
Don Burroughs - DB
Marion Campbell - DT
Stan Campbell - G
Jimmy Carr - DB
Irv Cross - DB
Ted Dean - HB
Bobby Freeman - DB
Gene Gossage - DE
Riley Gunnels - DT
King Hill - QB
Sonny Jurgensen - QB
Howard Keys - C
Ed Khayat - DT
Dick Lucas - E
Jim McCusker - T
Tommy McDonald - FL
John Nocera - LB
Don Oakes - T
Clarence Peaks - FB
Bob Pellegrini - LB
Will Renfro - DE
Pete Retzlaff - E
Jess Richardson - DT
Theron Sapp - FB
J.D. Smith - T
Leo Sugar - DE
Carl Taseff - DB
Jack Tracey - E
Bobby Walston - E
Chuck Weber - LB
John Wittenborn - G

1961 Pittsburgh

Ed Beatty - C
Charlie Bradshaw - T
Rudy Bukich - QB
Len Burnett - DB
Bill Butler - DB
Preston Carpenter - E
Henry Clement - E
Bob Coronado - E
Willie Daniel - DB
George Demko - DE
Dean Derby - DB
Buddy Dial - FL
Bobby Joe Green - K
Dick Haley - FL
Mike Henry - LB
Dick Hoak - HB
Dan James - T
John Johnson - FB
John Kapele - DE
Brady Keys - HB
Dick Klein - T
Joe Krupa - DT
Bobby Layne - QB
Gene Lipscomb - DT
Red Mack - HB
Steve Meilinger - E
Lou Michaels - DE
John Nisby - G
Terry Nofsinger - QB
Buzz Nutter - C
Myron Pottios - LB
John Reger - LB
Johnny Sample - DB
Mike Sandusky - G
Charlie Scales - FB
Bob Schmitz - LB
Bob Schnelker - E
Wilbert Scott - LB
Jackie Simpson - DB
Jack Stanton - HB
Ernie Stautner - DT
Ron Stehouwer - G
George Tarasovic - LB
Tom Tracy - HB

1961 St. Louis

Taz Anderson - E
Ted Bates - LB
Bobby Joe Conrad - HB
Ed Cook - T
John Crow - HB
Bob DeMarco - G
Joe Driskill - DB
Charley Ellzey - C
Sam Etcheverry - QB
Pat Fischer - HB
Frank Fuller - DT
Prentice Gautt - HB
Don Gillis - C
Charley Granger - T
Ken Gray - G
Bob Griffin - LB
Ralph Guglielmi - QB
Ken Hall - HB
Mal Hammack - FB
Ed Henke - DE
Jimmy Hill - DB
Charley Johnson - QB
Bill Koman - LB
Dick Lage - E
Monte Lee - LB
Ron McDole - DT
Mike McGee - G
Hugh McInnis - E
Ernie McMillan - T
Dale Meinert - LB
Dale Memmelaar - T
Frank Mestnik - FB
Jerry Norton - DB
Don Owens - DT
Luke Owens - DE
Ken Panfil - T
Gerry Perry - T
Sonny Randle - E
Tom Redmond - G
Joe Robb - DE
Billy Stacy - HB
Willie West - DB
Larry Wilson - DB

1961 San Francisco

Dave Baker - DB
Bruce Bosley - G
John Brodie - QB
Bernie Casey - E
Monte Clark - DT
Daniel Colchico - DE
Clyde Conner - E
Ted Connolly - G
Bill Cooper - FB
Lou Cordileone - DE
Tommy Davis - K
Eddie Dove - DB
Bob Harrison - LB
Matt Hazeltine - LB
Jim Johnson - DB
Carl Kammerer - LB
Gorden Kelley - LB
Billy Kilmer - QB
Charlie Krueger - DE
Roland Lakes - T
J. W. Lockett - FB
Bill Lopasky - G
Mike Magac - G
Don McIlhenny - HB
Jerry Mertens - DB
Dale Messer - HB
Frank Morze - C
Leo Nomellini - DT
Ray Norton - HB
R.C. Owens - E
Jimmy Ridlon - DB
C. R. Roberts - FB
Len Rohde - T
J. D. Smith - FB
Bob St. Clair - T
Monty Stickles - E
Aaron Thomas - E
John Thomas - LB
Bob Waters - QB
Abe Woodson - HB

1961 Washington

Bill Anderson - E
John Aveni - E
Ed Beatty - C
Don Bosseler - FB
Rod Breedlove - LB
Gene Cronin - LB
Jim Crotty - DB
Jim Cunningham - FB
Bernie Darre - G
Fred Dugan - E
Dale Hackbart - DB
Fred Hageman - C
Pat Heenan - DB
Sam Horner - DB
George Izo - QB
Dick James - DB
Steve Junker - E
Jim Kerr - DB
Joe Krakoski - DB
Dick Lasse - LB
Don Lawrence - DT
Ray Lemek - T
Lew Luce - HB
Riley Mattson - T
Fran O'Brien - T
Tom Osborne - E
John Paluck - DE
Vince Promuto - G
Joe Rutgens - DT
Doyle Schick - LB
Jim Schrader - C
Ben Scotti - DB
Norm Snead - QB
Mike Sommer - HB
Jim Steffen - DB
Andy Stynchula - DE
Bob Toneff - DT
Bob Whitlow - G
Roy Wilkins - LB
Jim Wulff - HB

1961 AFL

1961 Boston

Tom Addison - LB
Houston Antwine - DT
Walter Beach - DB
Fred Bruney - DB
Ron Burton - HB
Gino Cappelletti - FL
Jim Colclough - E
Jim Crawford - FB
Walt Cudzik - C
Bob Dee - DE
Jerry DeLucca - T
Larry Eisenhauer - DE
Larry Garron - HB
Milt Graham - T
Ron Hall - DB
Jim Hunt - DT
Harry Jacobs - LB
Harry Jagielski - DT
Joe Johnson - E
Bill Kimber - E
Dick Klein - T
Chuck Leo - G
Paul Lindquist - DT
Charley Long - T
Billy Lott - FB
Rommie Loudd - LB
Leroy Moore - DE
Ross O'Hanley - DB
Babe Parilli - QB
Willis Perkins - G
Ray Ratkowski - HB
Frank Robotti - LB
Al Romine - DB
Tony Sardisco - G
Gerhard Schwedes - HB
Chuck Shonta - DB
John Simerson - T
Robert Soltis - DB
Butch Songin - QB
Thomas Stephens - E
Bobby Towns - DB
Clyde Washington - HB
Don Webb - DB
Mel West - HB
Bob Yates - C
Tom Yewcic - HB

1961 Buffalo

Billy Atkins - DB
Art Baker - FB
Stew Barber - T
Glenn Bass - E
Al Bemiller - C
Dewey Bohling - HB
Fred Brown - HB
Wray Carlton - HB
Dan Chamberlain - HB
Don Chelf - T
Monte Crockett - E
Jim Crotty - DB
Tom Day - DE
John Dittrich - G
Elbert Dubenion - HB
Ralph Felton - LB
Willmer Fowler - HB
Johnny Green - QB
Joe Hergert - LB
Jack Johnson - DB
Cotton Letner - LB
Richie Lucas - DB
Billy Majors - DB
Archie Matsos - LB
Richie McCabe - DB
Don McDonald - DB
Chuck McMurtry - DT
Chuck Muelhaupt - G
Tommy O'Connell - QB
Harold Olson - T
Warren Rabb - QB
M.C. Reynolds - QB
Ken Rice - T
Perry Richards - E
Tom Rychlec - E
Jack Scott - DT
Billy Shaw - G
Bill Shockley - HB
Jim Sorey - DT
LaVerne Torczon - DE
Vern Valdez - DB
Jim Wagstaff - DB
Wayne Wolff - G
Mack Yoho - DE

1961 Dallas Texans

Ben Agajanian - K
Charlie Barnes - E
Max Boydston - E
Mel Branch - DE
Chris Burford - E
John Cadwell - G
Ray Collins - DT
Jerry Cornelison - T
Cotton Davidson - QB
Charley Diamond - T
Bo Dickinson - FB
Randy Duncan - QB
Don Flynn - DB
Sid Fournet - G
Jon Gilliam - C
Dave Grayson - DB
Ted Greene - LB
Tom Greene - QB
Abner Haynes - HB
Sherrill Headrick - LB
E.J. Holub - LB
Paul Hynes - DB
Frank Jackson - HB
Luther Jeralds - DE
Jack Johnson - DB
Edward Kelley - DB
Billy Krisher - G
Jerry Mays - DT
Paul Miller - DE
Walter Napier - DT
Doyle Nix - DB
Billy Pricer - FB
Al Reynolds - G
Johnny Robinson - HB
Paul Rochester - DT
Tony Romeo - E
Jack Spikes - FB
Smokey Stover - LB
Marvin Terrell - G
Jim Tyrer - T
Dave Webster - DB
Duane Wood - DB

1961 Denver

Ken Adamson - G
Buddy Allen - HB
Dave Ames - DB
Jim Barton - C
Fred Bukaty - FB
Al Carmichael - HB
John Cash - DE
Eldon Danenhauer - T
Jim Eifrid - LB
Dale Evans - HB
Al Frazier - HB
Chuck Gavin - DE
Goose Gonsoulin - DB
Buzz Guy - G
Art Hauser - DT
George Herring - QB
Jack Hill - HB
Gordy Holz - DT
Bob Hudson - LB
Bob Konovsky - DE
Pat Lamberti - LB
Carl Larpenter - G
Jack Mattox - DT
Wahoo McDaniel - LB
Bud McFadin - DT
Jim McMillin - DB
Bob McNamara - DB
Gene Mingo - HB
Mike Nichols - C
Phil Nugent - DB
Gene Prebola - E
Johnny Pyeatt - DB
Leo Reed - G
Bill Roehnelt - LB
Jimmy Sears - DB
Jackie Simpson - LB
Dan Smith - DB
Jerry Stalcup - LB
James Stinnette - LB
Donnie Stone - HB
Jerry Sturm - FB
Lionel Taylor - E
Jerry Traynham - HB
Frank Tripucka - QB
Joe Young - DE

1961 Houston

Dalva Allen - DE
Tony Banfield - DB
Byron Beams - DT
George Belotti - C
George Blanda - QB
Ron Botchan - LB
Billy Cannon - HB
Doug Cline - LB
Willard Dewveall - E
Mike Dukes - LB
Don Floyd - DE
Dick Frey - G
Fred Glick - DB
Bill Groman - E
Buzz Guy - G
John Guzik - LB
Ken Hall - HB
Charley Hennigan - FL
Ed Husmann - DT
Al Jamison - T
Mark Johnston - DB
Gene Jones - LB
Bob Kelly - T
Claude King - HB
Jack Laraway - LB
Jacky Lee - QB
Bob McLeod - E
Rich Michael - T
Charlie Milstead - DB
Dennit Morris - LB
Jim Norton - DB
Willis Perkins - G
Leo Reed - G
Bob Schmidt - C
George Shirkey - DT
Dave Smith - FB
Julian Spence - FL
Bob Talamini - G
Charley Tolar - FB
Orville Trask - DT
Hogan Wharton - G
John White - E
Gary Wisener - DB

1961 NY Titans

Don Allard - QB
Dave Ames - DB
Jim Apple - HB
Hubert Bobo - LB
Dewey Bohling - HB
Johnny Bookman - DB
Bob Brooks - FB
Tom Budrewicz - G
Dick Christy - HB
Gene Cockrell - T
Ed Cooke - DE
Thurlow Cooper - E
Al Dorow - QB
Roger Ellis - C
Dick Felt - DB
Jerry Fields - LB
Don Flynn - DB
Jim Furey - LB
Larry Grantham - LB
Moses Gray - T
Dick Guesman - DT
Mike Hudock - C
Paul Hynes - DB
Proverb Jacobs - DT
Dick Jamieson - QB
Curley Johnson - E
Jack Klotz - T
Pat Lamberti - LB
Bill Mathis - FB
Don Maynard - FL
John McMullan - G
Bob Mischak - G
Nick Mumley - DE
Bob O'Neil - G
Dainard Paulson - DB
Art Powell - E
Bert Rechichar - DB
Bob Reifsnyder - DE
Bob Renn - HB
Lee Riley - DB
Tom Saidock - DT
Bob Scrabis - QB
Bill Shockley - HB
Ed Walsh - T
Mel West - HB
Junior Wren - DB
Sid Youngelman - DE

1961 Oakland

Doug Asad - E
Al Bansavage - LB
Alex Bravo - DB
Jim Brewington - T
Jerry Burch - E
Joe Cannavino - DB
Bob Coolbaugh - E
Wayne Crow - HB
Clem Daniels - HB
Bob Dougherty - LB
George Fields - DT
Gary Finneran - DT
George Fleming - HB
Tom Flores - QB
Charley Fuller - HB
Bob Garner - DB
Charlie Hardy - E
John Harris - DB
Wayne Hawkins - G
Harry Jagielski - DT
Jon Jelacic - DE
Jim Jones - FB
Walt Kowalczyk - FB
Jack Larscheid - HB
Tom Louderback - LB
Alan Miller - FB
Riley Morris - LB
Jim Otto - C
Nick Papac - QB
Volney Peters - DT
Charley Powell - DE
Cliff Roberts - T
Herb Roedel - G
Ron Sabal - T
Hal Smith - DT
Willie Smith - G
Jack Stone - T
Bob Voight - T
Fred Williamson - DB

1961 San Diego

Chuck Allen - LB
Ernie Barnes - G
George Belotti - C
George Blair - DB
Howard Clark - E
Sam DeLuca - T
Hunter Enis - QB
Earl Faison - DE
Orlando Ferrante - G
Charlie Flowers - FB
Claude Gibson - DB
Dick Harris - DB
Luther Hayes - E
Bill Hudson - DT
Emil Karas - LB
Jack Kemp - QB
Dave Kocourek - E
Ernie Ladd - DT
Bob Laraba - HB
Keith Lincoln - HB
Paul Lowe - HB
Jacque MacKinnon - G
Paul Maguire - LB
Charlie McNeil - DB
Ron Mix - T
Ron Nery - DE
Don Norton - E
Sherman Plunkett - T
Bo Roberson - HB
Don Rogers - C
Bob Scarpitto - FL
Maury Schleicher - LB
Henry Schmidt - DT
Gene Selawski - T
Bud Whitehead - DB
Ernie Wright - T
Bob Zeman - DB

1962 NFL

1962 Baltimore

Raymond Berry - E
Dick Bielski - E
Bobby Boyd - HB
Ordell Braase - DE
Jackie Burkett - LB
Bob Clemens - HB
Jim Colvin - DT
John Diehl - DT
Wiley Feagin - G
Tom Gilburg - T
Wendell Harris - DB
Alex Hawkins - HB
Bill Kirchiro - G
Lenny Lyles - DB
Dee Mackey - E
Gino Marchetti - DE
Tom Matte - HB
Lamar McHan - QB
Lenny Moore - HB
Andy Nelson - DB
Jimmy Orr - FL
R.C. Owens - E
Jim Parker - G
Bill Pellington - LB
Joe Perry - FB
George Preas - T
Palmer Pyle - G
Alex Sandusky - G
Bill Saul - LB
Don Shinnick - LB
Billy Ray Smith Sr. - DT
Mark Smolinski - FB
Dan Sullivan - T
Dick Szymanski - C
Don Thompson - DE
Bake Turner - FL
Johnny Unitas - QB
Jim Welch - DB
Dave Yohn - LB

1962 Chi. Bears

John Adams - E
Art Anderson - T
Doug Atkins - DE
Charlie Bivins - HB
Rudy Bukich - QB
Ronnie Bull - HB
Jim Cadile - T
James Caroline - DB
Rick Casares - FB
Angelo Coia - E
Roger Davis - G
Mike Ditka - E
Stan Fanning - DT
Bo Farrington - E
Joe Fortunato - LB
Willie Galimore - HB
Bill George - LB
Bobby Joe Green - K
Stan Jones - G
Ted Karras - G
Bob Kilcullen - DT
Roger LeClerc - LB
Herman Lee - T
Earl Leggett - DT
Joe Marconi - FB
Billy Martin - HB
Bennie McRae - DB
Johnny Morris - FL
Larry Morris - LB
Don Mullins - DB
Tommy Neck - DB
Ed O'Bradovich - DE
Richie Petitbon - DB
Mike Pyle - C
Rosey Taylor - DB
Billy Wade - QB
Bob Wetoska - T
Dave Whitsell - DB
Fred Williams - DT
Maury Youmans - DE

1962 Cleveland

Johnny Brewer - E
Jim Brown - FB
John Brown - T
Hopalong Cassady - FL
Leon Clarke - E
Gary Collins - E
Vince Costello - LB
Bob Crespino - E
Ross Fichtner - DB
Galen Fiss - LB
Don Fleming - DB
Bobby Franklin - DB
Bob Gain - DT
Bill Glass - DE
Ernie Green - HB
Lou Groza - K
Gene Hickerson - G
Jim Houston - DE
Rich Kreitling - E
Mike Lucci - LB
Mike McCormack - T
John Morrow - C
Frank Morze - C
Jim Ninowski - QB
Frank Parker - DT
Bernie Parrish - DB
Floyd Peters - DT
Ray Renfro - FL
Frank Ryan - QB
Charlie Scales - HB
Dick Schafrath - T
Jim Shofner - DB
Jim Shorter - DB
Jim Ray Smith - G
Sam Tidmore - LB
Paul Wiggin - DE
Tommy Wilson - FB
John Wooten - G

1962 Dallas

George Andrie - DE
Sam Baker - K
Don Bishop - DB
Clyde Brock - T
Amos Bullocks - HB
Monte Clark - T
Frank Clarke - FL
Mike Connelly - C
Andy Cvercko - G
Donnie Davis - FL
Mike Dowdle - LB
Lee Folkins - E
Ken Frost - DT
Bob Fry - T
Mike Gaechter - DB
Cornell Green - DB
Glynn Gregory - DB
Chuck Howley - LB
Billy Howton - E
Lynn Hoyem - C
Joe Bob Isbell - G
Eddie LeBaron - QB
Bob Lilly - DE
Warren Livingston - DB
J. W. Lockett - FB
Bob Long - LB
Amos Marsh - FB
Dale Memmelaar - T
Don Meredith - QB
John Meyers - DT
Dick Nolan - DB
Pettis Norman - E
Jerry Norton - DB
Don Perkins - HB
Guy Reese - DT
Don Talbert - LB
Jerry Tubbs - LB

1962 Detroit

Terry Barr - FL
Carl Brettschneider - LB
Roger Brown - DT
Mike Bundra - DT
Gail Cogdill - E
Dick Compton - HB
Jim Gibbons - E
John Gonzaga - DT
John Gordy - T
Tom Hall - E
Harlon Hill - E
Alex Karras - DT
Night Train Lane - DB
Dan LaRose - T
Yale Lary - DB
Dick LeBeau - DB
Dan Lewis - HB
Dave Lloyd - C
John Lomakoski - T
Gary Lowe - DB
Bruce Maher - HB
Darris McCord - DE
Max Messner - LB
Dick Mills - G
Earl Morrall - QB
Nick Pietrosante - FB
Milt Plum - QB
Joe Schmidt - LB
Bob Scholtz - T
Harley Sewell - G
Pat Studstill - FL
Leo Sugar - DE
Larry Vargo - E
Wayne Walker - LB
Paul Ward - DT
Tom Watkins - HB
Ken Webb - FB
Bob Whitlow - C
Sam Williams - DE

1962 Green Bay

Herb Adderley - DB
Gary Barnes - E
Ed Blaine - G

Lew Carpenter - FL
Dan Currie - LB
Willie Davis - DE
Boyd Dowler - FL
Bill Forester - LB
Ron Gassert - DT
Forrest Gregg - T
Hank Gremminger - DB
Earl Gros - FB
Dave Hanner - DT
Paul Hornung - HB
Ken Iman - C
Henry Jordan - DT
Gary Knafelc - E
Ron Kostelnik - DT
Jerry Kramer - G
Ron Kramer - E
Norm Masters - T
Max McGee - E
Tom Moore - HB
Ray Nitschke - LB
Elijah Pitts - HB
Bill Quinlan - DE
Jim Ringo - C
John Roach - QB
Bob Skoronski - T
Bart Starr - QB
John Symank - DB
Jim Taylor - FB
Fuzzy Thurston - G
Nelson Toburen - LB
Jesse Whittenton - DB
Howie Williams - DB
Willie Wood - DB

1962 LA Rams

Duane Allen - E
Jon Arnett - HB
Pervis Atkins - HB
Dick Bass - FB
Jim Boeke - T
Zeke Bratkowski - QB
Charley Britt - DB
Doug Brown - DT
Joe Carollo - T
Lou Cordileone - DE
Charley Cowan - G
Lindon Crow - DB
Carroll Dale - E
Karl Finch - E
Roman Gabriel - QB
Alvin Hall - DB
Larry Hayes - C
Mike Henry - LB
Roy Hord - G
Art Hunter - C
Bill Jobko - LB
Deacon Jones - DE
John LoVetere - DT
Lamar Lundy - DE
Ollie Matson - FB
Marlin McKeever - LB
Ed Meador - DB
Ron Miller - QB
Merlin Olsen - DT
Jack Pardee - LB
Art Perkins - FB
Jim Phillips - E
Duane Putnam - G
Les Richter - LB
Joe Scibelli - G
Carver Shannon - DB
Glenn Shaw - FB
Bobby Smith - DB
Larry Stephens - DE
Frank Varrichione - T
Danny Villanueva - K

1962 Minnesota

Tom Adams - E
Grady Alderman - T
Larry Bowie - G
Bill Brown - FB
Bill Butler - DB
Jim Christopherson - LB
Bob Denton - DE
Dean Derby - DB
Paul Dickson - DT
Oscar Donahue - FL
Charley Ferguson - E
Tom Franckhauser - DB
Rip Hawkins - LB
Jerry Huth - G
Chuck Lamson - DB
Jim Leo - DE
Errol Linden - T
Cliff Livingston - LB
Jim Marshall - DE
Tommy Mason - HB
Doug Mayberry - FB
John McCormick - QB
Hugh McElhenny - HB
Mike Mercer - K
Clancy Osborne - LB
Jim Prestel - DT
Mike Rabold - G
Bobby Reed - HB
Jerry Reichow - E
Ed Sharockman - DB
Gordon Smith - E
Steve Stonebreaker - E
Charlie Sumner - DB
Fran Tarkenton - QB
Mick Tingelhoff - C

Mel Triplett - FB
Roy Winston - LB
Frank Youso - T

1962 NY Giants

Erich Barnes - DB
Reed Bohovich - G
Bookie Bolin - G
Rosey Brown - T
Ken Byers - DE
Don Chandler - K
Jim Collier - E
Johnny Counts - HB
Darrell Dess - G
Paul Dudley - HB
Bob Gaiters - HB
Frank Gifford - FL
Rosey Grier - DT
Ralph Guglielmi - QB
Sam Horner - DB
Sam Huff - LB
Chuck Janerette - DT
Jim Katcavage - DE
Phil King - HB
Greg Larson - C
Dick Lasse - LB
Dick Lynch - DB
Dick Modzelewski - DT
Joe Morrison - DB
Jimmy Patton - DB
Dick Pesonen - DB
Andy Robustelli - DE
Tom Scott - LB
Del Shofner - E
Bob Simms - LB
Jack Stroud - T
Aaron Thomas - E
Y. A. Tittle - QB
Mickey Walker - LB
Joe Walton - E
Allan Webb - DB
Alex Webster - FB
Ray Wietecha - C
Bill Winter - LB

1962 Philadelphia

John Baker - DE
Maxie Baughan - LB
Jim Beaver - DT
Chuck Bednarik - LB
Timmy Brown - HB
Frank Budd - FL
Don Burroughs - DB
Bob Butler - G
Jimmy Carr - DB
Pete Case - G
Hopalong Cassady - FL
Irv Cross - DB
Ted Dean - HB
Merrill Douglas - HB
Gene Gossage - G
Ken Gregory - E
Riley Gunnels - DT
Bob Harrison - LB
King Hill - QB
Roy Hord - G
Don Jonas - HB
Sonny Jurgensen - QB
John Kapele - DT
Howard Keys - T
Joe Lewis - DT
Dick Lucas - E
Mike McClellan - DB
Jim McCusker - T
Tommy McDonald - FL
John Nocera - LB
Don Oakes - DT
Clarence Peaks - FB
Pete Retzlaff - E
Bobby Richards - DE
Theron Sapp - HB
Jim Schrader - C
Ben Scotti - DB
J.D. Smith - T
Ralph Smith - E
Dick Stafford - DT
Bobby Walston - E
John Wittenborn - G
Mike Woulfe - LB

1962 Pittsburgh

Gary Ballman - HB
Tom Bettis - LB
Charlie Bradshaw - T
Ed Brown - QB
John Burrell - E
Preston Carpenter - E
Lou Cordileone - DE
Willie Daniel - DB
Buddy Dial - FL
Bob Ferguson - FB
Glenn Glass - DB
Dick Haley - DB
Rudy Hayes - LB
Harlon Hill - E
Dick Hoak - HB
Dan James - T
John Johnson - FB
John Kapele - DT
John Kenerson - DT
Brady Keys - DB
Ken Kirk - LB
Joe Krupa - DT

Bobby Layne - QB
Ray Lemek - G
Gene Lipscomb - DT
Red Mack - FL
Lou Michaels - DE
Terry Nofsinger - QB
Buzz Nutter - C
John Powers - E
John Reger - LB
Johnny Sample - DB
Mike Sandusky - G
Bob Schmitz - LB
Bob Simms - LB
Jackie Simpson - DB
Ernie Stautner - DE
Ron Stehouwer - G
George Strugar - DT
George Tarasovic - LB
Clendon Thomas - DB
Tom Tracy - HB
Joe Womack - HB

1962 St. Louis

Taz Anderson - E
Jim Bakken - K
Ted Bates - LB
Norm Beal - DB
Garland Boyette - LB
Chuck Bryant - E
Joe Childress - HB
Bobby Joe Conrad - FL
Ed Cook - T
John Crow - HB
Bob DeMarco - C
Fate Echols - T
Jack Elwell - E
Sam Etcheverry - QB
Pat Fischer - DB
Frank Fuller - DT
Prentice Gautt - FB
Irv Goode - T
Ken Gray - G
Mal Hammack - FB
Ed Henke - DE
Jimmy Hill - DB
George Hultz - DT
Roland Jackson - FB
Charley Johnson - QB
Bill Koman - LB
Mike McGee - G
Hugh McInnis - E
Ernie McMillan - T
Dale Meinert - LB
Don Owens - DT
Luke Owens - DE
Ken Panfil - T
Gerry Perry - G
Sonny Randle - E
Tom Redmond - G
Joe Robb - DE
Marion Rushing - LB
Billy Stacy - DB
Bill Triplett - DB
Larry Wilson - DB

1962 San Francisco

Bruce Bosley - G
John Brodie - QB
Bernie Casey - FL
Daniel Colchico - DE
Clyde Conner - E
Ted Connolly - G
Bill Cooper - FB
Tommy Davis - K
Leon Donohue - T
Eddie Dove - DB
Bob Gaiters - HB
Matt Hazeltine - LB
Jim Johnson - FL
Carl Kammerer - LB
Billy Kilmer - HB
Elbert Kimbrough - DB
Charlie Krueger - DT
Roland Lakes - T
Mike Magac - G
Kay McFarland - FL
John Mellekas - C
Jerry Mertens - DB
Dale Messer - DB
Clark Miller - DE
Leo Nomellini - DT
Ed Pine - LB
Jimmy Ridlon - DB
C. R. Roberts - FB
Len Rohde - DE
Karl Rubke - LB
J. D. Smith - FB
Bob St. Clair - T
Monty Stickles - E
John Sutro - T
Aaron Thomas - E
John Thomas - LB
Jim Vollenweider - FB
Bob Waters - QB
Lloyd Winston - FB
Abe Woodson - DB

1962 Washington

Bill Anderson - E
Billy Barnes - HB
Don Bosseler - FB
Rod Breedlove - LB
Claude Crabb - DB

Gene Cronin - DE
Jim Cunningham - FB
Ben Davidson - DT
Fred Dugan - E
Doug Elmore - DB
Bobby Freeman - DB
Dale Hackbart - DB
Fred Hageman - C
Galen Hall - QB
Ron Hatcher - FB
George Izo - QB
Leroy Jackson - HB
Dick James - HB
Steve Junker - E
Gorden Kelley - LB
Jim Kerr - DB
Ed Khayat - DE
Bob Khayat - G
Riley Mattson - T
Al Miller - LB
Bobby Mitchell - FL
Charlie Moore - G
John Nisby - G
Fran O'Brien - T
John Paluck - DE
Bob Pellegrini - LB
Vince Promuto - G
Joe Rutgens - DT
Hugh Smith - E
Norm Snead - QB
Jim Steffen - DB
Andy Stynchula - DE
Bob Toneff - DT

1962 AFL

1962 Boston

Tom Addison - LB
Don Allard - QB
Houston Antwine - DT
Fred Bruney - DB
Nick Buoniconti - LB
Ron Burton - HB
Gino Cappelletti - FL
Jim Colclough - E
Jim Crawford - HB
Walt Cudzik - C
Bob Dee - DE
Larry Eisenhauer - DE
Dick Felt - DB
Larry Garron - FB
Milt Graham - T
Ron Hall - DB
Jim Hunt - DE
Harry Jacobs - LB
Claude King - HB
Dick Klein - T
Chuck Leo - G
Charley Long - T
Billy Lott - FB
Rommie Loudd - LB
Leroy Moore - DE
Billy Neighbors - G
Ross O'Hanley - DB
Babe Parilli - QB
Jess Richardson - DT
Tony Romeo - E
Jack Rudolph - LB
Tony Sardisco - G
Chuck Shonta - DB
Thomas Stephens - E
Don Webb - HB
Bob Yates - C
Tom Yewcic - QB

1962 Buffalo

Ray Abruzzese - DB
Art Baker - FB
Stew Barber - T
Glenn Bass - E
Al Bemiller - C
Nate Borden - DE
Joe Cannavino - DB
Wray Carlton - HB
Carl Charon - DB
Monte Crockett - E
Jim Crotty - DB
Wayne Crow - HB
Tom Day - G
Jerry DeLucca - T
Al Dorow - QB
Elbert Dubenion - HB
Booker Edgerson - DB
Ralph Felton - LB
George Flint - G
Cookie Gilchrist - FB
Don Healy - DT
Carey Henley - HB
Frank Jackunas - C
Willie Jones - FB
Jack Kemp - QB
Tom Louderback - LB
Archie Matsos - LB
Marv Matuszak - LB
Tom Minter - DB
Leroy Moore - DE
Harold Olson - T
Warren Rabb - QB
Tom Rychlec - E
Tom Saidock - DT
Tom Sestak - DT
Billy Shaw - G
Jim Sorey - DT

Mike Stratton - LB
Carl Taseff - DB
LaVerne Torczon - DE
Jack Tracey - E
Ernie Warlick - E
Willie West - DB
Manch Wheeler - QB
John Yaccino - DB
Mack Yoho - DE
Sid Youngelman - DT

1962 Dallas Texans

Fred Arbanas - E
Sonny Bishop - G
Mel Branch - DE
Tommy Brooker - E
Chris Burford - E
Walt Corey - LB
Jerry Cornelison - T
Cotton Davidson - QB
Dick Davis - DE
Len Dawson - QB
Charley Diamond - T
Jon Gilliam - C
Dave Grayson - DB
Ted Greene - LB
Abner Haynes - HB
Sherrill Headrick - LB
E.J. Holub - C
Bill Hull - DE
Bobby Hunt - DB
Frank Jackson - HB
Edward Kelley - DB
Carl Larpenter - G
Jerry Mays - DE
Curtis McClinton - FB
Curt Merz - G
Bill Miller - E
Tom Pennington - K
Bobby Ply - DB
Al Reynolds - G
Johnny Robinson - HB
Paul Rochester - DT
Jimmy Saxton - HB
Jack Spikes - FB
Smokey Stover - LB
Marvin Terrell - G
Jim Tyrer - T
Eddie Wilson - QB
Duane Wood - DB

1962 Denver

Ken Adamson - G
Jim Barton - C
John Cash - DE
Eldon Danenhauer - T
John Denvir - G
Bo Dickinson - FB
Hunter Enis - QB
Tom Erlandson - LB
Jim Fraser - LB
Al Frazier - HB
Chuck Gavin - DE
Goose Gonsoulin - DB
Gordy Holz - DT
Larry Jordan - DE
Don Joyce - DE
Ike Lassiter - DE
Chuck Marshall - DB
Bob McCullough - G
Wahoo McDaniel - LB
Bud McFadin - G
John McGeever - DB
Jim McMillin - DB
Gene Mingo - HB
Tom Minter - DB
Johnny Olszewski - FB
Jim Perkins - T
Gene Prebola - E
Bill Roehnelt - LB
Justin Rowland - DB
Bob Scarpitto - FL
George Shaw - QB
Jerry Stalcup - LB
James Stinnette - FB
Donnie Stone - HB
Jerry Sturm - T
Jerry Tarr - HB
Lionel Taylor - E
Frank Tripucka - QB
Dick Wood - QB
Bob Zeman - DB

1962 Houston

Gene Babb - FB
Tony Banfield - DB
George Blanda - QB
Billy Cannon - HB
Doug Cline - LB
Ed Culpepper - DT
Gary Cutsinger - DE
Willard Dewveall - E
Mike Dukes - LB
Don Floyd - DE
Charley Frazier - E
John Frongillo - G
Fred Glick - DB
Tom Goode - LB
Bill Groman - E
Charley Hennigan - FL
Bill Herchman - DT
Ed Husmann - DT

Al Jamison - T
Bobby Jancik - DB
Mark Johnston - DB
Bob Kelly - DT
Dan Lanphear - DE
Jacky Lee - QB
Ron McDole - DE
Bob McLeod - E
Rich Michael - T
Bill Miller - DT
Jim Norton - DB
Larry Onesti - LB
Bob Schmidt - C
Dave Smith - FB
Bob Suci - DB
Walt Suggs - T
Bob Talamini - G
Charley Tolar - HB
Bucky Wegener - G
Hogan Wharton - G

1962 NY Titans

Billy Atkins - DB
Hubert Bobo - LB
Dick Christy - HB
Gene Cockrell - DE
Ed Cooke - LB
Thurlow Cooper - E
Roger Ellis - LB
Jerry Fields - LB
Charlie Flowers - FB
Wayne Fontes - DB
Sid Fournet - G
Bobby Fowler - FB
Larry Grantham - LB
Moses Gray - T
Johnny Green - QB
Lee Grosscup - QB
Dick Guesman - DT
Mike Hudock - C
Paul Hynes - DB
Proverb Jacobs - DT
Curley Johnson - HB
Karl Kaimer - DE
John Kenerson - DE
Jack Klotz - T
Ed Kovac - HB
Alex Kroll - C
Dean Look - QB
Bill Mathis - FB
Don Maynard - FL
Bob Mischak - G
Fran Morelli - T
Nick Mumley - DE
Dainard Paulson - DB
Art Powell - E
Perry Richards - E
Lee Riley - DB
Bob Scrabis - QB
Bill Shockley - HB
Butch Songin - QB
Harold Stephens - QB
George Strugar - DT
Jim Tiller - HB
LaVerne Torczon - DE
Bob Watters - DE
Mel West - HB

1962 Oakland

Ben Agajanian - K
Dalva Allen - DE
Dan Birdwell - DE
Max Boydston - E
George Boynton - DB
Charlie Brown - T
Stan Campbell - G
Dobie Craig - HB
Clem Daniels - HB
Cotton Davidson - QB
Dick Dorsey - E
Bob Dougherty - LB
Hunter Enis - QB
Dan Ficca - G
Charley Fuller - HB
Chon Gallegos - QB
Bob Garner - DB
Charlie Hardy - E
Wayne Hawkins - G
Don Heinrich - QB
Jon Jelacic - DE
Hal Lewis - HB
Chuck McMurtry - DT
Alan Miller - FB
Mel Montalbo - DB
Riley Morris - DE
Tommy Morrow - DB
Rich Mostardo - DB
Pete Nicklas - T
Jim Norris - T
Joe Novsek - DE
Jim Otto - C
M.C. Reynolds - QB
Charlie Rieves - LB
Hank Rivera - DB
Bo Roberson - HB
George Shirkey - DT
Jackie Simpson - LB
Willie Simpson - FB
Jack Stone - T
Orville Trask - DT
Vern Valdez - DB
Gene White - HB
Fred Williamson - DB

1962 San Diego

Chuck Allen - LB
Lance Alworth - E
Ernie Barnes - G
Bobby Bethune - DB
George Blair - DB
Hez Braxton - FB
Frank Buncom - LB
Reggie Carolan - E
Bert Coan - HB
Earl Faison - DE
Wayne Frazier - LB
Claude Gibson - DB
Fred Gillett - HB
Sam Gruneisen - LB
John Hadl - QB
Dick Harris - DB
Dick Hudson - T
Bill Hudson - DT
Bobby Jackson - FB
Emil Karas - LB
Val Keckin - QB
Jack Kemp - QB
Jack Klotz - T
Dave Kocourek - E
Ernie Ladd - DT
Keith Lincoln - HB
Jacque MacKinnon - FB
Paul Maguire - LB
Gerry McDougall - FB
Charlie McNeil - DB
Paul Miller - DE
Bob Mitinger - LB
Ron Mix - G
Ron Nery - DE
Don Norton - E
Sherman Plunkett - T
Jerry Robinson - E
Don Rogers - G
Maury Schleicher - LB
Henry Schmidt - DE
Pat Shea - G
Bud Whitehead - DB
Dick Wood - QB
Ernie Wright - T

1963 NFL

1963 Baltimore

Raymond Berry - E
Dick Bielski - E
Bobby Boyd - DB
Ordell Braase - DE
Jackie Burkett - LB
Jim Colvin - DT
Nate Craddock - FB
Gary Cuozzo - QB
John Diehl - DT
Tom Gilburg - T
Wendell Harris - DB
Alex Hawkins - E
Jerry Hill - FB
J. W. Lockett - FB
Jerry Logan - DB
Lenny Lyles - DB
John Mackey - E
Butch Maples - LB
Gino Marchetti - DE
Jim Martin - K
Tom Matte - HB
Lamar McHan - QB
Fred Miller - DT
Lenny Moore - HB
Andy Nelson - DB
Jimmy Orr - FL
R.C. Owens - E
Jim Parker - G
Bill Pellington - LB
George Preas - T
Palmer Pyle - G
Willie Richardson - FL
Alex Sandusky - G
Bill Saul - LB
Don Shinnick - LB
Dan Sullivan - G
Dick Szymanski - C
Don Thompson - DE
Johnny Unitas - QB
Bob Vogel - T
Jim Welch - DB
Butch Wilson - E

1963 Chi. Bears

Doug Atkins - DE
Steve Barnett - T
Tom Bettis - LB
Charlie Bivins - HB
Rudy Bukich - QB
Ronnie Bull - HB
Jim Cadile - G
James Caroline - DB
Rick Casares - FB
Angelo Coia - E
Roger Davis - G
Mike Ditka - E
Bo Farrington - E
Joe Fortunato - LB
Willie Galimore - HB
Bill George - LB
Larry Glueck - DB
Bobby Joe Green - K
Bob Jencks - E

John Johnson - FB
Stan Jones - DT
Ted Karras - G
Bob Kilcullen - DE
Roger LeClerc - LB
Herman Lee - T
Earl Leggett - DT
Joe Marconi - FB
Billy Martin - HB
Bennie McRae - DB
Johnny Morris - FL
Larry Morris - LB
Ed O'Bradovich - DE
Richie Petitbon - DB
Mike Pyle - C
Rosey Taylor - DB
Billy Wade - QB
Bob Wetoska - T
Dave Whitsell - DB
Fred Williams - DT

1963 Cleveland

Walter Beach - DB
Larry Benz - DB
Johnny Brewer - E
Jim Brown - FB
John Brown - T
Monte Clark - T
Gary Collins - FL
Ted Connolly - G
Vince Costello - LB
Bob Crespino - E
Andy Cverko - G
Ross Fichtner - DB
Galen Fiss - LB
Bobby Franklin - HB
Bob Gain - DT
Bill Glass - DE
Tom Goosby - LB
Ernie Green - HB
Lou Groza - K
Gene Hickerson - G
Jim Houston - LB
Tom Hutchinson - E
Jim Kanicki - DT
Rich Kreitling - E
Mike Lucci - LB
Jim McCusker - T
John Morrow - C
Frank Morze - C
Jim Ninowski - QB
Frank Parker - DT
Bernie Parrish - DB
Ray Renfro - FL
Frank Ryan - QB
Charlie Scales - HB
Dick Schafrath - T
Stan Sczurek - LB
Roger Shoals - T
Jim Shofner - DB
Jim Shorter - DB
Sam Tidmore - LB
Ken Webb - HB
Paul Wiggin - DE
John Wooten - G

1963 Dallas

George Andrie - DE
Sam Baker - K
Gary Barnes - E
Don Bishop - DB
Clyde Brock - T
Amos Bullocks - HB
Frank Clarke - FL
Mike Connelly - C
Dave Edwards - LB
Lee Folkins - E
Bob Fry - T
Mike Gaechter - DB
Cornell Green - DB
Wendell Hayes - HB
Harold Hays - LB
Chuck Howley - LB
Billy Howton - E
Lynn Hoyem - G
Joe Bob Isbell - G
Lee Roy Jordan - LB
Eddie LeBaron - QB
Bob Lilly - DT
Tony Liscio - T
Warren Livingston - DB
Amos Marsh - HB
Dale Memmelaar - G
Don Meredith - QB
John Meyers - DT
Pettis Norman - E
Ed Nutting - T
Jerry Overton - DB
Don Perkins - FB
Lance Poimbeouf - G
Guy Reese - DT
Jimmy Ridlon - DB
Ray Schoenke - T
Jim Ray Smith - T
Larry Stephens - DE
Jim Stiger - HB
Jerry Tubbs - LB

1963 Detroit

Terry Barr - FL
Carl Brettschneider - LB
Roger Brown - DT
Mike Bundra - DT
Hopalong Cassady - HB
Ernie Clark - LB
Gail Cogdill - E
Dick Compton - HB
Larry Ferguson - HB
Dennis Gaubatz - LB
Jim Gibbons - E
John Gonzaga - T
John Gordy - G
Al Greer - E
Tom Hall - E
Night Train Lane - DB
Dan LaRose - G
Yale Lary - DB
Dick LeBeau - DB
Monte Lee - LB
Dan Lewis - HB
Gary Lowe - DB
Bruce Maher - DB
Ollie Matson - HB
Darris McCord - DE
Max Messner - LB
Earl Morrall - QB
Floyd Peters - DT
Nick Pietrosante - FB
Milt Plum - QB
Lucien Reeberg - T
Nick Ryder - FB
Daryl Sanders - T
Joe Schmidt - LB
Bob Scholtz - T
Jim Simon - LB
Larry Vargo - E
Wayne Walker - LB
Tom Watkins - HB
Bob Whitlow - C
Sam Williams - DE

1963 Green Bay

Herb Adderley - DB
Lionel Aldridge - DE
Jan Barrett - E
Zeke Bratkowski - QB
Lew Carpenter - HB
Dan Currie - LB
Willie Davis - DE
Boyd Dowler - FL
Marv Fleming - E
Bill Forester - LB
Forrest Gregg - T
Hank Gremminger - DB
Dan Grimm - G
Earl Gros - FB
Dave Hanner - DT
Urban Henry - DT
Ed Holler - LB
Ken Iman - C
Bob Jeter - FL
Henry Jordan - DE
Ron Kostelnik - DT
Jerry Kramer - G
Ron Kramer - E
Norm Masters - T
Max McGee - E
Frank Mestnik - FB
Tom Moore - HB
Ray Nitschke - LB
Jerry Norton - DB
Elijah Pitts - HB
Jim Ringo - C
John Roach - QB
Dave Robinson - LB
Bob Skoronski - C
Bart Starr - QB
Jim Taylor - FB
Fuzzy Thurston - G
Jesse Whittenton - DB
Howie Williams - DB
Willie Wood - DB

1963 LA Rams

John Adams - E
Duane Allen - E
Jon Arnett - HB
Pervis Atkins - HB
Terry Baker - QB
Dick Bass - HB
Jim Boeke - T
Zeke Bratkowski - QB
Charley Britt - DB
Joe Carollo - T
Don Chuy - G
Charley Cowan - G
Lindon Crow - DB
Carroll Dale - E
Stan Fanning - DE
Roman Gabriel - QB
Rosey Grier - DT
John Griffin - DB
Alvin Hall - DB
Larry Hayes - C
Mike Henry - LB
Art Hunter - C
Deacon Jones - DE
Ken Kirk - C
Cliff Livingston - LB
Lamar Lundy - DE
Marlin McKeever - E
Ed Meador - DB
Merlin Olsen - DT
Jack Pardee - LB
Art Perkins - FB
Jim Phillips - FL
Joe Scibelli - G
Harley Sewell - G
Carver Shannon - HB
Bobby Smith - DB
Bill Swain - LB
Frank Varrichione - T
Danny Villanueva - K
Nat Whitmyer - DB
Ben Wilson - FB

1963 Minnesota

Grady Alderman - T
Jim Battle - G
Larry Bowie - G
Jim Boylan - FL
Bill Brown - FB
Bill Butler - HB
Lee Calland - DB
John Campbell - LB
Leon Clarke - FL
Fred Cox - K
Bob Denton - DE
Paul Dickson - DT
Terry Dillon - DB
Bob Ferguson - FB
Paul Flatley - E
Tom Franckhauser - DB
Rip Hawkins - LB
Don Hultz - DE
Jerry Huth - G
Bill Jobko - LB
Karl Kassulke - DB
Terry Kosens - DB
Chuck Lamson - DB
Errol Linden - T
Jim Marshall - DE
Tommy Mason - HB
Dave O'Brien - G
Ray Poage - FL
Jim Prestel - DT
Bobby Reed - HB
Jerry Reichow - E
Pat Russ - DT
Ed Sharockman - DB
Gordon Smith - E
Steve Stonebreaker - LB
Fran Tarkenton - QB
Mick Tingelhoff - C
Ron Vander Kelen - QB
Tommy Wilson - HB
Roy Winston - LB

1963 NY Giants

Bob Anderson - HB
Erich Barnes - DB
Bookie Bolin - G
Rosey Brown - T
Ken Byers - DE
Don Chandler - K
Johnny Counts - HB
Darrell Dess - G
Eddie Dove - DB
Frank Gifford - FL
Glynn Griffing - QB
Ralph Guglielmi - QB
Al Gursky - LB
Louis Guy - FL
Jerry Hillebrand - LB
Lane Howell - T
Sam Huff - LB
Jim Katcavage - DE
Charlie Killett - HB
Phil King - HB
Lou Kirouac - T
Greg Larson - C
John LoVetere - DT
Dick Lynch - DB
Hugh McElhenny - HB
Dick Modzelewski - DT
Joe Morrison - FL
Jimmy Patton - DB
Dick Pesonen - DB
Andy Robustelli - DE
Tom Scott - LB
Del Shofner - E
Jack Stroud - T
Bob Taylor - DE
Aaron Thomas - E
Y. A. Tittle - QB
Mickey Walker - LB
Joe Walton - E
Allan Webb - DB
Alex Webster - FB
Bill Winter - LB

1963 Philadelphia

Maxie Baughan - LB
Ed Blaine - G
Timmy Brown - HB
Don Burroughs - DB
Bill Byrne - G
Lee Roy Caffey - LB
Jimmy Carr - DB
Pete Case - G
Mike Clark - K
Irv Cross - DB
Ted Dean - FB
Paul Dudley - HB
Frank Fuller - DT
Ron Goodwin - FL
Dave Graham - T
Ralph Guglielmi - QQB
Riley Gunnels - DT
Bob Harrison - LB
Ralph Heck - LB
Gary Henson - E
King Hill - QB
Sonny Jurgensen - QB
Howard Keys - G
Dave Lloyd - LB
Dick Lucas - E
Ray Mansfield - DT
Jerry Mazzanti - DE
Mike McClellan - DB
Tommy McDonald - FL
John Mellekas - DT
Clarence Peaks - FB
Bill Quinlan - DE
Nate Ramsey - DB
Pete Retzlaff - E
Bobby Richards - DE
Theron Sapp - HB
Jim Schrader - C
Ben Scotti - DB
Jim Skaggs - G
J.D. Smith - T
Ralph Smith - E
Dick Stafford - DE
George Tarasovic - LB
Tom Woodeshick - HB

1963 Pittsburgh

Art Anderson - T
Frank Atkinson - DT
John Baker - DE
Gary Ballman - FL
Charlie Bradshaw - T
Jim Bradshaw - DB
Ed Brown - QB
John Burrell - E
Preston Carpenter - E
Lou Cordileone - DT
Roy Curry - FL
Willie Daniel - DB
Buddy Dial - E
Bob Ferguson - FB
Glenn Glass - DB
Dick Haley - DB
Dick Hoak - HB
Dan James - T
John Johnson - FB
Brady Keys - DB
Joe Krupa - DT
Ray Lemek - G
Red Mack - E
Lou Michaels - DE
Bill Nelsen - QB
Terry Nofsinger - QB
Buzz Nutter - C
Myron Pottios - LB
John Powers - E
John Reger - LB
Bob Rowley - LB
Andy Russell - LB
Mike Sandusky - G
Theron Sapp - HB
Bob Schmitz - LB
Ernie Stautner - DT
Ron Stehouwer - G
George Tarasovic - LB
Clendon Thomas - DB
Tom Tracy - HB

1963 St. Louis

Taz Anderson - E
Jim Bakken - K
Garland Boyette - LB
Don Brumm - DE
Jimmy Burson - DB
Joe Childress - FB
Bobby Joe Conrad - FL
Ed Cook - G
John Crow - HB
Bob DeMarco - C
Fate Echols - DT
Pat Fischer - DB
Billy Gambrell - E
Prentice Gautt - FB
Irv Goode - T
Ken Gray - G
Mal Hammack - E
Ed Henke - DE
Jimmy Hill - DB
John Houser - G
Buddy Humphrey - QB
Charley Johnson - QB
Bill Koman - LB
Ernie McMillan - T
Dave Meggyesy - LB
Dale Meinert - LB
Don Owens - DT
Luke Owens - DT
Bob Paremore - HB
Sonny Randle - E
Tom Redmond - DE
Bob Reynolds - T
Joe Robb - DE
Marion Rushing - LB
Sam Silas - DT
Jackie Smith - E
Billy Stacy - DB
Larry Stallings - LB
Jerry Stovall - DB
John Symank - DB
Bill Thornton - FB
Bill Triplett - HB
Larry Wilson - DB

1963 San Francisco

Kermit Alexander - DB
Bruce Bosley - G
Clyde Brock - T
John Brodie - QB
Bernie Casey - FL
Daniel Colchico - DE
Clyde Conner - E
Bill Cooper - LB
Tommy Davis - K
Leon Donohue - G
Eddie Dove - DB
Mike Dowdle - LB
Matt Hazeltine - LB
Jim Johnson - FL
Elbert Kimbrough - DB
Gary Knafelc - E
Charlie Krueger - DT
Roland Lakes - DT
Mike Lind - FB
Don Lisbon - HB
Mike Magac - G
Kay McFarland - FL
Lamar McHan - QB
Dale Messer - HB
Clark Miller - DE
Leo Nomellini - DT
Joe Perry - FB
Ed Pine - LB
Walt Rock - DT
Len Rohde - T
Karl Rubke - DE
Chuck Sieminski - DT
J. D. Smith - FB
Bob St. Clair - T
Monty Stickles - E
John Thomas - G
Jim Vollenweider - HB
Bob Waters - QB
Howie Williams - DB
Roy Williams - DT
Lloyd Winston - FB
Abe Woodson - DB

1963 Washington

Bill Anderson - E
Billy Barnes - HB
Don Bosseler - FB
Rod Breedlove - LB
Frank Budd - FL
Harry Butsko - LB
Jim Collier - E
Claude Crabb - DB
Jim Cunningham - FB
Andy Cvercko - G
Ben Davidson - DT
Fred Dugan - E
Wiley Feagin - G
Dave Francis - FB
Dale Hackbart - DB
Fred Hageman - C
George Izo - QB
Leroy Jackson - HB
Dick James - DB
Carl Kammerer - LB
Gorden Kelley - LB
Ed Khayat - DT
Bob Khayat - K
Riley Mattson - T
Al Miller - LB
Bobby Mitchell - FL
John Nisby - G
Fran O'Brien - T
John Paluck - DE
Bob Pellegrini - LB
Vince Promuto - G
Pat Richter - E
Joe Rutgens - DT
Ted Rzempoluch - DB
Johnny Sample - DB
Lonnie Sanders - DB
Norm Snead - QB
Ron Snidow - DE
Jim Steffen - DB
Andy Stynchula - DE
Bob Toneff - DT
Tom Tracy - HB

1963 AFL

1963 Boston

Tom Addison - LB
Houston Antwine - DT
Nick Buoniconti - LB
Ron Burton - HB
Gino Cappelletti - E
Jim Colclough - FL
Jim Crawford - HB
Harry Crump - FB
Walt Cudzik - C
Bob Dee - DE
Jerry DeLucca - DT
Larry Eisenhauer - DE
Dick Felt - DB
Larry Garron - FB
Art Graham - E
Milt Graham - DT
Ron Hall - DB
Bill Hudson - DT
Jim Hunt - DE
Charley Long - G
Billy Lott - FB
Don McKinnon - LB
Billy Neighbors - G
Tom Neumann - HB
Don Oakes - T
Ross O'Hanley - DB
Babe Parilli - QB
Jess Richardson - DT
Tony Romeo - E
Jack Rudolph - LB
Chuck Shonta - DB
Thomas Stephens - E
Bob Suci - DB
Dave Watson - G
Bob Yates - T
Tom Yewcic - QB

1963 Buffalo

Ray Abruzzese - DB
Billy Atkins - DB
Stew Barber - T
Glenn Bass - HB
Dave Behrman - T
Al Bemiller - C
Hez Braxton - HB
Fred Brown - HB
Wray Carlton - HB
Carl Charon - DB
Wayne Crow - HB
Tom Day - G
Jerry DeLucca - DT
Elbert Dubenion - FL
Jim Dunaway - DT
Booker Edgerson - DB
Charley Ferguson - E
George Flint - G
Cookie Gilchrist - FB
Dick Hudson - G
Harry Jacobs - LB
Jack Kemp - QB
Roger Kochman - HB
Daryle Lamonica - QB
Chuck Leo - G
Marv Matuszak - LB
Ron McDole - DE
Bill Miller - E
Leroy Moore - DE
Jesse Murdock - FB
Herb Paterra - LB
Ken Rice - G
Hank Rivera - DB
Ed Rutkowski - HB
George Saimes - HB
Tom Sestak - DT
Billy Shaw - G
Mike Stratton - LB
Eugene Sykes - DB
Jack Tracey - LB
Ernie Warlick - E
Willie West - DB
Mack Yoho - DE
Sid Youngelman - DT

1963 Denver

Ernie Barnes - G
Don Breaux - QB
Willie Brown - DB
Don Coffey - FL
Eldon Danenhauer - T
Bo Dickinson - FB
Hewritt Dixon - HB
Tom Erlandson - LB
Jim Fraser - LB
Al Frazier - FL
Bob Gaiters - HB
Chuck Gavin - DE
Goose Gonsoulin - DB
Bill Groman - FL
Gordy Holz - DT
Jerry Hopkins - LB
Ray Jacobs - DE
Tom Janik - DB
Billy Joe - FB
Ike Lassiter - DE
John McCormick - QB
Bob McCullough - G
Wahoo McDaniel - LB
Bud McFadin - DT
John McGeever - DB
Gene Mingo - HB
Charley Mitchell - DB
Ron Nery - DE
John Nocera - LB
Tom Nomina - G
Harold Olson - T
Jim Perkins - T
Anton Peters - DT
Gene Prebola - E
Tom Rychlec - E
Bob Scarpitto - FL
Leon Simmons - LB
John Sklopan - DB
Mickey Slaughter - QB
Donnie Stone - HB
Jerry Sturm - C
Lionel Taylor - E
Frank Tripucka - QB
Clarence Walker - HB
Bob Zeman - DB

1963 Houston

Gene Babb - FB
Johnny Baker - LB
Tony Banfield - DB
George Blanda - QB
Danny Brabham - LB
Bobby Brezina - HB
Billy Cannon - HB
Doug Cline - LB
Ed Culpepper - DT
Gary Cutsinger - DE
Willard Dewveall - E
Bo Dickinson - FB
Mike Dukes - LB
Don Floyd - DE
Charley Frazier - E
John Frongillo - C
Fred Glick - DB
Tom Goode - LB
Charley Hennigan - FL
Ed Husmann - DT
Bobby Jancik - DB
Mark Johnston - DB
Bob Kelly - T
Randy Kerbow - FL
Jacky Lee - QB
Bob McLeod - E
Dudley Meredith - DT
Rich Michael - T
Ron Nery - DE
Jim Norton - DB
Larry Onesti - LB
Willis Perkins - DE
Bob Schmidt - C
Dave Smith - FB
Walt Suggs - T
Bob Talamini - G
Bill Tobin - HB
Charley Tolar - FB
Bucky Wegener - G
Hogan Wharton - G

1963 Kansas City

Fred Arbanas - E
Bobby Bell - LB
Denny Biodrowski - G
Mel Branch - DE
Tommy Brooker - E
Buck Buchanan - DT
Ed Budde - G
Chris Burford - E
Bert Coan - HB
Walt Corey - LB
Len Dawson - QB
Charley Diamond - T
Bill Diamond - G
Curt Farrier - DT
Jon Gilliam - C
Dave Grayson - DB
Abner Haynes - HB
Sherrill Headrick - LB
Dave Hill - T
E.J. Holub - C
Bobby Hunt - DB
Frank Jackson - FL
Dick Johnson - E
Jerry Mays - DE
Curtis McClinton - FB
Curt Merz - G
Bobby Ply - DB
Al Reynolds - G
Johnny Robinson - DB
Paul Rochester - DT
Jack Spikes - FB
Smokey Stover - LB
Marvin Terrell - G
Jim Tyrer - T
Charley Warner - DB
Eddie Wilson - QB
Jerrel Wilson - LB
Duane Wood - DB

1963 NY Jets

Billy Atkins - DB
Bill Baird - DB
Ted Bates - LB
Bob Butler - G
Ed Chlebek - QB
Dick Christy - HB
Ed Cooke - LB
Roger Ellis - LB
Dan Ficca - G
Sid Fournet - G
Larry Grantham - LB
Johnny Green - QB
Ken Gregory - E
Dick Guesman - DT
Galen Hall - QB
Gene Heeter - E
Winston Hill - T
Roy Hord - G
Mike Hudock - C
Chuck Janerette - DT
Curley Johnson - FB
Jack Klotz - T
Dee Mackey - E
Bill Mathis - HB
Don Maynard - FL
Bob McAdams - DT
Walt Michaels - LB
Dainard Paulson - DB
Bill Perkins - HB
Pete Perreault - G
Sherman Plunkett - T
Jim Price - LB
Paul Rochester - DT
Mark Smolinski - FB

Marshall Starks - DB
Tony Stricker - DB
George Strugar - DT
LaVerne Torczon - DE
Bake Turner - E
Clyde Washington - DB
Bob Watters - DE
Dave West - DB
Dick Wood - QB
Bill Wood - DB
Dave Yohn - LB

1963 Oakland

Dalva Allen - DE
Jan Barrett - E
Dan Birdwell - DE
Sonny Bishop - G
Dave Costa - DT
Dobie Craig - E
Clem Daniels - HB
Cotton Davidson - QB
Bob Dougherty - LB
Tom Flores - QB
Claude Gibson - DB
Wayne Hawkins - G
Ken Herock - E
Proverb Jacobs - T
Jon Jelacic - DE
Dick Klein - T
Joe Krakoski - DB
Archie Matsos - LB
Doug Mayberry - FB
Jim McMillin - DB
Chuck McMurtry - DT
Mike Mercer - K
Alan Miller - FB
Bob Mischak - E
Tommy Morrow - DB
Jesse Murdock - FB
Jim Norris - DT
Clancy Osborne - LB
Jim Otto - C
Art Powell - E
Warren Powers - DB
Charlie Rieves - LB
Bo Roberson - HB
Glenn Shaw - FB
Jackie Simpson - LB
Mike Sommer - HB
Ollie Spencer - G
Herm Urenda - E
Fred Williamson - DB
Frank Youso - T

1963 San Diego

Chuck Allen - LB
Lance Alworth - FL
George Blair - DB
Frank Buncom - LB
Reggie Carolan - E
Sam DeLuca - G
Earl Faison - DE
Gary Glick - DB
George Gross - DT
Sam Gruneisen - G
John Hadl - QB
Dick Harris - DB
Bobby Jackson - FB
Emil Karas - LB
Keith Kinderman - FB
Dave Kocourek - E
Ernie Ladd - DT
Bobby Lane - LB
Keith Lincoln - FB
Paul Lowe - HB
Jacque MacKinnon - E
Paul Maguire - LB
Gerry McDougall - FB
Charlie McNeil - DB
Bob Mitinger - LB
Ron Mix - T
Don Norton - E
Ernie Park - T
Bob Petrich - DE
Jerry Robinson - E
Don Rogers - C
Tobin Rote - QB
Henry Schmidt - DT
Pat Shea - G
Walt Sweeney - G
Dick Westmoreland - DB
Bud Whitehead - DB
Ernie Wright - T

1964 NFL

1964 Baltimore

Raymond Berry - E
Bobby Boyd - HB
Ordell Braase - DE
Jackie Burkett - LB
Gary Cuozzo - QB
Ted Davis - LB
John Diehl - DT
Tom Gilburg - T
Wendell Harris - DB
Alex Hawkins - E
Alvin Haymond - DB
Jerry Hill - FB
Lou Kirouac - T
Jerry Logan - DB
Joe Don Looney - FB
Tony Lorick - FB
Lenny Lyles - DB
John Mackey - E
Gino Marchetti - DE
Tom Matte - HB
Lou Michaels - DE
Fred Miller - DT
Lenny Moore - HB
Jimmy Orr - FL
Jim Parker - G
Bill Pellington - LB
Neal Petties - E
George Preas - T
Guy Reese - DT
Willie Richardson - FL
Alex Sandusky - G
Don Shinnick - LB
Billy Ray Smith Sr. - DT
Steve Stonebreaker - LB
Dan Sullivan - T
Dick Szymanski - C
Johnny Unitas - QB
Bob Vogel - T
Jim Welch - DB
Butch Wilson - E

1964 Chi. Bears

Jon Arnett - HB
Doug Atkins - DE
Gary Barnes - E
Charlie Bivins - HB
Rudy Bukich - QB
Ronnie Bull - HB
George Burman - T
Jim Cadile - G
James Caroline - DB
Rick Casares - FB
Mike Ditka - E
Dick Evey - G
Joe Fortunato - LB
Bill George - LB
Larry Glueck - DB
Bobby Joe Green - K
Bob Jencks - E
John Johnson - DT
Stan Jones - DT
Ted Karras - G
Bob Kilcullen - DE
Rich Kreitling - E
Roger LeClerc - LB
Herman Lee - T
Earl Leggett - DT
Andy Livingston - HB
Joe Marconi - FB
Billy Martin - E
Billy Martin - HB
Bennie McRae - DB
Johnny Morris - FL
Larry Morris - LB
Ed O'Bradovich - DE
Richie Petitbon - DB
Jim Purnell - LB
Mike Pyle - C
Mike Rabold - G
Mike Reilly - LB
John Sisk - DB
Rosey Taylor - DB
Billy Wade - QB
Bob Wetoska - T
Dave Whitsell - HB

1964 Cleveland

Walter Beach - DB
Larry Benz - DB
Ed Bettridge - LB
Johnny Brewer - E
Jim Brown - FB
John Brown - T
Mike Bundra - DT
Lowell Caylor - DB
Monte Clark - T
Gary Collins - FL
Vince Costello - LB
Ross Fichtner - DB
Galen Fiss - LB
Bobby Franklin - DB
Bob Gain - DT
Bill Glass - DE
Ernie Green - HB
Lou Groza - K
Gene Hickerson - G
Jim Houston - LB
Tom Hutchinson - E
Jim Kanicki - DT
Leroy Kelly - HB
Mike Lucci - LB
Clifton McNeil - FL
Dale Memmelaar - G
Dick Modzelewski - DT
John Morrow - C
Jim Ninowski - QB
Frank Parker - DT
Bernie Parrish - DB
Dave Raimey - DB
Walter Roberts - FL
Frank Ryan - QB
Charlie Scales - FB
Dick Schafrath - T
Stan Sczurek - LB
Roger Shoals - G
Paul Warfield - E
Paul Wiggin - DE
Sid Williams - DE
John Wooten - G

1964 Dallas

George Andrie - DE
Don Bishop - DB
Jim Boeke - T
Amos Bullocks - HB
Frank Clarke - FL
Jim Colvin - DT
Mike Connelly - C
Buddy Dial - FL
Perry Lee Dunn - HB
Dave Edwards - LB
Lee Folkins - E
Bill Frank - T
Bob Fry - T
Mike Gaechter - DB
Pete Gent - E
Cornell Green - DB
Harold Hays - LB
Chuck Howley - LB
Joe Bob Isbell - G
Lee Roy Jordan - LB
Jake Kupp - G
Bob Lilly - DT
Tony Liscio - T
Warren Livingston - DB
Billy Lothridge - QB
Dave Manders - C
Amos Marsh - HB
Tommy McDonald - FL
Don Meredith - QB
Pettis Norman - E
Don Perkins - FB
Mel Renfro - DB
Jimmy Ridlon - DB
John Roach - QB
Ray Schoenke - T
Jim Ray Smith - G
Larry Stephens - DE
Jim Stiger - FB
Jerry Tubbs - LB
Dick Van Raaphorst - K
Maury Youmans - DE

1964 Detroit

Terry Barr - FL
Pat Batten - FB
Roger Brown - DT
Ernie Clark - LB
Gail Cogdill - E
Dick Compton - HB
Dennis Gaubatz - LB
Jim Gibbons - E
Sonny Gibbs - QB
John Gonzaga - G
John Gordy - G
Wally Hilgenberg - LB
Alex Karras - DT
Roger LaLonde - DT
Night Train Lane - DB
Yale Lary - DB
Dick LeBeau - DB
Monte Lee - LB
Dan Lewis - HB
Gary Lowe - HB
Bruce Maher - DB
Darris McCord - DE
Hugh McElhenny - HB
Hugh McInnis - E
Earl Morrall - QB
Nick Pietrosante - FB
Milt Plum - QB
Bill Quinlan - DE
Wayne Rasmussen - DB
Nick Ryder - FB
Daryl Sanders - T
Joe Schmidt - LB
Bob Scholtz - T
Jim Simon - G
J.D. Smith - T
Pat Studstill - FL
Bobby Thompson - DB
Wayne Walker - LB
Tom Watkins - HB
Warren Wells - E
Bob Whitlow - C
Sam Williams - DE

1964 Green Bay

Herb Adderley - DB
Lionel Aldridge - DE
Ken Bowman - C
Zeke Bratkowski - QB
Gene Breen - LB
Tom Brown - DB
Lee Roy Caffey - LB
Tommy Crutcher - FB
Dan Currie - LB
Willie Davis - DE
Boyd Dowler - FL
Marv Fleming - E
Forrest Gregg - T
Hank Gremminger - DB
Dan Grimm - G
Dave Hanner - DT
Doug Hart - DB
Paul Hornung - HB
Bob Jeter - E
Henry Jordan - DT
Ron Kostelnik - DT
Jerry Kramer - G
Ron Kramer - E
Bob Long - FL
Norm Masters - T
John McDowell - T
Max McGee - E
Tom Moore - HB
Ray Nitschke - LB
Jerry Norton - DB
Elijah Pitts - HB
Dave Robinson - LB
Bob Skoronski - C
Bart Starr - QB
Jim Taylor - FB
Fuzzy Thurston - G
Lloyd Voss - DE
Jesse Whittenton - DB
Willie Wood - DB
Steve Wright - T

1964 LA Rams

Duane Allen - E
Terry Baker - HB
Dick Bass - FB
Willie Brown - FL
Frank Budka - DB
Joe Carollo - T
Don Chuy - G
Charley Cowan - G
Lindon Crow - DB
Carroll Dale - E
Roger Davis - G
Roman Gabriel - QB
Bruce Gossett - K
Rosey Grier - DT
Marv Harris - LB
Mike Henry - LB
Art Hunter - C
Deacon Jones - DE
Les Josephson - FB
Gary Larsen - DT
Cliff Livingston - LB
Lamar Lundy - DE
Aaron Martin - DB
Marlin McKeever - E
Ed Meador - DB
Bill Munson - QB
Merlin Olsen - DT
Jack Pardee - LB
Jim Phillips - FL
Bucky Pope - FL
Jerry Richardson - DB
Joe Scibelli - G
Carver Shannon - HB
Bobby Smith - DB
Billy Truax - E
Frank Varrichione - T
Danny Villanueva - K
Andy Von Sonn - LB
Joe Wendryhoski - C
Fred Whittingham - G
Ben Wilson - HB

1964 Minnesota

Grady Alderman - T
Hal Bedsole - E
Larry Bowie - G
Charley Britt - DB
Bill Brown - FB
Mike Bundra - DT
Bill Butler - HB
Ken Byers - G
Lee Calland - DB
John Campbell - LB
Fred Cox - K
Ted Dean - HB
Bob Denton - DE
Paul Dickson - DT
Carl Eller - DE
Paul Flatley - E
Tom Hall - FL
Rip Hawkins - LB
Bill Jobko - LB
Karl Kassulke - DB
John Kirby - LB
Bob Lacey - E
Darrell Lester - FB
Errol Linden - T
Jim Marshall - DE
Tommy Mason - HB
Bill McWatters - FB
Tom Michel - HB
Dave O'Brien - DT
Jim Prestel - DT
Palmer Pyle - G
Jerry Reichow - E
George Rose - DB
Ed Sharockman - DB
Howard Simpson - DE
Gordon Smith - E
Milt Sunde - G
Bill Swain - LB
Fran Tarkenton - QB
Mick Tingelhoff - C
Ron Vander Kelen - QB
Larry Vargo - E
Bobby Walden - K
Roy Winston - LB

1964 NY Giants

Roger Anderson - T
Erich Barnes - DB
Bookie Bolin - G
Rosey Brown - T
Ken Byers - G
Don Chandler - K
Clarence Childs - HB
John Contoulis - DT
Tom Costello - LB
Bob Crespino - E
Darrell Dess - G
Frank Gifford - FL
Jerry Hillebrand - LB
Lane Howell - T
Dick James - DB
Homer Jones - FL
Jim Katcavage - DE
Greg Larson - C
Frank Lasky - T
John LoVetere - DT
Dick Lynch - DB
Max Messner - LB
Jim Moran - DT
Joe Morrison - HB
Andy Nelson - DB
R.C. Owens - FL
Jimmy Patton - DB
Dick Pesonen - DB
Andy Robustelli - DE
Henry Schichtle - QB
Tom Scott - LB
Del Shofner - E
Lou Slaby - LB
Jack Stroud - T
Andy Stynchula - DT
Bob Taylor - DE
Aaron Thomas - FL
Steve Thurlow - HB
Y. A. Tittle - QB
Mickey Walker - C
Allan Webb - DB
Alex Webster - FB
Ernie Wheelwright - FB
Bill Winter - LB
Gary Wood - QB

1964 Philadelphia

Sam Baker - K
Maxie Baughan - LB
Ed Blaine - G
Bob Brown - T
Timmy Brown - HB
Don Burroughs - DB
Pete Case - G
Jack Concannon - QB
Claude Crabb - FL
Irv Cross - DB
Roger Gill - HB
Glenn Glass - DB
Ron Goodwin - E
Dave Graham - T
Earl Gros - FB
Riley Gunnels - DE
Ralph Heck - LB
King Hill - QB
Lynn Hoyem - C
Don Hultz - DE
Ed Khayat - DT
Izzy Lang - FB
Dave Lloyd - LB
Red Mack - FL
Ollie Matson - HB
John Meyers - DT
Mike Morgan - LB
Floyd Peters - DT
Ray Poage - E
Nate Ramsey - DB
Pete Retzlaff - E
Bobby Richards - DE
Jim Ringo - C
Joe Scarpati - DB
Jim Schrader - C
Jim Skaggs - T
Ralph Smith - DB
Norm Snead - QB
George Tarasovic - DE
Don Thompson - DE
Tom Woodeshick - FB

1964 Pittsburgh

John Baker - DE
Gary Ballman - E
Charlie Bradshaw - T
Jim Bradshaw - DB
Ed Brown - QB
John Burrell - E
Mike Clark - K
Willie Daniel - DB
Dick Haley - DB
Bob Harrison - LB
Urban Henry - DT
Chuck Hinton - DT
Dick Hoak - HB
Ed Holler - LB
Dan James - T
John Johnson - FB
Jim Kelly - E
Brady Keys - DB
Phil King - HB
Joe Krupa - DT
Dan LaRose - DE
Ray Lemek - G
Chuck Logan - E
Ray Mansfield - DT
Paul Martha - E
Ben McGee - DE
Max Messner - LB
Bill Nelsen - QB
Terry Nofsinger - QB
Buzz Nutter - C
Clarence Peaks - FB
Myron Pottios - LB
John Powers - E
Mike Sandusky - G
Theron Sapp - HB
Bill Saul - LB
Bob Schmitz - LB
Bob Sherman - DB
Robert Soleau - LB
Ron Stehouwer - G
Clendon Thomas - DB
Tommy Wade - QB
Marv Woodson - HB

1964 St. Louis

Taz Anderson - E
Monk Bailey - DB
Jim Bakken - K
Don Brumm - DE
Jimmy Burson - DB
Joe Childress - HB
Bobby Joe Conrad - FL
Ed Cook - G
Willis Crenshaw - FB
John Crow - FB
Bob DeMarco - C
Pat Fischer - DB
Billy Gambrell - E
Prentice Gautt - FB
Irv Goode - G
Ken Gray - G
Mal Hammack - LB
Jimmy Hill - DB
Buddy Humphrey - QB
Charley Johnson - QB
Bill Koman - LB
Ken Kortas - DT
Ernie McMillan - T
Dave Meggyesy - LB
Dale Meinert - LB
Luke Owens - DT
Bob Paremore - HB
Sonny Randle - E
Tom Redmond - DE
Bob Reynolds - T
Joe Robb - DE
Marion Rushing - LB
Sam Silas - DT
Jackie Smith - E
Rick Sortun - G
Larry Stallings - LB
Jerry Stovall - DB
Bill Thornton - FB
Herschel Turner - T
Chuck Walker - DE
Larry Wilson - DB

1964 San Francisco

Kermit Alexander - DB
Bruce Bosley - C
John Brodie - QB
Bernie Casey - FL
Daniel Colchico - DE
Bill Cooper - LB
Tommy Davis - K
Floyd Dean - LB
Leon Donohue - G
Mike Dowdle - LB
Matt Hazeltine - LB
Jim Johnson - DB
Rudy Johnson - HB
Billy Kilmer - HB
Elbert Kimbrough - DB
Dave Kopay - HB
Charlie Krueger - DT
Roland Lakes - DT
Gary Lewis - FB
Mike Lind - FB
Don Lisbon - HB
Mike Magac - G
Kay McFarland - E
Jerry Mertens - DB
Dale Messer - FL
Clark Miller - DE
George Mira - QB
Frank Morze - C
Howard Mudd - G
Dave Parks - E
Ed Pine - LB
Bob Poole - E
Walt Rock - T
Len Rohde - T
Karl Rubke - DE
Ben Scotti - DB
Chuck Sieminski - DT
J. D. Smith - FB
Monty Stickles - E
John Thomas - G
Dave Wilcox - LB
Abe Woodson - DB

1964 Washington

Pervis Atkins - HB
Steve Barnett - T
Don Bosseler - FB
Rod Breedlove - LB
Preston Carpenter - E
Jimmy Carr - LB
Ozzie Clay - FL
Angelo Coia - E
Fred Hageman - C
Len Hauss - C
Joe Hernandez - FL
Sam Huff - LB
George Izo - QB
Sonny Jurgensen - QB
Carl Kammerer - DE
Paul Krause - DB
J. W. Lockett - FB
Jim Martin - K
Riley Mattson - T
Bobby Mitchell - FL
John Nisby - G
Fran O'Brien - T
John Paluck - DE
Bob Pellegrini - LB
Vince Promuto - G
John Reger - LB
Pat Richter - E
Joe Rutgens - DT
Johnny Sample - DB
Lonnie Sanders - DB
George Seals - G
Dick Shiner - QB
Jim Shorter - DB
Ron Snidow - DE
Jim Steffen - DB
Charley Taylor - HB
Bob Toneff - DT
Tom Tracy - HB
Tom Walters - DB
Fred Williams - DT

1964 AFL

1964 Boston

Tom Addison - LB
Houston Antwine - DT
Nick Buoniconti - LB
Ron Burton - HB
Gino Cappelletti - E
Dave Cloutier - DB
Jim Colclough - FL
Jim Crawford - FB
Bob Dee - DE
Jerry DeLucca - DT
Mike Dukes - LB
Larry Eisenhauer - DE
Lonnie Farmer - LB
Dick Felt - DB
J.D. Garrett - HB
Larry Garron - FB
Art Graham - E
Ron Hall - DB
Jim Hunt - DE
Charley Long - G
Don McKinnon - C
Jon Morris - C
Billy Neighbors - G
Don Oakes - T
Ross O'Hanley - DB
Babe Parilli - QB
Jess Richardson - DT
Tony Romeo - E
Jack Rudolph - LB
Bob Schmidt - T
Chuck Shonta - DB
Al Snyder - FL
Thomas Stephens - E
Len St. Jean - DE
Dave Watson - G
Don Webb - DB
Bob Yates - T
Tom Yewcic - QB

1964 Buffalo

Ray Abruzzese - DB
Joe Auer - HB
Stew Barber - T
Glenn Bass - E
Al Bemiller - G
Butch Byrd - DB
Wray Carlton - HB
Hagood Clarke - DB
Walt Cudzik - C
Tom Day - DE
Ollie Dobbins - DB
Elbert Dubenion - FL
Jim Dunaway - DT
Booker Edgerson - DB
George Flint - G
Cookie Gilchrist - FB
Pete Gogolak - K
Bill Groman - E
Dick Hudson - T
Harry Jacobs - LB
Tom Keating - DT
Jack Kemp - QB
Daryle Lamonica - QB
Paul Maguire - LB
Ron McDole - DE
Dudley Meredith - DT
Joe O'Donnell - T
Hatch Rosdahl - DT
Willie Ross - FB
Ed Rutkowski - FL
George Saimes - DB
Tom Sestak - DT
Billy Shaw - G
Bobby Smith - HB
Mike Stratton - LB
Eugene Sykes - DB
Jack Tracy - LB
Ernie Warlick - E
Charley Warner - DB

1964 Denver

Billy Atkins - DB
Frank Atkinson - DT
Ernie Barnes - G
Odell Barry - E
Norm Bass - DB
Willie Brown - DB
Ed Cooke - DE
Eldon Danenhauer - T
Al Denson - FL
Hewritt Dixon - HB
Tom Erlandson - LB
Stan Fanning - DE
Jim Fraser - LB
Goose Gonsoulin - DB
John Griffin - DB
Dick Guesman - DT
Gary Henson - E
Jerry Hopkins - LB
Ray Jacobs - DT
Chuck Janerette - DT
Tom Janik - DB
Billy Joe - FB
Larry Jordan - LB
Ray Kubala - C
Ike Lassiter - DE
Jacky Lee - QB
Marv Matuszak - LB
Bob McCullough - G
John McGeever - DB
Jim McMillin - DB
Gene Mingo - HB
Charley Mitchell - HB
Leroy Moore - DE
Tom Nomina - G
Harold Olson - T
Jim Perkins - T
Jim Price - LB
Bob Scarpitto - FL
Don Shackelford - G
Mickey Slaughter - QB
Matt Snorton - E
Donnie Stone - FB
Jerry Sturm - C
Lionel Taylor - E
Willie West - DB
Jim Wright - DB

1964 Houston

Scott Appleton - DT
Johnny Baker - E
Sonny Bishop - G
George Blanda - QB
Sid Blanks - HB
Danny Brabham - LB
Ode Burrell - HB
Doug Cline - LB
Dobie Craig - E
Gary Cutsinger - DE
Willard Dewveall - E
Stan Fanning - DE
Staley Faulkner - T
Don Floyd - DE
Jerry Fowler - T
Charley Frazier - E
Willie Frazier - E
John Frongillo - G
Fred Glick - DB
Tom Goode - C
Charley Hennigan - FL
W.K. Hicks - DB
Dalton Hoffman - FB
Ed Husmann - DT
Bobby Jackson - FB
Bobby Jancik - FL
Pete Jaquess - DB
Bob Kelly - T
Jack Klotz - T
Bud McFadin - DT
Bob McLeod - E
Benny Nelson - DB
Jim Norton - DB
Sammy Odom - LB
Larry Onesti - LB
Charlie Rieves - LB
Dave Smith - FB
Walt Suggs - T
Bob Talamini - G
Charley Tolar - FB
Don Trull - QB
John Wittenborn - G

1964 Kansas City

Fred Arbanas - E
Pete Beathard - QB
Bobby Bell - DE
Denny Biodrowski - G
Mel Branch - DE
Tommy Brooker - E
Buck Buchanan - DT
Ed Budde - G
Chris Burford - E
Reggie Carolan - E
Bert Coan - HB
Walt Corey - LB
Jerry Cornelison - T
Len Dawson - QB
Curt Farrier - DT
Jon Gilliam - C
Dave Grayson - DB
Abner Haynes - HB
Sherrill Headrick - LB
Dave Hill - T
Mack Lee Hill - FB
E.J. Holub - LB
Bobby Hunt - DB
Frank Jackson - FL
Ed Lothamer - DE
John Maczuzak - DT
Jerry Mays - DT
Curtis McClinton - FB
Curt Merz - G
Willie Mitchell - DB
Bobby Ply - DB
Al Reynolds - G
Johnny Robinson - DB
Hatch Rosdahl - DT
Jack Spikes - FB
Smokey Stover - LB
Jim Tyrer - T
Charley Warner - DB
Eddie Wilson - QB
Jerrel Wilson - HB
Duane Wood - DB

1964 NY Jets

Bill Baird - HB
Ralph Baker - LB
Ed Cummings - LB
Sam DeLuca - G
Jim Evans - FL
Dan Ficca - G
Larry Grantham - LB
Gene Heeter - E
Dave Herman - G
Winston Hill - T
Gordy Holz - DT
Mike Hudock - C
Curley Johnson - HB
Mark Johnston - DB
Al Lawson - FL
Pete Liske - DB
Dee Mackey - E
Bill Mathis - HB
Don Maynard - FL
Bob McAdams - DT
Jim McCusker - T
Wahoo McDaniel - LB
Bill Pashe - DB
Dainard Paulson - DB
Pete Perreault - G
Gerry Philbin - DE
Sherman Plunkett - T
Bill Rademacher - DB
Paul Rochester - DT
Bob Rowley - LB
John Schmitt - C
Mark Smolinski - FB
Matt Snell - FB
Marshall Starks - DB
Mike Taliaferro - QB
LaVerne Torczon - DE
Jim Turner - K
Bake Turner - E
Vince Turner - DB
Clyde Washington - DB
Bob Watters - DE
Willie West - DB
Bert Wilder - DE
Dick Wood - QB

1964 Oakland

Dalva Allen - DE
Jan Barrett - E
Dan Birdwell - DT
Doug Brown - DT
Bill Budness - LB
Billy Cannon - FB
Dan Conners - LB
Dave Costa - DT
Clem Daniels - HB
Ben Davidson - DE
Cotton Davidson - QB
Bo Dickinson - FB
Tom Flores - QB
Claude Gibson - DB
Fred Gillett - E
Louis Guy - DB
Wayne Hawkins - G
Ken Herock - E
Bobby Jackson - FB
Proverb Jacobs - T
Jon Jelacic - DE
Mark Johnston - DB
Dick Klein - T
Joe Krakoski - DB
Archie Matsos - LB
Jim McMillin - DB
Mike Mercer - K
Bill Miller - E
Gene Mingo - HB
Rex Mirich - DT
Bob Mischak - G
Tommy Morrow - DB
Jim Norris - DT
Clancy Osborne - LB
Jim Otto - C
Art Powell - E
Warren Powers - DB
Ken Rice - T
Bo Roberson - FL
Glenn Shaw - FB
Jackie Simpson - LB
Howie Williams - DB
Fred Williamson - DB
J.R. Williamson - LB
Frank Youso - T

1964 San Diego

Ben Agajanian - K
Chuck Allen - LB
Lance Alworth - FL
George Blair - DB
Frank Buncom - LB
Ron Carpenter - LB
Speedy Duncan - DB
Earl Faison - DE
Kenny Graham - DB
George Gross - DT
Sam Gruneisen - G
John Hadl - QB
Dick Harris - DB
Bob Horton - LB
Emil Karas - LB
Keith Kinderman - FB
Gary Kirner - T
Dave Kocourek - E
Ernie Ladd - DT
Bobby Lane - LB
Keith Lincoln - FB
Paul Lowe - HB
Jacque MacKinnon - FB
Lloyd McCoy - G
Gerry McDougall - FB
Charlie McNeil - DB
Mario Mendez - HB
Bob Mitinger - DE
Ron Mix - T
Fred Moore - DT
Don Norton - E
Ernie Park - T
Bob Petrich - DE
Jerry Robinson - E
Don Rogers - C
Tobin Rote - QB
Henry Schmidt - DT
Pat Shea - G
Walt Sweeney - G
Herb Travenio - K
Jimmy Warren - DB
Dick Westmoreland - DB
Bud Whitehead - FL
Ernie Wright - T

1965 NFL

1965 Baltimore

Raymond Berry - E
Bobby Boyd - DB
Ordell Braase - DE
Ed Brown - QB
Jackie Burkett - LB
Gary Cuozzo - QB
Mike Curtis - FB
Ted Davis - LB
Bobby Felts - HB
Dennis Gaubatz - LB
Tom Gilburg - T
Wendell Harris - DB
Alex Hawkins - FL
Alvin Haymond - DB
Jerry Hill - FB
Roy Hilton - DE
Monte Lee - LB
Jerry Logan - DB
Tony Lorick - FB
Lenny Lyles - DB
John Mackey - TE
Tom Matte - QB
Lou Michaels - DE
Fred Miller - DT
Lenny Moore - HB
Buzz Nutter - C
Jimmy Orr - FL
Jim Parker - G
Neal Petties - FL
George Preas - T
Guy Reese - DT
Glenn Ressler - C
Willie Richardson - FL
Alex Sandusky - G
Don Shinnick - LB
Billy Ray Smith Sr. - DT
Steve Stonebreaker - LB
Mike Strofolino - LB
Dan Sullivan - G
Dick Szymanski - C
Johnny Unitas - QB
Bob Vogel - T
Jim Welch - DB
Butch Wilson - TE

1965 Chi. Bears

Jon Arnett - HB
Doug Atkins - DE
Charlie Bivins - HB
Rudy Bukich - QB
Ronnie Bull - HB
Dick Butkus - LB
Jim Cadile - G
James Caroline - DB
Mike Ditka - TE
Dick Evey - DE
Joe Fortunato - LB
Bill George - LB
Larry Glueck - DB
Dick Gordon - E
Bobby Joe Green - K
John Johnson - DT
Jim Jones - E
Stan Jones - DT
Bob Kilcullen - DE
Ralph Kurek - FB
Roger LeClerc - LB
Herman Lee - T
Dick Leeuwenburg - T
Earl Leggett - DT
Andy Livingston - FB
Joe Marconi - FB
Billy Martin - TE
Bennie McRae - DB
Johnny Morris - FL
Larry Morris - LB
Dennis Murphy - DT
Ed O'Bradovich - DE
Richie Petitbon - DB
Jim Purnell - LB
Mike Pyle - C
Mike Rabold - G
Mike Reilly - LB
Gale Sayers - HB
George Seals - DT
Ron Smith - DB
Rosey Taylor - DB
Billy Wade - QB
Bob Wetoska - T
Dave Whitsell - DB

1965 Cleveland

Erich Barnes - DB
Walter Beach - DB
Larry Benz - DB
Johnny Brewer - TE
Jim Brown - FB
John Brown - T
Jamie Caleb - FB
Monte Clark - T
Gary Collins - FL
Vince Costello - LB
Ross Fichtner - DB
Galen Fiss - LB
Bobby Franklin - DB
Jim Garcia - DE
Bill Glass - DE
Ernie Green - HB
Lou Groza - K
Gene Hickerson - G
Jim Houston - LB
Mike Howell - DB
Tom Hutchinson - E
Walter Johnson - DT
Jim Kanicki - DT
Leroy Kelly - HB
Dale Lindsey - LB
Clifton McNeil - FL
Dale Memmelaar - G
Dick Modzelewski - DT
John Morrow - C
Jim Ninowski - QB
Bernie Parrish - DB
Walter Roberts - E
Frank Ryan - QB
Charlie Scales - FB
Dick Schafrath - T
Stan Sczurek - LB
Ralph Smith - TE
Paul Warfield - E
Paul Wiggin - DE
Sid Williams - LB
John Wooten - G

1965 Dallas

George Andrie - DE
Don Bishop - DB
Jim Boeke - T
Frank Clarke - E
Jim Colvin - DT
Mike Connelly - G
Buddy Dial - FL
Leon Donohue - G
Perry Lee Dunn - HB
Dave Edwards - LB
Mike Gaechter - DB
Pete Gent - FL
Cornell Green - DB
Bob Hayes - E
Harold Hays - LB
Chuck Howley - LB
Mitch Johnson - G
Lee Roy Jordan - LB
Jake Kupp - G
Bob Lilly - DT
Warren Livingston - DB
Obert Logan - DB
Dave Manders - C
Don Meredith - QB
Craig Morton - QB
Ralph Neely - T
Pettis Norman - TE
Don Perkins - FB
Garry Porterfield - DE
Jethro Pugh - DE
Dan Reeves - HB
Mel Renfro - HB
Jerry Rhome - QB
Colin Ridgway - K
J. D. Smith - FB
Larry Stephens - DT
Jim Stiger - FB
Don Talbert - T
Jerry Tubbs - LB
Danny Villanueva - K
Russell Wayt - LB
A.D. Whitfield - FB
Maury Youmans - DE

1965 Detroit

Terry Barr - FL
Roger Brown - DT
Ernie Clark - LB
Gail Cogdill - E
Bobby Felts - HB
Ed Flanagan - C
Jim Gibbons - TE
John Gonzaga - G
John Gordy - G
Larry Hand - DE
John Henderson - E
Wally Hilgenberg - LB
Jimmy Hill - DB
George Izo - QB
Alex Karras - DT
Ted Karras - G
Jim Kearney - DB
Ron Kramer - TE
Night Train Lane - DB
Dick LeBeau - DB
Joe Don Looney - HB
Mike Lucci - LB
Bruce Maher - DB
Amos Marsh - HB
Darris McCord - DE
Tom Myers - QB
Tom Nowatzke - FB
Nick Pietrosante - FB
Milt Plum - QB
Wayne Rasmussen - DB
Jerry Rush - DT
Daryl Sanders - T
Joe Schmidt - LB
Roger Shoals - T
Jim Simon - G
Bobby Smith - DB
Pat Studstill - FL
Bobby Thompson - DB
Tom Vaughn - DB
Wayne Walker - LB
Tom Watkins - HB
Bob Whitlow - C
Sam Williams - DE

1965 Green Bay

Herb Adderley - DB
Lionel Aldridge - DE
Bill Anderson - TE
Ken Bowman - C
Zeke Bratkowski - QB
Tom Brown - DB
Lee Roy Caffey - LB
Don Chandler - K
Dennis Claridge - QB
Junior Coffey - HB
Tommy Crutcher - LB
Bill Curry - C
Carroll Dale - FL
Willie Davis - DE
Boyd Dowler - E
Marv Fleming - TE
Forrest Gregg - G
Hank Gremminger - DB
Dan Grimm - G
Doug Hart - DB
Paul Hornung - HB
Allen Jacobs - FB
Bob Jeter - DB
Henry Jordan - DT
Ron Kostelnik - DT
Jerry Kramer - G
Bob Long - FL
Bud Marshall - DT
Max McGee - E
Tom Moore - HB
Ray Nitschke - LB
Elijah Pitts - HB
Dave Robinson - LB
Bob Skoronski - T
Bart Starr - QB
Jim Taylor - FB
Fuzzy Thurston - G
Lloyd Voss - DE
Willie Wood - DB
Steve Wright - T

1965 LA Rams

Terry Baker - HB
Dick Bass - FB
Fred Brown - LB
Willie Brown - FL
Mac Byrd - LB
Joe Carollo - T
Don Chuy - G
Charley Cowan - T
Dan Currie - LB
Roman Gabriel - QB
Bruce Gossett - K
Rosey Grier - DT
Tony Guillory - LB
Steve Heckard - E
Ken Iman - C
Deacon Jones - DE
Les Josephson - HB
Jon Kilgore - K
Chuck Lamson - DB
Cliff Livingston - LB
Billy Lothridge - K
Lamar Lundy - DE
Frank Marchlewski - C
Aaron Martin - DB
Tommy McDonald - FL
Danny McIlhany - DB
Marlin McKeever - TE
Ed Meador - DB
Frank Molden - DT
Bill Munson - QB
Merlin Olsen - DT
Roger Pillath - T
Tim Powell - DE
Jerry Richardson - DB
Joe Scibelli - G
Bobby Smith - DB
Ron Smith - QB
Jack Snow - E
Jim Stiger - FB
Mike Strofolino - LB
Billy Truax - TE
Frank Varrichione - T
Joe Wendryhoski - C
Clancy Williams - HB
Ben Wilson - FB
Doug Woodlief - LB

1965 Minnesota

Grady Alderman - T
Billy Barnes - HB
Hal Bedsole - TE
Bob Berry - QB
Larry Bowie - G
Bill Brown - FB
Ken Byers - G
Lee Calland - DB
Fred Cox - K
Paul Dickson - DT
Carl Eller - DE
Paul Flatley - E
Tom Hall - E
Rip Hawkins - LB
Gary Hill - DB
Dick James - HB
Bill Jobko - LB
Jeff Jordan - DB
Karl Kassulke - DB
Phil King - HB
John Kirby - LB
Gary Larsen - DT
Errol Linden - T
Earsell Mackbee - DB
Jim Marshall - DE
Tommy Mason - HB
Dave Osborn - HB
Jim Phillips - FL
Jim Prestel - DT
Lance Rentzel - HB
George Rose - DB
Ed Sharockman - DB
Gordon Smith - E
Milt Sunde - C
Archie Sutton - T
Fran Tarkenton - QB
Mick Tingelhoff - C
Ron Vander Kelen - QB
Larry Vargo - DB
Bobby Walden - K
Lonnie Warwick - LB
Roy Winston - LB
Jim Young - HB

1965 NY Giants

Ed Adamchik - C
Roger Anderson - DT
Bookie Bolin - G
Rosey Brown - T
Mike Bundra - DT
Henry Carr - DB
Jim Carroll - LB
Pete Case - G
Clarence Childs - DB
Glen Condren - DE
Tom Costello - LB
Bob Crespino - TE
Roger Davis - G
Rosey Davis - DE
Tucker Frederickson
Jerry Hillebrand - LB
Homer Jones - FL
Jim Katcavage - DE
Ernie Koy - HB
Bob Lacey - E
Roger LaLonde - DT
Greg Larson - C
Frank Lasky - T
Carl Lockhart - DB
John LoVetere - DT
Dick Lynch - DB
John McDowell - T
Chuck Mercein - FB
Earl Morrall - QB
Joe Morrison - FL
Dave O'Brien - DT
Jimmy Patton - DB
Smith Reed - HB
Bob Scholtz - C
Del Shofner - E
Lou Slaby - DT
Andy Stynchula - DE
Bill Swain - LB
Aaron Thomas - FL
Steve Thurlow - HB
Bob Timberlake - QB
Olen Underwood - LB
Mickey Walker - G
Allan Webb - DB
Ernie Wheelwright - FB
Willie Williams - DB
Gary Wood - QB

1965 Philadelphia

Sam Baker - K
Maxie Baughan - LB
Ed Blaine - G
Bob Brown - T
Timmy Brown - HB
Jack Concannon - QB
Claude Crabb - FL
Bill Cronin - TE
Irv Cross - DB
Roger Gill - TE
Glenn Glass - FL
Ron Goodwin - E
Dave Graham - T
Earl Gros - FB
Ralph Heck - LB
Fred Hill - E
King Hill - QB
Lane Howell - T
Lynn Hoyem - C
Don Hultz - LB
Jim Kelly - TE
Ed Khayat - DT
Izzy Lang - FB
Dave Lloyd - LB
Ollie Matson - HB
John Meyers - DT
Mike Morgan - LB
Al Nelson - DB
Jim Nettles - DB
Floyd Peters - DT
Ray Poage - E
Nate Ramsey - DB
Dave Recher - C
Pete Retzlaff - TE
Bobby Richards - DE
Jim Ringo - C
Joe Scarpati - HB
Bob Shann - DB
Jim Skaggs - T
Norm Snead - QB
George Tarasovic - DE
Harold Wells - LB
Erwin Will - DT
Tom Woodeshick - FB

1965 Pittsburgh

Ed Adamchik - C
Duane Allen - E
John Baker - DE
Gary Ballman - E
Charlie Bradshaw - T
Jim Bradshaw - DB
Rod Breedlove - LB
Gene Breen - LB
Ed Brown - QB
Cannonball Butler - HB
John Campbell - LB
Mike Clark - K
Willie Daniel - DB
Lee Folkins - TE
Riley Gunnels - DT
Ken Henson - C
John Hilton - TE
Chuck Hinton - DT
Dick Hoak - HB
Bob Hohn - DB
Art Hunter - C
Dan James - T
Roy Jefferson - E
John Johnson - FB
Brady Keys - DB
Ken Kortas - DT
Frank Lambert - K
Ray Lemek - G
Mike Lind - FB
Red Mack - FL
Mike Magac - G
Fran Mallick - DT
Ray Mansfield - DT
Paul Martha - HB
Ben McGee - DE
Max Messner - LB
Bill Nelsen - QB
Bob Nichols - T
Clarence Peaks - FB
Ed Pine - LB
Myron Pottios - LB
John Powers - LB
Mike Sandusky - G
Theron Sapp - FB
Bob Schmitz - LB
Bob Sherman - DB
Jerry Simmons - E
Clendon Thomas - DB
Tommy Wade - QB
Marv Woodson - DB

1965 St. Louis

Mike Alford - C
Monk Bailey - DB
Jim Bakken - K
Don Brumm - DE
Jimmy Burson - DB
Joe Childress - FB
Bobby Joe Conrad - FL

Ed Cook - G
Willis Crenshaw - FB
Bob DeMarco - C
Pat Fischer - DB
Billy Gambrell - E
Prentice Gautt - HB
Irv Goode - G
Ken Gray - G
Mal Hammack - TE
Buddy Humphrey - QB
Charley Johnson - QB
Bill Koman - LB
Chuck Logan - TE
Ernie McMillan - T
Ed McQuarters - DT
Dave Meggyesy - LB
Dale Meinert - LB
Mike Melinkovich - DE
Terry Nofsinger - QB
Ray Ogden - E
Luke Owens - DT
Sonny Randle - E
Tom Redmond - DE
Bob Reynolds - T
Joe Robb - DE
Marion Rushing - LB
Sam Silas - DT
Carl Silvestri - DB
Dave Simmons - LB
Jackie Smith - TE
Rick Sortun - G
Larry Stallings - LB
Jerry Stovall - DB
Bill Thornton - FB
Bill Triplett - HB
Herschel Turner - T
Chuck Walker - DT
Larry Wilson - DB
Abe Woodson - DB

1965 San Francisco

Kermit Alexander - DB
Ed Beard - LB
Bruce Bosley - C
John Brodie - QB
Vern Burke - E
Bernie Casey - FL
Joe Cerne - C
Jack Chapple - LB
Daniel Colchico - DE
John Crow - HB
Tommy Davis - K
Floyd Dean - LB
George Donnelly - DB
Mike Dowdle - LB
Bob Harrison - LB
Matt Hazeltine - LB
Jim Johnson - DB
Rudy Johnson - HB
Elbert Kimbrough - DB
Dave Kopay - HB
Charlie Krueger - DT
Roland Lakes - DT
Dan LaRose - DE
Gary Lewis - FB
Kay McFarland - E
Jerry Mertens - DB
Dale Messer - FL
Clark Miller - DE
George Mira - QB
Howard Mudd - G
Jim Norton - T
Dave Parks - E
Bob Poole - TE
Walt Rock - T
Len Rohde - T
Karl Rubke - DE
Chuck Sieminski - DT
Monty Stickles - TE
Wayne Swinford - DB
John Thomas - G
Dave Wilcox - LB
Ken Willard - FB
Jim Wilson - G

1965 Washington

Willie Adams - LB
Pervis Atkins - HB
Bob Briggs - FB
Preston Carpenter - E
Jimmy Carr - LB
Rick Casares - FB
Angelo Coia - E
Don Croftcheck - G
Dave Crossan - C
Darrell Dess - G
Chris Hanburger - LB
Rickie Harris - DB
Len Hauss - C
Sam Huff - LB
George Hughley - HB
Billy Hunter - DB
Bob Jencks - E
Sonny Jurgensen - QB
Carl Kammerer - DE
Paul Krause - FL
Dan Lewis - HB
Fred Mazurek - DB
Bobby Mitchell - FL
Fran O'Brien - T
John Paluck - DE
Bob Pellegrini - LB
Vince Promuto - G
Bill Quinlan - DE

Robert Reed - G
John Reger - LB
Pat Richter - E
Joe Rutgens - DT
Johnny Sample - DB
Lonnie Sanders - DB
John Seedborg - K
Dick Shiner - QB
Jim Shorter - DB
Jerry Smith - TE
Ron Snidow - DE
Jim Snowden - DE
Jim Steffen - DB
Charley Taylor - HB
Tom Walters - DB
Fred Williams - DT

1965 AFL

1965 Boston

Tom Addison - LB
Houston Antwine - DT
Joe Bellino - HB
Nick Buoniconti - LB
Ron Burton - HB
Justin Canale - G
Gino Cappelletti - E
Jim Colclough - FL
Jay Cunningham - DB
Bill Dawson - E
Bob Dee - DE
Mike Dukes - LB
Larry Eisenhauer - DE
Lonnie Farmer - LB
Dick Felt - DB
J.D. Garrett - HB
Larry Garron - FB
Art Graham - E
White Graves - DB
Ron Hall - DB
Tom Hennessey - DB
Jim Hunt - DE
Ellis Johnson - HB
Charley Long - G
Ed Meixler - LB
Jon Morris - C
Jim Nance - FB
Billy Neighbors - G
Tom Neville - T
Don Oakes - T
Ross O'Hanley - DB
Babe Parilli - QB
George Pyne - DT
Tony Romeo - E
Jack Rudolph - LB
Chuck Shonta - DB
Len St. Jean - DE
Don Webb - DB
Jim Whalen - E
Eddie Wilson - QB
Bob Yates - T
Tom Yewcic - QB

1965 Buffalo

Joe Auer - HB
Stew Barber - T
Glenn Bass - E
Dave Behrman - C
Al Bemiller - G
Butch Byrd - DB
Wray Carlton - HB
Hagood Clarke - DB
Paul Costa - E
Tom Day - DE
Elbert Dubenion - FL
Jim Dunaway - DT
Booker Edgerson - DB
Charley Ferguson - E
George Flint - G
Pete Gogolak - K
Bill Groman - E
Floyd Hudlow - FL
Dick Hudson - T
Harry Jacobs - LB
Tom Janik - DB
Billy Joe - FB
Tom Keating - DT
Jack Kemp - QB
Daryle Lamonica - QB
Bill Laskey - LB
Paul Maguire - LB
Ron McDole - DE
Dudley Meredith - DT
Pete Mills - E
Joe O'Donnell - T
Bo Roberson - FL
Ed Rutkowski - FL
George Saimes - DB
Henry Schmidt - DT
Marty Schottenheimer - LB
Tom Sestak - T
Billy Shaw - G
Bobby Smith - HB
Donnie Stone - FB
Mike Stratton - LB
Eugene Sykes - DB
Jack Tracey - E
Ernie Warlick - E
Charley Warner - HB

1965 Denver

Odell Barry - E
Lee Bernet - T
John Bramlett - LB
Bob Breitenstein - T
Willie Brown - DB
Gerry Bussell - DB
Paul Carmichael - HB
Ed Cooke - DE
Ed Cummings - LB
Eldon Danenhauer - T
Al Denson - FL
Hewritt Dixon - E
Tom Erlandson - LB
Miller Farr - DB
Cookie Gilchrist - FB
Goose Gonsoulin - DB
John Griffin - DB
Wendell Hayes - HB
Abner Haynes - HB
John Hohman - G
Jerry Hopkins - LB
Ray Jacobs - DT
Chuck Janerette - DT
Gene Jeter - LB
Gary Kroner - DB
Ray Kubala - C
Jacky Lee - QB
Max Leetzow - DT
Darrell Lester - FB
John McCormick - QB
Bob McCullough - G
John McGeever - DB
Jim McMillin - DB
Charley Mitchell - HB
Leroy Moore - DE
Tom Nomina - G
Charlie Parker - G
Bob Scarpitto - FL
Mickey Slaughter - QB
Jerry Sturm - G
Lionel Taylor - E
Jim Thibert - LB
Jim Thompson - DT
Nemiah Wilson - DB

1965 Houston

Scott Appleton - DT
Johnny Baker - LB
Tony Banfield - DB
Sonny Bishop - G
George Blanda - QB
Danny Brabham - LB
Ode Burrell - HB
B.W. Cheeks - HB
Doug Cline - LB
Dick Compton - E
Gary Cutsinger - DE
Norm Evans - T
Bob Evans - DE
Don Floyd - DE
Charley Frazier - E
Wayne Frazier - C
Willie Frazier - E
John Frongillo - G
Fred Glick - DB
Tom Goode - C
Jim Hayes - DT
Charley Hennigan - FL
W.K. Hicks - DB
Dalton Hoffman - FB
Harry Hooligan - FB
Ed Husmann - DT
Bobby Jackson - FB
Bobby Jancik - DB
Pete Jaquess - DB
Keith Kinderman - FB
George Kinney - DE
Bobby Maples - LB
Bud McFadin - DT
Bob McLeod - E
Rich Michael - T
Jim Norton - DB
Larry Onesti - LB
Charlie Rieves - LB
Jack Spikes - FB
Art Strahan - DE
Walt Suggs - T
Bob Talamini - G
Charley Tolar - FB
Don Trull - QB
Sammy Weir - FL
Maxie Williams - T
John Wittenborn - G

1965 Kansas City

Fred Arbanas - E
Pete Beathard - QB
Bobby Bell - DE
Denny Biodrowski - G
Mel Branch - DE
Solomon Brannan - HB
Tommy Brooker - E
Buck Buchanan - DT
Ed Budde - G
Chris Burford - E
Reggie Carolan - E
Ronnie Caveness - LB
Bert Coan - HB
Walt Corey - LB
Jerry Cornelison - T
Len Dawson - QB

Al Dotson - DT
Curt Farrier - DT
Jim Fraser - LB
Jon Gilliam - C
Sherrill Headrick - LB
Dave Hill - T
Mack Lee Hill - HB
E.J. Holub - LB
Bobby Hunt - DB
Chuck Hurston - DE
Frank Jackson - FL
Ed Lothamer - DE
Jerry Mays - DT
Curtis McClinton - FB
Curt Merz - G
Willie Mitchell - DB
Frank Pitts - FL
Bobby Ply - DB
Al Reynolds - G
Johnny Robinson - DB
Hatch Rosdahl - DT
Smokey Stover - LB
Otis Taylor - E
Jim Tyrer - T
Fred Williamson - DB
Jerrel Wilson - HB

1965 NY Jets

Ray Abruzzese - DB
Al Atkinson - LB
Bill Baird - DB
Ralph Baker - LB
Verlon Biggs - DT
Charlie Browning - HB
Kern Carson - HB
Nick DeFelice - T
Sam DeLuca - G
Mike Dukes - LB
Jim Evans - FL
Dan Ficca - G
Cornell Gordon - DB
Larry Grantham - LB
Jim Harris - DT
Gene Heeter - E
Dave Herman - G
Winston Hill - T
Mike Hudock - C
Jim Hudson - HB
Cosmo Iacovazzi - HB
Curley Johnson - HB
Dee Mackey - E
Bill Mathis - HB
Don Maynard - FL
Wahoo McDaniel - LB
Joe Namath - QB
Jim O'Mahoney - LB
Dainard Paulson - DB
Pete Perreault - G
Gerry Philbin - DE
Sherman Plunkett - T
Bill Rademacher - DB
Jerry Robinson - E
Paul Rochester - DT
George Sauer - E
John Schmitt - C
Bob Schweickert - HB
Arnie Simkus - DT
Mark Smolinski - FB
Matt Snell - FB
Mike Taliaferro - QB
LaVerne Torczon - DE
Jim Turner - K
Bake Turner - E
Clyde Washington - DB
Willie West - DB
Bert Wilder - DE

1965 Oakland

Pervis Atkins - E
Fred Biletnikoff - FL
Dan Birdwell - DT
Bill Budness - LB
Billy Cannon - E
Dan Conners - LB
Dave Costa - DT
Clem Daniels - HB
Ben Davidson - DE
Cotton Davidson - QB
John Diehl - DT
Tom Flores - QB
Claude Gibson - DB
Dave Grayson - DB
Roger Hagberg - FB
Wayne Hawkins - G
Dick Hermann - LB
Ken Herock - E
Joe Krakoski - DB
Ike Lassiter - DE
Marv Marinovich - G
Archie Matsos - LB
Kent McCloughan - DB
Mike Mercer - K
Alan Miller - FB
Gene Mingo - HB
Rex Mirich - DT
Bob Mischak - G
Carleton Oats - DE
Gus Otto - LB
Jim Otto - C
Art Powell - E
Warren Powers - DB
Ken Rice - G
Bo Roberson - FL
Harry Schuh - G

Bob Svihus - T
Larry Todd - HB
Howie Williams - DB
J.R. Williamson - LB
Dick Wood - QB
Frank Youso - T
Rich Zecher - T

1965 San Diego

Chuck Allen - LB
Jim Allison - FB
Lance Alworth - FL
Don Breaux - QB
Frank Buncom - LB
Ron Carpenter - LB
Kern Carson - HB
Dick Degen - LB
Steve DeLong - DE
Speedy Duncan - DB
Earl Faison - DE
Miller Farr - DB
John Farris - G
Gene Foster - FB
Kenny Graham - DB
George Gross - DT
Sam Gruneisen - C
John Hadl - QB
Dick Harris - DB
Bob Horton - LB
Jack Jacobson - DB
Howard Kindig - DE
Gary Kirner - T
Dave Kocourek - E
Ernie Ladd - DT
Keith Lincoln - FB
Paul Lowe - HB
Jacque MacKinnon - E
Ed Mitchell - G
Ron Mix - T
Fred Moore - DT
Don Norton - E
Ernie Park - T
Bob Petrich - DE
Rick Redman - LB
Pat Shea - G
Walt Sweeney - G
Sammie Taylor - FL
Steve Tensi - QB
Herb Travenio - K
Jimmy Warren - DB
Dick Westmoreland - DB
Bud Whitehead - DB
Ernie Wright - T
Bob Zeman - DB

1966 NFL

1966 Atlanta

Taz Anderson - TE
Gary Barnes - E
Vern Burke - E
Lee Calland - DB
Dennis Claridge - QB
Junior Coffey - HB
Angelo Coia - E
Ed Cook - G
Perry Lee Dunn - HB
Glenn Glass - FL
Dan Grimm - G
Alex Hawkins - E
Ralph Heck - LB
Tom Hutchinson - E
Bill Jobko - LB
Randy Johnson - QB
Rudy Johnson - HB
Jerry Jones - DT
Lou Kirouac - G
Dick Koeper - T
Errol Linden - T
Billy Lothridge - K
Red Mack - FL
Frank Marchlewski - C
Bud Marshall - DT
Billy Martin - TE
Larry Morris - LB
Tommy Nobis - LB
Nick Rassas - DB
Ken Reaves - DB
Ron Rector - HB
Guy Reese - DT
Bobby Richards - DE
Jerry Richardson - DB
Preston Ridlehuber - HB
Bob Riggle - DB
Karl Rubke - DE
Marion Rushing - LB
Charlie Scales - FB
Bob Sherlag - FL
Jimmy Sidle - TE
Chuck Sieminski - DT
Carl Silvestri - DB
Jim Simon - T
Steve Sloan - QB
Ron Smith - HB
Joe Szczecko - DT
Don Talbert - T
Tommy Tolleson - DB
Wade Traynham - K
Ernie Wheelwright - FB
Bob Whitlow - C
Sam Williams - DE
Bill Wolski - FB

1966 Baltimore

Jerry Allen - HB
Bob Baldwin - FB
Sam Ball - T
Raymond Berry - E
Tom Bleick - DB
Bobby Boyd - DB
Ordell Braase - DE
Barry Brown - LB
Jackie Burkett - LB
Gary Cuozzo - QB
Mike Curtis - LB
Ted Davis - LB
Dennis Gaubatz - LB
George Harold - DB
Alvin Haymond - DB
Jerry Hill - FB
Roy Hilton - DE
David Lee - K
Jerry Logan - DB
Tony Lorick - FB
Lenny Lyles - DB
John Mackey - TE
Gino Marchetti - DE
Tom Matte - HB
Dale Memmelaar - G
Lou Michaels - DE
Fred Miller - DT
Lenny Moore - FL
Jimmy Orr - FL
Jim Parker - T
Neal Petties - E
Glenn Ressler - C
Willie Richardson - FL
Alex Sandusky - G
Don Shinnick - LB
Billy Ray Smith Sr. - DT
Al Snyder - FL
Steve Stonebreaker - LB
Andy Stynchula - DE
Dan Sullivan - G
Dick Szymanski - C
Johnny Unitas - QB
Bob Vogel - T
Jim Welch - DB
Butch Wilson - TE

1966 Chi. Bears

Duane Allen - TE
Jon Arnett - HB
Doug Atkins - DE
Charlie Bivins - TE
Charlie Brown - DB
Doug Buffone - LB
Rudy Bukich - QB
Ronnie Bull - HB
Dick Butkus - LB
Jim Cadile - G
Frank Cornish - DT
Mike Ditka - TE
Dick Evey - DT
Joe Fortunato - LB
Curt Gentry - DB
Dick Gordon - E
Bobby Joe Green - K
John Johnson - DT
Jim Jones - E
Bob Kilcullen - DT
Ralph Kurek - FB
Roger LeClerc - C
Herman Lee - T
Joe Marconi - FB
Riley Mattson - T
Bennie McRae - DB
Johnny Morris - FL
Ed O'Bradovich - DE
Richie Petitbon - DB
Brian Piccolo - FB
Jim Purnell - LB
Mike Pyle - C
Mike Rabold - G
Larry Rakestraw - QB
Mike Reilly - LB
Gale Sayers - HB
Brian Schweda - DE
George Seals - T
Rosey Taylor - DB
Billy Wade - QB
Bob Wetoska - T
Dave Whitsell - DB

1966 Cleveland

Erich Barnes - DB
Jim Battle - T
Walter Beach - DB
Johnny Brewer - LB
John Brown - T
Monte Clark - T
Gary Collins - FL
Vince Costello - LB
Ross Fichtner - DB
Galen Fiss - LB
Bobby Franklin - DB
Bill Glass - DE
Ernie Green - FB
Lou Groza - K
Charlie Harraway - FB
Gene Hickerson - G
Fred Hoaglin - C
Jim Houston - TE
Mike Howell - DB
Joe Bob Isbell - G
Walter Johnson - DT

Jim Kanicki - DT
Ernie Kellermann - DB
Leroy Kelly - HB
Gary Lane - QB
Dale Lindsey - LB
Clifton McNeil - FL
Dick Modzelewski - DT
Milt Morin - TE
John Morrow - C
Jim Ninowski - QB
Frank Parker - DT
Bernie Parrish - DB
Nick Pietrosante - FB
Walter Roberts - FL
Frank Ryan - QB
Dick Schafrath - T
Randy Schultz - FB
Ralph Smith - TE
Paul Warfield - E
Paul Wiggin - DE
Sid Williams - LB
John Wooten - G

1966 Dallas

George Andrie - DE
Jim Boeke - T
Frank Clarke - TE
Jim Colvin - DT
Mike Connelly - T
Dick Daniels - DB
Buddy Dial - FL
Leon Donohue - G
Dave Edwards - LB
Mike Gaechter - DB
Walt Garrison - FB
Pete Gent - FL
Cornell Green - DB
Bob Hayes - E
Harold Hays - LB
Chuck Howley - LB
Mike Johnson - DB
Lee Roy Jordan - LB
Bob Lilly - DT
Tony Liscio - G
Warren Livingston - DB
Obert Logan - DB
Dave Manders - C
Don Meredith - QB
Craig Morton - QB
Ralph Neely - T
John Niland - G
Pettis Norman - TE
Don Perkins - FB
Jethro Pugh - DT
Dan Reeves - HB
Mel Renfro - HB
Jerry Rhome - QB
Bill Sandeman - DT
Les Shy - HB
J. D. Smith - FB
Larry Stephens - DE
Willie Townes - DE
Jerry Tubbs - LB
Danny Villanueva - K
Malcolm Walker - T
John Wilbur - DT

1966 Detroit

Mike Alford - C
Roger Brown - DT
Ernie Clark - LB
Bill Cody - LB
Gail Cogdill - E
Bobby Felts - HB
Ed Flanagan - C
Jim Gibbons - TE
John Gordy - G
Larry Hand - DE
John Henderson - FL
Wally Hilgenberg - LB
Alex Karras - DT
Jim Kearney - DB
Bob Kowalkowski - G
Ron Kramer - TE
Dick LeBeau - DB
Joe Don Looney - HB
Mike Lucci - LB
Bruce Maher - DB
Bill Malinchak - E
Amos Marsh - HB
Jerry Mazzanti - DE
Darris McCord - DE
Bruce McLenna - HB
Tom Myers - QB
Tom Nowatzke - FB
Milt Plum - QB
Wayne Rasmussen - DB
Johnnie Robinson - DB
Jerry Rush - DT
Daryl Sanders - T
Roger Shoals - T
Lou Slaby - LB
J.D. Smith - T
Bobby Smith - DB
Pat Studstill - FL
Karl Sweetan - QB
Bobby Thompson - DB
Jim Todd - HB
Doug Van Horn - G
Tom Vaughn - DB
Wayne Walker - LB
Willie Walker - FL
Garo Yepremian - K

1966 Green Bay

Herb Adderley - DB
Lionel Aldridge - DE
Donny Anderson - HB
Bill Anderson - TE
Ken Bowman - C
Zeke Bratkowski - QB
Allen Brown - TE
Robert Brown - DE
Tom Brown - DB
Lee Roy Caffey - LB
Don Chandler - K
Tommy Crutcher - LB
Bill Curry - C
Carroll Dale - FL
Willie Davis - DE
Boyd Dowler - E
Marv Fleming - TE
Gale Gillingham - G
Jim Grabowski - FB
Forrest Gregg - G
Doug Hart - DB
Dave Hathcock - DB
Paul Hornung - HB
Bob Jeter - DB
Henry Jordan - DT
Ron Kostelnik - DT
Jerry Kramer - G
Bob Long - FL
Red Mack - FL
Max McGee - E
Ray Nitschke - LB
Elijah Pitts - HB
Dave Robinson - LB
Bob Skoronski - T
Bart Starr - QB
Jim Taylor - FB
Fuzzy Thurston - G
Phil Vandersea - LB
Jim Weatherwax - DT
Willie Wood - DB
Steve Wright - T

1966 LA Rams

Bruce Anderson - DE
Dick Bass - FB
Maxie Baughan - LB
Joe Carollo - T
Don Chuy - G
Charley Cowan - T
Claude Crabb - FL
Irv Cross - DB
Dan Currie - LB
Henry Dyer - FB
Roman Gabriel - QB
Bill George - LB
Bruce Gossett - K
Hank Gremminger - DB
Rosey Grier - DT
Steve Heckard - E
Ken Iman - C
Deacon Jones - DE
Les Josephson - HB
Ted Karras - G
Jon Kilgore - K
Chuck Lamson - DB
Earl Leggett - DT
Lamar Lundy - DE
Tom Mack - G
Tommy McDonald - FL
Marlin McKeever - TE
Ed Meador - DB
Tom Moore - HB
Bill Munson - QB
Bob Nichols - T
Merlin Olsen - DT
Jack Pardee - LB
Dave Pivec - TE
Bucky Pope - FL
Myron Pottios - LB
Joe Scibelli - G
Jack Snow - E
Jim Stiger - FB
Billy Truax - TE
Joe Wendryhoski - C
Clancy Williams - DB
Doug Woodlief - LB
George Youngblood - DB

1966 Minnesota

Grady Alderman - T
Chuck Arrobio - T
Billy Barnes - HB
Hal Bedsole - TE
Bob Berry - QB
Larry Bowie - G
Bill Brown - FB
Preston Carpenter - TE
Fred Cox - K
Doug Davis - T
Paul Dickson - DT
Carl Eller - DE
Mike Fitzgerald - DB
Paul Flatley - E
Dale Hackbart - DB
Tom Hall - FL
Don Hansen - LB
Jeff Jordan - DB
Karl Kassulke - DB
Phil King - HB
John Kirby - LB
Gary Larsen - DT
Jim Lindsey - HB
Earsell Mackbee - DB
Jim Marshall - DE
Tommy Mason - HB
Dave Osborn - HB
Jim Phillips - FL
John Powers - TE
Lance Rentzel - E
George Rose - DB
Bob Schmitz - LB
Ed Sharockman - DB
Jerry Shay - DT
Milt Sunde - G
Archie Sutton - T
Fran Tarkenton - QB
Mike Tilleman - DT
Mick Tingelhoff - C
Dave Tobey - LB
Ron Vander Kelen - QB
Jim Vellone - G
Bobby Walden - K
Lonnie Warwick - LB
Jeff Williams - HB
Roy Winston - LB
Jim Young - HB

1966 NY Giants

Bookie Bolin - G
Steve Bowman - HB
Henry Carr - DB
Jim Carroll - LB
Pete Case - G
Clarence Childs - DB
Mike Ciccolella - LB
Glen Condren - DE
Bob Crespino - TE
Don Davis - DT
Roger Davis - T
Rosey Davis - DE
Darrell Dess - G
Jim Garcia - DE
Pete Gogolak - K
Charlie Harper - G
Phil Harris - DB
Wendell Harris - DB
Jerry Hillebrand - LB
Allen Jacobs - FB
Homer Jones - FL
Jim Katcavage - DE
Tom Kennedy - QB
Ernie Koy - FB
Greg Larson - C
Dan Lewis - HB
Carl Lockhart - DB
Dick Lynch - DB
Bill Matan - DE
Pep Menefee - FL
Chuck Mercein - FB
Jim Moran - DT
Earl Morrall - QB
Joe Morrison - HB
Jimmy Patton - DB
Francis Peay - T
Jim Prestel - DT
Smith Reed - HB
Bob Scholtz - C
Stan Sczurek - LB
Del Shofner - E
Jeff Smith - LB
Aaron Thomas - TE
Steve Thurlow - HB
Larry Vargo - LB
Joe Wellborn - C
Freeman White - LB
Gary Wood - QB
Willie Young - T

1966 Philadelphia

Sam Baker - K
Randy Beisler - DE
Ed Blaine - G
Bob Brown - T
Timmy Brown - HB
Willie Brown - FL
Dave Cahill - DT
Jack Concannon - QB
Ron Goodwin - E
Dave Graham - T
Earl Gros - FB
Ben Hawkins - FL
Fred Hill - E
King Hill - QB
Lane Howell - T
Lynn Hoyem - C
Don Hultz - DE
T.J. Jackson - FL
Ike Kelley - LB
Izzy Lang - FB
Dave Lince - TE
Dave Lloyd - LB
Aaron Martin - DB
Ollie Matson - HB
Ron Medved - DB
John Meyers - DT
Mike Morgan - LB
Al Nelson - DB
Jim Nettles - DB
Floyd Peters - DT
Gary Pettigrew - DE
Nate Ramsey - DB
Dave Recher - C
Pete Retzlaff - TE
Jim Ringo - C
Ray Rissmiller - T
Joe Scarpati - DB
Jim Skaggs - G
Norm Snead - QB
Bruce Van Dyke - G
Arunas Vasys - LB
Harold Wells - LB
Fred Whittingham - LB
Tom Woodeshick - HB

1966 Pittsburgh

Willie Asbury - FB
John Baker - DE
Gary Ballman - FL
Charlie Bradshaw - T
Jim Bradshaw - DB
Rod Breedlove - LB
Gene Breen - LB
Amos Bullocks - HB
Cannonball Butler - HB
John Campbell - LB
Mike Clark - K
Willie Daniel - DB
Larry Gagner - G
Riley Gunnels - DT
John Hilton - TE
Chuck Hinton - DT
Dick Hoak - HB
Bob Hohn - DB
George Izo - QB
Dan James - T
Roy Jefferson - FL
Tony Jeter - TE
Brady Keys - DB
Pat Killorin - C
Ken Kortas - DT
Frank Lambert - K
Dick Leftridge - FB
Mike Lind - FB
Mike Magac - G
Ray Mansfield - C
Paul Martha - DB
Ben McGee - DE
Ron Meyer - QB
Bill Nelsen - QB
Fran O'Brien - T
Roger Pillath - T
Tim Powell - DE
Andy Russell - LB
Bill Saul - LB
Bob Schmitz - LB
Jerry Simmons - E
Bobby Smith - HB
Ron Smith - QB
Steve Smith - TE
Eli Strand - G
Clendon Thomas - DB
Lloyd Voss - DT
Ralph Wenzel - G
J.R. Wilburn - E
Marv Woodson - DB

1966 St. Louis

Jim Bakken - K
Don Brumm - DE
Charlie Bryant - HB
Jimmy Burson - DB
Bobby Joe Conrad - FL
Willis Crenshaw - FB
Bob DeMarco - C
Pat Fischer - DB
Billy Gambrell - FL
Prentice Gautt - HB
Irv Goode - C
Ken Gray - G
Mal Hammack - TE
Jim Hart - QB
Jimmy Heidel - DB
Fred Heron - DE
Charley Johnson - QB
Dick Kasperek - C
Bill Koman - LB
Dave Long - DT
John McDowell - T
Ernie McMillan - T
Dave Meggyesy - LB
Dale Meinert - LB
Mike Melinkovich - DE
Terry Nofsinger - QB
Dave O'Brien - G
Ray Ogden - TE
Sonny Randle - E
Bob Reynolds - T
Joe Robb - DE
Johnny Roland - FB
Frank Roy - G
Roy Shivers - HB
Sam Silas - DT
Dave Simmons - LB
Jackie Smith - TE
Rick Sortun - G
Larry Stallings - LB
Jerry Stovall - DB
Mike Strofolino - LB
Bill Triplett - HB
Chuck Walker - DT
Bobby Williams - DB
Larry Wilson - DB
Abe Woodson - DB

1966 San Francisco

Kermit Alexander - DB
Ed Beard - LB
Bruce Bosley - C
John Brodie - QB
Bernie Casey - FL
Joe Cerne - C
John Crow - HB
Bob Daugherty - HB
Tommy Davis - K
George Donnelly - DB
Mike Dowdle - LB
Bob Harrison - LB
Matt Hazeltine - LB
Stan Hindman - DE
Jim Jackson - HB
Charlie Johnson - DT
Jim Johnson - DB
Billy Kilmer - QB
Elbert Kimbrough - DB
Dave Kopay - HB
Kent Kramer - TE
Charlie Krueger - DT
Roland Lakes - DT
Gary Lewis - FB
Dave McCormick - T
Kay McFarland - FL
Clark Miller - DE
George Mira - QB
Howard Mudd - G
Jim Norton - DT
Dave Parks - E
Mel Phillips - DB
Al Randolph - DB
Walt Rock - T
Len Rohde - T
Monty Stickles - TE
Wayne Swinford - E
John Thomas - G
Dave Wilcox - LB
Ken Willard - FB
Jim Wilson - G
Dick Witcher - FL

1966 Washington

Willie Adams - DE
Jim Avery - TE
Walt Barnes - DT
Tom Barrington - FB
Bill Briggs - DE
John Burrell - FL
Preston Carpenter - TE
Jim Carroll - LB
Billy Clay - DB
Don Croftcheck - LB
Dave Crossan - C
Darrell Dess - G
Charlie Gogolak - K
Tom Goosby - G
Chris Hanburger - LB
Rickie Harris - DB
Len Hauss - C
Pat Hodgson - E
Sam Huff - LB
Steve Jackson - LB
Mitch Johnson - T
Stan Jones - DT
Sonny Jurgensen - QB
Carl Kammerer - DE
Joe Kantor - FB
John Kelly - T
Paul Krause - DB
Jake Kupp - G
Joe Don Looney - HB
Bud Marshall - DT
Fred Mazurek - FL
Bobby Mitchell - FL
Fran O'Brien - T
Brig Owens - DB
Vince Promuto - G
Ron Rector - HB
John Reger - LB
Pat Richter - TE
Joe Rutgens - DT
Lonnie Sanders - DB
Ray Schoenke - G
Dick Shiner - QB
Jim Shorter - DB
Jerry Smith - TE
Ron Snidow - DE
Jim Snowden - T
Charley Taylor - HB
Steve Thurlow - HB
Tom Walters - DB
A.D. Whitfield - FB

1966 AFL

1966 Boston

Tom Addison - LB
Houston Antwine - DT
Joe Avezzano - C
Joe Bellino - FL
Jim Boudreaux - DE
Nick Buoniconti - LB
Justin Canale - G
Bob Cappadona - FB
Gino Cappelletti - FL
Jim Colclough - E
Jay Cunningham - DB
Bob Dee - DE
Larry Eisenhauer - DE
Lonnie Farmer - LB
Dick Felt - DB
Jim Fraser - LB
J.D. Garrett - HB
Larry Garron - HB
Art Graham - E
White Graves - DB
Ron Hall - DB
Tom Hennessey - DB
John Huarte - QB
Jim Hunt - DT
Ellis Johnson - E
Billy Johnson - DB
Ed Khayat - DT
Charley Long - G
John Mangum - DT
Jon Morris - C
Jim Nance - FB
Tom Neville - T
Don Oakes - T
Babe Parilli - QB
Vic Purvis - DB
Tony Romeo - TE
Doug Satcher - LB
Chuck Shonta - DB
Karl Singer - T
Len St. Jean - G
Don Webb - DB
Jim Whalen - TE
Tom Yewcic - QB

1966 Buffalo

Stew Barber - T
Glenn Bass - E
Al Bemiller - G
Bobby Burnett - HB
Butch Byrd - DB
Wray Carlton - FB
Hagood Clarke - DB
Dave Costa - DT
Paul Costa - TE
Bobby Crockett - E
Tom Day - DE
Wayne DeSutter - T
Elbert Dubenion - FL
Jim Dunaway - DT
Booker Edgerson - DB
Charley Ferguson - E
Doug Goodwin - FB
Paul Guidry - LB
Dick Hudson - T
Harry Jacobs - LB
Tom Janik - DB
Jack Kemp - QB
Charlie King - DB
Daryle Lamonica - QB
Booth Lusteg - K
Paul Maguire - LB
Ron McDole - DE
Dudley Meredith - DT
Pete Mills - E
Joe O'Donnell - G
Remi Prudhomme - G
Ed Rutkowski - E
George Saimes - DB
Bob Schmidt - T
Marty Schottenheimer - LB
Tom Sestak - DT
Billy Shaw - G
Allen Smith - HB
Jack Spikes - FB
Mike Stratton - LB
Jack Tracey - LB
Charley Warner - DB

1966 Denver

Lee Bernet - T
John Bramlett - LB
Bob Breitenstein - T
Willie Brown - DB
Sam Brunelli - G
Max Choboian - QB
Larry Cox - DT
Eric Crabtree - E
Marvin Davis - DE
Al Denson - TE
Billy Fletcher - DB
Jason Franci - E
Scotty Glacken - QB
Glenn Glass - E
Goose Gonsoulin - DB
John Gonzaga - G
John Griffin - DB
Don Gulseth - LB
Wendell Hayes - HB
Abner Haynes - HB
John Hohman - G
Jerry Hopkins - LB
Jerry Inman - DT
Ray Jacobs - DT
Gene Jeter - LB
Larry Kaminski - C
Bill Keating - G
Mike Kellogg - FB
Gary Kroner - K
Ray Kubala - C
Dan LaRose - DE
Max Leetzow - DE
Darrell Lester - FB
Pat Matson - G
Archie Matsos - LB
John McCormick - QB
Charley Mitchell - HB
Bob Richardson - DB
Tobin Rote - QB
Ronald Sbranti - LB
Bob Scarpitto - FL
Lew Scott - DB
Goldie Sellers - DB
Mickey Slaughter - QB
Jerry Sturm - G
George Tarasovic - DE
Lionel Taylor - E
Max Wettstein - TE
Nemiah Wilson - DB
Lonnie Wright - DB
Bob Young - DT

1966 Houston

George Allen - T
Scott Appleton - DT
Johnny Baker - LB
Sonny Bishop - G
George Blanda - QB
Sid Blanks - HB
Garland Boyette - LB
Danny Brabham - LB
Ode Burrell - HB
John Carrell - LB
Ronnie Caveness - LB
Doug Cline - LB
Gary Cutsinger - DE
Larry Elkins - FL
Don Floyd - DE
Charley Frazier - E
John Frongillo - C
Fred Glick - DB
Hoyle Granger - FB
Jim Hayes - DT
Charley Hennigan - FL
W.K. Hicks - DB
Glen Ray Hines - T
Pat Holmes - DT
Buddy Humphrey - QB
Bobby Jancik - DB
John Johnson - FB
Ernie Ladd - DT
Jacky Lee - QB
Bobby Maples - LB
Bob McLeod - TE
John Meyer - LB
Rich Michael - T
Jim Norton - DB
Bernie Parrish - DB
Bob Poole - TE
George Rice - G
Ed Scrutchins - DE
Donnie Stone - FB
Walt Suggs - T
Mickey Sutton - DB
Bob Talamini - G
Charley Tolar - FB
Allen Trammel - DB
Don Trull - QB
Olen Underwood - LB
Theo Viltz - DB
John Wittenborn - G

1966 Kansas City

Bud Abell - LB
Fred Arbanas - TE
Pete Beathard - QB
Bobby Bell - LB
Denny Biodrowski - G
Solomon Brannan - DB
Tommy Brooker - K
Aaron Brown - DE
Buck Buchanan - DT
Ed Budde - G
Chris Burford - E
Reggie Carolan - E
Bert Coan - HB
Walt Corey - LB
Len Dawson - QB
Tony DiMidio - T
Wayne Frazier - C
Mike Garrett - HB
Jon Gilliam - C
Sherrill Headrick - LB
Dave Hill - T
Jimmy Hill - DB
E.J. Holub - LB
Bobby Hunt - DB
Chuck Hurston - DE
Ed Lothamer - DT
Jerry Mays - DE
Curtis McClinton - FB
Mike Mercer - K
Curt Merz - G
Willie Mitchell - DB
Frank Pitts - E
Bobby Ply - DB
Al Reynolds - G
Andy Rice - DT
Johnny Robinson - DB
Hatch Rosdahl - G
Fletcher Smith - DB
Smokey Stover - LB
Otis Taylor - FL
Emmitt Thomas - DB
Gene Thomas - HB
Jim Tyrer - T
Fred Williamson - DB
Jerrel Wilson - FB

1966 Miami

Joe Auer - HB
Mel Branch - DE
Bob Bruggers - LB
Whit Canale - DE
Rick Casares - FB
George Chesser - FB
Ed Cooke - DE
Bill Cronin - TE
Al Dotson - DT
Frank Emanuel - LB
Tom Erlandson - LB
Norm Evans - T
Earl Faison - DE
Cookie Gilchrist - FB
Tom Goode - C
Jim Higgins - T
John Holmes - DE
Mike Hudock - C
Billy Hunter - HB
Frank Jackson - FL
Pete Jaquess - DB
Billy Joe - FB
Dave Kocourek - TE
Wes Matthews - E
Wahoo McDaniel - LB
John McGeever - DB
Gene Mingo - HB
Stan Mitchell - E
Doug Moreau - E
Bob Neff - DB
Billy Neighbors - G
Tom Nomina - DT
Karl Noonan - E
Rick Norton - QB
Ernie Park - T
Bob Petrella - DB
Sammy Price - FB
Ken Rice - G
Bo Roberson - FL
John Roderick - FL
Jack Rudolph - LB
John Stofa - QB
Jack Thornton - LB
LaVerne Torczon - DE
Howard Twilley - E
Hal Wantland - DB
Jimmy Warren - DB
Willie West - DT
Dick Westmoreland - DB
Maxie Williams - T
George Wilson - QB
Dick Wood - QB
Rich Zecher - DT

1966 NY Jets

Ray Abruzzese - DB
Al Atkinson - LB
Bill Baird - DB
Ralph Baker - LB
Verlon Biggs - DE
Emerson Boozer - HB
Steve Chomyszak - C
Earl Christy - HB
Paul Crane - LB
Nick DeFelice - T
Sam DeLuca - G
Mitch Dudek - T
Dan Ficca - G
Cornell Gordon - DB
Larry Grantham - LB
Jim Gray - DB
Pat Gucciardo - DB
Jim Harris - DT
Dave Herman - G
Winston Hill - T
Jim Hudson - DB
Curley Johnson - K
Pete Lammons - TE
Sherman Lewis - DB
Bill Mathis - HB
Don Maynard - FL
Joe Namath - QB
Jim O'Mahoney - LB
Dainard Paulson - DB
Pete Perreault - G
Gerry Philbin - DE
Sherman Plunkett - T
Bill Rademacher - E
Paul Rochester - DT
Johnny Sample - DB
George Sauer - E
Henry Schmidt - DT
John Schmitt - C
Allen Smith - HB
Mark Smolinski - FB
Matt Snell - FB
Mike Taliaferro - QB
Jim Turner - K
Bake Turner - E
Jim Waskiewicz - C
Sammy Weir - FL
Bob Werl - G
Bert Wilder - DT
Bill Yearby - DE

1966 Oakland

Pervis Atkins - HB
Pete Banaszak - HB
Fred Biletnikoff - FL
Rodger Bird - DB
Dan Birdwell - DT
Bill Budness - LB
Billy Cannon - TE
Dan Conners - LB
Clem Daniels - HB
Dave Daniels - DT
Ben Davidson - DE
Cotton Davidson - QB

Hewritt Dixon - HB
Mike Eischeid - K
Tom Flores - QB
Dave Grayson - DB
Charlie Green - QB
Roger Hagberg - FB
Jim Harvey - T
Wayne Hawkins - G
Rich Jackson - LB
Tom Keating - DT
Greg Kent - DE
Joe Krakoski - DB
Bill Laskey - LB
Ike Lassiter - DE
Kent McCloughan - DB
Mike Mercer - K
Bill Miller - E
Rex Mirich - DT
Tom Mitchell - TE
Carleton Oats - DT
Gus Otto - LB
Jim Otto - C
Art Powell - E
Warren Powers - DB
Palmer Pyle - G
Ray Schmautz - LB
Harry Schuh - T
Bob Svihus - T
Larry Todd - E
Dick Tyson - G
Howie Williams - DB
Willie Williams - DB
J.R. Williamson - LB

1966 San Diego

Chuck Allen - LB
Jim Allison - FB
Lance Alworth - FL
Joe Beauchamp - DB
Frank Buncom - LB
Doug Cline - LB
Dick Degen - LB
Steve DeLong - DT
Speedy Duncan - DB
Don Estes - G
Earl Faison - DE
Miller Farr - DB
John Farris - G
Gene Foster - FB
Willie Frazier - TE
Gary Garrison - E
Tom Good - LB
Kenny Graham - DB
Jim Griffin - DE
George Gross - DT
Sam Gruneisen - C
John Hadl - QB
Dan Henning - QB
Emil Karas - LB
Howard Kindig - DE
Gary Kirner - T
Paul Latzke - C
Keith Lincoln - FB
Mike London - LB
Paul Lowe - HB
Jacque MacKinnon - TE
Larry Martin - DT
Archie Matsos - LB
John Milks - LB
Ed Mitchell - G
Bob Mitinger - LB
Ron Mix - T
Fred Moore - DE
Don Norton - E
Terry Owens - T
Bob Petrich - DE
Dave Plump - DB
Rick Redman - LB
Houston Ridge - DE
Walt Sweeney - G
Steve Tensi - QB
Jim Tolbert - DB
John Travis - FB
Dick Van Raaphorst - K
Bud Whitehead - DB
Nat Whitmyer - DB
Ernie Wright - T
Bob Zeman - DB

1967 NFL

1967 Atlanta

Dick Absher - LB
Taz Anderson - TE
Gary Barnes - E
Tom Bleick - DB
Andy Bowling - LB
Lee Calland - DB
Junior Coffey - FB
Ed Cook - G
Perry Lee Dunn - HB
Mike Fitzgerald - DB
Dan Grimm - G
Tom Harmon - G
Alex Hawkins - FL
Ralph Heck - LB
Floyd Hudlow - DB
Bob Hughes - DE
Randy Johnson - QB
Lou Kirouac - G
Jake Kupp - G
Errol Linden - T
Billy Lothridge - K
Jim Mankins - FB
Frank Marchlewski - C
Billy Martin - TE
Tommy McDonald - FL
Tom Moore - HB
Tommy Nobis - LB
Terry Nofsinger - QB
Jim Norton - DT
Ray Ogden - TE
Nick Rassas - DB
Ken Reaves - DB
Ron Rector - HB
Bobby Richards - DE
Jerry Richardson - DB
Bob Riggle - DB
Karl Rubke - DT
Marion Rushing - LB
Bill Sandeman - T
Bob Sanders - LB
Chuck Sieminski - DT
Jerry Simmons - E
Jim Simon - G
Steve Sloan - QB
Ron Smith - DB
Joe Szczecko - DT
Don Talbert - T
Wade Traynham - K
Ernie Wheelwright - FB
Sam Williams - DE
Jim Wilson - G
Bo Wood - DE

1967 Baltimore

Don Alley - FL
Sam Ball - T
Raymond Berry - E
Bobby Boyd - DB
Ordell Braase - DE
Barry Brown - LB
Bill Curry - LB
Mike Curtis - LB
Norman Davis - G
Dennis Gaubatz - LB
George Harold - DB
Alex Hawkins - FL
Alvin Haymond - DB
Jerry Hill - FB
Roy Hilton - DE
David Lee - K
Jerry Logan - DB
Tony Lorick - FB
Lenny Lyles - DB
John Mackey - TE
Tom Matte - HB
Dale Memmelaar - G
Lou Michaels - DE
Fred Miller - DT
Lenny Moore - HB
Jimmy Orr - FL
Jim Parker - T
Preston Pearson - DB
Ray Perkins - E
Ron Porter - LB
Glenn Ressler - G
Willie Richardson - FL
Don Shinnick - LB
Billy Ray Smith Sr. - DT
Bubba Smith - DE
Charles Stukes - DB
Andy Stynchula - DE
Dan Sullivan - G
Dick Szymanski - C
Johnny Unitas - QB
Bob Vogel - T
Rick Volk - DB
Jim Ward - QB
Jim Welch - HB
Butch Wilson - TE

1967 Chi. Bears

Duane Allen - TE
Marty Amsler - DE
Charlie Brown - DB
Doug Buffone - LB
Rudy Bukich - QB
Ronnie Bull - FB
Dick Butkus - LB
Jim Cadile - G
Jack Concannon - QB
Frank Cornish - DT
Don Croftcheck - G
Austin Denney - TE
Al Dodd - DB
Dick Evey - DT
Curt Gentry - DB
Dick Gordon - E
Bobby Joe Green - K
Randy Jackson - T
Dan James - T
John Johnson - DT
Jim Jones - E
Bob Jones - E
Doug Kriewald - G
Rudy Kuechenberg - LB
Ralph Kurek - FB
Andy Livingston - FB
Bennie McRae - DB
Frank McRae - DT
Johnny Morris - FL
Ed O'Bradovich - DE
Mac Percival - K
Richie Petitbon - DB
Loyd Phillips - DE
Brian Piccolo - HB
Bob Pickens - T
Jim Purnell - LB
Mike Pyle - C
Mike Rabold - G
Larry Rakestraw - QB
Mike Reilly - LB
Gale Sayers - HB
George Seals - T
Terry Stoepel - TE
Joe Taylor - DB
Rosey Taylor - DB
Bob Wetoska - T

1967 Cleveland

Billy Andrews - LB
Erich Barnes - DB
Eppie Barney - FL
Johnny Brewer - LB
Monte Clark - T
Gary Collins - FL
Larry Conjar - FB
Jim Copeland - G
Ben Davis - DB
John Demarie - T
Ron Duncan - TE
Ross Fichtner - DB
Bill Glass - DE
Ernie Green - FB
Ron Green - FL
Jack Gregory - DE
Lou Groza - K
Charlie Harraway - FB
Gene Hickerson - G
Fred Hoaglin - C
Jim Houston - LB
Mike Howell - DB
Walter Johnson - DT
Jim Kanicki - DT
Ernie Kellermann - DB
Leroy Kelly - HB
Gary Lane - QB
Dale Lindsey - LB
Bob Matheson - LB
Clifton McNeil - FL
Milt Morin - TE
Frank Parker - DT
Nick Pietrosante - FB
Frank Ryan - QB
Dick Schafrath - T
Dick Shiner - QB
Ralph Smith - TE
Joe Taffoni - G
Carl Ward - DB
Paul Warfield - E
Paul Wiggin - DE
John Wooten - G
George Youngblood - DB

1967 Dallas

George Andrie - DE
Craig Baynham - HB
Jim Boeke - T
Phil Clark - DB
Frank Clarke - TE
Mike Connelly - C
Dick Daniels - DB
Harold Deters - K
Leon Donohue - G
Ron East - DT
Dave Edwards - LB
Mike Gaechter - DB
Walt Garrison - HB
Pete Gent - FL
Cornell Green - DB
Bob Hayes - E
Harold Hays - LB
Chuck Howley - LB
Mike Johnson - DB
Lee Roy Jordan - LB
Bob Lilly - DT
Tony Liscio - T
Don Meredith - QB
Craig Morton - QB
Ralph Neely - T
John Niland - G
Pettis Norman - TE
Don Perkins - FB
Jethro Pugh - DT
Dan Reeves - HB
Mel Renfro - DB
Lance Rentzel - E
Jerry Rhome - QB
Les Shy - HB
Larry Stephens - DE
Sims Stokes - E
Willie Townes - DE
Danny Villanueva - K
Malcolm Walker - T
John Wilbur - G
Rayfield Wright - TE

1967 Detroit

Lem Barney - DB
Mike Bass - DB
Charlie Bradshaw - T
Ernie Clark - LB
Gail Cogdill - E
Bill Cottrell - T
Mel Farr - HB
Bobby Felts - HB
Ed Flanagan - C
Frank Gallagher - G
Jim Gibbons - TE
Ron Goovert - LB
John Gordy - G
Larry Hand - DE
John Henderson - E
Lew Kamanu - DE
Alex Karras - DT
Bob Kowalkowski - G
Ron Kramer - TE
Dick LeBeau - DB
Mike Lucci - LB
Bruce Maher - DB
Bill Malinchak - E
Amos Marsh - FB
John McCambridge - DE
Darris McCord - DE
Mike Melinkovich - DE
Denis Moore - DT
Paul Naumoff - LB
Tom Nowatzke - FB
Milt Plum - QB
Wayne Rasmussen - DB
Jerry Rush - DT
Roger Shoals - T
Pat Studstill - FL
Karl Sweetan - QB
Bobby Thompson - DB
Tom Vaughn - DB
Wayne Walker - LB
Chuck Walton - G
Tom Watkins - HB
Mike Weger - DB
Randy Winkler - T
Garo Yepremian - K
Jerry Zawadzkas - TE

1967 Green Bay

Herb Adderley - DB
Lionel Aldridge - DE
Donny Anderson - HB
Ken Bowman - C
Zeke Bratkowski - QB
Allen Brown - TE
Robert Brown - DE
Tom Brown - DB
Lee Roy Caffey - LB
Dick Capp - TE
Don Chandler - K
Tommy Crutcher - LB
Carroll Dale - FL
Willie Davis - DE
Boyd Dowler - E
Jim Flanigan - LB
Marv Fleming - TE
Gale Gillingham - G
Jim Grabowski - FB
Forrest Gregg - T
Doug Hart - DB
Don Horn - QB
Bob Hyland - G
Claudis James - HB
Bob Jeter - DB
Henry Jordan - DT
Ron Kostelnik - DT
Jerry Kramer - G
Bob Long - FL
Max McGee - E
Chuck Mercein - FB
Ray Nitschke - LB
Elijah Pitts - HB
Dave Robinson - LB
John Rowser - DB
Bob Skoronski - T
Bart Starr - QB
Fuzzy Thurston - G
Jim Weatherwax - DT
Travis Williams - HB
Ben Wilson - FB
Willie Wood - DB
Steve Wright - T

1967 LA Rams

Dick Bass - FB
Maxie Baughan - LB
Gene Breen - LB
Roger Brown - DT
George Burman - G
Dave Cahill - DE
Joe Carollo - T
Bernie Casey - FL
Don Chuy - G
Charley Cowan - T
Claude Crabb - DB
Irv Cross - DB
Willie Daniel - DB
Willie Ellison - HB
Roman Gabriel - QB
Bruce Gossett - K
Tony Guillory - LB
Ken Iman - C
Deacon Jones - DE
Les Josephson - HB
Jon Kilgore - K
Chuck Lamson - DB
Lamar Lundy - DE
Tom Mack - G
Tommy Mason - HB
Ed Meador - DB
Bill Munson - QB
Bob Nichols - T
Merlin Olsen - DT
Jack Pardee - LB
Dave Pivec - LB
Bucky Pope - E
Myron Pottios - LB
Gregg Schumacher - DE
Joe Scibelli - G
Jack Snow - E
Jim Stiger - FB
Diron Talbert - DT
Billy Truax - TE
Wendell Tucker - E
Clancy Williams - DB
Kelton Winston - DB
Doug Woodlief - LB

1967 Minnesota

Grady Alderman - T
John Beasley - TE
Bob Berry - QB
Larry Bowie - G
Bob Breitenstein - T
Bill Brown - FB
Al Coleman - DB
Fred Cox - K
Doug Davis - T
Earl Denny - HB
Paul Dickson - DT
Carl Eller - DE
Paul Faust - LB
Mike Fitzgerald - DB
Paul Flatley - E
Bob Grim - DB
Dale Hackbart - DB
Don Hansen - LB
Jim Hargrove - LB
Clint Jones - HB
Jeff Jordan - DB
Joe Kapp - QB
Karl Kassulke - DB
Brady Keys - DB
John Kirby - LB
Gary Larsen - DT
Jim Lindsey - HB
Earsell Mackbee - DB
Jim Marshall - DE
Marlin McKeever - TE
Dave Osborn - HB
Alan Page - DT
John Pentecost - G
Jim Phillips - FL
Ed Sharockman - DB
Jerry Shay - DT
Arnie Simkus - DE
Milt Sunde - G
Archie Sutton - T
Pete Tatman - HB
Mick Tingelhoff - C
Dave Tobey - LB
Ron Vander Kelen - QB
Jim Vellone - T
Bobby Walden - K
Lonnie Warwick - LB
Gene Washington - E
Roy Winston - LB

1967 New Orleans

Danny Abramowicz - E
Dick Anderson - T
Doug Atkins - DE
Tom Barrington - HB
Charlie Brown - HB
Vern Burke - TE
Jackie Burkett - LB
Bo Burris - DB
Bill Cody - LB
Lou Cordileone - DT
Bruce Cortez - DB
Gary Cuozzo - QB
Ted Davis - LB
John Douglas - DB
Charlie Durkee - K
Jim Garcia - DE
John Gilliam - HB
Tom Hall - E
Ben Hart - DB
George Harvey - T
Jimmy Heidel - DB
Jimmy Hester - TE
Jerry Jones - T
Jimmy Jordan - HB
Les Kelley - LB
Billy Kilmer - QB
Kent Kramer - TE
Jake Kupp - G
Earl Leggett - DT
Obert Logan - DB
Don McCall - HB
Dave McCormick - T
Tom McNeill - K
Elijah Nevett - FL
Ray Ogden - TE
Ray Poage - E
Ray Rissmiller - T
Walter Roberts - FL
George Rose - DB
Dave Rowe - DT
Bill Sandeman - T
Roy Schmidt - G
Randy Schultz - FB
Brian Schweda - DE
Dave Simmons - LB
Jerry Simmons - E
Steve Stonebreaker - LB
Eli Strand - G
Jerry Sturm - T
Jim Taylor - FB
Mike Tilleman - DT
Phil Vandersea - LB
Joe Wendryhoski - C
Ernie Wheelwright - FB
Dave Whitsell - DB
Fred Whittingham - LB
Del Williams - G
Gary Wood - QB
George Youngblood - DB

1967 NY Giants

Bruce Anderson - DT
Roger Anderson - DT
Ken Avery - LB
Bookie Bolin - G
Henry Carr - DB
Pete Case - G
Clarence Childs - DB
Mike Ciccolella - LB
Jim Colvin - DT
Glen Condren - DE
Vince Costello - LB
Bob Crespino - TE
Rosey Davis - DE
Darrell Dess - G
Scott Eaton - DB
Mike Fitzgerald - DB
Tucker Frederickson - FB
Pete Gogolak - K
Andy Gross - G
Charlie Harper - G
Wendell Harris - DB
Dave Hathcock - DB
Chuck Hinton - C
Allen Jacobs - HB
Homer Jones - FL
Jim Katcavage - DE
Rich Kotite - LB
Ernie Koy - FB
Greg Larson - C
Carl Lockhart - DB
Bob Lurtsema - DT
Chuck Mercein - FB
Randy Minniear - HB
Jim Moran - DT
Earl Morrall - QB
Joe Morrison - HB
Les Murdock - K
Francis Peay - T
Bobby Post - DB
Del Shofner - E
Randy Staten - DE
Bill Swain - LB
Fran Tarkenton - QB
Aaron Thomas - TE
Bill Triplett - HB
Ed Weisacosky - LB
Freeman White - DB
Willie Williams - DB
Willie Young - T

1967 Philadelphia

Sam Baker - K
Gary Ballman - FL
Randy Beisler - DE
Fred Brown - LB
Bob Brown - T
Timmy Brown - HB
Benjy Dial - QB
Mike Ditka - TE
Ron Goodwin - E
Jim Gray - DB
Dick Hart - G
Ben Hawkins - E
Fred Hill - E
King Hill - QB
Lane Howell - T
Lynn Hoyem - C
Chuck Hughes - FL
Don Hultz - DE
Harry Jones - HB
Ike Kelley - LB
Jim Kelly - TE
Izzy Lang - FB
Dave Lince - TE
Dave Lloyd - LB
Aaron Martin - DB
Ron Medved - DB
John Meyers - DT
Mike Morgan - LB
Al Nelson - DB
Jim Nettles - DB
Floyd Peters - DT
Gary Pettigrew - DE
Nate Ramsey - DB
Dave Recher - C
Taft Reed - DB
Jim Ringo - C
Joe Scarpati - DB
Bob Shann - DB
Jim Skaggs - G
Norm Snead - QB
Bill Stetz - G
Mel Tom - DE
Arunas Vasys - LB
Harold Wells - LB
Harry Wilson - HB
Dean Wink - DE
Tom Woodeshick - HB
Gordon Wright - G

1967 Pittsburgh

Chet Anderson - TE
Dick Arndt - DT
Willie Asbury - FB
Richie Badar - QB
John Baker - DE
Charlie Bivins - HB
Jim Bradshaw - DB
Rod Breedlove - LB
John Brown - T
Cannonball Butler - HB
John Campbell - LB
Mike Clark - K
Dick Compton - E
Marshall Cropper - E
Sam Davis - T
Jim Elliott - K
John Foruria - DB
Larry Gagner - G
Earl Gros - FB
Mike Haggerty - T
John Hilton - TE
Chuck Hinton - DT
Dick Hoak - HB
Bob Hohn - DB
Roy Jefferson - FL
Brady Keys - DB
Ken Kortas - DT
Ray Mansfield - C
Jerry Marion - FL
Paul Martha - DB
Ray May - LB
Jerry Mazzanti - DE
Ben McGee - DE
Bobby Morgan - DB
Bill Nelsen - QB
Kent Nix - QB
Fran O'Brien - T
Andy Russell - LB
Bill Saul - LB
Don Shy - HB
Clendon Thomas - DB
Bruce Van Dyke - G
Lloyd Voss - DE
Ralph Wenzel - G
J.R. Wilburn - E
Marv Woodson - DB

1967 St. Louis

Jim Bakken - K
Mike Barnes - DB
Don Brumm - DE
Charlie Bryant - HB
Jimmy Burson - DB
Bobby Joe Conrad - FL
Willis Crenshaw - FB
Bob DeMarco - C
Pat Fischer - DB
Billy Gambrell - FL
Prentice Gautt - HB
Irv Goode - C
Ken Gray - G
Jim Hart - QB
Fred Heron - DE
Jerry Hillebrand - LB
Charley Johnson - QB
Dick Kasperek - C
Bill Koman - LB
Chuck Latourette - DB
Chuck Logan - TE
Dave Long - DT
Ed Marcontell - G
Ernie McMillan - T
Dave Meggyesy - LB
Dale Meinert - LB
Dave O'Brien - G
Bob Reynolds - T
Joe Robb - DE
Johnny Roland - FB
Bob Rowe - DE
Roy Shivers - HB
Sam Silas - DT
Jackie Smith - TE
Rick Sortun - G
Philip Spiller - DB
Larry Stallings - LB
Jerry Stovall - DB
Mike Strofolino - LB
Bill Thornton - FB
Chuck Walker - DT
Ted Wheeler - TE
Bobby Williams - DB
Clyde Williams - T
Dave Williams - FL
Larry Wilson - DB

1967 San Francisco

Kermit Alexander - DB
Ed Beard - LB
Bruce Bosley - C
John Brodie - QB
Joe Cerne - C
Elmer Collett - G
John Crow - HB
Doug Cunningham - HB
Tommy Davis - K
George Donnelly - DB
Goose Gonsoulin - DB
Bob Harrison - LB
Matt Hazeltine - LB
Dave Hettema - T
Stan Hindman - DE
Tom Holzer - DE
Jim Jackson - DB
Charlie Johnson - DT
Jim Johnson - DB

Walter Johnson - DE
Dave Kopay - HB
Charlie Krueger - DT
Roland Lakes - DT
Gary Lewis - FB
Clark Miller - DE
George Mira - QB
Howard Mudd - G
Chip Myers - FL
Frank Nunley - LB
Dave Olerich - TE
Don Parker - G
Dave Parks - E
Mel Phillips - DB
Sonny Randle - E
Al Randolph - DB
Walt Rock - T
Len Rohde - T
Steve Spurrier - QB
Monty Stickles - TE
Wayne Swinford - FL
John Thomas - G
Wayne Trimble - DB
Bill Tucker - FB
Dave Wilcox - LB
Ken Willard - FB
Bob Windsor - TE
Dick Witcher - TE

1967 Washington

Dick Absher - LB
Bruce Alford - K
Jerry Allen - HB
Don Bandy - G
Walt Barnes - DT
Ed Breding - LB
Bill Briggs - DE
John Burrell - FL
Jim Carroll - LB
Dave Crossan - C
Charlie Gogolak - K
Chris Hanburger - LB
Rickie Harris - DB
Len Hauss - C
Larry Hendershot - LB
Sam Huff - LB
Steve Jackson - LB
T.J. Jackson - DB
Mitch Johnson - T
Sonny Jurgensen - QB
Carl Kammerer - DE
John Kelly - T
Paul Krause - DB
Pete Larson - HB
Joe Don Looney - FB
John Love - DB
Ray McDonald - FB
Gene Mingo - K
Bobby Mitchell - HB
Spain Musgrove - DT
Jim Ninowski - QB
Brig Owens - DB
Jim Prestel - DT
Vince Promuto - G
Pat Richter - TE
Joe Rutgens - DT
Lonnie Sanders - DB
Ray Schoenke - G
Jim Shorter - DB
Jerry Smith - TE
Dick Smith - E
Ron Snidow - DE
Jim Snowden - T
Charley Taylor - E
Steve Thurlow - HB
Tom Walters - DB
A.D. Whitfield - FB
Sid Williams - LB
Heath Wingate - C

1967 AFL

1967 Boston

Tom Addison - LB
Houston Antwine - DT
Joe Bellino - HB
Jim Boudreaux - T
Nick Buoniconti - LB
Justin Canale - G
Bob Cappadona - FB
Gino Cappelletti - FL
John Charles - DB
Jim Colclough - E
Jay Cunningham - DB
Bob Dee - DE
Larry Eisenhauer - DE
Tom Fussell - DE
J.D. Garrett - HB
Larry Garron - HB
Art Graham - E
White Graves - DB
Ron Hall - DB
John Huarte - QB
Jim Hunt - DT
Ray Ilg - LB
Billy Johnson - DB
Bobby Leo - HB
Charley Long - G
John Mangum - DT
Leroy Mitchell - DB
Jon Morris - C
Jim Nance - FB
Tom Neville - T
Bobby Nichols - TE
Don Oakes - T
Babe Parilli - QB
Ed Philpott - LB
Vic Purvis - DB
Tony Romeo - TE
Doug Satcher - LB
Chuck Shonta - DB
Karl Singer - T
Len St. Jean - G
Terry Swanson - K
Ed Toner - LB
Don Trull - QB
Don Webb - DB
Jim Whalen - TE
Mel Witt - DT

1967 Buffalo

Teddy Bailey - HB
Stew Barber - T
Al Bemiller - C
Charlie Bivins - HB
Gary Bugenhagen - G
Bobby Burnett - HB
Butch Byrd - DB
Wray Carlton - HB
Hagood Clarke - DB
Paul Costa - TE
Dick Cunningham - T
Gene Donaldson - HB
Elbert Dubenion - FL
Jim Dunaway - DT
Booker Edgerson - DB
Tom Flores - QB
Wayne Frazier - C
Paul Guidry - LB
Dick Hudson - T
Harry Jacobs - LB
Tom Janik - DB
Jack Kemp - QB
Howard Kindig - DE
Charlie King - DB
Tony King - FL
Monte Ledbetter - FL
Jim LeMoine - LB
Keith Lincoln - FB
Paul Maguire - LB
Billy Masters - TE
Ron McDole - DE
Mike Mercer - K
Dudley Meredith - DT
Joe O'Donnell - G
Bob Petrich - DE
John Pitts - DB
Bobby Ply - DB
Art Powell - E
Remi Prudhomme - DE
Ed Rutkowski - FL
George Saimes - DB
Bob Schmidt - C
Marty Schottenheimer - LB
Tom Sestak - DT
Billy Shaw - G
Allen Smith - HB
Jack Spikes - FB
Mike Stratton - LB
Jack Tracey - TE
Rich Zecher - DT

1967 Denver

Lou Andrus - LB
Tom Beer - TE
Dave Behrman - T
Bob Breitenstein - T
Sam Brunelli - T
Tom Cassese - HB
Tom Cichowski - T
Dave Costa - DT
Larry Cox - DT
Eric Crabtree - E
Carl Cunningham - LB
Mike Current - T
Al Denson - FL
Rick Duncan - K
Pete Duranko - DE
Cookie Gilchrist - FB
Scotty Glacken - QB
George Goeddeke - C
Wendell Hayes - FB
Bo Hickey - FB
John Huard - LB
Bob Humphreys - K
Jerry Inman - DT
Rich Jackson - DE
Pete Jaquess - DB
Gene Jeter - LB
Larry Kaminski - C
Bill Keating - DT
Mike Kellogg - FB
Gary Kroner - K
Ray Kubala - C
Jim LeClair - QB
Roger LeClerc - C
Jack Lentz - DB
Floyd Little - HB
Fran Lynch - HB
Pat Matson - G
Rex Mirich - DE
Charley Mitchell - HB
Chip Myrtle - LB
Ernie Park - G
Bobby Ply - DB
Errol Prisby - DB
Frank Richter - LB
Bob Scarpitto - FL
Goldie Sellers - DB
Don Smith - G
Henry Sorrell - LB
Jim Summers - DB
Neal Sweeney - E
Eugene Sykes - DB
Steve Tensi - QB
Dick Tyson - G
Andre White - TE
Nemiah Wilson - DB
Lonnie Wright - DB
Bob Young - G

1967 Houston

Billy Anderson - QB
Pete Barnes - LB
Glenn Bass - FL
Pete Beathard - QB
Sonny Bishop - G
Sid Blanks - HB
Garland Boyette - LB
Danny Brabham - LB
Ode Burrell - FL
Woody Campbell - HB
Larry Carwell - DB
Ronnie Caveness - LB
Bob Davis - QB
Larry Elkins - FL
Miller Farr - DB
Don Floyd - DE
Charley Frazier - E
Hoyle Granger - FB
W.K. Hicks - DB
Glen Ray Hines - T
Pat Holmes - DE
Roy Hopkins - FB
Ken Houston - DB
Bobby Jancik - DB
Pete Johns - DB
Willie Jones - DE
Ernie Ladd - DT
Monte Ledbetter - FL
Jacky Lee - QB
Bobby Maples - C
Ed Marcontell - G
Bud Marshall - DT
Zeke Moore - DB
Jim Norton - DB
Willie Parker - DT
Bob Poole - TE
Alvin Reed - TE
Tom Regner - G
Andy Rice - DT
George Rice - DT
Carel Stith - DE
Walt Suggs - T
Bob Talamini - G
Lionel Taylor - E
Don Trull - QB
Olen Underwood - LB
George Webster - LB
John Wittenborn - K

1967 Kansas City

Bud Abell - LB
Fred Arbanas - TE
Pete Beathard - QB
Bobby Bell - LB
Denny Biodrowski - G
Buck Buchanan - DT
Ed Budde - G
Chris Burford - E
Reggie Carolan - TE
Bert Coan - HB
Len Dawson - QB
Tony DiMidio - C
Wayne Frazier - C
Mike Garrett - HB
Jon Gilliam - C
Sherrill Headrick - LB
Dave Hill - T
E.J. Holub - C
Mike Hudock - C
Bobby Hunt - DB
Chuck Hurston - LB
Jim Kearney - DB
Bob Kelly - T
Ernie Ladd - DT
Willie Lanier - LB
Jacky Lee - QB
Sam Longmire - DB
Ed Lothamer - DE
Jim Lynch - LB
Jerry Mays - DE
Curtis McClinton - FB
Curt Merz - G
Willie Mitchell - DB
Frank Pitts - E
Bobby Ply - DB
Al Reynolds - G
Andy Rice - DT
Gloster Richardson - FL
Johnny Robinson - DB
Fletcher Smith - DB
Noland Smith - FL
Jan Stenerud - K
Otis Taylor - FL
Emmitt Thomas - DB
Gene Thomas - HB
Gene Trosch - DT
Jim Tyrer - T
Wayne Walker - K
Fred Williamson - DB
Jerrel Wilson - FB

1967 Miami

Joe Auer - HB
Tom Beier - FL
John Bramlett - LB
Mel Branch - DE
Claude Brownlee - DT
Bob Bruggers - LB
Preston Carpenter - TE
George Chesser - FB
Jack Clancy - FL
Ed Cooke - DE
Mike Current - T
Frank Emanuel - LB
Tom Erlandson - LB
Norm Evans - T
Charlie Fowler - G
Tom Goode - C
Bob Griese - QB
Jack Harper - HB
Abner Haynes - HB
Jerry Hopkins - LB
Frank Jackson - FL
Ray Jacobs - DT
Pete Jaquess - DB
Bill Keating - DT
Mack Lamb - DB
Booth Lusteg - K
Wahoo McDaniel - LB
Gene Mingo - K
Stan Mitchell - FB
Doug Moreau - TE
Bob Neff - DB
Billy Neighbors - G
Tom Nomina - DT
Karl Noonan - E
Rick Norton - QB
Bob Petrella - DB
Sammy Price - HB
Jack Pyburn - T
Ken Rice - G
John Richardson - DT
Jim Riley - DE
Archie Roberts - QB
John Roderick - FL
Larry Seiple - HB
John Stofa - QB
Howard Twilley - E
Jimmy Warren - DB
Willie West - DB
Dick Westmoreland - DB
Maxie Williams - T
Freddie Woodson - G
Rich Zecher - DT

1967 NY Jets

Al Atkinson - LB
Bill Baird - DB
Ralph Baker - LB
Randy Beverly - DB
Verlon Biggs - DE
Emerson Boozer - HB
Solomon Brannan - DB
Earl Christy - HB
Paul Crane - LB
John Elliott - LB
Cornell Gordon - DB
Larry Grantham - LB
Jim Harris - T
Abner Haynes - HB
Dave Herman - G
Winston Hill - T
Jim Hudson - DB
Billy Joe - FB
Curley Johnson - TE
Henry King - DB
Pete Lammons - TE
Sherman Lewis - DB
Bill Mathis - HB
John Matlock - C
Don Maynard - FL
Carl McAdams - LB
Joe Namath - QB
Pete Perreault - G
Gerry Philbin - DE
Sherman Plunkett - T
Bill Rademacher - DB
Dennis Randall - DT
Randy Rasmussen - G
Jeff Richardson - G
Paul Rochester - DT
Johnny Sample - DB
George Sauer - E
John Schmitt - C
Bob Schweickert - FL
Paul Seiler - G
Mark Smolinski - FB
Matt Snell - FB
Mike Taliaferro - QB
Jim Turner - QB
Bake Turner - E
Jim Waskiewicz - T
Bert Wilder - DT

1967 Oakland

Dan Archer - G
Pete Banaszak - HB
Estes Banks - HB
Duane Benson - LB
Fred Biletnikoff - FL
Rodger Bird - DB
Dan Birdwell - DT
George Blanda - QB
Willie Brown - DB
Bill Budness - LB
Billy Cannon - TE
Dan Conners - LB
Clem Daniels - HB
Ben Davidson - DE
Hewritt Dixon - HB
Mike Eischeid - K
Bill Fairband - LB
Dave Grayson - DB
Roger Hagberg - FB
Jim Harvey - G
Wayne Hawkins - G
Ken Herock - E
Tom Keating - DT
Dave Kocourek - TE
Bob Kruse - G
Daryle Lamonica - QB
Bill Laskey - LB
Ike Lassiter - DE
Kent McCloughan - DB
Bill Miller - E
Carleton Oats - DE
Gus Otto - LB
Jim Otto - C
Warren Powers - DB
Harry Schuh - T
Rod Sherman - FL
Richard Sligh - DT
Bob Svihus - T
Larry Todd - HB
Gene Upshaw - T
Warren Wells - E
Howie Williams - DB
J.R. Williamson - LB

1967 San Diego

Harold Akin - T
Chuck Allen - LB
Jim Allison - FB
Lance Alworth - FL
Scott Appleton - DT
Johnny Baker - LB
Joe Beauchamp - DB
Ron Billingsley - DT
Frank Buncom - LB
Olie Cordill - E
Tom Day - DE
Steve DeLong - DT
Speedy Duncan - DB
Bernie Erickson - LB
Gene Foster - HB
Willie Frazier - TE
Gary Garrison - E
Kenny Graham - DB
Jim Griffin - DE
George Gross - DT
Sam Gruneisen - C
John Hadl - QB
Bob Howard - DB
Brad Hubbert - FB
Howard Kindig - DE
Gary Kirner - T
Paul Latzke - C
Larry Little - DT
Paul Lowe - HB
Jacque MacKinnon - TE
Frank Marsh - DB
Ron McCall - LB
Ed Mitchell - G
Ron Mix - T
Steve Newell - E
Terry Owens - T
Dickie Post - HB
Bob Print - LB
Rick Redman - LB
Houston Ridge - DT
Russ Smith - HB
Jeff Staggs - LB
Kay Stephenson - QB
Walt Sweeney - G
Jim Tolbert - DB
Dick Van Raaphorst - K
Bud Whitehead - HB
Ernie Wright - T

1968 NFL

1968 Atlanta

Dick Absher - LB
Ron Acks - LB
Grady Allen - LB
Joe Auer - HB
Bob Berry - QB
Greg Brezina - LB
Charlie Bryant - HB
Jimmy Burson - DB
Cannonball Butler - HB
Lee Calland - DB
Rick Cash - DE
Joe Cerne - C
Olie Cordill - DB
Carlton Dabney - DT
Mike Donohoe - TE
Steve Duich - G
Dave Dunaway - WR
Perry Lee Dunn - HB
Rick Eber - WR
Bob Etter - K
Paul Flatley - WR
Mike Freeman - DB
Jim Garcia - DT
Doug Goodwin - FB
Dan Grimm - G
Billy Harris - HB
Ralph Heck - LB
Floyd Hudlow - DB
Claude Humphrey - DE
Randy Johnson - QB
Dwight Lee - HB
Bruce Lemmerman - QB
Errol Linden - T
Bob Long - WR
Billy Lothridge - DB
Frank Marchlewski - C
Brendan McCarthy - FB
Tommy Nobis - LB
Jim Norton - DT
Ray Ogden - TE
Nick Rassas - DB
Ken Reaves - DB
Marion Rushing - LB
Bill Sandeman - T
Jerry Shay - DT
Jerry Simmons - WR
Jim Simon - G
Philip Sobocinski - C
Philip Spiller - DB
Art Strahan - DT
Larry Suchy - DB
Joe Szczecko - DT
Don Talbert - T
Harmon Wages - HB
Randy Winkler - T
John Wright - WR

1968 Baltimore

Ocie Austin - DB
Sam Ball - T
Bobby Boyd - DB
Ordell Braase - DE
Timmy Brown - HB
Gail Cogdill - WR
Terry Cole - FB
Bill Curry - C
Mike Curtis - LB
Dennis Gaubatz - LB
Bob Grant - LB
Alex Hawkins - WR
Jerry Hill - FB
Roy Hilton - DE
Cornelius Johnson - G
David Lee - K
Jerry Logan - DB
Lenny Lyles - DB
John Mackey - TE
Tom Matte - HB
Lou Michaels - DE
Fred Miller - DT
Tom Mitchell - TE
Earl Morrall - QB
Jimmy Orr - WR
Preston Pearson - HB
Ray Perkins - WR
Ron Porter - LB
Glenn Ressler - G
Willie Richardson - WR
Don Shinnick - LB
Billy Ray Smith Sr. - DT
Bubba Smith - DE
Charles Stukes - DB
Dan Sullivan - G
Dick Szymanski - C
Johnny Unitas - QB
Bob Vogel - T
Rick Volk - DB
Jim Ward - QB
John Williams - DE
Sid Williams - LB

1968 Chi. Bears

Doug Buffone - LB
Rudy Bukich - QB
Ronnie Bull - HB
Dick Butkus - LB
Jim Cadile - G
Virgil Carter - QB
Clarence Childs - DB
Jack Concannon - QB
Frank Cornish - DT
Austin Denney - TE
Dick Evey - DT
Curt Gentry - DB
Dick Gordon - WR
Bobby Joe Green - K
Major Hazelton - DB
Willie Holman - DT
Mike Hull - TE
Randy Jackson - T
John Johnson - DT
Bob Jones - WR
Jon Kilgore - K
Doug Kriewald - G
Rudy Kuechenberg - LB
Ralph Kurek - FB
Andy Livingston - FB
Garry Lyle - HB
Wayne Mass - T
Bennie McRae - DB
Ed O'Bradovich - DE
Mac Percival - K
Richie Petitbon - DB
Loyd Phillips - DE
Brian Piccolo - HB
Bob Pickens - T
Dan Pride - LB
Jim Purnell - LB
Mike Pyle - C
Larry Rakestraw - QB
Mike Reilly - LB
Gale Sayers - HB
George Seals - G
Joe Taylor - DB
Rosey Taylor - DB
Cecil Turner - WR
Emilio Vallez - TE
Bob Wallace - WR
Bob Wetoska - C

1968 Cleveland

Billy Andrews - LB
Erich Barnes - DB
Eppie Barney - WR
Monte Clark - T
Don Cockroft - K
Gary Collins - WR
Jim Copeland - G
Ben Davis - DB
John Demarie - G
John Garlington - LB
Bill Glass - DE
Ernie Green - FB
Ron Green - WR
Jack Gregory - DE
Charlie Harraway - FB
Gene Hickerson - G
Fred Hoaglin - C
Jim Houston - LB
Mike Howell - DB
Nate James - DB
Walter Johnson - DT
Jim Kanicki - DT
Ernie Kellermann - DB
Leroy Kelly - HB
Charlie Leigh - FB
Dale Lindsey - LB
Bob Matheson - LB
Tommy McDonald - WR
Wayne Meylan - LB
Alvin Mitchell - DB
Milt Morin - TE
Reece Morrison - HB
Bill Nelsen - QB
Frank Ryan - QB
Bill Sabatino - DT
Dick Schafrath - T
Ralph Smith - TE
Ron Snidow - DE
Joe Taffoni - T
Marv Upshaw - DE
Carl Ward - DB
Paul Warfield - WR
Bob Whitlow - C

1968 Dallas

George Andrie - DE
Craig Baynham - HB
Jackie Burkett - LB
Mike Clark - K
Phil Clark - DB
Larry Cole - DE
Dick Daniels - DB
Ron East - DT
Dave Edwards - LB
Mike Gaechter - DB
Walt Garrison - FB
Pete Gent - TE
Cornell Green - DB
Bob Hayes - WR
Dennis Homan - WR
Chuck Howley - LB
Mike Johnson - DB
Lee Roy Jordan - LB
D. D. Lewis - LB
Bob Lilly - DT
Tony Liscio - T
Dave Manders - C
Dave McDaniels - WR
Don Meredith - QB
Craig Morton - QB
Ralph Neely - T
John Niland - G
Pettis Norman - TE
Blaine Nye - G
Don Perkins - FB
Jethro Pugh - DT
Sonny Randle - WR
Dan Reeves - HB
Mel Renfro - DB
Lance Rentzel - WR
Jerry Rhome - QB
Les Shy - HB
Dave Simmons - LB
Andy Stynchula - DT
Willie Townes - DE
Malcolm Walker - T
Ron Widby - K
John Wilbur - G
Rayfield Wright - TE

1968 Detroit

John Baker - DE
Lem Barney - DB
Charlie Bradshaw - T
Mike Campbell - HB
Gail Cogdill - WR

Bill Cottrell - T
Jerry DePoyster - K
Nick Eddy - HB
Mel Farr - HB
Ed Flanagan - C
Rocky Freitas - T
Frank Gallagher - G
Billy Gambrell - WR
Jim Gibbons - TE
Larry Hand - DE
Lew Kamanu - DE
Alex Karras - DT
Greg Kent - T
Dave Kopay - FB
Bob Kowalkowski - G
Greg Landry - QB
Dick LeBeau - DB
Mike Lucci - LB
Bill Malinchak - WR
Earl McCullouch - WR
Ed Mooney - LB
Denis Moore - DT
Bill Munson - QB
Paul Naumoff - LB
Tom Nowatzke - FB
Phil Odle - WR
Wayne Rasmussen - DB
Joe Robb - DE
Jerry Rush - DT
Charlie Sanders - TE
Roger Shoals - T
Chuck Sieminski - DT
Bill Swain - LB
Bobby Thompson - DB
Bill Triplett - HB
Tom Vaughn - DB
Wayne Walker - LB
Chuck Walton - G
Mike Weger - DB
Jim Welch - HB

1968 Green Bay

Herb Adderley - DB
Lionel Aldridge - DE
Donny Anderson - HB
Ken Bowman - C
Zeke Bratkowski - QB
Robert Brown - DE
Tom Brown - DB
Lee Roy Caffey - LB
Fred Carr - LB
Leo Carroll - DE
Leon Crenshaw - DT
Carroll Dale - WR
Willie Davis - DE
Boyd Dowler - WR
Dave Dunaway - WR
Jim Flanigan - LB
Marv Fleming - TE
Gale Gillingham - G
Jim Grabowski - FB
Forrest Gregg - T
Doug Hart - DB
Dick Himes - T
Don Horn - QB
Bob Hyland - G
Claudis James - WR
Bob Jeter - DB
Henry Jordan - DT
Ron Kostelnik - DT
Jerry Kramer - G
Bill Lueck - G
Errol Mann - K
Chuck Mercein - FB
Mike Mercer - K
Ray Nitschke - LB
Francis Peay - T
Elijah Pitts - HB
Bucky Pope - WR
Dave Robinson - LB
John Rowser - DB
Gordon Rule - DB
Bob Skoronski - T
Bart Starr - QB
Bill Stevens - QB
Phil Vandersea - TE
Travis Williams - HB
Francis Winkler - DE
Willie Wood - DB

1968 LA Rams

Coy Bacon - DT
Dick Bass - FB
Maxie Baughan - LB
Gene Breen - LB
Roger Brown - DT
George Burman - C
Joe Carollo - T
Bernie Casey - WR
Don Chuy - G
Charley Cowan - T
Claude Crabb - DB
Irv Cross - DB
Willie Daniel - DB
Mike Dennis - HB
Henry Dyer - FB
Willie Ellison - HB
Vilnis Ezerins - FB
Roman Gabriel - QB
Bruce Gossett - K
Tony Guillory - LB
Dean Halverson - LB
Ken Iman - C
Harold Jackson - WR
Deacon Jones - DE
Lamar Lundy - DE
Tom Mack - G
Frank Marchlewski - C
Tommy Mason - FB
Ed Meador - DB
Merlin Olsen - DT
Jack Pardee - LB
Dave Pivec - TE
Milt Plum - QB
Myron Pottios - LB
Gregg Schumacher - DE
Joe Scibelli - G
Ron Smith - DB
Jack Snow - WR
Pat Studstill - WR
Diron Talbert - DT
Billy Truax - TE
Wendell Tucker - WR
Clancy Williams - DB
Jim Wilson - T
Kelton Winston - DB
Doug Woodlief - LB

1968 Minnesota

Grady Alderman - T
John Beasley - TE
Bookie Bolin - G
Larry Bowie - G
Bill Brown - FB
Bobby Bryant - DB
Fred Cox - K
Gary Cuozzo - QB
Doug Davis - T
Earl Denny - HB
Paul Dickson - DT
Carl Eller - DE
Bob Goodridge - WR
Bob Grim - WR
Dale Hackbart - DB
Tom Hall - WR
John Henderson - WR
Wally Hilgenberg - LB
King Hill - QB
Clint Jones - HB
Joe Kapp - QB
Karl Kassulke - DB
John Kirby - LB
Paul Krause - DB
Gary Larsen - DT
Jim Lindsey - FB
Earsell Mackbee - DB
Jim Marshall - DE
Billy Martin - TE
Mike McGill - LB
Dave Osborn - HB
Alan Page - DT
Art Powell - WR
Oscar Reed - HB
Ed Sharockman - DB
Steve Smith - DE
Milt Sunde - G
Mick Tingelhoff - C
Jim Vellone - G
Lonnie Warwick - LB
Gene Washington - WR
Charlie West - DB
Roy Winston - LB
Ron Yary - T

1968 New Orleans

Danny Abramowicz - WR
Doug Atkins - DE
Tony Baker - FB
Tom Barrington - FB
Jim Boeke - T
Johnny Brewer - LB
Charlie Brown - HB
Bo Burris - DB
Tom Carr - DT
Bill Cody - LB
Lou Cordileone - DT
Ted Davis - LB
John Douglas - DB
Charlie Durkee - K
Jim Ferguson - LB
Ross Fichtner - DB
Jim Fraser - K
John Gilliam - WR
Ross Gwinn - G
Jimmy Hester - TE
Gene Howard - DB
Jerry Jones - T
Les Kelley - LB
Billy Kilmer - QB
Elbert Kimbrough - DB
Jake Kupp - G
Earl Leggett - DT
Tony Lorick - FB
Don McCall - HB
Tom McNeill - K
Elijah Nevett - DB
Dave Parks - WR
Ray Poage - TE
Dave Rowe - DT
Roy Schmidt - G
Randy Schultz - HB
Brian Schweda - DE
Ronnie Lee South - QB
Monty Stickles - TE
Steve Stonebreaker - LB
Jerry Sturm - T
Karl Sweetan - QB
Dave Szymakowski - WR
Mike Tilleman - DE
Joe Wendryhoski - C
Ernie Wheelwright - FB
Dave Whitsell - DB
Fred Whittingham - LB
Del Williams - G
George Youngblood - DB

1968 NY Giants

Bruce Anderson - DE
Roger Anderson - DT
Ken Avery - LB
Ronnie Blye - HB
McKinley Boston - DE
Barry Brown - LB
Rich Buzin - T
Pete Case - G
Mike Ciccolella - LB
Vince Costello - LB
Bob Crespino - TE
Tommy Crutcher - LB
Henry Davis - LB
Darrell Dess - G
Bobby Duhon - HB
Scott Eaton - DB
Tucker Frederickson - FB
Pete Gogolak - K
Andy Gross - G
Charlie Harper - T
Chuck Hinton - C
Jim Holifield - DB
Homer Jones - WR
Jim Katcavage - DE
Joe Koontz - WR
Ernie Koy - FB
Gary Lane - QB
Greg Larson - C
Carl Lockhart - DB
Bob Lurtsema - DT
Bruce Maher - DB
Randy Minniear - HB
Joe Morrison - WR
Sam Silas - DT
Fran Tarkenton - QB
Aaron Thomas - WR
Doug Van Horn - G
Freeman White - TE
Willie Williams - DB
Butch Wilson - TE
Gary Wood - QB
Steve Wright - T
Willie Young - T

1968 Philadelphia

Sam Baker - K
Gary Ballman - WR
Randy Beisler - DE
Fred Brown - LB
Bob Brown - T
Gene Ceppetelli - C
Wayne Colman - LB
Larry Conjar - FB
Mike Dirks - G
Mike Ditka - TE
Rick Duncan - K
Mike Evans - C
Ron Goodwin - WR
Dave Graham - T
Dick Hart - G
Ben Hawkins - WR
Alvin Haymond - DB
Fred Hill - TE
King Hill - QB
Lane Howell - T
John Huarte - QB
Chuck Hughes - WR
Don Hultz - DE
Harry Jones - HB
Izzy Lang - HB
Dave Lloyd - LB
John Mallory - DB
Ron Medved - DB
Frank Molden - DT
Al Nelson - DB
Jim Nettles - DB
Mark Nordquist - G
Jim Norton - DT
Floyd Peters - DT
Gary Pettigrew - DE
Cyril Pinder - HB
Nate Ramsey - DB
Dave Recher - C
Tim Rossovich - DE
Joe Scarpati - HB
Norm Snead - QB
Mel Tom - DE
Arunas Vasys - LB
Harold Wells - LB
Dean Wink - DT
Tom Woodeshick - FB
Adrian Young - LB

1968 Pittsburgh

Dick Arndt - DT
Willie Asbury - FB
Rocky Bleier - HB
John Brown - T
John Campbell - LB
Dick Capp - LB
Dick Compton - WR
Mike Connelly - C
Marshall Cropper - WR
Sam Davis - G
John Foruria - LB
Larry Gagner - G
Earl Gros - FB
Mike Haggerty - T
Lou Harris - DB
Ken Hebert - WR
Jon Henderson - DB
Jerry Hillebrand - LB
John Hilton - TE
Chuck Hinton - DT
Dick Hoak - HB
Bob Hohn - DB
Roy Jefferson - WR
Tony Jeter - TE
Ken Kortas - DT
Rich Kotite - TE
Booth Lusteg - K
Ray Mansfield - C
Paul Martha - DB
Ray May - LB
Ben McGee - DE
Kent Nix - QB
Fran O'Brien - T
Frank Parker - DT
Ernie Ruple - T
Andy Russell - LB
Bill Saul - LB
Dick Shiner - QB
Bill Shockley - K
Don Shy - HB
Mike Taylor - T
Clendon Thomas - DB
Bruce Van Dyke - G
Lloyd Voss - DE
Bob Wade - DB
Bobby Walden - K
Tom Watkins - HB
Ralph Wenzel - G
J.R. Wilburn - WR
Marv Woodson - DB

1968 St. Louis

Bob Atkins - DB
Jim Bakken - K
Mike Barnes - DB
Don Brumm - DE
Ernie Clark - LB
Bobby Joe Conrad - WR
Willis Crenshaw - FB
Jerry Daanen - WR
Bob DeMarco - C
Bob Duncum - T
Cid Edwards - FB
Irv Goode - C
Ken Gray - G
Jim Hart - QB
Fred Heron - DT
Fred Hyatt - WR
Charley Johnson - QB
Dick Kasperek - C
Brady Keys - DB
MacArthur Lane - HB
Chuck Latourette - DB
Bobby Lee - WR
Chuck Logan - TE
Dave Long - DE
Ernie McMillan - T
Dave Meggyesy - LB
Bob Reynolds - T
Jamie Rivers - LB
Johnny Roland - HB
Rocky Rosema - LB
Bob Rowe - DT
Lonnie Sanders - DB
Mack Sauls - DB
Joe Schmiesing - DE
Roy Shivers - HB
Jackie Smith - TE
Rick Sortun - G
Larry Stallings - LB
Jerry Stovall - DB
Mike Strofolino - LB
Chuck Walker - DE
Ted Wheeler - G
Clyde Williams - G
Dave Williams - WR
Larry Wilson - DB

1968 San Francisco

Kermit Alexander - DB
Cas Banaszek - T
Ed Beard - LB
Bill Belk - DE
Forrest Blue - T
Bruce Bosley - C
John Brodie - QB
Elmer Collett - G
John Crow - HB
Doug Cunningham - HB
Clem Daniels - HB
Tommy Davis - K
Johnny Fuller - DB
Kevin Hardy - DE
Tommy Hart - LB
Harold Hays - LB
Matt Hazeltine - LB
Stan Hindman - DE
Charlie Johnson - DT
Jim Johnson - DB
Charlie Krueger - DT
Roland Lakes - DT
Dwight Lee - HB
Gary Lewis - HB
Kay McFarland - WR
Clifton McNeil - WR
Clark Miller - DE
George Mira - QB
Howard Mudd - G
Frank Nunley - LB
Dave Olerich - TE
Lance Olssen - T
Dennis Patera - K
Woody Peoples - G
Mel Phillips - DB
Sonny Randle - WR
Al Randolph - DB
Len Rohde - T
Steve Spurrier - QB
Bill Tucker - FB
Dave Wilcox - LB
Ken Willard - FB
Bob Windsor - TE
Dick Witcher - WR
John Woitt - DB

1968 Washington

Jerry Allen - HB
Don Bandy - G
Willie Banks - G
Ken Barefoot - TE
Walt Barnes - DT
Gary Beban - HB
Frank Bosch - DT
Mike Bragg - K
Ed Breding - LB
Bob Brunet - HB
Jim Carroll - LB
Dennis Crane - DT
Dave Crossan - C
Pat Fischer - DB
Charlie Gogolak - K
Chris Hanburger - LB
George Harold - DB
Rickie Harris - DB
Len Hauss - C
Sonny Jurgensen - QB
Carl Kammerer - DE
Pete Larson - HB
Aaron Martin - DB
Ray McDonald - FB
Marlin McKeever - TE
Bobby Mitchell - WR
Mike Morgan - LB
Spain Musgrove - DT
Jim Ninowski - QB
Brig Owens - DB
Vince Promuto - G
Pat Richter - TE
Walt Rock - T
Tom Roussel - LB
Joe Rutgens - DT
Ray Schoenke - G
Jerry Smith - TE
Jim Smith - DB
Dick Smith - HB
Jim Snowden - T
Charley Taylor - WR
Harry Theofiledes - QB
Steve Thurlow - FB
Fred Washington - T
A.D. Whitfield - FB
John Wooten - G

1968 AFL

1968 Boston

Houston Antwine - DT
Jim Boudreaux - T
Nick Buoniconti - LB
Dennis Byrd - DE
Whit Canale - DT
Justin Canale - G
Gino Cappelletti - WR
John Charles - DB
Jim Cheyunski - LB
Jim Colclough - WR
King Corcoran - QB
Larry Eisenhauer - DE
Paul Feldhausen - T
Tom Funchess - T
R. C. Gamble - FB
Larry Garron - HB
Art Graham - WR
Jim Hunt - DT
Ray Ilg - LB
Daryl Johnson - DB
Preston Johnson - FB
Billy Johnson - DB
Ed Koontz - LB
Bobby Leo - WR
Charley Long - G
Aaron Marsh - WR
Art McMahon - DB
Leroy Mitchell - DB
Jon Morris - C
Bill Murphy - WR
Jim Nance - FB
Tom Neville - T
Bobby Nichols - TE
Don Oakes - T
Ed Philpott - LB
Willie Porter - DB
Doug Satcher - LB
Bob Scarpitto - WR
Tom Sherman - QB
Karl Singer - T
Len St. Jean - G
Terry Swanson - K
Mike Taliaferro - QB
Gene Thomas - HB
Ed Toner - DT
Don Webb - DB
Jim Whalen - TE
J.R. Williamson - LB
Mel Witt - DE

1968 Buffalo

Bruce Alford - K
Max Anderson - HB
Stew Barber - T
Al Bemiller - C
Charlie Brown - HB
Butch Byrd - DB
Bob Cappadona - FB
Edgar Chandler - LB
Hagood Clarke - DB
Paul Costa - T
Bobby Crockett - WR
Dick Cunningham - T
Dan Darragh - QB
Tom Day - DE
Elbert Dubenion - WR
Jim Dunaway - DT
Booker Edgerson - DB
George Flint - G
Tom Flores - QB
Jack Frantz - C
Ben Gregory - FB
Paul Guidry - LB
Harry Jacobs - LB
Tom Janik - DB
Bob Kalsu - G
Howard Kindig - C
Jerry Lawson - DB
Monte Ledbetter - WR
Keith Lincoln - HB
Paul Maguire - LB
Billy Masters - TE
Mike McBath - DE
Gary McDermott - HB
Ron McDole - DE
Mike Mercer - K
Dudley Meredith - DT
Charley Mitchell - HB
Haven Moses - WR
Wayne Patrick - FB
John Pitts - DB
Ray Rissmiller - T
Benny Russell - QB
Ed Rutkowski - WR
George Saimes - DB
Marty Schottenheimer - LB
Tom Sestak - DT
Billy Shaw - G
Kay Stephenson - QB
Mike Stratton - LB
Bob Tatarek - DT
Richard Trapp - WR

1968 Cincinnati

Dan Archer - G
Marty Baccaglio - DE
Estes Banks - FB
Al Beauchamp - LB
Danny Brabham - LB
Frank Buncom - LB
Steve Chomyszak - DT
Paul Elzey - LB
Bernie Erickson - LB
Howard Fest - T
Curt Frazier - DB
White Graves - DB
Jim Griffin - DE
Harry Gunner - DE
Sherrill Headrick - LB
Ken Herock - TE
Mike Hibler - LB
Bobby Hunt - HB
Essex Johnson - HB
Bob Johnson - C
Willie Jones - DE
Rex Keeling - DB
Bob Kelly - T
Bill Kindricks - DT
Charlie King - DB
Ron Lamb - FB
Dale Livingston - K
John Matlock - T
Pat Matson - G
Ed McCall - WR
Wayne McClure - LB
Warren McVea - HB
Dave Middendorf - G
John Neidert - LB
Pete Perreault - G
Bill Peterson - TE
Jess Phillips - HB
Dennis Randall - DE
Andy Rice - DT
Paul Robinson - HB
Saint Saffold - WR
Bill Scott - DB
Rod Sherman - WR
Tommie Smiley - FB
Fletcher Smith - DB
Philip Spiller - DB
Bill Staley - DT
John Stofa - QB
Bob Trumpy - WR
Dewey Warren - QB
Teddy Washington - HB
Andre White - TE
Monk Williams - WR
Ernie Wright - T
Sam Wyche - QB

1968 Denver

Jay Bachman - C
Tom Beer - TE
Marlin Briscoe - QB
Sam Brunelli - T
Tom Cichowski - T
Dave Costa - DT
Larry Cox - DT
Eric Crabtree - WR
Carl Cunningham - LB
Mike Current - T
Al Denson - WR
Wallace Dickey - T
Joe DiVito - QB
Pete Duranko - DE
Terry Erwin - HB
Garrett Ford - FB
Fred Forsberg - LB
George Gaiser - T
Drake Garrett - DB
George Goeddeke - G
Charlie Greer - DB
Mike Haffner - WR
Buzz Highsmith - G
Gus Hollomon - DB
Bobby Howfield - K
John Huard - LB
Bob Humphreys - K
Jerry Inman - DT
Rich Jackson - DE
Pete Jaquess - DB
Jim Jones - WR
Larry Kaminski - C
Ron Lamb - FB
Gordon Lambert - LB
Jim LeClair - QB
Jack Lentz - DB
Hal Lewis - DB
Hub Lindsey - HB
Floyd Little - HB
Tommy Luke - DB
Fran Lynch - HB
Brendan McCarthy - FB
John McCormick - QB
Rex Mirich - DT
Alex Moore - DB
Bobby Moten - WR
Chip Myrtle - TE
Tom Oberg - DB
Frank Richter - LB
Paul Smith - DE
Jesse Stokes - DB
Steve Tensi - QB
Dave Tobey - LB
Bill Van Heusen - WR
Bob Vaughn - G
Dave Washington - TE
Bob Young - G

1968 Houston

Pete Barnes - LB
Glenn Bass - WR
Pete Beathard - QB
Jim Beirne - WR
Elvin Bethea - DE
Sonny Bishop - G
Sid Blanks - HB
Garland Boyette - LB
Ode Burrell - HB
Woody Campbell - HB
Ed Carrington - TE
Larry Carwell - DB
Ronnie Caveness - LB
Gary Cutsinger - DE
Bob Davis - QB
Tom Domres - DE
Miller Farr - DB
Charley Frazier - WR
Hoyle Granger - FB
Mac Haik - WR
W.K. Hicks - DB
Glen Ray Hines - T
Pat Holmes - DE
Roy Hopkins - FB
Ken Houston - DB
Pete Johns - DB
Jim LeMoine - TE
Bobby Maples - C
Bud Marshall - DT
Dudley Meredith - DT
Zeke Moore - DB
Jim Norton - DB
Willie Parker - DT
Steve Quinn - C
Alvin Reed - TE
Tom Regner - G
George Rice - DT
Bob Robertson - T
Marion Rushing - LB
Bob Smith - DB
Carel Stith - DT
Richard Stotter - LB
Walt Suggs - T
Richard Swatland - G

Lionel Taylor - WR
Don Trull - QB
Olen Underwood - LB
Wayne Walker - K
George Webster - LB
John Wittenborn - K

1968 Kansas City

Bud Abell - LB
Fred Arbanas - TE
Bobby Bell - LB
Ceasar Belser - DB
Aaron Brown - DE
Buck Buchanan - DT
Ed Budde - G
Reggie Carolan - TE
Bert Coan - HB
Curley Culp - G
George Daney - G
Len Dawson - QB
Mike Garrett - HB
Jack Gehrke - WR
Wendell Hayes - FB
Dave Hill - T
Robert Holmes - FB
E.J. Holub - C
Chuck Hurston - LB
Jim Kearney - DB
Ernie Ladd - DT
Willie Lanier - LB
Jacky Lee - QB
Mike Livingston - QB
Sam Longmire - WR
Ed Lothamer - DT
Paul Lowe - HB
Jim Lynch - LB
Dave Martin - LB
Jerry Mays - DE
Curtis McClinton - FB
Curt Merz - G
Willie Mitchell - DB
Mo Moorman - G
Frank Pitts - WR
Remi Prudhomme - DT
Gloster Richardson - WR
Johnny Robinson - DB
Goldie Sellers - DB
Noland Smith - WR
Jan Stenerud - K
Otis Taylor - WR
Emmitt Thomas - DB
Jim Tyrer - T
Jerrel Wilson - K

1968 Miami

Dick Anderson - DB
Rudy Barber - LB
John Bramlett - LB
Mel Branch - DE
Bob Bruggers - LB
Jim Cox - TE
Doug Crusan - T
Larry Csonka - FB
Bill Darnall - WR
Randy Edmunds - LB
Frank Emanuel - LB
Norm Evans - T
Manny Fernandez - DE
Charlie Fowler - G
Tom Goode - C
Bob Griese - QB
Kim Hammond - QB
Jack Harper - HB
Ray Jacobs - DT
Bob Joswick - DE
Jimmy Keyes - LB
Jim Kiick - HB
Mack Lamb - DB
Wahoo McDaniel - LB
Gene Milton - WR
Stan Mitchell - HB
Doug Moreau - TE
Bob Neff - DB
Billy Neighbors - G
Tom Nomina - DT
Karl Noonan - WR
Rick Norton - QB
Bob Petrella - DB
Sammy Price - HB
Jack Pyburn - T
John Richardson - DT
Jim Riley - DE
Larry Seiple - TE
Gary Tucker - HB
Howard Twilley - WR
Jim Urbanek - DT
Jimmy Warren - DB
Dick Washington - DB
Ed Weisacosky - LB
Willie West - DB
Dick Westmoreland - DB
Maxie Williams - G
Freddie Woodson - DE

1968 NY Jets

Al Atkinson - LB
Bill Baird - DB
Ralph Baker - LB
Randy Beverly - DB
Verlon Biggs - DE
Emerson Boozer - HB
Earl Christy - DB
Paul Crane - LB
Mike D'Amato - DB
John Dockery - DB
John Elliott - DT
Cornell Gordon - DB
Larry Grantham - LB
Ray Hayes - DT
Karl Henke - DT
Dave Herman - T
Winston Hill - T
Jim Hudson - DB
Billy Joe - FB
Curley Johnson - TE
Pete Lammons - TE
Bill Mathis - HB
Don Maynard - WR
Carl McAdams - DE
Joe Namath - QB
John Neidert - LB
Babe Parilli - QB
Gerry Philbin - DE
Bill Rademacher - WR
Randy Rasmussen - G
Jim Richards - DB
Jeff Richardson - C
Paul Rochester - DT
Johnny Sample - DB
George Sauer - WR
John Schmitt - C
Mark Smolinski - TE
Matt Snell - FB
Mike Stromberg - LB
Bob Talamini - G
Steve Thompson - DE
Jim Turner - QB
Bake Turner - WR
Sam Walton - T
Lee White - FB

1968 Oakland

Butch Atkinson - DB
Pete Banaszak - HB
Duane Benson - LB
Fred Biletnikoff - WR
Rodger Bird - DB
Dan Birdwell - DT
George Blanda - QB
Willie Brown - DB
Bill Budness - LB
Billy Cannon - TE
Dan Conners - LB
Ben Davidson - DE
Cotton Davidson - QB
Eldridge Dickey - WR
Hewritt Dixon - FB
Al Dotson - DT
John Eason - WR
Mike Eischeid - K
Bill Fairband - LB
Dave Grayson - DB
Roger Hagberg - FB
Jim Harvey - G
Wayne Hawkins - G
Jerry Hopkins - LB
Dave Kocourek - TE
Bob Kruse - G
Daryle Lamonica - QB
Ike Lassiter - DE
Kent McCloughan - DB
Bill Miller - WR
Carleton Oats - DE
Dave Ogas - LB
Chip Oliver - LB
Gus Otto - LB
Jim Otto - C
Warren Powers - DB
Preston Ridlehuber - HB
John Roderick - WR
Karl Rubke - C
Harry Schuh - T
Art Shell - T
Charlie Smith - HB
Bob Svihus - T
Larry Todd - HB
Gene Upshaw - G
Warren Wells - WR
Howie Williams - DB
Nemiah Wilson - DB

1968 San Diego

Harold Akin - T
Chuck Allen - LB
Jim Allison - FB
Lance Alworth - WR
Scott Appleton - DT
Marty Baccaglio - DE
Joe Beauchamp - DB
Ron Billingsley - DT
Bob Briggs - DT
Jon Brittenum - QB
Bob Bruggers - LB
Steve DeLong - DE
Speedy Duncan - DB
Ken Dyer - WR
Bernie Erickson - LB
Tom Erlandson - LB
Dick Farley - DB
Lane Fenner - WR
Jim Fetherston - LB
Gene Foster - FB
Willie Frazier - TE
Gary Garrison - WR
Kenny Graham - DB
Sam Gruneisen - C
John Hadl - QB
Bob Howard - DB
Brad Hubbert - FB
Curtis Jones - LB
Gary Kirner - G
Paul Latzke - C
Bill Lenkaitis - C
Keith Lincoln - HB
Larry Little - G
Paul Lowe - HB
Jacque MacKinnon - TE
Ron McCall - LB
Bob Mitinger - LB
Ron Mix - T
Terry Owens - T
Dennis Partee - K
Dickie Post - HB
Bob Print - LB
Rick Redman - LB
Houston Ridge - DE
Jim Schmedding - G
Russ Smith - HB
Dick Speights - DB
Jeff Staggs - LB
Walt Sweeney - G
Jim Tolbert - DB
Phil Tuckett - WR
Russ Washington - DT
Bob Wells - T
Andre White - TE
Bud Whitehead - DB

1969 NFL

1969 Atlanta

Ron Acks - LB
Grady Allen - LB
Bob Berry - QB
Bruce Bosley - C
Bob Breitenstein - G
Greg Brezina - LB
Charlie Bryant - HB
Cannonball Butler - HB
Dave Cahill - DT
Junior Coffey - FB
Gail Cogdill - WR
Glen Condren - DT
Ted Cottrell - LB
Dick Enderle - G
Bob Etter - K
Jim Ferguson - C
Paul Flatley - WR
Mike Freeman - DB
Paul Gipson - FB
Don Hansen - LB
Bob Hughes - DE
Claude Humphrey - DE
Randy Johnson - QB
George Kunz - T
Al Lavan - DB
Monte Ledbetter - WR
Bobby Lee - WR
Bruce Lemmerman - QB
Billy Lothridge - K
John Mallory - DB
Tom McCauley - WR
Gary McDermott - HB
Jim Mitchell - TE
Tommy Nobis - LB
Ken Reaves - DB
Rudy Redmond - DB
Bill Sabatino - DT
Bill Sandeman - T
Roy Schmidt - T
Jerry Shay - DT
Jerry Simmons - WR
Ralph Smith - TE
Mal Snider - G
Jeff Stanciel - HB
Jeff Van Note - LB
Harmon Wages - FB
Jim Waskiewicz - C
Jim Weatherford - DB
Nate Wright - DB
John Zook - DE

1969 Baltimore

Ocie Austin - DB
Sam Ball - T
John Campbell - LB
Terry Cole - FB
Larry Conjar - FB
Bill Curry - C
Mike Curtis - LB
Jim Duncan - DB
Perry Lee Dunn - FB
Dennis Gaubatz - LB
Bob Grant - LB
Dan Grimm - G
Sam Havrilak - DB
Ted Hendricks - LB
Jerry Hill - FB
Roy Hilton - DE
Eddie Hinton - WR
Cornelius Johnson - G
Ron Kostelnik - DT
David Lee - K
Jerry Logan - DB
Lenny Lyles - DB
John Mackey - TE
Tom Matte - HB
Carl Mauck - C
Tommy Maxwell - DB
Lou Michaels - DE
Fred Miller - DT
Tom Mitchell - TE
Earl Morrall - QB
Roland Moss - TE
Jimmy Orr - WR
Preston Pearson - HB
Ray Perkins - WR
Ron Porter - LB
Glenn Ressler - G
Willie Richardson - WR
Butch Riley - LB
Don Shinnick - LB
Billy Ray Smith Sr. - DT
Bubba Smith - DE
Charles Stukes - DB
Dan Sullivan - G
Johnny Unitas - QB
Bob Vogel - T
Rick Volk - DB
John Williams - G

1969 Chi. Bears

Marty Amsler - DE
Doug Buffone - LB
Ronnie Bull - FB
Dick Butkus - LB
Jim Cadile - G
Lee Calland - DB
Virgil Carter - QB
Tim Casey - LB
Jack Concannon - QB
Ron Copeland - WR
Frank Cornish - DT
Dick Daniels - DB
Austin Denney - TE
Bobby Douglass - QB
Dick Evey - DT
Jim Ferguson - C
Dick Gordon - WR
Bobby Joe Green - K
Dave Hale - DE
Major Hazelton - DB
Willie Holman - DE
Mike Hull - FB
Randy Jackson - T
Ken Kortas - DT
Rudy Kuechenberg - LB
Ralph Kurek - FB
Garry Lyle - HB
Dave Martin - LB
Wayne Mass - T
Rufus Mayes - T
Bennie McRae - DB
Ross Montgomery - FB
Howard Mudd - G
Ed O'Bradovich - DE
Ray Ogden - WR
Mac Percival - K
Loyd Phillips - DE
Brian Piccolo - FB
Bob Pickens - T
Dan Pride - LB
Mike Pyle - C
Gale Sayers - HB
George Seals - G
Jerry Simmons - WR
Joe Taylor - DB
Rosey Taylor - DB
Cecil Turner - WR
Emilio Vallez - TE
Bob Wallace - WR
Bob Wetoska - C
George Youngblood - DB

1969 Cleveland

Billy Andrews - LB
Erich Barnes - DB
Dean Brown - DB
Monte Clark - T
Don Cockroft - K
Gary Collins - WR
Jim Copeland - G
Ben Davis - DB
John Demarie - G
John Garlington - LB
Chip Glass - TE
Jack Gregory - DE
Gene Hickerson - G
Fred Hoaglin - C
Fair Hooker - WR
Jim Houston - LB
Mike Howell - DB
Al Jenkins - DE
Ron Johnson - HB
Walter Johnson - DT
Dave Jones - WR
Jim Kanicki - DT
Ernie Kellermann - DB
Leroy Kelly - HB
Charlie Leigh - FB
Dale Lindsey - LB
Bob Matheson - LB
Wayne Meylan - LB
Alvin Mitchell - DB
Milt Morin - TE
Reece Morrison - HB
Bill Nelsen - QB
Bob Oliver - T
Chuck Reynolds - G
Jerry Rhome - QB
Joe Righetti - DT
Dick Schafrath - T
Bo Scott - FB
Ron Snidow - DE
Freddie Summers - DB
Walt Sumner - DB
Joe Taffoni - T
Marv Upshaw - DT
Paul Warfield - WR

1969 Dallas

George Andrie - DE
Craig Baynham - HB
Otto Brown - DB
Jackie Burkett - LB
Mike Clark - K
Phil Clark - DB
Larry Cole - DE
Bobby Joe Conrad - WR
Mike Ditka - TE
Ron East - DT
Dave Edwards - LB
Richmond Flowers - WR
Mike Gaechter - DB
Walt Garrison - FB
Cornell Green - DB
Halvor Hagen - T
Bob Hayes - WR
Calvin Hill - HB
Dennis Homan - WR
Chuck Howley - LB
Mike Johnson - DB
Lee Roy Jordan - LB
Bob Lilly - DT
Tony Liscio - T
Dave Manders - C
Craig Morton - QB
Ralph Neely - T
John Niland - G
Pettis Norman - TE
Blaine Nye - G
Jethro Pugh - DT
Dan Reeves - FB
Mel Renfro - DB
Lance Rentzel - WR
Les Shy - HB
Roger Staubach - QB
Thomas Stincic - LB
Malcolm Walker - C
Claxton Welch - HB
Fred Whittingham - LB
Ron Widby - K
John Wilbur - G
Rayfield Wright - TE

1969 Detroit

Lem Barney - DB
Greg Barton - QB
Craig Cotton - TE
Bill Cottrell - G
Rick Duncan - K
Nick Eddy - HB
Mel Farr - HB
Ed Flanagan - C
Rocky Freitas - T
Frank Gallagher - G
Dan Goich - DE
Larry Hand - DE
Alex Karras - DT
Bob Kowalkowski - G
Greg Landry - QB
Dick LeBeau - DB
Mike Lucci - LB
Bill Malinchak - WR
Errol Mann - K
Earl McCullouch - WR
Ed Mooney - LB
Denis Moore - DT
Bill Munson - QB
Paul Naumoff - LB
Tom Nowatzke - LB
Phil Odle - WR
Rocky Rasley - G
Wayne Rasmussen - DB
Joe Robb - DE
Jerry Rush - DT
Charlie Sanders - TE
Roger Shoals - T
Bill Swain - LB
Altie Taylor - HB
Bill Triplett - FB
Tom Vaughn - DB
Wayne Walker - LB
Chuck Walton - G
Larry Walton - WR
Larry Watkins - FB
Mike Weger - DB
Bobby Williams - DB
John Wright - WR
Jim Yarbrough - T

1969 Green Bay

Herb Adderley - DB
Lionel Aldridge - DE
Donny Anderson - HB
Ken Bowman - C
Dave Bradley - G
Robert Brown - DT
Lee Roy Caffey - LB
Fred Carr - LB
Carroll Dale - WR
Willie Davis - DE
Boyd Dowler - WR
Jim Flanigan - LB
Marv Fleming - TE
Gale Gillingham - G
Jim Grabowski - FB
Forrest Gregg - T
Dave Hampton - HB
Doug Hart - DB
Bill Hayhoe - T
Dick Himes - T
Don Horn - QB
Bob Hyland - G
Bob Jeter - DB
Ron Jones - TE
Henry Jordan - DT
Bill Lueck - G
Booth Lusteg - K
Chuck Mercein - FB
Mike Mercer - K
Rich Moore - DT
Ray Nitschke - LB
Francis Peay - T
Elijah Pitts - HB
Dave Robinson - LB
John Rowser - DB
Gordon Rule - DB
John Spilis - WR
Bart Starr - QB
Bill Stevens - QB
Phil Vandersea - DE
Jim Weatherwax - DT
Perry Williams - FB
Travis Williams - HB
Francis Winkler - DE
Willie Wood - DB

1969 LA Rams

Coy Bacon - DT
Dick Bass - FB
Maxie Baughan - LB
Bob Brown - T
Roger Brown - DT
George Burman - C
Rick Cash - DE
Charley Cowan - T
Pat Curran - TE
Willie Daniel - DB
Mike Dennis - HB
Willie Ellison - HB
Roman Gabriel - QB
Bruce Gossett - K
Alvin Haymond - DB
Ken Iman - C
Mitch Johnson - T
Deacon Jones - DE
Les Josephson - FB
Bob Klein - TE
Mike LaHood - G
Izzy Lang - FB
Lamar Lundy - DE
Tom Mack - G
Frank Marchlewski - C
Tommy Mason - HB
Ed Meador - DB
Jim Nettles - DB
Merlin Olsen - DT
Jack Pardee - LB
John Pergine - LB
Richie Petitbon - DB
Myron Pottios - LB
Jim Purnell - LB
David Ray - WR
Joe Scibelli - G
Nate Shaw - DB
Ron Smith - DB
Larry Smith - HB
Jack Snow - WR
Pat Studstill - WR
Karl Sweetan - QB
Diron Talbert - DE
Billy Truax - TE
Wendell Tucker - WR
Clancy Williams - DB
Doug Woodlief - LB

1969 Minnesota

Grady Alderman - T
John Beasley - TE
Bookie Bolin - G
Bill Brown - FB
Bobby Bryant - DB
Fred Cox - K
Gary Cuozzo - QB
Doug Davis - T
Paul Dickson - DT
Carl Eller - DE
Bob Grim - WR
Dale Hackbart - LB
Tom Hall - WR
Jim Hargrove - LB
Billy Harris - HB
John Henderson - WR
Wally Hilgenberg - LB
Clint Jones - HB
Joe Kapp - QB
Karl Kassulke - DB
John Kirby - LB
Kent Kramer - TE
Paul Krause - DB
Gary Larsen - DT
Bob Lee - QB
Jim Lindsey - HB
Earsell Mackbee - DB
Jim Marshall - DE
Mike McGill - LB
Dave Osborn - HB
Alan Page - DT
Oscar Reed - HB
Mike Reilly - LB
Ed Sharockman - DB
Steve Smith - DE
Milt Sunde - G
Mick Tingelhoff - C
Jim Vellone - G
Lonnie Warwick - LB
Gene Washington - WR
Charlie West - DB
Ed White - G
Roy Winston - LB
Ron Yary - T

1969 New Orleans

Danny Abramowicz - WR
Dick Absher - LB
Doug Atkins - DE
Tony Baker - FB
Tom Barrington - FB
Johnny Brewer - LB
Bo Burris - DB
Bill Cody - LB
Daniel Colchico - DE
Wayne Colman - LB
Olie Cordill - DB
Norman Davis - G
Ted Davis - LB
Tom Dempsey - K
Al Dodd - WR
Edd Hargett - QB
Jimmy Hester - TE
Gene Howard - DB
Jerry Jones - T
Les Kelley - LB
Billy Kilmer - QB
Jake Kupp - G
Errol Linden - T
Andy Livingston - FB
Dave Long - DE
Joe Don Looney - HB
Tony Lorick - FB
Tom McNeill - K
Mike Morgan - LB
Richard Neal - DE
Elijah Nevett - DB
Jim Ninowski - QB
Dave Parks - TE
Ray Poage - TE
Steve Preece - DB
Mike Rengel - DT
Dave Rowe - DT
Bill Saul - LB
John Shinners - G
Don Shy - HB
Jerry Sturm - C
Don Talbert - T
Mike Taylor - T
Bobby Thompson - DB
Mike Tilleman - DT
Carl Ward - DB
Ernie Wheelwright - FB
Dave Whitsell - DB
Del Williams - G
Marv Woodson - DB

1969 NY Giants

Bruce Anderson - DE
McKinley Boston - LB
Al Brenner - DB
Rich Buzin - T
Pete Case - G
Gene Ceppetelli - C
Junior Coffey - FB
Tommy Crutcher - LB
Henry Davis - LB
Darrell Dess - G
Fred Dryer - DE
Dave Dunaway - WR
Scott Eaton - DB
Tucker Frederickson - FB
John Fuqua - HB
Pete Gogolak - K
Charlie Harper - T
Ralph Heck - LB
Don Herrmann - WR
Ray Hickl - LB
Chuck Hinton - C
Jim Holifield - DB
Rich Houston - WR
Curley Johnson - K
John Johnson - DT
Homer Jones - WR
John Kirby - LB
Rich Kotite - TE
Ernie Koy - FB
Greg Larson - C
Carl Lockhart - DB
Tom Longo - DB
Bob Lurtsema - DE
Bruce Maher - DB
Tim McCann - DT
Randy Minniear - HB
Frank Molden - DT
Joe Morrison - WR
Frank Parker - DT
Milt Plum - QB
Joe Szczecko - DT
Fran Tarkenton - QB
Aaron Thomas - WR

Doug Van Horn - G
Freeman White - TE
Willie Williams - DB
Butch Wilson - TE
Gary Wood - QB
Steve Wright - T
Willie Young - T

1969 Philadelphia

Sam Baker - K
Gary Ballman - WR
Ronnie Blye - HB
Bill Bradley - DB
Fred Brown - TE
Ernie Calloway - DT
Joe Carollo - T
Gene Ceppetelli - C
Don Chuy - G
Wayne Colman - LB
Irv Cross - DB
Mike Dirks - DT
Mike Evans - C
Dave Graham - T
Tony Guillory - LB
Dick Hart - G
Ben Hawkins - WR
Fred Hill - TE
Bill Hobbs - LB
Lane Howell - T
Chuck Hughes - WR
Don Hultz - DE
Harold Jackson - WR
Jay Johnson - LB
Harry Jones - HB
Ike Kelley - LB
Leroy Keyes - HB
Kent Lawrence - WR
Dave Lloyd - LB
Ron Medved - DB
George Mira - QB
Al Nelson - DB
Mark Nordquist - C
Floyd Peters - DT
Gary Pettigrew - DE
Cyril Pinder - FB
Ron Porter - LB
Nate Ramsey - DB
Jimmy Raye - DB
Tim Rossovich - DE
Joe Scarpati - DB
Jim Skaggs - G
Norm Snead - QB
Mel Tom - DE
Harry Wilson - HB
Tom Woodeshick - FB
Adrian Young - LB

1969 Pittsburgh

Bob Adams - TE
Don Alley - WR
Dick Arndt - DT
Warren Bankston - FB
Chuck Beatty - DB
John Brown - T
Lee Calland - DB
John Campbell - LB
Bob Campbell - HB
Marshall Cropper - WR
Sam Davis - G
Doug Fisher - LB
Larry Gagner - G
Joe Greene - DT
L. C. Greenwood - DE
Earl Gros - FB
Mike Haggerty - T
Terry Hanratty - QB
Jon Henderson - WR
Jerry Hillebrand - LB
John Hilton - TE
Chuck Hinton - DT
Dick Hoak - HB
Bob Hohn - DB
Roy Jefferson - WR
Jon Kolb - C
Ray Mansfield - C
Paul Martha - DB
Ray May - LB
Don McCall - HB
Ben McGee - DE
Gene Mingo - K
Kent Nix - QB
Clancy Oliver - DB
Andy Russell - LB
Dick Shiner - QB
Jim Shorter - DB
Brian Stenger - LB
Mike Taylor - T
Bruce Van Dyke - G
Lloyd Voss - DE
Bobby Walden - K
Clarence Washington - DT
Ralph Wenzel - G
J.R. Wilburn - WR
Erwin Williams - WR
Sid Williams - LB
Marv Woodson - DB

1969 St. Louis

Bob Atkins - DB
Jim Bakken - K
Robert Brown - TE
Terry Brown - WR
Don Brumm - DE
Willis Crenshaw - FB
Jerry Daanen - WR
Bob DeMarco - C
Cid Edwards - FB
Vern Emerson - T
John Gilliam - WR
Irv Goode - G
Ken Gray - G
Jim Hart - QB
Chip Healy - LB
Fred Heron - DT
King Hill - QB
Fred Hyatt - WR
Charley Johnson - QB
Rolf Krueger - DE
MacArthur Lane - HB
Ernie McMillan - T
Dave Meggyesy - LB
Wayne Mulligan - C
Dave Olerich - LB
Bob Reynolds - T
Jamie Rivers - LB
Johnny Roland - HB
Rocky Rosema - LB
Bob Rowe - DT
Lonnie Sanders - DB
Mack Sauls - DB
Joe Schmiesing - DT
Roy Shivers - HB
Jackie Smith - TE
Cal Snowden - DE
Rick Sortun - G
Larry Stallings - LB
Jerry Stovall - DB
Chuck Walker - DE
Roger Wehrli - DB
Clyde Williams - T
Dave Williams - WR
Larry Wilson - DB
Mike Wilson - DB
Nate Wright - DB

1969 San Francisco

Kermit Alexander - DB
Cas Banaszek - T
Ed Beard - LB
Randy Beisler - T
Bill Belk - DE
Forrest Blue - C
John Brodie - QB
Elmer Collett - G
Doug Cunningham - HB
Tommy Davis - K
Earl Edwards - DT
Johnny Fuller - DB
Momcilo Gavric - K
Fritz Greenlee - LB
Tommy Hart - DE
Harold Hays - LB
Stan Hindman - DE
Jim Johnson - DB
Lee Johnson - WR
Jon Kilgore - K
Charlie Krueger - DT
Ted Kwalick - TE
Roland Lakes - DT
Gary Lewis - FB
Clifton McNeil - WR
Gene Moore - HB
Howard Mudd - G
Frank Nunley - LB
Lance Olssen - T
Woody Peoples - G
Mel Phillips - DB
Al Randolph - DB
Len Rohde - T
Sam Silas - DE
Noland Smith - HB
Jim Sniadecki - LB
Steve Spurrier - QB
Rosey Taylor - DB
Jimmy Thomas - HB
Bill Tucker - FB
Skip Vanderbundt - LB
Gene Washington - WR
Dave Wilcox - LB
Ken Willard - FB
Bob Windsor - TE
Dick Witcher - WR
John Woitt - DB
Bill Wondolowski - WR

1969 Washington

Jerry Allen - HB
Willie Banks - G
Mike Bass - DB
Gary Beban - WR
Frank Bosch - DT
Mike Bragg - K
Larry Brown - HB
Tom Brown - DB
Leo Carroll - DE
Dennis Crane - DT
Dave Crossan - C
John Didion - C
Steve Duich - G
Henry Dyer - FB
Pat Fischer - DB
Dan Grimm - G
Chris Hanburger - LB
Charlie Harraway - FB
Rickie Harris - DB
Len Hauss - C
John Hoffman - DE
Sam Huff - LB
Sonny Jurgensen - QB
Carl Kammerer - DE
Curt Knight - K
Dave Kopay - FB
Bob Long - WR
Marlin McKeever - LB
Harold McLinton - LB
Clark Miller - DE
Spain Musgrove - DT
Jim Norton - DT
Brig Owens - DB
Vince Promuto - G
Pat Richter - TE
Walter Roberts - WR
Walt Rock - T
Tom Roussel - LB
Joe Rutgens - DT
Frank Ryan - QB
Ray Schoenke - C
Jerry Smith - TE
Jim Snowden - T
Charley Taylor - WR
Ted Vactor - DB
Bob Wade - DB

1969 AFL

1969 Boston

Houston Antwine - DT
Teddy Bailey - HB
Ron Berger - DE
Sid Blanks - HB
John Bramlett - LB
Barry Brown - LB
Johnny Cagle - DE
Gino Cappelletti - WR
Larry Carwell - DB
John Charles - DB
Jim Cheyunski - LB
Larry Eisenhauer - DE
Charley Frazier - WR
Tom Funchess - T
R. C. Gamble - HB
Carl Garrett - HB
Bob Gladieux - HB
Kim Hammond - QB
Karl Henke - DT
Ken Herock - TE
Jim Hunt - DT
Ray Jacobs - DT
Tom Janik - DB
Daryl Johnson - DB
Ezell Jones - T
Charley Long - G
Aaron Marsh - WR
Art McMahon - DB
Mike Montler - C
Jon Morris - C
Jim Nance - FB
Tom Neville - T
John Outlaw - DB
Ed Philpott - LB
Bill Rademacher - WR
Tom Richardson - WR
Marty Schottenheimer - LB
Clarence Scott - DB
Ron Sellers - WR
Tom Sherman - QB
Len St. Jean - G
Mike Taliaferro - QB
Ed Toner - DT
Don Webb - DB
Jim Whalen - TE
J.R. Williamson - LB
Mel Witt - DE

1969 Buffalo

Bruce Alford - K
Max Anderson - HB
Stew Barber - T
Al Bemiller - C
Marlin Briscoe - WR
Butch Byrd - DB
Edgar Chandler - LB
Jerald Collins - LB
Paul Costa - T
Hilton Crawford - DB
Bobby Crockett - WR
Dan Darragh - QB
Chuck DeVliegher - DT
Jim Dunaway - DT
Booker Edgerson - DB
Bill Enyart - FB
Charley Ferguson - TE
Tom Flores - QB
Willie Grate - TE
Paul Guidry - LB
James Harris - QB
Waddey Harvey - DT
Harry Jacobs - LB
Robert James - WR
Jack Kemp - QB
Howard Kindig - T
Bob Kruse - DT
Monte Ledbetter - WR
Angelo Loukas - G
Paul Maguire - LB
Billy Masters - TE
Mike McBath - DE
Ron McDole - DE
Haven Moses - WR
Julian Nunamaker - DE
Joe O'Donnell - G
Dave Ogas - LB
Wayne Patrick - FB
John Pitts - DB
Roy Reeves - WR
Pete Richardson - DB
Mike Richey - T
Preston Ridlehuber - HB
George Saimes - DB
Billy Shaw - G
Tom Sherman - QB
O.J. Simpson - HB
Mike Stratton - LB
Bob Tatarek - DT
Bubba Thornton - WR

1969 Cincinnati

Ken Avery - LB
Marty Baccaglio - DE
Al Beauchamp - LB
Bill Bergey - LB
Royce Berry - DE
Tim Buchanan - LB
Justin Canale - G
Steve Chomyszak - DT
Al Coleman - DB
Greg Cook - QB
Bruce Coslet - TE
Eric Crabtree - WR
Guy Dennis - G
Howard Fest - T
Jack Gehrke - WR
John Guillory - DB
Harry Gunner - DE
Ed Harmon - LB
Bobby Hunt - DB
Essex Johnson - HB
Jim Johnson - DB
Bob Johnson - C
Charlie King - DB
Ron Lamb - FB
Dale Livingston - K
Pat Matson - G
Dave Middendorf - G
Horst Muhlmann - K
Chip Myers - WR
Ernie Park - G
Frank Peters - T
Bill Peterson - LB
Jess Phillips - HB
Andy Rice - DT
Ken Riley - DB
Paul Robinson - HB
Fletcher Smith - DB
Tommie Smith - WR
Bill Staley - DT
Terry Swanson - K
Speedy Thomas - WR
Bob Trumpy - WR
Clem Turner - FB
Mike Wilson - G
Ernie Wright - T
Sam Wyche - QB

1969 Denver

Ted Alflen - HB
Jay Bachman - C
Walt Barnes - DE
Tom Beer - TE
Phil Brady - DB
Sam Brunelli - T
Tom Buckman - TE
Bobby Burnett - HB
George Burrell - DB
Tim Casey - LB
Grady Cavness - DB
Dave Costa - DT
Gary Crane - LB
Ken Criter - LB
Carl Cunningham - LB
Mike Current - T
Al Denson - WR
Wallace Dickey - T
Pete Duranko - DE
John Embree - WR
George Goeddeke - G
Charlie Greer - DB
Mike Haffner - WR
Buzz Highsmith - G
Gus Hollomon - DB
Bobby Howfield - K
John Huard - LB
Jerry Inman - DT
Rich Jackson - DE
Pete Jaquess - DB
Henry Jones - FB
Larry Kaminski - C
Gordon Lambert - LB
Pete Liske - QB
Floyd Little - HB
Fran Lynch - HB
Brendan McCarthy - FB
Rex Mirich - DT
Chip Myrtle - LB
Tom Oberg - DB
Chuck Pastrana - QB
Dave Pivec - TE
Frank Quayle - HB
Frank Richter - LB
Mike Schnitker - G
Tommie Smiley - FB
Jimmy Smith - DB
Paul Smith - DT
Steve Tensi - QB
Billy Thompson - DB
Bill Van Heusen - WR
Wandy Williams - HB
Bob Young - G

1969 Houston

Hank Autry - C
Pete Beathard - QB
Jim Beirne - WR
Elvin Bethea - DE
Sonny Bishop - G
Garland Boyette - LB
Ode Burrell - HB
Woody Campbell - HB
Ed Carrington - TE
Bob Davis - QB
Tom Domres - DT
John Douglas - DB
Elbert Drungo - T
Miller Farr - DB
Roy Gerela - K
Hoyle Granger - FB
Mac Haik - WR
W.K. Hicks - DB
Glen Ray Hines - T
Pat Holmes - DE
Roy Hopkins - FB
Ken Houston - DB
Rich Johnson - HB
Charlie Joiner - WR
Jim LeMoine - G
Jerry LeVias - WR
Bobby Maples - C
Ben Mayes - DT
Zeke Moore - DB
Willie Parker - DT
Johnny Peacock - DB
Ron Pritchard - LB
Alvin Reed - TE
Tom Regner - G
George Rice - DT
Mike Richardson - HB
Carel Stith - DT
Walt Suggs - T
Don Trull - QB
Olen Underwood - LB
Loyd Wainscott - LB
Ed Watson - LB
George Webster - LB
Glenn Woods - DE
Paul Zaeske - WR

1969 Kansas City

Fred Arbanas - T
Bobby Bell - LB
Ceasar Belser - DB
Aaron Brown - DE
Buck Buchanan - DT
Ed Budde - G
Curley Culp - DT
George Daney - G
Len Dawson - QB
Tom Flores - QB
Mike Garrett - HB
Wendell Hayes - FB
Dave Hill - T
Robert Holmes - FB
E.J. Holub - C
Chuck Hurston - LB
Jim Kearney - DB
Willie Lanier - LB
Jacky Lee - QB
Mike Livingston - QB
Ed Lothamer - DT
Paul Lowe - HB
Jim Lynch - LB
Jim Marsalis - DB
Jerry Mays - DE
Mickey McCarty - TE
Curtis McClinton - TE
Warren McVea - HB
Willie Mitchell - DB
Mo Moorman - G
Frank Pitts - WR
Ed Podolak - HB
Remi Prudhomme - C
Gloster Richardson - WR
Johnny Robinson - DB
Goldie Sellers - DB
Noland Smith - HB
Bob Stein - LB
Jan Stenerud - K
Otis Taylor - WR
Emmitt Thomas - DB
Gene Trosch - DE
Jim Tyrer - T
Jerrel Wilson - K

1969 Miami

Dick Anderson - DB
Tom Beier - DB
Tommy Boutwell - QB
John Boynton - T
Nick Buoniconti - LB
Jack Clancy - WR
Doug Crusan - T
Larry Csonka - FB
Bill Darnall - WR
Randy Edmunds - LB
Frank Emanuel - LB
Norm Evans - T
Manny Fernandez - DT
Tom Goode - C
Garry Grady - DB
Bob Griese - QB
Bob Heinz - DT
Jimmy Hines - WR
Bob Joswick - DT
Jimmy Keyes - LB
Jim Kiick - HB
Karl Kremser - K
Larry Little - T
Norm McBride - DE
Dale McCullers - LB
Jim Mertens - TE
Gene Milton - WR
Stan Mitchell - FB
Doug Moreau - TE
Mercury Morris - HB
Lloyd Mumphord - DB
Billy Neighbors - G
Karl Noonan - WR
Rick Norton - QB
Willie Pearson - DB
Bob Petrella - DB
Jesse Powell - LB
Barry Pryor - HB
Jeff Richardson - T
John Richardson - DT
Jim Riley - DE
Larry Seiple - TE
Bill Stanfill - DE
John Stofa - QB
Howard Twilley - WR
Jimmy Warren - DB
Ed Weisacosky - LB
Dick Westmoreland - DB
Maxie Williams - G
Freddie Woodson - G

1969 NY Jets

Al Atkinson - LB
Bill Baird - DB
Ralph Baker - LB
Mike Battle - DB
Randy Beverly - DB
Verlon Biggs - DE
Emerson Boozer - HB
Jim Carroll - LB
Paul Crane - LB
John Dockery - DB
John Elliott - DT
Roger Finnie - T
Dave Foley - T
Cornell Gordon - DB
Larry Grantham - LB
Dave Herman - G
Winston Hill - T
Jim Hudson - DB
Billy Joe - FB
Jimmie Jones - DE
Pete Lammons - TE
Cecil Leonard - DB
Bill Mathis - HB
Don Maynard - WR
Carl McAdams - DT
Joe Namath - QB
John Neidert - LB
George Nock - HB
Steve O'Neal - WR
Babe Parilli - QB
Pete Perreault - G
Gerry Philbin - DE
Randy Rasmussen - G
Jim Richards - DB
Paul Rochester - DT
George Sauer - WR
John Schmitt - C
Paul Seiler - C
Matt Snell - FB
Wayne Stewart - TE
Steve Thompson - DT
Jim Turner - QB
Bake Turner - WR
Sam Walton - T
Lee White - FB
Al Woodall - QB
Gordon Wright - G

1969 Oakland

Jackie Allen - DB
Butch Atkinson - DB
Pete Banaszak - FB
Duane Benson - LB
Fred Biletnikoff - WR
Dan Birdwell - DT
George Blanda - QB
Willie Brown - DB
Bill Budness - LB
George Buehler - G
Drew Buie - WR
Billy Cannon - TE
Dan Conners - LB
Ben Davidson - DE
Hewritt Dixon - FB
Al Dotson - DT
Lloyd Edwards - TE
Mike Eischeid - K
Dave Grayson - DB
Roger Hagberg - TE
Jim Harvey - G
Wayne Hawkins - G
Marv Hubbard - FB
Tom Keating - DT
Daryle Lamonica - QB
Bill Laskey - LB
Ike Lassiter - DE
Kent McCloughan - DB
Carleton Oats - DT
Chip Oliver - LB
Gus Otto - LB
Jim Otto - C
Harry Schuh - T
Art Shell - T
Rod Sherman - WR
Charlie Smith - HB
Bob Svihus - T
Art Thoms - DT
Larry Todd - HB
Gene Upshaw - G
Warren Wells - WR
Howie Williams - DB
Nemiah Wilson - DB

1969 San Diego

Chuck Allen - LB
Lance Alworth - WR
Pete Barnes - LB
Joe Beauchamp - DB
Ron Billingsley - DE
Bob Briggs - DT
Bob Bruggers - LB
Jim Campbell - LB
Levert Carr - DT
Steve DeLong - DE
Marty Domres - QB
Speedy Duncan - DB
Rick Eber - WR
Dick Farley - DB
Gene Ferguson - T
Jim Fetherston - LB
Gene Foster - FB
Willie Frazier - TE
Gary Garrison - WR
Kenny Graham - DB
Sam Gruneisen - C
John Hadl - QB
Jim Hill - DB
Bob Howard - DB
Brad Hubbert - FB
Gene Huey - DB
Gary Kirner - G
Bill Lenkaitis - G
Jacque MacKinnon - TE
Pete Mikolajewski - QB
Ron Mix - T
Terry Owens - T
Dennis Partee - K
Dickie Post - HB
Jeff Queen - TE
Rick Redman - LB
Larry Rentz - DB
Houston Ridge - DE
Dan Sartin - DT
Ron Sayers - HB
Jim Schmedding - G
Russ Smith - FB
Jeff Staggs - LB
Walt Sweeney - G
Jim Tolbert - DB
Richard Trapp - WR
Russ Washington - DT
Bob Wells - T

1970 Atlanta

Ron Acks - LB
Grady Allen - LB
Bob Berry - QB
Bob Breitenstein - T
Mike Brunson - WR
Cannonball Butler - HB
Sonny Campbell - HB
Grady Cavness - DB
Gail Cogdill - WR
Glen Condren - DT
Ted Cottrell - LB
Mike Donohoe - TE
Dick Enderle - G
Paul Flatley - WR
Mike Freeman - DB
Paul Gipson - FB
Dean Halverson - LB
Don Hansen - LB
Dave Hettema - T
Claude Humphrey - DE
Randy Johnson - QB
George Kunz - T
Al Lavan - DB
Kent Lawrence - WR
Greg Lens - DT
Billy Lothridge - K
John Mallory - DB
Art Malone - HB
Randy Marshall - DE
John Matlock - C
Andy Maurer - G
Tom McCauley - DB
Jim Mitchell - TE
Tommy Nobis - LB
Ken Reaves - DB
Rudy Redmond - DB
Gary Roberts - G
Bill Sandeman - T
John Small - LB
Mal Snider - T
Todd Snyder - WR

Jim Sullivan - DE
Jeff Van Note - C
Ken Vinyard - K
Harmon Wages - FB
John Zook - DE

1970 Baltimore

Jim Bailey - DT
Sam Ball - T
Norm Bulaich - FB
Larry Conjar - FB
Bill Curry - C
Mike Curtis - LB
Tom Curtis - DB
Jim Duncan - DB
Ron Gardin - DB
Tom Goode - C
Bob Grant - LB
Sam Havrilak - HB
Ted Hendricks - LB
Jerry Hill - FB
Roy Hilton - DE
Eddie Hinton - WR
Roy Jefferson - WR
Cornelius Johnson - G
David Lee - K
Jerry Logan - DB
John Mackey - TE
Jack Maitland - HB
Tom Matte - HB
Tommy Maxwell - DB
Ray May - LB
Fred Miller - DT
Tom Mitchell - TE
Earl Morrall - QB
Dennis Nelson - T
Billy Newsome - DE
Robbie Nichols - LB
Tom Nowatzke - FB
Jim O'Brien - WR
Jimmy Orr - WR
Ray Perkins - WR
Glenn Ressler - G
Billy Ray Smith Sr. - DT
Bubba Smith - DE
Charles Stukes - DB
Dan Sullivan - G
Johnny Unitas - QB
Bob Vogel - T
Rick Volk - DB
John Williams - G
George Wright - DT

1970 Boston

Houston Antwine - DT
Mike Ballou - LB
Tom Beer - TE
Ron Berger - DE
Randy Beverly - DB
Sid Blanks - HB
John Bramlett - LB
Barry Brown - TE
Gary Bugenhagen - T
Gino Cappelletti - WR
Larry Carwell - DB
Jim Cheyunski - LB
Charley Frazier - WR
Tom Funchess - T
Carl Garrett - HB
Bob Gladieux - HB
Charlie Gogolak - K
Jim Hunt - DT
Tom Janik - DB
Daryl Johnson - DB
Ezell Jones - T
Joe Kapp - QB
Dan Kecman - LB
Gayle Knief - WR
Ike Lassiter - DE
Odell Lawson - HB
Angelo Loukas - T
Art McMahon - DB
Rex Mirich - DT
Mike Montler - G
Jon Morris - C
Jim Nance - FB
Tom Neville - T
John Outlaw - DB
Ed Philpott - LB
Bill Rademacher - WR
Eddie Ray - TE
Tom Richardson - WR
Marty Schottenheimer - LB
Clarence Scott - DB
Ron Sellers - WR
Len St. Jean - G
Mike Taliaferro - QB
Bake Turner - WR
Don Webb - DB
Fred Whittingham - LB
J.R. Williamson - LB
Dennis Wirgowski - DE
Mel Witt - DE

1970 Buffalo

Glenn Alexander - WR
Jackie Allen - DB
Al Andrews - LB
Marlin Briscoe - WR
Butch Byrd - DB
Levert Carr - T
Edgar Chandler - LB
Richard Cheek - G
Jerald Collins - LB
Paul Costa - T
Al Cowlings - DE
Dick Cunningham - LB
Dan Darragh - QB
Austin Denney - TE
Jim Dunaway - DT
Bill Enyart - FB
Wayne Fowler - C
Jerry Gantt - T
Bob Gladieux - HB
Clyde Glosson - WR
Willie Grate - TE
Paul Guidry - LB
Grant Guthrie - K
James Harris - QB
Waddey Harvey - DT
Ike Hill - DB
Robert James - DB
Greg Jones - HB
Howard Kindig - C
Art Laster - T
Paul Maguire - K
Frank Marchlewski - C
Mike McBath - DE
Mike McCaffrey - LB
Ron McDole - DE
Jim McFarland - TE
Haven Moses - WR
Roland Moss - HB
Julian Nunamaker - DT
Joe O'Donnell - G
Lloyd Pate - HB
Wayne Patrick - FB
Tommy Pharr - DB
John Pitts - DB
Jim Reilly - G
Pete Richardson - DB
Dennis Shaw - QB
O.J. Simpson - HB
Mike Stratton - LB
Bob Tatarek - DT

1970 Chi. Bears

Craig Baynham - HB
Ross Brupbacher - LB
Doug Buffone - LB
Ronnie Bull - FB
Dick Butkus - LB
Jim Cadile - G
Lee Roy Caffey - LB
Phil Clark - DB
Rich Coady - C
Linzy Cole - WR
Jack Concannon - QB
Jeff Curchin - T
Dick Daniels - DB
Butch Davis - DB
Bobby Douglass - QB
George Farmer - WR
Dick Gordon - WR
Bobby Joe Green - K
Jimmy Gunn - LB
Harry Gunner - DE
Dave Hale - DT
Jimmy Hester - TE
Glen Holloway - G
Willie Holman - DT
Mike Hull - FB
Bob Hyland - C
Randy Jackson - T
Ralph Kurek - FB
Garry Lyle - HB
Wayne Mass - T
Bennie McRae - DB
Ross Montgomery - FB
Howard Mudd - G
John Neidert - LB
Kent Nix - QB
Ed O'Bradovich - DE
Ray Ogden - TE
Mac Percival - K
Gale Sayers - HB
George Seals - DT
Jim Seymour - WR
Don Shy - HB
Ron Smith - DB
Bill Staley - DT
Joe Taylor - DB
Cecil Turner - WR
Bob Wallace - TE
Ted Wheeler - G

1970 Cincinnati

Marty Amsler - DE
Ken Avery - LB
Marty Baccaglio - DE
Al Beauchamp - LB
Bill Bergey - LB
Royce Berry - DE
Ron Carpenter - DE
Virgil Carter - QB
Steve Chomyszak - DT
Al Coleman - DB
Frank Cornish - DT
Bruce Coslet - TE
Eric Crabtree - WR
Guy Dennis - G
Doug Dressler - FB
Paul Dunn - FB
Sandy Durko - DB
Ken Dyer - DB
Larry Ely - LB
Howard Fest - T
Kenny Graham - DB
John Guillory - DB
Essex Johnson - HB
Bob Johnson - C
Willie Jones - DT
Mike Kelly - TE
Ron Lamb - FB
Dave Lewis - QB
Pat Matson - G
Rufus Mayes - T
Wayne McClure - LB
Horst Muhlmann - K
Chip Myers - WR
Lemar Parrish - DB
Bill Peterson - LB
Jess Phillips - HB
Mike Reid - DT
Ken Riley - DB
Paul Robinson - HB
Nick Roman - DE
Fletcher Smith - DB
Speedy Thomas - WR
Bob Trumpy - TE
Mike Wilson - T
Ernie Wright - T
Sam Wyche - QB

1970 Cleveland

Billy Andrews - LB
Erich Barnes - DB
Tom Beutler - LB
Ken Brown - HB
Don Cockroft - K
Gary Collins - WR
Jim Copeland - G
Ben Davis - DB
John Demarie - G
Steve Engel - HB
John Garlington - LB
Don Gault - QB
Chip Glass - TE
Jack Gregory - DE
Gene Hickerson - G
Fred Hoaglin - C
Fair Hooker - WR
Jim Houston - LB
Mike Howell - DB
Al Jenkins - T
Walter Johnson - DT
Dave Jones - WR
Homer Jones - WR
Joe Jones - DE
Ernie Kellermann - DB
Leroy Kelly - HB
Rudy Kuechenberg - LB
Dale Lindsey - LB
Bob Matheson - LB
Bob McKay - T
Randy Minniear - HB
Milt Morin - TE
Reece Morrison - HB
Bill Nelsen - QB
Mike Phipps - QB
Chuck Reynolds - C
Joe Righetti - DT
Dick Schafrath - T
Tom Schoen - DB
Bo Scott - FB
Jerry Sherk - DT
Ron Snidow - DE
Ricky Stevenson - DB
Freddie Summers - DB
Walt Sumner - DB
Joe Taffoni - T
Bill Yanchar - DT

1970 Dallas

Herb Adderley - DB
Margene Adkins - WR
George Andrie - DE
Bob Asher - T
Mike Clark - K
Larry Cole - DE
Mike Ditka - TE
Ron East - DT
Dave Edwards - LB
Richmond Flowers - DB
Walt Garrison - FB
Cornell Green - DB
Halvor Hagen - C
Cliff Harris - DB
Bob Hayes - WR
Calvin Hill - FB
Dennis Homan - WR
Chuck Howley - LB
Lee Roy Jordan - LB
Steve Kiner - LB
D. D. Lewis - LB
Bob Lilly - DT
Tony Liscio - T
Dave Manders - C
Craig Morton - QB
Ralph Neely - T
John Niland - G
Pettis Norman - TE
Blaine Nye - G
Jethro Pugh - DT
Dan Reeves - HB
Mel Renfro - DB
Lance Rentzel - WR
Reggie Rucker - WR
Roger Staubach - QB
Thomas Stincic - LB
Duane Thomas - FB
Pat Toomay - DE
Mark Washington - DB
Charlie Waters - DB
Claxton Welch - HB
Ron Widby - K
Rayfield Wright - T

1970 Denver

Steve Alexakos - G
Bobby Anderson - FB
Jay Bachman - C
Walt Barnes - DE
Sam Brunelli - T
Bill Butler - LB
Dave Costa - DT
Willis Crenshaw - FB
Ken Criter - LB
Carl Cunningham - LB
Mike Current - T
Dick Davis - FB
Al Denson - WR
Pete Duranko - DE
Booker Edgerson - DB
John Embree - WR
Fred Forsberg - LB
Drake Garrett - DB
George Goeddeke - G
Cornell Gordon - DB
Charlie Greer - DB
Mike Haffner - WR
Jerry Hendren - WR
Bobby Howfield - K
Jerry Inman - DT
Rich Jackson - DE
Pete Jaquess - DB
Larry Kaminski - C
Pete Liske - QB
Floyd Little - HB
Fran Lynch - HB
Paul Martha - DB
Billy Masters - TE
Bill McKoy - LB
Alvin Mitchell - WR
Chip Myrtle - LB
Chuck Pastrana - QB
Alden Roche - DE
George Saimes - DB
Mike Schnitker - G
Paul Smith - DT
Steve Tensi - QB
Billy Thompson - DB
Clem Turner - FB
Bill Van Heusen - WR
Bob Wade - DB
Dave Washington - LB
Jim Whalen - TE
Wandy Williams - HB
Bob Young - G

1970 Detroit

Lem Barney - DB
Charlie Brown - WR
Craig Cotton - TE
Bill Cottrell - C
Nick Eddy - HB
Mel Farr - FB
Ed Flanagan - C
Rocky Freitas - T
Frank Gallagher - G
Dan Goich - DT
Larry Hand - DE
Dave Haverdick - DT
Chuck Hughes - WR
Alex Karras - DT
Bob Kowalkowski - G
Greg Landry - QB
Dick LeBeau - DB
Mike Lucci - LB
Errol Mann - K
Bruce Maxwell - HB
Earl McCullouch - WR
Terry Miller - LB
Jim Mitchell - DE
Ed Mooney - LB
Bill Munson - QB
Paul Naumoff - LB
Phil Odle - WR
Steve Owens - FB
Rocky Rasley - G
Wayne Rasmussen - DB
Joe Robb - DE
Jerry Rush - DT
Charlie Sanders - TE
Bill Saul - LB
Roger Shoals - T
Altie Taylor - HB
Bill Triplett - FB
Tom Vaughn - DB
Wayne Walker - LB
Chuck Walton - G
Larry Walton - WR
Herman Weaver - K
Mike Weger - DB
Bobby Williams - DB
Jim Yarbrough - T

1970 Green Bay

Lionel Aldridge - DE
Marty Amsler - DE
Donny Anderson - HB
Ken Bowman - C
Dave Bradley - G
Robert Brown - DE
Fred Carr - LB
Jim Carter - LB
Mike Carter - WR
Jack Clancy - WR
Carroll Dale - WR
Ken Ellis - DB
Jim Flanigan - LB
Gale Gillingham - G
Jim Grabowski - FB
Forrest Gregg - T
Dave Hampton - HB
Lee Harden - DB
Kevin Hardy - DT
Doug Hart - DB
Bill Hayhoe - T
John Hilton - TE
Dick Himes - T
Don Horn - QB
Ervin Hunt - DB
Bob Jeter - DB
Larry Krause - HB
Rudy Kuechenberg - LB
Dale Livingston - K
Bill Lueck - G
Al Matthews - DB
Mike McCoy - DT
Rich McGeorge - TE
Rich Moore - DT
Ray Nitschke - LB
Rick Norton - QB
Frank Patrick - QB
Francis Peay - T
Dave Robinson - LB
John Spilis - WR
Bart Starr - QB
Cleo Walker - C
Malcolm Walker - T
Sweeny Williams - DE
Perry Williams - FB
Travis Williams - HB
Willie Wood - DB

1970 Houston

Bob Atkins - DB
Hank Autry - C
Jim Beirne - WR
Elvin Bethea - DE
Garland Boyette - LB
Lee Brooks - DT
Woody Campbell - HB
Donnie Davis - TE
Joe Dawkins - FB
Tom Domres - DT
Elbert Drungo - T
Roy Gerela - K
Hoyle Granger - FB
Ken Gray - G
Mac Haik - WR
Claude Harvey - LB
Glen Ray Hines - T
Pat Holmes - DE
Roy Hopkins - FB
Ken Houston - DB
Benny Johnson - DB
Charley Johnson - QB
Charlie Joiner - WR
Spike Jones - K
Jerry LeVias - WR
Jess Lewis - LB
Bobby Maples - C
Leroy Mitchell - DB
Zeke Moore - DB
Spain Musgrove - DT
Bob Naponic - QB
Willie Parker - DT
Johnny Peacock - DB
Ron Pritchard - LB
Alvin Reed - TE
Tom Regner - G
Jerry Rhome - QB
Mike Richardson - HB
Ron Saul - G
Tommie Smiley - FB
Terry Stoepel - TE
Walt Suggs - T
Olen Underwood - LB
Loyd Wainscott - LB
George Webster - LB
Doug Wilkerson - G
Paul Zaeske - WR

1970 Kansas City

Fred Arbanas - TE
Bobby Bell - LB
Ceasar Belser - DB
Aaron Brown - DE
Buck Buchanan - DT
Ed Budde - G
Billy Cannon - TE
Curley Culp - DT
George Daney - G
Len Dawson - QB
Mike Garrett - HB
David Hadley - DB
Wendell Hayes - FB
Dave Hill - T
Jimmy Hines - WR
Robert Holmes - FB
E.J. Holub - C
John Huarte - QB
Chuck Hurston - LB
Jim Kearney - DB
Willie Lanier - LB
Bob Liggett - DT
Mike Livingston - QB
Jim Lynch - LB
Jim Marsalis - DB
Jerry Mays - DE
Warren McVea - HB
Willie Mitchell - DB
Mo Moorman - G
Mike Oriard - C
Frank Pitts - WR
Ed Podolak - HB
Lew Porter - WR
Gloster Richardson - WR
Johnny Robinson - DB
Jack Rudnay - C
Sid Smith - T
Bob Stein - LB
Jan Stenerud - K
Morris Stroud - TE
Otis Taylor - WR
Emmitt Thomas - DB
Jim Tyrer - T
Marv Upshaw - DE
Clyde Werner - LB
Jerrel Wilson - K

1970 LA Rams

Kermit Alexander - DB
Coy Bacon - DE
Maxie Baughan - LB
Bob Brown - T
George Burman - G
Rick Cash - DE
Charley Cowan - T
Pat Curran - FB
Willie Ellison - HB
Dick Evey - DT
Roman Gabriel - QB
Alvin Haymond - DB
Ken Iman - C
Mitch Johnson - T
Deacon Jones - DE
Jeff Jordan - HB
Les Josephson - FB
Bob Klein - TE
Bob Long - WR
Tom Mack - G
Tommy Mason - FB
Ed Meador - DB
Clark Miller - DE
Jim Nettles - DB
Merlin Olsen - DT
Jack Pardee - LB
John Pergine - LB
Richie Petitbon - DB
Elijah Pitts - HB
Myron Pottios - LB
Jim Purnell - LB
David Ray - WR
Jack Reynolds - LB
Rich Saul - LB
Joe Scibelli - G
Nate Shaw - DB
Larry Smith - HB
Jack Snow - WR
Pat Studstill - WR
Karl Sweetan - QB
Diron Talbert - DT
Billy Truax - TE
Wendell Tucker - WR
John Wilbur - G
Donnie Williams - WR
Clancy Williams - DB

1970 Miami

Dick Anderson - DB
Dean Brown - DB
Nick Buoniconti - LB
Frank Cornish - DT
Doug Crusan - T
Larry Csonka - FB
Ted Davis - LB
Bob DeMarco - C
Norm Evans - T
Manny Fernandez - DT
Marv Fleming - TE
Tim Foley - DB
Hubert Ginn - HB
Bob Griese - QB
Bob Heinz - DT
Curtis Johnson - DB
Jim Kiick - HB
Mike Kolen - LB
Karl Kremser - K
Bob Kuechenberg - G
Jim Langer - G
Larry Little - G
Jim Mandich - TE
Carl Mauck - C
Norm McBride - DE
Stan Mitchell - FB
Wayne Moore - T
Mercury Morris - HB
Lloyd Mumphord - DB
Karl Noonan - WR
Dick Palmer - LB
Bob Petrella - DB
Jesse Powell - LB
Barry Pryor - HB
John Richardson - DT
Willie Richardson - WR
Jim Riley - DE
Jake Scott - DB
Larry Seiple - TE
Bill Stanfill - DE
John Stofa - QB
Doug Swift - LB
Howard Twilley - WR
Paul Warfield - WR
Ed Weisacosky - LB
Maxie Williams - G
Garo Yepremian - K

1970 Minnesota

Grady Alderman - T
John Beasley - TE
Bill Brown - FB
Bobby Bryant - DB
Bill Cappleman - QB
John Charles - DB
Fred Cox - K
Gary Cuozzo - QB
Doug Davis - T
Paul Dickson - DT
Carl Eller - DE
Hap Farber - LB
Bob Grim - WR
Dale Hackbart - DB
Jim Hargrove - LB
John Henderson - WR
Wally Hilgenberg - LB
Clint Jones - HB
Karl Kassulke - DB
Kent Kramer - TE
Paul Krause - DB
Gary Larsen - DT
Bob Lee - QB
Jim Lindsey - HB
Jim Marshall - DE
Mike McGill - LB
Tom McNeill - K
Wayne Meylan - LB
Dave Osborn - HB
Alan Page - DT
Ted Provost - DB
Oscar Reed - HB
Ed Sharockman - DB
Steve Smith - T
Milt Sunde - G
Mick Tingelhoff - C
Jim Vellone - G
Stu Voigt - TE
John Ward - DE
Lonnie Warwick - LB
Gene Washington - WR
Charlie West - DB
Ed White - G
Roy Winston - LB
Ron Yary - T

1970 New Orleans

Danny Abramowicz - WR
Dick Absher - LB
Tony Baker - FB
Tom Barrington - FB
Johnny Brewer - LB
Jackie Burkett - LB
Ken Burrough - WR
Bill Cody - LB
Wayne Colman - LB
Dick Davis - FB
Tom Dempsey - K
Al Dodd - WR
Bill Dusenbery - HB
Frank Emanuel - LB
Larry Estes - DE
Julian Fagan - K
Hap Farber - LB
Earl Gros - FB
Edd Hargett - QB
Major Hazelton - DB
Hugo Hollas - DB
Gene Howard - DB
Delles Howell - DB
Harry Jacobs - LB
Billy Kilmer - QB
Jake Kupp - G
Gary Lewis - HB
Errol Linden - T
Andy Livingston - FB
Dave Long - DE
Dicky Lyons - DB
Don McCall - HB
Mike Morgan - LB
Richard Neal - DE
Elijah Nevett - DB
Vic Nyvall - HB
Jim Otis - FB
Dave Parks - TE
Elijah Pitts - HB
Ray Poage - TE
Steve Ramsey - QB
Mike Richey - T
Dave Rowe - DT
Joe Scarpati - DB
Bob Shaw - WR
John Shinners - G
Jerry Sturm - C
Doug Sutherland - G
Clovis Swinney - DT
Don Talbert - T
Mike Taylor - T
Mike Tilleman - DT
Willie Townes - DT
Claxton Welch - HB
Ernie Wheelwright - FB

Del Williams - C
Doug Wyatt - DB

1970 NY Giants

John Baker - DE
Willie Banks - G
Al Brenner - DB
Otto Brown - DB
Rich Buzin - T
Pete Case - G
Dennis Crane - T
John Douglas - LB
Fred Dryer - DE
Bobby Duhon - HB
Scott Eaton - DB
Jim Files - LB
Tucker Frederickson - FB
Pete Gogolak - K
Joe Green - DB
Charlie Harper - G
Matt Hazeltine - LB
Ralph Heck - LB
Don Herrmann - WR
Ray Hickl - LB
Rich Houston - WR
Pat Hughes - C
Len Johnson - C
Ron Johnson - HB
Bill Johnson - K
Jim Kanicki - DT
John Kirby - LB
Ernie Koy - HB
Greg Larson - C
Carl Lockhart - DB
Tom Longo - DB
Bob Lurtsema - DE
Clifton McNeil - WR
Joe Morrison - FB
Jim Norton - DT
Kenny Parker - DB
Jerry Shay - DT
Dick Shiner - QB
Les Shy - HB
Fran Tarkenton - QB
Aaron Thomas - WR
Bob Tucker - TE
Doug Van Horn - G
Willie Williams - DB
Willie Young - T

1970 NY Jets

Gary Arthur - TE
Al Atkinson - LB
Ralph Baker - LB
Mike Battle - DB
Tom Bayless - G
Eddie Bell - WR
Verlon Biggs - DE
Emerson Boozer - HB
Rich Caster - WR
Paul Crane - LB
Bob Davis - QB
John Dockery - DB
John Ebersole - LB
John Elliott - DT
Roger Finnie - G
Dave Foley - T
Larry Grantham - LB
Dave Herman - G
W.K. Hicks - DB
Winston Hill - T
Gus Hollomon - DB
Jim Hudson - DB
Jimmie Jones - DE
Pete Lammons - TE
Cecil Leonard - DB
John Little - DE
Mark Lomas - DT
Don Maynard - WR
Cliff McClain - HB
Chuck Mercein - FB
Dave Middendorf - G
Joe Namath - QB
George Nock - HB
Steve O'Neal - WR
Dennis Onkotz - LB
Pete Perreault - T
Gerry Philbin - DE
Randy Rasmussen - G
George Sauer - WR
John Schmitt - C
Matt Snell - FB
Wayne Stewart - TE
Steve Tannen - DB
Earlie Thomas - DB
Steve Thompson - DE
Jim Turner - QB
Lee White - FB
Al Woodall - QB

1970 Oakland

Butch Atkinson - DB
Pete Banaszak - HB
Duane Benson - LB
Fred Biletnikoff - WR
George Blanda - QB
Willie Brown - DB
Bill Budness - LB
George Buehler - G
Drew Buie - WR
Raymond Chester - TE
Tony Cline - DE
Dan Conners - LB
Ben Davidson - DE
Hewritt Dixon - FB
Al Dotson - DT
Mike Eischeid - K
Dave Grayson - DB
Jim Harvey - G
Don Highsmith - HB
Marv Hubbard - FB
Gerald Irons - LB
Tom Keating - DT
Ted Koy - TE
Daryle Lamonica - QB
Bill Laskey - LB
Jacque MacKinnon - TE
Kent McCloughan - DB
Carleton Oats - DT
Gus Otto - LB
Jim Otto - C
Harry Schuh - T
Art Shell - T
Rod Sherman - WR
Charlie Smith - HB
Ken Stabler - QB
Bob Svihus - T
Art Thoms - DT
Larry Todd - HB
Gene Upshaw - G
Jimmy Warren - DB
Carl Weathers - LB
Warren Wells - WR
Nemiah Wilson - DB
Alvin Wyatt - DB

1970 Philadelphia

Rick Arrington - QB
Gary Ballman - WR
Lee Bouggess - FB
Bill Bradley - DB
Don Brumm - DE
Ernie Calloway - DE
Joe Carollo - T
Norman Davis - G
Mike Dirks - DT
Mike Evans - C
Carl Gersbach - LB
Dick Hart - G
Richard Harvey - DB
Ben Hawkins - WR
Ed Hayes - DB
Fred Hill - WR
Bill Hobbs - LB
Don Hultz - DE
Calvin Hunt - C
Harold Jackson - WR
Jay Johnson - LB
Harry Jones - HB
Ray Jones - DB
Ike Kelley - LB
Wade Key - T
Leroy Keyes - HB
Dave Lloyd - LB
Ron Medved - DB
Denis Moore - DT
Mark Moseley - K
Al Nelson - DB
Mark Nordquist - C
Gary Pettigrew - DT
Cyril Pinder - HB
Ron Porter - LB
Steve Preece - DB
Nate Ramsey - DB
Tim Rossovich - LB
Jim Skaggs - G
Norm Snead - QB
Dick Stevens - T
Jim Thrower - DB
Mel Tom - DE
Billy Walik - WR
Larry Watkins - FB
Harry Wilson - HB
Tom Woodeshick - FB
Adrian Young - LB
Steve Zabel - TE

1970 Pittsburgh

Bob Adams - TE
Chuck Allen - LB
Dick Arndt - DT
Ocie Austin - DB
Warren Bankston - FB
Fred Barry - DB
Chuck Beatty - DB
Mel Blount - DB
Terry Bradshaw - QB
John Brown - T
Hubie Bryant - WR
Lee Calland - DB
Terry Cole - FB
Carl Crennel - LB
Henry Davis - LB
Sam Davis - G
Doug Fisher - LB
John Fuqua - FB
Kenny Graham - DB
Joe Greene - DT
L. C. Greenwood - DE
Mike Haggerty - T
Terry Hanratty - QB
Jerry Hillebrand - LB
Chuck Hinton - DT
Dick Hoak - HB
Dennis Hughes - TE
Dave Kalina - WR
Jon Kolb - T
Ray Mansfield - C
Ben McGee - DE
Gene Mingo - K
Clancy Oliver - DB
Preston Pearson - HB
John Rowser - DB
Andy Russell - LB
Ron Shanklin - WR
Rick Sharp - T
Dave Smith - WR
John Sodaski - DB
Jon Staggers - WR
Brian Stenger - LB
Bruce Van Dyke - G
Lloyd Voss - DE
Bobby Walden - K
Clarence Washington - DT
Allan Watson - K
Ralph Wenzel - G
J.R. Wilburn - WR

1970 St. Louis

Jim Bakken - K
Pete Beathard - QB
Robert Brown - TE
Terry Brown - DB
Jerry Daanen - WR
Cid Edwards - FB
Vern Emerson - T
Miller Farr - DB
John Gilliam - WR
Irv Goode - G
Jim Hart - QB
Chip Healy - LB
Fred Heron - DT
Chuck Hutchison - G
Fred Hyatt - WR
Rolf Krueger - DE
Mike LaHood - G
MacArthur Lane - FB
Chuck Latourette - DB
Jim McFarland - TE
Ernie McMillan - T
Wayne Mulligan - C
Dave Olerich - LB
Don Parish - LB
Charlie Pittman - HB
Tony Plummer - DB
Bob Reynolds - T
Jamie Rivers - LB
Johnny Roland - HB
Rocky Rosema - LB
Bob Rowe - DT
Joe Schmiesing - DT
Roy Shivers - HB
Mike Siwek - DT
Jackie Smith - TE
Cal Snowden - DE
Larry Stallings - LB
Jerry Stovall - DB
Chuck Walker - DE
Roger Wehrli - DB
Paul White - HB
Clyde Williams - G
Dave Williams - WR
Larry Wilson - DB
Nate Wright - DB

1970 San Diego

Lance Alworth - WR
Bob Babich - LB
Pete Barnes - LB
Joe Beauchamp - DB
Ron Billingsley - DT
Bob Briggs - DE
Bob Bruggers - LB
Wayne Clark - QB
Steve DeLong - DT
Chuck Detwiler - DB
Marty Domres - QB
Speedy Duncan - DB
Rick Eber - WR
Gene Ferguson - DT
Chris Fletcher - DB
Gene Foster - HB
Willie Frazier - TE
Mike Garrett - HB
Gary Garrison - WR
Walker Gillette - WR
Ira Gordon - G
Sam Gruneisen - C
John Hadl - QB
Jim Hill - DB
Bob Howard - DB
Brad Hubbert - FB
Bill Lenkaitis - G
Mike Mercer - K
Roland Moss - TE
Joe Owens - DE
Terry Owens - T
Dennis Partee - K
Dickie Post - HB
Jack Protz - LB
Jeff Queen - FB
Rick Redman - LB
Andy Rice - DT
Jim Schmedding - G
Dave Smith - HB
Russ Smith - FB
Jeff Staggs - DE
Art Strozier - TE
Walt Sweeney - G
Jim Tolbert - DB
Russ Washington - T
Bob Wells - T
Tom Williams - DT
Cal Withrow - C

1970 San Francisco

Cas Banaszek - T
Ed Beard - LB
Randy Beisler - G
Bill Belk - DE
Forrest Blue - C
John Brodie - QB
Carter Campbell - LB
Elmer Collett - G
Doug Cunningham - HB
Earl Edwards - DT
Johnny Fuller - DB
Bruce Gossett - K
Cedrick Hardman - DE
Tommy Hart - DE
Stan Hindman - DE
Bob Hoskins - G
John Isenbarger - HB
Jim Johnson - DB
Lee Johnson - WR
Charlie Krueger - DT
Ted Kwalick - TE
Roland Lakes - DT
Frank Nunley - LB
Woody Peoples - G
Mel Phillips - DB
Al Randolph - DB
Preston Riley - WR
Len Rohde - T
Sam Silas - DE
Mike Simpson - DB
Jim Sniadecki - LB
Steve Spurrier - QB
Jim Strong - HB
Bruce Taylor - DB
Rosey Taylor - DB
Jimmy Thomas - WR
Bill Tucker - HB
Skip Vanderbundt - LB
Gene Washington - WR
Dave Wilcox - LB
Ken Willard - FB
Bob Windsor - TE
Dick Witcher - WR

1970 Washington

Mack Alston - TE
Bruce Anderson - DE
Mike Bass - DB
Frank Bosch - DT
Mike Bragg - K
Larry Brown - HB
Bill Brundige - DE
Bob Brunet - HB
Leo Carroll - DE
John Didion - C
Henry Dyer - FB
Pat Fischer - DB
Gene Hamlin - C
Chris Hanburger - LB
Charlie Harraway - FB
Jim Harris - DB
Rickie Harris - DB
Len Hauss - C
Jon Henderson - WR
Terry Hermeling - DE
John Hoffman - DE
Jon Jaqua - DB
Sonny Jurgensen - QB
Curt Knight - K
Dave Kopay - HB
Paul Laaveg - G
Bill Malinchak - WR
Marlin McKeever - LB
Harold McLinton - LB
Brig Owens - DB
Floyd Peters - DT
Danny Pierce - FB
Vince Promuto - G
Pat Richter - TE
Walter Roberts - WR
Walt Rock - T
Tom Roussel - LB
Frank Ryan - QB
Roy Schmidt - G
Ray Schoenke - G
Manny Sistrunk - DT
Jerry Smith - TE
Jim Snowden - T
Charley Taylor - WR
Rusty Tillman - LB
Ted Vactor - DB
Steve Wright - T

1971 Atlanta

Ron Acks - LB
Grady Allen - LB
Bill Bell - K
Willie Belton - HB
Bob Berry - QB
John Bramlett - LB
Greg Brezina - LB
Ray Brown - DB
Ken Burrow - WR
Cannonball Butler - HB
Sonny Campbell - HB
Wes Chesson - WR
Glen Condren - DT
Mike Donohoe - TE
Dick Enderle - G
Don Hansen - LB
Leo Hart - QB
Tom Hayes - DB
Claude Humphrey - DE
Ray Jarvis - WR
Rudy Kuechenberg - LB
George Kunz - T
Greg Lens - DT
Mike Lewis - DE
Billy Lothridge - K
John Mallory - DB
Art Malone - FB
Randy Marshall - DE
John Matlock - C
Andy Maurer - G
Tom McCauley - DB
Jim Miller - G
Jim Mitchell - TE
Tommy Nobis - LB
Tony Plummer - DB
Ray Poage - TE
Joe Profit - HB
Ken Reaves - DB
Rudy Redmond - DB
Bill Sandeman - T
Larry Shears - DB
Dick Shiner - QB
John Small - LB
Mal Snider - T
Todd Snyder - WR
Jeff Van Note - C
Harmon Wages - FB
Cleo Walker - LB
John Zook - DE

1971 Baltimore

Jim Bailey - DT
Tom Beutler - LB
Norm Bulaich - HB
Bill Curry - C
Mike Curtis - LB
Tom Curtis - DB
Jim Duncan - DB
Lenny Dunlap - DB
Rusty Ganas - DT
Ron Gardin - WR
Sam Havrilak - WR
Ted Hendricks - LB
Lonnie Hepburn - DB
Roy Hilton - DE
Eddie Hinton - WR
Cornelius Johnson - G
Rex Kern - DB
Lynn Larson - T
Bill Laskey - LB
David Lee - K
Jerry Logan - DB
John Mackey - LB
Tom Matte - HB
Ray May - LB
Don McCauley - HB
Ken Mendenhall - C
Fred Miller - DT
Tom Mitchell - TE
Earl Morrall - QB
Dennis Nelson - T
Billy Newsome - DE
Robbie Nichols - LB
Don Nottingham - FB
Tom Nowatzke - FB
Jim O'Brien - WR
Ray Perkins - WR
Charlie Pittman - HB
Glenn Ressler - G
Willie Richardson - WR
Bubba Smith - DE
Charles Stukes - DB
Dan Sullivan - G
Johnny Unitas - QB
Bob Vogel - T
Rick Volk - DB
John Williams - G
George Wright - DT

1971 Buffalo

Jackie Allen - DB
Al Andrews - LB
Tim Beamer - DB
Jim Braxton - FB
Marlin Briscoe - WR
Levert Carr - T
Edgar Chandler - LB
Bob Chandler - WR
Dave Chapple - K
Jerald Collins - LB
Paul Costa - T
Al Cowlings - DE
Dick Cunningham - LB
Austin Denney - TE
Jim Dunaway - DT
Wes Grant - DE
Donnie Green - T
Tony Greene - DB
Paul Guidry - LB
Grant Guthrie - K
James Harris - QB
Bob Hews - DE
J. D. Hill - WR
Ike Hill - DB
Chuck Hurston - LB
Robert James - DB
Bruce Jarvis - C
Greg Jones - HB
Spike Jones - K
Howard Kindig - T
Ted Koy - TE
John Leypoldt - K
Mike McBath - DE
Bill McKinley - LB
Haven Moses - WR
Joe O'Donnell - G
Wayne Patrick - FB
John Pitts - DB
Jim Reilly - G
Pete Richardson - DB
Louis Ross - DE
Dennis Shaw - QB
O.J. Simpson - HB
Cal Snowden - DE
Mike Stratton - LB
Bob Tatarek - DT
Jan White - TE
Mike Wilson - G
Alvin Wyatt - DB
Willie Young - T

1971 Chi. Bears

Ross Brupbacher - LB
Doug Buffone - LB
Dick Butkus - LB
Jim Cadile - G
Rich Coady - C
Jack Concannon - QB
Jeff Curchin - T
Bobby Douglass - QB
George Farmer - WR
Charlie Ford - DB
Dick Gordon - WR
Jim Grabowski - FB
Bobby Joe Green - K
Jimmy Gunn - LB
Dave Hale - DT
Gene Hamlin - C
Cliff Hardy - DB
Jim Harrison - FB
John Hoffman - DE
Glen Holloway - G
Willie Holman - DE
Randy Jackson - T
Bob Jeter - DB
Garry Lyle - DB
Tony McGee - DE
Jerry Moore - DB
Joe Moore - HB
Bob Newton - T
Kent Nix - QB
Ed O'Bradovich - DE
Ray Ogden - TE
Mac Percival - K
Cyril Pinder - HB
Larry Rowden - LB
Gale Sayers - HB
George Seals - DT
Jim Seymour - WR
Don Shy - HB
Ron Smith - DB
Bill Staley - DT
Joe Taylor - DB
Earl Thomas - TE
Bill Tucker - FB
Cecil Turner - WR
Bob Wallace - TE
Steve Wright - T

1971 Cincinnati

Doug Adams - LB
Ken Anderson - QB
Ken Avery - LB
Al Beauchamp - LB
Bill Bergey - LB
Royce Berry - DE
Ron Carpenter - DE
Virgil Carter - QB
Steve Chomyszak - DT
Al Coleman - DB
Bruce Coslet - TE
Eric Crabtree - WR
Neal Craig - DB
Guy Dennis - G
Doug Dressler - FB
Sandy Durko - DB
Ken Dyer - DB
Larry Ely - LB
Howard Fest - T
Mike Haffner - WR
Jim Harris - DB
Vern Holland - T
Essex Johnson - HB
Ken Johnson - DE
Bob Johnson - C
Willie Jones - DT
Mike Kelly - TE
Ron Lamb - FB
Steve Lawson - G
Dave Lewis - QB
Ed Marshall - WR
Pat Matson - G
Rufus Mayes - T
Horst Muhlmann - K
Chip Myers - WR
Lemar Parrish - DB
Bill Peterson - LB
Jess Phillips - HB
Mike Reid - DT
Ken Riley - DB
Paul Robinson - HB
Nick Roman - DE
Fletcher Smith - DB
Speedy Thomas - WR
Bob Trumpy - TE
Fred Willis - FB
Ernie Wright - T

1971 Cleveland

Billy Andrews - LB
Erich Barnes - DB
Bob Briggs - DT
Stan Brown - WR
Ken Brown - HB
Don Cockroft - K
Gary Collins - WR
Jim Copeland - G
Bo Cornell - FB
Ben Davis - DB
John Demarie - G
Doug Dieken - T
John Garlington - LB
Chip Glass - TE
Jack Gregory - DE
Charlie Hall - LB
Gene Hickerson - G
Fred Hoaglin - C
Fair Hooker - WR
Jim Houston - LB
Mike Howell - DB
Mitch Johnson - T
Walter Johnson - DT
Dave Jones - WR
Joe Jones - DE
Ernie Kellermann - DB
Leroy Kelly - HB
Rick Kingrea - LB
Dale Lindsey - LB
Bob McKay - T
Milt Morin - TE
Reece Morrison - HB
Bill Nelsen - QB
Mike Phipps - QB
Frank Pitts - WR
Dick Schafrath - T
Clarence Scott - DB
Bo Scott - FB
Jerry Sherk - DT
Mike Sikich - G
Ron Snidow - DT
Freddie Summers - DB
Walt Sumner - DB

1971 Dallas

Herb Adderley - DB
Margene Adkins - WR
Lance Alworth - WR
George Andrie - DE
Lee Roy Caffey - LB
Mike Clark - K
Larry Cole - DE
Mike Ditka - TE
Dave Edwards - LB
John Fitzgerald - C
Richmond Flowers - DB
Toni Fritsch - K
Walt Garrison - FB
Cornell Green - DB
Forrest Gregg - T
Bill Gregory - DT
Cliff Harris - DB
Bob Hayes - WR
Calvin Hill - FB
Chuck Howley - LB
Lee Roy Jordan - LB
D. D. Lewis - LB
Bob Lilly - DT
Tony Liscio - T
Dave Manders - C
Craig Morton - QB
Ralph Neely - T
John Niland - G
Blaine Nye - G
Jethro Pugh - DT
Dan Reeves - HB
Mel Renfro - DB
Gloster Richardson - WR
Reggie Rucker - WR
Tody Smith - DE
Roger Staubach - QB
Thomas Stincic - LB
Don Talbert - T
Duane Thomas - FB
Ike Thomas - DB
Pat Toomay - DE
Billy Truax - TE
Rodney Wallace - G
Mark Washington - DB
Charlie Waters - DB
Claxton Welch - HB
Ron Widby - K
Joe Williams - HB
Rayfield Wright - T

1971 Denver

Lyle Alzado - DE
Bobby Anderson - HB
Jay Bachman - C
Walt Barnes - DE
Gordon Bowdell - WR
Sam Brunelli - T
Butch Byrd - DB

Carter Campbell - LB
Dave Costa - DT
Ken Criter - LB
Mike Current - T
Joe Dawkins - HB
Tom Domres - DT
Fred Forsberg - LB
Jack Gehrke - WR
George Goeddeke - G
Cornell Gordon - DB
Charlie Greer - DB
Dwight Harrison - WR
Don Horn - QB
Jerry Inman - DT
Larron Jackson - T
Rich Jackson - DE
Larry Kaminski - C
Floyd Little - HB
Fran Lynch - FB
Tommy Lyons - C
Billy Masters - TE
Bill McKoy - LB
Leroy Mitchell - DB
Marv Montgomery - T
Randy Montgomery - DB
John Mosier - TE
Chip Myrtle - LB
Dickie Post - HB
Steve Ramsey - QB
George Saimes - DB
Mike Schnitker - G
Roger Shoals - T
Jerry Simmons - WR
Paul Smith - DT
Billy Thompson - DB
Clem Turner - FB
Jim Turner - K
Olen Underwood - LB
Bill Van Heusen - WR
Dave Washington - LB
Jim Whalen - TE

1971 Detroit

Lem Barney - DB
Bob Bell - DT
Al Clark - DB
Craig Cotton - TE
Dick Evey - DT
Mel Farr - FB
Ed Flanagan - C
Rocky Freitas - T
Frank Gallagher - G
Paul Gipson - FB
Larry Hand - DE
Chuck Hughes - WR
Ron Jessie - WR
Bob Kowalkowski - G
Greg Landry - QB
Dick LeBeau - DB
Ken Lee - LB
Mike Lucci - LB
Errol Mann - K
Earl McCullouch - WR
Jim Mitchell - DE
Ed Mooney - LB
Bill Munson - QB
Paul Naumoff - LB
Steve Owens - FB
Ray Parson - T
Wayne Rasmussen - DB
Joe Robb - DE
Jerry Rush - DT
Charlie Sanders - TE
Altie Taylor - HB
Dave Thompson - C
Bill Triplett - FB
Tom Vaughn - DB
Wayne Walker - LB
Chuck Walton - G
Larry Walton - WR
Charlie Weaver - LB
Herman Weaver - K
Mike Weger - DB
Bobby Williams - DB
Larry Woods - DT
Jim Yarbrough - T
Mickey Zofko - HB

1971 Green Bay

Lionel Aldridge - DE
Donny Anderson - HB
Ken Bowman - C
Dave Bradley - G
Zeke Bratkowski - QB
John Brockington - FB
Robert Brown - DT
Fred Carr - LB
Jim Carter - LB
Dave Conway - K
Tommy Crutcher - LB
Carroll Dale - WR
Dave Davis - WR
Jim DeLisle - DT
Ken Duncan - K
Ken Ellis - DB
Len Garrett - TE
Gale Gillingham - G
Charlie Hall - DB
Dave Hampton - FB
Doug Hart - DB
Bill Hayhoe - T
Dick Himes - T
Scott Hunter - QB
Larry Krause - HB
Bill Lueck - G
Al Matthews - DB
Mike McCoy - DT
Rich McGeorge - TE
Lou Michaels - K
Ray Nitschke - LB
Frank Patrick - QB
Francis Peay - T
Elijah Pitts - HB
Al Randolph - DB
Dave Robinson - LB
Alden Roche - DE
Donnell Smith - DE
John Spilis - WR
Bart Starr - QB
Tim Webster - K
Sweeny Williams - DE
Perry Williams - FB
Randy Winkler - G
Richard Winther - C
Cal Withrow - C
Willie Wood - DB

1971 Houston

Allen Aldridge - DE
Willie Alexander - DB
Bob Atkins - DB
Braden Beck - K
Jim Beirne - WR
Bruce Bergey - DE
Elvin Bethea - DE
Ron Billingsley - DT
Garland Boyette - LB
Lee Brooks - DT
Ken Burrough - WR
Woody Campbell - HB
John Charles - DB
Linzy Cole - WR
Phil Croyle - LB
Joe Dawkins - HB
Lynn Dickey - QB
Tom Domres - DT
Elbert Drungo - G
Gene Ferguson - T
Willie Frazier - TE
Tom Funchess - T
Mac Haik - WR
Pat Holmes - DE
Robert Holmes - FB
Andy Hopkins - HB
Ken Houston - DB
Leroy Howard - DB
Benny Johnson - DB
Charley Johnson - QB
Charlie Joiner - WR
Zeke Moore - DB
Mark Moseley - K
Dave Olerich - LB
Dan Pastorini - QB
Dickie Post - HB
Ron Pritchard - LB
Alvin Reed - TE
Tom Regner - G
Floyd Rice - TE
Mike Richardson - HB
Ron Saul - G
Leroy Sledge - FB
Jerry Sturm - C
Walt Suggs - C
Mike Tilleman - DT
Ward Walsh - HB
Sam Walton - T
George Webster - LB
Bob Young - G

1971 Kansas City

Mike Adamle - HB
Nate Allen - DB
Bobby Bell - LB
Ceasar Belser - DB
Bruce Bergey - DE
Aaron Brown - DE
Buck Buchanan - DT
Ed Budde - G
Curley Culp - DT
George Daney - G
Len Dawson - QB
Willie Frazier - TE
David Hadley - DB
Wendell Hayes - FB
Dave Hill - T
Robert Holmes - FB
Dennis Homan - WR
John Huarte - QB
Bruce Jankowski - WR
Jim Kearney - DB
Willie Lanier - LB
Mike Livingston - QB
Ed Lothamer - DT
Jim Lynch - LB
Jim Marsalis - DB
Warren McVea - HB
Mo Moorman - G
Mike Oriard - C
Jim Otis - WR
Ed Podolak - HB
Kerry Reardon - DB
Johnny Robinson - DB
Jack Rudnay - C
Mike Sensibaugh - DB
Sid Smith - T
Bob Stein - DE
Jan Stenerud - K
Morris Stroud - TE
Otis Taylor - WR
Emmitt Thomas - DB
Jim Tyrer - T
Marv Upshaw - DE
Jerrel Wilson - K
Elmo Wright - WR
Wilbur Young - DT

1971 LA Rams

Kermit Alexander - DB
Coy Bacon - DT
Rich Buzin - T
Joe Carollo - T
Charley Cowan - T
Pat Curran - TE
Willie Ellison - HB
Dave Elmendorf - DB
Roman Gabriel - QB
Ken Geddes - LB
Dean Halverson - LB
Alvin Haymond - DB
Gene Howard - DB
Ken Iman - C
Deacon Jones - DE
Les Josephson - FB
Bob Klein - TE
Mike LaHood - G
Tom Mack - G
Matt Maslowski - WR
Marlin McKeever - LB
Bill Nelson - DT
Jim Nettles - DB
Merlin Olsen - DT
Phil Olsen - DT
Don Parish - LB
John Pergine - LB
Jim Purnell - LB
David Ray - WR
Lance Rentzel - WR
Jack Reynolds - LB
Jerry Rhome - QB
Isiah Robertson - LB
Rich Saul - G
Harry Schuh - T
Joe Scibelli - G
Larry Smith - HB
Jack Snow - WR
Pat Studstill - WR
Bob Thomas - HB
Lee White - FB
Clancy Williams - DB
Roger Williams - WR
Travis Williams - HB
Gregory Wojcik - DT
Jack Youngblood - DE

1971 Miami

Dick Anderson - DB
Nick Buoniconti - LB
Terry Cole - FB
Frank Cornish - DT
Doug Crusan - T
Larry Csonka - FB
Bob DeMarco - C
Vern Den Herder - DE
Norm Evans - T
Dale Farley - LB
Manny Fernandez - DT
Marv Fleming - TE
Tim Foley - DB
Hubert Ginn - HB
Bob Griese - QB
Bob Heinz - DE
Curtis Johnson - DB
Ray Jones - DB
Jim Kiick - HB
Mike Kolen - LB
Bob Kuechenberg - G
Jim Langer - G
Charlie Leigh - FB
Larry Little - G
Jim Mandich - TE
Wayne Mass - T
Bob Matheson - LB
George Mira - QB
Wayne Moore - T
Mercury Morris - HB
Lloyd Mumphord - DB
Karl Noonan - WR
Bob Petrella - DB
Jesse Powell - LB
John Richardson - DT
Jim Riley - DE
Jake Scott - DB
Larry Seiple - TE
Bill Stanfill - DE
Otto Stowe - WR
Doug Swift - LB
Howard Twilley - WR
Paul Warfield - WR
Garo Yepremian - K

1971 Minnesota

Grady Alderman - T
Robert Brown - TE
Bill Brown - FB
Bobby Bryant - DB
Fred Cox - K
Gary Cuozzo - QB
Doug Davis - T
Al Denson - WR
Carl Eller - DE
Carl Gersbach - LB
Bob Grim - WR
Leo Hayden - HB
John Henderson - WR
Wally Hilgenberg - LB
John Hilton - TE
Noel Jenke - LB
Clint Jones - HB
Karl Kassulke - DB
Paul Krause - DB
Gary Larsen - DT
Bob Lee - QB
Jim Lindsey - HB
Jim Marshall - DE
Dave Osborn - HB
Alan Page - DT
Jerry Patton - DT
Pete Perreault - G
Oscar Reed - HB
Roy Schmidt - G
Ed Sharockman - DB
Norm Snead - QB
Milt Sunde - G
Doug Sutherland - G
Mick Tingelhoff - C
Stu Voigt - TE
John Ward - DE
Lonnie Warwick - LB
Gene Washington - WR
Charlie West - DB
Ed White - G
Chuck Winfrey - LB
Roy Winston - LB
Jeff Wright - DB
Nate Wright - DB
Ron Yary - T
Godfrey Zaunbrecher - C

1971 New England

Julius Adams - DT
Houston Antwine - DT
Bill Atessis - DE
Tom Beer - G
Ron Berger - DT
Randy Beverly - DB
Hubie Bryant - WR
Larry Carwell - DB
Jim Cheyunski - LB
Phil Clark - DB
Dennis Coleman - LB
Eric Crabtree - WR
Randy Edmunds - LB
Ron Gardin - WR
Carl Garrett - HB
Bob Gladieux - HB
Charlie Gogolak - K
Halvor Hagen - C
Mike Haggerty - T
Rickie Harris - DB
Tom Janik - DB
Steve Kiner - LB
Ike Lassiter - DE
Odell Lawson - FB
Bill Lenkaitis - G
Jack Maitland - HB
Irvin Mallory - DB
Art May - DE
Mike Montler - T
Jon Morris - C
Roland Moss - TE
Jim Nance - FB
Tom Neville - T
John Outlaw - DB
Ed Philpott - LB
Jim Plunkett - QB
Kenny Price - LB
Perry Pruett - DB
Dave Rowe - DT
Reggie Rucker - WR
Clarence Scott - DB
Ron Sellers - WR
Len St. Jean - G
Al Sykes - WR
Randy Vataha - WR
Don Webb - DB
Ed Weisacosky - LB
Dennis Wirgowski - DE

1971 New Orleans

Danny Abramowicz - WR
Dick Absher - LB
Tony Baker - FB
Carlos Bell - TE
Don Burchfield - TE
Skip Butler - K
Wayne Colman - LB
Carl Cunningham - LB
John Didion - C
Al Dodd - WR
Charlie Durkee - K
Larry Estes - DE
Julian Fagan - K
Jim Flanigan - LB
James Ford - FB
Dan Goich - DT
Hoyle Granger - FB
Bob Gresham - HB
Edd Hargett - QB
Billy Harris - HB
Richard Harvey - DB
Ray Hester - LB
Glen Ray Hines - T
Sam Holden - T
Hugo Hollas - DB
Delles Howell - DB
John Huard - LB
Dave Kopay - HB
Jake Kupp - G
Bivian Lee - DB
Dave Long - DT
Archie Manning - QB
Dee Martin - DB
Doug Mooers - DE
Reynaud Moore - DB
Don Morrison - T
Richard Neal - DE
Bob Newland - WR
Joe Owens - DE
Dave Parks - TE
Bob Pollard - DT
Remi Prudhomme - C
Virgil Robinson - HB
Tom Roussel - LB
John Shinners - G
Jim Strong - HB
Mike Walker - DE
Del Williams - C
Doug Wyatt - DB

1971 NY Giants

Steve Alexakos - G
Pete Athas - WR
Tom Blanchard - K
Otto Brown - DB
Skip Butler - K
Junior Coffey - HB
John Douglas - LB
Fred Dryer - DE
Bobby Duhon - HB
Scott Eaton - DB
Charlie Evans - FB
Jim Files - LB
Richmond Flowers - DB
Tucker Frederickson - FB
Pete Gogolak - K
Joe Green - DB
Dick Hanson - DT
Charlie Harper - G
Ralph Heck - LB
Don Herrmann - WR
Ron Hornsby - LB
Rich Houston - WR
Pat Hughes - LB
Bob Hyland - G
Randy Johnson - QB
Ron Johnson - HB
Jim Kanicki - DT
Rich Kotite - TE
Roland Lakes - DT
Greg Larson - C
Carl Lockhart - DB
Bob Lurtsema - DE
Clifton McNeil - WR
Bennie McRae - DB
Joe Morrison - HB
Henry Reed - DE
Dave Roller - DT
Reggie Rucker - WR
Jerry Shay - DT
Fran Tarkenton - QB
Rocky Thompson - HB
Dave Tipton - DE
Bob Tucker - TE
Doug Van Horn - G
Vern Vanoy - DT
Wayne Walton - G
Willie Williams - DB
Willie Young - T
Coleman Zeno - WR

1971 NY Jets

Gary Arthur - TE
Al Atkinson - LB
Ralph Baker - LB
Eddie Bell - WR
Emerson Boozer - HB
Rich Caster - WR
Paul Crane - LB
Bob Davis - QB
John Dockery - DB
John Ebersole - LB
John Elliott - DT
Chris Farasopoulos - DB
Roger Finnie - DT
Dave Foley - C
Larry Grantham - LB
Steve Harkey - HB
Dave Herman - G
W.K. Hicks - DB
Winston Hill - T
Chuck Hinton - DT
Gus Hollomon - DB
Bobby Howfield - K
Roy Kirksey - G
Pete Lammons - TE
John Little - DT
Mark Lomas - DE
Don Maynard - WR
Cliff McClain - FB
John Mooring - T
Joe Namath - QB
George Nock - HB
Steve O'Neal - WR
Scott Palmer - DT
Gerry Philbin - DE
Randy Rasmussen - G
John Riggins - FB
John Schmitt - C
Matt Snell - FB
Rich Sowells - DB
Wayne Stewart - TE
Vern Studdard - WR
Bob Svihus - T
Clovis Swinney - DT
Steve Tannen - DB
Earlie Thomas - DB
Phillip Wise - DB
Al Woodall - QB
Willie Zapalac - DE

1971 Oakland

Butch Atkinson - DB
Pete Banaszak - FB
Duane Benson - LB
Fred Biletnikoff - WR
George Blanda - QB
Bob Brown - T
Willie Brown - DB
George Buehler - G
Drew Buie - WR
Raymond Chester - TE
Tony Cline - DE
Dan Conners - LB
Ben Davidson - DE
Clarence Davis - HB
Jerry DePoyster - K
Eldridge Dickey - WR
Mike Eischeid - K
Glenn Ellison - FB
Bill Enyart - FB
Tom Gipson - DT
Jim Harvey - G
Don Highsmith - HB
Marv Hubbard - FB
Gerald Irons - LB
Horace Jones - DE
Tom Keating - DT
Warren Koegel - C
Daryle Lamonica - QB
Tommy Maxwell - DB
Terry Mendenhall - LB
Ron Mix - T
Bob Moore - TE
Carleton Oats - DT
Gus Otto - LB
Jim Otto - C
Harold Rice - DE
Paul Seiler - C
Art Shell - T
Rod Sherman - WR
Greg Slough - LB
Charlie Smith - HB
Ken Stabler - QB
Jack Tatum - DB
Art Thoms - DT
Gene Upshaw - G
Phil Villapiano - LB
Jimmy Warren - DB
Carl Weathers - LB
Nemiah Wilson - DB

1971 Philadelphia

Hank Allison - G
Rick Arrington - QB
Tom Bailey - HB
Tony Baker - FB
Gary Ballman - WR
Lee Bouggess - FB
Bill Bradley - DB
Don Brumm - DE
Ronnie Bull - FB
Ernie Calloway - DE
Harold Carmichael - WR
Bob Creech - LB
Sonny Davis - FB
Vern Davis - DB
Tom Dempsey - K
Mike Dirks - DT
Mike Evans - C
Happy Feller - K
Richard Harris - DE
Ben Hawkins - WR
Fred Hill - WR
Bill Hobbs - LB
Don Hultz - DT
Harold Jackson - WR
Ike Kelley - LB
Wade Key - T
Leroy Keyes - DB
Kent Kramer - TE
Pete Liske - QB
Tom McNeill - K
Al Nelson - DB
Mark Nordquist - G
Gary Pettigrew - DT
Ron Porter - LB
Steve Preece - DB
Nate Ramsey - DB
Tim Rossovich - LB
Jim Skaggs - G
Jack Smith - DB
Steve Smith - T
Dick Stevens - T
Jim Thrower - DB
Mel Tom - DE
Tuufuli Uperesa - G
Billy Walik - WR
Jim Ward - QB
Larry Watkins - FB
Jim Whalen - TE
Fred Whittingham - LB
Tom Woodeshick - FB
Adrian Young - LB
Steve Zabel - TE

1971 Pittsburgh

Bob Adams - TE
Chuck Allen - LB
Ralph Anderson - DB
Bert Askson - DE
Ocie Austin - DB
Warren Bankston - FB
Chuck Beatty - DB
Rocky Bleier - HB
Mel Blount - DB
Terry Bradshaw - QB
John Brown - T
Larry Brown - TE
Jim Brumfield - HB
Lee Calland - DB
Jim Clack - C
Henry Davis - LB
Sam Davis - G
Glen Edwards - DB
John Fuqua - FB
Roy Gerela - K
Joe Greene - DT
L. C. Greenwood - DE
Jack Ham - LB
Terry Hanratty - QB
Mel Holmes - G
Dennis Hughes - TE
Jon Kolb - C
Bob Leahy - QB
Frank Lewis - WR
Ray Mansfield - C
Bobby Maples - C
Ben McGee - DT
Gerry Mullins - G
Preston Pearson - HB
John Rowser - DB
Andy Russell - LB
Ron Shanklin - WR
Rick Sharp - T
Dave Smith - WR
Jon Staggers - WR
Brian Stenger - LB
Bruce Van Dyke - G
Lloyd Voss - DT
Mike Wagner - DB
Bobby Walden - K
Dwight White - DE
Al Young - WR

1971 St. Louis

Jeff Allen - DB
Jim Bakken - K
Tom Banks - C
Pete Beathard - QB
Paul Dickson - DT
Dan Dierdorf - G
Cid Edwards - FB
Vern Emerson - T
Miller Farr - DB
John Gilliam - WR
Irv Goode - G
Mel Gray - WR
Dale Hackbart - DB
Jim Hargrove - LB
Jim Hart - QB
Fred Heron - DT
George Hoey - DB
Chuck Hutchison - G
Fred Hyatt - WR
Rolf Krueger - DT
MacArthur Lane - FB
Chuck Latourette - WR
Tom Longo - DB
Jim McFarland - TE
Mike McGill - LB
Ernie McMillan - T
Terry Miller - LB
Wayne Mulligan - C
Rick Ogle - LB
Don Parish - LB
Ted Provost - DB
Bob Reynolds - T
Jamie Rivers - LB
Johnny Roland - HB
Rocky Rosema - LB
Bob Rowe - DT
Joe Schmiesing - DE
Roy Shivers - HB
Jackie Smith - TE
Larry Stallings - LB
Larry Stegent - HB
Jerry Stovall - DB
Norm Thompson - DB
Chuck Walker - DE
Roger Wehrli - DB
Paul White - HB
Clyde Williams - G
Dave Williams - WR
Larry Willingham - DB
Larry Wilson - DB
Ron Yankowski - DE

1971 San Diego

Bob Babich - LB
Pete Barnes - LB
Joe Beauchamp - DB

Bob Bruggers - LB
Leon Burns - FB
Steve DeLong - DT
Chuck Detwiler - DB
Chuck Dicus - WR
Marty Domres - QB
Ron East - DT
Chris Fletcher - DB
Mike Garrett - HB
Gary Garrison - WR
Walker Gillette - WR
Ira Gordon - G
Wes Grant - DE
Sam Gruneisen - C
John Hadl - QB
Kevin Hardy - DT
Jim Hill - DB
Bob Howard - DB
Harris Jones - G
Jerry LeVias - WR
Carl Mauck - C
Mike Montgomery - HB
Pettis Norman - TE
Gary Nowak - DT
Terry Owens - T
Billy Parks - WR
Dennis Partee - K
Jack Porter - C
Jeff Queen - FB
Eddie Ray - FB
Rick Redman - LB
Andy Rice - DT
Mel Rogers - LB
Bryant Salter - DB
Jeff Staggs - DE
Art Strozier - TE
Walt Sweeney - G
John Tanner - LB
Lee Thomas - DE
Jim Tolbert - DB
Russ Washington - T
Ray White - LB
Doug Wilkerson - G
Tom Williams - DT

1971 San Francisco

Cas Banaszek - T
Ed Beard - LB
Randy Beisler - G
Bill Belk - DE
Forrest Blue - C
John Brodie - QB
Elmer Collett - G
Doug Cunningham - HB
Earl Edwards - DT
Johnny Fuller - DB
Bruce Gossett - K
Cedrick Hardman - DE
Tony Harris - DB
Tommy Hart - DE
Stan Hindman - DE
Bob Hoskins - G
John Isenbarger - HB
Jim Johnson - DB
Charlie Krueger - DT
Ted Kwalick - TE
Jim McCann - K
Frank Nunley - LB
Woody Peoples - G
Mel Phillips - DB
Preston Riley - WR
Len Rohde - T
Larry Schreiber - HB
Mike Simpson - DB
Jim Sniadecki - LB
Steve Spurrier - QB
Bruce Taylor - DB
Rosey Taylor - DB
Jimmy Thomas - HB
Skip Vanderbundt - LB
Gene Washington - WR
Vic Washington - HB
John Watson - T
Dave Wilcox - LB
Ken Willard - FB
Bob Windsor - TE
Dick Witcher - WR

1971 Washington

Mack Alston - TE
Mike Bass - DB
Verlon Biggs - DE
Mike Bragg - K
Larry Brown - HB
Bill Brundige - DT
Bob Brunet - HB
George Burman - C
Boyd Dowler - WR
Speedy Duncan - DB
Pat Fischer - DB
Bob Grant - LB
Chris Hanburger - LB
Charlie Harraway - FB
Len Hauss - C
Terry Hermeling - T
Mike Hull - FB
Jon Jaqua - DB
Roy Jefferson - WR
Jimmie Jones - DE
Jeff Jordan - HB
Sonny Jurgensen - QB
Billy Kilmer - QB
Curt Knight - K
Paul Laaveg - G
Bill Malinchak - WR
Tommy Mason - FB
Ron McDole - DE
Harold McLinton - LB
Clifton McNeil - WR
Brig Owens - DB
Jack Pardee - LB
Richie Petitbon - DB
Myron Pottios - LB
Walt Rock - T
Ray Schoenke - G
Manny Sistrunk - DT
Jerry Smith - TE
Jim Snowden - T
Diron Talbert - DT
Charley Taylor - WR
Mike Taylor - T
Rusty Tillman - LB
Ted Vactor - DB
John Wilbur - G
Sam Wyche - QB

1972 Atlanta

Grady Allen - LB
Bill Bell - K
Willie Belton - HB
Duane Benson - LB
Bob Berry - QB
Greg Brezina - LB
Ray Brown - DB
Ken Burrow - WR
Wes Chesson - WR
Glen Condren - DT
Ray Easterling - DB
Clarence Ellis - DB
Ted Fritsch - C
Willie Germany - DB
Len Gotshalk - T
Dave Hampton - HB
Don Hansen - LB
Dennis Havig - G
Tom Hayes - DB
Claude Humphrey - DE
John James - K
Ray Jarvis - WR
Noel Jenke - LB
George Kunz - T
Ron Lamb - FB
Mike Lewis - DE
Art Malone - FB
Rosie Manning - DT
Andy Maurer - G
Larry Mialik - TE
Jim Miller - G
Jim Mitchell - TE
Tommy Nobis - LB
Tony Plummer - DB
Joe Profit - HB
Eddie Ray - FB
Ken Reaves - DB
Bill Sandeman - T
Larry Shears - DB
John Small - DT
Todd Snyder - WR
Pat Sullivan - QB
Jeff Van Note - G
Chuck Walker - DT
John Zook - DE

1972 Baltimore

Dick Amman - DE
Jim Bailey - DE
Norm Bulaich - HB
Bill Curry - C
Mike Curtis - LB
Marty Domres - QB
Glenn Doughty - WR
Tom Drougas - T
Randy Edmunds - LB
Willie Franklin - WR
Sam Havrilak - WR
Ted Hendricks - LB
Lonnie Hepburn - DB
Roy Hilton - DE
Chuck Hinton - DT
Eddie Hinton - WR
Cornelius Johnson - G
Rex Kern - DB
Bruce Laird - DB
Bill Laskey - LB
David Lee - K
Jerry Logan - DB
Tom Matte - HB
Ray May - LB
Don McCauley - HB
Ken Mendenhall - C
Jack Mildren - DB
Fred Miller - DT
Lydell Mitchell - HB
Tom Mitchell - TE
John Mosier - TE
Nelson Munsey - DB
Dennis Nelson - T
Billy Newsome - DE
Don Nottingham - FB
Tom Nowatzke - FB
Jim O'Brien - WR
Glenn Ressler - G
John Shinners - G
Boris Shlapak - K
Cotton Speyrer - WR
Charles Stukes - DB
Dan Sullivan - G
Johnny Unitas - QB
Bob Vogel - T
Rick Volk - DB
Stan White - LB

1972 Buffalo

Bill Adams - G
Tom Beard - C
Jim Braxton - FB
Edgar Chandler - LB
Bob Chandler - WR
Bob Christiansen - TE
Linzy Cole - WR
Frank Cornish - DT
Paul Costa - T
Al Cowlings - DT
Don Croft - DT
Dick Cunningham - LB
Jeff Curchin - T
Dale Farley - LB
Dave Foley - T
Leon Garror - DB
Donnie Green - T
Tony Greene - DB
Paul Guidry - LB
Dwight Harrison - WR
Leo Hart - QB
Dick Hart - G
J. D. Hill - WR
Randy Jackson - HB
Robert James - DB
Bruce Jarvis - C
Spike Jones - K
Ted Koy - FB
Ken Lee - LB
John Leypoldt - K
Jeff Lyman - LB
John Matlock - C
Mike McBath - DE
Reggie McKenzie - G
Haven Moses - WR
Steve Okoniewski - DT
Dick Palmer - LB
Wayne Patrick - FB
Jerry Patton - DT
Walt Patulski - DE
Bob Penchion - G
John Pitts - DB
Remi Prudhomme - C
Louis Ross - DE
John Saunders - DB
Andy Selfridge - LB
Dennis Shaw - QB
O.J. Simpson - HB
Mike Stratton - LB
Mike Taliaferro - QB
Bob Tatarek - DT
Maurice Tyler - DB
Dave Washington - TE
Jan White - TE
Alvin Wyatt - DB
Willie Young - T

1972 Chi. Bears

Lionel Antoine - T
Bob Asher - G
Ross Brupbacher - LB
Doug Buffone - LB
Dick Butkus - C
Rich Buzin - T
Jim Cadile - G
Craig Clemons - DB
Rich Coady - C
Steve DeLong - DE
Bobby Douglass - QB
George Farmer - WR
Charlie Ford - DB
Bobby Joe Green - K
Jimmy Gunn - LB
Jim Harrison - FB
Glen Holloway - G
Willie Holman - DE
Larry Horton - DT
John Huarte - QB
Randy Jackson - T
Ernie Janet - G
Bob Jeter - DB
Gary Kosins - FB
Roger Lawson - HB
Bill Line - DT
Garry Lyle - DB
Matt Maslowski - WR
Tony McGee - DE
Bill McKinney - LB
Jerry Moore - DB
Bob Newton - G
Jim Osborne - DT
Bob Parsons - TE
Mac Percival - K
Bob Pifferini - LB
Cyril Pinder - HB
Andy Rice - DT
Larry Rowden - LB
Jim Seymour - WR
Don Shy - FB
Ron Smith - DB
Bill Staley - DT
Joe Taylor - DB
Earl Thomas - TE
Cecil Turner - WR
Bob Wallace - TE

1972 Cincinnati

Doug Adams - LB
Ken Anderson - QB
Ken Avery - LB
Al Beauchamp - LB
Bill Bergey - LB
Royce Berry - DE
Drew Buie - WR
Ron Carpenter - DE
Virgil Carter - QB
Tommy Casanova - DB
Steve Chomyszak - DT
Steve Conley - LB
Bruce Coslet - TE
Neal Craig - DB
Tom DeLeone - C
Guy Dennis - G
Doug Dressler - FB
Howard Fest - T
Vern Holland - T
Bernard Jackson - DB
Essex Johnson - HB
Ken Johnson - DT
Bob Johnson - C
Charlie Joiner - WR
Tim Kearney - LB
Ernie Kellermann - DB
Mike Kelly - TE
Steve Lawson - G
Jim LeClair - LB
Dave Lewis - QB
Pat Matson - G
Rufus Mayes - G
Reece Morrison - HB
Horst Muhlmann - K
Chip Myers - WR
Lemar Parrish - DB
Bill Peterson - LB
Jess Phillips - HB
Ron Pritchard - LB
Al Randolph - DB
Mike Reid - DT
Ken Riley - DB
Paul Robinson - HB
Speedy Thomas - WR
Bob Trumpy - TE
Stan Walters - T
Pete Watson - TE
Sherman White - DE
Fred Willis - FB

1972 Cleveland

Billy Andrews - LB
Bob Briggs - DT
Charlie Brinkman - WR
Cliff Brooks - DB - DB
Ken Brown - FB
Joe Carollo - T
Don Cockroft - K
Jim Copeland - C
Bo Cornell - FB
Fest Cotton - DT
Thom Darden - DB
Ben Davis - DB
Bob DeMarco - C
John Demarie - C
Doug Dieken - T
John Garlington - LB
Chip Glass - TE
Wes Grant - DE
Charlie Hall - LB
Gene Hickerson - G
Fred Hoaglin - C
Fair Hooker - WR
Jim Houston - DE
Mike Howell - DB
Rich Jackson - DE
Walter Johnson - DT
Leroy Kelly - HB
Rick Kingrea - LB
Billy Lefear - HB
Dale Lindsey - LB
Mel Long - LB
Bobby Majors - DB
Bob McKay - T
Milt Morin - TE
Chris Morris - T
Reece Morrison - HB
Bill Nelsen - QB
Bubba Pena - G
Mike Phipps - QB
Frank Pitts - WR
Gloster Richardson - WR
Nick Roman - DE
Clarence Scott - DB
Bo Scott - FB
Jerry Sherk - DE
Ron Snidow - DE
Paul Staroba - WR
Walt Sumner - DB
George Wright - DT
Craig Wycinsky - G

1972 Dallas

Herb Adderley - DB
Lance Alworth - WR
George Andrie - DE
John Babinecz - LB
Benny Barnes - DB
Marv Bateman - K
Larry Cole - DE
Ralph Coleman - LB
Mike Ditka - TE
Dave Edwards - LB
John Fitzgerald - C
Toni Fritsch - K
Jean Fugett - TE
Walt Garrison - FB
Cornell Green - DB
Bill Gregory - DT
Cliff Harris - DB
Bob Hayes - WR
Calvin Hill - FB
Chuck Howley - LB
Lee Roy Jordan - LB
Mike Keller - LB
D. D. Lewis - LB
Bob Lilly - DT
Dave Manders - C
Mike Montgomery - HB
Craig Morton - QB
Ralph Neely - T
Robert Newhouse - FB
John Niland - G
Blaine Nye - G
Billy Parks - WR
Jethro Pugh - DT
Dan Reeves - HB
Mel Renfro - DB
Ron Sellers - WR
Tody Smith - DE
Roger Staubach - QB
Bill Thomas - FB
Pat Toomay - DE
Billy Truax - TE
Rodney Wallace - G
Mark Washington - DB
Charlie Waters - DB
Rayfield Wright - T

1972 Denver

Lyle Alzado - DE
Bobby Anderson - HB
Bill Cottrell - G
Ken Criter - LB
Mike Current - T
Joe Dawkins - HB
Tom Domres - DT
Pete Duranko - DE
Mike Ernst - QB
Fred Forsberg - LB
Bob Geddes - LB
George Goeddeke - G
Cornell Gordon - DB
Tom Graham - LB
Charlie Greer - DB
Dwight Harrison - WR
John Hoffman - DE
Don Horn - QB
Larron Jackson - G
Rich Jackson - DE
Charley Johnson - QB
Larry Kaminski - C
Jim Krieg - WR
Floyd Little - HB
Fran Lynch - FB
Tommy Lyons - C
Bobby Maples - C
Billy Masters - TE
Bill McKoy - LB
Leroy Mitchell - DB
Marv Montgomery - T
Randy Montgomery - DB
Haven Moses - WR
Chip Myrtle - LB
Riley Odoms - TE
Don Parish - LB
Steve Preece - DB
Steve Ramsey - QB
George Saimes - DB
Mike Schnitker - G
Rick Sharp - T
Rod Sherman - WR
Jerry Simmons - WR
Mike Simone - LB
Paul Smith - DT
Billy Thompson - DB
Clem Turner - FB
Jim Turner - K
Bill Van Heusen - WR
Lloyd Voss - DT
Bill West - DB

1972 Detroit

Al Barnes - WR
Lem Barney - DB
Bob Bell - DT
Craig Cotton - TE
Nick Eddy - HB
Mel Farr - HB
Ed Flanagan - C
Rocky Freitas - T
Frank Gallagher - G
John Gordon - DT
Gene Hamlin - C
Larry Hand - DE
John Hilton - TE
Leon Jenkins - DB
Ron Jessie - WR
Gordon Jolley - T
Bob Kowalkowski - G
Greg Landry - QB
Dick LeBeau - DB
Mike Lucci - LB
Errol Mann - K
Earl McCullouch - WR
Jim Mitchell - DE
Bill Munson - QB
Paul Naumoff - LB
Rick Ogle - LB
Herb Orvis - DE
Steve Owens - FB
Charlie Potts - DB
Al Randolph - DB
Rocky Rasley - G
Wayne Rasmussen - DB
Rudy Redmond - DB
Charlie Sanders - TE
Ken Sanders - DE
Joe Schmiesing - DT
Bob Tatarek - DT
Altie Taylor - HB
Dave Thompson - T
Bill Triplett - FB
Wayne Walker - LB
Chuck Walton - G
Larry Walton - WR
Charlie Weaver - LB
Herman Weaver - K
Mike Weger - DB
Larry Woods - DT
Jim Yarbrough - T
Adrian Young - LB
Mickey Zofko - HB

1972 Green Bay

Ken Bowman - C
John Brockington - FB
Robert Brown - DT
Willie Buchanon - DB
Fred Carr - LB
Jim Carter - LB
Tommy Crutcher - LB
Carroll Dale - WR
Dave Davis - WR
Ken Ellis - DB
Len Garrett - TE
Paul Gibson - DB
Gale Gillingham - DT
Leland Glass - WR
Charlie Hall - DB
Bill Hayhoe - T
Larry Hefner - LB
Jim Hill - DB
Dick Himes - T
Bob Hudson - HB
Kevin Hunt - T
Scott Hunter - QB
Dave Kopay - FB
Bob Kroll - DB
Pete Lammons - TE
MacArthur Lane - HB
Bill Lueck - G
Chester Marcol - K
Al Matthews - DB
Mike McCoy - DT
Rich McGeorge - TE
Ray Nitschke - LB
Frank Patrick - QB
Francis Peay - T
Dave Pureifory - DE
Dave Robinson - LB
Alden Roche - DE
Mal Snider - G
Jon Staggers - WR
Jerry Tagge - QB
Ike Thomas - DB
Vern Vanoy - DT
Ward Walsh - HB
Ron Widby - K
Sweeny Williams - DE
Perry Williams - FB
Cal Withrow - C
Keith Wortman - G

1972 Houston

Allen Aldridge - DE
Willie Alexander - DB
Bob Atkins - DB
Ed Baker - QB
Jim Beirne - WR
Elvin Bethea - DE
Ron Billingsley - DT
Garland Boyette - LB
Lee Brooks - DT
Ken Burrough - WR
Skip Butler - K
Levert Carr - T
John Charles - DB
Linzy Cole - WR
Phil Croyle - LB
Rhett Dawson - WR
Gene Ferguson - T
Solomon Freelon - G
Tom Funchess - T
Hoyle Granger - FB
Buzz Highsmith - C
Pat Holmes - DT
Robert Holmes - FB
Ken Houston - DB
Calvin Hunt - C
Al Johnson - HB
Benny Johnson - DB
Charlie Joiner - WR
Lewis Jolley - HB
Rich Lewis - LB
Ralph Miller - G
Zeke Moore - DB
Mark Moseley - K
Guy Murdock - C
Kent Nix - QB
Dan Pastorini - QB
Ron Pritchard - LB
Alvin Reed - TE
Tom Regner - G
Floyd Rice - LB
Guy Roberts - LB
Paul Robinson - HB
Willie Rodgers - HB
Council Rudolph - DE
Greg Sampson - DE
Ron Saul - G
Dave Smith - WR
Mike Tilleman - DT
Jim Tolbert - DB
Ward Walsh - HB
George Webster - LB
Fred Willis - FB

1972 Kansas City

Mike Adamle - HB
Nate Allen - DB
Bobby Bell - LB
Keith Best - LB
Aaron Brown - DE
Buck Buchanan - DT
Ed Budde - G
Curley Culp - DT
George Daney - G
Len Dawson - QB
Willie Frazier - TE
Larry Gagner - G
Wendell Hayes - FB
Dave Hill - T
Dennis Homan - WR
Bruce Jankowski - WR
Jim Kearney - DB
Jeff Kinney - HB
Willie Lanier - LB
Mike Livingston - QB
Ed Lothamer - DT
Jim Lynch - LB
Jim Marsalis - DB
Larry Marshall - DB
Mo Moorman - G
Mike Oriard - C
Jim Otis - FB
Ed Podolak - HB
Kerry Reardon - DB
Jack Rudnay - C
George Seals - DT
Mike Sensibaugh - DB
Sid Smith - T
Bob Stein - LB
Jan Stenerud - K
Morris Stroud - TE
Otis Taylor - WR
Emmitt Thomas - DB
Jim Tyrer - T
Marv Upshaw - DE
Clyde Werner - LB
Bob West - WR
Jerrel Wilson - K
Elmo Wright - WR
Wilbur Young - DT

1972 LA Rams

Coy Bacon - DE
Pete Beathard - QB
Jim Bertelsen - HB
Larry Brooks - DT
Dave Chapple - K
Al Clark - DB
Charley Cowan - T
Pat Curran - TE
Fred Dryer - DE
Willie Ellison - HB
Dave Elmendorf - DB
Roman Gabriel - QB
Ken Geddes - LB
Dick Gordon - WR
Dean Halverson - LB
Gene Howard - DB
Ken Iman - C
Les Josephson - FB
Bob Klein - TE
Mike LaHood - G
John Love - WR
Tom Mack - G
Lawrence McCutcheon - HB
Marlin McKeever - LB
Bill Nelson - DT
Jim Nettles - DB
Merlin Olsen - DT
Phil Olsen - DT
John Pergine - LB
Jim Purnell - LB
David Ray - WR
Lance Rentzel - WR
Jack Reynolds - LB
Isiah Robertson - LB
Rich Saul - G
Harry Schuh - T
Joe Scibelli - G
Larry Smith - HB
Jack Snow - WR
Joe Sweet - WR
Bob Thomas - HB
Clancy Williams - DB
John Williams - G
Roger Williams - DB
Jack Youngblood - DE

1972 Miami

Dick Anderson - DB
Charlie Babb - DB
Larry Ball - LB
Marlin Briscoe - WR
Nick Buoniconti - LB
Doug Crusan - T
Larry Csonka - FB
Jim Del Gaizo - QB
Vern Den Herder - DE
Jim Dunaway - DT
Norm Evans - T
Manny Fernandez - DT
Marv Fleming - TE
Tim Foley - DB
Hubert Ginn - HB
Bob Griese - QB
Bob Heinz - DE
Mike Howell - DB
Al Jenkins - T
Ed Jenkins - HB
Curtis Johnson - DB
Jim Kiick - HB
Howard Kindig - T
Mike Kolen - LB
Bob Kuechenberg - G
Jim Langer - C
Charlie Leigh - FB
Larry Little - G
Billy Lothridge - K
Jim Mandich - TE
Bob Matheson - LB
Maulty Moore - DT
Wayne Moore - T
Earl Morrall - QB
Mercury Morris - HB
Lloyd Mumphord - DB
Jesse Powell - LB
Jake Scott - DB
Larry Seiple - TE
Bill Stanfill - DE
Otto Stowe - WR
Henry Stuckey - DB
Doug Swift - LB
Howard Twilley - WR
Paul Warfield - WR
Garo Yepremian - K

1972 Minnesota

Grady Alderman - T
John Beasley - TE
Terry Brown - DB
Bill Brown - FB
Bobby Bryant - DB
Fred Cox - K
Doug Davis - T
Calvin Demery - WR
Mike Eischeid - K
Carl Eller - DE
Carl Gersbach - LB
John Gilliam - WR
John Henderson - WR
Wally Hilgenberg - LB
Clint Jones - HB
Karl Kassulke - DB
Paul Krause - DB
Gary Larsen - DT
Bob Lee - QB
Jim Lindsey - HB
Bob Lurtsema - DT
Ed Marinaro - FB
Jim Marshall - DE
Amos Martin - LB
Dave Osborn - HB
Alan Page - DT
Oscar Reed - HB
Ed Sharockman - DB
Jeff Siemon - LB
Milt Sunde - C
Doug Sutherland - DE
Fran Tarkenton - QB
Mick Tingelhoff - C
Stu Voigt - TE
John Ward - DE
Lonnie Warwick - LB
Gene Washington - WR
Charlie West - DB
Ed White - G
Roy Winston - LB
Jeff Wright - DB
Nate Wright - DB
Ron Yary - T
Godfrey Zaunbrecher - C

1972 New England

Ron Acks - LB
Julius Adams - DE
Sam Adams - G
Josh Ashton - HB
Tom Beer - TE
Ron Berger - DE
Dick Blanchard - LB
Ron Bolton - DB
Hubie Bryant - WR
Larry Carwell - DB
Rick Cash - DT
Jim Cheyunski - LB
Ralph Cindrich - LB
Brian Dowling - QB
Carl Garrett - HB
Bob Gladieux - HB
Charlie Gogolak - K
Halvor Hagen - G
Rickie Harris - DB
George Hoey - DB
Honor Jackson - DB
Ron Kadziel - LB
Bill Lenkaitis - C
Jack Maitland - HB
Wayne Mass - T
Henry Matthews - HB
Art McMahon - DB
Mike Montler - T
Jon Morris - C
Tom Neville - T
John Outlaw - DB
Jim Plunkett - QB
Tom Reynolds - WR
Bob Reynolds - T
Dave Rowe - DT
Reggie Rucker - WR
Clarence Scott - DB
Len St. Jean - G
Pat Studstill - WR
John Tarver - FB
Randy Vataha - WR
Mike Walker - K
Ed Weisacosky - LB
Jim White - DE
Bob Windsor - TE
Dennis Wirgowski - DT

1972 New Orleans

Danny Abramowicz - WR
Margene Adkins - WR
Robert Brown - TE
Bill Butler - FB
Wayne Colman - LB
Mike Crangle - DE
John Didion - C
Charlie Durkee - K
Julian Fagan - K
Joe Federspiel - LB
Happy Feller - K
James Ford - FB
Arthur Green - HB
Bob Gresham - HB
Willie Hall - LB
Edd Hargett - QB
Billie Hayes - DB
Ray Hester - LB
Glen Ray Hines - T
Bill Hobbs - LB
Hugo Hollas - DB
Delles Howell - DB
Ernie Jackson - DB
Carl Johnson - G
Jake Kupp - G
Bob Kuziel - C
Bivian Lee - DB
Toni Linhart - K
Dave Long - DT
Archie Manning - QB
Doug Mooers - DT
Don Morrison - T
Tom Myers - DB
Richard Neal - DE
Bob Newland - WR
Joe Owens - DE
Dick Palmer - LB
Dave Parks - TE
Bob Pollard - DT
Remi Prudhomme - C
Craig Robinson - T
Virgil Robinson - HB
Tom Roussel - LB
Royce Smith - G
Thomas Stincic - LB
Jim Strong - FB
Faddie Tillman - DT
Cephus Weatherspoon - WR
Creston Whitaker - WR
Del Williams - G
Joe Williams - HB
Richard Winther - C
Doug Wyatt - DB

1972 NY Giants

Pete Athas - DB
Tom Blanchard - K
Otto Brown - DB
Carter Campbell - LB
Vince Clements - FB
Chuck Crist - DB
John Douglas - LB
Bobby Duhon - HB
Mark Ellison - G
Dick Enderle - G
Charlie Evans - FB
Jim Files - LB
Richmond Flowers - DB
Tom Gatewood - WR
Pete Gogolak - K
Dan Goich - DT
Jack Gregory - DE
Bob Grim - WR
Charlie Harper - DT
Don Herrmann - WR
John Hill - C
Ron Hornsby - LB
Rich Houston - WR
Pat Hughes - LB
Bob Hyland - C
Larry Jacobson - DT
Randy Johnson - QB
Ron Johnson - HB
Rich Kotite - TE
Greg Larson - C
Carl Lockhart - DB
John Mendenhall - DT
Joe Morrison - HB
Joe Orduna - HB
Henry Reed - DE
Eldridge Small - DB
Norm Snead - QB
Joe Taffoni - T
Rocky Thompson - HB
Dave Tipton - DE
Bob Tucker - TE
Doug Van Horn - G
Willie Williams - DB
Willie Young - T

1972 NY Jets

Al Atkinson - LB
Ralph Baker - LB
Jerome Barkum - WR
Eddie Bell - WR
Hank Bjorklund - HB
Emerson Boozer - HB
Rich Caster - TE
Paul Crane - C
Bob Davis - QB
John Ebersole - LB
John Elliott - DT
Chris Farasopoulos - DB
Roger Finnie - G
Ed Galigher - DE
Larry Grantham - LB
Steve Harkey - HB
Dave Herman - G
W.K. Hicks - DB
Winston Hill - T
Gus Hollomon - DB
Bobby Howfield - K
Joey Jackson - DT
Roy Kirksey - DT
John Little - DT
Mark Lomas - DT
Don Maynard - WR
Cliff McClain - HB
John Mooring - C
Joe Namath - QB
Steve O'Neal - K
Gerry Philbin - DE
Randy Rasmussen - G
John Riggins - FB
John Schmitt - C
Matt Snell - FB
Rich Sowells - DB
Wayne Stewart - TE
Bob Svihus - T
Steve Tannen - DB
Michael Taylor - LB
Earlie Thomas - DB
Steve Thompson - DT
Rocky Turner - WR
Phillip Wise - DB
Willie Zapalac - DE

1972 Oakland

Butch Atkinson - DB
Pete Banaszak - HB
Fred Biletnikoff - WR
George Blanda - QB
Cliff Branch - WR
Bob Brown - T
Willie Brown - DB
George Buehler - G
Joe Carroll - LB
Raymond Chester - TE
Tony Cline - DE
Dan Conners - LB
Dave Dalby - G
Clarence Davis - HB
Jerry DePoyster - K
Don Highsmith - HB
Marv Hubbard - FB
Gerald Irons - LB
Horace Jones - DE
Tom Keating - DT
Daryle Lamonica - QB
Tommy Maxwell - DB
Terry Mendenhall - LB
Bob Moore - TE
Carleton Oats - DT
Gus Otto - LB
Jim Otto - C
Jeff Queen - TE
Paul Seiler - C
Art Shell - T
Mike Siani - WR
Otis Sistrunk - DE
Greg Slough - LB
Charlie Smith - HB
Ken Stabler - QB
Jack Tatum - DB
Skip Thomas - DB
Art Thoms - DT
Gene Upshaw - G
John Vella - G
Phil Villapiano - LB
Jimmy Warren - DB
Nemiah Wilson - DB

1972 Philadelphia

Dick Absher - LB
Kermit Alexander - DB
Chuck Allen - LB
Jackie Allen - DB
Hank Allison - G
Houston Antwine - DT
Rick Arrington - QB
Tom Bailey - HB
Tony Baker - FB
Gary Ballman - WR
Bill Bradley - DB
John Bunting - LB
Ernie Calloway - DE
Harold Carmichael - WR
Bill Cody - LB
Al Coleman - DB
Bob Creech - LB
Larry Crowe - HB
Tom Dempsey - K
Larry Estes - DE
Mike Evans - C
Pat Gibbs - DB
Richard Harris - DE
Ben Hawkins - WR
Clark Hoss - TE
Don Hultz - DT
Harold Jackson - WR
Po James - HB
Wade Key - T
Leroy Keyes - DB
Kent Kramer - TE
Pete Liske - QB
Tom Luken - G
Wayne Mass - T
Tom McNeill - K
Al Nelson - DB
Mark Nordquist - C
Bill Overmyer - LB
Gary Pettigrew - DT
Ron Porter - LB
Steve Preece - DB
Nate Ramsey - DB
John Reaves - QB
Jim Skaggs - G
Steve Smith - T
John Sodaski - LB
Dick Stevens - T
Jerry Sturm - C
Tom Sullivan - HB
Jim Thrower - DB
Mel Tom - DE
Billy Walik - WR
Larry Watkins - FB
Vern Winfield - G
Adrian Young - LB
Steve Zabel - LB

1972 Pittsburgh

Ralph Anderson - DB
Warren Bankston - FB
Chuck Beatty - DB
Rocky Bleier - HB
Mel Blount - DB
Ed Bradley - LB
Terry Bradshaw - QB
Larry Brown - TE
Lee Calland - DB
Jim Clack - C
Henry Davis - LB
Sam Davis - G
Steve Davis - HB
John Dockery - DB
Glen Edwards - DB
John Fuqua - HB
Steve Furness - DT
Roy Gerela - K
Joe Gilliam - QB
Gordon Gravelle - T
Joe Greene - DT
L. C. Greenwood - DE
Jack Ham - LB
Craig Hanneman - DE
Terry Hanratty - QB
Franco Harris - FB
Ernie Holmes - DT
Mel Holmes - T
Jon Kolb - T
Frank Lewis - WR
Ray Mansfield - C
Ben McGee - DT
John McMakin - TE
Gerry Mullins - G
Barry Pearson - WR
Preston Pearson - HB
John Rowser - DB
Andy Russell - LB
Ron Shanklin - WR
Dave Smith - WR
Brian Stenger - LB
Bruce Van Dyke - G
Mike Wagner - DB
Bobby Walden - K
George Webster - LB
Dwight White - DE
Chuck Winfrey - LB
Al Young - WR

1972 St. Louis

Donny Anderson - HB
Mark Arneson - LB
Jim Bakken - K
Tom Banks - G
Craig Baynham - HB
Chuck Beatty - DB
Tom Beckman - DE
Dave Bradley - G
Don Brumm - DE
Leon Burns - FB
Cannonball Butler - HB
Steve Conley - LB
Gary Cuozzo - QB
Dan Dierdorf - G
Conrad Dobler - G
Miller Farr - DB
Walker Gillette - WR
Mel Gray - WR
Dale Hackbart - DB
Jim Hargrove - LB
Jim Hart - QB
Leo Hayden - FB
Don Heater - FB
Fred Heron - DT
John Hoffman - DE
Chuck Hutchison - G
Fred Hyatt - WR
Martin Imhof - DE
Jeff Lyman - LB
Jim McFarland - TE
Mike McGill - LB
Ernie McMillan - T
Terry Miller - LB
Wayne Mulligan - C
Scott Palmer - DT
Don Parish - LB
Ara Person - TE
Ahmad Rashad - WR
John Richardson - DT
Jamie Rivers - LB
Johnny Roland - HB
Bob Rowe - DT
Roy Shivers - HB
Jackie Smith - TE
Jeff Staggs - LB
Larry Stallings - LB
Norm Thompson - DB
Tim Van Galder - QB
Chuck Walker - DT
Eric Washington - DB
Roger Wehrli - DB
Bob Wicks - WR
Larry Willingham - DB
Larry Wilson - DB
Tom Woodeshick - FB
Steve Wright - T
Ron Yankowski - DE
Bob Young - G

1972 San Diego

Lionel Aldridge - DE
John Andrews - LB
Bob Babich - LB
Pete Barnes - LB
Joe Beauchamp - DB
Reggie Berry - DB
Lee Roy Caffey - LB
Mike Carter - WR
Wayne Clark - QB
Dave Costa - DT
Chuck Detwiler - DB
Chuck Dicus - WR
Oscar Dragon - FB
Lenny Dunlap - DB
Ron East - DT
Cid Edwards - FB
Chris Fletcher - DB
Mike Garrett - HB
Gary Garrison - WR
Ira Gordon - T
Sam Gruneisen - C
John Hadl - QB
Kevin Hardy - DT
Bob Howard - DB
Deacon Jones - DE
Ray Jones - DB
Pete Lazetich - LB
Jerry LeVias - WR
John Mackey - TE
Carl Mauck - C
Bill McClard - K
Pettis Norman - TE
Terry Owens - T
Dennis Partee - K
Rick Redman - LB
Tim Rossovich - LB
Bryant Salter - DB
Cal Snowden - DE
Walt Sweeney - G
John Sykes - HB
Jesse Taylor - HB
Lee Thomas - DE
Russ Washington - T
Ralph Wenzel - G
Lee White - FB
Ray White - LB
Doug Wilkerson - G
Dave Williams - WR
Gregory Wojcik - DT
Ernie Wright - T

1972 San Francisco

Cas Banaszek - C
Ed Beard - LB
Terry Beasley - WR
Randy Beisler - G
Bill Belk - DE
Forrest Blue - C
John Brodie - QB
Elmer Collett - G
Doug Cunningham - HB
Earl Edwards - DT
Johnny Fuller - DB
Bruce Gossett - K
Windlan Hall - DB
Cedrick Hardman - DE
Tommy Hart - DE
Bob Hoskins - DT
Marty Huff - LB
John Isenbarger - HB
Jim Johnson - DB
Charlie Krueger - DT
Rolf Krueger - DT
Ted Kwalick - TE
Jim McCann - K
Ralph McGill - DB
Frank Nunley - LB
Dave Olerich - LB
Woody Peoples - G
Mel Phillips - DB
Joe Reed - QB
Preston Riley - WR
Len Rohde - T
Larry Schreiber - HB
Mike Simpson - DB
Jim Sniadecki - LB
Steve Spurrier - QB
Bruce Taylor - DB
Jimmy Thomas - HB
Skip Vanderbundt - LB
Gene Washington - WR
Vic Washington - HB
John Watson - T
Dave Wilcox - LB
Ken Willard - FB
Dick Witcher - TE

1972 Washington

Mack Alston - TE
Mike Bass - DB
Verlon Biggs - DE
Mike Bragg - K
Larry Brown - HB
Bill Brundige - DT
Bob Brunet - HB
George Burman - G
Speedy Duncan - DB
Mike Fanucci - DE
Pat Fischer - DB
Chris Hanburger - LB
Charlie Harraway - FB
Len Hauss - C
Alvin Haymond - DB
Terry Hermeling - T
Mike Hull - FB
Jon Jaqua - DB
Roy Jefferson - WR
Jimmie Jones - DE
Jeff Jordan - HB
Sonny Jurgensen - QB
Billy Kilmer - QB
Curt Knight - K
Paul Laaveg - G
Bill Malinchak - WR
Ron McDole - DT
Harold McLinton - LB
Clifton McNeil - WR
Herb Mul-key - BB
George Nock - HB
Brig Owens - DB
Jack Pardee - LB
Richie Petitbon - DB
Myron Pottios - LB
Walt Rock - T
Ray Schoenke - T
Jeff Severson - DB
Manny Sistrunk - DT
Jerry Smith - TE
Diron Talbert - DT
Charley Taylor - WR
Rosey Taylor - DB
Rusty Tillman - LB
Ted Vactor - DB
John Wilbur - G
Sam Wyche - QB

1973 Atlanta

Nick Bebout - T
Duane Benson - LB
Greg Brezina - LB
Ray Brown - DB
Ken Burrow - WR
Wes Chesson - WR
Al Dodd - WR
Ray Easterling - DB
Clarence Ellis - DB
Ted Fritsch - C
Frank Gallagher - G
Tom Geredine - WR
Len Gotshalk - T
Dave Hampton - HB
Don Hansen - LB
Dennis Havig - G
Tom Hayes - DB
Claude Humphrey - DE
John James - K
George Kunz - T
Rolland Lawrence - DB
Bob Lee - QB
Mike Lewis - DT
Art Malone - FB
Rosie Manning - DT
Greg Marx - DE
Henry Matthews - HB
Andy Maurer - G
Larry Mialik - TE
Nick Mike-Mayer - K
Jim Mitchell - TE
Ken Mitchell - LB
Louis Neal - WR
Tommy Nobis - LB
Tony Plummer - DB
Joe Profit - HB
Eddie Ray - FB
Ken Reaves - DB
Bill Sandeman - T
Dick Shiner - QB
Pat Sullivan - QB
Mike Tilleman - DT
Jeff Van Note - C
Harmon Wages - FB
Chuck Walker - DT
Lonnie Warwick - LB
Joe Washington - HB
John Zook - DE

1973 Baltimore

Dick Amman - DT
John Andrews - TE
Jim Bailey - DT
Mike Barnes - DE
Stan Cherry - LB
Raymond Chester - TE
Elmer Collett - G
Mike Curtis - LB
Marty Domres - QB
Glenn Doughty - WR
Tom Drougas - T
Joe Ehrmann - DT
Hubert Ginn - HB
Sam Havrilak - WR
Ted Hendricks - LB
Brian Herosian - DB
Roy Hilton - DE
Fred Hoaglin - C
George Hunt - K
Cornelius Johnson - G
Bert Jones - QB
Mike Kaczmarek - LB
Rex Kern - DB
Bruce Laird - DB
David Lee - K
Ray May - LB
Don McCauley - HB
Ken Mendenhall - C
Jack Mildren - DB
Lydell Mitchell - HB
Tom Mitchell - TE
Ed Mooney - LB
Nelson Munsey - DB
Dan Neal - C
Dennis Nelson - T
Don Nottingham - FB
Ray Oldham - DB
Bill Olds - FB
Glenn Ressler - G
Joe Schmiesing - DE
Ollie Smith - WR
Cotton Speyrer - WR
David Taylor - T
Rick Volk - DB
Stan White - LB
Bill Windauer - DT

1973 Buffalo

Jim Braxton - FB
Bill Cahill - DB
Bob Chandler - WR
Jim Cheyunski - LB
Bo Cornell - FB
Phil Croyle - LB
Joe DeLamielleure - G
Earl Edwards - DE
Dale Farley - LB
Joe Ferguson - QB
Dave Foley - T
Fred Forsberg - LB
Wally Francis - WR
Leon Garror - DB
Donnie Green - T
Tony Greene - DB
Halvor Hagen - DE
Dwight Harrison - DB
J. D. Hill - WR
Robert James - DB
Bruce Jarvis - C
Ray Jarvis - WR
Spike Jones - K
Steve Jones - HB
Mike Kadish - DT
Bob Kampa - DT
Ernie Kellermann - DB
Rick Kingrea - LB
Ted Koy - TE
Merv Krakau - LB
Rich Lewis - LB
John Leypoldt - K
Brian McConnell - LB
Reggie McKenzie - G
Mike Montler - C
Steve Okoniewski - DT
Willie Parker - G
Jerry Patton - DT
Walt Patulski - DE
Bob Penchion - G
John Pitts - DB

Paul Seymour - TE
Dennis Shaw - QB
O.J. Simpson - HB
John Skorupan - LB
Ken Stone - DB
Pete Van Valkenberg - HB
Donnie Walker - DB
Dave Washington - TE
Larry Watkins - FB
Jeff Winans - DT

1973 Chi. Bears

Lionel Antoine - T
Bob Asher - T
Doug Buffone - LB
Dick Butkus - LB
Wally Chambers - DT
Gail Clark - LB
Craig Clemons - DB
Rich Coady - C
Craig Cotton - TE
Bobby Douglass - QB
Allan Ellis - DB
George Farmer - WR
Charlie Ford - DB
Carl Garrett - HB
Bobby Joe Green - K
Jimmy Gunn - LB
Dave Hale - DT
Jim Harrison - FB
Ike Hill - WR
Glen Holloway - G
Willie Holman - DE
Gary Hrivnak - DE
Gary Huff - QB
Randy Jackson - T
Ernie Janet - G
Bob Jeter - DB
Dave Juenger - WR
Steve Kinney - T
Gary Kosins - FB
Roger Lawson - HB
Garry Lyle - DB
Tony McGee - DE
Joe Moore - HB
Bob Newton - G
Jim Osborne - DT
Bob Parsons - TE
Mac Percival - K
Bob Pifferini - LB
Mike Reppond - WR
Tom Reynolds - WR
Andy Rice - DT
Don Rives - LB
Willie Roberts - DB
Mirro Roder - K
Reggie Sanderson - HB
Joe Taylor - DB
Earl Thomas - WR
Mel Tom - DE
Cecil Turner - WR
Adrian Young - LB

1973 Cincinnati

Doug Adams - LB
Ken Anderson - QB
Ken Avery - LB
Al Beauchamp - LB
Bill Bergey - LB
Royce Berry - DE
Lyle Blackwood - DB
Ron Carpenter - DT
Tommy Casanova - DB
Al Chandler - TE
Steve Chomyszak - DT
Boobie Clark - FB
Greg Cook - QB
Bruce Coslet - TE
Neal Craig - DB
Isaac Curtis - WR
Tom DeLeone - C
Lenvil Elliott - HB
Mike Ernst - QB
Howard Fest - G
Tim George - WR
Vern Holland - T
Bernard Jackson - DB
Essex Johnson - HB
Ken Johnson - DE
Bob Johnson - C
Charlie Joiner - WR
Bob Jones - DB
Tim Kearney - LB
Jim LeClair - LB
Dave Lewis - K
Pat Matson - G
Rufus Mayes - T
Reece Morrison - HB
Horst Muhlmann - K
Chip Myers - WR
Lemar Parrish - DB
Ron Pritchard - LB
Mike Reid - DT
Ken Riley - DB
John Shinners - G
Lee Thomas - DE
Bob Trumpy - TE
Stan Walters - T
Sherman White - DE
Joe Wilson - HB

1973 Cleveland

Billy Andrews - LB
Bob Babich - LB
Carl Barisich - DT
Bob Briggs - DE
Cliff Brooks - DB - DB
Ken Brown - HB
Joe Carollo - T
Don Cockroft - K
Jim Copeland - C
Thom Darden - DB
Ben Davis - DB
Bob DeMarco - C
John Demarie - G
Doug Dieken - T
John Garlington - LB
Chip Glass - TE
Van Green - DB
Charlie Hall - LB
Gene Hickerson - G
Steve Holden - WR
Fair Hooker - WR
Don Horn - QB
Chuck Hutchison - G
Walter Johnson - DT
Joe Jones - DE
Leroy Kelly - HB
Billy Lefear - HB
Mel Long - LB
Bob McKay - T
Hugh McKinnis - FB
Milt Morin - TE
Chris Morris - T
Mike Phipps - QB
Frank Pitts - WR
Greg Pruitt - HB
Gloster Richardson - WR
Nick Roman - DE
Jim Romaniszyn - LB
Clarence Scott - DB
Bo Scott - FB
Jerry Sherk - DT
Ken Smith - TE
Jim Stienke - DB
Dave Sullivan - WR
Walt Sumner - DB

1973 Dallas

Jim Arneson - C
John Babinecz - LB
Benny Barnes - DB
Rodrigo Barnes - LB
Marv Bateman - K
Mike Clark - K
Larry Cole - DE
Billy Joe DuPree - TE
Dave Edwards - LB
John Fitzgerald - C
Toni Fritsch - K
Jean Fugett - TE
Walt Garrison - FB
Cornell Green - DB
Bill Gregory - DT
Cliff Harris - DB
Bob Hayes - WR
Calvin Hill - FB
Chuck Howley - LB
Lee Roy Jordan - LB
D. D. Lewis - LB
Bob Lilly - DT
Dave Manders - C
Harvey Martin - DE
Mike Montgomery - WR
Craig Morton - QB
Ralph Neely - T
Robert Newhouse - HB
John Niland - G
Blaine Nye - G
Drew Pearson - WR
Cyril Pinder - HB
Jethro Pugh - DT
Mel Renfro - DB
Golden Richards - WR
Larry Robinson - HB
Roger Staubach - QB
Otto Stowe - WR
Les Strayhorn - HB
Pat Toomay - DE
Billy Truax - TE
Rodney Wallace - T
Bruce Walton - C
Mark Washington - DB
Charlie Waters - DB
Rayfield Wright - T

1973 Denver

Lyle Alzado - DE
Bobby Anderson - HB
Otis Armstrong - HB
Mike Askea - T
Barney Chavous - DE
Ken Criter - LB
Mike Current - T
Joe Dawkins - FB
Pete Duranko - DT
Fred Forsberg - LB
Tom Graham - LB
John Grant - DE
Charlie Greer - DB
Dale Hackbart - DB
Paul Howard - G
Jerry Inman - DT
Larron Jackson - T
Tom Jackson - LB
Charley Johnson - QB
Calvin Jones - DB
Larry Kaminski - C
Bill Laskey - LB
Floyd Little - HB
Fran Lynch - HB
Tommy Lyons - G
Bobby Maples - C
Billy Masters - TE
Ray May - LB
Leroy Mitchell - DB
Marv Montgomery - T
Randy Montgomery - DB
Haven Moses - WR
Riley Odoms - TE
Jim O'Malley - LB
John Pitts - DB
Steve Ramsey - QB
Oliver Ross - FB
Mike Schnitker - G
Jerry Simmons - WR
Mike Simone - LB
Ed Smith - DE
Paul Smith - DT
Billy Thompson - DB
Jim Turner - K
Maurice Tyler - DB
Bill Van Heusen - WR
Gene Washington - WR

1973 Detroit

Al Barnes - WR
Lem Barney - DB
Bob Bell - DT
Bill Cappleman - QB
Leon Crosswhite - FB
Guy Dennis - G
Mel Farr - HB
Miller Farr - DB
Ed Flanagan - C
Rocky Freitas - T
Willie Germany - DB
Mike Haggerty - T
Larry Hand - DE
Mike Hennigan - LB
John Hilton - TE
Jim Hooks - FB
Dick Jauron - DB
Ron Jessie - WR
Levi Johnson - DB
Gordon Jolley - T
Bob Kowalkowski - G
Greg Landry - QB
Jim Laslavic - LB
Mike Lucci - LB
Errol Mann - K
Earl McCullouch - WR
Jim Mitchell - DE
Bill Munson - QB
Paul Naumoff - LB
Jim O'Brien - WR
Herb Orvis - DT
Steve Owens - FB
Ernie Price - DT
Rocky Rasley - G
Charlie Sanders - TE
Ken Sanders - DE
John Small - DT
Altie Taylor - HB
Jim Teal - LB
Dave Thompson - G
Jim Thrower - DB
Chuck Walton - G
Larry Walton - WR
Charlie Weaver - LB
Herman Weaver - K
Mike Weger - DB
Doug Wyatt - DB
Jim Yarbrough - T
Mickey Zofko - HB

1973 Green Bay

Hise Austin - DB
Ken Bowman - C
Kent Branstetter - T
John Brockington - FB
Aaron Brown - DE
Robert Brown - DT
Willie Buchanon - DB
Fred Carr - LB
Jim Carter - LB
Jim Del Gaizo - QB
Mike Donohoe - TE
Ken Ellis - DB
Len Garrett - TE
Gale Gillingham - G
Leland Glass - WR
Les Goodman - FB
Dick Gordon - WR
Charlie Hall - DB
Bill Hayhoe - T
Larry Hefner - LB
Don Highsmith - HB
Jim Hill - DB
Dick Himes - T
Scott Hunter - QB
Noel Jenke - LB
Larry Krause - HB
MacArthur Lane - HB
Bill Lueck - G
Tom MacLeod - LB
Chester Marcol - K
Al Matthews - DB
Ron McBride - HB
Larry McCarren - C
Mike McCoy - DT
Rich McGeorge - TE
Carleton Oats - DT
Dave Pureifory - DE
Alden Roche - DE
Barry Smith - WR
Perry Smith - DB
Mal Snider - G
Jon Staggers - WR
Paul Staroba - WR
Jerry Tagge - QB
Ike Thomas - WR
Tom Toner - LB
Ron Widby - K
Sweeny Williams - DE
Perry Williams - FB
Cal Withrow - C
Keith Wortman - G

1973 Houston

Willie Alexander - DB
Mack Alston - TE
George Amundson - FB
Bob Atkins - DB
Jim Beirne - WR
Elvin Bethea - DE
Gregg Bingham - LB
Joe Blahak - DB
Ken Burrough - WR
Skip Butler - K
Levert Carr - T
John Charles - DB
Ralph Cindrich - LB
Al Cowlings - DT
Phil Croyle - LB
Dick Cunningham - LB
Bill Curry - C
Lynn Dickey - QB
Elbert Drungo - T
Larry Eaglin - DB
Mike Fanucci - DE
Solomon Freelon - G
Tom Funchess - T
Brian Goodman - G
Wes Grant - DT
Dave Green - K
Bob Gresham - HB
Sam Gruneisen - C
Paul Guidry - LB
Edd Hargett - QB
Alvin Haymond - DB
Eddie Hinton - WR
Calvin Hunt - C
Kevin Hunt - T
Al Jenkins - G
Al Johnson - HB
Benny Johnson - DB
Lewis Jolley - FB
Harris Jones - G
Ron Lou - C
John Matuszak - DT
Ron Mayo - TE
Brian McConnell - LB
Clifton McNeil - WR
Ralph Miller - G
Zeke Moore - DB
Dave Parks - TE
Billy Parks - WR
Dan Pastorini - QB
Floyd Rice - LB
Guy Roberts - LB
Paul Robinson - HB
Greg Sampson - DT
Ron Saul - G
Jeff Severson - DB
Tody Smith - DE
Bill Thomas - FB
Vern Vanoy - DT
Ted Washington - LB
Fred Willis - FB
Alvin Wyatt - DB

1973 Kansas City

Nate Allen - DB
Pete Beathard - QB
Bobby Bell - LB
Buck Buchanan - DT
Ed Budde - G
Gary Butler - TE
Curley Culp - DT
George Daney - G
Len Dawson - QB
Willie Ellison - FB
Andy Hamilton - WR
Wendell Hayes - FB
Dave Hill - T
Pat Holmes - DE
Doug Jones - DB
Jim Kearney - DB
Leroy Keyes - DB
Jeff Kinney - HB
Dan Kratzer - WR
Willie Lanier - LB
Mike Livingston - QB
John Lohmeyer - DE
Jim Lynch - LB
Jim Marsalis - DB
Larry Marshall - DB
Warren McVea - HB
Mo Moorman - T
Mike Oriard - G
Al Palewicz - LB
Francis Peay - T
Ed Podolak - HB
Kerry Reardon - DB
Jack Rudnay - C
George Seals - DT
Mike Sensibaugh - DB
Dave Smith - WR
Jan Stenerud - K
Morris Stroud - TE
Otis Taylor - WR
Emmitt Thomas - DB
Jim Tyrer - T
Marv Upshaw - DE
Wayne Walton - T
Clyde Werner - LB
Bob West - WR
Jerrel Wilson - K
Elmo Wright - WR
Wilbur Young - DE

1973 LA Rams

Tony Baker - FB
Jim Bertelsen - HB
Larry Brooks - DT
Cullen Bryant - DB
Dave Chapple - K
Al Clark - DB
Charley Cowan - T
Pat Curran - TE
Bill Drake - WR
Fred Dryer - DE
Dave Elmendorf - DB
Ken Geddes - LB
Dick Gordon - WR
John Hadl - QB
James Harris - QB
Ken Iman - C
Harold Jackson - WR
Les Josephson - FB
Rick Kay - LB
Bob Klein - TE
Tom Mack - G
Lawrence McCutcheon - HB
Eddie McMillan - DB
Terry Nelson - TE
Bill Nelson - DT
Merlin Olsen - DT
Phil Olsen - DT
Steve Preece - DB
David Ray - WR
Jack Reynolds - LB
Isiah Robertson - LB
Rich Saul - C
Harry Schuh - T
Joe Scibelli - G
Rob Scribner - HB
Rod Sherman - WR
Larry Smith - HB
Jack Snow - WR
Bob Stein - LB
Charles Stukes - DB
Joe Sweet - WR
John Williams - T
Jack Youngblood - DE
Jim Youngblood - LB

1973 Miami

Dick Anderson - DB
Charlie Babb - DB
Larry Ball - LB
Bruce Bannon - LB
Marlin Briscoe - WR
Nick Buoniconti - LB
Doug Crusan - T
Larry Csonka - FB
Vern Den Herder - DE
Norm Evans - T
Manny Fernandez - DT
Marv Fleming - TE
Tim Foley - DB
Hubert Ginn - HB
Irv Goode - G
Bob Griese - QB
Bob Heinz - DT
Curtis Johnson - DB
Jim Kiick - HB
Mike Kolen - LB
Bob Kuechenberg - G
Jim Langer - C
Charlie Leigh - FB
Larry Little - G
Jim Mandich - TE
Bob Matheson - LB
Maulty Moore - DT
Wayne Moore - T
Earl Morrall - QB
Mercury Morris - HB
Lloyd Mumphord - DB
Ed Newman - G
Don Nottingham - FB
Jesse Powell - LB
Bo Rather - WR
Jake Scott - DB
Larry Seiple - TE
Ron Sellers - WR
Tom Smith - HB
Bill Stanfill - DE
Henry Stuckey - DB
Doug Swift - LB
Howard Twilley - WR
Paul Warfield - WR
Larry Woods - DT
Garo Yepremian - K
Willie Young - T

1973 Minnesota

Grady Alderman - T
Gary Ballman - TE
John Beasley - TE
Bob Berry - QB
Terry Brown - DB
Bill Brown - FB
Bobby Bryant - DB
Fred Cox - K
Carroll Dale - WR
Rhett Dawson - WR
Mike Eischeid - K
Carl Eller - DE
Chuck Foreman - FB
Frank Gallagher - G
John Gilliam - WR
Charlie Goodrum - G
Wally Hilgenberg - LB
Doug Kingsriter - TE
Paul Krause - DB
Gary Larsen - DT
Jim Lash - WR
Steve Lawson - G
Bob Lurtsema - DT
Ed Marinaro - HB
Jim Marshall - DE
Amos Martin - LB
Brent McClanahan - HB
Dave Osborn - HB
Alan Page - DT
Ron Porter - LB
Al Randolph - DB
Oscar Reed - HB
Jeff Siemon - LB
Milt Sunde - G
Doug Sutherland - DT
Fran Tarkenton - QB
Mick Tingelhoff - C
Stu Voigt - TE
John Ward - G
Charlie West - DB
Ed White - G
Roy Winston - LB
Jeff Wright - DB
Nate Wright - DB
Ron Yary - T
Godfrey Zaunbrecher - C

1973 New England

Ron Acks - LB
Julius Adams - DT
Bob Adams - TE
Sam Adams - T
Ralph Anderson - DB
Josh Ashton - HB
Willie Banks - G
Bruce Barnes - K
Bill Bell - K
Ron Bolton - DB
Greg Boyd - DB
Rick Cash - DT
Edgar Chandler - LB
Sam Cunningham - FB
Nate Dorsey - DE
Brian Dowling - QB
Doug Dumler - C
Sandy Durko - DB
Will Foster - LB
Bob Geddes - LB
Paul Gipson - FB
Leon Gray - T
Ray Hamilton - DE
John Hannah - G
Mack Herron - HB
George Hoey - DB
Kevin Hunt - T
Honor Jackson - DB
Steve Kiner - LB
Steve King - LB
Bill Lenkaitis - G
Mel Lunsford - DT
Don Martin - DB
Dave Mason - DB
Bob McCall - HB
Art Moore - DT
Jon Morris - C
Tom Neville - T
Jim Plunkett - QB
Bob Reynolds - T
Dave Rowe - DT
Reggie Rucker - WR
Dick Shiner - QB
Donnell Smith - DE
Brian Stenger - LB
Darryl Stingley - WR
Len St. Jean - G
John Tanner - LB
John Tarver - FB
Randy Vataha - WR
Claxton Welch - HB
Jeff White - K
Bob Windsor - TE

1973 New Orleans

Danny Abramowicz - WR
Bert Askson - TE
Steve Baumgartner - DE
John Beasley - TE
Robert Brown - TE
Bill Butler - FB
Wayne Colman - LB
Bob Creech - LB
Bob Davis - QB
John Didion - C
Andy Dorris - DE
Jubilee Dunbar - WR
Joe Federspiel - LB
Happy Feller - K
Paul Fersen - T
Mike Fink - DB
Johnny Fuller - DB
Len Garrett - TE
Willie Hall - LB
Ray Hester - LB
Fred Hyatt - WR
Ernie Jackson - DB
Carl Johnson - T
Ray Jones - DB
Mike Kelly - TE
Rick Kingrea - LB
Jake Kupp - G
Odell Lawson - FB
Bivian Lee - DB
Dale Lindsey - LB
Archie Manning - QB
Henry Matthews - HB
Bill McClard - K
Jim Merlo - LB
Lincoln Minor - HB
Derland Moore - DT
Jerry Moore - DB
Don Morrison - T
Tom Myers - DB
Bob Newland - WR
Billy Newsome - DE
Steve O'Neal - K
Joe Owens - DE
Dick Palmer - LB
Jess Phillips - FB
Bob Pollard - DT
Elex Price - DT
Joe Profit - HB
Nate Ramsey - DB
Preston Riley - WR
Craig Robinson - T
Bobby Scott - QB
Royce Smith - G
Howard Stevens - HB
Speedy Thomas - WR
Del Williams - G
Doug Winslow - WR
John Wood - DT

1973 NY Giants

Pete Athas - DB
Gary Ballman - TE
Tom Blanchard - K
Otto Brown - DB
Bart Buetow - T
Carter Campbell - DE
Vince Clements - FB
Chuck Crist - DB
John Douglas - LB
Mark Ellison - G
Dick Enderle - G
Charlie Evans - FB
Jim Files - LB
Richmond Flowers - DB
Tom Gatewood - TE
Rich Glover - DT
Pete Gogolak - K
Dan Goich - DT
Jack Gregory - DE
Bob Grim - WR
Don Herrmann - WR
John Hill - T
Ron Hornsby - LB
Rich Houston - WR
Pat Hughes - LB
Bob Hyland - T
Honor Jackson - DB
Larry Jacobson - DT
Randy Johnson - QB
Ron Johnson - HB
Brian Kelley - LB
Greg Larson - C
Carl Lockhart - DB
Walt Love - WR
Ron Lumpkin - DB
Jim McCann - K
John Mendenhall - DT
Joe Orduna - FB
Henry Reed - LB
Jack Rizzo - HB
Johnny Roland - HB
Eldridge Small - DB
Norm Snead - QB
Joe Taffoni - T
Rocky Thompson - HB
Dave Tipton - DE
Bob Tucker - TE
Doug Van Horn - G
Brad Van Pelt - LB
Willie Williams - DB
Willie Young - T

1973 NY Jets

Mike Adamle - HB
Margene Adkins - WR
Al Atkinson - LB
Ralph Baker - LB

Jerome Barkum - WR
Eddie Bell - WR
Hank Bjorklund - HB
Emerson Boozer - HB
Dennis Cambal - TE
Rich Caster - TE
Bill Demory - QB
John Ebersole - LB
John Elliott - DE
Julian Fagan - K
Chris Farasopoulos - DB
Bill Ferguson - LB
Ed Galigher - DE
Rick Harrell - C
Dave Herman - G
Winston Hill - T
Delles Howell - DB
Bobby Howfield - K
Joey Jackson - DT
David Knight - WR
John Little - DT
Mark Lomas - DE
Cliff McClain - HB
John Mooring - C
Joe Namath - QB
Jim Nance - FB
Richard Neal - DT
Burgess Owens - DB
Garry Puetz - T
Randy Rasmussen - G
John Riggins - FB
John Schmitt - C
Rich Sowells - DB
Rob Spicer - LB
Bob Svihus - T
Steve Tannen - DB
Michael Taylor - LB
Earlie Thomas - DB
Steve Thompson - DT
Rocky Turner - DB
Phillip Wise - DB
Al Woodall - QB
Robert Woods - T
Willie Zapalac - LB

1973 Oakland

Butch Atkinson - DB
Pete Banaszak - HB
Warren Bankston - TE
Fred Biletnikoff - WR
George Blanda - QB
Cliff Branch - WR
Bob Brown - T
Willie Brown - DB
George Buehler - G
Joe Carroll - LB
Tony Cline - DE
Dan Conners - LB
Dave Dalby - C
Clarence Davis - HB
Ray Guy - K
Marv Hubbard - FB
Bob Hudson - HB
Gerald Irons - LB
Monte Johnson - LB
Horace Jones - DE
Kelvin Korver - DT
Daryle Lamonica - QB
Tommy Maxwell - DB
Bob Moore - TE
Jim Otto - C
Jeff Queen - TE
Paul Seiler - C
Art Shell - T
Mike Siani - WR
Otis Sistrunk - DT
Bubba Smith - DE
Charlie Smith - HB
Ken Stabler - QB
Steve Sweeney - WR
Jack Tatum - DB
Skip Thomas - DB
Art Thoms - DT
Gene Upshaw - G
John Vella - T
Phil Villapiano - LB
Jimmy Warren - DB
Gary Weaver - LB
Nemiah Wilson - DB

1973 Philadelphia

Kermit Alexander - DB
Tom Bailey - FB
Lee Bouggess - FB
Bill Bradley - DB
Norm Bulaich - HB
John Bunting - LB
Harold Carmichael - WR
Wes Chesson - WR
Al Coleman - DB
Dick Cunningham - LB
Stan Davis - WR
Tom Dempsey - K
Bill Dunstan - DT
Mike Evans - C
Roman Gabriel - QB
Dean Halverson - LB
Richard Harris - DE
Ben Hawkins - WR
Don Hultz - DT
Po James - HB
Wade Key - G
Roy Kirksey - G
Kent Kramer - TE
Joe Lavender - DB
Randy Logan - DB
Tom Luken - G
Marlin McKeever - LB
Tom McNeill - K
Guy Morriss - C
Al Nelson - DB
Mark Nordquist - G
Greg Oliver - HB
John Outlaw - DB
Gary Pettigrew - DT
Gerry Philbin - DE
Bob Picard - WR
John Reaves - QB
Kevin Reilly - LB
Tom Roussel - LB
Jerry Sisemore - T
Steve Smith - T
John Sodaski - LB
Dick Stevens - T
Tom Sullivan - HB
Mel Tom - DE
Vern Winfield - G
Dennis Wirgowski - DE
Will Wynn - DE
Charle Young - TE
Steve Zabel - LB
Don Zimmerman - WR

1973 Pittsburgh

Rocky Bleier - HB
Mel Blount - DB
Ed Bradley - LB
Terry Bradshaw - QB
Larry Brown - TE
Jim Clack - C
Dave Davis - WR
Henry Davis - LB
Sam Davis - G
Steve Davis - HB
John Dockery - DB
Glen Edwards - DB
John Fuqua - HB
Steve Furness - DT
Roy Gerela - K
Joe Gilliam - QB
Gordon Gravelle - T
Joe Greene - DT
L. C. Greenwood - DE
Jack Ham - LB
Craig Hanneman - DT
Terry Hanratty - QB
Franco Harris - FB
Glen Ray Hines - T
Ernie Holmes - DT
Mel Holmes - G
Tom Keating - DT
Jon Kolb - T
Frank Lewis - WR
Ray Mansfield - C
John McMakin - TE
Dennis Meyer - DB
Gerry Mullins - T
Barry Pearson - WR
Preston Pearson - HB
John Rowser - DB
Andy Russell - LB
Glenn Scolnik - WR
Ron Shanklin - WR
J.T. Thomas - DB
Loren Toews - LB
Bruce Van Dyke - G
Mike Wagner - DB
Bobby Walden - K
George Webster - LB
Dwight White - DE
Dave Williams - WR

1973 St. Louis

Donny Anderson - HB
Mark Arneson - LB
Jim Bakken - K
Tom Banks - G
Pete Barnes - LB
Willie Belton - HB
Tom Brahaney - C
Lee Brooks - DT
Dave Butz - DT
Dwayne Crump - DB
Ron Davis - G
Chuck Detwiler - DB
Dan Dierdorf - T
Conrad Dobler - G
Andy Dorris - DE
Clarence Duren - DB
Roger Finnie - G
Walker Gillette - WR
Mel Gray - WR
Gary Hammond - HB
Jim Hart - QB
Leo Hayden - HB
Gary Keithley - QB
Warren Koegel - C
Jack LeVeck - LB
Don Maynard - WR
Jim McFarland - TE
Ernie McMillan - T
Terry Metcalf - HB
Terry Miller - LB
Eddie Moss - HB
Wayne Mulligan - C
Clancy Oliver - DB
Jim Otis - FB
Marv Owens - WR
Ahmad Rashad - WR
Bob Reynolds - T
John Richardson - DT
Jamie Rivers - LB
Bob Rowe - DT
Council Rudolph - DE
Don Shy - HB
Bonnie Sloan - DT
Jackie Smith - TE
Jeff Staggs - LB
Larry Stallings - LB
Mike Taylor - T
Norm Thompson - DB
Jim Tolbert - DB
Eric Washington - DB
Roger Wehrli - DB
Ron Yankowski - DE
Bob Young - G

1973 San Diego

Lionel Aldridge - DE
Coy Bacon - DE
Joe Beauchamp - DB
Reggie Berry - DB
Wayne Clark - QB
Dave Costa - DT
Al Dennis - G
Jay Douglas - C
Lenny Dunlap - DB
Ron East - DT
Cid Edwards - FB
Chris Fletcher - DB
Dan Fouts - QB
Mike Garrett - HB
Gary Garrison - WR
Carl Gersbach - LB
Ira Gordon - T
Ron Holliday - WR
Robert Holmes - FB
Bob Howard - DB
Clint Jones - HB
Deacon Jones - DE
Pete Lazetich - DE
Jerry LeVias - WR
Carl Mauck - C
Willie McGee - DB
Pettis Norman - TE
Terry Owens - T
Gary Parris - TE
Dennis Partee - K
Rick Redman - LB
Floyd Rice - LB
Mel Rogers - LB
Tim Rossovich - LB
Bryant Salter - DB
Ron Smith - DB
Cal Snowden - DE
Mike Stratton - LB
Walt Sweeney - G
Jim Thaxton - TE
Bob Thomas - HB
Johnny Unitas - QB
Russ Washington - T
Ralph Wenzel - G
Ray Wersching - K
Doug Wilkerson - G
Dave Williams - WR
Gregory Wojcik - DT

1973 San Francisco

Danny Abramowicz - WR
Dave Atkins - HB
Cas Banaszek - T
Jean Barrett - T
Randy Beisler - G
Bill Belk - DE
Ed Beverly - WR
Forrest Blue - C
John Brodie - QB
Doug Cunningham - HB
Bruce Gossett - K
Windlan Hall - DB
Cedrick Hardman - DE
Ed Hardy - G
Willie Harper - LB
Tommy Hart - DE
Bob Hoskins - DT
Charlie Hunt - LB
John Isenbarger - WR
Randy Jackson - HB
Jim Johnson - DB
Charlie Krueger - DT
Rolf Krueger - DT
Ted Kwalick - TE
Ralph McGill - DB
Frank Nunley - LB
Dave Olerich - LB
Woody Peoples - G
Mel Phillips - DB
Joe Reed - QB
Len Rohde - T
Larry Schreiber - HB
Mike Simpson - DB
Jim Sniadecki - LB
Steve Spurrier - QB
Bruce Taylor - DB
Jimmy Thomas - HB
Skip Vanderbundt - LB
Gene Washington - WR
Vic Washington - HB
John Watson - G
Dave Wilcox - LB
Ken Willard - FB
Dick Witcher - TE
Tom Wittum - K

1973 Washington

Mike Bass - DB
Verlon Biggs - DE
Mike Bragg - K
Larry Brown - HB
Bill Brundige - DT
Bob Brunet - HB
Speedy Duncan - DB
Pat Fischer - DB
Frank Grant - WR
Chris Hanburger - LB
Mike Hancock - TE
Charlie Harraway - FB
Len Hauss - C
Terry Hermeling - T
Willie Holman - DE
Ken Houston - DB
Mike Hull - FB
Fred Hyatt - WR
Roy Jefferson - WR
Jimmie Jones - DE
Sonny Jurgensen - QB
Billy Kilmer - QB
Curt Knight - K
Paul Laaveg - G
Bill Malinchak - WR
Ron McDole - DE
Harold McLinton - LB
Herb Mul-key - RB
Brig Owens - DB
John Pergine - LB
Myron Pottios - LB
Alvin Reed - TE
Dave Robinson - LB
Walt Rock - T
Dan Ryczek - C
Ray Schoenke - G
Manny Sistrunk - DT
Jerry Smith - TE
George Starke - T
Ken Stone - DB
Diron Talbert - DT
Charley Taylor - WR
Duane Thomas - HB
Rusty Tillman - LB
Ted Vactor - DB
John Wilbur - G
Larry Willis - DB

1974 Atlanta

Larry Bailey - DT
Nick Bebout - T
Greg Brezina - LB
Ray Brown - DB
Ken Burrow - WR
Rick Byas - DB
Henry Childs - TE
Al Dodd - WR
Ray Easterling - DB
Clarence Ellis - DB
Ted Fritsch - C
Tom Geredine - WR
Len Gotshalk - T
Dave Hampton - HB
Don Hansen - LB
Dennis Havig - G
Tom Hayes - DB
Rudy Holmes - DB
Claude Humphrey - DE
John James - K
Vince Kendrick - FB
George Kunz - T
Rolland Lawrence - DB
Bob Lee - QB
Mike Lewis - DT
Art Malone - HB
Rosie Manning - DT
Molly McGee - HB
Kim McQuilken - QB
Larry Mialik - TE
Nick Mike-Mayer - K
Jim Miller - G
Jim Mitchell - TE
Ken Mitchell - LB
Louis Neal - WR
Tommy Nobis - LB
Dick Palmer - LB
Eddie Ray - FB
Paul Ryczek - C
Royce Smith - G
Haskel Stanback - HB
Pat Sullivan - QB
Mike Tilleman - DT
Gerald Tinker - WR
Jeff Van Note - C
Chuck Walker - DT
Lonnie Warwick - LB
John Zook - DE

1974 Baltimore

John Andrews - TE
Jim Bailey - DT
Mike Barnes - DE
Tim Berra - WR
Tony Bertuca - LB
Roger Carr - WR
Raymond Chester - TE
Elmer Collett - G
Fred Cook - DE
Mike Curtis - LB
Dan Dickel - LB
Marty Domres - QB
Glenn Doughty - WR
John Dutton - DE
Joe Ehrmann - DT
Randy Hall - DB
Bert Jones - QB
Bruce Laird - DB
David Lee - K
Toni Linhart - K
Tom MacLeod - LB
Ron Mayo - TE
Don McCauley - HB
Ken Mendenhall - C
Lydell Mitchell - HB
Nelson Munsey - DB
Dan Neal - C
Dennis Nelson - T
Doug Nettles - DB
Ray Oldham - DB
Bill Olds - FB
Joe Orduna - HB
Bob Pratt - G
Glenn Ressler - G
Danny Rhodes - LB
Tim Rudnick - DB
Freddie Scott - WR
Dave Simonson - T
Ollie Smith - WR
Cotton Speyrer - WR
David Taylor - T
Bill Troup - QB
Bob Van Duyne - G
Rick Volk - DB
Stan White - LB
Steven Williams - DE
Bill Windauer - DT

1974 Buffalo

Bill Adams - G
Doug Allen - LB
Marv Bateman - K
Jim Braxton - FB
Bill Cahill - DB
Don Calhoun - HB
Bob Chandler - WR
Jim Cheyunski - LB
Bo Cornell - FB
Dave Costa - DE
Neal Craig - DB
Don Croft - DT
Joe DeLamielleure - G
Earl Edwards - DE
Joe Ferguson - QB
Dave Foley - T
Wally Francis - WR
Reuben Gant - TE
Donnie Green - T
Tony Greene - DB
Halvor Hagen - T
Dwight Harrison - DB
Clint Haslerig - HB
Gary Hayman - HB
J. D. Hill - WR
Scott Hunter - QB
Robert James - DB
Bruce Jarvis - C
Ed Jenkins - HB
Spike Jones - K
Steve Jones - HB
Mike Kadish - DT
Bob Kampa - DT
Rex Kern - DB
Ted Koy - TE
Merv Krakau - LB
Rich Lewis - LB
John Leypoldt - K
Gary Marangi - QB
Reggie McKenzie - G
Dave Means - DE
Mike Montler - T
Wayne Mosley - HB
Nick Nighswander - C
Willie Parker - G
Walt Patulski - DE
Al Randolph - DB
Ahmad Rashad - WR
Paul Seymour - TE
O.J. Simpson - HB
John Skorupan - LB
Donnie Walker - DB
Dave Washington - TE
Larry Watkins - FB
Jeff Yeates - DT

1974 Chi. Bears

Lionel Antoine - T
Bob Asher - T
Joe Barnes - QB
Waymond Bryant - LB
Doug Buffone - LB
Wally Chambers - DT
Craig Clemons - DB
Rich Coady - C
Bobby Douglass - QB
Allan Ellis - DB
George Farmer - WR
Tom Forrest - G
Dave Gagnon - HB
Dave Gallagher - DT
Carl Garrett - HB
Ken Grandberry - HB
Jimmy Gunn - LB
Richard Harris - DT
Jim Harrison - FB
Clint Haslerig
Ike Hill - WR
Mike Hoban - G
Norm Hodgins - DB
Gary Hrivnak - DE
Gary Huff - QB
Don Hultz - DT
Randy Jackson - T
Ernie Janet - G
Jim Kelly - TE
Steve Kinney - T
Bill Knox - DB
Gary Kosins - FB
Garry Lyle - DB
Randy Montgomery - DB
Bob Newton - G
Jim Osborne - DT
Fred Pagac - TE
Bob Parsons - TE
Bob Pifferini - LB
Bo Rather - WR
Don Rives - LB
Mirro Roder - K
Hurles Scales - DB
Cliff Taylor - HB
Joe Taylor - DB
Mel Tom - DE
Pete Van Valkenberg - HB
Charlie Wade - WR
Wayne Wheeler - WR
Perry Williams - FB

1974 Cincinnati

Doug Adams - LB
Ken Anderson - QB
Ken Avery - LB
Al Beauchamp - LB
Royce Berry - DE
Lyle Blackwood - DB
Ron Carpenter - DT
Tommy Casanova - DB
Al Chandler - TE
Boobie Clark - FB
Wayne Clark - QB
Bruce Coslet - TE
Isaac Curtis - WR
Charlie Davis - HB
Doug Dressler - FB
Lenvil Elliott - HB
Howard Fest - G
Dave Green - K
Vern Holland - T
Bernard Jackson - DB
Essex Johnson - HB
Ken Johnson - DE
Bob Johnson - C
Charlie Joiner - WR
Evan Jolitz - LB
Bob Jones - DB
Tim Kearney - LB
Vic Koegel - LB
Bill Kollar - DT
Dave Lapham - T
Jim LeClair - LB
Bob Maddox - DE
Pat Matson - G
Rufus Mayes - T
John McDaniel - WR
Horst Muhlmann - K
Chip Myers - WR
Lemar Parrish - DB
Ron Pritchard - LB
Mike Reid - DT
Ken Riley - DB
Ken Sawyer - DB
John Shinners - G
Bob Trumpy - TE
Stan Walters - T
Sherman White - DE
Ed Williams - FB

1974 Cleveland

Pete Adams - G
Allen Aldridge - DE
Preston Anderson - DB
Billy Andrews - LB
Bob Babich - LB
Carl Barisich - DT
Cliff Brooks - DB - DB
Ken Brown - HB
Eddie Brown - DB
Don Cockroft - K
Jim Copeland - G
Thom Darden - DB
Barry Darrow - T
Tom DeLeone - C
Bob DeMarco - C
John Demarie - G
Doug Dieken - T
Jubilee Dunbar - WR
John Garlington - LB
Chris Gartner - K
Tim George - WR
Van Green - DB
Charlie Hall - LB
Ben Hawkins - WR
Steve Holden - WR
Glen Holloway - G
Fair Hooker - WR
Bob Hunt - HB
Chuck Hutchison - G
Mark Ilgenfritz - DE
Walter Johnson - DT
Billy Lefear - WR
Mel Long - LB
Bob McKay - T
Hugh McKinnis - FB
Milt Morin - TE
Mike Phipps - QB
Greg Pruitt - HB
Ernie Richardson - TE
Gloster Richardson - WR
Nick Roman - DE
Jim Romaniszyn - LB
Clarence Scott - DB
Bo Scott - FB
Mike Seifert - DE
Jerry Sherk - DT
Brian Sipe - QB
Dave Sullivan - WR
Gerry Sullivan - T
Walt Sumner - DB
Jim Thaxton - TE

1974 Dallas

Jim Arneson - C
Benny Barnes - DB
Rodrigo Barnes - LB
Marv Bateman - K
Duane Carrell - K
Larry Cole - DE
Doug Dennison - HB
Billy Joe DuPree - TE
Dave Edwards - LB
John Fitzgerald - C
Jean Fugett - TE
Walt Garrison - FB
Cornell Green - DB
Bill Gregory - DT
Cliff Harris - DB
Bob Hayes - WR
Efren Herrera - K
Calvin Hill - FB
Bill Houston - WR
Ron Howard - TE
Ken Hutcherson - LB
Too Tall Jones - DE
Lee Roy Jordan - LB
Gene Killian - G
D. D. Lewis - LB
Bob Lilly - DT
Clint Longley - QB
Dave Manders - C
Harvey Martin - DE
Dennis Morgan - HB
Craig Morton - QB
Ralph Neely - T
Robert Newhouse - HB
John Niland - G
Blaine Nye - G
Drew Pearson - WR
Mac Percival - K
Cal Peterson - LB
Jethro Pugh - DT
Mel Renfro - DB
Golden Richards - WR
Roger Staubach - QB
Les Strayhorn - HB
Pat Toomay - DE
Louie Walker - LB
Bruce Walton - T
Mark Washington - DB
Charlie Waters - DB
Rayfield Wright - T
Charley Young - HB

1974 Denver

Lyle Alzado - DE
Otis Armstrong - HB
LeFrancis Arnold - G
Boyd Brown - TE
Barney Chavous - DE
Ralph Cindrich - LB
Steve Coleman - DE
Ken Criter - LB
Mike Current - T
Tom Drougas - T
Pete Duranko - DT
Randy Gradishar - LB
Tom Graham - LB
John Grant - DE
Charlie Greer - DB
Lonnie Hepburn - DB
Paul Howard - G
John Hufnagel - QB
Larron Jackson - T
Tom Jackson - LB
Charley Johnson - QB
Calvin Jones - DB
Bob Kampa - DT
Jon Keyworth - FB
Bill Laskey - LB
Floyd Little - HB
Fran Lynch - HB
Tommy Lyons - G
Bobby Maples - C
Billy Masters - TE
Ray May - LB
Claudie Minor - T
Marv Montgomery - T
Haven Moses - WR
Riley Odoms - TE
Jim O'Malley - LB

John Pitts - DB
Steve Ramsey - QB
Joe Rizzo - LB
Oliver Ross - HB
John Rowser - DB
Mike Schnitker - G
Jerry Simmons - WR
Mike Simone - LB
Ed Smith - DE
Paul Smith - DT
Larry Steele - K
Otto Stowe - WR
Billy Thompson - DB
Jim Turner - K
Maurice Tyler - DB
Bill Van Heusen - WR

1974 Detroit

Lem Barney - DB
Thomas Blair - TE
Dexter Bussey - HB
Carl Capria - DB
Leon Crosswhite - FB
Ben Davis - DB
Guy Dennis - C
Ed Flanagan - C
Rocky Freitas - T
Bill Frohbose - DB
Larry Hand - DE
Mike Hennigan - LB
Jim Hooks - FB
Billy Howard - DT
Ray Jarvis - WR
Dick Jauron - DB
Ron Jessie - WR
Levi Johnson - DB
Gordon Jolley - T
Jimmie Jones - HB
Bob Kowalkowski - G
Greg Landry - QB
Jim Laslavic - LB
Errol Mann - K
Jim Mitchell - DE
Bill Munson - QB
Paul Naumoff - LB
Ed O'Neil - LB
Herb Orvis - DT
Steve Owens - FB
Bob Pickard - WR
Ernie Price - DT
Fred Rothwell - C
Charlie Sanders - TE
Ken Sanders - DE
John Small - LB
Altie Taylor - HB
Jim Thrower - DB
Chuck Walton - G
Larry Walton - WR
Charlie Weaver - LB
Herman Weaver - K
Charlie West - DB
Daryl White - G
Doug Wyatt - DB
Sam Wyche - QB
Jim Yarbrough - T
Mickey Zofko - HB

1974 Green Bay

Ron Acks - LB
Michael Basinger - DT
John Brockington - FB
Aaron Brown - DE
Willie Buchanon - DB
Fred Carr - LB
Jim Carter - LB
Jack Concannon - QB
Mark Cooney - LB
Mike Donohoe - TE
Ken Ellis - DB
Mike Fanucci - DE
Gale Gillingham - G
Les Goodman - FB
John Hadl - QB
Charlie Hall - DB
Larry Hefner - LB
Ted Hendricks - LB
Jim Hill - DB
Dick Himes - T
Noel Jenke - LB
Larry Krause - HB
MacArthur Lane - HB
Charlie Leigh - FB
Bill Lueck - G
Chester Marcol - K
Dave Mason - DB
Al Matthews - DB
Larry McCarren - C
Mike McCoy - DT
Rich McGeorge - TE
Lee Nystrom - T
Steve Odom - WR
Steve Okoniewski - DT
Ken Payne - WR
Dave Pureifory - DE
Alden Roche - DE
John Schmitt - C
Harry Schuh - T
Barry Smith - WR
Barty Smith - FB
Perry Smith - DB
Mal Snider - T
Jon Staggers - WR
Jerry Tagge - QB
Eric Torkelson - HB
Bruce Van Dyke - G
Pete Van Valkenberg - HB
Carl Wafer - DE
Randy Walker - K
Bob Wicks - WR
Sweeny Williams - DE
Keith Wortman - G

1974 Houston

Willie Alexander - DB
Mack Alston - TE
George Amundson - FB
Bob Atkins - DB
Duane Benson - LB
Elvin Bethea - DE
David Beverly - K
Gregg Bingham - LB
Jerry Broadnax - TE
Ken Burrough - WR
Skip Butler - K
Ronnie Carroll - G
John Charles - DB
Ralph Cindrich - LB
Ronnie Coleman - HB
Al Cowlings - LB
Curley Culp - DT
Marvin Davis - LB
Lynn Dickey - QB
Elbert Drungo - T
Leonard Fairley - DB
Ed Fisher - DE
Solomon Freelon - G
Brian Goodman - G
Bob Gresham - HB
Fred Hoaglin - C
Kevin Hunt - T
Al Johnson - DB
Billy Johnson - WR
Harris Jones - G
Steve Kiner - LB
Tommy Maxwell - DB
Bubba McCollum - DT
Mike Montgomery - WR
Zeke Moore - DB
Billy Parks - WR
Dan Pastorini - QB
Jeff Queen - TE
Guy Roberts - LB
Willie Rodgers - HB
Greg Sampson - T
Ron Saul - G
Jeff Severson - DB
Tody Smith - DE
Sid Smith - T
Ted Washington - LB
Vic Washington - HB
Terry Wells - HB
Jim White - DE
C.L. Whittington - DB
Fred Willis - FB

1974 Kansas City

Nate Allen - DB
Bobby Bell - LB
Bob Briggs - DE
Larry Brunson - WR
Buck Buchanan - DT
Ed Budde - G
Dean Carlson - QB
Tom Condon - G
Curley Culp - DT
George Daney - G
Len Dawson - QB
Fred DeBernardi - DE
Tom Drougas - T
Willie Ellison - FB
Charlie Getty - T
Tom Graham - LB
Woody Green - HB
Andy Hamilton - WR
Wendell Hayes - FB
Dave Hill - T
Tom Humphrey - C
David Jaynes - QB
Doug Jones - DB
Jim Kearney - DB
Tom Keating - DT
Jeff Kinney - HB
Willie Lanier - LB
Mike Livingston - QB
Jim Lynch - LB
Jim Marsalis - DB
John Matuszak - DT
Cleo Miller - HB
Donnie Joe Morris - HB
Jim Nicholson - T
Willie Osley - DB
Al Palewicz - LB
Barry Pearson - WR
Francis Peay - T
Ed Podolak - HB
Kerry Reardon - DB
Jack Rudnay - C
Mike Sensibaugh - DB
Jan Stenerud - K
John Strada - TE
Morris Stroud - TE
Otis Taylor - WR
Emmitt Thomas - DB
Bill Thomas - FB
Bob Thornbladh - LB
Marv Upshaw - DE
Wayne Walton - G
Clyde Werner - LB
Jerrel Wilson - K
Elmo Wright - WR
Wilbur Young - DE

1974 LA Rams

Tony Baker - FB
Jim Bertelsen - HB
Larry Brooks - DT
Cullen Bryant - HB
Mike Burke - K
John Cappelletti - HB
Dave Chapple - K
Al Clark - DB
Charley Cowan - T
Pat Curran - TE
Bill Curry - C
Bill Drake - DB
Fred Dryer - DE
Dave Elmendorf - DB
Ken Geddes - LB
John Hadl - QB
James Harris - QB
Ken Iman - C
Harold Jackson - WR
Ron Jaworski - QB
Cody Jones - DT
Les Josephson - FB
Bob Klein - TE
Tom Mack - G
Lawrence McCutcheon - HB
Willie McGee - WR
Eddie McMillan - DB
Terry Nelson - TE
Bill Nelson - DT
Merlin Olsen - DT
Phil Olsen - DT
Jim Peterson - LB
Tony Plummer - DB
Steve Preece - DB
David Ray - K
Lance Rentzel - WR
Jack Reynolds - LB
Isiah Robertson - LB
Rich Saul - C
Joe Scibelli - G
Rob Scribner - HB
Bill Simpson - DB
Jack Snow - WR
Bob Stein - LB
Timothy Stokes - T
Charles Stukes - DB
John Williams - T
Jack Youngblood - DE
Jim Youngblood - LB

1974 Miami

Dick Anderson - DB
Charlie Babb - DB
Melvin Baker - WR
Larry Ball - LB
Bruce Bannon - LB
Marlin Briscoe - WR
Nick Buoniconti - LB
Randy Crowder - DT
Doug Crusan - T
Larry Csonka - FB
Vern Den Herder - DE
Norm Evans - T
Manny Fernandez - DT
Marv Fleming - TE
Tim Foley - DB
Tom Funchess - T
Hubert Ginn - HB
Irv Goode - G
Bob Griese - QB
Bob Heinz - DE
Curtis Johnson - DB
Jim Kiick - HB
Mike Kolen - LB
Bob Kuechenberg - T
Jim Langer - C
Charlie Leigh - FB
Larry Little - G
Benny Malone - HB
Jim Mandich - TE
Bob Matheson - LB
Maulty Moore - DT
Nat Moore - WR
Wayne Moore - T
Earl Morrall - QB
Mercury Morris - HB
Lloyd Mumphord - DB
Ed Newman - G
Don Nottingham - FB
Don Reese - DT
Jake Scott - DB
Larry Seiple - TE
Bill Stanfill - DE
Don Strock - QB
Henry Stuckey - DB
Doug Swift - LB
Howard Twilley - WR
Paul Warfield - WR
Jeris White - DB
Tom Wickert - T
Garo Yepremian - K

1974 Minnesota

Grady Alderman - T
Scott Anderson - C
Bob Berry - QB
Joe Blahak - DB
Matt Blair - LB
Dave Boone - DE
Terry Brown - DB
Bill Brown - FB
Bobby Bryant - DB
Fred Cox - K
Steve Craig - TE
Mike Eischeid - K
Carl Eller - DE
Chuck Foreman - FB
John Gilliam - WR
Charlie Goodrum - T
Wally Hilgenberg - LB
John Holland - WR
Doug Kingsriter - TE
Paul Krause - DB
Gary Larsen - DT
Jim Lash - WR
Steve Lawson - G
Bob Lurtsema - DT
Ed Marinaro - HB
Jim Marshall - DE
Larry Marshall - DB
Amos Martin - LB
Andy Maurer - G
Brent McClanahan - HB
Sam McCullum - WR
Fred McNeill - LB
Dave Osborn - HB
Alan Page - DT
Randy Poltl - DB
Oscar Reed - HB
Steve Riley - T
Jeff Siemon - LB
Milt Sunde - G
Doug Sutherland - DT
Fran Tarkenton - QB
Mick Tingelhoff - C
Stu Voigt - TE
Jackie Wallace - DB
Ed White - G
Roy Winston - LB
Jeff Wright - DB
Nate Wright - DB
Ron Yary - T

1974 New England

Julius Adams - DT
Bob Adams - TE
Sam Adams - G
Josh Ashton - HB
Bruce Barnes - K
Rodrigo Barnes - LB
Ron Bolton - DB
Kent Carter - LB
Dave Chapple - K
Gail Clark - LB
Sam Cunningham - FB
Maury Damkroger - LB
Bill DuLac - G
Doug Dumler - C
Sandy Durko - DB
Will Foster - LB
Allen Gallaher - T
Bob Geddes - LB
Noe Gonzalez - HB
Neil Graff - QB
Leon Gray - T
Ray Hamilton - NT
John Hannah - G
Craig Hanneman - DE
Mack Herron - HB
Eddie Hinton - WR
Sam Hunt - LB
Ed Jenkins - HB
Andy Johnson - HB
Steve King - LB
Bill Lenkaitis - G
Mel Lunsford - DT
Al Marshall - WR
Jim Massey - DB
Prentice McCray - DB
Dave McCurry - DB
Tony McGee - DE
Jack Mildren - DB
Art Moore - NT
Jon Morris - C
Steve Nelson - LB
Tom Neville - T
Willie Osley - DB
Jim Plunkett - QB
Ken Pope - DB
Reggie Rucker - WR
Deac Sanders - DB
Steve Schubert - WR
Dick Shiner - QB
Donnell Smith - DE
John Smith - K
Darryl Stingley - WR
Joe Sweet - WR
John Tanner - TE
John Tarver - FB
Randy Vataha - WR
George Webster - LB
Joe Wilson - HB
Bob Windsor - TE

1974 New Orleans

Steve Baumgartner - DE
John Beasley - TE
Tom Blanchard - K
Greg Boyd - DB
Bill Butler - FB
Henry Childs - TE
Larry Cipa - QB
Don Coleman - LB
Wayne Colman - LB
Dave Davis - WR
Jack DeGrenier - FB
John Didion - C
Andy Dorris - DE
Chris Farasopoulos - DB
Joe Federspiel - LB
Paul Fersen - T
Johnny Fuller - DB
Len Garrett - TE
Donnie Gibbs - K
Sam Havrilak - WR
Ernie Jackson - DB
Rick Kingrea - LB
Jake Kupp - G
Phil LaPorta - T
Odell Lawson - FB
Bivian Lee - DB
Archie Manning - QB
Andy Maurer - G
Alvin Maxson - HB
Bill McClard - K
Earl McCullouch - WR
Rod McNeill - FB
Jim Merlo - LB
Rick Middleton - LB
Derland Moore - DT
Jerry Moore - DB
John Mooring - T
Don Morrison - T
Tom Myers - DB
Bob Newland - WR
Billy Newsome - DE
Joe Owens - DE
Joel Parker - WR
Jess Phillips - FB
Bob Pollard - DE
Elex Price - DT
Rocky Rasley - G
Ken Reaves - DB
Terry Schmidt - DB
Bobby Scott - QB
Paul Seal - TE
Mo Spencer - DB
Howard Stevens - HB
Speedy Thomas - WR
Dave Thompson - T
Bob Wicks - WR
Richard Williams - WR
Emanuel Zanders - G

1974 NY Giants

Pete Athas - DB
Bobby Brooks - DB
Karl Chandler - C
Don Clune - WR
Chuck Crist - DB
Steve Crosby - HB
Joe Dawkins - FB
Jim Del Gaizo - QB
Rick Dvorak - DE
Dick Enderle - G
Walker Gillette - WR
Chip Glass - TE
Pete Gogolak - K
Jack Gregory - DE
Bob Grim - WR
George Hasenohrl - DT
Don Herrmann - WR
John Hicks - G
John Hill - T
Roy Hilton - DE
Ron Hornsby - LB
Pat Hughes - LB
Bob Hyland - C
Honor Jackson - DB
Larry Jacobson - DT
Ed Jenkins - HB
Dave Jennings - K
Ron Johnson - HB
Brian Kelley - LB
Doug Kotar - HB
Carl Lockhart - DB
Leon McQuay - HB
John Mendenhall - DT
Craig Morton - QB
Tom Mullen - G
Gary Pettigrew - DT
Jim Pietrzak - DT
Clyde Powers - DB
Henry Reed - LB
Ray Rhodes - WR
Andy Selfridge - LB
Bill Singletary - LB
Eldridge Small - DB
Norm Snead - QB
Jim Stienke - DB
John Strada - TE
Carl Summerell - QB
Bob Tucker - TE
Doug Van Horn - T
Brad Van Pelt - LB
Carl Wafer - DT
Willie Young - T
Mickey Zofko - HB

1974 NY Jets

Mike Adamle - HB
Al Atkinson - LB
Ralph Baker - LB
Jerome Barkum - WR
Carl Barzilauskas - DT
Eddie Bell - WR
Roger Bernhardt - G
Hank Bjorklund - HB
Emerson Boozer - HB
Willie Brister - TE
Gordie Browne - T
Bob Burns - FB
Rich Caster - TE
Bill Demory - QB
John Ebersole - LB
Bill Ferguson - LB
Ed Galigher - DE
Greg Gantt - K
Winston Hill - T
Delles Howell - DB
Bobby Howfield - K
Jazz Jackson - HB
Howard Kindig - C
David Knight - WR
Warren Koegel - C
Pat Leahy - K
John Little - DT
Mark Lomas - DE
Wayne Mulligan - C
Joe Namath - QB
Richard Neal - DE
Burgess Owens - DB
Marv Owens - WR
Lou Piccone - WR
Garry Puetz - T
Randy Rasmussen - G
Steve Reese - LB
John Riggins - FB
Jamie Rivers - LB
Travis Roach - G
Joe Schmiesing - DE
Rich Sowells - DB
Steve Tannen - DB
Earlie Thomas - DB
Phillip Wise - DB
Al Woodall - QB
Larry Woods - DT
Robert Woods - T
Roscoe Word - DB

1974 Oakland

Butch Atkinson - DB
Pete Banaszak - HB
Warren Bankston - FB
Fred Biletnikoff - WR
George Blanda - QB
Morris Bradshaw - WR
Cliff Branch - WR
Willie Brown - DB
George Buehler - G
Dave Casper - TE
Tony Cline - DE
Dan Conners - LB
Dave Dalby - G
Clarence Davis - HB
Mike Dennery - LB
Ray Guy - K
Harold Hart - HB
Marv Hubbard - FB
Bob Hudson - HB
Gerald Irons - LB
George Jakowenko - K
Monte Johnson - LB
Horace Jones - DE
Kelvin Korver - DT
Daryle Lamonica - QB
Henry Lawrence - T
Larry Lawrence - QB
Dan Medlin - G
Bob Moore - TE
Jim Otto - C
Frank Pitts - WR
Bob Prout - DB
Art Shell - T
Mike Siani - WR
Otis Sistrunk - DT
Bubba Smith - DE
Charlie Smith - HB
Ron Smith - DB
Ken Stabler - QB
Jack Tatum - DB
Skip Thomas - DB
Art Thoms - DT
Gene Upshaw - G
Mark van Eeghen - FB
John Vella - T
Phil Villapiano - LB
Jimmy Warren - DB
Gary Weaver - LB
Nemiah Wilson - DB

1974 Philadelphia

Tom Bailey - FB
Bill Bergey - LB
Mike Boryla - QB
Bill Bradley - DB
Norm Bulaich - FB
John Bunting - LB
Jim Cagle - DT
Harold Carmichael - WR
Wes Chesson - WR
Willie Cullars - DE
Tom Dempsey - K
Herb Dobbins - T
Bill Dunstan - DT
Charlie Ford - DB
Roman Gabriel - QB
Dean Halverson - LB
Randy Jackson - FB
Po James - HB
Joe Jones - DE
Merritt Kersey - K
Wade Key - G
Roy Kirksey - G
Kent Kramer - TE
Joe Lavender - DB
Frank LeMaster - LB
Randy Logan - DB
Tom Luken - G
Larry Marshall - DB
Guy Morriss - C
Mark Nordquist - G
Greg Oliver - HB
John Outlaw - DB
Artimus Parker - DB
Jerry Patton - DT
Gary Pettigrew - DT
Bob Picard - WR
John Reaves - QB
Marion Reeves - DB
Kevin Reilly - LB
Jerry Sisemore - T
Charlie Smith - WR
Steve Smith - T
Dick Stevens - T
Tom Sullivan - HB
Mitch Sutton - DT
Will Wynn - DE
Charle Young - TE
Steve Zabel - LB
Don Zimmerman - WR

1974 Pittsburgh

Jimmy Allen - DB
Rocky Bleier - HB
Mel Blount - DB
Ed Bradley - LB
Terry Bradshaw - QB
Larry Brown - TE
Jim Clack - C
Dick Conn - DB
Charles Davis - DT
Sam Davis - G
Steve Davis - HB
Rich Druschel - G
Glen Edwards - DB
John Fuqua - HB
Steve Furness - DE
Reggie Garrett - WR
Roy Gerela - K
Joe Gilliam - QB
Gordon Gravelle - T
Joe Greene - DT
L. C. Greenwood - DE
Randy Grossman - TE
Jack Ham - LB
Terry Hanratty - QB
Franco Harris - FB
Reggie Harrison - FB
Ernie Holmes - DT
Marv Kellum - LB
Jon Kolb - T
Jack Lambert - LB
Frank Lewis - WR
Ray Mansfield - C
John McMakin - TE
Gerry Mullins - T
Preston Pearson - HB
Dave Reavis - T
Andy Russell - LB
Ron Shanklin - WR
Donnie Shell - DB
John Stallworth - WR
Lynn Swann - WR
J.T. Thomas - DB
Loren Toews - LB
Mike Wagner - DB
Bobby Walden - K
Mike Webster - G
Dwight White - DE
Jim Wolf - DE

1974 St. Louis

Sergio Albert - K
Donny Anderson - HB
Mark Arneson - LB
Jim Bakken - K
Tom Banks - C
Pete Barnes - LB
Bob Bell - DT
Willie Belton - HB
Tom Brahaney - C
Lee Brooks - DT
Dave Butz - DT
J.V. Cain - WR
Bob Crum - DE
Dwayne Crump - DB
Dan Dierdorf - T
Conrad Dobler - G
Clarence Duren - DB
Roger Finnie - DT
Steve George - DT
Mel Gray - WR
Gary Hammond - WR
Reggie Harrison - FB
Jim Hart - QB
Greg Hartle - LB
Steve Jones - HB
Greg Kindle - T
Jack LeVeck - LB
Jim McFarland - TE

Ernie McMillan - T
Terry Metcalf - HB
Terry Miller - LB
Eddie Moss - HB
Steve Neils - LB
Jim Otis - FB
Ken Reaves - DB
Hal Roberts - K
Bob Rowe - DT
Council Rudolph - DE
Hurles Scales - DB
Dennis Shaw - QB
Jackie Smith - TE
Mo Spencer - DB
Larry Stallings - LB
Scott Stringer - DB
Earl Thomas - WR
Norm Thompson - DB
Jim Tolbert - DB
Roger Wehrli - DB
Ken Willard - FB
Cal Withrow - C
Ron Yankowski - DE
Bob Young - G

1974 San Diego

Charles Anthony - LB
Coy Bacon - DE
Raymond Baylor - DE
Joe Beauchamp - DB
Jim Beirne - WR
Reggie Berry - DB
Bon Boatwright - DT
Glen Bonner - HB
Robert Brown - DT
Danny Colbert - DB
Harrison Davis - WR
Jay Douglas - C
Lenny Dunlap - DB
Cid Edwards - FB
Chris Fletcher - DB
Fred Forsberg - LB
Dan Fouts - QB
Jesse Freitas - QB
Gary Garrison - WR
Blenda Gay - DE
Carl Gersbach - LB
Don Goode - LB
Ira Gordon - T
Dick Gordon - WR
Dave Grannell - TE
George Hoey - DB
Don Horn - QB
Bob Howard - DB
Pete Lazetich - DE
Mike Lee - LB
Jerry LeVias - WR
Mark Markovich - G
Bo Matthews - FB
Carl Mauck - C
Chip Myrtle - LB
Terry Owens - T
Gary Parris - TE
Dennis Partee - K
Harold Paul - T
Floyd Rice - LB
Mel Rogers - LB
Dave Rowe - DT
Jeff Staggs - LB
Wayne Stewart - TE
John Teerlinck - DT
Jim Thaxton - TE
Bob Thomas - HB
Tommy Thompson - HB
Dave Tipton - DE
Brian Vertefeuille - T
Russ Washington - T
Ray Wersching - K
Doug Wilkerson - G
Sam Williams - DB
Don Woods - HB

1974 San Francisco

Danny Abramowicz - WR
Dave Atkins - HB
Cas Banaszek - T
Jean Barrett - C
Terry Beasley - WR
Randy Beisler - T
Bill Belk - DT
Ceasar Belser - DB
Mike Bettiga - WR
Forrest Blue - C
Dennis Bragonier - DB
Keith Fahnhorst - T
Bruce Gossett - K
Windlan Hall - DB
Cedrick Hardman - DE
Willie Harper - LB
Tommy Hart - DE
Stan Hindman - DT
Hugo Hollas - DB
Mike Holmes - DB
Bob Hoskins - DT
Tom Hull - LB
Wilbur Jackson - HB
Jim Johnson - DB
Sammy Johnson - FB
Rolf Krueger - DT
Ted Kwalick - WR
Ralph McGill - DB
Bill McKoy - LB
Tom Mitchell - TE

Manfred Moore - HB
Dennis Morrison - QB
Frank Nunley - LB
Tom Owen - QB
Bob Penchion - G
Woody Peoples - G
Mel Phillips - DB
Mike Raines - DT
Al Randolph - DB
Joe Reed - QB
Len Rohde - T
Bill Sandifer - DT
John Saunders - DB
Larry Schreiber - HB
Norm Snead - QB
Steve Spurrier - QB
Bruce Taylor - DB
Skip Vanderbundt - LB
Gene Washington - WR
John Watson - T
Bob West - WR
Dave Wilcox - LB
Delvin Williams - HB
Tom Wittum - K

1974 Washington

Mike Bass - DB
Maxie Baughan - LB
Verlon Biggs - DE
Mike Bragg - K
Larry Brown - HB
Bill Brundige - DT
Doug Cunningham - HB
Moses Denson - FB
Speedy Duncan - DB
Brad Dusek - LB
Charlie Evans - FB
Pat Fischer - DB
Frank Grant - WR
Chris Hanburger - LB
Mike Hancock - TE
Len Hauss - C
Ken Houston - DB
Mike Hull - FB
Martin Imhof - DE
Roy Jefferson - WR
Dennis Johnson - DT
Deacon Jones - DE
Larry Jones - DB
Sonny Jurgensen - QB
Billy Kilmer - QB
Paul Laaveg - G
Bill Malinchak - WR
Ron McDole - DE
Harold McLinton - LB
Mark Moseley - K
Herb Mul-key - RB
Stu O'Dell - LB
Brig Owens - DB
John Pergine - LB
Alvin Reed - TE
Dave Robinson - LB
Dan Ryczek - C
Bryant Salter - DB
Ray Schoenke - G
Manny Sistrunk - DT
Jerry Smith - TE
Larry Smith - HB
George Starke - T
Ken Stone - DB
Fred Sturt - T
Walt Sweeney - G
Diron Talbert - DT
Charley Taylor - WR
Joe Theismann - QB
Duane Thomas - HB
Rusty Tillman - LB
Jim Tyrer - T
Mike Varty - LB
John Wilbur - G

1975 Atlanta

Brent Adams - T
Steve Bartkowski - QB
Nick Bebout - T
Greg Brezina - LB
Ray Brown - DB
Ken Burrow - WR
Rick Byas - DB
Larry Crowe - HB
Brad Davis - FB
Ray Easterling - DB
Monroe Eley - FB
Wally Francis - WR
Len Gotshalk - T
Dave Hampton - HB
Don Hansen - LB
Dennis Havig - G
Tom Hayes - DB
Mack Herron - HB
Roy Hilton - DE
Larron Jackson - G
John James - K
Alfred Jenkins - WR
Bob Jones - DB
Fulton Kuykendall - LB
Rolland Lawrence - DB
Mike Lewis - DT
Ron Mabra - DB
Rosie Manning - DT
Greg McCrary - TE
Kim McQuilken - QB
Jeff Merrow - DT
Nick Mike-Mayer - K

Jim Mitchell - TE
Tommy Nobis - LB
Ralph Ortega - LB
Oscar Reed - HB
Carl Russ - LB
Paul Ryczek - C
Royce Smith - G
Haskel Stanback - HB
Pat Sullivan - QB
Woody Thompson - FB
Mike Tilleman - DT
Gerald Tinker - WR
Jeff Van Note - C
Chuck Walker - DT
John Zook - DE

1975 Baltimore

Mike Barnes - DT
Forrest Blue - C
Roger Carr - WR
Raymond Chester - TE
Jim Cheyunski - LB
Elmer Collett - G
Fred Cook - DE
Mike Curtis - LB
Dan Dickel - LB
Marty Domres - QB
Glenn Doughty - WR
John Dutton - DE
Joe Ehrmann - DT
Ed George - T
Ken Huff - G
Marshall Johnson - HB
Bert Jones - QB
Jimmie Kennedy - TE
George Kunz - T
Bruce Laird - DB
Roosevelt Leaks - FB
David Lee - K
Toni Linhart - K
Derrel Luce - LB
Tom MacLeod - LB
Don McCauley - HB
Ken Mendenhall - C
Lydell Mitchell - HB
Lloyd Mumphord - DB
Nelson Munsey - DB
Doug Nettles - DB
Ray Oldham - DB
Bill Olds - FB
Dave Pear - DT
Bob Pratt - G
Glenn Robinson - DE
Freddie Scott - WR
Howard Stevens - HB
David Taylor - T
Bob Van Duyne - G
Mike Varty - LB
Rick Volk - DB
Jackie Wallace - DB
Stan White - LB

1975 Buffalo

Bill AdamsG
Doug Allen - LB
Marv Bateman - K
Jim Braxton - FB
Don Calhoun - HB
Bob Chandler - WR
Bo Cornell - LB
Don Croft - DT
Joe DeLamielleure - G
Earl Edwards - DT
Joe Ferguson - QB
Dave Foley - T
Charlie Ford - DB
Steve Freeman - DB
Reuben Gant - TE
Donnie Green - T
Tony Greene - DB
Halvor Hagen - T
Dwight Harrison - DB
Clint Haslerig - WR
Gary Hayman - HB
J. D. Hill - WR
John Holland - WR
Mark Johnson - DE
Ed Jones - DB
Mike Kadish - DT
Merv Krakau - LB
John Leypoldt - K
Gary Marangi - QB
John McCrumbly - LB
Reggie McKenzie - G
Royce McKinney - DB
Mike Montler - C
Frank Oliver - DB
Willie Parker - C
Walt Patulski - DE
Tom Ruud - LB
Steve Schnarr - FB
Paul Seymour - TE
O.J. Simpson - HB
John Skorupan - LB
Ike Thomas - DB
Pat Toomay - DE
Vic Washington - DB
Jeff Winans - DE
Jeff Yeates - DT

1975 Chi. Bears

Mike Adamle - FB
Lionel Antoine - T

Bob Asher - T
Bob Avellini - QB
John Babinecz - LB
Waymond Bryant - LB
Doug Buffone - LB
Gary Butler - TE
Wally Chambers - DT
Craig Clemons - DB
Tom Donchez - FB
Bobby Douglass - QB
Earl Douthitt - DB
Cid Edwards - FB
Allan Ellis - DB
Larry Ely - LB
George Farmer - WR
Carl Gersbach - LB
Bob Grim - WR
Jimmy Gunn - LB
Roland Harper - HB
Richard Harris - DE
Mike Hartenstine - DE
Gary Hrivnak - DE
Gary Huff - QB
Noah Jackson - G
Bill Knox - DB
Greg Latta - TE
Virgil Livers - DB
Johnny Musso - HB
Dan Neal - C
Bob Newton - G
Mark Nordquist - C
Jim Osborne - DT
Bob Parsons - TE
Walter Payton - HB
Dan Peiffer - C
Bob Pifferini - LB
Doug Plank - DB
Bo Rather - WR
Don Rives - LB
Ron Rydalch - DT
Steve Schubert - WR
Jeff Sevy - T
Revie Sorey - G
Roger Stillwell - DT
Bob Thomas - K
Mel Tom - DE
Ted Vactor - DB
Nemiah Wilson - DB

1975 Cincinnati

Ken Anderson - QB
Al Beauchamp - LB
Lyle Blackwood - DB
Robert Brown - DT
Glenn Cameron - LB
Ron Carpenter - DT
Tommy Casanova - DB
Boobie Clark - FB
Marvin Cobb - DB
Bruce Coslet - TE
Brad Cousino - LB
Isaac Curtis - WR
Ricky Davis - DB
Chris Devlin - LB
Lenvil Elliott - HB
Howard Fest - G
Stan Fritts - HB
Dave Green - K
Bo Harris - LB
Champ Henson - FB
Vern Holland - T
Bernard Jackson - DB
Essex Johnson - HB
Ken Johnson - DE
Bob Johnson - C
Charlie Joiner - WR
Bill Kollar - DT
Al Krevis - T
Dave Lapham - G
Jim LeClair - LB
Rufus Mayes - T
John McDaniel - WR
Maulty Moore - DT
Chip Myers - WR
Jack Novak - TE
Lemar Parrish - DB
Ron Pritchard - LB
John Reaves - QB
Ken Riley - DB
John Shinners - G
Bob Trumpy - TE
Sherman White - DE
Ed Williams - FB

1975 Cleveland

Dick Ambrose - LB
Pete Athas - DB
Bob Babich - LB
Carl Barisich - DT
Ken Brown - HB
Eddie Brown - DB
Don Cockroft - K
Neal Craig - DB
Will Cureton - QB
Barry Darrow - T
Tom DeLeone - C
John Demarie - C
Doug Dieken - T
Ron East - DE
John Garlington - LB
Dave Graf - LB
Van Green - DB
Charlie Hall - LB
Jim Hill - DB

Steve Holden - WR
Chuck Hutchison - G
Henry Hynoski - FB
Robert Jackson - T
Walter Johnson - DT
Joe Jones - DE
Billy Lefear - WR
Jack LeVeck - LB
Stan Lewis - DE
Bob McKay - G
Hugh McKinnis - FB
Cleo Miller - HB
Willie Miller - WR
Mack Mitchell - DE
Milt Morin - TE
Gary Parris - TE
Tony Peters - DB
Mike Phipps - QB
John Pitts - DB
Larry Poole - HB
Billy Pritchett - FB
Greg Pruitt - HB
Oscar Roan - TE
Reggie Rucker - WR
Clarence Scott - DB
Jerry Sherk - DT
Brian Sipe - QB
Gerry Sullivan - T

1975 Dallas

Benny Barnes - DB
Bob Breunig - LB
Warren Capone - LB
Larry Cole - DT
Kyle Davis - C
Doug Dennison - FB
Pat Donovan - T
Billy Joe DuPree - TE
Dave Edwards - LB
John Fitzgerald - C
Toni Fritsch - K
Jean Fugett - WR
Bill Gregory - DT
Cliff Harris - DB
Tom Henderson - LB
Mitch Hoopes - K
Percy Howard - WR
Ron Howard - TE
Randy Hughes - DB
Too Tall Jones - DE
Lee Roy Jordan - LB
Scott Laidlaw - FB
Burton Lawless - G
D. D. Lewis - LB
Clint Longley - QB
Harvey Martin - DE
Ralph Neely - T
Robert Newhouse - FB
Blaine Nye - G
Drew Pearson - WR
Preston Pearson - HB
Cal Peterson - LB
Jethro Pugh - DT
Mel Renfro - DB
Golden Richards - WR
Herbert Scott - G
Roger Staubach - QB
Bruce Walton - T
Mark Washington - DB
Charlie Waters - DB
Randy White - LB
Roland Woolsey - DB
Rayfield Wright - T
Charley Young - HB

1975 Denver

Bob Adams - TE
Lyle Alzado - DT
Otis Armstrong - HB
Boyd Brown - TE
Rubin Carter - DT
Barney Chavous - DE
Mike Current - T
Jack Dolbin - WR
Mike Franckowiak - FB
Randy Gradishar - LB
John Grant - DT
Steve Haggerty - DB
Al Haywood - FB
George Hoey - DB
Paul Howard - G
John Hufnagel - QB
Tom Jackson - LB
Charley Johnson - QB
Calvin Jones - DB
Jon Keyworth - FB
Mike Lemon - LB
Floyd Little - HB
Fran Lynch - FB
Tommy Lyons - G
Bobby Maples - C
Ray May - LB
Claudie Minor - T
Marv Montgomery - T
Haven Moses - WR
Riley Odoms - TE
Phil Olsen - DT
Jim O'Malley - LB
John Pitts - DB
Randy Poltl - DB
Steve Ramsey - QB
Joe Rizzo - LB
Stan Rogers - T
Oliver Ross - HB

John Rowser - DB
Carl Schaukowitch - G
Jeff Severson - DB
Paul Smith - DT
Bob Swenson - LB
Earlie Thomas - DB
Billy Thompson - DB
Jim Turner - K
Rick Upchurch - WR
Bill Van Heusen - WR
Louis Wright - DB

1975 Detroit

Larry Ball - LB
Lem Barney - DB
Lynn Boden - G
Marlin Briscoe - WR
Dexter Bussey - HB
Jack Concannon - QB
Ben Davis - DB
Guy Dennis - C
Lenny Dunlap - DB
Doug English - DT
George Farmer - WR
Dennis Franklin - WR
Rocky Freitas - T
Larry Hand - DT
Mike Hennigan - LB
Craig Hertwig - T
R.W. Hicks - C
Jim Hooks - FB
Billy Howard - DE
Ray Jarvis - WR
Dick Jauron - DB
Levi Johnson - DB
Gordon Jolley - T
Horace King - FB
Bob Kowalkowski - G
Greg Landry - QB
Jim Laslavic - LB
Errol Mann - K
John McMakin - TE
Jim Mitchell - DE
Jon Morris - C
Bill Munson - QB
Paul Naumoff - LB
Ed O'Neil - LB
Herb Orvis - DT
Ernie Price - DE
Alan Pringle - K
Joe Reed - QB
Charlie Sanders - TE
Ken Sanders - DE
Jon Staggers - WR
Altie Taylor - HB
Bobby Thompson - HB
Leonard Thompson - WR
Charlie Weaver - LB
Herman Weaver - K
Mike Weger - DB
Charlie West - DB
Jim Yarbrough - T

1975 Green Bay

Ron Acks - LB
Bert Askson - TE
Bill Bain - G
David Beverly - K
John Brockington - FB
Steve Broussard - K
Carlos Brown - QB
Willie Buchanon - DB
Fred Carr - LB
Jim Carter - LB
Bill Cooke - DE
Joe Danelo - K
Ken Ellis - DB
Kent Gaydos - WR
Johnnie Gray - DB
John Hadl - QB
Charlie Hall - DB
Willard Harrell - HB
Larry Hefner - LB
Dick Himes - T
Tom Hull - LB
Ernie Janet - G
Steve Luke - DB
Chester Marcol - K
Pat Matson - G
Al Matthews - DB
Bob McCaffrey - C
Larry McCarren - C
Mike McCoy - DT
Rich McGeorge - TE
Ernie McMillan - T
Don Milan - QB
Steve Odom - WR
Steve Okoniewski - DT
Ken Payne - WR
Dave Pureifory - DE
Alden Roche - DE
Dave Roller - DT
Hurles Scales - DB
Barry Smith - WR
Barty Smith - FB
Perry Smith - DB
Gerald Tinker - WR
Tom Toner - LB
Eric Torkelson - HB
Bruce Van Dyke - G
Charlie Wade - WR
Gary Weaver - LB
Terry Wells - HB

Sweeny Williams - DE
Keith Wortman - G

1975 Houston

Willie Alexander - DB
Mack Alston - TE
Bob Atkins - DB
Jim Beirne - WR
Duane Benson - LB
Elvin Bethea - DE
David Beverly - K
Gregg Bingham - LB
Robert Brazile - LB
Ken Burrough - WR
Skip Butler - K
Ralph Cindrich - LB
Ronnie Coleman - HB
Mark Cotney - DB
Curley Culp - G
Lynn Dickey - QB
Elbert Drungo - T
Emmett Edwards - WR
Ed Fisher - G
Willie Frazier - TE
Willie Germany - DB
Don Hardeman - FB
Nate Hawkins - WR
Conway Hayman - G
Fred Hoaglin - C
Robert Holmes - FB
Kevin Hunt - T
Billy Johnson - WR
Steve Kiner - LB
John Little - DE
Carl Mauck - C
Zeke Moore - DB
Billy Parks - WR
Dan Pastorini - QB
Guy Roberts - LB
Willie Rodgers - HB
Greg Sampson - T
Ron Saul - G
John Sawyer - TE
Bubba Smith - DT
Tody Smith - DE
Greg Stemrick - DB
Ted Thompson - LB
Ted Washington - LB
Jim White - DE
C.L. Whittington - DB
Fred Willis - FB
Elmo Wright - WR

1975 Kansas City

Tony Adams - QB
Charlie Ane - C
Hise Austin - DB
Ken Avery - LB
Randy Beisler - G
Roger Bernhardt - G
Larry Brunson - WR
Buck Buchanan - DT
Ed Budde - G
Wayne Clark - QB
Tom Condon - G
Reggie Craig - WR
Len Dawson - QB
Doug Dressler - FB
Larry Estes - DT
Charlie Getty - T
Woody Green - HB
Jim Kearney - DB
Tim Kearney - LB
Tom Keating - DT
Jeff Kinney - HB
Morris LaGrand - FB
MacArthur Lane - FB
Willie Lanier - LB
Mike Livingston - QB
John Lohmeyer - DE
Jim Lynch - LB
Bob Maddox - DE
Jim Marsalis - DB
Don Martin - DB
Billy Masters - TE
John Matuszak - DE
Jim McCann - K
Cleo Miller - HB
Jim Nicholson - T
Al Palewicz - LB
Gery Palmer - T
Barry Pearson - WR
Bill Peterson - LB
Ed Podolak - HB
Rocky Rasley - G
Kerry Reardon - DB
Louis Ross - DE
Jack Rudnay - C
Mike Sensibaugh - DB
Jan Stenerud - K
Bill Story - T
Otis Taylor - WR
Charlie Thomas - HB
Emmitt Thomas - DB
Marv Upshaw - DT
Walter White - TE
Jerrel Wilson - K
Mike Wilson - G
Wilbur Young - DE

1975 LA Rams

Jim Bertelsen - FB
Larry Brooks - DT

Cullen Bryant - FB
John Cappelletti - HB
Duane Carrell - K
Al Clark - DB
Charley Cowan - T
Al Cowlings - DE
Bob DeMarco - C
Tom Dempsey - K
Fred Dryer - DE
Dave Elmendorf - DB
Mike Fanning - DE
Doug France - T
Ken Geddes - LB
Dennis Harrah - G
James Harris - QB
Harold Jackson - WR
Monte Jackson - DB
Ron Jaworski - QB
Ron Jessie - WR
Cody Jones - DT
Rick Kay - LB
Bob Klein - TE
Tom Mack - G
Lawrence McCutcheon - HB
Willie McGee - WR
Eddie McMillan - DB
Terry Nelson - TE
Bill Nelson - DT
Merlin Olsen - DT
Rod Perry - DB
Jim Peterson - LB
Rod Phillips - TE
Steve Preece - DB
Jack Reynolds - LB
Isiah Robertson - LB
Rich Saul - C
Joe Scibelli - G
Rob Scribner - HB
Bill Simpson - DB
Jack Snow - WR
John Williams - T
Jack Youngblood - DE
Jim Youngblood - LB

1975 Miami

John Andrews - DE
Charlie Babb - DB
Rodrigo Barnes - LB
Norm Bulaich - FB
Darryl Carlton - T
Randy Crowder - DT
Vern Den Herder - DE
Tom Drougas - G
Bruce Elia - LB
Norm Evans - T
Manny Fernandez - DT
Tim Foley - DB
Hubert Ginn - HB
Bob Griese - QB
Barry Hill - DB
Curtis Johnson - DB
Mike Kolen - LB
Bob Kuechenberg - G
Jim Langer - C
Larry Little - G
Benny Malone - HB
Jim Mandich - TE
Bob Matheson - LB
Jim McFarland - TE
Nat Moore - WR
Wayne Moore - T
Earl Morrall - QB
Mercury Morris - HB
Ed Newman - G
Don Nottingham - FB
Morris Owens - WR
Don Reese - DE
Earnest Rhone - LB
Jake Scott - DB
Larry Seiple - HB
Freddie Solomon - HB
Cotton Speyrer - WR
Bill Stanfill - DE
Don Strock - QB
Doug Swift - LB
Andre Tillman - TE
Steve Towle - LB
Howard Twilley - WR
Jeris White - DB
Stan Winfrey - FB
Garo Yepremian - K

1975 Minnesota

Pete Athas - DB
Autry Beamon - DB
Bob Berry - QB
Joe Blahak - DB
Matt Blair - LB
Terry Brown - DB
Bobby Bryant - DB
Neil Clabo - K
Fred Cox - K
Steve Craig - TE
Carl Eller - DE
Chuck Foreman - HB
John Gilliam - WR
Charlie Goodrum - T
Clint Haslerig - WR
Wally Hilgenberg - LB
Doug Kingsriter - TE
Paul Krause - DB
Jim Lash - WR
Steve Lawson - G
Bob Lee - QB
Bob Lurtsema - DE
Ed Marinaro - FB
Jim Marshall - DE
Amos Martin - LB
Andy Maurer - G
Brent McClanahan - FB
Sam McCullum - WR
Fred McNeill - LB
Robert Miller - FB
Mark Mullaney - DE
Dave Osborn - FB
Alan Page - DT
Steve Riley - T
Jeff Siemon - LB
Bob Stein - LB
Doug Sutherland - DT
Fran Tarkenton - QB
Mick Tingelhoff - C
Stu Voigt - TE
John Ward - G
Ed White - G
Roy Winston - LB
Jeff Wright - DB
Nate Wright - DB
Ron Yary - T

1975 New England

Julius Adams - DE
Sam Adams - G
Bobby Anderson - FB
Melvin Baker - WR
Rodrigo Barnes - LB
Ron Bolton - DB
Steve Burks - WR
Don Calhoun - HB
Allen Carter - FB
Dick Conn - DB
Steve Corbett - G
Sam Cunningham - FB
Pete Cusick - NT
Maury Damkroger - LB
Doug Dressler - FB
Bill DuLac - G
Doug Dumler - C
Russ Francis - TE
Bob Geddes - LB
Neil Graff - QB
Leon Gray - T
Steve Grogan - QB
Ray Hamilton - NT
John Hannah - G
Craig Hanneman - G
Mack Herron - HB
Bob Howard - DB
Sam Hunt - LB
Martin Imhof - DE
Andy Johnson - HB
Shelby Jordan - T
Durwood Keeton - DB
Steve King - LB
Bill Lenkaitis - C
Mel Lunsford - DE
Jim Massey - DB
Prentice McCray - DB
Tony McGee - DE
Leon McQuay - HB
Steve Nelson - LB
Mike Patrick - K
Jerry Patton - DT
Jim Plunkett - QB
Kevin Reilly - LB
Deac Sanders - DB
Rod Shoate - LB
John Smith - K
Darryl Stingley - WR
Dave Tipton - DT
Randy Vataha - WR
George Webster - LB
Bob Windsor - TE
Elmo Wright - WR
Steve Zabel - LB

1975 New Orleans

Melvin Baker - WR
Steve Baumgartner - DE
Tom Blanchard - K
Larry Burton - WR
Rusty Chambers - LB
Gil Chapman - WR
Henry Childs - TE
Larry Cipa - QB
Don Coleman - LB
Chuck Crist - DB
Sylvester Croom - C
Jim DeRatt - DB
Andy Dorris - DE
Joe Federspiel - LB
Johnny Fuller - DB
Len Garrett - TE
Elois Grooms - DE
Lee Gross - C
Andy Hamilton - WR
Don Herrmann - WR
John Hill - T
Ernie Jackson - DB
Andrew Jones - FB
Rick Kingrea - LB
Jake Kupp - G
Morris LaGrand - FB
Phil LaPorta - T
Bivian Lee - DB
Mike Lemon - LB
Archie Manning - QB
Alvin Maxson - HB
Bill McClard - K
Rod McNeill - FB
Rick Middleton - LB
Derland Moore - DT
Chris Morris - T
Don Morrison - T
Tom Myers - DB
Joe Owens - DE
Joel Parker - WR
Bob Pollard - DT
Elex Price - DT
Steven Rogers - HB
Terry Schmidt - DB
Kurt Schumacher - T
Bobby Scott - QB
Paul Seal - TE
Mo Spencer - DB
Mike Strachan - HB
Richie Szaro - K
Dave Thompson - C
Greg Westbrooks - LB
Tom Wickert - T
Emanuel Zanders - G

1975 NY Giants

Bobby Brooks - DB
Danny Buggs - WR
Karl Chandler - C
Don Clune - WR
Rondy Colbert - DB
Steve Crosby - HB
Joe Dawkins - FB
Rick Dvorak - DE
Dick Enderle - G
Charlie Ford - DB
Dave Gallagher - DE
Robert Giblin - DB
Walker Gillette - WR
Jack Gregory - DE
Jimmy Gunn - LB
John Hicks - G
Pat Hughes - LB
George Hunt - K
Bob Hyland - C
Dave Jennings - K
Ron Johnson - HB
Brian Kelley - LB
Doug Kotar - HB
Carl Lockhart - DB
George Martin - DE
John Mendenhall - DT
Craig Morton - QB
Tom Mullen - G
Jim Obradovich - TE
Jim Pietrzak - DT
Clyde Powers - DB
Ray Rhodes - WR
Bob Schmit - LB
Andy Selfridge - LB
Dave Simonson - T
Al Simpson - T
Jim Stienke - DB
Henry Stuckey - DB
Carl Summerell - QB
Bob Tucker - TE
Doug Van Horn - T
Brad Van Pelt - LB
Larry Watkins - FB
Marsh White - FB
Bill Windauer - DT
Willie Young - T

1975 NY Jets

Darrell Austin - T
Jim Bailey - DT
Jerome Barkum - WR
Carl Barzilauskas - DT
Eddie Bell - WR
Kenneth Bernich - LB
Emerson Boozer - HB
Willie Brister - TE
Gordie Browne - T
Carl Capria - DB
Rich Caster - TE
Jerry Davis - DB
Steve Davis - HB
John Ebersole - LB
Joe Fields - G
Ed Galigher - DT
Greg Gantt - K
Carl Garrett - HB
Bob Gresham - HB
Winston Hill - T
George Hoey - DB
Delles Howell - DB
Jazz Jackson - HB
John Jones - QB
David Knight - WR
Pat Leahy - K
Rich Lewis - LB
Wayne Mulligan - C
Joe Namath - QB
Richard Neal - DE
Billy Newsome - DE
Burgess Owens - DB
Lou Piccone - WR
Bob Prout - DB
Garry Puetz - G
Randy Rasmussen - G
Steve Reese - LB
John Riggins - FB
Jamie Rivers - LB
Rich Sowells - DB
Ed Taylor - DB
Godwin Turk - LB
Donnie Walker - DB
Phillip Wise - DB
Richard Wood - LB
Larry Woods - DT
Robert Woods - T
Roscoe Word - DB

1975 Oakland

Butch Atkinson - DB
Pete Banaszak - HB
Warren Bankston - FB
Fred Biletnikoff - WR
George Blanda - QB
Morris Bradshaw - WR
Cliff Branch - WR
Willie Brown - DB
George Buehler - G
Louis Carter - HB
Dave Casper - TE
Tony Cline - DE
Neal Colzie - DB
Dave Dalby - C
Clarence Davis - HB
Mike Dennery - LB
Ray Guy - K
Willie Hall - LB
Harold Hart - HB
Ted Hendricks - LB
Marv Hubbard - FB
David Humm - QB
Gerald Irons - LB
Monte Johnson - LB
Horace Jones - DE
Kelvin Korver - DT
Ted Kwalick - TE
Henry Lawrence - T
Larry Lawrence - QB
Dan Medlin - G
Bob Moore - TE
Charlie Phillips - DB
Jess Phillips - FB
Dave Rowe - DT
Art Shell - T
Mike Siani - WR
Otis Sistrunk - DT
Ken Stabler - QB
Steve Sylvester - G
Jack Tatum - DB
Skip Thomas - DB
Art Thoms - DT
Gene Upshaw - G
Mark van Eeghen - FB
John Vella - T
Phil Villapiano - LB

1975 Philadelphia

George Amundson - HB
Bill Bergey - LB
Jeff Bleamer - T
Mike Boryla - QB
Bill Bradley - DB
Cliff Brooks - DB - DB
John Bunting - LB
Harold Carmichael - WR
Steve Colavito - LB
Bill Dunstan - DT
Tom Ehlers - LB
Roman Gabriel - QB
Blenda Gay - DE
Rich Glover - DT
Dean Halverson - LB
Po James - HB
Ernie Janet - G
Spike Jones - K
Joe Jones - DE
Merritt Kersey - HB
Wade Key - G
Keith Krepfle - TE
Joe Lavender - DB
Frank LeMaster - LB
Randy Logan - DB
Ron Lou - C
Bill Lueck - G
Tom Luken - G
Art Malone - FB
Rosie Manning - DT
Larry Marshall - DB
James McAlister - HB
Dennis Morgan - HB
Guy Morriss - C
Horst Muhlmann - K
John Niland - G
Jim Opperman - LB
John Outlaw - DB
Artimus Parker - DB
Bob Picard - WR
Don Ratliff - DE
Jerry Sisemore - T
Charlie Smith - WR
Tom Sullivan - FB
Mitch Sutton - DT
John Tarver - FB
Stan Walters - T
Will Wynn - DE
Charle Young - TE
Don Zimmerman - WR

1975 Pittsburgh

Jimmy Allen - DB
John Banaszak - DE
Rocky Bleier - HB
Mel Blount - DB
Ed Bradley - LB
Terry Bradshaw - QB
Dave Brown - DB
Larry Brown - TE
Jim Clack - C
Mike Collier - HB
Sam Davis - G
Glen Edwards - DB
John Fuqua - HB
Steve Furness - DE
Reggie Garrett - WR
Roy Gerela - K
Joe Gilliam - QB
Gordon Gravelle - T
Joe Greene - DT
L. C. Greenwood - DE
Randy Grossman - TE
Jack Ham - LB
Terry Hanratty - QB
Franco Harris - FB
Reggie Harrison - FB
Ernie Holmes - DT
Marv Kellum - LB
Jon Kolb - T
Jack Lambert - LB
Frank Lewis - WR
Ray Mansfield - C
Gerry Mullins - T
Dave Reavis - T
Andy Russell - LB
Donnie Shell - DB
John Stallworth - WR
Lynn Swann - WR
J.T. Thomas - DB
Loren Toews - LB
Mike Wagner - DB
Bobby Walden - K
Mike Webster - G
Dwight White - DE

1975 St. Louis

Hank Allison - G
Mark Arneson - LB
Josh Ashton - HB
Jim Bakken - K
Tom Banks - G
Pete Barnes - LB
Bob Bell - DE
Tom Brahaney - C
Lee Brooks - DT
J.V. Cain - TE
Dwayne Crump - DB
Charles Davis - DT
Dan Dierdorf - T
Conrad Dobler - G
Clarence Duren - DB
Roger Finnie - G
Mel Gray - WR
Tim Gray - DB
Gary Hammond - WR
Ike Harris - WR
Jim Hart - QB
Greg Hartle - LB
Steve Jones - HB
Greg Kindle - G
Jerry Latin - HB
Terry Metcalf - HB
Eddie Moss - FB
Steve Neils - LB
Jim Otis - FB
Ken Reaves - DB
Bob Rowe - DT
Council Rudolph - DE
Dennis Shaw - QB
Jackie Smith - TE
Larry Stallings - LB
Earl Thomas - WR
Norm Thompson - DB
Jim Tolbert - DB
Roger Wehrli - DB
Jeff West - TE
Ray White - LB
Ron Yankowski - DE
Bob Young - G

1975 San Diego

Billy Andrews - LB
Dave Atkins - HB
Coy Bacon - DE
Melvin Baker - WR
Tony Baker - FB
Joe Beauchamp - DB
Glen Bonner - HB
Chuck Bradley - TE
Marlin Briscoe - WR
Booker Brown - G
Virgil Carter - QB
Danny Colbert - DB
Craig Cotton - TE
Pat Curran - TE
Fred Dean - DE
Bobby Douglass - HB
Ed Flanagan - C
Chris Fletcher - DB
Dan Fouts - QB
Jesse Freitas - QB
Mike Fuller - DB
Gary Garrison - WR
Don Goode - LB
Ira Gordon - G
Tom Graham - LB
Ken Hutcherson - LB
Gary Johnson - DT
Louie Kelcher - DT
Drew Mahalic - LB
Mark Markovich - C
Bo Matthews - FB
Dwight McDonald - WR
Terry Owens - T
Dennis Partee - K
Ralph Perretta - G
Floyd Rice - LB
Dave Rowe - DT
Sam Scarber - FB
Billy Shields - T
Charlie Smith - HB
Bob Stein - LB
Hal Stringert - DB
Joe Sweet - WR
Franklin Tate - LB
John Teerlinck - DT
Dave Tipton - DT
Maurice Tyler - DB
Russ Washington - T
Ray Wersching - K
Doug Wilkerson - G
Mike Williams - DB
Sam Williams - DB
Gregory Wojcik - DT
Don Woods - HB
Rickey Young - HB

1975 San Francisco

Nate Allen - DB
William Anderson - DB
Wayne Baker - DT
Cas Banaszek - T
Jean Barrett - G
Terry Beasley - WR
Greg Collins - LB
Cleveland Elam - DE
Keith Fahnhorst - T
Len Garrett - TE
Windlan Hall - DB
Cedrick Hardman - DE
Willie Harper - LB
Jeff Hart - T
Tommy Hart - DE
Bob Hayes - WR
Mike Holmes - WR
Bob Hoskins - DT
Wilbur Jackson - HB
Jim Johnson - DB
Kermit Johnson - HB
Sammy Johnson - FB
Bill Larson - TE
Ralph McGill - DB
Steve Mike-Mayer - K
Tom Mitchell - TE
Manfred Moore - HB
Frank Nunley - LB
Tom Owen - QB
Bob Penchion - G
Woody Peoples - G
Mel Phillips - DB
Bill Reid - C
Bill Sandifer - DT
John Saunders - DB
Larry Schreiber - FB
Norm Snead - QB
Steve Spurrier - QB
Bruce Taylor - DB
Skip Vanderbundt - LB
Dave Washington - LB
Gene Washington - WR
John Watson - T
Jimmy Webb - DT
Delvin Williams - HB
Tom Wittum - K

1975 Washington

Bobby Anderson - FB
Jim Arneson - C
Mike Bass - DB
Mike Bragg - K
Larry Brown - HB
Eddie Brown - DB
Bill Brundige - DT
Bob Brunet - FB
Dave Butz - DE
Moses Denson - FB
Brad Dusek - LB
Pat Fischer - DB
Frank Grant - WR
Chris Hanburger - LB
Len Hauss - C
Terry Hermeling - T
Ken Houston - DB
Roy Jefferson - WR
Dennis Johnson - DT
Randy Johnson - QB
Larry Jones - WR
Billy Kilmer - QB
Bob Kuziel - C
Paul Laaveg - G
Ron McDole - DE
Harold McLinton - LB
Mark Moseley - K
Ralph Nelson - HB
Brig Owens - DB
John Pergine - LB
Alvin Reed - TE
Dan Ryczek - C
Bryant Salter - DB
Ray Schoenke - T
Manny Sistrunk - DT
Jerry Smith - TE
George Starke - T
Timothy Stokes - T
Ken Stone - DB
Walt Sweeney - G
Diron Talbert - DT
Charley Taylor - WR
Joe Theismann - QB
Mike Thomas - HB
Spencer Thomas - DB
Rusty Tillman - LB
Pete Wysocki - LB

1976 Atlanta

Brent Adams - T
Bob Adams - TE
Jim Bailey - DE
Steve Bartkowski - QB
Bubba Bean - HB
Greg Brezina - LB
Ray Brown - DB
Rick Byas - DB
Sonny Collins - HB
Jim Cope - LB
Brad Davis - FB
Ron East - DT
Ray Easterling - DB
Mike Esposito - HB
Karl Farmer - WR
Wally Francis - WR
Steve George - DT
John Gilliam - WR
Len Gotshalk - G
Dave Hampton - HB
Claude Humphrey - DE
Scott Hunter - QB
Larron Jackson - G
John James - K
Alfred Jenkins - WR
Bob Jones - DB
Greg Kindle - T
Fulton Kuykendall - LB
Rolland Lawrence - DB
Mike Lewis - DT
Ron Mabra - DB
Greg Marderian - DT
Dewey McClain - LB
Phil McKinnely - T
Kim McQuilken - QB
Jeff Merrow - DE
Nick Mike-Mayer - K
Jim Mitchell - TE
Tommy Nobis - LB
Ralph Ortega - LB
Wally Pesuit - G
Scott Piper - WR
Billy Pritchett - FB
Frank Reed - DB
Guy Roberts - LB
Paul Ryczek - C
Dave Scott - T
Royce Smith - G
Haskel Stanback - HB
Woody Thompson - FB
Mike Tilleman - DT
Jeff Van Note - C
Jim Weatherly - C
Bill Windauer - DT
Jeff Yeates - DT

1976 Baltimore

Mike Barnes - DT
Tim Baylor - DB
Forrest Blue - C
Roger Carr - WR
Raymond Chester - TE
Jim Cheyunski - LB
Elmer Collett - G
Fred Cook - DE
Dan Dickel - LB
Glenn Doughty - WR
John Dutton - DE
Joe Ehrmann - DT
Ron Fernandes - DE
Randy Hall - DB
Ken Huff - G
Bert Jones - QB
Jimmie Kennedy - TE
George Kunz - T
Bruce Laird - DB
Roosevelt Leaks - FB
David Lee - K
Ron Lee - FB
Toni Linhart - K
Derrel Luce - LB
Don McCauley - FB
Ken Mendenhall - C
Lydell Mitchell - HB
Lloyd Mumphord - DB
Nelson Munsey - DB
Ken Novak - DT
Ray Oldham - DB
Bob Pratt - G
Bryant Salter - DB
Freddie Scott - WR
Sanders Shiver - LB
Ed Simonini - LB
Howard Stevens - HB
David Taylor - T
Spencer Thomas - DB
Ricky Thompson - WR
Bill Troup - QB
Bob Van Duyne - G
Jackie Wallace - DB
Stan White - LB

1976 Buffalo

Bill Adams - G
William Anderson - DB
Marv Bateman - K
Jim Braxton - FB
Cliff Brooks - DB
Bob Chandler - WR
Mario Clark - DB
Fred Coleman - TE
Bo Cornell - LB
Joe DeLamielleure - G
Joe Devlin - T
Emmett Edwards - WR
Joe Ferguson - QB
Dave Foley - T
Steve Freeman - DB
Robert Gaddis - WR
Reuben Gant - TE
Donnie Green - T
Van Green - DB
Tony Greene - DB
Dwight Harrison - DB
Clayton Heath - HB
John Holland - WR
Mike Holmes - DB
Roland Hooks - HB
George Jakowenko - K
Dan Jilek - LB
Mark Johnson - DE
Doug Jones - DB
Ken Jones - DE
Mike Kadish - DT
Jeff Kinney - FB
Merv Krakau - LB
John Leypoldt - K
Jeff Lloyd - DE
Gary Marangi - QB
Reggie McKenzie - G
Mike Montler - C
Keith Moody - DB
Bob Nelson - LB
Willie Parker - C
Bob Patton - C
Darnell Powell - HB
Eddie Ray - FB
Andy Reid - HB
Benny Ricardo - K
Tom Ruud - LB
Paul Seymour - TE
O.J. Simpson - HB
John Skorupan - LB
Tody Smith - DE
Marty Smith - DE
Vic Washington - HB
Sherman White - DE
Ben Williams - DT
Roscoe Word - DB
Jeff Yeates - DT

1976 Chi. Bears

Mike Adamle - HB
Lionel Antoine - T
Bob Avellini - QB
Brian Baschnagel - WR
Royce Berry - DE
Ross Brupbacher - LB
Waymond Bryant - LB
Doug Buffone - LB
Randy Burks - WR
Virgil Carter - QB
Wally Chambers - DT
Craig Clemons - DB
Allan Ellis - DB
Gary Fencik - DB
Roland Harper - HB
Mike Hartenstine - DE
Tom Hicks - LB
Gary Huff - QB
Noah Jackson - G
Dan Jiggetts - T
Bill Knox - DB
Greg Latta - TE
Dennis Lick - T
Virgil Livers - DB
Jerry Meyers - DE
Jerry Muckensturm - LB
Johnny Musso - HB
Dan Neal - C
Mark Nordquist - G
Jim Osborne - DT
Bob Parsons - TE
Walter Payton - HB
Dan Peiffer - C
Doug Plank - DB
Bo Rather - WR
Don Rives - LB
Ron Rydalch - DT
Terry Schmidt - DB
Larry Schreiber - FB
Steve Schubert - WR
James Scott - WR
Jeff Sevy - T
Ron Shanklin - WR
Revie Sorey - G
Roger Stillwell - DE
Bob Thomas - K
John Ward - G

1976 Cincinnati

Ken Anderson - QB
Coy Bacon - DE
Chris Bahr - K
Billy Brooks - WR
Robert Brown - DT
Glenn Bujnoch - G
Gary Burley - DE
Glenn Cameron - LB
Ron Carpenter - DT
Tommy Casanova - DB
Boobie Clark - FB
Marvin Cobb - DB
Bruce Coslet - TE
Isaac Curtis - WR
Tony Davis - HB
Chris Devlin - LB
Lenvil Elliott - HB
Greg Fairchild - G
Stan Fritts - FB
Archie Griffin - HB
Bo Harris - LB
Vern Holland - T
Ron Hunt - T
Bernard Jackson - DB
Ken Johnson - DE
Bob Johnson - C
Bill Kollar - DT
Dave Lapham - G
Jim LeClair - LB
Rufus Mayes - T
John McDaniel - WR
Pat McInally - WR
Melvin Morgan - DB
Chip Myers - WR
Lemar Parrish - DB
Scott Perry - DB
Ron Pritchard - LB
John Reaves - QB
Ken Riley - DB
Willie Shelby - HB
John Shinners - G
Bob Trumpy - TE
Reggie Williams - LB

1976 Cleveland

Pete Adams - G
Dick Ambrose - LB
Bob Babich - LB
Ron Bolton - DB
Terry Brown - DB
Don Cockroft - K
Neal Craig - DB
Bill Craven - DB
Thom Darden - DB
Barry Darrow - T
Tom DeLeone - C
Al Dennis - G
Doug Dieken - T
Brian Duncan - HB
Earl Edwards - DE
Ricky Feacher - WR
John Garlington - LB
Dave Graf - LB
Van Green - DB
Charlie Hall - LB
Steve Holden - WR
Gerald Irons - LB
Robert Jackson - G
Walter Johnson - DT
Joe Jones - DE
Dave Logan - WR
Dave Mays - QB
Cleo Miller - HB
Willie Miller - WR
Mack Mitchell - DE
Gary Parris - TE
Tony Peters - DB
Mike Phipps - QB
Larry Poole - HB
Greg Pruitt - HB
Mike Pruitt - FB
Oscar Roan - TE
Reggie Rucker - WR
Clarence Scott - DB
Henry Sheppard - T
Jerry Sherk - DT
Brian Sipe - QB
Mike St. Clair - DE
Gerry Sullivan - C
Paul Warfield - WR

1976 Dallas

Benny Barnes - DB
Bob Breunig - LB
Larry Cole - DT
Doug Dennison - HB
Pat Donovan - T
Billy Joe DuPree - TE
Jim Eidson - G
John Fitzgerald - C
Bill Gregory - DT
Cliff Harris - DB
Mike Hegman - LB
Tom Henderson - LB
Efren Herrera - K
Randy Hughes - DB
Jim Jensen - FB
Butch Johnson - WR
Too Tall Jones - DE
Lee Roy Jordan - LB
Aaron Kyle - DB
Scott Laidlaw - FB
Burton Lawless - G
D. D. Lewis - LB
Harvey Martin - DE
Ralph Neely - T
Robert Newhouse - FB
Blaine Nye - G
Drew Pearson - WR
Preston Pearson - HB
Jethro Pugh - DT
Tom Rafferty - G
Beasley Reece - DB
Mel Renfro - DB
Golden Richards - WR
Jay Saldi - TE
Greg Schaum - DE
Herbert Scott - G
Roger Staubach - QB
Mark Washington - DB
Charlie Waters - DB
Randy White - LB
Danny White - QB
Rayfield Wright - T
Charley Young - HB

1976 Denver

Lyle Alzado - DT
Otis Armstrong - HB
Bill Bain - T
Rich Baska - LB
Boyd Brown - TE
Rubin Carter - DT
Barney Chavous - DE
Jack Dolbin - WR
Larry Evans - LB
Steve Foley - DB
Mike Franckowiak - FB
Tom Glassic - G
Harvey Goodman - G
Randy Gradishar - LB
John Grant - DT
Wayne Hammond - DT
Billy Hardee - DB
Glenn Hyde - T
Martin Imhof - DT
Tom Jackson - LB
Calvin Jones - DB
Jon Keyworth - FB
Jim Kiick - HB
Tommy Lyons - G
Bobby Maples - C
Claudie Minor - T
Marv Montgomery - T
Randy Moore - DT
Haven Moses - WR
Riley Odoms - TE
Phil Olsen - C
Chris Pane - DB
Craig Penrose - QB
Lonnie Perrin - FB
Randy Poltl - DB
Steve Ramsey - QB
Joe Rizzo - LB
John Rowser - DB
John Schultz - WR
Paul Smith - DE
Bob Swenson - LB
Billy Thompson - DB
Godwin Turk - LB
Jim Turner - K
Rick Upchurch - WR
Bill Van Heusen - WR
Norris Weese - QB
Jim White - DE
Louis Wright - DB

1976 Detroit

Lem Barney - DB
Lynn Boden - G
Russ Bolinger - T
Andy Bolton - HB
Dexter Bussey - HB
Don Croft - DT
Gary Danielson - QB
Ben Davis - DB
Doug English - DT
Dennis Franklin - WR
Rocky Freitas - T
Lawrence Gaines - FB
Larry Hand - DT
Craig Hertwig - T
David Hill - TE
J. D. Hill - WR
Jim Hooks - FB
Billy Howard - DE
James Hunter - DB
Ray Jarvis - WR
Dick Jauron - DB
Levi Johnson - DB
Horace King - FB
Bob Kowalkowski - G
Greg Landry - QB
Jim Laslavic - LB
Ken Long - G
Errol Mann - K
Mark Markovich - C
Jim Mitchell - DE
Jon Morris - C
Paul Naumoff - LB
Ed O'Neil - LB
Herb Orvis - DT
Bob Picard - WR
Reggie Pierson - DB
Ernie Price - DE
Joe Reed - QB
Benny Ricardo - K
Charlie Sanders - TE
Ken Sanders - DE
Ian Sunter - K
Garth Ten Napel - LB
Bobby Thompson - HB
Leonard Thompson - WR
Maurice Tyler - DB
Larry Walton - WR
Charlie Weaver - LB
Herman Weaver - K
Charlie West - DB
John Woodcock - LB
Jim Yarbrough - T

1976 Green Bay

Ron Acks - LB
Bert Askson - TE
Bob Barber - DE
David Beverly - K
John Brockington - FB
Carlos Brown - QB
Willie Buchanon - DB
Jim Burrow - DB
Fred Carr - LB
Lynn Dickey - QB
Dick Enderle - G
Gale Gillingham - G
Johnnie Gray - DB
Jessie Green - WR
Jim Gueno - LB
Charlie Hall - DB
Don Hansen - LB
Willard Harrell - HB
Dick Himes - T
Bob Hyland - C
Melvin Jackson - G
Randy Johnson - QB
Steve Knutson - G
Mark Koncar - T
Bob Lally - LB
Steve Luke - DB
Chester Marcol - K
Larry McCarren - C
Mike McCoy - DB
Mike McCoy - DT
Rich McGeorge - TE
Steve Odom - WR
Dave Osborn - HB
Ken Payne - WR
Tom Perko - LB
Dave Pureifory - DE
Alden Roche - DE
Dave Roller - DT
Barty Smith - FB
Perry Smith - DB
Ollie Smith - WR
Ken Starch - FB
Cliff Taylor - HB
Tom Toner - LB
Eric Torkelson - HB
Bruce Van Dyke - G
Steve Wagner - DB
Gary Weaver - LB
Sweeny Williams - DE
Don Zimmerman - WR

1976 Houston

Willie Alexander - DB
Mack Alston - TE
Bob Atkins - DB
Melvin Baker - WR
Mike Barber - WR
Jim Beirne - WR
Duane Benson - LB
Elvin Bethea - DE
Gregg Bingham - LB
Robert Brazile - LB
Ken Burrough - WR
Albert Burton - DE
Skip Butler - K
Leroy Clark - K
Ronnie Coleman - HB
Curley Culp - NT
Al Darby - TE
Joe Dawkins - FB
Elbert Drungo - T
Emmett Edwards - WR
Ken Ellis - DB
Ed Fisher - G
John Hadl - QB
Don Hardeman - FB
Dennis Havig - G
Conway Hayman - G
Mitch Hoopes - K
Kevin Hunt - T
Al Johnson - HB
Billy Johnson - WR
Steve Kiner - LB
John Little - NT
Ron Lou - C
Carl Mauck - C
Zeke Moore - DB
Joe Owens - DE
Dan Pastorini - QB
Mike Reinfeldt - DB
Tim Rossovich - LB
Greg Sampson - T
John Sawyer - TE
Dave Simonson - T
Bubba Smith - DE
Tody Smith - DE
Greg Stemrick - DB
Altie Taylor - HB
Earl Thomas - WR
Ted Thompson - LB
Ted Washington - LB
Mike Weger - DB
C.L. Whittington - DB
Sam Williams - DB
Fred Willis - FB

1976 Kansas City

Tony Adams - QB
Billy Andrews - LB
Charlie Ane - C
Gary Barbaro - DB
Larry Brunson - WR
Ed Budde - G
Tim Collier - DB
Tom Condon - G
Reggie Craig - WR
Jimbo Elrod - LB
Larry Estes - DE
Charlie Getty - T
Tim Gray - DB
Woody Green - HB
Glynn Harrison - FB
Matt Herkenhoff - T
Jeff Kinney - FB
MacArthur Lane - FB
Willie Lanier - LB
Willie Lee - DT
Mike Livingston - QB
John Lohmeyer - DE
Jim Lynch - LB
Bob Maddox - DT
Henry Marshall - WR
Billy Masters - TE
Pat McNeil - FB
Jim Nicholson - T
Mike Nott - QB
Orrin Olsen - C
Whitney Paul - DE
Barry Pearson - WR
Ed Podolak - HB
Tommy Reamon - HB
Kerry Reardon - DB
Dave Rozumek - LB
Jack Rudnay - C
Keith Simons - DT
Jan Stenerud - K
Steve Taylor - DB
Emmitt Thomas - DB
Rod Walters - G
Clyde Werner - LB
Walter White - TE
Lawrence Williams - WR
Jerrel Wilson - K
Jim Wolf - DE
Wilbur Young - DE

1976 LA Rams

Jim Bertelsen - FB
Larry Brooks - DT
Cullen Bryant - FB
John Cappelletti - HB
Tom Dempsey - K
Fred Dryer - DE
Carl Ekern - LB
Dave Elmendorf - DB
Mike Fanning - DE
Doug France - T
Tom Geredine - WR
Pat Haden - QB
Dennis Harrah - G
James Harris - QB
Greg Horton - G
Rusty Jackson - K
Harold Jackson - WR
Monte Jackson - DB
Ron Jaworski - QB
Ron Jessie - WR
Freeman Johns - WR
Cody Jones - DT
Rick Kay - LB
Bob Klein - TE
Tom Mack - G
Lawrence McCutcheon - HB
Kevin McLain - LB
Terry Nelson - TE
Merlin Olsen - DT
Rod Perry - DB
Rod Phillips - FB
Steve Preece - DB
Geoff Reece - C
Jack Reynolds - LB
Isiah Robertson - LB
Mel Rogers - LB
Rich Saul - C
Dwight Scales - WR
Rob Scribner - HB
Bill Simpson - DB
Jackie Slater - T
Pat Thomas - DB
John Williams - T
Jack Youngblood - DE
Jim Youngblood - LB

1976 Miami

Dick Anderson - DB
John Andrews - DE
Charlie Babb - DB
Ted Bachman - DB
Norm Bulaich - FB
Nick Buoniconti - LB
Darryl Carlton - T
Rusty Chambers - LB
Randy Crowder - DT
Gary Davis - HB
Vern Den Herder - DE
Mike Dennery - LB
Tom Drougas - T
Ken Ellis - DB
Tim Foley - DB
Larry Gordon - LB
Bob Griese - QB
Duriel Harris - WR
Clayton Heath - HB
Bob Heinz - DT
Barry Hill - DB
Ike Hill - WR
Mike Holmes - DB
Curtis Johnson - DB
Bob Kuechenberg - G
Jim Langer - C
Larry Little - G
Benny Malone - HB
Jim Mandich - TE
Bob Matheson - LB
Loaird McCreary - TE
Mel Mitchell - G
Nat Moore - WR
Wayne Moore - T
Earl Morrall - QB
Ed Newman - G
Don Nottingham - FB
Morris Owens - WR
Don Reese - DE
Bryant Salter - DB
Larry Seiple - TE
Andy Selfridge - LB
Freddie Solomon - WR
Bill Stanfill - DE
Don Strock - QB
Andre Tillman - TE
Steve Towle - LB
Howard Twilley - WR
Jeris White - DB
Stan Winfrey - FB
Garo Yepremian - K

1976 Minnesota

Nate Allen - DB
Scott Anderson - C
Autry Beamon - DB
Bob Berry - QB
Matt Blair - LB
Bobby Bryant - DB
Bart Buetow - T
Neil Clabo - K
Fred Cox - K
Steve Craig - TE
Doug Dumler - C
Carl Eller - DE
Chuck Foreman - HB
Charlie Goodrum - T
Bob Grim - WR
Ron Groce - FB
Windlan Hall - DB
Wes Hamilton - G
Wally Hilgenberg - LB
Sammy Johnson - FB
Mark Kellar - FB
Paul Krause - DB
Jim Lash - WR
Bob Lee - QB
Bob Lurtsema - DE
Jim Marshall - DE
Amos Martin - LB
Brent McClanahan - HB
Fred McNeill - LB
Robert Miller - HB
Mark Mullaney - DE
Alan Page - DT
Ahmad Rashad - WR
Steve Riley - T
Jeff Siemon - LB
Willie Spencer - FB
Doug Sutherland - DT
Fran Tarkenton - QB
Mick Tingelhoff - C
Stu Voigt - TE
Ed White - G
James White - DT
Sammy White - WR
Leonard Willis - WR
Roy Winston - LB
Jeff Wright - DB
Nate Wright - DB
Ron Yary - T

1976 New England

Julius Adams - DE
Sam Adams - G
Pete Barnes - LB
Doug Beaudoin - DB
Richard Bishop - NT
Joe Blahak - DB
Marlin Briscoe - WR
Pete Brock - C
Steve Burks - WR
Don Calhoun - HB
Allen Carter - FB
Al Chandler - TE
Dick Conn - DB
Sam Cunningham - FB
Ricky Feacher - WR
Ike Forte - HB
Tim Fox - DB
Russ Francis - TE
Willie Germany - DB
Leon Gray - T
Steve Grogan - QB
Ray Hamilton - NT
John Hannah - G
Mike Haynes - DB
Bob Howard - DB
Sam Hunt - LB
Andy Johnson - HB
Steve King - LB
Bill Lenkaitis - C
Mel Lunsford - DE
Prentice McCray - DB
Tony McGee - DE
Bob McKay - T
Art Moore - NT
Steve Nelson - LB
Tom Neville - T
Tom Owen - QB
Mike Patrick - K
Jess Phillips - HB
Jim Romaniszyn - LB
Deac Sanders - DB
John Smith - K
Darryl Stingley - WR
Fred Sturt - G
Donnie Thomas - LB
Dave Tipton - NT
Randy Vataha - WR
George Webster - LB
Steve Zabel - LB

1976 New Orleans

Pete Athas - DB
Steve Baumgartner - DE
Tom Blanchard - K
Ken Bordelon - LB
Larry Burton - WR
Warren Capone - LB
Rusty Chambers - LB
Clarence Chapman - WR
Henry Childs - TE
Wayne Colman - LB
Chuck Crist - DB
Andy Dorris - DE
Bobby Douglass - QB
Joe Federspiel - LB
Tony Galbreath - FB
Elois Grooms - DE
Lee Gross - C
Jeff Hart - T
Don Herrmann - WR
John Hill - C
Ernie Jackson - DB
Benny Johnson - DB
Andrew Jones - FB
Kim Jones - FB
Jim Kearney - DB
Rick Kingrea - LB
Alvin Maxson - HB
Leon McQuay - HB
Jim Merlo - LB
Marv Montgomery - T
Derland Moore - DT
Don Morrison - T
Chuck Muncie - FB
Tom Myers - DB
Tinker Owens - WR
Bob Pollard - DT
Elex Price - DT
Kurt Schumacher - T
Bobby Scott - QB
Paul Seal - TE
Mo Spencer - DB
Terry Stieve - G
Mike Strachan - HB
Richie Szaro - K
Jim Thaxton - TE
Greg Westbrooks - LB
Tom Wickert - G
Jeff Winans - DE
Emanuel Zanders - G

1976 NY Giants

Troy Archer - DE
Gordon Bell - HB
Bobby Brooks - DB
Bill Bryant - DB
Danny Buggs - WR
Harry Carson - LB
Karl Chandler - C
Rondy Colbert - DB
Brad Cousino - LB
Steve Crosby - HB
Larry Csonka - FB
Joe Danelo - K
Rick Dvorak - DE
Bill Ellenbogen - G
Dave Gallagher - DT
Mike Gibbons - T
Walker Gillette - WR
Jack Gregory - DE
Bobby Hammond - HB
John Hicks - G
Ralph Hill - C
Pat Hughes - LB
Dave Jennings - K
Brian Kelley - LB
Doug Kotar - HB
Dan Lloyd - LB
Larry Mallory - DB
Ed Marshall - WR
George Martin - DE
John Mendenhall - DT
Ron Mikolajczyk - G
Craig Morton - QB
Tom Mullen - G

Clyde Powers - DB
Ray Rhodes - WR
Jim Robinson - WR
Bob Schmit - LB
Gary Shirk - TE
Al Simpson - G
Norm Snead - QB
Jim Stienke - DB
Henry Stuckey - DB
John Tate - LB
Bob Tucker - TE
Doug Van Horn - T
Brad Van Pelt - LB
Rick Volk - DB
Roger Wallace - WR
Larry Watkins - FB
Marsh White - FB
Roscoe Word - DB

1976 NY Jets

Darrell Austin - C
Jerome Barkum - WR
Carl Barzilauskas - DT
Cliff Brooks - DB
Don Buckey - WR
Greg Buttle - LB
Duane Carrell - K
Rich Caster - TE
Steve Davis - FB
Keith Denson - WR
John Ebersole - LB
Joe Fields - C
Clark Gaines - HB
Ed Galigher - DT
Louie Giammona - HB
Bob Gresham - HB
Clint Haslerig - WR
Mike Hennigan - LB
Winston Hill - T
Harry Howard - DB
Jazz Jackson - HB
Steve Joachim - QB
Larry Keller - LB
David Knight - WR
Al Krevis - T
Pat Leahy - K
Ed Marinaro - FB
Bob Martin - LB
Tommy Marvaso - DB
Joe Namath - QB
Richard Neal - DE
Billy Newsome - DE
Richard Osborne - TE
Burgess Owens - DB
Lou Piccone - WR
Lawrence Pillers - DE
Steve Poole - LB
Garry Puetz - G
Randy Rasmussen - G
Steven Rogers - HB
John Roman - T
James Rosecrans - LB
Carl Russ - LB
Abdul Salaam - DT
Howard Satterwhite - WR
Rich Sowells - DB
Shafer Suggs - DB
Ed Taylor - DB
Richard Todd - QB
Phillip Wise - DB
Robert Woods - T
Roscoe Word - DB

1976 Oakland

Butch Atkinson - DB
Pete Banaszak - HB
Warren Bankston - TE
Rodrigo Barnes - LB
Fred Biletnikoff - WR
Greg Blankenship - LB
Rik Bonness - LB
Morris Bradshaw - WR
Cliff Branch - WR
Willie Brown - DB
George Buehler - G
Dave Casper - TE
Neal Colzie - DB
Dave Dalby - C
Clarence Davis - HB
Carl Garrett - HB
Hubert Ginn - HB
Ray Guy - K
Willie Hall - LB
Ted Hendricks - LB
David Humm - QB
Rick Jennings - HB
Monte Johnson - LB
Terry Kunz - FB
Ted Kwalick - TE
Henry Lawrence - T
Errol Mann - K
John Matuszak - DE
Herb McMath - DE
Dan Medlin - G
Manfred Moore - HB
Charlie Phillips - DB
Charles Philyaw - DE
Mike Rae - QB
Mike Reinfeldt - DB
Floyd Rice - LB
Dave Rowe - DT
Art Shell - T
Mike Siani - WR

Otis Sistrunk - DT
Ken Stabler - QB
Fred Steinfort - K
Steve Sylvester - C
Jack Tatum - DB
Skip Thomas - DB
Gene Upshaw - G
Mark van Eeghen - FB
John Vella - T
Phil Villapiano - LB

1976 Philadelphia

Bill Bergey - LB
Jeff Bleamer - G
Mike Boryla - QB
Bill Bradley - DB
Cliff Brooks - DB
John Bunting - LB
Mark Burke - DB
Tommy Campbell - DB
Harold Carmichael - WR
Al Clark - DB
Bill Dunstan - DT
Tom Ehlers - LB
Dennis Franks - C
Roman Gabriel - QB
Blenda Gay - DE
Ed George - T
Carl Hairston - DE
Dave Hampton - HB
Mike Hogan - HB
Spike Jones - K
Wade Key - G
Keith Krepfle - TE
Pete Lazetich - DT
Frank LeMaster - LB
Randy Logan - DB
Herb Lusk - HB
Drew Mahalic - LB
Art Malone - FB
Larry Marshall - DB
James McAlister - HB
Guy Morriss - C
Horst Muhlmann - K
Dennis Nelson - T
Bill Olds - FB
Richard Osborne - TE
John Outlaw - DB
Vince Papale - WR
Artimus Parker - DB
Bob Picard - WR
Jerry Sisemore - G
Manny Sistrunk - DT
Charlie Smith - WR
Tom Sullivan - HB
Terry Tautolo - LB
Stan Walters - T
John Walton - QB
Will Wynn - DE
Charle Young - TE
Don Zimmerman - WR

1976 Pittsburgh

Jimmy Allen - DB
John Banaszak - DE
Theo Bell - WR
Greg Blankenship - LB
Rocky Bleier - HB
Mel Blount - DB
Terry Bradshaw - QB
Larry Brown - TE
Jim Clack - G
Bennie Cunningham - TE
Sam Davis - G
Jack Deloplaine - HB
Gary Dunn - DT
Glen Edwards - DB
John Fuqua - HB
Steve Furness - DT
Roy Gerela - K
Gordon Gravelle - T
Joe Greene - DT
L. C. Greenwood - DE
Randy Grossman - TE
Jack Ham - LB
Franco Harris - FB
Reggie Harrison - FB
Ernie Holmes - DT
Marv Kellum - LB
Jon Kolb - T
Mike Kruczek - QB
Jack Lambert - LB
Frank Lewis - WR
Ray Mansfield - C
Gerry Mullins - G
Ray Pinney - C
Ernest Pough - WR
Andy Russell - LB
Donnie Shell - DB
John Stallworth - WR
Lynn Swann - WR
J.T. Thomas - DB
Loren Toews - LB
Mike Wagner - DB
Bobby Walden - K
Mike Webster - C
Dwight White - DE

1976 St. Louis

Hank Allison - G
Mark Arneson - LB
Jim Bakken - K

Tom Banks - C
Al Beauchamp - LB
Bob Bell - DE
Tom Brahaney - C
Lee Brooks - DT
J.V. Cain - WR
Dwayne Crump - DB
Charles Davis - DT
Mike Dawson - DT
Dan Dierdorf - T
Conrad Dobler - G
Billy Donckers - QB
Clarence Duren - DB
Roger Finnie - T
Carl Gersbach - LB
Mel Gray - WR
Gary Hammond - WR
Ike Harris - WR
Jim Hart - QB
Greg Hartle - LB
Steve Jones - HB
Terry Joyce - TE
Tim Kearney - LB
Jerry Latin - HB
Mike McDonald - LB
Mike McGraw - LB
Terry Metcalf - HB
Wayne Morris - HB
Eddie Moss - FB
Steve Neils - LB
Lee Nelson - DB
Brad Oates - T
Steve Okoniewski - DT
Jim Otis - FB
Ken Reaves - DB
Mike Sensibaugh - DB
Jeff Severson - DB
Jackie Smith - TE
Larry Stallings - LB
Norm Thompson - DB
Pat Tilley - WR
Marv Upshaw - DT
Roger Wehrli - DB
Ray White - LB
Keith Wortman - G
Sam Wyche - QB
Ron Yankowski - DE
Bob Young - G
John Zook - DE

1976 San Diego

Charles Aiu - G
Eddie Bell - WR
Chuck Bradley - TE
Danny Colbert - DB
Pat Curran - TE
Fred Dean - DE
Charles DeJurnett - DT
Larry Dorsey - WR
Ed Flanagan - C
Chris Fletcher - DB
Dan Fouts - QB
Toni Fritsch - K
Mike Fuller - DB
Gary Garrison - WR
Don Goode - LB
Tom Graham - LB
Tom Hayes - DB
Mitch Hoopes - K
Bob Horn - LB
Neal Jeffrey - QB
Gary Johnson - DT
Charlie Joiner - WR
Leroy Jones - DE
Louie Kelcher - DT
John Lee - DE
Clint Longley - QB
Woodrow Lowe - LB
Don Macek - G
Bo Matthews - FB
Dwight McDonald - WR
Larry Mialik - TE
Rick Middleton - LB
Mercury Morris - HB
Artie Owens - WR
Ralph Perretta - G
Ray Preston - LB
Sam Scarber - FB
Billy Shields - T
Ron Singleton - T
Hal Stringert - DB
Jim Tolbert - DB
Russ Washington - T
Ray Wersching - K
Jeff West - TE
Doug Wilkerson - G
Mike Williams - DB
Don Woods - FB
Rickey Young - HB

1976 San Francisco

Cas Banaszek - T
Jean Barrett - T
Scott Bull - QB
Tony Cline - DE
Bill Cooke - T
Randy Cross - C
Marty Domres - QB
Cleveland Elam - DT
Bruce Elia - LB
Dick Enderle - G
Keith Fahnhorst - T
Bob Ferrell - FB
Cedrick Hardman - DE

Willie Harper - LB
Kenny Harrison - WR
Tommy Hart - DE
Paul Hofer - HB
Wilbur Jackson - FB
Jim Johnson - DB
Kermit Johnson - HB
Sammy Johnson - FB
Jim Lash - WR
Steve Lawson - G
Tony Leonard - DB
Eddie Lewis - DB
Andy Maurer - G
Willie McGee - WR
Ralph McGill - DB
Steve Mike-Mayer - K
Dale Mitchell - LB
Tom Mitchell - TE
Frank Nunley - LB
Jim Obradovich - TE
Mel Phillips - DB
Jim Plunkett - QB
Rocky Rasley - G
Bruce Rhodes - DB
Steve Rivera - WR
Bill Sandifer - DE
Bruce Taylor - DB
Skip Vanderbundt - LB
Dave Washington - LB
Gene Washington - WR
John Watson - G
Jimmy Webb - DT
Delvin Williams - HB
Tom Wittum - K

1976 Seattle

Ted Bachman - DB
Carl Barisich - DT
Nick Bebout - T
Don Bitterlich - K
Lyle Blackwood - DB
Andy Bolton - HB
Ed Bradley - LB
Dave Brown - DB
Don Clune - WR
Ron Coder - G
Randy Coffield - LB
Greg Collins - LB
Al Cowlings - DE
Mike Curtis - LB
Al Darby - TE
John Demarie - G
Don Dufek - DB
Rick Engles - K
Norm Evans - T
Ken Geddes - LB
Sammy Green - LB
Don Hansen - LB
Richard Harris - DE
Fred Hoaglin - C
Ron Howard - TE
Gordon Jolley - T
Ernie Jones - DB
Art Kuehn - C
Steve Largent - WR
John Leypoldt - K
Bob Lurtsema - DE
Al Matthews - DB
Sam McCullum - WR
Hugh McKinnis - FB
John McMakin - TE
Eddie McMillan - DB
Bill Munson - QB
Ralph Nelson - HB
Bob Newton - G
Steve Niehaus - DT
Bill Olds - FB
Bob Penchion - G
Steve Raible - WR
Oliver Ross - HB
Dave Simonson - T
Sherman Smith - FB
Don Testerman - FB
Dave Tipton - DE
Jim White - DE
Larry Woods - DT
Roland Woolsey - DB
Jim Zorn - QB

1976 Tampa Bay

Tom Alward - G
Larry Ball - LB
Joe Blahak - DB
Cedric Brown - DB
Louis Carter - HB
Bert Cooper - LB
Mark Cotney - DB
Mike Current - T
Charlie Davis - HB
Ricky Davis - DB
Parnell Dickinson - QB
Freddie Douglas - WR
Jimmy DuBose - FB
Howard Fest - G
Dave Green - K
Jimmy Gunn - LB
Isaac Hagins - WR
Terry Hanratty - QB
Charlie Hunt - LB
Larry Jameson - DT
Essex Johnson - HB
Curtis Jordan - DB
Vince Kendrick - FB
Larry Lawrence - QB

Mike Lemon - LB
Everett Little - G
Don Martin - DB
Ed McAleney - DE
Lee McGriff - WR
John McKay - WR
Rod McNeill - FB
Manfred Moore - HB
Maulty Moore - DT
Bob Moore - TE
Jack Novak - TE
Frank Oliver - DB
Morris Owens - WR
Fred Pagac - TE
Dave Pear - DT
Cal Peterson - LB
Jim Peterson - LB
Reggie Pierson - DB
Dave Reavis - T
Danny Reece - DB
Steve Reese - LB
Glenn Robinson - LB
Mirro Roder - K
Council Rudolph - DE
Dan Ryczek - C
Dewey Selmon - DT
Lee Roy Selmon - DE
Jimmy Sims - LB
Barry Smith - WR
Steve Spurrier - QB
Ken Stone - DB
Pat Toomay - DE
John Ward - G
Mike Washington - DB
Ed Williams - FB
Steven Wilson - T
Richard Wood - LB
Roscoe Word - DB
Randy Young - T
Steve Young - T

1976 Washington

Mike Bragg - K
Larry Brown - HB
Eddie Brown - DB
Bill Brundige - DT
Bob Brunet - HB
Danny Buggs - WR
Dave Butz - DT
Brad Dusek - LB
Pat Fischer - DB
Ted Fritsch - C
Brian Fryer - WR
Jean Fugett - TE
Frank Grant - WR
Chris Hanburger - LB
Len Hauss - C
Terry Hermeling - T
Dallas Hickman - DE
Calvin Hill - FB
Ken Houston - DB
Roy Jefferson - WR
Dennis Johnson - DT
Larry Jones - WR
Billy Kilmer - QB
Bob Kuziel - C
Joe Lavender - DB
Karl Lorch - DE
Bill Malinchak - WR
Ron McDole - DE
Harold McLinton - LB
Mark Moseley - K
Dan Nugent - G
Stu O'Dell - LB
Brig Owens - DB
John Riggins - FB
Ron Saul - G
Jake Scott - DB
Jerry Smith - TE
George Starke - T
Timothy Stokes - T
Diron Talbert - DT
Joe Theismann - QB
Mike Thomas - HB
Rusty Tillman - LB
Gerard Williams - DB
Doug Winslow - WR
Pete Wysocki - LB

1977 Atlanta

Brent Adams - T
Jim Bailey - DT
Steve Bartkowski - QB
Greg Brezina - LB
Ray Brown - DB
Warren Bryant - T
Rick Byas - DB
Ray Easterling - DB
Monroe Eley - FB
Mike Esposito - HB
Karl Farmer - WR
Wilson Faumuina - DT
Edgar Fields - DE
Wally Francis - WR
Claude Humphrey - DE
Scott Hunter - QB
John James - K
Alfred Jenkins - WR
June Jones - QB
Rick Kay - LB
Greg Kindle - G
Fulton Kuykendall - LB
Rolland Lawrence - DB
Mike Lewis - DT

Ron McCartney - LB
Dewey McClain - LB
Greg McCrary - TE
Secdrick McIntyre - HB
Phil McKinnely - T
Kim McQuilken - QB
Jeff Merrow - DE
Nick Mike-Mayer - K
Jim Mitchell - TE
Tom Moriarty - DB
Ralph Ortega - LB
Robert Pennywell - LB
Billy Pritchett - FB
Frank Reed - DB
Billy Ryckman - WR
Paul Ryczek - C
Dave Scott - G
Andy Spiva - DB
Haskel Stanback - HB
Fred Steinfort - K
R.C. Thielemann - G
Woody Thompson - FB
Jeff Van Note - G
Jeff Yeates - DE

1977 Baltimore

Mack Alston - TE
Mike Barnes - DT
Tim Baylor - DB
Lyle Blackwood - DB
Forrest Blue - C
Roger Carr - WR
Raymond Chester - TE
Elmer Collett - G
Fred Cook - DE
Dan Dickel - LB
Glenn Doughty - WR
John Dutton - DE
Joe Ehrmann - DT
Ron Fernandes - DE
Wade Griffin - T
Perry Griggs - WR
Ken Huff - G
Greg Johnson - DT
Marshall Johnson - WR
Bert Jones - QB
Jimmie Kennedy - TE
George Kunz - T
Bruce Laird - LB
Roosevelt Leaks - FB
David Lee - K
Ron Lee - FB
Toni Linhart - K
Derrel Luce - LB
Tom MacLeod - LB
Don McCauley - HB
Ken Mendenhall - C
Lydell Mitchell - HB
Lloyd Mumphord - DB
Nelson Munsey - DB
Doug Nettles - DB
Ken Novak - DT
Ray Oldham - DB
Bob Pratt - G
Howard Satterwhite - WR
Freddie Scott - WR
Sanders Shiver - LB
Ed Simonini - LB
Howard Stevens - HB
David Taylor - T
Norm Thompson - DB
Ricky Thompson - WR
Bill Troup - QB
Bob Van Duyne - G
Stan White - LB

1977 Buffalo

Bill Adams - G
Marv Bateman - K
Jim Braxton - FB
Curtis Brown - HB
Bob Chandler - WR
Mario Clark - DB
Mike Collier - HB
Greg Collins - LB
Bo Cornell - LB
Reggie Craig - WR
Joe DeLamielleure - G
Joe Devlin - T
Phil Dokes - DE
Bill Dunstan - DT
Joe Ferguson - QB
Dave Foley - T
Mike Franckowiak - FB
Steve Freeman - DB
Reuben Gant - TE
Tony Greene - DB
Dwight Harrison - DB
John Holland - WR
Roland Hooks - HB
Dan Jilek - LB
Doug Jones - DB
Ken Jones - T
Mike Kadish - DT
John Kimbrough - WR
Merv Krakau - LB
John Little - DT
Carson Long - K
Reggie McKenzie - G
Keith Moody - DB
Greg Morton - DE
Shane Nelson - LB
Bob Nelson - LB

Neil O'Donoghue - K
Willie Parker - C
Lou Piccone - WR
Charles Romes - DB
Tom Ruud - LB
Paul Seymour - TE
O.J. Simpson - HB
John Skorupan - LB
Sherman White - DE
Ben Williams - DE
Leonard Willis - WR
Connie Zelencik - C

1977 Chi. Bears

Ted Albrecht - T
Bob Avellini - QB
Brian Baschnagel - WR
Art Best - HB
Chuck Bradley - TE
Waymond Bryant - LB
Doug Buffone - LB
Gary Campbell - LB
Wally Chambers - DT
Craig Clemons - DB
Fred Dean - G
Robin Earl - FB
Allan Ellis - DB
Vince Evans - QB
Gary Fencik - DB
John Gilliam - WR
Roland Harper - FB
Mike Hartenstine - DE
Tom Hicks - LB
Noah Jackson - G
Dan Jiggetts - T
Greg Latta - TE
Dennis Lick - T
Virgil Livers - DB
Jerry Meyers - DE
Jerry Muckensturm - LB
Johnny Musso - HB
Dan Neal - C
Billy Newsome - DE
Jim Osborne - DT
Bob Parsons - TE
Walter Payton - HB
Dan Peiffer - C
Mike Phipps - QB
Doug Plank - DB
Bo Rather - WR
Steve Rivera - WR
Don Rives - LB
Mel Rogers - LB
Ron Rydalch - DT
Terry Schmidt - DB
Steve Schubert - WR
James Scott - WR
Jeff Sevy - T
Revie Sorey - G
Mike Spivey - DB
Roger Stillwell - DT
Bob Thomas - K
Len Walterscheid - DB

1977 Cincinnati

Jerry Anderson - DB
Ken Anderson - QB
Coy Bacon - DE
Chris Bahr - K
Billy Brooks - WR
Glenn Bujnoch - G
Gary Burley - DE
Glenn Cameron - LB
Tommy Casanova - DB
Boobie Clark - FB
Marvin Cobb - DB
Mike Cobb - TE
James Corbett - TE
Isaac Curtis - WR
Tony Davis - FB
Eddie Edwards - DT
Lenvil Elliott - HB
Greg Fairchild - G
Archie Griffin - HB
Bo Harris - LB
Steve Holden - WR
Vern Holland - T
Ron Hunt - T
Pete Johnson - FB
Ken Johnson - DE
Bob Johnson - C
Walter Johnson - DT
Dave Lapham - G
Jim LeClair - LB
Rufus Mayes - T
John McDaniel - WR
Pat McInally - WR
Melvin Morgan - DB
Lemar Parrish - DB
Scott Perry - DB
Ray Phillips - LB
Ron Pritchard - LB
John Reaves - QB
Ken Riley - DB
Willie Shelby - HB
John Shinners - G
Bob Trumpy - TE
Rick Walker - TE
Mike Wells - QB
Wilson Whitley - DT
Reggie Williams - LB

1977 Cleveland

Dick Ambrose - LB
Bob Babich - LB
Ron Bolton - DB
Don Cockroft - K
Greg Coleman - K
Reggie Craig - WR
Thom Darden - DB
Barry Darrow - T
Oliver Davis - DB
Tom DeLeone - C
Al Dennis - G
Doug Dieken - T
Brian Duncan - FB
Earl Edwards - DT
Ken Ellis - DB
Ricky Feacher - WR
John Garlington - LB
Dave Graf - LB
Charlie Hall - LB
Gerald Irons - LB
Robert Jackson - G
Mark Johnson - LB
Ricky Jones - DB
Joe Jones - DE
Bob Lingenfelter - T
Dave Logan - WR
Terry Luck - QB
Dave Mays - QB
Cleo Miller - FB
Mack Mitchell - DE
Gary Parris - TE
Eddie Payton - HB
Tony Peters - DB
Larry Poole - HB
Greg Pruitt - HB
Mike Pruitt - FB
Oscar Roan - TE
Reggie Rucker - WR
Clarence Scott - DB
Henry Sheppard - G
Jerry Sherk - DT
Mickey Sims - DT
Brian Sipe - QB
Mike St. Clair - DE
Gerry Sullivan - C
Paul Warfield - WR
Lawrence Williams - WR
Roland Woolsey - DB

1977 Dallas

Benny Barnes - DB
Bob Breunig - LB
Larry Brinson - FB
Guy Brown - LB
Larry Cole - DT
Jim Cooper - G
Doug Dennison - HB
Pat Donovan - T
Tony Dorsett - HB
Billy Joe DuPree - TE
John Fitzgerald - C
Andy Frederick - T
Bill Gregory - DT
Cliff Harris - DB
Mike Hegman - LB
Tom Henderson - LB
Efren Herrera - K
Tony Hill - WR
Randy Hughes - DB
Bruce Huther - LB
Butch Johnson - WR
Too Tall Jones - DE
Aaron Kyle - DB
Scott Laidlaw - FB
Burton Lawless - G
D. D. Lewis - LB
Harvey Martin - DE
Ralph Neely - T
Robert Newhouse - FB
Drew Pearson - WR
Preston Pearson - HB
Jethro Pugh - DT
Tom Rafferty - G
Mel Renfro - DB
Golden Richards - WR
Jay Saldi - TE
Herbert Scott - G
Dave Stalls - DE
Roger Staubach - QB
Mark Washington - DB
Charlie Waters - DB
Randy White - DT
Danny White - QB
Rayfield Wright - T

1977 Denver

Hank Allison - T
Lyle Alzado - DE
Otis Armstrong - HB
Rich Baska - LB
Billy Bryan - G
Rubin Carter - NT
Barney Chavous - DE
Bucky Dilts - K
Jack Dolbin - WR
Ron Egloff - TE
Larry Evans - LB
Steve Foley - DB
Tom Glassic - G
Randy Gradishar - LB
John Grant - NT
Paul Howard - G
Glenn Hyde - T
Bernard Jackson - DB
Tom Jackson - LB
Jim Jensen - FB
Jon Keyworth - FB
Jim Kiick - HB
Rob Lytle - HB
Brison Manor - DE
Bobby Maples - C
Andy Maurer - T
Claudie Minor - T
Mike Montler - C
Craig Morton - QB
Haven Moses - WR
Rob Nairne - LB
Riley Odoms - TE
Chris Pane - DB
Craig Penrose - QB
Lonnie Perrin - FB
Randy Poltl - DB
Randy Rich - DB
Larry Riley - DB
Joe Rizzo - LB
Steve Schindler - G
John Schultz - WR
Paul Smith - DE
Bob Swenson - LB
Billy Thompson - DB
Godwin Turk - LB
Jim Turner - K
Rick Upchurch - WR
Norris Weese - QB
Louis Wright - DB

1977 Detroit

Gary Anderson - G
Lem Barney - DB
Luther Blue - WR
Lynn Boden - G
Russ Bolinger - G
Andy Bolton - HB
Dexter Bussey - HB
Gary Danielson - QB
Tony Daykin - LB
Doug English - DT
Rocky Freitas - T
Larry Hand - DT
Craig Hertwig - T
David Hill - TE
J. D. Hill - WR
Mitch Hoopes - K
Marv Hubbard - FB
James Hunter - DB
Ray Jarvis - WR
Dick Jauron - DB
Levi Johnson - DB
Rick Kane - HB
Horace King - FB
Greg Landry - QB
Bill Larson - TE
Jim Laslavic - LB
Mark Markovich - G
Mike McGraw - LB
Steve Mike-Mayer - K
Jim Mitchell - DE
Mel Mitchell - G
Jon Morris - C
Paul Naumoff - LB
Ed O'Neil - LB
Herb Orvis - DT
Eddie Payton - HB
Reggie Pinkney - DB
Ernie Price - DE
Joe Reed - QB
Randy Rich - DB
Charlie Sanders - TE
Ken Sanders - DE
Dave Simonson - T
Wilbur Summers - K
Garth Ten Napel - LB
Leonard Thompson - WR
Charlie Weaver - LB
Charlie West - DB
Tom Wickert - T
Walt Williams - DB
John Woodcock - DE
Jim Yarbrough - T

1977 Green Bay

Bert Askson - TE
Bob Barber - DE
David Beverly - K
John Brockington - FB
Willie Buchanon - DB
Mike Butler - DE
Fred Carr - LB
Jim Carter - LB
Jim Culbreath - FB
Lynn Dickey - QB
Brian Dowling - QB
Derrel Gofourth - C
Johnnie Gray - DB
Jim Gueno - LB
Don Hansen - LB
Willard Harrell - HB
Keith Hartwig - WR
Dennis Havig - G
Dick Himes - T
Melvin Jackson - G
Ezra Johnson - DE
Steve Knutson - T
Greg Koch - T
Mark Koncar - T
Bob Kowalkowski - G
Steve Luke - DB
Chester Marcol - K
Larry McCarren - C
Mike McCoy - DB
Rich McGeorge - TE
Herb McMath - DT
Terdell Middleton - HB
Tim Moresco - DB
Steve Odom - WR
Ken Payne - WR
Dave Pureifory - DT
Terry Randolph - DB
Dave Roller - DT
Nate Simpson - HB
Barty Smith - FB
Blane Smith - LB
Ollie Smith - WR
Aundra Thompson - WR
Tom Toner - LB
Eric Torkelson - FB
Randy Vataha - WR
Steve Wagner - DB
Gary Weaver - LB
David Whitehurst - QB
Sweeny Williams - DE

1977 Houston

Willie Alexander - DB
Warren Anderson - WR
Mike Barber - TE
Steve Baumgartner - DE
Elvin Bethea - DE
Gregg Bingham - LB
Robert Brazile - LB
Ken Burrough - WR
Albert Burton - DE
Skip Butler - K
Rob Carpenter - FB
David Carter - C
Ronnie Coleman - HB
Curley Culp - NT
Bill Currier - DB
Tom Dempsey - K
Andy Dorris - DE
Elbert Drungo - G
Tom Duniven - QB
Ed Fisher - G
Eddie Foster - WR
Toni Fritsch - K
Gary Garrison - WR
Jimmie Giles - TE
John Hadl - QB
Don Hardeman - FB
Conway Hayman - T
Kevin Hunt - T
Al Johnson - DB
Billy Johnson - WR
Ken Kennard - NT
Steve Kiner - LB
Ernest Kirk - DE
Kurt Knoff - DB
Carl Mauck - C
Zeke Moore - DB
Cliff Parsley - K
Dan Pastorini - QB
George Reihner - G
Mike Reinfeldt - DB
Greg Sampson - T
Rich Sowells - DB
Greg Stemrick - DB
Art Stringer - LB
Ted Thompson - LB
Morris Towns - T
Mike Voight - HB
Ted Washington - LB
Mike Weger - DB
Tim Wilson - FB
Jim Young - DE

1977 Kansas City

Tony Adams - QB
Billy Andrews - LB
Charlie Ane - C
Mark Bailey - FB
Gary Barbaro - DB
Ed Beckman - TE
John Brockington - FB
Larry Brunson - WR
Ray Burks - LB
Tim Collier - DB
Tom Condon - G
Ricky Davis - DB
Jimbo Elrod - LB
Cliff Frazier - DT
Charlie Getty - G
Chris Golub - DB
Tim Gray - DB
Gary Green - DB
Darius Helton - G
Matt Herkenhoff - T
Tom Howard - LB
MacArthur Lane - FB
Willie Lanier - LB
Willie Lee - DT
Mike Livingston - QB
John Lohmeyer - DE
Jim Lynch - LB
Henry Marshall - WR
Ted McKnight - HB
Pat McNeil - FB
Arnold Morgado - HB
Jim Nicholson - T
Whitney Paul - DE
Ed Podolak - HB
Tony Reed - HB
Dave Rozumek - LB
Jack Rudnay - C
Tony Samuels - TE
Bob Simmons - G
Keith Simons - DT
Jan Stenerud - K
Emmitt Thomas - DB
Charlie Wade - WR
Ricky Wesson - DB
Walter White - TE
Tom Wickert - T
Lawrence Williams - WR
Jerrel Wilson - K
Wilbur Young - DE

1977 LA Rams

Larry Brooks - DT
Bob Brudzinski - LB
Cullen Bryant - FB
John Cappelletti - FB
Al Cowlings - DE
Nolan Cromwell - DB
Fred Dryer - DE
Carl Ekern - LB
Dave Elmendorf - DB
Mike Fanning - DT
Vince Ferragamo - QB
Doug France - T
Pat Haden - QB
Dennis Harrah - G
Winston Hill - T
Greg Horton - G
Harold Jackson - WR
Monte Jackson - DB
Ron Jessie - WR
Jim Jodat - FB
Freeman Johns - WR
Cody Jones - DT
Rick Kay - LB
Tom Mack - G
Lawrence McCutcheon - HB
Kevin McLain - LB
Joe Namath - QB
Terry Nelson - TE
Rick Nuzum - C
Rod Perry - DB
Rod Phillips - FB
Bob Pifferini - LB
Jack Reynolds - LB
Isiah Robertson - LB
Rich Saul - C
Dwight Scales - WR
Rafael Septien - K
Bill Simpson - DB
Jackie Slater - G
Pat Thomas - DB
Wendell Tyler - HB
Billy Waddy - WR
Glen Walker - K
Jackie Wallace - DB
Jeff Williams - T
John Williams - T
Charle Young - TE
Jack Youngblood - DE
Jim Youngblood - LB

1977 Miami

John Alexander - DE
Dick Anderson - DB
Terry Anderson - WR
Charlie Babb - DB
Larry Ball - LB
Carl Barisich - NT
Bob Baumhower - NT
Kim Bokamper - LB
Wade Bosarge - DB
Norm Bulaich - FB
Rusty Chambers - LB
Charles Cornelius - DB
Mike Current - T
Gary Davis - HB
Vern Den Herder - DE
A. J. Duhe - DE
Rick Dvorak - DE
Tim Foley - DB
Larry Gordon - LB
Bob Griese - QB
Duriel Harris - WR
Leroy Harris - FB
Bob Heinz - NT
Curtis Johnson - DB
Mike Kolen - LB
Bob Kuechenberg - G
Jim Langer - C
Larry Little - G
Benny Malone - HB
Jim Mandich - TE
Bob Matheson - LB
Loaird McCreary - TE
Mike Michel - K
Mel Mitchell - G
Nat Moore - HB
Wayne Moore - T
Ed Newman - G
Don Nottingham - FB
Wally Pesuit - G
Earnest Rhone - LB
Vern Roberson - DB
Guy Roberts - LB
Larry Seiple - TE
Freddie Solomon - WR
Don Strock - QB
Norris Thomas - DB
Andre Tillman - TE
Steve Towle - LB
Rick Volk - DB
Stan Winfrey - FB
Garo Yepremian - K
Steve Young - T

1977 Minnesota

Nate Allen - DB
Joe Blahak - DB
Matt Blair - LB
Bobby Bryant - DB
Neil Clabo - K
Fred Cox - K
Steve Craig - TE
Rick Danmeier - K
Doug Dumler - C
Carl Eller - DE
Chuck Foreman - HB
Charlie Goodrum - G
Bob Grim - WR
Windlan Hall - DB
Wes Hamilton - G
Tom Hannon - DB
Wally Hilgenberg - LB
Joey Jackson - DE
Sammy Johnson - HB
Mark Kellar - FB
Tommy Kramer - QB
Paul Krause - DB
Bob Lee - QB
Jim Marshall - DE
Brent McClanahan - FB
Fred McNeill - LB
Robert Miller - FB
Manfred Moore - HB
Mark Mullaney - DE
Alan Page - DT
Ahmad Rashad - WR
Steve Riley - T
Jeff Siemon - LB
Scott Studwell - LB
Doug Sutherland - DT
Dennis Swilley - G
Fran Tarkenton - QB
Mick Tingelhoff - C
Bob Tucker - TE
Stu Voigt - TE
Ed White - G
James White - DT
Sammy White - WR
Phillip Wise - DB
Jeff Wright - DB
Nate Wright - DB
Ron Yary - T

1977 New England

Julius Adams - DE
Sam Adams - G
Pete Barnes - LB
Doug Beaudoin - DB
Richard Bishop - NT
Greg Boyd - DE
Pete Brock - G
Steve Burks - WR
Don Calhoun - HB
Al Chandler - TE
Raymond Clayborn - DB
Dick Conn - DB
Ray Costict - LB
Sam Cunningham - FB
Ike Forte - HB
Tim Fox - DB
Russ Francis - TE
Leon Gray - T
Steve Grogan - QB
Ray Hamilton - NT
John Hannah - G
Don Hasselbeck - TE
Mike Haynes - DB
Bob Howard - DB
Sam Hunt - LB
Bob Hyland - C
Horace Ivory - HB
Shelby Jordan - T
Steve King - LB
Bill Lenkaitis - C
Mel Lunsford - DE
Prentice McCray - DB
Tony McGee - DE
Bob McKay - T
Art Moore - NT
Stanley Morgan - WR
Steve Nelson - LB
Tom Neville - T
Mike Patrick - K
Jess Phillips - FB
Rod Shoate - LB
John Smith - K
Darryl Stingley - WR
Fred Sturt - G
Donald Westbrook - WR
Steve Zabel - LB

1977 New Orleans

Steve Baumgartner - DE
Tom Blanchard - K
Ken Bordelon - LB
Wade Bosarge - DB
Greg Boykin - HB
Larry Burton - WR
Joe Campbell - DE
Craig Cassady - DB
Clarence Chapman - DB
Henry Childs - TE
Chuck Crist - DB
Oakley Dalton - DT
Bobby Douglass - QB
Joe Federspiel - LB
Mike Fultz - DT
Tony Galbreath - FB
John Gilliam - WR
Elois Grooms - DE
Lee Gross - C
Don Herrmann - WR
John Hill - C
Dave Hubbard - T
Pat Hughes - LB
Ernie Jackson - DB
Kim Jones - FB
Rick Kingrea - LB
Dave Lafary - T
Archie Manning - QB
Jim Marsalis - DB
Rich Mauti - WR
Jim Merlo - LB
Marv Montgomery - T
Derland Moore - DT
Don Morrison - T
Chuck Muncie - HB
Tom Myers - DB
Joel Parker - WR
Bob Pollard - DE
Elex Price - DT
Kurt Schumacher - G
Bobby Scott - QB
Jimmy Stewart - DB
Terry Stieve - G
Mike Strachan - HB
Richie Szaro - K
Jim Thaxton - TE
John Watson - C
Greg Westbrooks - LB
Leonard Willis - WR
Robert Woods - T
Emanuel Zanders - G

1977 NY Giants

Troy Archer - DT
Gordon Bell - HB
Boyd Brown - TE
Bill Bryant - DB
Harry Carson - LB
Karl Chandler - C
Larry Csonka - FB
Joe Danelo - K
Randy Dean - QB
Al Dixon - TE
Rick Dvorak - DE
Bill Ellenbogen - G
Mike Gibbons - T
Jerry Golsteyn - QB
Gordon Gravelle - T
Jack Gregory - DE
Bobby Hammond - HB
Harold Hart - HB
John Hicks - G
Ralph Hill - C
Dave Jennings - K
Gary Jeter - DE
Ernie Jones - DB
Brian Kelley - LB
Doug Kotar - HB
Dan Lloyd - LB
Larry Mallory - DB
Frank Marion - LB
Ed Marshall - WR
George Martin - DE
John Mendenhall - DT
Ron Mikolajczyk - G
Emery Moorehead - WR
Tom Mullen - T
Johnny Perkins - WR
Jim Pietrzak - DT
Joe Pisarcik - QB
Clyde Powers - DB
Beasley Reece - DB
Ray Rhodes - DB
Jim Robinson - WR
Andy Selfridge - LB
Gary Shirk - TE
Willie Spencer - FB
Jim Stienke - DB
Bob Tucker - TE
J. T. Turner - DT
Doug Van Horn - G
Brad Van Pelt - LB
Larry Watkins - FB

1977 NY Jets

Dan Alexander - G
Darrell Austin - G
Jerome Barkum - TE
Carl Barzilauskas - DT
Jeff Bleamer - T
Greg Buttle - LB
Duane Carrell - K
Rich Caster - WR
Scott Dierking - FB
Shelton Diggs - WR
Marty Domres - QB
John Ebersole - LB
Joe Fields - C
Clark Gaines - FB
Billy Hardee - DB
Bruce Harper - HB
John Hennessy - DE
Mike Hennigan - LB
Larry Keller - LB
Joe Klecko - DT
David Knight - WR
Pat Leahy - K
Kevin Long - HB
Ron Mabra - DB
Tank Marshall - DT
Bob Martin - LB
Tommy Marvaso - DB
Richard Neal - DE
Tom Newton - FB
Burgess Owens - DB
Al Palewicz - LB
Artimus Parker - DB
Lawrence Pillers - DE
Marvin Powell - T
Garry Puetz - T
Bob Raba - TE
Chuck Ramsey - K
Randy Rasmussen - G
Matt Robinson - QB
John Roman - G
Carl Russ - LB
Abdul Salaam - DT
Ken Schroy - DB
Shafer Suggs - DB
Ed Taylor - DB
Richard Todd - QB
Maurice Tyler - DB
Wesley Walker - WR
Charlie White - HB
Robert Woods - T

1977 Oakland

Butch Atkinson - DB
Pete Banaszak - FB
Warren Bankston - TE
Jeff Barnes - LB
Fred Biletnikoff - WR
Morris Bradshaw - WR
Cliff Branch - WR
Willie Brown - DB
George Buehler - G
Dave Casper - TE
Neal Colzie - DB
Dave Dalby - C
Clarence Davis - HB
Carl Garrett - HB
Hubert Ginn - HB
Ray Guy - K
Willie Hall - LB
Lester Hayes - DB
Ted Hendricks - LB
David Humm - QB
Steve Jackson - DB
Rick Jennings - WR
Monte Johnson - LB
Ted Kwalick - TE
Henry Lawrence - T
Errol Mann - K
Rod Martin - LB
Mickey Marvin - G
John Matuszak - DE
Randy McClanahan - LB
Mike McCoy - NT
Charlie Phillips - DB
Charles Philyaw - DE
Mike Rae - QB
Floyd Rice - LB
Terry Robiskie - FB
Dave Rowe - NT
Art Shell - T
Mike Siani - WR
Otis Sistrunk - DE
Ken Stabler - QB
Steve Sylvester - C
Jack Tatum - DB
Skip Thomas - DB
Pat Toomay - DE
Gene Upshaw - G
Mark van Eeghen - FB
John Vella - T
Phil Villapiano - LB
Jimmy Warren - DB

1977 Philadelphia

Bill Bergey - LB
James Betterson - FB
John Bunting - LB
Lem Burnham - DE
Harold Carmichael - WR
Herman Edwards - DB
Tom Ehlers - LB
Cleveland Franklin - FB
Dennis Franks - C
Roman Gabriel - QB
Ed George - T
Donnie Green - T
Carl Hairston - DE
Wally Henry - WR
Mike Hogan - FB
Johnny Jackson - NT
Ron Jaworski - QB
Ove Johansson - K
Charlie Johnson - NT
Eric Johnson - DB
Spike Jones - K
Wade Key - G
Keith Krepfle - TE
Pete Lazetich - NT
Frank LeMaster - LB

Randy Logan - DB
Tom Luken - G
Herb Lusk - HB
Drew Mahalic - LB
Larry Marshall - DB
Nick Mike-Mayer - K
Mark Mitchell - DB
Wilbert Montgomery - HB
Guy Morriss - C
Horst Muhlmann - K
Dennis Nelson - T
Richard Osborne - TE
John Outlaw - DB
Vince Papale - WR
James Reed - LB
Deac Sanders - DB
Jerry Sisemore - G
Manny Sistrunk - DE
Charlie Smith - WR
Tom Sullivan - HB
Terry Tautolo - LB
Art Thoms - DE
Stan Walters - T

1977 Pittsburgh

Jimmy Allen - DB
John Banaszak - DE
Rocky Bleier - HB
Mel Blount - DB
Terry Bradshaw - QB
Larry Brown - T
Jim Clack - G
Robin Cole - LB
Brad Cousino - LB
Bennie Cunningham - TE
Sam Davis - G
Jack Deloplaine - HB
Tony Dungy - DB
Glen Edwards - DB
Rick Engles - K
Steve Furness - DT
Roy Gerela - K
Neil Graff - QB
Joe Greene - DT
L. C. Greenwood - DE
Randy Grossman - TE
Jack Ham - LB
Franco Harris - FB
Reggie Harrison - FB
Ernie Holmes - DT
Jon Kolb - T
Mike Kruczek - QB
Dave LaCrosse - LB
Jack Lambert - LB
Frank Lewis - WR
Alvin Maxson - HB
Gerry Mullins - G
Ted Petersen - C
Ray Pinney - C
Ernest Pough - WR
Brent Sexton - DB
Donnie Shell - DB
Jim Smith - WR
Laverne Smith - HB
John Stallworth - WR
Lynn Swann - WR
J.T. Thomas - DB
Sidney Thornton - FB
Loren Toews - LB
Mike Wagner - DB
Bobby Walden - K
Mike Webster - C
Dwight White - DE
Dennis Winston - LB

1977 St. Louis

Carl Allen - DB
Kurt Allerman - LB
Hank Allison - T
Mark Arneson - LB
Dan Audick - G
Jim Bakken - K
Tom Banks - C
Bob Bell - DE
Tim Black - LB
Bill Bradley - DB
Tom Brahaney - C
J.V. Cain - TE
Duane Carrell - K
Rondy Colbert - DB
Charles Davis - DT
Mike Dawson - DT
Dan Dierdorf - T
Conrad Dobler - G
Billy Donckers - QB
Roger Finnie - T
Robert Giblin - DB
Mel Gray - WR
Ike Harris - WR
Jim Hart - QB
Steve Jones - HB
Terry Joyce - K
Tim Kearney - LB
Marv Kellum - LB
Jerry Latin - HB
Terry Metcalf - HB
Wayne Morris - FB
Steve Neils - LB
Lee Nelson - DB
Brad Oates - T
Steve Okoniewski - DT
Jim Otis - FB
Walt Patulski - DT
Ken Reaves - DB
Mike Sensibaugh - DB
Jeff Severson - DB
Perry Smith - DB
Jackie Smith - TE
Ken Stone - WR
Pat Tilley - WR
Roger Wehrli - DB
Eric Williams - LB
Keith Wortman - G
Ron Yankowski - DE
Bob Young - G
John Zook - DE

1977 San Diego

Charles Aiu - G
Larry Barnes - FB
Hank Bauer - HB
Rolf Benirschke - K
Chuck Bradley - TE
Booker Brown - T
Pat Curran - TE
Fred Dean - DE
Charles DeJurnett - DT
Larry Dorsey - WR
Jerome Dove - DB
Clarence Duren - DB
Dan Fouts - QB
Mike Fuller - DB
Don Goode - LB
Tom Graham - LB
James Harris - QB
Bob Horn - LB
Gary Johnson - DT
Charlie Joiner - WR
Leroy Jones - DE
Louie Kelcher - DT
Bob Klein - TE
John Lee - DE
Woodrow Lowe - LB
Don Macek - G
Bo Matthews - FB
Dwight McDonald - WR
Rick Middleton - LB
Bill Munson - QB
Cliff Olander - QB
Artie Owens - WR
Ralph Perretta - C
Ray Preston - LB
Johnny Rodgers - WR
Bob Rush - C
Pete Shaw - DB
Billy Shields - T
Hal Stringert - DB
Joe Washington - HB
Russ Washington - T
Jeff West - TE
Doug Wilkerson - G
Clarence Williams - FB
Mike Williams - DB
Don Woods - FB
Rickey Young - HB

1977 San Francisco

John Ayers - T
Mike Baldassin - LB
Cas Banaszek - T
Jean Barrett - T
Stan Black - DB
Ed Bradley - LB
Scott Bull - QB
Mike Burns - DB
Tony Cline - DE
Bill Cooke - DT
Randy Cross - C
Cleveland Elam - DT
Bruce Elia - LB
Keith Fahnhorst - T
Bob Ferrell - FB
Ed Galigher - DT
Cedrick Hardman - DE
Willie Harper - LB
Kenny Harrison - WR
Tommy Hart - DE
Paul Hofer - HB
Wilbur Jackson - FB
Rick Jennings - WR
Jim Lash - WR
Steve Lawson - G
Tony Leonard - DB
Eddie Lewis - DB
Al Matthews - DB
Willie McGee - WR
Ralph McGill - DB
Johnny Miller - G
Dale Mitchell - LB
Tom Mitchell - TE
Jim Obradovich - TE
Woody Peoples - G
Mel Phillips - DB
Jim Plunkett - QB
Steve Rivera - WR
Paul Seal - TE
Ron Singleton - T
Howard Stidham - LB
Bruce Taylor - DB
Skip Vanderbundt - LB
Dave Washington - LB
Gene Washington - WR
Jimmy Webb - DT
Ray Wersching - K
Dave Williams - HB
Delvin Williams - HB
Tom Wittum - K

1977 Seattle

Sam Adkins - QB
Steve August - T
Autry Beamon - DB
Nick Bebout - T
Terry Beeson - LB
Tony Benjamin - FB
Dennis Boyd - DE
Dave Brown - DB
Ron Coder - G
Pete Cronan - LB
Andy Dorris - DE
Don Dufek - DB
Ron East - DT
Rick Engles - K
Norm Evans - T
Duke Fergerson - WR
Ken Geddes - LB
Sammy Green - LB
Richard Harris - DE
Ron Howard - TE
Al Hunter - HB
Gordon Jolley - G
Horace Jones - DE
Mike Jones - LB
Art Kuehn - C
Steve Largent - WR
John Leypoldt - K
Doug Long - DB
Bob Lurtsema - DT
Tom Lynch - G
Ed Marinaro - FB
Amos Martin - LB
Sam McCullum - WR
Eddie McMillan - DB
Charles McShane - LB
Steve Myer - QB
Bob Newton - G
Steve Niehaus - DT
Walter Packer - DB
Steve Preece - DB
Steve Raible - WR
Fred Rayhle - TE
Geoff Reece - C
Alden Roche - DE
Bill Sandifer - DT
John Sawyer - TE
David Sims - HB
Sherman Smith - HB
Don Testerman - FB
Herman Weaver - K
Cornell Webster - DB
John Yarno - C
Jim Zorn - QB

1977 Tampa Bay

Ricky Bell - FB
Jeb Blount - QB
Rik Bonness - LB
Cedric Brown - DB
Gary Butler - TE
Darryl Carlton - T
Blanchard Carter - T
Louis Carter - HB
Mark Cotney - DB
Anthony Davis - HB
Jimmy DuBose - FB
Howard Fest - G
Dave Green - K
Isaac Hagins - WR
Charley Hannah - DE
Paul Harris - LB
Randy Hedberg - QB
Gary Huff - QB
Cecil Johnson - LB
Greg Johnson - DT
Randy Johnson - G
Curtis Jordan - DB
Bill Kollar - NT
Allan Leavitt - K
Mike Lemon - LB
Dave Lewis - LB
John McKay - WR
Dan Medlin - G
Bob Moore - TE
Larry Mucker - WR
Dana Nafziger - TE
Jack Novak - TE
Morris Owens - WR
Walter Packer - DB
Dave Pear - NT
George Ragsdale - WR
Dave Reavis - T
Danny Reece - DB
Glenn Robinson - DE
Council Rudolph - DE
Dan Ryczek - C
Dewey Selmon - LB
Lee Roy Selmon - DE
Mike Washington - DB
Jack Wender - HB
Jeris White - DB
Ed Williams - FB
Steven Wilson - G
Jeff Winans - G
Stan Winfrey - FB
Richard Wood - LB

1977 Washington

Mike Bragg - K
Eddie Brown - DB
Bill Brundige - DT
Bob Brunet - HB
Danny Buggs - WR
Dave Butz - DT
Mike Curtis - LB
Brad Dusek - LB
Pat Fischer - DB
Ted Fritsch - C
Jean Fugett - TE
Frank Grant - WR
Windlan Hall - DB
Chris Hanburger - LB
Clarence Harmon - HB
Joe Harris - LB
Len Hauss - C
Terry Hermeling - G
Dallas Hickman - DE
Calvin Hill - FB
Ken Houston - DB
Dennis Johnson - DE
Larry Jones - WR
Jim Kiick - HB
Billy Kilmer - QB
Bob Kuziel - C
Bill Larson - TE
Joe Lavender - DB
Karl Lorch - DE
Ron McDole - DE
Harold McLinton - LB
Mark Moseley - K
Eddie Moss - FB
Mark Murphy - DB
Dan Nugent - G
Stu O'Dell - LB
Brig Owens - DB
John Riggins - FB
Ron Saul - G
Jake Scott - DB
Jerry Smith - TE
George Starke - T
Timothy Stokes - T
Diron Talbert - DT
Charley Taylor - WR
Joe Theismann - QB
Mike Thomas - HB
Rusty Tillman - LB
Gerard Williams - DB
Will Wynn - DE
Pete Wysocki - LB

1978 Atlanta

Jim Bailey - DT
Steve Bartkowski - QB
Bubba Bean - HB
Greg Brezina - LB
Warren Bryant - T
Rick Byas - DB
Ray Easterling - DB
Mike Esposito - HB
Wilson Faumuina - DT
Edgar Fields - DE
Wally Francis - WR
George Franklin - FB
Lewis Gilbert - TE
Bob Glazebrook - DB
Claude Humphrey - DE
Alfred Jackson - WR
Ernie Jackson - DB
John James - K
Alfred Jenkins - WR
June Jones - QB
Mike Kenn - T
Fulton Kuykendall - LB
Rolland Lawrence - DB
Mike Lewis - DT
Tim Mazzetti - K
Ron McCartney - LB
Dewey McClain - LB
Phil McKinnely - T
Jeff Merrow - DE
Jim Mitchell - TE
Marv Montgomery - T
Ken Moore - TE
Tom Moriarty - DB
Ralph Ortega - LB
Ricky Patton - HB
Dennis Pearson - WR
Robert Pennywell - LB
Tom Pridemore - DB
Frank Reed - DB
Billy Ryckman - WR
Paul Ryczek - C
Dave Scott - G
Haskel Stanback - FB
Fred Steinfort - K
Steve Stewart - LB
Jim Stienke - DB
Ray Strong - HB
Garth Ten Napel - LB
R.C. Thielemann - G
Jeff Van Note - C
James Wright - TE
Jeff Yeates - DE

1978 Baltimore

Mack Alston - TE
Ron Baker - G
Mike Barnes - DT
Tim Baylor - DB
Lyle Blackwood - DB
Forrest Blue - C
Randy Burke - WR
Roger Carr - WR
Fred Cook - DE
Glenn Doughty - WR
John Dutton - DE
Joe Ehrmann - DT
Wade Griffin - T
Don Hardeman - FB
Dwight Harrison - DB
Ken Huff - G
Marshall Johnson - WR
Bert Jones - QB
Mike Kirkland - QB
George Kunz - T
Bruce Laird - DB
Roosevelt Leaks - FB
David Lee - K
Ron Lee - FB
Toni Linhart - K
Derrel Luce - LB
Tom MacLeod - LB
Greg Marshall - DT
Reese McCall - TE
Don McCauley - HB
Ken Mendenhall - C
Don Morrison - T
Lloyd Mumphord - DB
Doug Nettles - DB
Stu O'Dell - LB
Ray Oldham - DB
Calvin O'Neal - LB
Herb Orvis - DT
Mike Ozdowski - DE
Bob Pratt - G
Dave Rowe - DT
Sanders Shiver - LB
Mike Siani - WR
Ed Simonini - LB
Norm Thompson - DB
Bill Troup - QB
Bob Van Duyne - T
Joe Washington - HB
Stan White - LB

1978 Buffalo

Bill Adams - G
Doug Becker - LB
Jim Braxton - FB
Curtis Brown - FB
Mario Celotto - LB
Bob Chandler - WR
Mario Clark - DB
Joe DeLamielleure - G
Tom Dempsey - K
Joe Devlin - T
Phil Dokes - DT
Elbert Drungo - T
Tom Ehlers - LB
Joe Ferguson - QB
Mike Franckowiak - TE
Steve Freeman - DB
Reuben Gant - TE
Tom Graham - LB
Will Grant - C
Tony Greene - DB
Dee Hardison - DT
Roland Hooks - HB
Scott Hutchinson - DE
Mekeli Ieremia - DT
Rusty Jackson - K
Dan Jilek - LB
Dennis Johnson - FB
Dennis Johnson - DT
Doug Jones - DB
Ken Jones - T
Mike Kadish - DT
Merv Krakau - LB
Mike Levenseller - WR
Frank Lewis - WR
Dave Mays - QB
Randy McClanahan - LB
Reggie McKenzie - G
Eddie McMillan - DB
Terry Miller - HB
Keith Moody - DB
Bill Munson - QB
Shane Nelson - LB
Willie Parker - C
Lou Piccone - WR
Steve Powell - HB
Charles Romes - DB
Lucius Sanford - LB
Marvin Switzer - DB
Larry Walton - WR
Sherman White - DE
Ben Williams - DE
Leonard Willis - WR

1978 Chi. Bears

Ted Albrecht - T
Lionel Antoine - T
Bob Avellini - QB
Brian Baschnagel - WR
Doug Becker - LB
Art Best - HB
Doug Buffone - LB
Gary Campbell - LB
Mike Cobb - TE
Chris Devlin - LB
Robin Earl - FB
Vince Evans - QB
Gary Fencik - DB
Wentford Gaines - DB
Roland Harper - FB
Tommy Hart - DE
Mike Hartenstine - DE
Bruce Herron - LB
Tom Hicks - LB
Noah Jackson - G
Dan Jiggetts - T
Greg Latta - TE
Dennis Lick - T
Virgil Livers - DB
Jerry Meyers - DT
Mike Morgan - FB
Jon Morris - C
Jerry Muckensturm - LB
Dan Neal - C
Jim Osborne - DT
Alan Page - DT
Bob Parsons - TE
Walter Payton - HB
Mike Phipps - QB
Doug Plank - DB
Bo Rather - WR
Golden Richards - WR
Don Rives - LB
Ron Rydalch - DT
Terry Schmidt - DB
Steve Schubert - WR
James Scott - WR
Jeff Sevy - G
Brad Shearer - DT
John Skibinski - FB
Revie Sorey - G
Mike Spivey - DB
Bob Thomas - K
Len Walterscheid - DB

1978 Cincinnati

Ken Anderson - QB
Chris Bahr - K
Don Bass - TE
Louis Breeden - DB
Billy Brooks - WR
Ross Browner - DE
Glenn Bujnoch - G
Gary Burley - DE
Blair Bush - C
Glenn Cameron - LB
Boobie Clark - FB
Marvin Cobb - DB
James Corbett - TE
Isaac Curtis - WR
Tony Davis - FB
Tom DePaso - LB
Chris Devlin - LB
Tom Dinkel - LB
Mark Donahue - G
Eddie Edwards - DT
Lenvil Elliott - HB
Archie Griffin - HB
Ray Griffin - DB
Bo Harris - LB
Rob Hertel - QB
Vern Holland - T
Ron Hunt - T
Dick Jauron - DB
Pete Johnson - FB
Bob Johnson - C
Dave Lapham - G
Dennis Law - WR
Jim LeClair - LB
Rufus Mayes - T
Pat McInally - WR
Melvin Morgan - DB
Scott Perry - DB
Ray Phillips - LB
Dave Pureifory - DE
John Reaves - QB
Ken Riley - DB
Tom Ruud - LB
Ron Shumon - LB
Deacon Turner - HB
Ted Vincent - DT
Rick Walker - TE
Wilson Whitley - DT
Reggie Williams - LB
Mike Wilson - T

1978 Cleveland

Dick Ambrose - LB
Bob Babich - LB
Leo Biedermann - T
Ron Bolton - DB
George Buehler - G
Don Cockroft - K
Larry Collins - HB
Thom Darden - DB
Barry Darrow - T
Oliver Davis - DB
Tom DeLeone - C
Doug Dieken - T
Earl Edwards - DT
Johnny Evans - QB
Greg Fairchild - G
Ricky Feacher - WR
Dave Graf - LB
Charlie Hall - LB
Calvin Hill - FB
Gerald Irons - LB
Robert Jackson - LB
Robert Jackson - G
Ricky Jones - DB
Joe Jones - DE
Dave Logan - WR
Tom London - DB
Clay Matthews - LB
Cleo Miller - HB
Mark Miller - QB
Mack Mitchell - DE
Ozzie Newsome - TE
Gary Parris - TE
Tony Peters - DB
Greg Pruitt - HB
Mike Pruitt - FB
Randy Rich - DB
Oscar Roan - TE
Reggie Rucker - WR
Clarence Scott - DB
Henry Sheppard - G
Jerry Sherk - DT
Mickey Sims - DT
Brian Sipe - QB
Mike St. Clair - DE
Gerry Sullivan - C
Tom Sullivan - HB
Leo Tierney - C
Jesse Turnbow - DT
Keith Wright - WR

1978 Dallas

Benny Barnes - DB
Larry Bethea - DT
Alois Blackwell - HB
Bob Breunig - LB
Larry Brinson - FB
Guy Brown - LB
Glenn Carano - QB
Larry Cole - DT
Jim Cooper - C
Doug Dennison - HB
Pat Donovan - T
Tony Dorsett - HB
Billy Joe DuPree - TE
John Fitzgerald - C
Andy Frederick - T
Cliff Harris - DB
Mike Hegman - LB
Tom Henderson - LB
Tony Hill - WR
Randy Hughes - DB
Bruce Huther - LB
Butch Johnson - WR
Too Tall Jones - DE
Aaron Kyle - DB
Scott Laidlaw - FB
Burton Lawless - G
D. D. Lewis - LB
Harvey Martin - DE
Robert Newhouse - FB
Drew Pearson - WR
Preston Pearson - HB
Jethro Pugh - DT
Tom Rafferty - G
Tom Randall - G
Golden Richards - WR
Jay Saldi - TE
Herbert Scott - G
Rafael Septien - K
Jackie Smith - TE
Dave Stalls - DT
Roger Staubach - QB
Robert Steele - WR
Dennis Thurman - DB
Mark Washington - DB
Charlie Waters - DB
Randy White - DT
Danny White - QB
Rayfield Wright - T

1978 Denver

Lyle Alzado - DE
Otis Armstrong - HB
Bill Bain - T
Billy Bryan - C
Larry Canada - FB
Rubin Carter - NT
Barney Chavous - DE
Bucky Dilts - K
Jack Dolbin - WR
Ron Egloff - TE
Larry Evans - LB
Steve Foley - DB
Tom Glassic - G
Randy Gradishar - LB
John Grant - NT
Maurice Harvey - DB
Paul Howard - G
Glenn Hyde - T
Bernard Jackson - DB
Tom Jackson - LB
Jon Keyworth - FB
Vince Kinney - WR
Don Latimer - NT
Rob Lytle - HB
Brison Manor - DE
Bobby Maples - C
Claudie Minor - T
Bob Moore - TE
Craig Morton - QB
Haven Moses - WR
Rob Nairne - LB
Tom Neville - T
Riley Odoms - TE
Chris Pane - DB
Craig Penrose - QB
Lonnie Perrin - FB
Dave Preston - HB
Joe Rizzo - LB
Steve Schindler - G
John Schultz - WR
Paul Smith - DE
Bob Swenson - LB
Billy Thompson - DB

Godwin Turk - LB
Jim Turner - K
Rick Upchurch - WR
Norris Weese - QB
Charlie West - DB
Louis Wright - DB

1978 Detroit

Jimmy Allen - DB
Gary Anderson - G
Al Baker - DE
Karl Baldischwiler - T
Luther Blue - WR
Lynn Boden - G
Andy Bolton - HB
Luther Bradley - DB
Willie Brock - C
Mike Burns - DB
Dexter Bussey - HB
Ken Callicutt - HB
Karl Chandler - C
Bill Cooke - DT
Gary Danielson - QB
Tony Daykin - LB
Dan Dickel - LB
Homer Elias - G
Doug English - DT
Bill Fifer - T
Amos Fowler - G
Lawrence Gaines - FB
Dave Gallagher - DT
Bill Gay - TE
Dan Gray - DT
Donnie Green - T
Donnie Hickman - G
David Hill - TE
James Hunter - DB
Ray Jarvis - WR
Rick Kane - HB
Horace King - FB
Greg Landry - QB
Tony Leonard - DB
Willie McGee - WR
Mike Montler - C
Paul Naumoff - LB
Brad Oates - T
Ed O'Neil - LB
Reggie Pinkney - DB
Ernie Price - DE
Dave Pureifory - DE
Joe Reed - QB
Bruce Rhodes - DB
Benny Ricardo - K
Ken Sanders - DE
Freddie Scott - WR
Tom Skladany - K
John Sokolosky - C
Tony Sumler - DB
Larry Tearry - C
Nat Terry - DB
Jesse Thompson - WR
Leonard Thompson - WR
Dave Washington - LB
Charlie Weaver - LB
Walt Williams - DB
John Woodcock - DT

1978 Green Bay

John Anderson - LB
Bob Barber - DE
Carl Barzilauskas - DT
David Beverly - K
Elmo Boyd - WR
Willie Buchanon - DB
Mike Butler - DE
Jim Carter - LB
Frank Chesley - LB
Paul Coffman - TE
Jim Culbreath - FB
Mike Douglass - LB
Bobby Douglass - QB
Derrel Gofourth - G
Johnnie Gray - DB
Jim Gueno - LB
Leotis Harris - G
Estus Hood - DB
Mike Hunt - LB
Melvin Jackson - G
Danny Johnson - LB
Ezra Johnson - DE
Terry Jones - DT
Greg Koch - T
Walt Landers - FB
James Lofton - WR
Steve Luke - DB
Chester Marcol - K
Larry McCarren - C
Mike McCoy - DB
Rich McGeorge - TE
Terdell Middleton - HB
Rick Nuzum - C
Steve Odom - WR
Dave Roller - DT
Paul Rudzinski - LB
Howard Sampson - DB
Nate Simpson - HB
Gerald Skinner - T
Barty Smith - FB
Dennis Sproul - QB
Timothy Stokes - T
Willie Taylor - WR
Aundra Thompson - WR
Eric Torkelson - HB
Walter Tullis - WR
Steve Wagner - DB
Gary Weaver - LB
David Whitehurst - QB

1978 Houston

Willie Alexander - DB
Mike Barber - TE
Steve Baumgartner - DE
Elvin Bethea - DE
Gregg Bingham - LB
Robert Brazile - LB
Ken Burrough - WR
Earl Campbell - HB
Rob Carpenter - FB
David Carter - C
Rich Caster - WR
Ronnie Coleman - HB
Curley Culp - NT
Bill Currier - DB
Anthony Davis - HB
Jimmy Dean - DE
Johnnie Dirden - WR
Andy Dorris - DE
Brian Duncan - HB
Ed Fisher - G
Toni Fritsch - K
Conway Hayman - T
Al Johnson - DB
Billy Johnson - WR
Ken Kennard - NT
Steve Kiner - LB
Kurt Knoff - DB
Carl Mauck - C
Alvin Maxson - HB
Guido Merkens - WR
Gifford Nielsen - QB
Cliff Parsley - K
Dan Pastorini - QB
Larry Poole - HB
George Reihner - G
Mike Reinfeldt - DB
Mike Renfro - WR
Conrad Rucker - TE
Greg Sampson - T
John Schuhmacher - G
Greg Stemrick - DB
Art Stringer - LB
Ted Thompson - LB
Morris Towns - T
Robert Turner - HB
Ted Washington - LB
C.L. Whittington - DB
J. C. Wilson - DB
Tim Wilson - FB
Robert Woods - WR
Jim Young - DE

1978 Kansas City

Tony Adams - QB
Zenon Andrusyshyn - K
Charlie Ane - C
Mark Bailey - FB
Gary Barbaro - DB
Ed Beckman - TE
Horace Belton - HB
Larry Brown - T
Ted Burgmeier - DB
Tim Collier - DB
Tom Condon - G
Larry Dorsey - WR
Jimbo Elrod - LB
Charlie Getty - T
Tim Gray - DB
Gary Green - DB
Matt Herkenhoff - T
Sylvester Hicks - DE
Tom Howard - LB
Charles Jackson - LB
Stan Johnson - NT
Bill Kellar - ER
MacArthur Lane - FB
Dave Lindstrom - DE
Mike Livingston - QB
Jeff Lloyd - NT
Henry Marshall - WR
Larry Marshall - HB
Ted McKnight - HB
Jerrold McRae - WR
Ray Milo - DB
Arnold Morgado - FB
Jim Nicholson - T
Ricky Odom - DB
Don Parrish - NT
Whitney Paul - LB
Eddie Payton - HB
Clyde Powers - DB
Tony Reed - HB
Dave Rozumek - LB
Jack Rudnay - C
Tony Samuels - TE
Clarence Sanders - LB
Bob Simmons - G
J. T. Smith - WR
Gary Spani - LB
Jan Stenerud - K
Art Still - DE
Emmitt Thomas - DB
Rod Walters - G
Walter White - TE

1978 LA Rams

Larry Brooks - DT
Eddie Brown - DB
Bob Brudzinski - LB
Cullen Bryant - FB
John Cappelletti - HB
Frank Corral - K
Nolan Cromwell - DB
Anthony Davis - HB
Preston Dennard - WR
Reggie Doss - DE
Fred Dryer - DE
Carl Ekern - LB
Dave Elmendorf - DB
Mike Fanning - DT
Vince Ferragamo - QB
Doug France - T
Ed Fulton - G
Pat Haden - QB
Dennis Harrah - G
Greg Horton - G
Ron Jessie - WR
Jim Jodat - FB
Cody Jones - DT
Jerry Latin - HB
Tom Mack - G
Larry Marshall - HB
Lawrence McCutcheon - HB
Kevin McLain - LB
Willie Miller - WR
Terry Nelson - TE
Dwayne O'Steen - DB
Rod Perry - DB
Rod Phillips - FB
Jack Reynolds - LB
Isiah Robertson - LB
Dan Ryczek - C
Rich Saul - C
Dwight Scales - WR
Bill Simpson - DB
Jackie Slater - T
Doug Smith - C
Ron Smith - WR
Pat Thomas - DB
Wendell Tyler - HB
Billy Waddy - WR
Glen Walker - K
Jackie Wallace - DB
John Williams - T
Charle Young - TE
Jack Youngblood - DE
Jim Youngblood - LB

1978 Miami

John Alexander - DE
Terry Anderson - WR
Charlie Babb - DB
Larry Ball - LB
Carl Barisich - NT
Bob Baumhower - NT
Guy Benjamin - QB
Doug Betters - DE
Kim Bokamper - LB
Jim Braxton - FB
Norm Bulaich - FB
Jimmy Cefalo - WR
Rusty Chambers - LB
Sean Clancy - LB
Charles Cornelius - DB
Mike Current - T
Gary Davis - HB
Vern Den Herder - DE
A. J. Duhe - DE
Tim Foley - DB
Larry Gordon - LB
Bob Griese - QB
Bruce Hardy - TE
Duriel Harris - WR
Leroy Harris - FB
Curtis Johnson - DB
Bob Kuechenberg - G
Eric Laakso - T
Jim Langer - C
Larry Little - G
Benny Malone - HB
Bob Matheson - LB
Loaird McCreary - TE
Mel Mitchell - G
Nat Moore - WR
Wayne Moore - T
Ed Newman - G
Wally Pesuit - G
Bo Rather - WR
Earnest Rhone - LB
George Roberts - K
Bob Simpson - DE
Gerald Small - DB
Don Strock - QB
Norris Thomas - DB
Andre Tillman - TE
Steve Towle - LB
Rick Volk - DB
Delvin Williams - HB
Garo Yepremian - K

1978 Minnesota

Nate Allen - DB
Matt Blair - LB
Bobby Bryant - DB
Greg Coleman - K
Steve Craig - TE
Rick Danmeier - K
Carl Eller - DE
Chuck Foreman - FB
Charlie Goodrum - G
Wes Hamilton - G
Tom Hannon - DB
Paul Harris - LB
Wally Hilgenberg - LB
Randy Holloway - DE
Jim Hough - C
Sammy Johnson - FB
Mark Kellar - FB
Tommy Kramer - QB
Paul Krause - DB
Bob Lee - QB
Bob Lingenfelter - G
Jim Marshall - DE
Brent McClanahan - HB
Fred McNeill - LB
Kevin Miller - WR
Robert Miller - HB
Mark Mullaney - DE
Frank Myers - T
Alan Page - DT
Ahmad Rashad - WR
Steve Riley - T
Jeff Siemon - LB
Lyman Smith - DT
Scott Studwell - LB
Doug Sutherland - DT
Dennis Swilley - G
Fran Tarkenton - QB
Mick Tingelhoff - C
Bob Tucker - TE
John Turner - DB
Stu Voigt - TE
Harry Washington - WR
James White - DT
Sammy White - WR
Phillip Wise - DB
Mike Wood - K
Nate Wright - DB
Ron Yary - T
Rickey Young - HB

1978 New England

Julius Adams - DE
Sam Adams - G
Doug Beaudoin - DB
Richard Bishop - DE
Greg Boyd - DE
Pete Brock - C
Sidney Brown - DB
Don Calhoun - FB
Al Chandler - TE
Raymond Clayborn - DB
Dick Conn - DB
Ray Costict - LB
Bob Cryder - G
Sam Cunningham - FB
Terry Falcon - G
Tim Fox - DB
Russ Francis - TE
Leon Gray - T
Steve Grogan - QB
Ray Hamilton - NT
John Hannah - G
Don Hasselbeck - TE
Mike Hawkins - LB
Mike Haynes - DB
Ernie Holmes - NT
Sam Hunt - LB
Horace Ivory - HB
Harold Jackson - WR
Andy Johnson - HB
Shelby Jordan - T
Steve King - LB
Merv Krakau - LB
Bill Lenkaitis - C
Nick Lowery - K
Mel Lunsford - DE
James McAlister - HB
Prentice McCray - DB
Tony McGee - DE
Bob McKay - T
Stanley Morgan - WR
Steve Nelson - LB
Tom Owen - QB
Mike Patrick - K
Carlos Pennywell - WR
David Posey - K
Greg Schaum - DE
Rod Shoate - LB
John Smith - K
Fred Sturt - G
Mosi Tatupu - FB
Donald Westbrook - WR
Dwight Wheeler - T
Jerrel Wilson - K
Steve Zabel - LB

1978 New Orleans

Gary Anderson - G
Barry Bennett - DT
Tom Blanchard - K
Ray Brown - DB
Joe Campbell - DE
Wes Chandler - WR
Clarence Chapman - DB
Henry Childs - TE
Ron Crosby - LB
Conrad Dobler - G
Joe Federspiel - LB
Eric Felton - DB
Bill Fifer - T
Mike Fultz - DT
Tony Galbreath - FB
Elois Grooms - DE
Larry Hardy - TE
Ike Harris - WR
John Hill - C
Jack Holmes - FB
Pat Hughes - LB
Kevin Hunt - T
Kim Jones - FB
Tom Jurich - K
Rick Kingrea - LB
Dave Lafary - G
John Leypoldt - K
Archie Manning - QB
Rich Mauti - WR
Ralph McGill - DB
Jim Merlo - LB
Mark Meseroll - T
Steve Mike-Mayer - K
Derland Moore - DT
Chuck Muncie - HB
Tom Myers - DB
Richard Neal - DE
Tinker Owens - WR
Elex Price - DT
Rusty Rebowe - LB
Don Reese - DE
Floyd Rice - LB
Donald Schwartz - DB
Bobby Scott - QB
Mo Spencer - DB
Mike Strachan - HB
Fred Sturt - G
Richie Szaro - K
J.T. Taylor - T
Skip Vanderbundt - LB
James Van Wagner - HB
John Watson - T
Brooks Williams - TE
Robert Woods - T
Emanuel Zanders - G

1978 NY Giants

Troy Archer - DT
Brad Benson - T
Bill Bryant - DB
Harry Carson - LB
Jim Clack - C
Randy Coffield - LB
Larry Csonka - FB
Joe Danelo - K
Randy Dean - QB
Al Dixon - TE
Dan Doornink - FB
Jerry Golsteyn - QB
Gordon Gravelle - T
Jack Gregory - DE
Bobby Hammond - HB
Terry Jackson - DB
Dave Jennings - K
Gary Jeter - DT
Ernie Jones - DB
Brian Kelley - LB
Gordon King - T
Doug Kotar - HB
Jim Krahl - DT
Dan Lloyd - LB
Larry Mallory - DB
Frank Marion - LB
George Martin - DE
Alvin Maxson - HB
Odis McKinney - DB
John Mendenhall - DT
Ron Mikolajczyk - T
Emery Moorehead - WR
Johnny Perkins - WR
Jim Pietrzak - T
Joe Pisarcik - QB
Ernest Pough - WR
Beasley Reece - DB
Ray Rhodes - DB
Jim Robinson - WR
Gary Shirk - TE
John Skorupan - LB
Willie Spencer - FB
Billy Taylor - HB
James Thompson - WR
Leo Tierney - C
J. T. Turner - G
Maurice Tyler - DB
Doug Van Horn - G
Brad Van Pelt - LB

1978 NY Jets

Dan Alexander - G
Darrell Austin - G
Jerome Barkum - TE
Kevin Bell - WR
Greg Buttle - LB
Scott Dierking - FB
Jim Earley - FB
Joe Fields - C
Derrick Gaffney - WR
Clark Gaines - FB
Reggie Grant - DB
Bruce Harper - HB
John Hennessy - LB
Mike Hennigan - LB
Mark Iwanowski - TE
Bobby Jackson - DB
Bobby Jones - WR
Larry Keller - LB
Joe Klecko - DE
Pat Leahy - K
Kevin Long - HB
Bob Martin - LB
Mark Merrill - LB
Mike Mock - LB
Joe Moreino - NT
Tim Moresco - DB
Tom Newton - FB
Burgess Owens - DB
Joe Pellegrini Jr. - NT
Lawrence Pillers - DE
Darnell Powell - HB
Marvin Powell - T
Garry Puetz - G
Bob Raba - TE
Chuck Ramsey - K
Randy Rasmussen - G
Larry Riley - DB
Gregg Robinson - DE
Matt Robinson - QB
John Roman - T
Pat Ryan - QB
Abdul Salaam - NT
Ken Schroy - DB
Mickey Shuler - TE
Bruce Stephens - WR
Shafer Suggs - DB
Ed Taylor - DB
Richard Todd - QB
Stan Waldemore - G
Wesley Walker - WR
Chris Ward - T
Blake Whitlatch - LB

1978 Oakland

Pete Banaszak - HB
Warren Bankston - TE
Jeff Barnes - LB
Fred Biletnikoff - WR
Morris Bradshaw - WR
Cliff Branch - WR
Willie Brown - DB
Dave Browning - DE
Larry Brunson - WR
George Buehler - G
Dave Casper - TE
Raymond Chester - TE
Neal Colzie - DB
Dave Dalby - C
Clarence Davis - HB
Mike Davis - DB
Hubert Ginn - HB
Ray Guy - K
Willie Hall - LB
Harold Hart - HB
Lester Hayes - DB
Ted Hendricks - LB
John Huddleston - LB
David Humm - QB
Monte Jackson - DB
Monte Johnson - LB
Henry Lawrence - T
Errol Mann - K
Rod Martin - LB
Mickey Marvin - G
Lindsey Mason - T
John Matuszak - DE
Mike McCoy - NT
Charlie Phillips - DB
Charles Philyaw - DE
Derrick Ramsey - TE
Randy Rich - DB
Terry Robiskie - FB
Dave Rowe - DT
Booker Russell - FB
Art Shell - T
Otis Sistrunk - NT
Ken Stabler - QB
Joe Stewart - WR
Steve Sylvester - C
Jack Tatum - DB
Pat Toomay - DE
Gene Upshaw - G
Mark van Eeghen - FB
Phil Villapiano - LB
Robert Watts - LB
Greg Westbrooks - LB
Art Whittington - HB

1978 Philadelphia

Larry Barnes - FB
Bill Bergey - LB
James Betterson - FB
Bill Bryant - DB
John Bunting - LB
Lem Burnham - DE
Billy Campfield - HB
Harold Carmichael - WR
Ken Clarke - NT
Herman Edwards - DB
Rick Engles - K
Cleveland Franklin - FB
Dennis Franks - C
Ed George - T
Louie Giammona - HB
Carl Hairston - DE
Dennis Harrison - DE
Wally Henry - WR
Mike Hogan - FB
Bob Howard - DB
Ron Jaworski - QB
Charlie Johnson - NT
Eric Johnson - DB
Wade Key - G
Keith Krepfle - TE
Bill Larson - TE
Frank LeMaster - LB
Randy Logan - DB
Tom Luken - G
Herb Lusk - HB
Drew Mahalic - LB
Mike Michel - K
Oren Middlebrook - WR
Nick Mike-Mayer - K
Wilbert Montgomery - HB
Guy Morriss - C
Mike Osborn - LB
Richard Osborne - TE
John Outlaw - DB
Vince Papale - WR
Ken Payne - WR
Woody Peoples - G
Ray Phillips - LB
Deac Sanders - DB
John Sciarra - DB
Jerry Sisemore - T
Manny Sistrunk - DE
Charlie Smith - WR
Terry Tautolo - LB
Stan Walters - T
John Walton - QB
Reggie Wilkes - LB
Charles Williams - DB

1978 Pittsburgh

Fred Anderson - DE
Larry Anderson - DB
John Banaszak - DT
Tom Beasley - DT
Theo Bell - WR
Rocky Bleier - HB
Mel Blount - DB
Terry Bradshaw - QB
Larry Brown - T
Robin Cole - LB
Craig Colquitt - K
Steve Courson - G
Bennie Cunningham - TE
Sam Davis - G
Jack Deloplaine - HB
Tony Dungy - DB
Gary Dunn - DT
Steve Furness - DT
Wentford Gaines - DB
Roy Gerela - K
Joe Greene - DT
L. C. Greenwood - DE
Randy Grossman - TE
Jack Ham - LB
Franco Harris - FB
Ron Johnson - DB
Jon Kolb - T
Mike Kruczek - QB
Jack Lambert - LB
Jim Mandich - TE
Alvin Maxson - HB
Rick Moser - HB
Gerry Mullins - G
Ray Oldham - DB
Ted Petersen - C
Ray Pinney - T
Randy Reutershan - WR
Donnie Shell - DB
Jim Smith - WR
John Stallworth - WR
Lynn Swann - WR
Nat Terry - DB
Sidney Thornton - HB
Loren Toews - LB
Mike Wagner - DB
Mike Webster - C
Dwight White - DE
Dennis Winston - LB

1978 St. Louis

Carl Allen - DB
Kurt Allerman - LB
Warren Anderson - WR
Mark Arneson - LB
Jim Bakken - K
Tom Banks - C
John Barefield - LB
Larry Barnes - FB
Gordon Bell - HB
Bob Bell - DE
Tom Brahaney - C
Al Chandler - TE
Jimmy Childs - WR
George Collins - G
Charles Davis - NT
Mike Dawson - NT
Dan Dierdorf - T
Teddy Farmer - HB
Roger Finnie - T
Randy Gill - LB
Mel Gray - WR
Doug Greene - DB
Ken Greene - DB
Willard Harrell - HB
Jim Hart - QB
Steve Jones - HB
Tim Kearney - LB
Jerry Latin - HB
Steve Little - K
Mark Manges - QB
Wayne Morris - HB
Tom Mullen - G
Steve Neils - LB
Lee Nelson - DB

Jim Otis - FB
Steve Pisarkiewicz - QB
Bob Pollard - DE
Eason Ramson - TE
Mike Sensibaugh - DB
Willie Shelby - HB
Keith Simons - NT
Perry Smith - DB
Tommy Southard - WR
Dave Stief - WR
Terry Stieve - G
Ken Stone - DB
Jim Thaxton - TE
Pat Tilley - WR
Curtis Townsend - LB
Roger Wehrli - DB
Greg Westbrooks - LB
Eric Williams - LB
Mike Wood - K
Roland Woolsey - DB
Keith Wortman - T
Ron Yankowski - DE
Bob Young - G
John Zook - DE

1978 San Diego

Charles Aiu - G
Rickey Anderson - FB
Dan Audick - G
Larry Barnes - FB
Hank Bauer - HB
Rolf Benirschke - K
Larry Burton - WR
Pat Curran - TE
Fred Dean - DE
Charles DeJurnett - DT
Jerome Dove - DB
Glen Edwards - DB
Dan Fouts - QB
Mike Fuller - DB
Don Goode - LB
Buddy Hardaway - T
James Harris - QB
Bob Horn - LB
John Jefferson - WR
Gary Johnson - DT
Charlie Joiner - WR
Leroy Jones - DE
Louie Kelcher - DT
Linden King - DB
Bob Klein - TE
Jim Laslavic - LB
John Lee - DE
Woodrow Lowe - LB
Don Macek - C
Bo Matthews - FB
Greg McCrary - TE
Dwight McDonald - WR
Rick Middleton - LB
Lydell Mitchell - HB
Cliff Olander - QB
Artie Owens - WR
Ralph Perretta - C
Ray Preston - LB
Johnny Rodgers - WR
Pete Shaw - DB
Billy Shields - T
Mark Slater - C
Hal Stringert - DB
Russ Washington - T
Jeff West - TE
Ed White - G
Doug Wilkerson - G
Clarence Williams - HB
Mike Williams - DB
Don Woods - FB
Wilbur Young - DE

1978 San Francisco

John Ayers - T
Mike Baldassin - LB
Elmo Boyd - WR
Lon Boyett - TE
Greg Boykin - FB
Ed Bradley - LB
Scott Bull - QB
Dan Bunz - LB
Earl Carr - FB
Mike Connell - K
Chuck Crist - DB
Randy Cross - C
Kyle Davis - C
Steve DeBerg - QB
Walt Downing - G
Cleveland Elam - DT
Bruce Elia - LB
Keith Fahnhorst - T
Bob Ferrell - FB
Ed Galigher - DT
Cedrick Hardman - DE
Joe Harris - LB
Kenny Harrison - WR
Paul Hofer - HB
Ernie Hughes - G
Larry Jones - WR
Bob Jury - DB
Steve Knutson - G
Terry LeCount - WR
Tony Leonard - DB
Eddie Lewis - DB
Ken MacAfee - TE
Willie McCray - DE
Wonder Monds - DB
Dean Moore - LB
Mark Nichols - LB
Ricky Odom - DB
Fred Quillan - C
Archie Reese - DE
Vern Roberson - DB
Paul Seal - TE
Mike Shumann - WR
O.J. Simpson - HB
Ron Singleton - T
Freddie Solomon - WR
Jack Steptoe - WR
Bruce Threadgill - DB
Elliot Walker - HB
Jimmy Webb - DT
Ray Wersching - K
Dave Williams - HB

1978 Seattle

Charles Aiu - G
Steve August - T
Autry Beamon - DB
Nick Bebout - T
Terry Beeson - LB
Tony Benjamin - FB
Dennis Boyd - DT
Dave Brown - DB
Louis Bullard - T
Keith Butler - LB
Bill Cooke - DT
Rufus Crawford - HB
Pete Cronan - LB
Norm Evans - T
Duke Fergerson - WR
Ken Geddes - LB
Sammy Green - LB
Bill Gregory - DE
John Harris - DB
Efren Herrera - K
Ron Howard - TE
Al Hunter - HB
Kerry Justin - DB
Dave Kraayeveld - DE
Art Kuehn - C
Steve Largent - WR
John Leypoldt - K
Doug Long - DB
Tom Lynch - G
Sam McCullum - WR
Charles McShane - LB
Steve Myer - QB
Bob Newton - G
Steve Niehaus - DT
Brian Peets - TE
Ernie Price - DE
Steve Raible - WR
Alden Roche - DE
Bill Sandifer - DT
John Sawyer - TE
Keith Simpson - DB
David Sims - HB
Sherman Smith - FB
Don Testerman - FB
Herman Weaver - K
Cornell Webster - DB
John Yarno - C
Jim Zorn - QB

1978 Tampa Bay

Jerry Anderson - DB
Ricky Bell - HB
Rik Bonness - LB
Mike Boryla - QB
Aaron Brown - LB
Cedric Brown - DB
Darryl Carlton - T
Louis Carter - HB
Billy Cesare - DB
Wally Chambers - DE
Mark Cotney - DB
Randy Crowder - NT
Al Darby - TE
Johnny Davis - FB
Jimmy DuBose - FB
Dave Farmer - HB
Karl Farmer - WR
Larry Franklin - WR
Rocky Freitas - T
Jimmie Giles - TE
Randy Gill - LB
Frank Grant - WR
Dave Green - K
Isaac Hagins - WR
Charley Hannah - DE
Paul Harris - LB
Greg Horton - G
Gary Huff - QB
Earl Inmon - LB
Cecil Johnson - LB
Randy Johnson - G
Curtis Jordan - DB
Bill Kollar - DE
Mike Levenseller - WR
Dave Lewis - LB
Alvin Maxson - HB
John McKay - WR
Dan Medlin - G
Brett Moritz - G
Larry Mucker - WR
Dana Nafziger - LB
Jim Obradovich - TE
Neil O'Donoghue - K
Morris Owens - WR
Dave Pear - NT
Garry Puetz - G
Mike Rae - QB
George Ragsdale - HB
Dave Reavis - T
Danny Reece - DB
Kurt Schumacher - G
Dewey Selmon - LB
Lee Roy Selmon - DE
Mike Washington - DB
Charlie White - HB
Jeris White - DB
Doug Williams - QB
Steven Wilson - C
Jeff Winans - G
Richard Wood - LB

1978 Washington

Terry Anderson - WR
Coy Bacon - DE
Mike Bragg - K
Perry Brooks - DT
Danny Buggs - WR
Dave Butz - DT
Mike Curtis - LB
Fred Dean - G
Jack Deloplaine - HB
Brad Dusek - LB
Ike Forte - HB
Ted Fritsch - C
Jean Fugett - TE
Frank Grant - WR
Tony Green - HB
Chris Hanburger - LB
Jim Harlan - T
Clarence Harmon - HB
Don Harris - DB
Reggie Haynes - TE
Bob Heinz - DT
Terry Hermeling - T
Dallas Hickman - LB
Donnie Hickman - G
Ken Houston - DB
Don Hover - LB
Billy Kilmer - QB
Bob Kuziel - C
Joe Lavender - DB
Karl Lorch - DE
Benny Malone - HB
Greg McCrary - TE
John McDaniel - WR
Ron McDole - DE
Harold McLinton - LB
Mark Moseley - K
Mark Murphy - DB
Dan Nugent - G
Lemar Parrish - DB
John Riggins - FB
Ron Saul - G
Jake Scott - DB
J. T. Smith - WR
George Starke - T
Diron Talbert - DT
Joe Theismann - QB
Mike Thomas - HB
Ricky Thompson - WR
Gerard Williams - DB
Jeff Williams - T
Pete Wysocki - LB

1979 Atlanta

William Andrews - FB
Steve Bartkowski - QB
Bubba Bean - HB
Greg Brezina - LB
Warren Bryant - T
Rick Byas - DB
Brian Cabral - LB
Lynn Cain - HB
Tony Daykin - LB
Ray Easterling - DB
Wilson Faumuina - DT
Edgar Fields - DT
Wally Francis - WR
Bob Glazebrook - DB
Pat Howell - G
Alfred Jackson - WR
John James - K
Alfred Jenkins - WR
June Jones - QB
Mike Kenn - T
Jerome King - DB
Fulton Kuykendall - LB
Rolland Lawrence - DB
Mike Lewis - DT
James Mayberry - FB
Tim Mazzetti - K
Ron McCartney - LB
Dewey McClain - LB
Phil McKinnely - T
Jeff Merrow - DE
Russ Mikeska - TE
Jim Mitchell - TE
Tom Moriarty - DB
Mike Moroski - QB
Ricky Patton - HB
Dennis Pearson - WR
Robert Pennywell - LB
Tom Pridemore - DB
Frank Reed - DB
Billy Ryckman - WR
Paul Ryczek - C
Dave Scott - G
Don Smith - DE
Haskel Stanback - HB
Ray Strong - HB
R.C. Thielemann - G
Jeff Van Note - C
Joel Williams - LB
Jeff Yeates - DE
Mike Zele - DT

1979 Baltimore

Mack Alston - TE
Ron Baker - G
Mike Barnes - DT
Lyle Blackwood - DB
Larry Braziel - DB
Randy Burke - WR
Roger Carr - WR
Fred Cook - DE
Brian DeRoo - WR
Bucky Dilts - K
Glenn Doughty - WR
Joe Ehrmann - DT
Ron Fernandes - DE
Greg Fields - DE
Ben Garry - FB
Nesby Glasgow - DB
Jerry Golsteyn - QB
Wade Griffin - T
Lee Gross - C
Don Hardeman - FB
Dwight Harrison - DB
Jeff Hart - T
Ken Huff - G
Bert Jones - QB
Jim Krahl - DT
Barry Krauss - LB
Bruce Laird - DB
Greg Landry - QB
Roosevelt Leaks - FB
Toni Linhart - K
Reese McCall - TE
Don McCauley - HB
Ken Mendenhall - C
Steve Mike-Mayer - K
Doug Nettles - DB
Herb Orvis - DT
Mike Ozdowski - DE
Reggie Pinkney - DB
Bob Pratt - G
Sanders Shiver - LB
Mike Siani - WR
Ed Simonini - LB
David Taylor - T
Norm Thompson - DB
Bob Van Duyne - G
Joe Washington - HB
Stan White - LB
Mike Woods - LB
Steve Zabel - LB

1979 Buffalo

Jon Borchardt - T
Curtis Brown - FB
Jerry Butler - WR
Bob Chandler - WR
Mario Clark - DB
Mike Collier - FB
Joe DeLamielleure - G
Tom Dempsey - K
Joe Devlin - T
Joe Ferguson - QB
Steve Freeman - DB
Danny Fulton - WR
Ed Fulton - G
Reuben Gant - TE
Will Grant - C
Tony Greene - DB
Doug Greene - DB
Dee Hardison - DE
Jim Haslett - LB
Tom Higgins - LB
Roland Hooks - HB
Ron Howard - TE
Scott Hutchinson - DE
Rusty Jackson - K
Dan Jilek - LB
Dennis Johnson - FB
Ken Johnson - DE
Ken Jones - T
Mike Kadish - NT
Chris Keating - LB
Frank Lewis - WR
Dan Manucci - QB
Reggie McKenzie - G
Nick Mike-Mayer - K
Terry Miller - HB
Keith Moody - DB
Bill Munson - QB
Shane Nelson - LB
Jeff Nixon - DB
Willie Parker - C
Lou Piccone - WR
Steve Powell - HB
Isiah Robertson - LB
Charles Romes - DB
Lucius Sanford - LB
Joseph Shipp - TE
Fred Smerlas - NT
Tim Vogler - C
Sherman White - DE
Ben Williams - DE
Leonard Willis - WR

1979 Chi. Bears

Ted Albrecht - T
Tony Ardizzone - C
Bob Avellini - QB
Brian Baschnagel - WR
Lynn Boden - G
Doug Buffone - LB
Gary Campbell - LB
Mike Cobb - TE
Jack Deloplaine - HB
Robin Earl - FB
Allan Ellis - DB
Vince Evans - QB
Gary Fencik - DB
Wentford Gaines - DB
Kris Haines - WR
Dan Hampton - DE
Al Harris - DE
Tommy Hart - DE
Mike Hartenstine - DE
Bruce Herron - LB
Tom Hicks - LB
Noah Jackson - G
Dan Jiggetts - T
Lee Kunz - LB
Greg Latta - TE
Dennis Lick - T
Virgil Livers - DB
Willie McClendon - HB
Mark Merrill - LB
Jerry Meyers - DT
Jerry Muckensturm - LB
Dan Neal - C
Jim Osborne - DT
Alan Page - DT
Bob Parsons - TE
Walter Payton - HB
Lonnie Perrin - FB
Mike Phipps - QB
Doug Plank - DB
Golden Richards - WR
Ron Rydalch - DT
Terry Schmidt - DB
Steve Schubert - WR
James Scott - WR
John Skibinski - FB
Revie Sorey - G
Mike Spivey - DB
Bob Thomas - K
Len Walterscheid - DB
Harry Washington - WR
Rickey Watts - WR
Dave Williams - FB

1979 Cincinnati

Charles Alexander - HB
Ken Anderson - QB
Chris Bahr - K
Don Bass - WR
Louis Breeden - DB
Billy Brooks - WR
Jim Browner - DB
Ross Browner - DE
Glenn Bujnoch - G
Scott Burk - DB
Gary Burley - DE
Blair Bush - C
Glenn Cameron - LB
Marvin Cobb - DB
James Corbett - TE
Barney Cotton - G
Isaac Curtis - WR
Tom Dinkel - LB
Mark Donahue - G
Eddie Edwards - DT
Archie Griffin - HB
Ray Griffin - DB
Bo Harris - LB
Vern Holland - T
Dick Jauron - DB
Pete Johnson - FB
Bob Johnson - C
Steve Kreider - WR
Howie Kurnick - LB
Dave Lapham - G
Jim LeClair - LB
Mike Levenseller - WR
Vaughn Lusby - DB
Pat McInally - WR
Mack Mitchell - DE
Max Montoya - T
Scott Perry - DB
Nathan Poole - HB
Ken Riley - DB
Dan Ross - TE
Tom Ruud - LB
Jack Thompson - QB
Deacon Turner - HB
Rick Walker - TE
Mike White - DT
Wilson Whitley - DT
Reggie Williams - LB
Mike Wilson - T

1979 Cleveland

Willis Adams - WR
Lyle Alzado - DE
Dick Ambrose - LB
Ron Bolton - DB
Henry Bradley - DT
George Buehler - G
Clinton Burrell - DB
Don Cockroft - K
Thom Darden - DB
Oliver Davis - DB
Tom DeLeone - C
Doug Dieken - T
Rich Dimler - DT
Johnny Evans - QB
Ricky Feacher - WR
Dave Graf - LB
Jack Gregory - DE
Charlie Hall - LB
Dino Hall - HB
Calvin Hill - HB
Gerald Irons - LB
Robert Jackson - LB
Robert Jackson - G
Lawrence Johnson - DB
Ricky Jones - DB
Dave Logan - WR
Clay Matthews - LB
Cleo Miller - HB
Mark Miller - QB
Matt Miller - T
Pat Moriarty - HB
Ozzie Newsome - TE
Greg Pruitt - HB
Mike Pruitt - FB
Randy Rich - DB
Cody Risien - G
Reggie Rucker - WR
Clarence Scott - DB
Henry Sheppard - T
Jerry Sherk - DT
Mickey Sims - DT
Brian Sipe - QB
John Smith - WR
Mike St. Clair - DE
Gerry Sullivan - C
Curtis Weathers - TE
Keith Wright - WR

1979 Dallas

Benny Barnes - DB
Larry Bethea - DT
Alois Blackwell - HB
Bob Breunig - LB
Larry Brinson - FB
Guy Brown - LB
Glenn Carano - QB
Larry Cole - DE
Jim Cooper - T
Doug Cosbie - TE
Pat Donovan - T
Tony Dorsett - HB
Billy Joe DuPree - TE
John Dutton - DE
John Fitzgerald - C
Andy Frederick - T
Cliff Harris - DB
Mike Hegman - LB
Tom Henderson - LB
Tony Hill - WR
Randy Hughes - DB
Bruce Huther - LB
Butch Johnson - WR
Aaron Kyle - DB
Scott Laidlaw - FB
Burton Lawless - G
D. D. Lewis - LB
Wade Manning - DB
Harvey Martin - DE
Aaron Mitchell - DB
Robert Newhouse - FB
Drew Pearson - WR
Preston Pearson - HB
Tom Rafferty - G
Jay Saldi - TE
Herbert Scott - G
Rafael Septien - K
Robert Shaw - C
Ron Springs - HB
Dave Stalls - DT
Roger Staubach - QB
Bruce Thornton - DE
Dennis Thurman - DB
Randy White - DT
Danny White - QB
Steve Wilson - WR
Rayfield Wright - T

1979 Denver

Otis Armstrong - HB
Butch Atkinson - DB
Ken Brown - C
Billy Bryan - C
Larry Canada - FB
Rubin Carter - NT
Barney Chavous - DE
Kelvin Clark - T
Zachary Dixon - HB
Jack Dolbin - WR
Ron Egloff - TE
Larry Evans - LB
Steve Foley - DB
Tom Glassic - G
Randy Gradishar - LB
John Grant - DE
Paul Howard - G
Glenn Hyde - G
Bernard Jackson - DB
Tom Jackson - LB
Jim Jensen - FB
Jon Keyworth - FB
Vince Kinney - WR
Kit Lathrop - NT
Don Latimer - NT
Rob Lytle - HB
Brison Manor - DE
Claudie Minor - T
Craig Morton - QB
Haven Moses - WR
Rob Nairne - LB
Riley Odoms - TE
Chris Pane - DB
Craig Penrose - QB
Dave Preston - HB
Luke Prestridge - K
Bruce Radford - DE
Joe Rizzo - LB
Jim Ryan - LB
Fred Steinfort - K
Dave Studdard - T
Bob Swenson - LB
Billy Thompson - DB
Jim Turner - K
Rick Upchurch - WR
Steve Watson - WR
Norris Weese - QB
Charlie West - DB
Louis Wright - DB

1979 Detroit

Jimmy Allen - DB
Nate Allen - DB
John Arnold - WR
Al Baker - DE
Karl Baldischwiler - T
Luther Blue - WR
Russ Bolinger - G
Luther Bradley - DB
Jon Brooks - LB
Dexter Bussey - HB
Ken Callicutt - HB
Karl Chandler - C
Garry Cobb - LB
Eddie Cole - LB
Keith Dorney - T
Cleveland Elam - DT
Homer Elias - G
Ken Ellis - DB
Doug English - DT
Ken Fantetti - LB
Amos Fowler - G
Dennis Franks - C
Lawrence Gaines - FB
Dave Gallagher - DT
Bill Gay - DE
Jerry Golsteyn - QB
James Harrell - LB
David Hill - TE
James Hunter - DB
Scott Hunter - QB
Ernie Jackson - DB
Doug Jones - DB
Rick Kane - HB
Horace King - FB
Jeff Komlo - QB
Tony Leonard - DB
Eddie Lewis - DB
Don Morrison - T
Ulysses Norris - TE
Ed O'Neil - LB
Dave Parkin - DB
Don Patterson - DB
Wally Pesuit - G
Dave Pureifory - DE
Joe Reed - QB
Benny Ricardo - K
Bo Robinson - FB
Ken Sanders - DE
Freddie Scott - WR
Tom Skladany - K
Jimmy Stewart - DB
Larry Swider - K
Larry Tearry - C
Leonard Thompson - WR
Dave Washington - LB
Gene Washington - WR
Charlie Weaver - LB
Walt Williams - DB
Robert Woods - WR

1979 Green Bay

John Anderson - LB
Steve Atkins - FB
Bob Barber - DE
Carl Barzilauskas - DT
David Beverly - K
Tom Birney - K
Mike Butler - DE
Ron Cassidy - WR
Paul Coffman - TE
Jim Culbreath - FB
Lynn Dickey - QB
Mike Douglass - LB
Earl Edwards - DT
Derrel Gofourth - G
Johnnie Gray - DB
Jim Gueno - LB
Leotis Harris - G
Estus Hood - DB
Mike Hunt - LB
Eddie Lee Ivery - FB
Melvin Jackson - G
Charles Johnson - DT
Ezra Johnson - DE
Sammy Johnson - FB
Terry Jones - DT
Bobby Kimball - WR
Greg Koch - T
Mark Koncar - T
Walt Landers - FB

Kit Lathrop - NT
James Lofton - WR
Steve Luke - DB
Chester Marcol - K
Larry McCarren - C
Mike McCoy - DB
Joe McLaughlin - LB
Casey Merrill - DT
Terdell Middleton - HB
Henry Monroe - DB
Steve Odom - WR
Ricky Patton - HB
Paul Rudzinski - LB
Howard Sampson - DB
Dave Simmons - LB
Nate Simpson - HB
Barty Smith - FB
Steve Stewart - LB
Timothy Stokes - T
Aundra Thompson - WR
John Thompson - TE
Eric Torkelson - FB
Walter Tullis - WR
Wylie Turner - DB
Steve Wagner - DB
Gary Weaver - LB
Mike Wellman - C
David Whitehurst - QB
Rich Wingo - LB

1979 Houston

Willie Alexander - DB
Jesse Baker - DE
Mike Barber - TE
Steve Baumgartner - LB
Elvin Bethea - DE
Gregg Bingham - LB
Robert Brazile - LB
Ken Burrough - WR
Earl Campbell - HB
Rob Carpenter - FB
David Carter - C
Rich Caster - WR
Boobie Clark - FB
Ronnie Coleman - HB
Curley Culp - NT
Bill Currier - DB
Andy Dorris - DE
Rich Ellender - WR
Jimbo Elrod - LB
Ed Fisher - G
Eddie Foster - WR
Toni Fritsch - K
Leon Gray - T
Jeff Groth - WR
Carter Hartwig - DB
Conway Hayman - G
Daryl Hunt - LB
Charles Jefferson - DB
Billy Johnson - WR
Ken Kennard - NT
Kenny King - HB
Carl Mauck - C
Guido Merkens - WR
Mike Murphy - LB
Gifford Nielsen - QB
Cliff Parsley - K
Dan Pastorini - QB
Vernon Perry - DB
Wes Phillips - T
Tom Randall - G
George Reihner - G
Mike Reinfeldt - DB
Mike Renfro - WR
Conrad Rucker - TE
Greg Stemrick - DB
Mike Stensrud - NT
Art Stringer - LB
Ted Thompson - LB
Morris Towns - T
Ted Washington - LB
J. C. Wilson - DB
Tim Wilson - FB
Jim Young - DE

1979 Kansas City

Curtis Anderson - DE
Charlie Ane - C
Gary Barbaro - DB
Ed Beckman - TE
Mike Bell - DE
Horace Belton - HB
Jerry Blanton - LB
Larry Brown - T
M.L. Carter - DB
Herb Christopher - DB
Tim Collier - DB
Tom Condon - G
Johnnie Dirden - WR
Al Dixon - TE
Steve Fuller - QB
Earl Gant - HB
Steve Gaunty - WR
Charlie Getty - T
Gary Green - DB
Bob Grupp - K
Wilbert Haslip - FB
Matt Herkenhoff - T
Sylvester Hicks - DE
Tom Howard - LB
Charles Jackson - LB
Gerald Jackson - DB
Ken Kremer - NT
Dave Lindstrom - DE

Mike Livingston - QB
Frank Manumaleuga - LB
Henry Marshall - WR
Ted McKnight - FB
Arnold Morgado - FB
Jim Nicholson - T
Don Parrish - NT
Whitney Paul - LB
Horace Perkins - DB
Cal Peterson - LB
Tony Reed - HB
Jerry Reese - DB
Stan Rome - WR
Dave Rozumek - LB
Jack Rudnay - C
Tony Samuels - TE
Bob Simmons - G
J. T. Smith - WR
Gary Spani - LB
Jan Stenerud - K
Art Still - DE
Rod Walters - G
Walter White - TE
Mike Williams - FB

1979 LA Rams

George Andrews - LB
Bill Bain - G
Larry Brooks - DT
Eddie Brown - DB
Bob Brudzinski - LB
Cullen Bryant - FB
Ken Clark - K
Frank Corral - K
Nolan Cromwell - DB
Preston Dennard - WR
Reggie Doss - DE
Fred Dryer - DE
Bill Dunstan - DT
Ken Ellis - DB
Dave Elmendorf - DB
Mike Fanning - DT
Vince Ferragamo - QB
Doug France - T
Gordon Gravelle - T
Pat Haden - QB
Dennis Harrah - G
Joe Harris - LB
Drew Hill - WR
Eddie Hill - HB
Kent Hill - G
Ron Jessie - WR
Jim Jodat - FB
Sidney Justin - DB
Bob Lee - QB
Lawrence McCutcheon - HB
Kevin McLain - LB
Willie Miller - WR
Terry Nelson - TE
Ricky Odom - DB
Dwayne O'Steen - DB
Elvis Peacock - FB
Rod Perry - DB
Jack Reynolds - LB
Jeff Rutledge - QB
Dan Ryczek - C
Rich Saul - C
Jeff Severson - DB
Jackie Slater - T
Doug Smith - C
Ron Smith - WR
Ivory Sully - DB
Pat Thomas - DB
Wendell Tyler - HB
Billy Waddy - WR
Jackie Wallace - DB
Greg Westbrooks - LB
Jerry Wilkinson - DE
John Williams - T
Charle Young - TE
Jack Youngblood - DE
Jim Youngblood - LB

1979 Miami

Charlie Babb - DB
Carl Barisich - NT
Bob Baumhower - NT
Guy Benjamin - QB
Don Bessillieu - DB
Doug Betters - DE
Glenn Blackwood - DB
Kim Bokamper - LB
Norm Bulaich - FB
Jimmy Cefalo - WR
Rusty Chambers - LB
Neal Colzie - DB
Larry Csonka - FB
Mike Current - T
Gary Davis - HB
Vern Den Herder - DE
Mark Dennard - C
A. J. Duhe - DE
Tim Foley - DB
Jon Giesler - T
Larry Gordon - LB
Cleveland Green - T
Bob Griese - QB
Jeff Groth - WR
Bruce Hardy - TE
Duriel Harris - WR
Steve Howell - FB
Mike Kozlowski - DB

Bob Kuechenberg - T
Eric Laakso - G
Mel Land - LB
Jim Langer - C
Ronnie Lee - TE
Larry Little - G
Bob Matheson - LB
Nat Moore - WR
Tony Nathan - HB
Ed Newman - G
Ralph Ortega - LB
Earnest Rhone - LB
George Roberts - K
Gerald Small - DB
Don Strock - QB
Ed Taylor - DB
Norris Thomas - DB
Jeff Toews - G
Bob Torrey - FB
Steve Towle - LB
Uwe von Schamann - K
Delvin Williams - HB

1979 Minnesota

Nate Allen - DB
Tim Baylor - DB
Matt Blair - LB
Ted Brown - FB
Bobby Bryant - DB
Greg Coleman - K
Douglas Cunningham - WR
Rick Danmeier - K
Steve Dils - QB
Jimmy Edwards - HB
Chuck Foreman - FB
Charlie Goodrum - G
Wes Hamilton - G
Tom Hannon - DB
Joe Harris - LB
Wally Hilgenberg - LB
Randy Holloway - DE
Jim Hough - G
Dave Huffman - C
Kurt Knoff - DB
Tommy Kramer - QB
Paul Krause - DB
Terry LeCount - WR
Derrel Luce - LB
Jim Marshall - DE
Brent McClanahan - HB
Fred McNeill - LB
Kevin Miller - WR
Robert Miller - HB
Mark Mullaney - DE
Frank Myers - T
Steve Niehaus - DT
Keith Nord - DB
Ahmad Rashad - WR
Steve Riley - T
Dave Roller - DT
Jeff Siemon - LB
Robert Steele - WR
Scott Studwell - LB
Doug Sutherland - DT
Dennis Swilley - C
Bob Tucker - TE
John Turner - DB
Stu Voigt - TE
James White - DT
Sammy White - WR
Phillip Wise - DB
Nate Wright - DB
Ron Yary - T
Rickey Young - HB

1979 New England

Julius Adams - DE
Sam Adams - G
Doug Beaudoin - DB
Richard Bishop - DE
Pete Brock - C
Mark Buben - DE
Don Calhoun - FB
Matt Cavanaugh - QB
Al Chandler - TE
Allan Clark - HB
Raymond Clayborn - DB
Dick Conn - DB
Ray Costict - LB
Bob Cryder - G
Sam Cunningham - FB
Terry Falcon - G
Tim Fox - DB
Russ Francis - TE
Bob Golic - LB
Steve Grogan - QB
Ray Hamilton - NT
John Hannah - G
Eddie Hare - K
Don Hasselbeck - TE
Mike Hawkins - LB
Mike Haynes - DB
Sam Hunt - LB
Horace Ivory - HB
Harold Jackson - WR
Ray Jarvis - WR
Andy Johnson - HB
Shelby Jordan - T
Steve King - LB
Bill Lenkaitis - C
Mel Lunsford - DE
Bill Matthews - LB
Prentice McCray - DB

Tony McGee - DE
Stanley Morgan - WR
Steve Nelson - LB
Tom Owen - QB
Carlos Pennywell - WR
Garry Puetz - T
Rick Sanford - DB
Rod Shoate - LB
John Smith - K
Mosi Tatupu - FB
Mark Washington - DB
Donald Westbrook - WR
Dwight Wheeler - T
John Zamberlin - LB

1979 New Orleans

Barry Bennett - DT
Ken Bordelon - LB
Ray Brown - DB
Ed Burns - QB
Joe Campbell - DE
Wes Chandler - WR
Clarence Chapman - DB
Henry Childs - TE
Conrad Dobler - G
Russell Erxleben - K
Joe Federspiel - LB
Eric Felton - DB
Roger Finnie - T
Mike Fultz - DT
Tony Galbreath - FB
David Gray - DB
Elois Grooms - DE
Larry Hardy - TE
Ike Harris - WR
John Hill - C
Jack Holmes - FB
Pat Hughes - LB
Kim Jones - FB
Jim Kovach - LB
Dave Lafary - G
Archie Manning - QB
Reggie Mathis - LB
Rich Mauti - WR
Ralph McGill - DB
Jim Merlo - LB
Derland Moore - DT
Chuck Muncie - HB
Tom Myers - DB
Tinker Owens - WR
Rick Partridge - K
Jim Pietrzak - C
Elex Price - DT
Ricky Ray - DB
Don Reese - DE
Donald Schwartz - DB
Bobby Scott - QB
Mike Strachan - HB
Fred Sturt - G
J.T. Taylor - T
John Watson - T
Brooks Williams - TE
Wayne Wilson - HB
Robert Woods - T
Garo Yepremian - K
Emanuel Zanders - G

1979 NY Giants

Brad Benson - T
Alan Caldwell - DB
Harry Carson - LB
Todd Christensen - FB
Jim Clack - C
Randy Coffield - LB
Gus Coppens - T
Joe Danelo - K
Randy Dean - QB
Al Dixon - TE
Zachary Dixon - HB
Keith Eck - C
Dan Fowler - G
Gordon Gravelle - T
Earnest Gray - WR
Tony Green - HB
Bobby Hammond - HB
Eddie Hicks - FB
Cleveland Jackson - TE
Terry Jackson - DB
Dave Jennings - K
Gary Jeter - DE
Ken Johnson - FB
Ernie Jones - DB
Brian Kelley - LB
Gordon King - T
Doug Kotar - HB
Dan Lloyd - LB
Frank Marion - LB
George Martin - DE
Mike McCoy - DT
Loaird McCreary - TE
Odis McKinney - DB
John Mendenhall - DT
Ron Mikolajczyk - T
Calvin Miller - DT
Emery Moorehead - HB
Tom Mullady - TE
Tom Neville - T
Steve Odom - WR
Ray Oldham - DB
Johnny Perkins - WR
Jim Pietrzak - C
Joe Pisarcik - QB
Beasley Reece - DB
Ray Rhodes - DB

Jim Robinson - WR
Dwight Scales - WR
Gary Shirk - TE
Roy Simmons - G
Phil Simms - QB
John Skorupan - LB
Philip Tabor - DT
Billy Taylor - FB
Bob Torrey - FB
J. T. Turner - G
Doug Van Horn - G
Brad Van Pelt - LB
Gene Washington - WR
Jeff Weston - DT

1979 NY Jets

Dan Alexander - G
Jerome Barkum - TE
Woody Bennett - HB
Stan Blinka - LB
Greg Buttle - LB
Ron Crosby - LB
Eric Cunningham - G
Paul Darby - WR
Scott Dierking - HB
Donald Dykes - DB
Roger Farmer - WR
Joe Fields - C
Derrick Gaffney - WR
Clark Gaines - FB
Mark Gastineau - DE
Bruce Harper - HB
John Hennessy - LB
Bobby Jackson - DB
Dave Jacobs - K
Bobby Jones - WR
Joe Klecko - DT
Pat Leahy - K
Toni Linhart - K
Kevin Long - FB
Johnny Lynn - DB
Marty Lyons - DE
Bob Martin - LB
Ed McGlasson - C
Mike McKibben - LB
Mark Merrill - LB
Tim Moresco - DB
Tom Newton - FB
Burgess Owens - DB
Joe Pellegrini Jr. - DT
Lawrence Pillers - DE
Marvin Powell - T
Bob Raba - TE
Chuck Ramsey - K
Randy Rasmussen - G
Matt Robinson - QB
John Roman - T
Pat Ryan - QB
Abdul Salaam - DT
Ken Schroy - DB
Mickey Shuler - TE
Shafer Suggs - DB
John Sullivan - LB
Richie Szaro - K
Ed Taylor - DB
Richard Todd - QB
Stan Waldemore - G
Wesley Walker - WR
Chris Ward - T
Bob Winkel - DT

1979 Oakland

Jeff Barnes - LB
Joe Bell - DE
Rufus Bess - DB
Morris Bradshaw - WR
Cliff Branch - WR
Jim Breech - K
Dave Browning - DE
Larry Brunson - WR
Dave Casper - TE
Raymond Chester - TE
Todd Christensen - FB
Dave Dalby - C
Bruce Davis - T
Mike Davis - DB
Ray Guy - K
Clarence Hawkins - HB
Lester Hayes - DB
Ted Hendricks - LB
John Huddleston - LB
David Humm - QB
Monte Jackson - DB
Derrick Jensen - HB
Monte Johnson - LB
Willie Jones - DE
Reggie Kinlaw - NT
Henry Lawrence - T
Rod Martin - LB
Rich Martini - WR
Mickey Marvin - G
Ira Matthews - HB
John Matuszak - DE
Dan Medlin - G
Dave Pear - NT
Charlie Phillips - DB
Charles Philyaw - DE
Jim Plunkett - QB
Derrick Ramsey - TE
Terry Robiskie - HB
Booker Russell - FB
Art Shell - T
Ken Stabler - QB
Joe Stewart - WR

Steve Sylvester - G
Jack Tatum - DB
Pat Toomay - DE
Gene Upshaw - G
Mark van Eeghen - FB
John Vella - T
Phil Villapiano - LB
Greg Westbrooks - LB
Art Whittington - HB
Henry Williams - DB

1979 Philadelphia

Larry Barnes - FB
Bill Bergey - LB
Richard Blackmore - DB
John Bunting - LB
Lem Burnham - DE
Billy Campfield - HB
Harold Carmichael - WR
Earl Carr - FB
Al Chesley - LB
Ken Clarke - NT
Herman Edwards - DB
Scott Fitzkee - WR
Tony Franklin - K
Louie Giammona - HB
Carl Hairston - DE
Leroy Harris - FB
Dennis Harrison - DE
Wally Henry - WR
Bob Howard - DB
Claude Humphrey - DE
Ron Jaworski - QB
Charlie Johnson - NT
Wade Key - G
Keith Krepfle - TE
Al Latimer - DB
Frank LeMaster - LB
Randy Logan - DB
Rufus Mayes - T
Jerrold McRae - WR
Henry Monroe - DB
Wilbert Montgomery - HB
Guy Morriss - C
Woody Peoples - G
Petey Perot - G
Ray Phillips - LB
Garry Puetz - T
Jerry Robinson - LB
Max Runager - K
Deac Sanders - DB
John Sciarra - DB
Jerry Sisemore - T
Manny Sistrunk - DE
Mark Slater - C
Charlie Smith - WR
John Spagnola - TE
Terry Tautolo - LB
Stan Walters - T
John Walton - QB
Reggie Wilkes - LB
Brenard Wilson - DB

1979 Pittsburgh

Anthony Anderson - HB
Larry Anderson - DB
Matt Bahr - K
John Banaszak - DE
Tom Beasley - DT
Theo Bell - WR
Rocky Bleier - HB
Mel Blount - DB
Terry Bradshaw - QB
Larry Brown - T
Robin Cole - LB
Craig Colquitt - K
Steve Courson - G
Bennie Cunningham - TE
Sam Davis - G
Jack Deloplaine - HB
Thom Dornbrook - C
Gary Dunn - DT
Steve Furness - DT
Tom Graves - LB
Joe Greene - DT
L. C. Greenwood - DE
Randy Grossman - TE
Jack Ham - LB
Franco Harris - FB
Greg Hawthorne - FB
Ron Johnson - DB
Jon Kolb - T
Mike Kruczek - QB
Jack Lambert - LB
Rick Moser - HB
Gerry Mullins - G
Ted Petersen - T
Donnie Shell - DB
Jim Smith - WR
John Stallworth - WR
Lynn Swann - WR
J.T. Thomas - DB
Sidney Thornton - HB
Loren Toews - LB
Zack Valentine - LB
Mike Wagner - DB
Mike Webster - C
Dwight White - DE
Dennis Winston - LB
Dwayne Woodruff - DB

1979 St. Louis

Carl Allen - DB
Kurt Allerman - LB
Ottis Anderson - HB
Mark Arneson - LB
Tom Banks - C
John Barefield - LB
Joe Bostic - T
Tom Brahaney - C
Chuck Brown - C
Theotis Brown - FB
Al Chandler - TE
Jimmy Childs - WR
Sean Clancy - LB
George Collins - G
Charles Davis - NT
Mike Dawson - DE
Dan Dierdorf - T
Calvin Favron - LB
Chris Garlich - LB
Mel Gray - WR
Roy Green - DB
Ken Greene - DB
Willard Harrell - HB
Jim Hart - QB
Steve Henry - DB
Tim Kearney - LB
Steve Little - K
Thomas Lott - HB
Randy Love - HB
Wayne Morris - FB
Bill Murrell - TE
Steve Neils - LB
Lee Nelson - DB
Brad Oates - T
Richard Osborne - TE
Gary Parris - TE
Rod Phillips - FB
Steve Pisarkiewicz - QB
Bob Pollard - DE
Jim Ramey - DE
Bob Rozier - DE
Keith Simons - NT
Perry Smith - DB
Dave Stief - WR
Terry Stieve - G
Ken Stone - DB
Pat Tilley - WR
Roger Wehrli - DB
Eric Williams - LB
Mike Wood - K
Keith Wortman - T
Ron Yankowski - DE
Bob Young - G
John Zook - DE

1979 San Diego

Dan Audick - T
Hank Bauer - HB
Rolf Benirschke - K
Willie Buchanon - DB
Larry Burton - WR
Fred Dean - DE
Charles DeJurnett - DT
Jerome Dove - DB
Frank Duncan - DB
Glen Edwards - DB
John Floyd - WR
Dan Fouts - QB
Mike Fuller - DB
Roy Gerela - K
Don Goode - LB
James Harris - QB
Bob Horn - LB
John Jefferson - WR
Gary Johnson - DT
Charlie Joiner - WR
Leroy Jones - DE
Louie Kelcher - DT
Linden King - LB
Bob Klein - TE
John Lee - DE
Woodrow Lowe - LB
Don Macek - G
Bo Matthews - FB
Greg McCrary - TE
Lydell Mitchell - HB
Cliff Olander - QB
Artie Owens - HB
Ralph Perretta - C
Ray Preston - LB
Bob Rush - C
Pete Shaw - DB
Billy Shields - T
Hal Stringert - DB
Mike Thomas - HB
Cliff Thrift - LB
Russ Washington - T
Jeff West - TE
Ed White - G
Doug Wilkerson - G
Clarence Williams - FB
Mike Williams - DB
Kellen Winslow - TE
Mike Wood - K
Don Woods - FB
Wilbur Young - DT

1979 San Francisco

John Ayers - G
Jean Barrett - T
Dwaine Board - DE
John Bristor - DB

Bob Bruer - TE
Dan Bunz - LB
Gordy Ceresino - LB
Dwight Clark - WR
Charles Cornelius - DB
Al Cowlings - DE
Randy Cross - G
Steve DeBerg - QB
Walt Downing - G
Tony Dungy - DB
Lenvil Elliott - HB
Keith Fahnhorst - T
Bob Ferrell - FB
Phil Francis - HB
Tim Gray - DB
Cedrick Hardman - DE
Willie Harper - LB
Dwight Hicks - DB
Scott Hilton - LB
Paul Hofer - HB
Mike Hogan - FB
Wilbur Jackson - FB
Charles Johnson - DB
Eric Johnson - DB
Terry LeCount - WR
Eddie Lewis - DB
Ken MacAfee - TE
Bob Martin - LB
Jeff McIntyre - LB
Dan Melville - K
Joe Montana - QB
Melvin Morgan - DB
Dave Morton - LB
Bob Nelson - LB
James Owens - WR
Fred Quillan - C
Eason Ramson - TE
Archie Reese - DE
Thomas Seabron - LB
Paul Seal - TE
Mike Shumann - WR
Ron Shumon - LB
O.J. Simpson - HB
Ron Singleton - T
Freddie Solomon - WR
Ruben Vaughan - DT
Ted Vincent - DT
Jimmy Webb - DT
Ray Wersching - K
Gerard Williams - DB

1979 Seattle

Sam Adkins - QB
Steve August - T
Autry Beamon - DB
Nick Bebout - T
Terry Beeson - LB
Mark Bell - TE
Tony Benjamin - FB
Dennis Boyd - DE
Dave Brown - DB
Louis Bullard - T
Keith Butler - LB
Ron Coder - G
Bill Cooke - DT
Pete Cronan - LB
Dan Doornink - FB
Don Dufek - DB
Carl Eller - DE
Duke Fergerson - WR
Tony Green - HB
Jessie Green - WR
Sammy Green - LB
Bill Gregory - DE
Robert Hardy - DT
John Harris - DB
Efren Herrera - K
Al Hunter - HB
Michael Jackson - LB
Kerry Justin - DB
Art Kuehn - C
Steve Largent - WR
Tom Lynch - G
Sam McCullum - WR
Charles McShane - LB
Jeff Moore - HB
Steve Myer - QB
Bob Newton - G
Joe Norman - LB
Mike O'Brien - DB
Brian Peets - TE
Larry Polowski - LB
Ernie Price - DE
Steve Raible - WR
Jeff Sevy - T
Keith Simpson - DB
David Sims - HB
Sherman Smith - HB
Manu Tuiasosopo - DT
Herman Weaver - K
Cornell Webster - DB
John Yarno - C
Jim Zorn - QB

1979 Tampa Bay

Darrell Austin - G
Ricky Bell - FB
Rick Berns - HB
Tom Blanchard - K
Rik Bonness - LB
Aaron Brown - LB
Cedric Brown - DB
Darryl Carlton - T
Billy Cesare - DB
Wally Chambers - DE
Mark Cotney - DB
Randy Crowder - NT
Johnny Davis - FB
Tony Davis - FB
Jerry Eckwood - HB
Chuck Fusina - QB
Jimmie Giles - TE
Isaac Hagins - WR
Charley Hannah - T
Greg Horton - G
Cecil Johnson - LB
Gordon Jones - WR
Curtis Jordan - DB
Bill Kollar - DE
Dave Lewis - LB
Reggie Lewis - DE
David Logan - NT
Larry Mucker - WR
Dana Nafziger - LB
Jim Obradovich - TE
Neil O'Donoghue - K
Morris Owens - WR
Mike Rae - QB
George Ragsdale - HB
Dave Reavis - T
Danny Reece - DB
Greg Roberts - G
Gene Sanders - DE
Dewey Selmon - LB
Lee Roy Selmon - DE
Mike Washington - DB
Jeris White - DB
Doug Williams - QB
Steven Wilson - C
Richard Wood - LB
George Yarno - G

1979 Washington

Coy Bacon - DE
Mike Bragg - K
Perry Brooks - DT
Danny Buggs - WR
Dave Butz - DT
Monte Coleman - LB
Fred Dean - G
Chris DeFrance - WR
Greg Dubinetz - G
Phil DuBois - TE
Brad Dusek - LB
Ike Forte - HB
Ted Fritsch - C
Jean Fugett - TE
Kris Haines - WR
Bobby Hammond - HB
Buddy Hardeman - HB
Clarence Harmon - HB
Don Harris - DB
Terry Hermeling - T
Dallas Hickman - LB
Ken Houston - DB
Don Hover - LB
Joe Jones - DE
Bob Kuziel - C
Joe Lavender - DB
Karl Lorch - DE
Benny Malone - HB
John McDaniel - WR
Kim McQuilken - QB
Rich Milot - LB
Mark Moseley - K
Mark Murphy - DB
Neal Olkewicz - LB
Lemar Parrish - DB
Lonnie Perrin - FB
Tony Peters - DB
Grady Richardson - TE
John Riggins - FB
Ron Saul - G
Paul Smith - DE
George Starke - T
Diron Talbert - DT
Joe Theismann - QB
Ricky Thompson - WR
Ray Waddy - DB
Don Warren - TE
Jeff Williams - G
Pete Wysocki - LB

1980 Atlanta

Anthony Anderson - HB
William Andrews - FB
Steve Bartkowski - QB
Jon Brooks - LB
Warren Bryant - T
Rick Byas - DB
Lynn Cain - HB
Chuck Correal - C
Buddy Curry - LB
Tony Daykin - LB
Wilson Faumuina - NT
Edgar Fields - DE
Wally Francis - WR
Bob Glazebrook - DB
Chuck Herman - G
Pat Howell - G
Alfred Jackson - WR
John James - K
Alfred Jenkins - WR
Kenny Johnson - DB
Earl Jones - DB
Mike Kenn - T
Jerome King - DB
Fulton Kuykendall - LB
Jim Laughlin - LB
Rolland Lawrence - DB
James Mayberry - FB
Tim Mazzetti - K
Dewey McClain - LB
Phil McKinnely - T
Jeff Merrow - DE
Russ Mikeska - TE
Calvin Miller - NT
Junior Miller - TE
Mike Moroski - QB
Robert Pennywell - LB
Tom Pridemore - DB
Frank Reed - DB
Al Richardson - LB
Dave Scott - G
Don Smith - NT
Mike Smith - WR
Reggie Smith - WR
Ray Strong - HB
Stan Sytsma - LB
R.C. Thielemann - G
Jeff Van Note - C
Joel Williams - LB
Jeff Yeates - DE
Mike Zele - NT

1980 Baltimore

Mack Alston - TE
Kim Anderson - DB
Mike Barnes - DT
Lyle Blackwood - DB
Mike Bragg - K
Larry Braziel - DB
Randy Burke - WR
Ray Butler - WR
Roger Carr - WR
Fred Cook - DE
Brian DeRoo - WR
Curtis Dickey - HB
Zachary Dixon - HB
Ray Donaldson - C
Joe Ehrmann - DT
Greg Fields - DE
Chris Foote - G
Cleveland Franklin - FB
Ben Garry - FB
Nesby Glasgow - DB
Wade Griffin - T
Jeff Hart - T
Derrick Hatchett - DB
Steve Heimkreiter - LB
Ken Huff - G
Bert Jones - QB
Ricky Jones - LB
Jim Krahl - DT
Barry Krauss - LB
George Kunz - T
Bruce Laird - DB
Greg Landry - QB
Ron LaPointe - TE
Reese McCall - TE
Don McCauley - HB
Ken Mendenhall - C
Steve Mike
Herb Orvis - DT
Mike Ozdowski - DE
Reggie Pinkney - DB
Bob Pratt - G
Bob Raba - TE
Sanders Shiver - LB
Mike Siani - WR
Ed Simonini - LB
Marvin Sims - FB
Ed Smith - LB
Bob Van Duyne - G
Joe Washington - HB
Mike Woods - LB

1980 Buffalo

Rufus Bess - DB
Jon Borchardt - G
Mark Brammer - TE
Curtis Brown - FB
Jerry Butler - WR
Greg Cater - K
Mario Clark - DB
Joe Cribbs - HB
Joe Devlin - T
Conrad Dobler - G
Duke Fergerson - WR
Joe Ferguson - QB
Steve Freeman - DB
Reuben Gant - TE
Will Grant - C
Doug Greene - DB
Dee Hardison - T
Jim Haslett - LB
Roland Hooks - HB
David Humm - QB
Scott Hutchinson - DE
Darrell Irvin - DE
Ron Jessie - WR
Ken Johnson - DE
Ken Jones - T
Mike Kadish - NT
Chris Keating - LB
Rod Kush - DB
Roosevelt Leaks - FB
Frank Lewis - WR
Dan Manucci - QB
Reggie McKenzie - G
Nick Mike
Terry Miller - HB
Shane Nelson - LB
Jeff Nixon - DB
Artie Owens - WR
Ervin Parker - LB
Lou Piccone - WR
Jim Ritcher - C
Isiah Robertson - LB
Charles Romes - DB
Lucius Sanford - LB
Bill Simpson - DB
Fred Smerlas - NT
Roland Solomon - DB
Phil Villapiano - LB
Tim Vogler - C
Sherman White - DE
Ben Williams - DE

1980 Chi. Bears

Ted Albrecht - T
Brian Baschnagel - WR
Dave Becker - DB
Gary Campbell - LB
Mike Cobb - TE
Robin Earl - TE
Allan Ellis - DB
Vince Evans - QB
Gary Fencik - DB
Bob Fisher - TE
Wentford Gaines - DB
Kris Haines - WR
Dan Hampton - DE
Roland Harper - FB
Al Harris - DE
Mike Hartenstine - DE
Bruce Herron - LB
Tom Hicks - LB
Jonathan Hoke - DB
Noah Jackson - G
Dan Jiggetts - T
Lee Kunz - LB
Dennis Lick - T
Vaughn Lusby - DB
Willie McClendon - HB
Rocco Moore - G
Jerry Muckensturm - LB
Dan Neal - C
Jim Osborne - DT
Alan Page - DT
Bob Parsons - TE
Walter Payton - HB
Mike Phipps - QB
Doug Plank - DB
Ron Rydalch - DT
Terry Schmidt - DB
James Scott - WR
Brad Shearer - DT
John Skibinski - FB
Revie Sorey - G
Matt Suhey - FB
Paul Tabor - C
Bob Thomas - K
Mike Ulmer - DB
Len Walterscheid - DB
Rickey Watts - WR
Dave Williams - FB
Otis Wilson - LB

1980 Cincinnati

Charles Alexander - HB
Alton Alexis - WR
Ken Anderson - QB
Don Bass - WR
Jim Breech - K
Louis Breeden - DB
Greg Bright - DB
Jim Browner - DB
Ross Browner - DE
Glenn Bujnoch - G
Gary Burley - DE
Blair Bush - C
Glenn Cameron - LB
James Corbett - TE
Isaac Curtis - WR
Tom Dinkel - LB
Eddie Edwards - DE
William Glass - G
Archie Griffin - HB
Ray Griffin - DB
Bo Harris - LB
M. L. Harris - TE
Jo Jo Heath - DB
Bryan Hicks - DB
Rod Horn - NT
Dick Jauron - DB
Pete Johnson - FB
Steve Kreider - WR
Dave Lapham - G
Jim LeClair - LB
Mike Levenseller - WR
Pat McInally - WR
Andrew Melontree - LB
Cleo Montgomery - WR
Max Montoya - G
Blake Moore - C
Anthony Munoz - T
Nathan Poole - FB
Rick Razzano - LB
Ken Riley - DB
Dan Ross - TE
Ron Simpkins - LB
Mike St. Clair - DE
Shafer Suggs - DB
Ian Sunter - K
Jack Thompson - QB
Deacon Turner - HB
Sandro Vitiello - K
Mike White - DE
Wilson Whitley - NT
Reggie Williams - LB
Mike Wilson - T

1980 Cleveland

Willis Adams - WR
Lyle Alzado - DE
Dick Ambrose - LB
Autry Beamon - DB
Ron Bolton - DB
Henry Bradley - NT
Clinton Burrell - DB
Don Cockroft - K
Bill Cowher - LB
Ron Crews - NT
Thom Darden - DB
Oliver Davis - DB
Joe DeLamielleure - G
Tom DeLeone - C
Doug Dieken - T
Johnny Evans - QB
Ricky Feacher - WR
Judson Flint - DB
Elvis Franks - DE
Don Goode - LB
Charlie Hall - LB
Dino Hall - HB
Marshall Harris - DE
Calvin Hill - HB
Robert Jackson - LB
Robert Jackson - G
Lawrence Johnson - DB
Dave Logan - WR
Clay Matthews - LB
Paul McDonald - QB
Cleo Miller - FB
John Mohring - LB
Ozzie Newsome - TE
McDonald Oden - TE
Cliff Odom - LB
Joel Patten - T
Greg Pruitt - HB
Mike Pruitt - FB
Cody Risien - T
Reggie Rucker - WR
Clarence Scott - DB
Henry Sheppard - G
Jerry Sherk - DE
Brian Sipe - QB
Gerry Sullivan - C
Curtis Weathers - TE
Charles White - HB
Jerry Wilkinson - DE
Keith Wright - WR

1980 Dallas

Benny Barnes - DB
Larry Bethea - DT
Bob Breunig - LB
Guy Brown - LB
Glenn Carano - QB
Dextor Clinkscale - DB
Larry Cole - DT
Jim Cooper - T
Doug Cosbie - TE
Anthony Dickerson - LB
Pat Donovan - T
Tony Dorsett - HB
Billy Joe DuPree - TE
John Dutton - DT
John Fitzgerald - C
Andy Frederick - T
Mike Hegman - LB
Tony Hill - WR
Gary Hogeboom - QB
Randy Hughes - DB
Eric Hurt - DB
Bruce Huther - LB
Butch Johnson - WR
Too Tall Jones - DE
James Jones - HB
D. D. Lewis - LB
Harvey Martin - DE
Aaron Mitchell - DB
Robert Newhouse - FB
Timmy Newsome - FB
Drew Pearson - WR
Preston Pearson - HB
Kurt Petersen - G
Tom Rafferty - G
Bill Roe - LB
Jay Saldi - TE
Herbert Scott - G
Rafael Septien - K
Robert Shaw - C
Roland Solomon - DB
Ron Springs - FB
Bruce Thornton - DE
Dennis Thurman - DB
Charlie Waters - DB
Norm Wells - G
Randy White - DT
Danny White - QB
Steve Wilson - DB

1980 Denver

Otis Armstrong - HB
Keith Bishop - C
Greg Boyd - DE
Greg Bracelin - LB
Larry Brunson - WR
Billy Bryan - C
Rubin Carter - NT
Barney Chavous - DE
Kelvin Clark - T
Ron Egloff - TE
Larry Evans - LB
Steve Foley - DB
Tom Glassic - G
Randy Gradishar - LB
Mike Harden - DB
Maurice Harvey - DB
Paul Howard - G
Glenn Hyde - G
Bernard Jackson - DB
Tom Jackson - LB
Jim Jensen - FB
Rulon Jones - DE
Jon Keyworth - FB
Jeff Knapple - QB
Aaron Kyle - DB
Bill Larson - TE
Don Latimer - NT
Rob Lytle - HB
Brison Manor - DE
Lawrence McCutcheon
Claudie Minor - T
Emery Moorehead - WR
Craig Morton - QB
Haven Moses - WR
Rob Nairne - LB
Ben Norman - HB
Riley Odoms - TE
Dave Preston - HB
Luke Prestridge - K
Joe Rizzo - LB
Matt Robinson - QB
Jim Ryan - LB
Laval Short - NT
Art Smith - LB
Perry Smith - DB
Fred Steinfort - K
Dave Studdard - T
Arland Thompson - G
Billy Thompson - DB
Rick Upchurch - WR
Steve Watson - WR
James Wright - TE
Louis Wright - DB

1980 Detroit

Jimmy Allen - DB
John Arnold - WR
Al Baker - DE
Karl Baldischwiler - T
Russ Bolinger - G
Luther Bradley - DB
Dexter Bussey - FB
Ken Callicutt - HB
Garry Cobb - LB
Eddie Cole - LB
Curley Culp - NT
Gary Danielson - QB
Chris Dieterich - T
Keith Dorney - T
Homer Elias - G
Ken Fantetti - LB
Amos Fowler - C
Mike Friede - WR
Bill Gay - DT
Tommie Ginn - G
James Harrell - LB
David Hill - TE
Eric Hipple - QB
Vern Holland - T
James Hunter - DB
Rick Kane - HB
Horace King - FB
Jeff Komlo - QB
Burton Lawless - G
Eddie Lewis - DB
Alva Liles - NT
Derrel Luce - LB
Mike McCoy - DT
Prentice McCray - DB
John Mendenhall - DT
John Mohring - LB
Eddie Murray - K
Ulysses Norris - TE
Ray Oldham - DB
Willie Parker - C
Wally Pesuit - C
Dave Pureifory - DE
Bo Robinson - FB
Freddie Scott - WR
Dave Simmons - LB
Billy Sims - HB
Tom Skladany - K
Wayne Smith - DB
Jesse Thompson - WR
Leonard Thompson - WR
Tom Tuinei - DT
Tom Turnure - C
Rod Walters - G
Charlie Weaver - LB
Stan White - LB
Mike Whited - T
Ray Williams - WR
Walt Williams - DB
John Woodcock - DT

1980 Green Bay

Kurt Allerman - LB
John Anderson - LB
Vickey Ray Anderson - FB
Steve Atkins - FB
Buddy Aydelette - T
Bruce Beekley - LB
David Beverly - K
Tom Birney - K
Ken Brown - C
Mike Butler - DE
Brian Cabral - LB
Ron Cassidy - WR
Paul Coffman - TE
George Cumby - LB
Lynn Dickey - QB
Rich Dimler - NT
Mike Douglass - LB
Gerry Ellis - FB
Derrel Gofourth - G
Johnnie Gray - DB
Jim Gueno - LB
Leotis Harris - G
Estus Hood - DB
Harlan Huckleby - HB
Mike Hunt - LB
Eddie Lee Ivery - HB
Melvin Jackson - G
Charles Johnson - NT
Ezra Johnson - DE
Mike Jolly - DB
Terry Jones - NT
Bobby Kimball - WR
Syd Kitson - G
Greg Koch - T
Mark Koncar - T
Bill Larson - TE
Kit Lathrop - DE
Mark Lee - DB
Mike Lewis - NT
James Lofton - WR
Steve Luke - DB
Chester Marcol - K
Larry McCarren - C
Mike McCoy - DB
Casey Merrill - DE
Terdell Middleton - HB
Mark Murphy - DB
Fred Nixon - WR
Ed O'Neil - LB
Steve Pisarkiewicz - QB
Paul Rudzinski - LB
Barty Smith - FB
Jan Stenerud - K
Timothy Stokes - T
Karl Swanke - T
Aundra Thompson - WR
John Thompson - TE
Bill Troup - QB
Wylie Turner - DB
Mike Wellman - C
David Whitehurst - QB

1980 Houston

Adger Armstrong - FB
Jesse Baker - DE
Mike Barber - TE
Elvin Bethea - DE
Gregg Bingham - LB
Craig Bradshaw - QB
Robert Brazile - LB
Ken Burrough - WR
Earl Campbell - HB
Rob Carpenter - FB
David Carter - G
Dave Casper - TE
Rich Caster - TE
Boobie Clark - FB
Ronnie Coleman - HB
John Corker - LB
Curley Culp - NT
Greg Davidson - C
Charles Davis - NT
Andy Dorris - DE
Angelo Fields - T
Ed Fisher - G
Toni Fritsch - K
Leon Gray - T
Sammy Green - LB
Jeff Groth - WR
Carter Hartwig - DB
Conway Hayman - T
Tom Henderson - LB
Daryl Hunt - LB
Billy Johnson - WR
Ken Kennard - NT
Chester Marcol - K
Carl Mauck - C
Guido Merkens - WR
Gifford Nielsen - QB
Cliff Parsley - K
Vernon Perry - DB
Mike Reinfeldt - DB
Mike Renfro - WR
Carl Roaches - WR
Tim Smith - WR
Ken Stabler - QB
Greg Stemrick - DB
Mike Stensrud - DE
Art Stringer - LB
Jack Tatum - DB
Ted Thompson - LB
Morris Towns - T
Ted Washington - LB
J. C. Wilson - DB

Tim Wilson - FB
Bob Young - G

1980 Kansas City

Charlie Ane - C
Gary Barbaro - DB
Ed Beckman - TE
Mike Bell - DE
Horace Belton - HB
Jerry Blanton - LB
Brad Budde - G
Carlos Carson - WR
M.L. Carter - DB
Herb Christopher - DB
Tom Clements - QB
Tom Condon - G
Al Dixon - TE
Paul Dombroski - DB
Steve Fuller - QB
Earl Gant - HB
Bubba Garcia - WR
Charlie Getty - T
Gary Green - DB
Bob Grupp - K
Jim Hadnot - FB
Eric Harris - DB
Matt Herkenhoff - T
Sylvester Hicks - DE
Tom Howard - LB
Charles Jackson - LB
Bill Kenney - QB
Kelly Kirchbaum - LB
Ken Kremer - NT
Dave Lindstrom - DE
Nick Lowery - K
Dino Mangiero - NT
Frank Manumaleuga - LB
Henry Marshall - WR
Ted McKnight - FB
Jerry Meyers - DE
Arnold Morgado - FB
Brad Oates - T
Don Parrish - NT
Whitney Paul - LB
Cal Peterson - LB
Tony Reed - HB
Jerry Reese - DB
Stan Rome - WR
Donovan Rose - DB
Jim Rourke - T
Jack Rudnay - C
Tony Samuels - TE
Clarence Sanders - LB
Bob Simmons - G
Franky Smith - T
J. T. Smith - WR
Gary Spani - LB
Art Still - DE
Ken Talton - HB
Rod Walters - G
Mike Williams - TE

1980 LA Rams

George Andrews - LB
Walt Arnold - TE
Bill Bain - G
Larry Brooks - DT
Bob Brudzinski - LB
Cullen Bryant - FB
Frank Corral - K
Nolan Cromwell - DB
Jeff Delaney - DB
Preston Dennard - WR
Reggie Doss - DE
Fred Dryer - DE
Carl Ekern - LB
Mike Fanning - DT
Vince Ferragamo - QB
Doug France - T
Mike Guman - HB
Pat Haden - QB
Dennis Harrah - G
Joe Harris - LB
Victor Hicks - TE
Drew Hill - WR
Eddie Hill - HB
Kent Hill - G
Greg Horton - G
LeRoy Irvin - DB
Johnnie Johnson Jr. - DB
Cody Jones - DT
Bob Lee - QB
Ed McGlasson - G
Willie Miller - WR
Lydell Mitchell - HB
Jeff Moore - WR
Phil Murphy - DT
Terry Nelson - TE
Irvin Pankey - T
Elvis Peacock - HB
Rod Perry - DB
Jack Reynolds - LB
Conrad Rucker - TE
Jeff Rutledge - QB
Rich Saul - C
Jackie Slater - T
Doug Smith - G
Lucious Smith - DB
Ivory Sully - DB
Jewerl Thomas - HB
Pat Thomas - DB
Wendell Tyler - HB

Billy Waddy - WR
Greg Westbrooks - LB
Jack Youngblood - DE
Jim Youngblood - LB

1980 Miami

Jeffrey Allen - DB
Elmer Bailey - WR
Carl Barisich - NT
Bill Barnett - DE
Bob Baumhower - NT
Doug Beaudoin - DB
Woody Bennett - FB
Don Bessillieu - DB
Doug Betters - DE
Glenn Blackwood - DB
Kim Bokamper - LB
Jimmy Cefalo - WR
Billy Cesare - DB
Rusty Chambers - LB
Vern Den Herder - DE
Mark Dennard - C
Thom Dornbrook - G
A. J. Duhe - LB
Tim Foley - DB
Nick Giaquinto - HB
Jon Giesler - T
Larry Gordon - LB
Cleveland Green - T
Bob Griese - QB
Bruce Hardy - TE
Duriel Harris - WR
Steve Howell - FB
Bob Kuechenberg - G
Eric Laakso - T
Ronnie Lee - TE
Larry Little - G
Don McNeal - DB
Nat Moore - WR
Rick Moser - HB
Tony Nathan - HB
Ed Newman - G
Ralph Ortega - LB
Earnest Rhone - LB
George Roberts - K
Terry Robiskie - FB
Joe Rose - TE
Steve Shull - LB
Gerald Small - DB
Dwight Stephenson - C
Don Strock - QB
Ed Taylor - DB
Don Testerman - FB
Jeff Toews - G
Steve Towle - LB
Uwe von Schamann - K
Rod Walters - G
Delvin Williams - HB
David Woodley - QB

1980 Minnesota

Nick Bebout - T
Matt Blair - LB
Brent Boyd - G
Ted Brown - FB
Bob Bruer - TE
Larry Brune - DB
Bobby Bryant - DB
Marvin Cobb - DB
Greg Coleman - K
Rick Danmeier - K
Steve Dils - QB
Wes Hamilton - G
Tom Hannon - DB
Randy Holloway - DE
Jim Hough - G
Dave Huffman - T
Dennis Johnson - LB
Henry Johnson - LB
Kurt Knoff - DB
Tommy Kramer - QB
Jim Langer - C
Terry LeCount - WR
Derrel Luce - LB
Doug Martin - DE
Fred McNeill - LB
Kevin Miller - WR
Robert Miller - HB
Mel Mitchell - G
Mark Mullaney - DE
Keith Nord - DB
Doug Paschal - FB
Eddie Payton - HB
Ahmad Rashad - WR
Steve Riley - T
Dave Roller - DT
Ken Sanders - DE
Joe Senser - TE
Jeff Siemon - LB
Scott Studwell - LB
Doug Sutherland - DT
Dennis Swilley - C
Willie Teal - DB
Bob Tucker - TE
John Turner - DB
John Vella - T
Stu Voigt - TE
James White - DT
Sammy White - WR
Nate Wright - DB
Ron Yary - T
Rickey Young - HB

1980 New England

Julius Adams - DE
Sam Adams - G
Richard Bishop - NT
Pete Brock - C
Preston Brown - WR
Don Calhoun - FB
Matt Cavanaugh - QB
Allan Clark - HB
Raymond Clayborn - DB
Bob Cryder - G
Bill Currier - DB
Vagas Ferguson - HB
Chuck Foreman - FB
Tim Fox - DB
Russ Francis - TE
Bob Golic - LB
Steve Grogan - QB
Ray Hamilton - NT
John Hannah - G
Don Hasselbeck - TE
Mike Hawkins - LB
Mike Haynes - DB
Mike Hubach - K
Horace Ivory - HB
Harold Jackson - WR
Roland James - DB
Andy Johnson - HB
Shelby Jordan - T
Steve King - LB
Bill Lenkaitis - C
Mel Lunsford - DE
Bill Matthews - LB
Prentice McCray - DB
Doug McDougald - DE
Tony McGee - DE
Larry McGrew - LB
Steve McMichael - NT
Stanley Morgan - WR
Steve Nelson - LB
Carlos Pennywell - WR
Garry Puetz - T
Rick Sanford - DB
Rod Shoate - LB
John Smith - K
Mosi Tatupu - FB
Donald Westbrook - WR
Dwight Wheeler - T
John Zamberlin - LB

1980 New Orleans

Gordon Banks - WR
Guy Benjamin - QB
Barry Bennett - DT
Ken Bordelon - LB
Stan Brock - T
Ray Brown - DB
Ed Burns - QB
Joe Campbell - DE
Wes Chandler - WR
Clarence Chapman - DB
Henry Childs - TE
Larry Collins - HB
Larry Coombs - G
Tom Donovan - WR
Russell Erxleben - K
Chuck Evans - LB
Joe Federspiel - LB
Mike Fultz - DT
Tony Galbreath - FB
Elois Grooms - DE
Larry Hardy - TE
Ike Harris - WR
Tommy Hart - DE
John Hill - C
Stan Holloway - LB
Jack Holmes - HB
Jim Kovach - LB
Dave Lafary - T
Archie Manning - QB
James Marshall - DB
Reggie Mathis - LB
Rich Mauti - WR
Guido Merkens - WR
Derland Moore - DT
Chuck Muncie - FB
Tom Myers - DB
Artie Owens - WR
Tinker Owens - WR
Steve Parker - DE
Jim Pietrzak - C
Elex Price - DT
Ricky Ray - DB
Don Reese - DE
Benny Ricardo - K
Jimmy Rogers - HB
Donald Schwartz - DB
Bobby Scott - QB
Mike Spivey - DB
Mike Strachan - HB
Fred Sturt - G
J.T. Taylor - T
Dave Washington - LB
Dave Waymer - DB
Brooks Williams - TE
Wayne Wilson - FB
Robert Woods - G
Emanuel Zanders - G

1980 NY Giants

Ben Apuna - LB
Brad Benson - T
Art Best - HB

Tony Blount - DB
Scott Brunner - QB
Phil Cancik - LB
Harry Carson - LB
Jim Clack - C
Jim Culbreath - FB
Joe Danelo - K
Mike Dennis - DB
Terry Falcon - G
Eric Felton - DB
Mike Friede - WR
Alvin Garrett - HB
Earnest Gray - WR
Don Harris - DB
Mark Haynes - DB
Larry Heater - HB
Bud Hebert - DB
Steve Henry - DB
Eddie Hicks - FB
Mike Hogan - FB
Vern Holland - T
Terry Jackson - DB
Dave Jennings - K
Gary Jeter - DE
Dennis Johnson - TE
Nate Johnson - WR
Brian Kelley - LB
Gordon King - T
Jerome King - DB
Scott Laidlaw - FB
Myron Lapka - NT
Chris Linnin - DE
Frank Marion - LB
Dale Markham - DE
George Martin - DE
Bo Matthews - FB
Mike McCoy - DT
Curtis McGriff - NT
Joe McLaughlin - LB
Tom Mullady - TE
Doug Nettles - DB
Don Patterson - DB
Johnny Perkins - WR
Ralph Perretta - G
Leon Perry - FB
Danny Pittman - WR
Beasley Reece - DB
Nate Rivers - FB
Kelly Saalfeld - C
Gary Shirk - TE
Roy Simmons - G
Phil Simms - QB
John Skorupan - LB
George Small - NT
Philip Tabor - NT
Billy Taylor - HB
Steven Tobin - C
J. T. Turner - G
Kevin Turner - LB
Brad Van Pelt - LB
Whip Walton - LB
Jeff Weston - T
Mike Whittington - LB
Gary Woolford - DB
Kervin Wyatt - LB

1980 NY Jets

Dan Alexander - G
Jerome Barkum - TE
Bobby Batton - HB
Woody Bennett - FB
Guy Bingham - G
Stan Blinka - LB
Greg Buttle - LB
Steve Carpenter - DB
Gerald Carter - WR
Ron Crosby - LB
Eric Cunningham - G
Paul Darby - WR
Scott Dierking - HB
Donald Dykes - DB
Joe Fields - C
Derrick Gaffney - WR
Clark Gaines - FB
Mark Gastineau - DE
Chris Godfrey - DE
Bruce Harper - HB
Jerry Holmes - DB
Bobby Jackson - DB
Jesse Johnson - DB
Lam Jones - WR
Bobby Jones - WR
Joe Klecko - DE
Pat Leahy - K
Kenny Lewis - HB
Kevin Long - FB
Marty Lyons - DT
Saladin Martin - DB
Mike McKibben - LB
Lance Mehl - LB
Tim Moresco - DB
Tom Newton - FB
Lawrence Pillers - DE
Marvin Powell - T
Chuck Ramsey - K
Randy Rasmussen - G
Darrol Ray - DB
Wes Roberts - DE
John Roman - T
Pat Ryan - QB
Abdul Salaam - DT
Ken Schroy - DB
Mickey Shuler - TE
Shafer Suggs - DB
John Sullivan - LB

Richard Todd - QB
Stan Waldemore - G
Wesley Walker - WR
Chris Ward - T
Bob Winkel - DT

1980 Oakland

Chris Bahr - K
Jeff Barnes - LB
Morris Bradshaw - WR
Cliff Branch - WR
Dave Browning - DE
Joe Campbell - DE
Dave Casper - TE
Mario Celotto - LB
Bob Chandler - WR
Raymond Chester - TE
Todd Christensen - FB
Dave Dalby - C
Bruce Davis - T
Mike Davis - DB
Ray Guy - K
Cedrick Hardman - DE
Dwight Harrison - DB
Lester Hayes - DB
Ted Hendricks - LB
I.M. Hipp - HB
Monte Jackson - DB
Derrick Jensen - FB
Willie Jones - DE
Kenny King - HB
Reggie Kinlaw - NT
Henry Lawrence - T
Alva Liles - NT
Rod Martin - LB
Rich Martini - WR
Mickey Marvin - G
Lindsey Mason - T
Ira Matthews - HB
John Matuszak - DE
Randy McClanahan - LB
Odis McKinney - DB
Matt Millen - LB
Keith Moody - DB
Bob Nelson - LB
Dwayne O'Steen - DB
Burgess Owens - DB
Dan Pastorini - QB
Dave Pear - NT
Jim Plunkett - QB
Derrick Ramsey - TE
Art Shell - T
Mike Spivey - DB
Steve Sylvester - G
Gene Upshaw - G
Mark van Eeghen - FB
Greg Westbrooks - LB
Art Whittington - HB
Marc Wilson - QB

1980 Philadelphia

Ron Baker - G
Bill Bergey - LB
Richard Blackmore - DB
Luther Blue - WR
Thomas Brown - DE
John Bunting - LB
Billy Campfield - HB
Harold Carmichael - WR
Al Chesley - LB
Ken Clarke - NT
Jim Culbreath - FB
Zachary Dixon - HB
Ken Dunek - TE
Herman Edwards - DB
Scott Fitzkee - WR
Tony Franklin - K
Louie Giammona - HB
Lewis Gilbert - TE
Carl Hairston - DE
Perry Harrington - FB
Leroy Harris - FB
Dennis Harrison - DE
Zac Henderson - DB
Wally Henry - WR
Mike Hogan - FB
Claude Humphrey - DE
Ron Jaworski - QB
Charlie Johnson - NT
Steve Kenney - T
Keith Krepfle - TE
Frank LeMaster - LB
Randy Logan - DB
Wilbert Montgomery - HB
Guy Morriss - C
Rod Parker - WR
Woody Peoples - G
Petey Perot - G
Ray Phillips - LB
Joe Pisarcik - QB
Jerry Robinson - LB
Max Runager - K
John Sciarra - DB
Jerry Sisemore - T
Mark Slater - C
Charlie Smith - WR
John Spagnola - TE
Bob Torrey - FB
Steve Wagner - DB
Stan Walters - T
Reggie Wilkes - LB
Brenard Wilson - DB
Roynell Young - DB

1980 Pittsburgh

Larry Anderson - DB
Matt Bahr - K
John Banaszak - DE
Tom Beasley - DE
Theo Bell - WR
Rocky Bleier - HB
Mel Blount - DB
Terry Bradshaw - QB
Larry Brown - T
Marvin Cobb - DB
Robin Cole - LB
Craig Colquitt - K
Steve Courson - G
Bennie Cunningham - TE
Russell Davis - FB
Gary Dunn - DT
Steve Furness - DT
Joe Greene - DT
L. C. Greenwood - DE
Randy Grossman - TE
Jack Ham - LB
Franco Harris - FB
Greg Hawthorne - HB
Tunch Ilkin - G
Ron Johnson - DB
Jon Kolb - T
Jack Lambert - LB
Mark Malone - QB
Tyrone McGriff - G
Tom Moriarty - DB
Ted Petersen - T
Ray Pinney - G
Frank Pollard - HB
Donnie Shell - DB
Jim Smith - WR
John Stallworth - WR
Cliff Stoudt - QB
Lynn Swann - WR
Calvin Sweeney - WR
J.T. Thomas - DB
Sidney Thornton - HB
Loren Toews - LB
Zack Valentine - LB
Mike Wagner - DB
Mike Webster - C
Dwight White - DE
Dennis Winston - LB
Craig Wolfley - G
Dwayne Woodruff - DB

1980 St. Louis

Bill Acker - NT
Carl Allen - DB
Ottis Anderson - HB
Mark Arneson - LB
Charles Baker - LB
Tom Banks - G
John Barefield - LB
Mark Bell - WR
Joe Bostic - G
Tom Brahaney - C
Jon Brooks - LB
Rush Brown - NT
Theotis Brown - FB
Randy Clark - C
Ron Coder - G
Tim Collier - DB
George Collins - T
Chris Combs - TE
Barney Cotton - G
Kirby Criswell - LB
Mike Dawson - NT
Dan Dierdorf - T
Calvin Favron - LB
Mark Goodspeed - T
Mel Gray - WR
Roy Green - DB
Ken Greene - DB
Curtis Greer - DE
Willard Harrell - HB
Jim Hart - QB
Tim Kearney - LB
Jeff Lee - WR
Oudious Lee - NT
Rusty Lisch - QB
Steve Little - K
Randy Love - HB
Mike Loyd - QB
Doug Marsh - TE
Stafford Mays - DE
Jeff McIntyre - LB
Wayne Morris - FB
Steve Neils - LB
Lee Nelson - DB
Brad Oates - T
Neil O'Donoghue - K
Gary Parris - TE
Rod Phillips - FB
Bob Pollard - DE
Thomas Seabron - LB
Dave Stief - WR
Ken Stone - DB
Larry Swider - K
Pat Tilley - WR
Roger Wehrli - DB
Eric Williams - LB
Gerard Williams - DB
Keith Wortman - T
Ron Yankowski - DE

1980 San Diego

Dan Audick - T

Hank Bauer - HB
Rolf Benirschke - K
Willie Buchanon - DB
John Cappelletti - FB
Fred Dean - DE
Charles DeJurnett - DT
Jerome Dove - DB
Frank Duncan - DB
Glen Edwards - DB
John Floyd - WR
Dan Fouts - QB
Mike Fuller - DB
LaRue Harrington - FB
Bob Horn - LB
Bernard Jackson - DB
John Jefferson - WR
Gary Johnson - DT
Charlie Joiner - WR
Leroy Jones - DE
Louie Kelcher - DT
Linden King - LB
Jim Laslavic - LB
John Lee - DE
Chuck Loewen - T
Woodrow Lowe - LB
Ed Luther - QB
Don Macek - C
Greg McCrary - TE
Carl McGee - LB
Chuck Muncie - FB
Rick Partridge - K
Ralph Perretta - G
Scott Perry - DB
Ray Preston - LB
Bob Rush - C
Booker Russell - FB
Pete Shaw - DB
Billy Shields - T
Ron Smith - WR
Hal Stringert - DB
Mike Thomas - HB
Cliff Thrift - LB
Russ Washington - T
Ed White - G
Doug Wilkerson - G
Clarence Williams - HB
Mike Williams - DB
Kellen Winslow - TE
Mike Wood - K
Don Woods - HB
Wilbur Young - DE

1980 San Francisco

Jerry Aldridge - FB
Terry Anderson - WR
John Ayers - G
Jean Barrett - T
Dwaine Board - DE
Bob Bruer - TE
Ken Bungarda - T
Dan Bunz - LB
Mike Calhoun - DT
Ricky Churchman - DB
Dwight Clark - WR
Earl Cooper - FB
Charles Cornelius - DB
Randy Cross - G
Steve DeBerg - QB
Walt Downing - G
Lenvil Elliott - HB
Keith Fahnhorst - T
Bob Ferrell - FB
Phil Francis - FB
Lewis Gilbert - TE
Willie Harper - LB
Tom Henderson - LB
Dwight Hicks - DB
Scott Hilton - LB
Paul Hofer - HB
Ernie Hughes - G
Charles Johnson - DB
Jim Krahl - DT
Mel Land - DE
Bobby Leopold - LB
Jim Miller - K
Joe Montana - QB
Melvin Morgan - DB
James Owens - WR
Ricky Patton - HB
Scott Perry - DB
Lawrence Pillers - DE
Craig Puki - LB
Fred Quillan - C
Eason Ramson - TE
Archie Reese - DT
Ray Rhodes - DB
Jim Robinson - WR
Thomas Seabron - LB
Ron Singleton - T
Freddie Solomon - WR
Jim Stuckey - DE
Terry Tautolo - LB
Ken Times - DT
Keena Turner - LB
Ted Vincent - DT
George Visger - DT
Jimmy Webb - DE
Ray Wersching - K
Jerry Wilkinson - DE
Gerard Williams - DB
Herb Williams - DB
Don Woods - HB
Charle Young - TE

1980 Seattle

Sam Adkins - QB
Fred Anderson - DE
Steve August - T
Terry Beeson - LB
Mark Bell - TE
Larry Brinson - FB
Dave Brown - DB
Louis Bullard - T
Keith Butler - LB
Bill Cooke - DT
Terry Dion - DE
Dan Doornink - HB
Don Dufek - DB
Ron Essink - T
Jacob Green - DE
Jessie Green - WR
Bill Gregory - DE
Robert Hardy - DT
John Harris - DB
Efren Herrera - K
Andre Hines - T
Al Hunter - HB
Michael Jackson - LB
Jim Jodat - FB
Kerry Justin - DB
Dave Krieg - QB
Art Kuehn - C
Steve Largent - WR
Will Lewis - DB
Tom Lynch - G
Sam McCullum - WR
Lawrence McCutcheon
Vic Minor - DB
Jeff Moore - HB
Bob Newton - G
Joe Norman - LB
Steve Raible - WR
Terry Rennaker - LB
John Sawyer - TE
Jeff Sevy - G
Keith Simpson - DB
Sherman Smith - HB
Manu Tuiasosopo - DT
Tim Walker - LB
Jim Walsh - FB
Herman Weaver - K
Cornell Webster - DB
John Yarno - C
Jim Zorn - QB

1980 Tampa Bay

Darrell Austin - T
Ricky Bell - FB
Rick Berns - HB
Tom Blanchard - K
Scot Brantley - LB
Aaron Brown - LB
Cedric Brown - DB
Mike Calhoun - DT
Neal Colzie - DB
Mark Cotney - DB
Randy Crowder - NT
Gary Davis - HB
Johnny Davis - FB
Tony Davis - FB
Jerry Eckwood - HB
Chuck Fusina - QB
Jimmie Giles - TE
Isaac Hagins - WR
Charley Hannah - T
Andy Hawkins - LB
Kevin House - WR
Cecil Johnson - LB
Gordon Jones - WR
Curtis Jordan - DB
Bill Kollar - DE
Jim Leonard - C
Dave Lewis - LB
Reggie Lewis - DE
David Logan - NT
Larry Mucker - WR
Jim Obradovich - TE
Bruce Radford - NT
Dave Reavis - T
Danny Reece - DB
Greg Roberts - G
Conrad Rucker - TE
Tony Samuels - TE
Gene Sanders - G
Dewey Selmon - LB
Lee Roy Selmon - DE
Mike Shumann - WR
Ray Snell - G
Dave Stalls - DE
Norris Thomas - DB
Mike Washington - DB
Doug Williams - QB
Steven Wilson - C
Richard Wood - LB
George Yarno - G
Garo Yepremian - K

1980 Washington

Gary Anderson - G
Coy Bacon - DE
Jeff Bostic - C
Perry Brooks - DT
Dave Butz - DT
Rickey Claitt - HB
Monte Coleman - LB
Mike Connell - K
Fred Dean - G
Phil DuBois - TE
Brad Dusek - LB
Ike Forte - HB
Bobby Hammond - HB
Buddy Hardeman - HB
Clarence Harmon - HB
Kenny Harrison - WR
Terry Hermeling - T
Dallas Hickman - DE
Ken Houston - DB
Wilbur Jackson - FB
Joe Jones - DE
Mike Kruczek - QB
Bob Kuziel - C
Joe Lavender - DB
Karl Lorch - DE
John McDaniel - WR
Zion McKinney - WR
Rich Milot - LB
Art Monk - WR
Mark Moseley - K
Mark Murphy - DB
Mike Nelms - DB
Dan Nugent - G
Neal Olkewicz - LB
Lemar Parrish - DB
Dan Peiffer - C
Tony Peters - DB
Grady Richardson - TE
Ron Saul - G
Jerry Scanlan - T
Paul Smith - DT
George Starke - T
Diron Talbert - DT
Joe Theismann - QB
Ricky Thompson - WR
Ray Waddy - DB
Rick Walker - TE
Don Warren - TE
Jeris White - DB
Jeff Williams - G
Pete Wysocki - LB

1981 Atlanta

William Andrews - FB
Steve Bartkowski - QB
Warren Bryant - T
Bobby Butler - DB
Lynn Cain - HB
Buddy Curry - LB
Paul Davis - LB
Tony Daykin - LB
Wilson Faumuina - DE
Mickey Fitzgerald - FB
Wally Francis - WR
Blane Gaison - DB
Bob Glazebrook - DB
Pat Howell - G
Alfred Jackson - WR
John James - K
Alfred Jenkins - WR
Kenny Johnson - DB
Earl Jones - DB
June Jones - QB
Mike Kenn - T
Fulton Kuykendall - LB
Jim Laughlin - LB
Mick Luckhurst - K
James Mayberry - FB
Jeff Merrow - DE
Russ Mikeska - TE
Junior Miller - TE
Tom Moriarty - DB
Mike Moroski - QB
Neal Musser - LB
Tom Pridemore - DB
Al Richardson - LB
Bo Robinson - FB
Eric Sanders - T
Dave Scott - G
John Scully - C
Don Smith - NT
Reggie Smith - WR
Ray Strong - HB
Matthew Teague - DE
R.C. Thielemann - G
Jeff Van Note - C
Lyman White - LB
Joel Williams - LB
Scott Woerner - DB
Jeff Yeates - DE
Mike Zele - NT

1981 Baltimore

Kim Anderson - DB
Mike Barnes - DT
Larry Braziel - DB
Randy Burke - WR
Ray Butler - WR
Roger Carr - WR
Brian DeRoo - WR
Curtis Dickey - HB
Zachary Dixon - HB
Ray Donaldson - C
Joe Federspiel - LB
Tim Foley - T
Chris Foote - C
Cleveland Franklin - FB
Mike Fultz - DT
Mike Garrett - K
Nesby Glasgow - DB
Bubba Green - DT
Wade Griffin - T
Jeff Hart - T
Derrick Hatchett - DB
Steve Henry - DB
Dallas Hickman - DE
Ken Huff - G
David Humm - QB
Bert Jones - QB
Ricky Jones - LB
Barry Krauss - LB
Bruce Laird - DB
Greg Landry - QB
Reese McCall - TE
Don McCauley - HB
Randy McMillan - FB
Jimmy Moore - G
Herb Orvis - DT
Mike Ozdowski - DE
Reggie Pinkney - DB
Bob Pratt - G
Tim Sherwin - TE
Sanders Shiver - LB
David Shula - WR
Ed Simonini - LB
Marvin Sims - FB
Ed Smith - LB
Hosea Taylor - DE
Donnell Thompson - DE
Randy Van Divier - T
Daryl Wilkerson - DE
Kevin Williams - WR
Mike Wood - K
Mike Woods - LB

1981 Buffalo

Steve Alvers - TE
Buster Barnett - TE
Rufus Bess - DB
Jon Borchardt - T
Mark Brammer - TE
Curtis Brown - FB
Jerry Butler - WR
Greg Cater - K
Mario Clark - DB
Joe Cribbs - HB
Joe Devlin - T
Conrad Dobler - G
Joe Ferguson - QB
Byron Franklin - WR
Steve Freeman - DB
Will Grant - C
Jim Haslett - LB
Roland Hooks - HB
Mike Humiston - LB
Darrell Irvin - DE
Ron Jessie - WR
Ken Johnson - DE
Ken Jones - T
Mike Kadish - NT
Chris Keating - LB
Rod Kush - DB
Roosevelt Leaks - FB
Frank Lewis - WR
Tom Lynch - G
Lawrence McCutcheon - FB
Reggie McKenzie - G
Mike-Mayer - K
Shane Nelson - LB
Jeff Nixon - DB
Ervin Parker - LB
Lou Piccone - WR
Robb Riddick - HB
Jim Ritcher - G
Isiah Robertson - LB
Matt Robinson - QB
Charles Romes - DB
Lucius Sanford - LB
Bill Simpson - DB
Fred Smerlas - NT
Phil Villapiano - LB
Tim Vogler - C
Sherman White - DE
Chris Williams - DB
Ben Williams - DE

1981 Chi. Bears

Ted Albrecht - T
Marcus Anderson - WR
Bob Avellini - QB
Brian Baschnagel - WR
Todd Bell - DB
Brian Cabral - LB
Gary Campbell - LB
Mike Cobb - TE
Robin Earl - TE
Vince Evans - QB
Gary Fencik - DB
Jeff Fisher - DB
Bob Fisher - TE
Leslie Frazier - DB
Kris Haines - WR
Dan Hampton - DE
Roland Harper - FB
Al Harris - DE
Mike Hartenstine - DE
Reuben Henderson - DB
Bruce Herron - LB
Jay Hilgenberg - C
Noah Jackson - G
Dan Jiggetts - T
Lee Kunz - LB
Dennis Lick - T
Ken Margerum - WR
Willie McClendon - HB
Steve McMichael - DT
Emery Moorehead - WR
Dan Neal - C
Hans Nielsen - K
Jim Osborne - DT
Alan Page - DT
Bob Parsons - TE
Walter Payton - HB
Mike Phipps - QB
Doug Plank - DB
John Roveto - K
Terry Schmidt - DB
Brad Shearer - DT
Mike Singletary - LB
John Skibinski - FB
Revie Sorey - G
Matt Suhey - FB
Bob Thomas - K
Keith Van Horne - T
Len Walterscheid - DB
Rickey Watts - WR
Dave Williams - FB
Brooks Williams - TE
Otis Wilson - LB
Emanuel Zanders - G

1981 Cincinnati

Charles Alexander - HB
Ken Anderson - QB
Don Bass - WR
Jim Breech - K
Louis Breeden - DB
Greg Bright - DB
Ross Browner - DE
Glenn Bujnoch - G
Gary Burley - DE
Blair Bush - C
Glenn Cameron - LB
Clarence Chapman - DB
Cris Collinsworth - WR
Isaac Curtis - WR
Oliver Davis - DB
Tom Dinkel - LB
Eddie Edwards - DE
Guy Frazier - LB
Mike Fuller - DB
Archie Griffin - HB
Ray Griffin - DB
Jim Hargrove - FB
Bo Harris - LB
M. L. Harris - TE
Bryan Hicks - DB
Rod Horn - NT
Pete Johnson - FB
Bobby Kemp - DB
Steve Kreider - WR
Dave Lapham - G
Jim LeClair - LB
Pat McInally - WR
Max Montoya - G
Blake Moore - C
Anthony Munoz - T
Brad Oates - G
Mike Obrovac - T
Elvis Peacock - HB
Rick Razzano - LB
Ken Riley - DB
Dan Ross - TE
Turk Schonert - QB
Jeff Schuh - LB
John Simmons - DB
Mike St. Clair - DE
Jack Thompson - QB
David Verser - WR
Wilson Whitley - NT
Bobby Whitten - G
Reggie Williams - LB
Mike Wilson - T

1981 Cleveland

Willis Adams - WR
Lyle Alzado - DE
Dick Ambrose - LB
Matt Bahr - K
Autry Beamon - DB
Ron Bolton - DB
Henry Bradley - NT
Thomas Brown - DE
Clinton Burrell - DB
Steve Cox - K
Thom Darden - DB
Joe DeLamielleure - G
Tom DeLeone - C
Doug Dieken - T
Hanford Dixon - DB
Ricky Feacher - WR
Judson Flint - DB
Elvis Franks - DE
Danny Fulton - WR
Don Goode - LB
Dino Hall - HB
Marshall Harris - DE
Calvin Hill - HB
Bruce Huther - LB
Robert Jackson - LB
Robert Jackson - G
Dave Jacobs - K
Eddie Johnson - LB
Lawrence Johnson - DB
Dave Logan - WR
Clay Matthews - LB
Paul McDonald - QB
Cleo Miller - HB
Matt Miller - T
Cleo Montgomery - WR
Ozzie Newsome - TE
McDonald Oden - TE
Greg Pruitt - HB
Mike Pruitt - FB
Cody Risien - T
Mike Robinson - DE
Reggie Rucker - WR
Clarence Scott - DB
Henry Sheppard - G
Jerry Sherk - NT
Brian Sipe - QB
Gerry Sullivan - C
Rick Trocano - QB
Curtis Weathers - LB
Charles White - HB

1981 Dallas

Benny Barnes - DB
Larry Bethea - DT
Bob Breunig - LB
Guy Brown - LB
Glenn Carano - QB
Jim Cooper - T
Doug Cosbie - TE
Anthony Dickerson - LB
Doug Donley - WR
Pat Donovan - T
Tony Dorsett - HB
Michael Downs - DB
Billy Joe DuPree - TE
John Dutton - DT
Ron Fellows - DB
Andy Frederick - T
Mike Hegman - LB
Tony Hill - WR
Gary Hogeboom - QB
Butch Johnson - WR
Too Tall Jones - DE
James Jones - HB
Angelo King - LB
D. D. Lewis - LB
Harvey Martin - DE
Robert Newhouse - FB
Timmy Newsome - FB
Drew Pearson - WR
Kurt Petersen - G
Tom Rafferty - C
Howard Richards - G
Jay Saldi - TE
Herbert Scott - G
Rafael Septien - K
Robert Shaw - C
Don Smerek - DE
Danny Spradlin - LB
Ron Springs - FB
Bruce Thornton - DE
Dennis Thurman - DB
Glen Titensor - G
Everson Walls - DB
Charlie Waters - DB
Randy White - DT
Danny White - QB
Steve Wilson - DB
Steve Wright - T

1981 Denver

Greg Boyd - DE
Billy Bryan - C
Steve Busick - LB
Larry Canada - FB
Rubin Carter - NT
Barney Chavous - DE
Kelvin Clark - T
Steve DeBerg - QB
Ron Egloff - TE
Larry Evans - LB
Steve Foley - DB
Tom Glassic - G
Randy Gradishar - LB
Mike Harden - DB
Paul Howard - G
Glenn Hyde - G
Tom Jackson - LB
Rulon Jones - DE
Aaron Kyle - DB
Ken Lanier - T
Don Latimer - NT
Rob Lytle - HB
Wade Manning - WR
Brison Manor - DE
Mark Merrill - LB
Claudie Minor - T
Craig Morton - QB
Haven Moses - WR
Riley Odoms - TE
Rick Parros - FB
Dave Preston - HB
Luke Prestridge - K
Tony Reed - HB
Jim Ryan - LB
Dennis Smith - DB
Perry Smith - DB
Roland Solomon - DB
Fred Steinfort - K
Dave Studdard - T
Bob Swenson - LB
Billy Thompson - DB
Steve Trimble - DB
Rick Upchurch - WR
Steve Watson - WR
James Wright - TE
Louis Wright - DB

1981 Detroit

Jimmy Allen - DB
Al Baker - DE
Karl Baldischwiler - T
Russ Bolinger - G
Luther Bradley - DB
Dexter Bussey - FB
Ken Callicutt - HB
Garry Cobb - LB
Curley Culp - DT
Gary Danielson - QB
Jeff Delaney - DB
Chris Dieterich - T
Keith Dorney - T
Joe Ehrmann - DT
Homer Elias - G
Doug English - DT
Ken Fantetti - LB
Edgar Fields - DT
Amos Fowler - C
Steve Furness - DT
Bill Gay - DT
Tommie Ginn - G
Hector Gray - DB
Curtis Green - DT
Alvin Hall - DB
James Harrell - LB
David Hill - TE
Eric Hipple - QB
James Hunter - DB
Rick Kane - HB
Horace King - FB
Jeff Komlo - QB
Larry Lee - G
Robbie Martin - WR
Eddie Murray - K
Mark Nichols - WR
Bob Niziolek - TE
Ulysses Norris - TE
Ray Oldham - DB
Tracy Porter - WR
Dave Pureifory - DE
Freddie Scott - WR
Billy Sims - HB
Tom Skladany - K
Wayne Smith - DB
Terry Tautolo - LB
Leonard Thompson - WR
Vince Thompson - FB
Tom Turnure - C
Charlie Weaver - LB
Stan White - LB

1981 Green Bay

Kurt Allerman - LB
John Anderson - LB
Charlie Ane - C
Steve Atkins - HB
Byron Braggs - DE
Mike Butler - DE
Rich Campbell - QB
Ron Cassidy - WR
Paul Coffman - TE
George Cumby - LB
Lynn Dickey - QB
Mike Douglass - LB
Gerry Ellis - FB
Derrel Gofourth - G
Johnnie Gray - DB
Leotis Harris - G
Maurice Harvey - DB
Estus Hood - DB
Harlan Huckleby - HB
Tim Huffman - T
Eddie Lee Ivery - HB
John Jefferson - WR
Jim Jensen - FB
Ezra Johnson - DE
Terry Jones - NT
Syd Kitson - G
Greg Koch - T
Mark Koncar - T
Mark Lee - DB
Cliff Lewis - LB
Gary Lewis - TE
James Lofton - WR
Larry McCarren - C
Mike McCoy - DB
Casey Merrill - DE
Terdell Middleton - HB
Mark Murphy - DB
Fred Nixon - WR
Brad Oates - G
David Petway - DB
Guy Prather - LB
Randy Scott - LB
Ray Stachowicz - K
Jan Stenerud - K
Timothy Stokes - T
Karl Swanke - T
Arland Thompson - G
Aundra Thompson - WR
John Thompson - TE
Eric Torkelson - FB
Richard Turner - NT
Bill Whitaker - DB
David Whitehurst - QB
Delvin Williams - HB
Rich Wingo - LB

1981 Houston

Adger Armstrong - FB
Harold Bailey - WR
Jesse Baker - DE
Mike Barber - TE
Elvin Bethea - DE
Gregg Bingham - LB
Robert Brazile - LB
Billy Brooks - WR
Ken Burrough - WR
Earl Campbell - HB
Rob Carpenter - FB
David Carter - G
Dave Casper - TE
Ronnie Coleman - HB
John Corker - LB
Greg Davidson - C
Andy Dorris - DE
Nick Eyre - T
Angelo Fields - T
Ed Fisher - G
Toni Fritsch - K
Leon Gray - T
Carter Hartwig - DB
Mike Holston - WR
Daryl Hunt - LB
Bill Kay - DB
Ken Kennard - NT
Carl Mauck - C
Gifford Nielsen - QB
Cliff Parsley - K
Vernon Perry - DB
John Reaves - QB
Mike Reinfeldt - DB
Mike Renfro - WR
Avon Riley - LB
Carl Roaches - WR
John Schuhmacher - G
Daryle Skaugstad - NT
Tim Smith - WR
Ken Stabler - QB
Greg Stemrick - DB
Mike Stensrud - DE
Art Stringer - LB
Rich Thomaselli - HB
Ted Thompson - LB
Morris Towns - T
Willie Tullis - DB
Ted Washington - LB
J. C. Wilson - DB
Tim Wilson - FB

1981 Kansas City

Gary Barbaro - DB
Ed Beckman - TE
Mike Bell - DE
Jerry Blanton - LB
Curtis Bledsoe - HB
Brad Budde - G
Lloyd Burruss - DB
Phil Cancik - LB
Carlos Carson - WR
M.L. Carter - DB
Frank Case - DE
Deron Cherry - DB
Herb Christopher - DB
Tom Condon - G
Joe Delaney - HB
Al Dixon - TE
Paul Dombroski - DB
Steve Fuller - QB
Clark Gaines - HB
Bubba Garcia - WR
Charlie Getty - T
Jeff Gossett - K
Gary Green - DB
Bob Grupp - K
Jim Hadnot - FB
Eric Harris - DB
Marvin Harvey - TE
Matt Herkenhoff - T
Sylvester Hicks - DE
Tom Howard - LB
Billy Jackson - FB
Charles Jackson - LB
Bill Kenney - QB
Dave Klug - LB
Ken Kremer - NT
Dave Lindstrom - DE
Nick Lowery - K
Dino Mangiero - NT
Frank Manumaleuga - LB
Henry Marshall - WR
Ted McKnight - HB
Rick Moser - HB
James Murphy - WR
John Olenchalk - LB
Don Parrish - NT
Whitney Paul - LB
Cal Peterson - LB
Stan Rome - WR
Jim Rourke - G
Jack Rudnay - C
Willie Scott - TE
Bob Simmons - G
J. T. Smith - WR
Gary Spani - LB
Art Still - DE
Roger Taylor - T
Todd Thomas - C
Mike Williams - FB

1981 LA Rams

George Andrews - LB
Walt Arnold - TE
Bill Bain - G
Ron Battle - TE
Larry Brooks - DT
Cullen Bryant - FB
Howard Carson - LB
Mario Celotto - LB
Henry Childs - TE
Bob Cobb - DE
Kirk Collins - DB
Jim Collins - LB
Frank Corral - K
Nolan Cromwell - DB
Preston Dennard - WR
Reggie Doss - DT
Fred Dryer - DE
Carl Ekern - LB
Mike Fanning - DT
Doug France - T
Lewis Gilbert - TE
Mike Guman - FB
Pat Haden - QB
Dennis Harrah - G
Joe Harris - LB
Drew Hill - WR
Kent Hill - G
LeRoy Irvin - DB
Johnnie Johnson Jr. - DB
Cody Jones - DE
Jeff Kemp - QB
Phil McKinnely - T
Greg Meisner - DT
Willie Miller - WR
Jeff Moore - WR
Phil Murphy - DT
Mel Owens - LB
Irvin Pankey - T
Dan Pastorini - QB
Jairo Penaranda - FB
Rod Perry - DB
Jeff Rutledge - QB
Rich Saul - C
Jackie Slater - T
Doug Smith - G
Lucious Smith - DB
Ivory Sully - DB
Jewerl Thomas - HB
Pat Thomas - DB
Wendell Tyler - HB
Billy Waddy - WR
Jack Youngblood - DE
Jim Youngblood - LB

1981 Miami

Elmer Bailey - WR
Bill Barnett - DE
Bob Baumhower - NT
Woody Bennett - FB
Don Bessillieu - DB
Doug Betters - DE
Glenn Blackwood - DB
Lyle Blackwood - DB
Kim Bokamper - DE
Bob Brudzinski - LB
Jimmy Cefalo - WR
Vern Den Herder - DE
Mark Dennard - C
A. J. Duhe - LB
Andra Franklin - FB
Mike Fultz - DT
Nick Giaquinto - HB
Jon Giesler - T
Larry Gordon - LB
Cleveland Green - T
Bruce Hardy - TE
Duriel Harris - WR
Eddie Hill - HB
Steve Howell - FB
Jim Jensen - QB
Mike Kozlowski - DB
Bob Kuechenberg - G
Eric Laakso - T
Ronnie Lee - TE
Bo Matthews - FB
Don McNeal - DB
Nat Moore - WR
Tony Nathan - HB
Ed Newman - G
Tom Orosz - K
Ken Poole - DE
Steve Potter - LB
Ricky Ray - DB
Earnest Rhone - LB
Terry Robiskie - FB
Joe Rose - TE
Steve Shull - LB
Gerald Small - DB
Dwight Stephenson - C
Don Strock - QB
Ed Taylor - DB
Rodell Thomas - LB
Jeff Toews - G
Tommy Vigorito - HB
Uwe von Schamann - K
Fulton Walker - DB
David Woodley - QB

1981 Minnesota

Matt Blair - LB
Brent Boyd - G
Ted Brown - FB
Bob Bruer - TE
Greg Coleman - K
Rick Danmeier - K
Steve Dils - QB
Neil Elshire - DE
Tony Galbreath - FB
Wes Hamilton - G
Tom Hannon - DB
Sam Harrell - FB
Randy Holloway - DE
Jim Hough - G
Dave Huffman - G
Tim Irwin - T
Dennis Johnson - LB
Henry Johnson - LB
Kurt Knoff - DB
Tommy Kramer - QB
Jim Langer - C
Terry LeCount - WR
Leo Lewis - WR
Doug Martin - DE
Mardye McDole - WR
Fred McNeill - LB
Mark Mullaney - DE
Keith Nord - DB
Eddie Payton - HB
Ahmad Rashad - WR
Jarvis Redwine - HB
Steve Riley - T
Ken Sanders - DE
Robin Sendlein - LB
Joe Senser - TE
Jeff Siemon - LB
Scott Studwell - LB
John Swain - DB
Dennis Swilley - C
Willie Teal - DB
John Turner - DB
James White - NT
Sammy White - WR
Walt Williams - DB
Wade Wilson - QB
Ray Yakavonis - NT
Ron Yary - T
Rickey Young - HB

1981 New England

Julius Adams - DE
Richard Bishop - NT
Don Blackmon - LB
Pete Brock - C
Mark Buben - DE
Don Calhoun - FB
Rich Camarillo - K
Matt Cavanaugh - QB
Steven Clark - DE
Raymond Clayborn - DB
Tony Collins - HB
Bob Cryder - G
Sam Cunningham - FB
Lin Dawson - TE
Paul Dombroski - DB
Kevin Donnalley - DB
Vagas Ferguson - HB
Tim Fox - DB
Bob Golic - LB
Steve Grogan - QB
Ray Hamilton - NT
John Hannah - G
Ken Hartley - K
Don Hasselbeck - TE
Mike Hawkins - LB
Mike Haynes - DB
Brian Holloway - T
Mike Hubach - K
Horace Ivory - HB
Harold Jackson - WR
Roland James - DB
Andy Johnson - HB
Shelby Jordan - T
Steve King - LB
John Lee - DE
Keith Lee - DB
Bill Lenkaitis - C
Bill Matthews - LB
Tony McGee - DE
Stanley Morgan - WR
Steve Nelson - LB
Tom Owen - QB
Carlos Pennywell - WR
Garry Puetz - G
Rick Sanford - DB
Rod Shoate - LB
John Smith - K
Mosi Tatupu - FB
Kenneth Toler - WR
Donald Westbrook - WR
Dwight Wheeler - T
Darrell Wilson - DB
John Zamberlin - LB

1981 New Orleans

Sam Adams - G
Gordon Banks - WR
Barry Bennett - NT
Monte Bennett - NT
Ken Bordelon - LB
Jerry Boyarsky - NT
Hoby Brenner - TE
Stan Brock - T
Rich Caster - TE
Wes Chandler - WR
Russell Erxleben - K
Chuck Evans - LB
Russell Gary - DB
Elois Grooms - DE
Jeff Groth - WR
Larry Hardy - TE
Ike Harris - WR
John Hill - C
Jack Holmes - FB
Nat Hudson - G
Rickey Jackson - LB
Jim Kovach - LB
Dave Lafary - T
Archie Manning - QB
Rich Martini - WR
Guido Merkens - WR
Derland Moore - DE
Tom Myers - DB
Rob Nairne - LB
Scott Pelluer - LB
Jim Pietrzak - C
Johnnie Poe - DB
Ricky Ray - DB
Glen Redd - LB
Benny Ricardo - K
George Rogers - HB
Jimmy Rogers - HB
Paul Ryczek - C
Bobby Scott - QB
Mike Spivey - DB
Scott Stauch - HB
Fred Sturt - G
J.T. Taylor - T
Aundra Thompson - WR
Toussaint Tyler - FB
Frank Warren - DE
Frank Wattelet - DB
Dave Waymer - DB
Jim Wilks - DE
Brooks Williams - TE
Dave Wilson - QB
Wayne Wilson - HB
Bob Young - G

1981 NY Giants

Billy Ard - G
Carl Barisich - NT
Brad Benson - T
Leon Bright - HB
Scott Brunner - QB
Jim Burt - NT
Rob Carpenter - FB
Harry Carson - LB
Jim Clack - C
Bill Currier - DB
Joe Danelo - K
Mike Dennis - DB
Larry Flowers - DB
Ike Forte - HB
Mike Friede - WR
Alvin Garrett - HB
Earnest Gray - WR
Dee Hardison - DE
Mark Haynes - DB
Ernie Hughes - C
Byron Hunt - LB
Louis Jackson - HB
Terry Jackson - DB
Dave Jennings - K
Gary Jeter - DE
Brian Kelley - LB
Gordon King - T
Doug Kotar - HB
Frank Marion - LB
George Martin - DE
Bo Matthews - FB
Ed McGlasson - C
Curtis McGriff - DE
Joe McLaughlin - LB
John Mistler - WR
Tom Mullady - TE
Bill Neill - NT
Johnny Perkins - WR
Leon Perry - FB
Danny Pittman - WR
Beasley Reece - DB
Gary Shirk - TE
Roy Simmons - G
Phil Simms - QB
Timothy Stokes - T
Philip Tabor - DE
Lawrence Taylor - LB
Billy Taylor - HB
J. T. Turner - G
Brad Van Pelt - LB
Jeff Weston - T
Mike Whittington - LB
Dave Young - TE

1981 NY Jets

Dan Alexander - G
Mike Augustyniak - FB
Jerome Barkum - TE
Guy Bingham - C
Stan Blinka - LB
Greg Buttle - LB
Ron Crosby - LB
Ralph DeLoach - DE
Scott Dierking - HB
Donald Dykes - DB
Joe Fields - C
Derrick Gaffney - WR
Mark Gastineau - DE
Bruce Harper - HB
Jerry Holmes - DB
Bobby Jackson - DB
Jesse Johnson - DB
Lam Jones - WR
Bobby Jones - WR
Joe Klecko - DE
Pat Leahy - K
Kenny Lewis - HB
Kevin Long - FB
Johnny Lynn - DB
Marty Lyons - DT
Freeman McNeil - HB
Lance Mehl - LB
Kenny Neil - DE
Tom Newton - FB
Marvin Powell - T
Chuck Ramsey - K
Randy Rasmussen - G
Darrol Ray - DB
John Roman - T
Ben Rudolph - DT
Pat Ryan - QB
Abdul Salaam - DT
Ken Schroy - DB
Mickey Shuler - TE
Kurt Sohn - WR
Kirk Springs - DB
Steve Stephens - TE
Billy Taylor - HB
Richard Todd - QB
Stan Waldemore - G
Wesley Walker - WR
Chris Ward - T
Al Washington - LB
Marty Wetzel - LB
John Woodring - LB

1981 Oakland

Chris Bahr - K
Jeff Barnes - LB
Malcolm Barnwell - WR
Greg Bracelin - LB
Morris Bradshaw - WR
Cliff Branch - WR
Dave Browning - DE
Joe Campbell - DE
Mario Celotto - LB
Bob Chandler - WR
Raymond Chester - TE
Todd Christensen - TE
Dave Dalby - C
Bruce Davis - G
Mike Davis - DB
Ray Guy - K
Cedrick Hardman - DE
Frank Hawkins - FB
Lester Hayes - DB
Ted Hendricks - LB
Kenny Hill - DB
Monte Jackson - DB
Derrick Jensen - FB
Willie Jones - DE
Kenny King - HB
Reggie Kinlaw - NT
Henry Lawrence - T
Howie Long - NT
Curt Marsh - G
Rod Martin - LB
Mickey Marvin - G
Lindsey Mason - T
Ira Matthews - WR
John Matuszak - DE
Randy McClanahan - LB
Odis McKinney - DB
Matt Millen - LB
Cleo Montgomery - WR
Dwayne O'Steen - DB
Burgess Owens - DB
Jim Plunkett - QB
Derrick Ramsey - TE
Johnny Robinson - NT
Art Shell - T
Steve Sylvester - C
Gene Upshaw - G
Mark van Eeghen - FB
Ted Watts - DB
Greg Westbrooks - LB
Art Whittington - HB
Chester Willis - HB
Marc Wilson - QB

1981 Philadelphia

Steve Atkins - HB
Ron Baker - G
Richard Blackmore - DB
Greg Brown - DE
John Bunting - LB
Billy Campfield - HB
Harold Carmichael - WR
Al Chesley - LB
Ken Clarke - NT
Mike Curcio - LB
Herman Edwards - DB
Ray Ellis - DB
Mickey Fitzgerald - FB
Steve Folsom - TE
Tony Franklin - K
Louie Giammona - HB
Frank Giddens - T
Carl Hairston - DE
Perry Harrington - FB
Dennis Harrison - DE
Jo Jo Heath - DB
Wally Henry - WR
Alvin Hooks - WR
Claude Humphrey - DE
Ron Jaworski - QB
Charlie Johnson - NT
Steve Kenney - G
Keith Krepfle - TE
Frank LeMaster - LB
Randy Logan - DB
Leonard Mitchell - DE
Wilbert Montgomery - HB
Guy Morriss - C
Calvin Murray - HB
Hubie Oliver - FB
Rod Parker - WR
Petey Perot - G
Ray Phillips - LB
Joe Pisarcik - QB
Jerry Robinson - LB
Max Runager - K
Booker Russell - FB
John Sciarra - DB
Jerry Sisemore - T
Mark Slater - C
Charlie Smith - WR
Ron Smith - WR
John Spagnola - TE
Stan Walters - T
Reggie Wilkes - LB
Brenard Wilson - DB
Roynell Young - DB

1981 Pittsburgh

Larry Anderson - DB
John Banaszak - DE
Tom Beasley - DT
Mel Blount - DB
Terry Bradshaw - QB
Larry Brown - T
Robin Cole - LB
Craig Colquitt - K
Steve Courson - G
Bennie Cunningham - TE
Russell Davis - FB
Johnnie Dirden - WR
Gary Dunn - DT
John Goodman - DE
Joe Greene - DT
L. C. Greenwood - DE
Randy Grossman - TE
Jack Ham - LB
Franco Harris - FB
Greg Hawthorne - HB
Tunch Ilkin - T
Ron Johnson - DB
Bob Kohrs - DE
Jon Kolb - T
Jack Lambert - LB
David Little - LB
Mark Malone - QB
Tyrone McGriff - G
Rick Moser - HB
Ted Petersen - T
Ray Pinney - T
Frank Pollard - HB
Donnie Shell - DB
Jim Smith - WR
John Stallworth - WR
Cliff Stoudt - QB
Lynn Swann - WR
Calvin Sweeney - WR
J.T. Thomas - DB
Sidney Thornton - HB
Loren Toews - LB
David Trout - K
Zack Valentine - LB
Anthony Washington - DB
Mike Webster - C
Dennis Winston - LB
Craig Wolfley - G
Dwayne Woodruff - DB

1981 St. Louis

Bill Acker - NT
Dave Ahrens - LB
Carl Allen - DB
Ottis Anderson - HB
Charles Baker - LB
Mark Bell - WR
Carl Birdsong - K
Joe Bostic - G
Tom Brahaney - C
Rush Brown - DE
Theotis Brown - HB
Steve Carpenter - DB
Randy Clark - C
Ralph Clayton - WR
Tim Collier - DB
George Collins - T
Chris Combs - TE
Barney Cotton - G
Kirby Criswell - DE
Mike Dawson - NT
Dan Dierdorf - T
Calvin Favron - LB
Doak Field - LB
Mike Fisher - WR
John Floyd - WR
John Gillen - LB
Mel Gray - WR
Roy Green - WR
Ken Greene - DB
Curtis Greer - DE
Jeff Griffin - DB
Willard Harrell - HB
Jim Hart - QB
Charles Johnson - DB
E. J. Junior - LB
Tim Kearney - LB
Greg LaFleur - TE
Rusty Lisch - QB
Neil Lomax - QB
Randy Love - FB
Dale Markham - T
Doug Marsh - TE
Stafford Mays - DE
Stump Mitchell - HB
Wayne Morris - FB
Lee Nelson - DB
Neil O'Donoghue - K
Art Plunkett - T
Bob Pollard - DE
Bruce Radford - NT
Donald Schwartz - DB
Dave Stief - WR
Terry Stieve - G
Pat Tilley - WR
Ken Times - NT
Roger Wehrli - DB
Eric Williams - LB
Herb Williams - DB
Keith Wortman - T

1981 San Diego

Hank Bauer - HB
Doug Beaudoin - DB
Rolf Benirschke - K
Carlos Bradley - LB
James Brooks - HB
Billy Brooks - WR
Willie Buchanon - DB
John Cappelletti - FB
Wes Chandler - WR
Sam Claphan - T
Fred Dean - DE
Frank Duncan - DB
Glen Edwards - DB
Allan Ellis - DB
Keith Ferguson - DE
Scott Fitzkee - WR
Dan Fouts - QB
Bob Gregor - DB
Wyatt Henderson - DB
Pete Holohan - TE
Bob Horn - LB
Gary Johnson - DT
Charlie Joiner - WR
Leroy Jones - DE
Louie Kelcher - DT
Linden King - LB
Jim Laslavic - LB
Chuck Loewen - T
Woodrow Lowe - LB
Ed Luther - QB
Don Macek - C
Chuck Muncie - FB
Irvin Phillips - DB
Ray Preston - LB
Don Reese - DE
George Roberts - K
Bob Rush - C
Dwight Scales - WR
Pete Shaw - DB
Billy Shields - T
Eric Sievers - TE
Ron Smith - WR
Aundra Thompson - WR
Cliff Thrift - LB
Russ Washington - T
Jimmy Webb - DT
Ed White - G
Doug Wilkerson - G
Clarence Williams - HB
Jeff Williams - G
Mike Williams - DB
Kellen Winslow - TE
John Woodcock - DE
Wilbur Young - DT

1981 San Francisco

Dan Audick - T
John Ayers - G
Matt Bahr - K
Guy Benjamin - QB
Dwaine Board - DE
Matt Bouza - WR
Dan Bunz - LB
John Choma - G
Ricky Churchman - DB
Dwight Clark - WR
Earl Cooper - FB
Randy Cross - G
Johnny Davis - FB
Fred Dean - DE
Walt Downing - C
Walt Easley - FB
Lenvil Elliott - HB
Keith Fahnhorst - T
Rick Gervais - DB
Willie Harper - LB
John Harty - NT
Dwight Hicks - DB
Paul Hofer - HB
Arrington Jones - FB
Allan Kennedy - T
Pete Kugler - NT
Amos Lawrence - HB
Bobby Leopold - LB
Jim Looney - LB
Ronnie Lott - DB
Saladin Martin - DB
Milt McColl - LB
Jim Miller - K
Joe Montana - QB
Ricky Patton - HB
Brian Peets - TE
Lawrence Pillers - DE
Craig Puki - LB
Fred Quillan - C
Eason Ramson - TE
Archie Reese - NT
Jack Reynolds - LB
Bill Ring - HB
Mike Shumann - WR
Freddie Solomon - WR
Jim Stuckey - DE
Terry Tautolo - LB
Lynn Thomas - DB
Keena Turner - LB
Ray Wersching - K
Carlton Williamson - DB
Mike Wilson - WR
Eric Wright - DB
Charle Young - TE

1981 Seattle

Sam Adkins - QB
Wilson Alvarez - K
Fred Anderson - DE
Steve August - T
Edwin Bailey - G
Terry Beeson - LB
Dennis Boyd - T
Dave Brown - DB
Theotis Brown - HB
Keith Butler - LB
Pete Cronan - LB
Dan Doornink - FB
Don Dufek - DB
Bill Dugan - G
Kenny Easley - DB
Ron Essink - T
Brian Flones - LB
Greg Gaines - LB
Frank Garcia - K
Jacob Green - DE
Robert Hardy - DT
John Harris - DB
Efren Herrera - K
David Hughes - FB
Horace Ivory - HB
Michael Jackson - LB
Jim Jodat - FB
Paul Johns - WR
Gregg Johnson - DB
Kerry Justin - DB
Dave Krieg - QB
Art Kuehn - C
Eric Lane - HB
Steve Largent - WR
Will Lewis - DB
Sam McCullum - WR
Mark McGrath - WR
Terry Miller - HB
Vic Minor - DB
Jeff Moore - HB
Bob Newton - G
Joe Norman - LB
Steve Raible - WR
John Sawyer - TE
Keith Simpson - DB
Sherman Smith - HB
Doug Sutherland - DT
Rodell Thomas - LB
Mike Tice - TE
Manu Tuiasosopo - DT
Kevin Turner - LB
Jeff West - K
Mike White - DE
John Yarno - C
Jim Zorn - QB

1981 Tampa Bay

Ricky Bell - HB
Theo Bell - WR
Tom Blanchard - K
Scot Brantley - LB
Cedric Brown - DB
Joe Campbell - DE
Bill Capece - K
Gerald Carter - WR
Billy Cesare - DB
Neal Colzie - DB
Gary Davis - HB
Tony Davis - FB
Jeff Delaney - DB
Jerry Eckwood - HB
Chuck Fusina - QB
Jimmie Giles - TE
Hugh Green - LB
Charley Hannah - T
Andy Hawkins - LB
John Holt - DB
Kevin House - WR
Scott Hutchinson - DE
Cecil Johnson - LB
Gordon Jones - WR
Bill Kollar - DE
Jim Leonard - G
Dave Lewis - LB
David Logan - NT

Aaron Mitchell - DB
Dana Nafziger - LB
Jim Obradovich - TE
James Owens - HB
Dave Reavis - T
Greg Roberts - G
Gene Sanders - T
Lee Roy Selmon - DE
Laval Short - NT
Ray Snell - G
Dave Stalls - DE
Larry Swider - K
Norris Thomas - DB
Mike Washington - DB
Brad White - NT
James Wilder - FB
Doug Williams - QB
Steven Wilson - C
Richard Wood - LB
George Yarno - G
Garo Yepremian - K

1981 Washington

Coy Bacon - DE
Jeff Bostic - C
Perry Brooks - DT
Trent Bryant - DB
Dave Butz - DT
Rich Caster - TE
Rickey Claitt - HB
Mike Clark - DE
Monte Coleman - LB
Mike Connell - K
Cris Crissy - DB
Pete Cronan - LB
Brad Dusek - LB
Tom Flick - QB
Alvin Garrett - HB
Nick Giaquinto - HB
Dave Graf - LB
Darryl Grant - G
Russ Grimm - G
Clarence Harmon - HB
Dallas Hickman - DE
Wilbur Jackson - FB
Joe Jacoby - T
Melvin Jones - G
Curtis Jordan - DB
Mel Kaufman - LB
Joe Lavender - DB
Karl Lorch - DE
Quentin Lowry - LB
Dexter Manley - DE
Mark May - T
Greg McCrary - TE
LeCharls McDaniel - DB
Mat Mendenhall - DE
Terry Metcalf - WR
Rich Milot - LB
Art Monk - WR
Mark Moseley - K
Mark Murphy - DB
Mike Nelms - DB
Pat Ogrin - DT
Neal Olkewicz - LB
Lemar Parrish - DB
Tony Peters - DB
Bob Raba - TE
John Riggins - FB
Ron Saul - G
Jerry Scanlan - T
Virgil Seay - WR
George Starke - T
Joe Theismann - QB
Ricky Thompson - WR
Kevin Turner - LB
Rick Walker - TE
Don Warren - TE
Joe Washington - HB
Charlie Weaver - LB
Jeris White - DB
Otis Wonsley - FB
Wilbur Young - DT

1982 Atlanta

William Andrews - FB
Stacey Bailey - WR
Steve Bartkowski - QB
Clay Brown - TE
Reggie Brown - FB
Warren Bryant - T
Bobby Butler - DB
Lynn Cain - HB
Willie Curran - WR
Buddy Curry - LB
Paul Davis - LB
Blane Gaison - DB
Bob Glazebrook - DB
Floyd Hodge - WR
Pat Howell - G
Alfred Jackson - WR
Robert Jackson - LB
Alfred Jenkins - WR
Kenny Johnson - DB
Billy Johnson - WR
Earl Jones - DB
Mike Kenn - T
Keith Krepfle - TE
Fulton Kuykendall - LB
Jim Laughlin - LB
Mick Luckhurst - K
Jeff Merrow - DE
Russ Mikeska - TE
Junior Miller - TE

Mike Moroski - QB
Neal Musser - LB
Mike Perko - NT
Tom Pridemore - DB
Al Richardson - LB
Gerald Riggs - FB
George Roberts - K
Bo Robinson - FB
Doug Rogers - DE
Eric Sanders - T
Dave Scott - G
John Scully - C
Dave Smigelsky - K
Don Smith - NT
Mike Spivey - DB
Ray Strong - HB
R.C. Thielemann - G
Jeff Van Note - C
Lyman White - LB
Joel Williams - LB
Jeff Yeates - DE
Mike Zele - NT

1982 Baltimore

Kim Anderson - DB
Larry Anderson - DB
Elmer Bailey - WR
Pat Beach - TE
Matt Bouza - WR
Greg Bracelin - LB
James Burroughs - DB
Ray Butler - WR
Johnie Cooks - LB
Cleveland Crosby - DE
Terry Crouch - G
Jeff Delaney - DB
Curtis Dickey - HB
Zachary Dixon - HB
Ray Donaldson - C
Steve Durham - DE
Cleveland Franklin - FB
Nesby Glasgow - DB
Joe Harris - LB
Jeff Hart - T
Derrick Hatchett - DB
Darryl Hemphill - DB
Bernard Henry - WR
Nat Hudson - G
Ken Huff - G
Mike Humiston - LB
David Humm - QB
James Hunter - NT
Glenn Hyde - C
Fletcher Jenkins - DE
Ricky Jones - LB
Sidney Justin - DB
Barry Krauss - LB
Reese McCall - TE
Randy McMillan - FB
Danny Miller - K
Greg Murtha - T
Cliff Odom - LB
Dwayne O'Steen - DB
Gary Padjen - LB
Mike Pagel - QB
Art Schlichter - QB
Tim Sherwin - TE
Sanders Shiver - LB
Dave Simmons - LB
John Sinnott - T
Holden Smith - WR
Harry Stanback - DE
Rohn Stark - K
Arland Thompson - G
Donnell Thompson - DE
Ben Utt - G
Leo Wisniewski - NT
Mike Wood - K
Johnnie Wright - FB

1982 Buffalo

Buster Barnett - TE
Jon Borchardt - G
Mark Brammer - TE
Curtis Brown - FB
Jerry Butler - WR
Greg Cater - K
Allan Clark - HB
Mario Clark - DB
Joe Cribbs - HB
Justin Cross - T
Joe Devlin - T
Joe Ferguson - QB
Steve Freeman - DB
Will Grant - C
Jim Haslett - LB
Efren Herrera - K
Robert Holt - WR
Roland Hooks - HB
Darrell Irvin - DE
Ken Johnson - DE
Ken Jones - T
Chris Keating - LB
Matt Kofler - QB
Rod Kush - DB
Roosevelt Leaks - FB
Frank Lewis - WR
Joey Lumpkin - LB
Tom Lynch - G
Eugene Marve - LB
Reggie McKenzie - G
Ted McKnight - FB
Nick Mike
Booker Moore - FB

Mike Mosley - WR
Shane Nelson - LB
Jeff Nixon - DB
Ervin Parker - LB
Lemar Parrish - DB
Lou Piccone - WR
Jim Ritcher - G
Isiah Robertson - LB
Matt Robinson - QB
Charles Romes - DB
Mark Roopenian - NT
Lucius Sanford - LB
Bill Simpson - DB
Fred Smerlas - NT
Perry Tuttle - WR
Phil Villapiano - LB
Tim Vogler - C
Sherman White - DE
Art Whittington - HB
Chris Williams - DB
Ben Williams - DE

1982 Chi. Bears

Bob Avellini - QB
Brian Baschnagel - WR
Kurt Becker - G
Todd Bell - DB
Brian Cabral - LB
Gary Campbell - LB
Al Chesley - LB
Jerry Doerger - T
Robin Earl - TE
Vince Evans - QB
Gary Fencik - DB
Jeff Fisher - DB
Leslie Frazier - DB
Dennis Gentry - HB
Dan Hampton - DT
Roland Harper - FB
Al Harris - DE
Mike Hartenstine - DE
Perry Hartnett - G
Reuben Henderson - DB
Bruce Herron - LB
Jay Hilgenberg - C
Bruce Huther - LB
Noah Jackson - G
Dan Jiggetts - T
Ken Margerum - WR
Willie McClendon - FB
Phil McKinnely - T
Jim McMahon - QB
Steve McMichael - DT
Emery Moorehead - TE
Jerry Muckensturm - LB
Dan Neal - C
Jim Osborne - DT
Bob Parsons - K
Walter Payton - HB
Doug Plank - DB
Dan Rains - LB
John Roveto - K
Terry Schmidt - DB
James Scott - WR
Mike Singletary - LB
Matt Suhey - FB
Calvin Thomas - FB
Bob Thomas - K
Keith Van Horne - T
Henry Waechter - DE
Len Walterscheid - DB
Rickey Watts - WR
Jeff Williams - G
Brooks Williams - TE
Walt Williams - DB
Otis Wilson - LB

1982 Cincinnati

Charles Alexander - FB
Ken Anderson - QB
Jerry Boyarsky - NT
Jim Breech - K
Louis Breeden - DB
Ross Browner - DE
Glenn Bujnoch - G
Gary Burley - DE
Blair Bush - C
Glenn Cameron - LB
Glen Collins - DE
Cris Collinsworth - WR
Isaac Curtis - WR
Oliver Davis - DB
Tom Dinkel - LB
Eddie Edwards - DE
Guy Frazier - LB
Mike Fuller - DB
Archie Griffin - HB
Ray Griffin - DB
Bo Harris - LB
M. L. Harris - TE
Bryan Hicks - DB
Rodney Holman - TE
Robert Jackson - DB
Pete Johnson - FB
Bobby Kemp - DB
Steve Kreider - WR
Dave Lapham - G
Jim LeClair - LB
Pat McInally - K
Max Montoya - G
Blake Moore - C
Anthony Munoz - T
Mike Obrovac - T

Rick Razzano - LB
Ken Riley - DB
Dan Ross - TE
Turk Schonert - QB
Jeff Schuh - LB
John Simmons - DB
Ron Simpkins - LB
Mike St. Clair - DE
Rodney Tate - HB
Jack Thompson - QB
David Verser - WR
Ray Wagner - T
Emanuel Weaver - NT
Wilson Whitley - NT
Reggie Williams - LB
Mike Wilson - T

1982 Cleveland

Willis Adams - WR
Dick Ambrose - LB
Mike Baab - C
Matt Bahr - K
Keith Baldwin - DE
Chip Banks - LB
Ron Bolton - DB
Henry Bradley - NT
Larry Braziel - DB
Mark Buben - NT
Clinton Burrell - DB
Tom Cousineau - LB
Bill Cowher - LB
Steve Cox - K
Johnny Davis - FB
Joe DeLamielleure - G
Tom DeLeone - C
Doug Dieken - T
Hanford Dixon - DB
Ricky Feacher - WR
Judson Flint - DB
Elvis Franks - DE
Andy Frederick - T
Danny Fulton - WR
Bob Golic - NT
David Green - HB
Dino Hall - HB
Marshall Harris - DE
Robert Jackson - G
Bill Jackson - DB
Eddie Johnson - LB
Lawrence Johnson - DB
Mark Kafentzis - DB
Dave Logan - WR
Clay Matthews - LB
Paul McDonald - QB
Cleo Miller - FB
Matt Miller - T
Ozzie Newsome - TE
Scott Nicolas - LB
McDonald Oden - TE
Mike Pruitt - FB
Cody Risien - T
Mike Robinson - DE
Clarence Scott - DB
Brian Sipe - QB
Rick Trocano - QB
Kevin Turner - LB
Dwight Walker - HB
Curtis Weathers - LB
Charles White - HB
Mike Whitwell - WR

1982 Dallas

Brian Baldinger - C
Benny Barnes - DB
Larry Bethea - DE
Bob Breunig - LB
Guy Brown - LB
Glenn Carano - QB
Dextor Clinkscale - DB
Jim Cooper - T
Doug Cosbie - TE
Anthony Dickerson - LB
Doug Donley - WR
Pat Donovan - T
Tony Dorsett - HB
Michael Downs - DB
Billy Joe DuPree - TE
John Dutton - DT
Ron Fellows - DB
Mike Hegman - LB
Tony Hill - WR
Rod Hill - DB
Gary Hogeboom - QB
Monty Hunter - DB
Butch Johnson - WR
Too Tall Jones - DE
James Jones - HB
Angelo King - LB
Harvey Martin - DE
Robert Newhouse - FB
Timmy Newsome - FB
Drew Pearson - WR
George Peoples - FB
Kurt Petersen - G
Phil Pozderac - T
Tom Rafferty - C
Howard Richards - G
Jeff Rohrer - LB
Jay Saldi - TE
Herbert Scott - G
Rafael Septien - K
Don Smerek - DT
Danny Spradlin - LB
Ron Springs - FB

Dennis Thurman - DB
Glen Titensor - G
Everson Walls - DB
Randy White - DT
Danny White - QB
Steve Wright - G

1982 Denver

Keith Bishop - C
Greg Boyd - DE
Billy Bryan - C
Steve Busick - LB
Rubin Carter - NT
Barney Chavous - DE
Darren Comeaux - LB
Steve DeBerg - QB
Rick Dennison - LB
Ron Egloff - TE
Larry Evans - LB
Steve Foley - DB
Tom Glassic - G
Randy Gradishar - LB
Mike Harden - DB
Mark Herrmann - QB
Paul Howard - G
Roger Jackson - DB
Tom Jackson - LB
Rulon Jones - DE
Rich Karlis - K
Aaron Kyle - DB
Ken Lanier - T
Don Latimer - NT
Rob Lytle - FB
Wade Manning - WR
Brison Manor - DE
Orlando McDaniel - WR
Mark Merrill - LB
Claudie Minor - T
Craig Morton - QB
Riley Odoms - TE
Rick Parros - FB
Nathan Poole - FB
Dave Preston - HB
Luke Prestridge - K
Jim Ryan - LB
Dennis Smith - DB
Dave Studdard - T
Bob Swenson - LB
J.T. Thomas - DB
Steve Trimble - DB
Keith Uecker - T
Rick Upchurch - WR
Steve Watson - WR
Gerald Willhite - HB
Steve Wilson - DB
Sammy Winder - HB
Ken Woodard - LB
James Wright - TE
Louis Wright - DB

1982 Detroit

Al Baker - DE
Karl Baldischwiler - T
Roosevelt Barnes - LB
Russ Bolinger - G
Dexter Bussey - FB
Ken Callicutt - HB
Billy Cesare - DB
Garry Cobb - LB
Gary Danielson - QB
Chris Dieterich - T
Steve Doig - LB
Keith Dorney - T
Joe Ehrmann - DT
Homer Elias - G
Doug English - DT
Ken Fantetti - LB
Amos Fowler - C
Bill Gay - DE
William Graham - DB
Hector Gray - DB
Don Greco - G
Curtis Green - DE
Alvin Hall - DB
James Harrell - LB
David Hill - TE
Eric Hipple - QB
James Hunter - DB
John James - K
Rick Kane - HB
Horace King - FB
Al Latimer - DB
Edward Lee - WR
Larry Lee - G
Robbie Martin - WR
Bruce McNorton - DB
Martin Moss - DT
Eddie Murray - K
Mark Nichols - WR
Ulysses Norris - TE
Ray Oldham - DB
Rick Porter - HB
Tracy Porter - WR
Dave Pureifory - DE
Rob Rubick - TE
Freddie Scott - WR
Billy Sims - HB
Tom Skladany - K
Wayne Smith - DB
Terry Tautolo - LB
Bob Thomas - K
Leonard Thompson - WR
Tom Turnure - C

Dan Wagoner - DB
Bobby Watkins - DB
Stan White - LB
Jimmy Williams - LB

1982 Green Bay

John Anderson - LB
Byron Braggs - DE
Robert Brown - DE
Mike Butler - DE
Rich Campbell - QB
Allan Clark - HB
Paul Coffman - TE
George Cumby - LB
Lynn Dickey - QB
Mike Douglass - LB
Gerry Ellis - FB
Phil Epps - WR
Angelo Fields - T
Derrel Gofourth - G
Johnnie Gray - DB
Ron Hallstrom - G
Leotis Harris - G
Maurice Harvey - DB
Estus Hood - DB
Harlan Huckleby - HB
Tim Huffman - G
Eddie Lee Ivery - HB
John Jefferson - WR
Jim Jensen - FB
Ezra Johnson - DE
Mike Jolly - DB
Terry Jones - NT
Greg Koch - T
Jim Laslavic - LB
Mark Lee - DB
Cliff Lewis - LB
Gary Lewis - TE
James Lofton - WR
Larry McCarren - C
Mike McCoy - DB
Mike Meade - FB
Mark Merrill - LB
Casey Merrill - DE
Mark Murphy - DB
Guy Prather - LB
Del Rodgers - HB
Larry Rubens - C
Randy Scott - LB
Ray Stachowicz - K
Jan Stenerud - K
Timothy Stokes - T
Karl Swanke - T
John Thompson - TE
Richard Turner - NT
Bill Whitaker - DB
David Whitehurst - QB
Rich Wingo - LB

1982 Houston

Robert Abraham - LB
Gary Allen - HB
Adger Armstrong - FB
Walt Arnold - TE
Harold Bailey - WR
Jesse Baker - DE
Elvin Bethea - DE
Gregg Bingham - LB
Robert Brazile - LB
Steve Bryant - WR
Earl Campbell - HB
David Carter - C
Dave Casper - TE
John Corker - LB
Donnie Craft - FB
Greg Davidson - C
Stan Edwards - FB
Ed Fisher - G
Carter Hartwig - DB
Mike Holston - WR
Daryl Hunt - LB
John James - K
Bill Kay - DB
Florian Kempf - K
Ken Kennard - DE
Mark Koncar - T
Archie Manning - QB
Mike Munchak - G
Gifford Nielsen - QB
Cliff Parsley - K
Vernon Perry - DB
Tate Randle - DB
George Reihner - G
Mike Reinfeldt - DB
Mike Renfro - WR
Avon Riley - LB
Carl Roaches - WR
John Schuhmacher - T
Daryle Skaugstad - NT
Tim Smith - WR
Greg Stemrick - DB
Mike Stensrud - NT
Malcolm Taylor - DE
Rich Thomaselli - FB
Ted Thompson - LB
Morris Towns - T
Willie Tullis - DB
Ted Washington - LB
Ralph Williams - T
J. C. Wilson - DB
Tim Wilson - TE

1982 Kansas City

Bill Acker - NT
Gary Barbaro - DB
Ed Beckman - TE
Mike Bell - DE
Robert Blakely - WR
Jerry Blanton - LB
Curtis Bledsoe - HB
Trent Bryant - DB
Brad Budde - G
Lloyd Burruss - DB
Carlos Carson - WR
Deron Cherry - DB
Herb Christopher - DB
Tom Condon - G
Calvin Daniels - LB
Case deBruijn - K
Joe Delaney - HB
Al Dixon - TE
Steve Fuller - QB
Bob Gagliano - QB
Clark Gaines - FB
Charlie Getty - T
Jeff Gossett - K
Gary Green - DB
Jim Hadnot - FB
Anthony Hancock - WR
Eric Harris - DB
Louis Haynes - LB
Matt Herkenhoff - T
Tom Howard - LB
Billy Jackson - FB
Charles Jackson - LB
Bill Kenney - QB
Dave Klug - LB
Ken Kremer - NT
Dave Lindstrom - DE
Nick Lowery - K
Dino Mangiero - NT
Henry Marshall - WR
John Olenchalk - LB
Don Parrish - NT
Dean Prater - DE
Stan Rome - WR
Durwood Roquemore - DB
Jim Rourke - T
Jack Rudnay - C
Willie Scott - TE
Bob Simmons - G
J. T. Smith - WR
Gary Spani - LB
Al Steinfeld - C
Art Still - DE
Les Studdard - C
Del Thompson - HB
Tim Washington - DB

1982 LA Raiders

Marcus Allen - HB
Lyle Alzado - DE
Chris Bahr - K
Jeff Barnes - LB
Malcolm Barnwell - WR
Rick Berns - HB
Cliff Branch - WR
Dave Browning - DE
Bob Chandler - WR
Todd Christensen - TE
Dave Dalby - C
Bruce Davis - T
James Davis - DB
Mike Davis - DB
Ray Guy - K
Frank Hawkins - FB
Mike Hawkins - LB
Lester Hayes - DB
Ted Hendricks - LB
Kenny Hill - DB
Monte Jackson - DB
Derrick Jensen - FB
Kenny King - HB
Reggie Kinlaw - NT
Henry Lawrence - T
Howie Long - DE
Curt Marsh - G
Rod Martin - LB
Mickey Marvin - G
Randy McClanahan - LB
Vann McElroy - DB
Odis McKinney - DB
Matt Millen - LB
Cleo Montgomery - HB
Calvin Muhammad - WR
Ed Muransky - T
Bob Nelson - LB
Burgess Owens - DB
Cal Peterson - LB
Jim Plunkett - QB
Greg Pruitt - HB
Derrick Ramsey - TE
Archie Reese - NT
Johnny Robinson - NT
Jim Romano - C
Art Shell - T
Jack Squirek - LB
Steve Sylvester - C
Billy Taylor - HB
Ruben Vaughan - NT
Ted Watts - DB
Chester Willis - HB
Marc Wilson - QB

1982 LA Rams

Robert Alexander - HB
George Andrews - LB
Bill Bain - G
Mike Barber - TE
Doug Barnett - DE
Ron Battle - TE
Larry Brooks - DT
Cullen Bryant - FB
Howard Carson - LB
Kirk Collins - DB
Jim Collins - LB
Nolan Cromwell - DB
Charles DeJurnett - DT
Preston Dennard - WR
Reggie Doss - DE
Carl Ekern - LB
Mike Fanning - DT
George Farmer - WR
Vince Ferragamo - QB
Mike Guman - FB
Dennis Harrah - G
Drew Hill - WR
Kent Hill - G
LeRoy Irvin - DB
Johnnie Johnson Jr. - DB
A. J. Jones - FB
Bert Jones - QB
Cody Jones - DT
Wally Kersten - T
Mike Lansford - K
Myron Lapka - DT
George Lilja - C
Kerry Locklin - TE
Greg Meisner - DE
Willie Miller - WR
John Misko - K
Mel Owens - LB
Irvin Pankey - T
Rod Perry - DB
Barry Redden - HB
Mike Reilly - LB
Jackie Slater - T
Doug Smith - C
Lucious Smith - DB
Ivory Sully - DB
Jewerl Thomas - HB
Pat Thomas - DB
Wendell Tyler - HB
Billy Waddy - WR
Eric Williams - LB
Ron Yary - T
Jack Youngblood - DE
Jim Youngblood - LB

1982 Miami

Bill Barnett - DE
Bob Baumhower - NT
Woody Bennett - FB
Doug Betters - DE
Richard Bishop - NT
Glenn Blackwood - DB
Lyle Blackwood - DB
Kim Bokamper - DE
Charles Bowser - LB
Bob Brudzinski - LB
Jimmy Cefalo - WR
Steve Clark - NT
Larry Cowan - HB
Vern Den Herder - DE
Mark Dennard - C
Rich Diana - FB
A. J. Duhe - LB
Mark Duper - WR
Roy Foster - G
Andra Franklin - FB
Jon Giesler - T
Larry Gordon - LB
Cleveland Green - T
Bruce Hardy - TE
Duriel Harris - WR
Vince Heflin - WR
Ron Hester - LB
Eddie Hill - HB
Jim Jensen - QB
William Judson - DB
Mike Kozlowski - DB
Bob Kuechenberg - G
Eric Laakso - T
Paul Lankford - DB
Ronnie Lee - TE
Don McNeal - DB
Nat Moore - WR
Tony Nathan - HB
Ed Newman - G
Tom Orosz - K
Steve Potter - LB
Earnest Rhone - LB
Joe Rose - TE
Steve Shull - LB
Gerald Small - DB
Dwight Stephenson - C
Don Strock - QB
Jeff Toews - G
Tommy Vigorito - HB
Uwe von Schamann - K
Fulton Walker - DB
David Woodley - QB

1982 Minnesota

Rufus Bess - DB
Matt Blair - LB
Brent Boyd - G
Ted Brown - HB
Bob Bruer - TE
Greg Coleman - K
Rick Danmeier - K
Steve Dils - QB
Neil Elshire - DE
Tony Galbreath - FB
Wes Hamilton - G
Tom Hannon - DB
Sam Harrell - FB
Randy Holloway - DE
Jim Hough - G
Bryan Howard - DB
Dave Huffman - G
Tim Irwin - T
Harold Jackson - WR
Charlie Johnson - NT
Dennis Johnson - LB
Henry Johnson - LB
Steve Jordan - TE
Kurt Knoff - DB
Tommy Kramer - QB
Terry LeCount - WR
Leo Lewis - WR
Doug Martin - DE
Sam McCullum - WR
Mardye McDole - WR
Fred McNeill - LB
Mark Mullaney - DE
Darrin Nelson - HB
Keith Nord - DB
Eddie Payton - HB
Ahmad Rashad - WR
Jarvis Redwine - HB
Steve Riley - T
Curtis Rouse - G
Robin Sendlein - LB
Joe Senser - TE
Jeff Siemon - LB
Scott Studwell - LB
John Swain - DB
Dennis Swilley - C
Terry Tausch - T
Willie Teal - DB
John Turner - DB
James White - NT
Sammy White - WR
Walt Williams - DB
Ray Yakavonis - NT
Rickey Young - HB

1982 New England

Julius Adams - DE
Don Blackmon - LB
Morris Bradshaw - WR
Pete Brock - C
Preston Brown - WR
Rich Camarillo - K
Matt Cavanaugh - QB
Raymond Clayborn - DB
Tony Collins - HB
Larry Cowan - HB
George Crump - DE
Bob Cryder - G
Sam Cunningham - FB
Lin Dawson - TE
Paul Dombroski - DB
Vagas Ferguson - HB
Tom Flick - QB
Tim Golden - LB
Steve Grogan - QB
Darryl Haley - T
John Hannah - G
Don Hasselbeck - TE
Mike Haynes - DB
Luther Henson - NT
Brian Holloway - T
Brian Ingram - LB
Roland James - DB
Cedric Jones - WR
Shelby Jordan - T
Keith Lee - DB
Fred Marion - DB
Larry McGrew - LB
Danny Miller - K
Stanley Morgan - WR
Steve Nelson - LB
Dennis Owens - NT
Rex Robinson - K
Rick Sanford - DB
Kenneth Sims - DE
John Smith - K
Ricky Smith - DB
Ron Spears - DE
Mosi Tatupu - FB
Greg Taylor - HB
Andre Tippett - LB
Kenneth Toler - WR
Mark van Eeghen - FB
Robert Weathers - FB
Clayton Weishuhn - LB
Dwight Wheeler - C
Brian Williams - TE
Lester Williams - NT
Ron Wooten - G
John Zamberlin - LB

1982 New Orleans

Morten Andersen - K
Don Bass - TE
Ken Bordelon - LB
Hoby Brenner - TE
Stan Brock - T
Bruce Clark - DE
Kelvin Clark - G
Kenny Duckett - WR
Brad Edelman - G
Tony Elliott - NT
Russell Erxleben - K
Toni Fritsch - K
Hokie Gajan - FB
Russell Gary - DB
Kevin Gray - DB
Leon Gray - T
Jeff Groth - WR
Larry Hardy - TE
John Hill - C
Jack Holmes - FB
Bill Hurley - DB
Rickey Jackson - LB
Jim Kovach - LB
John Krimm - DB
Dave Lafary - T
Marvin Lewis - FB
Reggie Lewis - DE
Rodney Lewis - DB
Archie Manning - QB
Rich Mauti - WR
Guido Merkens - QB
Derland Moore - NT
Rob Nairne - LB
Louis Oubre - G
Whitney Paul - LB
Scott Pelluer - LB
Jim Pietrzak - C
Johnnie Poe - DB
George Rogers - HB
Jimmy Rogers - HB
Lindsay Scott - WR
Ed Simonini - LB
Chuck Slaughter - T
Ken Stabler - QB
Aundra Thompson - WR
Toussaint Tyler - FB
Frank Warren - DE
Frank Wattelet - DB
Dave Waymer - DB
Jim Wilks - DE
Wayne Wilson - FB
Dennis Winston - LB

1982 NY Giants

Billy Ard - G
Rich Baldinger - T
Brad Benson - T
Leon Bright - HB
Scott Brunner - QB
Jim Burt - NT
Brian Carpenter - DB
Rob Carpenter - FB
Harry Carson - LB
Cliff Chatman - FB
Bill Currier - DB
Joe Danelo - K
Mike Dennis - DB
Floyd Eddings - WR
Larry Flowers - DB
Chris Foote - C
Earnest Gray - WR
Dee Hardison - DE
Mark Haynes - DB
Larry Heater - HB
Ernie Hughes - C
Byron Hunt - LB
Terry Jackson - DB
Dave Jennings - K
Gary Jeter - DE
Brian Kelley - LB
Bruce Kimball - G
Gordon King - T
Frank Marion - LB
George Martin - DE
Mike Mayock - DB
Curtis McGriff - DE
Joe McLaughlin - LB
John Mistler - WR
Joe Morris - HB
Tom Mullady - TE
Bill Neill - NT
Johnny Perkins - WR
Leon Perry - FB
Danny Pittman - WR
Beasley Reece - DB
Jerome Sally - NT
Pete Shaw - DB
Gary Shirk - TE
Philip Tabor - DE
John Tautolo - G
Lawrence Taylor - LB
J. T. Turner - G
Rich Umphrey - C
Brad Van Pelt - LB
Jeff Weston - T
Mike Whittington - LB
Butch Woolfolk - HB

1982 NY Jets

Dan Alexander - G
Steve Alvers - TE
Mike Augustyniak - FB
Marion Barber - FB
Jerome Barkum - TE
Barry Bennett - DT
Guy Bingham - G
Stan Blinka - LB
Greg Buttle - LB
Tom Coombs - TE
Bob Crable - LB
Ron Crosby - LB
Dwayne Crutchfield - FB
Scott Dierking - HB
Joe Fields - C
George Floyd - DB
Derrick Gaffney - WR
Mark Gastineau - DE
Rusty Guilbeau - DE
Bruce Harper - HB
Jerry Holmes - DB
Bobby Jackson - DB
Jesse Johnson - DB
Lam Jones - WR
Bobby Jones - WR
Joe Klecko - DE
Pat Leahy - K
Jim Luscinski - T
Johnny Lynn - DB
Marty Lyons - DT
Freeman McNeil - HB
Lance Mehl - LB
Kenny Neil - DE
Tom Newton - FB
Joseph Pellegrini - C
Marvin Powell - T
Chuck Ramsey - K
Darrol Ray - DB
John Roman - T
Ben Rudolph - DT
Pat Ryan - QB
Abdul Salaam - DT
Ken Schroy - DB
Mickey Shuler - TE
Kurt Sohn - WR
Kirk Springs - DB
Richard Todd - QB
Stan Waldemore - G
Wesley Walker - WR
Chris Ward - T
John Woodring - LB

1982 Philadelphia

Harvey Armstrong - NT
Ron Baker - G
Richard Blackmore - DB
Greg Brown - DE
John Bunting - LB
Don Calhoun - FB
Billy Campfield - HB
Harold Carmichael - WR
Al Chesley - LB
Ken Clarke - NT
Mike Curcio - LB
Dennis DeVaughn - DB
Herman Edwards - DB
Ray Ellis - DB
Tony Franklin - K
Louie Giammona - HB
Frank Giddens - T
Anthony Griggs - LB
Carl Hairston - DE
Perry Harrington - FB
Leroy Harris - FB
Dennis Harrison - DE
Wally Henry - WR
Melvin Hoover - WR
Ron Jaworski - QB
Vyto Kab - TE
Steve Kenney - G
Frank LeMaster - LB
Randy Logan - DB
Von Mansfield - DB
Dean Miraldi - G
Leonard Mitchell - DE
Wilbert Montgomery - HB
Guy Morriss - C
Calvin Murray - HB
Petey Perot - G
Joe Pisarcik - QB
Mike Quick - WR
Jerry Robinson - LB
Max Runager - K
Lawrence Sampleton - TE
John Sciarra - DB
Jerry Sisemore - T
Mark Slater - C
Ron Smith - WR
John Spagnola - TE
Zack Valentine - LB
Stan Walters - T
Reggie Wilkes - LB
Brenard Wilson - DB
Tony Woodruff - WR
Roynell Young - DB

1982 Pittsburgh

Walter Abercrombie - HB
Gary Anderson - K
Tom Beasley - DE
Craig Bingham - LB
Mel Blount - DB
Fred Bohannon - DB
Emil Boures - C
Terry Bradshaw - QB
Larry Brown - T
Robin Cole - LB
Steve Courson - G
Bennie Cunningham - TE
Russell Davis - FB
Rick Donnalley - C
Gary Dunn - NT
Ernest French - DB
John Goodman - DE
John Goodson - K
Jack Ham - LB
Franco Harris - FB
Greg Hawthorne - HB
Bryan Hinkle - LB
Tunch Ilkin - T
Ron Johnson - DB
Bob Kohrs - LB
Jack Lambert - LB
David Little - LB
Tyrone McGriff - G
Mike Merriweather - LB
Rick Moser - HB
Ed Nelson - NT
Ted Petersen - T
Ray Pinney - T
Frank Pollard - HB
John Rodgers - TE
Guy Ruff - LB
Donnie Shell - DB
Jim Smith - WR
John Stallworth - WR
Cliff Stoudt - QB
Lynn Swann - WR
Calvin Sweeney - WR
Willie Sydnor - WR
Sidney Thornton - FB
Loren Toews - LB
Anthony Washington - DB
Sam Washington - DB
Mike Webster - C
Keith Willis - DE
Frank Wilson - TE
Craig Wolfley - G
Dwayne Woodruff - DB
Rick Woods - DB

1982 St. Louis

Dave Ahrens - LB
Carl Allen - DB
Kurt Allerman - LB
Ottis Anderson - HB
Charles Baker - LB
Vance Bedford - DB
Don Bessillieu - DB
Carl Birdsong - K
Joe Bostic - G
Rush Brown - DT
Randy Clark - C
Tim Collier - DB
George Collins - G
Mike Dawson - DT
Dan Dierdorf - C
Calvin Favron - LB
Earl Ferrell - FB
David Galloway - DT
John Gillen - LB
Mel Gray - WR
Roy Green - WR
Ken Greene - DB
Curtis Greer - DE
Jeff Griffin - DB
Elois Grooms - DE
Willard Harrell - HB
Jim Hart - QB
E. J. Junior - LB
Greg LaFleur - TE
Rusty Lisch - QB
Neil Lomax - QB
Randy Love - FB
Doug Marsh - TE
Stafford Mays - DE
Eddie McGill - TE
Stump Mitchell - HB
Wayne Morris - FB
Lee Nelson - DB
Neil O'Donoghue - K
Benny Perrin - DB
Art Plunkett - T
Craig Puki - LB
Tootie Robbins - T
Craig Shaffer - LB
Luis Sharpe - T
Mike Shumann - WR
Wayne Smith - DB
Dave Stief - DB
Terry Stieve - G
Ken Thompson - WR
Ricky Thompson - WR
Bruce Thornton - DT
Pat Tilley - WR
Roger Wehrli - DB
Herb Williams - DB

1982 San Diego

Rick Ackerman - DT
Jeffrey Allen - DB
Hank Bauer - FB
Ricky Bell - FB
Rolf Benirschke - K
Carlos Bradley - LB
James Brooks - HB
Willie Buchanon - DB
Maury Buford - K
John Cappelletti - FB
Wes Chandler - WR
Sam Claphan - T
Bobby Duckworth - WR
Donald Dykes - DB
Keith Ferguson - DE
Scott Fitzkee - WR
Dan Fouts - QB
Tim Fox - DB
Andrew Gissinger - T
Bob Gregor - DB
Pete Holohan - TE
Jim Jodat - HB
Gary Johnson - DT
Charlie Joiner - WR
Leroy Jones - DE
Louie Kelcher - DT
Linden King - LB
Bruce Laird - DB
Dave Lewis - LB
Chuck Loewen - G
Woodrow Lowe - LB
Ed Luther - QB
Don Macek - C
Dennis McKnight - C
Miles McPherson - DB
Chuck Muncie - HB
Ray Preston - LB
Bob Rush - C
Dwight Scales - WR
Dewey Selmon - LB
Billy Shields - T
Eric Sievers - TE
Cliff Thrift - LB
Russ Washington - T
Ed White - G
Doug Wilkerson - G
Mike Williams - DB
Kellen Winslow - TE
John Woodcock - DE
Andre Young - DB
Wilbur Young - DT

1982 San Francisco

Dan Audick - G
John Ayers - G
Terry Beeson - LB
Guy Benjamin - QB
Dwaine Board - DE
Dan Bunz - LB
John Choma - G
Dwight Clark - WR
Mike Clark - DE
Tim Collier - DB
Earl Cooper - FB
Randy Cross - G
Fred Dean - DE
Walt Downing - C
Walt Easley - FB
Keith Fahnhorst - T
Ron Ferrari - LB
Russ Francis - TE
Rick Gervais - DB
Willie Harper - LB
John Harty - NT
Dwight Hicks - DB
Bob Horn - LB
Ed Judie - LB
Pete Kugler - NT
Amos Lawrence - HB
Bobby Leopold - LB
Ronnie Lott - DB
Lindsey Mason - T
Milt McColl - LB
Dana McLemore - DB
Jim Miller - K
Joe Montana - QB
Jeff Moore - HB
Renaldo Nehemiah - WR
Ricky Patton - HB
Lawrence Pillers - NT
Fred Quillan - C
Eason Ramson - TE
Jack Reynolds - LB
Bill Ring - HB
Eric Scoggins - LB
Freddie Solomon - WR
Jeff Stover - DE
Jim Stuckey - DE
Lynn Thomas - DB
Keena Turner - LB
Tim Washington - DB
Ray Wersching - K
Newton Williams - HB
Vince Williams - FB
Carlton Williamson - DB
Mike Wilson - WR
Eric Wright - DB
Charle Young - TE

1982 Seattle

Fred Anderson - DE
Steve August - T
Edwin Bailey - G
Mark Bell - DE
Dennis Boyd - T
Dave Brown - DB
Theotis Brown - HB
Jeff Bryant - DE
Keith Butler - LB
Jack Campbell - T
Roger Carr - WR
Dan Doornink - FB
Don Dufek - DB
Bill Dugan - G
Kenny Easley - DB
Ron Essink - T
Brian Flones - LB
David Graham - DE
Jacob Green - DE
Robert Hardy - DT
John Harris - DB
David Hughes - FB
Horace Ivory - HB
Michael Jackson - LB
Paul Johns - WR
Gregg Johnson - DB
Norm Johnson - K
Kerry Justin - DB
Kani Kauahi - C
Dave Krieg - QB
Art Kuehn - C
Eric Lane - HB
Steve Largent - WR
Ken McAlister - DB
Pete Metzelaars - TE
Joe Nash - DT
Bob Pratt - G
Shelton Robinson - LB
John Sawyer - TE
Bruce Scholtz - LB
Keith Simpson - DB
Sherman Smith - HB
Rodell Thomas - LB
Mike Tice - TE
Manu Tuiasosopo - DT
Byron Walker - WR
Jeff West - K
Mike White - DT
Eugene Williams - LB
John Yarno - C
Jim Zorn - QB

1982 Tampa Bay

Dave Barrett - FB
Jerry Bell - TE
Theo Bell - WR
Scot Brantley - LB
Cedric Brown - DB
John Cannon - DE
Bill Capece - K
Gerald Carter - WR
Mel Carver - FB
Brian Clark - K
Bob Cobb - DE
Neal Colzie - DB
Mark Cotney - DB
Jeff Davis - LB
Sean Farrell - G
Jimmie Giles - TE
Jerry Golsteyn - QB
Hugh Green - LB
Charley Hannah - T
Andy Hawkins - LB
John Holt - DB
Kevin House - WR
Cecil Johnson - LB
Gordon Jones - WR
Jim Leonard - C
David Logan - NT
Terdell Middleton - HB
Tom Morris - DB
Michael Morton - HB
Rick Moser - HB
Dana Nafziger - LB
Jim Obradovich - TE
Dwayne O'Steen - DB
James Owens - HB
Dave Reavis - T
Booker Reese - DE
Greg Roberts - G
Gene Sanders - T
Lee Roy Selmon - DE
Johnny Ray Smith - DB
Ray Snell - G
Dave Stalls - DE
Larry Swider - K
Norris Thomas - DB
Mike Washington - DB
Brad White - NT
James Wilder - FB
Doug Williams - QB
Steven Wilson - C
Richard Wood - LB
George Yarno - G

1982 Washington

Stuart Anderson - LB
Jeff Bostic - C
Perry Brooks - DT
Charlie Brown - WR
Dave Butz - DT
Rich Caster - TE
Monte Coleman - LB
Pete Cronan - LB
Fred Dean - G
Vernon Dean - DB
Clint Didier - TE
Alvin Garrett - WR
Nick Giaquinto - HB
Darryl Grant - DT
Russ Grimm - G
Clarence Harmon - HB
Jeff Hayes - K
Bob Holly - QB
Wilbur Jackson - HB
Joe Jacoby - T
Curtis Jordan - DB
Mel Kaufman - LB
Larry Kubin - LB
Don Laster - T
Joe Lavender - DB

Todd Liebenstein - DE
Quentin Lowry - LB
Dexter Manley - DE
Mark May - G
LeCharls McDaniel - DB
Tony McGee - DE
Mat Mendenhall - DE
Rich Milot - LB
Art Monk - WR
Mark Moseley - K
Mark Murphy - DB
Mike Nelms - DB
Pat Ogrin - DT
Neal Olkewicz - LB
Tony Peters - DB
Garry Puetz - T
John Riggins - FB
Virgil Seay - WR
George Starke - T
Joe Theismann - QB
Rick Walker - TE
Don Warren - TE
Joe Washington - HB
Jeris White - DB
Greg Williams - DB
Mike Williams - TE
Otis Wonsley - FB

1983 Atlanta

William Andrews - FB
Stacey Bailey - WR
Steve Bartkowski - QB
Dan Benish - DT
Jim Britt - DB
Reggie Brown - FB
Warren Bryant - T
Bobby Butler - DB
Lynn Cain - HB
Arthur Cox - TE
Willie Curran - WR
Buddy Curry - LB
Rich Dixon - LB
Dan Dufour - G
David Frye - LB
Blane Gaison - DB
Ralph Giacomarro - K
Bob Glazebrook - DB
John Harper - LB
Steve Haworth - DB
Floyd Hodge - WR
Pat Howell - G
Alfred Jackson - WR
Alfred Jenkins - WR
Kenny Johnson - DB
Billy Johnson - WR
Earl Jones - DB
Mike Kenn - T
Fulton Kuykendall - LB
Ronnie Lee - G
Dave Levenick - LB
Mick Luckhurst - K
Allama Matthews - TE
Jeff Merrow - DE
Brett Miller - T
Junior Miller - TE
Mike Moroski - QB
Mike Pitts - DE
Tom Pridemore - DB
Andrew Provence - DT
John Rade - LB
Al Richardson - LB
Gerald Riggs - FB
Bo Robinson - FB
Doug Rogers - DE
Eric Sanders - T
John Scully - C
Don Smith - DT
R.C. Thielemann - G
Tom Tutson - DB
Jeff Van Note - C
Richard Williams - HB
Jeff Yeates - DE
Ben Young - TE
Mike Zele - DT

1983 Baltimore

Sid Abramowitz - T
Raul Allegre - K
Kim Anderson - DB
Larry Anderson - DB
Karl Baldischwiler - T
Quinton Ballard - NT
Earnest Barnes - NT
Pat Beach - TE
Mark Bell - DE
Matt Bouza - WR
Greg Bracelin - LB
James Burroughs - DB
Ray Butler - WR
Johnie Cooks - LB
Jeff Delaney - DB
Curtis Dickey - HB
Zachary Dixon - HB
Ray Donaldson - C
Grant Feasel - C
Nesby Glasgow - DB
Jeff Hart - T
Derrick Hatchett - DB
Bernard Henry - WR
Mark Herrmann - QB
Chris Hinton - G
Ricky Jones - LB
Mark Kafentzis - DB
Barry Krauss - LB

Lindsey Mason - T
Vernon Maxwell - LB
Randy McMillan - FB
Jim Mills - T
Alvin Moore - HB
Victor Oatis - WR
Cliff Odom - LB
Gary Padjen - LB
Mike Pagel - QB
Steve Parker - DE
Rick Porter - HB
Tracy Porter - WR
Tate Randle - DB
Mark Reed - QB
Tim Sherwin - TE
Sanders Shiver - LB
Phil Smith - WR
Rohn Stark - K
Hosea Taylor - DE
Jim Bob Taylor - QB
Donnell Thompson - DE
Marco Tongue - DB
Ben Utt - G
Henry Waechter - DE
Kendall Williams - DB
Newton Williams - HB
Leo Wisniewski - NT
Steve Wright - G
Dave Young - TE

1983 Buffalo

Bill Acker - NT
Buster Barnett - TE
Jon Borchardt - G
Mark Brammer - TE
Jerry Butler - WR
Darryl Caldwell - T
Greg Cater - K
Mario Clark - DB
Joe Cribbs - HB
Justin Cross - T
Joe Danelo - K
Julius Dawkins - WR
Joe Dufek - QB
Joe Ferguson - QB
Judson Flint - DB
Byron Franklin - WR
Steve Freeman - DB
Will Grant - C
Jim Haslett - LB
Tony Hunter - TE
Bill Hurley - DB
Scott Hutchinson - DE
Ken Johnson - DE
Ken Jones - T
Trey Junkin - LB
Chris Keating - LB
Mike Kennedy - DB
Dave Kilson - DB
Matt Kofler - QB
Rod Kush - DB
Roosevelt Leaks - FB
Frank Lewis - WR
Joey Lumpkin - LB
Tom Lynch - G
Eugene Marve - LB
Mark Merrill - LB
Booker Moore - FB
Mike Mosley - WR
Ervin Parker - LB
Robb Riddick - HB
Jim Ritcher - G
Charles Romes - DB
Mark Roopenian - NT
Lucius Sanford - LB
Fred Smerlas - NT
Fred Steinfort - K
Darryl Talley - LB
Gary Thompson - DB
Perry Tuttle - WR
Phil Villapiano - LB
Scott Virkus - DE
Tim Vogler - C
Len Walterscheid - DB
Sherman White - DE
Chris Williams - DB
Van Williams - HB
Ben Williams - DE

1983 Chi. Bears

Kelvin Atkins - LB
Bob Avellini - QB
Brian Baschnagel - WR
Kurt Becker - G
Todd Bell - DB
Mark Bortz - G
Brian Cabral - LB
Gary Campbell - LB
Jim Covert - T
Richard Dent - DE
Dave Duerson - DB
Pat Dunsmore - TE
Vince Evans - QB
Rob Fada - G
Gary Fencik - DB
Jeff Fisher - DB
Leslie Frazier - DB
Andy Frederick - T
Willie Gault - WR
Dennis Gentry - HB
Dan Hampton - DT
Al Harris - LB
Mike Hartenstine - DE
Perry Hartnett - G

Jay Hilgenberg - C
Anthony Hutchison - HB
Noah Jackson - G
John Janata - T
Tyrone Keys - DE
Ken Margerum - WR
Dennis McKinnon - WR
Jim McMahon - QB
Steve McMichael - DT
Emery Moorehead - TE
Jerry Muckensturm - LB
Dan Neal - C
Tim Norman - G
Jim Osborne - DT
Bob Parsons - K
Walter Payton - HB
Kevin Potter - DB
Dan Rains - LB
Mike Richardson - DB
Jay Saldi - TE
Terry Schmidt - DB
James Scott - WR
Dave Simmons - LB
Mike Singletary - LB
Revie Sorey - G
Ray Stachowicz - K
Matt Suhey - FB
Calvin Thomas - FB
Bob Thomas - K
Keith Van Horne - T
Rickey Watts - WR
Walt Williams - DB
Otis Wilson - LB

1983 Cincinnati

Charles Alexander - FB
Ken Anderson - QB
Jerry Boyarsky - NT
Jim Breech - K
Louis Breeden - DB
Ross Browner - DE
Gary Burley - DE
Glenn Cameron - LB
Jeff Christensen - QB
Glen Collins - DE
Cris Collinsworth - WR
Isaac Curtis - WR
Tom Dinkel - LB
Eddie Edwards - DE
Guy Frazier - LB
Andy Gibler - TE
James Griffin - DB
Ray Griffin - DB
Jim Hannula - T
M. L. Harris - TE
Rodney Holman - TE
Ray Horton - DB
Robert Jackson - DB
Pete Johnson - FB
Bobby Kemp - DB
Larry Kinnebrew - FB
Steve Kreider - WR
Tim Krumrie - NT
Dave Lapham - C
Jim LeClair - LB
Chris Lindstrom - DE
Steve Maidlow - LB
Mike Martin - WR
Pat McInally - K
Max Montoya - G
Blake Moore - C
Anthony Munoz - T
Mike Obrovac - G
Rick Razzano - LB
Ken Riley - DB
Dave Rimington - C
Dan Ross - TE
Turk Schonert - QB
Jeff Schuh - LB
John Simmons - DB
Ron Simpkins - LB
Rodney Tate - HB
Jimmy Turner - DB
David Verser - WR
Reggie Williams - LB
Stanley Wilson - HB
Mike Wilson - T

1983 Cleveland

Willis Adams - WR
Dick Ambrose - LB
Mike Baab - C
Matt Bahr - K
Keith Baldwin - DE
Chip Banks - LB
Rocky Belk - WR
Larry Braziel - DB
Thomas Brown - DE
Clinton Burrell - DB
Reggie Camp - DE
Dale Carver - LB
Bill Contz - T
Tom Cousineau - LB
Steve Cox - K
Johnny Davis - FB
Joe DeLamielleure - G
Tom DeLeone - C
Doug Dieken - T
Hanford Dixon - DB
Paul Farren - T
Ricky Feacher - WR
Vagas Ferguson - FB
Elvis Franks - DE
Bob Golic - NT

Jeff Gossett - K
Boyce Green - FB
Al Gross - DB
Dino Hall - HB
Harry Holt - TE
Thomas Hopkins - T
Robert Jackson - G
Eddie Johnson - LB
Lawrence Johnson - DB
Bobby Jones - WR
Dave Logan - WR
Clay Matthews - LB
Paul McDonald - QB
Ozzie Newsome - TE
Scott Nicolas - LB
Rod Perry - DB
Mike Pruitt - FB
Dave Puzzuoli - NT
Cody Risien - T
Clarence Scott - DB
Brian Sipe - QB
Tim Stracka - TE
Dwight Walker - HB
Curtis Weathers - LB
Mike Whitwell - DB

1983 Dallas

Gary Allen - HB
Brian Baldinger - G
Bill Bates - DB
Larry Bethea - DT
Bob Breunig - LB
Glenn Carano - QB
Dextor Clinkscale - DB
Jim Cooper - T
Doug Cosbie - TE
Anthony Dickerson - LB
Doug Donley - WR
Pat Donovan - T
Tony Dorsett - HB
Michael Downs - DB
Billy Joe DuPree - TE
John Dutton - DT
Ron Fellows - DB
Mike Hegman - LB
Tony Hill - WR
Rod Hill - DB
Gary Hogeboom - QB
Bruce Huther - LB
Jim Jeffcoat - DE
Butch Johnson - WR
Too Tall Jones - DE
Angelo King - LB
Harvey Martin - DE
Scott McLean - LB
Chuck McSwain - HB
Jim Miller - K
Robert Newhouse - FB
Timmy Newsome - FB
Drew Pearson - WR
Kurt Petersen - G
Phil Pozderac - T
Tom Rafferty - C
Howard Richards - T
Jeff Rohrer - LB
Chris Schultz - T
Herbert Scott - G
Rafael Septien - K
Cleo Simmons - TE
Don Smerek - DT
Ron Springs - FB
Dennis Thurman - DB
Glen Titensor - C
Mark Tuinei - DT
Everson Walls - DB
Michael Walter - LB
John Warren - K
Randy White - DT
Danny White - QB

1983 Denver

Jerry Baker - NT
Dean Barnett - TE
Keith Bishop - C
Walt Bowyer - DE
Clay Brown - TE
Billy Bryan - C
Steve Busick - LB
Rubin Carter - NT
Barney Chavous - DE
Darren Comeaux - LB
Mark Cooper - T
Steve DeBerg - QB
Rick Dennison - LB
Myron Dupree - DB
Ron Egloff - TE
John Elway - QB
Steve Foley - DB
Tom Glassic - G
Randy Gradishar - LB
Mike Harden - DB
Shawn Hollingsworth - T
Paul Howard - G
Roger Jackson - DB
Tom Jackson - LB
Rulon Jones - DE
Rich Karlis - K
Gary Kubiak - QB
Ken Lanier - T
Don Latimer - NT
Rob Lytle - HB
Brison Manor - DE
Karl Mecklenburg - LB
Wilbur Myers - DB

Jesse Myles - HB
Riley Odoms - TE
Rick Parros - FB
Nathan Poole - FB
Dave Preston - HB
Luke Prestridge - K
Jim Ryan - LB
Clint Sampson - WR
John Sawyer - TE
Dennis Smith - DB
Rich Stachowski - NT
Dave Studdard - T
Bob Swenson - LB
Zach Thomas - WR
Steve Trimble - DB
Keith Uecker - T
Rick Upchurch - WR
Steve Watson - WR
Gerald Willhite - FB
Steve Wilson - DB
Sammy Winder - HB
Ken Woodard - LB
James Wright - TE
Louis Wright - DB

1983 Detroit

Roosevelt Barnes - LB
Mike Black - K
Dexter Bussey - FB
James Caver - DB
Jeff Chadwick - WR
Garry Cobb - LB
Mike Cofer - DE
August Curley - LB
Gary Danielson - QB
Mike Dawson - DT
Chris Dieterich - T
Steve Doig - LB
Keith Dorney - T
Homer Elias - G
Doug English - DT
Mike Fanning - DT
Ken Fantetti - LB
Amos Fowler - C
Bill Gay - DE
William Graham - DB
Hector Gray - DB
Don Greco - G
Curtis Green - DE
Alvin Hall - DB
James Harrell - LB
Maurice Harvey - DB
Eric Hipple - QB
Ken Jenkins - HB
Demetrious Johnson - DB
James Jones - FB
Rick Kane - HB
Horace King - FB
Al Latimer - DB
Larry Lee - G
Robbie Martin - WR
Reese McCall - TE
Bruce McNorton - DB
Martin Moss - DT
Steve Mott - C
Eddie Murray - K
Mark Nichols - WR
Ulysses Norris - TE
Rob Rubick - TE
Freddie Scott - WR
Billy Sims - HB
Rich Strenger - T
Leonard Thompson - WR
Vince Thompson - FB
Tom Turnure - C
Dan Wagoner - DB
Bobby Watkins - DB
Jimmy Williams - LB

1983 Green Bay

John Anderson - LB
Greg Boyd - DE
Byron Braggs - DE
Robert Brown - DE
Rich Campbell - QB
Ron Cassidy - WR
Jessie Clark - FB
Paul Coffman - TE
George Cumby - LB
Mike Curcio - LB
Lynn Dickey - QB
Mike Douglass - LB
Dave Drechsler - G
Gerry Ellis - FB
Phil Epps - WR
Eddie Garcia - K
Charlie Getty - T
Johnnie Gray - DB
Ron Hallstrom - T
Leotis Harris - G
Maurice Harvey - DB
Estus Hood - DB
Harlan Huckleby - HB
Tim Huffman - G
Eddie Lee Ivery - HB
John Jefferson - WR
Charles Johnson - NT
Ezra Johnson - DE
Mike Jolly - DB
Terry Jones - NT
Syd Kitson - G
Greg Koch - T

Jim Laughlin - LB
Mark Lee - DB
Cliff Lewis - LB
Gary Lewis - TE
Tim Lewis - DB
James Lofton - WR
Larry McCarren - C
Mike McCoy - DB
Mike Meade - FB
Casey Merrill - DE
Mark Murphy - DB
Dwayne O'Steen - DB
Chet Parlavecchio - LB
Guy Prather - LB
Larry Rubens - C
Ron Sams - G
Randy Scott - LB
Bucky Scribner - K
Daryle Skaugstad - NT
Ron Spears - DE
Jan Stenerud - K
Karl Swanke - T
Richard Turner - NT
David Whitehurst - QB
Rich Wingo - LB
Chet Winters - HB

1983 Houston

Robert Abraham - LB
Gary Allen - HB
Walt Arnold - TE
Jesse Baker - DE
Elvin Bethea - DE
Gregg Bingham - LB
Keith Bostic - DB
Robert Brazile - LB
Curtis Brown - FB
Steve Brown - DB
Steve Bryant - WR
Earl Campbell - HB
David Carter - C
Dave Casper - TE
Donnie Craft - FB
Dwayne Crutchfield - FB
Chris Dressel - TE
Stan Edwards - FB
Vagas Ferguson - FB
Jerome Foster - DE
Doug France - T
Bob Hamm - DE
Carter Hartwig - DB
Derrick Hatchett - DB
Greg Hill - DB
Mike Holston - WR
Pat Howell - G
Daryl Hunt - LB
John James - K
Tim Joiner - LB
Bill Kay - DB
Florian Kempf - K
Oliver Luck - QB
Archie Manning - QB
Bruce Matthews - G
Mike McCloskey - TE
Darryl Meadows - DB
Larry Moriarty - FB
Mike Munchak - G
Gifford Nielsen - QB
Tate Randle - DB
Mike Reinfeldt - DB
Mike Renfro - WR
Avon Riley - LB
Carl Roaches - WR
Harvey Salem - T
John Schuhmacher - G
Tim Smith - WR
Brian Sochia - NT
Al Steinfeld - G
Mike Stensrud - NT
Les Studdard - C
Malcolm Taylor - DE
Ted Thompson - LB
Morris Towns - T
Willie Tullis - DB
Herkie Walls - WR
Ralph Williams - G
J. C. Wilson - DB

1983 Kansas City

Jim Arnold - K
Rich Baldinger - T
Ed Beckman - TE
Mike Bell - DE
Todd Blackledge - QB
Jerry Blanton - LB
Theotis Brown - FB
Trent Bryant - DB
Brad Budde - G
Lloyd Burruss - DB
Carlos Carson - WR
Deron Cherry - DB
Tom Condon - G
Calvin Daniels - LB
Bob Gagliano - QB
Ellis Gardner - T
Gary Green - DB
Jim Hadnot - FB
Anthony Hancock - WR
Louis Haynes - LB
Matt Herkenhoff - T
Tom Howard - LB
Billy Jackson - HB
Charles Jackson - LB
Van Jakes - DB

Bill Kenney - QB
Mark Kirchner - T
Dave Klug - LB
Ken Kremer - NT
Albert Lewis - DB
Dave Lindstrom - DE
Adam Lingner - C
Nick Lowery - K
Dave Lutz - T
Dino Mangiero - NT
Henry Marshall - WR
Stephone Paige - WR
Steve Potter - LB
Dean Prater - DE
Lawrence Ricks - HB
Durwood Roquemore - DB
Jim Rourke - T
Bob Rush - C
Willie Scott - TE
Bob Simmons - G
J. T. Smith - WR
Lucious Smith - DB
Gary Spani - LB
Art Still - DE
Jewerl Thomas - FB
Ken Thomas - HB
James Walker - LB
Ron Wetzel - TE
Ray Yakavonis - NT
John Zamberlin - LB

1983 LA Raiders

Marcus Allen - HB
Lyle Alzado - DE
Chris Bahr - K
Jeff Barnes - LB
Malcolm Barnwell - WR
Rick Berns - HB
Don Bessillieu - DB
Cliff Branch - WR
Darryl Byrd - LB
Tony Caldwell - LB
Todd Christensen - TE
Dave Dalby - C
Bruce Davis - T
James Davis - DB
Mike Davis - DB
Ray Guy - K
Charley Hannah - G
Don Hasselbeck - TE
Frank Hawkins - FB
Lester Hayes - DB
Mike Haynes - DB
Ted Hendricks - LB
Kenny Hill - DB
David Humm - QB
Derrick Jensen - FB
Shelby Jordan - T
Kenny King - HB
Reggie Kinlaw - NT
Henry Lawrence - T
Howie Long - DE
Rod Martin - LB
Mickey Marvin - G
Vann McElroy - DB
Odis McKinney - DB
Matt Millen - LB
Cleo Montgomery - HB
Don Mosebar - T
Calvin Muhammad - WR
Ed Muransky - T
Bob Nelson - LB
Irvin Phillips - DB
Bill Pickel - DE
Jim Plunkett - QB
Greg Pruitt - HB
Derrick Ramsey - TE
Archie Reese - NT
Johnny Robinson - NT
Jim Romano - C
Jack Squirek - LB
Dave Stalls - NT
Steve Sylvester - C
Greg Townsend - DE
Ted Watts - DB
Dokie Williams - WR
Chester Willis - HB
Marc Wilson - QB

1983 LA Rams

Robert Alexander - HB
George Andrews - LB
Bill Bain - T
Mike Barber - TE
Doug Barnett - DE
Richard Bishop - NT
Russ Bolinger - G
Howard Carson - LB
Kirk Collins - DB
Jim Collins - LB
Nolan Cromwell - DB
Charles DeJurnett - NT
Preston Dennard - WR
Eric Dickerson - FB
Reggie Doss - DE
Carl Ekern - LB
Henry Ellard - WR
George Farmer - WR
Vince Ferragamo - QB
Otis Grant - WR
Mike Guman - FB
Dennis Harrah - G
Eric Harris - DB

David Hill - TE
Kent Hill - G
LeRoy Irvin - DB
Monte Jackson - DB
Mark Jerue - LB
Gary Jeter - DE
Johnnie Johnson Jr. - DB
A. J. Jones - FB
Gordon Jones - WR
Jeff Kemp - QB
Gary Kowalski - T
Mike Lansford - K
Myron Lapka - NT
Dave Lewis - LB
James McDonald - TE
Greg Meisner - NT
John Misko - K
Chuck Nelson - K
Vince Newsome - DB
Mel Owens - LB
Barry Redden - HB
Joe Shearin - G
Jeff Simmons - WR
Jackie Slater - T
Doug Smith - C
Ivory Sully - DB
Mike Wilcher - LB
Eric Williams - LB
Henry Williams - DB
Mike Williams - DB
Jack Youngblood - DE
Jim Youngblood - LB

1983 Miami

Bill Barnett - DE
Bob Baumhower - NT
Woody Bennett - FB
Charles Benson - DE
Doug Betters - DE
Glenn Blackwood - DB
Lyle Blackwood - DB
Kim Bokamper - DE
Charles Bowser - LB
Mark Brown - LB
Bob Brudzinski - LB
Jimmy Cefalo - WR
Mike Charles - NT
Steve Clark - NT
Mark Clayton - WR
Mark Dennard - C
A. J. Duhe - LB
Mark Duper - WR
Roy Foster - G
Andra Franklin - FB
Jon Giesler - T
Cleveland Green - T
Bruce Hardy - TE
Duriel Harris - WR
Vince Heflin - WR
Eddie Hill - HB
Jim Jensen - QB
Dan Johnson - TE
William Judson - DB
Mike Kozlowski - DB
Bob Kuechenberg - G
Eric Laakso - T
Paul Lankford - DB
Dan Marino - QB
Nat Moore - WR
Tony Nathan - HB
Ed Newman - G
David Overstreet - HB
Earnest Rhone - LB
Reggie Roby - K
Joe Rose - TE
Gerald Small - DB
Robert Sowell - DB
Dwight Stephenson - C
Don Strock - QB
Terry Tautolo - LB
Rodell Thomas - LB
Emmett Tilley - LB
Jeff Toews - G
Tommy Vigorito - HB
Uwe von Schamann - K
Fulton Walker - DB
David Woodley - QB

1983 Minnesota

Walker Lee Ashley - LB
Rick Bell - HB
Rufus Bess - DB
Matt Blair - LB
Brent Boyd - G
Ted Brown - HB
Norris Brown - TE
Joey Browner - DB
Bob Bruer - TE
Dave Casper - TE
Greg Coleman - K
Steve Dils - QB
Neil Elshire - DE
Dennis Fowlkes - LB
Tony Galbreath - FB
Wes Hamilton - G
Tom Hannon - DB
Randy Holloway - DE
Jim Hough - G
Dave Huffman - G
Tim Irwin - T
Charlie Johnson - NT
Dennis Johnson - LB
Henry Johnson - LB
Mike Jones - WR
Steve Jordan - TE
Tommy Kramer - QB
Terry LeCount - WR
Carl Lee - DB
Leo Lewis - WR
Archie Manning - QB
Doug Martin - DE
Sam McCullum - WR
Mardye McDole - WR
Fred McNeill - LB
Mike Mularkey - TE
Mark Mullaney - DE
Darrin Nelson - HB
Keith Nord - DB
Jarvis Redwine - HB
Benny Ricardo - K
Steve Riley - T
Curtis Rouse - G
Robin Sendlein - LB
Scott Studwell - LB
John Swain - DB
Dennis Swilley - C
Terry Tausch - T
Willie Teal - DB
John Turner - DB
James White - NT
Sammy White - WR
Wade Wilson - QB
Ray Yakavonis - NT
Rickey Young - HB

1983 New England

Julius Adams - DE
Don Blackmon - LB
Pete Brock - C
Dave Browning - DE
Rich Camarillo - K
Raymond Clayborn - DB
Tony Collins - HB
Bob Cryder - T
Lin Dawson - TE
Paul Dombroski - DB
Tony Eason - QB
John Gillen - LB
Tim Golden - LB
Steve Grogan - QB
Darryl Haley - T
John Hannah - G
Marshall Harris - DE
Don Hasselbeck - TE
Luther Henson - NT
Brian Holloway - T
Brian Ingram - LB
Roland James - DB
Cedric Jones - WR
Mike Kerrigan - QB
Art Kuehn - C
Keith Lee - DB
Ronnie Lippett - DB
Fred Marion - DB
Larry McGrew - LB
Steve Moore - T
Stanley Morgan - WR
Steve Nelson - LB
Dennis Owens - NT
George Peoples - HB
Derrick Ramsey - TE
Johnny Rembert - LB
Ed Reynolds - LB
Doug Rogers - DE
Rick Sanford - DB
Kenneth Sims - DE
John Smith - K
Ricky Smith - DB
Ron Spears - DE
Stephen Starring - WR
Fred Steinfort - K
Mosi Tatupu - FB
Andre Tippett - LB
Mark van Eeghen - FB
Clarence Weathers - WR
Robert Weathers - FB
Clayton Weishuhn - LB
Dwight Wheeler - C
Brooks Williams - TE
Lester Williams - NT
Toby Williams - DE
Darryal Wilson - WR
Ron Wooten - G
Joaquin Zendejas - K

1983 New Orleans

Morten Andersen - K
Cliff Austin - HB
Hoby Brenner - TE
Stan Brock - T
Bruce Clark - DE
Kelvin Clark - G
Kenny Duckett - WR
Brad Edelman - G
Tony Elliott - NT
Russell Erxleben - K
Hokie Gajan - FB
Russell Gary - DB
Eugene Goodlow - WR
Leon Gray - T
Jeff Groth - WR
Larry Hardy - TE
John Hill - C
Bill Hurley - DB
Rickey Jackson - LB
Bobby Johnson - DB
Greg Knafelc - QB
Steve Korte - G
Jim Kovach - LB
Dave Lafary - T
Gary Lewis - NT
Reggie Lewis - DE
Rodney Lewis - DB
Chris Martin - LB
Rich Mauti - WR
Guido Merkens - QB
Derland Moore - NT
Rob Nairne - LB
Louis Oubre - G
Whitney Paul - LB
Scott Pelluer - LB
Vernon Perry - DB
Jim Pietrzak - C
Johnnie Poe - DB
Glen Redd - LB
George Rogers - HB
Jimmy Rogers - HB
Lindsay Scott - WR
Ken Stabler - QB
Greg Stemrick - DB
John Tice - TE
Frank Warren - DE
Frank Wattelet - DB
Dave Waymer - DB
Jim Wilks - DE
Dave Wilson - QB
Tim Wilson - FB
Wayne Wilson - HB
Dennis Winston - LB
Tyrone Young - WR

1983 NY Giants

Billy Ard - G
Rich Baldinger - T
Kevin Belcher - G
Brad Benson - T
Leon Bright - HB
Scott Brunner - QB
Jim Burt - NT
Billy Campfield - HB
Rob Carpenter - HB
Harry Carson - LB
Charles Cook - NT
Bill Currier - DB
Paul Davis - LB
Mike Dennis - DB
Floyd Eddings - WR
Larry Flowers - DB
Chris Foote - C
Earnest Gray - WR
Ali Haji-Sheikh - K
Dee Hardison - DE
Mark Haynes - DB
Andy Headen - LB
Larry Heater - HB
Ernie Hughes - C
Byron Hunt - LB
Terry Jackson - DB
Dave Jennings - K
Brian Kelley - LB
Terry Kinard - DB
Gordon King - T
Frank Marion - LB
Leonard Marshall - DE
George Martin - DE
Mike Mayock - DB
LeCharls McDaniel - DB
Curtis McGriff - DE
Joe McLaughlin - LB
Casey Merrill - DE
Mike Miller - WR
John Mistler - WR
Joe Morris - HB
Zeke Mowatt - TE
Tom Mullady - TE
Bill Neill - NT
Johnny Perkins - WR
Danny Pittman - WR
Beasley Reece - DB
Jeff Rutledge - QB
Jerome Sally - NT
Malcolm Scott - TE
Pete Shaw - DB
Phil Simms - QB
Al Steinfeld - C
John Tautolo - G
Lawrence Taylor - LB
John Tuggle - HB
J. T. Turner - G
Rich Umphrey - C
Brad Van Pelt - LB
Mike Whittington - LB
Byron Williams - WR
Butch Woolfolk - HB

1983 NY Jets

Dan Alexander - G
Mike Augustyniak - FB
Marion Barber - FB
Jerome Barkum - TE
Barry Bennett - DT
Guy Bingham - C
Stan Blinka - LB
Preston Brown - WR
Nick Bruckner - WR
Greg Buttle - LB
Tom Coombs - TE
Bob Crable - LB
Ron Crosby - LB
Dwayne Crutchfield - FB
Scott Dierking - HB
Jim Eliopulos - LB
Joe Fields - C
Derrick Gaffney - WR
Mark Gastineau - DE
Rusty Guilbeau - DE
Mike Harmon - WR
Bruce Harper - HB
Johnny Hector - HB
Jerry Holmes - DB
Bobby Jackson - DB
Jesse Johnson - DB
Lam Jones - WR
Joe Klecko - DT
Rocky Klever - FB
Pat Leahy - K
Kenny Lewis - FB
George Lilja - C
Johnny Lynn - DB
Marty Lyons - DT
Reggie McElroy - T
Freeman McNeil - HB
Lance Mehl - LB
Davlin Mullen - DB
Kenny Neil - DE
Joseph Pellegrini - C
Marvin Powell - T
Chuck Ramsey - K
Darrol Ray - DB
Ben Rudolph - DT
Pat Ryan - QB
Abdul Salaam - DT
Ken Schroy - DB
Mickey Shuler - TE
Kirk Springs - DB
Richard Todd - QB
Stan Waldemore - G
Wesley Walker - WR
Chris Ward - T
John Woodring - LB

1983 Philadelphia

Harvey Armstrong - NT
Ron Baker - G
Greg Brown - DE
Harold Carmichael - WR
Ken Clarke - NT
Bill Cowher - LB
Byron Darby - DE
Dennis DeVaughn - DB
Al Dixon - TE
Herman Edwards - DB
Ray Ellis - DB
Major Everett - FB
Gerry Feehery - C
Elbert Foules - DB
Tony Franklin - K
Jim Fritzsche - T
Anthony Griggs - LB
Michael Haddix - FB
Carl Hairston - DE
Perry Harrington - FB
Dennis Harrison - DE
Melvin Hoover - WR
Wes Hopkins - DB
Ron Jaworski - QB
Vyto Kab - TE
Steve Kenney - G
Rich Kraynak - LB
Randy Logan - DB
Dean Miraldi - T
Leonard Mitchell - T
Wilbert Montgomery - HB
Guy Morriss - C
Hubie Oliver - FB
Dan Pastorini - QB
Joe Pisarcik - QB
Mike Quick - WR
Jerry Robinson - LB
Max Runager - K
Lawrence Sampleton - TE
Jody Schulz - LB
John Sciarra - DB
Jerry Sisemore - T
Tom Skladany - K
Mark Slater - C
Ron Smith - WR
Thomas Strauthers - DE
Stan Walters - T
Reggie Wilkes - LB
Joel Williams - LB
Michael Williams - FB
Brenard Wilson - DB
Tony Woodruff - WR
Glen Young - WR
Roynell Young - DB

1983 Pittsburgh

Walter Abercrombie - HB
Gary Anderson - K
Tom Beasley - DE
Greg Best - DB
Craig Bingham - LB
Mel Blount - DB
Emil Boures - G
Terry Bradshaw - QB
Larry Brown - T
Wayne Capers - WR
Harvey Clayton - DB
Robin Cole - LB
Craig Colquitt - P
Steve Courson - G
Bennie Cunningham - TE
Russell Davis - FB
Rick Donnalley - C
Craig Dunaway - TE
Gary Dunn - NT
Gregg Garrity - WR
Keith Gary - DE
John Goodman - DE
Franco Harris - FB
Tim Harris - HB
Greg Hawthorne - WR
Bryan Hinkle - LB
Tunch Ilkin - T
Ron Johnson - DB
Mark Kirchner - T
Bob Kohrs - LB
Jack Lambert - LB
David Little - LB
Mark Malone - QB
Mike Merriweather - LB
Ed Nelson - NT
Henry Odom - HB
Ted Petersen - T
Frank Pollard - HB
Gabe Rivera - DT
John Rodgers - TE
Donnie Shell - DB
Paul Skansi - WR
John Stallworth - WR
Cliff Stoudt - QB
Calvin Sweeney - WR
Loren Toews - LB
Sam Washington - DB
Mike Webster - C
Eric Williams - DB
Keith Willis - DE
Blake Wingle - G
Craig Wolfley - G
Dwayne Woodruff - DB
Rick Woods - DB

1983 St. Louis

Dave Ahrens - LB
Kurt Allerman - LB
Ottis Anderson - HB
Dan Audick - G
Charles Baker - LB
Al Baker - DE
Steve Bird - WR
Carl Birdsong - P
Joe Bostic - G
Rush Brown - DT
Randy Clark - C
Paul Davis - LB
Dan Dierdorf - C
Mark Duda - DT
Jim Eliopulos - LB
Earl Ferrell - FB
David Galloway - DT
Roy Green - WR
Curtis Greer - DE
Jeff Griffin - DB
Elois Grooms - DT
Willard Harrell - HB
Bob Harris - LB
Jim Hart - QB
Victor Heflin - DB
Monty Hunter - DB
E. J. Junior - LB
Greg LaFleur - TE
Rusty Lisch - QB
Neil Lomax - QB
Randy Love - FB
Cedric Mack - DB
Doug Marsh - TE
Stafford Mays - DE
Eddie McGill - TE
Stump Mitchell - HB
Wayne Morris - FB
Lee Nelson - DB
Neil O'Donoghue - K
Chet Parlavecchio - LB
Benny Perrin - DB
Danny Pittman - WR
Art Plunkett - T
Tootie Robbins - T
George Schmitt - DB
Carlos Scott - DB
Craig Shaffer - LB
Luis Sharpe - T
Mike Shumann - WR
Leonard Smith - DB
Wayne Smith - DB
Terry Stieve - G
Ken Thompson - WR
Pat Tilley - WR
Lionel Washington - DB
Bill Whitaker - LB
Jamie Williams - TE

1983 San Diego

Rick Ackerman - NT
Rolf Benirschke - K
Carlos Bradley - LB
James Brooks - HB
Don Brown - T
Maury Buford - P
Gill Byrd - DB
John Cappelletti - FB
Roger Carr - WR
Wes Chandler - WR
Sam Claphan - T
Bobby Duckworth - WR
Chuck Ehin - DE
Bill Elko - G
Larry Evans - LB
Keith Ferguson - DE
Hosea Fortune - WR
Dan Fouts - QB
Tim Fox - DB
Andrew Gissinger - T
Derrel Gofourth - G
Mike Green - LB
Ken Greene - DB
Bob Gregor - DB
Reuben Henderson - DB
Pete Holohan - TE
Earnest Jackson - HB
Jim Jodat - FB
Gary Johnson - DE
Charlie Joiner - WR
Leroy Jones - DE
Louie Kelcher - DT
Linden King - LB
Bruce Laird - DB
Woodrow Lowe - LB
Ed Luther - QB
Don Macek - C
Bruce Mathison - QB
Dennis McKnight - C
Miles McPherson - DB
Chuck Muncie - FB
Derrie Nelson - LB
Darrell Pattillo - DB
Ray Preston - LB
Dwight Scales - WR
Billy Shields - T
Eric Sievers - TE
Billy Ray Smith Jr. - LB
Sherman Smith - FB
Cliff Thrift - LB
Danny Walters - DB
Ed White - G
Doug Wilkerson - G
Henry Williams - DB
Kellen Winslow - TE
Andre Young - DB

1983 San Francisco

John Ayers - G
Guy Benjamin - QB
Richard Blackmore - DB
Dwaine Board - DE
Dan Bunz - LB
Matt Cavanaugh - QB
John Choma - G
Dwight Clark - WR
Tim Collier - DB
Earl Cooper - TE
Roger Craig - FB
Randy Cross - G
Fred Dean - DE
Walt Downing - C
Riki Ellison - LB
Keith Fahnhorst - T
Ron Ferrari - LB
Russ Francis - TE
Rick Gervais - DB
Willie Harper - LB
John Harty - DT
Dwight Hicks - DB
Tom Holmoe - DB
Bob Horn - LB
Ed Judie - LB
Allan Kennedy - T
Pete Kugler - NT
Bobby Leopold - LB
Ronnie Lott - DB
Ken McAlister - LB
Milt McColl - LB
Dana McLemore - KR
Carl Monroe - HB
Joe Montana - QB
Blanchard Montgomery - LB
Jeff Moore - HB
Gary Moten - LB
Renaldo Nehemiah - WR
Tom Orosz - P
Bubba Paris - T
Lawrence Pillers - DT
Fred Quillan - C
Eason Ramson - TE
Jack Reynolds - LB
Bill Ring - HB
Jesse Sapolu - G
Daryle Skaugstad - NT
Freddie Solomon - WR
Jeff Stover - NT
Jim Stuckey - DE
Keena Turner - LB
Wendell Tyler - HB
Ray Wersching - K
Vince Williams - FB
Carlton Williamson - DB
Mike Wilson - WR
Eric Wright - DB

1983 Seattle

Steve August - T
Edwin Bailey - G
Jerome Boyd - LB
Dave Brown - DB
Theotis Brown - FB
Jeff Bryant - DE
Cullen Bryant - FB
Blair Bush - C
Keith Butler - LB
Chris Castor - WR
Sam Clancy - DE
Zachary Dixon - HB
Dan Doornink - FB
Don Dufek - DB
Bill Dugan - G
Kenny Easley - DB
Ron Essink - T
Greg Gaines - LB
Jacob Green - DE
John Harris - DB
Matt Hernandez - T
Mark Hicks - LB
David Hughes - FB
Darrell Irvin - DE
Harold Jackson - WR
Michael Jackson - LB
Paul Johns - WR
Gregg Johnson - DB
Norm Johnson - K
Kerry Justin - DB
Kani Kauahi - C
Dave Krieg - QB
Eric Lane - HB
Steve Largent - WR
Ken McAlister - DB
Reggie McKenzie - G
Sam Merriman - LB
Pete Metzelaars - TE
Paul Moyer - DB
Joe Nash - NT
Joe Norman - LB
Bob Pratt - G
Shelton Robinson - LB
Bruce Scholtz - LB
Keith Simpson - DB
Mike Tice - TE
Manu Tuiasosopo - NT
Byron Walker - WR
Curt Warner - HB
Jeff West - P
Eugene Williams - LB
Gary Wimmer - LB
Charle Young - TE
Jim Zorn - QB

1983 Tampa Bay

Hasson Arbubakrr - DE
Adger Armstrong - FB
Jerry Bell - TE
Theo Bell - WR
Scot Brantley - LB
Gene Branton - WR
Cedric Brown - DB
Glenn Bujnoch - G
John Cannon - DE
Bill Capece - K
Gerald Carter - WR
Mel Carver - FB
Jeremiah Castille - DB
Neal Colzie - DB
Mark Cotney - DB
Jeff Davis - LB
Sean Farrell - G
Frank Garcia - P
Jimmie Giles - TE
Jerry Golsteyn - QB
Hugh Green - LB
Randy Grimes - G
Andy Hawkins - LB
Bob Hewko - QB
John Holt - DB
Kevin House - WR
Cecil Johnson - LB
Ed Judie - LB
Jeff Komlo - QB
Sandy LaBeaux - DB
Jim Leonard - C
David Logan - NT
Quentin Lowry - LB
Terdell Middleton - HB
Tom Morris - DB
Michael Morton - HB
Jim Obradovich - TE
Dwayne O'Steen - DB
James Owens - HB
Dave Reavis - T
Beasley Reece - DB
Booker Reese - DE
Gene Sanders - T
Lee Roy Selmon - DE
Johnny Ray Smith - DB
Ray Snell - G
Danny Spradlin - LB
Dave Stalls - DE
Kelly Thomas - T
Norris Thomas - DB
Jack Thompson - QB
Robert Thompson - LB
Andre Tyler - WR
David Warnke - K
Mike Washington - DB
Brad White - NT
James Wilder - FB
Steven Wilson - C
Mark Witte - TE
Richard Wood - LB
George Yarno - G

1983 Washington

Stuart Anderson - LB

Jeff Bostic - C
Perry Brooks - DT
Charlie Brown - WR
Dave Butz - DT
Brian Carpenter - DB
Ken Coffey - DB
Monte Coleman - LB
Pete Cronan - LB
Vernon Dean - DB
Clint Didier - TE
Reggie Evans - HB
Alvin Garrett - WR
Nick Giaquinto - HB
Darryl Grant - DT
Darrell Green - DB
Russ Grimm - G
Jeff Hayes - P
Bob Holly - QB
Ken Huff - G
Joe Jacoby - T
Curtis Jordan - DB
Mel Kaufman - LB
Bruce Kimball - G
Larry Kubin - LB
Todd Liebenstein - DE
Quentin Lowry - LB
Dexter Manley - DE
Charles Mann - DE
Mark May - G
Tony McGee - DE
Mark McGrath - WR
Rich Milot - LB
Art Monk - WR
Mark Moseley - K
Mark Murphy - DB
Mike Nelms - WR
Neal Olkewicz - LB
John Riggins - FB
John Sawyer - TE
Virgil Seay - WR
Roy Simmons - G
George Starke - T
Dave Stief - WR
Joe Theismann - QB
Rick Walker - TE
Don Warren - TE
Anthony Washington - DB
Joe Washington - HB
Greg Williams - DB
Mike Williams - TE
Otis Wonsley - FB

1984 Atlanta

David Archer - QB
Cliff Austin - RB
Stacey Bailey - WR
Steve Bartkowski - QB
Dan Benish - DT
Cliff Benson - TE
Thomas Benson - LB
Jim Britt - DB
Rick Bryan - DE
Warren Bryant - T
Gary Burley - DT
Bobby Butler - DB
Lynn Cain - RB
Scott Case - DB
Mike Chapman - C
Arthur Cox - TE
Willie Curran - WR
Buddy Curry - LB
Dan Dufour - T
David Frye - LB
Blane Gaison - DB
Ralph Giacomarro - P
Roy Harris - DT
Steve Haworth - DB
Floyd Hodge - WR
Alfred Jackson - WR
Jeff Jackson - LB
Kenny Johnson - DB
Billy Johnson - WR
Mike Kenn - T
Fulton Kuykendall - LB
Mike Landrum - TE
Dave Levenick - LB
Mick Luckhurst - K
Rydell Malancon - LB
Allama Matthews - TE
Brett Miller - T
Mike Moroski - QB
Joseph Pellegrini - G
Mike Pitts - DT
Tom Pridemore - DB
Andrew Provence - DE
John Rade - LB
Al Richardson - LB
Gerald Riggs - RB
Eric Sanders - T
John Scully - G
Virgil Seay - WR
Gerald Small - DB
Don Smith - DE
Sylvester Stamps - RB
Rodney Tate - RB
Johnny Taylor - LB
R.C. Thielemann - G
Perry Tuttle - WR
Tim Tyrrell - RB
Jeff Van Note - C
Richard Williams - RB
Jeff Yeates - DE

1984 Buffalo

Bill Acker - NT
Joe Azelby - LB
Buster Barnett - TE
Martin Bayless - DB
Greg Bell - RB
Rodney Bellinger - DB
Jon Borchardt - G
Mark Brammer - TE
Mitchell Brookins - WR
Brian Carpenter - DB
Justin Cross - T
Joe Danelo - K
Stan David - LB
Julius Dawkins - WR
Preston Dennard - WR
Joe Devlin - T
Joe Dufek - QB
Joe Ferguson - QB
Byron Franklin - WR
Steve Freeman - DB
Will Grant - C
Jim Haslett - LB
Rod Hill - DB
Tony Hunter - TE
Ken Johnson - DE
Lawrence Johnson - DB
Ken Jones - T
Trey Junkin - LB
Chris Keating - LB
John Kidd - P
Matt Kofler - QB
Rod Kush - DB
Tom Lynch - G
Eugene Marve - LB
Sean McNanie - DE
Mark Merrill - LB
John Mistler - WR
Booker Moore - FB
Mike Mosley - WR
Speedy Neal - FB
Chuck Nelson - K
Ulysses Norris - TE
Steve Potter - LB
Dean Prater - DE
Robb Riddick - RB
Jim Ritcher - G
Charles Romes - DB
Lucius Sanford - LB
Fred Smerlas - NT
Lucious Smith - DB
Darryl Talley - LB
Gary Thompson - DB
Marco Tongue - DB
Scott Virkus - DE
Tim Vogler - C
Len Walterscheid - DB
Al Wenglikowski - LB
Craig White - WR
Van Williams - RB
Ben Williams - DE
Don Wilson - DB

1984 Chi. Bears

Brad Anderson - WR
Tom Andrews - C
Bob Avellini - QB
Brian Baschnagel - WR
Kurt Becker - G
Todd Bell - DB
Mark Bortz - G
Brian Cabral - LB
Jack Cameron - WR
Jim Covert - T
Richard Dent - DE
Dave Duerson - DB
Pat Dunsmore - TE
Rob Fada - G
Gary Fencik - DB
Dave Finzer - P
Jeff Fisher - DB
Leslie Frazier - DB
Andy Frederick - T
Steve Fuller - QB
Willie Gault - WR
Shaun Gayle - DB
Dennis Gentry - RB
Dan Hampton - DT
Al Harris - LB
Mike Hartenstine - DE
Jay Hilgenberg - C
Stefan Humphries - G
Anthony Hutchison - RB
Donald Jordan - RB
Tyrone Keys - DE
Mitch Krenk - TE
Greg Landry - QB
Rusty Lisch - QB
Wilber Marshall - LB
Dennis McKinnon - WR
Jim McMahon - QB
Steve McMichael - DT
Emery Moorehead - TE
Jim Osborne - DT
Walter Payton - RB
Kevin Potter - DB
Dan Rains - LB
Mike Richardson - DB
Ron Rivera - LB
Jay Saldi - TE
Terry Schmidt - DB
Mike Singletary - LB
Matt Suhey - RB
Calvin Thomas - RB
Bob Thomas - K
Keith Van Horne - T
Henry Waechter - DT
Otis Wilson - LB

1984 Cincinnati

Charles Alexander - RB
Ken Anderson - QB
Leo Barker - LB
Ralph Battle - DB
Brian Blados - T
Jerry Boyarsky - NT
Jim Breech - K
Louis Breeden - DB
James Brooks - RB
Ross Browner - DE
Glenn Cameron - LB
Bryan Clark - QB
Glen Collins - DE
Cris Collinsworth - WR
Isaac Curtis - WR
Eddie Edwards - DE
Boomer Esiason - QB
John Farley - RB
Guy Frazier - LB
James Griffin - DB
Ray Griffin - DB
M. L. Harris - TE
Rodney Holman - TE
Ray Horton - DB
Robert Jackson - DB
Stanford Jennings - RB
Bobby Kemp - DB
Don Kern - TE
Larry Kinnebrew - RB
Pete Koch - NT
Bruce Kozerski - C
Steve Kreider - WR
Tim Krumrie - NT
Steve Maidlow - LB
Mike Martin - WR
Pat McInally - P
Max Montoya - G
Anthony Munoz - T
Clay Pickering - WR
Brian Pillman - LB
Rick Razzano - LB
Bruce Reimers - T
Dave Rimington - C
Turk Schonert - QB
Jeff Schuh - LB
John Simmons - DB
Ron Simpkins - LB
Gary Smith - G
Jimmy Turner - DB
David Verser - WR
Gary Williams - WR
Reggie Williams - LB
Stanley Wilson - RB
Mike Wilson - T

1984 Cleveland

Willis Adams - TE
Stuart Anderson - LB
Mike Baab - C
Matt Bahr - K
Keith Baldwin - DE
Chip Banks - LB
Greg Best - DB
James Black - RB
Rickey Bolden - T
Larry Braziel - DB
Brian Brennan - WR
Preston Brown - KR
Clinton Burrell - DB
Earnest Byner - RB
Reggie Camp - DE
Bill Contz - T
Tom Cousineau - LB
Steve Cox - P
Bruce Davis - WR
Johnny Davis - FB
Joe DeLamielleure - G
Tom DeLeone - C
Doug Dieken - T
Hanford Dixon - DB
Jim Dumont - LB
Paul Farren - T
Ricky Feacher - WR
Tom Flick - QB
Elvis Franks - DE
Bob Golic - NT
Boyce Green - RB
Al Gross - DB
Carl Hairston - DE
Duriel Harris - WR
Harry Holt - TE
Robert Jackson - G
Eddie Johnson - LB
Lawrence Johnson - DB
Darryl Lewis - TE
George Lilja - T
David Marshall - LB
Clay Matthews - LB
Paul McDonald - QB
Frank Minnifield - DB
Ozzie Newsome - TE
Scott Nicolas - LB
Rod Perry - DB
Ted Petersen - T
Mike Pruitt - FB
Dave Puzzuoli - NT
Chris Rockins - DB
Don Rogers - DB
Tim Stracka - TE
Dwight Walker - WR
Curtis Weathers - LB
Charles White - RB
Glen Young - WR

1984 Dallas

Vince Albritton - DB
Gary Allen - RB
Dowe Aughtman - G
Brian Baldinger - G
Bill Bates - DB
Bob Breunig - LB
Billy Cannon Jr. - LB
Harold Carmichael - WR
Dextor Clinkscale - DB
Jim Cooper - T
Fred Cornwell - TE
Doug Cosbie - TE
Steve DeOssie - LB
Anthony Dickerson - LB
Doug Donley - WR
Tony Dorsett - RB
Michael Downs - DB
John Dutton - DT
Ron Fellows - DB
Norm Granger - RB
Duriel Harris - WR
Mike Hegman - LB
Tony Hill - WR
Gary Hogeboom - QB
Carl Howard - DB
John Hunt - G
Jim Jeffcoat - DE
Too Tall Jones - DE
James Jones - RB
Syd Kitson - G
Eugene Lockhart - LB
Chuck McSwain - RB
Jim Miller - P
Timmy Newsome - RB
Steve Pelluer - QB
Kurt Petersen - G
Kirk Phillips - WR
Phil Pozderac - T
Tom Rafferty - C
Mike Renfro - WR
Howard Richards - T
Jeff Rohrer - LB
Brian Salonen - TE
Herbert Scott - G
Victor Scott - DB
Rafael Septien - K
Don Smerek - DT
Waddell Smith - WR
Ron Springs - RB
Dennis Thurman - DB
Glen Titensor - DB
Mark Tuinei - DT
Jimmie Turner - LB
Everson Walls - DB
John Warren - P
Randy White - DT
Danny White - QB

1984 Denver

Ray Alexander - WR
Keith Bishop - G
Walt Bowyer - DE
Chris Brewer - RB
Billy Bryan - C
Steve Busick - LB
Rubin Carter - NT
Barney Chavous - DE
Darren Comeaux - LB
Mark Cooper - G
Rick Dennison - LB
John Elway - QB
Steve Foley - DB
Mike Freeman - G
Scott Garnett - NT
Marsharne Graves - T
Mike Harden - DB
Winford Hood - G
Paul Howard - G
Ricky Hunley - LB
Roger Jackson - DB
Tom Jackson - LB
Butch Johnson - WR
Rulon Jones - DE
Rich Karlis - K
Clarence Kay - TE
Gary Kubiak - QB
Gene Lang - RB
Ken Lanier - T
Tony Lilly - DB
Dave Logan - WR
Brison Manor - DE
Karl Mecklenburg - DE
Jesse Myles - RB
Chris Norman - P
Rick Parros - RB
Randy Robbins - DB
Jim Ryan - LB
Clint Sampson - WR
John Sawyer - TE
Aaron Smith - LB
Dennis Smith - DB
Scott Stankavage - QB
Dave Studdard - T
Don Summers - TE
Zach Thomas - WR
Andre Townsend - DE
Steve Watson - WR
Gerald Willhite - RB
Steve Wilson - DB
Sammy Winder - RB
Ken Woodard - LB
James Wright - TE
Louis Wright - DB

1984 Detroit

Steve Baack - T
Roosevelt Barnes - LB
Mike Black - P
Carl Bland - WR
Dexter Bussey - RB
Jeff Chadwick - WR
Garry Cobb - LB
Mike Cofer - DE
August Curley - LB
Dave D'Addio - FB
Gary Danielson - QB
Chris Dieterich - G
Kirk Dodge - LB
Steve Doig - LB
Keith Dorney - T
Homer Elias - G
Doug English - DT
Ken Fantetti - LB
Amos Fowler - C
William Frizzell - DB
Bill Gay - DE
William Graham - DB
Don Greco - G
Curtis Green - DT
Alvin Hall - DB
Eric Hipple - QB
Ken Jenkins - RB
Demetrious Johnson - DB
David Jones - C
James Jones - FB
Angelo King - LB
Don Laster - T
Al Latimer - DB
Larry Lee - G
David Lewis - TE
Mike Machurek - QB
Pete Mandley - WR
Robbie Martin - WR
Reese McCall - TE
Bruce McNorton - DB
Mike Meade - FB
Martin Moss - DE
Steve Mott - C
Eddie Murray - K
Mark Nichols - WR
Rob Rubick - TE
Billy Sims - RB
Rich Strenger - T
Terry Tautolo - LB
Leonard Thompson - WR
Dan Wagoner - DB
Bobby Watkins - DB
Eric Williams - DT
Gardner Williams - DB
Jimmy Williams - LB
John Witkowski - QB

1984 Green Bay

John Anderson - LB
Robert Brown - DE
Rich Campbell - QB
Mark Cannon - C
Alphonso Carreker - DE
Ron Cassidy - WR
Henry Childs - TE
Jessie Clark - FB
Paul Coffman - TE
Ray Crouse - RB
George Cumby - LB
Al Del Greco - K
Tony DeLuca - NT
Lynn Dickey - QB
John Dorsey - LB
Mike Douglass - LB
Dave Drechsler - G
Gerry Ellis - FB
Phil Epps - WR
Tom Flynn - DB
Eddie Garcia - K
Ron Hallstrom - T
Gary Hayes - DB
Gary Hoffman - T
Estus Hood - DB
Harlan Huckleby - RB
Tim Huffman - T
Donnie Humphrey - DE
Eddie Lee Ivery - RB
John Jefferson - WR
Ezra Johnson - DE
Boyd Jones - T
Daryll Jones - DB
Terry Jones - NT
Syd Kitson - G
Greg Koch - T
Mark Lee - DB
Cliff Lewis - LB
Gary Lewis - TE
Tim Lewis - DB
James Lofton - WR
Charles Martin - DE
Larry McCarren - C
Mike McLeod - DB
Blake Moore - C
Mark Murphy - DB
Bill Neill - NT
Dwayne O'Steen - DB
Guy Prather - LB
Del Rodgers - RB
Randy Scott - LB
Bucky Scribner - P
Karl Swanke - T
Lenny Taylor - WR
Keith Uecker - G
Ed West - TE
Rich Wingo - LB
Randy Wright - QB

1984 Houston

Robert Abraham - LB
Patrick Allen - DB
Jesse Baker - DE
Gregg Bingham - LB
Keith Bostic - DB
Robert Brazile - LB
Steve Brown - DB
Steve Bryant - WR
Bryan Caldwell - DE
Earl Campbell - RB
David Carter - C
Joe Cooper - K
Donnie Craft - RB
Jeff Donaldson - DB
Chris Dressel - TE
Bo Eason - DB
Stan Edwards - RB
Jerome Foster - DE
John Grimsley - LB
Bob Hamm - DE
Carter Hartwig - DB
Mike Holston - WR
Pat Howell - G
Daryl Hunt - LB
John James - P
Mike Johnson - DE
Tim Joiner - LB
Willie Joyner - RB
Florian Kempf - K
Mike Kennedy - DB
Oliver Luck - QB
Allen Lyday - DB
Robert Lyles - LB
Bruce Matthews - T
Mike McCloskey - TE
Darryl Meadows - DB
Johnny Meads - LB
Warren Moon - QB
Eric Moran - T
Larry Moriarty - RB
Eric Mullins - WR
Mike Munchak - G
Avon Riley - LB
Carl Roaches - KR
Jim Romano - C
Harvey Salem - T
John Schuhmacher - G
Tim Smith - WR
Brian Sochia - NT
Dean Steinkuhler - T
Mike Stensrud - NT
Mark Studaway - DE
Ted Thompson - LB
Willie Tullis - DB
Herkie Walls - WR
Jamie Williams - TE
Richard Williams - RB

1984 Indianapolis

Raul Allegre - K
Kim Anderson - DB
Larry Anderson - DB
Don Bailey - C
Mark Bell - TE
Dean Biasucci - K
Matt Bouza - WR
Greg Bracelin - LB
James Burroughs - DB
Ray Butler - WR
Kevin Call - T
Johnie Cooks - LB
Eugene Daniel - DB
Preston Davis - DB
Curtis Dickey - RB
Ray Donaldson - C
Andy Ekern - T
Grant Feasel - C
Ellis Gardner - T
Nesby Glasgow - DB
Steve Hathaway - LB
Bernard Henry - WR
Mark Herrmann - QB
Chris Hinton - G
Mike Humiston - LB
Mark Kafentzis - DB
Mark Kirchner - T
Barry Krauss - LB
Vernon Maxwell - LB
Randy McMillan - FB
Bo Metcalf - DB
Frank Middleton - RB
Jim Mills - T
Alvin Moore - RB
Cliff Odom - LB
Gary Padjen - LB
Mike Pagel - QB
Steve Parker - DE
Ted Petersen - T
Tracy Porter - WR
George Radachowsky - DB
Tate Randle - DB
Art Schlichter - QB
Chris Scott - DE
Tim Sherwin - TE
Byron Smith - DE
Phil Smith - WR
Ron Solt - G
Rohn Stark - P
Donnell Thompson - DE
Ben Utt - G
Scott Virkus - DE
Henry Waechter - DE
Brad White - NT
Vaughn Williams - DB
Blaise Winter - DE
Leo Wisniewski - NT
George Wonsley - RB
Steve Wright - G
Dave Young - TE

1984 Kansas City

John Alt - T
Jim Arnold - P
Walt Arnold - TE
Scott Auer - G
Rich Baldinger - T
Ed Beckman - TE
Mike Bell - DE
Todd Blackledge - QB
Jerry Blanton - LB
Theotis Brown - RB
Brad Budde - G
Lloyd Burruss - DB
Carlos Carson - WR
Deron Cherry - DB
Tom Condon - G
Calvin Daniels - LB
Mike Dawson - NT
Mike Gunter - RB
Anthony Hancock - WR
Herman Heard - RB
Matt Herkenhoff - T
Greg Hill - DB
Eric Holle - DE
Billy Jackson - RB
Charles Jackson - LB
Van Jakes - DB
Ken Jolly - LB
Bill Kenney - QB
Ken Kremer - NT
Ken Lacy - RB
Skip Lane - DB
Albert Lewis - DB
Dave Lindstrom - DE
Adam Lingner - C
Dave Little - TE
Nick Lowery - K
Dave Lutz - T
Bill Maas - NT
Henry Marshall - WR
Ken McAlister - LB
Sandy Osiecki - QB
Stephone Paige - WR
Jeff Paine - LB
Kerry Parker - DB
Scott Radecic - LB
Lawrence Ricks - RB
Mark Robinson - DB
Kevin Ross - DB
Jim Rourke - T
Bob Rush - C
Willie Scott - TE
J. T. Smith - WR
Gary Spani - LB
Art Still - DE
John Zamberlin - LB

1984 LA Raiders

Rick Ackerman - NT
Stan Adams - LB
Marcus Allen - RB
Lyle Alzado - DE
Chris Bahr - K
Jeff Barnes - LB
Malcolm Barnwell - WR
Greg Boyd - NT
Cliff Branch - WR
Warren Bryant - T
Darryl Byrd - LB
Tony Caldwell - LB
Dave Casper - TE
Todd Christensen - TE
Dave Dalby - C
Bruce Davis - T
James Davis - DB
Mike Davis - DB
Ray Guy - P
Charley Hannah - G
Frank Hawkins - RB
Lester Hayes - DB
Mike Haynes - DB
David Humm - QB
Derrick Jensen - TE
Sean Jones - DE
Shelby Jordan - T
Kenny King - RB
Reggie Kinlaw - NT
Henry Lawrence - T
Howie Long - DE
Curt Marsh - G
Rod Martin - LB
Mickey Marvin - G
Joe McCall - RB

Larry McCoy - LB
Vann McElroy - DB
Odis McKinney - DB
Mark Merrill - LB
Matt Millen - LB
Cleo Montgomery - WR
Don Mosebar - G
Ed Muransky - T
Bob Nelson - LB
Andy Parker - TE
Bill Pickel - NT
Jim Plunkett - QB
Greg Pruitt - RB
Jim Romano - C
Sam Seale - WR
Jimmy Smith - RB
Jack Squirek - LB
Stacey Toran - DB
Greg Townsend - DE
Brad Van Pelt - LB
Ted Watts - DB
Dwight Wheeler - C
Dokie Williams - WR
Chester Willis - RB
Marc Wilson - QB

1984 LA Rams

George Andrews - LB
Bill Bain - T
Mike Barber - TE
Russ Bolinger - G
Ed Brady - LB
Ron Brown - WR
Jim Collins - LB
Nolan Cromwell - DB
David Croudip - DB
Dwayne Crutchfield - RB
Charles DeJurnett - NT
Eric Dickerson - RB
Steve Dils - QB
Reggie Doss - DE
Carl Ekern - LB
Henry Ellard - WR
George Farmer - WR
Chris Faulkner - TE
Vince Ferragamo - QB
Otis Grant - WR
Gary Green - DB
Mike Guman - RB
Dennis Harrah - G
Eric Harris - DB
Drew Hill - WR
David Hill - TE
Kent Hill - G
LeRoy Irvin - DB
Mark Jerue - LB
Gary Jeter - DE
Johnnie Johnson Jr. - DB
A. J. Jones - RB
John Kamana - RB
Jeff Kemp - QB
Mike Lansford - K
Jim Laughlin - LB
James McDonald - TE
Mike McDonald - LB
Greg Meisner - NT
Shawn Miller - NT
John Misko - P
Vince Newsome - DB
Mel Owens - LB
Irvin Pankey - T
Mike Pleasant - DB
Barry Redden - RB
Doug Reed - DE
Booker Reese - DE
Joe Shearin - G
Jackie Slater - T
Doug Smith - C
Ivory Sully - DB
Norwood Vann - LB
Mike Wilcher - LB
Jack Youngblood - DE
Jim Youngblood - LB

1984 Miami

Bill Barnett - DE
Bob Baumhower - NT
Woody Bennett - FB
Charles Benson - DE
Doug Betters - DE
Glenn Blackwood - DB
Lyle Blackwood - DB
Kim Bokamper - DE
Charles Bowser - LB
Jay Brophy - LB
Bud Brown - DB
Mark Brown - LB
Bob Brudzinski - LB
Fernanza Burgess - WR
Joe Carter - RB
Jimmy Cefalo - WR
Mike Charles - NT
John Chesley - TE
Steve Clark - G
Mark Clayton - WR
A. J. Duhe - LB
Mark Duper - WR
Roy Foster - G
Andra Franklin - FB
Jon Giesler - T
Cleveland Green - T
Bruce Hardy - TE
Vince Heflin - WR
Eddie Hill - RB
Jim Jensen - WR
Dan Johnson - TE
Pete Johnson - FB
Ed Judie - LB
William Judson - DB
Mike Kozlowski - DB
Eric Laakso - T
Paul Lankford - DB
Ronnie Lee - G
Dan Marino - QB
Don McNeal - DB
Nat Moore - WR
Tony Nathan - RB
Ed Newman - G
Earnest Rhone - LB
Reggie Roby - P
Joe Rose - TE
Jackie Shipp - LB
Sanders Shiver - LB
Robert Sowell - DB
Dwight Stephenson - C
Don Strock - QB
Rodell Thomas - LB
Jeff Toews - G
Uwe von Schamann - K
Fulton Walker - DB

1984 Minnesota

Alfred Anderson - RB
Hasson Arbubakrr - DE
Walker Lee Ashley - LB
Rufus Bess - DB
Matt Blair - LB
Ted Brown - RB
Joey Browner - DB
Malcolm Carson - G
Bob Cobb - DE
Greg Coleman - P
Dwight Collins - WR
Jeff Colter - DB
Steve Dils - QB
Bill Dugan - G
Neil Elshire - DE
Grant Feasel - C
Dennis Fowlkes - LB
Marcellus Greene - DB
John Haines - NT
Wes Hamilton - G
Tom Hannon - DB
Don Hasselbeck - TE
Matt Hernandez - T
Randy Holloway - DE
Jim Hough - G
Tim Irwin - T
Charlie Johnson - NT
Dennis Johnson - LB
Mike Jones - WR
Steve Jordan - TE
Tommy Kramer - QB
Terry LeCount - WR
Carl Lee - DB
Leo Lewis - WR
Archie Manning - QB
Chris Martin - LB
Doug Martin - DE
Fred McNeill - LB
Mike Mularkey - TE
Mark Mullaney - DE
Darrin Nelson - RB
David Nelson - RB
Allen Rice - RB
Steve Riley - T
Curtis Rouse - G
Ron Sams - G
Robin Sendlein - LB
Joe Senser - TE
Greg Smith - NT
Jan Stenerud - K
Mark Stewart - LB
Scott Studwell - LB
Paul Sverchek - NT
John Swain - DB
Terry Tausch - T
Willie Teal - DB
Maurice Turner - RB
Ruben Vaughan - NT
Billy Waddy - WR
Dan Wagoner - DB
Sammy White - WR
Wade Wilson - QB

1984 New England

Julius Adams - DE
Don Blackmon - LB
Pete Brock - C
Rich Camarillo - P
Raymond Clayborn - DB
Tony Collins - RB
Lin Dawson - TE
Paul Dombroski - DB
Tony Eason - QB
Paul Fairchild - G
Tony Franklin - K
Irving Fryar - WR
Ernest Gibson - DB
Tim Golden - LB
Steve Grogan - QB
Darryl Haley - T
John Hannah - G
Greg Hawthorne - WR
Luther Henson - NT
Brian Holloway - T
Brian Ingram - LB
Craig James - RB
Roland James - DB
Cedric Jones - WR
Mike Kerrigan - QB
Keith Lee - DB
Ronnie Lippett - DB
Fred Marion - DB
Larry McGrew - LB
Rod McSwain - DB
Steve Moore - T
Stanley Morgan - WR
Guy Morriss - C
Steve Nelson - LB
Dennis Owens - NT
Luke Prestridge - P
Derrick Ramsey - TE
Johnny Rembert - LB
Ed Reynolds - LB
Bo Robinson - RB
Doug Rogers - DE
Rick Sanford - DB
Kenneth Sims - DE
Ricky Smith - KR
Stephen Starring - WR
Mosi Tatupu - RB
Andre Tippett - LB
Scott Virkus - DE
Clarence Weathers - WR
Robert Weathers - RB
Clayton Weishuhn - LB
Ed Williams - LB
Jon Williams - RB
Lester Williams - NT
Toby Williams - DE
Ron Wooten - G

1984 New Orleans

Morten Andersen - K
Edward Anthony - RB
Hoby Brenner - TE
Stan Brock - T
Earl Campbell - RB
David Carter - C
Bruce Clark - DE
Kelvin Clark - G
Kenny Duckett - WR
Brad Edelman - G
Tony Elliott - NT
Jitter Fields - DB
Hokie Gajan - FB
Russell Gary - DB
Jumpy Geathers - DE
Eugene Goodlow - WR
Jeff Groth - WR
Brian Hansen - P
Greg Harding - DB
Larry Hardy - TE
James Haynes - LB
Joel Hilgenberg - C
John Hill - C
Terry Hoage - DB
Rickey Jackson - LB
Bobby Johnson - DB
Steve Korte - C
Jim Kovach - LB
Dave Lafary - T
Reggie Lewis - DE
Rodney Lewis - DB
Guido Merkens - QB
Junior Miller - TE
Derland Moore - NT
Louis Oubre - G
Whitney Paul - LB
Scott Pelluer - LB
Jim Pietrzak - C
Johnnie Poe - DB
Glen Redd - LB
George Rogers - RB
Jimmy Rogers - RB
Lindsay Scott - WR
Ken Stabler - QB
Don Thorp - NT
John Tice - TE
Richard Todd - QB
Chris Ward - T
Frank Warren - DE
Frank Wattelet - DB
Dave Waymer - DB
Jim Wilks - DE
Dave Wilson - QB
Tim Wilson - FB
Wayne Wilson - RB
Dennis Winston - LB
Tyrone Young - WR

1984 NY Giants

Billy Ard - G
Carl Banks - LB
Kevin Belcher - G
Brad Benson - T
Jim Burt - NT
Rob Carpenter - RB
Harry Carson - LB
Frank Cephous - RB
Bill Currier - DB
Kenny Daniel - DB
Larry Flowers - DB
Tony Galbreath - RB
Chris Godfrey - G
Conrad Goode - T
Earnest Gray - WR
Ali Haji-Sheikh - K
Dee Hardison - DE
Mark Haynes - DB
Andy Headen - LB
Kenny Hill - DB
Byron Hunt - LB
Dave Jennings - P
Bobby Johnson - WR
Robbie Jones - LB
David Jordan - G
Terry Kinard - DB
Lionel Manuel - WR
Leonard Marshall - DE
George Martin - DE
Phil McConkey - WR
Curtis McGriff - DE
Joe McLaughlin - LB
Casey Merrill - DE
John Mistler - WR
Joe Morris - RB
Zeke Mowatt - TE
Tom Mullady - TE
Karl Nelson - T
Elvis Patterson - DB
Gary Reasons - LB
William Roberts - T
Jeff Rutledge - QB
Jerome Sally - NT
Pete Shaw - DB
Phil Simms - QB
Lawrence Taylor - LB
Rich Umphrey - C
Byron Williams - WR
Perry Williams - DB
Butch Woolfolk - RB

1984 NY Jets

Dan Alexander - G
Tom Baldwin - DT
Ted Banker - G
Marion Barber - FB
Bobby Bell - LB
Barry Bennett - DT
Guy Bingham - C
Dennis Bligen - RB
Nick Bruckner - WR
Fernanza Burgess - DB
Greg Buttle - LB
Russell Carter - DB
Kyle Clifton - LB
Bob Crable - LB
Chy Davidson - WR
Mike Dennis - DB
Glenn Dennison - TE
Jim Eliopulos - LB
Ron Faurot - DE
Joe Fields - C
George Floyd - DB
Derrick Gaffney - WR
Mark Gastineau - DE
Rusty Guilbeau - LB
Harry Hamilton - DB
Bruce Harper - RB
Johnny Hector - RB
Bobby Humphery - WR
Bobby Jackson - DB
Lam Jones - WR
Joe Klecko - DT
Rocky Klever - TE
Skip Lane - DB
Pat Leahy - K
George Lilja - C
Johnny Lynn - DB
Marty Lyons - DE
Reggie McElroy - T
Freeman McNeil - RB
Lance Mehl - LB
Cedric Minter - RB
Davlin Mullen - DB
Ken O'Brien - QB
Tony Paige - FB
Marvin Powell - T
Chuck Ramsey - P
Darrol Ray - DB
Ben Rudolph - DT
Pat Ryan - QB
Ken Schroy - DB
Mickey Shuler - TE
Kurt Sohn - WR
Kirk Springs - DB
Jim Sweeney - G
Stan Waldemore - G
Wesley Walker - WR
John Woodring - LB

1984 Philadelphia

Harvey Armstrong - NT
Ron Baker - G
Greg Brown - DE
Ken Clarke - NT
Evan Cooper - DB
Bill Cowher - LB
Byron Darby - DE
Mark Dennard - C
Herman Edwards - DB
Ray Ellis - DB
Major Everett - FB
Gerry Feehery - C
Elbert Foules - DB
Gregg Garrity - WR
Anthony Griggs - LB
Michael Haddix - FB
Andre Hardy - RB
Dennis Harrison - DE
Joe Hayes - WR
Melvin Hoover - WR
Wes Hopkins - DB
Mike Horan - P
Kenny Jackson - WR
Ron Jaworski - QB
Vyto Kab - TE
Steve Kenney - G
Rich Kraynak - LB
Dean May - QB
Paul McFadden - K
Dean Miraldi - T
Leonard Mitchell - T
Wilbert Montgomery - RB
Hubie Oliver - FB
Dave Pacella - G
Petey Perot - G
Joe Pisarcik - QB
Mike Quick - WR
Lou Rash - DB
Mike Reichenbach - LB
Jerry Robinson - LB
Rusty Russell - T
Lawrence Sampleton - TE
Jody Schulz - LB
Jerry Sisemore - T
John Spagnola - TE
Thomas Strauthers - DE
Andre Waters - DB
Reggie Wilkes - LB
Joel Williams - LB
Michael Williams - RB
Brenard Wilson - DB
Tony Woodruff - WR
Roynell Young - DB

1984 Pittsburgh

Walter Abercrombie - RB
Gary Anderson - K
Steve August - T
Craig Bingham - LB
Emil Boures - G
Chris Brown - DB
Larry Brown - T
Scott Campbell - QB
Wayne Capers - WR
Mark Catano - DE
Harvey Clayton - DB
Robin Cole - LB
Craig Colquitt - P
Anthony Corley - RB
Bennie Cunningham - TE
Gary Dunn - NT
Terry Echols - LB
Rich Erenberg - RB
Gregg Garrity - WR
Keith Gary - DE
Fernandars Gillespie - RB
John Goodman - DE
Bryan Hinkle - LB
Tunch Ilkin - T
Ron Johnson - DB
Bob Kohrs - LB
Chris Kolodziejski - TE
Jack Lambert - LB
Louis Lipps - WR
David Little - LB
Terry Long - G
Mark Malone - QB
Mike Merriweather - LB
Darrell Nelson - TE
Ed Nelson - NT
Frank Pollard - RB
Randy Rasmussen - C
John Rodgers - TE
Pete Rostosky - T
Todd Seabaugh - LB
Donnie Shell - DB
Ray Snell - T
Todd Spencer - RB
John Stallworth - WR
Calvin Sweeney - WR
Weegie Thompson - WR
Elton Veals - RB
Sam Washington - DB
Mike Webster - C
Eric Williams - DB
Robert Williams - DB
Keith Willis - DE
Blake Wingle - G
Craig Wolfley - G
David Woodley - QB
Dwayne Woodruff - DB
Rick Woods - DB

1984 St. Louis

Dave Ahrens - LB
Kurt Allerman - LB
Ottis Anderson - RB
Dan Audick - G
Charles Baker - LB
Al Baker - DE
Martin Bayless - DB
Steve Bird - WR
Carl Birdsong - P
Joe Bostic - G
Randy Clark - C
Ramsey Dardar - DT
Billy Davis - LB
Doug Dawson - G
Mark Duda - DT
Clyde Duncan - WR
Earl Ferrell - RB
David Galloway - DT
John Goode - TE
Roy Green - WR
Curtis Greer - DE
Jeff Griffin - DB
Elois Grooms - DT
Willard Harrell - RB
Perry Harrington - RB
Bob Harris - LB
Victor Heflin - DB
Randy Holloway - DE
Tom Howard - LB
E. J. Junior - LB
Bill Kay - DB
Greg LaFleur - TE
Neil Lomax - QB
Randy Love - RB
Cedric Mack - WR
Doug Marsh - TE
Stafford Mays - DE
Rick McIvor - QB
Stump Mitchell - RB
Lee Nelson - DB
Niko Noga - LB
Neil O'Donoghue - K
Benny Perrin - DB
Danny Pittman - WR
Art Plunkett - T
Dan Ralph - DT
Tootie Robbins - T
Carlos Scott - C
Craig Shaffer - LB
Luis Sharpe - T
Leonard Smith - DB
Wayne Smith - DB
Terry Stieve - G
Pat Tilley - WR
Quentin Walker - WR
Lionel Washington - DB
Bill Whitaker - DB

1984 San Diego

Rick Ackerman - NT
Jesse Bendross - WR
Rolf Benirschke - K
Steve Bird - WR
Carlos Bradley - LB
Maury Buford - P
Scott Byers - DB
Gill Byrd - DB
Wes Chandler - WR
Tony Chickillo - NT
Sam Claphan - T
Mike Dennis - DB
Bobby Duckworth - WR
Ron Egloff - TE
Chuck Ehin - DE
Bill Elko - NT
Keith Ferguson - DE
Dan Fouts - QB
Tim Fox - DB
Andrew Gissinger - C
Derrel Gofourth - G
Mike Green - LB
Ken Greene - DB
Bob Gregor - DB
Keith Guthrie - NT
Rickey Hagood - NT
Reuben Henderson - DB
Pete Holohan - TE
Earnest Jackson - RB
Lionel James - KR
Gary Johnson - NT
Pete Johnson - RB
Charlie Joiner - WR
Bill Kay - DB
Linden King - LB
Chuck Loewen - G
Woodrow Lowe - LB
Ed Luther - QB
Don Macek - C
Bruce Mathison - QB
Buford McGee - RB
Dennis McKnight - C
Miles McPherson - DB
Bobby Micho - TE
Wayne Morris - RB
Chuck Muncie - RB
Derrie Nelson - LB
Vince Osby - LB
Ray Preston - LB
Benny Ricardo - K
Fred Robinson - DE
Eric Sievers - TE
Billy Ray Smith Jr. - LB
Johnny Ray Smith - DB
Lucious Smith - DB
Jewerl Thomas - RB
Cliff Thrift - LB
John Turner - DB
Danny Walters - DB
Ed White - T
Doug Wilkerson - G
Eric Williams - LB
Lee Williams - DE
Kellen Winslow - TE
Andre Young - DB

1984 San Francisco

John Ayers - G
Dwaine Board - DE
Greg Boyd - DE
Dan Bunz - LB
Michael Carter - NT
Matt Cavanaugh - QB
Dwight Clark - WR
Mario Clark - DB
Earl Cooper - TE
Roger Craig - FB
Randy Cross - G
Fred Dean - DE
Al Dixon - TE
Riki Ellison - LB
Jim Fahnhorst - LB
Keith Fahnhorst - T
Ron Ferrari - LB
Russ Francis - TE
John Frank - TE
Jeff Fuller - DB
Derrick Harmon - RB
Dwight Hicks - DB
Tom Holmoe - DB
Gary Johnson - NT
Louie Kelcher - NT
Allan Kennedy - T
Ronnie Lott - DB
John Macaulay - C
Milt McColl - LB
Guy McIntyre - G
Dana McLemore - KR
Carl Monroe - RB
Joe Montana - QB
Blanchard Montgomery - LB
Renaldo Nehemiah - WR
Tom Orosz - P
Bubba Paris - T
Lawrence Pillers - NT
Fred Quillan - C
Jack Reynolds - LB
Bill Ring - RB
Max Runager - P
Jesse Sapolu - G
Todd Shell - LB
Billy Shields - T
Freddie Solomon - WR
Jeff Stover - NT
Jim Stuckey - DE
Manu Tuiasosopo - NT
Keena Turner - LB
Wendell Tyler - RB
Michael Walter - LB
Ray Wersching - K
Carlton Williamson - DB
Mike Wilson - WR
Eric Wright - DB

1984 Seattle

Sid Abramowitz - T
Steve August - T
Edwin Bailey - G
Dave Brown - DB
Jeff Bryant - DE
Cullen Bryant - FB
Blair Bush - C
Chuck Butler - LB
Keith Butler - LB
Chris Castor - WR
Bob Cryder - T
Zachary Dixon - RB
Dan Doornink - FB
Don Dufek - DB
Kenny Easley - DB
Randy Edwards - DE
Ron Essink - T
Mike Fanning - DE
Greg Gaines - LB
Jacob Green - DE
Franco Harris - FB
John Harris - DB
David Hughes - FB
Michael Jackson - LB
Terry Jackson - DB
Paul Johns - WR
Norm Johnson - K
John Kaiser - LB
Kani Kauahi - C
Dave Krieg - QB
Eric Lane - RB
Steve Largent - WR
Dino Mangiero - NT
Reggie McKenzie - G
Sam Merriman - LB
Pete Metzelaars - TE
Bryan Millard - T
Randall Morris - RB
Paul Moyer - DB
Joe Nash - NT
Bob Pratt - G
Shelton Robinson - LB
Dwight Scales - WR
Bruce Scholtz - LB
Adam Schreiber - G
Keith Simpson - DB
Paul Skansi - WR
Terry Taylor - DB
Mike Tice - TE
Daryl Turner - WR
Byron Walker - WR
Curt Warner - RB
Jeff West - P
Ray Wilmer - DB
Charle Young - TE
Fredd Young - LB
Jim Zorn - QB

1984 Tampa Bay

Fred Acorn - DB
Obed Ariri - K
Adger Armstrong - RB
Jerry Bell - TE
Theo Bell - WR
Byron Braggs - DE
Scot Brantley - LB
Leon Bright - RB
Cedric Brown - DB
Keith Browner - LB
Glenn Bujnoch - G
John Cannon - DE
Jay Carroll - TE
Gerald Carter - WR
Mel Carver - RB
Jeremiah Castille - DB
Randy Clark - DB
Mark Cotney - DB
Steve Courson - G
Craig Curry - DB
Phil Darns - DE
Jeff Davis - LB
Steve DeBerg - QB
Scott Dierking - RB
Dwayne Dixon - WR
Sean Farrell - G
Frank Garcia - P
Jimmie Giles - TE
Hugh Green - LB
Randy Grimes - C
Maurice Harvey - DB
Ron Heller - T
John Holt - DB
Kevin House - WR
Noah Jackson - G
Cecil Johnson - LB
Ken Kaplan - T
Blair Kiel - QB
David Logan - NT
Brison Manor - DE
Karl Morgan - NT
Michael Morton - RB
James Owens - RB
George Peoples - RB
Beasley Reece - DB
Booker Reese - DE
Gene Sanders - T
Lee Roy Selmon - DE
Danny Spradlin - LB
Kelly Thomas - T
Norris Thomas - DB
Zach Thomas - WR
Jack Thompson - QB
Robert Thompson - LB
Perry Tuttle - WR
Chris Washington - LB
Mike Washington - DB
James Wilder - RB
Steven Wilson - C
Mark Witte - TE
Richard Wood - LB

1984 Washington

Stuart Anderson - LB
Walt Arnold - TE
Tom Beasley - DE
Jeff Bostic - C
Perry Brooks - DT
Charlie Brown - WR
Dave Butz - DT
Brian Carpenter - DB
Ken Coffey - DB
Monte Coleman - LB
Pete Cronan - LB
Vernon Dean - DB
Clint Didier - TE
Rick Donnalley - C
Alvin Garrett - WR
Darryl Grant - DT
Darrell Green - DB
Keith Griffin - RB
Russ Grimm - G
Jim Hart - QB
Jeff Hayes - P
Ken Huff - G
Joe Jacoby - T
Anthony Jones - TE
Curtis Jordan - DB
Trey Junkin - LB
Rick Kane - RB
Mel Kaufman - LB
Bruce Kimball - G
Larry Kubin - LB
Todd Liebenstein - DE
Dexter Manley - DE
Charles Mann - DE
Rich Mauti - WR
Mark May - T
Tony McGee - DE
Mark McGrath - WR
Rich Milot - LB
Art Monk - WR
Jeff Moore - RB
Mark Moseley - K
Calvin Muhammad - WR
Mark Murphy - DB
Mike Nelms - KR
Neal Olkewicz - LB
Tony Peters - DB
John Riggins - RB
Virgil Seay - WR
Jimmy Smith - RB
Ricky Smith - DB
George Starke - T
Joe Theismann - QB
Morris Towns - T
J. T. Turner - G
Rick Walker - TE
Don Warren - TE
Anthony Washington - DB
Joe Washington - RB
Greg Williams - DB
Mike Williams - TE
Otis Wonsley - RB
Jim Youngblood - LB

1985 Atlanta

Anthony Allen - WR
David Archer - QB
Cliff Austin - RB
Stacey Bailey - WR
Steve Bartkowski - QB
Dan Benish - DT
Cliff Benson - TE
Thomas Benson - LB
Jim Britt - DB
Charlie Brown - WR
Rick Bryan - DE
Bobby Butler - DB
Scott Case - DB
Wendell Cason - DB
Arthur Cox - TE
David Croudip - DB
Buddy Curry - LB
Rick Donnelly - P
Bill Fralic - G
David Frye - LB
Mike Gann - DE
Ralph Giacomarro - P
Willard Goff - DT
George Greene - DB
Roy Harris - DT
Bob Holly - QB
Glen Howe - T
Jeff Jackson - LB
Kenny Johnson - DB
Billy Johnson - WR
Mike Kenn - T
Jeff Kiewel - G
Mick Luckhurst - K
Allama Matthews - TE
Brett Miller - T
Joseph Pellegrini - G
Lawrence Pillers - DE
Mike Pitts - DT
Reggie Pleasant - DB
Tom Pridemore - DB
Andrew Provence - DE
John Rade - LB
Wayne Radloff - C
Al Richardson - LB
Gerald Riggs - RB
Eric Sanders - T
John Scully - G
Sylvester Stamps - RB
Johnny Taylor - LB
Chuck Thomas - C
Sean Thomas - DB
Tim Tyrrell - RB
Jeff Van Note - C
Dan Wagoner - DB
Joe Washington - RB
Ronnie Washington - LB
Ken Whisenhunt - TE

1985 Buffalo

Martin Bayless - DB
Greg Bell - RB
Rodney Bellinger - DB
Mitchell Brookins - WR
Chris Burkett - WR
Derrick Burroughs - DB
Jerry Butler - WR
Greg Christy - G
Joe Cribbs - RB
Justin Cross - T
Joe DeLamielleure - G
Joe Devlin - T
Anthony Dickerson - LB
Vince Ferragamo - QB
Guy Frazier - LB
Steve Freeman - DB
Hal Garner - LB
Will Grant - C
Jim Haslett - LB
Dale Hellestrae - T
Rod Hill - DB
Anthony Hutchison - RB
Lawrence Johnson - DB
Ken Jones - T
John Kidd - P
Larry Kubin - LB
Steve Maidlow - LB
Eugene Marve - LB
Bruce Mathison - QB
Sean McNanie - DE
Pete Metzelaars - TE
Booker Moore - RB
Ulysses Norris - TE
Scott Norwood - K
Jim Perryman - DB
Dean Prater - DE
Mike Pruitt - RB
Eason Ramson - TE
Andre Reed - WR
Frank Reich - QB
Eric Richardson - WR
Jim Ritcher - G
Charles Romes - DB
Lucius Sanford - LB
Fred Smerlas - NT
Bruce Smith - DE
Don Smith - NT
Anthony Steels - RB
Darryl Talley - LB
Jimmy Teal - WR
Mark Traynowicz - G
Tim Vogler - G
Van Williams - RB
Ben Williams - DE
Don Wilson - DB
Eric Wilson - LB

1985 Chi. Bears

Brad Anderson - WR
Tom Andrews - C
Kurt Becker - G
Mark Bortz - G
Maury Buford - P
Kevin Butler - K
Brian Cabral - LB
Jim Covert - T
Richard Dent - DE
Dave Duerson - DB
Gary Fencik - DB
Leslie Frazier - DB
Andy Frederick - T
Steve Fuller - QB
Willie Gault - WR
Shaun Gayle - DB
Dennis Gentry - RB
Dan Hampton - DT
Mike Hartenstine - DE
Jay Hilgenberg - C
Stefan Humphries - G
Tyrone Keys - DE
James Maness - WR
Ken Margerum - WR
Wilber Marshall - LB
Dennis McKinnon - WR
Jim McMahon - QB
Steve McMichael - DT
Emery Moorehead - TE
Jim Morrissey - LB
Keith Ortego - WR
Walter Payton - RB
William Perry - DT
Reggie Phillips - DB
Mike Richardson - DB
Ron Rivera - LB
Thomas Sanders - RB
Mike Singletary - LB
Matt Suhey - RB
Ken Taylor - DB
Tom Thayer - G
Calvin Thomas - RB
Cliff Thrift - LB
Mike Tomczak - QB
Keith Van Horne - T
Henry Waechter - DT
Otis Wilson - LB
Tim Wrightman - TE

1985 Cincinnati

Charles Alexander - RB
Ken Anderson - QB
Leo Barker - LB
Brian Blados - T
Jerry Boyarsky - NT
Jim Breech - K
Louis Breeden - DB
James Brooks - RB
Eddie Brown - WR
Ross Browner - DE
Glenn Cameron - LB
Glen Collins - DE
Cris Collinsworth - WR
Lee Davis - DB
Tom Dinkel - LB
Eddie Edwards - DE
Boomer Esiason - QB
James Griffin - DB
M. L. Harris - TE
Rodney Holman - TE
Ray Horton - DB
Robert Jackson - DB
Stanford Jennings - RB
Bill Johnson - RB
Bobby Kemp - DB
Don Kern - TE
Emanuel King - LB
Larry Kinnebrew - RB
Bruce Kozerski - C
Steve Kreider - WR
Tim Krumrie - NT
Mike Martin - WR
Pat McInally - P
Max Montoya - G
Anthony Munoz - T
Clay Pickering - WR
Bruce Reimers - T
Dave Rimington - C
Dan Ross - TE
Turk Schonert - QB
Jeff Schuh - LB
John Simmons - DB
Ron Simpkins - LB
Sean Thomas - DB
Jimmy Turner - DB
Joe Walter - T
Sam Washington - DB
Reggie Williams - LB
Mike Wilson - WR
Carl Zander - LB

1985 Cleveland

Willis Adams - WR
Greg Allen - RB
Mike Baab - C
Matt Bahr - K
Keith Baldwin - DE
Fred Banks - WR
Chip Banks - LB
Rickey Bolden - T
Larry Braziel - DB
Brian Brennan - WR
Earnest Byner - RB
Reggie Camp - DE
Sam Clancy - DE
Bill Contz - T
Tom Cousineau - LB
Gary Danielson - QB
Johnny Davis - RB
Curtis Dickey - RB
Hanford Dixon - DB
Paul Farren - T
Dan Fike - G
Herman Fontenot - RB
Bob Golic - NT
Jeff Gossett - P
Boyce Green - RB
Al Gross - DB
Carl Hairston - DE
D.D. Hoggard - DB
Harry Holt - TE
Robert Jackson - G
John Jefferson - WR
Eddie Johnson - LB
Bernie Kosar - QB
Reggie Langhorne - WR
George Lilja - G
Kevin Mack - RB
Clay Matthews - LB
Paul McDonald - QB
Frank Minnifield - DB
Ozzie Newsome - TE
Scott Nicolas - LB
Dave Puzzuoli - NT
Cody Risien - T
Chris Rockins - DB
Don Rogers - DB
Travis Tucker - TE
Clarence Weathers - WR
Curtis Weathers - LB
Felix Wright - DB
Glen Young - WR

1985 Dallas

Vince Albritton - LB
Gordon Banks - WR
Bill Bates - DB
Kevin Brooks - DE
Dextor Clinkscale - DB
Jim Cooper - T
Fred Cornwell - TE
Doug Cosbie - TE
Steve DeOssie - LB
Tony Dorsett - RB
Michael Downs - DB
Kenny Duckett - WR
John Dutton - DT
Ricky Easmon - DB
Ron Fellows - DB
Todd Fowler - RB
Leon Gonzalez - WR
Mike Hegman - LB
Tony Hill - WR
Gary Hogeboom - QB
Jim Jeffcoat - DE
Too Tall Jones - DE
James Jones - RB
Crawford Ker - G
Robert Lavette - RB
Eugene Lockhart - LB
Timmy Newsome - RB
Steve Pelluer - QB
Jesse Penn - LB
Kurt Petersen - G
Dave Ponder - DT
Karl Powe - WR
Phil Pozderac - T
Tom Rafferty - C
Mike Renfro - WR
Howard Richards - G
Jeff Rohrer - LB
Brian Salonen - LB
Mike Saxon - P
Chris Schultz - T
Victor Scott - DB
Rafael Septien - K
Don Smerek - DT
Broderick Thompson - G
Dennis Thurman - DB
Glen Titensor - G
Mark Tuinei - C
Everson Walls - DB
Randy White - DT
Danny White - QB
John Williams - RB

1985 Denver

Mike Barber - TE
Keith Bishop - C
Billy Bryan - C
Steve Busick - LB
Rubin Carter - NT
Barney Chavous - DE
Darren Comeaux - LB
Mark Cooper - G
Rick Dennison - LB
John Elway - QB
Simon Fletcher - DE
Steve Foley - DB
Mike Harden - DB
Winford Hood - T
Paul Howard - G
Ricky Hunley - LB
Daniel Hunter - DB
Glenn Hyde - G
Roger Jackson - DB
Tom Jackson - LB
Butch Johnson - WR
Vance Johnson - WR
Rulon Jones - DE
Rich Karlis - K
Clarence Kay - TE
Greg Kragen - NT
Gary Kubiak - QB
Gene Lang - RB
Ken Lanier - T
Tony Lilly - DB
Keli McGregor - TE
Karl Mecklenburg - LB
Dean Miraldi - T
Chris Norman - P
Nathan Poole - RB
Randy Robbins - DB
Jim Ryan - LB
Clint Sampson - WR
Steven Sewell - RB
Dennis Smith - DB
Dave Studdard - T
Don Summers - TE
Andre Townsend - DE
Steve Watson - WR
Gerald Willhite - RB
Steve Wilson - DB
Sammy Winder - RB
Ken Woodard - LB
James Wright - TE
Louis Wright - DB

1985 Detroit

Kurt Allerman - LB
Steve Baack - NT
Roosevelt Barnes - LB
Mike Black - P
Carl Bland - WR
John Bostic - DB
Arnold Brown - DB
Lomas Brown - T
Dan Bunz - LB
Jeff Chadwick - WR
Clarence Chapman - DB
Mike Cofer - LB
August Curley - LB
Chris Dieterich - G
Keith Dorney - G
Doug English - DT
Leon Evans - DE
Ken Fantetti - LB
Joe Ferguson - QB
Keith Ferguson - DE
William Frizzell - DB
Duane Galloway - DB
Bill Gay - DE
Kevin Glover - C
William Graham - DB
Don Greco - G
Curtis Green - NT
Alvin Hall - DB
James Harrell - LB
Eric Hipple - QB
June James - LB
Demetrious Johnson - DB
A. J. Jones - RB
David Jones - C
James Jones - RB
Rick Kane - RB
Angelo King - LB
Larry Lee - G
David Lewis - TE
Pete Mandley - WR
Vernon Maxwell - LB
Reese McCall - TE
James McDonald - TE
Bruce McNorton - DB
Mike Meade - RB
Wilbert Montgomery - RB
Alvin Moore - RB
Martin Moss - DE
Steve Mott - C
Eddie Murray - K
Mark Nichols - WR
Rob Rubick - TE
Ray Snell - G
Hal Stephens - NT
Mark Stevenson - G
Rich Strenger - T
Leonard Thompson - WR
Tom Turnure - C
Bobby Watkins - DB
Eric Williams - NT
Jimmy Williams - LB

1985 Green Bay

John Anderson - LB
Don Bracken - P
Robert Brown - DE
Ronnie Burgess - DB
Mike Butler - DE
Mossy Cade - DB
Mark Cannon - C
Alphonso Carreker - DE
Chuck Clanton - DB
Jessie Clark - RB
Paul Coffman - TE
George Cumby - LB
Tony Degrate - DE
Al Del Greco - K
Preston Dennard - WR
Lynn Dickey - QB
John Dorsey - LB
Mike Douglass - LB
Gary Ellerson - RB
Gerry Ellis - RB
Phil Epps - WR
Tom Flynn - DB
Ron Hallstrom - G
Gary Hayes - DB
Harlan Huckleby - RB
Tim Huffman - T
Donnie Humphrey - DE
Eddie Lee Ivery - RB
Ezra Johnson - DE
Daryll Jones - DB
Greg Koch - T
Mark Lee - DB
Mark Lewis - TE
Tim Lewis - DB
James Lofton - WR
Charles Martin - DE
Mike McLeod - DB
Blake Moore - C
Rich Moran - C
Mark Murphy - DB
Brian Noble - LB
Guy Prather - LB
Joe Prokop - P
Ken Ruettgers - T
Randy Scott - LB
Mark Shumate - NT
Walter Stanley - WR
Ken Stills - DB
Karl Swanke - T
Maurice Turner - RB
Keith Uecker - G
Ed West - TE
Blake Wingle - G
Randy Wright - QB
Jim Zorn - QB

1985 Houston

Robert Abraham - LB
Mike Akiu - WR
Patrick Allen - DB
Jesse Baker - DE
Keith Bostic - DB
Tom Briehl - LB
Steve Brown - DB
Steve Bryant - WR
Frank Bush - LB
Richard Byrd - NT
Ray Childress - DE
Jeff Donaldson - DB
Chris Dressel - TE
Willie Drewrey - WR
Bo Eason - DB
Stan Edwards - RB
John Grimsley - LB
Drew Hill - WR
Mike Holston - WR
Pat Howell - G
Lee Johnson - P
Richard Johnson - DB
Mike Kelley - C
Rod Kush - DB
Oliver Luck - QB
Allen Lyday - DB
Robert Lyles - LB
Bruce Matthews - T
Mike McCloskey - TE
Audray McMillian - DB
Johnny Meads - LB
Warren Moon - QB
Eric Moran - T
Larry Moriarty - RB
Mike Moroski - QB
Mike Munchak - G
Avon Riley - LB
Jim Romano - C
Mike Rozier - RB
Harvey Salem - T
John Schuhmacher - G
Doug Smith - NT
Tim Smith - WR
Brian Sochia - NT
Mike Stensrud - NT
Steve Tasker - KR
Herkie Walls - WR
Jamie Williams - TE
Butch Woolfolk - RB
Tony Zendejas - K

1985 Indianapolis

George Achica - NT
Dave Ahrens - LB
Raul Allegre - K
Don Anderson - DB
Don Bailey - C
Karl Baldischwiler - T
Pat Beach - TE
Charles Benson - DE
Albert Bentley - RB
Duane Bickett - LB
Matt Bouza - WR
Mark Boyer - TE
Willie Broughton - DE
Ray Butler - WR
Kevin Call - T
Wayne Capers - WR
Roger Caron - T
Leonard Coleman - DB
Johnie Cooks - LB
Eugene Daniel - DB
Preston Davis - DB
Curtis Dickey - RB
Ray Donaldson - C
Owen Gill - RB
Nesby Glasgow - DB
Bernard Henry - WR
Chris Hinton - G
Lamonte Hunley - LB
Matt Kofler - QB
Barry Krauss - LB
Keith Lee - DB
Orlando Lowry - LB
Robbie Martin - WR
Keli McGregor - TE
Randy McMillan - RB
Frank Middleton - RB
Ricky Nichols - WR
Cliff Odom - LB
Mike Pagel - QB
George Radachowsky - DB
Tate Randle - DB
Art Schlichter - QB
Chris Scott - DE
Tim Sherwin - TE
Byron Smith - DE
Ron Solt - G
Rohn Stark - P
Donnell Thompson - DE
Ben Utt - G
Scott Virkus - DE
Brad White - NT
Oliver Williams - WR
George Wonsley - RB
Anthony Young - DB

1985 Kansas City

John Alt - T
Jim Arnold - P
Walt Arnold - TE
Scott Auer - G
Rich Baldinger - G
Mike Bell - DE
Todd Blackledge - QB
Jerry Blanton - LB
Brad Budde - G
Lloyd Burruss - DB
Carlos Carson - WR
Deron Cherry - DB
Sherman Cocroft - DB
Louis Cooper - LB
Calvin Daniels - LB
Rob Fada - G
Bob Hamm - DE
Anthony Hancock - WR
Jonathan Hayes - TE
Herman Heard - RB
Matt Herkenhoff - T
Greg Hill - DB
Eric Holle - DE
Mike Holston - WR
Ethan Horton - RB
Ken Jolly - LB
E. J. Jones - RB
Bill Kenney - QB
Bruce King - RB
Pete Koch - DE
Ken Lacy - RB
Garcia Lane - DB
Albert Lewis - DB
Dave Lindstrom - DE
Adam Lingner - C
Nick Lowery - K
Dave Lutz - T
Bill Maas - NT
Henry Marshall - WR
Odis McKinney - DB
Bob Olderman - G
Stephone Paige - WR
Jeff Paine - LB
Mike Pruitt - RB
Scott Radecic - LB
Mark Robinson - DB
Kevin Ross - DB
Bob Rush - C
Willie Scott - TE
Billy Shields - T
George Shorthose - WR
Jeff Smith - RB
Gary Spani - LB
Hal Stephens - DE
Art Still - DE

1985 LA Raiders

Marcus Allen - RB
Lyle Alzado - DE
Chris Bahr - K

Jeff Barnes - LB
Kevin Belcher - G
Don Bessillieu - DB
Cliff Branch - WR
Tony Caldwell - LB
Todd Christensen - TE
Dave Dalby - C
Bruce Davis - T
James Davis - DB
Mike Davis - DB
Elvis Franks - DE
Ray Guy - P
Charley Hannah - G
Frank Hawkins - RB
Lester Hayes - DB
Mike Haynes - DB
Jessie Hester - WR
Rusty Hilger - QB
Derrick Jensen - RB
Sean Jones - DE
Shelby Jordan - T
Trey Junkin - TE
Kenny King - RB
Henry Lawrence - T
Howie Long - DE
Curt Marsh - G
Rod Martin - LB
Mickey Marvin - G
Vann McElroy - DB
Reggie McKenzie - LB
Odis McKinney - DB
Matt Millen - LB
Tim Moffett - WR
Cleo Montgomery - WR
Don Mosebar - C
Andy Parker - TE
Bill Pickel - DT
Jim Plunkett - QB
Jerry Robinson - LB
Sam Seale - DB
Jim Smith - WR
Jack Squirek - LB
Dave Stalls - DT
Steve Strachan - RB
Stacey Toran - DB
Greg Townsend - DE
Brad Van Pelt - LB
Fulton Walker - DB
Dokie Williams - WR
Ricky Williams - DB
Mitch Willis - DT
Marc Wilson - QB

1985 LA Rams

Bill Bain - T
Mike Barber - TE
Russ Bolinger - G
Ed Brady - LB
Dieter Brock - QB
Ron Brown - WR
Lynn Cain - RB
Jim Collins - LB
Nolan Cromwell - DB
Charles DeJurnett - NT
Eric Dickerson - RB
Steve Dils - QB
Reggie Doss - DE
Bobby Duckworth - WR
Carl Ekern - LB
Henry Ellard - WR
Tim Fox - DB
Jerry Gray - DB
Gary Green - DB
Kevin Greene - LB
Mike Guman - RB
Dennis Harrah - G
Eric Harris - DB
Dennis Harrison - DE
Dale Hatcher - P
David Hill - TE
Kent Hill - G
Tony Hunter - TE
LeRoy Irvin - DB
Mark Jerue - LB
Gary Jeter - DE
Johnnie Johnson Jr. - DB
A. J. Jones - RB
Jeff Kemp - QB
Mike Lansford - K
Jim Laughlin - LB
Duval Love - G
James McDonald - TE
Greg Meisner - NT
Shawn Miller - NT
Vince Newsome - DB
Mel Owens - LB
Irvin Pankey - T
Barry Redden - RB
Doug Reed - DE
Booker Reese - DE
Jackie Slater - T
Tony Slaton - C
Doug Smith - C
Norwood Vann - LB
Charles White - RB
Mike Wilcher - LB
Mike Young - WR

1985 Miami

Bill Barnett - DE
Woody Bennett - RB
Doug Betters - DE
Glenn Blackwood - DB
Lyle Blackwood - DB
Kim Bokamper - DE
Charles Bowser - LB
Jay Brophy - LB
Bud Brown - DB
Mark Brown - LB
Bob Brudzinski - LB
Joe Carter - RB
Mike Charles - NT
Steve Clark - G
Mark Clayton - WR
Ron Davenport - RB
Jeff Dellenbach - T
Mark Duper - WR
Roy Foster - G
Jon Giesler - T
Cleveland Green - T
Hugh Green - LB
Lorenzo Hampton - RB
Bruce Hardy - TE
Duriel Harris - WR
Vince Heflin - WR
Jim Jensen - WR
Dan Johnson - TE
William Judson - DB
Mike Kozlowski - DB
Paul Lankford - DB
Larry Lee - G
Ronnie Lee - G
George Little - NT
Frank Lockett - WR
Dan Marino - QB
Don McNeal - DB
Mack Moore - DE
Nat Moore - WR
Alex Moyer - LB
Tony Nathan - RB
Fuad Reveiz - K
Reggie Roby - P
Joe Rose - TE
Robin Sendlein - LB
Jackie Shipp - LB
Sanders Shiver - LB
Mike Smith - DB
Robert Sowell - DB
Dwight Stephenson - C
Don Strock - QB
John Swain - DB
Jeff Toews - G
Tommy Vigorito - WR
Fulton Walker - DB

1985 Minnesota

Alfred Anderson - RB
Rufus Bess - DB
Matt Blair - LB
Steve Bono - QB
Brent Boyd - G
Ted Brown - RB
Joey Browner - DB
Jay Carroll - TE
Anthony Carter - WR
Greg Coleman - P
Chris Doleman - LB
Neil Elshire - DE
Dennis Fowlkes - LB
Issiac Holt - DB
Jim Hough - G
David Howard - LB
Dave Huffman - G
Tim Irwin - T
Dennis Johnson - LB
Mike Jones - WR
Steve Jordan - TE
Tommy Kramer - QB
Carl Lee - DB
Leo Lewis - WR
Kirk Lowdermilk - C
Mark MacDonald - G
Chris Martin - LB
Doug Martin - DE
Fred McNeill - LB
Tim Meamber - LB
Keith Millard - DE
Mike Mularkey - TE
Mark Mullaney - DE
Darrin Nelson - RB
Tim Newton - NT
Keith Nord - DB
Buster Rhymes - WR
Allen Rice - RB
Ted Rosnagle - DB
Curtis Rouse - G
Robert Smith - DE
Jan Stenerud - K
Scott Studwell - LB
Dennis Swilley - C
Terry Tausch - T
Willie Teal - DB
John Turner - DB
Maurice Turner - RB
Sammy White - WR
Wade Wilson - QB

1985 New England

Julius Adams - DE
Don Blackmon - LB
Jim Bowman - DB
Pete Brock - C
Rich Camarillo - P
Raymond Clayborn - DB
Tony Collins - RB
Tom Condon - G
Smiley Creswell - DE
Lin Dawson - TE
Tony Eason - QB
Paul Fairchild - G
Tony Franklin - K
Irving Fryar - WR
Ernest Gibson - DB
Steve Grogan - QB
John Hannah - G
Greg Hawthorne - WR
Brian Holloway - T
Brian Ingram - LB
Craig James - RB
Roland James - DB
Cedric Jones - WR
Ronnie Lippett - DB
Fred Marion - DB
Trevor Matich - C
Larry McGrew - LB
Rod McSwain - DB
Steve Moore - G
Stanley Morgan - WR
Guy Morriss - C
Steve Nelson - LB
Dennis Owens - NT
Art Plunkett - T
Derrick Ramsey - TE
Johnny Rembert - LB
Ed Reynolds - LB
Kenneth Sims - DE
Stephen Starring - WR
Mosi Tatupu - RB
Ben Thomas - DE
Andre Tippett - LB
Garin Veris - DE
Robert Weathers - RB
Derwin Williams - WR
Ed Williams - LB
Lester Williams - NT
Toby Williams - DE
Ron Wooten - G

1985 New Orleans

Morten Andersen - K
Edward Anthony - RB
Malcolm Barnwell - WR
Hoby Brenner - TE
Stan Brock - T
Earl Campbell - RB
David Carter - C
Bruce Clark - DE
Kelvin Clark - G
Jack Del Rio - LB
Kenny Duckett - WR
Brad Edelman - G
Tony Elliott - NT
Bobby Fowler - RB
Hokie Gajan - RB
Russell Gary - DB
Jumpy Geathers - DE
Daren Gilbert - T
Eugene Goodlow - WR
Jeff Groth - WR
Brian Hansen - P
Larry Hardy - TE
James Haynes - LB
Bobby Hebert - QB
Joel Hilgenberg - C
Terry Hoage - DB
Rickey Jackson - LB
Earl Johnson - DB
Joe Kohlbrand - LB
Steve Korte - C
Jim Kovach - LB
Dave Lafary - T
Eric Martin - WR
Brett Maxie - DB
Guido Merkens - QB
Mike Miller - WR
Derland Moore - NT
Whitney Paul - LB
Scott Pelluer - LB
Petey Perot - G
Johnnie Poe - DB
David Rackley - DB
Glen Redd - LB
Carl Roaches - WR
Jim Rourke - T
Adam Schreiber - G
Lindsay Scott - WR
John Tice - TE
Richard Todd - QB
Alvin Toles - LB
Willie Tullis - DB
Frank Warren - DE
Frank Wattelet - DB
Dave Waymer - DB
Jim Wilks - DE
Ralph Williams - T
Dave Wilson - QB
Wayne Wilson - RB
Dennis Winston - LB

1985 NY Giants

George Adams - RB
Billy Ard - G
Jess Atkinson - K
Carl Banks - LB
Mark Bavaro - TE
Brad Benson - T
Jim Burt - NT
Rob Carpenter - RB
Harry Carson - LB
Maurice Carthon - RB
Bill Currier - DB
Tyrone Davis - DB
Larry Flowers - DB
Tony Galbreath - RB
Chris Godfrey - G
Conrad Goode - T
Ali Haji-Sheikh - K
Dee Hardison - DE
Don Hasselbeck - TE
Mark Haynes - DB
Andy Headen - LB
Kenny Hill - DB
Jeff Hostetler - QB
Byron Hunt - LB
Bobby Johnson - WR
Robbie Jones - LB
David Jordan - G
Vyto Kab - TE
Terry Kinard - DB
Gordon King - T
Sean Landeta - P
Lionel Manuel - WR
Leonard Marshall - DE
George Martin - DE
Phil McConkey - WR
Curtis McGriff - DE
Casey Merrill - DE
Joe Morris - RB
Karl Nelson - T
Bart Oates - C
Elvis Patterson - DB
Gary Reasons - LB
Stacy Robinson - WR
Lee Rouson - RB
Jeff Rutledge - QB
Jerome Sally - NT
Eric Schubert - K
Phil Simms - QB
Lawrence Taylor - LB
Ted Watts - DB
Herb Welch - DB
Byron Williams - WR
Perry Williams - DB

1985 NY Jets

Sid Abramowitz - T
Dan Alexander - G
Tom Baldwin - DT
Ted Banker - T
Marion Barber - RB
Barry Bennett - DE
Guy Bingham - T
Dennis Bligen - RB
Nick Bruckner - WR
Russell Carter - DB
Kyle Clifton - LB
Bob Crable - LB
Chy Davidson - WR
Donnie Elder - DB
Jim Eliopulos - LB
Ron Faurot - LB
Joe Fields - C
Larry Flowers - DB
Mark Gastineau - DE
Kerry Glenn - DB
Billy Griggs - TE
Rusty Guilbeau - LB
Harry Hamilton - DB
Johnny Hector - RB
Carl Howard - DB
Bobby Humphery - WR
Charles Jackson - LB
Bobby Jackson - DB
Dave Jennings - P
Joe Klecko - DT
Rocky Klever - TE
Pat Leahy - K
Lester Lyles - DB
Johnny Lynn - DB
Marty Lyons - DE
Reggie McElroy - T
Freeman McNeil - RB
Lance Mehl - LB
Rich Miano - DB
Cedric Minter - RB
Matt Monger - LB
Davlin Mullen - DB
Ken O'Brien - QB
Tony Paige - RB
Marvin Powell - T
Ben Rudolph - DE
Pat Ryan - QB
Billy Shields - T
Mickey Shuler - TE
Mark Shumate - DE
Kurt Sohn - WR
Kirk Springs - DB
Jim Sweeney - G
Al Toon - WR
Jo-Jo Townsell - WR
Wesley Walker - WR
John Woodring - LB

1985 Philadelphia

Kevin Allen - T
Keith Baker - WR
Ron Baker - G
Aaron Brown - LB
Greg Brown - DE
Ken Clarke - DT
Garry Cobb - LB
Evan Cooper - DB
Smiley Creswell - DE
Randall Cunningham - QB
Byron Darby - DE
Mark Dennard - C
Joe Drake - DT
Herman Edwards - DB
Ray Ellis - DB
Major Everett - RB
Gerry Feehery - C
Elbert Foules - DB
Gregg Garrity - WR
Tim Golden - LB
John Goode - TE
Anthony Griggs - LB
Michael Haddix - RB
Wes Hopkins - DB
Mike Horan - P
Herman Hunter - RB
Earnest Jackson - RB
Kenny Jackson - WR
Ron Jaworski - QB
Tom Jelesky - T
Dwayne Jiles - LB
Ron Johnson - WR
Vyto Kab - TE
Steve Kenney - G
Jon Kimmel - LB
Rich Kraynak - LB
Dave Little - TE
Paul McFadden - K
Leonard Mitchell - T
Dwaine Morris - NT
Hubie Oliver - RB
Jairo Penaranda - RB
Tom Polley - LB
Mike Quick - WR
Ken Reeves - T
Mike Reichenbach - LB
John Spagnola - TE
Thomas Strauthers - DE
Andre Waters - DB
Reggie White - DT
Reggie Wilkes - LB
Joel Williams - LB
Brenard Wilson - DB
Roynell Young - DB

1985 Pittsburgh

Walter Abercrombie - RB
Gary Anderson - K
Emil Boures - G
Chris Brown - DB
Scott Campbell - QB
Gregg Carr - LB
Mark Catano - NT
Harvey Clayton - DB
Robin Cole - LB
Bennie Cunningham - TE
Gary Dunn - NT
Dave Edwards - DB
Rich Erenberg - RB
Keith Gary - DE
John Goodman - DE
Preston Gothard - TE
Bryan Hinkle - LB
Glen Howe - T
Tunch Ilkin - T
Bob Kohrs - LB
Louis Lipps - WR
David Little - LB
Terry Long - G
Mark Malone - QB
Mike Merriweather - LB
Steve Morse - RB
Darrell Nelson - TE
Ed Nelson - DE
Harry Newsome - P
Ray Pinney - T
Frank Pokorny - WR
Frank Pollard - RB
Randy Rasmussen - G
Pete Rostosky - T
Donnie Shell - DB
Darryl Sims - DE
Fred Small - LB
Ray Snell - T
Todd Spencer - RB
John Stallworth - WR
John Swain - DB
Calvin Sweeney - WR
Weegie Thompson - WR
Anthony Tuggle - DB
Dan Turk - C
Sam Washington - DB
Mike Webster - C
Eric Williams - DB
Keith Willis - DE
Blake Wingle - G
Dennis Winston - LB
Craig Wolfley - G
David Woodley - QB
Dwayne Woodruff - DB
Rick Woods - DB

1985 St. Louis

Ottis Anderson - RB
Jess Atkinson - K
Charles Baker - LB
Al Baker - DE
Scott Bergold - T
Carl Birdsong - P
Novo Bojovic - K
Joe Bostic - G
Scott Brunner - QB
Randy Clark - C
Doug Dawson - G
Mark Duda - DT
Clyde Duncan - WR
Earl Ferrell - RB
David Galloway - DT
Earnest Gray - WR
Roy Green - WR
Curtis Greer - DE
Jeff Griffin - DB
Elois Grooms - DT
Perry Harrington - RB
Bob Harris - LB
Liffort Hobley - DB
Tom Howard - LB
Bobby Johnson - DB
E. J. Junior - LB
Greg LaFleur - TE
Neil Lomax - QB
Randy Love - RB
Cedric Mack - DB
Doug Marsh - TE
Stafford Mays - DE
Rick McIvor - QB
Stump Mitchell - RB
Rob Monaco - C
Tony Mumford - RB
Lee Nelson - DB
Niko Noga - LB
Jay Novacek - WR
Freddie Joe Nunn - LB
Neil O'Donoghue - K
Benny Perrin - DB
Tootie Robbins - T
Carlos Scott - T
Luis Sharpe - T
J. T. Smith - WR
Lance Smith - G
Leonard Smith - DB
Wayne Smith - DB
Danny Spradlin - LB
Pat Tilley - WR
Lionel Washington - DB
Ron Wolfley - RB
Lonnie Young - DB

1985 San Diego

Curtis Adams - RB
Gary Anderson - RB
Jesse Bendross - WR
Rolf Benirschke - K
Craig Bingham - LB
Carlos Bradley - LB
Gill Byrd - DB
Wes Chandler - WR
Tony Chickillo - NT
Sam Claphan - T
Anthony Corley - RB
David Croudip - DB
Jeffery Dale - DB
Ken Dallafior - G
Wayne Davis - DB
Jerry Doerger - C
Chuck Ehin - NT
Chris Faulkner - TE
Mark Fellows - LB
Keith Ferguson - DE
Dan Fouts - QB
Scott Garnett - NT
Mike Green - LB
Mike Guendling - LB
John Hendy - DB
Mark Herrmann - QB
Pete Holohan - TE
Lionel James - RB
Trumaine Johnson - WR
Charlie Joiner - WR
David King - DB
Linden King - LB
Gary Kowalski - T
Jim Lachey - T
Jim Leonard - C
Terry Lewis - DB
Woodrow Lowe - LB
Don Macek - C
Buford McGee - RB
Dennis McKnight - C
Miles McPherson - DB
Ralf Mojsiejenko - P
Derrie Nelson - LB
Ronnie O'Bard - DB
Vince Osby - LB
Fred Robinson - DE
Jim Rockford - DB
Bill Searcey - G
Eric Sievers - TE
Tony Simmons - DE
Billy Ray Smith Jr. - LB
Lucious Smith - DB
Tim Spencer - RB
Anthony Steels - RB
Bob Thomas - K
Rich Umphrey - C
Danny Walters - DB
Ed White - G
Lee Williams - DE
Earl Wilson - DE
Kellen Winslow - TE

1985 San Francisco

John Ayers - G
Dwaine Board - DE
Michael Carter - NT
Matt Cavanaugh - QB
Dwight Clark - WR
Bruce Collie - T
Earl Cooper - TE
Roger Craig - RB
Randy Cross - G
Fred Dean - DE
Riki Ellison - LB
Jim Fahnhorst - LB
Keith Fahnhorst - T
Ron Ferrari - LB
Russ Francis - TE
John Frank - TE
Jeff Fuller - DB
Scott Garnett - NT
Derrick Harmon - RB
John Harty - DE
Dwight Hicks - DB
John Hill - C
Gary Johnson - DT
Jim Kovach - LB
Fulton Kuykendall - LB
Jim Leonard - C
Ronnie Lott - DB
Milt McColl - LB
Guy McIntyre - G
Dana McLemore - DB
Carl Monroe - RB
Joe Montana - QB
Tory Nixon - DB
Bubba Paris - T
Fred Quillan - C
Jerry Rice - WR
Bill Ring - RB
Max Runager - P
Todd Shell - LB
Freddie Solomon - WR
Jeff Stover - DE
Vince Stroth - T
Jim Stuckey - DE
Manu Tuiasosopo - NT
Keena Turner - LB
Wendell Tyler - RB
Michael Walter - LB
Ray Wersching - K
Carlton Williamson - DB
Mike Wilson - WR
Eric Wright - DB

1985 Seattle

Edwin Bailey - G
Jon Borchardt - G
Dave Brown - DB
Jeff Bryant - DE
Blair Bush - C
Keith Butler - LB
Ray Butler - WR
Jimmy Colquitt - P
Bob Cryder - T
Dan Doornink - RB
Kenny Easley - DB
Randy Edwards - DE
Ron Essink - T
Dave Finzer - P
Byron Franklin - WR
Greg Gaines - LB
Gale Gilbert - QB
Jacob Green - DE
Danny Greene - WR
Andre Hardy - RB
John Harris - DB
David Hughes - RB
Michael Jackson - LB
Terry Jackson - DB
Norm Johnson - K
John Kaiser - LB
Kani Kauahi - C
Reggie Kinlaw - NT
Dave Krieg - QB
Eric Lane - RB
Steve Largent - WR
Sam Merriman - LB
Bryan Millard - G
Randall Morris - RB
Paul Moyer - DB
Joe Nash - NT
Rick Parros - RB
Bob Pratt - G
Eugene Robinson - DB
Shelton Robinson - LB
Dan Ross - TE
Rick Sanford - DB
Bruce Scholtz - LB
Keith Simpson - DB
Paul Skansi - WR
Terry Taylor - DB
Mike Tice - TE
Daryl Turner - WR
Byron Walker - WR
Curt Warner - RB
Jeff West - P
John Williams - RB
Charle Young - TE
Fredd Young - LB

1985 Tampa Bay

Adger Armstrong - RB
Jerry Bell - TE
Theo Bell - WR
Scot Brantley - LB
Gene Branton - TE
Leon Bright - RB
Keith Browner - LB
John Cannon - DE
Gerald Carter - WR

Mel Carver - RB
Jeremiah Castille - DB
Steve Courson - G
Craig Curry - DB
Jeff Davis - LB
Steve DeBerg - QB
Paul Dombroski - DB
K. D. Dunn - TE
Ricky Easmon - DB
Sean Farrell - G
Don Fielder - DE
Phil Freeman - WR
Frank Garcia - P
Jimmie Giles - TE
Hugh Green - LB
David Greenwood - DB
Randy Grimes - C
Ron Heller - T
Ron Holmes - DE
John Holt - DB
Kevin House - WR
Carl Howard - DB
Donald Igwebuike - K
Cecil Johnson - LB
Dennis Johnson - LB
Ken Kaplan - T
Larry Kubin - LB
Chris Lindstrom - DE
David Logan - NT
Calvin Magee - TE
Rick Mallory - G
Karl Morgan - NT
George Peoples - RB
Mike Prior - DB
Ervin Randle - LB
Alan Risher - QB
Gene Sanders - T
Joe Shearin - G
Ron Springs - RB
Mark Studaway - DE
Ivory Sully - DB
David Verser - WR
Chris Washington - LB
James Wilder - RB
Steven Wilson - C
Mark Witte - TE
George Yarno - G
Steve Young - QB

1985 Washington

Stuart Anderson - LB
Doug Barnett - DE
Malcolm Barnwell - WR
Tom Beasley - DT
Jeff Bostic - C
Reggie Branch - RB
Dave Butz - DT
Raphel Cherry - DB
Gary Clark - WR
Monte Coleman - LB
Steve Cox - P
Pete Cronan - LB
Vernon Dean - DB
Clint Didier - TE
Rick Donnalley - C
Darryl Grant - DT
Darrell Green - DB
Keith Griffin - RB
Russ Grimm - G
Dean Hamel - DT
Steve Hamilton - DE
Jeff Hayes - P
Ken Huff - G
Joe Jacoby - T
Ken Jenkins - RB
Anthony Jones - TE
Curtis Jordan - DB
Mel Kaufman - LB
Chris Keating - LB
Todd Liebenstein - DE
Dexter Manley - DE
Charles Mann - DE
Mark May - T
Mark McGrath - WR
Raleigh McKenzie - G
Dan McQuaid - T
Rich Milot - LB
Art Monk - WR
Michael Morton - RB
Mark Moseley - K
Calvin Muhammad - WR
Neal Olkewicz - LB
Tony Peters - DB
Joe Phillips - WR
John Riggins - RB
George Rogers - RB
Jay Schroeder - QB
Joe Theismann - QB
R.C. Thielemann - G
Rick Walker - TE
Don Warren - TE
Barry Wilburn - DB
Greg Williams - DB
Kevin Williams - DB
Otis Wonsley - RB

1986 Atlanta

Anthony Allen - WR
William Andrews - RB
David Archer - QB
Cliff Austin - RB
Stacey Bailey - WR
Tony Baker - RB
Dan Benish - DT
Jim Britt - DB
Aaron Brown - LB
Charlie Brown - WR
Rick Bryan - DE
Bobby Butler - DB
Scott Campbell - QB
Scott Case - DB
Tony Casillas - NT
Wendell Cason - DB
Bret Clark - DB
Joe Costello - LB
Arthur Cox - TE
David Croudip - DB
Buddy Curry - LB
Floyd Dixon - WR
Rick Donnelly - P
Jamie Dukes - G
Herman Edwards - DB
Bill Fralic - T
Mike Gann - DE
Tim Green - LB
Ali Haji-Sheikh - K
Dennis Harrison - DE
Glen Howe - T
Kenny Johnson - DB
Billy Johnson - WR
Joey Jones - WR
Mike Kenn - T
Mick Luckhurst - K
Aubrey Matthews - WR
Ron Middleton - TE
Brett Miller - T
Robert Moore - DB
Joseph Pellegrini - G
Ray Phillips - LB
Mike Pitts - DE
Andrew Provence - DE
John Rade - LB
Wayne Radloff - C
Gerald Riggs - RB
Eric Sanders - T
Turk Schonert - QB
John Scully - G
Sylvester Stamps - RB
Johnny Taylor - LB
Jimmy Turner - DB
Tim Tyrrell - RB
Jeff Van Note - C
Ken Whisenhunt - TE
Reggie Wilkes - LB
Joel Williams - LB
Keith Williams - WR
Dennis Woodberry - DB

1986 Buffalo

Martin Bayless - DB
Greg Bell - RB
Rodney Bellinger - DB
Ray Bentley - LB
Jerry Boyarsky - NT
Walter Broughton - WR
Chris Burkett - WR
Derrick Burroughs - DB
Leonard Burton - C
Jerry Butler - WR
Carl Byrum - RB
Mark Catano - NT
Justin Cross - T
George Cumby - LB
Joe Devlin - T
Dwight Drane - DB
Guy Frazier - LB
Steve Freeman - DB
Tony Furjanic - LB
Hal Garner - LB
Mike Hamby - DE
Ronnie Harmon - RB
Dale Hellestrae - T
Rod Hill - DB
Kent Hull - C
Ken Jones - T
Jim Kelly - QB
Mark Kelso - DB
Don Kern - TE
John Kidd - P
Bruce King - RB
Eugene Marve - LB
Sean McNanie - DE
Pete Metzelaars - TE
Ricky Moore - RB
Scott Norwood - K
Ron Pitts - DB
Dean Prater - DE
Andre Reed - WR
Frank Reich - QB
Eric Richardson - WR
Robb Riddick - RB
Jim Ritcher - G
Butch Rolle - TE
Charles Romes - DB
Lucius Sanford - LB
Fred Smerlas - NT
Bruce Smith - DE
Don Smith - NT
Darryl Talley - LB
Steve Tasker - WR
Jimmy Teal - WR
Mark Traynowicz - G
Tim Vogler - G
Gary Wilkins - RB
Kevin Williams - DB
Will Wolford - G

1986 Chi. Bears

Neal Anderson - RB
Lew Barnes - WR
Kurt Becker - G
Todd Bell - DB
Paul Blair - T
Mark Bortz - G
Maury Buford - P
Kevin Butler - K
Brian Cabral - LB
Jim Covert - T
Richard Dent - DE
Maurice Douglass - DB
Dave Duerson - DB
Gary Fencik - DB
Doug Flutie - QB
Steve Fuller - QB
Willie Gault - WR
Shaun Gayle - DB
Dennis Gentry - WR
Dan Hampton - DE
Al Harris - LB
Mike Hartenstine - DE
Jay Hilgenberg - C
Stefan Humphries - G
Vestee Jackson - DB
Ken Margerum - WR
Wilber Marshall - LB
Jim McMahon - QB
Steve McMichael - DT
Emery Moorehead - TE
Jim Morrissey - LB
Keith Ortego - WR
Walter Payton - RB
William Perry - DT
Reggie Phillips - DB
Clay Pickering - WR
Dan Rains - LB
Mike Richardson - DB
Ron Rivera - LB
Larry Rubens - C
Thomas Sanders - RB
Mike Singletary - LB
Matt Suhey - RB
Tom Thayer - G
Calvin Thomas - RB
Mike Tomczak - QB
Keith Van Horne - T
Henry Waechter - DT
Otis Wilson - LB
Tim Wrightman - TE

1986 Cincinnati

Ken Anderson - QB
Leo Barker - LB
Lewis Billups - DB
Brian Blados - G
Ed Brady - LB
Jim Breech - K
Louis Breeden - DB
James Brooks - RB
Eddie Brown - WR
Ross Browner - DE
Barney Bussey - DB
Cris Collinsworth - WR
Kiki DeAyala - LB
David Douglas - T
Eddie Edwards - DE
Boomer Esiason - QB
David Fulcher - DB
Doug Gaynor - QB
Mike Hammerstein - DE
Jeff Hayes - P
Rodney Holman - TE
Ray Horton - DB
Robert Jackson - DB
Stanford Jennings - RB
Bill Johnson - RB
Eric Kattus - TE
Joe Kelly - LB
Bobby Kemp - DB
Emanuel King - LB
Larry Kinnebrew - RB
Bruce Kozerski - C
Steve Kreider - WR
Tim Krumrie - NT
Mike Martin - WR
Tim McGee - WR
Max Montoya - G
Anthony Munoz - T
Bruce Reimers - T
Dave Rimington - C
John Simmons - DB
Ron Simpkins - LB
Jim Skow - DE
Jimmy Turner - DB
Joe Walter - T
Leon White - LB
Reggie Williams - LB
Stanley Wilson - RB
Carl Zander - LB

1986 Cleveland

Mike Baab - C
Matt Bahr - K
Tony Baker - RB
Chip Banks - LB
Rickey Bolden - T
Brian Brennan - WR
Earnest Byner - RB
Reggie Camp - DE
Sam Clancy - DE
Bill Contz - T
Johnny Davis - RB
Curtis Dickey - RB
Hanford Dixon - DB
Ray Ellis - DB
Major Everett - RB
Paul Farren - T
Dan Fike - G
Herman Fontenot - RB
Bob Golic - NT
Jeff Gossett - P
Terry Greer - WR
Anthony Griggs - LB
Al Gross - DB
Carl Hairston - DE
Mark Harper - DB
D.D. Hoggard - DB
Harry Holt - TE
Eddie Johnson - LB
Mike Johnson - LB
Bernie Kosar - QB
Reggie Langhorne - WR
George Lilja - G
Kevin Mack - RB
Ralph Malone - DE
Clay Matthews - LB
Gerald McNeil - WR
Frank Minnifield - DB
Mark Moseley - K
Ozzie Newsome - TE
Scott Nicolas - LB
Mike Pagel - QB
Dave Puzzuoli - NT
Cody Risien - T
Chris Rockins - DB
Webster Slaughter - WR
Travis Tucker - TE
Brad Van Pelt - LB
Clarence Weathers - WR
Larry Williams - G
Jeff Wiska - G
Felix Wright - DB

1986 Dallas

Vince Albritton - DB
Jesse Baker - DE
Brian Baldinger - G
Gordon Banks - WR
Bill Bates - DB
Kevin Brooks - DE
Thornton Chandler - TE
Darryl Clack - RB
Reggie Collier - QB
Jim Cooper - T
Doug Cosbie - TE
Steve DeOssie - LB
Tony Dorsett - RB
Michael Downs - DB
John Dutton - DT
Ron Fellows - DB
Todd Fowler - RB
Cornell Gowdy - DB
Mike Hegman - LB
Manny Hendrix - DB
Tony Hill - WR
Johnny Holloway - DB
Garth Jax - LB
Jim Jeffcoat - DE
Too Tall Jones - DE
Crawford Ker - G
Robert Lavette - RB
Eugene Lockhart - LB
Paul McDonald - QB
Timmy Newsome - RB
Nate Newton - G
Bob Otto - DT
Steve Pelluer - QB
Jesse Penn - LB
Kurt Ploeger - DE
Karl Powe - WR
Phil Pozderac - T
Tom Rafferty - C
Mike Renfro - WR
Howard Richards - T
Jeff Rohrer - LB
Mike Saxon - P
Victor Scott - DB
Rafael Septien - K
Mike Sherrard - WR
Don Smerek - DT
Glen Titensor - G
Mark Tuinei - C
Herschel Walker - RB
Everson Walls - DB
Randy White - DT
Danny White - QB

1986 Denver

Ken Bell - RB
Keith Bishop - C
Tony Boddie - RB
Billy Bryan - C
Rubin Carter - NT
Tony Colorito - NT
Darren Comeaux - LB
Mark Cooper - G
Rick Dennison - LB
John Elway - QB
Simon Fletcher - DE
Steve Foley - DB
Mike Freeman - G
Freddie Gilbert - DE
Joey Hackett - TE
Mike Harden - DB
Mark Haynes - DB
Winford Hood - T
Mike Horan - P
Paul Howard - G
Ricky Hunley - LB
Daniel Hunter - DB
Mark Jackson - WR
Tom Jackson - LB
Vance Johnson - WR
Rulon Jones - DE
Rich Karlis - K
Clarence Kay - TE
Greg Kragen - NT
Gary Kubiak - QB
Gene Lang - RB
Ken Lanier - T
Tony Lilly - DB
Karl Mecklenburg - DE
Bobby Micho - TE
Orson Mobley - TE
Chris Norman - P
Dan Remsberg - T
Randy Robbins - DB
Jim Ryan - LB
Clint Sampson - WR
Steven Sewell - RB
Dennis Smith - DB
Dave Studdard - T
Andre Townsend - DE
Steve Watson - WR
Jack Weil - P
Gerald Willhite - RB
Steve Wilson - DB
Sammy Winder - RB
Ken Woodard - LB
Louis Wright - DB

1986 Detroit

Jim Arnold - P
Steve Baack - G
Scott Barrows - G
Mike Black - P
Carl Bland - WR
John Bostic - DB
Lomas Brown - T
Paul Butcher - LB
Jeff Chadwick - WR
Mike Cofer - LB
August Curley - LB
Chris Dieterich - G
Keith Dorney - G
Donnie Elder - DB
Leon Evans - DE
Joe Ferguson - QB
Keith Ferguson - DE
Duane Galloway - DB
Bill Gay - DE
Jimmie Giles - TE
Kevin Glover - C
William Graham - DB
Curtis Green - DE
James Griffin - DB
James Harrell - LB
Rod Hill - DB
Eric Hipple - QB
Herman Hunter - RB
Garry James - RB
Demetrious Johnson - DB
James Johnson - LB
James Jones - RB
Steve Kenney - G
Angelo King - LB
David Lewis - TE
Chuck Long - QB
Pete Mandley - WR
Vernon Maxwell - LB
Bruce McNorton - DB
Devon Mitchell - DB
Alvin Moore - RB
Steve Mott - C
Eddie Murray - K
Shelton Robinson - LB
Rob Rubick - TE
Harvey Salem - T
Eric Sanders - T
Oscar Smith - RB
Rich Strenger - T
Leonard Thompson - WR
Tom Turnure - G
Bobby Watkins - DB
Scott Williams - RB
Eric Williams - NT
Jimmy Williams - LB

1986 Green Bay

John Anderson - LB
Ed Berry - DB
Jerry Boyarsky - NT
Don Bracken - P
Robert Brown - DE
Mossy Cade - DB
Mark Cannon - C
Alphonso Carreker - DE
Paul Ott Carruth - RB
Bill Cherry - C
Jessie Clark - RB
Kenneth Davis - RB
Al Del Greco - K
Burnell Dent - LB
John Dorsey - LB
Gary Ellerson - RB
Gerry Ellis - RB
Phil Epps - WR
Greg Feasel - T
Vince Ferragamo - QB
Tom Flynn - DB
Nolan Franz - WR
Chuck Fusina - QB
George Greene - DB
David Greenwood - DB
Ron Hallstrom - G
Tim Harris - LB
Gary Hayes - DB
Donnie Humphrey - DE
Eddie Lee Ivery - WR
Ezra Johnson - DE
Matt Koart - DE
Mark Lee - DB
Bobby Leopold - LB
Mark Lewis - TE
Tim Lewis - DB
James Lofton - WR
Charles Martin - DE
Phil McConkey - WR
Ruben Mendoza - G
Mike Moffitt - TE
Rich Moran - C
Tom Neville - T
Brian Noble - LB
Kurt Ploeger - DE
Bill Renner - P
Dan Ross - TE
Ken Ruettgers - T
Jeff Schuh - LB
Randy Scott - LB
Joe Shield - QB
John Simmons - DB
Walter Stanley - WR
Ken Stills - DB
John Sullivan - DB
Karl Swanke - T
Ben Thomas - DE
Miles Turpin - LB
Alan Veingrad - T
Elbert Watts - DB
Mike Weddington - LB
Ed West - TE
Randy Wright - QB

1986 Houston

Robert Abraham - LB
Mike Akiu - WR
Patrick Allen - DB
Jesse Baker - DE
Chuck Banks - RB
Keith Bostic - DB
Steve Brown - DB
Frank Bush - LB
Richard Byrd - DE
Ray Childress - DE
Kirk Dodge - LB
Jeff Donaldson - DB
Chris Dressel - TE
Willie Drewrey - WR
Bo Eason - DB
Stan Edwards - RB
Eric Fairs - LB
William Fuller - DE
Ernest Givins - WR
Mike Golic - NT
Larry Griffin - DB
John Grimsley - LB
Drew Hill - WR
Kent Hill - G
Kenny Johnson - DB
Lee Johnson - P
Richard Johnson - DB
Oliver Luck - QB
Allen Lyday - DB
Robert Lyles - LB
Lynn Madsen - DE
Don Maggs - T
Bruce Matthews - T
Audray McMillian - DB
Johnny Meads - LB
Warren Moon - QB
Eric Moran - T
Karl Morgan - NT
Larry Moriarty - RB
Mike Munchak - G
Hubie Oliver - RB
Jeff Parks - TE
Jay Pennison - C
Allen Pinkett - RB
Avon Riley - LB
Jim Romano - C
Mike Rozier - RB
Harvey Salem - T
Doug Smith - NT
Tim Smith - WR
Dean Steinkuhler - T
Steve Tasker - WR
Malcolm Taylor - DE
Ray Wallace - RB
Doug Williams - T
Jamie Williams - TE
Butch Woolfolk - RB
Tony Zendejas - K

1986 Indianapolis

Dave Ahrens - LB
Harvey Armstrong - NT
Karl Baldischwiler - T
Pat Ballage - DB
Pat Beach - TE
Albert Bentley - RB
Dean Biasucci - K
Duane Bickett - LB
Matt Bouza - WR
Mark Boyer - TE
Bill Brooks - WR
Bob Brotzki - T
Willie Broughton - DE
Kevin Call - T
Wayne Capers - WR
Roger Caron - T
Dextor Clinkscale - DB
Leonard Coleman - DB
Johnie Cooks - LB
Eugene Daniel - DB
Kenny Daniel - DB
Preston Davis - DB
Ray Donaldson - C
Owen Gill - RB
Nesby Glasgow - DB
John Haines - NT
Jon Hand - DE
James Harbour - WR
Dwight Hicks - DB
Chris Hinton - G
Gary Hogeboom - QB
John Holt - DB
Lamonte Hunley - LB
Victor Jackson - DB
Scott Kellar - NT
Blair Kiel - QB
Mark Kirchner - T
Barry Krauss - LB
Greg LaFleur - TE
Jeff Leiding - LB
Orlando Lowry - LB
Mike Lush - DB
Robbie Martin - WR
Randy McMillan - RB
Walter Murray - WR
Cliff Odom - LB
Hubie Oliver - RB
Tate Randle - DB
Glen Redd - LB
Tim Sherwin - TE
Tommy Sims - DB
Ron Solt - G
Rohn Stark - P
Donnell Thompson - DE
Jack Trudeau - QB
Ben Utt - G
Oliver Williams - WR
George Wonsley - RB

1986 Kansas City

Mark Adickes - G
John Alt - T
Walt Arnold - TE
Gary Baldinger - DE
Rich Baldinger - G
Tom Baugh - C
Todd Blackledge - QB
Brad Budde - G
Lloyd Burruss - DB
Carlos Carson - WR
Deron Cherry - DB
Sherman Cocroft - DB
Paul Coffman - TE
Tim Cofield - LB
Lewis Colbert - P
Louis Cooper - LB
Rick Donnalley - C
Irv Eatman - T
Boyce Green - RB
Leonard Griffin - DE
Dino Hackett - LB
Anthony Hancock - WR
Emile Harry - WR
Jonathan Hayes - TE
Herman Heard - RB
Greg Hill - DB
Eric Holle - DE
Brian Jozwiak - T
Bill Kenney - QB
Bruce King - RB
Pete Koch - DE
Kit Lathrop - DE
Albert Lewis - DB
Adam Lingner - C
Nick Lowery - K
Dave Lutz - T
Bill Maas - NT
Henry Marshall - WR
Ken McAlister - LB
Larry Moriarty - RB
Stephone Paige - WR
Whitney Paul - LB
Aaron Pearson - LB
J. C. Pearson - DB
Mike Pruitt - RB
Scott Radecic - LB
Mark Robinson - DB
Kevin Ross - DB
Jim Rourke - G
Frank Seurer - QB
Chris Smith - RB
Jeff Smith - RB
Gary Spani - LB
Art Still - DE

1986 LA Raiders

Stefan Adams - DB
Marcus Allen - RB
Chris Bahr - K
Rod Barksdale - WR
Jeff Barnes - LB

Todd Christensen - TE
Earl Cooper - TE
Bruce Davis - T
James Davis - DB
Elvis Franks - DE
Ray Guy - P
Charley Hannah - G
Frank Hawkins - RB
Lester Hayes - DB
Mike Haynes - DB
Jessie Hester - WR
Rusty Hilger - QB
Derrick Jensen - TE
Sean Jones - DE
Shelby Jordan - T
Trey Junkin - TE
Jamie Kimmel - LB
Linden King - LB
Henry Lawrence - T
Bill Lewis - C
Howie Long - DE
Curt Marsh - G
Rod Martin - LB
Mickey Marvin - G
Napoleon McCallum - RB
Vann McElroy - DB
Reggie McKenzie - LB
Odis McKinney - DB
Matt Millen - LB
Tim Moffett - WR
Don Mosebar - C
Vance Mueller - RB
Andy Parker - TE
Mark Pattison - WR
Bill Pickel - DT
Jim Plunkett - QB
Chris Riehm - G
Jerry Robinson - LB
Sam Seale - DB
Steve Strachan - RB
Stacey Toran - DB
Greg Townsend - DE
Fulton Walker - DB
Dokie Williams - WR
Mitch Willis - DT
Marc Wilson - QB
Mike Wise - DE

1986 LA Rams

Steve Bartkowski - QB
Ron Brown - WR
Steve Busick - LB
Rob Carpenter - RB
Nolan Cromwell - DB
Charles DeJurnett - NT
Eric Dickerson - RB
Steve Dils - QB
Reggie Doss - DE
Bobby Duckworth - WR
Herman Edwards - DB
Carl Ekern - LB
Henry Ellard - WR
Jim Everett - QB
Tim Fox - DB
Jerry Gray - DB
Kevin Greene - LB
Mike Guman - RB
Dennis Harrah - G
Dale Hatcher - P
David Hill - TE
Kent Hill - G
Kevin House - WR
Tony Hunter - TE
LeRoy Irvin - DB
Mark Jerue - LB
Gary Jeter - DE
Damone Johnson - TE
Johnnie Johnson Jr. - DB
Mike Lansford - K
Jim Laughlin - LB
Darren Long - TE
Duval Love - G
Mike McDonald - LB
Greg Meisner - NT
Shawn Miller - NT
Tom Newberry - G
Vince Newsome - DB
Mel Owens - LB
Irvin Pankey - T
Mark Pattison - WR
Barry Redden - RB
Doug Reed - DE
Chuck Scott - WR
Jackie Slater - T
Tony Slaton - C
Doug Smith - C
Mickey Sutton - DB
Cliff Thrift - LB
Tim Tyrrell - RB
Norwood Vann - LB
Charles White - RB
Mike Wilcher - LB
Alvin Wright - NT
Mike Young - WR

1986 Miami

Bob Baumhower - NT
Woody Bennett - RB
Doug Betters - DE
Glenn Blackwood - DB
Lyle Blackwood - DB
Jay Brophy - LB

Bud Brown - DB
Donald Brown - DB
Mark Brown - LB
Bob Brudzinski - LB
Joe Carter - RB
Mike Charles - NT
Mark Clayton - WR
Ron Davenport - RB
Jeff Dellenbach - T
Mark Duper - WR
Craig Ellis - RB
Jerome Foster - NT
Roy Foster - G
David Frye - LB
Jon Giesler - T
Cleveland Green - T
Hugh Green - LB
Lorenzo Hampton - RB
Bruce Hardy - TE
Andy Hendel - LB
Jim Jensen - WR
Dan Johnson - TE
William Judson - DB
Greg Koch - T
Larry Kolic - LB
Mike Kozlowski - DB
Paul Lankford - DB
Larry Lee - G
Ronnie Lee - G
George Little - DE
Dan Marino - QB
Don McNeal - DB
Mack Moore - DE
Nat Moore - WR
Alex Moyer - LB
Tony Nathan - RB
John Offerdahl - LB
James Pruitt - WR
Fuad Reveiz - K
Fred Robinson - LB
Reggie Roby - P
Donovan Rose - DB
Jackie Shipp - LB
Mike Smith - DB
Brian Sochia - NT
Jack Squirek - LB
Dwight Stephenson - C
Don Strock - QB
Johnny Taylor - LB
Reyna Thompson - DB
Tom Toth - T
T. J. Turner - DE

1986 Minnesota

Alfred Anderson - RB
Walker Lee Ashley - LB
Rufus Bess - DB
Steve Bono - QB
Brent Boyd - G
Ted Brown - RB
Joey Browner - DB
Anthony Carter - WR
Greg Coleman - P
Chris Doleman - DE
Neil Elshire - DE
David Evans - DB
Neal Guggemos - DB
Jim Gustafson - WR
John Harris - DB
Carl Hilton - TE
Issiac Holt - DB
Jim Hough - G
David Howard - LB
Dave Huffman - G
Tim Irwin - T
Hassan Jones - WR
Steve Jordan - TE
Tommy Kramer - QB
Carl Lee - DB
Leo Lewis - WR
Kirk Lowdermilk - C
Mike Lush - DB
Mark MacDonald - G
Chris Martin - LB
Doug Martin - DE
Keith Millard - DT
Kyle Morrell - DB
Mike Mularkey - TE
Mark Mullaney - DE
Chuck Nelson - K
Darrin Nelson - RB
Tim Newton - DT
Joe Phillips - DT
Buster Rhymes - WR
Allen Rice - RB
Gerald Robinson - DE
Curtis Rouse - G
Jeff Schuh - LB
Jesse Solomon - LB
Mike Stensrud - DT
Scott Studwell - LB
Dennis Swilley - C
Terry Tausch - T
Willie Teal - DB
Wade Wilson - QB
Wayne Wilson - RB
Gary Zimmerman - T

1986 New England

Bill Bain - T
Greg Baty - TE
Mel Black - LB
Don Blackmon - LB
Jim Bowman - DB

Pete Brock - C
Rich Camarillo - P
Raymond Clayborn - DB
Tony Collins - RB
Steve Doig - LB
Reggie Dupard - RB
Tony Eason - QB
Paul Fairchild - G
Tony Franklin - K
Irving Fryar - WR
Ernest Gibson - DB
Vencie Glenn - DB
Steve Grogan - QB
Darryl Haley - T
Greg Hawthorne - TE
Milford Hodge - DE
Brian Holloway - T
Craig James - RB
Roland James - DB
Cedric Jones - WR
Ronnie Lippett - DB
Fred Marion - DB
Trevor Matich - C
Larry McGrew - LB
Rod McSwain - DB
Steve Moore - T
Stanley Morgan - WR
Guy Morriss - C
Steve Nelson - LB
Dennis Owens - NT
Gene Profit - DB
Tom Ramsey - QB
Johnny Rembert - LB
Ed Reynolds - LB
Mike Ruth - NT
Willie Scott - TE
Kenneth Sims - DE
Stephen Starring - WR
Mosi Tatupu - RB
Ben Thomas - DE
Andre Tippett - LB
Garin Veris - DE
Robert Weathers - RB
Clayton Weishuhn - LB
Brent Williams - DE
Derwin Williams - WR
Ed Williams - LB
Toby Williams - NT
Ron Wooten - G

1986 New Orleans

Morten Andersen - K
Sheldon Andrus - NT
Hoby Brenner - TE
Stan Brock - T
Bruce Clark - DE
Chuck Commiskey - G
Bill Contz - T
Jack Del Rio - LB
Jim Dombrowski - T
Jon Dumbauld - NT
Brad Edelman - G
Kelvin Edwards - WR
Tony Elliott - NT
Russell Gary - DB
Jumpy Geathers - DE
Antonio Gibson - DB
Daren Gilbert - T
Eugene Goodlow - WR
Mel Gray - RB
Brian Hansen - P
Herbert Harris - WR
James Haynes - LB
Bobby Hebert - QB
Joel Hilgenberg - C
Dalton Hilliard - RB
Milford Hodge - DE
Rickey Jackson - LB
Van Jakes - DB
Bobby Johnson - DB
Vaughan Johnson - LB
Mike Jones - WR
Buford Jordan - RB
Joe Kohlbrand - LB
Steve Korte - C
Babe Laufenberg - QB
Eric Martin - WR
Brett Maxie - DB
Rueben Mayes - RB
Dana McLemore - DB
Casey Merrill - DE
Sam Mills - LB
Johnnie Poe - DB
Glen Redd - LB
Pat Saindon - G
Pat Swilling - LB
John Tice - TE
Alvin Toles - LB
Willie Tullis - DB
Frank Warren - DE
Frank Wattelet - DB
Dave Waymer - DB
Jim Wilks - DE
John Williams - RB
Ralph Williams - G
Dave Wilson - QB
Wayne Wilson - RB

1986 NY Giants

Raul Allegre - K
Ottis Anderson - RB
Billy Ard - G
Carl Banks - LB
Mark Bavaro - TE

Brad Benson - T
Jim Burt - NT
Harry Carson - LB
Maurice Carthon - RB
Mark Collins - DB
Joe Cooper - K
Eric Dorsey - DE
Tom Flynn - DB
Tony Galbreath - RB
Chris Godfrey - G
Andy Headen - LB
Kenny Hill - DB
Jeff Hostetler - QB
Erik Howard - NT
Byron Hunt - LB
Bobby Johnson - WR
Damian Johnson - T
Pepper Johnson - LB
Brian Johnston - C
Robbie Jones - LB
Terry Kinard - DB
Sean Landeta - P
Greg Lasker - DB
Lionel Manuel - WR
Leonard Marshall - DE
George Martin - DE
Phil McConkey - WR
Solomon Miller - WR
Joe Morris - RB
Zeke Mowatt - TE
Karl Nelson - T
Bart Oates - C
Elvis Patterson - DB
Gary Reasons - LB
William Roberts - T
Stacy Robinson - WR
Lee Rouson - RB
Jeff Rutledge - QB
Jerome Sally - NT
Phil Simms - QB
Lawrence Taylor - LB
Bob Thomas - K
Vince Warren - WR
John Washington - DE
Herb Welch - DB
Perry Williams - DB

1986 NY Jets

Dan Alexander - G
Rogers Alexander - LB
Bill Bain - T
Tom Baldwin - DT
Ted Banker - G
Marion Barber - RB
Barry Bennett - DE
Troy Benson - LB
Guy Bingham - C
Dennis Bligen - RB
Russell Carter - DB
Kyle Clifton - LB
Bob Crable - LB
Robert Ducksworth - DB
Nuu Faaola - RB
Joe Fields - C
Jerome Foster - DE
Elvis Franks - DE
Mark Gastineau - DE
Kerry Glenn - DB
Billy Griggs - TE
Rusty Guilbeau - LB
Mike Haight - G
Harry Hamilton - DB
Michael Harper - WR
Johnny Hector - RB
Jerry Holmes - DB
Carl Howard - DB
Bobby Humphery - DB
Charles Jackson - LB
Dave Jennings - P
Gordon King - T
Joe Klecko - DT
Rocky Klever - TE
Pat Leahy - K
Lester Lyles - DB
Johnny Lynn - DB
Marty Lyons - DE
Kevin McArthur - LB
Reggie McElroy - T
Freeman McNeil - RB
Lance Mehl - LB
Rich Miano - DB
Matt Monger - LB
Derland Moore - DT
Davlin Mullen - DB
Ken O'Brien - QB
Tony Paige - RB
Ben Rudolph - DE
Pat Ryan - QB
Mickey Shuler - TE
Kurt Sohn - WR
Jim Stuckey - DE
Jim Sweeney - T
Al Toon - WR
Jo-Jo Townsell - WR
Wesley Walker - WR

1986 Philadelphia

Ron Baker - G
Mike Black - T
Greg Brown - DE
Keith Byars - RB
Matt Cavanaugh - QB
Ken Clarke - DT

Garry Cobb - LB
Joe Conwell - T
Evan Cooper - DB
Charles Crawford - RB
Randall Cunningham - QB
Byron Darby - TE
Matt Darwin - C
Bobby Duckworth - WR
Gerry Feehery - C
Elbert Foules - DB
William Frizzell - DB
Gregg Garrity - WR
Russell Gary - DB
Jim Gilmore - G
Michael Haddix - RB
Nick Haden - G
Terry Hoage - DB
Wes Hopkins - DB
Kenny Jackson - WR
Ron Jaworski - QB
Tom Jelesky - T
Dwayne Jiles - LB
Alonzo Johnson - LB
Ron Johnson - WR
Seth Joyner - LB
Rich Kraynak - LB
Bob Landsee - G
Byron Lee - LB
Dave Little - TE
Paul McFadden - K
Leonard Mitchell - T
Mike Quick - WR
Ken Reeves - T
Mike Reichenbach - LB
Adam Schreiber - G
Jody Schulz - LB
Clyde Simmons - DT
Reggie Singletary - G
Phil Smith - WR
John Spagnola - TE
Thomas Strauthers - DT
Junior Tautalatasi - RB
John Teltschik - P
Anthony Toney - RB
Jeff Tupper - DE
Andre Waters - DB
Mike Waters - RB
Reggie White - DE
Brenard Wilson - DB
Roynell Young - DB

1986 Pittsburgh

Walter Abercrombie - RB
Gary Anderson - K
Mark Behning - T
Bubby Brister - QB
Jessie Britt - WR
Scott Campbell - QB
Gregg Carr - LB
Harvey Clayton - DB
Robin Cole - LB
Gary Dunn - NT
Dave Edwards - DB
Donnie Elder - DB
Rich Erenberg - RB
Keith Gary - DE
Preston Gothard - TE
Anthony Henton - LB
Bryan Hinkle - LB
David Hughes - RB
Tunch Ilkin - T
Earnest Jackson - RB
Louis Lipps - WR
David Little - LB
Terry Long - G
Mark Malone - QB
Mike Merriweather - LB
Ed Nelson - DE
Harry Newsome - P
Ray Pinney - T
Frank Pollard - RB
Randy Rasmussen - C
Dan Reeder - RB
John Rienstra - G
Pete Rostosky - T
Lupe Sanchez - DB
Chuck Sanders - RB
Warren Seitz - TE
Chris Sheffield - DB
Donnie Shell - DB
Darryl Sims - DE
John Stallworth - WR
Larry Station - LB
John Swain - DB
Calvin Sweeney - WR
Weegie Thompson - WR
Dan Turk - C
Mike Webster - C
Eric Williams - DB
Gerald Williams - NT
Keith Willis - DE
Dennis Winston - LB
Craig Wolfley - G
Rick Woods - DB

1986 St. Louis

Ottis Anderson - RB
Evan Arapostathis - P
Kent Austin - QB
Charles Baker - LB
Al Baker - DE
Anthony Bell - LB

Cap Boso - TE
Joe Bostic - G
Ray Brown - T
Carl Carter - DB
Greg Cater - P
Gene Chilton - C
Randy Clark - C
Bob Clasby - DE
Doug Dawson - G
Rick DiBernardo - LB
Mark Duda - NT
Gary Dulin - DE
Earl Ferrell - RB
Chas Fox - WR
David Galloway - NT
Roy Green - WR
Scott Holman - WR
Don Holmes - WR
Van Hughes - DE
Bobby Johnson - DB
Troy Johnson - WR
E. J. Junior - LB
Derek Kennard - G
Greg LaFleur - TE
John Lee - K
Neil Lomax - QB
Cedric Mack - DB
Doug Marsh - TE
Stafford Mays - DE
Stump Mitchell - RB
Ron Monaco - LB
Niko Noga - LB
Jay Novacek - TE
Freddie Joe Nunn - LB
Tootie Robbins - T
Mike Ruether - C
Broderick Sargent - RB
Eric Schubert - K
Luis Sharpe - T
Vai Sikahema - RB
J. T. Smith - WR
Lance Smith - T
Leonard Smith - DB
Wayne Smith - DB
Robert Stallings - TE
Cliff Stoudt - QB
Eric Swanson - WR
Dennis Thurman - DB
Pat Tilley - WR
Lionel Washington - DB
Ron Wolfley - RB
Lonnie Young - DB

1986 San Diego

Curtis Adams - RB
Ty Allert - LB
Gary Anderson - RB
Rolf Benirschke - K
Thomas Benson - LB
Donald Brown - DB
Gill Byrd - DB
Wes Chandler - WR
Sam Claphan - T
Jeffery Dale - DB
Ken Dallafior - G
Wayne Davis - DB
Curt DiGiacomo - G
Mike Douglass - LB
Chuck Ehin - NT
Mark Fellows - LB
James FitzPatrick - T
Tom Flick - QB
Dan Fouts - QB
Vencie Glenn - DB
Dee Hardison - DE
Andy Hawkins - LB
Mark Herrmann - QB
Pete Holohan - TE
Daniel Hunter - DB
Lionel James - RB
Trumaine Johnson - WR
Charlie Joiner - WR
Gary Kowalski - G
Jim Lachey - T
Jim Leonard - C
Woodrow Lowe - LB
Don Macek - C
David Martin - DB
Bruce Mathison - QB
Buford McGee - RB
Dennis McKnight - C
Ralf Mojsiejenko - P
Mack Moore - DE
Derrie Nelson - LB
Leslie O'Neal - DE
Gary Plummer - LB
Fred Robinson - LB
Eric Sievers - TE
Billy Ray Smith Jr. - LB
Angelo Snipes - LB
Tim Spencer - RB
John Sullivan - DB
Ken Taylor - DB
Terry Unrein - NT
Jeff Walker - G
Danny Walters - DB
Timmie Ware - WR
Lee Williams - DE
Lester Williams - NT
Earl Wilson - DE
Kellen Winslow - TE
Blaise Winter - DE
Kevin Wyatt - DB

1986 San Francisco

John Ayers - G
Dwaine Board - DE
Michael Carter - NT
Tony Cherry - RB
Dwight Clark - WR
Bruce Collie - T
Tom Cousineau - LB
Roger Craig - RB
Derrick Crawford - WR
Joe Cribbs - RB
Randy Cross - G
Michael Durrette - G
Riki Ellison - LB
Jim Fahnhorst - LB
Keith Fahnhorst - T
Ron Ferrari - LB
Russ Francis - TE
John Frank - TE
Jeff Fuller - DB
Don Griffin - DB
Charles Haley - DE
Derrick Harmon - RB
Dennis Harrison - DT
John Harty - DE
Tom Holmoe - DB
Jeff Kemp - QB
Pete Kugler - NT
Ronnie Lott - DB
Ken Margerum - WR
Milt McColl - LB
Guy McIntyre - G
Tim McKyer - DB
Dana McLemore - DB
Carl Monroe - RB
Joe Montana - QB
Mike Moroski - QB
Tory Nixon - DB
Bubba Paris - T
Fred Quillan - C
Tom Rathman - RB
Jerry Rice - WR
Bill Ring - RB
Larry Roberts - DE
Doug Rogers - DE
Max Runager - P
Todd Shell - LB
Jeff Stover - DE
Jim Stuckey - DE
Manu Tuiasosopo - NT
Keena Turner - LB
Wendell Tyler - RB
Steve Wallace - T
Michael Walter - LB
Ray Wersching - K
Carlton Williamson - DB
Mike Wilson - WR
Eric Wright - DB

1986 Seattle

Eddie Anderson - DB
Edwin Bailey - G
Jon Borchardt - G
Dave Brown - DB
Jeff Bryant - DE
Blair Bush - C
Keith Butler - LB
Ray Butler - WR
Bob Cryder - T
Kenny Easley - DB
Bobby Joe Edmonds - RB
Randy Edwards - DE
Byron Franklin - WR
Greg Gaines - LB
Vince Gamache - P
Gale Gilbert - QB
Will Grant - C
Jacob Green - DE
Gordon Hudson - TE
Patrick Hunter - DB
Glenn Hyde - C
Michael Jackson - LB
Gregg Johnson - DB
Norm Johnson - K
Kerry Justin - DB
John Kaiser - LB
Kani Kauahi - C
Reggie Kinlaw - NT
Dave Krieg - QB
Eric Lane - RB
Steve Largent - WR
Jim Laughton - TE
Ron Mattes - T
Sam Merriman - LB
Bryan Millard - G
Alonzo Mitz - DE
Randall Morris - RB
Paul Moyer - DB
Joe Nash - NT
Eugene Robinson - DB
Bruce Scholtz - LB
Curt Singer - T
Paul Skansi - WR
Terry Taylor - DB
Mike Tice - TE
Daryl Turner - WR
Byron Walker - WR
Curt Warner - RB
John L. Williams - RB
Mike Wilson - T
Fredd Young - LB

1986 Tampa Bay

Greg Allen - RB
Jerry Bell - TE
Dennis Biigen - RB
Mack Boatner - RB
Scot Brantley - LB
Keith Browner - LB
John Cannon - DE
Gerald Carter - WR
Jeremiah Castille - DB
Craig Curry - DB
Jeff Davis - LB
Steve DeBerg - QB
K. D. Dunn - TE
Ricky Easmon - DB
Sean Farrell - G
Pat Franklin - RB
Phil Freeman - WR
Bobby Futrell - DB
Frank Garcia - P
Jimmie Giles - TE
Willie Gillespie - WR
Randy Grimes - C
Leonard Harris - WR
Vince Heflin - WR
Ron Heller - T
Ron Holmes - DE
Kevin House - WR
Bobby Howard - RB
Donald Igwebuike - K
Rod Jones - DB
Kevin Kellin - DE
Tyrone Keys - DE
David Logan - NT
J. D. Maarleveld - T
Calvin Magee - TE
Rick Mallory - G
Vito McKeever - DB
Karl Morgan - NT
Kevin Murphy - LB
Bob Nelson - NT
Marvin Powell - T
Ervin Randle - LB
Greg Robinson - T
Jeff Spek - LB
Ron Springs - RB
Ivory Sully - DB
Craig Swoope - DB
Rob Taylor - T
Jackie Walker - LB
Kevin Walker - DB
Chris Washington - LB
James Wilder - RB
David Williams - WR
Nathan Wonsley - RB
George Yarno - G
Steve Young - QB

1986 Washington

Jess Atkinson - K
Rick Badanjek - RB
Tom Beasley - DE
Jeff Bostic - C
Todd Bowles - DB
Reggie Branch - RB
Kelvin Bryant - RB
Shawn Burks - LB
Dave Butz - DT
Gary Clark - WR
Ken Coffey - DB
Monte Coleman - LB
Steve Cox - P
Calvin Daniels - LB
Vernon Dean - DB
Clint Didier - TE
Todd Frain - TE
Dwight Garner - RB
Darryl Grant - DT
Darrell Green - DB
Keith Griffin - RB
Russ Grimm - G
Dean Hamel - DT
Steve Hamilton - DE
Derek Holloway - WR
Joe Jacoby - T
Ken Jenkins - RB
Anthony Jones - TE
Curtis Jordan - DB
Mel Kaufman - LB
Markus Koch - DE
Joe Krakoski - LB
Dexter Manley - DE
Charles Mann - DE
Mark May - T
Raleigh McKenzie - G
Dan McQuaid - T
Rich Milot - LB
Art Monk - WR
Tim Morrison - DB
Mark Moseley - K
James Noble - WR
Neal Olkewicz - LB
Terry Orr - TE
Jeff Paine - LB
George Rogers - RB
Ricky Sanders - RB
Jay Schroeder - QB
Angelo Snipes - LB
R.C. Thielemann - G
Ron Tilton - G
Clarence Verdin - WR
Alvin Walton - DB
Don Warren - TE
Barry Wilburn - DB
Doug Williams - QB
Eric Yarber - WR
Max Zendejas - K

1987 Atlanta

David Archer - QB
Rick Badanjek - RB
Stacey Bailey - WR
Doug Barnett - C
Milton Barney - WR
Louis Berry - P
Dwight Bingham - DE
Ken Bowen - LB
Jim Britt - DB
Aaron Brown - LB
Charlie Brown - WR
Greg Brown - DE
Rick Bryan - DE
Jerry Butler - RB
Bobby Butler - DB
Sylvester Byrd - TE
Scott Campbell - QB
Scott Case - DB
Tony Casillas - NT
Wendell Cason - DB
Bret Clark - DB
Randy Clark - G
Joe Costello - LB
Arthur Cox - TE
David Croudip - DB
Buddy Curry - LB
Greg Davis - K
Floyd Dixon - WR
Rick Donnelly - P
Jamie Dukes - G
Larry Emery - RB
John Evans - TE
Major Everett - RB
Kenny Flowers - RB
Bill Fralic - T
Mike Gann - DE
Leon Gonzalez - WR
Tim Gordon - DB
Norm Granger - RB
Paul Gray - LB
Tim Green - LB
Steve Griffin - WR
Steve Griffin - WR
James Hall - LB
Kwante Hampton - WR
Dennis Harrison - DE
Jim Hendley - C
Charles Huff - DB
Lawrence Jackson - G
Billy Johnson - WR
Lyndell Jones - DB
John Kamana - RB
Mike Kenn - T
Jeff Kiewel - G
Leander Knight - DB
Erik Kramer - QB
Rich Kraynak - LB
Jim Laughlin - LB
Mick Luckhurst - K
Mike Lush - DB
Doug Mackie - T
Aubrey Matthews - WR
Joe McIntosh - RB
Ron Middleton - TE
Brett Miller - T
Chris Miller - QB
Leonard Mitchell - T
Buddy Moor - DE
Robert Moore - DB
Dwaine Morris - DE
Gary Moss - DB
Mark Mraz - DE
Jerome Norris - DB
Darryl Oliver - RB
Shelley Poole - RB
Art Price - LB
Andrew Provence - DE
Greg Quick - G
John Rade - LB
Wayne Radloff - C
Michael Reid - LB
Gerald Riggs - RB
Don Robinson - T
Pat Saindon - G
John Scully - G
John Settle - RB
Dan Sharp - TE
Elbert Shelley - DB
James Shibest - WR
Struggy Smith - DB
Herb Spencer - LB
Sylvester Stamps - RB
John Starnes - P
Mark Studaway - DE
Lenny Taylor - WR
Leon Thomasson - DB
Jessie Tuggle - LB
Jimmy Turner - DB
Jeff Van Raaphorst - QB
Emanuel Weaver - NT
Ken Whisenhunt - TE
Eric Wiegand - C
Reggie Wilkes - LB
Joel Williams - LB
Michael Williams - RB
Brenard Wilson - DB
Leonard Wingate - DE
Mitchell Young - DT
Geno Zimmerlink - TE

1987 Buffalo

Ira Albright - NT
John Armstrong - DB
Veno Belk - TE
Greg Bell - RB
Cornelius Bennett - LB
Ray Bentley - LB
Gerald Bess - DB
Joe Bock - C
Jack Bravyak - DE
Walter Broughton - WR
Tony Brown - T
Marc Brown - WR
Chris Burkett - WR
Derrick Burroughs - DB
Leonard Burton - T
Reggie Bynum - WR
Carl Byrum - RB
Bill Callahan - DB
Arnold Campbell - DE
Joe Chetti - RB
Steve Clark - DB
Will Cokeley - LB
Shane Conlan - LB
Wayne Davis - DB
Joe Devlin - T
Sean Dowling - T
Dwight Drane - DB
Mike Estep - G
Mitch Frerotte - G
Larry Friday - DB
Tony Furjanic - LB
Sheldon Gaines - WR
Scott Garnett - DE
Will Grant - C
Kris Haines - WR
Ronnie Harmon - RB
Scott Hernandez - NT
Kent Hull - C
Lawrence Johnson - DB
Trumaine Johnson - WR
Mike Jones - LB
John Kaiser - LB
Jim Kelly - QB
Mark Kelso - DB
John Kidd - P
Bruce King - RB
Kevin Lamar - G
Bob LeBlanc - LB
John Lewis - DB
Adam Lingner - C
Warren Loving - RB
Steve Maidlow - LB
Dan Manucci - QB
David Martin - DB
Eugene Marve - LB
Brian McClure - QB
Thad McFadden - WR
Joe McGrail - NT
Keith McKeller - TE
Sean McNanie - DE
Bruce Mesner - NT
Pete Metzelaars - TE
Mark Miller - QB
Roland Mitchell - DB
Jamie Mueller - RB
Scott Norwood - K
Chip Nuzzo - DB
Nate Odomes - DB
Mike Panepinto - RB
Kerry Parker - DB
Rick Partridge - P
Mark Pike - LB
Ron Pitts - DB
Kerry Porter - RB
Rick Porter - RB
Dean Prater - DE
Scott Radecic - LB
Andre Reed - WR
Robb Riddick - RB
Jim Ritcher - G
Butch Rolle - TE
Durwood Roquemore - DB
Erik Rosenmeier - C
Scott Schankweiler - LB
Todd Schlopy - K
Rick Schulte - G
Leon Seals - DE
Johnny Shepherd - RB
Mark Shupe - C
Joe Silipo - C
Fred Smerlas - NT
Bruce Smith - DE
Don Sommer - T
Darryl Talley - LB
Steve Tasker - WR
Richard Tharpe - DE
Willie Totten - QB
Mark Traynowicz - G
Tim Vogler - G
Mark Walczak - TE
Craig Walls - LB
Scott Watters - LB
Al Wenglikowski - LB
Gary Wilkins - TE
Leonard Williams - RB
Billy Witt - DE
Will Wolford - T

1987 Chi. Bears

John Adickes - C
Egypt Allen - DB
Jim Althoff - DT
Neal Anderson - RB
John Arp - T
Tommy Barnhardt - P
Kurt Becker - G
Bobby Bell - LB
Todd Bell - DB
Todd Black - WR
Paul Blair - T
Mark Bortz - G
Cap Boso - TE
Sam Bowers - TE
Steve Bradley - QB
Chris Brewer - RB
Kevin Brown - P
Kevin Butler - K
Dick Chapura - DT
Darryl Clark - RB
Jim Covert - T
Richard Dent - DE
Maurice Douglass - DB
George Duarte - DB
Dave Duerson - DB
Gary Fencik - DB
Greg Fitzgerald - DT
Doug Flutie - QB
Willie Gault - WR
Shaun Gayle - DB
Dennis Gentry - WR
Brian Glasgow - TE
Dan Hampton - DE
Jim Harbaugh - QB
Al Harris - LB
Chuck Harris - T
Frank Harris - RB
Lakei Heimuli - RB
Jay Hilgenberg - C
Mike Hintz - DB
Mike Hohensee - QB
Leonard Jackson - DE
Vestee Jackson - DB
Mike January - LB
Eric Jeffries - DB
Brent Johnson - C
Herbert Johnson - WR
Will Johnson - LB
Don Kindt - TE
Ken Knapczyk - WR
Glen Kozlowski - WR
Tim Lashar - K
Lorenzo Lynch - DB
Wilber Marshall - LB
Bruce McCray - DB
Sean McInerney - DT
Dennis McKinnon - WR
Jim McMahon - QB
Steve McMichael - DT
Paul Migliazzo - LB
Eldridge Milton - LB
Emery Moorehead - TE
Raymond Morris - LB
Ron Morris - WR
Jim Morrissey - LB
Anthony Mosley - RB
Gary Mullen - WR
Jon Norris - DE
Jay Norvell - LB
Jack Oliver - T
Keith Ortego - WR
Sean Payton - QB
Walter Payton - RB
William Perry - DT
Reggie Phillips - DB
Mike Richardson - DB
Stuart Rindy - G
Ron Rivera - LB
Garland Rivers - DB
Mark Rodenhauser - C
Jon Roehlk - G
Doug Rothschild - LB
Eugene Rowell - DT
Thomas Sanders - RB
Mike Singletary - LB
Sean Smith - DE
Mike Stoops - DB
Matt Suhey - RB
Guy Teafatiller - DT
Tom Thayer - G
Calvin Thomas - RB
Mike Tomczak - QB
Steve Trimble - DB
Keith Van Horne - T
Bryan Wagner - P
Lawrence White - WR
Otis Wilson - LB
John Wojciechowski - G
Al Wolden - RB

1987 Cincinnati

Doug Aronson - G
Chris Barber - DB
Leo Barker - LB
Len Bell - DB
Ben Bennett - QB
Bill Berthusen - NT
Lewis Billups - DB
Brian Blados - G
Nate Borders - DB
Ed Brady - LB
Jim Breech - K
Louis Breeden - DB
Adrian Breen - QB
James Brooks - RB
Eddie Brown - WR
Ken Brown - WR
Tom Brown - WR
Jason Buck - DE
Barney Bussey - DB
Toney Catchings - LB
Cris Collinsworth - WR
Keith Cupp - T
Kiki DeAyala - LB
David Douglas - T
James Eaddy - NT
Eddie Edwards - DE
Boomer Esiason - QB
Willie Fears - DE
Tom Flaherty - LB
John Fletcher - G
Pat Franklin - RB
David Fulcher - DB
Scott Fulhage - P
Mike Hammerstein - DE
Ira Hillary - WR
Rodney Holman - TE
Greg Horne - P
Ray Horton - DB
Gary Hunt - DB
Tim Inglis - LB
Robert Jackson - DB
Curtis Jeffries - TE
Stanford Jennings - RB
Mark Johnson - DB
Bill Johnson - RB
Eric Kattus - TE
Joe Kelly - LB
Emanuel King - LB
Larry Kinnebrew - RB
Bruce Kozerski - G
Tim Krumrie - NT
Marc Logan - RB
Massimo Manca - K
Aaron Manning - DB
Sam Manos - C
Mike Martin - WR
Skip McClendon - DE
David McCluskey - RB
Tim McGee - WR
Greg Meehan - WR
Max Montoya - G
Anthony Munoz - T
Rob Niehoff - DB
Marquis Pleasant - WR
Billy Poe - G
Bruce Reimers - T
Jeff Reinke - DE
Dan Rice - RB
Tom Richey - G
Jim Riggs - TE
Bob Riley - T
Dave Rimington - C
Dave Romasko - TE
Wade Russell - T
Turk Schonert - QB
Scott Schutt - LB
Lance Sellers - LB
Reggie Sims - TE
Jim Skow - DE
Daryl Smith - DB
Jeff Smith - DE
Ken Smith - G
Eric Thomas - DB
Mark Tigges - T
Rodney Tweet - WR
Dave Walter - QB
Joe Walter - T
David Ward - LB
Leon White - LB
Solomon Wilcots - DB
Reggie Williams - LB
Dana Wright - RB
Carl Zander - LB

1987 Cleveland

Mike Baab - C
Matt Bahr - K
Al Baker - DE
Vincent Barnett - DB
Clayton Beauford - WR
Rickey Bolden - T
Keith Bosley - T
Stephen Braggs - DB
Robert Brannon - DE
Brian Brennan - WR
Dave Butler - LB
Earnest Byner - RB
Reggie Camp - DE
James Capers - DE
Vince Carreker - DB
Alex Carter - DE
Jeff Christensen - QB
Sam Clancy - DE
Mike Crawford - RB
Tim Crawford - LB
Gary Danielson - QB
Johnny Davis - RB
Hanford Dixon - DB
Stacey Driver - RB
Brian Dudley - DB
Donnie Echols - TE
Ray Ellis - DB
Major Everett - RB
Paul Farren - T
Dan Fike - G
Herman Fontenot - RB
Brian Franco - K
Bob Golic - NT
Jeff Gossett - P
David Grayson - LB
Anthony Griggs - LB
Al Gross - DB
Rusty Guilbeau - LB
Carl Hairston - DE
Darryl Haley - T
Cliff Hannemann - LB
Mark Harper - DB
D.D. Hoggard - DB
Alvin Horn - DB
Enis Jackson - DB
Jeff Jaeger - K
Eddie Johnson - LB
Lee Johnson - P
Mike Johnson - LB
Marlon Jones - DE
Kirk Jones - RB
Mike Junkin - LB
Mike Katolin - C
Chris Kelley - TE
Perry Kemp - WR
Bernie Kosar - QB
Mike Kovaleski - LB
Mark Krerowicz - G
Reggie Langhorne - WR
Goran Lingmerth - K
Kevin Mack - RB
Tim Manoa - RB
Larry Mason - RB
Clay Matthews - LB
Gerald McNeil - WR
Nick Miller - LB
Frank Minnifield - DB
Aaron Moog - DE
Steve Nave - LB
Ozzie Newsome - TE
Mike Pagel - QB
Jerry Parker - LB
Steve Pierce - WR
Tom Polley - LB
Dave Puzzuoli - NT
Gregg Rakoczy - T
Cody Risien - T
Dejuan Robinson - DB
Billy Robinson - DB
Chris Rockins - DB
Mike Rusinek - NT
Lucius Sanford - LB
Darryl Sims - DE
Webster Slaughter - WR
Dave Sparenberg - G
George Swarn - RB
Mike Teifke - C
Derek Tennell - TE
Keith Tinsley - WR
Travis Tucker - TE
Ralph Van Dyke - T
David Verser - WR
Dale Walters - P
Louis Watson - WR
Remi Watson - WR
Clarence Weathers - WR
Larry Williams - G
Troy Wilson - DB
Blake Wingle - G
George Winslow - P
Frank Winters - C
Felix Wright - DB
Glen Young - WR

1987 Dallas

David Adams - RB
Vince Albritton - DB
Jimmy Armstrong - DB
Brian Baldinger - T
Gordon Banks - WR
Rod Barksdale - WR
Bill Bates - DB
Alvin Blount - RB
Rich Borresen - TE
Kerry Brady - K
Kevin Brooks - DE
Cornell Burbage - WR
Dave Burnette - T
Ron Burton - LB
Sal Cesario - G
Thornton Chandler - TE
Steve Cisowski - T
Darryl Clack - RB
Anthony Coleman - DB
Doug Cosbie - TE
Vince Courville - WR
Steve DeOssie - LB
Tony Dorsett - RB
Michael Downs - DB
Chris Duliban - LB
John Dutton - DT
Mike Dwyer - DT
Kelvin Edwards - WR
Harry Flaherty - LB
Steve Folsom - TE
Todd Fowler - RB
Ron Francis - DB
Kevin Gogan - T
Alex Green - DB
Tommy Haynes - DB
Mike Hegman - LB
Manny Hendrix - DB
Tim Hendrix - TE
Bill Hill - DB
Jeff Hurd - LB
Garth Jax - LB
Jim Jeffcoat - DE
Walt Johnson - DT
E. J. Jones - RB
Too Tall Jones - DE
Dale Jones - LB
Crawford Ker - G
Robert Lavette - RB
George Lilja - C
Bruce Livingston - DB
Eugene Lockhart - LB
Kelvin Martin - WR
Timmy Newsome - RB
Nate Newton - G
Danny Noonan - DT
Steve Pelluer - QB
Jesse Penn - LB
Ray Perkins - DE
Phil Pozderac - T
Tom Rafferty - C
Mike Renfro - WR
Jeff Rohrer - LB
Roger Ruzek - K
Buzz Sawyer - P
Mike Saxon - P
Chuck Scott - WR
Victor Scott - DB
Joe Shearin - C
Jon Shields - T
Victor Simmons - LB
Don Smerek - DT
Daryle Smith - T
Loren Snyder - QB
Sebron Spivey - WR
Russ Swan - LB
Kevin Sweeney - QB
Kirk Timmer - LB
Mark Tuinei - C
Mark Walen - DT
Gary Walker - T
Herschel Walker - RB
Everson Walls - DB
Randy Watts - DE
Gerald White - RB
Randy White - DT
Bob White - T
Danny White - QB
Robert Williams - DB
Luis Zendejas - K
Mike Zentic - C
Jeff Zimmerman - T

1987 Denver

Mitch Andrews - TE
John Ayers - G
Kevin Belcher - T
Ken Bell - RB
Keith Bishop - C
Tony Boddie - RB
Walt Bowyer - DE
Tyrone Braxton - DB
Michael Brooks - LB
Laron Brown - WR
Steve Bryan - NT
Billy Bryan - C
Scott Caldwell - RB
Jeremiah Castille - DB
Kevin Clark - DB
Mike Clendenen - K
Mark Cooper - G
Rick Dennison - LB
Kirk Dodge - LB
Joe Dudek - RB
John Elway - QB
Steve Fitzhugh - DB
Simon Fletcher - LB
Mike Freeman - G
Ralph Giacomarro - P
Freddie Gilbert - DE
Sam Graddy - WR
Mike Harden - DB
Archie Harris - G
Mark Haynes - DB
Winford Hood - G
Mike Horan - P
Stefan Humphries - G
Ricky Hunley - LB
Mark Jackson - WR
Roger Jackson - DB
Earl Johnson - DB
Vance Johnson - WR
Tim Joiner - LB
Daryll Jones - DB
David Jones - G
Leonard Jones - DB
Rulon Jones - DE
Ken Karcher - QB
Rich Karlis - K
Keith Kartz - T
Clarence Kay - TE
Bruce Klosterman - LB
Mike Knox - LB
Greg Kragen - NT
Gary Kubiak - QB
Gene Lang - RB
Ken Lanier - T
Larry Lee - G
Zeph Lee - RB
Tony Lilly - DB
Bill Lobenstein - DE
Kerry Locklin - TE
Tim Lucas - LB
Dan MacDonald - LB
Warren Marshall - RB
Rick Massie - WR
Dean May - QB
Monte McGuire - QB
Ron McLean - DE
Karl Mecklenburg - LB
Bobby Micho - RB
Orson Mobley - TE
Marc Munford - LB

Ricky Nattiel - WR
Russell Payne - TE
Jack Peavey - C
Lyle Pickens - DB
Bruce Plummer - DB
Nathan Poole - RB
Dan Remsberg - T
Randy Robbins - DB
Martin Rudolph - DB
Darryl Russell - DB
Jim Ryan - LB
Steven Sewell - RB
Dennis Smith - DB
Matt Smith - LB
Dave Studdard - T
Shane Swanson - WR
Bob Thompson - WR
Andre Townsend - DE
Jeff Tupper - NT
Steve Watson - WR
Gerald Willhite - RB
Steve Wilson - DB
Sammy Winder - RB
Bryant Winn - LB
Ray Woodard - DE

1987 Detroit

Earnest Adams - LB
Jim Arnold - P
Steve Baack - G
Jerry Ball - NT
Scott Barrows - G
Bob Beemer - DE
Charles Benson - DE
Karl Bernard - RB
Mike Black - P
Carl Bland - WR
Steve Boadway - LB
John Bostic - DB
Tom Boyd - LB
Danny Bradley - WR
Lomas Brown - T
Paul Butcher - LB
Patrick Cain - C
Carl Carr - LB
Jeff Chadwick - WR
Raphel Cherry - DB
Dexter Clark - DB
Mike Cofer - LB
Jerome Davis - NT
Jerry Diorio - TE
Tony Dollinger - RB
Keith Dorney - G
Stan Edwards - RB
Gary Ellerson - RB
Russell Erxleben - P
Creig Federico - DB
Joe Felton - G
Keith Ferguson - DE
Anthony Fields - DB
Brendan Folmar - QB
Duane Galloway - DB
Bill Gay - DE
Chris Geile - G
Dennis Gibson - LB
Jimmie Giles - TE
Kevin Glover - C
William Graham - DB
Curtis Green - DE
James Griffin - DB
Darrell Grymes - WR
Alvin Hall - DB
Maurice Harvey - DB
Ivan Hicks - DB
Mark Hicks - LB
Steve Hirsch - DB
Todd Hons - QB
Melvin Hoover - WR
Garry James - RB
George Jamison - LB
Gilvanni Johnson - WR
Rick Johnson - T
James Jones - RB
Vyto Kab - TE
Jeff Kacmarek - NT
Angelo King - LB
Matt Kinzer - P
Paul Kiser - G
Nick Kowgios - RB
Gary Lee - WR
Mark Lewis - TE
Danny Lockett - LB
Chuck Long - QB
Pete Mandley - WR
Vernon Maxwell - LB
Bob McDonough - DB
George McDuffie - DE
Bruce McNorton - DB
Joe Milinichik - G
John Misko - P
Steve Mott - C
Eddie Murray - K
Mark Nichols - WR
Tony Office - LB
Greg Orton - G
Tony Paige - RB
Mike Prindle - K
Jerry Quaerna - T
Derrick Ramsey - TE
Shelton Robinson - LB
Reggie Rogers - DE
Tim Ross - LB
Rob Rubick - TE
Dan Saleaumua - NT
Harvey Salem - G
Eric Sanders - T
Chris Sheffield - DB
Ricky Smith - WR
Chuck Steele - C
Rich Strenger - T
Ivory Sully - DB
Robert Thompson - LB
Stuart Tolle - NT
Eric Truvillion - WR
Jim Warne - T
Bobby Watkins - DB
Cleve Wester - RB
Mark Wheeler - TE
Scott Williams - RB
Eric Williams - NT
Eric Williams - DB
Jimmy Williams - LB
Mark Witte - TE
Butch Woolfolk - RB

1987 Green Bay

Aric Anderson - LB
John Anderson - LB
Todd Auer - LB
Warren Bone - LB
Jerry Boyarsky - NT
Don Bracken - P
Dave Brown - DB
Robert Brown - DE
Ross Browner - DE
David Caldwell - NT
Mark Cannon - C
Alphonso Carreker - DE
Paul Ott Carruth - RB
Bill Cherry - C
Putt Choate - LB
Jessie Clark - RB
Steve Collier - T
Chuck Compton - DB
Kelly Cook - RB
Kenneth Davis - RB
Al Del Greco - K
Burnell Dent - LB
John Dorsey - LB
Jeff Drost - NT
Tony Elliott - DB
Phil Epps - WR
Mike Estep - G
Kevin Fitzgerald - TE
Brent Fullwood - RB
Willie Gillus - QB
George Greene - DB
Bob Gruber - T
Joey Hackett - TE
Ron Hallstrom - G
Derrick Harden - WR
Jim Hargrove - RB
Tim Harris - LB
Anthony Harrison - DB
Perry Hartnett - G
Jim Hobbins - G
Johnny Holland - LB
Tony Hunter - RB
Craig Jay - TE
Norman Jefferson - DB
Greg Jensen - G
Ezra Johnson - DE
Kenneth Johnson - DB
Ken Jordan - LB
David King - DB
Don King - DB
Ed Konopasek - T
Mark Lee - DB
Tony Leiker - DE
Mark Lewis - TE
David Logan - NT
Don Majkowski - QB
Rydell Malancon - LB
Chris Mandeville - DB
Von Mansfield - DB
Charles Martin - DE
Stan Mataele - LB
John McGarry - G
Sylvester McGrew - DE
James Melka - LB
Jim Meyer - T
John Miller - LB
Ron Monaco - LB
Brent Moore - LB
Rich Moran - C
Larry Morris - RB
Jim Bob Morris - DB
Lee Morris - WR
Mark Murphy - DB
Frankie Neal - WR
Tom Neville - T
Brian Noble - LB
Freddie Parker - RB
Keith Paskett - WR
John Pointer - LB
Vince Rafferty - C
Lou Rash - DB
Corn Redick - WR
Bill Renner - P
Alan Risher - QB
Tommy Robison - G
Ken Ruettgers - T
Patrick Scott - WR
Travis Simpson - C
Wes Smith - WR
Walter Stanley - WR
Scott Stephen - LB
John Sterling - RB
Ken Stills - DB
Carl Sullivan - DE
Don Summers - TE
Lavale Thomas - RB
Keith Uecker - G
Alan Veingrad - T
Vince Villanucci - NT
Calvin Wallace - DE
Chuck Washington - DB
Mike Weddington - LB
Lee Weigel - RB
Clayton Weishuhn - LB
Ed West - TE
Kevin Willhite - RB
Randy Wright - QB
Max Zendejas - K

1987 Houston

Robert Abraham - LB
Earl Allen - DB
Patrick Allen - DB
Jesse Baker - DE
Craig Birdsong - DB
Keith Bostic - DB
Scott Boucher - T
Tom Briehl - LB
Sonny Brown - DB
Steve Brown - DB
Domingo Bryant - DB
Richard Byrd - DE
Toby Caston - LB
Ray Childress - DE
Charles Clinton - DB
Eric Cobble - RB
Rayford Cooks - DE
Chris Darrington - WR
Mitch Daum - TE
Bruce Davis - T
John Davis - T
John Diettrich - K
Joe Dixon - NT
Jeff Donaldson - DB
Willie Drewrey - WR
Curtis Duncan - WR
Bo Eason - DB
Scott Eccles - TE
Eric Fairs - LB
Scott Fox - LB
Jerrell Franklin - T
William Fuller - DE
Mark Gehring - TE
Ernest Givins - WR
Mike Golic - NT
Jeff Gossett - P
John Grimsley - LB
Leonard Harris - WR
Alonzo Highsmith - RB
Drew Hill - WR
Kent Hill - G
Herman Hunter - RB
Andrew Jackson - RB
Arrike James - TE
Thad Jefferson - LB
Haywood Jeffires - WR
Byron Johnson - LB
Kenny Johnson - DB
Lee Johnson - P
Richard Johnson - DB
Walter Johnson - LB
Larry Joyner - DB
Kurt Kafentzis - DB
Doug Kellermeyer - T
Mike Kelley - G
Billy Kidd - C
Eric Larkin - DE
Allen Lyday - DB
Robert Lyles - LB
Charles Martin - NT
Bruce Matthews - T
Keith McDonald - WR
Audray McMillian - DB
Johnny Meads - LB
Clay Miller - T
Warren Moon - QB
Ricky Moore - RB
Mike Munchak - G
Kenny Neil - DE
Tony Newsom - DB
Bob Otto - DE
Jeff Parks - TE
Brent Pease - QB
Jay Pennison - C
Brett Petersmark - G
Barry Pettyjohn - T
Allen Pinkett - RB
Mike Rozier - RB
Eugene Seale - LB
Donovan Small - DB
Al Smith - LB
Doug Smith - NT
Larry Smith - LB
Dean Steinkuhler - T
Vince Stroth - T
Steve Superick - P
Emmuel Thompson - DB
Spencer Tillman - RB
Dwain Turner - NT
Ira Valentine - RB
Paul Vogel - LB
Ray Wallace - RB
Joey Walters - WR
Bucky White - DB
Doug Williams - T
Jamie Williams - TE
Oliver Williams - WR
Almon Young - G
Tony Zendejas - K

1987 Indianapolis

Sid Abramowitz - T
Dave Ahrens - LB
Harvey Armstrong - NT
Pat Ballage - DB
Chuck Banks - RB
Roy Banks - WR
Pat Beach - TE
Mark Bellini - WR
Bill Benjamin - LB
Albert Bentley - RB
Dean Biasucci - K
Duane Bickett - LB
Mark Boggs - T
Matt Bouza - WR
Mark Boyer - TE
John Brandes - TE
Bill Brooks - WR
Bob Brotzki - T
Gordon Brown - RB
Steve Bryant - WR
Brian Bulluck - LB
Kevin Call - T
Milt Carthens - T
Mel Carver - RB
Ricky Chatman - LB
Leonard Coleman - DB
Craig Colquitt - P
Johnie Cooks - LB
Jeff Criswell - G
Craig Curry - DB
Eugene Daniel - DB
Kenny Daniel - DB
Byron Darby - DE
Lee Davis - DB
Eric Dickerson - RB
Randy Dixon - T
Ray Donaldson - C
Bill Elko - NT
Jitter Fields - DB
Nesby Glasgow - DB
Chris Goode - DB
Marsharne Graves - T
Ed Grimsley - LB
Bob Hamm - DE
Kevin Hancock - LB
Jon Hand - DE
Greg Hawthorne - WR
Shawn Heffern - T
Chris Hinton - G
Gary Hogeboom - QB
John Holt - DB
Marcus Jackson - NT
June James - LB
Kelley Johnson - WR
Bryant Jones - DB
Joe Jones - TE
Steve Jordan - K
Tim Kearse - WR
Scott Kellar - NT
Blair Kiel - QB
Steve Knight - G
Barry Krauss - LB
Jeff Leiding - LB
Keith Lester - TE
Orlando Lowry - LB
Frank Mattiace - NT
Chris McLemore - RB
Jim Merritts - NT
Walter Murray - WR
James Noble - WR
Terry Nugent - QB
Cliff Odom - LB
Bob Ontko - LB
Gary Padjen - LB
Joel Patten - T
Jim Perryman - DB
Ron Plantz - C
Mike Prior - DB
Roger Remo - LB
Freddie Robinson - DB
Brad Saar - LB
Sean Salisbury - QB
Jerome Sally - NT
Chris Scott - DE
Tim Sherwin - TE
John Simmons - DB
Pat Snyder - C
Ron Solt - G
Rohn Stark - P
Craig Swoope - DB
Donnell Thompson - DE
Don Thorp - NT
Jack Trudeau - QB
Willie Tullis - DB
Ben Utt - G
Mark Walczak - TE
John Williams - RB
George Wonsley - RB
Terry Wright - DB

1987 Kansas City

Bill Acker - NT
Mark Adickes - G
Kevin Adkins - C
John Alt - T
Walt Arnold - TE
Gary Baldinger - NT
Rich Baldinger - G
Tom Baugh - C
Mike Bell - DE
James Black - T
Todd Blackledge - QB
Eric Brown - WR
Trent Bryant - DB
Lloyd Burruss - DB
Carlos Carson - WR
Deron Cherry - DB
Mike Clemons - RB
Sherman Cocroft - DB
Paul Coffman - TE
Tim Cofield - LB
Darrell Colbert - WR
Lewis Colbert - P
Jeff Colter - DB
Louis Cooper - LB
Jack Del Rio - LB
Rick Donnalley - C
Dan Doubiago - T
Cornelius Dozier - DB
Irv Eatman - T
Jack Epps - DB
Alex Espinoza - QB
Richard Estell - WR
James Evans - RB
Jeff Faulkner - NT
Jitter Fields - DB
Randy Frazier - LB
Lee Getz - G
Kelly Goodburn - P
Leonard Griffin - DE
Steve Griffin - RB
Dino Hackett - LB
James Hamrick - K
James Harrell - LB
Bob Harris - LB
James Harvey - G
Jonathan Hayes - TE
Herman Heard - RB
Greg Hill - DB
Eric Hodges - WR
Eric Holle - NT
Tony Holloway - DE
Bruce Holmes - LB
Doug Hoppock - T
Todd Howard - LB
Doug Hudson - QB
Glenn Hyde - C
Byron Ingram - C
Ken Johnson - DE
Fred Jones - LB
Rod Jones - TE
Brian Jozwiak - G
Mark Keel - TE
Bill Kenney - QB
Pete Koch - DE
Stein Koss - TE
Ken Lacy - RB
Garcia Lane - DB
Albert Lewis - DB
Chris Lindstrom - DE
Nick Lowery - K
Dave Lutz - T
Bill Maas - NT
Henry Marshall - WR
Ken McAlister - LB
David Montagne - WR
Larry Moriarty - RB
Gary Moten - LB
Lloyd Mumphrey - NT
Kenny Nash - WR
Mark Nelson - T
Ted Nelson - DB
Christian Okoye - RB
Stephone Paige - WR
Paul Palmer - RB
Robert Parker - RB
Aaron Pearson - LB
J. C. Pearson - DB
Jim Pietrzak - C
Woodie Pippens - RB
Mark Robinson - DB
Steve Rogers - T
Kevin Ross - DB
Frank Seurer - QB
Eric Smith - DB
Chris Smith - RB
Angelo Snipes - LB
Gary Spann - LB
Matt Stevens - QB
Art Still - DE
Ralph Stockemer - RB
Carlton Thomas - DB
Arland Thompson - G
John Trahan - WR
John Walker - DE
Riley Walton - TE
Ray Woodard - DE
Kevin Wyatt - DB

1987 LA Raiders

Rick Ackerman - DT
Stefon Adams - DB
Carl Aikens - WR
Marcus Allen - RB
Eddie Anderson - DB
Chris Bahr - K
Jeff Barnes - LB
Brian Belway - DE
Barry Black - G
Ron Brown - DE
Jim Browne - RB
Keith Browner - LB
Bob Buczkowski - DE
Darryl Byrd - LB
Rick Calhoun - RB
Chetti Carr - DB
Ted Chapman - DE
Todd Christensen - TE
John Clay - T
Joe Cormier - LB
Bruce Davis - T
James Davis - DB
Andy Dickerson - G
Paul Dufault - C
Craig Ellis - RB
Jim Ellis - LB
Vince Evans - QB
Ron Fellows - DB
Mervyn Fernandez - WR
Ron Foster - DB
Vince Gamache - P
John Gesek - C
Rick Goltz - DE
Darryl Goodlow - LB
Phil Grimes - DE
Charley Hannah - G
David Hardy - K
Lance Harkey - DB
Rob Harrison - DB
Frank Hawkins - RB
Mike Haynes - DB
Jessie Hester - WR
Rusty Hilger - QB
Greg Hill - DB
Rod Hill - DB
Brian Holloway - T
Ethan Horton - RB
Leonard Jackson - LB
Victor Jackson - DB
Bo Jackson - RB
Sean Jones - DE
Trey Junkin - TE
Jamie Kimmel - LB
Linden King - LB
Greg Lathan - WR
Zeph Lee - RB
Bill Lewis - G
Wade Lockett - WR
James Lofton - WR
Howie Long - DE
Rod Martin - LB
Mickey Marvin - G
Vann McElroy - DB
Reggie McKenzie - LB
Chris McLemore - RB
Dan McMillen - LB
Matt Millen - LB
Dean Miraldi - G
Don Mosebar - C
Vance Mueller - RB
Mike Noble - LB
Andy Parker - TE
Mario Perry - TE
Bill Pickel - DT
David Pyles - T
Shawn Regent - C
Chris Riehm - G
Jerry Robinson - LB
Mike Rodriguez - DT
Sam Seale - DB
Steve Smith - RB
Steve Strachan - RB
Stan Talley - P
John Tautolo - T
Malcolm Taylor - DT
Willie Teal - DB
Tony Tillmon - DB
Stacey Toran - DB
Greg Townsend - DE
Lionel Washington - DB
Ronnie Washington - LB
Dwight Wheeler - G
Ron Wheeler - TE
Bruce Wilkerson - G
Dokie Williams - WR
David Williams - WR
Demise Williams - DB
Ricky Williams - DB
Mitch Willis - DT
Marc Wilson - QB
Chris Woods - WR
Scott Woolf - QB
Steve Wright - T
Jon Zogg - G

1987 LA Rams

Sam Anno - LB
David Aupiu - LB
Greg Baty - TE
Greg Bell - RB
Kyle Borland - LB
Richard Brown - LB
Ron Brown - WR
Cullen Bryant - RB
Dan Clark - LB
Jim Collins - LB
Tom Cox - T
Nolan Cromwell - DB
Rick DiBernardo - LB
Eric Dickerson - RB
Steve Dils - QB
Reggie Doss - DE
Dennis Edwards - NT
Carl Ekern - LB
Henry Ellard - WR
Jon Embree - TE
Donald Evans - DE
Jim Everett - QB
Jon Francis - RB
Owen Gill - RB
Hank Goebel - T
Jerry Gray - DB
Kevin Greene - LB
Mike Guman - RB
Darryl Hall - DB
Dennis Harrah - G
Dale Hatcher - P
Bernard Henry - WR
Cliff Hicks - DB
David Hill - TE
Neil Hope - LB
Kevin House - WR
LeRoy Irvin - DB
Kirby Jackson - DB
Robert Jenkins - T
Mark Jerue - LB
Gary Jeter - DE
Damone Johnson - TE
Holbert Johnson - DB
Johnnie Johnson Jr. - DB
Samuel Johnson - WR
Jim Kalafat - LB
Larry Kelm - LB
Marion Knight - NT
Mike Lansford - K
Duval Love - G
Chris Matau - G
James McDonald - TE
Mike McDonald - LB
Buford McGee - RB
Greg Meisner - NT
Hugh Millen - QB
Shawn Miller - NT
Stacey Mobley - WR
Malcolm Moore - TE
Joe Murray - G
Tom Newberry - G
Vince Newsome - DB
Don Noble - TE
Mel Owens - LB
Chris Pacheco - NT
Irvin Pankey - T
Dave Purling - NT
Bernard Quarles - QB
Doug Reed - DE
Reggie Richardson - DB
Joe Rose - TE
Craig Rutledge - DB
Mike Schad - G
Greg Sinnott - T
Jackie Slater - T
Tony Slaton - C
Doug Smith - C
Phil Smith - WR
Michael Stewart - DB
Fred Stokes - DE
Mickey Sutton - DB
Tom Taylor - LB
Kelly Thomas - T
Casey Tiumalu - RB
Navy Tuiasosopo - C
Tim Tyrrell - RB
Norwood Vann - LB
Frank Wattelet - DB
Charles White - RB
Cary Whittingham - LB
Kyle Whittingham - DB
Mike Wilcher - LB
Alonzo Williams - RB
Greg Williamson - DB
Alvin Wright - NT
Mike Young - WR
Ed Zeman - DB

1987 Miami

Clarence Bailey - RB
Fred Banks - WR
Bill Bealles - T
Willie Beecher - K
Charles Bennett - DE
Woody Bennett - RB
Doug Betters - DE
Glenn Blackwood - DB
John Bosa - DE
Bud Brown - DB
Mark Brown - LB
Tom Brown - RB
Bob Brudzinski - LB
Marvell Burgess - DB
Mike Caterbone - WR
Laz Chavez - LB
Eddie Chavis - WR
Mark Clayton - WR
Greg Cleveland - T
Jackie Cline - NT
Chris Conlin - G
Ron Davenport - RB
Jeff Dellenbach - T
Mark Dennis - T
Leland Douglas - WR
Mark Duper - WR
George Farmer - WR
Todd Feldman - WR
Roy Foster - G
Dennis Fowlkes - LB
David Frye - LB
Jon Giesler - T
Jim Gilmore - G
Stacy Gore - P
Rick Graf - LB
Hugh Green - LB
Lorenzo Hampton - RB
Bruce Hardy - TE
Jeff Hayes - P
Liffort Hobley - DB

Trell Hooper - DB
Mark Irvin - DB
Rickey Isom - FB
Steve Jacobson - G
Jim Jensen - WR
Dan Johnson - TE
Demetrious Johnson - DB
William Judson - DB
Scott Kehoe - T
Greg Koch - T
Larry Kolic - LB
Mark Konecny - RB
Mike Lambrecht - NT
Paul Lankford - DB
Ronnie Lee - T
David Lewis - TE
George Little - DE
Steve Lubischer - LB
Kyle Mackey - QB
Dan Marino - QB
Doug Marrone - G
David Marshall - LB
Don McNeal - DB
Victor Morris - LB
Tony Nathan - RB
Scott Nicolas - LB
John Offerdahl - LB
Louis Oubre - G
Greg Ours - C
Tim Pidgeon - LB
James Pruitt - WR
Floyd Raglin - DB
Tate Randle - DB
Ike Readon - NT
Dameon Reilly - WR
Fuad Reveiz - K
Reggie Roby - P
Donovan Rose - DB
Pete Roth - RB
Lawrence Sampleton - TE
Duke Schamel - LB
Scott Schwedes - WR
Ronald Scott - RB
Stanley Scott - DE
Jackie Shipp - LB
Rich Siler - TE
Mike Smith - DB
Willie Smith - TE
Brian Sochia - NT
Robert Sowell - DB
Scott Stankavage - QB
Dwight Stephenson - C
Greg Storr - LB
Troy Stradford - RB
Don Strock - QB
John Swain - DB
John Tagliaferri - RB
Reyna Thompson - DB
Van Tiffin - K
Tom Toth - G
T. J. Turner - DE
Joel Williams - TE
Derek Wimberly - DE
Jeff Wiska - G

1987 Minnesota

Steve Ache - LB
Tony Adams - QB
Alfred Anderson - RB
Sam Anno - LB
Walker Lee Ashley - LB
Ray Berry - LB
Rufus Bess - DB
Don Bramlett - DT
Jim Brim - WR
Larry Brown - WR
Joey Browner - DB
Dave Bruno - P
Tim Bryant - LB
Derek Burton - T
Anthony Carter - WR
Daniel Coleman - DE
Greg Coleman - P
Fabray Collins - LB
Ron Daugherty - WR
Dale Dawson - K
Jim Dick - LB
Chris Doleman - DE
D. J. Dozier - RB
Clifton Eley - TE
David Evans - DB
Rick Fenney - RB
Steve Finch - WR
Jamie Fitzgerald - DB
Chris Foote - C
Steve Freeman - DB
Phil Frye - RB
Rich Gannon - QB
Willie Gillespie - WR
Neal Guggemos - DB
Jim Gustafson - WR
Mark Hanson - G
Sam Harrell - RB
John Harris - DB
Steve Harris - RB
Mike Hartenstine - DE
Wymon Henderson - DB
Carl Hilton - TE
Issiac Holt - DB
David Howard - LB
Dave Huffman - G
Tim Irwin - T
Hassan Jones - WR

Wayne Jones - G
Steve Jordan - TE
Keith Kidd - WR
Greg Koch - T
Tommy Kramer - QB
Terry LeCount - WR
Carl Lee - DB
Leo Lewis - WR
Fletcher Louallen - DB
Terry Love - DB
Kirk Lowdermilk - C
Mark MacDonald - G
Chris Martin - LB
Doug Martin - DE
Marc May - TE
Stafford Mays - DE
Mike McCurry - G
Phil Micech - DE
Keith Millard - DT
Larry Miller - LB
Ted Million - G
Fred Molden - DT
Leonard Moore - RB
Mike Mularkey - TE
Najee Mustafaa - DB
Pete Najarian - LB
Chuck Nelson - K
Darrin Nelson - RB
Tim Newton - DT
Tony Norman - DE
Frank Ori - G
Rickey Parks - WR
Kurt Ploeger - DT
Kelly Quinn - LB
Randy Rasmussen - C
Allen Rice - RB
Greg Richardson - WR
Gerald Robinson - DE
Ted Rosnagle - DB
John Scardina - T
Ed Schenk - TE
Randy Scott - LB
Bucky Scribner - P
Ron Selesky - G
Mike Slaton - DB
Jimmy Smith - RB
Wayne Smith - DB
Jesse Solomon - LB
Timothy Starks - DB
Joe Stepanek - DT
Scott Studwell - LB
Dennis Swilley - C
Terry Tausch - T
Andre Thomas - RB
Henry Thomas - NT
Mike Turner - DB
John Turner - DB
Adam Walker - RB
Jimmy Walker - DT
Kevin Webster - C
Brad White - DT
Brett Wilson - RB
Wade Wilson - QB
Jeff Womack - RB
Gary Zimmerman - T

1987 New England

Julius Adams - DE
Rogers Alexander - LB
Bruce Armstrong - T
Ricky Atkinson - DB
Greg Baty - TE
Frank Bianchini - RB
Mel Black - LB
Don Blackmon - LB
Bob Bleier - QB
Jim Bowman - DB
Pete Brock - C
Rich Camarillo - P
Brian Carey - WR
Raymond Clayborn - DB
Duffy Cobbs - DB
Wayne Coffey - WR
Tony Collins - RB
George Colton - T
Rico Corsetti - LB
Elgin Davis - RB
Lin Dawson - TE
Steve Doig - LB
Reggie Dupard - RB
Tony Eason - QB
Paul Fairchild - G
Sean Farrell - G
Doug Flutie - QB
Todd Frain - TE
Russ Francis - TE
Tony Franklin - K
Arnold Franklin - TE
Irving Fryar - WR
Dennis Gadbois - WR
Ernest Gibson - DB
Steve Grogan - QB
John Guzik - NT
Bruce Hansen - RB
David Hendley - DB
Alan Herline - P
Milford Hodge - NT
Darryl Holmes - DB
Craig James - RB
Roland James - DB
Cedric Jones - WR
Tim Jordan - LB
Michael LeBlanc - RB
Larry Linne - WR
Ronnie Lippett - DB

Dino Mangiero - NT
Fred Marion - DB
Trevor Matich - C
Jerry McCabe - LB
Larry McGrew - LB
Joe McHale - LB
Chuck McSwain - RB
Rod McSwain - DB
Greg Moore - LB
Steve Moore - T
Stanley Morgan - WR
Guy Morriss - C
Steve Nelson - LB
Bob Perryman - RB
Joe Peterson - DB
Clay Pickering - WR
Art Plunkett - T
Tom Porell - NT
Gene Profit - DB
Tom Ramsey - QB
Ben Reed - DE
Johnny Rembert - LB
Ed Reynolds - LB
Greg Robinson - T
Mike Ruth - NT
Frank Sacco - LB
Todd Sandham - G
Jon Sawyer - DB
Eric Schubert - K
Willie Scott - TE
Randy Sealby - LB
Ron Shegog - DB
Kenneth Sims - DE
Stephen Starring - WR
Eric Stokes - G
Mosi Tatupu - RB
Andre Tippett - LB
Bill Turner - DE
Darren Twombly - C
Garin Veris - DE
Danny Villa - T
Todd Whitten - QB
Murray Wichard - DE
Steve Wilburn - DE
Brent Williams - DE
Derwin Williams - WR
Ed Williams - LB
Perry Williams - DB
Toby Williams - NT
Carl Woods - RB
Ron Wooten - G

1987 New Orleans

Michael Adams - DB
Vincent Alexander - RB
Morten Andersen - K
Sheldon Andrus - NT
Gene Atkins - DB
Tommy Barnhardt - P
Cliff Benson - TE
Dwight Beverly - RB
Robert Brannon - DE
Hoby Brenner - TE
Stan Brock - T
James Campen - C
Bruce Clark - DE
Robert Clark - WR
Mike Cofer - K
Chuck Commiskey - G
Bill Contz - T
Toi Cook - DB
Stacey Dawsey - WR
Joe DeForest - LB
Jim Dombrowski - T
Brad Edelman - G
Tony Elliott - NT
Ted Elliott - NT
John Fourcade - QB
Keith Fourcade - LB
Jumpy Geathers - DE
Antonio Gibson - DB
Daren Gilbert - T
Darren Gottschalk - TE
Mel Gray - RB
Brian Hansen - P
Herbert Harris - WR
Vic Harrison - WR
James Haynes - LB
Bobby Hebert - QB
Joel Hilgenberg - C
Lonzell Hill - WR
Dalton Hilliard - RB
Walt Housman - T
Kevin Ingram - QB
Rickey Jackson - LB
Van Jakes - DB
Phillip James - C
Garland Jean-Batiste - RB
Nate Johnson - RB
Vaughan Johnson - LB
Mike Jones - WR
Buford Jordan - RB
Ken Kaplan - T
Florian Kempf - K
Shawn Knight - DE
Joe Kohlbrand - LB
Steve Korte - C
Scott Leach - LB
Bill Leach - G
Greg Loberg - G
Milton Mack - DB
Ken Marchiol - LB
Eric Martin - WR
Brett Maxie - DB

Rueben Mayes - RB
Larry McCoy - LB
Sam Mills - LB
Ken O'Neal - TE
Mark Pattison - WR
Johnnie Poe - DB
Tim Riordan - QB
Jeff Rodenberger - RB
Bill Roe - LB
Malcolm Scott - TE
Jon Sutton - DB
Reggie Sutton - DB
Pat Swilling - LB
Patrick Swoopes - NT
Derrick Taylor - DB
Curtland Thomas - WR
Henry Thomas - G
Joe Thomas - WR
Junior Thurman - DB
John Tice - TE
Alvin Toles - LB
Darrel Toussaint - DB
Steve Trapilo - G
Dwight Walker - WR
Frank Warren - DE
Mike Waters - TE
Frank Wattelet - DB
Dave Waymer - DB
Ron Weissenhofer - LB
Jim Wilks - DE
Dave Wilson - QB
Scott Woerner - DB
Barry Word - RB
Kevin Young - DE

1987 NY Giants

George Adams - RB
Raul Allegre - K
Beau Almodobar - WR
Ottis Anderson - RB
Billy Ard - G
Stephen Baker - WR
Carl Banks - LB
Mark Bavaro - TE
Earl Beecham - RB
Lewis Bennett - WR
Brad Benson - T
George Benyola - K
Bill Berthusen - NT
Mike Black - T
Dennis Borcky - NT
Donald Brown - DB
Charlie Burgess - LB
Jim Burt - NT
Mike Busch - QB
Boris Byrd - DB
Reggie Carr - DE
Harry Carson - LB
Maurice Carthon - RB
Harvey Clayton - DB
Charles Coleman - TE
Mark Collins - DB
Jaime Covington - RB
Jim Crocicchia - QB
Mack Cummings - WR
Chris Davis - LB
Kelvin Davis - G
Dan DeRose - LB
Fred DiRenzo - RB
Robert DiRico - RB
Eric Dorsey - DE
Bill Dugan - G
Tom Flynn - DB
Tony Galbreath - RB
Curtis Garrett - DE
Chris Godfrey - G
Wayne Haddix - DB
Andy Headen - LB
Kenny Hill - DB
Anthony Howard - G
Erik Howard - NT
Byron Hunt - LB
Mark Ingram - WR
Damian Johnson - T
Pepper Johnson - LB
Brian Johnston - C
Chris Jones - C
Robbie Jones - LB
Jerry Kimmel - LB
Terry Kinard - DB
Sean Landeta - P
Greg Lasker - DB
Edwin Lovelady - WR
Lionel Manuel - WR
Leonard Marshall - DE
George Martin - DE
Phil McConkey - WR
Reggie McGowan - WR
Kevin Meuth - T
Jim Miller - P
Russell Mitchell - C
Dana Moore - P
Dan Morgan - G
Joe Morris - RB
Pat Morrison - DB
Zeke Mowatt - TE
Frank Nicholson - LB
Jimmy Norris - DB
Bart Oates - C
Kaulana Park - RB
Elvis Patterson - DB
Rob Porter - DB
Gary Reasons - LB
Steve Rehage - DB
Doug Riesenberg - T

William Roberts - T
Stacy Robinson - WR
Lee Rouson - RB
Jeff Rutledge - QB
Warren Seitz - WR
Phil Simms - QB
Brian Sisley - DE
Doug Smith - DB
Jeff Smith - TE
Torin Smith - DE
Frank Sutton - T
Gregg Swartwoudt - T
Joe Taibi - DE
Lawrence Taylor - LB
Warren Thompson - LB
Jeff Tootle - LB
Odessa Turner - WR
Scott Urch - G
John Washington - DE
Herb Welch - DB
Adrian White - DB
Van Williams - RB
Perry Williams - DB
Jim Yarbrough - DB

1987 NY Jets

Dan Alexander - G
Lynwood Alford - LB
Don Baldwin - DE
Ted Banker - G
Marion Barber - RB
Barry Bennett - DE
Troy Benson - LB
Guy Bingham - C
Dennis Bligen - RB
Walter Briggs - QB
Jay Brophy - LB
Chris Brown - LB
Joe Burke - RB
Russell Carter - DB
Tony Chickillo - DE
John Chirico - RB
Kyle Clifton - LB
Trent Collins - DB
Martin Cornelson - C
Anthony Corvino - G
Eric Coss - G
Bob Crable - LB
Sean Dykes - DB
Onzy Elam - LB
Nuu Faaola - RB
Joe Fields - C
Derrick Foster - RB
Jerome Foster - DE
Derrick Gaffney - WR
Tony Garbarczyk - DE
Mark Gastineau - DE
Kerry Glenn - DB
Alex Gordon - LB
Billy Griggs - TE
Mike Haight - G
Harry Hamilton - DB
Michael Harper - WR
Jim Haslett - LB
Jo Jo Heath - DB
Johnny Hector - RB
Marc Hogan - DB
Scott Holman - WR
Jerry Holmes - DB
Carl Howard - DB
Bobby Humphery - DB
Tom Humphrey - G
Eddie Hunter - RB
Stan Hunter - WR
Vince Jasper - G
Dave Jennings - P
Ken Jones - T
Gordon King - T
Joe Klecko - NT
Rocky Klever - TE
Jamie Kurisko - TE
Pat Leahy - K
Sid Lewis - DB
Lester Lyles - DB
Marty Lyons - DE
Tracy Martin - WR
Kevin McArthur - LB
Pete McCartney - G
Reggie McElroy - T
Freeman McNeil - RB
Lance Mehl - LB
Scott Mersereau - DE
Rich Miano - DB
Matt Monger - LB
Tim Newman - RB
Gerald Nichols - DT
David Norrie - QB
Ken O'Brien - QB
Tom O'Connor - P
George Radachowsky - DB
Pat Ragusa - K
Eric Riley - TE
Bobby Riley - WR
Larry Robinson - DB
Ken Rose - LB
Pat Ryan - QB
Mickey Shuler - TE
Don Smith - DE
Reggie Smith - WR
Kurt Sohn - WR
Treg Songy - DB
Jim Sweeney - T
Tony Sweet - TE
John Thomas - T

Al Toon - WR
Jo-Jo Townsell - WR
Maurice Turner - RB
Roger Vick - RB
Wesley Walker - WR
Henry Walls - LB
Ladell Wills - LB
Mike Witteck - LB
Mike Zordich - DB

1987 Philadelphia

David Alexander - T
Ty Allert - LB
Jim Angelo - G
Jim Auer - DE
Marvin Ayers - DE
Eric Bailey - TE
Ron Baker - G
Matt Battaglia - LB
Vic Bellamy - DB
Jesse Bendross - WR
Gary Bolden - DT
Kevin Bowman - WR
Carlos Bradley - LB
Cedrick Brown - DB
Dave Brown - LB
Jerome Brown - DT
Reggie Brown - RB
Keith Byars - RB
Cris Carter - WR
Tom Caterbone - DB
Matt Cavanaugh - QB
Ken Clarke - DT
Topper Clemons - RB
Garry Cobb - LB
Ray Conlin - DT
Joe Conwell - T
Evan Cooper - DB
Charles Crawford - RB
George Cumby - LB
Randall Cunningham - QB
Matt Darwin - T
Jon Dumbauld - DE
Byron Evans - LB
Ron Fazio - TE
Gerry Feehery - C
Elbert Foules - DB
William Frizzell - DB
Gregg Garrity - WR
Russell Gary - DB
Chris Gerhard - DB
Jimmie Giles - TE
Mike Golic - DE
Chuck Gorecki - LB
Otis Grant - WR
Jeff Griffin - DB
Elois Grooms - DE
Michael Haddix - RB
Skip Hamilton - DT
Greg Harding - DB
Terry Hoage - DB
Marty Horn - QB
Kenny Jackson - WR
Dave Jacobs - K
Angelo James - DB
Dwayne Jiles - LB
Alonzo Johnson - LB
Chris Johnson - DB
Ron Johnson - WR
Seth Joyner - LB
Kelly Kirchbaum - LB
John Klingel - DE
Michael Kullman - DB
Bob Landsee - G
Robert Lavette - RB
Byron Lee - LB
Scott Leggett - G
Greg Liter - DE
Dave Little - TE
Matt Long - C
Mike McCloskey - TE
Paul McFadden - K
Dan McMillen - DE
Guido Merkens - QB
Randall Mitchell - NT
Tim Mooney - DE
Bobby Morse - RB
Mike Nease - G
Mike Perrino - T
Ray Phillips - DE
Mike Pitts - DT
Mike Quick - WR
Ken Reeves - T
Mike Reichenbach - LB
Alan Reid - RB
Jay Repko - TE
Jacque Robinson - RB
Alvin Ross - RB
Mark Royals - P
Paul Ryczek - C
Adam Schreiber - G
Jody Schulz - LB
Mike Siano - WR
Clyde Simmons - DE
Reggie Singletary - G
Fred Smalls - LB
John Spagnola - TE
Ben Tamburello - C
Junior Tautalatasi - RB
John Teltschik - P
Scott Tinsley - QB
Anthony Toney - RB
Willie Turral - RB
Mike Ulmer - DB

Pete Walters - G
Andre Waters - DB
Jeff Wenzel - T
Troy West - DB
Reggie White - DE
Brenard Wilson - DB
Roynell Young - DB

1987 Pittsburgh

Walter Abercrombie - RB
Lyneal Alston - WR
Gary Anderson - K
Mel Anderson - WR
Steve Apke - LB
Buddy Aydelette - T
Craig Bingham - LB
Brian Blankenship - G
Steve Bono - QB
Jim Boyle - T
Bubby Brister - QB
Ralph Britt - TE
John Bruno - P
Gregg Carr - LB
Rodney Carter - RB
Spark Clark - RB
Jackie Cline - DE
Joey Clinkscales - WR
Robin Cole - LB
Reggie Collier - QB
Tommy Dawkins - DE
Charlie Dickey - G
Gary Dunn - NT
Dave Edwards - DB
Thomas Everett - DB
Moses Ford - WR
Lorenzo Freeman - NT
Keith Gary - DE
Preston Gothard - TE
Cornell Gowdy - DB
Larry Griffin - DB
Russell Hairston - WR
Delton Hall - DB
Bryan Hinkle - LB
Merril Hoge - RB
Alan Huff - NT
Tunch Ilkin - T
Earnest Jackson - RB
Tim Johnson - DE
Bruce Jones - DB
Daryl Knox - LB
Ben Lawrence - G
Danzell Lee - TE
Louis Lipps - WR
David Little - LB
Charles Lockett - WR
Terry Long - G
John Lott - C
Jeff Lucas - T
Mark Malone - QB
Mike Merriweather - LB
Kelvin Middleton - DB
Michael Minter - NT
Ed Nelson - NT
Harry Newsome - P
Hardy Nickerson - LB
Dave Opfar - NT
Paul Oswald - C
Ted Petersen - G
Ray Pinney - T
Frank Pollard - RB
Jerry Quick - T
Dan Reeder - RB
Rock Richmond - DB
John Rienstra - G
Avon Riley - LB
Cameron Riley - DB
Lupe Sanchez - DB
Chuck Sanders - RB
Chris Sheffield - DB
Donnie Shell - DB
Bret Shugarts - DE
John Stallworth - WR
Dwight Stone - RB
Tyronne Stowe - LB
Calvin Sweeney - WR
Weegie Thompson - WR
David Trout - K
Anthony Tuggle - DB
Xavier Warren - DE
Robert Washington - T
Mike Webster - C
Albert Williams - LB
Gerald Williams - DE
Joe Williams - LB
Ray Williams - DB
Keith Willis - DE
Craig Wolfley - G
Ken Woodard - LB
Dwayne Woodruff - DB
Rod Woodson - DB
Theo Young - TE

1987 St. Louis

Steve Alvord - DT
Dwayne Anderson - DB
Terrence Anthony - LB
Rob Awalt - TE
Charles Baker - LB
Anthony Bell - LB
Joe Bock - LB
Ron Bohm - DE
Joe Bostic - G
Ray Brown - G

Ron Brown - WR
Tony Buford - LB
Anthony Burke - DT
Victor Burnett - DT
Carl Carter - DB
Jimmie Carter - LB
Greg Cater - P
Gene Chilton - T
Bob Clasby - DT
Clarence Collins - WR
Travis Curtis - DB
Wayne Davis - LB
Al Del Greco - K
Mark Duda - DT
Gary Dulin - DE
Earl Ferrell - RB
Phil Forney - LB
Jim Gallery - K
David Galloway - DE
Mark Garalczyk - DT
Sammy Garza - QB
Don Goodman - RB
Roy Green - WR
Curtis Greer - DE
Shawn Halloran - QB
William Harris - TE
Johnny Holloway - DB
Don Holmes - WR
Greg Horne - P
Mark Jackson - DB
Ilia Jarostchuk - LB
Gregg Johnson - DB
Troy Johnson - WR
E. J. Junior - LB
Derek Kennard - C
Bob Keseday - TE
Neil Lomax - QB
Cedric Mack - DB
Terence Mack - LB
Mark Mathis - DB
Tony Mayes - DB
Derrick McAdoo - RB
Adrian McBride - WR
Tim McDonald - DB
Stump Mitchell - RB
Mike Morris - G
Niko Noga - LB
Peter Noga - LB
Jay Novacek - TE
Freddie Joe Nunn - DE
Jeff Paine - LB
Ron Pasquale - G
Todd Peat - G
Victor Perry - DT
John Preston - DB
Keith Radecic - C
Tootie Robbins - T
Mark Royals - P
Mike Ruether - C
Rod Saddler - DE
Broderick Sargent - RB
Ed Scott - DB
Colin Scotts - DT
Luis Sharpe - T
Vai Sikahema - RB
Ken Sims - DB
J. T. Smith - WR
Lance Smith - G
Leonard Smith - DB
Jason Staurovsky - K
Cliff Stoudt - QB
Charles Vatterott - G
Tom Welter - T
Ron Wolfley - RB
Charles Wright - DB
Lonnie Young - DB

1987 San Diego

Vince Abbott - K
Curtis Adams - RB
Ty Allert - LB
Anthony Anderson - DB
Gary Anderson - RB
Keith Baldwin - DE
Chip Banks - LB
Martin Bayless - DB
Monte Bennett - DE
Thomas Benson - LB
Rod Bernstine - TE
Ed Berry - DB
David Brandon - LB
Carl Brazley - DB
Lou Brock - DB
Steve Busick - LB
Gill Byrd - DB
Wes Chandler - WR
Mike Charles - NT
Sam Claphan - G
Ken Dallafior - G
Bruce Davis - WR
Mike Davis - DB
David Diaz-Infante - G
Chuck Ehin - NT
Chuck Faucette - LB
Greg Feasel - T
Kevin Ferguson - TE
James FitzPatrick - G
Dan Fouts - QB
Jeff Gaffney - K
Vencie Glenn - DB
Joe Goebel - C
Willard Goff - DE
Dee Hardison - DE
Walter Harris - DB
Andy Hawkins - LB
Mark Herrmann - QB
Jamie Holland - WR
Pete Holohan - TE
Harry Holt - TE
Darrel Hopper - DB
Mike Hudson - DB
Mike Humiston - LB
Daniel Hunter - DB
Brian Ingram - LB
Jeff Jackson - LB
Lionel James - WR
Keyvan Jenkins - RB
James Johnson - LB
Mike Kelley - QB
Randy Kirk - LB
Gary Kowalski - G
Jim Lachey - T
Don Macek - C
Dennis McKnight - C
Frank Middleton - RB
Pat Miller - LB
Les Miller - DE
Tim Moffett - WR
Ralf Mojsiejenko - P
Calvin Muhammad - WR
Rick Neuheisel - QB
Elvis Patterson - DB
Duane Pettitt - DE
Joe Phillips - DE
Gary Plummer - LB
Jeff Powell - RB
Stacy Price - LB
Joe Prokop - P
Barry Redden - RB
Tag Rome - WR
Charles Romes - DB
Dan Rosado - G
Curtis Rouse - G
Martin Sartin - RB
Eric Sievers - TE
Tony Simmons - DE
King Simmons - DB
Emil Slovacek - T
Billy Ray Smith Jr. - LB
Angelo Snipes - LB
Tim Spencer - RB
Todd Spencer - RB
John Stadnik - C
Anthony Steels - RB
Johnny Taylor - LB
Broderick Thompson - G
Terry Unrein - NT
Mark Vlasic - QB
Danny Walters - DB
Timmie Ware - WR
Ted Watts - DB
Dwight Wheeler - G
Al Williams - WR
Lee Williams - DE
Earl Wilson - DE
Karl Wilson - DE
Kellen Winslow - TE
Blaise Winter - NT
Ken Zachary - RB

1987 San Francisco

Jim Asmus - K
Harris Barton - T
Ed Blount - QB
Dwaine Board - DE
Jeff Bregel - G
Jeff Brockhaus - K
Ray Brown - RB
Keith Browner - LB
John Butler - DB
Michael Carter - NT
Tony Cherry - RB
Dwight Clark - WR
Mark Cochran - T
Bruce Collie - T
Glen Collins - DE
Darren Comeaux - LB
George Cooper - LB
Matt Courtney - DB
Tom Cousineau - LB
Roger Craig - RB
Joe Cribbs - RB
Randy Cross - G
Kevin Dean - LB
Joe Drake - NT
Chris Dressel - TE
Doug DuBose - RB
Michael Durrette - G
Riki Ellison - LB
Kevin Fagan - DE
Jim Fahnhorst - LB
Keith Fahnhorst - T
John Faylor - DB
Terrence Flagler - RB
Russ Francis - TE
John Frank - TE
Tracy Franz - T
Jeff Fuller - DB
Bob Gagliano - QB
Tony Gladney - WR
Clyde Glover - DE
Terry Greer - WR
Don Griffin - DB
Ron Hadley - LB
Charles Haley - DE
Andre Hardy - RB
Ron Heller - TE
Thomas Henley - WR
Gary Hoffman - T
Tom Holmoe - DB
James Johnson - LB
Brent Jones - TE
Jerry Keeble - LB
Carl Keever - LB
Mark Korff - LB
Pete Kugler - NT
Greg Liter - DE
Tim Long - C
Ronnie Lott - DB
Ken Margerum - WR
Derrick Martin - DB
Milt McColl - LB
Guy McIntyre - G
Tim McKyer - DB
Dana McLemore - DB
Doug Mikolas - NT
Carl Monroe - WR
Joe Montana - QB
Tory Nixon - DB
Bubba Paris - T
Limbo Parks - T
Reno Patterson - NT
Darryl Pollard - DB
Fred Quillan - C
Tom Rathman - RB
Kevin Reach - G
Jerry Rice - WR
Elston Ridgle - DE
Larry Roberts - DE
Del Rodgers - RB
Max Runager - P
Jesse Sapolu - G
Todd Shell - LB
Jonathan Shelley - DB
Mark Stevens - QB
Jeff Stover - DE
John Sullivan - DB
Harry Sydney - RB
John Taylor - WR
Chuck Thomas - C
Keena Turner - LB
Mike Varajon - RB
Steve Wallace - T
Michael Walter - LB
Mike Wells - TE
Ray Wersching - K
Carlton Williamson - DB
Mike Wilson - WR
Eric Wright - DB
Steve Young - QB

1987 Seattle

Harvey Allen - DB
Tom Andrews - C
Curt Baham - DB
Edwin Bailey - G
Roland Barbay - NT
Brant Bengen - WR
Tony Blue - DB
Jon Borchardt - T
Brian Bosworth - LB
Barry Bowman - P
Arnold Brown - DB
Jeff Bryant - DE
Tim Burnham - T
Tony Burse - RB
Blair Bush - C
Keith Butler - LB
Ray Butler - WR
Tony Caldwell - LB
Louis Clark - WR
Chris Corley - TE
Julio Cortes - LB
Fred Davis - DB
Rob DeVita - LB
Dale Dorning - DE
Wes Dove - DE
Kenny Easley - DB
Bobby Joe Edmonds - RB
Randy Edwards - DE
John Eisenhooth - NT
Russell Evans - WR
Don Fairbanks - DE
Grant Feasel - C
Byron Franklin - WR
Greg Gaines - LB
Charles Glaze - DB
David Graham - NT
Boyce Green - RB
Jacob Green - DE
Russ Griffith - P
Mike Hagen - RB
Scott Hagler - K
Matt Hanousek - G
Doug Hire - C
Doug Hollie - DE
Dave Hollis - DB
Van Hughes - DE
Patrick Hunter - DB
Joe Jackson - LB
Melvin Jenkins - DB
M. L. Johnson - LB
Norm Johnson - K
Kevin Juma - WR
Kerry Justin - DB
Mark Keel - TE
Jeff Kemp - QB
Dave Krieg - QB
Eric Lane - RB
Steve Largent - WR
Paul Lavine - LB
Kim Mack - DB
Bruce Mathison - QB
Ron Mattes - T
John McVeigh - LB
Sam Merriman - LB
Bryan Millard - G
Alonzo Mitz - DE
Alvin Moore - RB
Mark Moore - DB
Randall Morris - RB
Michael Morton - RB
Paul Moyer - DB
Joe Nash - NT
John O'Callaghan - TE
Fred Orns - LB
Curt Pardridge - WR
Rick Parros - RB
Dean Perriman - C
Alvin Powell - G
Greg Ramsey - DE
Howard Richards - T
Eugene Robinson - DB
Ruben Rodriguez - P
Ken Sager - TE
Bruce Scholtz - LB
Ron Scoggins - T
Jack Sims - G
Paul Skansi - WR
Dallis Smith - DB
Donald Snell - WR
Chad Stark - RB
Wilbur Strozier - TE
Terry Taylor - DB
Jimmy Teal - WR
Joe Terry - LB
Garth Thomas - G
Ricky Thomas - DB
Mike Tice - TE
Rico Tipton - LB
Daryl Turner - WR
Curt Warner - RB
Chris White - DB
Charles Wiley - NT
Jim Williams - RB
John L. Williams - RB
Lester Williams - NT
Mike Wilson - T
Tony Woods - LB
David Wyman - LB
Fredd Young - LB
Renard Young - DB

1987 Tampa Bay

Don Anderson - DB
Cliff Austin - RB
Steve Bartalo - RB
Greg Boone - RB
Scot Brantley - LB
Rufus Brown - G
John Cannon - DE
Mark Carrier - WR
Gerald Carter - WR
Steve Carter - WR
Walter Carter - DE
Mike Clark - DE
Torin Clark - DB
Mark Cooper - T
Ray Criswell - P
Ivory Curry - DB
Jeff Davis - LB
Steve DeBerg - QB
Dwayne Dixon - WR
Phil Freeman - WR
Bobby Futrell - DB
Brian Gant - LB
Frank Garcia - P
Jeff George - DB
Charles Gladman - RB
Conrad Goode - T
Sonny Gordon - DB
Don Graham - LB
Randy Grimes - C
Ron Hall - TE
Roy Harris - DE
Dave Heffernan - T
Ron Heller - T
Bruce Hill - WR
Mike Hold - QB
Derek Holloway - WR
Steve Holloway - TE
Ron Holmes - DE
Bobby Howard - RB
Jim Huddleston - G
John Hunt - G
Eddie Hunter - RB
Donald Igwebuike - K
Ray Isom - DB
David Jackson - WR
Cam Jacobs - LB
Curt Jarvis - NT
Hoss Johnson - T
Rod Jones - DB
David Jordan - G
Kevin Kellin - DE
Bobby Kemp - DB
Tyrone Keys - DE
Tim King - DB
Dan Land - RB
J. D. Maarleveld - T
Calvin Magee - TE
Rick Mallory - G
Fred McCallister - LB
Tom McHale - DE
Vito McKeever - DB
Solomon Miller - WR
Jeff Modesitt - TE
Sankar Montoute - LB
Winston Moss - LB
Kevin Murphy - LB
Fred Nordgren - NT
Paul O'Connor - G
Lee Paige - DB
Leon Pennington - LB
Chuck Pitcock - C
Marvin Powell - T
Don Pumphrey - T
Marcus Quinn - DB
Jim Ramey - DE
Ervin Randle - LB
John Reaves - QB
Ricky Reynolds - DB
Harold Ricks - RB
Charles Riggins - DE
Stanley Shakespeare - WR
Dan Sileo - NT
Jeff Smith - RB
Reggie Smith - T
Mike Stensrud - NT
Eric Streater - WR
Harry Swayne - DE
Craig Swoope - DB
Gene Taylor - WR
Rob Taylor - T
Pat Teague - LB
Vinny Testaverde - QB
Derrick Thomas - RB
Van Tiffin - K
Paul Tripoli - DB
Dan Turk - C
Calvin Turner - DE
Miles Turpin - LB
Jackie Walker - LB
Kevin Walker - DB
Herkie Walls - WR
Chris Washington - LB
Arthur Wells - TE
James Wilder - RB
Rick Woods - DB
Adrian Wright - RB
George Yarno - G
Jim Zorn - QB

1987 Washington

Anthony Allen - WR
Obed Ariri - K
Jess Atkinson - K
Dan Benish - DT
Cliff Benson - TE
Keiron Bigby - WR
Jeff Bostic - C
Todd Bowles - DB
Reggie Branch - RB
Darrick Brilz - G
Kelvin Bryant - RB
Derek Bunch - LB
Danny Burmeister - DB
Dave Butz - DT
Ravin Caldwell - LB
Joe Caravello - TE
Mark Carlson - T
Gary Clark - WR
Joe Cofer - DB
Monte Coleman - LB
Anthony Copeland - LB
John Cowne - C
Steve Cox - P
Eric Coyle - C
Bobby Curtis - LB
Brian Davis - DB
Vernon Dean - DB
Glenn Dennison - TE
Clint Didier - TE
K. D. Dunn - TE
Dave Etherly - DB
Frank Frazier - G
Steve Gage - DB
Alec Gibson - DT
Kurt Gouveia - LB
Darryl Grant - DT
Darrell Green - DB
Keith Griffin - RB
Russ Grimm - C
Ali Haji-Sheikh - K
Dean Hamel - DT
Steve Hamilton - DE
Allen Harvin - RB
Ray Hitchcock - C
Walter Holman - RB
Charles Jackson - DB
Joe Jacoby - T
Tim Jessie - RB
Richard Johnson - WR
Anthony Jones - TE
David Jones - C
Ted Karras - DT
Mel Kaufman - LB
Rick Kehr - G
Garry Kimble - DB
Jon Kimmel - LB
Markus Koch - DE
Skip Lane - DB
Kit Lathrop - DT
Dexter Manley - DE
Charles Mann - DE
Steve Martin - DE
Mark May - T
Craig McEwen - TE
Curtis McGriff - DT
Raleigh McKenzie - G
Dan McQuaid - T
Rich Milot - LB
Michael Mitchell - DB
Art Monk - WR
Tim Morrison - DB
Neal Olkewicz - LB
Terry Orr - TE
Phil Pettey - G
Joe Phillips - WR
Tony Robinson - QB
George Rogers - RB
Carlton Rose - LB
Ed Rubbert - QB
Anthony Sagnella - DT
Ricky Sanders - WR
Jay Schroeder - QB
Willard Scissum - G
Tony Settles - LB
Derrick Shepard - WR
Ed Simmons - T
Timmy Smith - RB
R.C. Thielemann - G
Steve Thompson - DT
Brendan Toibin - K
Dave Truitt - TE
Clarence Vaughn - DB
Clarence Verdin - WR
Lionel Vital - RB
Henry Waechter - DT
Alvin Walton - DB
Don Warren - TE
Jack Weil - P
Barry Wilburn - DB
Doug Williams - QB
Marvin Williams - TE
Eric Wilson - LB
Ted Wilson - WR
Wayne Wilson - RB
David Windham - LB
Dennis Woodberry - DB
Mike Wooten - C
Eric Yarber - WR

1988 Atlanta

Rick Badanjek - RB
Stacey Bailey - WR
Lew Barnes - WR
Greg Brown - DE
Aundray Bruce - LB
Rick Bryan - DE
Bobby Butler - DB
Reggie Camp - DE
Scott Case - DB
Tony Casillas - NT
Bret Clark - DB
Stan Clayton - T
Evan Cooper - DB
Joe Costello - LB
Marcus Cotton - LB
David Croudip - DB
Greg Davis - K
Steve Dils - QB
Charles Dimry - DB
Floyd Dixon - WR
Rick Donnelly - P
Jamie Dukes - G
Bill Fralic - G
Mike Gann - DE
Tim Gordon - DB
Tim Green - LB
Michael Haynes - WR
Jessie Hester - WR
Alex Higdon - TE
Houston Hoover - T
Mike Kenn - T
Leander Knight - DB
Gene Lang - RB
Danzell Lee - TE
Calvin Loveall - DB
Charles Martin - NT
Aubrey Matthews - WR
Hugh Millen - QB
Brett Miller - T
Chris Miller - QB
James Milling - WR
Robert Moore - DB
Paul Oswald - G
James Primus - RB
John Rade - LB
Wayne Radloff - C
Michael Reid - LB
Gerald Riggs - RB
John Scully - G
John Settle - RB
Elbert Shelley - DB
Vinson Smith - LB
Sylvester Stamps - RB
Jessie Tuggle - LB
Ken Whisenhunt - TE
Gary Wilkins - TE
Joel Williams - LB
Mitch Willis - NT
George Yarno - C

1988 Buffalo

Carlton Bailey - LB
Howard Ballard - T
Cornelius Bennett - LB
Ray Bentley - LB
Walter Broughton - WR
Chris Burkett - WR
Derrick Burroughs - DB
Leonard Burton - T
Carl Byrum - RB
Sherman Cocroft - DB
Shane Conlan - LB
Wayne Davis - DB
Joe Devlin - T
Dwight Drane - DB
Tom Erlandson Jr. - LB
Hal Garner - LB
Don Graham - LB
John Hagy - DB
Ronnie Harmon - RB
Dale Hellestrae - T
Kent Hull - C
Kirby Jackson - DB
Flip Johnson - WR
Trumaine Johnson - WR
Jim Kelly - QB
Mark Kelso - DB
John Kidd - P
Keith McKeller - TE
Pete Metzelaars - TE
Roland Mitchell - DB
Jamie Mueller - RB
Scott Norwood - K
Nate Odomes - DB
Mark Pike - DE
Dean Prater - DE
Scott Radecic - LB
Andre Reed - WR
Frank Reich - QB
Robb Riddick - RB
Jim Ritcher - G
Butch Rolle - TE
Leon Seals - DE
Fred Smerlas - NT
Bruce Smith - DE
Leonard Smith - DB
Art Still - DE
Darryl Talley - LB
Steve Tasker - WR
Thurman Thomas - RB
Mark Traynowicz - G
Erroll Tucker - KR
Tim Vogler - G
Will Wolford - T
Jeff Wright - NT

1988 Chi. Bears

John Adickes - C
Neal Anderson - RB
Kurt Becker - G
Mark Bortz - G
Cap Boso - TE
Kevin Butler - K
Dick Chapura - DT
Greg Clark - LB
Jim Covert - T
Wendell Davis - WR
Richard Dent - DE
Maurice Douglass - DB
Dave Duerson - DB
Shaun Gayle - DB
Dennis Gentry - WR
Dan Hampton - DE
Jim Harbaugh - QB
Al Harris - DE
Jay Hilgenberg - C
Vestee Jackson - DB
Troy Johnson - LB
Dante Jones - LB
Glen Kozlowski - WR
Todd Krumm - DB
Greg Lasker - DB
Lorenzo Lynch - DB
Dennis McKinnon - WR
Jim McMahon - QB
Steve McMichael - DT
Emery Moorehead - TE
Ron Morris - WR
Jim Morrissey - LB
Brad Muster - RB
Brent Novoselsky - TE
William Perry - DT
Mickey Pruitt - LB
Caesar Rentie - T
Mike Richardson - DB
Ron Rivera - LB
Thomas Sanders - RB
John Shannon - DT
Mike Singletary - LB
Sean Smith - DT
Lemuel Stinson - DB
Matt Suhey - RB
David Tate - DB
Tom Thayer - G
Calvin Thomas - RB
Jim Thornton - TE
Mike Tomczak - QB
Keith Van Horne - T
Bryan Wagner - P
John Wojciechowski - G

1988 Cincinnati

Leo Barker - LB
Lewis Billups - DB
Brian Blados - G
Ed Brady - LB
Jim Breech - K
James Brooks - RB
Eddie Brown - WR
Jason Buck - DE
Barney Bussey - DB
Cris Collinsworth - WR
Ellis Dillahunt - DB
Rickey Dixon - DB
David Douglas - T
Eddie Edwards - DE

Boomer Esiason - QB
David Fulcher - DB
Scott Fulhage - P
David Grant - NT
Ira Hillary - WR
Rodney Holman - TE
Ray Horton - DB
Tim Inglis - LB
Stanford Jennings - RB
Lee Johnson - P
Eric Kattus - TE
Joe Kelly - LB
Emanuel King - LB
Bruce Kozerski - C
Tim Krumrie - NT
Marc Logan - RB
Mike Martin - WR
Curtis Maxey - NT
Skip McClendon - DE
Tim McGee - WR
Max Montoya - G
Anthony Munoz - T
Mike Norseth - QB
Carl Parker - WR
Bruce Reimers - T
Jim Riggs - TE
Rich Romer - LB
Jim Rourke - T
Turk Schonert - QB
Jim Skow - DE
Daryl Smith - DB
Dave Smith - T
Eric Thomas - DB
Kevin Walker - LB
Joe Walter - T
Leon White - LB
Solomon Wilcots - DB
Reggie Williams - LB
Stanley Wilson - RB
Ickey Woods - RB
Carl Zander - LB

1988 Cleveland

Matt Bahr - K
Tony Baker - RB
Anthony Blaylock - DB
Rickey Bolden - T
Stephen Braggs - DB
Brian Brennan - WR
Charles Buchanan - DE
Earnest Byner - RB
Clifford Charlton - LB
Sam Clancy - DE
Gary Danielson - QB
Hanford Dixon - DB
Paul Farren - T
Dan Fike - G
Herman Fontenot - RB
Thane Gash - DB
Bob Golic - NT
David Grayson - LB
Anthony Griggs - LB
Carl Hairston - DE
Mark Harper - DB
Will Hill - DB
Eddie Johnson - LB
Lee Johnson - P
Mike Johnson - LB
Marlon Jones - DE
Tony Jones - T
Mike Junkin - LB
Bernie Kosar - QB
Reggie Langhorne - WR
Kevin Mack - RB
Tim Manoa - RB
Clay Matthews - LB
Gerald McNeil - WR
Frank Minnifield - DB
Ozzie Newsome - TE
Mike Pagel - QB
Michael Dean Perry - DE
Gregg Rakoczy - C
Cody Risien - T
Max Runager - P
Darryl Sims - DE
Webster Slaughter - WR
Don Strock - QB
Derek Tennell - TE
Van Waiters - LB
Brian Washington - DB
Clarence Weathers - WR
Larry Williams - G
Frank Winters - C
Felix Wright - DB
Glen Young - WR

1988 Dallas

Vince Albritton - DB
Ray Alexander - WR
Bill Bates - DB
Kevin Brooks - DT
Bob Brotzki - T
Cornell Burbage - DB
Ron Burton - LB
Thornton Chandler - TE
Darryl Clack - RB
Garry Cobb - LB
Doug Cosbie - TE
Steve DeOssie - LB
Michael Downs - DB
Kelvin Edwards - WR
Steve Folsom - TE
Todd Fowler - RB
Ron Francis - DB
Everett Gay - WR
Kevin Gogan - T
Manny Hendrix - DB
Mark Higgs - RB
Michael Irvin - WR
Garth Jax - LB
Jim Jeffcoat - DE
Too Tall Jones - DE
Crawford Ker - G
Eugene Lockhart - LB
Kelvin Martin - WR
Timmy Newsome - RB
Nate Newton - G
Danny Noonan - DT
Ken Norton - LB
Paul Oswald - C
Billy Owens - DB
Steve Pelluer - QB
Tom Rafferty - C
Roger Ruzek - K
Mike Saxon - P
Sean Scott - LB
Victor Scott - DB
Daryle Smith - T
Kevin Sweeney - QB
Glen Titensor - G
Mark Tuinei - C
Mark Walen - DT
Herschel Walker - RB
Everson Walls - DB
Randy White - DT
Bob White - C
Danny White - QB
Dave Widell - T
Robert Williams - DB
Charles Wright - DB
Luis Zendejas - K
Jeff Zimmerman - G

1988 Denver

Ken Bell - RB
Keith Bishop - C
Walt Bowyer - DE
Tyrone Braxton - DB
Michael Brooks - LB
Steve Bryan - NT
Billy Bryan - C
Jeremiah Castille - DB
Kevin Clark - DB
Rick Dennison - LB
Tony Dorsett - RB
John Elway - QB
Simon Fletcher - LB
Freddie Gilbert - DE
Sam Graddy - WR
Kevin Guidry - DB
Mike Harden - DB
Mark Haynes - DB
Winford Hood - G
Mike Horan - P
Stefan Humphries - G
Mark Jackson - WR
Jason Johnson - WR
Vance Johnson - WR
Rulon Jones - DE
Jim Juriga - G
Ken Karcher - QB
Rich Karlis - K
Keith Kartz - G
Clarence Kay - TE
Patrick Kelly - TE
Bruce Klosterman - LB
Shawn Knight - NT
Greg Kragen - NT
Gary Kubiak - QB
Ken Lanier - T
Larry Lee - C
Tim Lucas - LB
Rick Massie - WR
Karl Mecklenburg - LB
Orson Mobley - TE
Marc Munford - LB
Ricky Nattiel - WR
Gerald Perry - T
Bruce Plummer - DB
Randy Robbins - DB
Mike Ruether - C
Jim Ryan - LB
Steven Sewell - RB
Dennis Smith - DB
Dave Studdard - T
Calvin Thomas - RB
Andre Townsend - DE
Gerald Willhite - RB
Steve Wilson - DB
Sammy Winder - RB

1988 Detroit

Dave Ahrens - LB
Eric Andolsek - G
Jim Arnold - P
Jerry Ball - NT
Scott Barrows - G
Bennie Blades - DB
Carl Bland - WR
Lou Brock - DB
Lomas Brown - T
Paul Butcher - LB
Pat Carter - TE
Jeff Chadwick - WR
Raphel Cherry - DB
Jessie Clark - RB
Mike Cofer - LB
Paco Craig - WR
Keith Ferguson - DE
Dennis Gibson - LB
Kevin Glover - C
Curtis Green - DE
James Griffin - DB
Gary Hadd - DE
Rusty Hilger - QB
Eric Hipple - QB
Jerry Holmes - DB
Garry James - RB
George Jamison - LB
James Jones - RB
Gary Lee - WR
Mark Lewis - TE
Danny Lockett - LB
Chuck Long - QB
Pete Mandley - WR
Bruce McNorton - DB
Joe Milinichik - G
Devon Mitchell - DB
Randall Morris - RB
Steve Mott - C
Eddie Murray - K
Tony Paige - RB
Carl Painter - RB
Shelton Robinson - LB
Reggie Rogers - DE
Ray Roundtree - WR
Rob Rubick - TE
Dan Saleaumua - NT
Harvey Salem - T
Eric Sanders - T
Curt Singer - T
Chris Spielman - LB
Stephen Starring - WR
Thomas Strauthers - DE
Bobby Watkins - DB
William White - DB
Scott Williams - RB
Eric Williams - DE
Jimmy Williams - LB
John Witkowski - QB
Butch Woolfolk - RB

1988 Green Bay

John Anderson - LB
Albert Bell - WR
Scott Bolton - WR
Jerry Boyarsky - NT
Don Bracken - P
Dave Brown - DB
Robert Brown - DE
Curtis Burrow - K
Mark Cannon - C
Alphonso Carreker - DE
Paul Ott Carruth - RB
Chuck Cecil - DB
Patrick Collins - RB
John Corker - LB
Dave Croston - T
Kenneth Davis - RB
Dale Dawson - K
Burnell Dent - LB
Clint Didier - TE
Dean Dorsey - K
John Dorsey - LB
Phil Epps - WR
Brent Fullwood - RB
George Greene - DB
Joey Hackett - TE
Darryl Haley - T
Ron Hallstrom - G
Tim Harris - LB
Nate Hill - DE
Johnny Holland - LB
Norman Jefferson - DB
Kani Kauahi - C
Perry Kemp - WR
Blair Kiel - QB
Mark Lee - DB
Don Majkowski - QB
Chris Mandeville - DB
Larry Mason - RB
Aubrey Matthews - WR
Rich Moran - C
Mark Murphy - DB
Bob Nelson - NT
Tom Neville - T
Brian Noble - LB
Shawn Patterson - NT
Ron Pitts - DB
Gary Richard - DB
Ken Ruettgers - T
Patrick Scott - WR
Sterling Sharpe - WR
Ron Simpkins - LB
Walter Stanley - WR
Scott Stephen - LB
Ken Stills - DB
Lavale Thomas - RB
Keith Uecker - G
Mike Weddington - LB
Ed West - TE
Blaise Winter - DE
Keith Woodside - RB
Randy Wright - QB
Max Zendejas - K

1988 Houston

Patrick Allen - DB
Robert Banks - DE
Keith Bostic - DB
Steve Brown - DB
Domingo Bryant - DB
Richard Byrd - NT
Cody Carlson - QB
Toby Caston - LB
Ray Childress - DE
Bruce Davis - T
John Davis - T
Cris Dishman - DB
Jeff Donaldson - DB
Willie Drewrey - WR
Curtis Duncan - WR
Tracey Eaton - DB
Eric Fairs - LB
William Fuller - DE
Ernest Givins - WR
John Grimsley - LB
Leonard Harris - WR
Alonzo Highsmith - RB
Drew Hill - WR
Haywood Jeffires - WR
Kenny Johnson - DB
Richard Johnson - DB
Walter Johnson - LB
Sean Jones - DE
Quintin Jones - DB
Calvin Loveall - DB
Robert Lyles - LB
Don Maggs - T
Bruce Matthews - G
Johnny Meads - LB
Doug Mikolas - NT
Greg Montgomery - P
Warren Moon - QB
Mike Munchak - G
Brent Pease - QB
Jay Pennison - C
Allen Pinkett - RB
Mike Rozier - RB
Eugene Seale - LB
Al Smith - LB
Doug Smith - NT
Dean Steinkuhler - T
Vince Stroth - T
Spencer Tillman - RB
Chris Verhulst - TE
Lorenzo White - RB
Jamie Williams - TE
Tony Zendejas - K

1988 Indianapolis

O'Brien Alston - LB
Harvey Armstrong - NT
Jess Atkinson - K
Brian Baldinger - G
Michael Ball - DB
Roy Banks - WR
Pat Beach - TE
Mark Bellini - WR
Albert Bentley - RB
Dean Biasucci - K
Duane Bickett - LB
Matt Bouza - WR
Mark Boyer - TE
Kerry Brady - K
John Brandes - TE
Bill Brooks - WR
Bob Brotzki - C
Kevin Call - T
Chris Chandler - QB
Johnie Cooks - LB
Joe Cribbs - RB
Eugene Daniel - DB
Byron Darby - NT
Donnie Dee - TE
Eric Dickerson - RB
Randy Dixon - G
Ray Donaldson - C
Chris Gambol - T
Chris Goode - DB
Jon Hand - DE
Jeff Herrod - LB
Chris Hinton - T
Gary Hogeboom - QB
John Holt - DB
Ezra Johnson - DE
Joe Klecko - NT
Barry Krauss - LB
Orlando Lowry - LB
Dan McQuaid - T
Chuckie Miller - DB
Cliff Odom - LB
Joel Patten - T
Mike Prior - DB
James Pruitt - WR
Freddie Robinson - DB
Ron Solt - G
Rohn Stark - P
Craig Swoope - DB
Keith Taylor - DB
Donnell Thompson - DE
Don Thorp - NT
Jack Trudeau - QB
Willie Tullis - DB
Ricky Turner - QB
Ben Utt - G
Clarence Verdin - WR
George Wonsley - RB
Terry Wright - DB
Fredd Young - LB

1988 Kansas City

Mark Adickes - G
John Alt - T
Gary Baldinger - NT
Rich Baldinger - G
Tom Baugh - C
Mike Bell - DE
Lloyd Burruss - DB
Carlos Carson - WR
Deron Cherry - DB
Tim Cofield - LB
Darrell Colbert - WR
Louis Cooper - LB
Steve DeBerg - QB
Jack Del Rio - LB
Curt DiGiacomo - G
Irv Eatman - T
Gerry Feehery - C
Kenny Gamble - RB
Kelly Goodburn - P
Leonard Griffin - DE
Dino Hackett - LB
Dee Hardison - DE
Emile Harry - WR
James Harvey - G
Andy Hawkins - LB
Jonathan Hayes - TE
Herman Heard - RB
Greg Hill - DB
Dave Hollis - DB
Todd Howard - LB
Byron Ingram - G
Keyvan Jenkins - RB
Sidney Johnson - DB
Rod Jones - TE
Brian Jozwiak - G
Bill Kenney - QB
Albert Lewis - DB
Adam Lingner - C
Calvin Loveall - DB
Nick Lowery - K
Dave Lutz - T
Bill Maas - NT
Chris Martin - LB
Jerry McCabe - LB
Ron McLean - DE
Larry Moriarty - RB
Christian Okoye - RB
Stephone Paige - WR
Paul Palmer - RB
Aaron Pearson - LB
J. C. Pearson - DB
Kevin Porter - DB
Alfredo Roberts - TE
Kevin Ross - DB
Jerome Sally - NT
James Saxon - RB
Neil Smith - DE
Angelo Snipes - LB
Troy Stedman - LB
Mike Stensrud - NT
Kitrick Taylor - WR
Don Thorp - DE

1988 LA Raiders

Stefon Adams - DB
Marcus Allen - RB
Eddie Anderson - DB
Chris Bahr - K
Steve Beuerlein - QB
Ron Brown - LB
Tim Brown - WR
Russell Carter - DB
Todd Christensen - TE
Scott Davis - DE
Ron Fellows - DB
Mervyn Fernandez - WR
Mike Freeman - C
Willie Gault - WR
John Gesek - G
Jeff Gossett - P
Rory Graves - T
David Greenwood - DB
Charley Hannah - G
Mike Haynes - DB
Brian Holloway - G
Bo Jackson - RB
Trey Junkin - TE
Linden King - LB
Jim Lachey - T
Zeph Lee - DB
Bill Lewis - C
James Lofton - WR
Howie Long - DE
Rod Martin - LB
Milt McColl - LB
Terry McDaniel - DB
Vann McElroy - DB
Reggie McKenzie - LB
Chris McLemore - RB
Matt Millen - LB
Don Mosebar - C
Vance Mueller - RB
Andy Parker - TE
Bill Pickel - DT
Dennis Price - DB
Chris Riehm - G
Jerry Robinson - LB
Jay Schroeder - QB
Steve Smith - RB
Steve Strachan - RB
Malcolm Taylor - DT
Stacey Toran - DB
Greg Townsend - LB
Norwood Vann - LB
Lionel Washington - DB
Dwight Wheeler - C
Bruce Wilkerson - G
Mitch Willis - DT
Mike Wise - DE
Chris Woods - WR
Steve Wright - T

1988 LA Rams

Flipper Anderson - WR
Greg Bell - RB
Ron Brown - WR
Rich Camarillo - P
Jim Collins - LB
Aaron Cox - WR
Robert Delpino - RB
Carl Ekern - LB
Henry Ellard - WR
Jon Embree - TE
Jim Everett - QB
Brett Faryniarz - LB
Jerry Gray - DB
Gaston Green - RB
Kevin Greene - LB
Mike Guman - RB
Dale Hatcher - P
Mark Herrmann - QB
Cliff Hicks - DB
Pete Holohan - TE
LeRoy Irvin - DB
Robert Jenkins - T
Mark Jerue - LB
Gary Jeter - DE
Damone Johnson - TE
Johnnie Johnson Jr. - DB
Larry Kelm - LB
Mike Lansford - K
Duval Love - G
Mike McDonald - LB
Buford McGee - RB
Greg Meisner - NT
Shawn Miller - DE
Tom Newberry - G
Anthony Newman - DB
Vince Newsome - DB
Mel Owens - LB
Irvin Pankey - T
Doug Reed - DE
Mike Schad - G
Eric Sievers - TE
Jackie Slater - T
Tony Slaton - C
Doug Smith - C
Michael Stewart - DB
Fred Stokes - DE
Fred Strickland - LB
Mickey Sutton - DB
Tim Tyrrell - RB
James Washington - DB
Frank Wattelet - DB
Charles White - RB
Mike Wilcher - LB
Alvin Wright - NT
Mike Young - WR

1988 Miami

Fred Banks - WR
Woody Bennett - RB
John Bosa - DE
Bud Brown - DB
Mark Brown - LB
Bob Brudzinski - LB
Louis Cheek - T
Mark Clayton - WR
Jackie Cline - DE
Joe Cribbs - RB
Jeff Cross - DE
Ron Davenport - RB
Jeff Dellenbach - C
Mark Dennis - T
Mark Duper - WR
Ferrell Edmunds - TE
Roy Foster - G
Tony Franklin - K
David Frye - LB
Tony Furjanic - LB
Chris Gaines - LB
Harry Galbreath - G
Jon Giesler - T
Rick Graf - LB
Hugh Green - LB
Lorenzo Hampton - RB
Bruce Hardy - TE
Nate Hill - DE
Lifford Hobley - DB
Ilia Jarostchuk - LB
Ron Jaworski - QB
Jim Jensen - WR
Greg Johnson - G
William Judson - DB
Brian Kinchen - TE
Larry Kolic - LB
Eric Kumerow - DE
Mike Lambrecht - NT
Paul Lankford - DB
Ronnie Lee - T
Dan Marino - QB
Don McNeal - DB
John Offerdahl - LB
Bruce Plummer - DB
James Pruitt - WR
Fuad Reveiz - K
Reggie Roby - P
Scott Schwedes - WR
Jackie Shipp - LB
Brian Sochia - NT
Troy Stradford - RB
Rodney Thomas - DB
Reyna Thompson - DB
Tom Toth - G
T. J. Turner - DE
Jarvis Williams - DB

1988 Minnesota

Alfred Anderson - RB
Sam Anno - LB
Walker Lee Ashley - LB
Al Baker - DE
Barry Bennett - DE
Ray Berry - LB
Joey Browner - DB
Anthony Carter - WR
Paul Coffman - TE
Chris Doleman - DE
D. J. Dozier - RB
Brad Edwards - DB
Rick Fenney - RB
Chris Foote - C
Darrell Fullington - DB
Rich Gannon - QB
Bill Gay - DE
Jim Gustafson - WR
Darryl Harris - RB
John Harris - DB
Wymon Henderson - DB
Carl Hilton - TE
Issiac Holt - DB
David Howard - LB
Dave Huffman - G
Tim Irwin - T
Hassan Jones - WR
Steve Jordan - TE
Todd Kalis - G
Tommy Kramer - QB
Carl Lee - DB
Leo Lewis - WR
Kirk Lowdermilk - C
Mark MacDonald - G
Chris Martin - LB
Doug Martin - DE
Stafford Mays - DT
Randall McDaniel - G
Dan McQuaid - T
Keith Millard - DT
Mike Mularkey - TE
Najee Mustafaa - DB
Chuck Nelson - K
Darrin Nelson - RB
Tim Newton - DT
Al Noga - DT
Randy Rasmussen - C
Allen Rice - RB
Bucky Scribner - P
Jesse Solomon - LB
Scott Studwell - LB
Terry Tausch - G
Henry Thomas - NT
Wade Wilson - QB
Gary Zimmerman - T

1988 New England

Marvin Allen - RB
Bruce Armstrong - T
Mike Baab - C
Thomas Benson - LB
Jim Bowman - DB
Vincent Brown - LB
Raymond Clayborn - DB
Elgin Davis - RB
Lin Dawson - TE
Reggie Dupard - RB
Tony Eason - QB
Paul Fairchild - G
Sean Farrell - G
Jeff Feagles - P
Doug Flutie - QB
Russ Francis - TE
Irving Fryar - WR
Dennis Gadbois - WR
Teddy Garcia - K
Ernest Gibson - DB
Tim Goad - NT
Steve Grogan - QB
Milford Hodge - NT
Darryl Holmes - DB
Craig James - RB
Roland James - DB
Steve Johnson - TE
Cedric Jones - WR
Tim Jordan - LB
Ronnie Lippett - DB
Fred Marion - DB
Sammy Martin - WR
Trevor Matich - C
Larry McGrew - LB
Rod McSwain - DB
Stanley Morgan - WR
Eric Naposki - LB
Ed Nelson - DE
Bob Perryman - RB
Gene Profit - DB
Tom Ramsey - QB
Tom Rehder - T
Johnny Rembert - LB
Ed Reynolds - LB
Willie Scott - TE
Kenneth Sims - DE
Jason Staurovsky - K
John Stephens - RB
Mosi Tatupu - RB
Andre Tippett - LB
Garin Veris - DE

Danny Villa - T
Brent Williams - DE
Toby Williams - NT
Ron Wooten - G

1988 New Orleans

Michael Adams - DB
Morten Andersen - K
Gene Atkins - DB
Cliff Benson - TE
Dwaine Board - DE
Hoby Brenner - TE
Stan Brock - T
James Campen - C
Bruce Clark - DE
Robert Clark - WR
Chuck Commiskey - C
Bill Contz - T
Toi Cook - DB
Jim Dombrowski - T
Jon Dumbauld - DE
Brad Edelman - G
Tony Elliott - NT
Brian Forde - LB
John Fourcade - QB
Jumpy Geathers - DE
Antonio Gibson - DB
Daren Gilbert - T
Mel Gray - KR
Ted Gregory - NT
Brian Hansen - P
James Haynes - LB
Bobby Hebert - QB
Craig Heyward - RB
Joel Hilgenberg - C
Lonzell Hill - WR
Dalton Hilliard - RB
Rickey Jackson - LB
Van Jakes - DB
Vaughan Johnson - LB
Buford Jordan - RB
Joe Kohlbrand - LB
Steve Korte - C
Milton Mack - DB
Eric Martin - WR
Brett Maxie - DB
Rueben Mayes - RB
Sam Mills - LB
Mark Pattison - WR
Brett Perriman - WR
Greg Scales - TE
Reggie Sutton - DB
Pat Swilling - LB
John Tice - TE
Alvin Toles - LB
Steve Trapilo - G
Jeff Walker - T
Frank Warren - DE
Dave Waymer - DB
Jim Wilks - DE
Dave Wilson - QB
Barry Word - RB

1988 NY Giants

George Adams - RB
Raul Allegre - K
Ottis Anderson - RB
Billy Ard - G
Stephen Baker - WR
Carl Banks - LB
Mark Bavaro - TE
Brad Beckman - TE
Maury Buford - P
Jim Burt - NT
Harry Carson - LB
Maurice Carthon - RB
Mark Collins - DB
Johnie Cooks - LB
Eric Dorsey - DE
Jumbo Elliott - T
Joe Fields - C
Tom Flynn - DB
Neal Guggemos - DB
Wayne Haddix - DB
Andy Headen - LB
Kenny Hill - DB
Jeff Hostetler - QB
Erik Howard - NT
Byron Hunt - LB
Mark Ingram - WR
Damian Johnson - T
Pepper Johnson - LB
Terry Kinard - DB
Sean Landeta - P
Greg Lasker - DB
Lionel Manuel - WR
Leonard Marshall - DE
George Martin - DE
Phil McConkey - WR
Paul McFadden - K
Eric Moore - T
Joe Morris - RB
Zeke Mowatt - TE
Karl Nelson - T
Bart Oates - C
Gary Reasons - LB
Doug Riesenberg - T
William Roberts - T
Stacy Robinson - WR
Lee Rouson - RB
Jeff Rutledge - QB
Ricky Shaw - LB
Tim Sherwin - TE
Phil Simms - QB

Lawrence Taylor - LB
Odessa Turner - WR
John Washington - DE
Adrian White - DB
Robb White - DE
Sheldon White - DB
Perry Williams - DB

1988 NY Jets

Dan Alexander - G
Tom Baldwin - DE
Ted Banker - G
Marion Barber - RB
Barry Bennett - DE
Troy Benson - LB
Guy Bingham - C
John Booty - DB
Dave Cadigan - T
Kyle Clifton - LB
Robin Cole - LB
Jeff Criswell - T
K. D. Dunn - TE
Onzy Elam - LB
Nuu Faaola - RB
Paul Frase - DE
John Galvin - LB
Mark Garalczyk - DE
Mark Gastineau - DE
Alex Gordon - LB
Billy Griggs - TE
Mike Haight - G
Steve Hammond - LB
Michael Harper - WR
James Hasty - DB
Johnny Hector - RB
Carl Howard - DB
Bobby Humphery - DB
Pat Leahy - K
Marty Lyons - DE
Kevin McArthur - LB
Reggie McElroy - T
Erik McMillan - DB
Freeman McNeil - RB
Scott Mersereau - DT
Rich Miano - DB
Keith Neubert - TE
Gerald Nichols - DT
Ken O'Brien - QB
Joe Prokop - P
George Radachowsky - DB
Ken Rose - LB
Pat Ryan - QB
Adam Schreiber - C
Mickey Shuler - TE
Kurt Sohn - WR
Jim Sweeney - C
Al Toon - WR
Jo-Jo Townsell - WR
Roger Vick - RB
Wesley Walker - WR
Terry Williams - DB
Mike Withycombe - G
Mike Zordich - DB

1988 Philadelphia

Walter Abercrombie - RB
David Alexander - C
Eric Allen - DB
Ty Allert - LB
Ron Baker - G
Doug Bartlett - DT
Shawn Beals - WR
Todd Bell - DB
Jerome Brown - DT
Keith Byars - RB
Cris Carter - WR
Matt Cavanaugh - QB
Randall Cunningham - QB
Scott Curtis - LB
Matt Darwin - T
Dale Dawson - K
Dean Dorsey - K
Jon Dumbauld - DE
Byron Evans - LB
Donald Evans - DE
Eric Everett - DB
William Frizzell - DB
Gregg Garrity - WR
Jimmie Giles - TE
Mike Golic - DT
Michael Haddix - RB
Ron Heller - T
Terry Hoage - DB
Wes Hopkins - DB
Keith Jackson - TE
Kenny Jackson - WR
Izel Jenkins - DB
Dwayne Jiles - LB
Ron Johnson - WR
Seth Joyner - LB
John Klingel - DE
Mark Konecny - RB
Dave Little - TE
Mike Pitts - DT
Mike Quick - WR
Ken Reeves - T
Mike Reichenbach - LB
Dave Rimington - C
Adam Schreiber - G
Clyde Simmons - DE
Reggie Singletary - G

Ron Solt - G
Ben Tamburello - G
Junior Tautalatasi - RB
John Teltschik - P
Anthony Toney - RB
Andre Waters - DB
Reggie White - DE
Roynell Young - DB
Luis Zendejas - K

1988 Phoenix

Steve Alvord - DT
Rob Awalt - TE
Greg Baty - TE
Anthony Bell - LB
Joe Bostic - G
Michael Brim - DB
Ray Brown - G
Carl Carter - DB
Jessie Clark - RB
Bob Clasby - DT
Travis Curtis - DB
Wayne Davis - LB
Al Del Greco - K
Scott Dill - G
Earl Ferrell - RB
David Galloway - DE
Mark Garalczyk - DT
Roy Green - WR
Ken Harvey - LB
Don Holmes - WR
Greg Horne - P
Ricky Hunley - LB
Tony Jeffery - RB
Ernie Jones - WR
Tyrone Jones - LB
Tony Jordan - RB
E. J. Junior - LB
Derek Kennard - C
Greg Lasker - DB
Neil Lomax - QB
Lester Lyles - DB
Mark MacDonald - G
Cedric Mack - DB
Derrick McAdoo - RB
Tim McDonald - DB
Sean McNanie - DE
Stump Mitchell - RB
Roland Mitchell - DB
Ricky Moore - RB
Niko Noga - DE
Jay Novacek - TE
Freddie Joe Nunn - DE
Todd Peat - G
Reggie Phillips - DB
Tootie Robbins - T
Rod Saddler - DE
Andy Schillinger - WR
Luis Sharpe - T
Vai Sikahema - RB
J. T. Smith - WR
Lance Smith - T
Leonard Smith - DB
Cliff Stoudt - QB
Mark Traynowicz - G
Tom Tupa - QB
Mark Walczak - TE
Ron Wolfley - RB
Lonnie Young - DB

1988 Pittsburgh

Gary Anderson - K
Todd Blackledge - QB
Brian Blankenship - G
Steve Bono - QB
Jim Boyle - T
Bubby Brister - QB
Gregg Carr - LB
Rodney Carter - RB
Joey Clinkscales - WR
Dermontti Dawson - G
Thomas Everett - DB
Lorenzo Freeman - NT
Keith Gary - DE
Preston Gothard - TE
Cornell Gowdy - DB
Larry Griffin - DB
Delton Hall - DB
Anthony Henton - LB
Bryan Hinkle - LB
Mike Hinnant - TE
Merril Hoge - RB
Tunch Ilkin - T
Earnest Jackson - RB
John Jackson - T
Tim Johnson - DE
Troy Johnson - WR
Aaron Jones - DE
Darin Jordan - LB
Chuck Lanza - C
Greg Lee - DB
Louis Lipps - WR
David Little - LB
Greg Lloyd - LB
Charles Lockett - WR
Terry Long - G
Jeff Markland - TE
Harry Newsome - P
Hardy Nickerson - LB
Frank Pollard - RB
Rollin Putzier - NT
Jerry Reese - DE
John Rienstra - G
Lupe Sanchez - DB

Dwight Stone - RB
Tyronne Stowe - LB
Ben Thomas - DE
Weegie Thompson - WR
Mike Webster - C
Gerald Williams - NT
Warren Williams - RB
Craig Wolfley - T
Dwayne Woodruff - DB
Rod Woodson - DB

1988 San Diego

Vince Abbott - K
Curtis Adams - RB
Gary Anderson - RB
Keith Baldwin - DE
Martin Bayless - DB
Roy Bennett - DB
Rod Bernstine - TE
David Brandon - LB
Darrick Brilz - G
Keith Browner - DE
Gill Byrd - DB
Joseph Campbell - LB
Mike Charles - NT
John Clay - T
Leonard Coleman - DB
Arthur Cox - TE
Jeffery Dale - DB
Ken Dallafior - T
Steve DeLine - K
Quinn Early - WR
Chuck Faucette - LB
Cedric Figaro - LB
James FitzPatrick - G
Darren Flutie - WR
Chris Gambol - T
Vencie Glenn - DB
George Hinkle - DE
Jamie Holland - WR
Jeff Jackson - LB
Lionel James - RB
Anthony Jones - TE
Tyrone Keys - DE
Randy Kirk - LB
Gary Kowalski - G
Babe Laufenberg - QB
Don Macek - C
Mark Malone - QB
Dennis McKnight - C
Anthony Miller - WR
Pat Miller - DB
Les Miller - DE
Ralf Mojsiejenko - P
Leslie O'Neal - DE
Elvis Patterson - DB
Joe Phillips - DE
Gary Plummer - LB
Barry Redden - RB
David Richards - T
Dan Rosado - G
Kevin Scott - RB
Sam Seale - DB
Eric Sievers - TE
Billy Ray Smith Jr. - LB
Tim Spencer - RB
Wilbur Strozier - TE
Broderick Thompson - G
Mark Vlasic - QB
Lee Williams - DE
Karl Wilson - DE
Ken Woodard - LB

1988 San Francisco

Harris Barton - T
Dwaine Board - DE
Jeff Bregel - G
Chet Brooks - DB
Michael Carter - NT
Wes Chandler - WR
Mike Cofer - K
Bruce Collie - G
Greg Cox - DB
Roger Craig - RB
Randy Cross - C
Doug DuBose - RB
Riki Ellison - LB
Kevin Fagan - DE
Jim Fahnhorst - LB
Terrence Flagler - RB
John Frank - TE
Jeff Fuller - DB
Terry Greer - WR
Don Griffin - DB
Ron Hadley - LB
Charles Haley - LB
Ron Heller - TE
Barry Helton - P
Tom Holmoe - DB
Pierce Holt - NT
Brent Jones - TE
Sam Kennedy - LB
Pete Kugler - DE
Kevin Lilly - NT
Ronnie Lott - DB
Guy McIntyre - G
Tim McKyer - DB
Doug Mikolas - NT
Joe Montana - QB
Calvin Nicholas - WR
Tory Nixon - DB
Bubba Paris - T
Darryl Pollard - DB

Tom Rathman - RB
Jerry Rice - WR
Larry Roberts - DE
Del Rodgers - RB
Bill Romanowski - LB
Max Runager - P
Jesse Sapolu - G
Jeff Stover - DE
Danny Stubbs - DE
Harry Sydney - RB
John Taylor - WR
Chuck Thomas - C
Keena Turner - LB
Steve Wallace - T
Michael Walter - LB
Mike Wilson - WR
Eric Wright - DB
Steve Young - QB

1988 Seattle

Tommie Agee - RB
Edwin Bailey - G
Brian Blades - WR
Brian Bosworth - LB
Lou Brock - DB
Jeff Bryant - DE
Blair Bush - C
Ray Butler - WR
Louis Clark - WR
Ken Clarke - NT
Darren Comeaux - LB
Vernon Dean - DB
Bobby Joe Edmonds - KR
Stan Eisenhooth - C
Grant Feasel - C
Greg Gaines - LB
Nesby Glasgow - DB
Chris Godfrey - G
Jacob Green - DE
Kevin Harmon - RB
Dwayne Harper - DB
Doug Hollie - DE
Dave Hollis - DB
Patrick Hunter - DB
Melvin Jenkins - DB
M. L. Johnson - LB
Norm Johnson - K
Tommy Kane - WR
Jeff Kemp - QB
Dave Krieg - QB
Steve Largent - WR
Ron Mattes - T
Bryan Millard - G
Darrin Miller - LB
Alonzo Mitz - DE
Randall Morris - RB
Paul Moyer - DB
Joe Nash - NT
Rufus Porter - LB
Alvin Powell - G
Eugene Robinson - DB
Ruben Rodriguez - P
Bruce Scholtz - LB
Paul Skansi - WR
John Spagnola - TE
Kelly Stouffer - QB
Terry Taylor - DB
Jimmy Teal - WR
Mike Tice - TE
Curt Warner - RB
John L. Williams - RB
Mike Wilson - T
Tony Woods - LB
David Wyman - LB

1988 Tampa Bay

Selwyn Brown - DB
John Bruhin - G
John Cannon - DE
John Carney - K
Mark Carrier - WR
Joey Clinkscales - WR
Sidney Coleman - LB
Mark Cooper - T
Ray Criswell - P
Reuben Davis - DE
Donnie Elder - DB
Joe Ferguson - QB
Bobby Futrell - DB
Robert Goff - DE
Kerry Goode - RB
Randy Grimes - C
Paul Gruber - T
Ron Hall - TE
Harry Hamilton - DB
Odie Harris - DB
Bruce Hill - WR
Ron Holmes - DE
Bobby Howard - RB
William Howard - RB
Donald Igwebuike - K
Ray Isom - DB
Curt Jarvis - NT
Rod Jones - DB
Victor Jones - LB
Kevin Kellin - DE
Shawn Lee - NT
Calvin Magee - TE
Rick Mallory - G
Eugene Marve - LB
Derrick McAdoo - RB
Tom McHale - G
Winston Moss - LB

Kevin Murphy - LB
Pete Najarian - LB
Jeff Parks - TE
Frank Pillow - WR
Ervin Randle - LB
Ricky Reynolds - DB
Greg Richardson - WR
Mark Robinson - DB
Henry Rolling - LB
Don Smith - RB
Jeff Smith - RB
Stephen Starring - WR
Harry Swayne - DE
Lars Tate - RB
Gene Taylor - WR
Rob Taylor - T
Vinny Testaverde - QB
Kevin Thomas - C
Dan Turk - G
Jackie Walker - LB
Chris Washington - LB
James Wilder - RB
Charles Wright - DB

1988 Washington

Anthony Allen - WR
David Archer - QB
Tommy Barnhardt - P
Jeff Bostic - C
Todd Bowles - DB
Reggie Branch - RB
Kelvin Bryant - RB
Dave Butz - DT
Ravin Caldwell - LB
Joe Caravello - TE
Gary Clark - WR
Greg Coleman - P
Monte Coleman - LB
Steve Cox - P
Travis Curtis - DB
Brian Davis - DB
Steve Gage - DB
Kurt Gouveia - LB
Darryl Grant - DT
Darrell Green - DB
Keith Griffin - RB
Russ Grimm - G
Dean Hamel - DT
Steve Hamilton - DE
Dave Harbour - C
Joe Jacoby - T
Billy Johnson - WR
Anthony Jones - TE
Mel Kaufman - LB
Markus Koch - DE
Jim Lachey - T
Chip Lohmiller - K
Dexter Manley - DE
Charles Mann - DE
Greg Manusky - LB
Wilber Marshall - LB
Mark May - G
Craig McEwen - RB
Raleigh McKenzie - C
Ron Middleton - TE
Art Monk - WR
Jamie Morris - RB
Mike Oliphant - RB
Neal Olkewicz - LB
Terry Orr - TE
Mark Rypien - QB
Ricky Sanders - WR
Mike Scully - C
Derrick Shepard - WR
Ed Simmons - T
Timmy Smith - RB
R.C. Thielemann - G
Johnny Thomas - DB
Clarence Vaughn - DB
Alvin Walton - DB
Don Warren - TE
Barry Wilburn - DB
Doug Williams - QB
Kevin Williams - DB
Dennis Woodberry - DB

1989 Atlanta

Stacey Bailey - WR
Brad Beckman - TE
Guy Bingham - C
Tony Bowick - NT
Aundray Bruce - LB
Rick Bryan - DE
Bobby Butler - DB
Scott Campbell - QB
Scott Case - DB
Tony Casillas - NT
Stan Clayton - G
Shawn Collins - WR
Evan Cooper - DB
Marcus Cotton - LB
Greg Davis - K
Charles Dimry - DB
Floyd Dixon - WR
Jamie Dukes - C
Kenny Flowers - RB
Bill Fralic - G
Scott Fulhage - P
Mike Gann - DE
Tim Gordon - DB
Tim Green - LB
Michael Haynes - WR
Ron Heller - TE
Houston Hoover - T

John Hunter - T
Undra Johnson - WR
Keith Jones - RB
Brian Jordan - DB
Mike Kenn - T
Gene Lang - RB
Curtis Maxey - DE
Paul McFadden - K
Hugh Millen - QB
Chris Miller - QB
Robert Moore - DB
Ralph Norwood - T
Greg Paterra - RB
James Primus - RB
John Rade - LB
Wayne Radloff - G
Michael Reid - LB
Tommy Robison - G
Deion Sanders - DB
John Settle - RB
Elbert Shelley - DB
Malcolm Taylor - DE
Galand Thaxton - LB
Ben Thomas - DE
George Thomas - WR
Jessie Tuggle - LB
Gary Wilkins - TE
Joel Williams - LB
Tony Zackery - DB

1989 Buffalo

Carlton Bailey - LB
Howard Ballard - T
Don Beebe - WR
Cornelius Bennett - LB
Ray Bentley - LB
Kerry Brady - K
Chris Burkett - WR
Derrick Burroughs - DB
Leonard Burton - T
Tim Cofield - LB
Shane Conlan - LB
John Davis - T
Kenneth Davis - RB
Wayne Davis - DB
Joe Devlin - G
Dwight Drane - DB
Stan Gelbaugh - QB
John Hagy - DB
Chris Hale - DB
Ronnie Harmon - RB
Kent Hull - C
Kirby Jackson - DB
Flip Johnson - WR
Jim Kelly - QB
Mark Kelso - DB
John Kidd - K
Larry Kinnebrew - RB
Adam Lingner - C
James Lofton - WR
Keith McKeller - TE
Pete Metzelaars - TE
Matt Monger - LB
Jamie Mueller - RB
Scott Norwood - K
Nate Odomes - DB
Mark Pike - DE
Scott Radecic - LB
Andre Reed - WR
Frank Reich - QB
Elston Ridgle - DE
Jim Ritcher - G
Butch Rolle - TE
Leon Seals - DE
Fred Smerlas - NT
Bruce Smith - DE
Leonard Smith - DB
Art Still - DE
Mickey Sutton - DB
Darryl Talley - LB
Steve Tasker - WR
Thurman Thomas - RB
Erroll Tucker - DB
Will Wolford - T
Jeff Wright - NT

1989 Chi. Bears

Neal Anderson - RB
Trace Armstrong - DE
Mark Bortz - G
Cap Boso - TE
Maury Buford - P
Kevin Butler - K
Dick Chapura - T
Jim Covert - T
Wendell Davis - WR
Richard Dent - DE
Maurice Douglass - DB
Dave Duerson - DB
Chris Dyko - T
Jerry Fontenot - G
Shaun Gayle - DB
Dennis Gentry - WR
Mark Green - RB
Dan Hampton - DT
Jim Harbaugh - QB
LaSalle Harper - LB
Jay Hilgenberg - C
Steve Hyche - LB
Vestee Jackson - DB
Troy Johnson - LB
Dante Jones - LB
Glen Kozlowski - WR
Lorenzo Lynch - DB

Dennis McKinnon - WR
Steve McMichael - DT
Ron Morris - WR
Jim Morrissey - LB
Brad Muster - RB
Markus Paul - DB
William Perry - DT
Mickey Pruitt - LB
Ron Rivera - LB
John Roper - LB
Thomas Sanders - RB
John Shannon - DT
Mike Singletary - LB
Lemuel Stinson - DB
George Streeter - DB
Matt Suhey - RB
David Tate - DB
Brian Taylor - RB
Tom Thayer - G
Jim Thornton - TE
Mike Tomczak - QB
Keith Van Horne - T
Tom Waddle - WR
John Wojciechowski - G
Tony Woods - DE
Donnell Woolford - DB
Dave Zawatson - T

1989 Cincinnati

Eric Ball - RB
Chris Barber - DB
Leo Barker - LB
Lewis Billups - DB
Brian Blados - G
Ed Brady - LB
Jim Breech - K
James Brooks - RB
Eddie Brown - WR
Jason Buck - DE
Barney Bussey - DB
Richard Carey - DB
Rickey Dixon - DB
Boomer Esiason - QB
David Fulcher - DB
Jim Gallery - K
John Garrett - WR
David Grant - NT
Mike Hammerstein - DE
Ira Hillary - WR
John Holifield - RB
Rodney Holman - TE
Robert Jackson - DB
Stanford Jennings - RB
Paul Jetton - G
Lee Johnson - P
Scott Jones - T
Eric Kattus - TE
Joe Kelly - LB
Bruce Kozerski - C
Tim Krumrie - NT
Mike Martin - WR
Skip McClendon - DE
Tim McGee - WR
Max Montoya - G
Ken Moyer - T
Anthony Munoz - T
Carl Parker - WR
Bruce Reimers - T
Jim Riggs - TE
Rich Romer - LB
Turk Schonert
Jim Skow - DE
Kendal Smith - WR
Craig Taylor - RB
Eric Thomas - DB
Natu Tuatagaloa - DE
Kevin Walker - LB
Joe Walter - T
Dana Wells - NT
Leon White - LB
Solomon Wilcots - DB
Erik Wilhelm - QB
Reggie Williams - LB
Ickey Woods - RB
Carl Zander - LB

1989 Cleveland

Matt Bahr - K
Al Baker - DE
Ted Banker - G
Robert Banks - DE
Tom Baugh - C
Anthony Blaylock - DB
Rickey Bolden - T
Stephen Braggs - DB
Brian Brennan - WR
Clifford Charlton - LB
Hanford Dixon - DB
Paul Farren - T
Dan Fike - G
Thane Gash - DB
Tom Gibson - DT
Mike Graybill - T
David Grayson - LB
Carl Hairston - DT
Mark Harper - DB
Eddie Johnson - LB
Mike Johnson - LB
Vernon Joines - WR
Keith Jones - RB
Marlon Jones - DT
Tony Jones - T
Bernie Kosar - QB
Kyle Kramer - DB

Reggie Langhorne - WR
Robert Lyons - DB
Kevin Mack - RB
Tim Manoa - RB
Clay Matthews - LB
Gerald McNeil - WR
Eric Metcalf - RB
Ron Middleton - TE
Frank Minnifield - DB
Ozzie Newsome - TE
Mike Oliphant - WR
Mike Pagel - QB
Michael Dean Perry - DT
Chris Pike - DT
Gregg Rakoczy - G
Barry Redden - RB
Cody Risien - T
Kevin Robbins - T
Kevin Simons - T
Webster Slaughter - WR
Daryle Smith - T
Andrew Stewart - DE
Derek Tennell - TE
Lawyer Tillman - WR
Bryan Wagner - P
Van Waiters - LB
Felix Wright - DB

1989 Dallas

Troy Aikman - QB
Vince Albritton - DB
Ray Alexander - WR
Scott Ankrom - DB
Bill Bates - DB
Willie Broughton - DT
Eric Brown - DB
Cornell Burbage - WR
Ron Burton - LB
Jon Carter - DT
Thornton Chandler - TE
Darryl Clack - RB
Garry Cobb - LB
Jack Del Rio - LB
James Dixon - WR
Onzy Elam - LB
Steve Folsom - TE
Bernard Ford - WR
Ron Francis - DB
Kevin Gogan - T
Dean Hamel - DT
Steve Hendrickson - LB
Manny Hendrix - DB
Issiac Holt - DB
Ray Horton - DB
David Howard - LB
Michael Irvin - WR
Tim Jackson - DB
Jim Jeffcoat - DE
Keith Jennings - TE
Daryl Johnston - RB
Too Tall Jones - DE
Crawford Ker - G
Babe Laufenberg - QB
Kevin Lilly - DT
Eugene Lockhart - LB
Kelvin Martin - WR
Nate Newton - G
Danny Noonan - DT
Ken Norton - LB
Paul Palmer - RB
Tom Rafferty - C
Roger Ruzek - K
Broderick Sargent - RB
Mike Saxon - P
Kevin Scott - RB
Randy Shannon - LB
Derrick Shepard - WR
Sean Smith - DE
Jesse Solomon - LB
Mark Stepnoski - C
Curtis Stewart - RB
Junior Tautalatasi - RB
Ken Tippins - LB
Tony Tolbert - DE
Mark Tuinei - T
Herschel Walker - RB
Everson Walls - DB
Steve Walsh - QB
Bob White - C
Dave Widell - T
Robert Williams - DB
Luis Zendejas - K
Jeff Zimmerman - G

1989 Denver

Jeff Alexander - RB
Steve Atwater - DB
Ken Bell - WR
Keith Bishop - G
Mel Bratton - RB
Tyrone Braxton - DB
Michael Brooks - LB
Alphonso Carreker - DE
Darren Carrington - DB
Kip Corrington - DB
Scott Curtis - LB
Rick Dennison - LB
John Elway - QB
Simon Fletcher - LB
Paul Green - TE
Mark Haynes - DB
Wymon Henderson - DB
Brad Henke - DE
Ron Holmes - DE

Mike Horan - P
Bobby Humphrey - RB
Mark Jackson - WR
Vance Johnson - WR
Jim Juriga - G
Keith Kartz - C
Clarence Kay - TE
Patrick Kelly - TE
Bruce Klosterman - LB
Greg Kragen - NT
Gary Kubiak - QB
Ken Lanier - T
Tim Lucas - LB
Jake McCullough - DE
Karl Mecklenburg - LB
Orson Mobley - TE
Marc Munford - LB
Ricky Nattiel - WR
Gerald Perry - T
Warren Powers - DE
Randy Robbins - DB
Mike Ruether - C
Steven Sewell - RB
Richard Shelton - DB
Dennis Smith - DB
Monte Smith - G
Andre Townsend - DE
David Treadwell - K
Doug Widell - G
Sammy Winder - RB
Chris Woods - WR
Mike Young - WR

1989 Detroit

Bruce Alexander - DB
Eric Andolsek - G
Jim Arnold - P
Jerry Ball - NT
Bennie Blades - DB
Michael Brim - DB
Kevin Brooks - DE
Lomas Brown - T
Mark Brown - LB
Toby Caston - LB
Jeff Chadwick - WR
Robert Clark - WR
Mike Cofer - LB
James Cribbs - DE
Ray Crockett - DB
Ken Dallafior - G
Byron Darby - DE
Keith Ferguson - DE
John Ford - WR
Bob Gagliano - QB
Chris Gambol - T
Dennis Gibson - LB
Kevin Glover - C
Mel Gray - WR
Curtis Green - DE
James Griffin - DB
Eric Hipple - QB
Jerry Holmes - DB
George Jamison - LB
Richard Johnson - WR
Troy Johnson - WR
Victor Jones - LB
Keith Karpinski - LB
Chuck Long - QB
Trevor Matich - C
Keith McDonald - WR
Bruce McNorton - DB
Joe Milinichik - G
John Miller - DB
Stacey Mobley - WR
Eddie Murray - K
Niko Noga - LB
Tony Paige - RB
Carl Painter - RB
Paul Palmer - RB
Rodney Peete - QB
Lawrence Pete - NT
Jason Phillips - WR
Harvey Salem - T
Barry Sanders - RB
Eric Sanders - T
Chris Spielman - LB
Walter Stanley - WR
Terry Taylor - DB
Mike Utley - G
William White - DB
Eric Williams - DE
Jimmy Williams - LB
Mike Williams - WR
Jerry Woods - DB

1989 Green Bay

John Anderson - LB
Billy Ard - G
Mike Ariey - T
Carl Bland - WR
Jerry Boyarsky - NT
Don Bracken - P
Matt Brock - DE
Dave Brown - DB
Robert Brown - DE
Blair Bush - C
James Campen - C
Mark Cannon - C
Chuck Cecil - DB
Burnell Dent - LB
Clint Didier - TE
Anthony Dilweg - QB
Herman Fontenot - RB
Brent Fullwood - RB

George Greene - DB
Michael Haddix - RB
Mark Hall - DE
Ron Hallstrom - G
Tim Harris - LB
Johnny Holland - LB
Chris Jacke - K
Van Jakes - DB
Perry Kemp - WR
Mark Lee - DB
Don Majkowski - QB
Tony Mandarich - T
Aubrey Matthews - WR
Mike McGruder - DB
Rich Moran - G
Mark Murphy - DB
Bob Nelson - NT
Brian Noble - LB
Shawn Patterson - DE
Ron Pitts - DB
Jeff Query - WR
Ken Ruettgers - T
Sterling Sharpe - WR
John Spagnola - TE
Scott Stephen - LB
Ken Stills - DB
Mickey Sutton - DB
Alan Veingrad - T
Mike Weddington - LB
Ed West - TE
Blaise Winter - DE
Keith Woodside - RB
Vince Workman - RB

1989 Houston

Patrick Allen - DB
Steve Avery - RB
Billy Bell - DB
John Brantley - LB
Steve Brown - DB
Richard Byrd - DT
Cody Carlson - QB
Ray Childress - DT
Bruce Davis - T
Cris Dishman - DB
Jeff Donaldson - DB
Curtis Duncan - WR
Tracey Eaton - DB
Eric Fairs - LB
William Fuller - DE
Ernest Givins - WR
John Grimsley - LB
Leonard Harris - WR
Alonzo Highsmith - RB
Drew Hill - WR
Kenny Jackson - WR
Haywood Jeffires - WR
Kenny Johnson - DB
Richard Johnson - DB
Tracy Johnson - RB
Sean Jones - DE
Scott Kozak - LB
Robert Lyles - LB
Don Maggs - T
Bruce Matthews - G
Bubba McDowell - DB
Johnny Meads - LB
Glenn Montgomery - DT
Greg Montgomery - P
Warren Moon - QB
Bob Mrosko - TE
Mike Munchak - G
Jay Pennison - C
Allen Pinkett - RB
Mike Rozier - RB
Eugene Seale - LB
Al Smith - LB
Doug Smith - DT
Anthony Spears - DE
Dean Steinkuhler - T
Chris Verhulst - TE
Lorenzo White - RB
David Williams - T
George Yarno - C
Tony Zendejas - K

1989 Indianapolis

O'Brien Alston - LB
Harvey Armstrong - NT
Brian Baldinger - G
Michael Ball - DB
Chip Banks - LB
John Baylor - DB
Pat Beach - TE
Mitchell Benson - NT
Albert Bentley - RB
Dean Biasucci - K
Duane Bickett - LB
Matt Bouza - WR
Mark Boyer - TE
John Brandes - TE
Bill Brooks - WR
Kevin Call - T
Chris Chandler - QB
Sam Clancy - DE
Eugene Daniel - DB
Donnie Dee - TE
Eric Dickerson - RB
Randy Dixon - G
Titus Dixon - WR
Ray Donaldson - C
Stan Eisenhooth - C
Chris Goode - DB
Jon Hand - DE

Jeff Herrod - LB
Chris Hinton - T
Ivy Joe Hunter - RB
Ezra Johnson - DE
Kurt Larson - LB
Orlando Lowry - LB
Quintus McDonald - LB
Zefross Moss - T
Dan Murray - LB
Eric Naposki - LB
Cliff Odom - LB
Anthony Parker - DB
Bruce Plummer - DB
Mike Prior - DB
James Pruitt - WR
Tom Ramsey - QB
Andre Rison - WR
Rohn Stark - P
Keith Taylor - DB
Donnell Thompson - DE
Jack Trudeau - QB
Ben Utt - G
Clarence Verdin - WR
Charles Washington - DB
Ronnie Washington - LB
Clarence Weathers - WR
Fredd Young - LB

1989 Kansas City

Mark Adickes - G
Tommie Agee - RB
John Alt - T
Walker Lee Ashley - LB
Rich Baldinger - G
Lew Barnes - WR
Mike Bell - DE
Lloyd Burruss - DB
Mark Cannon - C
Paul Ott Carruth - RB
Carlos Carson - WR
Deron Cherry - DB
Gene Chilton - C
Bruce Clark - DE
Louis Cooper - LB
Danny Copeland - DB
Steve DeBerg - QB
Chris Dressel - TE
Irv Eatman - T
Mike Elkins - QB
Kenny Gamble - RB
Kelly Goodburn - P
Leonard Griffin - DE
Dino Hackett - LB
Michael Harris - C
Emile Harry - WR
Stacy Harvey - LB
Jonathan Hayes - TE
Herman Heard - RB
Kenny Hill - DB
Ron Jaworski - QB
Mike Junkin - LB
Albert Lewis - DB
Nick Lowery - K
Dave Lutz - G
Bill Maas - DE
Pete Mandley - WR
Chris Martin - LB
Rob McGovern - LB
Todd McNair - RB
Greg Meisner - NT
Mike Morris - C
Christian Okoye - RB
Stephone Paige - WR
J. C. Pearson - DB
Steve Pelluer - QB
Stan Petry - DB
Kevin Porter - DB
Alfredo Roberts - TE
Kevin Ross - DB
Dan Saleaumua - NT
James Saxon - RB
Neil Smith - DE
Angelo Snipes - LB
Derrick Thomas - LB
Robb Thomas - WR
Clarence Weathers - WR
Mike Webster - C
Naz Worthen - WR

1989 LA Raiders

Stefon Adams - WR
Mike Alexander - WR
Marcus Allen - RB
Eddie Anderson - DB
Thomas Benson - LB
Steve Beuerlein - QB
Tim Brown - WR
Russell Carter - DB
Joe Costello - LB
Derrick Crudup - RB
Scott Davis - DE
Mike Dyal - TE
Bobby Joe Edmonds - RB
Vince Evans - QB
Mervyn Fernandez - WR
Willie Gault - WR
John Gesek - G
Bob Golic - DT
Jeff Gossett - P
Rory Graves - T
Mike Harden - DB
Mike Haynes - DB
Ethan Horton - TE

Ricky Hunley - LB
Bo Jackson - RB
Jeff Jaeger - K
Trey Junkin - TE
Emanuel King - DE
Linden King - LB
Pete Koch - DE
Dan Land - DB
Zeph Lee - DB
Howie Long - DE
Terry McDaniel - DB
Vann McElroy - DB
Don Mosebar - C
Mark Mraz - DE
Vance Mueller - RB
Bill Pickel - DE
Kerry Porter - RB
Dennis Price - DB
Jerry Robinson - LB
Tim Rother - DT
Jay Schroeder - QB
Jackie Shipp - LB
Steve Smith - RB
Steve Strachan - RB
Greg Townsend - DE
Dan Turk - C
Timmie Ware - WR
Lionel Washington - DB
Bruce Wilkerson - T
Otis Wilson - LB
Mike Wise - DE
Steve Wisniewski - G
Steve Wright - G

1989 LA Rams

Flipper Anderson - WR
Kurt Becker - G
Greg Bell - RB
George Bethune - LB
Richard Brown - LB
Ron Brown - WR
Paul Butcher - LB
Pat Carter - TE
Aaron Cox - WR
Robert Delpino - RB
Henry Ellard - WR
Jim Everett - QB
Mel Farr Jr. - RB
Brett Faryniarz - LB
Cleveland Gary - RB
Jerry Gray - DB
Gaston Green - RB
Kevin Greene - DE
Dale Hatcher - P
Bill Hawkins - DE
Darryl Henley - DB
Mark Herrmann - QB
Cliff Hicks - DB
Pete Holohan - TE
LeRoy Irvin - DB
Alfred Jackson - DB
Robert Jenkins - T
Mark Jerue - LB
Damone Johnson - TE
Johnnie Johnson Jr. - DB
Larry Kelm - LB
Mike Lansford - K
Duval Love - G
Mike McDonald - LB
Buford McGee - RB
Mark Messner - LB
Shawn Miller - DT
Tom Newberry - C
Anthony Newman - DB
Vince Newsome - DB
Mel Owens - LB
Irvin Pankey - T
Mike Piel - DT
Doug Reed - DT
Jackie Slater - T
Tony Slaton - C
Brian Smith - DE
Doug Smith - C
Sean Smith - DT
Frank Stams - LB
Michael Stewart - DB
Fred Strickland - LB
James Washington - DB
Mike Wilcher - LB
Alvin Wright - DT

1989 Miami

Dave Ahrens - LB
Fred Banks - WR
John Bosa - DE
Andre Brown - WR
J.B. Brown - DB
Tom Brown - RB
Bob Brudzinski - LB
Louis Cheek - T
Greg Clark - LB
Mark Clayton - WR
Jackie Cline - DE
Jeff Cross - DE
Ron Davenport - RB
Jeff Dellenbach - T
Mark Dennis - T
Mark Duper - WR
Ferrell Edmunds - TE
Nuu Faaola - RB
Roy Foster - G
David Frye - LB
Harry Galbreath - G

Ernest Gibson - DB
Kerry Goode - RB
Rick Graf - LB
Hugh Green - LB
David Griggs - LB
Lorenzo Hampton - RB
Bruce Hardy - TE
Liffort Hobley - DB
Jim Jensen - WR
William Judson - DB
E. J. Junior - LB
Brian Kinchen - TE
Barry Krauss - LB
Eric Kumerow - LB
Mike Lambrecht - NT
Paul Lankford - DB
Ronnie Lee - T
Marc Logan - RB
Dan Marino - QB
Don McNeal - DB
John Offerdahl - LB
Louis Oliver - DB
Alvin Powell - G
Willard Reaves - RB
Reggie Roby - P
Scott Schwedes - WR
Scott Secules - QB
Sammie Smith - RB
Brian Sochia - NT
Cliff Stoudt - QB
Pete Stoyanovich - K
Troy Stradford - RB
Rodney Thomas - DB
Tom Toth - G
T. J. Turner - DE
Jeff Uhlenhake - C
Jarvis Williams - DB

1989 Minnesota

John Adickes - C
Alfred Anderson - RB
Rick Bayless - RB
Ray Berry - LB
David Braxton - LB
Michael Brim - DB
Joey Browner - DB
Anthony Carter - WR
Jessie Clark - RB
Ken Clarke - DT
Travis Curtis - DB
Chris Doleman - DE
D. J. Dozier - RB
Mark Dusbabek - LB
Brad Edwards - DB
Rick Fenney - RB
Chris Foote - DB
Darrell Fullington - DB
John Galvin - LB
Rich Gannon - QB
Teddy Garcia - K
Jim Gustafson - WR
Brian Habib - T
Carl Hilton - TE
Issiac Holt - DB
David Howard - LB
Dave Huffman - G
Darryl Ingram - TE
Tim Irwin - T
Ken Johnson - DB
Hassan Jones - WR
Steve Jordan - TE
Todd Kalis - G
Rich Karlis - K
Tommy Kramer - QB
Carl Lee - DB
Leo Lewis - WR
Kirk Lowdermilk - C
Doug Martin - DE
Randall McDaniel - G
Audray McMillian - DB
Mike Merriweather - LB
Keith Millard - DT
Najee Mustafaa - DB
Darrin Nelson - RB
Tim Newton - DT
Al Noga - DE
Brent Novoselsky - TE
Allen Rice - RB
Mark Rodenhauser - C
Bucky Scribner - K
Daryl Smith - DB
Jesse Solomon - LB
Thomas Strauthers - DE
Scott Studwell - LB
Henry Thomas - NT
Herschel Walker - RB
Wade Wilson - QB
Gary Zimmerman - T

1989 New England

Marvin Allen - RB
Glenn Antrum - WR
Bruce Armstrong - T
Mike Baab - C
Jim Bowman - DB
Vincent Brown - LB
Raymond Clayborn - DB
Eric Coleman - DB
Marv Cook - TE
Terrence Cooks - LB
Greg Davis - K
Lin Dawson - TE
David Douglas - G
Reggie Dupard - RB

Hart Lee Dykes - WR
Tony Eason - QB
Patrick Egu - RB
Paul Fairchild - G
Sean Farrell - G
Jeff Feagles - K
Howard Feggins - DB
Doug Flutie - QB
Irving Fryar - WR
Tim Goad - NT
Steve Grogan - QB
Milford Hodge - DE
Darryl Holmes - DB
Maurice Hurst - DB
Roland James - DB
Gary Jeter - DE
Cedric Jones - WR
Tim Jordan - LB
Orlando Lowry - LB
Fred Marion - DB
Sammy Martin - WR
Larry McGrew - LB
Emanuel McNeil - NT
Rod McSwain - DB
Stanley Morgan - WR
Mike Morris - C
Eric Naposki - LB
Bob Perryman - RB
Tom Rehder - T
Johnny Rembert - LB
Ed Reynolds - LB
Rodney Rice - DB
Bruce Scholtz - LB
Peter Shorts - DE
Eric Sievers - TE
Kenneth Sims - DE
Jason Staurovsky - K
John Stephens - RB
Mosi Tatupu - RB
Kitrick Taylor - WR
Michael Timpson - WR
Erroll Tucker - DB
David Viaene - T
Danny Villa - C
David Ward - LB
Brent Williams - DE
Marc Wilson - QB
George Wonsley - RB

1989 New Orleans

Morten Andersen - K
Gene Atkins - DB
Tommy Barnhardt - P
Hoby Brenner - TE
Stan Brock - T
Toi Cook - DB
Glenn Derby - T
Jim Dombrowski - T
Brad Edelman - G
Brian Forde - LB
John Fourcade - QB
Paul Frazier - RB
Jumpy Geathers - DE
Antonio Gibson - DB
Rod Harris - WR
Kevin Haverdink - T
James Haynes - LB
Bobby Hebert - QB
Craig Heyward - RB
Joel Hilgenberg - C
Lonzell Hill - WR
Dalton Hilliard - RB
Rickey Jackson - LB
Undra Johnson - WR
Vaughan Johnson - LB
Walter Johnson - LB
Mike Jones - WR
Buford Jordan - RB
Joe Kohlbrand - LB
Steve Korte - C
Milton Mack - DB
Doug Marrone - C
Eric Martin - WR
Wayne Martin - DE
Robert Massey - DB
Brett Maxie - DB
Michael Mayes - DB
Sam Mills - LB
Bobby Morse - RB
Calvin Nicholson - DB
Brett Perriman - WR
Kim Phillips - DB
Greg Scales - TE
Derrick Shepard - WR
Michael Simmons - DE
Pat Swilling - LB
Patrick Swoopes - NT
Bennie Thompson - DB
John Tice - TE
Steve Trapilo - G
Floyd Turner - WR
Jeff Walker - T
Frank Warren - DE
Dave Waymer - DB
Jim Wilks - NT
George Winslow - K

1989 NY Giants

George Adams - RB
Raul Allegre - K
Ottis Anderson - RB
Stephen Baker - WR
Carl Banks - LB
Mark Bavaro - TE
Maurice Carthon - RB
Mark Collins - DB
Johnie Cooks - LB
Greg Cox - DB
Howard Cross - TE
Steve DeOssie - LB
Eric Dorsey - DE
Mark Duckens - DE
Jumbo Elliott - T
Myron Guyton - DB
LaSalle Harper - LB
Jeff Hostetler - QB
Erik Howard - NT
Mark Ingram - WR
Greg Jackson - DB
Dwayne Jiles - LB
Damian Johnson - G
Pepper Johnson - LB
Terry Kinard - DB
Bob Kratch - G
Sean Landeta - P
Lionel Manuel - WR
Leonard Marshall - DE
Dave Meggett - RB
Eric Moore - T
Zeke Mowatt - TE
Bjorn Nittmo - K
Bart Oates - C
Gary Reasons - LB
Doug Riesenberg - T
William Roberts - T
Stacy Robinson - WR
Lee Rouson - RB
Jeff Rutledge - QB
Ricky Shaw - LB
Phil Simms - QB
Lawrence Taylor - LB
Reyna Thompson - DB
Lewis Tillman - RB
Odessa Turner - WR
John Washington - DE
Adrian White - DB
Robb White - DE
Sheldon White - DB
Brian Williams - C
Perry Williams - DB
Frank Winters - C

1989 NY Jets

Dan Alexander - G
Brad Baxter - RB
Sanjay Beach - WR
Troy Benson - LB
Adam Bob - LB
John Booty - DB
A. B. Brown - RB
Chris Burkett - WR
Dennis Byrd - DE
Dave Cadigan - G
Kyle Clifton - LB
Tim Cofield - LB
Jeff Criswell - T
Titus Dixon - WR
Chris Dressel - TE
K. D. Dunn - TE
Tony Eason - QB
Phil Epps - WR
Nuu Faaola - RB
Paul Frase - DE
Kerry Glenn - DB
Alex Gordon - LB
Billy Griggs - TE
Mike Haight - G
Michael Harper - WR
James Hasty - DB
Johnny Hector - RB
Carl Howard - DB
Bobby Humphery - DB
Leander Knight - DB
Jeff Lageman - DE
Pat Leahy - K
Marty Lyons - DE
Kyle Mackey - QB
Mark Malone - QB
Kevin McArthur - LB
Reggie McElroy - T
Erik McMillan - DB
Freeman McNeil - RB
Scott Mersereau - DT
Rich Miano - DB
Michael Mitchell - DB
Joe Mott - LB
Keith Neubert - TE
Gerald Nichols - DT
Ken O'Brien - QB
Jeff Oliver - T
Joe Prokop - P
George Radachowsky - DB
Ken Rose - LB
Pat Ryan - QB
Adam Schreiber - G
Mickey Shuler - TE
Curt Singer - T
Ron Stallworth - DE
Jim Sweeney - C
Al Toon - WR
Jo-Jo Townsell - WR
Roger Vick - RB
Wesley Walker - WR
Marvin Washington - DE
Greg Werner - TE
Terry Williams - DB
Mike Withycombe - G

1989 Philadelphia

David Alexander - C
Eric Allen - DB
Ty Allert - LB
Todd Bell - LB
Jerome Brown - DT
Keith Byars - RB
Carlos Carson - WR
Cris Carter - WR
Matt Cavanaugh - QB
Randall Cunningham - QB
Matt Darwin - T
Steve DeLine - K
Alan Dial - DB
Robert Drummond - RB
Anthony Edwards - WR
Byron Evans - LB
Eric Everett - DB
William Frizzell - DB
Gregg Garrity - WR
Jimmie Giles - TE
Mike Golic - DT
Britt Hager - LB
Al Harris - LB
Ron Heller - T
Mark Higgs - RB
Terry Hoage - DB
Wes Hopkins - DB
Keith Jackson - TE
Izel Jenkins - DB
Dwayne Jiles - LB
Ron Johnson - WR
Tyrone Jones - DB
Seth Joyner - LB
Steve Kaufusi - DE
Sammy Lilly - DB
Dave Little - TE
Mike Pitts - DT
Mike Quick - WR
Ken Reeves - T
Mike Reichenbach - LB
Dave Rimington - C
Max Runager - K
Roger Ruzek - K
Mike Schad - G
Ricky Shaw - LB
Heath Sherman - RB
Clyde Simmons - DE
Reggie Singletary - T
Jessie Small - LB
Ron Solt - G
Ben Tamburello - C
John Teltschik - P
Anthony Toney - RB
Rick Tuten - K
Andre Waters - DB
Reggie White - DE
Henry Williams - WR
Luis Zendejas - K

1989 Phoenix

Michael Adams - DB
Rob Awalt - TE
Tony Baker - RB
Anthony Bell - LB
Bob Buczkowski - DE
Ron Burton - LB
Rich Camarillo - P
Lydell Carr - RB
Carl Carter - DB
Jessie Clark - RB
Bob Clasby - NT
Al Del Greco - K
Scott Dill - G
Michael Downs - DB
Earl Ferrell - RB
David Galloway - DE
Freddie Gilbert - DE
Roy Green - WR
Kevin Guidry - DB
Gary Hadd - DT
Ken Harvey - LB
Eric Hill - LB
Gary Hogeboom - QB
Don Holmes - WR
Ilia Jarostchuk - LB
Garth Jax - LB
Ernie Jones - WR
Tony Jordan - RB
Kani Kauahi - C
Derek Kennard - G
Randy Kirk - LB
Shawn Knight - DE
Cedric Mack - DB
Phil McConkey - WR
Tim McDonald - DB
Stump Mitchell - RB
Roland Mitchell - DB
Jay Novacek - TE
Freddie Joe Nunn - LB
Todd Peat - G
Walter Reeves - TE
Tootie Robbins - T
Timm Rosenbach - QB
Rod Saddler - DE
Luis Sharpe - T
Vai Sikahema - RB
J. T. Smith - WR
Lance Smith - G
Jay Taylor - DB
Mark Traynowicz - G
Tom Tupa - QB
Marcus Turner - DB
Darryl Usher - WR
Jim Wahler - NT
Karl Wilson - DE
Joe Wolf - T
Ron Wolfley - RB
Lonnie Young - DB
Mike Zandofsky - G
Mike Zordich - DB

1989 Pittsburgh

Gary Anderson - K
David Arnold - DB
Todd Blackledge - QB
Brian Blankenship - G
Bubby Brister - QB
Rodney Carter - RB
Dermontti Dawson - C
Thomas Everett - DB
Lorenzo Freeman - NT
Larry Griffin - DB
Delton Hall - DB
Derek Hill - WR
Bryan Hinkle - LB
Mike Hinnant - TE
Merril Hoge - RB
Tunch Ilkin - T
John Jackson - T
A. J. Jenkins - LB
D. J. Johnson - DB
Jason Johnson - WR
Tim Johnson - DE
Aaron Jones - DE
Carnell Lake - DB
Chuck Lanza - C
Louis Lipps - WR
David Little - LB
Greg Lloyd - LB
Terry Long - G
Mike Mularkey - TE
Harry Newsome - K
Hardy Nickerson - LB
Jerry Olsavsky - LB
Terry O'Shea - TE
Tom Ricketts - T
John Rienstra - G
Tracy Simien - LB
Mark Stock - WR
Dwight Stone - WR
Tyronne Stowe - LB
Rick Strom - QB
Weegie Thompson - WR
Tim Tyrrell - RB
Ray Wallace - RB
Eric Wilkerson - RB
Gerald Williams - NT
Jerrol Williams - LB
Warren Williams - RB
Keith Willis - DE
Craig Wolfley - T
Dwayne Woodruff - DB
Rod Woodson - DB
Tim Worley - RB

1989 San Diego

Anthony Allen - WR
David Archer - QB
Chris Bahr - K
Martin Bayless - DB
Roy Bennett - DB
Rod Bernstine - RB
David Brandon - LB
Dana Brinson - WR
Michael A. Brooks - DB
Marion Butts - RB
Gill Byrd - DB
Joseph Campbell - LB
Joe Caravello - RB
Mike Charles - NT
Lewis Colbert - K
Leonard Coleman - DB
Jim Collins - LB
Arthur Cox - TE
Quinn Early - WR
Cedric Figaro - LB
James FitzPatrick - T
Victor Floyd - RB
Chris Gannon - TE
Vencie Glenn - DB
Burt Grossman - DE
Courtney Hall - G
George Hinkle - DE
Jamie Holland - WR
Joey Howard - T
Hank Ilesic - K
Lester Lyles - DB
Don Macek - C
Phil McConkey - WR
Craig McEwen - RB
Jim McMahon - QB
Brett Miller - T
Anthony Miller - WR
Les Miller - DT
Darrin Nelson - RB
Leslie O'Neal - LB
Andy Parker - TE
Joel Patten - T
Elvis Patterson - DB
Joe Phillips - NT
Gary Plummer - LB
David Richards - G
Gerald Robinson - DE
Sam Seale - DB
Billy Ray Smith Jr. - LB
Elliot Smith - DB
Tim Spencer - RB
Johnny Thomas - DB
Broderick Thompson - G
Billy Joe Tolliver - QB
Darryl Usher - WR
Mark Walczak - TE
Wayne Walker - WR
Lee Williams - DE
Ken Woodard - LB

1989 San Francisco

Michael Barber - WR
Harris Barton - G
Steve Bono - QB
Jeff Bregel - G
Chet Brooks - DB
Jim Burt - NT
Michael Carter - NT
Mike Cofer - K
Bruce Collie - G
Roger Craig - RB
Dave Cullity - T
Keith DeLong - LB
Kevin Fagan - DE
Jim Fahnhorst - LB
Terrence Flagler - RB
Jeff Fuller - DB
Antonio Goss - LB
Terry Greer - WR
Don Griffin - DB
Charles Haley - LB
Barry Helton - P
Keith Henderson - RB
Steve Hendrickson - LB
Tom Holmoe - DB
Pierce Holt - DE
Johnnie Jackson - DB
Brent Jones - TE
Pete Kugler - DE
Kevin Lilly - DT
Ronnie Lott - DB
Guy McIntyre - G
Tim McKyer - DB
Matt Millen - LB
Joe Montana - QB
Bubba Paris - T
Darryl Pollard - DB
Rollin Putzier - NT
Tom Rathman - RB
Jerry Rice - WR
Mike Richardson - DB
Larry Roberts - DE
Bill Romanowski - LB
Jesse Sapolu - C
Mike Sherrard - WR
Danny Stubbs - DE
Harry Sydney - RB
Terry Tausch - G
John Taylor - WR
Chuck Thomas - C
Spencer Tillman - RB
Keena Turner - LB
Steve Wallace - T
Wesley Walls - TE
Michael Walter - LB
Jamie Williams - TE
Mike Wilson - WR
Eric Wright - DB
Steve Young - QB

1989 Seattle

Edwin Bailey - G
Brian Blades - WR
Brian Bosworth - LB
Willie Bouyer - WR
Darrick Brilz - G
Jeff Bryant - DT
Joe Cain - LB
Jeff Chadwick - WR
Louis Clark - WR
Darren Comeaux - LB
Donnie Dee - TE
Grant Feasel - C
Derrick Fenner - RB
Jethro Franklin - DE
Nesby Glasgow - DB
Jacob Green - DE
Kevin Harmon - RB
Dwayne Harper - DB
Elroy Harris - RB
Roy Hart - NT
Andy Heck - T
Dave Hollis - DB
Patrick Hunter - DB
James Jefferson - DB
Melvin Jenkins - DB
Johnnie Johnson Jr. - DB
M. L. Johnson - LB
Norm Johnson - K
James Jones - RB
Rod Jones - TE
Tommy Kane - WR
Thom Kaumeyer - DB
Jeff Kemp - QB
Dave Krieg - QB
Steve Largent - WR
Harper LeBel - TE
Ron Mattes - T
Vernon Maxwell - LB
Travis McNeal - TE
Bryan Millard - G
Darrin Miller - LB
Alonzo Mitz - DE
Paul Moyer - DB
Joe Nash - DT
Rufus Porter - LB
Elston Ridgle - DE
Eugene Robinson - DB
Ruben Rodriguez - K
Paul Skansi - WR
Rod Stephens - LB
Kelly Stouffer - QB
Robert Tyler - TE
Curt Warner - RB
Warren Wheat - G
John L. Williams - RB
Mike Wilson - T
Tony Woods - DE
David Wyman - LB

1989 Tampa Bay

Sam Anno - LB
Carl Bax - G
John Bruhin - G
John Cannon - DE
John Carney - K
Mark Carrier - WR
Sherman Cocroft - DB
Sidney Coleman - LB
Mark Cooper - G
Reuben Davis - DE
Willie Drewrey - WR
Donnie Elder - DB
Joe Ferguson - QB
Bobby Futrell - DB
Robert Goff - DE
Randy Grimes - C
Paul Gruber - T
Ron Hall - TE
Harry Hamilton - DB
Odie Harris - DB
William Harris - TE
Bruce Hill - WR
William Howard - RB
Donald Igwebuike - K
Curt Jarvis - NT
Rod Jones - DB
Jamie Lawson - RB
Shawn Lee - NT
Eugene Marve - LB
Tom McHale - G
Alvin Mitchell - RB
Chris Mohr - K
Winston Moss - LB
Kevin Murphy - LB
Pete Najarian - LB
Danny Peebles - WR
Frank Pillow - WR
Ervin Randle - LB
Ricky Reynolds - DB
Mark Robinson - DB
Henry Rolling - LB
Ray Seals - DE
Mike Simmonds - G
Don Smith - RB
Sean Smith - DT
Sylvester Stamps - RB
Harry Swayne - T
Lars Tate - TB
Rob Taylor - T
Vinny Testaverde - QB
Broderick Thomas - LB
Jackie Walker - TE
Rhondy Weston - DE
James Wilder - RB

1989 Washington

Brian Bonner - LB
Jeff Bostic - C
Todd Bowles - DB
Reggie Branch - RB
Ray Brown - T
Earnest Byner - RB
Ravin Caldwell - LB
Gary Clark - WR
Monte Coleman - LB
Brian Davis - DB
Wayne Davis - DB
Reggie Dupard - RB
Kurt Gouveia - LB
Don Graham - LB
Darryl Grant - DT
Darrell Green - DB
Russ Grimm - G
Dave Harbour - C
Carl Harry - WR
Stan Humphries - QB
Joe Jacoby - G
A. J. Johnson - DB
Jimmie Johnson - TE
Joe Johnson - WR
Markus Koch - DE
Jim Lachey - T
Chip Lohmiller - K
Chris Mandeville - DB
Dexter Manley - DE
Charles Mann - DE
Greg Manusky - LB
Wilber Marshall - LB
Mark May - G
Martin Mayhew - DB
Raleigh McKenzie - C
Joe Mickles - RB
Ralf Mojsiejenko - P
Art Monk - WR
Jamie Morris - RB
Neal Olkewicz - LB
Terry Orr - TE
Willard Reaves - RB
Gerald Riggs - RB
Lybrant Robinson - DE
Tracy Rocker - DT
Mark Rypien - QB
Ricky Sanders - WR
Mark Schlereth - G
Ed Simmons - T
Mike Stensrud - DT
Fred Stokes - DE
Mike Tice - TE
Clarence Vaughn - DB
Alvin Walton - DB
Don Warren - TE
Herb Welch - DB
Barry Wilburn - DB
Doug Williams - QB

1990 Atlanta

Stacey Bailey - WR
Oliver Barnett - NT
Eric Bergeson - DB
Guy Bingham - C
Steve Broussard - RB
Aundray Bruce - LB
Rick Bryan - DE
Bobby Butler - DB
Scott Campbell - QB
Scott Case - DB
Tony Casillas - NT
Shawn Collins - WR
Darion Conner - LB
Marcus Cotton - LB
Greg Davis - K
Charles Dimry - DB
Floyd Dixon - WR
Jamie Dukes - C
Tory Epps - NT
William Evers - DB
Bill Fralic - G
Scott Fulhage - P
Mike Gann - DE
Tim Gordon - DB
Tim Green - DE
Michael Haynes - WR
Chris Hinton - T
Houston Hoover - G
John Hunter - T
Tracy Johnson - RB
Keith Jones - RB
Brian Jordan - DB
Mike Kenn - T
Gene Lang - RB
Robert Lyles - LB
Hugh Millen - QB
Chris Miller - QB
James Milling - WR
Roland Mitchell - DB
Mike Pringle - RB
John Rade - LB
Michael Reid - LB
Andre Rison - WR
Rickey Royal - DB
Mike Rozier - RB
Mike Ruether - C
Troy Sadowski - TE
Deion Sanders - DB
John Scully - G
John Settle - RB
Elbert Shelley - DB
George Thomas - WR
Ken Tippins - LB
Jessie Tuggle - LB
Gary Wilkins - TE

1990 Buffalo

Carlton Bailey - LB
Gary Baldinger - NT
Howard Ballard - T
Don Beebe - WR
Cornelius Bennett - LB
Ray Bentley - LB
Richard Carey - DB
Shane Conlan - LB
John Davis - T
Kenneth Davis - RB
Dwight Drane - DB
Al Edwards - WR
Mitch Frerotte - G
Carwell Gardner - RB
Hal Garner - LB
Gale Gilbert - QB
John Hagy - DB
Chris Hale - DB
Cliff Hicks - DB
Kent Hull - C
Jeff Hunter - DE
Kirby Jackson - DB
Jim Kelly - QB
Mark Kelso - DB
Larry Kinnebrew - RB
Adam Lingner - C
Mike Lodish - NT
James Lofton - WR
Keith McKeller - TE
Pete Metzelaars - TE
Matt Monger - LB
Jamie Mueller - RB
John Nies - K
Scott Norwood - K
Nate Odomes - DB
Glenn Parker - G

Marvcus Patton - LB
Kim Phillips - DB
Mark Pike - DE
David Pool - DB
Andre Reed - WR
Frank Reich - QB
Jim Ritcher - G
Butch Rolle - TE
Leon Seals - DE
Bruce Smith - DE
Don Smith - RB
Leonard Smith - DB
Darryl Talley - LB
Steve Tasker - WR
Thurman Thomas - RB
Vernon Turner - WR
Rick Tuten - P
James Williams - DB
Will Wolford - T
Jeff Wright - NT

1990 Chi. Bears

Neal Anderson - RB
Trace Armstrong - DE
Johnny Bailey - RB
Kurt Becker - G
Mark Bortz - G
Cap Boso - TE
Maury Buford - P
Kevin Butler - K
Mark Carrier - DB
James Coley - TE
Jim Covert - T
Ron Cox - LB
Wendell Davis - WR
Richard Dent - DE
Maurice Douglass - DB
Jerry Fontenot - G
Shaun Gayle - DB
Dennis Gentry - WR
Mark Green - RB
Dan Hampton - DT
Jim Harbaugh - QB
Jay Hilgenberg - C
Vestee Jackson - DB
Dante Jones - LB
Glen Kozlowski - WR
John Mangum - DB
Steve McMichael - DT
Ron Morris - WR
Jim Morrissey - LB
Brad Muster - RB
Markus Paul - DB
William Perry - DT
Terry Price - DT
Mickey Pruitt - LB
Ron Rivera - LB
John Roper - LB
James Rouse - RB
Tim Ryan - DE
Glenell Sanders - LB
Mike Singletary - LB
Quintin Smith - WR
Lemuel Stinson - DB
David Tate - DB
Lars Tate - RB
Tom Thayer - G
Jim Thornton - TE
Mike Tomczak - QB
Keith Van Horne - T
Tom Waddle - WR
Fred Washington - DT
Peter Tom Willis - QB
John Wojciechowski - G
Donnell Woolford - DB

1990 Cincinnati

Eric Ball - RB
Michael Barber - WR
Leo Barker - LB
Lewis Billups - DB
Brian Blados - G
Ed Brady - LB
Jim Breech - K
Mike Brennan - T
James Brooks - RB
Eddie Brown - WR
Jason Buck - DE
Barney Bussey - DB
Carl Carter - DB
Bernard Clark - LB
Rickey Dixon - DB
Boomer Esiason - QB
James Francis - LB
David Fulcher - DB
David Grant - NT
Harold Green - RB
Mike Hammerstein - DE
Rodney Holman - TE
Lynn James - WR
Stanford Jennings - RB
Paul Jetton - G
Lee Johnson - P
Rod Jones - DB
Eric Kattus - TE
Bruce Kozerski - C
Tim Krumrie - NT
Skip McClendon - DE
Tim McGee - WR
Ken Moyer - T
Anthony Munoz - T
Craig Ogletree - LB
Todd Philcox - QB
Mitchell Price - DB
Bruce Reimers - T
Jim Riggs - TE
Kirk Scrafford - T
Kendal Smith - WR
Craig Taylor - RB
Eric Thomas - DB
Natu Tuatagaloa - DE
Kevin Walker - LB
Joe Walter - T
Leon White - LB
Solomon Wilcots - DB
Erik Wilhelm - QB
Ickey Woods - RB
Carl Zander - LB

1990 Cleveland

Stefon Adams - DB
Mike Baab - C
Al Baker - DE
Robert Banks - DE
Harlon Barnett - DB
Anthony Blaylock - DB
Keith Bostic - DB
Stephen Braggs - DB
Brian Brennan - WR
Bob Buczkowski - DE
Rob Burnett - DT
Raymond Clayborn - DB
Marcus Cotton - LB
Paul Farren - T
Dan Fike - G
Jeff Francis - QB
Brent Fullwood - RB
Derrick Gainer - RB
Scott Galbraith - TE
Thane Gash - DB
Tom Gibson - DT
David Grayson - LB
Mark Harper - DB
Randy Hilliard - DB
Leroy Hoard - RB
Ben Jefferson - T
Eddie Johnson - LB
Mike Johnson - LB
Vernon Joines - WR
Jock Jones - LB
Tony Jones - T
Jerry Kauric - K
Bernie Kosar - QB
Reggie Langhorne - WR
Leo Lewis - DB
Kevin Mack - RB
Clay Matthews - LB
Eric Metcalf - RB
Frank Minnifield - DB
Mike Morris - C
Ozzie Newsome - TE
Mike Pagel - QB
Michael Dean Perry - DT
Chris Pike - DT
Anthony Pleasant - DE
Gregg Rakoczy - G
Barry Redden - RB
Ken Reeves - T
Kevin Robbins - T
Ken Rose - LB
Eugene Rowell - WR
Webster Slaughter - WR
John Talley - TE
Ralph Tamm - G
Bryan Wagner - P
Van Waiters - LB
Felix Wright - DB

1990 Dallas

Tommie Agee - RB
Troy Aikman - QB
Vince Albritton - DB
Rob Awalt - TE
Bill Bates - DB
Lester Brinkley - DE
Michael A. Brooks - DB
Willie Broughton - DT
Louis Cheek - T
Willis Crockett - LB
Jack Del Rio - LB
James Dixon - WR
Steve Folsom - TE
Ron Francis - DB
Kenneth Gant - DB
John Gesek - G
Kevin Gogan - T
Dean Hamel - DT
Dave Harper - LB
Rod Harris - WR
Dale Hellestrae - C
Manny Hendrix - DB
Alonzo Highsmith - RB
Issiac Holt - DB
Ray Horton - DB
David Howard - LB
Michael Irvin - WR
Jim Jeffcoat - DE
Daryl Johnston - RB
Jimmie Jones - DT
Crawford Ker - G
Babe Laufenberg - QB
Eugene Lockhart - LB
Kelvin Martin - WR
Dennis McKinnon - WR
Nate Newton - G
Danny Noonan - DT
Ken Norton - LB
Jay Novacek - TE
Mike Saxon - P
Randy Shannon - LB
Derrick Shepard - WR
Tony Slaton - G
Stan Smagala - DB
Emmitt Smith - RB
Timmy Smith - RB
Vinson Smith - LB
Jesse Solomon - LB
Mark Stepnoski - C
Danny Stubbs - DE
Tony Tolbert - DE
Mark Tuinei - T
Steve Walsh - QB
James Washington - DB
Robert Williams - DB
Mitch Willis - DT
Ken Willis - K
Alexander Wright - WR
Jeff Zimmerman - G

1990 Denver

Ty Allert - LB
Steve Atwater - DB
Scott Beavers - T
Mel Bratton - RB
Tyrone Braxton - DB
Michael Brooks - LB
Kevin Clark - DB
Kip Corrington - DB
Scott Curtis - LB
Jeff Davidson - G
Rick Dennison - LB
John Elway - QB
Blake Ezor - RB
Sean Farrell - G
Simon Fletcher - LB
David Galloway - DE
Ronnie Haliburton - LB
Darrell Hamilton - T
Wymon Henderson - DB
Ron Holmes - DE
Mike Horan - P
Bobby Humphrey - RB
Mark Jackson - WR
Vance Johnson - WR
Jim Juriga - G
Keith Kartz - C
Clarence Kay - TE
Greg Kragen - NT
Gary Kubiak - QB
Le-Lo Lang - DB
Ken Lanier - T
Tim Lucas - LB
Jake McCullough - DE
Karl Mecklenburg - LB
Jeff Mills - LB
Orson Mobley - TE
Alton Montgomery - DB
Marc Munford - LB
Ricky Nattiel - WR
Gerald Perry - T
Bruce Plummer - DB
Kerry Porter - RB
Warren Powers - DE
Randy Robbins - DB
Jeroy Robinson - LB
Steven Sewell - RB
Shannon Sharpe - WR
Dennis Smith - DB
Elliot Smith - DB
Tim Stallworth - WR
Jim Szymanski - DE
Anthony Thompson - LB
Andre Townsend - DE
David Treadwell - K
Chris Verhulst - TE
Dave Widell - T
Doug Widell - G
Sammy Winder - RB
Mike Young - WR

1990 Detroit

Bruce Alexander - DB
Eric Andolsek - G
Jim Arnold - P
Jerry Ball - NT
Bennie Blades - DB
Kevin Brooks - DE
Lomas Brown - T
Mark Brown - LB
Jeff Campbell - WR
Darren Carrington - DB
Toby Caston - LB
Robert Clark - WR
Jackie Cline - DE
Mike Cofer - LB
Ray Crockett - DB
Ken Dallafior - G
Mark Duckens - DE
Mike Farr - WR
Keith Ferguson - DE
Bob Gagliano - QB
Dennis Gibson - LB
Kevin Glover - C
Mel Gray - WR
Terry Greer - WR
Tracy Hayworth - LB
Jeff Hunter - DE
LeRoy Irvin - DB
George Jamison - LB
Richard Johnson - WR
Victor Jones - LB
Rich Karlis - K
Aubrey Matthews - WR
Dennis McKnight - C
Bruce McNorton - DB
John Miller - DB
Eddie Murray - K
Niko Noga - LB
Chris Oldham - DB
Dan Owens - DE
Rodney Peete - QB
Lawrence Pete - NT
Jason Phillips - WR
Harvey Salem - T
Barry Sanders - RB
Eric Sanders - T
Chris Spielman - LB
Marc Spindler - DT
Terry Taylor - DB
Mike Utley - G
Andre Ware - QB
Herb Welch - DB
Sheldon White - DB
William White - DB
James Wilder - RB
Jimmy Williams - LB

1990 Green Bay

Lester Archambeau - DE
Billy Ard - G
Tony Bennett - LB
Carl Bland - WR
Don Bracken - P
Matt Brock - DE
Robert Brown - DE
Blair Bush - C
LeRoy Butler - DB
James Campen - C
Chuck Cecil - DB
Burnell Dent - LB
Anthony Dilweg - QB
Herman Fontenot - RB
Brent Fullwood - RB
George Greene - DB
Michael Haddix - RB
Mark Hall - DE
Ron Hallstrom - G
Jackie Harris - TE
Tim Harris - LB
William Harris - TE
Johnny Holland - LB
Jerry Holmes - DB
Bobby Houston - LB
Chris Jacke - K
Perry Kemp - WR
Blair Kiel - QB
Mark Lee - DB
Don Majkowski - QB
Tony Mandarich - T
Rich Moran - G
Mark Murphy - DB
Bob Nelson - NT
Brian Noble - LB
Shawn Patterson - DE
Bryce Paup - LB
Ron Pitts - DB
Jeff Query - WR
Ken Ruettgers - T
Sterling Sharpe - WR
Scott Stephen - LB
Darrell Thompson - RB
Keith Uecker - G
Alan Veingrad - T
Clarence Weathers - WR
Mike Weddington - LB
Ed West - TE
Charles Wilson - WR
Blaise Winter - DE
Jerry Woods - DB
Keith Woodside - RB
Vince Workman - RB

1990 Houston

Patrick Allen - DB
Jeff Alm - DT
Steve Brown - DB
Cody Carlson - QB
Ray Childress - DT
Doug Dawson - G
Cris Dishman - DB
Curtis Duncan - WR
Eric Fairs - LB
Bernard Ford - WR
William Fuller - DE
Teddy Garcia - K
Ernest Givins - WR
John Grimsley - LB
Leonard Harris - WR
Drew Hill - WR
Haywood Jeffires - WR
Ezra Johnson - DE
Richard Johnson - DB
Tony Jones - WR
Sean Jones - DE
Quintin Jones - DB
Victor Jones - RB
Terry Kinard - DB
Leander Knight - DB
Scott Kozak - LB
Lamar Lathon - LB
Robert Lyles - LB
Don Maggs - T
Bruce Matthews - G
Bubba McDowell - DB
Gerald McNeil - WR
Johnny Meads - LB
Glenn Montgomery - DT
Greg Montgomery - P
Warren Moon - QB
Mike Munchak - G
Erik Norgard - C
Bo Orlando - DB
Willis Peguese - DE
Jay Pennison - C
Allen Pinkett - RB
Mike Rozier - RB
Eugene Seale - LB
Al Smith - LB
Doug Smith - DT
Dean Steinkuhler - T
Dee Thomas - DB
Lorenzo White - RB
David Williams - T
Tony Zendejas - K

1990 Indianapolis

Harvey Armstrong - NT
Brian Baldinger - G
Gary Baldinger - NT
Michael Ball - DB
Joey Banes - T
Chip Banks - LB
John Baylor - DB
Pat Beach - TE
Mitchell Benson - NT
Albert Bentley - RB
Dean Biasucci - K
Duane Bickett - LB
Bill Brooks - WR
Kevin Call - T
Sam Clancy - DE
Ken Clark - RB
Chris Conlin - G
Rick Cunningham - T
Eugene Daniel - DB
Eric Dickerson - RB
Randy Dixon - G
Ray Donaldson - C
Jeff Faulkner - DE
Joe Ferguson - QB
Jeff George - QB
Chris Goode - DB
Alan Grant - DB
Jon Hand - DE
Mark Herrmann - QB
Jeff Herrod - LB
Jessie Hester - WR
Cornell Holloway - DB
Ivy Joe Hunter - RB
Ralph Jarvis - DE
Anthony Johnson - RB
Kurt Larson - LB
Quintus McDonald - LB
Sean McNanie - DE
Stanley Morgan - WR
Zefross Moss - T
Mike Prior - DB
Scott Radecic - LB
Eugene Riley - TE
Bill Schultz - T
Stacey Simmons - WR
Tony Siragusa - NT
Rohn Stark - P
George Streeter - DB
Keith Taylor - DB
Donnell Thompson - DE
Pat Tomberlin - T
Jack Trudeau - QB
Matt Vanderbeek - DE
Clarence Verdin - WR
Tony Walker - LB
Fredd Young - LB

1990 Kansas City

John Alt - T
Rich Baldinger - T
Bryan Barker - P
Mike Bell - DE
J. J. Birden - WR
Lloyd Burruss - DB
Deron Cherry - DB
Louis Cooper - LB
Danny Copeland - DB
Steve DeBerg - QB
Jeff Donaldson - DB
Irv Eatman - T
Kenny Gamble - RB
Kelly Goodburn - P
Derrick Graham - T
Leonard Griffin - DE
Tim Grunhard - C
Dino Hackett - LB
Emile Harry - WR
Jonathan Hayes - TE
Fred Jones - WR
Bill Jones - RB
Albert Lewis - DB
Nick Lowery - K
Dave Lutz - G
Bill Maas - DE
Pete Mandley - WR
Chris Martin - LB
Rob McGovern - LB
Todd McNair - RB
Greg Meisner - NT
Christian Okoye - RB
Stephone Paige - WR
J. C. Pearson - DB
Steve Pelluer - QB
Stan Petry - DB
Kevin Porter - DB
Alfredo Roberts - TE
Tracy Rogers - LB
Kevin Ross - DB
Dan Saleaumua - NT
James Saxon - RB
Neil Smith - DE
Percy Snow - LB
David Szott - G
Derrick Thomas - LB
Robb Thomas - WR
Charles Washington - DB
Mike Webster - C
Danta Whitaker - TE
Frank Winters - G
Barry Word - RB
Naz Worthen - WR

1990 LA Raiders

Marcus Allen - RB
Eddie Anderson - DB
Rich Bartlewski - TE
Greg Bell - RB
Thomas Benson - LB
Ron Brown - DB
Tim Brown - WR
Ron Burton - LB
Mike Charles - DT
Scott Davis - DE
Torin Dorn - DB
Mike Dyal - TE
Riki Ellison - LB
Vince Evans - QB
Mervyn Fernandez - WR
James FitzPatrick - T
Willie Gault - WR
Bob Golic - DT
Alex Gordon - LB
Jeff Gossett - P
Sam Graddy - WR
Rory Graves - T
Mike Harden - DB
Jamie Holland - WR
Ethan Horton - TE
Ricky Hunley - LB
Bo Jackson - RB
Jeff Jaeger - K
A. J. Jimerson - LB
Darin Jordan - LB
Dan Land - DB
Garry Lewis - DB
Howie Long - DE
Napoleon McCallum - RB
Terry McDaniel - DB
Vann McElroy - DB
Max Montoya - G
Don Mosebar - C
Vance Mueller - RB
Andy Parker - TE
Elvis Patterson - DB
Todd Peat - G
Bill Pickel - DT
Jerry Robinson - LB
Tim Rother - DT
Jay Schroeder - QB
Steve Smith - RB
Greg Townsend - DE
Dan Turk - C
Aaron Wallace - LB
Lionel Washington - DB
Bruce Wilkerson - T
Mike Wise - DE
Steve Wisniewski - G
Steve Wright - G

1990 LA Rams

Flipper Anderson - WR
Richard Ashe - TE
Latin Berry - DB
George Bethune - LB
Bern Brostek - G
Paul Butcher - LB
John Carney - K
Pat Carter - TE
Greg Clark - LB
Aaron Cox - WR
Robert Delpino - RB
Marcus Dupree - RB
Henry Ellard - WR
Keith English - P
Jim Everett - QB
Derrick Faison - WR
Brett Faryniarz - LB
Cleveland Gary - RB
Jerry Gray - DB
Gaston Green - RB
Kevin Greene - DE
Bill Hawkins - DE
Darryl Henley - DB
Cliff Hicks - DB
Pete Holohan - TE
Bobby Humphery - DB
Alfred Jackson - DB
Robert Jenkins - T
Damone Johnson - TE
Larry Kelm - LB
Bruce Klosterman - LB
Mike Lansford - K
Tony Lomack - WR
Chuck Long - QB
Duval Love - G
Mike McDonald - LB
Buford McGee - RB
Jeff Mickel - G
Joe Milinichik - G
Tom Newberry - C
Anthony Newman - DB
Vince Newsome - DB
Irvin Pankey - T
Mike Piel - DT
Doug Reed - DT
Jackie Slater - T
Brian Smith - DE
Doug Smith - C
Frank Stams - LB
Michael Stewart - DB
Fred Strickland - LB
Mickey Sutton - DB
Pat Terrell - DB
Curt Warner - RB
Mike Wilcher - LB
Alvin Wright - DT

1990 Miami

Stefon Adams - DB
Fred Banks - WR
Greg Baty - TE
Andre Brown - WR
J.B. Brown - DB
Mark Clayton - WR
Tony Collins - RB
Jeff Cross - DE
Jeff Dellenbach - T
Mark Dennis - T
Mark Duper - WR
Ferrell Edmunds - TE
Roy Foster - G
Harry Galbreath - G
Kerry Glenn - DB
Rick Graf - LB
African Grant - DB
Hugh Green - LB
David Griggs - LB
Bobby Harden - DB
Mark Higgs - RB
Liffort Hobley - DB
Jim Jensen - WR
E. J. Junior - LB
Brian Kinchen - TE
Eric Kumerow - LB
Paul Lankford - DB
Shawn Lee - NT
Garrett Limbrick - RB
Marc Logan - RB
Dan Marino - QB
Greg Mark - DE
Tony Martin - WR
Mike McGruder - DB
Tim McKyer - DB
Stevon Moore - DB
Cliff Odom - LB
John Offerdahl - LB
Alfred Oglesby - NT
Louis Oliver - DB
Tony Paige - RB
James Pruitt - WR
Mike Reichenbach - LB
Reggie Roby - P
Scott Schwedes - WR
Scott Secules - QB
Keith Sims - G
Sammie Smith - RB
Brian Sochia - NT
Pete Stoyanovich - K
Troy Stradford - RB
Rodney Thomas - DB
T. J. Turner - DE
Jeff Uhlenhake - C
Richmond Webb - T
Bert Weidner - C
Jarvis Williams - DB
Karl Wilson - DE

1990 Minnesota

Alfred Anderson - RB
Walker Lee Ashley - LB
Ray Berry - LB
Paul Blair - T
David Braxton - LB
Michael Brim - DB
Joey Browner - DB
Anthony Carter - WR
Cris Carter - WR
Jessie Clark - RB
Ken Clarke - DT
Chris Doleman - DE
D. J. Dozier - RB
Mark Dusbabek - LB
Pat Eilers - DB
Willie Fears - DE
Rick Fenney - RB
Chris Foote - C
Darrell Fullington - DB
Jim Gallery - K
Rich Gannon - QB
Brian Habib - T
Alonzo Hampton - DB
Ira Hillary - WR
Dave Huffman - G
Donald Igwebuike - K
Tim Irwin - T
Ken Johnson - DB
Hassan Jones - WR
Mike Jones - TE
Steve Jordan - TE
Todd Kalis - G
William Kirksey - LB

Carl Lee - DB
Leo Lewis - WR
Kirk Lowdermilk - C
Randall McDaniel - G
Audray McMillian - DB
Mike Merriweather - LB
Keith Millard - DT
Najee Mustafaa - DB
Richard Newbill - LB
Harry Newsome - P
Al Noga - DE
Brent Novoselsky - TE
John Randle - DE
Fuad Reveiz - K
Allen Rice - RB
Adam Schreiber - C
Cedric Smith - RB
Ken Stills - DB
Thomas Strauthers - DE
Scott Studwell - LB
Henry Thomas - NT
Herschel Walker - RB
Jimmy Williams - LB
Wade Wilson - QB
Craig Wolfley - G
Gary Zimmerman - T

1990 New England

George Adams - RB
Ray Agnew - DE
Marvin Allen - RB
Bruce Armstrong - T
Vincent Brown - LB
Gene Chilton - C
Stan Clayton - T
Eric Coleman - DB
Pat Coleman - WR
Marv Cook - TE
Elbert Crawford - C
Lin Dawson - TE
Fred DeRiggi - NT
David Douglas - C
Hart Lee Dykes - WR
Paul Fairchild - G
Irving Fryar - WR
Chris Gambol - G
Chris Gannon - DE
Tim Goad - NT
Steve Grogan - QB
Brian Hansen - P
Richard Harvey - LB
Tim Hauck - DB
Marion Hobby - DE
Tom Hodson - QB
Maurice Hurst - DB
Brian Hutson - DB
Roland James - DB
Ilia Jarostchuk - LB
Damian Johnson - G
Cedric Jones - WR
Jamie Lawson - RB
Ronnie Lippett - DB
Fred Marion - DB
Sammy Martin - WR
Greg McMurtry - WR
Rod McSwain - DB
Jamie Morris - RB
Zeke Mowatt - TE
Don Overton - RB
Bob Perryman - RB
Johnny Rembert - LB
Ed Reynolds - LB
Junior Robinson - DB
Eric Sievers - TE
Chris Singleton - LB
Sean Smith - DE
Jason Staurovsky - K
John Stephens - RB
Richard Tardits - LB
Mosi Tatupu - RB
Michael Timpson - WR
Andre Tippett - LB
Garin Veris - DE
David Viaene - T
Danny Villa - C
Mickey Washington - DB
Brent Williams - DE
Ed Williams - LB
Marc Wilson - QB
Tony Zackery - DB

1990 New Orleans

Gerald Alphin - WR
Morten Andersen - K
Gene Atkins - DB
Tommy Barnhardt - P
Hoby Brenner - TE
Stan Brock - T
Vince Buck - DB
Toi Cook - DB
Richard Cooper - T
Travis Davis - NT
Glenn Derby - T
Jim Dombrowski - T
Gill Fenerty - RB
Brian Forde - LB
John Fourcade - QB
Robert Goff - NT
Kevin Haverdink - T
Craig Heyward - RB
Joel Hilgenberg - C
Lonzell Hill - WR
Dalton Hilliard - RB
Rickey Jackson - LB
Vaughan Johnson - LB
Buford Jordan - RB
Tommy Kramer - QB
Milton Mack - DB
Eric Martin - WR
Wayne Martin - DE
Robert Massey - DB
Brett Maxie - DB
Rueben Mayes - RB
Sam Mills - LB
Bobby Morse - RB
Brett Perriman - WR
Greg Scales - TE
Michael Simmons - DE
Joel Smeenge - DE
Ernest Spears - DB
Pat Swilling - LB
Bennie Thompson - DB
John Tice - TE
Steve Trapilo - G
Renaldo Turnbull - DE
Floyd Turner - WR
Steve Walsh - QB
Jim Wilks - NT
James Williams - LB
DeMond Winston - LB

1990 NY Giants

Bobby Abrams - LB
Raul Allegre - K
Ottis Anderson - RB
Matt Bahr - K
Stephen Baker - WR
Carl Banks - LB
Mark Bavaro - TE
Roger Brown - DB
Maurice Carthon - RB
Matt Cavanaugh - QB
Mark Collins - DB
Johnie Cooks - LB
Howard Cross - TE
Steve DeOssie - LB
Eric Dorsey - DE
Dave Duerson - DB
Jumbo Elliott - T
Mike Fox - DE
Myron Guyton - DB
Rodney Hampton - RB
Jeff Hostetler - QB
Erik Howard - NT
Mark Ingram - WR
Greg Jackson - DB
Pepper Johnson - LB
Bob Kratch - G
Troy Kyles - WR
Sean Landeta - P
Lionel Manuel - WR
Leonard Marshall - DE
Larry McGrew - LB
Dave Meggett - RB
Eric Moore - T
Bob Mrosko - TE
Bart Oates - C
Gary Reasons - LB
Tom Rehder - G
Doug Riesenberg - T
William Roberts - T
Stacy Robinson - WR
Lee Rouson - RB
Phil Simms - QB
Lawrence Taylor - LB
Reyna Thompson - DB
Lewis Tillman - RB
Odessa Turner - WR
Everson Walls - DB
John Washington - DE
Kent Wells - DT
David Whitmore - DB
Brian Williams - C
Perry Williams - DB

1990 NY Jets

Brad Baxter - RB
John Booty - DB
Mark Boyer - TE
A. B. Brown - RB
Chris Burkett - WR
Dennis Byrd - DE
Dave Cadigan - G
Kyle Clifton - LB
Jeff Criswell - T
Travis Curtis - DB
Darrell Davis - DE
Dale Dawkins - WR
Chris Dressel - TE
Roger Duffy - C
Tony Eason - QB
John Galvin - LB
Mike Haight - G
James Hasty - DB
Johnny Hector - RB
Carl Howard - DB
Ken Johnson - DB
Troy Johnson - LB
Scott Jones - T
Joe Kelly - LB
Patrick Kelly - TE
Jeff Lageman - DE
Pat Leahy - K
Terance Mathis - WR
Trevor Matich - C
Michael Mayes - DB
Erik McMillan - DB
Emanuel McNeil - DT
Freeman McNeil - RB
Scott Mersereau - DT
Brett Miller - T
Rob Moore - WR
Joe Mott - LB
Dan Murray - LB
Gerald Nichols - DT
Ken O'Brien - QB
Don Odegard - DB
Joe Prokop - P
Ron Stallworth - DE
Tony Stargell - DB
Mac Stephens - LB
Jim Sweeney - C
Troy Taylor - QB
Blair Thomas - RB
Al Toon - WR
Jo-Jo Townsell - WR
Brian Washington - DB
Marvin Washington - DE
Doug Wellsandt - TE
Dwayne White - G
Dave Zawatson - G

1990 Philadelphia

David Alexander - C
Eric Allen - DB
David Bailey - DE
Fred Barnett - WR
Mike Bellamy - WR
Jerome Brown - DT
Keith Byars - RB
Dick Chapura - DT
Louis Cheek - T
Bruce Collie - G
Randall Cunningham - QB
Matt Darwin - T
Robert Drummond - RB
Anthony Edwards - WR
Byron Evans - LB
Jeff Feagles - P
William Frizzell - DB
Mike Golic - DT
Cecil Gray - G
Britt Hager - LB
Marvin Hargrove - WR
Al Harris - LB
Rod Harris - WR
Ron Heller - T
Maurice Henry - LB
Terry Hoage - DB
Wes Hopkins - DB
Keith Jackson - TE
Kenny Jackson - WR
Izel Jenkins - DB
Seth Joyner - LB
Steve Kaufusi - DE
Harper LeBel - TE
Sammy Lilly - DB
Greg Mark - DE
Jim McMahon - QB
Mike Pitts - DT
Mike Quick - WR
Ken Rose - LB
Roger Ruzek - K
Thomas Sanders - RB
Mike Schad - G
Ricky Shaw - LB
Heath Sherman - RB
Mickey Shuler - TE
Clyde Simmons - DE
Reggie Singletary - T
Jessie Small - LB
Ben Smith - DB
Daryle Smith - T
Ron Solt - G
Ben Tamburello - C
Anthony Toney - RB
Roger Vick - RB
Andre Waters - DB
Reggie White - DE
Calvin Williams - WR

1990 Phoenix

David Bavaro - LB
Anthony Bell - LB
Stanley Blair - DB
David Braxton - LB
Rich Camarillo - P
Larry Centers - RB
Dick Chapura - DT
Bob Clasby - NT
Al Del Greco - K
Tracey Eaton - DB
Terrence Flagler - RB
Roy Green - WR
Carl Hairston - DT
Ken Harvey - LB
Eric Hill - LB
Don Holmes - WR
John Jackson - WR
Garth Jax - LB
Johnny Johnson - RB
Ernie Jones - WR
Tim Jorden - TE
Kani Kauahi - C
Derek Kennard - G
Bill Lewis - C
Dave Little - RB
Lorenzo Lynch - DB
Cedric Mack - DB
Dexter Manley - DE
Tim McDonald - DB
Freddie Joe Nunn - LB
Eldonta Osborne - LB
Ricky Proehl - WR
Walter Reeves - TE
Elston Ridgle - DE
Tootie Robbins - T
Jeroy Robinson - LB
Timm Rosenbach - QB
Rod Saddler - DE
Luis Sharpe - T
Vai Sikahema - RB
Dennis Smith - RB
J. T. Smith - WR
Lance Smith - G
Vernice Smith - G
Jay Taylor - DB
Anthony Thompson - RB
Tom Tupa - QB
Marcus Turner - DB
Jim Wahler - NT
Chris Washington - LB
Joe Wolf - T
Ron Wolfley - RB
Lonnie Young - DB
Mike Zordich - DB

1990 Pittsburgh

Gary Anderson - K
Richard Bell - RB
Brian Blankenship - G
Bubby Brister - QB
Chris Calloway - WR
Kenny Davidson - DE
Lorenzo Davis - WR
Dermontti Dawson - C
Donald Evans - DE
Thomas Everett - DB
Barry Foster - RB
Lorenzo Freeman - NT
Eric Green - TE
Larry Griffin - DB
Delton Hall - DB
Carlton Haselrig - G
Derek Hill - WR
Bryan Hinkle - LB
Merril Hoge - RB
Tunch Ilkin - T
John Jackson - T
A. J. Jenkins - LB
D. J. Johnson - DB
Aaron Jones - DE
Gary Jones - DB
Carnell Lake - DB
Louis Lipps - WR
David Little - LB
Greg Lloyd - LB
Terry Long - G
Eddie Miles - LB
Mike Mularkey - TE
Hardy Nickerson - LB
Jerry Olsavsky - LB
Terry O'Shea - TE
Tom Ricketts - T
John Rienstra - G
Richard Shelton - DB
Dwight Stone - WR
Tyronne Stowe - LB
Rick Strom - QB
Dan Stryzinski - P
Justin Strzelczyk - T
Craig Veasey - DT
Gerald Williams - NT
Jerrol Williams - LB
Warren Williams - RB
Keith Willis - DE
Dwayne Woodruff - DB
Rod Woodson - DB
Tim Worley - RB

1990 San Diego

Martin Bayless - DB
Rod Bernstine - RB
Michael A. Brooks - DB
Richard Brown - LB
Marion Butts - RB
Gill Byrd - DB
Joe Caravello - RB
John Carney - K
Frank Cornish - C
Arthur Cox - TE
Quinn Early - WR
Donnie Elder - DB
Cedric Figaro - LB
Eric Floyd - G
Donald Frank - DB
John Friesz - QB
Joe Fuller - DB
Vencie Glenn - DB
Leo Goeas - G
Burt Grossman - DE
Courtney Hall - G
Ronnie Harmon - RB
Steve Hendrickson - LB
George Hinkle - DE
John Kidd - P
Nate Lewis - WR
Sammy Lilly - DB
Lester Lyles - DB
Jerry Mays - RB
Craig McEwen - RB
Joe Mickles - RB
Anthony Miller - WR
Les Miller - DT
Jeff Mills - LB
Darrin Nelson - RB
Leslie O'Neal - LB
Terry Orr - RB
Joel Patten - T
Joe Phillips - NT
Gary Plummer - LB
Fuad Reveiz - K
David Richards - G
Gerald Robinson - DE
Mark Rodenhauser - C
Henry Rolling - LB
Tony Savage - NT
Scott Schwedes - WR
Sam Seale - DB
Junior Seau - LB
Anthony Shelton - DB
Billy Ray Smith Jr. - LB
Tim Spencer - RB
Kitrick Taylor - WR
Broderick Thompson - G
Billy Joe Tolliver - QB
Tom Toth - G
Mark Vlasic - QB
Derrick Walker - TE
Lee Williams - DE
Walter Wilson - WR
Mike Zandofsky - G

1990 San Francisco

Harris Barton - G
Chet Brooks - DB
Dennis Brown - DE
Jim Burt - NT
Dexter Carter - RB
Michael Carter - NT
Mike Cofer - K
Greg Cox - DB
Roger Craig - RB
Eric Davis - DB
Keith DeLong - LB
LeRoy Etienne - LB
Kevin Fagan - DE
Jim Fahnhorst - LB
Don Griffin - DB
Charles Haley - LB
Martin Harrison - LB
Barry Helton - P
Keith Henderson - RB
Pierce Holt - DE
Johnnie Jackson - DB
Brent Jones - TE
Pete Kugler - NT
Kevin Lewis - DB
Ron Lewis - WR
Ronnie Lott - DB
Guy McIntyre - G
Matt Millen - LB
Joe Montana - QB
Bubba Paris - T
Bruce Plummer - DB
Frank Pollack - T
Darryl Pollard - DB
Tom Rathman - RB
Jerry Rice - WR
Larry Roberts - DE
Bill Romanowski - LB
Jesse Sapolu - C
Mike Sherrard - WR
Ricky Siglar - T
Fred Smerlas - NT
Harry Sydney - RB
John Taylor - WR
Chuck Thomas - C
Spencer Tillman - RB
Keena Turner - LB
Steve Wallace - T
Wesley Walls - TE
Michael Walter - LB
Dave Waymer - DB
Jamie Williams - TE
Mike Wilson - WR
Eric Wright - DB
Steve Young - QB

1990 Seattle

Dave Ahrens - LB
Ty Allert - LB
Ricky Andrews - LB
Edwin Bailey - G
Robert Blackmon - DB
Brian Blades - WR
Ned Bolcar - LB
Darrick Brilz - G
Jeff Bryant - DT
Joe Cain - LB
Jeff Chadwick - WR
Louis Clark - WR
Darren Comeaux - LB
Rick Donnelly - P
Grant Feasel - C
Derrick Fenner - RB
Nesby Glasgow - DB
Jacob Green - DE
Dwayne Harper - DB
Eric Hayes - DT
Andy Heck - T
Ron Heller - TE
Patrick Hunter - DB
James Jefferson - DB
Melvin Jenkins - DB
Norm Johnson - K
James Jones - RB
Trey Junkin - TE
Tommy Kane - WR
Thom Kaumeyer - DB
Jeff Kemp - QB
Cortez Kennedy - DT
Dave Krieg - QB
Ronnie Lee - T
Derek Loville - RB
Ron Mattes - T
Vann McElroy - DB
Travis McNeal - TE
Bryan Millard - G
Donald Miller - LB
Mike Morris - T
Joe Nash - DT
Richard Newbill - LB
Rufus Porter - LB
Eugene Robinson - DB
Paul Skansi - WR
Rod Stephens - LB
Mike Tice - TE
Joe Tofflemire - C
Chris Warren - RB
John L. Williams - RB
Terry Wooden - LB
Tony Woods - DE
David Wyman - LB

1990 Tampa Bay

Gary Anderson - RB
Jesse Anderson - TE
Sam Anno - LB
Terry Anthony - WR
Carl Bax - G
Ian Beckles - G
John Bruhin - G
John Cannon - DE
Jeff Carlson - QB
Mark Carrier - WR
Chris Chandler - QB
Steve Christie - K
Reggie Cobb - RB
Sidney Coleman - LB
Reuben Davis - DE
Scott Dill - G
Willie Drewrey - WR
Eric Everett - DB
Chris Ford - WR
Bobby Futrell - DB
Randy Grimes - C
Paul Gruber - T
Wayne Haddix - DB
Ron Hall - TE
Harry Hamilton - DB
Odie Harris - DB
John Harvey - RB
Bruce Hill - WR
Curt Jarvis - NT
Jamie Lawson - RB
Eugene Marve - LB
Tony Mayberry - C
Keith McCants - LB
Tom McHale - G
Winston Moss - LB
Kevin Murphy - LB
Tim Newton - NT
Danny Peebles - WR
Bruce Perkins - RB
Frank Pillow - WR
Ervin Randle - LB
Ricky Reynolds - DB
Rodney Rice - DB
Mark Robinson - DB
Benji Roland - DE
Mark Royals - P
Ray Seals - DE
Jim Skow - DE
Harry Swayne - T
Rob Taylor - T
Vinny Testaverde - QB
Broderick Thomas - LB
Ed Thomas - TE
Robb White - DE
Willie Wyatt - DE

1990 Washington

Mark Adickes - G
Jeff Bostic - C
Todd Bowles - DB
John Brandes - TE
Ray Brown - T
Kelvin Bryant - RB
Earnest Byner - RB
Ravin Caldwell - LB
Gary Clark - WR
Monte Coleman - LB
Andre Collins - LB
Brian Davis - DB
Wayne Davis - DB
Reggie Dupard - RB
Brad Edwards - DB
Jumpy Geathers - DT
Kelly Goodburn - P
Kurt Gouveia - LB
Darryl Grant - DT
Darrell Green - DB
Russ Grimm - G
Stephen Hobbs - WR
Stan Humphries - QB
Joe Jacoby - G
A. J. Johnson - DB
Jimmie Johnson - TE
Joe Johnson - WR
Sidney Johnson - DB
Tim Johnson - DT
Randy Kirk - LB
Markus Koch - DE
Jim Lachey - T
Chip Lohmiller - K
Charles Mann - DE
Greg Manusky - LB
Wilber Marshall - LB
Martin Mayhew - DB
Alvoid Mays - DB
Raleigh McKenzie - C
Ron Middleton - TE
Brian Mitchell - RB
Ralf Mojsiejenko - P
Art Monk - WR
Terry Orr - TE
Gerald Riggs - RB
Tracy Rocker - DT
Jeff Rutledge - QB
Mark Rypien - QB
Ricky Sanders - WR
Mark Schlereth - G
Ed Simmons - T
Walter Stanley - WR
Fred Stokes - DE
Johnny Thomas - DB
Clarence Vaughn - DB
Alvin Walton - DB
Don Warren - TE
Ken Whisenhunt - TE
James Wilder - RB
Eric Williams - DT

1991 Atlanta

Oliver Barnett - NT
Rich Bartlewski - TE
Guy Bingham - C
Steve Broussard - RB
Aundray Bruce - LB
Rick Bryan - DE
Bobby Butler - DB
Scott Case - DB
Pat Chaffey - RB
Shawn Collins - WR
Darion Conner - LB
Brad Daluiso - K
Floyd Dixon - WR
Jeff Donaldson - DB
Jamie Dukes - C
Tracey Eaton - DB
Tory Epps - NT
William Evers - DB
Brett Favre - QB
Joe Fishback - DB
Bill Fralic - G
Scott Fulhage - P
Mike Gann - DE
Moe Gardner - NT
Tim Green - DE
Michael Haynes - WR
Chris Hinton - T
Houston Hoover - G
John Hunter - T
Norm Johnson - K
Tracy Johnson - RB
Keith Jones - RB
Brian Jordan - DB
Mike Kenn - T
Harper LeBel - TE
Robert Lyles - LB
Tim McKyer - DB
Chris Miller - QB
Brian Mitchell - DB
Erric Pegram - RB
Jason Phillips - WR
Bruce Pickens - DB
Mike Pritchard - WR
Wes Pritchett - LB
John Rade - LB
Reggie Redding - T
Michael Reid - LB
Andre Rison - WR
Mike Rozier - RB
Mike Ruether - C
Deion Sanders - DB
Elbert Shelley - DB
Joe Sims - T
George Thomas - WR
Ken Tippins - LB
Billy Joe Tolliver - QB
Jessie Tuggle - LB
Gary Wilkins - TE

1991 Buffalo

Mike Alexander - WR
Carlton Bailey - LB
Gary Baldinger - NT
Howard Ballard - T
David Bavaro - LB
Don Beebe - WR
Cornelius Bennett - LB
Ray Bentley - LB
Shane Conlan - LB
Brad Daluiso - K
John Davis - G
Kenneth Davis - RB
Dwight Drane - DB
Al Edwards - WR
Mitch Frerotte - G
Eddie Fuller - RB
Carwell Gardner - RB
Hal Garner - LB
Odell Haggins - NT

Chris Hale - DB
Phil Hansen - DE
Cliff Hicks - DB
Kent Hull - C
Kirby Jackson - DB
Henry Jones - DB
Jim Kelly - QB
Mark Kelso - DB
Adam Lingner - C
Mike Lodish - NT
James Lofton - WR
Keith McKeller - TE
Pete Metzelaars - TE
Chris Mohr - P
Scott Norwood - K
Nate Odomes - DB
Chris Oldham - DB
Glenn Parker - G
Marvcus Patton - LB
Mark Pike - DE
Andre Reed - WR
Frank Reich - QB
Jim Ritcher - G
Reggie Rogers - DE
Butch Rolle - TE
Leon Seals - DE
Bruce Smith - DE
Leonard Smith - DB
Joe Staysniak - T
Darryl Talley - LB
Steve Tasker - WR
Brian Taylor - DB
Thurman Thomas - RB
James Williams - DB
Will Wolford - T
Jeff Wright - NT

1991 Chi. Bears

Neal Anderson - RB
Trace Armstrong - DE
Johnny Bailey - RB
Mark Bortz - G
Cap Boso - TE
Maury Buford - P
Kevin Butler - K
Mark Carrier - DB
Ron Cox - LB
Wendell Davis - WR
Richard Dent - DE
Maurice Douglass - DB
Jerry Fontenot - C
Chris Gardocki - K
Shaun Gayle - DB
Dennis Gentry - WR
Mark Green - RB
Jim Harbaugh - QB
John Hardy - DB
Jay Hilgenberg - C
Keith Jennings - TE
Dante Jones - LB
Glen Kozlowski - WR
Darren Lewis - RB
John Mangum - DB
Ron Mattes - T
Steve McMichael - DT
Anthony Morgan - WR
Ron Morris - WR
Jim Morrissey - LB
Brad Muster - RB
Markus Paul - DB
William Perry - DT
Ron Rivera - LB
John Roper - LB
James Rouse - RB
Tim Ryan - DT
Mike Singletary - LB
Lemuel Stinson - DB
Mike Stonebreaker - LB
David Tate - DB
Tom Thayer - G
Stan Thomas - T
Jim Thornton - TE
Keith Van Horne - T
Tom Waddle - WR
James Williams - DE
Peter Tom Willis - QB
John Wojciechowski - G
Donnell Woolford - DB
Eric Wright - WR
Chris Zorich - DT

1991 Cincinnati

Mike Arthur - C
Eric Ball - RB
Michael Barber - WR
Leo Barker - LB
Antoine Bennett - DB
Lewis Billups - DB
Brian Blados - G
Ed Brady - LB
Jim Breech - K
Mike Brennan - T
James Brooks - RB
Eddie Brown - WR
Barney Bussey - DB
Bernard Clark - LB
Mike Dingle - RB
Rickey Dixon - DB
Boomer Esiason - QB
Richard Fain - DB
James Francis - LB
David Fulcher - DB
Shane Garrett - WR
Alex Gordon - LB
David Grant - NT
Harold Green - RB
Wayne Haddix - DB
Donald Hollas - QB
Rodney Holman - TE
Lynn James - WR
Paul Jetton - C
Lee Johnson - P
Scott Jones - T
Rod Jones - DB
Eric Kattus - TE
Joe King - DB
Bruce Kozerski - C
Tim Krumrie - NT
Skip McClendon - DE
Tim McGee - WR
Alonzo Mitz - DE
Ken Moyer - T
Anthony Munoz - T
Mitchell Price - DB
Bruce Reimers - G
Reggie Rembert - WR
Jim Riggs - TE
Lamar Rogers - DE
Rod Saddler - DE
Kirk Scrafford - T
Danny Stubbs - DE
Ralph Tamm - G
Craig Taylor - RB
Eric Thomas - DB
Natu Tuatagaloa - DE
Fernandus Vinson - DB
Kevin Walker - LB
Joe Walter - T
Leon White - LB
Erik Wilhelm - QB
Alfred Williams - LB
Mike Withycombe - T
Ickey Woods - RB
Carl Zander - LB

1991 Cleveland

Mike Baab - C
Harlon Barnett - DB
Latin Berry - DB
Anthony Blaylock - DB
Stephen Braggs - DB
David Brandon - LB
Brian Brennan - WR
Richard Brown - LB
Rob Burnett - DE
Raymond Clayborn - DB
Frank Conover - T
Johnie Cooks - LB
Arthur Cox - TE
Derrick Douglas - RB
Paul Farren - G
Cedric Figaro - LB
Dan Fike - G
Anthony Florence - DB
Scott Galbraith - TE
Brian Hansen - P
Odie Harris - DB
Randy Hilliard - DB
Leroy Hoard - RB
Darryl Ingram - DB
Alfred Jackson - DB
Michael Jackson - WR
Lynn James - WR
Mike Johnson - LB
James Jones - DE
Jock Jones - LB
Tony Jones - T
Brian Kinchen - TE
Ed King - G
Joe King - DB
Randy Kirk - LB
Bernie Kosar - QB
Reggie Langhorne - WR
Ernie Logan - DE
Kevin Mack - RB
Clay Matthews - LB
Bruce McGonnigal - TE
Eric Metcalf - RB
Frank Minnifield - DB
Joe Morris - RB
Vince Newsome - DB
Mike Oliphant - RB
Danny Peebles - WR
Michael Dean Perry - DT
Todd Philcox - QB
Anthony Pleasant - DE
John Rienstra - G
Lee Rouson - RB
Pio Sagapolutele - DE
Tyrone Shavers - WR
Webster Slaughter - WR
Matt Stover - K
John Talley - TE
Ralph Tamm - G
Chris Thome - C
John Thornton - DE
Eric Turner - DB
Van Waiters - LB
Mike Wise - DE
Rob Woods - T

1991 Dallas

Tommie Agee - RB
Troy Aikman - QB
Vince Albritton - DB
Rob Awalt - TE
Bill Bates - DB
Steve Beuerlein - QB
Ricky Blake - RB
Larry Brown - DB
Darrick Brownlow - LB
Tony Casillas - DT
Reggie Cooper - LB
Jack Del Rio - LB
James Dixon - WR
Dixon Edwards - LB
Kenneth Gant - DB
John Gesek - G
Kevin Gogan - G
Alvin Harper - WR
Dale Hellestrae - C
Manny Hendrix - DB
Alonzo Highsmith - RB
Tony Hill - DE
Issiac Holt - DB
Ray Horton - DB
Michael Irvin - WR
Jim Jeffcoat - DE
Daryl Johnston - RB
Jimmie Jones - DE
Leon Lett - DE
Kelvin Martin - WR
Russell Maryland - DT
Godfrey Myles - LB
Nate Newton - T
Danny Noonan - DT
Ken Norton - LB
Jay Novacek - TE
Mickey Pruitt - LB
Curvin Richards - RB
Alfredo Roberts - TE
Mike Saxon - P
Derrick Shepard - WR
Stan Smagala - DB
Donald Smith - DB
Emmitt Smith - RB
Vinson Smith - LB
Mark Stepnoski - C
Danny Stubbs - DE
Tony Tolbert - DE
Mark Tuinei - T
Alan Veingrad - G
James Washington - DB
Erik Williams - T
Robert Williams - DB
Ken Willis - K
Alexander Wright - WR

1991 Denver

Steve Atwater - DB
Tyrone Braxton - DB
Michael Brooks - LB
Alphonso Carreker - DE
Kevin Clark - DB
Mike Croel - LB
Jeff Davidson - G
Charles Dimry - DB
John Elway - QB
Sean Farrell - G
Simon Fletcher - LB
Gaston Green - RB
Ronnie Haliburton - LB
Darrell Hamilton - T
Wymon Henderson - DB
Ron Holmes - DE
Mike Horan - P
Bobby Humphrey - RB
Mark Jackson - WR
Barry Johnson - WR
Reggie Johnson - TE
Vance Johnson - WR
Keith Kartz - C
Clarence Kay - TE
Crawford Ker - G
Greg Kragen - NT
Gary Kubiak - QB
Le-Lo Lang - DB
Ken Lanier - T
Greg Lewis - RB
Tim Lucas - LB
Karl Mecklenburg - LB
Jeff Mills - LB
Alton Montgomery - DB
Mark Murray - LB
Ricky Nattiel - WR
Bob Perryman - RB
Warren Powers - DE
Reggie Rivers - RB
Randy Robbins - DB
Derek Russell - WR
Harvey Salem - T
Steven Sewell - RB
Shannon Sharpe - TE
Dennis Smith - DB
Brian Sochia - NT
Nick Subis - C
Jim Szymanski - DE
Keith Traylor - LB
David Treadwell - K
Kenny Walker - DE
Dave Widell - T
Doug Widell - G
Mike Young - WR

1991 Detroit

Bruce Alexander - DB
Eric Andolsek - G
Jim Arnold - P
Jerry Ball - NT
Reggie Barrett - WR
Anthony Bell - LB
Bennie Blades - DB
Shawn Bouwens - G
Lomas Brown - T
Mark Brown - LB
Jeff Campbell - WR
Toby Caston - LB
Robert Clark - WR
Mike Cofer - LB
Scott Conover - T
Ray Crockett - DB
Ken Dallafior - G
D. J. Dozier - RB
Mike Farr - WR
Roman Fortin - T
Dennis Gibson - LB
Kevin Glover - C
Mel Gray - WR
Willie Green - WR
Tracy Hayworth - LB
Jeff Hunter - DE
Cedric Jackson - RB
George Jamison - LB
Melvin Jenkins - DB
Victor Jones - LB
Erik Kramer - QB
Dave Little - TE
Chuck Long - QB
Aubrey Matthews - WR
Darryl Milburn - DE
Herman Moore - WR
Eddie Murray - K
Niko Noga - LB
Don Overton - RB
Dan Owens - DE
Bubba Paris - T
Rodney Peete - QB
Brett Perriman - WR
Lawrence Pete - NT
Kelvin Pritchett - DE
Eugene Riley - TE
Barry Sanders - RB
Eric Sanders - T
Kevin Scott - DB
Chris Spielman - LB
Marc Spindler - NT
Terry Taylor - DB
Derek Tennell - TE
Mike Utley - G
Andre Ware - QB
Herb Welch - DB
Sheldon White - DB
William White - DB

1991 Green Bay

Erik Affholter - WR
Lester Archambeau - DE
Billy Ard - G
Steve Avery - RB
Tony Bennett - LB
Matt Brock - DE
Robert Brown - DE
Reggie Burnette - LB
Blair Bush - C
LeRoy Butler - DB
James Campen - C
Chuck Cecil - DB
Louis Cheek - T
Greg Clark - LB
Vinnie Clark - DB
Don Davey - DE
Walter Dean - RB
Burnell Dent - LB
Joe Fuller - DB
Steve Gabbard - T
Ron Hallstrom - G
Jackie Harris - TE
Tim Hauck - DB
Johnny Holland - LB
Jerry Holmes - DB
Chris Jacke - K
Scott Jones - T
John Jurkovic - NT
Perry Kemp - WR
Blair Kiel - QB
Kurt Larson - LB
Don Majkowski - QB
Tony Mandarich - T
Paul McJulien - P
Roland Mitchell - DB
Rich Moran - G
Mark Murphy - DB
Brian Noble - LB
Shawn Patterson - DE
Bryce Paup - LB
Jeff Query - WR
Allen Rice - RB
Ken Ruettgers - T
Sterling Sharpe - WR
Vai Sikahema - RB
Scott Stephen - LB
Darrell Thompson - RB
Mike Tomczak - QB
Esera Tuaolo - NT
Keith Uecker - T
Clarence Weathers - WR
Chuck Webb - RB
Ed West - TE
Charles Wilson - WR
Keith Woodside - RB
Vince Workman - RB

1991 Houston

Jeff Alm - DT
Herbie Anderson - DB
Gary Brown - RB
Cody Carlson - QB
Ray Childress - DT
Pat Coleman - WR
Doug Dawson - C
Al Del Greco - K
Cris Dishman - DB
Kevin Donnalley - T
Mike Dumas - DB
Curtis Duncan - WR
Eric Fairs - LB
John Flannery - C
William Fuller - DE
Ernest Givins - WR
Rick Graf - LB
Leonard Harris - WR
Drew Hill - WR
Ian Howfield - K
Steve Jackson - DB
Haywood Jeffires - WR
Alex Johnson - WR
Ezra Johnson - DE
Richard Johnson - DB
Tony Jones - WR
Sean Jones - DE
Victor Jones - RB
Scott Kozak - LB
Lamar Lathon - LB
Darryll Lewis - DB
Don Maggs - G
Bruce Matthews - C
Bubba McDowell - DB
Johnny Meads - LB
Frank Miotke - WR
Glenn Montgomery - DT
Greg Montgomery - P
Warren Moon - QB
Mike Munchak - G
Bo Orlando - DB
Willis Peguese - DE
Allen Pinkett - RB
Marcus Robertson - DB
Eugene Seale - LB
Al Smith - LB
Doug Smith - DT
Dean Steinkuhler - T
Kent Sullivan - P
Lorenzo White - RB
David Williams - T
Lee Williams - DE

1991 Indianapolis

Mel Agee - DE
Brian Baldinger - G
Michael Ball - DB
Chip Banks - LB
John Baylor - DB
Pat Beach - TE
Albert Bentley - RB
Dean Biasucci - K
Duane Bickett - LB
Brian Blados - G
Bill Brooks - WR
Kevin Call - T
Mark Cannon - C
Kerry Cash - TE
Sam Clancy - DE
Ken Clark - RB
James Coley - TE
Chris Conlin - G
Shane Curry - DE
Eugene Daniel - DB
Travis Davis - NT
Eric Dickerson - RB
Randy Dixon - G
Ray Donaldson - C
Cedric Figaro - LB
Jeff George - QB
Frank Giannetti - LB
Chris Goode - DB
Alan Grant - DB
Jon Hand - DE
Mark Herrmann - QB
Jeff Herrod - LB
Jessie Hester - WR
Rusty Hilger - QB
Cornell Holloway - DB
Darvell Huffman - WR
Matt Jaworski - LB
Anthony Johnson - RB
Brian Jones - LB
Brian Lattimore - RB
Jack Linn - T
Tim Manoa - RB
Sammy Martin - WR
Dave McCloughan - DB
Quintus McDonald - LB
Zefross Moss - T
Bob Mrosko - TE
Irvin Pankey - T
Bubba Paris - T
Bruce Perkins - RB
Mike Prior - DB
Scott Radecic - LB
Bill Schultz - T
Darin Shoulders - T
Tony Siragusa - NT
Pat Snyder - C
Rohn Stark - P
Keith Taylor - DB
Donnell Thompson - DE
Reggie Thornton - WR
Jack Trudeau - QB
Matt Vanderbeek - LB
Mark Vander Poel - T
Clarence Verdin - WR
Tony Walker - LB

1991 Kansas City

John Alt - T
Kimble Anders - RB
Rich Baldinger - T
Bryan Barker - P
Tim Barnett - WR
Billy Bell - DB
Mike Bell - DE
J. J. Birden - WR
Lloyd Burruss - DB
Deron Cherry - DB
Willie Davis - WR
Steve DeBerg - QB
Eric Everett - DB
Derrick Graham - T
Leonard Griffin - DE
Tim Grunhard - C
Dino Hackett - LB
Emile Harry - WR
Jonathan Hayes - TE
Pete Holohan - TE
Fred Jones - WR
Bill Jones - RB
Albert Lewis - DB
Nick Lowery - K
Dave Lutz - G
Bill Maas - DE
Chris Martin - LB
Lonnie Marts - LB
Todd McNair - RB
Charles Mincy - DB
Christian Okoye - RB
Stephone Paige - WR
Anthony Parker - DB
J. C. Pearson - DB
Stan Petry - DB
Kevin Porter - DB
Ervin Randle - LB
Tracy Rogers - LB
Kevin Ross - DB
Troy Sadowski - TE
Dan Saleaumua - NT
James Saxon - RB
Tracy Simien - LB
Tom Sims - NT
Neil Smith - DE
Troy Stradford - RB
Patrick Swoopes - DE
David Szott - G
Derrick Thomas - LB
Robb Thomas - WR
Mark Vlasic - QB
Charles Washington - DB
Harvey Williams - RB
Frank Winters - C
Barry Word - RB

1991 LA Raiders

Marcus Allen - RB
Eddie Anderson - DB
Nick Bell - RB
Thomas Benson - LB
Tim Brown - WR
Roger Craig - RB
Derrick Crudup - DB
Scott Davis - DE
Torin Dorn - DB
Riki Ellison - LB
Vince Evans - QB
Mervyn Fernandez - WR
James FitzPatrick - G
Willie Gault - WR
Andrew Glover - TE
Bob Golic - DT
Jeff Gossett - P
Sam Graddy - WR
Rory Graves - T
Nolan Harrison - DT
Roy Hart - DT
Jamie Holland - WR
Ethan Horton - TE
Jeff Jaeger - K
A. J. Jimerson - DE
Mike Jones - LB
Dan Land - DB
Garry Lewis - DB
Doug Lloyd - RB
Howie Long - DE
Ronnie Lott - DB
Todd Marinovich - QB
Napoleon McCallum - RB
Terry McDaniel - DB
Reggie McElroy - T
Max Montoya - G
Don Mosebar - C
Winston Moss - LB
Joel Patten - T
Elvis Patterson - DB
Jerry Robinson - LB
Jay Schroeder - QB
Anthony Smith - DE
Steve Smith - RB
Greg Townsend - DE
Dan Turk - C
Aaron Wallace - LB
Lionel Washington - DB
Bruce Wilkerson - T
Marcus Wilson - RB
Steve Wisniewski - G
Steve Wright - T

1991 LA Rams

Flipper Anderson - WR
Robert Bailey - DB
Bern Brostek - C
Ron Brown - WR
Paul Butcher - LB
Pat Carter - TE
Mike Charles - DT
Aaron Cox - WR
Terry Crews - LB
Robert Delpino - RB
Marcus Dupree - RB
Henry Ellard - WR
Jim Everett - QB
Brett Faryniarz - LB
Cleveland Gary - RB
Tom Gibson - DE
Jerry Gray - DB
Kevin Greene - LB
Dale Hatcher - P
Bill Hawkins - DE
Barry Helton - P
Darryl Henley - DB
Robert Jenkins - T
Damone Johnson - TE
Larry Kelm - LB
David Lang - RB
Sammy Lilly - DB
Duval Love - G
Todd Lyght - DB
Mike McDonald - LB
Buford McGee - RB
Joe Milinichik - G
Tom Newberry - C
Anthony Newman - DB
Mike Pagel - QB
Jeff Pahukoa - G
Gerald Perry - T
Roman Phifer - LB
Mike Piel - DT
Chris Pike - DT
Jim Price - TE
Jimmy Raye - WR
Gerald Robinson - DE
David Rocker - DT
Glenell Sanders - LB
Jackie Slater - T
Doug Smith - C
Frank Stams - LB
Michael Stewart - DB
Fred Strickland - LB
Mosi Tatupu - RB
Pat Terrell - DB
Ben Thomas - DE
Rodney Thomas - DB
Ernie Thompson - RB
Vernon Turner - WR
Karl Wilson - DE
Alvin Wright - DT
Robert Young - DT
Tony Zendejas - K

1991 Miami

Fred Banks - WR
Greg Baty - TE
Charlie Baumann - K
Ned Bolcar - LB
J.B. Brown - DB
Mark Clayton - WR
Louis Cooper - LB
Arthur Cox - TE
Bryan Cox - LB
Aaron Craver - RB
Jeff Cross - DE
Jeff Dellenbach - T
Mark Dennis - T
Mark Duper - WR
Ferrell Edmunds - TE
Harry Galbreath - G
Donnie Gardner - DE
Kerry Glenn - DB
Chris Green - DB
Hugh Green - LB
David Griggs - LB
Bobby Harden - DB
Charles Henry - TE
Mark Higgs - RB
Randal Hill - WR
Mike Iaquaniello - DB
Vestee Jackson - DB
Jim Jensen - WR
E. J. Junior - LB
Chuck Klingbeil - NT
Paul Lankford - DB
Shawn Lee - NT
Marc Logan - RB
Dan Marino - QB
Tony Martin - WR
Mike McGruder - DB
Scott Miller - WR
Scott Mitchell - QB
Cliff Odom - LB
John Offerdahl - LB
Alfred Oglesby - NT
Louis Oliver - DB
Tony Paige - RB
James Pruitt - WR
Mike Reichenbach - LB
Reggie Roby - P
Scott Secules - QB
Keith Sims - G
Sammie Smith - RB
Brian Sochia - NT
Pete Stoyanovich - K

Patrick Swoopes - DE
T. J. Turner - DE
Jeff Uhlenhake - C
Richmond Webb - T
Bert Weidner - C
Gene Williams - G
Jarvis Williams - DB
Mike Williams - WR
Dave Zawatson - T

1991 Minnesota

Terry Allen - RB
Alfred Anderson - RB
Randy Baldwin - RB
Ray Berry - LB
Joey Browner - DB
Ivan Caesar - LB
Anthony Carter - WR
Cris Carter - WR
Ken Clarke - DT
Chris Doleman - DE
Mark Dusbabek - LB
Pat Eilers - DB
Rick Fenney - RB
Rich Gannon - QB
Brian Habib - T
Tim Irwin - T
Carlos Jenkins - LB
Hassan Jones - WR
Mike Jones - TE
Steve Jordan - TE
Todd Kalis - G
Carl Lee - DB
Leo Lewis - WR
Kirk Lowdermilk - C
Greg Manusky - LB
Michael Mayes - DB
Randall McDaniel - G
Audray McMillian - DB
Mike Merriweather - LB
Mike Morris - C
Najee Mustafaa - DB
Darrin Nelson - RB
Harry Newsome - P
Al Noga - DE
Brent Novoselsky - TE
Terry Obee - WR
John Randle - DT
Jake Reed - WR
Fuad Reveiz - K
Adam Schreiber - C
Todd Scott - DB
Mac Stephens - LB
Thomas Strauthers - DE
Mike Teeter - DT
Henry Thomas - DT
Herschel Walker - RB
Solomon Wilcots - DB
Jimmy Williams - LB
Wade Wilson - QB
Craig Wolfley - G
Felix Wright - DB
Gary Zimmerman - T

1991 New England

George Adams - RB
Ray Agnew - DE
Marvin Allen - RB
Bruce Armstrong - T
Charlie Baumann - K
Vincent Brown - LB
Rob Carpenter - WR
Freddie Childress - G
Gene Chilton - C
Ben Coates - TE
Harry Colon - DB
Marv Cook - TE
Elbert Crawford - G
Irving Fryar - WR
Darrell Fullington - DB
Chris Gannon - DE
Tim Goad - NT
Tim Gordon - DB
Pat Harlow - T
Richard Harvey - LB
Jerome Henderson - DB
Marion Hobby - DE
Tom Hodson - QB
David Howard - LB
Ivy Joe Hunter - RB
Maurice Hurst - DB
David Key - DB
Ronnie Lippett - DB
Eugene Lockhart - LB
Fred Marion - DB
Sammy Martin - WR
Shawn McCarthy - P
Greg McMurtry - WR
Jon Melander - G
Hugh Millen - QB
David Pool - DB
Gregg Rakoczy - C
Johnny Rembert - LB
Ed Reynolds - LB
Leonard Russell - RB
Chris Singleton - LB
Fred Smerlas - NT
Sean Smith - DE
Jason Staurovsky - K
John Stephens - RB
Richard Tardits - LB
Gene Taylor - WR
Michael Timpson - WR
Andre Tippett - LB
Jon Vaughn - RB
Garin Veris - DE
Danny Villa - G
Bryan Wagner - P
Mickey Washington - DB
Brent Williams - DE
Tony Zackery - DB

1991 New Orleans

Gerald Alphin - WR
Morten Andersen - K
Gene Atkins - DB
Tommy Barnhardt - P
Hoby Brenner - TE
Stan Brock - T
Mike Buck - QB
Vince Buck - DB
Wesley Carroll - WR
Toi Cook - DB
Richard Cooper - T
Jim Dombrowski - T
Quinn Early - WR
Gill Fenerty - RB
Brian Forde - LB
Vencie Glenn - DB
Robert Goff - NT
Kevin Haverdink - T
Bobby Hebert - QB
Craig Heyward - RB
Joel Hilgenberg - C
Dalton Hilliard - RB
Rickey Jackson - LB
Stanford Jennings - RB
Vaughan Johnson - LB
Reggie Jones - DB
Buford Jordan - RB
Derek Kennard - G
Mark Lee - DB
Brad Leggett - C
Milton Mack - DB
Eric Martin - WR
Wayne Martin - DE
Brett Maxie - DB
Fred McAfee - RB
Les Miller - DE
Sam Mills - LB
Bobby Morse - RB
Pat Newman - WR
Calvin Nicholson - DB
Stan Petry - DB
Chris Port - G
Scott Ross - LB
Greg Scales - TE
Joel Smeenge - DE
Cedric Smith - RB
Pat Swilling - LB
Bennie Thompson - DB
John Tice - TE
Renaldo Turnbull - DE
Floyd Turner - WR
Frank Wainright - TE
Steve Walsh - QB
Frank Warren - DE
Jim Wilks - NT
James Williams - LB
Larry Williams - G

1991 NY Giants

Bobby Abrams - LB
Raul Allegre - K
Ottis Anderson - RB
Matt Bahr - K
Stephen Baker - WR
Carl Banks - LB
Roger Brown - DB
Jarrod Bunch - RB
Maurice Carthon - RB
Matt Cavanaugh - QB
Mark Collins - DB
Howard Cross - TE
Steve DeOssie - LB
Eric Dorsey - DE
Jumbo Elliott - T
Mike Fox - DE
Lorenzo Freeman - NT
A. J. Greene - DB
Myron Guyton - DB
Rodney Hampton - RB
Jeff Hostetler - QB
Erik Howard - NT
Mark Ingram - WR
Greg Jackson - DB
Pepper Johnson - LB
Clarence Jones - T
Bob Kratch - G
Sean Landeta - P
Leonard Marshall - DE
Ed McCaffrey - WR
Kanavis McGhee - LB
Lamar McGriggs - DB
Dave Meggett - RB
Greg Meisner - NT
Corey Miller - LB
Eric Moore - T
Zeke Mowatt - TE
Bart Oates - C
Gary Reasons - LB
Doug Riesenberg - T
William Roberts - T
Phil Simms - QB
Joey Smith - WR
Lawrence Taylor - LB
Reyna Thompson - DB
Lewis Tillman - RB
Odessa Turner - WR
Everson Walls - DB
John Washington - DE
Adrian White - DB
Brian Williams - C
Perry Williams - DB

1991 NY Jets

Louie Aguiar - P
Raul Allegre - K
Brad Baxter - RB
Mark Boyer - TE
Michael Brim - DB
A. B. Brown - RB
Chris Burkett - WR
Dennis Byrd - DT
Dave Cadigan - G
Kyle Clifton - LB
Jeff Criswell - T
Darrell Davis - DE
Dale Dawkins - WR
Chris Dressel - TE
Roger Duffy - C
Irv Eatman - T
Paul Frase - DE
John Galvin - LB
Mark Gunn - DE
Mike Haight - G
James Hasty - DB
Johnny Hector - RB
Bobby Houston - LB
Troy Johnson - LB
Joe Kelly - LB
Patrick Kelly - TE
R. J. Kors - DB
Jeff Lageman - DE
Pat Leahy - K
Mo Lewis - LB
Terance Mathis - WR
Trevor Matich - C
Erik McMillan - DB
Freeman McNeil - RB
Scott Mersereau - DT
Brett Miller - T
Rob Moore - WR
Browning Nagle - QB
Ken O'Brien - QB
Don Odegard - DB
Bill Pickel - DT
Dennis Price - DB
Tony Stargell - DB
Jim Sweeney - C
Troy Taylor - QB
Blair Thomas - RB
Al Toon - WR
Brian Washington - DB
Marvin Washington - DE
Ken Whisenhunt - TE
Dwayne White - G
Lonnie Young - DB

1991 Philadelphia

David Alexander - C
Eric Allen - DB
Fred Barnett - WR
John Booty - DB
Jerome Brown - DT
Keith Byars - RB
Bruce Collie - G
Randall Cunningham - QB
Antone Davis - T
Robert Drummond - RB
Byron Evans - LB
Jeff Feagles - P
Mike Flores - DE
Brad Goebel - QB
Mike Golic - DT
Cecil Gray - G
Roy Green - WR
Britt Hager - LB
Andy Harmon - DE
Rod Harris - WR
Ron Heller - T
Wes Hopkins - DB
John Hudson - G
Keith Jackson - TE
Kenny Jackson - WR
Izel Jenkins - DB
Maurice Johnson - TE
James Joseph - RB
Seth Joyner - LB
Jeff Kemp - QB
Scott Kowalkowski - LB
Dennis McKnight - C
Jim McMahon - QB
Rich Miano - DB
Mike Pitts - DT
Bruce Plummer - DB
Ken Rose - LB
Roger Ruzek - K
Pat Ryan - QB
Thomas Sanders - RB
Rob Selby - G
Heath Sherman - RB
Mickey Shuler - TE
Clyde Simmons - DE
Jessie Small - LB
Ben Smith - DB
Daryle Smith - T
Otis Smith - DB
Ron Solt - G
William Thomas - LB
Andre Waters - DB
Reggie White - DE
Calvin Williams - WR

1991 Phoenix

David Braxton - LB
Rich Camarillo - P
Larry Centers - RB
Chris Chandler - QB
Sidney Coleman - LB
Dexter Davis - DB
Greg Davis - K
Dave Duerson - DB
Anthony Edwards - WR
Scott Evans - LB
Richard Fain - DB
Jeff Faulkner - DE
Amod Field - WR
Terrence Flagler - RB
Stan Gelbaugh - QB
Ken Harvey - LB
Eric Hill - LB
Randal Hill - WR
Steve Hyche - LB
John Jackson - WR
Garth Jax - LB
Johnny Johnson - RB
Ernie Jones - WR
Jock Jones - LB
Mike Jones - DE
Tim Jorden - TE
Kani Kauahi - C
Craig Kupp - QB
Bill Lewis - C
Steve Lofton - DB
Tony Lomack - WR
Lorenzo Lynch - DB
Robert Massey - DB
Tim McDonald - DB
Freddie Joe Nunn - LB
Chris Oldham - DB
Craig Patterson - NT
Ricky Proehl - WR
Walter Reeves - TE
Tootie Robbins - T
Rod Saddler - DE
Luis Sharpe - T
Lance Smith - G
Vernice Smith - G
Tyronne Stowe - LB
Eric Swann - DE
Jay Taylor - DB
Anthony Thompson - RB
Tom Tupa - QB
Marcus Turner - DB
Jim Wahler - NT
Aeneas Williams - DB
Chris Williams - NT
Willie Williams - T
Joe Wolf - G
Ron Wolfley - RB
Mike Zordich - DB

1991 Pittsburgh

Gary Anderson - K
Brian Blankenship - G
Jeff Brady - LB
Bubby Brister - QB
Dean Caliguire - G
Chris Calloway - WR
Keith Cash - TE
Adrian Cooper - TE
Kenny Davidson - DE
Dermontti Dawson - C
Donald Evans - DE
Thomas Everett - DB
Barry Foster - RB
Jeff Graham - WR
Eric Green - TE
Larry Griffin - DB
Delton Hall - DB
Carlton Haselrig - G
Bryan Hinkle - LB
Merril Hoge - RB
Tunch Ilkin - T
John Jackson - T
D. J. Johnson - DB
Aaron Jones - DE
Gary Jones - DB
Carnell Lake - DB
Louis Lipps - WR
David Little - LB
Greg Lloyd - LB
Terry Long - G
Rob McGovern - LB
Ernie Mills - WR
Mike Mularkey - TE
Hardy Nickerson - LB
Neil O'Donnell - QB
Jerry Olsavsky - LB
Huey Richardson - LB
Tom Ricketts - T
Richard Shelton - DB
Kevin Smith - DB
Ariel Solomon - T
Dwight Stone - RB
Rick Strom - QB
Dan Stryzinski - P
Justin Strzelczyk - T
Leroy Thompson - RB
Craig Veasey - DE
Shawn Vincent - DB
Sammy Walker - DB
Gerald Williams - NT
Jerrol Williams - LB
Warren Williams - RB
Keith Willis - DE
Mike Withycombe - C
Rod Woodson - DB
Tim Worley - RB

1991 San Diego

Martin Bayless - DB
Mitchell Benson - DT
Rod Bernstine - RB
Eric Bieniemy - RB
Anthony Blaylock - DB
Marion Butts - RB
Gill Byrd - DB
John Carney - K
Darren Carrington - DB
Greg Clark - LB
Frank Cornish - C
Arthur Cox - TE
Donnie Elder - DB
Floyd Fields - DB
Eric Floyd - T
Donald Frank - DB
John Friesz - QB
Bob Gagliano - QB
Leo Goeas - G
David Grayson - LB
Burt Grossman - DE
Courtney Hall - C
Ronnie Harmon - RB
Steve Hendrickson - RB
George Hinkle - DE
Shawn Jefferson - WR
John Kidd - P
Randy Kirk - LB
Nate Lewis - WR
Cedric Mack - DB
Mark May - G
Skip McClendon - DE
Craig McEwen - RB
Anthony Miller - WR
Eric Moten - G
Leslie O'Neal - DE
Joe Phillips - NT
Gary Plummer - LB
Stanley Richard - DB
David Richards - G
Mark Rodenhauser - C
Henry Rolling - LB
Chris Samuels - RB
Sam Seale - DB
Junior Seau - LB
Anthony Shelton - DB
Billy Ray Smith Jr. - LB
Harry Swayne - T
Kitrick Taylor - WR
Galand Thaxton - LB
Yancey Thigpen - WR
Broderick Thompson - G
George Thornton - DT
Mark Walczak - TE
Derrick Walker - TE
Mike Wilcher - LB
Duane Young - TE
Mike Zandofsky - C

1991 San Francisco

Harris Barton - G
Sanjay Beach - WR
Steve Bono - QB
Todd Bowles - DB
Dennis Brown - DE
Jim Burt - NT
Dean Caliguire - C
Dexter Carter - RB
Michael Carter - NT
Mike Cofer - K
Greg Cox - DB
Eric Davis - DB
Keith DeLong - LB
Mitch Donahue - LB
Kevin Fagan - DE
Roy Foster - G
Antonio Goss - LB
Don Griffin - DB
Charles Haley - LB
Merton Hanks - DB
Tim Harris - LB
Keith Henderson - RB
Pierce Holt - DE
Johnnie Jackson - DB
Greg Joelson - DE
John Johnson - LB
Brent Jones - TE
Darin Jordan - LB
Mark Lee - DB
Kevin Lewis - DB
Guy McIntyre - G
Ralf Mojsiejenko - P
Bill Musgrave - QB
Tom Neville - G
Frank Pollack - T
Joe Prokop - P
Tom Rathman - RB
Jerry Rice - WR
Larry Roberts - DE
Bill Romanowski - LB
Jesse Sapolu - C
Mike Sherrard - WR
Harry Sydney - RB
John Taylor - WR
Chuck Thomas - C
Spencer Tillman - RB
Steve Wallace - T
Wesley Walls - TE
Michael Walter - LB
Ted Washington - NT
Dave Waymer - DB
David Whitmore - DB
Jamie Williams - TE
Steve Young - QB

1991 Seattle

Edwin Bailey - G
Robert Blackmon - DB
Brian Blades - WR
Darrick Brilz - G
Jeff Bryant - DT
Joe Cain - LB
Jeff Chadwick - WR
Bernard Clark - LB
Louis Clark - WR
Darren Comeaux - LB
Marcus Cotton - LB
David Daniels - WR
Brian Davis - DB
Dedrick Dodge - DB
Rick Donnelly - P
Grant Feasel - C
Derrick Fenner - RB
Nesby Glasgow - DB
Jacob Green - DE
Dwayne Harper - DB
Eric Hayes - DT
Andy Heck - T
Bill Hitchcock - T
Patrick Hunter - DB
James Jefferson - DB
James Jones - RB
Trey Junkin - TE
Tommy Kane - WR
John Kasay - K
Jeff Kemp - QB
Cortez Kennedy - DT
Dave Krieg - QB
Ronnie Lee - T
Derek Loville - RB
Dan McGwire - QB
Travis McNeal - TE
Bryan Millard - G
Joe Nash - DT
Richard Newbill - LB
Rufus Porter - LB
Eugene Robinson - DB
Curt Singer - G
Paul Skansi - WR
Jim Skow - DE
Rod Stephens - LB
Kelly Stouffer - QB
Doug Thomas - WR
Mike Tice - TE
Rick Tuten - P
Alex Waits - P
Chris Warren - RB
Warren Wheat - G
John L. Williams - RB
Terry Wooden - LB
Tony Woods - DE
David Wyman - LB

1991 Tampa Bay

Gary Anderson - RB
Jesse Anderson - TE
Sam Anno - LB
Terry Anthony - WR
Ian Beckles - G
John Bruhin - G
Jeff Carlson - QB
Mark Carrier - WR
Carl Carter - DB
Marty Carter - DB
Al Chamblee - DE
Chris Chandler - QB
Steve Christie - K
Reggie Cobb - RB
Tony Covington - DB
Reuben Davis - DE
Lawrence Dawsey - WR
Scott Dill - T
Willie Drewrey - WR
William Frizzell - DB
Darrell Fullington - DB
Darryl Grant - DT
Paul Gruber - T
Wayne Haddix - DB
Rhett Hall - DE
Ron Hall - TE
Harry Hamilton - DB
Alonzo Hampton - DB
Robert Hardy - RB
Alonzo Highsmith - RB
Bruce Hill - WR
Roger Jones - DB
Dexter Manley - DE
Eugene Marve - LB
Tony Mayberry - C
Keith McCants - DE
Tom McHale - G
Charles McRae - T
Kevin Murphy - LB
Tim Newton - DE
Gerald Nichols - DE
Maurice Oliver - LB
Ricky Reynolds - DB
Glenn Rogers - DE
Mark Royals - P
Tim Ryan - G
Ray Seals - DE
Jesse Solomon - LB
Rob Taylor - T
Vinny Testaverde - QB
Broderick Thomas - LB
Ed Thomas - TE
Calvin Tiggle - LB
Chuck Weatherspoon - RB
Robert Wilson - RB

1991 Washington

Mark Adickes - G
Jeff Bostic - C
John Brandes - TE
Jason Buck - DE
Earnest Byner - RB
Ravin Caldwell - LB
Gary Clark - WR
Monte Coleman - LB
Andre Collins - LB
Danny Copeland - DB
Travis Curtis - DB
Brad Edwards - DB
Ricky Ervins - RB
Jumpy Geathers - DT
Kelly Goodburn - P
Kurt Gouveia - LB
Darrell Green - DB
Russ Grimm - G
Terry Hoage - DB
Stephen Hobbs - WR
Joe Jacoby - T
James Jenkins - TE
A. J. Johnson - DB
Jimmie Johnson - TE
Joe Johnson - WR
Sidney Johnson - DB
Tim Johnson - DT
Markus Koch - DE
Jim Lachey - T
Chip Lohmiller - K
Charles Mann - DE
Wilber Marshall - LB
Martin Mayhew - DB
Alvoid Mays - DB
Raleigh McKenzie - C
Ron Middleton - TE
Matt Millen - LB
Brian Mitchell - RB
Art Monk - WR
Terry Orr - TE
Gerald Riggs - RB
Jeff Rutledge - QB
Mark Rypien - QB
Ricky Sanders - WR
Mark Schlereth - G
Ed Simmons - T
Fred Stokes - DE
Ralph Tamm - G
Clarence Vaughn - DB
Alvin Walton - DB
Don Warren - TE
Eric Williams - DT
Bobby Wilson - DT

1992 Atlanta

Oliver Barnett - DE
Steve Broussard - RB
Bobby Butler - DB
Scott Case - DB
Darion Conner - LB
Jeff Donaldson - DB
Jamie Dukes - C
Tory Epps - NT
Eric Fairs - LB
Joe Fishback - DB
Roman Fortin - G
Bill Fralic - G
Scott Fulhage - P
Mike Gann - DE
Moe Gardner - NT
Bill Goldberg - NT
Tim Green - DE
Michael Haynes - WR
Drew Hill - WR
Chris Hinton - T
Houston Hoover - G
Norm Johnson - K
Tony Jones - WR
Keith Jones - RB
Mike Kenn - T
Harper LeBel - TE
Tim McKyer - DB
Chris Miller - QB
James Milling - WR
Brian Mitchell - DB
Erric Pegram - RB
Jason Phillips - WR
Bruce Pickens - DB
Mike Pritchard - WR
Terry Ray - DB
Michael Reid - LB
Louis Riddick - DB
Andre Rison - WR
Mike Ruether - C
Deion Sanders - DB
Elbert Shelley - DB
Chuck Smith - DE
Tony Smith - RB
Jesse Solomon - LB
George Thomas - WR

Ken Tippins - LB
Billy Joe Tolliver - QB
Jessie Tuggle - LB
Charles Washington - DB
John Washington - DE
Bob Whitfield - T
Wade Wilson - QB

1992 Buffalo

Rob Awalt - TE
Carlton Bailey - LB
Gary Baldinger - NT
Howard Ballard - T
Don Beebe - WR
Cornelius Bennett - LB
Steve Christie - K
Shane Conlan - LB
Jerry Crafts - T
Matt Darby - DB
John Davis - G
Kenneth Davis - RB
Al Edwards - WR
John Fina - T
Mitch Frerotte - G
Eddie Fuller - RB
Carwell Gardner - RB
Keith Goganious - LB
Chris Hale - DB
Phil Hansen - DE
Richard Harvey - LB
Cliff Hicks - DB
Kent Hull - C
Kirby Jackson - DB
Henry Jones - DB
Jim Kelly - QB
Mark Kelso - DB
Brad Lamb - WR
Adam Lingner - C
Mike Lodish - NT
James Lofton - WR
Mark Maddox - LB
Keith McKeller - TE
Pete Metzelaars - TE
Chris Mohr - P
Nate Odomes - DB
Glenn Parker - G
Marvcus Patton - LB
Mark Pike - DE
Andre Reed - WR
Frank Reich - QB
Jim Ritcher - G
Kurt Schulz - DB
Bruce Smith - DE
Darryl Talley - LB
Steve Tasker - WR
Thurman Thomas - RB
Chris Walsh - WR
James Williams - DB
Keith Willis - DE
Will Wolford - T
Jeff Wright - NT

1992 Chi. Bears

Louis Age - T
Neal Anderson - RB
Trace Armstrong - DE
Troy Auzenne - T
Kelly Blackwell - TE
Mark Bortz - G
Kevin Butler - K
Mark Carrier - DB
Bob Christian - RB
Ron Cox - LB
Wendell Davis - WR
Richard Dent - DE
Maurice Douglass - DB
Richard Fain - DB
Jerry Fontenot - G
Will Furrer - QB
Chris Gardocki - P
Shaun Gayle - DB
Dennis Gentry - WR
Mark Green - RB
Jim Harbaugh - QB
Keith Jennings - TE
Dante Jones - LB
Glen Kozlowski - WR
Jay Leeuwenburg - C
Darren Lewis - RB
John Mangum - DB
Steve McMichael - DT
Anthony Morgan - WR
Ron Morris - WR
Jim Morrissey - LB
Brad Muster - RB
Markus Paul - DB
William Perry - DT
Ron Rivera - LB
Mark Rodenhauser - C
John Roper - LB
Tim Ryan - DT
Jim Schwantz - LB
Mike Singletary - LB
Alonzo Spellman - DE
Lemuel Stinson - DB
David Tate - DB
Tom Thayer - G
Stan Thomas - T
Keith Van Horne - T
Tom Waddle - WR
Barry Wagner - WR
James Williams - DT
Peter Tom Willis - QB
John Wojciechowski - G

Donnell Woolford - DB
Eric Wright - WR
Chris Zorich - DT

1992 Cincinnati

Mike Arthur - C
Eric Ball - RB
Antoine Bennett - DB
Ray Bentley - LB
Jim Breech - K
Brian Brennan - WR
Barney Bussey - DB
Rickey Dixon - DB
Boomer Esiason - QB
Derrick Fenner - RB
James Francis - LB
Mike Frier - DE
David Fulcher - DB
Alex Gordon - LB
Harold Green - RB
Donald Hollas - QB
Rodney Holman - TE
Lee Johnson - P
Rod Jones - DB
Randy Kirk - LB
David Klingler - QB
Bruce Kozerski - G
Tim Krumrie - NT
Ricardo McDonald - LB
Tim McGee - WR
Jon Melander - G
Ostell Miles - RB
Alonzo Mitz - DE
Anthony Munoz - T
Roosevelt Nix - DE
Carl Pickens - WR
Mitchell Price - DB
Jeff Query - WR
Thomas Rayam - T
Gary Reasons - LB
Reggie Rembert - WR
Elston Ridgle - DE
Jim Riggs - TE
Frank Robinson - LB
Lamar Rogers - DE
Kevin Sargent - T
Tony Savage - NT
Kirk Scrafford - T
Eric Shaw - LB
Milt Stegall - WR
Danny Stubbs - DE
Eric Thomas - DB
Jeff Thomason - TE
Craig Thompson - TE
Brian Townsend - RB
Fernandus Vinson - DB
Kevin Walker - LB
Joe Walter - T
Leonard Wheeler - DB
Alfred Williams - LB
Darryl Williams - DB
Mike Withycombe - T

1992 Cleveland

Bobby Abrams - LB
Randy Baldwin - RB
Harlon Barnett - DB
Mark Bavaro - TE
Latin Berry - DB
David Brandon - LB
James Brooks - RB
Richard Brown - LB
Rob Burnett - DE
Freddie Childress - T
Shawn Collins - WR
Bob Dahl - G
Cedric Figaro - LB
Dan Fike - G
Fred Foggie - DB
Scott Galbraith - TE
Brad Goebel - QB
Alan Haller - DB
Brian Hansen - P
Odie Harris - DB
Jay Hilgenberg - C
Randy Hilliard - DB
Leroy Hoard - RB
Jamie Holland - WR
Pete Holohan - TE
Alfred Jackson - DB
Michael Jackson - WR
Mike Johnson - LB
Bill Johnson - DE
James Jones - DT
Tony Jones - T
Brian Kinchen - TE
Ed King - G
Bernie Kosar - QB
Ernie Logan - DE
Kevin Mack - RB
Clay Matthews - LB
Keenan McCardell - WR
Eric Metcalf - RB
Frank Minnifield - DB
Stevon Moore - DB
Vince Newsome - DB
Michael Dean Perry - DT
Todd Philcox - QB
Anthony Pleasant - DE
John Rienstra - G
Pio Sagapolutele - G
Rico Smith - WR
Frank Stams - LB
Matt Stover - K

Terry Taylor - DB
Chris Thome - C
Lawyer Tillman - WR
Mike Tomczak - QB
Eric Turner - DB
Tommy Vardell - RB
Everson Walls - DB
Barry Wilburn - DB
Ron Wolfley - RB
Alvin Wright - DT
Lance Zeno - C

1992 Dallas

Bobby Abrams - LB
Tommie Agee - RB
Troy Aikman - QB
Bill Bates - DB
Steve Beuerlein - QB
Larry Brown - DB
Tony Casillas - DT
Frank Cornish - C
Dixon Edwards - LB
Lin Elliott - K
Thomas Everett - DB
Derrick Gainer - RB
Kenneth Gant - DB
John Gesek - G
Kevin Gogan - G
Charles Haley - DE
Alvin Harper - WR
Dale Hellestrae - C
Chad Hennings - DE
Tony Hill - DE
Clayton Holmes - DB
Issiac Holt - DB
Ray Horton - DB
Michael Irvin - WR
Jim Jeffcoat - DE
Daryl Johnston - RB
Jimmie Jones - DE
Robert Jones - LB
Leon Lett - DE
Kelvin Martin - WR
Russell Maryland - DT
Godfrey Myles - LB
Nate Newton - G
Danny Noonan - DT
Ken Norton - LB
Jay Novacek - TE
Mickey Pruitt - LB
Curvin Richards - RB
Alfredo Roberts - TE
Mike Saxon - P
Emmitt Smith - RB
Jimmy Smith - WR
Kevin Smith - DB
Vinson Smith - LB
Mark Stepnoski - C
Derek Tennell - TE
Tony Tolbert - DE
Mark Tuinei - T
Alan Veingrad - G
James Washington - DB
Erik Williams - T
Robert Williams - DB
Darren Woodson - DB
Alexander Wright - WR

1992 Denver

Jeff Alexander - RB
Steve Atwater - DB
Tyrone Braxton - DB
Michael Brooks - DB
Mike Croel - LB
Brad Daluiso - K
Jeff Davidson - G
Charles Dimry - DB
Shane Dronett - DE
John Elway - QB
Simon Fletcher - LB
Russ Freeman - T
Ron Geater - NT
John Granby - WR
Gaston Green - RB
Wymon Henderson - DB
Ron Holmes - DE
Mike Horan - P
Mark Jackson - WR
Chuck Johnson - T
Reggie Johnson - TE
Vance Johnson - WR
Victor Jones - RB
John Kacherski - LB
Keith Kartz - C
Clarence Kay - TE
Greg Kragen - NT
Le-Lo Lang - DB
Ken Lanier - T
Greg Lewis - RB
Tim Lucas - LB
Tommy Maddox - QB
Arthur Marshall - WR
Karl Mecklenburg - LB
Jeff Mills - LB
Alton Montgomery - DB
Shawn Moore - QB
Ricky Nattiel - WR
Muhammad Oliver - DB
Daren Parker - P
Bob Perryman - RB
Reggie Rivers - RB
Frank Robinson - DB
Ruben Rodriguez - P
Derek Russell - WR

Shannon Sharpe - TE
Dennis Smith - DB
Sammie Smith - RB
Brian Sochia - NT
John Sullins - LB
Cedric Tillman - WR
Keith Traylor - LB
David Treadwell - K
Kenny Walker - DE
Dave Widell - C
Doug Widell - G
Mike Young - WR

1992 Detroit

Jim Arnold - P
Jerry Ball - NT
Reggie Barrett - WR
Bennie Blades - DB
Shawn Bouwens - G
Lomas Brown - T
Leonard Burton - C
Jeff Campbell - WR
Toby Caston - LB
Willie Clay - DB
Mike Cofer - LB
Harry Colon - DB
Scott Conover - T
Ray Crockett - DB
Ken Dallafior - G
John Derby - LB
Mike Farr - WR
Darryl Ford - LB
Dennis Gibson - LB
Kevin Glover - C
Mel Gray - WR
Willie Green - WR
Jason Hanson - K
Tracy Hayworth - LB
Mike Hinnant - TE
Jeff Hunter - DE
George Jamison - LB
Melvin Jenkins - DB
Jimmie Johnson - TE
Troy Johnson - LB
Andre Jones - LB
Victor Jones - LB
Erik Kramer - QB
Jack Linn - G
Eric Lynch - G
Aubrey Matthews - WR
Mike McDonald - LB
Dennis McKnight - C
Thomas McLemore - TE
Blake Miller - C
Herman Moore - WR
Don Overton - RB
Dan Owens - DE
Rodney Peete - QB
Brett Perriman - WR
Lawrence Pete - NT
Robert Porcher - DE
Kelvin Pritchett - DE
Junior Robinson - DB
Barry Sanders - RB
Eric Sanders - T
Kevin Scott - DB
Tracy Scroggins - LB
Chris Spielman - LB
Marc Spindler - DE
Troy Stradford - RB
Larry Tharpe - T
Ed Tillison - RB
Andre Ware - QB
Sheldon White - DB
William White - DB

1992 Green Bay

Lester Archambeau - DE
Sebastian Barrie - DE
Sanjay Beach - WR
Edgar Bennett - RB
Tony Bennett - LB
Lewis Billups - DB
Jeff Brady - LB
Matt Brock - DE
Robert Brooks - WR
Robert Brown - LB
Terrell Buckley - DB
LeRoy Butler - DB
James Campen - C
Carl Carter - DB
Chuck Cecil - DB
Vinnie Clark - DB
Brett Collins - LB
Don Davey - DE
Burnell Dent - LB
Mark D'Onofrio - LB
Brett Favre - QB
Cecil Gray - T
Ron Hallstrom - G
Corey Harris - DB
Jackie Harris - TE
Tim Hauck - DB
Johnny Holland - LB
Darryl Ingram - TE
Chris Jacke - K
Johnnie Jackson - DB
John Jurkovic - NT
George Koonce - LB
Ron Lewis - WR
Don Majkowski - QB
Dave McCloughan - DB
Buford McGee - RB
Paul McJulien - P

Dexter McNabb - RB
Keith Millard - DE
Roland Mitchell - DB
Rich Moran - G
Tom Neville - G
Brian Noble - LB
Danny Noonan - NT
Alfred Oglesby - NT
Bryce Paup - LB
Tootie Robbins - T
Ken Ruettgers - T
Harvey Salem - G
Sterling Sharpe - WR
Joe Sims - T
Harry Sydney - RB
Kitrick Taylor - WR
Darrell Thompson - RB
Esera Tuaolo - NT
David Viaene - T
Bryan Wagner - P
Ed West - TE
Adrian White - DB
Marcus Wilson - RB
Frank Winters - C
Vince Workman - RB

1992 Houston

Jeff Alm - DT
Joe Bowden - LB
Tony Brown - DB
Gary Brown - RB
Cody Carlson - QB
Ray Childress - DT
Pat Coleman - WR
Doug Dawson - G
Al Del Greco - K
Cris Dishman - DB
Kevin Donnalley - T
Mike Dumas - DB
Curtis Duncan - WR
John Flannery - G
William Fuller - DE
Ernest Givins - WR
Rick Graf - LB
Jerry Gray - DB
Corey Harris - WR
Leonard Harris - WR
Steve Jackson - DB
Haywood Jeffires - WR
Richard Johnson - DB
Sean Jones - DE
Scott Kozak - LB
Lamar Lathon - LB
Darryll Lewis - DB
Don Maggs - T
Bruce Matthews - C
Damon Mays - WR
Bubba McDowell - DB
Johnny Meads - LB
Glenn Montgomery - DT
Greg Montgomery - P
Warren Moon - QB
Mike Munchak - G
Erik Norgard - C
Bo Orlando - DB
Willis Peguese - DE
Bucky Richardson - QB
Tim Roberts - DT
Marcus Robertson - DB
Eddie Robinson - LB
Eugene Seale - LB
Webster Slaughter - WR
Al Smith - LB
Doug Smith - DT
Spencer Tillman - RB
Craig Veasey - DT
Gary Wellman - WR
Lorenzo White - RB
David Williams - T
Lee Williams - DE

1992 Indianapolis

Mel Agee - DE
Ashley Ambrose - DB
Charles Arbuckle - TE
Michael Ball - DB
Chip Banks - LB
John Baylor - DB
Jason Belser - DB
Dean Biasucci - K
Duane Bickett - LB
Bill Brooks - WR
Kevin Call - T
Maurice Carthon - RB
Kerry Cash - TE
Sam Clancy - DE
Ken Clark - RB
Quentin Coryatt - LB
Rodney Culver - RB
Eugene Daniel - DB
Randy Dixon - G
Ray Donaldson - C
Steve Emtman - DE
Jeff George - QB
Chris Goode - DB
Steve Grant - LB
Jon Hand - DE
Mark Herrmann - QB
Jeff Herrod - LB
Jessie Hester - WR
Cornell Holloway - DB
Anthony Johnson - RB
Reggie Langhorne - WR
Trevor Match - G

Ron Mattes - T
Skip McClendon - DE
Tony McCoy - NT
Eddie Miller - WR
Zefross Moss - T
Irvin Pankey - T
Willis Peguese - DE
Mike Prior - DB
Scott Radecic - LB
Tom Ricketts - G
Bill Schultz - T
Tony Siragusa - NT
Ron Solt - G
Tony Stargell - DB
Rohn Stark - P
Ed Toner - RB
Jack Trudeau - QB
Tom Tupa - QB
Matt Vanderbeek - LB
Mark Vander Poel - T
Clarence Verdin - WR
Tony Walker - LB

1992 Kansas City

John Alt - T
Kimble Anders - RB
Mike Baab - C
Rich Baldinger - T
Bryan Barker - P
Tim Barnett - WR
Martin Bayless - DB
J. J. Birden - WR
Dale Carter - DB
Keith Cash - TE
Willie Davis - WR
Tom Dohring - T
Mike Dyal - TE
Mike Evans - DT
Derrick Graham - T
Leonard Griffin - DE
Tim Grunhard - C
Tony Hargain - WR
Emile Harry - WR
Jonathan Hayes - TE
Fred Jones - WR
Bill Jones - RB
Kani Kauahi - C
Dave Krieg - QB
Albert Lewis - DB
Tahaun Lewis - DB
Nick Lowery - K
Dave Lutz - G
Bill Maas - DE
Cedric Mack - DB
Darrell Malone - DB
Chris Martin - LB
Lonnie Marts - LB
Todd McNair - RB
Darren Mickell - DE
Charles Mincy - DB
Eddie Murray - K
Christian Okoye - RB
J. C. Pearson - DB
Joe Phillips - DT
Kevin Porter - DB
Ervin Randle - LB
Tracy Rogers - LB
Kevin Ross - DB
Dan Saleaumua - DT
Tracy Simien - LB
Tom Sims - DT
Michael Smith - WR
Neil Smith - DE
Percy Snow - LB
Joe Staysniak - G
Kent Sullivan - P
David Szott - G
Doug Terry - DB
Derrick Thomas - LB
Bennie Thompson - DB
Joe Valerio - T
Harvey Williams - RB
Barry Word - RB

1992 LA Raiders

Marcus Allen - RB
Eddie Anderson - DB
Anthony Bell - LB
Nick Bell - RB
Thomas Benson - LB
Willie Broughton - DT
Tim Brown - WR
Aundray Bruce - DE
Eric Dickerson - RB
Torin Dorn - DB
Riki Ellison - LB
Vince Evans - QB
Mervyn Fernandez - WR
Derrick Gainer - RB
Willie Gault - WR
Andrew Glover - TE
Bob Golic - DT
Jeff Gossett - P
Sam Graddy - WR
Nolan Harrison - DT
Ethan Horton - TE
Derrick Hoskins - DB
Jeff Jaeger - K
David Jones - TE
Mike Jones - LB
Dan Land - DB
Howie Long - DE
Ronnie Lott - DB
Todd Marinovich - QB

Napoleon McCallum - RB
Terry McDaniel - DB
Reggie McElroy - T
Chester McGlockton - DT
Max Montoya - G
Don Mosebar - C
Winston Moss - LB
Elvis Patterson - DB
Todd Peat - G
Jay Schroeder - QB
Sam Seale - DB
Greg Skrepenak - G
Anthony Smith - DE
Kevin Smith - RB
Steve Smith - RB
Greg Townsend - DE
Dan Turk - C
Aaron Wallace - LB
Lionel Washington - DB
Dave Waymer - DB
Bruce Wilkerson - T
Steve Wisniewski - G
Alexander Wright - WR
Steve Wright - T

1992 LA Rams

Flipper Anderson - WR
Robert Bailey - DB
Marc Boutte - DT
Don Bracken - P
Bern Brostek - C
Blair Bush - C
Paul Butcher - LB
Pat Carter - TE
Jeff Chadwick - WR
Aaron Cox - WR
Chris Crooms - DB
Robert Delpino - RB
Henry Ellard - WR
Jim Everett - QB
Cleveland Gary - RB
Sean Gilbert - DT
Kevin Greene - LB
Emile Harry - WR
Bill Hawkins - DE
Eric Hayes - DT
Darryl Henley - DB
Steve Israel - DB
Robert Jenkins - T
Damone Johnson - TE
Larry Kelm - LB
Todd Kinchen - WR
David Lang - RB
Tim Lester - RB
Sammy Lilly - DB
Todd Lyght - DB
Travis McNeal - TE
Joe Milinichik - G
Tom Newberry - G
Anthony Newman - DB
Mike Pagel - QB
Jeff Pahukoa - G
Gerald Perry - T
Roman Phifer - LB
Mike Piel - DT
Warren Powers - DE
Jim Price - TE
Gerald Robinson - DE
David Rocker - DT
Jim Skow - DE
Jackie Slater - T
Scott Stephen - LB
Michael Stewart - DB
Troy Stradford - RB
Fred Strickland - LB
Pat Terrell - DB
Anthony Thompson - RB
Vernon Turner - WR
Leon White - LB
Alvin Wright - DT
Robert Young - DE
Tony Zendejas - K

1992 Miami

Bruce Alexander - DB
Fred Banks - WR
Greg Baty - TE
Stephen Braggs - DB
J.B. Brown - DB
Robert Clark - WR
Mark Clayton - WR
Marco Coleman - DE
Roosevelt Collins - LB
Bryan Cox - LB
Aaron Craver - RB
Jeff Cross - DE
Jeff Dellenbach - T
Mark Dennis - T
Mark Duper - WR
Ferrell Edmunds - TE
Harry Galbreath - G
Kerry Glenn - DB
Chris Green - DB
David Griggs - DE
John Grimsley - LB
Bobby Harden - DB
Mark Higgs - RB
Liffort Hobley - DB
Dwight Hollier - LB
Bobby Humphrey - RB
Jeff Hunter - DE

Keith Jackson - TE
Vestee Jackson - DB
Jim Jensen - WR
Chuck Klingbeil - NT
Darrell Malone - DB
Dan Marino - QB
Tony Martin - WR
Scott Miller - WR
Scott Mitchell - QB
Dave Moore - TE
Cliff Odom - LB
John Offerdahl - LB
Alfred Oglesby - NT
Louis Oliver - DB
Tony Paige - RB
Bernie Parmalee - RB
Joe Prokop - P
Reggie Roby - P
Mark Sander - LB
James Saxon - RB
Keith Sims - G
Pete Stoyanovich - K
T. J. Turner - NT
Jeff Uhlenhake - C
Troy Vincent - DB
Richmond Webb - T
Larry Webster - DT
Bert Weidner - G
Gene Williams - G
Jarvis Williams - DB
Mike Williams - WR

1992 Minnesota

Scott Adams - G
Terry Allen - RB
Roy Barker - DT
David Bavaro - LB
Ray Berry - LB
Anthony Carter - WR
Cris Carter - WR
Roger Craig - RB
Brad Culpepper - DT
Bernard Dafney - G
Jack Del Rio - LB
Chris Doleman - DE
Eric Everett - DB
Rich Gannon - QB
Vencie Glenn - DB
Brian Habib - G
Robert Harris - DE
Keith Henderson - RB
George Hinkle - DT
Tim Irwin - T
Carlos Jenkins - LB
Joe Johnson - WR
Hassan Jones - WR
Steve Jordan - TE
Carl Lee - DB
Kirk Lowdermilk - C
Greg Manusky - LB
Skip McClendon - DE
Ed McDaniel - LB
Randall McDaniel - G
Audray McMillian - DB
Mike Merriweather - LB
Mike Morris - C
Darrin Nelson - RB
Harry Newsome - P
Al Noga - DE
Brent Novoselsky - TE
Anthony Parker - DB
John Randle - DT
Jake Reed - WR
Fuad Reveiz - K
Sean Salisbury - QB
Adam Schreiber - C
Todd Scott - DB
Derek Tennell - TE
Henry Thomas - DT
Mike Tice - TE
Esera Tuaolo - DT
Van Waiters - LB
Tripp Welborne - DB
Ronnie West - WR
Danta Whitaker - WR
David Wilson - DB
Felix Wright - DB
Gary Zimmerman - T

1992 New England

Ray Agnew - DE
Darren Anderson - DB
Bruce Armstrong - T
Charlie Baumann - K
Roger Brown - DB
Vincent Brown - LB
Jeff Carlson - QB
Gene Chilton - C
Eugene Chung - T
Ben Coates - TE
Todd Collins - LB
Marv Cook - TE
Tim Edwards - DE
Irving Fryar - WR
Chris Gannon - DE
Sam Gash - RB
Tim Goad - NT
Tim Gordon - DB
Pat Harlow - T
Jerome Henderson - DB
Marion Hobby - DE
Tom Hodson - QB
David Howard - LB
Maurice Hurst - DB

Dion Lambert - DB
Eugene Lockhart - LB
Scott Lockwood - RB
Shawn McCarthy - P
Rob McGovern - LB
Greg McMurtry - WR
Hugh Millen - QB
David Pool - DB
Gregg Rakoczy - G
Reggie Redding - G
Johnny Rembert - LB
Randy Robbins - DB
Leonard Russell - RB
Dwayne Sabb - LB
Chris Singleton - LB
Fred Smerlas - NT
Rod Smith - DB
Walter Stanley - WR
Calvin Stephens - G
John Stephens - RB
Richard Tardits - LB
Michael Timpson - WR
Andre Tippett - LB
Kevin Turner - RB
Jon Vaughn - RB
Brent Williams - DE
Larry Williams - G
David Wilson - G
Scott Zolak - QB

1992 New Orleans

Morten Andersen - K
Gene Atkins - DB
Tommy Barnhardt - P
Hoby Brenner - TE
Stan Brock - T
Mike Buck - QB
Vince Buck - DB
Wesley Carroll - WR
Toi Cook - DB
Richard Cooper - T
Jim Dombrowski - T
Marcus Dowdell - WR
Vaughn Dunbar - RB
Quinn Early - WR
Antonio Gibson - DB
Robert Goff - NT
Bobby Hebert - QB
Craig Heyward - RB
Joel Hilgenberg - C
Dalton Hilliard - RB
Rickey Jackson - LB
Paul Jetton - C
Vaughan Johnson - LB
Reggie Jones - DB
Buford Jordan - RB
Derek Kennard - G
Tyrone Legette - DB
Louis Lipps - WR
Sean Lumpkin - DB
Cedric Mack - DB
Eric Martin - WR
Wayne Martin - DE
Brett Maxie - DB
Fred McAfee - RB
Les Miller - DE
Sam Mills - LB
Pat Newman - WR
Chris Port - G
Torrance Small - WR
Joel Smeenge - DE
Jimmy Spencer - DB
Tommie Stowers - TE
Pat Swilling - LB
Keith Taylor - DB
John Tice - TE
Steve Trapilo - G
Renaldo Turnbull - DE
Floyd Turner - WR
Frank Wainright - TE
Frank Warren - DE
Jim Wilks - NT
James Williams - LB
DeMond Winston - LB

1992 NY Giants

Bobby Abrams - LB
Ottis Anderson - RB
Matt Bahr - K
Stephen Baker - WR
Carl Banks - LB
John Brandes - TE
Dave Brown - QB
Derek Brown - TE
Jarrod Bunch - RB
Chris Calloway - WR
Jesse Campbell - DB
Mark Collins - DB
Howard Cross - TE
Steve DeOssie - LB
Stacey Dillard - DE
Eric Dorsey - DE
Jumbo Elliott - T
Mike Fox - DE
Kent Graham - QB
Myron Guyton - DB
Keith Hamilton - DE
Rodney Hampton - RB
Jeff Hostetler - QB
Erik Howard - NT
Mark Ingram - WR
Greg Jackson - DB
Pepper Johnson - LB
Clarence Jones - T

Bob Kratch - G
Sean Landeta - P
Leonard Marshall - DE
Ed McCaffrey - WR
Kanavis McGhee - LB
Lamar McGriggs - DB
Dave Meggett - RB
Corey Miller - LB
Eric Moore - T
Bart Oates - C
Aaron Pierce - TE
Joe Prokop - P
Corey Raymond - DB
Ed Reynolds - LB
Doug Riesenberg - T
William Roberts - G
Ruben Rodriguez - P
Phil Simms - QB
Joey Smith - WR
Phillippi Sparks - DB
Lawrence Taylor - LB
Reyna Thompson - DB
Lewis Tillman - RB
Everson Walls - DB
John Washington - DE
Corey Widmer - DE
Brian Williams - C
Perry Williams - DB
Ken Willis - K

1992 NY Jets

Louie Aguiar - P
Kurt Barber - LB
Brad Baxter - RB
Jeff Blake - QB
Cary Blanchard - K
Mark Boyer - TE
Michael Brim - DB
A. B. Brown - RB
Chris Burkett - WR
Dennis Byrd - DE
Dave Cadigan - G
Glenn Cadrez - LB
Sheldon Canley - RB
Rob Carpenter - WR
Pat Chaffey - RB
Kyle Clifton - LB
Keo Coleman - LB
Jeff Criswell - T
Dale Dawkins - WR
Cal Dixon - C
Roger Duffy - G
Irv Eatman - T
Joe Fishback - DB
Paul Frase - DT
Scottie Graham - RB
Mark Gunn - DT
James Hasty - DB
Johnny Hector - RB
Bobby Houston - LB
Mario Johnson - DT
Don Jones - LB
Eric Kattus - TE
Joe Kelly - LB
R. J. Kors - DB
Jeff Lageman - DE
Mo Lewis - LB
Siupeli Malamala - T
Terance Mathis - WR
Erik McMillan - DB
Freeman McNeil - RB
Scott Mersereau - DT
Brett Miller - T
Johnny Mitchell - TE
Rob Moore - WR
Browning Nagle - QB
Ken O'Brien - QB
Bill Pickel - DT
Kevin Porter - DB
Dennis Price - DB
Huey Richardson - LB
Troy Sadowski - TE
Jason Staurovsky - K
Jim Sweeney - C
Blair Thomas - RB
Al Toon - WR
Marcus Turner - DB
Brian Washington - DB
Marvin Washington - DE
Ken Whisenhunt - TE
Dwayne White - G
Karl Wilson - DT
Lonnie Young - DB

1992 Philadelphia

David Alexander - C
Eric Allen - DB
Brian Baldinger - G
Fred Barnett - WR
Ephesians Bartley - LB
Pat Beach - TE
John Booty - DB
Tony Brooks - RB
Keith Byars - TE
Randall Cunningham - QB
Antone Davis - T
Floyd Dixon - WR
Byron Evans - LB
Jeff Feagles - P
Mike Flores - DE
Eric Floyd - G
William Frizzell - DB
Tom Gerhart - DB

Mike Golic - DT
Roy Green - WR
Britt Hager - LB
Andy Harmon - DT
Ron Heller - T
Wes Hopkins - DB
John Hudson - G
Izel Jenkins - DB
Tommy Jeter - DT
Maurice Johnson - TE
James Joseph - RB
Seth Joyner - LB
Scott Kowalkowski - LB
Jim McMahon - QB
Mark McMillian - DB
Rich Miano - DB
Mike Pitts - DT
Ken Rose - LB
Roger Ruzek - K
Mike Schad - G
Leon Seals - DT
Rob Selby - G
Heath Sherman - RB
Vai Sikahema - WR
Clyde Simmons - DE
Daryle Smith - T
Otis Smith - DB
Siran Stacy - RB
Jeff Sydner - WR
William Thomas - LB
Herschel Walker - RB
Andre Waters - DB
Reggie White - DE
Calvin Williams - WR

1992 Phoenix

Johnny Bailey - RB
Michael Bankston - DE
Rob Baxley - T
Eric Blount - RB
David Braxton - LB
Ivory Lee Brown - RB
Rich Camarillo - P
Larry Centers - RB
Chris Chandler - QB
Ed Cunningham - C
Rick Cunningham - T
Dexter Davis - DB
Greg Davis - K
Reuben Davis - DE
Dave Duerson - DB
Anthony Edwards - WR
Jeff Faulkner - DE
Odie Harris - DB
Ken Harvey - LB
Eric Hill - LB
Randal Hill - WR
Steve Hyche - LB
John Jackson - WR
Garth Jax - LB
Johnny Johnson - RB
Ernie Jones - WR
Jock Jones - LB
Mike Jones - DE
Bill Lewis - C
Steve Lofton - DB
Lorenzo Lynch - DB
Robert Massey - DB
Mark May - G
Tim McDonald - DB
Freddie Joe Nunn - LB
Chris Oldham - DB
Mitchell Price - DB
Ricky Proehl - WR
Walter Reeves - TE
Butch Rolle - TE
Timm Rosenbach - QB
Keith Rucker - DE
Tony Sacca - QB
Luis Sharpe - T
Jessie Small - LB
Lance Smith - G
Vernice Smith - G
Tyronne Stowe - LB
Eric Swann - DE
Anthony Thompson - RB
Danny Villa - G
Jim Wahler - NT
Derek Ware - RB
Aeneas Williams - DB
Joe Wolf - G
Willie Wright - TE
Mike Zordich - DB

1992 Pittsburgh

Gary Anderson - K
Jesse Anderson - TE
Albert Bentley - RB
Bubby Brister - QB
Russ Campbell - TE
Adrian Cooper - TE
Charles Davenport - WR
Kenny Davidson - DE
Dermontti Dawson - C
Mark Didio - WR
Donald Evans - DE
Darryl Ford - LB
Barry Foster - RB
Kendall Gammon - C
Jeff Graham - WR
Eric Green - TE
Larry Griffin - DB
Alan Haller - DB

Carlton Haselrig - G
Bryan Hinkle - LB
Merril Hoge - RB
Garry Howe - NT
Tunch Ilkin - T
John Jackson - T
D. J. Johnson - DB
Aaron Jones - DE
Tim Jorden - TE
Levon Kirkland - LB
Carnell Lake - DB
David Little - LB
Greg Lloyd - LB
Duval Love - G
Ernie Mills - WR
Hardy Nickerson - LB
Neil O'Donnell - QB
Jerry Olsavsky - LB
Darrick Owens - WR
Darren Perry - DB
Mark Royals - P
Leon Searcy - T
Richard Shelton - DB
Ariel Solomon - C
Joel Steed - NT
Dwight Stone - WR
Justin Strzelczyk - T
Yancey Thigpen - WR
Leroy Thompson - RB
Sammy Walker - DB
Elnardo Webster - LB
Solomon Wilcots - DB
Gerald Williams - NT
Jerrol Williams - LB
Warren Williams - RB
Rod Woodson - DB

1992 San Diego

Sam Anno - LB
Johnnie Barnes - WR
Rod Bernstine - RB
Eric Bieniemy - RB
Anthony Blaylock - DB
Brian Brennan - WR
Marion Butts - RB
Gill Byrd - DB
John Carney - K
Darren Carrington - DB
Robert Claiborne - WR
Floyd Fields - DB
Donald Frank - DB
James Fuller - DB
Bob Gagliano - QB
Leo Goeas - G
Burt Grossman - DE
Courtney Hall - C
Delton Hall - DB
Ronnie Harmon - RB
Steve Hendrickson - RB
Stan Humphries - QB
Shawn Jefferson - WR
John Kidd - P
Shawn Lee - DT
Nate Lewis - WR
Eugene Marve - LB
Deems May - TE
Anthony Miller - WR
Chris Mims - DE
Eric Moten - G
Kevin Murphy - LB
Leslie O'Neal - DE
Gary Plummer - LB
Marquez Pope - DB
Alfred Pupunu - TE
Stanley Richard - DB
David Richards - G
Henry Rolling - LB
Tony Savage - NT
Junior Seau - LB
Jim Skow - DE
Billy Ray Smith Jr. - LB
Walter Stanley - WR
Harry Swayne - T
Broderick Thompson - G
George Thornton - DT
Peter Tuipulotu - RB
Sean Vanhorse - DB
Derrick Walker - TE
Reggie White - DT
Curtis Whitley - C
Blaise Winter - DT
Duane Young - TE
Mike Zandofsky - C

1992 San Francisco

Harris Barton - G
Harry Boatswain - T
Brian Bollinger - G
Steve Bono - QB
Dennis Brown - DE
Dexter Carter - RB
Michael Carter - NT
Mike Cofer - K
Eric Davis - DB
Keith DeLong - LB
Mitch Donahue - LB
Chris Dressel - TE
Kevin Fagan - DE
Roy Foster - G
Thane Gash - DB
Antonio Goss - LB
Alan Grant - DB
Jacob Green - DE

Don Griffin - DB
Dana Hall - DB
Merton Hanks - DB
Tim Harris - DE
Martin Harrison - LB
Keith Henderson - RB
Pierce Holt - DE
Johnnie Jackson - DB
John Johnson - LB
Brent Jones - TE
Darin Jordan - LB
Amp Lee - RB
Ron Lewis - WR
Marc Logan - RB
Mike McGruder - DB
Guy McIntyre - G
Reggie McKenzie - G
Joe Montana - QB
Tom Rathman - RB
Jerry Rice - WR
Larry Roberts - DE
Bill Romanowski - LB
Jesse Sapolu - C
Mike Sherrard - WR
Ralph Tamm - G
John Taylor - WR
Chuck Thomas - DE
Odessa Turner - WR
Garin Veris - DE
Adam Walker - RB
Steve Wallace - T
Michael Walter - LB
Ted Washington - NT
Ricky Watters - RB
David Whitmore - DB
David Wilkins - LB
Jamie Williams - TE
Klaus Wilmsmeyer - P
Steve Young - QB

1992 Seattle

Theo Adams - G
Robert Blackmon - DB
Brian Blades - WR
Darrick Brilz - G
Jeff Bryant - DE
Joe Cain - LB
Greg Clark - LB
Louis Clark - WR
David Daniels - WR
Brian Davis - DB
Dedrick Dodge - DB
Sean Farrell - G
Grant Feasel - C
Malcolm Frank - DB
Stan Gelbaugh - QB
Nesby Glasgow - DB
Paul Green - TE
Dwayne Harper - DB
Andy Heck - T
Ron Heller - TE
Bill Hitchcock - G
John Hunter - G
Patrick Hunter - DB
James Jefferson - DB
Tracy Johnson - RB
James Jones - RB
Mike Jones - TE
E. J. Junior - LB
Trey Junkin - TE
Tommy Kane - WR
John Kasay - K
Mike Keim - T
Cortez Kennedy - DT
Ronnie Lee - T
Rueben Mayes - RB
Dan McGwire - QB
Keith Millard - DT
Joe Nash - DT
Richard Newbill - LB
Rufus Porter - LB
Ray Roberts - T
Eugene Robinson - DB
Rafael Robinson - DB
Tyrone Rodgers - DT
Michael Sinclair - DE
Bob Spitulski - LB
Rod Stephens - LB
Kelly Stouffer - QB
Doug Thomas - WR
Robb Thomas - WR
Joe Tofflemire - C
Brian Treggs - WR
Natu Tuatagaloa - DE
Rick Tuten - P
Chris Warren - RB
John L. Williams - RB
Terry Wooden - LB
Tony Woods - DE
David Wyman - LB

1992 Tampa Bay

Elijah Alexander - LB
Darren Anderson - DB
Gary Anderson - RB
Jesse Anderson - TE
Tyji Armstrong - TE
Chris Barber - DB
Michael Barber - WR
Ian Beckles - G
Brian Blados - G
Ed Brady - LB
James Brooks - RB
Joey Browner - DB

Darrick Brownlow - LB
Reggie Burnette - LB
Mark Carrier - WR
Marty Carter - DB
Al Chamblee - DE
Reggie Cobb - RB
Sidney Coleman - LB
Tony Covington - DB
Willie Culpepper - WR
Reuben Davis - DE
Lawrence Dawsey - WR
Steve DeBerg - QB
Scott Dill - T
Santana Dotson - DE
Willie Drewrey - WR
Mark Duckens - DE
Craig Erickson - QB
Darrell Fullington - DB
David Grant - DE
Rogerick Green - DB
Randy Grimes - C
Paul Gruber - T
Rhett Hall - DE
Ron Hall - TE
Todd Harrison - TE
Courtney Hawkins - WR
Alonzo Highsmith - RB
Stanford Jennings - RB
Roger Jones - DB
E. J. Junior - LB
Joe King - DB
Garry Lewis - DB
Milton Mack - DB
Tony Mayberry - C
Corey Mayfield - DE
Keith McCants - DE
Anthony McDowell - RB
Tom McHale - G
Charles McRae - T
Dave Moore - TE
Eddie Murray - K
Jeff Parker - WR
Darryl Pollard - DB
Bruce Reimers - G
Ricky Reynolds - DB
Reggie Rogers - DE
Mazio Royster - RB
Tim Ryan - G
Ray Seals - DE
Dan Stryzinski - P
Mike Sullivan - G
Rob Taylor - T
Vinny Testaverde - QB
Broderick Thomas - LB
George Thomas - WR
Calvin Tiggle - LB
Mark Wheeler - NT
Jimmy Williams - LB
Ken Willis - K
Charles Wilson - WR

1992 Washington

Tony Barker - LB
Guy Bingham - C
Jeff Bostic - C
Todd Bowles - DB
John Brandes - TE
John Brantley - LB
Ray Brown - T
Jason Buck - DE
Earnest Byner - RB
Ravin Caldwell - LB
Gary Clark - WR
Monte Coleman - LB
Andre Collins - LB
Shane Collins - DE
Cary Conklin - QB
Danny Copeland - DB
Brad Edwards - DB
Pat Eilers - DB
Mohammed Elewonibi - T
Matt Elliott - C
Ricky Ervins - RB
Jumpy Geathers - DT
Kelly Goodburn - P
Kurt Gouveia - LB
Darrell Green - DB
Robert Green - RB
David Gulledge - DB
Mike Haight - T
Carl Harry - WR
Stephen Hobbs - WR
Desmond Howard - WR
Joe Jacoby - G
James Jenkins - TE
A. J. Johnson - DB
Sidney Johnson - DB
Tim Johnson - DT
Jim Lachey - T
Chip Lohmiller - K
Charles Mann - DE
Wilber Marshall - LB
Martin Mayhew - DB
Alvoid Mays - DB
Raleigh McKenzie - C
Johnny Meads - LB
Ron Middleton - TE
Brian Mitchell - RB
Art Monk - WR
Tom Myslinski - G
Terry Orr - TE
Huey Richardson - LB
Ray Rowe - TE
Jeff Rutledge - QB
Mark Rypien - QB

Ricky Sanders - WR
Mark Schlereth - G
Ed Simmons - T
Fred Stokes - WR
Johnny Thomas - DB
Jim Wahler - DT
Don Warren - TE
Mickey Washington - DB
Eric Williams - DT
Bobby Wilson - DT

1993 Atlanta

Mel Agee - DE
Keith Alex - G
Harold Alexander - P
Lester Archambeau - DE
Steve Broussard - RB
Rick Bryan - DE
Scott Case - DB
Vinnie Clark - DB
Darion Conner - LB
Eric Dickerson - RB
Howard Dinkins - LB
Jeff Donaldson - DB
Jamie Dukes - C
Tracey Eaton - DB
Tory Epps - NT
Roman Fortin - G
Mike Gann - DE
Moe Gardner - NT
Jumpy Geathers - DT
Ron George - LB
Bill Goldberg - NT
Dwayne Gordon - LB
Tim Green - DE
Roger Harper - DB
Michael Haynes - WR
Bobby Hebert - QB
Drew Hill - WR
Chris Hinton - T
Pierce Holt - DE
Melvin Jenkins - DB
Norm Johnson - K
Mike Kenn - T
Lincoln Kennedy - G
Harper LeBel - TE
Ernie Logan - DE
Mitch Lyons - TE
Chris Miller - QB
David Mims - WR
Brian Mitchell - DB
Alton Montgomery - DB
Erric Pegram - RB
Jason Phillips - WR
Bruce Pickens - DB
Mike Pritchard - WR
Andre Rison - WR
Mike Ruether - G
Deion Sanders - DB
Elbert Shelley - DB
Chuck Smith - LB
Tony Smith - RB
Jesse Solomon - LB
Ken Tippins - LB
Billy Joe Tolliver - QB
Jessie Tuggle - LB
Darnell Walker - DB
Charles Washington - DB
Bob Whitfield - T

1993 Buffalo

Rob Awalt - TE
Howard Ballard - T
Oliver Barnett - DE
Don Beebe - WR
Cornelius Bennett - LB
Bill Brooks - WR
Monty Brown - LB
Steve Christie - K
Russell Copeland - WR
Jerry Crafts - T
Matt Darby - DB
John Davis - G
Kenneth Davis - RB
Mike Devlin - C
John Fina - T
Eddie Fuller - RB
Carwell Gardner - RB
Gale Gilbert - QB
Keith Goganious - LB
Phil Hansen - DE
Richard Harvey - LB
Jerome Henderson - DB
Kent Hull - C
Henry Jones - DB
Jim Kelly - QB
Mark Kelso - DB
Brad Lamb - WR
Adam Lingner - C
Mike Lodish - NT
Mark Maddox - LB
Keith McKeller - TE
Pete Metzelaars - TE
Chris Mohr - P
Tom Myslinski - G
Nate Odomes - DB
Glenn Parker - G
John Parrella - DE
James Patton - DE
Marvcus Patton - LB
Mark Pike - DE
David Pool - DB
Andre Reed - WR

Frank Reich - QB
Jim Ritcher - G
Kurt Schulz - DB
Bruce Smith - DE
Thomas Smith - DB
Darryl Talley - LB
Steve Tasker - WR
Thurman Thomas - RB
Nate Turner - RB
Chris Walsh - WR
Mickey Washington - DB
James Williams - DB
Jeff Wright - NT

1993 Chi. Bears

Neal Anderson - RB
Trace Armstrong - DE
Troy Auzenne - T
Myron Baker - LB
Fred Banks - WR
Anthony Blaylock - DB
Mark Bortz - G
Kevin Butler - K
Joe Cain - LB
Mark Carrier - DB
Bob Christian - RB
Curtis Conway - WR
Ron Cox - LB
Wendell Davis - WR
Richard Dent - DE
Maurice Douglass - DB
Tory Epps - DT
Al Fontenot - DE
Jerry Fontenot - G
Chris Gardocki - P
Shaun Gayle - DB
Chris Gedney - TE
Robert Green - RB
Jim Harbaugh - QB
Craig Heyward - RB
John Ivlow - RB
Keith Jennings - TE
Keshon Johnson - DB
Dante Jones - LB
Jay Leeuwenburg - G
Darren Lewis - RB
Jeremy Lincoln - DB
John Mangum - DB
Gene McGuire - C
Steve McMichael - DT
Kevin Miniefield - DB
Barry Minter - LB
Anthony Morgan - WR
Jim Morrissey - LB
Tom Myslinski - G
Terry Obee - WR
Markus Paul - DB
Todd Perry - G
William Perry - DT
Tim Ryan - DT
Carl Simpson - DT
Vernice Smith - G
Vinson Smith - LB
Percy Snow - LB
Alonzo Spellman - DE
Keith Van Horne - T
Tom Waddle - WR
Ryan Wetnight - TE
Danta Whitaker - TE
James Williams - T
Peter Tom Willis - QB
John Wojciechowski - G
Donnell Woolford - DB
Tim Worley - RB
Chris Zorich - DT

1993 Cincinnati

Eric Ball - RB
Ryan Benjamin - RB
Chuck Bradley - T
Michael Brim - DB
Scott Brumfield - T
Ron Carpenter - DB
Wesley Carroll - WR
John Copeland - TE
Allen DeGraffenreid - WR
Derrick Fenner - RB
James Francis - LB
Mike Frier - DE
David Frisch - TE
Alex Gordon - LB
Alan Grant - DB
Harold Green - RB
Lance Gunn - DB
George Hinkle - DE
Garry Howe - NT
Donnell Johnson - T
Lee Johnson - P
Dan Jones - T
Rod Jones - DB
Randy Kirk - LB
David Klingler - QB
R. J. Kors - DB
Bruce Kozerski - G
Tim Krumrie - NT
Jack Linn - G
Ricardo McDonald - LB
Tony McGee - TE
Karmeeleyah McGill - LB
Ostell Miles - RB
Ken Moyer - T

Roosevelt Nix - DE
Ty Parten - NT
Doug Pelfrey - K
Carl Pickens - WR
Mitchell Price - DB
Jeff Query - WR
Thomas Rayam - G
Reggie Rembert - WR
Patrick Robinson - WR
Kevin Sargent - T
Jay Schroeder - QB
Tom Scott - T
Eric Shaw - LB
Marcello Simmons - DB
Brad Smith - LB
Milt Stegall - WR
Danny Stubbs - LB
Jeff Thomason - TE
Craig Thompson - TE
Reggie Thornton - WR
Steve Tovar - LB
Fernandus Vinson - DB
Joe Walter - T
Leonard Wheeler - DB
Sheldon White - DB
Erik Wilhelm - QB
Alfred Williams - LB
Darryl Williams - DB

1993 Cleveland

Herman Arvie - T
Randy Baldwin - RB
Jerry Ball - DT
David Brandon - LB
Rob Burnett - DE
Mike Caldwell - LB
Mark Carrier - WR
Bob Dahl - G
Gerald Dixon - LB
Steve Everitt - C
Dan Footman - DE
Stacey Hairston - DB
Brian Hansen - P
Randy Hilliard - DB
Leroy Hoard - RB
Houston Hoover - G
Michael Jackson - WR
Tim Jacobs - DB
Mike Johnson - LB
Pepper Johnson - LB
Bill Johnson - DE
James Jones - DT
Selwyn Jones - DB
Tony Jones - T
Brian Kinchen - TE
Ed King - T
Bernie Kosar - QB
Kevin Mack - RB
Clay Matthews - LB
Keenan McCardell - WR
Thomas McLemore - TE
Erik McMillan - DB
Eric Metcalf - RB
Stevon Moore - DB
Najee Mustafaa - DB
Michael Dean Perry - DT
Todd Philcox - QB
Anthony Pleasant - DE
Louis Riddick - DB
Patrick Rowe - WR
Pio Sagapolutele - DE
Rico Smith - WR
Del Speer - DB
Frank Stams - LB
Matt Stover - K
Eddie Sutter - LB
Terry Taylor - DB
Vinny Testaverde - QB
Lawyer Tillman - WR
Eric Turner - DB
Tommy Vardell - RB
Everson Walls - DB
Clarence Williams - TE
Gene Williams - T
Wally Williams - C
Ron Wolfley - RB
Lance Zeno - C

1993 Dallas

Bobby Abrams - LB
Tommie Agee - RB
Troy Aikman - QB
Bill Bates - DB
Kelly Blackwell - TE
Larry Brown - DB
Tony Casillas - DT
Lincoln Coleman - RB
Frank Cornish - C
Dixon Edwards - LB
Lin Elliott - K
Thomas Everett - DB
Joe Fishback - DB
Derrick Gainer - RB
Scott Galbraith - TE
Kenneth Gant - DB
Jason Garrett - QB
John Gesek - G
Kevin Gogan - G
Charles Haley - DE
Chris Hall - DB
Alvin Harper - WR
Dale Hellestrae - G
Chad Hennings - DT
Michael Irvin - WR

Jim Jeffcoat - DE
John Jett - P
Daryl Johnston - RB
Jimmie Jones - DT
Robert Jones - LB
Bernie Kosar - QB
Derrick Lassic - RB
Leon Lett - DE
Brock Marion - DB
Russell Maryland - DT
Joey Mickey - TE
Eddie Murray - K
Godfrey Myles - LB
Nate Newton - G
Ken Norton - LB
Jay Novacek - TE
Elvis Patterson - DB
Jim Price - TE
John Roper - LB
Darrin Smith - LB
Emmitt Smith - RB
Kevin Smith - DB
Mark Stepnoski - C
Dave Thomas - DB
Tony Tolbert - DE
Mark Tuinei - T
Matt Vanderbeek - LB
James Washington - DB
Erik Williams - T
Kevin Williams - WR
Robert Williams - DB
Tyrone Williams - WR
Darren Woodson - DB

1993 Denver

Elijah Alexander - LB
Steve Atwater - DB
Rod Bernstine - RB
Melvin Bonner - WR
Ronnie Bradford - DB
Tyrone Braxton - DB
Mike Croel - LB
Robert Delpino - RB
Charles Dimry - DB
Mitch Donahue - LB
Shane Dronett - DE
Darren Drozdov - NT
Jason Elam - K
John Elway - QB
Jerry Evans - TE
Simon Fletcher - LB
Russ Freeman - T
Brian Habib - G
Darryl Hall - DB
Reggie Johnson - TE
Vance Johnson - WR
Rondell Jones - DB
Keith Kartz - C
Tony Kimbrough - WR
Greg Kragen - NT
Le-Lo Lang - DB
Tim Lucas - LB
Anthony Lynn - RB
Tommy Maddox - QB
Don Maggs - T
Arthur Marshall - WR
Karl Mecklenburg - LB
Bob Meeks - G
Jon Melander - G
Glyn Milburn - RB
Jeff Mills - LB
Willie Oshodin - DE
David Pool - DB
Reggie Rivers - RB
Frank Robinson - DB
Jeff Robinson - DE
Barry Rose - WR
Tom Rouen - P
Derek Russell - WR
Kirk Scrafford - T
Shannon Sharpe - TE
Dennis Smith - DB
Alphonso Taylor - DT
Kitrick Taylor - WR
Cedric Tillman - WR
Dave Widell - G
Dan Williams - DE
David Wyman - LB
Gary Zimmerman - T

1993 Detroit

Gary Anderson - RB
Jim Arnold - P
Bennie Blades - DB
Shawn Bouwens - G
Lomas Brown - T
Jeff Campbell - WR
Toby Caston - LB
Willie Clay - DB
Harry Colon - DB
Mike Compton - C
Scott Conover - T
Ray Crockett - DB
Darryl Ford - LB
Bill Fralic - G
Dennis Gibson - LB
Kevin Glover - C
Mel Gray - WR
Willie Green - WR
Ty Hallock - TE
Jason Hanson - K
Tracy Hayworth - LB
Rodney Holman - TE
George Jamison - LB

Greg Jeffries - DB
Melvin Jenkins - DB
Jimmie Johnson - TE
Victor Jones - LB
Erik Kramer - QB
Jack Linn - T
Antonio London - LB
Dave Lutz - G
Eric Lynch - RB
Aubrey Matthews - WR
Tim McKyer - DB
Ryan McNeil - DB
Derrick Moore - RB
Herman Moore - WR
Dan Owens - DE
Rodney Peete - QB
Brett Perriman - WR
Lawrence Pete - NT
Robert Porcher - DE
Kelvin Pritchett - DE
Curvin Richards - RB
David Richards - G
Mark Rodenhauser - C
Barry Sanders - RB
Kevin Scott - DB
Tracy Scroggins - LB
Chris Spielman - LB
Marc Spindler - DE
Pat Swilling - LB
Larry Tharpe - T
Marty Thompson - TE
Mack Travis - NT
Vernon Turner - WR
Andre Ware - QB
William White - DB

1993 Green Bay

Edgar Bennett - RB
Tony Bennett - LB
Matt Brock - DE
Robert Brooks - WR
Gilbert Brown - NT
Terrell Buckley - DB
LeRoy Butler - DB
James Campen - C
Mark Chmura - TE
Mark Clayton - WR
Keo Coleman - LB
Brett Collins - WR
Shawn Collins - WR
Don Davey - DE
Ty Detmer - QB
Earl Dotson - T
Doug Evans - DB
Brett Favre - QB
Harry Galbreath - G
David Grant - DE
Corey Harris - DB
Jackie Harris - TE
Tim Hauck - DB
Johnny Holland - LB
Paul Hutchins - T
Tunch Ilkin - T
Darryl Ingram - TE
Chris Jacke - K
John Jurkovic - NT
George Koonce - LB
Ron Lewis - WR
Bill Maas - NT
Dexter McNabb - RB
Mike Merriweather - LB
Roland Mitchell - DB
Rich Moran - G
Anthony Morgan - WR
Jim Morrissey - LB
Joe Mott - LB
Brian Noble - LB
Muhammad Oliver - DB
Shawn Patterson - DE
Bryce Paup - LB
Bruce Pickens - DB
Mike Prior - DB
Tootie Robbins - T
Ken Ruettgers - T
Sterling Sharpe - WR
Wayne Simmons - LB
Joe Sims - T
John Stephens - RB
George Teague - DB
Darrell Thompson - RB
Keith Traylor - LB
Bryan Wagner - P
Sammy Walker - DB
Ed West - TE
Reggie White - DE
Doug Widell - G
Kevin Williams - RB
James Willis - LB
Marcus Wilson - RB
Frank Winters - C
Lance Zeno - C

1993 Houston

Melvin Aldridge - DB
Jeff Alm - DT
Micheal Barrow - LB
Blaine Bishop - DB
Joe Bowden - LB
Tony Brown - DB
Gary Brown - RB
Reggie Brown - WR
Cody Carlson - QB
Ray Childress - DT
Pat Coleman - WR

Doug Dawson - G
Al Del Greco - K
Cris Dishman - DB
Kevin Donnalley - T
Willie Drewrey - WR
Curtis Duncan - WR
William Fuller - DE
Ernest Givins - WR
Travis Hannah - WR
Leonard Harris - WR
Terry Hoage - DB
Brad Hopkins - T
Steve Jackson - DB
Haywood Jeffires - WR
Tony Jones - WR
Sean Jones - DE
Scott Kozak - LB
Lamar Lathon - LB
Darryll Lewis - DB
Wilber Marshall - LB
Emanuel Martin - DB
Le'Shai Maston - RB
Bruce Matthews - C
Damon Mays - WR
Keith McCants - DE
Bubba McDowell - DB
John Henry Mills - TE
Glenn Montgomery - DT
Greg Montgomery - P
Warren Moon - QB
Mike Munchak - G
Erik Norgard - C
Bo Orlando - DB
Bucky Richardson - QB
Tim Roberts - DT
Marcus Robertson - DB
Eddie Robinson - LB
Webster Slaughter - WR
Al Smith - LB
Kent Sullivan - P
Mike Teeter - DE
Stan Thomas - T
Spencer Tillman - RB
Craig Veasey - DE
Gary Wellman - WR
Lorenzo White - RB
David Williams - T
Lee Williams - DT

1993 Indianapolis

Ashley Ambrose - DB
Charles Arbuckle - TE
Michael Ball - DB
John Baylor - DB
Jason Belser - DB
Dean Biasucci - K
Duane Bickett - LB
Michael Brandon - DE
Ray Buchanan - DB
Paul Butcher - LB
Kevin Call - T
Kerry Cash - TE
Sam Clancy - DE
Quentin Coryatt - LB
Aaron Cox - WR
Rodney Culver - RB
Eugene Daniel - DB
Sean Dawkins - WR
Randy Dixon - G
Steve Emtman - DT
Jeff George - QB
Chris Goode - DB
Steve Grant - LB
Cecil Gray - T
Derwin Gray - DB
Jon Hand - DE
Jeff Herrod - LB
Jessie Hester - WR
Anthony Johnson - RB
Reggie Langhorne - WR
Kirk Lowdermilk - C
Don Majkowski - QB
Trevor Matich - C
Skip McClendon - DE
Tony McCoy - NT
Devon McDonald - LB
Eddie Miller - WR
Zefross Moss - T
Willis Peguese - DE
Roosevelt Potts - RB
Scott Radecic - LB
John Ray - T
Bill Schultz - T
Tom Sims - NT
Tony Siragusa - NT
Tony Stargell - DB
Rohn Stark - P
Joe Staysniak - T
Ed Toner - RB
Jack Trudeau - QB
Clarence Verdin - WR
Warren Williams - RB
Will Wolford - T

1993 Kansas City

Marcus Allen - RB
John Alt - T
Kimble Anders - RB
Erick Anderson - LB
Bryan Barker - P
Tim Barnett - WR
Mike Bartrum - TE
Martin Bayless - DB
J. J. Birden - WR

Matt Blundin - QB
Dale Carter - DB
Keith Cash - TE
Willie Davis - WR
Ron Dickerson - RB
Mike Dyal - TE
Jaime Fields - LB
Derrick Graham - T
Leonard Griffin - DE
Tim Grunhard - C
Jonathan Hayes - TE
Danan Hughes - WR
Fred Jones - WR
Hassan Jones - WR
Dave Krieg - QB
Albert Lewis - DB
Garry Lewis - DB
Nick Lowery - K
Lonnie Marts - LB
Pellom McDaniels - DE
Reggie McElroy - G
Erik McMillan - DB
Todd McNair - RB
Darren Mickell - DT
Charles Mincy - DB
Joe Montana - QB
Tim Newton - DT
Muhammad Oliver - DB
Joe Phillips - DT
Bruce Pickens - DB
Tom Ricketts - G
Tracy Rogers - LB
Kevin Ross - DB
Dan Saleaumua - DT
Will Shields - G
Ricky Siglar - T
Tracy Simien - LB
Neil Smith - DE
John Stephens - RB
Santo Stephens - LB
David Szott - G
Jay Taylor - DB
Doug Terry - DB
Derrick Thomas - LB
Bennie Thompson - DB
Ernie Thompson - RB
Joe Valerio - G
Danny Villa - G
Tim Watson - DB
David Whitmore - DB
Harvey Williams - RB
Robert Williams - DB
Felix Wright - DB

1993 LA Raiders

Eddie Anderson - DB
Patrick Bates - DB
Nick Bell - RB
Greg Biekert - LB
Willie Broughton - DT
Tim Brown - WR
Aundray Bruce - DE
Rickey Dixon - DB
Torin Dorn - DB
John Duff - TE
Vince Evans - QB
David Fulcher - LB
Willie Gault - WR
Andrew Glover - TE
Jeff Gossett - P
Nolan Harrison - DT
Daryl Hobbs - WR
Ethan Horton - TE
Derrick Hoskins - DB
Jeff Hostetler - QB
Raghib Ismail - WR
Jeff Jaeger - K
James Jett - WR
Mike Jones - LB
Randy Jordan - RB
Joe Kelly - LB
Dan Land - DB
Ken Lanier - T
Howie Long - DE
Napoleon McCallum - RB
Terry McDaniel - DB
Chester McGlockton - DT
Tyrone Montgomery - RB
Max Montoya - G
Don Mosebar - C
Winston Moss - LB
Elvis Patterson - DB
Todd Peat - G
Gerald Perry - T
Greg Robinson - RB
Anthony Smith - DE
Kevin Smith - TE
Steve Smith - RB
Richard Stephens - T
Greg Townsend - DE
James Trapp - DB
Dan Turk - C
Aaron Wallace - LB
Lionel Washington - DB
Bruce Wilkerson - T
Steve Wisniewski - G
Alexander Wright - WR

1993 LA Rams

Flipper Anderson - WR
Darryl Ashmore - T

Robert Bailey - DB
Jerome Bettis - RB
Marc Boutte - DT
Deral Boykin - DB
Don Bracken - P
Jeff Brady - LB
Bern Brostek - C
Richard Buchanan - WR
Blair Bush - C
Pat Carter - TE
Brett Collins - LB
Shane Conlan - LB
Dexter Davis - DB
Troy Drayton - TE
Irv Eatman - T
Henry Ellard - WR
Jim Everett - QB
Cleveland Gary - RB
Sean Gilbert - DT
Leo Goeas - G
Courtney Griffin - DB
Howard Griffith - RB
Wymon Henderson - DB
Darryl Henley - DB
Thomas Homco - LB
Steve Israel - DB
Robert Jenkins - T
Ernie Jones - WR
Todd Kinchen - WR
Sean LaChapelle - WR
Sean Landeta - P
David Lang - RB
Tim Lester - RB
James Lofton - WR
Keith Loneker - G
Todd Lyght - DB
Chris Martin - LB
Paul McJulien - P
Travis McNeal - TE
Tom Newberry - G
Anthony Newman - DB
Mike Pagel - QB
Jeff Pahukoa - G
Roman Phifer - LB
Mitchell Price - DB
Kevin Robbins - T
Gerald Robinson - TE
David Rocker - DT
Henry Rolling - LB
T. J. Rubley - QB
Sam Seale - DB
Jackie Slater - T
Michael Stewart - DB
Fred Stokes - DE
Pat Terrell - DB
Russell White - RB
Leon White - LB
Tony Woods - DE
Robert Young - DE
Tony Zendejas - K

1993 Miami

Bruce Alexander - DB
Fred Banks - WR
Greg Baty - TE
Stephen Braggs - DB
J.B. Brown - DB
Chuck Bullough - LB
Keith Byars - RB
Marco Coleman - DE
Bryan Cox - LB
Jeff Cross - DE
Steve DeBerg - QB
Jeff Dellenbach - T
Mark Dennis - T
Irving Fryar - WR
Mike Golic - NT
Chris Gray - G
Chris Green - DB
David Griggs - DE
John Grimsley - LB
Bobby Harden - DB
Dale Hatcher - P
Ron Heller - T
Mark Higgs - RB
Liffort Hobley - DB
Dwight Hollier - LB
Jeff Hunter - DE
Mark Ingram - WR
Keith Jackson - TE
Vestee Jackson - DB
Terry Kirby - RB
Chuck Klingbeil - NT
Darrell Malone - DB
Dan Marino - QB
Tony Martin - WR
O. J. McDuffie - WR
David Merritt - LB
Scott Miller - WR
Scott Mitchell - QB
Cliff Odom - LB
John Offerdahl - LB
Louis Oliver - DB
Bernie Parmalee - RB
Doug Pederson - QB
James Saxon - RB
Keith Sims - G
Chris Singleton - LB
Frankie Smith - DB
Pete Stoyanovich - K
Tom Thayer - C
Jeff Uhlenhake - C
Craig Veasey - NT
Troy Vincent - DB
Richmond Webb - T

Larry Webster - DT
Bert Weidner - G
Jarvis Williams - DB
Mike Williams - WR
Ronnie Williams - TE
Karl Wilson - DT

1993 Minnesota

Bobby Abrams - LB
Scott Adams - G
Roy Barker - DT
Ron Carpenter - DB
Anthony Carter - WR
Cris Carter - WR
Jeff Christy - C
Roger Craig - RB
Brad Culpepper - DT
Bernard Dafney - T
Jack Del Rio - LB
Chris Doleman - DE
Chuck Evans - RB
Dave Garnett - LB
John Gerak - G
Vencie Glenn - DB
Scottie Graham - RB
Eric Guliford - WR
James Harris - DE
Robert Harris - DE
Bruce Holmes - LB
Tim Irwin - T
Qadry Ismail - WR
Carlos Jenkins - LB
Izel Jenkins - DB
Shawn Jones - DB
Steve Jordan - TE
Todd Kalis - G
Carl Lee - DB
Everett Lindsay - G
Greg Manusky - LB
Ed McDaniel - LB
Randall McDaniel - G
Lamar McGriggs - DB
Jim McMahon - QB
Audray McMillian - DB
Mike Morris - C
Harry Newsome - P
Brent Novoselsky - TE
Anthony Parker - DB
J. C. Pearson - DB
John Randle - DT
Jake Reed - WR
Fuad Reveiz - K
Sean Salisbury - QB
Adam Schreiber - C
Todd Scott - DB
Ashley Sheppard - LB
Robert Smith - RB
Fred Strickland - LB
Derek Tennell - TE
Henry Thomas - DT
Mike Tice - TE
Gino Torretta - QB
Olanda Truitt - WR
Esera Tuaolo - DT
Barry Word - RB

1993 New England

Ray Agnew - DE
Bruce Armstrong - T
Mike Arthur - C
Matt Bahr - K
Rich Baldinger - G
Harlon Barnett - DB
David Bavaro - LB
Drew Bledsoe - QB
Vincent Brisby - WR
Corwin Brown - DB
Troy Brown - WR
Vincent Brown - LB
Jason Carthen - LB
Eugene Chung - G
Ben Coates - TE
Todd Collins - LB
Marv Cook - TE
Ray Crittenden - WR
Corey Croom - RB
Chris Gannon - DE
Sam Gash - RB
Mike Gisler - G
Tim Goad - NT
Rich Griffith - TE
Pat Harlow - T
Ronnie Harris - WR
Jerome Henderson - DB
Maurice Hurst - DB
Mario Johnson - NT
Aaron Jones - DE
Todd Jones - C
Dion Lambert - DB
Burnie Legette - RB
Vernon Lewis - DB
Bill Lewis - C
Scott Lockwood - RB
Greg McMurtry - WR
Brandon Moore - T
Mike Pitts - DE
Terry Ray - DB
Todd Rucci - G
Leonard Russell - RB
Dwayne Sabb - LB
Mike Saxon - P
Scott Secules - QB
Chris Singleton - LB
Scott Sisson - K

Chris Slade - LB
Rod Smith - DB
Reyna Thompson - DB
Michael Timpson - WR
Andre Tippett - LB
Kevin Turner - RB
John Washington - DE
Adrian White - LB
David White - LB
Brent Williams - DE
Darryl Wren - DB
Scott Zolak - QB

1993 New Orleans

Morten Andersen - K
Jesse Anderson - TE
Gene Atkins - DB
Tommy Barnhardt - P
Hoby Brenner - TE
Derek Brown - RB
Mike Buck - QB
Vince Buck - DB
Toi Cook - DB
Richard Cooper - T
Ronnie Dixon - NT
Jim Dombrowski - G
Marcus Dowdell - WR
Karl Dunbar - DE
Quinn Early - WR
Jeff Faulkner - DE
Reggie Freeman - LB
Robert Goff - NT
Othello Henderson - DB
Jay Hilgenberg - C
Joel Hilgenberg - C
Dalton Hilliard - RB
Tyrone Hughes - DB
Rickey Jackson - LB
Vaughan Johnson - LB
Reggie Jones - DB
Derek Kennard - G
Tyrone Legette - DB
Sean Lumpkin - DB
Cedric Mack - DB
Eric Martin - WR
Wayne Martin - DE
Brett Maxie - DB
Fred McAfee - RB
Les Miller - DE
Sam Mills - LB
Brad Muster - RB
Lorenzo Neal - RB
Derrick Ned - RB
Pat Newman - WR
Chris Port - G
Willie Roaf - T
Torrance Small - WR
Joel Smeenge - DE
Irv Smith - TE
Jimmy Spencer - DB
Tommie Stowers - TE
Keith Taylor - DB
Renaldo Turnbull - DE
Floyd Turner - WR
Frank Wainright - TE
Steve Walsh - QB
Frank Warren - DE
Jim Wilks - NT
James Williams - LB
Wade Wilson - QB
DeMond Winston - LB

1993 NY Giants

Jessie Armstead - LB
Carlton Bailey - LB
Willie Beamon - DB
Greg Bishop - T
Michael Brooks - LB
Dave Brown - QB
Derek Brown - TE
Marcus Buckley - LB
Jarrod Bunch - RB
Chris Calloway - WR
Jesse Campbell - DB
Mark Collins - DB
Keith Crawford - WR
Howard Cross - TE
Brad Daluiso - K
Scott Davis - G
Steve DeOssie - LB
Stacey Dillard - NT
Jumbo Elliott - T
Mark Flythe - DE
Mike Fox - DE
Kent Graham - QB
Myron Guyton - DB
Keith Hamilton - DE
Rodney Hampton - RB
Mike Horan - P
Erik Howard - NT
Greg Jackson - DB
Mark Jackson - WR
Izel Jenkins - DB
Clarence Jones - T
Bob Kratch - G
Sean Landeta - P
Ed McCaffrey - WR
Kanavis McGhee - LB
Dave Meggett - RB
Corey Miller - LB
Eric Moore - T
Bart Oates - C
Aaron Pierce - TE
Andre Powell - LB

Kenyon Rasheed - RB
Corey Raymond - DB
Doug Riesenberg - T
William Roberts - G
Mike Sherrard - WR
Phil Simms - QB
Phillippi Sparks - DB
Mike Strahan - DE
David Tate - DB
Lawrence Taylor - LB
George Thornton - DE
Lewis Tillman - RB
David Treadwell - K
Corey Widmer - LB
Brian Williams - C
Perry Williams - DB

1993 NY Jets

Louie Aguiar - P
Richie Anderson - RB
Kurt Barber - LB
Fred Baxter - TE
Brad Baxter - RB
Cary Blanchard - K
James Brown - T
Chris Burkett - WR
Dave Cadigan - G
Glenn Cadrez - LB
Rob Carpenter - WR
Pat Chaffey - RB
Kyle Clifton - LB
Jeff Criswell - T
Dale Dawkins - WR
Steve DeOssie - LB
Cal Dixon - C
Roger Duffy - G
Boomer Esiason - QB
Paul Frase - DT
Victor Green - DB
Mark Gunn - DT
James Hasty - DB
Cliff Hicks - DB
Bobby Houston - LB
Johnny Johnson - RB
Don Jones - LB
Marvin Jones - LB
Jeff Lageman - DE
Mo Lewis - LB
Ronnie Lott - DB
Siupeli Malamala - T
Leonard Marshall - DT
Terance Mathis - WR
Mike Merriweather - LB
Scott Mersereau - DT
Johnny Mitchell - TE
Rob Moore - WR
Adrian Murrell - RB
Browning Nagle - QB
Bill Pickel - DT
Damon Pieri - DB
Anthony Prior - DB
Coleman Rudolph - DE
Troy Sadowski - TE
Jim Sweeney - C
Blair Thomas - RB
Eric Thomas - DB
Jim Thornton - TE
Marcus Turner - DB
Brian Washington - DB
Marvin Washington - DE
Dwayne White - G
Matt Willig - T
Karl Wilson - DT
Lonnie Young - DB

1993 Philadelphia

David Alexander - C
Eric Allen - DB
Matt Bahr - K
Victor Bailey - WR
Brian Baldinger - G
Corey Barlow - DB
Fred Barnett - WR
Mark Bavaro - TE
Bubby Brister - QB
Mike Chalenski - DE
Louis Cooper - LB
Randall Cunningham - QB
Antone Davis - T
Byron Evans - LB
Jeff Feagles - P
Mike Flores - DE
Eric Floyd - G
William Frizzell - DB
Britt Hager - LB
Ron Hallstrom - G
Andy Harmon - DT
Tim Harris - DE
Vaughn Hebron - RB
Lester Holmes - G
Wes Hopkins - DB
John Hudson - G
Tommy Jeter - DT
Maurice Johnson - TE
James Joseph - RB
Seth Joyner - LB
Reggie Lawrence - WR
James Lofton - WR
Tom McHale - G
Erik McMillan - DB
Mark McMillian - DB
Rich Miano - DB
Keith Millard - DT

Gerald Nichols - DT
Ken O'Brien - QB
Derrick Oden - LB
William Perry - DT
Mike Reid - DB
Leonard Renfro - DT
Paul Richardson - WR
John Roper - LB
Ken Rose - LB
Roger Ruzek - K
Mike Schad - G
Rob Selby - G
Heath Sherman - RB
Vai Sikahema - RB
Clyde Simmons - DE
Ben Smith - DB
Otis Smith - DB
Jeff Sydner - WR
William Thomas - LB
Broderick Thompson - T
Herschel Walker - RB
Andre Waters - DB
Calvin Williams - WR
Mike Young - WR

1993 Phoenix

Johnny Bailey - RB
Michael Bankston - DE
Pat Beach - TE
Steve Beuerlein - QB
Eric Blount - RB
John Booty - DB
David Braxton - LB
Chad Brown - DE
Rich Camarillo - P
Chuck Cecil - DB
Larry Centers - RB
Chris Chandler - QB
Gary Clark - WR
Ben Coleman - G
Ed Cunningham - C
Rick Cunningham - T
Dexter Davis - DB
Greg Davis - K
Reuben Davis - DE
Dave Duerson - DB
Ernest Dye - G
Anthony Edwards - WR
Chad Fann - TE
Odie Harris - DB
Ken Harvey - LB
Garrison Hearst - RB
Eric Hill - LB
Randal Hill - WR
Steve Hyche - LB
Garth Jax - LB
Chuckie Johnson - DT
Jock Jones - LB
Mike Jones - DE
Kani Kauahi - C
Steve Lofton - DB
Lorenzo Lynch - DB
Robert Massey - DB
Mark May - G
David Merritt - LB
Ronald Moore - RB
Freddie Joe Nunn - LB
Chris Oldham - DB
Ricky Proehl - WR
Walter Reeves - TE
Butch Rolle - TE
Keith Rucker - DE
Luis Sharpe - T
Lance Smith - G
Tyronne Stowe - LB
Eric Swann - DE
Brett Wallerstedt - LB
Derek Ware - RB
Aeneas Williams - DB
Joe Wolf - G
Mike Zordich - DB

1993 Pittsburgh

Gary Anderson - K
Steve Avery - RB
Reggie Barnes - LB
Chad Brown - LB
Adrian Cooper - TE
Randy Cuthbert - RB
Charles Davenport - WR
Kenny Davidson - DE
Dermontti Dawson - C
Donald Evans - DE
Deon Figures - DB
Dan Fike - G
Barry Foster - RB
Kendall Gammon - C
Jeff Graham - WR
Eric Green - TE
Kevin Greene - LB
Larry Griffin - DB
Alan Haller - DB
Carlton Haselrig - G
Andre Hastings - WR
Kevin Henry - DE
Bryan Hinkle - LB
Dave Hoffmann - LB
Merril Hoge - RB
John Jackson - T
D. J. Johnson - DB
Gary Jones - DB
Victor Jones - RB
Tim Jorden - TE
Craig Keith - TE

Levon Kirkland - LB
Carnell Lake - DB
Greg Lloyd - LB
Duval Love - G
Rico Mack - LB
Ernie Mills - WR
Neil O'Donnell - QB
Jerry Olsavsky - LB
Lonnie Palelei - G
Darren Perry - DB
Mark Royals - P
Leon Searcy - T
Richard Shelton - DB
Ariel Solomon - C
Joel Steed - NT
Dwight Stone - WR
Justin Strzelczyk - T
Ricky Sutton - DE
Yancey Thigpen - WR
Leroy Thompson - RB
Mike Tomczak - QB
Gerald Williams - DE
Willie Williams - DB
Rod Woodson - DB
Tim Worley - RB
Jeff Zgonina - DT

1993 San Diego

Sam Anno - LB
Johnnie Barnes - WR
Eric Bieniemy - RB
Jeff Brady - LB
Stan Brock - T
Lewis Bush - LB
Marion Butts - RB
John Carney - K
Darren Carrington - DB
Eric Castle - DB
Joe Cocozzo - G
Terry Crews - LB
Brian Davis - DB
Mike Dyal - TE
Floyd Fields - DB
Donald Frank - DB
John Friesz - QB
James Fuller - DB
Darrien Gordon - DB
Burt Grossman - DE
Courtney Hall - C
Ronnie Harmon - RB
Steve Hendrickson - RB
Stan Humphries - QB
Shawn Jefferson - WR
Raylee Johnson - DE
Eric Jonassen - T
John Kidd - P
Shawn Lee - DT
Nate Lewis - WR
Deems May - TE
Natrone Means - RB
Joe Milinichik - G
Doug Miller - LB
Anthony Miller - WR
Chris Mims - DE
Mike Mooney - T
Eric Moten - G
Leslie O'Neal - DE
Gary Plummer - LB
Marquez Pope - DB
Alfred Pupunu - TE
Stanley Richard - DB
Junior Seau - LB
Mark Seay - WR
Raymond Smoot - G
Kent Sullivan - P
Harry Swayne - T
Sean Vanhorse - DB
Derrick Walker - TE
Reggie White - DT
Curtis Whitley - C
Jerrol Williams - LB
Blaise Winter - DT
Duane Young - TE
Mike Zandofsky - G

1993 San Francisco

Harris Barton - G
Sanjay Beach - WR
Harry Boatswain - T
Brian Bollinger - G
Steve Bono - QB
John Brandes - TE
Dennis Brown - DE
Ravin Caldwell - LB
Dexter Carter - RB
Mike Cofer - K
Chris Dalman - G
Eric Davis - DB
Keith DeLong - LB
Kevin Fagan - DE
Brett Faryniarz - LB
Roy Foster - G
Antonio Goss - LB
Alan Grant - DB
Don Griffin - DB
Dana Hall - DB
Merton Hanks - DB
Adrian Hardy - DB
Martin Harrison - DE
Terry Hoage - DB
John Johnson - LB
Brent Jones - TE
Darin Jordan - LB
Todd Kelly - LB

Larry Kelm - LB
Matt LaBounty - DE
Amp Lee - RB
Marc Logan - RB
Tim McDonald - DB
Mike McGruder - DB
Guy McIntyre - G
Bill Musgrave - QB
James Parrish - T
Tom Rathman - RB
Jerry Rice - WR
Larry Roberts - DE
Bill Romanowski - LB
Damien Russell - DB
Jesse Sapolu - C
Nate Singleton - WR
Artie Smith - DE
Dana Stubblefield - DT
Ralph Tamm - G
John Taylor - WR
Mark Thomas - DE
Odessa Turner - WR
Adam Walker - RB
Steve Wallace - T
Wesley Walls - TE
Michael Walter - LB
Ted Washington - NT
Ricky Watters - RB
Jamie Williams - TE
Klaus Wilmsmeyer - P
Karl Wilson - DE
Troy Wilson - DE
Steve Young - QB

1993 Seattle

Brian Allred - DB
Michael Bates - WR
Ray Berry - LB
Robert Blackmon - DB
Jeff Blackshear - G
Brian Blades - WR
David Brandon - LB
Darrick Brilz - G
Jeff Bryant - DE
Anthony Davis - LB
Ray Donaldson - C
Ferrell Edmunds - TE
Antonio Edwards - DE
Stan Gelbaugh - QB
Carlton Gray - DB
Paul Green - TE
Dino Hackett - LB
Dwayne Harper - DB
Andy Heck - T
Bill Hitchcock - G
Patrick Hunter - DB
James Jefferson - DB
Tracy Johnson - RB
E. J. Junior - LB
Trey Junkin - TE
John Kasay - K
Mike Keim - T
Cortez Kennedy - DT
Kelvin Martin - WR
Rueben Mayes - RB
Dave McCloughan - DB
Michael McCrary - DE
Dan McGwire - QB
Rick Mirer - QB
Kevin Murphy - LB
Joe Nash - DT
Rufus Porter - LB
Ray Roberts - T
Eugene Robinson - DB
Rafael Robinson - DB
Tyrone Rodgers - DT
Michael Sinclair - DE
Bob Spitulski - LB
Rod Stephens - LB
Doug Thomas - WR
Robb Thomas - LB
Natu Tuatagaloa - DE
Rick Tuten - P
Jon Vaughn - RB
Chris Warren - RB
Terrence Warren - WR
Dean Wells - LB
John L. Williams - RB
Terry Wooden - LB

1993 Tampa Bay

Theo Adams - T
Chidi Ahanotu - DE
Darren Anderson - DB
Gary Anderson - RB
Tyji Armstrong - TE
Ian Beckles - G
Ed Brady - LB
Darrick Brownlow - LB
Curtis Buckley - DB
Reggie Burnette - LB
Barney Bussey - DB
Marty Carter - DB
Robert Claiborne - WR
Reggie Cobb - RB
Horace Copeland - WR
Eric Curry - DE
Lawrence Dawsey - WR
Steve DeBerg - QB
Scott Dill - T
Santana Dotson - DE
Demetrius DuBose - LB
Craig Erickson - QB
Jerry Gray - DB

Paul Gruber - T
Rhett Hall - DE
Ron Hall - TE
Rudy Harris - RB
Courtney Hawkins - WR
Eric Hayes - DE
Michael Husted - K
Roger Jones - DB
Joe King - DB
Sean Love - G
John Lynch - DB
Milton Mack - DB
Tony Mayberry - C
Martin Mayhew - DB
Anthony McDowell - RB
Charles McRae - T
Dave Moore - TE
Hardy Nickerson - LB
Markus Paul - DB
Shawn Price - DE
Bruce Reimers - G
Ricky Reynolds - DB
Mazio Royster - RB
Tim Ryan - G
Ray Seals - DE
Dan Stryzinski - P
Mike Sullivan - G
Rob Taylor - T
Broderick Thomas - LB
Lamar Thomas - WR
Pat Tomberlin - G
Vernon Turner - WR
Casey Weldon - QB
Mark Wheeler - NT
Jimmy Williams - LB
Bernard Wilson - NT
Charles Wilson - WR
Vince Workman - RB

1993 Washington

Carl Banks - LB
Guy Bingham - C
Jeff Bostic - C
Todd Bowles - C
Reggie Brooks - RB
Ray Brown - T
Jason Buck - DE
Earnest Byner - RB
Tom Carter - DB
Greg Clifton - WR
Monte Coleman - LB
Andre Collins - LB
Shane Collins - DE
Cary Conklin - QB
Danny Copeland - DB
Brad Edwards - DB
Pat Eilers - DB
Mohammed Elewonibi - T
Ricky Ervins - RB
Jeff Faulkner - DE
Rich Gannon - QB
Kelly Goodburn - P
Kurt Gouveia - LB
Rick Graf - LB
Darrell Green - DB
Rick Hamilton - LB
Lamont Hollinquest - LB
Desmond Howard - WR
Greg Huntington - C
Joe Jacoby - G
James Jenkins - TE
A. J. Johnson - DB
Tim Johnson - DT
Chip Lohmiller - K
Charles Mann - DE
Alvoid Mays - DB
Tim McGee - WR
Raleigh McKenzie - C
Ron Middleton - TE
Brian Mitchell - RB
Art Monk - WR
Darryl Moore - G
Darryl Morrison - DB
Gerald Nichols - DT
Al Noga - DE
Terry Orr - TE
Sterling Palmer - DE
Marc Raab - C
Jim Riggs - TE
Reggie Roby - P
Ray Rowe - TE
Mark Rypien - QB
Ricky Sanders - WR
Mark Schlereth - G
Ed Simmons - T
Vernice Smith - G
Mark Stock - WR
Johnny Thomas - DB
Jim Wahler - DT
Eric Williams - DT
Keith Willis - DE
Bobby Wilson - DT
Frank Wycheck - RB

1994 Arizona

Brent Alexander - DB
Michael Bankston - DT
Sebastian Barrie - DT
Steve Beuerlein - QB
Michael Brandon - DE
Chad Brown - DE
Larry Centers - RB
Gary Clark - WR
Ben Coleman - T
Ed Cunningham - C
Rick Cunningham - T
Herschel Currie - DB
Greg Davis - K
Karl Dunbar - DT
Ernest Dye - G
Eric England - DE
Chad Fann - TE
Jeff Feagles - P
Odie Harris - DB
Frank Harvey - RB
Garrison Hearst - RB
Brian Henesey - RB
Mark Higgs - RB
Eric Hill - LB
Randal Hill - WR
Terry Hoage - DB
Terry Irving - LB
Garth Jax - LB
Seth Joyner - LB
Randy Kirk - LB
Kevin Knox - WR
Chuck Levy - RB
Lorenzo Lynch - DB
Wilber Marshall - LB
Fred McAfee - RB
Keith McCants - DE
Jim McMahon - QB
David Merritt - LB
Jamir Miller - LB
Ronald Moore - RB
Chris Oldham - DB
Todd Peterson - K
Ricky Proehl - WR
Anthony Redmon - G
Bryan Reeves - WR
Patrick Robinson - WR
Terry Samuels - TE
Jay Schroeder - QB
Luis Sharpe - T
Clyde Simmons - DE
Eric Swann - DT
Mark Tucker - C
Derek Ware - TE
Andre Waters - DB
Aeneas Williams - DB
James Williams - DB
Bernard Wilson - DT
Joe Wolf - G
Barry Word - RB

1994 Atlanta

Mel Agee - DT
Harold Alexander - P
Dunstan Anderson - DE
Jamal Anderson - RB
Lester Archambeau - DE
Scott Case - DB
Vinnie Clark - DB
Chris Doleman - DE
Irv Eatman - T
Brad Edwards - DB
Bert Emanuel - WR
Darryl Ford - LB
Roman Fortin - G
Moe Gardner - NT
Jumpy Geathers - DT
Jeff George - QB
Ron George - LB
Bill Goldberg - DT
Dwayne Gordon - LB
Roger Harper - DB
Leonard Harris - WR
Bobby Hebert - QB
Craig Heyward - RB
Pierce Holt - DT
Eric Jack - DB
D. J. Johnson - DB
Norm Johnson - K
Mike Kenn - T
Lincoln Kennedy - G
Perry Klein - QB
Harper LeBel - TE
Mitch Lyons - TE
Terance Mathis - WR
Clay Matthews - LB
Brett Maxie - DB
David Mims - WR
Alton Montgomery - DB
Erric Pegram - RB
Anthony Phillips - DB
David Richards - G
Andre Rison - WR
Jim Ritcher - G
Kevin Ross - DB
Ricky Sanders - WR
Elbert Shelley - DB
Chuck Smith - DE
Tony Smith - RB
Darryl Spencer - WR
Ken Tippins - LB
Robbie Tobeck - C
Jessie Tuggle - LB
Scott Tyner - K
Clarence Verdin - WR
Darnell Walker - DB
Charles Washington - DB
Bob Whitfield - T
Mike Zandofsky - C

1994 Buffalo

Oliver Barnett - DE
Don Beebe - WR
Cornelius Bennett - LB
Bucky Brooks - WR
Bill Brooks - WR
Monty Brown - LB
Jeff Burris - DB
Steve Christie - K
Russell Copeland - WR
Jerry Crafts - T
Matt Darby - DB
John Davis - G
Kenneth Davis - RB
Mike Devlin - G
Mike Dumas - DB
John Fina - T
Carwell Gardner - RB
Keith Goganious - LB
Phil Hansen - DE
Jerome Henderson - DB
Steve Hoyem - T
Kent Hull - C
Lonnie Johnson - TE
Henry Jones - DB
Yonel Jourdain - RB
Jim Kelly - QB
Corbin Lacina - T
Adam Lingner - C
Mike Lodish - NT
Mark Maddox - LB
Vince Marrow - TE
Pete Metzelaars - TE
Chris Mohr - P
Jerry Ostroski - G
Glenn Parker - G
James Patton - DE
Marvcus Patton - LB
Marlo Perry - LB
Ed Philion - NT
Mark Pike - DE
Andre Reed - WR
Frank Reich - QB
Sam Rogers - LB
Kurt Schulz - DB
Bruce Smith - DE
Thomas Smith - DB
Darryl Talley - LB
Steve Tasker - WR
Damon Thomas - WR
Thurman Thomas - RB
Nate Turner - RB
Mickey Washington - DB
Jeff Wright - NT

1994 Chi. Bears

Trace Armstrong - DE
Troy Auzenne - T
Myron Baker - LB
Mark Bortz - G
Todd Burger - G
James Burton - DB
Kevin Butler - K
Joe Cain - LB
Mark Carrier - DB
Tony Carter - RB
Bob Christian - RB
Trevor Cobb - RB
Curtis Conway - WR
Marv Cook - TE
Ron Cox - LB
Maurice Douglass - DB
Tory Epps - DT
Jim Flanigan - DT
Al Fontenot - DE
Jerry Fontenot - G
Chris Gardocki - P
Shaun Gayle - DB
Chris Gedney - TE
Jeff Graham - WR
Robert Green - RB
Raymont Harris - RB
Andy Heck - T
Merril Hoge - RB
Darwin Ireland - LB
Keith Jennings - TE
Keshon Johnson - DB
Dante Jones - LB
Erik Kramer - QB
Jay Leeuwenburg - G
Nate Lewis - WR
Jeremy Lincoln - DB
John Mangum - DB
Anthony Marshall - DB
Greg McMurtry - WR
Kevin Miniefield - DB
Barry Minter - LB
Tom Myslinski - G
Todd Perry - G
Greg Primus - WR
Carl Simpson - DT
Vinson Smith - LB
Alonzo Spellman - DE
John Thierry - DE
Lewis Tillman - RB
Tom Waddle - WR
Steve Walsh - QB
Ryan Wetnight - TE
James Williams - T
Donnell Woolford - DB
Tim Worley - RB
Chris Zorich - DT

1994 Cincinnati

Eric Ball - RB
Jeff Blake - QB
Rich Braham - T
David Braxton - LB
Darrick Brilz - G
Michael Brim - DB
Steve Broussard - RB
Scott Brumfield - T
Dave Cadigan - G
John Copeland - DE
Jeff Cothran - RB
Mark Dennis - T
Forey Duckett - DB
Derrick Fenner - RB
James Francis - LB
Mike Frier - DE
David Frisch - TE
Harold Green - RB
Adrian Hardy - DB
Jeff Hill - WR
Donald Hollas - QB
Kevin Jefferson - LB
John Johnson - LB
Lee Johnson - P
Dan Jones - T
Rod Jones - DB
Roger Jones - DB
David Klingler - QB
Bruce Kozerski - G
Tim Krumrie - DT
Ricardo McDonald - LB
Tim McGee - WR
Tony McGee - TE
Kanavis McGhee - DE
Eric Moore - G
Ken Moyer - C
Louis Oliver - DB
Ty Parten - DE
Doug Pelfrey - K
Carl Pickens - WR
Trent Pollard - T
Jeff Query - WR
Keith Rucker - DT
Troy Sadowski - TE
Kevin Sargent - T
Corey Sawyer - DB
Darnay Scott - WR
Eric Shaw - LB
Artie Smith - DE
Ramondo Stallings - DE
Milt Stegall - WR
Santo Stephens - LB
Steve Tovar - LB
Greg Truitt - C
Fernandus Vinson - DB
Kimo von Oelhoffen - DT
Bracey Walker - DB
Brett Wallerstedt - LB
Erik Wilhelm - QB
Dan Wilkinson - DT
Alfred Williams - DE
Darryl Williams - DB

1994 Cleveland

Derrick Alexander - WR
Herman Arvie - T
Randy Baldwin - RB
Carl Banks - LB
Issac Booth - DB
Orlando Brown - T
Rob Burnett - DE
Earnest Byner - RB
Mike Caldwell - LB
Mark Carrier - WR
Bob Dahl - G
Doug Dawson - G
Gerald Dixon - LB
Steve Everitt - C
Dan Footman - DE
Brad Goebel - QB
Don Griffin - DB
Stacey Hairston - DB
Frank Hartley - TE
Travis Hill - LB
Leroy Hoard - RB
Michael Jackson - WR
Tim Jacobs - DB
Pepper Johnson - LB
Bill Johnson - DE
James Jones - DT
Tony Jones - T
Brian Kinchen - TE
Antonio Langham - DB
Rick Lyle - DE
Keenan McCardell - WR
Thomas McLemore - WR
Eric Metcalf - RB
Stevon Moore - DB
Pat Newman - WR
Michael Dean Perry - DT
Anthony Pleasant - DE
Walter Reeves - TE
Louis Riddick - DB
Mark Rypien - QB
Pio Sagapolutele - DE
Rico Smith - WR
Del Speer - DB
Frank Stams - LB
Matt Stover - K
Eddie Sutter - LB
Vinny Testaverde - QB
Bennie Thompson - DB
Tom Tupa - P
Eric Turner - DB
Tommy Vardell - RB
Gene Williams - T
Wally Williams - C

1994 Dallas

Tommie Agee - RB
Troy Aikman - QB
Larry Allen - G
Bill Bates - DB
Chris Boniol - K
Larry Brown - DB
Darrick Brownlow - LB
Shante Carver - DE
Lincoln Coleman - RB
Frank Cornish - C
Dixon Edwards - LB
Joe Fishback - DB
Cory Fleming - WR
Scott Galbraith - TE
Kenneth Gant - DB
Jason Garrett - QB
Charles Haley - DE
Alvin Harper - WR
George Hegamin - T
Dale Hellestrae - G
Chad Hennings - DT
Clayton Holmes - DB
Michael Irvin - WR
Jim Jeffcoat - DE
John Jett - P
Daryl Johnston - RB
Robert Jones - LB
Derek Kennard - G
Leon Lett - DE
Brock Marion - DB
Russell Maryland - DT
Hurvin McCormack - DT
Godfrey Myles - LB
Nate Newton - G
Jay Novacek - TE
Rodney Peete - QB
Jim Schwantz - LB
Darrin Smith - LB
Emmitt Smith - RB
Kevin Smith - DB
Mark Stepnoski - C
Ron Stone - G
Darren Studstill - DB
Blair Thomas - RB
Dave Thomas - DB
Tony Tolbert - DE
Mark Tuinei - T
Matt Vanderbeek - LB
James Washington - DB
Erik Williams - T
Kevin Williams - WR
Robert Wilson - RB
Darren Woodson - DB

1994 Denver

Allen Aldridge - LB
Elijah Alexander - LB
Steve Atwater - DB
Rod Bernstine - RB
Ronnie Bradford - DB
Keith Burns - LB
Butler By'Not'e - DB
Jeff Campbell - WR
Dwayne Carswell - TE
Derrick Clark - RB
Ray Crockett - DB
Mike Croel - LB
Mitch Donahue - LB
Shane Dronett - DE
Jason Elam - K
John Elway - QB
Jerry Evans - TE
Simon Fletcher - LB
Russ Freeman - T
Randy Fuller - DB
Brian Habib - G
Darryl Hall - DB
Richard Harvey - LB
Harald Hasselbach - DE
Randy Hilliard - DB
Ray Jacobs - LB
Rondell Jones - DB
Tony Kimbrough - WR
Ken Lanier - T
Don Maggs - T
Karl Mecklenburg - LB
Jon Melander - G
Glyn Milburn - RB
Hugh Millen - QB
Anthony Miller - WR
Tom Nalen - C
Willie Oshodin - DE
Mike Pritchard - WR
Reggie Rivers - RB
Jeff Robinson - DE
Tom Rouen - P
Derek Russell - WR
Leonard Russell - RB
Glenell Sanders - LB
Kirk Scrafford - T
Shannon Sharpe - TE
Ben Smith - DB
Dennis Smith - DB
Deon Strother - RB
Charles Swann - WR
Cedric Tillman - WR
Ted Washington - NT
Dave Widell - G
Dan Williams - DE
David Wyman - LB
Gary Zimmerman - T

1994 Detroit

Tom Beer - LB
Bennie Blades - DB
Shane Bonham - DE
Jocelyn Borgella - DB
Shawn Bouwens - G
Lomas Brown - T
Anthony Carter - WR
Willie Clay - DB
Harry Colon - DB
Mike Compton - C
Scott Conover - T
Kevin Glover - C
Mel Gray - WR
Ron Hall - TE
Ty Hallock - TE
Jason Hanson - K
Tracy Hayworth - LB
Rodney Holman - TE
Greg Jeffries - DB
Mike Johnson - LB
Victor Jones - LB
Scott Kowalkowski - LB
Dave Krieg - QB
Antonio London - LB
Dave Lutz - G
Eric Lynch - RB
Milton Mack - DB
Van Malone - DB
Robert Massey - DB
Aubrey Matthews - WR
Ryan McNeil - DB
Scott Mitchell - QB
Greg Montgomery - P
Derrick Moore - RB
Herman Moore - WR
Johnnie Morton - WR
Dan Owens - DE
Brett Perriman - WR
Robert Porcher - DE
Kelvin Pritchett - DE
Mark Rodenhauser - C
Barry Sanders - RB
Tracy Scroggins - LB
Chris Spielman - LB
Marc Spindler - NT
Pat Swilling - LB
Broderick Thomas - LB
Mike Wells - DE
Doug Widell - G

1994 Green Bay

Edgar Bennett - RB
Matt Brock - DT
Robert Brooks - WR
Gary Brown - T
Gilbert Brown - DT
Mark Brunell - QB
Terrell Buckley - DB
LeRoy Butler - DB
Mark Chmura - TE
Reggie Cobb - RB
Don Davey - DE
Earl Dotson - T
Forey Duckett - DB
Jamie Dukes - C
Doug Evans - DB
Brett Favre - QB
Harry Galbreath - G
Ruffin Hamilton - LB
Corey Harris - DB
Tim Hauck - DB
Craig Hentrich - P
Charles Hope - G
Paul Hutchins - T
Chris Jacke - K
Keshon Johnson - DB
LeShon Johnson - RB
Reggie Johnson - TE
Sean Jones - DE
Charles Jordan - WR
John Jurkovic - NT
George Koonce - LB
Dorsey Levens - RB
Ron Lewis - WR
Lenny McGill - DB
Guy McIntyre - G
Steve McMichael - DT
Terry Mickens - WR
Roland Mitchell - DB
Anthony Morgan - WR
Bryce Paup - LB
Mike Prior - DB
Ken Ruettgers - T
Bill Schroeder - WR
Sterling Sharpe - WR
Wayne Simmons - LB
Joe Sims - G
Fred Strickland - LB
George Teague - DB
Darrell Thompson - RB
Ed West - TE
Reggie White - DE
Gabe Wilkins - DT
Mark Williams - LB
James Willis - LB
Jeff Wilner - TE
Marcus Wilson - RB
Ray Wilson - DB
Frank Winters - C

1994 Houston

Tomur Barnes - DB
Micheal Barrow - LB
Blaine Bishop - DB
Joe Bowden - LB
Gary Brown - RB
Reggie Brown - WR
Rich Camarillo - P
Cody Carlson - QB
Pat Carter - TE
Ray Childress - DT
Pat Coleman - WR
Kenny Davidson - DE
Mike Davis - DB
Al Del Greco - K
Cris Dishman - DB
Kevin Donnalley - G
Brett Faryniarz - LB
John Flannery - G
Malcolm Floyd - WR
Henry Ford - DE
Ernest Givins - WR
Travis Hannah - WR
Brad Hopkins - T
Steve Jackson - DB
Haywood Jeffires - WR
Lamar Lathon - LB
Darryll Lewis - DB
Roderick Lewis - TE
Le'Shai Maston - LB
Bruce Matthews - C
Keith McCants - DE
Bubba McDowell - DB
Todd McNair - RB
John Henry Mills - RB
Glenn Montgomery - DT
Erik Norgard - C
Jeremy Nunley - DE
Bo Orlando - DB
Bucky Richardson - QB
Tim Roberts - DE
Marcus Robertson - DB
Eddie Robinson - LB
Webster Slaughter - WR
Al Smith - LB
Mike Teeter - DT
Stan Thomas - T
Spencer Tillman - RB
Billy Joe Tolliver - QB
Gary Wellman - WR
Lorenzo White - RB
David Williams - T
Barron Wortham - LB

1994 Indianapolis

Trev Alberts - LB
Ashley Ambrose - DB
Charles Arbuckle - TE
Aaron Bailey - WR
Shannon Baker - WR
Bradford Banta - TE
Jason Belser - DB
Tony Bennett - LB
Dean Biasucci - K
Dewell Brewer - RB
Ray Buchanan - DB
Paul Butcher - LB
Kerry Cash - TE
Quentin Coryatt - LB
John Covington - DB
Eugene Daniel - DB
Sean Dawkins - WR
Randy Dixon - G
Steve Emtman - DE
Carlos Etheredge - TE
Marshall Faulk - RB
Steve Grant - LB
Cecil Gray - T
Derwin Gray - DB
Jon Hand - DE
Jim Harbaugh - QB
Jeff Herrod - LB
Garry Howe - DT
Ronald Humphrey - RB
Leonard Humphries - DB
Mark Jackson - WR
Kirk Lowdermilk - C
Eric Mahlum - G
Don Majkowski - QB
Jason Mathews - T
Tony McCoy - NT
Devon McDonald - LB
Zefross Moss - T
Browning Nagle - QB
Al Noga - DE
Freddie Joe Nunn - DE
Robert O'Neal - DB
Roosevelt Potts - RB
Scott Radecic - LB
Brian Ratigan - LB
Tom Sims - DT
Tony Siragusa - DT
Rohn Stark - P
Joe Staysniak - G
David Tate - DB
Lance Teichelman - DE
Ed Toner - RB
Floyd Turner - WR
Lamont Warren - RB
Damon Watts - DB
Bernard Whittington - DE
Will Wolford - T

1994 Kansas City

Louie Aguiar - P
Arnold Ale - LB
Marcus Allen - RB
John Alt - T
Kimble Anders - RB
Darren Anderson - DB
Donnell Bennett - RB
J. J. Birden - WR
Matt Blundin - QB
Steve Bono - QB
Vaughn Booker - DE
Dale Carter - DB
Keith Cash - TE
Mark Collins - DB
Anthony Davis - LB
Willie Davis - WR
Lake Dawson - WR
Ron Dickerson - RB
Lin Elliott - K
Jaime Fields - LB
Matt Gay - DB
Derrick Graham - T
Tracy Greene - TE
Monty Grow - DB
Tim Grunhard - C
Rick Hamilton - LB
Greg Hill - RB
Danan Hughes - WR
George Jamison - LB
Jimmie Johnson - TE
Victor Jones - RB
Lindsay Knapp - G
Greg Kragen - NT
Greg Manusky - LB
Eric Martin - WR
Pellom McDaniels - DE
Darren Mickell - DE
Charles Mincy - DB
Joe Montana - QB
Chris Penn - WR
Joe Phillips - DT
Tracy Rogers - LB
Dan Saleaumua - DT
Will Shields - G
Ricky Siglar - T
Tracy Simien - LB
Neil Smith - DE
Tommie Stowers - TE
David Szott - G
Jay Taylor - DB
Doug Terry - DB
Derrick Thomas - LB
Joe Valerio - G
Jon Vaughn - RB
Danny Villa - G
Rob Waldrop - NT
Bracey Walker - DB
Derrick Walker - TE
Tim Watson - DB
William White - DB
David Whitmore - DB
Jerrol Williams - LB
Mike Young - WR

1994 LA Raiders

Eddie Anderson - DB
Jerry Ball - DT
Patrick Bates - DB
Wes Bender - RB
Greg Biekert - LB
Cary Brabham - DB
Tim Brown - WR
Aundray Bruce - DE
Jarrod Bunch - RB
Scott Davis - DE
John Duff - TE
Vince Evans - QB
James Folston - LB
Donald Frank - DB
Rob Fredrickson - LB
Andrew Glover - TE
Kevin Gogan - G
Jeff Gossett - P
Nolan Harrison - DE
Daryl Hobbs - WR
Rob Holmberg - LB
Derrick Hoskins - DB
Jeff Hostetler - QB
Raghib Ismail - WR
Jeff Jaeger - K
Robert Jenkins - T
James Jett - WR
Calvin Jones - RB
Mike Jones - LB
Dan Land - DB
Albert Lewis - DB
Napoleon McCallum - RB
Terry McDaniel - DB
Chester McGlockton - DT
Tyrone Montgomery - WR
Max Montoya - G
Don Mosebar - C
Winston Moss - LB
Gerald Perry - T
Tom Rathman - RB
Austin Robbins - DT
Greg Skrepenak - T
Anthony Smith - DE
Kevin Smith - TE
James Trapp - DB
Dan Turk - C
Aaron Wallace - DE
Lionel Washington - DB
Alberto White - DE
Bruce Wilkerson - T
Harvey Williams - RB
Jamie Williams - TE
Steve Wisniewski - G
Alexander Wright - WR

1994 LA Rams

Flipper Anderson - WR
Darryl Ashmore - T
Johnny Bailey - RB
Robert Bailey - DB
Chuck Belin - G
Jerome Bettis - RB
Rickey Brady - TE
Chris Brantley - WR
Bern Brostek - C
Isaac Bruce - WR
Richard Buchanan - WR
Blair Bush - C
Chris Chandler - QB
Brett Collins - LB
Shane Conlan - LB
Dexter Davis - DB
Troy Drayton - TE
D'Marco Farr - DT
Brad Fichtel - G
Wayne Gandy - T
Sean Gilbert - DT
Leo Goeas - G
Howard Griffith - RB
Wymon Henderson - DB
Darryl Henley - DB
Jessie Hester - WR
Thomas Homco - LB
Steve Israel - DB
Clarence Jones - T
Jimmie Jones - DT
Joe Kelly - LB
Todd Kinchen - WR
Sean Landeta - P
David Lang - RB
Tim Lester - RB
Keith Loneker - G
Todd Lyght - DB
Keith Lyle - DB
Tommy Maddox - QB
Chris Martin - LB
Ron Middleton - TE
Chris Miller - QB
Tom Newberry - G
Anthony Newman - DB
Brad Ottis - DE
Roman Phifer - LB
Marquez Pope - DB
Gerald Robinson - DE
David Rocker - DT
Henry Rolling - LB
Jermaine Ross - WR
Jackie Slater - T
Fred Stokes - DE
Toby Wright - DB
Robert Young - DE
Tony Zendejas - K

1994 Miami

Jim Arnold - P
Gene Atkins - DB
Greg Baty - TE
Aubrey Beavers - LB
Tim Bowens - NT
Brant Boyer - LB
Tyrone Braxton - DB
J.B. Brown - DB
Chuck Bullough - LB
Keith Byars - RB
Marco Coleman - DE
Bryan Cox - LB
Aaron Craver - RB
Jeff Cross - DE
Jeff Dellenbach - C
DeWayne Dotson - LB
Dion Foxx - LB
Irving Fryar - WR
William Gaines - NT
Cleveland Gary - RB
Chris Gray - G
Chris Green - DB
Ron Heller - T
Mark Higgs - RB
Sean Hill - DB
Dwight Hollier - LB
Houston Hoover - G
Mark Ingram - WR
Tim Irwin - T
Calvin Jackson - DB
Keith Jackson - TE
Tyoka Jackson - LB
John Kidd - P
Terry Kirby - RB
Chuck Klingbeil - NT
Bernie Kosar - QB
Darrell Malone - DB
Dan Marino - QB
O. J. McDuffie - WR
Scott Miller - WR
Jeff Novak - G
Muhammad Oliver - DB
Bernie Parmalee - RB
David Pool - DB
Tim Ruddy - C
James Saxon - RB
Keith Sims - G
Chris Singleton - LB
Frankie Smith - DB
Jesse Solomon - LB
Irving Spikes - RB
Michael Stewart - DB
Pete Stoyanovich - K
Craig Veasey - NT
Troy Vincent - DB
Richmond Webb - T
Larry Webster - DE
Bert Weidner - G
Mike Williams - WR
Ronnie Williams - TE
Robert Wilson - RB

1994 Minnesota

Bobby Abrams - LB
Terry Allen - RB
Roy Barker - DE
Malik Boyd - DB
Richard Brown - LB
Cris Carter - WR
Jeff Christy - C
Adrian Cooper - TE
Frank Cornish - G
Bernard Dafney - T
Brian Davis - DB
Jack Del Rio - LB
David Dixon - G
Chuck Evans - RB
Dave Garnett - LB
John Gerak - G
Vencie Glenn - DB
Scottie Graham - RB
Robert Griffith - DB
Eric Guliford - WR
James Harris - DE
Robert Harris - DE
Martin Harrison - DE
Chris Hinton - T
Qadry Ismail - WR
Carlos Jenkins - LB
Brad Johnson - QB
Andrew Jordan - TE
Steve Jordan - TE
Amp Lee - RB
Ed McDaniel - LB
Randall McDaniel - G
Reggie McElroy - T
Lamar McGriggs - DB
Warren Moon - QB
Mike Morris - C
Roosevelt Nix - DE
Brent Novoselsky - TE
David Palmer - RB
Anthony Parker - DB
John Randle - DT
Jake Reed - WR
Fuad Reveiz - K
Sean Salisbury - QB
Mike Saxon - P
Todd Scott - DB
Ashley Sheppard - LB
William Sims - LB
Fernando Smith - DE
Robert Smith - RB
Todd Steussie - T
Henry Thomas - DT
Esera Tuaolo - DT
Chris Walsh - WR
Dewayne Washington - DB

1994 New England

Ray Agnew - DE
Bruce Armstrong - T
Mike Arthur - C
Matt Bahr - K
Harlon Barnett - DB
Troy Barnett - DE
David Bavaro - LB
Drew Bledsoe - QB
Vincent Brisby - WR
Corwin Brown - DB
Troy Brown - WR
Vincent Brown - LB
John Burke - TE
Marion Butts - RB
Jason Carthen - LB
Eugene Chung - G
Ben Coates - TE
Todd Collins - LB
Ray Crittenden - WR
Corey Croom - RB
Steve DeOssie - LB
Sam Gash - RB
Mike Gisler - G
Tim Goad - NT
Myron Guyton - DB
Pat Harlow - T
Ronnie Harris - WR
Steve Hawkins - WR
Maurice Hurst - DB
Aaron Jones - DE
Mike Jones - DE
Bob Kratch - G
Max Lane - T
Burnie Legette - RB
Vernon Lewis - DB
Willie McGinest - LB
Brandon Moore - T
Marty Moore - LB
Pat O'Neill - P
Mike Pitts - DE
Terry Ray - DB
Ricky Reynolds - DB
Todd Rucci - G
Dwayne Sabb - LB
Doug Skene - G
Chris Slade - LB
Rod Smith - DB
Sylvester Stanley - NT
Blair Thomas - RB
Leroy Thompson - RB
Michael Timpson - WR
Kevin Turner - RB
Larry Whigham - DB
Darryl Wren - DB
Scott Zolak - QB

1994 New Orleans

Scott Adams - G
Morten Andersen - K
Tommy Barnhardt - P
Mario Bates - RB
Kirk Botkin - TE
Derek Brown - RB
Vince Buck - DB
Israel Byrd - DB
Herman Carroll - DE
Vinnie Clark - DB
Darion Conner - LB
Richard Cooper - T
Ernest Dixon - LB
Jim Dombrowski - G
Vaughn Dunbar - RB
Quinn Early - WR
Jim Everett - QB
Robert Goff - DE
Jim Hanna - DT
Michael Haynes - WR
Othello Henderson - DB
Tyrone Hughes - DB
Joe Johnson - DT
Tyrone Johnson - WR
Reggie Jones - DB
Selwyn Jones - DB
Carl Lee - DB
Tyrone Legette - DB
Sean Lumpkin - DB
Wayne Martin - DE
J. J. McCleskey - DB
Les Miller - NT
Sam Mills - LB
Derrell Mitchell - WR
Brad Muster - RB
Lorenzo Neal - RB
Derrick Ned - RB
Craig Novitsky - C
Chris Port - G
Steve Rhem - WR
Willie Roaf - T
Torrance Small - WR
Joel Smeenge - LB
Irv Smith - TE
Jimmy Spencer - DB
Mike Stonebreaker - LB
Winfred Tubbs - LB
Renaldo Turnbull - DE
Jeff Uhlenhake - C
Wesley Walls - TE
Frank Warren - DE
James Williams - LB
Wade Wilson - QB
Ray Wilson - DB
DeMond Winston - LB

1994 NY Giants

Jessie Armstead - LB
Carlton Bailey - LB
Willie Beamon - DB
Greg Bishop - T
John Booty - DB
Chad Bratzke - DE
Michael Brooks - LB
Dave Brown - QB
Derek Brown - TE
Marcus Buckley - LB
Chris Calloway - WR
Jesse Campbell - DB
Howard Cross - TE
Brad Daluiso - K
Scott Davis - G
Stacey Dillard - DT
Omar Douglas - WR
Gary Downs - RB
Keith Elias - RB
Jumbo Elliott - T
Mike Fox - DE
Kent Graham - QB
Keith Hamilton - DE
Rodney Hampton - RB
Mike Horan - P
Erik Howard - DT
Mark Jackson - WR
Brian Kozlowski - TE
Thomas Lewis - WR
Arthur Marshall - WR
Chris Maumalanga - DT
Dave Meggett - RB
Corey Miller - LB
Aaron Pierce - TE
Andre Powell - LB
Thomas Randolph - DB
Kenyon Rasheed - RB
Corey Raymond - DB
Doug Riesenberg - T
William Roberts - G
Coleman Rudolph - DE
Adam Schreiber - C
Jason Sehorn - DB
Mike Sherrard - WR
Pete Shufelt - LB
Lance Smith - G
Phillippi Sparks - DB
Mike Strahan - DE
David Treadwell - K
Corey Widmer - LB
Brian Williams - C
Jarvis Williams - DB
Tito Wooten - DB

1994 NY Jets

Tuineau Alipate - LB
Richie Anderson - RB
Stevie Anderson - WR
Kurt Barber - DE
Fred Baxter - TE
Brad Baxter - RB
Lou Benfatti - DT
James Brown - T
Glenn Cadrez - LB
Rob Carpenter - WR
Tony Casillas - DT
Kyle Clifton - LB
Jeff Criswell - T
Cal Dixon - C
Roger Duffy - G
Boomer Esiason - QB
Donald Evans - DT
Glenn Foley - QB
Paul Frase - DT
Aaron Glenn - DB
Victor Green - DB
Mark Gunn - DT
Brian Hansen - P
James Hasty - DB
Cliff Hicks - DB
Bobby Houston - LB
Anthony Johnson - RB
Johnny Johnson - RB
Marvin Jones - LB
Jeff Lageman - DE
Mo Lewis - LB
Ronnie Lott - DB
Nick Lowery - K
Siupeli Malamala - T
Everett McIver - G
Johnny Mitchell - TE
Art Monk - WR
Rob Moore - WR
Adrian Murrell - RB
Alfred Oglesby - DT
Orlando Parker - WR
Bill Pickel - DT
Anthony Prior - DB
Jim Sweeney - C
Pat Terrell - DB
Eric Thomas - DB
Jim Thornton - TE
Jack Trudeau - QB
Marcus Turner - DB
Brian Washington - DB
Marvin Washington - DE
Dwayne White - G
Matt Willig - T
Ryan Yarborough - WR

1994 Philadelphia

David Alexander - C
Eric Allen - DB
Victor Bailey - WR
Bryan Barker - P
Fred Barnett - WR
Mark Bavaro - TE
Mitch Berger - P
Bubby Brister - QB
Randall Cunningham - QB
Antone Davis - T
Byron Evans - LB
Mike Flores - DE
Derrick Frazier - DB
William Fuller - DE
Charlie Garner - RB
Burt Grossman - DE
Britt Hager - LB
Andy Harmon - DT
Vaughn Hebron - RB
Lester Holmes - G
John Hudson - G
Al Jackson - DB
Greg Jackson - DB
Tommy Jeter - DT
Maurice Johnson - TE
Vaughan Johnson - LB
James Joseph - RB
Tom McHale - T
Mark McMillian - DB
Rich Miano - DB
Eddie Murray - K
Derrick Oden - LB
Brian O'Neal - RB
Joe Panos - G
William Perry - DT
Mike Reid - DB
Leonard Renfro - DT
Bill Romanowski - LB
Ken Rose - LB
Rob Selby - G
Otis Smith - DB
Jeff Sydner - WR
William Thomas - LB
Broderick Thompson - T
Greg Townsend - DE
Herschel Walker - RB
Jeff Wilkins - K
Bernard Williams - T
Calvin Williams - WR
Marc Woodard - LB
Eric Zomalt - DB
Mike Zordich - DB

1994 Pittsburgh

Gary Anderson - K
Steve Avery - RB
Myron Bell - DB
Chad Brown - LB
Brentson Buckner - DE
Reggie Clark - LB
Randy Cuthbert - RB
Anthony Daigle - RB
Charles Davenport - WR
Dermontti Dawson - C
Ta'ase Faumui - DE
Deon Figures - DB
Fred Foggie - DB
Barry Foster - RB
Kendall Gammon - C
Jason Gildon - LB
Eric Green - TE
Kevin Greene - LB
Andre Hastings - WR
Jonathan Hayes - TE
Kevin Henry - DE
John Jackson - T
Charles Johnson - WR
Gary Jones - DB
Victor Jones - RB
Todd Kalis - G
Craig Keith - TE
Levon Kirkland - LB
Carnell Lake - DB
Greg Lloyd - LB
Duval Love - G
Fred McAfee - RB
Tim McKyer - DB
Ernie Mills - WR
Bam Morris - RB
Neil O'Donnell - QB
Jerry Olsavsky - LB
Darren Perry - DB
Walter Rasby - TE
Eric Ravotti - LB
Ed Robinson - LB
Mark Royals - P
Ray Seals - DE
Leon Searcy - T
Tim Simpson - G
Ariel Solomon - C
Joel Steed - NT
Dwight Stone - WR
Justin Strzelczyk - G
Yancey Thigpen - WR
Mike Tomczak - QB
Gerald Williams - DE
John L. Williams - RB
Willie Williams - DB
Rod Woodson - DB
Jeff Zgonina - NT

1994 San Diego

Johnnie Barnes - WR
Eric Bieniemy - RB
David Binn - TE
Stan Brock - T
Lewis Bush - LB
John Carney - K
Darren Carrington - DB
Eric Castle - DB
Willie Clark - DB
Joe Cocozzo - G
Andre Coleman - WR
Rodney Culver - RB
Isaac Davis - G
Reuben Davis - DT
Dennis Gibson - LB
Gale Gilbert - QB
Darrien Gordon - DB
David Griggs - LB
Courtney Hall - C
Ronnie Harmon - RB
Dwayne Harper - DB
Rodney Harrison - DB
Steve Hendrickson - LB
Stan Humphries - QB
Shawn Jefferson - WR
Raylee Johnson - DE
Eric Jonassen - T
John Kidd - P
Aaron Laing - TE
Shawn Lee - DT
Tony Martin - WR
Deems May - TE
Natrone Means - RB
Joe Milinichik - G
Doug Miller - LB
Les Miller - DE
Chris Mims - DE
Shannon Mitchell - TE
Leslie O'Neal - DE
Vaughn Parker - T
John Parrella - DT
Alfred Pupunu - TE
Stanley Richard - DB
Junior Seau - LB
Mark Seay - WR
Harry Swayne - T
Cornell Thomas - DE
Sean Vanhorse - DB
Bryan Wagner - P
Reggie White - DT
Curtis Whitley - C
Blaise Winter - DT
Duane Young - TE
Lonnie Young - DB

1994 San Francisco

Harris Barton - G
Harry Boatswain - T
Brian Bollinger - T
Doug Brien - K
Dennis Brown - DE
Brett Carolan - TE
Dexter Carter - RB
Toi Cook - DB
Chris Dalman - G
Eric Davis - DB
Derrick Deese - G
Richard Dent - DE
Dedrick Dodge - DB
Tyronne Drakeford - DB
William Floyd - RB
Antonio Goss - LB
Elvis Grbac - QB
Dana Hall - DB
Rhett Hall - DT
Merton Hanks - DB
Adrian Hardy - DB
Tim Harris - DE
Rickey Jackson - LB
Brent Jones - TE
Darin Jordan - LB
Todd Kelly - DE
Marc Logan - RB
Derek Loville - RB
Charles Mann - DE
Ed McCaffrey - WR
Tim McDonald - DB
Rod Milstead - G
Kevin Mitchell - LB
Bill Musgrave - QB
Ken Norton - LB
Bart Oates - C
Tony Peterson - LB
Gary Plummer - LB
Frank Pollack - T
Ted Popson - TE
Jerry Rice - WR
Deion Sanders - DB
Jesse Sapolu - C
Nate Singleton - WR
Artie Smith - DE
Dana Stubblefield - DT
Ralph Tamm - G
John Taylor - WR
Mark Thomas - DE
Adam Walker - RB
Steve Wallace - T
Ricky Watters - RB
Klaus Wilmsmeyer - P
Troy Wilson - DE
Lee Woodall - LB
Bryant Young - DT
Steve Young - QB

1994 Seattle

Sam Adams - DT
James Atkins - T
Howard Ballard - T
Michael Bates - WR
Jay Bellamy - DB
Duane Bickett - LB
Robert Blackmon - DB
Jeff Blackshear - G
Brian Blades - WR
David Brandon - LB
Tony Brown - DB
Beno Bryant - RB
Carlester Crumpler - TE
Ray Donaldson - C
Forey Duckett - DB
Ferrell Edmunds - TE
Antonio Edwards - DE
Mike Frier - DT
Stan Gelbaugh - QB
Carlton Gray - DB
Paul Green - TE
Ronnie Harris - WR
Bill Hitchcock - G
Patrick Hunter - DB
Tracy Johnson - RB
Trey Junkin - TE
John Kasay - K
Mike Keim - T
Cortez Kennedy - DT
Dion Lambert - DB
Kelvin Martin - WR
Kevin Mawae - G
Dave McCloughan - DB
Michael McCrary - DE
Dan McGwire - QB
James McKnight - WR
Rick Mirer - QB
Joe Nash - DT
Rufus Porter - LB
Ray Roberts - T
Eugene Robinson - DB

Rafael Robinson - DB
Tyrone Rodgers - DE
Michael Sinclair - DE
Lamar Smith - RB
Steve Smith - RB
Del Speer - DB
Bob Spitulski - LB
Rod Stephens - LB
Mack Strong - RB
Terry Taylor - DB
Robb Thomas - WR
Joe Tofflemire - C
Rick Tuten - P
Jon Vaughn - RB
Chris Warren - RB
Terrence Warren - WR
Orlando Watters - DB
Dean Wells - LB
Brent Williams - DE
Terry Wooden - LB

1994 Tampa Bay

Chidi Ahanotu - DE
Tyji Armstrong - TE
Ian Beckles - G
Harold Bishop - TE
Ed Brady - LB
Jeff Brady - LB
Curtis Buckley - DB
Barney Bussey - DB
Marty Carter - DB
Horace Copeland - WR
Tony Covington - DB
Brad Culpepper - DT
Eric Curry - DE
Lawrence Dawsey - WR
Trent Dilfer - QB
Scott Dill - G
Charles Dimry - DB
Santana Dotson - DT
Demetrius DuBose - LB
Craig Erickson - QB
Thomas Everett - DB
Rogerick Green - DB
Willie Green - WR
Paul Gruber - T
Jackie Harris - TE
Rudy Harris - RB
Courtney Hawkins - WR
Jeff Hunter - DE
Michael Husted - K
Tim Irwin - T
Sean Love - G
John Lynch - DB
Lonnie Marts - LB
Tony Mayberry - C
Martin Mayhew - DB
Anthony McDowell - RB
Mike McGruder - DB
Toddrick McIntosh - DT
Charles McRae - G
Dave Moore - TE
Hardy Nickerson - LB
Keith Powe - DE
Shawn Price - DE
Errict Rhett - RB
Mazio Royster - RB
Tony Stargell - DB
Dan Stryzinski - P
Mike Sullivan - G
Lamar Thomas - WR
Vernon Turner - RB
Casey Weldon - QB
Mark Wheeler - DT
Bernard Wilson - DT
Charles Wilson - WR
Karl Wilson - DE
Vince Workman - RB

1994 Washington

Erick Anderson - LB
Martin Bayless - DB
William Bell - RB
Marc Boutte - DT
Deral Boykin - DB
Reggie Brooks - RB
Ray Brown - T
Tom Carter - DB
Monte Coleman - LB
Andre Collins - LB
Shane Collins - DE
Pat Eilers - DB
Henry Ellard - WR
Ricky Ervins - RB
Gus Frerotte - QB
John Friesz - QB
John Gesek - C
Kurt Gouveia - LB
Alan Grant - DB
Darrell Green - DB
Rick Hamilton - LB
Ken Harvey - LB
Kurt Haws - TE
Lamont Hollinquest - LB
Ethan Horton - RB
Desmond Howard - WR
James Jenkins - TE
A. J. Johnson - DB
Tre' Johnson - T
Tim Johnson - DT
Jim Lachey - T
Chip Lohmiller - K
Leonard Marshall - DE
Trevor Match - C

Alvoid Mays - DB
Raleigh McKenzie - G
Lamar Mills - DE
Brian Mitchell - RB
Darryl Morrison - DB
Dexter Nottage - DE
Sterling Palmer - DE
Joe Patton - G
Reggie Roby - P
Tyrone Rush - RB
Sebastian Savage - DB
Mark Schlereth - G
Leslie Shepherd - WR
Heath Shuler - QB
Ed Simmons - T
Cedric Smith - RB
Vernice Smith - G
Tyronne Stowe - LB
Keith Taylor - DB
Johnny Thomas - DB
Olanda Truitt - WR
Bobby Wilson - DT
Tydus Winans - WR
Tony Woods - DE
Frank Wycheck - RB

1995 Arizona

Melvin Aldridge - LB
Brent Alexander - DB
Stevie Anderson - WR
Michael Bankston - DE
Carlos Brooks - DB
Chad Brown - DE
Lance Brown - DB
Mike Buck - QB
Stoney Case - QB
Larry Centers - RB
Ben Coleman - T
Ed Cunningham - C
Bernard Dafney - T
Greg Davis - K
Marcus Dowdell - WR
Jerry Drake - DE
Jamie Dukes - C
Karl Dunbar - DT
Ernest Dye - T
Anthony Edwards - WR
Eric England - DE
Chad Fann - TE
Jeff Feagles - P
Eric Floyd - T
Wendall Gaines - TE
Cecil Gray - T
Darryl Hardy - LB
Garrison Hearst - RB
Mark Higgs - RB
Eric Hill - LB
Terry Hoage - DB
Patrick Hunter - DB
Terry Irving - LB
Garth Jax - LB
LeShon Johnson - RB
Tony Jones - DB
Seth Joyner - LB
Randy Kirk - LB
Dave Krieg - QB
Kwamie Lassiter - DB
Wesley Leasy - LB
Duval Love - G
Lorenzo Lynch - DB
Chris Maumalanga - DT
Oscar McBride - TE
Keith McCants - DE
David Merritt - LB
Jamir Miller - LB
Rob Moore - WR
Tito Paul - DB
Anthony Redmon - G
Bryan Reeves - WR
C.J. Richardson - DB
Terry Samuels - RB
Frank Sanders - WR
Rob Selby - G
Simon Shanks - LB
Clyde Simmons - DE
Ben Smith - DB
Eric Swann - DT
Ryan Terry - RB
Larry Tharpe - T
Andre Waters - DB
Aeneas Williams - DB
Bernard Wilson - DT
Joe Wolf - G

1995 Atlanta

Mel Agee - DT
Morten Andersen - K
Jamal Anderson - RB
Lester Archambeau - DE
J. J. Birden - WR
Tyrone Brown - WR
John Burrough - DT
Devin Bush - DB
Ron Davis - DB
Chris Doleman - DE
Brad Edwards - DB
Bert Emanuel - WR
Roman Fortin - C
Moe Gardner - NT
Jumpy Geathers - DT
Jeff George - QB
Ron George - LB
Travis Hall - DE
Roger Harper - DB

Bobby Hebert - QB
Craig Heyward - RB
Pierce Holt - DT
D. J. Johnson - DB
Lincoln Kennedy - G
Harper LeBel - TE
Mitch Lyons - TE
Terance Mathis - WR
Clay Matthews - LB
Eric Metcalf - WR
Rich Miano - DB
Alton Montgomery - DB
Jeff Pahukoa - G
Anthony Phillips - DB
Roell Preston - WR
David Richards - G
Jim Ritcher - G
Kevin Ross - DB
Ricky Sanders - WR
Elbert Shelley - DB
Chuck Smith - DE
Darryl Spencer - WR
Dan Stryzinski - P
Lorenzo Styles - LB
Darryl Talley - LB
Terry Taylor - DB
Ken Tippins - LB
Robbie Tobeck - G
Jessie Tuggle - LB
Darnell Walker - DB
Bob Whitfield - T
Gene Williams - G
Mike Zandofsky - G
Tony Zendejas - K

1995 Buffalo

Justin Armour - WR
Cornelius Bennett - LB
Bill Brooks - WR
Monty Brown - LB
Ruben Brown - G
Jeff Burris - DB
Steve Christie - K
Tony Cline - TE
Todd Collins - QB
Robert Coons - TE
Russell Copeland - WR
Damien Covington - LB
Matt Darby - DB
Mike Devlin - G
Greg Evans - DB
John Fina - T
Carwell Gardner - RB
Chris Green - DB
Phil Hansen - DE
John Holecek - LB
Darick Holmes - RB
Kent Hull - C
Ken Irvin - DB
Jim Jeffcoat - DE
Filmel Johnson - DB
Lonnie Johnson - TE
Henry Jones - DB
Yonel Jourdain - RB
Jim Kelly - QB
Marlon Kerner - DB
Corbin Lacina - G
Adam Lingner - C
Corey Louchiey - T
Mark Maddox - LB
Chris Mohr - P
Tom Nutten - C
Jerry Ostroski - G
Glenn Parker - G
Bryce Paup - LB
Marlo Perry - LB
Ed Philion - DT
Mark Pike - DE
Andre Reed - WR
Sam Rogers - LB
Kurt Schulz - DB
Bruce Smith - DE
Thomas Smith - DB
Steve Tasker - WR
Damon Thomas - WR
Thurman Thomas - RB
Tim Tindale - RB
Alex Van Pelt - QB
Ted Washington - NT
David White - LB
Karl Wilson - LB

1995 Carolina

Carlton Bailey - LB
Randy Baldwin - RB
Tommy Barnhardt - P
Don Beebe - WR
Blake Brockermeyer - T
Paul Butcher - LB
Butler By'Not'e - DB
Matthew Campbell - G
Mark Carrier - WR
Bob Christian - RB
Kerry Collins - QB
Darion Conner - LB
Chad Cota - DB
Mark Dennis - T
Matt Elliott - G
Brett Faryniarz - LB
Jeff Fields - DE
Mike Fox - DE
Frank Garcia - G
Derrick Graham - T
Willie Green - WR

Howard Griffith - RB
Eric Guliford - WR
Alan Haller - DB
Travis Hill - LB
Anthony Johnson - RB
Reggie Jones - WR
John Kasay - K
Shawn King - DE
Greg Kragen - NT
Lamar Lathon - LB
Steve Lofton - DB
Sean Love - G
Emerson Martin - G
Brett Maxie - DB
Bubba McDowell - DB
Tim McKyer - DB
Pete Metzelaars - TE
Sam Mills - LB
Derrick Moore - RB
Andrew Peterson - G
Dino Philyaw - RB
Tyrone Poole - DB
Shawn Price - DE
Walter Rasby - TE
Michael Reed - DB
Frank Reich - QB
Mark Rodenhauser - C
Andre Royal - LB
Rod Smith - DB
Dwight Stone - WR
Pat Terrell - DB
Blair Thomas - RB
Mark Thomas - DE
Lawyer Tillman - TE
Jack Trudeau - RB
Nate Turner - RB
Curtis Whitley - C
Gerald Williams - DE
Vince Workman - RB
Jeff Zgonina - DE

1995 Chi. Bears

Scott Adams - T
Troy Auzenne - T
Myron Baker - LB
Robert Bass - LB
Fabien Bownes - WR
Todd Burger - G
James Burton - DB
Kevin Butler - K
Joe Cain - LB
Mark Carrier - DB
Tony Carter - RB
Marty Carter - DB
Curtis Conway - WR
Ron Cox - LB
Richard Dent - DE
Pat Eilers - DB
Mike Faulkerson - RB
Jim Flanigan - DT
Al Fontenot - DE
Jerry Fontenot - C
Chris Gedney - TE
Jeff Graham - WR
Robert Green - RB
Raymont Harris - RB
Sean Harris - LB
Garland Hawkins - LB
Andy Heck - T
Darwin Ireland - LB
Keith Jennings - TE
Anthony Johnson - RB
Keshon Johnson - DB
Dwayne Joseph - DB
Erik Kramer - QB
Jay Leeuwenburg - G
Nate Lewis - WR
Jeremy Lincoln - DB
Dennis Lundy - RB
John Mangum - DB
Anthony Marshall - DB
Kevin Miniefield - DB
Barry Minter - LB
Pat O'Neill - P
Todd Perry - G
Andre President - TE
Greg Primus - WR
Pat Riley - DE
Rashaan Salaam - RB
Todd Sauerbrun - P
Carl Simpson - DT
Vinson Smith - LB
Alonzo Spellman - DE
John Thierry - DE
Lewis Tillman - RB
Michael Timpson - WR
Steve Walsh - QB
Ryan Wetnight - TE
James Williams - T
Donnell Woolford - DB
Chris Zorich - DT

1995 Cincinnati

Thomas Bailey - WR
Eric Bieniemy - RB
Jeff Blake - QB
Darrick Brilz - G
Michael Brim - DB
Anthony Brown - T
Scott Brumfield - G
Jason Burns - RB
Andre Collins - LB
Gerald Collins - LB
John Copeland - DE

Jeff Cothran - RB
David Dunn - WR
James Francis - LB
Harold Green - RB
Adrian Hardy - DB
Jeff Hill - WR
Kevin Jefferson - LB
Lee Johnson - P
Dan Jones - G
Rod Jones - DB
Roger Jones - DB
James Joseph - RB
Todd Kalis - G
Todd Kelly - DE
David Klingler - QB
Bruce Kozerski - G
James Logan - LB
Ricardo McDonald - LB
Tony McGee - TE
Randy Neal - LB
Alfred Oglesby - DT
Ty Parten - DE
Doug Pelfrey - K
Carl Pickens - WR
Trent Pollard - G
Jeff Query - WR
Keith Rucker - DT
Troy Sadowski - TE
Kevin Sargent - T
Corey Sawyer - DB
Darnay Scott - WR
Sam Shade - DB
Chris Shelling - DB
Artie Smith - DE
Ramondo Stallings - DE
Steve Tovar - LB
Greg Truitt - C
Melvin Tuten - T
Kimo von Oelhoffen - DT
Bracey Walker - DB
Brett Wallerstedt - LB
Joe Walter - T
Derek Ware - TE
Leonard Wheeler - DB
Dan Wilkinson - DT
Darryl Williams - DB

1995 Cleveland

Vashone Adams - DB
Derrick Alexander - WR
Herman Arvie - T
Carl Banks - LB
Michael Bates - WR
Harold Bishop - TE
Issac Booth - DB
Donny Brady - DB
Orlando Brown - T
Rob Burnett - DE
Earnest Byner - RB
Mike Caldwell - LB
Bob Dahl - G
Mike Davis - DB
Jed DeVries - G
Gerald Dixon - LB
Steve Everitt - C
Dan Footman - DE
Mike Frederick - DE
Tim Goad - NT
Don Griffin - DB
Dana Hall - DB
Frank Hartley - TE
Travis Hill - LB
Leroy Hoard - RB
Earnest Hunter - RB
Michael Jackson - WR
Tim Jacobs - DB
Pepper Johnson - LB
Tony Jones - T
Brian Kinchen - TE
Antonio Langham - DB
Keenan McCardell - WR
Rich McKenzie - LB
Eric Moore - T
Stevon Moore - DB
Anthony Pleasant - DE
Craig Powell - LB
Ricky Powers - RB
Walter Reeves - TE
Louis Riddick - DB
Andre Rison - WR
Pio Sagapolutele - DE
Rico Smith - WR
Frank Stams - LB
Matt Stover - K
Eddie Sutter - LB
Vinny Testaverde - QB
Johnny Thomas - DB
Bennie Thompson - DB
Tom Tupa - P
Eric Turner - DB
Tommy Vardell - RB
Larry Webster - DT
Lorenzo White - RB
Wally Williams - C
Eric Zeier - QB

1995 Dallas

Troy Aikman - QB
Larry Allen - G
Robert Bailey - DB
Jon Baker - K
Reggie Barnes - LB
Bill Bates - DB

Michael Batiste - G
Darren Benson - DT
Eric Bjornson - TE
Chris Boniol - K
Alundis Brice - DB
Greg Briggs - DB
Larry Brown - DB
Shante Carver - DE
Scott Case - DB
Billy Davis - WR
Ray Donaldson - C
Dixon Edwards - LB
Anthony Fieldings - DB
Cory Fleming - WR
Oronde Gadsden - WR
Jason Garrett - QB
Charles Haley - DE
Darryl Hardy - LB
George Hegamin - T
Dale Hellestrae - G
Chad Hennings - DT
Clayton Holmes - DB
Michael Irvin - WR
John Jett - P
Daryl Johnston - RB
Robert Jones - LB
Derek Kennard - G
David Lang - RB
Leon Lett - DT
Brock Marion - DB
Russell Maryland - DT
Hurvin McCormack - DT
Godfrey Myles - LB
Nate Newton - G
Jay Novacek - TE
Dominique Ross - RB
Deion Sanders - DB
Jim Schwantz - LB
Darrin Smith - LB
Emmitt Smith - RB
Kevin Smith - DB
Ron Stone - G
Oscar Sturgis - DE
Tony Tolbert - DE
Greg Tremble - DB
Mark Tuinei - T
Kendell Watkins - TE
Charlie Williams - DB
Erik Williams - T
Kevin Williams - WR
Sherman Williams - RB
Wade Wilson - QB
Darren Woodson - DB

1995 Denver

Allen Aldridge - LB
Elijah Alexander - LB
Steve Atwater - DB
Rod Bernstine - RB
Ronnie Bradford - DB
Tyrone Braxton - DB
Jamie Brown - T
Ken Brown - LB
Keith Burns - LB
Glenn Cadrez - LB
Dwayne Carswell - TE
Byron Chamberlain - WR
Aaron Craver - RB
Ray Crockett - DB
Terrell Davis - RB
Gary Downs - RB
Shane Dronett - DT
Jason Elam - K
John Elway - QB
Jerry Evans - TE
Simon Fletcher - DE
Dave Garnett - LB
Brian Habib - G
Britt Hager - LB
Harald Hasselbach - DE
Tim Hauck - DB
Cliff Hicks - DB
Randy Hilliard - DB
Ray Jacobs - LB
Vance Johnson - WR
Dante Jones - LB
James Jones - DT
Rondell Jones - DB
Mike Lodish - T
Ed McCaffrey - WR
Reggie McElroy - T
Glyn Milburn - RB
Hugh Millen - QB
Anthony Miller - WR
Bill Musgrave - QB
Tom Nalen - C
Willie Oshodin - DE
Michael Dean Perry - DT
Mike Pritchard - WR
Reggie Rivers - RB
Jeff Robinson - DE
Tom Rouen - P
Mark Schlereth - G
Bill Schultz - G
Shannon Sharpe - TE
Rod Smith - WR
Ralph Tamm - G
Maa Tanuvasa - DT
Eric Thomas - DB
Broderick Thompson - T
Lionel Washington - DB
Dan Williams - DE
Troy Wilson - DB
David Wyman - LB

Gary Zimmerman - T

1995 Detroit

Tom Beer - LB
Bennie Blades - DB
Shane Bonham - DE
Stephen Boyd - LB
Lomas Brown - T
Anthony Carter - WR
Willie Clay - DB
Mike Compton - C
Scott Conover - T
Luther Elliss - DE
Kevin Glover - C
Ron Hall - TE
Jason Hanson - K
Tracy Hayworth - LB
Hessley Hempstead - G
Kevin Hickman - TE
Rodney Holman - TE
Greg Jeffries - DB
Mike Johnson - LB
Jeff Jones - T
Scott Kowalkowski - LB
Antonio London - LB
Dave Lutz - G
Eric Lynch - RB
Don Majkowski - QB
Van Malone - DB
Robert Massey - DB
Aubrey Matthews - WR
Kez McCorvey - WR
Ryan McNeil - DB
Scott Mitchell - QB
Herman Moore - WR
Johnnie Morton - WR
Zefross Moss - T
Dan Owens - DE
Brett Perriman - WR
Robert Porcher - DE
Corey Raymond - DB
Ron Rivers - RB
Mark Royals - P
Barry Sanders - RB
Cory Schlesinger - RB
Tracy Scroggins - LB
Tony Semple - G
David Sloan - TE
Chris Spielman - LB
Henry Thomas - DT
Vernon Turner - RB
Sean Vanhorse - DB
Mike Wells - DE
Doug Widell - G
Allen Williams - RB

1995 Green Bay

Mike Arthur - C
Mike Bartrum - TE
Edgar Bennett - RB
Dirk Borgognone - K
Robert Brooks - WR
Gary Brown - T
Gilbert Brown - NT
LeRoy Butler - DB
Mark Chmura - TE
Shannon Clavelle - DE
Keith Crawford - DB
Ty Detmer - QB
Matthew Dorsett - DB
Earl Dotson - T
Doug Evans - DB
Brett Favre - QB
Antonio Freeman - WR
Harry Galbreath - G
Bernardo Harris - LB
William Henderson - RB
Craig Hentrich - P
Darius Holland - DT
Mark Ingram - WR
Chris Jacke - K
Keith Jackson - TE
Travis Jervey - RB
LeShon Johnson - RB
Sean Jones - DE
Charles Jordan - WR
John Jurkovic - NT
Joe Kelly - LB
George Koonce - LB
Bob Kuberski - NT
Matt LaBounty - DE
Dorsey Levens - RB
Lenny McGill - DB
Jim McMahon - QB
Terry Mickens - WR
Anthony Morgan - WR
Roderick Mullen - DB
Craig Newsome - DB
Mike Prior - DB
T. J. Rubley - QB
Ken Ruettgers - T
Wayne Simmons - LB
Joe Sims - G
Fred Strickland - LB
Aaron Taylor - G
George Teague - DB
Jeff Thomason - TE
Adam Timmerman - G
Reggie White - DE
Gabe Wilkins - DE
Brian Williams - LB
Jeff Wilner - TE
Marcus Wilson - RB
Frank Winters - C

1995 Houston

Tomur Barnes - DB
Micheal Barrow - LB
Blaine Bishop - DB
Joe Bowden - LB
Gary Brown - RB
Marion Butts - RB
Rich Camarillo - P
Chuck Cecil - DB
Chris Chandler - QB
Ray Childress - DT
Anthony Cook - DE
Kenny Davidson - DE
Al Del Greco - K
Cris Dishman - DB
Kevin Donnalley - G
Irv Eatman - T
Hicham El-Mashtoub - C
Josh Evans - DT
Malcolm Floyd - WR
Henry Ford - DE
Will Furrer - QB
Mel Gray - KR
Lemanski Hall - LB
Travis Hannah - WR
Odie Harris - DB
Steve Hendrickson - RB
Brad Hopkins - T
Torey Hunter - DB
Steve Jackson - DB
Haywood Jeffires - WR
Darryll Lewis - DB
Roderick Lewis - TE
James Logan - LB
Dennis Lundy - RB
Bruce Matthews - G
Kanavis McGhee - DE
Steve McNair - QB
Todd McNair - RB
John Henry Mills - LB
Glenn Montgomery - DT
Erik Norgard - G
Jim Reid - T
Michael Roan - TE
Marcus Robertson - DB
Eddie Robinson - LB
Derek Russell - WR
Chris Sanders - WR
Al Smith - LB
Mark Stepnoski - C
Rodney Thomas - RB
Jim Thornton - TE
Natu Tuatagaloa - DE
Craig Veasey - DT
Gary Walker - DT
David Williams - T
Barron Wortham - LB
Frank Wycheck - TE

1995 Indianapolis

Trev Alberts - LB
Ashley Ambrose - DB
Flipper Anderson - WR
Charles Arbuckle - TE
Aaron Bailey - WR
Bradford Banta - TE
Jason Belser - DB
Tony Bennett - LB
Cary Blanchard - K
Ben Bronson - WR
Ray Buchanan - DB
Conrad Clarks - DB
Mike Cofer - K
Quentin Coryatt - LB
Zack Crockett - RB
Eugene Daniel - DB
Sean Dawkins - WR
Ken Dilger - TE
Randy Dixon - G
Craig Erickson - QB
Marshall Faulk - RB
Chris Gardocki - P
Steve Grant - LB
Derwin Gray - DB
Clif Groce - RB
Jim Harbaugh - QB
Shawn Harper - T
Jeff Herrod - LB
Ronald Humphrey - RB
Ellis Johnson - DE
Paul Justin - QB
Kirk Lowdermilk - C
Eric Mahlum - G
Jason Mathews - T
Tony McCoy - DT
Devon McDonald - LB
Ray McElroy - DB
Thomas McLemore - TE
Steve Morrison - LB
Freddie Joe Nunn - DE
Bobby Olive - WR
Garin Patrick - G
Marcus Pollard - TE
Roosevelt Potts - RB
Scott Radecic - LB
Glenell Sanders - LB
Tony Siragusa - DT
Brian Stablein - WR
Joe Staysniak - G
David Tate - DB
Floyd Turner - WR
Kipp Vickers - G
Lamont Warren - RB
Damon Watts - DB
Derek West - T
Bernard Whittington - DE
Trevor Wilmot - LB
Will Wolford - T
Vince Workman - RB

1995 Jacksonville

Bryan Barker - P
Steve Beuerlein - QB
Tony Boselli - T
Shawn Bouwens - G
Brant Boyer - LB
Deral Boykin - DB
Mark Brunell - QB
Darren Carrington - DB
Bernard Carter - LB
Ryan Christopherson - RB
Eugene Chung - G
Reggie Clark - LB
Vinnie Clark - DB
Reggie Cobb - RB
Ben Coleman - G
Harry Colon - DB
Frank Cornish - G
Don Davey - DT
Travis Davis - DB
Brian DeMarco - G
Mike Dumas - DB
Vaughn Dunbar - RB
Paul Frase - DE
Ernest Givins - WR
Keith Goganious - LB
Rogerick Green - DB
Rich Griffith - TE
Monty Grow - DB
Ray Hall - DT
Mike Hollis - K
Desmond Howard - WR
Chris Hudson - DB
Greg Huntington - G
Willie Jackson - WR
Rob Johnson - QB
Tommy Johnson - DB
Randy Jordan - RB
Craig Keith - TE
Jeff Lageman - DE
Gordon Laro - TE
Ernie Logan - DE
Curtis Marsh - WR
Le'Shai Maston - RB
Corey Mayfield - DT
Tom McManus - LB
Bronzell Miller - DE
Pete Mitchell - TE
Tom Myslinski - G
Jeff Novak - G
Kelvin Pritchett - DT
Bryan Schwartz - LB
Ashley Sheppard - LB
Joel Smeenge - LB
Jimmy Smith - WR
Santo Stephens - LB
James Stewart - RB
Darren Studstill - DB
Dave Thomas - DB
Mike Thompson - DT
Cedric Tillman - WR
Mickey Washington - DB
Dave Widell - C
Bruce Wilkerson - T
James Williams - LB
Mark Williams - LB

1995 Kansas City

Louie Aguiar - P
Marcus Allen - RB
John Alt - T
Kimble Anders - RB
Darren Anderson - DB
Martin Bayless - DB
Donnell Bennett - RB
Steve Bono - QB
Vaughn Booker - DE
Dale Carter - DB
Perry Carter - DB
Keith Cash - TE
Mark Collins - DB
Jeff Criswell - T
Anthony Davis - LB
Willie Davis - WR
Lake Dawson - WR
Lin Elliott - K
Rich Gannon - QB
Tim Grunhard - C
James Hasty - DB
Greg Hill - RB
Danan Hughes - WR
George Jamison - LB
Trezelle Jenkins - T
Greg Manusky - LB
Pellom McDaniels - DE
Darren Mickell - DE
Chris Penn - WR
Joe Phillips - DT
Bryan Proby - DE
Tony Richardson - RB
Tracy Rogers - LB
Dan Saleaumua - DT
Will Shields - G
Ricky Siglar - T
Tracy Simien - LB
Webster Slaughter - WR
Neil Smith - DE
Frank Stams - LB
David Szott - G
Doug Terry - DB
Derrick Thomas - LB
Leroy Thompson - RB
Keith Traylor - DT
Joe Valerio - T
Tamarick Vanover - WR
Danny Villa - G
Derrick Walker - TE
Brian Washington - DB
Tim Watson - DB
William White - DB

1995 Miami

Ethan Albright - T
Antonio Armstrong - LB
Trace Armstrong - DE
Gene Atkins - DB
Aubrey Beavers - LB
Tim Bowens - DT
J.B. Brown - DB
Terrell Buckley - DB
Keith Byars - RB
Gary Clark - WR
Marco Coleman - DE
Bryan Cox - LB
Jeff Cross - DE
Kirby Dar Dar - WR
DeWayne Dotson - RB
Steve Emtman - DE
Dion Foxx - LB
Irving Fryar - WR
Chris Gray - G
Eric Green - TE
Andrew Greene - G
Ed Hawthorne - DT
Ron Heller - T
Randal Hill - WR
Sean Hill - DB
Dwight Hollier - LB
Calvin Jackson - DB
Pat Johnson - DB
John Kidd - P
Terry Kirby - RB
Chuck Klingbeil - NT
Jeff Kopp - LB
Bernie Kosar - QB
Dan Marino - QB
O. J. McDuffie - WR
Dan McGwire - QB
Tom McHale - G
Billy Milner - T
Eric Moore - T
Louis Oliver - DB
Bernie Parmalee - RB
Joe Planansky - TE
Tim Ruddy - C
Keith Sims - G
Chris Singleton - LB
Frankie Smith - DB
Irving Spikes - RB
Michael Stewart - DB
Pete Stoyanovich - K
Troy Vincent - DB
Frank Wainright - TE
Richmond Webb - T
Bert Weidner - C
Mike Williams - WR
Ronnie Williams - TE
Robert Wilson - RB

1995 Minnesota

Derrick Alexander - DE
Tuineau Alipate - LB
Roy Barker - DE
Harlon Barnett - DB
Pete Bercich - LB
Jeff Brady - LB
Richard Brown - LB
Cris Carter - WR
Jeff Christy - C
Adrian Cooper - TE
Rick Cunningham - T
Greg DeLong - TE
Jack Del Rio - LB
David Dixon - G
Chuck Evans - RB
Jason Fisk - DT
Donald Frank - DB
Corey Fuller - DB
John Gerak - G
Scottie Graham - RB
Robert Griffith - DB
Shelly Hammonds - DB
James Harris - DE
Martin Harrison - DE
Chris Hinton - G
Qadry Ismail - WR
Alfred Jackson - DB
Brad Johnson - QB
Andrew Jordan - TE
Amp Lee - RB
Everett Lindsay - G
Ed McDaniel - LB
Randall McDaniel - G
Charles Mincy - DB
Warren Moon - QB
Mike Morris - C
David Palmer - RB
Bobby Phillips - RB
John Randle - DT
Jake Reed - WR
Fuad Reveiz - K
Mike Saxon - P
Fernando Smith - DE
Robert Smith - RB
Todd Steussie - T
James Stewart - RB
Korey Stringer - T
Broderick Thomas - LB
Orlando Thomas - DB
Mike Tice - TE
Esera Tuaolo - DT
Chris Walsh - WR
Dewayne Washington - DB

1995 New England

Bobby Abrams - LB
Bruce Armstrong - T
Matt Bahr - K
Troy Barnett - DE
Drew Bledsoe - QB
Vincent Brisby - WR
Corwin Brown - DB
Troy Brown - WR
Vincent Brown - LB
John Burke - TE
Eddie Cade - DB
Alcides Catanho - LB
Ben Coates - TE
Ferric Collons - DE
Corey Croom - RB
Jeff Dellenbach - C
Steve DeOssie - LB
David Frisch - TE
Sam Gash - RB
Mike Gisler - G
Hason Graham - WR
Rupert Grant - RB
David Green - RB
Myron Guyton - DB
Pat Harlow - T
Jimmy Hitchcock - DB
Maurice Hurst - DB
Ted Johnson - LB
Aaron Jones - DE
Mike Jones - DE
Bob Kratch - G
Max Lane - T
Ty Law - DB
Kevin Lee - WR
Vernon Lewis - DB
Curtis Martin - RB
Willie McGinest - LB
Dave Meggett - RB
Brandon Moore - T
Marty Moore - LB
Will Moore - WR
Pat O'Neill - P
Andre President - TE
Terry Ray - DB
Ricky Reynolds - DB
Tim Roberts - DE
William Roberts - G
Todd Rucci - G
Dwayne Sabb - LB
Chris Slade - LB
Bryan Wagner - P
Bruce Walker - NT
Larry Whigham - DB
Reggie White - NT
Dave Wohlabaugh - C
Carlos Yancy - DB
Scott Zolak - QB

1995 New Orleans

Eric Allen - DB
Mario Bates - RB
Kirk Botkin - TE
Doug Brien - K
Willie Broughton - DT
Derek Brown - RB
Vince Buck - DB
Israel Byrd - DB
Ron Childs - LB
Richard Cooper - T
Lee DeRamus - WR
Ernest Dixon - LB
Jim Dombrowski - G
Vaughn Dunbar - RB
Quinn Early - WR
Tory Epps - DT
Jim Everett - QB
Mark Fields - LB
Robert Goff - DE
Richard Harvey - LB
Michael Haynes - WR
Tom Hodson - QB
Tyrone Hughes - DB
Dameian Jeffries - DE
Joe Johnson - DT
John Johnson - LB
Brian Jones - LB
Ernest Jones - DE
Ed King - G
Alan Kline - T
Tyrone Legette - DB
Chip Lohmiller - K
Sean Lumpkin - DB
Wayne Martin - DT
J. J. McCleskey - DB
Andy McCollum - C
Lorenzo Neal - RB
Derrick Ned - RB
Anthony Newman - DB
Craig Novitsky - C
Shane Pahukoa - DB
Chris Port - G
Rufus Porter - LB
Steve Rhem - WR
Willie Roaf - T
Torrance Small - WR
Irv Smith - TE
Jimmy Spencer - DB
Israel Stanley - DE
Winfred Tubbs - LB
Renaldo Turnbull - DE
Jeff Uhlenhake - C
Wesley Walls - TE
Klaus Wilmsmeyer - P
Ray Zellars - RB

1995 NY Giants

Ray Agnew - DT
Derek Allen - C
Jessie Armstead - LB
Willie Beamon - DB
Greg Bishop - T
Chad Bratzke - DE
Michael Brooks - LB
Dave Brown - QB
Marcus Buckley - LB
Chris Calloway - WR
Jesse Campbell - DB
Mike Croel - LB
Howard Cross - TE
Brad Daluiso - K
Stacey Dillard - DT
Omar Douglas - WR
Maurice Douglass - DB
Jamal Duff - DE
Keith Elias - RB
Jumbo Elliott - T
Vencie Glenn - DB
Scott Gragg - T
Keith Hamilton - DE
Rodney Hampton - RB
Gary Harrell - WR
Robert Harris - DE
Mike Horan - P
Brian Kozlowski - TE
Thomas Lewis - WR
Tommy Maddox - QB
Arthur Marshall - WR
Corey Miller - LB
Aaron Pierce - TE
Thomas Randolph - DB
Doug Riesenberg - T
Coleman Rudolph - DE
Adam Schreiber - C
Jason Sehorn - DB
Mike Sherrard - WR
Lance Smith - G
Phillippi Sparks - DB
Mike Strahan - DE
Ben Talley - LB
Herschel Walker - RB
Tim Watson - DB
Charles Way - RB
Tyrone Wheatley - RB
Corey Widmer - LB
Brian Williams - C
Tito Wooten - DB
Rodney Young - DB
Rob Zatechka - G

1995 NY Jets

Richie Anderson - RB
Kurt Barber - DE
Fred Baxter - TE
Brad Baxter - RB
Lou Benfatti - DT
John Bock - C
Kyle Brady - TE
Bubby Brister - QB
Matt Brock - DE
James Brown - T
Glenn Cadrez - LB
Ron Carpenter - DB
Dexter Carter - RB
Chad Cascadden - LB
Tony Casillas - DT
Curtis Ceaser - WR
Wayne Chrebet - WR
Kyle Clifton - LB
Tyrone Davis - WR
Cal Dixon - C
Hugh Douglas - DE
Roger Duffy - G
Boomer Esiason - QB
Donald Evans - DE
Glenn Foley - QB
Aaron Glenn - DB
Victor Green - DB
Carl Greenwood - DB
Brian Hansen - P
Carlton Haselrig - G
Melvin Hayes - T
Bobby Houston - LB
Erik Howard - DT
Gary Jones - DB
Marvin Jones - LB
Vance Joseph - DB
Mo Lewis - LB
Nick Lowery - K
Siupeli Malamala - G
Wilber Marshall - LB
Eddie Mason - LB
Sherriden May - RB
Everett McIver - G
Johnny Mitchell - TE
Ronald Moore - RB
Adrian Murrell - RB
Matt O'Dwyer - G
Anthony Prior - DB
Kenyon Rasheed - RB
Todd Scott - DB
Don Silvestri - K
Otis Smith - DB
Marc Spindler - DT
Jeff Sydner - WR
Marcus Turner - DB
Marvin Washington - DE
Matt Willig - T
Charles Wilson - WR
Terrence Wisdom - G
Ryan Yarborough - WR
Lonnie Young - DB

1995 Oakland

Eddie Anderson - DB
Joe Aska - RB
Eric Ball - RB
Jerry Ball - DT
Greg Biekert - LB
Tim Brown - WR
Aundray Bruce - DE
Kerry Cash - TE
Matt Dyson - DE
Vince Evans - QB
Derrick Fenner - RB
James Folston - LB
Cole Ford - K
Keith Franklin - LB
Rob Fredrickson - LB
Russ Freeman - T
Andrew Glover - TE
Kevin Gogan - G
Jeff Gossett - P
Nolan Harrison - DT
Daryl Hobbs - WR
Billy Joe Hobert - QB
Rob Holmberg - LB
Derrick Hoskins - DB
Jeff Hostetler - QB
Raghib Ismail - WR
Jeff Jaeger - K
Robert Jenkins - T
James Jett - WR
Calvin Jones - RB
Mike Jones - LB
Napoleon Kaufman - RB
Carl Kidd - DB
Joe King - DB
Jeff Kysar - T
Dan Land - DB
Albert Lewis - DB
Terry McDaniel - DB
Chester McGlockton - DT
Mike Morton - LB
Najee Mustafaa - DB
Gerald Perry - T
Bruce Pickens - DB
Austin Robbins - DT
Barret Robbins - C
Greg Skrepenak - T
Anthony Smith - DE
Richard Stephens - T
Pat Swilling - DE
James Trapp - DB
Dan Turk - C
Aaron Wallace - DE
Harvey Williams - RB
Steve Wisniewski - G

1995 Philadelphia

Gary Anderson - K
Fred Barnett - WR
Harry Boatswain - T
Barrett Brooks - T
Rob Carpenter - WR
Mike Chalenski - DT
Frank Cornish - C
Randall Cunningham - QB
Antone Davis - T
Nate Dingle - LB
Ronnie Dixon - DT
Troy Drake - T
Mohammed Elewonibi - T
Jay Fiedler - QB
Derrick Frazier - DB
William Fuller - DE
Charlie Garner - RB
Kurt Gouveia - LB
Mark Gunn - DE
Rhett Hall - DT
Andy Harmon - DT
Jerome Henderson - DB
Steve Hendrickson - LB
Lester Holmes - G
John Hudson - C
Tom Hutton - P
Greg Jackson - DB
Greg Jefferson - DE
Jimmie Johnson - TE
Kevin Johnson - DT
Reggie Johnson - TE
Chris T. Jones - WR
Mike Mamula - LB
Kelvin Martin - WR
Fred McCrary - RB
Guy McIntyre - G
Raleigh McKenzie - C
Mark McMillian - DB
Dexter McNabb - RB
Art Monk - WR
Derrick Oden - LB
Joe Panos - G
Rodney Peete - QB
Bill Romanowski - LB
Joe Rudolph - G
James Saxon - RB
Danny Stubbs - DE
Bobby Taylor - DB
William Thomas - LB
Greg Tremble - DB
Kevin Turner - RB
Frank Wainright - TE
Ricky Watters - RB
Ed West - TE
David Whitmore - DB
Barry Wilburn - DB
Calvin Williams - WR
James Willis - LB
Derrick Witherspoon - RB
Marc Woodard - LB
Sylvester Wright - LB
Eric Zomalt - DB
Mike Zordich - DB

1995 Pittsburgh

Steve Avery - RB
Johnnie Barnes - WR
Myron Bell - DB
Chad Brown - LB
Mark Bruener - TE
Brentson Buckner - DE
Dermontti Dawson - C
Ta'ase Faumui - DE
Deon Figures - DB
Lethon Flowers - DB
Randy Fuller - DB
Kendall Gammon - C
Oliver Gibson - DE
Jason Gildon - LB
Kevin Greene - LB
Tracy Greene - TE
Andre Hastings - WR
Jonathan Hayes - TE
Kevin Henry - DE
Corey Holliday - WR
John Jackson - T
Charles Johnson - WR
Norm Johnson - K
Bill Johnson - DE
Donta Jones - LB
Levon Kirkland - LB
Carnell Lake - DB
Tim Lester - RB
Greg Lloyd - LB
Alvoid Mays - DB
Fred McAfee - RB
Jim Miller - QB
Ernie Mills - WR
Bam Morris - RB
Tom Newberry - G
Neil O'Donnell - QB
Chris Oldham - DB
Jerry Olsavsky - LB
Lonnie Palelei - T
James Parrish - T
Erric Pegram - RB
Darren Perry - DB
Eric Ravotti - LB
Ray Seals - DE
Leon Searcy - T
Ariel Solomon - C
Brenden Stai - G
Rohn Stark - P
Joel Steed - NT
Kordell Stewart - QB
Justin Strzelczyk - G
Yancey Thigpen - WR
Mike Tomczak - QB
John L. Williams - RB
Willie Williams - DB
Rod Woodson - DB

1995 St. Louis

Darryl Ashmore - T
Johnny Bailey - RB
Dave Barr - QB
Chuck Belin - G
Jerome Bettis - RB
Dean Biasucci - K
Bern Brostek - C
Isaac Bruce - WR
Kevin Carter - DE
Pat Carter - TE
Shane Conlan - LB
Marv Cook - TE
Dexter Davis - DB
Paschall Davis - LB
Torin Dorn - DB
Troy Drayton - TE
D'Marco Farr - DT
Cedric Figaro - LB
Wayne Gandy - T
Sean Gilbert - DT
Leo Goeas - G
Jessie Hester - WR
Thomas Homco - LB

Dana Howard - LB
Jesse James - C
Carlos Jenkins - LB
Clarence Jones - T
Jimmie Jones - DT
Todd Kinchen - WR
Sean Landeta - P
Keith Loneker - G
Todd Lyght - DB
Keith Lyle - DB
Gerald McBurrows - DB
Steve McLaughlin - K
Chris Miller - QB
Brent Moss - RB
Brad Ottis - DE
Anthony Parker - DB
Roman Phifer - LB
Lovell Pinkney - TE
Jim Price - TE
John Reece - DB
Greg Robinson - RB
Leonard Russell - RB
Mark Rypien - QB
Mike Scurlock - DB
Ashley Sheppard - LB
Jackie Slater - T
Fred Stokes - DE
J.T. Thomas - WR
Alberto White - DE
Dwayne White - G
Zach Wiegert - T
Jay Williams - DT
Ron Wolfley - RB
Alexander Wright - WR
Toby Wright - DB
Robert Young - DE

1995 San Diego

Sebastian Barrie - DT
Darren Bennett - P
Tony Berti - G
David Binn - C
David Brandon - LB
Stan Brock - T
Lewis Bush - LB
John Carney - K
Eric Castle - DB
Willie Clark - DB
Joe Cocozzo - G
Andre Coleman - WR
Rodney Culver - RB
Isaac Davis - G
Reuben Davis - DT
'Omar Ellison - WR
Greg Engel - C
Terrell Fletcher - RB
Shaun Gayle - DB
Dennis Gibson - LB
Gale Gilbert - QB
Dwayne Gordon - LB
Courtney Hall - C
Ronnie Harmon - RB
Dwayne Harper - DB
Rodney Harrison - DB
Aaron Hayden - RB
David Hendrix - DB
Stan Humphries - QB
Shawn Jefferson - WR
A. J. Johnson - DB
Raylee Johnson - DE
Shawn Lee - DT
Tony Martin - WR
Deems May - TE
Natrone Means - RB
Ron Middleton - TE
Chris Mims - DE
Shannon Mitchell - TE
Mark Montreuil - DB
Eric Moten - G
Leslie O'Neal - DE
Bo Orlando - DB
Vaughn Parker - T
John Parrella - DT
Alfred Pupunu - TE
Don Sasa - DT
Junior Seau - LB
Mark Seay - WR
Terrance Shaw - DB
Harry Swayne - T
Duane Young - TE
Glen Young - LB

1995 San Francisco

Oliver Barnett - DE
Harris Barton - T
Michael Brandon - DE
Doug Brien - K
Dennis Brown - DE
Junior Bryant - DE
Mike Caldwell - WR
Brett Carolan - TE
Dexter Carter - RB
Cary Conklin - QB
Toi Cook - DB
Chris Dalman - C
Eric Davis - DB
Derrick Deese - G
Dedrick Dodge - DB
Tyronne Drakeford - DB
Ricky Ervins - RB
William Floyd - RB
Jamal Fountaine - DE
Antonio Goss - LB
Elvis Grbac - QB
Darryl Hall - DB
Merton Hanks - DB
Tim Harris - DE
Steve Israel - DB
Rickey Jackson - LB
Brent Jones - TE
Derek Loville - RB
Anthony Lynn - RB
Tim McDonald - DB
Rod Milstead - G
Kevin Mitchell - LB
Ken Norton - LB
Bart Oates - C
Brian O'Neal - RB
Tony Peterson - LB
Gary Plummer - LB
Frank Pollack - T
Marquez Pope - DB
Ted Popson - TE
Jerry Rice - WR
Jesse Sapolu - G
Kirk Scrafford - T
Nate Singleton - WR
J.J. Stokes - WR
Dana Stubblefield - DT
John Taylor - WR
Chris Thomas - LB
Tommy Thompson - P
Adam Walker - RB
Steve Wallace - T
Terrence Warren - WR
Jeff Wilkins - K
Alfred Williams - DE
Michael Williams - DB
Jamal Willis - RB
Lee Woodall - LB
Bryant Young - DT
Steve Young - QB
Tony Zendejas - K

1995 Seattle

Sam Adams - DT
James Atkins - T
Howard Ballard - T
Michael Barber - LB
Jay Bellamy - DB
Duane Bickett - LB
Robert Blackmon - DB
Jeff Blackshear - G
Brian Blades - WR
Steve Broussard - RB
Tony Brown - DB
Tony Covington - DB
Carlester Crumpler - TE
Antonio Edwards - DE
Christian Fauria - TE
John Friesz - QB
Joey Galloway - WR
Carlton Gray - DB
Corey Harris - DB
Ronnie Harris - WR
Tracy Johnson - RB
Selwyn Jones - DB
Matt Joyce - G
Trey Junkin - TE
Mike Keim - T
Cortez Kennedy - DT
Jason Kyle - LB
James Logan - LB
Kevin Mawae - C
Michael McCrary - DE
James McKnight - WR
Henry McMillian - DT
Rick Mirer - QB
Winston Moss - LB
Joe Nash - DT
Todd Peterson - K
Ricky Proehl - WR
Ray Roberts - T
Eugene Robinson - DB
Rafael Robinson - DB
Michael Sinclair - DE
Lamar Smith - RB
Steve Smith - RB
Tyronne Stowe - LB
Mack Strong - RB
Jim Sweeney - C
Robb Thomas - WR
Rick Tuten - P
Chris Warren - RB
Dean Wells - LB
Brent Williams - DE
Terry Wooden - LB

1995 Tampa Bay

Clifton Abraham - DB
Chidi Ahanotu - DE
Tyji Armstrong - TE
Ian Beckles - G
John Booty - DB
Tony Bouie - DB
Ed Brady - LB
Derrick Brooks - LB
Curtis Buckley - DB
Barney Bussey - DB
Horace Copeland - WR
Brad Culpepper - DT
Eric Curry - DE
Tyree Davis - WR
Lawrence Dawsey - WR
Trent Dilfer - QB
Scott Dill - T
Charles Dimry - DB
Santana Dotson - DT
Demetrius DuBose - LB
Bobby Joe Edmonds - RB
Jerry Ellison - RB
Thomas Everett - DB
Kenneth Gant - DB
Paul Gruber - T
Alvin Harper - WR
Jackie Harris - TE
Courtney Hawkins - WR
Michael Husted - K
Stephen Ingram - T
Melvin Johnson - DB
John Lynch - DB
Lonnie Marts - LB
Tony Mayberry - C
Martin Mayhew - DB
Mike McGruder - DB
Toddrick McIntosh - DT
Charles McRae - G
Dave Moore - TE
Hardy Nickerson - LB
Pete Pierson - T
Keith Powe - DE
Jim Pyne - G
Errict Rhett - RB
Reggie Roby - P
Wardell Rouse - LB
Warren Sapp - DT
Cedric Saunders - TE
Todd Scott - DB
Herman Smith - DE
Tony Stargell - DB
Darnell Stephens - LB
Mike Sullivan - C
Lamar Thomas - WR
Casey Weldon - QB
Mark Wheeler - DT

1995 Washington

Terry Allen - RB
Jamie Asher - TE
Robert Bailey - DB
Romeo Bandison - DT
Coleman Bell - TE
William Bell - RB
Marc Boutte - DT
Reggie Brooks - RB
Ray Brown - G
Darrick Brownlow - LB
Tom Carter - DB
Terry Crews - DE
Henry Ellard - WR
Mike Flores - DE
Dion Foxx - LB
Gus Frerotte - QB
William Gaines - DT
Scott Galbraith - TE
John Gesek - C
Darrell Green - DB
Ken Harvey - LB
James Jenkins - TE
Tre' Johnson - T
Tim Johnson - DT
Jim Lachey - T
Ron Lewis - G
Marc Logan - RB
Trevor Matich - C
Brian Mitchell - RB
Darryl Morrison - DB
Eddie Murray - K
Dexter Nottage - DE
Muhammad Oliver - DE
Rich Owens - DE
Sterling Palmer - DE
Joe Patton - G
Marvcus Patton - LB
Darryl Pounds - DB
Jeff Query - WR
Cory Raymer - C
Stanley Richard - DB
Sebastian Savage - DB
Leslie Shepherd - WR
Heath Shuler - QB
Ed Simmons - T
Cedric Smith - RB
Vernice Smith - G
Rod Stephens - LB
Keith Taylor - DB
Brian Thure - T
Olanda Truitt - WR
Matt Turk - P
Scott Turner - DB
Matt Vanderbeek - LB
James Washington - DB
Michael Westbrook - WR
Tydus Winans - WR
Tony Woods - DE

1996 Arizona

Brent Alexander - DB
Stevie Anderson - WR
Michael Bankston - DE
Tommy Bennett - DB
Ronnie Bradford - DB
Lance Brown - DB
Lomas Brown - T
Kevin Butler - K
Pat Carter - TE
Larry Centers - RB
Ryan Christopherson - RB
Matt Darby - DB
Greg Davis - K
Mike Devlin - C
James Dexter - G
Marcus Dowdell - WR
Jerry Drake - DT
Ernest Dye - G
Anthony Edwards - WR
Eric England - DE
Boomer Esiason - QB
Jeff Feagles - P
Aaron Graham - C
Kent Graham - QB
Jarius Hayes - TE
Eric Hill - LB
Terry Hoage - DB
Terry Irving - LB
D. J. Johnson - DB
LeShon Johnson - RB
Kevin Jordan - WR
Matt Joyce - G
Seth Joyner - LB
Trey Junkin - C
Kwamie Lassiter - DB
Wesley Leasy - LB
Duval Love - G
Chris Maumalanga - DT
Oscar McBride - TE
J. J. McCleskey - DB
Devon McDonald - LB
Leeland McElroy - RB
Ronald McKinnon - LB
Johnny McWilliams - TE
Jamir Miller - LB
Rob Moore - WR
Brad Ottis - DT
Tito Paul - DB
Anthony Redmon - G
Simeon Rice - DE
Frank Sanders - WR
Rob Selby - G
Ben Smith - DB
Cedric Smith - RB
Joe Staysniak - G
Eric Swann - DT
Ryan Terry - RB
Aeneas Williams - DB
Bernard Wilson - DT
Joe Wolf - G

1996 Atlanta

Morten Andersen - K
Jamal Anderson - RB
Lester Archambeau - DE
Patrick Bates - DB
Cornelius Bennett - LB
J. J. Birden - WR
Juran Bolden - DB
Sean Boyd - DB
David Brandon - LB
Ethan Brooks - T
Tyrone Brown - WR
John Burrough - DT
Devin Bush - DB
Antone Davis - T
Shane Dronett - DE
Brad Edwards - DB
Bert Emanuel - WR
Scott Fields - LB
Roman Fortin - C
Moe Gardner - DT
Jeff George - QB
Ron George - LB
Travis Hall - DE
Bobby Hebert - QB
Craig Heyward - RB
Richard Huntley - RB
D. J. Johnson - DB
Todd Kelly - DE
Harper LeBel - TE
Mitch Lyons - TE
Terance Mathis - WR
Clay Matthews - LB
Lenny McGill - DB
Tim McKyer - DB
Eric Metcalf - WR
Browning Nagle - QB
Nate Odomes - DB
Dan Owens - DT
Jeff Pahukoa - G
Anthony Phillips - DB
Roell Preston - WR
David Richards - T
Louis Riddick - DB
Craig Sauer - LB
Freddie Scott - WR
Elbert Shelley - DB
Chuck Smith - DE
Dan Stryzinski - P
Lorenzo Styles - LB
Robbie Tobeck - G
Jessie Tuggle - LB
Darnell Walker - DB
Bob Whitfield - T
Gene Williams - G
Matt Willig - G
Mike Zandofsky - G
Jeff Zgonina - DT

1996 Baltimore

Vashone Adams - DB
Derrick Alexander - WR
Herman Arvie - T
Randy Baldwin - RB
Harold Bishop - TE
Jeff Blackshear - G
Issac Booth - DB
Donny Brady - DB
Dorian Brew - DB
Orlando Brown - G
Rob Burnett - DE
Anthony Edwards - WR
Earnest Byner - RB
Mike Caldwell - LB
Sedric Clark - LB
Mike Croel - LB
Dexter Daniels - LB
Corey Dowden - DB
Ray Ethridge - WR
Steve Everitt - C
Dan Footman - DE
Elliott Fortune - DE
Mike Frederick - DE
Carwell Gardner - RB
Tim Goad - DT
Keith Goganious - LB
Eric Green - TE
Frank Hartley - TE
Leroy Hoard - RB
Earnest Hunter - RB
Sale Isaia - G
Michael Jackson - WR
DeRon Jenkins - DB
James Jones - DT
Tony Jones - T
Brian Kinchen - TE
Antonio Langham - DB
Jermaine Lewis - WR
Ray Lewis - LB
Rick Lyle - DE
Greg Montgomery - P
Stevon Moore - DB
Bam Morris - RB
Quentin Neujahr - G
Jonathan Ogden - G
Anthony Pleasant - DE
Craig Powell - LB
James Roe - WR
Matt Stover - K
Eddie Sutter - LB
Vinny Testaverde - QB
Bennie Thompson - DB
Eric Turner - DB
Floyd Turner - WR
Calvin Williams - WR
Jerrol Williams - LB
Wally Williams - G
Eric Zeier - QB

1996 Buffalo

Ethan Albright - G
Carey Bender - RB
Chris Brantley - WR
Jason Bratton - RB
Ruben Brown - G
Jeff Burris - DB
Steve Christie - K
Tony Cline - TE
Todd Collins - QB
Robert Coons - TE
Russell Copeland - WR
Damien Covington - LB
Quinn Early - WR
John Fina - T
Phil Hansen - DE
Darick Holmes - RB
Kent Hull - C
Ken Irvin - DB
Raymond Jackson - DB
Jim Jeffcoat - DE
Lonnie Johnson - TE
Henry Jones - DB
Jim Kelly - QB
Marlon Kerner - DB
Corbin Lacina - G
Corey Louchiey - T
Mark Maddox - LB
Emanuel Martin - DB
Chris Mohr - P
Sean Moran - DE
Eric Moulds - WR
Gabe Northern - DE
Jerry Ostroski - G
Glenn Parker - T
Bryce Paup - LB
Marlo Perry - LB
Mark Pike - DE
Shawn Price - DE
Andre Reed - WR
Sam Rogers - LB
Kurt Schulz - DB
Eric Smedley - DB
Bruce Smith - DE
Thomas Smith - DB
Chris Spielman - LB
Matt Stevens - DB
Steve Tasker - WR
Thurman Thomas - RB
Tim Tindale - RB
Alex Van Pelt - QB
Ted Washington - NT
David White - LB
Dusty Zeigler - C

1996 Carolina

Carlton Bailey - LB
Myron Baker - LB
Michael Bates - WR
Steve Beuerlein - QB
Tim Biakabutuka - RB
Duane Bickett - LB
Blake Brockermeyer - T
Matthew Campbell - T
Mark Carrier - WR
Kerry Collins - QB
Tim Colston - NT
Toi Cook - DB
Chad Cota - DB
Eric Davis - DB
Mark Dennis - T
Matt Elliott - G
Mike Fox - DE
Frank Garcia - G
Norberto Garrido - T
Willie Green - WR
Kevin Greene - LB
Scott Greene - RB
Howard Griffith - RB
Brandon Hayes - G
Leroy Hoard - RB
Raghib Ismail - WR
Tommy Jeter - DT
Anthony Johnson - RB
John Kasay - K
Shawn King - DE
Greg Kragen - NT
Lamar Lathon - LB
Steve Lofton - DB
Brett Maxie - DB
Emmanuel McDaniel - DB
Les Miller - DT
Sam Mills - LB
Muhsin Muhammad - WR
Winslow Oliver - RB
Dino Philyaw - RB
Damon Pieri - DB
Tyrone Poole - DB
Walter Rasby - TE
Michael Reed - DB
Mark Rodenhauser - C
Andre Royal - LB
Greg Skrepenak - G
Rod Smith - DB
Rohn Stark - P
Dwight Stone - WR
Pat Terrell - DB
Mark Thomas - DE
Wesley Walls - TE
Curtis Whitley - C
Gerald Williams - DE

1996 Chi. Bears

Clifton Abraham - DB
Greg Briggs - LB
Todd Burger - G
James Burton - DB
Joe Cain - LB
Mark Carrier - DB
Tony Carter - DB
Marty Carter - DB
Kerry Cash - TE
Jon Clark - T
Curtis Conway - WR
Bryan Cox - LB
Rob Davis - DT
Bobby Engram - WR
Mike Faulkerson - RB
Jim Flanigan - DT
Al Fontenot - DE
Jerry Fontenot - C
Marlon Forbes - DB
Paul Grasmanis - DT
Robert Green - RB
Raymont Harris - RB
Sean Harris - LB
Walt Harris - DB
Andy Heck - T
Michael Hicks - RB
Dana Howard - LB
Carlos Huerta - K
Jack Jackson - WR
John Jackson - WR
Jeff Jaeger - K
Keith Jennings - TE
Marcus Keyes - DT
Erik Kramer - QB
Dave Krieg - QB
Michael Lowery - LB
John Mangum - DB
Anthony Marshall - DB
Chris Martin - DB
Shane Matthews - QB
Kevin Miniefield - DB
Barry Minter - LB
Bobby Neely - TE
Todd Perry - G
Evan Pilgrim - G
Carl Reeves - DE
Rashaan Salaam - RB
Todd Sauerbrun - P
Carl Simpson - DT
Vinson Smith - LB
Marcus Spears - T
Alonzo Spellman - DE
Ryan Stenstrom - QB
John Thierry - DE
Michael Timpson - WR
Chris Villarrial - C
Ryan Wetnight - TE
James Williams - T
Donnell Woolford - DB

1996 Cincinnati

Ashley Ambrose - DB
Willie Anderson - T
Marco Battaglia - TE
Eric Bieniemy - RB
Ken Blackman - G
Jeff Blake - QB
Rich Braham - C
Darrick Brilz - C
Anthony Brown - T
Scott Brumfield - G
Ki-Jana Carter - RB
Andre Collins - LB
John Copeland - DE
Jeff Cothran - RB
Kenny Davidson - DE
Gerald Dixon - LB
David Dunn - WR
James Francis - LB
Garrison Hearst - RB
Jeff Hill - WR
James Hundon - WR
Lee Johnson - P
Tim Johnson - DT
Rod Jones - DB
Rod Jones - G
Roger Jones - DB
Todd Kelly - DE
Jevon Langford - DE
Ricardo McDonald - LB
Tony McGee - TE
Brian Milne - RB
Tim Morabito - DT
Greg Myers - DB
Randy Neal - LB
Bo Orlando - DB
Doug Pelfrey - K
Carl Pickens - WR
Troy Sadowski - TE
Corey Sawyer - DB
Darnay Scott - WR
Sam Shade - DB
Chris Shelling - DB
Artie Smith - DE
Jimmy Spencer - DB
Ramondo Stallings - DE
Steve Tovar - LB
Greg Truitt - C
Tom Tumulty - LB
Melvin Tuten - T
Kimo von Oelhoffen - DT
Bracey Walker - DB
Joe Walter - T
Leonard Wheeler - DB
Erik Wilhelm - QB
Dan Wilkinson - DT
Tydus Winans - WR

1996 Dallas

Troy Aikman - QB
Larry Allen - G
Tyji Armstrong - TE
Bill Bates - DB
Eric Bjornson - TE
Chris Boniol - K
Alundis Brice - DB
Alan Campos - LB
Shante Carver - DE
Tony Casillas - DT
Ray Childress - DT
Wendell Davis - DB
Billy Davis - WR
Ray Donaldson - C
John Flannery - C
Derrick Frazier - DB
Jason Garrett - QB
Randall Godfrey - LB
Charles Haley - DE
Roger Harper - DB
George Hegamin - T
Dale Hellestrae - C
Chad Hennings - DT
Michael Irvin - WR
John Jett - P
Daryl Johnston - RB
Derek Kennard - C
Leon Lett - DT
Brock Marion - DB
Kelvin Martin - WR
Hurvin McCormack - DE
Johnny Mitchell - TE
Godfrey Myles - LB
Nate Newton - G
Kavika Pittman - DE
Dominique Ross - RB
Deion Sanders - DB
Jim Schwantz - LB
Clay Shiver - C
Darrin Smith - LB
Emmitt Smith - RB
Kevin Smith - DB
Fred Strickland - LB
George Teague - DB
Broderick Thomas - DE
Tony Tolbert - DE
Mark Tuinei - T
Mike Ulufale - DT
Herschel Walker - RB
Derek Ware - TE
Charlie Williams - DB
Erik Williams - T
Kevin Williams - WR
Sherman Williams - RB

Stepfret Williams - WR
Wade Wilson - QB
Darren Woodson - DB

1996 Denver

Allen Aldridge - LB
Steve Atwater - DB
Tyrone Braxton - DB
Jamie Brown - T
Keith Burns - LB
Glenn Cadrez - LB
Dwayne Carswell - TE
Byron Chamberlain - TE
Aaron Craver - RB
Ray Crockett - DB
Terrell Davis - RB
David Diaz-Infante - G
Jason Elam - K
John Elway - QB
Jumpy Geathers - DT
Brian Habib - G
Britt Hager - LB
Harald Hasselbach - DE
Tim Hauck - DB
Vaughn Hebron - RB
Randy Hilliard - DB
Tory James - DB
Patrick Jeffers - WR
Darrius Johnson - DB
Ernest Jones - DE
Rondell Jones - DB
Todd Kinchen - WR
Jeff Lewis - QB
Mike Lodish - DT
Ed McCaffrey - WR
Reggie McElroy - T
Anthony Miller - WR
John Mobley - LB
Bill Musgrave - QB
Tom Nalen - C
Michael Dean Perry - DT
Reggie Rivers - RB
Jeff Robinson - DE
Bill Romanowski - LB
Tom Rouen - P
Mark Schlereth - G
Shannon Sharpe - TE
Mike Sherrard - WR
Detron Smith - RB
Rod Smith - WR
Ralph Tamm - G
Maa Tanuvasa - DT
Broderick Thompson - T
Lionel Washington - DB
Alfred Williams - DE
Dan Williams - DE
Gary Zimmerman - T

1996 Detroit

Tom Beer - LB
Bennie Blades - DB
Shane Bonham - DE
Jocelyn Borgella - DB
Stephen Boyd - LB
Michael Brooks - LB
Steve Brooks - TE
Reggie Brown - LB
Mike Compton - C
Scott Conover - T
Shane Dronett - DT
Luther Elliss - DT
Brad Ford - DB
Kevin Glover - C
Jason Hanson - K
Chris Harrison - G
Jeff Hartings - G
Hessley Hempstead - C
Greg Jeffries - DB
Pepper Johnson - LB
Jeff Jones - T
Scott Kowalkowski - LB
Antonio London - LB
Eric Lynch - RB
Don Majkowski - QB
Van Malone - DB
Aubrey Matthews - WR
Kez McCorvey - WR
Ryan McNeil - DB
Pete Metzelaars - TE
Glyn Milburn - RB
Scott Mitchell - QB
Herman Moore - WR
Johnnie Morton - WR
Zefross Moss - T
Brett Perriman - WR
Robert Porcher - DE
Derek Price - TE
Corey Raymond - DB
Ron Rice - DB
Ron Rivers - RB
Ray Roberts - T
Mark Royals - P
Barry Sanders - RB
Cory Schlesinger - RB
Tracy Scroggins - LB
Tony Semple - G
David Sloan - TE
Ryan Stewart - DB
Eric Stocz - TE
Henry Thomas - DT
Kerwin Waldroup - DE
Keith Washington - DE
Mike Wells - DE
Richard Woodley - DB

1996 Green Bay

Mike Arthur - C
Don Beebe - WR
Edgar Bennett - RB
Robert Brooks - WR
Bucky Brooks - DB
Gary Brown - T
Gilbert Brown - DT
LeRoy Butler - DB
Mark Chmura - TE
Shannon Clavelle - DE
Ron Cox - LB
Jeff Dellenbach - C
Earl Dotson - T
Santana Dotson - DT
Corey Dowden - DB
Doug Evans - DB
Brett Favre - QB
Antonio Freeman - WR
Bernardo Harris - LB
Chris Hayes - DB
William Henderson - RB
Craig Hentrich - P
Darius Holland - DT
Lamont Hollinquest - LB
Desmond Howard - WR
Chris Jacke - K
Keith Jackson - TE
Travis Jervey - RB
Calvin Jones - RB
Sean Jones - DE
Lindsay Knapp - G
George Koonce - LB
Bob Kuberski - DT
Dorsey Levens - RB
Derrick Mayes - WR
Gene McGuire - C
Keith McKenzie - LB
Jim McMahon - QB
John Michels - T
Terry Mickens - WR
Anthony Morgan - WR
Roderick Mullen - DB
Craig Newsome - DB
Doug Pederson - QB
Mike Prior - DB
Andre Rison - WR
Eugene Robinson - DB
Mike Robinson - DB
Ken Ruettgers - T
Brian Satterfield - RB
Wayne Simmons - LB
Kevin Smith - RB
Aaron Taylor - G
Jeff Thomason - TE
Adam Timmerman - G
Reggie White - DE
Bruce Wilkerson - T
Gabe Wilkins - DE
Brian Williams - LB
Tyrone Williams - DB
Frank Winters - C

1996 Houston

Mike Archie - RB
Tomur Barnes - DB
Micheal Barrow - LB
Blaine Bishop - DB
Joe Bowden - LB
Kendrick Burton - DE
Chris Chandler - QB
Lee Cole - DB
Anthony Cook - DE
Willie Davis - WR
Al Del Greco - K
Cris Dishman - DB
Kevin Donnalley - G
Anthony Dorsett - DB
Irv Eatman - T
Hicham El-Mashtoub - C
Josh Evans - DE
Malcolm Floyd - WR
Henry Ford - DE
Eddie George - RB
Mel Gray - KR
Mike Halapin - DT
Lemanski Hall - LB
Ronnie Harmon - RB
Brad Hopkins - T
Steve Jackson - DB
Lenoy Jones - LB
Terry Killens - LB
Jason Layman - T
Darryll Lewis - DB
Roderick Lewis - TE
Bruce Matthews - G
James McKeehan - TE
Steve McNair - QB
John Henry Mills - LB
Bryant Mix - DE
Erik Norgard - G
Michael Roan - TE
James Roberson - DE
Marcus Robertson - DB
Rafael Robinson - DB
Reggie Roby - P
Jon Runyan - T
Derek Russell - WR
Chris Sanders - WR
Al Smith - LB
Mark Stepnoski - C
Rayna Stewart - DB
Rodney Thomas - RB

Gary Walker - DE
Sheddrick Wilson - WR
Barron Wortham - LB
Frank Wycheck - TE
Robert Young - DE

1996 Indianapolis

Trev Alberts - LB
Elijah Alexander - LB
Troy Auzenne - T
Aaron Bailey - WR
Bradford Banta - TE
Kerwin Bell - QB
Jason Belser - DB
Tony Bennett - LB
Cary Blanchard - K
Ray Buchanan - DB
Sammie Burroughs - LB
Quentin Coryatt - LB
Zack Crockett - RB
Eugene Daniel - DB
Sean Dawkins - WR
Richard Dent - DE
Ken Dilger - TE
Chris Doering - WR
Marshall Faulk - RB
Derrick Frazier - DB
Chris Gardocki - P
Steve Grant - LB
Derwin Gray - DB
Clif Groce - RB
Steve Hall - DB
Jim Harbaugh - QB
Steve Hardin - G
Marvin Harrison - WR
Jeff Herrod - LB
Chris Hetherington - RB
Ellis Johnson - DE
Richard Jones - DB
Vance Joseph - DB
Paul Justin - QB
Jay Leeuwenburg - C
Kirk Lowdermilk - C
Eric Mahlum - G
Tony Mandarich - T
Steve Martin - DT
Jason Mathews - T
Dedric Mathis - DB
Tony McCoy - DT
Ray McElroy - DB
Arnold Mickens - RB
Steve Morrison - LB
Freddie Joe Nunn - DE
Bobby Olive - WR
Marcus Pollard - TE
Kendall Shello - DE
Tony Siragusa - DT
Scott Slutzker - TE
Brian Stablein - WR
Mark Stock - WR
David Tate - DB
Kipp Vickers - T
Lamont Warren - RB
Damon Watts - DB
Derek West - T
Bernard Whittington - DE
Doug Widell - G
Vince Workman - RB
Phil Yeboah-Kodie - LB

1996 Jacksonville

Bryan Barker - P
Reggie Barlow - WR
Aaron Beasley - DB
Ricky Bell - DB
Tony Boselli - T
Brant Boyer - LB
Tony Brackens - DE
Bucky Brooks - DB
Derek Brown - TE
Mark Brunell - QB
Kendricke Bullard - WR
Michael Cheever - C
Ryan Christopherson - RB
Reggie Clark - LB
Vinnie Clark - DB
Ben Coleman - G
Don Davey - DT
Andre Davis - DT
Travis Davis - DB
Brian DeMarco - G
Nate Dingle - LB
Paul Frase - DE
Rashid Gayle - DB
Roger Graham - RB
Rich Griffith - TE
Dana Hall - DB
Ty Hallock - LB
Kevin Hardy - LB
Mike Hollis - K
Chris Hudson - DB
Greg Huntington - C
Willie Jackson - WR
Rob Johnson - QB
Randy Jordan - RB
John Jurkovic - DT
Jeff Kopp - LB
Jeff Lageman - DE
Ernie Logan - DE
Curtis Marsh - WR
Robert Massey - DB
Le'Shai Maston - RB

Keenan McCardell - WR
Tom McManus - LB
Natrone Means - RB
Pete Mitchell - TE
Jeff Novak - G
Kelvin Pritchett - DT
Andre Rison - WR
Eddie Robinson - LB
Bryan Schwartz - LB
Leon Searcy - T
Clyde Simmons - DE
Joel Smeenge - LB
Jimmy Smith - WR
James Stewart - RB
Darren Studstill - DB
Dave Thomas - DB
Rich Tylski - G
Mickey Washington - DB
Dave Widell - C

1996 Kansas City

Louie Aguiar - P
Marcus Allen - RB
John Alt - T
Kimble Anders - RB
Darren Anderson - DB
Victor Bailey - WR
Tom Barndt - G
Martin Bayless - DB
Donnell Bennett - RB
Steve Bono - QB
Vaughn Booker - DE
John Browning - DE
Dale Carter - DB
Keith Cash - TE
Mark Collins - DB
Jeff Criswell - T
Anthony Davis - LB
Lake Dawson - WR
Troy Dumas - LB
Donnie Edwards - LB
Rich Gannon - QB
Tim Grunhard - C
James Hasty - DB
Greg Hill - RB
Joe Horn - WR
Danan Hughes - WR
George Jamison - LB
Trezelle Jenkins - T
Reggie Johnson - TE
Sean LaChapelle - WR
Greg Manusky - LB
Pellom McDaniels - DE
Todd McNair - RB
Chris Penn - WR
Joe Phillips - DT
Tony Richardson - RB
Tracy Rogers - LB
Dan Saleaumua - DT
Will Shields - G
Ricky Siglar - T
Tracy Simien - LB
Neil Smith - DE
Tony Stargell - DB
Pete Stoyanovich - K
David Szott - G
Derrick Thomas - LB
Reggie Tongue - DB
Keith Traylor - DT
Tamarick Vanover - WR
Danny Villa - G
Derrick Walker - TE
Brian Washington - DB
William White - DB
Jerome Woods - DB

1996 Miami

Karim Abdul-Jabbar - RB
Trace Armstrong - DE
Gene Atkins - DB
Robert Bailey - DB
Fred Barnett - WR
John Bock - G
Tim Bowens - DT
O.J. Brigance - LB
J.B. Brown - DB
James Brown - T
Jeff Buckey - T
Terrell Buckley - DB
Shane Burton - DT
Keith Byars - RB
Brett Carolan - TE
Kirby Dar Dar - WR
Cal Dixon - C
Troy Drayton - TE
Steve Emtman - DT
Craig Erickson - QB
Daryl Gardener - DT
Chris Gray - G
Norman Hand - DT
Anthony Harris - LB
Randal Hill - WR
Sean Hill - DB
Dwight Hollier - LB
Larry Izzo - LB
Calvin Jackson - DB
Tim Jacobs - DB
Aaron Jones - DE
Charles Jordan - WR
John Kidd - P
Bernie Kosar - QB
Dan Marino - QB

O. J. McDuffie - WR
Everett McIver - G
Jerris McPhail - RB
Scott Miller - WR
Billy Milner - T
Joe Nedney - K
Louis Oliver - DB
Bernie Parmalee - RB
Stanley Pritchett - RB
Tim Ruddy - C
Keith Sims - G
Chris Singleton - LB
Irving Spikes - RB
Michael Stewart - DB
Danny Stubbs - DE
Lamar Thomas - WR
Zach Thomas - LB
Frank Wainright - TE
Richmond Webb - T
Jerry Wilson - DB
Robert Wilson - RB
Shawn Wooden - DB

1996 Minnesota

Derrick Alexander - DE
Tomur Barnes - DB
Harlon Barnett - DB
Pete Bercich - LB
Mitch Berger - P
Jeff Brady - LB
Richard Brown - LB
Cris Carter - WR
Jeff Christy - C
Duane Clemons - DE
Greg DeLong - TE
Scott Dill - T
David Dixon - G
Dixon Edwards - LB
Chuck Evans - RB
Jason Fisk - DT
David Frisch - TE
Corey Fuller - DB
Dave Garnett - LB
John Gerak - G
Robert Goff - DE
Hunter Goodwin - TE
Scottie Graham - RB
Robert Griffith - DB
Steve Hall - DB
Ben Hanks - LB
Martin Harrison - DE
Leroy Hoard - RB
Qadry Ismail - WR
Alfred Jackson - DB
Chris Johnson - DB
Brad Johnson - QB
Andrew Jordan - TE
Amp Lee - RB
James Manley - DT
Randall McDaniel - G
Warren Moon - QB
Mike Morris - C
Harold Morrow - RB
David Palmer - WR
Anthony Prior - DB
John Randle - DT
Jake Reed - WR
Scott Sisson - K
Fernando Smith - DE
Robert Smith - RB
Ariel Solomon - T
Todd Steussie - T
Korey Stringer - T
Darryl Talley - LB
Orlando Thomas - DB
Esera Tuaolo - NT
Sean Vanhorse - DB
Jay Walker - QB
Chris Walsh - WR
Dewayne Washington - DB
Moe Williams - RB

1996 New England

Bruce Armstrong - T
Troy Barnett - DT
Mike Bartrum - TE
Drew Bledsoe - QB
Vincent Brisby - WR
Corwin Brown - DB
Monty Brown - LB
Troy Brown - WR
Tedy Bruschi - LB
John Burke - TE
Keith Byars - RB
Willie Clay - DB
Ben Coates - TE
Todd Collins - LB
Ferric Collons - DE
Jeff Dellenbach - C
Chad Eaton - DT
Sam Gash - RB
Mike Gisler - C
Terry Glenn - WR
Hason Graham - WR
Marrio Grier - RB
Jerome Henderson - DB
Jimmy Hitchcock - DB
Shawn Jefferson - WR
Dietrich Jells - WR
Ted Johnson - LB
Mike Jones - DE
Bob Kratch - G
Max Lane - T

Ty Law - DB
Vernon Lewis - DB
Ray Lucas - WR
Curtis Martin - RB
Willie McGinest - DE
Mike McGruder - DB
Dave Meggett - RB
Lawyer Milloy - DB
Marty Moore - LB
Will Moore - WR
Lovett Purnell - TE
Terry Ray - DB
Ricky Reynolds - DB
David Richards - T
William Roberts - G
Todd Rucci - G
Dwayne Sabb - LB
Pio Sagapolutele - DT
Walter Scott - DE
Chris Slade - LB
Otis Smith - DB
Chris Sullivan - DE
Tom Tupa - P
Adam Vinatieri - K
Mark Wheeler - DT
Larry Whigham - DB
Dave Wohlabaugh - C
Devin Wyman - DT
Scott Zolak - QB

1996 New Orleans

Tom Ackerman - C
Eric Allen - DB
Mario Bates - RB
Doug Brien - K
Willie Broughton - DT
Derek Brown - RB
Je'Rod Cherry - DB
Don Davis - LB
Lee DeRamus - WR
Ernest Dixon - LB
Jim Dombrowski - G
Jim Everett - QB
Mark Fields - LB
Kendall Gammon - C
Paul Green - TE
Terry Guess - WR
Richard Harvey - LB
Mercury Hayes - WR
Michael Haynes - WR
Keno Hills - T
Derrick Hoskins - DB
Tyrone Hughes - DB
Earnest Hunter - RB
Greg Jackson - DB
Haywood Jeffires - WR
Joe Johnson - DT
Tony Johnson - TE
Brian Jones - LB
Clarence Jones - T
Ed King - G
Sean Lumpkin - DB
Henry Lusk - TE
Wayne Martin - DT
J. J. McCleskey - DB
Andy McCollum - C
Mark McMillian - DB
Darren Mickell - DE
Alex Molden - DB
Lorenzo Neal - RB
Anthony Newman - DB
Craig Novitsky - G
Doug Nussmeier - QB
Emile Palmer - DT
Rufus Porter - LB
Willie Roaf - T
Austin Robbins - DT
Torrance Small - WR
Brady Smith - DE
Irv Smith - TE
Fred Stokes - DE
William Strong - DB
Winfred Tubbs - LB
Renaldo Turnbull - DE
Mike Verstegen - G
Ricky Whittle - RB
Donald Willis - C
Klaus Wilmsmeyer - P
Ray Zellars - RB

1996 NY Giants

Ray Agnew - DT
Kevin Alexander - WR
Jessie Armstead - LB
Willie Beamon - DB
Greg Bishop - T
Chad Bratzke - DE
Dave Brown - QB
Marcus Buckley - LB
Chris Calloway - WR
Jesse Campbell - DB
Doug Colman - LB
Howard Cross - TE
Brad Daluiso - K
Lawrence Dawsey - WR
Omar Douglas - WR
Maurice Douglass - DB
Gary Downs - RB
Keith Elias - RB
Percy Ellsworth - DB
Scott Galyon - LB
Scott Gragg - T
Conrad Hamilton - DB
Keith Hamilton - DE

Rodney Hampton - RB
Robert Harris - DE
Bernard Holsey - DT
Mike Horan - P
Cedric Jones - DE
Danny Kanell - QB
Brian Kozlowski - TE
Thomas Lewis - WR
Arthur Marshall - WR
Corey Miller - LB
Roman Oben - T
Aaron Pierce - TE
Thomas Randolph - DB
Moses Regular - LB
Jerry Reynolds - G
Coleman Rudolph - LB
Brian Saxton - TE
Adam Schreiber - C
Jason Sehorn - DB
Lance Smith - G
Phillippi Sparks - DB
Ron Stone - G
Mike Strahan - DE
Amani Toomer - WR
Robert Walker - RB
Charles Way - RB
Tyrone Wheatley - RB
Corey Widmer - LB
Brian Williams - C
Tito Wooten - DB
Rodney Young - DB
Rob Zatechka - G

1996 NY Jets

David Alexander - C
Richie Anderson - RB
Henry Bailey - WR
Fred Baxter - TE
Aubrey Beavers - LB
Harry Boatswain - T
Kyle Brady - TE
Matt Brock - DT
Ron Carpenter - DB
Chad Cascadden - LB
Mike Chalenski - DE
Wayne Chrebet - WR
Kyle Clifton - LB
Reggie Cobb - RB
Marcus Coleman - DB
Lou D'Agostino - RB
Tyrone Davis - TE
Hugh Douglas - DE
Roger Duffy - C
Jumbo Elliott - T
Kwame Ellis - DB
Jeff Faulkner - DT
Glenn Foley - QB
Harry Galbreath - G
Aaron Glenn - DB
Jeff Graham - WR
Victor Green - DB
Carl Greenwood - DB
Mark Gunn - DE
Bobby Hamilton - DE
Rick Hamilton - LB
Brian Hansen - P
Melvin Hayes - T
Bobby Houston - LB
Erik Howard - DE
John Hudson - C
Keyshawn Johnson - WR
Gary Jones - DB
Marvin Jones - LB
Brad Keeney - DT
Mo Lewis - LB
Nick Lowery - K
Siupeli Malamala - G
Sherriden May - RB
Ray Mickens - DB
Ronald Moore - RB
Adrian Murrell - RB
Neil O'Donnell - QB
Matt O'Dwyer - G
James Parrish - T
Frank Reich - QB
Phillip Riley - WR
Don Silvestri - K
Webster Slaughter - WR
Otis Smith - DB
Marc Spindler - DT
Alex Van Dyke - WR
Marvin Washington - DE
Brent Williams - DE
David Williams - T
Lonnie Young - DB
Eric Zomalt - DB

1996 Oakland

Eddie Anderson - DB
Leo Araguz - P
Joe Aska - RB
Jerry Ball - DT
Greg Biekert - LB
Larry Brown - DB
Tim Brown - WR
Aundray Bruce - DE
Paul Butcher - LB
Rich Camarillo - P
Darren Carrington - DB
Perry Carter - DB
Rick Cunningham - G
Jerone Davison - RB
Rickey Dudley - TE

Derrick Fenner - RB
James Folston - LB
Cole Ford - K
Rob Fredrickson - LB
Andrew Glover - TE
La'Roi Glover - DT
Kevin Gogan - T
Jeff Gossett - P
Tim Hall - RB
Pat Harlow - T
Nolan Harrison - DT
Marcus Hinton - TE
Daryl Hobbs - WR
Billy Joe Hobert - QB
Rob Holmberg - LB
Jeff Hostetler - QB
Robert Jenkins - T
James Jett - WR
Lance Johnstone - DE
Mike Jones - LB
Trey Junkin - TE
Napoleon Kaufman - RB
Lincoln Kennedy - T
Carl Kidd - DB
David Klingler - QB
Dan Land - DB
Albert Lewis - DB
Lorenzo Lynch - DB
Lamar Lyons - DB
Russell Maryland - DT
Terry McDaniel - DB
Chester McGlockton - DT
Charles McRae - T
Mike Morton - LB
Barret Robbins - C
Kenny Shedd - WR
Anthony Smith - DE
Pat Swilling - DE
James Trapp - DB
Olanda Truitt - WR
Dan Turk - C
Harvey Williams - RB
Steve Wisniewski - G

1996 Philadelphia

Gary Anderson - K
Deral Boykin - DB
Barrett Brooks - T
Darion Conner - DE
Richard Cooper - T
Brian Dawkins - DB
Ty Detmer - QB
Ronnie Dixon - DT
Troy Drake - T
Jason Dunn - TE
Ray Farmer - LB
Irving Fryar - WR
James Fuller - DB
William Fuller - DE
Charlie Garner - RB
Don Griffin - DB
Mark Gunn - DE
Rhett Hall - DT
Andy Harmon - DT
Lester Holmes - T
Bobby Hoying - QB
Tom Hutton - P
Mark Ingram - WR
Greg Jefferson - DE
Jimmie Johnson - TE
Kevin Johnson - DT
Chris T. Jones - WR
Joe Kelly - LB
Mike Mamula - LB
Whit Marshall - LB
Jermane Mayberry - G
Guy McIntyre - G
Raleigh McKenzie - C
Joe Panos - G
Rodney Peete - QB
Mark Rypien - QB
Michael Samson - DT
Mark Seay - WR
Freddie Solomon - WR
Bobby Taylor - DB
Hollis Thomas - DT
Johnny Thomas - DB
William Thomas - LB
Kevin Turner - RB
Morris Unutoa - C
Troy Vincent - DB
Adam Walker - RB
Ricky Watters - RB
Ed West - TE
Barry Wilburn - DB
Calvin Williams - WR
James Willis - LB
Derrick Witherspoon - RB
Marc Woodard - LB
Sylvester Wright - DE
Eric Zomalt - DB
Mike Zordich - DB

1996 Pittsburgh

Jahine Arnold - WR
Myron Bell - DB
Jerome Bettis - RB
Kirk Botkin - TE
Chad Brown - LB
Mark Bruener - TE
Brentson Buckner - DT
Steve Conley - LB
Bernard Dafney - T
Dermontti Dawson - C
Shayne Edge - P
Carlos Emmons - LB
John Farquhar - TE
Deon Figures - DB
Lethon Flowers - DB
Randy Fuller - DB
Oliver Gibson - DE
Jason Gildon - LB
Andre Hastings - WR
Jonathan Hayes - TE
Kevin Henry - DE
Corey Holliday - WR
Earl Holmes - LB
John Jackson - T
Charles Johnson - WR
Norm Johnson - K
Bill Johnson - DE
Donta Jones - LB
Levon Kirkland - LB
Carnell Lake - DB
Tim Lester - RB
Greg Lloyd - LB
Fred McAfee - RB
Jim Miller - QB
Josh Miller - P
Ernie Mills - WR
Tom Myslinski - T
Chris Oldham - DB
Jerry Olsavsky - LB
Erric Pegram - RB
Darren Perry - DB
Eric Ravotti - LB
Israel Raybon - DE
Terry Richardson - RB
Orpheus Roye - DE
Brenden Stai - G
Joel Steed - NT
Kordell Stewart - QB
Justin Strzelczyk - T
Jim Sweeney - C
Yancey Thigpen - WR
Mike Tomczak - QB
Willie Williams - DB
Jon Witman - RB
Will Wolford - G
Rod Woodson - DB

1996 St. Louis

Darryl Ashmore - T
Tony Banks - QB
Chuck Belin - G
Bern Brostek - C
Isaac Bruce - WR
Kevin Carter - DE
Hayward Clay - TE
Ernie Conwell - TE
Keith Crawford - WR
Paschall Davis - LB
Torin Dorn - DB
Troy Drayton - TE
D'Marco Farr - DT
Cedric Figaro - LB
Wayne Gandy - T
Percell Gaskins - LB
Leo Goeas - T
Antonio Goss - LB
Harold Green - RB
Mike Gruttadauria - C
James Harris - DE
Derrick Harris - RB
Marcus Holliday - RB
Thomas Homco - LB
Carlos Huerta - K
Jesse James - C
Carlos Jenkins - LB
Jimmie Jones - DT
Robert Jones - LB
Eddie Kennison - WR
Jon Kirksey - DT
Aaron Laing - TE
Sean Landeta - P
Jeremy Lincoln - DB
Chip Lohmiller - K
Todd Lyght - DB
Keith Lyle - DB
Jamie Martin - QB
Gerald McBurrows - DB
Fred Miller - T
Billy Milner - T
Jerald Moore - RB
Herman O'Berry - DB
Leslie O'Neal - DE
Chuck Osborne - DT
Anthony Parker - DB
Roman Phifer - LB
Lawrence Phillips - RB
Greg Robinson - RB
Jermaine Ross - WR
Mike Scurlock - DB
J.T. Thomas - WR
Joe Valerio - G
Marquis Walker - DB
Steve Walsh - QB
Alberto White - DE
Dwayne White - G
Zach Wiegert - T
Billy Williams - WR
Jay Williams - DT
Mark Williams - LB
Alexander Wright - WR
Toby Wright - DB

1996 San Diego

Arnold Ale - LB
Darren Bennett - P
Tony Berti - G
David Binn - TE
Kevin Bouie - RB
Freddie Bradley - RB
Lewis Bush - LB
John Carney - K
Eric Castle - DB
Willie Clark - DB
Joe Cocozzo - G
Andre Coleman - WR
Marco Coleman - DE
Joe Cummings - LB
Isaac Davis - G
Reuben Davis - DT
Vernon Edwards - DE
'Omar Ellison - WR
Greg Engel - C
Terrell Fletcher - RB
Darrien Gordon - DB
Dwayne Gordon - LB
Kurt Gouveia - LB
Courtney Hall - C
Dwayne Harper - DB
Rodney Harrison - DB
Aaron Hayden - RB
David Hendrix - DB
Stan Humphries - QB
Raylee Johnson - DE
Charlie Jones - WR
Shawn Lee - DT
Tony Martin - WR
Deems May - TE
Jim Mills - G
Chris Mims - DE
Shannon Mitchell - TE
Mark Montreuil - DB
Eric Moten - G
Vaughn Parker - T
John Parrella - DT
Alfred Pupunu - TE
Walter Reeves - TE
Brian Roche - TE
Kevin Ross - DB
Leonard Russell - RB
Sean Salisbury - QB
Patrick Sapp - LB
Don Sasa - DT
Junior Seau - LB
Terrance Shaw - DB
Troy Sienkiewicz - G
Bryan Still - WR
Bryan Stoltenberg - C
Harry Swayne - T
Glen Young - LB

1996 San Francisco

Roy Barker - DE
Harris Barton - T
Daved Benefield - LB
Michael Brandon - DE
Jeff Brohm - QB
Dennis Brown - DE
Ray Brown - G
Junior Bryant - DE
Curtis Buckley - DB
Mike Caldwell - WR
Dexter Carter - RB
Adrian Cooper - TE
Chris Dalman - C
Derrick Deese - G
Dedrick Dodge - DB
Chris Doleman - DE
Tyronne Drakeford - DB
William Floyd - RB
Elvis Grbac - QB
Merton Hanks - DB
Tim Hanshaw - G
Mark Harris - WR
Israel Ifeanyi - DE
Steve Israel - DB
Brent Jones - TE
Terry Kirby - RB
Randy Kirk - LB
Kevin Lee - WR
Derek Loville - RB
Anthony Lynn - RB
Sean Manuel - TE
Tim McDonald - DB
Rod Milstead - G
Kevin Mitchell - LB
Ken Norton - LB
Terrell Owens - WR
Tony Peterson - LB
Gary Plummer - LB
Frank Pollack - T
Marquez Pope - DB
Ted Popson - TE
Daryl Price - DE
Jerry Rice - WR
Jesse Sapolu - G
Kirk Scrafford - T
Nate Singleton - WR
Frankie Smith - DB
J.J. Stokes - WR
Dana Stubblefield - DT
Tommy Thompson - P
Iheanyi Uwaezuoke - WR
Tommy Vardell - RB
Steve Wallace - T
Jeff Wilkins - K
James Williams - DB
Lee Woodall - LB
Bryant Young - DT
Steve Young - QB

1996 Seattle

Sam Adams - DT
James Atkins - T
Howard Ballard - T
Michael Barber - LB
Frank Beede - C
Jay Bellamy - DB
Robert Blackmon - DB
Brian Blades - WR
Steve Broussard - RB
Reggie Brown - RB
Carlester Crumpler - TE
T.J. Cunningham - DB
Ed Cunningham - C
Phillip Daniels - DE
Antonio Edwards - DE
Christian Fauria - TE
John Friesz - QB
Joey Galloway - WR
Stan Gelbaugh - QB
Derrick Graham - G
Carlton Gray - DB
Oscar Gray - RB
Corey Harris - DB
Ronnie Harris - WR
Dou Innocent - RB
Selwyn Jones - DB
Pete Kendall - G
Cortez Kennedy - DT
Jason Kyle - LB
Matt LaBounty - DE
James Logan - LB
Kevin Mawae - C
Michael McCrary - DE
James McKnight - WR
Henry McMillian - DT
Rick Mirer - QB
Glenn Montgomery - DT
Winston Moss - LB
Joe Nash - DT
Todd Peterson - K
Mike Pritchard - WR
Ricky Proehl - WR
Dexter Seigler - DB
Michael Sinclair - DE
Lamar Smith - RB
Mack Strong - RB
Fred Thomas - DB
Gino Torretta - QB
Rick Tuten - P
Eric Unverzagt - LB
Chris Warren - RB
Dean Wells - LB
Darryl Williams - DB
Grant Williams - T
Ronnie Williams - TE
Terry Wooden - LB

1996 Tampa Bay

Donnie Abraham - DB
Scott Adams - G
Chidi Ahanotu - DE
Mike Alstott - RB
Eric Austin - DB
Tommy Barnhardt - P
Ian Beckles - G
Tony Bouie - DB
Derrick Brooks - LB
Reggie Brooks - RB
Joel Crisman - C
Brad Culpepper - DT
Eric Curry - DE
Jorge Diaz - G
Trent Dilfer - QB
Charles Dimry - DB
Kevin Dogins - LB
Demetrius DuBose - LB
Jerry Ellison - RB
John Farquhar - TE
Kenneth Gant - DB
Jeff Gooch - LB
Paul Gruber - T
Alvin Harper - WR
Jackie Harris - TE
Courtney Hawkins - WR
Michael Husted - K
Tyoka Jackson - DE
Melvin Johnson - DB
Tracy Johnson - RB
LaCurtis Jones - LB
Marcus Jones - DT
Tyrone Legette - DB
John Lynch - DB
Jason Maniecki - DT
Marvin Marshall - WR
Lonnie Marts - LB
Tony Mayberry - C
Martin Mayhew - DB
Scott Milanovich - QB
Charles Mincy - DB
Dave Moore - TE
Hardy Nickerson - LB
Jason Odom - T
Pete Pierson - T
Jim Pyne - G
Errict Rhett - RB
Doug Riesenberg - T
Reggie Rusk - DB
Larry Ryans - WR
Warren Sapp - DT
Todd Scott - DB
Nilo Silvan - WR
Herman Smith - DE
Robert Staten - RB
Darnell Stephens - LB
Willy Tate - TE
Robb Thomas - WR
Leroy Thompson - RB
Regan Upshaw - DE
Casey Weldon - QB
Steve White - DE
Karl Williams - WR

1996 Washington

Patrise Alexander - LB
Terry Allen - RB
Flipper Anderson - WR
Jamie Asher - TE
Darryl Ashmore - T
Romeo Bandison - DT
Tomur Barnes - DB
Troy Barnett - DT
William Bell - RB
Scott Blanton - K
Marc Boutte - DT
Larry Bowie - RB
Bill Brooks - WR
Darrick Brownlow - LB
Tom Carter - DB
Alcides Catanho - LB
Bob Dahl - G
Stephen Davis - RB
Henry Ellard - WR
Leomont Evans - DB
Gus Frerotte - QB
William Gaines - DT
Scott Galbraith - TE
Sean Gilbert - DT
Darrell Green - DB
Ken Harvey - LB
James Jenkins - TE
Tre' Johnson - G
Ryan Kuehl - DT
Marc Logan - RB
Trevor Matich - C
Brian Mitchell - RB
Darryl Morrison - DB
Dexter Nottage - DE
Rich Owens - DE
Sterling Palmer - DE
Joe Patton - G
Marvcus Patton - LB
Darryl Pounds - DB
Shar Pourdanesh - T
Cory Raymer - C
Stanley Richard - DB
Chris Sedoris - C
Leslie Shepherd - WR
Heath Shuler - QB
Ed Simmons - T
Rod Stephens - LB
Eric Sutton - DB
Keith Taylor - DB
Matt Turk - P
Scott Turner - DB
Jeff Uhlenhake - C
Matt Vanderbeek - LB
Brian Walker - DB
Marquis Walker - DB
Michael Westbrook - WR
Tony Woods - DE

1997 Arizona

Brent Alexander - FS
Michael Bankston - DE
Tommy Bennett - SS
Kevin Bouie - RB
Fred Brock - WR
Lomas Brown - T
Kevin Butler - K
Mike Caldwell - LB
Mark Campbell - DT
Pat Carter - TE
Stoney Case - QB
Larry Centers - FB
Lyron Cobbins - LB
Matt Darby - SS
Mike Devlin - C
James Dexter - T
Chris Dishman - G
Anthony Edwards - WR
Jeff Feagles - P
Chris Gedney - TE
Aaron Graham - C
Kent Graham - QB
Thomas Guynes - T
Kenny Harris - DB
Eric Hill - MLB
Ty Howard - CB
Terry Irving - OLB
LeShon Johnson - RB
Matt Joyce - G
Trey Junkin - TE
Tom Knight - CB
Kwamie Lassiter - DB
J. J. McCleskey - DB
Tony McCombs - LB
Leeland McElroy - RB
Ronald McKinnon - OLB
Johnny McWilliams - TE
Jamir Miller - OLB
Kevin Miniefield - DB
Rob Moore - WR
Ronald Moore - RB
Joe Nedney - K
Brad Ottis - DT
Tito Paul - DB
Jake Plummer - QB
Anthony Redmon - G
Simeon Rice - DE
Frank Sanders - WR
Rob Selby - G
Cedric Smith - FB
Mark Smith - DT
Eric Swann - DT
Rashod Swinger - DT
Aeneas Williams - CB
Kevin Williams - WR
Bernard Wilson - DT
Joe Wolf - T

1997 Atlanta

Scott Adams - T
Morten Andersen - K
Jamal Anderson - RB
Lester Archambeau - DE
Chris Bayne - DB
Cornelius Bennett - OLB
Scott Bentley - K
Juran Bolden - DB
Michael Booker - CB
Ronnie Bradford - CB
David Brandon - OLB
Ray Buchanan - CB
John Burrough - DT
Devin Bush - FS
Chris Chandler - QB
Bob Christian - FB
Calvin Collins - C
Henri Crockett - OLB
Antone Davis - T
Nathan Davis - DE
Scott Davis - G
Gary Downs - RB
Shane Dronett - DE
Bert Emanuel - WR
Roman Fortin - C
Jamal Fountaine - DE
Tony Graziani - QB
Harold Green - RB
Donovan Greer - CB
Travis Hall - DT
Ruffin Hamilton - LB
Byron Hanspard - RB
Mercury Hayes - WR
Michael Haynes - WR
Todd Kinchen - WR
Brian Kozlowski - TE
Terance Mathis - WR
Lenny McGill - DB
Nate Miller - T
Dan Owens - DT
Anthony Pleasant - DE
O.J. Santiago - TE
Craig Sauer - LB
Brian Saxton - TE
Adam Schreiber - G
Freddie Scott - WR
Chris Shelling - DB
Chuck Smith - DE
Ed Smith - TE
Dan Stryzinski - P
Eddie Sutter - LB
Robbie Tobeck - G
Billy Joe Tolliver - QB
Jessie Tuggle - MLB
Ed West - TE
William White - SS
Bob Whitfield - T
Gene Williams - G
Matt Willig - T
Marcus Wimberly - DB

1997 Baltimore

Derrick Alexander - WR
Jeff Blackshear - G
Peter Boulware - OLB
Donny Brady - CB
Dorian Brew - DB
Cornell Brown - LB
Orlando Brown - T
Rob Burnett - DE
Earnest Byner - RB
Ben Cavil - G
Kenyon Cotton - RB
Bernard Dafney - G
Eugene Daniel - CB
Ray Ethridge - WR
Spencer Folau - T
Mike Frederick - DE
Leo Goeas - G
Jay Graham - RB
Eric Green - TE
Kim Herring - FS
Priest Holmes - RB
Michael Jackson - WR
DeRon Jenkins - CB
James Jones - DT
Rondell Jones - FS
Brian Kinchen - TE
Antonio Langham - CB
Jermaine Lewis - WR
Ray Lewis - MLB
Lamar Lyons - DB
Tyrus McCloud - LB
Michael McCrary - DE
Greg Montgomery - P
Stevon Moore - SS
Bam Morris - FB
Quentin Neujahr - C
A.J. Ofodile - TE
Jonathan Ogden - T
Tyrell Peters - LB
James Roe - WR
Jamie Sharper - OLB
Nate Singleton - WR
Tony Siragusa - DT
Ralph Staten - DB
Matt Stover - K
Leland Taylor - DT
Vinny Testaverde - QB
Bennie Thompson - DB
Tony Vinson - RB
Chris Ward - DE
Keith Washington - DE
Larry Webster - DT
John Williams - DB
Wally Williams - C
Ryan Yarborough - WR
Eric Zeier - QB

1997 Buffalo

Ethan Albright - T
Dan Brandenburg - LB
Ruben Brown - G
Jeff Burris - CB
Steve Christie - K
Tony Cline - TE
Todd Collins - QB
Bill Conaty - C
Robert Coons - TE
Damien Covington - ILB
Quinn Early - WR
John Fina - T
Mitchell Galloway - WR
Phil Hansen - DE
Billy Joe Hobert - QB
John Holecek - MLB
Darick Holmes - RB
Ken Irvin - DB
Raymond Jackson - DB
Jim Jeffcoat - DE
Lonnie Johnson - TE
Henry Jones - SS
Marlon Kerner - DB
Corbin Lacina - G
Corey Louchiey - T
Mark Maddox - LB
Emanuel Martin - DB
Chris Mohr - P
Sean Moran - DT
Eric Moulds - WR
Jamie Nails - T
Gabe Northern - LB
Jerry Ostroski - T
Bryce Paup - OLB
Marlo Perry - LB
Mark Pike - DE
Shawn Price - DE
Andre Reed - WR
Jerry Reese - WR
Jay Riemersma - TE
Sam Rogers - OLB
Kurt Schulz - FS
Eric Smedley - DB
Antowain Smith - RB
Bruce Smith - DE
Thomas Smith - CB
Chris Spielman - ILB
Marcus Spriggs - T
Steve Tasker - WR
Thurman Thomas - RB
Tim Tindale - FB
Alex Van Pelt - QB
Ted Washington - NT
Marcellus Wiley - DE
Pat Williams - DT
Dusty Zeigler - C

1997 Carolina

Clifton Abraham - DB
Carlton Bailey - LB
Myron Baker - LB
Micheal Barrow - OLB
Michael Bates - WR
Steve Beuerlein - QB
Tim Biakabutuka - RB
Blake Brockermeyer - T
Matt Campbell - G
Mark Carrier - WR
Rae Carruth - WR
Kerry Collins - QB
Toi Cook - DB
Chad Cota - SS
Norbert Davidds-Garrido - T
Eric Davis - CB
Matt Elliott - G
Mike Fox - DE
Frank Garcia - C
Percell Gaskins - LB
Bucky Greeley - C
Scott Greene - FB
Raghib Ismail - WR
Anthony Johnson - RB
John Kasay - K
Shawn King - DE
Greg Kragen - NT
Fred Lane - RB
Lamar Lathon - OLB

Kris Mangum - TE
Les Miller - DE
Ernie Mills - WR
Sam Mills - ILB
Mike Minter - FS
Tim Morabito - DT
Muhsin Muhammad - WR
Winslow Oliver - RB
Damon Pieri - DB
Tyrone Poole - CB
Walter Rasby - TE
Israel Raybon - DE
Mark Rodenhauser - C
Andre Royal - ILB
Tarek Saleh - LB
Ray Seals - DE
Greg Skrepenak - G
Rod Smith - DB
Dwight Stone - WR
Kinnon Tatum - LB
Pat Terrell - FS
Renaldo Turnbull - LB
Wesley Walls - TE
Ken Walter - P
Gerald Williams - DE

1997 Chicago Bears

Tremayne Allen - TE
John Allred - TE
Darnell Autry - RB
Ricky Bell - DB
Fabien Bownes - WR
Todd Burger - G
James Burton - DB
Tony Carter - FB
Daryl Carter - LB
Marty Carter - SS
Tom Carter - CB
Jon Clark - T
Curtis Conway - WR
Terry Cousin - CB
Bryan Cox - MLB
Ron Cox - OLB
Corey Dowden - DB
Mike Dulaney - RB
Bobby Engram - WR
Jim Flanigan - DT
Marlon Forbes - DB
Paul Grasmanis - DT
Chris Gray - G
Ronnie Harmon - RB
Raymont Harris - RB
Sean Harris - LB
Walt Harris - CB
Andy Heck - T
Jimmy Herndon - T
Michael Hicks - RB
Van Hiles - DB
Tyrone Hughes - RB
Greg Huntington - G
Jeff Jaeger - K
Keith Jennings - TE
Erik Kramer - QB
Harper LeBel - TE
Michael Lowery - LB
John Mangum - FS
Anthony Marshall - DB
Barry Minter - OLB
Rick Mirer - QB
Chris Penn - WR
Todd Perry - G
Tony Peterson - LB
Evan Pilgrim - C
Ricky Proehl - WR
Carl Reeves - DE
Rashaan Salaam - RB
Todd Sauerbrun - P
Bill Schultz - G
Carl Simpson - DT
Eric Smith - WR
Alonzo Spellman - DE
Tony Stargell - DB
Steve Stenstrom - QB
John Thierry - DE
Mark Thomas - DE
Chris Villarrial - C
Ryan Wetnight - TE
Casey Wiegmann - C
James Williams - T
Tyrone Williams - DE
Chris Zorich - DT

1997 Cincinnati

Ashley Ambrose - CB
Willie Anderson - T
Marco Battaglia - TE
Eric Bieniemy - RB
Ken Blackman - G
Jeff Blake - QB
Rich Braham - G
Darrick Brilz - C
Anthony Brown - T
Scott Brumfield - G
Brentson Buckner - NT
Steve Bush - TE
Ki-Jana Carter - HB
Andre Collins - LB
John Copeland - DE
Canute Curtis - LB
Corey Dillon - HB
Gerald Dixon - OLB
Ty Douthard - RB
David Dunn - WR
Boomer Esiason - QB
James - Francis OLB
Cory Gilliard - DB
Scottie Graham - RB
Billy Granville - ILB
Brock Gutierrez - C
James Hundon - WR
Mike Jenkins - WR
Lee Johnson - P
Rod Jones - T
Jevon Langford - DE
Anthone Lott - CB
Tremain Mack - SS
Ricardo McDonald - ILB
Tony McGee - TE
Brian Milne - FB
Greg Myers - FS
Bo Orlando - DB
Tito Paul - CB
Doug Pelfrey - K
Carl Pickens - WR
Andre Purvis - DT
Kevin Sargent - T
Corey Sawyer - DB
Darnay Scott - WR
Sam Shade - SS
Jimmy Spencer - CB
Ramondo Stallings - DE
Tim Terry - LB
Steve Tovar - ILB
Greg Truitt - C
Tom Tumulty - ILB
Gunnard Twyner - WR
Kimo von Oelhoffen - NT
Joe Walter - T
Dan Wilkinson - DE
Reinard Wilson - OLB
Lawrence Wright - DB

1997 Dallas

Troy Aikman - QB
Larry Allen - G
Antonio Anderson - DT
Bill Bates - DB
Darren Benson - DT
Eric Bjornson - TE
Shante Carver - DE
Tony Casillas - DT
Dexter Coakley - OLB
Richie Cunningham - K
Wendell Davis - DB
Billy Davis - WR
John Flannery - G
Scott Galbraith - TE
Jason Garrett - QB
Randall Godfrey - OLB
Toby Gowin - P
Darryl Hardy - LB
George Hegamin - T
Dale Hellestrae - T
Nate Hemsley - LB
Chad Hennings - DT
Tony Hutson - G
Michael Irvin - WR
Daryl Johnston - FB
David LaFleur - TE
Leon Lett - DE
Brock Marion - FS
Kevin Mathis - CB
Hurvin McCormack - DT
Anthony Miller - WR
Singor Mobley - DB
Nate Newton - G
Kavika Pittman - DE
Deion Sanders - CB
Steve Scifres - G
Clay Shiver - C
Emmitt Smith - RB
Kevin Smith - CB
Vinson Smith - LB
Omar Stoutmire - DB
Fred Strickland - MLB
Nicky Sualua - RB
Broderick Thomas - LB
Tony Tolbert - DE
Mark Tuinei - T
Herschel Walker - FB
Kenny Wheaton - DB
Charlie Williams - DB
Erik Williams - T
Sherman Williams - RB
Stepfret Williams - WR
Wade Wilson - QB
Darren Woodson - SS

1997 Denver

Allen Aldridge - MLB
Flipper Anderson - WR
Steve Atwater - FS
Scott Bentley - K
Tyrone Braxton - SS
Bubby Brister - QB
Jamie Brown - T
Keith Burns - LB
Glenn Cadrez - LB
Dwayne Carswell - TE
Byron Chamberlain - TE
Ray Crockett - CB
Terrell Davis - RB
David Diaz-Infante - G
Dedrick Dodge - DB
Jason Elam - K
John Elway - QB
David Gamble - WR
Darrien Gordon - CB
Willie Green - WR
Howard Griffith - FB
Brian Habib - G
Harald Hasselbach - DE
Vaughn Hebron - RB
Randy Hilliard - DB
Patrick Jeffers - WR
Darrius Johnson - DB
Ernest Jones - DE
Tony Jones - T
Jeff Lewis - QB
Mike Lodish - NT
Derek Loville - RB
Anthony Lynn - RB
Ed McCaffrey - WR
Tim McKyer - DB
John Mobley - OLB
Tom Nalen - C
Dan Neil - G
Michael Dean Perry - DT
Trevor Pryce - DT
David Richie - NT
Bill Romanowski - OLB
Tom Rouen - P
Steve Russ - LB
Mark Schlereth - G
Shannon Sharpe - TE
Detron Smith - RB
Neil Smith - DE
Rod Smith - WR
Harry Swayne - T
Maa Tanuvasa - DT
Keith Traylor - DT
Tony Veland - DB
Alfred Williams - DE
Gary Zimmerman - T

1997 Detroit

Kevin Abrams - CB
Robert Bailey - DB
Matt Blundin - QB
Shane Bonham - DT
Stephen Boyd - MLB
Tommie Boyd - WR
Reggie Brown - OLB
Mark Carrier - FS
Pete Chryplewicz - TE
Harry Colon - DB
Mike Compton - G
Luther Elliss - DT
Kevin Glover - C
Ben Hanks - LB
Jason Hanson - K
Jeff Hartings - G
Hessley Hempstead - G
Kevin Hickman - TE
George Jamison - OLB
Greg Jeffries - DB
John Jett - P
Andre Johnson* - T
Richard Jordan - LB
Travis Kirschke - DT
Scott Kowalkowski - LB
Antonio London - OLB
Van Malone - SS
Kez McCorvey - WR
Pete Metzelaars - TE
Glyn Milburn - WR
Scott Mitchell - QB
Herman Moore - WR
Johnnie Morton - WR
Robert Porcher - DE
Daryl Porter - DB
Tony Ramirez - T
Corey Raymond - CB
Frank Reich - QB
Ron Rice - SS
Ron Rivers - RB
Ray Roberts - T
Juan Roque - T
Matt Russell - LB
Barry Sanders - HB
Cory Schlesinger - RB
Tracy Scroggins - DE
Tony Semple - G
David Sloan - TE
Marc Spindler - DE
Ryan Stewart - DB
Eric Stocz - TE
Larry Tharpe - T
Tommy Vardell - FB
Kerwin Waldroup - DE
Mike Wells - NT
Bryant Westbrook - CB
* Post

1997 Green Bay

Don Beebe - WR
Steve Bono - QB
Robert Brooks - WR
Bucky Brooks - DB
Gilbert Brown - DT
LeRoy Butler - SS
Mark Chmura - TE
Shannon Clavelle - DE
Mark Collins - DB
Chris Darkins - RB
Rob Davis - G
Tyrone Davis - TE
Jeff Dellenbach - C
Earl Dotson - T
Santana Dotson - DT
Doug Evans - CB
Brett Favre - QB
Paul Frase - DE
Antonio Freeman - WR
Bernardo Harris - MLB
Aaron Hayden - RB
William Henderson - FB
Craig Hentrich - P
Darius Holland - DT
Lamont Hollinquest - LB
Travis Jervey - RB
Reggie Johnson - TE
Seth Joyner - OLB
Randy Kinder - RB
George Koonce - LB
Bob Kuberski - DT
Dorsey Levens - RB
Ryan Longwell - K
Derrick Mayes - WR
Blaine McElmurry - DB
Keith McKenzie - DE
John Michels - T
Terry Mickens - WR
Roderick Mullen - DB
Craig Newsome - DB
Doug Pederson - QB
Roell Preston - WR
Mike Prior - DB
Marco Rivera - G
Eugene Robinson - FS
Bill Schroeder - WR
Darren Sharper - DB
Wayne Simmons - OLB
Jermaine Smith - DT
Aaron Taylor - G
Jeff Thomason - TE
Adam Timmerman - G
Ross Verba - T
Reggie White - DE
Bruce Wilkerson - T
Gabe Wilkins - DE
Brian Williams - OLB
Gerald Williams - DE
Tyrone Williams - CB
Frank Winters - C

1997 Indianapolis

Elijah Alexander - OLB
Aaron Bailey - WR
Brad Banta - TE
Jason Belser - FS
Tony Bennett - DE
Bert Berry - LB
Robert Blackmon - SS
Cary Blanchard - K
Sammie Burroughs - DB
Eugene Chung - G
Rico Clark - DB
Quentin Coryatt - OLB
Zack Crockett - RB
Sean Dawkins - WR
Ken Dilger - TE
Chris Doering - WR
Marshall Faulk - RB
Al Fontenot - DE
Dan Footman - DE
Chris Gardocki - P
Tarik Glenn - G
Steve Grant - MLB
Carlton Gray - CB
Derwin Gray - DB
Clif Groce - RB
Jim Harbaugh - QB
Marvin Harrison - WR
Chris Hetherington - RB
Kelly Holcomb - QB
Nate Jacquet - WR
Ellis Johnson - DT
Paul Justin - QB
Jay Leeuwenburg - C
Tony Mandarich - T
Steve Martin - DT
Jason Mathews - T
Dedric Mathis - CB
Tony McCoy - DT
Emmanuel McDaniel - DB
Ray McElroy - CB
Kaipo McGuire - WR
Adam Meadows - T
Monty Montgomery - DB
Steve Morrison - OLB
Leon Neal - RB
Marcus Pollard - TE
Roosevelt Potts - RB
Carl Powell - DE
Kendel Shello - DT
Scott Slutzker - TE
Brian Stablein - WR
David Tate - DB
Kipp Vickers - G
Scott Von der Ahe - LB
Lamont Warren - RB
Damon Watts - CB
Derek West - T
Bernard Whittington - DT
Doug Widell - G

1997 Jacksonville

Curtis Anderson - WR
Bryan Barker - P
Reggie Barlow - WR
Aaron Beasley - CB
Tony Boselli - T
Brant Boyer - LB
Tony Brackens - DE
Bucky Brooks - DB
Derek Brown - TE
Mark Brunell - QB
Michael Cheever - C
Ben Coleman - G
Don Davey - DT
Travis Davis - SS
Brian DeMarco - G
Kevin Devine - CB
Deon Figures - CB
Todd Fordham - T
Rich Griffith - TE
Dana Hall - DB
Ty Hallock - FB
James Hamilton - LB
Kevin Hardy - OLB
Mike Hollis - K
Chris Hudson - FS
Willie Jackson - WR
Rob Johnson - QB
Damon Jones - TE
Randy Jordan - RB
John Jurkovic - DT
Jeff Kopp - LB
Jeff Lageman - DE
Mike Logan - CB
Steve Matthews - QB
Keenan McCardell - WR
Natrone Means - RB
Pete Mitchell - TE
Will Moore - WR
Jeff Novak - G
Chris Parker - RB
Ricky Parker - DB
Seth Payne - DT
Kelvin Pritchett - DT
Eddie Robinson - OLB
Bryan Schwartz - MLB
Leon Searcy - T
Daimon Shelton - RB
Clyde Simmons - DE
Joel Smeenge - DE
Jimmy Smith - WR
James Stewart - RB
Dave Thomas - CB
Jabbar Threats - DE
Esera Tuaolo - NT
Rich Tylski - G
Jose White - LB
Dave Widell - C
Renaldo Wynn - DT

1997 Kansas City

Louie Aguiar - P
Marcus Allen - RB
Kimble Anders - FB
Darren Anderson - DB
Tom Barndt - DT
Donnell Bennett - RB
Vaughn Booker - DE
Bucky Brooks - DB
John Browning - DE
Dale Carter - CB
Shannon Clavelle - DE
Jeff Criswell - T
Anthony Davis - OLB
Lake Dawson - WR
Troy Dumas - LB
Donnie Edwards - ILB
Rich Gannon - QB
Tony Gonzalez - TE
Elvis Grbac - QB
Tim Grunhard - C
James Hasty - CB
Kerry Hicks - DE
Greg Hill - RB
Joe Horn - WR
Bobby Houston - LB
Danan Hughes - WR
Trezelle Jenkins - T
Clyde Johnson - CB
Kevin Lockett - WR
Greg Manusky - LB
Pellom McDaniels - OLB
Mark McMillian - DB
Dexter Nottage - DE
Glenn Parker - T
Ty Parten - DT
Brett Perriman - WR
Michael Dean Perry - DT
Joe Phillips - NT
Ted Popson - TE
Alfred Pupunu - TE
Tony Richardson - RB
Andre Rison - WR
Kevin Ross - DB
Todd Scott - DB
Will Shields - G
Tracy Simien - LB
Wayne Simmons - ILB
Jeff Smith - C
Marcus Spears - T
Pete Stoyanovich - K
David Szott - G
Ralph Tamm - G
Derrick Thomas - OLB
Billy Joe Tolliver - QB
Reggie Tongue - SS
Tamarick Vanover - WR
Derrick Walker - TE
Steve Wallace - T
Dan Williams - DE
Terry Wooden - ILB
Jerome Woods - FS

1997 Miami

Karim Abdul-Jabbar - RB
Dunstan Anderson - DE
Trace Armstrong - DE
Fred Barnett - WR
John Bock - C
Tim Bowens - DT
O.J. Brigance - LB
James Brown - T
Jeff Buckey - G
Terrell Buckley - CB
Shane Burton - DE
Mike Chalenski - DE
Mike Crawford - LB
DeWayne Dotson - LB
Troy Drayton - TE
Craig Erickson - QB
Daryl Gardener - DT
Anthony Harris - OLB
Corey Harris - FS
Dwight Hollier - LB
Qadry Ismail - WR
Calvin Jackson - CB
Tim Jacobs - DB
Charles Jordan - WR
John Kidd - P
Jim Kitts - LB
Sam Madison - CB
Brian Manning - WR
Olindo Mare - K
Dan Marino - QB
O. J. McDuffie - WR
Everett McIver - G
Jerris McPhail - RB
Ray Nealy - RB
Bernie Parmalee - FB
Brett Perriman - WR
Ed Perry - TE
Lawrence Phillips - RB
Roosevelt Potts - RB
Stanley Pritchett - FB
Kyle Richardson - P
Derrick Rodgers - OLB
Tim Ruddy - C
Mike Sheldon - T
Keith Sims - G
Irving Spikes - RB
Danny Stubbs - DE
Barron Tanner - DT
Jason Taylor - DE
George Teague - FS
Lamar Thomas - WR
Zach Thomas - MLB
Frank Wainright - TE
Bracey Walker - DB
Ronnie Ward - LB
Richmond Webb - T
Jerry Wilson - DB
Shawn Wooden - SS

1997 Minnesota

Derrick Alexander - DE
Jerry Ball - NT
Pete Bercich - LB
Mitch Berger - P
Tony Bland - WR
Orlando Bobo - G
Jeff Brady - MLB
Gregg Briggs - LB
Duane Butler - DB
Cris Carter - WR
Jeff Christy - C
Duane Clemons - DE
Stalin Colinet - DE
Randall Cunningham - QB
LeShun Daniels - G
Greg Davis - K
Greg DeLong - TE
Scott Dill - G
David Dixon - G
Dixon Edwards - OLB
Chuck Evans - FB
Jason Fisk - NT
Corey Fuller - CB
Ron George - LB
Andrew Glover - TE
Hunter Goodwin - TE
Torrian Gray - FS
Robert Green - RB
Robert Griffith - SS
Matt Hatchette - WR
Leroy Hoard - RB
Brad Johnson - QB
Andrew Jordan - TE
Everett Lindsay - C
Ed McDaniel - OLB
Randall McDaniel - G
Mike Morris - C
Harold Morrow - RB
Eddie Murray - K
David Palmer - RB
Anthony Prior - DB
John Randle - DT
Jake Reed - WR
Dwayne Rudd - LB
Bob Sapp - G
Fernando Smith - DE
Robert Smith - RB
Todd Steussie - T
Korey Stringer - T
Robert Tate - WR
Orlando Thomas - FS
Jay Walker* - QB
Chris Walsh - WR
Dewayne Washington - CB
Leonard Wheeler - DB
Moe Williams - RB
Tony Williams - DT
* Post

1997 New England

Bruce Armstrong - T
Mike Bartrum - TE
Drew Bledsoe - QB
Vincent Brisby - WR
Troy Brown - WR
Tedy Bruschi - LB
Keith Byars - FB
Chris Canty - DB
Chris Carter - DB
Willie Clay - FS
Ben Coates - TE
Todd Collins - OLB
Ferric Collons - DE
Vernon Crawford - LB
Derrick Cullors - RB
Damon Denson - G
Chad Eaton - DT
Ed Ellis - T
Tony Gaiter - WR
Sam Gash - RB
Mike Gisler - C
Terry Glenn - WR
Marrio Grier - RB
Jimmy Hitchcock - CB
Heath Irwin - G
Steve Israel - DB
Shawn Jefferson - WR
Dietrich Jells - WR
Ted Johnson - MLB
Mike D. Jones - DE
Max Lane - G
Ty Law - CB
Steve Lofton - DB
Curtis Martin - RB
Willie McGinest - DE
Mike McGruder - DB
Dave Meggett - RB
Lawyer Milloy - SS
Brandon Mitchell - DE
Marty Moore - LB
Zefross Moss - T
Lovett Purnell - TE
Scott Rehberg - T
Todd Rucci - G
Bernard Russ - LB
Sedrick Shaw - RB
Chris Slade - OLB
Chris Sullivan - DE
Henry Thomas - DT
Tom Tupa - QB
Danny Villa - T
Adam Vinatieri - K
Mark Wheeler - DT
Larry Whigham - DB
Dave Wohlabaugh - C
Devin Wyman - DT
Scott Zolak - QB

1997 New Orleans

Tom Ackerman - G
Vashone Adams - FS
Ink Aleaga - LB
Eric Allen - CB
Derrick Barnes - LB
Mario Bates - RB
Brett Bech - WR
Wes Bender - RB
Doug Brien - K
Je'Rod Cherry - DB
Don Davis - LB
Isaac Davis - G
Troy Davis - RB
Ernest Dixon - LB
John Farquhar - TE
Mark Fields - OLB
Jerry Fontenot - C
Kendall Gammon - C
La'Roi Glover - DT
Donovan Greer - CB
Eric Guliford - WR
Richard Harvey - OLB
Andre Hastings - WR
Mercury Hayes - WR
Chris Hewitt - DB
Randal Hill - WR
Keno Hills - G
Daryl Hobbs - WR
Billy Joe Hobert - QB
Joe Johnson - DE
Tony Johnson - TE
Clarence Jones - T
Rob Kelly - DB
Ed King - G
Sammy Knight - FS
Wayne Martin - DT
Andy McCollum - G
Fred McCrary - RB
Darren Mickell - DE
Keith Mitchell - LB
Alex Molden - CB

Chris Naeole - G
Anthony Newman - SS
Doug Nussmeier - QB
Keith Poole - WR
Willie Roaf - T
Austin Robbins - DT
Mark Royals - P
Pio Sagapolutele - DT
Nicky Savoie - TE
Heath Shuler - QB
Ricky Siglar - T
Brady Smith - DE
Irv Smith - TE
Jared Tomich - DE
Winfred Tubbs - MLB
Gunnard Twyner - WR
Mike Verstegen - G
Mickey Washington - DB
Danny Wuerffel - QB
Ray Zellars - FB

1997 New York Giants

Ray Agnew - DE
Kevin Alexander - WR
Jessie Armstead - OLB
Tiki Barber - RB
Greg Bishop - G
Chad Bratzke - DE
Dave Brown - QB
Marcus Buckley - LB
Chris Calloway - WR
Mike Cherry - QB
Doug Colman - LB
Howard Cross - TE
Brad Daluiso - K
Antonio Edwards - DE
Percy Ellsworth - DB
Derek Engler - C
Scott Galyon - LB
Sam Garnes - SS
Scott Gragg - T
Conrad Hamilton - DB
Keith Hamilton - DT
Rodney Hampton - RB
Robert Harris - DT
Ike Hilliard - WR
Bernard Holsey - DE
Cedric Jones - DE
Danny Kanell - QB
Eric Lane - RB
Thomas Lewis - WR
Robert Massey - DB
Brad Maynard - P
Corey Miller - OLB
Pete Monty - LB
Roman Oben - T
David Patten - WR
Erric Pegram - RB
Christian Peter - DT
Ryan Phillips - LB
Aaron Pierce - TE
Alfred Pupunu* - TE
Thomas Randolph - CB
Jerry Reynolds - T
Brandon Sanders - DB
Lance Scott - C
Jason Sehorn - CB
Phillippi Sparks - CB
Bryan Stoltenberg - C
Ron Stone - G
Michael Strahan - DE
Amani Toomer - WR
Charles Way - FB
Tyrone Wheatley - RB
Corey Widmer - MLB
Tito Wooten - FS
Rodney Young - DB
Rob Zatechka - G
*Post

1997 New York Jets

Richie Anderson - RB
Raymond Austin - DB
Fred Baxter - TE
Kyle Brady - TE
Corwin Brown - DB
John Burke - TE
Lamont Burns - G
Chad Cascadden - LB
Wayne Chrebet - WR
Chuck Clements - QB
Marcus Coleman - DB
J.R. Conrad - C
Terry Day - DE
Ronnie Dixon - NT
Hugh Douglas - DE
Roger Duffy - C
Jumbo Elliott - T
James Farrior - OLB
Jason Ferguson - DT
Matt Finkes - LB
Glenn Foley - QB
Aaron Glenn - CB
Dwayne Gordon - ILB
Jeff Graham - WR
Victor Green - SS
Jay Hagood - T
John Hall - K
Bobby Hamilton - DE
Brian Hansen - P
Chris Hayes - DB
Jerome Henderson - FS
John Hudson - C
Kerry Jenkins - T
Keyshawn Johnson - WR
Pepper Johnson - ILB
Leon Johnson - RB
Marvin Jones - ILB
Mo Lewis - OLB
Ernie Logan - NT
Ray Lucas - QB
Rick Lyle - DE
Siupeli Malamala - T
Ray Mickens - DB
Adrian Murrell - RB
Lorenzo Neal - RB
Neil O'Donnell - QB
Matt O'Dwyer - G
Lonnie Palelei - G
William Roberts - G
Otis Smith - CB
Jerald Sowell - RB
Rick Terry - DT
Alex Van Dyke - WR
Dedric Ward - WR
Casey Wiegmann - C
David Williams - T
Chris Wing - LB

1997 Oakland

Eddie Anderson - DB
Leo Araguz - P
Joe Aska - RB
Greg Biekert - MLB
Calvin Branch - CB
Larry Brown - DB
Tim Brown - WR
Aundray Bruce - DE
Perry Carter - CB
Rick Cunningham - T
Jerone Davison - RB
Rickey Dudley - TE
Derrick Fenner - RB
James Folston - OLB
Cole Ford - K
Rob Fredrickson - OLB
Jeff George - QB
Tim Hall - RB
Pat Harlow - T
Rob Holmberg - LB
Lester Holmes - G
Desmond Howard - WR
Grady Jackson - DE
James Jett - WR
Kevin Johnson - DT
Lance Johnstone - DE
Napoleon Kaufman - RB
Lincoln Kennedy - T
David Klingler - QB
Dan Land - DB
Chad Levitt - RB
Albert Lewis - CB
Lorenzo Lynch - DB
Russell Maryland - DT
Terry McDaniel - CB
Chester McGlockton - DT
John Henry Mills - LB
Mike Morton - OLB
Barret Robbins - C
Bob Rosenstiel - TE
Darrell Russell - DE
Kenny Shedd - WR
Anthony Smith - DE
Greg Townsend - DE
James Trapp - SS
Adam Treu - G
Olanda Truitt - WR
Eric Turner - FS
Aaron Wallace - LB
Lionel Washington - DB
Curtis Whitley - C
Harvey Williams - RB
Steve Wisniewski - G

1997 Philadelphia

Justin Armour - WR
Ian Beckles - G
Chris Boniol - K
Barrett Brooks - T
DeAuntae Brown - DB
Lonny Calicchio - P
Willie Clark - DB
Darion Conner - DE
Jerry Crafts - G
James Darling - OLB
Brian Dawkins - FS
Richard Dent - DE
Ty Detmer - QB
Charles Dimry - CB
Troy Drake - T
Jason Dunn - TE
Charles Emanuel - DB
Steve Everitt - C
Ray Farmer - OLB
DeShawn Fogle - LB
Irving Fryar - WR
Charlie Garner - RB
Mel Gray - RB
Rhett Hall - DT
Andy Harmon - DT
Jon Harris - DE
Jeff Herrod - LB
Bobby Hoying - QB
Tom Hutton - P
Edward Jasper - DT
Greg Jefferson - DE
Jimmie Johnson - TE
Chris Jones T. - WR
Jimmie Jones - DT
Ndukwe Kalu - DE
Randy Kinder - RB
Chad Lewis - TE
Mike Mamula - DE
Jermane Mayberry - T
Tim McTyer - DB
Bubba Miller - C
Joe Panos - G
Rodney Peete - QB
Mark Seay - WR
Darrin Smith - OLB
Freddie Solomon - WR
Duce Staley - RB
Matt Stevens - DB
Bobby Taylor - CB
Hollis Thomas - DT
William Thomas - OLB
Michael Timpson - WR
Kevin Turner - FB
Morris Unutoa - C
Troy Vincent - CB
Al Wallace - DE
Tim Watson - DB
Ricky Watters - RB
James Willis - MLB
Derrick Witherspoon - RB
Antwuan Wyatt - WR
Mike Zandofsky - G
Mike Zordich - SS

1997 Pittsburgh

Mike Adams - WR
Myron Bell - SS
Jerome Bettis - RB
Will Blackwell - WR
Kirk Botkin - TE
J.B. Brown - DB
Mark Bruener - TE
Andre Coleman - WR
Steven Conley - LB
Dermontti Dawson - C
Carlos Emmons - LB
Lethon Flowers - DB
Randy Fuller - DB
Oliver Gibson - DT
Jason Gildon - OLB
Nolan Harrison - DE
Courtney Hawkins - WR
Kevin Henry - DE
Corey Holliday - WR
Earl Holmes - ILB
John Jackson - T
Charles Johnson - WR
Norm Johnson - K
George Jones - RB
Donta Jones - OLB
Levon Kirkland - ILB
Carnell Lake - SS
Tim Lester - FB
Greg Lloyd - OLB
Mitch Lyons - TE
Rod Manuel - DE
Curtis Marsh - WR
Fred McAfee - RB
Josh Miller - P
Tom Myslinski - G
Chris Oldham - DB
Jerry Olsavsky - LB
Darren Perry - FS
Mike Quinn - QB
Orpheus Roye - DE
Troy Sadowski - TE
Chad Scott - CB
Brenden Stai - G
Joel Steed - NT
Jamain Stephens - T
Kordell Stewart - QB
Justin Strzelczyk - T
Jim Sweeney - C
Yancey Thigpen - WR
Mike Tomczak - QB
Mike Vrabel - DE
Paul Wiggins - T
Jon Witman - RB
Will Wolford - G
Donnell Woolford - CB

1997 St. Louis

Taje Allen - DB
Tony Banks - QB
Will Brice - P
Bern Brostek - C
Isaac Bruce - WR
Kevin Carter - DE
Charlie Clemons - LB
Ernie Conwell - TE
Keith Crawford - WR
Nate Dingle - LB
Troy Dumas - LB
Ernest Dye - T
D'Marco Farr - DT
Malcolm Floyd - WR
Wayne Gandy - T
John Gerak - G
Mike Gruttadauria - C
Britt Hager - LB
Craig Heyward - FB
Mike Horan - P
Mitch Jacoby - TE
Billy Jenkins - DB
Bill Johnson - DT
Mike A. Jones - OLB
Robert Jones - MLB
Muadianvita Kazadi - LB
Eddie Kennison - WR
Aaron Laing - TE
Amp Lee - RB
Todd Lyght - CB
Keith Lyle - FS
Gerald McBurrows - DB
Dexter McCleon - DB
Ryan McNeil - CB
Fred Miller - T
Jerald Moore - RB
Ronald Moore - RB
Leslie O'Neal - DE
Orlando Pace - T
Roman Phifer - OLB
Lawrence Phillips - RB
Bryan Robinson - DE
Jeff Robinson - DE
Jermaine Ross - WR
Joe Rowe - DB
Mark Rypien - QB
Mike Scurlock - DB
Torrance Small - WR
Vernice Smith - C
Lorenzo Styles - LB
J.T. Thomas - WR
David Thompson - RB
Ryan Tucker - C
Marquis Walker - CB
Brett Wallerstedt - LB
Zach Wiegert - G
Jeff Wilkins - K
Jay Williams - DE
Toby Wright - SS
Jeff Zgonina - DT

1997 San Diego

Darren Bennett - P
Tony Berti - T
David Binn - DB
Ben Bordelon - T
Paul Bradford - CB
Dorian Brew - DB
Gary Brown - RB
James Burgess - ILB
Lewis Bush - OLB
Kenny Bynum - RB
John Carney - K
Robert Chancey - RB
Joe Cocozzo - G
Marco Coleman - DE
Aaron Craver - FB
Ray Crittenden - WR
Greg Davis - K
Isaac Davis - G
Mike Dumas - FS
Greg Engel - C
Jim Everett - QB
Terrell Fletcher - RB
William Fuller - DE
Carwell Gardner - RB
Kurt Gouveia - ILB
Michael Hamilton - LB
Norman Hand - DT
Dwayne Harper - CB
Rodney Harrison - SS
Frank Hartley - TE
David Hendrix - DB
Bobby Houston - LB
Stan Humphries - QB
Greg Jackson - DB
Toran James - LB
Raylee Johnson - DE
Charlie Jones - WR
Freddie Jones - TE
Shawn Lee - DT
Tony Martin - WR
Raleigh McKenzie - C
Eric Metcalf - WR
Jim Mills - G
Shannon Mitchell - TE
Mike Mohring - DT
Mark Montreuil - DB
Vaughn Parker - T
John Parrella - DT
Erric Pegram - RB
Todd Philcox - QB
Marcus Price - T
Alfred Pupunu - TE
Latario Rachal - WR
Brian Roche - TE
Patrick Sapp - OLB
Junior Seau - ILB
Terrance Shaw - CB
Troy Sienkiewicz - G
Bryan Still - WR
Michael Swift - CB
Van Tuinei - DE
Craig Whelihan - QB
Gerome Williams - DB

1997 San Francisco

Gary Anderson - K
Roy Barker - DE
Jeff Brohm - QB
Zack Bronson - DB
Ray Brown - G
Junior Bryant - DE
Curtis Buckley - DB
Greg Clark - TE
Chris Dalman - C
Derrick Deese - T
Chris Doleman - DE
Tyronne Drakeford - DB
Jim Druckenmiller - QB
Marc Edwards - RB
Chad Fann - TE
William Floyd - FB
Kevin Gogan - G
Kevin Greene - DE
Merton Hanks - FS
Tim Hanshaw - G
Mark Harris - WR
Garrison Hearst - RB
Brent Jones - TE
Terry Kirby - RB
Randy Kirk - LB
Chuck Levy - RB
Brett Maxie - DB
Tim McDonald - SS
Rod Milstead - G
Kevin Mitchell - LB
Ken Norton - OLB
Terrell Owens - WR
Gary Plummer - MLB
Frank Pollack - T
Marquez Pope - CB
Daryl Price - DE
Albert Reese - DT
Jerry Rice - WR
Joe Rudolph - G
Mike Salmon - DB
Jesse Sapolu - C
Jim Schwantz - LB
Kirk Scrafford - T
Frankie Smith - DB
J.J. Stokes - WR
Dana Stubblefield - DT
Tommy Thompson - P
Iheanyi Uwaezuoke - WR
Darnell Walker - CB
Marvin Washington - DE
James Williams - LB
Lee Woodall - OLB
Rod Woodson - CB
Bryant Young - DT
Steve Young - QB

1997 Seattle

Sam Adams - DT
James Atkins - T
Howard Ballard - T
Mike Barber - LB
Frank Beede - G
Jay Bellamy - SS
Brian Blades - WR
Bennie Blades - SS
Greg Bloedorn - C
Steve Broussard - RB
Chad Brown - OLB
Reggie Brown - RB
Joe Cain - LB
Andre Coleman - WR
Carlester Crumpler - TE
Phillip Daniels - DE
Tyree Davis - WR
Antonio Edwards - DE
Christian Fauria - TE
John Friesz - QB
Joey Galloway - WR
Derrick Graham - G
Darryl Hardy - LB
Ronnie Harris - WR
Martin Harrison - DE
Tim Hauck - DB
Daryl Hobbs - WR
Walter Jones - T
Pete Kendall - G
Cortez Kennedy - DT
Jon Kitna - QB
Matt LaBounty - DE
Jeremy Lincoln - DB
James Logan - LB
Kevin Mawae - C
Deems May - TE
James McKnight - WR
Warren Moon - QB
Winston Moss - OLB
Riddick Parker - DT
Todd Peterson - K
Mike Pritchard - WR
C.J. Richardson - DB
Kyle Richardson - P
Reggie Rusk - CB
Dan Saleaumua - DT
Dexter Seigler - DB
Michael Sinclair - DE
Lamar Smith - RB
Shawn Springs - CB
Rohn Stark - P
Eric Stokes - DB
Mack Strong - FB
Fred Thomas - DB
Rick Tuten - P
Eric Unverzagt - LB
Chris Warren - RB
Dean Wells - MLB
Darryl Williams - FS
Grant Williams - T
Willie Williams - CB

1997 Tampa Bay

Donnie Abraham - CB
Chidi Ahanotu - DE
Mike Alstott - FB
Reidel Anthony - WR
Ronde Barber - CB
Tommy Barnhardt - P
Greg Bellisari - LB
Tony Bouie - S
Derrick Brooks - OLB
Horace Copeland - WR
Brad Culpepper - DT
Eric Curry - DE
John Davis - TE
Jorge Diaz - G
Trent Dilfer - QB
Kevin Dogins* - C
Warrick Dunn - RB
Jerry Ellison - RB
Kenneth Gant - S
Jeff Gooch - OLB
Paul Gruber - T
Patrick Hape - TE
Jackie Harris - TE
Brice Hunter - WR
Michael Husted - K
Tyoka Jackson - DE
Melvin Johnson - FS
Marcus Jones - DT
Andrew Jordan - TE
Sean Landeta - P
Tyrone Legette - CB
John Lynch - SS
Jason Maniecki - DT
Tony Mayberry - C
Frank Middleton - G
Charles Mincy - FS
Dave Moore - TE
Hardy Nickerson - MLB
Jason Odom - T
Anthony Parker - CB
Pete Pierson - T
Rufus Porter - OLB
Jim Pyne - G
Shelton Quarles - LB
Errict Rhett - RB
Reggie Rusk - CB
Warren Sapp - DT
Alshermond Singleton - LB
Robb Thomas - WR
Regan Upshaw - DE
Steve Walsh - QB
Steve White - DE
Karl Williams - WR
Jerry Wunsch - T
Floyd Young - CB
*Post

1997 Tennessee

Mike Archie - RB
Tomur Barnes - DB
Blaine Bishop - SS
Joe Bowden - OLB
Isaac Byrd - WR
Anthony Cook - DE
Willie Davis - WR
Al Del Greco - K
Kevin Donnalley - G
Anthony Dorsett - DB
Josh Evans - DT
Malcolm Floyd - WR
Henry Ford - DT
Eddie George - RB
Spencer George - RB
Mel Gray - RB
Mike Halapin - DT
Lemanski Hall - LB
Ronnie Harmon - RB
Kenny Holmes - DE
Brad Hopkins - T
Steve Jackson - CB
Lenoy Jones - LB
Roger Jones - DB
Joey Kent - WR
Terry Killens - LB
Dave Krieg - QB
Jason Layman - T
Darryll Lewis - CB
Roderick Lewis - TE
Pratt Lyons - DE
Lonnie Marts - OLB
Derrick Mason - WR
Bruce Matthews - G
George McCullough - DB
James McKeehan - TE
Steve McNair - QB
Bryant Mix - DE
Erik Norgard - G
James Ritchey - QB
Michael Roan - TE
James Roberson - DE
Marcus Robertson - FS
Rafael Robinson - DB
Reggie Roby - P
Jon Runyan - T
Derek Russell - WR
Chris Sanders - WR
Scott Sanderson - T
Dennis Stallings - LB
Mark Stepnoski - C
Rayna Stewart - SS
Rodney Thomas - RB
Denard Walker - CB
Gary Walker - DT
Armon Williams - DB
Barron Wortham - MLB
Frank Wycheck - TE

1997 Washington

Patrise Alexander - LB
Terry Allen - RB
Jamie Asher - TE
Darryl Ashmore - T
Brad Badger - G
Scott Blanton - K
Marc Boutte - DT
Larry Bowie - FB
Jesse Campbell - SS
Albert Connell - WR
Bob Dahl - G
Stephen Davis - RB
Cris Dishman - CB
Jamal Duff - DE
Henry Ellard - WR
Steve Emtman - DE
Leomont Evans - DB
Gus Frerotte - QB
David Frisch - TE
William Gaines - DT
Darrell Green - CB
Trent Green - QB
Alvin Harper - WR
Ken Harvey - OLB
Jeff Hostetler - QB
Chris Jacke - K
James Jenkins - TE
Tre' Johnson - G
Greg Jones - LB
Kelvin Kinney - DE
Ryan Kuehl - DT
Kenard Lang - DE
Marc Logan - RB
Chris Mims - DT
Brian Mitchell - RB
Rich Owens - DE
Joe Patton - G
Marvcus Patton - MLB
Darryl Pounds - DB
Shar Pourdanesh - T
Cory Raymer - C
Stanley Richard - FS
Keith Rucker - DT
Twan Russell - LB
Chris Sanders - TE
Don Sasa - DT
Leslie Shepherd - WR
Ed Simmons - T
Derek Smith - OLB
Keith Thibodeaux - DB
Chris Thomas - WR
James Thrash - WR
Dan Turk - C
Matt Turk - P
Jeff Uhlenhake - C
Brian Walker - DB
Michael Westbrook - WR
Williams Jamel - DB
Chris Zorich - DT

1998 Arizona

Ronnie Anderson - WR
Mario Bates - RB
Tommy Bennett - SS
Fred Brock - WR
Dave Brown - QB
J.B. Brown - CB
Lomas Brown - T
Larry Centers - FB
Corey Chavous - CB
Jon Clark - T
Anthony Clement - T
Jerome Daniels - G
Allen DeGraffenreid - T
Mike Devlin - C
James Dexter - T
Chris Dishman - G
Jerry Drake - DE
Chris Gedney - TE
Aaron Graham - C
Terry Hardy - TE
Jarius Hayes - TE
Lester Holmes - G
Ty Howard - DB
Terry Irving - LB
Chris Jacke - K
Matt Joyce - T
Trey Junkin - TE
Tom Knight - CB
Kwamie Lassiter - FS
Mark Maddox - LB
J.J. McCleskey - CB
Tony McCombs - OLB
Dell McGee - DB
Ronald McKinnon - MLB
Johnny McWilliams - TE
Eric Metcalf - WR
Jamir Miller - OLB
Rob Moore - WR
Mike Moten - DT
Adrian Murrell - RB
Joe Nedney - K
Michael Pittman - RB
Scott Player - P
Jake Plummer - QB
Simeon Rice - DE

Frank Sanders - WR
Patrick Sapp - LB
Carl Simpson - DT
Mark Smith - DT
Eric Swann - DT
Rashod Swinger - DT
Pat Tillman - FS
Andre Wadsworth - DE
Zack Walz - LB
Aeneas Williams - CB
Bernard Wilson - DT

1998 Atlanta

Morten Andersen - K
Darren Anderson - DB
Jamal Anderson - RB
Lester Archambeau - DE
Chris Bayne - DB
Cornelius Bennett - OLB
Juran Bolden - DB
Michael Booker - CB
Ronnie Bradford - CB
Keith Brooking - LB
Omar Brown - DB
Ray Buchanan - CB
John Burrough - DE
Devin Bush - DB
Chris Chandler - QB
Bob Christian - FB
Calvin Collins - G
Henri Crockett - OLB
Steve DeBerg - QB
Gary Downs - RB
Shane Dronett - DT
Tim Dwight - WR
Antonio Edwards - DE
Randy Fuller - DB
Jammi German - WR
Tony Graziani - QB
Harold Green - RB
Travis Hall - DT
Bob Hallen - C
Ruffin Hamilton - LB
Ronnie Harris - WR
Todd Kinchen - WR
Brian Kozlowski - TE
Tony Martin - WR
Terance Mathis - WR
Ken Oxendine - RB
Jose Portilla - T
Eugene Robinson - FS
Ephraim Salaam - T
O.J. Santiago - TE
Craig Sauer - OLB
Adam Schreiber - C
Chuck Smith - DE
Ed Smith - TE
Dan Stryzinski - P
Shawn Swayda - DE
Ben Talley - LB
Robbie Tobeck - C
Esera Tuaolo - NT
Jessie Tuggle - MLB
William White - SS
Bob Whitfield - T
Dave Widell - G
Elijah Williams - DB
Gene Williams - G

1998 Baltimore

James Atkins - G
Jeff Blackshear - G
Peter Boulware - OLB
Donny Brady - DB
Cornell Brown - LB
Orlando Brown - T
Rob Burnett - DE
Ben Cavil - G
Kenyon Cotton - RB
Lional Dalton - DT
Mike Flynn - T
Spencer Folau - T
Paul Frase - DE
Mike Frederick - DE
Jay Graham - RB
Eric Green - TE
Jim Harbaugh - QB
Corey Harris - FS
Kim Herring - FS
Priest Holmes - RB
Michael Jackson - WR
DeRon Jenkins - CB
Pat Johnson - WR
James Jones - DT
Brian Kinchen - TE
Jeff Kopp - LB
Harper LeBel - TE
Jermaine Lewis - WR
Ray Lewis - MLB
Tyrus McCloud - LB
Michael McCrary - DE
Jeff Mitchell - C
Stevon Moore - SS
A.J. Ofodile - TE
Jonathan Ogden - T
Jerry Olsavsky - LB
Tyrell Peters - LB
Roosevelt Potts - FB
Errict Rhett - RB
Kyle Richardson - P
Wally Richardson - QB
James Roe - WR
Jamie Sharper - OLB
Tony Siragusa - DT
Duane Starks - CB
Ralph Staten - DB
Matt Stover - K
Bennie Thompson - DB
Floyd Turner - WR
Keith Washington - DE
Larry Webster - DT
John Williams - DB
Wally Williams - G
Rod Woodson - CB
Ryan Yarborough - WR
Eric Zeier - QB

1998 Buffalo

Ethan Albright - T
Dan Brandenburg - LB
Ruben Brown - G
Steve Christie - K
Bill Conaty - C
Sam Cowart - ILB
Joe Cummings - LB
Quinn Early - WR
John Fina - T
Doug Flutie - QB
Cole Ford - K
Sam Gash - FB
Donovan Greer - CB
Phil Hansen - DE
Robert Hicks - T
Ray Hill - DB
John Holecek - ILB
Darick Holmes - RB
Ken Irvin - CB
Raymond Jackson - DB
Lonnie Johnson - TE
Rob Johnson - QB
Henry Jones - SS
Marlon Kerner - DB
Jonathan Linton - RB
Kamil Loud - WR
Emanuel Martin - FS
Chris Mohr - P
Sean Moran - DE
Eric Moulds - WR
Jamie Nails - T
Gabe Northern - OLB
Jerry Ostroski - T
Joe Panos - G
Marlo Perry - LB
Mark Pike - LB
Daryl Porter - DB
Shawn Price - DE
Andre Reed - WR
Jay Riemersma - TE
Sam Rogers - OLB
Kurt Schulz - FS
Wayne Simmons - ILB
Eric Smedley - DB
Antowain Smith - RB
Bruce Smith - DE
Thomas Smith - CB
Marcus Spriggs - T
Thurman Thomas - RB
Alex Van Pelt - QB
Ted Washington - NT
Marcellus Wiley - DE
Clarence Williams - RB
Kevin Williams - WR
Pat Williams - DT
Duane Young - TE
Dusty Zeigler - C

1998 Carolina

Brent Alexander - FS
Micheal Barrow - ILB
Michael Bates - WR
Steve Beuerlein - QB
Tim Biakabutuka - RB
Rob Bohlinger - T
Juran Bolden - DB
Jeff Brady - ILB
Blake Brockermeyer - T
Luther Broughton - TE
Matt Campbell - G
Mark Carrier - WR
Rae Carruth - WR
Kerry Collins - QB
Norbert Davidds-Garrido - T
Eric Davis - CB
Mike Dulaney - RB
Doug Evans - CB
William Floyd - FB
Mike Fox - NT
Frank Garcia - G
Sean Gilbert - DE
Derwin Gray - DB
Kevin Greene - OLB
Donald Hayes - WR
Raghib Ismail - WR
Paul Janus - T
Jerry Jensen - LB
Anthony Johnson - RB
Ernest Jones - DE
John Kasay - K
Corbin Lacina - G
Fred Lane - RB
Lamar Lathon - LB
Greg Lloyd - OLB
Steve Lofton - CB
Kris Mangum - TE
Lenny McGill - DB
Les Miller - DT
Mike Minter - SS
Tim Morabito - NT
Muhsin Muhammad - WR
Winslow Oliver - RB
Jason Peter - DE
Anthony Redmon - G
Spencer Reid - LB
Damien Richardson - SS
Tarek Saleh - LB
Don Sasa - DT
Steve Scifres - T
Ricky Siglar - T
Rod Smith - DB
Bryan Stoltenberg - C
Dwight Stone - WR
Ryan Sutter - DB
Kinnon Tatum - LB
Rick Terry - DT
Tony Veland - FS
Danny Villa - C
Wesley Walls - TE
Ken Walter - P
Leonard Wheeler - DB

1998 Chicago Bears

James Allen - RB
John Allred - TE
Raymond Austin - DB
Ricky Bell - DB
Edgar Bennett - RB
Fabien Bownes - WR
Marty Carter - SS
Tom Carter - CB
Robert Chancey - RB
Andre Collins - LB
Curtis Conway - WR
Terry Cousin - CB
Chris Draft - LB
Bobby Engram - WR
Curtis Enis - RB
Jim Flanigan - DT
Marlon Forbes - DB
Paul Grasmanis - DT
Lemanski Hall - LB
Ty Hallock - FB
Sean Harris - OLB
Walt Harris - CB
Andy Heck - T
Jimmy Herndon - T
Randy Hilliard - DB
Mike Horan - P
Greg Huntington - C
Jeff Jaeger - K
Erik Kramer - QB
Olin Kreutz - C
Shawn Lee - DE
John Mangum - DB
Patrick Mannelly - T
Alonzo Mayes - TE
Ricardo McDonald - OLB
Glyn Milburn - RB
Barry Minter - MLB
Moses Moreno - QB
Bam Morris - RB
Tony Parrish - FS
Chris Penn - WR
Todd Perry - G
Carl Reeves - DE
Bryan Robinson - DE
Marcus Robinson - WR
Todd Sauerbrun - P
Jim Schwantz - LB
Frankie Smith - DB
Steve Stenstrom - QB
John Thierry - DE
Mark Thomas - DE
Chris Villarrial - G
Mike Wells - DT
Ryan Wetnight - TE
Casey Wiegmann - C
James Williams - T

1998 Cincinnati

Ashley Ambrose - CB
Willie Anderson - T
Michael Bankston - DE
Marco Battaglia - TE
Myron Bell - DB
Brandon Bennett - RB
Eric Bieniemy - RB
Ken Blackman - G
Roosevelt Blackmon - CB
Michael Blair - RB
Jeff Blake - QB
Rich Braham - G
Darrick Brilz - C
Anthony Brown - G
Steve Bush - FB
Ki-Jana-Carter - RB
John Copeland - NT
Brad Costello - P
Canute Curtis - LB
Corey Dillon - HB
David Dunn - WR
Steve Foley - LB
James Francis - OLB
Damon Gibson - WR
Mike Goff - G
Billy Granville - LB
Brock Gutierrez - C
Artrell Hawkins - CB
James Hundon - WR
Willie Jackson - WR
Lee Johnson - P
Rod Jones - T
Paul Justin - QB
Eric Kresser - QB
Jevon Langford - DE
Tremain Mack - DB
Ric Mathias - DB
Tony McGee - TE
Brian Milne - FB
Kelvin Moore - DB
Greg Myers - FS
Neil O'Donnell - QB
Rod Payne - C
Doug Pelfrey - K
Carl Pickens - WR
Andre Purvis - DT
Thomas Randolph - DB
Adrian Ross - LB
Kevin Sargent - T
Corey Sawyer - DB
Darnay Scott - WR
Sam Shade - SS
Scott Shaw - G
Brian Simmons - ILB
Clyde Simmons - DE
Takeo Spikes - ILB
Jimmy Sprotte - LB
Glen Steele - DT
Mike Thompson - DT
Greg Truitt - C
Tom Tumulty - ILB
Kimo von Oelhoffen - NT
Stepfret Williams - WR
Reinard Wilson - OLB

1998 Dallas

Flozell Adams - G
Troy Aikman - QB
Larry Allen - T
Antonio Anderson - DE
Terry Billups - CB
Eric Bjornson - TE
Larry Brown - DB
Hayward Clay - TE
Dexter Coakley - OLB
Richie Cunningham - K
Billy Davis - WR
Greg Ellis - DE
Jason Garrett - QB
Randall Godfrey - OLB
Toby Gowin - P
Darren Hambrick - LB
Dale Hellestrae - G
Nate Hemsley - LB
Chad Hennings - NT
Tyrone Hughes - DB
Tony Hutson - T
Michael Irvin - WR
Patrick Jeffers - WR
Daryl Johnston - FB
Mike Kiselak - C
David LaFleur - TE
Leon Lett - DT
Kevin Mathis - CB
Hurvin McCormack - DT
Everett McIver - G
Ernie Mills - WR
Singor Mobley - DB
Michael Myers - DT
Nate Newton - G
Jeff Ogden - WR
Kavika Pittman - DE
Mike Quinn - QB
Izell Reese - DB
Oliver Ross - T
Deion Sanders - CB
Clay Shiver - C
Artie Smith - DE
Emmitt Smith - RB
Kevin Smith - CB
Omar Stoutmire - FS
Fred Strickland - MLB
Nicky Sualua - RB
George Teague - FS
Robert Thomas - LB
Chris Warren - RB
Kenny Wheaton - DB
Charlie Williams - DB
Erik Williams - T
Sherman Williams - RB
Darren Woodson - SS

1998 Denver

Justin Armour - WR
Steve Atwater - FS
Chris Banks - G
Tyrone Braxton - SS
Bubby Brister - QB
Cyron Brown - DE
Eric Brown - SS
Keith Burns - LB
Glenn Cadrez - MLB
Dwayne Carswell - TE
Byron Chamberlain - TE
George Coghill - DB
Ray Crockett - CB
Terrell Davis - RB
David Diaz-Infante - G
Jason Elam - K
John Elway - QB
Darrien Gordon - CB
Willie Green - WR
Brian Griese - QB
Howard Griffith - FB
Harald Hasselbach - DE
Vaughn Hebron - RB
Tory James - DB
Darrius Johnson - DB
Ernest Jones - DE
Tony Jones - T
Seth Joyner - LB
Matt Lepsis - T
Mike Lodish - NT
Derek Loville - RB
Anthony Lynn - RB
Ed McCaffrey - WR
John Mobley - OLB
Tom Nalen - C
Marcus Nash - WR
Dan Neil - G
Tito Paul - DB
Trevor Pryce - DT
Bill Romanowski - OLB
Tom Rouen - P
Mark Schlereth - G
Shannon Sharpe - TE
Detron Smith - RB
Neil Smith - DE
Rod Smith - WR
Harry Swayne - T
Maa Tanuvasa - DE
Keith Traylor - DT
Marvin Washington - DE
Nate Wayne - LB
Alfred Williams - DE

1998 Detroit

Kevin Abrams - CB
Allen Aldridge - OLB
Robert Bailey - DB
Charlie Batch - QB
Eric Beverly - C
Stephen Boyd - MLB
Tommie Boyd - WR
Lamar Campbell - DB
Mark Carrier - FS
Mike Chalenski - DE
Pete Chryplewicz - TE
Mike Compton - G
Germane Crowell - WR
Luther Elliss - DT
Terry Fair - CB
Rob Fredrickson - OLB
Jason Hanson - K
Jeff Hartings - G
Kevin Hickman - TE
Darius Holland - DT
George Jamison - LB
Greg Jeffries - DB
John Jett - P
Andre Johnson - T
Richard Jordan - MLB
John Kidd - P
Scott Kowalkowski - LB
Jerris McPhail - RB
Scott Mitchell - QB
Herman Moore - WR
Johnnie Morton - WR
Brock Olivo - RB
Kevin O'Neill - LB
Dan Owens - NT
Robert Porcher - DE
Jim Pyne - C
Tony Ramirez - T
Walter Rasby - TE
Travis Reece - FB
Frank Reich - QB
Ron Rice - SS
Ron Rivers - RB
Ray Roberts - T
Barry Sanders - HB
Don Sasa - DT
Cory Schlesinger - RB
Tracy Scroggins - DE
Tony Semple - G
David Sloan - TE
Marc Spindler - DT
Brian Stablein - WR
Ryan Stewart - DB
Kywin Supernaw - DB
Henry Taylor - DT
Larry Tharpe - T
Corey Thomas - WR
Marvin Thomas - DE
Tommy Vardell - FB
Kerwin Waldroup - DE
Bryant Westbrook - CB

1998 Green Bay

Joseph Andruzzi - G
Roosevelt Blackmon - CB
Michael Blair - RB
Juran Bolden - DB
Vaughn Booker - DE
Corey Bradford - WR
Robert Brooks - WR
Gilbert Brown - DT
Jonathan Brown - DE
LeRoy Butler - SS
Mark Chmura - TE
Kerry Cooks - DB
Russell Copeland - WR
Rob Davis - DT
Tyrone Davis - TE
Jeff Dellenbach - C
Earl Dotson - T
Santana Dotson - DT
Brett Favre - QB
Mike Flanagan - C
Antonio Freeman - WR
Scott Galbraith - TE
Bernardo Harris - MLB
Raymont Harris - RB
William Henderson - FB
Vonnie Holliday - DE
Lamont Hollinquest - LB
Darick Holmes - RB
Travis Jervey - RB
Jim Kitts - RB
George Koonce - OLB
Bob Kuberski - DT
Sean Landeta - P
Dorsey Levens - RB
Antonio London - LB
Ryan Longwell - K
Billy Lyon - DE
Brian Manning - WR
Derrick Mayes - WR
Scott McGarrahan - DB
Keith McKenzie - DE
Jim Nelson* - LB
Craig Newsome - CB
Doug Pederson - QB
Roell Preston - WR
Mike Prior - DB
Marco Rivera - G
Bill Schroeder - WR
Darren Sharper - FS
Rod Smith - DB
Pat Terrell - DB
Jeff Thomason - TE
Adam Timmerman - G
Ross Verba - T
Jude Waddy - LB
Mike Wahle - G
Reggie White - DE
Brian Williams - OLB
Tyrone Williams - CB
Matt Willig - T
Frank Winters - C
* Post

1998 Indianapolis

Elijah Alexander - OLB
Billy Austin - DB
Aaron Bailey - WR
Brad Banta - TE
Mike Barber - MLB
Jason Belser - FS
Bert Berry - DE
Robert Blackmon - SS
Tony Blevins - DB
Jeff Burris - CB
Larry Chester - DT
Jason Chorak - LB
Rico Clark - DB
Steven Conley - LB
Zack Crockett - RB
Ken Dilger - TE
Keith Elias - RB
Marshall Faulk - RB
Al Fontenot - DE
Dan Footman - DE
Chris Gardocki - P
Tarik Glenn - T
E.G. Green - WR
Scott Greene - RB
Marvin Harrison - WR
Tim Hauck - FS
Jeff Herrod - MLB
Chris Hetherington - RB
Craig Heyward - RB
Rob Holmberg - LB
Waverly Jackson - T
Ellis Johnson - DT
Jason Johnson - C
Antony Jordon - LB
Jay Leeuwenburg - C
Tony Mandarich - G
Peyton Manning - QB
Steve Martin - DT
Tony McCoy - DT
Ray McElroy - DB
Kaipo McGuire - WR
Steve McKinney - G
Adam Meadows - T
Monty Montgomery - CB
Larry Moore - G
Steve Morrison - OLB
Tom Myslinski - G
Jerome Pathon - WR
Marcus Pollard - TE
Tyrone Poole - CB
Andre Royal - OLB
Freddie Scott - WR
Kendel Shello - DT
Torrance Small - WR
Mark Thomas - DE
Ratcliff Thomas - LB
Van Tuinei - DE
Mike Vanderjagt - K
Lamont Warren - RB
Bernard Whittington - DE
Jeff Zgonina - DT

1998 Jacksonville

Tavian Banks - RB
Bryan Barker - P
Reggie Barlow - WR
Aaron Beasley - CB
Tony Boselli - T
Brant Boyer - LB
Tony Brackens - DE
Mark Brunell - QB
Ben Coleman - G
Zack Crockett - RB
Eric Curry - DE
Donovin Darius - SS
Travis Davis - FS
Brian DeMarco - G
Kevin Devine - DB
Deon Figures - CB
Todd Fordham - T
Rich Griffith - TE
James Hamilton - LB
Kevin Hardy - OLB
Mike Hollis - K
Chris Howard - RB
Chris Hudson - FS
Damon Jones - TE
George Jones - RB
John Jurkovic - DT
Jeff Kopp - LB
Jeff Lageman - DE
Mike Logan - DB
Reggie Lowe - DE
Jamie Martin - QB
Eddie Mason - LB
Keenan McCardell - WR
Blaine McElmurry - DB
Tom McManus - MLB
Pete Mitchell - TE
Will Moore - WR
Quentin Neujahr - C
Jeff Novak - G
Bryce Paup - OLB
Seth Payne - DT
Kelvin Pritchett - DT
Jonathan Quinn - QB
Troy Sadowski - TE
Bryan Schwartz - MLB
Leon Searcy - T
Tawambi Settles - DB
Daimon Shelton - FB
Joel Smeenge - DE
Fernando Smith - DE
Jimmy Smith - WR
James Stewart - RB
Erik Storz - LB
Cordell Taylor - CB
Fred Taylor - RB
Dave Thomas - CB
Jabbar Threats - DE
Rich Tylski - G
John Wade - C
Jose White - DT
Alvis Whitted - WR
Lamanzer Williams - DE
Renaldo Wynn - DE

1998 Kansas City

Louie Aguiar - P
Derrick Alexander - WR
Kimble Anders - FB
Tom Barndt - NT
Donnell Bennett - RB
Bucky Brooks - DB
John Browning - DE
Dale Carter - CB
Keith Crawford - DB
Jeff Criswell - T
Anthony Davis - OLB
Ernest Dixon - LB
Ronnie Dixon - DT
Donnie Edwards - MLB
Greg Favors - ILB
Rich Gannon - QB
Ron George - LB
Tony Gonzalez - TE
Elvis Grbac - QB
Tim Grunhard - C
James Hasty - CB
Eric Hicks - DE
Darius Holland - DT
Joe Horn - WR
Danan Hughes - WR
Melvin Johnson - DB
Jason Kaiser - CB
Kevin Lockett - WR
Greg Manusky - LB
Pellom McDaniels - DE
Chester McGlockton - DT
Mark McMillian - CB
Bam Morris - HB
Leslie O'Neal - DE
Glenn Parker - G
Ty Parten - DE
Ted Popson - TE
Derrick Ransom - DT
Tony Richardson - RB
Victor Riley - T
Andre Rison - WR
Brian Roche - TE
Rashaan Shehee - RB
Will Shields - G
Ricky Siglar - T
Wayne Simmons - ILB
Jeff Smith - C
Marcus Spears - T
Pete Stoyanovich - K
David Szott - G

Ralph Tamm - G
Willy Tate - TE
Derrick Thomas - OLB
Reggie Tongue - SS
Tamarick Vanover - WR
Bracey Walker - DB
Eric Warfield - DB
Jerrott Willard - LB
Robert Williams - DB
Jerome Woods - FS

1998 Miami

Karim Abdul-Jabbar - RB
Trace Armstrong - DE
John Avery - RB
John Bock - G
Tim Bowens - DT
O.J. Brigance - LB
Lorenzo Bromell - DE
James Brown - T
Jeff Buckey - G
Terrell Buckley - CB
Shane Burton - DT
Horace Copeland - WR
Kirby Dar Dar - WR
Mark Dixon - G
Kevin Donnalley - G
Todd Doxzon - QB
Troy Drayton - TE
Oronde Gadsden - WR
Daryl Gardener - DT
Anthony Harris - LB
Ray Hill - DB
Dwight Hollier - LB
Damon Huard - QB
Larry Izzo - LB
Calvin Jackson - SS
Nate Jacquet - WR
Robert Jones - OLB
Charles Jordan - WR
Henry Lusk - TE
Sam Madison - CB
Olindo Mare - K
Dan Marino - QB
Brock Marion - FS
O. J. McDuffie - WR
Kenny Mixon - DE
Ronald Moore - RB
Bernie Parmalee - RB
Ed Perry - TE
Stanley Pritchett - FB
Derrick Rodgers - OLB
Tim Ruddy - C
Mike Sheldon - T
Brent Smith - T
Rayna Stewart - DB
Barry Stokes - G
Danny Stubbs - DE
Patrick Surtain - DB
Barron Tanner - DT
Jason Taylor - DE
Lamar Thomas - WR
Zach Thomas - MLB
Iheanyi Uwaezuoke - WR
Frank Wainright - TE
Brian Walker - DB
Richmond Webb - T
Klaus Wilmsmeyer - P
Jerry Wilson - DB
Shawn Wooden - DB

1998 Minnesota

Derrick Alexander - DE
Gary Anderson - K
Obafemi Ayanbadejo - RB
Jerry Ball - DT
Antonio Banks - DB
Anthony Bass - DB
Pete Bercich - LB
Mitch Berger - P
Matt Birk - T
Tony Bland - WR
Orlando Bobo - G
Gregg Briggs* - DB
Duane Butler - DB
Cris Carter - WR
Jeff Christy - C
Duane Clemons - DE
Stalin Colinet - DE
Randall Cunningham - QB
Greg DeLong - TE
David Dixon - G
Dixon Edwards - OLB
Chuck Evans - FB
Jay Fiedler - QB
Jason Fisk - DT
Corey Fuller - CB
Andrew Glover - TE
Hunter Goodwin - TE
Torrian Gray - DB
Robert Griffith - SS
Matt Hatchette - WR
Jimmy Hitchcock - CB
Leroy Hoard - RB
Bobby Houston - LB
Brad Johnson - QB
Everett Lindsay - G
Chris Liwienski - T
Kivuusama Mays - LB
Ed McDaniel - MLB
Randall McDaniel - G
Ramos McDonald - CB
Mike Morris - C
Harold Morrow - RB
Randy Moss - WR
David Palmer - RB
Anthony Phillips - DB
John Randle - DE
Jake Reed - WR
Dwayne Rudd - OLB
Robert Smith - RB
Todd Steussie - T
Korey Stringer - T
Robert Tate - WR
Orlando Thomas - FS
Chris Walsh - WR
Ben Williams - DT
Moe Williams - RB
Tony Williams - DT
Kailee Wong - LB
*Post

1998 New England

Bruce Armstrong - T
Mike Bartrum - TE
Drew Bledsoe - QB
Vincent Brisby - WR
Troy Brown - WR
Tedy Bruschi - OLB
Chris Canty - CB
Tony Carter - FB
Chris Carter - DB
Willie Clay - FS
Ben Coates - TE
Todd Collins - OLB
Ferric Collons - DE
Dana Cottrell - LB
Vernon Crawford - LB
Derrick Cullors - RB
Damon Denson - G
Chad Eaton - DT
Robert Edwards - RB
Henry Ellard - WR
Ed Ellis - T
Chris Floyd - RB
Terry Glenn - WR
Heath Irwin - G
Steve Israel - CB
Shawn Jefferson - WR
Ted Johnson - MLB
Tebucky Jones - DB
Anthony Ladd - WR
Max Lane - G
Ty Law - CB
Steve Lofton - DB
Willie McGinest - DE
Lawyer Milloy - SS
Brandon Mitchell - DT
Marty Moore - LB
Zefross Moss - T
Lovett Purnell - TE
Scott Rehberg - T
Leonta Rheams - DT
Todd Rucci - G
Bernard Russ - LB
Rod Rutledge - TE
Harold Shaw - RB
Sedrick Shaw - RB
Tony Simmons - WR
Chris Slade - OLB
Greg Spires - DE
Shawn Stuckey - LB
Chris Sullivan - DE
Henry Thomas - DT
Tom Tupa - P
Adam Vinatieri - K
Mark Wheeler - DT
Larry Whigham - DB
Dave Wohlabaugh - C
Scott Zolak - QB

1998 New Orleans

Tom Ackerman - C
Ink Aleaga - LB
Brett Bech - WR
Chris Bordano - MLB
Doug Brien - K
Je'Rod Cherry - DB
Cameron Cleeland - TE
Kerry Collins - QB
Chad Cota - SS
Aaron Craver - RB
Don Davis - LB
Troy Davis - RB
Sean Dawkins - WR
Tyronne Drakeford - CB
John Farquhar - TE
Mark Fields - OLB
Jerry Fontenot - C
Kendall Gammon - C
La'Roi Glover - DT
Eric Guliford - WR
Andre Hastings - WR
Chris Hewitt - DB
Keno Hills - T
Billy Joe Hobert - QB
Qadry Ismail - WR
Alonzo Johnson - WR
Joe Johnson - DE
Tony Johnson - TE
Brian Jones - LB
Clarence Jones - T
Rob Kelly - DB
Sammy Knight - FS
Earl Little - CB
Wayne Martin - DT
Andy McCollum - G
Keith Mitchell - OLB
Kevin Mitchell - MLB
Alex Molden - CB
Chris Naeole - G
Wilmont Perry - RB
Julian Pittman - DE
Keith Poole - WR
Willie Roaf - T
Austin Robbins - DT
Mark Royals - P
Ricky Siglar - T
Scott Slutzker - TE
Brady Smith - DE
Lamar Smith - HB
Vinson Smith - LB
Billy Joe Tolliver - QB
Jared Tomich - DE
Kyle Turley - G
Ron Warner - LB
Fred Weary - DB
Josh Wilcox - TE
Troy Wilson - DE
Danny Wuerffel - QB
Ray Zellars - RB

1998 New York Giants

Brian Alford - WR
Jessie Armstead - OLB
Tiki Barber - RB
Greg Bishop - G
Kory Blackwell - CB
Chad Bratzke - DE
Gary Brown - RB
Curtis Buckley - DB
Marcus Buckley - OLB
Chris Calloway - WR
Mike Cherry - QB
Doug Colman - LB
Greg Comella - RB
Howard Cross - TE
Brad Daluiso - K
Percy Ellsworth - SS
Derek Engler - C
Scott Galyon - LB
Sam Garnes - SS
Scott Gragg - T
Kent Graham - QB
Carlton Gray - DB
Andy Haase - TE
Conrad Hamilton - CB
Keith Hamilton - DT
Robert Harris - DT
Ike Hilliard - WR
Bernard Holsey - DT
Cedric Jones - DE
Joe Jurevicius - WR
Danny Kanell - QB
Jeremy Lincoln - DB
Brad Maynard - P
Pete Monty - LB
Roman Oben - T
Lonnie Palelei - G
David Patten - WR
Christian Peter - DT
Ryan Phillips - LB
Alfred Pupunu - TE
Jerry Reynolds - G
Brandon Sanders - DB
Lance Scott - C
Phillippi Sparks - CB
Ron Stone - G
Michael Strahan - DE
Amani Toomer - WR
Charles Way - FB
Tyrone Wheatley - RB
Jason Whittle - G
Corey Widmer - MLB
George Williams - DT
Shaun Williams - DB
Tito Wooten - FS
Rodney Young - DB

1998 New York Jets

Richie Anderson - RB
Fred Baxter - TE
Dorian Boose - DE
Kyle Brady - TE
Corwin Brown - DB
Todd Burger - G
Keith Byars - FB
Chad Cascadden - LB
Wayne Chrebet - WR
Marcus Coleman - DB
Bryan Cox - OLB
Jumbo Elliott - T
Jason Fabini - T
James Farrior - LB
Jason Ferguson - DT
Glenn Foley - QB
Scott Frost - DB
Nick Gallery - P
Mike Gisler - G
Aaron Glenn - CB
Dwayne Gordon - OLB
Victor Green - SS
John Hall - K
Bobby Hamilton - DE
Brian Hansen - P
Carl Hansen - DT
Chris Hayes - DB
Jerome Henderson - FS
Rob Holmberg - LB
John Hudson - G
Kerry Jenkins - T
Keyshawn Johnson - WR
Pepper Johnson - MLB
Leon Johnson - RB
John Kidd - P
Mo Lewis - OLB
Ernie Logan - DT
Ray Lucas - QB
Rick Lyle - DE
Curtis Martin - RB
Kevin Mawae - C
Dave Meggett - RB
Ray Mickens - DB
Matt O'Dwyer - G
Eric Ogbogu - DE
Anthony Pleasant - DE
Craig Powell - LB
Otis Smith - CB
Jerald Sowell - RB
Blake Spence - TE
Vinny Testaverde - QB
Alex Van Dyke - WR
Dedric Ward - WR
Kevin Williams - FS

1998 Oakland

Eric Allen - CB
Vincent Amey - DE
Leo Araguz - P
Darryl Ashmore - G
Greg Biekert - MLB
Calvin Branch - DB
Jeremy Brigham - TE
Bucky Brooks - DB
Derek Brown - TE
Tim Brown - WR
Aundray Bruce - DE
Perry Carter - DB
Mo Collins - T
Rick Cunningham - T
Greg Davis - K
Ernest Dixon - LB
Rickey Dudley - TE
James Folston - OLB
Jeff George - QB
Derrick Graham - G
Pat Harlow - T
James Harris - DE
Richard Harvey - OLB
Donald Hollas - QB
Desmond Howard - WR
Grady Jackson - DE
James Jett - WR
Lance Johnstone - DE
Randy Jordan - RB
Napoleon Kaufman - RB
Lincoln Kennedy - T
Albert Lewis - FS
Russell Maryland - DT
Terry Mickens - WR
John Henry Mills - LB
Mike Morton - LB
Anthony Newman - SS
Chuck Osborne - DT
Anthony Prior - DB
Louis Riddick - DB
Jon Ritchie - RB
Barret Robbins - C
Darrell Russell - DT
Kenny Shedd - WR
Travian Smith - LB
Pat Swilling - DE
James Trapp - DB
Adam Treu - C
Eric Turner - FS
Marquis Walker - CB
Aaron Wallace - LB
Harvey Williams - RB
Jermaine Williams - RB
Rodney Williams - WR
Wade Wilson - QB
Steve Wisniewski - G
Terry Wooden - OLB
Charles Woodson - CB

1998 Philadelphia

Ian Beckles - G
Chris Boniol - K
James Bostic - RB
Barrett Brooks - T
Mike Caldwell - OLB
Richard Cooper - T
Russell Copeland - WR
Jerry Crafts - T
James Darling - OLB
Brian Dawkins - FS
Koy Detmer - QB
Hugh Douglas - DE
Jason Dunn - TE
Steve Everitt - C
Ray Farmer - LB
Chris Fontenot - TE
Irving Fryar - WR
Charlie Garner - RB
Jeff Graham - WR
Rhett Hall - DT
Karl Hankton - WR
Al Harris - CB
Jon Harris - DE
Aaron Hayden - RB
George Hegamin - G
Bobby Hoying - QB
Tom Hutton - P
Edward Jasper - DT
Greg Jefferson - DE
Dietrich Jells - WR
Jimmie Johnson - TE
Bill Johnson - DT
Andrew Jordan - TE
Chad Lewis - TE
Clarence Love - DB
Anthony Marshall - DB
Steve Martin - DT
Jermane Mayberry - G
Tim McTyer - DB
Bubba Miller - C
Rodney Peete - QB
Mike Reed - RB
Ike Reese - LB
Allen Rossum - DB
Kaseem Sinceno - TE
Henry Slay - DT
Freddie Solomon - WR
Duce Staley - RB
Matt Stevens - DB
Bobby Taylor - CB
Hollis Thomas - DT
Tra Thomas - T
William Thomas - OLB
Jeremiah Trotter - LB
Kevin Turner - FB
Morris Unutoa - C
Troy Vincent - CB
Corey Walker - RB
Al Wallace - DE
Brandon Whiting - DT
James Willis - MLB
Mike Zordich - SS

1998 Pittsburgh

Jahine Arnold - WR
Jerome Bettis - HB
Harold Bishop - TE
Will Blackwell - WR
Lance Brown - DB
Mark Bruener - TE
Andre Coleman - WR
Steven Conley - LB
Chris Conrad - T
Dermontti Dawson - C
Roger Duffy - G
David Dunn - WR
Carlos Emmons - OLB
Alan Faneca - G
John Fiala - LB
Lethon Flowers - SS
Chris Fuamatu-Ma'afala - RB
Matt George - K
Oliver Gibson - DT
Jason Gildon - OLB
Nolan Harrison - DE
Courtney Hawkins - WR
Kevin Henry - DE
Earl Holmes - ILB
Richard Huntley - RB
John Jenkins - DB
Charles Johnson - WR
Norm Johnson - K
Donta Jones - ILB
Carlos King - RB
Levon Kirkland - ILB
Carnell Lake - CB
Tim Lester - FB
Mitch Lyons - TE
Rod Manuel - DE
Fred McAfee - RB
Josh Miller - P
Chris Oldham - DB
Bo Orlando - DB
Darren Perry - FS
Mark Rodenhauser - C
Orpheus Roye - DE
Jason Simmons - DB
Jeremy Staat - DE
Brenden Stai - G
Joel Steed - NT
Jamain Stephens - T
Kordell Stewart - QB
Justin Strzelczyk - T
Jim Sweeney - C
Mike Tomczak - QB
Deshea Townsend - DB
Mike Vrabel - DE
Hines Ward - WR
Dewayne Washington - CB
Jon Witman - FB
Will Wolford - T

1998 San Diego

Darren Bennett - P
David Binn - TE
James Burgess - LB
John Burke - TE
Lewis Bush - OLB
Kenny Bynum - RB
John Carney - K
Willie Clark - DB
Marco Coleman - DE
Wendell Davis - HB
Charles Dimry - CB
Gerald Dixon - OLB
Dedrick Dodge - DB
Mike Dumas - DB
Terrell Fletcher - RB
Roman Fortin - C
William Fuller - DE
Tony Gaiter - WR
Kurt Gouveia - ILB
Michael Hamilton - LB
Norman Hand - DT
Dwayne Harper - DB
Rodney Harrison - SS
Frank Hartley - TE
Jon Haskins - LB
Greg Jackson - FS
John Jackson - T
Kendyl Jacox - G
Raylee Johnson - DE
Charlie Jones - WR
Freddie Jones - TE
Ryan Leaf - QB
Lloyd Lee - DB
Raleigh McKenzie - G
Natrone Means - RB
Chris Mims - DE
Mike Mohring - DT
Vaughn Parker - T
John Parrella - DT
Marcus Price - T
Marc Raab - C
Latario Rachal - WR
Mikhael Ricks - WR
Raleigh Roundtree - G
Junior Seau - ILB
Terrance Shaw - CB
Troy Sienkiewicz - G
Webster Slaughter - WR
Jimmy Spencer - CB
Tremayne Stephens - RB
Bryan Still - WR
Aaron Taylor - G
Ryan Thelwell - WR
Steve Tovar - LB
Craig Whelihan - QB
Jamal Williams - DT
Williams, Gerome - DB

1998 St. Louis

Ray Agnew - DT
Taje Allen - DB
Tyji Armstrong - TE
Tony Banks - QB
Steve Bono - QB
Ethan Brooks - G
Isaac Bruce - WR
Ron Carpenter - DB
Kevin Carter - DE
Charlie Clemons - LB
Ernie Conwell - TE
D'Marco Farr - DT
John Flannery - C
London Fletcher - LB
Wayne Gandy - T
Mike Gruttadauria - C
Az-zahir Hakim - WR
Derrick Harris - FB
June Henley - RB
Jon Hesse - LB
Eric Hill - MLB
Greg Hill - RB
Robert Holcombe - RB
Tony Horne - WR
Mitch Jacoby - TE
Billy Jenkins - SS
Mike A. Jones - OLB
Mike D. Jones - DE
Eddie Kennison - WR
Amp Lee - RB
Leonard Little - LB
Todd Lyght - CB
Keith Lyle - FS
Gerald McBurrows - DB
Dexter McCleon - CB
Ryan McNeil - CB
Fred Miller - G
Jerald Moore - RB
Tom Nutten - C
Orlando Pace - T
Roman Phifer - OLB
Joe Phillips - DT
Ricky Proehl - WR
Jeff Robinson - DE
Mike Scurlock - DB
Corey Sears - DT
Lorenzo Styles - LB
J.T. Thomas - WR
David Thompson - RB
Ryan Tucker - G
Rick Tuten - P
Phillip Ward - LB
Kurt Warner - QB
Zach Wiegert - G
Jeff Wilkins - K
Jay Williams - DE
Roland Williams - TE
Grant Wistrom - DE
Toby Wright - DB

1998 San Francisco

Roy Barker - DE
Fred Beasley - RB
Tony Blevins - DB
Shane Bonham - DT
Zack Bronson - DB
Jamie Brown - T
Ray Brown - G
Junior Bryant - DT
Curtis Buckley - DB
Brentson Buckner - DE
Greg Clark - TE
Chris Dalman - C
Derrick Deese - T
Ty Detmer - QB
Chris Doleman - DE
Jim Druckenmiller - QB
Marc Edwards - FB
Chad Fann - TE
Dave Fiore - T
Reggie Givens - LB
Kevin Gogan - G
Steve Gordon - C
Charles Haley* - DE
Merton Hanks - FS
Tim Hanshaw - G
Mark Harris - WR
Garrison Hearst - RB
Eddie Howard - P
Terry Kirby - RB
Randy Kirk - LB
Antonio Langham - CB
Tyrone Legette - DB
Chuck Levy - RB
Tim McDonald - SS
R.W. McQuarters - CB
Randy Neal - LB
Ken Norton - OLB
Terrell Owens - WR
Tony Peterson - LB
Marquez Pope - DB
Jeff Posey - DE
Jerry Rice - WR
Wade Richey - K
David Richie - NT
Reggie Roby - P
Chris Ruhman - T
Lance Schulters - DB
Kirk Scrafford - T
Irv Smith - TE
J.J. Stokes - WR
Winfred Tubbs - MLB
Iheanyi Uwaezuoke - WR
Darnell Walker - CB
Gabe Wilkins - DT
James Williams - LB
Lee Woodall - OLB
Bryant Young - DT
Steve Young - QB
* Post

1998 Seattle

Sam Adams - DT
Howard Ballard - T
Jay Bellamy - SS
Brian Blades - WR
Steve Broussard - RB
Chad Brown - OLB
Reggie Brown - RB
Hillary Butler - LB
Mark Collins - DB
Mike Croel - DE
Carlester Crumpler - TE
Phillip Daniels - DE
Joey Eloms - DB
Christian Fauria - TE
Jeff Feagles - P
John Friesz - QB
Joey Galloway - WR
Kevin Glover - C
Chris Gray - C
Ahman Green - RB
Andrew Greene - G
Brian Habib - G
Ronnie Harris - WR
Walter Jones - T
Kerry Joseph - DB
Pete Kendall - G
Cortez Kennedy - DT
Jon Kitna - QB
Jason Kyle - LB
Matt LaBounty - DE
James Logan - LB
Deems May - TE
Terry McDaniel - DB
Jason McEndoo - C
James McKnight - WR
Itula Mili - TE
Warren Moon - QB
DeShone Myles - MLB
Riddick Parker - DT
Todd Peterson - K
Mike Pritchard - WR
Dan Saleaumua - DT
Anthony Simmons - OLB
Michael Sinclair - DE
Darrin Smith - OLB
Shawn Springs - CB
Eric Stokes - DB
Mack Strong - FB
Fred Thomas - DB
Ricky Watters - RB
Todd Weiner - T
Dean Wells - MLB
Darryl Williams - FS
Grant Williams - T
Willie Williams - CB
Robert Wilson - WR

1998 Tampa Bay

Donnie Abraham - CB
Chidi Ahanotu - DE
Mike Alstott - FB
Reidel Anthony - WR
Ronde Barber - CB
Tommy Barnhardt - P
Greg Bellisari - LB
Tony Bouie - DB
Derrick Brooks - OLB
James Cannida - DT
Brad Culpepper - DT
Don Davis - LB
John Davis - TE
Jorge Diaz - G
Trent Dilfer - QB
Kevin Dogins - G
Jamie Duncan - MLB
Warrick Dunn - RB
Jerry Ellison - RB
Bert Emanuel - WR
Jeff Gooch - OLB
Jacquez Green - WR
Paul Gruber - T
Patrick Hape - TE
Brice Hunter - WR
Michael Husted - K
Tyoka Jackson - DE
Marcus Jones - DT
Brian Kelly - DB
John Lynch - SS
Jason Maniecki - DT
Tony Mayberry - C
Frank Middleton - G
Charles Mincy - FS
Dave Moore - TE
Lorenzo Neal - RB
Hardy Nickerson - MLB
Jason Odom - T
Mitch Palmer - LB
Anthony Parker - CB
Pete Pierson - T
Shelton Quarles - LB
Damien Robinson - DB
Warren Sapp - DT
Alshermond Singleton - LB
Shevin Smith - DB
Robb Thomas - WR
Regan Upshaw - DE
Eric Vance - DB
Steve Walsh - QB
Todd Washington - C
Steve White - DE
Williams, Karl - WR
Jerry Wunsch - T
Floyd Young - DB

1998 Tennessee

Mike Archie - RB
Blaine Bishop - SS
Joe Bowden - MLB
Isaac Byrd - WR
Anthony Cook - DE
Willie Davis - WR
Al Del Greco - K
Anthony Dorsett - DB
Kevin Dyson - WR
Josh Evans - DT
Henry Ford - DT
Eddie George - RB
Spencer George - RB
Jackie Harris - TE
Craig Hentrich - P
Kenny Holmes - DE
Brad Hopkins - T
Steve Jackson - FS
Lenoy Jones - LB
Joey Kent - WR
Terry Killens - LB
Dave Krieg - QB
Jason Layman - G
Darryll Lewis - CB
Kevin Long - C
Pratt Lyons - DE
Lonnie Marts - OLB
Derrick Mason - WR
Jason Mathews - T
Bruce Matthews - G
Steve Matthews - QB
George McCullough - DB
Steve McNair - QB
Erik Norgard - G
Benji Olson - G
Perry Phenix - DB
Evan Pilgrim - G
Michael Roan - TE
James Roberson - DE
Marcus Robertson - FS
Eddie Robinson - OLB
Samari Rolle - CB
Jon Runyan - T
Joe Salave'a - DT
Chris Sanders - WR
Scott Sanderson - T
Dainon Sidney - DB
Dennis Stallings - LB
Mark Stepnoski - C
Mike Sutton - DE
Yancey Thigpen - WR
Rodney Thomas - RB
Denard Walker - CB
Gary Walker - DT
Barron Wortham - LB
Frank Wycheck - TE

1998 Washington

David Akers - K
Patrise Alexander - LB
Stephen Alexander - TE
Terry Allen - RB
Jamie Asher - TE
Brad Badger - T
Shawn Barber - LB
Michael Batiste - G
Cary Blanchard - K
Scott Blanton - K
Marc Boutte - DT
Larry Bowie - FB
Doug Brown - DT
Chester Burnett - LB
Jesse Campbell - DB
Albert Connell - WR
Brett Conway - K
Buddy Crutchfield - CB
Stephen Davis - FB
Tim Denton - CB
Cris Dishman - CB
Troy Drake - T
Jamal Duff - DE
Henry Ellard - WR
Greg Evans - DB
Leomont Evans - SS
Mark Fischer - C
Gus Frerotte - QB
Darrell Green - CB
Trent Green - QB
Malcolm Hamilton - LB
Ken Harvey - OLB
Skip Hicks - RB
David Hoelscher - DE
James Jenkins - TE
Tre' Johnson - G
Greg Jones - OLB
Ndukwe Kalu - DE
Kelvin Kinney - DE
Jim Kitts - RB
Kenard Lang - DE
Le'Shai Maston - RB
Rod Milstead - G
Brian Mitchell - RB
Joe Patton - G
Marvcus Patton - MLB
Antwaune Ponds - LB
Darryl Pounds - DB
Shar Pourdanesh - T
Cory Raymer - C
Stanley Richard - FS
Twan Russell - LB
Mike Sellers - TE
Leslie Shepherd - WR
Keith Sims - G
Derek Smith - OLB
Matt Stevens - DB
Dana Stubblefield - DT
Chris Thomas - WR
James Thrash - WR
Dan Turk - C
Matt Turk - P
Michael Westbrook - WR
Paul Wiggins - T
Dan Wilkinson - DT
Jamel Williams - DB

The Annual Record

The Annual Record presents the standings and principal offensive and defensive statistics for each National Football League season since 1920, the American Football League of 1960-69, and the All-America Football Conference of 1946-49.

Starting at the left of each year is the list of teams for that year in the order of their league finish. Divisions, in effect since 1933 in the NFL, are indicated. Teams that did not win their division but qualified for the playoffs are marked with an asterisk.

Moving to the right, you'll find the team's won-lost-tied record, followed by its winning percentage. Until 1972, ties were ignored in computing a team's winning percentage. Since then, they have been counted as one-half win and one-half loss. Below the standings you'll find the total number of games played in the league during the year.

The next entry across the top is the total points scored by a team (OWN PTS), and the points scored against it by its opponents (OPP PTS) in two columns connected by a dash. The number at the bottom of these two columns gives the total number of points scored in the league that season.

No scoring is given for the year 1920, and teams and their won-lost records are given in alphabetical order. The 14 APFA teams played many games against non-APFA foes in that year. No standings were kept, and, in awarding the season's championship to Akron, the club owners appear to have considered all games played by its members. Several teams ran up huge scores against non-APFA opponents. Presenting team scoring records for 1920 (or individual scoring records for that year in the Players Register) would be misleading, whether all games or only certain games were included.

The next two columns list the points-per-game scored by a given team and the points scored by its opponents. These are derived by dividing the team's points scored by its number of games (including ties), and dividing its opponents points scored by the number of games. The number at the bottom of this column is the average total points scored by both the team and its opponents in a league game that season.

The remainder of the line gives the team's rushing and passing offensive and defensive record.

For rushing, the abbreviations at the top of the OWN-OPP columns:

- ATT = rushing attempts
- YARD = rushing yardage
- AVG = average gain per attempt
- TD = rushing touchdowns

For passing:

- ATT = passing attempts
- COM = completions
- PCT = completion percentage
- YARD = total yards gained
- AVG = average gain per attempt
- TD = touchdown passes
- IN = interceptions

Below the standings are the scores of playoff games, championship games, and Super Bowls.

Individual achievements are given next. These include the five leading rushers, passers, receivers, and scorers in the league (and, starting in 1970, in the conference). For interceptions, punting, punt returns, and kickoff returns, only the leaders are given.

SUPERLATIVES lists outstanding achievements that may or may not be included in the leaders sections. For example, the player with the highest yards per reception average may not have been one of the top five in total receptions.

LONGEST lists the longest plays of the year. A small "t" after the number indicates the play went for a touchdown.

1920 AMERICAN PROFESSIONAL FOOTBALL ASSOCIATION

Team	W	L	T	Pct.
Akr	8	0	3	1.000
Buf	9	1	1	.900
Can	7	4	2	.636
ChiC	6	2	2	.750
ChiT	2	5	1	.286
Cle	2	4	2	.333
Col	2	6	2	.250
Day	5	2	2	.714
Det	2	3	3	.400
Ham	2	5	0	.286
Mun	0	1	0	.000
Roch	6	3	2	.667
RI	6	2	2	.750
Sta	10	1	2	.909

1921 AMERICAN PROFESSIONAL FOOTBALL ASSOCIATION

Team	W	L	T	Pct.	PTS-OPP	PPG-OPP
Sta	9	1	1	.900	128- 53	11.6- 4.8
Buf	9	1	2	.900	211- 29	17.6- 2.4
Akr	8	3	1	.727	148- 31	12.3- 2.6
Can	5	2	3	.714	106- 55	10.6- 5.5
RI	4	2	1	.667	65- 30	9.3- 4.3
Eva	3	2	0	.600	87- 46	17.4- 9.2
GB	3	2	1	.600	70- 55	11.7- 9.2
Day	4	4	1	.500	96- 67	10.7- 7.4
ChiC	3	3	2	.500	54- 53	6.9- 6.6
Roch	2	3	0	.400	85- 76	17.0-15.2
Cle	3	5	0	.375	95- 58	11.9- 7.3
Was	1	2	0	.333	21- 28	7.0- 9.3
Cin	1	3	0	.250	14-117	3.5-29.3
Ham	1	3	1	.250	17- 45	3.4- 9.0
Min	1	3	1	.250	37- 41	9.3-10.3
Det	1	5	1	.167	19-106	2.7-15.1
Col	1	8	0	.111	47-222	5.2-24.7
Ton	0	1	0	.000	0- 45	0.0-45.0
Mun	0	2	0	.000	0- 28	0.0-14.0
Lou	0	2	0	.000	0- 27	0.0-13.5
NYG	0	2	0	.000	0- 72	0.0-36.0
66 games					1300	19.7

LEADING SCORERS	TD	FG	XP	PTS
Elmer Oliphant, Buf	1	5	26	47
Ockie Anderson, Buf	7	0	0	42
Fritz Pollard, Akr	7	0	0	42
Frank Bacon, Day	6	0	0	36
Jim Laird, Buf-Roch-Can	6	0	0	36
Dutch Sternaman, Sta	2	5	9	56

SUPERLATIVES

Touchdowns	7	Ockie Anderson, Buf Fritz Pollard, Akr
Field Goals	5	Dutch Sternaman, Sta Elmer Oliphant, Buf
Extra Points	26	Elmer Oliphant, Buf

1922 NATIONAL FOOTBALL LEAGUE

Team	W	L	T	Pct.	PTS-OPP	PPG-OPP
Can	10	0	2	1.000	184- 15	15.3- 1.3
ChiB	9	3	0	.750	123- 44	10.3- 3.7
ChiC	8	3	0	.727	96- 50	8.7- 4.5
Tol	5	2	2	.714	94- 59	10.4- 6.5
RI	4	2	1	.667	154- 27	22.0- 3.9
Rac	6	4	1	.600	122- 56	11.1- 5.1
Day	4	3	1	.571	80- 62	10.0- 7.8
GB	4	3	3	.571	70- 54	7.0- 5.4
Buf	5	4	1	.556	87- 41	8.7- 4.1
Akr	3	5	2	.375	146- 95	14.6- 9.5
Mil	2	4	3	.333	51- 71	5.7- 7.9
Oor	2	6	0	.250	69-190	8.6-23.8
Min	1	3	0	.250	19- 40	4.8-10.0
Lou	1	3	0	.250	13-140	3.3-35.0
Eva	0	3	0	.000	6- 88	2.0-29.3
Roch	0	4	1	.000	13- 76	2.6-15.2
Ham	0	5	1	.000	0- 69	0.0-11.5
Col	0	7	0	.000	24-174	3.4-24.9
73 games					1351	18.5

LEADING SCORERS	TD	FG	XP	PTS
Hank Gillo, Rac	5	6	4	52
Jimmy Conzelman, RI-Mil	7	2	0	48
Guy Chamberlin, Can	7	0	0	42
Dutch Sternaman, ChiB	3	6	5	41
Paddy Driscoll, ChiC	2	8	4	40

SUPERLATIVES

Touchdowns	7	Guy Chamberlin, Can Jimmy Conzelman, RI-Mil
Field Foals	8	Paddy Driscoll, ChiC
Extra Points	9	Russ Hathaway, Day-Can

1923 NATIONAL FOOTBALL LEAGUE

Team	W	L	T	Pct.	PTS-OPP	PPG-OPP
Can	11	0	1	1.000	246- 19	20.5- 1.6
ChiB	9	2	1	.818	123- 35	10.3- 2.9
GB	7	2	1	.778	85- 34	8.5- 3.4
Mil	7	2	3	.778	100- 49	8.3- 4.1
Cle	3	1	3	.750	52- 49	7.4- 7.0
ChiC	8	4	0	.667	161- 56	13.4- 4.7
Dul	4	3	0	.571	35- 33	5.0- 4.2
Col	5	4	1	.556	119- 35	11.9- 3.5
Buf	5	4	3	.500	81- 53	6.8- 4.4
Rac	4	4	2	.500	86- 76	8.6- 7.6
Tol	3	3	2	.400	41- 66	5.1- 8.3
RI	2	3	3	.400	84- 62	10.5- 7.8
Min	2	5	2	.286	48- 81	5.3- 9.0
StL	1	4	2	.200	14- 39	2.0- 5.6
Ham	1	5	1	.167	14- 59	2.0- 8.4
Day	1	6	1	.143	16- 95	2.0-11.9
Akr	1	6	0	.143	25- 74	3.6-10.6
Oor	1	10	0	.091	43-257	3.9-23.4
Roch	0	4	0	.000	6-141	1.5-35.3
Lou	0	3	0	.000	0- 83	0.0-27.3
88 games					1379	15.6

LEADING SCORERS	TD	FG	XP	PTS
Paddy Driscoll, ChiC	7	10	6	78
Wilbur Henry, Can	1	9	26	59
Dutch Sternaman, ChiB	5	5	7	52
Ben Winkelman, Mil	3	6	9	45
Hank Gillo, Rac	2	8	8	44

SUPERLATIVES

Touchdowns	7	Paddy Driscoll, ChiC Lou Smyth, Can
Field Goals	10	Paddy Driscoll, ChiC
Extra Points (kick)	25	Wilbur Henry, Can

1924 NATIONAL FOOTBALL LEAGUE

Team	W	L	T	Pct.	PTS-OPP	PPG-OPP
Cle	7	1	1	.875	229- 60	25.4- 6.7
ChiB	6	1	4	.857	136- 55	12.4- 5.0
Fra	11	2	1	.846	326-109	23.3- 7.8
Dul	5	1	0	.833	56- 16	6.2- 2.7
RI	6	2	2	.750	88- 38	8.8- 3.8
GB	7	4	0	.636	108- 38	9.8- 3.5
Rac	4	3	3	.571	69- 47	6.9- 4.7
ChiC	5	4	1	.556	90- 67	9.0- 6.7
Buf	6	5	0	.545	120-140	10.9-12.7
Col	4	4	0	.500	91- 68	11.4- 8.5
Ham	2	2	1	.500	18- 45	3.6- 9.0
Mil	5	8	0	.385	142-188	10.9-14.5
Akr	2	6	0	.333	59-132	7.4-16.5
Day	2	6	0	.333	45-148	5.6-18.5
KC	2	7	0	.222	46-124	5.1-13.8
Ken	0	4	1	.000	12-117	2.4-23.4
Min	0	6	0	.000	14-108	2.3-16.0
Roch	0	7	0	.000	7-156	1.0-22.3
81 games					1656	20.4

LEADING SCORERS	TD	FG	XP	PTS
Joey Sternaman, ChiB	6	9	12	75
Tex Hamer, Fra	12	0	0	72
Ben Boynton, Roch-Buf	6	4	11	59
Hank Gillo, Rac	3	8	6	48
Jack Storer, Fra	8	0	0	48

SUPERLATIVES

Touchdowns	12	Tex Hamer, Fra
Field Goals	9	Joey Sternaman, ChiB
Extra Points	17	Jim Welsh, Fra

1925 NATIONAL FOOTBALL LEAGUE

Team	W	L	T	Pct.	PTS-OPP	PPG-OPP
ChiC	11	2	1	.846	230- 65	16.4- 4.6
Pott	10	2	0	.833	270- 45	22.5- 3.8
Det	8	2	2	.800	129- 39	10.8- 3.3
NYG	8	4	0	.667	122- 67	10.2- 5.6
Akr	4	2	2	.667	65- 51	8.2- 4.3
Fra	13	7	0	.650	190-169	9.5- 8.5
ChiB	9	5	3	.643	158- 96	9.3- 5.6
RI	5	3	3	.625	99- 58	9.0- 5.3
GB	8	5	0	.615	151-110	11.6- 8.5
Prov	6	5	1	.545	111-101	9.3- 8.4
Can	4	4	0	.500	50- 73	6.3- 9.1
Cle	5	8	1	.385	75-135	5.4- 9.6

KC	2	5	1	.296	65- 97	8.1-12.1
Ham	1	4	0	.200	23- 87	4.6-17.4
Buf	1	6	2	.143	33-113	3.7-12.6
Dul	0	3	0	.000	6- 25	2.0- 8.3
Roch	0	6	0	.000	26-111	3.7-15.9
Mil	0	6	0	.000	7-191	1.2-31.8
Day	0	7	1	.000	3- 84	0.4-10.5
Col	0	9	0	.000	28-124	3.1-13.8
104 games					1841	17.7

LEADING SCORERS	TD	FG	XP	PTS
Charley Berry, Pott	6	3	29	74
Paddy Driscoll, ChiC	4	11	10	67
Joey Sternaman, ChiB	7	3	17	62
Tony Latone, Pott	7	0	0	48
Tex Hamer, Fra	7	0	3	45

SUPERLATIVES

Touchdowns	7	Hal Erickson, ChiC
		Hoot Flanagan, Pott
		Tex Hamer, Fra
		Tony Latone, Pott
		Joey Sternaman, ChiB
Field Goals	11	Paddy Driscoll, ChiC
Extra Points	29	Charley Berry, Pott

1926 NATIONAL FOOTBALL LEAGUE

Team	W	L	T	Pct.	PTS-OPP	PPG-OPP
Fra	14	1	2	.933	236- 49	13.9- 2.9
ChiB	12	1	3	.923	216- 63	13.5- 3.9
Pott	10	2	2	.833	155- 29	11.1- 2.1
KC	8	3	0	.727	76- 53	6.9- 4.8
GB	7	3	3	.700	151- 61	11.6- 4.7
LA	6	3	1	.667	67- 57	6.7- 5.7
NYG	8	4	1	.667	147- 51	11.3- 3.9
Dul	6	5	3	.545	113- 81	8.1- 5.8
Buf	4	4	2	.500	53- 62	5.3- 6.2
ChiC	5	6	1	.455	74- 98	6.1- 8.2
Prov	5	7	1	.417	99-103	7.6- 7.9
Det	4	6	2	.400	107- 60	8.9- 5.0
Har	3	7	0	.300	57- 99	5.7- 9.9
Bkn	3	8	0	.273	60-150	5.5-13.6
Mil	2	7	0	.222	41- 66	4.6- 7.3
Akr	1	4	3	.200	23- 89	2.9-11.1
Day	1	4	1	.200	15- 82	2.5-13.7
Rac	1	4	0	.200	8- 92	1.6-18.4
Col	1	6	0	.143	26- 93	3.7-13.3
Can	1	9	3	.100	46-161	3.5-12.4
Ham	0	4	0	.000	3- 56	0.8-14.0
Lou	0	4	0	.000	0-108	0.0-27.0
116 games					1773	15.3

LEADING SCORERS	TD	FG	XP	PTS
Paddy Driscoll, ChiB	6	12	14	86
Ernie Nevers, ChiC	8	4	11	71
Barney Wentz, Pott	10	0	0	60
Curly Oden, Prov	10	0	0	60
Bert Jones, Fra	9	0	0	54

SUPERLATIVES

Touchdowns	10	Curly Oden, Prov
		Barney Wentz, Pott
Field Goals	12	Paddy Driscoll, ChiB
Extra Points	15	Jack McBride, NYG
		Jim Welsh, Pott

1926 AMERICAN FOOTBALL LEAGUE

Team	W	L	T	Pct.	PTS-OPP	PPG-OPP
Phi	8	2	0	.800	93- 52	9.3- 5.2
NYY	10	5	0	.667	212- 82	14.1- 5.5
Cle	3	2	0	.600	62- 46	12.4- 9.2
LA	6	6	2	.500	105- 83	7.5- 6.9
Chi	5	6	3	.455	88- 69	6.3- 4.9
Bos	2	4	0	.333	20- 81	3.3-13.5
RI	2	6	1	.250	21-126	2.3-14.0
Bkn	1	3	0	.250	25- 68	6.3-17.0
Nwk	0	3	2	.000	7- 26	1.4- 5.2
41 games					633	15.4

AFL LEADING SCORERS	TD	FG	XP	PTS
Eddie Tryon, NYY	9	2	12	72
Joey Sternaman, Chi	4	9	7	52
Red Grange, NYY	8	0	2	50
Al Kreuz, Phi	1	8	4	34
Dave Noble, Cle	6	0	1	31

SUPERLATIVES

Touchdowns	9	Eddie Tryon, NYY
Field Goals	9	Joey Sternaman, Chi
Extra Points	12	Eddie Tryon, NYY

1927 NATIONAL FOOTBALL LEAGUE

Team	W	L	T	Pct.	PTS-OPP	PPG-OPP
NYG	11	1	1	.917	197- 20	15.2- 1.5
GB	7	2	1	.778	113- 43	11.3- 4.3
ChiB	9	3	2	.750	149- 98	10.6- 7.0
Cle	8	4	1	.667	209-107	16.1- 8.2
Prov	8	5	1	.615	105- 86	7.5- 6.1
NYY	7	8	1	.467	142-174	8.9-10.9
Fra	6	9	3	.400	152-166	8.4- 9.2
Pott	5	8	0	.385	80-163	6.2-12.5
ChiC	3	7	1	.300	60-134	5.5-12.2
Day	1	6	1	.143	15- 57	1.9- 7.1
Dul	1	8	0	.111	68-134	7.6-14.9
Buf	0	5	0	.000	8-123	1.6-24.6
72 games					1075	14.9

LEADING SCORERS	TD	FG	XP	PTS
Jack McBride, NYG	6	2	15	57
Bert Bloodgood, Cle	6	1	6	45
Eddie Tryon, NYY	6	0	8	44
Paddy Driscoll, ChiB	6	2	7	43
Ken Mercer, Fra	3	5	6	39

SUPERLATIVES

Touchdowns	6	Bert Bloodgood, Cle
		Paddy Driscoll, ChiB
		Hinkey Haines, NYG
		Jack McBride, NYG
		Bill Senn, ChiB
		Eddie Tryon, NYY
		Mule Wilson, NYG
Field Goals	5	Ken Mercer, Fra
Extra Points	15	Jack McBride, NYG

1928 NATIONAL FOOTBALL LEAGUE

Team	W	L	T	Pct.	PTS-OPP	PPG-OPP
Prov	8	1	2	.889	128- 42	11.6- 3.8
Fra	11	3	2	.786	175- 84	10.9- 5.3
Det	7	2	1	.778	189- 76	18.9- 7.6
GB	6	4	3	.600	120- 92	9.2- 7.1
ChiB	7	5	1	.583	182- 85	14.0- 6.5
NYG	4	7	2	.364	79-136	6.1-10.5
NYY	4	8	1	.333	103-179	7.9-13.8
Pott	2	8	0	.200	74-134	7.4-13.4
ChiC	1	5	0	.167	7-107	1.2-17.8
Day	0	7	0	.000	9-131	1.3-18.7
56 games					1066	19.0

LEADING SCORERS	TD	FG	XP	PTS
Benny Friedman, Det	6	0	19	55
Verne Lewellen, GB	9	0	0	54
Gibby Welch, NYY	8	0	0	48
Tiny Feather, Det	7	0	0	42
Ken Mercer, Fra	6	0	2	38

SUPERLATIVES

Touchdowns	9	Verne Lewellen, GB
Field Goals	3	Harry O'Boyle, GB
Extra Points	19	Benny Friedman, Det

1929 NATIONAL FOOTBALL LEAGUE

Team	W	L	T	Pct.	PTS-OPP	PPG-OPP
GB	12	0	1	1.000	198- 22	15.2- 1.7
NYG	13	1	1	.923	312- 86	20.8- 5.7
Fra	9	4	5	.692	129-128	7.2- 7.1
ChiC	6	6	1	.500	154- 83	11.8- 6.4
Bos	4	4	0	.500	98- 73	12.3- 9.1
Ora	3	4	4	.429	35- 80	3.2- 7.3
SI	3	4	3	.429	89- 65	8.9- 6.5
Prov	4	6	2	.400	107-117	8.9- 9.8
ChiB	4	9	2	.333	119-227	7.9-15.1
Buf	1	7	1	.125	48-142	5.3-15.8
Min	1	9	0	.100	48-185	4.8-18.5
Day	0	6	0	.000	7-136	1.2-22.7
70 games					1344	9.6

LEADING SCORERS	TD	FG	XP	PTS
Ernie Nevers, ChiC	12	1	10	85
Len Sedbrook, NYG	11	0	0	66
Tony Plansky, NYG	9	2	2	62
Tony Latone, Bos	9	0	0	54
Ray Flaherty, NYG	8	0	1	49

SUPERLATIVES

Touchdowns	12	Ernie Nevers, ChiC
Field Goals	3	Chuck Weimer, Buf
Extra Points	20	Benny Friedman, NYG

1930 NATIONAL FOOTBALL LEAGUE

Team	W	L	T	Pct.	PTS-OPP	PPG-OPP
GB	10	3	1	.769	234-111	16.7- 7.9
NYG	13	4	0	.765	308- 98	18.1- 5.8
ChiB	9	4	1	.692	169- 71	12.1- 5.1
Bkn	7	4	1	.636	154- 59	12.8- 4.9
Prov	6	4	1	.600	90-125	8.2-11.4
SI	5	5	2	.500	95-112	7.9- 9.3
ChiC	5	6	2	.455	128-132	9.8-10.2
Port	5	6	3	.455	176-161	12.6-11.5
Fra	4	13	1	.235	113-321	6.3-17.8
Min	1	7	1	.125	27-165	3.0-18.3
Nwk	1	10	1	.091	51-190	4.3-15.8
73 games					1545	21.2

LEADING SCORERS	TD	FG	XP	PTS
Jack McBride, Bkn	8	0	8	56
Verne Lewellen, GB	9	0	0	54
Ken Strong, SI	7	1	8	53
Benny Friedman, NYG	6	1	10	49
Red Grange, ChiB	8	0	1	49

SUPERLATIVES

Touchdowns	9	Verne Lewellen, GB
Field Goals	2	Frosty Peters, Prov-Port
Extra Points	14	Red Dunn, GB

1931 NATIONAL FOOTBALL LEAGUE

Team	W	L	T	Pct.	PTS-OPP	PPG-OPP
GB	12	2	0	.857	291- 87	20.8- 6.2
Port	11	3	0	.786	175- 77	12.5- 5.5
ChiB	8	5	0	.615	145- 92	11.2- 7.1
ChiC	5	4	0	.556	120-128	13.3-14.2
NYG	7	6	1	.538	154-100	11.0- 7.1
Prov	4	4	3	.500	78-127	7.1-11.5
SI	4	6	1	.400	79-118	7.2-10.7
Cle	2	8	0	.200	45-137	4.5-13.7
Bkn	2	12	0	.143	64-199	4.6-14.2
Fra	1	6	1	.143	13- 99	1.6-12.4
59 games					1164	19.7

LEADING SCORERS	TD	FG	XP	PTS
Johnny (Blood) McNally, GB	14	0	0	84
Ernie Nevers, ChiC	8	1	15	66
Dutch Clark, Port	9	0	6	60
Ken Strong, SI	7	2	5	53
Red Grange, ChiB	7	0	0	42

SUPERLATIVES

Touchdowns	14	Johnny (Blood) McNally, GB
Field Goals	2	Ken Strong, SI
Extra Points	15	Red Dunn, GB
		Ernie Nevers, ChiC

1932 NATIONAL FOOTBALL LEAGUE

					SCORING		RUSHING				PASSING						
Team	W	L	T	PCT	OWN-OPP PTS-PTS	OWN-OPP PPG-PPG	OWN-OPP ATT-ATT	OWN-OPP YARD-YARD	OWN-OPP AVG-AVG	ON-OP TD-TD	OWN-OPP ATT-ATT	OWN-OPP COM-COM	OWN-OPP PCT-PCT	OWN-OPP YARD-YARD	OWN-OPP AVG-AVG	ON-OP TD-TD	ON-OP IN-IN
ChiB*	7	1	6	.875	160- 44	11.4- 3.1	513-	1620-	3.7-	13-	148-	67-	45.3-	982-	6.6-	8-	7-
GB	10	3	1	.769	152- 63	10.8- 4.5	434-	1333-	3.1-	7-	134-	48-	35.8-	798-	6.0-	9-	14-
Port	6	2	4	.750	116- 71	9.7- 5.9	373-	1230-	3.3-	9-	113-	43-	38.1-	623-	5.5-	6-	12-
Bos	4	4	2	.500	55- 79	5.5- 7.9	304-	1249-	4.1-	4-	92-	17-	18.5-	216-	2.3-	1-	15-
NYG	4	6	2	.400	93-113	7.8- 9.4	423-	1311-	3.1-	3-	164-	82-	50.0-	949-	5.8-	9-	14-
Bkn	3	9	0	.250	63-131	5.3-10.9	391-	1109-	2.8-	4-	136-	42-	30.9-	586-	4.3-	5-	16-
ChiC	2	6	2	.250	72-114	7.2-11.4	310-	917-	3.0-	6-	126-	40-	31.7-	628-	5.0-	2-	4-
SI	2	7	3	.222	77-173	6.4-14.4	490-	1780-	3.6-	9-	131-	33-	25.2-	518-	4.0-	2-	16-
58 games					788	13.6	3238	10549	3.3	55	1044	372	35.6	5300	5.1	42	98

*Chicago Bears defeated Portsmouth in post-season playoff to break a tie for the championship. The result of the game was included in the regular season and statistics.

LEADING RUSHERS	ATT	YARD	AVG	TD
Cliff Battles, Bos	148	576	3.9	3
Bronko Nagurski, ChiB	121	533	4.3	4
Bob Campiglio, SI	104	504	4.8	2
Dutch Clark, Port	137	461	3.4	3
Doug Wycoff, SI	135	454	3.4	1

LEADING PASSERS	ATT	COM	YARD	TD	IN
Arnie Herber, GB	101	37	639	9	9
Walter Holmer, ChiC	78	25	449	2	1
Jack McBride, Bkn-NYG	74	36	363	6	9
Keith Molesworth, ChiB	64	25	346	3	4
Benny Friedman, Bkn	74	23	319	5	10

LEADING RECEIVERS	NO	YARD	AVG	TD
Ray Flaherty, NYG	21	350	16.7	5
Luke Johnsos, ChiB	19	321	16.9	2
Harry Ebding, Port	14	171	12.2	1
Johnny (Blood) McNally, GB	14	168	12.0	3
Red Grange, ChiB	11	168	15.3	4

LEADING SCORERS	TD	FG	XP	PTS
Dutch Clark, Det	6	3	10	55
Red Grange, ChiB	7	0	0	42
Ray Flaherty, NYG	5	0	0	30
Jack Grossman, Bkn	5	0	0	30
Luke Johnsos, ChiB	4	0	2	26

SUPERLATIVES

Touchdowns	6	Red Grange, ChiB
Field Goals	3	Dutch Clark, Port
Extra Points	10	Dutch Clark, Port
		Tiny Engebretsen, ChiB

1933 NATIONAL FOOTBALL LEAGUE

					SCORING		RUSHING				PASSING						
Team	W	L	T	PCT	OWN-OPP PTS-PTS	OWN-OPP PPG-PPG	OWN-OPP ATT-ATT	OWN-OPP YARD-YARD	OWN-OPP AVG-AVG	ON-OP TD-TD	OWN-OPP ATT-ATT	OWN-OPP COM-COM	OWN-OPP PCT-PCT	OWN-OPP YARD-YARD	OWN-OPP AVG-AVG	ON-OP TD-TD	ON-OP IN-IN
Eastern Division																	
NYG	11	3	0	.786	244-101	17.4- 7.2	476-493	1634-1777	3.4-3.6	15- 7	178-202	74- 62	41.6-30.7	1348- 809	7.6- 4.0	15- 6	19-40
Bkn	5	4	1	.556	93- 54	9.3- 5.4	356-339	1112- 964	3.1-2.8	4- 3	170-161	79- 55	46.5-34.2	1129- 813	6.6- 5.0	7- 2	21-22
Bos	5	5	2	.500	103- 97	8.5- 8.1	467-329	2260-1159	4.8-3.5	11- 6	106-162	33- 72	31.1-44.4	514- 1312	4.8- 8.1	1- 7	25-24
Phi	3	5	1	.375	77-158	8.6-17.6	354-308	1103-1083	3.1-3.5	6-11	149-176	40- 63	26.8-35.8	657- 1223	4.4- 6.9	4- 8	34-19
Pit	3	6	2	.333	67-208	6.1-18.9	338-441	914-1805	2.7-4.1	4-16	196-142	60- 57	30.6-40.1	1029- 930	5.3- 6.5	3- 8	40-19
Western Division																	
ChiB	10	2	1	.833	133- 82	10.2- 6.3	496-514	1734-1625	3.5-3.2	11- 4	212-187	74- 63	34.9-33.7	1229- 691	5.8- 3.7	11- 4	29-32
Port	6	5	0	.545	128- 87	11.6- 7.9	456-413	1720-1422	3.8-3.4	9- 5	170-107	65- 32	38.2-29.9	959- 558	5.6- 5.2	7- 5	18-22
GB	5	7	1	.423	170-107	13.1- 8.2	487-442	1513-1210	3.1-2.7	13- 4	209-179	89- 48	42.6-26.8	1186- 711	5.7- 4.0	6- 7	18-30
Cin	3	6	1	.333	38-110	3.8-11.0	320-417	795-1361	2.5-3.3	2- 7	102-162	25- 66	24.5-40.7	357- 980	3.5- 6.0	0- 6	15-22
ChiC	1	9	1	.100	52-101	4.7- 9.2	368-422	1017-1386	2.8-3.3	2- 6	139-153	37- 58	26.6-37.9	470- 851	3.4- 5.6	3- 4	30-19
57 games					1105	19.4	4118	13792	3.3	69	1631	576	35.3	8878	5.4	57	249

Championship: ChiB 23, NYG 21

LEADING RUSHERS	ATT	YARD	AVG	TD
Jim Musick, Bos	173	809	4.7	5
Cliff Battles, Bos	136	737	5.4	3
Bronko Nagurski, ChiB	128	533	4.2	1
Glenn Presnell, Port	118	522	4.4	6
Swede Hanson, Phi	133	475	3.6	3

LEADING PASSERS	ATT	COM	YARD	TD	IN
Harry Newman, NYG	136	53	973	11	17
Glenn Presnell, Port	125	50	774	6	12
Arnie Herber, GB	124	50	656	3	12
Benny Friedman, Bkn	80	42	594	5	7
Chris Cagle, Bkn	74	31	457	2	10

LEADING RECEIVERS	NO	YARD	AVG	TD
Shipwreck Kelly, Bkn	22	246	11.2	3
Roger Grove, GB	17	215	12.6	0
Bill Hewitt, ChiB	14	273	19.5	2
Ray Tesser, Pit	14	282	20.1	0
Lavie Dilweg, GB	13	225	17.3	0

LEADING SCORERS	TD	FG	PAT	PTS
Ken Strong, NYG	6	5	13	64
Glenn Presnell, Port	6	5	13	64
Jim Musick, Bos	5	1	12	45
Shipwreck Kelly, Bkn	7	0	1	43
Kink Richards, NYG	7	0	1	43

SUPERLATIVES

Rushing Avg.	6.2	Kink Richards, NYG
Receiving Avg.	21.8	Paul Moss, Pit
Completion Pct.	52.5	Benny Friedman, Bkn
Touchdowns	7	Kink Richards, NYG
		Shipwreck Kelly, Bkn
		Buckets Goldenberg, GB
Touchdown Passes	4	Dale Burnett, NYG
Field Goals	6	Jack Manders, ChiB
Extra Points	14	Jack Manders, ChiB

1934 NATIONAL FOOTBALL LEAGUE

					SCORING		RUSHING				PASSING						
Team	W	L	T	PCT	OWN-OPP PTS-PTS	OWN-OPP PPG-PPG	OWN-OPP ATT-ATT	OWN-OPP YARD-YARD	OWN-OPP AVG-AVG	ON-OP TD-TD	OWN-OPP ATT-ATT	OWN-OPP COM-COM	OWN-OPP PCT-PCT	OWN-OPP YARD-YARD	OWN-OPP AVG-AVG	ON-OP TD-TD	ON-OP IN-IN
Eastern Division																	
NYG	8	5	0	.615	147-107	11.3- 8.2	567-465	1935-1634	3.4-3.5	12- 7	149-184	64- 54	43.0-29.3	796- 744	5.3- 4.0	5- 5	17-22
Bos	6	6	0	.500	107- 94	8.9- 7.8	415-418	1668-1715	4.0-4.1	10- 5	138-159	35- 45	25.4-28.3	459- 682	3.3- 4.3	4- 4	22-18
Bkn	4	7	0	.364	61-153	5.5-13.9	309-496	980-2153	3.2-4.3	1-16	161-123	42- 41	26.1-33.3	577- 595	3.6- 4.8	5- 6	26-17
Phi	4	7	0	.364	127- 85	11.5- 7.7	460-411	1876-1658	4.1-4.0	11- 9	163-135	48- 41	29.4-30.4	576- 545	3.5- 4.0	7- 1	23-22
Pit	2	10	0	.167	51-206	4.3-17.2	418-517	1527-2569	3.6-5.0	2-15	186-133	58- 45	31.2-33.8	952- 610	5.1- 4.6	4-10	23-20
Western Division																	
ChiB	13	0	0	1.000	286- 86	22.0- 6.6	567-429	2847-1407	5.0-3.3	20- 9	192-226	57- 73	29.7-32.3	955- 806	5.0- 3.6	16- 2	24-27
Det	10	3	0	.769	238- 59	18.3- 4.5	632-437	2740-1231	4.3-2.8	27- 2	142-200	46- 53	32.4-26.5	747- 678	5.3- 3.4	3- 5	15-33
GB	7	6	0	.538	156-112	12.0- 8.6	456-517	1183-1564	2.6-3.0	8- 9	197-172	74- 56	37.6-32.6	1165- 686	5.9- 4.0	10- 3	19-25
ChiC	5	6	0	.455	80- 84	7.3- 7.6	316-360	1141- 954	3.6-2.7	7- 5	132-106	34- 37	25.8-34.9	302- 585	2.3- 5.5	1- 5	13-14
StL	1	2	0	.333	27- 61	9.0-20.3	104-136	339- 451	2.6-3.3	2- 5	58- 52	21- 14	46.2-26.9	340- 309	5.9- 5.9	1- 4	10- 3
Cin	0	8	0	.000	10-243	1.3-30.4	197-255	731-1631	3.7-6.4	1-19	88-116	26- 46	29.5-39.7	248- 877	2.8- 7.6	0-11	14- 5
60 games					1290	21.5	4441	16967	3.8	101	1606	505	31.4	7117	4.4	56	206

Championship: NYG 30, ChiB 13

LEADING RUSHERS	ATT	YARD	AVG	TD
Beattie Feathers, ChiB	119	1004	8.4	8
Swede Hanson, Phi	146	805	5.5	7
Dutch Clark, Det	123	763	6.2	8
Bronko Nagurski, ChiB	123	586	4.8	7
Ernie Caddel, Det	105	528	5.0	4

LEADING PASSERS	ATT	COM	YARD	TD	IN
Arnie Herber, GB	115	42	799	8	12
Warren Heller, Pit	112	31	511	2	15
Harry Newman, NYG	93	35	391	1	12
Dutch Clark, Det	50	23	383	0	3
Ed Matesic, Phi	60	20	278	2	5

LEADING RECEIVERS	NO	YARD	AVG	TD
Joe Carter, Phi	16	238	14.9	4
Red Badgro, NYG	16	206	12.9	1
Ben Smith, Pit	14	218	15.6	0
Jack Grossman, Bkn	11	161	14.6	1
Clarke Hinkle, GB	11	113	10.3	1
Bill Hewitt, ChiB	11	151	13.7	5
Charley Malone, Bos	11	131	11.9	2

LEADING SCORERS	TD	FG	PAT	PTS
Jack Manders, ChiB	3	10	28	76
Dutch Clark, Det	8	4	13	73
Glenn Presnell, Det	7	4	9	63
Ken Strong, NYG	6	4	8	56
Beattie Feathers, ChiB	9	0	1	55

SUPERLATIVES

Rushing Avg.	8.4	Beattie Feathers, ChiB
Receiving Avg.	26.4	Harry Ebding, Det
Completion Pct.	46.9	Ed Danowski, NYG
Touchdowns	9	Beattie Feathers, ChiB
Field Goals	10	Jack Manders, ChiB
Extra Points	31	Jack Manders, ChiB

1935 NATIONAL FOOTBALL LEAGUE

					SCORING		RUSHING				PASSING						
Team	W	L	T	PCT	OWN-OPP PTS-PTS	OWN-OPP PPG-PPG	OWN-OPP ATT-ATT	OWN-OPP YARD-YARD	OWN-OPP AVG-AVG	ON-OP TD-TD	OWN-OPP ATT-ATT	OWN-OPP COM-COM	OWN-OPP PCT-PCT	OWN-OPP YARD-YARD	OWN-OPP AVG-AVG	ON-OP TD-TD	ON-OP IN-IN
Eastern Division																	
NYG	9	3	0	.750	180- 96	15.0- 8.0	497-436	1453-1089	2.9-2.5	9- 4	154-205	69- 66	44.8-32.2	947- 962	6.1- 4.7	10- 5	19-26
Bkn	5	6	1	.455	90-141	7.5-11.8	367-531	1108-1810	3.0-3.4	6- 8	178-163	52- 55	29.2-33.7	718- 997	4.0- 6.1	5- 7	23-26
Pit	4	8	0	.333	100-209	8.3-17.4	327-543	508-1957	1.6-3.6	4-12	234-209	67- 68	28.6-32.5	996- 1208	4.3- 5.8	5-13	40-21
Bos	2	8	1	.200	65-123	5.9-11.2	448-404	1265- 998	2.8-2.5	5- 5	175-167	48- 68	27.4-40.7	767- 928	4.4- 5.6	3- 8	35-29
Phi	2	9	0	.182	60-179	5.5-16.3	411-443	1054-1697	2.6-3.8	2-15	169-168	46- 59	27.2-35.1	823- 871	4.9- 5.2	6- 6	30-23
Western Division																	
Det	7	3	2	.700	191-111	15.9- 9.3	532-443	1773-1039	3.3-2.3	15- 3	142-181	57- 58	40.1-32.0	920- 931	6.5- 5.1	9- 8	20-25
GB	8	4	0	.667	181- 96	15.1- 8.0	448-448	1562-1219	3.5-2.7	7- 6	230-190	93- 61	40.4-32.1	1449- 837	6.3- 4.4	11- 6	27-27
ChiB	6	4	2	.600	192-106	16.0- 8.8	539-448	2096-1270	3.9-2.8	13- 6	221-194	73- 59	33.0-30.4	1221- 926	5.5- 4.8	13- 7	21-37
ChiC	6	4	2	.600	99- 97	8.3- 8.1	547-420	1521-1261	2.8-3.0	6- 8	127-153	47- 58	37.0-37.9	612- 793	4.8- 5.2	2- 4	23-24
53 games					1158	21.8	4116	12340	3.0	67	1630	552	33.9	8453	5.2	64	238

Championship: Det 26, NYG 7

One game between Boston and Philadelphia canceled

LEADING RUSHERS	ATT	YARD	AVG	TD
Doug Russell, ChiC	140	499	3.6	0
Ernie Caddel, Det	87	450	5.2	6
Kink Richards, NYG	149	449	3.0	4
Dutch Clark, Det	120	427	3.6	4
Bill Shepherd, Bos-Det	143	425	3.0	4

LEADING PASSERS	ATT	COM	YARD	TD	IN
Ed Danowski, NYG	113	57	794	10	9
Arnie Herber, GB	109	40	729	8	14
Johnny Gildea, Pit	105	28	529	2	20
Bernie Masterson, ChiB	44	18	446	6	4
Bill Shepherd, Bos-Det	64	28	417	2	14

LEADING RECEIVERS	NO	YARD	AVG	TD
Tod Goodwin, NYG	26	432	16.6	4
Johnny (Blood) McNally, GB	25	404	16.2	3
Bill Smith, ChiC	24	318	13.3	2
Charley Malone, Bos	22	433	19.7	2
Luke Johnsos, ChiB	19	298	15.7	4

LEADING SCORERS	TD	FG	PAT	PTS
Dutch Clark, Det	6	1	16	55
Don Hutson, GB	7	0	1	43
Dale Burnett, NYG	6	0	0	36
Ernie Caddel, Det	6	0	0	36
Bill Karr, ChiB	6	0	0	36

SUPERLATIVES

Rushing Avg.	5.2	Ernie Caddell, Det
Receiving Avg.	23.6	Joe Carter, Phi
Completion Pct.	50.4	Ed Danowski, NYG
Touchdowns	7	Don Hutson, GB
Field Goals	6	Armand Niccolai, Pit
		Bill Smith, ChiC
Extra Points	16	Dutch Clark, Det

1936 NATIONAL FOOTBALL LEAGUE

					SCORING		RUSHING				PASSING						
Team	W	L	T	PCT	OWN-OPP PTS-PTS	OWN-OPP PPG-PPG	OWN-OPP ATT-ATT	OWN-OPP YARD-YARD	OWN-OPP AVG-AVG	ON-OP TD-TD	OWN-OPP ATT-ATT	OWN-OPP COM-COM	OWN-OPP PCT-PCT	OWN-OPP YARD-YARD	OWN-OPP AVG-AVG	ON-OP TD-TD	ON-OP IN-IN
Eastern Division																	
Bos	7	5	0	.583	149-110	12.4- 9.2	435-434	1454-1148	3.3-2.6	8- 3	214-198	77- 62	36.0-31.3	1102- 954	5.1- 4.8	5- 7	23-22
Pit	6	6	0	.500	98-187	8.2-15.6	472-543	1100-2150	2.3-4.0	4-11	198-164	81- 52	40.9-31.7	1078- 907	5.4- 5.5	5-13	28-25
NYG	5	6	1	.455	115-163	9.6-13.6	517-488	1837-1781	3.6-3.6	4-12	179-149	69- 60	38.5-40.3	887- 997	5.0- 6.7	10- 7	17-19

Team	W	L	T	PCT	SCORING OWN-OPP PTS-PTS	SCORING OWN-OPP PPG-PPG	RUSHING OWN-OPP ATT-ATT	RUSHING OWN-OPP YARD-YARD	RUSHING OWN-OPP AVG-AVG	RUSHING ON-OP TD-TD	PASSING OWN-OPP ATT-ATT	PASSING OWN-OPP COM-COM	PASSING OWN-OPP PCT-PCT	PASSING OWN-OPP YARD-YARD	PASSING OWN-OPP AVG-AVG	PASSING ON-OP TD-TD	PASSING ON-OP IN-IN
Bkn	3	8	1	.273	92-161	7.7-13.4	364-579	1300-1868	3.6-3.2	9-11	141-174	43- 65	30.5-37.4	621- 905	4.4- 5.2	2- 7	23-23
Phi	1	11	0	.083	51-206	4.3-17.2	473-468	1415-1973	3.0-4.2	2-12	170-147	39- 61	22.9-41.5	603- 853	3.5- 5.8	3-10	36-15
Western Division																	
GB	10	1	1	.909	248-118	20.7- 9.8	490-478	1664-1494	3.4-3.1	11- 5	255-227	108- 81	42.4-35.7	1629- 1170	6.4- 5.2	17- 7	19-31
ChiB	9	3	0	.750	222- 94	18.5- 7.8	552-510	2206-1822	4.0-3.6	12- 9	170-227	58- 86	34.1-37.9	1099- 1174	6.5- 5.2	16- 3	21-35
Det	8	4	0	.667	235-102	19.6- 8.5	591-446	2885-1427	4.9-3.2	22- 3	146-194	61- 70	41.8-36.1	818- 1027	5.6- 5.3	6- 6	23-22
ChiC	3	8	1	.273	74-143	6.2-11.9	559-507	1509-1707	2.7-3.4	5-11	183-176	68- 67	37.2-38.1	1123- 973	6.1- 5.5	3- 7	26-24
54 games					1284	23.8	4453	15370	3.5	166	1656	604	36.5	8960	5.4	67	216

Championship: GB 21, Bos 6

LEADING RUSHERS	ATT	YARD	AVG	TD
Tuffy Leemans, NYG	206	830	4.0	2
Ace Gutowsky, Det	191	827	4.3	6
Dutch Clark, Det	123	628	5.1	7
Cliff Battles, Bos	176	614	3.5	5
George Grosvenor, ChiB-ChiC	170	612	3.6	4

LEADING PASSERS	ATT	COM	YARD	TD	IN
Arnie Herber, GB	173	77	1239	11	13
Ed Matesic, Pit	138	64	850	4	16
Phil Sarboe, ChiC-Bos	114	47	680	3	13
Pug Vaughan, ChiC	79	30	546	2	10
Ed Danowski, NYG	104	47	515	5	10

LEADING RECEIVERS	NO	YARD	AVG	TD
Don Hutson, GB	34	536	15.8	8
Bill Smith, ChiC	20	414	20.7	1
Ernie Caddel, Det	19	150	7.9	1
Wayne Millner, Bos	18	211	11.7	0
Eggs Manske, Phi	17	325	19.1	0

LEADING SCORERS	TD	FG	PAT	PTS
Dutch Clark, Det	7	4	19	73
Jack Manders, ChiB	4	7	17	62
Don Hutson, GB	9	0	0	54
Bill Hewitt, ChiB	7	0	0	42
Cliff Battles, Bos	7	0	0	42

SUPERLATIVES

Rushing Avg.	6.4	Ernie Caddell, Det
Receiving Avg.	23.9	Bill Hewitt, ChiB
Completion Pct.	53.5	Dutch Clark, Det
Touchdowns	9	Don Hutson, GB
Field Goals	7	Jack Manders, ChiB Armand Niccolai, Pit
Extra Points	19	Dutch Clark, Det

1937 NATIONAL FOOTBALL LEAGUE

Team	W	L	T	PCT	SCORING OWN-OPP PTS-PTS	SCORING OWN-OPP PPG-PPG	RUSHING OWN-OPP ATT-ATT	RUSHING OWN-OPP YARD-YARD	RUSHING OWN-OPP AVG-AVG	RUSHING ON-OP TD-TD	PASSING OWN-OPP ATT-ATT	PASSING OWN-OPP COM-COM	PASSING OWN-OPP PCT-PCT	PASSING OWN-OPP YARD-YARD	PASSING OWN-OPP AVG-AVG	PASSING ON-OP TD-TD	PASSING ON-OP IN-IN
Eastern Division																	
Was	8	3	0	.727	195-120	17.7-10.9	450-352	1604-1149	3.6-3.3	11- 3	222-171	99- 66	44.6-38.6	1316- 946	5.9- 5.5	11-12	20-17
NYG	6	3	2	.667	128-109	11.6- 9.9	476-390	1519-1216	3.2-3.2	4- 6	203-182	83- 71	40.9-39.0	1024- 929	5.0- 5.1	10- 5	11-30
Pit	4	7	0	.364	122-145	11.1-13.2	493-405	1419-1311	2.9-3.2	5- 7	164-185	57- 60	34.8-32.4	918- 902	5.6- 4.9	9- 9	27-17
Bkn	3	7	1	.300	82-174	7.5-15.8	357-474	982-1764	2.8-3.7	5-10	179-165	64- 74	35.8-44.8	995- 990	5.6- 6.0	4-10	25-21
Phi	2	8	1	.200	86-177	7.8-16.1	285-502	884-1812	3.1-3.6	2- 6	207-196	63- 79	30.4-40.3	849- 1315	4.1- 6.7	8-15	15-24
Western Division																	
ChiB	9	1	1	.900	201-100	18.3- 9.1	479-412	1612- 933	3.4-2.3	5- 5	147-195	56- 78	38.1-40.0	1014- 1292	6.9- 6.6	17- 6	13-17
GB	7	4	0	.636	220-122	20.0-11.1	483-400	1786-1184	3.7-3.0	10- 8	216-197	95- 70	44.0-35.5	1398- 1115	6.5- 5.7	16- 7	26-22
Det	7	4	0	.636	180-105	16.4- 9.5	484-387	2074-1329	4.3-3.4	12- 8	120-165	44- 59	36.7-35.8	631- 804	5.3- 4.9	4- 4	18-24
ChiC	5	5	1	.500	135-165	12.3-15.0	385-475	1149-1457	3.0-3.1	7- 6	189-204	77- 73	40.7-35.8	1243- 1051	6.6- 5.2	8-13	21-24
Cle	1	10	0	.091	75-207	6.8-18.8	370-465	930-1804	2.5-3.9	6- 8	168-155	59- 67	35.1-43.2	839- 883	5.0- 5.7	3- 9	21-15
55 games					1424	25.9	4262	13959	3.3	67	1815	697	38.4	10227	5.6	90	206

Championship: Was 28, ChiB 21

LEADING RUSHERS	ATT	YARD	AVG	TD
Cliff Battles, Was	216	874	4.0	5
Clarke Hinkle, GB	129	552	4.3	5
John Karcis, Pit	128	513	4.0	3
Dutch Clark, Det	96	468	4.9	5
George Grosvenor, ChiC	143	461	3.2	2

LEADING PASSERS	ATT	COM	YARD	TD	IN
Sammy Baugh, Was	171	81	1127	8	14
Pat Coffee, ChiC	119	52	824	4	11
Ed Danowski, NYG	134	66	814	8	5
Arnie Herber, GB	104	47	684	7	10
Bernie Masterson, ChiB	72	26	615	9	7

LEADING RECEIVERS	NO	YARD	AVG	TD
Don Hutson, GB	41	552	13.5	7
Gaynell Tinsley, ChiC	36	675	18.8	5
Charley Malone, Was	28	419	15.0	4
Jeff Barrett, Bkn	20	461	23.1	3
Bill Hewitt, Phi	16	197	12.3	5

LEADING SCORERS	TD	FG	PAT	PTS
Jack Manders, ChiB	5	8	15	69
Clarke Hinkle, GB	7	2	9	57
Riley Smith, Was	3	5	22	55
Dutch Clark, Det	6	1	6	45
Cliff Battles, Was	7	0	0	42
Don Hutson, GB	7	0	0	42

SUPERLATIVES

Rushing Avg.	5.6	Ernie Caddell, Det
Receiving Avg.	23.1	Jeff Barrett, Bkn
Completion Pct.	50.7	Bob Monnett, GB
Touchdowns	7	Cliff Battles, Was Clark Hinkle, GB Don Hutson, GB
Field Goals	8	Jack Manders, ChiB
Extra Points	22	Riley Smith, Was

1938 NATIONAL FOOTBALL LEAGUE

Team	W	L	T	PCT	SCORING OWN-OPP PTS-PTS	SCORING OWN-OPP PPG-PPG	RUSHING OWN-OPP ATT-ATT	RUSHING OWN-OPP YARD-YARD	RUSHING OWN-OPP AVG-AVG	RUSHING ON-OP TD-TD	PASSING OWN-OPP ATT-ATT	PASSING OWN-OPP COM-COM	PASSING OWN-OPP PCT-PCT	PASSING OWN-OPP YARD-YARD	PASSING OWN-OPP AVG-AVG	PASSING ON-OP TD-TD	PASSING ON-OP IN-IN
Eastern Division																	
NYG	8	2	1	.800	194- 79	17.6- 7.2	466-373	1550-1114	3.3-3.0	12- 3	186-226	91- 77	48.9-34.1	1142- 914	6.1- 4.0	10- 5	19-34
Was	6	3	2	.667	148-154	13.5-14.0	388-427	1424-1231	3.7-2.9	10- 8	248-195	114- 69	46.0-35.4	1536- 943	6.2- 4.8	9- 9	28-19
Bkn	4	4	3	.500	131-161	11.9-14.6	381-410	1212-1509	3.2-3.7	9- 6	171-246	69-105	40.4-42.7	992- 1414	5.8- 5.7	6-13	9-28
Phi	5	6	0	.455	154-164	14.0-14.9	346-463	1011-1855	2.9-4.0	2-12	191-197	64- 97	33.5-49.2	917- 1396	4.8- 7.1	15- 7	19-16
Pit	2	9	0	.182	79-169	7.2-15.4	457-425	1414-1368	3.1-3.2	5- 7	194-185	72- 74	37.1-40.0	916- 1213	4.7- 6.6	5-13	32-14
Western Division																	
GB	8	3	0	.727	223-118	20.3-10.7	454-372	1571-1206	3.5-3.2	9- 8	210-232	91- 92	43.3-39.7	1466- 1343	7.0- 5.8	20- 5	20-22
Det	7	4	0	.636	119-108	10.8- 9.8	472-338	1893-1081	4.0-3.2	11- 6	148-205	49- 77	33.1-37.6	747- 1105	5.0- 5.4	3- 9	16-23
ChiB	6	5	0	.545	194-148	17.6-13.4	461-382	1686-1236	3.7-3.2	11- 8	197-190	72- 76	36.5-40.0	1222- 897	6.2- 4.7	12- 9	18-24
Cle	4	7	0	.364	131-215	11.9-19.5	336-500	798-1745	2.4-3.5	5-15	245-172	88- 77	35.9-44.8	1363- 1248	5.6- 7.3	9-12	34-23
ChiC	2	9	0	.182	111-168	10.1-15.3	382-453	1149-1363	3.0-3.0	9-10	240-182	114- 80	47.5-44.0	1340- 1168	5.6- 6.4	4-11	26-18
55 games					1484	27.0	4143	13708	3.3	83	2030	824	40.6	11641	5.7	93	221

Championship: NYG 23, GB 17

LEADING RUSHERS	ATT	YARD	AVG	TD
Whizzer White, Pit	152	567	3.7	4
Tuffy Leemans, NYG	121	463	3.8	4
Bill Shepherd, Det	100	455	4.6	3
Cecil Isbell, GB	85	445	5.2	2
Ace Gutowsky, Det	131	444	3.4	2

LEADING PASSERS	ATT	COM	YARD	TD	IN
Ace Parker, Bkn	148	63	865	5	7
Sammy Baugh, Was	128	63	853	6	11
Bernie Masterson, ChiB	112	46	848	5	9
Ed Danowski, NYG	129	70	848	7	8
Cecil Isbell, GB	91	37	659	8	10

LEADING RECEIVERS	NO	YARD	AVG	TD
Gaynell Tinsley, ChiC	41	516	12.6	1
Don Hutson, GB	32	548	17.1	9
Joe Carter, Phi	27	386	14.3	7
Charley Malone, Was	24	257	10.7	1
Jim Benton, Cle	21	418	19.9	5

LEADING SCORERS	TD	FG	PAT	PTS
Clarke Hinkle, GB	7	3	7	58
Don Hutson, GB	9	0	3	57
Joe Carter, Phi	8	0	0	48
Ward Cuff, NYG	2	5	18	45
Andy Farkas, Was	6	0	1	37
Jack Manders, ChiB	3	3	10	37

SUPERLATIVES

Rushing Avg.	5.2	Cecil Isbell, GB
Receiving Avg.	19.9	Jim Benton, Cle
Completion Pct.	54.4	Bob Monnett, GB
Touchdowns	9	Don Hutson, GB
Field Goals	5	Ward Cuff, NYG
		Ralph Kercheval, Bkn
Extra Points	18	Ward Cuff, NYG

1939 NATIONAL FOOTBALL LEAGUE

					SCORING		RUSHING				PASSING						
Team	W	L	T	PCT	OWN-OPP PTS-PTS	OWN-OPP PPG-PPG	OWN-OPP ATT-ATT	OWN - OPP YARD-YARD	OWN-OPP AVG-AVG	ON-OP TD-TD	OWN-OPP ATT-ATT	OWN-OPP COM-COM	OWN-OPP PCT-PCT	OWN - OPP YARD - YARD	OWN-OPP AVG-AVG	ON-OP TD-TD	ON-OP IN-IN
Eastern Division																	
NYG	9	1	1	.900	168- 85	15.3- 7.7	448-406	1281-1216	2.9-3.0	9- 5	177-222	75- 89	42.4-40.1	971- 1283	5.5- 5.8	8- 3	11-35
Was	8	2	1	.800	242- 94	22.0- 8.5	410-412	1693- 999	4.1-2.4	12- 5	201-243	117- 90	58.2-37.0	1795- 1116	8.9- 4.6	18- 6	18-24
Bkn	4	6	1	.400	108-219	9.8-19.9	407-427	1327-1488	3.3-3.5	7-13	176-195	77- 92	43.8-47.2	1024- 1599	5.9- 8.2	4-13	16-22
Phi	1	9	1	.100	105-200	9.5-18.2	329-455	631-1661	1.9-3.7	5-11	267-210	119- 98	44.6-46.7	1516- 1290	5.7- 6.1	7-11	22-17
Pit	1	9	1	.100	114-216	10.4-19.6	428-440	1138-1701	2.7-3.9	7-18	221-193	70- 88	31.7-45.6	1084- 1368	4.9- 7.1	8-10	34-11
Western Division																	
GB	9	2	0	.818	233-153	21.2-13.9	500-333	1574-1165	3.1-3.5	13-12	248-239	101-106	40.7-44.4	1871- 1602	7.5- 6.7	14- 9	15-26
ChiB	8	3	0	.727	298-157	27.1-14.3	439-353	2043- 812	4.7-2.3	21- 9	221-319	89-133	40.3-41.7	1965- 1768	8.9- 5.5	16- 9	19-25
Det	6	5	0	.545	145-150	13.2-13.6	406-375	1487-1203	3.7-3.2	10- 5	227-217	92- 92	40.5-42.4	1357- 1400	6.0- 6.5	7-13	20-14
Cle	5	5	1	.500	195-164	17.7-14.9	387-431	1260-1499	3.3-3.5	14-11	253-199	127- 78	50.2-39,2	1415- 1249	5.6- 6.3	12- 9	21-23
ChiC	1	10	0	.091	84-254	7.6-23.1	321-443	835-1525	2.6-3.4	4-13	247-201	85- 86	34.4-42.8	1170- 1493	4.7- 7.4	5-16	33-12
55 games					1692	30.8	4075	13269	3.3	102	2238	952	42.5	14168	6.3	99	209

Championship: GB 27, NYG 0

LEADING RUSHERS	ATT	YARD	AVG	TD
Bill Osmanski, ChiB	121	699	5.8	7
Andy Farkas, Was	139	547	3.9	5
Joe Maniaci, ChiB	77	544	7.1	4
Pug Manders, Bkn	114	482	4.2	2
Parker Hall, Cle	120	458	3.8	2

LEADING PASSERS	ATT	COM	YARD	TD	IN
Davey O'Brien, Phi	201	99	1324	6	17
Parker Hall, Cle	208	106	1227	9	13
Arnie Herber, GB	139	57	1107	8	9
Frank Filchock, Was	89	55	1094	11	7
Ace Parker, Bkn	157	72	977	4	13

LEADING RECEIVERS	NO	YARD	AVG	TD
Don Hutson, GB	34	846	24.9	6
Perry Schwartz, Bkn	33	550	16.7	3
Vic Spadaccini, Cle	32	292	9.1	1
Red Ramsey, Phi	31	359	11.6	1
Jim Benton, Cle	27	388	14.4	7

LEADING SCORERS	TD	FG	PAT	PTS
Andy Farkas, Was	11	0	2	68
Johnny Drake, Cle	9	0	0	54
Jack Manders, ChiB	4	3	17	50
Jim Benton, Cle	8	0	0	48
Bill Osmanski, ChiB	8	0	0	48

LEADING PUNTER	NO	AVG	Long
Parker Hall, Cle	58	40.8	80

SUPERLATIVES

Rushing Avg.	7.1	Joe Maniaci, ChiB
Receiving Avg.	27.3	Andy Farkas, Was
Completion Pct.	61.8	Frank Filchock, Was
Touchdowns	11	Andy Farkas, Was
Field Goals	7	Ward Cuff, NYG
Extra Points	18	Tiny Engebretsen, GB

1940 NATIONAL FOOTBALL LEAGUE

					SCORING		RUSHING				PASSING						
Team	W	L	T	PCT	OWN-OPP PTS-PTS	OWN-OPP PPG-PPG	OWN-OPP ATT-ATT	OWN - OPP YARD-YARD	OWN-OPP AVG-AVG	ON-OP TD-TD	OWN-OPP ATT-ATT	OWN-OPP COM-COM	OWN-OPP PCT-PCT	OWN - OPP YARD - YARD	OWN-OPP AVG-AVG	ON-OP TD-TD	ON-OP IN-IN
Eastern Division																	
Was	9	2	0	.818	245-142	22.3-12.9	400-362	1402-1075	3.5-3.0	15- 5	244-287	144-125	59.0-43.6	1887- 1782	7.7- 6.2	18-11	22-18
Bkn	8	3	0	.727	186-120	16.9-10.9	414-429	1546-1391	3.7-3.2	9- 7	191-259	80-113	41.9-43.6	1267- 1445	6.6- 5.6	14- 8	13-18
NYG	6	4	1	.600	131-133	11.9-12.1	454-413	1476- 977	3.3-2.4	6- 8	174-234	78- 91	44.8-38.9	1036- 1242	6.0- 5.3	9- 7	15-23
Pit	2	7	2	.222	60-178	5.5-16.2	403-438	1102-1491	2.7-3.4	2-12	189-192	58- 83	30.7-43.2	875- 1231	4.6- 6.4	4- 9	27- 8
Phi	1	10	0	.091	111-211	10.1-19.2	317-460	298-1778	0.9-3.9	8-18	362-151	152- 80	42.0-53.0	1855- 1012	5.1- 6.7	6- 9	20-12
Western Division																	
ChiB	8	3	0	.727	238-152	21.6-13.8	494-372	1818-1003	3.7-2.7	16- 7	171-269	68-133	39.8-49.4	1401- 1747	8.2- 6.5	10-14	15-27
GB	6	4	1	.600	238-155	21.6-14.1	463-387	1604-1040	3.5-2.7	10- 9	283-252	118- 98	41.7-38.9	1796- 1492	6.3- 5.9	18- 9	26-40
Det	5	5	1	.500	138-153	12.5-13.9	427-381	1457-1323	3.4-3.5	12-13	195-177	86- 77	44.1-43.5	1177- 1034	6.0- 5.8	3- 6	27-29
Cle	4	6	1	.400	171-191	15.5-17.4	364-467	1142-1612	3.1-3.5	11- 9	247-247	109- 99	44.1-40.1	1582- 1490	6.4- 6.0	12-13	25-25
ChiC	2	7	2	.222	139-222	12.6-20.2	400-427	1315-1470	3.3-3.4	11-12	198-186	75- 69	37.9-37.1	912- 1313	4.6- 7.1	6-14	33-23
55 games					1657	30.1	4136	13160	3.2	100	2254	968	42.9	13788	6.1	100	223

Championship: ChiB 73, Was 0

LEADING RUSHERS	ATT	YARD	AVG	TD
Whizzer White, Det	146	514	3.5	5
Johnny Drake, Cle	134	480	3.6	9
Tuffy Leemans, NYG	132	474	3.6	1
Banks McFadden, Bkn	85	411	4.8	1
Dick Todd, Was	76	408	5.4	4

LEADING PASSERS	ATT	COM	YARD	TD	IN
Sammy Baugh, Was	177	111	1367	12	10
Davey O'Brien, Phi	277	124	1290	5	17
Parker Hall, Cle	183	77	1108	7	16
Cecil Isbell, GB	150	68	1037	8	12
Sid Luckman, ChiB	105	48	941	4	9

LEADING RECEIVERS	NO	YARD	AVG	TD
Don Looney, Phi	58	707	12.2	4
Don Hutson, GB	45	664	14.8	7
Jimmy Johnston, Was	29	350	12.1	3
Jim Benton, Cle	22	351	16.0	3
Vic Spadaccini, Cle	22	276	12.5	2
Wayne Millner, Was	22	233	10.6	3

LEADING SCORERS	TD	FG	PAT	PTS
Don Hutson, GB	7	0	15	57
Johnny Drake, Cle	9	0	2	56
Dick Todd, Was	9	0	0	54
Ace Parker, Bkn	5	0	19	49
Clarke Hinkle, GB	3	9	3	48

LEADING INTERCEPTORS	NO	YDS	AVG	TD
Ace Parker, Bkn	6	146	24.3	1
Kent Ryan, Det	6	65	10.8	0
Don Hutson, GB	6	24	4.0	0

LEADING PUNTER	NO	AVG	Long
Sammy Baugh, Was	35	51.4	85

SUPERLATIVES

Rushing Avg.	5.4	Dick Todd, Was
Receiving Avg.	26.3	Paul McDonough, Cle
Completion Pct.	62.7	Sammy Baugh, Was
Touchdowns	9	Johnny Drake, Cle
		Dick Todd, Was
Field Goals	9	Clarke Hinkle, GB
Extra Points	19	Ace Parker, Bkn

1941 NATIONAL FOOTBALL LEAGUE

					SCORING		RUSHING				PASSING						
Team	W	L	T	PCT	OWN-OPP PTS-PTS	OWN-OPP PPG-PPG	OWN-OPP ATT-ATT	OWN-OPP YARD-YARD	OWN-OPP AVG-AVG	ON-OP TD-TD	OWN-OPP ATT-ATT	OWN-OPP COM-COM	OWN-OPP PCT-PCT	OWN-OPP YARD-YARD	OWN-OPP AVG-AVG	ON-OP TD-TD	ON-OP IN-IN
Eastern Division																	
NYG	8	3	0	.727	238-114	21.6-10.4	433-408	1318-1165	3.0-2.9	16- 9	156-218	68-103	43.6-47.2	1088- 1212	7.0- 5.6	11- 6	12-29
Bkn	7	4	0	.636	158-127	14.4-11.5	444-376	1665-1210	3.7-3.2	14- 6	202-189	90- 86	44.6-45.5	1134- 1169	5.6- 6.2	5- 6	18-20
Was	6	5	0	.545	176-174	16.0-15.8	406-410	1097-1110	2.7-2.7	7-16	262-229	134-103	51.1-45.0	1563- 1338	6.0- 5.8	11-14	30-23
Phi	2	8	1	.200	119-218	10.8-19.8	360-432	849-1498	2.4-3.5	6-14	249-238	115-100	46.2-42.0	1367- 1369	5.5- 5.8	10-13	27-21
Pit	1	9	1	.100	103-276	9.4-25.1	381-426	1223-1550	3.2-3.6	9-17	168-189	42- 84	25.0-44.4	654- 1168	3.8- 6.2	5-10	34-19
Western Division																	
ChiB	10	1	0	.909	396-147	36.0-13.4	495-373	2290-1076	4.6-2.9	30- 6	196-265	98-106	50.0-40.0	2002- 1463	10.2- 5.5	19- 9	11-34
GB	10	1	0	.909	258-120	23.5-10.9	467-356	1550-1221	3.3-3.4	13-10	253-233	133-104	52.6-44.6	1731- 1343	6.8- 5.8	17- 8	13-25
Det	4	6	1	.400	121-195	11.0-17.7	361-475	1009-1404	2.8-3.0	7- 8	187-247	58-112	31.0-45.3	848- 1605	4.5- 6.5	5- 8	20-18
ChiC	3	7	1	.300	127-197	11.5-17.9	386-384	1098-1301	2.8-3.4	8-13	252-196	117- 90	46.4-45.9	1658- 1305	6.6- 6.7	6-12	20-16
Cle	2	9	0	.182	116-244	10.5-22.2	343-436	984-1547	2.9-3.5	4-23	285-436	123- 90	43.2-43.7	1352- 1425	4.7- 6.9	10-14	35-15
55 games					1812	32.9	4076	13083	3.2	114	2210	978	44.3	13397	6.1	99	219

Western Division Playoff: ChiB 33, GB 14
Championship: ChiB 37, NYG 9

LEADING RUSHERS	ATT	YARD	AVG	TD
Pug Manders, Bkn	111	486	4.4	6
George McAfee, ChiB	65	474	7.3	6
Marshall Goldberg, ChiC	117	427	3.6	3
Norm Standlee, ChiB	81	414	5.1	5
Clarke Hinkle, GB	129	393	3.0	5

LEADING PASSERS	ATT	COM	YARD	TD	IN
Cecil Isbell, GB	206	117	1479	15	11
Sammy Baugh, Was	193	106	1236	10	19
Sid Luckman, ChiB	119	68	1181	9	6
Tommy Thompson, Phi	162	86	974	8	14
Ace Parker, Bkn	102	51	642	2	8

LEADING RECEIVERS	NO	YARD	AVG	TD
Don Hutson, GB	58	738	12.7	10
Dick Humbert, Phi	29	332	11.4	3
Bill Dewell, ChiC	28	262	9.4	1
Perry Schwartz, Bkn	25	362	14.5	2
Lou Brock, GB	22	307	14.0	2

LEADING SCORERS	TD	FG	PAT	PTS
Don Hutson, GB	12	1	20	95
George McAfee, ChiB	12	0	0	72
Hugh Gallarneau, ChiB	11	0	0	66
Clarke Hinkle, GB	6	6	2	56
Ward Cuff, NYG	2	5	19	46

LEADING INTERCEPTORS	NO	YDS	AVG	TD
Marshall Goldberg, ChiC	7	54	7.7	0
Art Jones, Pit	7	35	5.0	0

LEADING PUNTER	NO	AVG	Long
Sammy Baugh, Was	30	48.7	75

LEADING PUNT RETURNER	NO	YDS	AVG	Long	TD
Whizzer White, Det	19	262	13.8	64	0

LEADING KICKOFF RETURNER	NO	YDS	AVG	Long	TD
Marshall Goldberg, ChiC	12	290	24.2	41	0

SUPERLATIVES

Rushing Avg.	7.3	George McAfee, ChiB
Receiving Avg.	28.5	Ken Kavanaugh, ChiB
Completion Pct.	57.1	Sid Luckman, ChiB
Touchdowns	12	Don Hutson, GB
		George McAfee, ChiB
Field Goals	6	Clarke Hinkle, GB
Extra Points	20	Don Hutson, GB
	20	Bob Snyder, ChiB

LONGEST

Run	70	George McAfee, ChiB
Pass	80	Ray Mallouf to John Hall, ChiC
Interception	91	Hal Van Every, GB
Punt	75	Sammy Baugh, Was
Punt Return	90	Andy Uram, GB
Field Goal	43	Clarke Hinkle, GB

1942 NATIONAL FOOTBALL LEAGUE

					SCORING		RUSHING				PASSING						
Team	W	L	T	PCT	OWN-OPP PTS-PTS	OWN-OPP PPG-PPG	OWN-OPP ATT-ATT	OWN-OPP YARD-YARD	OWN-OPP AVG-AVG	ON-OP TD-TD	OWN-OPP ATT-ATT	OWN-OPP COM-COM	OWN-OPP PCT-PCT	OWN-OPP YARD-YARD	OWN-OPP AVG-AVG	ON-OP TD-TD	ON-OP IN-IN
Eastern Division																	
Was	10	1	0	.909	227-102	20.6- 9.3	413-367	1521- 848	3.7-2.3	9- 5	257-216	137- 81	53.3-37.5	1600- 1093	6.2- 5.1	16- 5	17-19
Pit	7	4	0	.636	167-119	15.2-10.8	490-366	1851-1205	3.8-3.3	15- 6	161-211	51-100	31.7-47.4	686- 1183	4.3- 5.6	2- 9	11-21
NYG	5	5	1	.500	155-139	14.1-12.6	401-486	1211-1485	3.0-3.2	10-13	148-228	67-114	45.3-50.0	957- 1401	6.5- 6.1	10- 4	14-15
Bkn	3	8	0	.273	100-168	9.1-15.3	431-426	1495-1630	3.5-3.8	9-13	159-199	56- 89	35.2-44.7	714- 1175	4.5- 5.9	3- 9	24-14
Phi	2	9	0	.182	134-239	12.2-21.7	407-464	1105-1727	2.7-3.7	8-20	213-178	96- 78	45.1-44.4	1416- 1241	6.6- 7.0	8-12	17-18
Western Division																	
ChiB	11	0	0	1.000	376- 84	34.2- 7.6	470-294	1911- 519	4.1-1.8	23- 3	194-280	94-111	48.5-39.6	1974- 1179	10.2- 4.2	21- 7	29-33
GB	8	2	1	.800	300-215	27.3-19.5	422-376	1274-1559	3.0-4.1	10-17	330-242	172-100	52.1-41.3	2407- 1471	7.3- 6.1	28- 8	18-33
Cle	5	6	0	.455	150-207	13.6-18.8	310-463	1035-1764	3.3-3.9	5-11	249-262	109-125	43.8-47.7	1537- 1740	6.2- 6.6	13-17	27-23
ChiC	3	8	0	.273	98-209	8.9-19.0	366-390	1021-1495	2.8-3.8	4-11	316-214	131- 84	41.5-39.3	1432- 1502	4.5- 7.0	6-15	29-25
Det	0	11	0	.000	38-263	3.5-23.9	342-440	1261-1463	3.7-3.3	4-13	222-219	73-103	32.9-47.0	885- 1623	4.0- 7.4	1-22	33-18
55 games					1745	31.7	4052	13685	3.4	97	2249	986	43.8	13608	5.3	108	219

Championship: Was 14, ChiB 6

LEADING RUSHERS	ATT	YARD	AVG	TD
Bill Dudley, Pit	162	696	4.3	5
Merlyn Condit, Bkn	129	647	5.0	3
Gary Famiglietti, ChiB	118	503	4.3	8
Andy Farkas, Was	125	468	3.7	4
Dick Riffle, Pit	115	467	4.1	4

LEADING PASSERS	ATT	COM	YARD	TD	IN
Cecil Isbell, GB	268	146	2021	24	14
Sammy Baugh, Was	225	132	1524	16	11
Sid Luckman, ChiB	105	57	1023	10	13
Tommy Thompson, Phi	203	95	1410	8	16
Wilson Schwenk, ChiC	295	126	1350	6	27

LEADING RECEIVERS	NO	YARD	AVG	TD
Don Hutson, GB	74	1211	16.4	17
Frank (Pop) Ivy, ChiC	27	259	9.6	0
Dante Magnani, Cle	24	276	11.5	4
Jim Benton, Cle	23	345	15.0	1
Dick Todd, Was	23	328	14.3	4

LEADING SCORERS	TD	FG	PAT	PTS
Don Hutson, GB	17	1	33	138
Ray McLean, ChiB	9	0	0	54
Gary Famiglietti, ChiB	8	0	0	48
Frank Maznicki, ChiB	2	4	21	45
Hugh Gallarneau, ChiB	7	0	0	42

LEADING INTERCEPTOR	NO	YDS	AVG	TD
Bulldog Turner, ChiB	8	96	12.0	1

LEADING PUNTER	NO	AVG	Long
Sammy Baugh, Was	37	48.2	74

LEADING PUNT RETURNER	NO	YDS	AVG	Long	TD
Merlyn Condit, Bkn	21	210	10.0	23	0

LEADING KICKOFF RETURNER	NO	YDS	AVG	Long	TD
Marshall Goldberg, ChiC	15	393	26.2	95	1

SUPERLATIVES

Rushing Avg.	6.4	Frank Maznicki, ChiB
Receiving Avg.	30.1	Ray McLean, ChiB
Completion Pct.	58.7	Sammy Baugh, Was
Touchdowns	17	Don Hutson, GB
Field Goals	5	Bill Daddio, ChiC
Extra Points	33	Don Hutson, GB

LONGEST

Run	80	Lloyd Cardwell, Det
Pass	73	Cecil Isbell to Don Hutson, GB
Interception	66	Neal Adams, NYG
Punt	74	Sammy Baugh, Was Dean McAdams, Bkn
Punt Return	89	Ray McLean, ChiB
Kickoff Return	98	Andy Uram, GB
Field Goal	46	Chet Adams, Cle

1943 NATIONAL FOOTBALL LEAGUE

Team	W	L	T	PCT	SCORING OWN-OPP PTS-PTS	SCORING OWN-OPP PPG-PPG	RUSHING OWN-OPP ATT-ATT	RUSHING OWN-OPP YARD-YARD	RUSHING OWN-OPP AVG-AVG	RUSHING ON-OP TD-TD	PASSING OWN-OPP ATT-ATT	PASSING OWN-OPP COM-COM	PASSING OWN-OPP PCT-PCT	PASSING OWN-OPP YARD-YARD	PASSING OWN-OPP AVG-AVG	PASSING ON-OP TD-TD	PASSING ON-OP IN-IN
Eastern Division																	
Was	6	3	1	.667	229-137	22.9-13.7	320-406	1069-1330	3.3-3.3	7-10	254-193	139- 77	54.7-39.9	1837- 1026	7.2- 5.3	24- 9	20-26
NYG	6	3	1	.667	197-170	19.7-17.0	386-366	1436-1006	3.7-2.7	14- 8	149-229	63-119	42.3-52.0	760- 1724	5.1- 7.5	8-16	9-18
PhPt	5	4	1	.556	225-230	22.5-23.0	459-312	1730- 793	3.8-2.5	18-18	175-221	65-102	37.1-46.2	1138- 1393	6.5- 6.3	11-15	20-22
Bkn	2	8	0	.200	65-234	6.5-23.4	333-404	610-1562	1.8-3.9	4-16	205-219	90- 86	43.9-39.3	969- 1552	4.7- 7.1	5-15	21-15
Western Division																	
ChiB	8	1	1	.889	303-157	30.3-15.7	424-332	1651-1282	3.9-3.9	14-14	229-203	117- 64	51.1-31.5	2310- 980	10.1- 4.8	28- 8	17-24
GB	7	2	1	.778	264-172	26.4-17.2	397-350	1442-1112	3.6-3.2	13- 9	253-242	114-111	45.1-45.9	1909- 1420	7.5- 5.9	21-16	19-42
Det	3	6	1	.333	178-218	17.8-21.8	294-381	817-1213	2.8-3.2	10-14	248-227	93-109	37.5-48.0	1290- 1606	5.2- 7.1	11-16	37-19
ChiC	0	10	0	.000	95-238	9.5-23.8	334-396	709-1166	2.1-2.9	5-13	219-198	88-101	40.2-51.0	1095- 1607	5.0- 8.1	6-21	39-16
40 games					1556	38.9	2947	9464	3.2	85	1732	769	44.4	11308	6.5	114	182

Eastern Division Playoff: Was 28, NYG 0

Championship: ChiB 41, Was 21

LEADING RUSHERS	ATT	YARD	AVG	TD
Bill Paschal, NYG	147	572	3.9	10
Clarke Hinkle, PhPt	116	571	4.9	4
Harry Clark, ChiB	120	556	4.6	3
Ward Cuff, NYG	80	523	6.5	3
Tony Canadeo, GB	94	489	5.2	3

LEADING PASSERS	ATT	COM	YARD	TD	IN
Sammy Baugh, Was	239	133	1754	23	19
Sid Luckman, ChiB	202	110	2194	28	12
Irv Comp, GB	92	46	662	7	4
Ron Cahill, ChiC	109	50	608	3	21
Dean McAdams, Bkn	75	37	315	0	7

LEADING RECEIVERS	NO	YARD	AVG	TD
Don Hutson, GB	47	776	16.5	11
Joe Aguirre, Was	37	420	11.4	7
Wilbur Moore, Was	30	537	17.9	7
Ed Rucinski, ChiC	26	398	15.3	3
Harry Jacunski, GB	24	528	22.0	3

LEADING SCORERS	TD	FG	PAT	PTS
Don Hutson, GB	12	3	36	117
Harry Clark, ChiB	10	0	0	60
Andy Farkas, Was	9	0	0	54
Harry Hopp, Det	9	0	0	54
Wilbur Moore, Was	9	0	0	54

LEADING INTERCEPTOR	NO	YDS	AVG	TD
Sammy Baugh, Was	11	112	10.2	0

LEADING PUNTER	NO	AVG	Long
Sammy Baugh, Was	50	45.9	81

LEADING PUNT RETURNER	NO	YDS	AVG	Long	TD
Andy Farkas, Was	15	168	11.2	33	0

LEADING KICKOFF RETURNER	NO	YDS	AVG	Long	TD
Ken Heineman, Bkn	16	444	27.8	69	0

SUPERLATIVES

Rushing Avg.	6.5	Ward Cuff, NYG
Receiving Avg.	24.6	Tony Bova, PhPt
Completion Pct.	57.7	Sammy Baugh, Was
Touchdowns	12	Don Hutson, GB Bill Paschal, NYG
Field Goals	3	Ward Cuff, NYG Don Hutson, GB
Extra Points	39	Bob Snyder, ChiB

LONGEST

Run	79	Dante Magnani, ChiB
Pass	86	Lou Brock to Harry Jacunski, GB
Interception	91	Clarke Hinkle, PhPt
Punt	81	Sammy Baugh, Was
Punt Return	77	Frank Sinkwich, Det
Kickoff Return	98	Ned Mathews, Det
Field Goal	45	Ward Cuff, NYG

1944 NATIONAL FOOTBALL LEAGUE

Team	W	L	T	PCT	SCORING OWN-OPP PTS-PTS	SCORING OWN-OPP PPG-PPG	RUSHING OWN-OPP ATT-ATT	RUSHING OWN-OPP YARD-YARD	RUSHING OWN-OPP AVG-AVG	RUSHING ON-OP TD-TD	PASSING OWN-OPP ATT-ATT	PASSING OWN-OPP COM-COM	PASSING OWN-OPP PCT-PCT	PASSING OWN-OPP YARD-YARD	PASSING OWN-OPP AVG-AVG	PASSING ON-OP TD-TD	PASSING ON-OP IN-IN
Eastern Division																	
NYG	8	1	1	.889	206- 75	20.6- 7.5	416-374	1532-1000	3.7-2.7	11- 6	125-258	47-114	37.6-44.2	857- 1290	6.9- 5.0	9- 3	17-34
Phi	7	1	2	.875	267-131	26.7-13.1	424-321	1661- 558	3.9-1.7	23- 7	136-231	55-105	40.4-45.5	941- 1379	6.9- 6.0	9-12	12-33
Was	6	3	1	.667	169-180	16.9-18.0	342-409	904-1492	2.6-3.7	6-15	299-188	170- 84	56.9-44.7	2021- 1166	6.8- 6.2	17- 9	17-19
Bos	2	8	0	.200	82-233	8.2-23.3	324-446	471-1575	1.5-3.5	3-20	197-166	85- 76	43.1-45.8	1030- 1131	5.2- 6.8	6-11	22-16
Bkn	0	10	0	.000	108-328	10.8-32.8	365-362	964-1181	2.6-3.3	6-14	213-181	76- 78	35.7-43.1	996- 1227	4.7- 6.8	3- 9	29-10
Western Division																	
GB	8	2	0	.800	238-141	23.8-14.1	395-357	1517-1130	3.8-3.2	16-10	253-227	105- 89	41.5-39.4	1471- 1224	5.8- 5.4	15-10	24-29
ChiB	6	3	1	.667	258-172	25.8-17.2	412-298	1562- 954	3.8-3.2	16-14	217-208	107- 69	49.3-33.2	1616- 1052	7.4- 5.1	21-10	18-24
Det	6	3	1	.667	216-151	21.6-15.1	326-403	1141-1216	3.5-3.0	14- 7	207-248	89-106	43.0-43.1	1475- 1442	7.1- 5.9	16-15	28-26
Cle	4	6	0	.400	188-224	18.8-22.4	358-387	1141-1412	3.2-3.7	11-16	209-206	85- 87	40.7-42.3	1261- 1434	6.0- 7.0	13-16	26-27
ChPt	0	10	0	.000	108-328	10.8-32.8	360-365	1019-1394	2.8-3.8	7-25	258-204	87- 98	33.7-48.0	1257- 1575	4.9- 7.7	8-22	41-16
50 games					1840	38.8	3722	11912	3.2	113	2114	906	42.9	12925	6.1	117	234

Championship: GB 14, NYG 7

LEADING RUSHERS	ATT	YARD	AVG	TD
Bill Paschal, NYG	196	737	3.8	9
John Grigas, ChPt	185	610	3.3	3
Frank Sinkwich, Det	150	563	3.8	6
Henry Margarita, ChiB	88	463	5.3	4
Steve Van Buren, Phi	80	444	5.6	5

LEADING PASSERS	ATT	COM	YARD	TD	IN
Frank Filchock, Was	147	84	1139	13	9
Sammy Baugh, Was	146	82	849	4	8
Sid Luckman, ChiB	143	71	1018	11	11
Irv Comp, GB	177	80	1159	12	21
Al Reisz, Cle	113	49	777	8	10

LEADING RECEIVERS	NO	YARD	AVG	TD
Don Hutson, GB	58	866	14.9	9
Jim Benton, Cle	39	505	12.9	6
Joe Aguirre, Was	34	410	12.1	4
Wilbur Moore, Was	33	424	12.8	5
Les Dye, Was	24	281	11.7	2
George Wilson, ChiB	24	265	11.0	4
Bob Masterson, Bkn	24	258	10.8	1

LEADING SCORERS	TD	FG	PAT	PTS
Don Hutson, GB	9	0	31	85
Frankie Sinkwich, Det	6	2	24	66
Roy Zimmerman, Phi	3	4	32	62
Bill Paschal, NYG	9	0	0	54
Joe Aguirre, Was	4	4	15	51

LEADING INTERCEPTOR	NO	YDS	AVG	TD
Howard Livingston, NYG	9	172	19.1	1

LEADING PUNTER	NO	AVG	Long
Frank Sinkwich, Det	45	41.0	73

LEADING PUNT RETURNER	NO	YDS	AVG	Long	TD
Steve Van Buren, Phi	15	230	15.3	55t	1

LEADING KICKOFF RETURNER	NO	YDS	AVG	Long	TD
Bob Thurbon, ChPt	12	291	24.3	55	0

SUPERLATIVES

Rushing Avg.	6.1	Al Grygo, ChiB
Receiving Avg.	37.3	Mel Bleeker, Phi
Completion Pct.	57.1	Frank Filchock, Was
Touchdowns	9	Don Hutson, GB
		Bill Paschal, NYG
Field Goals	6	Ken Strong, NYG
Extra Points	36	Pete Gudauskas, ChiB

LONGEST

Run	80	Bob Davis, Bos
Pass	86t	Sid Luckman to Ray McLean, ChiB
Interception	83t	Don Perkins, GB
Punt	76	Sammy Baugh, Was
		Cecil Johnson, Bkn
Punt Return	60	Frank Seno, Was
Kickoff Return	97t	Steve Van Buren, Phi
Field Goal	49	Roy Zimmerman, Phi

1945 NATIONAL FOOTBALL LEAGUE

					SCORING		RUSHING				PASSING						
Team	W	L	T	PCT	OWN-OPP PTS-PTS	OWN-OPP PPG-PPG	OWN-OPP ATT-ATT	OWN-OPP YARD-YARD	OWN-OPP AVG-AVG	ON-OP TD-TD	OWN-OPP ATT-ATT	OWN-OPP COM-COM	OWN-OPP PCT-PCT	OWN-OPP YARD-YARD	OWN-OPP AVG-AVG	ON-OP TD-TD	ON-OP IN-IN
Eastern Division																	
Was	8	2	0	.800	209-121	20.9-12.1	394-337	1708-1003	4.3-3.0	15- 8	228-209	146- 95	64.0-45.5	1838- 1121	8.1- 5.4	12- 9	11-16
Phi	7	3	0	.700	272-133	27.2-13.3	391-318	1647- 817	4.2-2.6	26- 8	192-205	98- 89	51.0-43.4	1321- 1243	6.9- 6.1	11-10	14-19
NYG	3	6	1	.333	179-198	17.9-19.8	317-395	791-1643	2.5-4.2	6-17	201-186	92- 99	45.8-53.2	1532- 1410	7.6- 7.6	16- 6	16-13
Bos	3	6	1	.333	123-211	12.3-21.1	345-387	846-1643	2.5-3.5	9-15	160-227	66-104	41.3-45.8	1000- 1427	6.3- 6.3	6-10	21-30
Pit	2	8	0	.200	79-220	7.9-22.0	367-363	951-1371	2.6-3.8	8-16	164-191	61-102	37.2-53.4	652- 1617	4.0- 8.5	0-14	21-13
Western Division																	
Cle	9	1	0	.900	244-136	24.4-13.6	372-349	1714-1026	4.6-2.9	19-10	199-253	100- 99	50.3-39.1	1767- 1463	8.9- 5.8	16- 9	20-28
Det	7	3	0	.700	195-194	19.5-19.4	313-356	857- 912	2.7-2.6	8- 7	238-227	87- 89	36.6-39.2	1544- 1615	6.5- 7.1	15-17	36-23
GB	6	4	0	.600	258-173	25.8-17.3	377-388	1325-1349	3.5-3.5	15-16	218-231	81-111	37.2-48.1	1536- 1708	7.0- 7.4	14- 9	24-24
ChiB	3	7	0	.300	192-235	19.2-23.5	422-357	1497-1464	3.5-4.1	13-20	244-195	128- 83	52.5-42.6	1857- 1283	7.6- 6.6	14-10	12-15
ChiC	1	9	0	.100	98-228	9.8-22.8	334-382	933-1320	2.8-3.5	8-17	267-187	99- 87	37.1-46.5	1328- 1490	5.0- 8.0	5-15	18-12
50 games					1849	37.0	3632	12269	3.4	127	2111	958	45.4	14375	6.8	109	193

Championship: Cle 15, Was 14

LEADING RUSHERS	ATT	YARD	AVG	TD
Steve Van Buren, Phi	143	832	5.8	15
Frank Akins, Was	147	797	5.4	6
Henry Margarita, ChiB	112	497	4.4	3
Fred Gehrke, Cle	74	467	6.3	7
Fred Gillette, Cle	63	390	6.2	1

LEADING PASSERS	ATT	COM	YARD	TD	IN
*Sammy Baugh, Was	182	128	1669	11	4
*Sid Luckman, ChiB	217	117	1725	14	10
Bob Waterfield, Cle	171	88	1609	14	16
Leroy Zimmerman, Phi	132	67	991	9	8
Paul Christman, ChiC	219	89	1147	5	12

**Tied for passing title.*

LEADING RECEIVERS	NO	YARD	AVG	TD
Don Hutson, GB	47	834	17.7	9
Jim Benton, Cle	45	1067	23.7	8
Steve Bagarus, Was	35	623	17.8	5
George Wilson, ChiB	28	259	9.3	3
John Greene, Det	26	550	21.2	4
Bill Dewell, ChiC	26	370	14.2	1

LEADING SCORERS	TD	FG	PAT	PTS
Steve Van Buren, Phi	18	0	2	110
Don Hutson, GB	10	2	31	97
Bob Waterfield, Cle	5	1	31	64
Frank Liebel, NYG	10	0	0	60
Ted Fritsch, GB	8	3	0	57

LEADING INTERCEPTOR	NO	YDS	AVG	TD
Roy Zimmerman, Phi	7	90	12.9	0

LEADING PUNTER	NO	AVG	Long
Roy Dale McKay, GB	44	41.2	73

LEADING PUNT RETURNER	NO	YDS	AVG	Long	TD
Dave Ryan, Det	15	220	14.7	56	0

LEADING KICKOFF RETURNER	NO	YDS	AVG	Long	TD
Steve Van Buren, Phi	13	373	28.7	98t	1

SUPERLATIVES

Rushing Avg.	6.3	Fred Gehrke, Cle
Receiving Avg.	26.9	Frank Liebel, NYG
Completion Pct.	70.3	Sammy Baugh, Was
Touchdowns	18	Steve Van Buren, Phi
Field Goals	7	Joe Aguirre, Was
Extra Points	31	Don Hutson, GB
		Bob Waterfield, Cle

LONGEST

Run	77t	Bill Paschal, NYG
Pass	84t	Bob Waterfield to Jim Benton, Cle
Interception	74	Sammy Baugh, Was
Punt	73	Roy Dale McKay, GB
Punt Return	81t	Chuck DeShane, Det
Kickoff Return	98t	Steve Van Buren, Phi
Field Goal	49	Ted Fritsch, GB

1946 NATIONAL FOOTBALL LEAGUE

					SCORING		RUSHING				PASSING						
Team	W	L	T	PCT	OWN-OPP PTS-PTS	OWN-OPP PPG-PPG	OWN-OPP ATT-ATT	OWN-OPP YARD-YARD	OWN-OPP AVG-AVG	ON-OP TD-TD	OWN-OPP ATT-ATT	OWN-OPP COM-COM	OWN-OPP PCT-PCT	OWN-OPP YARD-YARD	OWN-OPP AVG-AVG	ON-OP TD-TD	ON-OP IN-IN
Eastern Division																	
NYG	7	3	1	.700	236-162	21.5-14.7	413-394	1467-1289	3.6-3.3	15-12	194-258	100-128	51.5-49.6	1450- 1823	7.5- 7.7	14- 9	25-19
Phi	6	5	0	.545	231-220	21.0-17.4	422-418	1263-1123	3.0-2.7	12-19	217-220	116- 95	53.5-43.2	1641- 1360	7.6- 6.2	14-11	19-26
Was	5	5	1	.500	171-191	15.5-17.4	435-407	1492-1103	3.4-2.7	10-16	221-216	112-101	50.7-46.8	1613- 1342	7.3- 6.2	10-10	22-24
Pit	5	5	1	.500	136-117	12.4-10.6	414-466	1307-1754	3.2-3.8	13- 9	161-162	58- 64	36.0-39.5	970- 939	6.0- 5.8	4- 6	13-14
Bos	2	8	1	.200	189-273	17.2-24.8	365-452	1109-1852	3.0-4.1	10-22	239-227	103-106	43.1-46.7	1566- 1642	6.6- 7.3	15-15	18-17
Western Division																	
ChiB	8	2	1	.800	289-193	26.3-17.5	506-334	1762-1044	3.5-3.1	19-12	253-257	120-108	47.4-42.0	1950- 1610	7.7- 6.3	18-14	19-27
LARm	6	4	1	.600	277-257	25.2-23.4	404-402	1683-1325	4.2-3.3	15-14	326-265	153-112	46.9-42.3	2080- 2154	6.4- 8.1	19-21	24-23
GB	6	5	0	.545	148-158	13.5-14.4	561-367	1765-1372	3.1-3.7	12-15	178-214	54- 94	30.3-43.9	841- 1288	4.7- 6.0	4- 8	18-24
ChiC	6	5	0	.545	260-198	23.6-18.0	371-438	1529-1249	4.1-2.9	16-12	266-273	115-118	43.2-43.2	1951- 1603	7.3- 5.9	17-14	20-25
Det	1	10	0	.091	142-310	12.9-28.2	274-481	470-1698	1.7-3.5	7-21	287-249	119-123	41.5-49.4	1774- 1975	5.8- 7.9	11-20	33-13
55 games					2079	37.8	4165	13847	3.3	129	2342	1050	44.8	15836	6.8	126	211

Championship: ChiB 24, NYG 14

LEADING RUSHERS	ATT	YARD	AVG	TD
Bill Dudley, Pit	146	604	4.1	3
Pat Harder, ChiC	106	545	5.1	4
Steve Van Buren, Phi	116	529	4.6	5
Hugh Gallarneau, ChiB	112	476	4.3	7
Tony Canadeo, GB	122	476	3.9	0

LEADING PASSERS	ATT	COM	YARD	TD	IN
Bob Waterfield, LARm	251	127	1747	18	17
Sid Luckman, ChiB	229	110	1826	17	16
Paul Governali, Bos	192	83	1293	13	10
Paul Christman, ChiC	229	100	1656	13	18
Sammy Baugh, Was	161	87	1163	8	17

LEADING RECEIVERS	NO	YARD	AVG	TD
Jim Benton, LARm	63	981	15.5	6
Harold Crisler, Bos	32	385	12.0	5
Steve Bagarus, Was	31	438	14.1	3
Jack Ferrante, Phi	28	451	16.1	4
Bill Dewell, ChiC	27	643	23.8	7
Mal Kutner, ChiC	27	634	23.5	5

LEADING SCORERS	TD	FG	PAT	PTS
Ted Fritsch, GB	10	9	13	100
Bob Waterfield, LARm	1	6	37	61
Augie Lio, Phi	1	6	27	51
Bill Dudley, Pit	5	2	12	48
Hugh Gallarneau, ChiB	8	0	0	48

LEADING INTERCEPTOR	NO	YDS	AVG	TD
Bill Dudley, Pit	10	242	24.2	1

LEADING PUNTER	NO	AVG	Long
Roy Dale McKay, GB	64	42.7	64

LEADING PUNT RETURNER	NO	YDS	AVG	Long	TD
Bill Dudley, Pit	27	385	14.3	52	0

LEADING KICKOFF RETURNER	NO	YDS	AVG	Long	TD
Abe Karnofsky, Bos	21	599	28.5	97t	1

SUPERLATIVES		
Rushing Avg.	6.8	Elmer Angsman, ChiC
Receiving Avg.	23.8	Bill Dewell, ChiC
Completion Pct.	55.3	Tommy Thompson, Phi
Touchdowns	10	Ted Fritsch, GB
Field Goals	9	Ted Fritsch, GB
Extra Points	37	Bob Waterfield, LARm

LONGEST		
Run	84t	Tom Harmon, LARm
Pass	88t	Dave Ryan to John Greene, Det
Interception	85t	Tom Harmon, LARm
Punt	81	Bill deCorrevont, Det
Punt Return	70	Jack Wilson, LARm
Kickoff Return	105t	Frank Seno, ChiC
Field Goal	46	Ted Fritsch, GB

1946 ALL-AMERICAN FOOTBALL CONFERENCE

					SCORING		RUSHING				PASSING						
Team	W	L	T	PCT	OWN-OPP PTS-PTS	OWN-OPP PPG-PPG	OWN-OPP ATT-ATT	OWN-OPP YARD-YARD	OWN-OPP AVG-AVG	ON-OP TD-TD	OWN-OPP ATT-ATT	OWN-OPP COM-COM	OWN-OPP PCT-PCT	OWN-OPP YARD-YARD	OWN-OPP AVG-AVG	ON-OP TD-TD	ON-OP IN-IN
Western Division																	
CleA	12	2	0	.850	423-137	30.2- 9.8	494-546	2007-1616	4.1-3.0	27- 8	237-299	123-125	51.9-41.8	2266- 1317	9.6- 4.4	22- 8	7-41
SF-A	9	5	0	.643	307-189	21.9-13.5	582-426	2175- 873	3.7-2.1	22- 7	252-359	130-185	51.6-51.5	1721- 2150	6.8- 5.9	18-15	21-21
LA-A	7	5	2	.583	305-290	21.8-20.7	549-451	1949-1356	3.6-3.0	17-19	322-284	176-138	54.7-48.6	2193- 2101	6.8- 7.4	19-17	30-20
ChiA	5	6	3	.454	263-315	18.8-22.5	511-475	1559-1718	3.1-3.6	10-16	310-259	144-119	46.5-46.0	1898- 1618	6.1- 6.3	18-19	29-31
Eastern Division																	
NY-A	10	3	1	.769	270-192	19.3-13.7	512-449	1880-1055	3.7-2.3	17- 9	274-252	129-123	47.1-48.4	1645- 1564	6.0- 6.2	13-13	21-16
BknA	3	10	1	.230	226-339	16.1-24.2	374-575	1017-2458	2.7-4.3	9-24	327-255	162-132	49.5-51.9	2258- 2077	6.9- 8.2	17-19	23-12
BufA	3	10	1	.230	249-370	17.8-26.4	501-497	2046-2075	4.1-4.2	13-21	238-295	96-146	40.3-49.5	1367- 2370	5.7- 8.0	16-23	23-22
MiaA	3	11	0	.214	167-378	11.2-27.0	408-528	848-2248	2.1-4.3	13-24	295-252	131-123	44.4-48.4	1725- 1876	5.9- 7.4	10-19	33-24
56 games					2210	39.5	3931	13481	3.4	128	2255	1091	48.4	15073	6.7	133	187

Championship: CleA 14, NY-A 9

LEADING RUSHERS	ATT	YARD	AVG	TD
Spec Sanders, NY-A	140	709	5.1	6
Norm Standlee, SF-A	134	651	4.9	2
Vic Kulbitski, BufA	97	605	6.2	2
Marion Motley, CleA	73	601	8.2	5
Edgar Jones, CleA	77	539	7.0	4

LEADING PASSERS	ATT	COM	YARD	TD	IN
Glenn Dobbs, BknA	269	135	1886	13	15
Otto Graham, CleA	174	95	1834	17	5
Charley O'Rourke, LA-A	182	105	1250	12	14
Frankie Albert, SF-A	197	104	1404	14	14
Bob Hoernschemeyer, Chi	193	95	1266	14	14

LEADING RECEIVERS	NO	YARD	AVG	TD
Dante Lavelli, CleA	40	843	21.8	8
Alyn Beals, SF-A	40	586	14.7	10
Saxon Judd, BknA	34	443	13.0	4
Fay King, BufA	30	466	15.5	6
Elroy Hirsch, ChiA	27	347	12.9	3

LEADING SCORERS	TD	FG	PAT	PTS
Lou Groza, CleA	0	13	45	84
Spec Sanders, NY-A	12	0	0	72
Alyn Beals, SF-A	10	0	1	81
Steve Nemeth, ChiA	0	9	32	59
Joe Aguirre, LA-A	2	4	31	55

LEADING INTERCEPTOR	NO	YDS	AVG	TD
Tommy Colella, CleA	10	110	11.0	0

LEADING PUNTER	NO	AVG
Glenn Dobbs, BknA	80	47.8

LEADING PUNT RETURNER	NO	YDS	AVG	TD
Chuck Fenenbock, LA-A	16	299	18.7	0

LEADING KICKOFF RETURNER	NO	YDS	AVG	TD
Chuck Fenenbock, LA-A	17	479	28.2	1

SUPERLATIVES		
Rushing Avg.	8.4	Chuck Fenenbock, LA-A
Receiving Avg.	23.5	Mac Speedie, CleA
Completion Pct.	57.7	Charley O'Rourke, LA-A
Touchdowns	12	Spec Sanders, NY-A
Field Goals	13	Lou Groza, CleA
Extra Points	45	Lou Groza, CleA

1947 NATIONAL FOOTBALL LEAGUE

					SCORING		RUSHING				PASSING						
Team	W	L	T	PCT	OWN-OPP PTS-PTS	OWN-OPP PPG-PPG	OWN-OPP ATT-ATT	OWN-OPP YARD-YARD	OWN-OPP AVG-AVG	ON-OP TD-TD	OWN-OPP ATT-ATT	OWN-OPP COM-COM	OWN-OPP PCT-PCT	OWN-OPP YARD-YARD	OWN-OPP AVG-AVG	ON-OP TD-TD	ON-OP IN-IN
Eastern Division																	
Phi	8	4	0	.667	308-242	25.7-20.2	474-380	1971-1329	4.2-3.5	21-13	223-334	116-152	52.0-45.5	1761- 2410	7.9- 7.2	18-19	19-23
Pit	8	4	0	.667	240-259	20.0-21.6	496-403	1948-1622	3.9-4.0	15-11	209-244	86- 98	41.1-40.2	1410- 1847	6.8- 7.6	10-20	19-18
Bos	4	7	1	.364	168-256	14.0-21.3	343-483	973-2020	2.8-4.1	5-18	238-303	95-158	39.9-52.1	1661- 2042	6.9- 6.7	15-17	27-28
Was	4	8	0	.333	295-367	24.6-30.6	384-409	1343-1564	3.5-3.8	11-18	416-282	231-146	55.5-51.8	3336- 2422	8.0- 8.6	28-26	18-21
NYG	2	8	2	.200	190-309	15.8-25.8	366-457	1195-1836	3.3-4.0	7-18	293-276	123-121	42.0-43.8	1999- 2015	6.8- 7.3	17-19	26-27
Western Division																	
ChiC	9	3	0	.750	306-231	25.5-19.3	468-400	1735-1759	3.7-4.4	20-10	340-314	160-148	47.1-47.1	2580- 2206	7.6- 7.3	18-18	25-27
ChiB	8	4	0	.667	363-241	30.3-20.1	448-392	1958-1423	4.4-3.6	21- 6	378-345	194-161	51.3-46.7	3093- 2449	8.2- 7.1	29-20	35-27
GB	6	5	1	.545	274-210	22.8-17.5	510-433	2149-1606	4.2-3.7	14-13	253-277	112-122	44.3-44.0	1724- 1790	6.8- 6.5	17-14	19-30
LARm	6	6	0	.500	259-214	21.6-17.8	459-453	2171-1544	4.7-3.4	15-12	293-306	123-145	42.0-47.4	1660- 2059	5.7- 6.7	13-14	28-24
Det	3	9	0	.250	231-305	19.3-25.4	333-461	1234-1975	3.7-4.3	6-18	348-310	167-156	48.0-50.3	2446- 2430	7.1- 7.8	23-21	34-25
60 games					2634	43.9	4281	16677	3.9	135	2991	1407	47.0	21670	7.2	188	250

Eastern Division Playoff: Phi 21, Pit 0
Championship: ChiC 28, Phi 21

LEADING RUSHERS	ATT	YARD	AVG	TD
Steve Van Buren, Phi	217	1008	4.6	14
Johnny Clement, Pit	129	670	5.2	4
Tony Canadeo, GB	103	464	4.5	2
Kenny Washington, LARm	60	444	7.4	5
Walt Schlinkman, GB	115	439	3.8	2

LEADING PASSERS	ATT	COM	YARD	TD	IN
Sammy Baugh, Was	354	210	2938	25	15
Tommy Thompson, Phi	201	106	1680	16	15
Sid Luckman, ChiB	323	176	2712	24	31
Jack Jacobs, GB	242	108	1615	16	17
Paul Christman, ChiC	301	138	2191	17	22

LEADING RECEIVERS	NO	YARD	AVG	TD
Jim Keane, ChiB	64	910	14.2	10
Bob Nussbaumer, Was	47	597	12.7	4
Mal Kutner, ChiC	43	944	22.0	7
Nolan Luhn, GB	42	696	16.6	7
Bill Dewell, ChiC	42	576	13.7	4

LEADING SCORER	TD	FG	PAT	PTS
Pat Harder, ChiC	7	7	39	102
Dick Poillon, Was	6	4	37	85
Steve Van Buren, Phi	14	0	0	84
Ken Kavanaugh, ChiB	13	0	0	78
Bill Dudley, Det	11	0	0	66

LEADING INTERCEPTORS	NO	YDS	AVG	TD
Frank Reagan, NYG	10	203	20.3	0
Frank Seno, Bos	10	100	10.0	0

LEADING PUNTER	NO	AVG	Long
Jack Jacobs, GB	57	43.5	74

LEADING PUNT RETURNER	NO	YDS	AVG	Long	TD
Walt Slater, Pit	28	435	15.5	33	0

LEADING KICKOFF RETURNER	NO	YDS	AVG	Long	TD
Eddie Saenz, Was	29	797	27.5	94t	2

SUPERLATIVES

Rushing Avg.	7.4	Kenny Washington, LARm
Receiving Avg.	32.6	Don Currivan, Bos
Completion Pct.	59.3	Sammy Baugh, Was
Touchdowns	14	Steve Van Buren, Phi
Field Goals	7	Ward Cuff, GB
		Pat Harder, ChiC
		Bob Waterfield, LARm
Extra Points	44	Ray McLean, ChiB

LONGEST

Run	92t	Kenny Washington, LARm
Pass	88t	Frank Reagan to George Franck, NYG
Interception	96t	Bulldog Turner, ChiB
Punt	86	Bob Waterfield, LARm
Punt Return	88t	Tom Harmon, LARm
Kickoff Return	95t	Steve Van Buren, Phi
Field Goal	50	Ted Fritsch, GB

1947 ALL-AMERICAN FOOTBALL CONFERENCE

					SCORING		RUSHING				PASSING						
Team	W	L	T	PCT	OWN-OPP PTS-PTS	OWN-OPP PPG-PPG	OWN-OPP ATT-ATT	OWN-OPP YARD-YARD	OWN-OPP AVG-AVG	ON-OP TD-TD	OWN-OPP ATT-ATT	OWN-OPP COM-COM	OWN-OPP PCT-PCT	OWN-OPP YARD-YARD	OWN-OPP AVG-AVG	ON-OP TD-TD	ON-OP IN-IN
Western Division																	
CleA	12	1	1	.923	410-185	29.3-13.2	479-503	2557-2181	5.3-4.3	24-12	296-303	174-129	58.8-42.6	2990- 1707	10.1- 5.6	26-11	12-32
SF-A	8	4	2	.667	327-264	23.4-18.9	587-405	2767-1631	4.7-4.0	22-10	297-332	147-177	49.5-53.3	1993- 2502	6.7- 7.5	22-23	19-24
LA-A	7	7	0	.500	328-256	23.4-18.3	487-461	1780-1668	3.7-3.6	17- 9	300-310	141-157	47.0-50.6	2127- 2376	7.1- 7.7	19-24	25-24
ChiA	1	13	0	.071	263-425	18.8-30.4	401-564	1520-2752	3.8-4.9	9-34	341-288	157-140	46.0-48.6	2353- 2206	6.9- 7.7	23-20	26-19
EASTERN DIVISION																	
NY-A	11	2	1	.846	378-239	27.0-17.1	534-371	2930-1237	5.5-3.3	27-13	216-304	111-144	51.4-47.4	1795- 1910	8.3- 6.3	16-17	18-17
BufA	8	4	2	.667	320-288	22.9-20.6	496-507	2217-2218	4.5-4.4	18-22	267-260	129-133	48.3-51.2	1891- 1929	7.1- 7.4	24-14	23-18
BknA	3	10	1	.231	181-340	12.9-24.3	495-514	1936-2516	3.9-4.9	21-16	232-265	92-124	39.7-46.8	1060- 2130	4.6- 8.0	4-21	17-16
BalA	2	11	1	.154	167-377	11.9-26.9	417-571	1161-2665	2.8-4.7	7-29	352-239	177-124	50.3-51.9	2337- 1791	6.6- 7.5	13-17	24-14
56 games					2374	42.4	3896	18783	4.3	145	2301	1128	49.0	16551	7.1	147	164

Championship: CleA 14, NY-A 3

LEADING RUSHERS	ATT	YARD	AVG	TD
Spec Sanders, NY-A	231	1432	6.2	19
John Strzykalski, SF-A	143	906	6.3	5
Marion Motley, CleA	146	889	6.0	8
Chet Mutryn, BufA	140	868	6.2	9
Buddy Young, NY-A	116	712	6.1	3

LEADING PASSERS	ATT	COM	YARD	TD	IN
Otto Graham, CleA	269	163	2753	25	11
Bud Schwenk, BalA	327	168	2236	13	20
Frankie Albert, SF-A	242	128	1692	18	15
George Ratterman, BufA	244	124	1840	22	20
Spec Sanders, NY-A	171	93	1442	14	17

LEADING RECEIVERS	NO	YARD	AVG	TD
Mac Speedie, CleA	67	1146	17.1	6
Dante Lavelli, CleA	49	799	16.3	9
Alyn Beals, SF-A	47	655	13.9	10
Lamar Davis, BalA	46	515	11.2	2
Billy Hillenbrand, BalA	39	702	18.0	7

LEADING SCORER	TD	FG	PAT	PTS
Spec Sanders, NY-A	19	0	0	114
Ben Agajanian, LA-A	0	15	39	84
Chet Mutryn, BufA	12	0	1	73
Harvey Johnson, NY-A	0	7	49	70
John Kimbrough, LA-A	11	0	0	66

LEADING INTERCEPTORS	NO	YDS	AVG	TD
Tommy Colella, CleA	6	130	21.7	1
Bill Kellagher, ChiA	6	77	12.8	0
Len Eshmont, SF-A	6	72	12.0	0

LEADING PUNTER	NO	AVG
Mickey Colmer, BknA	56	44.7

LEADING PUNT RETURNER	NO	YDS	AVG	TD
Glenn Dobbs, BknA-LA-A	19	215	11.3	0

LEADING KICKOFF RETURNER	NO	YDS	AVG	TD
Chet Mutryn, BufA	21	691	32.9	1

SUPERLATIVES

Rushing Avg.	6.4	Edgar Jones, CleA
Receiving Avg.	21.9	Ray Ramsey, ChiA
Completion Pct.	60.6	Otto Graham, CleA
Touchdowns	19	Spec Sanders, NY-A
Field Goals	15	Ben Agajanian, LA-A
Extra Points	49	Harvey Johnson, NY-A

1948 NATIONAL FOOTBALL LEAGUE

					SCORING		RUSHING				PASSING						
Team	W	L	T	PCT	OWN-OPP PTS-PTS	OWN-OPP PPG-PPG	OWN-OPP ATT-ATT	OWN-OPP YARD-YARD	OWN-OPP AVG-AVG	ON-OP TD-TD	OWN-OPP ATT-ATT	OWN-OPP COM-COM	OWN-OPP PCT-PCT	OWN-OPP YARD-YARD	OWN-OPP AVG-AVG	ON-OP TD-TD	ON-OP IN-IN
Eastern Division																	
Phi	9	2	1	.818	376-156	31.3-13.0	528-376	2378-1209	4.5-3.2	21- 5	301-338	159-139	52.8-41.1	2241- 1951	7.5- 5.8	27-14	16-23
Was	7	5	0	.583	291-287	24.3-23.9	434-482	1603-1958	3.7-4.1	11-17	360-289	202-135	56.1-46.7	2861- 1953	7.9- 6.8	24-20	26-24
NYG	4	8	0	.333	297-388	24.8-32.3	362-481	1219-2168	3.4-4.5	12-26	363-311	191-157	52.6-50.5	2504- 2406	6.9- 7.7	24-25	16-39
Pit	4	8	0	.333	200-243	16.7-20.3	510-434	1934-1648	3.8-3.8	17- 7	266-279	108-149	40.6-53.4	1529- 1987	5.8- 7.1	8-18	29-13
Bos	3	9	0	.250	174-372	14.5-31.0	365-511	1170-2320	3.2-4.5	4-19	261-356	101-161	38.7-45.2	1308- 2463	5.0- 6.9	13-27	34-18
Western Division																	
ChiC	11	1	0	.917	395-226	32.9-18.8	531-408	2560-1516	4.8-3.7	25- 8	285-336	134-159	47.0-47.3	2134- 2520	7.5- 7.5	22-22	12-23
ChiB	10	2	0	.833	375-151	31.3-12.6	567-384	2452-1254	4.4-3.3	24- 8	287-336	142-139	49.5-41.4	1894- 1646	6.6- 4.9	22-12	19-30
LARm	6	5	1	.545	327-269	27.3-22.4	427-441	1743-1570	4.1-3.6	13-13	395-309	201-164	50.9-53.1	2748- 2143	7.0- 6.9	28-20	25-19
GB	3	9	0	.250	154-290	12.8-24.2	446-537	1759-2153	3.9-4.0	11-21	274-280	109-134	39.8-51.5	1364- 1626	5.0- 6.3	8-13	29-29
Det	2	10	0	.167	200-407	16.7-33.9	389-495	1360-2382	3.5-4.8	6-27	324-302	151-161	48.8-53.3	2288- 2176	7.1- 7.2	20-25	26-14
60 games					2789	46.5	4549	18178	4.0	151	3116	1498	48.0	20871	6.7	196	232

Championship: Phi 7, ChiC 0

LEADING RUSHERS	ATT	YARD	AVG	TD
Steve Van Buren, Phi	201	945	4.7	10
Charley Trippi, ChiC	128	690	5.4	6
Elmer Angsman, ChiC	131	638	4.9	8
Camp Wilson, Det	157	612	3.9	2
Tony Canadeo, GB	123	589	4.8	4

LEADING PASSERS	ATT	COM	YARD	TD	IN
Tommy Thompson, Phi	246	141	1965	25	11
Jim Hardy, LARm	211	112	1390	14	7
Charlie Conerly, NYG	299	162	2175	22	13
Sammy Baugh, Was	315	185	2599	22	23
Ray Mallouf, ChiC	143	73	1160	13	6

LEADING RECEIVERS	NO	YARD	AVG	TD
Tom Fears, LARm	51	698	13.7	4
Pete Pihos, Phi	46	766	16.7	11
Mal Kutner, ChiC	41	943	23.0	14
Val Jansante, Pit	39	623	16.0	3
Bill Swiacki, NYG	39	550	14.1	10

LEADING SCORERS	TD	FG	PAT	PTS
Pat Harder, ChiC	6	7	53	110
Mal Kutner, ChiC	15	0	0	90
Cliff Patton, Phi	0	8	50	74
Pete Pihos, Phi	11	0	0	66
Dick Poillon, Was	3	5	33	66

LEADING INTERCEPTOR	NO	YDS	AVG	TD
Dan Sandifer, Was	13	258	19.8	2

LEADING PUNTER	NO	AVG	Long
Joe Muha, Phi	57	47.3	82

LEADING PUNT RETURNER	NO	YDS	AVG	Long	TD
George McAfee, ChiB	30	417	13.9	60t	1

LEADING KICKOFF RETURNER	NO	YDS	AVG	Long	TD
Joe Scott, NYG	20	569	28.5	99t	1

SUPERLATIVES

Rushing Avg.	5.4	Charley Trippi, ChiC
Receiving Avg.	23.0	Mal Kutner, ChiC
Completion Pct.	58.7	Sammy Baugh, Was
Touchdowns	15	Mal Kutner, ChiC
Field Goals	8	Cliff Patton, Phi
Extra Points	53	Pat Harder, ChiC

LONGEST

Run	74t	Noah Mullins, ChiB
Pass	86t	Sammy Baugh to Dan Sandifer, Was
Interception	89t	Joe Golding, Bos
Punt	88	Bob Waterfield, LARm
Punt Return	70t	Jerome Davis, ChiC
Kickoff Return	99t	Joseph Scott, NYG
Field Goal	47	Bob Waterfield, LARm

1948 ALL-AMERICAN FOOTBALL CONFERENCE

					SCORING		RUSHING				PASSING						
Team	W	L	T	PCT	OWN-OPP PTS-PTS	OWN-OPP PPG-PPG	OWN-OPP ATT-ATT	OWN-OPP YARD-YARD	OWN-OPP AVG-AVG	ON-OP TD-TD	OWN-OPP ATT-ATT	OWN-OPP COM-COM	OWN-OPP PCT-PCT	OWN-OPP YARD-YARD	OWN-OPP AVG-AVG	ON-OP TD-TD	ON-OP IN-IN
Western Division																	
CleA	14	0	0	1.000	389-190	27.8-13.6	544-436	2557-1519	4.7-3.5	25-10	344-354	178-159	51.7-44.9	2809- 2097	8.2- 5.9	26-14	16-24
SF-A	12	2	0	.857	495-248	35.4-17.7	603-468	3663-1906	6.1-4.1	35-11	288-374	162-184	56.3-49.2	2104- 2615	7.3- 7.0	30-23	14-32
LA-A	7	7	0	.500	258-305	18.4-21.8	400-514	1554-1906	3.9-4.8	11-14	406-344	195-164	48.0-47.7	2497- 2473	6.2- 7.5	21-24	24-24
ChiA	1	13	0	.071	202-439	14.4-31.4	484-538	1719-2614	3.6-4.9	8-33	341-318	146-155	42.8-48.7	2290- 2588	6.7- 7.8	19-23	38-19
EASTERN DIVISION																	
BufA	7	7	0	.500	360-358	25.7-25.6	539-483	2738-1983	5.1-4.3	29-25	360-414	177-211	49.2-51.0	2683- 2829	7.5- 6.8	17-14	26-14
BalA	7	7	0	.500	333-327	23.8-23.4	532-504	2166-2522	4.1-5.0	22-21	340-364	185-177	54.4-48.6	2899- 2829	8.5- 6.7	19-18	13-22
NY-A	6	8	0	.429	265-301	18.9-21.5	464-467	1977-2015	4.3-4.3	20-18	316-341	139-160	44.0-48.9	1966- 2767	6.2- 8.1	15-19	24-27
BknA	2	12	0	.143	253-387	18.1-27.6	409-585	1787-3146	4.4-5.4	12-30	410-296	188-160	45.9-54.1	2524- 1985	6.2- 6.7	20-23	32-25
56 games					2555	45.6	3975	18161	4.6	185	2805	1370	48.8	19772	7.0	167	187

Division Playoff: BufA 28, BalA 17
Championship: CleA 49, BufA 7

LEADING RUSHERS	ATT	YARD	AVG	TD
Marion Motley, CleA	157	964	6.1	5
John Strzykalski, SF-A	141	915	6.5	4
Chet Mutryn, BufA	147	823	5.6	10
Spec Sanders, NY-A	169	759	4.5	9
Lou Tomasetti, BufA	134	716	5.3	7

LEADING PASSERS	ATT	COM	YARD	TD	IN
Otto Graham, CleA	333	173	2713	25	15
Glenn Dobbs, LA-A	369	185	2403	21	20
Y.A. Tittle, BalA	289	161	2522	16	9
George Ratterman, BufA	335	168	2577	16	22
Frankie Albert, SF-A	264	154	1990	29	10

LEADING RECEIVERS	NO	YARD	AVG	TD
Mac Speedie, CleA	58	816	14.1	4
Alton Baldwin, Buf	54	916	17.0	8
Billy Hillenbrand, BalA	50	970	19.4	6
Fay King, ChiA	50	647	12.9	7
Alyn Beals, SF-A	45	591	12.8	14

LEADING SCORERS	TD	FG	PAT	PTS
Chet Mutryn, BufA	16	0	0	96
Alyn Beals, SF-A	14	0	0	84
Joe Vetrano, SF-A	1	5	62	83
Billy Hillenbrand, BalA	13	0	0	78
Lou Groza, CleA	0	8	51	75

LEADING INTERCEPTOR	NO	YDS	AVG	TD
Otto Schnellbacher, NY-A	11	239	21.7	1

LEADING PUNTER	NO	AVG
Glenn Dobbs, LA-A	68	49.1

LEADING PUNT RETURNER	NO	YDS	AVG	TD
Herman Wedemeyer, LA-A	23	368	16.0	0

LEADING KICKOFF RETURNER	NO	YDS	AVG	TD
Monk Gafford, Bkn-A	23	559	19.5	0

SUPERLATIVES

Rushing Avg.	7.3	Joe Perry, SF-A
Receiving Avg.	20.4	Chet Mutryn, BufA
Completion Pct.	58.3	Frankie Albert, SF-A
Touchdowns	16	Chet Mutryn, BufA
Field Goals	10	Rex Grossman, BalA
Extra Points	62	Joe Vetrano, SF-A

1949 NATIONAL FOOTBALL LEAGUE

					SCORING		RUSHING				PASSING						
Team	W	L	T	PCT	OWN-OPP PTS-PTS	OWN-OPP PPG-PPG	OWN-OPP ATT-ATT	OWN-OPP YARD-YARD	OWN-OPP AVG-AVG	ON-OP TD-TD	OWN-OPP ATT-ATT	OWN-OPP COM-COM	OWN-OPP PCT-PCT	OWN-OPP YARD-YARD	OWN-OPP AVG-AVG	ON-OP TD-TD	ON-OP IN-IN
Eastern Division																	
Phi	11	1	0	.917	364-134	30.3-11.2	632-353	2607-1217	4.1-3.4	25- 5	251-303	130-121	51.8-39.9	1909- 1607	7.8- 5.3	18-11	14-29
Pit	6	5	1	.545	224-214	18.7-17.8	535-463	2209-1862	4.1-4.0	19-17	209-337	81-161	38.8-47.8	1310- 2043	6.3- 6.1	10- 9	10-22
NYG	6	6	0	.500	287-298	23.9-24.8	419-465	1404-1664	3.4-3.6	15-20	322-374	155-193	48.1-51.6	2157- 2460	6.7- 6.7	17-16	23-22
Was	4	7	1	.364	268-339	22.3-28.3	407-487	1579-2316	3.9-4.8	14-23	394-316	197-148	50.0-46.8	2816- 2409	7.1- 7.6	22-24	29-18
NYB	1	10	1	.091	153-368	12.8-30.7	353-535	1184-2360	3.4-4.4	9-20	343-303	172-147	50.1-48.5	2025- 2132	5.9- 7.0	10-25	23-14
Western Division																	
LARm	8	2	2	.800	360-239	30.0-19.9	445-472	1732-1679	3.9-3.6	17-14	366-335	192-144	52.5-43.0	2819- 2084	7.7- 6.2	23-16	27-30
ChiB	9	3	0	.750	332-218	27.7-18.2	483-428	1785-1196	3.7-2.8	18- 6	385-320	193-152	50.1-47.5	3055- 2147	7.9- 6.7	24-20	30-27
ChiC	6	5	1	.545	360-301	30.0-25.1	467-446	2130-1874	4.6-4.2	21-19	307-383	138-174	45.0-45.4	1763- 2617	5.8- 6.8	21-18	26-33
Det	4	8	0	.333	237-259	19.8-21.6	397-491	1381-1827	3.5-3.7	10-15	399-312	178-149	44.6-47.8	2291- 1814	5.8- 5.8	18-14	28-32
GB	2	10	0	.167	114-329	9.5-27.4	503-501	2061-2077	4.1-4.1	7-20	299-292	91-138	30.4-47.3	1291- 2123	4.3- 7.3	5-15	29-20
60 games					2699	45.0	4641	18072	3.9	152	3275	1527	56.6	21436	6.5	168	247

Championship: Phi 14, LARm 0

LEADING RUSHERS	ATT	YARD	AVG	TD
Steve Van Buren, Phi	263	1146	4.4	11
Tony Canadeo, GB	208	1052	5.1	4
Elmer Angsman, ChiC	125	674	5.4	6
Gene Roberts, NYG	152	634	4.2	9
Jerry Nuzum, Pit	139	611	4.4	5

LEADING PASSERS	ATT	COM	YARD	TD	IN
Sammy Baugh, Was	255	145	1903	18	14
Johnny Lujack, ChiB	312	162	2658	23	22
Tommy Thompson, Phi	214	116	1727	16	11
Bob Waterfield, LARm	296	154	2168	17	24
Charlie Conerly, NYG	305	152	2138	17	20

LEADING RECEIVERS	NO	YARD	AVG	TD
Tom Fears, LARm	77	1013	13.2	9
Bob Mann, Det	66	1014	15.4	4
Bill Chipley, NYB	57	631	11.1	2
Jim Keane, ChiB	47	696	14.8	6
Bill Swiacki, NYG	47	652	13.9	4

LEADING SCORERS	TD	FG	PAT	PTS
Pat Harder, ChiC	8	3	45	102
Gene Roberts, NYG	17	0	0	102
Bill Dudley, Det	6	5	30	81
Bob Waterfield, LARm	1	9	43	76
Steve Van Buren, Phi	12	0	0	72

LEADING INTERCEPTOR	NO	YDS	AVG	TD
Bob Nussbaumer, ChiC	12	157	13.1	0

LEADING PUNTER	NO	AVG	Long
Mike Boyda, NYB	56	44.2	61

LEADING PUNT RETURNER	NO	YDS	AVG	Long	TD
Vitamin T Smith, LARm	27	427	15.8	85	1

LEADING KICKOFF RETURNER	NO	YDS	AVG	Long	TD
Don Doll, Det	21	536	25.5	56	0

SUPERLATIVES

Rushing Avg.	6.0	Bosh Pritchard, Phi
Receiving Avg.	22.6	Ken Kavanaugh, ChiB
Completion Pct.	56.9	Sammy Baugh, Was
Touchdowns	17	Gene Roberts, NYG
Field Goals	9	Cliff Patton, Phi Bob Waterfield, LARm
Extra Points	45	Pat Harder, ChiC

LONGEST

Run	97t	Bob Gage, Pit
Pass	85t	Charlie Conerly to Gene Roberts, NYG
Interception	102t	Bob Smith, Det
Punt	82	Joe Geri, Pit
Punt Return	85	Vitamin T Smith, LARm
Kickoff Return	95t	Jack Salscheider, NYG
Field Goal	48	John Patton, Phi
Extra Points	45	Pat Harder, ChiC

1949 ALL-AMERICAN FOOTBALL CONFERENCE

					SCORING		RUSHING				PASSING						
Team	W	L	T	PCT	OWN-OPP PTS-PTS	OWN-OPP PPG-PPG	OWN-OPP ATT-ATT	OWN-OPP YARD-YARD	OWN-OPP AVG-AVG	ON-OP TD-TD	OWN-OPP ATT-ATT	OWN-OPP COM-COM	OWN-OPP PCT-PCT	OWN-OPP YARD-YARD	OWN-OPP AVG-AVG	ON-OP TD-TD	ON-OP IN-IN
Western Division																	
CleA	9	1	2	.900	339-171	28.3-14.3	403-437	1682-1905	4.2-4.4	24-13	296-304	166-120	56.1-39.5	2929- 1677	9.9- 6.5	21- 9	12-29
SF-A	9	3	0	.750	416-227	34.7-18.9	506-401	2798-1364	5.5-3.4	26-12	287-318	139-137	48.4-43.1	1995- 1949	7.0- 6.1	28-15	20-32
NY-A	8	4	0	.667	196-206	16.3-17.2	510-360	2143-1134	4.2-3.2	16- 8	199-316	66-159	33.2-50.3	1032- 2189	5.2- 6.9	5-13	22-24
BufA	5	5	2	.500	236-256	19.7-21.3	492-385	2047-1616	4.2-4.2	16-13	273-282	156-132	57.1-46.8	1873- 2109	6.9- 7.5	15-18	16- 9
ChiA	4	8	0	.333	179-268	14.9-22.3	342-467	1080-2309	3.2-4.9	9-24	297-197	129-107	43.4-54.3	2009- 1732	6.8- 8.8	12- 9	28-15
LA-A	4	8	0	.333	253-322	21.1-26.8	430-484	1838-2148	4.3-4.4	19-20	286-290	114-148	39.9-51.0	1728- 2414	6.0- 8.3	9-22	23-21
BalA	1	11	0	.083	172-341	14.3-28.4	362-511	1284-2396	3.5-4.7	8-28	325-256	160-127	49.2-49.6	2355- 1851	7.3- 7.2	14-18	22-13
42 games					1791	42.6	3045	13986	4.2	118	1963	930	47.4	13921	7.1	104	143

Playoff: CleA 31, BufA 21
Playoff: SF-A 17, NY-A 7
Championship Game: CleA 21, SF-A 7

LEADING RUSHERS	ATT	YARD	AVG	TD
Joe Perry, SF-A	115	783	6.8	8
Chet Mutryn, BufA	131	696	5.3	5
Marion Motley, CleA	113	570	5.0	8
Ollie Cline, BufA	125	518	4.1	3
Buddy Young, NY-A	76	495	6.5	5

LEADING PASSERS	ATT	COM	YARD	TD	IN
Otto Graham, CleA	285	161	2785	19	10
Y.A. Tittle, BalA	289	148	2209	14	18
George Ratterman, BufA	252	146	1777	14	13
Frankie Albert, SF-A	260	129	1862	27	16
Bob Hoernschemeyer, ChiA	167	69	1063	6	11

LEADING RECEIVERS	NO	YARD	AVG	TD
Mac Speedie, CleA	62	1028	16.6	7
Alton Baldwin, BufA	53	719	13.6	7
Alyn Beals, SF-A	44	678	15.4	12
Dan Edwards, ChiA	42	573	13.6	3
Lamar Davis, BalA	38	548	14.4	1

LEADING SCORERS	TD	FG	PAT	PTS
Alyn Beals, SF-A	12	0	1	73
Joe Perry, SF-A	11	0	0	66
Joe Vetrano, SF-A	0	3	56	65
Marion Motley, CleA	8	0	0	48
Billy Stone, BalA	8	0	0	48
Buddy Young, NY-A	8	0	0	48

LEADING INTERCEPTOR	NO	YDS	AVG	TD
Jim Cason, SF-A	9	152	16.9	0

LEADING PUNTER	NO	AVG
Frankie Albert, SF-A	31	48.2

LEADING PUNT RETURNER	NO	YDS	AVG	TD
Jim Cason, SF-A	21	351	16.7	0

LEADING KICKOFF RETURNER	NO	YDS	AVG	TD
Herman Wedemeyer, BalA	30	602	20.1	0

SUPERLATIVES

Rushing Avg.	6.8	Joe Perry, SF-A
Receiving Avg.	20.0	Billy Stone, BalA
Completion Pct.	57.9	George Ratterman, BufA
Touchdowns	12	Alyn Beals, SF-A
Field Goals	7	Harvey Johnson, NY-A
Extra Points	56	Joe Vetrano, SF-A

1950 NATIONAL FOOTBALL LEAGUE

					SCORING		RUSHING				PASSING						
Team	W	L	T	PCT	OWN-OPP PTS-PTS	OWN-OPP PPG-PPG	OWN-OPP ATT-ATT	OWN-OPP YARD-YARD	OWN-OPP AVG-AVG	ON-OP TD-TD	OWN-OPP ATT-ATT	OWN-OPP COM-COM	OWN-OPP PCT-PCT	OWN-OPP YARD-YARD	OWN-OPP AVG-AVG	ON-OP TD-TD	ON-OP IN-IN
American Conference																	
Cle	10	2	0	.833	310-144	25.8-12.0	457-451	2089-1573	4.6-3.5	20-10	260-292	139-121	53.5-41.4	1984- 1581	7.6- 5.4	15- 8	21-31
NYG	10	2	0	.833	268-150	22.3-12.5	515-473	2336-1387	4.5-2.9	21- 8	187-295	81-145	43.3-49.2	1338- 1848	7.2- 6.3	12-11	10-27
Phi	6	6	0	.500	254-141	21.2-11.8	581-391	2328-1603	4.0-4.1	13- 5	285-277	121-102	42.5-36.8	1836- 1621	6.4- 5.9	15-10	28-31
Pit	6	6	0	.500	180-195	15.0-16.3	477-460	1659-1889	3.5-4.1	12-12	255-300	100-146	39.2-48.7	1729- 1801	6.8- 6.0	10-10	29-22
ChiC	5	7	0	.417	233-287	19.4-23.9	386-525	1604-2132	4.2-4.1	14-21	368-269	165-130	44.8-48.3	2375- 2075	6.5- 7.7	21-14	31-22
Was	3	9	0	.250	232-326	19.3-27.2	410-462	1773-1944	4.3-4.2	10-17	314-328	154-145	49.0-44.2	2093- 2276	6.7- 6.9	18-19	25-19
National Conference																	
LARm	9	3	0	.750	466-309	38.8-25.8	404-431	1711-1882	4.2-4.4	28-12	453-385	253-165	55.8-42.9	3709- 2576	8.2- 6.7	31-26	27-31
ChiB	9	3	0	.750	279-207	23.3-17.3	574-388	2308-1449	4.0-3.7	25-14	296-354	135-169	45.6-47.7	1927- 2265	6.5- 6.4	5-11	24-16
NYY	7	5	0	.583	366-367	30.5-30.6	397-434	1832-2445	4.6-5.6	16-29	355-396	174-189	49.0-47.7	2894- 2775	8.2- 7.0	29-17	26-30
Det	6	6	0	.500	321-285	26.8-23.8	389-399	1626-1367	4.2-3.4	14-13	403-381	176-191	43.7-50.1	2772- 2580	6.9- 6.8	22-23	29-31
GB	3	9	0	.250	244-406	20.3-33.8	398-422	1706-1885	4.3-4.5	15-24	367-379	140-185	38.1-48.8	1831- 2818	5.0- 7.4	14-24	37-27
SF	3	9	0	.250	213-297	17.8-24.8	460-443	1955-1662	4.3-3.8	14-17	326-347	164-164	50.3-47.3	1875- 2289	5.8- 6.6	14-16	25-22
Bal	1	11	0	.083	213-462	17.8-38.5	345-514	1148-2857	3.3-5.6	12-29	438-304	206-156	47.0-51.3	2687- 2545	6.1- 8.4	14-31	31-34
78 games					3579	45.8	5793	24075	4.2	208	4307	2008	46.6	29050	6.7	220	343

American Conf. Playoff: Cle 8, NYG 3
National Conf. Playoff: LARm 24, ChiB 14
Championship: Cle 30, LARm 28

LEADING RUSHERS	ATT	YARD	AVG	Long	TD
Marion Motley, Cle	140	810	5.8	69t	3
Frank Ziegler, Phi	172	733	4.3	52	1
Joe Geri, Pit	188	705	3.8	47	2
Eddie Price, NYG	126	703	5.6	74	4
Joe Perry, SF	124	647	5.2	78t	5

LEADING PASSERS	ATT	COM	YARD	TD	IN
Norm Van Brocklin, LARm	233	127	2061	18	14
Otto Graham, Cle	253	137	1943	14	20
Joe Geri, Pit	113	41	866	6	15
George Ratterman, NYY	294	140	2251	22	24
Charlie Conerly, NYG	132	56	1000	8	7

LEADING RECEIVERS	NO	YARD	AVG	Long	TD
Tom Fears, LARm	84	1116	13.3	53t	7
Dan Edwards, NYY	52	775	14.9	82t	6
Cloyce Box, Det	50	1009	20.2	82t	11
Paul Salata, Bal	50	618	12.4	57t	4
Bob Shaw, ChiC	48	971	20.2	65t	12

LEADING SCORERS	TD	FG	PAT	PTS
Doak Walker, Det	11	8	38	128
Johnny Lujack, ChiB	11	3	34	109
Bob Waterfield, LARm	1	7	54	81
Lou Groza, Cle	1	13	29	74
Shaw, ChiC	12	0	0	72

LEADING INTERCEPTOR	NO	YDS	AVG	Long	TD
Spec Sanders, NYY	13	199	15.3	29	0

LEADING PUNTER	NO	AVG	Long
Curly Morrison, ChiB	57	43.3	65

LEADING PUNT RETURNER	NO	YDS	AVG	Long	TD
Herb Rich, Bal	12	276	23.0	86t	1

LEADING KICKOFF RETURNER	NO	YDS	AVG	Long	TD
Vitamin T Smith, LARm	22	742	33.7	97t	3

SUPERLATIVES

Rushing Avg.	6.3	Johnny Lujack, ChiB
Receiving Avg.	21.4	Hugh Taylor, Was
Completion Pct.	57.3	Bob Waterfield, LARm
Touchdowns	12	Bob Shaw, ChiC
Field Goals	13	Lou Groza, Cle
Extra Points	54	Bob Waterfield, LARm

LONGEST

Run	96t	Bob Hoernschemeyer, Det
Pass	96t	Tobin Rote to Billy Grimes, GB
Interception	94t	Roy Steiner, GB
Punt	76	Jim Hardy, ChiC
Punt Return	96t	Bill Dudley, Was
Kickoff Return	103t	Russ Craft, Phi
Field Goal	52	Ted Fritsch, GB

1951 NATIONAL FOOTBALL LEAGUE

Team	W	L	T	PCT	SCORING OWN-OPP PTS-PTS	SCORING OWN-OPP PPG-PPG	RUSHING OWN-OPP ATT-ATT	RUSHING OWN-OPP YARD-YARD	RUSHING OWN-OPP AVG-AVG	RUSHING ON-OP TD-TD	PASSING OWN-OPP ATT-ATT	PASSING OWN-OPP COM-COM	PASSING OWN-OPP PCT-PCT	PASSING OWN-OPP YARD-YARD	PASSING OWN-OPP AVG-AVG	PASSING ON-OP TD-TD	PASSING ON-OP IN-IN
American Conference																	
Cle	11	1	0	.917	331-152	27.6-12.7	415-428	1708-1454	4.1-3.4	20- 8	271-330	151-151	55.7-45.8	2273- 1978	8.4- 6.0	18-10	17-22
NYG	9	2	1	.818	254-161	21.1-13.4	491-392	1713- 913	3.5-2.3	10- 8	210-377	101-162	48.1-43.0	1432- 2337	6.8- 6.2	11-11	26-41
Was	5	7	0	.417	183-296	15.3-24.7	547-464	2151-2093	3.9-4.5	14-20	226-295	99-140	43.8-47.4	1508- 2104	6.8- 7.1	8-16	25-18
Pit	4	7	1	.364	183-235	15.3-19.6	425-499	1428-1859	3.4-3.7	9-13	330-266	130-136	39.4-51.1	1842- 1887	5.6- 6.3	10-12	26-30
Phi	4	8	0	.333	234-264	19.5-22.0	509-462	1562-1816	3.1-3.9	13-12	284-287	120-119	42.3-41.5	1713- 1748	6.0- 6.1	17-17	29-18
ChiC	3	9	0	.250	210-287	17.5-23.9	440-476	1963-1977	4.5-4.2	14-15	334-265	161-123	48.2-46.4	2244- 1973	6.7- 7.4	13-18	24-27
National Conference																	
LARm	8	4	0	.667	392-261	32.7-21.8	426-478	2210-2206	5.2-4.8	22-17	373-329	189-140	50.2-42.6	3296- 1992	8.8- 6.1	26-13	22-19
Det	7	4	1	.636	336-259	28.0-21.6	410-454	1841-1509	4.5-3.3	11-13	351-374	158-181	45.0-48.4	2500- 2608	7.1- 7.0	29-18	24-15
SF	7	4	1	.636	255-205	21.3-17.1	523-417	2366-1549	4.5-3.7	18- 9	281-353	154-158	54.8-44.7	1955- 2313	7.0- 6.5	14-15	19-33
ChiB	7	5	0	.583	286-282	23.8-23.5	539-372	2408-1958	4.5-5.3	24-15	315-337	143-160	45.4-47.5	2239- 2431	7.1- 7.2	12-21	20-21
GB	3	9	0	.250	254-375	21.2-31.3	313-496	1196-2152	3.8-4.3	8-22	478-313	231-157	48.3-50.2	2846- 2535	6.0- 8.1	26-25	29-22
NYY	1	9	2	.100	241-382	20.1-31.8	364-464	1337-2397	3.7-5.1	12-23	428-355	172-182	40.2-51.3	2634- 2776	6.2- 7.8	16-24	27-22
72 Games					3159	43.9	5402	21883	4.1	175	3881	1809	46.6	26482	6.8	200	288

Championship: LARm 24, Cle 17

LEADING RUSHERS	ATT	YARD	AVG	Long	TD
Eddie Price, NYG	271	971	3.6	80t	7
Rob Goode, Was	208	951	4.6	33	9
Dan Towler, LARm	126	854	6.8	79t	6
Bob Hoernschemeyer, Det	132	678	5.1	85t	2
Joe Perry, SF	136	677	5.0	58t	3

LEADING PASSERS	ATT	COM	YARD	TD	IN
Bob Waterfield, LARm	176	88	1566	13	10
Norm Van Brocklin, LARm	194	100	1725	13	11
Otto Graham, Cle	265	147	2205	17	16
Steve Romanik, ChiB	101	43	791	3	9
Bob Celeri, NYY	238	102	1797	12	15

LEADING RECEIVERS	NO	YARD	AVG	Long	TD
Elroy Hirsch, LARm	66	1495	22.7	91t	17
Gordy Soltau, SF	59	826	14.0	48t	7
Fran Polsfoot, ChiC	57	796	14.0	80t	4
Bob Mann, GB	50	696	13.9	52	8
Dante Lavelli, Cle	43	586	13.6	47	6

LEADING SCORERS	TD	FG	PAT	PTS
Elroy Hirsch, LARm	17	0	0	102
Bob Waterfield, LARm	3	13	41	98
Doak Walker, Det	6	6	43	97
Bob Walston, Phil	8	6	28	94
Gordy Soltau, SF	7	6	30	90

LEADING INTERCEPTOR	NO	YDS	AVG	Long	TD
Otto Schnellbacher, NYG	11	194	17.6	46t	2

LEADING PUNTER	NO	AVG	Long
Horace Gillom, Cle	73	45.5	66

LEADING PUNT RETURNER	NO	YDS	AVG	Long	TD
Buddy Young, NYY	12	231	19.3	79t	1

LEADING KICKOFF RETURNER	NO	YDS	AVG	Long	TD
Lynn Chandnois, Pit	12	390	32.5	55	0

SUPERLATIVES

Rushing Avg.	6.9	Tobin Rote, GB
Receiving Avg.	22.7	Elroy Hirsch, LARm
Completion Pct.	56.6	Bobby Thomason, GB
Touchdowns	17	Elroy Hirsch, LARm
Field Goals	13	Bob Waterfield, LARm
Extra Points	43	Lou Groza, Cle
		Doak Walker, Det

LONGEST

Run	85t	Bob Hoernschemeyer, Det
Pass	91t	Bob Waterfield to Elroy Hirsch, LARm
Interception	88t	Bob Summerhays, GB
Punt	75	Verl Lillywhite, SF
Punt Return	89t	Jack Christiansen, Det
Kickoff Return	100t	Emlen Tunnell, NYG
Field Goal	47	Bob Waterfield, LARm

1952 NATIONAL FOOTBALL LEAGUE

Team	W	L	T	PCT	SCORING OWN-OPP PTS-PTS	SCORING OWN-OPP PPG-PPG	RUSHING OWN-OPP ATT-ATT	RUSHING OWN-OPP YARD-YARD	RUSHING OWN-OPP AVG-AVG	RUSHING ON-OP TD-TD	PASSING OWN-OPP ATT-ATT	PASSING OWN-OPP COM-COM	PASSING OWN-OPP PCT-PCT	PASSING OWN-OPP YARD-YARD	PASSING OWN-OPP AVG-AVG	PASSING ON-OP TD-TD	PASSING ON-OP IN-IN
American Conference																	
Cle	8	4	0	.667	310-213	25.8-17.8	394-411	1786-1386	4.5-3.4	12-11	374-348	184-141	49.2-40.5	2839- 2028	7.6- 5.8	22-17	26-22
NYG	7	5	0	.583	234-231	19.5-19.3	442-404	1636-1303	3.7-3.2	11- 8	280-337	121-162	43.2-48.1	1713- 2514	6.1- 7.5	16-18	22-28
Phi	7	5	0	.583	252-271	21.0-22.6	434-408	1370-1396	3.2-3.4	10-12	361-343	154-157	42.7-45.8	2272- 2164	6.3- 6.3	13-19	19-20
Pit	5	7	0	.417	300-273	25.0-22.8	384-460	1204-1744	3.1-3.8	12- 8	365-369	167-167	45.8-45.3	2504- 2765	6.9- 7.5	21-24	23-27
ChiC	4	8	0	.333	172-221	14.3-18.4	477-455	1748-1588	3.7-3.5	10- 8	289-307	124-149	42.9-48.5	1512- 1942	5.2- 6.3	10-16	22-25
Was	4	8	0	.333	240-287	20.0-23.9	467-428	1655-1817	3.5-4.3	10-19	286-275	147-121	51.4-44.0	2127- 1817	7.4- 6.6	20-12	21-18
National Conference																	
Det	9	3	0	.750	344-192	28.7-16.0	442-353	1780-1145	4.0-3.2	14- 8	362-382	171-182	47.2-47.6	2495- 2421	6.9- 6.3	24-15	28-32
LARm	9	3	0	.750	349-234	29.1-19.5	411-441	1811-1613	4.4-3.7	11-10	329-360	167-161	50.8-44.7	2438- 2252	7.4- 6.3	17-18	31-38
SF	7	5	0	.583	285-221	23.8-18.4	421-412	1905-1566	4.5-3.8	16-10	342-342	177-151	51.8-44.2	2371- 1929	6.9- 5.6	19-15	23-17
GB	6	6	0	.500	295-312	24.6-26.0	405-415	1485-1507	3.7-3.6	11-16	337-340	161-162	47.8-47.6	2688- 2205	8.0- 6.5	26-17	25-22
ChiB	5	7	0	.417	245-326	20.4-27.2	411-463	1543-1921	3.8-4.1	11-20	347-311	141-160	40.6-51.4	2015- 2350	5.8- 7.6	18-16	27-20
Dal	1	11	0	.083	182-427	15.2-35.6	381-421	1397-2334	3.7-5.5	13-17	352-310	149-150	42.3-48.4	1807- 2394	5.1- 7.7	12-31	20-28
72 Games					3208	44.6	5069	19320	3.8	141	4024	1863	46.3	26781	6.7	218	287

National Conf. Playoff: Det 31, LARm 21
Championship: Det 17, Cle 7

LEADING RUSHERS	ATT	YARD	AVG	Long	TD
Dan Towler, LARm	156	894	5.7	44t	10
Eddie Price, NYG	183	748	4.1	75t	5
Joe Perry, SF	158	725	4.6	78t	8
Hugh McElhenny, SF	98	684	7.0	89t	6
Bob Hoernschemeyer, Det	106	457	4.3	41	4

LEADING PASSERS	ATT	COM	YARD	TD	IN
Norm Van Brocklin, LARm	205	113	1736	14	17
Tobin Rote, GB	157	82	1268	13	8
Babe Parilli, GB	177	77	1416	13	17
Otto Graham, Cle	364	181	2816	20	24
Frankie Albert, SF	129	71	964	8	10

LEADING RECEIVERS	NO	YARD	AVG	Long	TD
Mac Speedie, Cle	62	911	14.7	50	5
Bud Grant, Phi	56	997	17.8	84t	7
Elbie Nickel, Pit	55	884	16.1	54t	9
Gordy Soltau, SF	55	774	14.1	49t	7
Don Stonesifer, ChiC	54	617	11.4	26	0

LEADING SCORERS	TD	FG	PAT	PTS
Gordy Soltau, SF	7	6	34	94
Cloyce Box, Det	15	0	0	90
Lou Groza, Cle	0	19	32	89
Pat Harder, Det	3	11	34	85
Bob Waterfield, LARm	1	11	44	83

LEADING INTERCEPTOR	NO	YDS	AVG	Long	TD
Night Train Lane, LARm	14	298	21.3	80t	2

LEADING PUNTER	NO	AVG	Long
Horace Gillom, Cle	61	45.7	73

LEADING PUNT RETURNER	NO	YDS	AVG	Long	TD
Jack Christiansen, Det	15	322	21.5	79t	2

LEADING KICKOFF RETURNER	NO	YDS	AVG	Long	TD
Lynn Chandnois, Pit	17	599	35.2	93t	2

SUPERLATIVES

Rushing Avg.	7.0	Hugh McElhenny, SF
Receiving Avg.	23.4	Hugh Taylor, Was
Completion Pct.	55.1	Norm Van Brocklin, LARm
Touchdowns	15	Cloyce Box, Det
Field Goals	19	Lou Groza, Cle
Extra Points	44	Bob Waterfield, LARm

LONGEST

Run	89t	Hugh McElhenny, SF
Pass	90t	Babe Parilli to Billy Howton, GB
Interception	97t	Herb Rich, LARm
Punt	73	Horace Gillom, Cle
Punt Return	94t	Hugh McElhenny, SF
Kickoff Return	100t	Ollie Matson, ChiC
Field Goal	52	Lou Groza, Cle

1953 NATIONAL FOOTBALL LEAGUE

					SCORING		RUSHING				PASSING							
Team	W	L	T	PCT	OWN-OPP PTS-PTS	OWN-OPP PPG-PPG	OWN-OPP ATT-ATT	OWN-OPP YARD-YARD	OWN-OPP AVG-AVG	ON-OP TD-TD	OWN-OPP ATT-ATT	OWN-OPP COM-COM	OWN-OPP PCT-PCT	OWN-OPP YARD-YARD	OWN-OPP AVG-AVG	ON-OP TD-TD	ON-OP IN-IN
Eastern Conference																	
Cle	11	1	0	.917	348-162	29.0-13.5	379-374	1577-1560	4.2-4.2	20-11	303-389	191-164	63.0-42.2	3059- 2271	10.1- 5.8	16-10	9-25
Phi	7	4	1	.636	352-215	29.3-17.9	410-331	1722-1117	4.2-3.4	22- 6	438-374	224-167	51.1-44.7	3357- 2289	7.7- 6.1	25-17	31-24
Was	6	5	1	.545	208-215	17.3-17.9	413-455	1726-1886	4.2-4.1	10-15	278-350	107-171	38.5-48.9	1736- 1950	6.2- 5.8	12- 8	29-27
Pit	6	6	0	.500	211-263	17.6-21.9	432-366	1549-1125	3.6-3.1	13- 9	416-372	189-193	45.4-51.9	2014- 2413	4.8- 6.5	10-22	21-21
NYG	3	9	0	.250	179-277	14.9-23.1	398-385	1049-1360	2.6-3.5	6-12	345-368	158-173	45.8-47.0	1985- 2558	5.8- 6.5	16-20	34-23
ChiC	1	10	1	.091	190-337	15.8-28.1	322-440	1179-1662	3.7-3.8	7-24	408-341	181-176	44.4-51.6	2191- 2619	5.4- 7.7	14-17	27-24
Western Conference																	
Det	10	2	0	.833	271-205	22.6-17.1	427-404	1812-1580	4.2-3.9	12-10	316-354	144-159	45.6-44.9	2309- 2162	7.3- 6.1	18-13	27-38
SF	9	3	0	.750	372-237	31.0-19.8	443-398	2230-1548	5.0-3.9	26-12	322-358	174-173	54.0-48.6	2407- 2100	7.5- 5.9	22-17	19-23
LARm	8	3	1	.727	366-236	30.5-19.7	426-375	2148-1570	5.0-4.2	23-10	324-366	173-161	53.4-44.0	2772- 2181	8.6- 6.0	19-15	18-30
ChiB	3	8	1	.273	218-262	18.2-21.8	367-437	1129-1776	3.1-4.1	9-15	446-364	206-174	46.2-47.8	2637- 2530	5.9- 7.0	15-14	30-14
Bal	3	9	0	.250	182-350	15.2-29.2	376-445	1459-2315	3.9-5.2	7-21	319-321	126-165	39.5-51.4	1625- 2411	5.1- 7.5	13-21	27-23
GB	2	9	1	.182	200-338	16.7-28.2	424-407	1665-1748	3.9-4.3	14-24	352-312	147-144	41.8-46.2	1833- 2341	5.2- 7.5	9-15	34-28
72 games					3097	43.0	4817	19245	4.0	169	4267	2020	47.3	27925	6.5	189	306

Championship: Det 17, Cle 16

LEADING RUSHERS	ATT	YARD	AVG	Long	TD
Joe Perry, SF	192	1018	5.3	51t	10
Dan Towler, LARm	152	879	5.8	73t	7
Skeets Quinlan, LARm	97	705	7.3	74t	4
Charlie Justice, Was	115	616	5.4	43	2
Fran Rogel, Pit	137	527	3.8	58	2

LEADING PASSERS	ATT	COM	YARD	TD	IN
Otto Graham, Cle	258	167	2722	11	9
Norm Van Brocklin, LARm	286	156	2393	19	14
Y.A. Tittle, SF	259	149	2121	20	16
Bobby Thomason, Phi	304	162	2462	21	20
Bobby Layne, Det	273	125	2088	16	21

LEADING RECEIVERS	NO	YARD	AVG	Long	TD
Pete Pihos, Phi	63	1049	16.7	59	10
Elbie Nickel, Pit	62	743	12.0	40	4
Elroy Hirsch, LARm	61	941	15.4	70	4
Don Stonesifer, ChiC	56	684	12.2	46	2
Jim Dooley, ChiB	53	841	15.9	72	4

LEADING SCORERS	TD	FG	PAT	PTS
Gordy Soltau, SF	6	10	48	114
Lou Groza, Cle	0	23	39	108
Doak Walker, Det	5	12	27	93
Bobby Walston, Phi	5	4	45	87
Joe Perry, SF	13	0	0	78

LEADING INTERCEPTOR	NO	YDS	AVG	Long	TD
Jack Christiansen, Det	12	238	19.8	92t	1

LEADING PUNTER	NO	AVG	Long
Pat Brady, Pit	80	46.9	64

LEADING PUNT RETURNER	NO	YDS	AVG	Long	TD
Charley Trippi, ChiC	21	239	11.4	38	0

LEADING KICKOFF RETURNER	NO	YDS	AVG	Long	TD
Joe Arenas, SF	16	551	34.4	82	0

SUPERLATIVES

Rushing Avg.	7.3	Skeets Quinlan, LARm
Receiving Avg.	22.8	Bob Boyd, LARm
Completion Pct.	64.7	Otto Graham, Cle
Touchdowns	13	Joe Perry, SF
Field Goals	23	Lou Groza, Cle
Extra Points	48	Gordy Soltau, SF

LONGEST

Run	74t	Skeets Quinlan, LARm
Pass	97t	Bobby Layne to Cloyce Box, Det
Interception	92t	Jack Christiansen, Det
Punt	69	Clarence Avinger, NYG
Punt Return	78t	Woodley Lewis, LARm
Kickoff Return	104t	Buddy Young, Bal
Field Goal	56	Bert Rechichar, Bal

1954 NATIONAL FOOTBALL LEAGUE

					SCORING		RUSHING				PASSING						
					OWN-OPP	OWN-OPP	OWN-OPP	OWN-OPP	OWN-OPP	ON-OP	OWN-OPP	OWN-OPP	OWN-OPP	OWN - OPP	OWN-OPP	ON-OP	ON-OP
Team	W	L	T	PCT	PTS-PTS	PPG-PPG	ATT-ATT	YARD-YARD	AVG-AVG	TD-TD	ATT-ATT	COM-COM	PCT-PCT	YARD - YARD	AVG-AVG	TD-TD	IN-IN
Eastern Conference																	
Cle	9	3	0	.750	336-162	28.0-13.5	476-372	1793-1050	3.8-2.8	23- 4	295-300	174-126	59.0-42.0	2557- 1784	8.7- 5.9	14-15	22-23
Phi	7	4	1	.625	284-230	23.7-19.2	401-354	1196-1063	3.0-3.0	4- 8	401-345	206-143	51.4-41.4	2982- 2030	7.4- 5.9	33-13	30-28
NYG	7	5	0	.583	293-184	24.4-15.3	380-415	1482-1332	3.9-3.2	8- 9	334-352	163-164	48.8-46.6	2467- 2322	7.4- 6.6	27-11	22-33
Pit	5	7	0	.417	219-263	18.3-21.9	368-486	1282-2193	3.5-4.7	10-14	386-295	189-167	49.0-56.6	2321- 2458	6.0- 8.3	15-18	26-30
Was	3	9	0	.250	207-432	17.3-36.0	427-400	1626-1888	3.8-4.7	9-20	257-387	116-217	45.1-56.1	1813- 3060	7.1- 7.9	15-33	32-18
ChiC	2	10	0	.167	183-347	15.3-28.9	418-400	1612-1532	3.9-3.8	10-13	349-356	148-193	42.4-54.2	1903- 3006	5.5- 8.4	8-29	30-24
Western Conference																	
Det	9	2	1	.818	337-189	28.1-15.8	393-397	1608-1520	4.1-3.8	11-13	395-357	215-150	54.4-42.0	2972- 2390	7.5- 6.7	25-10	21-30
ChiB	8	4	0	.667	301-279	25.1-23.3	353-427	1142-1917	3.2-4.5	8-15	429-369	208-177	48.5-48.0	3299- 2432	7.7- 6.6	26-13	35-27
SF	7	4	1	.636	313-251	26.1-20.9	442-348	2498-1371	5.7-3.9	28- 8	340-374	187-193	55.0-51.6	2444- 3015	7.2- 8.1	15-24	12-19
LARm	6	5	1	.545	314-285	26.2-23.8	432-368	2140-1615	5.0-4.4	24-14	321-393	171-219	53.3-55.7	3180- 2697	9.9- 6.9	15-16	23-23
GB	4	8	0	.333	234-251	19.5-20.9	321-403	1328-1817	4.1-4.6	13-13	412-374	195-208	47.3-55.6	2454- 2690	6.0- 7.2	14-17	19-19
Bal	3	9	0	.250	131-279	10.9-23.3	364-425	1275-1630	3.5-3.8	4-21	313-330	163-178	52.1-53.9	2005- 2513	6.4- 7.6	9-12	22-20
72 games					3152	43.8	4775	18982	4.0	152	4232	2135	50.4	30397	7.2	216	294

Championship: Cle 56, Det 10

LEADING RUSHERS	ATT	YARD	AVG	Long	TD
Joe Perry, SF	173	1049	6.1	58	8
John Henry Johnson, SF	129	681	5.3	38t	9
Tank Younger, LARm	91	610	6.7	75t	8
Dan Towler, LARm	149	599	4.0	24	11
Maurice Bassett, Cle	144	588	4.1	22	6

LEADING PASSERS	ATT	COM	YARD	TD	IN
Norm Van Brocklin, LARm	260	139	2637	13	21
Otto Graham, Cle	240	142	2092	11	17
Zeke Bratkowski, ChiB	130	67	1087	8	17
Tom Dublinski, Det	138	77	1073	8	7
Bob Clatterbuck, NYG	101	50	781	6	7

LEADING RECEIVERS	NO	YARD	AVG	Long	TD
Pete Pihos, Phi	60	872	14.5	34	10
Billy Wilson, SF	60	830	13.8	43	5
Bob Boyd, LARm	53	1212	22.9	80t	6
Billy Howton, GB	52	768	14.8	59	2
Dante Lavelli, Cle	47	802	17.1	64	7

LEADING SCORERS	TD	FG	PAT	PTS
Bobby Walston, Phi	11	4	36	114
Doak Walker, Det	5	11	43	106
Lou Groza, Cle	0	16	37	85
Gordy Soltau, SF	2	11	31	76
Ben Agajanian, NYG	0	13	35	74

LEADING INTERCEPTOR	NO	YDS	AVG	Long	TD
Night Train Lane, ChiC	10	181	18.1	64	0

LEADING PUNTER	NO	AVG	Long
Pat Brady, Pit	66	43.2	72

LEADING PUNT RETURNER	NO	YDS	AVG	Long	TD
Veryl Switzer, GB	24	306	12.8	93t	1

LEADING KICKOFF RETURNER	NO	YDS	AVG	Long	TD
Billy Reynolds, Cle	14	413	29.5	51	0

SUPERLATIVES

Rushing Avg.	8.0	Hugh McElhenny, SF
Receiving Avg.	25.0	Harlon Hill, ChiB
Completion Pct.	59.2	Otto Graham, Cle
Touchdowns	12	Harlon Hill, ChiB
Field Goals	16	Lou Groza, Cle
Extra Points	43	Doak Walker, Det

LONGEST

Run	88t	Billy Wells, Was
Pass	84t	Adrian Burk to Jerry Williams, Phi
Interception	81t	Russ Craft, Pit
Punt	80	Horace Gillom, Cle
Punt Return	93t	Veryl Switzer, GB
Kickoff Return	100t	Bill Bowman, Det
Field Goal	50	Pat Summerall, ChiC

1955 NATIONAL FOOTBALL LEAGUE

					SCORING		RUSHING				PASSING						
					OWN-OPP	OWN-OPP	OWN-OPP	OWN - OPP	OWN-OPP	ON-OP	OWN-OPP	OWN-OPP	OWN-OPP	OWN - OPP	OWN-OPP	ON-OP	ON-OP
Team	W	L	T	PCT	PTS-PTS	PPG-PPG	ATT-ATT	YARD-YARD	AVG-AVG	TD-TD	ATT-ATT	COM-COM	PCT-PCT	YARD - YARD	AVG-AVG	TD-TD	IN-IN
Eastern Conference																	
Cle	9	2	1	.818	349-218	29.1-18.2	536-351	2020-1189	3.8-3.4	20-12	234-323	130-126	55.6-39.0	2225- 1775	9.5- 5.5	21-15	11-25
Was	8	4	0	.667	246-222	20.5-18.5	478-391	2000-1275	4.2-3.3	17- 8	257-340	101-165	39.3-48.5	1549- 2189	6.0- 6.4	11-17	21-19
NYG	6	5	1	.545	267-223	22.3-18.6	414-418	1693-1441	4.1-3.4	13-10	292-373	137-181	46.9-48.5	1865- 2543	6.4- 6.8	17-16	15-23
ChiC	4	7	1	.364	224-252	18.7-21.0	438-465	1626-1902	3.7-4.1	10-11	280-371	106-154	37.9-41.5	1520- 2146	5.4- 5.8	14-16	25-29
Phi	4	7	1	.364	248-231	20.7-19.3	392-455	1317-1637	3.4-3.8	9-12	400-272	198-124	49.5-45.6	2696- 1810	6.7- 6.7	19-12	24-16
Pit	4	8	0	.333	195-285	16.3-23.8	420-494	1284-1814	3.1-3.7	13-11	390-242	189-123	48.5-50.8	2550- 1530	6.5- 6.3	12-19	30-10
Western Conference																	
LARm	8	3	1	.727	260-231	21.7-19.3	451-423	1943-1624	4.3-3.8	17-10	344-351	175-198	50.9-55.0	2206- 2518	6.4- 7.2	9-18	18-31
ChiB	8	4	0	.667	294-251	24.5-20.9	487-398	2388-2100	4.9-5.3	19-17	306-354	145-177	47.4-50.0	2108- 2369	6.9- 6.7	17-14	23-19
GB	6	6	0	.500	258-276	21.5-23.0	433-475	1883-2174	4.3-4.6	11-18	348-259	159-118	45.7-45.6	2004- 1768	5.8- 6.8	17-13	19-31
Bal	5	6	1	.455	214-239	17.8-19.9	456-448	1833-2035	4.0-4.5	15-18	266-320	134-158	50.4-49.4	1795- 2288	6.7- 7.2	11-12	22-19
SF	4	8	0	.333	216-298	18.0-24.8	408-538	1713-2135	4.2-4.0	12-24	303-311	151-147	49.8-47.3	2225- 2045	7.3- 6.8	17-10	28-21
Det	3	9	0	.250	230-275	19.2-22.9	392-449	1477-1851	3.8-4.1	11-16	400-304	204-163	51.0-53.6	2542- 2304	6.4- 7.6	15-18	22-15
72 games					3001	41.7	5305	21177	4.0	167	3820	1829	47.9	25285	6.6	180	258

Championship: Cle 38, LARm 14

LEADING RUSHERS	ATT	YARD	AVG	Long	TD
Alan Ameche, Bal	213	961	4.5	79t	9
Howie Ferguson, GB	192	859	4.5	57	4
Curly Morrison, Cle	156	824	5.3	56	3
Ron Waller, LARm	151	716	4.7	55t	7
Joe Perry, SF	156	701	4.5	42	2

LEADING PASSERS	ATT	COM	YARD	TD	IN
Otto Graham, Cle	185	98	1721	15	8
Ed Brown, ChiB	164	85	1307	9	10
Bobby Thomason, Phi	171	88	1337	10	7
Y.A. Tittle, SF	287	147	2185	17	28
Eddie LeBaron, Was	178	79	1270	9	15

LEADING RECEIVERS	NO	YARD	AVG	Long	TD
Pete Pihos, Phi	62	864	13.9	40t	7
Billy Wilson, SF	53	831	15.7	72t	7
Billy Howton, GB	44	697	15.8	60	5
Dave Middleton, Det	44	663	15.1	77t	3
Tom Fears, LARm	44	569	12.9	31	2
Lew Carpenter, Det	44	312	7.1	34t	2

LEADING SCORERS	TD	FG	PAT	PTS
Doak Walker, Det	7	9	27	96
Vic Janowicz, Was	7	6	28	88
George Blanda, ChiB	2	11	37	82
Fred Cone, GB	0	16	30	78
Lou Groza, Cle	0	11	44	77

LEADING INTERCEPTOR	NO	YDS	AVG	Long	TD
Will Sherman, LARm	11	101	9.2	36	0

LEADING PUNTER	NO	AVG	Long
Norm Van Brocklin, LARm	60	44.6	61

LEADING PUNT RETURNER	NO	YDS	AVG	Long	TD
Ollie Matson, ChiC	13	245	18.8	78	2

LEADING KICKOFF RETURNER	NO	YDS	AVG	Long	TD
Al Carmichael, GB	14	418	29.9	100t	1

SUPERLATIVES

Rushing Avg.	5.4	Rick Casares, ChiB
Receiving Avg.	20.8	Ray Renfro, Cle
Completion Pct.	53.0	Otto Graham, Cle
Touchdowns	9	Alan Ameche, Bal Harlon Hill, ChiB
Field Goals	16	Fred Cone, GB
Extra Points	44	Lou Groza, Cle

LONGEST

Run	81t Rick Casares, ChiB
Pass	98t Ogden Compton to Night Train Lane, ChiC
Interception	92t Leo Sanford, ChiC
Punt	75 Adrian Burk, Phi
Punt Return	78t Ollie Matson, ChiC
Kickoff Return	100t Al Carmichael, GB
Field Goal	52 Bert Rechichar, Bal

1956 NATIONAL FOOTBALL LEAGUE

					SCORING		RUSHING				PASSING						
Team	W	L	T	PCT	OWN-OPP PTS-PTS	OWN-OPP PPG-PPG	OWN-OPP ATT-ATT	OWN-OPP YARD-YARD	OWN-OPP AVG-AVG	ON-OP TD-TD	OWN-OPP ATT-ATT	OWN-OPP COM-COM	OWN-OPP PCT-PCT	OWN-OPP YARD-YARD	OWN-OPP AVG-AVG	ON-OP TD-TD	ON-OP IN-IN
Eastern Conference																	
NYG	8	3	1	.727	264-197	22.0-16.4	499-415	2129-1443	4.3-3.5	18-10	275-297	133-149	48.4-50.2	1601- 1890	5.8- 6.4	17-12	14-17
ChiC	7	5	0	.583	240-182	20.0-15.2	527-478	2053-2075	3.9-4.3	14-14	214-287	100-129	46.7-44.9	1492- 1670	7.0- 5.8	13- 8	14-33
Was	6	6	0	.500	183-225	15.3-18.6	501-446	1743-1570	3.5-3.5	5-15	215-240	104-120	48.4-50.0	1335- 1739	6.2- 7.2	11-11	18-18
Cle	5	7	0	.417	167-177	13.9-14.8	480-463	1845-2032	3.8-4.4	8-13	202-226	105-107	52.0-47.3	1358- 1215	6.7- 5.4	8- 7	18-18
Pit	5	7	0	.417	217-250	18.1-20.8	413-468	1350-1743	3.3-3.7	14-14	318-234	136-128	42.8-54.7	1793- 1646	5.6- 6.8	14-14	24-18
Phi	3	8	1	.273	143-215	11.9-17.9	418-513	1377-1893	3.3-3.7	11-10	249-243	122-114	49.0-46.9	1556- 1506	6.2- 6.2	6-15	27-16
Western Conference																	
ChiB	9	2	1	.818	363-246	30.1-20.5	536-384	2468-1483	4.6-3.9	22-14	250-332	135-159	54.0-47.9	2193- 2413	8.8- 7.3	19-16	19-23
Det	9	3	0	.750	300-188	25.0-15.7	507-373	2011-1503	4.0-4.0	21- 9	301-297	160-138	53.2-46.5	2250- 2045	7.5- 6.9	13-11	23-28
SF	5	6	1	.455	233-284	19.4-23.7	419-481	1836-2192	4.4-4.6	17-23	297-279	162-147	54.5-52.7	2262- 2115	7.6- 7.6	8-12	19-17
Bal	5	7	0	.417	270-322	22.5-26.8	432-447	2202-1916	5.1-4.3	21-16	279-297	158-165	56.6-55.6	2210- 2463	7.9- 8.3	14-22	18-13
GB	4	8	0	.333	264-342	22.0-28.5	337-512	1421-2619	4.2-5.1	13-20	353-260	171-144	48.4-55.4	2591- 2166	7.3- 8.3	21-17	18-19
LARm	4	8	0	.333	291-307	24.3-25.6	384-473	1978-1944	5.2-4.1	15-21	329-290	170-156	51.7-53.8	2601- 2374	7.9- 8.2	18-17	28-20
72 games					2935	40.8	5453	22413	4.1	179	3282	1656	50.5	23242	7.1	162	240

Championship: NYG 47, ChiB 7

LEADING RUSHERS	ATT	YARD	AVG	Long	TD
Rick Casares, ChiB	234	1126	4.8	68t	12
Ollie Matson, ChiC	192	924	4.8	79t	5
Hugh McElhenny, SF	185	916	5.0	86t	8
Alan Ameche, Bal	178	858	4.8	43	8
Frank Gifford, NYG	159	819	5.2	69	5

LEADING PASSERS	ATT	COM	YARD	TD	IN
Ed Brown, ChiB	168	96	1667	11	12
Bill Wade, LARm	178	91	1461	10	13
Bobby Layne, Det	244	129	1909	9	17
Norm Van Brocklin, LARm	124	68	966	7	12
Lamar McHan, ChiC	152	72	1159	10	8

LEADING RECEIVERS	NO	YARD	AVG	Long	TD
Billy Wilson, SF	60	889	14.8	77t	5
Billy Howton, GB	55	1188	21.6	66t	12
Frank Gifford, NYG	51	603	11.8	48	4
Harlon Hill, ChiB	47	1128	24.0	79t	11
Jim Mutscheller, Bal	44	715	16.3	53t	6

LEADING SCORERS	TD	FG	PAT	PTS
Bobby Layne, Det	5	12	33	99
Rick Casares, ChiB	14	0	0	84
George Blanda, ChiB	0	12	45	81
Fred Cone, GB	4	5	33	72
Billy Howton, GB	12	0	0	72

LEADING INTERCEPTOR	NO	YDS	AVG	Long	TD
Lindon Crow, ChiC	11	170	15.5	42	0

LEADING PUNTER	NO	AVG	Long
Norm Van Brocklin, LARm	48	43.1	72

LEADING PUNT RETURNER	NO	YDS	AVG	Long	TD
Ken Konz, Cle	13	187	14.4	65t	1

LEADING KICKOFF RETURNER	NO	YDS	AVG	Long	TD
Tommy Wilson, LARm	15	477	31.8	103t	1

SUPERLATIVES

Rushing Avg.	7.5 Lenny Moore, Bal
Receiving Avg.	24.0 Harlon Hill, ChiB
Completion Pct.	57.1 Ed Brown, ChiB
Touchdowns	14 Rick Casares, ChiB
Field Goals	17 Sam Baker, Was
Extra Points	45 George Blanda, ChiB

LONGEST

Run	86t Hugh McElhenny,SF
Pass	79t Bill McColl to Harlon Hill, ChiB
Interception	95t Will Sherman, LARm
Punt	72 Norm Van Brocklin, LARm
Punt Return	95t Frank Bernardi, ChiC
Kickoff Return	106t Al Carmichael, Was
Field Goal	49 Sam Baker, Was

1957 NATIONAL FOOTBALL LEAGUE

					SCORING		RUSHING				PASSING						
Team	W	L	T	PCT	OWN-OPP PTS-PTS	OWN-OPP PPG-PPG	OWN-OPP ATT-ATT	OWN-OPP YARD-YARD	OWN-OPP AVG-AVG	ON-OP TD-TD	OWN-OPP ATT-ATT	OWN-OPP COM-COM	OWN-OPP PCT-PCT	OWN-OPP YARD-YARD	OWN-OPP AVG-AVG	ON-OP TD-TD	ON-OP IN-IN
Eastern Conference																	
Cle	9	2	1	.818	269-172	22.4-14.3	501-396	1958-1502	3.9-3.8	19-11	195-242	108-105	55.4-43.4	1873- 1511	9.6- 6.2	12- 8	14-19
NYG	7	5	0	.583	254-211	21.2-17.6	441-442	1649-1845	3.7-4.0	13-12	269-226	147-104	54.6-46.0	2158- 1596	8.0- 7.1	15-10	12-18
Pit	6	6	0	.500	161-178	13.4-14.8	390-412	1174-1425	3.0-3.5	7- 7	312-234	149-112	47.8-47.9	2013- 1523	6.5- 6.5	11-10	14-19
Was	5	6	1	.455	251-230	20.9-19.2	500-394	1873-1567	3.7-4.0	17-11	201-262	109-135	54.2-51.5	1741- 2193	8.7- 8.4	11-18	13-16
Phi	4	8	0	.333	173-230	14.4-19.2	424-451	1582-1714	3.7-3.8	9-15	204-257	99-133	48.5-51.8	1379- 2083	6.8- 8.1	10-10	23-17
ChiC	3	9	0	.250	200-299	16.7-24.9	365-521	1442-2201	4.0-4.2	12-19	271-233	111-117	41.0-50.2	1969- 2027	7.3- 7.2	12-17	22-12
Western Conference																	
Det	8	4	0	.667	251-231	20.9-19.3	409-406	1811-1521	4.4-3.7	12-13	361-290	163-163	45.2-56.2	2239- 2099	6.2- 7.2	17-15	22-25
SF	8	4	0	.667	260-264	21.7-22.0	377-434	1622-1847	4.3-4.3	15-18	305-332	191-182	62.6-54.8	2407- 2582	7.9- 7.8	17-13	18-18
Bal	7	5	0	.583	303-235	25.3-19.9	434-375	1735-1174	4.0-3.1	12-10	314-342	177-175	56.4-51.2	2608- 2548	8.3- 7.5	25-19	19-28
LARm	6	6	0	.500	307-278	25.6-23.2	474-440	2142-1845	4.5-4.2	15-15	296-301	144-153	48.6-50.8	2256- 2186	7.6- 7.3	21-15	23-14
ChiB	5	7	0	.417	203-211	16.9-17.6	457-419	1686-1383	3.7-3.3	15-10	286-306	130-153	45.5-50.0	1945- 2212	6.8- 7.2	7-15	28-15
GB	3	9	0	.250	218-311	18.2-25.9	380-462	1441-2159	3.8-4.7	13-18	325-314	157-153	48.3-48.7	2157- 2185	6.6- 7.0	12-18	23-30
72 games					2850	39.6	5152	20115	3.9	159	3339	1685	50.5	24745	7.4	170	231

Western Conf. Playoff: Det 31, SF 27
Championship: Det 59, Cle 14

LEADING RUSHERS	ATT	YARD	AVG	Long	TD
Jim Brown, Cle	202	942	4.7	69t	9
Rick Casares, ChiB	204	700	3.4	25t	6
Don Bosseler, Was	167	673	4.0	28	7
John Henry Johnson, Det	129	621	4.8	62	5
Tommy Wilson, LARm	127	616	4.9	46	3

LEADING PASSERS	ATT	COM	YARD	TD	IN
Tommy O'Connell, Cle	110	63	1229	9	8
Eddie LeBaron, Was	167	99	1508	11	10
Johnny Unitas, Bal	301	172	2550	24	17
Norm Van Brocklin, LARm	265	132	2105	20	21
Lamar McHan, ChiC	200	87	1568	10	15

LEADING RECEIVERS	NO	YARD	AVG	Long	TD
Billy Wilson, SF	52	757	14.6	40	6
Raymond Berry, Bal	47	800	17.0	67t	6
Jack McClairen, Pit	46	630	13.7	48t	2
Frank Gifford, NYG	41	588	14.3	63	4
Lenny Moore, Bal	40	687	17.2	82t	7

LEADING SCORERS	TD	FG	PAT	PTS
Sam Baker, Was	1	14	29	77
Lou Groza, Cle	0	15	32	77
Fred Cone, GB	2	12	26	74

Paige Cothren, LARm	0	11	38	71
George Blanda, ChiB	1	14	23	71

LEADING INTERCEPTORS	NO	YDS	AVG	Long	TD
Milt Davis, Bal	10	219	21.9	75t	2
Jack Christiansen, Det	10	137	13.7	52	1
Jack Butler, Pit	10	85	8.5	20	0

LEADING PUNTER	NO	AVG	Long
Don Chandler, NYG	60	44.6	61

LEADING PUNT RETURNER	NO	YDS	AVG	Long	TD
Bert Zagers, Was	14	217	15.5	76t	2

LEADING KICKOFF RETURNER	NO	YDS	AVG	Long	TD
Jon Arnett, LARm	18	504	28.0	98t	1

SUPERLATIVES

Rushing Avg.	5.0	Lenny Moore, Bal
Receiving Avg.	29.0	Ray Renfro, Cle
Completion Pct.	63.1	Y.A. Tittle, SF
Touchdowns	11	Lenny Moore, Bal
Field Goals	15	Lou Groza, Cle
Extra Points	38	Paige Cothren, LARm

LONGEST

Run	76	Ron Waller, LARm
Pass	83t	Lamar McHan to Gern Nagler, ChiC
Interception	99t	Jerry Norton, Phi
Punt	86	Larry Barnes, SF
Punt Return	76t	Bert Zagers, Was
Kickoff Return	98t	Jon Arnett, LARm
Field Goal	50	Ben Agajanian, NYG

1958 NATIONAL FOOTBALL LEAGUE

					SCORING		RUSHING				PASSING						
Team	W	L	T	PCT	OWN-OPP PTS-PTS	OWN-OPP PPG-PPG	OWN-OPP ATT-ATT	OWN-OPP YARD-YARD	OWN-OPP AVG-AVG	ON-OP TD-TD	OWN-OPP ATT-ATT	OWN-OPP COM-COM	OWN-OPP PCT-PCT	OWN - OPP YARD - YARD	OWN-OPP AVG-AVG	ON-OP TD-TD	ON-OP IN-IN
Eastern Conference																	
NYG	9	3	0	.750	246-183	20.5-15.3	450-399	1725-1440	3.8-3.6	14- 7	266-311	119-142	44.7-45.7	1718- 2130	6.5- 6.8	15-11	12-21
Cle	9	3	0	.750	302-217	25.2-18.1	475-369	2526-1448	5.3-3.9	24- 6	206-312	110-162	53.4-51.9	1758- 2387	8.5- 7.7	12-20	14-16
Pit	7	4	1	.636	261-230	21.8-19.2	394-403	1521-1491	3.9-3.7	14-14	336-334	156-173	46.4-51.8	2895- 2136	8.6- 6.4	16-11	21-24
Was	4	7	1	.364	214-268	17.8-22.3	480-396	1977-1734	4.1-4.4	11-13	251-300	121-153	48.2-51.0	1989- 2782	7.9- 9.3	14-21	17-16
ChiC	2	9	1	.182	261-356	21.8-29.7	366-449	1456-2133	4.0-4.8	9-26	407-337	198-171	48.6-50.7	2735- 2793	6.7- 8.3	23-18	27-15
Phi	2	9	1	.182	235-306	19.6-25.5	334-488	1093-1929	3.3-4.0	13-15	402-289	214-138	53.2-47.8	2772- 2244	6.9- 7.8	18-22	21-15
Western Conference																	
Bal	9	3	0	.750	381-203	31.8-16.9	456-331	2127-1291	4.7-3.9	24-13	354-363	178-168	50.3-46.3	2537- 2248	7.2- 6.2	26- 9	11-35
ChiB	8	4	0	.667	298-230	24.8-19.2	437-351	1770-1297	4.1-3.7	15-12	321-327	146-153	45.5-46.8	2021- 2142	6.3- 6.6	18-14	24-22
LARm	8	4	0	.667	344-278	28.7-23.2	345-405	1734-1777	5.0-4.4	18-12	358-381	186-188	52.0-49.3	2909- 2303	8.1- 6.0	19-21	26-28
SF	6	6	0	.500	257-324	21.4-27.0	359-380	1628-2038	4.5-5.4	18-15	383-341	223-163	58.2-47.8	2691- 2218	7.0- 6.5	15-25	29-16
Det	4	7	1	.364	261-276	21.8-23.0	364-407	1360-1720	3.7-4.2	9-19	319-320	141-167	44.2-52.2	2148- 2255	6.7- 7.0	20-15	14-22
GB	1	10	1	.091	193-382	16.1-31.8	345-427	1421-1720	4.1-4.8	7-24	348-336	161-175	46.3-52.1	2118- 2653	6.1- 7.9	15-24	27-13
72 games					3253	45.2	4805	20338	4.2	176	3951	1953	49.4	28291	7.2	211	243

Eastern Conf. Playoff: NYG 10, Cle 0
Championship: Bal 23, NYG 17 (OT)

LEADING RUSHERS	ATT	YARD	AVG	Long	TD
Jim Brown, Cle	257	1527	5.9	65t	17
Alan Ameche, Bal	171	791	4.6	28	8
Joe Perry, SF	125	758	6.1	73t	4
Tom Tracy, Pit	169	714	4.2	64	5
Jon Arnett, LARm	133	683	5.1	57	6

LEADING PASSERS	ATT	COM	YARD	TD	IN
Eddie LeBaron, Was	145	79	1365	11	10
Milt Plum, Cle	189	102	1619	11	11
Bobby Layne, Pit	294	145	2510	14	12
Bill Wade, LARm	341	181	2875	18	22
Johnny Unitas, Bal	263	136	2007	19	7

LEADING RECEIVERS	NO	YARD	AVG	Long	TD
Raymond Berry, Bal	56	794	14.2	54	9
Pete Retzlaff, Phi	56	766	13.7	49	2
Del Shofner, LARm	51	1097	21.5	92t	8
Lenny Moore, Bal	50	938	18.5	77t	7
Clyde Conner, SF	49	512	10.4	26	5

LEADING SCORERS	TD	FG	PAT	PTS
Jim Brown, Cle	18	0	0	108
Lenny Moore, Bal	14	0	0	84
Paige Cothren, LARm	0	14	42	84
Tom Miner, Pit	0	14	31	73
George Blanda, ChiB	0	11	36	69

LEADING INTERCEPTOR	NO	YDS	AVG	Long	TD
Jim Patton, NYG	11	183	16.6	42	0

LEADING PUNTER	NO	AVG	Long
Sam Baker, Was	48	45.4	64

LEADING PUNT RETURNER	NO	YDS	AVG	Long	TD
Jon Arnett, LARm	18	223	12.4	58	0

LEADING KICKOFF RETURNER	NO	YDS	AVG	Long	TD
Ollie Matson, ChiC	14	497	35.5	101t	2

SUPERLATIVES

Rushing Avg.	7.3	Lenny Moore, Bal
Receiving Avg.	27.6	Jimmy Orr, Pit
Completion Pct.	59.9	John Brodie, SF
Touchdowns	18	Jim Brown, Cle
Field Goals	14	Paige Cothren, LARm
		Tom Miner, Pit
Extra Points	48	Steve Myhra, Balt

LONGEST

Run	83t	John David Crow, ChiC
Pass	93t	Bill Wade to Red Phillips, LARm
Interception	70t	Will Sherman, LARm
Punt	67	Don Chandler, NYG
Punt Return	71t	Yale Lary, Det
Kickoff Return	103t	Lenny Lyles, Bal
Field Goal	49	Pat Summerall, NYG

1959 NATIONAL FOOTBALL LEAGUE

					SCORING		RUSHING				PASSING						
Team	W	L	T	PCT	OWN-OPP PTS-PTS	OWN-OPP PPG-PPG	OWN-OPP ATT-ATT	OWN-OPP YARD-YARD	OWN-OPP AVG-AVG	ON-OP TD-TD	OWN-OPP ATT-ATT	OWN-OPP COM-COM	OWN-OPP PCT-PCT	OWN - OPP YARD - YARD	OWN-OPP AVG-AVG	ON-OP TD-TD	ON-OP IN-IN
Eastern Conference																	
NYG	10	2	0	.833	284-170	23.7-14.2	433-379	1646-1261	3.8-3.3	11- 6	302-304	165-137	54.6-45.1	2633- 1811	8.7- 6.0	18-11	13-22
Cle	7	5	0	.583	270-214	22.5-17.8	457-360	2149-1422	4.7-4.0	20- 9	276-319	159-168	57.6-52.7	2033- 2457	7.4- 7.7	14-17	9-18
Phi	7	5	0	.583	268-278	22.3-23.2	391-429	1315-2068	3.4-4.8	13-15	352-292	194-141	55.1-49.3	2644- 2074	7.5- 7.1	17-17	16-20
Pit	6	5	1	.545	257-216	21.4-18.0	406-405	1543-1500	3.8-3.7	10-10	318-285	150-128	47.0-44.9	2298- 2014	7.2- 7.1	21-12	23-22
Was	3	9	0	.250	185-350	15.4-29.2	422-404	1964-2214	4.7-5.5	9-19	284-319	121-185	42.6-58.0	1824- 2606	6.4- 8.2	13-26	23-13
Chi	2	10	0	.167	234-324	19.5-27.0	367-477	1613-1874	4.4-3.9	10-15	280-266	125-138	44.6-51.9	1766- 2359	6.3- 8.9	14-22	19-15
Western Conference																	
Bal	9	3	0	.750	374-251	31.2-20.9	435-325	1705-1557	3.9-4.8	13-16	376-351	196-171	52.3-48.7	2938- 2497	7.8- 7.1	33-13	14-40
ChiB	8	4	0	.667	252-196	21.0-16.3	392-429	1438-1783	3.7-4.2	14-11	310-333	156-144	50.3-43.2	2284- 2147	7.4- 6.4	15-14	16-22
GB	7	5	0	.583	248-246	20.7-20.5	421-430	1907-1770	4.5-4.1	15-14	268-329	128-169	47.8-51.4	1963- 2030	7.3- 6.2	16-14	17-14
SF	7	5	0	.583	255-237	21.3-19.8	407-433	1839-1974	4.5-4.6	16-16	264-341	132-176	50.0-51.6	1685- 2272	6.4- 6.7	12-15	22-14
Det	3	8	1	.273	203-275	16.9-22.9	399-403	1792-1562	4.5-3.9	13-13	328-288	136-147	41.5-51.0	2131- 2340	6.5- 8.1	10-19	27-14
LARm	2	10	0	.167	242-315	20.2-26.3	371-427	1778-1704	4.8-4.0	15-15	356-287	196-151	55.1-52.8	2723- 2315	7.6- 8.1	14-17	22- 7
72 games					3072	42.7	4901	20689	4.2	159	3714	1858	50.0	26922	7.2	197	221

Championship: Bal 31, NYG 16

LEADING RUSHERS	ATT	YARD	AVG	Long	TD
Jim Brown, Cle	290	1329	4.6	70t	14
J.D. Smith, SF	207	1036	5.0	73t	10
Ollie Matson, LARm	161	863	5.4	50	6
Tom Tracy, Pit	199	794	4.0	51	3
Bobby Mitchell, Cle	131	743	5.7	90t	5

LEADING PASSERS	ATT	COM	YARD	TD	IN
Charlie Conerly, NYG	194	113	1706	14	4
Earl Morrall, Det	137	65	1102	5	6
Johnny Unitas, Bal	367	193	2899	32	14
Norm Van Brocklin, Phi	340	191	2617	16	14
Bill Wade, LARm	261	153	2001	12	17

LEADING RECEIVERS	NO	YARD	AVG	Long	TD
Raymond Berry, Bal	66	959	14.5	55t	14
Del Shofner, LARm	47	936	19.9	72t	7
Lenny Moore, Bal	47	846	18.0	71	6
Tommy McDonald, Phi	47	846	18.0	71	10
Jim Mutscheller, Bal	44	699	15.9	40t	8
Billy Wilson, SF	44	540	12.3	57t	4

LEADING SCORERS	TD	FG	PAT	PTS
Paul Hornung, GB	7	7	31	94
Pat Summerall, NYG	0	20	30	90
Ray Berry, Bal	14	0	0	84
Jim Brown, Cle	14	0	0	84
Bobby Joe Conrad, ChiC	6	6	30	84

LEADING INTERCEPTORS	NO	YDS	AVG	Long	TD
Dean Derby, Pit	7	127	18.1	24	0
Milt Davis, Bal	7	119	17.0	57t	1
Don Shinnick, Bal	7	70	10.0	23	0

LEADING PUNTER	NO	AVG	Long
Yale Lary, Det	45	47.1	67

LEADING PUNT RETURNER	NO	YDS	AVG	Long	TD
Johnny Morris, ChiB	14	171	12.2	78t	1

LEADING KICKOFF RETURNER	NO	YDS	AVG	Long	TD
Abe Woodson, SF	13	382	29.4	105t	1

SUPERLATIVES

Rushing Avg.	6.6	Johnny Olszewski, Was
Receiving Avg.	23.2	Max McGee, GB
Completion Pct.	58.6	Milt Plum, Cle
Touchdowns	14	Raymond Berry, Bal Jim Brown, Cle
Field Goals	20	Pat Summerall, NYG
Extra Points	50	Steve Myhra, Bal

LONGEST

Run	90t	Bobby Mitchell, Cle
Pass	88t	Ed Brown to Harlon Hill, ChiB
Interception	70t	Harland Svare, NYG
Punt	71	Tommy Davis, SF Rick Casares, ChiB
Punt Return	84t	Ken Hall, ChiC
Kickoff Return	105t	Abe Woodson, SF
Field Goal	50	Jim Martin, Det

1960 AMERICAN FOOTBALL LEAGUE

					SCORING		RUSHING				PASSING						
Team	W	L	T	PCT	OWN-OPP PTS-PTS	OWN-OPP PPG-PPG	OWN-OPP ATT-ATT	OWN-OPP YARD-YARD	OWN-OPP AVG-AVG	ON-OP TD-TD	OWN-OPP ATT-ATT	OWN-OPP COM-COM	OWN-OPP PCT-PCT	OWN-OPP YARD-YARD	OWN-OPP AVG-AVG	ON-OP TD-TD	ON-OP IN-IN
Eastern Division																	
Hou	10	4	0	.714	379-285	27.1-20.4	474-438	1565-1027	3.3-2.3	15-6	456-557	218-271	47.8-48.7	3371-3874	7.4-7.0	31-28	28-25
NYT	7	7	0	.500	382-399	27.3-28.5	485-449	1460-1378	3.0-3.1	14-20	474-450	238-216	49.8-48.0	3334-2919	7.0-6.5	32-27	28-24
Buf	5	8	1	.358	296-303	21.1-21.6	462-474	1211-1393	2.6-2.9	15-15	447-429	184-185	41.2-43.1	2689-2461	6.0-5.7	19-19	29-33
Bos	5	9	0	.357	286-349	20.4-24.9	401-477	1218-1513	3.0-3.2	11-21	475-429	223-210	46.9-49.0	2865-2958	6.0-6.9	25-19	23-25
Western Division																	
LAC	10	4	0	.714	373-336	26.6-24.0	437-414	1536-1750	3.5-4.2	24-24	441-467	229-227	51.9-48.6	3177-2851	7.2-6.1	21-21	29-28
DalT	8	6	0	.571	362-253	25.9-18.1	483-422	1814-980	3.8-2.3	24-14	435-503	209-261	48.0-51.2	2831-3002	6.5-6.0	16-19	19-32
Oak	6	8	0	.429	319-388	22.8-27.7	475-442	1785-1598	3.7-3.6	23-17	463-477	235-234	50.8-49.1	2923-3385	6.3-7.1	18-28	28-25
Den	4	9	1	.308	309-393	22.1-28.1	440-541	1195-2145	2.7-4.0	10-19	508-387	259-189	51.0-48.8	3247-2987	6.4-7.7	24-25	35-27
56 games					2706	48.3	3657	11784	3.2	136	3699	1795	48.5	24437	6.6	186	219

AFL Championship: Hou 24, LAC 16

LEADING RUSHERS	ATT	YARD	AVG	Long	TD
Abner Haynes, DalT	156	875	5.6	57	9
Paul Lowe, LAC	136	855	6.3	69	9
Billy Cannon, Hou	152	644	4.2	60	1
Dave Smith, Hou	154	643	4.2	65	5
Tony Teresa, Oak	139	608	4.4	83	6

LEADING PASSERS	ATT	COM	YARD	TD	IN
Jack Kemp, LAC	406	211	3018	20	25
Al Dorow, NYT	396	201	2748	26	26
Frank Tripucka, Den	478	248	3038	24	34
Butch Songin, Bos	392	187	2476	22	15
Cotton Davidson, DalT	379	179	2474	15	16

LEADING RECEIVERS	NO	YARD	AVG	Long	TD
Lionel Taylor, Den	92	1235	13.4	80	12
Bill Groman, Hou	72	1473	20.5	92	12
Don Maynard, NYT	72	1265	17.6	65	6
Art Powell, NYT	69	1167	16.9	76	14
Abner Haynes, DalT	55	576	10.5	34	3

LEADING SCORERS	TD	FG	PAT	PTS
Gene Mingo, Den	6	18	33	123
George Blanda, Hou	4	15	46	115
Jack Spikes, DalT	5	13	34	103
Bill Shockley, NYT	2	9	47	86
Ben Agajanian, LAC	0	13	46	85

LEADING INTERCEPTOR	NO	YDS	AVG	TD
Goose Gonsoulin, Den	11	98	8.9	0

LEADING PUNTER	NO	AVG	Long
Paul Maguire, LAC	43	40.5	61

LEADING PUNT RETURNER	NO	YDS	AVG	Long	TD
Abner Haynes, DalT	14	215	15.4	46	0

LEADING KICKOFF RETURNER	NO	YDS	AVG	Long	TD
Ken Hall, Hou	19	594	31.3	104	1

SUPERLATIVES

Rushing Avg.	6.3	Paul Lowe, LAC
Receiving Avg.	20.5	Bill Groman, Hou
Completion Pct.	54.0	Tom Flores, Oak
Touchdowns	14	Art Powell, NYT
Field Goals	18	Gene Mingo, Den

LONGEST

Run	87t	Jack Larscheid, Oak
Pass	92t	Jacky Lee to Bill Groman, Hou
Interception	80t	David Webster, DalT
Punt	72	Wayne Crow, Oak
Punt Return	76t	Gene Mingo, Den
Kickoff Return	104t	Ken Hall, Hou
Field Goal	53	George Blanda, Hou

1960 NATIONAL FOOTBALL LEAGUE

					SCORING		RUSHING				PASSING						
Team	W	L	T	PCT	OWN-OPP PTS-PTS	OWN-OPP PPG-PPG	OWN-OPP ATT-ATT	OWN-OPP YARD-YARD	OWN-OPP AVG-AVG	ON-OP TD-TD	OWN-OPP ATT-ATT	OWN-OPP COM-COM	OWN-OPP PCT-PCT	OWN-OPP YARD-YARD	OWN-OPP AVG-AVG	ON-OP TD-TD	ON-OP IN-IN
Eastern Conference																	
Phi	10	2	0	.833	321-246	26.8-20.5	351-449	1134-2200	3.2-4.9	9-14	331-283	177-139	53.5-49.1	2957-1984	8.9-7.0	29-14	20-30
Cle	8	3	1	.727	362-217	30.2-18.1	383-405	1930-1643	5.0-4.1	18-10	264-319	160-163	60.6-51.1	2343-2370	8.9-7.4	22-15	5-31
NYG	6	4	2	.600	271-261	22.6-21.8	406-396	1440-1267	3.5-3.2	10-8	322-297	156-142	48.4-47.8	2385-2010	7.4-6.8	20-19	23-22
StL	6	5	1	.545	288-230	24.0-19.2	484-344	2356-1212	4.9-3.5	13-8	285-300	126-156	44.2-52.0	1990-2147	7.0-7.2	20-20	25-21
Pit	5	6	1	.455	240-275	20.0-22.9	411-414	1623-1493	3.9-3.6	9-13	285-361	139-184	48.8-51.0	2511-3075	8.8-8.5	20-20	21-16
Was	1	9	2	.100	178-309	14.8-25.7	415-362	1313-1502	3.2-4.1	9-9	274-321	147-169	53.6-52.8	1816-2768	6.6-8.8	9-24	23-15
Western Conference																	
GB	8	4	0	.667	332-209	27.7-17.4	463-350	2150-1285	4.6-3.7	29-7	279-365	137-192	49.1-52.6	1993-2432	7.1-6.7	9-19	13-22
Det	7	5	0	.583	239-212	19.9-17.7	392-360	1714-1348	4.4-3.7	19-9	333-354	166-175	49.8-49.4	2022-2275	6.1-6.4	6-17	21-19
SF	7	5	0	.583	208-205	17.3-17.1	413-363	1681-1587	4.1-4.4	9-13	336-293	174-140	51.8-47.8	1866-2001	5.6-6.8	11-11	12-20
Bal	6	6	0	.500	288-234	24.0-19.5	345-379	1289-1591	3.7-4.2	10-17	392-298	196-144	50.0-48.3	3164-2068	8.1-6.9	26-8	24-30
ChiB	5	6	1	.455	194-299	16.2-24.9	373-403	1639-1679	4.4-4.2	11-17	324-291	146-146	45.1-50.2	2130-1808	6.6-6.2	13-14	32-10
LARm	4	7	1	.364	265-297	22.1-24.8	343-419	1449-1718	4.2-4.1	9-16	335-339	177-168	52.8-49.6	2188-2510	6.5-7.4	19-18	22-23
Dal	0	11	1	.000	177-369	14.8-30.8	312-447	1049-2242	3.4-5.0	6-20	354-293	163-146	46.0-49.8	2388-2305	6.7-7.9	17-22	33-15
78 games					3363	43.1	5091	20767	4.1	161	4114	2064	50.2	29753	7.2	221	274

NFL Championship: Phi 17, GB 13

LEADING RUSHERS	ATT	YARD	AVG	Long	TD
Jim Brown, Cle	215	1257	5.8	71t	9
Jim Taylor, GB	230	1101	4.8	32	11
John David Crow, StL	183	1071	5.9	57	6
Nick Pietrosante, Det	161	872	5.4	57	8
J.D. Smith, SF	174	780	4.5	41	5

LEADING PASSERS	ATT	COM	YARD	TD	IN
Milt Plum, Cle	250	151	2297	21	5
Norm Van Brocklin, Phi	284	153	2471	24	17
Johnny Unitas, Bal	378	190	3099	25	24
Bill Wade, LARm	182	106	1294	12	11
Bobby Layne, Pit	209	103	1814	13	17

LEADING RECEIVERS	NO	YARD	AVG	Long	TD
Raymond Berry, Bal	74	1298	17.5	70t	10
Sonny Randle, StL	62	893	14.4	57t	15
Red Phillips, LARm	52	883	17.0	61t	8
Jim Gibbons, Det	51	604	11.8	65t	2
Pete Retzlaff, Phi	46	826	18.0	57t	5

LEADING SCORERS	TD	FG	PAT	PTS
Paul Hornung, GB	15	15	41	176
Bobby Walston, Phi	4	14	39	103
Sonny Rnadle, StL	15	0	0	90
Sam Baker, Cle	0	12	44	80
Tommy McDonald, Phi	13	0	0	78
Lenny Moore, Bal	13	0	0	78
Tommy Davis, SF	0	19	21	78

LEADING INTERCEPTORS	NO	YDS	AVG	Long	TD
Dave Baker, SF	10	96	9.6	28	0
Jerry Norton, StL	10	96	9.6	26	0

LEADING PUNTER	NO	AVG	Long
Jerry Norton, StL	39	45.6	62

LEADING PUNT RETURNER	NO	YDS	AVG	Long	TD
Abe Woodson, SF	13	174	13.4	48	0

LEADING KICKOFF RETURNER	NO	YDS	AVG	Long	TD
Tom Moore, GB	12	397	33.1	84	0

SUPERLATIVES

Rushing Avg.	5.9	John David Crow, StL
Receiving Avg.	24.3	Buddy Dial, Pit
Completion Pct.	60.4	Milt Plum, Cle
Touchdowns	15	Paul Hornung, GB Sonny Randle, StL
Field Goals	19	Tommy Davis, SF

LONGEST

Run	87t	John Henry Johnson, Pit
Pass	91t	Bart Starr to Boyd Dowler, GB Ed Brown to Willard Dewveall, ChiB
Interception	92t	Bernie Parrish, Cle
Punt	75	Bob Greene, Pit
Punt Return	48	Abe Woodson, SF
Kickoff Return	97t	Lenny Lyles, Bal
Field Goal	52	Jim Martin, Det

1961 AMERICAN FOOTBALL LEAGUE

					SCORING		RUSHING				PASSING						
Team	W	L	T	PCT	OWN-OPP PTS-PTS	OWN-OPP PPG-PPG	OWN-OPP ATT-ATT	OWN-OPP YARD-YARD	OWN-OPP AVG-AVG	ON-OP TD-TD	OWN-OPP ATT-ATT	OWN-OPP COM-COM	OWN-OPP PCT-PCT	OWN-OPP YARD-YARD	OWN-OPP AVG-AVG	ON-OP TD-TD	ON-OP IN-IN
Eastern Division																	
Hou	10	3	1	.769	513-242	36.6-17.3	452-365	1896-1634	4.2-4.5	15-17	498-493	254-212	51.0-43.0	4568- 2750	9.2- 5.8	48-13	29-33
Bos	9	4	1	.692	413-313	29.5-22.4	389-350	1675-1041	4.3-3.0	15- 9	420-479	206-241	49.0-50.3	2795- 3490	6.7- 7.3	29-27	21-22
NYT	7	7	0	.500	301-390	21.5-27.9	426-414	1678-1880	3.9-4.5	17-20	460-462	204-211	44.3-45.7	2733- 3044	5.9- 6.6	20-26	32-25
Buf	6	8	0	.429	294-342	21.0-24.4	438-349	1606-1377	3.7-3.9	18- 9	439-430	194-206	44.2-47.3	2786- 3237	6.3- 7.5	15-28	25-29
Western Division																	
SD	12	2	0	.857	396-219	28.3-15.6	391-401	1466-1357	3.7-3.4	24- 7	423-485	190-234	44.9-46.2	3121- 2736	7.4- 5.6	17-16	25-49
DalT	6	8	0	.429	334-343	23.9-24.5	439-410	2183-1525	5.0-3.7	23-18	399-439	177-219	44.4-49.9	2815- 3077	7.1- 7.0	18-20	27-24
Den	3	11	0	.214	251-432	17.9-30.9	333-435	1091-1633	3.3-3.8	11-17	568-433	265-194	46.7-44.8	3004- 3060	5.3- 7.1	18-30	45-26
Oak	2	12	0	.143	237-458	16.9-32.7	350-494	1234-2382	3.5-4.8	10-36	423-409	209-192	49.4-46.9	2514- 2942	5.9- 7.2	17-22	28-24
56 games					2739	48.9	3218	12829	4.0	133	3630	1699	46.8	24336	6.7	182	232

AFL Championship: Hou 10, SD 3

LEADING RUSHERS	ATT	YARD	AVG	Long	TD
Billy Cannon, Hou	200	948	4.7	61	6
Bill Mathis, NYT	202	846	4.2	30	7
Abner Haynes, DalT	179	841	4.7	59	9
Paul Lowe, SD	175	767	4.4	87	9
Charlie Tolar, Hou	157	577	3.7	28	4

LEADING PASSERS	ATT	COM	YARD	TD	IN
George Blanda, Hou	362	187	3330	36	22
Tom Flores, Oak	366	190	2176	15	19
Jack Kemp, SD	364	165	2686	15	22
Al Dorow, NYT	438	197	2651	19	30
Babe Parilli, Bos	198	104	1314	13	9

LEADING RECEIVERS	NO	YDS	AVG	Long	TD
Lionel Taylor, Den	100	1176	11.8	52	4
Charley Hennigan, Hou	82	1746	21.3	80	12
Art Powell, NYT	71	881	12.4	48	5
Dave Kocourek, SD	55	1055	19.2	76	4
Chris Burford, DalT	51	850	16.7	54	5

LEADING SCORERS	TD	FG	PAT	PTS
Gino Cappelletti, Bos	8	17	48	147
George Blanda, Hou	0	16	64	112
Bill Groman, Hou	18	0	0	108
Bill Cannon, Hou	15	0	0	90
Abner Haynes, DalT	13	0	0	78

LEADING INTERCEPTOR	NO	YDS	AVG	Long	TD
Billy Atkins, Buf	10	158	15.8	29	0

LEADING PUNTER	NO	AVG	Long
Billy Atkins, Buf	85	44.5	70

LEADING PUNT RETURNER	NO	YDS	AVG	Long	TD
Dick Christy, NYT	18	383	21.3	70	2

LEADING KICKOFF RETURNER	NO	YDS	AVG	Long	TD
Dave Grayson, DalT	16	453	28.3	73	0

SUPERLATIVES

Rushing Avg.	8.6	Jack Spikes, DalT
Receiving Avg.	23.5	Bill Groman, Hou
Completion Pct.	52.5	Babe Parilli, Bos
Touchdowns	18	Bill Groman, Hou
Field Goals	17	Gino Cappelletti, Bos

LONGEST

Run	87t	Paul Lowe, SD
Pass	91t	Jack Kemp to Keith Lincoln, SD
Interception	99t	Dave Grayson, DalT
Punt	82	Paul Maguire, SD
Punt Return	70t	Dick Christy, NYT
Kickoff Return	93t	Fred Brown, Buf
Field Goal	55	George Blanda, Hou

1961 NATIONAL FOOTBALL LEAGUE

					SCORING		RUSHING				PASSING						
Team	W	L	T	PCT	OWN-OPP PTS-PTS	OWN-OPP PPG-PPG	OWN-OPP ATT-ATT	OWN-OPP YARD-YARD	OWN-OPP AVG-AVG	ON-OP TD-TD	OWN-OPP ATT-ATT	OWN-OPP COM-COM	OWN-OPP PCT-PCT	OWN-OPP YARD-YARD	OWN-OPP AVG-AVG	ON-OP TD-TD	ON-OP IN-IN
Eastern Conference																	
NYG	10	3	1	.769	368-220	26.3-15.7	464-419	1857-1761	4.0-4.2	13- 6	416-386	215-176	51.7-45.6	3035- 2600	7.3- 6.7	27-21	23-33
Phi	10	4	0	.714	361-297	25.8-21.2	373-474	1507-2007	4.0-4.2	10-12	429-383	241-224	56.2-58.5	3824- 3183	8.9- 8.3	34-23	26-17
Cle	8	5	1	.615	319-270	22.8-19.3	476-411	2163-1605	4.5-3.9	15-16	320-358	185-200	57.8-55.9	2538- 2831	7.9- 7.9	20-16	13-20
StL	7	7	0	.500	279-267	19.9-19.1	386-477	1405-1676	3.6-3.5	8- 9	351-389	168-187	47.9-48.1	2434- 2644	6.9- 6.8	21-18	23-24
Pit	6	8	0	.429	295-287	21.1-20.5	543-396	1761-1463	3.2-3.7	10-11	334-420	176-201	52.7-47.9	2622- 2780	7.9- 6.6	23-22	34-25
Dal	4	9	1	.308	236-380	16.9-27.1	416-454	1819-2161	4.4-4.8	6-20	422-326	215-168	50.9-51.5	2918- 2635	6.9- 8.1	23-21	27-25
Was	1	12	1	.077	174-392	12.4-28.0	361-412	1072-1550	3.0-3.8	9-10	420-409	189-238	45.0-58.2	2566- 3493	6.1- 8.5	12-37	28-26

Team	W	L	T	PCT	PTS-PTS	PPG-PPG	ATT-ATT	YARD-YARD	AVG-AVG	TD-TD	ATT-ATT	COM-COM	PCT-PCT	YARD-YARD	AVG-AVG	TD-TD	IN-IN
Western Conference																	
GB	11	3	0	.786	391-223	27.9-15.9	474-412	2350-1694	5.0-4.1	27-12	306-414	177-218	57.8-52.7	2502- 2630	8.2- 6.4	18-13	16-29
Det	8	5	1	.615	270-258	19.3-18.4	439-412	1868-1520	4.3-3.7	16-14	398-385	186-203	46.7-52.7	2830- 2744	7.1- 7.1	14-11	27-29
Bal	8	6	0	.571	302-307	21.6-21.9	456-418	2119-1869	4.6-4.5	17-17	438-351	232-161	53.0-45.9	3018- 2320	6.9- 6.6	17-18	29-16
ChiB	8	6	0	.571	326-302	23.3-21.6	436-401	1890-1652	4.3-4.1	16-10	349-398	186-209	53.3-52.5	3011- 3164	8.6- 7.9	26-27	24-24
SF	7	6	1	.538	346-272	24.7-19.4	448-419	2100-1701	4.7-4.1	27-13	346-380	187-196	54.0-51.6	3057- 2874	8.8- 7.8	15-18	19-19
LARm	4	10	0	.286	263-333	18.8-23.8	415-508	1958-2440	4.7-4.8	17-26	386-328	199-184	51.6-56.1	2709- 2642	7.0- 8.1	13-19	21-23
Min	3	11	0	.214	285-407	20.3-29.1	419-493	1897-2067	4.5-5.4	14-29	377-365	203-194	53.8-53.2	2527- 3051	6.7- 8.4	22-21	22-22
98 games					4215	43.0	6106	25766	4.2	205	5292	2759	52.1	39591	7.5	285	332

NFL Championship: GB 37, NYG 0

LEADING RUSHERS	ATT	YARD	AVG	Long	TD
Jim Brown, Cle	305	1408	4.6	38	8
Jim Taylor, GB	243	1307	5.4	53	15
Alex Webster, NYG	196	928	4.7	59	2
Nick Pietrosante, Det	201	841	4.2	42	5
J.D. Smith, SF	167	823	4.9	33	8

LEADING PASSERS	ATT	COM	YARD	TD	IN
Milt Plum, Cle	302	177	2416	18	10
Sonny Jurgensen, Phi	416	235	3723	32	24
Bart Starr, GB	295	172	2418	16	16
John Brodie, SF	283	155	2588	14	12
Bill Wade, ChiB	250	139	2258	22	13

LEADING RECEIVERS	NO	YARD	AVG	Long	TD
Red Phillips, LARm	78	1092	14.0	69t	5
Raymond Berry, Bal	75	873	11.6	44	0
Del Shofner, NYG	68	1125	16.5	46t	11
Tommy McDonald, Phi	64	1144	17.9	66	13
Mike Ditka, ChiB	56	1076	19.2	76t	12
Billy Howton, Dal	56	785	14.0	53	4

LEADING SCORER	TD	FG	PAT	PTS
Paul Hornung, GB	10	15	41	146
Bobby Watson, Phi	2	14	43	97
Steve Myhra, Bal	0	21	33	96
Lenny Moore, Bal	15	0	0	90
Pat Summerall, NYG	0	14	46	88

LEADING INTERCEPTOR	NO	YDS	AVG	Long	TD
Dick Lynch, NYG	9	60	6.7	36	0

LEADING PUNTER	NO	AVG	Long
Yale Lary, Det	52	48.4	71

LEADING PUNT RETURNER	NO	YDS	AVG	Long	TD
Willie Wood, GB	14	225	16.1	72t	2

LEADING KICKOFF RETURNER	NO	YDS	AVG	Long	TD
Dick Bass, LARm	23	698	30.3	64	0

SUPERLATIVES		
Rushing Avg.	7.0	Lenny Moore, Bal
Receiving Avg.	22.4	Frank Clarke, Dal
Completion Pct.	58.6	Milt Plum, Cle
Touchdowns	16	Jim Taylor, GB
Field Goals	21	Steve Myhra, Bal

LONGEST		
Run	73t	Dick Bass, LARm
Pass	98t	Bill Wade to John Farrington, ChiB
Interception	102t	Erich Barnes, NYG
Punt	78	Jerry Norton, StL
Punt Return	90t	Dick Bass, LARm
Kickoff Return	105t	Timmy Brown, Phi
		Jon Arnett, LARm
Field Goal	52	Steve Myhra, Bal
		John Aveni, Was

1962 AMERICAN FOOTBALL LEAGUE

					SCORING		RUSHING				PASSING						
Team	W	L	T	PCT	OWN-OPP PTS-PTS	OWN-OPP PPG-PPG	OWN-OPP ATT-ATT	OWN-OPP YARD-YARD	OWN-OPP AVG-AVG	ON-OP TD-TD	OWN-OPP ATT-ATT	OWN-OPP COM-COM	OWN-OPP PCT-PCT	OWN-OPP YARD-YARD	OWN-OPP AVG-AVG	ON-OP TD-TD	ON-OP IN-IN
Eastern Division																	
Hou	11	3	0	.786	387-270	27.6-19.3	457-362	1742-1569	3.8-4.3	15-10	475-486	227-213	47.8-43.8	3323- 2865	7.0- 5.9	32-18	48-35
Bos	9	4	1	.692	346-295	24.7-21.1	432-393	1970-1426	4.6-3.6	11-14	382-450	195-216	51.0-48.0	2930- 3435	7.7- 7.6	25-19	13-25
Buf	7	6	1	.538	309-272	22.1-19.4	501-373	2480-1687	5.0-4.5	20-10	351-440	150-215	42.7-48.9	2181- 2996	6.2- 6.8	15-24	26-36
NYT	5	9	0	.357	278-423	19.9-30.2	317-453	1213-2049	3.8-4.5	9-19	505-417	242-194	47.9-46.5	3161- 2929	6.3- 7.0	20-28	35-29
Western Division																	
DalT	11	3	0	.786	389-233	27.8-16.6	479-351	2407-1250	5.0-3.8	21-14	322-467	195-239	60.8-51.2	2824- 2953	8.8- 6.3	29-13	17-32
Den	7	7	0	.500	353-334	25.2-23.9	322-439	1298-1868	4.0-4.3	12-11	559-423	292-202	52.2-47.8	3739- 2894	6.7- 6.8	21-24	40-27
SD	4	10	0	.286	314-392	22.4-28.0	410-437	1647-1903	4.0-4.4	13-16	416-402	168-196	40.4-48.8	2686- 2926	6.5- 7.3	23-29	34-29
Oak	1	13	0	.071	213-370	15.2-26.4	367-477	1392-2397	3.8-5.0	14-21	446-371	175-169	39.2-45.6	2671- 2517	6.0- 6.8	11-21	29-29
56 games					2589	46.2	3285	14149	4.3	115	3456	1644	47.6	23515	6.8	176	242

AFL Championship: DalT 20, Hou 17 (OT)

LEADING RUSHERS	ATT	YARD	AVG	Long	TD
Cookie Gilchrist, Buf	214	1096	5.1	44	13
Abner Haynes, DalT	221	1049	4.7	71	13
Charley Tolar, Hou	244	1012	4.1	25	7
Clem Daniels, Oak	161	766	4.8	72	7
Curtis McClinton, DalT	111	604	5.4	69	2

LEADING PASSERS	ATT	COM	YARD	TD	IN
Len Dawson, DalT	310	189	2759	29	17
Babe Parilli, Bos	253	140	1988	18	8
Frank Tripucka, Den	440	240	2917	17	25
George Blanda, Hou	418	197	2810	27	42
Johnny Green, NYT	258	128	1741	10	18

LEADING RECEIVERS	NO	YARD	AVG	Long	TD
Lionel Taylor, Den	77	908	11.8	45	4
Art Powell, NYT	64	1130	17.7	80	8
Dick Christy, NYT	62	538	8.7	41	3
Bo Dickinson, Den	60	554	9.2	33	4
Don Maynard, NYT	56	1041	18.6	86	8

LEADING SCORERS	TD	FG	PAT	PTS
Gene Mingo, Den	4	27	32	137
Cookie Gilchrist, Buf	15	8	14	128
Gino Cappelletti, Bos	5	20	38	128
Abner Haynes, DalT	19	0	0	114
Tommy Brooker, DalT	3	12	33	87

LEADING INTERCEPTOR	NO	YDS	AVG	Long	TD
Lee Riley, NYT	11	122	11.1	30	0

LEADING PUNTER	NO	AVG	Long
Jim Fraser, Den	55	43.6	75

LEADING PUNT RETURNER	NO	YDS	AVG	Long	TD
Dick Christy, NYT	15	250	16.7	73	2

LEADING KICKOFF RETURNER	NO	YDS	AVG	Long	TD
Bobby Jancik, Hou	24	726	30.3	61	0

SUPERLATIVES		
Rushing Avg.	5.8	Larry Garron, Bos
Receiving Avg.	21.7	Jim Colclough, Bos
Completion Pct.	60.9	Len Dawson, DalT
Touchdowns	19	Abner Haynes, DalT
Field Goals	27	Gene Mingo, Den

LONGEST		
Run	86t	Keith Lincoln, SD
Pass	98t	Jacky Lee to Willard Dewveall, Hou
Interception	91t	Fred Williamson, Oak
Punt	75	Jim Fraser, Den
Punt Return	73t	Dick Christy, NYT
Kickoff Return	103t	Keith Lincoln, SD
Field Goal	54	George Blanda, Hou

1962 NATIONAL FOOTBALL LEAGUE

					SCORING		RUSHING				PASSING						
Team	W	L	T	PCT	OWN-OPP PTS-PTS	OWN-OPP PPG-PPG	OWN-OPP ATT-ATT	OWN-OPP YARD-YARD	OWN-OPP AVG-AVG	ON-OP TD-TD	OWN-OPP ATT-ATT	OWN-OPP COM-COM	OWN-OPP PCT-PCT	OWN-OPP YARD-YARD	OWN-OPP AVG-AVG	ON-OP TD-TD	ON-OP IN-IN
Eastern Conference																	
NYG	12	2	0	.857	398-283	28.4-20.2	430-413	1698-1677	3.9-4.1	11-13	411-450	215-223	52.3-49.6	3446- 3238	8.4- 7.2	35-21	22-26
Pit	9	5	0	.643	312-363	22.3-25.9	572-383	2333-1419	4.1-3.9	17-13	319-438	160-223	50.2-50.9	2419- 3490	7.6- 8.0	14-34	23-28
Cle	7	6	1	.538	291-257	20.8-18.4	414-466	1772-1940	4.3-4.2	18-17	370-341	200-189	54.1-55.4	2747- 2277	7.4- 6.7	17-15	16-24

Was	5	7	2	.417	305-376	21.8-26.9	371-411	1088-1636	2.9-4.0	10-12	428-412	223-247	52.1-60.0	3532- 3860	8.3- 9.4	27-35	27-28
Dal	5	8	1	.385	398-402	28.4-28.7	434-387	2040-1510	4.7-3.9	16-17	380-437	200-233	52.6-53.3	3115- 3904	8.2- 8.9	31-33	17-20
StL	4	9	1	.308	287-361	20.5-25.8	416-452	1698-1724	4.1-3.8	20-18	434-377	220-196	50.7-52.0	3388- 3302	7.8- 8.8	18-21	30-16
Phi	3	10	1	.231	282-356	20.1-25.4	324-576	1155-2126	3.6-4.0	13-23	428-363	228-198	53.3-54.5	3632- 3023	8.5- 8.3	23-16	31-26
Western Conference																	
GB	13	1	0	.929	415-148	29.6-10.8	518-404	2460-1531	4.7-3.8	36- 4	311-355	187-187	60.1-52.7	2621- 2084	8.4- 5.9	14-10	13-31
Det	11	3	0	.786	315-177	22.5-12.6	489-353	1922-1231	3.9-3.5	14- 6	379-367	211-187	55.7-51.0	2827- 2441	7.5- 6.7	19-11	24-24
ChiB	9	5	0	.643	321-287	22.9-20.5	386-438	1489-2073	3.9-4.7	17-17	430-363	229-170	53.3-46.8	3286- 2460	7.6- 6.8	20-14	28-23
Bal	7	7	0	.500	293-288	20.9-20.6	448-423	1601-1504	3.6-3.6	9-17	423-381	237-206	56.0-54.1	3330- 2975	7.9- 7.8	27-19	25-23
SF	6	8	0	.429	282-331	20.1-23.6	460-464	1873-2241	4.1-4.8	15-22	323-296	182-164	57.3-55.4	2491- 2494	7.7- 8.4	19-17	19-12
Min	2	11	1	.154	254-410	18.1-29.3	426-463	1864-1978	4.4-4.3	7-20	348-397	170-214	48.9-53.9	2699- 3365	7.8- 8.5	22-29	31-25
LARm	1	12	1	.077	220-334	15.7-23.9	376-501	1689-2092	4.5-4.2	10-14	372-379	189-217	50.8-57.3	2524- 3144	6.8- 8.3	14-25	19-19
98 games					4373	44.6	6064	24682	4.1	213	5356	2851	53.2	42057	7.9	300	325

NFL Championship: GB 16, NYG 7

LEADING RUSHERS	ATT	YARD	AVG	Long	TD
Jim Taylor, GB	272	1474	5.4	51	19
John Henry Johnson, Pit	251	1141	4.5	40	7
Dick Bass, LARm	196	1033	5.3	57	6
Jim Brown, Cle	230	996	4.3	31	13
Don Perkins, Dal	222	945	4.3	35	7

LEADING PASSERS	ATT	COM	YARD	TD	IN
Bart Starr, GB	285	178	2438	12	9
Y.A. Tittle, NYG	375	200	3224	33	20
Eddie LeBaron, Dal	166	95	1436	16	9
Frank Ryan, Cle	194	112	1541	10	7
Sonny Jurgensen, Phi	366	196	3261	22	26

LEADING RECEIVERS	NO	YARD	AVG	Long	TD
Bobby Mitchell, Was	72	1384	19.2	81t	11
Sonny Randle, StL	63	1158	18.4	86t	7
Bobby Joe Conrad, StL	62	954	15.4	72t	4
Red Phillips, LARm	60	875	14.6	65t	5
Tommy McDonald, Phi	58	1146	19.8	60t	10
Mike Ditka, ChiB	58	904	15.6	69t	5
Johnny Morris, ChiB	58	889	15.3	73t	5

LEADING SCORERS	TD	FG	PAT	PTS
Jim Taylor, GB	19	0	0	114
Lou Michaels, Pit	0	26	32	110
Jim Brown, Cle	18	0	0	108
Don Chandler, NYG	0	19	47	104
John David Crow, StL	17	0	0	102

LEADING INTERCEPTOR	NO	YDS	AVG	Long	TD
Willie Wood, GB	9	132	14.7	37	0

LEADING PUNTER	NO	AVG	Long
Tommy Davis, SF	48	45.6	82

LEADING PUNT RETURNER	NO	YDS	AVG	Long	TD
Pat Studstill, Det	29	457	15.8	44	0

LEADING KICKOFF RETURNER	NO	YDS	AVG	Long	TD
Abe Woodson, SF	37	1157	31.3	79	0

SUPERLATIVES

Rushing Avg.	5.6	Amos Marsh, Dal
Receiving Avg.	22.2	Frank Clarke, Dal
Completion Pct.	62.5	Bart Starr, GB
Touchdowns	19	Tim Taylor, GB
Field Goals	26	Lou Michaels, Pit

LONGEST

Run	77t	Willie Galimore, ChiB
Pass	89t	Fran Tarkenton to Charley Ferguson, Min
Interception	101t	Richie Petitbon, ChiB
Punt	82	Tommy Davis, SF
Punt Return	85t	Abe Woodson, SF
Kickoff Return	103t	Herb Adderley, GB
Field Goal	53	Sam Baker, Dal

1963 AMERICAN FOOTBALL LEAGUE

					SCORING		RUSHING				PASSING						
Team	W	L	T	PCT	OWN-OPP PTS-PTS	OWN-OPP PPG-PPG	OWN-OPP ATT-ATT	OWN - OPP YARD-YARD	OWN-OPP AVG-AVG	ON-OP TD-TD	OWN-OPP ATT-ATT	OWN-OPP COM-COM	OWN-OPP PCT-PCT	OWN - OPP YARD - YARD	OWN-OPP AVG-AVG	ON-OP TD-TD	ON-OP IN-IN
Eastern Division																	
Bos	7	6	1	.538	317-257	22.6-18.4	437-310	1618-1108	3.7-3.5	17-	410-477	184-230	44.9-48.2	2547- 2607	6.2- 5.5	17-21	29-29
Buf	7	6	1	.538	304-291	21.7-20.8	455-303	1838-1217	4.0-4.0	21-	457-472	227-218	49.7-46.1	3057- 2831	6.7- 6.0	16-24	24-22
Hou	6	8	0	.429	302-372	21.6-26.6	341-446	1209-1981	3.5-4.4	11-	501-424	261-190	52.0-44.8	3210- 2600	6.4- 6.1	26-24	33-36
NYJ	5	8	1	.385	249-399	17.8-28.5	306-460	969-2129	3.2-4.6	8-	480-417	209-223	43.5-53.4	2530- 3037	5.3- 7.3	21-25	29-21
Western Division																	
SD	11	3	0	.786	399-256	28.5-18.3	395-379	2201-1443	5.8-3.8	20-	357-472	202-232	56.6-49.1	2950- 2521	8.3- 5.3	28-17	24-29
Oak	10	4	0	.714	363-288	25.9-20.6	359-371	1595-1466	4.4-3.9	11-	442-440	191-208	43.2-47.2	2926- 2571	6.6- 5.8	31-23	24-35
KC	5	7	2	.417	347-263	24.8-18.8	400-387	1697-1558	4.2-4.0	12-	439-429	231-218	52.6-50.8	2651- 2629	6.0- 6.1	30-18	22-26
Den	2	11	1	.154	301-473	21.5-33.8	384-403	1508-1710	3.9-4.2	10-	453-408	217-204	47.9-50.0	2487- 3366	5.5- 8.3	23-40	28-16
56 games					2582	46.1	3077	12635	4.1	110	3539	1722	48.7	22358	6.3	192	213

Eastern Division Playoff: Bos 26, Buf 8
AFL Championship: SD 51, Bos 10

LEADING RUSHERS	ATT	YARD	AVG	Long	TD
Clem Daniels, Oak	215	1099	5.1	74	3
Paul Lowe, SD	177	1010	5.7	66	8
Cookie Gilchrist, Buf	232	979	4.2	32	12
Keith Lincoln, SD	128	826	6.5	76	5
Larry Garron, Bos	179	750	4.2	47	2

LEADING PASSERS	ATT	COM	YARD	TD	IN
Tobin Rote, SD	286	170	2510	20	17
Tom Flores, Oak	247	113	2101	20	13
Jack Kemp, Buf	384	194	2914	13	20
Len Dawson, KC	352	190	2389	26	19
George Blanda, Hou	423	224	3003	24	25

LEADING RECEIVERS	NO	YARD	AVG	Long	TD
Lionel Taylor, Den	78	1101	14.1	72	10
Art Powell, Oak	73	1304	17.8	85	16
Bake Turner, NYJ	71	1007	14.2	53	6
Bill Miller, Buf	69	860	12.5	36	3
Chris Burford, KC	68	824	12.1	69	9

LEADING SCORERS	TD	FG	PAT	PTS
Gino Cappelletti, Bos	2	22	35	113
George Blair, SD	0	17	44	95
Art Powell, Oak	16	0	0	96
Cookie Gilchrist, Buf	14	0	0	84
Gene Mingo, Den	0	16	35	83

LEADING INTERCEPTOR	NO	YDS	AVG	Long	TD
Fred Glick, Hou	12	180	15.0	45	1

LEADING PUNTER	NO	AVG	Long
Jim Fraser, Den	81	44.4	66

LEADING PUNT RETURNER	NO	YDS	AVG	Long	TD
Hoot Gibson, Oak	26	307	11.8	85	2

LEADING KICKOFF RETURNER	NO	YDS	AVG	Long	TD
Bobby Jancik, Hou	45	1317	29.3	53	0

SUPERLATIVES

Rushing Avg.	6.4	Keith Lincoln, SD
Receiving Avg.	22.8	Clem Daniels, Oak
Completion Pct.	59.4	Tobin Rote, SD
Touchdowns	16	Art Powell, Oak
Field Goals	22	Gino Cappelletti, Bos

LONGEST

Run	76	Keith Lincoln, SD
Pass	93t	Tom Flores to Dobie Craig, Oak
Interception	98t	Bob Suci, Bos
Punt	72	Jerrel Wilson, KC
Punt Return	93t	Bill Baird, NYJ
Kickoff Return	99t	Dave Grayson, KC
Field Goal	52	Gene Mingo, Den

1963 NATIONAL FOOTBALL LEAGUE

					SCORING		RUSHING				PASSING						
Team	W	L	T	PCT	OWN-OPP PTS-PTS	OWN-OPP PPG-PPG	OWN-OPP ATT-ATT	OWN-OPP YARD-YARD	OWN-OPP AVG-AVG	ON-OP TD-TD	OWN-OPP ATT-ATT	OWN-OPP COM-COM	OWN-OPP PCT-PCT	OWN-OPP YARD-YARD	OWN-OPP AVG-AVG	ON-OP TD-TD	ON-OP IN-IN
Eastern Conference																	
NYG	11	3	0	.786	448-280	32.0-20.0	453-411	1777-1669	3.9-4.1	12-14	426-368	243-176	57.0-47.8	3558- 2588	8.4- 7.0	39-22	21-34
Cle	10	4	0	.714	343-262	24.5-18.7	460-423	2639-1651	5.7-3.9	15-10	322-408	164-208	50.9-51.0	2449- 2718	7.5- 6.7	27-16	20-22
StL	9	5	0	.643	341-283	24.4-20.2	423-461	1839-1802	4.3-3.9	10-19	438-370	228-180	52.1-48.6	3403- 2519	7.8- 6.8	30-13	21-18
Pit	7	4	3	.636	321-295	22.9-21.1	578-419	2136-1728	3.7-4.1	14-14	368-384	170-191	46.2-49.7	3028- 3400	8.2- 8.9	21-21	20-25
Dal	4	10	0	.286	305-378	21.8-27.0	420-455	1795-2094	4.3-4.6	18-12	375-378	200-202	53.3-50.1	2799- 3392	7.5- 8.4	20-31	21-26
Was	3	11	0	.214	279-398	19.9-28.4	344-469	1289-1863	3.7-4.0	15-12	430-417	204-230	47.4-55.2	3525- 3484	8.2- 8.4	17-33	34-21
Phi	2	10	2	.167	242-381	17.3-27.2	376-466	1438-1985	3.8-4.1	8-17	380-375	193-211	50.8-56.3	3666- 3106	7.0- 8.3	22-28	31-15
Western Conference																	
ChiB	11	1	2	.917	301-144	21.5-10.3	487-412	1679-1442	3.4-3.5	15- 7	404-353	221-164	54.7-46.5	2670- 2045	6.6- 5.8	18-10	14-36
GB	11	2	1	.846	369-206	26.4-14.7	504-428	2248-1586	4.5-3.7	22-11	345-378	179-180	51.9-47.6	2711- 2340	7.9- 6.2	22- 9	21-22
Bal	8	6	0	.571	316-285	22.6-20.4	396-434	1642-1794	4.1-4.1	11-16	433-348	248-181	57.3-52.0	3605- 2589	8.3- 7.4	20-19	12-15
Det	5	8	1	.385	326-265	23.3-18.9	415-405	1601-1564	3.9-3.9	11-12	406-378	202-183	49.8-48.4	2997- 2597	7.4- 6.9	26-17	26-24
Min	5	8	1	.385	309-390	22.1-27.9	445-410	1842-1733	4.1-4.2	17-12	355-404	197-233	55.5-57.7	2687- 3362	7.6- 8.3	16-31	17-11
LARm	5	9	0	.357	210-350	15.0-25.0	405-431	1393-1785	3.5-4.1	14-14	384-379	186-208	48.4-54.9	2558- 3025	6.7- 8.0	11-25	22-19
SF	2	12	0	.143	198-391	14.1-27.9	406-488	1454-2076	3.6-4.3	8-20	349-450	156-244	44.7-54.2	2090- 3581	6.0- 8.0	13-27	22-14
98 games					4308	44.0	6112	24772	4.1	190	5415	2791	51.5	41746	7.7	302	302

NFL Championship: ChiB 14, NYG 10

LEADING RUSHERS	ATT	YARD	AVG	Long	TD
Jim Brown, Cle	291	1863	6.4	80t	12
Jim Taylor, GB	248	1018	4.1	40t	9
Timmy Brown, Phi	192	841	4.4	34	6
John Henry Johnson, Pit	186	773	4.2	48	4
Tommy Mason, Min	166	763	4.6	70t	7

LEADING PASSERS	ATT	COM	YARD	TD	IN
Y.A. Tittle, NYG	367	221	3145	36	14
Johnny Unitas, Bal	410	237	3481	20	12
Earl Morrall, Det	328	174	2621	24	14
Frank Ryan, Cle	256	135	2026	25	13
Charley Johnson, StL	423	222	3280	28	21

LEADING RECEIVERS	NO	YARD	AVG	Long	TD
Bobby Joe Conrad, StL	73	967	13.2	48	10
Bobby Mitchell, Was	69	1436	20.8	99t	7
Terry Barr, Det	66	1086	16.5	75t	13
Del Shofner, NYG	64	1181	18.5	70t	9
Buddy Dial, Pit	60	1295	21.6	83t	9

LEADING SCORERS	TD	FG	PAT	PTS
Don Chandler, NYG	0	18	52	106
Jim Martin, Bal	0	24	32	104
Lou Michaels, Pit	0	21	32	95
Jerry Kramer, GB	0	16	43	91
Jim Brown, Cle	15	0	0	90

LEADING INTERCEPTORS	NO	YDS	AVG	Long	TD
Dick Lynch, NYG	9	251	27.9	82t	3
Roosevelt Taylor, ChiB	9	172	19.1	46	1

LEADING PUNTER	NO	AVG	Long
Yale Lary, Det	35	48.9	73

LEADING PUNT RETURNER	NO	YDS	AVG	Long	TD
Dick James, Was	16	214	13.4	39	0

LEADING KICKOFF RETURNER	NO	YDS	AVG	Long	TD
Abe Woodson, SF	29	935	32.2	103t	3

SUPERLATIVES

Rushing Avg.	6.4	Jim Brown, Cle
Receiving Avg.	21.6	Buddy Dial, Pit
Completion Pct.	60.2	Y.A. Tittle, NYG
Touchdowns	15	Jim Brown, Cle
Field Goals	24	Jim Martin, Bal

LONGEST

Run	80t	Jim Brown, Cle
Pass	99t	George Izo to Bobby Mitchell, Was
Interception	87t	Leroy Caffey, Phi
Punt	73	Yale Lary, Det
		Gary Collins, Cle
Punt Return	90t	Tommy Watkins, Det
Kickoff Return	103t	Abe Woodson, SF
Field Goal	53	Don Chandler, NYG
		Sam Baker, Dal

1964 AMERICAN FOOTBALL LEAGUE

					SCORING		RUSHING				PASSING						
Team	W	L	T	PCT	OWN-OPP PTS-PTS	OWN-OPP PPG-PPG	OWN-OPP ATT-ATT	OWN-OPP YARD-YARD	OWN-OPP AVG-AVG	ON-OP TD-TD	OWN-OPP ATT-ATT	OWN-OPP COM-COM	OWN-OPP PCT-PCT	OWN-OPP YARD-YARD	OWN-OPP AVG-AVG	ON-OP TD-TD	ON-OP IN-IN
Eastern Division																	
Buf	12	2	0	.857	400-242	28.6-17.3	492-300	2040- 913	4.1-3.0	25- 4	397-517	174-241	43.8-46.6	3422- 3361	8.6- 6.5	19-24	34-28
Bos	10	3	1	.769	365-297	26.1-21.2	381-356	1361-1143	3.6-3.2	9-10	476-530	229-261	48.1-49.2	3467- 3645	7.3- 6.9	31-23	27-31
NYJ	5	8	1	.385	278-315	19.9-22.5	384-410	1457-1675	3.8-4.1	11-14	451-473	201-228	44.6-48.2	2694- 3472	6.0- 7.3	19-22	33-34
Hou	4	10	0	.286	310-355	22.1-25.4	327-438	1347-1961	4.1-4.5	14-18	592-433	299-229	50.5-52.9	3734- 3469	6.3- 8.0	19-24	29-30
Western Division																	
SD	8	5	1	.615	341-300	24.4-21.4	392-399	1522-1522	3.9-3.8	14-10	445-484	224-240	50.3-49.6	3363- 2926	7.6- 6.0	28-22	30-30
KC	7	7	0	.500	366-306	26.1-21.9	415-390	1825-1315	4.4-3.4	14- 9	412-440	228-218	55.3-49.5	3321- 2910	8.1- 6.6	32-25	21-28
Oak	5	7	2	.417	303-350	21.6-25.0	331-396	1480-1750	4.5-4.4	9-20	521-433	253-206	48.6-47.6	3886- 3292	7.5- 7.6	28-21	33-26
Den	2	11	1	.154	240-438	17.1-31.3	391-424	1311-2064	3.4-4.9	10-21	456-440	230-215	50.4-48.9	2541- 3353	5.6- 7.6	14-29	32-32
56 games					2603	46.5	3113	12343	4.0	106	3750	1838	49.0	26428	7.0	190	239

AFL Championship: Buf 20, SD 7

LEADING RUSHERS	ATT	YARD	AVG	Long	TD
Cookie Gilchrist, Buf	230	981	4.3	67	6
Matt Snell, NYJ	215	948	4.4	42	5
Clem Daniels, Oak	173	824	4.8	42	2
Sid Blanks, Hou	145	756	5.2	91	6
Abner Haynes, KC	139	697	5.0	80	4

LEADING PASSERS	ATT	COM	YARD	TD	IN
Len Dawson, KC	354	199	2879	30	18
Babe Parilli, Bos	473	228	3465	31	27
George Blanda, Hou	505	262	3287	17	27
John Hadl, SD	274	147	2157	18	15
Cotton Davidson, Oak	320	155	2497	21	19

LEADING RECEIVERS	NO	YARD	AVG	Long	TD
Charley Hennigan, Hou	101	1546	15.3	53	8
Art Powell, Oak	76	1361	17.9	77	11
Lionel Taylor, Den	76	873	11.5	57	7
Frank Jackson, KC	62	943	15.2	72	9
Lance Alworth, SD	61	1235	20.2	82	13

LEADING SCORERS	TD	FG	PAT	PTS
Gino Cappelletti, Bos	7	25	37#	155
Pete Gogolak, Buf	0	19	45	102
Lance Alworth, SD	15	0	0	90
Mike Mercer, Oak	0	15	34	79
George Blanda, Hou	0	13	37	76

#includes one two-point conversion

LEADING INTERCEPTOR	NO	YDS	AVG	Long	TD
Dainard Paulson, NYJ	12	157	13.1	42	1

LEADING PUNTER	NO	AVG	Long
Jim Fraser, Den	73	44.2	67

LEADING PUNT RETURNER	NO	YDS	AVG	Long	TD
Bobby Jancik, Hou	12	220	18.3	82	1

LEADING KICKOFF RETURNER	NO	YDS	AVG	Long	TD
Bo Roberson, Oak	36	975	27.1	59	0

SUPERLATIVES

Rushing Avg.	5.5	Mack Lee Hill, KC
Receiving Avg.	27.1	Elbert Dubenion, Buf
Completion Pct.	56.2	Len Dawson, KC
Touchdowns	15	Lance Alworth, SD
Field Goals	25	Gino Cappelletti, Bos

LONGEST

Run	91t	Sid Blanks, Hou
Pass	94t	Jack Kemp to Glenn Bass, Buf
Interception	98t	Pete Jaquess, Hou
Punt	79	Jim Norton, Hou
Punt Return	82t	Bobby Jancik, Hou
Kickoff Return	93t	Ode Burrell, Hou
Field Goal	51	Gino Cappelletti, Bos
		Gene Mingo, Den

1964 NATIONAL FOOTBALL LEAGUE

					SCORING		RUSHING				PASSING						
Team	W	L	T	PCT	OWN-OPP PTS-PTS	OWN-OPP PPG-PPG	OWN-OPP ATT-ATT	OWN-OPP YARD-YARD	OWN-OPP AVG-AVG	ON-OP TD-TD	OWN-OPP ATT-ATT	OWN-OPP COM-COM	OWN-OPP PCT-PCT	OWN-OPP YARD-YARD	OWN-OPP AVG-AVG	ON-OP TD-TD	ON-OP IN-IN
Eastern Conference																	
Cle	10	3	1	.769	415-293	29.6-20.9	435-465	2163-2012	5.0-4.3	14-18	344-401	181-230	52.6-57.4	2542- 2932	7.4- 7.3	28-18	19-19
StL	9	3	2	.750	357-331	25.5-23.6	456-414	1770-1800	3.9-4.0	12-13	422-389	223-193	52.8-49.6	3045- 2848	7.2- 7.3	21-21	24-25
Phi	6	8	0	.429	312-313	22.3-22.4	430-445	1922-1746	4.5-3.9	16-15	397-406	199-202	50.1-49.8	2746- 2950	6.9- 7.3	19-18	18-17
Was	6	8	0	.429	307-305	21.9-21.8	366-440	1237-1813	3.4-4.1	11-20	415-406	214-193	51.6-47.5	3071- 2600	7.4- 6.4	25-16	16-34
Dal	5	8	1	.385	250-289	17.9-20.6	421-439	1691-1504	4.0-3.4	15- 6	404-377	192-172	47.5-45.6	2516- 2571	6.2- 6.8	10-22	24-18
Pit	5	9	0	.357	253-315	18.1-22.5	516-454	2102-1994	4.1-4.4	14-15	323-378	141-185	43.7-48.9	2308- 2582	7.2- 6.8	14-16	24-12
NYG	2	10	2	.167	241-399	17.2-28.5	435-468	1404-1919	3.2-4.1	12-15	431-361	217-188	50.3-52.1	2848- 2799	6.6- 7.8	16-28	26-15
Western Conference																	
Bal	12	2	0	.857	428-225	30.6-16.1	456-422	2007-1798	4.4-4.3	29-13	345-385	176-217	51.0-56.4	3045- 2621	8.8- 6.8	22-14	9-23
GB	8	5	1	.615	342-260	24.4-18.6	495-417	2276-1532	4.6-3.7	23-15	321-318	186-173	57.9-54.4	2474- 1980	7.7- 6.2	16-11	6-16
Min	8	5	1	.615	355-339	25.4-24.2	519-389	2183-1616	4.2-4.2	14-10	326-375	179-182	54.9-48.5	2614- 2993	8.0- 8.0	23-23	26-19
Det	7	5	2	.583	280-289	20.0-20.6	412-429	1414-1638	3.4-3.8	7-10	385-406	206-226	53.4-55.7	2890- 2906	7.5- 7.2	23-14	21-22
LARm	5	7	2	.417	283-245	20.2-17.5	400-419	1629-1501	4.1-3.6	11-14	368-435	173-213	47.0-49.0	2769- 3094	7.5- 7.1	18-27	20-17
ChiB	5	9	0	.357	260-379	18.6-27.1	356-436	1166-1863	3.3-4.3	5-19	494-366	282-188	57.1-51.4	3056- 2897	6.2- 7.9	25-27	21-10
SF	4	10	0	.286	236-330	16.9-23.6	383-443	1332-1560	3.5-3.5	11-11	461-434	225-232	48.8-53.5	2990- 3141	6.5- 7.2	18-23	22-15
98 games					4319	44.1	6080	24296	4.0	194	5436	2794	51.4	38914	7.2	278	276

NFL Championship: Cle 27, Bal 0

LEADING RUSHERS	ATT	YARD	AVG	Long	TD
Jim Brown, Cle	280	1446	5.2	71	7
Jim Taylor, GB	235	1169	5.0	84t	12
John Henry Johnson, Pit	235	1048	4.5	45t	7
Bill Brown, Min	226	866	3.8	48	7
Don Perkins, Dal	174	768	4.4	59	6

LEADING PASSERS	ATT	COM	YARD	TD	IN
Bart Starr, GB	272	163	2144	15	4
Fran Tarkenton, Min	306	171	2506	22	11
Sonny Jurgensen, Was	385	207	2934	24	13
Johnny Unitas, Bal	305	158	2824	19	6
Milt Plum, Det	287	154	2241	18	15

LEADING RECEIVERS	NO	YARD	AVG	Long	TD
Johnny Morris, ChiB	93	1200	12.9	63t	10
Mike Ditka, ChiB	75	897	12.0	34	5
Frank Clarke, Dal	65	973	15.0	49	5
Bobby Joe Conrad, StL	61	780	12.8	53	6
Bobby Mitchell, Was	60	904	15.1	60	10

LEADING SCORER	TD	FG	PAT	PTS
Lenny Moore, Bal	20	0	0	120
Lou Groza, Cle	0	22	49	115
Jim Bakken, StL	0	25	40	115
Paul Hornung, GB	5	12	41	107
Fred Cox, Min	0	21	40	103

LEADING INTERCEPTOR	NO	YDS	AVG	Long	TD
Paul Krause, Was	12	140	11.7	35t	1

LEADING PUNTER	NO	AVG	Long
Bobby Walden, Min	72	46.4	73

LEADING PUNT RETURNER	NO	YDS	AVG	Long	TD
Tommy Watkins, Det	16	238	14.9	68t	2

LEADING KICKOFF RETURNER	NO	YDS	AVG	Long	TD
Clarence Childs, NYG	34	987	29.0	100t	1

SUPERLATIVES

Rushing Avg.	5.2	Jim Brown, Cle
Receiving Avg.	19.9	Gary Ballman, Phi
Completion Pct.	61.9	Rudy Bukich, ChiB
Touchdowns	20	Lenny Moore, Bal
Field Goals	25	Jim Bakken, StL

LONGEST

Run	84t	Jim Taylor, GB
Pass	95t	Bill Munson to Bucky Pope, LARm
Interception	97t	Bobby Smith, LARm
Punt	75	Billy Lothridge, Dal
Punt Return	90	Brady Keys, Pit
Kickoff Return	100t	Clarence Childs, NYG
Field Goal	53	Tommy Davis, SF

1965 AMERICAN FOOTBALL LEAGUE

					SCORING		RUSHING				PASSING						
Team	W	L	T	PCT	OWN-OPP PTS-PTS	OWN-OPP PPG-PPG	OWN-OPP ATT-ATT	OWN-OPP YARD-YARD	OWN-OPP AVG-AVG	ON-OP TD-TD	OWN-OPP ATT-ATT	OWN-OPP COM-COM	OWN-OPP PCT-PCT	OWN-OPP YARD-YARD	OWN-OPP AVG-AVG	ON-OP TD-TD	ON-OP IN-IN
Eastern Division																	
Buf	10	3	1	.769	313-226	22.4-16.1	392-360	1288-1114	3.3-3.1	16- 5	461-502	208-227	45.1-45.2	2744- 3416	6.0- 6.8	13-19	24-32
NYJ	5	8	1	.385	285-303	20.4-21.6	367-432	1476-1551	4.0-3.6	11-10	459-472	209-220	45.5-46.6	2751- 2900	6.0- 6.1	21-22	22-26
Bos	4	8	2	.333	244-302	17.4-21.6	373-425	1117-1531	3.0-3.6	8-10	473-431	193-206	40.8-47.8	2854- 2891	6.0- 6.7	19-17	29-21
Hou	4	10	0	.286	298-429	21.3-30.6	324-508	1175-2683	3.6-5.3	10-17	550-416	224-177	40.7-42.5	3070- 2643	5.6- 6.4	25-27	35-27
Western Division																	
SD	9	2	3	.818	340-227	24.3-16.2	486-306	1998-1094	4.1-3.6	13- 7	401-474	203-206	50.6-43.5	3379- 2480	8.4- 5.2	23-17	26-28
Oak	8	5	1	.615	298-239	21.3-17.1	390-407	1538-1487	3.9-3.7	8-10	431-466	195-199	45.2-42.7	2713- 2947	6.3- 6.3	22-20	17-24
KC	7	5	2	.583	322-285	23.0-20.4	418-381	1752-1376	4.2-3.6	15-12	395-451	199-216	50.4-47.9	2894- 2711	7.3- 6.0	22-18	20-20
Den	4	10	0	.286	303-392	21.6-28.0	453-384	1829-1337	4.0-3.5	14-24	482-440	222-202	46.1-45.9	2848- 3265	5.9- 7.4	18-23	30-25
56 games					2403	42.9	3203	12173	3.8	95	3652	1653	45.3	23253	6.4	163	203

AFL Championship: Buf 23, SD 0

LEADING RUSHERS	ATT	YARD	AVG	Long	TD
Paul Lowe, SD	222	1121	5.0	59	7
Cookie Gilchrist, Den	252	954	3.8	44	6
Clem Daniels, Oak	219	884	4.0	57	5
Matt Snell, NYJ	169	763	4.5	44	4
Curtis McClinton, KC	175	661	3.8	48	6

LEADING PASSERS	ATT	COM	YARD	TD	IN
John Hadl, SD	348	174	2798	20	21
Len Dawson, KC	305	163	2262	21	14
Joe Namath, NYJ	340	164	2220	18	15
Jack Kemp, Buf	391	179	2368	10	18
George Blanda, Hou	442	186	2542	20	30

LEADING RECEIVERS	NO	YARD	AVG	Long	TD
Lionel Taylor, Den	85	1131	13.3	63	6
Lance Alworth, SD	69	1602	23.2	85	14
Don Maynard, NYJ	68	1218	17.9	56	14
Ode Burrell, Hou	55	650	11.8	52	4
Art Powell, Oak	52	800	15.4	66	12

LEADING SCORERS	TD	FG	PAT	PTS
Gino Cappelletti, Bos	9	17	27	132
Pete Gogolak, Buf	0	28	31	115
Herb Travenio, SD	0	18	40	94
Jim Turner, NYJ	0	20	31	91
Lance Alworth, SD	14	0	0	84
Don Maynard, NYJ	14	0	0	84

LEADING INTERCEPTOR	NO	YDS	AVG	Long	TD
W.K. Hicks, Hou	9	156	17.3	31	0

LEADING PUNTER	NO	AVG	Long
Jerrel Wilson, KC	69	45.4	64

LEADING PUNT RETURNER	NO	YDS	AVG	Long	TD
Speedy Duncan, SD	30	464	15.5	66	2

LEADING KICKOFF RETURNER	NO	YDS	AVG	Long	TD
Abner Haynes, Den	34	901	26.5	60	0

SUPERLATIVES

Rushing Avg.	5.0	Paul Lowe, SD
Receiving Avg.	23.2	Lance Alworth, SD
Completion Pct.	53.4	Len Dawson, KC
Touchdowns	14	Lance Alworth, SD Don Maynard, NYJ
Field Goals	28	Pete Gogolak, Buf

LONGEST

Run	80t Wray Carlton, Buf	Punt	79 Jim Norton, Hou
Pass	95t George Blanda to Dick Compton, Hou	Punt Return	82t Bobby Jancik, Hou
Interception	79t Dave Grayson, Oak	Kickoff Return	102t Charley Warner, Buf
		Field Goal	53 Gino Cappelletti, Bos

1965 NATIONAL FOOTBALL LEAGUE

					SCORING		RUSHING				PASSING						
Team	W	L	T	PCT	OWN-OPP PTS-PTS	OWN-OPP PPG-PPG	OWN-OPP ATT-ATT	OWN-OPP YARD-YARD	OWN-OPP AVG-AVG	ON-OP TD-TD	OWN-OPP ATT-ATT	OWN-OPP COM-COM	OWN-OPP PCT-PCT	OWN-OPP YARD-YARD	OWN-OPP AVG-AVG	ON-OP TD-TD	ON-OP IN-IN
Eastern Conference																	
Cle	11	3	0	.786	363-325	25.9-23.2	476-412	2331-1866	4.9-4.5	19-11	329-419	160-204	48.6-48.7	2339-3153	7.1-7.5	23-31	16-24
Dal	7	7	0	.500	325-280	23.2-20.0	416-422	1608-1444	3.9-3.4	8-13	362-426	168-205	46.4-48.1	2756-3063	7.6-7.2	25-17	18-18
NYG	7	7	0	.500	270-338	19.3-24.1	423-447	1651-1956	3.9-4.4	12-20	342-393	171-208	50.0-52.9	2685-3251	7.9-8.3	23-18	16-16
Was	6	8	0	.429	257-301	18.4-21.5	354-486	1037-1753	2.9-3.6	7-16	427-318	220-161	51.5-50.6	2908-2539	6.8-8.0	20-15	20-27
Phi	5	9	0	.357	363-359	25.9-25.6	404-419	1824-1582	4.5-3.8	21-11	434-393	223-215	51.4-54.7	3442-3123	7.9-7.9	22-28	26-25
StL	5	9	0	.357	296-309	21.1-22.1	431-433	1619-1813	3.8-4.2	10-11	448-380	221-184	49.3-48.4	3222-2826	7.2-7.4	20-24	25-17
Pit	2	12	0	.143	202-397	14.4-28.4	407-483	1378-2080	3.4-4.3	10-19	354-353	161-173	45.5-49.0	2503-2703	7.1-7.7	10-25	35-12
Western Conference																	
GB	10	3	1	.769	316-224	22.6-16.0	432-480	1488-1988	3.4-4.1	14-10	306-383	166-187	54.2-48.8	2508-2316	8.2-6.0	19-11	14-27
Bal	10	3	1	.769	389-284	27.8-20.3	445-410	1593-1483	3.6-3.6	13-11	399-400	222-213	55.6-53.3	3330-2903	8.3-7.3	31-22	17-22
ChiB	9	5	0	.643	409-275	29.2-19.6	479-400	2131-1530	4.4-3.8	27-11	361-444	201-217	55.7-48.9	3020-3086	8.4-7.0	22-18	12-20
SF	7	6	1	.538	421-402	30.1-28.7	428-405	1783-1535	4.2-3.8	13-20	454-448	272-225	59.9-50.2	3633-3302	8.0-7.4	35-24	21-13
Min	7	7	0	.500	383-403	27.4-28.8	505-408	2278-1755	4.5-4.3	19-17	372-357	189-187	50.8-52.4	2861-2692	7.7-7.5	21-31	12-19
Det	6	7	1	.462	257-295	18.4-21.1	453-409	1469-1460	3.2-3.6	16-9	374-344	170-190	45.5-55.2	2083-2508	5.6-7.3	14-21	26-26
LARm	4	10	0	.286	269-328	19.2-23.4	378-417	1464-1409	3.9-3.4	8-16	445-349	230-205	51.7-58.7	3059-2884	6.9-8.3	22-22	19-11
98 games					4520	46.1	6031	23654	3.9	197	5407	2774	51.3	40349	7.5	307	277

Western Conf. Playoff: GB 13, Bal 10 (OT)
NFL Championship: GB 23, Cle 12

LEADING RUSHERS	ATT	YARD	AVG	Long	TD
Jim Brown, Cle	289	1544	5.3	67	17
Gale Sayers, ChiB	166	867	5.2	61t	14
Timmy Brown, Phi	158	861	5.4	54t	6
Ken Willard, SF	189	778	4.1	32	5
Jim Taylor, GB	207	734	3.5	35	4

LEADING PASSERS	ATT	COM	YARD	TD	IN
Rudy Bukich, ChiB	312	176	2641	20	9
Johnny Unitas, Bal	282	164	2530	23	12
John Brodie, SF	391	242	3112	30	16
Bart Starr, GB	251	140	2055	16	9
Earl Morrall, NYG	302	155	2446	22	12

LEADING RECEIVERS	NO	YARD	AVG	Long	TD
Dave Parks, SF	80	1344	16.8	53t	12
Tommy McDonald, LARm	67	1036	15.5	51	9
Pete Retzlaff, Phi	66	1190	18.0	78	10
Bobby Mitchell, Was	60	867	14.5	80t	6
Bernie Casey, SF	59	765	13.0	59t	8

LEADING SCORERS	TD	FG	PAT	PTS
Gale Sayers, ChiB	22	0	0	132
Jim Brown, Cle	21	0	0	126
Fred Cox, Min	0	23	44	113
Tommy Davis, SF	0	17	52	103
Jim Bakken, StL	0	21	33	96

LEADING INTERCEPTOR	NO	YDS	AVG	Long	TD
Bobby Boyd, Bal	9	78	8.7	24	1

LEADING PUNTER	NO	AVG	Long
Gary Collins, Cle	65	46.7	71

LEADING PUNT RETURNER	NO	YDS	AVG	Long	TD
Leroy Kelly, Cle	17	265	15.6	67t	2

LEADING KICKOFF RETURNER	NO	YDS	AVG	Long	TD
Tommy Watkins, Det	17	584	34.4	94	0

SUPERLATIVES

Rushing Avg.	5.4	Timmy Brown, Phi
Receiving Avg.	21.8	Bob Hayes, Dal
Completion Pct.	61.9	John Brodie, SF
Touchdowns	22	Gale Sayers, ChiB
Field Goals	23	Fred Cox, Min

LONGEST

Run	67	Jim Brown, Cle
Pass	89t	Earl Morrall to Homer Jones, NYG
Interception	96t	Larry Wilson, StL
Punt	90	Don Chandler, GB
Punt Return	85t	Gale Sayers, ChiB
Kickoff Return	101t	Lance Rentzel, Min
Field Goal	53	Fred Cox, Min
		Tommy Davis, SF

1966 AMERICAN FOOTBALL LEAGUE

					SCORING		RUSHING				PASSING						
Team	W	L	T	PCT	OWN-OPP PTS-PTS	OWN-OPP PPG-PPG	OWN-OPP ATT-ATT	OWN-OPP YARD-YARD	OWN-OPP AVG-AVG	ON-OP TD-TD	OWN-OPP ATT-ATT	OWN-OPP COM-COM	OWN-OPP PCT-PCT	OWN-OPP YARD-YARD	OWN-OPP AVG-AVG	ON-OP TD-TD	ON-OP IN-IN
Eastern Division																	
Buf	9	4	1	.692	358-255	25.6-18.2	455-344	1892-1051	4.2-3.0	19-6	473-466	199-205	42.1-44.0	3000-3307	6.3-7.1	15-22	21-29
Bos	8	4	2	.667	315-283	22.5-20.2	471-369	1963-1135	4.2-3.1	17-7	393-509	186-247	47.3-48.5	2784-3565	7.1-7.0	20-26	21-22
NYJ	6	6	2	.500	322-312	23.0-22.3	376-388	1442-1524	3.8-3.9	15-14	514-467	251-212	48.8-45.4	3556-3064	6.9-6.6	21-19	29-21
Hou	3	11	0	.214	335-396	23.9-28.3	413-422	1515-1833	3.7-4.3	11-10	485-438	226-209	46.6-47.7	3168-3390	6.5-7.7	29-35	28-18
Mia	3	11	0	.214	213-362	15.2-25.9	394-416	1410-1510	3.6-3.6	5-15	454-425	179-198	39.4-46.6	2374-3281	5.2-7.7	16-25	32-31
Western Division																	
KC	11	2	1	.846	448-276	32.0-19.7	439-353	2274-1356	5.2-3.8	19-10	377-494	199-226	52.8-45.8	3123-2876	8.3-5.8	31-18	15-33
Oak	8	5	1	.615	315-288	22.5-20.6	363-418	1427-1792	3.9-4.3	13-16	450-405	212-183	47.1-45.2	3425-2440	7.6-6.0	26-15	26-23
SD	7	6	1	.538	335-284	23.9-20.3	361-497	1537-2403	4.3-4.8	9-19	434-382	224-170	51.6-44.5	3347-2386	7.7-6.2	29-13	15-27
Den	4	10	0	.286	196-381	14.0-27.2	376-441	1173-2029	3.1-4.6	6-17	402-396	166-192	41.3-48.5	2351-2819	5.8-7.1	12-26	30-13
63 games					2837	45.0	3648	14633	4.0	114	3982	1842	46.3	27128	6.8	199	217

AFL Championship: KC 31, Buf 7

LEADING RUSHERS	ATT	YARD	AVG	Long	TD
Jim Nance, Bos	299	1458	4.9	65	11
Mike Garrett, KC	147	801	5.4	77	6
Clem Daniels, Oak	204	801	3.9	64	7
Bobby Burnett, Buf	187	766	4.1	32	4
Wray Carlton, Buf	156	696	4.5	23	6

LEADING PASSERS	ATT	COM	YARD	TD	IN
Len Dawson, KC	284	159	2527	26	10
John Hadl, SD	375	200	2846	23	14
Tom Flores, Oak	306	151	2638	24	14
Joe Namath, NYJ	471	232	3379	19	27
Babe Parilli, Bos	382	181	2721	20	20

LEADING RECEIVERS	NO	YARD	AVG	Long	TD
Lance Alworth, SD	73	1383	18.9	78	13
George Sauer, NYJ	63	1079	17.1	77	5
Otis Taylor, KC	58	1297	22.4	89	8
Chris Burford, KC	58	758	13.1	38	8
Willie Frazier, Hou	57	1129	19.8	79	12

LEADING SCORERS	TD	FG	PAT	PTS
Gino Cappelletti, Bos	6	16	35	119
Mike Mercer, KC	0	21	35	98
Booth Lusteg, Buf	0	19	41	98
Jim Turner, NYJ	0	18	34	88
George Blanda, Hou	0	16	39	87
Dick Van Raaphorst, SD	0	16	39	87

LEADING INTERCEPTORS	NO	YDS	AVG	Long	TD
Johnny Robinson, KC	10	136	13.6	29	1
Bobby Hunt, KC	10	113	11.3	33	0

LEADING PUNTER	NO	AVG	Long
Bob Scarpitto, Den	76	45.8	70

LEADING PUNT RETURNER	NO	YDS	AVG	Long	TD
Speedy Duncan, SD	18	238	13.2	81	1

LEADING KICKOFF RETURNER	NO	YDS	AVG	Long	TD
Goldie Sellers, SD	19	541	28.5	100	2

SUPERLATIVES

Rushing Avg.	5.4	Mike Garrett, KC
Receiving Avg.	22.4	Otis Taylor, KC
Completion Pct.	56.0	Len Dawson, KC
Touchdowns	13	Lance Alworth, SD
Field Goals	21	Mike Mercer, Oak-KC

LONGEST

Run	77t	Mike Garrett, KC
Pass	89t	Len Dawson to Otis Taylor, KC
Interception	87	Ron Hall, Bos
Punt	70	Bob Scarpitto, Den
Punt Return	81t	Speedy Duncan, SD
Kickoff Return	100t	Goldie Sellers, Den Nemiah Wilson, Den
Field Goal	51	George Blanda, Hou

1966 NATIONAL FOOTBALL LEAGUE

					SCORING		RUSHING				PASSING						
Team	W	L	T	PCT	OWN-OPP PTS-PTS	OWN-OPP PPG-PPG	OWN-OPP ATT-ATT	OWN-OPP YARD-YARD	OWN-OPP AVG-AVG	ON-OP TD-TD	OWN-OPP ATT-ATT	OWN-OPP COM-COM	OWN-OPP PCT-PCT	OWN-OPP YARD-YARD	OWN-OPP AVG-AVG	ON-OP TD-TD	ON-OP IN-IN
Eastern Conference																	
Dal	10	3	1	.769	445-239	31.8-17.1	471-356	2122-1176	4.5-3.3	24- 6	413-457	214-212	51.8-46.4	3331- 2802	8.1- 6.1	27-17	14-17
Cle	9	5	0	.643	403-259	28.8-18.5	415-450	2166-1894	5.2-4.2	18-12	402-406	212-221	52.7-54.4	3142- 2650	7.8- 6.5	33-14	15-30
Phi	9	5	0	.643	326-340	23.3-24.3	478-390	1859-1693	3.9-4.3	19-13	378-446	179-226	47.4-50.7	2159- 2964	5.7- 6.6	14-23	22-20
StL	8	5	1	.615	264-265	18.9-18.9	458-377	1601-1192	3.5-3.2	10-11	386-443	180-197	46.6-44.5	2292- 2733	5.9- 6.2	13-15	19-21
Was	7	7	0	.500	351-355	25.1-25.4	356-438	1377-1831	3.9-4.2	9-19	443-411	255-224	57.6-54.5	3230- 3237	7.3- 7.9	28-21	20-23
Pit	5	8	1	.385	316-347	22.6-24.8	375-468	1092-1786	2.9-3.8	13-11	401-397	188-192	46.9-48.4	2877- 2849	7.2- 7.2	18-27	22-24
Atl	3	11	0	.214	204-437	14.6-31.2	405-472	1519-2172	3.8-4.6	11-20	381-396	175-227	45.9-57.3	2362- 3376	6.2- 8.5	14-26	27-19
NYG	1	12	1	.077	263-501	18.8-35.8	380-480	1457-2053	3.8-4.3	7-23	424-357	208-194	49.1-54.3	2999- 3086	7.1- 8.6	20-36	31-17
Western Conference																	
GB	12	2	0	.857	335-163	23.9-11.6	475-446	1673-1644	3.5-3.7	18- 9	318-390	193-202	60.7-51.8	2831- 2316	8.9- 5.9	18- 7	5-28
Bal	9	5	0	.643	314-226	22.4-16.1	418-460	1556-1733	3.7-3.8	7- 7	401-425	221-240	55.1-56.5	3172- 2759	7.9- 6.5	26-14	27-22
LARm	8	6	0	.571	289-212	20.6-15.1	448-401	1742-1302	3.9-3.2	12-10	450-406	249-190	55.3-46.8	2891- 2830	6.4- 7.0	12-13	17-26
SF	6	6	2	.500	320-325	22.9-23.2	422-414	1790-1629	4.2-3.9	12-15	500-414	261-206	52.2-49.8	3239- 2895	6.5- 7.0	21-22	26-18
ChiB	5	7	2	.417	234-272	16.7-19.4	463-466	1927-1604	4.2-3.4	12-13	338-406	159-202	47.0-49.8	2016- 2600	5.0- 6.4	10-13	23-15
Det	4	9	1	.308	206-317	14.7-22.6	394-479	1429-2006	3.6-4.2	13-16	456-363	239-210	52.4-57.9	2752- 2702	6.0- 7.4	8-19	28-24
Min	4	9	1	.308	292-304	20.9-21.7	551-412	2091-1686	3.8-4.1	15-15	417-391	216-206	51.8-52.7	2932- 2426	7.0- 6.2	18-13	22-14
105 games					4562	43.4	6509	25401	3.9	200	6108	3149	51.6	42225	6.9	280	318

NFL Championship: GB 34, Dal 27
Super Bowl I: GB (NFL) 35, KC (AFL) 10

LEADING RUSHERS	ATT	YARD	AVG	Long	TD
Gale Sayers, ChiB	229	1231	5.4	58t	8
Leroy Kelly, Cle	209	1141	5.5	70t	15
Dick Bass, LARm	248	1090	4.4	50	8
Bill Brown, Min	251	829	3.3	33t	6
Ken Willard, SF	191	763	4.0	49	5

LEADING PASSERS	ATT	COM	YARD	TD	IN
Bart Starr, GB	251	156	2257	14	3
Sonny Jurgensen, Was	436	254	3209	28	19
Frank Ryan, Cle	382	200	2974	29	14
Don Meredith, Dal	344	177	2805	24	12
Johnny Unitas, Bal	348	195	2748	22	24

LEADING RECEIVERS	NO	YARD	AVG	Long	TD
Charley Taylor,Was	72	1119	15.5	86t	12
Pat Studstill, Det	67	1266	18.9	99t	5
Dave Parks, SF	66	974	14.8	65t	5
Bob Hayes, Dal	64	1232	19.3	95t	13
Tom Moore, LARm	60	433	7.2	30t	3

LEADING SCORERS	TD	FG	PAT	PTS
Bruce Gossett, LARm	0	28	29	113
Danny Villanueve, Dal	0	17	56	107
Charlie Gogolak, Was	0	22	39	105
Lou Michaels, Bal	0	21	35	98
Mike Clark, Pit	0	21	34	97

LEADING INTERCEPTOR	NO	YDS	AVG	Long	TD
Larry Wilson, StL	10	180	18.0	91t	2

LEADING PUNTER	NO	AVG	Long
David Lee, Bal	49	45.6	64

LEADING PUNT RETURNER	NO	YDS	AVG	Long	TD
Johnny Roland, StL	20	221	11.1	86t	1

LEADING KICKOFF RETURNER	NO	YDS	AVG	Long	TD
Gale Sayers, ChiB	23	718	31.2	93t	2

SUPERLATIVES

Rushing Avg.	5.5	Leroy Kelly, Cle
Receiving Avg.	21.8	Homer Jones, NYG
Completion Pct.	62.2	Bart Starr, GB
Touchdowns	16	Leroy Kelly, Cle Dan Reeves, Dal
Field Goals	28	Bruce Gossett, LARm

LONGEST

Run	70t	Leroy Kelly, Cle
Pass	99t	Karl Sweetan to Pat Studstill, Det
Interception	101t	Henry Carr, NYG
Punt	70	Bobby Walden, Min
Punt Return	86t	Johnny Roland, StL
Kickoff Return	94t	Roy Shivers, StL
	94	Dick Gordon, ChiB
Field Goal	51	Sam Baker, Phi

1967 AMERICAN FOOTBALL LEAGUE

					SCORING		RUSHING				PASSING						
Team	W	L	T	PCT	OWN-OPP PTS-PTS	OWN-OPP PPG-PPG	OWN-OPP ATT-ATT	OWN-OPP YARD-YARD	OWN-OPP AVG-AVG	ON-OP TD-TD	OWN-OPP ATT-ATT	OWN-OPP COM-COM	OWN-OPP PCT-PCT	OWN-OPP YARD-YARD	OWN-OPP AVG-AVG	ON-OP TD-TD	ON-OP IN-IN
Eastern Division																	
Hou	9	4	1	.692	258-199	18.4-14.2	476-424	2122-1637	4.5-3.9	12- 7	332-461	143-228	43.1-49.5	1532- 2619	4.6- 5.7	11-10	20-26
NYJ	8	5	1	.615	371-329	26.5-23.5	389-386	1307-1633	3.4-4.2	17-14	515-424	271-195	52.6-46.0	4128- 2489	8.0- 5.9	27-20	29-27
Buf	4	10	0	.286	237-285	16.9-20.4	371-437	1271-1622	3.4-3.7	9-11	434-377	183-162	42.2-43.0	2763- 2191	6.4- 5.8	14-17	34-27
Mia	4	10	0	.286	219-407	15.6-29.1	326-466	1323-2145	4.1-4.6	10-18	480-349	229-188	47.7-53.9	2741- 3082	5.7- 8.8	16-31	28-28
Bos	3	10	1	.231	280-389	20.0-27.8	391-417	1604-1350	4.1-3.2	10-12	434-423	191-211	44.0-49.9	2784- 3123	6.4- 7.4	20-28	32-17
Western Division																	
Oak	13	1	0	.929	468-233	33.4-16.6	458-352	1928-1129	4.2-3.2	19- 9	464-459	236-189	50.9-41.2	3541- 2831	7.6- 6.2	33-18	23-30
KC	9	5	0	.643	408-254	29.1-18.1	462-343	2018-1408	4.4-4.1	18-10	382-462	213-229	55.8-49.6	2773- 2890	7.3- 6.3	26-13	19-31
SD	8	5	1	.615	360-352	25.7-25.1	417-441	1715-1553	4.1-3.5	14-17	463-464	230-230	49.7-49.6	3517- 3455	7.6- 7.5	26-26	24-13
Den	3	11	0	.214	256-409	18.3-29.2	420-444	1265-2076	3.0-4.7	10-21	374-459	150-214	40.1-46.6	2190- 3289	5.9- 7.2	17-27	18-28
63 games					2857	45.3	3710	14553	3.9	119	3878	1846	47.6	25969	6.7	190	227

AFL Championship: Oak 40, Hou 7

LEADING RUSHERS	ATT	YARD	AVG	Long	TD
Jim Nance, Bos	269	1216	4.5	53	7
Hoyle Granger, Hou	236	1194	5.1	67	6
Mike Garrett, KC	236	1087	4.6	58	9
Dickie Post, SD	161	663	4.1	67t	7
Brad Hubbert, SD	116	643	5.5	80t	2

LEADING PASSERS	ATT	COM	YARD	TD	IN
Daryle Lamonica, Oak	425	220	3228	30	20
Len Dawson, KC	357	206	2651	24	17
Joe Namath, NYJ	491	258	4007	26	28
John Hadl, SD	427	217	3365	24	22
Bob Griese, Mia	331	166	2005	15	18

LEADING RECEIVERS	NO	YARD	AVG	Long	TD
George Sauer, NYJ	75	1189	15.9	61t	6
Don Maynard, NYJ	71	1434	20.2	75t	10
Jack Clancy, Mia	67	868	13.0	44t	2
Otis Taylor, KC	59	958	16.2	71t	11
Hewritt Dixon, Oak	59	563	9.5	48	2

LEADING SCORERS	TD	FG	PAT	PTS
George Blanda, Oak	0	20	56	116
Jan Stenerud, KC	0	21	45	108
Gino Cappelletti, Bos	3	16	29	95
Dick Van Raaphorst, SD	0	15	45	90
Jim Turner, NYJ	0	17	36	87

LEADING INTERCEPTOR	NO	YDS	AVG	Long	TD
Miller Farr, Hou	10	264	26.4	67	3
Tom Jancik, Buf	10	222	22.2	46	2
Dick Westmoreland, Mia	10	127	12.7	29	1

LEADING PUNTER	NO	AVG	Long
Bob Scarpitto, Den	105	44.9	73

LEADING PUNT RETURNER	NO	YDS	AVG	Long	TD
Floyd Little, Den	16	270	16.9	72t	1

LEADING KICKOFF RETURNER	NO	YDS	AVG	Long	TD
Zeke Moore, Hou	14	405	28.9	92t	1

SUPERLATIVES

Rushing Avg.	5.5	Brad Hubbert, SD
Receiving Avg.	20.2	Don Maynard, NYJ
Completion Pct.	57.7	Len Dawson, KC
Touchdowns	13	Emerson Boozer, NYJ
Field Goals	21	Jan Stenerud, KC

LONGEST

Run	80t	Brad Hubbert, SD
Pass	79t	Babe Parilli to Art Graham, Bos
Interception	100t	Speedy Duncan, SD
Punt	73	Bob Scarpitto, Den
Punt Return	78	Rodger Bird, Oak
Kickoff Return	106t	Noland Smith, KC
Field Goal	54	Jan Stenerud, KC

1967 NATIONAL FOOTBALL LEAGUE

					SCORING		RUSHING				PASSING						
Team	W	L	T	PCT	OWN-OPP PTS-PTS	OWN-OPP PPG-PPG	OWN-OPP ATT-ATT	OWN-OPP YARD-YARD	OWN-OPP AVG-AVG	ON-OP TD-TD	OWN-OPP ATT-ATT	OWN-OPP COM-COM	OWN-OPP PCT-PCT	OWN-OPP YARD-YARD	OWN-OPP AVG-AVG	ON-OP TD-TD	ON-OP IN-IN
EASTERN CONFERENCE																	
Capitol Division																	
Dal	9	5	0	.643	342-268	24.4-19.1	477-339	1900-1081	4.0-3.2	13-11	417-482	210-260	50.4-53.9	3093- 3167	7.4- 6.6	28-21	28-29
Phi	6	7	1	.462	351-409	25.1-29.2	328-434	1250-1741	3.8-4.0	12-16	445-480	244-255	54.8-53.1	3463- 3382	7.8- 7.0	30-29	24-21
Was	5	6	3	.455	347-353	24.8-25.2	345-431	1247-1852	3.6-4.3	13-19	527-468	301-468	57.1-55.8	3887- 3713	7.4- 7.9	31-20	17-20
NO	3	11	0	.214	233-379	16.6-27.1	334-469	1192-2092	3.6-4.5	9-22	478-410	237-207	49.6-50.5	2989- 3035	6.3- 7.4	13-25	23-22
Century Division																	
Cle	9	5	0	.643	334-297	23.9-21.2	444-459	2139-1767	4.8-3.8	15-15	333-454	160-250	48.0-55.1	2314- 3231	6.9- 7.1	22-19	18-22
NYG	7	7	0	.500	369-379	26.4-27.1	436-416	1864-1799	4.3-4.3	16-20	406-389	221-195	54.4-50.1	3382- 2731	8.3- 7.0	33-25	20-17
StL	6	7	1	.462	333-356	23.8-25.4	472-410	1397-1502	3.9-3.7	15-13	431-360	204-169	47.3-46.9	3170- 3023	7.4- 8.4	20-26	35-19
Pit	4	9	1	.308	281-320	20.1-22.9	431-418	1397-1377	3.2-3.3	13-12	442-397	214-201	48.4-50.6	2781- 2854	6.3- 7.2	19-22	29-26
WESTERN CONFERENCE																	
Coastal Division																	
LARm	11	1	2	.917	398-196	28.4-14.0	490-361	1906-1119	3.9-3.1	16- 6	390-445	206-212	52.8-47.6	2947- 2694	7.6- 6.1	28-14	16-32
Bal	11	1	2	.917	394-198	28.1-14.1	443-387	1645-1411	3.7-3.6	21- 5	457-395	265-221	58.0-55.9	3561- 2678	7.8- 6.8	22-13	17-32
SF	7	7	0	.500	273-337	19.5-24.1	434-407	1764-1698	4.1-4.2	16-17	469-403	228-212	48.6-52.6	2862- 2755	6.1- 6.8	16-19	26-16
Atl	1	12	1	.077	233-294	16.6-21.0	344-504	1303-2139	3.8-4.2	6-18	370-421	179-238	48.4-56.5	2144- 3588	5.8- 8.5	13-31	25-17
Central Division																	
GB	9	4	1	.692	332-209	23.7-14.9	474-443	1915-1923	4.0-4.3	18- 7	331-337	182-155	55.0-46.0	2758- 1644	8.3- 4.9	15-13	27-26
ChiB	7	6	1	.538	239-218	17.1-15.6	489-419	1852-1531	3.8-3.7	12-11	268-384	131-164	48.9-42.7	1673- 2146	6.2- 5.6	9-14	18-28
Det	5	7	2	.417	260-259	18.6-18.5	473-471	1907-1795	4.0-3.8	14-15	351-312	160-143	45.6-45.8	1826- 2089	5.2- 6.7	14-11	19-23
Min	3	8	3	.273	233-294	16.6-21.0	454-500	1811-2104	4.0-4.2	10-12	336-314	150-149	44.6-47.5	1951- 2071	5.8- 6.6	11-17	24-16
112 games					4952	44.2	6868	26489	3.9	219	6451	3292	51.0	44801	6.9	324	366

Conf. Championships: Dal 52, Cle 14
GB 18, LARm 7
NFL Championship: GB 21, Dal 17
Super Bowl II: GB (NFL) 33, Oak (AFL) 14

LEADING RUSHERS	ATT	YARD	AVG	Long	TD
Leroy Kelly, Cle	235	1205	5.1	42t	11
Dave Osborn, Min	215	972	4.5	73	2
Gale Sayers, ChiB	186	880	4.7	70	7
Johnny Roland, StL	234	876	3.7	70	10
Mel Farr, Det	206	860	4.2	57	3

LEADING PASSERS	ATT	COM	YARD	TD	IN
Sonny Jurgensen, Was	508	288	3747	31	16
Johnny Unitas, Bal	436	255	3428	20	16
Fran Tarkenton, NYG	377	204	3088	29	19
Roman Gabriel, LARm	371	196	2779	25	13
Norm Snead, Phi	434	240	3399	29	24

LEADING RECEIVERS	NO	YARD	AVG	Long	TD
Charley Taylor, Was	70	990	14.1	86t	9
Jerry Smith, Was	67	849	12.7	43	12
Willie Richardson, Bal	63	860	13.7	31t	8
Bobby Mitchell, Was	60	866	14.4	65t	6
Ben Hawkins, Phi	59	1265	21.4	87t	10

LEADING SCORERS	TD	FG	PAT	PTS
Jim Bakken, StL	0	27	36	117
Bruce Gossett, LARm	0	20	48	108
Don Chandler, GB	0	19	39	96
Homer Jones, NYG	14	0	0	84
Sam Baker, Phi	0	12	45	81

LEADING INTERCEPTOR	NO	YDS	AVG	Long	TD
Lem Barney, Det	10	232	23.2	71t	3
Dave Whitsell, NO	10	178	17.8	41t	2

LEADING PUNTER	NO	AVG	Long
Billy Lothridge, Atl	87	43.7	62

LEADING PUNT RETURNER	NO	YDS	AVG	Long	TD
Ben Davis, Cle	18	229	12.7	52t	1

LEADING KICKOFF RETURNER	NO	YDS	AVG	Long	TD
Travis Williams, GB	18	739	41.1	104t	4

SUPERLATIVES

Rushing Avg.	5.1	Leroy Kelly, Cle
Receiving Avg.	24.7	Homer Jones, NYG
Completion Pct.	58.5	John Unitas, Bal
Touchdowns	14	Homer Jones, NYG
Field Goals	27	Jim Bakken, StL

LONGEST

Run		
Pass		
Interception	4t	Rick Volk, Bal
Punt	78	Pat Studstill, Det
Punt Return	81	Bob Grim, Min
Kickoff Return	104t	Travis Williams, GB
Field Goal	53	Lou Michaels, Bal

1968 AMERICAN FOOTBALL LEAGUE

					SCORING		RUSHING				PASSING						
Team	W	L	T	PCT	OWN-OPP PTS-PTS	OWN-OPP PPG-PPG	OWN-OPP ATT-ATT	OWN-OPP YARD-YARD	OWN-OPP AVG-AVG	ON-OP TD-TD	OWN-OPP ATT-ATT	OWN-OPP COM-COM	OWN-OPP PCT-PCT	OWN-OPP YARD-YARD	OWN-OPP AVG-AVG	ON-OP TD-TD	ON-OP IN-IN
Eastern Division																	
NYJ	11	3	0	.786	419-280	29.9-20.0	467-368	1608-1195	3.4-3.2	22- 9	436-403	217-187	49.8-48.4	3574- 2567	8.2- 6.4	20-17	19-28
Hou	7	7	0	.500	303-248	21.6-17.7	462-462	1804-1704	3.9-3.7	16- 9	414-359	191-158	46.1-44.0	2864- 2003	6.9- 5.8	17-13	25-20
Mia	5	8	1	.385	276-355	19.7-25.4	417-445	1704-2172	4.1-4.9	12-19	423-342	216-179	51.1-52.3	2843- 2904	6.7- 8.5	21-23	22-22

Bos	4	10	0	.286	229-406	16.4-29.0	421-479	1362-1825	3.1-3.8	8-22	409-416	160-200	39.1-48.1	2121- 2826	5.2- 6.8	16-20	33-23
Buf	1	12	1	.077	199-367	14.2-26.2	400-505	1527-2021	3.8-4.0	9-15	405-340	168-143	41.5-42.1	1714- 2477	4.2- 7.3	7-19	28-22
Western Division																	
Oak	12	2	0	.857	453-233	32.4-16.6	471-442	2168-1804	4.6-4.1	16-12	468-446	237-189	50.6-42.4	3771- 2657	8.1- 6.0	31-13	18-25
KC	12	2	0	.857	276-170	19.7-12.1	537-365	2227-1266	4.1-3.5	16- 4	270-461	156-214	57.8-46.4	2492- 3562	9.2- 7.1	20-14	11-37
SD	9	5	0	.643	382-310	27.3-22.1	428-439	1765-1641	4.1-3.7	12-13	472-430	225-217	47.7-50.5	3813- 2896	8.1- 6.7	29-20	33-20
Den	5	9	0	.357	255-404	18.2-28.9	411-457	1614-1861	3.9-4.1	11-20	427-429	179-217	41.9-50.6	2826- 3419	6.6- 8.0	20-25	27-20
Cin	3	11	0	.214	215-329	15.4-23.5	421-473	1807-2097	4.3-4.4	14-13	313-411	167-212	53.4-51.6	1896- 2903	6.1- 7.1	8-25	11-10
70 games					3007	43.0	4435	17586	4.0	136	4037	1916	47.5	27914	6.9	189	227

Western Division Playoff: Oak 41, KC 6
AFL Championship: NYJ 27, Oak 23

LEADING RUSHERS	ATT	YARD	AVG	Long	TD
Paul Robinson, Cin	238	1023	4.3	87t	8
Robert Holmes, KC	174	866	5.0	76t	7
Hewritt Dixon, Oak	206	865	4.2	28	2
Hoyle Granger, Hou	202	848	4.2	47t	7
Dickie Post, SD	151	758	5.0	62t	3

LEADING PASSERS	ATT	COM	YARD	TD	IN
Len Dawson, KC	224	131	2019	17	9
Daryle Lamonica, Oak	416	206	3245	25	15
Joe Namath, NYJ	380	187	3147	15	17
Bob Griese, Mia	355	186	2473	21	16
John Hadl, SD	440	208	3473	27	32

LEADING RECEIVERS	NO	YARD	AVG	Long	TD
Lance Alworth, SD	68	1312	19.3	80t	10
George Sauer, NYJ	66	1141	17.3	43	3
Fred Biletnikoff, Oak	61	1037	17.0	82	6
Karl Noonan, Mia	58	760	13.1	50t	11
Don Maynard, NYJ	57	1297	22.8	87t	10

LEADING SCORERS	TD	FG	PAT	PTS
Jim Turner, NYJ	0	34	43	145
Jan Stenerud, KC	0	30	39	129
George Blanda, Oak	0	21	54	117
Dennis Partee, SD	0	22	40	106
Gino Cappelletti, Bos	2	15	26	83

LEADING INTERCEPTOR	NO	YDS	AVG	Long	TD
Dave Grayson, Oak	10	195	19.5	54	1

LEADING PUNTER	NO	AVG	Long
Jerrel Wilson, KC	63	45.1	70

LEADING PUNT RETURNER	NO	YDS	AVG	Long	TD
Noland Smith, KC	18	270	15.0	80t	1

LEADING KICKOFF RETURNER	NO	YDS	AVG	Long	TD
George Atkinson, Oak	32	802	25.1	60	0

SUPERLATIVES		
Rushing Avg.	5.0	Dickie Post, SD
Receiving Avg.	22.8	Don Maynard, NYJ
Completion Pct.	58.5	Len Dawson, KC
Touchdowns	12	Warren Wells, Oak
Field Goals	34	Jim Turner, NYJ

LONGEST		
Run	87t	Paul Robinson, Cin
Pass	94t	George Blanda to Warren Wells, Oak
Interception	100t	Tom Janik, Buf
Punt	87	Bob Scarpitto, Den
Punt Return	95t	Speedy Duncan, SD
Kickoff Return	100t	Max Anderson, Buf
Field Goal	52	Jan Stenerud, KC

1968 NATIONAL FOOTBALL LEAGUE

					SCORING		RUSHING				PASSING						
Team	W	L	T	PCT	OWN-OPP PTS-PTS	OWN-OPP PPG-PPG	OWN-OPP ATT-ATT	OWN-OPP YARD-YARD	OWN-OPP AVG-AVG	ON-OP TD-TD	OWN-OPP ATT-ATT	OWN-OPP COM-COM	OWN-OPP PCT-PCT	OWN - OPP YARD - YARD	OWN-OPP AVG-AVG	ON-OP TD-TD	ON-OP IN-IN
EASTERN DIVISION																	
Capitol Division																	
Dal	12	2	0	.857	431-186	30.8-13.3	480-369	2091-1195	4.4-3.2	22- 2	399-428	217-220	54.4-51.4	3295- 2838	8.3- 6.6	25-20	18-26
NYG	7	7	0	.500	294-325	21.0-23.2	474-425	1882-2001	4.0-4.7	13-22	366-364	195-191	53.3-52.5	2715- 2498	7.4- 6.9	21-18	17-26
Was	5	9	0	.357	249-358	17.8-25.6	360-497	1164-2194	3.2-4.4	6-18	408-359	227-202	55.6-56.3	2824- 2662	6.9- 7.4	23-16	18-21
Phi	2	12	0	.143	202-351	14.4-25.1	369-515	1411-2141	3.8-4.2	3-18	380-327	194-182	51.1-55.7	2357- 2557	6.2- 7.8	16-20	29-13
Century Division																	
Cle	10	4	0	.714	394-273	28.1-19.5	447-423	2031-1842	4.5-4.4	20-11	363-439	184-213	50.7-48.5	3039- 2447	8.4- 5.6	27-19	16-32
StL	9	4	1	.692	325-289	23.2-20.6	463-423	1996-1558	4.3-3.7	22-10	385-399	169-210	43.9-52.6	2389- 3261	6.2- 8.2	16-23	20-13
NO	4	9	1	.308	246-327	17.6-23.4	409-439	1527-2105	3.7-4.8	7-13	439-366	210-153	47.8-41.8	2549- 2483	5.8- 6.8	17-25	29-16
Pit	2	11	1	.154	244-397	17.4-28.4	399-441	1721-1624	4.3-3.7	7-14	451-413	211-220	46.8-53.3	2764- 3360	6.1- 8.1	22-29	26-17
WESTERN CONFERENCE																	
Coastal Division																	
Bal	13	1	0	.929	402-144	28.7-10.3	463-375	1809-1339	3.9-3.6	16- 6	359-432	196-224	54.6-51.9	3094- 2405	8.6- 5.6	28- 9	22-29
LARm	10	3	1	.769	312-200	22.3-14.3	503-397	1932-1305	3.8-3.3	14- 9	384-353	189-158	49.2-44.8	2413- 2196	6.3- 6.2	20-12	17-25
SF	7	6	1	.538	303-310	21.6-22.1	443-445	1784-1776	4.0-4.0	11-12	417-416	239-201	57.3-48.3	3107- 2548	7.5- 6.1	24-19	23-20
Atl	2	12	0	.143	170-389	12.1-27.8	366-518	1305-2235	3.6-4.3	9-17	326-389	158-248	48.5-63.8	2386- 3306	7.3- 8.5	9-30	24-14
Central Division																	
Min	8	6	0	.571	282-242	20.1-17.3	500-432	1921-1903	3.8-4.4	19- 8	282-315	154-185	54.6-58.7	1995- 2162	7.1- 6.9	11-16	17-16
ChiB	7	7	0	.500	250-333	17.9-23.8	500-427	2377-1704	4.8-4.0	14-17	343-333	158-172	46.1-51.7	1868- 2893	5.4- 8.7	27-25	21-18
GB	6	7	1	.462	281-227	20.1-16.2	450-476	1749-1800	3.9-3.8	12-11	318-327	188-157	59.1-48.0	2651- 2031	8.3- 6.2	21-14	15-17
Det	4	8	2	.333	207-241	14.8-17.2	433-457	1702-1680	3.9-3.7	6-13	377-337	204-157	54.1-46.6	2649- 2448	7.0- 7.3	17-12	15-24
112 games					4592	41.0	7059	28402	4.0	201	5997	3093	51.6	42095	7.0	324	327

Conference championships: Cle 31, Dal 20;
Bal 24, Min 14
NFL Championship: Bal 34, Cle 0
Super Bowl III: NYJ (AFL) 16, Bal (NFL) 7

LEADING RUSHERS	ATT	YARD	AVG	Long	TD
Leroy Kelly, Cle	248	1239	5.0	65	16
Ken Willard, SF	227	967	4.3	69t	7
Tom Woodeshick, Phi	217	947	4.4	54t	3
Dick Hoak, Pit	175	858	4.9	77t	3
Gale Sayers, ChiB	138	856	6.2	63	2

LEADING PASSERS	ATT	COM	YARD	TD	IN
Earl Morrall, Bal	317	182	2909	26	17
Don Meredith, Dal	309	171	2500	21	12
John Brodie, SF	404	234	3020	22	21
Bart Starr, GB	171	109	1617	15	8
Fran Tarkenton, NYG	337	182	2555	21	12

LEADING RECEIVERS	NO	YARD	AVG	Long	TD
Clifton McNeil, SF	71	994	14.0	65t	7
Roy Jefferson, Pit	58	1074	18.5	62	11
Lance Rentzel, Dal	54	1009	18.7	65t	6
Dan Abramowicz, NO	54	890	16.5	47t	7
Bob Hayes, Dal	53	909	17.2	54t	10

LEADING SCORERS	TD	FG	PAT	PTS
Leroy Kelly, Cle	20	0	0	120
Mike Clark Dal	0	17	54	105
Mac Percival, ChiB	0	25	25	100
Dan Cockroft, Cle	0	18	46	100
Bruce Gossett, LARm	0	17	37	88
Fred Cox, Min	0	19	31	88

LEADING INTERCEPTOR	NO	YDS	AVG	Long	TD
Willie Williams, NYG	10	103	10.3	24	0

LEADING PUNTER	NO	AVG	Long
Billy Lothridge, Atl	75	44.3	70

LEADING PUNT RETURNER	NO	YDS	AVG	Long	TD
Bob Hayes, Dal	15	312	20.8	90t	2

LEADING KICKOFF RETURNER	NO	YDS	AVG	Long	TD
Preston Pearson, Bal	15	527	35.1	102t	2

SUPERLATIVES		
Rushing Avg.	6.2	Gale Sayers, ChiB
Receiving Avg.	23.5	Homer Jones, NYG
Completion Pct.	63.7	Bart Starr, GB
Touchdowns	20	Leroy Kelly, Cle
Field Goals	25	Mac Percival, ChiB

LONGEST

Run	77t Dick Hoak, Pit	Punt Return	98t Charlie West, Min
Pass	99t Sonny Jurgensen to Gerry Allen, Was	Kickoff Return	102t Preston Pearson, Bal
Interception	96t Roosevelt Taylor, ChiB	Field Goal	50 Mike Clark, Dal
Punt	84 Ron Widby, Dal		Don Cockroft, Cle

1969 AMERICAN FOOTBALL LEAGUE

					SCORING		RUSHING				PASSING						
Team	W	L	T	PCT	OWN-OPP PTS-PTS	OWN-OPP PPG-PPG	OWN-OPP ATT-ATT	OWN-OPP YARD-YARD	OWN-OPP AVG-AVG	ON-OP TD-TD	OWN-OPP ATT-ATT	OWN-OPP COM-COM	OWN-OPP PCT-PCT	OWN-OPP YARD-YARD	OWN-OPP AVG-AVG	ON-OP TD-TD	ON-OP IN-IN
Eastern Division																	
NYJ	10	4	0	.714	353-269	25.2-19.2	469-343	1782-1326	3.8-3.9	14- 7	394-437	203-232	51.5-53.1	2939- 3086	7.5- 7.1	21-22	20-29
Hou	6	6	2	.500	278-279	19.9-19.9	440-430	1706-1556	3.9-3.6	12-10	489-371	239-167	48.9-45.0	3147- 2495	6.4- 6.7	15-18	31-23
Bos	4	10	0	.286	266-316	19.0-22.6	367-528	1489-2359	4.1-4.5	11-18	338-348	162-203	47.9-58.3	2191- 2610	6.5- 7.5	19-18	18-20
Buf	4	10	0	.286	230-359	16.4-25.6	384-454	1522-1858	4.0-4.5	7-17	442-368	215-175	48.6-47.6	2716- 2772	6.1- 7.5	17-21	30-19
Mia	3	10	1	.231	233-332	16.6-23.7	401-422	1513-1489	3.8-3.5	12- 9	424-404	201-196	47.4-48.5	2558- 2845	6.0- 7.0	12-25	29-18
Western Division																	
Oak	12	1	1	.923	377-242	26.9-17.3	459-438	1765-1661	3.8-3.8	4-13	439-422	227-164	51.7-38.9	3375- 2511	7.7- 6.0	36-15	26-26
KC	11	3	0	.786	359-177	25.6-12.6	522-314	2220-1091	4.3-3.5	19- 8	351-426	196-200	55.8-46.9	2638- 2491	7.5- 5.8	16-10	20-32
SD	8	6	0	.571	288-276	20.6-19.7	455-366	1985-1442	4.4-3.9	18-11	444-423	208-241	46.8-57.0	2927- 3075	6.6- 7.3	13-22	21-31
Den	5	8	1	.385	297-344	21.2-24.6	394-436	1637-1709	4.2-3.9	12-15	403-437	192-223	47.6-51.0	2835- 3295	7.0- 7.5	23-19	23-14
Cin	4	9	1	.308	280-367	20.0-26.2	363-523	1523-2651	4.2-5.1	10-13	308-396	163-205	52.9-51.8	2720- 2866	8.8- 7.2	22-24	15-21
70 games					2961	42.3	4254	17142	4.0	119	4032	2006	49.8	28046	7.0	194	233

Divisional Playoffs: KC 13, NYJ 6;
Oak 56, Hou 7

AFL Championship: KC 17, Oak 7

LEADING RUSHERS	ATT	YARD	AVG	Long	TD
Dickie Post, SD	182	873	4.8	60	6
Jim Nance, Bos	193	750	3.9	43	6
Hoyle Granger, Hou	186	740	4.0	23	3
Mike Garrett, KC	168	732	4.4	34t	6
Floyd Little, Den	146	729	5.0	48t	6

LEADING PASSERS	ATT	COM	YARD	TD	IN
Greg Cook, Cin	197	106	1854	15	11
Joe Namath, NYJ	361	185	2734	19	17
Daryle Lamonica, Oak	426	221	3302	34	25
Mike Livingston, KC	161	84	1123	4	6
John Hadl, SD	324	158	2253	10	11

LEADING RECEIVERS	NO	YARD	AVG	Long	TD
Lance Alworth, SD	64	1003	15.7	76t	4
Fred Biletnikoff, Oak	54	837	15.5	53t	12
Moses Denson, Den	53	809	15.3	62t	10
Alvin Reed, Hou	51	664	13.0	43t	2
Warren Wells, Oak	47	1260	26.8	80t	14
Don Maynard, NYJ	47	938	20.0	60t	6

LEADING SCORERS	TD	FG	PAT	PTS
Jim Turner, NYJ	0	32	33	129
Jan Stenerud, KC	0	27	38	119
George Blanda, Oak	0	20	45	105
Roy Gerela, Hou	0	19	29	86
Warren Wells, Oak	14	0	0	84

LEADING INTERCEPTOR	NO	YDS	AVG	Long	TD
Emmitt Thomas, KC	9	146	16.2	45t	1

LEADING PUNTER	NO	AVG	Long
Dennis Partee, SD	71	44.6	62

LEADING PUNT RETURNER	NO	YDS	AVG	Long	TD
Billy Thompson, Den	25	288	11.5	40	0

LEADING KICKOFF RETURNER	NO	YDS	AVG	Long	TD
Billy Thompson, Den	18	513	28.5	63	0

SUPERLATIVES

Rushing Avg.	5.0	Carl Garrett, Bos
Receiving Avg.	26.8	Warren Wells, Oak
Completion Pct.	59.0	Len Dawson, KC
Touchdowns	14	Warren Wells, Oak
Field Goals	32	Jim Turner, NYJ

LONGEST

Run	83	Jess Phillips, Cin
Pass	86t	Pete Beathard to Jerry LeVias, Hou
Interception	76t	Dave Grayson, Oak
Punt	98	Steve O'Neal, NYJ
Punt Return	64	Noland Smith, KC
Kickoff Return	105t	Mercury Morris, Mia
Field Goal	54	Jan Stenerud, KC

1969 NATIONAL FOOTBALL LEAGUE

					SCORING		RUSHING				PASSING						
Team	W	L	T	PCT	OWN-OPP PTS-PTS	OWN-OPP PPG-PPG	OWN-OPP ATT-ATT	OWN-OPP YARD-YARD	OWN-OPP AVG-AVG	ON-OP TD-TD	OWN-OPP ATT-ATT	OWN-OPP COM-COM	OWN-OPP PCT-PCT	OWN-OPP YARD-YARD	OWN-OPP AVG-AVG	ON-OP TD-TD	ON-OP IN-IN
EASTERN CONFERENCE																	
Capitol Division																	
Dal	11	2	1	.846	369-223	26.4-15.9	532-313	2276-1050	4.3-3.4	17- 3	355-458	189-235	53.2-51.3	3212- 3109	9.0- 6.8	24-23	18-24
Was	7	5	2	.583	307-319	21.9-22.8	377-511	1532-2299	4.1-4.5	11-26	444-369	275-192	61.9-52.0	3106- 2316	7.0- 6.3	22-11	16-16
NO	5	9	0	.357	311-393	22.2-28.1	399-419	1705-1835	4.3-4.4	12-15	453-382	245-200	54.1-52.4	3215- 3382	7.1- 8.9	22-32	20-12
Phi	4	9	1	.308	279-377	19.9-26.9	395-467	1563-1909	4.0-4.1	10-15	458-444	216-243	47.2-54.7	3022- 3250	6.6- 7.3	20-23	28-15
Century Division																	
Cle	10	3	1	.769	351-300	25.1-21.4	447-417	1788-1990	4.0-4.8	17-18	378-387	199-202	52.6-52.2	2830- 2787	7.5- 7.2	24-19	21-19
NYG	6	8	0	.429	264-298	18.9-21.2	397-466	1593-2053	4.0-4.4	8-14	435-340	234-171	53.8-50.3	3076- 2430	7.1- 7.1	24-18	8-19
StL	4	9	1	.308	314-389	22.4-27.8	382-438	1446-1644	3.8-3.8	17-10	430-465	216-260	50.2-55.9	2940- 3752	6.8- 8.1	19-38	25-15
Pit	1	13	0	.071	218-404	15.6-28.9	400-455	1542-1732	3.9-3.8	8-17	391-410	176-227	45.0-55.4	2458- 2973	6.3- 7.3	17-27	29-25
WESTERN CONFERENCE																	
Coastal Division																	
LARm	11	3	0	.786	320-243	22.9-17.4	382-415	1413-1475	3.7-3.6	8- 8	416-430	222-202	53.4-47.0	2650- 2919	6.4- 6.8	25-18	7-26
Bal	8	5	1	.615	279-268	19.9-19.1	417-399	1490-1400	3.6-3.5	16- 8	429-459	225-271	52.4-59.0	3143- 3499	7.3- 7.6	17-20	27-15
Atl	6	8	0	.429	276-268	19.7-19.1	455-475	2058-2032	4.5-4.3	9-14	282-383	149-225	52.8-58.7	2230- 2536	7.9- 6.6	20-13	12-19
SF	4	8	2	.333	277-319	19.8-22.8	391-422	1536-1704	3.9-4.0	13-14	496-402	278-205	56.0-51.0	3379- 2726	6.8- 6.8	22-22	26-20
Central Division																	
Min	12	2	0	.857	379-133	27.1- 9.5	489-337	1850-1089	3.8-3.2	15- 4	346-410	176-213	50.9-52.0	2498- 2035	7.2- 5.0	24- 8	18-30
Det	9	4	1	.692	259-188	18.5-13.4	474-372	1755-1223	3.7-3.3	11- 7	329-350	165-167	50.2-47.7	1958- 3109	6.0- 6.4	12-15	18-21
GB	8	6	0	.571	269-221	19.2-15.8	432-485	1692-1982	3.9-4.1	11- 7	319-360	182-177	57.1-49.2	2678- 2133	8.4- 5.9	20-13	17-19
ChiB	1	13	0	.071	210-339	15.0-24.2	462-440	2078-1900	4.5-4.3	14-17	384-296	193-150	50.3-50.7	1929- 2239	5.0- 7.6	11-23	21-16
112 games					4682	41.8	6831	27317	4.0	197	6345	3340	52.6	44324	7.0	323	311

Conference Championships: Cle 38, Dal 14;
Min 23, LARm 20

NFL Championship: Min 27, Cle 7

Super Bowl IV: KC (AFL) 23, Min (NFL) 7

LEADING RUSHERS	ATT	YARD	AVG	Long	TD
Gale Sayers, ChiB	236	1032	4.4	28	8
Calvin Hill, Dal	204	942	4.6	55	8
Tom Matte, Bal	235	909	3.9	26	11
Larry Brown, Was	202	888	4.4	57	4
Tom Woodeshick, Phi	186	831	4.5	21	4

LEADING PASSERS	ATT	COM	YARD	TD	IN
Sonny Jurgensen, Was	442	274	3102	22	15
Bart Starr, GB	148	92	1161	9	6
Fran Tarkenton, NYG	409	220	2918	23	8
Roman Gabriel, LARm	399	217	2549	24	7
Craig Morton, Dal	302	162	2619	21	15

LEADING RECEIVERS	NO	YARD	AVG	Long	TD
Dan Abramowicz, NO	73	1015	13.9	49t	7
Charley Taylor, Was	71	883	12.4	88t	8
Roy Jefferson, Pit	67	1079	16.1	63	9
Harold Jackson, Phi	65	1116	17.2	65t	9
Dave Williams, StL	56	702	12.5	61	7

LEADING SCORERS	TD	FG	PAT	PTS
Fred Cox, Min	0	26	43	121
Mike Clark, Dal	0	20	43	103
Bruce Gossett, LARm	0	22	36	102
Errol Mann, Det	0	25	26	101
Tom Dempsey, NO	0	22	33	99

LEADING INTERCEPTOR	NO	YDS	AVG	Long	TD
Mel Renfro, Dal	10	118	11.8	41	0

LEADING PUNTER	NO	AVG	Long
David Lee, Bal	57	45.3	66

LEADING PUNT RETURNER	NO	YDS	AVG	Long	TD
Alvin Haymond, LARm	33	435	13.2	52	0

LEADING KICKOFF RETURNER	NO	YDS	AVG	Long	TD
Bobby Williams, Det	17	563	33.1	96t	1

SUPERLATIVES

Rushing Avg.	4.8	Tony Baker, NO
Receiving Avg.	22.3	Lance Rentzel, Dal
Completion Pct.	62.2	Bart Starr, GB
Touchdowns	13	Tom Matte, Bal
		Lance Rentzel, Dal
Field Goals	26	Fred Cox, Min

LONGEST

Run	80t	Clint Jones, Min
Pass	93t	Roman Gabriel to Wendell Tucker, LARm
Interception	85t	Doug Hart, GB
Punt	81	Tom McNeill, NO
Punt Return	86t	Rickie Harris, Was
Kickoff Return	101t	Don McCall, Pit
Field Goal	55	Tom Dempsey, NO

1970 AMERICAN FOOTBALL CONFERENCE

					SCORING		RUSHING				PASSING						
Team	W	L	T	PCT	OWN-OPP PTS-PTS	OWN-OPP PPG-PPG	OWN-OPP ATT-ATT	OWN-OPP YARD-YARD	OWN-OPP AVG-AVG	ON-OP TD-TD	OWN-OPP ATT-ATT	OWN-OPP COM-COM	OWN-OPP PCT-PCT	OWN-OPP YARD-YARD	OWN-OPP AVG-AVG	ON-OP TD-TD	ON-OP IN-IN
Eastern Division																	
Bal	11	2	1	.846	321-234	22.9-16.7	411-390	1336-1439	3.3-3.7	9- 6	416-452	219-238	52.6-52.7	3087- 2780	7.4- 6.2	23-16	22-25
Mia*	10	4	0	.714	297-228	21.2-16.3	492-387	2082-1453	4.2-3.8	14- 8	299-403	159-234	53.2-58.1	2284- 2708	7.6- 6.7	15-17	19-23
NYJ	4	10	0	.286	255-286	18.2-20.4	463-408	1653-1283	3.6-3.1	11- 7	386-383	193-165	50.0-43.1	2592- 2680	6.7- 7.0	14-20	22-23
Buf	3	10	0	.231	204-337	14.6-24.1	367-484	1465-1718	4.0-3.5	8-16	402-338	213-157	53.0-46.4	2916- 2334	7.3- 6.9	13-15	26-11
Bos	2	12	0	.143	149-361	10.6-25.8	334-503	1040-2074	3.1-4.1	11-20	382-334	176-177	44.9-53.0	1975- 2430	5.0- 7.3	7-19	28- 8
Central Division																	
Cin	8	6	0	.571	312-255	22.3-18.2	461-418	2057-1543	4.5-3.7	16-11	339-428	172-209	50.7-48.8	2097- 2885	6.2- 6.7	12-18	11-23
Cle	7	7	0	.500	286-265	20.4-18.9	462-451	1579-2006	3.4-4.4	14-10	392-357	190-186	48.5-52.1	2752- 2528	7.0- 7.1	17-16	24-19
Pit	5	9	0	.357	210-272	15.0-19.4	432-487	1715-1679	4.0-3.4	13- 8	384-393	150-191	39.1-48.6	2312- 2555	6.0- 6.5	12-21	32-23
Hou	3	10	1	.231	217-352	15.5-25.1	419-466	1556-1793	3.7-3.8	10-16	470-344	238-164	50.6-47.7	2768- 2851	5.9- 8.3	12-25	23-18
Western Division																	
Oak	8	4	2	.667	300-293	21.4-20.9	471-460	1964-2027	4.2-4.4	7-10	418-339	210-157	50.2-46.3	3029- 2386	7.2- 7.0	28-22	21-19
KC	7	5	2	.583	372-244	26.6-17.4	448-418	1858-1657	4.1-4.0	11-10	289-408	154-195	53.3-47.8	2038- 2280	7.1- 5.6	13-15	16-31
SD	5	6	3	.455	282-278	20.1-19.9	395-480	1450-1967	3.7-4.1	9-15	387-365	192-207	49.6-56.7	2936- 2422	7.6- 6.6	24-13	19- 9
Den	5	8	1	.385	253-264	18.1-18.9	436-409	1802-1351	4.1-3.3	17- 7	403-379	183-191	45.4-50.4	23582- 810	5.9- 7.4	11-20	28-16

1970 NATIONAL FOOTBALL CONFERENCE

Team	W	L	T	PCT	OWN-OPP PTS-PTS	OWN-OPP PPG-PPG	OWN-OPP ATT-ATT	OWN-OPP YARD-YARD	OWN-OPP AVG-AVG	ON-OP TD-TD	OWN-OPP ATT-ATT	OWN-OPP COM-COM	OWN-OPP PCT-PCT	OWN-OPP YARD-YARD	OWN-OPP AVG-AVG	ON-OP TD-TD	ON-OP IN-IN
Eastern Division																	
Dal	10	4	0	.714	299-221	21.4-15.8	522-415	2300-1856	4.4-4.0	16-10	297-399	149-193	50.2-48.4	2445- 2226	8.2- 5.6	18-10	16-24
NYG	9	5	0	.643	301-270	21.5-19.3	465-419	1799-1692	3.9-4.0	11-11	403-364	230-186	57.1-51.1	2892- 2650	7.2- 7.3	19-19	12-17
StL	8	5	1	.615	325-228	23.2-16.3	429-472	1998-1762	4.7-3.7	18-10	390-382	178-183	45.6-47.9	2689- 2416	6.9- 6.3	16-16	19-21
Was	6	8	0	.429	297-314	21.2-22.4	444-468	2021-2068	4.6-4.4	11-19	342-374	203-205	59.4-54.8	2357- 2434	6.9- 6.5	23-14	10-15
Phi	3	10	1	.231	241-332	17.2-23.7	450-457	1539-2064	3.4-4.5	11-16	410-313	218-161	53.2-51.4	2651- 2176	6.5- 7.0	16-16	23-10
Central Division																	
Min	12	2	0	.857	335-143	23.9-10.2	508-398	1634-1365	3.2-3.4	16- 4	344-367	173-195	50.3-53.1	2378- 1798	6.9- 4.9	12- 6	15-28
Det*	10	4	0	.714	347-202	24.8-14.4	514-362	2127-1152	4.1-3.2	16- 7	394-371	167-194	56.8-52.3	2121- 2491	7.2- 6.7	19-14	12-28
ChiB	6	8	0	.429	256-261	18.3-18.6	353-459	1092-1471	3.1-3.2	3-11	422-394	210-233	49.8-59.1	2431- 2925	5.8- 7.4	21-18	22-17
GB	6	8	0	.429	196-293	14.0-20.9	453-453	1595-1829	3.5-4.0	8-14	351-369	177-177	50.4-48.0	2196- 2496	6.3- 6.8	11-13	24-20
Western Division																	
SF	10	3	1	.769	352-267	25.1-19.1	471-425	1580-1799	3.4-4.2	13-12	383-384	226-185	59.0-48.2	2990- 2434	7.8- 6.3	25-19	10-22
LARm	9	4	1	.692	325-202	23.2-14.4	430-395	1763-1359	4.1-3.4	12- 6	426-378	218-196	51.2-51.9	2658- 2615	6.2- 6.9	17-15	13-19
Atl	4	8	2	.333	206-261	14.7-18.6	431-479	1600-1722	3.7-3.6	4-14	342-348	197-191	57.6-54.9	2262- 2397	6.6- 6.9	18-11	21-19
NO	2	11	1	.154	172-347	12.3-24.8	371-469	1215-1891	3.3-4.0	4-15	415-430	213-238	51.3-55.3	2690- 3197	6.5- 7.4	11-19	22-22
League 182 games					7010	38.5	11432	48820	3.8	293	9796	5008	51.1	65904	6.7	427	510

*Wild Card qualifier for playoffs
AFC Divisional Playoffs: Bal 17, Cin 0; Oak 21, Mia 14
NFC Divisional Playoffs: Dal 5, Det 0; SF 17, Min 14
AFC Championship: Bal 27, Oak 17
NFC Championship: Dal 17, SF 10
Super Bowl V: Bal (AFC) 16, Dal (NFC) 13

LEADING RUSHERS AFC	ATT	YARD	AVG	Long	TD
Floyd Little, Den	209	901	4.3	80t	3
Larry Csonka, Mia	193	874	4.5	53	6
Hewritt Dixon, Oak	197	861	4.4	39t	1
Ed Podolak, KC	168	749	4.5	65t	3
Frenchy Fuqua, Pit	138	691	5.0	85t	7

LEADING RUSHERS NFC	ATT	YARD	AVG	Long	TD
Larry Brown, Was	237	1125	4.7	75t	5
Ron Johnson, NYG	263	1027	3.9	68t	8
MacArthur Lane, StL	206	977	4.7	75	11
Donny Anderson, GB	222	853	3.8	54	5
Duane Thomas, Dal	151	803	5.3	47t	5

LEADING PASSERS AFC	ATT	COM	YARD	TD	IN
Daryle Lamonica, Oak	356	179	2516	22	15
John Hadl, SD	327	162	2388	22	15
Len Dawson, KC	262	141	1876	13	14
Bob Griese, Mia	245	142	2019	12	17
Dennis Shaw, Buf	321	178	2507	10	20

LEADING PASSERS NFC	ATT	COM	YARD	TD	IN
John Brodie, SF	378	223	2941	24	10
Sonny Jurgensen, Was	337	202	2354	23	10
Fran Tarkenton, NYG	389	219	2777	19	12
Bob Berry, Atl	269	156	1806	16	13
Craig Morton, Dal	207	102	1819	15	7

LEADING RECEIVERS AFC	NO	YARD	AVG	Long	TD
Marlin Brisco, Buf	57	1036	18.2	48	8
Eddie Hinton, Bal	47	733	15.6	40	5
Al Denson, Den	47	646	13.7	42	2
Alvin Reed, Hou	47	604	12.9	34	2
Fred Biletnikoff, Oak	45	768	17.1	51	7

LEADING RECEIVERS NFC	NO	YARD	AVG	Long	TD
Dick Gordon, ChiB	71	1026	14.5	69t	13
Dan Abramowicz, NO	55	906	16.5	48	5
Gene Washington, SF	53	1100	20.8	79t	12
Jack Snow, LARm	51	859	16.8	71	7
Clifton McNeil, NYG	50	764	15.3	59	4
Lee Bougess, Phi	50	401	8.0	34	2

LEADING SCORERS AFC	TD	FG	PAT	PTS
Jan Stenerud, KC	0	30	26	116
Horst Muhlmann, Cin	0	25	33	106
Garo Yepremian, Mia	0	22	31	97
Jim O'Brien, Bal	0	19	36	93
Jim Turner, NYJ	0	19	28	85

LEADING SCORERS NFC	TD	FG	PAT	PTS
Fred Cox, Min	0	30	35	125
David Ray, LARm	0	29	34	121
Pete Gogolak, NYG	0	25	32	107
Bruce Gossett, SF	0	21	39	102
Errol Mann, Det	0	20	41	101

LEADING INTERCEPTOR	NO	YARD	AVG	Long	TD
Johnny Robinson, KC (AFC)	10	155	15.5	57	0
Dick LeBeau, Det (NFC)	9	96	10.7	43	0

LEADING PUNTER	NO	AVG	Long
Dave Lewis, Cin (AFC)	79	46.2	63
Julian Fagan, NO (NFC)	77	42.5	64

LEADING PUNT RETURNER	NO	YDS	AVG	Long	TD
Ed Podolak, KC (AFC)	23	311	13.5	60	0
Bruce Taylor, SF (NFC)	43	516	12.0	76	0

LEADING KICKOFF RETURNER	NO	YDS	AVG	Long	TD
Jim Duncan, Bal (AFC)	20	707	35.4	99t	1
Cecil Turner, ChiB (NFC)	23	752	32.7	96t	4

SUPERLATIVES AFC		
Rushing Avg.	5.0	Frenchy Fuqua, Pit
Receiving Avg.	22.9	Gary Garrison, SD
Completion Pct.	58.0	Bob Griese, Mia
Touchdowns	12	Gary Garrison, SD
Field Goals	30	Jan Stenerud, KC

SUPERLATIVES NFC		
Rushing Avg.	5.3	Duane Thomas, Dal
Receiving Avg.	21.2	John Gilliam, StL
Completion Pct.	59.9	Sonny Jurgensen, Was
Touchdowns	13	MacArthur Lane, StL
		Dick Gordon, ChiB
Field Goals	30	Fred Cox, Min

LONGEST AFC		
Run	85t	Frenchy Fuqua, Pit
Pass	87t	Terry Bradshaw to Dave Smith, Pit
	87t	Jerry Rhome to Charlie Joiner, Hou
Interception	86	Dick Anderson, Mia
Punt	73	Spike Jones, Hou
Punt Return	80t	Ron Gardin, Bal
Kickoff Return	99t	Jim Duncan, Bal
Field Goal	55	Jan Stenerud, KC

LONGEST NFC		
Run	76	Greg Landry, Det
Pass	89t	Don Horn to Carroll Dale, GB
		Craig Morton to Bob Hayes, Dal
Interception	76t	Doug Hart, GB
Punt	68	Bill Johnson, NYG
Punt Return	77t	Tom McCauley, Atl
Kickoff Return	101t	Dave Hampton, GB
Field Goal	63	Tom Dempsey, NO

1971 AMERICAN FOOTBALL CONFERENCE

					SCORING		RUSHING				PASSING						
Team	W	L	T	PCT	OWN-OPP PTS-PTS	OWN-OPP PPG-PPG	OWN-OPP ATT-ATT	OWN-OPP YARD-YARD	OWN-OPP AVG-AVG	ON-OP TD-TD	OWN-OPP ATT-ATT	OWN-OPP COM-COM	OWN-OPP PCT-PCT	OWN-OPP YARD-YARD	OWN-OPP AVG-AVG	ON-OP TD-TD	ON-OP IN-IN
Eastern Division																	
Mia	10	3	1	.769	315-174	22.5-12.4	486-403	2429-1661	5.0-4.1	11-10	293-363	156-206	53.2-56.7	2248- 2293	7.7- 6.3	20-10	10-17
Bal*	10	4	0	.714	313-140	22.4-10.0	512-352	2149-1113	4.2-3.2	23- 8	344-361	176-185	51.2-51.2	2152- 2027	6.3- 5.6	10- 9	21-28
NE	6	8	0	.429	238-325	17.0-23.2	419-481	1669-1918	4.0-4.0	7-14	330-350	159-170	48.2-48.6	2206- 2403	6.7- 6.9	19-16	16-15
NYJ	6	8	0	.429	212-299	15.1-21.4	485-472	1888-2302	3.9-4.9	12-18	278-342	119-163	42.8-47.7	1556- 2285	5.6- 6.7	15-17	16-13
Buf	1	13	0	.071	184-394	13.1-28.1	320-562	1337-2496	4.2-4.4	6-21	401-303	202-157	50.4-51.8	2410- 2333	6.0- 7.7	12-20	32-11
Central Division																	
Cle	9	5	0	.643	285-273	20.4-19.5	461-484	1558-2227	3.4-4.6	19-14	376-339	188-156	50.0-46.0	2521- 2170	6.7- 6.4	14-12	27-24
Pit	6	8	0	.429	246-292	17.6-20.9	416-440	1758-1482	4.2-3.4	10-13	414-408	214-235	51.7-57.6	2446- 3060	5.9- 7.5	15-16	26-17
Hou	4	9	1	.308	251-330	17.9-23.6	361-489	1106-1723	3.1-3.5	10-22	423-354	194-180	45.9-50.8	2643- 2416	6.2- 6.8	12-11	37-23
Cin	4	10	0	.286	284-265	20.3-18.9	462-489	2142-1778	4.6-4.0	14-11	365-335	214-157	58.6-46.9	2427- 2382	6.6- 7.1	15-19	11-27
Western Division																	
KC	10	3	1	.769	302-208	21.6-14.9	487-367	1843-1300	3.8-3.5	14- 9	337-418	183-209	54.3-50.0	2694- 2703	8.0- 6.5	15-11	13-27
Oak	8	4	2	.667	344-278	24.6-19.9	473-480	2130-1751	4.5-3.6	19-14	348-359	174-184	50.0-51.3	2363- 2609	6.8- 7.3	21-15	26-23
SD	6	8	0	.429	311-341	22.2-24.4	390-493	1604-2296	4.1-4.7	11-25	450-347	244-193	54.2-55.6	3305- 2439	7.3- 7.0	23-15	28-22
Den	4	9	1	.308	203-275	14.5-19.6	512-426	2093-1834	4.1-4.3	9-11	358-356	175-150	48.9-42.1	2243- 2420	6.3- 6.8	8-18	27-20

1971 NATIONAL FOOTBALL CONFERENCE

Team	W	L	T	PCT	OWN-OPP PTS-PTS	OWN-OPP PPG-PPG	OWN-OPP ATT-ATT	OWN-OPP YARD-YARD	OWN-OPP AVG-AVG	ON-OP TD-TD	OWN-OPP ATT-ATT	OWN-OPP COM-COM	OWN-OPP PCT-PCT	OWN-OPP YARD-YARD	OWN-OPP AVG-AVG	ON-OP TD-TD	ON-OP IN-IN
Eastern Division																	
Dal	11	3	0	.786	406-222	29.0-15.9	512-363	2249-1144	4.4-3.2	25- 8	361-421	206-209	57.1-49.6	3037- 2660	8.4- 6.3	22-15	14-26
Was*	9	4	1	.692	276-190	19.7-13.6	477-408	1757-1396	3.7-3.4	8- 7	334-411	182-191	54.5-46.5	2391- 2448	7.2- 6.0	13-11	15-29
Phi	6	7	1	.462	221-302	15.8-21.6	407-450	1248-1962	3.1-4.4	6-16	390-407	200-220	51.3-54.1	2552- 2971	6.5- 7.3	13-16	20-22
StL	4	9	1	.308	231-279	16.5-19.9	417-486	1530-1985	3.7-4.1	8-10	385-375	170-212	44.2-56.5	2656- 2546	6.9- 6.8	14-12	26-17
NYG	4	10	0	.286	228-362	16.3-25.9	394-449	1461-2059	3.7-4.6	11-12	462-333	268-173	58.0-52.0	3062- 2458	6.6- 7.4	14-25	25-15
Central Division																	
Min	11	3	0	.786	245-139	17.5- 9.9	484-447	1695-1600	3.5-3.6	14- 2	334-405	157-206	47.0-50.9	1910- 2022	5.7- 5.0	9-10	18-27
Det	7	6	1	.538	341-286	24.4-20.4	532-432	2376-1842	4.5-4.3	15-15	299-306	157-163	52.5-53.3	2453- 2163	8.2- 7.1	17-17	14-22
ChiB	6	8	0	.429	185-276	13.2-19.7	365-509	1434-2116	3.9-4.2	6-14	443-362	186-192	42.0-53.0	2294- 2607	5.4- 7.2	12-12	28-22
GB	4	8	2	.333	274-298	19.6-21.3	500-489	2229-1707	4.5-3.5	18- 7	254-353	121-186	47.6-52.7	1842- 2469	7.3- 7.0	12-21	24-16
Western Division																	
SF	9	5	0	.643	300-216	21.4-15.4	498-408	2129-1668	4.3-4.1	12- 4	391-341	209-152	53.5-44.8	2688- 2309	6.9- 6.8	18-17	24-14
LARm	8	5	1	.615	313-260	22.4-18.6	460-455	2139-1658	4.7-3.6	15-11	370-387	185-200	50.0-51.7	2304- 2693	6.2- 7.0	18-15	11-27
Atl	7	6	1	.538	274-277	19.6-19.8	494-500	1703-2149	3.4-4.3	12-19	285-343	167-164	58.6-47.8	2495- 1895	8.8- 5.5	16- 9	21-20
NO	4	8	2	.333	266-347	19.0-24.8	452-495	1711-2200	3.8-4.4	18-18	387-333	182-175	47.0-52.6	2355- 2472	6.1- 7.4	12-20	14-20
League 182 games					7048	38.7	11776	47367	4.0	168	9412	4788	50.9	63253	6.7	289	544

*Wild Card qualifier for playoffs
AFC Divisional playoff: Mia 27, KC 24 (OT); Bal 20, Cle 3
NFC Divisional Playoffs: Dal 20, Min 12; SF 24, Was 20
AFC Championship: Mia 21, Bal 0
NFC Championship: Dal 14, SF 3
Super Bowl VI: Dal (NFC) 24, Mia (AFC) 3

LEADING RUSHERS AFC	ATT	YARD	AVG	Long	TD
Floyd Little, Den	284	1133	4.0	40	6
Larry Csonka, Mia	195	1051	5.4	28	7
Marv Hubbard, Oak	181	867	4.8	20	5
Leroy Kelly, Cle	234	865	3.7	35	10
Carl Garrett, NE	181	784	4.3	38	1

LEADING RUSHERS NFC	ATT	YARD	AVG	Long	TD
John Brockington, GB	216	1105	5.1	52t	4
Steve Owens Det	246	1035	4.2	23	8
Willie Ellison, LARm	211	1000	4.7	80t	4
Larry Brown, Was	253	948	3.7	34	4
Ken Willard, SF	216	855	4.0	49	4

LEADING PASSERS AFC	ATT	COM	YARD	TD	IN
Bob Griese, Mia	263	145	2089	19	9
Len Dawson, KC	301	167	2504	15	13
Virgil Carter, Cin	222	138	1624	10	7
John Hadl, SD	431	233	3075	21	25
Bill Nelson, Cle	325	174	2319	13	23

LEADING PASSERS NFC	ATT	COM	YARD	TD	IN
Roger Staubach, Dal	211	126	1882	15	4
Greg Landry, Det	261	136	2237	16	13
Billy Kilmer, Was	306	166	2221	13	13
Bob Berry, Atl	226	136	2005	11	16
Roman Gabriel, LARm	352	180	2238	17	10

LEADING RECEIVERS AFC	NO	YARD	AVG	Long	TD
Fred Biletnikoff, Oak	61	929	15.2	49	9
Otis Taylor, KC	57	1110	19.5	82	7
Randy Vataha, NE	51	872	17.1	88t	9
Ron Shanklin, Pit	49	652	13.3	42	6
Frenchy Fuqua, Pit	49	427	8.7	40t	1

LEADING RECEIVERS NFC	NO	YARD	AVG	Long	TD
Bob Tucker, NYG	59	791	13.4	63t	4
Ted Kwalick, SF	52	664	12.8	42t	5
Harold Jackson, Phi	47	716	15.2	69t	3
Roy Jefferson, Was	47	701	14.9	70t	4
Gene Washington, SF	46	884	19.2	71t	4
George Farmer, ChiB	46	737	16.0	64	5

LEADING SCORERS AFC	TD	FG	PAT	PTS
Garo Yepremian, Mia	0	28	33	117
Jan Stenerud, KC	0	26	32	110
Jim O'Brien, Bal	0	20	35	95
Jim Turner, NYJ	0	25	18	93
Horst Muhlmann, Cin	0	20	31	91

LEADING SCORERS NFC	TD	FG	PAT	PTS
Curt Knight, Was	0	29	27	114
Errol Mann, Det	0	22	37	103
Bruce Gossett, SF	0	23	32	101
Fred Cox, Min	0	22	25	91
David Ray, LARm	0	18	37	91

LEADING INTERCEPTOR	NO	YARD	AVG	Long	TD
Ken Houston, Hou (AFC)	9	220	24.4	48t	4
Bill Bradley, Phi (NFC)	11	248	22.5	51	0

LEADING PUNTER	NO	AVG	Long
Dave Lewis, Cin (AFC)	72	44.8	56
Tom McNeill, Phi (NFC)	73	42.0	64

LEADING PUNT RETURNER	NO	YDS	AVG	Long	TD
Leroy Kelly, Cle (AFC)	30	292	9.7	74	0
Speedy Duncan, Was (NFC)	22	233	10.6	33	0

LEADING KICKOFF RETURNER	NO	YDS	AVG	Long	TD
Mercury Morris, Mia (AFC)	15	423	28.2	94t	1
Travis Williams, LARm (NFC)	25	743	29.7	105t	1

SUPERLATIVES AFC		
Rushing Avg.	5.4	Larry Csonka, Mia
Receiving Avg.	23.2	Paul Warfield, Mia
Completion Pct.	62.2	Virgil Carter, Cin
Touchdowns	12	Leroy Kelly, Cle
Field Goals	28	Garo Yepremian, Mia

SUPERLATIVES NFC		
Rushing Avg.	5.1	John Brockington, GB
Receiving Avg.	24.0	Bob Hayes, Dal
Completion Pct.	60.2	Bob Berry, Atl
Touchdowns	13	Duane Thomas, Dal
Field Goals	29	Curt Knight, Was

LONGEST AFC		
Run	86t	Essex Johnson, Cin
Pass	90t	Virgil Carter to Speedy Thomas, Cin
Interception	70t	John Rowser, Pit
Punt	76	David Lee, Bal
Punt Return	74	Leroy Kelly, Cle
Kickoff Return	94t	Mercury Morris, Mia
Field Goal	54	Jan Stenerud, KC

LONGEST NFC		
Run	80t	Willie Ellison, LARm
Pass	85t	Roger Staubach to Bob Hayes, Dal
Interception	89	Charlie West, Min
Punt	64	Julian Fagan, NO Tom McNeill, Phi
Punt Return	50	Bill Walik, Phi
Kickoff Return	105t	Travis Williams, LARm
Field Goal	54	Tom Dempsey, Phi

1972 AMERICAN FOOTBALL CONFERENCE

					SCORING		RUSHING				PASSING						
Team	W	L	T	PCT	OWN-OPP PTS-PTS	OWN-OPP PPG-PPG	OWN-OPP ATT-ATT	OWN-OPP YARD-YARD	OWN-OPP AVG-AVG	ON-OP TD-TD	OWN-OPP ATT-ATT	OWN-OPP COM-COM	OWN-OPP PCT-PCT	OWN-OPP YARD-YARD	OWN-OPP AVG-AVG	ON-OP TD-TD	ON-OP IN-IN
Eastern Division																	
Mia	14	0	0	1.000	385-171	27.5-12.2	613-389	2960-1548	4.8-4.0	26- 8	259-348	144-178	55.6-51.1	2235- 2029	8.6- 5.8	17-10	12-26
NYJ	7	7	0	.500	367-324	26.2-23.1	461-476	2010-2072	4.4-4.4	18-16	347-363	172-186	49.6-51.2	2930- 2888	8.4- 8.0	21-18	22-19
Bal	5	9	0	.429	235-252	16.8-18.0	462-515	1894-1989	4.1-3.9	10-15	381-313	203-178	53.3-56.9	2503- 2555	6.6- 8.2	15-15	12-23
Buf	4	9	1	.321	257-377	18.4-26.9	512-532	2132-2241	4.2-4.2	11-26	316-308	164-131	51.9-42.5	2012- 2148	6.4- 7.0	16-19	24-23
NE	3	11	0	.214	192-446	13.7-31.9	386-548	1532-2717	4.0-5.0	13-27	412-326	198-175	48.1-53.7	2579- 2634	6.3- 8.1	10-24	28-10
Central Division																	
Pit	11	3	0	.786	343-175	24.5-12.5	497-445	2520-1715	5.1-3.9	22- 6	324-411	156-206	48.1-50.1	1958- 2383	6.0- 5.8	12- 9	12-28
Cle*	10	4	0	.714	268-249	19.1-17.8	453-520	1793-2333	4.0-4.5	13-13	337-310	158-160	46.9-51.6	2135- 1994	6.3- 6.4	13-14	19-13
Cin	8	6	0	.571	299-229	21.4-16.4	491-406	1996-1815	4.1-4.5	16-11	384-350	219-167	57.0-47.7	2513- 2033	6.5- 5.8	10-11	11-20
Hou	1	13	0	.071	164-380	11.7-27.1	397-546	1518-2591	3.8-4.7	7-23	375-324	181-174	48.3-53.7	2045- 2315	5.5- 7.1	10-12	23- 6
Western Division																	
Oak	10	3	1	.750	365-248	26.1-17.7	521-469	2376-1764	4.6-3.8	20- 9	370-348	198-166	53.5-47.7	2599- 2363	7.0- 6.8	23-14	15-25
KC	8	6	0	.571	287-254	20.5-18.1	476-453	1915-1805	4.0-4.0	6-12	384-368	217-186	56.5-50.5	2335- 2483	6.1- 6.7	20-17	20-24
Den	5	9	0	.357	325-350	23.2-25.0	409-439	1838-1668	4.5-3.8	17-15	384-397	201-206	52.3-51.9	2900- 2540	7.6- 6.4	19-19	23-10
SD	4	9	1	.321	264-344	18.9-24.6	504-436	1995-1673	4.0-3.8	12-18	377-358	192-201	50.9-56.1	2516- 2441	6.7- 6.8	15-18	28-24

1972 NATIONAL FOOTBALL CONFERENCE

Team	W	L	T	PCT	OWN-OPP PTS-PTS	OWN-OPP PPG-PPG	OWN-OPP ATT-ATT	OWN-OPP YARD-YARD	OWN-OPP AVG-AVG	ON-OP TD-TD	OWN-OPP ATT-ATT	OWN-OPP COM-COM	OWN-OPP PCT-PCT	OWN-OPP YARD-YARD	OWN-OPP AVG-AVG	ON-OP TD-TD	ON-OP IN-IN
Eastern Division																	
Was	11	3	0	.786	336-218	24.0-15.6	513-427	2082-1733	4.1-4.1	17-12	284-367	159-186	56.0-50.7	2281- 2130	8.0- 5.8	21-10	15-17
Dal*	10	4	0	.714	319-240	22.8-17.1	499-428	2124-1515	4.3-3.5	17- 7	367-382	196-187	53.4-49.0	2580- 2508	7.0- 6.6	16-18	23-16
NYG	8	6	0	.571	331-247	23.6-17.6	524-402	2022-1855	3.9-4.6	16- 9	344-333	206-182	50.9-54.7	2537- 2571	7.4- 7.7	20-19	15-23
StL	4	9	1	.321	193-303	13.8-21.6	361-548	1229-2189	3.4-4.0	9-11	363-365	171-221	47.1-60.5	2259- 2733	6.2- 7.5	11-15	23-11
Phi	2	11	1	.179	145-352	10.4-25.1	398-544	1393-2266	3.5-4.2	2-22	375-318	184-175	49.1-55.0	2527- 2615	6.7- 8.2	10-20	20-19
Central Division																	
GB	10	4	0	.714	304-226	21.7-16.1	544-443	2127-1517	3.9-3.4	17-14	237-340	101-174	42.6-51.2	1536- 2209	6.5- 6.5	7- 7	9-17
Det	8	5	1	.607	339-290	24.2-20.7	473-491	2021-2204	4.3-4.5	20-14	305-312	155-171	50.8-54.8	2283- 2146	7.5- 6.9	19-18	18-12
Min	7	7	0	.500	301-252	21.5-18.0	472-454	1740-2002	3.7-4.4	11-13	385-331	218-169	56.6-51.1	2726- 1791	7.1- 5.4	19-13	13-26
ChiB	4	9	1	.321	225-275	16.1-19.6	536-476	2360-1751	4.4-3.7	15-11	205-342	78-180	38.0-52.6	1283- 2345	6.3- 6.9	9-16	13-21
Western Division																	
SF	8	5	1	.607	353-249	25.2-17.8	445-446	1616-1847	3.6-4.1	11-12	380-366	217-169	57.1-46.2	2888- 2582	7.6- 7.1	27-14	24-19
Atl	7	7	0	.500	269-274	19.2-19.6	500-504	2092-2063	4.2-4.1	16-16	296-301	157-137	53.0-45.5	2202- 1911	7.4- 6.3	13-13	15-18
LARm	6	7	1	.464	291-286	20.8-20.4	472-438	2209-1762	4.7-4.0	17- 9	371-363	184-181	49.6-49.9	2282- 2472	6.2- 6.8	13-20	22-16
NO	2	11	1	.179	215-361	15.4-25.8	337-482	1230-2089	3.6-4.3	5-15	449-367	230-213	51.2-58.0	2781- 2596	6.2- 7.1	18-21	21-14
League 182 games					7372	40.5	12256	50724	4.1	364	9011	4659	51.7	61425	6.8	404	480

*Wild Card qualifier for playoffs
AFC Divisional Playoffs: Pit 13, Oak 7; Mia 20, Cle 14
NFC Divisional Playoffs: Dal 30, SF 28; Was 16, GB 3
AFC Championship: Mia 21, Pit 17
NFC Championship: Was 26, Dal 3
Super Bowl VII: Mia (AFC) 14, Was (NFC) 7

LEADING RUSHERS AFC	ATT	YARD	AVG	Long	TD
O.J. Simpson, Buf	292	1251	4.3	94t	6
Larry Csonka, Mia	213	1117	5.2	45	6
Marv Hubbard, Oak	219	1100	5.0	39	4
Franco Harris, Pit	188	1055	5.6	75t	10
Mike Garrett, SD	272	1031	3.8	41t	6

LEADING RUSHERS NFC	ATT	YARD	AVG	Long	TD
Larry Brown, Was	285	1216	4.3	38t	8
Ron Johnson, NYG	298	1182	4.0	35t	9
Calvin Hill, Dal	245	1036	4.2	26	6
John Brockington, GB	274	1027	3.7	30t	8
Dave Hampton, Atl	230	995	4.3	56t	6

LEADING PASSERS AFC	ATT	COM	YARD	TD	IN
Earl Morrall, Mia	150	83	1360	11	7
Daryle Lamonica, Oak	281	149	1998	18	12
Charley Johnson, Den	238	132	1783	14	14
Johnny Unitas, Bal	157	88	1111	4	6
Ken Anderson, Cin	301	171	1918	7	7

LEADING PASSERS NFC	ATT	COM	YARD	TD	IN
Norm Snead, NYG	325	196	2307	17	12
Bob Berry, Atl	277	154	2158	13	12
Fran Tarkenton, Min	378	215	2651	18	13
Bill Kilmer, Was	225	120	1648	19	11
Steve Spurrier, SF	269	147	1983	18	16

LEADING RECEIVERS AFC	NO	YARD	AVG	Long	TD
Fred Biletnikoff, Oak	58	802	13.8	39t	7
Chris Taylor, KC	57	821	14.4	44	6
Chip Myers, Cin	57	792	13.9	42	3
J.D. Hill, Buf	52	754	14.5	58t	5
Gary Garrison, SD	52	744	14.3	52t	7

LEADING RECEIVERS NFC	NO	YARD	AVG	Long	TD
Harold Jackson, Phi	62	1048	16.9	77t	4
Bob Tucker, NYG	55	764	13.9	39	4
Art Malone, Atl	50	585	11.7	57t	2
Charley Taylor, Was	49	673	13.7	70t	7
John Gilliam, Min	47	1035	22.0	66t	7
Bob Newland, NO	47	579	12.3	42t	2

LEADING SCORERS AFC	TD	FG	PAT	PTS
Bobby Howfield, NYJ	0	27	40	121
Roy Gerela, Pit	0	28	35	119
Garo Yepremian, Mia	0	24	43	115
Horst Muhlmann, Cin	0	27	30	111
Jim Turner, Den	0	20	37	97

LEADING SCORERS NFC	TD	FG	PAT	PTS
Chester Marcol, GB	0	33	29	128
David Ray, LARm	0	24	31	103
Toni Fritsch, Dal	0	21	36	99
Errol Mann, Det	0	20	38	98
Fred Cox, Min	0	21	34	97
Pete Gogolak, NYG	0	21	34	97

LEADING INTERCEPTOR	NO	YARD	AVG	Long	TD
Mike Sensibaugh, KC (AFC)	8	65	8.1	35	0
Bill Bradley, Phi (NFC)	9	73	8.1	21	0

LEADING PUNTER	NO	AVG	Long
Jerrel Wilson, KC (AFC)	66	44.8	69
Dave Chapple, LARm (NFC)	53	44.2	70

LEADING PUNT RETURNER	NO	YDS	AVG	Long	TD
Chris Farasopoulos, NYJ (AFC)	17	179	10.5	65t	1
Ken Ellis, GB (NFC)	14	215	15.4	80t	1

LEADING KICKOFF RETURNER	NO	YDS	AVG	Long	TD
Bruce Laird, Bal (AFC)	29	843	29.1	73	0
Ron Smith, ChiB (NFC)	30	924	30.8	94t	1

SUPERLATIVES AFC

Rushing Avg.	5.6	Franco Harris, Pit
Receiving Avg.	21.4	Rich Caster, NYJ
Completion Pct.	57.4	Len Dawson, KC
Touchdowns	14	Emerson Boozer, NYJ
Field Goals	28	Roy Gerela, Pit

SUPERLATIVES NFC

Rushing Avg.	6.9	Bobby Douglass, ChiB
Receiving Avg.	22.0	John Gilliam, Min
Completion Pct.	60.3	Norm Snead, NYG
Touchdowns	14	Ron Johnson, NYG
Field Goals	33	Chester Marcol, GB

LONGEST AFC

Run	94t	O.J. Simpson, Buf
Pass	83t	Joe Namath to Eddie Bell, NYJ
Interception	82t	Phil Villapiano, Oak
Punt	72	Bobby Walden, Pit
Punt Return	66t	Tommy Casanova, Cin
Kickoff Return	94t	Randy Montgomery, Den
Field Goal	57	Don Cockroft, Cle

LONGEST NFC

Run	68	Larry Smith, LARm
Pass	98	Jim Hart to Bobby Moore, StL
Interception	88t	Rudy Redmond, Det
Punt	71	Julian Fagan, NO
Punt Return	85t	Jon Staggers, GB
Kickoff Return	98t	Vic Washington, SF
Field Goal	54	Toni Fritsch, Dal

1973 AMERICAN FOOTBALL CONFERENCE

					SCORING		RUSHING				PASSING						
Team	W	L	T	PCT	OWN-OPP PTS-PTS	OWN-OPP PPG-PPG	OWN-OPP ATT-ATT	OWN-OPP YARD-YARD	OWN-OPP AVG-AVG	ON-OP TD-TD	OWN-OPP ATT-ATT	OWN-OPP COM-COM	OWN-OPP PCT-PCT	OWN-OPP YARD-YARD	OWN-OPP AVG-AVG	ON-OP TD-TD	ON-OP IN-IN
Eastern Division																	
Mia	12	2	0	.857	343-150	24.5-10.7	507-511	2521-1991	5.0-3.9	16- 9	256-320	133-151	52.0-47.2	1675- 1604	6.5- 5.0	17- 5	12-21
Buf	9	5	0	.643	259-230	18.5-16.4	605-455	3088-1797	5.1-3.9	20-11	213-368	96-166	45.1-45.1	1236- 2394	5.8- 6.5	4-12	14-14
NE	5	9	0	.357	258-300	18.4-21.4	454-560	1612-2850	3.6-5.1	15-16	380-240	195-134	51.3-55.8	2581- 1600	6.8- 6.7	13-11	17-13
Bal	4	10	0	.286	226-341	16.1-24.4	536-491	2031-2089	3.8-4.3	9-15	300-331	137-199	45.7-60.1	1746- 2599	5.8- 7.9	14-16	25-15
NYJ	4	10	0	.286	240-306	17.1-21.9	453-538	1864-2228	4.1-4.1	7-12	373-296	181-150	48.5-50.7	2353- 2148	6.3- 7.3	16-18	22-19
Central Division																	
Cin	10	4	0	.714	286-231	20.4-16.5	515-459	2236-1807	4.3-3.9	13-15	332-338	180-182	54.2-53.8	2439- 2240	7.3- 6.6	18- 9	12-18
Pit*	10	4	0	.714	347-210	24.8-15.0	555-488	2143-1652	3.9-3.4	12- 8	309-359	140-164	45.3-45.7	2157- 1923	7.0- 5.4	20-11	26-37
Cle	7	5	2	.571	234-255	16.7-18.2	506-513	1968-2091	3.9-4.1	12- 7	308-312	152-144	49.4-46.2	1741- 1984	5.7- 6.4	10-16	20-12
Hou	1	13	0	.071	199-447	14.2-31.9	386-576	1388-2410	3.6-4.2	9-19	411-326	225-178	54.7-54.6	2370- 2466	5.8- 7.6	11-26	27-17
Western Division																	
Oak	9	4	1	.679	292-175	20.9-12.5	547-435	2510-1470	4.6-3.4	14- 5	353-370	205-170	58.1-45.9	2611- 1995	7.4- 5.4	16-12	18-17
Den	7	5	2	.571	354-296	25.3-21.1	487-455	1954-1795	4.0-3.9	16-14	378-387	196-202	51.9-52.2	2708- 2766	7.2- 7.1	22-15	20-14
KC	7	5	2	.571	231-192	16.5-13.7	511-493	1793-1956	3.5-4.0	11-11	313-324	173-157	55.3-48.5	2039- 1942	6.5- 6.0	10-11	13-21
SD	2	11	1	.179	188-386	13.4-27.6	431-559	1814-2264	4.2-4.1	9-23	363-341	161-177	44.4-51.9	2129- 2473	5.9- 7.3	9-18	30-16

1973 NATIONAL FOOTBALL CONFERENCE

Team	W	L	T	PCT	OWN-OPP PTS-PTS	OWN-OPP PPG-PPG	OWN-OPP ATT-ATT	OWN-OPP YARD-YARD	OWN-OPP AVG-AVG	ON-OP TD-TD	OWN-OPP ATT-ATT	OWN-OPP COM-COM	OWN-OPP PCT-PCT	OWN-OPP YARD-YARD	OWN-OPP AVG-AVG	ON-OP TD-TD	ON-OP IN-IN
Eastern Division																	
Dal	10	4	0	.714	382-203	27.3-14.5	542-435	2418-1471	4.5-3.4	17- 5	321-352	192-187	59.8-53.1	2602- 2301	8.1- 6.5	26-15	16-18
Was*	10	4	0	.714	325-198	23.2-14.1	459-480	1439-1603	3.1-3.3	9- 8	372-406	209-203	56.2-50.0	2560- 2531	6.9- 6.2	20-12	14-26
Phi	5	8	1	.393	310-393	22.1-28.1	417-513	1791-2423	4.3-4.7	9-22	479-370	275-219	57.4-59.2	3236- 2789	6.8- 7.5	23-22	13-15
StL	4	9	1	.321	286-365	20.4-26.1	416-504	1671-2120	4.0-4.2	13-16	394-417	210-252	53.3-60.4	2592- 3226	6.6- 7.7	16-23	15-10
NYG	2	11	1	.179	226-362	16.1-25.9	456-497	1478-2174	3.2-4.4	11-21	412-275	230-161	55.8-58.5	2762- 2252	6.7- 8.2	14-17	30-20
Central Division																	
Min	12	2	0	.857	296-168	21.1-12.0	538-450	2275-1974	4.2-4.4	14- 5	298-377	179-198	60.1-52.5	2234- 2124	7.5- 5.6	16- 8	9-21
Det	6	7	1	.464	271-247	19.4-17.6	496-501	2133-2117	4.3-4.2	17-10	325-332	171-173	52.6-52.1	2105- 2058	6.4- 6.2	12-15	19-22
GB	5	7	2	.429	202-259	14.4-18.5	527-506	1973-1999	3.7-4.0	10-13	255-327	119-180	46.7-56.0	1503- 2050	5.9- 6.3	7-14	17-15
ChiB	3	11	0	.214	195-334	13.9-23.9	496-563	1907-2509	3.8-4.5	11-19	303-303	136-156	44.9-51.5	1617- 1978	5.3- 6.5	8-17	16-14
Western Division																	
LARm	12	2	0	.857	388-178	27.7-12.7	659-368	2925-1270	4.4-3.5	18- 5	271-328	144-179	53.1-54.6	2107- 2023	7.8- 6.2	22-10	11-20
Atl	9	5	0	.643	318-224	22.7-16.0	518-520	2037-2129	3.9-4.1	18-12	320-324	168-151	52.5-46.6	2362- 1619	7.4- 5.0	14-11	12-22
NO	5	9	0	.357	163-312	11.6-22.3	497-556	1842-2402	3.7-4.3	5-17	338-337	163-176	48.2-52.2	1901- 2333	5.6- 6.9	11-15	17-16
SF	5	9	0	.357	262-319	18.7-22.8	422-513	1743-1963	4.1-3.8	15-11	466-383	233-194	50.0-50.7	2645- 2591	5.7- 6.8	9-19	25-17
League 182 games					7081	38.9	12936	52544	4.1	330	8845	4603	52.0	58009	6.6	378	470

*Wild Card qualifier for playoffs
AFC Divisional Playoffs: Oak 33, Pit 14; Mia 34, Cin 16
NFC Divisional Playoffs: Min 27, Was 20; Dal 27, LARm 16
AFC Championship: Mia 27, Oak 10
NFC Championship: Min 27, Dal 10
Super Bowl VIII: Mia (AFC) 24, Min (NFC) 7

LEADING RUSHERS AFC	ATT	YARD	AVG	Long	TD
O.J. Simpson, Buf	332	2003	6.0	80t	12
Larry Csonka, Mia	219	1003	4.6	25	5
Essex Johnson, Cin	195	997	5.1	46	4
Boobie Clark, Cin	254	988	3.9	26	8
Floyd Little, Den	256	979	3.8	47	12

LEADING RUSHERS NFC	ATT	YARD	AVG	Long	TD
John Brockington, GB	265	1144	4.3	53	3
Calvin Hill, Dal	273	1142	4.2	21	6
Lawrence McCutcheon, LARm	210	1097	5.2	37	2
Dave Hampton, Atl	263	997	3.8	25	4
Tom Sullivan, Phi	217	968	4.5	37	4

LEADING PASSERS AFC	ATT	COM	YARD	TD	IN
Ken Stabler, Oak	260	163	1997	14	10
Bob Griese, Mia	218	116	1422	17	8
Ken Anderson, Cin	329	179	2428	18	12
Charley Johnson, Den	346	184	2465	20	17
Al Woodall, NYJ	201	101	1228	9	8

LEADING PASSERS NFC	ATT	COM	YARD	TD	IN
Roger Staubach, Dal	286	179	2428	23	15
Fran Tarkenton, Min	274	169	2113	15	7
John Hadl, LARm	258	135	2008	22	11
Roman Gabriel, Phi	460	270	3219	23	12
Bill Kilmer, Was	227	122	1656	14	9

LEADING RECEIVERS AFC	NO	YARD	AVG	Long	TD
Fred Willis, Hou	57	371	6.5	50	1
Ed Podolak, KC	55	445	8.1	25	0
Reggie Rucker, NE	53	743	14.0	64	3
Fred Biletnikoff, Oak	48	660	13.8	32	4
Isaac Curtis, Cin	45	843	18.7	77t	9
Mike Siani, Oak	45	742	16.5	80t	3
Boobie Clark, Cin	45	347	7.7	39	0

LEADING RECEIVERS NFC	NO	YARD	AVG	Long	TD
Harold Carmichael, Phi	67	1116	16.7	73	9
Charley Taylor, Was	59	801	13.6	53	7
Charle Young, Phi	55	854	15.5	80t	6
Bob Tucker, NYG	50	681	13.6	33	5
Tom Sullivan, Phi	50	322	6.4	29	1

LEADING SCORERS AFC	TD	FG	PAT	PTS
Roy Gerela, Pit	0	29	36	123
Garo Yepremian, Mia	0	25	38	113
Jim Turner, Den	0	22	40	106
George Blanda, Oak	0	23	31	100
Horst Muhlmann, Cin	0	21	31	94

LEADING SCORERS NFC	TD	FG	PAT	PTS
David Ray, LARm	0	30	40	130
Nick Mike-Mayer, Atl	0	26	34	112
Tom Dempsey, Phi	0	24	34	106
Bruce Gossett, SF	0	26	26	104
Curt Knight, Was	0	22	37	103

LEADING INTERCEPTOR	NO	YARD	AVG	Long	TD
Dick Anderson, Mia (AFC)	8	163	20.4	38t	2
Mike Wagner, Pit (AFC)	8	134	16.8	38	0
Bobby Bryant, Min (NFC)	7	105	15.0	46t	1

LEADING PUNTER	NO	AVG	Long
Jerrel Wilson, KC (AFC)	80	45.5	68
Tom Wittum, SF (NFC)	79	43.7	62

LEADING PUNT RETURNER	NO	YDS	AVG	Long	TD
Ron Smith, SD (AFC)	27	352	13.0	84t	2
Bruce Taylor, SF (NFC)	15	207	13.8	61	0

LEADING KICKOFF RETURNER	NO	YDS	AVG	Long	TD
Wallace Francis, Buf (AFC)	23	687	29.9	101t	2
Carl Garrett, ChiB (NFC)	16	486	30.4	67	0

SUPERLATIVES AFC

Rushing Avg.	6.4	Mercury Morris, Mia
Receiving Avg.	18.7	Isaac Curtis, Cin
Completion Pct.	62.7	Ken Stabler, Oak
Touchdowns	13	Floyd Little, Den
Gield Goals	29	Roy Gerela, Pit

SUPERLATIVES NFC

Rushing Avg.	5.2	Lawrence McCutcheon, LARm
Receiving Avg.	21.9	Harold Jackson, LARm
Completion Pct.	62.6	Roger Staubach, Dal
Touchdowns	14	Larry Brown, Was
Field Goals	30	David Ray, LARm

LONGEST AFC

Run	80t	O.J. Simpson, Buf
Pass	80t	Ken Stabler to Mike Siani, Oak
Interception	87	Joe Blahak, Hou
Punt	78	Bill Van Heusen, Den
Punt Return	84t	Ron Smith, SD
Kickoff Return	103t	Bob Gresham, Hou
Field Goal	53	Garo Yepremian, Mia

LONGEST NFC

Run	63	Tom Wittum, SF
Pass	84t	Greg Landry to Ron Jessie, Det
Interception	95t	Dick Jauron, Det
Punt	72	John James, Atl
Punt Return	72	Ike Hill, ChiB
Kickoff Return	97t	Herb Mul-Key, Was
		Don Shy, StL
Field Goal	54	Bruce Gossett, SF

1974 AMERICAN FOOTBALL CONFERENCE

					SCORING		RUSHING				PASSING						
Team	W	L	T	PCT	OWN-OPP PTS-PTS	OWN-OPP PPG-PPG	OWN-OPP ATT-ATT	OWN - OPP YARD-YARD	OWN-OPP AVG-AVG	ON-OP TD-TD	OWN-OPP ATT-ATT	OWN-OPP COM-COM	OWN-OPP PCT-PCT	OWN - OPP YARD - YARD	OWN-OPP AVG-AVG	ON-OP TD-TD	ON-OP IN-IN
Eastern Division																	
Mia	11	3	0	.786	327-216	23.4-15.4	570-404	2191-1624	3.8-4.0	25- 7	283-372	171-200	60.4-53.8	2313- 2452	8.2- 6.6	18-14	18-16
Buf*	9	5	0	.643	264-244	18.9-17.4	545-489	2094-1878	3.8-3.8	11-19	251-311	128-146	51.0-46.9	1728- 1898	6.9- 6.1	14-11	15-20
NE	7	7	0	.500	348-289	24.9-20.6	520-467	2134-1587	4.1-3.4	21-16	359-374	177-210	49.3-56.1	2514- 2774	7.0- 7.4	19-17	23-24
NYJ	7	7	0	.500	279-300	19.9-21.4	444-539	1625-2240	3.7-4.2	12-20	369-347	194-186	52.6-53.6	2631- 2249	7.1- 6.5	20-14	24-17
Bal	2	12	0	.143	190-329	13.6-23.5	450-516	1818-1961	4.0-3.8	13-20	425-312	221-180	52.0-57.7	2424- 2348	5.7- 7.5	9-16	24-10
Central Division																	
Pit	10	3	1	.750	305-189	21.8-13.5	546-472	2417-1608	4.4-3.4	19- 7	386-339	166-147	43.0-43.4	2154- 1872	5.6- 5.5	12-14	21-25
Cin	7	7	0	.500	283-259	20.2-18.5	445-497	1978-2152	4.4-4.3	14-16	353-359	224-186	63.5-51.8	2804- 2110	7.9- 5.9	18-13	13- 9
Hou	7	7	0	.500	236-282	16.9-20.1	421-474	1361-2050	3.2-4.3	16-15	363-405	203-231	55.9-57.0	2275- 2724	6.3- 6.7	12-19	19-21
Cle	4	10	0	.286	251-344	17.9-24.6	461-555	1924-2415	4.2-4.4	14-17	367-308	179-139	48.8-45.1	2129- 2259	5.8- 7.3	12-22	24-24
Western Division																	
Oak	12	2	0	.857	355-228	25.4-16.3	561-459	2334-2108	4.2-4.6	15-12	335-367	186-175	55.5-47.7	2561- 2425	7.6- 6.6	28-12	18-27
Den	7	6	1	.536	302-294	21.6-21.0	486-487	2157-1808	4.4-3.7	20-17	329-426	184-237	55.9-55.6	2660- 2805	8.1- 6.6	18-14	17-22
KC	5	9	0	.357	233-293	16.6-20.9	469-502	1720-1801	3.7-3.6	10-16	395-408	211-206	53.4-50.5	2421- 2838	6.1- 7.0	11-22	25-28
SD	5	9	0	.357	212-285	15.1-20.4	508-508	2111-2160	4.2-4.3	15-21	349-367	165-222	47.3-60.5	2479- 2815	7.1- 7.7	12-13	22-15

1974 NATIONAL FOOTBALL CONFERENCE

Team	W	L	T	PCT	OWN-OPP PTS-PTS	OWN-OPP PPG-PPG	OWN-OPP ATT-ATT	OWN - OPP YARD-YARD	OWN-OPP AVG-AVG	ON-OP TD-TD	OWN-OPP ATT-ATT	OWN-OPP COM-COM	OWN-OPP PCT-PCT	OWN - OPP YARD - YARD	OWN-OPP AVG-AVG	ON-OP TD-TD	ON-OP IN-IN
Eastern Division																	
StL	10	4	0	.714	285-218	20.4-15.6	466-461	1956-1888	3.3-4.1	12-15	391-413	201-230	51.4-55.7	2492- 2581	6.4- 6.2	20-11	8-16
Was*	10	4	0	.714	320-196	22.9-14.0	470-414	1443-1439	3.1-3.5	11- 7	413-399	254-197	61.5-49.4	2978- 2102	7.2- 5.3	22-13	11-25
Dal	8	6	0	.571	297-235	21.2-16.8	542-417	2454-1344	4.5-3.2	22- 8	385-349	206-178	53.5-51.0	2856- 2451	7.4- 7.0	14-17	15-13
Phi	7	7	0	.500	242-217	17.3-15.5	415-460	1385-1797	3.3-3.9	13-14	461-434	258-230	56.0-53.0	2531- 2684	5.5- 6.2	14- 9	17-18
NYG	2	12	0	.143	195-299	13.9-21.4	441-521	1496-1916	3.4-3.7	11-15	393-415	207-245	52.7-59.0	2349- 2688	6.0- 6.5	12-22	26-15
Central Division																	
Min	10	4	0	.714	310-195	22.1-13.9	488-437	1856-1605	3.8-3.7	17-12	400-396	234-214	58.5-54.0	2909- 2569	7.3- 6.5	22- 8	13-22
Det	7	7	0	.500	256-270	18.3-19.3	397-486	1433-2102	3.6-4.3	13-17	377-405	216-219	57.3-54.1	2475- 2423	6.6- 6.0	11-13	11-17
GB	6	8	0	.429	210-206	15.0-14.7	482-465	1571-1641	3.3-3.5	10-10	385-383	187-188	48.6-49.1	2162- 2254	5.6- 5.9	5-10	21-23
ChiB	4	10	0	.286	152-279	10.9-19.9	434-519	1480-1739	3.4-3.4	10-17	396-329	185-174	46.7-52.9	2079- 2250	5.3- 6.8	8-12	22-18
Western Division																	
LARm	10	4	0	.714	263-181	18.8-12.9	566-381	2125-1302	3.8-3.4	16- 4	338-381	169-194	50.0-50.9	2368- 2465	7.0- 6.7	16-16	13-22
SF	6	8	0	.429	226-236	16.1-16.9	477-503	1981-2033	4.2-4.0	10-13	361-339	170-178	47.1-52.5	2281- 2178	6.3- 6.5	15-14	28-20
NO	5	9	0	.357	166-263	11.9-18.8	503-447	1983-1758	3.9-3.9	9-11	389-369	185-193	47.6-52.3	2037- 2330	5.2- 6.3	10-17	21-16
Atl	3	11	0	.214	111-271	7.9-19.4	400-627	1493-2564	3.7-4.1	6-19	356-302	160-136	44.9-45.0	1781- 1847	5.0- 6.1	4-13	31-17
League 182 games					6618	36.4	12507	48520	3.9	365	9609	5041	52.5	62391	6.5	376	500

*Wild Card qualifier for playoffs
AFC Divisional Playoffs: Oak 28, Mia 26; Pit 32, Buf 14
NFC Divisional Playoffs: Min 30, StL 14; LARm 19, Was 10
AFC Championship: Pit 24, Oak 13
NFC Championship: Min 14, LARm 10
Super Bowl IX: Pit (AFC) 16, Min (NFC) 6

LEADING RUSHERS AFC	ATT	YARD	AVG	Long	TD
Otis Armstrong, Den	263	1407	5.3	43	9
Don Woods, SD	227	1162	5.1	56t	7
O.J. Simpson, Buf	270	1125	4.2	41t	3
Franco Harris, Pit	208	1006	4.8	54	5
Marv Hubbard, Oak	188	865	4.6	32	4

LEADING RUSHERS NFC	ATT	YARD	AVG	Long	TD
Lawrence McCutcheon, LARm	236	1109	4.7	23t	3
John Brockington, GB	266	883	3.3	33	5
Calvin Hill, Dal	185	844	4.6	27	7
Chuck Foreman, Min	199	777	3.9	32	9
Tom Sullivan, Phi	244	760	3.1	28t	11

LEADING PASSERS AFC	ATT	COM	YARD	TD	IN
Ken Anderson, Cin	328	213	2667	18	10
Ken Stabler, Oak	310	178	2469	26	12
Charley Johnson, Den	244	136	1969	13	9
Bob Griese, Mia	253	152	1968	16	15
Dan Pastorini, Hou	247	140	1571	10	10

LEADING PASSERS NFC	ATT	COM	YARD	TD	IN
Sonny Jurgensen, Was	167	107	1185	11	5
James Harris, LARm	198	106	1544	11	6
Billy Kilmer, Was	234	137	1632	10	6
Fran Tarkenton, Min	351	199	2598	17	12
Jim Hart, StL	388	200	2411	20	8

LEADING RECEIVERS AFC	NO	YARD	AVG	Long	TD
Lydell Mitchell, Bal	72	544	7.6	24	2
Cliff Branch, Oak	60	1092	18.2	67t	13
Ed Podolak, KC	43	306	7.1	26	1
Riley Odoms, Den	42	639	15.2	41	6
Fred Biletnikoff, Oak	42	593	14.1	46	7

LEADING RECEIVERS NFC	NO	YARD	AVG	Long	TD
Charle Young, Phi	63	696	11.0	29	3
Drew Pearson, Dal	62	1087	17.5	50t	2
Harold Carmichael, Phi	56	649	11.6	39	8
Ron Jessie, Det	54	761	14.1	46	3
Charley Taylor, Was	54	738	13.7	51	5

LEADING SCORERS AFC	TD	FG	PAT	PTS
Roy Gerela, Pit	0	20	33	93
John Smith, NE	0	16	42	90
John Leypoldt, Buf	0	19	25	82
Cliff Branch, Oak	13	0	0	78
George Blanda, Oak	0	11	44	77

LEADING SCORERS NFC	TD	FG	PAT	PTS
Chester Marcol, GB	0	25	19	94
Errol Mann, Det	0	23	23	92
Chuck Foreman, Min	15	0	0	90
Mark Moseley, Was	0	18	27	81
Tom Sullivan, Phi	12	0	0	72

LEADING INTERCEPTOR	NO	YARD	AVG	Long	TD
Emmitt Thomas, KC (AFC)	12	214	17.8	73t	2
Ray Brown, Atl (NFC)	8	164	20.5	59t	1

LEADING PUNTER	NO	AVG	Long
Ray Guy, Oak (AFC)	74	42.2	66
Tom Blanchard, NO (NFC)	88	42.1	71

LEADING PUNT RETURNER	NO	YDS	AVG	Long	TD
Lemar Parrish, Cin (AFC)	18	338	18.8	90t	2
Dick Jauron, Det (NFC)	17	286	16.8	58	0

LEADING KICKOFF RETURNER	NO	YDS	AVG	Long	TD
Greg Pruitt, Cle (AFC)	22	606	27.5	88t	1
Terry Metcalf, StL (NFC)	20	623	31.2	94t	1

SUPERLATIVES AFC

Rushing Avg.	5.3	Otis Armstrong, Den
Receiving Avg.	21.1	Isaac Curtis, Cin
Completion Pct.	64.9	Ken Anderson, Cin
Touchdowns	13	Cliff Branch, Oak
Field Goals	20	Roy Gerela, Pit

SUPERLATIVES NFC

Rushing Avg.	4.7	Terry Metcalf, StL
Receiving Avg.	21.2	Gene Washington, SF
Completion Pct.	64.1	Sonny Jurgensen, Was
Touchdowns	15	Chuck Foreman, Min
Field Goals	25	Chester Marcol, GB

LONGEST AFC

Run	75t	Sam Cunningham, NO
Pass	89t	Joe Namath to Rich Caster, NYJ
Interception	73t	Emmitt Thomas, KC
Punt	69	David Beverly, Hou
Punt Return	90t	Lemar Parrish, Cin
Kickoff Return	88t	Greg Pruitt, Cle
Field Goal	50	Jan Stenerud, KC

LONGEST NFC

Run	75t	Terry Metcalf, StL
Pass	81	Gary Hammond to Jackie Smith, StL
Interception	59t	Ray Brown, Atl
Punt	71	Tom Blanchard, NO
Punt Return	98t	Dennis Morgan, Dal
Kickoff Return	102t	Larry Jones, Was
Field Goal	52	Chester Marcol, GB
		Bill McClard, NO

1975 AMERICAN FOOTBALL CONFERENCE

					SCORING		RUSHING				PASSING						
Team	W	L	T	PCT	OWN-OPP PTS-PTS	OWN-OPP PPG-PPG	OWN-OPP ATT-ATT	OWN-OPP YARD-YARD	OWN-OPP AVG-AVG	ON-OP TD-TD	OWN-OPP ATT-ATT	OWN-OPP COM-COM	OWN-OPP PCT-PCT	OWN-OPP YARD-YARD	OWN-OPP AVG-AVG	ON-OP TD-TD	ON-OP IN-IN
Eastern Division																	
Bal	10	4	0	.714	395-269	28.2-19.2	536-453	2217-1821	4.1-4.0	28-17	354-393	211-193	59.6-49.1	2606-2317	7.4-5.9	19-17	8-29
Mia	10	4	0	.714	357-222	25.5-15.9	594-443	2500-1768	4.2-4.0	26-14	279-375	170-200	60.9-53.3	2196-2335	7.8-6.2	19-9	17-21
Buf	8	6	0	.571	420-355	30.0-25.4	588-480	2974-1993	5.1-4.2	26-21	354-431	182-237	51.4-55.0	2661-3355	7.5-7.6	28-25	19-25
NE	3	11	0	.214	258-358	18.4-25.6	472-555	1845-2220	3.9-4.0	14-20	401-368	193-213	48.1-57.9	2768-2515	6.9-6.8	16-18	28-13
NYJ	3	11	0	.214	258-433	18.4-30.9	501-574	2079-2737	4.1-4.8	15-25	384-316	174-180	45.3-57.0	2468-2860	6.4-9.1	16-26	33-15
Central Division																	
Pit	12	2	0	.857	373-162	26.6-11.6	581-431	2633-1825	4.5-4.2	22-8	337-396	191-183	56.7-46.2	2544-2194	6.7-5.5	21-9	12-27
Cin*	11	3	0	.786	340-246	24.3-17.6	499-473	1819-2194	3.6-4.6	20-15	433-389	255-175	58.9-45.0	3497-2001	8.1-5.1	23-11	14-22
Hou	10	4	0	.714	293-226	20.9-16.1	526-498	2068-1680	3.9-3.4	14-13	347-409	165-235	47.6-57.5	2099-2800	6.0-6.9	14-14	17-24
Cle	3	11	0	.214	218-372	15.6-26.6	440-544	1850-2032	4.2-3.7	14-21	437-361	220-202	49.2-56.0	2297-2889	5.3-8.0	7-25	23-10
Western Division																	
Oak	11	3	0	.786	375-255	26.8-18.2	643-475	2573-1785	4.0-3.8	28-15	350-398	196-171	56.0-43.0	2625-2318	7.5-5.8	19-14	28-35
Den	6	8	0	.429	254-307	18.1-21.9	490-526	1993-1974	4.1-3.8	9-19	427-348	210-181	49.2-52.0	2900-2245	7.0-6.5	15-14	34-16
KC	5	9	0	.357	282-341	20.1-24.4	487-562	1847-2724	3.8-4.0	14-24	395-325	217-186	54.9-57.2	2785-2703	7.1-8.3	15-18	16-20
SD	2	12	0	.143	189-345	13.5-24.6	434-606	1801-2442	4.1-4.0	14-21	337-390	165-237	49.0-60.8	1998-2719	5.9-7.0	7-16	17-20

1975 NATIONAL FOOTBALL CONFERENCE

Team	W	L	T	PCT	OWN-OPP PTS-PTS	OWN-OPP PPG-PPG	OWN-OPP ATT-ATT	OWN-OPP YARD-YARD	OWN-OPP AVG-AVG	ON-OP TD-TD	OWN-OPP ATT-ATT	OWN-OPP COM-COM	OWN-OPP PCT-PCT	OWN-OPP YARD-YARD	OWN-OPP AVG-AVG	ON-OP TD-TD	ON-OP IN-IN
Eastern Division																	
StL	11	3	0	.786	356-276	25.4-19.7	555-487	2402-1925	4.3-4.0	19-16	355-446	187-233	52.7-52.2	2619-2862	7.4-6.4	20-16	20-22
Dal*	10	4	0	.714	350-268	25.0-19.1	571-474	2432-1699	4.3-3.6	17-13	376-373	207-162	55.1-43.4	2835-2328	7.5-6.2	19-19	17-25
Was	8	6	0	.571	325-276	23.2-19.7	444-525	1752-2047	3.9-3.9	9-11	448-389	229-217	51.1-55.8	3092-2714	6.9-7.0	28-17	29-18
NYG	5	9	0	.357	216-306	15.4-21.9	482-555	1627-2422	3.4-4.4	17-16	379-365	193-196	50.9-53.7	2457-2539	6.5-6.6	11-20	18-16
Phi	4	10	0	.286	225-302	16.1-21.6	461-529	1702-2233	3.7-4.2	3-20	394-369	238-226	52.0-53.3	2640-2658	5.8-6.3	19-13	23-26
Central Division																	
Min	12	2	0	.857	377-180	26.9-12.9	556-383	2094-1532	3.8-4.0	18-7	446-360	281-175	63.0-48.6	3121-1994	7.0-5.5	27-14	14-28
Det	7	7	0	.500	245-262	17.5-18.7	532-480	2147-1929	4.0-4.0	10-12	362-360	183-181	50.6-50.3	2240-2377	6.2-6.6	15-16	12-20
ChiB	4	10	0	.286	191-379	13.6-27.1	441-547	1653-2070	3.7-3.8	11-25	356-399	191-208	53.7-52.1	2169-2825	6.1-7.1	9-22	23-13
GB	4	10	0	.286	226-285	16.1-20.4	431-580	1547-2339	3.6-4.0	14-14	394-369	212-192	53.8-52.0	2400-2474	6.1-6.7	11-13	22-14
Western Division																	
LARm	12	2	0	.857	312-135	22.3-9.6	585-423	2371-1533	4.1-3.6	18-4	334-387	181-187	54.2-48.3	2450-2126	7.3-5.5	14-11	17-22
SF	5	9	0	.357	255-286	18.2-20.4	422-518	1598-1829	3.8-3.5	12-14	450-411	234-228	52.0-55.5	2806-2521	6.2-6.1	15-15	19-11
Atl	4	10	0	.286	240-289	17.1-20.6	465-571	1794-2277	3.9-4.0	12-13	388-437	165-227	42.5-51.9	2361-2810	6.1-6.4	18-16	29-25
NO	2	12	0	.143	165-360	11.8-25.7	463-507	1642-1930	3.5-3.8	9-15	392-354	181-206	46.2-58.2	1961-2587	5.0-7.3	8-25	24-16
League 182 games					7495	41.2	13199	52960	4.0	413	9973	5231	52.5	66595	6.7	433	533

*Wild Card qualifier for playoffs
AFC Divisional Playoffs: Pit 28, Bal 10; Oak 31, Cin 28
NFC Divisional playoffs: LARm 35, StL 23; Dal 17, Min 14
AFC Championship: Pit 16, Oak 10
NFC Championship: Dal 37, LARm 7
Super Bowl X: Pit (AFC) 21, Dal (NFC) 17

LEADING RUSHERS AFC	ATT	YARD	AVG	Long	TD
O.J. Simpson, Buff	329	1817	5.5	88t	16
Franco Harris, Pit	262	1246	4.8	36	10
Lydell Mitchell, Bal	289	1193	4.1	70t	11
Greg Pruitt, Cle	217	1067	4.9	50	8
John Riggins, NYJ	238	1005	4.2	42	8

LEADING RUSHERS NFC	ATT	YARD	AVG	Long	TD
Jim Otis, StL	269	1076	4.0	30	5
Chuck Foreman, Min	280	1070	3.8	31t	13
Dave Hampton, Atl	250	1002	4.0	22	5
Robert Newhouse, Dal	209	930	4.4	29	2
Mike Thomas, Was	235	919	3.9	34	4

LEADING PASSERS AFC	ATT	COM	YARD	TD	IN
Ken Anderson, Cin	377	228	3169	21	11
Len Dawson, KC	140	93	1095	5	4
Bert Jones, Bal	344	203	2483	18	8
Terry Bradshaw, Pit	286	165	2055	18	9
Bob Griese, Mia	191	118	1693	14	13

LEADING PASSERS NFC	ATT	COM	YARD	TD	IN
Fran Tarkenton, Min	425	273	2994	25	13
Roger Staubach, Dal	348	198	2666	17	16
Billy Kilmer, Was	346	178	2440	23	16
James Harris, LARm	285	157	2148	14	15
Norm Snead, SF	189	108	1337	9	10

LEADING RECEIVERS AFC	NO	YARD	AVG	Long	TD
Reggie Rucker, Cle	60	770	12.8	40t	3
Lydell Mitchell, Bal	60	544	9.1	35t	4
Bob Chandler, Buf	55	746	13.6	35	6
Ken Burrough, Hou	53	1063	20.1	77t	8
Cliff Branch, Oak	51	893	17.5	53	9

LEADING RECEIVERS NFC	NO	YARD	AVG	Long	TD
Chuck Foreman, Min	73	691	9.5	33	9
Ken Payne, GB	58	766	13.2	54	0
Ed Marinaro, Min	54	462	8.6	25	3
Charley Taylor, Was	53	744	14.0	64	6
John Gilliam, Min	50	777	15.5	46	7

LEADING SCORERS AFC	TD	FG	PAT	PTS
O.J. Simpson, Buf	23	0	0	138
Pete Banaszak, Oak	16	0	0	96
Jan Stenerud, KC	0	22	30	96
Roy Gerela, Pit	0	17	44	95
Lydell Mitchell, Bal	15	0	0	90

LEADING SCORERS NFC	TD	FG	PAT	PTS
Chuck Foreman, Min	22	0	0	132
Toni Fritsch, Dal	0	22	38	104
Jim Bakken, StL	0	19	40	97
Tom Dempsey, LARm	0	21	31	94
Fred Cox, Min	0	13	46	85
Mark Moseley, Was	0	16	37	85

LEADING INTERCEPTOR	NO	YARD	AVG	Long	TD
Mel Blount, Pit (AFC)	11	121	11.0	47	0
Paul Krause, Min (NFC)	10	201	20.1	81	0

LEADING PUNTER	NO	AVG	Long
Ray Guy, Oak (AFC)	68	43.8	64
Herman Weaver, Det (NFC)	80	42.0	61

LEADING PUNT RETURNER	NO	YDS	AVG	Long	TD
Billy Johnson, Hou (AFC)	40	612	15.3	83t	3
Terry Metcalf, StL (NFC)	23	285	12.4	69t	1

LEADING KICKOFF RETURNER	NO	YDS	AVG	Long	TD
Harold Hart, Oak (AFC)	17	518	30.5	102t	1
Walter Payton, ChiB (NFC)	14	444	31.7	70	0

SUPERLATIVES AFC

Rushing Avg.	5.5	O.J. Simpson, Buf
Receiving Avg.	21.2	Isaac Curtis, Cin
Completion Pct.	66.4	Len Dawson, KC
Touchdowns	23	O.J. Simpson, Buf
Field Goals	22	Jan Stenerud, KC

SUPERLATIVES NFC

Rushing Avg.	5.4	Delvin Williams, SF
Receiving Avg.	20.2	Alfred Jenkins, Atl
Completion Pct.	64.2	Fran Tarkenton, Min
Touchdowns	22	Chuck Foreman, Min
Field Goals	22	Toni Fritsch, Dal

LONGEST AFC

Run	88t	O.J. Simpson, Buf
Pass	91	Joe Namath to Rich Caster, NYJ
Interception	74	Zeke Moore, Hou
Punt	74	Marv Bateman, Buf
Punt Return	83t	Billy Johnson, Hou
Kickoff Return	102t	Harold Hart, Oak
Field Goal	53	Jim Turner, Den

LONGEST NFC

Run	57t	Jerry Latin, StL
Pass	96t	Billy Kilmer to Frank Grant, Was
Interception	89t	Frank LeMaster, Phi
Punt	75	John James, Atl
Punt Return	69t	Terry Metcalf, StL
Kickoff Return	97t	Thomas Henderson, Dal
Field Goal	55	Bob Thomas, ChiB

1976 AMERICAN FOOTBALL CONFERENCE

					SCORING		RUSHING				PASSING						
Team	W	L	T	PCT	OWN-OPP PTS-PTS	OWN-OPP PPG-PPG	OWN-OPP ATT-ATT	OWN-OPP YARD-YARD	OWN-OPP AVG-AVG	ON-OP TD-TD	OWN-OPP ATT-ATT	OWN-OPP COM-COM	OWN-OPP PCT-PCT	OWN-OPP YARD-YARD	OWN-OPP AVG-AVG	ON-OP TD-TD	ON-OP IN-IN
Eastern Division																	
Bal	11	3	0	.786	417-246	29.8-17.6	565-438	2303-1844	4.1-4.2	26-11	361-372	215-192	59.6-51.6	3221- 2804	8.9- 7.5	24-16	10-15
NE*	11	3	0	.786	376-236	26.9-16.9	591-462	2948-1847	5.0-4.0	24-12	309-437	146-229	47.2-52.4	1910- 2604	8.2- 6.0	18-16	20-23
Mia	6	8	0	.429	263-264	18.8-18.9	491-525	2118-2411	4.3-4.6	15-14	346-347	193-195	55.8-56.2	2604- 2863	7.5- 8.3	15-20	15-11
NYJ	3	11	0	.214	169-383	12.1-27.4	438-582	1924-2592	4.4-4.5	10-14	393-374	180-204	45.8-54.5	1989- 2468	5.1- 6.6	7-25	20-11
Buf	2	12	0	.143	245-363	17.5-25.9	548-533	2566-2465	4.7-4.6	11-19	383-337	156-163	40.7-48.4	2084- 2475	5.4- 7.3	16-18	17-19
Central Division																	
Pit	10	4	0	.714	342-138	24.4- 9.9	653-452	2971-1467	4.5-3.2	33- 5	277-373	143-158	51.6-42.4	1935- 2179	7.0- 5.8	10- 9	12-22
Cin	10	4	0	.714	335-210	23.9-15.0	481-520	2109-1912	4.4-3.7	15-11	360-364	187-177	51.9-48.6	2443- 2202	6.8- 6.0	21-13	15-26
Cle	9	5	0	.643	267-287	19.1-20.5	533-445	2295-1761	4.3-4.0	9-15	373-392	209-225	56.0-57.4	2399- 2353	6.4- 6.0	21-18	15-21
Hou	5	9	0	.357	222-273	15.9-19.5	416-540	1498-2072	3.6-3.8	6-13	423-345	227-173	53.7-50.1	2429- 2259	5.7- 6.5	17-17	19-11
Western Division																	
Oak	13	1	0	.929	350-237	25.0-16.9	567-478	2285-1903	4.1-4.0	14-17	361-389	232-197	64.3-50.6	3195- 2848	8.9- 7.3	33-13	18-16
Den	9	5	0	.643	315-206	22.5-14.7	500-496	1932-1709	3.9-3.4	14-14	353-391	168-214	47.6-54.7	2510- 2265	7.1- 5.8	15- 8	22-24
SD	6	8	0	.429	248-285	17.7-20.4	473-516	2040-2048	4.3-4.0	13-10	388-386	223-219	57.5-56.7	2687- 2822	6.9- 7.3	17-21	18-20
KC	5	9	0	.357	290-376	20.7-26.9	498-565	1873-2861	3.8-5.2	18-24	419-375	229-215	54.7-57.3	3303- 2684	7.9- 7.2	15-25	17-23
TB	0	14	0	.000	125-412	8.9-29.4	433-588	1503-2560	3.5-4.4	5-23	376-321	181-178	48.1-55.5	1926- 2412	5.1- 7.5	9-19	20- 9
1976 NATIONAL FOOTBALL CONFERENCE																	
Eastern Division																	
Dal	11	3	0	.786	296-194	21.1-13.9	538-484	2147-1821	4.0-3.8	16-12	390-391	222-187	56.9-47.8	2967- 2236	7.6- 5.7	17-12	13-16
Was*	10	4	0	.714	291-217	20.8-15.5	548-555	2111-2205	3.9-4.0	10-12	370-354	187-146	50.5-41.2	2288- 2241	6.2- 6.3	20-11	20-26
StL	10	4	0	.714	309-267	22.1-19.1	580-491	2301-1979	4.0-4.0	17-19	392-342	220-176	56.1-51.5	2967- 2358	7.6- 6.9	18-13	13-19
Phi	4	10	0	.286	165-286	11.8-20.4	505-532	2080-2053	4.1-3.9	8-16	369-404	182-237	49.3-58.7	1844- 2688	5.0- 6.7	11-17	18- 9
NYG	3	11	0	.214	170-250	12.1-17.9	530-560	1904-2203	3.6-3.9	11-14	326-330	175-189	53.7-57.3	2104- 2230	6.5- 6.8	9-11	24-12
Central Division																	
Min	11	2	1	.821	305-176	21.8-12.6	540-487	2003-2096	3.7-4.3	18-14	442-323	270-158	61.1-48.9	3117- 1907	7.1- 5.9	17- 8	10-19
ChiB	7	7	0	.500	253-216	18.1-15.4	578-522	2363-1984	4.1-3.8	20-10	278-401	123-200	44.2-49.9	1705- 2612	6.1- 6.5	9-15	15-24
Det	6	8	0	.429	262-220	18.7-15.7	516-496	2213-1901	4.3-3.8	9-13	356-313	201-137	56.5-43.8	2630- 1904	7.4- 6.1	20-11	12-24
GB	5	9	0	.357	218-299	15.6-21.4	485-546	1722-2288	3.6-4.2	15-17	357-354	164-196	45.9-55.4	2105- 2192	5.9- 6.2	10-13	22-11
Western Division																	
LARm	10	3	1	.750	351-190	25.1-13.6	613-429	2528-1564	4.1-3.6	23-11	315-397	171-199	54.3-50.1	2629- 2487	8.3- 6.3	17-11	15-32
SF	8	6	0	.571	270-190	19.3-13.6	576-487	2447-1786	4.2-3.7	14-10	306-374	155-180	50.7-48.1	1963- 2349	6.4- 6.3	15-13	21- 9
Atl	4	10	0	.286	172-312	12.3-22.3	470-574	1689-2577	3.6-4.5	10-22	354-340	157-184	44.4-54.1	1809- 2276	5.1- 6.7	10-14	24-18
NO	4	10	0	.286	253-346	18.1-24.7	431-554	1775-2280	4.1-4.1	16-22	403-367	206-200	51.1-54.5	2353- 2514	5.8- 6.9	8-18	14-12
Sea	2	12	0	.000	229-429	16.4-30.6	374-614	1416-2876	3.8-4.7	14-20	480-367	229-223	47.7-60.8	2874- 2770	6.0- 7.5	13-27	30-15
League 196 games					7508	38.3	14461	59064	4.1	414	10260	5351	52.2	67990	6.6	432	497

*Wild Card qualifier for playoffs

AFC Divisional Playoffs: Oak 24, NE 21; Pit 40, Bal 14

NFC Divisional Playoffs: Min 35, Was 20; LARm 14, Dal 12

AFC Championship: Oak 24, Pit 7

NFC Championship: Min 24, LARm 13

Super Bowl XI: Oak (AFC) 32, Min (NFC) 14

LEADING RUSHERS AFC	ATT	YARD	AVG	Long	TD
O.J. Simpson, Buf	290	1503	5.2	75t	8
Lydell Mitchell, Bal	289	1200	4.2	43	5
Franco Harris, Pit	289	1128	3.9	30	14
Rocky Bleier, Pit	220	1036	4.7	28	5
Mark van Eeghen, Oak	233	1012	4.3	21	3

LEADING RUSHERS NFC	ATT	YARD	AVG	Long	TD
Walter Payton, ChiB	311	1390	4.5	60	13
Delvin Williams, SF	248	1203	4.9	80t	7
Lawrence McCutcheon, LARm	291	1168	4.0	40	9
Chuck Foreman, Min	278	1155	4.2	46	13
Mike Thomas, Was	254	1101	4.3	28	5

LEADING PASSERS AFC	ATT	COM	YARD	TD	IN
Ken Stabler, Oak	291	194	2737	27	17
Bert Jones, Bal	343	207	3104	24	9
Joe Ferguson, Buf	151	74	1086	9	1
Bob Griese, Mia	272	162	2097	11	12
Mike Livingston, KC	338	189	2682	12	13

LEADING PASSERS NFC	ATT	COM	YARD	TD	IN
James Harris, LARm	158	91	1460	8	6
Greg Landry, Det	291	168	2191	17	8
Fran Tarkenton, Min	412	255	2961	17	8
Jim Hart, StL	388	218	2946	18	13
Roger Staubach, Dal	369	208	2715	14	11

LEADING RECEIVERS AFC	NO	YARD	AVG	Long	TD
MacArthur Lane, KC	66	686	10.4	44	1
Bob Chandler, Buf	61	824	13.5	58t	10
Lydell Mitchell, Bal	60	555	9.3	40t	3
Dave Casper, Oak	53	691	13.0	30t	10
Ken Burrough, Hou	51	932	18.3	69t	7

LEADING RECEIVERS NFC	NO	YARD	AVG	Long	TD
Drew Pearson, Dal	58	806	13.9	40t	6
Chuck Foreman, Min	55	567	10.3	41t	1
Steve Largent, Sea	54	705	13.1	45	4
Tony Galbreath, NO	54	420	7.8	35	1
Ahmad Rashad, Min	53	671	12.7	47	3

LEADING SCORERS AFC	TD	FG	PAT	PTS
Toni Linhart, Bal	0	20	49	109
Jan Stenerud, KC	0	21	27	90
John Smith, NE	0	15	42	87
Franco Harris, Pit	14	0	0	84
Roy Gerela, Pit	0	14	40	82

LEADING SCORERS NFC	TD	FG	PAT	PTS
Mark Moseley, Was	0	22	31	97
Jim Bakken, StL	0	20	33	93
Fred Cox, Min	0	19	32	89
Efren Herrera, Dal	0	18	34	88
Tom Dempsey, LARm	0	17	36	87

LEADING INTERCEPTOR	NO	YARD	AVG	Long	TD
Ken Riley, Cin (AFC)	9	141	15.7	53t	1
Monte Jackson, LARm (NFC)	10	173	17.3	46t	3

LEADING PUNTER	NO	AVG	Long
Marv Bateman, Buf (AFC)	86	42.8	78
John James, Atl	(NFC)101	42.1	67

LEADING PUNT RETURNER	NO	YDS	AVG	Long	TD
Rick Upchurch, Den (AFC)	39	536	13.7	92t	4
Eddie Brown, Was (NFC)	48	646	13.5	71t	1

LEADING KICKOFF RETURNER	NO	YDS	AVG	Long	TD
Duriel Harris, Mia (AFC)	17	559	32.9	69	0
Cullen Bryant, LARm (NFC)	16	459	28.7	90t	1

SUPERLATIVES AFC		
Rushing Avg.	5.6	Don Calhoun, NE
Receiving Avg.	25.9	Roger Carr, Bal
Completion Pct.	66.7	Ken Stabler, Oak
Touchdowns	14	Franco Harris, Pit
Field Goals	21	Jan Stenerud, KC

SUPERLATIVES NFC		
Rushing Avg.	4.9	Delvin Williams, SF
Receiving Avg.	22.9	Ron Jessie, LARm
Completion Pct.	61.9	Fran Tarkenton, Min
Touchdowns	14	Chuck Foreman, Min
Field Goals	22	Mark Moseley, Was

LONGEST AFC		
Run	77t	Archie Griffin, Cin
Pass	88t	Ken Stabler to Cliff Branch, Oak
Interception	101t	Tony Greene, Buf
Punt	78	Marv Bateman, Buf
Punt Return	92t	Rick Upchurch, Den
Kickoff Return	97t	Willie Shelby, Cin
Field Goal	54	Skip Butler, Hou

LONGEST NFC		
Run	80t	Delvin Williams, SF
Pass	85t	Jim Plunkett to Delvin Williams, SF
Interception	83t	Jim Merlo, NO
Punt	69	Herman Weaver, Det
Punt Return	71t	Eddie Brown, Was
Kickoff Return	90t	Cullen Bryant, LARm
Field Goal	50	Joe Danelo, NYG
		Rich Szaro, NO

1977 AMERICAN FOOTBALL CONFERENCE

					SCORING		RUSHING				PASSING						
Team	W	L	T	PCT	OWN-OPP PTS-PTS	OWN-OPP PPG-PPG	OWN-OPP ATT-ATT	OWN-OPP YARD-YARD	OWN-OPP AVG-AVG	ON-OP TD-TD	OWN-OPP ATT-ATT	OWN-OPP COM-COM	OWN-OPP PCT-PCT	OWN-OPP YARD-YARD	OWN-OPP AVG-AVG	ON-OP TD-TD	ON-OP IN-IN
Eastern Division																	
Bal	10	4	0	.714	295-221	21.1-15.8	586-423	2123- 798	3.8-4.3	17-11	395-382	224-181	56.7-47.4	2686- 2549	6.8- 6.7	17-10	12-30
Mia	10	4	0	.714	313-197	22.4-14.1	519-467	2366-1749	4.6-3.7	18-12	311-414	182-226	58.5-54.6	2264- 2393	7.3- 5.8	22-10	14-15
NE	9	5	0	.643	278-217	19.9-15.5	603-452	2303-1605	3.8-3.6	13- 8	305-356	160-188	52.5-52.8	2162- 2504	7.1- 7.0	17-16	21-19
NYJ	3	11	0	.214	191-300	13.6-21.4	437-575	1618-2245	3.7-3.9	6-14	360-377	170-215	47.2-57.0	2286- 2587	6.4- 6.9	14-23	26-11
Buf	3	11	0	.214	160-313	11.4-22.4	450-589	1861-2405	4.1-4.1	3-21	458-316	221-155	48.3-49.1	2803- 2213	6.1- 7.0	12-17	24-21
Central Division																	
Pit	9	5	0	.643	283-243	20.2-17.4	581-493	2258-1723	3.9-3.5	20- 9	341-357	173-157	50.7-40.0	2632- 2254	7.7- 6.3	17-16	21-31
Hou	8	6	0	.571	299-230	21.4-16.4	509-522	1989-1815	3.9-3.5	15-11	347-379	181-192	52.2-50.7	2107- 2431	6.1- 6.4	14-12	21-26
Cin	8	6	0	.571	238-235	17.0-16.8	488-525	1861-1897	3.8-3.6	10-15	385-351	192-196	49.9-55.8	2550- 2453	6.6- 7.0	12-14	16-16
Cle	6	8	0	.429	269-267	19.2-19.1	510-524	2200-2098	4.3-4.0	9-14	377-340	208-184	55.2-54.1	2374- 2298	6.3- 6.8	19-15	31-23
Western Division																	
Den	12	2	0	.857	274-148	19.6-10.6	523-470	2043-1531	3.9-3.3	16- 5	313-426	163-235	52.1-55.2	2265- 2556	7.2- 6.0	15-11	12-25
Oak*	11	3	0	.786	351-230	25.1-16.4	681-408	2627-1754	3.9-4.3	20- 7	324-367	184-177	56.8-48.2	2338- 2503	7.2- 6.8	21-17	24-26
SD	7	7	0	.500	222-205	15.9-14.6	488-508	1761-1927	3.6-3.8	10-11	369-380	206-172	55.8-45.3	2442- 2088	6.6- 5.5	11-14	20-21
Sea	5	9	0	.357	282-373	20.1-26.6	461-596	1964-2485	4.3-4.2	12-21	387-349	175-199	45.2-57.0	2459- 2464	6.4- 7.1	23-19	32-25
KC	2	12	0	.143	225-349	16.1-24.9	456-632	1843-2971	4.0-4.7	13-23	374-333	190-175	50.8-52.7	2514- 2244	6.7- 6.7	11-15	26-21

1977 NATIONAL FOOTBALL CONFERENCE

Team	W	L	T	PCT	OWN-OPP PTS-PTS	OWN-OPP PPG-PPG	OWN-OPP ATT-ATT	OWN-OPP YARD-YARD	OWN-OPP AVG-AVG	ON-OP TD-TD	OWN-OPP ATT-ATT	OWN-OPP COM-COM	OWN-OPP PCT-PCT	OWN-OPP YARD-YARD	OWN-OPP AVG-AVG	ON-OP TD-TD	ON-OP IN-IN
Eastern Division																	
Dal	12	2	0	.857	345-212	24.6-15.1	564-457	2369-1651	4.2-3.6	21- 9	372-371	215-154	57.8-41.5	2689- 1991	7.2- 5.4	18-14	10-21
Was	9	5	0	.643	196-189	14.0-13.5	502-537	1752-2039	3.5-3.8	4- 8	383-380	183-167	47.8-43.9	2284- 2430	6.0- 6.4	15-12	16-21
StL	7	7	0	.500	272-287	19.4-20.5	507-513	2042-2235	4.0-4.4	19-11	366-376	195-198	53.3-52.7	2608- 2476	7.1- 6.6	14-22	21-19
Phi	5	9	0	.357	220-207	15.7-14.8	484-523	1722-1917	3.6-3.7	10-10	349-358	167-183	47.9-51.1	2198- 2192	6.3- 6.1	18-14	21-21
NYG	5	9	0	.357	181-265	12.9-18.9	548-519	1897-1777	3.5-3.4	11-16	311-328	134-185	43.1-56.4	1762- 2399	5.7- 7.3	6-12	22-12
Central Division																	
Min	9	5	0	.643	231-227	16.5-16.2	510-548	1821-2222	3.6-4.1	9-11	388-312	228-149	58.8-47.8	2692- 1835	6.9- 5.9	19-15	22-16
ChiB*	9	5	0	.643	255-253	18.2-18.1	599-541	2811-2157	4.7-4.0	18-14	305-377	161-182	52.8-48.3	2070- 2334	6.8- 6.2	11- 7	18-18
Det	6	8	0	.429	183-252	13.1-18.0	479-521	1706-1905	3.6-3.7	11-13	384-302	191-161	49.7-53.3	1959- 2123	5.1- 7.0	7-14	16-19
GB	4	10	0	.286	134-219	9.6-15.6	469-583	1464-2317	3.1-4.0	5-16	327-319	164-186	50.2-58.3	2013- 2042	6.2- 6.4	6-10	21-13
TB	2	12	0	.143	103-223	7.4-15.9	465-581	1424-2031	3.1-3.5	4-13	321-337	131-190	40.8-56.4	1714- 2141	5.3- 6.4	3-10	30-23
Western Division																	
LARm	10	4	0	.714	302-146	21.6-10.4	621-462	2575-1698	4.1-3.7	19- 7	339-370	182-180	53.7-48.6	2253- 2236	6.6- 6.0	16-11	11-25
Atl	7	7	0	.500	179-129	12.8- 9.2	582-504	1890-1858	3.2-3.7	9- 5	297-320	140-141	47.1-44.1	1740- 1775	5.9- 5.5	8- 9	16-26
SF	5	9	0	.357	220-260	15.7-18.6	564-551	2086-1869	3.7-3.4	16-16	277-270	136-139	49.1-51.5	1797- 1948	6.5- 7.2	9-14	17- 8
NO	3	11	0	.214	232-336	16.6-24.0	484-623	2024-2729	4.2-4.4	14-21	321-290	166-154	51.7-53.1	1933- 2127	6.0- 7.3	13-15	21-10
League 186 games					6733	36.2	14650	56400	3.8	352	9786	5022	51.3	63594	6.5	388	562

*Wild Card qualifier for playoffs
AFC Divisional Playoffs: Den 34, Pit 21; Oak 37, Bal 31 (OT)
Divisional Playoffs: Dal 37, ChiB 7; Min 14, LARm 7
AFC Championship: Den 20, Oak 17
NFC Championship: Dal 23, Min 6
Super Bowl XII: Dal (NFC) 27, Den (AFC) 10

LEADING RUSHERS AFC	ATT	YARD	AVG	Long	TD
Mark van Eeghen, Oak	324	1273	3.9	27	7
Franco Harris, Pit	300	1162	3.9	61t	11
Lydell Mitchell, Bal	301	1159	3.9	64t	3
Greg Pruitt, Cle	236	1086	4.6	78t	3
Sam Cunningham, NE	270	1015	3.8	31t	4

LEADING RUSHERS NFC	ATT	YARD	AVG	Long	TD
Walter Payton, ChiB	339	1852	5.5	73	14
Lawrence McCutcheon, LARm	294	1238	4.2	48	7
Chuck Foreman, Min	270	1112	4.1	51	6
Tony Dorsett, Dal	208	1007	4.8	84t	12
Delvin Williams, SF	268	931	3.5	40	7

LEADING PASSERS AFC	ATT	COM	YARD	TD	IN
Bob Griese, Mia	307	180	2252	22	13
Craig Morton, Den	254	131	1929	14	8
Bert Jones, Bal	393	224	2686	17	11
Ken Stabler, Oak	294	169	2176	20	20
Terry Bradshaw, Pit	314	162	2523	17	19

LEADING PASSERS	NFC	ATT	COM	YARD	TD
Roger Staubach, Dal	361	210	2620	18	9
Pat Haden, LARm	216	122	1551	11	6
Fran Tarkenton, Min	258	155	1734	9	14
Greg Landry, Det	240	135	1359	6	7
Archie Manning, NO	205	113	1284	8	9

LEADING RECEIVERS AFC	NO	YARD	AVG	Long	TD
Lydell Mitchell, Bal	71	620	8.7	38	4
Bob Chandler, Buf	60	745	12.4	31	4
Clark Gaines, NYJ	55	469	8.5	31	1
Nat Moore, Mia	52	765	14.7	73t	12
Don McCauley, Bal	51	495	9.7	34t	2

LEADING RECEIVERS NFC	NO	YARD	AVG	Long	TD
Ahmad Rashad, Min	51	681	13.4	48t	2
James Scott, ChiB	50	809	16.2	72t	3
Drew Pearson, Dal	48	870	18.1	67	2
Harold Jackson, LARm	48	666	13.9	58	6
Harold Carmichael, Phi	46	665	14.5	50t	7
Preston Pearson, Dal	46	535	11.6	36t	4

LEADING SCORERS AFC	TD	FG	PAT	PTS
Errol Mann, Oak	0	20	39	99
Toni Linhart, Bal	0	17	32	83
Chris Bahr, Cin	0	19	25	82
Don Cockroft, Cle	0	17	30	81
Nat Moore, Mia	13	0	0	78
John Smith, NE	0	15	33	78

LEADING SCORERS NFC	TD	FG	PAT	PTS
Walter Payton, ChiB	16	0	0	96
Efren Herrera, Dal	0	18	39	93
Rafael Septien, LARm	0	18	32	86
Mark Moseley, Was	0	21	19	82
Tony Dorsett, Dal	13	0	0	78

LEADING INTERCEPTOR	NO	YARD	AVG	Long	TD
Lyle Blackwood, Bal (AFC)	10	163	16.3	37	0
Rolland Lawrence, Atl (NFC)	7	138	19.7	36	0

LEADING PUNTER	NO	AVG	Long
Ray Guy, Oak (AFC)	59	43.3	74
Tom Blanchard, NO (NFC)	82	42.4	66

LEADING PUNT RETURNER	NO	YDS	AVG	Long	TD
Billy Johnson, Hou (AFC)	35	539	15.4	87t	2
Larry Marshall, Phi (NFC)	46	489	10.6	48	0

LEADING KICKOFF RETURNER	NO	YDS	AVG	Long	TD
Raymond Clayborn, NE (AFC)	28	869	31.0	101t	3
Wilbert Montgomery, Phi (NFC)	23	619	26.9	99t	1

SUPERLATIVES AFC

Rushing Avg.	4.8	Benny Malone, Mia
Receiving Avg.	21.1	Wesley Walker, NYJ
Completion Pct.	58.6	Bob Griese, Mia
Touchdowns	13	Nat Moore, Mia
Field Goals	20	Errol Mann, Oak

SUPERLATIVES NFC

Rushing Avg.	5.5	Walter Payton, ChiB
Receiving Avg.	20.6	Mel Gray, StL
Completion Pct.	60.1	Fran Tarkenton, Min
Touchdowns	16	Walter Payton, ChiB
Field Goals	21	Mark Moseley, Was

LONGEST AFC

Run	78t	Greg Pruitt, Cle
Pass	94t	Ken Anderson to Billy Brooks, Cin
Interception	102t	Gary Barbaro, KC
Punt	75	Marv Bateman, Buf
Punt Return	91t	Keith Moody, Buf
Kickoff Return	101t	Raymond Clayborn, NE
Field Goal	51	John Leypoldt, Sea

LONGEST NFC

Run	84t	Tony Dorsett, Dal
Pass	95t	Lynn Dickey to Steve Odom, GB
Interception	79t	Thomas Henderson, Dal
		Mike Sensibaugh, StL
Punt	70	Dave Green, TB
Punt Return	87t	Eddie Payton, Det
Kickoff Return	99t	Wilbert Montgomery, Phi
Field Goal	54	Mark Moseley, Was
		Rich Szaro, NO

1978 AMERICAN FOOTBALL CONFERENCE

					SCORING		RUSHING				PASSING						
Team	W	L	T	PCT	OWN-OPP PTS-PTS	OWN-OPP PPG-PPG	OWN-OPP ATT-ATT	OWN-OPP YARD-YARD	OWN-OPP AVG-AVG	ON-OP TD-TD	OWN-OPP ATT-ATT	OWN-OPP COM-COM	OWN-OPP PCT-PCT	OWN - OPP YARD - YARD	OWN-OPP AVG-AVG	ON-OP TD-TD	ON-OP IN-IN
Eastern Division																	
NE	11	5	0	.688	358-286	22.4-17.9	671-511	3165-1852	4.7-3.6	30-14	390-425	196-235	50.3-55.3	3006- 3059	6.8- 6.0	15-21	25-22
Mia*	11	5	0	.688	372-254	23.3-15.9	548-543	2366-2261	4.3-4.2	18-15	379-437	226-256	59.6-58.6	2707- 3251	6.1- 6.1	24-15	18-32
NYJ	8	8	0	.500	359-364	22.4-22.8	562-600	2250-2701	4.0-4.5	21-20	388-447	193-260	49.7-58.2	2957- 3052	6.1- 6.0	19-21	28-23
Buf	5	11	0	.313	302-354	18.9-22.1	556-677	2381-3228	4.3-4.8	15-23	388-317	203-167	52.3-52.7	2503- 2156	5.4- 5.8	21-20	17-14
Bal	5	11	0	.313	239-421	14.9-26.3	532-662	2044-3010	3.8-4.5	9-21	383-357	202-191	52.7-53.5	2543- 3125	4.8- 7.5	17-29	30-17
Central Division																	
Pit	14	2	0	.875	356-195	22.3-12.2	641-513	2297-1774	3.6-3.5	16-11	380-442	212-221	55.8-50.0	2961- 2755	6.7- 4.9	28-10	22-27
Hou*	10	6	0	.625	283-298	17.7-18.6	603-556	2476-2072	4.1-3.7	19-14	373-428	201-240	53.9-56.1	2473- 3125	6.0- 6.1	16-17	17-17
Cle	8	8	0	.500	334-356	20.9-22.3	559-563	2488-2149	4.5-3.8	17-19	442-489	236-265	53.4-54.2	3137- 3435	6.0- 6.2	22-20	21-27
Cin	4	12	0	.250	252-284	15.8-17.8	526-607	2131-2396	4.1-3.9	10-16	470-396	250-193	53.2-48.7	3039- 2520	5.4- 5.2	14-14	30-20
Western Division																	
Den	10	6	0	.625	282-198	17.6-12.4	601-549	2451-1979	4.1-3.6	15-12	391-438	217-246	55.5-56.2	2710- 2712	5.4- 5.3	17- 9	17-31
Oak	9	7	0	.563	311-283	19.4-17.7	577-583	2186-2183	3.8-3.7	18-15	433-448	251-234	58.0-52.2	3095- 2916	5.8- 5.7	16-17	31-28
Sea	9	7	0	.563	345-358	21.6-22.4	561-551	2394-2513	4.3-4.6	28-20	467-460	261-263	55.9-57.2	3401- 3225	6.1- 6.2	15-21	22-22
SD	9	7	0	.563	355-309	22.2-19.3	590-510	2096-2208	3.6-4.3	16-12	477-441	271-237	56.8-53.7	3566- 2825	6.6- 4.8	26-23	30-22
KC	4	12	0	.250	243-327	15.2-20.4	663-602	2986-2384	4.5-4.0	19-21	370-365	204-219	55.1-60.0	2032- 2820	4.7- 6.6	7-17	16-21

1978 NATIONAL FOOTBALL CONFERENCE

Team	W	L	T	PCT	OWN-OPP PTS-PTS	OWN-OPP PPG-PPG	OWN-OPP ATT-ATT	OWN-OPP YARD-YARD	OWN-OPP AVG-AVG	ON-OP TD-TD	OWN-OPP ATT-ATT	OWN-OPP COM-COM	OWN-OPP PCT-PCT	OWN - OPP YARD - YARD	OWN-OPP AVG-AVG	ON-OP TD-TD	ON-OP IN-IN
Eastern Division																	
Dal	12	4	0	.750	384-288	24.0-18.0	625-477	2783-1721	4.5-3.6	22-13	449-432	251-202	55.9-46.8	3405- 2730	6.6- 4.7	25-11	17-23
Phi*	9	7	0	.563	270-250	16.9-15.6	587-505	2456-1862	4.2-3.7	16-11	401-443	207-228	51.6-51.5	2485- 2986	5.0- 5.9	16-17	16-28
Was	8	8	0	.500	273-283	17.1-17.7	537-625	2082-2538	3.9-4.1	10-15	438-409	212-197	48.4-48.2	2978- 2701	5.3- 5.4	17-11	21-22
StL	6	10	0	.375	248-296	15.5-18.5	554-588	1954-2396	3.5-4.1	14-15	508-428	252-212	49.6-49.5	3357- 2641	6.0- 5.1	16-19	21-26
NYG	6	10	0	.375	264-298	16.5-18.6	580-640	2304-2656	4.0-4.2	12-25	382-443	176-210	46.1-47.4	2428- 2637	5.1- 5.1	13-10	27-21
Central Division																	
Min	8	7	1	.531	294-306	18.4-19.1	505-559	1536-2116	3.0-3.8	10-20	592-442	352-240	59.5-54.3	3528- 2917	5.2- 5.7	25-15	34-22
GB	8	7	1	.531	249-269	15.6-16.8	550-620	2023-2439	3.7-3.9	16-19	357-463	180-254	50.4-54.9	2358- 2910	5.3- 4.9	11-16	18-27

Det	7	9	0	.438	290-300	18.1-18.8	525-565	2163-2184	4.1 -3.9	12-18	429-350	247-191	57.6-54.6	2746- 2781	4.8- 5.7	19-19	18-22
ChiB	7	9	0	.438	253-274	15.8-17.1	634-568	2526-2174	4.0 -3.8	19-15	352-436	186-239	52.8-54.8	2221- 2857	5.0- 5.3	7-16	28-17
TB	5	11	0	.313	241-259	15.1-16.2	549-595	2098-2049	3.8 -3.4	16-12	361-419	151-241	41.8-57.5	2171- 2535	4.1- 5.0	12-13	18-29
Western Division																	
LARm	12	4	0	.750	316-245	19.8-15.3	609-505	2308-1845	3.8 -3.7	12-11	466-399	236-188	50.6-47.1	3109- 2449	5.8- 4.5	13-15	22-28
Atl*	9	7	0	.563	240-290	15.0-18.1	533-578	1660-2067	3.1 -3.6	13-21	449-444	221-215	49.2-48.4	2883- 2789	4.8- 4.8	11-11	23-12
NO	7	9	0	.438	281-298	17.6-18.6	512-579	1845-2420	3.6 -4.2	17- 9	479-418	294-215	61.4-51.4	3452- 2700	6.1- 5.5	17-21	16-21
SF	2	14	0	.125	219-350	13.7-21.9	585-649	2091-2365	3.6 -3.6	14-17	435-413	190-219	43.7-53.0	2306- 2948	4.1- 5.9	9-20	36-18
League 224 games					8213	36.7	16075	63540	4.0	454	11829	6278	53.1	79557	6.7	468	639

*Wild Card qualifier for playoffs
AFC Wild Card Game: Hou 17, Mia 9
NFC Wild Card game: Atl 14, Phi 13
AFC Divisional Playoffs: Pit 33, Den 10; Hou 31, NE 14
NFC Divisional Playoffs: Dal 27, Atl 20; LARm 34, Min 10
AFC Championship: Pit 34, Hou 5
NFC Championship: Dal 28, LARm 0
Super Bowl XIII: Pit (AFC) 35, Dal (NFC) 31

LEADING RUSHERS AFC	ATT	YARD	AVG	Long	TD
Earl Campbell, Hou	302	1450	4.8	81t	13
Delvin Williams, Mia	272	1258	4.6	58	8
Franco Harris, Pit	310	1082	3.5	37	8
Mark van Eeghen, Oak	270	1080	4.0	34	9
Terry Miller, Buf	238	1060	4.5	60t	7

LEADING RUSHERS NFC	ATT	YARD	AVG	Long	TD
Walter Payton, ChiB	333	1395	4.2	76	11
Tony Dorsett, Dal	290	1325	4.6	63	7
Wilbert Montgomery, Phi	259	1220	4.7	47	9
Terdell Middleton, GB	284	1116	3.9	76t	11
John Riggins, Was	248	1014	4.1	31	5

LEADING PASSERS AFC	ATT	COM	YARD	TD	IN
Terry Bradshaw, Pit	368	207	2915	28	20
Dan Fouts, SD	381	224	2999	24	20
Bob Griese, Mia	235	148	1791	11	11
Brian Sipe, Cle	399	222	2906	21	15
Craig Morton, Den	267	146	1802	11	8

LEADING PASSERS NFC	ATT	COM	YARD	TD	IN
Roger Staubach, Dal	413	231	3190	25	16
Archie Manning, NO	471	291	3416	17	16
Gary Danielson, Det	351	199	2294	18	17
Fran Tarkenton, Min	572	345	3468	25	32
Ron Jaworski, Phi	398	206	2487	16	16

LEADING RECEIVERS AFC	NO	YARD	AVG	Long	TD
Steve Largent, Sea	71	1168	16.5	57t	8
Dave Casper, Oak	62	852	13.7	44	9
Lynn Swann, Pit	61	880	14.4	62	11
Lydell Mitchell, SD	57	500	8.8	55t	2
John Jefferson, SD	56	1001	17.9	46t	13

LEADING RECEIVERS NFC	NO	YARD	AVG	Long	TD
Rickey Young, Min	88	704	8.0	48	5
Tony Galbreath, NO	74	582	7.9	35	2
Ahmad Rashad, Min	66	769	11.7	58t	8
Pat Tilley, StL	62	900	14.5	43	3
Chuck Foreman, Min	61	396	6.5	20	2

LEADING SCORERS AFC	TD	FG	PAT	PTS
Pat Leahy, NYJ	0	22	41	107
Garo Yepremian, Mia	0	19	41	98
Don Cockroft, Cle	0	19	37	94
Rolf Benirschke, SD	0	18	37	91
David Sims, Sea	15	0	0	90

LEADING SCORERS NFC	TD	FG	PAT	PTS
Frank Corral, LARm	0	29	31	118
Rafael Septien, Dal	0	16	46	94
Benny Ricardo, Det	0	20	32	92
Joe Danelo, NYG	0	21	27	90
Mark Moseley, Was	0	19	30	87

LEADING INTERCEPTOR	NO	YARD	AVG	Long	TD
Thom Darden, Cle (AFC)	10	200	20.0	46	0
Ken Stone, StL (NFC)	9	139	15.4	33	0
Willie Buchanon, GB (NFC)	9	93	10.3	77t	1

LEADING PUNTER	NO	AVG	Long
Pat McInally, Cin (AFC)	91	43.1	65
Tom Skladany, Det (NFC)	86	42.5	63

LEADING PUNT RETURNER	NO	YDS	AVG	Long	TD
Rick Upchurch, Den (AFC)	36	493	13.7	75t	1
Jackie Wallace, LARm (NFC)	52	618	11.9	58	0

LEADING KICKOFF RETURNER	NO	YDS	AVG	Long	TD
Keith Wright, Cle (AFC)	30	789	26.3	86	0
Steve Odom, GB (NFC)	25	677	27.1	95t	1

SUPERLATIVES AFC

Rushing Avg.	6.0	Ted McKnight, KC
Receiving Avg.	24.4	Wesley Walker, NYJ
Completion Pct.	63.0	Bob Griese, Mia
Touchdowns	15	David Sims, Sea
Field Goals	22	Pat Leahy, NYJ

SUPERLATIVES NFC

Rushing Avg.	4.7	Wilbert Montgomery, Phi
Receiving Avg.	20.0	Morris Owens, TB
Completion Pct.	61.8	Archie Manning, NO
Touchdowns	12	Terdell Middleton, GB
Field Goals	29	Frank Corral, LARm

LONGEST AFC

Run	81t	Earl Campbell, Hou
Pass	92t	Joe Ferguson to Frank Lewis, Buf
Interception	85t	Charles Romes, Buf
Punt	79	Chuck Ramsey, NYJ
Punt Return	82t	Bruce Harper, NYJ
		Keith Moody, Buf
Kickoff Return	102t	Curtis Brown, Buf
Field Goal	52	Chris Bahr, Cin

LONGEST NFC

Run	76t	Terdell Middleton, GB
	76	Walter Payton, ChiB
Pass	91t	Roger Staubach to Tony Dorsett, Dal
Interception	97t	Tommy Myers, NO
Punt	81	Mike Wood, StL
Punt Return	80t	Tony Green, Was
Kickoff Return	100t	Dennis Pearson, Atl
Field Goal	52	Mark Moseley, Was

1979 AMERICAN FOOTBALL CONFERENCE

					SCORING		RUSHING				PASSING						
Team	W	L	T	PCT	OWN-OPP PTS-PTS	OWN-OPP PPG-PPG	OWN-OPP ATT-ATT	OWN - OPP YARD-YARD	OWN-OPP AVG-AVG	ON-OP TD-TD	OWN-OPP ATT-ATT	OWN-OPP COM-COM	OWN-OPP PCT-PCT	OWN - OPP YARD - YARD	OWN-OPP AVG-AVG	ON-OP TD-TD	ON-OP IN-IN
Eastern Division																	
Mia	10	6	0	.625	341-257	21.3-16.1	561-484	2187-1702	3.9 -3.5	19- 9	416-418	235-230	56.5-55.0	3018- 3051	6.2- 6.0	20-17	22-23
NE	9	7	0	.563	411-326	25.7-20.4	604-495	2252-1770	3.7 -3.6	16-22	475-467	237-246	49.9-52.7	3600- 3065	6.1- 4.9	30-13	23-20
NYJ	8	8	0	.500	337-383	21.1-23.9	634-502	2646-1706	4.2 -3.4	23-13	369-570	190-339	51.5-59.5	2664- 4288	6.5- 7.0	16-31	25-21
Buf	7	9	0	.438	268-279	16.8-17.4	474-617	1621-2481	3.4 -4.0	11-18	465-382	241-193	51.8-50.5	3603- 2713	6.3- 6.3	14-14	15-24
Bal	5	11	0	.313	271-351	16.9-21.9	515-559	1674-2306	3.3 -4.1	12-15	550-411	313-203	56.9-49.4	3575- 3080	5.3- 6.2	18-23	19-23
Central Division																	
Pit	12	4	0	.750	416-262	26.0-16.4	561-506	2603-1709	4.6 -3.4	25- 9	492-480	272-226	55.3-47.1	3877- 2912	7.0- 4.8	26-19	26-27
Hou*	11	5	0	.688	362-331	22.6-20.7	616-522	2571-2225	4.2 -4.3	24-19	386-465	195-242	50.5-52.0	2494- 3186	5.4- 5.4	17-18	21-34
Cle	9	7	0	.563	359-352	22.4-22.0	504-577	2281-2604	4.5 -4.5	16-25	545-468	289-271	53.0-57.9	3838- 3289	5.9- 6.1	28-14	27-16
Cin	4	12	0	.250	337-421	21.1-26.3	560-528	2329-2219	4.2 -4.2	23-22	426-492	228-275	53.5-55.9	2821- 3908	4.7- 7.1	17-27	15-20
Western Division																	
SD	12	4	0	.750	411-246	25.7-15.4	481-475	1668-1907	3.5 -4.0	25-19	541-472	338-261	62.5-55.3	4138- 2881	6.8- 5.0	24-11	25-28
Den*	10	6	0	.625	289-262	18.1-16.4	525-502	2036-1693	3.9 -3.4	13-16	476-512	260-271	54.6-57.9	3433- 3321	6.0- 6.0	18-11	23-19
Sea	9	7	0	.563	378-372	23.6-23.3	500-533	1967-2375	3.9 -4.5	24-23	523-508	292-317	55.8-62.4	3791- 3739	6.6- 6.4	20-21	18-17
Oak	9	7	0	.563	365-337	22.8-21.1	491-534	1763-2374	3.5 -4.4	13-17	513-471	311-247	60.6-52.4	3704- 3366	6.2- 6.2	27-21	23-24
KC	7	9	0	.438	238-262	14.9-16.4	569-522	2316-1847	4.1 -3.5	18- 8	361-528	190-296	52.6-56.1	1953- 3404	4.1- 5.5	7-22	18-23

1979 NATIONAL FOOTBALL CONFERENCE

Team	W	L	T	PCT													
Eastern Division																	
Dal	11	5	0	.688	371-313	23.2-19.6	578-500	2375-2115	4.1-4.2	15-15	503-435	287-207	57.1-47.6	3883- 2833	6.6- 5.2	29-21	13-13
Phi*	11	5	0	.688	339-282	21.2-17.6	567-515	2421-2271	4.3-4.4	17-16	410-459	209-243	51.0-52.9	2882- 2798	5.9- 4.9	21-18	13-22
Was	10	6	0	.625	348-295	21.8-18.4	609-541	2328-2154	3.8-4.0	17-21	401-470	235-234	58.6-49.8	2839- 3339	5.9- 5.8	20-18	15-26
NYG	6	10	0	.375	237-323	14.8-20.2	498-618	1820-2452	3.7-4.0	12-14	401-463	190-253	47.4-54.6	2419- 3154	4.3- 5.9	15-22	22-21
StL	5	11	0	.313	307-358	19.2-22.4	566-567	2582-2204	4.6-3.9	24-18	492-478	248-258	50.4-54.0	2870- 3067	4.9- 5.7	12-22	24-18
Central Division																	
TB	10	6	0	.625	273-237	17.1-14.8	609-539	2437-1873	4.0-3.5	13-13	434-436	183-250	42.2-57.3	2700- 2405	5.9- 4.4	19-14	26-14
ChiB*	10	6	0	.625	306-249	19.1-15.6	627-519	2486-1978	4.0-3.8	17- 9	373-458	195-222	52.3-48.5	2429- 2908	5.3- 5.0	16-21	16-29
Min	7	9	0	.438	259-337	16.2-21.1	487-583	1764-2526	3.6-4.3	9-24	566-424	315-229	55.7-54.0	3397- 2965	5.2- 5.9	23-14	24-22
GB	5	11	0	.313	246-316	15.4-19.8	483-639	1861-2885	3.9-4.5	14-14	444-440	240-249	54.1-56.6	3057- 3041	5.5- 5.8	15-21	22-18
Det	2	14	0	.125	219-365	13.7-22.8	441-638	1677-2515	3.8-3.9	11-22	452-402	218-220	50.4-54.0	2775- 2787	4.6- 5.5	14-15	27-14
Western Division																	
LARm	9	7	0	.563	323-309	20.2-19.3	592-548	2460-1997	4.2-3.6	16-13	456-454	242-220	53.1-48.5	3032- 3007	5.4- 5.1	19-24	29-25
NO	8	8	0	.500	370-360	23.1-22.5	551-521	2476-2469	4.5-4.7	28-22	428-488	257-265	60.0-54.3	3291- 3457	7.1- 5.7	16-24	22-26
Atl	6	10	0	.375	300-388	18.8-24.3	500-555	2200-2163	4.4-3.9	15-29	479-487	251-268	52.4-55.0	3127- 3799	5.1- 7.0	19-17	23-15
SF	2	14	0	.125	308-416	19.3-26.0	480-544	1932-2213	4.0-4.1	17-24	602-441	361-262	60.0-59.4	3760- 3407	5.9- 6.8	18-25	21-15
League 224 games					8989	40.1	15183	60733	4.0	487	12979	7022	54.1	89170	6.9	538	597

*Wild Card qualifier for playoffs
AFC Wild Card Game: Hou 13, Den 7
NFC Wild Card game: Phi 27, ChiB 17
AFC Divisional Playoffs: Hou 17, SD 14; Pit 34, Mia 14
NFC Divisional Playoffs: TB 24, Phi 17; LARm 21, Dal 19
AFC Championship: Pit 27, Hou 13
NFC Championship: LARm 9, TB 0
Super Bowl XIV: Pit (AFC) 31, LARm (NFC) 19

LEADING RUSHERS AFC	ATT	YARD	AVG	Long	TD
Earl Campbell, Hou	368	1697	4.6	61t	19
Mike Pruitt, Cle	264	1294	4.9	77t	9
Franco Harris, Pit	267	1186	4.4	71t	11
Clark Gaines, NYJ	186	905	4.9	52	0
Joe Washington, Bal	242	884	3.7	26	4

LEADING RUSHERS NFC	ATT	YARD	AVG	Long	TD
Walter Payton, ChiB	369	1610	4.4	43t	14
Ottis Anderson, StL	331	1605	4.8	76t	8
Wilbert Montgomery, Phi	338	1512	4.5	62t	9
Ricky Bell, TB	283	1263	4.5	49	7
Chuck Muncie, NO	238	1198	5.0	69t	11

LEADING PASSERS AFC	ATT	COM	YARD	TD	IN
Dan Fouts, SD	530	332	4082	24	24
Ken Stabler, Oak	498	304	3615	26	22
Ken Anderson, Cin	339	189	2340	16	10
Jim Zorn, Sea	505	285	3661	20	18
Steve Grogan, NE	423	206	3286	28	20

LEADING PASSERS NFC	ATT	COM	YARD	TD	IN
Roger Staubach, Dal	461	267	3586	27	11
Joe Theismann, Was	395	233	2797	20	13
Ron Jaworski, Phi	374	190	2669	18	12
Archie Manning, NO	420	252	3169	15	20
Steve DeBerg, SF	578	347	3652	17	21

LEADING RECEIVERS AFC	NO	YARD	AVG	Long	TD
Joe Washington, Bal	82	750	9.1	43t	3
Charlie Joiner, SD	72	1008	14.0	39	4
John Stallworth, Pit	70	1183	16.9	65t	8
Steve Largent, Sea	66	1237	18.7	55t	9
Rick Upchurch, Den	64	937	14.6	47	7

LEADING RECEIVERS NFC	NO	YARD	AVG	Long	TD
Ahmad Rashad, Min	80	1156	14.5	52t	9
Wallace Francis, Atl	74	1013	13.7	42	8
Rickey Young, Min	72	519	7.2	18	4
Wes Chandler, NO	65	1069	16.4	85	6
Freddie Scott, Det	62	929	15.0	50	5

LEADING SCORERS AFC	TD	FG	PAT	PTS
John Smith, NE	0	23	46	115
Earl Campbell, Hou	19	0	0	114
Matt Bahr, Pit	0	18	50	104
Toni Fritsch, Hou	0	21	41	104
Efren Herrera, Sea	0	19	43	100

LEADING SCORERS NFC	TD	FG	PAT	PTS
Mark Moseley, Was	0	25	39	114
Tony Franklin, Phi	0	23	36	105
Rafael Septien, Dal	0	19	40	97
Walter Payton, ChiB	16	0	0	96
Ray Wersching, SF	0	20	32	92

LEADING INTERCEPTOR	NO	YARD	AVG	Long	TD
Mike Reinfeldt, Hou (AFC)	12	205	17.1	39	0
Lemar Parrish, Was (NFC)	9	65	7.2	23	0

LEADING PUNTER	NO	AVG	Long
Bob Grupp, KC (AFC)	89	43.6	74
Dave Jennings, NYG (NFC)	104	42.7	72

LEADING PUNT RETURNER	NO	YDS	AVG	Long	TD
Tony Nathan, Mia (AFC)	28	306	10.9	86t	1
John Sciarra, Phi (NFC)	16	182	11.4	38	0

LEADING KICKOFF RETURNER	NO	YDS	AVG	Long	TD
Larry Brunson, Oak	(AFC)	17	441	25.9	89
Jimmy Edwards, Min	(NFC)	44	1103	25.1	83

SUPERLATIVES AFC

Rushing Avg.	5.0	Sidney Thornton, Pit
Receiving Avg.	22.8	Stanley Morgan, NE
Completion Pct.	62.6	Dan Fouts, SD
Touchdowns	19	Earl Campbell, Hou
Field Goals	23	John Smith, NE

SUPERLATIVES NFC

Rushing Avg.	5.1	Wendell Tyler, LARm
Receiving Avg.	18.7	Drew Pearson, Dal
Completion Pct.	60.0	Steve DeBerg, SF
Touchdowns	16	Walter Payton, ChiB
Field Goals	25	Mark Moseley, Was

LONGEST AFC

Run	84t	Ted McKnight, KC
Pass	84t	Joe Ferguson to Curtis Brown, Buf
Interception	96t	Ray Griffin, Cin
Punt	74	Bob Grupp, KC
Punt Return	88t	J.T. Smith, KC
Kickoff Return	104t	Ira Matthews, Oak
Field Goal	55	Chris Bahr, Cin

LONGEST NFC

Run	80	Leroy Harris, Phi
Pass	85	Archie Manning to Wes Chandler, NO
Interception	78	Carl Allen, StL
Punt	74	Mike Bragg, Was
Punt Return	77t	Steve Schubert, ChiB
	77	Lee Nelson, StL
Kickoff Return	106t	Roy Green, StL
Field Goal	59	Tony Franklin, Phi

1980 AMERICAN FOOTBALL CONFERENCE

					SCORING		RUSHING				PASSING						
Team	W	L	T	PCT	OWN-OPP PTS-PTS	OWN-OPP PPG-PPG	OWN-OPP ATT-ATT	OWN-OPP YARD-YARD	OWN-OPP AVG-AVG	ON-OP TD-TD	OWN-OPP ATT-ATT	OWN-OPP COM-COM	OWN-OPP PCT-PCT	OWN - OPP YARD - YARD	OWN-OPP AVG-AVG	ON-OP TD-TD	ON-OP IN-IN
Eastern Division																	
Buf	11	5	0	.688	320-260	20.0-16.3	603-486	2222-1819	3.7-3.7	17-14	461-433	262-240	56.8-55.4	2936- 2561	5.7- 4.9	20-15	19-24
NE	10	6	0	.625	441-325	27.6-20.3	588-482	2240-1876	3.8-3.9	19-12	413-458	240-266	58.1-58.1	3395- 3232	7.3- 5.8	27-28	27-24
Mia	8	8	0	.500	266-305	16.6-19.1	492-530	1876-2018	3.8-3.8	9-13	492-505	267-290	54.3-57.4	2953- 3439	5.1- 6.0	21-21	26-28
Bal	7	9	0	.438	355-387	22.2-24.2	527-574	2078-2210	3.9-3.9	20-20	493-476	272-260	55.2-54.6	3409- 3576	5.9- 6.6	25-21	24-17
NYJ	4	12	0	.250	302-395	18.9-24.7	470-508	1873-1951	4.0-3.8	17-20	481-544	265-337	55.1-61.9	3335- 3899	5.8- 6.4	17-27	30-23
Central Division																	
Cle	11	5	0	.688	357-310	22.3-19.4	436-485	1673-1761	3.8-3.6	15-12	554-536	337-336	60.8-62.7	4132- 4089	6.8- 6.8	30-23	14-22
Hou*	11	5	0	.688	295-251	18.4-15.7	573-444	2635-1811	4.6-4.1	18- 8	463-454	296-246	63.9-54.2	3271- 3053	6.1- 5.7	15-16	28-26

Pit	9	7	0	.563	352-313	22.0-19.6	512-486	1986-1762	3.9-3.6	15- 9	484-532	250-280	51.7-52.6	3832- 3517	6.9- 6.1	26-25	24-26
Cin	6	10	0	.375	244-312	15.3-19.5	513-469	2069-1680	4.0-3.6	9-13	510-491	281-284	55.1-57.8	3102- 3426	5.2- 7.0	17-22	25-20
Western Division																	
SD	11	5	0	.688	418-327	26.1-20.4	509-478	1879-1842	3.7-3.9	18-18	594-519	350-300	58.9-57.8	4741- 3324	7.2- 4.9	30-18	26-20
Oak*	11	5	0	.688	364-306	22.8-19.1	541-501	2146-1726	4.0-3.4	14-19	456-524	235-296	51.5-56.5	3294- 3731	5.8- 5.7	23-17	24-35
KC	8	8	0	.500	319-336	19.9-21.0	552-536	1873-2206	3.4-4.1	15-17	401-523	237-278	59.1-53.2	2869- 3393	5.3- 5.6	15-25	14-28
Den	8	8	0	.500	310-323	19.4-20.2	480-554	1865-2120	3.9-3.8	16-10	467-448	262-270	56.1-60.3	3107- 3449	5.4- 6.4	14-20	25-16
Sea	4	12	0	.250	291-408	18.2-25.5	456-550	1783-2067	3.9-3.8	13-17	517-462	287-267	55.5-57.8	3494- 3280	5.5- 6.4	18-28	23-23

1980 NATIONAL FOOTBALL CONFERENCE

Eastern Division																	
Phi	12	4	0	.750	384-222	24.0-13.9	527-445	1995-1618	3.8-3.6	19- 8	477-543	275-265	57.7-48.8	3771- 3180	6.9- 4.8	28-16	12-25
Dal*	12	4	0	.750	454-311	28.4-19.4	595-469	2378-2069	4.0-4.4	26-15	449-484	265-231	59.0-47.7	3356- 3568	6.5- 6.1	30-21	25-27
Was	6	10	0	.375	261-293	16.3-18.3	517-585	2016-2524	3.9-4.3	12-16	486-392	284-187	58.4-47.7	3171- 2504	5.4- 5.0	17-17	18-33
StL	5	11	0	.313	299-350	18.7-21.9	519-547	2183-2059	4.2-3.8	19-17	470-531	239-287	50.9-54.0	3063- 3616	5.2- 5.8	16-23	24-20
NYG	4	12	0	.250	249-425	15.6-26.6	483-584	1730-2507	3.6-4.3	10-31	514-448	245-255	47.7-56.9	2931- 3469	4.7- 6.8	19-22	25-18
Central Division																	
Min	9	7	0	.563	317-308	19.8-19.3	433-531	1642-2456	3.8-4.6	14-15	574-499	331-283	57.7-56.7	3934- 3644	6.0- 6.4	22-24	23-24
Det	9	7	0	.563	334-272	20.9-17.0	572-449	2599-1599	4.5-3.8	21- 9	423-462	248-256	58.6-55.4	3287- 3234	6.3- 5.8	13-14	12-23
ChiB	7	9	0	.438	304-264	19.0-16.5	579-506	2440-2015	4.2-4.0	22-10	404-451	209-238	51.7-52.8	2669- 3271	5.5- 5.8	13-20	25-17
TB	5	10	1	.344	271-341	16.9-21.3	477-548	1839-2101	3.9-3.8	9-20	530-516	256-328	48.3-63.6	3414- 3477	5.8- 6.1	20-17	17-15
GB	5	10	1	.344	231-371	14.4-23.2	493-565	1806-2399	3.7-4.2	13-19	511-460	289-259	56.6-56.3	3651- 3617	5.9- 6.9	15-19	29-13
Western Division																	
Atl	12	4	0	.750	405-272	25.3-17.0	559-441	2405-1670	4.3-3.8	15- 8	467-564	259-333	55.5-59.0	3568- 3990	6.5- 5.9	31-24	17-26
LARm*	11	5	0	.688	424-289	26.5-18.1	615-445	2799-1945	4.6-4.4	17-13	451-510	261-245	57.9-48.0	3441- 3097	6.7- 4.6	31-23	23-25
SF	6	10	0	.375	320-415	20.0-25.9	415-556	1743-2218	4.2-4.0	10-20	597-495	363-327	60.8-66.1	3799- 3958	5.7- 8.0	27-29	26-17
NO	1	15	0	.063	291-487	18.2-30.4	348-630	1362-3106	3.9-4.9	9-28	566-445	334-255	59.0-57.3	4010- 3341	6.0- 6.6	26-31	22-12
League 224 games					9178	41.0	14384	57135	4.0	431	12705	7699	56.2	95935	7.6	606	627

*Wild Card qualifiers for playoffs
AFC Wild Card playoff: Oak 27, Hou 7
NFC Wild Card playoff: Dal 34, LARm 13
AFC Divisional playoffs: SD 20, Buf 14; Oak 14, Cle 12
NFC Divisional playoffs: Phi 31, Min 16; Dal 30, Atl 27
AFC championship: Oak 34, SD 27
NFC championship: Phi 20, Dal 7
Super Bowl XV: Oak (AFC) 27, Phi (NFC) 10

LEADING RUSHERS AFC	ATT	YARD	AVG	Long	TD
Earl Campbell, Hou	373	1934	5.2	55t	13
Joe Cribbs, Buf	306	1185	3.9	48	11
Mike Pruitt, Cle	249	1034	4.2	56t	6
Mark van Eeghen, Oak	222	838	3.8	34	5
Chuck Muncie, SD-NO	175	827	4.7	53	6

LEADING RUSHERS NFC	ATT	YARD	AVG	Long	TD
Walter Payton, ChiB	317	1460	4.6	69t	6
Ottis Anderson, StL	301	1352	4.5	52	9
William Andrews, Atl	265	1308	4.9	33	4
Billy Sims, Det	313	1303	4.2	52	13
Tony Dorsett, Dal	278	1185	4.3	56	11

LEADING PASSERS AFC	ATT	COM	YARD	TD	IN
Brian Sipe, Cle	554	337	4132	30	14
Dan Fouts, SD	589	348	4715	30	24
Craig Morton, Den	301	183	2150	12	13
Steve Fuller, KC	320	193	2250	10	12
Bert Jones, Bal	446	248	3134	23	21

LEADING PASSERS NFC	ATT	COM	YARD	TD	IN
Ron Jaworski, Phi	451	257	3529	27	12
Vince Ferragamo, LARm	404	240	3199	30	19
Steve Bartkowski, Atl	463	257	3544	31	16
Joe Montana, SF	273	176	1795	15	9
Gary Danielson, Det	417	244	3223	13	11

LEADING RECEIVERS AFC	NO	YARD	AVG	Long	TD
Kellen Winslow, SD	89	1290	14.5	65	9
John Jefferson, SD	82	1340	16.3	58t	13
Charlie Joiner, SD	71	1132	15.9	51	4
Steve Largent, Sea	66	1064	16.1	67t	6
Mike Pruitt, Cle	63	471	7.5	28	0

LEADING RECEIVERS NFC	NO	YARD	AVG	Long	TD
Earl Cooper, SF	83	567	6.8	66t	4
Dwight Clark, SF	82	991	12.1	71t	8
James Lofton, GB	71	1226	17.3	47	4
Ahmad Rashad, Min	69	1095	15.9	76t	5
Pat Tilley, StL	68	966	14.2	60t	6

LEADING SCORERS AFC	TD	FG	PAT	PTS
John Smith, NE	0	26	51	129
Rolf Benirschke, SD	0	24	46	118
Fred Steinfort, Den	0	26	32	110
Chris Bahr, Oak	0	19	41	98
Nick Lowery, KC	0	20	37	97

LEADING SCORERS NFC	TD	FG	PAT	PTS
Ed Murray, Det	0	27	35	116
Tim Mazzetti, Atl	0	19	46	103
Frank Corral, LARm	0	16	51	99
Tony Franklin, Phi	0	16	48	96
Billy Sims, Det	16	0	0	96

LEADING INTERCEPTOR	NO	YARD	AVG	Long	TD
Lester Hayes, Oak (AFC)	13	273	21.0	61	1
Nolan Cromwell, LARm (NFC)	8	140	17.5	34	1

LEADING PUNTER	NO	AVG	Long
Luke Prestridge, Den (AFC)	70	43.9	57
Dave Jennings, NYG (NFC)	94	44.8	63

LEADING PUNT RETURNER	NO	YDS	AVG	Long	TD
J.T. Smith, KC (AFC)	40	581	14.5	75t	2
Kenny Johnson, Atl (NFC)	23	281	12.2	56	0

LEADING KICKOFF RETURNER	NO	YDS	AVG	Long	TD
Horace Ivory, NE (AFC)	36	992	27.6	98t	1
Rich Mauti, NO (NFC)	31	798	25.7	52	0

SUPERLATIVES AFC

Rushing Avg.	5.2	Earl Campbell, Hou
Receiving Avg.	22.0	Stanley Morgan, NE
Completion Pct.	64.1	Ken Stabler, Hou
Touchdowns	13	Earl Campbell, Hou
		Curtis Dickey, Bal
		John Jefferson, SD
Field Goals	26	John Smith, NE
		Fred Steinfort, Den

SUPERLATIVES NFC

Rushing Avg.	5.0	Dexter Bussey, Det
Receiving Avg.	19.3	James Scott, ChiB
Completion Pct.	64.5	Joe Montana, SF
Touchdowns	16	Billy Sims, Det
Field Goals	27	Ed Murray, Det

LONGEST AFC

Run	89t	Kenny King, Oak
Pass	86t	Jim Plunkett to Cliff Branch, Oak
Interception	93t	Randy Gradishar, Den
Punt	71	George Roberts, Mia
Punt Return	75t	Roland James, NE
		Will Lewis, Sea
		J.T. Smith, KC
Kickoff Return	98t	Horace Ivory, NE
Field Goal	57	Nick Lowery, KC
		Fred Steinfort, Den

LONGEST NFC

Run	72t	Wilbert Montgomery, Phi
Pass	93t	Steve DeBerg to Freddie Solomon, SF
Interception	99t	Johnnie Johnson, LARm
Punt	67	Tom Skladany, Det
Punt Return	66	Alvin Garrett, NYG
Kickoff Return	101t	James Owens, SF
Field Goal	52	Ed Murray, Det
		Mark Moseley, Was
		Rafael Septien, Dal

1981 AMERICAN FOOTBALL CONFERENCE

Team	W	L	T	PCT	SCORING OWN-OPP PTS-PTS	OWN-OPP PPG-PPG	RUSHING OWN-OPP ATT-ATT	OWN-OPP YARD-YARD	OWN-OPP AVG-AVG	ON-OP TD-TD	PASSING OWN-OPP ATT-ATT	OWN-OPP COM-COM	OWN-OPP PCT-PCT	OWN-OPP YARD-YARD	OWN-OPP AVG-AVG	ON-OP TD-TD	ON-OP IN-IN
Eastern Division																	
Mia	11	4	1	.719	345-275	21.6-17.2	535-492	2173-2032	4.1-4.1	18-10	498-509	271-297	54.4-58.3	3385- 3645	6.0- 6.1	18-23	21-18
NYJ*	10	5	1	.656	355-287	22.2-17.9	571-465	2341-1867	4.1-4.0	11-19	507-505	283-275	55.8-54.5	3279- 3522	5.7- 5.3	26-15	14-21
Buf*	10	6	0	.625	311-276	19.4-17.3	524-516	2125-2075	4.1-4.0	13- 7	503-474	253-367	50.3-56.3	3661- 3243	6.8- 5.5	25-21	20-19
Bal	2	14	0	.125	259-533	16.2-33.3	441-607	1850-2665	4.2-4.4	11-30	479-491	265-301	55.3-61.3	3379- 4228	5.9- 8.2	21-37	23-16
NE	2	14	0	.125	322-370	20.1-23.1	499-644	2040-2950	4.1-4.6	23-20	482-439	254-243	52.7-55.4	3904- 3052	6.8- 6.3	17-18	34-16
Central Division																	
Cin	12	4	0	.750	421-304	26.3-19.0	493-465	1973-1881	4.0-4.0	19-12	550-548	332-316	60.4-57.7	4200- 3757	6.8- 5.8	30-24	12-19
Pit	8	8	0	.500	356-297	22.3-18.6	554-500	2372-1869	4.3-3.7	21-10	461-544	247-302	53.6-55.5	3457- 4108	6.8- 6.5	25-22	19-30
Hou	7	9	0	.438	281-355	17.6-22.2	466-549	1734-2411	3.7-4.4	11-16	441-502	258-295	58.5-58.8	3119- 3554	5.8- 6.2	21-22	23-18
Cle	5	11	0	.313	276-375	17.3-23.4	474-516	1929-2078	4.1-4.0	11-14	624-469	348-275	55.8-58.6	4339- 3512	6.0- 6.6	21-28	27-15
Western Division																	
SD	10	6	0	.625	478-390	29.9-24.4	481-491	2005-1825	4.2-3.7	26-25	629-571	368-313	58.5-54.8	4873- 4695	7.3- 7.0	34-22	18-23
Den	10	6	0	.625	321-289	20.1-18.1	515-467	1895-2005	3.7-4.3	12-17	485-497	289-267	59.6-53.7	3992- 3168	6.5- 5.4	27-13	21-23
KC	9	7	0	.563	343-290	21.4-18.1	610-207	2633-1747	4.3-3.4	22-17	410-567	224-291	54.6-51.3	2917- 3821	5.9- 6.1	12-16	22-26
Oak	7	9	0	.438	273-343	17.1-21.4	493-524	2058-1832	4.2-3.5	11-15	545-537	267-289	49.0-53.8	3356- 4011	4.9- 6.2	18-24	28-13
Sea	6	10	0	.375	322-388	20.1-24.3	440-588	1594-2806	3.6-4.8	14-20	524-502	307-294	58.6-58.6	3727- 3394	6.1- 5.8	21-25	15-21

1981 NATIONAL FOOTBALL CONFERENCE

Team	W	L	T	PCT	SCORING OWN-OPP PTS-PTS	OWN-OPP PPG-PPG	RUSHING OWN-OPP ATT-ATT	OWN-OPP YARD-YARD	OWN-OPP AVG-AVG	ON-OP TD-TD	PASSING OWN-OPP ATT-ATT	OWN-OPP COM-COM	OWN-OPP PCT-PCT	OWN-OPP YARD-YARD	OWN-OPP AVG-AVG	ON-OP TD-TD	ON-OP IN-IN
Eastern Division																	
Dal	12	4	0	.750	367-277	22.9-17.3	630-468	2711-2049	4.3-4.4	15-16	439-511	241-236	54.9-46.2	3414- 3717	6.7- 6.1	24-17	15-37
Phi*	10	6	0	.625	368-221	23.0-13.8	559-476	2509-1751	4.5-3.7	17-11	476-507	258-248	54.2-48.9	3249- 3050	6.1- 4.9	25-12	22-26
NYG*	9	7	0	.563	295-257	18.4-16.1	481-553	1685-1891	3.5-3.4	11-10	506-544	251-294	49.6-54.0	3009- 3318	4.8- 5.0	16-14	20-17
Was	8	8	0	.500	347-349	21.7-21.8	532-532	2157-2161	4.1-4.1	19-17	525-452	307-214	58.5-47.3	3743- 3310	6.3- 6.3	19-21	22-24
StL	7	9	0	.438	315-408	19.7-25.5	519-509	2213-2428	4.3-4.8	20-20	477-495	253-282	53.0-57.0	3269- 3547	5.5- 6.3	15-29	24-21
Central Division																	
TB	9	7	0	.563	315-268	19.7-16.8	458-551	1731-2172	3.8-3.9	13-16	473-541	239-317	50.5-58.6	3565- 3297	7.0- 5.6	20-10	14-32
Det	8	8	0	.500	397-322	24.8-20.1	596-469	2795-1623	4.7-3.5	26-14	463-475	228-261	52.3-54.9	3474- 3596	6.5- 6.2	18-22	23-24
GB	8	8	0	.500	324-361	20.3-22.6	478-546	1670-2098	3.5-3.8	11-21	514-505	286-284	55.6-56.2	3576- 3353	5.6- 5.7	24-18	24-30
Min	7	9	0	.438	325-369	20.3-23.1	391-540	1512-2045	3.9-3.8	8-15	709-481	382-265	53.9-55.1	4567- 3599	5.9- 6.5	27-26	29-16
ChiB	6	10	0	.375	253-324	15.8-20.3	608-521	2171-2146	3.6-4.1	13-13	489-525	222-233	45.4-44.4	2728- 3527	4.7- 5.8	14-23	23-18
Western Division																	
SF	13	3	0	.813	357-250	22.3-15.6	560-464	1941-1918	3.5-4.1	17-10	517-514	328-273	63.4-53.1	3766- 3135	6.5- 5.2	20-16	13-27
Atl	7	9	0	.438	426-355	26.6-22.2	495-459	1965-1666	4.0-3.6	15-10	563-565	311-322	55.2-57.0	3986- 3927	6.2- 6.2	30-30	24-25
LARm	6	10	0	.375	303-351	18.9-21.9	559-585	2236-2397	4.0-4.1	17-19	477-439	235-204	49.3-46.5	3008- 3057	4.9- 5.7	15-17	32-17
NO	4	12	0	.250	207-378	12.9-23.6	546-504	2286-1916	4.2-3.8	16-17	441-471	238-287	54.0-60.9	2778- 3578	5.0- 6.7	8-26	27-17
League 224 games					9262	41.3	14508	58304	4.0	441	14180	7745	54.6	99721	7.0	591	609

*Wild Card qualifiers for playoffs
AFC Wild Card playoff: Buf 31, NYJ 27
NFC Wild Card playoff: NYG 27, Phi 21
AFC Divisional playoffs: SD 41, Mia 38 (OT); Cin 28, Buf 21
NFC Divisional playoffs: Dal 38, TB 0 ; SF 38, NYG 24
AFC championship: Cin 27, SD 7
NFC championship: SF 28, Dal 7
Super Bowl XVI: SF (NFC) 26, Cin (AFC) 21

LEADING RUSHERS AFC	ATT	YARD	AVG	Long	TD
Earl Campbell, Hou	361	1376	3.8	43	10
Chuck Muncie, SD	251	1144	4.6	73t	19
Joe Delaney, KC	234	1121	4.8	82t	3
Mike Pruitt, Cle	247	1103	4.5	21	7
Joe Cribbs, Buf	257	1097	4.3	35	3

LEADING RUSHERS NFC	ATT	YARD	AVG	Long	TD
George Rogers, NO	378	1674	4.4	79t	13
Tony Dorsett, Dal	342	1646	4.8	75t	4
Billy Sims, Det	296	1437	4.9	51	13
W. Montgomery, Phi	286	1402	4.9	41	8
Ottis Anderson, StL	328	1376	4.2	28	9

LEADING PASSERS AFC	ATT	COM	YARD	TD	IN
Ken Anderson, Cin	479	300	3754	29	10
Craig Morton, Den	376	225	3195	21	14
Dan Fouts, SD	609	360	4802	33	17
Terry Bradshaw, Pit	370	201	2887	22	14
Jim Zorn, Sea	397	236	2788	13	9

LEADING PASSERS NFC	ATT	COM	YARD	TD	IN
Joe Montana, SF	488	311	3565	19	12
Danny White, Dal	391	223	3098	22	13
Steve Bartkowski, Atl	533	297	3829	30	23
Lynn Dickey, GB	354	204	2593	17	15
Joe Theismann, Was	496	293	3568	19	20

LEADING RECEIVERS AFC	NO	YARD	AVG	Long	TD
Kellen Winslow, SD	88	1075	12.2	67t	10
Steve Largent, Sea	75	1224	16.3	57t	9
Dan Ross, Cin	71	910	12.8	37	5
Frank Lewis, Buf	70	1244	17.8	33	4
Charlie Joiner, SD	70	1188	17.0	57	7

LEADING RECEIVERS NFC	NO	YARD	AVG	Long	TD
Dwight Clark, SF	85	1105	13.0	78t	4
Ted Brown, Min	83	694	8.4	63	2
William Andrews, Atl	81	735	9.1	70t	2
Joe Senser, Min	79	1004	12.7	53	8
James Lofton, GB	71	1294	18.2	75t	8

LEADING SCORERS AFC	TD	FG	PAT	PTS
Jim Breech, Cin	0	22	49	115
Nick Lowery, KC	0	26	37	115
Chuck Muncie, SD	19	0	0	114
Pat Leahy, NYJ	0	25	38	113
Rolf Benirschke, SD	0	19	55	112

LEADING SCORERS NFC	TD	FG	PAT	PTS
Ed Murray, Det	0	25	46	121
Rafael Septien, Dal	0	27	40	121
Mick Luckhurst, Atl	0	21	51	114
Joe Danelo, NYG	0	24	31	103
Wendell Tyler, LARm	17	0	0	102

LEADING INTERCEPTOR	NO	YARD	AVG	Long	TD
John Harris, Sea (AFC)	10	155	15.5	42t	2
Everson Walls, Dal (NFC)	11	133	12.2	33	0

LEADING PUNTER	NO	AVG	Long
Pat McInally, Cin (AFC)	72	45.4	62
Tom Skladany, Det (NFC)	64	43.5	74

LEADING PUNT RETURNER	NO	YDS	AVG	Long	TD
James Brooks, SD (AFC)	22	290	13.2	42	0
LeRoy Irvin, LARm (NFC)	46	615	13.4	84t	3

LEADING KICKOFF RETURNER	NO	YDS	AVG	Long	TD
Carl Roaches, Hou (AFC)	28	769	27.5	96t	1
Mike Nelms, Was (NFC)	37	1099	29.7	84	0

SUPERLATIVES AFC		
Rushing Avg.	5.3	Tony Nathan, Mia
Receiving Avg.	23.4	Stanley Morgan, NE
Completion Pct.	62.6	Ken Anderson, Cin
Touchdowns	19	Chuck Muncie, SD
Field Goals	26	Nick Lowery, KC

SUPERLATIVES NFC		
Rushing Avg.	4.9	Wilbert Montgomery, Phi
Receiving Avg.	21.0	Kevin House, TB
Completion Pct.	63.7	Joe Montana, SF
Touchdowns	17	Wendell Tyler, LARm
Field Goals	27	Rafael Septien, Dal

LONGEST AFC		
Run	82t	Joe Delaney, KC
Pass	95t	Craig Morton to Steve Watson, Den
Interception	102t	Louis Breeden, Cin
Punt	75	Rich Camarillo, NE
Punt Return	87t	Tommy Vigorito, Mia
Kickoff Return	96t	Carl Roaches, Hou
Field Goal	54	Efren Herrera, Sea

LONGEST NFC

Run	79t George Rogers, NO	Punt	75 Carl Birdsong, StL
Pass	94t Eric Hipple to Leonard Thompson, Det	Punt Return	94t Mark Lee, GB
Interception	101t Tom Pridemore, Atl	Kickoff Return	99t Eddie Payton, Min
		Field Goal	55 Joe Danelo, NYG

1982 AMERICAN FOOTBALL CONFERENCE

					SCORING		RUSHING				PASSING						
Team	W	L	T	PCT	OWN-OPP PTS-PTS	OWN-OPP PPG-PPG	OWN-OPP ATT-ATT	OWN-OPP YARD-YARD	OWN-OPP AVG-AVG	ON-OP TD-TD	OWN-OPP ATT-ATT	OWN-OPP COM-COM	OWN-OPP PCT-PCT	OWN-OPP YARD-YARD	OWN-OPP AVG-AVG	ON-OP TD-TD	ON-OP IN-IN
LARd*	8	1	0	.889	260-200	28.9-22.2	292-234	1080- 778	3.7-3.3	15-12	267-375	154-193	57.7-51.5	2086- 2617	6.5- 5.5	14-11	15-18
Mia*	7	2	0	.778	198-131	22.0-14.6	333-293	1344-1285	4.0-4.4	11- 7	238-226	129-119	54.2-52.7	1401- 1281	5.3- 4.0	8- 7	13-19
Cin*	7	2	0	.778	232-177	25.8-19.7	269-223	949- 850	3.5-3.8	13- 8	310-306	219-187	70.6-61.1	2501- 2250	6.9- 6.2	12-12	9-14
Pit*	6	3	0	.667	204-146	22.7-16.2	289-236	1187- 762	4.1-3.2	7- 5	275-329	141-176	51.3-53.5	1922- 2385	6.1- 5.8	17-12	16-17
SD*	6	3	0	.667	288-221	32.0-24.6	267-230	1121- 961	4.2-4.2	15-10	338-342	208-233	61.5-68.1	3021- 2437	8.7- 6.4	19-10	12-13
NYJ*	6	3	0	.667	245-166	27.2-18.4	304-269	1317- 983	4.3-3.7	13- 5	279-298	165-159	59.1-53.4	2107- 1817	6.3- 5.2	16-10	9-17
NE*	5	4	0	.556	143-157	15.9-17.4	324-315	1347-1289	4.2-4.1	3- 9	187-267	93-142	49.7-53.2	1420- 1691	6.4- 5.3	12- 9	9-12
Cle*	4	5	0	.444	140-182	15.6-20.2	256-306	873-1292	3.4-4.2	7-13	334-266	174-144	52.1-54.1	2057- 1967	5.1- 6.3	9- 9	16-17
Buf	4	5	0	.444	150-154	16.7-17.1	319-268	1371-1034	4.3-3.9	9- 6	273-256	149-114	54.6-44.5	1671- 1382	5.5- 4.9	8- 8	17-13
Sea	4	5	0	.444	127-147	14.1-16.3	227-337	795-1461	3.5-4.3	4-12	326-246	176-138	54.0-56.1	2068- 1468	5.0- 5.1	9- 4	13-13
KC	3	6	0	.333	176-184	19.6-20.4	269-280	943-1065	3.5-3.8	3- 7	264-262	145-155	54.9-59.2	1864- 1787	5.1- 6.0	10-12	8-12
Den	2	7	0	.222	148-226	16.4-25.1	257-293	1018- 935	4.0-3.2	6- 8	311-307	181-172	58.2-56.0	2019- 2350	5.4- 6.9	8-14	19-12
Hou	1	8	0	.111	136-245	15.1-27.2	225-298	799-1225	3.6-4.1	5-10	287-284	153-179	53.3-63.0	1882- 2453	4.8- 7.0	12-18	15- 3
Bal	0	8	1	.056	113-236	12.6-26.2	293-348	1044-1473	3.6-4.2	4-10	283-246	142-138	50.2-56.1	1613- 1920	4.8- 7.1	6-18	10- 5

1982 NATIONAL FOOTBALL CONFERENCE

Team	W	L	T	PCT	OWN-OPP PTS-PTS	OWN-OPP PPG-PPG	OWN-OPP ATT-ATT	OWN-OPP YARD-YARD	OWN-OPP AVG-AVG	ON-OP TD-TD	OWN-OPP ATT-ATT	OWN-OPP COM-COM	OWN-OPP PCT-PCT	OWN-OPP YARD-YARD	OWN-OPP AVG-AVG	ON-OP TD-TD	ON-OP IN-IN
Was*	8	1	0	.889	190-128	21.1-14.2	315-247	1140- 946	3.6-3.8	5- 8	253-275	162-146	54.0-53.1	2068- 1870	6.5- 5.3	13- 8	9-11
Dal*	6	3	0	.667	226-145	25.1-16.1	296-260	1313-1011	4.4-3.9	10- 5	258-289	160-152	62.0-52.6	2150- 2002	6.7- 5.4	16-10	14-15
GB*	5	3	1	.611	226-169	25.1-18.8	283-275	1081- 932	3.8-3.4	12- 9	267-327	143-177	53.6-54.1	2068- 1950	6.1- 5.1	12- 9	15-12
Min*	5	4	0	.556	187-198	20.8-22.0	245-260	912-1020	3.7-3.9	6- 8	334-292	187-157	56.0-53.8	2105- 2106	5.5- 5.8	15-11	12-12
Atl*	5	4	0	.556	183-199	20.3-22.1	310-253	1181-1044	3.8-4.1	12-13	275-280	176-157	64.0-56.1	1992- 1945	5.9- 6.1	9-12	11-10
StL*	5	4	0	.556	135-170	15.0-18.9	307-256	1209- 995	3.9-3.9	10- 5	240-291	129-174	53.8-59.8	1576- 2035	4.9- 5.9	6-16	6- 6
TB*	5	4	0	.556	158-178	17.6-19.8	268-285	952-1058	3.6-3.7	6- 9	308-254	164-145	53.2-57.1	2071- 1608	6.1- 5.0	9-10	11-11
Det*	4	5	0	.444	181-176	20.1-19.6	283-271	1022- 854	3.6-3.2	5- 6	285-288	136-155	47.7-53.8	1754- 2098	4.8- 5.8	12-11	18-18
NO	4	5	0	.444	129-160	14.3-17.8	331-255	1257- 974	3.8-3.8	8- 8	248-245	137-149	55.2-60.8	1571- 1864	5.2- 5.9	8-11	14- 9
NYG	4	5	0	.444	164-160	18.2-17.8	244-301	842-1118	3.5-3.7	7- 7	298-244	161-148	54.0-60.7	2017- 1810	6.0- 5.7	10-10	9-12
SF	3	6	0	.333	209-206	23.2-22.9	219-303	740-1199	3.4-4.0	6- 9	348-278	215-158	61.8-56.8	2668- 1949	6.8- 6.3	17-14	11- 9
ChiB	3	6	0	.333	141-174	15.7-19.3	276-261	988- 902	3.6-3.5	5- 4	262-294	141-164	53.8-55.8	1749- 2189	5.1- 6.0	10-14	11-13
Phi	3	6	0	.333	191-195	21.2-21.7	211-299	829-1031	3.9-3.4	11- 5	288-285	168-168	58.3-58.9	2100- 2136	5.8- 6.1	12-14	13-15
LARm	2	7	0	.222	200-250	22.2-27.8	251-307	1025-1202	4.1-3.9	13-13	297-281	166-175	55.9-62.3	2136- 2290	6.4- 7.1	11-16	14-11
League 126 games					5080	40.3	7763	29679	3.8	8.3	7933	4474	56.4	55657	7.0	320	349

*Qualifiers for playoffs
AFC First round playoffs: LARd 27, Cle 10; Mia 28, NE 13; NYJ 44, Cin 17; SD 31, Pit 28
NFC First round playoffs: Was 31, Det 7; GB 41, StL 16; Dal 30, TB 17; Min 30, Atl 24
AFC Second round playoffs: NYJ 17, LARd 14; Mia 34, SD 13
NFC Second round playoffs: Was 21, Min 7; Dal 37, GB 26
AFC championship: Mia 14, NYJ 0
NFC championship: Was 31, Dal 17
Super Bowl XVII: Was (NFC) 27, Mia (AFC) 17

LEADING RUSHERS AFC	ATT	YARD	AVG	Long	TD
Freeman McNeil, NYJ	151	786	5.2	48	6
Andra Franklin, Mia	177	701	4.0	25t	7
Marcus Allen, LARd	160	697	4.4	53	11
Joe Cribbs, Buf	134	633	4.9	62t	3
Tony Collins, NE	164	632	3.9	54	1

LEADING RUSHERS NFC	ATT	YARD	AVG	Long	TD
Tony Dorsett, Dal	177	745	4.2	99t	5
Billy Sims, Det	172	639	3.7	29	4
Walter Payton, ChiB	148	596	4.0	26	1
Ottis Anderson, StL	145	587	4.0	64	3
William Andrews, Alt	139	573	4.1	19t	5

LEADING PASSERS AFC	ATT	COM	YARD	TD	IN
Ken Anderson, Cin	309	218	2495	12	9
Dan Fouts, SD	330	204	2883	17	11
Richard Todd, NYJ	261	153	1961	14	8
Steve Grogan, NE	122	66	930	7	4
Terry Bradshaw, Pit	240	127	1768	17	11

LEADING PASSERS NFC	ATT	COM	YARD	TD	IN
Joe Theismann, Was	252	161	2033	13	9
Danny White, Dal	247	156	2079	16	12
Joe Montana, SF	346	213	2613	17	11
Jim McMahon, ChiB	210	120	1501	9	7
Steve Bartkowski, Atl	262	166	1905	8	11

LEADING RECEIVERS AFC	NO	YARD	AVG	Long	TD
Kellen Winslow, SD	54	721	13.4	40	6
Wes Chandler, SD	49	1032	21.1	66t	9
Cris Collinsworth, Cin	49	700	14.3	50	1
Ozzie Newsome, Cle	49	633	12.9	54	3
Dan Ross, Cin	47	508	10.8	28	3

LEADING RECEIVERS NFC	NO	YARD	AVG	Long	TD
Dwight Clark, SF	60	913	15.2	51	5
James Wilder, TB	53	466	8.8	32	1
William Andrews, Atl	42	503	12.0	86t	2
Wendell Tyler, LARm	38	375	9.9	40	4
Jeff Moore, SF	37	405	10.9	55	4

LEADING SCORERS AFC	TD	FG	PAT	PTS
Marcus Allen, LARd	14	0	0	84
Rolf Benirschke, SD	0	16	32	80
Nick Lowery, KC	0	19	17	74
Jim Breech, Cin	0	14	25	67
Uwe von Schamann, Mia	0	15	21	66

LEADING SCORERS NFC	TD	FG	PAT	PTS
Wendell Tyler, LARm	13	0	0	78
Mark Moseley, Was	0	20	16	76
Bill Capece, TB	0	18	14	68
Jan Stenerud, KC	0	13	25	64
Eddie Lee Ivery, GB	10	0	0	60

LEADING INTERCEPTOR	NO	YARD	AVG	Long	TD
Ken Riley, Cin (AFC)	5	88	17.6	56t	1
Bobby Jackson, NYJ (AFC)	5	84	16.8	77t	1
Dwayne Woodruff, Pit (AFC)	5	53	10.6	30	0
Donnie Shell, Pit (AFC)	5	27	5.4	18	0
Everson Walls, Dal (NFC)	7	61	8.7	37	0

LEADING PUNTER	NO	AVG	Long
Luke Prestridge, Den (AFC)	45	45.0	65
Carl Birdsong, StL (NFC)	54	43.8	65

LEADING PUNT RETURNER	NO	YDS	AVG	Long	TD
Rick Upchurch, Den (AFC)	15	242	16.1	78t	2
Billy Johnson, Atl (NFC)	24	273	11.4	71	0

LEADING KICKOFF RETURNER	NO	YDS	AVG	Long	TD
Mike Mosley, Buf (AFC)	18	487	27.1	66	0
Alvin Hall, Det (NFC)	16	426	26.6	96t	1

SUPERLATIVES AFC

Rushing Avg.	5.2	Freeman McNeil, NYJ
Receiving Avg.	21.1	Wes Chandler, SD
Completion Pct.	70.6	Ken Anderson, Cin
Touchdowns	14	Marcus Allen, LARd
Field Goals	19	Nick Lowery, KC
Sacks	7.5	Jesse Baker, Hou

SUPERLATIVES NFC

Rushing Avg.	4.5	Wilbert Montgomery, Phi
Receiving Avg.	21.6	Charlie Brown, Was
Completion Pct.	63.9	Joe Theismann, Was
Touchdowns	13	Wendell Tyler, LARm
Field Goals	20	Mark Moseley, Was
Sacks	11.5	Doug Martin, Min

LONGEST AFC		
Run	62t	Joe Cribbs, Buf
Pass	75t	Matt Cavanaugh to Stanley Morgan, NE
Interception	99t	Rick Sanford, NE
Punt	76	Rich Camarillo, NE
Punt Return	78t	Rick Upchurch, Den
Kickoff Return	98t	Ricky Smith, NE
Field Goal	58	Dan Miller, Bal

LONGEST NFC		
Run	99t	Tony Dorsett, Dal
Pass	86t	Steve Bartkowski to William Andrews, Atl
Interception	97t	Lawrence Taylor, NYG
Punt	81	Bob Parsons, ChiB
Punt Return	93t	Dana McLemore, SF
Kickoff Return	96t	Alvin Hall, Det
Field Goal	53	Rafael Septien, Dal

1983 AMERICAN FOOTBALL CONFERENCE

					SCORING		RUSHING				PASSING						
Team	W	L	T	PCT	OWN-OPP PTS-PTS	OWN-OPP PPG-PPG	OWN-OPP ATT-ATT	OWN-OPP YARD-YARD	OWN-OPP AVG-AVG	ON-OP TD-TD	OWN-OPP ATT-ATT	OWN-OPP COM-COM	OWN-OPP PCT-PCT	OWN-OPP YARD-YARD	OWN-OPP AVG-AVG	ON-OP TD-TD	ON-OP IN-IN
Eastern Division																	
Mia	12	4	0	.750	389-250	24.3-15.6	568-460	2150-2037	3.8-4.4	16-11	442-480	254-277	57.6-57.7	3235- 3365	6.6- 5.7	26-19	11-26
NE	8	8	0	.500	274-289	17.1-18.1	538-549	2605-2281	4.8-4.2	19- 9	412-514	220-277	53.3-53.9	3040- 3365	7.4- 6.0	16-19	18-17
Buf	8	8	0	.500	283-351	17.7-21.9	415-566	1736-2503	4.2-4.4	4-14	571-480	317-286	55.5-59.6	3438- 3553	5.1- 6.5	30-22	28-13
Bal	7	9	0	.438	264-354	16.5-22.1	601-516	2695-2118	4.5-4.1	10-13	377-488	188-281	49.9-57.6	2663- 3832	5.5- 6.7	12-31	22-20
NYJ	7	9	0	.438	313-331	19.6-20.7	474-547	2068-2378	4.4-4.3	11-13	559-488	330-269	59.0-58.1	3742- 3301	5.7- 5.7	21-22	28-22
Central Division																	
Pit	10	6	0	.625	355-303	22.2-18.9	614-509	2610-1833	4.3-3.6	17-14	409-447	211-238	51.6-53.2	2754- 3260	5.2- 5.8	15-19	23-28
Cle	9	7	0	.563	356-342	22.3-21.4	465-509	1922-2065	4.1-3.9	13-15	567-469	324-280	57.1-50.7	3932- 3316	6.1- 6.1	27-22	28-22
Cin	7	9	0	.438	346-302	21.6-18.9	542-430	2104-1499	3.9-3.5	24-16	454-502	290-288	63.9-57.4	3492- 3163	6.4- 5.2	14-17	18-23
Hou	2	14	0	.125	288-460	18.0-28.8	502-576	1998-2787	4.0-4.8	16-23	482-424	260-252	53.9-59.4	3286- 3095	6.8- 6.3	16-26	29-14
Western Division																	
LARd	12	4	0	.750	442-338	27.6-21.1	542-436	2240-1586	4.1-3.6	18-13	504-531	301-282	59.7-53.1	3910- 3646	6.2- 5.4	31-20	24-20
Sea*	9	7	0	.563	356-342	22.3-21.4	546-511	2119-2198	3.9-4.3	19-14	449-521	251-311	55.9-59.7	3316- 4182	6.0- 6.8	25-33	18-26
Den*	9	7	0	.563	302-327	18.9-20.4	471-509	1784-1938	3.8-3.8	15-14	499-552	254-307	50.9-55.6	3466- 3988	5.5- 6.2	17-18	22-27
SD	6	10	0	.375	358-462	22.4-28.9	423-552	1536-2173	3.6-3.9	16-26	635-544	369-330	58.1-60.7	4891- 4051	7.0- 6.6	27-28	33-16
KC	6	10	0	.375	386-367	24.1-22.9	387-554	1254-2275	3.2-4.1	13-18	641-500	369-261	57.6-52.2	4664- 3361	6.3- 5.8	29-21	19-30

1983 NATIONAL FOOTBALL CONFERENCE

Team	W	L	T	PCT	OWN-OPP PTS-PTS	OWN-OPP PPG-PPG	OWN-OPP ATT-ATT	OWN-OPP YARD-YARD	OWN-OPP AVG-AVG	ON-OP TD-TD	OWN-OPP ATT-ATT	OWN-OPP COM-COM	OWN-OPP PCT-PCT	OWN-OPP YARD-YARD	OWN-OPP AVG-AVG	ON-OP TD-TD	ON-OP IN-IN
Eastern Division																	
Was	14	2	0	.875	541-332	33.8-20.8	629-349	2625-1289	4.2-3.7	30- 9	463-570	278-301	60.0-52.8	3765- 4377	7.1- 6.4	29-28	11-34
Dal*	12	4	0	.750	479-360	29.9-22.5	519-410	2117-1499	4.1-3.7	21-12	554-558	346-299	62.5-53.6	4156- 4365	6.5- 6.4	31-27	25-27
StL	8	7	1	.531	374-428	23.4-26.8	525-443	2277-1838	4.3-4.1	15-23	460-519	267-290	58.0-55.9	3309- 3635	5.5- 5.5	29-24	21-28
Phi	5	11	0	.313	233-322	14.6-20.1	402-633	1417-2655	3.5-4.2	5-14	486-430	252-247	51.9-57.4	3532- 3048	5.7- 6.0	22-20	18- 8
NYG	3	12	1	.219	267-347	16.7-21.7	506-502	1794-1733	3.5-3.5	9-10	575-493	284-283	49.4-57.4	3854- 3584	6.7- 6.1	12-26	31-23
Central Division																	
Det	9	7	0	.563	347-286	21.7-17.9	513-503	2181-2104	4.3-4.2	18-11	503-515	263-297	52.3-57.7	3297- 3401	5.4- 5.6	19-21	23-22
GB	8	8	0	.500	429-439	26.8-27.4	439-597	1807-2641	4.1-4.4	15-28	526-518	311-300	59.1-57.9	4688- 4033	7.7- 6.7	33-20	32-19
ChiB	8	8	0	.500	311-301	19.4-18.8	583-482	2727-2000	4.7-4.1	14-20	447-490	255-249	57.0-50.8	3461- 3516	6.2- 5.8	21-15	22-21
Min	8	8	0	.500	316-348	19.8-21.8	470-579	1806-2584	3.8-4.5	17-16	555-478	310-263	55.9-55.0	3514- 3229	5.4- 5.5	15-23	22-25
TB	2	14	0	.125	241-380	15.1-23.8	428-561	1794-1733	3.2-3.7	9-19	528-490	300-300	56.8-61.2	3854- 3584	5.4- 6.2	18-15	24-23
Western Division																	
SF	10	6	0	.625	432-293	27.0-18.3	511-449	2257-1936	4.4-4.3	17-10	528-526	339-322	64.2-61.2	4021- 3701	6.8- 5.6	27-23	12-24
LARm*	9	7	0	.563	361-344	22.6-21.5	511-489	2253-1781	4.4-3.6	20-21	489-556	286-319	58.5-57.4	3411- 3869	6.3- 6.1	23-18	23-24
NO	8	8	0	.500	319-337	19.9-21.1	595-472	2461-2000	4.1-4.2	19-11	425-496	243-271	57.2-54.6	2782- 3128	5.4- 4.9	14-20	25-23
Atl	7	9	0	.438	370-389	23.1-24.3	492-499	2224-2309	4.5-4.6	17-20	507-493	321-313	63.3-63.5	3793- 3734	6.1- 6.7	24-28	10-15
League 224 games					9779	43.7	14211	58122	4.1	437	14047	7993	56.9	100922	7.2	625	620

*Wild Card qualifiers for playoffs
AFC Wild Card playoff: Sea 31, Den 7
NFC Wild Card playoff: LARm 24, Dal 17
AFC Divisional playoffs: Sea 27, Mia 20; LARd 38, Pit 10
NFC Divisional playoffs: SF 24, Det 23; Was 51, LARm 7
AFC championship: LARd 30, Sea 14
NFC championship: Was 24, SF 21
Super Bowl XVIII: LARd (AFC) 38, Was (NFC) 9

LEADING RUSHERS AFC	ATT	YARD	AVG	Long	TD
Curt Warner, Sea	335	1449	4.3	60	13
Earl Campbell, Hou	322	1301	4.0	42	12
Mike Pruitt, Cle	293	1184	4.0	27	10
Joe Cribbs, Buf	263	1131	4.3	45	3
Curtis Dickey, Bal	254	1122	4.4	56	4

LEADING RUSHERS NFC	ATT	YARD	AVG	Long	TD
Eric Dickerson, LARm	390	1808	4.6	85t	18
William Andrews, Atl	331	1567	4.7	27	7
Walter Payton, ChiB	314	1421	4.5	49t	6
John Riggins, Was	375	1347	3.6	44	24
Tony Dorsett, Dal	289	1321	4.6	77	8

LEADING PASSERS AFC	ATT	COM	YARD	TD	IN
Dan Marino, Mia	296	173	2210	20	6
Dave Krieg, Sea	243	147	2139	18	11
Dan Fouts, SD	340	215	2975	20	15
Ken Anderson, Cin	297	198	2333	12	13
Jim Plunkett, LARd	379	230	2935	20	18

LEADING PASSERS NFC	ATT	COM	YARD	TD	IN
Steve Bartkowski, Atl	432	274	3167	22	5
Joe Theismann, Was	459	276	3714	29	11
Joe Montana, SF	515	332	2910	26	12
Neil Lomax, StL	354	209	2636	24	11
Lynn Dickey, GB	484	289	4458	32	29

LEADING RECEIVERS AFC	NO	YARD	AVG	Long	TD
Todd Christensen, LARd	92	1247	13.6	45	12
Ozzie Newsome, Cle	89	970	10.9	66t	6
Kellen Winslow, SD	88	1172	13.3	46	8
Tim Smith, Hou	83	1176	14.2	47t	6
Carlos Carson, KC	80	1351	16.9	50t	7

LEADING RECEIVERS NFC	NO	YARD	AVG	Long	TD
Roy Green, StL	78	1227	15.7	71t	14
Charlie Brown, Was	78	1125	15.7	75t	8
Earnest Gray, NYG	78	1139	14.6	62	5
Ron Springs, Dal	73	589	8.1	80t	1
Dwight Clark, SF	70	840	12.0	46t	8

LEADING SCORERS AFC	TD	FG	PAT	PTS
Gary Anderson, Pit	0	27	38	119
Nick Lowery, KC	0	24	44	116
Chris Bahr, LARd	0	21	51	114
Raul Allegre, Bal	0	30	22	112
Norm Johnson, Sea	0	18	49	103

LEADING SCORERS NFC	TD	FG	PAT	PTS
Mark Moseley, Was	0	33	62	161
John Riggins, Was	24	0	0	144
Ali Haji-Sheikh, NYG	0	35	22	127
Ray Wersching, SF	0	25	51	126
Rafael Septien, Dal	0	22	57	123

LEADING INTERCEPTOR	NO	YARD	AVG	Long	TD
Ken Riley, Cin (AFC)	8	89	11.1	42t	2
Vann McElroy, LARd (AFC)	8	68	8.5	28	0
Mark Murphy, Was (NFC)	9	127	14.1	48	0

LEADING PUNTER	NO	AVG	Long
Rohn Stark, Bal (AFC)	91	45.3	68
Frank Garcia, TB (NFC)	95	42.2	64

LEADING PUNT RETURNER	NO	YDS	AVG	Long	TD
Kirk Springs, NYJ (AFC)	23	287	12.5	76t	1
Henry Ellard, LARm (NFC)	16	217	13.6	72t	1

LEADING KICKOFF RETURNER	NO	YDS	AVG	Long	TD
Fulton Walker, Mia (AFC)	36	962	26.7	78	0
Darrin Nelson, Min (NFC)	18	445	24.7	50	0

SUPERLATIVES AFC		
Rushing Avg.	5.5	Mosi Tatupu, NE
Receiving Avg.	19.7	Mark Duper, Mia
Completion Pct.	66.7	Ken Anderson, Cin
Touchdowns	14	Pete Johnson, Cin
		Curt Warner, Sea
Field Goals	30	Raul Allegre, Bal
Sacks	19.0	Mark Gastineau, NYJ

SUPERLATIVES NFC		
Rushing Avg.	5.3	Joe Washington, Was
Receiving Avg.	22.4	James Lofton, GB
Completion Pct.	64.5	Joe Montana, SF
Touchdowns	24	John Riggins, Was
Field Goals	35	Ali-Haji-Sheikh, NYG
Sacks	17.5	Fred Dean, SF

LONGEST AFC		
Run	80	Larry Moriarty, Hou
Pass	99t	Jim Plunkett to Cliff Branch, LARd
Interception	73t	Jacob Green, Sea
Punt	70	Rich Camarillo, NE
Punt Return	97t	Greg Pruitt, LARd
Kickoff Return	97t	Carl Roaches, Hou
Field Goal	58	Nick Lowery, KC
		Steve Cox, Cle

LONGEST NFC		
Run	85t	Eric Dickerson, LARm
Pass	87t	Jim McMahon to Willie Gault, ChiB
Interception	70t	Bobby Johnson, NO
		Mel Kaufman, Was
	70	Roosevelt Barnes, Det
Punt	70	Bucky Scribner, GB
Punt Return	90t	Phillip Epps, GB
Kickoff Return	66	Stump Mitchell, StL
Field Goal	56	Ali Haji-Sheikh, NYG (twice)

1984 AMERICAN FOOTBALL CONFERENCE

					SCORING		RUSHING				PASSING						
Team	W	L	T	PCT	OWN-OPP PTS-PTS	OWN-OPP PPG-PPG	OWN-OPP ATT-ATT	OWN-OPP YARD-YARD	OWN-OPP AVG-AVG	ON-OP TD-TD	OWN-OPP ATT-ATT	OWN-OPP COM-COM	OWN-OPP PCT-PCT	OWN-OPP YARD-YARD	OWN-OPP AVG-AVG	ON-OP TD-TD	ON-OP IN-IN
Eastern Division																	
Mia	14	2	0	.875	513-298	32.1-18.6	484-458	1918-2155	4.0-4.7	18-16	572-551	367-310	64.2-56.3	5146- 3604	9.0- 6.5	49-22	18-24
NE	9	7	0	.563	362-352	22.6-22.0	482-498	2032-1886	4.2-3.8	15-11	500-513	292-283	58.4-55.2	3685- 3666	7.4- 7.1	26-25	14-17
NYJ	7	9	0	.438	332-364	20.8-22.8	504-497	2189-2064	4.3-4.2	17-16	488-511	272-312	55.7-61.1	3341- 3862	6.9- 7.6	20-24	21-15
Ind	4	12	0	.250	239-414	14.9-25.9	510-559	2025-2007	4.0-3.6	13-16	411-515	206-298	50.1-57.9	2543- 3890	6.2- 7.6	13-31	22-18
Buf	2	14	0	.125	250-454	15.6-28.4	398-531	1643-2108	4.1-4.0	9-19	588-495	298-300	50.7-60.6	3252- 3667	5.5- 7.4	18-32	30-16
Central Division																	
Pit	9	7	0	.563	387-310	24.2-19.4	574-454	2179-1617	3.8-3.6	13-12	443-515	240-299	54.2-58.1	3519- 3689	7.9- 7.2	25-19	25-31
Cin	8	8	0	.500	339-339	21.2-21.2	540-477	2179-1868	4.0-3.9	18-21	496-517	306-302	61.7-58.4	3659- 3689	7.4- 7.1	17-15	22-25
Cle	5	11	0	.313	250-297	15.6-18.6	489-494	1696-1945	3.5-3.9	10-10	495-458	273-261	55.2-57.0	3490- 3049	7.1- 6.7	14-15	23-20
Hou	2	14	0	.125	240-437	15.0-27.3	433-596	1656-2789	3.8-4.7	13-27	487-447	282-271	57.9-60.6	3610- 3446	7.4- 7.7	14-23	15-13
Western Division																	
Den	13	3	0	.813	353-241	22.1-15.1	508-435	2076-1664	4.1-3.8	12-10	475-631	263-346	55.4-54.8	3116- 4453	6.6- 7.1	22-16	17-31
Sea*	12	4	0	.750	418-282	26.1-17.6	495-475	1645-1789	3.3-3.8	10-11	497-521	283-265	56.9-50.9	3751- 3572	7.6- 6.9	32-18	26-38
LARd*	11	5	0	.688	368-278	22.5-17.4	516-517	1886-1892	3.7-3.7	19-12	491-508	266-254	54.2-50.0	3718- 3268	7.6- 6.4	21-19	28-20
KC	8	8	0	.500	314-324	19.6-20.3	408-523	1527-1980	3.7-3.8	12-10	593-586	305-332	51.4-56.7	3869- 4009	6.5- 6.8	21-19	22-30
SD	7	9	0	.438	394-413	24.6-25.8	456-457	1654-1851	3.6-4.1	18-23	662-531	401-323	60.6-60.8	4928- 4303	7.4- 8.1	25-27	21-19

1984 NATIONAL FOOTBALL CONFERENCE

Team	W	L	T	PCT	OWN-OPP PTS-PTS	OWN-OPP PPG-PPG	OWN-OPP ATT-ATT	OWN-OPP YARD-YARD	OWN-OPP AVG-AVG	ON-OP TD-TD	OWN-OPP ATT-ATT	OWN-OPP COM-COM	OWN-OPP PCT-PCT	OWN-OPP YARD-YARD	OWN-OPP AVG-AVG	ON-OP TD-TD	ON-OP IN-IN
Eastern Division																	
Was	11	5	0	.688	426-310	26.6-19.4	588-390	2274-1589	3.9-4.1	20-13	485-575	286-318	59.0-55.3	3417- 4301	7.1- 7.5	24-25	13-21
NYG*	9	7	0	.563	299-301	18.7-18.8	493-474	1680-1818	3.4-3.8	12-10	535-529	288-288	53.8-54.4	4066- 3736	7.6- 7.1	22-20	18-19
StL	9	7	0	.563	423-345	26.4-21.6	488-442	2088-1923	4.3-4.4	21-11	566-494	347-251	61.3-50.8	4634- 3574	8.2- 6.9	28-26	16-21
Dal	9	7	0	.563	308-308	19.3-19.3	469-510	1714-2226	3.7-4.4	12- 8	604-527	322-250	53.3-47.4	3995- 3200	6.6- 6.1	19-23	26-28
Phi	6	9	0	.406	278-320	17.4-20.0	381-556	1338-2189	3.5-3.9	6-12	606-492	331-262	54.6-53.3	3823- 3506	6.3- 7.1	19-22	17-20
Central Division																	
ChiB	10	6	0	.625	325-248	20.3-15.5	674-378	2974-1377	4.4-3.6	22-10	390-435	226-198	57.9-45.5	2695- 3069	6.9- 7.1	14-14	15-21
GB	8	8	0	.500	390-309	24.4-19.3	461-545	2019-2145	4.4-3.9	18-14	506-551	281-315	55.5-57.2	3740- 3470	7.4- 6.3	30-16	30-27
TB	6	10	0	.375	335-380	20.9-25.1	483-511	1776-2233	3.7-4.4	17-27	563-490	334-286	59.3-58.4	3907- 3480	6.9- 7.1	22-20	23-18
Det	4	11	1	.281	283-408	17.7-25.5	446-519	2017-1808	4.5-3.5	13-17	531-466	298-288	56.1-61.8	3787- 3782	7.1- 8.1	19-27	22-14
Min	3	13	0	.188	276-484	17.3-30.3	444-547	1844-2573	4.2-4.7	10-20	533-490	281-319	52.7-65.1	3337- 3954	6.3- 8.1	18-35	25-11
Western Division																	
SF	15	1	0	.938	475-227	14.2-14.2	534-432	2465-1795	4.6-4.2	21-10	496-546	312-298	62.0-54.6	4079- 3744	8.2- 6.9	32-14	10-25
LARm*	10	6	0	.625	346-316	21.6-19.8	541-449	2864-1600	5.3-3.6	16-15	358-566	176-346	49.2-61.1	2382- 3964	6.7- 7.0	16-18	17-17
NO	7	9	0	.438	298-361	18.6-22.6	523-549	2171-2461	4.2-4.5	9-13	476-422	246-239	51.7-56.6	3198- 2873	6.7- 6.8	21-23	28-13
Atl	4	12	0	.250	281-382	17.6-23.9	489-538	1994-2153	4.1-4.0	16-16	478-443	294-262	61.5-59.1	3546- 3413	7.4- 7.7	14-27	20-12
League 224 games					9502	42.4	13811	55503	4.0	410	14325	8076	56.4	102233	7.1	615	584

*Wild Card qualifiers for playoffs
AFC Wild Card playoff: Sea 13, LARd 7
NFC Wild Card playoff: NYG 16, LARm 13
AFC Divisional playoffs: Mia 13, Sea 10; Pit 24, Den 17
NFC Divisional playoffs: SF 21, NYG 10; ChiB 23, Was 10
AFC championship: Mia 45, Pit 28
NFC championship: SF 23, ChiB 0
Super Bowl XIX: SF (NFC) 38, Mia (AFC) 16

LEADING RUSHERS AFC	ATT	YARD	AVG	Long	TD
Earnest Jackson, SD	296	1179	4.0	32t	8
Marcus Allen, LARd	275	1168	4.2	52t	13
Sammy Winder, Den	296	1153	3.9	24	4
Greg Bell, Buf	262	1100	4.2	85t	7
Freeman McNeil, NYJ	229	1070	4.7	53	5

LEADING RUSHERS NFC	ATT	YARD	AVG	Long	TD
Eric Dickerson, LARm	379	2105	5.6	66	14
Walter Payton, ChiB	381	1684	4.4	72t	11
James Wilder, TB	407	1544	3.8	37	13
Gerald Riggs, Atl	353	1486	4.2	57	13
Wendell Tyler, SF	246	1262	5.1	40	7

LEADING PASSERS AFC	ATT	COM	YARD	TD	IN
Dan Marino, Mia	564	362	5084	48	17
Tony Eason, NE	431	259	3228	23	8
Dan Fouts, SD	507	317	3740	19	17
Dave Krieg, Sea	480	276	3671	32	24
Ken Anderson, Cin	275	175	2107	10	12

LEADING PASSERS NFC	ATT	COM	YARD	TD	IN
Joe Montana, SF	432	279	3630	28	10
Neil Lomax, StL	560	345	4614	28	16
Steve Bartkowski, Atl	269	181	2158	11	10
Joe Theismann, Was	477	283	3391	24	13
Lynn Dickey, GB	401	237	3195	25	19

LEADING RECEIVERS AFC	NO	YARD	AVG	Long	TD
Ozzie Newsome, Cle	89	1001	11.2	52	5
John Stallworth, Pit	80	1395	17.4	51	11
Todd Christensen, LARd	80	1007	12.6	38	7
Steve Largent, Sea	74	1164	15.7	65	12
Mark Clayton, Mia	73	1389	19.0	65t	18

LEADING RECEIVERS NFC	NO	YARD	AVG	Long	TD
Art Monk, Was	106	1372	12.9	72	7
James Wilder, TB	85	685	8.1	50	0
Roy Green, StL	78	1555	19.9	83t	12
James Jones, Det	77	662	8.6	39	5
Kevin House, TB	76	1005	13.2	55	5

LEADING SCORERS AFC	TD	FG	PAT	PTS
Gary Anderson, Pit	0	24	45	117
Norm Johnson, Sea	0	20	50	110
Marcus Allen, LARd	18	0	0	108
Mark Clayton, Mia	18	0	0	108
Tony Franklin, NE	0	22	42	108

LEADING SCORERS NFC	TD	FG	PAT	PTS
Ray Wersching, SF	0	25	56	131
Mark Moseley, Was	0	24	48	120
Neil O'Donoghue, StL	0	23	48	117
Paul McFadden, Phi	0	30	26	116
Mike Lansford, LARm	0	25	37	112

LEADING INTERCEPTOR	NO	YARD	AVG	Long	TD
Ken Easley, Sea (AFC)	10	126	12.6	58t	2
Tom Flynn, GB (NFC)	9	106	11.8	31	0

LEADING PUNTER	NO	AVG	Long
Jim Arnold, KC (AFC)	98	44.9	63
Brian Hansen, NO (NFC)	69	43.8	66

LEADING PUNT RETURNER	NO	YDS	AVG	Long	TD
Mike Martin, Cin (AFC)	24	376	15.7	55	0
Henry Ellard, LARm (NFC)	30	403	13.4	83t	2

LEADING KICKOFF RETURNER	NO	YDS	AVG	Long	TD
Bobby Humphery, NYJ (AFC)	22	675	30.7	97t	1
Barry Redden, LARm (NFC)	23	530	23.0	40	0

SUPERLATIVES AFC

Rushing Avg.	5.0	Joe Carter, Mia
Receiving Avg.	20.4	Daryl Turner, Sea
Completion Pct.a	64.2	Dan Marino, Mia
Touchdowns	18	Marcus Allen, LARd Mark Clayton, Mia
Field Goals	24	Gary Anderson, Pit Matt Bahr, Cle
Sacks	22.0	Mark Gastineau, NYJ

SUPERLATIVES NFC

Rushing Avg.	6.0	Hokie Gajan, NO
Receiving Avg.	22.0	James Lofton, GB
Completion Pct.	67.3	Steve Bartkowski, Atl
Touchdowns	14	Eric Dickerson, LARm John Riggins, Was
Field Goals	30	Paul McFadden, Phi
Sacks	17.5	Richard Dent, ChiB

LONGEST AFC

Run	85t	Greg Bell, Buf
Pass	92	Marc Wilson to Marcus Allen, LARd
Interception	99t	Gill Byrd, SD
Punt	89	Luke Prestridge, NE
Punt Return	76t	Louis Lipps, Pit
Kickoff Return	97t	Bobby Humphery, NYJ
Field Goal	60	Steve Cox, Cle

LONGEST NFC

Run	81	Billy Sims, Det
Pass	90t	Ron Jaworski to Mike Quick, Phi
Interception	99t	Tim Lewis, GB
Punt	87	David Finzer, ChiB
Punt Return	83t	Henry Ellard, LARm
Kickoff Return	97t	Del Rodgers, GB
Field Goal	54	Jan Stenerud, Min

1985 AMERICAN FOOTBALL CONFERENCE

					SCORING		RUSHING				PASSING						
Team	W	L	T	PCT	OWN-OPP PTS-PTS	OWN-OPP PPG-PPG	OWN-OPP ATT-ATT	OWN-OPP YARD-YARD	OWN-OPP AVG-AVG	ON-OP TD-TD	OWN-OPP ATT-ATT	OWN-OPP COM-COM	OWN-OPP PCT-PCT	OWN-OPP YARD-YARD	OWN-OPP AVG-AVG	ON-OP TD-TD	ON-OP IN-IN
Eastern Division																	
Mia	12	4	0	.750	428-320	26.8-20.0	444-509	1729-2256	3.9-4.4	19-15	576-487	343-257	59.5-52.8	4278- 3789	6.9- 6.7	31-21	21-23
NYJ*	11	5	0	.688	393-264	24.6-16.5	564-433	2312-1516	4.1-3.5	18-10	497-507	303-267	61.0-52.7	3963- 3626	6.4- 5.3	25-17	8-22
NE*	11	5	0	.688	362-290	22.6-18.1	565-466	2331-1655	4.1-3.6	15-15	457-525	255-262	55.8-49.9	3483- 3393	6.4- 5.3	20-14	22-23
Ind	5	11	0	.313	320-386	20.0-24.1	485-539	2439-2145	5.0-4.0	22-20	468-504	235-275	50.2-54.6	2811- 3721	5.1- 6.4	15-24	20-16
Buf	2	14	0	.125	200-381	12.5-23.8	412-569	1611-2462	3.9-4.3	13-20	517-477	263-265	50.9-55.6	3331- 3301	5.3- 6.1	9-24	31-20
Central Division																	
Cle	8	8	0	.500	287-294	17.9-18.4	533-497	2285-1851	4.3-3.7	16-14	414-509	222-289	53.6-56.8	2865- 3460	5.9- 5.6	17-18	13-18
Cin	7	9	0	.438	441-437	27.6-27.3	503-461	2183-1999	4.3-4.3	20-23	518-518	302-297	58.3-57.3	4082- 3998	6.7- 6.6	31-26	13-19
Pit	8	9	0	.438	379-355	23.7-22.2	541-470	2177-1876	4.0-4.0	14-19	512-484	254-287	49.6-59.3	3397- 3088	5.8- 6.8	23-18	27-20
Hou	5	11	0	.313	284-412	17.8-25.8	428-588	1570-2814	3.7-4.8	13-21	512-462	277-260	54.1-56.3	3523- 3654	5.4- 6.6	18-29	22-15
Western Division																	
LARd	12	4	0	.750	354-308	22.1-19.3	532-461	2262-1605	4.3-3.5	18- 7	506-511	269-251	53.2-49.1	3481- 3486	5.7- 5.2	20-22	24-17
Den	11	5	0	.688	380-329	23.8-20.6	497-475	1851-1973	3.7-4.2	20-10	617-547	329-277	53.3-50.6	3952- 3654	5.6- 5.4	23-22	23-24
Sea	8	8	0	.500	349-303	21.8-18.9	462-473	1644-1837	3.6-3.9	9-12	575-496	304-273	52.9-55.0	3820- 3787	5.4- 6.0	28-22	23-24
SD	8	8	0	.500	467-435	29.2-27.2	440-470	1665-1972	3.8-4.2	20-25	632-595	386-357	61.1-60.0	5175- 4597	7.3- 6.8	37-28	30-26
KC	6	10	0	.375	317-360	19.8-22.5	428-513	1486-2169	3.5-4.2	10-18	511-576	267-332	52.3-57.6	3726- 3752	6.1- 5.7	23-22	23-27

1985 NATIONAL FOOTBALL CONFERENCE

Team	W	L	T	PCT	OWN-OPP PTS-PTS	OWN-OPP PPG-PPG	OWN-OPP ATT-ATT	OWN-OPP YARD-YARD	OWN-OPP AVG-AVG	ON-OP TD-TD	OWN-OPP ATT-ATT	OWN-OPP COM-COM	OWN-OPP PCT-PCT	OWN-OPP YARD-YARD	OWN-OPP AVG-AVG	ON-OP TD-TD	ON-OP IN-IN
Eastern Division																	
Dal	10	6	0	.625	357-333	22.3-20.8	462-465	1741-1853	3.8-4.0	11-18	587-549	344-279	58.6-50.8	4236- 4214	6.1- 6.2	27-20	25-33
NYG*	10	6	0	.625	399-283	24.9-17.7	581-419	2451-1482	4.2-3.5	24- 9	497-535	275-278	56.3-52.0	3829- 3377	6.3- 4.7	22-20	20-24
Was	10	6	0	.625	297-312	18.6-19.5	571-424	2523-1734	4.4-4.1	20-11	512-465	280-239	54.7-51.4	3243- 3124	5.0- 5.3	13-19	21-23
Phi	7	9	0	.438	286-310	17.9-19.4	428-526	1630-2205	3.8-4.2	8-17	567-478	290-251	51.1-52.5	4036- 3289	5.8- 5.5	19-18	28-18
StL	5	11	0	.313	278-414	17.4-25.9	417-562	1974-2378	4.7-4.3	14-11	534-461	296-253	55.4-54.0	3581- 3257	5.2- 6.1	19-34	18-13
Central Division																	
ChiB	15	1	0	.938	456-198	28.5-12.4	610-359	2781-1319	4.5-3.7	27- 6	432-522	237-249	54.9-47.7	3303- 3299	6.5- 4.8	17-16	16-34
GB	8	8	0	.500	337-355	21.1-22.2	470-494	2208-2047	4.7-4.1	16-17	513-509	267-295	52.0-58.0	3552- 3509	5.6- 5.6	21-22	27-15
Min	7	9	0	.438	346-359	21.6-22.4	406-542	1516-2223	3.7-4.1	19-16	576-490	311-280	54.0-57.1	3931- 3464	5.9- 6.2	22-20	29-22
Det	7	9	0	.438	307-366	19.2-22.9	452-560	1538-2665	3.4-4.8	13-19	462-478	254-283	55.0-59.2	3316- 3242	5.7- 5.6	19-16	21-18
TB	2	14	0	.125	294-448	18.4-28.0	434-547	1644-2430	3.8-4.4	11-28	508-505	269-318	53.0-63.0	3423- 3955	5.7- 6.8	22-18	26-18
Western Division																	
LARm	11	5	0	.688	340-277	21.3-17.3	503-444	2057-1586	4.1-3.6	15- 9	403-548	234-296	58.1-54.0	2872- 3483	5.4- 5.1	16-19	14-29
SF*	10	6	0	.625	411-263	25.7-16.4	477-435	2232-1683	4.7-3.9	20-10	550-621	331-346	60.2-56.7	3987- 3965	6.2- 5.2	26-11	14-18
NO	5	11	0	.313	294-401	18.4-25.1	431-508	1683-2162	3.9-4.3	4-19	508-529	260-306	51.2-57.8	3257- 3975	4.9- 6.4	20-26	23-21
Atl	4	12	0	.250	282-452	17.6-28.3	560-437	2466-2052	4.4-4.7	14-24	462-535	254-289	55.0-54.0	3025- 4129	4.7- 6.6	13-32	20-22
League 224 games					9645	43.1	13636	55969	4.1	443	14423	7911	54.8	101518	7.0	598	602

*Wild Card qualifiers for playoffs
AFC Wild Card playoff: NE 26, NYJ 14
NFC Wild Card playoff: NYG 17, SF 3
AFC Divisional playoffs: Mia 24, Cle 21; NE 27, LARd 20
NFC Divisional playoffs: LARm 20, Dal 0; ChiB 21, NYG 0
AFC championship: NE 31, Mia 14
NFC championship: ChiB 24, LARm 0
Super Bowl XX: ChiB (NFC) 46, NE (AFC) 10

LEADING RUSHERS AFC	ATT	YARD	AVG	Long	TD
Marcus Allen, LARd	380	1759	4.6	61t	11
Freeman McNeil, NYJ	294	1331	4.5	69	3
Craig James, NE	263	1227	4.7	65t	5
Kevin Mack, Cle	222	1104	5.0	61	7
Curt Warner, Sea	291	1094	3.8	38	8

LEADING RUSHERS NFC	ATT	YARD	AVG	Long	TD
Gerald Riggs, Atl	397	1719	4.3	50	10
Walter Payton, ChiB	324	1551	4.8	40t	9
Joe Morris, NYG	294	1336	4.5	65t	21
Tony Dorsett, Dal	305	1307	4.3	60t	7
James Wilder, TB	365	1300	3.6	28	10

LEADING PASSERS AFC	ATT	COM	YARD	TD	IN
Ken O'Brien, NYJ	488	297	3888	25	8
Boomer Esiason, Cin	431	251	3443	27	12
Dan Fouts, SD	430	254	3638	27	20
Dan Marino, Mia	567	336	4137	30	21
Bill Kenney, KC	338	181	2536	17	9

LEADING PASSERS NFC	ATT	COM	YARD	TD	IN
Joe Montana, SF	494	303	3653	27	13
Jim McMahon, ChiB	318	178	2392	15	11
Dieter Brock, LARm	365	218	2658	16	13
Danny White, Dal	450	267	3157	21	17
Neil Lomax, StL	471	265	3214	18	12

LEADING RECEIVERS AFC	NO	YARD	AVG	Long	TD
Lionel James, SD	86	1027	11.9	67t	6
Todd Christensen, LARd	82	987	12.0	48	6
Butch Woolfolk, Hou	80	814	10.2	80t	4
Steve Largent, Sea	79	1287	16.3	43	6
Mickey Shuler, NYJ	76	879	11.6	35	7

LEADING RECEIVERS NFC	NO	YARD	AVG	Long	TD
Roger Craig, SF	92	1016	11.0	73	6
Art Monk, Was	91	1226	13.5	53	2
Tony Hill, Dal	74	1113	15.0	53t	7
Mike Quick, Phi	73	1247	17.1	99t	11
Gary Clark, Was	72	926	12.9	55	5

LEADING SCORERS AFC	TD	FG	PAT	PTS
Gary Anderson, Pit	0	33	40	139
Pat Leahy, NYJ	0	26	45	121
Jim Breech, Cin	0	24	48	120
Fuad Reveiz, Mia	0	22	50	116
Tony Franklin, NE	0	24	40	112

LEADING SCORERS NFC	TD	FG	PAT	PTS
Kevin Butler, ChiB	0	31	51	144
Joe Morris, NYG	21	0	0	126
Morten Andersen, NO	0	31	27	120
Ed Murray, Det	0	26	31	109
Mike Lansford, LARm	0	22	38	104
Paul McFadden, Phi	0	25	29	104

LEADING INTERCEPTOR	NO	YARD	AVG	Long	TD
Albert Lewis, KC	(AFC)	8	59	7.4	16
Eugene Daniel, Ind	(AFC)	8	53	6.6	29
Everson Walls, Dal	(NFC)	9	31	3.4	19

LEADING PUNTER	NO	AVG	Long
Rohn Stark, Ind (AFC)	78	45.9	68
Dick Donnelly, Atl (NFC)	59	43.6	68

LEADING PUNT RETURNER	NO	YDS	AVG	Long	TD
Irving Fryar, NE (AFC)	37	520	14.1	85t	2
Henry Ellard, LARm (NFC)	37	501	13.5	80t	1

LEADING KICKOFF RETURNER	NO	YDS	AVG	Long	TD
Glen Young, Cle (AFC)	35	898	25.7	63	0
Ron Brown, LARm (NFC)	28	918	32.8	98t	3

SUPERLATIVES AFC

Rushing Avg.	5.2	George Wonsley, Ind
Receiving Avg.	21.9	Stephone Paige, KC
Completion Pct.	60.9	Ken O'Brien, NYJ
Touchdowns	15	Louis Lipps, Pit
Field Goals	33	Gary Anderson, Pit
Sacks	16.5	Andre Tippett, NE

SUPERLATIVES NFC

Rushing Avg.	5.5	Stump Mitchell, StL
Receiving Avg.	21.3	Willie Gault, ChiB
Completion Pct.	61.3	Joe Montana, SF
Touchdowns	21	Joe Morris, NYG
Field Goals	31	Morten Andersen, NO Kevin Butler, ChiB
Sacks	17.0	Richard Dent, ChiB

LONGEST AFC

Run	77t	Greg Bell, Buf
Pass	96t	Ken O'Brien to Wesley Walker, NYJ
Interception	83	Fred Marion, NE
Punt	75	Rich Camarillo, NE
Punt Return	85t	Irving Fryar, NE
Kickoff Return	98t	Gary Anderson, SD
Field Goal	58	Nick Lowery, KC

LONGEST NFC

Run	80	Jessie Clark, GB
Pass	99t	Ron Jaworski to Mike Quick, Phi
Interception	90	Mike Richardson, ChiB
Punt	75	Mike Horan, Phi
Punt Return	80t	Henry Ellard, LARm
Kickoff Return	99t	Willie Gault, ChiB
Field Goal	55	Morten Andersen, NO

1986 AMERICAN FOOTBALL CONFERENCE

					SCORING		RUSHING				PASSING						
Team	W	L	T	PCT	OWN-OPP PTS-PTS	OWN-OPP PPG-PPG	OWN-OPP ATT-ATT	OWN-OPP YARD-YARD	OWN-OPP AVG-AVG	ON-OP TD-TD	OWN-OPP ATT-ATT	OWN-OPP COM-COM	OWN-OPP PCT-PCT	OWN-OPP YARD-YARD	OWN-OPP AVG-AVG	ON-OP TD-TD	ON-OP IN-IN
Eastern Division																	
NE	11	5	0	.688	412-307	25.8-19.2	469-510	1373-2203	2.9-4.3	10-19	557-473	340-255	61.0-53.9	4321- 3324	6.6- 5.7	29-15	13-21
NYJ*	10	6	0	.625	364-386	22.8-24.1	590-450	1729-1661	3.5-3.7	16-12	537-603	334-348	62.2-57.7	4032- 4567	6.3- 7.0	27-35	21-20
Mia	8	8	0	.500	430-405	26.9-25.3	349-540	1545-2483	4.4-4.6	9-23	645-485	392-290	60.8-59.8	4898- 3825	7.2- 6.9	46-22	23-13
Buf	4	12	0	.250	287-348	17.9-21.8	419-465	1654-1721	3.9-3.7	9-18	499-570	294-343	58.9-60.2	3697- 4069	6.2- 6.3	22-21	19-10
Ind	3	13	0	.188	229-400	14.3-25.0	407-517	1491-1962	3.7-3.8	10-14	586-510	300-306	51.2-60.0	3615- 3933	5.0- 7.0	16-28	24-16
Central Division																	
Cle	12	4	0	.750	391-310	24.4-19.4	470-494	1650-1981	3.5-4.0	20-12	536-518	315-291	56.6-56.2	4018- 3546	6.5- 5.0	18-21	11-18
Cin	10	6	0	.625	409-394	25.6-24.6	521-514	2533-2122	4.9-4.1	24-23	497-495	287-278	57.7-56.2	4160- 3520	7.5- 5.9	25-17	20-17
Pit	6	10	0	.375	307-336	19.2-21.0	564-471	2223-1872	3.9-4.0	16-10	491-536	238-311	48.5-58.0	2747- 3669	5.1- 5.8	16-22	20-20
Hou	5	11	0	.313	274-329	17.1-20.6	490-532	1700-2035	3.5-3.8	13-13	561-490	286-228	52.3-46.5	3843- 3200	5.8- 5.8	14-25	31-16
Western Division																	
Den	11	5	0	.688	378-327	23.6-20.4	456-432	1678-1891	3.7-3.8	17-13	549-545	306-301	56.7-55.2	3811- 3755	6.0- 5.6	22-21	16-18
KC*	10	6	0	.625	358-326	22.4-20.4	432-485	1468-1739	3.4-3.6	10-13	521-569	257-303	49.3-53.3	3122- 3555	4.8- 5.2	23-21	18-31
Sea	10	6	0	.625	366-293	22.9-18.3	513-471	2300-1750	4.5-3.7	15-12	453-535	268-301	59.2-56.3	3424- 3888	6.3- 6.2	24-20	14-22
LARd	8	8	0	.500	323-346	20.2-21.6	475-439	1790-1726	3.8-3.9	6-19	530-501	281-271	53.0-54.1	3973- 3539	5.9- 5.5	27-21	25-26
SD	4	12	0	.250	335-396	20.9-24.8	471-475	1576-1678	3.3-3.5	19-14	604-509	339-288	56.1-56.6	4045- 4128	5.9- 6.5	21-27	33-15

1986 NATIONAL FOOTBALL CONFERENCE

Team	W	L	T	PCT	OWN-OPP PTS-PTS	OWN-OPP PPG-PPG	OWN-OPP ATT-ATT	OWN-OPP YARD-YARD	OWN-OPP AVG-AVG	ON-OP TD-TD	OWN-OPP ATT-ATT	OWN-OPP COM-COM	OWN-OPP PCT-PCT	OWN-OPP YARD-YARD	OWN-OPP AVG-AVG	ON-OP TD-TD	ON-OP IN-IN
Eastern Division																	
NYG	14	2	0	.875	371-236	23.2-14.8	558-350	2255-1284	4.0-3.7	18-10	472-587	260-334	55.1-56.9	3500- 3887	6.1- 5.4	22-15	22-24
Was*	12	4	0	.750	368-296	23.0-18.5	474-459	1732-1805	3.7-3.9	23-14	542-532	276-302	50.9-56.8	4109- 3916	6.8- 6.0	22-21	22-19
Dal	7	9	0	.438	346-337	21.6-21.1	447-500	1969-2200	4.4-4.4	21-17	547-464	319-226	58.3-48.7	4003- 3149	5.8- 5.4	21-21	24-17
Phi	5	10	1	.344	256-312	16.0-19.5	499-458	2002-1989	4.0-4.3	8-14	514-532	268-260	52.1-48.3	3248- 3641	4.1- 5.5	19-21	17-23
StL	4	11	1	.281	218-351	13.6-21.9	419-560	1787-2227	4.3-4.0	8-17	516-436	293-215	56.8-49.3	3140- 2992	4.7- 5.5	17-21	19-10
Central Division																	
ChiB	14	2	0	.875	352-187	22.0-11.7	606-427	2700-1463	4.5-3.4	21- 4	415-513	208-243	50.1-47.4	2912- 3170	6.3- 4.6	12-12	25-31
Min	9	7	0	.563	398-273	24.9-17.1	461-481	1738-1796	3.8-3.7	14-10	519-494	290-276	55.9-55.9	4185- 3475	7.0- 6.1	31-16	15-24
Det	5	11	0	.313	277-326	17.3-20.4	470-519	1771-2349	3.8-4.5	13-15	500-468	286-279	57.2-59.6	3107- 3090	5.2- 5.5	18-14	20-22
GB	4	12	0	.250	254-418	15.9-26.1	424-565	1614-2095	3.8-3.7	8-16	565-448	305-267	54.0-59.6	3708- 3142	5.7- 6.1	18-31	27-20
TB	2	14	0	.125	239-473	14.9-29.6	455-558	1863-2648	4.1-4.7	12-31	459-484	245-289	53.4-59.7	2892- 3838	4.9- 7.3	13-23	25-13
Western Division																	
SF	10	5	1	.656	374-247	23.4-15.4	510-406	1986-1555	3.9-3.8	16- 8	582-604	353-324	60.7-53.6	4299- 3773	6.7- 5.1	21-18	20-39
LARm*	10	6	0	.625	309-267	19.3-16.7	578-460	2457-1681	4.3-3.7	16- 9	403-539	194-313	48.1-58.1	2380- 3482	5.9- 5.5	15-17	15-28
Atl	7	8	1	.469	280-280	17.5-17.5	578-485	2524-1916	4.4-4.0	12-10	452-453	246-241	54.4-53.2	3046- 3169	5.1- 6.3	14-19	17-22
NO	7	9	0	.438	288-287	18.0-17.9	505-486	2074-1559	4.1-3.2	15-11	425-576	232-331	54.6-57.5	2893- 3886	5.9- 5.7	13-21	25-26
League 224 games					9193	41.0	13509	53172	3.9	401	14469	8014	55.4	101128	7.0	586	581

*Wild Card qualifiers for playoffs
AFC Wild Card playoff: NYJ 35, KC 15
NFC Wild Card playoff: Was 19, LARm 7
AFC Divisional playoffs: Cle 23, NYJ 20 (OT); Den 22, NE 17
NFC Divisional playoffs: Was 27, Chi 13; NYG 49, SF 3
AFC championship: Den 23, Cle 20 (OT)
NFC championship: NYG 17, Was 0
Super Bowl XXI: NYG (NFC) 39, Den (AFC) 20

LEADING RUSHERS AFC	ATT	YARD	AVG	Long	TD
Curt Warner, Sea	319	1481	4.6	60t	13
James Brooks, Cin	205	1087	5.3	56t	5
Earnest Jackson, Pit	216	910	4.2	31	5
Walter Abercrombie, Pit	214	877	4.1	38t	6
Freeman McNeil, NYJ	214	856	4.0	40	5

LEADING RUSHERS NFC	ATT	YARD	AVG	Long	TD
Eric Dickerson, LARm	404	1821	4.5	42t	11
Joe Morris, NYG	341	1516	4.4	54	14
Rueben Mayes, NO	286	1353	4.7	50	8
Walter Payton, ChiB	321	1333	4.2	41	8
Gerald Riggs, Atl	343	1327	3.9	31	9

LEADING PASSERS AFC	ATT	COM	YARD	TD	IN
Dan Marino, Mia	623	378	4746	44	23
Dave Krieg, Sea	375	225	2921	21	11
Tony Eason, NE	448	276	3328	19	10
Boomer Esiason, Cin	469	273	3959	24	17
Ken O'Brien, NYJ	482	300	3690	25	20

LEADING PASSERS NFC	ATT	COM	YARD	TD	IN
Tommy Kramer, Min	372	208	3000	24	10
Joe Montana, SF	307	191	2236	8	9
Eric Hipple, Det	305	192	1919	9	11
Phil Simms, NYG	468	259	3487	21	22
Neil Lomax, StL	421	240	2583	13	12

LEADING RECEIVERS AFC	NO	YARD	AVG	Long	TD
Todd Christensen, LARd	95	1153	12.1	35	8
Al Toon, NYJ	85	1176	13.8	62t	8
Stanley Morgan, NE	84	1491	17.8	44t	10
Gary Anderson, SD	80	871	10.9	65t	8
Tony Collins, NE	77	684	8.9	49	5

LEADING RECEIVERS NFC	NO	YARD	AVG	Long	TD
Jerry Rice, SF	86	1570	18.3	66t	15
Roger Craig, SF	81	624	7.7	48	0
J.T. Smith, StL	80	1014	12.8	45	6
Herschel Walker, Dal	76	837	11.0	84t	2
Gary Clark, Was	74	1265	17.1	55	7

LEADING SCORERS AFC	TD	FG	PAT	PTS
Tony Franklin, NE	0	32	44	140
Norm Johnson, Sea	0	22	42	108
Rich Karlis, Den	0	20	44	104
Jim Breech, Cin	0	17	50	101
Nick Lowery, KC	0	19	43	100

LEADING SCORERS NFC	TD	FG	PAT	PTS
Kevin Butler, ChiB	0	28	36	120
Ray Wersching, SF	0	25	41	116
Chuck Nelson, Min	0	22	44	110
Morten Andersen, NO	0	26	30	108
George Rogers, Was	18	0	0	108

LEADING INTERCEPTOR	NO	YARD	AVG	Long	TD
Deron Cherry, KC (AFC)	9	150	16.7	49	0
Ronnie Lott, SF (NFC)	10	134	13.4	57t	1

LEADING PUNTER	NO	AVG	Long
Rohn Stark, Ind (AFC)	76	45.2	63
Sean Landeta, NYG (NFC)	79	44.8	61

LEADING PUNT RETURNER	NO	YDS	AVG	Long	TD
Bobby Joe Edmonds, Sea (AFC)	34	419	12.3	75t	1
Vai Sikahema, StL (NFC)	43	522	12.1	71t	2

LEADING KICKOFF RETURNER	NO	YDS	AVG	Long	TD
Lupe Sanchez, Pit (AFC)	25	591	23.6	64	0
Dennis Gentry, ChiB (NFC)	20	576	28.8	91t	1

SUPERLATIVES AFC

Rushing Avg.	5.3	James Brooks, Cin
Receiving Avg.	22.9	Chris Burkett, Buf
Completion Pct.	62.2	Ken O'Brien, NYJ
Touchdowns	14	Samuel Winder, Den
Field Goals	32	Tony Franklin, NE
Sacks	15.5	Sean Jones, LARd

SUPERLATIVES NFC

Rushing Avg.	4.9	Herschel Walker, Dal
Receiving Avg.	20.7	Walter Stanley, GB
Completion Pct.	63.0	Eric Hipple, Det
Touchdowns	18	George Rogers, Was
Field Goals	28	Kevin Butler, ChiB
Sacks	20.5	Lawrence Taylor, NYG

LONGEST AFC

Run	70t	Albert Bentley, Ind
Pass	85t	Dan Marino to Mark Duper, Mia
Interception	80	John Holt, Ind
Punt	73	Reggie Roby, Mia (twice)
Punt Return	84t	Gerald McNeil, Cle
Kickoff Return	100t	Gerald McNeil, Cle
Field Goal	54	Norm Johnson, Sea

LONGEST NFC

Run	84t	Herschel Walker, Dal
Pass	85	Mike Tomczak to Emery Moorehead, ChiB
Interception	88t	Tory Nixon, SF
Punt	71	Rick Donnelly, Atl
Punt Return	83t	Walter Stanley, GB
Kickoff Return	101t	Mel Gray, NO
Field Goal	57	Steve Cox, Was

1987 AMERICAN FOOTBALL CONFERENCE

					SCORING		RUSHING				PASSING						
Team	W	L	T	PCT	OWN-OPP PTS-PTS	OWN-OPP PPG-PPG	OWN-OPP ATT-ATT	OWN-OPP YARD-YARD	OWN-OPP AVG-AVG	ON-OP TD-TD	OWN-OPP ATT-ATT	OWN-OPP COM-COM	OWN-OPP PCT-PCT	OWN - OPP YARD - YARD	OWN-OPP AVG-AVG	ON-OP TD-TD	ON-OP IN-IN
Eastern Division																	
Ind	9	6	0	.600	300-238	20.0-15.9	497-463	2143-1790	4.3-3.9	14- 6	447-501	255-250	57.0-49.9	3042- 3073	6.8- 6.1	16-19	16-20
NE	8	7	0	.533	320-293	21.3-19.5	513-490	1771-1778	3.5-3.6	12-13	440-520	236-273	53.6-52.5	2929- 3438	6.7- 6.6	22-17	18-21
Mia	8	7	0	.533	362-335	24.1-22.3	408-498	1662-2198	4.1-4.4	16-18	584-494	338-295	57.9-59.7	3977- 3430	6.8- 6.9	29-21	20-16
Buf	7	8	0	.467	270-305	18.0-20.3	465-541	1840-2052	4.0-3.8	9-11	516-447	292-249	56.6-55.7	3246- 3121	6.3- 7.0	21-25	19-17
NYJ	6	9	0	.400	334-360	22.3-24.0	458-476	1671-1835	3.6-3.9	17-15	517-488	302-260	58.4-53.3	3402- 3412	6.6- 7.0	18-27	15-18
Central Division																	
Cle	10	5	0	.667	390-239	26.0-15.9	474-401	1745-1433	3.7-3.6	16- 7	482-467	291-246	60.4-52.7	3625- 3088	7.5- 6.6	27-15	12-23
Hou*	9	6	0	.600	345-349	23.0-23.3	486-446	1923-1848	4.0-4.1	12-10	482-495	240-266	49.8-53.7	3534- 3416	7.3- 6.9	24-25	23-23
Pit	8	7	0	.533	285-299	19.0-19.9	517-455	2144-1610	4.1-3.5	11- 8	429-481	198-290	46.2-60.3	2464- 3506	5.7- 7.3	13-22	27-26
Cin	4	11	0	.267	285-370	19.0-24.7	538-441	2164-1641	4.0-3.7	13-15	475-456	255-267	53.7-58.6	3468- 3359	7.3- 7.4	17-24	20-14
Western Division																	
Den	10	4	1	.700	379-288	25.3-19.2	510-454	1920-2017	3.9-4.4	18-16	530-456	285-261	53.8-57.2	3874- 3040	7.3- 6.7	24-15	19-28
Sea*	9	6	0	.600	371-314	24.7-20.9	496-472	2023-2201	4.1-4.7	13-14	405-445	237-255	58.5-57.3	3028- 3196	7.5- 7.2	31-20	21-17
SD	8	7	0	.533	253-317	16.9-21.1	396-522	1308-2171	3.3-4.2	11-14	516-441	303-227	58.7-51.5	3602- 3080	7.0- 7.0	13-19	23-13
LARd	5	10	0	.333	301-289	20.1-19.3	475-469	2197-1637	4.6-3.5	13-12	457-425	247-224	54.0-52.7	3429- 3088	7.5- 7.3	19-18	18-13
KC	4	11	0	.267	273-388	18.2-25.9	419-535	1799-2333	4.3-4.4	7-16	432-484	236-279	54.6-57.6	2985- 3473	6.9- 7.2	17-25	17-11
1987 NATIONAL FOOTBALL CONFERENCE																	
Eastern Division																	
Was	11	4	0	.733	379-285	25.3-19.0	500-441	2102-1679	4.2-3.8	18-10	478-527	247-276	51.7-52.4	3718- 3767	7.8- 7.1	27-19	18-23
Dal	7	8	0	.467	340-348	22.7-23.2	465-459	1865-1617	4.0-3.5	17-19	500-502	288-269	57.6-53.6	3594- 3781	7.2- 7.5	19-21	20-23
StL	7	8	0	.467	362-368	24.1-24.5	462-492	1873-2001	4.1-4.1	15-16	529-490	305-276	57.7-56.3	3850- 3668	7.3- 7.5	25-30	15-14
Phi	7	8	0	.467	337-380	22.5-25.3	509-428	2027-1643	4.0-3.8	12-16	520-561	283-305	54.4-54.4	3561- 4058	6.8- 7.2	26-29	16-21
NYG	6	9	0	.400	280-312	18.7-20.8	440-493	1457-1768	3.3-3.6	4-14	499-508	265-292	53.1-57.5	3645- 3272	7.3- 6.4	26-17	22-20
Central Division																	
ChiB	11	4	0	.733	356-282	23.7-18.8	485-412	1954-1413	4.0-3.4	13- 5	493-507	272-255	55.2-50.3	3420- 3286	6.9- 6.5	23-24	24-13
Min*	8	7	0	.533	336-335	22.4-22.3	482-440	1983-1724	4.1-3.9	20- 9	446-498	232-278	52.0-55.8	3185- 3407	7.1- 6.8	21-24	23-26
GB	5	9	1	.367	255-300	17.0-20.0	464-521	1801-1920	3.9-3.7	13-15	455-469	234-279	51.4-59.5	2977- 3200	6.5- 6.8	15-14	17-18
TB	4	11	0	.267	286-360	19.1-24.0	394-500	1365-2038	3.5-4.1	7-18	517-457	264-271	51.1-59.3	3377- 3255	6.5- 7.1	22-23	17-16
Det	4	11	0	.267	269-384	17.9-25.6	398-504	1435-2070	3.6-4.1	9-18	509-459	275-259	54.0-56.4	3150- 3558	6.2- 7.8	16-23	26-19
Western Division																	
SF	13	2	0	.867	459-253	30.6-16.9	524-429	2237-1611	4.3-3.8	11- 8	501-467	322-224	64.3-48.0	3955- 2771	7.9- 5.9	44-13	14-25
NO*	12	3	0	.800	422-283	28.1-18.9	569-388	2190-1550	3.8-4.0	20- 6	411-489	227-246	55.2-50.3	2987- 3155	7.3- 6.5	23-25	12-30
LARm	6	9	0	.400	317-361	21.1-24.1	512-419	2097-1732	4.1-4.1	15- 8	420-504	220-281	52.4-55.8	2750- 3693	6.5- 7.3	16-31	18-16
Atl	3	12	0	.200	205-436	13.7-29.1	333-600	1298-2734	3.9-4.6	5-24	501-453	247-243	49.3-53.6	3108- 3291	6.2- 7.3	17-26	32-15
League 210 games					9071	43.2	13189	52044	3.9	361	13491	7396	54.8	93822	7.0	611	540

*Wild Card qualifiers for playoffs
AFC Wild Card playoff: Hou 23, Sea 20, overtime
NFC Wild Card playoff: Min 44, NO 10
AFC Divisional playoffs: Cle 38, Ind 21; Den 34, Hou 10
NFC Divisional playoffs: Min 36, SF 24; Was 21, Chi 17
AFC championship: Den 38, Cle 33
NFC championship: Was 17, Min 10
Super Bowl XXII: Was (NFC) 42, Den (AFC) 10

LEADING RUSHERS AFC	ATT	YARD	AVG	Long	TD
Eric Dickerson, LARm-Ind	283	1288	4.6	57	6
Curt Warner, Sea	234	985	4.2	57t	8
Mike Rozier, Hou	229	957	4.2	41	3
Marcus Allen, LARd	200	754	3.8	44	5
Sammy Winder, Den	196	741	3.8	19	6

LEADING RUSHERS NFC	ATT	YARD	AVG	Long	TD
Charles White, LARm	324	1374	4.2	58	11
Rueben Mayes, NO	243	917	3.8	38	5
Herschel Walker, Dal	209	891	4.3	60t	7
Gerald Riggs, Atl	203	875	4.3	44	2
Roger Craig, SF	215	815	3.8	25	3

LEADING PASSERS AFC	ATT	COM	YARD	TD	IN
Bernie Kosar, Cle	389	241	3033	22	9
Dan Marino, Mia	444	263	3245	26	13
Dave Krieg, Sea	294	178	2131	23	16
Bill Kenney, KC	273	154	2107	15	9
Marc Wilson, LARd	266	152	2070	12	8

LEADING PASSERS NFC	ATT	COM	YARD	TD	IN
Joe Montana, SF	398	266	3954	31	13
Phil Simms, NYG	282	163	2230	17	9
Neil Lomax, StL	463	275	3387	24	12
Jim McMahon, ChiB	210	125	1639	12	8
Steve DeBerg, TB	275	159	1891	14	7

LEADING RECEIVERS AFC	NO	YARD	AVG	Long	TD
Al Toon, NYJ	68	976	14.4	58t	5
Steve Largent, Sea	58	912	15.7	55	8
Andre Reed, Buf	57	752	13.2	40	5
Chris Burkett, Buf	56	765	13.7	47	4
Ronnie Harmon, Buf	56	477	8.5	42	2

LEADING RECEIVERS NFC	NO	YARD	AVG	Long	TD
J.T. Smith, StL	91	1117	12.3	38	8
Roger Craig, SF	66	492	7.5	35t	1
Jerry Rice, SF	65	1078	16.6	57t	22
Herschel Walker, Dal	60	715	11.9	44	1
Pete Mandley, Det	58	720	12.4	41	7

LEADING SCORERS AFC	TD	FG	PAT	PTS
Jim Breech, Cin	0	24	25	97
Dean Biasucci, Ind	0	24	24	96
Tony Zendejas, Hou	0	20	32	92
Rich Karlis, Den	0	18	37	91
Gary Anderson, Pit	0	22	21	87

LEADING SCORERS NFC	TD	FG	PAT	PTS
Jerry Rice, SF	23	0	0	138
Morten Andersen, NO	0	28	37	121
Roger Ruzek, Dal	0	22	26	92
Mike Lansford, LARm	0	17	36	87
Kevin Butler, ChiB	0	19	28	85

LEADING INTERCEPTOR	NO	YARD	AVG	Long	TD
Mike Prior, Ind (AFC)	6	57	9.5	38	0
Mark Kelso, Buf (AFC)	6	25	4.2	12	0
Keith Bostic, Hou (AFC)	6	14	2.3	7	0
Barry Wilburn, Was (NFC)	9	135	15.0	100t	1

LEADING PUNTER	NO	AVG	Long
Ralf Mojsiejenko, SD (AFC)	67	42.9	57
Rick Donnelly, Atl (NFC)	61	44.0	62

LEADING PUNT RETURNER	NO	YDS	AVG	Long	TD
Bobby Joe Edmonds, Sea (AFC)	20	251	12.6	40	0
Mel Gray, NO (NFC)	24	352	14.7	80	0

LEADING KICKOFF RETURNER	NO	YDS	AVG	Long	TD
Paul Palmer, KC (AFC)	38	923	24.3	95t	2
Sylvester Stamps, Atl (NFC)	24	660	27.5	97t	1

SUPERLATIVES AFC

Rushing Avg.	4.5	Eric Dickerson, Ind
Receiving Avg.	21.5	James Lofton, LARd
Completion Pct.	62.0	Bernie Kosar, Cle
Touchdowns	11	Johnny Hector, NYJ
Field Goals	24	Dean Biasucci, Ind Jim Breech, Cin
Sacks	12.5	Andre Tippett, NE

SUPERLATIVES NFC

Rushing Avg.	4.9	Darrin Nelson, Min
Receiving Avg.	24.3	Anthony Carter, Min
Completion Pct.	66.8	Joe Montana, SF
Touchdowns	23	Jerry Rice, SF
Field Goals	28	Morten Andersen, NO
Sacks	21.0	Reggie White, Phi

LONGEST AFC

Run	91t	Bo Jackcon, LARd
Pass	83t	Warren Moon to Ernest Givins, Hou
Interception	103t	Vencie Glenn, SD
Punt	77	Reggie Roby, Mia
Punt Return	91t	Jo-Jo Townsell, NYJ
Kickoff Return	95t	Paul Palmer, KC
Field Goal	54	Nick Lowery, KC

LONGEST NFC

Run	72	Darrin Nelson, Min
Pass	88t	Ed Rubbert to Anthony Allen, Was
Interception	100t	Barry Wilburn, Min
Punt	77	Steve Cox, Was
Punt Return	94t	Dennis McKinnon, ChiB
Kickoff Return	97t	Sylvester Stamps, Atl
Field Goal	53	Raul Allegre, NYG Ed Murray, Det

1988 AMERICAN FOOTBALL CONFERENCE

					SCORING		RUSHING				PASSING						
Team	W	L	T	PCT	OWN-OPP PTS-PTS	OWN-OPP PPG-PPG	OWN-OPP ATT-ATT	OWN-OPP YARD-YARD	OWN-OPP AVG-AVG	ON-OP TD-TD	OWN-OPP ATT-ATT	OWN-OPP COM-COM	OWN-OPP PCT-PCT	OWN - OPP YARD - YARD	OWN-OPP AVG-AVG	ON-OP TD-TD	ON-OP IN-IN
Eastern Division																	
Buf	12	4	0	.750	329-237	20.6-14.8	528-477	2133-1854	4.0-3.9	15-14	454-448	271-250	59.7-55.8	3411- 3046	7.5- 6.8	15-14	17-15
Ind	9	7	0	.563	354-315	22.1-19.7	545-447	2249-1694	4.1-3.8	23-14	403-539	222-321	55.1-59.6	2865- 3803	7.1- 7.1	15-21	22-15
NE	9	7	0	.563	250-284	15.6-17.8	588-496	2120-2099	3.6-4.2	17-20	389-436	199-234	51.2-53.7	2333- 2801	6.0- 6.4	12-13	28-20
NYJ	8	7	1	.531	372-354	23.3-22.1	514-517	2132-2124	4.1-4.1	19-15	538-476	299-244	55.6-51.3	3374- 3823	6.3- 8.0	20-28	11-24
Mia	6	10	0	.375	319-380	19.9-23.8	335-557	1205-2506	3.6-4.5	11-22	621-491	363-298	58.5-60.7	4557- 3442	7.3- 7.0	29-19	23-16
Central Division																	
Cin	12	4	0	.750	448-329	28.0-20.6	563-493	2710-2048	4.8-4.2	27-18	392-524	225-283	57.4-54.0	3592- 3508	9.2- 6.7	28-19	14-22
Cle*	10	6	0	.625	304-288	19.0-18.0	440-498	1575-1920	3.6-3.9	10-13	537-474	313-245	58.3-51.7	3686- 3102	6.9- 6.5	19-13	17-20
Hou*	10	6	0	.625	424-365	26.5-22.8	558-431	2249-1592	4.0-3.7	26-20	428-512	218-281	50.9-54.9	3166- 3619	7.4- 7.1	21-22	18-22
Pit	5	11	0	.313	336-421	21.0-26.3	499-516	2228-1864	4.5-3.6	17-20	489-532	226-309	46.2-58.1	3307- 4086	6.8- 7.7	15-25	20-20
Western Division																	
Sea	9	7	0	.563	339-329	21.2-20.6	517-509	2086-2286	4.0-4.5	14-14	437-501	245-280	56.1-55.9	2979- 3618	6.8- 7.2	22-21	20-22
Den	8	8	0	.500	327-352	20.4-22.0	464-552	1815-2538	3.9-4.6	13-21	581-467	324-262	55.8-56.1	3941- 3168	6.8- 6.8	24-18	22-16
LARd	7	9	0	.438	325-369	20.3-23.1	493-533	1852-2208	3.8-4.1	15-17	496-483	219-265	44.2-54.9	3503- 3471	7.1- 7.2	21-23	20-17
SD	6	10	0	.375	231-332	14.4-20.8	438-521	2041-2133	4.7-4.1	11-15	468-517	241-274	51.5-53.0	2628- 3525	5.6- 6.8	11-22	20-16
KC	4	11	1	.281	254-320	15.9-20.0	448-609	1713-2592	3.8-4.3	8-23	528-410	282-214	53.4-52.2	3484- 2591	6.6- 6.3	16-12	21-18

1988 NATIONAL FOOTBALL CONFERENCE

Team	W	L	T	PCT	OWN-OPP PTS-PTS	OWN-OPP PPG-PPG	OWN-OPP ATT-ATT	OWN-OPP YARD-YARD	OWN-OPP AVG-AVG	ON-OP TD-TD	OWN-OPP ATT-ATT	OWN-OPP COM-COM	OWN-OPP PCT-PCT	OWN - OPP YARD - YARD	OWN-OPP AVG-AVG	ON-OP TD-TD	ON-OP IN-IN
Eastern Division																	
Phi	10	6	0	.625	379-319	23.7-19.9	464-466	1945-1652	4.2-3.5	17-11	581-578	309-309	53.2-53.5	3927- 4443	6.8- 7.7	25-23	17-32
NYG	10	6	0	.625	359-304	22.4-19.0	493-454	1689-1759	3.4-3.9	15- 8	525-566	290-294	55.2-51.9	3716- 3755	7.1- 6.6	22-23	14-15
Was	7	9	0	.438	345-387	21.6-24.2	437-442	1543-1745	3.5-3.9	8-17	592-497	327-261	55.2-52.5	4339- 3744	7.3- 7.5	33-24	25-14
Pho	7	9	0	.438	344-398	21.5-24.9	480-467	2027-1925	4.2-4.1	15-19	562-508	322-264	57.3-52.0	4191- 3539	7.5- 7.0	26-30	19-16
Dal	3	13	0	.188	265-381	16.6-23.8	469-454	1995-1858	4.3-4.1	10-13	555-523	307-264	55.3-50.5	3727- 3883	6.7- 7.4	21-30	27-10
Central Division																	
ChiB	12	4	0	.750	312-215	19.5-13.4	555-389	2319-1326	4.2-3.4	25- 5	461-545	248-245	53.8-45.0	3173- 3399	6.9- 6.2	13-18	15-26
Min*	11	5	0	.688	406-233	25.4-14.6	501-435	1806-1602	3.6-3.7	22-10	520-480	294-219	56.5-45.6	4100- 2763	7.9- 5.8	20-12	18-36
TB	5	11	0	.313	261-350	16.3-21.9	452-478	1753-1551	3.9-3.2	11-21	512-527	253-304	49.4-57.7	3608- 3744	7.0- 7.1	16-19	36-21
Det	4	12	0	.250	220-313	13.8-19.6	391-511	1243-2037	3.2-4.0	7-16	477-513	213-337	44.7-65.7	2572- 3672	5.4- 7.2	13-17	18-15
GB	4	12	0	.250	240-315	15.0-19.7	385-514	1379-2110	3.6-4.1	14-17	582-474	319-256	54.8-54.0	3609- 2949	6.2- 6.2	13-12	24-20
Western Division																	
SF	10	6	0	.625	369-294	23.1-18.4	527-441	2523-1588	4.8-3.6	18- 8	502-530	293-292	58.4-55.1	3675- 3284	7.3- 6.2	21-25	14-22
LARm*	10	6	0	.625	407-293	25.4-18.3	507-414	2003-1686	4.0-4.1	16-12	522-571	312-307	59.8-53.8	4002- 3694	7.7- 6.5	31-17	18-22
NO	10	6	0	.625	312-283	19.5-17.7	512-442	2046-1779	4.0-4.0	9- 7	498-505	286-277	57.4-54.9	3256- 3579	6.5- 7.1	21-19	16-17
Atl	5	11	0	.313	244-315	15.3-19.7	478-518	2016-2319	4.2-4.5	11-14	481-504	250-281	52.0-55.8	2914- 3584	6.1- 7.1	13-17	19-24
League 224 games					9075	40.5	13581	54395	4.0	424	14131	7670	54.3	97635	6.9	556	553

*Wild Card qualifiers for playoffs
AFC Wild Card playoff: Hou 24, Cle 23
NFC Wild Card playoff: Min 28, LARm 17
AFC Divisional playoffs: Cin 21, Sea 13; Buf 17, Hou 10
NFC Divisional playoffs: ChiB 20, Phi 12; SF 34, Min 9
AFC championship: Cin 21, Buf 10
NFC championship: SF 28, ChiB 3
Super Bowl XXIII: SF (NFC) 20, Cin (AFC) 16

LEADING RUSHERS AFC	ATT	YARD	AVG	Long	TD
Eric Dickerson, Ind	388	1659	4.3	41t	14
John Stephens, NE	297	1168	3.9	52	4
Gary Anderson, SD	225	1119	5.0	36	3
Ickey Woods, Cin	203	1066	5.3	56	15
Curt Warner, Sea	266	1025	3.9	29	10

LEADING RUSHERS NFC	ATT	YARD	AVG	Long	TD
Herschel Walker, Dal	361	1514	4.2	38	5
Roger Craig, SF	310	1502	4.8	46t	9
Greg Bell, LARm	288	1212	4.2	44	16
Neal Anderson, ChiB	249	1106	4.4	80t	12
Joe Morris, NYG	307	1083	3.5	27	5

LEADING PASSERS AFC	ATT	COM	YARD	TD	IN
Boomer Esiason, Cin	388	223	3572	28	14
Dave Krieg, Sea	228	134	1741	18	8
Warren Moon, Hou	294	160	2327	17	8
Bernie Kosar, Cle	259	156	1890	10	7
Dan Marino, Mia	606	354	4434	28	23

LEADING PASSERS NFC	ATT	COM	YARD	TD	IN
Wade Wilson, Min	332	204	2746	15	9
Jim Everett, LARm	517	308	3964	31	18
Joe Montana, SF	397	238	2981	18	10
Neil Lomax, Pho	443	255	3395	20	11
Phil Simms, NYG	479	263	3359	21	11

LEADING RECEIVERS AFC	NO	YARD	AVG	Long	TD
Al Toon, NYJ	93	1067	11.5	42	5
Mark Clayton, Mia	86	1129	13.1	45t	14
Drew Hill, Hou	72	1141	15.8	57t	10
Andre Reed, Buf	71	968	13.6	65t	6
Mickey Shuler, NYJ	70	805	11.5	42t	5

LEADING RECEIVERS NFC	NO	YARD	AVG	Long	TD
Henry Ellard, LARm	86	1414	16.4	68	10
Eric Martin, NO	85	1083	12.7	40t	7
J.T. Smith, Pho	83	986	11.9	29	5
Keith Jackson, Phi	81	869	10.7	41	6
Roger Craig, SF	76	534	7.0	22	1

LEADING SCORERS AFC	TD	FG	PAT	PTS
Scott Norwood, Buf	0	32	33	129
Gary Anderson, Pit	0	28	34	118
Dean Biasucci, Ind	0	25	39	114
Tony Zendejas, Hou	0	22	48	114
Pat Leahy, NYJ	0	23	43	112

LEADING SCORERS NFC	TD	FG	PAT	PTS
Mike Cofer, SF	0	27	40	121
Mike Lansford, LARm	0	24	45	117
Morten Andersen, NO	0	26	32	110
Greg Bell, LARm	18	0	0	108
Chuck Nelson, Min	0	20	48	108

LEADING INTERCEPTOR	NO	YARD	AVG	Long	TD
Erik McMillan, NYJ (AFC)	8	168	21.0	55t	2
Scott Case, Atl (NFC)	10	47	4.7	12	0

LEADING PUNTER	NO	AVG	Long
Harry Newsome, Pit (AFC)	65	45.4	62
Jim Arnold, Det (NFC)	97	42.4	69

LEADING PUNT RETURNER	NO	YDS	AVG	Long	TD
JoJo Townsell, NYJ (AFC)	35	409	11.7	59t	1
John Taylor, SF (NFC)	44	556	12.6	95t	2

LEADING KICKOFF RETURNER	NO	YDS	AVG	Long	TD
Tim Brown, LARd (AFC)	41	1098	26.8	97t	1
Donnie Elder, TB (NFC)	34	772	22.7	51	0

SUPERLATIVES AFC

Rushing Avg.	5.3	Ickey Woods, Cin
Receiving Avg.	24.0	Eddie Brown, Cin
Completion Pct.	60.2	Bernie Kosar, Cle
Touchdowns	15	Eric Dickerson, Ind
		Ickey Woods, Cin
Field Goals	32	Scott Norwood, Buf
Sacks	11.5	Greg Townsend, LARd

SUPERLATIVES NFC

Rushing Avg.	4.8	Roger Craig, SF
Receiving Avg.	20.4	Michael Irvin, Dal
Completion Pct.	61.4	Wade Wilson, Min
Touchdowns	18	Greg Bell, LARm
Field Goals	27	Mike Cofer, SF
Sacks	18.0	Reggie White, Phi

LONGEST AFC

Run	65	Kevin Mack, Cle
Pass	89t	Bubby Brister to Louis Lipps, Pit
Interception	86t	Greg Townsend, LARd
Punt	74	Jeff Feagles, NE
Punt Return	73t	Clarence Verdin, Ind
Kickoff Return	98t	Stanford Jennings, Cin
Field Goal	53	Dean Biasucci, Ind

LONGEST NFC

Run	80t	Neal Anderson, ChiB
Pass	96t	Joe Montana to Jerry Rice, SF
Interception	94t	Walker Lee Ashley, Min
Punt	70	John Teltschik, Phi
		Bryan Wagner, ChiB
Punt Return	95t	John Taylor, SF
Kickoff Return	73	Ron Brown, LARm
Field Goal	53	Donald Igwebuike, TB

1989 AMERICAN FOOTBALL CONFERENCE

					SCORING		RUSHING				PASSING						
Team	W	L	T	PCT	OWN-OPP PTS-PTS	OWN-OPP PPG-PPG	OWN-OPP ATT-ATT	OWN-OPP YARD-YARD	OWN-OPP AVG-AVG	ON-OP TD-TD	OWN-OPP ATT-ATT	OWN-OPP COM-COM	OWN-OPP PCT-PCT	OWN - OPP YARD - YARD	OWN-OPP AVG-AVG	ON-OP TD-TD	ON-OP IN-IN
Eastern Division																	
Buf	9	7	0	.563	409-317	25.6-19.8	532-484	2264-1840	4.3-3.8	15-15	478-508	281-255	58.8-50.2	3831- 3495	8.0- 6.9	32-14	20-23
Ind	8	8	0	.500	298-301	18.6-18.8	458-507	1853-2077	4.0-4.1	11-10	493-556	253-322	51.3-57.9	3134- 3918	6.4- 7.0	18-15	17-21
Mia	8	8	0	.500	331-379	20.7-23.7	400-493	1330-2153	3.3-4.4	10-19	601-513	331-315	55.1-61.4	4302- 3811	7.2- 7.4	26-21	25-15
NE	5	11	0	.313	297-391	18.6-24.4	485-495	1749-1978	3.6-4.0	12-19	610-449	302-259	49.5-57.7	3972- 3905	6.5- 8.7	17-27	27-16
NYJ	4	12	0	.250	253-411	15.8-25.7	400-517	1596-2136	4.0-4.1	11-16	570-514	338-282	59.3-54.9	3892- 4035	6.8- 7.9	14-31	24-15
Central Division																	
Cle	9	6	1	.594	334-254	20.9-15.9	448-446	1609-1670	3.6-3.7	14- 8	529-540	309-269	58.4-49.8	3625- 3520	6.9- 6.5	20-20	15-27
Hou*	9	7	0	.563	365-412	22.8-25.8	495-437	1928-1669	3.9-3.8	16-20	496-467	295-260	59.5-57.6	3786- 3819	7.6- 8.2	23-28	16-21
Pit*	9	7	0	.563	265-326	16.6-20.4	500-498	1818-2008	3.6-4.0	17-16	404-548	210-290	52.0-52.9	2662- 3721	6.6- 6.8	10-17	13-21
Cin	8	8	0	.500	404-285	25.3-17.8	529-482	2483-2162	4.7-4.5	17- 9	513-482	288-258	56.1-53.1	3950- 3383	7.7- 7.0	32-22	13-21
Western Division																	
Den	11	5	0	.688	362-226	22.6-14.1	554-426	2092-1580	3.0-3.7	15-10	474-504	256-268	54.0-53.2	3352- 3201	7.1- 6.4	21-13	20-21
KC	8	7	1	.531	318-286	19.9-17.9	559-445	2227-1766	4.5-4.0	9- 9	414-471	259-236	59.5-50.1	3220- 2821	7.8- 6.0	14-16	23-15
LARd	8	8	0	.500	315-297	19.7-18.6	454-504	2038-1940	4.5-3.8	9-15	414-506	201-277	48.6-54.7	3277- 3311	7.9- 6.5	21-18	22-18
Sea	7	9	0	.438	241-327	15.1-20.4	405-520	1392-2118	3.4-4.1	5-11	559-445	316-252	56.5-56.6	3583- 3332	6.4- 7.5	21-23	23- 9
SD	6	10	0	.375	266-290	16.6-18.1	432-479	1873-1813	4.3-3.8	13-13	515-513	270-283	52.4-55.2	3291- 3311	6.4- 6.5	15-15	19-25

1989 NATIONAL FOOTBALL CONFERENCE

Team	W	L	T	PCT	OWN-OPP PTS-PTS	OWN-OPP PPG-PPG	OWN-OPP ATT-ATT	OWN-OPP YARD-YARD	OWN-OPP AVG-AVG	ON-OP TD-TD	OWN-OPP ATT-ATT	OWN-OPP COM-COM	OWN-OPP PCT-PCT	OWN - OPP YARD - YARD	OWN-OPP AVG-AVG	ON-OP TD-TD	ON-OP IN-IN
Eastern Division																	
NYG	12	4	0	.750	348-252	21.8-15.8	556-421	1889-1539	3.4-3.7	17-10	444-486	248-273	55.9-56.2	3355- 3427	7.6- 7.1	17-16	16-22
Phi*	11	5	0	.688	342-274	21.4-17.1	540-426	2208-1605	4.1-3.8	14- 6	538-520	294-258	54.6-48.8	3455- 3713	6.4- 7.1	23-26	16-30
Was	10	6	0	.625	386-308	24.1-19.3	514-384	1904-1344	3.7-3.5	14- 9	581-530	337-277	58.0-52.3	4476- 3875	7.7- 7.3	24-25	17-27
Pho	5	11	0	.313	258-377	16.1-23.6	407-539	1361-2302	3.3-4.3	10-12	523-531	279-286	53.3-53.9	3659- 3794	7.0- 7.1	17-24	30-16
Dal	1	15	0	.063	204-393	12.8-24.6	355-543	1409-1991	4.0-3.7	7-17	513-488	266-301	51.9-61.7	3124- 3748	6.1- 7.7	14-21	27- 7

Central Division																				
Min	10	6	0	.625	351-275	21.9-17.2	514-462	2066-1683	4.0-3.6	12-14	499-488	272-252	54.5-51.6	3468- 3003	6.9- 6.2	17-18	19-18
GB	10	6	0	.625	362-356	22.6-22.3	397-460	1732-2008	4.4-4.4	13-15	600-476	354-302	59.0-63.4	4325- 3553	7.2- 7.5	27-22	20-25
Det	7	9	0	.438	312-364	19.5-22.8	421-454	2053-1521	4.9-3.6	23-18	450-570	229-370	50.9-64.9	3282- 4193	7.3- 7.4	11-19	24-16
ChiB	6	10	0	.375	358-377	22.4-23.6	516-446	2287-1897	4.4-4.3	22-21	484-554	267-307	55.2-59.3	3262- 4079	6.7- 7.4	14-21	27-26
TB	5	11	0	.313	320-419	20.0-26.2	412-479	1507-2023	3.7-4.2	10-18	570-515	302-301	53.0-58.4	3666- 3659	6.4- 7.1	23-29	28-21
Western Division																	
SF	14	2	0	.875	442-253	27.6-15.8	493-372	1966-1383	4.0-3.7	14- 9	483-564	339-316	70.2-56.0	4584- 3568	9.5- 6.3	35-15	11-21
LARm*	11	5	0	.688	426-344	26.6-21.5	472-404	1909-1543	4.0-3.8	19-13	523-577	308-345	58.9-59.8	4369- 4302	8.4- 7.5	29-24	18-21
NO	9	7	0	.563	386-301	24.1-18.8	502-373	1948-1326	3.9-3.6	19-10	461-577	284-320	61.6-55.5	3651- 4222	7.9- 7.3	23-23	19-21
Atl	3	13	0	.188	279-437	17.4-27.3	318-572	1155-2471	3.6-4.3	11-26	578-437	312-259	54.0-59.3	3903- 3737	6.8- 8.6	17-19	12-20
League 224 games					9232	41.2	13068	61646	4.0	388	14338	8000	55.8	102456	7.1	582	559

*Wild Card qualifiers for playoffs
AFC Wild Card playoff: Pit 26, Hou 23, overtime
NFC Wild Card playoff: LARm 21, Phi 7
AFC Divisional playoffs: Cle 34, Buf 30; Den 24, Pit 23
NFC Divisional playoffs: LARm 19, NYG 13 (OT); SF 41, Min 13
AFC championship: Den 37, Cle 21
NFC championship: SF 30, LARm 3
Super Bowl XXIV: SF (NFC) 55, Den (AFC) 10

LEADING RUSHERS AFC	ATT	YARD	AVG	Long	TD
Christian Okoye, KC	370	1480	4.0	59	12
Eric Dickerson, Ind	314	1311	4.2	21t	7
Thurman Thomas, Buff	298	1244	4.2	38	6
James Brooks, Cin	221	1239	5.6	65t	7
Bobby Humphrey, Den	294	1151	3.9	40	7

LEADING RUSHERS NFC	ATT	YARD	AVG	Long	TD
Barry Sanders, Det	280	1470	5.3	34	14
Neal Anderson, ChiB	274	1275	4.7	73	11
Dalton Hilliard, NO	344	1262	3.7	40	13
Greg Bell, LARm	272	1137	4.2	47	15
Roger Craig, SF	271	1054	3.9	27	6

LEADING PASSERS AFC	ATT	COM	YARD	TD	IN
Boomer Esiason, Cin	455	258	3525	28	11
Warren Moon, Hou	464	280	3631	23	14
Jim Kelly, Buf	391	228	3130	25	18
Bernie Kosar, Cle	513	303	3533	18	14
Dan Marino, Mia	550	308	3997	24	22

LEADING PASSERS NFC	ATT	COM	YARD	TD	IN
Joe Montana, SF	386	271	3521	26	8
Jim Everett, LARm	518	304	4310	29	17
Mark Rypien, Was	476	280	3768	22	13
Bobby Hebert, NO	353	222	2686	15	15
Don Majkowski, GB	599	353	4318	27	20

LEADING RECEIVERS AFC	NO	YARD	AVG	Long	TD
Andre Reed, Buf	88	1312	14.9	78t	9
Brian Blades, Sea	77	1063	13.8	60t	5
Vance Johnson, Den	76	1095	14.4	69	7
John L. Williams, Sea	76	657	8.6	51t	6
Anthony Miller, SD	75	1252	16.7	69t	10

LEADING RECEIVERS NFC	NO	YARD	AVG	Long	TD
Sterling Sharpe, GB	90	1423	15.8	79t	12
Mark Carrier, TB	86	1422	16.5	78t	9
Art Monk, Was	86	1186	13.8	60t	8
Jerry Rice, SF	82	1483	18.1	68t	17
Ricky Sanders, Was	80	1138	14.2	68	4

LEADING SCORERS AFC	TD	FG	PAT	PTS
David Treadwell, Den	0	27	39	120
Scott Norwood, Buf	0	23	46	115
Tony Zendejas, Hou	0	25	40	115
Nick Lowery, KC	0	24	34	106
Jeff Jaeger, LARd	0	23	34	103

LEADING SCORERS NFC	TD	FG	PAT	PTS
Mike Cofer, SF	0	29	49	136
Ralf Mojsiejenko, Was	0	29	41	128
Rich Karlis, Min	0	31	27	120
Dalton Hilliard, NO	18	0	0	108
Chris Jacke, GB	0	22	42	108
Mike Lansford, LARm	0	23	51	120

LEADING INTERCEPTOR	NO	YARD	AVG	Long	TD
Felix Wright, Cle (AFC)	9	91	10.1	27t	1
Eric Allen, Phi (NFC)	8	38	4.8	18	0

LEADING PUNTER	NO	AVG	Long
Greg Montgomery, Hou (AFC)	56	43.3	63
Rich Camarillo, Pho (NFC)	76	43.4	58

LEADING PUNT RETURNER	NO	YDS	AVG	Long	TD
Clarence Verdin, Ind (AFC)	23	296	12.9	49t	1
Walter Stanley, Det (NFC)	36	496	13.8	74	0

LEADING KICKOFF RETURNER	NO	YDS	AVG	Long	TD
Rod Woodson, Pit (AFC)	36	982	27.3	84t	1
Mel Gray, Det (NFC)	24	640	26.7	57	0

SUPERLATIVES AFC

Rushing Avg.	5.6	James Brooks, Cin
Receiving Avg.	19.0	Webster Slaughter, Cle
Completion Pct.	60.5	Steve DeBerg, KC
Touchdowns	12	Christian Okoye, KC
		Thurman Thomas, Buf
Field Goals	27	David Treadwell, Den
Sacks	14.0	Lee Williams, SD

SUPERLATIVES NFC

Rushing Avg.	6.0	Randall Cunningham, Phi
Receiving Avg.	26.0	Willie Anderson, LARm
Completion Pct.	70.2	Joe Montana, SF
Touchdowns	18	Dalton Hilliard, NO
Field Goals	31	Rich Karlis, Min
Sacks	21.0	Chris Doleman, Min

LONGEST AFC

Run	92t	Bo Jackson, LARd
Pass	97t	Bernie Kosar to Webster Slaughter, Cle
Interception	92t	Erik McMillan, NYJ
Punt	76	Joe Prokop, NYJ
Punt Return	70t	Scott Schwedes, Mia
Kickoff Return	97t	Mark Logan, Mia
		James Jefferson, Sea
Field Goal	59	Pete Stoyanovich, Mia

LONGEST NFC

Run	73	Neal Anderson, ChiB
Pass	95t	Joe Montana to John Taylor, SF
Interception	90	Issiac Holt, Min
Punt	91	Randall Cunningham, Phi
Punt Return	76t	Dave Meggett, NYG
Kickoff Return	99t	Joe Howard, Was
		Bobby Morse, NO
Field Goal	54	Paul McFadden, Atl

1990 AMERICAN FOOTBALL CONFERENCE

					SCORING		RUSHING				PASSING							
Team	W	L	T	PCT	OWN-OPP PTS-PTS	OWN-OPP PPG-PPG	OWN-OPP ATT-ATT	OWN-OPP YARD-YARD	OWN-OPP AVG-AVG	ON-OP TD-TD	OWN-OPP ATT-ATT	OWN-OPP COM-COM	OWN-OPP PCT-PCT	OWN - OPP YARD - YARD	OWN-OPP AVG-AVG	ON-OP TD-TD	ON-OP IN-IN
Eastern Division																	
Buf	13	3	0	.813	428-263	26.8-16.4	479-483	2080-1808	4.3-3.7	20-13	425-455	263-254	61.9-55.8	3404- 3125	8.0- 6.9	28-17	11-18
Mia*	12	4	0	.750	336-242	21.0-15.1	420-461	1535-1831	3.7-4.0	13-11	539-462	310-257	57.5-55.6	3611- 3064	6.7- 6.6	21-14	12-19
Ind	7	9	0	.438	281-353	17.6-22.1	335-513	1282-2212	3.8-4.3	9-12	488-492	269-301	55.1-61.2	3297- 3605	6.8- 7.3	22-20	21- 9
NYJ	6	10	0	.375	295-345	18.4-21.6	476-423	2127-2018	4.5-4.8	16-15	451-516	246-311	54.5-60.3	3059- 3745	6.8- 7.3	14-23	11-18
NE	1	15	0	.063	181-446	11.3-27.9	383-565	1398-2676	3.7-4.7	4-29	514-374	274-218	53.3-58.3	3208- 3245	6.2- 8.7	14-21	20-14
Central Division																	
Cin	9	7	0	.563	360-352	22.5-22.0	484-442	2120-2085	4.4-4.7	16-15	425-543	237-300	55.8-55.2	3152- 3725	7.4- 6.9	25-24	23-15
Hou*	9	7	0	.563	405-307	25.3-19.2	328-392	1417-1575	4.3-4.0	10-12	639-460	399-267	62.4-58.0	5072- 3332	7.9- 7.2	37-18	15-21
Pit	9	7	0	.563	292-240	18.3-15.0	456-446	1880-1615	4.1-3.6	11-13	408-460	237-236	58.1-51.3	2887- 2728	7.1- 5.9	20- 9	15-24
Cle	3	13	0	.188	228-462	14.3-28.9	345-511	1120-2105	3.5-4.1	10-21	573-444	301-253	52.5-57.0	3407- 3296	6.0- 7.4	13-32	23-13

Western Division																	
LARd	12	4	0	.750	337-268	21.1-16.8	496-439	2028-1716	4.1-3.9	20- 4	336-437	183-236	54.5-56.3	2885- 3032	8.6- 6.9	19-20	10-13
KC*	11	5	0	.688	369-257	23.1-16.1	504-373	1948-1640	3.9-4.4	11-12	449-512	260-267	57.9-52.1	3458- 3662	7.7- 7.2	23-16	5-20
Sea	9	7	0	.563	306-286	19.1-17.9	457-413	1749-1605	3.8-3.9	18- 7	448-504	265-300	59.2-59.5	3194- 3256	7.1- 6.5	15-19	20-12
SD	6	10	0	.375	315-281	19.7-17.6	484-424	2257-1515	4.7-3.6	14-10	472-462	246-264	52.1-55.0	2840- 3255	6.0- 7.0	18-22	19-19
Den	5	11	0	.313	331-374	20.7-23.4	462-456	1872-1963	4.1-4.3	19-16	527-479	305-284	57.9-59.3	3671- 3671	7.0- 7.7	15-22	18-10

1990 NATIONAL FOOTBALL CONFERENCE

Eastern Division																	
NYG	13	3	0	.813	335-211	20.9-13.2	541-388	2049-1459	3.8-3.8	19- 9	398-496	231-278	58.0-56.0	2898- 2933	7.3- 5.9	18-12	5-13
Phi*	10	6	0	.625	396-299	24.8-18.7	540-336	2556-1172	4.7-3.5	10- 9	479-566	281-273	58.7-48.2	3582- 3771	7.5- 6.7	34-23	13-19
Was*	10	6	0	.625	381-301	23.8-18.8	515-382	2083-1587	4.0-4.2	16- 8	536-514	301-281	56.2-54.7	3611- 3483	6.7- 6.8	22-21	22-21
Dal	7	9	0	.438	244-308	15.3-19.3	393-482	1500-1976	3.8-4.1	13-18	475-470	254-271	53.5-57.7	2898- 2931	6.1- 6.2	12-12	24-11
Pho	5	11	0	.313	268-396	16.8-24.8	451-521	1915-2318	4.2-4.4	13-20	439-402	238-233	54.2-58.0	3118- 3130	7.1- 7.8	16-29	18-16
Central Division																	
ChiB	11	5	0	.688	348-280	21.8-17.5	551-391	2436-1572	4.4-4.0	22-10	430-495	229-258	53.3-52.1	2827- 3220	6.6- 6.5	14-19	12-31
TB	6	10	0	.375	264-367	16.5-22.9	410-496	1626-2223	4.0-4.5	7-20	448-471	245-263	54.7-55.8	3282- 3460	7.3- 7.3	18-22	24-25
Det	6	10	0	.375	373-413	23.3-25.8	366-532	1927-2388	5.3-4.5	19-22	460-507	242-319	52.6-62.9	3328- 3625	7.2- 7.1	24-21	20-17
GB	6	10	0	.375	271-347	16.9-21.7	350-475	1369-2059	3.9-4.3	5-16	541-479	302-256	55.8-53.4	3696- 3555	6.8- 7.4	20-20	21-16
Min	6	10	0	.375	351-326	21.9-20.4	455-503	1867-2074	4.1-4.1	10-12	497-422	265-218	53.3-51.7	3445- 2920	6.9- 6.9	25-20	24-22
Western Division																	
SF	14	2	0	.875	353-239	22.1-14.9	454-353	1718-1258	3.8-3.6	12- 7	583-522	360-265	61.7-50.8	4371- 3278	7.5- 6.3	28-17	16-17
NO*	8	8	0	.500	274-275	17.1-17.2	464-410	1850-1559	4.0-3.8	14- 8	447-534	226-316	50.6-59.2	2757- 3584	6.2- 8.5	15-21	23- 8
LARm	5	11	0	.313	345-412	21.6-25.8	422-418	1612-1649	3.8-3.9	17-17	561-501	310-296	55.3-59.1	4016- 3942	7.2- 7.9	24-30	17-12
Atl	5	11	0	.313	348-365	21.8-22.8	420-413	1594-1357	3.8-3.3	11-11	528-537	293-297	55.5-55.3	3726- 4127	7.1- 7.7	21-31	18-17
League 224 games					9015	40.2	12442	51012	4.1	377	13516	7572	56.0	94700	7.0	575	480

*Wild Card qualifiers for playoffs
AFC Wild Card playoffs: Mia 17, KC 16; Cin 41, Hou 14
NFC Wild Card playoffs: Was 20, Phi 6; ChiB 16, NO 6
AFC Divisional playoffs: Buf 44, Mia 34; LARd 20, Cin 10
NFC Divisional playoffs: SF 28, Was 10; NYG 31, ChiB 3
AFC championship: Buf 51, LARd 3
NFC championship: NYG 15, SF 13
Super Bowl XXV: NYG (NFC) 20, Buf (AFC) 19

LEADING RUSHERS AFC	ATT	YARD	AVG	Long	TD
Thurman Thomas, Buf	271	1297	4.8	80t	11
Marion Butts, SD	265	1225	4.6	52	8
Bobby Humphrey, Den	288	1202	4.2	37t	7
Barry Word, KC	204	1015	5.0	53t	4
James Brooks, Cin	195	1004	5.1	56t	5

LEADING RUSHERS NFC	ATT	YARD	AVG	Long	TD
Barry Sanders, Det	255	1304	5.1	45t	13
Earnest Byner, Was	297	1219	4.1	22	6
Neal Anderson, ChiB	260	1078	4.1	52	10
Randall Cunningham, Phi	118	942	8.0	52t	5
Emmitt Smith, Dal	241	937	3.9	48t	11

LEADING PASSERS AFC	ATT	COM	YARD	TD	IN
Jim Kelly, Buf	346	219	2829	24	9
Warren Moon, Hou	584	362	4689	33	13
Steve DeBerg, KC	444	258	3444	23	4
Jay Schroeder, LARd	334	182	2849	19	9
Dan Marino, Mia	531	306	3563	21	11

LEADING PASSERS NFC	ATT	COM	YARD	TD	IN
Phil Simms, NYG	311	184	2284	15	4
Randall Cunningham, Phi	465	271	3466	30	13
Joe Montana, SF	520	321	3944	26	16
Jim Harbaugh, ChiB	312	180	2178	10	6
Rodney Peete, Det	271	142	1974	13	8

LEADING RECEIVERS AFC	NO	YARD	AVG	Long	TD
Haywood Jeffires, Hou	74	1048	14.2	87t	8
Drew Hill, Hou	74	1019	13.8	57	5
John L. Williams, Sea	73	699	9.6	60	0
Ernest Givins, Hou	72	979	13.6	80t	9
Andre Reed, Buf	71	945	13.3	56t	8
Albert Bentley, Ind	71	664	9.4	73	2

LEADING RECEIVERS NFC	NO	YARD	AVG	Long	TD
Jerry Rice, SF	100	1502	15.0	64t	13
Andre Rison, Atl	82	1208	14.7	75t	10
Keith Byars, Phi	81	819	10.1	54	3
Henry Ellard, LARm	76	1294	17.0	50t	4
Gary Clark, Was	75	1112	14.8	53t	8

LEADING SCORERS AFC	TD	FG	PAT	PTS
Nick Lowery, KC	0	34	37	139
Scott Norwood, Buf	0	20	50	110
David Treadwell, Den	0	25	34	109
Norm Johnson, Sea	0	23	33	102
Pat Leahy, NYJ	0	23	32	101

LEADING SCORERS NFC	TD	FG	PAT	PTS
Chip Lohmiller, Was	0	30	41	131
Kevin Butler, ChiB	0	26	36	114
Mike Cofer, SF	0	24	39	111
Roger Ruzek, Phi	0	21	45	108
Greg Davis, Atl	0	22	40	106

LEADING INTERCEPTOR	NO	YARD	AVG	Long	TD
Richard Johnson, Hou (AFC)	8	100	12.5	35	1
Mark Carrier, ChiB (NFC)	10	39	3.9	14	0

LEADING PUNTER	NO	AVG	Long
Mike Horan, Den (AFC)	58	44.4	67
Sean Landeta, NYG (NFC)	75	44.1	67

LEADING PUNT RETURNER	NO	YDS	AVG	Long	TD
Clarence Verdin, Ind (AFC)	31	396	12.8	36	0
Johnny Bailey, ChiB (NFC)	36	399	11.1	95t	1

LEADING KICKOFF RETURNER	NO	YDS	AVG	Long	TD
Kevin Clark, Den (AFC)	20	505	25.3	75	0
David Meggett, NYG (NFC)	21	492	23.4	58	0

SUPERLATIVES AFC		
Rushing Avg.	5.6	Bo Jackson, LARd
Receiving Avg.	20.3	James Lofton, Buf
Completion Pct.	63.3	Jim Kelly, Buf
Touchdowns	15	Derrick Fenner, Sea
Field Goals	34	Nick Lowery, KC
Sacks	20.0	Derrick Thomas, KC

SUPERLATIVES NFC		
Rushing Avg.	8.0	Randall Cunningham, Phi
Receiving Avg.	21.5	Willie Anderson, LARm
Completion Pct.	61.7	Joe Montana, SF
Touchdowns	16	Barry Sanders, Det
Field Goals	30	Chip Lohmiller, Was
Sacks	16.0	Charles Haley, SF

LONGEST AFC		
Run	88	Bo Jackson, LARd
Pass	90	Bubby Brister to Dwight Stone, Pit
	90t	Steve DeBerg to J.J. Birden, KC
Interception	73	Ronnie Lippett, NE
Punt	70	Lee Johnson, Cin (twice)
Punt Return	98t	Terrence Mathis, NYJ
Kickoff Return	101t	Eric Metcalf, Cle
Field Goal	55	Dean Biasucci, Ind

LONGEST NFC		
Run	74t	Dexter Carter, SF
Pass	95t	Randall Cunningham to Fred Barnett, Phi
Interception	82t	Deion Sanders, Atl
Punt	67	Sean Landeta, NYG
Punt Return	95t	Johnny Bailey, ChiB
Kickoff Return	99t	Gaston Green, LARm
Field Goal	56	Mike Cofer, SF
		Chip Lohmiller, Was

1991 AMERICAN FOOTBALL CONFERENCE

Team	W	L	T	PCT	SCORING		RUSHING				PASSING						
					OWN-OPP PTS-PTS	OWN-OPP PPG-PPG	OWN-OPP ATT-ATT	OWN-OPP YARD-YARD	OWN-OPP AVG-AVG	ON-OP TD-TD	OWN-OPP ATT-ATT	OWN-OPP COM-COM	OWN-OPP PCT-PCT	OWN-OPP YARD-YARD	OWN-OPP AVG-AVG	ON-OP TD-TD	ON-OP IN-IN
Eastern Division																	
Buf	13	3	0	.813	458-318	28.6-19.9	505-519	2381-2044	4.7-3.9	16-20	516-536	332-299	64.3-55.8	4140- 3660	8.0- 6.8	39-12	19-23
NYJ*	8	8	0	.500	314-293	19.6-18.3	523-379	2160-1442	4.1-3.8	17- 8	503-540	295-331	58.6-61.3	3429- 3765	6.8- 7.0	12-21	12-18
Mia	8	8	0	.500	343-349	21.4-21.8	379-499	1352-2301	3.6-4.6	8-17	563-485	327-300	58.1-61.9	4077- 3353	7.2- 6.9	26-18	14-12
NE	6	10	0	.375	211-305	13.2-19.1	433-460	1467-1579	3.4-3.4	9- 5	481-565	284-335	59.0-59.3	3442- 4035	7.2- 7.1	11-25	22-12
Ind	1	15	0	.063	143-381	8.9-23.8	354-544	1169-2327	3.3-4.3	3-23	512-388	305-240	59.6-61.9	3066- 3002	6.0- 7.7	10-22	16-15
Central Division																	
Hou	11	5	0	.688	386-251	24.1-15.7	331-407	1366-1540	4.1-3.8	16- 8	667-532	411-310	61.6-58.3	4804- 3522	7.2- 6.6	24-17	21-20
Pit	7	9	0	.438	292-344	18.3-21.5	394-466	1627-1582	4.1-3.4	8-14	476-535	259-334	54.4-62.4	3313- 3843	7.0- 7.2	20-21	16-19
Cle	6	10	0	.375	293-298	18.3-18.6	389-447	1360-1875	3.5-4.2	12-12	503-522	312-312	62.0-59.8	3547- 3445	7.1- 6.6	19-20	10-15
Cin	3	13	0	.188	263-435	16.4-27.2	449-454	1811-1662	4.0-3.7	11-20	511-505	290-303	56.8-60.0	3413- 4119	6.7- 8.2	14-26	22-17
Western Division																	
Den	12	4	0	.750	304-235	19.0-14.7	507-411	2015-1794	4.0-4.4	16- 8	459-476	246-246	53.6-51.7	3310- 3101	7.0- 6.5	13-12	12-23
KC*	10	6	0	.625	322-252	20.1-15.8	521-417	2217-1770	4.3-4.2	14- 8	479-471	284-279	59.3-59.2	3281- 3532	6.9- 7.5	19-17	14-15
LARd*	9	7	0	.563	298-297	18.6-18.6	446-447	1706-1889	3.8-4.2	8-13	414-513	220-295	53.1-57.5	2977- 3559	7.2- 6.9	20-18	18-18
Sea	7	9	0	.438	276-261	17.3-16.3	394-435	1426-1684	3.6-3.9	11- 4	488-517	290-296	59.4-57.3	3371- 3288	6.9- 6.4	15-18	26-18
SD	4	12	0	.250	274-342	17.1-21.4	464-430	2248-1666	4.8-3.9	16-15	511-503	272-300	53.2-59.6	2983- 3628	5.8- 7.2	13-22	16-19

1991 NATIONAL FOOTBALL CONFERENCE

Team	W	L	T	PCT	PTS-PTS	PPG-PPG	ATT-ATT	YARD-YARD	AVG-AVG	TD-TD	ATT-ATT	COM-COM	PCT-PCT	YARD-YARD	AVG-AVG	TD-TD	IN-IN
Eastern Division																	
Was	14	2	0	.875	485-224	30.3-14.0	540-348	2049-1346	3.8-3.9	21-11	447-549	261-292	58.4-53.2	3771- 3292	8.4- 6.0	30-13	11-27
Dal*	11	5	0	.688	342-310	21.4-19.4	433-400	1711-1571	4.0-3.9	15-11	500-540	305-320	61.0-59.3	3663- 3646	7.3- 6.8	16-17	12-12
Phi	10	6	0	.625	285-244	17.8-15.3	446-383	1396-1136	3.1-3.0	8- 4	513-467	285-206	55.6-44.1	3169- 2807	6.2- 6.0	17-16	27-26
NYG	8	8	0	.500	281-297	17.6-18.6	487-414	2064-1726	4.2-4.2	16-11	428-440	261-251	61.0-57.0	3025- 3128	7.1- 7.1	13-17	8-12
Pho	4	12	0	.250	196-344	12.3-21.5	391-493	1295-2136	3.3-4.3	6-27	492-447	254-268	51.6-60.0	3039- 3069	6.2- 6.9	10-12	25-17
Central Division																	
Det	12	4	0	.750	339-295	21.2-18.4	454-444	1930-1760	4.3-4.0	19-16	459-534	252-315	54.9-59.0	2974- 3523	6.5- 6.6	16-16	17-19
ChiB*	11	5	0	.688	299-269	18.7-16.8	502-389	1949-1580	3.9-4.1	18- 9	497-513	286-286	57.5-55.8	3292- 3184	6.6- 6.2	16-19	17-17
Min	8	8	0	.500	301-306	18.8-19.1	464-456	2201-1837	4.7-4.0	18-17	477-499	284-286	59.5-57.3	3016- 3396	6.3- 6.8	16-16	16-17
GB	4	12	0	.250	273-313	17.1-19.6	381-457	1389-1546	3.6-3.4	12-10	514-531	272-305	52.9-57.4	3213- 3573	6.3- 6.7	17-20	19-15
TB	3	13	0	.188	199-365	12.4-22.8	371-512	1429-2107	3.9-4.1	9-21	495-438	250-257	50.5-58.7	2955- 3130	6.0- 7.1	13-15	29-11
Western Division																	
NO	11	5	0	.688	341-211	15.1-13.2	438-334	1709-1213	3.5-3.6	15- 6	506-491	292-259	57.7-52.7	3419- 3057	6.8- 6.2	20-12	15-29
Atl*	10	6	0	.625	361-338	22.6-21.1	410-466	1664-1953	4.1-4.2	6-13	500-481	260-252	52.0-52.4	3634- 3532	7.3- 7.3	30-28	22-19
SF	10	6	0	.625	393-239	24.6-14.9	440-399	1861-1512	4.2-3.8	19- 8	522-499	325-267	62.3-53.5	4167- 3254	8.0- 6.5	29-16	12-12
LARm	3	13	0	.188	234-390	14.6-24.4	388-469	1285-1659	3.3-3.5	11-19	518-434	289-259	55.8-59.7	3610- 3657	7.0- 8.4	13-25	20-11
League 224 games					8506	38.0	12279	48237	3.9	358	13951	8003	57.4	96100	6.9	511	488

*Wild Card qualifiers for playoffs
AFC Wild Card playoffs: KC 10, LARd 6; Hou 17, NYJ 10
NFC Wild Card playoffs: Atl 27, NO 20; Dal 17, ChiB 13
AFC Divisional playoffs: Den 26, Hou 24; Buf 37, KC 14
NFC Divisional playoffs: Was 24, Atl 7; Det 38, Dal 6
AFC championship: Buf 10, Den 7
NFC championship: Was 41, Det 10
Super Bowl XXVI: Was (NFC) 37, Buf (AFC) 24

LEADING RUSHERS AFC	ATT	YARD	AVG	Long	TD
Thurman Thomas, Buf	288	1407	4.9	33	7
Gaston Green, Den	261	1037	4.0	63t	4
Christian Okoye, KC	225	1031	4.6	48	9
Leonard Russell, NE	266	959	3.6	24	4
Mark Higgs, Mia	231	905	3.9	24	4

LEADING RUSHERS NFC	ATT	YARD	AVG	Long	TD
Emmitt Smith, Dal	365	1563	4.3	75t	12
Barry Sanders, Det	342	1548	4.5	69t	16
Rodney Hampton, NYG	256	1059	4.1	44	10
Earnest Byner, Was	274	1048	3.8	32	5
Herschel Walker, Min	198	825	4.2	71t	10

LEADING PASSERS AFC	ATT	COM	YARD	TD	IN
Jim Kelly, Buf	474	304	3844	33	17
Bernie Kosar, Cle	494	307	3487	18	9
Dan Marino, Mia	549	318	3970	25	12
Dave Krieg, Sea	285	187	2080	11	12
Warren Moon, Hou	655	404	4690	23	21

LEADING PASSERS NFC	ATT	COM	YARD	TD	IN
Steve Young, SF	279	180	2517	17	8
Mark Rypien, Was	421	249	3564	28	11
Steve Bono, SF	237	141	1617	11	4
Troy Aikman, Dal	363	237	2754	11	10
Jeff Hostetler, NYG	285	179	2032	5	4

LEADING RECEIVERS AFC	NO	YARD	AVG	Long	TD
Haywood Jeffires, Hou	100	1181	11.8	44	7
Drew Hill, Hou	90	1109	12.3	61t	4
Marv Cook, NE	82	808	9.9	49	3
Andre Reed, Buf	81	1113	13.7	55	10
Al Toon, NYJ	74	963	13.0	32	0

LEADING RECEIVERS NFC	NO	YARD	AVG	Long	TD
Michael Irvin, Dal	93	1523	16.4	66t	8
Andre Rison, Atl	81	976	12.0	39t	12
Jerry Rice, SF	80	1206	15.1	73t	14
Cris Carter, Min	72	962	13.4	50	5
Art Monk, Was	71	1049	14.8	64t	8

LEADING SCORERS AFC	TD	FG	PAT	PTS
Pete Stoyanovich, Mia	0	31	28	121
Jeff Jaeger, LARd	0	29	29	116
David Treadwell, Den	0	27	31	112
Nick Lowery, KC	0	25	35	110
Scott Norwood, Buf	0	18	56	110

LEADING SCORERS NFC	TD	FG	PAT	PTS
Chip Lohmiller, Was	0	31	56	149
Ken Willis, Dal	0	27	37	118
Morten Andersen, NO	0	25	38	113
Roger Ruzek, Phi	0	28	27	111
Barry Sanders, Det	17	0	0	102

LEADING INTERCEPTOR	NO	YARD	AVG	Long	TD
Ronnie Lott, LARd (AFC)	8	52	6.5	27	0
Ray Crockett, Det (NFC)	6	141	23.5	96t	1

LEADING PUNTER	NO	AVG	Long
Reggie Roby, Mia (AFC)	54	45.7	64
Harry Newsome, Min (NFC)	68	45.5	65

LEADING PUNT RETURNER	NO	YDS	AVG	Long	TD
Rod Woodson, Pit (AFC)	28	320	11.4	40	0
Mel Gray, Det (NFC)	25	385	15.4	78t	1

LEADING KICKOFF RETURNER	NO	YDS	AVG	Long	TD
Nate Lewis, SD (AFC)	23	578	25.1	95t	1
Mel Gray, Det (NFC)	36	929	25.8	71	0

SUPERLATIVES AFC

Rushing Avg.	4.9	Thurman Thomas, Buf
Receiving Avg.	20.3	Dwight Stone, Pit
Completion Pct.	65.6	Dave Kreig, Sea
Touchdowns	12	Mark Clayton, Mia
		Thurman Thomas, Buf
Field Goals	31	Pete Stoyanovich, Mia
Sacks	15.0	William Fuller, Hou

SUPERLATIVES NFC

Rushing Avg.	4.7	Terry Allen, Min
Receiving Avg.	22.4	Michael Haynes, Atl
Completion Pct.	65.3	Troy Aikman, Dal
Touchdowns	17	Barry Sanders, Det
Field Goals	31	Chip Lohmiller, Ws
Sacks	17.0	Pat Swilling, NO

LONGEST AFC

Run	78t	Kenneth Davis, Den
Pass	89t	Neil O'Donnell to Dwight Stone, Pit
Interception	83	Erik McMillan, NYJ
		Lloyd Burruss, KC
Punt	93	Shawn McCarthy, NE
Punt Return	78t	Mitchell Price, Cin
Kickoff Return	99t	Jon Vaughn, NE
Field Goal	55	Matt Stover, Cle

LONGEST NFC

Run	75t	Emmitt Smith, Dal
Pass	97t	Steve Young to John Taylor, SF
Interception	97	Reggie Rutland, Min
Punt	77	Jeff Feagles, Phi
Punt Return	85t	Kevin Martin, Dal
Kickoff Return	102t	Alexander Wright, Dal
Field Goal	60	Morten Andersen, NO

1992 AMERICAN FOOTBALL CONFERENCE

					SCORING		RUSHING				PASSING						
Team	W	L	T	PCT	OWN-OPP PTS-PTS	OWN-OPP PPG-PPG	OWN-OPP ATT-ATT	OWN-OPP YARD-YARD	OWN-OPP AVG-AVG	ON-OP TD-TD	OWN-OPP ATT-ATT	OWN-OPP COM-COM	OWN-OPP PCT-PCT	OWN-OPP YARD-YARD	OWN-OPP AVG-AVG	ON-OP TD-TD	ON-OP IN-IN
Eastern Division																	
Mia	11	5	0	.688	340-281	21.3-17.6	407-428	1525-1600	3.7-3.7	9-9	563-512	332-294	59.0-57.4	4148-3266	7.4-6.4	24-16	17-18
Buf*	11	5	0	.688	381-283	23.8-17.7	549-427	2436-1395	4.4-3.3	18-8	509-520	293-305	57.6-58.7	3678-3560	7.2-6.8	23-19	21-23
Ind	9	7	0	.563	216-302	13.5-18.9	379-495	1102-2174	2.9-4.4	8-16	546-470	305-260	55.9-55.3	3584-3236	6.6-6.9	13-14	26-20
NYJ	4	12	0	.250	220-315	13.8-19.7	424-460	1752-1919	4.1-4.2	8-13	495-465	251-527	50.7-55.3	2962-3201	6.0-6.9	12-19	24-21
NE	2	14	0	.125	205-363	12.8-22.7	419-521	1550-1951	3.7-3.7	6-15	444-459	244-258	55.0-56.2	2492-3211	5.6-7.0	13-22	19-14
Central Division																	
Pit	11	5	0	.688	299-225	18.7-14.1	518-436	2156-1841	4.2-4.2	13-6	431-478	249-252	57.8-52.7	3046-3065	7.1-6.4	15-15	14-22
Hou*	10	6	0	.625	352-258	22.0-16.1	353-412	1626-1634	4.6-4.0	10-6	573-445	373-248	65.1-55.7	4231-2898	7.4-6.5	27-20	23-20
Cle	7	9	0	.438	272-275	17.0-17.2	451-429	1607-1605	3.6-3.7	7-5	398-486	238-291	59.8-59.9	3102-3467	7.8-7.1	18-23	16-13
Cin	5	11	0	.313	274-364	17.1-22.8	454-490	1976-2007	4.4-4.1	11-15	435-489	227-288	52.2-58.9	2284-3620	5.3-7.4	16-24	17-16
Western Division																	
SD	11	5	0	.688	335-241	20.9-15.1	489-365	1875-1395	3.8-3.8	18-10	496-491	282-271	56.9-55.2	3614-3188	7.3-6.5	16-17	21-25
KC*	10	6	0	.625	348-282	21.8-17.6	446-441	1352-1787	3.4-4.1	14-12	413-458	230-253	55.7-55.2	3115-2928	7.5-6.4	15-19	12-24
Den	8	8	0	.500	262-329	16.4-20.6	403-489	1500-1963	3.7-4.0	11-10	473-462	258-268	54.5-58.0	3312-3437	7.0-7.4	16-21	29-15
LARd	7	9	0	.438	249-281	15.6-17.6	434-478	1794-1684	4.1-3.5	7-17	471-450	233-243	49.5-54.0	2950-3153	6.3-7.0	20-11	23-12
Sea	2	14	0	.125	140-312	8.8-19.5	402-513	1596-1922	4.0-3.7	4-14	476-428	230-251	48.3-58.6	2323-2978	4.9-7.0	9-11	23-20

1992 NATIONAL FOOTBALL CONFERENCE

Team	W	L	T	PCT	OWN-OPP PTS-PTS	OWN-OPP PPG-PPG	OWN-OPP ATT-ATT	OWN-OPP YARD-YARD	OWN-OPP AVG-AVG	ON-OP TD-TD	OWN-OPP ATT-ATT	OWN-OPP COM-COM	OWN-OPP PCT-PCT	OWN-OPP YARD-YARD	OWN-OPP AVG-AVG	ON-OP TD-TD	ON-OP IN-IN
Eastern Division																	
Dal	13	3	0	.813	409-243	25.6-15.2	500-345	2120-1244	4.2-3.6	20-11	491-484	314-263	64.0-54.3	3597-3034	7.3-6.3	23-16	15-17
Phi*	11	5	0	.688	354-245	22.1-15.3	516-387	2388-1481	4.6-3.8	19-4	429-517	255-263	59.4-50.9	3054-3316	7.1-6.4	20-20	13-24
Was*	9	7	0	.563	300-255	18.8-15.9	483-406	1727-1696	3.6-4.2	10-11	485-466	272-258	56.1-55.4	3339-3021	6.9-6.5	15-15	17-23
NYG	6	10	0	.375	306-367	19.1-22.9	458-458	2077-2012	4.5-4.4	20-17	433-440	232-270	53.6-61.4	2628-3228	6.1-7.3	14-22	10-14
Pho	4	12	0	.250	243-332	15.2-20.8	395-436	1491-1635	3.8-3.8	11-13	517-452	298-276	57.6-61.1	3334-3687	6.5-8.2	15-24	24-16
Central Division																	
Min	11	5	0	.688	374-249	23.4-15.6	497-438	2030-1733	4.1-4.0	19-11	458-508	258-320	56.3-63.0	3162-3124	6.9-6.1	18-12	15-28
GB	9	7	0	.563	276-296	17.3-18.5	420-406	1555-1821	3.7-4.5	7-12	527-483	340-277	64.5-57.3	3498-3496	6.6-7.2	20-16	15-15
TB	5	11	0	.313	267-365	16.7-22.8	438-441	1706-1675	3.9-3.8	12-15	511-508	299-293	58.5-57.7	3399-3740	6.7-7.4	17-25	20-20
ChiB	5	11	0	.313	295-361	18.4-22.6	427-468	1871-1948	4.4-4.2	15-14	479-442	266-261	55.5-59.0	3334-3290	7.0-7.4	17-20	24-14
Det	5	11	0	.313	273-332	17.1-20.8	378-460	1644-1841	4.3-4.0	9-14	406-487	231-296	56.9-60.8	3150-3402	7.8-7.0	16-20	21-21
Western Division																	
SF	14	2	0	.875	431-236	26.9-14.8	482-351	2315-1418	4.8-4.0	22-5	480-551	319-320	66.5-58.1	4054-3642	8.5-6.6	29-20	9-17
NO*	12	4	0	.750	330-202	20.6-12.6	454-381	1628-1605	3.6-4.2	10-8	426-511	251-287	58.9-56.2	3297-2846	7.7-5.6	19-13	16-18
Atl	6	10	0	.375	327-414	20.4-25.9	322-464	1270-2294	3.9-4.9	3-20	548-439	336-277	61.3-63.1	3892-3496	7.1-8.0	33-24	15-11
LARm	6	10	0	.375	313-383	19.6-23.9	393-467	1659-2230	4.2-4.8	12-22	495-507	289-305	58.4-60.2	3422-3481	6.9-6.9	23-18	20-18
League 224 games					8391	37.4	12291	49509	4.0	333	13408	7705	57.5	92011	6.9	516	519

*Wild Card qualifiers for playoffs
AFC Wild Card playoffs: SD 17, KC 0; Buf 41, Hou 38 (OT)
NFC Wild Card playoffs: Was 24, Min 7; Phi 36, NO 20
AFC Divisional playoffs: Buf 24, Pit 3; Mia 31, SD 0
NFC Divisional playoffs: SF 20, Was 13; Dal 34, Phi 10
AFC championship: Buf 29, Mia 10
NFC championship: Dal 30, SF 20
Super Bowl XXVII: Dal (NFC) 52, Buf (AFC) 17

LEADING RUSHERS AFC	ATT	YARD	AVG	Long	TD
Barry Foster, Pit	390	1690	4.3	69	11
Thurman Thomas, Buf	312	1487	4.8	44	9
Lorenzo White, Hou	265	1226	4.6	44	7
Harold Green, Cin	265	1170	4.4	53	2
Chris Warren, Sea	223	1017	4.6	52	3

LEADING RUSHERS NFC	ATT	YARD	AVG	Long	TD
Emmitt Smith, Dal	373	1713	4.6	68t	18
Barry Sanders, Det	312	1352	4.3	55t	9
Terry Allen, Min	266	1201	4.5	51	13
Reggie Cobb, TB	310	1171	3.8	25	9
Rodney Hampton, NYG	257	1141	4.4	63t	14

LEADING PASSERS AFC	ATT	COM	YARD	TD	IN
Warren Moon, Hou	346	224	2521	18	12
Dan Marino, Mia	554	330	4116	24	16
Neil O'Donnell, Pit	313	185	2283	13	9
Jim Kelly, Buf	462	269	3457	23	19
Cody Carlson, Hou	227	149	1710	9	11

LEADING PASSERS NFC	ATT	COM	YARD	TD	IN
Steve Young, SF	402	268	3465	25	7
Chris Miller, Atl	253	152	1739	15	6
Troy Aikman, Dal	473	302	3445	23	14
Randall Cunningham, Phi	384	233	2775	19	11
Brett Favre, GB	471	302	3227	18	13

LEADING RECEIVERS AFC	NO	YARD	AVG	Long	TD
Haywood Jeffires, Hou	90	913	10.1	47	9
Curtis Duncan, Hou	82	954	11.6	72	1
Ronnie Harmon, SD	79	914	11.6	55	1
John L. Williams, Sea	74	556	7.5	27	2
Anthony Miller, SD	72	1060	14.7	67t	7

LEADING RECEIVERS NFC	NO	YARD	AVG	Long	TD
Sterling Sharpe, GB	108	1461	13.5	76t	13
Andre Rison, Atl	93	1119	12.0	71t	11
Jerry Rice, SF	84	1201	14.3	80t	10
Michael Irvin, Dal	78	1396	17.9	87t	7
Mike Pritchard, Atl	77	827	11.7	38t	5

LEADING SCORERS AFC	TD	FG	PAT	PTS
Pete Stoyanovich, Mia	0	30	34	124
Steve Christie, Buf	0	24	43	115
Gary Anderson, Pit	0	28	29	113
John Carney, SD	0	26	35	113
Nick Lowery, KC	0	22	39	105

LEADING SCORERS NFC	TD	FG	PAT	PTS
Morten Andersen, NO	0	29	33	120
Chip Lohmiller, Was	0	30	30	120
Lin Elliott, Dal	0	24	47	119
Emmitt Smith, Dal	19	0	0	114
Mike Cofer, SF	0	18	53	107

LEADING INTERCEPTOR	NO	YARD	AVG	Long	TD
Henry Jones, Buf (AFC)	8	263	32.9	82t	2
Audray McMillian, Min (NFC)	8	157	19.6	51t	2

LEADING PUNTER	NO	AVG	Long
Greg Montgomery, Hou (AFC)	53	46.9	66
Harry Newsome, Min (NFC)	72	45.0	84

LEADING PUNT RETURNER	NO	YDS	AVG	Long	TD
Rod Woodson, Pit (AFC)	32	364	11.4	80t	1
Johnny Bailey, Pho (NFC)	20	263	13.2	65	0

LEADING KICKOFF RETURNER	NO	YDS	AVG	Long	TD
Jon Vaughn, NE (AFC)	20	564	28.2	100t	1
Deion Sanders, Atl (NFC)	40	1067	26.7	99t	2

SUPERLATIVES AFC		
Rushing Avg.	4.8	Thurman Thomas, Buf
Receiving Avg.	21.0	Willie Davis, KC
Completion Pct.	65.6	Cody Carlson, Hou
Touchdowns	12	Thurman Thomas, Buf
Field Goals	30	Pete Stoyanovich, Mia
Sacks	17.0	Leslie O'Neal, SD

SUPERLATIVES NFC		
Rushing Avg.	5.2	Heath Sherman, Phi
Receiving Avg.	18.9	Herman Moore, Det
Completion Pct.	66.7	Steve Young, SF
Touchdowns	19	Emmitt Smith, Dal
Field Goals	30	Chip Lohmiller, Was
Sacks	19.0	Clyde Simmons, Phi

LONGEST AFC		
Run	69	Barry Foster, Pit
Pass	83t	David Klingler to Jeff Query, Cin
Interception	103t	Louis Oliver, Mia
Punt	73	Brian Hansen, Cle
Punt Return	95t	Carl Pickens, Cin
Kickoff Return	100t	Jon Vaughn, NE
Field Goal	54	Al Del Greco, Hou
		Jeff Jaeger, LARd
		Steve Christie, Buf

LONGEST NFC		
Run	71	David Lang, LARm
Pass	89t	Chris Miller to Michael Haynes, Atl
Interception	84t	Jack Del Rio, Min
Punt	84	Harry Newsome, Min
Punt Return	87t	Val Sikahema, Phi
Kickoff Return	99t	Deion Sanders, Atl
Field Goal	54	Norm Johnson, Atl (twice)

1993 AMERICAN FOOTBALL CONFERENCE

					SCORING		RUSHING				PASSING						
Team	W	L	T	PCT	OWN-OPP PTS-PTS	OWN-OPP PPG-PPG	OWN-OPP ATT-ATT	OWN-OPP YARD-YARD	OWN-OPP AVG-AVG	ON-OP TD-TD	OWN-OPP ATT-ATT	OWN-OPP COM-COM	OWN-OPP PCT-PCT	OWN-OPP YARD-YARD	OWN-OPP AVG-AVG	ON-OP TD-TD	ON-OP IN-IN
Eastern Division																	
Buf	12	4	0	.750	329-242	20.6-15.1	550-500	1943-1921	3.5-3.8	12- 7	497-582	304-323	61.2-55.5	3535- 3889	7.1- 6.7	20-18	18-23
Mia	9	7	0	.563	349-351	21.8-21.9	419-460	1459-1665	3.5-3.6	10-12	581-572	342-350	58.9-61.2	4564- 3682	7.9- 6.4	27-26	18-13
NYJ	8	8	0	.500	270-247	16.9-15.4	521-420	1880-1473	3.6-3.5	14- 8	489-497	294-296	60.1-59.6	3492- 3434	7.1- 6.9	16-15	12-19
NE	5	11	0	.313	238-286	14.9-17.9	502-505	1780-1951	3.5-3.9	9- 9	566-474	289-280	51.1-59.1	3412- 3087	6.0- 6.5	17-20	24-13
Ind	4	12	0	.250	189-378	11.8-23.6	365-575	1288-2521	3.5-4.4	4-20	594-454	332-270	55.9-59.5	3623- 3238	6.1- 7.1	10-22	15-10
Central Division																	
Hou	12	4	0	.750	368-238	23.0-14.9	409-369	1792-1273	4.4-3.4	11- 9	614-582	357-302	58.1-51.9	4145- 3914	6.8- 6.7	23-16	25-26
Pit*	9	7	0	.563	308-281	19.3-17.6	491-399	2003-1368	4.1-3.4	13- 6	540-521	299-277	55.4-53.2	3606- 3440	6.7- 6.6	16-16	12-24
Cle	7	9	0	.438	304-307	19.0-19.2	425-451	1701-1654	4.0-3.7	8- 9	478-541	262-306	54.8-56.6	3328- 3466	7.0- 6.4	23-19	19-13
Cin	3	13	0	.188	187-319	11.7-19.9	423-521	1511-2220	3.6-4.3	3-15	510-457	272-251	53.3-54.9	2830- 2952	5.6- 6.5	11-20	11-12
Western Division																	
KC	11	5	0	.688	328-291	20.5-18.2	445-453	1655-1620	3.7-3.6	14-11	490-525	287-312	58.6-59.4	3384- 3379	6.9- 6.4	20-18	10-21
LARd*	10	6	0	.625	306-326	19.1-20.4	433-494	1425-1865	3.3-3.8	10-17	495-457	281-258	56.8-56.5	3882- 3141	7.8- 6.9	17-17	14-14
Den*	9	7	0	.563	373-284	23.3-17.8	468-397	1693-1418	3.6-3.6	13- 6	553-562	350-314	63.3-55.9	4061- 3969	7.3- 7.1	27-21	10-18
SD	8	8	0	.500	322-290	20.1-18.1	455-414	1824-1314	4.0-3.2	14-10	563-556	301-329	53.5-59.2	3383- 3958	6.0- 7.1	18-17	14-22
Sea	6	10	0	.375	280-314	17.5-19.6	473-452	2015-1660	4.3-3.7	13-12	498-595	280-333	56.2-56.0	2896- 3897	5.8- 6.5	13-16	18-22

1993 NATIONAL FOOTBALL CONFERENCE

Team	W	L	T	PCT	OWN-OPP PTS-PTS	OWN-OPP PPG-PPG	OWN-OPP ATT-ATT	OWN-OPP YARD-YARD	OWN-OPP AVG-AVG	ON-OP TD-TD	OWN-OPP ATT-ATT	OWN-OPP COM-COM	OWN-OPP PCT-PCT	OWN-OPP YARD-YARD	OWN-OPP AVG-AVG	ON-OP TD-TD	ON-OP IN-IN
Eastern Division																	
Dal	12	4	0	.750	376-229	23.5-14.3	490-423	2161-1651	4.4-3.9	20- 7	475-555	317-334	66.7-60.2	3617- 3347	7.6- 6.0	18-14	6-14
NYG*	11	5	0	.688	288-205	18.0-12.8	560-395	2210-1547	3.9-3.9	11- 7	424-514	257-298	60.6-58.0	3180- 3354	7.5- 6.5	17-13	9-18
Phi	8	8	0	.500	293-315	18.3-19.7	456-467	1761-2080	3.9-4.5	7-11	556-463	328-251	59.0-54.2	3463- 3153	6.2- 6.8	23-22	13-20
Pho	7	9	0	.438	326-269	20.4-16.8	452-433	1809-1861	4.0-4.3	12-13	522-495	310-281	59.4-56.8	3635- 3511	7.0- 7.1	21-14	20- 9
Was	4	12	0	.250	230-345	14.4-21.6	396-513	1728-2112	4.4-4.1	11-14	533-483	287-291	53.8-60.2	2764- 3584	5.2- 7.4	11-24	21-17
Central Division																	
Det	10	6	0	.625	298-292	18.6-18.3	456-433	1944-1649	4.3-3.8	9-12	435-514	264-309	60.7-60.1	2943- 3273	6.8- 6.4	15-19	19-19
Min*	9	7	0	.563	277-290	17.3-18.1	447-415	1624-1536	3.6-3.7	8-14	526-478	315-310	59.9-64.9	3381- 3146	6.4- 6.6	18-11	14-24
GB*	9	7	0	.563	340-282	21.3-17.6	448-424	1619-1582	3.6-3.7	14- 6	528-529	322-290	61.0-54.8	3330- 3201	6.3- 6.1	19-16	24-18
ChiB	7	9	0	.438	234-230	14.6-14.4	477-476	1677-1835	3.5-3.9	10- 9	388-504	230-306	59.3-60.7	2270- 3105	5.9- 6.2	7-12	16-18
TB	5	11	0	.313	237-376	14.8-23.5	402-479	1290-1994	3.2-4.2	6-15	508-503	262-300	51.6-59.6	3295- 3384	6.5- 6.7	19-22	25- 9
Western Division																	
SF	10	6	0	.625	473-295	29.6-18.4	463-404	2133-1800	4.6-4.5	26- 6	524-564	354-314	67.6-55.7	4480- 3513	8.6- 6.2	29-23	17-19
NO	8	8	0	.500	317-343	19.8-21.4	414-513	1766-2090	4.3-4.1	10- 7	481-444	274-259	57.0-58.3	3183- 2924	6.6- 6.6	18-22	21-10
Atl	6	10	0	.375	316-385	19.8-24.1	395-419	1590-1784	4.0-4.3	4-14	573-505	334-308	58.3-61.0	3787- 3786	6.6- 7.5	28-27	25-13
LARm	5	11	0	.313	221-367	13.8-22.9	449-480	2014-1851	4.5-3.9	8-18	473-488	247-299	52.2-61.3	3021- 3763	6.4- 7.7	16-17	19-11
League 224 games					8377	37.4	12684	49295	3.9	304	14414	8351	57.9	96490	6.7	517	469

*Wild Card qualifiers for playoffs
AFC Wild Card playoffs: KC 27, Pit 24 (OT); LARd 42, Den 24
NFC Wild Card playoffs: GB 28, Det 24; NYG 17, Min 10
AFC Divisional playoffs: Buf 29, LARd 23; KC 28, Hou 20
NFC Divisional playoffs: SF 44, NYG 3; Dal 27, GB 17
AFC championship: Buf 30, KC 13
NFC championship: Dal 38, SF 21
Super Bowl XXVIII: Dal (NFC) 30, Buf (AFC) 13

LEADING RUSHERS AFC	ATT	YARD	AVG	Long	TD
Thurman Thomas, Buf	355	1315	3.7	27	6
Leonard Russell, NE	300	1088	3.6	21	7
Chris Warren, Sea	273	1072	3.9	45t	7
Gary Brown, Hou	195	1002	5.1	26	6
Johnny Johnson, NYJ	198	821	4.1	57t	3

LEADING RUSHERS NFC	ATT	YARD	AVG	Long	TD
Emmitt Smith, Dal	283	1486	5.3	62t	9
Jerome Bettis, LARm	294	1429	4.9	71t	7
Erric Pegram, Atl	292	1185	4.1	29	3
Barry Sanders, Det	243	1115	4.6	42	3
Rodney Hampton, NYG	292	1077	3.7	20	5

LEADING PASSERS AFC	ATT	COM	YARD	TD	IN
John Elway, Den	551	348	4030	25	10
Joe Montana, KC	298	181	2144	13	7
Vinny Testaverde, Cle	230	130	1797	14	9
Boomer Esiason, NYJ	473	288	3421	16	11
Scott Mitchell, Mia	233	133	1773	12	8

LEADING PASSERS NFC	ATT	COM	YARD	TD	IN
Steve Young, SF	462	314	4023	29	16
Troy Aikman, Dal	392	271	3100	15	6
Phil Simms, NYG	400	247	3038	15	9
Bubby Brister, Phi	309	181	1905	14	5
Bobby Hebert, Atl	430	263	2978	24	17

LEADING RECEIVERS AFC	NO	YARD	AVG	Long	TD
Reggie Langhorne, Ind	85	1038	12.2	72t	3
Anthony Miller, SD	84	1162	13.8	66t	7
Shannon Sharpe, Den	81	995	12.3	63	9
Tim Brown, LARd	80	1180	14.8	71t	7
Brian Blades, Sea	80	945	11.8	41	3

LEADING RECEIVERS NFC	NO	YARD	AVG	Long	TD
Sterling Sharpe, GB	112	1274	11.4	54	11
Jerry Rice, SF	98	1503	15.3	80t	15
Michael Irvin, Dal	88	1330	15.1	61t	7
Andre Rison, Atl	86	1242	14.4	53t	15
Cris Carter, Min	86	1071	12.5	58	9

LEADING SCORERS AFC	TD	FG	PAT	PTS
Jeff Jaeger, LARd	0	35	27	132
Al Del Greco, Hou	0	29	39	126
John Carney, SD	0	31	31	124
Jason Elam, Den	0	26	41	119
Gary Anderson, Pit	0	28	32	116

LEADING SCORERS NFC	TD	FG	PAT	PTS
Jason Hanson, Det	0	34	28	130
Chris Jacke, GB	0	31	35	128
Ed Murray, Dal	0	28	38	122
Morten Andersen, NO	0	28	33	117
Norm Johnson, Atl	0	26	34	112

LEADING INTERCEPTOR	NO	YARD	AVG	Long	TD
Eugene Robinson, Sea (AFC)	9	80	8.9	28	0
Deion Sanders, Atl (NFC)	7	91	13.0	41	0

LEADING PUNTER	NO	AVG	Long
Greg Montgomery, Hou (AFC)	54	45.6	77
Jim Arnold, Det (NFC)	72	44.5	68

LEADING PUNT RETURNER	NO	YDS	AVG	Long	TD
Eric Metcalf, Cle (AFC)	36	464	12.9	91t	2
Tyrone Hughes, NO (NFC)	37	503	13.6	83t	2

LEADING KICKOFF RETURNER	NO	YDS	AVG	Long	TD
Raghib Ismail, LARd (AFC)	25	605	24.2	66	0
Robert Brooks, GB (NFC)	23	611	26.6	95t	1

SUPERLATIVES AFC

Rushing Avg.	5.1	Gary Brown, Hou
Receiving Avg.	23.4	James Jett, LARd
Completion Pct.	63.2	John Elway, Den
Touchdowns	15	Marcus Allen, KC
Field Goals	35	Jeff Jaeger, LARd
Sacks	15.0	Neil Smith, KC

SUPERLATIVES NFC

Rushing Avg.	5.3	Emmitt Smith, Dal
Receiving Avg.	21.6	Alvin Harper, Dal
Completion Pct.	69.1	Troy Aikman, Dal
Touchdowns	16	Jerry Rice, SF
Field Goals	34	Jason Hanson, Det
Sacks	13.0	Renaldo Turnbull, NO
		Reggie White, GB

LONGEST AFC

Run	77t	Keith Byars, Mia
Pass	82	Scott Secules to Kevin Turner & lateral to Leonard Russell, NE
Interception	102t	Donald Frank, SD
Punt	77	Greg Montgomery, Hou
Punt Return	91t	Eric Metcalf, Cle
Kickoff Return	66	Raghib Ismail, LARd
Field Goal	59	Steve Christie, Buf

LONGEST NFC

Run	85t	Reggie Brooks, Was
Pass	98t	Bobby Hebert to Michael Haynes, Atl
Interception	94t	Eric Allen, Phi
Punt	75	Harold Alexander, Atl
Punt Return	83t	Tyrone Hughes, NO
Kickoff Return	99t	Tyrone Hughes, NO
Field Goal	57	Michael Husted, TB

1994 AMERICAN FOOTBALL CONFERENCE

					SCORING		RUSHING				PASSING						
Team	W	L	T	PCT	OWN-OPP PTS-PTS	OWN-OPP PPG-PPG	OWN-OPP ATT-ATT	OWN-OPP YARD-YARD	OWN-OPP AVG-AVG	ON-OP TD-TD	OWN-OPP ATT-ATT	OWN-OPP COM-COM	OWN-OPP PCT-PCT	OWN-OPP YARD-YARD	OWN-OPP AVG-AVG	ON-OP TD-TD	ON-OP IN-IN
Eastern Division																	
Mia	10	6	0	.625	389-327	24.3-20.4	434-394	1658-1430	3.8-3.6	13-14	627-577	392-334	62.5-57.9	4533- 3954	7.2- 6.9	31-23	18-23
NE*	10	6	0	.625	351-312	21.9-19.5	478-422	1332-1760	2.8-4.2	12-11	699-545	405-298	57.9-54.7	4583- 3737	6.6- 6.9	25-21	27-22
Ind	8	8	0	.500	307-320	19.2-20.0	495-463	2060-1646	4.2-3.6	15- 8	376-598	217-354	57.7-59.2	2519- 3897	6.7- 6.5	15-24	14-18
Buf	7	9	0	.438	340-356	21.3-22.3	483-447	1831-1515	3.8-3.4	14-10	542-535	342-314	63.1-58.7	3714- 3812	6.9- 7.1	23-26	21-16
NYJ	6	10	0	.375	264-320	16.5-20.0	416-463	1566-1809	3.8-3.9	8-17	539-522	310-333	57.5-63.8	3323- 3730	6.2- 7.1	18-19	18-17
Central Division																	
Pit	12	4	0	.750	316-234	19.8-14.6	546-421	2180-1452	4.0-3.4	15- 7	463-532	266-280	57.5-52.6	3247- 3256	7.0- 6.1	17-12	9-17
Cle*	11	5	0	.688	340-204	21.3-12.8	449-465	1657-1669	3.7-3.6	12- 9	507-587	266-325	52.5-55.4	3269- 3425	6.5- 5.8	20-13	21-18
Cin	3	13	0	.188	276-406	17.3-25.4	404-517	1556-1906	3.9-3.7	5-16	542-505	289-294	53.3-58.2	3541- 3458	6.5- 6.8	21-22	19-10
Hou	2	14	0	.125	226-352	14.1-22.0	417-540	1682-2120	4.0-3.9	10-17	554-399	274-221	49.5-55.4	3216- 2963	5.8- 7.4	13-18	17-14
Western Division																	
SD	11	5	0	.688	381-306	23.8-19.1	482-385	1852-1404	3.8-3.6	13-11	522-577	305-363	58.4-62.9	3619- 3911	6.9- 6.8	20-20	14-17
KC*	9	7	0	.563	319-298	19.9-18.6	464-446	1732-1734	3.7-3.9	12-11	615-504	366-300	59.5-59.5	4092- 3500	6.7- 6.9	20-23	14-12
LARd	9	7	0	.563	303-327	18.9-20.4	428-444	1512-1543	3.5-3.5	7-11	487-564	281-306	57.7-54.3	3556- 3684	7.3- 6.5	22-24	16-12
Den	7	9	0	.438	347-396	21.7-24.8	431-432	1470-1752	3.4-4.1	19-12	626-568	388-322	62.0-56.7	4383- 4296	7.0- 7.6	18-28	13-12
Sea	6	10	0	.375	287-323	17.9-20.2	480-511	2084-1952	4.3-3.8	16-15	498-537	253-313	50.8-58.3	2809- 3603	5.6- 6.7	13-15	9-19

1994 NATIONAL FOOTBALL CONFERENCE

Team	W	L	T	PCT	PTS-PTS	PPG-PPG	ATT-ATT	YARD-YARD	AVG-AVG	TD-TD	ATT-ATT	COM-COM	PCT-PCT	YARD-YARD	AVG-AVG	TD-TD	IN-IN
Eastern Division																	
Dal	12	4	0	.750	414-248	25.9-15.5	550-437	1953-1561	3.6-3.6	26- 8	448-522	282-269	62.9-51.5	3461- 3051	7.7- 5.8	19-19	14-22
NYG	9	7	0	.563	279-305	17.4-19.1	525-447	1754-1728	3.3-3.9	12-11	405-500	226-289	55.8-57.8	2847- 3391	7.0- 6.8	16-16	18-16
Ariz	8	8	0	.500	235-267	14.7-16.7	480-409	1560-1370	3.3-3.3	12- 7	538-465	287-234	53.3-50.3	3284- 3310	6.1- 7.1	11-19	19-23
Phi	7	9	0	.438	308-308	19.3-19.3	432-449	1761-1616	4.1-3.6	14-11	566-490	316-251	55.8-51.2	3736- 3359	6.6- 6.9	18-20	14-21
Was	3	13	0	.188	320-412	20.0-25.8	407-556	1415-1975	3.5-3.6	5-24	546-496	271-300	49.6-60.5	3524- 3799	6.5- 7.7	25-22	27-17
Central Division																	
Min	10	6	0	.625	356-314	22.3-19.6	419-355	1524-1090	3.6-3.1	11- 9	673-597	409-368	60.8-61.6	4570- 3902	6.8- 6.5	18-25	20-18
GB*	9	7	0	.563	382-287	23.9-17.9	417-381	1543-1363	3.7-3.6	11- 9	609-605	375-337	61.6-55.7	3977- 3677	6.5- 6.1	33-20	14-21
Det*	9	7	0	.563	357-342	22.3-21.4	406-512	2080-1859	5.1-3.6	12-15	459-547	250-370	54.5-67.6	3085- 3745	6.7- 6.8	24-21	14-12
ChiB*	9	7	0	.563	271-307	16.9-19.2	487-432	1588-1922	3.3-4.4	10-10	502-522	308-295	61.4-56.5	3230- 3262	6.4- 6.2	19-16	16-12
TB	6	10	0	.375	251-351	15.7-21.9	430-468	1489-1964	3.5-4.2	8-13	491-498	271-303	55.2-60.8	3436- 3486	7.0- 7.0	17-25	16- 9
Western Division																	
SF	13	3	0	.813	505-296	31.6-18.5	491-375	1897-1338	3.9-3.6	23-16	511-583	359-329	70.3-56.4	4362- 3756	8.5- 6.4	37-15	11-23
NO	7	9	0	.438	348-407	21.8-25.4	373-458	1336-1758	3.6-3.8	11-10	569-559	366-353	64.3-63.1	4027- 4007	7.1- 7.2	22-28	18-17
Atl	7	9	0	.438	317-385	19.8-24.1	480-409	1560-1370	3.3-3.3	12- 7	538-465	287-234	53.3-50.3	3284- 3310	6.9- 7.1	11-19	19-23
LARm	4	12	0	.250	286-365	17.9-22.8	397-496	1389-1781	3.5-3.6	6-12	512-541	291-320	56.8-59.1	3597- 3548	7.0- 6.6	23-23	18-14
League 224 games					9075	40.5	12550	46710	3.7	340	15056	8739	58.0	101884	6.8	583	474

*Wild Card qualifiers for playoffs
AFC Wild Card playoffs: Mia 27, KC 17; Cle 20, NE 13
NFC Wild Card playoffs: GB 16, Det 12; ChiB 35, Min 18
AFC Divisional playoffs: Pit 29, Cle 9; SD 22, Mia 21
NFC Divisional playoffs: SF 44, ChiB 15; Dal 35, GB 9
AFC championship: SD 17, Pit 13
NFC championship: SF 38, Dal 28
Super Bowl XXIX: SF (NFC) 49, SD (AFC) 26

LEADING RUSHERS AFC	ATT	YARD	AVG	Long	TD
Chris Warren, Sea	333	1545	4.6	41	9
Natrone Means, SD	343	1350	3.9	25	12
Marshall Faulk, Ind	314	1282	4.1	52	11
Thurman Thomas, Buf	287	1093	3.8	29	7
Harvey Williams, LARd	282	983	3.5	28	4

LEADING RUSHERS NFC	ATT	YARD	AVG	Long	TD
Barry Sanders, Det	331	1883	5.7	85	7
Emmitt Smith, Dal	368	1484	4.0	46	21
Rodney Hampton, NYG	327	1075	3.3	27t	6
Terry Allen, Min	255	1031	4.0	45	8
Jerome Bettis, LARm	319	1025	3.2	19	3

LEADING PASSERS AFC	ATT	COM	YARD	TD	IN
Dan Marino, Mia	615	385	4453	30	17
John Elway, Den	494	307	3490	16	10
Jim Kelly, Buf	448	285	3114	22	17
Joe Montana, KC	493	299	3283	16	9
Stan Humphries, SD	453	264	3209	17	12

LEADING PASSERS NFC	ATT	COM	YARD	TD	IN
Steve Young, SF	461	324	3969	35	10
Brett Favre, GB	582	363	3882	33	14
Jim Everett, NO	540	346	3855	22	18
Troy Aikman, Dal	361	233	2676	13	12
Jeff George, Atl	524	322	3734	23	18

LEADING RECEIVERS AFC	NO	YARD	AVG	Long	TD
Ben Coates, NE	96	1174	12.2	62t	7
Andre Reed, Buf	90	1303	14.5	83t	8
Tim Brown, LARd	89	1309	14.7	77t	9
Shannon Sharpe, Den	87	1010	11.6	44	4
Brian Blades, Sea	81	1086	13.4	45	4

LEADING RECEIVERS NFC	NO	YARD	AVG	Long	TD
Cris Carter, Min	122	1256	10.3	65t	7
Jerry Rice, SF	112	1499	13.4	69t	13
Terance Mathis, Atl	111	1342	12.1	81	11
Sterling Sharpe, GB	94	1119	11.9	49	18
Jake Reed, Min	85	1175	13.8	59	4

LEADING SCORERS AFC	TD	FG	PAT	PTS
John Carney, SD	0	34	33	135
Jason Elam, Den	0	30	29	119
Matt Bahr, NE	0	27	36	117
Steve Christie, Buf	0	24	38	110
Matt Stover, Cle	0	26	32	110

LEADING SCORERS NFC	TD	FG	PAT	PTS
Fuad Reveiz, Min	0	34	30	132
Emmitt Smith, Dal	22	0	0	132
Morten Andersen, NO	0	28	32	116
Chris Boniol, Dal	0	22	48	114
Sterling Sharpe, GB	18	0	0	108

LEADING INTERCEPTOR	NO	YARD	AVG	Long	TD
Eric Turner, Cle (AFC)	9	199	22.1	93t	1
Aeneas Williams, Ariz (NFC)	9	89	9.9	43	0

LEADING PUNTER	NO	AVG	Long
Jeff Gossett, LARd (AFC)	77	43.9	65
Sean Landeta, LARm (NFC)	78	44.8	62

LEADING PUNT RETURNER	NO	YDS	AVG	Long	TD
Darrien Gordon, SD (AFC)	36	475	13.2	90t	2
Brian Mitchell, Was (NFC)	32	452	14.1	78t	2

LEADING KICKOFF RETURNER	NO	YDS	AVG	Long	TD
Randy Baldwin, Cle (AFC)	28	753	26.9	85t	1
Mel Gray, Det (NFC)	45	1276	28.4	102t	3

SUPERLATIVES AFC

Rushing Avg.	4.6	Chris Warren, Sea
Receiving Avg.	18.8	Darnay Scott, Cin
Completion Pct.	63.6	Jim Kelly, Buf
Touchdowns	12	Marshall Faulk, Ind
		Natrone Means, SD
Field Goals	34	John Carney, SD
Sacks	14.0	Kevin Greene, Pit

SUPERLATIVES NFC

Rushing Avg.	5.7	Barry Sanders, Det
Receiving Avg.	24.9	Alvin Harper, Dal
Completion Pct.	70.3	Steve Young, SF
Touchdowns	22	Emmitt Smith, Dal
Field Goals	34	Fuad Reveiz, Min
Sacks	13.5	Ken Harvey, Was
		John Randle, Min

LONGEST AFC

Run	90	Johnny Johnson, NYJ
Pass	99t	Stan Humphries to Tony Martin, SD
Interception	99t	Stanley Richard, SD
Punt	71	Chris Mohr, Buf
Punt Return	92t	Eric Metcalf, Cle
Kickoff Return	95t	Ronald Humphrey, Ind
Field Goal	54	Jason Elam, Den
		Doug Pelfrey, Cin

LONGEST NFC

Run	91t	Herschel Walker, Phi
Pass	93	Randall Cunningham to Herschel Walker, Phi
Interception	94t	Darrin Woodson, Dal
Punt	80	Randall Cunningham, Phi
Punt Return	103t	Robert Bailey, LARm
Kickoff Return	102t	Mel Gray, Det
Field Goal	54	Chip Lohmiller, Was

1995 AMERICAN FOOTBALL CONFERENCE

					SCORING		RUSHING				PASSING						
Team	W	L	T	PCT	OWN-OPP PTS-PTS	OWN-OPP PPG-PPG	OWN-OPP ATT-ATT	OWN-OPP YARD-YARD	OWN-OPP AVG-AVG	ON-OP TD-TD	OWN-OPP ATT-ATT	OWN-OPP COM-COM	OWN-OPP PCT-PCT	OWN-OPP YARD-YARD	OWN-OPP AVG-AVG	ON-OP TD-TD	ON-OP IN-IN
Eastern Division																	
Buf	10	6	0	.625	350-335	21.9-20.9	521-453	1993-1626	3.8-3.6	10-16	506-582	279-310	55.1-53.3	3348- 3864	6.6- 6.6	24-14	14-17
Ind*	9	7	0	.563	331-316	20.7-19.8	478-418	1855-1457	3.9-3.5	14- 8	434-569	270-336	62.2-59.1	3373- 3739	7.8- 6.6	20-23	11-13
Mia*	9	7	0	.563	398-332	24.9-20.8	413-415	1506-1675	3.6-4.0	16- 7	592-556	384-327	64.9-58.8	4398- 3756	7.4- 6.8	28-30	20-14
NE	6	10	0	.375	294-377	18.4-23.6	474-448	1866-1878	3.9-4.2	16-12	686-549	351-342	51.2-62.3	3789- 4107	5.5- 6.9	14-29	16-15
NYJ	3	13	0	.188	233-384	14.6-24.0	365-526	1279-2016	3.5-3.8	2-15	589-497	330-263	56.0-52.9	3129- 3055	5.3- 6.1	20-21	24-17
Central Division																	
Pit	11	5	0	.689	407-327	25.4-20.4	494-370	1852-1321	3.7-3.6	17- 9	592-531	348-314	58.8-59.1	4093- 3512	6.9- 6.6	21-24	21-22
Cin	7	9	0	.438	349-374	21.8-23.4	364-483	1439-2104	4.0-4.4	7-10	586-602	334-364	57.0-60.5	3915- 4512	6.7- 7.5	29-25	18-12
Hou	7	9	0	.438	348-324	21.8-20.3	478-400	1664-1526	3.5-3.8	12-11	536-553	314-289	58.6-52.3	3512- 3325	6.6- 6.0	22-24	18-21
Cle	5	11	0	.313	289-356	18.1-22.3	398-480	1482-1826	3.7-3.8	5-15	555-573	324-360	58.4-62.8	3772- 4013	6.8- 7.0	21-23	20-17
Jac	4	12	0	.250	275-404	17.2-25.3	410-504	1705-2003	4.2-4.0	9-17	495-509	275-304	55.6-59.7	3144- 3584	6.4- 7.0	19-28	15-13
Western Division																	
KC	13	3	0	.813	358-241	22.4-15.1	507-404	2222-1327	4.4-3.3	14- 7	531-596	300-329	56.5-55.2	3178- 3569	6.0- 6.0	21-16	10-16
SD*	9	7	0	.563	321-323	20.1-20.2	479-441	1747-1691	3.6-3.8	14-15	540-543	318-321	58.9-59.1	3706- 3605	6.9- 6.6	17-16	18-17
Sea	8	8	0	.500	363-366	22.7-22.9	477-496	2178-2130	4.6-4.3	20-11	511-554	273-310	53.4-56.0	3359- 3706	6.6- 6.7	19-26	23-16
Den	8	8	0	.500	388-345	24.3-21.6	440-451	1995-1895	4.5-4.2	14-19	594-529	350-297	58.9-56.1	4260- 3518	7.2- 6.7	27-20	14- 8
Oak	8	8	0	.500	348-332	21.8-20.8	463-446	1932-1794	4.2-4.0	10-16	543-527	317-301	58.4-57.1	3787- 3642	7.0- 6.9	25-14	21-11

1995 NATIONAL FOOTBALL CONFERENCE

Team	W	L	T	PCT	OWN-OPP PTS-PTS	OWN-OPP PPG-PPG	OWN-OPP ATT-ATT	OWN-OPP YARD-YARD	OWN-OPP AVG-AVG	ON-OP TD-TD	OWN-OPP ATT-ATT	OWN-OPP COM-COM	OWN-OPP PCT-PCT	OWN-OPP YARD-YARD	OWN-OPP AVG-AVG	ON-OP TD-TD	ON-OP IN-IN
Eastern Division																	
Dal	12	4	0	.750	435-291	27.2-18.2	495-442	2201-1772	4.4-4.0	29-13	494-523	322-293	65.2-56.0	3741- 3491	7.4- 6.7	18-17	10-19
Phi*	10	6	0	.625	318-338	19.9-21.1	508-466	2121-1822	4.2-3.9	19-14	496-499	284-268	57.3-53.7	2931- 3121	5.9- 6.3	11-14	19-19
Was	6	10	0	.375	326-359	20.4-22.4	469-483	1956-2132	4.2-4.4	15-18	521-546	265-338	50.9-61.9	3496- 3403	6.7- 6.2	16-20	20-16
NYG	5	11	0	.313	290-340	18.1-21.3	478-500	1833-2109	3.8-4.2	17-17	479-508	260-299	54.3-58.9	2863- 3361	6.0- 6.6	11-17	13-16
Ariz	4	12	0	.250	275-422	17.2-26.4	387-503	1363-2249	3.5-4.5	3-14	560-461	327-264	58.4-57.3	3893- 3655	7.0- 7.9	17-33	24-19
Central Division																	
GB	11	5	0	.689	404-314	25.3-19.6	410-374	1428-1515	3.5-4.1	9-12	593-616	372-351	62.7-57.0	4539- 3915	7.7- 6.4	39-25	15-13
Det*	10	6	0	.625	436-336	27.3-21.0	387-409	1753-1795	4.5-4.4	16-15	605-580	362-354	59.8-61.0	4510- 4121	7.5- 7.1	33-17	12-22
ChiB	9	7	0	.563	392-360	24.5-22.5	492-405	1930-1441	3.9-3.6	15- 9	523-595	315-374	60.2-62.9	3838- 4240	7.3- 7.1	29-27	10-16
Min	8	8	0	.500	412-385	25.8-24.1	433-352	1733-1329	4.0-3.8	10-11	642-620	402-369	62.6-59.5	4500- 4416	7.0- 7.1	33-29	16-25
TB	7	9	0	.438	238-335	14.9-20.9	398-449	1587-1754	4.0-3.9	19-14	507-557	267-346	52.7-62.1	3341- 4098	6.6- 7.4	5-19	20-14
Western Division																	
SF	11	5	0	.688	457-258	28.6-16.1	415-348	1479-1061	3.6-3.0	19- 5	644-611	432-330	67.1-54.0	4779- 3577	7.4- 5.9	29-19	16-26
Atl*	9	7	0	.563	362-349	22.6-21.8	337-404	1393-1547	4.1-3.8	8-12	603-650	364-405	60.4-62.3	4456- 4751	7.4- 7.3	26-28	12-18
StL	7	9	0	.438	309-418	19.3-26.1	392-410	1431-1677	3.7-4.1	5-14	632-534	366-320	57.9-59.9	4113- 3699	6.5- 6.9	27-27	23-22
Car	7	9	0	.438	289-325	18.1-20.3	454-450	1573-1576	3.5-3.5	10-17	537-586	263-310	49.0-52.9	3046- 3716	6.2- 6.3	16-15	25-21
NO	7	9	0	.438	319-348	19.9-21.8	383-469	1390-1838	3.6-3.9	11-13	573-543	349-329	60.9-60.6	4002- 3998	7.0- 7.4	26-23	14-17
League 240 games					10314	43.0	13191	51886	3.9	385	16699	9717	58.2	113069	6.8	663	512

*Wild Card qualifiers for playoffs
AFC Wild Card playoffs: Buf 37, Mia 22; Ind 35, SD 20
NFC Wild Card playoffs: Phi 58, Det 37; GB 37, Atl 20
AFC Divisional playoffs: Pit 40, Buf 21; Ind 10, KC 7
NFC Divisional playoffs: GB 27, SF 17; Dal 30, Phi 11
AFC championship: Pit 20, Ind 16
NFC championship: Dal 38, GB 27
Super Bowl XXX: Dal (NFC) 27, Pit (AFC) 17

LEADING RUSHERS AFC	ATT	YARD	AVG	Long	TD
Curtis Martin, NE	368	1487	4.0	49	14
Chris Warren, Sea	310	1346	4.3	52	15
Terrell Davis, Den	237	1117	4.7	60t	7
Harvey Williams, Oak	255	1114	4.4	60	9
Marshall Faulk, Ind	289	1078	3.7	40	11

LEADING RUSHERS NFC	ATT	YARD	AVG	Long	TD
Emmitt Smith, Dal	377	1773	4.7	60t	25
Barry Sanders, Det	314	1500	4.8	75t	11
Terry Allen, Was	338	1309	3.9	28	10
Ricky Watters, Phi	337	1273	3.8	57	11
Errict Rhett, TB	332	1207	3.6	21	11

LEADING PASSERS AFC	ATT	COM	YARD	TD	IN
Jim Harbaugh, Ind	314	200	2575	17	5
Dan Marino, Mia	482	309	3668	24	15
Vinny Testaverde, Cle	392	241	2883	17	10
Chris Chandler, Hou	356	225	2460	17	10
Neil O'Donnell, Pit	416	246	2970	17	7

LEADING PASSERS NFC	ATT	COM	YARD	TD	IN
Brett Favre, GB	570	359	4413	38	13
Troy Aikman, Dal	432	280	3304	16	7
Erik Kramer, ChiB	522	315	3838	29	10
Steve Young, SF	447	299	3200	20	11
Scott Mitchell, Det	583	346	4338	32	12

LEADING RECEIVERS AFC	NO	YARD	AVG	Long	TD
Carl Pickens, Cin	99	1234	12.5	68t	17
Tony Martin, SD	90	1224	13.6	51t	6
Tim Brown, Oak	89	1342	15.1	80t	10
Yancey Thigpen, Pit	85	1307	15.4	43	5
Ben Coates, NE	84	915	10.9	35	6

LEADING RECEIVERS NFC	NO	YARD	AVG	Long	TD
Herman Moore, Det	123	1686	13.7	69t	14
Jerry Rice, SF	122	1848	15.1	81t	15
Cris Carter, Min	122	1371	11.2	60t	17
Isaac Bruce, StL	119	1781	15.0	72	13
Michael Irvin, Dal	111	1603	14.4	50	10

LEADING SCORERS AFC	TD	FG	PAT	PTS
Norm Johnson, Pit	0	34	39	141
Jason Elam, Den	0	31	39	132
Steve Christie, Buf	0	31	33	126
Doug Pelfrey, Cin	0	29	34	121
Pete Stoyanovich, Mia	0	27	37	118

LEADING SCORERS NFC	TD	FG	PAT	PTS
Emmitt Smith, Dal	25	0	0	150
Jason Hanson, Det	0	28	48	132
Chris Boniol, Dal	0	27	46	127
Morten Andersen, Atl	0	31	29	122
Fuad Reveiz, Min	0	26	44	122

LEADING INTERCEPTOR	NO	YARD	AVG	Long	TD
Willie Williams, Pit (AFC)	7	122	17.4	63t	1
Orlando Thomas, Min (NFC)	9	108	12.0	45t	1

LEADING PUNTER	NO	AVG	Long
Rick Tuten, Sea (AFC)	83	45.0	73
Sean Landeta, StL (NFC)	83	44.3	63

LEADING PUNT RETURNER	NO	YDS	AVG	Long	TD
Andre Coleman, SD (AFC)	28	326	11.6	88t	1
David Palmer, Min (NFC)	26	342	13.2	74t	1

LEADING KICKOFF RETURNER	NO	YDS	AVG	Long	TD
Ron Carpenter, NYJ (AFC)	20	553	27.7	58	0
Brian Mitchell, Was (NFC)	55	1408	25.6	59	0

SUPERLATIVES AFC

Rushing Avg.	4.7	Terrell Davis, Den
Receiving Avg.	23.5	Chris Sanders, Hou
Completion Pct.	64.1	Dan Marino, Mia
Touchdowns	17	Carl Pickens, Cin
Field Goals	34	Norm Johnson, Pit
Sacks	17.5	Bryce Paup, Buf

SUPERLATIVES NFC

Rushing Avg.	5.4	Charlie Garner, Phi
Receiving Avg.	18.8	Willie Green, Car
Completion Pct.	66.9	Steve Young, SF
Touchdowns	17	Cris Carter, Min
Field Goals	31	Morten Andersen, Atl
Sacks	13.0	William Fuller, Phi
		Wayne Martin, NO

LONGEST AFC

Run	86t	Joey Galloway, Sea
Pass	88t	Jeff Blake to Darnay Scott, Cin
Interception	99t	Shaun Gayle, SD
Punt	73	Rick Tuten, Sea
Punt Return	89t	Joey Galloway, Sea
Kickoff Return	99t	Tamarick Vanover, KC
Field Goal	56	Jason Elam, Den

LONGEST NFC

Run	75t	Barry Sanders, Det
	75	Jerry Ellison, TB
Pass	99t	Brett Favre to Robert Brooks, GB
Interception	96t	Tim McKyer, Car
Punt	69	Mark Royals, Det
Punt Return	78t	Dexter Carter, SF
Kickoff Return	91t	Thomas Lewis, NYG
Field Goal	59	Morten Andersen, Atl

1996 AMERICAN FOOTBALL CONFERENCE

					SCORING		RUSHING				PASSING						
Team	W	L	T	PCT	OWN-OPP PTS-PTS	OWN-OPP PPG-PPG	OWN-OPP ATT-ATT	OWN - OPP YARD-YARD	OWN-OPP AVG-AVG	ON-OP TD-TD	OWN-OPP ATT-ATT	OWN-OPP COM-COM	OWN-OPP PCT-PCT	OWN - OPP YARD - YARD	OWN-OPP AVG-AVG	ON-OP TD-TD	ON-OP IN-IN
Eastern Division																	
NE	11	5	0	.687	419-313	26.2-19.6	427-434	1468-1502	3.4-3.5	15-14	628-596	374-322	59.6-54.0	4091- 4055	6.5- 6.8	27-17	15-23
Buf*	10	6	0	.625	319-266	19.9-16.6	563-495	1901-1669	3.4-3.4	14-12	483-562	279-292	57.8-52.0	3558- 3409	7.4- 6.1	18-11	24-14
Ind*	9	7	0	.562	317-334	19.8-20.9	420-459	1448-1760	3.4-3.8	9-12	537-534	311-318	57.9-59.6	3544- 3825	6.6- 7.2	16-25	11-13
Mia	8	8	0	.500	339-325	21.2-20.3	460-411	1622-1536	3.5-3.7	14-10	504-539	300-337	59.5-62.5	3783- 3888	7.5- 7.2	22-29	11-20
NYJ	1	15	0	.063	279-454	17.4-28.4	407-539	1565-2200	3.8-4.1	8-19	629-456	339-257	53.9-56.4	3911- 3542	6.2- 7.8	22-33	30-11
Central Division																	
Pit	10	6	0	.625	344-257	21.5-16.1	525-411	2299-1415	4.4-3.4	18- 7	456-547	246-322	53.9-58.9	2990- 3316	6.6- 6.1	15-17	19-23
Jac*	9	7	0	.562	325-335	20.3-20.9	431-447	1650-1781	3.8-4.0	13- 9	557-509	353-291	63.4-57.2	4387- 3551	7.8- 7.0	19-24	20-13
Cin	8	8	0	.500	372-369	23.3-23.1	478-444	1793-1643	3.8-3.7	14-15	563-571	316-319	56.1-55.9	3726- 4028	6.6- 7.1	25-22	16-34
Hou	8	8	0	.500	345-319	21.6-19.9	475-397	1950-1385	4.1-3.5	12- 5	463-524	272-312	58.7-59.5	3296- 3467	7.1- 6.6	22-24	15-12
Bal	4	12	0	.250	371-441	23.2-27.6	416-508	1745-1920	4.2-3.8	10-18	570-537	335-350	58.8-65.2	4274- 4115	7.5- 7.7	34-27	20-15
Western Division																	
Den	13	3	0	.813	391-275	24.4-17.2	525-345	2362-1331	4.5-3.9	20- 5	536-566	327-302	61.0-53.4	3662- 3413	6.8- 6.0	26-22	17-23
KC	9	7	0	.562	297-300	18.6-18.8	488-441	2009-1666	4.1-3.8	15-11	530-536	290-289	54.7-53.9	3093- 3731	5.8- 7.0	18-19	14-17
SD	8	8	0	.500	310-376	19.4-23.5	412-431	1312-1755	3.2-4.1	7-10	577-636	314-369	54.4-58.0	3654- 3867	6.3- 6.1	23-28	21-22
Oak	7	9	0	.438	340-293	21.3-18.3	457-463	2172-1676	4.8-3.6	7- 7	533-513	311-284	58.3-55.4	3327- 3273	6.2- 6.4	28-22	19-17
Sea	7	9	0	.438	317-376	19.8-23.5	442-507	1997-2096	4.5-4.1	16-15	494-512	261-303	52.8-59.2	3216- 3624	6.5- 7.1	14-25	17-14

1996 NATIONAL FOOTBALL CONFERENCE

Eastern Division																	
Dal	10	6	0	.625	286-250	17.9-15.6	475-437	1641-1576	3.5-3.6	14-10	487-484	307-271	63.0-56.0	3249- 3025	6.7- 6.3	12-10	14-19
Phi*	10	6	0	.625	363-341	22.7-21.3	489-421	1882-1565	3.8-3.7	16-12	548-500	328-271	59.9-54.2	3979- 3243	7.3- 6.5	19-18	18-19
Was	9	7	0	.562	364-312	22.8-19.5	467-520	1910-2275	4.1-4.4	27-20	471-560	270-325	57.3-58.0	3453- 3655	7.3- 6.5	12-12	11-21
Ariz	7	9	0	.438	300-397	18.8-24.8	401-514	1502-1862	3.7-3.6	8-18	613-520	336-311	54.8-59.8	3917- 3684	6.4- 7.1	23-21	21-11
NYG	6	10	0	.375	242-297	15.1-18.6	485-487	1603-1748	3.3-3.6	4-14	459-533	238-317	51.9-59.5	2663- 3477	5.8- 6.5	14-15	21-22
Central Division																	
GB	13	3	0	.813	456-210	28.5-13.1	485-400	1838-1460	4.0-3.5	9- 7	548-544	328-283	59.9-52.0	3938- 2942	7.2- 5.4	39-12	13-26
Min*	9	7	0	.562	298-315	18.6-19.7	435-445	1546-1966	3.6-4.4	7-15	561-537	331-314	59.0-58.5	3899- 3384	7.0- 6.3	24-18	19-22
ChiB	7	9	0	.438	283-305	17.7-19.1	472-427	1720-1617	3.6-3.8	9-13	551-524	318-314	57.7-59.9	3350- 3476	6.1- 6.6	19-21	18-17
TB	6	10	0	.375	221-293	13.8-18.3	472-438	1589-1889	3.4-4.3	8-13	494-503	274-311	55.5-61.8	2944- 3132	6.0- 6.2	12-17	20-17
Det	5	11	0	.313	302-368	18.9-23.0	389-510	1810-2007	4.7-3.9	15-12	541-502	309-311	57.1-62.0	3463- 3577	6.4- 7.1	20-28	21-11
Western Division																	
Car	12	4	0	.750	367-218	22.9-13.6	502-374	1729-1562	3.4-4.2	9- 6	487-556	273-307	56.1-55.2	3333- 3585	6.8- 6.5	22-17	11-22
SF*	12	4	0	.750	398-257	24.9-16.1	454-418	1847-1497	4.1-3.6	17- 4	550-558	358-287	65.1-51.4	3859- 3461	7.0- 6.2	24-21	16-20

StL	6	10	0	.375	303-409	18.9-25.6	448-478	1607-1854	3.6-3.9	10-22	481-558	249-341	51.8-61.1	3144- 3856	6.5- 6.9	18-23	23-26
Atl	3	13	0	.188	309-465	19.3-29.1	329-473	1461-2041	4.4-4.3	9-18	601-485	357-302	59.4-62.3	3919- 3953	6.5- 8.2	26-26	30- 6
NO	3	13	0	.188	229-339	14.3-21.2	386-521	1308-2076	3.4-4.0	10-11	515-465	295-267	57.3-57.4	3069- 3117	6.0- 6.7	13-22	17-12
League 224 games					9806	43.8	13605	52286	3.8	464	15967	9199	57.6	106691	6.7	726	540

*Wild Card qualifiers for playoffs
AFC Wild Card playoffs: Jac 30, Buf 27; Pit 42, Ind 14
NFC Wild Card playoffs: Dal 40, Min 15; SF 14, Phi 0
AFC Divisional playoffs: Jac 30, Den 27; NE 28, Pit 3
NFC Divisional playoffs: GB 35, SF 14; Car 26, Dal 17
AFC championship: NE 20, Jac 6
NFC championship: GB 35, NE 21
Super Bowl XXXI: GB (NFC) 35, NE (AFC) 21

LEADING RUSHERS AFC	ATT	YARD	AVG	Long	TD
Terrell Davis, Den	345	1538	4.5	71t	13
Jerome Bettis, Pit	320	1431	4.5	50t	11
Eddie George, Hou	335	1368	4.1	76	8
Adrian Murrell, NYJ	301	1249	4.2	78	6
Curtis Martin, NE	316	1152	3.6	57	14

LEADING RUSHERS NFC	ATT	YARD	AVG	Long	TD
Barry Sanders, Det	307	1553	5.1	54t	11
Ricky Watters, Phi	353	1411	4.0	56t	13
Terry Allen, Was	347	1353	3.9	49t	21
Emmitt Smith, Dal	327	1204	3.7	42	12
Anthony Johnson, Car	300	1120	3.7	29	6

LEADING PASSERS AFC	ATT	COM	YARD	TD	IN
John Elway, Den	466	287	3328	26	14
Vinny Testaverde, Bal	549	325	4177	33	19
Dan Marino, Mia	373	221	2795	17	9
Mark Brunell, Jac	557	353	4367	19	20
Drew Bledsoe, NE	623	373	4086	27	15

LEADING PASSERS NFC	ATT	COM	YARD	TD	IN
Steve Young, SF	316	214	2410	14	6
Brett Favre, GB	543	325	3899	39	13
Brad Johnson, Min	311	195	2258	17	10
Ty Detmer, Phi	401	238	2911	15	13
Troy Aikman, Dal	465	296	3126	12	13

LEADING RECEIVERS AFC	NO	YARD	AVG	Long	TD
Carl Pickens, Cin	100	1180	11.8	61t	12
Terry Glenn, NE	90	1132	12.6	37t	6
Tim Brown, Oak	90	1104	12.3	42t	9
Tony Martin, SD	85	1171	13.8	55	14
Keenan McCardell, Jac	85	1129	13.3	52	3

LEADING RECEIVERS NFC	NO	YARD	AVG	Long	TD
Jerry Rice, SF	108	1254	11.6	39	8
Herman Moore, Det	106	1296	12.2	50	9
Larry Centers, Ariz	99	766	7.7	39	7
Cris Carter, Min	96	1163	12.1	43	10
Brett Perriman, Det	94	1021	10.9	44	5

LEADING SCORERS AFC	TD	FG	PAT	PTS
Cary Blanchard, Ind	0	36	27	135
Al Del Greco, Hou	0	32	35	131
Adam Vinatiera, NE	0	27	39	120
John Carney, SD	0	29	31	118
Mike Hollis, Jac	0	30	27	117

LEADING SCORERS NFC	TD	FG	PAT	PTS
John Kasay, Car	0	37	34	145
Jeff Wilkins, SF	0	30	40	130
Terry Allen, Was	21	0	0	126
Chris Boniol, Dal	0	32	24	122
Scott Blanton, Was	0	26	40	118

LEADING INTERCEPTOR	NO	YARD	AVG	Long	TD
Tyrone Braxton, Den (AFC)	9	128	14.2	69t	1
Keith Lyle, StL (NFC)	9	152	16.9	68	0

LEADING PUNTER	NO	AVG	Long
Chris Gardocki, Ind (AFC)	68	45.7	61
Matt Turk, Was (NFC)	75	45.1	63

LEADING PUNT RETURNER	NO	YDS	AVG	Long	TD
Darien Gordon, SD (AFC)	36	537	14.9	81t	1
Desmond Howard, GB (NFC)	58	875	15.1	92t	2

LEADING KICKOFF RETURNER	NO	YDS	AVG	Long	TD
Tamarick Vanover, KC (AFC)	20	553	27.7	58	0
Michael Bates, Car (NFC)	33	998	30.2	93t	1

SUPERLATIVES AFC

Rushing Avg.	5.8	Napoleon Kaufman, Oak
Receiving Avg.	18.4	Chris Sanders, Hou
Completion Pct.	63.4	Mark Brunell, Jac
Touchdowns	17	Curtis Martin, NE
Field Goals	36	Cary Blanchard, Ind
Sacks	13.5	Bruce Smith, Buf
		Michael McCrary, Sea

SUPERLATIVES NFC

Rushing Avg.	5.1	Barry Sanders, Det
Receiving Avg.	19.5	Henry Ellard, Was
Completion Pct.	67.7	Steve Young, SF
Touchdowns	21	Terry Allen, Was
Field Goals	37	John Kasay. Car
Sacks	14.5	Kevin Greene, Car

LONGEST AFC

Run	80	Kordell Stewart, Pit
Pass	95	Todd Collins to Quinn Early, Buf
Interception	100t	Vencie Glenn, NYJ
Punt	80	Chris Mohr, Buf
Punt Return	88t	Joey Galloway, Sea
Kickoff Return	97t	Tamarick Vanover, KC
Field Goal	56	Al Del Greco, Hou

LONGEST NFC

Run	80t	LeShon Johnson, Ariz
Pass	99t	Brad Johnson to Jake Reed, Min
Interception	98t	Bennie Blades, Det
Punt	72	Todd Sauerbrun, ChiB
Punt Return	92t	Desmond Howard, GB
Kickoff Return	97t	Derrick Witherspoon, Phi
Field Goal	55	Scott Blanton, Was

1997 AMERICAN FOOTBALL CONFERENCE

					SCORING		RUSHING				PASSING						
Team	W	L	T	PCT	OWN-OPP PTS-PTS	OWN-OPP PPG-PPG	OWN-OPP ATT-ATT	OWN-OPP YARD-YARD	OWN-OPP AVG-AVG	ON-OP TD-TD	OWN-OPP ATT-ATT	OWN-OPP COM-COM	OWN-OPP PCT-PCT	OWN - OPP YARD - YARD	OWN-OPP AVG-AVG	ON-OP TD-TD	ON-OP IN-IN
Eastern Division																	
NE	10	6	0	.625	369-289	23.1-18.1	398-436	1464-1616	3.7-3.7	6-16	532-619	321-368	60.3-59.5	3808- 3772	7.2- 6.1	31-14	15-19
Mia*	9	7	0	.563	339-327	21.2-20.4	430-443	1343-1813	3.1-4.1	18- 9	576-530	332-329	57.6-62.1	3945- 3782	6.8- 7.1	16-23	12-10
NYJ	9	7	0	.563	348-287	21.8-17.9	431-470	1485-1899	3.4-4.0	10- 9	564-558	319-304	56.6-54.5	3555- 3663	6.3- 6.6	20-23	10-18
Buf	6	10	0	.375	255-367	15.9-22.9	422-470	1782-1690	4.2-3.6	12-11	546-502	293-287	53.7-57.2	3213- 3405	5.9- 6.8	12-17	25-15
Ind	3	13	0	.188	313-401	19.6-25.1	450-493	1727-1690	3.8-3.6	10-18	523-453	317-261	60.6-57.6	3560- 3067	6.8- 6.8	16-26	16-12
Central Division																	
Pit	11	5	0	.688	372-307	23.2-19.2	572-403	2479-1318	4.3-3.3	19- 5	466-554	253-295	54.3-53.2	3215- 3681	6.9- 6.6	22-24	19-20
Jac*	11	5	0	.688	394-318	24.6-19.8	454-455	1720-1734	3.8-3.8	20-12	504-532	313-320	62.1-60.2	3922- 3835	7.8- 7.2	20-24	9-14
Ten	8	8	0	.500	333-310	20.8-19.4	541-414	2414-1573	4.5-3.8	17-12	420-543	220-321	52.4-59.1	2704- 3898	6.4- 7.2	15-21	13-14
Cin	7	9	0	.438	355-405	22.2-25.3	452-514	1966-2223	4.3-4.3	23-15	504-542	302-309	59.9-57.0	3603- 3668	7.1- 6.8	21-30	9-13
Bal	6	9	1	.406	326-345	20.4-21.6	420-470	1589-1690	3.8-3.6	7-17	586-556	338-332	57.7-59.7	3929- 3966	6.7- 7.1	25-20	16-17
Western Division																	
KC	13	3	0	.813	375-232	23.4-14.5	529-413	2171-1621	4.1-3.9	15- 8	493-507	281-271	57.0-53.5	3129- 3618	6.3- 7.2	20-15	10-21
Den*	12	4	0	.750	472-287	29.5-17.9	520-381	2378-1803	4.6-4.7	18-10	513-526	287-290	55.9-55.1	3704- 3166	7.2- 6.0	27-20	11-18
Sea	8	8	0	.500	365-362	22.8-22.6	404-455	1800-1731	4.5-3.8	13-10	609-462	359-276	58.9-59.7	4187- 3356	6.9- 7.3	26-19	21-13
Oak	4	12	0	.250	324-419	20.3-26.2	360-525	1588-2246	4.4-4.3	9-19	529-552	294-324	55.6-58.7	3944- 4109	7.5- 7.4	29-21	10-10
SD	4	12	0	.250	266-425	16.6-26.6	409-453	1416-1698	3.5-3.7	5-12	565-568	291-297	51.5-52.3	3475- 3632	6.1- 6.4	12-31	21-15

1997 NATIONAL FOOTBALL CONFERENCE

Eastern Division																	
NYG	10	5	1	.656	307-265	19.1-16.6	521-432	1988-1451	3.8-3.4	14-17	474-596	249-325	52.5-54.5	2763- 3957	5.8- 6.6	14-10	12-27
Was	8	7	1	.531	327-289	20.4-18.1	453-508	1615-2212	3.6-4.4	12-15	547-513	283-267	51.7-52.0	3581- 3098	6.5- 6.0	12-14	22-16
Phi	6	9	1	.406	317-372	19.8-23.3	465-476	1943-2009	4.2-4.2	11-16	587-490	330-259	56.2-52.9	4009- 3201	6.8- 6.5	22-20	16-14
Dal	6	10	0	.375	304-314	19.0-19.6	423-511	1637-1994	3.9-3.9	6-12	553-473	314-253	56.8-53.5	3454- 2717	6.2- 5.7	19-20	12- 7
Ariz	4	12	0	.250	283-379	17.7-23.7	395-524	1255-2180	3.2-4.2	9-13	602-491	317-279	52.7-56.8	3953- 3461	6.6- 7.0	19-23	22-15
Central Division																	
GB	13	3	0	.813	422-282	26.4-17.6	459-443	1909-1876	4.2-4.2	9-16	523-563	309-288	59.1-51.2	3896- 3225	7.4- 5.7	35-10	16-21
TB*	10	6	0	.625	299-263	18.7-16.4	479-420	1934-1617	4.0-3.9	15-10	404-518	224-325	55.4-62.7	2638- 3342	6.5- 6.5	21-13	12-13
Det*	9	7	0	.563	379-306	23.7-19.1	447-471	2464-1833	5.5-3.9	19-15	540-507	304-281	56.3-55.4	3605- 3401	6.7- 6.7	19-15	17-17
Min*	9	7	0	.563	354-359	22.1-22.4	449-442	2041-1983	4.5-4.5	14-13	540-542	319-336	59.1-62.0	3537- 3957	6.6- 7.3	26-28	16-12
Chi	4	12	0	.250	263-421	16.4-26.3	490-421	1746-1858	3.6-4.4	14-18	595-476	336-273	56.5-57.4	3501- 3289	5.9- 6.9	14-18	22-13
Western Division																	
SF	13	3	0	.813	375-265	23.4-16.6	523-386	1969-1366	3.8-3.5	16- 5	432-509	278-258	64.4-50.7	3432- 3011	7.9- 5.9	20-23	11-25
Car	7	9	0	.438	265-314	16.5-19.6	441-497	1770-1973	4.0-4.0	11-12	534-490	289-260	54.1-53.1	3156- 3253	5.9- 6.6	11-17	24-11
Atl	7	9	0	.438	320-361	20.0-22.6	442-409	1643-1666	3.7-4.1	8-18	484-496	273-275	56.4-55.4	3445- 3794	7.1- 7.6	26-24	11-18
NO	6	10	0	.375	237-327	14.8-20.4	417-496	1461-1764	3.5-3.6	9-11	458-518	228-293	49.8-56.6	2901- 3289	6.3- 6.3	13-21	33-16
StL	5	11	0	.313	299-359	18.7-22.4	443-440	1563-1687	3.5-3.8	15-10	526-543	271-288	51.5-53.0	3524- 3675	6.7- 6.8	14-10	15-25
League 240 games					9957	41.4	13639	54260	4.0	384	15729	8844	56.2	96875	6.2	617	479

*Wild Card qualifiers for playoffs
AFC Wild Card playoffs: Den 42, Jac 17; NE 17, Mia 3
NFC Wild Card playoffs: Min 23, NYG 22; TB 20, Det 10
AFC Divisional playoffs: Pit 7, NE 6; Den 14, KC 10
NFC Divisional playoffs: SF 38, Min 22; GB 21, TB 7
AFC championship: Den 24, Pit 21
NFC championship: GB 23, SF 10
Super Bowl XXXII: Den (AFC) 31, GB (NFC) 24

LEADING RUSHERS AFC	ATT	YARD	AVG	Long	TD
Terrell Davis, Den	369	1750	4.7	50t	15
Jerome Bettis, Pit	375	1665	4.4	34	7
Eddie George, Ten	357	1399	3.9	30	6
Napoleon Kaufman	272	1294	4.8	83t	6
Curtis Martin	274	1160	4.2	70t	4

LEADING RUSHERS NFC	ATT	YARD	AVG	Long	TD
Barry Sanders, Det	335	2053	6.1	82t	11
Dorsey Levens, GB	329	1435	4.4	52t	7
Robert Smith, Min	232	1266	5.5	78t	6
Ricky Watters, Phi	285	1110	3.9	28	7
Emmitt Smith, Dal	261	1074	4.1	44	4

LEADING PASSERS AFC	ATT	COMP	YARD	TD	IN
Mark Brunell, Jac	435	264	3281	18	7
Jeff George, Oak	521	290	3917	29	9
Drew Bledsoe, NE	522	314	3706	28	15
John Elway, Den	502	280	3635	27	11
Jim Harbaugh, Ind	309	189	2060	10	4

LEADING PASSERS NFC	ATT	COMP	YARD	TD	IN
Steve Young, SF	356	241	3029	19	6
Chris Chandler, Atl	342	202	2692	20	7
Brett Favre, GB	513	304	3867	35	16
Brad Johnson, Min	452	275	3036	20	12
Bobby Hoying, Phi	225	128	1573	11	6

LEADING RECEIVERS AFC	NO	YARD	AVG	Long	TD
Tim Brown, Oak	104	1408	13.5	59t	5
Keenan McCardell, Jac	85	1164	13.7	60	5
Jimmy Smith, Jac	82	1324	16.1	75	4
Yancey Thigpen, Pit	79	1398	17.7	69t	7
O.J. McDuffie, Mia	76	943	12.4	55	1

LEADING RECEIVERS NFC	NO	YARD	AVG	Long	TD
Herman Moore, Det	104	1293	12.4	79	8
Rob Moore, Ariz	97	1584	16.3	47t	8
Cris Carter, Min	89	1069	12.0	43	13
Irving Fryer, Phi	86	1316	15.3	72t	6
Antonio Freeman, GB	81	1243	15.3	58t	12

LEADING SCORERS AFC	TD	FG	PAT	PTS
Mike Hollis, Jac	0	31	41	134
Jason Elam, Den	0	26	46	124
John Hall, NYJ	0	28	36	120
Cary Blanchard, Ind	0	32	21	117
Olindo Mare, Mia	0	28	33	117

LEADING SCORERS NFC	TD	FG	PAT	PTS
Richie Cunningham, Dal	0	34	24	126
Gary Anderson, SF	0	29	38	125
Ryan Longwell, GB	0	24	48	120
Jason Hanson, Det	0	26	39	117
Jeff Wilkins, StL	0	25	32	107

LEADING INTERCEPTOR	NO	YARD	AVG	Long	TD
Mark McMillian, KC (AFC)	8	274	34.3	87t	3
Darryl Williams, Sea (AFC)	8	172	21.5	44t	1
Ryan McNeil, StL (NFC)	9	127	14.1	75t	1

LEADING PUNTER	NO	AVG	Long
Tom Tupa, NE (AFC)	78	45.8	73
Mark Royals, NO (NFC)	88	45.9	66

LEADING PUNT RETURNER	NO	YDS	AVG	Long	TD
Jermaine Lewis, Bal (AFC)	28	437	15.6	89t	2
David Palmer, Min (NFC)	34	444	13.1	57	0

LEADING KICKOFF RETURNER	NO	YDS	AVG	Long	TD
Aaron Glenn, NYJ (AFC)	28	741	26.5	96t	1
Michael Bates, Car (NFC)	47	1281	27.3	56	0

SUPERLATIVES AFC		
Rushing Avg.	6.7	Steve McNair, Ten
Receiving Avg.	18.7	James McKnight, Sea
Completion Pct.	61.2	Jim Harbaugh, Ind
Touchdowns	16	Karim Abdul-Jabbar, Mia
Field Goals	32	Cary Blanchard, Ind
Sacks	14.0	Bruce Smith, Buf

SUPERLATIVES NFC		
Rushing Avg.	6.1	Barry Sanders, Det
Receiving Avg.	16.8	Robert Brooks, GB
Completion Pct.	67.7	Steve Young, SF
Touchdowns	14	Barry Sanders, Det
Field Goals	34	Richie Cunningham, Dal
Sacks	15.5	John Randle, Min

LONGEST AFC		
Run	83t	Napoleon Kaufman, Oakland
Pass	92	Eric Zeier to Derrick Alexander, Bal
Interception	100t	Jimmy Hitchcock, NE
Punt	73	Tom Tupa, NE
Punt Return	94t	Darrien Gordon, Den
Kickoff Return	102t	Eric Bieniemy, Cin
Field Goal	55	Steve Christie, Buf
		John Hall, NYJ

LONGEST NFC		
Run	82t	Barry Sanders, Det
Pass	89t	Heath Shuler to Randall Hill, NO
Interception	95t	Sam Garnes, NYG
Punt	74	Sean Landeta, TB
Punt Return	83t	Deion Sanders, Dal
Kickoff Return	102	Eric Guilford, NO
Field Goal	55	Morten Anderson, Atl
		Jason Hanson, Det

1998 AMERICAN FOOTBALL CONFERENCE

					SCORING		RUSHING				PASSING						
Team	W	L	T	PCT	OWN-OPP PTS-PTS	OWN-OPP PPG-PPG	OWN-OPP ATT-ATT	OWN-OPP YARD-YARD	OWN-OPP AVG-AVG	ON-OP TD-TD	OWN-OPP ATT-ATT	OWN-OPP COM-COM	OWN-OPP PCT-PCT	OWN - OPP YARD - YARD	OWN-OPP AVG-AVG	ON-OP TD-TD	ON-OP IN-IN
Eastern Division																	
NYJ	12	4	0	.750	416-266	26.0-16.6	500-400	1879-1659	3.8-4.1	12-11	532-544	318-285	59.8-52.4	3836- 3040	7.2- 5.6	33-16	13-21
Mia*	10	6	0	.625	321-265	20.0-16.6	458-395	1535-2924	3.4-3.8	10- 6	546-504	316-252	57.9-50.0	3395- 2924	6.2- 5.8	23-17	16-29
Buf*	10	6	0	.625	400-333	25.0-20.8	530-375	2175-1493	4.1-4.0	13-11	461-531	269-294	58.4-55.4	3366- 3198	7.3- 6.0	28-27	14-18
NE*	9	7	0	.563	337-329	21.0-20.6	403-447	1480-1547	3.7-3.5	9- 8	556-570	295-336	53.1-58.9	3660- 3635	6.6- 6.4	23-26	17-24
Ind	3	13	0	.188	310-444	19.4-27.8	384-544	1486-2566	3.9-4.7	7-20	576-461	326-275	56.2-59.7	3739- 3266	6.5- 7.1	33-27	28- 8

Central Division																	
Jac	11	5	0	.688	392-338	24.5-21.1	487-450	2102-2000	4.3-4.4	19- 9	463-577	269-325	58.1-56.3	3112- 3559	6.7- 6.2	24-23	12-13
Tenn	8	8	0	.500	330-320	20.6-20.0	462-414	1970-1610	4.3-3.9	12- 9	519-511	305-319	58.8-62.4	3291- 3511	6.4- 6.9	16-24	10-12
Pit	7	9	0	.438	263-303	16.4-18.9	490-479	2034-1642	4.2-3.4	8- 8	489-482	274-268	56.0-55.6	2552- 3321	5.2- 6.2	13-17	20-16
Bal	6	10	0	.375	269-335	16.8-20.9	408-472	1629-1705	4.0-3.6	7-12	477-539	272-316	57.0-58.6	3152- 3592	6.6- 6.7	16-20	15-17
Cin	3	13	0	.188	268-452	16.8-28.3	405-558	1639-2612	4.0-4.7	7-23	521-406	307-233	58.9-57.4	3545- 3151	6.8- 7.7	20-23	12-13
Western Division																	
Den	14	2	0	.875	501-309	31.3-19.3	525-356	2468-1287	4.7-3.6	26- 8	491-544	290-285	59.1-57.9	3624- 3648	7.4- 6.7	32-28	14-19
Oak	8	8	0	.500	288-356	18.0-22.3	449-482	1727-1674	3.8-3.5	6- 8	519-497	282-291	54.3-58.6	3088- 2876	5.9- 5.8	21-22	25-21
Sea	8	8	0	.500	372-310	23.3-19.4	426-487	1626-1999	3.8-4.1	11-13	480-597	273-343	56.9-57.5	3000- 3690	6.3- 6.2	21-18	18-24
KC	7	9	0	.438	327-363	20.4-22.7	433-491	1548-1869	3.6-3.8	19-17	543-479	305-259	56.2-54.1	3260- 2985	6.0- 6.8	15-17	18-13
SD	5	11	0	.313	241-342	15.1-21.4	460-422	1728-1140	3.8-2.7	11-12	566-530	261-271	46.1-51.1	2864- 3068	5.1- 5.8	11-21	34-20

1998 NATIONAL FOOTBALL CONFERENCE

Eastern Division																	
Dal	10	6	0	.625	381-275	23.8-17.2	499-401	2014-1619	4.0-4.0	21-10	474-553	279-290	58.9-52.4	3436- 3545	7.2- 6.4	17-21	8-14
Ariz*	9	7	0	.563	325-378	20.3-23.6	450-492	1627-1989	3.6-4.0	18-18	552-518	326-299	59.1-57.7	3482- 3276	6.3- 5.9	17-21	20-20
NYG	8	8	0	.500	287-309	17.9-19.3	474-476	1889-2004	4.0-4.2	10-13	507-521	265-282	52.3-54.1	2566- 3167	5.1- 6.1	18-17	15-19
Was	6	10	0	.375	319-421	19.9-26.3	401-531	1685-2436	4.2-4.6	15-24	565-493	304-281	53.8-57.0	3325- 2918	5.9- 5.9	24-21	14-13
Phi	3	13	0	.188	161-344	10.0-21.5	427-528	1775-2416	4.2-4.6	10-18	534-449	282-249	52.8-55.5	2413- 2720	4.5- 6.1	7-18	18- 9
Central Division																	
Min	15	1	0	.938	556-296	34.8-18.5	450-404	1936-1614	4.3-4.0	17-12	533-555	327-320	61.4-57.7	4328- 3452	8.1- 6.2	41-17	16-19
GB*	11	5	0	.688	408-319	25.5-19.9	447-390	1526-1442	3.4-3.7	7-23	575-540	361-296	62.8-54.8	4110- 3065	7.1- 5.7	33-23	23-13
TB	8	8	0	.500	314-295	19.6-18.4	523-415	2148-1583	4.1-3.8	12-12	449-473	234-274	52.1-57.9	2606- 2762	5.8- 5.8	21-15	18-12
Det	5	11	0	.313	306-378	19.1-23.6	441-487	1955-2102	4.4-4.3	12-15	489-474	274-284	56.0-59.9	3130- 3015	6.4- 6.4	17-23	13-12
ChiB	4	12	0	.250	276-368	17.3-23.0	454-479	1713-1875	3.8-3.9	9-12	494-456	284-292	57.5-64.0	3053- 3228	6.2- 6.5	16-12	13-14
Western Division																	
Atl	14	2	0	.875	442-289	27.6-18.1	516-361	2101-1203	4.1-3.3	18- 7	424-551	237-311	55.9-56.4	3386- 3531	8.0- 6.4	28-22	15-19
SF*	12	4	0	.750	479-328	29.9-20.5	491-395	2544-1610	5.2-4.1	19- 7	556-566	347-294	62.4-51.9	4256- 3733	7.6- 6.6	41-25	15-21
NO	6	10	0	.375	305-359	19.0-22.4	374-466	1325-1714	3.5-3.7	6-13	534-539	278-328	52.1-60.9	3138- 3954	5.9- 7.3	19-24	19-21
Car	4	12	0	.250	336-413	21.0-25.8	405-491	1454-2133	3.6-4.3	11-14	507-501	292-298	57.6-59.5	3322- 3709	6.6- 7.4	25-30	18-19
StL	4	12	0	.250	285-378	17.8-23.6	395-479	1385-2049	3.5-4.3	17-11	556-475	314-256	56.5-53.9	3087- 2831	5.1- 6.0	12-28	18-16
League 240 games					10215	42.6	13567	54103	4.0	379	15488	8766	56.6	99122	6.4	665	509

*Wild Card qualifiers for playoffs
AFC Wild Card playoffs: Mia 24, Buf 17; Jac 25, NE 10
NFC Wild Card playoffs: Ariz 20, Dal 7; SF 30, GB 27
AFC Divisional playoffs: Den 38, Mia 3; NYJ 34, Jac 24
NFC Divisional playoffs: Atl 20, SF 18; Min 41, Ariz 21
AFC championship: Den 23, NYJ 10
NFC championship: Atl 30, Min 27 (OT)
Super Bowl XXXIII: Den (AFC) 34, Atl (NFC) 19

LEADING RUSHERS AFC	ATT	YARD	AVG	Long	TD
Terrell Davis, Den	392	2008	5.1	70	21
Marshall Faulk, Ind	324	1319	4.1	68t	6
Eddie George, Tenn	348	1294	3.7	37t	5
Curtis Martin, NYJ	369	1287	3.5	60t	8
Ricky Watters, Sea	319	1239	3.9	39t	9

LEADING RUSHERS NFC	ATT	YARD	AVG	Long	TD
Jamal Anderson, Atl	410	1846	4.5	48	14
Garrison Hearst, SF	310	1570	5.1	96t	7
Barry Sanders, Det	343	1491	4.3	73t	4
Emmitt Smith, Dal	319	1332	4.2	32	13
Robert Smith, Min	249	1187	4.8	74t	6

LEADING PASSERS AFC	ATT	COM	YARD	TD	IN
Vinny Testaverde, NYJ	421	259	3256	29	7
John Elway, Den	356	210	2806	22	10
Neil O'Donnell, Cin	343	212	2216	15	4
Mark Brunell, Jac	354	208	2601	20	9
Doug Flutie, Buf	354	202	2711	20	11

LEADING PASSERS NFC	ATT	COM	YARD	TD	IN
Randall Cunningham, Min	425	259	3704	34	10
Steve Young, SF	517	322	4170	36	12
Chris Chandler, Atl	327	190	3154	25	12
Troy Aikman, Dal	315	187	2330	12	5
Steve Beuerlein, Car	343	216	2613	17	12

LEADING RECEIVERS AFC	NO	YARD	AVG	Long	TD
O.J. McDuffie, Mia	90	1050	11.7	61t	7
Rod Smith, Den	86	1222	14.2	58	6
Marshall Faulk, Ind	86	908	10.6	78t	4
Keyshawn Johnson	83	1131	13.6	41t	10
Carl Pickens, Cin	82	1023	12.5	67t	5

LEADING RECEIVERS NFC	NO	YARD	AVG	Long	TD
Frank Sanders, Ariz	89	1145	12.9	42	3
Antonio Freeman, GB	84	1424	17.0	84t	14
Jerry Rice, SF	82	1157	14.1	75t	9
Herman Moore, Det	82	983	12.0	36	5
Cris Carter, Min	78	1011	13.0	54t	12

LEADING SCORERS AFC	TD	FG	PAT	PTS
Steve Christie, Buf	0	33	41	140
Terrell Davis, Den	23	0	0	138
Al Del Greco, Tenn	0	36	28	136
Jason Elam, Den	0	23	58	127
Adam Vinatieri, NE	0	31	32*	127

*also scored 2-point conversion

LEADING SCORERS NFC	TD	FG	PAT	PTS
Gary Anderson, Min	0	35	59	164
Ryan Longwell, GB	0	29	41	128
Richie Cunningham, Dal	0	29	40	127
Morten Andersen, Atl	0	23	51	120
Jason Hanson, Det	0	29	27	114

LEADING INTERCEPTOR	NO	YARD	AVG	Long	TD
Ty Law, NE (AFC)	9	133	14.8	59t	1
Kwamie Lassiter, Ariz (NFC)	8	80	10.0	29	0

LEADING PUNTER	NO	AVG	Long
Craig Hentrich, Tenn (AFC)	69	47.2	71
Mark Royals, NO (NFC)	88	45.6	64

LEADING PUNT RETURNER	NO	YDS	AVG	Long	TD
Reggie Barlow, Jac (AFC)	43	555	12.9	85t	1
Deion Sanders, Dal (NFC)	24	375	15.6	69t	2

LEADING KICKOFF RETURNER	NO	YDS	AVG	Long	TD
Corey Harris, Bal (AFC)	35	965	27.6	95t	1
Terry Fair, Det	51	1428	28.0	105t	2

SUPERLATIVES AFC		
Rushing Avg.	5.1	Terrell Davis, Den
Receiving Avg.	22.7	Shawn Jefferson, NE
Completion Pct.	61.8	Neil O'Donnell, Cin
Touchdowns	23	Terrell Davis, Den
Field Goals	36	Al Del Greco, Tenn
Sacks	16.5	Michael Sinclair, Sea

SUPERLATIVES NFC		
Rushing Avg.	5.1	Garrison Hearst, SF
Receiving Avg.	19.0	Randy Moss, Min
Completion Pct.	63.0	Brett Favre, GB
Touchdowns	17	Randy Moss, Min
Field Goals	35	Gary Anderson, Min
Sacks	16	Reggie White, GB

LONGEST AFC		
Run	80t	Napoleon Kaufman, Oak
Pass	86t	Drew Bledsoe to Terry Glenn, NE
Interception	94	Eric Turner, Oak
Punt	76	Tom Rouen, Den
Punt Return	87t	Jermaine Lewis, Bal
Kickoff Return	97t	Tremain Mack, Cin
		Pat Johnson, Bal
Field Goal	63	Jason Elam, Den

LONGEST NFC		
Run	96t	Garrison Hearst, SF
Pass	98t	Charlie Batch to Johnnie Morton, Det
Interception	91	Sammy Knight, NO
Punt	72	Sean Landeta, GB
Punt Return	95t	Jacquez Green, TB
Kickoff Return	105t	Terry Fair, Det
Field Goal	57	Jeff Wilkins, StL

The All-Time Leaders

The Records Section contains the NFL career leaders in various statistical categories, such as passing attempts, rushing yards, and interceptions. It should be remembered that statistics for other leagues are not commingled with NFL statistics. Hence, players such as Cleveland's Otto Graham, who played the first four of his ten professional seasons in the AAFC, does not appear on most career passing lists in this section.

Following the Career Leaders, we include the top 25 Season Leaders in selected statistical categories. These lists change greatly with each season. Because we have included the top 25, the reader will be able to see when a current player nears a meaningful mark.

Career Rushing Records

RUSHING ATTEMPTS

	Player	Year	Atts.
1	Walter Payton	1975-87	3838
2	Barry Sanders	1989-98	3062
3	Marcus Allen	1982-97	3022
4	Eric Dickerson	1983-93	2996
5	Franco Harris	1972-84	2949
6	Tony Dorsett	1977-88	2936
7	John Riggins	1971-79, 81-85	2916
8	Emmitt Smith	1990-98	2914
9	Thurman Thomas	1988-98	2813
10	Ottis Anderson	1979-92	2562
11	O.J. Simpson	1969-79	2404
12	Jim Brown	1957-65	2359
13	Earl Campbell	1978-85	2187
14	Earnest Byner	1984-97	2095
15	Roger Craig	1983-93	1991
16	Gerald Riggs	1982-91	1989
17	Herschel Walker	1986-97	1954
18	Ricky Watters	1992-98	1947
19	Jim Taylor	1958-67	1941
20	Larry Csonka	1968-74, 76-79	1891
21	Mike Pruitt	1976-86	1844
22	Rodney Hampton	1990-97	1824
23	Jerome Bettis	1993-98	1807
24	Freeman McNeil	1981-92	1798
25	Joe Perry	1950-63	1737
26	Leroy Kelly	1964-73	1727
27	Curt Warner	1983-90	1698
28	George Rogers	1981-87	1692
29	James Brooks	1981-92	1685
30	Terry Allen	1991-92, 94-98	1684
31	Lydell Mitchell	1972-80	1675
32	Mark van Eeghen	1974-83	1652
33	Bill Brown	1961-74	1649
34	Floyd Little	1967-75	1641
35	Ken Willard	1965-74	1622
36	Chris Warren	1990-98	1618
37	James Wilder	1981-90	1586
38	John Henry Johnson	1954-66	1571
39	Chuck Muncie	1976-84	1561
40	Chuck Foreman	1973-80	1556
41	Wilbert Montgomery	1977-85	1540
42	Larry Brown	1969-76	1530
43	Lawrence McCutcheon	1972-81	1521
44	Neal Anderson	1986-93	1515
45	Don Perkins	1961-68	1500
46	Sammy Winder	1982-90	1495
47	Pete Johnson	1977-84	1489
48	Calvin Hill	1969-74, 76-81	1452
49	Rick Casares	1955-66	1431
50	Joe Morris	1982-88, 91	1411
51	Marshall Faulk	1994-98	1389
52	Sam Cunningham	1973-79, 81-82	1385
53	John Brockington	1971-77	1347
54	Marion Butts	1989-95	1345
55	Wendell Tyler	1977-86	1344
56	Terrell Davis	1995-98	1343
57	Jim Nance	1965-71, 73	1341
58	Curtis Martin	1995-98	1327
59	Steve Van Buren	1944-51	1320
60	William Andrews	1979-83, 86	1315
61	Delvin Williams	1974-81	1312
62	Joe Cribbs	1980-83, 85-88	1309
63	Mike Garrett	1966-73	1308
64	Natrone Means	1993-98	1297
65	Emerson Boozer	1966-75	1291
	Kevin Mack	1985-93	1291
67	Christian Okoye	1987-92	1246
68	John L. Williams	1986-95	1245
69	Dick Bass	1960-69	1218
70	MacArthur Lane	1968-78	1206
71	Greg Bell	1984-90	1204
	Ron Johnson	1969-75	1204
73	Dexter Bussey	1974-84	1203
74	Tom Matte	1961-72	1200
75	Donny Anderson	1966-74	1197
76	Greg Pruitt	1973-84	1196
	Alex Webster	1955-64	1196
78	Joe Washington	1977-85	1195
79	Tony Collins	1981-87, 90	1191
80	Dave Osborn	1965-76	1179
81	Rob Carpenter	1977-86	1172
82	Clarke Hinkle	1932-41	1171
83	Ollie Matson	1952, 54-66	1170
	Altie Taylor	1969-76	1170
85	Garrison Hearst	1993-98	1166
86	Leonard Russell	1991-96	1164
87	Robert Newhouse	1972-83	1160
	Jim Otis	1970-78	1160
89	Mike Rozier	1985-91	1159
90	John David Crow	1958-68	1157
	Ed Podolak	1969-77	1157
92	Harold Green	1990-98	1151
93	Dave Hampton	1969-76	1148
94	Clem Daniels	1960-68	1146
95	Adrian Murrell	1993-98	1134
96	Dick Hoak	1961-70	1132
97	Billy Sims	1980-84	1131
98	Dalton Hilliard	1986-93	1126
99	Hugh McElhenny	1952-64	1124
100	Ted Brown	1979-86	1117
101	Edgar Bennett	1992-96, 98	1109
102	J.D. Smith	1956-66	1100
103	Mike Thomas	1975-80	1087
104	Lenny Moore	1956-67	1069
105	Reggie Cobb	1990-96	1065
106	Lorenzo White	1988-95	1062
107	Earnest Jackson	1983-88	1059
108	Matt Snell	1964-72	1057
109	Johnny Hector	1983-92	1051
110	Johnny Johnson	1990-94	1046
111	Bill Mathis	1960-69	1044
112	Eddie George	1996-98	1040
	Tommy Mason	1961-71	1040
114	Abner Haynes	1960-67	1036
115	Tony Galbreath	1976-87	1031
	Carl Garrett	1969-77	1031
	Craig Heyward	1988-98	1031
118	Jim Kiick	1968-74, 76-77	1029
119	Paul Lowe	1960-61, 63-69	1026
120	Tony Canadeo	1941-44, 46-52	1025
121	Otis Armstrong	1973-80	1023
122	Harvey Williams	1991-98	1021
123	Darrin Nelson	1982-92	1020
124	Johnny Roland	1966-73	1015
125	Rickey Young	1975-83	1011
126	Cookie Gilchrist	1962-67	1010
	James Jones	1983-92	1010

RUSHING YARDS

	Player	Year	Yds.
1	Walter Payton	1975-87	16726
2	Barry Sanders	1989-98	15269
3	Eric Dickerson	1983-93	13259
4	Tony Dorsett	1977-88	12739
5	Emmitt Smith	1990-98	12566
6	Jim Brown	1957-65	12312
7	Marcus Allen	1982-97	12243
8	Franco Harris	1972-84	12120
9	Thurman Thomas	1988-98	11786
10	John Riggins	1971-79, 81-85	11352
11	O.J. Simpson	1969-79	11236
12	Ottis Anderson	1979-92	10273
13	Earl Campbell	1978-85	9407
14	Jim Taylor	1958-67	8597
15	Joe Perry	1950-63	8378
16	Earnest Byner	1984-97	8261
17	Herschel Walker	1986-97	8225
18	Roger Craig	1983-93	8189
19	Gerald Riggs	1982-91	8188
20	Larry Csonka	1968-74, 76-79	8081
21	Freeman McNeil	1981-92	8074
22	James Brooks	1981-92	7962
23	Ricky Watters	1992-98	7873
24	Mike Pruitt	1976-86	7378
25	Jerome Bettis	1993-98	7372
26	Leroy Kelly	1964-73	7274
27	George Rogers	1981-87	7176
28	Chris Warren	1990-98	6997
29	Rodney Hampton	1990-97	6897
30	Terry Allen	1991-92, 94-98	6881
31	Curt Warner	1983-90	6844
32	John Henry Johnson	1954-66	6803
33	Wilbert Montgomery	1977-85	6789
34	Chuck Muncie	1976-84	6702
35	Mark van Eeghen	1974-83	6651
36	Lawrence McCutcheon	1972-81	6578
37	Lydell Mitchell	1972-80	6534
38	Terrell Davis	1995-98	6413
39	Wendell Tyler	1977-86	6378
40	Floyd Little	1967-75	6323
41	Don Perkins	1961-68	6217
42	Neal Anderson	1986-93	6166
43	Ken Willard	1965-74	6105
44	Calvin Hill	1969-74, 76-81	6083
45	James Wilder	1981-90	6008
46	William Andrews	1979-83, 86	5986
47	Chuck Foreman	1973-80	5950
48	Larry Brown	1969-76	5875
49	Steve Van Buren	1944-51	5860
50	Bill Brown	1961-74	5838
51	Rick Casares	1955-66	5797
52	Greg Pruitt	1973-84	5672
53	Pete Johnson	1977-84	5626
54	Delvin Williams	1974-81	5598
55	Joe Morris	1982-88, 91	5585
56	Mike Garrett	1966-73	5481
57	Sam Cunningham	1973-79, 81-82	5453
58	Sammy Winder	1982-90	5427
59	Dick Bass	1960-69	5417
60	Jim Nance	1965-71, 73	5401
61	Joe Cribbs	1980-83, 85-88	5356
62	Marshall Faulk	1994-98	5320
63	Hugh McElhenny	1952-64	5281

Player	Year	Yds.
64 John Brockington	1971-77	5185
Marion Butts	1989-95	5185
66 Lenny Moore	1956-67	5174
67 Ollie Matson	1952, 54-66	5173
68 Clem Daniels	1960-68	5138
69 Emerson Boozer	1966-75	5135
70 Kevin Mack	1985-93	5123
71 Billy Sims	1980-84	5106
72 Dexter Bussey	1974-84	5105
73 Curtis Martin	1995-98	5086
74 John L. Williams	1986-95	5006
75 Paul Lowe	1960-61, 63-69	4995
76 John David Crow	1958-68	4963
77 Greg Bell	1984-90	4959
78 Gale Sayers	1965-71	4956
79 Garrison Hearst	1993-98	4939
80 Natrone Means	1993-98	4938
81 Christian Okoye	1987-92	4897
82 Joe Washington	1977-85	4839
83 Robert Newhouse	1972-83	4784
84 Randall Cunningham	1985-95, 97-98	4741
85 Donny Anderson	1966-74	4696
86 J.D. Smith	1956-66	4672
87 MacArthur Lane	1968-78	4656
88 Stump Mitchell	1981-89	4649
89 Tony Collins	1981-87, 90	4647
90 Tom Matte	1961-72	4646
91 Alex Webster	1955-64	4638
92 Abner Haynes	1960-67	4630
93 Ted Brown	1979-86	4546
94 Marv Hubbard	1969-75, 77	4544
95 Dave Hampton	1969-76	4536
96 Adrian Murrell	1993-98	4489
97 Mike Rozier	1985-91	4462
98 Otis Armstrong	1973-80	4453
99 Ed Podolak	1969-77	4451
100 Darrin Nelson	1982-92	4442
101 Harold Green	1990-98	4365
102 Rob Carpenter	1977-86	4363
103 Jim Otis	1970-78	4350
104 Dave Osborn	1965-76	4336
105 Ron Johnson	1969-75	4308
Altie Taylor	1969-76	4308
107 Craig Heyward	1988-98	4301
108 Cookie Gilchrist	1962-67	4293
109 Matt Snell	1964-72	4285
110 Robert Smith	1993-98	4282
111 Johnny Hector	1983-92	4280
112 Lorenzo White	1988-95	4242
113 Tommy Mason	1961-71	4203
114 Tony Canadeo	1941-44, 46-52	4197
Carl Garrett	1969-77	4197
116 Mike Thomas	1975-80	4196
117 Steve Young	1985-98	4182
118 Earnest Jackson	1983-88	4167
119 Dalton Hilliard	1986-93	4164
120 Mercury Morris	1969-76	4133
121 Gary Brown	1991-95, 97-98	4123
122 Johnny Johnson	1990-94	4078
123 Tony Galbreath	1976-87	4072
124 Jamal Anderson	1994-98	4063
125 Eddie George	1996-98	4061
126 Alan Ameche	1955-60	4045
127 Nick Pietrosante	1959-67	4026
128 Curtis Dickey	1980-86	4019
129 Frank Pollard	1980-88	3989
130 Leonard Russell	1991-96	3973
131 Dick Hoak	1961-70	3965
132 Edgar Bennett	1992-96, 98	3964
133 Harvey Williams	1991-98	3952
134 Barry Foster	1990-94	3943
135 Walt Garrison	1966-74	3886
136 Randy McMillan	1981-86	3876
137 Rocky Bleier	1968, 71-80	3865
138 Timmy Brown	1959-68	3862
139 Clarke Hinkle	1932-41	3860
140 Wilbur Jackson	1974-77, 79-82	3852
141 Jon Arnett	1957-66	3833
142 Gerry Ellis	1980-86	3826

AVERAGE GAIN
(Minimum 750 Rushing Attempts)

Player	Year	Avg.
1 Jim Brown	1957-65	5.22
2 Mercury Morris	1969-76	5.14
3 Gale Sayers	1965-71	5.00
4 Barry Sanders	1989-98	4.99
5 Paul Lowe	1960-61, 63-69	4.87
6 Lenny Moore	1956-67	4.84
7 Joe Perry	1950-63	4.82
8 Robert Smith	1993-98	4.78
9 Marv Hubbard	1969-75, 77	4.78
10 Terrell Davis	1995-98	4.78
11 Wendell Tyler	1977-86	4.75
12 Greg Pruitt	1973-84	4.74
13 Paul Younger	1949-58	4.73
14 James Brooks	1981-92	4.73
15 Stump Mitchell	1981-89	4.72
16 Hugh McElhenny	1952-64	4.70
17 O.J. Simpson	1969-79	4.67
18 Gerry Ellis	1980-86	4.58
19 Terry Metcalf	1973-77, 81	4.57
20 William Andrews	1979-83, 86	4.55
21 Hoyle Granger	1966-72	4.54
22 Clarence Davis	1971-78	4.53
23 Billy Sims	1980-84	4.51
24 Freeman McNeil	1981-92	4.49
25 Clem Daniels	1960-68	4.48
26 Abner Haynes	1960-67	4.47
27 Keith Lincoln	1961-68	4.46
28 Dick Bass	1960-69	4.45
29 Steve Van Buren	1944-51	4.44
30 Jim Taylor	1958-67	4.43
31 Eric Dickerson	1983-93	4.43
32 Ollie Matson	1952, 54-66	4.42
33 Wilbert Montgomery	1977-85	4.41
34 John Elway	1983-98	4.40
35 Walter Payton	1975-87	4.36
36 Darrin Nelson	1982-92	4.35
37 Otis Armstrong	1973-80	4.35
38 Timmy Brown	1959-68	4.34
39 Tony Dorsett	1977-88	4.34
40 John Henry Johnson	1954-66	4.33
41 Lawrence McCutcheon	1972-81	4.32
42 Chris Warren	1990-98	4.32
43 Walt Garrison	1966-74	4.32
44 Emmitt Smith	1990-98	4.31
45 Barry Foster	1990-94	4.31
46 Earl Campbell	1978-85	4.30
47 Frank Gifford	1952-60, 62-64	4.30
48 Amos Marsh	1961-67	4.30
49 Chuck Muncie	1976-84	4.29
50 John David Crow	1958-68	4.29
51 Curtis Dickey	1980-86	4.29
52 Tom Woodeshick	1963-72	4.28
53 Willie Ellison	1967-74	4.28
54 Les Josephson	1964-67, 69-74	4.27
55 Larry Csonka	1968-74, 76-79	4.27
56 Kenneth Davis	1986-94	4.27
57 Delvin Williams	1974-81	4.27
58 Cookie Gilchrist	1962-67	4.25
59 J.D. Smith	1956-66	4.25
60 Dexter Bussey	1974-84	4.24
61 George Rogers	1981-87	4.24
62 Garrison Hearst	1993-98	4.24
63 Sherman Smith	1976-83	4.22
64 Gary Brown	1991-95, 97-98	4.22
65 Nick Pietrosante	1959-67	4.22
66 Leroy Kelly	1964-73	4.21
67 Herschel Walker	1986-97	4.21

RUSHING TOUCHDOWNS

Player	Year	TDs
1 Emmitt Smith	1990-98	125
2 Marcus Allen	1982-97	123
3 Walter Payton	1975-87	110
4 Jim Brown	1957-65	106
5 John Riggins	1971-79, 81-85	104
6 Barry Sanders	1989-98	99
7 Franco Harris	1972-84	91
8 Eric Dickerson	1983-93	90
9 Jim Taylor	1958-67	83
10 Ottis Anderson	1979-92	81
11 Tony Dorsett	1977-88	77
12 Pete Johnson	1977-84	76
13 Earl Campbell	1978-85	74
Leroy Kelly	1964-73	74
15 Chuck Muncie	1976-84	71
16 Gerald Riggs	1982-91	69
Steve Van Buren	1944-51	69
18 Thurman Thomas	1988-98	65
Ricky Watters	1992-98	65
20 Larry Csonka	1968-74, 76-79	64
21 Lenny Moore	1956-67	63
22 O.J. Simpson	1969-79	61
Herschel Walker	1986-97	61
24 Terry Allen	1991-92, 94-98	60
25 Earnest Byner	1984-97	56
Roger Craig	1983-93	56
Terrell Davis	1995-98	56
Curt Warner	1983-90	56
29 George Rogers	1981-87	54
30 Chuck Foreman	1973-80	53
Joe Perry	1950-63	53
32 Emerson Boozer	1966-75	52
Bill Brown	1961-74	52
34 Neal Anderson	1986-93	51
Greg Bell	1984-90	51
Mike Pruitt	1976-86	51
37 Paul Hornung	1957-62, 64-66	50
Joe Morris	1982-88, 91	50
Wendell Tyler	1977-86	50
40 James Brooks	1981-92	49
Rick Casares	1955-66	49
Rodney Hampton	1990-97	49
43 John Henry Johnson	1954-66	48
Chris Warren	1990-98	48
45 Pete Banaszak	1966-78	47
46 Abner Haynes	1960-67	46
Kevin Mack	1985-93	46
48 Tom Matte	1961-72	45
Wilbert Montgomery	1977-85	45
Jim Nance	1965-71, 73	45
Ken Willard	1965-74	45
52 Larry Kinnebrew	1983-87, 89-90	44
53 Marion Butts	1989-95	43
Sam Cunningham	1973-79, 81-82	43
Floyd Little	1967-75	43
Dan Towler	1950-55	43
Steve Young	1985-98	43
58 Marshall Faulk	1994-98	42
Calvin Hill	1969-74, 76-81	42
Don Perkins	1961-68	42
Billy Sims	1980-84	42
62 Donny Anderson	1966-74	41
Johnny Hector	1983-92	41
Natrone Means	1993-98	41
65 Alan Ameche	1955-60	40
Ted Brown	1979-86	40
Ron Johnson	1969-75	40
Jack Kemp	1957, 60-67, 69	40
Curtis Martin	1995-98	40
Ollie Matson	1952, 54-66	40
Don McCauley	1971-81	40
Christian Okoye	1987-92	40
J.D. Smith	1956-66	40
74 Dalton Hilliard	1986-93	39
Gale Sayers	1965-71	39
Alex Webster	1955-64	39
Sammy Winder	1982-90	39
78 John David Crow	1958-68	38
Paul Lowe	1960-61, 63-69	38
Hugh McElhenny	1952-64	38
Freeman McNeil	1981-92	38
Wayne Morris	1976-84	38
Ernie Nevers	1926-27, 29-31	38
84 Cookie Gilchrist	1962-67	37
Verne Lewellen	1924-32	37
Bill Mathis	1960-69	37
Tobin Rote	1950-59, 63-64, 66	37
Mark van Eeghen	1974-83	37
James Wilder	1981-90	37
90 Dutch Clark	1931-32, 34-38	36
91 Brad Baxter	1989-95	35
Larry Brown	1969-76	35
Mike Garrett	1966-73	35
Steve Grogan	1975-90	35
Clarke Hinkle	1932-41	35

Career Passing

PASSING ATTEMPTS

Player	Year	Atts.
1 Dan Marino	1983-98	7989
2 John Elway	1983-98	7250
3 Warren Moon	1984-98	6786
4 Fran Tarkenton	1961-78	6467
5 Dan Fouts	1973-87	5604
6 Joe Montana	1979-90, 92-94	5391
7 Dave Krieg	1980-98	5311
8 Boomer Esiason	1984-97	5205
9 Johnny Unitas	1956-73	5186
10 Jim Hart	1966-84	5076
11 Steve DeBerg	1978-93, 98	5024
12 Jim Everett	1986-97	4923
13 Jim Kelly	1986-96	4779
14 John Hadl	1962-77	4687
15 Phil Simms	1979-81, 83-93	4647
16 Vinny Testaverde	1987-98	4598
17 Joe Ferguson	1973-86, 88-90	4519
18 Roman Gabriel	1962-77	4498
19 John Brodie	1957-73	4491
20 Ken Anderson	1971-86	4475
21 Norm Snead	1961-76	4353
22 Sonny Jurgensen	1957-74	4262
23 Ron Jaworski	1974-86, 88-89	4117

24 Steve Young	1985-98	4065
25 Troy Aikman	1989-98	4011
26 George Blanda	1949-58, 60-75	4007
27 Terry Bradshaw	1970-83	3901
28 Randall Cunningham	1985-95, 97-98	3875
29 Y.A. Tittle	1950-64	3817
30 Ken Stabler	1970-84	3793
31 Craig Morton	1965-82	3786
32 Joe Namath	1965-77	3762
33 Brett Favre	1991-98	3757
34 Len Dawson	1957-75	3741
35 Jim Plunkett	1971-77, 79-86	3701
36 Bobby Layne	1948-62	3700
37 Tommy Kramer	1977-90	3651
38 Archie Manning	1971-75, 77-84	3642
39 Ken O'Brien	1984-93	3602
Joe Theismann	1974-85	3602
41 Steve Grogan	1975-90	3593
42 Steve Bartkowski	1975-86	3456
43 Brian Sipe	1974-83	3439
44 Bob Griese	1967-80	3429
45 Jeff George	1990-98	3402
46 Charley Johnson	1961-75	3392
47 Drew Bledsoe	1993-98	3382
48 Bernie Kosar	1985-96	3365
49 Babe Parilli	1952-53, 56-58, 60-69	3330
50 Jim Harbaugh	1987-98	3282
51 Neil Lomax	1981-88	3153
52 Bart Starr	1956-71	3149
Jim Zorn	1976-85, 87	3149
54 Lynn Dickey	1971, 73-77, 79-85	3125
55 Bobby Hebert	1985-89, 91-96	3121
56 Jack Kemp	1957, 60-67, 69	3073
57 Dan Pastorini	1971-81, 83	3055
58 Sammy Baugh	1937-52	2995
59 Billy Kilmer	1961-62, 64, 66-78	2984
60 Richard Todd	1976-85	2967
61 Roger Staubach	1969-79	2958
62 Danny White	1976-88	2950
63 Tobin Rote	1950-59, 63-64, 66	2907
64 Norm Van Brocklin	1949-60	2895
65 Neil O'Donnell	1991-98	2862
66 Charlie Conerly	1948-61	2833
67 Chris Miller	1987-95	2811
68 Jay Schroeder	1985-94	2808
69 Earl Morrall	1956-76	2689
70 Mark Rypien	1988-97	2604
71 Daryle Lamonica	1963-74	2601
72 Chris Chandler	1988-98	2587
73 Jim McMahon	1982-96	2573
74 Bert Jones	1973-82	2551
75 Billy Wade	1954-66	2523
76 Stan Humphries	1989-90, 92-97	2516
77 Doug Williams	1978-82, 86-89	2507
78 Bill Kenney	1980-88	2430
79 Wade Wilson	1981, 83-98	2428
80 Milt Plum	1957-69	2419
81 Jeff Hostetler	1985-86, 88-97	2338
82 Don Meredith	1960-68	2308
83 Greg Landry	1968-81, 84	2300
84 Bubby Brister	1986-95, 97-98	2172
85 Erik Kramer	1987, 91-98	2158
86 Frank Ryan	1958-70	2133
87 Scott Mitchell	1991-98	2091
88 Marc Wilson	1980-87, 89-90	2081

PASSING COMPLETIONS

Player	Year	Comps.
1 Dan Marino	1983-98	4763
2 John Elway	1983-98	4123
3 Warren Moon	1984-98	3972
4 Fran Tarkenton	1961-78	3686
5 Joe Montana	1979-90, 92-94	3409
6 Dan Fouts	1973-87	3297
7 Dave Krieg	1980-98	3105
8 Boomer Esiason	1984-97	2969
9 Steve DeBerg	1978-93, 98	2874
Jim Kelly	1986-96	2874
11 Jim Everett	1986-97	2841
12 Johnny Unitas	1956-73	2830
13 Ken Anderson	1971-86	2654
14 Steve Young	1985-98	2622
15 Jim Hart	1966-84	2593
16 Phil Simms	1979-81, 83-93	2576
17 Vinny Testaverde	1987-98	2559
18 Troy Aikman	1989-98	2479
19 John Brodie	1957-73	2469
20 Sonny Jurgensen	1957-74	2433
21 Joe Ferguson	1973-86, 88-90	2369
22 Roman Gabriel	1962-77	2366
23 John Hadl	1962-77	2363
24 Brett Favre	1991-98	2318
25 Norm Snead	1961-76	2276
26 Ken Stabler	1970-84	2270
27 Ron Jaworski	1974-86, 88-89	2187
28 Randall Cunningham	1985-95, 97-98	2177
29 Len Dawson	1957-75	2136
30 Y.A. Tittle	1950-64	2118
31 Ken O'Brien	1984-93	2110
32 Craig Morton	1965-82	2053
33 Joe Theismann	1974-85	2044
34 Terry Bradshaw	1970-83	2025
35 Tommy Kramer	1977-90	2012
36 Archie Manning	1971-75, 77-84	2011
37 Bernie Kosar	1985-96	1994
38 Jeff George	1990-98	1971
39 Brian Sipe	1974-83	1944
40 Jim Plunkett	1971-77, 79-86	1943
41 Jim Harbaugh	1987-98	1933
42 Steve Bartkowski	1975-86	1932
43 Bob Griese	1967-80	1926
44 George Blanda	1949-58, 60-75	1911
45 Drew Bledsoe	1993-98	1887
46 Joe Namath	1965-77	1886
47 Steve Grogan	1975-90	1879
48 Bobby Hebert	1985-89, 91-96	1839
49 Neil Lomax	1981-88	1817
50 Bobby Layne	1948-62	1814
51 Bart Starr	1956-71	1808
52 Danny White	1976-88	1761
53 Lynn Dickey	1971, 73-77, 79-85	1747
54 Charley Johnson	1961-75	1737
55 Sammy Baugh	1937-52	1693
56 Roger Staubach	1969-79	1685
57 Jim Zorn	1976-85, 87	1669
58 Neil O'Donnell	1991-98	1650
59 Richard Todd	1976-85	1610
60 Billy Kilmer	1961-62, 64, 66-78	1585
61 Dan Pastorini	1971-81, 83	1556
62 Norm Van Brocklin	1949-60	1553
63 Babe Parilli	1952-53, 56-58, 60-69	1552
64 Chris Miller	1987-95	1534
65 Chris Chandler	1988-98	1494
66 Jim McMahon	1982-96	1492
67 Mark Rypien	1988-97	1461
68 Jack Kemp	1957, 60-67, 69	1436
69 Stan Humphries	1989-90, 92-97	1431
70 Bert Jones	1973-82	1430
71 Jay Schroeder	1985-94	1426
72 Charlie Conerly	1948-61	1418
73 Wade Wilson	1981, 83-98	1391
74 Earl Morrall	1956-76	1379
75 Billy Wade	1954-66	1370
76 Jeff Hostetler	1985-86, 88-97	1357
77 Bill Kenney	1980-88	1330
78 Tobin Rote	1950-59, 63-64, 66	1329
79 Milt Plum	1957-69	1306
80 Daryle Lamonica	1963-74	1288
81 Greg Landry	1968-81, 84	1276
82 Doug Williams	1978-82, 86-89	1240
83 Erik Kramer	1987, 91-98	1239
84 Bubby Brister	1986-95, 97-98	1185
85 Scott Mitchell	1991-98	1184
86 Don Meredith	1960-68	1170
87 Steve Beuerlein	1988-89, 91-98	1126
88 Mike Tomczak	1985-98	1109
89 Rodney Peete	1989-98	1108
90 Gary Danielson	1976-78, 80-85, 87-88	1105

COMPLETION PERCENTAGE
(minimum 1500 Pass Attempts)

Player	Year	Pct.
1 Steve Young	1985-98	64.50
2 Joe Montana	1979-90, 92-94	63.24
3 Troy Aikman	1989-98	61.81
4 Brett Favre	1991-98	61.70
5 Mark Brunell	1994-98	60.38
6 Jim Kelly	1986-96	60.14
7 Ken Stabler	1970-84	59.85
8 Danny White	1976-88	59.69
9 Dan Marino	1983-98	59.62
10 Ken Anderson	1971-86	59.31
11 Bernie Kosar	1985-96	59.26
12 Bobby Hebert	1985-89, 91-96	58.92
13 Jim Harbaugh	1987-98	58.90
14 Dan Fouts	1973-87	58.83
15 Ken O'Brien	1984-93	58.58
16 Warren Moon	1984-98	58.53
17 Dave Krieg	1980-98	58.46
18 Tony Eason	1983-90	58.25
19 Jeff Hostetler	1985-86, 88-97	58.04
20 Jim McMahon	1982-96	57.99
21 Jeff George	1990-98	57.94
22 Chris Chandler	1988-98	57.75
23 Jim Everett	1986-97	57.71
24 Neil O'Donnell	1991-98	57.65
25 Neil Lomax	1981-88	57.63
26 Bart Starr	1956-71	57.42
27 Erik Kramer	1987, 91-98	57.41
28 Wade Wilson	1981, 83-98	57.29
29 Steve DeBerg	1978-93, 98	57.21
30 Rodney Peete	1989-98	57.20
31 Gary Danielson	1976-78, 80-85, 87-88	57.19
32 Len Dawson	1957-75	57.10
33 Sonny Jurgensen	1957-74	57.09
34 Boomer Esiason	1984-97	57.04
35 Fran Tarkenton	1961-78	57.00
36 Roger Staubach	1969-79	56.96
37 Rich Gannon	1987-88, 90-93, 95-98	56.88
38 Stan Humphries	1989-90, 92-97	56.88
39 John Elway	1983-98	56.87
40 Joe Theismann	1974-85	56.75
41 Scott Mitchell	1991-98	56.62
42 Brian Sipe	1974-83	56.53
43 Sammy Baugh	1937-52	56.53
44 Randall Cunningham	1985-95, 97-98	56.18
45 Bob Griese	1967-80	56.17
46 Mark Rypien	1988-97	56.11
47 Bert Jones	1973-82	56.06
48 Lynn Dickey	1971, 73-77, 79-85	55.90
49 Steve Bartkowski	1975-86	55.90
50 Jeff Blake	1992, 94-98	55.89
51 Vince Ferragamo	1977-80, 82-86	55.85
52 Drew Bledsoe	1993-98	55.80
53 Otto Graham	1950-55	55.72
54 Vinny Testaverde	1987-98	55.65
55 Y.A. Tittle	1950-64	55.49
56 Greg Landry	1968-81, 84	55.48
57 Phil Simms	1979-81, 83-93	55.43
58 Don Majkowski	1987-96	55.43
59 Archie Manning	1971-75, 77-84	55.22
60 Tommy Kramer	1977-90	55.11
61 Steve Beuerlein	1988-89, 91-98	55.09
62 John Brodie	1957-73	54.98
63 Steve Bono	1985-89, 91-98	54.94
64 Bill Kenney	1980-88	54.73
65 Chris Miller	1987-95	54.57
66 Johnny Unitas	1956-73	54.57
67 Bubby Brister	1986-95, 97-98	54.56
68 Billy Wade	1954-66	54.30
69 Richard Todd	1976-85	54.26
70 Craig Morton	1965-82	54.23
71 Trent Dilfer	1994-98	54.12
72 Milt Plum	1957-69	53.99
73 Bill Munson	1964-79	53.99
74 Eric Hipple	1980-86, 88-89	53.69
75 Norm Van Brocklin	1949-60	53.64
76 Mike Tomczak	1985-98	53.34
77 Rick Mirer	1993-97	53.32

78 Ron Jaworski	1974-86, 88-89	53.12
79 Billy Kilmer	1961-62, 64, 66-78	53.12
80 Jack Trudeau	1986-95	53.10
81 Jim Zorn	1976-85, 87	53.00
82 Roman Gabriel	1962-77	52.60
83 Jim Plunkett	1971-77, 79-86	52.50
84 Joe Ferguson	1973-86, 88-90	52.42
85 Steve Grogan	1975-90	52.30
86 Norm Snead	1961-76	52.29
87 Marc Wilson	1980-87, 89-90	52.14
88 Mike Livingston	1968-79	52.08
89 Terry Bradshaw	1970-83	51.91
90 Sid Luckman	1939-50	51.83
91 Kerry Collins	1995-98	51.47
92 Earl Morrall	1956-76	51.28
93 Charley Johnson	1961-75	51.21
94 Frank Ryan	1958-70	51.10
95 Jim Hart	1966-84	51.08
96 Dan Pastorini	1971-81, 83	50.93
97 Mark Malone	1980-81, 83-89	50.91
98 Jay Schroeder	1985-94	50.78
99 Don Meredith	1960-68	50.69
100 Bill Nelsen	1963-72	50.55
101 John Hadl	1962-77	50.42
102 Frank Tripucka	1949-52, 60-63	50.37
103 Bob Waterfield	1945-52	50.34
104 Joe Namath	1965-77	50.13
105 Mike Pagel	1982-93	50.10
106 Charlie Conerly	1948-61	50.05
107 Eddie LeBaron	1952-53, 55-63	50.00
108 Daryle Lamonica	1963-74	49.52
109 Doug Williams	1978-82, 86-89	49.46
110 Mike Phipps	1970-81	49.25
111 Bobby Layne	1948-62	49.03
112 Tom Flores	1960-61, 63-69	48.86
113 Ed Brown	1954-65	47.76
114 George Blanda	1949-58, 60-75	47.69
115 Jack Kemp	1957, 60-67, 69	46.73
116 Babe Parilli	1952-53, 56-58, 60-69	46.61
117 Tobin Rote	1950-59, 63-64, 66	45.72
118 Cotton Davidson	1954, 57, 60-66, 68	43.95

PASSING YARDS

Player	Year	Yds.
1 Dan Marino	1983-98	58913
2 John Elway	1983-98	51475
3 Warren Moon	1984-98	49097
4 Fran Tarkenton	1961-78	47003
5 Dan Fouts	1973-87	43040
6 Joe Montana	1979-90, 92-94	40551
7 Johnny Unitas	1956-73	40239
8 Dave Krieg	1980-98	38147
9 Boomer Esiason	1984-97	37920
10 Jim Kelly	1986-96	35467
11 Jim Everett	1986-97	34837
12 Jim Hart	1966-84	34665
13 Steve DeBerg	1978-93, 98	34241
14 John Hadl	1962-77	33503
15 Phil Simms	1979-81, 83-93	33462
16 Ken Anderson	1971-86	32838
17 Steve Young	1985-98	32678
18 Vinny Testaverde	1987-98	32479
19 Sonny Jurgensen	1957-74	32224
20 John Brodie	1957-73	31548
21 Norm Snead	1961-76	30797
22 Joe Ferguson	1973-86, 88-90	29817
23 Roman Gabriel	1962-77	29444
24 Len Dawson	1957-75	28711
25 Troy Aikman	1989-98	28346
26 Y.A. Tittle	1950-64	28339
27 Ron Jaworski	1974-86, 88-89	28190
28 Terry Bradshaw	1970-83	27989
29 Ken Stabler	1970-84	27938
30 Craig Morton	1965-82	27908
31 Joe Namath	1965-77	27663
32 Randall Cunningham	1985-95, 97-98	27082
33 George Blanda	1949-58, 60-75	26920
34 Steve Grogan	1975-90	26886
35 Brett Favre	1991-98	26803
36 Bobby Layne	1948-62	26768
37 Jim Plunkett	1971-77, 79-86	25882
38 Joe Theismann	1974-85	25206
39 Ken O'Brien	1984-93	25094
40 Bob Griese	1967-80	25092
41 Tommy Kramer	1977-90	24777
42 Bart Starr	1956-71	24718
43 Charley Johnson	1961-75	24410
44 Steve Bartkowski	1975-86	24124
45 Archie Manning	1971-75, 77-84	23911
46 Brian Sipe	1974-83	23713
47 Norm Van Brocklin	1949-60	23611
48 Lynn Dickey	1971, 73-77, 79-85	23322
49 Bernie Kosar	1985-96	23301
50 Jeff George	1990-98	23229
51 Neil Lomax	1981-88	22771
52 Roger Staubach	1969-79	22700
53 Babe Parilli	1952-53, 56-58, 60-69	22681
54 Jim Harbaugh	1987-98	22111
55 Drew Bledsoe	1993-98	21981
56 Danny White	1976-88	21959
57 Sammy Baugh	1937-52	21886
58 Bobby Hebert	1985-89, 91-96	21683
59 Jack Kemp	1957, 60-67, 69	21218
60 Jim Zorn	1976-85, 87	21115
61 Earl Morrall	1956-76	20809
62 Richard Todd	1976-85	20610
63 Billy Kilmer	1961-62, 64, 66-78	20495
64 Jay Schroeder	1985-94	20063
65 Charlie Conerly	1948-61	19488
66 Daryle Lamonica	1963-74	19154
67 Neil O'Donnell	1991-98	19026
68 Tobin Rote	1950-59, 63-64, 66	18850
69 Chris Miller	1987-95	18793
70 Billy Wade	1954-66	18530
71 Chris Chandler	1988-98	18526
72 Dan Pastorini	1971-81, 83	18515
73 Mark Rypien	1988-97	18416
74 Bert Jones	1973-82	18190
75 Jim McMahon	1982-96	18148
76 Milt Plum	1957-69	17536
77 Wade Wilson	1981, 83-98	17283
78 Bill Kenney	1980-88	17277
79 Don Meredith	1960-68	17199
80 Stan Humphries	1989-90, 92-97	17191
81 Doug Williams	1978-82, 86-89	16998
82 Jeff Hostetler	1985-86, 88-97	16430
83 Greg Landry	1968-81, 84	16052
84 Frank Ryan	1958-70	16042
85 Ed Brown	1954-65	15600
86 Sid Luckman	1939-50	14686
87 Steve Beuerlein	1988-89, 91-98	14566
88 Erik Kramer	1987, 91-98	14549
89 Mike Tomczak	1985-98	14454
90 Scott Mitchell	1991-98	14452
91 Marc Wilson	1980-87, 89-90	14391
92 Bubby Brister	1986-95, 97-98	14276
93 Bill Nelsen	1963-72	14165

PASSING YARDS PER ATTEMPT
(minimum 1500 Pass Attempt)

Player	Year	Yds.
1 Otto Graham	1950-55	8.63
2 Sid Luckman	1939-50	8.42
3 Norm Van Brocklin	1949-60	8.16
4 Steve Young	1985-98	8.04
5 Ed Brown	1954-65	7.85
6 Bart Starr	1956-71	7.85
7 Johnny Unitas	1956-73	7.76
8 Earl Morrall	1956-76	7.74
9 Dan Fouts	1973-87	7.68
10 Len Dawson	1957-75	7.67
11 Roger Staubach	1969-79	7.67
12 Sonny Jurgensen	1957-74	7.56
13 Joe Montana	1979-90, 92-94	7.52
14 Frank Ryan	1958-70	7.52
15 Steve Grogan	1975-90	7.48
16 Lynn Dickey	1971, 73-77, 79-85	7.46
17 Eddie LeBaron	1952-53, 55-63	7.46
18 Don Meredith	1960-68	7.45
19 Danny White	1976-88	7.44
20 Bill Nelsen	1963-72	7.44
21 Y.A. Tittle	1950-64	7.42
22 Jim Kelly	1986-96	7.42
23 Dan Marino	1983-98	7.37
24 Craig Morton	1965-82	7.37
25 Ken Stabler	1970-84	7.37
26 Daryle Lamonica	1963-74	7.36
27 Joe Namath	1965-77	7.35
28 Billy Wade	1954-66	7.34
29 Ken Anderson	1971-86	7.34
30 Bob Waterfield	1945-52	7.33
31 Bob Griese	1967-80	7.32
32 Sammy Baugh	1937-52	7.31
33 Boomer Esiason	1984-97	7.29
34 Mark Brunell	1994-98	7.28
35 Fran Tarkenton	1961-78	7.27
36 Milt Plum	1957-69	7.25
37 Warren Moon	1984-98	7.24
38 Bobby Layne	1948-62	7.23
39 Neil Lomax	1981-88	7.22
40 Phil Simms	1979-81, 83-93	7.20
41 Charley Johnson	1961-75	7.20
42 Dave Krieg	1980-98	7.18
43 Terry Bradshaw	1970-83	7.17
44 Chris Chandler	1988-98	7.16
45 John Hadl	1962-77	7.15
46 Jay Schroeder	1985-94	7.14
47 Brett Favre	1991-98	7.13
48 Bert Jones	1973-82	7.13
49 Steve Beuerlein	1988-89, 91-98	7.13
50 Gary Danielson	1976-78, 80-85, 87-88	7.12
51 Tony Eason	1983-90	7.12
52 Wade Wilson	1981, 83-98	7.12
53 Bill Kenney	1980-88	7.11
54 John Elway	1983-98	7.10
55 Jim Everett	1986-97	7.08
56 Norm Snead	1961-76	7.07
57 Mark Rypien	1988-97	7.07
58 Troy Aikman	1989-98	7.07
59 Vinny Testaverde	1987-98	7.06
60 Jim McMahon	1982-96	7.05
61 Jeff Hostetler	1985-86, 88-97	7.03
62 John Brodie	1957-73	7.02
63 Vince Ferragamo	1977-80, 82-86	7.02
64 Rodney Peete	1989-98	7.01
65 Joe Theismann	1974-85	7.00
66 Jim Plunkett	1971-77, 79-86	6.99
67 Randall Cunningham	1985-95, 97-98	6.99
68 Steve Bartkowski	1975-86	6.98
69 Greg Landry	1968-81, 84	6.98
70 Tom Flores	1960-61, 63-69	6.97
71 Ken O'Brien	1984-93	6.97
72 Mike Tomczak	1985-98	6.95
73 Bobby Hebert	1985-89, 91-96	6.95
74 Richard Todd	1976-85	6.95
75 Eric Hipple	1980-86, 88-89	6.93
76 Bernie Kosar	1985-96	6.92
77 Marc Wilson	1980-87, 89-90	6.92
78 Scott Mitchell	1991-98	6.91
79 Jack Kemp	1957, 60-67, 69	6.90
80 Brian Sipe	1974-83	6.90
81 Charlie Conerly	1948-61	6.88
82 Billy Kilmer	1961-62, 64, 66-78	6.87
83 Ron Jaworski	1974-86, 88-89	6.85
84 Stan Humphries	1989-90, 92-97	6.83
85 Jim Hart	1966-84	6.83
86 Jeff George	1990-98	6.83
87 Steve DeBerg	1978-93, 98	6.82
88 Babe Parilli	1952-53, 56-58, 60-69	6.81
89 Jeff Blake	1992, 94-98	6.79
90 Tommy Kramer	1977-90	6.79
91 Doug Williams	1978-82, 86-89	6.78
92 Erik Kramer	1987, 91-98	6.74
93 Jim Harbaugh	1987-98	6.74
94 George Blanda	1949-58, 60-75	6.72

	Player	Year	
95	Cotton Davidson	1954, 57, 60-66, 68	6.71
96	Jim Zorn	1976-85, 87	6.71
97	Chris Miller	1987-95	6.69
98	Don Majkowski	1987-96	6.67
99	Neil O'Donnell	1991-98	6.65
100	Joe Ferguson	1973-86, 88-90	6.60
101	Bubby Brister	1986-95, 97-98	6.57
102	Archie Manning	1971-75, 77-84	6.57
103	Roman Gabriel	1962-77	6.55
104	Bill Munson	1964-79	6.51
105	Drew Bledsoe	1993-98	6.50
106	Tobin Rote	1950-59, 63-64, 66	6.48
107	Mike Livingston	1968-79	6.45
108	Rich Gannon	1987-88, 90-93, 95-98	6.35
109	Trent Dilfer	1994-98	6.33
110	Mike Pagel	1982-93	6.24
111	Jack Trudeau	1986-95	6.23
112	Kerry Collins	1995-98	6.21
113	Mark Malone	1980-81, 83-89	6.17
114	Steve Bono	1985-89, 91-98	6.14
115	Dan Pastorini	1971-81, 83	6.06
116	Frank Tripucka	1949-52, 60-63	5.89
117	Rick Mirer	1993-97	5.85
118	Mike Phipps	1970-81	5.84

TOUCHDOWN PASSES

	Player	Year	TDs
1	Dan Marino	1983-98	408
2	Fran Tarkenton	1961-78	342
3	John Elway	1983-98	300
4	Warren Moon	1984-98	290
	Johnny Unitas	1956-73	290
6	Joe Montana	1979-90, 92-94	273
7	Dave Krieg	1980-98	261
8	Sonny Jurgensen	1957-74	255
9	Dan Fouts	1973-87	254
10	Boomer Esiason	1984-97	247
11	John Hadl	1962-77	244
12	Len Dawson	1957-75	239
13	Jim Kelly	1986-96	237
14	George Blanda	1949-58, 60-75	236
15	Steve Young	1985-98	229
16	John Brodie	1957-73	214
17	Brett Favre	1991-98	213
18	Terry Bradshaw	1970-83	212
	Y.A. Tittle	1950-64	212
20	Jim Hart	1966-84	209
21	Vinny Testaverde	1987-98	204
22	Jim Everett	1986-97	203
23	Roman Gabriel	1962-77	201
24	Phil Simms	1979-81, 83-93	199
25	Ken Anderson	1971-86	197
26	Steve DeBerg	1978-93, 98	196
	Joe Ferguson	1973-86, 88-90	196
	Bobby Layne	1948-62	196
	Norm Snead	1961-76	196
30	Ken Stabler	1970-84	194
31	Bob Griese	1967-80	192
32	Randall Cunningham	1985-95, 97-98	190
33	Sammy Baugh	1937-52	187
34	Craig Morton	1965-82	183
35	Steve Grogan	1975-90	182
36	Ron Jaworski	1974-86, 88-89	179
37	Babe Parilli	1952-53, 56-58, 60-69	178
38	Charlie Conerly	1948-61	173
	Joe Namath	1965-77	173
	Norm Van Brocklin	1949-60	173
41	Charley Johnson	1961-75	170
42	Daryle Lamonica	1963-74	164
	Jim Plunkett	1971-77, 79-86	164
44	Earl Morrall	1956-76	161
45	Joe Theismann	1974-85	160
46	Tommy Kramer	1977-90	159
47	Steve Bartkowski	1975-86	156
48	Danny White	1976-88	155
49	Brian Sipe	1974-83	154
50	Roger Staubach	1969-79	153
51	Billy Kilmer	1961-62, 64, 66-78	152
	Bart Starr	1956-71	152
53	Frank Ryan	1958-70	149
54	Tobin Rote	1950-59, 63-64, 66	148
55	Troy Aikman	1989-98	141
	Lynn Dickey	1971, 73-77, 79-85	141
57	Sid Luckman	1939-50	137
58	Neil Lomax	1981-88	136
59	Bobby Hebert	1985-89, 91-96	135
	Don Meredith	1960-68	135

PASSING INTERCEPTIONS

	Player	Year	Ints.
1	George Blanda	1949-58, 60-75	277
2	John Hadl	1962-77	268
3	Fran Tarkenton	1961-78	266
4	Norm Snead	1961-76	257
5	Johnny Unitas	1956-73	253
6	Jim Hart	1966-84	247
7	Bobby Layne	1948-62	243
8	Dan Fouts	1973-87	242
9	Dan Marino	1983-98	235
10	Warren Moon	1984-98	232
11	John Elway	1983-98	226
12	John Brodie	1957-73	224
13	Ken Stabler	1970-84	222
14	Y.A. Tittle	1950-64	221
15	Joe Namath	1965-77	220
	Babe Parilli	1952-53, 56-58, 60-69	220
17	Terry Bradshaw	1970-83	210
18	Joe Ferguson	1973-86, 88-90	209
19	Steve Grogan	1975-90	208
20	Steve DeBerg	1978-93, 98	204
21	Sammy Baugh	1937-52	203
22	Dave Krieg	1980-98	199
23	Jim Plunkett	1971-77, 79-86	198
24	Tobin Rote	1950-59, 63-64, 66	191
25	Vinny Testaverde	1987-98	190
26	Sonny Jurgensen	1957-74	189
27	Craig Morton	1965-82	187
28	Boomer Esiason	1984-97	184
29	Len Dawson	1957-75	183
	Jack Kemp	1957, 60-67, 69	183
31	Charley Johnson	1961-75	181
32	Lynn Dickey	1971, 73-77, 79-85	179
33	Norm Van Brocklin	1949-60	178
34	Jim Everett	1986-97	175
	Jim Kelly	1986-96	175
36	Archie Manning	1971-75, 77-84	173
37	Bob Griese	1967-80	172
38	Charlie Conerly	1948-61	167
39	Ron Jaworski	1974-86, 88-89	164
40	Dan Pastorini	1971-81, 83	161
	Richard Todd	1976-85	161
42	Ken Anderson	1971-86	160

LOWEST INTERCEPTION PERCENTAGE
(minimum 1500 Pass Attempts)

	Player	Year	Pct.
1	Neil O'Donnell	1991-98	1.99
2	Steve Bono	1985-89, 91-98	2.47
3	Mark Brunell	1994-98	2.50
4	Steve Young	1985-98	2.53
5	Joe Montana	1979-90, 92-94	2.58
6	Bernie Kosar	1985-96	2.59
7	Jeff George	1990-98	2.70
8	Ken O'Brien	1984-93	2.72
9	Jeff Blake	1992, 94-98	2.77
10	Jim Harbaugh	1987-98	2.83
11	Neil Lomax	1981-88	2.85
12	Troy Aikman	1989-98	2.87
13	Dan Marino	1983-98	2.94
14	Drew Bledsoe	1993-98	3.02
15	Jeff Hostetler	1985-86, 88-97	3.04
16	Randall Cunningham	1985-95, 97-98	3.07
17	Rich Gannon	1987-88, 90-93, 95-98	3.07
18	John Elway	1983-98	3.12
19	Brett Favre	1991-98	3.14
20	Scott Mitchell	1991-98	3.16
21	Erik Kramer	1987, 91-98	3.20
22	Tony Eason	1983-90	3.26
23	Roman Gabriel	1962-77	3.31
24	Stan Humphries	1989-90, 92-97	3.34
25	Steve Beuerlein	1988-89, 91-98	3.38
26	Phil Simms	1979-81, 83-93	3.38
27	Mark Rypien	1988-97	3.38
28	Bubby Brister	1986-95, 97-98	3.41
29	Warren Moon	1984-98	3.42
30	Chris Chandler	1988-98	3.48
31	Jim McMahon	1982-96	3.50
32	Don Majkowski	1987-96	3.52
33	Boomer Esiason	1984-97	3.54
34	Bill Kenney	1980-88	3.54
35	Jim Everett	1986-97	3.55
36	Ken Anderson	1971-86	3.58
37	Chris Miller	1987-95	3.59
38	Jim Kelly	1986-96	3.66
39	Roger Staubach	1969-79	3.68
40	Doug Williams	1978-82, 86-89	3.71
41	Dave Krieg	1980-98	3.75
42	Rick Mirer	1993-97	3.81
43	Joe Theismann	1974-85	3.83
44	Jay Schroeder	1985-94	3.85
	Trent Dilfer	1994-98	3.85
46	Bert Jones	1973-82	3.96
47	Bobby Hebert	1985-89, 91-96	3.97
48	Rodney Peete	1989-98	3.98
49	Ron Jaworski	1974-86, 88-89	3.98
50	Bill Munson	1964-79	4.04
51	Gary Danielson	1976-78, 80-85, 87-88	4.04
52	Steve DeBerg	1978-93, 98	4.06
53	Fran Tarkenton	1961-78	4.11
54	Vinny Testaverde	1987-98	4.13
55	Steve Bartkowski	1975-86	4.17
56	Mike Pagel	1982-93	4.17
57	Kerry Collins	1995-98	4.18
58	Jack Trudeau	1986-95	4.20
59	Wade Wilson	1981, 83-98	4.20
60	Dan Fouts	1973-87	4.32
61	Tommy Kramer	1977-90	4.33
62	Brian Sipe	1974-83	4.33
63	Bart Starr	1956-71	4.38
64	Sonny Jurgensen	1957-74	4.43
65	Danny White	1976-88	4.47
66	Jim Zorn	1976-85, 87	4.48
67	Greg Landry	1968-81, 84	4.48
68	Eric Hipple	1980-86, 88-89	4.53
69	Joe Ferguson	1973-86, 88-90	4.62
70	Mike Tomczak	1985-98	4.71
71	Mike Livingston	1968-79	4.74
72	Archie Manning	1971-75, 77-84	4.75
73	Don Meredith	1960-68	4.81
74	Jim Hart	1966-84	4.87
75	Johnny Unitas	1956-73	4.88
76	Len Dawson	1957-75	4.89
77	Billy Kilmer	1961-62, 64, 66-78	4.89
78	Marc Wilson	1980-87, 89-90	4.90
79	Mark Malone	1980-81, 83-89	4.92
80	Craig Morton	1965-82	4.94
81	John Brodie	1957-73	4.99
82	Bob Griese	1967-80	5.02
83	Frank Ryan	1958-70	5.20
84	Milt Plum	1957-69	5.25
85	Dan Pastorini	1971-81, 83	5.27
86	Bill Nelsen	1963-72	5.30
87	Daryle Lamonica	1963-74	5.31
88	Billy Wade	1954-66	5.31
89	Charley Johnson	1961-75	5.34
90	Jim Plunkett	1971-77, 79-86	5.35
91	Tom Flores	1960-61, 63-69	5.36
92	Terry Bradshaw	1970-83	5.38
93	Richard Todd	1976-85	5.43
94	Earl Morrall	1956-76	5.50
95	Vince Ferragamo	1977-80, 82-86	5.63
96	John Hadl	1962-77	5.72
97	Lynn Dickey	1971, 73-77, 79-85	5.73
98	Steve Grogan	1975-90	5.79
99	Y.A. Tittle	1950-64	5.79
100	Joe Namath	1965-77	5.85
101	Ken Stabler	1970-84	5.85
102	Charlie Conerly	1948-61	5.89
103	Norm Snead	1961-76	5.90

104 Jack Kemp	1957, 60-67, 69	5.96
105 Mike Phipps	1970-81	6.00
106 Otto Graham	1950-55	6.01
107 Norm Van Brocklin	1949-60	6.15
108 Cotton Davidson	1954, 57, 60-66, 68	6.16
109 Bobby Layne	1948-62	6.57
110 Tobin Rote	1950-59, 63-64, 66	6.57
111 Babe Parilli	1952-53, 56-58, 60-69	6.61
112 Sammy Baugh	1937-52	6.78
113 George Blanda	1949-58, 60-75	6.91
114 Ed Brown	1954-65	6.95
115 Frank Tripucka	1949-52, 60-63	7.11
116 Sid Luckman	1939-50	7.57
117 Eddie LeBaron	1952-53, 55-63	7.85
118 Bob Waterfield	1945-52	7.92

Career Pass Receiving

RECEPTIONS

Player	Year	Recs.
1 Jerry Rice	1985-98	1139
2 Art Monk	1980-95	940
3 Andre Reed	1985-98	889
4 Cris Carter	1987-98	834
5 Steve Largent	1976-89	819
6 Henry Ellard	1983-98	814
7 Irving Fryar	1984-98	784
8 James Lofton	1978-93	764
9 Charlie Joiner	1969-86	750
10 Michael Irvin	1988-98	740
11 Gary Clark	1985-95	699
12 Andre Rison	1989-98	681
13 Tim Brown	1988-98	680
14 Ozzie Newsome	1978-90	662
15 Charley Taylor	1964-75, 77	649
16 Drew Hill	1979-82, 84-93	634
17 Don Maynard	1958, 60-73	633
18 Raymond Berry	1955-67	631
19 Keith Byars	1986-98	610
Herman Moore	1991-98	610
21 Anthony Miller	1988-97	595
Sterling Sharpe	1988-94	595
23 Rob Moore	1990-98	591
24 Harold Carmichael	1971-84	590
25 Fred Biletnikoff	1965-78	589
26 Marcus Allen	1982-97	587
27 Bill Brooks	1986-96	583
28 Mark Clayton	1983-93	582
Ronnie Harmon	1986-97	582
30 Brian Blades	1988-98	581
31 Harold Jackson	1968-83	579
32 Ernest Givins	1986-95	571
33 Mark Carrier	1987-98	569
34 Lionel Taylor	1959-68	567
35 Roger Craig	1983-93	566
36 Webster Slaughter	1986-96, 98	563
37 Wes Chandler	1978-88	559
Roy Green	1979-92	559
39 Stanley Morgan	1977-90	557
40 Eric Martin	1985-94	553
41 John L. Williams	1986-95	546
42 J.T. Smith	1978-90	544
43 Lance Alworth	1962-72	542
44 Kellen Winslow	1979-87	541
45 John Stallworth	1974-87	537
46 Larry Centers	1990-98	535
Haywood Jeffires	1987-96	535
48 Shannon Sharpe	1990-98	529
49 Eric Metcalf	1989-98	526
50 Brett Perriman	1988-97	525
51 Bobby Mitchell	1958-68	521
52 Al Toon	1985-92	517
53 Earnest Byner	1984-97	512
Herschel Walker	1986-97	512
55 Mark Duper	1982-92	511
56 Nat Moore	1974-86	510
57 Dwight Clark	1979-87	506
58 Billy Howton	1952-63	503
59 Cliff Branch	1972-85	501
60 Steve Jordan	1982-94	498
61 Tommy McDonald	1957-68	495
Ahmad Rashad	1972-74, 76-82	495
63 Walter Payton	1975-87	492
64 Tony Galbreath	1976-87	490
65 Drew Pearson	1973-83	489
66 Don Hutson	1935-45	488
67 Anthony Carter	1985-95	486
68 Ricky Sanders	1986-95	483
69 Jackie Smith	1963-78	480
70 Tony Hill	1977-86	479
Art Powell	1959-68	479
72 Terance Mathis	1990-98	477
73 Boyd Dowler	1959-69, 71	474
74 Carl Pickens	1992-98	473
75 Pat Tilley	1976-86	468
76 Tony Martin	1990-98	463
77 Mickey Shuler	1978-91	462
78 Todd Christensen	1979-88	461
79 Ben Coates	1991-98	458
80 Quinn Early	1988-98	454
81 Thurman Thomas	1988-98	453
82 Pete Retzlaff	1956-66	452
83 Roy Jefferson	1965-76	451
84 Haven Moses	1968-81	448
85 Reggie Rucker	1970-81	447
86 Keith Jackson	1988-96	441
87 Carroll Dale	1960-73	438
Wesley Walker	1977-89	438
89 Ricky Proehl	1990-98	433
90 James Wilder	1981-90	431
91 Michael Haynes	1988-97	428
92 Mike Ditka	1961-72	427
Paul Warfield	1964-74, 76-77	427
94 Bobby Joe Conrad	1958-69	422
Jay Novacek	1985-95	422
Bob Tucker	1970-80	422
97 Ken Burrough	1970-81	421
Jerry Smith	1965-77	421
99 Charle Young	1973-85	418
100 Cris Collinsworth	1981-88	417
Brent Jones	1987-97	417
102 Isaac Curtis	1973-84	416
Henry Marshall	1976-87	416
104 Vance Johnson	1985-93, 95	415
Emmitt Smith	1990-98	415
106 Reggie Langhorne	1985-93	411
107 Charley Hennigan	1960-66	410
Otis Taylor	1965-75	410

RECEIVING YARDS

Player	Year	Yds.
1 Jerry Rice	1985-98	17612
2 James Lofton	1978-93	14004
3 Henry Ellard	1983-98	13777
4 Steve Largent	1976-89	13089
5 Art Monk	1980-95	12721
6 Andre Reed	1985-98	12559
7 Charlie Joiner	1969-86	12146
8 Irving Fryar	1984-98	11983
9 Don Maynard	1958, 60-73	11834
10 Michael Irvin	1988-98	11737
11 Gary Clark	1985-95	10856
12 Stanley Morgan	1977-90	10716
13 Cris Carter	1987-98	10447
14 Harold Jackson	1968-83	10372
15 Lance Alworth	1962-72	10266
16 Drew Hill	1979-82, 84-93	9831
17 Tim Brown	1988-98	9600
18 Andre Rison	1989-98	9381
19 Raymond Berry	1955-67	9275
20 Anthony Miller	1988-97	9148
21 Charley Taylor	1964-75, 77	9110
22 Harold Carmichael	1971-84	8985
23 Fred Biletnikoff	1965-78	8974
Mark Clayton	1983-93	8974
25 Wes Chandler	1978-88	8966
26 Roy Green	1979-92	8965
27 Mark Duper	1982-92	8869
28 Mark Carrier	1987-98	8763
29 Rob Moore	1990-98	8747
30 John Stallworth	1974-87	8723
31 Cliff Branch	1972-85	8685
32 Paul Warfield	1964-74, 76-77	8565
33 Herman Moore	1991-98	8467
34 Billy Howton	1952-63	8459
35 Tommy McDonald	1957-68	8410
36 Wesley Walker	1977-89	8306
37 Carroll Dale	1960-73	8277
38 Ernest Givins	1986-95	8215
39 Eric Martin	1985-94	8161
40 Sterling Sharpe	1988-94	8134
41 Webster Slaughter	1986-96, 98	8111
42 Haven Moses	1968-81	8091
43 Art Powell	1959-68	8046
44 Bill Brooks	1986-96	8001
45 Don Hutson	1935-45	7991
46 Tony Hill	1977-86	7988
47 Ozzie Newsome	1978-90	7980
48 Bobby Mitchell	1958-68	7954
49 Jackie Smith	1963-78	7918
50 Jimmy Orr	1958-70	7914
51 Drew Pearson	1973-83	7822
52 Anthony Carter	1985-95	7733
53 Brian Blades	1988-98	7620
54 Nat Moore	1974-86	7546
55 Roy Jefferson	1965-76	7539
56 Gary Garrison	1966-77	7538
57 Bob Hayes	1965-75	7414
58 Pete Retzlaff	1956-66	7412
59 Otis Taylor	1965-75	7306
60 Boyd Dowler	1959-69, 71	7270
61 Lionel Taylor	1959-68	7195
62 Ken Burrough	1970-81	7102
63 Isaac Curtis	1973-84	7101
64 Tony Martin	1990-98	7087
65 Reggie Rucker	1970-81	7065
66 John Gilliam	1967-77	7056
67 Pat Tilley	1976-86	7005
68 J.T. Smith	1978-90	6974
69 Gene Washington	1969-77, 79	6856
70 Ahmad Rashad	1972-74, 76-82	6831
71 Charley Hennigan	1960-66	6823
72 Shannon Sharpe	1990-98	6759
73 Dwight Clark	1979-87	6750
74 Kellen Winslow	1979-87	6741
75 Frank Lewis	1971-83	6724
76 Cris Collinsworth	1981-88	6698
77 Mel Gray	1971-82	6644
78 Willie Gault	1983-93	6635
79 Al Toon	1985-92	6605
80 Brett Perriman	1988-97	6589
81 Michael Haynes	1988-97	6588
82 Henry Marshall	1976-87	6545
83 Ricky Sanders	1986-95	6477
84 Del Shofner	1957-67	6470
85 Mike Quick	1982-90	6464
86 Sammy White	1976-85	6400
87 Carlos Carson	1980-89	6372
88 Quinn Early	1988-98	6365
89 Max McGee	1954, 57-67	6346
90 Stephone Paige	1983-91	6341
91 Haywood Jeffires	1987-96	6334
92 Terance Mathis	1990-98	6332
93 Steve Jordan	1982-94	6307

AVERAGE GAIN
(minimum 200 Receptions)

Player	Year	Avg.
1 Homer Jones	1964-70	22.26
2 Buddy Dial	1959-66	20.83
3 Harlon Hill	1954-62	20.24
4 Flipper Anderson	1988-97	20.06
5 Paul Warfield	1964-74, 76-77	20.06
6 Bob Hayes	1965-75	19.98
7 Willie Gault	1983-93	19.92
8 Jimmy Orr	1958-70	19.79
9 Ray Renfro	1952-63	19.60
10 Hugh Taylor	1947-54	19.24
11 Stanley Morgan	1977-90	19.24
12 Wesley Walker	1977-89	18.96
13 Lance Alworth	1962-72	18.94
14 Mel Gray	1971-82	18.93
15 Carroll Dale	1960-73	18.90
16 Roger Carr	1974-83	18.71
17 Don Maynard	1958, 60-73	18.70
18 Frank Clarke	1957-67	18.65
19 Gary Garrison	1966-77	18.61
20 Del Shofner	1957-67	18.54
21 John Gilliam	1967-77	18.47
22 Max McGee	1954, 57-67	18.39
23 Crazy Legs Hirsch	1949-57	18.36
24 James Lofton	1978-93	18.33
25 Ben Hawkins	1966-74	18.25
26 Haven Moses	1968-81	18.06
27 Carlos Carson	1980-89	18.05
28 Mervyn Fernandez	1987-92	18.01
29 Lance Rentzel	1965-72, 74	18.01
30 Elbert Dubenion	1960-68	18.01
31 Harold Jackson	1968-83	17.91
32 Pete Brewster	1952-60	17.90
33 Otis Taylor	1965-75	17.82
34 Gene Washington	1969-77, 79	17.81
35 Mike Quick	1982-90	17.81
36 Jack Snow	1965-75	17.68
37 Jim Colclough	1960-68	17.67
38 Alfred Jenkins	1975-83	17.41
39 Aaron Thomas	1961-70	17.38
40 Bob Schnelker	1953-61	17.38
41 Mark Duper	1982-92	17.36
42 Cliff Branch	1972-85	17.34
43 Steve Watson	1979-87	17.31
44 Jim Doran	1951-61	17.30
45 Kevin House	1980-87	17.29
46 Bobby Walston	1951-62	17.24
47 Rich Caster	1970-82	17.13
48 Isaac Curtis	1973-84	17.07
49 Ray Mathews	1951-60	17.01
50 Tommy McDonald	1957-68	16.99
51 Lionel Manuel	1984-90	16.99
52 Derrick Alexander	1994-98	16.98
53 Frank Lewis	1971-83	16.94
54 Henry Ellard	1983-98	16.93
55 Leonard Thompson	1975-86	16.90
56 Eddie Brown	1985-91	16.90
57 Ernie Jones	1988-93	16.88

58 Ken Burrough	1970-81	16.87
59 Stephone Paige	1983-91	16.82
60 Billy Howton	1952-63	16.82
61 Art Powell	1959-68	16.80
62 Terry Barr	1957-65	16.78
63 Louis Lipps	1984-92	16.77
64 Jim Mutscheller	1954-61	16.75
65 Duriel Harris	1976-85	16.74
66 Roy Jefferson	1965-76	16.72
67 Hassan Jones	1986-93	16.70
68 Tony Hill	1977-86	16.68
69 Charley Frazier	1962-70	16.68
70 Jim Benton	1938-40, 42-47	16.67
71 Charley Hennigan	1960-66	16.64
72 Lenny Moore	1956-67	16.64
73 Gary Ballman	1962-73	16.61
74 Stacey Bailey	1982-90	16.61
75 Ray Butler	1980-88	16.52
76 Jackie Smith	1963-78	16.50
77 Al Denson	1964-71	16.44
78 Sonny Randle	1959-68	16.43
79 Dave Kocourek	1960-68	16.43
80 Pete Retzlaff	1956-66	16.40
81 Don Hutson	1935-45	16.38
82 Rick Upchurch	1975-83	16.36
83 Clem Daniels	1960-68	16.33
84 Freddie Scott	1974-83	16.30
85 Sammy White	1976-85	16.28
86 John Jefferson	1978-85	16.28
87 Lynn Swann	1974-82	16.26
88 John Stallworth	1974-87	16.24
89 Mark Jackson	1986-94	16.23
90 Tim McGee	1986-94	16.21

RECEIVING TOUCHDOWNS

Player	Year	TDs
1 Jerry Rice	1985-98	164
2 Cris Carter	1987-98	101
3 Steve Largent	1976-89	100
4 Don Hutson	1935-45	99
5 Don Maynard	1958, 60-73	88
6 Lance Alworth	1962-72	85
Andre Reed	1985-98	85
Paul Warfield	1964-74, 76-77	85
9 Mark Clayton	1983-93	84
Tommy McDonald	1957-68	84
11 Art Powell	1959-68	81
12 Harold Carmichael	1971-84	79
Charley Taylor	1964-75, 77	79
14 Andre Rison	1989-98	78
15 Irving Fryar	1984-98	77
16 Fred Biletnikoff	1965-78	76
Harold Jackson	1968-83	76
18 James Lofton	1978-93	75
19 Nat Moore	1974-86	74
20 Stanley Morgan	1977-90	72
21 Bob Hayes	1965-75	71
Wesley Walker	1977-89	71
23 Gary Collins	1962-71	70
24 Tim Brown	1988-98	69
25 Raymond Berry	1955-67	68
Art Monk	1980-95	68
27 Cliff Branch	1972-85	67
28 Roy Green	1979-92	66
Jimmy Orr	1958-70	66
30 Gary Clark	1985-95	65
Henry Ellard	1983-98	65
Charlie Joiner	1969-86	65
Bobby Mitchell	1958-68	65
Sonny Randle	1959-68	65
Sterling Sharpe	1988-94	65
36 Anthony Miller	1988-97	63
John Stallworth	1974-87	63
38 Michael Irvin	1988-98	62
39 Billy Howton	1952-63	61
Pete Pihos	1947-55	61
Mike Quick	1982-90	61
42 Drew Hill	1979-82, 84-93	60
Jerry Smith	1965-77	60
Gene Washington	1969-77, 79	60
45 Mark Duper	1982-92	59
46 Gary Garrison	1966-77	58
Hugh Taylor	1947-54	58
48 Herman Moore	1991-98	57
Carl Pickens	1992-98	57
Otis Taylor	1965-75	57
51 Wes Chandler	1978-88	56
Haven Moses	1968-81	56
53 Chris Burford	1960-67	55
Anthony Carter	1985-95	55
55 Isaac Curtis	1973-84	53
Crazy Legs Hirsch	1949-57	53
57 Dave Casper	1974-84	52
Carroll Dale	1960-73	52
Roy Jefferson	1965-76	52
60 Charley Hennigan	1960-66	51
Tony Hill	1977-86	51
Del Shofner	1957-67	51
Lynn Swann	1974-82	51
64 Frank Clarke	1957-67	50
Haywood Jeffires	1987-96	50
Ken Kavanaugh	1940-41, 45-50	50
Max McGee	1954, 57-67	50
Ray Renfro	1952-63	50
Sammy White	1976-85	50
70 Ken Burrough	1970-81	49
Ernest Givins	1986-95	49
Keith Jackson	1988-96	49
Eric Martin	1985-94	49
Stephone Paige	1983-91	49
Billy Wilson	1951-60	49

Career Interceptions

Player	Year	Ints.
1 Paul Krause	1964-79	81
2 Emlen Tunnell	1948-61	79
3 Night Train Lane	1952-65	68
4 Ken Riley	1969-83	65
5 Ronnie Lott	1981-94	63
6 Dave Brown	1975-89	62
Dick LeBeau	1959-72	62
8 Emmitt Thomas	1966-78	58
9 Mel Blount	1970-83	57
Bobby Boyd	1960-68	57
Johnny Robinson	1960-71	57
Everson Walls	1981-93	57
13 Lem Barney	1967-77	56
Pat Fischer	1961-77	56
15 Willie Brown	1963-78	54
16 Eugene Robinson	1985-98	53
17 Jack Butler	1951-59	52
Bobby Dillon	1952-59	52
Jimmy Patton	1955-66	52
Mel Renfro	1964-77	52
Larry Wilson	1960-72	52
22 Bobby Bryant	1968-80	51
Donnie Shell	1974-87	51
24 Don Burroughs	1955-64	50
Deron Cherry	1981-91	50
John Harris	1978-88	50
Yale Lary	1952-53, 56-64	50
28 Ken Houston	1967-80	49
Jake Scott	1970-78	49
30 Herb Adderley	1961-72	48
Dave Grayson	1961-70	48
Richie Petitbon	1959-72	48
Dave Waymer	1980-92	48
Willie Wood	1960-71	48
35 Darrell Green	1983-98	47
Jim Johnson	1961-76	47
Lemar Parrish	1970-82	47
Rod Woodson	1987-98	47
39 Jack Christiansen	1951-58	46
Goose Gonsoulin	1960-67	46
Mike Haynes	1976-89	46
Ed Meador	1959-70	46
Dave Whitsell	1958-69	46
44 Erich Barnes	1958-71	45
Thom Darden	1972-74, 76-81	45
Jim Norton	1960-68	45
47 Eric Allen	1988-98	44
Steve Foley	1976-86	44
49 Kermit Alexander	1963-73	43
50 Gill Byrd	1983-92	42
Bobby Hunt	1962-69	42
Albert Lewis	1983-98	42
53 Don Doll	1949-54	41
Carl Lockhart	1965-75	41
Johnny Sample	1958-68	41
Deion Sanders	1989-98	41
Charlie Waters	1970-78, 80-81	41
58 Butch Byrd	1964-71	40
W.K. Hicks	1964-72	40
Tom Keane	1948-55	40
Warren Lahr	1950-59	40
Ed Sharockman	1961-72	40
Billy Thompson	1969-81	40
Roger Wehrli	1969-82	40
65 Gary Barbaro	1976-82	39
Glen Edwards	1971-81	39
Lester Hayes	1977-86	39
Rolland Lawrence	1973-80	39
Clarence Scott	1971-83	39
Aeneas Williams	1991-98	39
71 Ray Brown	1971-80	38
Lindon Crow	1955-64	38
Eugene Daniel	1984-97	38
Gary Fencik	1976-87	38
Mike Harden	1980-90	38
Tim McDonald	1987-98	38
Kevin Ross	1984-97	38
Rick Volk	1967-78	38
79 Joey Browner	1983-92	37
Nolan Cromwell	1977-87	37
Cris Dishman	1988-98	37
Tony Greene	1971-79	37
Bob Howard	1967-79	37
Dick Lynch	1958-66	37
Ken Reaves	1966-77	37
Don Shinnick	1957-69	37
Jack Tatum	1971-80	37
Lionel Washington	1983-97	37
Dwayne Woodruff	1979-85, 87-90	37

Career Punting

PUNTING AVERAGE
(minimum 250 Punts)

Player	Year	Avg.
1 Sammy Baugh	1937-52	45.10
2 Darren Bennett	1995-98	44.71
3 Tommy Davis	1959-69	44.68
4 Yale Lary	1952-53, 56-64	44.29
5 Matt Turk	1995-98	44.22
6 Bob Scarpitto	1961-68	43.84
7 Horace Gillom	1950-56	43.82
8 Jerry Norton	1954-64	43.77
9 Tom Rouen	1993-98	43.72
10 Dave Lewis	1970-73	43.67
11 Craig Hentrich	1994-98	43.61
12 Sean Landeta	1985-98	43.58
13 Greg Montgomery	1988-94, 96-97	43.57
14 Tom Tupa	1988-92, 94-98	43.51
15 Rick Tuten	1989-98	43.49
16 Don Chandler	1956-67	43.45
17 Rohn Stark	1982-97	43.36
18 Reggie Roby	1983-98	43.30
19 Jerrel Wilson	1963-78	43.04
20 Norm Van Brocklin	1949-60	42.85
21 Danny Villanueva	1960-67	42.75
22 Bryan Barker	1990-98	42.75
23 Rich Camarillo	1981-96	42.74
24 Bobby Joe Green	1960-73	42.59
25 Tommy Barnhardt	1987-98	42.59
26 Sam Baker	1953, 56-69	42.59
27 Lee Johnson	1985-98	42.58
28 Harry Newsome	1985-93	42.50
29 Mark Royals	1987, 90-98	42.50
30 Chris Gardocki	1991-98	42.47
31 Ralf Mojsiejenko	1985-91	42.45
32 Bob Waterfield	1945-52	42.43
33 Ray Guy	1973-86	42.41
34 Tom Hutton	1995-98	42.37
35 John Jett	1993-98	42.33
36 Curley Johnson	1960-69	42.31
37 Brian Hansen	1984-88, 90-98	42.31
38 Jim Arnold	1983-94	42.31
39 Jim Fraser	1962-66, 68	42.22
40 Mike Horan	1984-98	42.21
41 Tom Skladany	1978-83	42.12
42 Rick Donnelly	1985-88, 90-91	42.10
43 Jim Norton	1960-68	42.07
44 Steve Cox	1981-88	42.00
45 Ron Widby	1968-73	41.98
46 Pat Richter	1963-70	41.96
47 Luke Prestridge	1979-84	41.90
48 Pat McInally	1976-85	41.87
49 Fred Morrison	1950-56	41.75
50 Jeff Feagles	1988-98	41.73
51 Billy Van Heusen	1968-76	41.70
52 Paul Maguire	1960-70	41.68
53 Mike Saxon	1985-95	41.68
54 Bobby Walden	1964-77	41.61
55 Louie Aguiar	1991-98	41.60
56 Max McGee	1954, 57-67	41.59
57 John Kidd	1984-98	41.50
58 Carl Birdsong	1981-85	41.43
59 Scott Fulhage	1987-92	41.39
60 Maury Buford	1982-86, 88-91	41.36
61 Jeff Gossett	1981-83, 85-96	41.31
62 Larry Swider	1979-82	41.30
63 Craig Colquitt	1978-81, 83-84, 87	41.29
64 Dennis Partee	1968-75	41.27
65 Tom Blanchard	1971-81	41.26
66 King Hill	1958-69	41.25
67 Mike Eischeid	1966-74	41.23
68 Dave Jennings	1974-87	41.22
69 Tom McNeill	1967-73	41.13
70 Frank Garcia	1981, 83-87	41.11
71 Mike Black	1983-87	41.11
72 Klaus Wilmsmeyer	1992-96, 98	41.05
73 Bucky Scribner	1983-84, 87-89	41.04
74 George Roberts	1978-82	40.99
75 Gary Collins	1962-71	40.96
76 Billy Lothridge	1964-72	40.96
77 Chris Mohr	1989, 91-98	40.92

78 Marv Bateman	1972-77	40.88
79 Adrian Burk	1950-56	40.85
80 Bryan Wagner	1987-95	40.80
81 Tom Wittum	1973-77	40.77
82 Steve O'Neal	1969-73	40.73
83 Pat Studstill	1961-62, 64-72	40.65
84 Russell Erxleben	1979-83, 87	40.65
85 John James	1972-84	40.62
86 David Lee	1966-78	40.60
87 Greg Coleman	1977-88	40.59
88 Ed Brown	1954-65	40.56
89 Mike Mercer	1961-70	40.50
90 Julian Fagan	1970-73	40.47
91 Tom Landry	1950-55	40.39
92 Don Cockroft	1968-80	40.34
93 Herman Weaver	1970-80	40.26
94 Max Runager	1979-89	40.21
95 Danny White	1976-88	40.18
96 Dan Stryzinski	1990-98	40.13
97 Jug Girard	1948-57	40.12
98 Dave Green	1973-78	40.10
99 John Teltschik	1986-89	40.08
100 Larry Seiple	1967-77	40.04
101 Chuck Ramsey	1977-84	40.01
102 Dale Hatcher	1985-89, 91, 93	40.01
103 Kelly Goodburn	1987-93	39.92
104 Don Bracken	1985-90, 92-93	39.86
105 Mike Bragg	1968-80	39.83
106 Roy Zimmerman	1940-48	39.80
107 Cliff Parsley	1977-82	39.76
108 Dan Pastorini	1971-81, 83	39.65
109 Donny Anderson	1966-74	39.60
110 Spike Jones	1970-77	39.26
111 Tom Janik	1963-71	39.09
112 Joe Prokop	1985, 87-92	39.06
113 Duane Carrell	1974-77	38.90
114 Greg Cater	1980-83, 86-87	38.74
115 Mike Connell	1978, 80-81	38.73
116 Bob Parsons	1972-83	38.67
117 Rusty Jackson	1976, 78-79	38.65
118 Tom Yewcic	1961-66	38.60
119 Jeff Hayes	1982-87	38.22
120 Cotton Davidson	1954, 57, 60-66, 68	38.14
121 David Beverly	1974-80	38.13
122 Jeff West	1975-79, 81-85	38.07
123 Bucky Dilts	1977-79	37.46

CAREER PUNTS

Player	Year	Punts
1 Dave Jennings	1974-87	1154
2 Rohn Stark	1982-97	1141
3 John James	1972-84	1083
4 Jerrel Wilson	1963-78	1072
5 Ray Guy	1973-86	1049
6 Brian Hansen	1984-88, 90-98	1048
7 Rich Camarillo	1981-96	1027
8 Reggie Roby	1983-98	992
9 Lee Johnson	1985-98	984
10 Jeff Gossett	1981-83, 85-96	982
11 Mike Bragg	1968-80	978
12 Mike Horan	1984-98	977
13 Bobby Walden	1964-77	974
14 Bobby Joe Green	1960-73	970
15 John Kidd	1984-98	957
16 Sean Landeta	1985-98	926
17 Jeff Feagles	1988-98	896
18 Bob Parsons	1972-83	884
19 Jim Arnold	1983-94	866
20 David Lee	1966-78	838
21 Greg Coleman	1977-88	820
22 Tom Blanchard	1971-81	819
23 Mike Saxon	1985-95	813
24 Paul Maguire	1960-70	795
25 Tommy Barnhardt	1987-98	729
26 Mark Royals	1987, 90-98	728
27 Rick Tuten	1989-98	709
28 Sam Baker	1953, 56-69	703
29 Pat McInally	1976-85	700
30 Herman Weaver	1970-80	693
31 Chris Mohr	1989, 91-98	685
32 Harry Newsome	1985-93	683
Dan Stryzinski	1990-98	683
34 Max Runager	1979-89	661
35 Don Chandler	1956-67	660
36 Don Cockroft	1968-80	651
37 Bryan Barker	1990-98	640
38 Larry Seiple	1967-77	633
39 Louie Aguiar	1991-98	631
40 Jeff West	1975-79, 81-85	621
41 Danny White	1976-88	610

Career Kick Returns

PUNT RETURNS

Player	Year	Rets.
1 Dave Meggett	1989-98	349
2 Tim Brown	1988-98	304
3 Vai Sikahema	1986-93	292
4 Billy Johnson	1974-80, 82-88	282
5 Eric Metcalf	1989-98	281
6 Brian Mitchell	1990-98	277
7 J.T. Smith	1978-90	267
8 Emlen Tunnell	1948-61	262
9 Kelvin Martin	1987-96	261
10 Rod Woodson	1987-98	258
11 Alvin Haymond	1964-73	253
12 Mike Fuller	1975-82	252
Mel Gray	1986-97	252
14 Rick Upchurch	1975-83	248
15 Ron Smith	1965-74	235
16 Phil McConkey	1984-89	228
17 Danny Reece	1976-80	222
18 Glyn Milburn	1993-98	218
19 Mike Nelms	1980-84	212
20 Irving Fryar	1984-98	206
21 Speedy Duncan	1964-74	202
22 Leo Lewis	1981-91	201
23 Greg Pruitt	1973-84	194
24 Willie Drewrey	1985-93	192
25 Gerald McNeil	1986-90	191
26 Theo Bell	1976, 78-85	189
27 Willie Wood	1960-71	187
28 Bruce Harper	1977-84	183
29 Clarence Verdin	1986-94	178
30 Darrien Gordon	1993-94, 96-98	177
Freddie Solomon	1975-85	177
32 Robbie Martin	1981-86	175
Walter Stanley	1985-90, 92	175
34 Eddie Brown	1974-79	172
Kevin Williams	1993-98	172
36 Neal Colzie	1975-83	170
37 Desmond Howard	1992-98	164
Todd Kinchen	1992-98	164
39 Howard Stevens	1973-77	163
40 Tyrone Hughes	1993-98	162
Pete Mandley	1984-90	162
Larry Marshall	1972-78	162
43 Charlie West	1968-79	158
44 Billy Thompson	1969-81	157
45 Stump Mitchell	1981-89	156
Eddie Payton	1977-78, 80-82	156
47 Carl Roaches	1980-85	155
48 Dana McLemore	1982-87	152
Deion Sanders	1989-98	152
50 John Taylor	1987-95	149
51 Butch Atkinson	1968-77, 79	148
Johnny Bailey	1990-95	148
Wally Henry	1977-82	148
54 LeRoy Irvin	1980-90	147
55 Butch Johnson	1976-85	146
56 Fulton Walker	1981-86	145

PUNT RETURN YARDS

Player	Year	Yds.
1 Dave Meggett	1989-98	3708
2 Billy Johnson	1974-80, 82-88	3317
3 Vai Sikahema	1986-93	3169
4 Brian Mitchell	1990-98	3144
5 Tim Brown	1988-98	3106
6 Rick Upchurch	1975-83	3008
7 Eric Metcalf	1989-98	2804
8 J.T. Smith	1978-90	2764
9 Mel Gray	1986-97	2753
10 Mike Fuller	1975-82	2660
11 Kelvin Martin	1987-96	2567
12 Rod Woodson	1987-98	2362
13 Darrien Gordon	1993-94, 96-98	2329
14 Emlen Tunnell	1948-61	2217
15 Speedy Duncan	1964-74	2201
16 Glyn Milburn	1993-98	2166
17 Alvin Haymond	1964-73	2148
18 Irving Fryar	1984-98	2055
19 Greg Pruitt	1973-84	2007
20 Desmond Howard	1992-98	1981
21 Mike Nelms	1980-84	1948
22 Leo Lewis	1981-91	1868
23 Phil McConkey	1984-89	1832
24 Billy Thompson	1969-81	1814
25 Ron Smith	1965-74	1788
26 Bruce Harper	1977-84	1784
27 Neal Colzie	1975-83	1759
28 Kevin Williams	1993-98	1744
29 Gerald McNeil	1986-90	1717
30 Robbie Martin	1981-86	1670
31 Clarence Verdin	1986-94	1650
32 Deion Sanders	1989-98	1629
33 Walter Stanley	1985-90, 92	1619
34 Freddie Solomon	1975-85	1614
35 Dana McLemore	1982-87	1598
36 Willie Drewrey	1985-93	1597
37 Howard Stevens	1973-77	1559
38 Danny Reece	1976-80	1554
39 Henry Ellard	1983-98	1527
40 John Taylor	1987-95	1517
41 Bill Dudley	1942, 45-51, 53	1515
42 Theo Bell	1976, 78-85	1511
Eddie Brown	1974-79	1511
Pete Mandley	1984-90	1511
45 Todd Kinchen	1992-98	1493
46 David Palmer	1994-98	1484
47 Bobby Joe Edmonds	1986-89, 95	1471
48 Larry Marshall	1972-78	1466
49 LeRoy Irvin	1980-90	1457
50 Fulton Walker	1981-86	1437
51 George McAfee	1940-41, 45-50	1431
52 Johnny Bailey	1990-95	1420
53 Tyrone Hughes	1993-98	1411

PUNT RETURN AVERAGE
(minimum 75 Punt Returns)

Player	Year	Avg.
1 Darrien Gordon	1993-94, 96-98	13.16
2 George McAfee	1940-41, 45-50	12.78
3 Jack Christiansen	1951-58	12.75
4 Claude Gibson	1961-65	12.55
5 Jermaine Lewis	1996-98	12.30
6 Reggie Barlow	1996-98	12.24
7 Bill Dudley	1942, 45-51, 53	12.22
8 Rick Upchurch	1975-83	12.13
9 Desmond Howard	1992-98	12.08
10 Billy Johnson	1974-80, 82-88	11.76
11 Mack Herron	1973-75	11.69
12 Billy Thompson	1969-81	11.55
13 Brian Mitchell	1990-98	11.35
14 Henry Ellard	1983-98	11.31
15 Rodger Bird	1966-68	11.31
16 Bosh Pritchard	1942, 46-49, 51	11.28
17 Terry Metcalf	1973-77, 81	11.14
18 Bob Hayes	1965-75	11.13
19 Floyd Little	1967-75	11.02
20 Louis Lipps	1984-92	11.02
21 Bobby Joe Edmonds	1986-89, 95	10.98
22 Mel Gray	1986-97	10.92
23 Speedy Duncan	1964-74	10.90
24 Vitamin Smith	1949-53	10.85
25 Vai Sikahema	1986-93	10.85
26 Deion Sanders	1989-98	10.72
27 Jo-Jo Townsell	1985-90	10.71
28 Winslow Oliver	1996-98	10.66
29 Dave Meggett	1989-98	10.62
30 David Palmer	1994-98	10.60
31 Mike Fuller	1975-82	10.56
32 Eddie Kennison	1996-98	10.53
33 Leroy Kelly	1964-73	10.53
34 Dana McLemore	1982-87	10.51
35 Tommy Vigorito	1981-83, 85	10.51
36 Keith Moody	1976-80	10.45
37 Jeff Burris	1994-98	10.45
38 Jake Scott	1970-78	10.44
39 Stanley Morgan	1977-90	10.43
40 Mike Haynes	1976-89	10.43
41 J.T. Smith	1978-90	10.35
42 Neal Colzie	1975-83	10.35
43 Greg Pruitt	1973-84	10.35
44 Abner Haynes	1960-67	10.29
45 Leon Johnson	1997-98	10.28
46 Jackie Wallace	1974-79	10.27
47 Tim Brown	1988-98	10.22
48 John Taylor	1987-95	10.18
49 Kevin Williams	1993-98	10.14
50 Joey Galloway	1995-98	10.12
51 Tom Watkins	1961-65, 67-68	10.10
52 Amani Toomer	1996-98	10.05
53 Tamarick Vanover	1995-98	10.02
54 Gerald Willhite	1982-88	10.02
55 Eric Metcalf	1989-98	9.98
56 Irving Fryar	1984-98	9.98
57 Glyn Milburn	1993-98	9.94
58 LeRoy Irvin	1980-90	9.91
59 Fulton Walker	1981-86	9.91
60 Ken Jenkins	1983-86	9.91
61 Mike Martin	1983-89	9.86
62 Dexter Carter	1990-96	9.84
63 Kelvin Martin	1987-96	9.84

64	Bruce Harper	1977-84	9.75
65	Eric Guliford	1993-95, 97-98	9.70
66	Bill Butler	1959-64	9.66
67	Lionel James	1984-88	9.62
68	Johnny Bailey	1990-95	9.59
69	Howard Stevens	1973-77	9.56
70	Scott Schwedes	1987-90	9.56
71	Robbie Martin	1981-86	9.54
72	Dale Carter	1992-98	9.48
73	Andre Hastings	1993-98	9.42
74	Jeff Fisher	1981-84	9.38
75	Jeff Query	1989-95	9.37
76	Pete Mandley	1984-90	9.33
77	Bruce Taylor	1970-77	9.32
78	Cliff Hicks	1987-95	9.30
79	Al Dodd	1967, 69-71, 73-74	9.30
80	Leo Lewis	1981-91	9.29
81	Clarence Verdin	1986-94	9.27
82	Walter Stanley	1985-90, 92	9.25
83	Dennis McKinnon	1983-85, 87-90	9.23
84	Glen Edwards	1971-81	9.22
85	Lemar Parrish	1970-82	9.20
86	Mike Nelms	1980-84	9.19
87	Lem Barney	1967-77	9.17
88	Rod Woodson	1987-98	9.16
89	Mickey Sutton	1986-90	9.14
90	Ralph McGill	1972-79	9.14
91	Freddie Solomon	1975-85	9.12
92	Todd Kinchen	1992-98	9.10
93	Derrick Shepard	1987-91	9.05
94	Larry Marshall	1972-78	9.05
95	Butch Johnson	1976-85	8.99
96	Paul Skansi	1983-91	8.99
97	Gerald McNeil	1986-90	8.99
98	Bill Baird	1963-69	8.94
99	Lew Barnes	1986, 88-89	8.92
100	Pete Athas	1971-76	8.89
101	Eddie Payton	1977-78, 80-82	8.89
102	O.J. McDuffie	1993-98	8.88
103	Stump Mitchell	1981-89	8.83
104	Eddie Brown	1974-79	8.78
105	Manfred Moore	1974-77	8.75
106	Tyrone Hughes	1993-98	8.71
107	Chris Warren	1990-98	8.65
108	Tommy Casanova	1972-77	8.62
109	Vernon Turner	1990-95	8.60
110	Ed Podolak	1969-77	8.59
111	Johnny Morris	1958-67	8.59
112	Virgil Livers	1975-79	8.58
113	Vance Johnson	1985-93, 95	8.51
114	Alvin Haymond	1964-73	8.49
115	Emlen Tunnell	1948-61	8.46
116	James Jones	1980-82, 84-85	8.46
117	Jeff Groth	1979-85	8.45
118	Butch Atkinson	1968-77, 79	8.43
119	Jon Staggers	1970-75	8.43
120	Steve Schubert	1974-79	8.41
121	Larry Brunson	1974-80	8.40
122	Willie Drewrey	1985-93	8.32
123	Wally Henry	1977-82	8.32
124	Bobby Futrell	1986-90	8.30
125	Phil Epps	1982-89	8.19
126	Jon Arnett	1957-66	8.18
127	Leon Bright	1981-85	8.15
128	Nesby Glasgow	1979-92	8.14
129	Dino Hall	1979-83	8.12
130	Rich Mauti	1977-80, 82-84	8.05
131	Rickie Harris	1965-72	8.04
132	Phil McConkey	1984-89	8.04
133	Theo Bell	1976, 78-85	7.99
134	Don Paul	1950-58	7.98
135	Dick James	1956-65	7.93
136	Tony Leonard	1976-79	7.82
137	Bill Bradley	1969-77	7.81
138	Jerry LeVias	1969-74	7.81
139	Abe Woodson	1958-66	7.77
140	John Sciarra	1978-83	7.77
141	Kenny Johnson	1980-89	7.76
142	Larry Anderson	1978-84	7.76
143	Mel Renfro	1964-77	7.72
144	Johnnie Gray	1975-83	7.72
145	Rod Harris	1989-91	7.65
146	Ron Smith	1965-74	7.61
147	Evan Cooper	1984-89	7.55
148	Jim Smith	1977-82, 85	7.52
149	Al Carmichael	1953-58, 60-61	7.48
150	Willie Wood	1960-71	7.44
151	Woodley Lewis	1950-60	7.43
152	Hugh McElhenny	1952-64	7.30
153	Carl Taseff	1951, 53-62	7.26
154	Carl Roaches	1980-85	7.20
155	Ira Matthews	1979-81	7.14
156	Patrick Robinson	1993-94	7.02
157	Danny Reece	1976-80	7.00
158	Butch Byrd	1964-71	6.98
159	Charlie West	1968-79	6.96
160	Willard Harrell	1975-84	6.94
161	Rolland Lawrence	1973-80	6.73
162	Rick Volk	1967-78	6.52
163	Kermit Alexander	1963-73	6.28
164	Joe Arenas	1951-57	6.24
165	Ike Hill	1970-71, 73-74, 76	6.10
166	Yale Lary	1952-53, 56-64	6.02
167	Keith Wright	1978-80	5.99
168	Billy Reynolds	1953-54, 57-58, 60	5.35
169	Elijah Pitts	1961-71	5.25
170	Bert Rechichar	1952-61	3.66

PUNT RETURN TOUCHDOWNS

	Player	Year	TDs
1	Eric Metcalf	1989-98	9
2	Jack Christiansen	1951-58	8
	Rick Upchurch	1975-83	8
4	Dave Meggett	1989-98	7
	Brian Mitchell	1990-98	7
6	Darrien Gordon	1993-94, 96-98	6
	Desmond Howard	1992-98	6
	Billy Johnson	1974-80, 82-88	6
9	Curly Oden	1925-28, 30-32	5
	Deion Sanders	1989-98	5
	Emlen Tunnell	1948-61	5
12	Dick Christy	1958, 60-63	4
	Speedy Duncan	1964-74	4
	Henry Ellard	1983-98	4
	Joey Galloway	1995-98	4
	LeRoy Irvin	1980-90	4
	Jermaine Lewis	1996-98	4
	Dana McLemore	1982-87	4
	Lemar Parrish	1970-82	4
	Vai Sikahema	1986-93	4
	J.T. Smith	1978-90	4
	Freddie Solomon	1975-85	4
	Clarence Verdin	1986-94	4

KICKOFF RETURNS

	Player	Year	Rets.
1	Mel Gray	1986-97	421
2	Brian Mitchell	1990-98	378
3	Tyrone Hughes	1993-98	283
4	Glyn Milburn	1993-98	277
5	Ron Smith	1965-74	275
6	Eric Metcalf	1989-98	273
7	Dave Meggett	1989-98	252
8	Dexter Carter	1990-96	250
	Kevin Williams	1993-98	250
10	Bruce Harper	1977-84	243
11	Clarence Verdin	1986-94	237
12	Vai Sikahema	1986-93	235
13	Rod Woodson	1987-98	220
14	Herschel Walker	1986-97	215
15	Michael Bates	1993-98	204
16	Ron Brown	1984-91	199
17	Steve Odom	1974-79	194
18	Andre Coleman	1994-98	193
	Abe Woodson	1958-66	193
20	Dennis Gentry	1982-92	192
21	Al Carmichael	1953-58, 60-61	191
22	Larry Anderson	1978-84	189
	Dick James	1956-65	189
24	Desmond Howard	1992-98	185
25	Timmy Brown	1959-68	184
26	Qadry Ismail	1993-98	183
27	Speedy Duncan	1964-74	180
28	Stump Mitchell	1981-89	177
29	Steve Broussard	1990-98	175
	Mike Nelms	1980-84	175
31	Bobby Joe Edmonds	1986-89, 95	173
32	Drew Hill	1979-82, 84-93	172
33	Alvin Haymond	1964-73	170
34	Nate Lewis	1990-95	169
35	Tamarick Vanover	1995-98	168
36	Fulton Walker	1981-86	167
37	Darrin Nelson	1982-92	163
38	Vaughn Hebron	1993-94, 96-98	158
	Bobby Jancik	1962-67	158
40	Eddie Payton	1977-78, 80-82	156
41	Carl Garrett	1969-77	154
	Carl Roaches	1980-85	154
43	Kermit Alexander	1963-73	153
	Aaron Bailey	1994-98	153
45	Bruce Laird	1972-83	152
46	Dino Hall	1979-83	151
47	Donnie Elder	1985-86, 88-91	150
	Corey Harris	1992-98	150
	Deion Sanders	1989-98	150
50	Albert Bentley	1985-92	149
51	Stanford Jennings	1984-92	148

KICKOFF RETURN YARDS

	Player	Year	Yds.
1	Mel Gray	1986-97	10250
2	Brian Mitchell	1990-98	8693
3	Tyrone Hughes	1993-98	6999
4	Ron Smith	1965-74	6922
5	Glyn Milburn	1993-98	6742
6	Kevin Williams	1993-98	5933
7	Eric Metcalf	1989-98	5691
8	Dave Meggett	1989-98	5566
9	Abe Woodson	1958-66	5538
10	Dexter Carter	1990-96	5412
11	Bruce Harper	1977-84	5407
12	Herschel Walker	1986-97	5084
13	Michael Bates	1993-98	5046
14	Vai Sikahema	1986-93	4933
15	Clarence Verdin	1986-94	4930
16	Rod Woodson	1987-98	4894
17	Al Carmichael	1953-58, 60-61	4798
18	Timmy Brown	1959-68	4781
19	Dick James	1956-65	4676
20	Speedy Duncan	1964-74	4539
21	Ron Brown	1984-91	4493
22	Andre Coleman	1994-98	4466
23	Steve Odom	1974-79	4451
24	Alvin Haymond	1964-73	4438
25	Dennis Gentry	1982-92	4353
26	Larry Anderson	1978-84	4217
27	Tamarick Vanover	1995-98	4213
28	Bobby Jancik	1962-67	4185
29	Mike Nelms	1980-84	4128
30	Steve Broussard	1990-98	4060
31	Qadry Ismail	1993-98	4029
32	Stump Mitchell	1981-89	4007
33	Desmond Howard	1992-98	3863
34	Nate Lewis	1990-95	3825
35	Vaughn Hebron	1993-94, 96-98	3802
36	Joe Arenas	1951-57	3798
37	Fulton Walker	1981-86	3779
38	Bruce Laird	1972-83	3748
39	Ollie Matson	1952, 54-66	3746
40	Carl Garrett	1969-77	3704
41	Eddie Payton	1977-78, 80-82	3676
42	Darrin Nelson	1982-92	3659
43	Bobby Joe Edmonds	1986-89, 95	3646
44	Kermit Alexander	1963-73	3586
45	Corey Harris	1992-98	3543
46	Aaron Bailey	1994-98	3501
47	Drew Hill	1979-82, 84-93	3460
48	Clarence Childs	1964-68	3454
49	Deion Sanders	1989-98	3437
50	Larry Marshall	1972-78	3396
51	Carl Roaches	1980-85	3352
52	Vic Washington	1971-76	3341
53	Woodley Lewis	1950-60	3325
54	Albert Bentley	1985-92	3192
55	Dino Hall	1979-83	3185
56	Cannonball Butler	1965-72	3131
57	Jon Arnett	1957-66	3110
58	Terry Metcalf	1973-77, 81	3087
59	Herb Adderley	1961-72	3080
60	Bo Roberson	1961-66	3057

KICKOFF RETURN AVERAGE
(minimum 75 Kickoff Returns)

	Player	Year	Avg.
1	Gale Sayers	1965-71	30.56
2	Lynn Chandnois	1950-56	29.57
3	Abe Woodson	1958-66	28.69
4	Buddy Young	1950-55	27.93
5	Travis Williams	1967-71	27.46
6	Joe Arenas	1951-57	27.32
7	Clarence Davis	1971-78	27.09
8	Steve Van Buren	1944-51	26.71
9	Lenny Lyles	1958-69	26.68
10	Mercury Morris	1969-76	26.55
11	Bobby Jancik	1962-67	26.49
12	Mel Renfro	1964-77	26.42
13	Bobby Mitchell	1958-68	26.37
14	Ollie Matson	1952, 54-66	26.20
15	Alvin Haymond	1964-73	26.11
16	Noland Smith	1967-69	26.06
17	Al Nelson	1965-73	25.99
18	Timmy Brown	1959-68	25.98
19	Vic Washington	1971-76	25.90
20	Dave Hampton	1969-76	25.87
21	Larry Garron	1960-68	25.83
22	Clarence Childs	1964-68	25.78
23	Herb Adderley	1961-72	25.67
24	Pat Studstill	1961-62, 64-72	25.65
25	Terry Metcalf	1973-77, 81	25.51

	Player	Year	Avg.
26	Walter Roberts	1964-67, 69-70	25.50
27	Dave Grayson	1961-70	25.44
28	Charley Warner	1963-66	25.43
29	Don Shy	1967-73	25.27
30	Speedy Duncan	1964-74	25.22
31	Ron Smith	1965-74	25.17
32	Al Carmichael	1953-58, 60-61	25.12
33	Bobby Williams	1966-67, 69-71	25.12
34	Tamarick Vanover	1995-98	25.08
35	Charlie West	1968-79	25.02
36	Abner Haynes	1960-67	25.00
37	Butch Atkinson	1968-77, 79	24.91
38	Tom Watkins	1961-65, 67-68	24.85
39	Rick Upchurch	1975-83	24.79
40	Dick James	1956-65	24.74
41	Michael Bates	1993-98	24.74
42	Tyrone Hughes	1993-98	24.73
43	Wally Francis	1973-81	24.73
44	Jon Arnett	1957-66	24.68
45	Bruce Laird	1972-83	24.66
46	Larry Marshall	1972-78	24.61
47	Preston Pearson	1967-80	24.57
48	Clint Jones	1967-73	24.51
49	Charlie Bivins	1960-67	24.50
50	Dick Gordon	1965-74	24.37
51	Mel Gray	1986-97	24.35
52	Glyn Milburn	1993-98	24.34
53	Woodley Lewis	1950-60	24.27
54	Floyd Little	1967-75	24.26
55	Cecil Turner	1968-73	24.22
56	Mack Herron	1973-75	24.21
57	Eddie Brown	1974-79	24.16
58	Vaughn Hebron	1993-94, 96-98	24.06
59	Carl Garrett	1969-77	24.05
60	Frank Seno	1943-49	23.95
61	Roell Preston	1995-98	23.94
62	Billy Johnson	1974-80, 82-88	23.91
63	Aaron Glenn	1994-98	23.78
64	Derrick Witherspoon	1995-97	23.76
65	Kevin Williams	1993-98	23.73
66	Greg Pruitt	1973-84	23.72
67	Dick Christy	1958, 60-63	23.68
68	Herschel Walker	1986-97	23.65
69	Corey Harris	1992-98	23.62
70	Brian Baschnagel	1976-84	23.62
71	Mike Nelms	1980-84	23.59
72	Eddie Payton	1977-78, 80-82	23.56
73	Eddie Saenz	1946-51	23.56
74	Jerry LeVias	1969-74	23.54
75	Cannonball Butler	1965-72	23.54
76	Bo Roberson	1961-66	23.52
77	Leroy Kelly	1964-73	23.47
78	Kermit Alexander	1963-73	23.44
79	Larry Brunson	1974-80	23.24
80	Glen Young	1983-85, 87-88	23.24
81	Jon Vaughn	1991-94	23.20
82	Steve Broussard	1990-98	23.20
83	Butch Johnson	1976-85	23.19
84	Sammy Martin	1988-91	23.17
85	Tony Canadeo	1941-44, 46-52	23.15
86	Hugh McElhenny	1952-64	23.14
87	Andre Coleman	1994-98	23.14
88	Irving Spikes	1994-97	23.12
89	David Dunn	1995-98	23.09
90	Lou Piccone	1974-82	23.05
91	Brian Mitchell	1990-98	23.00
92	Bernard Jackson	1972-80	22.96
93	Steve Odom	1974-79	22.94
94	Dave Williams	1977-81	22.94
95	O.J. McDuffie	1993-98	22.92
96	James Dixon	1989-91	22.92
97	Deion Sanders	1989-98	22.91
98	Aaron Bailey	1994-98	22.88
99	Bobby Humphery	1984-90	22.88
100	Rich Mauti	1977-80, 82-84	22.82
101	Manfred Moore	1974-77	22.82
102	Rickie Harris	1965-72	22.80
103	Ernie Mills	1991-98	22.73
104	Howard Stevens	1973-77	22.68
105	Dennis Gentry	1982-92	22.67
106	Stump Mitchell	1981-89	22.64
107	Nate Lewis	1990-95	22.63
108	Fulton Walker	1981-86	22.63
109	David Palmer	1994-98	22.62
110	Sylvester Stamps	1984-89	22.60
111	Ron Brown	1984-91	22.58
112	Reggie Smith	1980-81, 87	22.57
113	Gary Davis	1976-81	22.51
114	Bake Turner	1962-70	22.51
115	Roy Green	1979-92	22.49
116	Ken Jenkins	1983-86	22.47
117	Artie Owens	1976-80	22.45
118	Darrin Nelson	1982-92	22.45
119	Nesby Glasgow	1979-92	22.42
120	Wally Henry	1977-82	22.41
121	Eric Moulds	1996-98	22.38
122	Pervis Atkins	1961-66	22.36
123	Bill Dudley	1942, 45-51, 53	22.35
124	Larry Anderson	1978-84	22.31
125	Randy Baldwin	1991-96	22.28
126	Charles Wilson	1990-95	22.26
127	Bruce Harper	1977-84	22.25
128	Rod Woodson	1987-98	22.25
129	Dave Meggett	1989-98	22.09
130	James Owens	1979-84	22.06
131	Margene Adkins	1970-73	22.02
132	Alvin Hall	1981-85, 87	22.02
133	Qadry Ismail	1993-98	22.02
134	Al Hunter	1977-80	22.01
135	Jermaine Lewis	1996-98	21.97
136	Mike Martin	1983-89	21.91
137	Bill Butler	1959-64	21.86
138	Carl Monroe	1983-87	21.84
139	Jimmy Rogers	1980-84	21.79
140	Carl Roaches	1980-85	21.77
141	Darryl Clack	1986-89	21.71
142	Dexter Carter	1990-96	21.65
143	Mike Fuller	1975-82	21.53
144	Eric Ball	1989-95	21.51
145	Albert Bentley	1985-92	21.42
146	Don Beebe	1989-97	21.42
147	Raghib Ismail	1993-98	21.41
148	Ken Bell	1986-89	21.33
149	Alexander Wright	1990-96	21.28
150	Keith Moody	1976-80	21.27
151	Michael Morton	1982-85, 87	21.22
152	Del Rodgers	1982, 84, 87-88	21.16
153	Lionel James	1984-88	21.15
154	Herman Hunter	1985-87	21.12
155	Phil Freeman	1985-87	21.10
156	Jamie Holland	1987-92	21.10
157	Lorenzo Hampton	1985-89	21.09
158	Dino Hall	1979-83	21.09
159	Bobby Joe Edmonds	1986-89, 95	21.08
160	Johnny Bailey	1990-95	21.04
161	George Taliaferro	1950-55	21.00
162	Vai Sikahema	1986-93	20.99
163	James Brooks	1981-92	20.92
164	Jo-Jo Townsell	1985-90	20.90
165	Desmond Howard	1992-98	20.88
166	Eric Metcalf	1989-98	20.85
167	Clarence Verdin	1986-94	20.80
168	Stephen Starring	1983-88	20.77
169	Chris Warren	1990-98	20.70
170	Hopalong Cassady	1956-63	20.70
171	Zachary Dixon	1979-84	20.58
172	Troy Brown	1993-98	20.57
173	Marc Logan	1987-97	20.56
174	Willie Drewrey	1985-93	20.56
175	Cleo Montgomery	1980-85	20.50
176	Gerald McNeil	1986-90	20.35
177	Donnie Elder	1985-86, 88-91	20.27
178	Dwight Stone	1987-98	20.17
179	Drew Hill	1979-82, 84-93	20.12
180	Chuck Levy	1994, 97-98	20.11
181	Leon Bright	1981-85	20.05
182	Stanford Jennings	1984-92	20.03
183	Art Whittington	1978-82	19.91
184	Willard Harrell	1975-84	19.80
185	Randall Morris	1984-88	19.79
186	Allen Pinkett	1986-91	19.71
187	Robert Lavette	1985-87	19.61
188	Vernon Turner	1990-95	19.60
189	Gary Anderson	1985-88, 90-93	19.43
190	Jeff Smith	1985-88	19.16
191	Kelvin Martin	1987-96	19.12
192	Thomas Sanders	1985-91	18.81
193	Erric Pegram	1991-97	18.70
194	Walter Stanley	1985-90, 92	18.63
195	Ronnie Harmon	1986-97	18.62
196	Robbie Martin	1981-86	18.61
197	Terance Mathis	1990-98	18.50

KICKOFF RETURN TOUCHDOWNS

	Player	Year	TDs
1	Mel Gray	1986-97	6
	Ollie Matson	1952, 54-66	6
	Gale Sayers	1965-71	6
	Travis Williams	1967-71	6
5	Timmy Brown	1959-68	5
	Bobby Mitchell	1958-68	5
	Abe Woodson	1958-66	5
8	Ron Brown	1984-91	4
	Andre Coleman	1994-98	4
	Cecil Turner	1968-73	4
	Tamarick Vanover	1995-98	4
	Jon Vaughn	1991-94	4
13	Cullen Bryant	1973-84, 87	3
	Lynn Chandnois	1950-56	3
	Raymond Clayborn	1977-91	3
	Dennis Gentry	1982-92	3
	Dave Hampton	1969-76	3
	Tyrone Hughes	1993-98	3
	Lenny Lyles	1958-69	3
	Mercury Morris	1969-76	3
	Deion Sanders	1989-98	3
	Ron Smith	1965-74	3
	Vitamin Smith	1949-53	3
	Steve Van Buren	1944-51	3
	Charley Warner	1963-66	3
	Dave Williams	1977-81	3
	Derrick Witherspoon	1995-97	3

Career Scoring and Placekicking

POINTS

	Player	Year	Pts.
1	George Blanda	1949-58, 60-75	2002
2	Gary Anderson	1982-98	1845
3	Morten Andersen	1982-98	1761
4	Nick Lowery	1978, 80-96	1711
5	Jan Stenerud	1967-85	1699
6	Norm Johnson	1982-98	1657
7	Eddie Murray	1980-95, 97	1532
8	Pat Leahy	1974-91	1470
9	Jim Turner	1964-79	1439
10	Matt Bahr	1979-95	1422
11	Mark Moseley	1970-72, 74-86	1382
12	Jim Bakken	1962-78	1380
13	Fred Cox	1963-77	1365
14	Al Del Greco	1984-98	1360
15	Lou Groza	1950-59, 61-67	1349
16	Jim Breech	1979-92	1246
17	Chris Bahr	1976-89	1213
18	Kevin Butler	1985-97	1208
19	Gino Cappelletti	1960-70	1130
20	Ray Wersching	1973-87	1122
21	Pete Stoyanovich	1989-98	1087
22	Don Cockroft	1968-80	1080
23	Garo Yepremian	1966-67, 70-81	1074
24	Jerry Rice	1985-98	1058
25	Bruce Gossett	1964-74	1031
26	Jeff Jaeger	1987, 89-98	995
27	Sam Baker	1953, 56-69	977
28	Greg Davis	1987-98	962
29	Rafael Septien	1977-86	960
30	Steve Christie	1990-98	957
31	Lou Michaels	1958-69, 71	955
32	Fuad Reveiz	1985-88, 90-95	931
33	Chip Lohmiller	1988-96	913
34	Roy Gerela	1969-79	903
35	John Carney	1988-98	892
36	Bobby Walston	1951-62	881
37	Tony Zendejas	1985-95	874
38	Marcus Allen	1982-97	872
	Tony Franklin	1979-88	872
40	Pete Gogolak	1964-74	863
41	Chris Jacke	1989-98	861
42	Errol Mann	1968-78	846
43	Dean Biasucci	1984, 86-95	823
	Don Hutson	1935-45	823
45	Emmitt Smith	1990-98	806
46	Rich Karlis	1982-90	799
47	Mike Lansford	1982-90	789
48	John Kasay	1991-98	774
49	Matt Stover	1991-98	768
50	Rolf Benirschke	1977-86	766
51	Paul Hornung	1957-62, 64-66	760
52	Toni Fritsch	1971-73, 75-82	758
53	Jim Brown	1957-65	756
	Bob Thomas	1975-86	756
55	Jason Hanson	1992-98	751
56	Walter Payton	1975-87	750
57	Tommy Davis	1959-69	738
58	Jason Elam	1993-98	730
59	Tom Dempsey	1969-79	729
60	Mike Clark	1963-71, 73	724
61	Horst Muhlmann	1969-77	707
62	Mike Cofer	1987-93, 95	702
63	John Riggins	1971-79, 81-85	696
64	John Smith	1974-83	692
65	Lenny Moore	1956-67	678
66	Scott Norwood	1985-91	670
67	Barry Sanders	1989-98	654

68	Gordie Soltau	1950-58	644
69	Joe Danelo	1975-84	639
70	Gene Mingo	1960-67, 69-70	629
71	Cris Carter	1987-98	622
72	Steve Largent	1976-89	608
73	Efren Herrera	1974, 76-82	604
74	Franco Harris	1972-84	600
75	Raul Allegre	1983-91	594
	Mike Mercer	1961-70	594
77	David Treadwell	1989-94	587
78	Doug Pelfrey	1993-98	579
79	Eric Dickerson	1983-93	576
	Neil O'Donoghue	1977-85	576
81	Bob Waterfield	1945-52	573
82	Nick Mike-Mayer	1973-82	571
83	Roger Ruzek	1987-93	566
84	Pat Summerall	1952-61	563
85	Mick Luckhurst	1981-87	558
	Jim Taylor	1958-67	558
87	Tony Dorsett	1977-88	546
	Bobby Mitchell	1958-68	546
89	Cary Blanchard	1992-93, 95-98	544
90	Leroy Kelly	1964-73	540
	Charley Taylor	1964-75, 77	540
	Uwe von Schamann	1979-84	540
93	Doak Walker	1950-55	534
94	Don Maynard	1958, 60-73	532
95	Pat Harder	1946-53	531
96	Don Chandler	1956-67	530
97	Ben Agajanian	1945, 49, 53-57, 60-62, 64	525
	Chester Marcol	1972-80	525
99	Lance Alworth	1962-72	524
100	Paul McFadden	1984-89	520
101	Chris Boniol	1994-98	517
102	Ottis Anderson	1979-92	516
	Andre Reed	1985-98	516
	Thurman Thomas	1988-98	516
	Paul Warfield	1964-74, 76-77	516
106	Mark Clayton	1983-93	510
	Tommy McDonald	1957-68	510

POINT AFTER TOUCHDOWN ATTEMPTS

	Player	Year	Atts.
1	George Blanda	1949-58, 60-75	958
2	Lou Groza	1950-59, 61-67	657
3	Norm Johnson	1982-98	620
4	Jan Stenerud	1967-85	601
5	Gary Anderson	1982-98	590
6	Pat Leahy	1974-91	584
7	Nick Lowery	1978, 80-96	568
8	Morten Andersen	1982-98	566
9	Jim Bakken	1962-78	553
10	Jim Turner	1964-79	543
11	Jim Breech	1979-92	539
	Fred Cox	1963-77	539
13	Matt Bahr	1979-95	534
14	Eddie Murray	1980-95, 97	527
15	Chris Bahr	1976-89	519
16	Mark Moseley	1970-72, 74-86	512
17	Ray Wersching	1973-87	477
18	Al Del Greco	1984-98	470
19	Garo Yepremian	1966-67, 70-81	464
20	Don Cockroft	1968-80	457
21	Sam Baker	1953, 56-69	444
22	Rafael Septien	1977-86	433
23	Kevin Butler	1985-97	426
24	Lou Michaels	1958-69, 71	401
25	Bobby Walston	1951-62	384
26	Bruce Gossett	1964-74	383
27	Fuad Reveiz	1985-88, 90-95	378
28	Roy Gerela	1969-79	365
29	Tony Franklin	1979-88	355
30	Pete Gogolak	1964-74	354
	Pete Stoyanovich	1989-98	354
32	Gino Cappelletti	1960-70	353
33	Rolf Benirschke	1977-86	352
34	Tommy Davis	1959-69	350
35	Mike Clark	1963-71, 73	338
36	Bob Waterfield	1945-52	336
37	Errol Mann	1968-78	333
38	Bob Thomas	1975-86	330
39	Tony Zendejas	1985-95	327
40	Mike Lansford	1982-90	325
41	John Smith	1974-83	323
42	Jeff Jaeger	1987, 89-98	320
43	Chris Jacke	1989-98	317
44	Mike Cofer	1987-93, 95	312
45	Chip Lohmiller	1988-96	309
46	Gordie Soltau	1950-58	303
47	Toni Fritsch	1971-73, 75-82	300
48	Steve Christie	1990-98	298
49	Greg Davis	1987-98	296
50	Mike Mercer	1961-70	295
51	Rich Karlis	1982-90	294

POINTS AFTER TOUCHDOWN

	Player	Year	Pts.
1	George Blanda	1949-58, 60-75	942
2	Lou Groza	1950-59, 61-67	641
3	Norm Johnson	1982-98	613
4	Gary Anderson	1982-98	585
5	Jan Stenerud	1967-85	580
6	Nick Lowery	1978, 80-96	562
7	Morten Andersen	1982-98	558
	Pat Leahy	1974-91	558
9	Jim Bakken	1962-78	534
10	Matt Bahr	1979-95	522
11	Eddie Murray	1980-95, 97	521
	Jim Turner	1964-79	521
13	Fred Cox	1963-77	519
14	Jim Breech	1979-92	517
15	Chris Bahr	1976-89	490
16	Mark Moseley	1970-72, 74-86	482
17	Al Del Greco	1984-98	463
18	Ray Wersching	1973-87	456
19	Garo Yepremian	1966-67, 70-81	444
20	Don Cockroft	1968-80	432
21	Sam Baker	1953, 56-69	428
22	Rafael Septien	1977-86	420
23	Kevin Butler	1985-97	413
24	Lou Michaels	1958-69, 71	385
25	Bruce Gossett	1964-74	374
26	Fuad Reveiz	1985-88, 90-95	367
27	Bobby Walston	1951-62	365
28	Roy Gerela	1969-79	351
29	Pete Stoyanovich	1989-98	349
30	Tommy Davis	1959-69	348
31	Pete Gogolak	1964-74	344
32	Gino Cappelletti	1960-70	342
33	Tony Franklin	1979-88	341
34	Rolf Benirschke	1977-86	328
35	Mike Clark	1963-71, 73	325
36	Tony Zendejas	1985-95	316
37	Mike Lansford	1982-90	315
	Errol Mann	1968-78	315
	Bob Waterfield	1945-52	315
40	Jeff Jaeger	1987, 89-98	314
41	Chris Jacke	1989-98	312
42	John Smith	1974-83	308
43	Mike Cofer	1987-93, 95	303
	Bob Thomas	1975-86	303
45	Chip Lohmiller	1988-96	301
46	Steve Christie	1990-98	294
47	Greg Davis	1987-98	290
48	Mike Mercer	1961-70	288
49	Toni Fritsch	1971-73, 75-82	287
50	Gordie Soltau	1950-58	284
51	Rich Karlis	1982-90	283

FIELD GOALS

	Player	Year	FGs
1	Gary Anderson	1982-98	420
2	Morten Andersen	1982-98	401
3	Nick Lowery	1978, 80-96	383
4	Jan Stenerud	1967-85	373
5	Norm Johnson	1982-98	348
6	Eddie Murray	1980-95, 97	337
7	George Blanda	1949-58, 60-75	335
8	Pat Leahy	1974-91	304
	Jim Turner	1964-79	304
10	Matt Bahr	1979-95	300
	Mark Moseley	1970-72, 74-86	300
12	Al Del Greco	1984-98	299
13	Jim Bakken	1962-78	282
	Fred Cox	1963-77	282
15	Kevin Butler	1985-97	265
16	Pete Stoyanovich	1989-98	246
17	Jim Breech	1979-92	243
18	Chris Bahr	1976-89	241
19	Lou Groza	1950-59, 61-67	234
20	Jeff Jaeger	1987, 89-98	227
21	Greg Davis	1987-98	224
22	Ray Wersching	1973-87	222
23	Steve Christie	1990-98	221
24	Bruce Gossett	1964-74	219
25	Don Cockroft	1968-80	216
26	John Carney	1988-98	214
27	Garo Yepremian	1966-67, 70-81	210
28	Chip Lohmiller	1988-96	204
29	Fuad Reveiz	1985-88, 90-95	188
30	Lou Michaels	1958-69, 71	187
31	John Kasay	1991-98	186
	Tony Zendejas	1985-95	186
33	Dean Biasucci	1984, 86-95	185
34	Roy Gerela	1969-79	184
35	Chris Jacke	1989-98	183
36	Rafael Septien	1977-86	180
37	Sam Baker	1953, 56-69	179
38	Tony Franklin	1979-88	177
	Errol Mann	1968-78	177
40	Gino Cappelletti	1960-70	176
41	Matt Stover	1991-98	174
42	Pete Gogolak	1964-74	173
43	Rich Karlis	1982-90	172
44	Jason Hanson	1992-98	168
45	Tom Dempsey	1969-79	159
46	Mike Lansford	1982-90	158
47	Jason Elam	1993-98	157
	Toni Fritsch	1971-73, 75-82	157
49	Horst Muhlmann	1969-77	154
50	Bob Thomas	1975-86	151
51	Rolf Benirschke	1977-86	146
52	Raul Allegre	1983-91	137
53	Doug Pelfrey	1993-98	135
	David Treadwell	1989-94	135
55	Mike Clark	1963-71, 73	133
	Mike Cofer	1987-93, 95	133
	Joe Danelo	1975-84	133
	Scott Norwood	1985-91	133
59	Cary Blanchard	1992-93, 95-98	131
60	Tommy Davis	1959-69	130
61	John Smith	1974-83	128

FIELD GOAL ATTEMPTS

	Player	Year	Atts.
1	George Blanda	1949-58, 60-75	637
2	Jan Stenerud	1967-85	558
3	Gary Anderson	1982-98	525
4	Morten Andersen	1982-98	510
5	Jim Turner	1964-79	489
6	Nick Lowery	1978, 80-96	479
7	Mark Moseley	1970-72, 74-86	457
8	Fred Cox	1963-77	455
9	Norm Johnson	1982-98	452
10	Jim Bakken	1962-78	447
11	Eddie Murray	1980-95, 97	445
12	Pat Leahy	1974-91	426
13	Matt Bahr	1979-95	415
14	Lou Groza	1950-59, 61-67	405
15	Al Del Greco	1984-98	391
16	Chris Bahr	1976-89	381
17	Kevin Butler	1985-97	361
18	Bruce Gossett	1964-74	360
19	Lou Michaels	1958-69, 71	341
20	Jim Breech	1979-92	340
21	Gino Cappelletti	1960-70	334
22	Ray Wersching	1973-87	329
23	Don Cockroft	1968-80	328
24	Greg Davis	1987-98	325
25	Sam Baker	1953, 56-69	316
26	Garo Yepremian	1966-67, 70-81	313
27	Roy Gerela	1969-79	306
28	Pete Stoyanovich	1989-98	305
29	Jeff Jaeger	1987, 89-98	301
30	Pete Gogolak	1964-74	294
31	Chip Lohmiller	1988-96	284
32	Steve Christie	1990-98	277
33	Tommy Davis	1959-69	276
	Errol Mann	1968-78	276
35	John Carney	1988-98	264
	Tony Franklin	1979-88	264
37	Dean Biasucci	1984, 86-95	262
38	Tom Dempsey	1969-79	258
39	Rafael Septien	1977-86	256
40	Tony Zendejas	1985-95	252
41	Fuad Reveiz	1985-88, 90-95	250
42	Rich Karlis	1982-90	239
	Horst Muhlmann	1969-77	239

	Player	Year	FGs
	Bob Thomas	1975-86	239
45	Chris Jacke	1989-98	238
46	John Kasay	1991-98	235
47	Mike Clark	1963-71, 73	232
48	Toni Fritsch	1971-73, 75-82	231
49	Joe Danelo	1975-84	228
50	Matt Stover	1991-98	221
51	Gene Mingo	1960-67, 69-70	219
52	Mike Lansford	1982-90	217
53	Pat Summerall	1952-61	212
54	Jason Hanson	1992-98	209
55	Rolf Benirschke	1977-86	208
56	Nick Mike-Mayer	1973-82	204
57	Mike Cofer	1987-93, 95	201
	Jason Elam	1993-98	201
59	Chester Marcol	1972-80	196
60	Mike Mercer	1961-70	193
61	Jim Martin	1950-61, 63-64	192
62	John Smith	1974-83	191
63	Mac Percival	1967-74	190
64	Neil O'Donoghue	1977-85	189
65	Raul Allegre	1983-91	186
66	Scott Norwood	1985-91	184
67	David Ray	1969-74	178
68	Curt Knight	1969-73	175
	David Treadwell	1989-94	175
70	Efren Herrera	1974, 76-82	171
	Doug Pelfrey	1993-98	171
72	Cary Blanchard	1992-93, 95-98	170

FIELD GOAL PERCENTAGE
(minimum 100 Field Goals Attempted)

	Player	Year	FGs	Atts.	Pct.
1	Mike Hollis	1995-98	102	125	81.60
2	John Carney	1988-98	214	264	81.06
3	Chris Boniol	1994-98	117	145	80.69
4	Pete Stoyanovich	1989-98	246	305	80.66
5	Adam Vinatieri	1996-98	83	103	80.58
6	Jason Hanson	1992-98	168	209	80.38
7	Gary Anderson	1982-98	420	525	80.00
8	Nick Lowery	1978, 80-96	383	479	79.96
9	Steve Christie	1990-98	221	277	79.78
10	Doug Brien	1994-98	98	123	79.67
11	Todd Peterson	1994-98	94	118	79.66
12	John Kasay	1991-98	186	235	79.15
13	Jeff Wilkins	1994-98	87	110	79.09
14	Doug Pelfrey	1993-98	135	171	78.95
15	Matt Stover	1991-98	174	221	78.73
16	Morten Andersen	1982-98	401	510	78.63
17	Jason Elam	1993-98	157	201	78.11
18	David Treadwell	1989-94	135	175	77.14
19	Cary Blanchard	1992-93, 95-98	131	170	77.06
20	Norm Johnson	1982-98	348	452	76.99
21	Chris Jacke	1989-98	183	238	76.89
22	Brad Daluiso	1991-98	101	132	76.52
23	Al Del Greco	1984-98	299	391	76.47
24	Eddie Murray	1980-95, 97	337	445	75.73
25	Donald Igwebuike	1985-90	108	143	75.52
26	Jeff Jaeger	1987, 89-98	227	301	75.42
27	Fuad Reveiz	1985-88, 90-95	188	250	75.20
28	Tony Zendejas	1985-95	186	252	73.81
29	Raul Allegre	1983-91	137	186	73.66
30	Paul McFadden	1984-89	120	163	73.62
31	Kevin Butler	1985-97	265	361	73.41
32	Michael Husted	1993-98	117	160	73.13
33	Mike Lansford	1982-90	158	217	72.81
34	Matt Bahr	1979-95	300	415	72.29
	Roger Ruzek	1987-93	120	166	72.29
36	Scott Norwood	1985-91	133	184	72.28
37	Rich Karlis	1982-90	172	239	71.97
38	Chip Lohmiller	1988-96	204	284	71.83
39	Jim Breech	1979-92	243	340	71.47
40	Pat Leahy	1974-91	304	426	71.36
41	Dean Biasucci	1984, 86-95	185	262	70.61
42	Rafael Septien	1977-86	180	256	70.31
43	Rolf Benirschke	1977-86	146	208	70.19
44	Mick Luckhurst	1981-87	115	164	70.12
45	Greg Davis	1987-98	224	325	68.92
46	Ali Haji-Sheikh	1983-87	76	111	68.47
47	Toni Fritsch	1971-73, 75-82	157	231	67.97
48	Efren Herrera	1974, 76-82	116	171	67.84
49	Uwe von Schamann	1979-84	101	149	67.79
50	Ray Wersching	1973-87	222	329	67.48
51	Garo Yepremian	1966-67, 70-81	210	313	67.09
52	Tony Franklin	1979-88	177	264	67.05
53	John Smith	1974-83	128	191	67.02
54	Jan Stenerud	1967-85	373	558	66.85
55	Mike Cofer	1987-93, 95	133	201	66.17
56	Rick Danmeier	1977-82	70	106	66.04
57	Don Cockroft	1968-80	216	328	65.85
58	Mark Moseley	1970-72, 74-86	300	457	65.65
59	Benny Ricardo	1976, 78-81, 83-84	92	142	64.79
60	Horst Muhlmann	1969-77	154	239	64.44
61	Errol Mann	1968-78	177	276	64.13
62	Chris Bahr	1976-89	241	381	63.25
63	Bob Thomas	1975-86	151	239	63.18
64	Jim Bakken	1962-78	282	447	63.09
65	Jim Turner	1964-79	304	489	62.17
66	Fred Cox	1963-77	282	455	61.98
67	David Ray	1969-74	110	178	61.80
68	Chester Marcol	1972-80	121	196	61.73
69	Tom Dempsey	1969-79	159	258	61.63
70	Bruce Gossett	1964-74	219	360	60.83
71	Frank Corral	1978-81	75	124	60.48
72	John Leypoldt	1971-78	93	154	60.39
73	Roy Gerela	1969-79	184	306	60.13
74	Neil O'Donoghue	1977-85	112	189	59.26
75	Toni Linhart	1972, 74-79	75	127	59.06
76	Bobby Howfield	1968-74	98	166	59.04
77	Pete Gogolak	1964-74	173	294	58.84
78	Dennis Partee	1968-75	71	121	58.68
79	Don Chandler	1956-67	94	161	58.39
80	Joe Danelo	1975-84	133	228	58.33
81	Fred Cone	1951-57, 60	59	102	57.84
82	Lou Groza	1950-59, 61-67	234	405	57.78
83	Curt Knight	1969-73	101	175	57.71
84	Mike Clark	1963-71, 73	133	232	57.33
85	Sam Baker	1953, 56-69	179	316	56.65
86	Nick Mike-Mayer	1973-82	115	204	56.37
87	Skip Butler	1971-77	71	127	55.91
88	Jim O'Brien	1970-73	60	108	55.56
89	Fred Steinfort	1976-81, 83	63	114	55.26
90	Lou Michaels	1958-69, 71	187	341	54.84
91	Bob Waterfield	1945-52	60	110	54.55
92	Mac Percival	1967-74	101	190	53.16
93	Danny Villanueva	1960-67	85	160	53.13
94	Mike Mercer	1961-70	102	193	52.85
95	Gino Cappelletti	1960-70	176	334	52.69
96	George Blanda	1949-58, 60-75	335	637	52.59
97	Charlie Durkee	1967-68, 71-72	52	101	51.49
98	Steve Mike-Mayer	1975-80	67	131	51.15
99	Gene Mingo	1960-67, 69-70	112	219	51.14
100	Bobby Walston	1951-62	80	157	50.96
101	Ben Agajanian	1945, 49, 53-57, 60-62, 64	84	165	50.91
102	Gordie Soltau	1950-58	70	139	50.36
103	Roger LeClerc	1960-67	76	152	50.00
104	Jim Martin	1950-61, 63-64	92	192	47.92
105	Pat Summerall	1952-61	100	212	47.17
106	Paul Hornung	1957-62, 64-66	66	140	47.14
107	Tommy Davis	1959-69	130	276	47.10
108	Wayne Walker	1958-72	53	131	40.46

The All-Time Leaders: Season

MOST RUSHING ATTEMPTS

	Player	Year	Atts.
1	Jamal Anderson, Atl	1998	410
2	James Wilder, TB	1984	407
3	Eric Dickerson, LARm	1986	404
4	Gerald Riggs, Atl	1985	397
5	Terrell Davis, Den	1998	392
6	Eric Dickerson, LARm	1983	390
	Barry Foster, Pit	1992	390
8	Eric Dickerson, Ind	1988	388
9	Walter Payton, ChiB	1984	381
10	Marcus Allen, LARd	1985	380
11	Eric Dickerson, LARm	1984	379
12	George Rogers, NO	1981	378
13	Emmitt Smith, Dal	1995	377
14	John Riggins, Was	1983	375
	Jerome Bettis, Pit	1997	375
16	Earl Campbell, Hou	1980	373
	Emmitt Smith, Dal	1992	373
18	Christian Okoye, KC	1989	370
19	Walter Payton, ChiB	1979	369
	Terrell Davis, Den	1997	369
	Curtis Martin, NYJ	1998	369
22	Earl Campbell, Hou	1979	368
	Emmitt Smith, Dal	1994	368
	Curtis Martin, NE	1995	368
25	James Wilder, TB	1985	365
	Emmitt Smith, Dal	1991	365

MOST RUSHING YARDS

	Player	Year	Yds.
1	Eric Dickerson, LARm	1984	2105
2	Barry Sanders, Det	1997	2053
3	Terrell Davis, Den	1998	2008
4	O.J. Simpson, Buf	1973	2003
5	Earl Campbell, Hou	1980	1934
6	Barry Sanders, Det	1994	1883
7	Jim Brown, Cle	1963	1863
8	Walter Payton, ChiB	1977	1852
9	Jamal Anderson, Atl	1998	1846
10	Eric Dickerson, LARm	1986	1821
11	O.J. Simpson, Buf	1975	1817
12	Eric Dickerson, LARm	1983	1808
13	Emmitt Smith, Dal	1995	1773
14	Marcus Allen, LARd	1985	1759
15	Terrell Davis, Den	1997	1750
16	Gerald Riggs, Atl	1985	1719
17	Emmitt Smith, Dal	1992	1713
18	Earl Campbell, Hou	1979	1697
19	Barry Foster, Pit	1992	1690
20	Walter Payton, ChiB	1984	1684
21	George Rogers, NO	1981	1674
22	Jerome Bettis, Pit	1997	1665
23	Eric Dickerson, Ind	1988	1659
24	Tony Dorsett, Dal	1981	1646
25	Walter Payton, ChiB	1979	1610

HIGHEST RUSHING AVERAGE
(100 or more attempts)

	Player	Year	Att.	Avg.
1	Beattie Feathers, ChiB	1934	119	8.44
2	Randall Cunningham, Phi	1990	118	7.98
3	Bobby Douglass, ChiB	1972	141	6.87
4	Dan Towler, LARm	1951	126	6.78
5	Steve McNair, Ten	1997	101	6.67
6	Keith Lincoln, SD	1963	128	6.45
7	Mercury Morris, Mia	1973	149	6.40
8	Jim Brown, Cle	1963	291	6.40
9	Paul Lowe, LAC	1960	136	6.29
10	Dutch Clark, Det	1934	123	6.20
11	Gale Sayers, ChiB	1968	138	6.20
12	Barry Sanders, Det	1997	335	6.13
13	Joe Perry, SF	1958	125	6.06
14	Joe Perry, SF	1954	173	6.06
15	O.J. Simpson, Buf	1973	332	6.03
16	Hokie Gajan, NO	1984	102	6.03
17	Ted McKnight, KC	1978	104	6.03
18	Randall Cunningham, Phi	1989	104	5.97
19	Jim Brown, Cle	1958	257	5.94
20	John David Crow, StL	1960	183	5.85
21	Jim Brown, Cle	1960	215	5.85
22	Napoleon Kaufman, Oak	1996	150	5.83
23	Steve Van Buren, Phi	1945	143	5.82
24	Marion Motley, Cle	1950	140	5.79
25	Dan Towler, LARm	1953	152	5.78
26	Bill Osmanski, ChiB	1939	121	5.78

MOST RUSHING TOUCHDOWNS

	Player	Year	TDs
1	Emmitt Smith, Dal	1995	25
2	John Riggins, Was	1983	24
3	Joe Morris, NYG	1985	21
	Emmitt Smith, Dal	1994	21
	Terry Allen, Was	1996	21
	Terrell Davis, Den	1998	21
7	Jim Taylor, GB	1962	19
	Earl Campbell, Hou	1979	19
	Chuck Muncie, SD	1981	19
10	Eric Dickerson, LARm	1983	18
	George Rogers, Was	1986	18
	Emmitt Smith, Dal	1992	18
13	Jim Brown, Cle	1958	17
	Jim Brown, Cle	1965	17
15	Lenny Moore, Bal	1964	16
	Leroy Kelly, Cle	1968	16
	Pete Banaszak, Oak	1975	16
	O.J. Simpson, Buf	1975	16
	Greg Bell, LARm	1988	16
	Barry Sanders, Det	1991	16
21	Steve Van Buren, Phi	1945	15
	Jim Taylor, GB	1961	15
	Leroy Kelly, Cle	1966	15
	Ickey Woods, Cin	1988	15
	Greg Bell, LARm	1989	15
	Chris Warren, Sea	1995	15
	Karim Abdul-Jabbar, Mia	1997	15
	Terrell Davis, Den	1997	15

MOST PASS COMPLETIONS

	Player	Year	Comps.
1	Warren Moon, Hou	1991	404
2	Drew Bledsoe, NE	1994	400
3	Dan Marino, Mia	1994	385
4	Dan Marino, Mia	1986	378
5	Warren Moon, Min	1995	377
6	Drew Bledsoe, NE	1996	373
7	Warren Moon, Min	1994	371
8	Brett Favre, GB	1994	363
9	Dan Marino, Mia	1984	362
	Warren Moon, Hou	1990	362
11	Dan Fouts, SD	1981	360
12	Brett Favre, GB	1995	359
13	Dan Marino, Mia	1988	354
14	Don Majkowski, GB	1989	353
	Mark Brunell, Jac	1996	353
16	Dan Fouts, SD	1980	348
	John Elway, Den	1993	348
18	Steve DeBerg, SF	1979	347
	Brett Favre, GB	1998	347
20	Bill Kenney, KC	1983	346
	Jim Everett, NO	1994	346
	Scott Mitchell, Det	1995	346
23	Fran Tarkenton, Min	1978	345
	Neil Lomax, StL	1984	345
	Jim Everett, NO	1995	345

HIGHEST COMPLETION PERCENTAGE
(150 or more attempts)

	Player	Year	Att.	Pct.
1	Ken Anderson, Cin	1982	309	70.6
2	Sammy Baugh, Was	1945	182	70.3
3	Steve Young, SF	1994	461	70.3
4	Joe Montana, SF	1989	386	70.2
5	Elvis Grbac, SF	1995	183	69.4
6	Troy Aikman, Dal	1993	392	69.1
7	Wade Wilson, Atl	1992	163	68.1
8	Steve Young, SF	1993	462	68.0
9	Steve Young, SF	1996	316	67.7
10	Steve Young, SF	1997	356	67.7
11	Steve Bartkowski, Atl	1984	269	67.3
12	Steve Young, SF	1995	447	66.9
13	Joe Montana, SF	1987	398	66.8
14	Steve Young, SF	1992	402	66.7
	Ken Stabler, Oak	1976	291	66.7
	Ken Anderson, Cin	1983	297	66.7
17	Bernie Kosar, Cle	1992	155	66.5
18	Mark Herrmann, SD	1985	201	65.7
19	Cody Carlson, Hou	1992	227	65.6
20	Dave Krieg, Sea	1991	285	65.6
21	Troy Aikman, Dal	1991	363	65.3
22	Ken Anderson, Cin	1974	328	64.9
23	Troy Aikman, Dal	1995	432	64.8
24	Warren Moon, Hou	1992	346	64.7
25	Otto Graham, Cle	1953	258	64.7

MOST YARDS GAINED PASSING

	Player	Year	Yds.
1	Dan Marino, Mia	1984	5084
2	Dan Fouts, SD	1981	4802
3	Dan Marino, Mia	1986	4746
4	Dan Fouts, SD	1980	4715
5	Warren Moon, Hou	1991	4690
6	Warren Moon, Hou	1990	4689
7	Neil Lomax, StL	1984	4614
8	Drew Bledsoe, NE	1994	4555
9	Lynn Dickey, GB	1983	4458
10	Dan Marino, Mia	1994	4453
11	Dan Marino, Mia	1988	4434
12	Brett Favre, GB	1995	4413
13	Mark Brunell, Jac	1996	4367
14	Bill Kenney, KC	1983	4348
15	Scott Mitchell, Det	1995	4338
16	Don Majkowski, GB	1989	4318
17	Jim Everett, LARm	1989	4310
18	Warren Moon, Min	1994	4264
19	Warren Moon, Min	1995	4228
20	Brett Favre, GB	1998	4212
21	Vinny Testaverde, Bal	1996	4177
22	Steve Young, SF	1998	4170
23	Jeff George, Atl	1995	4143
24	Dan Marino, Mia	1985	4137
25	Brian Sipe, Cle	1980	4132

HIGHEST AVERAGE YARDS PER ATTEMPT
(100 or more attempts)

	Player	Year	Att.	YPA
1	Tommy O'Connell, Cle	1957	110	11.17
2	Sid Luckman, ChiB	1943	202	10.86
3	Otto Graham, Cle	1953	258	10.55
4	Norm Van Brocklin, LARm	1954	260	10.14
5	Bill Nelsen, Pit	1966	112	10.02
6	Sid Luckman, ChiB	1941	119	9.92
	Ed Brown, ChiB	1956	168	9.92
8	Sid Luckman, ChiB	1942	105	9.75
9	Chris Chandler, Atl	1998	327	9.65
10	Steve Grogan, NE	1986	102	9.57
11	Jacky Lee, Hou	1961	127	9.49
12	Bart Starr, GB	1968	171	9.46
13	Len Dawson, KC	1968	224	9.42
14	Eddie LeBaron, Was	1958	145	9.41
	Greg Cook, Cin	1969	197	9.41
	Bob Waterfield, Cle	1945	171	9.41
	Ken Stabler, Oak	1976	291	9.41
18	Bob Berry, Atl	1968	153	9.37
19	Otto Graham, Cle	1955	185	9.30
20	Johnny Unitas, Bal	1964	305	9.26
21	James Harris, LARm	1976	158	9.24
22	Lynn Dickey, GB	1983	484	9.21
	Boomer Esiason, Cin	1988	388	9.21
24	George Blanda, Hou	1961	362	9.20
25	Milt Plum, Cle	1960	250	9.19

MOST TOUCHDOWN PASSES

	Player	Year	TDs
1	Dan Marino, Mia	1984	48
2	Dan Marino, Mia	1986	44
3	Brett Favre, GB	1996	39
4	Brett Favre, GB	1995	38
5	George Blanda, Hou	1961	36
	Y.A. Tittle, NYG	1963	36
	Steve Young, SF	1998	36
8	Steve Young, SF	1994	35
	Brett Favre, GB	1997	35
10	Daryle Lamonica, Oak	1969	34
	Randall Cunningham, Min	1998	34
12	Y.A. Tittle, NYG	1962	33
	Dan Fouts, SD	1981	33
	Warren Moon, Hou	1990	33
	Jim Kelly, Buf	1991	33
	Brett Favre, GB	1994	33
	Warren Moon, Min	1995	33
	Vinny Testaverde, Bal	1996	33
19	Johnny Unitas, Bal	1959	32
	Sonny Jurgensen, Phi	1961	32
	Lynn Dickey, GB	1983	32
	Dave Krieg, Sea	1984	32
	Scott Mitchell, Det	1995	32
24	Babe Parilli, Bos	1964	31
	Sonny Jurgensen, Was	1967	31
	Steve Bartkowski, Atl	1980	31
	Joe Montana, SF	1987	31
	Jim Everett, LARm	1988	31
	Brett Favre, GB	1998	31

MOST PASS RECEPTIONS

	Player	Year	Rec.
1	Herman Moore, Det	1995	123
2	Cris Carter, Min	1994	122
	Cris Carter, Min	1995	122
	Jerry Rice, SF	1995	122
5	Isaac Bruce, StL	1995	119
6	Sterling Sharpe, GB	1993	112
	Jerry Rice, SF	1994	112
8	Terance Mathis, Atl	1994	111
	Michael Irvin, Dal	1995	111
10	Sterling Sharpe, GB	1992	108
	Brett Perriman, Det	1995	108
	Jerry Rice, SF	1996	108
13	Art Monk, Was	1984	106
	Herman Moore, Det	1996	106
15	Eric Metcalf, Atl	1995	104
	Tim Brown, Oak	1997	104
	Herman Moore, Det	1997	104
18	Robert Brooks, GB	1995	102
19	Charley Hennigan, Hou	1964	101
	Larry Centers, Ariz	1995	101
21	Lionel Taylor, Den	1961	100
	Jerry Rice, SF	1990	100
	Haywood Jeffires, Hou	1991	100
	Carl Pickens, Cin	1996	100
25	Carl Pickens, Cin	1995	99
	Larry Centers, Ariz	1996	99

MOST YARDS RECEIVING

	Player	Year	Yds.
1	Jerry Rice, SF	1995	1848
2	Isaac Bruce, StL	1995	1781
3	Charley Hennigan, Hou	1961	1746
4	Herman Moore, Det	1995	1686
5	Michael Irvin, Dal	1995	1603
6	Lance Alworth, SD	1965	1602
7	Rob Moore, Ariz	1997	1584
8	Jerry Rice, SF	1986	1570
9	Roy Green, StL	1984	1555
10	Charley Hennigan, Hou	1964	1546
11	Michael Irvin, Dal	1991	1523
12	Jerry Rice, SF	1993	1503

13 Jerry Rice, SF	1990	1502
14 Jerry Rice, SF	1994	1499
15 Robert Brooks, GB	1995	1497
16 Crazy Legs Hirsch, LARm	1951	1495
17 Stanley Morgan, NE	1986	1491
18 Brett Perriman, Det	1995	1488
19 Jerry Rice, SF	1989	1483
20 Bill Groman, Hou	1960	1473
21 Sterling Sharpe, GB	1992	1461
22 Bobby Mitchell, Was	1963	1436
23 Don Maynard, NYJ	1967	1434
24 Antonio Freeman, GB	1998	1424
25 Sterling Sharpe, GB	1989	1423

HIGHEST AVERAGE GAIN PER RECEPTION
(20 or more receptions)

Player	Year	Rec.	Avg.
1 Don Currivan, Bos	1947	24	32.6
2 Bucky Pope, LARm	1964	25	31.4
3 Bobby Duckworth, SD	1984	25	28.6
4 Ray Renfro, Cle	1957	21	28.0
5 Jimmy Orr, Pit	1958	33	27.6
6 Jessie Hester, LARd	1986	23	27.5
7 Homer Jones, NYG	1965	26	27.3
8 Elbert Dubenion, Buf	1964	42	27.1
9 Frank Liebel, NYG	1945	22	27.0
10 Warren Wells, Oak	1969	47	26.8
11 Earl McCullouch, Det	1971	21	26.3
12 Jack Snow, LARm	1967	28	26.3
13 Art Graham, Bos	1963	21	26.2
14 Bob Hayes, Dal	1970	34	26.1
15 Ron Sellers, Bos	1969	27	26.1
16 Flipper Anderson, LARm	1989	44	26.0
17 Mervyn Fernandez, LARd	1988	31	26.0
18 Roger Carr, Bal	1976	43	25.9
19 Theo Bell, Pit	1980	29	25.8
20 Jimmy Orr, Bal	1968	29	25.6
21 Ken Kavanaugh, ChiB	1947	32	25.6
22 Paul Warfield, Mia	1970	28	25.1
23 Harlon Hill, ChiB	1954	45	25.0
24 Don Hutson, GB	1939	34	24.9
25 Alvin Harper, Dal	1994	33	24.9

MOST TOUCHDOWN RECEPTIONS

Player	Year	Rec.
1 Jerry Rice, SF	1987	22
2 Mark Clayton, Mia	1984	18
Sterling Sharpe, GB	1994	18
4 Don Hutson, GB	1942	17
Crazylegs Hirsch, LARm	1951	17
Bill Groman, Hou	1961	17
Jerry Rice, SF	1989	17
Cris Carter, Min	1995	17
Carl Pickens, Cin	1995	17
Randy Moss, Min	1998	17
11 Art Powell, Oak	1963	16
12 Cloyce Box, Det	1952	15
Sonny Randle, StL	1960	15
Jerry Rice, SF	1986	15
Jerry Rice, SF	1993	15
Andre Rison, Atl	1993	15
Jerry Rice, SF	1995	15
18 Mal Kutner, ChiC	1948	14
Raymond Berry, Bal	1959	14
Art Powell, NYT	1960	14
Frank Clarke, Dal	1962	14
Lance Alworth, SD	1965	14
Don Maynard, NYJ	1965	14
Warren Wells, Oak	1969	14
Roy Green, StL	1983	14
Mark Clayton, Mia	1988	14
Jerry Rice, SF	1991	14
Anthony Miller, Den	1995	14
Herman Moore, Det	1995	14
Michael Jackson, Bal	1996	14
Tony Martin, SD	1996	14
Antonio Freeman, GB	1998	14
Terrell Owens, SF	1998	14

MOST POINTS

Player	Year	Avg.
1 Paul Hornung, GB	1960	176
2 Gary Anderson, Min	1998	164
3 Mark Moseley, Was	1983	161
4 Gino Cappelletti, Bos	1964	155
5 Emmitt Smith, Dal	1995	150
6 Chip Lohmiller, Was	1991	149
7 Gino Cappelletti, Bos	1961	147
8 Paul Hornung, GB	1961	146
9 Jim Turner, NYJ	1968	145
John Kasay, Car	1996	145
11 John Riggins, Was	1983	144
Kevin Butler, ChiB	1985	144
13 Norm Johnson, Pit	1995	141
14 Tony Franklin, NE	1986	140
Steve Christie, Buf	1998	140
16 Gary Anderson, Pit	1985	139
Nick Lowery, KC	1990	139
18 Don Hutson, GB	1942	138
O.J. Simpson, Buf	1975	138
Jerry Rice, SF	1987	138
Terrell Davis, Den	1998	138
22 Gene Mingo, Den	1962	137
23 Mike Cofer, SF	1989	136
Al Del Greco, Ten	1998	136
25 John Carney, SD	1994	135
Cary Blanchard, Ind	1996	135

MOST FIELD GOALS

Player	Year	FGs
1 John Kasay, Car	1996	37
2 Cary Blanchard, Ind	1996	36
Al Del Greco, Ten	1998	36
4 Ali Haji-Sheikh, NYG	1983	35
Jeff Jaeger, LARd	1993	35
Gary Anderson, Min	1998	35
7 Jim Turner, NYJ	1968	34
Nick Lowery, KC	1990	34
Jason Hanson, Det	1993	34
John Carney, SD	1994	34
Fuad Reveiz, Min	1994	34
Norm Johnson, Pit	1995	34
Richie Cunningham, Dal	1997	34
14 Chester Marcol, GB	1972	33
Mark Moseley, Was	1983	33
Gary Anderson, Pit	1985	33
Steve Christie, Buf	1998	33
18 Jim Turner, NYJ	1969	32
Tony Franklin, NE	1986	32
Scott Norwood, Buf	1988	32
Chris Boniol, Dal	1996	32
Al Del Greco, Hou	1996	32
Cary Blanchard, Ind	1997	32
24 Morten Andersen, NO	1985	31
Kevin Butler, ChiB	1985	31
Rich Karlis, Min	1989	31
Chip Lohmiller, Was	1991	31
Pete Stoyanovich, Mia	1991	31
John Carney, SD	1993	31
Chris Jacke, GB	1993	31
Morten Andersen, Atl	1995	31
Steve Christie, Buf	1995	31
Jason Elam, Den	1995	31
Mike Hollis, Jac	1997	31
Adam Vinatieri, NE	1998	31

MOST INTERCEPTIONS

Player	Year	Int.
1 Night Train Lane, LARm	1952	14
2 Dan Sandifer, Was	1948	13
Spec Sanders, NYY	1950	13
Lester Hayes, Oak	1980	13
5 Bob Nussbaumer, ChiC	1949	12
Don Doll, Det	1950	12
Woodley Lewis, LARm	1950	12
Jack Christiansen, Det	1953	12
Fred Glick, Hou	1963	12
Paul Krause, Was	1964	12
Dainard Paulson, NYJ	1964	12
Emmitt Thomas, KC	1974	12
Mike Reinfeldt, Hou	1979	12
14 Sammy Baugh, Was	1943	11
Don Doll, Det	1949	11
Otto Schnellbacher, NYG	1951	11
Tom Keane, Bal	1953	11
Will Sherman, LARm	1955	11
Lindon Crow, ChiC	1956	11
Jimmy Patton, NYG	1958	11
Goose Gonsoulin, Den	1960	11
Lee Riley, NYT	1962	11
Ron Hall, Bos	1964	11
Bill Bradley, Phi	1971	11
Mel Blount, Pit	1975	11
Everson Walls, Dal	1981	11

HIGHEST PUNTING AVERAGE
(30 or more Punts)

Player	Year	Punts	Avg.
1 Sammy Baugh, Was	1940	35	51.4
2 Yale Lary, Det	1963	35	48.9
3 Sammy Baugh, Was	1941	30	48.7
4 Yale Lary, Det	1961	52	48.4
5 Sammy Baugh, Was	1942	37	48.2
6 Joe Muha, Phi	1948	57	47.3
7 Craig Hentrich, Ten	1998	69	47.2
8 Yale Lary, Det	1959	45	47.1
9 Bobby Joe Green, Pit	1961	73	47.0
10 Greg Montgomery, Hou	1992	53	46.9
11 Tom Rouen, Den	1998	66	46.9
12 Pat Brady, Pit	1953	80	46.9
13 Gary Collins, Cle	1965	65	46.7
14 Don Chandler, NYG	1959	55	46.6
15 Bobby Joe Green, ChiB	1963	64	46.5
16 Bobby Walden, Min	1964	72	46.4
17 John Kidd, Mia	1996	78	46.3
18 Yale Lary, Det	1964	67	46.3
19 Dave Lewis, Cin	1970	79	46.2
20 Rohn Stark, Ind	1985	78	45.9
21 Sammy Baugh, Was	1943	50	45.9
22 Mark Royals, NO	1997	88	45.9
23 Tommy Davis, SF	1965	54	45.8
24 Tom Tupa, NE	1997	78	45.8
25 Horace Gillom, Cle	1952	61	45.7

The Head Coaches Register

Bob Carroll, Pete Fierle, and David Neft

The Head Coaches Register is the product of many years of research at the Pro Football Hall of Fame. Using a variety of sources, researchers at the Hall assembled the basic list on a number of file cards. As new information came to light, the cards were updated. A continuing problem for researchers is that, in the early years of the NFL, many teams used co-head coaches. Since it's impossible to say which of two individuals were responsible for games won or lost in a given year under the two-coach system, those years are marked with a single asterisk (*), and the co-coaches are named.

Men who coached AAFC teams as well as NFL teams are in the main register, although their AAFC records are not counted as NFL marks. A second register provides the records of those men who were head coaches in the AAFC only.

Prior to 1972, tie games were discounted when figuring winning percentage. Since then, ties have counted as half a win and half a loss. In all cases, ties count as half a win and half a loss in a coach's career totals.

For this edition, the editors have added demographic information (birth date, college) for every NFL coach. Three asterisks (***) next to a coach's name indicate that his demographic information can be found in the Player Register. A number sign (#) signifies that the coach won a championship, and a caret (^) indicates additional information. P stands for postseason record.

	W	L	T	Pct.	Place	P
FAYE ABBOTT* **						
1928 Day	0	7	0	.000	10 NFL	—
1929 Day	0	6	0	.000	12 NFL	—
	0	13	0	.000		—

FRANKIE ALBERT***

	W	L	T	Pct.	Place	P
1956 SF	5	6	1	.455	3 NFL-W	—
1957 SF	8	4	0	.667	2 NFL-W	0-1
1958 SF	6	6	0	.500	4 NFL-W	—
	19	16	1	.542		0-1

DOC ALEXANDER***

	W	L	T	Pct.	Place	P
1922 Roch	0	4	1	.000	16 NFL	—
1926 NYG	8	4	1	.667	7 NFL	—
	8	8	2	.500		—

GEORGE ALLEN Allen, George Herbert
Col: Alma; Marquette; Michigan B: 4/29/1922, Grosse Point Woods, MI D: 12/31/1990, Rancho Palos Verdes, CA

	W	L	T	Pct.	Place	P
1966 LARm	8	6	0	.571	3 NFL-W	—
1967 LARm	11	1	2	.917	1 NFL-Coa	0-1
1968 LARm	10	3	1	.769	2 NFL-Coa	—
1969 LARm	11	3	0	.786	1 NFL-Coa	0-1
1970 LARm	9	4	1	.692	2 NFC-W	—
1971 Was	9	4	1	.692	2 NFC-E	0-1
1972 Was#	11	3	0	.786	1 NFC-E	2-1
1973 Was	10	4	0	.714	2 NFC-E	0-1
1974 Was	10	4	0	.714	2 NFC-E	0-1
1975 Was	8	6	0	.571	3 NFC-E	—
1976 Was	10	4	0	.714	2 NFC-E	0-1
1977 Was	9	5	0	.643	2 NFC-E	—
	116	47	5	.705		2-7

\# NFC Champion

HUNK ANDERSON***

	W	L	T	Pct.	Place	P
1942 ChiB*	6	0	0	1.000	1 NFL-W	0-1
1943 ChiB*#	8	1	1	.889	1 NFL-W	1-0
1944 ChiB*	6	3	1	.667	2 NFL-W	—
1945 ChiB*	3	7	0	.300	4 NFL-W	—
	23	11	2	.667		1-1

* co-coach with Luke Johnsos
\# NFL Champion

ROY ANDREWS***

	W	L	T	Pct.	Place	P
1924 KC	2	7	0	.222	15 NFL	—
1925 KC	2	5	1	.286	13 NFL	—
1926 KC	8	3	0	.727	4 NFL	—
1927 Cle	8	4	1	.667	4 NFL	—
1928 Det	7	2	1	.778	3 NFL	—
1929 NYG	13	1	1	.929	2 NFL	—
1930 NYG	11	4	0	.733	2 NFL	—
1931 ChiC	0	2	0	.000	4 NFL	—
	51	28	4	.639		—

JOHN ARMSTRONG***

	W	L	T	Pct.	Place	P
1924 RI	5	2	2	.714	5 NFL	—

NEILL ARMSTRONG***

	W	L	T	Pct.	Place	P
1978 ChiB	7	9	0	.438	4 NFC-C	—
1979 ChiB	10	6	0	.625	2 NFC-C	0-1
1980 ChiB	7	9	0	.438	3 NFC-C	—
1981 ChiB	6	10	0	.375	5 NFC-C	—
	30	34	0	.469		0-1

BILL ARNSPARGER Arnsparger, William Stephen
Col: Miami (OH) B: 12/16/1926, Paris, KY

	W	L	T	Pct.	Place	P
1974 NYG	2	12	0	.143	5 NFC-E	—
1975 NYG	5	9	0	.357	4 NFC-E	—
1976 NYG	0	7	0	.000	5 NFC-E	—
	7	28	0	.200		—

BILL AUSTIN***

	W	L	T	Pct.	Place	P
1966 Pit	5	8	1	.385	6 NFL-E	—
1967 Pit	4	9	1	.308	4 NFL-Cny	—
1968 Pit	2	11	1	.154	4 NFL-Cny	—
1970 Was	6	8	0	.429	4 NFC-E	—
	17	36	3	.330		—

JOE BACH Bach, Joseph Anthony
Col: Carleton; Notre Dame B: 1/17/1901, Tower, MN D: 10/24/1966, Pittsburgh, PA

	W	L	T	Pct.	Place	P
1935 Pit	4	8	0	.333	3 NFL-E	—
1936 Pit	6	6	0	.500	2 NFL-E	—
1952 Pit	5	7	0	.417	4 NFL-A	—
1953 Pit	6	6	0	.500	4 NFL-E	—
	21	27	0	.438		—

HERMAN BALL Ball, Herman
Col: Davis & Elkins B: 5/9/1910, Kingsville, WV D: 1/12/1998, Paoli, PA

	W	L	T	Pct.	Place	P
1949 Was	1	4	0	.200	4 NFL-E	—
1950 Was	3	9	0	.250	6 NFL-A	—
1951 Was	0	3	0	.000	3 NFL-A	—
	4	16	0	.200		—

SHORTY BARR***

	W	L	T	Pct.	Place	P
1926 Rac	1	2	0	.333	18 NFL	—

NORM BARRY***

	W	L	T	Pct.	Place	P
1925 ChiC#	11	2	1	.846	1 NFL	—
1926 ChiC	5	6	1	.455	10 NFL	—
	16	8	2	.654		—

NFL Champion

DIM BATTERSON Batterson, George W.
B: 10/—/1882, NY Deceased

	W	L	T	Pct.	Place	P
1927 Buf	0	5	0	.000	12 NFL	—

SAMMY BAUGH***

	W	L	T	Pct.	Place	P
1960 NYT	7	7	0	.500	2 AFL-E	—
1961 NYT	7	7	0	.500	3 AFL-E	—
1964 Hou	4	10	0	.286	4 AFL-E	—
	18	24	0	.429		—

BULL BEHMAN***

	W	L	T	Pct.	Place	P
1929 Fra	10	4	5	.714	3 NFL	—
1930 Fra	21	0	1	.167	9 NFL	—
1931 Fra	1	6	1	.143	10 NFL	—
	13	20	7	.413		—

BILL BELICHICK Belichick, William
Col: Wesleyan B: 4/16/1952, Nashville, TN

	W	L	T	Pct.	Place	P
1991 Cle	61	0	0	.375	3 AFC-C	—
1992 Cle	7	9	0	.438	3 AFC-C	—
1993 Cle	7	9	0	.438	3 AFC-C	—
1994 Cle	11	5	0	.688	2 AFC-C	1-1
1995 Cle	5	11	0	.438	4 AFC-C	—
	36	44	0	.450		1-1

BERT BELL Bell, De Benneville
Col: Pennsylvania B: 2/25/1895, Philadelphia, PA
D: 10/11/1959, Philadelphia, PA

	W	L	T	Pct.	Place	P
1936 Phi	1	11	0	.083	5 NFL-E	—
1937 Phi	2	8	1	.200	5 NFL-E	—
1938 Phi	5	6	0	.455	4 NFL-E	—
1939 Phi	1	9	1	.100	4 NFL-E	—
1940 Phi	1	10	0	.091	5 NFL-E	—
1941 Pit	0	2	0	.000	5 NFL-E	—
	10	46	2	.190		—

PHIL BENGTSON Bengtson, John Phillip
Col: Minnesota B: 7/17/1913, Rosseau, MN D: 12/18/1994, San Diego, CA

	W	L	T	Pct.	Place	P
1968 GB	6	7	1	.462	3 NFL-C	—
1969 GB	8	6	0	.571	3 NFL-C	—
1970 GB	6	8	0	.429	4 NFC-C	—
1972 NE	1	4	0	.200	5 AFC-E	—
	21	25	1	.457		—

LEEMAN BENNETT Bennett, Leeman
Col: Kentucky B: 6/20/1938, Paducah, KY

	W	L	T	Pct.	Place	P
1977 Atl	7	7	0	.500	2 NFC-W	—
1978 Atl	9	7	0	.563	2 NFC-W	1-1
1979 Atl	6	10	0	.375	3 NFC-W	—
1980 Atl	12	4	0	.750	1 NFC-W	0-1
1981 Atl	7	9	0	.438	2 NFC-W	—
1982 Atl	5	4	0	.556	5 NFC	0-1
1985 TB	2	14	0	.125	5 NFC-C	—
1986 TB	2	14	0	.125	5 NFC-C	—
	50	69	0	.420		1-3

DUTCH BERGMAN Bergman, Arthur J.
Col: Notre Dame; Detroit B: 2/23/1895, Peru, IN D: 8/18/1972, Washington, DC

	W	L	T	Pct.	Place	P
1943 Was	6	3	1	.667	1 NFL-E	1-1

RAYMOND BERRY***

	W	L	T	Pct.	Place	P
1984 NE	4	4	0	.500	2 AFC-E	—
1985 NE#	11	5	0	.688	3 AFC-E	3-1
1986 NE	11	5	0	.688	1 AFC-E	0-1
1987 NE	8	7	0	.533	2 AFC-E	—
1988 NE	9	7	0	.563	3 AFC-E	—
1989 NE	5	11	0	.313	4 AFC-E	—
	48	39	0	.552		3-2

AFC Champion

PUNK BERRYMAN Berryman, Robert Norman
Col: Penn State B: 12/13/1893 D: 5/20/1988, Philadelphia, PA

	W	L	T	Pct.	Place	P
1924 Fra	11	2	1	.846	3 NFL	—
1926 Bkn*	3	8	0	.273	14 NFL	—
	14	10	1	.580		—

* Combined with AFL Horsemen for final three games (0-3)

TOM BETTIS***

	W	L	T	Pct.	Place	P
1977 KC	1	6	0	.143	5 AFC-W	—

HUGO BEZDEK Bezdek, Hugo Francis
Col: Chicago B: 3/1/1883, Prague, Czech Republic
D: 9/19/1952, Ventor City, NJ

	W	L	T	Pct.	Place	P
1937 Cle	1	10	0	.091	5 NFL-W	—
1938 Cle	0	3	0	.000	4 NFL-W	—
	1	13	0	.071		—

SCOTTY BIERCE***

	W	L	T	Pct.	Place	P
1925 Akr	4	2	2	.667	5 NFL	—

ED BILES Biles, Edward G.
Col: Miami (OH) B: 10/18/1931, Cincinnati, OH

	W	L	T	Pct.	Place	P
1981 Hou	7	9	0	.438	3 AFC-C	—
1982 Hou	1	8	0	.111	13 AFC	—
1983 Hou	0	6	0	.000	4 AFC-C	—
	8	23	0	.258		—

LISLE BLACKBOURN Blackbourn, Lisle William
Col: Lawrence B: 6/3/1899, Beetown, WI D: 6/14/1983 Lancaster, WI

	W	L	T	Pct.	Place	P
1954 GB	4	8	0	.333	5 NFL-W	—
1955 GB	6	6	0	.500	3 NFL-W	—
1956 GB	4	8	0	.333	5 NFL-W	—
1957 GB	3	9	0	.250	6 NFL-W	—
	17	31	0	.354		—

JOE BRANDY Brandy, Joseph Ralph Jr.
Col: Notre Dame B: 11/6/1897, Ogdensburg, NY D: 7/-/1971, Ogdensburg, NY

	W	L	T	Pct.	Place	P
1924 Min	0	6	0	.000	17 NFL	—

WAYNE BRENKERT***

	W	L	T	Pct.	Place	P
1923 Akr	1	1	0	.500	17 NFL	—
1924 Akr	2	6	0	.250	13 NFL	—
	3	7	0	.300		—

UNTZ BREWER***

	W	L	T	Pct.	Place	P
1922 Akr	3	5	2	.375	10 NFL	—

CHARLIE BRICKLEY Brickley, Charles Edward
Col: Harvard B: 11/6/1897, Boston, MA D: 12/28/1949, New York, NY

	W	L	T	Pct.	Place	P
1921 NYG	0	2	0	.000	21 NFL	—

FRANK BRIDGES Bridges, Frank D.
Col: Harvard B: 7/4/1890, Savannah, GA D: 6/10/1970, San Antonio, TX

	W	L	T	Pct.	Place	P
1944 Bkn*	0	5	0	.000	5 NFL-E	—

* co-coach with Ed Kubale

MARTY BRILL Brill, Martin
Col: Pennsylvania; Notre Dame B: 3/13/1906, Philadelphia, PA D: 4/30/1973, Whittier, CA

	W	L	T	Pct.	Place	P
1931 SI	3	3	1	.500	7 NFL	—

RICH BROOKS Brooks, Richard L.
Col: Oregon State B: 8/10/1941, Forest, CA

	W	L	T	Pct.	Place	P
1995 StL	7	9	0	.438	3 NFC-W	—
1996 StL	6	10	0	.375	3 NFC-W	—
	13	19	0	.406		—

PAUL BROWN Brown, Paul Eugene
Col: Ohio State; Miami (OH) B: 9/7/1908, Norwalk, OH D: 8/5/1991, Cincinnati, OH

	W	L	T	Pct.	Place	P
AAFC						
1946 CleA#	12	2	0	.857	1 AAFC-W	1-0
1947 CleA#	12	1	1	.923	1 AAFC-W	1-0
1948 CleA#	14	0	0	1.000	1 AAFC-W	1-0
1949 CleA#	9	1	2	.900	1 AAFC-W	2-0
	47	4	3	.898		5-0
NFL						
1950 Cle#	10	2	0	.833	1 NFL-A	2-0
1951 Cle	11	1	0	.917	1 NFL-A	0-1
1952 Cle	8	4	0	.667	1 NFL-A	0-1
1953 Cle	11	1	0	.917	1 NFL-E	0-1
1954 Cle#	9	3	0	.750	1 NFL-E	1-0
1955 Cle#	9	2	1	.818	1 NFL-E	1-0
1956 Cle	5	7	0	.417	4 NFL-E	—
1957 Cle	9	2	1	.818	1 NFL-E	0-1
1958 Cle	9	3	0	.750	2 NFL-E	0-1
1959 Cle	7	5	0	.583	2 NFL-E	—
1960 Cle	8	3	1	.727	2 NFL-E	—
1961 Cle	8	5	1	.615	3 NFL-E	—
1962 Cle	7	6	1	.538	3 NFL-E	—
1968 Cin	3	11	0	.214	5 AFL-W	—
1969 Cin	4	9	1	.308	5 AFL-W	—
1970 Cin	8	6	0	.571	1 AFC-C	0-1
1971 Cin	4	10	0	.286	4 AFC-C	—
1972 Cin	8	6	0	.571	3 AFC-C	—
1973 Cin	10	4	0	.714	1 AFC-C	0-1
1974 Cin	7	7	0	.500	2 AFC-C	—
1975 Cin	11	3	0	.786	2 AFC-C	0-1
	166	100	6	.621		4-8

\# league champion

FRED BRUNEY***

	W	L	T	Pct.	Place	P
1985 Phi	1	0	0	1.000	4 NFC-E	—

JOHNNY BRYAN***

	W	L	T	Pct.	Place	P
1925 Mil	0	6	0	.000	18 NFL	—
1926 Mil	2	7	0	.222	15 NFL	—
	2	13	0	.133		—

JOE BUGEL Bugel, Joseph John
Col: Western Kentucky B: 3/10/1940, Pittsburgh, PA

	W	L	T	Pct.	Place	P
1990 Pho	5	11	0	.313	5 NFC-E	—
1991 Pho	4	12	0	.250	5 NFC-E	—
1992 Pho	4	12	0	.250	5 NFC-E	—
1993 Pho	7	9	0	.438	4 NFC-E	—
1997 Oak	4	12	0	.333	4 AFC-W	—
	24	56	0	.300		—

HANK BULLOUGH***

	W	L	T	Pct.	Place	P
1978 NE*	0	1	0	.000	1 AFC-E	0-1
1985 Buf	2	10	0	.167	5 AFC-E	—
1986 Buf	2	7	0	.222	4 AFC-E	—
	4	18	0	.182		0-1

* co-coach with Ron Erhardt

JERRY BURNS Burns, Jerome Monahan
Col: Michigan B: 1/24/1927, Detroit, MI

	W	L	T	Pct.	Place	P
1986 Min	9	7	0	.563	2 NFC-C	—
1987 Min	8	7	0	.533	2 NFC-C	2-1
1988 Min	11	5	0	.688	2 NFC-C	1-1
1989 Min	10	6	0	.625	1 NFC-C	0-1
1990 Min	6	10	0	.375	5 NFC-C	—
1991 Min	8	8	0	.500	3 NFC-C	—
	52	43	0	.547		3-3

HUGH CAMPBELL Campbell, Hugh Thomas
Col: Washington State B: 5/21/1941, San Jose, CA

	W	L	T	Pct.	Place	P
1984 Hou	3	13	0	.188	4 AFC-C	—
1985 Hou	5	9	0	.357	4 AFC-C	—
	8	22	0	.267		—

MARION CAMPBELL***

	W	L	T	Pct.	Place	P
1974 Atl	1	5	0	.167	4 NFC-W	—
1975 Atl	4	10	0	.286	3 NFC-W	—
1976 Atl	1	4	0	.200	3 NFC-W	—
1983 Phi	5	11	0	.313	4 NFC-E	—
1984 Phi	6	9	1	.406	5 NFC-E	—
1985 Phi	6	9	0	.400	4 NFC-E	—
1987 Atl	3	12	0	.200	4 NFC-W	—
1988 Atl	5	11	0	.313	4 NFC-W	—
1989 Atl	3	9	0	.250	4 NFC-W	—
	34	80	1	.300		—

DOM CAPERS Capers, Dominic
Col: Mount Union B: 8/5/1950, Cambridge, OH

	W	L	T	Pct.	Place	P
1995 Car	7	9	0	.438	4 NFC-W	—
1996 Car	12	4	0	.750	1 NFC-W	1-1
1997 Car	7	9	0	.438	2 NFC-W	—
1998 Car	4	12	0	.250	4 NFC-W	—
	30	34	0	.469		1-1

PETE CARROLL Carroll, Peter C.
Col: U. of Pacific B: 9/15/1951, San Francisco, CA

	W	L	T	Pct.	Place	P
1994 NYJ	6	10	0	.375	5 AFC-E	—
1997 NE	10	6	0	.625	1 AFC-E	1-1
1998 NE	9	7	0	.563	4 AFC-E	0-1
	25	23	0	.521		1-2

BUD CARSON Carson, Leon H. *Col:* North Carolina Coll. B: 4/28/1931, Brackenridge, PA

	W	L	T	Pct.	Place	P
1989 Cle	9	6	1	.594	1 AFC-C	1-1
1990 Cle	2	7	0	.222	4 AFC-C	—
	11	13	1	.460		1-1

EDDIE CASEY***

	W	L	T	Pct.	Place	P
1935 Bos	2	8	1	.200	4 NFL-E	—

PETE CAWTHON Cawthon, Peter Willis
Col: Southwestern (TX) B: 3/24/1898, Houston, TX

	W	L	T	Pct.	Place	P
1943 Bkn	2	8	0	.200	4 NFL-E	—
1944 Bkn	0	5	0	.000	5 NFL-E	—
	2	13	0	.133		—

GUY CHAMBERLIN***

	W	L	T	Pct.	Place	P
1922 Can#	10	0	2	1.000	1 NFL	—
1923 Can#	11	0	1	1.000	1 NFL	—
1924 Cle#	7	1	1	.875	1 NFL	—
1925 Fra	13	7	0	.650	6 NFL	—
1926 Fra#	14	1	2	.933	1 NFL	—
1927 ChiC	3	7	1	.300	9 NFL	—
	58	16	7	.759		—

\# NFL Champion

COONIE CHECKAYE***

	W	L	T	Pct.	Place	P
1921 Mun	0	2	0	.000	19 NFL	—

JACK CHEVIGNY Chevigny, John Edward
Col: Notre Dame B: 8/14/1906, Hammond, IN D: 2/19/1945, Iwo Jima

	W	L	T	Pct.	Place	P
1932 ChiC	2	6	2	.250	4 NFL	—

JACK CHRISTIANSEN***

	W	L	T	Pct.	Place	P
1963 SF	2	9	0	.182	7 NFL-W	—
1964 SF	4	10	0	.286	7 NFL-W	—
1965 SF	7	6	1	.538	4 NFL-W	—
1966 SF	6	6	2	.500	4 NFL-W	—
1967 SF	7	7	0	.500	3 NFL-Coa	—
5 yrs	26	38	3	.410		—

ALGY CLARK***

	W	L	T	Pct.	Place	P
1934 Cin	0	8	0	.000	6 NFL-W	—

DUTCH CLARK***

	W	L	T	Pct.	Place	P
1937 Det	7	4	0	.636	3 NFL-W	—
1938 Det	7	4	0	.636	2 NFL-W	—
1939 Cle	5	5	1	.500	4 NFL-W	—
1940 Cle	4	6	1	.400	4 NFL-W	—
1941 Cle	2	9	0	.182	5 NFL-W	—
1942 Cle	5	6	0	.455	3 NFL-W	—
	30	34	2	.470		—

MONTE CLARK***

	W	L	T	Pct.	Place	P
1976 SF	8	6	0	.571	2 NFC-W	—
1978 Det	7	9	0	.438	3 NFC-C	—
1979 Det	2	14	0	.125	5 NFC-C	—
1980 Det	9	7	0	.563	2 NFC-C	—
1981 Det	8	8	0	.500	2 NFC-C	—
1982 Det	4	5	0	.444	8 NFC	0-1
1983 Det	9	7	0	.563	1 NFC-C	0-1
1984 Det	4	11	1	.281	4 NFC-C	—
	51	67	1	.433		0-2

POTSY CLARK Clark, George (Little Colonel)
Col: William & Vashti; Illinois B: 3/20/1894, Carthage, IL
D: 11/8/1972, La Jolla, CA

	W	L	T	Pct.	Place	P
1931 Port	11	3	0	.786	2 NFL	—
1932 Port	6	2	4	.750	3 NFL	—
1933 Port	6	5	0	.545	2 NFL-W	—
1934 Det	10	3	0	.769	2 NFL-W	—
1935 Det#	7	3	2	.700	1 NFL-W	1-0
1936 Det	8	4	0	.667	3 NFL-W	—
1937 Bkn	3	7	1	.300	4 NFL-E	—
1938 Bkn	4	4	3	.500	3 NFL-E	—
1939 Bkn	4	6	1	.400	3 NFL-E	—
1940 Det	5	5	1	.500	3 NFL-W	—
	64	42	12	.593		1-0

NFL Champion

STAN COFALL***

	W	L	T	Pct.	Place	P
1920 Cle	0	2	1	.000	10 NFL	—

BLANTON COLLIER Collier, Blanton Long
Col: Georgetown (KY) B: 7/2/1906, Millersburg, KY
D: 3/22/1983, Houston, TX

	W	L	T	Pct.	Place	P
1963 Cle	10	4	0	.714	2 NFL-E	—
1964 Cle#	10	3	1	.769	1 NFL-E	1-0
1965 Cle	11	3	0	.786	1 NFL-E	0-1
1966 Cle	9	5	0	.643	2 NFL-E	—
1967 Cle	9	5	0	.643	1 NFL-Cty	0-1
1968 Cle	10	4	0	.714	1 NFL-Cty	1-1
1969 Cle	10	3	1	.769	1 NFL-Cty	1-1
1970 Cle	7	7	0	.500	2 AFC-C	—
	76	34	2	.688		3-4

NFL Champion

JOE COLLIER Collier, Joel Dale
Col: Northwestern B: 6/7/1932, Rock Island, IL

	W	L	T	Pct.	Place	P
1966 Buf	9	4	1	.692	1 AFL-E	0-1
1967 Buf	4	10	0	.286	3 AFL-E	—
1968 Buf	0	2	0	.000	5 AFL-E	—
	13	16	1	.450		0-1

RED CONKRIGHT***

	W	L	T	Pct.	Place	P
1962 Oak	1	8	0	.111	4 AFL-W	—

JIMMY CONZELMAN***

	W	L	T	Pct.	Place	P
1921 RI	4	1	0	.800	5 NFL	—
1922 RI	4	2	1	.667	5 NFL	—
1922 Mil	0	3	0	.000	11 NFL	—
1923 Mil	7	2	3	.778	4 NFL	—
1925 Det	8	2	2	.800	3 NFL	—
1926 Det	4	6	2	.400	12 NFL	—
1927 Prov	8	5	1	.615	5 NFL	—
1928 Prov#	8	1	2	.889	1 NFL	—
1929 Prov	4	6	2	.400	7 NFL	—
1930 Prov	6	4	1	.600	5 NFL	—
1940 ChiC	2	7	2	.222	5 NFL-W	—
1941 ChiC	3	7	1	.300	4 NFL-W	—
1942 ChiC	3	8	0	.273	4 NFL-W	—
1946 ChiC	6	5	0	.545	4 NFL-W	—
1947 ChiC#	9	3	0	.750	1 NFL-W	1-0
1948 ChiC	11	1	0	.917	1 NFL-W	0-1
	87	63	17	.572		1-1

NFL Champion

AL CORNSWEET***

	W	L	T	Pct.	Place	P
1931 Cle*	2	8	0	.200	8 NFL	—

* co-coach with Hoge Workman

DON CORYELL Coryell, Donald David
Col: Washington B: 10/17/1924, Seattle, WA

	W	L	T	Pct.	Place	P
1973 StL	4	9	1	.321	4 NFC-E	—
1974 StL	10	4	0	.714	1 NFC-E	0-1
1975 StL	11	3	0	.786	1 NFC-E	0-1
1976 StL	10	4	0	.714	3 NFC-E	—
1977 StL	7	7	0	.500	3 NFC-E	—
1978 SD	8	4	0	.667	4 AFC-W	—
1979 SD	12	4	0	.750	1 AFC-W	0-1
1980 SD	11	5	0	.688	1 AFC-W	1-1
1981 SD	10	6	0	.625	1 AFC-W	1-1
1982 SD	6	3	0	.667	5 AFC	1-1
1983 SD	6	10	0	.375	4 AFC-W	—
1984 SD	7	9	0	.438	5 AFC-W	—
1985 SD	8	8	0	.500	4 AFC-W	—
1986 SD	1	7	0	.125	5 AFC-W	—
	111	83	1	.572		3-6

BRUCE COSLET***

	W	L	T	Pct.	Place	P
1990 NYJ	6	10	0	.375	4 AFC-E	—
1991 NYJ	8	8	0	.500	2 AFC-E	0-1
1992 NYJ	4	12	0	.250	4 AFC-E	—
1993 NYJ	8	8	0	.500	3 AFC-E	—
1996 Cin	7	2	0	.778	3 AFC-C	—
1997 Cin	7	9	0	.438	4 AFC-C	—
1998 Cin	3	13	0	.188	5 AFC-C	—
	43	62	0	.410		0-1

FRANK COUGHLIN***

	W	L	T	Pct.	Place	P
1921 RI	0	1	1	.000	5 NFL	—

TOM COUGHLIN Coughlin, Thomas Richard
Col: Syracuse B: 8/31/1946, Waterloo, NY

	W	L	T	Pct.	Place	P
1995 Jac	4	12	0	.250	5 AFC-C	—
1996 Jac	9	7	0	.563	2 AFC-C	2-1
1997 Jac	11	5	0	.688	2 AFC-C	0-1
1998 Jac	11	5	0	.688	1 AFC-C	1-1
	35	29	0	.547		3-3

BILL COWHER***

	W	L	T	Pct.	Place	P
1992 Pit	11	5	0	.688	1 AFC-C	0-1
1993 Pit	9	7	0	.563	2 AFC-C	0-1
1994 Pit	12	4	0	.750	1 AFC-C	1-1
1995 Pit#	11	5	0	.688	1 AFC-C	2-1
1996 Pit	10	6	0	.625	1 AFC-C	1-1
1997 Pit	11	5	0	.688	1 AFC-C	1-1
1998 Pit	7	9	0	.438	3 AFC-C	—
	71	41	0	.634		5-6

AFC Champion

MILAN CREIGHTON***

	W	L	T	Pct.	Place	P
1935 ChiC	6	4	2	.600	4 NFL-W	—
1936 ChiC	3	8	1	.273	4 NFL-W	—
1937 ChiC	5	5	1	.500	4 NFL-W	—
1938 ChiC	2	9	0	.182	5 NFL-W	—
	16	26	4	.391		—

CLEM CROWE Crowe, Clem Frederick
Col: Notre Dame B: 10/18/1903, Lafayette, IN D: 4/13/1983, Rochester, NY

	W	L	T	Pct.	Place	P
AAFC						
1949 BufA	4	1	1	.800		0-1
NFL						

	W	L	T	Pct.	Place	P
1950 Balt	1	11	0	.083	7 NFL-N	—

RUSS DAUGHERITY***

	W	L	T	Pct.	Place	P
1927 Fra*	4	4	2	.500	7 NFL	—

* co-coach with Charley Rogers, Ed Weir, and Swede Youngstrom

AL DAVIS Davis, Allen
Col: Wittenberg; Syracuse B: 7/4/1929, Brockton, MA

	W	L	T	Pct.	Place	P
1963 Oak	10	4	0	.714	2 AFL-W	—
1964 Oak	5	7	2	.417	3 AFL-W	—
1965 Oak	8	5	1	.615	2 AFL-W	—
	23	16	3	.583		—

DUD DEGROOT DeGroot, Dudley Sargent
Col: Stanford B: 11/20/1899, Chicago, IL D: 5/5/1970, El Cajon, CA

	W	L	T	Pct.	Place	P
NFL						
1944 Was	6	3	1	.667	3 NFL-E	—
1945 Was	8	2	0	.800	1 NFL-E	0-1
	14	5	1	.725		0-1
AAFC						
1946 LA-A	7	5	2	.583	AAC-W	—
1947 LA-A	5	6	0	.455	AAC-W	—
	12	11	2	.520		—

HERB DELL Dell, Herbert
B: 1/—/1889, OH Deceased

	W	L	T	Pct.	Place	P
1922 Col	0	8	0	.000	18 NFL	—

JACK DEPLER***

	W	L	T	Pct.	Place	P
1929 Ora	3	5	4	.375	8 NFL	—
1930 Bkn	7	4	1	.636	4 NFL	—
1931 Bkn	2	12	0	.143	9 NFL	—
	12	21	5	.382		—

DAN DEVINE Devine, Daniel John
Col: Minnesota-Duluth B: 12/23/1924, Augusta, WI

	W	L	T	Pct.	Place	P
1971 GB	4	8	2	.333	4 NFC-C	—
1972 GB	10	4	0	.714	1 NFC-C	0-1
1973 GB	5	7	2	.429	3 NFC-C	—
1974 GB	6	8	0	.429	3 NFC-C	—
	25	27	4	.482		0-1

HUGH DEVORE Devore, Hugh John
Col: Notre Dame B: 11/25/1910, Newark, NJ D: 12/8/1992, Edmond, OK

	W	L	T	Pct.	Place	P
1953 GB*	0	2	0	.000	6 NFL-W	—
1956 Phi	3	8	1	.273	6 NFL-E	—
1957 Phi	4	8	0	.333	5 NFL-E	—
	7	18	1	.288		—

* co-coach with Ray McLean

LONE STAR DIETZ Dietz, William H.
Col: Friends; Carlisle B: 8/17/1884, Pine Ridge, SD D: 7/20/1964, PA

	W	L	T	Pct.	Place	P
1933 Bos	5	5	2	.500	3 NFL-E	—
1934 Bos	6	6	0	.500	2 NFL-E	—
	11	11	2	.500		—

LUBY DIMEOLO DiMeolo, Albert
Col: Pittsburgh B: 10/27/1903, Youngstown, OH D: 6//1966

	W	L	T	Pct.	Place	P
1934 Pit	2	10	0	.167	5 NFL-E	—

MIKE DITKA***

	W	L	T	Pct.	Place	P
1982 ChiB	3	6	0	.333	12 NFC	—
1983 ChiB	8	8	0	.500	3 NFC-C	—
1984 ChiB	10	6	0	.625	1 NFC-C	1-1
1985 ChiB#	15	1	0	.938	1 NFC-C	3-0
1986 ChiB	14	2	0	.875	1 NFC-C	0-1
1987 ChiB	11	4	0	.733	1 NFC-C	0-1
1988 ChiB	12	4	0	.750	1 NFC-C	1-1
1989 ChiB	6	10	0	.375	4 NFC-C	—
1990 ChiB	11	5	0	.688	1 NFC-C	1-1
1991 ChiB	11	5	0	.688	2 NFC-C	0-1
1992 ChiB	5	11	0	.313	4 NFC-C	—
1997 NO	6	10	0	.375	4 NFC-W	—
1998 NO	6	10	0	.375	3 NFC-W	—
	118	82	0	.590		6-6

\# NFC Champion; won Super Bowl

MEL DOHERTY***

	W	L	T	Pct.	Place	P
1921 Cin	1	3	0	.250	13 NFL	—

BUFF DONELLI Donelli, Aldo T.
Col: Duquesne B: 7/22/1907, Morgan, PA D: 8/9/1994, Ft. Lauderdale, FL

	W	L	T	Pct.	Place	P
1941 Pit	0	5	0	.000	5 NFL-E	—
1944 Cle	4	6	0	.400	4 NFL-W	—
	4	11	0	.267		—

JIM DOOLEY***

	W	L	T	Pct.	Place	P
1968 ChiB	7	7	0	.500	2 NFL-C	—
1969 ChiB	1	13	0	.071	4 NFL-C	—
1970 ChiB	6	8	0	.429	3 NFL-C	—
1971 ChiB	6	8	0	.429	3 NFL-C	—
	20	36	0	.357		—

GUS DORAIS Dorais, Charles Emile
Col: Notre Dame B: 7/2/1891, Chippewa Falls, WI D: 1/3/1954, Birmingham, MI

	W	L	T	Pct.	Place	P
1943 Det	3	6	1	.333	3 NFL-W	—
1944 Det	6	3	1	.667	3 NFL-W	—
1945 Det	7	3	0	.700	2 NFL-W	—
1946 Det	1	10	0	.091	5 NFL-W	—
1947 Det	3	9	0	.250	5 NFL-W	—
	20	31	2	.396		—

JAP DOUDS***

	W	L	T	Pct.	Place	P
1933 Pit	3	6	2	.333	5 NFL-E	—

ROD DOWHOWER Dowhower, Rodney Douglas
Col: San Diego State B: 4/15/1943, Ord, NE

	W	L	T	Pct.	Place	P
1985 Ind	5	11	0	.313	4 AFC-E	—
1986 Ind	0	13	0	.000	5 AFC-E	—
	5	24	0	.172		—

PADDY DRISCOLL***

	W	L	T	Pct.	Place	P
1920 ChiC	6	2	2	.750	4 NFL	—
1921 ChiC	3	3	2	.500	9 NFL	—
1922 ChiC	8	3	0	.727	3 NFL	—
1956 ChiB	9	2	1	.818	1 NFL-W	0-1
1957 ChiB	5	7	0	.417	5 NFL-W	—
	31	17	5	.632		0-1

CHUCK DRULIS***

	W	L	T	Pct.	Place	P
1961 StL*	2	0	0	1.000	4 NFL-E	—

* co-coach with Ray Prochaska and Ray Willsey

TONY DUNGY***

	W	L	T	Pct.	Place	P
1996 TB	6	10	0	.375	4 NFC-C	—
1997 TB	10	6	0	.625	2 NFC-C	1-1
1998 TB	8	8	0	.500	3 NFC-C	—
	24	24	0	.500		1-1

BILL EDWARDS Edwards, William Miller (Big Bill)
Col: Ohio State; Wittenberg B: 6/21/1905, Massillon, OH D: 6/12/1987, Springfield, OH

	W	L	T	Pct.	Place	P
1941 Det	4	6	1	.400	3 NFL-W	—
1942 Det	0	3	0	.000	5 NFL-W	—
	4	9	1	.321		—

TURK EDWARDS***

	W	L	T	Pct.	Place	P
1946 Was	5	5	1	.500	3 NFL-E	—
1947 Was	4	8	0	.333	4 NFL-E	—
1948 Was	7	5	0	.583	2 NFL-E	—
	16	18	1	.471		—

CAP EDWARDS***

	W	L	T	Pct.	Place	P
1921 Can	5	2	3	.714	4 NFL	—
1923 Cle	3	1	3	.750	5 NFL	—

	W	L	T	Pct.	Place	P
1925 Cle	5	8	1	.385	12 NFL	—
	13	11	7	.532		—

EDDIE ERDELATZ Erdelatz, Edward Joseph
Col: St. Mary's B: 4/21/1913, San Francisco, CA
D: 11/11/1966, Burlingame, CA

	W	L	T	Pct.	Place	P
1960 Oak	6	8	0	.429	3 AFL-W	—
1961 Oak	0	2	0	.000	4 AFL-W	—
	6	10	0	.375		—

RON ERHARDT Erhardt, Ronald Peter
Col: Jamestown (ND) B: 2/27/1932, Mandan, ND

	W	L	T	Pct.	Place	P
1978 NE *	0	1	0	.000	1 AFC-E	0-1
1979 NE	9	7	0	.563	2 AFC-E	—
1980 NE	10	6	0	.625	2 AFC-E	—
1981 NE	2	14	0	.125	5 AFC-E	—
	21	28	0	.429		0-1

* co-coach with Hank Bullough

DENNIS ERICKSON Erickson, Dennis
Col: Montana State B: 3/24/1947, Everett, WA

	W	L	T	Pct.	Place	P
1995 Sea	8	8	0	.500	3 AFC-W	—
1996 Sea	7	9	0	.438	5 AFC-W	—
1997 Sea	8	8	0	.500	3 AFC-W	—
1998 Sea	8	8	0	.500	3 AFC-W	—
	31	33	0	.484		—

HAL ERICKSON***

	W	L	T	Pct.	Place	P
1924 Mil	5	8	0	.385	12 NFL	—

CHARLIE EWART Ewart, Charles Diven
Col: Yale B: 10/16/1915, Lynn, MA D: 4/30/1990,
Elk Grove, IL

	W	L	T	Pct.	Place	P
1949 NYB	1	10	1	.091	5 NFL-E	—

WEEB EWBANK Ewbank, Wilbur Charles
Col: Miami (OH) B: 5/6/1907, Richmond, IN D: 11/17/1998,
Oxford, OH

	W	L	T	Pct.	Place	P
1954 Bal	3	9	0	.250	6 NFL-W	—
1955 Bal	5	6	1	.455	4 NFL-W	—
1956 Bal	5	7	0	.417	4 NFL-W	—
1957 Bal	7	5	0	.583	3 NFL-W	—
1958 Bal#	9	3	0	.750	1 NFL-W	1-0
1959 Bal#	9	3	0	.750	1 NFL-W	1-0
1960 Bal	6	6	0	.500	4 NFL-W	—
1961 Bal	8	6	0	.571	3 NFL-W	—
1962 Bal	7	7	0	.500	4 NFL-W	—
1963 NYJ	5	8	1	.385	4 AFL-E	—
1964 NYJ	5	8	1	.385	3 AFL-E	—
1965 NYJ	5	8	1	.385	2 AFL-E	—
1966 NYJ	6	6	2	.500	3 AFL-E	—
1967 NYJ	8	5	1	.615	2 AFL-E	—
1968 NYJ+	11	3	0	.786	1 AFL-E	2-0
1969 NYJ	10	4	0	.714	1 AFL-E	0-1
1970 NYJ	4	10	0	.286	3 AFC-E	—
1971 NYJ	6	8	0	.429	4 AFC-E	—
1972 NYJ	7	7	0	.500	2 AFC-E	—
1973 NYJ	4	10	0	.286	5 AFC-E	—
	130	129	7	.502		4-1

\# NFL Champion
\+ AFL Champion; won Super Bowl

CHUCK FAIRBANKS Fairbanks, Charles Leo
Col: Michigan State B: 6/10/1933, Detroit, MI

	W	L	T	Pct.	Place	P
1973 NE	5	9	0	.357	3 AFC-E	—
1974 NE	7	7	0	.500	3 AFC-E	—
1975 NE	3	11	0	.214	4 AFC-E	—
1976 NE	11	3	0	.786	2 AFC-E	0-1
1977 NE	9	5	0	.643	3 AFC-E	—
1978 NE	11	4	0	.733	1 AFC-E	—
	46	39	0	.541		0-1

GUIL FALCON***

	W	L	T	Pct.	Place	P
1920 ChiT	2	5	1	.286	11 NFL	—
1922 Tol	5	2	2	.714	4 NFL	—
1923 Tol	3	3	2	.500	11 NFL	—
	10	10	5	.500		—

JIM FASSEL Fassel, James
Col: Fullerton JC (CA); Southern California B: 8/31/1949,
Anaheim, CA

	W	L	T	Pct.	Place	P
1997 NYG	10	5	1	.656	1 NFC-E	0-1
1998 NYG	8	8	0	.500	3 NFC-E	—
	18	13	1	.578		0-1

JACK FAULKNER Faulkner, Jack T.
Col: Miami (OH) B: 4/4/1926, Youngstown, OH

	W	L	T	Pct.	Place	P
1962 Den	7	7	0	.500	2 AFL-W	—
1963 Den	2	11	1	.154	4 AFL-W	—
1964 Den	0	4	0	.000	4 AFL-W	—
	9	22	1	.297		—

FRANK FAUSCH***

	W	L	T	Pct.	Place	P
1921 Eva	3	2	0	.600	6 NFL	—
1922 Eva	0	3	0	.000	15 NFL	—
	3	5	0	.375		—

TOM FEARS***

	W	L	T	Pct.	Place	P
1967 NO	3	11	0	.214	4 NFL-Cap	—
1968 NO	4	9	1	.308	3 NFL-Cty	—
1969 NO	5	9	0	.357	3 NFL-Cap	—
1970 NO	1	5	1	.167	4 NFC-W	—
	13	34	2	.286		—

MARTY FELDMAN Feldman, Martin
Col: Oregon; Stanford B: 9/12/1922, Los Angeles, CA

	W	L	T	Pct.	Place	P
1961 Oak	2	10	0	.167	4 AFL-W	—
1962 Oak	0	5	0	.000	4 AFL-W	—
	2	15	0	.118		—

FRANKIE FILCHOCK***

	W	L	T	Pct.	Place	P
1960 Den	4	9	1	.308	4 AFL-W	—
1961 Den	3	11	0	.214	3 AFL-W	—
	7	20	1	.268		—

JACK FISH Fish, John

	W	L	T	Pct.	Place	P
1930 Nwk	1	4	1	.200	11 NFL	—

JEFF FISHER***

	W	L	T	Pct.	Place	P
1994 Hou	1	5	0	.167	4 AFC-C	—
1995 Hou	7	9	0	.438	3 AFC-C	—
1996 Hou	8	8	0	.500	4 AFC-C	—
1997 Ten	8	8	0	.500	3 AFC-C	—
1998 Ten	8	8	0	.500	2 AFC-C	—
	32	38	0	.457		—

RAY FLAHERTY***

	W	L	T	Pct.	Place	P
NFL						
1936 Bos	7	5	0	.583	1 NFL-E	0-1
1937 Was#	8	3	0	.727	1 NFL-E	1-0
1938 Was	6	3	2	.667	2 NFL-E	—
1939 Was	8	2	1	.800	2 NFL-E	—
1940 Was	9	2	0	.818	1 NFL-E	0-1
1941 Was	6	5	0	.545	3 NFL-E	—
1942 Was#	10	1	0	.909	1 NFL-E	1-0
	54	21	3	.712		2-2
AAFC						
1946 NY-A	10	3	1	.769		0-1
1947 NY-A	11	2	1	.846		0-1
1948 NY-A	1	3	0	.250		—
1949 Ch-A	4	8	0	.333		—
	26	16	2	.614		0-2

\# NFL Champion

TOM FLORES***

	W	L	T	Pct.	Place	P
1979 Oak	9	7	0	.563	4 AFC-W	—
1980 Oak#	11	5	0	.688	2 AFC-W	4-0
1981 Oak	7	9	0	.438	4 AFC-W	—
1982 LARd	8	1	0	.889	1 AFC	1-1
1983 LARd#	12	4	0	.750	1 AFC-W	3-0
1984 LARd	11	5	0	.688	3 AFC-W	0-1
1985 LARd	12	4	0	.750	1 AFC-W	0-1
1986 LARd	8	8	0	.500	4 AFC-W	—
1987 LARd	5	10	0	.333	4 AFC-W	—

	W	L	T	Pct.	Place	P
1992 Sea	2	14	0	.125	5 AFC-W	—
1993 Sea	6	10	0	.375	5 AFC-W	—
1994 Sea	6	10	0	.375	5 AFC-W	—
	97	87	0	.527		8-3

AFC Champion; won Super Bowl

BOB FOLWELL Folwell, Robert Cook Jr.
Col: Pennsylvania B: 2/17/1885, Mullica Hill, NJ D: 1/8/1928, Philadelphia, PA

	W	L	T	Pct.	Place	P
1925 NYG	8	4	0	.667	4 NFL	—

WAYNE FONTES***

	W	L	T	Pct.	Place	P
1988 Det	2	3	0	.400	4 NFC-C	—
1989 Det	7	9	0	.438	3 NFC-C	—
1990 Det	6	10	0	.375	3 NFC-C	—
1991 Det	12	4	0	.750	1 NFC-C	1-1
1992 Det	5	11	0	.313	5 NFC-C	—
1993 Det	10	6	0	.625	1 NFC-C	0-1
1994 Det	9	7	0	.563	3 NFC-C	0-1
1995 Det	10	6	0	.625	2 NFC-C	0-1
1996 Det	5	11	0	.313	5 NFC-C	—
	66	67	0	.496		1-4

JACK FORSYTH Forsyth, Walter Scott
Col: Rochester B: 5/4/1892, Rochester, NY D: 12/19/1966, Rochester, NY

	W	L	T	Pct.	Place	P
1920 Roch	6	3	2	.667	7 NFL	—
1921 Roch	2	3	0	.400	10 NFL	—
	8	6	2	.563		—

RICK FORZANO Forzano, Richard Edward
Col: Kent State B: 11/20/1928, Akron, OH

	W	L	T	Pct.	Place	P
1974 Det	7	7	0	.500	2 NFC-C	—
1975 Det	7	7	0	.500	2 NFC-C	—
1976 Det	1	3	0	.250	3 NFC-C	—
	15	17	0	.469		—

BENNY FRIEDMAN***

	W	L	T	Pct.	Place	P
1930 NYG*	2	0	0	1.000	2 NFL	—
1932 Bkn	3	9	0	.250	6 NFL	—
	5	9	0	.357		—

* co-coach with Steve Owen

CHAN GAILEY Gailey, Thomas Chandler
Col: Florida B: 1/5/1952, Gainesville, FL

	W	L	T	Pct.	Place	P
1998 Dal	10	6	0	.625	1 NFC-E	0-1

FRANK GANSZ Gansz, Francis von Rensselaer
Col: Navy B: 11/22/1938, Altoona, PA

	W	L	T	Pct.	Place	P
1987 KC	4	11	0	.267	5 AFC-W	—
1988 KC	4	11	1	.267	5 AFC-W	—
	8	22	1	.274		—

BUDGE GARRETT***

	W	L	T	Pct.	Place	P
1922 Mil	2	1	3	.667	11 NFL	—

MIKE GETTO Getto, Michael
Col: Pittsburgh B: 9/18/1905, Irwin, PA D: 8/27/1960, Lawrence, KS

	W	L	T	Pct.	Place	P
1942 Bkn	3	8	0	.273	4 NFL-E	—

JOE GIBBS Gibbs, Joe Jackson
Col: Cerritos JC (CA); San Diego State B: 11/25/1940, Mocksville, NC

	W	L	T	Pct.	Place	P
1981 Was	8	8	0	.500	4 NFC-E	—
1982 Was #	8	1	0	.889	1 NFC	4-0
1983 Was+	14	2	0	.875	1 NFC-E	2-1
1984 Was	11	5	0	.688	1 NFC-E	0-1
1985 Was	10	6	0	.625	3 NFC-E	—
1986 Was	12	4	0	.750	2 NFC-E	2-1
1987 Was#	11	4	0	.733	1 NFC-E	3-0
1988 Was	7	9	0	.438	3 NFC-E	—
1989 Was	10	6	0	.625	3 NFC-E	—
1990 Was	10	6	0	.625	3 NFC-E	1-1
1991 Was#	14	2	0	.875	1 NFC-E	3-0
1992 Was	9	7	0	.563	3 NFC-E	1-1
	124	60	0	.674		16-5

NFC Champion; won Super Bowl
+ NFC Champion

ABE GIBRON***

	W	L	T	Pct.	Place	P
1972 ChiB	4	9	1	.321	4 NFC-C	—
1973 ChiB	3	11	0	.214	4 NFC-C	—
1974 ChiB	4	10	0	.286	4 NFC-C	—
	10	30	1	.256		—

GEORGE GIBSON***

	W	L	T	Pct.	Place	P
1930 Min	1	7	1	.125	10 NFL	—
1930 Fra	2	3	0	.400	9 NFL	—
	3	10	1	.250		—

KEVIN GILBRIDE Gilbride, Kevin
Col: Southern Connecticut State B: 8/27/1951, New Haven, CT

	W	L	T	Pct.	Place	P
1997 SD	4	12	0	.250	5 AFC-W	—
1998 SD	2	4	0	.333	5 AFC-W	—
	6	16	0	.273		—

FRED GILLIES***

	W	L	T	Pct.	Place	P
1928 ChiC	1	5	0	.167	9 NFL	—

SID GILLMAN Gillman, Sidney
Col: Ohio State B: 10/26/1911, Minneapolis, MN

	W	L	T	Pct.	Place	P
1955 LARm	8	3	1	.727	1 NFL-W	0-1
1956 LARm	4	8	0	.333	6 NFL-W	—
1957 LARm	6	6	0	.500	4 NFL-W	—
1958 LARm	8	4	0	.667	3 NFL-W	—
1959 LARm	2	10	0	.167	6 NFL-W	—
1960 LAC	10	4	0	.714	1 AFL-W	0-1
1961 SD	12	2	0	.857	1 AFL-W	0-1
1962 SD	4	10	0	.286	3 AFL-W	—
1963 SD#	11	3	0	.786	1 AFL-W	1-0
1964 SD	8	5	1	.615	1 AFL-W	0-1
1965 SD	9	2	3	.818	1 AFL-W	0-1
1966 SD	7	6	1	.538	3 AFL-W	—
1967 SD	8	5	1	.615	3 AFL-W	—
1968 SD	9	5	0	.643	3 AFL-W	—
1969 SD	4	5	0	.444	3 AFL-W	—
1971 SD	4	6	0	.400	3 AFC-W	—
1973 Hou	1	8	0	.111	4 AFC-C	—
1974 Hou	7	7	0	.500	3 AFC-C	—
	122	99	7	.550		1-5

AFL Champion

HANK GILLO***

	W	L	T	Pct.	Place	P
1920 Ham	2	5	0	.286	12 NFL	—

HARRY GILMER***

	W	L	T	Pct.	Place	P
1965 Det	6	7	1	.462	6 NFL-W	—
1966 Det	4	9	1	.308	6 NFL-W	—
	10	16	2	.393		—

JERRY GLANVILLE Glanville, Jerry Michael
Col: Northern Michigan B: 10/14/1941, Detroit, MI

	W	L	T	Pct.	Place	P
1985 Hou	0	2	0	.000	4 AFC-C	—
1986 Hou	5	11	0	.313	4 AFC-C	—
1987 Hou	9	6	0	.600	2 AFC-C	1-1
1988 Hou	10	6	0	.625	3 AFC-C	1-1
1989 Hou	9	7	0	.563	2 AFC-C	0-1
1990 Atl	5	11	0	.313	4 NFC-W	—
1991 Atl	10	6	0	.625	2 NFC-W	1-1
1992 Atl	6	10	0	.375	3 NFC-W	—
1993 Atl	6	10	0	.375	3 NFC-W	—
	60	69	0	.465		3-4

ARCHIE GOLEMBESKI***

	W	L	T	Pct.	Place	P
1925 Prov	6	5	1	.545	10 NFL	—

OTTO GRAHAM***

	W	L	T	Pct.	Place	P
1966 Was	7	7	0	.500	5 NFL-E	—
1967 Was	5	6	3	.455	3 NFL-Cap	—

	W	L	T	Pct.	Place	P
1968 Was	5	9	0	.357	3 NFL-Cap	—
	17	22	3	.440		—

BUD GRANT***

	W	L	T	Pct.	Place	P
1967 Min	3	8	3	.273	4 NFL-C	—
1968 Min	8	6	0	.571	1 NFL-C	0-1
1969 Min#	12	2	0	.857	1 NFL-C	2-1
1970 Min	12	2	0	.857	1 NFC-C	0-1
1971 Min	11	3	0	.786	1 NFC-C	0-1
1972 Min	7	7	0	.500	3 NFC-C	—
1973 Min+	12	2	0	.857	1 NFC-C	2-1
1974 Min+	10	4	0	.714	1 NFC-C	2-1
1975 Min	12	2	0	.857	1 NFC-C	0-1
1976 Min+	11	2	1	.821	1 NFC-C	2-1
1977 Min	9	5	0	.643	1 NFC-C	1-1
1978 Min	8	7	1	.531	1 NFC-C	0-1
1979 Min	7	9	0	.438	3 NFC-C	—
1980 Min	9	7	0	.563	1 NFC-C	0-1
1981 Min	7	9	0	.438	4 NFC-C	—
1982 Min	5	4	0	.556	4 NFC	1-1
1983 Min	8	8	0	.500	4 NFC-C	—
1985 Min	7	9	0	.438	3 NFC-C	—
	158	96	5	.620		10-12

NFL Champion
+ NFC Champion

DENNIS GREEN Green, Dennis
Col: Iowa B: 2/17/1949, Harrisburg, PA

	W	L	T	Pct.	Place	P
1992 Min	11	5	0	.688	1 NFC-C	0-1
1993 Min	9	7	0	.563	2 NFC-C	0-1
1994 Min	10	6	0	.625	1 NFC-C	0-1
1995 Min	8	8	0	.500	4 NFC-C	—
1996 Min	9	7	0	.563	2 NFC-C	0-1
1997 Min	9	7	0	.563	4 NFC-C	1-1
1998 Min	15	1	0	.938	1 NFC-C	1-1
	71	41	0	.634		2-6

FORREST GREGG***

	W	L	T	Pct.	Place	P
1975 Cle	3	11	0	.214	4 AFC-C	—
1976 Cle	9	5	0	.643	3 AFC-C	—
1977 Cle	6	7	0	.462	4 AFC-C	—
1980 Cin	6	10	0	.375	4 AFC-C	—
1981 Cin#	12	4	0	.750	1 AFC-C	2-1
1982 Cin	7	2	0	.778	3 AFC	0-1
1983 Cin	7	9	0	.438	3 AFC-C	—
1984 GB	8	8	0	.500	2 NFC-C	—
1985 GB	8	8	0	.500	2 NFC-C	—
1986 GB	4	12	0	.250	4 NFC-C	—
1987 GB	5	9	1	.367	3 NFC-C	—
	75	85	1	.469		2-2

AFC Champion

HAL GRIFFEN***

	W	L	T	Pct.	Place	P
1930 Port	5	6	3	.455	8 NFL	—

TEX GRIGG***

	W	L	T	Pct.	Place	P
1925 Roch	0	6	1	.000	17 NFL	—

JON GRUDEN Gruden, Jon
Col: Dayton B: 8/17/1963, Sandusky, OH

	W	L	T	Pct.	Place	P
1998 Oak	8	8	0	.500	2 AFC-W	—

HINKEY HAINES***

	W	L	T	Pct.	Place	P
1931 SI	1	3	0	.250	7 NFL	—

GEORGE HALAS***

	W	L	T	Pct.	Place	P
1920 Sta	10	1	2	.909	2 NFL	—
1921 Sta#	9	1	1	.900	1 NFL	—
1922 ChiB	9	3	0	.750	2 NFL	—
1923 ChiB	9	2	1	.818	2 NFL	—
1924 ChiB	6	1	4	.857	2 NFL	—
1925 ChiB	9	5	3	.643	7 NFL	—
1926 ChiB	12	1	3	.923	2 NFL	—
1927 ChiB	9	3	2	.750	3 NFL	—
1928 ChiB	7	5	1	.583	5 NFL	—
1929 ChiB	4	9	2	.308	9 NFL	—
1933 ChiB#	10	2	1	.833	1 NFL-W	1-0
1934 ChiB	13	0	0	1.000	1 NFL-W	0-1
1935 ChiB	6	4	2	.600	3 NFL-W	—
1936 ChiB	9	3	0	.750	2 NFL-W	—
1937 ChiB	9	1	1	.900	1 NFL-W	0-1
1938 ChiB	6	5	0	.545	3 NFL-W	—
1939 ChiB	8	3	0	.727	2 NFL-W	—
1940 ChiB#	8	3	0	.727	1 NFL-W	1-0
1941 ChiB#	10	1	0	.909	1 NFL-W	2-0
1942 ChiB	5	0	0	1.000	1 NFL-W	—
1946 ChiB#	8	2	1	.800	1 NFL-W	1-0
1947 ChiB	8	4	0	.667	2 NFL-W	—
1948 ChiB	10	2	0	.833	2 NFL-W	—
1949 ChiB	9	3	0	.750	2 NFL-W	—
1950 ChiB	9	3	0	.750	2 NFL-N	0-1
1951 ChiB	7	5	0	.583	4 NFL-N	—
1952 ChiB	5	7	0	.417	5 NFL-N	—
1953 ChiB	3	8	1	.273	4 NFL-W	—
1954 ChiB	8	4	0	.667	2 NFL-W	—
1955 ChiB	8	4	0	.667	2 NFL-W	—
1958 ChiB	8	4	0	.667	2 NFL-W	—
1959 ChiB	8	4	0	.667	2 NFL-W	—
1960 ChiB	5	6	1	.455	5 NFL-W	—
1961 ChiB	8	6	0	.571	4 NFL-W	—
1962 ChiB	9	5	0	.643	3 NFL-W	—
1963 ChiB#	11	1	2	.917	1 NFL-W	1-0
1964 ChiB	5	9	0	.357	6 NFL-W	—
1965 ChiB	9	5	0	.643	3 NFL-W	—
1966 ChiB	5	7	2	.417	5 NFL-W	—
1967 ChiB	7	6	1	.538	2 NFL-C	—
	318	148	31	.671		6-3

NFL Champion

PHIL HANDLER***

	W	L	T	Pct.	Place	P
1943 ChiC	0	10	0	.000	4 NFL-W	—
1944 ChPt*	0	10	0	.000	5 NFL-W	—
1945 ChiC	1	9	0	.100	5 NFL-W	—
1949 ChiC**	2	4	0	.333	3 NFL-W	—
1951 ChiC^	1	1	0	.500	6 NFL-E	—
	4	34	0	.105		—

* co-coach with Walt Kiesling
** co-coach with Buddy Parker for first 6 games
^ co-coach with Cecil Isbell

RAY HANDLEY Handley, Robert Ray
Col: Stanford B: 10/8/1944, Artesia, NM

	W	L	T	Pct.	Place	P
1991 NYG	8	8	0	.500	4 NFC-E	—
1992 NYG	6	10	0	.375	4 NFC-E	—
	14	18	0	.438		—

JIM HANIFAN Hanifan, James Martin Michael
Col: California B: 9/21/1933, Compton, CA

	W	L	T	Pct.	Place	P
1980 StL	5	11	0	.313	4 NFC-E	—
1981 StL	7	9	0	.438	5 NFC-E	—
1982 StL	5	4	0	.556	6 NFC	0-1
1983 StL	8	7	1	.531	3 NFC-E	—
1984 StL	9	7	0	.563	3 NFC-E	—
1985 StL	5	11	0	.313	5 NFC-E	—
1989 Atl	0	4	0	.000	4 NFC-W	—
	39	53	1	.476		0-1

BO HANLEY***

	W	L	T	Pct.	Place	P
1924 Ken*	0	4	1	.000	16 NFL	—

* co-coach with Earl Potteiger

HAL HANSON***

	W	L	T	Pct.	Place	P
1932 SI	2	7	3	.222	8 NFL	—

NORB HECKER***

	W	L	T	Pct.	Place	P
1966 Atl	3	11	0	.214	7 NFL-E	—
1967 Atl	1	12	1	.077	4 NFL-Coa	—
1968 Atl	0	3	0	.000	4 NFL-Coa	—
	4	26	1	.145		—

ERNIE HEFFERLE Hefferle, Ernest
Col: Duquesne B: 1/12/1915, Herminie, PA

	W	L	T	Pct.	Place	P
1975 NO	1	7	0	.125	4 NFC-W	—

JACK HEGARTY Hegarty, John Edward
Col: Holy Cross; Georgetown B: 6/9/1888, Newburyport, MA Deceased

	W	L	T	Pct.	Place	P
1921 Was	1	2	0	.333	12 NFL	—

JACK HELDT***

	W	L	T	Pct.	Place	P
1926 Col	1	6	0	.143	19 NFL	—

GUS HENDERSON Henderson, Elmer Clinton (Gloomy Gus)
Col: Oberlin B: 3/10/1889, Oberlin, OH D: 12/16/1965, Desert Hot Springs, CA

	W	L	T	Pct.	Place	P
1939 Det	6	5	0	.545	3 NFL-W	—

DUTCH HENDRIAN***

	W	L	T	Pct.	Place	P
1923 Akr	0	5	0	.000	17 NFL	—

DAN HENNING***

	W	L	T	Pct.	Place	P
1983 Atl	7	9	0	.438	4 NFC-W	—
1984 Atl	4	12	0	.250	4 NFC-W	—
1985 Atl	4	12	0	.250	4 NFC-W	—
1986 Atl	7	8	1	.469	3 NFC-W	—
1989 SD	6	10	0	.375	5 AFC-W	—
1990 SD	6	10	0	.375	4 AFC-W	—
1991 SD	4	12	0	.250	5 AFC-W	—
	38	73	1	.344		—

PETE HENRY***

	W	L	T	Pct.	Place	P
1926 Can*	1	9	3	.100	20 NFL	—
1928 Pott	2	8	0	.200	8 NFL	—
	3	17	3	.196		—

* co-coach with Harry Robb

WALLY HESS***

	W	L	T	Pct.	Place	P
1922 Ham	0	5	1	.000	17 NFL	—
1923 Ham	1	5	1	.167	15 NFL	—
1924 Ham	2	2	1	.500	11 NFL	—
	3	12	3	.250		—

RED HICKEY***

	W	L	T	Pct.	Place	P
1959 SF	7	5	0	.583	4 NFL-W	—
1960 SF	7	5	0	.583	3 NFL-W	—
1961 SF	7	6	1	.538	5 NFL-W	—
1962 SF	6	8	0	.429	5 NFL-W	—
1963 SF	0	3	0	.000	7 NFL-W	—
	27	27	1	.500		—

MAX HICKS***

	W	L	T	Pct.	Place	P
1921 Ham	1	3	1	.250	14 NFL	—

AUSTIN HIGGINS***

	W	L	T	Pct.	Place	P
1921 Lou	0	2	0	.000	20 NFL	—

BOB HOLLWAY Hollway, Robert
Col: Michigan B: 1/29/1926, Ann Arbor, MI

	W	L	T	Pct.	Place	P
1971 StL	4	9	1	.308	4 NFC-E	—
1972 StL	4	9	1	.308	4 NFC-E	—
	8	18	2	.321		—

MIKE HOLMGREN Holmgren, Michael George
Col: Southern California B: 6/15/1948, San Francisco, CA

	W	L	T	Pct.	Place	P
1992 GB	9	7	0	.563	2 NFC-C	—
1993 GB	9	7	0	.563	3 NFC-C	1-1
1994 GB	9	7	0	.563	2 NFC-C	1-1
1995 GB	11	5	0	.688	1 NFC-C	2-1
1996 GB#	13	3	0	.813	1 NFC-C	3-0
1997 GB*	13	3	0	.813	1 NFC-C	2-1
1998 GB	11	5	0	.688	2 NFC-C	0-1
	75	37	0	.670		9-5

\# NFL Champion; won Super Bowl
* NFC Champion

MIKE HOLOVAK***

	W	L	T	Pct.	Place	P
1961 Bos	7	1	1	.875	2 AFL-E	—
1962 Bos	9	4	1	.692	2 AFL-E	—
1963 Bos	7	6	1	.538	1 AFL-E	1-1
1964 Bos	10	3	1	.769	2 AFL-E	—
1965 Bos	4	8	2	.333	3 AFL-E	—
1966 Bos	8	4	2	.677	2 AFL-E	—
1967 Bos	3	10	1	.231	5 AFL-E	—
1968 Bos	4	10	0	.286	4 AFL-E	—
1976 NYJ	0	1	0	.000	4 AFC-E	—
	52	47	9	.523		1-1

LOU HOLTZ Holtz, Louis Leo
Col: Kent State B: 1/16/1937, Follansbee, WV

	W	L	T	Pct.	Place	P
1976 NYJ	3	10	0	.231	4 AFC-E	—

ARNIE HORWEEN***

	W	L	T	Pct.	Place	P
1923 ChiC	8	4	0	.667	6 NFL	—
1924 ChiC	5	4	1	.556	8 NFL	—
	13	8	1	.614		—

JIM LEE HOWELL***

	W	L	T	Pct.	Place	P
1954 NYG	7	5	0	.583	3 NFL-E	—
1955 NYG	6	5	1	.545	3 NFL-E	—
1956 NYG#	8	3	1	.727	1 NFL-E	1-0
1957 NYG	7	5	0	.583	2 NFL-E	—
1958 NYG	9	3	0	.750	1 NFL-E	1-1
1959 NYG	10	2	0	.833	1 NFL-E	0-1
1960 NYG	6	4	2	.600	3 NFL-E	—
	53	27	4	.655		2-2

\# NFL Champion

TOMMY HUDSPETH Hudspeth, Tommy Joe
Col: Tulsa B: 9/14/31, Cherryvail, KS

	W	L	T	Pct.	Place	P
1976 Det	5	5	0	.500	3 NFC-C	—
1977 Det	6	8	0	.429	3 NFC-C	—
	11	13	0	.470		—

KEN HUFFINE***

	W	L	T	Pct.	Place	P
1920 Mun	0	1	0	.000	14 NFL	—

ED HUGHES***

	W	L	T	Pct.	Place	P
1971 Hou	4	9	1	.308	3 AFC-C	—

TOMMY HUGHITT***

	W	L	T	Pct.	Place	P
1920 Buf	9	1	1	.900	3 NFL	—
1921 Buf	9	1	2	.900	2 NFL	—
1922 Buf	5	4	1	.556	9 NFL	—
1923 Buf	5	4	3	.556	8 NFL	—
1924 Buf	6	5	0	.545	9 NFL	—
	34	15	7	.670		—

HAL HUNTER***

	W	L	T	Pct.	Place	P
1984 Ind	0	1	0	.000	4 AFC-E	—

TUT IMLAY***

	W	L	T	Pct.	Place	P
1926 LA*	6	3	1	.667	6 NFL	—

* co-coach with Brick Muller

LINDY INFANTE Infante, Gelindo
Col: Florida B: 5/27/1940, Miami, FL

	W	L	T	Pct.	Place	P
1988 GB	4	12	0	.250	5 NFC-C	—
1989 GB	10	6	0	.625	2 NFC-C	—
1990 GB	6	10	0	.375	4 NFC-C	—
1991 GB	4	12	0	.250	4 NFC-C	—
1996 Ind	9	7	0	.563	3 AFC-E	0-1
1997 Ind	3	13	0	.188	5 AFC-E	—
	36	60	0	.375		0-1

CECIL ISBELL***

	W	L	T	Pct.	Place	P
AAFC						
1947 BalA	2	11	1	.154		—
1948 BalA	7	7	0	.500		—
1949 BalA	0	4	0	.000		—
	9	22	1	.297		—

	W	L	T	Pct.	Place	P
NFL						
1951 ChiC*	1	1	0	.500	6 NFL-A	—

* co-coach with Phil Handler

POP IVY***

	W	L	T	Pct.	Place	P
1958 ChiC	2	9	1	.182	5 NFL-E	—
1959 ChiC	2	10	0	.167	6 NFL-E	—
1960 StL	6	5	1	.545	4 NFL-E	—
1961 StL	5	7	0	.417	4 NFL-E	—
1962 Hou	11	3	0	.786	1 AFL-E	0-1
1963 Hou	6	8	0	.429	3 AFL-E	—
	32	42	2	.434		0-1

HERB JOESTING***

	W	L	T	Pct.	Place	P
1929 Min	1	9	0	.100	11 NFL	—

BILL JOHNSON***

	W	L	T	Pct.	Place	P
1976 Cin	10	4	0	.714	2 AFC-C	—
1977 Cin	8	6	0	.571	3 AFC-C	—
1978 Cin	0	5	0	.000	4 AFC-C	—
	18	15	0	.545		—

HARVEY JOHNSON***

	W	L	T	Pct.	Place	P
1968 Buf	1	10	1	.091	5 AFL-E	—
1971 Buf	1	13	0	.071	5 AFC-E	—
	2	23	1	.096		—

JIMMY JOHNSON Johnson, James William
Col: Arkansas B: 7/16/1943, Port Arthur, TX

	W	L	T	Pct.	Place	P
1989 Dal	1	15	0	.063	5 NFC-E	—
1990 Dal	7	9	0	.438	4 NFC-E	—
1991 Dal	11	5	0	.688	2 NFC-E	1-1
1992 Dal#	13	3	0	.813	1 NFC-E	3-0
1993 Dal#	12	4	0	.750	1 NFC-E	3-0
1996 Mia	8	8	0	.500	4 AFC-E	—
1997 Mia	9	7	0	.563	2 AFC-E	0-1
1998 Mia	10	6	0	.625	2 AFC-E	1-1
	71	57	0	.555		8-3

\# NFC Champion; won Super Bowl

LUKE JOHNSOS***

	W	L	T	Pct.	Place	P
1942 ChiB*	6	0	0	1.000	1 NFL-W	0-1
1943 ChiB*#	8	1	1	.889	1 NFL-W	1-0
1944 ChiB*	6	3	1	.667	2 NFL-W	—
1945 ChiB*	3	7	0	.300	4 NFL-W	—
	23	11	2	.667		1-1

* co-coach with Hunk Anderson
\# NFL Champion

AL JOLLEY***

	W	L	T	Pct.	Place	P
1929 Buf	1	7	1	.125	10 NFL	—
1933 Cin*	3	6	1	.333	4 NFL-W	—
	4	13	2	.263		—

* Jolley was coach at the beginning of the season with Mike Palm as assistant. Evidence suggests Palm became coach sometime before season's end. Cincinnati's season record is given here because it is unclear which games should be credited to which man.

JUNE JONES***

	W	L	T	Pct.	Place	P
1994 Atl	7	9	0	.438	3 NFC-W	—
1995 Atl	9	7	0	.563	2 NFC-W	0-1
1996 Atl	3	13	0	.188	4 NFC-W	—
1998 SD	3	7	0	.300	5 AFC-W	—
	22	36	0	.379		0-1

RALPH JONES Jones, Ralph Robert
Col: Wabash B: -/-/1880 D: 7/25/1951, Boulder, CO

	W	L	T	Pct.	Place	P
1930 ChiB	9	4	1	.692	3 NFL	—
1931 ChiB	8	5	0	.615	3 NFL	—
1932 ChiB #	7	1	6	.875	1 NFL	—
	24	10	7	.671		—

\# NFL Champion

JOHN KARCIS***

	W	L	T	Pct.	Place	P
1942 Det	0	8	0	.000	5 NFL-W	—

JIM KENDRICK***

	W	L	T	Pct.	Place	P
1923 Lou	0	3	0	.000	19 NFL	—
1926 Buf	4	4	2	.500	9 NFL	—
	4	7	2	.385		—

JACK KEOGH Keogh, John Joseph
Col: Amherst; Pennsylvania B: 6/17/1886, South Hadley Falls, MA D: 2/13/1955, Holyoke, MA

	W	L	T	Pct.	Place	P
1926 Har	3	7	0	.300	13 NFL	—

ED KHAYAT***

	W	L	T	Pct.	Place	P
1971 Phi	6	4	1	.462	3 NFC-E	—
1972 Phi	2	11	1	.179	5 NFC-E	—
	8	15	2	.360		—

WALT KIESLING***

	W	L	T	Pct.	Place	P
1939 Pit	1	6	1	.143	5 NFL-E	—
1940 Pit	2	7	2	.222	4 NFL-E	—
1941 Pit	1	2	1	.333	5 NFL-E	—
1942 Pit	7	4	0	.636	2 NFL-E	—
1943 PhPt*	5	4	1	.556	3 NFL-E	—
1944 ChPt**	0	10	0	.000	5 NFL-W	—
1954 Pit	5	7	0	.417	4 NFL-E	—
1955 Pit	4	8	0	.333	6 NFL-E	—
1956 Pit	5	7	0	.417	5 NFL-E	—
	30	55	5	.361		—

* co-coach with Greasy Neale
** co-coach with PhilHandler

CHUCK KNOX Knox, Charles Robert
Col: Juniata B: 4/27/1932, Sewickley, PA

	W	L	T	Pct.	Place	P
1973 LARm	12	2	0	.857	1 NFC-W	0-1
1974 LARm	10	4	0	.714	1 NFC-W	1-1
1975 LARm	12	2	0	.857	1 NFC-W	1-1
1976 LARm	10	3	1	.750	1 NFC-W	1-1
1977 LARm	10	4	0	.714	1 NFC-W	0-1
1978 Buf	5	11	0	.313	4 AFC-E	—
1979 Buf	7	9	0	.438	4 AFC-E	—
1980 Buf	11	5	0	.688	1 AFC-E	0-1
1981 Buf	10	6	0	.625	3 AFC-E	1-1
1982 Buf	4	5	0	.444	9 AFC	—
1983 Sea	9	7	0	.563	2 AFC-W	2-1
1984 Sea	12	4	0	.750	2 AFC-W	1-1
1985 Sea	8	8	0	.500	3 AFC-W	—
1986 Sea	10	6	0	.625	3 AFC-W	—
1987 Sea	9	6	0	.600	2 AFC-W	0-1
1988 Sea	9	7	0	.563	1 AFC-W	0-1
1989 Sea	7	9	0	.438	4 AFC-W	—
1990 Sea	9	7	0	.563	3 AFC-W	—
1991 Sea	7	9	0	.438	4 AFC-W	—
1992 LARm	6	10	0	.375	4 NFC-W	—
1993 LARm	5	11	0	.313	4 NFC-W	—
1994 LARm	4	12	0	.250	4 NFC-W	—
	186	147	1	.558		7-11

HERB KOPF Kopf, Herbert Mark
Col: Washington & Jefferson B: 2/3/1895, Winstead, CT D: 1/-/1967, Caldwell, NJ

	W	L	T	Pct.	Place	P
1944 Bos	2	8	0	.200	4 NFL-E	—
1945 Bos	3	6	1	.333	4 NFL-E	—
1946 Bos	2	8	1	.200	5 NFL-E	—
	7	22	2	.258		—

WALT KOPPISCH***

	W	L	T	Pct.	Place	P
1925 Buf	1	6	2	.143	15 NFL	—

RICH KOTITE***

	W	L	T	Pct.	Place	P
1991 Phi	10	6	0	.625	3 NFC-E	—
1992 Phi	11	5	0	.688	2 NFC-E	1-1
1993 Phi	8	8	0	.500	3 NFC-E	—
1994 Phi	7	9	0	.438	4 NFC-E	—
1995 NYJ	3	13	0	.188	5 AFC-E	—
1996 NYJ	1	15	0	.063	5 AFC-E	—
	40	56	0	.417		1-1

OLLIE KRAEHE***

	W	L	T	Pct.	Place	P
1923 StL	1	4	2	.200	14 NFL	—

	W	L	T	Pct.	Place	P

ED KUBALE Kubale, Edwin
Col: Centre B: 11/22/1899, Fort Smith, AR D: 2/4/1971, Danville, KY

	W	L	T	Pct.	Place	P
1944 Bkn*	0	5	0	.000	5 NFL-E	—

* co-coach with Frank Bridges

JOE KUHARICH***

	W	L	T	Pct.	Place	P
1952 ChiC	4	8	0	.333	5 NFL-A	—
1954 Was	3	9	0	.250	5 NFL-E	—
1955 Was	8	4	0	.667	2 NFL-E	—
1956 Was	6	6	0	.500	3 NFL-E	—
1957 Was	5	6	1	.455	4 NFL-E	—
1958 Was	4	7	1	.364	4 NFL-E	—
1964 Phi	6	8	0	.429	3 NFL-E	—
1965 Phi	5	9	0	.357	4 NFL-E	—
1966 Phi	9	5	0	.643	3 NFL-E	—
1967 Phi	6	7	1	.462	2 NFL-Cap	—
1968 Phi	2	12	0	.143	4 NFL-Cap	—
	58	81	3	.419		—

HANK KUHLMANN Kuhlmann, Henry Norman
Col: Missouri B: 10/6/1937, St. Louis, MO

	W	L	T	Pct.	Place	P
1989 Pho	0	5	0	.000	4 NFC-E	—

FRANK KUSH Kush, Frank Joseph
Col: Michigan State B: 1/20/1929, Windber, PA

	W	L	T	Pct.	Place	P
1982 Bal	0	8	1	.000	9 AFC	—
1983 Bal	7	9	0	.438	4 AFC-E	—
1984 Ind	4	11	0	.267	4 AFC-E	—
	11	28	1	.288		—

JIM LAIRD***

	W	L	T	Pct.	Place	P
1926 Prov	5	7	1	.417	11 NFL	—

CURLY LAMBEAU***

	W	L	T	Pct.	Place	P
1921 GB	3	2	1	.600	7 NFL	—
1922 GB	4	3	3	.571	8 NFL	—
1923 GB	7	2	1	.778	3 NFL	—
1924 GB	7	4	0	.636	6 NFL	—
1925 GB	8	5	0	.615	9 NFL	—
1926 GB	7	3	3	.700	5 NFL	—
1927 GB	7	2	1	.778	2 NFL	—
1928 GB	6	4	3	.600	4 NFL	—
1929 GB#	12	0	1	1.000	1 NFL	—
1930 GB#	10	3	1	.769	1 NFL	—
1931 GB#	12	2	0	.857	1 NFL	—
1932 GB	10	3	1	.769	2 NFL	—
1933 GB	5	7	1	.417	3 NFL-W	—
1934 GB	7	6	0	.538	3 NFL-W	—
1935 GB	8	4	0	.667	2 NFL-W	—
1936 GB#	10	1	1	.909	1 NFL-W	1-0
1937 GB	7	4	0	.636	2 NFL-W	—
1938 GB	8	3	0	.727	1 NFL-W	0-1
1939 GB#	9	2	0	.818	1 NFL-W	1-0
1940 GB	6	4	1	.600	2 NFL-W	—
1941 GB	10	1	0	.909	2 NFL-W	0-1
1942 GB	8	2	1	.800	2 NFL-W	—
1943 GB	7	2	1	.778	2 NFL-W	—
1944 GB#	8	2	0	.800	1 NFL-W	1-0
1945 GB	6	4	0	.600	3 NFL-W	—
1946 GB	6	5	0	.545	3 NFL-W	—
1947 GB	6	5	1	.545	3 NFL-W	—
1948 GB	3	9	0	.250	4 NFL-W	—
1949 GB	2	10	0	.167	5 NFL-W	—
1950 ChiC	5	7	0	.417	5 NFL-A	—
1951 ChiC	2	8	0	.200	6 NFL-A	—
1952 Was	4	8	0	.333	6 NFL-A	—
1953 Was	6	5	1	.545	3 NFL-E	—
	226	132	22	.624		3-2

\# NFL Champion

TOM LANDRY***

	W	L	T	Pct.	Place	P
1960 Dal	0	11	1	.000	7 NFL-E	—
1961 Dal	4	9	1	.308	6 NFL-E	—
1962 Dal	5	8	1	.385	5 NFL-E	—
1963 Dal	4	10	0	.286	5 NFL-E	—
1964 Dal	5	8	1	.385	5 NFL-E	—
1965 Dal	7	7	0	.500	2 NFL-E	—
1966 Dal	10	3	1	.769	1 NFL-E	0-1
1967 Dal	9	5	0	.643	1 NFL-Cap	1-1
1968 Dal	12	2	0	.857	1 NFL-Cap	0-1
1969 Dal	11	2	1	.846	1 NFL-Cap	0-1
1970 Dal+	10	4	0	.714	1 NFC-E	2-1
1971 Dal#	11	3	0	.786	1 NFC-E	3-0
1972 Dal	10	4	0	.714	2 NFC-E	1-1
1973 Dal	10	4	0	.714	1 NFC-E	1-1
1974 Dal	8	6	0	.571	3 NFC-E	—
1975 Dal+	10	4	0	.714	2 NFC-E	2-1
1976 Dal	11	3	0	.786	1 NFC-E	0-1
1977 Dal#	12	2	0	.857	1 NFC-E	3-0
1978 Dal+	12	4	0	.750	1 NFC-E	2-1
1979 Dal	11	5	0	.688	1 NFC-E	0-1
1980 Dal	12	4	0	.750	2 NFC-E	2-1
1981 Dal	12	4	0	.750	1 NFC-E	1-1
1982 Dal	6	3	0	.667	2 NFC	2-1
1983 Dal	12	4	0	.750	2 NFC-E	0-1
1984 Dal	9	7	0	.563	4 NFC-E	—
1985 Dal	10	6	0	.625	1 NFC-E	0-1
1986 Dal	7	9	0	.438	3 NFC-E	—
1987 Dal	7	8	0	.467	2 NFC-E	—
1988 Dal	3	13	0	.188	5 NFC-E	—
29 yrs	250	162	6	.605		20-16

\+ NFC Champion
\# NFC Champion; won Super Bowl

WALLY LEMM Lemm, Walter Homer
Col: Carroll B: 10/23/1919, Chicago, IL D: 10/2/1988, Waukesha, WI

	W	L	T	Pct.	Place	P
1961 Hou#	9	0	0	1.000	1 AFL-E	1-0
1962 StL	4	9	1	.308	6 NFL-E	—
1963 StL	9	5	0	.643	3 NFL-E	—
1964 StL	9	3	2	.750	2 NFL-E	—
1965 StL	5	9	0	.357	6 NFL-E	—
1966 Hou	3	11	0	.214	4 AFL-E	—
1967 Hou	9	4	1	.692	1 AFL-E	0-1
1968 Hou	7	7	0	.500	2 AFL-E	—
1969 Hou	6	6	2	.500	2 AFL-E	0-1
1970 Hou	3	10	1	.231	4 AFC-C	—
	64	64	7	.500		1-2

\# AFL Champion

JIM LEONARD***

	W	L	T	Pct.	Place	P
1945 Pit	2	8	0	.200	5 NFL-E	—

MARV LEVY Levy, Marvin Daniel
Col: Coe B: 8/3/1926, Chicago, IL

	W	L	T	Pct.	Place	P
1978 KC	4	12	0	.250	5 AFC-W	—
1979 KC	7	9	0	.438	5 AFC-W	—
1980 KC	8	8	0	.500	3 AFC-W	—
1981 KC	9	7	0	.563	3 AFC-W	—
1982 KC	3	6	0	.333	11 AFC	—
1986 Buf	2	5	0	.286	4 AFC-E	—
1987 Buf	7	8	0	.467	4 AFC-E	—
1988 Buf	12	4	0	.750	1 AFC-E	1-1
1989 Buf	9	7	0	.563	1 AFC-E	0-1
1990 Buf#	13	3	0	.813	1 AFC-E	2-1
1991 Buf#	13	3	0	.813	1 AFC-E	2-1
1992 Buf#	11	5	0	.688	2 AFC-E	3-1
1993 Buf#	12	4	0	.750	1 AFC-E	2-1
1994 Buf	7	9	0	.438	4 AFC-E	—
1995 Buf	10	6	0	.625	1 AFC-E	1-1
1996 Buf	10	6	0	.625	2 AFC-E	0-1
1997 Buf	6	10	0	.375	4 AFC-E	—
	143	112	0	.561		11-8

\# AFC Champion

ART LEWIS***

	W	L	T	Pct.	Place	P
1938 Cle	4	4	0	.500	4 NFL-W	—

VINCE LOMBARDI Lombardi, Vincent Thomas
Col: Fordham B: 6/11/1913, Brooklyn, NY D: 9/3/1970, Washington, DC

	W	L	T	Pct.	Place	P
1959 GB	7	5	0	.583	3 NFL-W	—
1960 GB	8	4	0	.667	1 NFL-W	0-1
1961 GB#	11	3	0	.786	1 NFL-W	1-0
1962 GB#	13	1	0	.929	1 NFL-W	1-0
1963 GB	11	2	1	.846	2 NFL-W	—

	W	L	T	Pct.	Place	P
1964 GB	8	5	1	.615	2 NFL-W	—
1965 GB#	10	3	1	.769	1 NFL-W	2-0
1966 GB+	12	2	0	.857	1 NFL-W	2-0
1967 GB+	9	4	1	.692	1 NFL-C	3-0
1969 Was	7	5	2	.583	2 NFL-Cap	—
	96	34	6	.728		9-1

\# NFL Champion
\+ NFL Champion; won Super Bowl

LEO LYONS Lyons, Leo V.
No college B: 3/11/1892, Fairport, NY D: 5/18/1976, Rochester, NY

	W	L	T	Pct.	Place	P
1923 Roch	0	4	0	.000	20 NFL	—
1924 Roch	0	3	0	.000	18 NFL	—
	0	7	0	.000		—

JOHN MACKOVIC Mackovic, John
Col: Wake Forest B: 10/1/1943, Barberton, OH

	W	L	T	Pct.	Place	P
1983 KC	6	10	0	.375	5 AFC-W	—
1984 KC	8	8	0	.500	4 AFC-W	—
1985 KC	6	10	0	.375	5 AFC-W	—
1986 KC	10	6	0	.625	2 AFC-W	0-1
	30	34	0	.469		0-1

DICK MACPHERSON MacPherson, Richard F.
Col: Springfield B: 11/4/1930, Old Town, ME

	W	L	T	Pct.	Place	P
1991 NE	6	10	0	.375	4 AFC-E	—
1992 NE	2	14	0	.125	5 AFC-E	—
	8	24	0	.250		—

JOHN MADDEN Madden, John Earl
Col: Cal-Poly SLO B: 4/10/1936, Daly City, CA

	W	L	T	Pct.	Place	P
1969 Oak	12	1	1	.923	1 AFL-W	1-1
1970 Oak	8	4	2	.667	1 AFC-W	1-1
1971 Oak	8	4	2	.667	2 AFC-W	—
1972 Oak	10	3	1	.750	1 AFC-W	0-1
1973 Oak	9	4	1	.679	1 AFC-W	1-1
1974 Oak	12	2	0	.857	1 AFC-W	1-1
1975 Oak	11	3	0	.786	1 AFC-W	1-1
1976 Oak#	13	1	0	.929	1 AFC-W	3-0
1977 Oak	11	3	0	.786	2 AFC-W	1-1
1978 Oak	9	7	0	.563	2 AFC-W	—
	103	32	7	.750		9-7

\# AFC Champion; won Super Bowl

LOU MAHRT***

	W	L	T	Pct.	Place	P
1927 Day	1	6	1	.143	10 NFL	—

RAY MALAVASI Malavasi, Raymond Giovanni Baptiste
Col: Army; Mississippi State B: 11/8/1930, Passaic, NJ
D: 12/15/1987, Santa Ana, CA

	W	L	T	Pct.	Place	P
1966 Den	4	8	0	.333	4 AFL-W	—
1978 LARm	12	4	0	.750	1 NFC-W	1-1
1979 LARm#	9	7	0	.563	1 NFC-W	2-1
1980 LARm	11	5	0	.688	2 NFC-W	0-1
1981 LARm	6	10	0	.375	3 NFC-W	—
1982 LARm	2	7	0	.222	14 NFC	—
	44	41	0	.518		3-3

\# NFC Champion

TED MARCHIBRODA***

	W	L	T	Pct.	Place	P
1975 Bal	10	4	0	.714	1 AFC-E	0-1
1976 Bal	11	3	0	.786	1 AFC-E	0-1
1977 Bal	10	4	0	.714	1 AFC-E	0-1
1978 Bal	5	11	0	.313	5 AFC-E	—
1979 Bal	5	11	0	.313	5 AFC-E	—
1992 Ind	9	7	0	.563	3 AFC-E	—
1993 Ind	4	12	0	.250	5 AFC-E	—
1994 Ind	8	8	0	.500	3 AFC-E	—
1995 Ind	9	7	0	.563	2 AFC-E	2-1
1996 Bal	4	12	0	.250	5 AFC-C	—
1997 Bal	6	9	1	.406	5 AFC-C	—
1998 Bal	6	10	0	.375	4 AFC-C	—
	83	86	1	.491		2-4

STEVE MARIUCCI Mariucci, Steven
Col: Northern Michigan B: 11/4/1955, Iron Mountain, MI

	W	L	T	Pct.	Place	P
1997 SF	13	3	0	.813	1 NFC-W	1-1
1998 SF	12	4	0	.750	2 NFC-W	1-1
	25	7	0	.781		2-2

BILLY MARSHALL Marshall, William H.
Col: Detroit Mercy

	W	L	T	Pct.	Place	P
1920 Det	2	3	3	.400	9 NFL	—
1921 Det	1	5	1	.167	16 NFL	—
	3	8	4	.333		—

JOHN MAZUR Mazur, John
Col: Notre Dame B: 6/17/1930, Plymouth, PA

	W	L	T	Pct.	Place	P
1970 Bos	1	6	0	.143	5 AFC-E	—
1971 NE	6	8	0	.429	3 AFC-E	—
1972 NE	2	7	0	.222	5 AFC-E	—
	9	21	0	.300		—

DON MCCAFFERTY***

	W	L	T	Pct.	Place	P
1970 Bal#	11	2	1	.846	1 AFC-E	3-0
1971 Bal	10	4	0	.714	2 AFC-E	1-1
1972 Bal	1	4	0	.200	3 AFC-E	—
1973 Det	6	7	1	.464	2 NFC-C	—
	28	17	2	.617		4-1

\# AFC Champion; won Super Bowl

MIKE MCCORMACK***

	W	L	T	Pct.	Place	P
1973 Phi	5	8	1	.393	3 NFC-E	—
1974 Phi	7	7	0	.500	4 NFC-E	—
1975 Phi	4	10	0	.286	5 NFC-E	—
1980 Bal	7	9	0	.438	4 AFC-E	—
1981 Bal	2	14	0	.125	4 AFC-E	—
1982 Sea	4	3	0	.571	10 AFC	—
	29	51	1	.364		—

PETE MCCULLEY McCulley, Peter
Col: Louisiana Tech B: 11/29/1931, Franklin, MS Deceased

	W	L	T	Pct.	Place	P
1978 SF	1	8	0	.111	4 NFC-W	—

CAP MCEWAN McEwan, John James
Col: Minnesota; Army B: 2/18/1893, Alexandria, MN
D: 8/9/1970, New York, NY

	W	L	T	Pct.	Place	P
1933 Bkn	5	4	1	.556	2 NFL-E	—
1934 Bkn	4	7	0	.364	3 NFL-E	—
	9	11	1	.452		—

AL MCGALL *(No biographical information available.)*

	W	L	T	Pct.	Place	P
1930 Nwk	0	3	0	.000	11 NFL	—

WALLY MCILWAIN***

	W	L	T	Pct.	Place	P
1926 Rac	0	2	0	.000	18 NFL	—

JOHN MCKAY McKay, John Harvey
Col: Purdue; Oregon B: 7/5/1923, Everettsville, WV

	W	L	T	Pct.	Place	P
1976 TB	0	14	0	.000	5 AFC-W	—
1977 TB	2	12	0	.143	5 NFC-C	—
1978 TB	5	11	0	.313	5 NFC-C	—
1979 TB	10	6	0	.625	1 NFC-C	1-1
1980 TB	5	10	1	.344	4 NFC-C	—
1981 TB	9	7	0	.563	1 NFC-C	0-1
1982 TB	5	4	0	.556	7 NFC	0-1
1983 TB	2	14	0	.125	5 NFC-C	—
1984 TB	6	10	0	.375	3 NFC-C	—
	44	88	1	.335		1-3

RAY MCLEAN***

	W	L	T	Pct.	Place	P
1953 GB*	0	2	0	.000	6 NFL-W	—
1958 GB	1	10	1	.091	6 NFL-W	—
	1	12	1	.107		—

* co-coach with Hugh Devore

BO MCMILLIN***

	W	L	T	Pct.	Place	P
1948 Det	2	10	0	.167	5 NFL-W	—
1949 Det	4	8	0	.333	4 NFL-W	—
1950 Det	6	6	0	.500	4 NFL-N	—
1951 Phi	2	0	0	1.000	5 NFL-N	—
	14	24	0	.368		—

	W	L	T	Pct.	Place	P
JOHNNY (BLOOD) MCNALLY* **						
1937 Pit	4	7	0	.364	3 NFL-E	—
1938 Pit	2	9	0	.182	5 NFL-E	—
1939 Pit	0	3	0	.000	5 NFL-E	—
	6	19	0	.240		—

	W	L	T	Pct.	Place	P
BILL MCPEAK* **						
1961 Was	1	12	1	.077	7 NFL-E	—
1962 Was	5	7	2	.417	4 NFL-E	—
1963 Was	3	11	0	.214	6 NFL-E	—
1964 Was	6	8	0	.429	4 NFL-E	—
1965 Was	6	8	0	.429	4 NFL-E	—
	21	46	3	.321		—

JOHN MCVAY McVay, John E.
Col: Miami (OH) B: 1/5/1931, Bellaire, OH

	W	L	T	Pct.	Place	P
1976 NYG	3	4	0	.429	5 NFC-E	—
1977 NYG	5	9	0	.357	5 NFC-E	—
1978 NYG	6	10	0	.375	5 NFC-E	—
	14	23	0	.378		—

HARRY MEHRE***

	W	L	T	Pct.	Place	P
1923 Min	2	5	2	.286	13 NFL	—

KEN MEYER Meyer, Ken
Col: Denison B: 7/14/1925, Erie, PA

	W	L	T	Pct.	Place	P
1977 SF	5	9	0	.357	3 NFC-W	—

RON MEYER Meyer, Ronald Shaw
Col: Purdue B: 2/17/1941, Westerville, OH

	W	L	T	Pct.	Place	P
1982 NE	5	4	0	.556	7 AFC	0-1
1983 NE	8	8	0	.500	2 AFC-E	—
1984 NE	5	3	0	.625	2 AFC-E	—
1986 Ind	3	0	0	1.000	5 AFC-E	—
1987 Ind	9	6	0	.600	1 AFC-E	0-1
1988 Ind	9	7	0	.563	2 AFC-E	—
1989 Ind	8	8	0	.500	2 AFC-E	—
1990 Ind	7	9	0	.438	3 AFC-E	—
1991 Ind	0	5	0	.000	5 AFC-E	—
	54	50	0	.519		0-2

WALT MICHAELS***

	W	L	T	Pct.	Place	P
1977 NYJ	3	11	0	.214	4 AFC-E	—
1978 NYJ	8	8	0	.500	3 AFC-E	—
1979 NYJ	8	8	0	.500	3 AFC-E	—
1980 NYJ	4	12	0	.250	5 AFC-E	—
1981 NYJ	10	5	1	.656	2 AFC-E	0-1
1982 NYJ	6	3	0	.667	6 AFC	2-1
	39	47	1	.454		2-2

JOHN MICHELOSEN Michelosen, John P.
Col: Pittsburgh B: 2/13/1916, Ambridge, PA D: 10/17/1982, San Diego, CA

	W	L	T	Pct.	Place	P
1948 Pit	4	8	0	.333	4 NFL-E	—
1949 Pit	6	5	1	.545	2 NFL-E	—
1950 Pit	6	6	0	.500	4 NFL-A	—
1951 Pit	4	7	1	.364	4 NFL-A	—
	20	26	2	.438		—

RED MILLER Miller, Robert N.
Col: Western Illinois B: 10/31/1927, Macomb, IL

	W	L	T	Pct.	Place	P
1977 Den#	12	2	0	.857	1 AFC-W	2-1
1978 Den	10	6	0	.625	1 AFC-W	0-1
1979 Den	10	6	0	.625	2 AFC-W	0-1
1980 Den	8	8	0	.500	4 AFC-W	—
	40	22	0	.645		2-3

\# AFC Champion

WAYNE MILLNER***

	W	L	T	Pct.	Place	P
1951 Phi	2	8	0	.200	5 NFL-A	—

DICK MODZELEWSKI***

	W	L	T	Pct.	Place	P
1977 Cle	0	1	0	.000	4 AFC-W	—

KEITH MOLESWORTH***

	W	L	T	Pct.	Place	P
1953 Bal	3	9	0	.250	5 NFL-W	—

JIM MORA Mora, James Ernest
Col: Occidental B: 5/24/1935, Glendale, CA

	W	L	T	Pct.	Place	P
1986 NO	7	9	0	.438	4 NFC-W	—
1987 NO	12	3	0	.800	2 NFC-W	0-1
1988 NO	10	6	0	.625	3 NFC-W	—
1989 NO	9	7	0	.563	3 NFC-W	—
1990 NO	8	8	0	.500	2 NFC-W	0-1
1991 NO	11	5	0	.688	1 NFC-W	0-1
1992 NO	12	4	0	.750	2 NFC-W	0-1
1993 NO	8	8	0	.500	2 NFC-W	—
1994 NO	7	9	0	.438	2 NFC-W	—
1995 NO	7	9	0	.438	5 NFC-W	—
1996 NO	2	6	0	.250	5 NFC-W	—
1998 Ind	3	13	0	.188	5 AFC-E	—
	96	87	0	.525		0-4

CHARLEY MORAN Moran, Charles Barthell (Uncle Charley)
Col: Bethel (KY) B: 2/22/1878, Nashville, TN D: 6/14/1949, Horse Cave, KY

	W	L	T	Pct.	Place	P
1927 Fra	2	5	1	.286	7 NFL	—

BRICK MULLER***

	W	L	T	Pct.	Place	P
1926 LA*	6	3	1	.667	6 NFL	—

* co-coach with Tut Imlay

JOHNNY MURPHY
(No biographical information available.)

	W	L	T	Pct.	Place	P
1924 Roch	0	4	0	.000	18 NFL	—

GREASY NEALE Neale, Alfred Earle
Col: West Virginia Wesleyan B: 11/3/1891, Parkersburg, WV D: 11/2/1973, Lake Worth, FL

	W	L	T	Pct.	Place	P
1941 Phi	2	8	1	.200	4 NFL-E	—
1942 Phi	2	9	0	.182	5 NFL-E	—
1943 PhPt	5	4	1	.556	3 NFL-E	—
1944 Phi	7	1	2	.875	2 NFL-E	—
1945 Phi	7	3	0	.700	2 NFL-E	—
1946 Phi	6	5	0	.545	2 NFL-E	—
1947 Phi	8	4	0	.667	1 NFL-E	1-1
1948 Phi#	9	2	1	.818	1 NFL-E	1-0
1949 Phi#	11	1	0	.917	1 NFL-E	1-0
1950 Phi	6	6	0	.500	3 NFL-A	—
	63	43	5	.590		3-1

\# NFL Champion

AL NESSER***

	W	L	T	Pct.	Place	P
1926 Akr	0	1	1	.000	16 NFL	—

TED NESSER***

	W	L	T	Pct.	Place	P
1920 Col	2	6	2	.250	13 NFL	—
1921 Col	1	8	0	.111	17 NFL	—
	3	14	2	.211		—

ERNIE NEVERS***

	W	L	T	Pct.	Place	P
1927 Dul	1	8	0	.111	11 NFL	—
1930 ChiC	5	6	2	.455	7 NFL	—
1931 ChiC	5	2	0	.714	4 NFL	—
1939 ChiC	1	10	0	.091	5 NFL-W	—
	12	26	2	.325		—

FRANK NIED Nied, Francis Theodore
No college B: 8/14/1894, Akron, OH D: 5/13/1969, Fort Lauderdale, FL

	W	L	T	Pct.	Place	P
1926 Akr	1	3	2	.250	16 NFL	—

MIKE NIXON***

	W	L	T	Pct.	Place	P
1959 Was	3	9	0	.250	5 NFL-E	—
1960 Was	1	9	2	.100	6 NFL-E	—
1965 Pit	2	12	0	.143	7 NFL-E	—
	6	30	2	.184		—

DICK NOLAN***

	W	L	T	Pct.	Place	P
1968 SF	7	6	1	.538	3 NFL-Coa	—
1969 SF	4	8	2	.333	4 NFL-Coa	—
1970 SF	10	3	1	.769	1 NFC-W	1-1
1971 SF	9	5	0	.643	1 NFC-W	1-1

	W	L	T	Pct.	Place	P
1972 SF	8	5	1	.607	1 NFC-W	0-1
1973 SF	5	9	0	.357	4 NFC-W	—
1974 SF	6	8	0	.429	2 NFC-W	—
1975 SF	5	9	0	.357	2 NFC-W	—
1978 NO	7	9	0	.438	3 NFC-W	—
1979 NO	8	8	0	.500	2 NFC-W	—
1980 NO	0	12	0	.000	4 NFC-W	—
	69	82	5	.458		2-3

CHUCK NOLL***

	W	L	T	Pct.	Place	P
1969 Pit	1	13	0	.071	4 NFL-Cty	—
1970 Pit	5	9	0	.357	3 AFC-C	—
1971 Pit	6	8	0	.429	2 AFC-C	—
1972 Pit	11	3	0	.786	1 AFC-C	1-1
1973 Pit	10	4	0	.714	2 AFC-C	0-1
1974 Pit#	10	3	1	.750	1 AFC-C	3-0
1975 Pit#	12	2	0	.857	1 AFC-C	3-0
1976 Pit	10	4	0	.714	1 AFC-C	1-1
1977 Pit	9	5	0	.643	1 AFC-C	0-1
1978 Pit#	14	2	0	.875	1 AFC-C	3-0
1979 Pit#	12	4	0	.750	1 AFC-C	3-0
1980 Pit	9	7	0	.563	3 AFC-C	—
1981 Pit	8	8	0	.500	2 AFC-C	—
1982 Pit	6	3	0	.667	4 AFC	0-1
1983 Pit	10	6	0	.625	1 AFC-C	0-1
1984 Pit	9	7	0	.563	1 AFC-C	1-1
1985 Pit	7	9	0	.438	3 AFC-C	—
1986 Pit	6	10	0	.375	3 AFC-C	—
1987 Pit	8	7	0	.533	3 AFC-C	—
1988 Pit	5	11	0	.313	4 AFC-C	—
1989 Pit	9	7	0	.563	3 AFC-C	1-1
1990 Pit	9	7	0	.563	3 AFC-C	—
1991 Pit	7	9	0	.438	2 AFC-C	—
	193	148	1	.566		16-8

\# AFC Champion; won Super Bowl

JOHN NORTH North, John Puckett
Col: Vanderbilt B: 6/17/1921, Old Hickory, TN

	W	L	T	Pct.	Place	P
1973 NO	5	9	0	.357	3 NFC-W	—
1974 NO	5	9	0	.357	3 NFC-W	—
1975 NO	1	5	0	.167	4 NFC-W	—
	11	23	0	.324		—

FRED O'CONNOR O'Connor, Fred
Col: E. Stroudsburg State B: 9/1/1939, Brooklyn, NY

	W	L	T	Pct.	Place	P
1978 SF	1	6	0	.143	4 NFC-W	—

STEVE OWEN***

	W	L	T	Pct.	Place	P
1930 NYG*	2	0	0	1.000	2 NFL	—
1931 NYG	7	6	1	.538	5 NFL	—
1932 NYG	4	6	2	.400	5 NFL	—
1933 NYG	11	3	0	.786	1 NFL-E	0-1
1934 NYG#	8	5	0	.615	1 NFL-E	1-0
1935 NYG	9	3	0	.750	1 NFL-E	0-1
1936 NYG	5	6	1	.455	3 NFL-E	—
1937 NYG	6	3	2	.667	2 NFL-E	—
1938 NYG#	8	2	1	.800	1 NFL-E	1-0
1939 NYG	9	1	1	.900	1 NFL-E	0-1
1940 NYG	6	4	1	.600	3 NFL-E	—
1941 NYG	8	3	0	.727	1 NFL-E	0-1
1942 NYG	5	5	1	.500	3 NFL-E	—
1943 NYG	6	3	1	.667	2 NFL-E	0-1
1944 NYG	8	1	1	.889	1 NFL-E	0-1
1945 NYG	3	6	1	.333	3 NFL-E	—
1946 NYG	7	3	1	.700	1 NFL-E	0-1
1947 NYG	2	8	2	.200	5 NFL-E	—
1948 NYG	4	8	0	.333	3 NFL-E	—
1949 NYG	6	6	0	.500	3 NFL-E	—
1950 NYG	10	2	0	.833	2 NFL-A	0-1
1951 NYG	9	2	1	.818	2 NFL-A	—
1952 NYG	7	5	0	.583	2 NFL-A	—
1953 NYG	3	9	0	.250	5 NFL-E	—
	153	100	17	.598		2-8

* co-coach with Benny Friedman
\# NFL Champion

MIKE PALM***

	W	L	T	Pct.	Place	P
1933 CinN^	3	6	1	.333	4 NFL-W	—

^ Al Jolley was coach at beginning of season with Palm as assistant. Evidence suggests Palm became coach sometime before season's end. Cincinnati's season record is given here because it is unclear which games should be credited to which man.

BILL PARCELLS Parcells, Duane Charles (Tuna)
Col: Wichita State B: 8/22/1941, Englewood, NJ

	W	L	T	Pct.	Place	P
1983 NYG	3	12	1	.219	5 NFC-E	—
1984 NYG	9	7	0	.563	2 NFC-E	1-1
1985 NYG	10	6	0	.625	2 NFC-E	1-1
1986 NYG#	14	2	0	.875	1 NFC-E	3-0
1987 NYG	6	9	0	.400	5 NFC-E	—
1988 NYG	10	6	0	.625	2 NFC-E	—
1989 NYG	12	4	0	.750	1 NFC-E	0-1
1990 NYG#	13	3	0	.813	1 NFC-E	3-0
1993 NE	5	11	0	.313	4 AFC-E	—
1994 NE	10	6	0	.625	2 AFC-E	0-1
1995 NE	6	10	0	.375	4 AFC-E	—
1996 NE+	11	5	0	.688	1 AFC-E	2-1
1997 NYJ	9	7	0	.563	3 AFC-E	—
1998 NYJ	12	4	0	.750	1 AFC-E	1-1
	130	92	1	.585		11-6

\# NFL Champion; won Super Bowl
\+ AFC Champion

JACK PARDEE***

	W	L	T	Pct.	Place	P
1975 ChiB	4	10	0	.286	3 NFC-C	—
1976 ChiB	7	7	0	.500	2 NFC-C	—
1977 ChiB	9	5	0	.643	2 NFC-C	0-1
1978 Was	8	8	0	.500	3 NFC-E	—
1979 Was	10	6	0	.625	3 NFC-E	—
1980 Was	6	10	0	.375	3 NFC-E	—
1990 Hou	9	7	0	.563	2 AFC-C	0-1
1991 Hou	11	5	0	.688	1 AFC-C	1-1
1992 Hou	10	6	0	.625	2 AFC-C	0-1
1993 Hou	12	4	0	.750	1 AFC-C	0-1
1994 Hou	1	9	0	.100	4 AFC-C	—
	87	77	0	.530		1-5

BUDDY PARKER***

	W	L	T	Pct.	Place	P
1949 ChiC*	2	4	0	.333	3 NFL-W	—
1949 ChiC	4	1	1	.800	3 NFL-W	—
1951 Det	7	4	1	.636	2 NFL-N	—
1952 Det#	9	3	0	.750	1 NFL-N	2-0
1953 Det#	10	2	0	.833	1 NFL-W	1-0
1954 Det	9	2	1	.818	1 NFL-W	0-1
1955 Det	3	9	0	.250	6 NFL-W	—
1956 Det	9	3	0	.750	2 NFL-W	—
1957 Pit	6	6	0	.500	3 NFL-E	—
1958 Pit	7	4	1	.636	3 NFL-E	—
1959 Pit	6	5	1	.545	4 NFL-E	—
1960 Pit	5	6	1	.455	5 NFL-E	—
1961 Pit	6	8	0	.429	5 NFL-E	—
1962 Pit	9	5	0	.643	2 NFL-E	—
1963 Pit	7	4	3	.636	4 NFL-E	—
1964 Pit	5	9	0	.357	6 NFL-E	—
	104	75	9	.577		3-1

* co-coach with Phil Handler
\# NFL Champion

JACK PATERA***

	W	L	T	Pct.	Place	P
1976 Sea	2	12	0	.143	5 NFC-W	—
1977 Sea	5	9	0	.357	4 AFC-W	—
1978 Sea	9	7	0	.563	3 AFC-W	—
1979 Sea	9	7	0	.563	3 AFC-W	—
1980 Sea	4	12	0	.250	5 AFC-W	—
1981 Sea	6	10	0	.375	5 AFC-W	—
1982 Sea	0	2	0	.000	10 AFC	—
	35	59	0	.372		—

	W	L	T	Pct.	Place	P
PAT PEPPLER Peppler, Albert						
Col: Michigan State B: 4/16/1922, Baltimore, MD						
1976 Atl	3	6	0	.333	3 NFC-W	—
RAY PERKINS***						
1979 NYG	6	10	0	.375	4 NFC-E	—
1980 NYG	4	12	0	.250	5 NFC-E	—
1981 NYG	9	7	0	.563	3 NFC-E	1-1
1982 NYG	4	5	0	.444	10 NFC	—
1987 TB	4	11	0	.267	4 NFC-C	—
1988 TB	5	11	0	.313	3 NFC-C	—
1989 TB	5	11	0	.313	5 NFC-C	—
1990 TB	5	8	0	.385	2 NFC-C	—
	42	75	0	.359		1-1
BILL PETERSON Peterson, William E.						
Col: Ohio Northern B: 5/14/1923, Toronto, OH						
1972 Hou	1	13	0	.071	4 AFC-C	—
1973 Hou	0	5	0	.000	4 AFC-C	—
	1	18	0	.053		—
RICHIE PETITBON***						
1993 Was	4	12	0	.250	5 NFC-E	—
JIM PHELAN Phelan, James Michael						
Col: Notre Dame B: 12/5/1893, Portland, OR D: 11/14/1974, Honolulu, HI						
AAFC						
1948 LA-A	7	7	0	.500		—
1949 LA-A	4	8	0	.333		—
	11	15	0	.423		—
NFL						
1952 Dal	1	11	0	.083	6 NFL-N	—
BUM PHILLIPS Phillips, Oail Andrews						
Col: Lamar JC (TX); Stephen F. Austin B: 9/29/1923, Orange, TX						
1975 Hou	10	4	0	.714	3 AFC-C	—
1976 Hou	5	9	0	.357	4 AFC-C	—
1977 Hou	8	6	0	.571	2 AFC-C	—
1978 Hou	10	6	0	.625	2 AFC-C	2-1
1979 Hou	11	5	0	.688	2 AFC-C	2-1
1980 Hou	11	5	0	.688	2 AFC-C	0-1
1981 NO	4	12	0	.250	4 NFC-W	—
1982 NO	4	5	0	.444	9 NFC	—
1983 NO	8	8	0	.500	3 NFC-W	—
1984 NO	7	9	0	.438	3 NFC-W	—
1985 NO	4	8	0	.333	3 NFC-W	—
	82	77	0	.516		4-3
WADE PHILLIPS Phillips, Wade						
Col: Houston B: 6/21/1947, Orange, TX						
1985 NO	1	3	0	.250	3 NFC-W	—
1993 Den	9	7	0	.563	3 AFC-W	0-1
1994 Den	7	9	0	.438	4 AFC-W	—
1998 Buf	10	6	0	.625	3 AFC-E	0-1
	27	25	0	.519		0-2
AL PIEROTTI***						
1920 Cle	2	2	1	.500	10 NFL	—
FRITZ POLLARD***						
1921 Akr*	8	3	1	.727	3 NFL	—
1925 Ham	0	1	0	.000	14 NFL	—
	8	4	1	.654		—

* co-coach with Elgie Tobin

	W	L	T	Pct.	Place	P
HAMP POOL***						
AAFC						
1946 MiaA A	2	6	0	.250		—
1947 ChiA A	1	3	0	.250		—
	3	9	0	.250		—
NFL						
1952 LARm	9	3	0	.750	2 NFL-N	0-1
1953 LARm	8	3	1	.727	3 NFL-W	—
1954 LARm	6	5	1	.545	4 NFL-W	—
	23	10	2	.686		0-1
EARL POTTEIGER***						
1924 Ken*	0	4	1	.000	16 NFL	—
1927 NYG#	11	1	1	.917	1 NFL	—
1928 NYG	4	7	2	.364	6 NFL	—
	15	12	4	.548		—

* co-coach with Bo Hanley
\# NFL Champion

	W	L	T	Pct.	Place	P
RAY PROCHASKA***						
1961 StL*	2	0	0	1.000	4 NFL-E	—

* co-coach with Chuck Drulis and Ray Willsey

	W	L	T	Pct.	Place	P
TOMMY PROTHO Prothro, James Thompson						
Col: Duke B: 7/20/1920, Memphis, TN D: 5/14/1995, Memphis, TN						
1971 LARm	8	5	1	.615	2 NFC-W	—
1972 LARm	6	7	1	.464	3 NFC-W	—
1974 SD	5	9	0	.357	4 AFC-W	—
1975 SD	2	12	0	.143	4 AFC-W	—
1976 SD	6	8	0	.429	3 AFC-W	—
1977 SD	7	7	0	.500	3 AFC-W	—
1978 SD	1	3	0	.250	4 AFC-W	—
	35	51	2	.409		—
JOHN RALSTON Ralston, John R.						
Col: California B: 4/26/1927, Oakland, CA						
1972 Den	5	9	0	.357	3 AFC-W	—
1973 Den	7	5	2	.571	2 AFC-W	—
1974 Den	7	6	1	.536	2 AFC-W	—
1975 Den	6	8	0	.429	2 AFC-W	—
1976 Den	9	5	0	.643	2 AFC-W	—
	34	33	3	.507		—
BUSTER RAMSEY***						
1960 Buf	5	8	1	.385	3 AFL-E	—
1961 Buf	6	8	0	.429	4 AFL-E	—
	11	16	1	.411		—
DICK RAUCH***						
1925 Pott	10	2	0	.833	2 NFL	—
1926 Pott	10	2	2	.833	3 NFL	—
1927 Pott	5	8	0	.385	8 NFL	—
1928 NYY	4	8	1	.333	7 NFL	—
1929 Bos	4	4	0	.500	5 NFL	—
	33	24	3	.575		—
JOHN RAUCH***						
1966 Oak	8	5	1	.615	2 AFL-W	—
1967 Oak#	13	1	0	.929	1 AFL-W	1-1
1968 Oak	12	2	0	.857	1 AFL-W	1-1
1969 Buf	4	10	0	.286	4 AFL-E	—
1970 Buf	3	10	1	.231	4 AFC-E	—
	40	28	2	.586		2-2

\# AFL Champion

	W	L	T	Pct.	Place	P
DAN REEVES***						
1981 Den	10	6	0	.625	2 AFC-W	—
1982 Den	2	7	0	.222	12 AFC	—
1983 Den	9	7	0	.563	3 AFC-W	0-1
1984 Den	13	3	0	.813	1 AFC-W	0-1
1985 Den	11	5	0	.688	2 AFC-W	—
1986 Den*	11	5	0	.688	1 AFC-W	2-1
1987 Den*	10	4	1	.700	1 AFC-W	2-1
1988 Den	8	8	0	.500	2 AFC-W	—
1989 Den*	11	5	0	.688	1 AFC-W	2-1
1990 Den	5	11	0	.313	5 AFC-W	—
1991 Den	12	4	0	.750	1 AFC-W	1-1
1992 Den	8	8	0	.500	3 AFC-W	—
1993 NYG	11	5	0	.688	2 NFC-E	1-1
1994 NYG	9	7	0	.563	2 NFC-E	—
1995 NYG	5	11	0	.313	4 NFC-E	—
1996 NYG	6	10	0	.375	5 NFC-E	—
1997 Atl	7	9	0	.438	3 NFC-W	—

	W	L	T	Pct.	Place	P
1998 Atl#	14	2	0	.875	1 NFC-W	2-1
	162	117	1	.580		10-8

* AFC Champion
# NFC Champion

RAY RHODES***

	W	L	T	Pct.	Place	P
1995 Phi	10	6	0	.625	2 NFC-E	1-1
1996 Phi	10	6	0	.625	2 NFC-E	0-1
1997 Phi	6	9	1	.406	3 NFC-E	—
1998 Phi	3	13	0	.188	5 NFC-E	—
	29	34	1	.461		1-2

HOMER RICE Rice, Homer C.
Col: Centre B: 2/20/1927, Bellevue, KY

	W	L	T	Pct.	Place	P
1978 Cin	4	7	0	.364	4 AFC-C	—
1979 Cin	4	12	0	.250	4 AFC-C	—
	8	19	0	.296		—

RAY RICHARDS***

	W	L	T	Pct.	Place	P
1955 ChiC	4	7	1	.364	4 NFL-E	—
1956 ChiC	7	5	0	.583	2 NFL-E	—
1957 ChiC	3	9	0	.250	6 NFL-E	—
	14	21	1	.403		—

JIM RINGO***

	W	L	T	Pct.	Place	P
1976 Buf	0	9	0	.000	5 AFC-E	—
1977 Buf	3	11	0	.214	5 AFC-E	—
	3	20	0	.130		—

HARRY ROBB***

	W	L	T	Pct.	Place	P
1925 Can	4	4	0	.500	11 NFL	—
1926 Can*	1	9	3	.100	20 NFL	—
	5	13	3	.310		—

* co-coach with Wilbur Henry

J.D. ROBERTS Roberts, John David
Col: Oklahoma B: 10/24/1932, Oklahoma City, OK

	W	L	T	Pct.	Place	P
1970 NO	1	6	0	.143	4 NFC-W	—
1971 NO	4	8	2	.333	4 NFC-W	—
1972 NO	2	11	1	.179	4 NFC-W	—
	7	25	3	.243		—

ED ROBINSON Robinson, Edward North
Col: Brown B: 10/15/1873, Lynn, MA D: 3/10/1995, Boston, MA

	W	L	T	Pct.	Place	P
1931 Prov	4	4	3	.500	6 NFL	—

JOHN ROBINSON Robinson, John Alexander
Col: Oregon B: 7/25/1935, Chicago, IL

	W	L	T	Pct.	Place	P
1983 LARm	9	7	0	.563	2 NFC-W	1-1
1984 LARm	10	6	0	.625	2 NFC-W	0-1
1985 LARm	11	5	0	.688	1 NFC-W	1-1
1986 LARm	10	6	0	.625	2 NFC-W	0-1
1987 LARm	6	9	0	.400	3 NFC-W	—
1988 LARm	10	6	0	.625	2 NFC-W	0-1
1989 LARm	11	5	0	.688	2 NFC-W	2-1
1990 LARm	5	11	0	.313	3 NFC-W	—
1991 LARm	3	13	0	.188	4 NFC-W	—
	75	68	0	.524		4-6

CHARLEY ROGERS***

	W	L	T	Pct.	Place	P
1927 Fra*	4	4	2	.500	7 NFL	—

* co-coach with Russ Daugherty, Ed Weir, and Swede Youngstrom

DARRYL ROGERS Rogers, Darryl D.
Col: Fresno State B: 5/28/1935, Los Angeles, CA

	W	L	T	Pct.	Place	P
1985 Det	7	9	0	.438	4 NFC-C	—
1986 Det	5	11	0	.313	3 NFC-C	—
1987 Det	4	11	0	.267	5 NFC-C	—
1988 Det	2	9	0	.182	4 NFC-C	—
	18	40	0	.310		—

GENE RONZANI***

	W	L	T	Pct.	Place	P
1950 GB	3	9	0	.250	5 NFL-N	—
1951 GB	3	9	0	.250	5 NFL-N	—
1952 GB	6	6	0	.500	4 NFL-N	—
1953 GB	2	7	1	.222	6 NFL-W	—
	14	31	1	.315		—

TAM ROSE***

	W	L	T	Pct.	Place	P
1921 Ton	0	1	0	.000	18 NFL	—

BOBBY ROSS Ross, Robert Joseph
Col: VMI B: 12/23/1935, Richmond, VA

	W	L	T	Pct.	Place	P
1992 SD	11	5	0	.688	1 AFC-W	1-1
1993 SD	8	8	0	.500	4 AFC-W	—
1994 SD	11	5	0	.688	1 AFC-W	2-1
1995 SD	9	7	0	.563	2 AFC-W	0-1
1996 SD	8	8	0	.500	3 AFC-W	—
1997 Det	9	7	0	.563	3 NFC-C	0-1
1998 Det	5	11	0	.313	4 NFC-C	—
	61	51	0	.545		3-4

BABE RUETZ Ruetz, George Gerhard
No college B: 9/23/1893, Racine, WI D: 5/24/1997, Racine, WI

	W	L	T	Pct.	Place	P
1922 Rac	6	4	1	.600	6 NFL	—
1923 Rac	4	4	2	.500	10 NFL	—
1924 Rac	4	3	3	.571	7 NFL	—
	14	11	6	.548		—

CLIVE RUSH***

	W	L	T	Pct.	Place	P
1969 Bos	4	10	0	.286	3 AFL-E	—
1970 Bos	1	6	0	.143	5 AFC-E	—
	5	16	0	.238		—

ROD RUST Rust, Rodney A.
Col: Iowa State B: 8/2/1928, Webster City, IA

	W	L	T	Pct.	Place	P
1990 NE	1	15	0	.063	5 AFC-E	—

SAM RUTIGLIANO **Rutigliano, Samuel**
Col: Tulsa B: 7/1/1932, Brooklyn, NY

	W	L	T	Pct.	Place	P
1978 Cle	8	8	0	.500	3 AFC-C	—
1979 Cle	9	7	0	.563	3 AFC-C	—
1980 Cle	11	5	0	.688	1 AFC-C	0-1
1981 Cle	5	11	0	.313	4 AFC-C	—
1982 Cle	4	5	0	.444	8 AFC	0-1
1983 Cle	9	7	0	.563	2 AFC-C	—
1984 Cle	1	7	0	.125	3 AFC-C	—
	47	50	0	.485		0-2

BUDDY RYAN Ryan, James David
Col: Oklahoma State B: 2/16/1934, Frederick, OK

	W	L	T	Pct.	Place	P
1986 Phi	5	10	1	.344	4 NFC-E	—
1987 Phi	7	8	0	.467	4 NFC-E	—
1988 Phi	10	6	0	.625	1 NFC-E	0-1
1989 Phi	11	5	0	.688	2 NFC-E	0-1
1990 Phi	10	6	0	.625	2 NFC-E	0-1
1994 Ariz	8	8	0	.500	3 NFC-E	—
1995 Ariz	4	12	0	.250	5 NFC-E	—
	55	55	1	.500		0-3

LOU RYMKUS***

	W	L	T	Pct.	Place	P
1960 Hou#	10	4	0	.714	1 AFL-E	1-0
1961 Hou#	1	3	1	.250	1 AFL-E	—
	11	7	1	.605		1-0

AFL Champion

LOU SABAN***

	W	L	T	Pct.	Place	P
1960 Bos	5	9	0	.357	4 AFL-E	—
1961 Bos	2	3	0	.400	2 AFL-E	—
1962 Buf	7	6	1	.538	3 AFL-E	—
1963 Buf	7	6	1	.538	2 AFL-E	0-1
1964 Buf#	12	2	0	.857	1 AFL-E	1-0
1965 Buf#	10	3	1	.769	1 AFL-E	1-0
1967 Den	3	11	0	.214	4 AFL-W	—
1968 Den	5	9	0	.357	4 AFL-W	—
1969 Den	5	8	1	.385	4 AFL-W	—
1970 Den	5	8	1	.385	4 AFC-W	—
1971 Den	2	6	1	.250	4 AFC-W	—
1972 Buf	4	9	1	.321	4 AFC-E	—
1973 Buf	9	5	0	.643	2 AFC-E	—
1974 Buf	9	5	0	.643	2 AFC-E	0-1

	W	L	T	Pct.	Place	P
1975 Buf	8	6	0	.571	3 AFC-E	—
1976 Buf	2	3	0	.400	5 AFC-E	—
	95	99	7	.490		2-2

AFL Champion

LEN SACHS***

	W	L	T	Pct.	Place	P
1926 Lou	0	4	0	.000	22 NFL	—

ANDY SALATA***

	W	L	T	Pct.	Place	P
1930 Nwk	0	3	0	.000	11 NFL	—

JOHN SANDUSKY***

	W	L	T	Pct.	Place	P
1972 Bal	4	5	0	.444	3 AFC-E	—

AL SAUNDERS Saunders, Alan Keith
Col: San Jose State B: 2/1/1947, London, England

	W	L	T	Pct.	Place	P
1986 SD	3	5	0	.375	5 AFC-W	—
1987 SD	8	7	0	.533	3 AFC-W	—
1988 SD	6	10	0	.375	4 AFC-W	—
	17	22	0	.436		—

DEWEY SCANLON Scanlon, Dewey D.
Col: Valparaiso B: 8/16/1899, West Duluth, MN Deceased

	W	L	T	Pct.	Place	P
1924 Dul	5	1	0	.833	4 NFL	—
1925 Dul	0	3	0	.000	16 NFL	—
1926 Dul	6	5	3	.545	8 NFL	—
1929 ChiC	6	6	1	.500	4 NFL	—
	17	15	4	.528		—

PAUL SCHISSLER Schissler, Paul John Jr.
Col: Doane; Hastings; Nebraska B: 11/11/1893, Hastings, NE D: 4/17/1963, Hastings, NE

	W	L	T	Pct.	Place	P
1933 ChiC	1	9	1	.100	5 NFL-W	—
1934 ChiC	5	6	0	.455	4 NFL-W	—
1935 Bkn	5	6	1	.455	2 NFL-E	—
1936 Bkn	3	8	1	.273	4 NFL-E	—
	14	29	3	.337		—

JOE SCHMIDT***

	W	L	T	Pct.	Place	P
1967 Det	5	7	2	.417	3 NFL-C	—
1968 Det	4	8	2	.333	4 NFL-C	—
1969 Det	9	4	1	.692	2 NFL-C	—
1970 Det	10	4	0	.714	2 NFC-C	0-1
1971 Det	7	6	1	.538	2 NFC-C	—
1972 Det	8	5	1	.607	2 NFC-C	—
	43	34	7	.554		0-1

HOWARD SCHNELLENBERGER Schnellenberger, Howard
Col: Kentucky B: 3/16/1934, Louisville, KY

	W	L	T	Pct.	Place	P
1973 Bal	4	10	0	.286	4 AFC-E	—
1974 Bal	0	3	0	.000	5 AFC-E	—
	4	13	0	.235		—

MARTY SCHOTTENHEIMER***

	W	L	T	Pct.	Place	P
1984 Cle	4	4	0	.500	3 AFC-C	—
1985 Cle	8	8	0	.500	1 AFC-C	0-1
1986 Cle	12	4	0	.750	1 AFC-C	1-1
1987 Cle	10	5	0	.667	1 AFC-C	1-1
1988 Cle	10	6	0	.625	2 AFC-C	0-1
1989 KC	8	7	1	.531	2 AFC-W	—
1990 KC	11	5	0	.688	2 AFC-W	0-1
1991 KC	10	6	0	.625	2 AFC-W	1-1
1992 KC	10	6	0	.625	2 AFC-W	0-1
1993 KC	11	5	0	.688	1 AFC-W	2-1
1994 KC	9	7	0	.563	2 AFC-W	0-1
1995 KC	13	3	0	.813	1 AFC-W	0-1
1996 KC	9	7	0	.563	2 AFC-W	—
1997 KC	13	3	0	.813	1 AFC-W	0-1
1998 KC	7	9	0	.438	4 AFC-W	—
	145	85	1	.630		5-11

RALPH SCOTT***

	W	L	T	Pct.	Place	P
1927 NYY	7	8	1	.467	6 NFL	—

GEORGE SEIFERT Seifert, George Gerald
Col: Utah B: 1/22/1940, San Francisco, CA

	W	L	T	Pct.	Place	P
1989 SF#	14	2	0	.875	1 NFC-W	3-0
1990 SF	14	2	0	.875	1 NFC-W	1-1
1991 SF	10	6	0	.625	3 NFC-W	—
1992 SF	14	2	0	.875	1 NFC-W	1-1
1993 SF	10	6	0	.625	1 NFC-W	1-1
1994 SF#	13	3	0	.813	1 NFC-W	3-0
1995 SF	11	5	0	.688	1 NFC-W	0-1
1996 SF	12	4	0	.750	2 NFC-W	1-1
	98	30	0	.766		10-5

NFC Champion; won Super Bowl

MIKE SHANAHAN Shanahan, Michael
Col: Eastern Illinois B: 8/24/1952, Oak Park, IL

	W	L	T	Pct.	Place	P
1988 LARd	7	9	0	.438	3 AFC-W	—
1989 LARd	1	3	0	.250	3 AFC-W	—
1995 Den	8	8	0	.500	4 AFC-W	—
1996 Den	13	3	0	.813	1 AFC-W	0-1
1997 Den#	12	4	0	.750	2 AFC-W	4-0
1998 Den#	14	2	0	.875	1 AFC-W	3-0
	55	29	0	.655		7-1

AFC Champion; won Super Bowl

CLARK SHAUGHNESSY Shaughnessy, Clark Daniel
Col: Minnesota B: 3/6/1892, St. Cloud, MN D: 5/15/1970, Santa Clara, CA

	W	L	T	Pct.	Place	P
1948 LARm	6	5	1	.545	3 NFL-W	—
1949 LARm	8	2	2	.800	1 NFL-W	0-1
	14	7	3	.646		0-1

BUCK SHAW Shaw, Lawrence Timothy
Col: Creighton; Notre Dame B: 3/28/1899, Mitchellville, IA D: 3/19/1977, Menlo Park, CA

	W	L	T	Pct.	Place	P
AAFC						
1946 SF-A	9	5	0	.642	2AAFC-W	—
1947 SF-A	8	4	2	.667	2AAFC-W	—
1948 SF-A	12	2	0	.857	2AAFC-W	—
1949 SF-A	9	3	0	.750	2AAFC	1-1
	38	14	2	.722		1-1
NFL						
1950 SF	3	9	0	.250	6 NFL-N	—
1951 SF	7	4	1	.636	3 NFL-N	—
1952 SF	7	5	0	.583	3 NFL-N	—
1953 SF	9	3	0	.750	2 NFL-W	—
1954 SF	7	4	1	.636	3 NFL-W	—
1958 Phi	2	9	1	.182	6 NFL-W	—
1959 Phi	7	5	0	.583	2 NFL-W	—
1960 Phi#	10	2	0	.833	1 NFL-W	1-0
	52	41	3	.557		1-0

NFL Champion

ART SHELL***

	W	L	T	Pct.	Place	P
1989 LARd	7	5	0	.583	3 AFC-W	—
1990 LARd	12	4	0	.750	1 AFC-W	1-1
1991 LARd	9	7	0	.563	3 AFC-W	0-1
1992 LARd	7	9	0	.438	4 AFC-W	—
1993 LARd	10	6	0	.625	2 AFC-W	1-1
1994 LARd	9	7	0	.563	3 AFC-W	—
	54	38	0	.587		2-3

ALLIE SHERMAN***

	W	L	T	Pct.	Place	P
1961 NYG	10	3	1	.769	1 NFL-E	0-1
1962 NYG	12	2	0	.857	1 NFL-E	0-1
1963 NYG	11	3	0	.786	1 NFL-E	0-1
1964 NYG	2	10	2	.167	7 NFL-E	—
1965 NYG	7	7	0	.500	3 NFL-E	—
1966 NYG	1	12	1	.077	8 NFL-E	—
1967 NYG	7	7	0	.500	2 NFL-Cty	—
1968 NYG	7	7	0	.500	2 NFL-Cap	—
	57	51	4	.527		0-3

KEN SHIPP***

	W	L	T	Pct.	Place	P
1975 NYJ	1	4	0	.200	5 AFC-E	—

JIM SHOFNER***

	W	L	T	Pct.	Place	P
1990 Cle	1	6	0	.143	4 AFC-C	—

DAVID SHULA Shula, David Donald
Col: Dartmouth B: 5/28/1959, Lexington, KY

	W	L	T	Pct.	Place	P
1992 Cin	5	11	0	.313	4 AFC-C	—
1993 Cin	3	13	0	.188	4 AFC-C	—
1994 Cin	3	13	0	.188	3 AFC-C	—
1995 Cin	7	9	0	.438	2 AFC-C	—
1996 Cin	1	6	0	.143	3 AFC-C	—
	19	52	0	.268		—

DON SHULA***

	W	L	T	Pct.	Place	P
1963 Bal	8	6	0	.571	3 NFL-W	—
1964 Bal	12	2	0	.857	1 NFL-W	0-1
1965 Bal	10	3	1	.769	2 NFL-W	0-1
1966 Bal	9	5	0	.643	2 NFL-W	—
1967 Bal	11	1	2	.917	2 NFL-Coa	—
1968 Bal*	13	1	0	.929	1 NFL-Coa	2-1
1969 Bal	8	5	1	.615	2 NFL-Coa	—
1970 Mia	10	4	0	.714	2 AFC-E	0-1
1971 Mia#	10	3	1	.769	1 AFC-E	2-1
1972 Mia+	14	0	0	1.000	1 AFC-E	3-0
1973 Mia+	12	2	0	.857	1 AFC-E	3-0
1974 Mia	11	3	0	.786	1 AFC-E	0-1
1975 Mia	10	4	0	.714	2 AFC-E	—
1976 Mia	6	8	0	.429	3 AFC-E	—
1977 Mia	10	4	0	.714	2 AFC-E	—
1978 Mia	11	5	0	.688	2 AFC-E	0-1
1979 Mia	10	6	0	.625	1 AFC-E	0-1
1980 Mia	8	8	0	.500	3 AFC-E	—
1981 Mia	11	4	1	.719	1 AFC-E	0-1
1982 Mia#	7	2	0	.778	2 AFC	3-1
1983 Mia	12	4	0	.750	1 AFC-E	0-1
1984 Mia#	14	2	0	.875	1 AFC-E	2-1
1985 Mia	12	4	0	.750	1 AFC-E	1-1
1986 Mia	8	8	0	.500	3 AFC-E	—
1987 Mia	8	7	0	.533	3 AFC-E	—
1988 Mia	6	10	0	.375	5 AFC-E	—
1989 Mia	8	8	0	.500	3 AFC-E	—
1990 Mia	12	4	0	.750	2 AFC-E	1-1
1991 Mia	8	8	0	.500	3 AFC-E	—
1992 Mia	11	5	0	.688	1 AFC-E	1-1
1993 Mia	9	7	0	.563	2 AFC-E	—
1994 Mia	10	6	0	.625	1 AFC-E	1-1
1995 Mia	9	7	0	.563	3 AFC-E	0-1
	328	156	6	.676		19-17

* NFL Champion
\# AFC Champion
\+ AFC Champion; won Super Bowl

HERB SIES***

	W	L	T	Pct.	Place	P
1923 RI	2	3	3	.400	12 NFL	—

NICK SKORICH***

	W	L	T	Pct.	Place	P
1961 Phi	10	4	0	.714	2 NFL-E	—
1962 Phi	3	10	1	.231	7 NFL-E	—
1963 Phi	2	10	2	.167	7 NFL-E	—
1971 Cle	9	5	0	.643	1 AFC-C	0-1
1972 Cle	10	4	0	.714	2 AFC-C	0-1
1973 Cle	7	5	2	.571	3 AFC-C	—
1974 Cle	4	10	0	.286	4 AFC-C	—
	45	48	5	.485		0-2

JERRY SMITH***

	W	L	T	Pct.	Place	P
1971 Den	2	3	0	.400	4 AFC-W	—

CLIPPER SMITH Smith, Maurice Francis
Col: Notre Dame B: 10/15/1898, Manteno, IL D: 3/18/1984, Laguna Beach, CA

	W	L	T	Pct.	Place	P
1947 Bos	4	7	1	.364	3 NFL-E	—
1948 Bos	3	9	0	.250	5 NFL-E	—
	7	16	1	.313		—

BOB SNYDER***

	W	L	T	Pct.	Place	P
1947 LARm	6	6	0	.500	4 NFL-W	—

MAC SPEEDIE***

	W	L	T	Pct.	Place	P
1964 Den	2	7	1	.222	4 AFL-W	—
1965 Den	4	10	0	.286	4 AFL-W	—
1966 Den	0	2	0	.000	4 AFL-W	—
	6	19	1	.250		—

GENE STALLINGS Stallings, Eugene Clifton
Col: Texas A&M B: 3/2/1935, Paris, TX

	W	L	T	Pct.	Place	P
1986 StL	4	11	1	.281	5 NFC-E	—
1987 StL	7	8	0	.467	3 NFC-E	—
1988 Pho	7	9	0	.438	4 NFC-E	—
1989 Pho	5	6	0	.455	4 NFC-E	—
	23	34	1	.405		—

DICK STANFEL***

	W	L	T	Pct.	Place	P
1980 NO	1	3	0	.250	4 NFC-W	—

BART STARR***

	W	L	T	Pct.	Place	P
1975 GB	4	10	0	.286	4 NFC-C	—
1976 GB	5	9	0	.357	4 NFC-C	—
1977 GB	4	10	0	.286	4 NFC-C	—
1978 GB	8	7	1	.531	2 NFC-C	—
1979 GB	5	11	0	.313	4 NFC-C	—
1980 GB	5	10	1	.344	5 NFC-C	—
1981 GB	8	8	0	.500	3 NFC-C	—
1982 GB	5	3	1	.611	3 NFC	1-1
1983 GB	8	8	0	.500	2 NFC-C	—
	52	76	3	.408		1-1

LES STECKEL Steckel, Leslie Todd
Col: Kansas B: 7/1/1946, Whitehall, PA

	W	L	T	Pct.	Place	P
1984 Min	3	13	0	.188	5 NFC-C	—

KAY STEPHENSON***

	W	L	T	Pct.	Place	P
1983 Buf	8	8	0	.500	3 AFC-E	—
1984 Buf	2	14	0	.125	5 AFC-E	—
1985 Buf	0	4	0	.000	5 AFC-E	—
	10	26	0	.278		—

JOEY STERNAMAN***

	W	L	T	Pct.	Place	P
1923 Dul	4	3	0	.571	7 NFL	—

GAYLORD STINCHCOMB***

	W	L	T	Pct.	Place	P
1923 Col	3	3	1	.500	9 NFL	—

CARL STORCK Storck, Carl H.
Col: George Williams YMCA College B: 11/14/1892, Dayton, OH D: 3/13/1950, Dayton, OH

	W	L	T	Pct.	Place	P
1922 Day	4	3	1	.571	7 NFL	—
1923 Day	1	6	1	.143	16 NFL	—
1924 Day	2	6	0	.250	14 NFL	—
1925 Day	0	7	1	.000	19 NFL	—
1926 Day	1	4	1	.200	17 NFL	—
	8	26	4	.263		—

RED STRADER***

	W	L	T	Pct.	Place	P
AAFC						
1948 NY-A	5	5	0	.500	3 AAFC-E	—
1949 NY-A	8	4	0	.667	3 AAFC	0-1
	13	9	0	.619		0-1
NFL						
1950 NYY	7	5	0	.583	3 NFL-N	—
1951 NYY	1	9	2	.100	6 NFL-N	—
1955 SF	4	8	0	.333	5 NFL-W	—
	12	22	2	.361		—

HANK STRAM Stram, Henry Willis
Col: Purdue B: 1/3/1924, Chicago, IL

	W	L	T	Pct.	Place	P
1960 DalT	8	6	0	.571	2 AFL-W	—
1961 DalT	6	8	0	.429	2 AFL-W	—
1962 DalT#	11	3	0	.786	1 AFL-W	1-0
1963 KC	5	7	2	.417	3 AFL-W	—
1964 KC	7	7	0	.500	2 AFL-W	—

	W	L	T	Pct.	Place	P
1965 KC	7	5	2	.583	3 AFL-W	—
1966 KC#	11	2	1	.846	1 AFL-W	1-1
1967 KC	9	5	0	.643	2 AFL-W	—
1968 KC	12	2	0	.857	2 AFL-W	0-1
1969 KC+	11	3	0	.786	2 AFL-W	3-0
1970 KC	7	5	2	.583	2 AFC-W	—
1971 KC	10	3	1	.769	1 AFC-W	0-1
1972 KC	8	6	0	.571	2 AFC-W	—
1973 KC	7	5	2	.583	3 AFC-W	—
1974 KC	5	9	0	.357	3 AFC-W	—
1976 NO	4	10	0	.286	4 NFC-W	—
1977 NO	3	11	0	.214	4 NFC-W	—
	131	97	10	.571		5-3

AFL Champion
+ AFL Champion; won Super Bowl

CHUCK STUDLEY Studley, Charles
Col: Illinois B: 1/17/1929, Maywood, IL

	W	L	T	Pct.	Place	P
1983 Hou	2	8	0	.200	4 AFC-C	—

JOE STYDAHAR***

	W	L	T	Pct.	Place	P
1950 LARm	9	3	0	.750	1 NFL-N	1-1
1951 LARm#	8	4	0	.667	1 NFL-N	1-0
1952 LARm	0	1	0	.000	2 NFL-N	—
1953 ChiC	1	10	1	.091	6 NFL-E	—
1954 ChiC	2	10	0	.167	6 NFL-E	—
	20	28	1	.418		2-1

NFL Champion

JOCK SUTHERLAND Sutherland, John Bain
Col: Pittsburgh B: 3/21/1889, Coupar-Angus, Scotland
D: 4/11/1948, Pittsburgh, PA

	W	L	T	Pct.	Place	P
1940 Bkn	8	3	0	.727	2 NFL-E	—
1941 Bkn	7	4	0	.636	2 NFL-E	—
1946 Pit	5	5	1	.500	4 NFL-E	—
1947 Pit	8	4	0	.667	2 NFL-E	0-1
	28	16	1	.633		0-1

HARLAND SVARE***

	W	L	T	Pct.	Place	P
1962 LARm	0	5	1	.000	7 NFL-W	—
1963 LARm	5	9	0	.357	6 NFL-W	—
1964 LARm	5	7	2	.417	5 NFL-W	—
1965 LARm	4	10	0	.286	7 NFL-W	—
1971 SD	2	2	0	.500	3 AFC-W	—
1972 SD	4	9	1	.321	4 AFC-W	—
1973 SD	1	6	1	.143	4 AFC-W	—
	21	48	5	.318		—

BARRY SWITZER Switzer, Barry
Col: Arkansas B: 10/5/1937, Crossett, AR

	W	L	T	Pct.	Place	P
1994 Dal	12	4	0	.750	1st NFC-E	1-1
1995 Dal#	12	4	0	.750	1st NFC-E	3-0
1996 Dal	10	6	0	.625	1st NFC-E	1-1
1997 Dal	6	10	0	.375	4th NFC-E	—
	40	24	0	.625		5-2

NFC Champion; won Super Bowl

NELSON TALBOT Talbot, Nelson Strobridge
Col: Yale B: 6/10/1892, Dayton, OH D: 7/6/1952, Dayton, OH

	W	L	T	Pct.	Place	P
1920 Day	5	2	2	.714	6 NFL	—
1921 Day	4	4	1	.500	8 NFL	—
	9	6	3	.583		—

HUGH TAYLOR***

	W	L	T	Pct.	Place	P
1965 HouA	4	10	0	.286	4 AFL-E	—

GUS TEBELL***

	W	L	T	Pct.	Place	P
1923 Col	2	1	0	.667	9 NFL	—

JOE THOMAS Thomas, Joseph
Col: Ohio Northern B: 3/18/1921, Warren, OH

	W	L	T	Pct.	Place	P
1974 Bal	2	9	0	.182	5 AFC-E	—

JIM THORPE***

	W	L	T	Pct.	Place	P
1920 Can	7	4	2	.636	8 NFL	—
1921 Cle	3	5	0	.375	11 NFL	—
1922 Oor	3	6	0	.333	12 NFL	—
1923 Oor	1	10	0	.091	18 NFL	—
	14	25	2	.366		—

ELGIE TOBIN***

	W	L	T	Pct.	Place	P
1920 Akr	#	8	0	31.000	1 NFL	—
1921 Akr *	8	3	1	.727	3 NFL	—
	16	3	4	.783		—

NFL Champion
* co-coach with Fritz Pollard

VINCE TOBIN Tobin, Vincent Michael
Col: Missouri B: 9/29/1943, Burlington Junction, MO

	W	L	T	Pct.	Place	P
1996 Ariz	7	9	0	.438	4 NFC-E	—
1997 Ariz	4	12	0	.250	5 NFC-E	—
1998 Ariz	9	7	0	.563	2 NFC-E	1-1
	20	28	0	.417		1-1

DICK TODD***

	W	L	T	Pct.	Place	P
1951 Was	5	4	0	.556	3 NFL-A	—

RUSSELL TOLLEFSON Tollefson, Russell I.
Col: Minnesota B: 9/27/1891, Minneapolis, MN Deceased

	W	L	T	Pct.	Place	P
1922 Min	1	3	0	.250	13 NFL	—

JIM TRIMBLE Trimble, James William
Col: Indiana B: 5/29/1918, McKeesport, PA

	W	L	T	Pct.	Place	P
1952 Phi	7	5	0	.583	3 NFL-A	—
1953 Phi	7	4	1	.636	2 NFL-E	—
1954 Phi	7	4	1	.636	2 NFL-E	—
1955 Phi	4	7	1	.364	5 NFL-E	—
	25	20	3	.552		—

BULLDOG TURNER***

	W	L	T	Pct.	Place	P
1962 NYT	5	9	0	.357	4 AFL-E	—

NORV TURNER Turner, Norval Eugene
Col: Oregon B: 5/17/1952, Camp Lejeune, NC

	W	L	T	Pct.	Place	P
1994 Was	3	13	0	.188	5 NFC-E	—
1995 Was	6	10	0	.375	3 NFC-E	—
1996 Was	9	7	0	.563	3 NFC-E	—
1997 Was	8	7	1	.531	2 NFC-E	—
1998 Was	6	10	0	.375	4 NFC-E	—
	32	47	1	.406		—

RUBE URSELLA***

	W	L	T	Pct.	Place	P
1920 RI	6	2	2	.750	5 NFL	—
1921 Min	1	3	0	.250	15 NFL	—
1925 RI	5	3	3	.625	8 NFL	—
	12	8	4	.583		—

NORM VAN BROCKLIN***

	W	L	T	Pct.	Place	P
1961 Min	3	11	0	.214	7 NFL-W	—
1962 Min	2	11	1	.154	6 NFL-W	—
1963 Min	5	8	1	.385	5 NFL-W	—
1964 Min	8	5	1	.615	3 NFL-W	—
1965 Min	7	7	0	.500	5 NFL-W	—
1966 Min	4	9	1	.308	7 NFL-W	—
1968 Atl	2	9	0	.182	4 NFL-Coa	—
1969 Atl	6	8	0	.429	3 NFL-Coa	—
1970 Atl	4	8	2	.333	3 NFC-W	—
1971 Atl	7	6	1	.538	3 NFC-W	—
1972 Atl	7	7	0	.500	2 NFC-W	—
1973 Atl	9	5	0	.643	2 NFC-W	—
1974 Atl	2	6	0	.250	4 NFC-W	—
	66	100	7	.402		—

RICK VENTURI Venturi, Richard
Col: Northwestern B: 2/23/1946, Taylorville, IL

	W	L	T	Pct.	Place	P
1991 Ind	1	10	0	.091	5 AFC-E	—
1996 NO	1	7	0	.125	5 NFC-W	—
	2	17	0	.105		—

DICK VERMEIL Vermeil, Richard Albert
Col: San Jose State B: 10/30/1936, Calistoga, CA

	W	L	T	Pct.	Place	P
1976 Phi	4	10	0	.286	4 NFC-E	—
1977 Phi	5	9	0	.357	4 NFC-E	—

	W	L	T	Pct.	Place	P
1978 Phi	9	7	0	.563	2 NFC-E	0-1
1979 Phi	11	5	0	.688	2 NFC-E	1-1
1980 Phi#	12	4	0	.750	1 NFC-E	2-1
1981 Phi	10	6	0	.625	2 NFC-E	0-1
1982 Phi	3	6	0	.333	13 NFC	—
1997 StL	5	11	0	.313	5 NFC-W	—
1998 StL	4	12	0	.250	5 NFC-W	—
	63	70	0	.474		3-4

NFC Champion

CHARLIE WALLER Waller, Charles
Col: Georgia; Oglethorpe B: 12/26/1921, Griffin, GA

	W	L	T	Pct.	Place	P
1969 SD	4	1	0	.800	3 AFL-W	—
1970 SD	5	6	3	.455	3 AFC-W	—
	9	7	3	.553		—

RON WALLER***

	W	L	T	Pct.	Place	P
1973 SD	1	5	0	.167	4 AFC-W	—

ADAM WALSH Walsh, Adam James
Col: Notre Dame B: 12/4/1901, Churchville, IA D: 1/13/1985, Los Angeles, CA

	W	L	T	Pct.	Place	P
1945 Cle#	9	1	0	.900	1 NFL-W	1-0
1946 LARm	6	4	1	.600	2 NFL-W	—
	15	5	1	.738		—

NFL Champion

BILL WALSH Walsh, William Ernest
Col: San Jose State B:11/30/1931, Los Angeles, CA

	W	L	T	Pct.	Place	P
1979 SF	2	14	0	.125	4 NFC-W	—
1980 SF	6	10	0	.375	3 NFC-W	—
1981 SF#	13	3	0	.813	1 NFC-W	3-0
1982 SF	3	6	0	.333	11 NFC	—
1983 SF	10	6	0	.625	1 NFC-W	1-1
1984 SF#	15	1	0	.938	1 NFC-W	3-0
1985 SF	10	6	0	.625	2 NFC-W	0-1
1986 SF	10	5	1	.656	1 NFC-W	0-1
1987 SF	13	2	0	.867	1 NFC-W	0-1
1988 SF#	10	6	0	.625	1 NFC-W	3-0
	92	59	1	.609		10-4

NFC Champion; won Super Bowl

CHILE WALSH Walsh, Charles Francis
Col: Notre Dame B: 2/4/1903, Des Moines, IA D: 9/4/1971, Los Angeles, CA

	W	L	T	Pct.	Place	P
1934 StL	1	2	0	.333	5 NFL-W	—

JOE WALTON***

	W	L	T	Pct.	Place	P
1983 NYJ	7	9	0	.438	5 AFC-E	—
1984 NYJ	7	9	0	.438	3 AFC-E	—
1985 NYJ	11	5	0	.688	2 AFC-E	0-1
1986 NYJ	10	6	0	.625	2 AFC-E	1-1
1987 NYJ	6	9	0	.400	5 AFC-E	—
1988 NYJ	8	7	1	.531	4 AFC-E	—
1989 NYJ	4	12	0	.250	5 AFC-E	—
	53	57	1	.482		1-2

DAVE WANNSTEDT Wannstedt, David Raymond
Col: Pittsburgh B: 5/21/1952, Pittsburgh, PA

	W	L	T	Pct.	Place	P
1993 ChiB	7	9	0	.438	4 NFC-C	—
1994 ChiB	9	7	0	.563	4 NFC-C	1-1
1995 ChiB	9	7	0	.563	3 NFC-C	—
1996 ChiB	7	9	0	.438	3 NFC-C	—
1997 ChiB	4	12	0	.250	5 NFC-C	—
1998 ChiB	4	12	0	.250	5 NFC-C	—
	40	56	0	.417		1-1

BOB WATERFIELD***

	W	L	T	Pct.	Place	P
1960 LARm	4	7	1	.364	6 NFL-W	—
1961 LARm	4	10	0	.286	6 NFL-W	—
1962 LARm	1	7	0	.125	7 NFL-W	—
	9	24	1	.279		—

RED WEAVER***

	W	L	T	Pct.	Place	P
1924 Col	4	4	0	.500	10 NFL	—
1925 Col	0	9	0	.000	20 NFL	—
	4	13	0	.235		—

ALEX WEBSTER***

	W	L	T	Pct.	Place	P
1969 NYG	6	8	0	.429	2 NFL-Cty	—
1970 NYG	9	5	0	.643	2 NFC-E	—
1971 NYG	4	10	0	.286	5 NFC-E	—
1972 NYG	8	6	0	.571	3 NFC-E	—
1973 NYG	2	11	1	.179	5 NFC-E	—
	29	40	1	.421		—

ED WEIR***

	W	L	T	Pct.	Place	P
1927 Fra*	4	4	2	.500	7 NFL	—
1928 Fra	11	3	2	.786	2 NFL	—
	15	7	4	.654		—

* co-coach with Russ Daugherty, Charley Rogers, and Swede Youngstrom

JOHN E. WHELCHEL Whelchel, John Esten
Col: Navy B: 4/1/1898, Hogansville, GA D: 11/5/1973, Portsmouth, VA

	W	L	T	Pct.	Place	P
1949 Was	3	3	1	.500	4 NFL-E	—

MIKE WHITE White, Michael
Col: California B: 1/4/1936, Berkeley, CA

	W	L	T	Pct.	Place	P
1995 Oak	8	8	0	.500	5 AFC-W	—
1996 Oak	7	9	0	.438	4 AFC-W	—
	15	17	0	.469		—

PAUL WIGGIN***

	W	L	T	Pct.	Place	P
1975 KC	5	9	0	.357	3 AFC-W	—
1976 KC	5	9	0	.357	4 AFC-W	—
1977 KC	1	6	0	.143	5 AFC-W	—
	11	24	0	.314		—

HUBERT WIGGS***

	W	L	T	Pct.	Place	P
1922 Lou	1	3	0	.250	14 NFL	—

BUD WILKINSON Wilkinson, Charles Burnham
Col: Minnesota B: 4/23/1916, Minneapolis, MN D: 2/9/1994, St. Louis, MO

	W	L	T	Pct.	Place	P
1978 StL	6	10	0	.375	4 NFC-E	—
1979 StL	3	10	0	.231	5 NFC-E	—
	9	20	0	.310		—

JERRY WILLIAMS***

	W	L	T	Pct.	Place	P
1969 Phi	4	9	1	.308	4 NFL-Cap	—
1970 Phi	3	10	1	.231	5 NFC-E	—
1971 Phi	0	3	0	.000	3 NFC-E	—
	7	22	2	.258		—

RICHARD WILLIAMSON Williamson, Richard
Col: Alabama B: 4/13,1941, Ft. Deposit, AL

	W	L	T	Pct.	Place	P
1990 TB	1	2	0	.333	2 NFC-C	—
1991 TB	3	13	0	.188	5 NFC-C	—
	4	15	0	.211		—

RAY WILLSEY Willsey, Raymond
Col: California B: 9/30/1928, Regina, Canada

	W	L	T	Pct.	Place	P
1961 StL*	2	0	0	1.000	4 NFL-E	—

* co-coach with Chuck Drulis and Ray Prochaska

GEORGE WILSON***

	W	L	T	Pct.	Place	P
1957 Det#	8	4	0	.667	1 NFL-W	2-0
1958 Det	4	7	1	.364	5 NFL-W	—
1959 Det	3	8	1	.273	5 NFL-W	—
1960 Det	7	5	0	.583	2 NFL-W	—
1961 Det	8	5	1	.615	2 NFL-W	—
1962 Det	11	3	0	.786	2 NFL-W	—
1963 Det	5	8	1	.385	4 NFL-W	—
1964 Det	7	5	2	.583	4 NFL-W	—
1966 Mia	3	11	0	.214	3 AFL-E	—
1967 Mia	4	10	0	.286	4 AFL-E	—
1968 Mia	5	8	1	.385	3 AFL-E	—
1969 Mia	3	10	1	.231	5 AFL-E	—
	68	84	8	.450		2-0

NFL Champion

LARRY WILSON***

	W	L	T	Pct.	Place	P
1979 StL	2	1	0	.667	5 NFC-E	—

CHARLEY WINNER Winner, Charles Height
Col: Southeast Missouri State; Washington (StL) B: 7/2/1924, Somerville, NJ

	W	L	T	Pct.	Place	P
1966 StL	8	5	1	.615	4 NFL-E	—
1967 StL	6	7	1	.462	3 NFL-Cty	—
1968 StL	9	4	1	.692	2 NFL-Cty	—
1969 StL	4	9	1	.308	3 NFL-Cty	—
1970 StL	8	5	1	.615	3 NFC-E	—
1974 NYJ	7	7	0	.500	4 AFC-E	—
1975 NYJ	2	7	0	.222	5 AFC-E	—
	44	44	5	.500		—

HOGE WORKMAN***

	W	L	T	Pct.	Place	P
1931 Cle*	2	8	0	.200	8 NFL	—

* co-coach with Al Cornsweet

LUD WRAY***

	W	L	T	Pct.	Place	P
1932 Bos	4	4	2	.500	4 NFL	—
1933 Phi	3	5	1	.375	4 NFL-E	—
1934 Phi	4	7	0	.364	4 NFL-E	—
1935 Phi	2	9	0	.182	5 NFL-E	—
	13	25	3	.354		—

SAM WYCHE***

	W	L	T	Pct.	Place	P
1984 Cin	8	8	0	.500	2 AFC-C	—
1985 Cin	7	9	0	.438	2 AFC-C	—
1986 Cin	10	6	0	.625	2 AFC-C	—
1987 Cin	4	11	0	.267	4 AFC-C	—
1988 Cin#	12	4	0	.750	1 AFC-C	2-1
1989 Cin	8	8	0	.500	4 AFC-C	—
1990 Cin	9	7	0	.563	1 AFC-C	1-1
1991 Cin	3	13	0	.188	4 AFC-C	—
1992 TB	5	11	0	.313	3 NFC-C	—
1993 TB	5	11	0	.313	5 NFC-C	—
1994 TB	6	10	0	.375	5 NFC-C	—
1995 TB	7	9	0	.438	5 NFC-C	—
	84	107	0	.440		3-2

AFC Champion

DOUG WYCOFF***

	W	L	T	Pct.	Place	P
1929 SI	3	4	3	.429	6 NFL	—
1930 SI	5	5	2	.500	6 NFL	—
	8	9	5	.477		—

DOC YOUNG Young, Alva Andrew
Col: Indiana U. Medical College B: 12/18/1881, Hamilton Co., IN D: 7/2/1971, Chicago, IL

	W	L	T	Pct.	Place	P
1925 Ham	1	3	0	.250	14 NFL	—
1926 Ham	0	4	0	.000	21 NFL	—
	1	7	0	.125		—

SWEDE YOUNGSTROM***

	W	L	T	Pct.	Place	P
1927 Fra*	4	4	2	.500	7 NFL	—

* co-coach with Russ Daugherty, Charley Rogers, and Ed Weir

AAFC-only Coaches

CLIFF BATTLES***

	W	L	T	Pct.	Place	P
1946 BknA*	1	6	0	.143		—
1947 BknA	3	10	1	.231		—
	4	16	1	.214		—

* co coach with Tom Scott

PAT BOLAND Boland, Patrick Henry
Col: Minnesota B: 10/12/1906, Duluth, MN D: 7/2/1971, Duluth, MN

	W	L	T	Pct.	Place	P
1946 ChiA	2	3	1	.400		—

JIM CROWLEY***

	W	L	T	Pct.	Place	P
1947 ChiA	0	10	0	.000		—

RED DAWSON Dawson, Lowell Potter
Col: Wisconsin-River Falls; Tulane B: 12/20/1906, Minneapolis, MN D: 6/10/1983, Ocala, FL

	W	L	T	Pct.	Place	P
1946 BufA	3	10	1	.231		—
1947 BufA	8	4	2	.667		—
1948 BufA	7	7	0	.500		1-1
1949 BufA	1	4	1	.200		—
	19	25	4	.438		1-1

BOB DOVE***

	W	L	T	Pct.	Place	P
1946 ChiA*	2	2	1	.500		—

* co-coach with Ned Mathews and Willie Wilkin

WALT DRISKILL Driskill, Walter Scott
Col: Colorado

	W	L	T	Pct.	Place	P
1949 BalA	1	7	0	.125		—

DICK HANLEY***

	W	L	T	Pct.	Place	P
1946 ChiA	1	1	1	.500		—

MEL HEIN***

	W	L	T	Pct.	Place	P
1947 LA-A*	2	1	0	.667		—

* co coach with Ted Shipkey

NED MATHEWS***

	W	L	T	Pct.	Place	P
1946 ChiA*	2	2	1	.500		—

* co-coach with Bob Dove and Willie Wilkin

ED MCKEEVER McKeever, Edward Clark Timothy
Col: Notre Dame; Texas Tech B: 8/25/1910, San Antonio, TX D: 9/12/1974, Baton Rouge, LA

	W	L	T	Pct.	Place	P
1948 ChiA	1	13	0	.071		—

JACK MEAGHER***

	W	L	T	Pct.	Place	P
1946 MiaA	1	5	0	.167		—

TOM SCOTT

	W	L	T	Pct.	Place	P
1946 BknA*	1	6	0	.143		—

* co coach with Cliff Battles

TED SHIPKEY Shipkey, Theodore Edwin
Col: Stanford B: 9/23/1904, Great Falls, MT D: 7/18/1978, Placentia, CA

	W	L	T	Pct.	Place	P
1947 LA-A*	2	1	0	.667		—

* co coach with Mel Hein

MAL STEVENS Stevens, Marvin Allen
Col: Washburn; Yale B: 4/14/1900, Stockton, KS D: 12/6/1979, New York, NY

	W	L	T	Pct.	Place	P
1946 BknA	2	4	1	.333		—

CARL VOYLES Voyles, Carl Marvin (Dutch)
Col: Oklahoma State B: 8/11/1898, McLoud, OK D: 1/11/1932, Fort Myers, FL

	W	L	T	Pct.	Place	P
1948 BknA	2	12	0	.143		—

WILLIE WILKIN***

	W	L	T	Pct.	Place	P
1946 ChiA*	2	2	1	.500		—

* co-coach with Bob Dove and Ned Mathews

APPENDIXES

APPENDIX 1

Famous Pro Football Firsts

Michael Gershman

First Pro

November 12, 1892 - William (Pudge) Heffelfinger was paid $500 to play for the Allegheny Athletic Association.

First Indoor Game

December 28, 1902 - The Syracuse Athletic Club defeated New York 5-0 in Madison Square Garden.

First African-American Pro Player

September 16, 1904 - Halfback Charles Follis signed a contract to play with the Shelby Athletic Club.

First Major League Organized

August 20, 1920 - Pro football's first major league, the American Professional Football Conference, was formed in Canton, Ohio. Four weeks later, the league changed its name to the American Professional Football Association, and in 1922 became the National Football League. The APFA's first president was Jim Thorpe, and the first games between league members took place October 3, 1920. The Dayton Triangles beat the Columbus Panhandles 14-0 that day, while the Rock Island Independents shut out the Muncie Flyers 45-0.

First APFA Champion

Akron Pros, 1920

First NFL Night Game

November 6, 1929 - The Chicago Cardinals defeated the Providence Steam Roller 16-0 at Providence.

First NFL Rules

February 25, 1933 - The NFL discontinued the use of the collegiate rulebook and began to develop its own rules. The most significant change was that the forward pass became legal anywhere behind the scrimmage line.

First Official NFL Championship Game

December 17, 1933 - In 1933, the NFL was divided into two divisions for the first time. The Chicago Bears defeated the New York Giants 23-21 in the first official championship game.

First Player Picked in the First NFL Draft

February 8, 1936 - The Philadelphia Eagles selected University of Chicago halfback Jay Berwanger, who also won the first Heisman Trophy. The Eagles traded the rights to Berwanger to the Bears, but he did not agree to terms with Chicago and never played pro football.

First Pro Bowl

January 15, 1939 - The New York Giants defeated the Pro All-Stars 13-10 at Wrigley Field in Los Angeles.

First Divisional Playoff Game

December 14, 1941 - The Chicago Bears defeated the Green Bay Packers 33-14 in an NFL Western Division playoff. One week later, Chicago beat the New York Giants 37-9 to win the NFL championship.

First Adoption of Free Substitution

April 7, 1943 - Free substitution was adopted because of the wartime manpower emergency. Limited substitution returned in 1946, but free substitution permanently was adopted in 1949.

First Modern African-American Player

March 21, 1946 - The Los Angeles Rams signed halfback Kenny Washington. Woody Strode also played for the Rams in 1946, while Marion Motley and Bill Willis played for the AAFC's Cleveland Browns.

First Use of Penalty Flag by NFL Officials

September 17, 1948 - The penalty flag first was used in Green Bay's 31-0 victory over the Boston Yanks.

First Overtime Game

August 28, 1955 - The Los Angeles Rams defeated the New York Giants 23-17 after three minutes of overtime in a preseason game at Portland, Oregon.

First Overtime Championship Game

December 28, 1958 - The Baltimore Colts defeated the New York Giants 23-17 in what many call "the Greatest Game Ever Played."

First Super Bowl

January 15 1967 - The Green Bay Packers defeated the Kansas City Chiefs 35-10 at the Los Angeles Memorial Coliseum.

APPENDIX 2

Game Scores 1920-1998

Paul Bennett, Bob Carroll, Pete Fierle, John Hogrogian, David Neft, and Pete Palmer

The paramount question may always be "Who won?" But other queries immediately follow: what was the score? Where and when was the game played? How big was the crowd? The following should answer most of those questions. In preparing this section, the researchers primarily used newspaper stories and media guides for the years 1920-1969. Particularly in the first two decades, published game attendance figures, when they were given at all, were often estimates made by friendly sportswriters or optimistic team officials. At best, they should be considered "ball park figures." Additionally, until 1974 when the Elias Sports Bureau began publishing actual turnstile counts in its record books, game attendance figures often represented the number of tickets sold rather than the actual number of people in the stadium.

When games were played in locations other than the home team's city or home field, that information is given in italics under the score. Night games are marked N. Overtime games are marked #.

Non-APFA Teams (1920 only)

In 1920, the APFA did not keep standings. It appears that all games—whether against APFA members or not—were counted in a team's record when it came time to award the first championship. For 1920 only, so-called "non-league" games are included in this record, using the following abbreviations to identify non-APFA teams that played APFA members.

*Abu = All-Buffalo (NY)
*Boo = Chicago (IL) Boosters
*Cha = Champaign (IL) Legion
*Cin = Cincinnati (OH) Celts
*Ely = Elyria (OH) Athletics
*FtP = Ft. Porter (NY)
*FtW = Ft. Wayne (IN) Friars
*Gar = Gary (IN) Elks
*Kew = Kewanee (IL) Walworths
*Lan = Lansing (MI) Oldsmobile
*Log = Logan Square (Chicago, IL)
*Mar = Detroit (MI) Maroons
*McK = McKeesport (PA) Olympics
*Min = Minneapolis (MN) Marines
*Mol = Moline (IL) Indians
*Pan = Cleveland (OH) Panthers
*Pir = Columbus (OH) Wagner Pirates
*Pit = Pitcairn (PA) Quakers
*Pul = Pullman Thorns (Chicago, IL)
*Ric = Richmond (VA) Athletics
*Roc = Rockford (IL) A.C.
*Sca = Rochester (NY) Scalpers
*Stm = Chicago (IL) Staysm
*StP = St. Paul (MN) Ideals
*Tho = Thorn Tornadoes (Chicago, IL)
*Tol = Toledo (OH) Maroons
*Ton = All-Tonawanda (NY)
*Uni = Union A.A. (Phila., PA)
*Uti = Utica (NY) K. of C.
*Was = Washington Glee Club (New Haven, CT)
*W&J = Wash. & Jeff. Collegians
*WBu = West (NY) Buffalo
*Zan = Zanesville (OH) Mark Grays

American Professional Football Association 1920

Sun 09/26
*StP 0 at RI 48 800

Sun 10/03
*Whg 0 at Akr 43 4,000
*WBu 6 at Buf 32 n/a
*Pit 0 at Can 48 n/a
Col 0 at Day 14 4,000
*Mol 0 at DecS 20 1,500
Mun 0 at RI 45 3,110
*Abu 0 at Roch 10 2,000

Sun 10/10
Col 0 at Akr 37 n/a
*Abu 0 at Buf 51 n/a
*Tol 0 at Can 42 n/a
ChiC 0 at ChiT 0 5,000
Cle 0 at Day 0 n/a
*Kew 7 at DecS 25 1,500
*Pan 14 at Det 40 n/a
Ham 0 at RI 26 2,554
*FtP 0 at Roch 66 n/a

Sun 10/17
*Cin 0 at Akr 13 n/a
*McK 7 at Buf 28 n/a
Cle 0 at Can 7 7,000
*Mol 3 at ChiC 33 n/a
Det 0 at ChiT 12 5,000
Col 0 at *FtW 14 5,000
Ham 0 at Day 44 2,000
DecS 7 at RI 0 7,000
*Uti 0 at Roch 0 n/a

Sun 10/24
Cle 0 at Akr 7 n/a
*Tol 0 at Buf 38 n/a
Can 20 at Day 20 5,000
ChiC 0 at RI 7 4,000
DecS 10 at ChiT 0 5,000
Col 0 at Det 6 n/a
*Syr 7 at Roch 21 a/a

Sun 10/31
Akr 10 at Can 0 10,000
Roch 6 at Buf 17 7,500
Det 0 at ChiC 21 3,000
at Cubs Park, Chicago
ChiT 7 at RI 20 n/a
Col 0 at Cle 7 5,000
*Cin 7 at Day 23 n/a
DecS 29 at *Roc 0 n/a
Ham 14 at *Log 9 3,000

Sun 11/07
*Ton 0 at Buf 35 n/a
Can 18 at Cle 0 n/a
ChiC 6 at ChiT 3 7,000
Col 10 at *Zan 0 n/a
DecS 0 at RI 0 4,991
Ham 14 at *Pul 13 n/a
*Uti 7 at Roch 27 n/a

Thu 11/11
DecS 20 at *Cha 0 n/a
RI 7 at *Tho 7 n/a

Sun 11/14
Akr 7 at Cle 7 8,000
Col 7 at Buf 43 9,000
ChiT 0 at Can 21 8,000
*Cin 0 at ChiC 20 5,000
Day 21 at RI 0 n/a
DecS 3 at *Min 0 n/a
Det 0 at *FtW 0 n/a
Ham 6 at *Gar 7 2,000
*Ton 6 at Roch 0 n/a

Sun 11/21
Day 0 at Akr 13 n/a
Can 3 at Buf 0 15,000
*Lan 0 at ChiC 14 3,500
*Tol 0 at Cle 14 n/a
Col 0 at *Zan 0 n/a
Ham 7 at DecS 28 3,000
*Sca 0 at Roch 16 n/a

Thu 11/25
Can 0 at Akr 7 n/a
DecS 6 at ChiT 0 8,000
Col 0 at *Ely 0 n/a
Det 0 at Day 28 n/a
Ham 0 at *Boo 27 n/a
*Ton 14 at Roch 3 n/a

Sun 11/28
Akr 14 at Day 0 n/a
Cle 0 at Buf 7 5,000
DecS 6 at ChiC 7 5,000
*Tho 0 at ChiT 27 n/a
*Lan 0 at Det 0 n/a
*Sca 6 at Roch 7 n/a
*W&J 7 at RI 48 n/a

Sat 12/04
Can 3 at Buf 7 10,000
at Polo Grounds, New York

Sun 12/05
Akr 0 at Buf 0 3,000
Can 0 at *Was 0 3,000
ChiC 0 at DecS 10 11,000
at Cubs Park, Chicago
*Pir 0 at Col 24 2,000
*Mar 7 at Det 7 n/a
*Sca 0 at Roch 0 n/a

Sat 12/11
Can 7 at *Uni 13 17,000

Sun 12/12
Akr 0 at DecS 0 12,000
at Cubs Park, Chicago

Sat 12/18
Can 39 at *Ric 0 n/a

American Professional Football Association 1921

Sun 09/25
Col 0 at Akr 14 2,000

Sun 10/02
Ham 0 at Buf 17 3,500
Cin 0 at Akr 41 2,500
Min 0 at ChiC 20 4,000
Col 13 at Day 42 n/a
Det 0 at RI 0 3,304
Lou 0 at Eva 21 2,000

Sun 10/09
Akr 23 at ChiC 0 6,000
Col 0 at Buf 38 n/a
Ham 7 at Can 7 n/a
Day 7 at Det 10 n/a
Mun 0 at Eva 14 n/a

Mon 10/10
RI 10 at DecS 14 5,000
at Decatur, IL

Sun 10/16
RI 14 at ChiC 7 4,000
Can 14 at Day 14 n/a
Akr 20 at Det 0 n/a
Roch 13 at DecS 16 8,000
at Chicago, IL
Col 9 at Cle 35 n/a
NYBG 0 at Buf 55 7,500
Ham 3 at Eva 0 n/a
Cin 14 at Mun 0 n/a

Sun 10/23
Akr 3 at Can 0 8,000
Col 6 at ChiC 17 6,000
Roch 0 at Buf 28 10,000
Cin 0 at Cle 28 n/a
Min 6 at GB 7 6,000
RI 14 at Det 0 3,000
Day 0 at DecS 7 8,000
at Chicago, IL

Sun 10/30
Roch 0 at Akr 19 4,000
Det 0 at Buf 21 7,000
Cle 2 at Day 3 4,000
RI 13 at GB 3 6,000
Col 0 at Min 28 n/a

Sun 11/06
Cle 6 at Buf 10 n/a
Ham 0 at ChiC 7 n/a
Akr 21 at Col 0 n/a
Det 9 at DecS 20 6,000
at Chicago, IL
Eva 6 at GB 43 n/a
Day 0 at Can 14 n/a
Min 3 at RI 14 2,000
Ton 0 at Roch 45 3,000

Sun 11/13
Akr 0 at Buf 0 n/a
RI 0 at DecS 3 4,000
at Chicago, IL
Det 0 at Day 27 n/a
Ham 7 at GB 14 n/a
Can 7 at Cle 0 n/a

Sun 11/20
GB 3 at ChiC 3 2,000
Akr 0 at Day 3 n/a
Col 13 at Roch 27 2,500
Cle 7 at DecS 22 10,000
at Chicago, IL
Can 7 at Buf 7 n/a

Thu 11/24
Can 14 at Akr 0 n/a
Buf 7 at DecS 6 n/a
at Chicago, IL

Sun 11/27
Can 15 at Was 0 4,000
Day 0 at Buf 7 n/a
GB 0 at DecS 20 7,000
at Chicago, IL
Cin 0 at Eva 48 n/a

Sat 12/03
Akr 0 at Buf 14 n/a
Cle 17 at NYBG 0 3,000

Sun 12/04
Akr 7 at ChiC 0 3,500
Buf 7 at DecS 10 n/a
at Chicago, IL
Col 6 at Lou 0 n/a

Sun 12/11
Can 0 at DecS 10 3,000
at Chicago, IL
Cle 0 at Was 7 5,000

Sun 12/18
ChiC 0 at DecS 0 2,000
at Chicago, IL
Can 28 at Was 14 6,000

National Football League 1922

Sun 10/01
Col 0 at Akr 36 3,000
Ham 0 at Buf 7 4,500
Lou 0 at Can 38 3,000
Mil 0 at ChiC 3 3,500
Oor 0 at Day 36 n/a
ChiB 6 at Rac 0 4,000
GB 14 at RI 19 3,500
Eva 0 at Tol 15 2,000

Sun 10/08
Can 0 at Day 0 3,000
Rac 10 at GB 6 3,603
Col 6 at Oor 20 1,200
ChiB 10 at RI 6 4,749
Mil 12 at Tol 12 2,000

Thu 10/12
Roch 13 at Akr 13 2,000

Sun 10/15
Ham 0 at Tol 14 2,000
Eva 0 at RI 60 n/a
Rac 0 at Mil 20 6,000
Min 0 at Day 17 n/a
Roch 0 at ChiB 7 n/a
Col 0 at Buf 19 n/a
Oor 0 at Can 14 n/a
GB 3 at ChiC 16 3,500

Sun 10/22
Buf 0 at ChiB 7 6,500
Can 22 at Akr 0 n/a
Tol 7 at Rac 0 3,500
Roch 0 at RI 26 n/a
Ham 0 at Day 20 n/a
GB 0 at Mil 0 6,000
Min 0 at ChiC 3 4,000

Sun 10/29
Buf 7 at Day 0 5,000
Can 7 at ChiB 6 10,000
Col 6 at ChiC 37 5,000
RI 0 at GB 0 8,000
Ham 0 at Mil 0 n/a
Roch 0 at Rac 9 n/a
Oor 0 at Akr 62 n/a
Lou 0 at Tol 39 2,500

Sun 11/05
Tol 0 at Can 0 n/a
Day 0 at ChiB 9 n/a
Buf 7 at ChiC 9 4,000
Oor 6 at Min 13 4,000
Lou 0 at Rac 57 n/a
Col 0 at GB 3 2,000
Ham 0 at Akr 22 n/a

Sat 11/11
Col 0 at Rac 34 n/a

Sun 11/12
Day 0 at RI 43 n/a
Buf 0 at Can 3 n/a
Min 6 at GB 14 2,000
Akr 0 at ChiC 7 2,000
Oor 6 at ChiB 33 n/a
Eva 6 at Lou 13 n/a

Sun 11/19
Can 7 at ChiC 0 7,500
GB 3 at Rac 3 3,000
RI 0 at ChiB 3 n/a
Akr 3 at Buf 3 n/a
Oor 0 at Mil 13 6,500

Sun 11/26
ChiC 3 at Can 20 2,500
Akr 10 at ChiB 20 6,000
Col 6 at Tol 7 1,700
Ham 0 at Rac 6 n/a
Mil 0 at GB 13 n/a
Oor 19 at Buf 7 n/a

Thu 11/30
Buf 21 at Roch 0 n/a
ChiB 0 at ChiC 6 14,000
Mil 0 at Rac 3 3,500
Oor 18 at Col 6 n/a
Akr 0 at Can 14 n/a

Sun 12/03
Mil 6 at Can 40 n/a
Tol 0 at ChiB 22 n/a
GB 14 at Rac 0 4,500
at Milaukee, WI
Day 7 at ChiC 3 3,000
Akr 0 at Buf 16 n/a

Sun 12/10
Can 19 at Tol 0 5,000
ChiB 0 at ChiC 9 15,000

National Football League 1923

Sun 09/30
Ham 0 at Can 17 5,000
ChiB 0 at RI 3 3,500
Min 0 at GB 12 3,008
Oor 2 at Mil 13 4,000
Buf 0 at ChiC 3 n/a
Akr 7 at Dul 10 n/a
Col 6 at Day 7 6,000
Tol 7 at Rac 7 n/a

Sun 10/07
Lou 0 at Can 37 n/a
ChiB 3 at Rac 0 5,000
StL 0 at GB 0 2,831
Col 0 at Mil 0 2,000
Cle 0 at RI 0 3,500
Roch 0 at ChiC 60 n/a
Dul 10 at Min 0 n/a
Akr 0 at Buf 9 n/a
Oor 0 at Tol 7 5,000
Day 0 at Ham 7 n/a

Sun 10/14
Day 0 at Can 30 n/a
ChiB 3 at GB 0 4,451
Rac 7 at Mil 7 4,000
Akr 0 at ChiC 19 n/a
Buf 3 at Col 0 3,500
Roch 0 at RI 56 2,500
Oor 0 at Min 23 4,000
Ham 0 at StL 0 719

Sun 10/21
Can 6 at ChiB 0 n/a
Mil 0 at GB 12 5,000
StL 0 at Cle 6 7,000
Min 0 at ChiC 9 4,000
Ham 0 at Dul 3 4,000
Lou 0 at Col 34 n/a
Oor 0 at Buf 57 n/a
Akr 7 at Rac 9 n/a
Day 3 at Tol 6 3,000

Sun 10/28
Akr 3 at Can 7 2,500
Buf 3 at ChiB 18 n/a
Rac 24 at GB 3 2,800
StL 0 at Mil 6 4,700
Oor 0 at Cle 27 n/a
Day 3 at ChiC 13 5,000
Min 0 at Dul 9 3,000
Col 3 at Tol 0 5,000

Sun 11/04
Can 7 at ChiC 3 6,000
Oor 0 at ChiB 26 1,000
GB 3 at StL 0 750
Mil 14 at RI 3 2,500
Cle 0 at Buf 0 n/a
Rac 6 at Min 13 1,200

Sun 11/11
Can 3 at Buf 3 10,000
Akr 6 at ChiB 20 4,000
GB 16 at Rac 0 3,500
Dul 3 at Mil 6 n/a
Day 0 at Cle 0 11,000
Ham 0 at ChiC 6 3,500
Tol 0 at Col 16 n/a
RI 6 at Min 6 n/a
Oor 0 at StL 14 5,000

Sun 11/18
Oor 0 at Can 41 5,000
RI 3 at ChiB 7 6,500
GB 10 at Mil 7 5,400
Col 3 at Cle 9 6,000
Dul 0 at ChiC 10 5,500
Day 0 at Buf 3 3,500

Sat 11/24
Tol 12 at Roch 6 n/a
Mil 17 at StL 0 2,395

Sun 11/25
Can 46 at Cle 10 17,000
Ham 7 at ChiB 14 3,500
Dul 0 at GB 10 n/a
Rac 10 at ChiC 4 7,000
Oor 3 at Col 27 n/a
Tol 3 at Buf 3 n/a
Min 6 at RI 6 n/a

Thu 11/29
Tol 0 at Can 28 3,000
ChiC 0 at ChiB 3 13,500
Ham 0 at GB 19 n/a
Mil 16 at Rac 0 n/a
Buf 0 at Akr 2 1,700

Sat 12/01
Buf 13 at Roch 0 n/a

Sun 12/02
Buf 0 at Can 14 4,000
Mil 0 at ChiB 0 n/a
Oor 19 at ChiC 22 1,200
Day 3 at Col 30 n/a
Min 0 at Rac 23 n/a

Sun 12/09
Can 10 at Col 0 1,700
RI 7 at ChiB 29 6,000
Mil 14 at ChiC 12 6,000
Oor 19 at Lou 0 1,200

National Football League 1924

Sat 09/27
Roch 0 at Fra 21 7,000

Sun 09/28
ChiB 0 at RI 0 4,500
GB 3 at Dul 6 2,200
Ham 0 at Rac 10 3,000
Mil 7 at ChiC 17 4,000

Sat 10/04
Ken 6 at Fra 31 7,000

Sun 10/05
Akr 3 at Roch 0 1,200
ChiB 14 at Cle 16 n/a
Col 0 at Buf 13 5,000
Dul 3 at Min 0 3,000
Fra 7 at Day 19 4,000
GB 0 at ChiC 3 2,852
KC 0 at Mil 3 n/a
Rac 0 at RI 9 3,500

Sat 10/11
Cle 3 at Fra 3 n/a

Sun 10/12
Akr 14 at Cle 29 n/a
Col 15 at Roch 7 2,000
Day 7 at Buf 0 6,000
KC 0 at GB 16 2,800
Ken 0 at Mil 21 1,000
Min 0 at ChiC 13 n/a
Rac 10 at ChiB 10 10,000
Ham 0 at RI 26 3,000

Sat 10/18
Col 7 at Fra 23 10,000

Sun 10/19
ChiC 0 at ChiB 6 12,000
Mil 0 at GB 17 4,150
Ham 6 at Ken 6 600
KC 3 at Rac 13 n/a
Roch 0 at Buf 26 3,500
Day 0 at RI 20 4,500

Sun 10/26
Akr 13 at Buf 17 8,000
Col 17 at Day 6 3,000
Fra 3 at ChiB 33 8,000
Min 0 at GB 19 2,500
Rac 10 at Mil 0 4,000
Ham 6 at ChiC 3 3,500
RI 7 at KC 23 n/a
Ken 0 at Dul 32 n/a
Roch 0 at Cle 59 n/a

Sat 11/01
Akr 0 at Fra 23 6,000

Sun 11/02
Akr 0 at Col 30 3,000
Day 0 at Cle 35 n/a
Dul 6 at Min 0 n/a
Fra 24 at Buf 0 6,000
Rac 3 at GB 6 4,000
Ham 6 at KC 0 n/a
Mil 17 at ChiC 8 3,000
RI 3 at ChiB 3 10,000

Sat 11/08
KC 7 at Fra 42 10,000

Sun 11/09
Cle 20 at Akr 7 5,000
Col 6 at ChiB 12 7,000
Day 0 at ChiC 23 2,500
Dul 0 at GB 13 2,700
Min 7 at Mil 28 n/a
Ken 0 at Buf 27 n/a

RI 6 at Rac 3 3,500

Tue 11/11
Mil 3 at KC 7 3,000

Sat 11/15
Min 7 at Fra 39 8,000

Sun 11/16
Akr 0 at ChiC 13 2,500
Day 6 at Buf 14 2,700
Fra 12 at Cle 7 n/a
GB 17 at Mil 10 3,800
Rac 3 at ChiB 3 6,500
Roch 0 at Col 16 2,500
KC 0 at RI 17 3,000

Sat 11/22
Buf 16 at Roch 0 n/a
Mil 6 at Fra 21 5,000

Sun 11/23
GB 0 at ChiB 3 6,000
Col 0 at Cle 7 n/a
Dul 9 at RI 0 2,500
Rac 10 at ChiC 10 4,000

Mil 23 at Buf 0 n/a

Thu 11/27
Buf 0 at Akr 22 n/a
ChiB 21 at ChiC 0 13,000
Day 7 at Fra 32 15,000
Mil 10 at Cle 53 4,000
at Canton, OH
GB 17 at KC 6 1,542

Fri 11/29
Buf 7 at Fra 45 7,000

Sun 11/30
GB 0 at Rac 7 2,200
Mil 14 at ChiB 31 1,000

National Football League 1925

Sun 09/20
ChiB 0 at RI 0 n/a
Ham 0 at GB 14 3,000

Sat 09/26
Buf 7 at Fra 27 15,000

Sun 09/27
Buf 0 at Pott 28 3,500
ChiB 10 at GB 14 5,389
Col 0 at Det 7 3,500
Ham 10 at ChiC 6 n/a
Cle 0 at Akr 7 2,000
KC 3 at Dul 0 n/a
Roch 7 at Can 14 n/a
Day 0 at RI 0 3,000

Sat 10/03
Prov 0 at Fra 7 8,000

Sun 10/04
ChiB 0 at Det 0 3,342
Col 0 at Cle 3 4,000
Day 0 at Can 14 n/a
GB 0 at RI 3 3,000
KC 7 at Akr 14 n/a
Mil 0 at ChiC 34 2,500
Prov 6 at Pott 0 5,000
Roch 0 at Buf 0 5,000

Sat 10/10
Can 7 at Fra 12 15,000

Sun 10/11
Col 9 at ChiC 19 n/a

Can 0 at Pott 28 n/a
Fra 0 at Det 3 n/a
KC 13 at Cle 16 n/a
Ham 7 at ChiB 28 n/a
NYG 0 at Prov 14 8,000
Mil 0 at GB 31 2,300
RI 12 at Dul 0 4,000
Akr 0 at Buf 0 n/a

Sat 10/17
NYG 3 at Fra 5 15,000

Sun 10/18
Akr 20 at Can 3 5,000
KC 7 at ChiC 20 n/a
Cle 0 at ChiB 7 n/a
Col 6 at Buf 17 4,500
Day 0 at Det 6 4,132
Fra 14 at NYG 0 27,000
Pott 34 at Prov 0 7,500
RI 0 at GB 20 5,000

Sat 10/24
Day 0 at Fra 3 2,000

Sun 10/25
Akr 0 at Det 0 5,400
ChiB 0 at ChiC 9 13,000
Roch 13 at GB 33 2,700
KC 3 at RI 3 1,500

Sat 10/31
Col 0 at Fra 19 5,000

Sun 11/01
Cle 0 at NYG 19 18,000
Col 0 at Pott 20 3,000
Day 3 at Akr 17 2,500
Dul 6 at ChiC 10 n/a
Fra 12 at Buf 3 8,000
GB 6 at Mil 0 2,300
Ham 6 at Det 26 n/a
Roch 0 at Prov 17 n/a
RI 0 at ChiB 6 8,000

Tue 11/03
Buf 0 at NYG 7 20,000

Sat 11/07
Akr 7 at Fra 17 12,000

Sun 11/08
Akr 0 at Pott 21 n/a
Buf 0 at Prov 10 n/a
Cle 0 at Can 6 2,000
Col 0 at NYG 19 4,000
Mil 0 at Det 21 n/a
Fra 0 at ChiB 19 5,000
GB 6 at ChiC 9 3,000

Thu 11/11
Cle 13 at Det 22 n/a
Roch 0 at NYG 13 10,000

Sat 11/14
Pott 0 at Fra 20 15,000

Sun 11/15
Buf 6 at ChiC 23 4,000

Day 0 at GB 7 3,000
Det 0 at ChiB 14 6,200
KC 12 at RI 35 1,500
Prov 12 at NYG 13 20,000
Roch 6 at Pott 14 n/a

Sat 11/21
Cle 14 at Fra 0 7,000

Sun 11/22
Day 0 at ChiC 14 3,000
Col 0 at Can 6 n/a
Cle 6 at Pott 24 n/a
Fra 7 at Prov 20 14,000
GB 0 at ChiB 21 6,898
KC 3 at NYG 9 28,000
Roch 0 at Det 20 n/a
Mil 7 at RI 40 1,200

Thu 11/26
ChiC 0 at ChiB 0 39,000
KC 17 at Cle 0 1,000
at Hartford, CT
RI 6 at Det 3 n/a
GB 0 at Pott 31 3,500

Sat 11/28
GB 7 at Fra 13 10,000

Sun 11/29
Cle 7 at Prov 7 7,000
Day 0 at NYG 23 18,000
Fra 0 at Pott 49 9,000
Col 13 at ChiB 14 28,000
RI 0 at ChiC 7 3,000

Sat 12/05
ChiB 14 at Fra 7 36,000

Sun 12/06
Can 0 at Cle 6 n/a
GB 13 at Prov 10 7,000
Pott 21 at ChiC 7 5,000
ChiB 19 at NYG 7 68,000

Wed 12/09
ChiB 6 at Prov 9 15,000
at Boston, MA

Thu 12/10
Mil 0 at ChiC 59 ***
No admission charged

Sat 12/12
Cle 3 at Fra 0 7,000
ChiB 0 at Det 21 6,000
Ham 0 at ChiC 13 n/a

Sun 12/13
Fra 14 at Prov 6 n/a
NYG 9 at ChiB 0 18,000

Sun 12/20
Fra 13 at Cle 7 1,000

National Football League 1926

Sun 09/19
Col 0 at ChiC 14 2,500
Det 0 at GB 21 4,500
ChiB 10 at Mil 7 n/a
KC 0 at Dul 7 6,000

Sat 09/25
Akr 6 at Fra 6 5,000

Sun 09/26
NYG 21 at Har 0 6,500
Bkn 0 at Prov 13 7,000
Akr 0 at Buf 7 2,500
Col 14 at Can 2 2,500
LA 0 at ChiC 15 7,500
Ham 3 at Rac 6 2,500
ChiB 6 at GB 6 7,000
Det 0 at Mil 6 2,500

Sat 10/02
Har 0 at Fra 13 15,000

Sun 10/03
Fra 10 at Har 0 3,000
Day 3 at Buf 0 5,000
Col 0 at Pott 3 n/a
NYG 7 at Prov 6 7,500
Ham 0 at Akr 17 n/a
Lou 0 at Can 13 3,000
ChiB 10 at Det 7 10,000
Rac 0 at ChiC 20 3,500
LA 6 at Mil 0 n/a
Dul 0 at GB 0 2,500

Sat 10/09
Buf 0 at Fra 30 6,000

Sun 10/10
KC 0 at Det 10 n/a
Har 0 at Bkn 6 1,000
Day 6 at Pott 24 n/a
NYG 0 at ChiB 7 8,000
Can 0 at Akr 0 n/a
Col 0 at Prov 19 n/a
Mil 13 at Rac 2 1,500
ChiC 13 at GB 7 5,000
Dul 26 at Ham 0 n/a

Sat 10/16
KC 9 at Col 0 5,000
Pott 21 at Bkn 0 8,000
NYG 0 at Fra 6 7,000

Sun 10/17
Lou 0 at Det 47 n/a
Buf 7 at Day 6 1,500
Fra 6 at NYG 0 15,000
Bkn 0 at Pott 14 8,000
LA 16 at Can 13 5,000
ChiB 16 at ChiC 0 12,000
Dul 21 at Rac 0 2,600
Mil 0 at GB 7 3,000

Sat 10/23
Col 12 at Bkn 20 8,000
Can 0 at Fra 17 4,000

Sun 10/24
Bkn 6 at Har 16 1,000

LA 0 at Buf 0 3,000
KC 0 at NYG 13 10,000
Pott 0 at Prov 14 1,500
Akr 0 at Det 25 n/a
Dul 6 at ChiB 24 12,000
ChiC 3 at Mil 2 n/a
Rac 0 at GB 35 n/a

Sat 10/30
Prov 7 at Fra 6 n/a

Sun 10/31
GB 3 at ChiC 0 2,500
Buf 0 at Pott 14 n/a
Fra 6 at Prov 3 n/a
Dul 7 at Mil 6 n/a
Akr 0 at ChiB 17 6,500
Can 0 at Det 6 n/a
KC 7 at Har 2 500

Tue 11/02
Can 7 at NYG 7 4,000

Sat 11/06
ChiC 7 at Fra 33 8,000

Sun 11/07
KC 10 at Bkn 9 4,000
ChiC 0 at NYG 20 5,000
Akr 0 at Pott 34 n/a
Dul 0 at Det 0 21,000
LA 7 at Prov 6 n/a
GB 21 at Mil 0 4,300
Lou 0 at ChiB 34 7,000
Col 0 at Buf 26 3,500

Can 7 at Har 16 4,500

Thu 11/11
Dul 13 at NYG 14 5,000
LA 0 at Pott 10 3,000
ChiC 0 at ChiB 10 10,000
Can 2 at Prov 21 4,000

Sat 11/13
Dul 0 at Fra 10 6,000

Sun 11/14
Day 0 at Det 0 n/a
LA 6 at NYG 0 20,000
Mil 7 at ChiB 10 3,500
Can 0 at Bkn 19 7,000
Dul 0 at Pott 13 n/a
Lou 0 at GB 14 1,300
Buf 13 at Har 7 n/a
KC 22 at Prov 0 n/a

Sat 11/20
Day 0 at Fra 35 6,000

Sun 11/21
Dul 10 at Can 2 n/a
KC 2 at Buf 0 n/a
LA 20 at Bkn 0 10,000
Prov 0 at NYG 21 10,000
Ham 0 at Pott 7 n/a
Day 0 at Har 16 n/a
GB 13 at ChiB 19 7,500

Thu 11/25
NYG 17 at Bkn 0 10,000

LA 9 at Det 6 7,000
ChiC 0 at ChiB 0 8,000
GB 14 at Fra 20 10,000
Prov 0 at Pott 8 n/a
Akr 0 at Can 0 n/a

Sat 11/27
Det 6 at Fra 7 6,000
Dul 16 at Har 0 n/a

Sun 11/28
GB 7 at Det 0 1,000
Bkn 0 at NYG 27 7,000
KC 7 at ChiC 2 12,000
Pott 0 at Buf 0 n/a
Dul 0 at Prov 0 n/a
Can 0 at ChiB 35 5,000

Sat 12/04
ChiB 6 at Fra 7 10,000

Sun 12/05
LA 3 at KC 7 3,000

Sat 12/11
Prov 0 at Fra 24 4,500

Sun 12/12
Dul 7 at KC 12 n/a
Pott 7 at ChiB 9 5,500
Pott 0 at Fra 0 2,000

Sun 12/19
GB 3 at ChiB 3 10,000

National Football League 1927

Sun 09/18
Day 0 at GB 14 3,600

Sat 09/24
Day 6 at Fra 3 7,000

Sun 09/25
ChiB 9 at ChiC 0 4,000
Buf 0 at Pott 22 n/a
NYG 8 at Prov 0 7,500
Cle 7 at GB 12 4,500

Sun 10/02
NYY 6 at Day 3 6,000
Buf 0 at Prov 5 3,500
Pott 7 at ChiC 19 2,000
ChiB 7 at GB 6 5,500
NYG 0 at Cle 0 3,000

Sat 10/08
Day 0 at Fra 0 4,000

Sun 10/09
Day 0 at ChiC 7 2,500
NYG 19 at Pott 0 5,000
Dul 0 at GB 20 4,000

NYY 13 at Cle 7 20,000

Wed 10/12
NYY 19 at Buf 8 3,500

Sat 10/15
Buf 0 at Fra 54 5,000

Sun 10/16
Fra 23 at Buf 0 1,500
Cle 6 at NYG 0 25,000
Pott 6 at Prov 3 7,500
ChiC 0 at GB 13 4,500
NYY 0 at ChiB 12 30,000

Sat 10/22
NYG 13 at Fra 0 9,000

Sun 10/23
Fra 0 at NYG 27 15,000
Day 0 at Prov 7 6,500
NYY 0 at GB 13 11,000
Cle 12 at ChiB 14 20,000
Dul 27 at Pott 0 n/a

Sat 10/29
Prov 20 at Fra 7 15,000

Sun 10/30
Day 6 at ChiB 14 8,000
Fra 0 at Prov 14 9,000
NYY 7 at ChiC 6 15,000
Dul 20 at Cle 21 12,000
Pott 0 at NYG 16 20,000

Sat 11/05
Pott 0 at Fra 10 6,000

Sun 11/06
GB 6 at ChiC 6 3,500
Fra 0 at Pott 9 n/a
Prov 0 at ChiB 0 15,000
NYY 0 at Cle 15 2,500
Dul 0 at NYG 21 15,000

Tue 11/08
ChiB 6 at NYY 26 10,000
Prov 0 at NYG 25 38,000

Fri 11/11
NYY 19 at Pott 12 n/a

Sat 11/12
Cle 0 at Fra 22 6,000

Sun 11/13
Pott 12 at ChiB 30 8,000
Day 0 at GB 6 2,500
Fra 0 at Cle 37 5,000
ChiC 6 at NYY 20 10,000
Dul 7 at Prov 13 n/a

Sat 11/19
ChiC 8 at Fra 12 6,000

Sun 11/20
ChiC 7 at NYG 28 10,000
GB 6 at ChiB 14 6,000
Dul 0 at Pott 6 n/a
Cle 22 at Prov 0 12,000

Thu 11/24
ChiC 3 at ChiB 0 6,000
Prov 0 at Pott 6 4,000
GB 17 at Fra 9 9,000
Cle 30 at NYY 19 15,000

Sat 11/26
Dul 0 at Fra 6 n/a

Sun 11/27
ChiB 7 at NYG 13 15,000
NYY 7 at Prov 14 10,000
Cle 32 at ChiC 7 5,000

Sat 12/03
ChiB 0 at Fra 0 4,000
Prov 9 at NYY 0 5,000
at Syracuse, NY
Dul 0 at Cle 20 n/a

Sun 12/04
Pott 0 at Prov 20 1,500
Fra 0 at ChiB 9 2,500
NYY 0 at NYG 14 10,000

Sat 12/10
NYY 6 at Fra 6 4,500

Sun 12/11
Dul 14 at ChiB 27 2,500
NYG 13 at NYY 0 8,000

National Football League 1928

Sun 09/23
Fra 19 at GB 9 6,500
ChiB 15 at ChiC 0 4,000

Sat 09/29
Day 0 at Fra 6 4,000

Sun 09/30
ChiB 12 at GB 12 8,500
NYG 12 at Pott 6 7,000
NYY 7 at Prov 20 4,000

Sun 10/07
NYY 7 at Pott 9 5,000
NYG 6 at GB 0 7,000
Day 0 at ChiC 7 n/a
Fra 10 at Prov 6 6,000

Sat 10/13
NYY 13 at Fra 0 6,000

Sun 10/14
ChiC 0 at GB 20 4,200
Day 0 at Prov 28 7,000
Det 35 at NYY 12 10,000
NYG 0 at ChiB 13 15,000

Sat 10/20
Day 9 at Fra 13 7,000

Sun 10/21
Prov 12 at NYY 6 7,000
GB 16 at ChiB 6 15,000
NYG 0 at Det 28 n/a

Sun 10/28
Day 0 at GB 17 3,100
Pott 6 at Prov 13 8,000
Det 6 at ChiB 0 20,000
NYG 10 at NYY 7 25,000

Sat 11/03
Det 7 at Fra 25 8,000

Sun 11/04
Det 0 at Prov 7 8,500
GB 26 at Pott 14 5,000
NYY 0 at ChiB 27 10,000
Fra 0 at NYG 0 3,000

Tue 11/06
Pott 7 at NYG 13 20,000

Sat 11/10
Pott 0 at Fra 19 n/a

Sun 11/11
Day 0 at ChiB 27 5,000
Fra 24 at Pott 0 n/a
NYY 0 at GB 0 5,000
Det 19 at NYG 19 25,000

Sat 11/17
Prov 6 at Fra 6 9,000

Sun 11/18
Fra 0 at Prov 6 12,000
Pott 6 at ChiB 13 5,000
NYY 0 at Det 13 8,000
GB 7 at NYG 0 12,000

Sat 11/24
ChiC 0 at Fra 19 8,000

Sun 11/25
ChiC 0 at NYY 19 7,000
GB 0 at Pott 26 1,600
ChiB 7 at Det 14 15,000
NYG 0 at Prov 16 13,000

Thu 11/29
Prov 7 at Pott 0 n/a
Day 0 at Det 33 n/a

GB 0 at Fra 2 8,000
ChiC 0 at ChiB 34 10,000

Sun 12/02
Fra 6 at ChiB 28 12,000
NYY 19 at NYG 13 20,000
GB 7 at Prov 7 9,000

Sat 12/08
NYG 0 at Fra 7 3,500

Sun 12/09
GB 6 at ChiB 0 14,000
Det 34 at NYY 6 2,500

Sat 12/15
ChiB 0 at Fra 19 7,000

Sun 12/16
NYG 6 at NYY 7 15,000

National Football League 1929

Sun 09/22
Day 0 at GB 9 5,000
ChiB 19 at Min 6 6,000
at Madison, WI

Sat 09/28
Day 7 at Fra 14 7,000

Sun 09/29
ChiB 0 at GB 23 13,000
NYG 0 at Ora 0 9,000
Day 0 at Prov 41 8,500
ChiC 9 at Buf 3 4,000

Sat 10/05
Buf 0 at Fra 19 6,000

Sun 10/06
ChiB 7 at Min 6 6,000
Fra 13 at Buf 0 n/a
Bos 0 at Ora 7 7,000
NYG 7 at Prov 0 14,000
Day 0 at SI 12 6,000
ChiC 2 at GB 9 6,000

Sun 10/13
Fra 2 at GB 14 9,000
ChiB 16 at Buf 0 n/a
ChiC 7 at Min 14 10,000
Ora 0 at Prov 7 10,000
SI 9 at NYG 19 30,000
Day 0 at Bos 41 800

Sat 10/19
Ora 6 at Fra 6 6,000

Sun 10/20
Fra 0 at NYG 32 30,000
Min 0 at GB 24 6,000
Buf 7 at Prov 7 8,500
Ora 19 at Bos 13 6,000
ChiC 0 at ChiB 0 20,000

Sat 10/26
SI 6 at Fra 6 7,000

Sun 10/27
Fra 3 at SI 0 10,000
Min 0 at ChiB 27 9,500
Buf 6 at Bos 14 n/a
at Pottsville, PA

Prov 0 at NYG 19 25,000
GB 7 at ChiC 6 8,000

Tue 10/29
Ora 0 at Bos 6 n/a
at Pottsville, PA

Sat 11/02
ChiC 0 at Fra 8 5,000

Sun 11/03
GB 16 at Min 6 3,000
Ora 0 at SI 0 3,500
NYG 26 at ChiB 14 26,000

Tue 11/05
NYG 45 at Buf 6 n/a
Prov 7 at SI 7 10,000

Wed 11/06
N ChiC 16 at Prov 0 6,000

Sat 11/09
Prov 0 at Fra 7 6,000

Sun 11/10
Fra 7 at Prov 6 n/a
Ora 0 at NYG 22 20,000
Bos 6 at SI 14 7,500
GB 14 at ChiB 0 13,000
Min 0 at ChiC 8 1,000

Sat 11/16
ChiB 14 at Fra 20 9,000

Sun 11/17
Fra 0 at Ora 0 1,500
Buf 7 at Bos 12 n/a
ChiB 0 at NYG 34 15,000
Min 16 at Prov 19 n/a
GB 12 at ChiC 0 10,000

Sat 11/23
Min 0 at Fra 24 5,000

Sun 11/24
GB 20 at NYG 6 25,000
Bos 6 at Prov 20 n/a
Buf 19 at ChiB 7 3,500
Day 0 at ChiC 19 300
Min 0 at SI 34 2,000

Thu 11/28
NYG 21 at SI 7 12,000
GB 0 at Fra 0 8,500
ChiC 40 at ChiB 6 7,000

Sun 12/01
Fra 0 at ChiB 0 1,500
GB 25 at Prov 0 6,500
SI 0 at Ora 0 8,000
ChiC 21 at NYG 24 5,000

Sat 12/07
NYG 12 at Fra 0 7,000

Sun 12/08
Fra 0 at NYG 31 20,000
GB 25 at ChiB 0 6,000
ChiC 26 at Ora 0 n/a

Sat 12/14
Ora 0 at Fra 10 3,000

Sun 12/15
NYG 14 at ChiB 9 5,000

National Football League 1930

Sun 09/14
Nwk 6 at Port 13 4,000

Wed 09/17
N NYG 32 at Nwk 0 10,000

Sun 09/21
Bkn 0 at ChiB 0 10,000
at Mills Stadium, Chi.
ChiC 0 at GB 14 8,000

Nwk 6 at SI 12 7,000

Wed 09/24
N Fra 13 at Nwk 6 2,000

N Bkn 0 at Port 12 6,000

Sat 09/27
SI 3 at Fra 7 6,000

Sun 09/28
ChiB 0 at GB 7 10,000
NYG 27 at Prov 7 12,000
ChiC 7 at Min 7 n/a
Fra 0 at SI 21 6,000

Wed 10/01
N SI 7 at Nwk 7 8,000
N Fra 0 at Prov 14 3,500

Sat 10/04
Nwk 19 at Fra 0 5,000

Sun 10/05
ChiC 0 at Port 0 6,500
ChiB 20 at Min 0 7,000
NYG 7 at GB 14 11,000
Nwk 0 at Prov 14 4,500
Bkn 20 at SI 0 3,500

Wed 10/08
N Fra 7 at Port 39 n/a
N ChiC 13 at Nwk 0 5,000

Sun 10/12
Port 0 at Min 13 2,000
Nwk 0 at Bkn 32 7,000
NYG 12 at ChiB 0 12,000
ChiC 7 at Prov 9 6,500
Fra 12 at GB 27 8,000

Thu 10/16
N ChiC 12 at NYG 25 15,000

Sat 10/18
Bkn 14 at Fra 7 3,000

Sun 10/19
Bkn 14 at Nwk 0 n/a
Fra 0 at NYG 53 10,000
GB 13 at Min 0 n/a
SI 6 at Prov 7 5,000
ChiB 32 at ChiC 6 7,000

Wed 10/22
N ChiB 6 at Port 7 7,500

Sat 10/25
ChiC 34 at Fra 7 n/a

Sun 10/26
Port 13 at ChiC 23 8,000
Prov 0 at NYG 25 10,000
SI 6 at Nwk 0 n/a
Fra 7 at ChiB 13 5,000
Min 0 at GB 19 6,000

Wed 10/29
N Nwk 7 at NYG 34 5,000

Sun 11/02
Port 13 at GB 47 7,500
Fra 0 at ChiC 6 3,000
SI 7 at NYG 9 18,000
Bkn 0 at Prov 3 n/a
Min 7 at ChiB 20 4,000

Wed 11/05
N NYG 19 at Port 6 7,000

Sat 11/08
Prov 7 at Fra 20 4,000

Sun 11/09
Port 13 at SI 13 5,000
NYG 13 at ChiC 7 4,000
Fra 7 at Prov 7 n/a
Min 0 at Bkn 34 12,000
GB 13 at ChiB 12 22,000

Sat 11/15
Port 6 at Fra 7 3,500

Sun 11/16
GB 6 at ChiC 13 12,000
ChiB 12 at NYG 0 5,000

Sat 11/22
ChiB 13 at Fra 6 6,500

Sun 11/23
GB 6 at NYG 13 37,000
Min 0 at Prov 10 n/a
SI 6 at Bkn 0 15,000

Thu 11/27
NYG 6 at SI 7 12,000
Prov 12 at Bkn 33 8,000
GB 25 at Fra 7 5,000
ChiC 0 at ChiB 6 8,000

Sun 11/30
Port 6 at ChiB 14 6,000
Bkn 7 at NYG 6 25,000
GB 37 at SI 7 9,500

Sat 12/06
NYG 14 at Fra 6 4,000

Sun 12/07
Min 0 at Port 42 3,500
GB 0 at ChiB 21 20,000
NYG 13 at Bkn 0 20,000

Sun 12/14
GB 6 at Port 6 4,500

National Football League 1931

Sun 09/13
Bkn 0 at Port 14 7,000
Cle 0 at GB 26 5,000

Fri 09/18
N Cle 0 at ChiB 21 6,000
at Loyola Stad., Chi.

Sun 09/20
Bkn 6 at GB 32 7,000

Wed 09/23
N ChiC 3 at Port 13 8,000

Sat 09/26
N Bkn 0 at Cle 6 2,000

Sun 09/27
ChiB 0 at GB 7 13,500
NYG 14 at Prov 6 8,000

Wed 09/30
N NYG 6 at Port 14 10,000

Fri 10/02
N Bkn 20 at Fra 0 2,000
at Municipal Stad., Phila.

Sun 10/04
Fra 0 at Prov 0 n/a
NYG 7 at GB 27 14,000
Bkn 7 at SI 9 12,000

Wed 10/07
Cle 0 at Port 6 n/a

Sat 10/10
Prov 6 at Fra 0 3,000

Sun 10/11
SI 6 at Bkn 18 15,000
ChiC 7 at GB 26 8,000
NYG 0 at ChiB 6 7,500

Thu 10/15
N Fra 0 at Port 19 5,000

Sun 10/18
Fra 0 at GB 15 6,000
Cle 13 at Prov 6 6,000
ChiC 13 at ChiB 26 8,000
SI 0 at NYG 7 25,000
Port 19 at Bkn 0 10,000

Sun 10/25
Port 20 at SI 7 12,000
Prov 20 at GB 48 n/a
Bkn 0 at NYG 27 22,000
Fra 13 at ChiB 12 26,000

Sun 11/01
Port 0 at NYG 14 32,500
ChiC 14 at Bkn 7 15,000
Prov 7 at SI 7 3,500
GB 6 at ChiB 2 30,000

Wed 11/04
N Bkn 0 at SI 13 6,000

Sun 11/08
Fra 0 at NYG 13 25,000
Bkn 0 at Prov 7 4,000
SI 0 at GB 26 7,000
ChiC 14 at Cle 6 10,000
Port 6 at ChiB 9 25,000

Wed 11/11
N SI 12 at Port 14 n/a

Sun 11/15
ChiB 12 at NYG 6 20,000
Cle 6 at Port 14 10,000
at Cincinnati, OH
SI 0 at Prov 6 2,000
GB 13 at ChiC 21 8,000

Sat 11/21
Cle 7 at Prov 13 n/a

Sun 11/22
Port 19 at ChiC 20 5,000
Cle 7 at SI 16 n/a
ChiB 26 at Bkn 0 25,000
GB 14 at NYG 10 35,000

Thu 11/26
GB 38 at Prov 7 5,000
NYG 6 at SI 9 10,000
ChiC 7 at ChiB 18 14,000

Sat 11/28
Cle 0 at ChiC 21 1,500

Sun 11/29
ChiB 0 at Port 3 9,000
Prov 0 at NYG 0 10,000
GB 7 at Bkn 0 10,000

Sun 12/06
GB 6 at ChiB 7 18,000
NYG 19 at Bkn 6 25,000

Sun 12/13
NYG 25 at ChiB 6 8,000

National Football League 1932

Sun 09/18
ChiC 7 at GB 15 3,500

Sun 09/25
NYG 0 at Port 7 6,000
ChiB 0 at GB 0 13,000
Bkn 7 at SI 0 9,000

Sun 10/02
ChiC 7 at Port 7 n/a
NYG 0 at GB 13 5,500
ChiB 0 at SI 0 8,000
Bkn 14 at Bos 0 8,000

Sun 10/09
Port 10 at GB 15 5,500
ChiB 0 at ChiC 0 8,000
NYG 6 at Bos 14 10,000
SI 7 at Bkn 6 15,000

Sun 10/16
Port 7 at SI 7 7,500
GB 2 at ChiB 0 17,500
ChiC 9 at Bos 0 15,000
Bkn 12 at NYG 20 25,000

Thu 10/20
N Port 13 at SI 6 5,000

Sun 10/23
SI 7 at ChiB 27 27,540
Bkn 0 at GB 13 5,000
Bos 0 at NYG 0 15,000

Sun 10/30
Port 6 at NYG 0 20,000
ChiB 7 at Bos 7 18,000
SI 0 at GB 26 n/a
Bkn 7 at ChiC 27 5,000

Sun 11/06
Port 17 at Bkn 7 25,000
ChiB 28 at NYG 8 12,000
GB 19 at ChiC 9 8,323
SI 6 at Bos 19 12,000

Sun 11/13
Port 13 at ChiB 13 5,500
GB 21 at Bos 0 16,500
SI 7 at NYG 27 15,000
ChiC 0 at Bkn 3 15,000

Sun 11/20
Bos 0 at Port 10 5,000
Bkn 0 at ChiB 20 6,500
GB 0 at NYG 6 17,000
ChiC 7 at SI 21 5,000

Thu 11/24
ChiC 0 at ChiB 34 6,800
GB 7 at Bkn 0 17,000
NYG 13 at SI 13 8,000

Sun 11/27
ChiB 7 at Port 7 7,000
GB 21 at SI 3 3,500
Bos 8 at ChiC 6 6,200
NYG 13 at Bkn 7 10,000

Sun 12/04
GB 0 at Port 19 10,000
NYG 0 at ChiB 6 n/a
Bos 7 at Bkn 0 20,000

Sun 12/11
GB 0 at ChiB 9 5,000

League Championship Playoff

Sun 12/18
Port 0 at ChiB 9 12,000
at Chicago Stadium, indoors

National Football League 1933

Sun 09/17
Bos 7 at GB 7 5,000
Cin 0 at Port 21 5,000

Wed 09/20
N NYG 23 at Pit 2 20,000

Sun 09/24
ChiB 14 at GB 7 12,000
NYG 7 at Port 17 7,000

Wed 09/27
N ChiC 13 at Pit 14 5,000

Sun 10/01
NYG 10 at GB 7 12,467
at Milwaukee, WI
Bos 0 at ChiB 7 9,000
at Soldier Field, Chi.
ChiC 6 at Port 7 n/a

Wed 10/04
N Bos 21 at Pit 6 15,000

Sun 10/08
Port 0 at GB 17 5,200
ChiB 10 at Bkn 0 20,000
NYG 20 at Bos 21 15,000
ChiC 3 at Cin 0 1,500

Wed 10/11
N Cin 3 at Pit 17 5,000

Sun 10/15
Pit 0 at GB 47 4,000
ChiC 9 at ChiB 12 12,000
Port 13 at Bos 0 20,000
Phi 0 at NYG 56 18,000
Cin 0 at Bkn 27 12,000

Wed 10/18
N Port 25 at Phi 0 1,750

Sun 10/22
GB 7 at ChiB 10 19,000
ChiC 0 at Bos 10 16,000
Bkn 7 at NYG 21 35,000
Pit 0 at Cin 0 n/a

Sun 10/29
Phi 9 at GB 35 3,007
Pit 16 at Bos 14 7,500
NYG 10 at ChiB 14 28,000
ChiC 0 at Bkn 7 18,000

Sun 11/05
GB 14 at ChiC 6 5,000
ChiB 0 at Bos 10 22,820
Phi 6 at Cin 0 n/a
Port 10 at NYG 13 15,000
Pit 3 at Bkn 3 15,000

Sun 11/12
GB 0 at Port 7 7,500
ChiB 3 at Phi 3 17,850
Bos 0 at NYG 7 17,601
Bkn 32 at Pit 0 12,000
Cin 12 at ChiC 9 6,000

Sun 11/19
GB 7 at Bos 20 16,399
ChiB 0 at NYG 3 22,000
Pit 6 at Phi 25 6,000
Bkn 3 at ChiC 0 4,000
Port 7 at Cin 10 n/a

Sun 11/26
GB 6 at NYG 17 17,000
Port 14 at ChiB 17 9,000
Bos 0 at Bkn 14 15,000
Cin 3 at Phi 20 10,000

Thu 11/30
ChiB 22 at ChiC 6 n/a
NYG 10 at Bkn 0 28,000

Sun 12/03
GB 10 at Phi 0 9,500
ChiB 17 at Port 7 10,000
Bos 0 at ChiC 0 7,000
Pit 3 at NYG 27 10,000
Bkn 0 at Cin 10 3,500

Sun 12/10
GB 6 at ChiB 7 7,000
NYG 20 at Phi 14 8,000

1933 NFL Championship

Sun 12/17
NYG 21 at ChiB 23 26,000

National Football League 1934

Sun 09/09
CiSL 0 at Pit 13 14,164

Sun 09/16
Phi 6 at GB 19 5,000
Bos 7 at Pit 0 17,171

Sun 09/23
ChiC 9 at CiSL 0 6,000
at Dayton, OH
NYG 0 at Det 9 12,000
ChiB 24 at GB 10 13,500

Wed 09/26
N Phi 17 at Pit 0 11,500

Sun 09/30
NYG 6 at GB 20 11,000
at Milwaukee, WI
Bos 6 at Bkn 10 12,500
ChiC 0 at Det 6 18,000
ChiB 21 at CiSL 3 5,500

Wed 10/03
N NYG 14 at Pit 12 13,000

Sun 10/07
NYG 16 at Bos 13 20,000
Pit 9 at Phi 7 9,000
N ChiC 16 at CiSL 0 2,500
Det 3 at GB 0 7,500
ChiB 21 at Bkn 7 20,000

Wed 10/10
N ChiB 28 at Pit 0 20,000

Sun 10/14
Bkn 0 at NYG 14 30,000
Det 10 at Phi 0 9,860
CiSL 0 at GB 41 3,000
ChiB 20 at ChiC 0 15,000
Pit 0 at Bos 39 15,500

Wed 10/17
N Bos 0 at Det 24 12,000

Sun 10/21
Phi 0 at Bos 6 10,000
Pit 7 at NYG 17 11,000
ChiC 0 at GB 15 4,000
CiSL 7 at ChiB 41 11,000

Mon 10/22
N Bkn 0 at Det 28 10,000

Sun 10/28
Phi 0 at NYG 17 8,500
ChiC 0 at Bos 9 10,000
Det 38 at CiSL 0 4,800
at Portsmouth, OH
Pit 3 at Bkn 21 8,000
GB 14 at ChiB 27 11,000

Sun 11/04
NYG 7 at ChiB 27 25,000
GB 10 at Bos 0 23,722
Pit 7 at Det 40 6,000

Tue 11/06
CiSL 0 at Phi 64 n/a
at Temple, Stad., Phila.
N ChiC 21 at Bkn 0 7,000

Sun 11/11
GB 3 at NYG 17 22,000
Pit 0 at CiSL 6 13,700
ChiB 21 at Bos 0 26,000
Bkn 10 at Phi 7 8,000
Det 17 at ChiC 13 7,000

Sun 11/18
ChiC 9 at GB 0 3,000
at Milwaukee, WI
Bos 14 at Phi 7 n/a
ChiB 10 at NYG 9 55,000

Sun 11/18
Bkn 10 at Pit 0 10,000
CiSL 7 at Det 40 13,000

Sun 11/25
Bos 0 at NYG 3 20,000
Phi 13 at Bkn 0 8,000
ChiC 6 at ChiB 17 13,800
GB 3 at Det 0 12,000

Thu 11/29
NYG 27 at Bkn 0 15,000
ChiB 19 at Det 16 25,000
GB 0 at ChiC 6 1,738

Sun 12/02
Bkn 3 at Bos 13 13,000
NYG 0 at Phi 6 12,471
Det 7 at ChiB 10 34,412
GB 21 at CiSL 14 6,300

1934 NFL Championship

Sun 12/09
ChiB 13 at NYG 30 35,059

National Football League 1935

Fri 09/13
N Pit 17 at Phi 7 20,000
at Temple Stad., Phila.

Sun 09/15
ChiC 7 at GB 6 10,000

Fri 09/20
N Phi 0 at Det 35 10,000

Sun 09/22
ChiB 0 at GB 7 13,600
NYG 42 at Pit 7 24,000

Sun 09/29
Bkn 3 at Bos 7 18,000
ChiC 10 at Det 10 8,200
NYG 7 at GB 16 10,000
ChiB 23 at Pit 7 11,858

Sun 10/06
NYG 20 at Bos 12 8,000
Det 10 at Bkn 12 10,000
Pit 0 at GB 27 5,000

Wed 10/09
N Phi 17 at Pit 6 6,271

Sun 10/13
Det 17 at Bos 7 18,737
ChiC 3 at GreB 0 13,000
at Milwaukee, WI
Bkn 7 at NYG 10 30,000
ChiB 39 at Phi 0 20,000

Sun 10/20
Bkn 14 at ChiB 24 18,000
Det 9 at GB 13 9,500
at Milwaukee, WI
Bos 6 at NYG 17 20,000
ChiC 13 at Pit 17 7,000

Sun 10/27
Phi 6 at Bkn 17 20,000
GB 17 at ChiB 14 29,386
ChiC 14 at NYG 13 32,000
Bos 0 at Pit 6 12,000

Wed 10/30
N Bos 0 at Det 14 14,000

Sun 11/03
Phi 7 at Bos 6 10,000
Det 7 at ChiC 6 5,000
ChiB 20 at NYG 3 40,000
Bkn 13 at Pit 7 13,390

Tue 11/05
N Bkn 3 at Phi 0 10,000

Sun 11/10
ChiB 30 at Bos 14 16,000
Pit 16 at Bkn 7 18,000
Phi 3 at ChiC 12 6,000
Det 7 at GB 31 12,000

Sun 11/17
NYG 3 at ChiB 0 19,000
GB 10 at Det 20 12,500
N ChiC 12 at Bkn 14 18,000

Sun 11/24
ChiC 6 at Bos 0 5,000
Det 20 at ChiB 20 14,624
Phi 0 at NYG 10 n/a
GB 34 at Pit 14 12,902

Thu 11/28
NYG 21 at Bkn 0 25,000
GB 7 at ChiC 9 7,500
ChiB 2 at Det 14 18,000

Sun 12/01
Pit 3 at Bos 13 5,000
ChiC 7 at ChiB 7 12,167
Bkn 0 at Det 28 12,000
NYG 21 at Phi 14 6,500

Sun 12/08
Bos 0 at Bkn 0 5,000
Pit 0 at NYG 13 7,000
GB 13 at Phi 6 4,000
ChiB 13 at ChiC 0 17,373

1935 NFL Championship

Sun 12/15
NYG 7 at Det 26 15,000

National Football League 1936

Sun 09/13
ChiC 7 at GB 10 8,900
Bos 0 at Pit 10 15,622
NYG 7 at Phi 10 20,000

Sun 09/20
ChiB 30 at GB 3 14,312
Bos 26 at Phi 3 n/a

Wed 09/23
N Pit 10 at Bkn 6 10,000

Sun 09/27
Bos 14 at Bkn 3 15,000
NYG 7 at Pit 10 25,800
ChiB 17 at Phi 0 25,000

Mon 09/28
N ChiC 0 at Det 39 15,000

Sun 10/04
ChiC 0 at GB 24 11,000
at Milwaukee, WI
N Phi 0 at Bkn 18 10,000
ChiB 27 at Pit 9 29,000
NYG 7 at Bos 0 15,000

Sun 10/11
Bos 2 at GB 31 6,100
ChiC 3 at ChiB 7 16,288
Bkn 10 at NYG 10 25,000
Det 23 at Phi 0 15,000

Wed 10/14
N Det 14 at Bkn 7 8,000
N Phi 0 at Pit 17 10,042

Sun 10/18
Det 18 at GB 20 13,500
Pit 7 at ChiB 26 20,000
ChiC 6 at NYG 14 17,000
Phi 7 at Bos 17 4,000

Sun 10/25
Pit 10 at GB 42 10,000
at Milwaukee, WI
Det 10 at ChiB 12 27,424
Phi 17 at NYG 21 15,000
ChiC 0 at Bkn 9 20,000

Sun 11/01
GB 21 at ChiB 10 31,346
Det 7 at NYG 14 26,243
Bkn 7 at Pit 10 10,000
ChiC 10 at Bos 13 7,000

Thu 11/05
N Pit 6 at Phi 0 7,891
at Johnstown, PA

Sun 11/08
Pit 3 at Det 28 20,000
Phi 0 at ChiC 13 1,500
ChiB 25 at NYG 7 25,325
GB 7 at Bos 3 11,220

Sun 11/15
NYG 0 at Det 38 20,000
Pit 6 at ChiC 14 3,856
GB 38 at Bkn 7 25,325
ChiB 26 at Bos 0 12,000

Sun 11/22
Det 14 at ChiC 7 7,579
GB 26 at NYG 14 20,000
Bkn 6 at Bos 30 5,000
ChiB 28 at Phi 7 10,000

Thu 11/26
ChiB 7 at Det 13 22,000
NYG 14 at Bkn 0 18,000

Sun 11/29
GB 26 at Det 17 22,000
ChiB 7 at ChiC 14 13,704
Pit 0 at Bos 30 7,000
Bkn 13 at Phi 7 5,000

Sun 12/06
Bkn 6 at Det 14 10,000
GB 0 at ChiC 0 4,793
Bos 14 at NYG 0 18,000

1936 NFL Championship

Sun 12/13
GB 21 at Bos 6 29,545
at Polo Grounds, NY

National Football League 1937

Sun 09/05
Phi 14 at Pit 27 8,588

Fri 09/10
N Bkn 13 at Phi 7 5,221
N Det 28 at Cle 0 24,800
at Municipal Stad., Phil.

Sun 09/12
ChiC 14 at GB 7 10,000

Thu 09/16
N NYG 3 at Was 13 24,500

Sun 09/19
ChiB 14 at GB 2 16,658
ChiC 7 at Det 16 18,000
Pit 21 at Bkn 0 18,000

Tue 09/21
N Cle 21 at Phi 3 3,107

Fri 09/24
N ChiC 21 at Was 14 22,367

Sun 09/26
NYG 10 at Pit 7 33,095
Cle 7 at Bkn 9 12,000
ChiC 6 at Phi 6 3,912

Sun 10/03
NYG 16 at Phi 7 4,878
Det 6 at GB 26 17,553
Bkn 7 at Was 11 16,000
ChiC 6 at Cle 0 10,400

Mon 10/04
N ChiB 7 at Pit 0 22,511

Sun 10/10
Phi 14 at Was 0 7,320
ChiC 13 at GB 34 16,181
at Milwaukee, WI

ChiB 20 at Cle 2 5,000
Pit 3 at Det 7 16,000

Sun 10/17
Phi 0 at NYG 21 20,089
Pit 20 at Was 34 12,835
ChiC 7 at ChiB 16 23,000
GB 35 at Cle 10 12,100
Bkn 0 at Det 30 18,000

Sun 10/24
Bkn 0 at NYG 21 25,000

Was 10 at Phi 7 6,580
ChiC 13 at Pit 7 8,963
Cle 7 at GB 35 3,600
Det 20 at ChiB 28 34,530

Sun 10/31
GB 14 at Det 13 21,311
ChiB 3 at NYG 3 50,449
Phi 7 at Pit 16 2,772
Was 21 at Bkn 0 22,500
Cle 7 at ChiC 13 9,923

Sun 11/07
Pit 0 at NYG 17 21,447
GB 24 at ChiB 14 44,977
Phi 14 at Bkn 10 8,373
Cle 7 at Det 27 15,500

Sun 11/14
Det 17 at NYG 0 35,790
Bkn 7 at ChiB 29 7,065
Was 13 at Pit 21 12,000
Phi 7 at GB 37 13,340
at Milwaukee, WI

Sun 11/21
Bkn 23 at Pit 0 3,700
GB 0 at NYG 10 38,965
Det 16 at ChiC 7 8,576
Was 16 at Cle 7 3,500

Thu 11/25
ChiB 13 at Det 0 24,173
NYG 13 at Bkn 13 27,000

Sun 11/28
GB 6 at Was 14 30,000

Cle 7 at ChiB 15 4,188

Sun 12/05
ChiB 42 at ChiC 28 7,313
Was 49 at NYG 14 58,285

1937 NFL Championship

Sun 12/12
Was 28 at ChiB 21 15,878

National Football League 1938

Fri 09/09
N Pit 7 at Det 16 17,000
at Titan Stadium, Detroit

Sun 09/11
ChiC 13 at ChiB 16 20,000
at Soldier Field, Chicago
Cle 17 at GB 26 8,247
Was 26 at Phi 23 20,000
NYG 27 at Pit 14 17,340

Fri 09/16
N Phi 27 at Pit 7 19,749
at Buffalo, NY

Sat 09/17
ChiC 7 at Cle 6 7,448

Sun 09/18
ChiB 2 at GB 0 15,172
Bkn 16 at Was 16 23,000

Fri 09/23
N Pit 17 at Bkn 3 21,494

Sun 09/25
NYG 10 at Phi 14 23,877
Cle 13 at Was 37 27,000
ChiC 7 at GB 28 18,000
at Milwaukee, WI

Wed 09/29
N GB 24 at ChiC 22 10,678
at Buffalo, NY

Sun 10/02
ChiB 28 at Phi 6 22,245
Det 17 at Cle 21 8,012
ChiC 0 at Bkn 13 17,129

Mon 10/03
N Pit 13 at NYG 10 18,805

Sun 10/09
NYG 10 at Was 7 37,500

Det 17 at GB 7 21,968
Bkn 17 at Pit 7 n/a
ChiB 7 at Cle 14 8,000

Sun 10/16
ChiB 34 at ChiC 28 21,614
Was 7 at Det 5 42,855
Phi 7 at NYG 17 33,187
Bkn 7 at GB 35 11,892
at Milwaukee, WI

Sun 10/23
ChiC 0 at Det 10 17,917
Cle 23 at ChiB 21 18,705
Phi 14 at Was 20 3,000
Pit 0 at GB 20 12,142
Bkn 14 at NYG 28 36,228

Wed 10/26
N Phi 7 at ChiC 0 15,000
at Erie, PA

Sun 10/30
Det 13 at ChiB 7 24,346
GB 28 at Cle 7 18,843
Was 6 at Bkn 6 29,913

Sun 11/06
GB 24 at ChiB 17 40,208
Cle 0 at Det 6 31,140
Bkn 10 at Phi 7 11,477
ChiC 0 at NYG 6 19,648
Was 7 at Pit 0 12,910

Sun 11/13
GB 28 at Det 7 45,139
at Briggs Stadium, Detroit
Was 7 at ChiB 31 21,817
Phi 14 at Bkn 32 13,052
Cle 0 at NYG 28 25,000

Sun 11/20
Phi 14 at Pit 7 6,500
at Charleston, WV
GB 3 at NYG 15 48,279

ChiB 24 at Bkn 6 26,416
Det 7 at ChiC 3 8,279

Thu 11/24
ChiB 7 at Det 14 26,278
NYG 7 at Bkn 7 17,400

Sun 11/27
Cle 17 at ChiC 31 2,200
Pit 0 at Was 15 22,000

Sun 12/04
Phi 21 at Det 7 18,985
Cle 13 at Pit 7 7,500
at New Orleans, LA
Was 0 at NYG 36 57,461

1938 NFL Championship

Sun 12/11
GB 17 at NYG 23 48,120

National Football League 1939

Sun 09/10
ChiC 13 at Det 21 15,075
at Titan Stadium Detroit

Thu 09/14
N Pit 7 at Bkn 12 19,444

Fri 09/15
N Cle 21 at ChiB 30 10,000

Sun 09/17
Was 7 at Phi 0 33,258
ChiC 10 at GB 14 11,792

Wed 09/20
N Cle 12 at Bkn 23 12,423

Sun 09/24
ChiC 10 at Pit 0 19,008
ChiB 16 at GB 21 19,192

Bkn 7 at Det 27 15,515
at Titan Stadium, Detroit
NYG 13 at Phi 3 30,864

Sun 10/01
Cle 27 at GB 24 9,988
Bkn 0 at Phi 0 1,880
NYG 0 at Was 0 26,342
N Det 17 at ChiC 3 11,000
at Soldier Field, Chicago

Mon 10/02
N ChiB 32 at Pit 0 10,325

Sun 10/08
ChiB 35 at Cle 21 18,209
Bkn 13 at Was 41 27,092
NYG 14 at Pit 7 9,663
ChiC 20 vs GB 27 18,965
at Milwaukee, WI

Sun 10/15
Phi 10 at NYG 27 34,471
ChiC 7 at ChiB 44 29,592
Pit 14 at Was 44 25,982
Cle 7 at Det 15 30,096

Sun 10/22
Cle 24 at ChiC 0 10,043
Det 7 at GB 26 22,558
Was 21 at Pit 14 8,602
ChiB 13 at NYG 16 58,963
Phi 14 at Bkn 23 13,057

Sun 10/29
Det 10 at ChiB 0 30,903
Was 14 vs GB 24 24,308
at Milwaukee, WI
NYG 7 at Bkn 6 34,032
Pit 14 at Cle 14 11,579

Sun 11/05
GB 27 at ChiB 30 40,537
Phi 6 at Was 7 20,444
NYG 14 at Det 18 47,492
ChiC 0 at Cle 14 8,378

Mon 11/06
N Pit 13 at Bkn 17 8,951

Sun 11/12
ChiC 7 at NYG 17 28,217
GB 23 at Phi 16 23,862
ChiB 23 at Det 13 42,684
Was 42 at Bkn 0 28,541

Sun 11/19
Det 3 at Cle 14 28,142
Phi 14 at ChiB 27 21,398
ChiC 7 at Was 28 26,667
GB 28 at Bkn 0 19,843
Pit 7 at NYG 23 19,372

Thu 11/23
Pit 14 at Phi 17 20,000

Sun 11/26
Bkn 7 at NYG 28 30,144
Det 7 at Was 31 36,183
ChiB 48 at ChiC 7 16,055
GB 7 at Cle 6 30,691
Phi 12 at Pit 24 8,788

Sun 12/03
Was 7 at NYG 9 62,404
GB 12 at Det 7 30,699
Phi 13 at Cle 35 9,189
at Colorado Springs, CO

1939 NFL Championship

Sun 12/10
NYG vs 0 GB 27 32,279
at Milwaukee, WI

National Football League 1940

Sun 09/08
ChiC 7 at Pit 7 22,000

Sun 09/15
Phi 20 at GB 27 11,657
Det 0 at ChiC 0 18,048
at Buffalo, NY
Bkn 17 at Was 24 32,763
NYG 10 at Pit 10 18,601

Sun 09/22
ChiB 41 at GB 10 22,557
Pit 10 at Det 7 15,310
Phi 13 at Cle 21 15,941
NYG 7 at Was 21 34,712

Wed 09/25
N ChiB 7 at ChiC 21 23,181

Sat 09/28
N NYG 20 at Phi 14 26,431

Sun 09/29
ChiC 6 at GB 31 20,234
at Milwaukee, WI
Cle 0 at Det 6 15,347
Bkn 10 at Pit 3 26,618

Fri 10/04
N Phi 17 at Bkn 30 24,008

Sat 10/05
N ChiC 14 at Det 43 20,619

Sun 10/06
ChiB 21 at Cle 14 18,998
Was 40 at Pit 10 25,213

Sun 10/13
Cle 14 at GB 31 16,299
Det 0 at ChiB 7 34,217
ChiC 21 at Was 28 33,691
Pit 0 at Bkn 21 19,468

Phi 7 at NYG 17 30,317

Sun 10/20
Det 23 at GB 14 21,001
ChiC 14 at Cle 26 13,363
Was 34 at Phi 17 25,062
Bkn 7 at ChiB 16 31,101
Pit 0 at NYG 12 19,798

Sat 10/26
N Bkn 21 at Phi 7 6,500

Sun 10/27
Pit 3 at GB 24 13,703
at Milwaukee, WI
Was 20 at Det 14 28,809
Cle 7 at ChiC 17 10,313
ChiB 37 at NYG 21 44,219

Sun 11/03
GB 7 at ChiB 14 45,434

Det 0 at Cle 34 18,881
Pit 10 at Was 37 31,204
NYG 10 at Bkn 7 32,958

Sun 11/10
GB 28 at ChiC 7 11,364
ChiB 14 at Det 17 21,735
Cle 13 at NYG 0 23,614
Was 14 at Bkn 16 33,846
Phi 3 at Pit 10 9,556

Sun 11/17
GB 3 at NYG 7 28,262
Det 0 at Phi 17 6,327
Cle 14 at Bkn 29 19,212
ChiB 3 at Was 7 35,331

Sun 11/24
GB 50 at Det 7 26,019
Cle 25 at ChiB 47 20,717
ChiC 9 at Bkn 14 16,619

Was 7 at NYG 21 46,439

Thu 11/28
Pit 7 at Phi 0 4,200

Sun 12/01
GB 13 at Cle 13 16,249
ChiC 20 at ChiB 31 13,902
Phi 6 at Was 13 25,838
Bkn 14 at NYG 6 54,993

1940 NFL Championship

Sun 12/08
ChiB 73 at Was 0 36,034

National Football League 1941

Sun 09/07
Pit 14 at Cle 17 23,720
at Akron, OH

Sat 09/13
N NYG 24 at Phi 0 25,478
at Municipal Stadium, Phila.

Sun 09/04
Det 0 at GB 23 16,734

Tue 09/16
N Cle 10 at ChiC 6 15,000

Sun 09/21
Cle 7 at GB 24 18,463
at Milwaukee, WI
Phi 10 at Pit 7 12,893
Det 7 at Bkn 14 19,269

Sat 09/27
N Bkn 24 at Phi 13 16,341
Det 14 at ChiC 14 17,458

Sun 09/28
ChiB 25 at GB 17 24,876
NYG 17 at Was 10 35,677

Sun 10/05
NYG 37 at Pit 10 13,458
ChiB 48 at Cle 21 23,850
ChiC 13 at GB 14 10,000
at Milwaukee, WI
Bkn 0 at Was 3 32,642

Sun 10/12
Phi 0 at NYG 16 30,842
Was 24 at Pit 20 18,733
ChiC 7 at ChiB 53 34,668
Bkn 7 at GB 30 15,621
at Milwaukee, WI

Cle 7 at Det 17 26,481

Sun 10/19
GB 17 at Cle 14 13,086
Pit 7 at NYG 28 34,604
Det 0 at ChiB 49 29,980
ChiC 20 at Bkn 6 12,054
Was 21 at Phi 17 19,071

Sun 10/26
ChiC 14 at Phi 21 12,683
NYG 13 at Bkn 16 28,675
Pit 7 at ChiB 34 17,217
GB 24 at Det 7 30,269
Cle 13 at Was 17 32,820

Sun 11/02
ChiC 10 at NYG 7 29,289
GB 16 at ChiB 14 46,484
Pit 3 at Was 23 30,755
Det 14 at Cle 0 10,554

Phi 6 at Bkn 15 15,899

Sun 11/09
Det 13 at NYG 20 27,875
Cle 13 at ChiB 31 18,102
Pit 7 at Phi 7 15,601
Was 7 at Bkn 13 31,713

Sun 11/16
Cle 14 at NYG 49 32,740
ChiC 9 at GB 17 15,495
Bkn 7 at Pit 14 20,843
Phi 17 at Det 21 16,306
Was 21 at ChiB 35 30,095

Sun 11/23
Was 13 at NYG 20 49,317
ChiC 7 at Cle 0 5,000
ChiB 24 at Det 7 28,657
GB 54 at Pit 7 15,202

Sun 11/30
Pit 7 at Bkn 35 12,336
GB 22 at Was 17 35,594
ChiB 49 at Phi 14 32,608
ChiC 3 at Det 21 17,051

Sun 12/07
ChiB 34 at ChiC 24 18,879
Bkn 21 at NYG 7 55,051
Phi 14 at Was 20 27,102

Western Division Playoff

Sun 12/14
GB 14 at ChiB 33 43,425

1941 NFL Championship

Sun 12/21
NYG 9 at ChiB 37 13,341

National Football League 1942

Sun 09/13
Phi 24 at Pit 14 13,349
Cle 0 at ChiC 7 18,698
at Buffalo, NY

Sun 09/20
N Det 0 at ChiC 13 14,742
Phi 14 at Cle 24 6,434
at Akron, OH
Pit 14 at Was 28 25,000

Sun 09/27
ChiB 44 at GB 28 20.007
Cle 14 at Det 0 14,646
NYG 14 at Was 7 34,700
Bkn 35 at Phi 14 5,682
at Buffalo, NY

Sun 10/04
ChiB 21 at Cle 7 17,167
N GB 17 at ChiC 13 24,897
Bkn 28 at Det 7 12,598
NYG 10 at Pit 13 9,600
Was 14 at Phi 10 15,500

Sun 10/11
ChiC 14 at ChiB 41 38,500
Det 7 at GB 38 19,500
at Milwaukee, WI
Cle 14 at Was 33 33,250
Phi 17 at NYG 35 28,264
Pit 7 at Bkn 0 17,689

Sun 10/18
NYG 7 at ChiB 26 32,000
ChiC 7 at Det 0 14,100

Cle 28 at GB 45 12,847
Was 21 at Bkn 10 25,635
Pit 14 at Phi 0 12,500

Sun 10/25
Phi 14 at ChiB 45 15,372
ChiC 3 at Cle 7 7,896
GB 28 at Det 7 19,097
NYG 7 at Bkn 17 23,234
Was 14 at Pit 0 37,764

Sun 11/01
Det 0 at ChiB 16 12,205
ChiC 24 at GB 55 14,782
Cle 17 at Bkn 0 6,329
Pit 17 at NYG 9 19,346
Phi 27 at Was 30 32,658

Sun 11/08
ChiB 35 at Bkn 0 31,643
ChiC 0 at Was 28 35,425
GB 30 at Cle 12 16,473
Pit 35 at Det 7 16,679
NYG 14 at Phi 0 13,548

Sun 11/15
GB 7 at ChiB 38 42,787
Det 7 at Cle 27 4,029
Was 14 at NYG 7 30,879
Phi 14 at Bkn 7 3,858

Sun 11/22
ChiB 42 at Det 0 17,348
ChiC 3 at Pit 19 20,711
GB 21 at NYG 21 30,246
Bkn 3 at Was 23 34,450

Sun 11/29
Cle 0 at ChiB 47 13,195
ChiC 7 at NYG 21 20,354
GB 7 at Phi 0 13,700
Was 15 at Det 3 6,044
Bkn 0 at Pit 13 4,593

Sun 12/06
ChiB 21 at ChiC 7 8,251
Pit 21 at GB 24 5,138
at Milwaukee, WI
Bkn 0 at NYG 10 27,449

1942 NFL Championship

Sun 12/13
ChiB 6 at Was 14 36,006

National Football League 1943

Sun 09/19
ChiC 17 at Det 35 23,408

Sun 09/26
Bkn 0 at Det 27 23,768
ChiB 21 at GB 21 23,675

Sat 10/02
N Bkn 0 at PhPt 17 11,131
at Philadelphia, PA

Sun 10/03
GB 28 at ChiC 7 15,563
ChiB 27 at Det 21 48,118

Sat 10/09
N NYG 14 at PhPt 28 15,340
at Philadelphia, PA

Sun 10/10
ChiC 0 at ChiB 20 24,658
Det 14 at GB 35 21,396
Bkn 0 at Was 27 35,540

Sun 10/17
NYG 20 at Bkn 0 18,361
Det 7 at ChiC 0 15,072
at Buffalo, NY
Was 33 at GB 7 23,058
at Milwaukee, WI
PhPt 21 at ChiB 48 21,744

Sun 10/24
Bkn 21 at ChiB 33 9,600
GB 27 at Det 6 41,463
PhPt 14 at NYG 42 42,681
ChiC 7 at Was 13 35,540

Sun 10/31
GB 35 at NYG 21 46,208
Was 48 at Bkn 10 11,471
Det 14 at ChiB 35 25,187
ChiC 13 at PhPt 34 16,351
at Pittsburgh, PA

Sun 11/07
GB 7 at ChiB 21 43,425
NYG 0 at Det 0 16,992
ChiC 0 at Bkn 7 13,340
Was 14 at PhPt 14 28,893
at Philadelphia, PA

Sun 11/14
Det 20 at Was 42 35,540
PhPt 7 at Bkn 13 7,614
ChiB 56 at NYG 7 56,591

ChiC 14 at GB 35 10,831
at Milwaukee, WI

Sun 11/21
ChiC 13 at NYG 24 19,804
GB 31 at Bkn 7 18,992
ChiB 7 at Was 21 35,672
Det 34 at PhPt 35 23,338
at Pittsburgh, PA

Sun 11/28
PhPt 27 at Was 14 35,826
Bkn 7 at NYG 24 28,706
ChiB 35 at ChiC 24 17,219

Sun 12/05
GB 38 at PhPt 28 34,294
at Philadelphia, PA

Was 10 at NYG 14 51,308

Sun 12/12
NYG 31 at Was 7 35,540

Eastern Division Playoff

Sun 12/19
Was 28 at NYG 0 42,800

1943 NFL Championship

Sun 12/26
Was 21 at ChiB 41 34,320

National Football League 1944

Sun 09/17
Bkn 7 at GB 14 12,994
at Milwaukee, WI

Sun 09/24
Cle 30 at ChPi 28 20,968
at Pittsburgh, PA
ChiB 20 at GB 42 24,362

Tue 09/26
N Phi 28 at Bos 7 19,851

Sun 10/01
Det 6 at GB 27 18,556
at Milwaukee, WI

Sun 10/08
NYG 22 at Bos 10 17,463

Bkn 14 at Det 19 15,702
ChPi 7 at GB 34 16,535
ChiB 7 at Cle 19 15,750
Was 31 at Phi 31 32,549

Sun 10/15
Was 21 at Bos 14 17,758
NYG 14 at Bkn 7 24,854
ChPi 7 at ChiB 34 29,940
Cle 20 at Det 17 21,115

Sun 10/22
Bos 0 at Phi 38 24,638
Bkn 14 at Was 17 35,540
ChPi 0 at NYG 23 40,734
Det 21 at ChiB 21 23,835
Cle 21 at GB 30 18,780

Sun 10/29
Bos 17 at Bkn 14 13,237
ChPi 20 at Was 42 35,540
Cle 21 at ChiB 28 23,644
GB 14 at Det 0 30,844
Phi 24 at NYG 17 42,639

Sun 11/05
Bos 0 at NYG 31 28,364
Phi 21 at Bkn 7 15,289
Det 27 at ChPi 6 17,743
at Pittsburgh, PA
GB 0 at ChiB 21 45,553
Cle 10 at Was 14 35,540

Sun 11/12
Bos 7 at ChiB 21 19,374
Was 10 at Bkn 0 20,404

ChPi 7 at Det 21 13,239
GB 42 at Cle 7 17,166
NYG 21 at Phi 21 33,248

Sun 11/19
Bkn 6 at Bos 13 15,666
ChiB 21 at Det 41 21,960
Cle 33 at ChPi 6 14,732
at Chicago, IL
GB 0 at NYG 24 56,481
Phi 37 at Was 7 35,540

Sun 11/26
Bos 7 at Was 14 35,540
Bkn 0 at NYG 7 29,387
GB 35 at ChPi 20 7,158
at Chicago, IL
ChiB 28 at Phi 7 34,035

Det 26 at Cle 14 7,452

Sun 12/03
Bos 7 at Det 38 15,027
Bkn 0 at Phi 34 13,467
ChiB 49 at ChPi 7 9,069
at Pittsburgh, PA
Was 13 at NYG 16 47,457

Sun 12/10
Cle 13 at Phi 26 24,123
NYG 31 at Was 0 35,540

1944 NFL Championship

Sun 12/17
GB 14 at NYG 7 46,015

National Football League 1945

Sun 09/23
Det 10 at ChiC 0 5,461
at Milwaukee, WI

Tue 09/25
N Pit 7 at Bos 28 27,502

Sun 09/30
ChiB 21 at GB 31 24,525
ChiC 0 at Cle 21 10,872

Sun 10/07
Det 21 at GB 57 20,463
at Milwaukee, WI
ChiB 0 at Cle 17 19,580
ChiC 6 at Phi 21 25,581
Was 20 at Bos 28 21,333
NYG 34 at Pit 6 20,097

Sun 10/14
ChiC 16 at ChiB 7 20,784
Cle 27 at GB 14 24,607
Phi 24 at Det 28 22,580
NYG 13 at Bos 13 30,988
at Yankee Stadium, New York
Was 14 at Pit 0 14,050

Sun 10/21
Cle 41 at ChiB 21 28,273
Bos 14 at GB 38 20,846
at Milwaukee, WI
ChiC 0 at Det 26 32,644
Pit 21 at NYG 7 43,070
Phi 14 at Was 24 34,778

Sun 10/28
ChiC 14 at GB 33 19,221
ChiB 10 at Det 16 37,260
Was 24 at NYG 14 55,461
Cle 14 at Phi 28 38,149
Bos 10 at Pit 6 25,447

Sun 11/04
GB 24 at ChiB 28 45,527
Cle 21 at NYG 17 46,219
Det 10 at Bos 9 17,631
Phi 45 at Pit 3 23,018
ChiC 21 at Was 24 35,000

Sun 11/11
Det 35 at ChiB 28 24,798
GB 7 at Cle 20 28,686
NYG 17 at Phi 38 30,047
ChiC 0 at Pit 23 13,153
Bos 7 at Was 34 34,788

Sun 11/18
Cle 35 at ChiC 21 18,000
Det 14 at NYG 35 38,215
Pit 6 at Phi 30 23,838
GB 28 at Bos 0 31,923
ChiB 21 at Was 28 34,788

Thu 11/22
Cle 28 at Det 21 40,017

Sun 11/25
Pit 7 at ChiB 28 20,689
GB 23 at NYG 14 52,681
Was 0 at Phi 16 37,306

Sun 12/02
ChiB 28 at ChiC 20 13,925
Bos 7 at Cle 20 18,470
GB 3 at Det 14 23,468
Phi 21 at NYG 28 45,372
Pit 0 at Was 24 34,788

Sun 12/09
Bos 7 at Phi 35 27,905
NYG 0 at Was 17 34,788

1945 NFL Championship

Sun 12/16
Was 14 at Cle 15 32,178
at Municipal Stadium, Cleve.

National Football League 1946

Fri 09/20
N ChiC 7 at Pit 14 32,951

Sun 09/29
ChiB 30 at GB 7 25,049
Phi 25 at LARm 14 30,500
Pit 14 at Was 14 33,620

Mon 09/30
N Det 14 at ChiC 34 26,842

Tue 10/01
N NYG 17 at Bos 0 16,500

Sun 10/06
LARm 21 at GB 17 27,049
at Milwaukee, WI
ChiB 34 at ChiC 17 39,263
Det 16 at Was 17 33,589
Bos 25 at Phi 49 33,986
NYG 17 at Pit 14 33,702

Sun 10/13
LARm 28 at ChiB 28 44,211
ChiC 36 at Det 14 21,906
NYG 14 at Was 24 33,651
GB 19 at Phi 7 36,127
Bos 7 at Pit 16 34,297

Sun 10/20
Phi 14 at ChiB 21 41,221
Pit 7 at GB 17 22,588
Det 14 at LARm 35 27,926
ChiC 24 at NYG 28 50,581
Was 14 at Bos 6 22,544

Sun 10/27
Det 7 at GB 10 23,564
at Milwaukee, WI
LARm 10 at ChiC 34 38,180
Phi 28 at Was 24 33,691
ChiB 0 at NYG 14 62,349
Pit 33 at Bos 7 13,797

Sun 11/03
GB 7 at ChiB 10 46,321
LARm 41 at Det 20 34,447
NYG 14 at Phi 24 40,059
Was 7 at Pit 14 36,995
ChiC 28 at Bos 14 10,556

Sun 11/10
GB 19 at ChiC 7 30,681
Pit 7 at Det 17 13,621
ChiB 27 at LARm 21 68,381
Bos 14 at Was 17 33,691
Phi 17 at NYG 45 60,874

Sun 11/17
Was 20 at ChiB 24 43,315
GB 9 at Det 0 21,055
ChiC 14 at LARm 17 38,271
Bos 28 at NYG 28 35,583
Phi 7 at Pit 10 38,882

Sun 11/24
Det 6 at ChiB 42 31,169
ChiC 24 at GB 6 16,150
Pit 0 at NYG 7 45,347
Was 27 at Phi 10 36,633
LARm 21 at Bos 40 23,689

Thu 11/28
Bos 34 at Det 10 13,010

Sun 12/01
ChiC 35 at ChiB 28 47,511
GB 20 at Was 7 33,691
LARm 31 at NYG 21 47,366
Pit 7 at Phi 10 29,943

Sun 12/08
ChiB 45 at Det 24 19,579
GB 17 at LARm 38 46,838
Was 0 at NYG 31 60,337
Phi 40 at Bos 14 29,555

1946 NFL Championship

Sun 12/15
ChiB 24 at NYG 14 58,346

All-America Football Conference 1946

Fri 09/06
N MiaA 0 at CleA 44 60,135

Sun 09/08
BknA 27 at BufA 14 24,489
NY-A 21 at SF-A 7 35,000

Fri 09/13
N CleA 20 at ChiA 6 51,962
N BknA 14 at LA-A 20 19,500

Sat 09/14
N BufA 10 at NY-A 21 40,606

Sun 09/15
MiaA 14 at SF-A 21 25,000

Fri 09/20
N NY-A 17 at ChiA 17 25,000
N MiaA 14 at LA-A 30 23,000

Sun 09/22
CleA 28 at BufA 0 30,302
BknA 13 at SF-A 32 35,000

Wed 09/25
N BufA 35 at ChiA 38 20,768

Sun 09/29
LA-A 21 at BufA 21 18,163
SF-A 7 at ChiA 24 26,875
NY-A 7 at CleA 24 57,084

Fri 10/04
N NY-A 21 at BufA 13 17,101

Sat 10/05
N LA-A 21 at ChiA 9 31,076

Sun 10/06
BknA 7 at CleA 26 43,713

Tue 10/08
N SF-A 34 at MiaA 7 7,621

Fri 10/11
N ChiA 21 at BknA 21 16,211
N MiaA 17 at BufA 14 5,040

Sat 10/12
N CleA 7 at NY-A 0 34,252

Sun 10/13
SF-A 23 at LA-A 14 12,500

Fri 10/18
N MiaA 7 at ChiA 28 20,172

Sat 10/19
N BknA 10 at NY-A 21 30,212
N SF-A 14 at BufA 17 6,101

Sun 10/20
LA-A 14 at CleA 31 71,134

Fri 10/25
N MiaA 7 at BknA 30 15,200

Sun 10/27
ChiA 17 at BufA 49 15,758
SF-A 34 at CleA 20 70,385
NY-A 31 at LA-A 17 15,000

Sat 11/02
N BknA 21 at ChiA 14 17,924
N BufA 14 at SF-A 27 12,500

Sun 11/03
CleA 16 at LA-A 17 24,800
MiaA 21 at NY-A 24 18,800

Sun 11/10
BufA 17 at BknA 14 12,820
CleA 14 at SF-A 7 41,061
LA-A 12 at NY-A 17 30,765

Mon 11/11
N ChiA 20 at MiaA 7 7,438

Sun 11/17
LA-A 19 at BknA 14 7,500
ChiA 14 at CleA 51 60,457
SF-A 9 at NY-A 10 18,695

Mon 11/18
N BufA 14 at MiaA 21 5,592

Sun 11/24
SF-A 30 at BknA 14 15,100
BufA 17 at CleA 42 37,054
ChiA 38 at NY-A 28 21,270

Mon 11/25
N LA-A 34 at MiaA 21 9,987

Thu 11/28
NY-A 21 at BknA 7 16,240

Sat 11/30
N ChiA 0 at SF-A 14 12,000

Sun 12/01
BufA 14 at LA-A 62 27,000

Tue 12/03
N CleA 34 at MiaA 0 9,083

Sun 12/08
CleA 66 at BknA 14 14,600
LA-A 7 at SF-A 48 25,000

Mon 12/09
N NY-A 31 at MiaA 0 7,000

Fri 12/13
N BknA 20 at MiaA 31 2,340

Sun 12/15
ChiA 17 at LA-A 17 22,515

1946 AAFC Championship

Sun 12/22
NY-A 9 at CleA 14 41,181

National Football League 1947

Sat 09/21
N Det 10 at Pit 17 34,691

Sat 09/28
N ChiB 20 at GB 29 25,461
N Det 21 at ChiC 45 22,245
N Was 28 at Phi 45 35,406

Sun 09/29
LARm 48 at Pit 7 35,658
NYG 7 at Bos 7 21,905

Sun 10/05
ChiB 7 at ChiC 31 39,263
LARm 14 at GB 17 31,613
at Milwaukee, WI
Det 21 at Bos 7 15,097
Phi 23 at NYG 0 29,823
Pit 26 at Was 27 36,565

Sun 10/12
ChiC 14 at GB 10 25,562
LARm 27 at Det 13 42,955
Phi 7 at ChiB 40 34,338
Pit 30 at Bos 14 18,894
NYG 20 at Was 28 36,533

Sun 10/19
ChiC 7 at LARm 27 69,631
Det 24 at ChiB 33 31,960
Phi 24 at Pit 35 33,538
Bos 14 at NYG 0 37,144
Was 10 at GB 27 28,572
at Milwaukee, WI

Sun 10/26
ChiB 56 at Was 20 36,591
LARm 7 at Phi 14 36,364
Det 17 at GB 34 25,179
Pit 38 at NYG 21 41,736
Bos 7 at ChiC 27 22,286

Sun 11/02
ChiB 28 at Bos 24 24,894
LARm 10 at ChiC 17 40,075
Phi 38 at Was 14 36,591
Pit 18 at GB 17 30,073
at Milwaukee, WI
NYG 7 at Det 35 28,812

Sun 11/09
ChiC 17 at Det 7 25,296
GB 17 at ChiB 20 46,112
Phi 41 at NYG 24 29,016
Bos 27 at LARm 16 19,715
Was 14 at Pit 21 36,257

Sun 11/16
ChiB 41 at LARm 21 37,934
GB 20 at ChiC 21 40,086
Bos 0 at Phi 32 26,498
Was 21 at Det 38 17,003
NYG 7 at Pit 24 35,000

Sun 11/23
ChiC 21 at Was 45 35,362
GB 24 at NYG 24 27,939
Det 17 at LARm 28 17,693
Phi 14 at Bos 21 15,628
Pit 7 at ChiB 49 34,142

Thu 11/27
ChiB 34 at Det 14 27,214

Sun 11/30
ChiC 31 at NYG 35 28,744
GB 30 at LARm 10 31,040
Pit 0 at Phi 21 37,218
Was 27 at Bos 24 24,800

Sun 12/07
ChiC 45 at Phi 21 32,322
GB 35 at Det 14 14,055
LARm 17 at ChiB 14 34,215
Bos 7 at Pit 17 31,398
Was 10 at NYG 35 25,594

Sun 12/14
ChiC 30 at ChiB 21 48,632
GB 14 at Phi 28 24,216
Bos 13 at Was 40 33,226
NYG 10 at LARm 35 24,050

Eastern Division Playoff

Sun 12/21
Phi 21 at Pit 0 36,729

1947 NFL Championship

Sun 12/28
Phi 21 at ChiC 28 30,759

All-America Football Conference 1947

Fri 08/29
N LA-A 24 at ChiA 21 41,182

Sun 08/31
BknA 7 at SF-A 23 31,874
NY-A 24 at BufA 28 32,385

Fri 09/05
N BufA 14 at CleA 30 63,263
N ChiA 26 at NY-A 48 36,777

Sun 09/07
BknA 7 at BalA 16 27,418
LA-A 14 at SF-A 17 31,298

Fri 09/12
N CleA 55 at BknA 7 18,876
N NY-A 30 at LA-A 14 82,675

Sun 09/14
BalA 7 at SF-A 14 25,787
ChiA 20 at BufA 28 33,648

Fri 09/19
N BknA 21 at LA-A 48 38,817
N BufA 31 at ChiA 14 22,685

Sun 09/21
BalA 0 at CleA 28 44,257
NY-A 21 at SF-A 16 52,819

Fri 09/26
N CleA 41 at ChiA 21 18,450

Sun 09/28
NY-A 21 at BalA 7 51,583
SF-A 41 at BufA 24 36,099

Fri 10/03
N BknA 35 at ChiA 31 16,844

Sun 10/05
SF-A 28 at BalA 28 29,556
BufA 27 at LA-A 25 36,087
NY-A 17 at CleA 26 80,067

Sun 10/12
BalA 15 at BufA 20 27,345
ChiA 28 at SF-A 42 23,300
BknA 7 at NY-A 31 21,882
LA-A 13 at CleA 10 63,124

Fri 10/17
N BufA 14 at BknA 14 9,792

Sun 10/19
LA-A 38 at BalA 10 36,852
ChiA 28 at CleA 31 35,266

Fri 10/24
N NY-A 28 at ChiA 7 20,310

Sun 10/26
BalA 0 at LA-A 56 27,000
BknA 7 at BufA 35 23,762
CleA 14 at SF-A 7 54,483

Fri 10/31
N ChiA 3 at BknA 7 2,960

Sun 11/02
BalA 21 at NY-A 35 21,714
SF-A 26 at LA-A 16 53,726
CleA 28 at BufA 7 43,167

Fri 11/07
N BalA 21 at ChiA 27 5,395

Sun 11/09
BknA 12 at CleA 13 30,279
SF-A 16 at NY-A 24 37,342
LA-A 0 at BufA 25 21,293

Sun 11/16
BalA 14 at BknA 21 9,604
SF-A 14 at CleA 37 76,504
LA-A 13 at NY-A 16 37,625

Fri 11/21
N SF-A 41 at ChiA 16 5,791

Sun 11/23
BufA 33 at BalA 14 19,593
CleA 28 at NY-A 28 70,060
LA-A 16 at BknA 21 11,866

Thu 11/27
SF-A 21 at BknA 7 9,837
CleA 27 at LA-A 17 45,009

Sun 11/30
ChiA 7 at BA-A 14 14,085
BufA 13 at NY-A 35 39,012

Sun 12/07
CleA 42 at BalA 0 20,574
BufA 21 at SF-A 21 22,943
ChiA 14 at LA-A 34 20,856
NY-A 20 at BknA 17 14,166

1947 AAFC Championship

Sun 12/14
CleA 14 at NY-A 3 61,879

National Football League 1948

Fri 09/17
N GB 31 at Bos 0 15,443

Wed 09/22
N Det 7 at LARm 44 17,271

Thu 09/23
N NYG 27 at Bos 7 7,428

Fri 09/24
N Phi 14 at ChiC 21 25,875

Sun 09/26
Pit 14 at Was 17 32,084
ChiB 45 at GB 7 25,546

Sun 10/03
Phi 28 at LARm 28 36,884
NYG 10 at Was 41 32,593
Bos 14 at Pit 24 26,216
Det 21 at GB 33 24,206

Mon 10/04
N ChiB 28 at ChiC 17 52,765

Sat 10/09
N Bos 17 at Det 14 18,747

Sun 10/10
Was 7 at Pit 10 28,969
NYG 0 at Phi 45 22,804
ChiC 17 at GB 7 34,369
at Milwaukee, WI
LARm 21 at ChiB 42 43,707

Sun 10/17
Phi 45 at Was 0 35,584
Pit 7 at Bos 13 7,208
ChiC 63 at NYG 35 35,584
LARm 0 at GB 16 25,119
Det 0 at ChiB 28 35,425

Sun 10/24
Was 23 at GB 7 13,433
at Milwaukee, WI
Pit 27 at NYG 34 13,443
Bos 27 at ChiC 49 23,423
ChiB 7 at Phi 12 36,227
LARm 34 at Det 27 17,444

Sun 10/31
Phi 34 at Pit 7 32,474
NYG 14 at ChiB 35 41,608
Bos 21 at Was 59 29,758
ChiC 27 at LARm 22 32,149
GB 20 at Det 24 16,174

Sun 11/07
Phi 35 at NYG 14 24,983
Was 23 at Bos 7 13,659
ChiB 21 at LARm 6 56,263
GB 7 at Pit 38 26,058
Det 20 at ChiC 56 24,051

Sun 11/14
Bos 0 at Phi 45 22,958
ChiC 24 at Pit 7 33,364
LARm 52 at NYG 37 22,766
GB 6 at ChiB 7 48,113
Det 21 at Was 46 32,528

Sun 11/21
Was 21 at Phi 42 36,254
Pit 14 at Det 17 16,189
NYG 49 at GB 3 12,639
at Milwaukee, WI
ChiB 51 at Bos 17 18,048
LARm 24 at ChiC 27 29,031

Thu 11/25
ChiC 28 at Det 14 22,957

Sun 11/28
Was 13 at ChiB 48 42,299
Pit 0 at Phi 17 22,001
Bos 14 at NYG 28 19,636
GB 10 at LARm 24 23,874

Sun 12/05
Phi 14 at Bos 37 9,652
NYG 28 at Pit 38 27,645
ChiB 42 at Det 14 27,485
LARm 41 at Was 13 32,970
GB 7 at ChiC 42 26,072

Sun 12/12
Was 28 at NYG 21 23,156
Pit 14 at LARm 31 27,967
ChiC 24 at ChiB 21 51,283
Det 21 at Phi 45 15,322

1948 NFL Championship

Sun 12/19
ChiC 0 at Phi 7 28,864

All-America Football Conference 1948

Fri 08/27
N LA-A 7 at ChiA 0 26,479
N NY-A 21 at BknA 3 16,411

Sun 08/29
BufA 14 at SF-A 35 33,946

Fri 09/03
N LA-A 14 at CleA 19 60,193

Sun 09/05
BknA 20 at SF-A 36 32,606
NY-A 28 at BalA 45 31,800

Mon 09/06
N ChiA 7 at BufA 42 25,816

Fri 09/10
N BknA 7 at LA-A 17 35,246
N BalA 14 at ChiA 21 14,642

Sun 09/12
CleA 42 at BufA 13 35,340
NY-A 0 at SF-A 41 60,927

Thu 09/16
N BalA 27 at NY-A 14 18,959

Fri 09/17
N CleA 28 at ChiA 7 30,874

Sun 09/19
LA-A 14 at SF-A 36 45,420

Sun 09/26
ChiA 10 at CleA 21 37,190
SF-A 38 at BufA 28 31,103
BknA 20 at BalA 35 34,554

Wed 09/29
N NY-A 10 at LA-A 20 35,655

Fri 10/01
N SF-A 31 at ChiA 14 14,553

Sun 10/03
BknA 21 at BufA 31 17,694

Tue 10/05
N CleA 14 at BalA 10 22,359

Fri 10/08
N ChiA 28 at LA-A 49 31,119

Sun 10/10
BknA 17 at CleA 30 31,187
NY-A 14 at BufA 13 18,825
SF-A 56 at BalA 14 37,209

Fri 10/15
N BalA 29 at LA-A 14 40,019
N ChiA 7 at BknA 21 8,671

Sun 10/17
BufA 14 at CleA 31 28,054
SF-A 21 at NY-A 7 29,743

Sun 10/24
NY-A 7 at CleA 35 46,912
BknA 35 at Ch-a 14 5,964
BufA 35 at LA-A 21 26,818
BalA 10 at SF-A 21 27,978

Sun 10/31
LA-A 17 at BknA 0 12,825
BalA 17 at BufA 35 23,694
NY-A 42 at ChiA 7 13,239

Sun 11/07
BalA 7 at CleA 28 32,314
LA-A 6 at NY-A 38 17,386
BufA 26 at BknA 21 7,805
ChiA 21 at SF-A 44 25,306

Sun 11/14
SF-A 7 at CleA 14 82,769
ChiA 24 at BalA 38 21,899
LA-A 27 at BufA 20 23,725
BknA 7 at NY-A 21 17,642

Sun 11/21
CleA 34 at NY-A 21 52,518
LA-A 17 at BalA 14 25,228
SF-A 63 at BknA 40 9,336

Thu 11/25
CleA 31 at LA-A 14 60,031
BufA 39 at ChiA 35 6,305

Sun 11/28
CleA 31 at SF-A 28 59,785
BufA 35 at NY-A 14 18,376
BalA 38 at BknA 20 7,629

Sun 12/05
CleA 31 at BknA 21 9,821
ChiA 7 at NY-A 28 4,930
SF-A 38 at LA-A 21 51,460
BufA 15 at BalA 35 33,090

Eastern Division Playoff

Sun 12/12
BufA 28 at BalA 17 27,325

1948 AAFC Championship

Sun 12/19
BufA 7 at CleA 49 22,981

National Football League 1949

Thu 09/22
N Phi 7 at NYB 0 8,426

Fri 09/23
N Det 24 at LARm 27 17,878

Sun 09/25
NYG 7 at Pit 28 20,957
ChiB 17 at GB 0 25,571

Mon 09/26
N Was 7 at ChiC 38 24,136

Fri 09/30
N NYG 38 at NYB 14 17,704

Sun 10/02
LARm 48 at GB 7 24,308
ChiB 17 at ChiC 7 52,867

Mon 10/03
N Phi 22 at Det 14 25,012

N Was 27 at Pit 14 30,000

Fri 10/07
N GB 19 at NYB 0 5,099

Sat 10/08
N ChiC 3 at Phi 28 34,597
N Det 7 at Pit 14 21,355

Sun 10/09
NYG 45 at Was 35 30,073
LARm 31 at ChiB 16 42,124

Sun 10/16
Phi 21 at ChiB 38 50,129
Pit 21 at NYG 17 29,911
NYB 14 at Was 38 26,278
LARm 21 at Det 10 19,839
ChiC 39 at GB 17 18,464
at Milwaukee, WI

Sun 10/23
Was 14 at Phi 49 28,885
NYB 13 at Pit 24 22,042
ChiB 28 at NYG 35 30,587
Det 24 at ChiC 7 23,215
GB 7 at LARm 35 37,546

Sun 10/30
Phi 38 at Pit 7 37,903
NYG 41 at ChiC 38 21,339
Was 14 at NYB 14 3,678
ChiB 24 at LARm 27 86,080
Det 14 at GB 16 10,855
at Milwaukee, WI

Sun 11/06
Pit 14 at Was 27 26,038
NYB 31 at NYG 24 23,222
LARm 14 at Phi 38 38,830
ChiC 42 at Det 19 22,479
GB 3 at ChiB 24 47,218

Sun 11/13
Phi 44 at Was 21 31,170
NYG 30 at GB 10 20,151
LARm 7 at Pit 7 20,510
ChiC 65 at NYB 20 9,072
GB 24 at ChiB 27 37,303

Sun 11/20
Pit 30 at GB 7 5,483
at Milwaukee, WI
NYB 0 at Phi 42 22,165
LARm 28 at ChiC 28 34,100
ChiB 31 at Was 21 30,418
Det 45 at NYG 21 21,338

Thu 11/24
ChiB 28 at Det 7 24,385

Sun 11/27
Pit 17 at Phi 34 22,191
Was 7 at NYG 23 12,985

NYB 20 at LARm 42 38,052
GB 21 at ChiC 41 16,787

Sun 12/04
Phi 24 at NYG 3 25,446
Pit 21 at ChiB 30 36,071
NYB 27 at Det 28 11,956
ChiC 31 at LARm 27 74,673
GB 0 at Was 30 23,200

Sun 12/11
Pit 27 at NYB 0 4,028
NYG 3 at Phi 17 21,022
Was 27 at LARm 53 44,899
ChiC 21 at ChiB 52 50,101
GB 7 at Det 21 12,576

1949 NFL Championship

Sun 12/18
Phi 14 at LARm 0 22,245

All-America Football Conference 1949

Fri 08-26
N BufA 14 at ChiA 17 23,800

Sun 08/28
BalA 17 at SF-A 31 29,095

Fri 09/02
N BalA 17 at LA-A 49 20,211

Sun 09/04
ChiA 7 at SF-A 42 28,311

Mon 09/05
N CleA 28 at BufA 28 31,839

Fri 09/09
N ChiA 10 at LA-A 7 30,193

Sun 09/11
BalA 0 at CleA 21 21,621
NY-A 17 at BufA 14 30,410

Fri 09/16
N BalA 7 at ChiA 35 18,483

Sun 09/18
NY-A 3 at CleA 14 26,312
LA-A 14 at SF-A 42 31,960

Thu 09/22
N LA-A 7 at NY-A 10 14,437

Sun 09/25
CleA 28 at BalA 20 36,837
SF-A 17 at BufA 28 32,097

Fri 09/30
N SF-A 42 at ChiA 24 31,561

Sun 10/02
LA-A 7 at CleA 42 30,465
BalA 35 at BufA 28 25,692

Fri 10/07
N NY-A 38 at ChiA 24 17,098

Sun 10/09
CleA 28 at SF-A 56 59,720
BufA 28 at LA-A 42 16,575

Fri 10/14
N CleA 61 at LA-A 14 27,427

Sun 10/16
BufA 7 at SF-A 51 35,476
NY-A 24 at BalA 21 32,645

Sun 10/23
SF-A 3 at NY-A 24 38,187
LA-A 14 at BufA 17 21,310
ChiA 17 at BalA 7 23,107

Fri 10/28
N LA-A 24 at ChiA 14 11,249

Sun 10/30
SF-A 28 at CleA 30 72,189
BalA 14 at NY-A 21 10,692

Sun 11/06
ChiA 2 at CleA 35 16,506
BufA 17 at NY-A 14 16,758
SF-A 28 at BalA 10 23,704

Sun 11/13
BufA 7 at CleA 7 22,511
SF-A 41 at LA-A 24 17,880
ChiA 10 at NY-A 14 9,091

Sun 11/20
CleA 31 at NY-A 0 50,711
ChiA 0 at BufA 10 18,494
LA-A 21 at BalA 10 19,503

Thu 11/24
CleA 14 at ChiA 6 5,031

NY-A 17 at LA-A 16 20,096

Sun 11/27
NY-A 14 at SF-A 35 44,828
BufA 38 at BalA 14 16,323

AAFC Playoffs

Sun 12/04
BufA 21 at CleA 31 17,270
NY-A 7 at SF-A 14 41,393

1949 AAFC Championship

Sun 12/11
SF-A 7 at CleA 21 22,550

National Football League 1950

Sat 09/16
N Cle 35 at Phi 10 71,237

Sun 09/17
ChiB 24 at LARm 20 21,000
Det 45 at GB 7 22,096
NYG 18 at Pit 7 24,699
NYY 21 at SF 17 29,600
Was 38 at Bal 14 29,000

Fri 09/22
N NYY 28 at LARm 45 23,768

Sun 09/24
Cle 31 at Bal 0 15,201
ChiB 32 at SF 20 35,558
Phi 45 at ChiC 7 24,914
Pit 7 at Det 10 19,600
Was 21 at GB 35 14,109
at Milwaukee, WI

Fri 09/29
N Det 21 at NYY 44 11,096

Sun 10/01
ChiB 21 at GB 31 24,893
LARm 35 at SF 14 27,262
NYG 6 at Cle 0 37,647

Pit 26 at Was 7 25,008

Mon 10/02
N Bal 13 at ChiC 55 14,439

Sat 10/07
N LARm 20 at Phi 56 24,134
N Cle 30 at Pit 17 35,590

Sun 10/08
ChiC 6 at ChiB 27 48,025
NYY 44 at GB 31 23,871
NYG 21 at Was 17 19,288
SF 7 at Det 24 17,337

Thu 10/12
N SF 24 at NYY 29 5,740

Sun 10/15
ChiC 24 at Cle 34 33,774
GB 14 at ChiB 28 51,065
LARm 30 at Det 28 35,589
Phi 24 at Bal 14 14,413
Pit 17 at NYG 6 21,725

Thu 10/19
N GB 17 at NYY 35 13,661

Sun 10/22
Bal 27 at LARm 70 16,025
ChiC 38 at Was 28 27,856
Cle 13 at NYG 17 41,734
Det 27 at SF 28 27,350
Phi 17 at Pit 10 35,662

Sun 10/29
Bal 14 at SF 17 14,800
ChiB 27 at NYY 38 50,178
Det 24 at LARm 65 27,475
NYG 3 at ChiC 17 23,964
Pit 7 at Cle 45 40,714
Was 3 at Phi 35 33,707

Sun 11/05
ChiB 35 at Det 21 32,000
Cle 10 at ChiC 7 38,456
GB 21 at Bal 41 12,971
Pit 9 at Phi 7 24,629
SF 21 at LARm 28 33,234
Was 21 at NYG 24 23,909

Sun 11/12
Bal 7 at Pit 17 24,141
ChiC 21 at NYG 51 22,380
LARm 45 at GB 14 20,456
at Milwaukee, WI

NYY 20 at ChiB 28 50,102
Phi 33 at Was 0 29,407
SF 14 at Cle 34 28,786

Sun 11/19
ChiC 14 at Phi 10 28,368
GB 21 at Det 24 17,752
LARm 43 at NYY 35 45,213
NYG 55 at Bal 20 14,573
SF 0 at ChiB 17 35,105
Was 14 at Cle 20 21,908

Thu 11/23
Pit 28 at ChiC 17 11,622
NYY 14 at Det 49 28,000

Sun 11/26
Bal 28 at Was 38 21,275
LARm 14 at ChiB 24 43,678
Phi 3 at NYG 7 24,093
SF 21 at GB 25 13,196

Sun 12/03
ChiB 10 at ChiC 20 31,919
Det 45 at Bal 21 12,058
GB 14 at LARm 51 39,323
NYY 7 at NYG 51 41,630
Phi 7 at Cle 13 37,490

Was 24 at Pit 7 19,741

Sun 12/10
Bal 14 at NYY 51 6,836
ChiC 7 at Pit 28 18,301
Cle 45 at Was 21 30,143
Det 3 at ChiB 6 34,604
GB 14 at SF 30 19,204
NYG 9 at Phi 7 26,440

American Conference Playoff

Sun 12/17
NYG 3 at Cle 8 33,054

National Conference Playoff

Sun 12/17
ChiB 20 at LARm 24 83,501

1950 NFL Championship

Sun 12/24
LARm 28 at Cle 30 29,751

National Football League 1951

Fri 09/28
N NYY 14 at LARm 54 30,315

Sun 09/30
ChiB 31 at GB 20 24,666
Cle 10 at SF 24 48,263
Phi 17 at ChiC 14 16,129

Was 17 at Det 35 27,831

Mon 10/01
N NYG 13 at Pit 13 27,984

Sat 10/06
N SF 14 at Phi 21 23,432

Sun 10/07
ChiB 14 at ChiC 28 33,781
Cle 38 at LARm 23 67,186
NYG 35 at Was 14 23,800
Pit 33 at GB 35 8,324
at Milwaukee, WI

Mon 10/08
N NYY 10 at Det 37 24,194

Sun 10/14
ChiC 17 at NYG 28 28,095
LARm 27 at Det 21 52,907
NYY 21 at ChiB 24 37,697

Phi 24 at GB 37 18,489
SF 28 at Pit 24 27,124
Was 0 at Cle 45 33,968

Sun 10/21
ChiC 3 at Was 7 22,960

LARm 28 at GB 0 21,393
at Milwaukee, WI
NYY 24 at Det 24 21,807
Phi 24 at NYG 26 28,656
Pit 0 at Cle 17 32,409
SF 7 at ChiB 13 42,296

Sun 10/28
ChiB 28 at Det 23 34,778
GB 29 at NYY 27 7,351
LARm 17 at SF 44 49,538
NYG 13 at Cle 14 56,947
Pit 28 at ChiC 14 14,373
Was 27 at Phi 23 20,437

Sun 11/04
ChiB 27 at Was 0 31,737
Cle 34 at ChiC 17 19,742
Det 24 at GB 17 18,800
NYY 31 at NYG 37 25,682
Phi 34 at Pit 13 19,649
SF 16 at LARm 23 54,346

Sun 11/11
ChiC 21 at LARm 45 29,995
Det 41 at ChiB 28 43,709
GB 7 at Pit 28 20,080
NYY 14 at SF 19 25,538
Phi 17 at Cle 20 36,571
Was 14 at NYG 28 21,242

Sun 11/18
ChiC 27 at SF 21 19,658
Cle 10 at NYG 0 52,215
Det 28 at Phi 10 25,350
GB 13 at ChiB 24 36,771
NYY 21 at LARm 48 34,717
Was 22 at Pit 7 15,060

Thu 11/22
GB 35 at Det 52 32,247

Sun 11/25
Pit 17 at Phi 13 15,537
ChiB 21 at Cle 42 40,969
LARm 21 at Was 31 26,307
NYG 10 at ChiC 0 11,892
SF 10 at NYY 10 10,184

Sun 12/02
ChiC 28 at Cle 49 30,550
LARm 42 at ChiB 17 50,286
NYY 31 at GB 28 14,297
Phi 35 at Was 21 23,738
Pit 0 at NYG 14 18,186
SF 20 at Det 10 45,757

Sun 12/09
ChiB 45 at NYY 21 13,075
Cle 28 at Pit 0 24,229
Det 24 at LARm 22 52,937
GB 19 at SF 31 15,121
NYG 23 at Phi 7 19,322
Was 20 at ChiC 17 9,459

Sun 12/16
ChiC 24 at ChiB 14 15,085
Cle 24 at Phi 9 16,263
Det 17 at SF 21 27,276
GB 14 at LARm 42 23,698
NYG 27 at NYY 17 6,658
Pit 20 at Was 10 18,096

1951 NFL Championship

Sun 12/23
Cle 17 at LARm 24 57,522

National Football League 1952

Sun 09/28
ChiB 24 at GB 14 24,656
Det 3 at SF 17 54,761
LARm 7 at Cle 37 57,832
NYG 24 at Dal 6 17,500
Phi 31 at Pit 25 24,501
Was 23 at ChiC 7 17,837

Fri 10/03
N Det 17 at LARm 14 42,743

Sat 10/04
N Cle 21 at Pit 20 27,923
N NYG 31 at Phi 7 22,512

Sun 10/05
ChiB 10 at ChiC 21 34,697
SF 37 at Dal 14 12,566
Was 20 at GB 35 9,657
at Milwaukee, WI

Sun 10/12
ChiC 17 at Was 6 24,600
Dal 20 at ChiB 38 35,429
LARm 30 at GB 28 21,693
at Milwaukee, WI
NYG 17 at Cle 9 51,858
Pit 21 at Phi 26 18,648
SF 28 at Det 0 56,822

Sat 10/18
N GB 24 at Dal 14 14,000

Sun 10/19
ChiC 24 at NYG 23 41,182
Cle 49 at Phi 7 27,874
LARm 16 at Det 24 40,152
SF 40 at ChiB 16 46,338
Was 28 at Pit 24 22,605

Sun 10/26
ChiB 7 at LARm 31 43,574
Dal 21 at SF 48 26,887
Det 52 at GB 17 24,656
Phi 14 at NYG 10 21,458
Pit 34 at ChiC 28 20,395
Was 15 at Cle 19 32,496

Sun 11/02
ChiB 20 at SF 17 58,255
Cle 6 at Det 17 56,029
Dal 20 at LARm 42 30,702
NYG 28 at ChiC 6 27,195
Phi 10 at GB 12 10,149
at Milwaukee, WI
Pit 24 at Was 23 25,866

Sun 11/09
ChiC 13 at Cle 28 34,097
Det 31 at Pit 6 26,170
GB 41 at ChiB 28 41,751
LARm 27 at Dal 6 10,000
SF 14 at NYG 23 54,230
Was 20 at Phi 38 16,932

Sun 11/16
ChiC 7 at Phi 10 18,906
Dal 13 at Det 43 33,304
GB 17 at NYG 3 26,723
LARm 40 at ChiB 24 40,737
Pit 28 at Cle 29 34,973
SF 23 at Was 17 30,863

Sun 11/23
ChiC 14 at Pit 17 18,330
Dal 14 at GB 42 16,340
Det 23 at ChiB 24 37,508
NYG 14 at Was 10 21,125
Phi 28 at Cle 20 28,948
SF 9 at LARm 35 77,698

Thu 11/27
GB 24 at Det 48 39,101
ChiB 23 at Dal 27 3,000
at Akron, OH

Sun 11/30
Cle 48 at Was 24 22,679
LARm 34 at SF 21 49,420
NYG 7 at Pit 63 15,140
Phi 22 at ChiC 28 13,577

Sun 12/07
ChiB 21 at Det 45 50,410
Cle 10 at ChiC 0 24,541
Dal 21 at Phi 38 18,376
GB 27 at LARm 45 49,822
Pit 24 at SF 7 13,886
Was 27 at NYG 17 21,237

Sat 12/13
Dal 6 at Det 41 12,252

Sun 12/14
ChiC 7 at ChiB 10 32,578
Cle 34 at NYG 37 41,610
GB 14 at SF 24 17,579
Phi 21 at Was 27 22,468
Pit 14 at LARm 28 74,130

Western Division Playoff

Sun 12/21
LARm 21 at Det 31 47,645

1952 NFL Championship

Sun 12/28
Det 17 at Cle 7 50,934

National Football League 1953

Sun 09/27
ChiB 9 at Bal 13 23,715
Cle 27 at GB 0 22,604
at Milwaukee, WI
NYG 7 at LARm 21 49,579
Phi 21 at SF 31 27,819
Pit 21 at Det 38 44,587
Was 24 at ChiC 13 16,055

Fri 10/02
N Was 21 at Phi 21 19,099

Sat 10/03
N Det 27 at Bal 17 25,159
N NYG 14 at Pit 24 31,500

Sun 10/04
ChiB 17 at GB 13 24,835
Cle 27 at ChiC 7 24,374
LARm 30 at SF 31 43,922

Sat 10/10
N Phi 13 at Cle 37 45,802

Sun 10/11
Bal 16 at ChiB 14 35,316
ChiC 28 at Pit 31 25,935
LARm 38 at GB 20 23,353
at Milwaukee, WI
NYG 9 at Was 13 26,241
SF 21 at Det 24 58,079

Sat 10/17
N Pit 7 at Phi 23 18,681

Sun 10/18
Bal 14 at GB 37 18,713
ChiC 7 at NYG 21 30,301
Cle 30 at Was 14 33,963
LARm 31 at Det 19 55,772
SF 35 at ChiB 28 36,909

Sat 10/24
N GB 14 at Pit 31 22,918

Sun 10/25
ChiB 24 at LARm 38 49,546
Cle 7 at NYG 0 30,773
Det 14 at SF 10 52,300
Phi 56 at ChiC 17 22,064
Was 17 at Bal 27 34,031

Sat 10/31
N GB 35 at Bal 24 33,797

Sun 11/01
ChiB 14 at SF 24 26,308
Det 24 at LARm 37 93,751
NYG 23 at ChiC 20 17,499
Phi 35 at Pit 7 27,547
Was 3 at Cle 27 47,845

Sat 11/07
N Bal 7 at Det 17 46,508

Sun 11/08
ChiC 17 at Was 28 19,654
GB 21 at ChiB 21 39,889
NYG 7 at Phi 30 24,331
Pit 16 at Cle 34 35,592
SF 31 at LARm 27 85,865

Sun 11/15
Bal 14 at Phi 45 27,813
ChiB 27 at Was 24 21,392
Det 14 at GB 7 20,834
LARm 24 at ChiC 24 26,674
Pit 14 at NYG 10 20,411
SF 21 at Cle 23 80,698

Sat 11/21
N ChiC 0 at Phi 38 19,402

Sun 11/22
Cle 20 at Pit 16 32,904
Det 20 at ChiB 16 36,165
LARm 21 at Bal 13 27,268
SF 37 at GB 7 16,378
at Milwaukee, WI
Was 24 at NYG 21 16,887

Thu 11/26
GB 15 at Det 34 52,607

Sun 11/29
ChiC 16 at Cle 27 24,499
LARm 21 at ChiB 24 31,626
Phi 28 at NYG 37 20,294
SF 38 at Bal 21 26,005
Was 17 at Pit 9 17,026

Sat 12/05
Bal 2 at LARm 45 26,656

Sun 12/06
ChiB 7 at Det 13 58,056
GB 14 at SF 48 31,337
NYG 14 at Cle 62 40,235
Phil 0 at Was 10 21,579
Pit 21 at ChiC 17 14,138

Sat 12/12
GB 17 at LARm 33 23,069

Sun 12/13
Bal 14 at SF 45 23,923
ChiC 24 at ChiB 17 38,059
Cle 27 at Phi 42 38,897
Det 27 at NYG 16 28,390
Pit 14 at Was 13 22,057

1953 NFL Championship

Sun 12/27
Cle 16 at Det 17 54,577

National Football League 1954

Sun 09/26
ChiB 23 at Det 48 52,343
Cle 10 at Phi 28 26,546
LARm 48 at Bal 0 36,215
NYG 41 at ChiC 10 16,780
Pit 21 at GB 20 20,675
Was 7 at SF 41 32,085

Sat 10/02
N NYG 14 at Bal 20 27,088
N Was 7 at Pit 37 22,492

Sun 10/03
ChiB 10 at GB 3 24,414
Phi 35 at ChiC 16 17,084
SF 24 at LARm 24 93,621

Sat 10/09
N Pit 22 at Phi 24 37,322

Sun 10/10
Bal 9 at ChiB 28 27,845
ChiC 7 at Cle 31 24,101
LARm 3 at Det 21 56,523
NYG 51 at Was 21 21,217
SF 23 at GB 17 15,571
at Milwaukee, WI

Sat 10/16
N Bal 0 at Det 35 48,272

Sun 10/17
ChiC 17 at NYG 31 31,256
Cle 27 at Pit 55 33,262
LARm 17 at GB 35 17,455
at Milwaukee, WI
Phi 49 at Was 21 22,051
SF 31 at ChiB 24 42,935

Sat 10/23
N Phi 7 at Pit 17 39,075

Sun 10/24
ChiB 38 at LARm 42 48,204
Cle 35 at ChiC 3 23,823
Det 31 at SF 37 58,891
GB 7 at Bal 6 28,680
Was 7 at NYG 24 22,597

Sat 10/30
N GB 37 at Phi 14 25,378

Sun 10/31
Bal 21 at Was 24 23,566
ChiB 31 at SF 27 49,833
Det 27 at LARm 24 74,315
NYG 14 at Cle 24 30,448
Pit 14 at ChiC 17 18,765

Sat 11/06
N Det 27 at Bal 3 25,287

Sun 11/07
ChiC 14 at Phi 30 21,963
GB 23 at ChiB 28 47,038
LARm 42 at SF 34 58,758
NYG 30 at Pit 6 36,358
Was 3 at Cle 62 25,158

Sat 11/13
N Bal 13 at GB 24 19,786
at Milwaukee, WI

Sun 11/14
ChiC 17 at LARm 28 40,786
Cle 39 at ChiB 10 48,773
Phi 14 at NYG 27 46,565
Pit 14 at Was 17 19,388
SF 7 at Det 48 58,431

Sat 11/20
N SF 31 at Pit 3 37,001

Sun 11/21
ChiB 28 at Bal 13 23,093
Det 21 at GB 17 20,767
LARm 17 at NYG 16 27,077
Phi 0 at Cle 6 41,537
Was 16 at ChiC 38 15,619

Thu 11/25
GB 24 at Det 28 55,532

Sun 11/28
ChiC 17 at Pit 20 14,460
Cle 16 at NYG 7 45,936
LARm 13 at ChiB 24 32,338
SF 13 at Bal 17 23,875
Was 33 at Phi 41 18,517

Sat 12/04
Bal 22 at LARm 21 30,821

Sun 12/05
ChiB 29 at ChiC 7 33,594
Cle 34 at Was 14 21,761
GB 0 at SF 35 32,012
Phi 13 at Det 13 54,939
Pit 3 at NYG 24 16,856

Sat 12/11
Bal 7 at SF 10 25,456

Sun 12/12
ChiC 20 at Was 37 18,107
Det 24 at ChiB 28 37,240
GB 27 at LARm 35 38,839
NYG 14 at Phi 29 28,449
Pit 7 at Cle 42 28,064

Sun 12/19
Det 14 at Cle 10 34,168

1954 NFL Championship

Sun 12/26
Det 10 at Cle 56 43,827

National Football League 1955

Sat 09/24
N NYG 17 at Phi 27 29,597

Sun 09/25
ChiB 17 at Bal 23 36,167
Det 17 at GB 20 22,217
LARm 23 at SF 14 58,722
Was 27 at Cle 17 30,041

Mon 09/26
N ChiC 7 at Pit 14 26,359

Sat 10/01
N Det 13 at Bal 28 40,030
N Was 31 at Phi 30 31,891

Sun 10/02
ChiB 3 at GB 24 24,662
Cle 38 at SF 3 43,595
NYG 17 at ChiC 28 9,555
Pit 26 at LARm 27 45,816

Sat 10/08
N Bal 24 at GB 20 40,199
at Milwaukee, WI

Sun 10/09
ChiC 24 at Was 10 26,337
LARm 17 at Det 10 54,836
NYG 23 at Pit 30 29,422
Phi 17 at Cle 21 43,974
SF 20 at ChiB 19 41,651

Sat 10/15
N Phi 7 at Pit 13 33,413

Sun 10/16
Bal 10 at ChiB 38 40,184
ChiC 0 at NYG 10 7,000
Cle 24 at Was 14 29,168
LARm 28 at GB 30 26,960
at Milwaukee, WI
SF 27 at Det 24 51,438

Sun 10/23
ChiB 34 at SF 23 56,350
Det 13 at LARm 24 68,690
GB 10 at Cle 41 51,482
Phi 24 at ChiC 24 24,620
Pit 19 at NYG 17 27,365
Was 14 at Bal 13 51,587

Sat 10/29
N GB 10 at Bal 14 34,411

Sun 10/30
ChiB 31 at LARm 20 69,587
Cle 26 at ChiC 20 29,471
Det 21 at SF 38 44,831
Pit 0 at Phi 24 31,164
Was 7 at NYG 35 17,402

Sat 11/05
N Bal 14 at Det 24 53,874
N Pit 13 at ChiC 27 23,310

Sun 11/06
GB 31 at ChiB 52 48,890
NYG 14 at Cle 24 46,524
Phi 21 at Was 34 25,741
SF 14 at LARm 27 85,302

Sun 11/13
Bal 7 at NYG 17 33,982
ChiC 14 at GB 31 20,104
Cle 17 at Phi 33 39,303
Det 31 at Pit 28 34,441
LARm 3 at ChiB 24 50,187
SF 0 at Was 7 25,112

Sun 11/20
ChiB 24 at Det 14 53,610
LARm 17 at Bal 17 41,146
Phi 7 at NYG 31 22,075
Pit 14 at Cle 41 53,509
SF 21 at GB 27 19,099
at Milwaukee, WI
Was 31 at ChiC 0 16,901

Thu 11/24
GB 10 at Det 24 51,685

Sun 11/27
ChiB 14 at ChiC 53 47,314
Cle 35 at NYG 35 45,699
LARm 23 at Phi 21 31,648
SF 14 at Bal 26 33,485
Was 23 at Pit 14 21,760

Sun 12/04
Bal 14 at LARm 20 37,024
ChiC 3 at Phi 27 19,478
Cle 30 at Pit 7 31,101
Det 20 at ChiB 21 39,388
GB 28 at SF 7 32,897
NYG 27 at Was 20 28,556

Sun 12/11
Bal 24 at SF 35 33,471
ChiC 24 at Cle 35 25,914
GB 17 at LARm 31 90,535
NYG 24 at Det 19 45,929
Phi 10 at ChiB 17 34,783
Pit 17 at Was 28 20,547

1955 NFL Championship

Mon 12/26
Cle 38 at LARm 14 85,693

National Football League 1956

Sun 09/30
Cle 7 at ChiC 9 20,966
NYG 38 at SF 21 41,751
Phi 7 at LARm 27 54,412
Was 13 at Pit 30 27,718
ChiB 21 at Bal 28 45,221
Det 20 at GB 16 24,668

Sat 10/06
N Cle 14 at Pit 10 35,398
N Was 9 at Phi 13 26,607
N Det 31 at Bal 14 42,622

Sun 10/07
NYG 27 at ChiC 35 21,799
ChiB 37 at GB 21 24,668
LARm 30 at SF 33 56,489

Sun 10/14
ChiC 31 at Was 3 25,794
NYG 21 at Cle 9 60,042
Phi 35 at Pit 21 31,375
Bal 33 at GB 38 24,214
at Milwaukee, WI
SF 7 at ChiB 31 47,526
LARm 21 at Det 24 56,281

Sun 10/21
ChiC 20 at Phi 6 36,545
Cle 9 at Was 20 23,332
Pit 10 at NYG 38 48,108
Bal 27 at ChiB 58 48,364
SF 17 at Det 20 55,662
LARm 17 at GB 42 24,200
at Milwaukee, WI

Sun 10/28
Was 17 at ChiC 14 30,533
Pit 24 at Cle 16 50,358
Phi 3 at NYG 20 40,960
GB 21 at Bal 28 40,086
ChiB 38 at SF 21 52,612
Det 16 at LARm 7 76,758

Sun 11/04
Phi 17 at ChiC 28 27,609
Cle 24 at GB 7 28,590
at Milwaukee, WI
NYG 17 at Pit 14 31,240
ChiB 35 at LARm 24 69,894
Det 17 at SF 13 46,708

Sun 11/11
ChiC 10 at NYG 23 62,410
Bal 21 at Cle 7 42,404
Pit 7 at Phi 14 22,652
Det 17 at Was 18 28,003
GB 14 at ChiB 38 49,172
SF 6 at LARm 30 69,828

Sun 11/18
ChiC 7 at Pit 14 24,086
Cle 16 at Phi 0 25,894
NYG 7 at Was 33 26,261
Bal 3 at Det 27 55,788
LARm 21 at ChiB 30 48,102
SF 17 at GB 16 17,986

Thu 11/22
GB 24 at Det 20 54,087

Sun 11/25
Pit 27 at ChiC 38 17,224
Was 20 at Cle 17 22,878
ChiB 17 at NYG 17 55,191
SF 10 at Phi 10 19,326
LARm 21 at Bal 56 40,321

Sun 12/02
GB 24 at ChiC 21 22,620
Phi 14 at Cle 17 20,654
Was 14 at NYG 28 46,361
LARm 13 at Pit 30 20,450
SF 20 at Bal 17 37,227
ChiB 10 at Det 42 57,024

Sat 12/08
GB 20 at SF 38 32,433

Sun 12/09
ChiC 3 at ChiB 10 48,606
Cle 24 at NYG 7 27,707
Phi 17 at Was 19 22,333
Pit 7 at Det 45 52,124
Bal 7 at LARm 31 51,037

Sat 12/15
NYG 21 at Phi 7 16,562

Sun 12/16
ChiC 24 at Cle 7 25,312
Pit 23 at Was 0 21,097
Bal 17 at SF 30 43,791
Det 21 at ChiB 38 49,086
GB 21 at LARm 49 45,209

Sun 12/23
Was 17 at Bal 19 32,944

1956 NFL Championship

Sun 12/30
ChiB 7 at NYG 47 56,836

National Football League 1957

Sun 09/29
ChiB 17 at GB 21 32,132
ChiC 20 at SF 10 35,743
Det 14 at Bal 34 40,112
NYG 3 at Cle 6 58,095
Phi 13 at LARm 17 62,506
Was 7 at Pit 28 27,452

Sat 10/05
N ChiB 10 at Bal 21 46,558
N Cle 23 at Pit 12 35,570
N NYG 24 at Phi 20 28,342

Sun 10/06
Det 24 at GB 14 32,120
LARm 20 at SF 23 59,637
Was 37 at ChiC 14 18,278

Sun 10/13
Bal 45 at GB 17 26,322
at Milwaukee, WI
ChiC 20 at Pit 29 29,446
LARm 7 at Det 10 55,914
NYG 24 at Was 20 39,086
Phi 7 at Cle 24 53,493
SF 21 at ChiB 17 45,310

Sun 10/20
Bal 27 at Det 31 55,764
ChiC 44 at Was 14 23,159
Cle 7 at Phi 17 22,443
LARm 26 at ChiB 34 47,337
Pit 0 at NYG 35 52,589
SF 24 at GB 14 18,919
at Milwaukee, WI

Sun 10/27
ChiB 17 at SF 21 56,693
Cle 17 at ChiC 7 26,341
Det 17 at LARm 35 77,314
GB 24 at Bal 21 48,510
Phi 0 at Pit 6 27,016
Was 31 at NYG 14 40,416

Sun 11/03
ChiB 16 at LARm 10 80,456
Det 31 at SF 35 59,702
NYG 31 at GB 17 32,070
Phi 38 at ChiC 21 18,718
Pit 19 at Bal 13 42,575
Was 17 at Cle 21 52,936

Sun 11/10
Bal 21 at Was 17 33,149
ChiC 14 at NYG 27 46,402
Det 27 at Phi 16 29,320
GB 14 at ChiB 21 47,153
Pit 0 at Cle 24 53,709
SF 24 at LARm 37 102,368

Sun 11/17
Bal 29 at ChiB 14 47,168
Cle 30 at Was 30 27,722
LARm 31 at GB 27 19,540
at Milwaukee, WI
Phi 0 at NYG 13 42,845
SF 10 at Det 31 56,915

Sun 11/24
ChiB 27 at Det 7 55,769
GB 27 at Pit 10 29,701
LARm 31 at Cle 45 65,407
NYG 28 at ChiC 21 19,200
SF 21 at Bal 27 50,073
Was 12 at Phi 21 20,730

Thu 11/28
GB 6 at Det 18 54,301

Sun 12/01
ChiC 0 at Cle 31 40,525
LARm 14 at Bal 31 52,060
Pit 6 at Phi 7 16,364
SF 27 at NYG 17 54,121
Was 14 at ChiB 3 39,148

Sat 12/07
NYG 10 at Pit 21 19,772

Sun 12/08
Bal 13 at SF 17 59,950
ChiB 14 at ChiC 6 43,735
Cle 7 at Det 20 55,814
GB 17 at LARm 42 70,572
Phi 7 at Was 42 21,304

Sat 12/14
ChiC 31 at Phi 27 12,555

Sun 12/15
Bal 21 at LARm 37 52,560
Cle 34 at NYG 28 54,294
Det 21 at ChiB 13 41,088
GB 20 at SF 27 59,100
Pit 3 at Was 10 22,577

Sun 12/22
Pit 27 at ChiC 2 10,084

Western Division Playoff

Sun 12/22
Det 31 at SF 27 60,118

1957 NFL Championship

Sun 12/29
Cle 59 at Det 14 55,263

National Football League 1958

Sun 09/28
ChiB 34 at GB 20 32,150
Cle 30 at LARm 27 69,993
Det 15 at Bal 28 48,377
NYG 37 at ChiC 7 21,923
at Buffalo, NY
Pit 20 at SF 23 51,856
Was 24 at Phi 14 36,850

Sat 10/04
N ChiB 38 at Bal 51 52,622
N Was 10 at ChiC 37 21,824

Sun 10/05
Cle 45 at Pit 12 31,130
Det 13 at GB 13 32,053
LARm 33 at SF 3 59,826
NYG 24 at Phi 27 23,178

Sun 10/12
Bal 24 at GB 17 24,553
at Milwaukee, WI
ChiC 28 at Cle 35 65,403
LARm 42 at Det 28 55,648
NYG 21 at Was 14 30,348
Phi 3 at Pit 24 23,153
SF 6 at ChiB 28 43,310

Sun 10/19
Bal 40 at Det 14 55,190
ChiC 23 at NYG 6 52,684
GB 21 at Was 37 25,228
LARm 10 at ChiB 31 41,387
Pit 10 at Cle 27 66,852
SF 30 at Phi 24 33,110

Sun 10/26
ChiB 27 at SF 14 59,441
Cle 38 at ChiC 24 30,933
Det 41 at LARm 24 81,703
Phi 35 at GB 38 31,043
Pit 6 at NYG 17 25,007
Was 10 at Bal 35 54,403

Sun 11/02
ChiB 35 at LARm 41 100,470
Det 21 at SF 24 59,350
GB 0 at Bal 56 51,333
NYG 21 at Cle 17 78,404
Phi 21 at ChiC 21 17,486
Was 16 at Pit 24 19,525

Sun 11/09
Bal 21 at NYG 24 71,164
ChiC 31 at Was 45 26,196
Det 30 at Cle 10 75,363
GB 10 at ChiB 24 48,424
Pit 31 at Phi 24 26,306
SF 7 at LARm 56 95,082

Sun 11/16
Bal 17 at ChiB 0 48,664
ChiC 21 at Phi 49 18,315
Cle 20 at Was 10 32,372
LARm 20 at GB 7 28,051
NYG 10 at Pit 31 30,030
SF 21 at Det 35 54,523

Sun 11/23
ChiB 20 at Det 7 55,280
LARm 7 at Bal 34 57,557
Phi 14 at Cle 28 51,319
Pit 27 at ChiC 20 15,946
SF 33 at GB 12 19,786
at Milwaukee, WI
Was 0 at NYG 30 46,752

Thu 11/27
GB 14 at Det 24 50,971

Sun 11/30
ChiB 10 at Pit 24 20,094
LARm 20 at ChiC 14 13,014
Phi 10 at NYG 24 35,438
SF 27 at Bal 35 57,557
Was 14 at Cle 21 33,240

Sat 12/06
Bal 28 at LARm 30 100,202

Sun 12/07
ChiC 14 at ChiB 30 41,617
Cle 21 at Phi 14 36,773
GB 21 at SF 48 50,793
NYG 19 at Det 17 50,115
Pit 14 at Was 14 23,370

Sat 12/13
ChiC 21 at Pit 38 16,660

Sun 12/14
Bal 12 at SF 21 58,334
Cle 10 at NYG 13 63,192
Det 16 at ChiB 21 38,346
GB 20 at LARm 34 54,634
Phi 0 at Was 20 22,621

Eastern Division Playoff

Sun 12/21
Cle 0 at NYG 10 61,174

1958 NFL Championship

Sun 12/28
Bal 23 at NYG 17# 64,185

National Football League 1959

Sat 09/26
N NYG 23 at LARm 21 71,297
N Cle 7 at Pit 17 33,884

Sun 09/27
ChiB 6 at GB 9 32,150
Det 9 at Bal 21 55,588
Phi 14 at SF 24 41,697
Was 21 at ChiC 49 21,892

Sat 10/03
N ChiB 26 at Bal 21 57,557

Sun 10/04
Cle 34 at ChiC 7 19,935
Det 10 at GB 28 32,150
LARm 0 at SF 34 56,028
NYG 21 at Phi 49 27,023
Was 23 at Pit 17 26,570

Sun 10/11
Bal 31 at Det 24 54,197
ChiC 14 at Was 23 25,937
LARm 28 at ChiB 21 47,036
NYG 10 at Cle 6 65,534
Pit 24 at Phi 28 27,343
SF 20 at GB 21 32,150

Sun 10/18
Bal 21 at ChiB 7 48,430
ChiC 7 at Cle 17 46,422
LARm 45 at GB 6 36,194
at Milwaukee, WI
Phi 7 at NYG 24 68,783
Pit 27 at Was 6 28,218
SF 34 at Det 13 52,585

Sun 10/25
ChiB 17 at SF 20 59,045
Det 17 at LARm 7 74,288
GB 21 at Bal 38 57,557
NYG 21 at Pit 16 33,596
Phi 28 at ChiC 24 20,112
at Minneapolis, MN
Was 7 at Cle 34 42,732

Sun 11/01
ChiB 26 at LARm 21 77,943
Cle 38 at Bal 31 57,557
Det 7 at SF 33 59,064
GB 3 at NYG 20 68,837
Pit 24 at ChiC 45 23,187
Was 23 at Phi 30 39,854

Sun 11/08
Bal 24 at Was 27 32,773
ChiC 3 at NYG 9 56,779
Det 10 at Pit 10 24,618
GB 17 at ChiB 28 46,205
Phi 7 at Cle 28 58,275
SF 24 at LARm 16 94,376

Sun 11/15
Bal 28 at GB 24 25,521
at Milwaukee, WI
ChiC 17 at Phi 27 28,887
Cle 31 at Was 17 32,266
LARm 17 at Det 23 52,217
Pit 14 at NYG 9 66,786
SF 3 at ChiB 14 42,157

Sun 11/22
ChiB 24 at Det 14 54,059
LARm 20 at Phi 23 47,425
NYG 30 at ChiC 20 26,625
at Minneapolis, MN
Pit 21 at Cle 20 68,563
SF 14 at Bal 45 57,557
Was 0 at GB 21 31,853

Thu 11/26
GB 24 at Det 17 49,221

Sun 11/29
ChiB 31 at ChiC 7 48,687
LARm 21 at Bal 35 57,557
Phi 0 at Pit 31 22,191
SF 21 at Cle 20 56,854
Was 14 at NYG 45 60,982

Sat 12/05
Bal 34 at SF 14 59,075

Sun 12/06
ChiC 21 at Det 45 45,811
Cle 7 at NYG 48 68,436
GB 38 at LARm 20 61,044
Phi 34 at Was 14 24,325
Pit 21 at ChiB 27 41,476

Sat 12/12
Bal 45 at LARm 26 65,528

Sun 12/13
ChiC 20 at Pit 35 19,011
Cle 28 at Phi 21 45,952
Det 14 at ChiB 25 40,890
GB 36 at SF 14 55,997
NYG 24 at Was 10 26,198

1959 NFL Championship

Sun 12/27
NYG 16 at Bal 31 57,545

American Football League 1960

Fri 09/09
N Den 13 at Bos 10 21,597

Sat 09/10
N DalT 20 at LAC 21 17,724

Sun 09/11
Hou 37 at Oak 22 12,703
Buf 3 at NYT 27 10,200

Fri 09/16
N DalT 34 at Oak 16 8,021

Sat 09/17
N Bos 28 at NYT 24 19,200

Sun 09/18
LAC 28 at Hou 38 20,156
Den 27 at Buf 21 15,229

Fri 09/23
N Buf 13 at Bos 0 20,732
N Den 24 at NYT 28 20,482

Sun 09/25
Oak 14 at Hou 13 16,421
LAC 0 at DalT 17 42,000

Sun 10/02
LAC 24 at Buf 10 15,821
NYT 37 at DalT 35 37,500
Oak 14 at Den 31 18,372

Sat 10/08
N Bos 35 at LAC 0 18,226

Sun 10/09
NYT 21 at Hou 27 16,156
Oak 20 at DalT 19 21,000

Sun 10/16
Bos 14 at Oak 27 11,500
DalT 10 at Hou 20 19,026
NYT 17 at Buf 13 14,988
LAC 23 at Den 19 19,141

Sun 10/23
Bos 24 at Den 31 12,683
Hou 42 at NYT 28 21,000
Oak 9 at Buf 38 8,876

Fri 10/28
N LAC 45 at Bos 16 13,988
N Oak 28 at NYT 27 10,000

Sun 10/30
Hou 24 at Buf 25 23,001
DalT 17 at Den 14 13,102

Fri 11/04
N Oak 28 at Bos 34 8,446
N LAC 21 at NYT 7 19,402

Sun 11/06
Hou 45 at Den 25 20,778
DalT 45 at Buf 28 19,610

Fri 11/11
N NYT 21 at Bos 38 11,653

Sun 11/13
Hou 21 at LAC 24 21,085
Buf 7 at Oak 20 8,800
Den 7 at DalT 34 21,000

Fri 11/18
N DalT 14 at Bos 42 14,721

Sun 11/20
Den 10 at Hou 20 14,489
Buf 32 at LAC 3 16,161

Thu 11/24
DalT 35 at NYT 41 14,344

Fri 11/25
Hou 24 at Bos 10 27,123

Sun 11/27
Buf 38 at Den 38 7,785
Oak 28 at LAC 52 15,075

Sun 12/04
Bos 14 at Buf 38 14,335
Hou 0 at DalT 24 20,000
LAC 41 at Oak 17 12,061
NYT 30 at Den 27 5,861

Sat 12/10
Den 33 at LAC 41 9,928

Sun 12/11
Bos 0 at DalT 34 12,000
Buf 23 at Hou 31 25,243
NYT 31 at Oak 28 9,037

Sat 12/17
Den 10 at Oak 48 5,159

Sun 12/18
Bos 21 at Hou 37 22,352
Buf 7 at DalT 24 18,000
NYT 43 at LAC 50 11,457

1960 AFL Championship

Sun 01/01
LAC 16 at Hou 24 32,183

National Football League 1960

Fri 09/23
N StL 43 at LARm 21 47,448

Sat 09/24
N Pit 35 at Dal 28 30,000

Sun 09/25
ChiB 17 at GB 14 32,150
Cle 41 at Phi 24 56,303
NYG 21 at SF 19 44,598
Was 0 at Bal 20 53,818

Fri 09/30
N Phi 27 at Dal 25 18,500

Sun 10/02
ChiB 7 at Bal 42 57,808
Det 9 at GB 28 32,150
LARm 9 at SF 13 53,633
NYG 35 at StL 14 26,089
Pit 20 at Cle 28 67,692

Sun 10/09
Bal 21 at GB 35 32,150
Dal 14 at Was 26 21,142
LARm 27 at ChiB 34 47,776
NYG 19 at Pit 17 40,323
StL 27 at Phi 31 33,701
SF 14 at Det 10 49,825

Sun 10/16
Cle 48 at Dal 7 28,500
Det 10 at Phi 28 38,065
LARm 17 at Bal 31 57,808
StL 14 at Pit 27 22,971
SF 10 at ChiB 27 48,226
Was 24 at NYG 24 60,625

Sun 10/23
Bal 17 at Det 30 53,854
ChiB 24 at LARm 24 63,838
Dal 10 at StL 12 23,128
Phi 31 at Cle 29 64,850
Pit 27 at Was 27 25,292
SF 14 at GB 41 39,914
at Milwaukee, WI

Sun 10/30
Bal 45 at Dal 7 25,500
ChiB 7 at SF 25 55,071
Cle 31 at Was 10 32,086
Det 35 at LARm 48 53,295
GB 19 at Pit 13 30,155
StL 20 at NYG 13 58,516

Sun 11/06
Det 24 at SF 0 48,447
GB 24 at Bal 38 57,808
LARm 38 at Dal 13 16,000
NYG 17 at Cle 13 82,872
Pit 7 at Phi 34 58,324
Was 7 at StL 44 22,458

Sun 11/13
Bal 24 at ChiB 20 48,713
Dal 7 at GB 41 32,294
LARm 10 at Det 12 54,019
Pit 24 at NYG 27 63,321
StL 27 at Cle 28 49,192
Was 13 at Phi 19 39,361

Sun 11/20
Cle 10 at Pit 14 35,215
Det 7 at ChiB 28 46,267
LARm 33 at GB 31 35,763
at Milwaukee, WI
Phi 17 at NYG 10 63,571
StL 26 at Was 14 23,848
SF 26 at Dal 14 10,000

Thu 11/24
GB 10 at Det 23 51,123

Sun 11/27
Cle 17 at StL 17 26,146
Dal 7 at ChiB 17 39,951
NYG 23 at Phi 31 60,547
SF 30 at Bal 22 57,808
Was 10 at Pit 22 22,334

Sun 12/04
Dal 31 at NYG 31 55,033
Det 20 at Bal 15 57,808
GB 41 at ChiB 13 46,406
Phi 20 at StL 6 21,358
SF 23 at LARm 7 77,254
Was 16 at Cle 27 35,211

Sat 12/10
GB 13 at SF 0 53,612

Sun 12/11
Bal 3 at LARm 10 75,461
ChiB 0 at Cle 42 38,155
Dal 14 at Det 23 43,272
NYG 17 at Was 3 14,077
Phi 21 at Pit 27 22,101

Sat 12/17
GB 35 at LARm 21 53,445

Sun 12/18
Bal 10 at SF 34 57,269
ChiB 0 at Det 36 51,017
Cle 48 at NYG 34 56,517
Phi 38 at Was 28 20,558
Pit 7 at StL 38 20,840

1960 NFL Championship

Mon 12/26
GB 13 at Phi 17 67,325

American Football League 1961

Sat 09/09
N NYT 21 at Bos 20 16,683
N Oakl 0 at Hou 55 16,231

Sun 09/10
SD 26 at DalT 10 24,500
Den 22 at Buf 10 16,636

Sat 09/16
N Den 17 at Bos 45 14,479

Sun 09/17
Oak 0 at SD 44 20,216
NYT 31 at Buf 41 15,584

Sat 09/23
N Bos 23 at Buf 21 21,504

Sun 09/24
Hou 24 at SD 34 29,210
DalT 42 at Oak 35 6,700
Den 28 at NYT 35 14,381

Sat 09/30
N SD 19 at Buf 11 20,742

Sun 10/01
Den 19 at Oak 33 8,361
Hou 21 at DalT 26 28,000
Bos 30 at NYT 37 15,189

Sat 10/07
N SD 38 at Bos 27 17,748

Sun 10/08
DalT 19 at Den 12 14,500
Buf 22 at Hou 12 22,761

Fri 10/13
N Hou 31 at Bos 31 15,070

Sun 10/15
SD 25 at NYT 10 25,136
Oak 24 at Den 27 11,129
DalT 24 at Buf 27 20,678

Sun 10/22
Buf 21 at Bos 52 9,398
SD 41 at Oak 10 12,014
NYT 10 at Den 27 12,508
DalT 7 at Hou 38 23,228

Sun 10/29
Den 0 at SD 37 32,584
NYT 14 at Oak 6 7,138
Bos 18 at DalT 17 20,500
Hou 28 at Buf 16 21,237

Fri 11/03
N DalT 21 at Bos 28 25,063

Sun 11/05
NYT 13 at SD 48 33,391
Oak 31 at Buf 22 17,027
Hou 55 at Den 14 11,564

Sat 11/11
N Oak 12 at NYT 23 16,811

Sun 11/12
SD 19 at Den 16 7,859
Buf 30 at DalT 20 15,000
Bos 15 at Hou 27 35,649

Fri 11/17
N Oak 17 at Bos 20 18,169

Sun 11/19
DalT 14 at SD 24 33,786
Buf 23 at Den 10 7,645
NYT 13 at Hou 49 33,428

Thu 11/23
Buf 14 at NYT 21 12,023

Sun 11/26
Oak 11 at DalT 43 14,500
Den 14 at Hou 45 27,864

Sun 12/03
SD 13 at Hou 33 37,854
Buf 26 at Oak 21 8,011
Bos 28 at Den 24 9,303
DalT 7 at NYT 28 14,117

Sat 12/09
Bos 35 at Oak 21 6,500

Sun 12/10
Buf 10 at SD 28 24,486
Den 21 at DalT 49 8,000
Hou 48 at NYT 21 9,462

Sun 12/17
Bos 41 at SD 0 21,339
Hou 47 at Oak 16 4,821
NYT 24 at DalT 35 12,500

1961 AFL Championship

Sun 12/24
Hou 10 at SD 3 29,556

National Football League 1961

Sun 09/17
ChiB 13 at Min 37 32,236
Cle 20 at Phi 27 60,671
Det 17 at GB 13 44,307
at Milwaukee, WI
LARm 24 at Bal 27 54,259
Pit 24 at Dal 27 23,500
StL 21 at NYG 10 58,059
Was 3 at SF 35 43,412

Sat 09/23
N ChiB 21 at LARm 17 53,315

Sun 09/24
Det 16 at Bal 15 54,259
Min 7 at Dal 21 20,500
NYG 17 at Pit 14 35,587
StL 17 at Cle 20 50,433
SF 10 at GB 30 38,669
Was 7 at Phi 14 50,108

Sun 10/01
ChiB 0 at GB 24 38,669
Dal 7 at Cle 25 43,638
Min 33 at Bal 34 54,259
NYG 24 at Was 21 36,767
Pit 14 at LARm 24 40,707
StL 30 at Phi 27 59,399
SF 49 at Det 0 53,155

Sun 10/08
Bal 7 at GB 45 38,669
ChiB 31 at Det 17 50,521
Dal 28 at Min 0 33,070
LARm 0 at SF 35 59,004
NYG 24 at StL 9 23,713
Pit 16 at Phi 21 60,671
Was 7 at Cle 31 46,186

Sun 10/15
Bal 10 at ChiB 24 48,719
GB 49 at Cle 17 75,049
LARm 13 at Det 14 45,873
NYG 31 at Dal 10 41,500
Phi 20 at StL 7 20,262
SF 38 at Min 24 34,415
Was 0 at Pit 20 15,072

Sun 10/22
Bal 17 at Det 14 53,016
Cle 30 at Pit 28 29,296
GB 33 at Min 7 42,007
LARm 14 at NYG 24 63,053
Phi 43 at Dal 7 25,000
StL 24 at Was 0 28,037
SF 0 at ChiB 31 49,070

Sun 10/29
ChiB 21 at Bal 20 57,641
Cle 21 at StL 10 26,696
Dal 17 at NYG 16 60,254
Det 28 at LARm 10 49,123
Min 10 at GB 28 44,116
at Milwaukee, WI
Phi 27 at Was 24 31,066
SF 10 at Pit 20 19,686

Sun 11/05
ChiB 14 at Phi 16 60,671
Det 20 at SF 20 56,878
GB 21 at Bal 45 57,641
Min 17 at LARm 31 38,594
Pit 17 at Cle 13 62,723
StL 31 at Dal 17 20,500
Was 0 at NYG 53 56,055

Sun 11/12
Bal 20 at Min 28 38,010
Cle 17 at Was 6 28,975
Dal 7 at Pit 37 17,519
Det 45 at StL 14 20,320
GB 31 at ChiB 28 49,711
Phi 21 at NYG 38 62,800
SF 7 at LARm 17 63,766

Sun 11/19
ChiB 31 at SF 41 52,972
Det 37 at Min 10 32,296
LARm 7 at GB 35 38,669
Phi 24 at Cle 45 68,399
Pit 21 at NYG 42 62,592
StL 0 at Bal 16 56,112
Was 28 at Dal 28 17,500

Thu 11/23
GB 17 at Det 9 55,662

Sun 11/26
Bal 27 at Was 6 41,062
Dal 13 at Phi 35 60,127
LARm 24 at ChiB 28 45,965
Min 28 at SF 38 48,905
NYG 37 at Cle 21 80,455
StL 27 at Pit 30 17,090

Sun 12/03
Cle 38 at Dal 17 23,500
Det 16 at ChiB 15 47,394
LARm 21 at Min 42 30,068
NYG 17 at GB 20 47,012
at Milwaukee, WI
Phi 35 at Pit 24 21,653
SF 17 at Bal 20 57,641
Was 24 at StL 38 16,204

Sat 12/09
N Bal 17 at LARm 34 41,268

Sun 12/10
Cle 14 at ChiB 17 38,717
Dal 13 at StL 31 15,384
GB 21 at SF 22 55,722
Min 7 at Det 13 42,655
NYG 28 at Phi 24 60,671
Pit 30 at Was 14 21,134

Sat 12/16
N Bal 27 at SF 24 45,517

Sun 12/17
Cle 7 at NYG 7 61,084
Dal 24 at Was 34 21,451
GB 24 at LARm 17 49,169
Min 35 at ChiB 52 34,539
Phi 27 at Det 24 44,231
Pit 0 at StL 20 16,298

1961 NFL Championship

Sun 12/31
NYG 0 at GB 37 39,029

American Football League 1962

Fri 09/07
N SD 21 at Den 30 28,000

Sat 09/08
N Bos 28 at DalT 42 32,000

Sun 09/09
Hou 28 at Buf 23 31,236
NYT 28 at Oak 17 12,893

Sat 09/15
N Den 23 at Buf 20 30,577

Sun 09/16
Hou 21 at Bos 34 32,276
NYT 14 at SD 40 22,003

Fri 09/21
N Den 16 at Bos 41 21,038

Sat 09/22
N NYT 17 at Buf 6 24,024

Sun 09/23
Hou 42 at SD 17 28,061
DalT 26 at Oak 16 12,500

Sun 09/30
SD 42 at Oak 33 13,000
Den 32 at NYT 10 5,729
Buf 21 at DalT 41 25,500

Fri 10/05
N Oak 7 at Den 44 22,452

Sat 10/06
N Bos 43 at NYT 14 4,719

Sun 10/07
DalT 28 at SD 32 23,092
Buf 14 at Hou 17 26,350

Fri 10/12
N DalT 27 at Bos 7 23,874

Sat 10/13
N SD 10 at Buf 35 20,074

Sun 10/14
NYT 17 at Hou 56 20,650
Den 23 at Oak 6 7,000

Fri 10/19
N SD 20 at Bos 24 20,888

Sat 10/20
N Oak 6 at Buf 14 21,037

Sun 10/21
Hou 10 at Den 20 34,496
NYT 17 at DalT 20 17,814

Fri 10/26
N Oak 16 at Bos 26 12,514

Sun 10/28
DalT 31 at Hou 7 31,750
SD 3 at NYT 23 7,175
Buf 45 at Den 38 26,051

Sat 11/03
N Bos 28 at Buf 28 33,247

Sun 11/04
Oak 21 at NYT 31 4,728
Hou 14 at DalT 6 29,017
Den 23 at SD 20 20,827

Sun 11/11
DalT 52 at NYT 31 5,974
Bos 33 at Den 29 28,187
Hou 28 at Oak 20 11,000
Buf 40 at SD 20 22,204

Sun 11/18
DalT 24 at Den 3 23,523
Bos 17 at Hou 21 35,250
Buf 10 at Oak 6 11,700

Thu 11/22
NYT 46 at Den 45 15,776

Fri 11/23
N Buf 10 at Bos 21 12,023

Sun 11/25
SD 27 at Hou 33 28,235
Oak 7 at DalT 35 13,557

Fri 11/30
N NYT 17 at Bos 24 20,015

Sun 12/02
DalT 14 at Buf 23 35,261
Den 17 at Hou 34 30,650
Oak 21 at SD 31 17,834

Sat 12/08
Buf 20 at NYT 3 4,011

Sun 12/09
Oak 17 at Hou 32 27,400
Den 10 at DalT 17 19,137
Bos 20 at SD 14 19,887

Sat 12/15
Hou 44 at NYT 10 3,828

Sun 12/16
SD 17 at DalT 26 18,384
Bos 0 at Oak 20 8,000

1962 AFL Championship

Sun 12/23
DalT 20 at Hou 17# 37,981

National Football League 1962

Sun 09/16
ChiB 30 at SF 14 46,052
LARm 27 at Bal 30 54,796
Min 7 at GB 34 38,669
NYG 7 at Cle 17 81,115
Pit 7 at Det 45 46,441
StL 27 at Phi 21 58,910
Was 35 at Dal 35 15,730

Sun 09/23
Bal 34 at Min 7 30,787
ChiB 27 at LARm 23 44,376
NYG 29 at Phi 13 60,671
Pit 30 at Dal 28 19,478
StL 0 at GB 17 44,885
at Milwaukee, WI
SF 24 at Det 45 51,032
Was 17 at Cle 16 57,491

Sun 09/30
ChiB 0 at GB 49 38,669
Cle 7 at Phi 35 60,671
Dal 27 at LARm 17 26,907
Det 29 at Bal 20 57,966
Min 7 at SF 21 38,407
NYG 31 at Pit 27 40,916
StL 14 at Was 24 37,419

Sat 10/06
N Phi 7 at Pit 13 22,164

Sun 10/07
ChiB 13 at Min 0 33,141
Dal 10 at Cle 19 44,040
Det 7 at GB 9 38,669
LARm 14 at Was 20 38,264
NYG 31 at StL 14 20,327
SF 21 at Bal 13 54,148

Sun 10/14
Bal 36 at Cle 14 80,132
GB 48 at Min 21 41,475
LARm 10 at Det 13 53,714
Phi 19 at Dal 41 18,645
Pit 20 at NYG 17 62,808
SF 34 at ChiB 27 48,902
Was 17 at StL 17 18,104

Sun 10/21
Bal 15 at ChiB 35 49,066
Cle 34 at StL 7 23,256
Dal 42 at Pit 27 23,106
Det 14 at NYG 17 62,856
Min 38 at LARm 14 33,071
SF 13 at GB 31 46,010
at Milwaukee, WI
Was 27 at Phi 21 60,671

Sun 10/28
ChiB 3 at Det 11 53,342
Cle 41 at Pit 14 35,417
GB 17 at Bal 6 57,966
LARm 28 at SF 14 51,033
Phi 21 at Min 31 30,071
StL 28 at Dal 24 16,027
Was 34 at NYG 49 62,884

Sun 11/04
Bal 22 at SF 3 44,875
Dal 38 at Was 10 49,888
Det 12 at LARm 3 44.241
GB 38 at ChiB 7 48,753
Min 31 at Pit 39 14,642
Phi 14 at Cle 14 63,848
StL 28 at NYG 31 62,775

Sun 11/11
Bal 14 at LARm 2 39,502
Cle 9 at Was 17 48,169
Det 38 at SF 24 43,449
GB 49 at Phi 0 60,671
Min 30 at ChiB 31 46,984
NYG 41 at Dal 10 45,668
Pit 26 at StL 17 20,284

Sun 11/18
Bal 13 at GB 17 38,669
ChiB 34 at Dal 33 12,692
Det 17 at Min 6 31,257
Phi 14 at NYG 19 62,705
StL 14 at Cle 38 41,815
SF 24 at LARm 17 42,554
Was 21 at Pit 23 21,231

Thu 11/22
GB 14 at Det 26 57,578

Sun 11/25
ChiB 57 at Bal 0 56,164
Dal 14 at Phi 28 58,070
LARm 24 at Min 24 26.728
NYG 42 at Was 24 49,129
Pit 14 at Cle 35 53,601
SF 24 at StL 17 17,532

Sun 12/02
Bal 14 at Det 21 53,012
Cle 21 at Dal 45 24,226
LARm 10 at GB 41 46,833
at Milwaukee, WI
NYG 26 at ChiB 24 49,043
Phi 37 at Was 14 32,229
StL 7 at Pit 19 17,265
SF 35 at Min 12 33,076

Sat 12/08
Was 21 at Bal 34 56,964

Sun 12/09
Cle 13 at NYG 17 62,794
Dal 20 at StL 52 14,102
GB 31 at SF 21 53,769
LARm 14 at ChiB 30 38,685
Min 23 at Det 37 42,256
Pit 26 at Phi 17 60,671

Sat 12/15
Cle 13 at SF 10 35,274

Sun 12/16
Dal 31 at NYG 41 62,694
Det 0 at ChiB 3 44,948
GB 20 at LARm 17 60,389
Min 17 at Bal 42 53,645
Phi 35 at StL 45 14,989
Pit 27 at Was 24 34,508

1962 NFL Championship

Sun 12/30
GB 16 at NYG 7 64,892

American Football League 1963

Sat 09/07
N KC 59 at Den 7 21,115
N Oak 24 at Hou 13 24,749

Sun 09/08
Buf 10 at SD 14 22,344
NYJ 14 at Bos 38 24,120

Sat 09/14
N Bos 13 at SD 17 26,097
N Den 14 at Hou 20 23,147

Sun 09/15
Buf 17 at Oak 35 17,568

Sun 09/22
Hou 17 at NYJ 24 9,336
Bos 20 at Oak 14 17,131
KC 27 at Buf 27 33,487

Sat 09/28
N Oak 7 at NYJ 10 17,100
N Hou 31 at Buf 20 32,340

Sun 09/29
KC 10 at SD 24 22,654
Bos 10 at Den 14 18,636

Sat 10/05
N Oak 0 at Buf 12 24,846
N Bos 24 at NYJ 31 16,769

Sun 10/06
Hou 7 at KC 28 27,801
SD 34 at Den 50 18,428

Fri 10/11
N Oak 14 at Bos 20 26,494

Sun 10/13
NYJ 20 at SD 24 27,189
Hou 33 at Den 24 24,087
Buf 35 at KC 26 25,519

Fri 10/18
N Den 21 at Bos 40 25,418

Sun 10/20
SD 38 at KC 17 30,107
NYJ 26 at Oak 49 15,557
Buf 14 at Hou 28 23,948

Sat 10/26
N Den 35 at NYJ 35 22,553
N Bos 21 at Buf 28 27,243

Sun 10/27
Oak 34 at SD 33 20,182
KC 7 at Hou 28 26,331

Fri 11/01
N Hou 3 at Bos 45 31,185

Sat 11/02
N SD 53 at NYJ 7 20,798

Sun 11/03
Buf 30 at Den 28 19,424
KC 7 at Oak 10 18,919

Fri 11/08
N Oak 22 at KC 7 24,897

Sat 11/09
N Den 17 at Buf 27 30,989

Sun 11/10
SD 7 at Bos 6 28,402
NYJ 27 at Hou 31 23,619

Sun 11/17
NYJ 14 at Den 9 14,247
SD 23 at Buf 13 38,592
KC 24 at Bos 24 17,270

Thu 11/28
Oak 26 at Den 10 14,763

Sun 12/01
Hou 0 at SD 27 31,613
Buf 7 at Bos 17 16,981
KC 0 at NYJ 17 18,824

Sun 12/08
Den 21 at KC 52 17,443
SD 27 at Oak 41 20,249
Bos 46 at Hou 28 23,462
NYJ 14 at Buf 45 20,222

Sat 12/14
Buf 19 at NYJ 10 6,526
Bos 3 at KC 35 12,598

Sun 12/15
Den 31 at Oak 35 15,223
SD 20 at Hou 14 18,540

Sun 12/22
NYJ 0 at KC 48 12,202
Hou 49 at Oak 52 17,401
Den 20 at SD 58 31,312

Eastern Division Playoff

Sat 12/28
Bos 20 at Buf 14 33,044

1963 AFL Championship

Sun 01/05
Bos 10 at SD 51 31,270

National Football League 1963

Sat 09/14
N Det 23 at LARm 2 49,342
N StL 34 at Dal 7 36,432

Sun 09/15
ChiB 10 at GB 3 42,327
Min 24 at SF 20 30,781
NYG 37 at Bal 28 60,029
Pit 21 at Phi 21 58,205
Was 14 at Cle 37 57,618

Sat 09/21
N Was 37 at LARm 14 29,295

Sun 09/22
Bal 20 at SF 14 31,006
ChiB 28 at Min 7 33,923
Cle 41 at Dal 24 28,710

Det 10 at GB 31 45,912
at Milwaukee, WI
NYG 0 at Pit 31 46,068
StL 28 at Phi 24 60,671

Sun 09/29
Bal 20 at GB 31 42,327
ChiB 37 at Det 21 55,400
Dal 17 at Was 21 40,101
LARm 6 at Cle 20 54,713
NYG 37 at Phi 14 60,671
StL 10 at Pit 23 28,225
SF 14 at Min 45 28,564

Sat 10/05
N Pit 23 at Cle 35 84,684

Sun 10/06
Bal 3 at ChiB 10 48,998
Dal 21 at Phi 24 60,671
LARm 10 at GB 42 42,327
NYG 24 at Was 14 49,219
StL 56 at Min 14 30,220
SF 3 at Det 26 44,088

Sun 10/13
ChiB 52 at LARm 14 40,476
Cle 35 at NYG 24 62,986
Det 14 at Dal 17 27,264
GB 37 at Min 28 42,567
Phi 37 at Was 24 42,219
Pit 23 at StL 24 23,715
SF 3 at Bal 20 56,962

Sun 10/20
Bal 25 at Det 21 51,901
ChiB 14 at SF 20 35,837
Dal 21 at NYG 37 62,889
GB 30 at StL 7 32,224
Min 24 at LARm 27 30,565
Phi 7 at Cle 37 75,174
Was 27 at Pit 38 56,962

Sun 10/27
Dal 21 at Pit 27 19,047
GB 34 at Bal 20 60,065
Min 10 at Det 28 44,509
NYG 33 at Cle 6 84,213
Phi 7 at ChiB 16 48,514
StL 21 at Was 7 46,921
SF 21 at LARm 28 45,532

Sun 11/03
ChiB 17 at Bal 7 60,065
Cle 23 at Phi 17 60,671
Det 45 at SF 7 33,511
LARm 13 at Min 21 33,567
NYG 38 at StL 21 29,482
Pit 14 at GB 33 46,293
at Milwaukee, WI
Was 20 at Dal 35 18,838

Sun 11/10
Cle 7 at Pit 9 54,497
Dal 24 at SF 31 29,563
Det 21 at Bal 24 59,758
LARm 0 at ChiB 6 48,312
Min 7 at GB 28 42,327
Phi 14 at NYG 42 62,936
Was 20 at StL 24 18,197

Sun 11/17
Bal 37 at Min 34 33,136
GB 7 at ChiB 26 49,166
LARm 28 at Det 21 44,951
Phi 20 at Dal 27 23,694
Pit 34 at Was 28 49,219
StL 20 at Cle 14 75,232
SF 14 at NYG 48 62,982

Sun 11/24
Bal 16 at LARm 17 48,555
ChiB 17 at Pit 17 36,465
Dal 17 at Cle 27 55,096
Det 31 at Min 34 28,763
StL 24 at NYG 17 62,992
SF 10 at GB 28 49,905
at Milwaukee, WI
Was 13 at Phi 10 60,671

Thu 11/28
GB 13 at Det 13 54,016

Sun 12/01
Bal 36 at Was 20 44,006
Cle 24 at StL 10 32,531
LARm 21 at SF 17 33,321
Min 17 at ChiB 17 47,249
NYG 34 at Dal 27 29,653
Phi 20 at Pit 20 16,721

Sat 12/07
GB 31 at LARm 14 52,357
Cle 10 at Det 38 51,382
Min 10 at Bal 41 54,122
Phi 14 at StL 38 15,979
Pit 24 at Dal 19 24,136
SF 7 at ChiB 27 46,994
Was 14 at NYG 44 62,992

Sat 12/14
GB 21 at SF 17 31,031

Sun 12/15
Cle 27 at Was 20 40,865
Dal 28 at StL 24 12,695
Det 14 at ChiB 24 45,317
LARm 16 at Bal 19 52,834
Min 34 at Phi 13 57,403
Pit 17 at NYG 33 63,240

1963 NFL Championship

Sun 12/29
NYG 10 at ChiB 14 45,801

American Football League 1964

Sat 09/12
N Den 6 at NYJ 30 44,497
N Hou 21 at SD 27 20,611

Sun 09/13
KC 17 at Buf 34 30,157
Bos 17 at Oak 14 21,126

Sat 09/19
N Oak 28 at Hou 42 26,482

Sun 09/20
Den 13 at Buf 30 28,501
Bos 33 at SD 28 20,568

Sat 09/26
N SD 3 at Buf 30 40,167

Sun 09/27
NYJ 10 at Bos 26 22,716
Hou 38 at Den 17 22,651
KC 21 at Oak 9 18,163

Sat 10/03
N SD 17 at NYJ 17 50,222
N Oak 20 at Buf 23 36,461

Sun 10/04
Bos 39 at Den 10 15,485
Hou 7 at KC 28 22,727

Fri 10/09
N SD 26 at Bos 17 35,006

Sat 10/10
N Oak 13 at NYJ 35 36,499

Sun 10/11
KC 27 at Den 33 16,285
Buf 48 at Hou 17 26,218

Fri 10/16
N Oak 43 at Bos 43 23,279

Sat 10/17
N Hou 21 at NYJ 24 35,819

Sun 10/18
Buf 35 at KC 22 20,904
Den 14 at SD 42 23,332

Fri 10/23
N KC 7 at Bos 24 27,400

Sat 10/24
N NYJ 24 at Buf 34 39,621

Sun 10/25
SD 20 at Hou 17 21,671
Den 7 at Oak 40 17,858

Sat 10/31
N Bos 14 at NYJ 35 45,033

Sun 11/01
Den 39 at KC 49 15,053
Oak 17 at SD 31 25,557
Hou 10 at Buf 24 40,119

Fri 11/06
N Hou 24 at Bos 25 28,161

Sun 11/08
Buf 20 at NYJ 7 61,929
Oak 7 at KC 42 21,023
SD 31 at Den 20 19,670

Sun 11/15
Bos 36 at Buf 28 42,308
NYJ 16 at Den 20 11,309
SD 28 at KC 14 19,792
Hou 10 at Oak 20 16,375

Fri 11/20
N Den 7 at Bos 12 24,979

Sun 11/22
KC 28 at Hou 19 17,782
NYJ 26 at Oak 35 15,589

Thu 11/26
Buf 27 at SD 24 34,865

Sun 11/29
KC 14 at NYJ 27 46,597
Bos 34 at Hou 17 17,560
Oak 20 at Den 20 15,958

Sun 12/06
Bos 31 at KC 24 13,166
NYJ 3 at SD 38 25,753
Buf 13 at Oak 16 18,134

Sun 12/13
KC 49 at SD 6 26,562
Buf 30 at Den 19 14,431
NYJ 17 at Hou 33 16,225

Sun 12/20
Buf 24 at Bos 14 38,021
NYJ 7 at KC 24 14,316
Den 15 at Hou 34 15,839
SD 20 at Oak 21 20,124

1964 AFL Championship

Sat 12/26
SD 7 at Buf 20 40,242

National Football League 1964

Sat 09/12
N StL 16 at Dal 6 36,605

Sun 09/13
Bal 24 at Min 34 35,563
ChiB 12 at GB 23 42,327
Cle 27 at Was 13 47,577
Det 26 at SF 17 33,204
LARm 26 at Pit 14 33,988
NYG 7 at Phi 38 60,671

Sat 09/19
N Det 17 at LARm 17 52,001

Sun 09/20
Bal 21 at GB 20 42,327
ChiB 34 at Min 28 41,387
NYG 24 at Pit 27 35,053
StL 33 at Cle 33 76,954
SF 28 at Phi 24 57,353
Was 18 at Dal 24 25,158

Fri 09/25
N Was 10 at NYG 13 62,996

Sun 09/27
ChiB 0 at Bal 52 56,537
Cle 28 at Phi 20 60,671
Dal 17 at Pit 23 35,594
Min 13 at LARm 22 50,009
StL 23 at SF 13 30,969

Mon 09/28
N GB 14 at Det 10 59,203

Sun 10/04
ChiB 21 at SF 31 33,132
Dal 6 at Cle 27 72,062
LARm 20 at Bal 35 56,537
Min 24 at GB 23 42,327
NYG 3 at Det 26 54,836
Pit 7 at Phi 21 59,354
StL 23 at Was 17 49,219

Sat 10/10
N Pit 23 at Cle 7 80,530

Sun 10/11
Det 24 at Min 20 40,840
LARm 17 at ChiB 38 47,358
NYG 13 at Dal 13 33,324
Phi 20 at Was 35 49,219
SF 14 at GB 24 47,380
at Milwaukee, WI

Mon 10/12
N Bal 47 at StL 27 60,213

Sun 10/18
Cle 20 at Dal 16 37,456
Det 10 at ChiB 0 47,567
GB 21 at Bal 24 60,213
Phi 23 at NYG 17 62,978
Pit 10 at Min 30 39,873
SF 14 at LARm 42 54,355
Was 24 at StL 38 23,748

Sun 10/25
Bal 34 at Det 0 57,814
ChiB 20 at Was 27 49,219
Dal 31 at StL 13 28,253
LARm 27 at GB 17 47,617
at Milwauee, WI
Min 27 at SF 22 31,845
NYG 20 at Cle 42 81,050
Phi 34 at Pit 10 38,393

Sun 11/01
Cle 30 at Pit 17 49,568
Dal 24 at ChiB 10 47,527
GB 42 at Min 13 44,278
LARm 17 at Det 37 52,064
StL 17 at NYG 34 63,072
SF 7 at Bal 37 60,213
Was 21 at Phi 10 60,671

Sun 11/08
Bal 40 at ChiB 24 47,891
Dal 31 at NYG 21 63,031
Det 7 at GB 30 42,327
Phi 10 at LARm 20 53,994
Pit 30 at StL 34 28,245
SF 7 at Min 24 40,408
Was 24 at Cle 34 76,385

Sun 11/15
ChiB 34 at LARm 24 61,115
Det 21 at Cle 37 83,064
GB 14 at SF 24 38,483
Min 14 at Bal 17 60,213
NYG 10 at StL 10 29,608
Phi 17 at Dal 14 55,972
Was 30 at Pit 0 31,587

Sun 11/22
Bal 24 at LARm 7 72,137
Cle 21 at GB 28 48,065
at Milwaukee, WI
Dal 16 at Was 28 49,218
Min 23 at Det 23 48,291
Pit 44 at NYG 17 62,961
StL 38 at Phi 13 60,671
SF 21 at ChiB 23 46,772

Thu 11/26
ChiB 27 at Det 24 52,231

Sun 11/29
Bal 14 at SF 3 33,642
GB 45 at Dal 21 44,975
LARm 13 at Min 34 31,677
NYG 21 at Was 36 49,219
Phi 24 at Cle 38 79,289
StL 21 at Pit 20 27,807

Sat 12/05
GB 17 at ChiB 3 43,636

Sun 12/06
Cle 19 at StL 28 31,585
Dal 14 at Phi 24 60,671
Det 31 at Bal 14 60,213
LARm 7 at SF 28 31,791
Min 30 at NYG 21 62,802
Pit 14 at Was 7 49,219

Sat 12/12
Cle 52 at NYG 20 63,007

Sun 12/13
GB 24 at LARm 24 40,735
Min 41 at ChiB 14 46,486
Phi 34 at StL 36 24,636
Pit 14 at Dal 17 35,271
SF 7 at Det 24 41,854
Was 17 at Bal 45 60,213

1964 NFL Championship

Sun 12/27
Bal 0 at Cle 27 79,544

American Football League 1965

Sat 09/11
N Bos 7 at Buf 24 45,502
N Den 31 at SD 34 27,022

Sun 09/12
KC 10 at Oak 37 18,659
NYJ 21 at Hou 27 52,680

Sat 09/18
N KC 14 at NYJ 10 53,658

Sun 09/19
SD 17 at Oak 6 21,406
Buf 30 at Den 15 30,682
Bos 10 at Hou 31 32,445

Fri 09/24
N Den 27 at Bos 10 26,782

Sun 09/26
KC 10 at SD 10 28,126
Hou 17 at Oak 21 18,116
NYJ 21 at Buf 33 45,056

Sun 10/03
Hou 14 at SD 31 28,190
NYJ 13 at Den 16 34,988
Bos 17 at KC 27 26,773
Oak 12 at Buf 17 41,246

Fri 10/08
N Oak 24 at Bos 10 24,824

Sun 10/10
KC 31 at Den 23 31,001
SD 34 at Buf 3 45,260

Sat 10/16
N Oak 24 at NYJ 24 54,890

Sun 10/17
Hou 17 at Den 28 32,492
Buf 23 at KC 7 26,941
SD 13 at Bos 13 20,924

Sat 10/23
N SD 34 at NYJ 9 60,679

Sun 10/24
Bos 21 at Oak 30 20,585
KC 36 at Hou 38 34,620
Den 13 at Buf 31 45,046

Sun 10/31
Bos 22 at SD 6 33,366
Oak 7 at KC 14 18,354
Hou 19 at Buf 17 44,267
Den 10 at NYJ 45 55,572

Sun 11/07
SD 35 at Den 21 33,073
NYJ 13 at KC 10 25,523
Oak 33 at Hou 21 35,729
Buf 23 at Bos 7 24,415

Sun 11/14
Buf 17 at Oak 14 19,352
SD 7 at KC 31 21,968
Den 31 at Hou 21 28,126
NYJ 30 at Bos 20 18,589

Sun 11/21
Oak 28 at Den 20 30,369
Hou 14 at NYJ 41 55,312
KC 10 at Bos 10 13,056

Thu 11/25
Buf 20 at SD 20 27,473

Sun 11/28
Hou 21 at KC 52 16,459
Bos 27 at NYJ 23 59,344

Sat 12/04
NYJ 7 at SD 38 32,167

Sun 12/05
Den 13 at Oak 24 19,023
Buf 29 at Hou 18 23,087

Sun 12/12
NYJ 14 at Oak 24 19,013
Bos 28 at Den 20 27,207
SD 37 at Hou 26 24,120
KC 25 at Buf 34 40,298

Sat 12/18
Hou 14 at Bos 42 14,508

Sun 12/19
Oak 14 at SD 24 26,056
Den 35 at KC 45 14,421
Buf 12 at NYJ 14 57,396

1965 AFL Championship

Sun 12/26
Buf 23 at SD 0 30,361

National Football League 1965

Sun 09/19
ChiB 24 at SF 52 31,211
Cle 17 at Was 7 48,208
GB 41 at Pit 9 38,383
LARm 0 at Det 20 46,941
Min 16 at Bal 35 56,562
NYG 2 at Dal 31 59,366
StL 27 at Phi 34 54,260

Sat 09/25
N ChiB 28 at LARm 30 36,359

Sun 09/26
Bal 17 at GB 20 48,130
at Milwaukee, WI
Det 31 at Min 29 46,826
NYG 16 at Phi 14 57,154
Pit 17 at SF 27 28,161
StL 49 at Cle 13 80,161
Was 7 at Dal 27 61,577

Sun 10/03
ChiB 14 at GB 23 50,852
Cle 35 at Phi 17 60,759
Min 38 at LARm 35 36,755
NYG 23 at Pit 13 31,871
SF 24 at Bal 27 57,342
Was 10 at Det 14 52,627

Mon 10/04
Dal 13 at StL 20 32,034

Sat 10/09
N Pit 19 at Cle 24 80,187

Sun 10/10
Det 7 at Bal 31 60,238
LARm 6 at ChiB 31 45,760
NYG 14 at Min 40 44,283
Phi 35 at Dal 24 56,249
StL 37 at Was 16 50,205
SF 10 at GB 27 50,852

Sun 10/17
Bal 38 at Was 7 50,405
ChiB 45 at Min 37 47,426
Dal 17 at Cle 23 80,451
GB 31 at Det 21 56,712
Phi 27 at NYG 35 62,815
StL 20 at Pit 7 31,085
SF 45 at LARm 21 38,615

Sun 10/24
Cle 38 at NYG 14 62,864
Dal 3 at GB 13 48,311
at Milwaukee, WI
Det 10 at ChiB 38 45,658
LARm 20 at Bal 35 60,238
Min 42 at SF 41 40,673
Pit 20 at Phi 14 56,515
Was 24 at StL 20 32,228

Sun 10/31
Bal 34 at SF 28 43,575
Dal 13 at Pit 22 37,804
Det 31 at LARm 7 35,187
GB 10 at ChiB 31 45,664
Min 27 at Cle 17 83,505
Phi 21 at Was 23 50,301
StL 10 at NYG 14 62,807

Sun 11/07
Bal 26 at ChiB 21 45,656
Det 12 at GB 7 50,852
LARm 13 at Min 24 47,426
Phi 34 at Cle 38 72,807
Pit 17 at StL 21 31,899
SF 31 at Dal 39 39,677
Was 23 at NYG 7 62,788

Sun 11/14
Bal 41 at Min 21 47,426
LARm 3 at GB 6 48,485
at Milwaukee, WI
NYG 21 at Cle 34 82,426
Pit 17 at Dal 24 57,293
StL 13 at ChiB 34 45,663
SF 27 at Det 21 52,570
Was 14 at Phi 21 60,444

Sun 11/21
ChiB 17 at Det 10 51,499
Cle 24 at Dal 17 76,251
GB 38 at Min 13 47,426
LARm 27 at SF 30 39,253
NYG 28 at StL 15 31,704
Phi 24 at Bal 34 60,238
Was 31 at Pit 3 25,052

Thu 11/25
Bal 24 at Det 24 55,036

Sun 11/28
ChiB 35 at NYG 14 62,933
Cle 42 at Pit 21 42,757
Dal 31 at Was 34 50,205
GB 10 at LARm 21 39,733
Phi 28 at StL 24 28,706
SF 45 at Min 24 36,748

Sun 12/05
ChiB 13 at Bal 0 60,238
Dal 21 at Phi 19 54,714
Det 14 at SF 17 38,483
LARm 27 at StL 3 27,943
Min 19 at GB 24 50,852
Pit 10 at NYG 35 62,735
Was 16 at Cle 24 77,765

Sat 12/11
StL 13 at Dal 27 38,499

Sun 12/12
Cle 7 at LARm 42 49,048
GB 42 at Bal 27 60,238
Min 29 at Det 7 45,420
NYG 27 at Was 10 50,373
Phi 47 at Pit 13 22,002
SF 20 at ChiB 61 43,400

Sat 12/18
Bal 20 at LARm 17 46,646

Sun 12/19
Cle 27 at StL 24 29,348
Dal 38 at NYG 20 62,871
Det 35 at Phi 28 56,718
GB 24 at SF 24 45,710
Min 24 at ChiB 17 46,604
Pit 14 at Was 35 49,806

Western Division Playoff

Sun 12/26
Bal 10 at GB 13# 50,484

1965 Championship Game

Sun 01/02
Cle 12 at GB 23 50,777

America Football League 1966

Fri 09/02
N Oak 23 at Mia 14 26,276

Sat 09/03
N Den 7 at Hou 45 30,156

Sun 09/04
Buf 7 at SD 27 27,252

Fri 09/09
N NYJ 19 at Mia 14 34,402

Sat 09/10
N Oak 0 at Hou 31 31,763
N Bos 0 at SD 24 29,539

Sun 09/11
KC 42 at Buf 20 42,023

Sun 09/18
KC 32 at Oak 10 50,746
Mia 24 at Buf 58 37,546
Hou 13 at NYJ 52 54,681
Bos 24 at Den 10 25,337

Sun 09/25
KC 43 at Bos 24 22,641
SD 29 at Oak 20 37,183
NYJ 16 at Den 7 29,878
Hou 20 at Buf 27 42,526

Sun 10/02
Hou 38 at Den 40 27,203
NYJ 24 at Bos 24 27,255
Mia 10 at SD 44 26,444
Buf 29 at KC 14 43,885

Sat 10/08
N Bos 20 at Buf 10 45,542
N Den 10 at KC 37 33,929
N SD 16 at NYJ 17 63,497

Sun 10/09
Mia 10 at Oak 21 30,787

Sun 10/16
Den 7 at Mia 24 23,393
Oak 34 at KC 13 33,057
NYJ 0 at Hou 24 30,823
SD 17 at Buf 17 45,169

Sun 10/23
Mia 20 at Hou 13 23,173
Oak 24 at NYJ 21 58,135
KC 56 at Den 10 26,196
SD 17 at Bos 35 32,371

Sun 10/30
Buf 33 at NYJ 23 61,552
Oak 21 at Bos 24 26,941
Den 17 at SD 24 25,819
Hou 23 at KC 48 31,676

Sun 11/06
Hou 23 at Oak 38 34,102
SD 14 at KC 24 40,986
Den 17 at Bos 10 18,154
Buf 29 at Mia 0 37,177

Sun 11/13
Oak 41 at SD 19 26,230
Mia 16 at KC 34 34,063
Hou 21 at Bos 27 23,426
NYJ 3 at Buf 14 45,738

Sun 11/20
Bos 27 at KC 27 41,475
Buf 42 at Hou 20 27,312
Oak 17 at Den 3 26,703
Mia 13 at NYJ 30 58,664

Thu 11/24
Buf 31 at Oak 10 36,781

Sun 11/27
KC 32 at NYJ 24 60,318
SD 17 at Den 20 24,860
Bos 20 at Mia 14 22,754

Sat 12/03
NYJ 28 at Oak 28 32,144

Sun 12/04
Mia 7 at Den 17 32,592
SD 28 at Hou 22 17,569
Buf 3 at Bos 14 39,350

Sun 12/11
NYJ 27 at SD 42 25,712
Bos 38 at Hou 14 17,100
Den 10 at Oak 28 31,765
KC 19 at Mia 18 17,881

Sat 12/17
Bos 28 at NYJ 38 58,921

Sun 12/18
KC 27 at SD 17 28,348
Hou 28 at Mia 29 20,045
Den 21 at Buf 38 40,583

1966 AFL Championship

Sun 01/01
KC 31 at Buf 7 42,080

National Football League 1966

Sat 09/10
N Bal 3 at GB 24 48,650
at Milwaukee, WI

Sun 09/11
Min 20 at SF 20 29,312
Phi 13 at StL 16 39,065
LARm 19 at Atl 14 54,418
NYG 34 at Pit 34 37,693
Cle 38 at Was 14 48,643
ChiB 3 at Det 14 52,225

Fri 09/16
N ChiB 17 at LARm 31 58,916

Sun 09/18
Atl 10 at Phi 23 54,049
Bal 38 at Min 23 47,426
Det 3 at Pit 17 35,473
NYG 7 at Dal 52 60,010
Was 7 at StL 23 40,198
GB 21 at Cle 20 83,943

Sun 09/25
LARm 13 at GB 24 50,861
Was 33 at Pit 27 37,505
Atl 10 at Det 28 47,615
SF 14 at Bal 36 56,715
StL 34 at Cle 28 74,814
Min 17 at Dal 28 64,116
NYG 17 at Phi 35 60,177

Fri 09/30
N SF 3 at LARm 34 45,642

Sun 10/02
ChiB 13 at Min 10 47,426
StL 41 at Phi 10 59,305
Dal 47 at Atl 14 56,990
Pit 10 at Was 24 47,360
Det 14 at GB 23 50,861
Cle 28 at NYG 7 62,916

Sat 10/08
N Pit 10 at Cle 41 82,687

Sun 10/09
Phi 7 at Dal 56 69,372
Bal 17 at ChiB 27 47,452
LARm 14 at Det 7 52,793
NYG 19 at StL 24 43,893
Atl 20 at Was 33 50,116
GB 20 at SF 21 39,290

Sun 10/16
GB 17 at ChiB 0 48,573
Was 10 at NYG 13 62,825
LARm 7 at Min 35 47,426
Phi 31 at Pit 14 28,233
Dal 10 at StL 10 50,673
Det 14 at Bal 45 60,238
SF 44 at Atl 7 54,788

Sun 10/23
Dal 21 at Cle 30 84,721
LARm 10 at ChiB 17 47,475
Min 17 at Bal 20 60,238
Phi 31 at NYG 3 63,018
Atl 3 at GB 56 48,623
at Milwaukee, WI
StL 20 at Was 26 50,154
Det 24 at SF 27 36,745

Sun 10/30
Pit 21 at Dal 52 58,453
Cle 49 at Atl 17 57,235
SF 3 at Min 28 45,007
Was 27 at Phi 13 60,652
Bal 17 at LARm 3 57,898
GB 31 at Det 7 56,954

Mon 10/31
N ChiB 17 at StL 24 49,516

Sun 11/06
StL 20 at NYG 17 62,967
Was 10 at Bal 37 60,238
Cle 6 at Pit 16 39,690
Dal 23 at Phi 24 60,658
Det 10 at ChiB 10 47,041
LARm 13 at SF 21 35,372
Min 20 at GB 17 50,861

Sun 11/13
Bal 19 at Atl 7 58,850
Det 32 at Min 31 43,939
Phi 7 at Cle 27 77,968
StL 9 at Pit 30 28,552
NYG 14 at LARm 55 34,746
SF 30 at ChiB 30 47,079
Dal 31 at Was 30 50,927

Sun 11/20
Atl 27 at NYG 16 62,746
Bal 14 at Det 20 52,383
Phi 35 at SF 34 31,993
ChiB 6 at GB 13 50,861
Dal 20 at Pit 7 42,185
Min 6 at LARm 21 38,775
Was 3 at Cle 14 78,466

Thu 11/24
Cle 14 at Dal 26 80,259
SF 41 at Det 14 53,189

Sun 11/27
Atl 6 at ChiB 23 44,777
GB 28 at Min 16 47,426
LARm 23 at Bal 7 60,238
Pit 3 at StL 6 46,099
NYG 41 at Was 72 50,439

Sun 12/04
Atl 20 at Min 13 37,117
ChiB 16 at Bal 21 60,238
StL 17 at Dal 31 76,965
NYG 40 at Cle 49 61,651
Det 3 at LARm 23 40,039
SF 7 at GB 20 48,725
at Milwaukee, WI
Pit 23 at Phi 27 54,275

Sat 12/10
GB 14 at Bal 10 60,238

Sun 12/11
ChiB 14 at SF 41 37,170
Cle 21 at Phi 33 58,074
Min 28 at Det 16 43,002
StL 10 at Atl 16 57,169
Was 34 at Dal 31 64,198
Pit 47 at NYG 28 62,658

Sat 12/17
Cle 38 at StL 10 47,721

Sun 12/18
Min 28 at ChiB 41 45,191
Bal 30 at SF 14 40,005
Phi 37 at Was 28 50,405
Pit 57 at Atl 33 56,229
Dal 17 at NYG 7 62,735
GB 27 at LARm 23 72,416

1966 NFL Championship

Sun 01/01
GB 34 at Dal 27 74,152

Super Bowl I

Sun 01/15
KC 10 vs GB 35 61,946
at Los Angeles, CA

American Football League 1967

Sun 09/03
Bos 21 at Den 26

Sat 09/09
N KC 25 at Hou 20 28,003
N Bos 14 at SD 28 39,337

Sun 09/10
NYJ 17 at Buf 20 45,748
Den 0 at Oak 51 25,423

Sun 09/17
Den 21 at Mia 35 29,381
Bos 7 at Oak 35 26,289
Hou 20 at Buf 3 41,384

Sun 09/24
NYJ 38 at Den 24 36,272
Hou 3 at SD 13 36,032
Bos 23 at Buf 0 45,748
KC 24 at Mia 0 36,272

Sun 10/01
KC 21 at Oak 23 50,268
Den 6 at Hou 10 21,798
SD 37 at Buf 17 39,310
Mia 7 at NYJ 29 61,240

Sat 10/07
N Oak 14 at NYJ 27 63,106

Sun 10/08
Bos 31 at SD 31 23,620
Buf 17 at Den 16 35,188
Mia 0 at KC 41 45,291

Sun 10/15
Hou 28 at NYJ 28 62,729
KC 31 at SD 45 45,365
Mia 10 at Bos 41 23,955
Oak 24 at Buf 20 45,758

Sun 10/22
SD 38 at Den 21 34,465
Oak 48 at Bos 14 25,057
NYJ 33 at Mia 14 30,049
Hou 24 at KC 19 46,365

Sun 10/29
Buf 3 at Hou 10 30,060
Den 9 at KC 52 44,002
Bos 23 at NYJ 30 62,784
SD 10 at Oak 51 53,474

Sun 11/05
Hou 7 at Bos 18 19,422
Oak 21 at Den 17 29,043
Mia 13 at Buf 35 31,622
NYJ 18 at KC 42 46,642

Sun 11/12
Buf 10 at NYJ 20 62,671
Mia 0 at SD 24 34,760
Hou 20 at Den 18 30,392
KC 33 at Bos 10 23,010

Sun 11/19
Den 21 at Buf 20 30,891
Mia 17 at Oak 31 37,295
SD 17 at KC 16 46,738
NYJ 29 at Bos 24 26,790

Thu 11/23
Oak 44 at KC 22 44,020
Den 20 at SD 24 34,586

Sun 11/26
Bos 6 at Hou 27 28,044
Buf 14 at Mia 17 27,050

Sun 12/03
Mia 14 at Hou 17 20,979
Oak 41 at SD 21 53,474
Buf 13 at KC 23 41,943
Den 33 at NYJ 24 61,615

Sat 12/09
Buf 44 at Bos 16 20,627

Sun 12/10
Oak 19 at Hou 7 36,375
KC 21 at NYJ 7 62,891
SD 24 at Mia 41 23,007

Sat 12/16
SD 17 at Hou 24 19,870

Sun 12/17
NYJ 29 at Oak 38 53,011
Bos 32 at Mia 41 25,969
KC 38 at Den 24 31,660

Sat 12/23
Hou 41 at Mia 10 25,982

Sun 12/24
NYJ 42 at SD 31 34,580
Buf 21 at Oak 28 30,738

1967 AFL Championship

Sun 12/31
Hou 7 at Oak 40 53,330

National Football League 1967

Sun 09/17
Dal 21 at Cle 14 81,039
Det 17 at GB 17 50,861
Atl 31 at Bal 38 56,715
Was 24 at Phi 35 60,709
ChiB 13 at Pit 41 53,365
NYG 37 at StL 20 40,801
LARm 27 at NO 13 80,579
SF 27 at Min 21 39,638

Fri 09/22
N Min 3 at LARm 39 52,255

Sun 09/24
StL 28 at Pit 14 45,579
NYG 24 at Dal 38 66,209
Cle 14 at Det 31 57,383
ChiB 10 at GB 13 50,861
Bal 38 at Phi 6 60,755
Atl 7 at SF 38 30,207
Was 30 at NO 10 74,937

Sun 10/01
Cle 42 at NO 7 77,045
ChiB 17 at Min 7 44,868
Atl 0 at GB 23 49,467
at Milwaukee, WI
Det 28 at StL 38 43,821
SF 7 at Bal 41 60,238
Pit 24 at Phi 34 60,335
LARm 35 at Dal 13 75,229
NYG 34 at Was 38 50,266

Sat 10/07
N Pit 10 at Cle 21 82,949

Sun 10/08
GB 27 at Det 17 57,877
StL 34 at Min 24 40,017
Bal 24 at ChiB 3 47,190
SF 27 at LARm 24 60,424
Dal 17 at Was 14 50,566
NO 21 at NYG 27 62,670
Phi 38 at Atl 7 53,868

Sun 10/15
Det 3 at ChiB 14 46,024
Min 10 at GB 7 49,601
at Milwaukee, WI
LARm 24 at Bal 24 60,238
NO 10 at Dal 14 64,128
NYG 27 at Pit 24 39,782
StL 16 at Cle 20 77,813
SF 28 at Phi 27 60,825
Was 20 at Atl 20 56,238

Sun 10/22
ChiB 0 at Cle 24 83,183
Dal 24 at Pit 21 39,641
Phi 14 at StL 48 46,562
GB 48 at NYG 21 62,585
Was 28 at LARm 28 55,381
NO 13 at SF 27 34,285
Bal 20 at Min 20 47,693
Atl 3 at Det 24 50,601

Sun 10/29
Bal 17 at Was 13 50,574
Cle 34 at NYG 38 62,903
Dal 14 at Phi 21 60,740
Det 45 at SF 3 37,990
LARm 28 at ChiB 17 46,073
Min 20 at Atl 21 52,859
Pit 14 at NO 10 68,911

Mon 10/30
N GB 31 at StL 23 49,792

Sun 11/05
GB 10 at Bal 13 60,238
Atl 7 at Dal 37 54,751
LARm 17 at SF 7 53,194
NYG 24 at Min 27 44,950
Cle 34 at Pit 14 47,131
ChiB 27 at Det 13 55,606
Phi 24 at NO 31 59,596
StL 27 at Was 21 50,480

Sun 11/12
Bal 49 at Atl 7 58,850
Cle 7 at GB 55 50,074
at Milwaukee, WI
Dal 27 at NO 10 83,437
Det 10 at Min 10 40,032
Pit 14 at StL 14 46,994
SF 28 at Was 31 50,326
NYG 7 at ChiB 34 46,223
Phi 17 at LARm 33 57,628

Sun 11/19
Det 7 at Bal 41 60,238
LARm 31 at Atl 3 56,871
Min 10 at Cle 14 68,431
SF 0 at GB 13 50,861
NO 21 at Phi 48 60,751
StL 3 at ChiB 30 47,417
Pit 20 at NYG 28 62,892
Was 27 at Dal 20 75,538

Thu 11/23
StL 21 at Dal 46 68,787
LARm 31 at Det 7 54,389

Sun 11/26
Atl 24 at NO 27 83,437
Bal 26 at SF 9 44,815
GB 17 at ChiB 13 47,513
Min 41 at Pit 27 23,773
Phi 7 at NYG 44 63,027
Was 37 at Cle 42 72,798

Sun 12/03
NO 20 at StL 31 41,171
NYG 14 at Cle 24 78,594
Phi 35 at Was 35 50,451
GB 30 at Min 27 47,693
Atl 3 at LARm 20 40,395
ChiB 28 at SF 14 25,613
Dal 17 at Bal 23 60,238
Pit 24 at Det 14 47,713

Sat 12/09
GB 24 at LARm 27 76,637

Sun 12/10
Phi 17 at Dal 38 55,834
Cle 20 at StL 16 47,782
Det 30 at NYG 7 63,011
Min 10 at ChiB 10 40,110
NO 10 at Bal 30 60,238
SF 34 at Atl 28 51,798
Was 15 at Pit 10 22,251

Sat 12/16
Dal 16 at SF 24 27,182

Sun 12/17
Min 3 at Det 14 44,874
NO 30 at Was 14 50,486
Bal 10 at LARm 34 77,277
StL 14 at NYG 37 62,955
ChiB 23 at Atl 14 54,107
Pit 24 at GB 17 50,861
Cle 24 at Phi 28 60,858

Conference Championships

Sat 12/23
LARm 7 at GB 28 49,861
at Milwaukee, WI

Sun 12/24
Cle 14 at Dal 52 70,786

1967 NFL Championship

Sun 12/31
Dal 17 at GB 21 50,861

Super Bowl II

Sun 01/14
GB 33 vs Oak 14 75,546
at Miami, FL

American Football League 1968

Fri 09/06
N Cin 13 at SD 29 33,686

Sun 09/08
Bos 16 at Buf 7 38,865

Mon 09/09
N KC 26 at Hou 21 45,083

Sat 09/14
N Hou 24 at Mia 10 40,067

Sun 09/15
NYJ 20 at KC 19 48,871
Oak 48 at Buf 6 43,056
Den 10 at Cin 24 25,049

Sat 09/21
N Hou 14 at SD 30 46,217
N Oak 47 at Mia 21 30,021

Sun 09/22
Den 2 at KC 34 48,871
NYJ 47 at Bos 31 29,192
at Birmingham, AL
Buf 23 at Cin 34 24,405

Sat 09/28
N KC 48 at Mia 3 28,501

Sun 09/29
Bos 20 at Den 17 37,024
Oak 24 at Hou 15 46,098
SD 31 at Cin 10 28,642
NYJ 35 at Buf 37 38,044

Sat 10/05
N SD 20 at NYJ 23 63,786
N KC 18 at Buf 7 40,748

Sun 10/06
Cin 7 at Den 10 41,257
Mia 24 at Hou 7 36,109
Bos 10 at Oak 41 44,253

Sat 10/12
N Buf 14 at Mia 14 25,559

Sun 10/13
SD 23 at Oak 14 53,257
Den 21 at NYJ 13 63,052
Cin 3 at KC 13 47,096
Hou 16 at Bos 0 32,502

Sun 10/20
Den 24 at SD 55 42,953
Buf 6 at Bos 23 21,082
Oak 10 at KC 24 50,015
Mia 24 at Cin 22 25,076
NYJ 20 at Hou 14 51,710

Sun 10/27
SD 20 at KC 27 50,344
Bos 14 at NYJ 48 62,351
Mia 14 at Den 21 44,115
Cin 10 at Oak 31 37,083
Hou 30 at Buf 7 34,339

Sun 11/03
Mia 28 at SD 34 37,284
Den 35 at Bos 14 18,304
Buf 21 at NYJ 25 61,452
Hou 27 at Cin 17 24,012
KC 21 at Oak 38 53,357

Sun 11/10
Hou 7 at NYJ 26 60,242
KC 16 at Cin 9 25,537
Mia 21 at Buf 17 28,751
Oak 43 at Den 7 50,002
SD 27 at Bos 17 19,278

Sun 11/17
SD 21 at Buf 6 27,993
NYJ 32 at Oak 43 53,318
Den 17 at Hou 38 36,075
Cin 38 at Mia 21 30,304
Bos 17 at KC 31 48,271

Sun 11/24
NYJ 37 at SD 15 51,175
Buf 32 at Den 34 35,142
Oak 34 at Cin 0 27,116
Mia 34 at Bos 10 18,305

Thu 11/28
Buf 10 at Oak 13 39,883
Hou 10 at KC 24 49,493

Sun 12/01
Cin 14 at Bos 33 17,796
Mia 17 at NYJ 35 61,766
SD 47 at Den 23 35,212

Sat 12/07
Buf 6 at Hou 35 34,110

Sun 12/08
Bos 7 at Mia 38 24,242
Cin 14 at NYJ 27 61,111
Den 27 at Oak 33 47,754
KC 40 at SD 3 51,174

Sat 12/14
KC 30 at Den 7 38,463

Sun 12/15
Bos 17 at Hou 45 34,198
NYJ 31 at Mia 7 32,843
Oak 34 at SD 27 40,698

Western Division Playoff

Sun 12/22
KC 6 at Oak 41 53,357

1968 AFL Championship

Sun 12/29
Oak 23 at NYJ 27 62,627

National Football League 1968

Sat 09/14
N Atl 7 at Min 47 45,563

Sun 09/15
Det 13 at Dal 59 61,382
Cle 24 at NO 10 74,215
NYG 34 at Pit 20 45,698
SF 10 at Bal 27 56,864
Was 38 at ChiB 28 41,321
Phi 13 at GB 30 50,861

Mon 09/16
N LARm 24 at StL 13 49,757

Sun 09/22
ChiB 0 at Det 42 50,688
Bal 28 at Atl 20 50,428
StL 17 at SF 35 27,557
Pit 10 at LARm 45 49,647
NYG 34 at Phi 25 60,858
Was 17 at NO 37 65,941
Min 26 at GB 13 49,346
at Milwaukee, WI
Cle 7 at Dal 28 68,733

Sun 09/29
Was 21 at NYG 48 62,979
ChiB 27 at Min 17 47,644
Det 23 at GB 17 50,861
Dal 45 at Phi 13 60,858
LARm 24 at Cle 6 82,514
Atl 13 at SF 28 27,477
StL 21 at NO 20 79,021
Bal 41 at Pit 7 44,480

Sat 10/05
N Pit 24 at Cle 31 81,865

Sun 10/06
ChiB 7 at Bal 28 60,238
Dal 27 at StL 10 48,296
GB 38 at Atl 7 58,850
Phi 14 at Was 17 50,816
SF 10 at LARm 24 69,520
Det 10 at Min 24 44,289
NO 21 at NYG 38 62,967

Sun 10/13
Min 17 at NO 20 71,105
LARm 16 at GB 14 49,646
at Milwaukee, WI
Det 28 at ChiB 10 46,996
Bal 42 at SF 14 32,822
NYG 21 at Atl 24 49,962
StL 27 at Cle 21 79,349
Phi 14 at Dal 34 72,083
Pit 13 at Was 16 50,659

Sun 10/20
Cle 30 at Bal 20 60,238
Was 14 at StL 41 46,456
Atl 14 at LARm 27 54,443
ChiB 29 at Phi 16 60,858
GB 14 at Det 14 57,302
NO 16 at Pit 12 32,303
SF 26 at NYG 10 62,958
Dal 20 at Min 7 47,644

Sun 10/27
NYG 13 at Was 10 50,839
NO 17 at StL 31 45,476
Min 24 at ChiB 26 46,562
LARm 10 at Bal 27 20,238
SF 14 at Det 7 53,555
Atl 7 at Cle 30 67,732
Phi 3 at Pit 6 26,098

Mon 10/28
N GB 28 at Dal 17 74,604

Sun 11/03
Dal 17 at NO 3 84,728
Cle 33 at SF 21 31,359
StL 45 at Phi 17 59,208
Was 14 at Min 27 47,644
Bal 26 at NYG 0 62,973
ChiB 13 at GB 10 50,861
Pit 41 at Atl 21 47,727
Det 7 at LARm 10 77,982

Sun 11/10
LARm 17 at Atl 10 53,979
NYG 27 at Dal 21 72,163
Pit 28 at StL 28 45,432
SF 19 at ChiB 27 46,978
Was 16 at Phi 10 59,133
Bal 27 at Det 10 55,170
NO 17 at Cle 35 70,125
GB 10 at Min 14 47,644

Sun 11/17
LARm 20 at SF 20 41,815
NO 7 at GB 29 49,644
at Milwaukee, WI
Cle 45 at Pit 24 41,572
Dal 44 at Was 24 50,816
Min 13 at Det 6 48,654
Phi 6 at NYG 7 62,896
StL 0 at Bal 27 60,238
Atl 16 at ChiB 13 44,214

Sun 11/24
SF 45 at Pit 28 21,408
Atl 12 at StL 17 43,246
Dal 34 at ChiB 3 46,667
Min 9 at Bal 21 60,238
GB 27 at Was 7 50,621
Phi 13 at Cle 47 62,338
NO 20 at Det 20 46,152
NYG 21 at LARm 24 68,534

Thu 11/28
Phi 12 at Det 0 47,909
Was 20 at Dal 29 66,076

Sun 12/01
Atl 0 at Bal 44 60,238
LARm 31 at Min 3 47,644
ChiB 23 at NO 17 78,285
GB 20 at SF 27 47,218
StL 20 at Pit 10 22,682
NYG 10 at Cle 45 83,193

Sat 12/07
Bal 16 at GB 3 50,861

Sun 12/08
NO 17 at Phi 29 57,128
ChiB 17 at LARm 16 66,368
Cle 24 at Was 21 50,661
Det 24 at Atl 7 49,437
Min 30 at SF 20 29,049
Pit 7 at Dal 28 55,069
StL 28 at NYG 21 62,709

Sat 12/14
Cle 16 at StL 27 39,746

Sun 12/15
GB 28 at ChiB 27 46,435
Min 24 at Phi 17 54,530
Det 3 at Was 14 50,123
Pit 14 at NO 24 66,131
SF 14 at Atl 12 44,977
Bal 28 at LARm 24 69,397
Dal 28 at NYG 10 62,617

Conference Championships

Sat 12/21
Dal 20 at Cle 31 81,497

Sun 12/22
Min 14 at Bal 24 60,238

1968 NFL Championship

Sun 12/29
Bal 34 at Cle 0 80,628

Super Bowl III

Sun 01/12
NYJ 16 vs Bal 7 75,389
at Miami, FL

American Football League 1969

Sun 09/14
Bos 7 at Den 35 43,679
NYJ 33 at Buf 19 46,165
Mia 21 at Cin 27 24,487
Hou 17 at Oak 21 49,361
KC 27 at SD 9 47,988

Sat 09/20
N Mia 17 at Oak 20 50,277

Sun 09/21
Hou 17 at Buf 3 40,146
SD 20 at Cin 34 26,243
NYJ 19 at Den 21 50,583
KC 31 at Bos 0 22,002

Sun 09/28
Den 28 at Buf 41 40,302
NYJ 27 at SD 34 54,042
Oak 38 at Bos 23 19,069
KC 19 at Cin 24 27,812
Mia 10 at Hou 22 41,086

Sat 10/04
N Oak 20 at Mia 20 35,614
N Cin 14 at SD 21 52,748

Sun 10/05
KC 26 at Den 13 50,564
Buf 14 at Hou 28 46,485
NYJ 23 at Bos 14 25,584

Sat 10/11
N SD 21 at Mia 14 34,585
N Bos 16 at Buf 23 46,201

Sun 10/12
Hou 0 at KC 24 45,805
Oak 24 at Den 14 49,511
NYJ 21 at Cin 7 27,927

Sun 10/19
SD 13 at Bos 10 18,346
Mia 10 at KC 17 48,809
Den 30 at Cin 23 27,920
Buf 21 at Oak 50 54,418

Mon 10/20
Hou 17 at NYJ 26 63,841

Sun 10/26
Cin 22 at KC 42 50,934
Den 21 at Hou 24 45,348
Buf 6 at Mia 24 39,837
Oak 24 at SD 12 54,008
Bos 17 at NYJ 23 62,298

Sun 11/02
Hou 0 at Bos 24 19,006
KC 29 at Buf 7 45,844
SD 0 at Den 13 45,511
Oak 17 at Cin 31 27,927
Mia 31 at NYJ 34 61,761

Sun 11/09
Cin 31 at Hou 31 45,298
SD 3 at KC 27 51,104
Den 10 at Oak 41 54,416
Mia 17 at Bos 16 19,821
Buf 6 at NYJ 16 62,680

Sun 11/16
Hou 20 at Den 20 45,002
SD 16 at Oak 21 54,372
Mia 3 at Buf 28 32,686
Bos 25 at Cin 14 27,927
KC 34 at NYJ 16 63,849

Sun 11/23
Cin 7 at NYJ 40 62,128
Den 24 at SD 45 34,664
Hou 32 at Mia 7 27,281
Buf 21 at Bos 35 25,584
Oak 27 at KC 24 51,982

Thu 11/27
Den 17 at KC 31 48,773
SD 21 at Hou 17 40,065

Sun 11/30
Bos 38 at Mia 23 32,121
at Tampa, FL
Cin 13 at Buf 16 35,122
Oak 27 at NYJ 14 63,865

Sat 12/06
NYJ 34 at Hou 26 51,923

Sun 12/07
Cin 17 at Oak 37 54,427
Den 24 at Mia 27 25,332
Buf 19 at KC 22 47,112
Bos 18 at SD 28 33,146

Sat 12/13
KC 6 at Oak 10 54,443

Sun 12/14
Bos 23 at Hou 27 39,215
Cin 16 at Den 27 42,198
Buf 6 at SD 45 47,582
NYJ 27 at Mia 9 48,108

Divisional Playoffs

Sat 12/20
KC 13 at NYJ 6 62,977

Sun 12/21
Hou 7 at Oak 56 53,539

1969 AFL Championship

Sun 01/04
KC 17 at Oak 7 54,444

National Football League 1969

Sun 09/21
LARm 27 at Bal 20 56,864
Was 26 at NO 20 73,147
Min 23 at NYG 24 62,900
Cle 27 at Phi 20 60,658
StL 3 at Dal 24 62,134
ChiB 0 at GB 17 50,861
SF 12 at Atl 24 45,940
Det 13 at Pit 16 51,360

Sun 09/28
Was 23 at Cle 27 82,581
Pit 27 at Phi 41 60,658
NYG 0 at Det 24 54,358
Bal 14 at Min 52 47,900
Atl 7 at LARm 17 51,031
ChiB 17 at StL 20 50,039
SF 7 at GB 14 48,184
at Milwaukee, WI
Dal 21 at NO 17 79,567

Sun 10/05
Det 28 at Cle 21 82,933
Was 17 at SF 17 35,184
StL 27 at Pit 14 45,011
NO 17 at LARm 36 54,879
Dal 38 at Phi 7 60,658
Bal 21 at Atl 14 57,806
GB 7 at Min 19 60,740
ChiB 24 at NYG 28 62,583

Sun 10/12
Pit 7 at NYG 10 62,987
LARm 27 at SF 21 45,995
Dal 24 at Atl 17 54,833
Cle 27 at NO 17 71,274
GB 28 at Det 17 58,384
StL 17 at Was 33 50,481
Min 31 at ChiB 0 45,757

Mon 10/13
N Phi 20 at Bal 24 56,864

Sat 10/18
N Pit 31 at Cle 42 84,078

Sun 10/19
Atl 21 at SF 7 28,684
NYG 14 at Was 20 50,352
Bal 30 at NO 10 80,636
GB 21 at LARm 34 78,947
Phi 14 at Dal 49 71,509
ChiB 7 at Det 13 54,732
Min 27 at StL 10 49,430

Sun 10/26
SF 24 at Bal 21 60,238
StL 21 at Cle 21 81,186
NO 10 at Phi 13 60,658
Was 14 at Pit 7 36,557
Atl 10 at GB 28 50,861
Det 10 at Min 24 47,900
LARm 9 at ChiB 7 45,985

Mon 10/27
N NYG 3 at Dal 25 58,964

Sun 11/02
GB 38 at Pit 34 46,403
Det 26 at SF 14 35,100
Phi 23 at NYG 20 62,912
NO 51 at StL 42 46,718
LARm 38 at Atl 6 58,850
Was 17 at Bal 41 60,238
ChiB 14 at Min 31 47,900
Dal 10 at Cle 42 84,850

Sun 11/09
GB 6 at Bal 14 60,238
Atl 21 at Det 27 53,242
NO 17 at Dal 33 68,282
SF 30 at LARm 41 73,975
Phi 28 at Was 28 50,502
Pit 7 at ChiB 38 45,856
Cle 3 at Min 51 47,900
NYG 17 at StL 42 49,194

Sun 11/16
StL 0 at Det 20 51,749
ChiB 31 at Atl 48 53,722
Cle 24 at Pit 3 47,670
Dal 41 at Was 28 50,474
NO 25 at NYG 24 62,927
LARm 23 at Phi 17 60,658
Min 9 at GB 7 48,321
at Milwaukee, WI
Bal 17 at SF 20 38,472

Sun 11/23
Bal 24 at ChiB 21 45,455
Det 16 at GB 10 50,861
Atl 20 at Was 27 50,345
Dal 23 at LARm 24 79,105
Pit 14 at Min 52 47,202
NYG 17 at Cle 28 80,595
SF 38 at NO 43 71,448
Phi 34 at StL 30 45,512

Thu 11/27
Min 27 at Det 0 57,906
SF 24 at Dal 24 62,348

Sun 11/30
Cle 28 at ChiB 24 45,050
NYG 10 at GB 20 48,156
at Milwaukee, WI
Phi 17 at NO 26 72,805
Atl 6 at Bal 13 60,238
LARm 24 at Was 13 50,352
Pit 10 at StL 47 43,721

Sat 12/06
ChiB 21 at SF 42 32,826

Sun 12/07
Was 34 at Phi 29 60,658
GB 7 at Cle 20 82,137
Dal 10 at Pit 7 24,990
NO 17 at Atl 45 51,021
Det 17 at Bal 17 60,238
StL 6 at NYG 49 62,973
Min 20 at LARm 13 80,430

Sat 12/13
Bal 10 at Dal 27 63,191

Sun 12/14
Cle 27 at StL 21 44,924
Atl 27 at Phi 3 60,658
GB 21 at ChiB 3 45,216
NO 14 at Was 17 50,354
NYG 21 at Pit 17 21,067
LARm 0 at Det 28 53,256
SF 7 at Min 10 43,028

Sun 12/21
StL 28 at GB 45 50,861
Phi 13 at SF 14 25,391
Bal 13 at LARm 7 73,326
Was 10 at Dal 20 56,924
Pit 24 at NO 27 72,256
Min 3 at Atl 10 52,872
Det 20 at ChiB 3 41,879
Cle 14 at NYG 27 62,966

Conference Championships

Sat 12/27
LARm 20 at Min 23 47,900

Sun 12/28
Cle 38 at Dal 14 69,321

1969 NFL Championship

Sun 01/04
Cle 7 at Min 27 47,900

Super Bowl IV

Sun 01/11
Min 7 vs KC 23 80,562
at New Orleans, LA

National Football League 1970

Fri 09/18
N StL 13 at LARm 34 63,130

Sat 09/19
N ChiB 24 at NYG 16 62,936

Sun 09/20
Atl 14 at NO 3 77,042
Dal 17 at Phi 7 59,728
KC 10 at Min 27 47,900
Den 25 at Buf 10 34,882
Mia 14 at Bos 27 32,607
Oak 21 at Cin 31 56,616
Det 40 at GB 0 56,263
Bal 16 at SD 14 47,782
Hou 19 at Pit 7 45,538
Was 17 at SF 26 34,984

Mon 09/21
N NYJ 21 at Cle 31 85,703

Sun 09/27
Cle 31 at SF 34 37,502
Atl 24 at GB 27 56,263
NYG 10 at Dal 28 57,236
LARm 19 at Buf 0 46,206
Pit 13 at Den 16 50,705
Phi 16 at ChiB 20 53,643
Was 17 at StL 27 44,246
Cin 3 at Det 38 58,202
NO 0 at Min 26 47,900
Mia 20 at Hou 10 39,840
NYJ 31 at Bos 21 36,040
Oak 27 at SD 27 42,109

Mon 09/28
N KC 44 at Bal 24 53,911

Sat 10/03
N Pit 7 at Cle 15 84,349
N Oak 13 at Mia 20 57,140

Sun 10/04
Dal 7 at StL 20 50,780
Min 10 at GB 13 47,967
at Milwaukee, WI
NYG 10 at NO 14 69,126
Bal 14 at Bos 6 38,235
KC 13 at Den 26 50,705
Hou 20 at Cin 13 55,094
NYJ 31 at Buf 34 46,206
SD 10 at LARm 37 69,564
SF 20 at Atl 21 58,850
Was 33 at Phi 21 60,658

Mon 10/05
N ChiB 14 at Det 28 58,210

Sat 10/10
N Mia 20 at NYJ 6 62,712

Sun 10/11
Atl 0 at Dal 13 53,611
SF 20 at LARm 6 77,272
Bos 10 at KC 23 50,698
NO 17 at StL 24 45,294
Bal 24 at Hou 20 48,050
Det 10 at Was 31 50,414
Cin 27 at Cle 30 83,520
Den 23 at Oak 35 53,436
Phi 23 at NYG 30 62,820
Buf 10 at Pit 23 42,140
Min 24 at ChiB 0 45,485

Mon 10/12
N GB 22 at SD 20 53,064

Sun 10/18
Bal 29 at NYJ 22 63,301
SD 20 at ChiB 7 45,278
KC 27 at Cin 19 57,265
NO 20 at SF 20 39,446
LARm 31 at GB 21 56,263
Mia 33 at Buf 14 41,312
Pit 7 at Hou 3 42,799
Det 41 at Cle 24 83,577
StL 35 at Phi 20 59,002
NYG 16 at Bos 0 39,091
Dal 13 at Min 54 47,900
Atl 10 at Den 24 50,705

Mon 10/19
N Was 20 at Oak 34 54,471

Sun 10/25
Det 16 at ChiB 10 45,632
Phi 17 at GB 30 48,022
at Milwaukee, WI
Cin 0 at Was 20 50,415
Dal 27 at KC 16 51,158
StL 17 at NYG 35 62,984
Den 14 at SF 19 39,515
Buf 10 at NYJ 6 62,712
Hou 31 at SD 31 41,427
NO 14 at Atl 32 58,850
Cle 28 at Mia 0 75,313
Bos 3 at Bal 27 60,240
Pit 14 at Oak 31 54,423

Mon 10/26
N LARm 3 at Min 13 47,900

Sun 11/01
Mia 0 at Bal 35 60,240
Hou 0 at StL 44 47,911
Was 19 at Den 3 50,705
Phi 17 at Dal 21 55,736
NYG 22 at NYJ 10 63,903
Min 30 at Det 17 58,210
Buf 45 at Bos 10 31,148
LARm 30 at NO 17 77,861
GB 10 at SF 26 59,335
ChiB 23 at Atl 14 58,850
SD 27 at Cle 10 80,047
Oak 17 at KC 17 51,334

Mon 11/02
N Cin 10 at Pit 21 38,968

Sun 11/08
SF 37 at ChiB 16 45,607
Hou 9 at KC 24 49,810
NYJ 17 at Pit 21 50,028
Cin 43 at Buf 14 43,587
Min 19 at Was 10 50,415
Den 21 at SD 24 48,327
Mia 17 at Phi 24 58,171
Atl 10 at LARm 10 67,232
Cle 20 at Oak 23 54,463
Bos 0 at StL 31 46,466
Det 17 at NO 19 66,910
Dal 20 at NYG 23 62,938

Mon 11/09
N Bal 13 at GB 10 48,063
at Milwaukee, WI

Sun 11/15
Atl 13 at Phi 13 55,425
Buf 17 at Bal 17 60,240
Det 20 at Min 24 47,900
KC 31 at Pit 14 50,081
Cle 10 at Cin 14 60,007

SD 16 at Bos 14 30,597
ChiB 19 at GB 20 56,263
SF 30 at Hou 20 43,040
NO 10 at Mia 21 42,866
Was 33 at NYG 35 62,915
Oak 24 at Den 19 50,959
NYJ 31 at LARm 20 76,378

Mon 11/16
N StL 38 at Dal 0 69,323

Sun 11/22
GB 3 at Min 10 47,900
Bos 3 at NYJ 17 61,822
Den 31 at NO 6 66,837
SF 7 at Det 28 56,232
Bal 17 at Mia 34 67,699
LARm 17 at Atl 7 58,850
StL 6 at KC 6 50,711
Dal 45 at Was 21 50,415
SD 17 at Oak 20 54,594
Buf 13 at ChiB 31 41,015
Pit 7 at Cin 34 59,276
Hou 14 at Cle 28 74,723

Mon 11/23
N NYG 20 at Phi 23 59,117

Thu 11/26
Oak 14 at Det 28 56,597
GB 3 at Dal 16 67,182

Sun 11/29
Bos 14 at Buf 10 31,427
Min 10 at NYJ 20 62,333
NO 6 at Cin 26 59,342
NYG 27 at Was 24 50,415
SD 14 at KC 26 50,315
LARm 30 at SF 13 59,602
Phi 14 at StL 23 46,581
Den 21 at Hou 31 35,733
ChiB 20 at Bal 21 60,240
Cle 9 at Pit 28 50,214

Mon 11/30
N Mia 20 at Atl 7 54,036

Sat 12/05
ChiB 13 at Min 16 47,900

Sun 12/06
NO 16 at LARm 34 66,410
Den 0 at KC 16 50,454
Buf 6 at NYG 20 62,870
Bos 20 at Mia 37 51,032
StL 3 at Det 16 56,362
GB 20 at Pit 12 46,418
Was 0 at Dal 34 57,936
Oak 14 at NYJ 13 62,905
Phi 10 at Bal 29 60,240
Atl 20 at SF 24 41,387
Cin 17 at SD 14 41,461

Mon 12/07
N Cle 21 at Hou 10 50,582

Sat 12/12
KC 6 at Oak 20 54,596
Dal 6 at Cle 2 75,458

Sun 12/13
SF 38 at NO 27 61,940
Phi 6 at Was 24 50,415
NYG 34 at StL 17 50,845
Pit 16 at Atl 27 54,162
Cin 30 at Hou 20 34,435
SD 17 at Den 17 50,959
NYJ 10 at Mia 16 75,099
Bal 20 at Buf 14 34,346
Min 35 at Bos 14 37,819
GB 17 at ChiB 35 44,957

Mon 12/14
N Det 28 at LARm 23 79,441

Sat 12/19
NYJ 20 at Bal 35 60,240

Sun 12/20
GB 0 at Det 20 57,387
ChiB 24 at NO 3 63,518
Cle 27 at Den 13 51,001
SF 38 at Oak 7 54,535
Min 37 at Atl 7 57,992
KC 13 at SD 31 41,379
Bos 7 at Cin 45 60,157
Pit 20 at Phi 30 55,252
Hou 10 at Dal 52 50,504
Buf 7 at Mia 45 70,990
StL 27 at Was 28 50,415
LARm 31 at NYG 3 62,870

AFC/NFC Divisional Playoffs

Sat 12/26
Cin 0 at Bal 17 51,127
Det 0 at Dal 5 73,167

Sun 12/27
SF 17 at Min 14 41,050
Mia 14 at Oak 21 54,401

1970 AFC/NFC Championships

Sun 01/03
Oak 17 at Bal 27 56,368
Dal 17 at SF 10 59,625

Super Bowl V

Sun 01/17
Bal 16 vs Dal 13 79,204
at Miami, FL

National Football League 1971

Sun 09/19
KC 14 at SD 21 54,061
LARm 20 at NO 24 70,915
Phi 14 at Cin 37 55,880
Pit 15 at ChiB 17 55,049
Mia 10 at Den 10 51,228
Hou 0 at Cle 31 73,387
NYG 42 at GB 40 56,263
Was 24 at StL 17 46,805
SF 17 at Atl 20 56,990
Dal 49 at Buf 37 46,206
NYJ 0 at Bal 22 56,458
Oak 6 at NE 20 55,405

Mon 09/20
N Min 16 at Det 13 54,418

Sun 09/26
ChiB 20 at Min 17 47,900
Atl 20 at LARm 20 57,895
Cle 14 at Bal 13 56,837
Was 30 at NYG 3 62,795
SF 38 at NO 20 81,595
KC 20 at Hou 16 46,498
Mia 29 at Buf 14 45,139
Cin 10 at Pit 21 44,448
Det 34 at NE 7 61,057
Oak 34 at SD 0 54,084
Den 13 at GB 34 47,957
at Milwaukee, WI
Dal 42 at Phi 7 65,358

Mon 09/27
N NYJ 10 at StL 17 50,358

Sun 10/03
SF 31 at Phi 3 65,358
ChiB 3 at LARm 17 66,957
NYG 21 at StL 20 49,571
SD 17 at Pit 21 44,339
Atl 38 at Det 41 54,418
NYJ 14 at Mia 10 70,670
NO 13 at Hou 13 47,966
Buf 0 at Min 19 47,900
Cin 17 at GB 20 56,263
Bal 23 at NE 3 61,232
Was 20 at Dal 16 61,554
KC 16 at Den 3 51,200

Mon 10/04
N Oak 34 at Cle 20 84,285

Sun 10/10
Pit 17 at Cle 27 83,391
Bal 43 at Buf 0 46,206
NO 14 at ChiB 35 55,049
Hou 13 at Was 22 53,041
NYJ 0 at NE 20 61,357
StL 26 at Atl 9 58,850
SD 10 at KC 31 50,514
LARm 20 at SF 13 44,000
GB 28 at Det 31 54,418
Mia 23 at Cin 13 60,099
Oak 27 at Den 16 51,200
Min 13 at Phi 0 65,358

Mon 10/11
N NYG 13 at Dal 20 63,378

Sun 10/17
ChiB 0 at SF 13 44,133
StL 0 at Was 20 53,041
Det 31 at Hou 7 45,885
NE 3 at Mia 41 58,822
Phi 10 at Oak 34 54,615
LARm 24 at Atl 16 58,850
Bal 31 at NYG 7 62,860
Buf 17 at NYJ 28 61,948
SD 16 at Den 20 51,200
Min 24 at GB 13 56,263
Cle 27 at Cin 24 60,284
Dal 14 at NO 24 83,088

Mon 10/18
N Pit 16 at KC 38 49,533

Sat 10/23
N Buf 3 at SD 20 49,261

Sun 10/24
Cin 27 at Oak 31 54,699
Was 20 at KC 27 51,989
Den 27 at Cle 0 75,674
Mia 30 at NYJ 14 62,130
GB 13 at LARm 30 75,351
SF 26 at StL 14 50,419
NO 6 at Atl 28 58,850
ChiB 28 at Det 23 54,418
Hou 16 at Pit 23 45,872
NYG 7 at Phi 23 65,358
NE 21 at Dal 44 65,708

Mon 10/25
N Bal 3 at Min 10 49,784

Sun 10/31
NYJ 21 at SD 49 44,786
Min 17 at NYG 10 62,829
Dal 19 at ChiB 23 55,049
StL 28 at Buf 23 40,040
Mia 20 at LARm 14 72,903
NO 14 at Was 24 53,041
Den 16 at Phi 17 65,358
NE 10 at SF 27 45,092
Atl 31 at Cle 14 76,825
KC 20 at Oak 20 54,715
Pit 21 at Bal 34 60,238
Cin 6 at Hou 10 37,947

Mon 11/01
N Det 14 at GB 14 47,961
at Milwaukee, WI

Sun 11/07
Buf 0 at Mia 34 61,016
Phi 7 at Was 7 53,041
Atl 9 at Cin 6 59,604
SD 17 at NYG 35 62,905
Dal 16 at StL 13 50,486
SF 13 at Min 9 49,784
Oak 21 at NO 21 83,102
Cle 9 at Pit 26 50,202
Det 24 at Den 20 51,200
KC 10 at NYJ 13 62,812
Hou 20 at NE 28 53,155
GB 17 at ChiB 14 55,049

Mon 11/08
N LARm 17 at Bal 24 57,722

Sun 11/14
NYG 21 at Atl 17 58,850
Hou 21 at Oak 41 54,705
Pit 21 at Mia 24 66,435
Buf 33 at NE 38 57,446
Cle 7 at KC 13 50,388
Bal 14 at NYJ 13 63,947
LARm 21 at Det 13 54,418
Phi 7 at Dal 20 60,178
Was 15 at ChiB 16 55,049
Cin 24 at Den 10 51,200
NO 26 at SF 20 45,138
GB 0 at Min 3 49,784

Mon 11/15
N StL 17 at SD 20 46,486

Sun 11/21
SD 33 at Oak 34 54,681
SF 6 at LARm 17 80,050
Dal 13 at Was 0 53,041
Den 10 at KC 28 49,945
NYJ 20 at Buf 7 41,577
Min 23 at NO 10 83,130
NYG 13 at Pit 17 50,008
Phi 37 at StL 20 48,658
Hou 13 at Cin 28 59,390
NE 7 at Cle 27 65,238
Det 28 at ChiB 3 55,049
Bal 14 at Mia 17 75,312

Mon 11/22
N GB 21 at Atl 28 58,850

Thu 11/25
LARm 21 at Dal 28 66,595
KC 21 at Det 32 54,418

Sun 11/28
Atl 7 at Min 24 49,784
Den 22 at Pit 10 39,710
StL 24 at NYG 7 62,878
Was 20 at Phi 13 65,358
NE 20 at Buf 27 27,166
SF 24 at NYJ 21 63,936
SD 0 at Cin 31 59,580
Cle 37 at Hou 24 37,921
Bal 37 at Oak 14 54,689
NO 29 at GB 21 48,035
at Milwaukee, WI

Mon 11/29
N ChiB 3 at Mia 34 75,312

Sat 12/04
NYJ 10 at Dal 52 66,689

Sun 12/05
Phi 23 at Det 20 54,418
NO 28 at LARm 45 73,610
GB 16 at StL 16 50,443
Cin 27 at Cle 31 82,705
ChiB 3 at Den 6 51,200
NYG 7 at Was 23 53,041
Mia 13 at NE 34 61,457
Buf 0 at Bal 24 58,476
Pit 3 at Hou 29 37,778
Min 14 at SD 30 54,505
Oak 13 at Atl 24 58,850

Mon 12/06
N KC 26 at SF 17 45,306

Sat 12/11
Mia 3 at Bal 14 60,238
Det 10 at Min 29 49,784

Sun 12/12
Cle 21 at NO 17 72,794
ChiB 10 at GB 31 56,263
Dal 42 at NYG 14 62,815
StL 7 at Phi 19 65,358
Atl 3 at SF 24 44,582
Pit 21 at Cin 13 60,022
Oak 14 at KC 16 51,215
Den 17 at SD 45 44,347
Hou 20 at Buf 14 28,107
NE 6 at NYJ 13 63,175

Mon 12/13
N Was 38 at LARm 24 80,402

Sat 12/18
StL 12 at Dal 31 66,672

Sun 12/19
Cle 20 at Was 13 53,041
SD 33 at Hou 49 35,959
Buf 9 at KC 22 48,121
Cin 21 at NYJ 35 63,151
Den 13 at Oak 21 56,651
GB 6 at Mia 27 76,812
Phi 41 at NYG 28 62,774
Det 27 at SF 31 45,580
LARm 23 at Pit 14 45,233
Min 27 at ChiB 10 55,049
Atl 24 at NO 20 75,554
NE 21 at Bal 17 57,942

Divisional Playoffs

Sat 12/25
Dal 20 at Min 12 47,307
Mia 27 at KC 24# 45,822

Sun 12/26
Bal 20 at Cle 3 70,734
Was 20 at SF 24 45,327

1971 AFC/NFC Championships

Sun 01/02
SF 3 at Dal 14 63,409
Bal 0 at Mia 21 76,622

Super Bowl VI

Sun 01/16
Dal 24 vs Mia 3 81,023
at New Orleans, LA

National Football League 1972

Sun 09/17
GB 26 at Cle 10 75,771
NYJ 41 at Buf 24 46,206
NYG 16 at Det 30 54,418
StL 10 at Bal 3 53,625
Phi 6 at Dal 28 55,850
Oak 28 at Pit 34 51,141
Hou 17 at Den 30 51,656
Mia 20 at KC 10 79,829
Cin 31 at NE 7 60,999
NO 14 at LARm 34 66,303
Atl 37 at ChiB 21 55,701
SD 3 at SF 34 59,438

Mon 09/18
N Was 24 at Min 21 47,900

Sun 09/24
NYJ 44 at Bal 34 56,626
Dal 23 at NYG 14 62,725
StL 10 at Was 24 53,039
Den 14 at SD 37 49,048
Min 34 at Det 10 54,418
Hou 13 at Mia 34 77,821

Cle 27 at Phi 17 65,720
SF 20 at Buf 27 45,845
Pit 10 at Cin 15 54,292
Atl 20 at NE 21 60,999
LARm 13 at ChiB 13 55,701
Oak 20 at GB 14 56,263

Mon 09/25
N KC 20 at NO 17 70,793

Sun 10/01
LARm 3 at Atl 31 57,122
Cin 6 at Cle 27 81,564
Dal 13 at GB 16 47,103
at Milwaukee, WI
KC 45 at Den 24 51,656
SF 37 at NO 2 69,840
Was 23 at NE 24 60,999
Mia 16 at Min 14 47,900
Det 38 at ChiB 24 55,701
Pit 25 at StL 19 49,140
Bal 17 at Buf 0 46,206
SD 17 at Oak 17 53,455
NYJ 20 at Hou 26 51,423

Mon 10/02
N NYG 27 at Phi 12 65,720

Sun 10/08
SF 7 at LARm 31 77,382
Den 10 at Cin 21 55,812
Phi 0 at Was 14 53,039
NE 14 at Buf 38 41,749
Mia 27 at NYJ 17 63,841
ChiB 17 at GB 20 56,263
Pit 13 at Dal 17 65,682
StL 19 at Min 17 49,687
KC 31 at Cle 7 83,819
Det 26 at Atl 23 58,850
SD 23 at Bal 20 55,459
NO 21 at NYG 45 62,507

Mon 10/09
N Oak 34 at Hou 0 51,378

Sun 10/15
LARm 34 at Phi 3 65,720
Dal 21 at Bal 0 58,992
NYG 23 at SF 17 58,606

Min 23 at Den 20 51,656
Atl 21 at NO 14 66,294
ChiB 17 at Cle 0 72,339
NYJ 41 at NE 13 60,999
Cin 23 at KC 16 79,068
Was 33 at StL 3 50,454
Buf 16 at Oak 28 53,501
Hou 7 at Pit 24 42,929
SD 10 at Mia 24 78,212

Mon 10/16
N GB 24 at Det 23 54,418

Sun 10/22
Atl 10 at GB 9 47,967
at Milwaukee, WI
Buf 23 at Mia 24 78,175
NO 20 at SF 20 59,167
Cin 12 at LARm 15 73,385
Cle 23 at Hou 17 38,113
Dal 20 at Was 24 53,039
StL 21 at NYG 27 62,756
SD 20 at Det 34 54,371
NE 3 at Pit 33 46,081
Den 30 at Oak 23 53,551
Phi 21 at KC 20 78,389
Bal 20 at NYJ 24 62,948

Mon 10/23
N Min 10 at ChiB 13 55,701

Sun 10/29
Phi 3 at NO 21 65,664
Pit 38 at Buf 21 45,882
Hou 7 at Cin 30 59,409
Cle 27 at Den 20 51,656
ChiB 27 at StL 10 50,464
SF 49 at Atl 14 58,850
KC 26 at SD 14 54,533
LARm 17 at Oak 45 54,660
Mia 23 at Bal 0 60,000
Min 27 at GB 13 56,263
Was 23 at NYG 16 62,878
NE 10 at NYJ 34 62,867

Mon 10/30
N Det 24 at Dal 28 65,378

Sun 11/05
StL 6 at Phi 6 65,720
Hou 0 at Cle 20 61,985
Dal 34 at SD 28 54,476
NO 6 at Min 37 49,784
Mia 30 at Buf 16 46,206
ChiB 0 at Det 14 54,418
Atl 7 at LARm 20 75,018
Oak 14 at KC 27 82,094
Den 17 at NYG 29 62,689
Cin 17 at Pit 40 50,350
SF 24 at GB 34 47,897
at Milwaukee, WI
Was 35 at NYJ 17 62,692

Mon 11/06
N Bal 24 at NE 17 60,999

Sun 11/12
Buf 3 at NYJ 41 62,853
KC 7 at Pit 16 50,350
Det 14 at Min 16 49,784
NO 20 at Atl 36 58,850
Phi 18 at Hou 17 34,175
StL 24 at Dal 33 65,218
Bal 21 at SF 24 61,214
Oak 20 at Cin 14 59,485
GB 23 at ChiB 17 55,701
NYG 13 at Was 27 53,039
Den 16 at LARm 10 65,398
NE 0 at Mia 52 78,148

Mon 11/13
N Cle 21 at SD 17 54,205

Sun 11/19
Dal 28 at Phi 7 65,720
Bal 20 at Cin 19 49,512
NYG 13 at StL 7 48,014
SD 27 at KC 17 79,011
NYJ 24 at Mia 28 78,166
NO 14 at Det 27 53,752
GB 23 at Hou 10 41,752
SF 34 at ChiB 21 65,201
Min 45 at LARm 41 77,982
Pit 24 at Cle 26 83,009
Buf 27 at NE 24 60,999
Oak 37 at Den 20 51,656

Mon 11/20
N Atl 13 at Was 24 53,039

Thu 11/23
SF 31 at Dal 10 65,124
NYJ 20 at Det 37 54,418

Sun 11/26
GB 16 at Was 21 53,039
Min 10 at Pit 23 50,348
Phi 10 at NYG 62 62,586
KC 3 at Oak 26 54,801
LARm 16 at NO 19 64,325
Buf 10 at Cle 27 70,104
NE 0 at Bal 31 54,907
Den 20 at Atl 23 58,850
Cin 13 at ChiB 3 55,701
Hou 20 at SD 34 46,289

Mon 11/27
N StL 10 at Mia 31 78,190

Sun 12/03
Den 21 at KC 24 66,725
NYG 10 at Cin 13 59,523
Cle 0 at Pit 30 50,350
NO 17 at NYJ 18 62,496
Buf 7 at Bal 35 55,390
ChiB 10 at Min 23 49,784
Det 7 at GB 33 56,263
Mia 37 at NE 21 60,999
Dal 27 at StL 6 49,797
Hou 10 at Atl 20 58,850
Was 23 at Phi 7 65,720
Oak 21 at SD 19 54,611

Mon 12/04
N LARm 26 at SF 16 61,214

Sat 12/09
Cle 27 at Cin 24 59,524
Was 24 at Dal 34 65,136

Sun 12/10
SD 13 at Den 38 51,478
Mia 23 at NYG 13 62,728
ChiB 21 at Phi 12 65,720
GB 23 at Min 7 49,784
Atl 0 at SF 20 61,214

Det 21 at Buf 21 41,583
LARm 14 at StL 24 36,873
NE 17 at NO 10 64,889
Pit 9 at Hou 3 36,528
Bal 10 at KC 24 44,175

Mon 12/11
N NYJ 16 at Oak 24 54,843

Sat 12/16
Bal 0 at Mia 16 78,202
Min 17 at SF 20 61,214

Sun 12/17
NYG 23 at Dal 3 64,602
KC 17 at Atl 14 58,860
Cle 26 at NYJ 10 62,614
NE 21 at Den 45 51,656
Det 34 at LARm 17 71,761
Pit 24 at SD 2 52,873
ChiB 21 at Oak 28 54,711
Buf 24 at Was 17 53,039
Cin 61 at Hou 17 32,428
GB 30 at NO 20 65,881
Phi 23 at StL 24 34,872

AFC/NFC Divisional Playoffs

Sat 12/23
Dal 30 at SF 28 61,214
Oak 7 at Pit 13 50,350

Sun 12/24
GB 3 at Was 16 53,140
Cle 14 at Mia 20 78,196

1972 AFC/NFC Championships

Sun 12/31
Dal 3 at Was 26 53,129
Mia 21 at Pit 17 50,350

Super Bowl VII

Sun 01/14
Mia 14 vs Was 7 90,182
at Los Angeles, CA

National Football League 1973

Sun 09/16
Atl 62 at NO 7 66,428
StL 34 at Phi 23 61,103
LARm 23 at KC 13 62,315
Buf 31 at NE 13 56,119
Cin 10 at Den 28 49,059
SD 0 at Was 38 52,718
SF 13 at Mia 21 68,275
Hou 14 at NYG 34 57,979
Oak 16 at Min 24 44,818
Bal 14 at Cle 24 74,303
Det 10 at Pit 24 48,913
Dal 20 at ChiB 17 49,790

Mon 09/17
N NYJ 7 at GB 23 47,124
at Milwaukee, WI

Sun 09/23
Mia 7 at Oak 12 74,121
Atl 0 at LARm 31 61,197
Hou 10 at Cin 24 51,823
KC 10 at NE 7 57,918
Phi 23 at NYG 23 57,138
NYJ 34 at Bal 10 55,942
Det 13 at GB 13 55,495
Was 27 at StL 34 50,316
Min 22 at ChiB 13 52,035
SF 36 at Den 34 51,706
Cle 6 at Pit 33 49,396
Buf 7 at SD 34 47,588

Mon 09/24
N NO 3 at Dal 40 52,715

Sun 09/30
NYG 10 at Cle 12 76,065
Was 28 at Phi 7 64,147

NE 23 at Mia 44 62,508
Oak 3 at KC 16 72,631
NO 10 at Bal 14 52,393
StL 10 at Dal 45 64,729
NYJ 7 at Buf 9 77,425
Cin 20 at SD 13 46,733
GB 3 at Min 11 48,176
LARm 40 at SF 20 57,487
Pit 36 at Hou 7 39,331
ChiB 33 at Den 14 51,159

Mon 10/01
N Atl 6 at Det 31 45,599

Sun 10/07
Cin 10 at Cle 17 70,805
Bal 16 at NE 24 57,044
SF 13 at Atl 9 51,107
NYJ 3 at Mia 31 63,850
Den 14 at KC 16 71,414
SD 21 at Pit 38 48,795
Min 23 at Det 9 49,544
LARm 31 at Hou 26 34,875
Oak 17 at StL 10 49,051
GB 16 at NYG 14 70,050
at New Haven, CT
Phi 26 at Buf 27 72,364
ChiB 16 at NO 21 56,561

Mon 10/08
N Dal 7 at Was 14 54,314

Sun 10/14
Den 48 at Hou 20 32,801
Pit 7 at Cin 19 55,819
Det 13 at NO 20 57,810
Phi 27 at StL 24 44,400
Dal 31 at LARm 37 81,428

NYJ 9 at NE 7 57,781
Bal 13 at Buf 31 78,875
Min 17 at SF 13 56,438
KC 10 at GB 10 46,583
at Milwaukee, WI
ChiB6 at Atl 46 47,342
Oak 27 at SD 17 50,672
Was 21 at NYG 3 70,168

Mon 10/15
N Mia 17 at Cle 9 72,070

Sun 10/21
NYG 28 at Dal 45 58,741
StL 13 at Was 31 54,381
KC 6 at Cin 14 56,397
NYJ 14 at Pit 26 48,682
Bal 29 at Det 27 48,058
Buf 6 at Mia 27 65,241
Atl 41 at SD 0 41,527
NE 13 at ChiB 10 47,643
Hou 13 at Cle 42 61,146
NO 0 at SF 40 52,881
GB 7 at LARm 24 80,558
Phi 21 at Min 28 47,478

Mon 10/22
N Oak 23 at Den 23 51,270

Sun 10/28
Was 3 at NO 19 66,315
Oak 34 at Bal 21 54,147
Den 40 at NYJ 28 55,108
Hou 14 at ChiB 35 43,755
Atl 17 at SF 3 56,825
Dal 16 at Phi 30 63,300
SD 16 at Cle 16 68,244
Cin 13 at Pit 20 45,761

Mia 30 at NE 14 57,919
NYG 27 at StL 35 47,589
GB 0 at Det 34 43,616
LARm 9 at Min 10 47,787

Mon 10/29
N KC 14 at Buf 23 76,071

Sun 11/04
Cin 10 at Dal 38 54,944
NE 23 at Phi 24 65,070
Den 17 at StL 17 46,565
Hou 31 at Bal 27 46,207
Cle 3 at Min 26 46,722
KC 19 at SD 0 50,234
ChiB 31 at GB 17 53,231
LARm 13 at Atl 15 55,837
SF 20 at Det 30 49,310
Buf 0 at NO 13 74,770
NYG 0 at Oak 42 51,200
Mia 24 at NYJ 14 57,491

Mon 11/05
N Was 16 at Pit 21 49,220

Sun 11/11
StL 21 at GB 25 52,922
Bal 0 at Mia 44 60,332
Dal 23 at NYG 10 70,128
NE 13 at NYJ 33 51,034
Pit 17 at Oak 9 47,535
Cin 16 at Buf 13 76,927
Atl 44 at Phi 27 63,114
Cle 23 at Hou 13 37,230
Det 7 at Min 28 47,911
SF 9 at Was 33 54,267
SD 19 at Den 30 51,034
NO 7 at LARm 29 70,358

Mon 11/12
N ChiB 7 at KC 19 70,664

Sun 11/18
NYJ 14 at Cin 20 55,745
StL 13 at NYG 24 65,795
SF 13 at LARm 31 78,358
Hou 14 at KC 38 68,444
Cle 7 at Oak 3 47,398
GB 24 at NE 33 60,525
Phi 10 at Dal 31 59,375
Det 30 at ChiB 7 48,625
Den 23 at Pit 13 48,580
Bal 14 at Was 22 52,675
Mia 17 at Buf 0 77,138
NO 14 at SD 17 34,848

Mon 11/19
Min 14 at Atl 20 56,519

Thu 11/22
Was 20 at Det 0 46,807
Mia 14 at Dal 7 58,0889

Sun 11/25
Buf 24 at Bal 17 52,250
SD 3 at Oak 31 40,195
NE 32 at Hou 0 27,344
StL 24 at Cin 42 50,918
Pit 16 at Cle 21 67,773
NYG 16 at Phi 20 63,086
Atl 28 at NYJ 20 61,327
ChiB 13 at Min 31 48,503
LARm 24 at NO 13 67,192
KC 10 at Den 14 51,331

Mon 11/26
GB 6 at SF 20 49,244

Sun 12/02
Cle 20 at KC 20 70,296
Phi 28 at SF 38 51,155
Dal 22 at Den 10 51,508
NYG 24 at Was 27 52,036
Buf 17 at Atl 6 54,607
Min 0 at Cin 27 57,859
LARm 26 at ChiB 0 47,620
SD 14 at NE 30 58,150
Bal 17 at NYJ 20 51,167
Oak 17 at Hou 6 25,801
NO 10 at GB 30 46,092
Det 20 at StL 16 44,982

Mon 12/03
N Pit 26 at Mia 30 68,901

Sat 12/08
Min 31 at GB 7 53,830
KC 7 at Oak 37 53,061

Sun 12/09
NE 13 at Buf 37 72,470
Mia 3 at Bal 16 41,005
ChiB 7 at Det 40 41,729
SF 10 at NO 16 62,490
Cle 17 at Cin 34 58,266
StL 32 at Atl 10 48,030
Hou 7 at Pit 33 38,004
NYJ 23 at Phi 24 34,621
Den 42 at SD 28 44,954
Was 7 at Dal 27 62,195

Mon 12/10
N NYG 6 at LARm 40 73,328

Sat 12/15
Pit 37 at SF 14 52,252
Det 7 at Mia 34 53,375

Sun 12/16
Buf 34 at NYJ 14 47,740
NE 13 at Bal 18 52,065
Cle 17 at LARm 30 73,948
Dal 30 at StL 3 43,946
Cin 27 at Hou 24 21,955
NO 10 at Atl 14 34,147
Min 31 at NYG 7 70,041
at New Haven, CT
Phi 20 at Was 38 49,484
GB 21 at ChiB 0 29,157
SD 6 at KC 33 43,755
Den 17 at Oak 21 51,910

AFC/NFC Divisional Playoffs

Sat 12/22
Was 20 at Min 27 46,065
Pit 14 at Oak 33 50,094

Sun 12/23
Cin 16 at Mia 34 74,651
LARm 16 at Dal 27 62,081

1973 AFC/NFC Championships

Sun 12/30
Oak 10 at Mia 27 74,384
Min 27 at Dal 10 59,688

Super Bowl VIII

Sun 01/13
Min 7 vs Mia 24 68,142
at Houston, TX

National Football League 1974

Sun 09/15
Mia 24 at NE 34 51,508
NYJ 16 at KC 24 73,959
Det 9 at ChiB 17 48,134
Min 32 at GB 17 55,131
Phi 3 at StL 7 40,322
Dal 24 at Atl 0 52,322
SD 14 at Hou 21 25,317
LARm 17 at Den 10 56,981
Bal 0 at Pit 30 48,890
Was 13 at NYG 10 49,849
SF 17 at NO 13 59,945
Cle 7 at Cin 33 53,113

Mon 09/16
N Oak 20 at Buf 21 79,791

Sun 09/22
NO 0 at LARm 24 57,314
GB 20 at Bal 13 35,873
NE 28 at NYG 20 44.082
NYJ 23 at ChiB 21 50,213
Min 7 at Det 6 44,546
SF 16 at Atl 10 47,686
Hou 7 at Cle 20 55,242
Pit 35 at Den 35# 50,858
KC 7 at Oak 27 48,108
Mia 24 at Buf 16 78,990
StL 17 at Was 10 53,888
SD 20 at Cin 17 51,178

Mon 09/23
N Dal 10 at Phi 13 64,089

Sun 09/29
Cle 7 at StL 29 43,472
Bal 10 at Phi 30 64,205
KC 17 at Hou 7 28,538
ChiB 7 at Min 11 46,217
Oak 17 at Pit 0 48,304
NYJ 12 at Buf 16 76,866
Atl 13 at NO 14 55,025
Cin 21 at SF 3 49,895
LARm 14 at NE 20 59,712
Mia 28 at SD 21 44,706
Det 19 at GB 21 45,970
at Milwaukee, WI
NYG 14 at Dal 6 45,841

Mon 09/30
N Den 3 at Was 30 54,395

Sun 10/06
Was 17 at Cin 28 56,175
Den 17 at KC 14 67,298
Atl 14 at NYG 7 42,379
Bal 3 at NE 42 55,820
Buf 27 at GB 7 51,919
StL 34 at SF 9 47,675
Min 23 at Dal 21 57,847
Phi 13 at SD 7 36,013
Pit 13 at Hou 7 30,049
NO 10 at ChiB 24 45,818
Det 13 at LARm 16 56,599
Oak 40 at Cle 24 65,247

Mon 10/07
N NYJ 17 at Mia 21 61,527

Sun 10/13
NO 17 at Den 33 50,751
ChiB 10 at Atl 13 47,835
NE 24 at NYJ 0 57,828
Oak 14 at SD 10 40,013
Pit 34 at KC 24 65,517
Cin 34 at Cle 24 70,897
Buf 27 at Bal 14 36,314
Mia 17 at Was 20 54,395
Hou 10 at Min 51 48,006
Dal 28 at StL 31 49,885
LARm 6 at GB 17 45,938
at Milwaukee, WI
NYG 7 at Phi 35 64,801

Mon 10/14
N SF 13 at Det 17 45,199

Sun 10/20
SD 7 at Den 27 50,748
NE 28 at Buf 30 78,926
Cin 27 at Oak 30 51,821
Cle 16 at Pit 20 48,100
Bal 35 at NYJ 20 51,745
KC 3 at Mia 9 67,779
Det 20 at Min 16 47,807
SF 14 at LARm 37 67,319
NO 13 at Atl 3 47,217
NYG 3 at Was 24 53,879
StL 31 at Hou 27 26,371
Phi 24 at Dal 31 43,586

Mon 10/21
N GB 9 at ChiB 10 50,623

Sun 10/27
Oak 35 at SF 24 58,542
NE 17 at Min 14 48,177
Den 21 at Cle 23 60,478
ChiB 6 at Buf 16 78,084
Hou 34 at Cin 21 55,434
Bal 7 at Mia 17 65,868
LARm 20 at NYJ 13 56,110
KC 24 at SD 14 33,898
Was 20 at StL 23 49,410
Dal 21 at NYG 7 57,381
GB 17 at Det 19 51,775
Phi 10 at NO 14 57,136

Mon 10/28
N Atl 17 at Pit 24 48,094

Sun 11/03
Hou 27 at NYJ 22 47,218
Oak 28 at Den 17 45,766
Was 17 at GB 6 55,288
Cin 24 at Bal 14 35,110
StL 14 at Dal 17 64,146
NYG 33 at KC 27 61,437
Min 17 at ChiB 0 33,343
Buf 29 at NE 28 58,932
Cle 35 at SD 36 34,087
NO 14 at Det 19 43,256
Phi 0 at Pit 27 47,996
Atl 7 at Mia 42 64,399

Mon 11/04
N LARm 15 at SF 13 57,526

Sun 11/10
SD 14 at KC 7 48,551
Den 17 at Bal 6 32,244
SF 14 at Dal 20 50,018
Det 13 at Oak 35 51,973
NYJ 26 at NYG 20# 64,327
Pit 10 at Cin 17 57,532
Mia 21 at NO 0 68,339
Cle 21 at NE 14 57,263
Was 27 at Phi 20 65,947
ChiB 3 at GB 20 46,567
in Milwaukee, WI
Hou 21 at Buf 9 79,144
Atl 0 at LARm 21 62,133

Mon 11/11
N Min 28 at StL 24 50,183

Sun 11/17
Buf 28 at Mia 35 68,313
Dal 21 at Was 28 54,395
LARm 7 at NO 20 35,727
SF 34 at ChiB 0 42,686
SD 10 at Oak 17 50,178
NYG 19 at Det 20 40,431
Bal 17 at Atl 7 41,278
Pit 26 at Cle 16 77,195
GB 19 at Min 7 47,924
StL 13 at Phi 3 61,982
Cin 3 at Hou 20 44,054
NYJ 21 at NE 16 57,115

Mon 11/18
N KC 42 at Den 34 50,236

Sun 11/24
StL 23 at NYG 21 40,615
Phi 7 at Was 26 54,395
Min 17 at LARm 20 87,138
KC 6 at Cin 33 49,777
Buf 15 at Cle 10 66,504
Den 20 at Oak 17 51,224
Mia 14 at NYJ 17 57,162
Atl 0 at SF 27 45,435
ChiB 17 at Det 34 40,930
SD 0 at GB 34 50,321
NE 27 at Bal 17 33,782
Dal 10 at Hou 0 49,775

Mon 11/25
N Pit 28 at NO 7 69,010

Thu 11/28
Was 23 at Dal 24 63,243
Den 31 at Det 27 51,157

Sun 12/01
NO 9 at Min 29 44,202
GB 14 at Phi 36 42,030
SF 0 at Cle 7 24,559
SD 14 at NYJ 27 44,888
NYG 13 at ChiB 16 18,802
NE 26 at Oak 41 50,120
KC 17 at StL 13 41,863
Bal 0 at Buf 6 75,325
LARm 30 at Atl 7 18,648
Hou 13 at Pit 10 41,195

Mon 12/02
N Cin 3 at Mia 24 71,962

Sat 12/07
Cle 17 at Dal 41 48,754
Atl 10 at Min 23 47,105

Sun 12/08
Mia 17 at Bal 16 33,320
Phi 20 at NYG 7 21,170
GB 6 at SF 7 47,475
StL 0 at NO 14 47,172
Det 23 at Cin 19 45,159
ChiB 21 at SD 28 33,662
Pit 21 at NE 17 52,107
Hou 14 at Den 37 46,942
Buf 10 at NYJ 20 31,982
Oak 7 at KC 6 60,577

Mon 12/09
N Was 23 at LARm 17 84,327

Sat 12/14
Dal 23 at Oak 27 45,840
Min 35 at KC 15 35,480
Cin 3 at Pit 27 42,878

Sun 12/15
Cle 24 at Hou 28 33,299
NO 21 at SF 35 40,418
Den 0 at SD 17 35,756
GB 3 at Atl 10 10,020
NYG 14 at StL 26 47,414
Det 17 at Phi 28 57,157
ChiB 0 at Was 42 52,085
Buf 14 at LARm 19 78,967
NE 27 at Mia 34 56,920
NYJ 45 at Bal 38 31,651

AFC/NFC Divisional Playoffs

Sat 12/21
StL 14 at Min 30 44,626
Mia 26 at Oak 28 52,817

Sun 12/22
Buf 14 at Pit 32 48,321
Was 10 at LARm 19 80,118

1974 AFC/NFC Championships

Sun 12/29
LARm 10 at Min 14 47,404
Pit 24 at Oak 13 53,515

Super Bowl IX

Sun 01/12
Pit 16 vs Min 6 80,997
at New Orleans, LA

National Football League 1975

Sun 09/21
NO 3 at Was 41 54,414
KC 33 at Den 37 51,858
SF 17 at Min 27 46,479
Atl 20 at StL 23 42,172
Pit 37 at SD 0 35,853
Cle 17 at Cin 24 52,874
NYG 23 at Phi 14 60,798
Bal 35 at ChiB 7 51,678
Det 30 at GB 16 50,781
at Milwaukee, WI
NYJ 14 at Buf 42 77,837
Hou 7 at NE 0 51,934
LARm 7 at Dal 18 49,091

Mon 09/22
N Oak 31 at Mia 21 78,744

Sun 09/28
Det 17 at Atl 14 45,218
Buf 30 at Pit 21 49,438
SD 17 at Hou 33 33,765
Cin 21 at NO 0 52,637
StL 31 at Dal 37# 52,417
LARm 23 at SF 14 55,072
Min 42 at Cle 10 63,163
NYJ 30 at KC 24 73,939
Mia 22 at NE 14 59,967
Phi 13 at ChiB 15 48,071
Oak 31 at Bal 20 39,084
NYG 13 at Was 49 54,953

Mon 09/29
N GB 13 at Den 23 52,491

Sun 10/05
NYG 14 at StL 26 44,919
Bal 13 at LARm 24 60,011
NO 7 at Atl 14 29,444
Den 14 at Buf 38 79,798
NE 7 at NYJ 36 57,365
Was 10 at Phi 26 64,397
ChiB 3 at Min 28 47,578
Cin 21 at Hou 19 42,412
SF 20 at KC 3 54,490
Oak 6 at SD 0 31,095
Mia 31 at GB 7 55,396
Pit 42 at Cle 6 73,217

Mon 10/06
N Dal 36 at Det 10 79,384

Sun 10/12
GB 19 at NO 20 51,371
Dal 13 at NYG 7 56,511
NYJ 21 at Min 29 47,739
Atl 17 at SF 3 44,043
Hou 40 at Cle 10 46,531
NE 10 at Cin 27 51,220
Buf 38 at Bal 31 43,907
Den 9 at Pit 20 49,164
ChiB 7 at Det 27 73,477
Oak 10 at KC 42 60,425
Phi 16 at Mia 24 60,127
LARm 13 at SD 10# 37,382

Mon 10/13
N StL 17 at Was 27 54,693

Sun 10/19
Phi 20 at StL 31 45,242
Mia 43 at NYJ 0 47,191
KC 12 at SD 10 26,469
GB 19 at Dal 17 64,189
Atl 7 at LARm 22 60,581

Oak 10 at Cin 14 48,122
Det 19 at Min 25 47,872
Was 10 at Hou 13 49,566
Cle 15 at Den 16 52,540
Bal 10 at NE 21 51,417
NO 21 at SF 35 39,990
ChiB 3 at Pit 34 47,579

Mon 10/20
N NYG 17 at Buf 14 79,426

Sat 10/25
N StL 20 at NYG 13 49,598

Sun 10/26
SD 0 at Oak 25 42,796
SF 16 at NE 24 60,358
Mia 35 at Buf 30 79,080
Cin 21 at Atl 14 45,811
Bal 45 at NYJ 28 55,137
Was 23 at Cle 7 56,702
Dal 20 at Phi 17 64,889
Pit 16 at GB 13 52,258
at Milwaukee, WI
Det 8 at Hou 24 46,904
Den 13 at KC 26 70,043
NO 14 at LARm 38 54,723

Mon 10/27
N Min 13 at ChiB 9 51,259

Sat 11/01
N SD 24 at NYG 35 52,032

Sun 11/02
Pit 30 at Cin 24 58,418
Min 28 at GB 17 55,378
Buf 24 at NYJ 23 58,343
NE 17 at StL 24 45,907
Hou 17 at KC 13 62,989
Cle 7 at Bal 21 35,235
Dal 24 at Was 30# 55,004
Mia 46 at ChiB 13 51,298
Oak 42 at Den 17 52,330
Atl 7 at NO 23 49,342
Det 28 at SF 17 43,209

Mon 11/03
N LARm 42 at Phi 3 64,601

Sun 11/09
Atl 0 at Min 38 43,751
Hou 17 at Pit 24 49,460
Cle 10 at Det 21 74,653
GB 14 at ChiB 27 48,738
Cin 17 at Den 16 49,702
NE 33 at SD 19 24,161
SF 24 at LARm 23 74,064
Was 21 at NYG 13 57,242
Bal 42 at Buf 35 77,320
NO 10 at Oak 48 51,267
NYJ 7 at Mia 27 72,896
StL 24 at Phi 23 60,277

Mon 11/10
N KC 34 at Dal 31 63,539

Sun 11/16
GB 10 at Det 13 76,356
Cle 17 at Oak 38 50,461
Min 20 at NO 7 52,765
Was 17 at StL 20# 49,919
KC 3 at Pit 28 48,803
NYJ 19 at Bal 52 52,097
Den 27 at SD 17 26,048
Mia 19 at Hou 20 48,892
Dal 34 at NE 31 60,905
LARm 16 at Atl 7 44,595
Phi 13 at NYG 10 53,434
ChiB 3 at SF 31 41,728

Mon 11/17
N Buf 24 at Cin 33 56,666

Sun 11/23
SF 16 at NO 6 40,328
NYG 14 at GB 40 50,150
at Milwaukee, WI
Den 21 at Atl 35 28,686
SD 13 at Min 28 43,737
NE 31 at Buf 45 65,655
Bal 33 at Mia 17 61,986
ChiB 10 at LARm 38 58,690
Cin 23 at Cle 35 56,427
Phi 17 at Dal 27 57,893
Oak 26 at Was 23# 53,582
StL 37 at NYJ 6 53,169
Det 21 at KC 24# 55,161

Mon 11/24
N Pit 32 at Hou 9 49,947

Thu 11/27
LARm 20 at Det 0 69,552
Buf 32 at StL 14 41,899

Sun 11/30
NYG 3 at Dal 14 53,329
Pit 20 at NYJ 7 52,618
Hou 19 at Cin 23 46,128
NO 16 at Cle 17 44,753
ChiB 7 at GB 28 46,821
KC 14 at Bal 28 42,122
SD 10 at Den 13# 44,982
SF 17 at Phi 27 56,694
Min 30 at Was 31 54,498
Atl 34 at Oak 37# 50,860

Mon 12/01
N NE 7 at Mia 20 61,963

Sun 12/07
SD 28 at KC 20 46,888
GB 3 at Min 24 46,147
Dal 17 at StL 31 49,701
NYJ 30 at NE 28 53,989
Bal 21 at NYG 0 49,863
Buf 21 at Mia 31 74,573
Cin 31 at Phi 0 56,984
Hou 27 at SF 13 44,015
Det 21 at ChiB 25 37,772
LARm 14 at NO 7 39,958
Cle 17 at Pit 31 47,962
Was 30 at Atl 27 52,809

Mon 12/08
N Den 10 at Oak 17 51,075

Sat 12/13
Was 10 at Dal 31 61,091
Cin 14 at Pit 35 48,889

Sun 12/14
KC 14 at Cle 40 44,368
Buf 34 at NE 14 58,393
Mia 7 at Bal 10# 59,398
StL 34 at ChiB 20 35,052
Phi 10 at Den 25 36,860
NO 14 at NYG 28 40,150
Min 10 at Det 17 72,742
GB 5 at LARm 22 59,312
SF 9 at Atl 31 38,501
Hou 27 at Oak 26 50,719

Mon 12/15
N NYJ 16 at SD 24 49,706

Sat 12/20
Min 35 at Buf 13 54,993
Pit 3 at LARm 10 69,389
Den 13 at Mia 14 43,064

Sun 12/21
KC 20 at Oak 28 48,604
Cle 10 at Hou 21 43,770
SD 17 at Cin 47 46,474
NE 21 at Bal 34 51,926
Dal 31 at NYJ 21 37,279
NYG 26 at SF 23 34,354
Atl 13 at GB 22 38,565
StL 24 at Det 13 64,272
ChiB 42 at NO 17 33,371
Phi 26 at Was 3 49,385

AFC/NFC Divisional Playoffs

Sat 12/27
Bal 10 at Pit 28 49,557
StL 23 at LARm 35 73,459

Sun 12/28
Dal 17 at Min 14 48,050
Cin 28 at Oak 31 53,030

1975 AFC/NFC Championships

Sun 01/04
Dal 37 at LARm 7 88,919
Oak 10 at Pit 16 50,609

Super Bowl X

Sun 01/18
Dal 17 vs Pit 21 80,187
at Miami, FL

National Football League 1976

Sun 09/12
Pit 28 at Oak 31 51,371
Det 3 at ChiB 10 54,125
StL 30 at Sea 24 58,441
Min 40 at NO 9 58,156
NYG 17 at Was 19 54,245
Phi 7 at Dal 27 53,540
Den 7 at Cin 17 53,464
SF 26 at GB 14 54,628
SD 30 at KC 16 53,133
Bal 27 at NE 13 39,512
LARm 30 at Atl 14 53,607
TB 0 at Hou 20 42,228
NYJ 17 at Cle 38 67,496

Mon 09/13
N Mia 30 at Buf 21 77,683

Sun 09/19
ChiB 19 at SF 12 44,158
Mia 14 at NE 30 41,879
GB 0 at StL 29 48,842
Hou 13 at Buf 3 61,364
Cin 27 at Bal 28 50,621
LARm 10 at Min 10# 47,310
Atl 10 at Det 24 50,115
SD 23 at TB 0 38,276
NYG 7 at Phi 20 60,643
Dal 24 at NO 6 61,413
NYJ 3 at Den 46 62,519
Cle 14 at Pit 31 49,169
Sea 7 at Was 31 53,174

Mon 09/20
N Oak 24 at KC 21 60,884

Sun 09/26
Atl 10 at ChiB 0 41,029
Cle 13 at Den 44 62,758
StL 24 at SD 43 39,911
Buf 14 at TB 9 42,805
NYG 10 at LARm 24 60,698
Min 10 at Det 9 76,914
SF 37 at Sea 21 59,108
NYJ 0 at Mia 16 49,754
NO 27 at KC 17 53,918
NE 30 at Pit 27 47,379
Bal 27 at Dal 30 63,725
Oak 14 at Hou 13 42,338
GB 7 at Cin 28 44,103

Mon 09/27
N Was 20 at Phi 17# 60,131

Sun 10/03
NYG 21 at StL 27 48,039
NYJ 6 at SF 17 42,961
Dal 28 at Sea 13 62,027
TB 17 at Bal 42 40,453
SD 0 at Den 26 62,486
Was 7 at ChiB 33 52,105
Oak 17 at NE 48 61,068
Cin 45 at Cle 24 75,817
Phi 14 at Atl 13 45,535
LARm 31 at Mia 28 60,753
Hou 31 at NO 26 51,973
Det 14 at GB 24 54,758
KC 17 at Buf 50 51,909

Mon 10/04
N Pit 6 at Min 17 47,809

Sun 10/10
NE 10 at Det 30 59,730
Atl 0 at NO 30 51,521
Pit 16 at Cle 18 75,769
Buf 14 at NYJ 17 52,416
Den 3 at Hou 17 47,928
Mia 14 at Bal 28 58,832
ChiB 19 at Min 20 47,948
Sea 20 at GB 27 54,983
at Milwaukee, WI
KC 33 at Was 30 53,060
TB 0 at Cin 21 49,700
Dal 24 at NYG 14 76,042
Oak 27 at SD 17 50,223
Phi 14 at StL 33 44,933

Mon 10/11
N SF 16 at LARm 0 80,532

Sun 10/17
Cin 6 at Pit 23 48,311
Dal 17 at StL 21 50,317
ChiB 12 at LARm 20 71,751
Det 7 at Was 20 45,908
Cle 20 at Atl 17 32,837
Bal 31 at Buf 13 71,009
NO 3 at SF 33 43,160
Hou 27 at SD 30 31,950
KC 20 at Mia 17# 43,325
Sea 13 at TB 10 41,112
Phi 13 at GB 28 55,115
Oak 17 at Den 10 63,241
NYG 7 at Min 24 47,156

Mon 10/18
N NYJ 7 at NE 41 50,883

Sat 10/23
N Atl 0 at SF 15 50,240

Sun 10/24
ChiB 21 at Dal 31 60,790
Det 41 at Sea 14 61,280
Cin 27 at Hou 7 45,499
Mia 23 at TB 20 59,115
GB 14 at Oak 18 52,232
SD 17 at Cle 21 60,018
Bal 20 at NYJ 0 49,768
LARm 16 at NO 10 51,984
Pit 27 at NYG 0 69,783
Min 31 at Phi 12 56,233
Den 35 at KC 26 57,961
NE 26 at Buf 22 45,144

Mon 10/25
N StL 10 at Was 20 48,325

Sun 10/31
KC 28 at TB 19 40,079
Den 6 at Oak 19 52,169
Min 13 at ChiB 14 53,602
Phi 10 at NYG 0 68,690
SF 20 at StL 23# 50,365
Dal 20 at Was 7 55,004
NO 20 at Atl 23 33,702
Sea 6 at LARm 45 52,035
GB 6 at Det 27 74,582
SD 0 at Pit 23 45,484
NYJ 19 at Buf 14 41,285
Cle 6 at Cin 21 54,776
NE 3 at Mia 10 52,863

Mon 11/01
N Hou 14 at Bal 38 59,732

Sun 11/07
StL 17 at Phi 14 60,760
Atl 13 at Sea 30 57,985
Was 24 at SF 21 56,134
Det 23 at Min 31 46,735
NYG 3 at Dal 9 58,230
TB 13 at Den 48 62,503
NO 27 at GB 32 52,936
at Milwaukee, WI
Cle 21 at Hou 7 39,828
Buf 10 at NE 20 61,157
Mia 27 at NYJ 7 53,344
Bal 37 at SD 21 42,827
Pit 45 at KC 0 71,516
Oak 28 at ChiB 27 53,585

Mon 11/08
N LARm 12 at Cin 20 52,480

Sun 11/14
Det 16 at NO 17 42,048
TB 0 at NYJ 34 46,427
Den 17 at SD 0 32,017
SF 16 at Atl 21 19,733
NE 21 at Bal 14 58,226
GB 13 at ChiB 24 52,907
Mia 3 at Pit 14 48,945
Was 9 at NYG 12 72,975
KC 10 at Oak 21 48,859
Sea 21 at Min 27 45,087
Phi 3 at Cle 24 62,120
Hou 27 at Cin 31 52,243
StL 30 at LARm 28 64,698

Mon 11/15
N Buf 10 at Dal 17 51,779

Sun 11/21
Min 17 at GB 10 53,104
at Milwaukee, WI
SD 34 at Buf 13 36,539
Was 16 at StL 10 49,833
Hou 16 at Pit 32 47,947
Cin 27 at KC 24 46,259
Cle 24 at TB 7 34,948
NYG 13 at Den 14 62,961
NE 38 at NYJ 24 49,983
LARm 23 at SF 3 58,573
Dal 10 at Atl 17 54,992
ChiB 10 at Det 14 77,731
NO 51 at Sea 27 61,865
Oak 26 at Phi 7 62,113

Mon 11/22
N Bal 17 at Mia 16 62,104

Thu 11/25
StL 14 at Dal 19 62,498
Buf 14 at Det 27 66,569

Sun 11/28
Phi 0 at Was 24 54,292
Pit 7 at Cin 3 55,142
TB 16 at Oak 49 49,990
ChiB 16 at GB 10 56,267
Den 14 at NE 38 61,128
KC 23 at SD 20 29,272
Sea 16 at NYG 28 65,111
NYJ 16 at Bal 33 43,823
Atl 14 at Hou 20 25,838
Mia 13 at Cle 17 74,715
NO 14 at LARm 33 54,906

Mon 11/29
N Min 16 at SF 20 56,775

Sat 12/04
Bal 17 at StL 24 48,282
Atl 0 at LARm 59 57,336

Sun 12/05
GB 9 at Min 20 43,700
Det 10 at NYG 24 66,069
Hou 10 at Cle 13 56,025
Was 37 at NYJ 16 46,638
Dal 26 at Phi 7 55,072
ChiB 34 at Sea 7 60,510
KC 16 at Den 17 57,995
TB 0 at Pit 42 43,385
Buf 27 at Mia 45 43,475
NO 6 at NE 27 53,592
SF 7 at SD 13# 33,539

Mon 12/06
N Cin 20 at Oak 35 52,430

Sat 12/11
Min 29 at Mia 7 46,543

LARm 20 at Det 17 73,470
Pit 21 at Hou 0 52,437

Sun 12/12
Was 27 at Dal 14 59,916
StL 17 at NYG 14 60,553
Sea 10 at Phi 27 37,949
SF 27 at NO 7 42,536
Buf 20 at Bal 58 50,451

Cin 42 at NYJ 3 31,067
NE 31 at TB 14 39,606
Cle 14 at KC 39 34,340
SD 0 at Oak 24# 50,102
GB 24 at Atl 20 23,116
Den 28 at ChiB 14 44,459

AFC/NFC Divisional Playoffs

Sat 12/18
NE 21 at Oak 24 53,045
Was 20 at Min 35 47,221

Sun 12/19
Pit 29 at Bal 40 60,020
LARm 14 at Dal 12 62,436

1976 AFC/NFC Championships

Sun 12/26
Pit 7 at Oak 24 53,739
LARm 13 at Min 24 47,191

Super Bowl XI

Sun 01/09
Oak 32 vs Min 14 100,421
at Pasadena, CA

National Football League 1977

Sun 09/18
Dal 16 at Min 10# 47,678
GB 24 at NO 20 56,250
TB 3 at Phi 13 61,549
StL 0 at Den 7 75,002
Det 20 at ChiB 30 51,530
Mia 13 at Buf 0 76,097
SD 0 at Oak 24 51,022
KC 17 at NE 21 58,185
Cle 13 at Cin 3 52,847
Bal 29 at Sea 14 58,991
Was 17 at NYG 20 76,086
NYJ 0 at Hou 20 39,488
LARm 6 at Atl 17 55,956

Mon 09/19
N SF 0 at Pit 27 48,046

Sat 09/24
N Min 9 at TB 3 66,272

Sun 09/25
Mia 19 at SF 15 40,503
Phi 0 at LARm 20 46,031
Atl 6 at Was 10 55,031
Sea 20 at Cin 42 45,579
Bal 20 at NYJ 12 43,439
SD 23 at KC 7 56,146
NO 19 at Det 23 51,458
Buf 6 at Den 26 74,737
Hou 16 at GB 10 55,071
ChiB 13 at StL 16 49,878
Oak 16 at Pit 7 50,398
NYG 21 at Dal 41 64,215

Mon 09/26
N NE 27 at Cle 30# 76,418

Sun 10/02
NYG 3 at Atl 17 46,174
TB 7 at Dal 23 55,316
NO 42 at ChiB 24 51,488
Cin 3 at SD 24 40,352
SF 14 at LARm 34 55,466
StL 14 at Was 24 55,031
Pit 28 at Cle 14 79,021
Buf 14 at Bal 17 47,717
GB 7 at Min 19 47,143
NE 27 at NYJ 30 38,277
Den 24 at Sea 13 53,108
Phi 13 at Det 17 56,877
Hou 7 at Mia 27 46,619

Mon 10/03
N Oak 37 at KC 28 60,684

Sun 10/09
Atl 7 at SF 0 38,009
Mia 28 at Bal 45 57,005
Phi 28 at NYG 10 48,824
Det 7 at Min 14 45,860
Cin 17 at GB 7 53,653
at Milwaukee, WI
Was 10 at TB 0 58,571
SD 14 at NO 0 53,942
Dal 30 at StL 24 50,129
NYJ 24 at Buf 19 32,046
Sea 0 at NE 31 45,927
Oak 26 at Cle 10 79,178
KC 7 at Den 23 74,718
Pit 10 at Hou 27 47,777

Mon 10/10
N LARm 23 at ChiB 24 51,412

Sun 10/16
GB 6 at Det 10 78,452
StL 21 at Phi 17 65,507
Bal 17 at KC 6 63,076
Cle 24 at Hou 23 47,888
SF 17 at NYG 20 70,366
ChiB 16 at Min 22# 47,709
Atl 0 at Buf 3 27,348
Den 30 at Oak 7 53,616
Was 16 at Dal 34 62,115
NE 24 at SD 20 50,327
NO 7 at LARm 14 46,045
TB 23 at Sea 30 54,783
NYJ 17 at Mia 21 43,446

Mon 10/17
N Cin 14 at Pit 20 47,950

Sun 10/23
Sea 13 at Mia 31 29,855
Hou 10 at Pit 27 48,517
KC 21 at SD 16 33,010
Atl 16 at ChiB 10 49,407
Bal 3 at NE 17 60,958
Oak 28 at NYJ 27 56,734
NO 31 at StL 49 48,417
Dal 16 at Phi 10 65,507
NYG 17 at Was 6 53,903
Cle 27 at Buf 16 60,905
Det 7 at SF 28 39,392
Den 24 at Cin 13 54,395
GB 13 at TB 0 47,635

Mon 10/24
N Min 3 at LARm 35 62,414

Sun 10/30
Pit 21 at Bal 31 60,225
Phi 17 at Was 23 55,031
Buf 17 at Sea 56 61,180
SD 14 at Mia 13 40,670
ChiB 26 at GB 0 56,002
KC 7 at Cle 44 60,381
Oak 24 at Den 14 75,007
Det 0 at Dal 37 63,160
Min 14 at Atl 7 59,257
LARm 26 at NO 27 59,023
TB 10 at SF 20 34,700
Hou 10 at Cin 13# 53,194
NYJ 13 at NE 24 61,042

Mon 10/31
N NYG 0 at StL 28 50,323

Sun 11/06
Cin 10 at Cle 7 81,932
GB 10 at KC 20 62,687
SD 0 at Det 20 72,559
SF 10 at Atl 3 46,577
Dal 24 at NYG 10 74,532
Sea 7 at Oak 44 50,929
ChiB 0 at Hou 47 47,226
StL 27 at Min 7 47,066
Buf 24 at NE 14 60,263
TB 0 at LARm 31 45,493
Pit 7 at Den 21 74,967
Mia 14 at NYJ 10 51,582
NO 7 at Phi 28 53,482

Mon 11/07
N Was 3 at Bal 10 57,740

Sun 11/13
Sea 17 at NYJ 0 42,923
LARm 24 at GB 6 52,948
at Milwaukee, WI
Bal 31 at Buf 13 39,444
Was 17 at Phi 14 60,702
NYG 10 at TB 0 46,518
Det 6 at Atl 17 47,461
Hou 29 at Oak 34 53,667
Den 17 at SD 14 45,211
NE 5 at Mia 17 67,502
SF 10 at NO 7# 41,564
Cin 10 at Min 42 45,371
Cle 31 at Pit 35 47,055
KC 27 at ChiB 28 49,543

Mon 11/14
N StL 24 at Dal 17 64,038

Sun 11/20
TB 7 at Det 16 49,751
LARm 23 at SF 10 56,779
Dal 13 at Pit 28 49,761
Hou 22 at Sea 10 61,519
Phi 16 at StL 21 48,768
Min 7 at ChiB 10 49,563
Mia 17 at Cin 23 46,733
Atl 20 at NO 21 43,135
Cle 21 at NYG 7 72,576
Oak 7 at SD 12 50,887
Den 14 at KC 7 54,050
NYJ 12 at Bal 33 50,957
NE 20 at Buf 7 27,598

Mon 11/21
N GB 9 at Was 10 51,498

Thu 11/24
N Mia 55 at StL 14 50,269
ChiB 31 at Det 14 71,373

Sun 11/27
Min 13 at GB 6 56,267
LARm 9 at Cle 0 70,352
NYG 13 at Cin 30 32,705
NO 17 at SF 20 33,702
Atl 17 at TB 0 43,592
SD 30 at Sea 28 47,338
KC 20 at Hou 34 42,994
Phi 6 at NE 14 57,893
Bal 13 at Den 27 74,939
Dal 14 at Was 7 55,031
Pit 23 at NYJ 20 47,385

Mon 11/28
N Buf 13 at Oak 34 51,558

Sun 12/04
NYJ 16 at NO 13 40,464
Was 10 at Buf 0 22,975
SF 27 at Min 28 40,745
Sea 20 at Pit 30 45,429
Oak 14 at LARm 20 67,075
Phi 14 at Dal 24 60,289
StL 7 at NYG 27 71,826
Cin 27 at KC 7 38,488
Det 9 at GB 10 56,267
Den 24 at Hou 14 46,875
Cle 14 at SD 37 37,312
NE 16 at Atl 10 57,911
ChiB 10 at TB 0 48,948

Mon 12/05
N Bal 6 at Mia 17 68,977

Sat 12/10
Was 26 at StL 20 36,067
Pit 10 at Cin 17 36,133

Sun 12/11
NYG 14 at Phi 17 47,731
Min 13 at Oak 35 52,771
SD 9 at Den 17 74,905
Hou 19 at Cle 15 30,898
Buf 14 at NYJ 10 31,929
GB 10 at ChiB 21 33,557
Mia 10 at NE 14 61,064
Det 13 at Bal 10 45,124
TB 33 at NO 14 40,124
Sea 34 at KC 31 22,262
Atl 7 at LARm 23 52,574

Mon 12/12
N Dal 42 at SF 35 55,851

Sat 12/17
Buf 14 at Mia 31 39,626
LARm 14 at Was 17 54,208
Min 30 at Det 21 78,572

Sun 12/18
NE 24 at Bal 30 42,250
KC 20 at Oak 21 50,304
Cin 16 at Hou 21 46,212
Den 6 at Dal 14 63,752
Cle 19 at Sea 20 61,583
NYJ 0 at Phi 27 19,241
StL 7 at TB 17 56,922
NO 7 at Atl 35 36,895
Pit 10 at SD 9 50,727
SF 14 at GB 16 44,902
at Milwaukee, WI
ChiB 12 at NYG 9# 50,152

AFC/NFC Divisional Playoffs

Sat 12/24
Oak 37 at Bal 31# 60,763
Pit 21 at Den 34 75,011

Mon 12/26
Min 14 at LARm 7 62,538
ChiB 7 at Dal 37 62,920

1977 AFC/NFC Championships

Sun 01/01
Oak 17 at Den 20 74,982
Min 6 at Dal 23 61,968

Super Bowl XII

Sun 01/15
Dal 27 vs Den 10 75,583
at New Orleans, LA

National Football League 1978

Sat 09/02
N NYG 19 at TB 13 67,456

Sun 09/03
StL 10 at ChiB 17 52,791
SD 24 at Sea 20 55,778
Pit 28 at Buf 17 64,147
Min 24 at NO 31 54,187
Oak 6 at Den 14 74,904
Was 16 at NE 14 55,037
KC 24 at Cin 23 41,810
GB 13 at Det 7 51,187
Mia 20 at NYJ 33 49,598
LARm 16 at Phi 14 64,721
SF 7 at Cle 24 68,973
Hou 14 at Atl 20 57,328

Mon 09/04
N Bal 0 at Dal 38 55,037

Sat 09/09
N Det 15 at TB 7 64,445

Sun 09/10
NYJ 21 at Buf 20 40,985
Oak 21 at SD 20 51,653
Cin 10 at Cle 13# 72,691
Atl 0 at LARm 10 46,201
Phi 30 at Was 35 54,380
NO 17 at GB 28 54,336
at Milwaukee, WI
NE 16 at StL 6 48,233
Dal 34 at NYG 24 73,265
Sea 10 at Pit 21 48,277
ChiB 16 at SF 13 49,502
Mia 42 at Bal 0 47,730
Hou 20 at KC 17 40,213

Mon 09/11
N Den 9 at Min 12# 46,508

Sun 09/17
Dal 14 at LARm 27 65,749
Phi 24 at NO 17 49,242
Oak 28 at GB 3 55,903
ChiB 19 at Det 0 65,982
TB 16 at Min 10 46,152
Cle 24 at Atl 16 56,648
SF 19 at Hou 20 46,161
Sea 24 at NYJ 17 46,911
Buf 24 at Mia 31 48,373
Was 28 at StL 10 49,282
Pit 28 at Cin 3 50,260
SD 14 at Den 27 74,983
KC 10 at NYG 26 70,546

Mon 09/18
N Bal 34 at NE 27 57,284

Sun 09/24
NO 20 at Cin 18 40,455
Cle 9 at Pit 15# 49,573
LARm 10 at Hou 6 45,749
Mia 3 at Phi 17 62,998
Atl 9 at TB 14 58,073
NYJ 3 at Was 23 54,729
Bal 17 at Buf 24 55,270
GB 24 at SD 3 42,755
NE 21 at Oak 14 52,904
StL 12 at Dal 21 62,760
Den 23 at KC 17# 60,593
Det 16 at Sea 28 56,781
SF 10 at NYG 27 71,536

Mon 09/25
N Min 24 at ChiB 20 53,561

Sun 10/01
StL 10 at Mia 24 43,882
SD 23 at NE 28 60,781
Pit 28 at NYJ 17 52,058
Cin 12 at SF 28 41,107
Sea 7 at Den 28 74,989
Oak 25 at ChiB 19# 52,848

Det 14 at GB 35 54,601
at Milwaukee, WI
LARm 26 at NO 20 61,654
NYG 20 at Atl 23 47,765
KC 13 at Buf 28 47,310
Min 24 at TB 7 65,972
Hou 16 at Cle 13 72,776
Phi 17 at Bal 14 50,314

Mon 10/02
N Dal 5 at Was 9 55,031

Sun 10/08
Den 0 at SD 23 50,077
Atl 7 at Pit 31 48,202
NYG 3 at Dal 24 63,420
Bal 30 at StL 17 47,479
ChiB 14 at GB 24 56,267
Phi 14 at NE 24 61,016
Buf 14 at NYJ 45 44,545
Hou 17 at Oak 21 52,550
Was 21 at Det 19 60,555
TB 30 at KC 13 38,201
SF 10 at LARm 27 59,337
Min 28 at Sea 29 62,031
Cle 24 at NO 16 50,158

Mon 10/09
N Cin 0 at Mia 21 54,729

Sun 10/15
Pit 34 at Cle 14 81,302
KC 6 at Oak 28 50,759
Buf 10 at Hou 17 47,727
Sea 28 at GB 45 52,712
at Milwaukee, WI
TB 14 at NYG 17 68,025
LARm 34 at Min 17 46,551
NYJ 33 at Bal 10 45,563
Mia 28 at SD 21 50,637
NO 14 at SF 7 37,671
Dal 24 at StL 21# 48,991
Det 0 at Atl 14 51,172
NE 10 at Cin 3 48,699
Was 10 at Phi 17 65,722

Mon 10/16
N ChiB 7 at Den 16 75,008

Sun 10/22
Den 6 at Bal 7 54,057
Cin 0 at Buf 5 47,754
NO 10 at LARm 3 47,574
StL 10 at NYJ 23 49,244
ChiB 19 at TB 33 68,146
Atl 20 at SF 17 34,133
Was 6 at NYG 17 76,192
Oak 7 at Sea 27 62,529
SD 14 at Det 31 54,031
Cle 3 at KC 17 41,157
Mia 24 at NE 33 60,424
GB 7 at Min 21 47,411
Phi 7 at Dal 14 60,525

Mon 10/23
N Hou 24 at Pit 17 48,021

Thu 10/26
N Min 21 at Dal 10 61,848

Sun 10/29
TB 7 at GB 9 55,108
StL 16 at Phi 10 62,989
NYJ 21 at NE 55 60,585
Bal 8 at Mia 26 53,542
Buf 20 at Cle 41 51,409
KC 24 at Pit 27 48,185
Hou 13 at Cin 28 50,532
SF 20 at Was 38 55,031
Det 21 at ChiB 17 53,378
SD 27 at Oak 23 52,612
NYG 17 at NO 28 58,806
Den 20 at Sea 17# 62,948

Mon 10/30
N LARm 7 at Atl 15 57,250

Sun 11/05
Det 7 at Min 17 46,008
GB 3 at Phi 10 64,214
NE 14 at Buf 10 44,897
Cle 10 at Hou 14 45,827
SF 10 at Atl 21 55,468
TB 23 at LARm 26 55,182
NYG 10 at StL 20 48,820
Cin 13 at SD 22 43,639
NO 14 at Pit 20 48,525
Sea 31 at ChiB 29 50,697
Dal 16 at Mia 23 69,414

Oak 20 at KC 10 75,418
NYJ 31 at Den 28 74,983

Mon 11/06
N Was 17 at Bal 21 57,831

Sun 11/12
Bal 17 at Sea 14 61,905
NYG 13 at Was 16 55,031
NYJ 9 at Phi 17 65,950
Pit 7 at LARm 10 63,089
TB 23 at Det 34 60,320
Atl 20 at NO 17 70,323
ChiB 14 at Min 17 43,286
Dal 42 at GB 14 55,256
Den 19 at Cle 7 70,856
StL 16 at SF 10 33,155
KC 23 at SD 29# 41,395
Hou 26 at NE 23 60,356
Mia 25 at Buf 24 48,623

Mon 11/13
N Oak 34 at Cin 21 51,374

Sun 11/19
NO 7 at Dal 27 57,920
StL 27 at Was 17 52,460
NE 19 at NYJ 17 55,568
Sea 13 at KC 10 35,252
Atl 7 at ChiB 13 46,022
Cle 45 at Bal 24 45,341
Buf 10 at TB 31 61,383
Det 17 at Oak 29 44,517
Phi 19 at NYG 17 70,318
LARm 31 at SF 28 45,022
Cin 6 at Pit 7 47,578
SD 13 at Min 7 38,859
GB 3 at Den 16 74,965

Mon 11/20
Mia 30 at Hou 35 50,290

Thu 11/23
Den 14 at Det 17 71,785
Was 10 at Dal 37 64,905

Sun 11/26
NO 17 at Atl 20 55,121
NYG 17 at Buf 41 28,496
SD 0 at KC 23 26,248

Phi 14 at StL 10 39,693
TB 3 at ChiB 14 42,373
NYJ 24 at Mia 13 49,255
Sea 17 at Oak 16 52.978
Min 10 at GB 10# 51,737
LARm 19 at Cle 30 55,158
NE 35 at Bal 14 42,828
Cin 10 at Hou 17 43,245

Mon 11/27
N Pit 24 at SF 7 51,657

Sun 12/03
GB 17 at TB 7 67,754
Phi 27 at Min 28 38,772
LARm 20 at NYG 17 62,629
Bal 16 at NYJ 24 50,248
Buf 10 at KC 14 25,781
Cle 24 at Sea 47 62,262
Det 14 at StL 21 39,200
SF 13 at NO 24 50,068
Den 21 at Oak 6 53,932
Atl 7 at Cin 37 25,336
NE 10 at Dal 17 63,263
Pit 13 at Hou 3 54,261
Mia 16 at Was 0 52,860

Mon 12/04
N ChiB 7 at SD 40 48,492

Sat 12/09
Bal 13 at Pit 35 41,957
Min 14 at Det 45 78,685

Sun 12/10
KC 3 at Den 24 74,149
Oak 6 at Mia 23 73,003
Buf 24 at NE 26 59,598
GB 0 at ChiB 14 34,306
StL 0 at NYG 17 52,226
TB 3 at SF 6 30,931
Dal 31 at Phi 13 64,667
Was 17 at Atl 20 54,178
NYJ 34 at Cle 37# 36,881
Hou 17 at NO 12 63,169
Sea 10 at SD 37 49,975

Mon 12/11
N Cin 20 at LARm 19 47,471

Sat 12/16
Pit 21 at Den 17 74,104
ChiB 14 at Was 10 49,774

Sun 12/17
KC 19 at Sea 23 58,490
SD 45 at Hou 24 49,554
Dal 30 at NYJ 7 52,532
Atl 21 at StL 42 40,022
GB 14 at LARm 31 42,500
NO 17 at TB 10 51,207
NYG 3 at Phi 20 56,396
Buf 21 at Bal 14 25,415
Cle 16 at Cin 48 46,985
SF 14 at Det 33 56,674
Min 20 at Oak 27 44,643

Mon 12/18
N NE 3 at Mia 23 72,071

Wild-Card Playoffs

Sun 12/24
Hou 17 at Mia 9 70,036
Phi 13 at Atl 14 49,447

AFC/NFC Divisional Playoffs

Sat 12/30
Atl 20 at Dal 27 60,338
Den 10 at Pit 33 48,921

Sun 12/31
Min 10 at LARm 34 69,631
Hou 31 at NE 14 60,881

1978 AFC/NFC Championships

Sun 01/07
Hou 5 at Pit 34 49,417
Dal 28 at LARm 0 67,470

Super Bowl XIII

Sun 01/21
Pit 35 vs Dal 31 79,484
at Miami, Fl

National Football League 1979

Sat 09/01
N Det 16 at TB 31 68,225

Sun 09/02
Dal 22 at StL 21 50,855
Cle 25 at NYJ 22# 48,472
Atl 40 at NO 34# 70,940
GB 3 at ChiB 6 56,515
Bal 0 at KC 14 50,442
Mia 9 at Buf 7 69,441
Oak 24 at LARm 17 59,000
Hou 29 at Was 27 54,582
SF 22 at Min 28 46,539
Cin 0 at Den 10 74,788
SD 33 at Sea 16 62,287
NYG 17 at Phi 23 67,366

Mon 09/03
N Pit 16 at NE 13# 60,978

Thu 09/06
N LARm 13 at Den 9 74,884

Sun 09/09
Cle 27 at KC 24 42,181
Sea 10 at Mia 19 56,233
Hou 7 at Pit 38 49,792
Cin 24 at Buf 51 43,504
Dal 21 at SF 13 56,728
Was 27 at Det 24 54,991
StL 27 at NYG 14 71,370
Min 7 at ChiB 26 53,231
TB 29 at Bal 26# 36,374
NO 19 at GB 28 53,184
at Milwaukee, WI
NYJ 3 at NE 56 53,113
Oak 10 at SD 30 50,255

Mon 09/10
N Atl 14 at Phi 10 66,935

Sun 09/16
Bal 10 at Cle 13 72,070
KC 6 at Hou 20 45,684
TB 21 at GB 10 55,498
Den 20 at Atl 17# 57,677
Pit 24 at StL 21 50,416
Buf 19 at SD 27 50,709
Mia 27 at Min 12 46,187
Oak 10 at Sea 27 61,602
ChiB 20 at Dal 24 64,056
SF 24 at LARm 27 44,303
Phi 26 at NO 14 54,212
Det 10 at NYJ 31 49,612
NE 20 at Cin 14 41,805

Mon 09/17
N NYG 0 at Was 27 54,672

Sun 09/23
ChiB 16 at Mia 31 66,011
Atl 23 at Det 24 56,249
GB 21 at Min 27# 46,524
SD 21 at NE 27 60,916
NYJ 31 at Buf 46 68,731
Oak 7 at KC 35 67,821
Hou 30 at Cin 27# 45,615
Was 17 at StL 7 50,680
Sea 34 at Den 37 74,879
LARm 6 at TB 21 69,497
Phi 17 at NYG 13 74,265
Bal 13 at Pit 17 49,483
NO 30 at SF 21 39,727

Mon 09/24
N Dal 7 at Cle 26 80,123

Sun 09/30
StL 0 at LARm 21 48,160
Cle 10 at Hou 31 48,915
NYG 14 at NO 24 51,543
Was 16 at Atl 7 56,819
Min 13 at Det 10 75,295
Den 3 at Oak 27 52,632
SF 9 at SD 31 50,893
Cin 13 at Dal 38 63,179
KC 24 at Sea 6 61,169
Buf 31 at Bal 13 31,904
TB 17 at ChiB 13 55,258
Pit 14 at Phi 17 70,352
Mia 27 at NYJ 33 51,496

Mon 10/01
N NE 14 at GB 27 52,842

Sun 10/07
Dal 36 at Min 20 45,572
LARm 35 at NO 17 68,986
ChiB 7 at Buf 0 73,383
SD 0 at Den 7 74,997
NYJ 8 at Bal 10 32,142
KC 10 at Cin 7 40,041
Was 17 at Phi 28 69,142
TB 14 at NYG 17 72,841
GB 7 at Atl 25 56,184
StL 24 at Hou 17 53,043
Det 17 at NE 24 60,629
Pit 51 at Cle 35 81,250
Sea 35 at SF 24 44,592

Mon 10/08
N Mia 3 at Oak 13 52,419

Sun 10/14
SF 16 at NYG 32 70,352
NO 42 at TB 14 67,640

Det 16 at GB 24 53,950
at Milwaukee, WI
Atl 19 at Oak 50 52,900
Pit 10 at Cin 34 52,381
NE 27 at ChiB 7 54,128
Phi 24 at StL 20 48,367
Hou 28 at Bal 16 45,021
Was 13 at Cle 9 63,323
Buf 7 at Mia 17 45,597
Sea 10 at SD 20 50,007
LARm 6 at Dal 30 64,462
Den 24 at KC 10 74,292

Mon 10/15
N Min 7 at NYJ 14 54,479

Sun 10/21
Det 7 at NO 17 57,428
SD 40 at LARm 16 62,245
StL 13 at Dal 22 64,300
Hou 14 at Sea 34 60,705
NYG 21 at KC 17 44,362
Phi 7 at Was 17 54,442
GB 3 at TB 21 67,186
Oak 19 at NYJ 28 55,802
Mia 13 at NE 28 61,096
Cin 27 at Cle 28 75,119
Bal 14 at Buf 13 50,581
ChiB 27 at Min 30 41,164
Atl 15 at SF 20 33,952

Mon 10/22
N Den 7 at Pit 42 49,699

Thu 10/25
N SD 22 at Oak 45 53,709

Sun 10/28
Dal 3 at Pit 14 50,199

Cle 38 at StL 20 47,845
NO 14 at Was 10 53,133
Buf 20 at Det 17 61,911
NE 26 at Bal 31 41,029
NYJ 24 at Hou 27# 45,825
TB 12 at Min 10 46,906
KC 3 at Den 20 74,908
Phi 13 at Cin 37 43,036
ChiB 28 at SF 27 42,773
NYG 20 at LARm 14 43,376
GB 7 at Mia 27 47,741

Mon 10/29
N Sea 31 at Atl 28 52,566

Sun 11/04
SD 20 at KC 14 59,353
Min 7 at StL 37 47,213
NYJ 27 at GB 22 54,201
Cle 24 at Phi 19 69,019
Det 7 at ChiB 35 50,108
TB 14 at Atl 17 55,150
Dal 16 at NYG 14 76,490
LARm 24 at Sea 0 62,048
NO 3 at Den 10 74,482
NE 26 at Buf 6 67,935
Cin 28 at Bal 38 37,740
SF 10 at Oak 23 52,764
Was 7 at Pit 38 49,462

Mon 11/05
N Hou 9 at Mia 6 72,073

Sun 11/11
LARm 23 at ChiB 27 51,483
StL 28 at Was 30 50,868
Atl 3 at NYG 24 60,860
Sea 29 at Cle 24 72,440
Oak 17 at Hou 31 48,000

TB 16 at Det 14 70,461
Bal 0 at Mia 19 50,193
Buf 14 at NYJ 12 50,647
Min 7 at GB 19 52,706
at Milwaukee, WI
Pit 30 at KC 3 70,132
SF 20 at NO 31 65,551
NE 10 at Den 45 74,379
SD 26 at Cin 24 40,782

Mon 11/12
N Phi 31 at Dal 21 62,417

Sun 11/18
Pit 7 at SD 35 52,426
NYG 3 at TB 31 70,261
KC 24 at Oak 21 53,596
NO 24 at Sea 38 60,055
Det 7 at Min 14 43,650
StL 13 at Phi 16 70,235
GB 12 at Buf 19 39,679
Dal 20 at Was 34 55,031
Cin 21 at Hou 42 49,829
NYJ 13 at ChiB 23 53,635
Den 38 at SF 28 42,910
Bal 21 at NE 50 60,879
Mia 24 at Cle 30# 80,374

Mon 11/19
N Atl 14 at LARm 20 54,097

Thu 11/22
Hou 30 at Dal 24 63,897
ChiB 0 at Det 20 66,219

Sun 11/25
Phi 21 at GB 10 50,023
Min 23 at TB 22 70,039
Cle 30 at Pit 33# 48,773
KC 7 at SD 28 50,078
Mia 28 at Bal 24 38,016
StL 28 at Cin 34 25,103
NO 37 at Atl 6 42,815
Oak 14 at Den 10 74,186
LARm 26 at SF 20 49,282
Buf 16 at NE 13# 60,991
Was 6 at NYG 14 72,641

Mon 11/26
N NYJ 7 at Sea 30 59,977

Thu 11/29
N NE 24 at Mia 39 69,174

Sun 12/02
Atl 28 at SD 26 50,198
ChiB 14 at TB 0 69,508
Hou 7 at Cle 14 69,112
GB 21 at Was 38 51,682
Det 7 at Phi 44 66,128
NYG 7 at Dal 28 63,787
SF 10 at StL 13 41,593
Cin 17 at Pit 37 46,521
Min 21 at LARm 27# 56,700
Bal 17 at NYJ 30 47,744
Den 19 at Buf 16 37,886
Sea 21 at KC 37 42,160

Mon 12/03
N Oak 42 at NO 35 65,541

Sat 12/08
Dal 24 at Phi 17 71,434
Den 23 at Sea 28 60,038

Sun 12/09
Mia 28 at Det 10 78,087
NE 26 at NYJ 27 45,131
Cin 14 at Was 28 52,882
Cle 14 at Oak 19 52,641
TB 7 at SF 23 44,506
LARm 34 at Atl 13 49,236
ChiB 15 at GB 14 54,207
SD 35 at NO 0 61,059
Buf 3 at Min 10 42,239
NYG 20 at StL 29 39,802
KC 10 at Bal 7 37,226

Mon 12/10
N Pit 17 at Hou 20 55,293

Sat 12/15
NYJ 27 at Mia 24 49,915
GB 18 at Det 13 57,376

Sun 12/16
Buf 0 at Pit 28 48,002
Phi 26 at Hou 20 49,407
KC 0 at TB 3 63,624
Was 34 at Dal 35 62,867
StL 6 at ChiB 42 42,810
NO 29 at LARm 14 53,879
Min 23 at NE 27 54,719
Cle 12 at Cin 16 42,183
Sea 29 at Oak 24 53,177
Bal 31 at NYG 7 58,711
SF 21 at Atl 31 37,211

Mon 12/17
N Den 7 at SD 17 51,906

Wild-Card Games

Sun 12/23
ChiB 17 at Phi 27 69,397
Den 7 at Hou 13 48,776

AFC/NFC Divisional Playoffs

Sat 12/29
Phi 17 at TB 24 71,402
Hou 17 at SD 14 51,192

Sun 12/30
LARm 21 at Dal 19 64,792
Mia 14 at Pit 34 50,214

AFC/NFC Championship

Sun 01/06
Hou 13 at Pit 27 50,475
LARm 9 at TB 0 72,033

Super Bowl XIV

Sun 01/20
LARm 19 vs Pit 31 103,985
at Pasadena, CA

National Football League 1980

Sun 09/07
ChiB 6 at GB 12# 54,381
NYG 41 at StL 35 49,122
TB 17 at Cin 12 55,551
Atl 23 at Min 24 44,773
Det 41 at LARm 20 64,892
SD 34 at Sea 13 62,042
Hou 17 at Pit 31 54,386
SF 26 at NO 23 58,621
Den 6 at Phi 27 70,307
Oak 27 at KC 14 54,269
Cle 17 at NE 34 49,222
Bal 17 at NYJ 14 50,777
Mia 7 at Buf 17 79,598

Mon 09/08
N Dal 17 at Was 3 55,045

Thu 09/11
N LARm 9 at TB 10 66,576

Sun 09/14
NO 3 at ChiB 22 62,523
Sea 17 at KC 16 42,403
Dal 20 at Den 41 74,919
Det 29 at GB 7 53,099
at Milwaukee, WI
StL 21 at SF 24# 49,999
Pit 20 at Bal 17 54,914
Cin 16 at Mia 17 38,322
NYJ 10 at Buf 20 65,315
Oak 24 at SD 30# 51,943
Phi 42 at Min 7 46,460
Was 23 at NYG 21 73,343
Atl 37 at NE 21 48,321

Mon 09/15
N Hou 16 at Cle 7 80,243

Sun 09/21
Pit 28 at Cin 30 52,490
StL 7 at Det 20 80,027
KC 13 at Cle 20 63,614
TB 17 at Dal 28 62,750
GB 21 at LARm 51 63,850
Buf 35 at NO 26 65,551
Min 34 at ChiB 14 59,983
SF 37 at NYJ 27 50,608
Bal 16 at Hou 21 47,878
SD 30 at Den 13 74,970
Was 21 at Oak 24 45,163
Mia 20 at Atl 17 55,479
NE 37 at Sea 31 61,035

Mon 09/22
NYG 3 at Phi 35 70,767

Sun 09/28
NO 16 at Mia 21 40,946
LARm 28 at NYG 7 73,414
Oak 7 at Buf 24 77,259
SD 24 at KC 7 45,161
Cle 34 at TB 27 65,540
Phi 14 at StL 24 49,079
NYJ 21 at Bal 35 33,373
ChiB 3 at Pit 38 53,987
Hou 13 at Cin 10 50,413
Atl 20 at SF 17 56,518
Min 7 at Det 27 80,219
Dal 28 at GB 7 54,776
at Milwaukee, WI
Sea 14 at Was 0 55,045

Mon 09/29
N Den 14 at NE 23 60,153

Sun 10/05
Det 28 at Atl 43 57,652
StL 40 at NO 7 45,388
Buf 26 at SD 24 51,982
Den 19 at Cle 16 81,065
KC 31 at Oak 17 40,153
Cin 9 at GB 14 55,006
Was 14 at Phi 24 69,044
SF 26 at LARm 48 62,188
NYG 3 at Dal 24 59,126
NE 21 at NYJ 11 53,603
Bal 30 at Mia 17 50,631
Pit 23 at Min 17 47,583
Sea 26 at Hou 7 46,860

Mon 10/06
N TB 0 at ChiB 23 61,350

Sun 10/12
SD 24 at Oak 38 44,826
NYJ 14 at Atl 7 57,458
Phi 31 at NYG 16 71,051
SF 14 at Dal 59 63,399
Mia 0 at NE 34 60,777
Cle 27 at Sea 3 61,366
Bal 17 at Buf 12 73,634
NO 13 at Det 24 78,147
Cin 17 at Pit 16 53,668
Hou 20 at KC 21 75,048
ChiB 7 at Min 13 46,751
GB 14 at TB 14# 64,854
LARm 21 at StL 13 50,230

Mon 10/13
N Was 17 at Den 20 74,657

Sun 10/19
Sea 27 at NYJ 17 52,496
NE 37 at Bal 21 53,924
GB 21 at Cle 26 75,548
Min 0 at Cin 14 44,487
StL 0 at Was 23 55,045
Dal 10 at Phi 17 70,696
NYG 7 at SD 44 50,397
LARm 31 at SF 17 55,360
Atl 41 at NO 14 62,651
TB 14 at Hou 20 48,167
KC 23 at Den 17 74,459
Det 7 at ChiB 24 58,508
Buf 14 at Mia 17 41,636

Mon 10/20
N Oak 45 at Pit 34 53,940

Sun 10/26
Pit 26 at Cle 27 79,095
NE 13 at Buf 31 75,092
SD 31 at Dal 42 60,639
Den 14 at NYG 9 67,598
Min 3 at GB 16 55,361
TB 24 at SF 23 51,925
StL 17 at Bal 10 33,506
Sea 14 at Oak 33 50,185
NO 14 at Was 22 51,375
ChiB 14 at Phi 17 68,752
Det 17 at KC 20 59,391
LARm 10 at Atl 13 57,401
Cin 3 at Hou 23 49,189

Mon 10/27
N Mia 14 at NYJ 17 53,046

Sun 11/02
Atl 30 at Buf 14 57,959
Hou 20 at Den 16 74,717
Dal 27 at StL 24 50,701
Min 39 at Was 14 52,060
NYG 13 at TB 30 68,256
Phi 27 at Sea 20 61,047
Mia 10 at Oak 16 46,378
NYJ 21 at NE 34 60,834
NO 31 at LARm 45 59,909
GB 20 at Pit 22 52,165
SD 31 at Cin 14 46,406
Bal 31 at KC 24 52,283
SF 13 at Det 17 78,845

Mon 11/03
N ChiB 21 at Cle 27 83,224

Sun 11/09
Dal 35 at NYG 38 68,343
Atl 33 at StL 27# 48,662
Den 20 at SD 13 51,435
Was 21 at ChiB 35 57,159
Cin 17 at Oak 28 44,132
Mia 35 at LARm 14 62,198
Det 0 at Min 34 46,264
SF 16 at GB 23 54,475
at Milwaukee, WI
Phi 34 at NO 21 44,340
Buf 31 at NYJ 24 45,677
Cle 28 at Bal 27 45,369
KC 31 at Sea 30 58,976
Pit 24 at TB 21 71,636

Mon 11/10
N NE 34 at Hou 38 51,524

Sun 11/16
Phi 24 at Was 0 51,897
LARm 17 at NE 14 60,609
NYJ 24 at Den 31 72,114
StL 21 at Dal 31 52,567
SF 13 at Mia 17 45,135
Bal 10 at Det 9 77,677
Hou 10 at ChiB 6 53,390
NO 13 at Atl 31 53,871
TB 30 at Min 38 46,032
Cle 13 at Pit 16 54,563
KC 7 at SD 20 50,248
GB 21 at NYG 27 72,368
Buf 14 at Cin 0 40,836

Mon 11/17
N Oak 19 at Sea 17 60,480

Thu 11/20
N SD 27 at Mia 24# 63,013

Sun 11/23
Pit 13 at Buf 28 79,659
Hou 28 at NYJ 31# 52,358
GB 25 at Min 13 47,234
Was 10 at Dal 14 58,809
ChiB 17 at Atl 28 49,156
KC 21 at StL 13 42,871
Sea 20 at Den 36 73,274
NYG 0 at SF 12 38,574
Det 24 at TB 10 64,976
Oak 7 at Phi 10 68,535
Cin 7 at Cle 31 79,253
Bal 21 at NE 47 61,297

Mon 11/24
N LARm 27 at NO 7 53,448

Thu 11/27
Sea 7 at Dal 51 57,540
ChiB 23 at Det 17# 75,397

Sun 11/30
Was 6 at Atl 10 55,665
StL 23 at NYG 7 65,852
Cle 17 at Hou 14 51,514
Cin 20 at KC 6 41,594
Min 23 at NO 20 30,936
Phi 21 at SD 22 51,567
Mia 10 at Pit 23 51,384
TB 20 at GB 17 54,225
at Milwaukee, WI
NYJ 13 at LARm 38 59,743
Buf 24 at Bal 28 36,184
NE 17 at SF 21 45,254

Mon 12/01
N Den 3 at Oak 9 51,593

Thu 12/04
N Pit 0 at Hou 6 53,960

Sun 12/07
SD 17 at Was 40 48,556
Det 23 at StL 24 46,966
Atl 20 at Phi 17 70,205
LARm 7 at Buf 10# 77,133
NYJ 14 at Cle 17 78,454
Bal 33 at Cin 34 35,651
Min 21 at TB 10 65,649
NO 35 at SF 38# 37,949
GB 7 at ChiB 61 57,176
Dal 19 at Oak 13 53,194
Den 14 at KC 31 40,237
NYG 27 at Sea 21 51,617

Mon 12/08
N NE 13 at Mia 16# 63,282

Sat 12/13
Sea 14 at SD 21 49,980
NYG 13 at Was 16 44,443

Sun 12/14
SF 10 at Atl 35 55,767
NO 21 at NYJ 20 38,077
Cin 17 at ChiB 14# 48,808
KC 16 at Pit 21 50,013
StL 3 at Phi 17 68,969
TB 14 at Det 27 77,098
Oak 24 at Den 21 73,974
Buf 2 at NE 24 63,292
Cle 23 at Min 28 42,202
Hou 22 at GB 3 53,201
Mia 24 at Bal 14 30,564

Mon 12/15
N Dal 14 at LARm 38 65,154

Sat 12/20
NYJ 24 at Mia 17 41,854
ChiB 14 at TB 13 55,298

Sun 12/21
Cle 27 at Cin 24 50,058
Oak 33 at NYG 17 61,287
Den 25 at Sea 17 51,853
Phi 27 at Dal 35 62,548
NE 38 at NO 27 38,277
Buf 18 at SF 13 37,476
KC 38 at Bal 28 16,941
Min 16 at Hou 20 51,064
GB 3 at Det 24 75,111
Atl 17 at LARm 20# 62,469
Was 31 at StL 7 35,942

Mon 12/22
N Pit 17 at SD 26 51,785

Wild-Card Playoffs

Sun 12/28
Hou 7 at Oak 27 52,762
LARm 13 at Dal 34 64,533

AFC/NFC Divisional Playoffs

Sat 01/03
Buf 14 at SD 20 52,028
Min 16 at Phi 31 68,434

Sun 01/04
Oak 14 at Cle 12 77,655
Dal 30 at Atl 27 60,022

1980 AFC/NFC Championships

Sun 01/11
Oak 34 at SD 27 52,438
Dal 7 at Phi 20 70,696

Super Bowl XV

Sun 01/25
Oak 27 vs Phi 10 75,500
at New Orleans, LA

National Football League 1981

Sun 09/06
Hou 27 at LARm 20 63,198
KC 37 at Pit 33 53,305
Oak 7 at Den 9 74,796
Phi 24 at NYG 10 72,459
Bal 29 at NE 28 49,572
SF 17 at Det 24 62,123
Dal 26 at Was 10 55,045
NO 0 at Atl 27 57,406
Min 13 at TB 21 66,287
NYJ 0 at Buf 31 79,754
GB 16 at ChiB 9 62,411
Sea 21 at Cin 27 41,177
Mia 20 at StL 7 50,351

Mon 09/07
N SD 44 at Cle 14 78,904

Thu 09/10
N Pit 10 at Mia 30 74,190

Sun 09/13
StL 17 at Dal 30 63,602
Cin 31 at NYJ 30 49,454
Buf 35 at Bal 3 44,950
ChiB 17 at SF 28 49,520
Atl 31 at GB 17 55,382
NE 3 at Phi 13 71,089
Den 10 at Sea 13 58,513
Det 23 at SD 28 51,624
Hou 9 at Cle 3 79,483
NYG 17 at Was 7 53,343
LARm 17 at NO 23 62,063
TB 10 at KC 19 50,555

Mon 09/14
N Oak 36 at Min 10 47,186

Thu 09/17
N Phi 20 at Buf 14 78,331

Sun 09/20
SF 17 at Atl 34 56,653
Mia 16 at Hou 10 47,379
Bal 10 at Den 28 74,804
SD 42 at KC 31 63,866
Det 24 at Min 26 45,350
NYJ 10 at Pit 38 52,973
Cle 20 at Cin 17 52,170
Was 30 at StL 40 47,592
GB 23 at LARm 35 61,286
NO 7 at NYG 20 69,814
TB 17 at ChiB 28 60,130
Sea 10 at Oak 20 45,725

Mon 09/21
N Dal 35 at NE 21 60,311

Sun 09/27
NO 14 at SF 21 44,433
Min 30 at GB 13 55,012
at Milwaukee, WI
SD 24 at Den 42 74,844
NYG 10 at Dal 18 63,449
Oak 0 at Det 16 77,919
StL 10 at TB 20 65,850
NE 21 at Pit 27# 53,344
Atl 17 at Cle 28 78,283
Hou 17 at NYJ 33 50,309
Mia 31 at Bal 28 41,630
Was 13 at Phi 36 70,664
KC 20 at Sea 14 59,255
Buf 24 at Cin 27# 46,418

Mon 09/28
N LARm 24 at ChiB 7 62,461

Sun 10/04
NYJ 28 at Mia 28# 68,723
KC 17 at NE 33 55,931
Den 17 at Oak 0 51,035
Bal 17 at Buf 23 77,813
Pit 20 at NO 6 64,578
Sea 10 at SD 24 51,463
Det 10 at TB 28 71,733
SF 30 at Was 17 51,843
Cle 16 at LARm 27 63,924
ChiB 21 at Min 24 43,827
Cin 10 at Hou 17 44,350
GB 27 at NYG 14 73,684
Dal 17 at StL 20 49,477

Mon 10/05
N Atl 13 at Phi 16 71,488

Sun 10/11
Min 33 at SD 31 50,708
StL 14 at NYG 34 67,128
Dal 14 at SF 45 57,574
NE 24 at NYJ 28 55,093
Was 24 at ChiB 7 57,683
Det 21 at Den 27 74,509
Phi 31 at NO 14 52,728
LARm 37 at Atl 35 57,841
Sea 17 at Hou 35 42,671
Cle 7 at Pit 13 53,250
TB 21 at GB 10 55,264
Cin 41 at Bal 19 33,860
Oak 0 at KC 27 76,543

Mon 10/12
N Mia 21 at Buf 31 78,576

Sun 10/18
NO 17 at Cle 20 76,059
Buf 14 at NYJ 33 54,607
SD 43 at Bal 14 41,921
SF 13 at GB 3 50,171
at Milwaukee, WI
Pit 7 at Cin 34 57,090
Den 14 at KC 28 74,672
Was 10 at Mia 13 47,367
NYG 32 at Sea 0 56,134
LARm 17 at Dal 29 64,649
TB 16 at Oak 18 42,288
Hou 10 at NE 38 60,474
StL 20 at Atl 41 51,428
Phi 23 at Min 35 45,459

Mon 10/19
N ChiB 17 at Det 48 71,273

Sun 10/25
GB 27 at Det 31 76,063
LARm 17 at SF 20 59,190
NYG 27 at Atl 24# 60,749
TB 10 at Phi 20 70,714
SD 17 at ChiB 20# 52,906
Den 7 at Buf 9 77,757
Sea 19 at NYJ 3 49,678
Cin 7 at NO 17 46,336
Min 17 at StL 30 48,039
Bal 28 at Cle 42 78,986
KC 28 at Oak 17 42,194
NE 22 at Was 24 50,394
Mia 27 at Dal 28 64,221

Mon 10/26
N Hou 13 at Pit 26 52,732

Sun 11/01
Hou 21 at Cin 34 54,736
StL 21 at Was 42 55,045
NE 17 at Oak 27 44,246
NYJ 26 at NYG 7 74,740
KC 20 at SD 22 51,307
Atl 41 at NO 10 63,637
SF 17 at Pit 14 52,878
Bal 10 at Mia 27 46,061
Cle 13 at Buf 22 78,226
Sea 24 at GB 34 49,467
ChiB 10 at TB 20 63,688
Det 13 at LARm 20 61,814
Dal 17 at Phi 14 72,111

Mon 11/02
N Min 17 at Den 19 74,834

Sun 11/08
Phi 52 at StL 10 48,421
Cle 20 at Den 23# 74,859
Oak 16 at Hou 17 45,519
ChiB 16 at KC 13# 60,605
Cin 40 at SD 17 51,259
Pit 21 at Sea 24 59,058
Atl 14 at SF 17 59,127
Det 31 at Was 33 52,096
Mia 30 at NE 27# 60,436
NYG 24 at GB 26 54,138
at Milwaukee, WI
TB 10 at Min 25 47,038
NO 21 at LARm 13 61,068
NYJ 41 at Bal 14 31,521

Mon 11/09
N Buf 14 at Dal 27 62,583

Sun 11/15
Pit 34 at Atl 20 57,485
Cle 15 at SF 12 52,455
NYJ 17 at NE 6 45,342
Buf 0 at StL 24 46,214
Bal 13 at Phi 38 68,618
Dal 24 at Det 27 79,694
ChiB 17 at GB 21 55,338
Den 24 at TB 7 64,518
NO 10 at Min 20 45,215
LARm 10 at Cin 24 56,836
Was 30 at NYG 27# 63,133
Oak 33 at Mia 17 67,531
Hou 10 at KC 23 73,984

Mon 11/16
N SD 23 at Sea 44 58,628

Sun 11/22
Mia 15 at NYJ 16 59,962
Den 21 at Cin 38 57,207
NYG 20 at Phi 10 66,827
Det 23 at ChiB 7 50,082
Pit 32 at Cle 10 77,958
Was 10 at Dal 24 64,583
NE 17 at Buf 20 71,593
NO 27 at Hou 24 49,581
SF 33 at LARm 31 63,456
SD 55 at Oak 21 50,199
Sea 13 at KC 40 49,002
GB 3 at TB 37 63,251
StL 35 at Bal 24 24,784

Mon 11/23
N Min 30 at Atl 31 60,749

Thu 11/26
ChiB 9 at Dal 10 63,499
KC 10 at Det 27 76,735

Sun 11/29
Oak 32 at Sea 31 57,147
Atl 31 at Hou 27 40,201
TB 31 at NO 14 62,209
Was 14 at Buf 21 59,624
Cin 41 at Cle 21 75,186
Den 17 at SD 34 51,533
GB 35 at Min 23 46,025
StL 27 at NE 20 39,946
Bal 0 at NYJ 25 53,593
LARm 0 at Pit 24 51,854
NYG 10 at SF 17 57,186

Mon 11/30
Phi 10 at Mia 13 67,797

Thu 12/03
Cle 13 at Hou 17 44,502

Sun 12/06
Buf 28 at SD 27 51,488
KC 13 at Den 16 74,744
Dal 37 at Bal 13 54,871
NE 14 at Mia 24 50,421
SF 21 at Cin 3 56,796
Min 9 at ChiB 10 50,766
LARm 7 at NYG 10 59,659
NYJ 23 at Sea 27 53,105
Det 17 at GB 31 54,481
Atl 23 at TB 24 69,221
Phi 13 at Was 15 52,206
NO 3 at StL 30 46,923

Mon 12/07
N Pit 27 at Oak 30 51,769

Sat 12/12
Minn 7 at Det 45 79,428
NYJ 14 at Cle 13 56,866

Sun 12/13
Hou 6 at SF 28 55,707
SD 24 at TB 23 67,388
Sea 13 at Den 23 74,527
GB 35 at NO 7 45,518
ChiB 23 at Oak 6 40,384
Bal 14 at Was 38 46,706
NYG 20 at StL 10 47,358
Mia 17 at KC 7 57,407
Buf 19 at NE 10 42,549
Phi 10 at Dal 21 64,955
Cin 17 at Pit 10 50,623

Mon 12/14
N Atl 16 at LARm 21 57,054

Sat 12/19
Buf 6 at Mia 16 72,956
Dal 10 at NYG 13# 73,009

Sun 12/20
GB 3 at NYJ 28 56,340
SF 21 at NO 17 43,639
Cin 30 at Atl 28 35,972
StL 0 at Phi 38 56,656
Cle 21 at Sea 42 51,435
KC 10 at Min 6 41,110
Den 24 at ChiB 35 40,125
NE 21 at Bal 23 17,073
Pit 20 at Hou 21 41,056
Was 30 at LARm 7 52,224
TB 20 at Det 17 80,444

Mon 12/21
N Oak 10 at SD 23 52,279

Wild-Card Playoffs

Sun 12/27
Buf 31 at NYJ 27 57,050
NYG 27 at Phi 21 71,611

AFC/NFC Divisional Playoffs

Sat 01/02
SD 41 at Mia 38# 73,735
TB 0 at Dal 38 64,848

Sun 01/03
Buf 21 at Cin 28 55,420
NYG 24 at SF 38 58,360

1981 AFC/NFC Championships

Sun 01/10
SD 7 at Cin 27 46,302
Dal 27 at SF 28 60,525

Super Bowl XVI

Sun 01/24
SF 26 at Cin 21 81,270
at Pontiac, MI

National Football League 1982

Sun 09/12
SD 23 at Den 3 73,564
Mia 45 at NYJ 28 53,360
LARd 23 at SF 17 59,748
LARm 23 at GB 35 53,694
at Milwaukee, WI
Cle 21 at Sea 7 55,907
KC 9 at Buf 14 78,746
Was 37 at Phi 34# 68,885
TB 10 at Min 17 58,540
Hou 6 at Cin 27 52,268
ChiB 10 at Det 17 71,337
NE 24 at Bal 13 39,055
Atl 16 at NYG 14 74,286
StL 21 at NO 7 58,673

Mon 09/13
N Pit 36 at Dal 28 63,431

Thu 09/16
N Min 22 at Buf 23 77,753

Sun 09/19
Was 21 at TB 13 66,187
Sea 21 at Hou 23 43,117
Det 19 at LARm 14 59,470
LARd 38 at Atl 14 54,774
Bal 20 at Mia 24 51,999
NYJ 31 at NE 7 53,515
Phi 24 at Cle 21 78,830
Dal 24 at StL 7 50,705
NO 10 at ChiB 0 56,600
Cin 20 at Pit 26# 53,973
SF 21 at Den 24 73,889
SD 12 at KC 19 60,514

Mon 09/20
N GB 27 at NYG 19 68,405

Season interrupted: Players strike for 57 days, from midnight September 20 to November 17.

Sun 11/21
TB 9 at Dal 14 49,578
NE 7 at Cle 10 51,781
Mia 9 at Buf 7 52,945
Bal 0 at NYJ 37 46,970
Pit 24 at Hou 10 42,336
Min 7 at GB 26 44,681
at Milwaukee, WI
Det 17 at ChiB 20 46,783
Cin 18 at Phi 14 65,172
KC 17 at NO 27 39,341
SF 31 at StL 20 38,064
Was 27 at NYG 17 70,766
LARm 17 at Atl 34 39,686
Sea 17 at Den 10 73,916

Mon 11/22
N SD 24 at LARd 28 42,162

Thu 11/25
NYG 13 at Det 6 64,348
Cle 14 at Dal 31 46,267

Sun 11/28
Hou 21 at NE 29 33,602
ChiB 7 at Min 35 54,724
Phi 9 at Was 13 48,313
NO 23 at SF 20 51,611
StL 23 at Atl 20 33,411
LARd 17 at Cin 31 53,330
Pit 0 at Sea 16 55,553
Bal 0 at Buf 20 33,985
GB 13 at NYJ 15 53,872
Den 20 at SD 30 47,629
KC 14 at LARm 20 45,793

Mon 11/29
N Mia 17 at TB 23 65,854

Thu 12/02
N SF 30 at LARm 24 58,574

Sun 12/05
SD 30 at Cle 13 54,064
KC 14 at Pit 35 52,090
Sea 23 at LARd 28 42,170
StL 23 at Phi 20 63,622
Buf 21 at GB 33 46,655
at Milwaukee, WI
Atl 34 at Den 27 73,984
Min 14 at Mia 22 45,721
NE 13 at ChiB 26 36,973
Cin 20 at Bal 17 23,598
TB 13 at NO 10 61,709
Hou 14 at NYG 17 71,184
Dal 24 at Was 10 54,633

Mon 12/06
N NYJ 28 at Det 13 79,361

Sat 12/11
SD 41 at SF 37 55,988
Phi 7 at NYG 23 66,053

Sun 12/12
ChiB 14 at Sea 20 52,826
NO 0 at Atl 35 39,535
Pit 0 at Buf 13 58,391
Mia 0 at NE 3 25,716
Was 12 at StL 7 35,308
LARd 21 at KC 16 26,307
TB 17 at NYJ 32 28,147
Det 30 at GB 10 51,875
Bal 10 at Min 13 53,981
Cle 10 at Cin 23 54,305
Den 27 at LARm 24 48,112

Mon 12/13
N Dal 37 at Hou 7 51,808

Sat 12/18
NYJ 19 at Mia 20 67,702
LARm 31 at LARd 37 56,646

Sun 12/19
Atl 17 at SF 7 53,234
NE 16 at Sea 0 53,457
Pit 9 at Cle 10 67,139
StL 10 at ChiB 7 43,270
Buf 23 at TB 24 62,510
GB 20 at Bal 20# 25,920
Hou 14 at Phi 35 44,119
Min 34 at Det 31 73,058
KC 37 at Den 16 74,192
NO 7 at Dal 21 64,506
NYG 14 at Was 15 50,030

Mon 12/20
N Cin 34 at SD 50 51,296

Sun 12/26
SF 26 at KC 13 24,319
NYJ 42 at Min 14 58,672
ChiB 34 at LARm 26 46,502
Det 21 at TB 23 65,997
Phi 24 at Dal 20 46,199
Den 10 at LARd 27 44,160
NE 14 at Pit 37 51,515
GB 38 at Atl 7 50,245
NYG 21 at StL 24 39,824
Bal 26 at SD 44 49,711
Was 27 at NO 10 48,667
Cle 20 at Hou 14 36,599
Sea 10 at Cin 24 55,330

Mon 12/27
N Buf 10 at Mia 27 73,924

Sun 01/02
Atl 6 at NO 35 47,336
StL 0 at Was 28 52,544
Den 11 at Sea 13 43,145
NYJ 13 at KC 37 11,902
ChiB 23 at TB 26# 68,112
LARd 41 at SD 34 51,612
Buf 19 at NE 30 36,218
Cle 21 at Pit 37 52,312
GB 24 at Det 27 64,377
NYG 26 at Phi 24 63,917
Cin 35 at Hou 27 26,522
Mia 34 at Bal 7 19,073
LARm 21 at SF 20 54,256

Mon 01/03
N Dal 27 at Min 31 60,007

First Round Playoffs

Sat 01/08
Det 7 at Was 31 55,045
StL 16 at GB 41 54,282
NE 13 at Mia 28 68,842
Cle 10 at LARd 27 56,555

Sun 01/09
Atl 24 at Min 30 60,560
TB 17 at Dal 30 65,042
SD 31 at Pit 28 53,546
NYJ 44 at Cin 17 57,560

Second Round Playoffs

Sat 01/15
Min 7 at Was 21 54,593
NYJ 17 at LARd 14 90,037

Sun 01/16
SD 13 at Mia 34 71,383
GB 26 at Dal 37 63,972

1982 AFC/NFC Championships

Sat 01/22
Dal 17 at Was 31 55,045

Sun 01/23
NYJ 0 at Mia 14 67,396

Super Bowl XVII

Sun 01/30
Mia 17 at Was 27 103,667
at Pasadena, CA

National Football League 1983

Sat 09/03
N Phi 22 at SF 17 55,775

Sun 09/04
Atl 20 at ChiB 17 60,165
Bal 29 at NE 23# 45,526
Den 14 at Pit 10 58,233
Det 11 at TB 0 62,154
GB 41 at Hou 38# 44,073
LARd 21 at Cin 10 50,956
LARm 16 at NYG 6 75,281
Mia 12 at Buf 0 78,715
Min 27 at Cle 21 70,087
NYJ 41 at SD 29 51,004
StL 17 at NO 28 60,430
Sea 13 at KC 17 42,531

Mon 09/05
N Dal 31 at Was 30 55,045

Thu 09/08
N SF 48 at Min 17 58,162

Sun 09/11
Buf 10 at Cin 6 46,839
Cle 31 at Det 26 60,095
Dal 34 at StL 17 48,532
Den 17 at Bal 10 52,613
Hou 6 at LARd 20 37,526
NE 24 at Mia 34 59,343
NO 27 at LARm 30 45,572
NYG 16 at Atl 13# 52,850
Pit 25 at GB 21 55,154
Sea 17 at NYJ 10 54,972
TB 10 at ChiB 17 58,186
Was 23 at Phi 13 69,542

Mon 09/12
N SD 17 at KC 14 62,150

Thu 09/15
N Cin 7 at Cle 17 79,700

Sun 09/18
Atl 30 at Det 14 54,622
Bal 23 at Buf 28 40,937
ChiB 31 at NO 34# 64,692
KC 12 at Was 27 55,045
LARm 24 at GB 27 54,037
at Milwaukee, WI
Min 19 at TB 16# 57,567
NYG 13 at Dal 28 62,347
NYJ 13 at NE 23 43,182
Phi 13 at Den 10 74,202
Pit 40 at Hou 28 44,150
SD 31 at Sea 34 61,714
SF 42 at StL 27 38,132

Mon 09/19
N Mia 14 at LARd 27 57,796

Sun 09/25
Atl 20 at SF 24 57,814
ChiB 19 at Bal 22# 34,350
Cin 23 at TB 17 56,023
Cle 30 at SD 24# 49,482
Det 17 at Min 20 58,254
Hou 13 at Buf 30 60,070
KC 6 at Mia 14 50,785
LARd 22 at Den 7 74,289
LARm 24 at NYJ 27# 52,070
NE 28 at Pit 23 58,282
NO 20 at Dal 21 62,136
StL 14 at Phi 11 64,465
Was 27 at Sea 17 60,718

Mon 09/26
N GB 3 at NYG 27 75,308

Sun 10/02
Bal 34 at Cin 31 48,104
Dal 37 at Min 24 60,774
Den 14 at ChiB 31 58,210
Det 10 at LARm 21 49,403
Hou 10 at Pit 17 56,901
LARd 35 at Was 37 54,016
Mia 7 at NO 17 66,489
Phi 28 at Atl 24 50,621
StL 14 at KC 38 58,975
SD 41 at NYG 34 73,892
SF 33 at NE 13 54,293
Sea 24 at Cle 9 75,446
TB 14 at GB 55 54,272

Mon 10/03
N NYJ 34 at Buf 10 79,933

Sun 10/09
Buf 38 at Mia 35# 59,948
Den 26 at Hou 14 44,209
GB 14 at Det 38 67,738
KC 20 at LARd 21 40,492
LARm 10 at SF 7 59,119
Min 23 at ChiB 14 59,632
NE 7 at Bal 12 37,013
NO 19 at Atl 17 51,654
NYJ 7 at Cle 10 78,235
Phi 17 at NYG 13 73,291
Sea 21 at SD 28 49,132
TB 24 at Dal 27# 63,308
Was 38 at StL 14 42,698

Mon 10/10
N Pit 24 at Cin 14 56,086

Sun 10/16
Atl 21 at LARm 27 50,404
Buf 30 at Bal 7 38,565
ChiB 17 at Det 31 66,709
Cin 17 at Den 24 74,305
Cle 17 at Pit 44 59,263
Hou 14 at Min 34 58,910
LARd 36 at Sea 38 60,967
Mia 32 at NYJ 14 58,615
NYG 17 at KC 38 55,449
Phi 7 at Dal 37 63,070
StL 34 at TB 27 48,224
SD 21 at NE 37 59,016
SF 32 at NO 13 68,154

Mon 10/17
N Was 47 at GB 48 55,255

Sun 10/23
Atl 27 at NYJ 21 46,878
ChiB 7 at Phi 6 45,263
Cle 21 at Cin 28 50,047
Det 17 at Was 38 43,189
KC 13 at Hou 10# 39,462
LARd 40 at Dal 38 64,991
Mia 21 at Bal 7 32,343
Min 20 at GB 17# 55,236
NE 31 at Buf 0 60,424
NO 24 at TB 21 48,242
Pit 27 at Sea 21 61,615
SD 6 at Den 14 74,581
SF 45 at LARm 35 66,070

Mon 10/24
N NYG 20 at StL 20# 45,630

Sun 10/30
Bal 22 at Phi 21 59,150
Dal 38 at NYG 20 76,142
Det 38 at ChiB 17 58,764
GB 14 at Cin 34 53,349
Hou 19 at Cle 25# 66,955
KC 24 at Den 27 74,640
LARm 14 at Mia 30 72,175
Min 31 at StL 41 38,796
NE 13 at Atl 24 47,546
NO 21 at Buf 27 49,413
NYJ 27 at SF 13 54,796
Sea 34 at LARd 21 49,708
TB 12 at Pit 17 57,648

Mon 10/31
N Was 27 at SD 24 46,114

Sun 11/06
Atl 10 at NO 27 67,062
Bal 17 at NYJ 14 53,323
Buf 7 at NE 21 42,604
ChiB 14 at LARm 21 53,010
Cin 55 at Hou 14 39,706
Cle 21 at GB 35 54,089
at Milwaukee, WI
Den 19 at Sea 27 61,189
LARd 28 at KC 20 75,497
Mia 20 at SF 17 57,832
Dal 27 at Phi 20 71,236
StL 7 at Was 45 51,380
SD 3 at Pit 26 58,191
TB 17 at Min 12 59,239

Mon 11/07
N NYG 9 at Det 15 68,985

Sun 11/13
Buf 24 at NYJ 17 48,513
Cin 15 at KC 20 44,711
Dal 23 at SD 24 46,192
Den 20 at LARd 22 51,945
Det 17 at Hou 27 40,660
GB 29 at Min 21 60,113
Mia 6 at NE 17 60,771
NO 0 at SF 27 40,022
Phi 14 at ChiB 17 47,524
Pit 24 at Bal 13 57,319
Sea 28 at StL 33 33,280
TB 0 at Cle 20 56,091
Was 33 at NYG 17 71,482

Mon 11/14
N LARm 36 at Atl 13 31,202

Sun 11/20
Bal 0 at Mia 37 54,482
ChiB 27 at TB 0 36,816
Cle 30 at NE 0 40,987
Det 23 at GB 20# 50,050
at Milwaukee, WI
Hou 10 at Cin 38 46,375
KC 21 at Dal 41 64,103
LARd 27 at Buf 24 72,393
Min 17 at Pit 14 58,417
NYG 23 at Phi 0 57,977
SD 14 at StL 44 40,644
SF 24 at Atl 28 32,782
Sea 27 at Den 38 74,710
Was 42 at LARm 20 63,031

Mon 11/21
N NYJ 31 at NO 28 68,606

Thu 11/24
Pit 3 at Det 45 77,724
StL 17 at Dal 35 60,974

Sun 11/27
Bal 23 at Cle 41 65,812
Buf 17 at LARm 41 48,246
Den 7 at SD 31 43,650
GB 41 at Atl 47# 35,688
Hou 24 at TB 33 38,625
KC 48 at Sea 51# 56,793
Min 16 at NO 17 59,502
NE 3 at NYJ 26 48,620
NYG 12 at LARd 27 41,473
Phi 24 at Was 28 54,324
SF 3 at ChiB 13 40,483

Mon 11/28
N Cin 14 at Mia 38 74,506

Thu 12/01
N LARd 42 at SD 10 47,760

Sun 12/04
Atl 21 at Was 37 52,074
Buf 14 at KC 9 27,104
ChiB 28 at GB 31 51,147
Cin 23 at Pit 10 55,832
Cle 6 at Den 27 70,912
Dal 35 at Sea 10 63,352
LARm 9 at Phi 13 32,867
Mia 24 at Hou 17 39,434
NO 0 at NE 7 24,579
NYJ 10 at Bal 6 29,431
StL 10 at NYG 6 25,156

TB 21 at SF 35 49,773

Mon 12/05
N Min 2 at Det 13 79,169

Sat 12/10
Atl 24 at Mia 31 56,725
Pit 34 at NYJ 7 53,996

Sun 12/11
Bal 19 at Den 21 74,864
ChiB 19 at Min 13 57,880
Cle 27 at Hou 34 29,746
Det 9 at Cin 17 45,728
KC 38 at SD 41 35,510
NE 21 at LARm 7 46,503

NO 20 at Phi 17# 45,182
StL 34 at LARd 24 32,111
SF 23 at Buf 10 38,039
Sea 17 at NYG 12 48,942
Was 31 at Dal 10 65,074

Mon 12/12
N GB 12 at TB 9# 50,763

Fri 12/16
N NYJ 14 at Mia 34 59,975

Sat 12/17
Cin 14 at Min 20 51,565
NYG 22 at Was 31 53,874

Sun 12/18
Buf 14 at Atl 31 31,015
Den 17 at KC 48 11,377
GB 21 at ChiB 23 35,807
Hou 10 at Bal 20 20,418
LARm 26 at NO 24 70,148
NE 6 at Sea 24 59,688
Phi 7 at StL 31 21,902
Pit 17 at Cle 30 72,313
SD 14 at LARd 30 57,325
TB 20 at Det 23 78,392

Mon 12/19
N Dal 17 at SF 42 59,957

Wild-Card Playoffs

Sat 12/24
Den 7 at Sea 31 64,275

Mon 12/26
LARm 24 at Dal 17 62,118

AFC/NFC Divisional Playoffs

Sat 12/31
Sea 27 at Mia 20 74,136
Det 23 at SF 24 59,979

Sun 01/01
LARm 7 at Was 51 54,440
Pit 10 at LARd 38 90,380

1983 AFC/NFC Championships

Sun 01/08
SF 21 at Was 24 55,363
Sea 14 at LARd 30 88,734

Super Bowl XVIII

Sun 01/22
Was 9 at LARd 38 72,920
at Tampa, FL

National Football League 1984

Sun 09/02
Atl 36 at NO 28 66,652
TB 14 at ChiB 34 58,789
Cin 17 at Den 20 74,178
StL 23 at GB 24 53,738
KC 37 at Pit 27 56,709
LARd 24 at Hou 14 49,092
Mia 35 at Was 17 52,683
NE 21 at Buf 17 48,528
Phi 27 at NYG 28 71,520
NYJ 23 at Ind 14 60,398
SD 42 at Min 13 57,276
SF 30 at Det 27 56,782

Mon 09/03
Cle 0 at Sea 33 59,540
N Dal 20 at LARm 13 65,403

Thu 09/06
N Pit 23 at NYJ 17 70,564

Sun 09/09
Denv 0 at ChiB 27 54,335
Det 27 at Atl 24# 49,878
Ind 35 at Hou 21 43,820
KC 27 at Cin 22 47,111
GB 7 at LARd 28 46,269
Cle 17 at LARm 20 43,043
NE 7 at Mia 28 66,083
TB 13 at NO 17 54,686
Dal 7 at NYG 28 75,921
Min 17 at Phi 19 55,942
Buf 7 at StL 37 35,785
SD 17 at Sea 31 61,314

Mon 09/10
N Was 31 at SF 37 59,707

Sun 09/16
ChiB 9 at GB 7 55,942
Phi 17 at Dal 23 64,521
Den 24 at Cle 14 61,980
LARd 22 at KC 20 75,111
Atl 20 at Min 27 53,955
Sea 23 at NE 38 43,140
Cin 23 at NYJ 43 64,193
LARm 14 at Pit 24 58,104
StL 34 at Ind 33 60,274
Hou 14 at SD 31 52,266
NO 20 at SF 30 57,611
Det 17 at TB 21 44,560
NYG 14 at Was 30 52,997

Mon 09/17
N Mia 21 at Buf 17 65,455

Sun 09/23
Hou 10 at Atl 42 45,248
Pit 10 at Cle 20 77,312
GB 6 at Dal 20 64,222
KC 0 at Den 21 74,263
LARm 24 at Cin 14 45,406
Ind 7 at Mia 44 55,415
Min 29 at Det 28 57,511
StL 24 at NO 34 58,723
TB 14 at NYG 17 72,650
NYJ 28 at Buf 26 48,330

SF 21 at Phi 9 62,771
ChiB 9 at Sea 38 61,520
Was 26 at NE 10 60,503

Mon 09/24
N SD 30 at LARd 33 76,131

Sun 09/30
Dal 23 at ChiB 14 63,623
LARd 13 at Den 16 74,833
Buf 17 at Ind 31 60,032
Cle 6 at KC 10 40,785
NYG 12 at LARm 33 53,417
Mia 36 at StL 28 46,991
NE 28 at NYJ 21 68,978
NO 27 at Hou 10 43,108
Det 24 at SD 27 53,509
Atl 5 at SF 14 57,990
Sea 20 at Min 12 57,171
GB 27 at TB 30# 47,487
Phi 0 at Was 20 53,064

Mon 10/01
N Cin 17 at Pit 38 57,098

Sun 10/07
Atl 30 at LARm 28 47,832
NO 7 at ChiB 20 53,752
Hou 3 at Cin 13 43,637
Den 28 at Det 7 55,836
Sea 14 at LARd 28 77,904
Mia 31 at Pit 7 59,103
NE 17 at Cle 16 53,036
NYJ 17 at KC 16 51,843
Phi 27 at Buf 17 37,555
StL 31 at Dal 20 61,438
SD 34 at GB 28 54,045
Min 31 at TB 35 47,405
Was 35 at Ind 7 60,012

Mon 10/08
N SF 31 at NYG 10 76,112

Sun 10/14
TB 7 at Det 13# 44,308
SD 13 at KC 31 62,233
Min 20 at LARd 23 49,276
LARm 28 at NO 10 63,161
Hou 10 at Mia 28 52,435
Cin 14 at NE 20 48,154
NYG 19 at Atl 7 50,268
NYJ 24 at Cle 20 55,673
Ind 7 at Phi 16 50,277
Pit 20 at SF 17 59,110
ChiB 21 at StL 38 49,554
Buf 28 at Sea 31 59,034
Dal 14 at Was 34 55,431

Mon 10/15
N GB 14 at Den 17 62,546

Sun 10/21
ChiB 44 at TB 9 60,003
Cle 9 at Cin 12 50,667
NO 27 at Dal 30# 50,966
Den 37 at Buf 7 31,204
Det 16 at Min 14 59,953

Pit 16 at Ind 17 60,026
LARd 44 at SD 37 57,442
Mia 44 at NE 24 60,711
KC 7 at NYJ 28 66,782
NYG 10 at Phi 24 64,677
Was 24 at StL 26 50,262
SF 34 at Hou 21 39,900
Sea 30 at GB 24 52,286
at Milwaukee, WI

Mon 10/22
N LARm 24 at Atl 10 52,681

Sun 10/28
Min 7 at ChiB 16 57,517
Cin 31 at Hou 13 34,010
Ind 3 at Dal 22 58,724
Den 22 at LARd 19# 91,020
Det 9 at GB 41 54,289
TB 20 at KC 24 41,710
Buf 7 at Mia 38 58,824
NYJ 20 at NE 30 60,513
NO 16 at Cle 14 52,489
Was 13 at NYG 37 76,192
Atl 10 at Pit 35 55,971
StL 34 at Phi 14 54,310
SF 33 at LARm 0 65,481

Mon 10/29
N Sea 24 at SD 0 53,974

Sun 11/04
LARd 6 at ChiB 17 59,858
Cle 13 at Buf 10 33,343
NE 19 at Den 26 74,908
GB 23 at NO 13 57,426
LARm 16 at StL 13 50,950
Mia 31 at NYJ 17 72,655
TB 24 at Min 27 54,949
NYG 19 at Dal 7 60,235
Phi 23 at Det 23# 59,141
Hou 7 at Pit 35 48,892
SD 38 at Ind 10 60,143
Cin 17 at SF 23 58,324
KC 0 at Sea 45 61,396

Mon 11/05
N Atl 14 at Was 27 51,301

Sun 11/11
Pit 20 at Cin 22 52,497
Dal 24 at StL 17 48,721
Den 16 at SD 13 53,162
Min 17 at GB 45 52,931
at Milwaukee, WI
Hou 17 at KC 16 44,464
ChiB 13 at LARm 29 62,021
Ind 9 at NYJ 5 51,066
Phi 23 at Mia 24 70,227
Buf 10 at NE 38 43,313
NO 17 at Atl 13 40,590
SF 41 at Cle 7 60,092
Det 14 at Was 28 50,212
NYG 17 at TB 20 46,534

Mon 11/12
N LARd 14 at Sea 17 64,001

Sun 11/18
Dal 3 at Buf 14 74,391
Det 14 at ChiB 16 54,911
Cle 23 at Atl 7 28,280
Min 21 at Den 42 74,716
LARm 6 at GB 31 52,031
at Milwaukee, WI
NYJ 20 at Hou 31 40,141
KC 7 at LARd 17 48,575
NE 50 at Ind 17 60,009
StL 10 at NYG 16 73,428
Was 10 at Phi 16 63,117
Mia 28 at SD 34# 53,041
TB 17 at SF 24 57,704
Sea 26 at Cin 6 50,280

Mon 11/19
N Pit 24 at NO 27 66,005

Thu 11/22
NE 17 at Dal 20 55,341
GB 28 at Det 31 63,698

Sun 11/25
ChiB 34 at Min 3 56,881
Atl 14 at Cin 35 44,678
Hou 10 at Cle 27 46,077
Ind 7 at LARd 21 40,289
LARm 34 at TB 33 42,242
KC 27 at NYG 28 74,383
SD 24 at Pit 52 55,856
Phi 16 at StL 17 39,858
SF 35 at NO 3 65,177
Sea 27 at Den 24 74,922
Buf 14 at Was 41 51,513

Mon 11/26
N NYJ 17 at Mia 28 74,884

Thu 11/29
N Was 31 at Min 17 55,017

Sun 12/02
Ind 15 at Buf 21 20,693
Cin 20 at Cle 17# 51,774
Dal 26 at Phi 10 66,322
TB 14 at GB 27 46,800
Pit 20 at Hou 23# 39,781
Den 13 at KC 16 38,494
LARd 45 at Mia 34 71,222
NO 21 at LARm 34 49,348
NYG 20 at NYJ 10 74,975
StL 33 at NE 10 53,558
SF 35 at Atl 17 29,644
Det 17 at Sea 38 62,441

Mon 12/03
N ChiB 7 at SD 20 45,470

Sat 12/08
Buf 17 at NYJ 21 45,378
Min 7 at SF 51 56,670

Sun 12/09
Cin 24 at NO 21 40,855
SD 13 at Den 16 74,867
GB 20 at ChiB 14 59,374

Sea 7 at KC 34 34,855
Hou 16 at LARm 27 49,092
Mia 35 at Ind 17 60,411
NE 17 at Phi 27 41,581
Cle 20 at Pit 23 55,825
NYG 21 at StL 31 49,973
Atl 6 at TB 23 33,808
Was 30 at Dal 28 64,286

Mon 12/10
N LARd 24 at Det 3 66,710

Fri 12/14
N LARm 16 at SF 19 59,743

Sat 12/15
Den 31 at Sea 14 64,411
NO 10 at NYG 3 63,739

Sun 12/16
Phi 10 at Atl 26 15,582
ChiB 30 at Det 13 53,252
Buf 21 at Cin 52 55,771
Cle 27 at Hou 20 33,676
GB 38 at Min 14 51,197
KC 42 at SD 21 40,221
Ind 10 at NE 16 22,383
Pit 13 at LARd 7 83,056
NYJ 21 at TB 41 43,817
StL 27 at Was 29 54,299

Mon 12/17
N Dal 21 at Mia 28 74,139

Wild-Card Playoffs

Sat 12/22
LARd 7 at Sea 13 62,049

Sun 12/23
NYG 16 at LARm 13 67,037

AFC/NFC Divisional Playoffs

Sat 12/29
Sea 10 at Mia 31 73,469
NYG 10 at SF 21 60,303

Sun 12/30
ChiB 23 at Was 19 55,431
Pit 24 at Den 17 74,981

1984 AFC/NFC Championships

Sun 01/06
Pit 28 at Mia 45 76,029
ChiB 0 at SF 23 61,040

Super Bowl XIX

Sun 01/20
Mia 16 at SF 38 84,059
at Stanford, CA

National Football League 1985

Sun 09/08
Ind 3 at Pit 45 57,259
Mia 23 at Hou 26 47,656
Phi 0 at NYG 21 76,141
NYJ 0 at LARd 31 57,123
SD 14 at Buf 9 67,597
Sea 28 at Cin 24 51,625
TB 28 at ChiB 38 57,828
StL 27 at Cle 24# 62,107
Det 28 at Atl 27 37,785
KC 47 at NO 27 57,760
Den 16 at LARm 20 52,522
SF 21 at Min 28 57,375
GB 20 at NE 26 49,488

Mon 09/09
N Was 14 at Dal 44 62,292

Thu 09/12
N LARd 20 at KC 36 72,686

Sun 09/15
Sea 49 at SD 35 54,420
LARm 17 at Phi 6 60,920
Hou 13 at Was 16 53,553
Min 31 at TB 16 46,188
Ind 13 at Mia 30 53,693
Buf 3 at NYJ 42 63,449
Cin 27 at StL 41 46,321
NYG 20 at GB 23 56,144
Dal 21 at Det 26 72,985
Atl 16 at SF 35 58,923
NO 23 at Den 34 74,488
NE 7 at ChiB 20 60,533

Mon 09/16
N Pit 7 at Cle 17 79,042

Thu 09/19
N ChiB 33 at Min 24 61,242

Sun 09/22
Cle 7 at Dal 20 61,456
NE 17 at Buf 14 45,320
Den 44 at Atl 28 37,903
NYJ 24 at GB 3 53,667
at Milwaukee, WI
Phi 19 at Was 6 53,748
KC 0 at Mia 31 69,791
SD 44 at Cin 41 52,270
SF 34 at LARd 10 87,006
Hou 0 at Pit 20 58,752
Det 6 at Ind 14 60,042
StL 17 at NYG 27 74,987
TB 13 at NO 20 45,320

Mon 09/23
N LARm 35 at Sea 24 63,292

Sun 09/29
Mia 30 at Den 26 73,614
Ind 20 at NYJ 25 61,987
Atl 6 at LARm 17 49,870
Dal 17 at Hou 10 39,686
NYG 16 at Phi 10# 66,696
LARd 35 at NE 20 60,686
TB 9 at Det 30 45,023
NO 20 at SF 17 58,053
Was 10 at ChiB 45 63,708
GB 28 at StL 43 48,598
Cle 21 at SD 7 52,107
Sea 7 at KC 28 50,485
Min 27 at Buf 20 45,667

Mon 09/30
N Cin 37 at Pit 24 59,541

Sun 10/06
ChiB 27 at TB 19 51,795
SF 38 at Atl 17 44,740
Dal 30 at NYG 29 74,981
SD 21 at Sea 26 61,300
Det 10 at GB 43 55,914
NYJ 29 at Cin 20 51,785
Hou 20 at Den 31 74,699
Buf 17 at Ind 49 60,003
Pit 20 at Mia 24 72,820
NE 20 at Cle 24 62,139
Min 10 at LARm 13 61,139
KC 10 at LARd 19 55,133
Phi 21 at NO 23 56,364

Mon 10/07
N StL 10 at Was 27 53,134

Sun 10/13
NYG 30 at Cin 35 53,112
ChiB 26 at SF 10 60,523
StL 7 at Phi 30 48,186
LARm 31 at TB 27 39,607
Atl 26 at Sea 30 60,430
Pit 13 at Dal 27 62,932
NO 13 at LARd 23 48,152
KC 20 at SD 31 50,067
Min 17 at GB 20 54,647
at Milwaukee, WI
Buf 3 at NE 14 40,462
Den 15 at Ind 10 60,128
Cle 21 at Hou 6 38,386
Det 3 at Was 24 52,845

Mon 10/14
N Mia 7 at NYJ 23 73,807

Sun 10/20
Cin 27 at Hou 44 35,590
SF 21 at Det 23 67,715
SD 17 at Min 21 61,670
StL 10 at Pit 23 56,478
Sea 10 at Den 13# 74,899
Was 3 at NYG 17 74,389
LARd 21 at Cle 20 77,928
LARm 16 at KC 0 64,474
TB 38 at Mia 41 62,335
Dal 14 at Phi 16 70,114
NYJ 13 at NE 20 58,163
NO 24 at Atl 31 44,784
Ind 9 at Buf 21 28,430

Mon 10/21
N GB 7 at ChiB 23 65,095

Sun 10/27
Min 9 at ChiB 27 63,815
GB 10 at Ind 37 59,708
Was 14 at Cle 7 78,540
Hou 20 at StL 10 43,190
Sea 14 at NYJ 17 69,320
SF 28 at LARm 14 65,939
NYG 21 at NO 13 54,082
Mia 21 at Det 31 75,291
NE 32 at TB 14 34,661
Den 30 at KC 10 68,249
Buf 17 at Phi 21 60,987
Pit 21 at Cin 26 55,421
Atl 10 at Dal 24 57,941

Mon 10/28
N SD 21 at LARd 34 69,297

Sun 11/03
LARd 3 at Sea 33 64,060
KC 20 at Hou 23 41,238
TB 20 at NYG 22 72,031
Den 10 at SD 30 57,312
NYJ 35 at Ind 17 59,683
Cle 9 at Pit 10 51,976
Was 44 at Atl 10 42,209
Cin 23 at Buf 17 25,640
Mia 13 at NE 17 58,811
ChiB 16 at GB 10 55,343
Det 13 at Min 16 58,012
Phi 13 at SF 24 58,383
NO 10 at LARm 28 49,030

Mon 11/04
N Dal 10 at StL 21 49,347

Sun 11/10
GB 27 at Min 17 59,970
LARm 19 at NYG 24 74,663
Sea 27 at NO 3 47,365
LARd 34 at SD 40# 58,566
NYJ 17 at Mia 21 73,965
Atl 17 at Phi 23# 63,694
Pit 36 at KC 28 46,126
Ind 15 at NE 34 54,176
Cle 10 at Cin 27 57,293
Det 3 at ChiB 24 53,467
StL 0 at TB 16 34,736
Dal 13 at Was 7 55,750
Hou 0 at Buf 20 21,831

Mon 11/11
N SF 16 at Den 17 73,173

Sun 11/17
Pit 30 at Hou 7 45,977
LARm 14 at Atl 30 29,960
Buf 7 at Cle 17 50,764
Cin 6 at LARd 13 52,501
NE 20 at Sea 13 60,345
TB 28 at NYJ 62 65,344
NO 14 at GB 38 52,104
at Milwaukee, WI
Min 21 at Det 41 54,647
KC 3 at SF 31 56,447
Mia 34 at Ind 20 59,666
SD 24 at Den 30# 74,376
ChiB 44 at Dal 0 63,855
Phi 24 at StL 14 39,032

Mon 11/18
N NYG 21 at Was 23 53,371

Sun 11/24
Atl 0 at ChiB 36 61,769
NO 30 at Min 23 54,117
Was 30 at Pit 23 59,293
NE 13 at NYJ 16# 74,100
Mia 23 at Buf 14 50,474
Det 16 at TB 19# 43,471
Den 28 at LARd 31# 63,131
NYG 34 at StL 3 41,248
GB 17 at LARm 34 52,710
SD 35 at Hou 37 34,336
Phi 17 at Dal 34 54,047
Ind 7 at KC 20 21,762
Cin 6 at Cle 24 74,439

Mon 11/25
N Sea 6 at SF 19 57,482

Thu 11/28
NYJ 20 at Det 31 65,531
StL 17 at Dal 35 54,125

Sun 12/01
TB 0 at GB 21 19,856
KC 6 at Sea 24 52,655
LARm 3 at NO 29 44,122
SF 35 at Was 8 51,321
NE 38 at Ind 31 56,740
Hou 27 at Cin 45 46,140
Den 31 at Pit 23 56,797
Buf 7 at SD 40 45,487
Cle 35 at NYG 33 66,482
LARd 34 at Atl 24 20,585
Min 28 at Phi 23 54,688

Mon 12/02
N ChiB 24 at Mia 38 75,594

Sun 12/08
Det 6 at NE 23 59,078
Ind 10 at ChiB 17 59,997
Was 17 at Phi 12 60,373
NYJ 27 at Buf 7 23,122
Dal 24 at Cin 50 56,936
Pit 44 at SD 54 52,098
LARd 17 at Den 14# 75,042
TB 7 at Min 26 51,593
Atl 10 at KC 38 18,199
NYG 35 at Hou 14 36,576
NO 16 at StL 28 29,527
Cle 13 at Sea 31 58,477
Mia 34 at GB 24 52,671

Mon 12/09
N LARm 27 at SF 20 60,581

Sat 12/14
KC 13 at Den 14 69,209
ChiB 19 at NYJ 6 74,752

Sun 12/15
Phi 14 at SD 20 45,569
StL 14 at LARm 46 52,052
Sea 3 at LARd 13 77,425
SF 31 at NO 19 46,065
NYG 21 at Dal 28 62,310
Hou 21 at Cle 28 50,793
Cin 24 at Was 27 50,544
Ind 31 at TB 23 25,577
GB 26 at Det 23 49,379
Buf 24 at Pit 30 35,953
Min 13 at Atl 14 14,167

Mon 12/16
N NE 27 at Mia 30 69,489

Fri 12/20
N Den 27 at Sea 24 56,283

Sat 12/21
Pit 10 at NYG 28 66,785
Was 27 at StL 16 28,090

Sun 12/22
SD 34 at KC 38 18,178
GB 20 at TB 17 33,992
Buf 0 at Mia 28 64,811
Atl 16 at NO 10 31,717
Cin 23 at NE 34 57,953
Phi 37 at Min 35 49,722
ChiB 37 at Det 17 74,042
Cle 10 at NYJ 37 59,073
Hou 16 at Ind 34 55,818
Dal 16 at SF 31 60,114

Mon 12/23
N LARd 16 at LARm 6 66,676

Wild-Card Playoffs

Sat 12/28
NE 26 at NYJ 14 75,945

Sun 12/29
SF 3 at NYG 17 75,131

AFC/NFC Divisional Playoffs

Sat 01/04
Cle 21 at Mia 24 74,667
Dal 0 at LARm 20 66,581

Sun 01/05
NYG 0 at ChiB 21 65,670
NE 27 at LARd 20 87,163

1985 AFC/NFC Championships

Sun 01/12
LARm 0 at ChiB 24 66,030
NE 31 at Mia 14 75,662

Super Bowl XX

Sun 01/26
ChiB 46 at NE 10 73,818
at New Orleans, LA

National Football League 1986

Sun 09/07
Atl 31 at NO 10 67,950
Cin 14 at KC 24 43,430
Cle 31 at ChiB 41 61,975
Det 13 at Min 10 54,851
Hou 31 at GB 3 54,065
Ind 3 at NE 33 55,208
LARd 36 at Den 38 75,695
LARm 16 at StL 10 40,347
Mia 28 at SD 50 57,726
NYJ 28 at Buf 24 79,951
Phi 14 at Was 41 53,982
Pit 0 at Sea 30 61,461
SF 31 at TB 7 50,780

Mon 09/08
N NYG 28 at Dal 31 59,804

Thu 09/11
N NE 20 at NYJ 6 72,422

Sun 09/14
Buf 33 at Cin 36# 52,714
Cle 23 at Hou 20 46,049
Dal 31 at Det 7 73,812
GB 10 at NO 24 46,383
Ind 10 at Mia 30 51,848
KC 17 at Sea 23 61,068
LARd 6 at Was 10 55,235
Min 23 at TB 10 34,579
Phi 10 at ChiB 13# 65,130
StL 13 at Atl 33 46,463
SD 7 at NYG 20 74,921
SF 13 at LARm 16 65,195

Mon 09/15
N Den 21 at Pit 10 57,305

Thu 09/18
N Cin 30 at Cle 13 78,779

Sun 09/21
Atl 37 at Dal 35 62,880
Den 33 at Phi 7 63,839
Hou 13 at KC 27 43,699
LARm 24 at Ind 7 59,012
Mia 45 at NYJ 51# 71,025
NO 17 at SF 26 58,927
NYG 14 at LARd 9 71,164
Pit 7 at Min 31 56,795
StL 10 at Buf 17 65,762
Sea 38 at NE 31 58,977
TB 24 at Det 20 38,453
Was 30 at SD 27 57,853

Mon 09/22
N ChiB 25 at GB 12 55,527

Sun 09/28
Atl 23 at TB 20# 38,950
ChiB 44 at Cin 7 55,146
Det 21 at Cle 24 72,029
GB 7 at Min 42 60,478
KC 20 at Buf 17 67,555
LARm 20 at Phi 34 65,646
NE 20 at Den 27 75,804
NO 17 at NYG 20 72,765
NYJ 26 at Ind 7 56,075
Pit 22 at Hou 16# 42,001
SD 13 at LARd 17 63,153
SF 31 at Mia 16 70,264
Sea 14 at Was 19 54,157

Mon 09/29
N Dal 31 at StL 7 49,077

Sun 10/05
Buf 13 at NYJ 14 69,504
Cin 34 at GB 28 51,230
at Milwaukee, WI
Cle 27 at Pit 24 57,327
Dal 14 at Den 29 76,082
Hou 13 at Det 24 41,960
Ind 14 at SF 35 57,252
LARd 24 at KC 17 74,430
Mia 7 at NE 34 60,689
Min 0 at ChiB 23 63,921
NYG 13 at StL 6 40,562
Phi 16 at Atl 0 57,104
TB 20 at LARm 26# 50,585
Was 14 at NO 6 57,317

Mon 10/06
N SD 7 at Sea 33 63,207

Sun 10/12
Buf 14 at Mia 27 49,467
ChiB 20 at Hou 7 46,026
Den 31 at SD 14 55,662
Det 21 at GB 14 52,290
KC 7 at Cle 20 71,278
LARm 14 at Atl 26 51,662
Min 27 at SF 24# 58,637
NO 17 at Ind 14 53,512
NYJ 31 at NE 24 60,342
Phi 3 at NYG 35 74,221
StL 30 at TB 19 33,307
Sea 10 at LARd 14 70,635
Was 6 at Dal 30 63,264

Mon 10/13
N Pit 22 at Cin 24 54,283

Sun 10/19
ChiB 7 at Min 23 62,851
Dal 17 at Phi 14 68,572
Det 10 at LARm 14 50,992
GB 17 at Cle 14 76,438
Hou 28 at Cin 31 53,844
Ind 13 at Buf 24 50,050
LARd 30 at Mia 28 53,421
NE 34 at Pit 0 54,743
NYG 12 at Sea 17 62,282
StL 21 at Was 28 53,494
SD 41 at KC 42 55,767
SF 10 at Atl 10# 55,306
TB 7 at NO 38 43,355

Mon 10/20
N Den 10 at NYJ 22 73,759

Sun 10/26
Atl 7 at LARm 14 56,993
Cin 9 at Pit 30 50,816
Cle 23 at Min 20 59,133
Det 7 at ChiB 13 62,064
LARd 28 at Hou 17 41,641
Mia 17 at Ind 13 58,350
NE 23 at Buf 3 77,808
NO 23 at NYJ 28 44,246
StL 6 at Dal 37 60,756
SD 7 at Phi 23 41,469
SF 31 at GB 17 50,557
at Milwaukee, WI
Sea 13 at Den 20 76,089
TB 20 at KC 27 36,230

Mon 10/27
N Was 20 at NYG 27 75,923

Sun 11/02
Atl 17 at NE 25 60,597
Buf 28 at TB 34 32,806
Cin 24 at Det 17 52,423
Cle 24 at Ind 9 57,962
Dal 14 at NYG 17 74,871
Den 21 at LARd 10 90,131
GB 3 at Pit 27 52,831
Hou 7 at Mia 28 43,804
KC 24 at SD 23 48,518
Min 38 at Was 44# 51,928
NYJ 38 at Sea 7 62,497
Phi 10 at StL 13 33,051
SF 10 at NO 23 53,234

Mon 11/03
N LARm 20 at ChiB 17 64,877

Sun 11/09
ChiB 23 at TB 3 70,097
Cin 28 at Hou 32 32,120
LARd 17 at Dal 13 61,706
LARm 0 at NO 6 62,352
Min 24 at Det 10 53,725
NE 30 at Ind 21 56,890
NYG 17 at Phi 14 60,601
NYJ 28 at Atl 14 53,476
Pit 12 at Buf 16 72,000
StL 17 at SF 43 59,172
SD 9 at Den 3 75,012
Sea 7 at KC 27 53,268
Was 16 at GB 7 47,728

Mon 11/10
N Mia 16 at Cle 26 77,949

Sun 11/16
ChiB 13 at Atl 10 55,520
Cle 14 at LARd 27 65,461
Dal 24 at SD 21 55,622
Det 13 at Phi 11 54,568
Hou 10 at Pit 21 49,724
Ind 16 at NYJ 31 65,149
KC 17 at Den 38 75,745
NE 30 at LARm 28 64,339
Mia 34 at Buf 24 76,474
NYG 22 at Min 20 62,003
NO 16 at StL 7 32,069
Sea 7 at Cin 34 54,410
TB 7 at GB 31 48,271
at Milwaukee, WI

Mon 11/17
N SF 6 at Was 14 54,774

Thu 11/20
N LARd 37 at SD 31# 56,031

Sun 11/23
Atl 0 at SF 20 58,747
Buf 19 at NE 22 60,455
Dal 14 at Was 41 55,642
Den 16 at NYG 19 75,116
Det 38 at TB 17 30,029
GB 10 at ChiB 12 59,291
Ind 17 at Hou 31 31,702
KC 14 at StL 23 29,680
Min 20 at Cin 24 53,003
NO 13 at LARm 26 58,600
Phi 20 at Sea 24 55,786
Pit 31 at Cle 37# 76,452

Mon 11/24
N NYJ 3 at Mia 45 70,206

Thu 11/27
GB 44 at Det 40 61,199
Sea 31 at Dal 14 58,023

Sun 11/30
Atl 20 at Mia 14 53,762
Buf 17 at KC 14 31,492
Cin 28 at Den 34 58,705
Hou 10 at Cle 13# 62,309
LARm 17 at NYJ 3 70,539
NE 21 at NO 20 58,259
Phi 33 at LARd 27# 53,338
Pit 10 at ChiB 13# 61,425
SD 17 at Ind 3 47,950
TB 13 at Min 45 56,235
Was 20 at StL 17 35,637

Mon 12/01
N NYG 21 at SF 17 59,777

Sun 12/07
Cin 31 at NE 7 59,639
Cle 21 at Buf 17 47.488
Den 10 at KC 37 62,402
Det 17 at Pit 27 57,961
Hou 0 at SD 27 50,120
Ind 28 at Atl 23 40,003
Mia 31 at NO 27 68,239
Min 32 at GB 6 47,637
NYG 24 at Was 14 54,651
NYJ 10 at SF 24 60,946
StL 10 at Phi 10# 59,074
TB 14 at ChiB 48 65,130
Dal 10 at LARm 29 67,839

Mon 12/08
N LARd 0 at Sea 37 64,060

Sat 12/13
Pit 45 at NYJ 24 76,025
Was 30 at Den 31 75,265

Sun 12/14
Buf 14 at Ind 24 56,972
Cle 34 at Cin 3 58,669
GB 21 at TB 7 40,382
KC 20 at LARd 17 63,145
Mia 37 at LARm 31# 67,153
Min 10 at Hou 23 32,738
NO 14 at Atl 9 55,630
Phi 23 at Dal 21 62,079
StL 7 at NYG 27 75,760
SF 29 at NE 24 59,798
Sea 34 at SD 24 54,804

Mon 12/15
N ChiB 16 at Det 13 75,602

Fri 12/19
N LARm 14 at SF 24 60,366

Sat 12/20
Den 16 at Sea 41 63,697
GB 24 at NYG 55 71,351

Sun 12/21
Atl 20 at Det 6 35,255
Buf 7 at Hou 16 31,049
ChiB 24 at Dal 10 57,256
Ind 30 at LARd 24 41,349
KC 24 at Pit 19 47,150
NO 17 at Min 33 51,209
NYJ 21 at Cin 52 51,619
SD 17 at Cle 47 68,505
TB 17 at StL 21 23,957
Was 21 at Phi 14 61,816

Mon 12/22
N NE 34 at Mia 27 74,516

Wild-Card Playoffs

Sun 12/28
KC 15 at NYJ 35 75,210
LARm 7 at Was 19 54,567

AFC/NFC Divisional Playoffs

Sat 01/03
NYJ 20 at Cle 23# 79,720
Was 27 at ChiB 13 65,524

Sun 01/04
NE 17 at Den 22 75,262
SF 3 at NYG 49 75,691

1986 AFC/NFC Championships

Sun 01/11
Den 23 at Cle 20# 79,973
Was 0 at NYG 17 76,891

Super Bowl XXI

Sun 01/25
Den 20 vs NYG 39 101,063
at Pasadena, CA

National Football League 1987

Sun 09/13
Det 19 at Min 34 57,061
SF 17 at Pit 30 55,735
Dal 13 at StL 24 42,241
Phi 24 at Was 34 52,188
Sea 17 at Den 40 75,999
NYJ 31 at Buf 28 75,718
Mia 21 at NE 28 54,642
Cle 21 at NO 28 62,339
LARd 20 at GB 0 54,983
Atl 10 at TB 48 51,250
LARm 16 at Hou 20 33,186
Cin 23 at Ind 21 59,387
SD 13 at KC 20 59,940

Mon 09/14
N NYG 19 at ChiB 34 65,704

Sun 09/20
Min 21 at LARm 16 63,567
Dal 16 at NYG 14 73,426
Was 20 at Atl 21 63,567
SF 27 at Cin 26 53,498
KC 14 at Sea 43 61,667
Den 17 at GB 17# 50,624
at Milwaukee, WI
NO 17 at Phi 27 57,485
Hou 30 at Buf 34 56,534
Mia 23 at Ind 10 57,524
TB 3 at ChiB 20 63,551
StL 24 at SD 28 47,988
Pit 10 at Cle 34 79,543
Det 7 at LARd 27 50,300

Mon 09/21
N NE 24 at NYJ 43 70,847

The season was reduced from a 16-game season to 15 as a result of a 24-day players' strike called by the NFLPA on September 22. Games scheduled for the third weekend were cancelled but the games of weeks four, five, and six were played with replacement teams. Striking players returned for the seventh week of the season, October 25.

Sun 10/04
LARm 10 at NO 37 29,745
Hou 40 at Den 10 38,494
GB 23 at Min 16 13,911
StL 21 at Was 28 27,728
ChiB 35 at Phi 3 4,074
Ind 47 at Buf 6 9,860
TB 31 at Det 27 4,919
KC 17 at LARd 35 10,708
SD 10 at Cin 9 18,074
Dal 38 at NYJ 24 12,370
Mia 20 at Sea 24 19,448
Pit 28 at Atl 12 16,667
Cle 20 at NE 10 14,830

Mon 10/05
N SF 41 at NYG 21 16,471

Sun 10/11
Det 19 at GB 16# 35,779
NYJ 0 at Ind 6 34,927
Phi 22 at Dal 41 40,622
Pit 21 at LARm 31 20,218
NO 19 at StL 24 11,795
Buf 7 at NE 14 11,878
KC 0 at Mia 42 25,867
Was 38 at NYG 12 9,123
Cin 17 at Sea 10 31,739
Hou 15 at Cle 10 38,927
SD 17 at TB 13 23,878
Min 7 at ChiB 27 32,113
SF 25 at Atl 17 8,684

Mon 10/12
N LARd 14 at Den 30 61,230

Sun 10/18
Min 10 at TB 20 20,850
Ind 7 at Pit 21 34,627
Sea 37 at Det 14 8,310
SD 23 at LARd 17 23,541
LARm 20 at Atl 24 15,813
Cle 34 at Cin 0 40,179
NO 19 at ChiB 17 46,813
NE 21 at Hou 7 28,294
Mia 31 at NYJ 37# 18,249
Den 26 at KC 17 20,296
StL 28 at SF 34 38,094
NYG 3 at Buf 6# 15,737
Phi 10 at GB 16# 35,842

Mon 10/19
N Was 13 at Dal 7 60,415

Sun 10/25
NE 16 at Ind 30 48,850
Buf 34 at Mia 31# 61,295
ChiB 27 at TB 26 70,747
SF 24 at NO 22 60,497
Sea 35 at LARd 13 52,735
KC 21 at SD 42 47,972
Dal 20 at Phi 37 60,497
NYJ 16 at Was 17 53,497
Cin 20 at Pit 23 53,692
Atl 33 at Hou 37 29,062
GB 34 at Det 33 27,278
StL 7 at NYG 30 74,391

Mon 10/26
N LARm 17 at Cle 30 76,933
N Den 27 at Min 34 51,011

Sun 11/01
Pit 24 at Mia 35 52,578
Was 27 at Buf 7 71,640
LARd 23 at NE 26 60,664
Det 0 at Den 34 75,172
NO 38 at Atl 0 42,196
SF 31 at LARm 10 55,328
TB 23 at GB 17 50,308
at Milwaukee, WI
Cle 24 at SD 27# 55,381
Ind 19 at NYJ 14 60,863
Phi 28 at StL 23 24,586
Hou 31 at Cin 29 52,700
KC 28 at ChiB 31 63,498
Min 17 at Sea 28 61,134

Mon 11/02
N NYG 24 at Dal 33 55,730

Sun 11/08
Den 14 at Buf 21 63,698
SD 16 at Ind 13 60,459
Pit 17 at KC 16 45,249
Dal 17 at Det 27 45,325
LARd 20 at Min 31 57,150
ChiB 26 at GB 24 53,320
NE 10 at NYG 17 73,817
Mia 20 at Cin 14 53,848
Was 27 at Phi 31 66,398
TB 28 at StL 31 22,449
NO 31 at LARm 14 43,379
Atl 3 at Cle 38 71,135
Hou 20 at SF 27 59,740

Mon 11/09
N Sea 14 at NYJ 30 60,452

Sun 11/15
NYG 20 at Phi 17 66,172
NYJ 16 at KC 9 40,718
TB 17 at Min 23 48,605
Dal 23 at NE 17# 60,567
LARm 27 at StL 24 27,730
Det 13 at Was 20 50,593
Cin 16 at Atl 10 25,758
Hou 23 at Pit 3 56,177
GB 13 at Sea 24 60,963
NO 26 at SF 24 68,436
Buf 21 at Cle 27 78,409
LARd 14 at SD 16 60,639
Ind 40 at Mia 21 65,433

Mon 11/16
N ChiB 29 at Den 31 75,783

Sun 11/22
Buf 17 at NYJ 14 58,407
StL 31 at Phi 19 55,592
SD 3 at Sea 34 62,444
Det 10 at ChiB 30 63,357
Mia 20 at Dal 14 56,519
Atl 13 at Min 24 53,866
SF 24 at TB 10 63,211
Ind 0 at NE 24 56,906
Den 23 at LARd 17 61,318
NYG 14 at NO 23 67,739
Cle 40 at Hou 7 51,161
Pit 30 at Cin 16 52,795
GB 23 at KC 3 34,611

Mon 11/23
N LARm 30 at Was 26 53,614

Thu 11/26
Min 44 at Dal 38# 54,229
KC 27 at Det 20 43,820

Sun 11/29
NO 20 at Pit 16 47,896
Cle 24 at SF 38 60,248
StL 34 at Atl 21 15,909
NYG 19 at Was 23 45,818
Hou 27 at Ind 51 54,009
GB 10 at ChiB 23 61,638
TB 3 at LARm 35 45,188
Den 31 at SD 17 61,880
Cin 20 at NYJ 27 41,135
Mia 0 at Buf 27 68,055
Phi 34 at NE 31# 54,198

Mon 11/30
N LARd 37 at Sea 14 62,802

Sun 12/06
KC 27 at Cin 30# 46,489
TB 34 at NO 44 66,471
Atl 21 at Dal 10 40,103
Sea 9 at Pit 13 48,881
ChiB 30 at Min 24 62,331
Buf 21 at LARd 34 43,143
SF 23 at GB 12 51,118
Phi 20 at NYG 23# 65,874
SD 18 at Hou 33 31,714
LARm 37 at Det 16 33,413
Ind 9 at Cle 7 70,661
Was 34 at StL 17 31,324
NE 20 at Den 31 75,794

Mon 12/07
N NYJ 28 at Mia 37 58,879

Sun 12/13
Mia 28 at Phi 10 63,841
NYG 24 at StL 27 29,623
Atl 0 at LARm 33 43,310
Hou 10 at NO 24 68,257
Min 10 at GB 16 47,059
at Milwaukee, WI
LARd 10 at KC 16 63,834
Buf 27 at Ind 3 60,253
Dal 20 at Was 24 54,882
Pit 20 at SD 16 51,605
Den 21 at Sea 28 61,759
Cin 24 at Cle 38 77,331
NYJ 20 at NE 42 60,617
Det 20 at TB 10 41,669

Mon 12/14
N ChiB 0 at SF 41 63,509

Sat 12/19
KC 17 at Den 20 75,053
GB 10 at NYG 20 51,013

Sun 12/20
Ind 20 at SD 7 46,211
NE 13 at Buf 7 74,945
Phi 38 at NYJ 27 30,572
Pit 16 at Hou 24 38,683
Cle 24 at LARd 17 40,275
Atl 7 at SF 35 54,275
Sea 34 at ChiB 21 62,518
StL 31 at TB 14 32,046
NO 41 at Cin 24 43,424
Min 17 at Det 14 27,693
Was 21 at Mia 23 65,715

Mon 12/21
Dal 29 at LARm 21 60,700

Sat 12/26
Cle 19 at Pit 13 56,394
Was 27 at Min 24# 59,160

Sun 12/27
GB 24 at NO 33 68,364
TB 6 at Ind 24 60,468
NYJ 7 at NYG 20 68,318
Cin 17 at Hou 21 49,275
StL 16 at Dal 21 36,788
SD 0 at Den 24 37,500
LARm 0 at SF 48 57,950
ChiB 6 at LARd 3 78,019
Buf 7 at Phi 17 57,547
Sea 20 at KC 41 20,370
Det 30 at Atl 13 13,906

Mon 12/28
N NE 24 at Mia 10 61,192

Wild-Card Playoffs

Sun 01/03
Min 44 at NO 10 68,546
Sea 20 at Hou 23# 50,519

AFC/NFC Divisional Playoffs

Sat 01/09
Ind 21 at Cle 38 79,372
Min 36 at SF 24 63,008

Sun 01/10
Was 21 at ChiB 17 65,268
Hou 10 at Den 34 75,440

1987 AFC/NFC Championships

Sun 01/17
Min 10 at Was 17 55,212
Cle 33 at Den 38 76,197

Super Bowl XXII

Sun 01/31
Was 42 at Den 10 73,302
at San Diego, CA

National Football League 1988

Sun 09/04
Dal 21 at Pit 24 56,813
Hou 17 at Ind 14# 57,251
Phi 41 at TB 14 43,502
Pho 14 at Cin 21 50,404
NYJ 3 at NE 28 44,027
LARm 34 at GB 7 53,460
Atl 17 at Det 31 31,075
SF 34 at NO 33 69,145
SD 13 at LARd 24 39,029
Sea 21 at Den 14 75,986
Min 10 at Buf 13 76,783
Cle 6 at KC 3 55,654
Mia 7 at ChiB 34 63,330

Mon 09/05
N Was 20 at NYG 27 76,417

Sun 09/11
ChiB 17 at Ind 13 60,503
NO 29 at Atl 21 48,901
Mia 6 at Buf 9 79,529
TB 13 at GB 10 52,583
Det 10 at LARm 17 46,262
Pit 29 at Was 30 54,083
NYJ 23 at Cle 3 74,434
KC 10 at Sea 31 61,512
NE 6 at Min 36 55,545
SD 3 at Den 34 75,359
Cin 28 at Phi 24 66,459
LARd 35 at Hou 38 46,050
SF 20 at NYG 17 75,943

Mon 09/12
N Dal 17 at Pho 14 67,132

Sun 09/18
Den 13 at KC 20 63,268
NYG 12 at Dal 10 55,325
Pho 30 at TB 24 35,034
Phi 10 at Was 17 53,920
LARm 22 at LARd 17 84,870
Hou 3 at NYJ 45 64,683
Atl 34 at SF 17 60,168
NO 22 at Det 14 32,943
Sea 6 at SD 17 44,449
Cin 17 at Pit 12 56,647
GB 17 at Mia 24 54,409
Buf 16 at NE 14 55,945
Min 31 at ChiB 7 63,990

Mon 09/19
N Ind 17 at Cle 23 75,148

Sun 09/25
Pit 28 at Buf 36 78,735
ChiB 24 at GB 6 56,492
TB 9 at NO 13 66,671
NE 6 at Ind 31 38,636
LARm 45 at NYG 31 75,617
Phi 21 at Min 23 56,012
NYJ 17 at Det 10 29,250
SD 24 at KC 23 45,498
Was 21 at Pho 30 61,973
Atl 20 at Dal 26 39,702
Mia 13 at Ind 15 59,638
Cle 17 at Cin 24 56,397
SF 38 at Sea 7 62,382

Mon 09/26
N LARd 30 at Den 27# 75,964

Sun 10/02
Buf 3 at ChiB 24 62,793
GB 24 at TB 27 40,003
KC 17 at NYJ 17# 66,110
Cin 45 at LARd 21 42,594
NYG 24 at Was 23 54,601
Pho 41 at LARm 27 49,830
Cle 23 at Pit 9 56,410
Sea 31 at Atl 20 28,619
Den 12 at SD 0 55,763
Min 7 at Mia 24 59,867
Det 13 at SF 20 58,285
Hou 23 at Phi 32 64,692
Ind 17 at NE 21 58,050

Mon 10/03
N Dal 17 at NO 20 68,474

Sun 10/09
Sea 16 at Cle 10 78,605
KC 6 at Hou 7 39,135
NO 23 at SD 17 42,693
ChiB 24 at Det 7 64,526
Den 16 at SF 13# 61,711
Pit 14 at Pho 31 53,278
NE 3 at GB 45 51,932
at Milwaukee, WI
TB 13 at Min 14 55,274
Was 35 at Dal 17 63,235
Ind 23 at Buf 34 76,018
LARm 33 at Atl 0 30,852
Mia 24 at LARd 14 50,751
NYJ 19 at Cin 36 57,482

Mon 10/10
N NYG 13 at Phi 24 63,736

Sun 10/16
GB 34 at Min 14 59,053
Det 10 at NYG 30 74,813
Dal 7 at ChiB 17 64,759
Hou 34 at Pit 14 52,229
Pho 17 at Was 33 54,402
LARd 27 at KC 17 77,078
NO 20 at Sea 19 63,569
Cin 21 at NE 27 59,969
SF 24 at LARm 21 65,450
Phi 3 at Cle 19 78,787
TB 31 at Ind 35 53,135
SD 28 at Mia 31 58,972
Atl 14 at Den 30 75,287

Mon 10/17
N Buf 37 at NYJ 14 70,218

Sun 10/23
Min 49 at TB 20 48,020
Sea 10 at LARm 31 57,033
Den 21 at Pit 39 49,811
Det 7 at KC 6 66,926
Cle 29 at Pho 21 61,261
Ind 16 at SD 0 37,722
NYG 23 at Atl 16 45,092
NYJ 44 at Mia 30 68,292
Dal 23 at Phi 24 66,309
Was 20 at GB 17 51,767
at Milwaukee, WI
Hou 21 at Cin 44 54,659
NE 20 at Buf 23 76,824
LARd 6 at NO 20 66,249

Mon 10/24
N SF 9 at ChiB 10 65,293

Sun 10/30
KC 10 at LARd 17 36,103
NYG 13 at Det 10# 38,354
Cin 16 at Cle 23 79,147
Atl 27 at Phi 24 65,244
ChiB 7 at NE 30 60,821
Min 21 at SF 24 60,738
LARm 12 at NO 10 68,238
GB 0 at Buf 28 79,176
Pit 20 at NYJ 24 64,862
Mia 17 at TB 14 67,352
Pho 16 at Dal 10 42,196
SD 14 at Sea 17 59,641
Was 17 at Hou 41 48,781

Mon 10/31
N Den 23 at Ind 55 60,544

Sun 11/06
SF 23 at Pho 24 64,544
NYJ 14 at Ind 38 59,233
Mia 10 at NE 21 60,840
LARm 24 at Phi 30 66,469
KC 11 at Den 17 74,227
NO 24 at Was 27 54,183
GB 0 at Atl 20 29,952
LARd 13 at SD 3 54,134
Pit 7 at Cin 42 56,403
TB 10 at ChiB 28 56,892
Det 17 at Min 44 55,573
Buf 13 at Sea 3 61,074
Dal 21 at NYG 29 75,826

Mon 11/07
N Cle 17 at Hou 24 51,467

Sun 11/13
Min 43 at Dal 3 57,830
Phi 27 at Pit 26 46,026
NYG 17 at Pho 24 65,324
Hou 24 at Sea 27 60,446
LARd 9 at SF 3 54,448
SD 10 at Atl 7 26,326
Cle 7 at Den 30 75,806
NE 14 at NYJ 13 48,358
ChiB 34 at Was 14 52,418
TB 23 at Det 20 25,956
Cin 28 at KC 31 34,614
Ind 20 at GB 13 53,492
NO 14 at LARm 10 63,305

Mon 11/14
N Buf 31 at Mia 6 67,091

Sun 11/20
SD 38 at LARm 24 45,462
Pit 7 at Cle 27 77,131
Det 19 at GB 9 44,327
at Milwaukee, WI
NE 6 at Mia 3 53,526
Sea 24 at KC 27 33,152
Cin 38 at Dal 24 37,865
Ind 3 at Min 12 58,342
NYJ 6 at Buf 9# 78,389
Den 0 at NO 42 68,075
ChiB 27 at TB 15 67,070
Phi 23 at NYG 17# 43,621
Atl 12 at LARd 6 40,967
Pho 20 at Hou 38 43,843

Mon 11/21
N Was 21 at SF 37 59,268

Thu 11/24
Min 23 at Det 0 46,379
Hou 25 at Dal 17 50,845

Sun 11/27
SF 48 at SD 10 51,484
NE 21 at Ind 24 58,157
Cle 17 at Was 13 51,604
Mia 34 at NYJ 38 52,752
Pho 21 at Phi 31 57,918
TB 10 at Atl 17 14,020
GB 0 at ChiB 16 62,026
KC 10 at Pit 16 42,057
NYG 13 at NO 12 66,526
Buf 21 at Cin 35 58,672
LARm 24 at Den 35 74,141

Mon 11/28
LARd 27 at Sea 35 62,641

Sun 12/04
Sea 7 at NE 13 59,068
Pit 37 at Hou 34 47,471
Buf 5 at TB 10 49,498
Pho 7 at NYG 44 73,429
GB 14 at Det 30 28,124
SD 10 at Cin 27 58,866
Was 20 at Phi 19 65,847
Ind 31 at Mia 28 45,236
Dal 21 at Cle 24 77,683
Den 20 at LARd 21 65,561
NO 3 at Min 45 61,215
NYJ 34 at KC 38 30,059
SF 13 at Atl 3 44,048

Mon 12/05
N ChiB 3 at LARm 23 65,579

Sat 12/10
Ind 16 at NYJ 34 46,284
Phi 23 at Pho 17 54,832

Sun 12/11
Pit 14 at SD 20 33,816
TB 7 at NE 10# 39,889
Den 14 at Sea 42 62,839
Cin 6 at Hou 41 50,269
NO 17 at SF 30 62,977
Atl 7 at LARm 22 42,828
Min 6 at GB 18 48,892
Dal 24 at Was 17 51,526
Det 12 at ChiB 13 55,010
LARd 21 at Buf 37 77,348
KC 12 at NYG 28 69,809

Mon 12/12
N Cle 31 at Mia 38 61,884

Sat 12/17
NE 10 at Den 21 70,910
Was 17 at Cin 20# 52,157

Sun 12/18
Det 10 at TB 21 37,778
Buf 14 at Ind 17 59,908
LARm 38 at SF 16 62,444
Sea 43 at LARd 37 61,127
NYG 21 at NYJ 27 69,770
Phi 23 at Dal 7 46,131
Hou 23 at Cle 28 74,610
Atl 9 at NO 10 60,566
KC 13 at SD 24 26,339
GB 26 at Pho 17 44,586
Mia 24 at Pit 40 36,051

Mon 12/19
N ChiB 27 at Min 28 62,067

Wild-Card Playoffs

Sat 12/24
Hou 24 at Cle 23 74,977

Mon 12/26
LARm 17 at Min 28 57,666

AFC/NFC Divisional Playoffs

Sat 12/31
Phi 12 at ChiB 20 65,534
Sea 13 at Cin 21 58,560

Sun 01/01
Hou 10 at Buf 17 79,532
Min 9 at SF 34 61,848

1988 AFC/NFC Championships

Sun 01/08
Buf 10 at Cin 21 59,747
SF 28 at ChiB 3 66,946

Super Bowl XXIII

Sun 01/22
Cin 16 at SF 20 75,129
at Miami, FL

National Football League 1989

Sun 09/10
LARm 31 at Atl 21 38,708
NE 27 at NYJ 24 64,541
Sea 7 at Phi 31 64,287
KC 20 at Den 34 74,284
Hou 7 at Min 38 54,015
Buf 27 at Mia 24 54,541
Cle 51 at Pit 0 57,982
Dal 0 at NO 28 66,977
TB 23 at GB 21 55,650
SD 14 at LARd 40 40,237
Pho 16 at Det 13 36,735
SF 30 at Ind 24 60,111
Cin 14 at ChiB 17 64,730

Mon 09/11
N NYG 27 at Was 24 54,160

Sun 09/17
Pho 34 at Sea 24 60,444
Pit 10 at Cin 41 53,885
NYJ 24 at Cle 38 73,516
SF 20 at TB 16 64,087
Mia 24 at NE 10 57,043
Ind 17 at LARm 31 63,995
Dal 21 at Atl 27 55,825
Hou 34 at SD 27 42,013
LARd 19 at KC 24 71,741
Phi 42 at Was 37 53,493
Det 14 at NYG 24 76,021
Min 7 at ChiB 38 66,475
NO 34 at GB 35 55,809

Mon 09/18
N Den 28 at Buf 14 78,176

Sun 09/24
KC 6 at SD 21 40,128
Min 14 at Pit 27 50,744
Sea 24 at NE 3 48,025
Atl 9 at Ind 13 57,816
NO 10 at TB 20 44,053
Was 30 at Dal 7 53,200
NYJ 40 at Mia 33 65,908
ChiB 47 at Det 27 71,418
Buf 47 at Hou 41# 57,278
SF 38 at Phi 28 66,042
Pho 7 at NYG 35 75,742
LARd 21 at Den 31 75,754
GB 38 at LARm 41 57,701

Mon 09/25
N Cle 14 at Cin 21 55,996

Sun 10/01
Den 13 at Cle 16 78,637
SD 24 at Pho 13 44,201
NYG 30 at Dal 13 51,785
NE 10 at Buf 31 78,921
Was 16 at NO 14 46,358
Ind 17 at NYJ 10 65,542
Atl 21 at GB 23 54,647
at Milwaukee, WI
LARm 13 at SF 12 64,250
Mia 7 at Hou 39 53,326
Cin 21 at KC 17 60,165
Sea 24 at LARd 20 44,319
Pit 23 at Det 3 43,804
TB 3 at Min 17 54,817

Mon 10/02
N Phi 13 at ChiB 27 66,625

Sun 10/08
Buf 14 at Ind 37 58,890
Hou 13 at NE 23 59,828
Dal 13 at GB 31 56,656
Cin 26 at Pit 16 52,785
Atl 14 at LARm 26 52,182
SD 10 at Den 16 75,222
Det 17 at Min 24 55,380
ChiB 35 at TB 42 72,077
NYG 19 at Phi 21 65,688
Pho 28 at Was 30 55,692
SF 24 at NO 20 60,488
Cle 10 at Mia 13# 58,444
KC 20 at Sea 16 60,715

Mon 10/09
N LARd 14 at NYJ 7 68,040

Sun 10/15
Mia 20 at Cin 13 58,184
KC 14 at LARd 20 40,453
Pit 17 at Cle 7 78,840
Hou 33 at ChiB 28 64,383
SF 31 at Dal 14 61,077
Det 17 at TB 16 46,255
NYJ 14 at NO 29 59,521
Was 17 at NYG 20 76,245
GB 14 at Min 26 62,075
Phi 17 at Pho 5 42,620
Sea 17 at SD 16 50,079
NE 15 at Atl 16 39,697
Ind 3 at Den 14 74,600

Mon 10/16
N LARm 20 at Buf 23 76,231

Sun 10/22
Den 24 at Sea 21# 62,353
GB 20 at Mia 23 56,624
LARd 7 at Phi 10 64,019
Min 20 at Det 7 51,579
Dal 28 at KC 36 76,841
NYG 20 at SD 13 48,566
NE 20 at SF 37 70,000
TB 28 at Was 32 52,862
NYJ 3 at Buf 34 76,811
Atl 20 at Pho 34 33,894
Ind 23 at Cin 12 57,642
Pit 0 at Hou 27 59,091
NO 40 at LARm 21 57,567

Mon 10/23
N ChiB 7 at Cle 27 78,722

Sun 10/29
Pho 19 at Dal 10 44,431
KC 17 at Pit 23 54,194
LARm 10 at ChiB 20 65,506
Phi 28 at Den 24 75,065
Mia 17 at Buf 31 80,208
NE 23 at Ind 20# 59,356
TB 23 at Cin 56 57,225
Det 20 at GB 23# 53,731
at Milwaukee, WI
SD 7 at Sea 10 59,691
Atl 13 at NO 20 65,153
Hou 17 at Cle 28 78,765
SF 23 at NYJ 10 62,805
Was 24 at LARd 37 52,781

Mon 10/30
N Min 14 at NYG 24 76,041

Sun 11/05
Sea 10 at KC 20 54,488
ChiB 13 at GB 14 56,556
Pit 7 at Den 34 74,739
Phi 17 at SD 20 47,019
NYG 20 at Pho 13 46,588
Cin 7 at LARd 28 51,080
LARm 21 at Min 23# 59,600
Buf 28 at Atl 30 45,267
Det 31 at Hou 35 48,056
Ind 13 at Mia 19 52.680
NYJ 27 at NE 26 53,366
Cle 42 at TB 31 69,162
Dal 13 at Was 3 53,187

Mon 11/06
NO 13 at SF 31 60,667

Sun 11/12
GB 22 at Det 31 44,324
LARd 12 at SD 14 59,151
Dal 20 at Pho 24 49,657
Atl 3 at SF 45 59,914
ChiB 20 at Pit 0 56,505
Cle 17 at Sea 7 58,978
Was 10 at Phi 3 65,443
Mia 31 at NYJ 23 65,923
Den 16 at KC 13 76,245
Min 24 at TB 10 56,271
Ind 7 at Buf 30 79,256
NO 28 at NE 24 47,680
NYG 10 at LARm 31 65,127

Mon 11/13
Cin 24 at Hou 26 60,694

Sun 11/19
Pho 14 at LARm 37 53,176
KC 10 at Cle 10# 77,922
Buf 24 at NE 33 49,663
Mia 17 at Dal 14 58,738
NYJ 10 at Ind 27 58,236
SD 17 at Pit 20 44,203
Sea 3 at NYG 15 75,014
TB 32 at ChiB 31 63,826
NO 26 at Atl 17 53,173
LARd 7 at Hou 23 59,198
Min 9 at Phi 10 65,944
GB 21 at SF 17 62,219
Det 7 at Cin 42 55,720

Mon 11/20
N Den 14 at Was 10 52,975

Thu 11/23
Phi 27 at Dal 0 54,444
Cle 10 at Det 13 65,624

Sun 11/26
Hou 0 at KC 34 51,342
Pit 34 at Mia 14 59,936
SD 6 at Ind 10 58,822
Atl 7 at NYJ 27 40,429
Min 19 at GB 20 55,592
at Milwaukee, WI
Cin 7 at Buf 24 80,074
TB 14 at Pho 13 33,297
NE 21 at LARd 24 38,747
Sea 14 at Den 41 75,117
ChiB 14 at Was 38 50,044
LARm 20 at NO 17# 64,274

Mon 11/27
N NYG 24 at SF 34 63,471

Sun 12/03
Mia 21 at KC 26 54,610
Cin 21 at Cle 0 76,236
NYJ 20 at SD 17 38,954
Was 29 at Pho 10 38,870
LARm 35 at Dal 31 46,100
Den 13 at LARd 16# 87,560
SF 23 at Atl 10 43,128
GB 17 at TB 16 58,120
NO 14 at Det 21 38,550
Hou 23 at Pit 16 40,541
Phi 24 at NYG 17 74,809
Ind 16 at NE 22 32,234
ChiB 16 at Min 27 60,664

Mon 12/04
N Buf 16 at Sea 17 57,682

Sun 12/10
Cle 17 at Ind 23# 58,550
NYG 14 at Den 7 63,283
KC 21 at GB 3 56,694
NO 22 at Buf 19 70,037
Pit 13 at NYJ 0 41,037
Det 27 at ChiB 17 52,650
Sea 24 at Cin 17 54,744
TB 17 at Hou 20 54,532
Atl 17 at Min 43 58,116
Pho 14 at LARd 16 41,785
Dal 10 at Phi 20 66,769
SD 21 at Was 26 47,693
NE 10 at Mia 31 62,127

Mon 12/11
N SF 30 at LARm 27 68,936

Sat 12/16
Den 37 at Pho 0 56,071
Dal 0 at NYG 15 72,141

Sun 12/17
Buf 10 at SF 21 60,927
NE 10 at Pit 28 26,594
Min 17 at Cle 23# 70,777
GB 40 at ChiB 28 44,781
NYJ 14 at LARm 38 53,063
Mia 13 at Ind 42 55,665
TB 7 at Det 33 40,362
SD 20 at KC 13 40,623
Hou 7 at Cin 61 47,510
Was 31 at Atl 30 37,501
LARd 17 at Sea 23 61,076

Mon 12/18
N Phi 20 at NO 30 68,561

Sat 12/23
Cle 24 at Hou 20 58,342
Buf 37 at NYJ 0 21,148
Was 29 at Sea 0 60,294

Sun 12/24
Den 16 at SD 19 50,524
GB 20 at Dal 10 41,265
Det 31 at Atl 24 7,092
Pit 31 at TB 22 29,690
Pho 14 at Phi 31 43,287
ChiB 0 at SF 26 58,829
LARm 24 at NE 20 27,940
Ind 6 at NO 41 49,009
KC 27 at Mia 24 43,612
LARd 17 at NYG 34 70,306

Mon 12/25
N Cin 21 at Min 29 58,829

Wild-Card Playoffs

Sun 12/31
LARm 21 at Phi 7 65,479
Pit 26 at Hou 23# 59,406

AFC/NFC Divisional Playoffs

Sat 01/06
Buf 30 at Cle 34 78,921
Min 13 at SF 41 64,918

Sun 01/07
LARm 19 at NYG 13# 76,526
Pit 23 at Den 24 75,477

1989 AFC/NFC Championships

Sun 01/14
Cle 21 at Den 37 76,046
LARm 3 at SF 30 65,634

Super Bowl XXIV

Sun 01/28
SF 55 at Den 10 72,919
at New Orleans, LA

National Football League 1990

Sun 09/09
Den 9 at LARd 14 54,206
Mia 27 at NE 24 45,305
Hou 27 at Atl 47 56,222
NYJ 20 at Cin 25 56,167
Ind 10 at Buf 26 78,899
Pit 3 at Cle 13 78,298
Sea 0 at ChiB 17 64,400
LARm 24 at GB 36 57,685
Min 21 at KC 24 68,363
SD 14 at Dal 17 48,063
Pho 0 at Was 31 52,649
TB 38 at Det 21 56,692
N Phi 20 at NYG 27 76,202

Mon 09/10
N SF 13 at NO 12 68,629

Sun 09/16
Buf 7 at Mia 30 68,490
Cin 21 at SD 16 48,098
LARd 17 at Sea 13 61,889
Cle 21 at NYJ 24 67,354
NE 16 at Ind 14 49,256
Atl 14 at Det 21 48,961
NYG 28 at Dal 7 61,090
NO 3 at Min 32 56,272
Pho 23 at Phi 21 64,396
Was 13 at SF 26 64,287
ChiB 31 at GB 13 58,938
LARm 35 at TB 14 59,705
N Hou 9 at Pit 20 54,814

Mon 09/17
N KC 23 at Den 24 75,277

Sun 09/23
KC 17 at GB 3 58,817
Mia 3 at NYG 20 76,483
NE 7 at Cin 41 56,470
Pit 3 at LARd 20 50,657
SD 24 at Cle 14 77,429
Sea 31 at Den 34# 75,290
Ind 10 at Hou 24 50,093
Pho 7 at NO 28 61,110
Atl 13 at SF 19 62,858
Dal 15 at Was 19 53,804
Min 16 at ChiB 19 65,420
Phi 27 at LARm 21 63,644
N Det 20 at TB 23 55,075

Mon 09/24
N Buf 30 at NYJ 7 69,927

Sun 09/30
Cle 0 at KC 34 75,462
Den 28 at Buf 29 74,393
Hou 17 at SD 7 48,762
Dal 17 at NYG 31 75,923
NYJ 37 at NE 13 36,724
GB 24 at Det 21 64,509
Mia 28 at Pit 6 54,691
TB 23 at Min 20# 54,462
ChiB 10 at LARd 24 80,156
Ind 24 at Phi 23 62,067
N Was 38 at Pho 10 49,303

Mon 10/01
N Cin 16 at Sea 31 60,135

Sun 10/07
Cin 34 at LARm 31 62,619
KC 19 at Ind 23 54,950
NYJ 16 at Mia 20 69,678
SD 14 at Pit 36 53,486
NO 27 at Atl 28 57,401
SF 24 at Hou 21 59,931
GB 13 at ChiB 27 59,929
Det 34 at Min 27 57,586
Sea 33 at NE 20 39,735
TB 10 at Dal 14 60,076
N LARd 24 at Buf 38 80,076

Mon 10/08
N Cle 30 at Den 29 74,814

Sun 10/14
Cin 17 at Hou 48 53,501
Cle 20 at NO 25 68,608
Pit 34 at Den 17 74,285
SD 39 at NYJ 3 63,311
Sea 17 at LARd 24 50,624
Dal 3 at Pho 20 45,235
Det 24 at KC 43 74,312
GB 14 at TB 26 64,472
NYG 24 at Was 20 54,737
SF 45 at Atl 35 57,921
N LARm 9 at ChiB 38 59,383

Mon 10/15
N Min 24 at Phi 32 66,296

Thu 10/18
NE 10 at Mia 17 62,630

Sun 10/21
Den 27 at Ind 17 59,850
KC 7 at Sea 19 60,358
Pit 7 at SF 27 64,301
Dal 17 at TB 13 68,315
NO 10 at Hou 23 57,908
Phi 7 at Was 13 53,567
Pho 19 at NYG 20 76,518
LARd 24 at SD 9 60,569
NYJ 27 at Buf 30 79,002
Atl 24 at LARm 44 54,761

Mon 10/22
N Cin 34 at Cle 13 78,567

Sun 10/28
Cle 17 at SF 20 63,672
Mia 27 at Ind 7 59,213
TB 10 at SD 41 40,653
ChiB 31 at Pho 21 71,233
Buf 27 at NE 10 51,959
Min 10 at GB 24 55,125
at Milwaukee, WI
Phi 21 at Dal 20 62,605
NYJ 17 at Hou 12 56,337
Det 27 at NO 10 64,368
Was 10 at NYG 21 75,351
N Cin 17 at Atl 38 53,214

Mon 10/29
N LARm 10 at Pit 41 56,466

Sun 11/04
Buf 42 at Cle 0 78,331
Hou 13 at LARm 17 52,628
LARd 7 at KC 9 70,951
NE 20 at Phi 48 65,514
SD 31 at Sea 14 59,646
Atl 9 at Pit 21 57,093
SF 24 at GB 20 58,835
Was 41 at Det 38 69,326
ChiB 26 at TB 6 68,575
Dal 9 at NYJ 24 68,086
Pho 3 at Mia 23 54,924
NO 21 at Cin 7 60,067
N Den 22 at Min 27 57,331

Mon 11/05
N NYG 24 at Ind 7 58,688

Sun 11/11
Atl 24 at ChiB 30 62,855
Den 7 at SD 19 59,557
Ind 13 at NE 10 28,924
Mia 17 at NYJ 3 68,362
Sea 17 at KC 16 71,285
GB 29 at LARd 16 50,855
Min 17 at Det 7 68,264
NYG 31 at LARm 7 64,632
TB 7 at NO 35 67,865
Pho 14 at Buf 45 74,904
N SF 24 at Dal 6 62,966

Mon 11/12
N Was 14 at Phi 28 65,857

Sun 11/18
Hou 35 at Cle 23 76,726
NE 0 at Buf 14 74,720
NYJ 14 at Ind 17 47,283
SD 10 at KC 27 63,717
ChiB 16 at Den 13 75,013
Dal 24 at LARm 21 58,589
Det 0 at NYG 20 76,109
GB 24 at Pho 21 46,876
Min 24 at Sea 21 59,735
NO 17 at Was 31 52,573
TB 7 at SF 31 62,221
Phi 24 at Atl 23 53,755
N Pit 3 at Cin 27 60,064

Mon 11/19
N LARd 13 at Mia 10 75,553

Thu 11/22
Den 27 at Det 40 73,896
Was 17 at Dal 27 60,355

Sun 11/25
Ind 34 at Cin 20 60,051
KC 27 at LARd 24 65,170
Mia 30 at Cle 13 70,225
NE 14 at Pho 34 30,110
Pit 24 at NYJ 7 57,806
Atl 7 at NO 10 68,229
LARm 28 at SF 17 62,633
NYG 13 at Phi 31 66,706
TB 10 at GB 20 53,677
at Milwaukee, WI
ChiB 13 at Min 41 58,666
N Sea 13 at SD 10 50,096

Mon 11/26
N Buf 24 at Hou 27 60,130

Sun 12/02
Cin 16 at Pit 12 58,200
Hou 10 at Sea 13 57,692
Mia 20 at Was 42 53,599
NYJ 17 at SD 38 40,877
Ind 17 at Pho 20 31,885
KC 37 at NE 7 26,280
LARd 23 at Den 20 74,162
LARm 38 at Cle 23 61,981
NO 13 at Dal 17 60,087
Phi 23 at Buf 30 79,320
Atl 17 at TB 23 42,839
Det 17 at ChiB 23 66,946
N GB 7 at Min 23 62,058

Mon 12/03
N NYG 3 at SF 7 66,413

Sun 12/09
Den 20 at KC 31 74,347
Buf 31 at Ind 7 53,268
Cle 14 at Hou 58 54,469
Min 15 at NYG 23 76,121
NO 24 at LARm 20 65,844
NE 3 at Pit 24 48,354
Sea 20 at GB 14 52,015
at Milwaukee, WI
Pho 24 at Atl 13 36,222
SF 20 at Cin 17 60,084
ChiB 9 at Was 10 53,920
N Phi 20 at Mia 23 67,034

Mon 12/10
N LARd 38 at Det 31 72,190

Sat 12/15
Buf 17 at NYG 13 66,893
Was 25 at NE 10 22,286

Sun 12/16
Cin 7 at LARd 24 54,132
Pit 9 at NO 6 68,582
SD 10 at Den 20 64,919
Hou 27 at KC 10 61,756
Min 13 at TB 26 47,272
Pho 10 at Dal 41 60,190
Ind 29 at NYJ 21 41,423
Atl 10 at Cle 13 46,536
Sea 17 at Mia 24 57,851
GB 0 at Phi 31 66,627
N ChiB 21 at Det 38 67,559

Mon 12/17
N SF 26 at LARm 10 65,619

Sat 12/22
LARd 28 at Min 24 63,314
Det 24 at GB 17 46,700
N Was 28 at Ind 35 58,173

Sun 12/23
Cle 0 at Pit 35 51,665
Hou 20 at Cin 40 60,044
KC 24 at SD 21 45,135
NE 7 at NYJ 42 46,641
Dal 3 at Phi 17 63,895
Mia 14 at Buf 24 80,235
LARm 13 at Atl 20 30,021
NO 13 at SF 10 60,112
NYG 24 at Pho 21 41,212
TB 14 at ChiB 27 46,456
N Den 12 at Sea 17 55,845

Sat 12/29
KC 21 at ChiB 10 60,262
Phi 23 at Pho 21 31,796

Sun 12/30
Buf 14 at Was 29 52,397
Cle 14 at Cin 21 60,041
SD 12 at LARd 17 62,583
Dal 7 at Atl 26 50,097
Det 10 at Sea 30 50,681
GB 13 at Den 22 46,943
NYG 13 at NE 10 60,410
SF 20 at Min 17 51,590
NYJ 16 at TB 14 46,543
Ind 17 at Mia 23 59,547
N Pit 14 at Hou 34 56,906

Mon 12/31
N LARm 17 at NO 20 68,647

First-Round Playoffs

Sat 01/05
KC 16 at Mia 17 62,276
Was 20 at Phi 6 65,287

Sun 01/06
Hou 14 at Cin 41 60,012
NO 6 at ChiB 16 60,767

AFC/NFC Divisional Playoffs

Sat 01/12
Mia 34 at Buf 44 77,087
Was 10 at SF 28 65,292

Sun 01/13
Cin 10 at LARd 20 92,045
ChiB 3 at NYG 31 77,025

1990 AFC/NFC Championships

Sun 01/20
LARd 3 at Buf 51 80,325
NYG 15 at SF 13 65,750

Super Bowl XXV

Sun 01/27
Buf 19 at NYG 20 73,813
at Tampa, FL

National Football League 1991

Sun 09/01
Phi 20 at GB 3 59,991
Mia 31 at Buf 35 80,252
SD 20 at Pit 26 55,848
TB 13 at NYJ 16 61,204
Cin 14 at Den 45 72,855
Pho 24 at LARm 14 47,069
Sea 24 at NO 27 68,492
Dal 26 at Cle 14 78,860
Min 6 at ChiB 10 64,112
NE 16 at Ind 7 49,961
LARd 17 at Hou 47 61,367
Atl 3 at KC 14 74,246
N Det 0 at Was 45 55,671

Mon 09/02
N SF 14 at NYG 16 76,319

Sun 09/08
Min 20 at Atl 19 50,936
Cle 20 at NE 0 35,377
GB 14 at Det 23 43,132
LARm 19 at NYG 13 76,541
ChiB 21 at TB 20 62,409
Ind 6 at Mia 17 51,155
Pit 34 at Buf 52 79,545
Pho 26 at Phi 10 63,818
Den 13 at LARd 16 48,569
SD 14 at SF 34 60,753
NO 17 at KC 10 74,916
NYJ 13 at Sea 20 56,770
N Hou 30 at Cin 7 56,463

Mon 09/09
N Was 33 at Dal 31 63,025

Sun 09/15
NYG 17 at ChiB 20 64,829
Pho 0 at Was 34 54,622
Atl 13 at SD 10 44,804
NE 6 at Pit 20 53,703
TB 13 at GB 15 58,114
Cin 13 at Cle 14 78,269
Buf 23 at NYJ 20 65,309
Sea 10 at Den 16 74,152
Mia 13 at Det 17 56,896
Ind 0 at LARd 16 40,287
Phi 24 at Dal 0 62,656
SF 14 at Min 17 59,148
N LARm 7 at NO 24 68,583

Mon 09/16
N KC 7 at Hou 17 61,058

Sun 09/22
Det 33 at Ind 24 53,396
Was 34 at Cin 27 52,038
LARm 10 at SF 27 63,871
GB 13 at Mia 16 56,583
Buf 17 at TB 10 57,323
Hou 20 at NE 24 30,702
Pit 14 at Phi 23 65,511
Min 0 at NO 26 68,591
SD 19 at Den 27 73,258
LARd 17 at Atl 21 53,615
Sea 13 at KC 20 57,323
Cle 10 at NYG 13 75,891
N Dal 17 at Pho 9 68,814

Mon 09/23
N NYJ 13 at ChiB 19 65,256

Sun 09/29
KC 14 at SD 13 44,907
Mia 23 at NYJ 41 71,170
TB 3 at Det 31 44,479
ChiB 20 at Buf 35 80,366
SF 6 at LARd 12 91,494
GB 21 at LARm 23 54,736
NO 27 at Atl 6 56,556
Ind 3 at Sea 31 56,656
NE 10 at Pho 24 26,043
NYG 16 at Dal 21 64,010
N Den 13 at Min 6 55,031

Mon 09/30
N Phi 0 at Was 23 55,198

Sun 10/06
Mia 20 at NE 10 55,075
Dal 20 at GB 17 55,031
at Milwaukee, WI
Sea 13 at Cin 7 60,010
SD 21 at LARd 13 42,787
Den 14 at Hou 42 59,145
NYJ 17 at Cle 14 71,042
Was 20 at ChiB 7 64,941
Phi 13 at TB 14 41,219
Min 20 at Det 24 63,423
Pho 9 at NYG 20 75,891
N Pit 21 at Ind 3 55,383

Mon 10/07
N Buf 6 at KC 33 76,120

Sun 10/13
SD 24 at LARm 30 47,433
Atl 39 at SF 34 57,343
Pho 7 at Min 34 51,029
Cin 23 at Dal 35 63,275
Ind 6 at Buf 42 79,015
Hou 23 at NYJ 20 70,758
Cle 17 at Was 42 54,715
Mia 7 at KC 42 76,021
NO 13 at Phi 6 64,224
N LARd 23 at Sea 20 61,974

Mon 10/14
N NYG 23 at Pit 20 57,608

Thu 10/17
ChiB 10 at GB 0 58,435

Sun 10/20
Cle 30 at SD 24 48,440
Atl 10 at Pho 16 24,124
Hou 17 at Mia 13 60,705
Det 3 at SF 35 61,240
TB 7 at NO 23 68,591
Sea 27 at Pit 7 54,678
LARm 17 at LARd 20 85,102
KC 16 at Den 19 75,866
Min 23 at NE 26 45,367
NYJ 17 at Ind 6 53,025

Mon 10/21
N Cin 16 at Buf 35 80,131

Sun 10/27
SF 23 at Phi 7 65,796
Pit 14 at Cle 17 78,285
Cin 3 at Hou 35 58,634
Dal 10 at Det 34 74,506
Den 9 at NE 6 43,994
SD 9 at Sea 20 58,025
ChiB 20 at NO 17 68,591
Min 28 at Pho 0 45,447
LARm 14 at Atl 31 50,187
GB 27 at TB 0 40,275
N Was 17 at NYG 13 76,627

Mon 10/28
N LARd 21 at KC 24 77,111

Sun 11/03
Hou 13 at Was 16 55,096
NE 17 at Buf 22 78,278
GB 16 at NYJ 19 67,435
Mia 10 at Ind 6 55,899
NO 24 at LARm 17 58,213
TB 13 at Min 28 35,737
Pho 7 at Dal 27 61,190
SF 14 at Atl 17 51,259
Det 10 at ChiB 20 57,281
Cle 21 at Cin 23 55,077
N Pit 13 at Den 20 70,973

Mon 11/04
N NYG 7 at Phi 30 65,816

Sun 11/10
Det 21 at TB 30 37,742
Sea 14 at SD 17 43,597
SF 3 at NO 10 68,591
Buf 34 at GB 24 52,175
at Milwaukee, WI
Ind 28 at NYJ 27 44,792

Atl 17 at Was 56 52,641
Pit 33 at Cin 27 55,503
NYG 21 at Pho 14 50,048
Dal 23 at Hou 26 63,001
KC 27 at LARm 20 52,511
LARd 17 at Den 16 75,896
Phi 32 at Cle 30 72,086
N NE 20 at Mia 30 56,065

Mon 11/11
N ChiB 34 at Min 17 59,001

Sun 11/17
ChiB 31 at Ind 17 60,519
Was 41 at Pit 14 56,813
Pho 10 at SF 14 50,180
NO 21 at SD 24 48,420
Min 35 at GB 21 57,614
Sea 7 at LARd 31 49,317
Den 24 at KC 20 74,661
TB 7 at Atl 43 41,274
Dal 9 at NYG 22 76,410
LARm 10 at Det 21 60,873
Cin 10 at Phi 17 63,189
NYJ 28 at NE 21 30,743
N Cle 24 at Hou 28 58,155

Mon 11/18
N Buf 41 at Mia 27 71,062

Sun 11/24
Mia 16 at ChiB 13 58,288
Det 34 at Min 14 51,644
Ind 10 at GB 14 42,132
at Milwaukee, WI
Dal 24 at Was 21 55,561
Den 10 at Sea 13 60,430
Hou 14 at Pit 26 45,795
NYG 21 at TB 14 63,698
SD 3 at NYJ 24 59,025
KC 15 at Cle 20 63,991
Buf 13 at NE 16 47,053
Phi 34 at Pho 14 32,568
LARd 38 at Cin 14 52,044
N Atl 23 at NO 20 68,591

Mon 11/25
N SF 33 at LARm 10 61,881

Thu 11/28
Pit 10 at Dal 20 62,253
ChiB 6 at Det 16 78,879

Sun 12/01
NYG 24 at Cin 27 45,063
NO 24 at SF 38 62,092
NYJ 13 at Buf 24 80,243
TB 14 at Mia 33 51,036
NE 3 at Den 20 67,116
KC 19 at Sea 6 57,248
Was 27 at LARm 6 55,027
Cle 31 at Ind 0 57,539
GB 31 at Atl 35 43,270
N LARd 9 at SD 7 56,780

Mon 12/02
N Phi 13 at Hou 6 62,141

Sun 12/08
Ind 17 at NE 23 20,131
Pitt 6 at Hou 31 59,225
SD 17 at KC 20 73,330
Den 17 at Cle 7 73,539
Buf 30 at LARd 27 85,081
Atl 31 at LARm 14 35,315
Was 20 at Pho 14 48,373
GB 13 at ChiB 27 62,353
NO 14 at Dal 23 64,530
Phi 19 at NYG 14 76,099
NYJ 20 at Det 34 69,304
SF 24 at Sea 22 64,677
N Min 26 at TB 24 41,091

Mon 12/09
N Cin 13 at Mia 37 60,616

Sat 12/14
TB 0 at ChiB 27 54,719
KC 14 at SF 28 62,672

Sun 12/15
Pho 19 at Den 24 74,098
NE 6 at NYJ 3 55,869
Dal 25 at Phi 13 65,854
Cin 10 at Pit 17 35,420
Hou 17 at Cle 14 55,680
NYG 17 at Was 34 54,722
Sea 13 at Atl 26 55,834
Mia 30 at SD 38 47,731
LARm 14 at Min 20 46,312
Det 21 at GB 17 43,881
N Buf 35 at Ind 7 48,286

Mon 12/16
N LARd 0 at NO 27 68,625

Sat 12/21
GB 27 at Min 7 52,860
Hou 20 at NYG 24 63,421

Sun 12/22
Was 22 at Phi 24 58,988
KC 27 at LARd 21 65,144
Det 17 at Buf 14 78,059
NO 27 at Pho 3 30,928
Atl 27 at Dal 31 60,962
Den 17 at SD 14 51,449
Ind 3 at TB 17 28,043
NYJ 23 at Mia 20 69,636
Cle 10 at Pit 17 47,070
NE 7 at Cin 29 46,394
N LARm 9 at Sea 23 51,100

Mon 12/23
N ChiB 14 at SF 52 60,419

First-Round Playoffs

Sat 12/28
LARd 6 at KC 10 75,827
Atl 27 at NO 20 68,794

Sun 12/29
NYJ 19 at Hou 17 61,485
Dal 17 at ChiB 13 62,594

AFC/NFC Divisional Playoffs

Sat 01/04
Hou 24 at Den 26 75,301
Atl 7 at Was 24 55,181

Sun 01/05
KC 14 at Buf 37 80,182
Dal 6 at Det 38 79,835

1991 AFC/NFC Championships

Sun 01/12
Den 7 at Buf 10 80,272
Det 10 at Was 41 55,585

Super Bowl XXVI

Sun 01/26
Was 37 at Buf 24 63,130
at Minneapolis, MN

National Football League 1992

Sun 09/06
Pit 29 at Hou 24 63,713
NYJ 17 at Atl 20 65,585
NO 13 at Phi 15 63,513
Min 23 at GB 20 58,617
Det 24 at ChiB 27 63,672
Cin 21 at Sea 3 65,851
LARm 7 at Buf 40 79,001
Cle 3 at Ind 14 50,766
Pho 7 at TB 23 41,315
KC 24 at SD 10 45,024
SF 31 at NYG 14 74,519
N LARd 13 at Den 17 75,418

Mon 09/07
N Was 10 at Dal 23 63,538

Sun 09/13
ChiB 6 at NO 28 68,591
NE 0 at LARm 14 40,402
Min 17 at Det 31 57,519
SD 13 at Den 21 74,367
Buf 34 at SF 31 64,053
Hou 20 at Ind 10 44,851
NYJ 10 at Pit 27 56,050
Sea 7 at KC 26 75,125
Dal 34 at NYG 28 76,430
GB 3 at TB 31 50,051
LARd 21 at Cin 24 54,240
Atl 17 at Was 24 54,343
N Phi 31 at Pho 14 42,533

Mon 09/14
N Mia 27 at Cle 23 74,765

Sun 09/20
Den 0 at Phi 30 65,833
Cin 23 at GB 24 57,272
SF 31 at NYJ 14 71,020
NO 10 at Atl 7 67,328
LARm 10 at Mia 26 55,945
Pho 20 at Dal 31 62,575
Det 10 at Was 13 55,818
KC 20 at Hou 23 60,955
Cle 28 at LARd 16 48,102
Pit 23 at SD 6 46,127
Sea 10 at NE 6 42,327
TB 20 at Min 26 48,113
Ind 0 at Buf 38 77,781

Mon 09/21
N NYG 27 at ChiB 14 63,444

Sun 09/27
Atl 31 at ChiB 41 63,528
Buf 41 at NE 7 52,527
TB 27 at Det 23 51,374
NYJ 10 at LARm 18 42,005
Pit 3 at GB 17 58,743
SD 0 at Hou 27 57,491
Den 12 at Cle 0 78,064
Min 42 at Cin 7 53,847
Mia 19 at Sea 17 59,674
N SF 16 at NO 10 68,591

Mon 09/28
N LARd 7 at KC 27 77,486

Sun 10/04
Mia 37 at Buf 10 80,368
NO 13 at Det 7 66,971
ChiB 20 at Min 21 60,992
GB 10 at Atl 24 63,769
Ind 24 at TB 14 56,585
KC 19 at Den 20 75,629
NYG 10 at LARd 13 43,103
Was 24 at Pho 27 34,488
LARm 24 at SF 27 63,071
Sea 6 at SD 17 36,783
N NE 21 at NYJ 30 60,180

Mon 10/05
N Dal 7 at Phi 31 66,572

Sun 10/11
SF 24 at NE 12 54,126
Phi 17 at KC 24 76,626
Pho 21 at NYG 31 70,042
Sea 0 at Dal 27 62,311
Pit 9 at Cle 17 78,080
Atl 17 at Mia 21 68,633
Hou 38 at Cin 24 54,254
Buf 3 at LARd 20 52,287
NYJ 3 at Ind 6 48,393
N LARm 10 at NO 13 68,591

Mon 10/12
N Den 3 at Was 34 56,371

Thu 10/15
Det 14 at Min 31 52,816

Sun 10/18
GB 6 at Cle 17 69,268
NE 17 at Mia 38 57,282
SD 34 at Ind 14 48,552
Phi 12 at Was 16 55,198
KC 10 at Dal 17 64,115
LARd 19 at Sea 0 56,904
Hou 21 at Den 27 74,827
NYG 17 at LARm 38 53,541
NO 30 at Pho 21 27,735
Atl 17 at SF 56 63,302
TB 14 at ChiB 31 61,412

Mon 10/19
N Cin 0 at Pit 20 55,411

Sun 10/25
Sea 10 at NYG 23 67,399
Ind 31 at Mia 20 61,117
ChiB 30 at GB 10 59,435
Dal 28 at LARd 13 91,505
Den 21 at SD 24 53,576
Was 15 at Min 13 59,098
Cin 10 at Hou 26 58,701
Det 38 at TB 7 53,985
Cle 19 at NE 17 32,219
Phoe 3 at Phi 7 64,676
N Pit 27 at KC 3 76,175

Mon 10/26
N Buf 24 at NYJ 20 68,181

Sun 11/01
Mia 14 at NYJ 26 69,313
TB 21 at NO 23 68,591
LARm 28 at Atl 30 62,168
Cle 10 at Cin 30 54,765
SF 14 at Pho 24 47,642
GB 27 at Det 13 60,594
NE 7 at Buf 16 78,268
Hou 20 at Pit 21 58,074
Phi 10 at Dal 20 65,015
Ind 0 at SD 26 40,324
N NYG 24 at Was 7 53,647

Mon 11/02
N Min 38 at ChiB 10 61,257

Sun 11/08
NO 31 at NE 14 45,413
Mia 28 at Ind 0 59,892
GB 7 at NYG 27 72,038
Min 35 at TB 7 49,095
LARd 10 at Phi 31 65,388
Dal 37 at Det 3 74,816
Cle 24 at Hou 14 57,348
SD 14 at KC 16 72,876
NYJ 16 at Den 27 74,678
Pit 20 at Buf 28 80,294
Pho 20 at LARm 14 40,788
Was 16 at Sea 3 53,616
N Cin 31 at ChiB 28 56,120

Mon 11/09
N SF 41 at Atl 3 67,404

Sun 11/15
NE 37 at Ind 34 42,631
Det 14 at Pit 17 52,242
Cin 14 at NYJ 17 60,196
Phi 24 at GB 27 52,689
at Milwaukee, WI
Was 16 at KC 35 75,238
Pho 17 at Atl 20 58,477
Hou 17 at Min 13 56,726
SD 14 at Cle 13 58,396
Sea 3 at LARd 20 46,862
ChiB 17 at TB 20 69,102
NO 20 at SF 21 64,895
LARm 27 at Dal 23 63,690
N NYG 13 at Den 27 75,269

Mon 11/16
N Buf 26 at Mia 20 70,629

Sun 11/22
Phi 47 at NYG 34 68,153
Cle 13 at Min 17 53,323
Hou 16 at Mia 19 63,597
GB 17 at ChiB 3 56,170
Atl 14 at Buf 41 80,004
Det 19 at Cin 13 48,574
Ind 14 at Pit 30 51,501
TB 14 at SD 29 43,197
SF 27 at LARm 10 65,858
Dal 16 at Pho 10 72,439
Den 0 at LARd 24 50,011
NYJ 3 at NE 24 27,642
N KC 24 at Sea 14 49,867

Mon 11/23
N Was 3 at NO 20 68,591

Thu 11/26
Hou 24 at Det 21 73,711
NYG 3 at Dal 30 62,416

Sun 11/29
KC 23 at NYJ 7 57,375
Mia 13 at NO 24 68,591
Pho 3 at Was 41 53,541
Pit 21 at Cinc 9 54,253
NE 0 at Atl 34 54,494
Phi 14 at SF 20 64,374
Min 31 at LARm 17 54,831
TB 14 at GB 19 52,347
at Milwaukee, WI
Buf 13 at Ind 16 50,221
ChiB 14 at Cle 27 73,578
N LARd 3 at SD 27 59,894

Mon 11/30
N Den 13 at Sea 16 51,612

Thu 12/03
N Atl 14 at NO 22 68,591

Sun 12/06
Ind 6 at NE 0 19,429
NYJ 24 at Buf 17 75,876
Cin 21 at Cle 37 68,368
Sea 14 at Pit 20 47,015
Min 17 at Phi 28 65,280
Det 10 at GB 38 49,469
at Milwaukee, WI
Dal 31 at Den 27 74,946
SD 27 at Pho 21 26,880
Was 28 at NYG 10 62,998
KC 7 at LARd 28 45,227
Mia 3 at SF 27 58,474
N LARm 31 at TB 27 38,387

Mon 12/07
N ChiB 7 at Hou 24 62,193

Sat 12/12
NYG 0 at Pho 19 28,452
Den 17 at Buf 27 71,740

Sun 12/13
Phi 20 at Sea 17 65,902
Ind 10 at NYJ 6 33,684
Dal 17 at Was 20 56,437
NO 37 at LARm 14 47,355
Atl 35 at TB 7 38,208
Cle 14 at Det 24 65,970
NE 20 at KC 27 52,208
Cin 10 at SD 27 50,579
SF 20 at Min 17 60,685
Pit 6 at ChiB 30 52,904
N GB 16 at Hou 14 57,285

Mon 12/14
N LARd 7 at Mia 20 67,098

Sat 12/19
TB 14 at SF 21 60,519
KC 21 at NYG 35 53,418

Sun 12/20
SD 36 at LARd 14 40,152
ChiB 3 at Det 16 72,777
Pho 13 at Ind 16 46,763
Sea 6 at Den 10 72,570
Min 6 at Pit 3 53,613
NE 10 at Cin 20 45,355
Hou 17 at Cle 14 59,898

Buf 20 at NO 16 68,591
LARm 13 at GB 28 57,796
Was 13 at Phi 17 65,841
N NYJ 17 at Mia 19 68,275

Mon 12/21
N Dal 41 at Atl 17 67,036

Sat 12/26
LARd 21 at Was 20 53,032
NO 20 at NYJ 0 45,614

Sun 12/27
SD 31 at Sea 14 49,324
Mia 16 at NE 13 34,726
Den 20 at KC 42 76,240
Cle 13 at Pit 23 53,776
GB 7 at Min 27 61,461
Atl 27 at LARm 38 37,706
Ind 21 at Cin 17 47,837
NYG 10 at Phi 20 64,266
ChiB 14 at Dal 27 63,101
TB 7 at Pho 3 29,645
N Buf 3 at Hou 27 61,742

Mon 12/28
N Det 6 at SF 24 55,907

First-Round Playoffs

Sat 01/02
KC 0 at SD 17 58,278
Was 24 at Min 7 57,353

Sun 01/03
Hou 38 at Buf 41 75,141
Phi 36 at NO 20 68,591

AFC/NFC Divisional Playoffs

Sat 01/09
Buf 24 at Pit 3 60,407
Was 13 at SF 20 64,991

Sun 01/10
SD 0 at Mia 31 71,224
Phi 10 at Dal 34 68,591

1992 AFC/NFC Championships

Sun 01/17
Buf 29 at Mia 10 72,703
Dal 30 at SF 20 64,920

Super Bowl XXVII

Sun 01/31
Buf 17 at Dal 52 98,374
at Pasadena, CA

National Football League 1993

Sun 09/05
SF 24 at Pit 13 57,502
NE 14 at Buf 38 79,751
Den 26 at NYJ 20 68,130
Mia 24 at Ind 20 51,858
Cin 14 at Cle 27 75,508
NYG 26 at ChiB 20 66,900
Min 7 at LARd 24 45,136
LARm 6 at GB 36 54,648
at Milwaukee, WI
Sea 12 at SD 18 58,039
KC 27 at TB 3 63,378
Atl 13 at Det 30 56,216
Pho 17 at Phi 23 59,831
N Hou 21 at NO 33 69,029

Mon 09/06
N Dal 16 at Was 35 56,345

Sun 09/12
NO 34 at Atl 31 64,287
NYJ 24 at Mia 14 70,314
ChiB 7 at Min 10 56,285
Pit 0 at LARm 27 50,588
KC 0 at Hou 30 59,780
Buf 13 at Dal 10 63,226
Pho 17 at Was 10 53,525
TB 7 at NYG 23 75,891
Phi 20 at GB 17 59,061
SD 17 at Den 34 75,074
Det 19 at NE 16 54,151
Ind 9 at Cin 6 50,299
N LARd 17 at Sea 13 58,836

Mon 09/13
N SF 13 at Cle 23 78,512

Sun 09/19
Sea 17 at NE 14 50,392
LARm 10 at NYG 20 76,213
Hou 17 at SD 18 58,519
Det 3 at NO 14 69,039
Cle 19 at LARd 16 48,617
Was 31 at Phi 34 65,435
Cin 7 at Pit 34 53,682
Atl 30 at SF 37 63,032
N Dal 17 at Pho 10 73,025

Mon 09/20
N Den 7 at KC 15 78,453

Sun 09/26
LARm 28 at Hou 13 53,072
GB 13 at Min 15 61,077
Cle 10 at Ind 23 59,654
Mia 22 at Buf 13 79,635
SF 13 at NO 16 69,041
Sea 19 at Cin 10 46,880
Pho 20 at Det 26 57,180
TB 17 at ChiB 47 58,329
N NE 7 at NYJ 45 64,836

Mon 09/27
N Pit 45 at Atl 17 65,477

Sun 10/03
Ind 13 at Den 35 74,953
NO 37 at LARm 6 50,709
Min 19 at SF 38 63,071
Phi 35 at NYJ 30 72,593
SD 14 at Sea 31 54,778
GB 14 at Dal 36 63,568
Atl 0 at ChiB 6 57,441
LARd 9 at KC 24 77,395
Det 10 at TB 27 40,794
N NYG 14 at Buf 17 79,813

Mon 10/04
N Was 10 at Mia 17 68,568

Sun 10/10
NYG 41 at Was 7 53,715
TB 0 at Min 15 53,562
Cin 15 at KC 17 75,394
SD 3 at Pit 16 55,264
Dal 27 at Ind 3 60,453
Mia 24 at Cle 14 78,138
NYJ 20 at LARd 24 41,627
ChiB 17 at Phi 6 63,601
NE 23 at Pho 21 36,115
N Den 27 at GB 30 58,943

Mon 10/11
N Hou 7 at Buf 35 79,928

Thu 10/14
N LARm 24 at Atl 30 45,231

Sun 10/17
KC 17 at SD 14 60,729
Phi 10 at NYG 21 76,050
Hou 28 at NE 14 51,037
Cle 28 at Cin 17 55,647
Was 6 at Pho 36 48,143
SF 17 at Dal 26 65,099
Sea 10 at Det 30 60,801
NO 14 at Pit 37 56,056

Mon 10/18
N LARd 23 at Den 20 75,712

Sun 10/24
GB 37 at TB 14 47,354
Cin 12 at Hou 28 50,039
Buf 19 at NYJ 10 71,541
Pho 14 at SF 28 62,020
NE 9 at Sea 10 56,526
Det 16 at LARm 13 43,850
Pit 23 at Cle 28 78,118
Atl 26 at NO 15 69,043
N Ind 27 at Mia 41 57,301

Mon 10/25
N Min 19 at ChiB 12 64,677

Sun 10/31
Dal 23 at Phi 10 61,912
Sea 17 at Den 28 73,644
ChiB 3 at GB 17 58,945
NYJ 10 at NYG 6 71,659
TB 31 at Atl 24 50,647
SD 30 at LARd 23 45,122
LARm 17 at SF 40 63,417
NO 20 at Pho 17 36,778
KC 10 at Mia 30 67,765
NE 6 at Ind 9 46,522
N Det 30 at Min 27 53,739

Mon 11/01
N Was 10 at Buf 24 79,106

Sun 11/07
Den 29 at Cle 14 77,818
Buf 13 at NE 10 54,326
SD 30 at Min 17 54,960
Phi 3 at Pho 16 41,634
LARd 16 at ChiB 14 59,750
NYG 9 at Dal 31 64,735
Mia 10 at NYJ 27 71,306
Sea 14 at Hou 24 50,447
Pit 24 at Cin 16 51,202
TB 0 at Det 23 65,295
N Ind 24 at Was 30 50,523

Mon 11/08
N GB 16 at KC 23 76,742

Sun 11/14
Mia 19 at Phi 14 64,213
GB 19 at NO 17 69,043
SF 45 at TB 21 43,835
Atl 13 at LARm 0 37,073
Hou 38 at Cin 3 42,347
NYJ 31 at Ind 17 47,351
Min 26 at Den 23 67,329
Cle 5 at Sea 22 54,622
KC 31 at LARd 20 66,553
Pho 15 at Dal 20 64,224
Was 6 at NYG 20 76,606
N ChiB 16 at SD 13 58,459

Mon 11/15
N Buf 0 at Pit 23 60,265

Sun 11/21
Hou 27 at Cle 20 71,668
Wash 6 at LARm 10 45,546
Pit 13 at Den 37 74,840
NYG 7 at Phi 3 62,928
LARd 12 at SD 7 60,615
ChiB 19 at KC 17 76,872
Ind 9 at Buf 23 79,101
Cin 12 at NYJ 17 64,264
Dal 14 at Atl 27 71,253
NE 13 at Mia 17 59,982
Det 17 at GB 26 55,119
at Milwaukee, WI
N Min 10 at TB 23 40,848

Mon 11/22
N NO 7 at SF 42 66,500

Thu 11/25
Mia 16 at Dal 14 60,198
ChiB 10 at Det 6 76,699

Sun 11/28
Den 17 at Sea 9 57,812
Pho 17 at NYG 19 59,979
NYJ 6 at NE 0 42,810
TB 10 at GB 13 56,995
Cle 14 at Atl 17 54,510
LARd 10 at Cin 16 43,272
Buf 7 at KC 23 74,452
NO 17 at Min 14 53,030
SF 35 at LARm 10 62,143
Phi 17 at Was 14 46,663
N Pit 3 at Hou 23 61,238

Mon 11/29
N SD 31 at Ind 0 54,110

Sun 12/05
KC 31 at Sea 16 58,551
Den 10 at SD 13 60,233
Atl 17 at Hou 33 58,186
Ind 9 at NYJ 6 45,799
NYG 19 at Mia 14 72,161
LARm 10 at Pho 38 33,964
LARd 25 at Buf 24 79,478
Was 23 at TB 17 49,035
NO 13 at Cle 17 60,388
Min 13 at Det 0 63,216
GB 17 at ChiB 30 62,236
NE 14 at Pit 17 51,358
N Cin 8 at SF 21 60,039

Mon 12/06
N Phi 17 at Dal 23 64,521

Sat 12/11
SF 24 at Atl 27 64,688
NYJ 3 at Was 0 47,970

Sun 12/12
KC 21 at Den 27 75,822
Dal 37 at Min 20 63,321
Sea 23 at LARd 27 38,161
Buf 10 at Phi 7 60,769
ChiB 10 at TB 13 56,667
Det 21 at Pho 14 39,393
LARm 23 at NO 20 69,033
Cle 17 at Hou 19 63,016
Ind 6 at NYG 20 70,411
Cin 2 at NE 7 29,794
N GB 20 at SD 13 57,930

Mon 12/13
N Pit 21 at Mia 20 73,882

Sat 12/18
Den 13 at ChiB 3 53,056
Dal 28 at NYJ 7 73,109

Sun 12/19
Pho 30 at Sea 27 45,737
SD 24 at KC 28 74,778
TB 20 at LARd 27 40,532
SF 55 at Det 17 77,052
NE 20 at Cle 17 48,618
Hou 26 at Pit 17 57,592
LARm 3 at Cin 15 36,612
Atl 17 at Was 30 50,192
Min 21 at GB 17 54,773
at Milwaukee, WI
Buf 47 at Mia 34 71,597
N Phi 20 at Ind 10 44,952

Mon 12/20
N NYG 24 at NO 14 69,036

Sat 12/25
Hou 10 at SF 7 61,744

Sun 12/26
Cle 42 at LARm 14 34,155
Det 20 at ChiB 14 43,443
Was 3 at Dal 38 64,497
NYG 6 at Pho 17 53,414
TB 17 at Den 10 73,434
Pit 6 at Sea 16 51,814
NYJ 14 at Buf 16 70,817
Ind 0 at NE 38 26,571
Atl 17 at Cin 21 47,014
LARd 0 at GB 28 54,482
NO 26 at Phi 37 50,085
N KC 10 at Min 30 59,236

Mon 12/27
N Mia 20 at SD 45 60,311

Fri 12/31
Min 14 at Was 9 42,836

Sun 01/02
Den 30 at LARd 33 66,904
Sea 24 at KC 34 72,136
ChiB 6 at LARm 20 39,147
Buf 30 at Ind 10 43,028
GB 20 at Det 30 77,510
Dal 16 at NYG 13 77,356
SD 32 at TB 17 35,587
Pho 27 at Atl 10 44,360
Mia 27 at NE 33 53,883
Cin 13 at NO 20 58,036
Cle 9 at Pit 16 49,208
N NYJ 0 at Hou 24 61,040

Mon 01/03
N Phi 37 at SF 34 61,653

First-Round Playoffs

Sat 01/08
KC 24 at Pit 27 74,515
GB 28 at Det 24 68,479

Sun 01/09
LARd 24 at Den 42 65,314
Min 10 at NYG 17 75,089

AFC/NFC Divisional Playoffs

Sat 01/15
LARd 23 at Buf 29 61,923
NYG 3 at SF 44 67,143

Sun 01/16
KC 28 at Hou 20 64,011
GB 17 at Dal 27 64,790

1993 AFC/NFC Championships

Sun 01/23
KC 13 at Buf 30 76,642
SF 21 at Dal 38 64,902

Super Bowl XXVIII

Sun 01/30
Dal 30 at Buf 13 72,817
at Atlanta, GA

National Football League 1994

Sun 09/04
Hou 21 at Ind 45 47,372
Atl 28 at Det 31 60,740
Ariz 12 at LARm 14 32,969
Dal 26 at Pitt 9 60,156
Cle 28 at Cin 20 52,778
TB 9 at ChiB 21 61,844
Phi 23 at NYG 28 76,130
NYJ 23 at Buff 3 79,460
KC 30 at NO 17 69,362
Sea 28 at Was 7 56,454
Min 10 at GB 16 59,487
NE 35 at Mia 39 69,613
N SD 37 at Den 34 74,032

Mon 09/05
N LARd 14 at SF 44 68,032

Sun 09/11
Mia 24 at GB 14 55,011
at Milwaukee, WI
Pit 17 at Cle 10 77,774
Sea 38 at LARd 9 47,319
Ind 10 at TB 24 36,631
Buf 38 at NE 35 60,274
LARm 13 at Atl 31 55,378
Den 22 at NYJ 25 73,436
Cin 10 at SD 27 53,217
Was 38 at NO 24 58,049
Det 3 at Min 10 57,349
SF 17 at KC 24 79,907
Hou 17 at Dal 20 64,402
N NYG 20 at Ariz 17 60,066

Mon 09/12
N ChiB 22 at Phi 30 64,890

Sun 09/18
SF 34 at LARm 19 56,479
Was 23 at NYG 31 77,298
NE 31 at Cin 28 46,640
SD 24 at Sea 10 65,536
NYJ 14 at Mia 28 68,192
Buf 15 at Hou 7 55,424
Min 42 at ChiB 14 61,073
LARd 48 at Den 16 75,764
GB 7 at Phi 13 63,922
Ariz 0 at Cle 32 62,818
Ind 21 at Pit 31 54,040
NO 9 at TB 7 45,522
N KC 30 at Atl 10 67,357

Mon 09/19
N Det 20 at Dal 17 64,102

Sun 09/25
Mia 35 at Min 38 64,035
Cin 13 at Hou 20 44,253
Pit 13 at Sea 30 59,637
NE 23 at Det 17 59,618
Atl 27 at Was 20 53,238
NO 13 at SF 24 63,971
SD 26 at LARd 24 55,385
TB 3 at GB 30 58,551
Cle 21 at Ind 14 55,821
LARm 16 at KC 0 78,184
N ChiB 19 at NYJ 7 70,806

Mon 09/26
N Den 20 at Buf 27 75,373

Sun 10/02
Phi 40 at SF 8 64,771
Dal 34 at Was 7 55,394
Det 14 at TB 24 38,012
Min 7 at Ariz 17 67,950
Sea 15 at Ind 17 49,876
NYJ 7 at Cle 27 76,188
NYG 22 at NO 27 55,076
Atl 8 at LARm 5 34,599
GB 16 at NE 17 57,522
Buf 13 at ChiB 20 62,406
N Mia 23 at Cin 7 55,056

Mon 10/03
N Hou 14 at Pit 30 57,274

Sun 10/09
LARd 21 at NE 17 59,869
NO 7 at ChiB 17 63,822
TB 13 at Atl 34 52,633
Den 16 at Sea 9 63,872
Ariz 3 at Dal 38 64,518
KC 6 at SD 20 62,923
LARm 17 at GB 24 58,911
Mia 11 at Buf 21 79,491
SF 27 at Det 21 77,340
Ind 6 at NYJ 16 66,244
N Was 17 at Phi 21 63,947

Mon 10/10
N Min 27 at NYG 10 77,294

Thu 10/13
N Cle 11 at Hous 8 50,364

Sun 10/16
SF 42 at Atl 3 67,298
NE 17 at NYJ 24 71,123
Ind 27 at Buf 17 79,404
Phi 13 at Dal 24 64,703
Ariz 19 at Was 16 50,019
NYG 10 at LARm 17 40,474
Cin 10 at Pit 14 55,353
SD 36 at NO 22 50,565
LARd 17 at Mia 20 69,380

Mon 10/17
N KC 31 at Den 28 75,151

Thu 10/20
N GB 10 at Min 13 63,041

Sun 10/23
Sea 23 at KC 38 78,847
Cin 13 at Cle 37 77,588
Was 41 at Ind 27 57,879
Atl 17 at LARd 30 42,192
Pit 10 at NYG 6 71,819
ChiB 16 at Det 21 73,574
Den 20 at SD 15 61,626
TB 16 at SF 41 62,741
Dal 28 at Ariz 21 71,023
LARm 34 at NO 37 47,908

Mon 10/24
N Hous 6 at Phi 21 65,233

Sun 10/30
KC 10 at Buf 44 79,501
Min 36 at TB 13 42,110
Sea 15 at SD 35 59,001
NYJ 25 at Ind 28 44,350
Cle 14 at Den 26 73,190
Mia 23 at NE 3 59,167
Det 28 at NYG 25 75,124
Hou 14 at LARd 17 40,473
Phi 31 at Was 29 53,530
Dal 23 at Cin 20 57,096
N Pit 17 at Ariz 20 73,400

Mon 10/31
N GB 33 at ChiB 6 47,381

Sun 11/06
NO 20 at Min 21 57,564
Cin 20 at Sea 17 46,630
Buf 17 at NYJ 22 67,030
Ariz 7 at Phi 17 64,952
ChiB 20 at TB 6 60,821
Pit 12 at Hous 9 47,822
Ind 21 at Mia 22 67,863
SF 37 at Was 22 54,335
SD 9 at Atl 10 59,217
Den 21 at LARm 27 48,103
NE 6 at Cle 13 73,878
Det 30 at GB 38 54,995
at Milwaukee, WI
N LARd 3 at KC 13 78,709

Mon 11/07
N NYG 10 at Dal 38 64,836

Sun 11/13
SD 14 at KC 13 76,997
Hou 31 at Cin 34 54,908
Min 20 at NE 26 58,382
Atl 32 at NO 33 60,313
Sea 10 at Den 17 71,290
LARd 20 at LARm 17 65,208
NYJ 10 at GB 17 58,307
Dal 14 at SF 21 69,014
ChiB 17 at Mia 14 65,006
Cle 26 at Phil 7 65,233
Ariz 10 at NYG 9 71,719
N TB 9 at Det 14 50,814

Mon 11/14
N Buf 10 at Pit 23 59,019

Sun 11/20
Phil 6 at Ariz 12 62,779
Cle 13 at KC 20 66,129
Atl 28 at Den 32 70,594
Det 10 at ChiB 20 55,035
SD 17 at NE 23 59,690
NO 19 at LARd 24 41,722
NYJ 31 at Min 21 60,687
Wash 7 at Dal 31 64,644
GB 20 at Buf 29 79,029
TB 21 at Sea 22 37,466
Ind 17 at Cin 13 55,566
Mia 13 at Pit 16 59,148
N LARm 27 at SF 31 62,774

Mon 11/21
N NYG 13 at Hou 10 53,201

Thu 11/24
Buf 21 at Det 35 75,672
GB 31 at Dal 42 64,597

Sun 11/27
Cin 13 at Den 15 69,714
LARm 17 at SD 31 59,579
KC 9 at Sea 10 54,120
ChiB 19 at Ariz 16 65,922
NYG 21 at Was 19 43,384
Hou 10 at Cle 34 65,088
TB 20 at Min 17 47,259
Mia 28 at NYJ 24 75,606
Pit 21 at LARd 3 58,327
Phi 21 at Atl 28 60,008
N NE 12 at Ind 10 43,839

Mon 11/28
N SF 35 at NO 14 61,304

Thu 12/01
N ChiB 27 at Min 33 61,483

Sun 12/04
Was 21 at TB 26 45,121
NYG 16 at Cle 13 72,068
NO 31 at LARm 15 34,960
Pit 38 at Cin 15 59,997
NYJ 13 at NE 24 60,138
Ariz 30 at Hou 12 39,821
Atl 14 at SF 50 60,549
Dal 31 at Phi 19 65,974
Ind 31 at Sea 19 39,574
Den 20 at KC 17 77,631
GB 31 at Det 34 76,338
N Buf 42 at Mia 31 69,358

Mon 12/05
N LARd 24 at SD 17 63,012

Sat 12/10
Cle 19 at Dal 14 64,286
Det 18 at NYJ 7 56,080

Sun 12/11
ChiB 3 at GB 40 57,927
Ind 13 at NE 28 57,656
SF 38 at SD 15 62,105
Cin 20 at NYG 27 67,530
Sea 16 at Hou 14 31,453
Was 15 at Ariz 17 53,790
Min 21 at Buf 17 66,501
Phi 3 at Pit 14 55,474
Den 13 at LARd 23 60,016
LARm 14 at TB 24 34,150
N NO 29 at Atl 20 61,307

Mon 12/12
N KC 28 at Mia 45 71,578

Sat 12/17
Min 19 at Det 41 73,881
Den 19 at SF 42 64,884

Sun 12/18
SD 21 at NYJ 6 48,213
NYG 16 at Phi 13 64,540
Clev 7 at Pit 17 60,808
Cinc 7 at Ariz 28 50,110
Hous 9 at KC 31 74,474
LARm 13 at ChiB 27 56,276
Miam 6 at Ind 10 58,867
Atl 17 at GB 21 54,885
at Milwaukee, WI
NE 41 at Buf 17 56,784
TB 17 at Was 14 47,315
N LARd 17 at Sea 16 53,301

Mon 12/19
N Dal 24 at NO 16 67,323

Sat 12/24
NYJ 10 at Hou 24 31,176
Pit 34 at SD 37 58,379
Dal 10 at NYG 15 66,943
Buf 9 at Ind 10 38,458
Ariz 6 at Atl 10 35,311
Sea 9 at Cle 35 54,180
Was 24 at LARm 21 25,705
NO 30 at Den 28 64,445
Phi 30 at Cin 33 39,923
NE 13 at ChiB 3 60,178
GB 34 at TB 19 65,076
KC 19 at LARd 9 64,130

Sun 12/25
N Det 20 at Mia 27 70,980

Mon 12/26
N SF 14 at Min 21 63,326

First-Round Playoffs

Sat 12/31
Det 12 at GB 16 58,125
KC 17 at Mia 27 67,487

Sun 01/01
NE 13 at Cle 20 77,452
ChiB 35 at Min 18 60,347

AFC/NFC Divisional Playoffs

Sat 01/07
Clev 9 at Pit 29 58,185
ChiB 15 at SF 44 64,644

Sun 01/08
GB 9 at Dal 35 64,745
Mia 21 at SD 22 63,381

1994 AFC/NFC Championship

Sun 01/15
SD 17 at Pit 13 61,545
Dal 28 at SF 38 69,125

Super Bowl XXIX

Sun 01/29
SD 26 at SF 49 74,107
at Miami, FL

National Football League 1995

Sun 09/03
Ariz 7 at Was 27 52,731
Car 20 at Atl 23 58,808
Cin 24 at Ind 21 42,445
Cle 14 at NE 17 60,126
Det 20 at Pit 23 58,002
Hou 10 at Jack 3 72,363
KC 34 at Sea 10 54,062
Min 14 at ChiB 31 63,036
NYJ 14 at Mia 52 71,317
StL 17 at GB 14 60,104
SD 7 at Oak 17 50,323
SF 24 at NO 22 66,627
TB 21 at Phil 6 66,266
N Buff 7 at Den 22 75,743

Mon 09/04
N Dal 35 at NYG 0 77,454

Sun 09/10
Atl 10 at SF 41 63,627
Car 9 at Buf 31 79,190
Den 21 at Dal 31 64,576
Det 10 at Min 20 52,234
Ind 27 at NYJ 24 65,134
Jac 17 at Cin 24 48,318
Mia 20 at NE 3 60,239
NO 13 at StL 17 58,186
NYG 17 at KC 20 77,962
Oak 20 at Wash 8 54,548
Pit 34 at Hou 17 44,122
Sea 10 at SD 14 54,420
N Phi 31 at Ariz 19 45,004

Mon 09/11
N GB 27 at ChiB 24 64,855

Sun 09/17
Ariz 20 at Det 17 58,727
Atl 27 at NO 24 57,442
ChiB 25 at TB 6 71,507
Cin 21 at Sea 24 39,492
Cle 14 at Hou 7 36,077
Ind 14 at Buf 20 62,499
Jac 10 at NYJ 27 49,970
NYG 6 at GB 14 60,117
Oak 17 at KC 23 78,696
StL 31 at Car 10 54,060
SD 27 at Phi 21 63,081
Was 31 at Den 38 71,930
N Dal 23 at Min 17 60,088

Mon 09/18
N Pit 10 at Mia 23 72,874

Sun 09/24
Ariz 20 at Dal 34 64,560
ChiB 28 at StL 34 59,679
Den 6 at SD 17 58,978
Hou 38 at Cin 28 46,332
KC 17 at Cle 35 74,280
Min 44 at Pit 24 57,853
NO 29 at NYG 45 72,619
NYJ 3 at Atl 13 40,778
Phi 17 at Oak 48 48,875
Was 6 at TB 14 49,234
N GB 24 at Jac 14 66,744

Mon 09/25
N SF 24 at Det 27 76,236

Sun 10/01
Dal 23 at Was 27 55,489
Den 10 at Sea 27 56,483
Jac 17 at Hou 16 36,346
KC 24 at Ariz 3 50,211
Mia 26 at Cin 23 52,671
NE 17 at Atl 30 47,114
NYG 6 at SF 20 65,536
Phi 15 at NO 10 43,938
StL 18 at Ind 21 58,616
SD 16 at Pit 31 57,012
TB 20 at Car 13 50,076
N Oak 47 at NYJ 10 68,941

Mon 10/02
N Buf 22 at Cle 19 76,211

Sun 10/08
Ariz 21 at NYG 27 68,463
Car 27 at ChiB 31 59,668
Cin 16 at TB 19 41,732
Cle 20 at Det 38 74,171
GB 24 at Dal 34 64,806
Hou 17 at Min 23 56,430
Ind 27 at Mia 24 68,471
NYJ 10 at Buf 29 79,485
Pit 16 at Jac 20 72,042
Sea 14 at Oak 34 60,213
Was 34 at Phi 37 65,498
N Den 37 at NE 3 60,074

Mon 10/09
N SD 23 at KC 29 79,288

Thu 10/12
Atl 19 at StL 21 59,700

Sun 10/15
ChiB 30 at Jac 27 72,020
Dal 23 at SD 9 62,664
Det 21 at GB 30 60,302
NE 26 at KC 31 77,992
NYJ 15 at Car 26 52,613
Phi 17 at NYG 14 74,252
SF 17 at Ind 18 60,273
Min 17 at TB 20 55,703
Mia 30 at NO 33 55,628
Sea 21 at Buf 27 74,362
Was 20 at Ariz 24 42,370

Mon 10/16
N Oakl 0 at Den 27 75,491

Thu 10/19
Cin 27 at Pitt 9 56,684

Sun 10/22
Atl 24 at TB 21 66,135
Det 30 at Was 36 52,332
Hou 32 at ChiB 35 63,545
Ind 17 at Oak 30 53,543
Jac 23 at Cle 15 64,405
KC 21 at Den 7 71,044
Mia 16 at NYJ 17 67,228
Min 21 at GB 38 60,332
NO 3 at Car 20 55,484
SD 35 at Sea 25 45,821
SF 44 at StL 10 59,915

Mon 10/23
N Buf 14 at NE 27 60,203

Sun 10/29
Buf 6 at Mia 23 71,060
Car 20 at NE 17 60,064
Cle 29 at Cin 26 58,632
Dal 28 at Atl 13 70,089
GB 16 at Det 24 73,462
Jac 7 at Pit 24 54,516
NO 11 at SF 7 65,272
NYJ 10 at Ind 17 49,250
StL 9 at Phi 20 62,172
Sea 14 at Ariz 20 39,600
TB 7 at Hou 19 31,489
N NYG 24 at Was 15 53,310

Mon 10/30
N ChiB 14 at Min 6 58,217

Sun 11/05
Ariz 6 at Den 38 71,488
Buf 16 at Ind 10 59,612
Car 13 at SF 7 61,722
Det 22 at Atl 34 49,619
GB 24 at Min 27 62,839
Hou 37 at Cle 10 57,881
NE 20 at NYJ 7 61,462
NYG 28 at Sea 30 42,100
Oak 20 at Cin 17 51,265
Pit 37 at ChiB 34 61,838
StL 10 at NO 19 43,120
Was 3 at KC 24 77,821
N Mia 24 at SD 14 61,966

Mon 11/06
N Phi 12 at Dal 34 64,876

Sun 11/12
Atl 17 at Buf 23 62,690
Car 17 at StL 28 65,598
ChiB 28 at GB 35 59,996
Cin 32 at Hou 25 32,998
Ind 14 at NO 17 44,122
KC 22 at SD 7 59,285
Min 30 at Ariz 24 51,342
NE 34 at Mia 17 70,399
Oak 17 at NYG 13 71,160
SF 38 at Dal 20 65,180
Sea 47 at Jac 30 71,290
TB 24 at Det 27 60,644
N Den 13 at Phi 31 60,842

Mon 11/13
N Cle 3 at Pit 20 58,675

Sun 11/19
Ariz 7 at Car 27 49,582
Buf 28 at NYJ 26 54,436
Dal 34 at Oak 21 54,444
Det 24 at ChiB 17 61,779
GB 31 at Cle 20 55,388
Ind 24 at NE 10 59,544
Jac 16 at TB 17 71,629
NO 24 at Min 43 58,108
NYG 19 at Phi 28 63,562
Pit 49 at Cin 31 54,636
StL 6 at Atl 31 46,309
SD 27 at Den 30 74,681
Sea 27 at Was 20 51,298
N Hou 13 at KC 20 77,576

Mon 11/20
N SF 44 at Mia 20 73,080

Thu 11/23
KC 12 at Dal 24 64,901
Min 38 at Det 44 74,559

Sun 11/26
Atl 37 at Ariz 40 35,147
ChiB 27 at NYG 24 70,015
Cin 17 at Jac 13 68,249
Den 33 at Hou 42 36,113
Mia 28 at Ind 36 60,414
NE 35 at Buf 25 69,384
NYJ 16 at Sea 10 41,160
Phi 14 at Was 7 50,539
Pit 20 at Cle 17 67,269
StL 13 at SF 41 66,049
TB 13 at GB 35 59,218
N Car 26 at NO 34 39,580

Mon 11/27
N Oak 6 at SD 12 60,607

Thu 11/30
NYG 10 at Ariz 6 44,246

Sun 12/03
Atl 20 at Mia 21 63,395
Cin 10 at GB 24 60,318
Cle 13 at SD 31 56,358
Hou 7 at Pit 21 56,013
Ind 10 at Car 13 49,841
Jac 23 at Den 31 72,231
KC 29 at Oak 23 53,930
NO 31 at NE 17 59,876
Phi 14 at Sea 26 39,893
StL 23 at NYJ 20 52,023
TB 17 at Min 31 52,879
Was 24 at Dal 17 64,866
N Buf 17 at SF 27 65,568

Mon 12/04
N ChiB 7 at Det 27 77,230

Sat 12/09
Ariz 25 at SD 28 55,258
Cle 11 at Min 27 47,984

Sun 12/10
Buf 45 at StL 27 64,623
ChiB 10 at Cin 16 38,642
Dal 17 at Phi 20 66,198
Det 24 at Hou 17 35,842
Ind 41 at Jac 31 66,099
NO 14 at Atl 19 54,603
NYJ 28 at NE 31 46,617
Pit 29 at Oak 10 53,516
SF 31 at Car 10 76,136
Sea 31 at Den 27 71,488
Was 13 at NYG 20 48,247
N GB 10 at TB 13 67,557

Mon 12/11
N KC 6 at Mia 13 70,321

Sat 12/16
GB 34 at NO 23 50,132
NE 27 at Pit 41 57,158

Sun 12/17
Ariz 20 at Phi 21 62,076
Atl 17 at Car 21 53,833
Cin 10 at Cle 26 55,875
Den 17 at KC 20 75,061
Jac 0 at Det 44 70,204
Mia 20 at Buf 23 79,531
NYG 20 at Dal 21 64,400
NYJ 6 at Hou 23 35,873
SD 27 at Ind 24 55,318
TB 10 at ChiB 31 49,475
Was 35 at StL 23 63,760
N Oak 10 at Sea 44 58,428

Mon 12/18
N Min 30 at SF 37 64,975

Sat 12/23
SD 27 at NYG 17 50,243
Det 37 at TB 10 50,049
N NE 7 at Ind 10 54,685

Sun 12/24
Car 17 at Was 20 42,903
Cle 21 at Jac 24 66,007
Den 31 at Oak 28 50,074
Hou 28 at Buf 17 45,253
Mia 41 at StL 22 63,876
Min 24 at Cin 27 34,568
NO 12 at NYJ 0 28,885
Phi 14 at ChiB 20 52,391
Pit 19 at GB 24 60,649
SF 27 at Atl 28 51,785
Sea 3 at KC 26 75,784

Mon 12/25
N Dal 37 at Ariz 13 72,394

Wild-Card Playoffs

Sat 12/30
Det 37 at Phi 58 66,099
Mia 22 at Buf 37 73,103

Sun 12/31
Atl 20 at GB 37 60,453
Ind 35 at SD 20 61,182

AFC/NFC Divisional Playoffs

Sat 01/06
Buf 21 at Pit 40 59,072
GB 27 at SF 17 69,311

Sun 01/07
Ind 10 at KC 7 77,594
Phi 11 at Dal 30 64,371

1995 AFC/NFC Championship

Sun 01/14
GB 27 at Dal 38 65,135
Ind 16 at Pit 20 61,062

Super Bowl XXX

Sun 01/28
Dal 27 vs Pit 17 76,347
at Tempe, AZ

National Football League 1996

Sun 09/01
Ariz 13 at Ind 20 48,133
Atl 6 at Car 29 69,522
Cin 16 at StL 26 62,659
Det 13 at Min 17 52,972
GB 34 at TB 3 54,102
KC 20 at Hou 19 27,725
NE 10 at Mia 24 71,542
NO 11 at SF 27 63,970
NYJ 6 at Den 31 70,595
Oak 14 at Bal 19 64,124
Phi 17 at Was 14 53,415
Pit 9 at Jac 24 70,210
Sea 7 at SD 29 58,780
N Buf 23 at NYG 20 74,218

Mon 09/02
N Dal 6 at ChiB 22 63,076

Sun 09/08
Bal 17 at Pit 31 57,241
Car 22 at NO 20 43,228
ChiB 3 at Was 10 56,454
Cin 14 at SD 27 55,880
Den 30 at Sea 20 43,671
Hou 34 at Jac 27 66,468
Ind 21 at NYJ 7 63,534
Min 23 at Atl 17 42,688
NE 10 at Buf 17 78,104
NYG 0 at Dal 27 63,069
Oak 3 at KC 19 79,281
StL 0 at SF 34 63,624
TB 6 at Det 21 57,469
N Mia 38 at Ariz 10 55,444

Mon 09/09
N Phi 13 at GB 39 60,666

Sun 09/15
Ariz 0 at NE 31 59,118
Bal 13 at Hou 29 20,082
Det 17 at Phi 24 66,007
Ind 25 at Dal 24 63,021
Jac 3 at Oak 17 46,291
KC 35 at Sea 17 39,790
Min 20 at ChiB 14 61,301
NO 15 at Cin 30 45,412
NYJ 27 at Mia 36 68,137
SD 10 at GB 42 60,584
Was 31 at NYG 10 71,693
N TB 23 at Den 27 71,535

Mon 09/16
N Buf 6 at Pit 24 59,002

Sun 09/22
Ariz 28 at NO 14 34,316
ChiB 16 at Det 35 70,022
Dal 7 at Buf 10 78,098
Den 14 at KC 17 79,439
GB 21 at Min 30 64,168
Jac 25 at NE 28 59,446
NYG 13 at NYJ 6 58,339
SD 40 at Oak 34 49,097
SF 7 at Car 23 72,224
Sea 17 at TB 13 30,212
Was 17 at StL 10 62,303
N Phi 33 at Atl 18 40,107

Mon 09/23
N Mia 6 at Ind 10 60,891

Sun 09/29
Atl 17 at SF 39 62,995
Car 14 at Jac 24 71,537
Den 14 at Cin 10 51,798
Det 27 at TB 0 34,961
GB 31 at Sea 10 59,973
Hou 16 at Pit 30 58,608
KC 19 at SD 22 59,384
Min 10 at NYG 15 70,970
NO 10 at Bal 17 61,063
Oak 17 at ChiB 19 57,062
StL 28 at Ariz 31 33,116
N NYJ 16 at Was 31 52,068

Mon 09/30
N Dal 23 at Phi 19 67,201

Sun 10/06
Atl 24 at Det 28 58,666
Car 12 at Min 14 60,894
GB 37 at ChiB 6 65,480
Ind 13 at Buf 16 79,401
Jac 13 at NO 17 34,231
NE 46 at Bal 38 63,569
Oak 34 at NYJ 13 63,611
SD 17 at Den 28 75,058
SF 28 at StL 11 61,260
Sea 22 at Mia 15 59,539
N Hou 30 at Cin 27 51,610

Mon 10/07
N Pit 17 at KC 7 79,189

Sun 10/13
Ariz 3 at Dal 17 64,096
ChiB 24 at NO 27 43,512
Cin 10 at Pit 20 58,875
Det 21 at Oak 37 50,037
Hou 23 at Atl 13 35,401
Mia 21 at Buf 7 79,642
Min 13 at TB 24 32,175
NYJ 17 at Jac 21 65,699
Phi 19 at NYG 10 72,729
StL 13 at Car 45 70,535
Was 27 at NE 22 59,638
N Bal 21 at Ind 26 56,978

Mon 10/14
N SF 20 at GB 23 60,716

Thu 10/17
N Sea 16 at KC 34 76,057

Sun 10/20
Atl 28 at Dal 32 64,091
Bal 34 at Den 45 70,453
Buf 25 at NYJ 22 49,775
Cin 21 at SF 28 63,218
Jac 14 at StL 17 60,066
Mia 28 at Phi 35 66,240
NE 27 at Ind 9 58,725
NO 7 at Car 19 70,888
NYG 21 at Was 31 52,684
Pit 13 at Hou 23 50,337
TB 9 at Ariz 13 27,738

Mon 10/21
N Oak 23 at SD 14 62,350

Sun 10/27
Car 9 at Phi 20 65,982
Dal 29 at Mia 10 75,283
Ind 16 at Was 31 54,254
Jac 21 at Cin 28 45,890
KC 7 at Den 34 75,852
NYG 35 at Det 7 63,501
NYJ 31 at Ariz 21 28,088
Pit 20 at Atl 17 58,760
StL 31 at Bal 37 60,256
SD 13 at Sea 32 38,143
SF 10 at Hou 9 53,644
TB 7 at GB 13 60,790
N Buf 25 at NE 28 59,858

Mon 10/28
N ChiB 15 at Min 13 58,143

Sun 11/03
Ariz 8 at NYG 16 68,262
Car 17 at Atl 20 42,726
Cin 24 at Bal 21 60,743
Det 18 at GB 28 60,695
Hou 16 at Sea 23 36,320
KC 21 at Min 6 59,552
Mia 23 at NE 42 58,942
Phi 31 at Dal 21 64,952
StL 6 at Pit 42 58,148
SD 26 at Ind 19 58,484
TB 10 at ChiB 13 58,727
Was 13 at Buf 38 78,002
N SF 24 at NO 17 53,297

Mon 11/04
N Den 22 at Oak 21 61,179

Sun 11/10
Ariz 37 at Was 34 51,929
Atl 16 at StL 59 65,690
Bal 27 at Jac 30 64,628
Buf 24 at Phi 17 66,613
ChiB 12 at Den 17 75,555
Dal 20 at SF 17 68,919
GB 20 at KC 27 79,281
Hou 31 at NO 14 34,121
Ind 13 at Mia 37 66,623
Min 23 at Sea 42 50,794
NE 31 at NYJ 27 61,715
Oak 17 at TB 20 45,392
Pit 24 at Cin 34 57,265
N NYG 17 at Car 27 70,298

Mon 11/11
N Det 21 at SD 27 60,425

Sun 11/17
Bal 20 at SF 38 51,596
Car 20 at StL 10 60,652
ChiB 10 at KC 14 76,762
Cin 17 at Buf 31 75,549
Den 34 at NE 8 59,452
Jac 3 at Pit 28 58,879
Mia 23 at Hou 20 47,358
NO 15 at Atl 17 43,119
NYG 23 at Ariz 31 34,924
NYJ 29 at Ind 34 48,322
Sea 16 at Det 17 51,194
TB 25 at SD 17 57,526
Was 26 at Phi 21 66,834
N Min 16 at Oak 13 41,183

Mon 11/18
N GB 6 at Dal 21 65,032

Sun 11/24
Atl 31 at Cin 41 44,868
Car 31 at Hou 6 20,107
Dal 6 at NYG 20 77,081
Den 21 at Min 17 59,142
Det 14 at ChiB 31 55,864
Ind 13 at NE 27 58,226
Jac 28 at Bal 25 57,384
NO 7 at TB 13 40,203
NYJ 10 at Buf 35 60,854
Oak 27 at Sea 21 47,506
Phi 30 at Ariz 36 36,175
SD 28 at KC 14 69,472
SF 19 at Was 16 54,235
N GB 24 at StL 9 61,499

Mon 11/25
N Pit 24 at Mia 17 73,489

Thu 11/28
KC 28 at Det 24 75,079
Was 10 at Dal 21 64,995

Sun 12/01
Ariz 17 at Min 41 46,767
Buf 10 at Ind 13 53,804
ChiB 17 at GB 28 59,682
Cin 27 at Jac 30 57,408
Hou 35 at NYJ 10 21,723
Mia 7 at Oak 17 60,591
NYG 0 at Phi 24 51,468
Pit 17 at Bal 31 51,822
StL 26 at NO 10 26,310
Sea 7 at Den 34 74,982
TB 0 at Car 24 57,623
N NE 45 at SD 7 59,209

Mon 12/02
N SF 34 at Atl 10 46,318

Thu 12/05
N Phi 10 at Ind 37 52,689

Sun 12/08
Atl 31 at NO 15 32,923
Bal 14 at Cin 21 43,022
Buf 18 at Sea 26 41,373
Car 30 at SF 24 66,291
Dal 10 at Ariz 6 70,763
Den 6 at GB 41 60,712
Jac 23 at Hou 17 20,196
NYG 17 at Mia 7 63,889
NYJ 10 at NE 34 54,621
StL 9 at ChiB 35 45,075
SD 3 at Pit 16 56,368
Was 10 at TB 24 44,733
N Min 24 at Det 22 46,043

Mon 12/09
N KC 7 at Oak 26 57,082

Sat 12/14
Phi 21 at NYJ 20 29,178
SD 14 at ChiB 27 49,763

Sun 12/15
Bal 16 at Car 27 70,075
Cin 21 at Hou 13 15,131
GB 31 at Det 3 73,214
Ind 24 at KC 19 71,136
NE 6 at Dal 12 64,578
NO 17 at NYG 3 52,530
Oak 19 at Den 24 75,466
StL 34 at Atl 27 26,519
SF 25 at Pit 15 59,823
TB 10 at Min 21 49,202
Was 26 at Ariz 27 34,260
N Sea 20 at Jac 20 66,134

Mon 12/16
N Buf 14 at Mia 16 67,016

Sat 12/21
NE 23 at NYG 22 65,387
NO 13 at StL 14 57,681

Sun 12/22
Ariz 19 at Phi 29 63,658
Atl 17 at Jac 19 71,449
ChiB 19 at TB 34 51,572
Dal 10 at Was 37 50,454
Hou 24 at Bal 21 52,704
Ind 31 at Cin 24 49,389
KC 9 at Buf 20 68,671
Mia 31 at NYJ 28 47,271
Min 10 at GB 38 59,306
Pit 14 at Car 18 72,217
Sea 28 at Oak 21 33,455
N Den 10 at SD 16 46,801

Mon 12/23
N Det 14 at SF 24 61,921

Wild-Card Playoffs

Sat 12/28
Jac 30 at Buf 27 70,213
Min 15 at Dal 40 64,682

Sun 12/29
Ind 14 at Pit 42 58,078
Phi 0 at SF 14 56,460

AFC/NFC Divisional Playoffs

Sat 01/04
Jac 30 at Den 27 75,678
SF 14 at GB 35 60,787

Sun 01/05
Pit 3 at NE 28 60,188
Dal 17 at Car 26 72,808

1996 AFC/NFC Championships

Sun 01/12
Jac 6 at NE 20 60,190
Car 13 at GB 30 60,216

Super Bowl XXXI

Sun 01/26
GB 35 vs NE 21 72,301
at New Orleans, LA

National Football League 1997

Sun 08/31
Jac 28 at Bal 27 61,018
Dal 37 at Pit 7 60,397
N Was 24 at Car 10 72,633
Ariz 21 at Cin 24 50,298
Phi 17 at NYG 31 70,296
NYJ 41 at Sea 3 53,893
Ind 10 at Mia 16 70,813
Atl 17 at Det 28 61,244
NO 24 at StL 38 64,575
SF 6 at TB 13 62,544
KC 3 at Den 19 75,600
Oak 21 at Ten 24# 30,171
SD 7 at NE 41 60,190
Min 34 at Buf 13 79,139

Mon 09/01
N ChiB 24 at GB 38 60,766

Sun 09/07
Buf 28 at NYJ 22 72,988
Car 9 at Atl 6 51,829
Cin 10 at Bal 23 52,968
Den 35 at Sea 14 55,859
GB 9 at Phi 10 66,803
Min 27 at ChiB 24 59,263
NE 31 at Ind 6 53,632
NYG 13 at Jac 40 70,581
SD 20 at NO 6 65,760
SF 15 at StL 12 64,630
TB 24 at Det 17 58,234
Ten 13 at Mia 16# 64,439
Was 13 at Pit 14 58,059
N Dal 22 at Ariz 25# 71,578

Mon 09/08
N KC 28 at Oak 27 61,523

Sun 09/14
Ariz 13 at Was 19# 78,270
Bal 24 at NYG 23 69,768
Buf 16 at KC 22 78,169
Car 26 at SD 7 70,813
Det 32 at ChiB 7 59,147
Mia 18 at GB 23 60,075
NO 7 at SF 33 61,838
Oak 36 at Atl 31 47,922
StL 14 at Den 35 74,338
Sea 31 at Ind 3 49,194
TB 28 at Min 14 63,697
N NYJ 24 at NE 27# 60,072

Mon 09/15
N Phi 20 at Dal 21 63,942

Sun 09/21
Atl 7 at SF 34 60,404
Bal 36 at Ten 10 17,737
ChiB 3 at NE 31 59,873
Cin 20 at Den 38 73,871
Det 17 at NO 35 50,116
Ind 35 at Buf 37 55,340
KC 35 at Car 14 67,402
Min 32 at GB 38 60,115
NYG 3 at StL 13 64,642
Oak 22 at NYJ 23 72,586
SD 22 at Sea 26 51,110
N Mia 21 at TB 31 73,314

Mon 09/22
N Pit 21 at Jac 30 73,016

Sun 09/28
Ariz 18 at TB 19 53,804
Bal 17 at SD 21 54,094
ChiB 3 at Dal 27 64,082
Den 29 at Atl 21 48,211
GB 15 at Det 26 78,110
Jac 12 at Was 24 74,421
NO 9 at NYG 14 68,891
NYJ 31 at Cin 14 57,209
StL 17 at Oak 35 42,506
Sea 17 at KC 20# 77,877
Ten 24 at Pit 37 57,507
N Phi 19 at Min 28 55,149

Mon 09/29
N SF 34 at Car 21 70,972

Sun 10/05
Cin 13 at Jac 21 67,728
Dal 17 at NYG 20 77,137
Det 13 at Buf 22 78,025
KC 14 at Mia 17 71,794
Min 20 at Ariz 19 45,550
NYJ 16 at Ind 12 48,295
Pit 42 at Bal 34 64,421
SD 25 at Oak 10 43,648
TB 16 at GB 21 60,100
Ten 13 at Sea 16 49,897
Was 10 at Phi 24 67,008
N NO 20 at ChiB 17 58,865

Mon 10/06
N NE 13 at Den 34 75,821

Sun 10/12
Atl 23 at NO 17 65,619
Buf 6 at NE 33 59,802
Car 14 at Min 21 62,625
Cin 7 at Ten 30 17,071
Det 27 at TB 9 72,095
GB 24 at ChiB 23 62,212
Mia 31 at NYJ 20 75,601
NYG 27 at Ariz 13 38,959
Phi 21 at Jac 38 69,150
StL 10 at SF 30 63,825
N Ind 22 at Pit 24 57,925

Mon 10/13
N Dal 16 at Was 21 76,159

Thu 10/16
SD 3 at KC 31 77,196

Sun 10/19
Ariz 10 at Phi 13# 66,860
Car 13 at NO 0 50,963
Den 25 at Oak 28 57,006
Jac 22 at Dal 26 64,464
Mia 24 at Bal 13 64,354
NE 19 at NYJ 24 77,716
NYG 26 at Det 20# 70,069
Pit 26 at Cin 10 60,020
SF 35 at Atl 28 53,378
Sea 17 at StL 9 64,819
Was 14 at Ten 28 31,042

Mon 10/20
N Buf 9 at Ind 6 61,139

Sun 10/26
Bal 20 at Was 17 75,067
Cin 27 at NYG 29 72,584
Dal 12 at Phi 13 67,106
Den 23 at Buf 20# 78,458
Ind 19 at SD 35 63,177
Jac 17 at Pit 23# 57,011
KC 28 at StL 20 64,864
Min 10 at TB 6 66,815
Oak 34 at Sea 45 66,264
SF 23 at NO 0 60,443
Ten 41 at Ariz 14 44,030
N Atl 12 at Car 21 54,675

Mon 10/27
N GB 28 at NE 10 59,972
N ChiB 36 at Mia 33# 73,156

Sun 11/02
Bal 16 at NYJ 19# 59,524
Dal 10 at SF 17 68,657
Jac 30 at Ten 24 27,208
Mia 6 at Buf 9 78,011
NE 18 at Min 23 62,197
Oak 14 at Car 38 71,064
Phi 21 at Ariz 31 39,549
StL 31 at Atl 34 36,583
SD 31 at Cin 38 53,754
Sea 27 at Den 30 74,212
TB 31 at Ind 28 58,512
Was 31 at ChiB 8 53,032
N Det 10 at GB 20 60,126

Mon 11/03
N Pit 10 at KC 13 78,301

Sun 11/09
Ariz 6 at Dal 24 64,302
Car 0 at Den 34 71,408
ChiB 22 at Min 29 63,443
Cin 28 at Ind 13 58,473
Det 7 at Was 30 75,261
KC 10 at Jac 24 70,444
NE 31 at Buf 10 65,783
NO 13 at Oak 10 40,091
NYG 6 at Ten 10 26,744
NYJ 17 at Mia 24 73,809
StL 7 at GB 17 60,093
Sea 37 at SD 31 64,616
TB 31 at Atl 10 46,018
N Bal 0 at Pit 37 56,669

Mon 11/10
N SF 24 at Phi 12 67,133

Sun 11/16
Ariz 10 at NYG 19 68,316
Atl 27 at StL 21 64,299
Car 19 at SF 27 61,500
Cin 3 at Pit 20 55,226
Den 22 at KC 24 77,963
GB 38 at Ind 41 60,928
Min 15 at Det 38 68,910
NE 7 at TB 27 70,479
NYJ 23 at ChiB 15 45,642
Phi 10 at Bal 10# 63,546
Sea 17 at NO 20# 50,493
Ten 9 at Jac 17 70,070
Was 14 at Dal 17 64,559
N Oak 38 at SD 13 65,714

Mon 11/17
N Buf 13 at Mia 30 74,155

Sun 11/23
Ariz 16 at Bal 13 53,976
Buf 14 at Ten 31 23,571
Car 16 at StL 10 64,609
Dal 17 at GB 45 60,111
Ind 10 at Det 32 62,803
Jac 26 at Cin 31 55,158
KC 19 at Sea 14 66,264
Mia 24 at NE 27 59,002
Min 21 at NYJ 23 70,131
NO 3 at Atl 20 48,620
Pit 20 at Phi 23 67,166
SD 10 at SF 17 61,905
TB 7 at ChiB 13 43,955
N NYG 7 at Was 7# 75,703

Mon 11/24
N Oak 3 at Den 31 75,307

Thu 11/27
ChiB 20 at Det 55 77,904
Ten 27 at Dal 14 63,421

Sun 11/30
Atl 24 at Sea 17 52,584
Bal 27 at Jac 29 63,712
Cin 42 at Phi 44 66,623
Ind 17 at NE 20 58,507
Mia 34 at Oak 16 50,569
NO 16 at Car 13 57,957
NYJ 10 at Buf 20 47,776
Pit 26 at Ariz 20# 66,341
STL 23 at Was 20 74,772
SF 9 at KC 44 77,535
TB 20 at NYG 8 77,859
N Den 38 at SD 28 54,245

Mon 12/01
N GB 27 at Min 11 64,001

Thu 12/04
Ten 14 at Cin 41 49,086

Sun 12/07
Atl 14 at SD 3 46,317
Buf 3 at ChiB 20 39,784
Den 24 at Pit 35 59,739
GB 17 at TB 6 73,523
Ind 22 at NYJ 14 61,168
Min 17 at SF 28 55,761
NE 26 at Jac 20 73,446
NYG 31 at Phi 21 67,084
Oak 0 at KC 30 76,379
StL 34 at NO 27 54,803
Sea 24 at Bal 31 54,395
Was 38 at Ariz 28 41,537
N Det 30 at Mia 33 72,266

Mon 12/08
N Car 23 at Dal 13 63,251

Sat 12/13
Pit 24 at NE 21# 60,013
Was 10 at NYG 30 77,571

Sun 12/14
Ariz 10 at NO 27 45,517
Dal 24 at Cin 31 60,043
Det 14 at Min 13 60,982
GB 31 at Car 10 70,887
Jac 20 at Buf 14 41,231
KC 29 at SD 7 54,594
Mia 0 at Ind 41 61,282
Phi 17 at Atl 20 42,866
Sea 22 at Oak 21 40,124
TB 0 at NYJ 31 60,122
Ten 19 at Bal 21 60,558
N ChiB 13 at Mia 10 66,030

Mon 12/15
N Den 17 at SF 34 68,461

Sat 12/20
Buf 21 at GB 31 60,108
StL 30 at Car 18 58,101

Sun 12/21
Atl 26 at Ariz 29 32,003
Bal 14 at Cin 16 60,719
ChiB 15 at TB 31 70,930
Ind 28 at Min 39 54,107
Jac 20 at Oak 9 40,032
NO 13 at KC 25 66,772
NYG 20 at Dal 7 63,746
NYJ 10 at Det 13 77,624
Phi 32 at Was 35 75,932
Pit 6 at Ten 16 50,677
SD 3 at Den 38 69,632
N SF 9 at Sea 38 66,253

Mon 12/22
N NE 14 at Mia 12 74,379

Wild-Card Playoffs

Sat 12/27
Min 23 at NYG 22 77,710
Jac 17 at Den 42 74,481

Sun 12/28
Mia 3 at NE 17 60,041
Det 10 at TB 20 73,361

AFC/NFC Divisional Playoffs

Sat 01/03
NE 6 at Pit 7 61,228
Min 22 at SF 38 65,018

Sun 01/04
TB 7 at GB 21 60,327
Den 14 at KC 10 76,965

1997 AFC/NFC Championships

Sun 01/11
Den 24 at Pit 21 61,382
GB 23 at SF 10 68,987

Super Bowl XXXII

Sun 01/25
GB 24 vs Den 31 68,912
at San Diego, CA

National Football League 1998

Sun 09/06
Ariz 10 at Dal 38 63,602
Atl 19 at Car 14 65,129
Buf 14 at SD 16 64,037
Det 19 at GB 38 60,102
Jac 24 at ChiB 23 55,614
Mia 24 at Ind 15 60,587
NO 24 at StL 17 56,943
NYJ 30 at SF 36# 64,419
Pit 20 at Bal 13 68,847
Sea 38 at Phi 0 66,418
TB 7 at Min 31 62,538
Ten 23 at Cin 14 55,848
Was 24 at NYG 31 76,629
N Oak 8 at KC 28 78,945

Mon 09/07
N NE 21 at Den 27 74,745

Sun 09/13
Ariz 14 at Sea 33 57,678
Bal 24 at NYJ 10 70,063
Buf 7 at Mia 13 73,097
Car 14 at NO 19 51,915
ChiB 12 at Pit 17 59,084
Cin 34 at Det 28# 66,354
Dal 23 at Den 42 75,013
KC 16 at Jac 21 69,821
Min 38 at StL 31 56,234
NYG 17 at Oak 20 40,545
Phi 12 at Atl 17 46,456
SD 13 at Ten 7 41,089
TB 15 at GB 23 60,124
N Ind 6 at NE 29 60,068

Mon 09/14
N SF 45 at Was 10 76,798

Sun 09/20
Bal 10 at Jac 24 70,384
ChiB 15 at TB 27 64,328
Den 34 at Oak 17 56,578
Det 6 at Min 29 63,107
GB 13 at Cin 6 56,346
Ind 6 at NYJ 44 79,469
Pit 0 at Mia 21 73,948
StL 34 at Buf 33 65,199
SD 7 at KC 23 73,730
Ten 16 at NE 27 59,973
Was 14 at Sea 24 63,336
N Phi 3 at Ariz 17 39,782

Mon 09/21
N Dal 31 at NYG 7 78,039

Sun 09/27
Ariz 20 at StL 17 55,832
Atl 20 at SF 31 62,296
Den 38 at Was 16 71,880
GB 37 at Car 30 69,723
Jac 27 at Ten 22 34,656
KC 24 at Phi 21 66,675
Min 31 at ChiB 28 57,783
NO 19 at Ind 13# 48,480
NYG 34 at SD 16 55,672
Oak 13 at Dal 12 63,544
Sea 10 at Pit 13 58,413
N Cin 24 at Bal 31 68,154

Mon 09/28
N TB 6 at Det 27 74,724

Sun 10/04
Car 23 at Atl 51 50,724
Dal 31 at Was 10 72,284
Det 27 at ChiB 31 55,562
Mia 9 at NYJ 20 75,257
NE 30 at NO 27 56,172
NYG 3 at TB 20 64,989
Oak 23 at Ariz 20 53,240
Phi 16 at Den 41 73,218
SD 12 at Ind 17 51,988
SF 21 at Buf 26 76,615
N Sea 6 at KC 17 66,418

Mon 10/05
N Min 37 at GB 24 59,849

Sun 10/11
Buf 31 at Ind 24 52,938
Car 20 at Dal 27 64,181
ChiB 7 at Ariz 20 50,495
Den 21 at Sea 16 66,258
KC 10 at NE 40 59,749
NYJ 10 at StL 30 55,938
Pit 20 at Cin 25 59,979
SD 6 at Oak 7 42,467
SF 31 at NO 0 62,811
Ten 12 at Bal 8 68,561
Was 12 at Phi 17 66,183
N Atl 34 at NYG 20 71,173

Mon 10/12
N Mia 21 at Jac 28 74,051

Thu 10/15
N GB 20 at Det 27 77,932

Sun 10/18
Ariz 7 at NYG 34 70,456
Bal 6 at Pit 16 58,620
Car 13 at TB 16 63,600
Cin 14 at Ten 44 33,288
Dal 12 at ChiB 13 59,201
Ind 31 at SF 34 68,486
Jac 16 at Buf 17 77,635
NO 23 at Atl 31 60,774
Phi 10 at SD 13 56,967
StL 0 at Mia 14 65,418
Was 7 at Min 41 64,004

Mon 10/19
N NYJ 24 at NE 14 60,062

Sun 10/25
Atl 3 at NYJ 28 71,573
Bal 10 at GB 28 59,860
ChiB 23 at Ten 20 40,089
Cin 10 at Oak 27 40,089
Jac 24 at Den 37 75,217
Min 34 at Det 13 77,885
NE 9 at Mia 12# 73,973
SF 28 at StL 10 58,563
Sea 27 at SD 20 58,512
TB 3 at NO 9 52,695
N Buf 30 at Car 14 64,050

Mon 10/26
N Pit 20 at KC 13 79,431

Sun 11/01
Ariz 17 at Det 15 66,087
Den 33 at Cin 26 59,974
Jac 45 at Bal 19 68,915
Mia 24 at Buf 30 79,011
Min 24 at TB 27 64,979
NE 21 at Ind 16 58,056
NO 17 at Car 31 62,514
NYG 14 at Was 21 67,976
NYJ 20 at KC 17 65,104
StL 15 at Atl 37 37,996
SF 22 at GB 36 59,794
Ten 41 at Pit 31 58,222
N Oak 31 at Sea 18 66,246

Mon 11/02
N Dal 34 at Phi 0 67,002

Sun 11/08
Atl 41 at NE 10 59,790
Buf 12 at NYJ 34 75,043
Car 23 at SF 25 68,572
Cin 11 at Jac 24 67,040
Det 9 at Phi 10 66,785
Ind 14 at Mia 27 73,400
KC 12 at Sea 24 66,251
NO 24 at Min 31 63,779
NYG 6 at Dal 16 64,316
Oak 10 at Bal 13 69,037
StL 20 at ChiB 12 50,263
SD 10 at Den 27 74,925
Was 27 at Ariz 29 45,950
N Ten 31 at TB 22 65,054

Mon 11/09
N GB 20 at Pit 27 60,507

Sun 11/15
Bal 14 at SD 13 54,388
Cin 3 at Min 24 64,232
Dal 35 at Ariz 28 71,670
GB 37 at NYG 3 76,272
Mia 13 at Car 9 67,887
NE 10 at Buf 13 72,020
NYJ 23 at Ind 24 55,520
Phi 3 at Was 28 67,704
Pit 14 at Ten 23 41,104
StL 3 at NO 24 46,430
SF 19 at Atl 31 69,828
Sea 17 at Oak 20 51,527
TB 24 at Jac 29 72,974
N ChiB 3 at Det 26 63,152

Mon 11/16
N Den 30 at KC 7 78,100

Sun 11/22
Ariz 45 at Was 42 63,435
Bal 20 at Cin 13 52,571
Car 24 at StL 20 50,716
ChiB 13 at Atl 20 60,804
Det 28 at TB 25 64,265
GB 14 at Min 28 64,471
Ind 11 at Buf 34 49,032
Jac 15 at Pit 30 59,124
KC 37 at SD 38 59,894
NYJ 24 at Ten 3 37,084
Oak 14 at Den 40 75,325
Phi 0 at NYG 20 65,763
Sea 22 at Dal 30 64,142
N NO 20 at SF 31 68,429

Mon 11/23
N Mia 23 at NE 26 58,729

Thu 11/26
Min 46 at Dal 36 64,336
Pit 16 at Det 19# 78,139

Sun 11/29
Ariz 24 at KC 34 69,613
Atl 21 at StL 10 47,971
Buf 21 at NE 25 58,304
Car 21 at NYJ 48 71,501
Ind 31 at Bal 38 68,898
Jac 34 at Cin 17 55,432
NO 10 at Mia 30 73,216
Phi 16 at GB 24 59,862
TB 31 at ChiB 17 51,938
Ten 18 at Sea 20 59,048
Was 29 at Oak 19 41,409
N Den 31 at SD 16 66,532

Mon 11/30
N NYG 7 at SF 31 68,212

Thu 12/03
N StL 14 at Phi 17 66,155

Sun 12/06
Bal 14 at Ten 16 31,124
Buf 33 at Cin 20 54,359
Dal 3 at NO 22 65,065
Det 22 at Jac 37 70,717
Ind 21 at Atl 28 61,141
KC 31 at Den 35 74,962
Mia 27 at Oak 17 61,254
NE 23 at Pit 9 58,362
NYG 23 at Ariz 19 46,128
SD 20 at Was 24 65,713
SF 31 at Car 28# 63,332
Sea 31 at NYJ 32 72,200
N ChiB 22 at Min 48 64,247

Mon 12/07
N GB 22 at TB 24 65,497

Sun 12/13
Ariz 20 at Phi 17# 62,176
Atl 27 at NO 17 61,678
ChiB 20 at GB 26 59,813
Cin 26 at Ind 39 55,179
Dal 17 at KC 20 77,697
Den 16 at NYG 20 72,336
Min 38 at Bal 28 69,074
NE 18 at StL 32 48,946
Oak 21 at Buf 44 62,002
Pit 3 at TB 16 65,335
SD 17 at Sea 38 62,690
Ten 16 at Jac 13 65,657
Was 28 at Car 25 46,940
N NYJ 21 at Mia 16 74,369

Mon 12/14
N Det 13 at SF 35 68,585

Sat 12/19
NYJ 17 at Buf 10 79,056
TB 16 at Was 20 66,309

Sun 12/20
Atl 24 at Det 17 67,143
Bal 3 at ChiB 24 40,853
Cin 25 at Pit 24 52,017
Ind 23 at Sea 27 58,703
KC 7 at NYG 28 66,040
NO 17 at Ariz 19 51,617
Oak 17 at SD 10 60,716
Phi 9 at Dal 13 62,722
StL 13 at Car 20 50,047
SF 21 at NE 24 59,153

Ten 22 at GB 30	59,888
N Jac 10 at Min 50	64,363

Mon 12/21

N Den 21 at Mia 31	74,363

Sat 12/26

KC 31 at Oak 21	52,769
Min 26 at Ten 16	41,121

Sun 12/27

Buf 45 at NO 33	39,707
Car 27 at Ind 19	58,182
Det 10 at Bal 19	68,405
GB 16 at ChiB 13	58,393
Mia 16 at Atl 38	69,754
NE 10 at NYJ 31	74,302
NYG 20 at Phi 10	66,596
StL 19 at SF 38	68,386
SD 16 at Ariz 13	71,670
Sea 21 at Den 28	74,057
TB 35 at Cin 0	49,826
N Was 7 at Dal 23	63,565

Mon 12/28

N Pit 3 at Jac 21	74,143

AFC/NFC Wild-Card Playoffs

Sat 01/02

Buf 17 at Mia 24	72,698
Ariz 20 at Dal 7	62,969

Sun 01/03

NE 10 at Jac 25	71,139
GB 27 at SF 30	66,506

AFC/NFC Divisional Playoffs

Sat 01/09

SF 18 at Atl 20	70,262
Mia 3 at Den 38	75,729

Sun 01/10

Jac 24 at NYJ 34	78,817
Ariz 21 at Min 41	63,760

1998 AFC/NFC Championships

Sun 01/17

Atl 30 at Min 27#	64,060
NYJ 10 at Den 23	75,402

Super Bowl XXXIII

Sun 01/31

Atl 19 vs Den 34	74,803
at Miami, FL	

APPENDIX 3

Football Quotations

Bob Carroll and Michael Gershman

Coaches

"A gambler is a coach who uses a number-one draft choice on an untested, inexperienced lineman or receiver from Illinois Normal. A conservative is a man who trades his number-one choices for established veterans. In my opinion, the odds are against gamblers, innovators, and pacesetters in football. Call me a conservative."

—*George Allen*

"[George Allen's] father gave him a six-week-old puppy when he was four, and he traded it away for two twelve-year-old cats."

—*Redskins president Edward Bennett Williams*

"There are coaches who spend eighteen hours a day coaching the perfect game, and they lose because the ball is oval and they can't control the bounce."

—*Bud Grant*

"Every coach is in the last year of his contract. Some just don't know it."

—*Dan Henning*

"Winning is a habit. Unfortunately, so is losing."

—*Vince Lombardi*

"One night, after a long, cold, difficult day, Lombardi came home late and tumbled into bed. 'God,' his wife said, 'your feet are cold.' And Lombardi answered, 'Around the house, dear, you may call me Vince.' "

—*Paul Hornung*

"When I got into the coaching business, I knew I was getting into a high-risk, high-profile profession, so I adopted a philosophy I've never wavered from. Yesterday is a canceled check, today is cash on the line, tomorrow is a promissory note."

—*Hank Stram*

Asked about his operation: "It was a brain transplant. I got a sportswriter's brain so I could be sure I had one that hadn't been used."

—*Norm Van Brocklin*

About 49ers coach Bill Walsh: "You half expect his headset is playing Mozart."

—Los Angeles Times *columnist Jim Murray*

"Being in politics is like being a football coach. You have to be smart enough to understand the game and dumb enough to think it's important."

—*Wisconsin senator Eugene McCarthy*

"Football was invented by a mean son of a bitch, and that's the way the game's supposed to be played."

—*Steve Owen*

"Whoever calls the signals in a football game has the coach's life in his two bare hands."

—*John McKay*

Players

On Paul Hornung: "You know what made him great inside the five-yard line like no other player? He loved the glory. He loved the glory like no other player I've ever coached."

—*Vince Lombardi*

"Actually, I was only at Iowa two terms—Truman's and Eisenhower's."

—*Alex Karras*

"There's nothing wrong with reading the game plan by the light of a jukebox."

—*Kenny Stabler*

Reporter: "As a football player, what is your primary weakness?" Perry: "Cheeseburgers."

—*William (Refrigerator) Perry*

"My great awakening came in my second year when I got hurt and finally realized, hey, they're shooting real bullets out there."

—*John Riggins*

"When you're as slow as I am, you don't lose any steps as you grow older."

—*Howard Twilley*

Asked what record he would treasure most: "Probably the Beatles' White album."

—*Steve Largent*

"The hole is never where it's supposed to be."

—*Franco Harris*

On Larry Csonka: "When he goes on safari, the lions roll up their windows."

—*Monte Clark*

Asked if he had majored in basket weaving at Alabama: "Naw, man, journalism—it was easier."

—*Joe Namath*

"A quarterback hasn't arrived until he can tell the coach to go to hell."

—Johnny Unitas

"I'd like the body of Jim Brown, the moves of Gale Sayers, the strength of Earl Campbell and the acceleration of O.J. Simpson. And just once I would like to run and feel the wind in my hair."

—Balding running back Rocky Bleier

Upon first meeting Joe Montana: "Who is this, the punter?"

—Dwight Clark

"I'm an artist. Only my art is to assault people."

—Howie Long

"By the time you learn all the handshakes, the season is over."

—Johnny Unitas

Fans

"The Redskins are the only thing in Washington that the people think of as 'ours.' Nobody in Washington gives a tinker's damn about the Kennedy Center or the Washington Symphony."

—Richard M. Nixon

"How could Nixon know so little about Watergate and so much about football?"

—Penn State coach Joe Paterno

"Fans sometimes don't understand. The other team gets paid, too."

—Fran Tarkenton

"My definition of a fan is the kind of guy who will scream at you from the sixtieth row of the bleachers because he thinks you missed a marginal holding call in the center of the interior line, and then after the game won't be able to find his car in the parking lot."

—NFL referee Jim Tunney

The Game

"Football combines two grim features of American Life—violence and committee meetings [huddles]."

—Commentator George Will

"Football is a game designed to keep coal miners off the streets."

—Writer Jimmy Breslin

On instructions he received on special teams: "Kid, just go down and throw yourself on the fire."

—Steve Raible

"Pro football is like nuclear warfare. There are no winners, only survivors."

—Frank Gifford

"Passing is timing. It's the ability to stand in there and take a chance on a beating by Deacon Jones or Carl Eller until the right time comes to let of go of the ball. Nothing is important except releasing the ball at the right instant. Therefore, accuracy means less than guts."

—John Hadl

On playing middle linebacker: "Playing middle linebacker is like walking through a lion's cage in a three piece pork-chop suit."

—Cecil Johnson

"You have to prove your manhood more times in one season than most men do in a lifetime. When you don't make it, when you can't perform or you get beat or you get cut, you're cut as a man."

—Dan Goich

Winning

On winning the 1952 title: "We never got a ring for winning. We got a nine-dollar blue blanket that said, 'World Champions.' "

—Bobby Layne

"You take the best team and the worst team and line them up and you would find very little physical difference. You would find an emotional difference. The winning team has a dedication. It will have at its core a group of veteran players who set the standards. They will not accept defeat."

—Merlin Olsen

"You can go to the bank and borrow money, but you can't go to the bank and borrow a Super Bowl ring."

—Joe Greene

APPENDIX 4

Special Teams

Ted Brock

Not even Dick Vermeil, the NFL's first special-teams coach, can tell you who first used the term "special teams," or where and when it took the place of "kicking teams" as the label of choice. Vermeil joined the staff of the Los Angeles Rams in 1968, under head coach George Allen and began working exclusively with all phases of the kicking game—kickoff coverage and return, punt coverage and return, and placekicking.

Vermeil, looking back over three decades, says it hardly matters where the term got started. The main thing, he says, is that "George Allen was the first coach to make special teams special. [Before], teams used to work on the kicking game on Saturday morning the day before a game, with no pads."

Vermeil, a meticulous gatherer of data, helped Allen—and every head coach since 1969—change all that. Years later, as a color commentator for ABC-TV, Vermeil kept extensive charts on all aspects of the kicking game, college and professional.

Allen moved special teams up another notch on the status scale by giving Vermeil almost full access to the Rams' roster. "There were very few people who were excluded from full participation, or at least a backup role, on special teams," Vermeil says. "George gave you the personnel to make sure you had a good eleven-man unit on the field.

"George also allowed you time on the practice field and in meetings. He said you never could use 'I didn't have enough time' as an excuse. He told me the Rams had lost three games in 1968 because of breakdowns in special teams. George ran practice sessions that lasted three to four hours—so dedicating serious time to evaluating and preparing special teams made perfect sense to him."

With time on his side, Vermeil even could venture beyond coaching the technical sides of the game and set about grading the upcoming opponent's special teams, finding obvious weaknesses in their scheme and player performance.

"The third thing about George Allen," Vermeil says, "is that he was a big seller of the kicking game to the players. When you had the reinforcement of the boss in regard to that, it made you a more effective assistant coach. So he was part of the motivational force, and that really helped." Finally, Vermeil says, Allen made special teams a priority in building his team's roster. He traded for kickoff returner Ron Smith in 1968 and punt returner Alvin Haymond in 1969.

"He wanted the best kick returner, as anyone else would want the best receiver," Vermeil says. "He wanted the best punt returner, when someone else would want the best running back. And if it came down to a close decision between a new player and another player, even though George was a veteran-oriented guy, chances were the player who was better on special teams was going to make the roster."

Two cases in point were Pat Curran, a Single-Wing tailback from Lakeland College, and another Allen favorite, Rusty Tillman, a linebacker from Northern Arizona who had played a year with Washington before Allen arrived there as head coach in 1971.

"Curran was really green," Vermeil says. "He was on the verge of being cut, because he was just raw. And I convinced George, 'You've got to keep this guy. He is a great special-teams player.' " Curran excelled on special teams with the Rams from 1969-1974 and with San Diego from 1975-78.

Tillman, meanwhile, made his name synonymous with special-teams play, first as a self-described "wedge-buster," the football equivalent of a kamikaze pilot on punt- and kickoff-coverage units. Tillman plied his trade with Washington (1970-77). After retirement, he became a special-teams guru as an assistant with Seattle (1979-1994). He has also coached at Tampa Bay (1995), Oakland (1996-97), and Indianapolis (1998).

Tillman and Allen spent seven seasons together. "George was an innovator," Tillman says. "He was always looking for an edge. He brought a legacy of special teams to Washington. His Rams teams had dominated the league in all special-teams categories. He got us to believe it."

Allen's Washington teams became known as the Over-the-Hill Gang, for his commitment to stocking the Redskins with veteran players. He brought in players older than most people's furniture—quarterback Billy Kilmer, wide receiver Roy Jefferson, defensive tackle Diron Talbert, linebacker Jack Pardee, and defensive ends Ron McDole and Verlon Biggs.

Just as important were Allen's acquisitions of kick returner Leslie (Speedy) Duncan and special-teams standout Jeff Jordan, a former Ram. Punt returner Haymond came from the Rams to the Redskins the following season.

The same character traits that convinced Vermeil and Allen to keep Curran are the traits Tillman looks for in a special-teams player today. Excluding the specialists—the return men, the punter, the kicker, the holder, and the long snapper for punts and kicks—there are as many as 10 players on the field whose abilities, Tillman says, must meet the same criteria as the players on the starting offensive and defensive units.

This is a case where Tillman's fire as a player meshes with Allen's and Vermeil's love of preparation and evaluation—and gives special teams' importance another boost.

"There are 1,400 to 1,500 guys in the National Football League," Tillman says. "They're fortunate to be the best at what they do. The good special-teams players are the ones who want to perform. They rise above the rest.

"The Arabs have a saying: 'Don't give in to the sun.' It can be 140 degrees on the desert, and they live by that. Special-teams players are the same way. These are guys who don't give in to weakness."

In the mid-to late-1980s, Seattle's Fredd Young and Rufus Porter were the AFC's preeminent special-teams players. In the NFC, Dallas's Bill Bates, Minnesota's Joey Browner, and the Cardinals' Ron Wolfley were premier players. Following the 1984 season—15 years after George Allen hired Vermeil as the league's first special-teams coach—the NFL made room for one special-teams player on each conference's Pro Bowl team.

Then, as the 1990s began, a player emerged who would set the standard for special-teams play. "The best special-teams player of all time is Steve Tasker," Tillman says. "He's phenomenal."

Tasker, only 5 feet 9 inches and 183 pounds, was picked up by the Buffalo Bills after being waived by Houston in 1986. He'd played for Northwestern teams that owned title to the Big Ten cellar. Despite only average speed, Tasker soon became a constant menace, covering kicks and blocking punts. Prior to his retirement in 1997, he played in seven Pro Bowls for the Bills.

"What I found out about kickoff coverage, and I really studied it," says Tasker, who currently works as a commentator for CBS, "is speed is not the most important thing. I can remember initially with the Rams, the ball would be kicked and everyone's downfield. You'd look twenty-five to thirty yards downfield and a guy who runs the forty-yard dash in four-point-nine seconds is two steps ahead of a guy who runs it in four-point-six. The difference was not the speed. The difference was the intent to do a good job."

In 13 years as the NFL's premier special-teams player, Tasker became every bit as scholarly as Vermeil and Tillman in describing the basics of his craft. "All of what football entails is in special teams," Tasker says, adding that the good special-teams players have multiple talents.

"If you're a guard, say, on punt coverage, you have to block," he says. "Then you have to be a world-class sprinter. You have to run through traffic, around officials, looking up at a ball fifty feet in the air, trying to figure out where it's going to come down. Then you've got to be a linebacker and make the tackle."

To support his point (and Tillman's) about "multiple talents," Tasker recalls the 1988 AFC Championship Game, which the Bills lost to Cincinnati, thereby missing a trip to Super Bowl XXIII.

"On a punt return, 999 times out of 1,000, all you have to do is try to block the punt and 'block away' during the return," he says. "But in that game, the Bengals shifted out of punt formation into an offensive formation, and all of a sudden we were a first-string defense."

The play came late in the game, with the Bengals leading 14-10. On fourth down at the Bills' 33, Cincinnati's Stanley Wilson picked up a first down, leading to the touchdown that ensured Cincinnati's 21-10 victory. (There's a touch of irony in Tasker's voice when he notes that the Bengals were the last team to hire a full-time special-teams coach in the late 1980s.)

Consistency and familiarity among players on special teams is difficult, if not impossible, in the free-agency-driven NFL of the 1990s. As any season progresses, injuries to starting offensive and defensive players are inevitable, and each replacement changes the special-teams lineup.

An offensive lineman playing 50 or 60 downs a game (let alone mentally adjusting to his new role in the starting unit) can't be careening downfield on punts and/or kickoffs. Consequently, the built-in chaos of a kick coverage or return is heightened as each new face joins the unit.

"If you just go down [a club's special teams lineup] game by game, by the fourth or fifth game you'll see three or four changes," Tasker says.

It's important to note Bills coach Marv Levy's place in the special-teams coaching chain. There was Allen, then there was Vermeil, who credits Howard Schnellenberger, the long-time NFL assistant and later head coach at Louisville and Oklahoma, with having given him a crash course on the professional kicking game when he came to the Rams in 1969.

When Vermeil was lured from the Rams to be Tommy Prothro's offensive coordinator in 1970, Levy moved in as the Rams' special-teams coach. The Rams fired Allen at the end of the 1970 season. When the Redskins hired Allen in 1971, he brought in Levy as his special-teams coach. Tillman was his prize pupil.

In the end, when foot meets ball and the downfield surge of opposing special-teams units turns into the game's closest thing to mayhem, there really isn't that much to choose between Tasker's blend of courage and wit, the hellfire of Tillman, or the analysis of Vermeil.

"You have a skill guy as your punt-return man, a skill guy as your kick returner, your punter, your kicker," Tasker says. "You might consider your long snapper part of that group. They're specialists. You've got to have guys on your team with those skills.

"But being a football player on special teams is not as important as being an athlete. And being a professional is the bottom line."

APPENDIX 5

Life in the Trenches

Phil Barber

We all do it, so it must be human nature. The quarterback takes the snap and drops back, and we watch the ball. Whether the passer hands off to a teammate, throws downfield, or gets dumped in the backfield, we follow that ball like a pea in a shell game.

Such a strategy immediately shows us the outcome of each play, but it neglects a world of action that rages along the line of scrimmage. It is called "the pit," or "the trenches," and the men who work there are as anonymous as big-time professional athletes can be. Gene Upshaw, the great Raiders guard of the 1970s, likened it to being Paul Revere's horse: do all the work, get lost in the historical shuffle. Even the Hogs, the Washington Redskins' popular crew of the 1980s, were like big, cuddly mascots. Once the game began, nobody focused on them.

So it is that even serious fans sometimes miss the complex interactions that take place along the front wall. The linemen of the 1990s must deal with cross blocking and zone blocking, option blocks and chop blocks (usually by the tight end), overshifts, undershifts, stunts, traps, and varied splits. It's a far cry from the days when chunky guards and tackles would fire straight across the line to grapple with chunky tackles and ends, or maybe conspire on a double-team block.

To be fair, the era of the Single Wing did have a few wrinkles not seen today. Tackles sometimes carried the ball, for example. But skilled pass protection was unheard of until Paul Brown taught his Cleveland Browns to form a cup around quarterback Otto Graham in the late 1940s.

In the early years of pro football, of course, the linemen played both offense and defense, as did all their teammates. The specialization that emerged in the 1950s had a profound effect upon the trenches. Vince Lombardi, the patron saint of blockers everywhere, claimed he could take one look at a big man and size him up for offense or defense. "If he combs his hair and says 'Sir' a lot, and 'I'd really like to become an outstanding professional football player,' he'll end up on offense," Lombardi said. "But if he shows up in a beat-up leather jacket and a two-day growth of beard, spits on the floor, and demands, 'How much you gonna pay me?' he's got to play defense."

The coach's descriptions weren't too far-fetched. Ask anyone who has interviewed a number of football players and they will tell you that offensive linemen generally are the most cerebral and articulate men on the team. One NFL personnel director told writer Paul Zimmerman that the positions that consistently rank highest on pre-draft intelligence tests are (1) offensive tackle, (2) center, (3) quarterback, and (4) guard.

Responsibilities

Offensive linemen have to be smart to learn their convoluted assignments. They must be patient because they are taught to accept the aggression of the defenders while pass blocking. And they had better display some humility because they are the only athletes in any major American sport who are utterly without individual statistics. Offensive linemen are graded by their coaches on every play, but there are no personal numbers to which a fan can point admiringly. Beyond the mental attributes, the most important traits for a blocker are quick feet and short speed—that is, speed off the ball and within a five-yard area of the snap.

In terms of longevity, offensive line might be the safest position in football. It is not uncommon for blockers to play past their twelfth season, and tackle Jackie Slater recently retired after 20 years with the Rams. Yet, while they avoid the high-speed collisions that end so many careers at other positions, offensive linemen consistently are subjected to a brutal pounding.

It starts with a torturously compact and uncomfortable stance: legs directly under the torso, spine bent at a 90-degree angle at the neck, weight largely supported by one hand. After that come banged knees, bent fingers (especially for centers, who can't tape their hands), and forearms to the throat or sternum. At least the offensive linemen don't have to live with the head slap anymore; that was outlawed in 1977.

The offensive tackles are huge, tall men whose primary responsibility is pass blocking. Height is critical because it provides leverage, making it harder for the defensive ends to pull them off balance. The tackle's job was altered radically in 1978, when offensive linemen were allowed to open their hands and extend their arms while blocking. Some have complained that the rule change took the skill out of the position and turned one-on-one battles between linemen into shoving matches. Others say it simply legalized what had been happening for a long time. In any case, it removed what had been a huge disadvantage for pass blockers, and opened the way for an era of passing. (For the linemen, it was the most significant development since the advent of face masks in the 1950s; that one allowed blockers to keep their heads up, and it improved the quality of their play immensely.)

The guards aren't so isolated, but they must be more versatile. A guard has to be strong enough to block straight-up against a 300-pound defensive tackle and fast enough to get outside—to "pull"—and lead the interference on a sweep or a pitchout.

How hard is the center's job? It depends on the defensive alignment he is facing, which often depends on the era of play. Against an even front, such as the standard 4-3 defense popular throughout much of NFL history, the center has it relatively easy. Ron Mix, the tackle who was regarded as the AFL's best offensive lineman, called center "a place to hide a weak brother" and "a racket." Indeed, with no one positioned in front of him, the center is free to chase after the middle linebacker or double up on one of the defensive linemen.

Against an odd front, though—such as the 5-4 of the 1940s or the 3-4 of the late 1970s and early 1980s (and which we occasionally see today)—the center is a glorified punching bag for a nose tackle. He is vulnerable because he has to snap the ball backwards while attempting to move forward. It's why Jack Rudnay, who centered for the Chiefs from 1970-1982, once listed his position as "prone" on a team questionnaire.

The defensive line spots need less explanation. They are "defensive" in name only; in truth, they usually are on the attack. The defensive tackles always have been the most massive players on defense. The bigger they are, the harder they are to move on running plays.

Defensive ends must help contain the outside rush and thwart off-tackle plays, but their number-one concern is rushing the passer. (Some are specialists who play only on passing downs, a trend sparked by the 49ers' Fred Dean in 1981.) They tend to be tall, quick, strong-armed, and ornery.

Action and Reaction

Of course, tight ends, fullbacks, linebackers, and safeties also jump into the trenches with more or less regularity, but the action of the interior linemen alone is enough to boggle the senses. Every break of a huddle sets in motion a jumbled series of responsibilities and maneuvers, a chain of action and reaction that is difficult to break down into component parts.

Just as the quarterback can change the play with an audible, the center may call a new blocking scheme before the snap. He may think the placement of one or more defensive linemen threatens the blocking angles, or he may not like the "splits," the spaces between offensive linemen. Narrow splits can take away an inside rush; wide splits help blockers get outside.

Each offensive lineman would love to alter his stance to fit the play. He would set his rear foot farther back and his butt high for a hard forward thrust, or align his feet parallel to pull. But he can't afford to tip off his enemy, so he seeks to maintain consistent form.

With the quarterback still barking signals, the defensive linemen all can move one slot to the strong side (an overshift) or the weak side (an undershift) to confuse the blockers. After the snap, especially in a passing situation, two (or more) defensive linemen may "stunt," or trade rush lanes. In an end-tackle stunt, for example, the defensive end will charge across and attempt to tie up both his man (the offensive tackle) and the guard on that side. The defensive tackle will then shoot behind the end, into what should be an open gap.

The offensive linemen can counter by zone blocking—protecting an area rather than fighting off one man—or cross blocking, which entails trading assignments. And if one of the defensive tackles has been getting too much penetration, they can "trap" him—that is, a guard from the opposite side of the center can move parallel to the line and nail the defensive tackle from the side.

If all of this sounds a bit complicated, rest assured that it actually is a gross oversimplification. Every lineman, on either side of the line of scrimmage, is responsible for either moving or avoiding a well-trained mountain of flesh and bones in a matter of seconds, and everyone's assignment is directly affected by everyone else's. And that's to say nothing of individual technique, or of scrambling quarterbacks, screen passes, draws, or misdirection plays. Small wonder the fans wind up watching the ball.

Size Counts

If NFL line play is a cat-and-mouse game, the felines and rodents are getting bigger all the time. Look at the average weight in pounds of interior linemen on the official all-pro teams of each decade, as voted by a Pro Football Hall of Fame selection committee:

Decade	Offense	Defense
1920s	230	230
1930s	227	227
1940s	228	228
1950s	248.5	251
1960s	258	258
1970s	265	254.5
1980s	269	270.5

The reasons for the growth spurts can be seen at other positions, too: more extensive nationwide scouting, weightlifting, and better diet. Before these things were commonplace, Gino Marchetti was a terror at 240 pounds. His coaches thought defensive ends should go 245 or more, so Gino stuffed his jock with lead weights before stepping on the scale.

Linemen aren't the only things growing larger. Their wallets are expanding, too. Players at every position have benefited from free agency, but none more so than offensive linemen. Pushed into bidding wars, management has been forced to acknowledge how important those big bulls are.

Better to be an obscure millionaire, a lineman might console himself, than a bankrupt celebrity.

APPENDIX 6

Quarterbacks: A History

Beau Riffenburgh

During professional football's early days, quarterbacks did not exist. In fact, neither did the forward pass. That all changed at the instigation of President Theodore Roosevelt. Horrified by a college sport that resulted in 18 deaths and 149 major injuries in 1905 alone, the President stated, "Brutality and foul play should receive the same summary punishment given to a man who cheats at cards." T.R. threatened to ban the sport by presidential decree if those in charge did not clean it up.

In December, 1905, the Intercollegiate Athletic Association of the United States (later renamed the National Collegiate Athletic Association) was organized to govern intercollegiate athletics, particularly football. At a meeting on January 12, 1906, the association's new rules committee dramatically changed the focus of the sport from a plodding, brutal, and unimaginative attack featuring popular but dangerous mass formations, such as the flying wedge, to one with more daring and offensive potential. The changes included:

- legalizing the forward pass;
- reducing the game from 70 to 60 minutes;
- establishing a neutral zone separating the teams by the length of the ball;
- increasing the distance to be gained for a first down from 5 to 10 yards;
- requiring six (later changed to seven) men to be on the line of scrimmage.

The new rules, which also affected the pro sport because it had not yet developed any rules of its own, eliminated the mass plays, forced the development of outside running attacks, and led to the popularization of the first of the modern offensive formations, the T. In the early years of the century, Amos Alonzo Stagg used the T-formation at the University of Chicago. In the next decade, Bob Zuppke at the University of Illinois utilized the T while serving as the mentor to George Halas and Ralph Jones. Elsewhere, Glenn (Pop) Warner developed the Single-Wing, which soon became the most popular formation.

The passing game, however, didn't immediately catch on, largely because of severe restrictions. For example, a pass could not be thrown to a receiver within five yards of either side of where the ball was put in play (that is, the center). In addition, a passer had to be at least five yards behind the line of scrimmage. Thus, the new passing game was confined to simple corner routes. Nevertheless, on October 27, 1906, in a game against a combined team from Benwood and Moundsville, West Virginia, George (Peggy) Parratt, the quarterback of the Massillon Tigers, completed a forward pass to end (Bullet) Dan Riley. It was the first authenticated pass completion in pro football history.

Still, passes remained few and far between in the professional game, until Green Bay's Earl (Curly) Lambeau began throwing out of his Notre Dame Box formation during the 1920s. But even the success of Lambeau and the Packers' other passers—halfback Verne Lewellen and tailback Red Dunn—didn't cause the real acceptance of the passing game. That was accomplished by former Michigan All-America Benny Friedman, who entered the NFL in 1927 with the Cleveland Bulldogs and immediately eclipsed Lambeau's passing records. Friedman also shocked fans and players alike by calling passes on first down, previously a rarity.

The next year the passing game made another important stride forward when Pop Warner's Stanford team easily defeated Army in New York, causing Warner's Double-Wing formation to be widely imitated. With two backs spread out and close to the line of scrimmage, the Double-Wing laid the foundation for the spread formations used today. It also provided the basis of many of the first formations built around the passing game.

T for Eleven

Two developments in the 1930s—the renewed popularity of the T-formation and the appearance of pro football's first great receiver—paved the way for the emergence of the modern quarterback and today's passing game.

Although the T had been used since the turn of the century, most coaches considered it a moribund formation by 1930. But the most popular formations—the Notre Dame Box and the Single-Wing—never were effective for the passing game, and the T, with its quarterback dropping straight back, ultimately proved ideal for reading defenses and picking up receivers.

In 1930, George Halas took a three-year break from coaching the Bears to concentrate on running the club and drumming up fan interest. His replacement was Ralph Jones, who immediately started tinkering with the Bears' T-formation. Jones widened the splits between Chicago's interior offensive linemen, giving them and the backs more room to maneuver. Jones also moved the ends out wide, spaced the halfbacks wider, and placed one of the halfbacks in motion. These changes turned out to be revolutionary.

With these splits and his man in motion, Jones not only spread the game horizontally, but also vertically, because players were out wide they could easily get downfield for passes. Moreover, the man in motion initially gave tremendous problems to the defenses, which were not nearly as sophisticated as the offenses of the time. The back could turn in and make a crack-back block on the defensive end, lure a linebacker out of position—opening up a running lane—or pull a defensive back out of position, opening up areas to pass.

By 1932, Jones' efforts paid dividends. That year the Bears finished 6-1-6, tying the Portsmouth Spartans (6-1-4) for first place (ties did not count). For the NFL's first 12 seasons, the team with the best winning percentage has been declared champion. Since this was the first time teams had tied in winning percentage, a special playoff game was set up to determine the champion. Because of snowstorms, it was played indoors at Chicago Stadium, and the Bears won 9-0, with the big play being a 2-yard touchdown pass from Bronko Nagurski to Red Grange.

That "special" game spawned a host of changes in the NFL, most notably the creation of two divisions in order to have a postseason championship game every year. It also produced a host of new rules that were the NFL's first real breakaway from the college game. Among the new rules were the use of inbounds lines (now called hashmarks), placed 10 yards from each sideline; the legalization of passing from anywhere behind the line of scrimmage; moving the goal posts from the back of the end zone to the goal line; and slimming the ball down to facilitate passing.

These changes not only opened up the passing game, they proved to be the first of many revisions. In the next several years, the football was again streamlined, the hashmarks were moved another five yards from the sideline, passing was encouraged by dropping the rule that an incomplete pass into the end zone was a touchback, and rules to protect the passer were implemented.

Hutson and Baugh

The Packers, coached by Lambeau (his playing career ended in 1929), were the first team to take full advantage of these rules. Green Bay had two outstanding passers in tailback Arnie Herber and his successor Cecil Isbell, but the key to the Packers' success was Don Hutson, a slim, lightning-fast end who had moves that were vastly ahead of any others in the game. Hutson was, and remains, the most dominant player at one position in football history. When he entered the NFL in 1935, the record for receptions in a season was 24 (which increased to 26 that year). He caught 34 in 1936, increased the record to 41 the next year, made 58 catches in 1941, and broke that mark with 74 in 1942.

Hutson also increased the yardage mark for a single season from 432 yards in 1935 to 1,211 and improved the touchdown reception record from 5 to 17.

What Hutson did for receiving, Sammy Baugh did for passing. Not only was Baugh arguably the best overall player in the history of pro football, he was far ahead of his contemporaries as a passer. As a rookie in 1937, "Slingin' Sammy" led the Redskins to the NFL Championship Game, where he passed for 354 yards and 3 touchdowns in a 28-21 victory over the Bears. He set an NFL record that season with 81 completions, a mark he eventually raised to 210. Baugh helped make the forward pass an integral part of the pro game. He was one of the first advocates of the short passing game, and, with his ability to see the entire field, to comprehend defensive reactions instantly, and to fire the ball without hesitation, he made the primitive defenses of his day obsolete.

"He would cock the ball, bring it down, and drift off as if about to run, cock again, make a mock throw to one side, and shoot a touchdown to the other," New York Giants head coach Steve Owen wrote of Baugh. "He was never committed until he was flat on the ground and the ball with him. I have seen him make bullet-like throws with his tremendous wrist action as he was nailed by a hard tackle and falling."

After eight years as a tailback in the Double-Wing, in 1945 Baugh made the transition to a T-formation quarterback, and he proved to be even more devastating. He immediately broke his own NFL completion percentage record of 62.7 by hitting 70.3 percent, a mark that lasted until 1982.

Shaughnessy Shows the Way

Baugh's move was symbolic of a shift to the T-formation in the 1940s. The focal point in this shift was the Chicago Bears, with Clark Shaughnessy and Sid Luckman leading the way. By 1939, the Bears' T had grown more complex, to counter teams such as the Lions and Packers, who had solved it by rotating their defensive backs to the side of the motion. All that complexity required a special quarterback, and the Bears found one that year in Luckman, an All-America tailback at Columbia and the club's top pick. In Chicago, he came under the tutelage of Shaughnessy, who was the head coach at the University of Chicago and a volunteer assistant for the Bears.

Luckman was one of the great technicians of the game. He was a masterful ball-handler and an excellent passer, but, most importantly, he was perfect for the new system that Shaughnessy had installed. Luckman spun from under center and faked, handed off, or pitched on quick-opening plays, quite a contrast from the slowly developing plays of the traditional Single-Wing. Because of Luckman's speed, double-team blocking was no longer necessary, so linemen could move out fast, brush block their opponents, and move downfield to block someone else.

Shaughnessy also put in the same system at Stanford, where he became head coach in 1940, and his team went 10-0 behind another wizard of the T, Frankie Albert. But during the break before Stanford played in the Rose Bowl, Shaughnessy returned to Chicago to revamp the Bears' offense before the 1940 NFL Championship Game. His major change was to add a counter play, in which the Bears split one man wide, sent another man in motion to the opposite side, and then ran back to the side of the spread end. The counter was as old as football itself, but Shaughnessy realized that it would be devastatingly effective against the Washington defense, which predictably shifted its linebackers toward the man in motion.

"I drew up the entire offense," Shaughnessy said later. "I threw out all the junk that wasn't working. Then I looked at the pictures of the Redskins-Bears game of two weeks earlier [the Redskins had won 7-3]. It was obvious that Washington was going to use a certain defense and wasn't going to change."

On the first play of the game, Bears halfback George McAfee went in motion. Washington's linebackers moved with him, just as Shaughnessy knew they would. The Bears ran the same motion on the next play, but fullback Bill Osmanski swept around end in the opposite direction and ran 68 yards for a touchdown that started a 73-0 rout, the biggest margin of victory in NFL history.

Several weeks later, when Stanford defeated Nebraska in the Rose Bowl, the T was hailed as the offensive wave of the future. Indeed, in the next eight years, every NFL team except Pittsburgh went to the T full time. Modern football—and the modern quarterback—had arrived.

Shaughnessy wasn't done refining the T-formation, however. In 1948, he became head coach of the Los Angeles Rams. The next year, the Rams acquired halfback Elroy (Crazylegs) Hirsch. Shaughnessy wanted to get Hirsch into the lineup, but he was concerned about whether he could take the pounding a halfback received. So, despite having two outstanding ends in NFL receiving leader Tom Fears and Bob Shaw, Shaughnessy split Hirsch out wide as a flanker, creating the first full-time player at that position.

The result was devastating. By combining with star quarterback Bob Waterfield and rookie Norm Van Brocklin, Fears broke Hutson's NFL record with 77 receptions, while the Rams roared into the NFL Championship Game. However, on a rain-soaked, muddy field that nullified their superior speed, the Rams lost to the Eagles. A power struggle within the organization claimed Shaughnessy, who was fired.

Shaughnessy's replacement was Joe Stydahar, who hired Hamp Pool as his offensive coach. Pool further refined Shaughnessy's offense, benefiting from working with four future Hall of Fame members: Fears, Hirsch, Waterfield, and Van Brocklin.

"We had all kinds of formations," Pool later said. "We used quite a lot of slot formation—with the halfback just outside the linemen and off the line of scrimmage. Then we'd put the other halfback in motion the other way. This would leave us only one setback, the fullback, to block on pass protection. But we would get four men into deep patterns in a hurry, and we would just eat them up. The defenses we were facing were exclusively man-to-man, and no one person could stay with Hirsch or Fears."

With perhaps the most electrifying offense the NFL has ever seen, the Rams scored an amazing 38.8 points per game in 1950. Fears broke his own record with 84 catches. But the Rams again lost in the NFL title game, with the Cleveland Browns winning on a last-minute field goal. The next year, the Rams were back again, as it was Hirsch who led the league with 66 receptions for a record 1,495 yards and 17 touchdowns. And the big-play attack finally carried through the postseason, as Los Angeles defeated the Browns 24-17 in the NFL Championship Game when Fears scored on a 73-yard pass from Van Brocklin in the fourth quarter.

Professor Brown

The Browns might not have been as exciting as the Rams, but no team has ever put together a decade like Cleveland did from 1946 to 1955. With Paul Brown as head coach and Otto Graham at quarterback, they appeared in 10 consecutive championship games—four in the All-America Football Conference and six in the NFL—winning seven times.

Brown was the first coach to bring a true sense of science to professional football. Many routine parts of the pro game today—full-time coaching staffs, the study of game films, calling plays via messengers, classroom study, intelligence testing, using playbooks, and extensive college scouting—were either Brown's innovations or were brought to a new level of efficiency by him.

"I don't think it's stretching the truth to say Paul Brown redesigned the game," Graham said. "He was the first to make football a year-round job for his coaches and players. He was the first to take his players to a hotel the night before a game in their hometown, to get them away from the kids and the noise and neighbors and distractions.

"We were the first team to carry notebooks. We'd start off each year talking about the most basic fundamentals. He'd dictate to us, and we'd write it down, things like how to do your calisthenics, the right way to touch your toes, how to form a huddle. After ten years I was still writing it all down. It was like being in the Navy and hearing the same lecture on how to make hospital corners on your bed sheets. But you remembered.

"And Paul was an innovator on the field. He took advantage of the fact that the defenses of the time were pretty basic and non-mobile. There were no blitzes, no stunts, no zones. So he took advantage of the defenses by developing the draw play for Marion Motley and the sideline pass—break to the side and come back for the ball—for [Mac] Speedie, [Dante] Lavelli, and myself."

Brown's insistence on running precise pass routes rather than the somewhat sloppy routes of the time may have been his most important innovation.

"We had never seen such a spot-passing program as they had," Philadelphia defensive back Russ Craft later said when recalling how the Browns made their NFL debut by picking apart the 1949 NFL champion Eagles. "We would be on top of the receivers, but they caught the ball anyway because the pass was so well timed."

It helped that the Browns possessed one of the best pairs of receivers ever—Speedie and Lavelli—catching those passes, but even more important was "Mr. Automatic," Otto Graham. The finest passing technician of his time, Graham led either the AAFC or the National Football League in passing five times, while finishing second three more times in his 10 years.

"Otto Graham was the key to the whole team," Brown later said. "He had the finest peripheral vision I've ever witnessed, and that is a very big factor in a quarterback. He had total composure on the field, the ability to find whatever receiver was going to come open, and the arm and athletic ability to get the ball to him. His hand-eye coordination was most unusual, and he was bigger than you'd think and faster than you'd think.

"Otto was my greatest player because he played the most important position, and he played it to perfection. He was the crux of how we got things done. I don't discount Marion Motley, Dante Lavelli, or Jim Brown. But the guy who was the engineer, the guy with the touch that pulled us out of so many situations, was Otto Graham. To put it simply, find me another quarterback who took his team to as many championships."

Not Just a Sideline

If there was one area where the Brown-Graham partnership lost a little of its sparkle, it was over another of Brown's contributions to quarterbacking: calling the plays from the sidelines. "When Paul began calling the plays from the bench, I disagreed, but the whole thing was exaggerated over the years," Graham once said. "I didn't like it, but I didn't resent it.

"Calling a play is nothing more than a guess. You see those movies where the quarterback raises up from the huddle, looks at the defense, then ducks down and calls the play. Well, that's baloney. Paul could see as much or more from the sideline than I could from the huddle. My complaint was that he didn't want me to audible. He did let me check off now and then, but I had to be right. The rest of the time, Paul called the plays, and the record shows he called 'em pretty good."

Brown was firm in his views about this issue. "Otto was one of the brightest players you could imagine," he said. "But nobody under pressure of performing can give as much thought to play selection as he should. We were feeding in information from all our coaches in the press box—and we always had a coach sitting in the end zone. I was a quarterback myself—not a very good one—and in those days when you couldn't think of anything else, you'd run off tackle. What does a quarterback see when he makes a handoff? What part of the defense does he see? He doesn't see much. Field level is the worst vantage point in the stadium.

"Besides, a coach calling the plays takes a lot of heat off the quarterback—and a lot of coaches don't want this responsibility. I didn't care. The players perform and get the credit. If people wanted to blast me for a dumb call, I could take it."

Pass First

While Brown and Graham were enjoying their greatest success, on the other side of the country another coach who never received the same level of acclaim was developing the passing game in a different way. Chuck Taylor had been a little-known offensive lineman for Shaughnessy's 1940 Stanford team before serving as the school's freshman coach for several years. He then moved on to the San Francisco 49ers, where he coached under Buck Shaw, before returning to Stanford as head coach in 1951. That very year, he led Stanford to the Rose Bowl.

"I learned fast that Stanford wasn't going to run over anybody," Taylor later said. "But passing could keep us in almost every game, and could allow us to upset a team that was physically stronger than we were. So we made the decision to go to a style of passing that was unique at the time. We would establish the passing game first. We wouldn't run to establish the pass, but the other way around. It was the real start of that strategy in football."

Not only was Taylor's pass-first philosophy the forerunner of today's playbooks, but he also added sophistication to what had been rather primitive concepts.

"The traditional passing game had had the receiver run down ten yards and turn around," Taylor remarked. "There never was any deviation from the pattern. But we changed that. We divided the field up into nine zones and called zone patterns instead of specific routes. That way, it was up to the receivers to get open, and it was the quarterback's responsibility to be able to read the defense and his own receiver."

Taylor not only allowed for deviation on a play, but before the play. His adoption of a sophisticated set of audibles, and his quarterbacks' success with them, helped popularize the practice of changing of plays at the line of scrimmage. Meanwhile, in the huddle, most professional quarterbacks called their own plays during the 1960s. However, that began to change in the following decade when the Cowboys made five Super Bowl appearances during the 1970's, with coach Tom Landry calling the plays. This system is still in use for most NFL teams today; virtually all teams send in the plays from the sidelines—now via radio waves instead of sending in substitutes or wig-wagging signals—although quarterbacks usually have permission to change the play at the line of scrimmage if the situation necessitates.

The Master

One of the more vitriolic debates over play-calling occurred in Los Angeles, where one of the best quarterbacks ever, Norm Van Brocklin, linked up with one of the great offensive coaching minds, Sid Gillman. Though Gillman had posted an impressive record at Miami of Ohio and the University of Cincinnati, he had not yet developed all of the theories and nuances that later earned him selection to the Pro Football Hall of Fame. When he joined Los Angeles in 1955, his intermittent calling of plays quickly soured his relationship with his all-pro quarterback.

"The coach really shouldn't call the plays," Van Brocklin later said. "It is not good for the quarterback because he becomes an automaton. He stops thinking. He comes to depend upon the coach and can't depend upon himself. Then, when a coach who has been calling all the plays starts doing it in fits and starts, it makes the whole situation difficult. I never objected to taking a suggestion from the bench, but I did object to play-calling becoming a divisive force on the team."

Despite this conflict, the Rams won the Western Conference in Gillman's first season, before being thrashed by the Browns in the 1955 NFL Championship Game, Graham's last game. But more importantly, the season served as a training ground for Gillman, who would go on to be a leader in the use of the short-passing game.

"At that point, it wasn't a question of innovations," Gillman said. "We simply had great talent—we had Dutch Van Brocklin and Tom Fears and Elroy Hirsch and Ron Waller. The main thing was Fears. We were just beginning to understand how moves are made by a receiver. Fears was one of the greatest 'move' men in the history of the game. He didn't have much speed, but he could turn 'em on their heads. We studied Fears and we began coaching what he was doing."

But it was Gillman's association with Van Brocklin that helped Gillman develop the theories that would alter the passing philosophy for many quarterbacks to come. "Just watching what Van Brocklin did in practice was a learning experience," Gillman said. "How he played and how he thought helped contribute enormously to the development of the passing game." In later years, Gillman helped develop an enormous range of successful quarterbacks—Bill Wade, Zeke Bratkowski, Frank Ryan, Jack Kemp, John Hadl, and Ron Jaworski—with theories gleaned at least in part from his association with Van Brocklin.

In 1960, Gillman became the head coach of the Los Angeles Chargers of the new American Football League. Not only did he lend the AFL a certain amount of credibility, he developed one of pro football's most explosive offenses. In fact, Gillman's teams epitomized "AFL-style" football, which mixed deep passes to speedy wide receivers with short, safe passes to tight ends and backs.

Others Catch On

Gillman had truly talented receivers with great speed—such as Lance Alworth and Gary Garrison—and turned them into all-pro pass-catchers, or, in Alworth's case, a Hall of Fame receiver. Gillman also started training other football minds, including Jack Faulkner, Chuck Noll, and Don Klosterman.

But none of Gillman's assistants added more to the passing game than Al Davis, who became head coach of the Oakland Raiders in 1963. Davis became a major influence in the passing game of the 1960s and early 1970s. His "vertical passing game" emphasized huge offensive lines that could protect quarterbacks for a long time, and deep passing to speedy wide receivers, such as Warren Wells and Cliff Branch. Of course, having Fred Biletnikoff constantly open short helped the Raiders' deep passing game, but Davis's scheme helped make Daryle Lamonica and Kenny Stabler among the most feared passers in pro football.

Meanwhile, Van Brocklin moved into the coaching ranks, taking over the expansion Minnesota Vikings in 1961, and he immediately found out what a coach-quarterback disagreement looked like from the other side. Van Brocklin had earlier commented that a quarterback should run the ball only if his life were in immediate danger. Who should be Van Brocklin's first quarterback at Minnesota but Fran Tarkenton, a rookie in 1961. Tarkenton, of course, went on to play 18 years and establish numerous NFL passing records, but it was his scrambling that so distressed Van Brocklin.

"With Tarkenton," Van Brocklin said after they had been together several seasons, "you need to have an exceptionally good third-and-forty offense." At a time when NFL quarterbacks did not run the ball a great deal, Tarkenton started the swing in the other direction. Within the next decade, youngsters such as Greg Landry and Bobby Douglass were breaking quarterback running marks left and right. But while Douglass and Landry did their thing, the passing game followed Tarkenton's lead and reversed upon itself.

Air Coryell

The coach most responsible for the shift to the ball-control passing attack was Don Coryell. Coryell had made previously little-known San Diego State a national power, while developing a host of quarterbacks who would play in the NFL: Rod Dowhower, Don Horn, Dennis Shaw, Brian Sipe, and Jesse Freitas. When he joined the St Louis Cardinals in 1973, they had not made the playoffs in 25 years. But after one rebuilding year, with Coryell masterminding the offense and Jim Hart leading it on the field, the Cardinals won two division titles in a row. Coryell then moved to San Diego, where he joined with Dan Fouts to produce an era of aerial success even greater than the Chargers had enjoyed under Gillman.

"It was the system," Fouts later said. "If you check back through Don Coryell's history as a coach, you'll find he had success throwing the ball wherever he went. We believed in his system, and that's what was most important. From the head man down to the waterboys, everybody knew we were going to throw the ball and be successful doing it."

Coryell's system relied on spot passes and mismatches, which made it unique at the time. Coryell's quarterbacks—and both Hart and Fouts were great ones—didn't throw to where receivers were, but to where the receiver figured to end up. They threw to spots. That allowed them to deliver the ball quickly, using two- and three-step drops rather than the common five- or seven-step drops. The ball was put in the air so quickly that the defensive line did not have the time to pressure the quarterback nor did the linebackers or defensive backs have time to react, which cut down on the number of interceptions, increased the number of short passes, and fashioned a new offensive dimension: the ball-control passing game.

Coryell became the first coach to extensively use two tight ends in a one-back offense, a formation that became popular throughout football after Washington won Super Bowl XVII using it. This formation forced the defense to give single coverage to either a wide receiver or to San Diego's Hall of Fame tight end Kellen Winslow, who possessed the speed and receiving talents of a wide receiver.

"We like to line up two tight ends and work over the

middle," Dan Fouts observed while he was still playing for Coryell. "That forces teams to cover a tight end with a safety or linebacker. Our tight ends should have a speed advantage against linebackers and a size advantage against safeties, so we should get a completion. We can also get an advantage in numbers. We'll flood zones or overload zones. We'll put two guys in an area where there is one defender or three guys in an area where there are two defenders.

"We're tough to defend. If you play us zone, you can't blitz and the quarterback has time to throw. If you play us man-to-man, you might get beat long. There's always the threat that someone's going deep in our offense. We look to him first."

It was Coryell's system, but he was fortunate to have a man perfectly suited to it. Fouts was virtually a machine, able to make three, four, even five reads before deciding on his target. And that choice also had to take into account decisions by the receivers, a concept initiated by Chuck Taylor but perfected by Coryell.

"Not only is a receiver at liberty to make adjustments in his route, he is expected to," Fouts continued with his explanation. "I have my reads and the receiver has his—and we're both reading the same thing. I'm expecting the adjustment to come. If the defense is in zone coverage, I know what's coming from my receiver. Guys like Charlie Joiner, Wes Chandler, and Kellen Winslow have instant recognition. That's what separates the great ones from the guys selling cars."

Fouts and Coryell—and all other recent offensive coaches and personnel—benefited greatly from the rules changes that were adopted to open up the passing game and make pro football more exciting. In 1974, defensive players were limited to bumping or chucking a pass receiver only once, and rolling blocks by wide receivers were made illegal.

Four years later, National Football League rules changes permitted a defender to maintain contact with a receiver within five yards of the line of scrimmage, but outlawed contact beyond that point.

League officials also interpreted the pass-blocking rule to permit the extending of arms and open hands, which allowed the offensive line to better protect the quarterback.

The West Coast Offense Arrives

These new rules particularly favored the creative, and none more so than Bill Walsh during his 10 years as head coach of San Francisco. A former assistant to both Paul Brown in Cincinnati (Brown founded the Bengals after leaving Cleveland) and Coryell in San Diego, Walsh popularized the ball-control passing game even more than Coryell because Walsh's teams went one step further: they won three Super Bowls.

Walsh certainly didn't invent the pass in the flat, but no one had ever used it so consistently, or effectively. He made the short pass a large part of his running game. Perhaps the most remarked-upon aspect of Walsh's offense was that he scripted the first 20-25 plays of each game, running them in precise order. If a drive stalled, the 49ers would simply pick up where they left off the next time they got the ball. Conventional wisdom said a team should probe for a weakness in the defense and then hammer it again and again. But, when Walsh finished his script, he knew exactly what plays would work and what adjustments to make for the failed plays to succeed. His arsenal was still full by the fourth quarter. Small wonder the 49ers achieved an unsurpassed reputation for coming from behind in the final moments.

In Walsh's rookie season as an NFL coach in 1979—after having tutored Guy Benjamin and Steve Dils at Stanford, each of whom led the nation in passing as a senior—Steve DeBerg set NFL records for pass attempts and completions for the 49ers.

But the next year, DeBerg lost his job to second-year pro Joe Montana, who proved to be the perfect operative for Walsh's theories. Montana's pinpoint passing, timely running, and ability to pull out wins when all seemed lost helped make the 49ers the team of the decade in the 1980s. Montana's magic continued even after Walsh as the 49ers won a fourth Super Bowl after the 1989 season under Walsh's successor, George Seifert.

"Unlike the Steelers, who won their first two Super Bowls with a magnificent defense, the 49ers won primarily because of Montana," said former New York Jets personnel director Mike Hickey. "He was the key to their team all along. As a guy who can get the job done that a quarterback is supposed to do—win—Montana is one of the two or three best ever."

Remarkably, despite Montana's success, some people called for his removal in favor of Steve Young as early as 1988. One of the greatest physical talents to play quarterback in the NFL, Young had to wait his turn until 1991 and 1992, when Montana missed most of two successive seasons with injuries. But Young made the most of his chances, leading the NFL in passing both years, as he did again in 1993 (after Montana was traded to Kansas City), 1994, 1996, and 1997. Young shares Sammy Baugh's record of six league passing titles.

"Young is clearly one of the greatest quarterbacks ever," Seifert said. "It is not just that he is such a phenomenal athlete and one of the best runners ever from his position, but he is also statistically the most proficient passer in league history.

"He has suffered some by popular comparisons to Montana, but on an individual level he has produced even more than Joe did. Certainly no other player has led the league in passing five times in six years. They were different stylistically, but it would be hard to take one over the other. Either could make a claim as the best ever."

The Best Ever

The same could be said about a number of other quarterbacks. A survey was done several years ago of personnel directors and scouts—men who had been around professional football for up to 50 years and had therefore seen virtually all of the greats—attempting to determine the finest quarterback ever.

At that time, five different quarterbacks received mention as the best ever. Then, in 1994, four quarterbacks were put on the NFL's 75th Anniversary All-Time Team, voted on by media and NFL personnel. Three players received the nod from just one of these panels—Montana, the master of the come-from-behind victory; Layne, the greatest leader of men; and Sonny Jurgensen, the best pure passer ever.

Three other quarterbacks received mention from both—Baugh, arguably the most complete football player ever; Graham, the greatest winner; and Johnny Unitas, who had been elected as the all-time choice in 1969 on the National Football League's 50th Anniversary Team.

"Sammy Baugh might be the best overall football player in NFL history," one of the scouts said at the time of the voting. "But Johnny Unitas stands alone as a quarterback. He was cool, he was daring, he was flawless. He had perfect passing form. He was the ultimate thinker and leader. He could fire up a team or keep them cold and calculating. He could do anything and everything. I don't think there will be another like him."

Each of these six, established himself as a ferocious competitor, a superior athlete, a leader with a drive to win. Each worked to succeed in that most vital, most glamorous, and most difficult of positions—NFL quarterback.

APPENDIX 7

Quarterbacks on the Run

Beau Riffenburgh

Maybe the most obvious difference between the National Football League and collegiate football is that no professional teams subscribe to Darrell Royal's famous adage, "Only three things can happen when you pass, and two of them are bad." In college football, where Royal, Bud Wilkinson, Woody Hayes, and many like-minded coaches long avoided the pass, quarterbacks who run better than they pass often flourish. Indeed, teams such as Air Force regularly have quarterbacks who rush for more than 1,000 yards in a season, and there have been numerous college quarterbacks who have both passed for and run for more than 1,000 yards in the same year.

Not in the NFL. "The best way to cripple your team in a hurry is to have your quarterback running the ball regularly on designed plays," Super Bowl winning coach Hank Stram said. "Any defensive player loves to tee off on a quarterback, and with the size and strength of defensive linemen and linebackers today, quarterbacks wouldn't last long if they expose themselves as runners. Enough get hurt just trying to throw the ball."

According to NFL personnel wizard Tom Braatz, a tendency to run the ball is not exactly a bonus in a college quarterback. "When NFL scouts look for a potential quarterback from the college ranks, running ability is not the first quality that comes to mind," Braatz said. "The NFL quarterback must have arm strength, size, intelligence, accuracy, touch, anticipation, timing, judgment, leadership, poise, and, hopefully, mobility to avoid the rush. But mobility is a bonus, not a necessity, and we normally translate it to mean scrambling, not running. Most quarterbacks who like to run first or who take off—instead of staying in the pocket to allow that receiver to come open—will not impress many scouts because they probably will not remain healthy very long in the atmosphere of the NFL."

Many of the most successful running quarterbacks didn't make the NFL at all—such as Johnny Bright, James Street, Condredge Holloway, and Turner Gill. Others did make it but had brief and disappointing stays—such as Terry Baker, Jimmy Sidle, Gary Beban, Rex Kern, and Jack Mildren. In fact, the star college runners who have been the most successful in pro football generally did so at positions other than quarterback, such as Dan Reeves (halfback), Freddie Solomon (wide receiver), and Nolan Cromwell (safety).

Yet, despite the doubts of coaches and scouts about quarterbacks becoming ball carriers, and despite the numbers of running quarterbacks who have not made it, the NFL has had many quarterbacks who have run successfully. Coincidentally, most of the league's finest running quarterbacks were not outstanding college runners. This has been the case both in an era of mobile quarterbacks (such as the 1980s) and the time of classic dropback passers who rarely strayed from the pocket (such as during the 1960s).

Regardless of when they played, running quarterbacks usually put more pressure on defenses than predominantly pocket passers.

The Men with the Golden Feet

"Let's be realistic," Bucko Kilroy, the great personnel expert for New England once said. "In their respective time periods, Joe Namath and Dan Marino had the golden arms, but neither put the same kind of pressure on defenses that contemporaries like Fran Tarkenton or John Elway did, guys who could roll out, scramble, or run. With quarterbacks like that, defenders have to play a guessing game because the quarterback has a much wider selection of options." Quarterbacks who offer the added dimension of moving the chains by running the ball have used their talents in different ways. Bobby Douglass preferred to run first and throw second. Roger Staubach would move around until he saw either an open receiver or a running lane for himself. Fran Tarkenton almost seemed to run around for the fun of it. Roman Gabriel ran on third-and-short, when he was like a fullback going straight at the defense. And Archie Manning ran out of sheer necessity.

The effectiveness of quarterbacks as runners was simply not an issue in the NFL until the 1940s. The introduction of the T-formation with man in motion—as revolutionized by Clark Shaughnessy, Sid Luckman, and the Chicago Bears—took the game by storm and, to a great extent, drove out the Single-Wing and Double-Wing formations. In that decade, most of the league started using the T, and the quarterback position became more and more pass-oriented. The average passing yards per game rose from 211.6 in 1938, the year before Luckman joined the Bears, to 361.2 in 1947, an increase of 71 percent in a decade.

The Bears, Rams, and Browns—three of the greatest teams in pro football history—revolutionized the NFL with their sophisticated pass offenses in the 1940s and 1950s. But one of the earliest of the effective running quarterbacks came from a surprising source. Tobin Rote joined Green Bay in 1950 out of Rice. The next year, the 3-9 Packers not only led the NFL in pass attempts, but Rote became the major part of the team's ground game, running for 523 yards (the most ever by a quarterback) with a league-leading 6.9-yard average.

Five years later, Rote was still at it, not only leading the league in pass attempts, completions, yards, and touchdown passes, but running for 11 touchdowns. By the time he retired in 1966 after three years in the American Football League, Rote had increased his career rushing totals to 3,128 yards and 37 touchdowns, both tops among quarterbacks.

Two of Rote's greatest contemporaries could also carry the football. Bobby Layne had led the Texas Longhorns in rushing in college, and he continued his tough-guy performance in the NFL, where he ran for 2,451 yards and 25 touchdowns in 15 seasons. His best year rushing was 1952, when he gained 411 yards, then scored the first touchdown in Detroit's 17-7 NFL Championship Game victory over Cleveland. Layne's opposing quarterback in that game, Otto Graham, was no slouch himself as a runner. Graham never rolled up the yardage that some did, but he was always a threat, particularly on short yardage and near the goal line. In his 10 years in pro football (four in the AAFC and six in the NFL), not only did Graham run for 44 touchdowns (still the most ever by a quarterback), he also scored 5 touchdowns in his final two NFL title games, both easy victories.

It wasn't until the 1970s that Rote's position as the dominant running quarterback in the history of pro football was challenged. In 1970, Greg Landry, in his first year as a starter for Detroit, ran for 350 yards with a 10.0-yard average. The next season he broke Rote's mark by gaining 530 yards, while averaging 7.0 yards per carry. His passing didn't suffer, as he finished second in the National Football Conference in that category. Landry came close to surpassing that mark the next year, with 524 yards and 9 touchdowns, but injuries slowed his rushing productivity for the rest of his long career.

Chicago Bears rookie Bobby Douglass burst onto the scene with 408 rushing yards on an 8.0-yard average in 1969. Perhaps the former Kansas All-America should have changed to running back because with his power, speed, and size (6 feet 4 inches, 225 pounds) he could have been an outstanding back. Instead, he remained at quarterback, and in 1972 he truly broke loose, rushing for 968 yards (still the most ever by an NFL quarterback) on a 6.9-yard average, which remains the third highest in NFL history. Douglass added 525 yards in 1973, but he didn't pass proficiently enough to maintain a starting position, and he never played a full season again.

The Minnesota Scrambler

In 1961, rookie Fran Tarkenton joined the Minnesota Vikings. "Frantic Fran" not only made an immediate impact as one of the league's best passers, but established himself as perhaps the best-ever scrambler.

"It used to drive you crazy," said Don Shula, who was the coach of the Baltimore Colts when Tarkenton was in his first of two stints with the Vikings. "Tarkenton would scramble all around the backfield, giving ground and going farther and farther back toward his own goal line. Then, just when you thought your defensive lineman had him, he'd duck away and start going back to the line of scrimmage. He'd wander all over the field, just waiting for a receiver to come open. Then he'd complete a pass."

When receivers didn't come open, Tarkenton would just take off, and he managed to gain more than 300 yards rushing in seven of his first eight seasons. Tarkenton ran less as he got older, but he still ran enough to finish his career with 3,674 yards and a 5.4-yard average.

"There have been better runners than Tarkenton, but no one has been a better scrambler," said Graham, who had a close view of Tarkenton as head coach of the Washington Redskins. "I will forever have a picture of him just running willy-nilly around the backfield, defensive linemen huffing and puffing, slowing down as they tire, and then being wiped out by a block from an offensive player. Meanwhile, when he started dodging around, his receivers broke off their normal routes and went to a second set of patterns that emphasized hooks and comebacks. No matter how good a defensive back is, he can't cover someone for 15 seconds, so Tarkenton would hit the guy coming open. It was remarkable."

A similar, and equally remarkable, performer—as a passer, a runner, and a winner—was Roger Staubach. When he was winning the Heisman Trophy at the U.S. Naval Academy, Staubach loved to run, and he showed the same passion when he joined the Cowboys in 1969. He drove defenses crazy—and sometimes his coach, Tom Landry—with his routine practice of dropping back, looking, and taking off up the field. He averaged almost 8 yards per carry in his first three years in the NFL, but Staubach was injured on a run in a preseason game against the Rams in 1972. He became a more controlled scrambler after that, but he still finished with 2,264 yards and a 5.5-yard average in 11 years.

"It is remarkable how similar the careers of Roger Staubach and Terry Bradshaw were," NFL personnel expert Joel Bussert said. "Each came in with huge talent and, very early on, with a chance to be a starter. Each had outstanding potential as a passer but seemed to love to run the ball almost more than to throw it. Staubach was cured of it by his injury in 1972, and Bradshaw was cured of it by his benching in favor of Joe Gilliam in 1973 and 1974. When he concentrated on leading the team first, on passing second, and on running only when he had to, rather than when he wanted to, Bradshaw developed into one of the greats. Of course, he and Staubach also each led their teams to the Super Bowl four times, and the only time one came out a loser was the two times when the Steelers beat the Cowboys. And, it was Bradshaw's brain and his arm that won those games, not his legs."

Grogan Takes Off

In 1973, when Chuck Fairbanks became the head coach and general manager of New England, one of the first things he talked about was his desire to run the Wishbone, as he had so successfully at the University of Oklahoma. His quarterback, Jim Plunkett, was not hugely mobile, however, so Fairbanks went shopping for someone who could tuck the ball in and run. The result was Steve Grogan, a lanky, tough customer from Kansas State.

When Plunkett was injured in 1975, the fearless rookie took over and established himself as one of the more effective runners in the league. (Fortunately for Grogan, Fairbanks had abandoned the potentially disastrous concept of the Wishbone in the NFL.) In 1976, his first year as a full-time starter, Grogan ran for 397 yards and 12 touchdowns; two years later, he pounded out 539 yards, as the Patriots became the first team in history to have four players each rush for more than 500 yards. Like Landry, Staubach, Archie Manning, Joe Montana, and many other quarterbacks, Grogan ran less in his later years.

"Many quarterbacks who do run early in their careers begin to realize as they pick up small injuries that they will not continue to play at the same level if they do not redefine their game and cut back on putting themselves at risk," Braatz said. "That is why so many of them who seem able to do everything early on end up being conservative dropback passers. If they keep trying to run, it will catch up with them, like it did with Randall Cunningham, who had established himself as probably the best running quarterback in league history."

Cunningham certainly had the numbers to back up Braatz's viewpoint. After spending his rookie year as a backup, he used pure athleticism to establish himself as one of the most dangerous weapons in the NFL. For five consecutive years he rushed for more than 500 yards in a season. He netted 942 yards on only 118 carries in 1990, his 8.0 yards per carry being the second-best figure in NFL history for a season, and his yardage was second among quarterbacks only behind Douglass. Meanwhile, he also passed for more than 3,400 yards in three of those seasons. Then in 1991, Cunningham suffered a season-ending knee injury in the first quarter of the first game of the season.

"It was truly remarkable how Randall came back in 1992 after his knee injury," said then Philadelphia coach Rich Kotite. "One would have thought that he hadn't had any problem at all." That year Cunningham again gained more than 500 yards, while averaging 6.3 yards per carry. But the next year another injury forced him to miss most of the season, and ended his stint as the game's premier quarterback running threat. Nevertheless, through the 1998 season, Cunningham had gained 4,741 yards while averaging 6.5 yards per carry. Both numbers are the best ever by an NFL quarterback.

"I am not sure that there have been any quarterbacks in the past 20 years who are as multitalented as Cunningham," Kotite said. "But if there have been any who could equal that pure overall ability, they would have to be John Elway and Steve Young. They are both remarkable from the running standpoint because they are among the few quarterbacks ever who have been outstanding runners throughout their entire career."

Again, the statistics back up the statement. Elway carried the ball 774 times in his 16-year career, more than any other quarterback in NFL history, while gaining 3,407 yards and scoring 33 touchdowns. This while passing for more than 3,000 yards 12 times. Young, on the other hand, despite spending much of his career as a backup to Joe Montana, has netted the second-most rushing yards (4,182) ever by a quarterback while scoring 43 times. Both Young and Elway learned to scramble to buy time rather than to gain yards.

"Young and Elway both had to learn patience and to try to overcome their almost unbelievable natural talents," said football guru Tom Bass. "Young's passing skills, in particular, are second to none, and he needed to be able to protect himself from being hurt again and missing substantial parts of a season. This is a very difficult thing to do when a player has always had the ability to just take off and make big gains. But they both have worked on it very successfully, and the results have been long careers and successful entries into the playoffs. If they had run more, they would have had more yards, but their teams might not have been so successful.

"Like a lot of the other most successful quarterbacks, guys who ran less as their careers went on, Young and Elway showed that they understood that while they want to do everything they can to win the game or even to move the chains, in this game there is always next week or next season to come back to. Ultimately it is nice to be a running threat, but it is better for a quarterback to not run, than literally to run himself out of the game."

APPENDIX 8

The Great Receivers

Beau Riffenburgh

Great receivers aren't born, they are made. There have been enough butterfingered track stars and plenty of muscular, well-built ball-droppers to disprove the theory that those leaping, diving, one-handed catches are not just automatic. The men making those catches have trained for years to pull in the ball whenever it is thrown in their direction. But there is a lot more to being an outstanding receiver than just being able to catch a pass.

Just like their quarterbacks, receivers come in all sizes and styles and emphasize widely varying strengths. They can be sprinters who are deep threats, possession receivers who succeed because of outstanding hands and moves that allow them to separate from defenders, or ball carriers who are most dangerous after they make the reception.

Nor can a great receiver be measured strictly by the number of passes he catches or the yards he produces. Such yardsticks ignore the dynamics of the team for which any receiver plays. It is considerably easier to catch a lot of passes if a team regularly throws the ball and isn't wedded to the ground game. Simply comparing reception totals also doesn't take into account the fact that recent players have had 16 games per season, as opposed to 10, 12, or 14 of earlier eras. Moreover, in recent years, the rules have encouraged the passing game and hindered defenders. In previous eras defensive backs could virtually beat up the receivers at will, making every pass considerably more difficult to haul in than those of today.

One receiver who could grab a lot of passes simply because he could outrun every defender was Bob Hayes, the fastest of the NFL's speed burners. After setting a world record in the 100-meter dash at the Tokyo Olympics in 1964, Hayes led the NFL with a 21.8-yard average and 12 touchdown receptions as a rookie in 1965; he repeated with 13 touchdown catches the next year.

When Dallas became more run-oriented as Duane Thomas, Walt Garrison, and Calvin Hill led the Cowboys to Super Bowls V and VI, Hayes's receptions dropped, but he remained just as frightening to defensive backs, averaging 26.1 yards per reception in 1970 and an NFL-high 24.0 yards the following year.

"For more than three decades now, other teams have tried to turn track stars into NFL players, like the Cowboys did with Hayes," former Dallas personnel director Gil Brandt said. "The difference is that Hayes was not just a track athlete, he was a great football player. He frequently is thought of simply for his speed, but he was just as talented in his way as Paul Warfield."

Although Homer Jones, Buddy Dial, and Warren Wells were other Hayes-like deep threats, perhaps the single greatest of that genre of receiver actually played for the run-oriented Chicago Cardinals from 1946-1950. Mal Kutner finished in the NFL's top-five receivers each of his first three seasons, each time averaging 22 or more yards per reception. But he was a lot more than just a bombs-away target.

"Kutner was the first consistent deep threat in NFL history," said a long-time scout who played against Kutner when he helped lead the Cardinals to back-to-back appearances in the NFL title game. "He was one of the fastest players in the league, had marvelous moves, and was incredibly dangerous once he had the ball. If he could play with the rules today, he would be just as dangerous and just as productive as Jerry Rice. If both Kutner and his quarterback, Paul Christman, hadn't suffered debilitating injuries in 1949, they would have been the greatest passing combination of the fifties."

The AFL and AAFC Influence

At the other end of the spectrum from Hayes and Kutner was Lionel Taylor, a receiver who didn't possess such native ability, but who somehow still managed to lead the American Football League in career receptions (567), led that league in receiving five of its first six years, and in 1961 became the first pro football player to record 100 receptions in a season.

"This guy didn't have the speed to play pro football," says a long-time NFL scout. "It was almost an insult to defensive backs to send him up against them. Yet when he was with the Broncos, he ended up catching more than seventy-five passes six years in a row. There has not been a better example of what can be achieved by hard work, competitiveness, and heart."

Taylor's last year of leading the AFL in receptions (he had 85 catches in 1965) marked the emergence of another inordinately productive receiver who was not blessed with great speed, but who had the hands and moves to be deadly efficient as a short receiver. "The image of Fred Biletnikoff will always be of him rubbing stickum on his hands, arms, and uniform," one AFC personnel director says of the Pro Football Hall of Fame enshrinee who made 589 receptions with the Raiders, leading the AFC in that category in 1971 and 1972. "But it wasn't just the stickum. I think Fred was actually an octopus. I don't see any other way he could have made all of those unbelievable catches.

"And it wasn't just his hands. Fred could go over the middle, and he could turn defensive backs inside out with his moves. Most people remember his performance in Super Bowl XI , but the game I associate with Fred is when he personally destroyed the best secondary in pro football, catching seven passes for 180 yards and three first-half touchdowns in a 1968 playoff game against the Chiefs."

Biletnikoff benefited from having a speed merchant as the Raiders' other wide receiver for much of his NFL career, first Warren Wells and then Cliff Branch. It has not been unusual that outstanding receivers have come in pairs, and that has made them even more difficult for defenses to cover. Perhaps the first great example of this was the two unknowns that coach Paul Brown helped turn into all-pros with the Cleveland Browns: Dante Lavelli and Mac Speedie.

Lavelli had played for Brown at Ohio State before joining the newly formed Browns of the newly formed All-America Football Conference in 1946. That same year, Speedie entered the pros, having been spotted by Brown playing service football. In the next eight seasons (1946-1953), not a year passed without at least one of these two (and sometimes both) being named all-league. Speedie led the AAFC in receiving three times and Lavelli once. When the Browns moved to the NFL in 1950, the pair continued to be productive. Speedie led that the NFL in receptions in 1952, while Lavelli, known as "Gluefingers," caught at least 30 passes in five of his first six seasons after the Browns joined—and dominated—the NFL.

"There have been a lot of great pairs of wide receivers," Weeb Ewbank, an assistant on those Browns teams and later head coach of the Baltimore Colts and New York Jets, said shortly after his induction into the Pro Football Hall of Fame. "I had Don Maynard and George Sauer, and there was Lance Alworth and Gary Garrison out in San Diego, but until now few have really been able to equal Lavelli and Speedie. They were, quite simply, the best two receivers in the AAFC, and when they came into the NFL they immediately became the best in that league."

Stallworth and Swann

One of the greatest receiving tandems came from a franchise that turned around its loser's image with an impressive ground game. Pittsburgh's solid running game made Lynn Swann and John Stallworth even more lethal, and vice versa.

During the late 1970s and early 1980s, these two exceptional receivers combined grace, speed, and exceptional athletic ability to terrorize defenses, particularly in big games. In Super Bowl X, Swann was named most valuable player after he made 4 receptions for 161 yards. One catch—a spectacular sideline grab—set up the Steelers' first touchdown and another clinched the game on a 64-yard scoring strike from Terry Bradshaw in the final period. Three years later, Swann again caught the clinching touchdown in Super Bowl XIII against Dallas, but only after Stallworth had already hauled in 28- and 75-yard scores from Bradshaw in the first half.

The pair completed their championship heroics when, trailing the Los Angeles Rams in Super Bowl XIV, Swann caught a 47-yard scoring pass and then Stallworth hauled in the game winner on a 73-yard bomb from Bradshaw at the Rose Bowl.

"Swann and Stallworth didn't have the regular-season numbers that some of their contemporaries did," Steelers head coach Chuck Noll later said about his star receivers. "But then, the other teams didn't have the running production that we had from Franco Harris and Rocky Bleier. Having two players on the outside like that not only gave us the quick-hitting big play that was so important in some of our postseason victories, but it helped open up the running game. If the secondary ignored our receivers for even a moment, they could be burned badly, and they all knew it, so they couldn't come up and help with stopping the run. One mark of a great receiver is what he does for the entire offense, not just the passing game, and those two really helped open up the run."

Coincidentally, two of the greatest, and most productive, receivers only became so after they moved to wideout from running back. Bobby Mitchell and Charley Taylor played together for the Washington Redskins, where the offense was based almost totally on Sonny Jurgensen's arm. Mitchell garnered NFL rookie of the year honors in 1958 as a halfback, playing next to Jim Brown in Cleveland, but he moved to flanker when he was traded to the Redskins in 1962. Mitchell responded by leading the NFL in receiving yards in 1962 and 1963. Taylor earned unanimous acclaim as NFL rookie of the year in 1964, after rushing for 755 yards and catching passes for 814 more.

Taylor proved to be so adept at catching passes that he moved to wide receiver in his third season and led the NFL in receptions in 1966 and 1967. When Mitchell retired after the 1968 season, he had 521 receptions for 7,954 yards and 65 touchdowns. Taylor played until 1977, retiring as pro football's all-time leading receiver, with 649 catches for 9,140 yards and 79 touchdowns. Mitchell entered the Pro Football Hall of Fame in 1983, followed the next year by Taylor.

"Mitchell and Taylor both would have made the Hall of Fame if they had been left at halfback," said Bill McPeak, who coached both players with Washington. "But they were even more dangerous as receivers. The frightening thing about them was that they had wide receiver speed and ball-catching ability, but they had running back ability once they caught a pass. These were no skinny little receivers, but tough backs who could run through defensive backs."

Largent and Berry

These receivers were some of the greatest ever, yet there are another half dozen who stand out above them and all of the rest. As with the other receivers in the game, these six have been linked by their success rather than by the similarity of their talents.

"Consistency is the word for Steve Largent," a former

scout remarked shortly after the Seattle Seahawks star retired following the 1989 season. "He wanted to be the best in pro football, and he constantly played at a level of intensity and effort that he hoped would make him so. Sheer effort made him the best receiver in the NFL for more than a decade."

Largent set NFL records (since broken) with 819 receptions, 13,089 yards, 100 touchdown catches, and 177 consecutive games with a reception. In 14 years, he made 50 or more receptions 10 times and surpassed 1,000 yards receiving eight times. Not bad for a guy who was a fourth-round draft pick by the Houston Oilers in 1976, but the Tulsa graduate played only four preseason games for Houston before being traded to the expansion Seahawks for an eighth-round selection.

Similar accolades have been given to Raymond Berry. He wasn't selected until the twentieth round of the NFL draft, but Berry went on to earn a place in the Pro Football Hall of Fame.

From 1955 through 1967 with the Baltimore Colts, Berry made 40 or more receptions 10 times; led the NFL in receptions three consecutive seasons (1958-1960); and made 631 receptions for 9,275 yards and 68 touchdowns, finishing his career as the leading receiver in pro football history. Of course, it didn't hurt that he was teamed with Johnny Unitas for all but his rookie season.

"Berry wasn't particularly big, had only average speed, and couldn't move with the ball overly well, but he might have been the most intelligent receiver ever," Ewbank later said. "He worked on his moves and on the psychological aspects of the game until he could catch short passes, particularly down-and-outs, against any defensive back in the world. Berry's strength was his work ethic: he was a perfectionist, and it showed. For example, he fumbled only twice in thirteen years."

Absolutely Everything

At the opposite end of the spectrum from Largent and Berry was Paul Warfield, a remarkably physically gifted player with the speed to be a sprinter, the toughness to have played halfback at Ohio State for Woody Hayes, and a grace rarely equaled in the history of the sport. He was the deep threat for two great running teams, first the Browns, when they featured Jim Brown and then Leroy Kelly, and then the Dolphins, when Larry Csonka, Jim Kiick, and Mercury Morris bashed their way to consecutive Super Bowl titles.

In 13 years with these run-oriented teams, he only once caught as many as 50 passes, finishing with a solid, but not remarkable, total of 427 receptions. However, he averaged more than 20 yards per reception seven consecutive years, and he completed his career with 8,565 yards, a 20.1-yard average, and 85 touchdowns.

"Warfield had absolutely everything, the entire package," said an opposing coach shortly after Warfield was selected to the Hall of Fame in his first year of eligibility. "He could just glide down the field with that blistering speed, yet he had the remarkable ability to stop in a step or to cut without slowing down. He also had fabulous hands and great moves with and without the ball. But the word that best fits Warfield is grace. It is just lucky for his opponents that the Browns had Brown and Kelly and the Dolphins Csonka, because if those teams had decided to throw the ball, Warfield would have been in the end zone about every other minute."

The Top Three

The man who actually seems to have been in the end zone just about that frequently is one of three receivers whom most experts actually rate above Warfield as one of the three best ever: Jerry Rice. The all-time leader in catches, yards, and touchdowns, Rice has set himself apart from the rest of the field. This is a man who, after all, has four times caught 100 or more passes in a season, totaled 1,000 or more receiving yards in a season 12 times, and six times led the league in yards.

"There is no part of his game that is not remarkable," observed Rice's former coach Bill Walsh. "He is most unusual in that he is both a great possession receiver and a deadly deep threat. The reason is his unfathomable ability once he latches onto the ball. I've never seen anyone who can move around, through, and away from defensive backs like he can."

Despite the fact that Rice has eclipsed virtually every major receiving record, there are two receivers who can't be left behind when it comes to pass-catching ability: Lance Alworth and Don Hutson.

Alworth, nicknamed "Bambi" because of his boyish looks, speed (9.5 seconds in the 100-yard dash), fluid movement, and leaping ability, was the first player from the American Football League to be inducted into the Pro Football Hall of Fame. No receiver in the history of the game—not even Warfield or Rice—could make the spectacular catch like the two-time All-America from Arkansas.

In nine years with San Diego, Alworth caught passes in a then-record 96 consecutive games, led the AFL in receiving three times, and gained more than 1,000 yards for seven consecutive years. In 1965, he caught 69 passes for an AFL-record 1,602 yards, an amazing 23.2 yards per reception, and 14 touchdowns.

"When I used to dream about what I would take if I could have anything in the world given to me, I used to start with the chance to play with Lance Alworth," Hall of Fame quarterback Joe Namath once commented. "I know a lot of people would expect me to go after something wild and crazy. No; I just wanted Bambi on the other side of my passes."

"Alworth was almost certainly the most exciting player ever," echoes a former NFL scout and offensive coach. "If I had to start a team with any player I ever saw play, my first selection—before Jim Brown or Dick Butkus or Merlin Olsen—would be Lance Alworth."

Hutson was even more dominating than Alworth, Rice, or any other receiver in National Football League history. In 11 years, he led the NFL in receptions eight times, in yardage seven times, and in touchdown receptions nine times. Seemingly able to do anything, he also led the league in scoring five consecutive seasons, in field goals once, and interceptions once.

But the most impressive thing about Hutson was the amount that the former Alabama All-America outdistanced his rivals. In 1942, when Hutson set NFL records with 74 receptions, 1,211 yards, and 17 touchdowns, the second-highest figures in the league were 27 receptions, 345 yards, and 4 touchdowns. In fact, before Hutson came on the scene, the record for touchdown receptions in a season was only 5; he moved the record further and further up the ladder, setting the mark with 6 in 1935, then 8 in 1936, 9 in 1938, 10 in 1941, and then, finally, 17 in 1942.

"No matter how many receptions modern receivers make, they will never be able to rival Hutson," all-time great scout Bucko Kilroy once said. "He had nine-eight speed for the hundred-yard dash more than half a century ago. He had simply amazing hands. He made moves that no one had ever seen before in pro football. There is no one in the annals of the game at any position—not even Jim Brown—who is comparable to him."

"Hutson is the man all other receivers will be measured against," Brandt said. "He was unbelievably far ahead of his contemporaries, and he would be better than anyone else if he could be transferred to any other era. All I can say is, Hayes might have been the fastest, Berry the hardest working, Rice the most productive, and Alworth the most dynamic, but Hutson—and nobody but Hutson—was the best of all time."

Notes on Contributors

Phil Barber is a former senior editor for NFL Properties, where he managed *GameDay* magazine, the annual Super Bowl program, and *75 Seasons,* a coffee-table history of the league. Now he contributes to the league's various publications from his home in Calistoga, California. He also writes for *The Sporting News* and the *San Francisco Chronicle* on a freelance basis, and he produces a weekly column for *The Napa Valley Register.*

Tom Barnidge is a senior editor for NFL Properties Publishing and has spent most of his adult life in sports journalism. He covered the NFL from 1974-1981 as a reporter and, later, as a columnist, for the *St. Louis Post-Dispatch.* He was named managing editor of *The Sporting News* in 1982 and became editor-in-chief in 1985. From 1985-86, he also hosted *Sports Page,* a weekly TV show for which he won three Emmy awards. He oversees the *Official Super Bowl Game Program* and *NFL Kickoff,* the league's preseason magazine.

Ted Brock lives in Modesto, California, and is sports editor of *The Modesto Bee.* He grew up in the shadow of Berkeley's Memorial Stadium, where he first learned about football as a fan of Lynn (Pappy) Waldorf's Golden Bears in the 1950s. A graduate of Occidental College, Brock was a senior editor and staff writer with NFL Properties from 1977-1985 and helped produce *GameDay* and *PRO!* magazines. He co-authored *25 Years: The NFL Since 1960* in 1985 and *75 Seasons* in 1994. He has also taught sportswriting at the University of Southern California.

Joel Bussert is the senior director of player personnel/football operations for the NFL. He is responsible for supervision of the NFL's college draft each year and serves as liaison to the league's Competition Committee. He also has contributed research to the Elias Sports Bureau and *The Sporting News.*

Jim J. Campbell has followed the football scene closely since 1943, when he spent his entire weekly allowance (25 cents) for a copy of *Illustrated Football Annual.* Campbell has written a dozen books, including *Golden Years of Pro Football,* dozens of magazine articles, countless newspaper columns, and has contributed "Trivia Timeout" to *Pro Football Weekly* for many years. He worked in and around the NFL for 15 years, with the Pittsburgh Steelers, at the Pro Football Hall of Fame, with NFL Properties, and with the NFL Alumni. Currently, he is director of the Bison Club at Bucknell University.

Bob Carroll is the founder and executive director of the Professional Football Researchers Association (PFRA) and edits the group's newsletter, *The Coffin Corner.* His many sports books include *Pro Football: When the Grass Was Real and Baseball Between the Lies,* and he was a contributor to *Biographical Encyclopedia of American Sports: Football* (1988).

Jack Clary is an award-winning sports media specialist and author of some 55 sports books, including nearly three dozen on pro football. His book, *Pro Football's Great Moments,* was published in 11 different editions, and he worked with Hall of Fame coaches Paul Brown, Chuck Noll, Don Shula, and Tom Landry to produce *The Gamemakers,* a primer on the art of managing people. He spent 17 years as a sports writer and columnist for the *Associated Press* and is a regular contributor to programs for the Cincinnati Bengals, for whom he also handles special assignments.

Ray Didinger covered pro football for the *Philadelphia Bulletin* and *Philadelphia Daily News* for 26 years before joining NFL Films in 1996 as a producer. The 1995 winner of the Dick McCann Award for distinguished coverage of pro football, Didinger's name was added to the Writers' Honor Roll in the Pro Football Hall of Fame in Canton, Ohio. Didinger was named Pennsylvania Sportswriter of the Year five times. He won three Associated Press awards for column writing, the Pro Football Writers of America award for best feature story in 1991, and wrote the script for the documentary, *Football America.*

Jerry Di Paolo has been a sports writer for 23 years. He graduated from Point Park College in Pittsburgh in 1976 and began working for several newspapers, most notably the *Pittsburgh Press* from 1986 until its sale in 1992. He has been with the *Pittsburgh Tribune-Review* since 1993 and been its Steelers beat reporter since 1994. He contributed to the *Total Football* spin-off book, *Total Steelers,* in 1998, and his work is included in the 300 Greatest Players Plus section in this edition of *Total Football.*

Elias Sports Bureau is the official statistician for the NFL, a function it has performed since 1961. The New

York City-based information company collects, verifies, processes, and distributes the league's official statistics, in forms both printed and electronic, to various media ranging from the press box to the Internet. In addition to supplying the vast bulk of the statistical material for this book, Elias also serves as official statistician for Major League Baseball and the National Basketball Association.

Pete Fierle joined the Pro Football Hall of Fame in April, 1988, as a researcher in the Library-Research Center. In November, 1996, he was named information services manager. Fierle also oversees the Hall's photo archive and Internet web site (www.profootballhof.com). From 1990-93, he was responsible for the Hall of Fame's Educational Outreach Program. Before he joined the Hall of Fame, Fierle worked in the programming department at ESPN in Bristol, Connecticut, and the Buffalo Bills public relations department in Orchard Park, New York.

David Fischer worked as a writer/producer for NBC sports on the Internet, directing football coverage for nbcsports.com from 1995-97. He contributed to four of the *Total Football* spin-off books in 1998, namely *Total Super Bowl, Total Quarterbacks, Total Steelers,* and *Total Cowboys.* A native of Philadelphia (and die-hard Eagles fan) he now lives in Washington, D.C.

Michael Gershman was editor-in-chief of *Total Football Online* for AT&T Interchange. A long-time PFRA member, he is also a co-editor of *Total Baseball,* co-author of *Twentieth Century Sports,* and a founding partner in Total Sports. He also wrote *Diamonds: The Evolution of the Ballpark,* winner of the Casey Award as "the best baseball book of 1993."

Jim Gigliotti has been an associate editor at NFL Properties since 1989. Prior to that he spent five years in the sports information office of the University of Southern California, initially as assistant sports information director and, later, as director of publications. He is in his sixth season as editor of the national edition of *NFL Insider,* the league's in-stadium magazine.

Ed Gruver is the author of *The Foolish Club: A History of the American Football League* and *The Ice Bowl.* Born and raised in northern New Jersey, he has been a sportswriter for 13 years. He is a member of the Pro Football Researchers Association and a contributing writer for the PFRA newsletter/magazine. A lifelong Packers and Browns fan, he lives in central Pennsylvania.

John Hogrogian is a veteran pro football researcher who has contributed historical articles on the Providence Steam Roller, Staten Island Stapletons, and Hartford Blues to *PRO!* magazine and on the New York Titans to the PFRA newsletter/magazine. He has spent several years researching the long lost all-pro teams of the 1920s. A former president of the Pro Football Researchers Association, Hogrogian received its Ralph Hay Award for lifetime achievement in the field of pro football historiography in 1995.

Joe Horrigan is a 20-year employee of the Pro Football Hall of Fame. Currently the Hall's vice president communications/exhibits, he previously served as its curator/director of research information. Horrigan, who has written several articles on pro football and pro football history, is the author of *The Pro Football Hall of Fame Answer Book* and *Football Legends of All-Time* (with Bob Carroll). A charter member and past president of the Pro Football Researchers Association, he was the 1991 recipient of that organization's Ralph Hay Award.

Rick Korch is the manager of publications of the Jacksonville Jaguars and has spent 20 years in and around the National Football League. Korch was previously the editor-in- chief of *Pro Football Weekly,* the public relations director for the NFL Alumni, and a public relations assistant for the Miami Dolphins. Korch is the author of several other books, including *The Truly Great, The Official Pro Football Hall of Fame Playbook,* and *The Fantasy Football Guide.* Korch has won six awards from the Professional Football Writers of America, including one for the best feature story in 1990.

Kevin Lamb covered the NFL and Chicago Bears full-time for 16 years for the *Chicago Daily News* and *Chicago Sun-Times.* A 1973 graduate of Northwestern University's Medill School of Journalism, he covered sports for the *Milwaukee Journal* and *Newsday* before going to Chicago. Lamb has written five books about pro football and contributed to five others, as well as the last 22 *Encyclopedia Britannica's Books of the Year.* In addition to pro football, he has won national awards for enterprise reporting and articles about children's issues, crime, mental health, and general features.

Bob McGinn has been covering the Green Bay Packers since 1979, including the last 15 seasons as a beat writer on a daily basis for the *Milwaukee Journal Sentinel.* An award-winning sportswriter and a native of Escanaba, Michigan, and a journalism graduate of the University of Michigan, his peers have named him Wisconsin Sportswriter of the Year on four separate occasions. He contributed to the *Total Football* spin-off book, *Total Packers,* in 1998, and his work is included in the 300 Greatest Players Plus section in this edition of *Total Football.*

David Neft is a co-author of *The Sports Encyclopedia: Pro Football,* which has appeared in 15 editions, and also co-wrote *The Scrapbook History of Pro Football.* Neft served as editor-in-chief for the first edition of *The Baseball Encyclopedia* and is vice president of research for the Gannett Company, Inc.

David Pietrusza, former president of the Society for American Baseball Research (SABR) and Editor-in-

Chief of Total Sports, is the author of *Judge and Jury: The Life and Times of Judge Kenesaw Mountain Landis*, winner of SABR's Casey Award as the best baseball book of 1998. He is also author of *Lights On!: The Wild Century-Long Saga of Night Baseball; Minor Miracles: The Legend and Lure of Minor League Baseball; Major Leagues;* and *Baseball's Canadian-American League.* He co-edited *Total Mets, Total Braves,* and *Total Indians,* as well as seven books on football and served as managing editor of the first edition of *Total Football.* Pietrusza served as producer for the documentary *Local Heroes* for PBS-television station WMHT and as consultant for the Baseball Online segment of the PBS LearningLink system. A columnist for *Oldtyme Baseball News,* he has written for such other periodicals as *USA Today, Baseball Weekly, Baseball America, Elysian Fields Quarterly, The National Pastime, New Mexico Magazine,* and *The Baseball Research Journal*. Pietrusza was also a writer for Microsoft's multimedia product. A former member of the Amsterdam (N.Y.) City Council, he serves as Public Information Officer for the NYS Governor's Office of Regulatory Reform and has written extensively on American and world history.

Beau Riffenburgh is editor-in-chief for Total Sports. He was on the public relations staff of the Los Angeles Lakers before serving eight years as an associate editor and senior writer for NFL Properties. He then spent 11 years in Cambridge, England, as a lecturer in the History Faculty at the University of Cambridge and as editor of *Polar Record,* the world's oldest journal of polar research. In Britain, he also coached "American football" for eight years at the university level, posting an overall record of 68-12-2 and winning three national titles.

Matthew Silverman is a senior editor for Total Sports and co-edited the most recent edition of *Total Baseball.* In addition to *Total Football* and six of its recent spin-offs, he created football content for the company's AT&T Interchange site. Formerly a part-time editor at *Variety* in New York, he worked at three New England newspapers following his graduation from Roanoke College.

Don Smith retired in 1997 as vice-president/public relations director at the Pro Football Hall of Fame after 29 years. He administered the Hall's selection process for electing new members, was the official scorer for every Super Bowl except the first, and invented the forward passing statistical rating system used by the NFL since 1973. In his 47-year sports career, Smith, a 1950 University of Denver Phi Beta Kappa graduate, worked in sports administration with the Denver Bears baseball team, the Western Athletic Conference, the Denver Broncos, and the New Orleans Saints.

John Thorn edited *The Armchair Quarterback* and co-authored *The Hidden Game of Football* and *The Football Abstract* with Bob Carroll and Pete Palmer. A long-time member and past president of the PFRA, Thorn is also a co-editor of *Total Baseball* and the publisher of Total Sports.

Team and League Abbreviations

These are the franchises and leagues, and their abbreviations as used throughout this book.

Akr	Akron Pros 1920-25; Indians 1926
Ariz	Arizona Cardinals 1994-98
Atl	Atlanta Falcons 1966-98
BalA	Baltimore Colts AAFC 1947-49
Bal	Baltimore Colts 1950,1953-83; Ravens 1996-98
Bkn	Brooklyn Lions 1926; Dodgers 1930-43; Tigers 1944
BknA	Brooklyn Dodgers AAFC 1946-48
Bos	Boston Bulldogs 1929; Braves 1932; Redskins 1933-36; Boston Yanks 1944-48; Boston Patriots 1960-70
Buf	Buffalo All-Americans 1920-23; Bisons 1924-25, Rangers 1926; Bisons 1927, 1929; Bills 1960-98
BufA	Buffalo Bisons AAFC 1946; Bills AAFC 1947-49
Can	Canton Bulldogs 1920-23, 1925-26
Car	Carolina Panthers 1995-98
ChiB	Chicago Bears 1922-98
ChiC	Chicago Cardinals 1920-59
ChiA	Chicago Rockets AAFC 1946-48; Hornets 1949
ChiT	Chicago Tigers 1920
ChPt	Chicago Cardinals-Pittsburgh Steelers Combine 1944
Cin	Cincinnati Celts 1921; Reds 1933; Bengals 1968-98
CiSL	Cincinnati Reds-St. Louis Gunners 1934
Cle	Cleveland Tigers 1920-21; Indians 1923; Bulldogs 1924-25,1927; Indians 1931; Rams 1937-42, 1944-45; Browns 1950-95
CleA	Cleveland Browns AAFC 1946-49
Col	Columbus Panhandles 1920-22; Tigers 1923-26
Dal	Dallas Texans 1952; Cowboys 1970-98
DalT	AFL Dallas Texans 1960-62
Day	Dayton Triangles 1920-29
Den	Denver Broncos 1970-98
Det	Detroit Heralds 1920; Tigers 1921; Panthers 1925-26; Wolverines 1928; Lions 1934-98
Dul	Duluth Kelleys 1923-25; Eskimos 1926-27
Eva	Evansville Crimson Giants 1921-22
Fra	Frankford Yellow Jackets 1924-31
GB	Green Bay Packers 1921-98
Ham	Hammond Pros 1920-26
Har	Hartford Blues 1926
Hou	Houston Oilers 1960-96
Ind	Indianapolis Colts 1984-98
Jac	Jacksonville Jaguars 1995-98
KC	Kansas City Blues 1924; Cowboys 1925-26; Chiefs 1963-98
Ken	Kenosha Maroons 1924
LA	Los Angeles Buccaneers 1926
LAC	Los Angeles Chargers 1970
LARd	Los Angeles Raiders 1982-94
LARm	Los Angeles Rams 1946-94
LA-A	Los Angeles Dons AAFC 1946-49
Lou	Louisville Brecks 1921-23; Colonels 1926
MiaA	Miami Seahawks AAFC 1946
Mia	Miami Dolphins 1976-98
Mil	Milwaukee Badgers 1922-26
Min	Minneapolis Marines 1921-24; Red Jackets 1929-30; Vikings 1961-98
Mun	Muncie Flyers 1920-21
NE	New England Patriots 1971-98
NO	New Orleans Saints 1967-98
Nwk	Newark Tornadoes 1930
NYB	New York Bulldogs 1949
NYG	New York Brickley Giants 1921; New York Giants 1925-98
NY-A	New York Yankees AAFC 1946-49
NYY	New York Yankees 1927-28; New York Yanks 1950-51
NYT	New York Titans 1960-62
NYJ	New York Jets 1963-98
Oak	Oakland Raiders 1960-81; 1995-98
Oor	Oorang Indians 1922-23
Ora	Orange Tornadoes 1929
Phi	Philadelphia Eagles 1933-42, 1944-98
Pho	Phoenix Cardinals 1988-93
Pit	Pittsburgh Pirates 1933-39; Steelers 1940-42, 1945-98
PhPt	Philadelphia Eagles-Pittsburgh Steelers Combine 1943
Port	Portsmouth Spartans 1930-33
Pott	Pottsville Maroons 1925-28
Prov	Providence Steam Roller 1925-31
Rac	Racine Legion 1922-24; Racine Tornadoes 1926
RI	Rock Island Independents 1920-25
Roch	Rochester Jeffersons 1920-25
SD	San Diego Chargers 1961-98
Sea	Seattle Seahawks 1977-98
SF-A	San Francisco 49ers AAFC 1946-49
SF	San Francisco 49ers 1950-98
SI	Staten Island Stapletons 1929-32
StL	St. Louis All-Stars 1923; Cardinals 1960-87; Rams 1995-98
TB	Tampa Bay Buccaneers 1976-98
Ten	Tennessee Oilers, 1997-98
Tol	Toledo Maroons 1922-23
Ton	Tonawanda Kardex 1921
Was	Washington Senators 1921; Redskins 1937-98